2024

2024 STANDARD CATALOG OF

FIREARMS

34th Edition

EDITED BY

Jim Supica

Published by

Gun Digest® Books, an imprint of Caribou Media Group, LLC
Gun Digest Media
5583 W. Waterford Ln., Suite D
Appleton, WI 54913
gundigest.com

To order books or other products call 920.471.4522 ext. 104
or visit us online at **gundigeststore.com**

ISBN-13: 978-1-959265-03-0

Edited by Jim Supica and Corey Graff
Cover by Gene Coo

Printed in the United States of America

10 9 8 7 6 5 4 3 2 1

CONTENTS

INTRODUCTION

The *Standard Catalog of Firearms* is the leading illustrated firearms price guide, featuring over 15,000 guns. Each model is described and listed with estimated values in up to six different condition grades. Over the years, it has drawn on the expertise of hundreds of prominent firearms historians, dealers and collectors to compile an essential reference for anyone interested in guns and considering buying or selling them.

The prices listed are estimates of the fair market value of a particular gun model and variation in a specific condition. The condition makes a significant difference in value, which can take knowledge and experience to assess accurately. Widely different standards apply to modern and antique guns. Knowing which set of definitions applies to the arm being evaluated is essential.

The values listed are not carved in stone. Prices may fluctuate regionally. They may rise or fall with the time of year, the threat of new restrictive gun laws or even when featured in the latest movie or video game. However, the listed values should give the interested buyer or seller a good starting point in determining what a gun is worth.

Reader input is welcome for future editions. Send your corrections, value observations and suggestions to JimSupica@outlook.com or Jim Supica, PO Box 82, Olathe, KS 66051.

SCOPE & SUPPLEMENTAL REFERENCES

The *Standard Catalog of Firearms* tackles an extensive range of firearms, including many types that other general gun references have traditionally ignored. It includes extensive listings of significant manufacturers of antique and modern sporting arms, including obscure makers not covered in other works, some commemorative and limited-edition guns and modern blackpowder guns. In addition, it covers some antique firearms by 19th-century American individual gunsmiths, many antique military and some 20th-century military firearms.

The descriptions and illustrations are as important as the value estimates, making this book an essential reference for firearms identification.

Other firearms guides are handy and recommended for supplementing this book. The best of these include:

- *Standard Catalog of Military Firearms* edited by Phillip Peterson, an essential companion to this volume.
- *Blue Book of Gun Values* by Zachary R. Fjestad and Lisa Beuning, a classic price guide rating guns by the percentage of original finish remaining, updated annually.
- *Flayderman's Guide to Antique American Firearms and their Values* by Norm Flayderman, the classic reference for antique firearm identification. However, note that values were last updated in 2007 as of this writing.

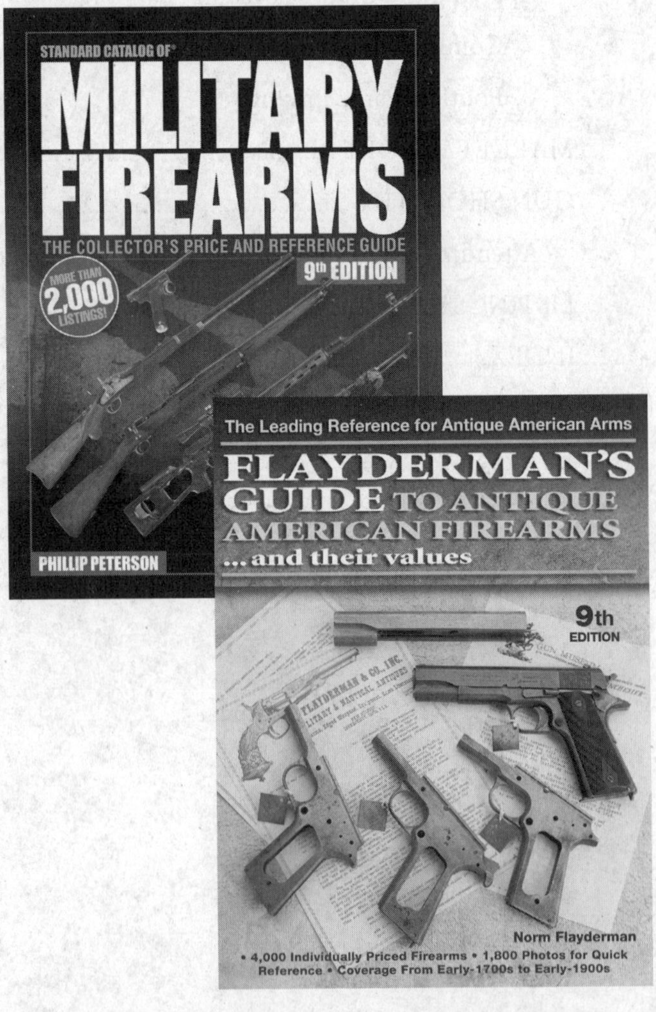

ABOUT THE EDITOR

Jim Supica is an AGI-Certified Firearms Appraiser and the owner of Supica Consulting, LLC (GunHeritage.com), providing firearms appraisals, consulting, writing, media and collection liquidation assistance. Until retiring in January 2020, he spent a dozen years as Director of the NRA Museums Division overseeing the NRA National Firearms Museum at NRA Headquarters in Fairfax, VA, and the NRA National Sporting Arms Museum at Bass Pro Shops in Springfield, MO. Before that, he spent 20 years as a full-time collectible arms dealer and auctioneer. He has served on the NRA Board of Directors and as President of the Smith & Wesson Collectors Association and Missouri Valley Arms Collectors Association. He holds a Juris Doctorate from the University of Kansas School of Law.

Supica is the editor or co-author of 10 books on firearms history and gun collecting and has written numerous articles on the topics. He has appeared as a firearms expert on hundreds of television show episodes, including *American Guns* on Amazon Prime, *NRA Gun Gurus, Gun Stories* and *American Rifleman Television.*

GUN DIGEST STAFF

Layout, value updates, and new model listings are provided by *Gun Digest* staff members, including:

- Jim Schlender, publisher
- Corey Graff, managing editor
- Todd Woodard (ARs)
- Robert Sadowski (Semi-Auto Pistols)
- Shane Jahn (Revolvers)
- Kristin Alberts (Shotguns & Rifles)
- Jamie Olsen (Online gun values & database)
- Michelle Graff, data entry specialist

ACKNOWLEDGMENTS

This book is an accumulation of over three decades of effort and research by an impressive group of firearms values and history experts. They include:

PREVIOUS EDITORS OF THE *STANDARD CATALOG OF FIREARMS*:

- Dan Brdlik, 1991
- Ned Schwing, 1992–2006
- Herbert Houze, 1992, 1993, 1996
- M. Howard Madaus, 1992–1993
- Dan Shideler, 2007–2011
- Jerry Lee, 2012–2020

CONTRIBUTORS

James Brewster, Jim Cate, Val Forgett, Rick Hacker, Rex Halfpenny, Kurt House, Stoney Roberts, Jackie Smith, Michael Tenny, Blaine Wade, Mike Allee, Richard Nahas, Ed Cornett, David Nowak, Gaston Comeau, Dr. Steven Rettke, John Thomas, Bruce Mower, Robert Vivas, Lee Jarrett, Mike Helms, Randy Jones, James Briesacher, Mike Dwyer, Tamara Hoover, David Royal, Tom Rowe and the members of smith-wessonforum.com.

PREVIOUS CONTRIBUTORS

Bailey Brower, Lisa Beuning, John Eckert, Michael Wozniak, Joe Pittenger, Bob Kaesta, Al Owens, George Layman, Tony Miele, Tom Boyer, J. B. Barnes, Bill Saska, Ed Tinker, Joe Cornell, Jeff John, Al Novak, Tim Olson, Kenneth Wilkinson, Kermit Feuge, Don Criswell, Rod Fuller, John Dougan, Jim Rankin, John Gallo, Duke McCaw, Otis Spigelmyer, Dave Kidd, Don Combs, Larry Orr, Don Stika, Robert R. Anderson, Philip Schreier, Roy Jinks, Harrison Carroll, Orvel Reichert, Dave Kidd, C.W. Slagle, John Kronschnabl, Eric Larson, Simeon Stoddard, Jerry Cummings, Pete Harvey, David Tinker, Robert M. Hausman, Patrick Hogan, Douglas Tate, J.R. Moody, Bob Ball, Thomas Barker, Scott Bennett, David Bichrest, Douglas Carlson, Kevin Cherry, Don Criswell, Bert O'Neill, Jeff Faintich, Richard Freer, David Hunter,

Clive Law, Roger Lenzmeier, Karl Lippard, Duke McCaa, Rich Machniak, Gale Morgan, J.R. Moody, Doug Murray, Nick Niles, Dean Rinehart, Richard M. Kumor, Sr., Dan Sheil, Walt Snider, Allan Wilson, Joe Gaddini, David Moore, Harold Hamilton, Michael McIntosh, Ed Buehlman, Joe McBride, Walt Snyder, Tom Turpin, Horst Held, Dave Banducci, Bob Lancaster, Judy Voss, Rick Sapp, Fred Baumann, Phillip Peterson, Tom Caceci, Jim Stark, LCDR James Dodd USN (ret.), David Rachwal, Bud Bugni, John Callahan, Jason Devine, Ken Durham, Gene Guilaroff, William Hammond, Karl Karash, Chuck Karwan, Karl Lippard, Dr. Daniel Menser, Jeff Munnel, Bob Rayburn, Ron Schmidt, Joe Schroeder, Dan Shell, Don Stika, John Stimson Jr., Adam Trieschmann, Michael Wamsher, Geraldine Brophy, Garry James, Steve Gash, J.B. Wood, Holt Bodinson, John Taffin, Rodney James, Alan Heldreth, Mike Clark, Paul Thompson, Joe Morton, Dwight Van Brunt, Linda Powell, Jessica Kallam, Ken Jorgensen, Bud Fini, Paul Pluff, Scott Grange, Jennifer Pearsall, Wes Dillon, Kevin Hogan, Dave LaRue, Jim Ciolli Jr., Marc Murphy, Jay Hansen, Rick Verzal, Roy Marcot, John Powell, Steve Poulin, Dave Sanders, John Puglisi, Payton Miller, Nick Sisley, Terry Wieland, Bart Skelton, Jon Sundra, Wayne van Zwoll, Don Findley, Jim Wilson, Dick Williams, Tom Tabor, Jim Dickson, Paul Scarlata, John Malloy, Layne Simpson, Larry Sterett, Kevin Muramatsu, Patrick Sweeney, Charlie Petty, Mac Prasac, Jim Foral, Wiley Clapp, Bill Hamm, Stan Trzoniec, Jason Morton, Keith Bernkrant, Jamie Harvey, Mike Nischalke, Karen Lutto, Barbara Fausti, Wes Lang, Val Forgett, Greg Krueger, Robert K. Campbell, Don Findley, John Haviland, Doug Wicklund, Jon W. Miller, Earl Minot, Lee Newton, L.P. Brezny, Jeff Quinn, Walt Hampton, Jim Floral, Jordan Matuszak, Kevin Van Cleave, Tone Moe, Bob Axelrod, Josh Lowensteiner, Ron Fouty, Ted Pollard, John Swift and Michael Wood.

AUCTION HOUSES, DEALERS, and SHOWS
The following sources have been beneficial in researching current market firearms values:

- Rock Island Auction Company—the world's largest firearms specialty auction house. Previous sales are easily searchable by auction date. Excellent source for high-end firearms values. *rockislandauction.com*
- Morphy Auctions—with its database of compiled previous sales, makes it easy to search prices realized for all previous auctions. It also includes prices realized for James D. Julia firearms auctions. *morphyauctions.com*
- Collectors Firearms, Houston, Texas—has an extensive inventory of antique and collectible firearms for sale with prices listed. *collectorsfirearms.com*
- Cowan's—website includes prices realized from previous auctions. *cowanauctions.com*
- Kull's Old Town Station, Topeka, Kansas. *armsbid.com*
- Amoskeag Auction. *amoskeagauction.com*
- Other auction house websites including Czerny, Heritage Auctions, Pot of Gold Auction, Christie's, Bonham's, Leland Little, Carol Watson's Orange Coast Auction, Poulin Antiques and Auctions, Little John's Auction, Milestone Auction, Skinner Auctioneers & Appraisers, Centurion, North American Auction Co., Milestone Auction, French Broad River Auction Co., Pook & Pook, Affiliated Auctions, CT Firearms Auction, Holt's Auctioneers, and Lock Stock & Barrel (*LSBauctions.com*).
- Online auction-tracking websites, including *liveauctioneers.com, invaluable.com, bidsquare.com, icollector.com, lotsearch.net* and *proxibid.com*. These websites accumulate prices for various auctions, including the most significant firearms auctioneers.
- Other collectible arms dealers' websites, including Joe Salter, Leroy Merz, David Condon, Monty Whitley and O.C. Young.
- *Gunauction.com*—an online firearms auction site that includes sold prices.
- *Gunbroker.com, gunsinternational.com,*

gunsamerica.com—leading online firearms auction sites often show current bid and buy-it-now prices for firearms listed for sale. However, prices for sold items are not shown, limiting the usefulness of value research.

- Wanenmacher's Tulsa Arms Show, every April and November. *tulsaarmsshow.com*
- MVACA Kansas City National Gun Show, every July. *mvaca.org*

GRADING SYSTEM

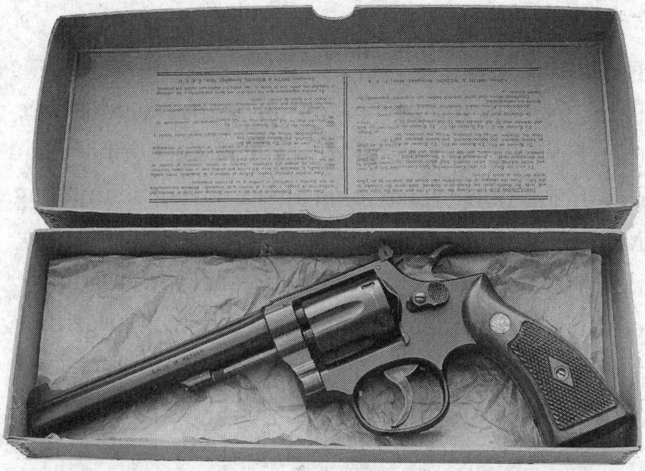

NIB – NEW IN BOX

100% original finish. The gun is exactly as it left the manufacturer. It has not been fired and has no wear. It is in its original factory carton or case with all the paperwork and accessories that originally came with the gun. All original parts. In this book, NIB values are listed only for modern guns. Antique firearms in New in Box condition are scarce and will bring a substantial premium over an Antique Excellent specimen.

EXCELLENT

An Excellent condition modern or antique gun must be in perfect working order with unmarred stock or grips. It will have an excellent bore and sharp markings and decorations and must be factory original with no refinish, repair, alterations or additions of any kind with original factory sights.

Modern Excellent – At least 98% original metal and wood finish.

Antique Excellent – At least 80% original finish.

FINE (Antiques only)

Antique Fine – 30% to 80% original finish. Minor marks on the wood. Good bore. Sharp original lettering, markings and designs. "Fine" is not used to describe modern guns.

VERY GOOD

A Very Good condition modern or antique firearm must have all factory original major parts and be in good working order. It may have some minor blemishes, repairs, alterations or non-factory additions. Markings and decorations are distinct and sharp. No pitting or corrosion.

Modern Very Good – 90% to 98% original finish. No refinishing. Good bore.

Antique Very Good – 0% to 30% original finish or most of a period-of-use professional or factory refinish. The wood may be slightly scratched or dinged. Bore condition is disregarded.

GOOD

A Good condition modern or antique gun may have minor repairs, alterations or non-factory additions. It should be in safe working condition. Central markings should be visible.

Modern Good – Over half the original finish or most of a professional refinish. The bore may have some wear or corrosion.

Antique Good – Usually no original finish. Metal may be smoothly rusted or lightly pitted in places or have been lightly cleaned or professionally refinished. The stock or grips may be scratched or dinged with repaired minor cracks or a correct well-fit replacement. Bore condition is disregarded.

FAIR

Fair condition modern or antique guns include those that show heavy use and cosmetic neglect or have had significant non-professional alterations or refinishing. Markings may not be legible, with the critical exception that possessing a modern firearm with an obliterated serial number is not legal. The stock or grips may be replaced, show heavy use or repair cracks.

Modern Fair – Generally has some finish remaining. It must be in good working order and safe to shoot.

Antique Fair – May be lightly pitted overall, vigorously cleaned or refinished with rounded edges. If not working, it must be repairable. If working, it must be safe to shoot.

POOR

Modern and antique guns will have little to no finish and may show pitting and rust. Parts may be broken or missing. They may not be working and may not be safe to shoot.

Modern Poor – Usually, these guns are so far gone that they are valued primarily for their salvageable parts.

Antique Poor – Some heavily worn or rusted antique guns may have value as conversation piece relics or representative examples of a rare specimen.

Example prices are shown for the conditions described above in this format:

Modern guns:

NIB	Exc.	V.G.	Good	Fair	Poor
2250	1800	1500	1250	1000	700

Antique guns:

Antique

Exc.	Fine	V.G.	Good	Fair	Poor
4000	2850	1700	950	400	250

APPLYING THE GRADING SYSTEM

For the values listed in this guide to have any meaning, it is essential to correctly evaluate the firearm's condition—a difference in condition may halve or double its value. Each of the condition grades used in this book has a specific meaning. Antique firearms (usually those manufactured before 1899) have different standards for a particular grade than recent guns. The *Standard Catalog of Firearms* grading system is an expanded version of the widely known and used NRA Condition Rating System.

We revised the *Standard Catalog of Firearms* antique condition definitions in the 2022 edition to be compatible with the NRA system. If you're familiar with the NRA system, you should be able to safely assume that *Standard Catalog* grades have the same meaning that you're used to. If you're accustomed to the old system used in earlier editions of *Standard Catalog*, you should closely review the antique definitions above.

WARNING! An Antique label on a gun's listing does not automatically mean that all examples of that model are legally antiques and exempt from the legal restrictions on sales of modern firearms. Many models' production eras span the 1898/1899 cutoff date. On these antique/modern transition models, we've tried to use the grading system that applies to most of the gun's production. For example, we'll probably use modern condition grades if the gun was made from 1895 to 1930. For one made from 1870 to 1910, we'd be more likely to use antique grades. To determine whether a gun purchase is subject to legal restrictions, research its antique/modern status.

The Grading System is a widely accepted set of guidelines but is not intended to be precise. A case could be made that many knowledgeable folks, consciously or unconsciously, apply a sliding scale based on age. Let's speculate that it might be something like this:

UNOFFICIAL SLIDING SCALE BY YEAR OF PRODUCTION	
PERCENT ORIGINAL FINISH REQUIRED FOR EXCELLENT GRADE	
Pre-1875	80%
1875–1885	85%
1885–1915	90%
1915–1945	95%
Post-1945	98%

Type of finish – Various types of finish wear differently, affecting a gun's visual appeal and the perceived condition and corresponding values. It's impossible to rate the "percentage of original finish" on a stainless steel or polymer-frame gun with no additional finish applied to the surfaces. The overall wear must be evaluated to determine its condition.

For earlier traditional finishes, the fact that bluing wears differently than nickel impacts a gun's overall condition rating. Bluing can fade to a pleasing and well-blended plum patina, whereas when nickel plating wears off, the underlying metal may darken, giving the gun a splotchy appearance.

The *Standard Catalog of Smith & Wesson* offers the following table suggesting different percentages of finish required for an "Excellent" rating for nickel vs. blued guns based on the date of production:

EXCELLENT RATING BY TYPE OF FINISH		
ERA	BLUED	NICKEL
Pre-1865	80%	85%
1865–1890	85%	90%
1890–1920	90%	95%
1920–1945	95%	98%
Post-1945	98%	99%+

COMMON SENSE

Finally, condition grading must be approached with a healthy dose of common sense. Condition definitions were originally developed chiefly by and for gun collectors. The definitions generally work best for guns that are sought for their rarity, age, history and originality. When considering the value of a firearm intended to be used as a shooter, the definitions may need some mental adjustment.

An obvious example is the grading requirement concerning "factory original" or "no additions or alterations." For a WWI military Mauser that has been "sporterized" with the stock and barrel cut, bolt turned down, scope mounted, and fully refinished, those modifications destroy the collector value of the gun. However, it still has value as a shooter, based primarily on the quality of the work.

On the other hand, if you have an Excellent or NIB current production rifle worth $900 with a $1,100 non-factory scope added, the value has usually not been reduced by that addition. The value has increased, assuming no physical rifle modification was necessary to mount the scope. It may not be worth the combined value of the rifle and scope separately, but the addition will have enhanced the value of the package.

The whole point of having a grading system is to have memorable and understandable shorthand terminology to summarize the condition of a gun for valuation purposes. There will be additional varying factors by necessity, but it makes a good starting place.

POLITICAL PANIC PRICING

Certain firearms and related items are subject to price fluctuations in response to politics, production shortages and other events. This variance can apply to so-called "assault weapons" (a bullshit political term incorrectly applied to semi-automatic rifles with detachable magazines and modern features such as pistol-grip stocks and use of synthetic materials), semi-auto pistols with a magazine capacity of over 10 rounds, ammunition, magazines, or even any type handgun potentially used for personal defense, depending on current events and shifting political tides.

Price spikes for those items usually happen when certain events occur. Most common causes:

- There is a plausible political threat to restrict or prohibit certain types of firearms, often the election of an anti-gun president or congress.
- Current events create the perception that the average individual may be more likely to need a personal-defense firearm to protect themselves, their family and their property.
- There is a mass shooting or other event that stimulates political rhetoric supporting gun bans.

Historically, these events have resulted in increased demand, scarcity of supply and corresponding pricing increases from 10% or less to as much as 25% or more. The panic's duration is usually unpredictable, and prices generally drift back to previous values. For this reason, we are slow to raise published estimated values in response to current events. Still, buyers and sellers should know these real (usually temporary) price fluctuations.

MARKET REPORT

Just like a new car's value drops when you drive it off the dealer's lot, the value of a new gun diminishes when you walk out of the gun shop door with it. Unlike automobiles, however, firearm values tend to stabilize and slowly increase as years pass. Wear and tear from handling and use will reduce the gun's value, but if kept in the same condition, the overall pricing trend tends to be upward over time. As decades pass, most guns bought as "shooters" eventually become "collectibles," valued for their utility, rarity, history and nostalgia. Old guns don't seem to experience market crashes that affect other collectibles, such as Beanie Babies and antique china. Maybe this is partially because a vintage gun retains its usefulness.

There are trends in firearms values. For shooting pieces, these can be impacted by military and police armament choices, technical improvements, trends in competition shooting or being featured in the latest Netflix series.

Among collectible guns, certain types may tend to see value spurts. Since WWII, the most popular collectibles have generally followed a historical timeline, beginning with early Kentucky rifles and other muzzleloaders, followed by Civil War-era arms, then Old West sixguns and lever-actions during the height of TV western popularity, and moving toward mid-20th century military arms in more recent years. However, as a trend passes, values don't tend to crash. More often, they become stagnant, and a piece becomes more difficult to sell.

Individual gun owners and collectors must remember that firearm values usually estimate what the gun will sell for at retail. The folks doing the selling are in it to make money and need to buy the guns at a price lower than what they will sell for. Realize that unless you can find the end consumer to buy your gun or collection, a dealer will offer you less than retail or take a percentage-based commission if they sell it.

Although the panic buying of the Covid and riot era of 2020–2021 has settled down, overall gun buyer interest has remained strong in 2022 and 2023, with prices steady and increasing. Values during 2024 will doubtless be influenced by political trends, most notably the election. Prices rise when an anti-gun government seems probable and slow when a Second Amendment-friendly administration appears likely.

Several prominent gun collectors, historians and dealers shared their thoughts on the current market.

Michael Tenny, CEO of Cheaper Than Dirt!, has noticed the following:

- *Deep-pocket, serious collectors are still active in 2023 and 2024, while bargain-hunting buyers have softened with the challenges of the economy.*
- *Military weapons and historically significant firearms are strong sellers and have been doing better for the last three years as buyers seek 'history' as a category.*
- *The top trend that still has lots of strength is NFA Class III items, especially U.S. Military and high-condition specimens.*
- *As the U.S. Population ages, there are more buyers with money who want to relive their youth; they cherish the fast cars and great guns they remember. This market is offset by our youth, who have little interest in anything older than themselves and prefer function over quality, and price over durability.*

Jackie Smith summarizes current gun show trends:

From what I can see, the used firearms market is very strong, with modern automatics like Glock, H&K,

SIG, etc., selling for as much as the manufacturer's suggested retail. New guns are selling for premium prices depending on which model it is.

C&R guns are bringing 15-20% more than last year.

Antiques are still bringing 20% more than the last time we chatted.

Collectible ammo is very strong, with 1950s 22 boxes bringing $20 per box and the stuff from the '60-'80s bringing $15-20 per box of 50 rds.

Blaine Wade, Chairman of the NRA Gun Collector Committee, points out possible buying opportunities early in the year:

I have perceived a lull in the market for sellers each year from January through March. I typically look for the more collectible firearms that would usually bring 15% to 25% more during an optimum market time. This 1st quarter of the year is what I believe to be a "Buyer's Market" and is probably due to the after-Christmas effect and tax time. I typically will purchase 50%–75% of the year's collectible purchases during that time period.

Prominent gun writer and NRA Publications Field Editor Rick Hacker provides a broad view of trends:

This year's collecting scene is pretty much a repeat of last year—priceless vintage collectibles are still miraculously coming onto the market as older collectors either die off or decide to cash in on their long-held collectible firearms. Vintage Winchesters, along with Colt and early-20th century Smith & Wesson revolvers, continue to be the gold standard.

The fact that 2023 was the 150th anniversary of both the Colt Single Action Army and the Winchester '73 has focused an increased amount of attention on these long-time favorites, with Second Generation SAA's having already assumed their own collecting niche, with some prices for as-new Second Generation guns rivaling those of First Generation Colts. While the Third Generation Colt SAA is still being made, they are difficult to obtain due to limited production and availability. In response, Tony Galazan's Standard Manufacturing company was inspired to produce a well-made American copy of the SAA completely machined from 4140 steel. Those who remember the excellent U.S. Fire Ams SAAs, which are no longer made and have escalated in value, are taking notice, even though Tony's single-action is priced on a par with a Colt, whose value is already historically well-established.

WWII military firearms without import marks continue to be in demand, especially authentic trench guns (fakes abound) as well as civilian riot shotguns. Likewise. the market for personal defense and EDC pistols remains active, with revolvers now getting a slight uptick in attention over semi-autos, which nonetheless continue to dominate the new gun list.

Some 19th- and 20th-century British guns are starting to bring higher prices, but the muzzleloading market continues to remain soft. Replica guns are relatively underpriced, although this is changing with the cost of materials constantly rising. They probably won't be any cheaper than they are today, with the no-longer-made Colt blackpowder cap and ball revolvers of a few years ago starting to inch up in value if they are NIB. In addition, the uncertainty of the elections, as of this writing, is also fueling the new gun market, especially for ARs.

With more new collectors and first-time gun buyers entering the market, my overall advice is to buy quality over cheapness, only deal with reputable sources, and if it is a historical or rare gun, get provenance or factory letters. Factory letters are worth the extra cost, as they add to a gun's value and resale potential.

James Brewster and Dan Diedrich of SARAH15 Guns, Ltd., give an overall view of the market:

Collector-grade, complete examples continue to be king. The completeness, condition, and extras add exponential value to any package. This seems to be across all makes, models and vintages. Specific to the Smith & Wesson market, the trends seem to show a softening of the pre- and early post-war revolver markets. While scarce configurations will still bring a premium, that premium is not what it once was. We suspect this is mostly impacted by generational factors. Top values seem to be creeping into collector-grade packages from the 1960s and 1970s. The big-bores and magnums still continue to fetch top dollar, with the 29s being the undisputed winner. Paraphrasing Dirty Harry, these are making everyone's day. The prices of S&W semi-autos, including the performance center guns, also appear to be softening. Obviously, there are exceptions in all categories, but the prices as a whole seem to be lower than 3 to 5 years ago. Aside from the Smith & Wesson firearms market, S&W accessories are on the rise. Top-condition target stocks and Lew Horton combat stocks are seeing an all-time high in the market.

Beyond the S&W markets, we would make the following generalities. The Winchester market is softening, and the 1980s HK (Heckler & Koch) market is booming. With the recent sellout of Remington, their prices took a sharp incline and now seem to be leveling off. Colt is Colt and will always fetch good results. The "stock" 1911 market is hurting with the commonality of the semi-custom (Cabot, Alchemy Custom Weaponry, Wilson Combat, Ed Brown, Nighthawk Custom, and Guncrafter Industries) 1911 market ramping up. WWII and military collectors are still hot after their niche interests, and the market continues to see an uprise in authentic items.

Kurt House provides insights into collectible gun trends:

Everyone understands that Texas is a good place to collect guns, so I am aware of that bias. Thus, my perspective is influenced not only by the Texas geopolitical arena, which is much in the national news lately, but also and perhaps more importantly, by over 60 years of blissful antique arms collecting. The present climate here is hot, both in temperature and in some areas of gun collecting. Like many collectors, I am ever amazed at auction prices and private exchanges, which seem to indicate that demand is not decreasing, in spite of my observation that many in my age group are either dispersing their collections or their collections are being dispersed by their heirs, if you know what I mean. I can't imagine how, in spite of the passing of so many of my friends lately, the gun market is sustaining stability, even increasing. Invoking the old law of supply and demand, it would seem that a lowered demand would decrease prices, yet the opposite seems true in today's market, if only in certain sectors. However, if this is true, how do we explain an ascending market? Here are some over-simplified possible explanations:

1. *The demand is not really decreasing.*
2. *The supply is decreasing.*
3. *Population increase accounting for the loss of old collectors.*
4. *Geo-political climate; remember when a certain anti-gun president was the best gun salesman of the year?*

It appears that, in general, demand could be waning for the former gold standard arms in favor of later-made double-action pistols, automatics, fancy shotguns, big-bore double rifles and such arms, even Class III arms that formerly carried a barrier due to the license required, are selling well. As supporting evidence, interest in matchlock, wheel-lock, flintlock, and percussion guns, that is, guns from former eras, is translating into lower prices for those categories. For another example, prices of Colt Single Actions, once likened to the price of a $20 U.S. gold piece, are beginning to feel pressure, maybe because the old guy buyers are dying and more stellar collections are being dispersed. But who can explain this market? The Colt Single Action that killed Billy the Kid just set a world record, selling at over $6 million, so somebody understands history.

Rex Halfpenny, Event Coordinator for the S&W Collectors Association, notes:

I like revolvers, beautiful wood, bright blue, nickel and stainless. So while walking through the 2023 NRA Annual Meeting exhibit hall in Indianapolis, I was overwhelmed by all the modern sporting rifles. This is certainly not new, but I was still surprised by how many manufacturers, old and new, are adding models to an already flooded marketplace. Keep in mind that, for the most part, these models are not unique. They are all interchangeable. Second to all the MSRs are the increasing number of higher-end, feature-rich, railed, ported, optic-ready semi-auto pistols, with an expanding number offered in a variety of attractive colors, many with gold bling.

Stoney Roberts, Supreme Sasquatch and Master of the Outdoors reports on ammo and reloading components and closes us out with an investment perspective and advice for the future:

For the first time in years, I had to deal with the current markets for reloading component parts. It went something like this.

Dies: I happened to be attending one of the largest gun shows in America in Tulsa, Oklahoma. I was there for three days and must have looked at a thousand tables to locate the only set of .32 H&R magnum dies at the show. At least, they were bargain-priced for a set of custom dies. Returning home, I looked for dies at all of the better gun shops in my hometown of Springfield, MO., to find none available. As a friend of mine would say, "Unobtainium."

Primers: Small pistol primers were easier to come by, and I found a box of 1,000 at the same Tulsa gun show for about twice the price I had paid previously (several years ago) for the same quantity. I thought this might be a gun show thing; however, after checking a significant number of local stores, the pricing seemed to have been in line with the current markets.

Powder: The preferred powder for this loading is Unique. I searched almost all local gun shops, including one of the largest sporting goods shops in America located here in Springfield, to find that Unique was unavailable. So, after recommendations from several friends and local reloaders, I settled on Hodgden CFE Pistol. There was no reference to this powder in any of the numerous reloading manuals I have. However, the store had a pamphlet with load information for the powder, and there was information online on Hodgdon's website. Once again, the price was roughly twice what I had paid for the last pound of Unique I had purchased several years ago.

Bullets: I visited every sporting goods store in the Springfield area to find that the preferred 85-grain hollowpoint bullets I was looking for were unavailable at any price. I then began my Internet search, finding that most suppliers were out of stock. I finally found a couple of sources with bullets in stock. Prices for the bullets were reasonable, by current pricing standards, around $30 per 100. One source wanted $15 for shipping and the other $9.

This review may not be indicative of all markets as it was confined mostly to my local area. However, it is a far cry from my previous experience in acquiring the components necessary for safe and accurate load development. This makes me long for the days when you could walk into your favorite Liar's Club (gun shop) and walk out with all of the needed loading components and more advice than asked for. So, why do we reload? Loading your own is certainly no longer a cost savings compared to the price of over-the-counter cartridges. Most standard cartridges are readily available at your local discount stores, but what if you want to shoot something more exotic or want a specific result from your loads?

I fairly regularly attend several different gun shows within my geographic area and have noted the vast sea of gray heads (including mine) that are attending these events, all in search of unidentified treasures hidden and undervalued on thousands of display tables. My first impressions are that these baby boomers are aging out of the firearms market, posing the possibility that there will be a flood of estates containing wonderful gun collections entering the markets over a relatively short period of time. We all know the economic theory of excess inventories causing values to fall. So, who will be purchasing from these estates?

On a more positive side, during these gun shows, I am selling significantly huge numbers of editions of the Standard Catalog of Firearms, *and by far, the majority of purchasers are from a younger generation. If they have an interest in the current firearms values and collections and are entering the markets at somewhat lower costs, they become buyers, and buyers raise values (another economic theory).*

I believe quality firearms are, and will remain, great long-term investments.

Gun Show Tips

Attending a gun show can sharpen your gun collecting chops, and it's a lot of fun, too!

By Jim Supica

If you like guns enough to be reading this book, you owe it to yourself to check out a gun show or two if you haven't already. Gun shows can range from well-armed fleamarkets to elaborate national convention-style professional exhibitions. COVID hit gun shows hard, and for a year or more, nearly all were canceled. Now, they are building their way back, some faster than others.

How Gun Shows Work

At most gun shows, dealers rent tables from the promoter to display and sell their wares. Of course, the emphasis is on guns and related items, including accessories, accouterments, militaria, ammo, parts, knives, hunting gear, related books and art, collectibles, various gimcracks and geegaws. Depending on the show rules, other sales tables may be permitted with products such as jewelry, coins, purses, beef jerky and camping gear. The best shows will limit what type of merchandise can be offered, keeping the overall firearms theme, but you never know what you'll find.

Most gun shows are weekend affairs held at a rented convention center-type public facility. Some shows are annual, while others may be regularly scheduled as often as monthly. Vendors rent 8-foot folding tables from the promoter, laid out in rows to display merchandise. Usually, setup is Friday, with only tableholders permitted entry; teardown is typically Sunday at the show's end. Tables can cost from $50 to $200, depending on the size and popularity of the show.

The public pays for admission on Saturday and Sunday, usually $8 to $20 daily. Most venues, but not all, have free parking. Most attendees are shopping or browsing. They can bring personal firearms to sell, usually load-checked at the door and tied inoperable with a plastic zip tie.

Gun Show Tips, Practices and Etiquette

Some basic guidelines for how to fit in, enjoy yourself, get a good deal, and go with the flow:

- Ask before touching or handling an item on a table. In general, don't handle guns unless you're seriously considering buying. Also, ask before taking pictures.
- Ask before working the action, dry-firing, disassembling or even load-checking a gun that's on a table. This is a bit of a departure from standard safety protocols since, in many cases, it's customary to load-check a gun when you first pick it up. However, manipulating a gun's action can damage an antique gun, add usage marks to a pristine as-new gun, or leave sweaty fingerprints that start rust, all of which reduce its value.
- Be sure any gun you bring into the show is unloaded. This is usually a show requirement and applies to concealed carry guns as well. Negligent discharges at gun shows are very rare, but when they do occur, it is often the result of someone foolishly getting out a concealed carry piece to get a value estimate, trying it in a holster, passing it to someone else to look at or other thoughtless handling. Don't be That Guy.
- And *do* follow all other basic firearms safety rules. At a show, it's easy to start thinking of guns as merchandise and forget their basic function. Treat every gun as if it were loaded, and do

not let the muzzle point at others.

- Be considerate of others. Don't stand in front of a vendor's table blocking the view of others unless you're actively looking. Don't have conversations in the middle of an aisle, impeding the flow of traffic. Never put food, drink or personal items on a dealer's table. If you're carrying a long gun, be careful not to whack others with the barrel.
- Don't talk on the phone while examining a gun. The dealer may assume that you are making an illegal "strawman" purchase for another individual who is ineligible to own a firearm. In general, if you're making a cell phone call, do it out of the way so as not to block others from tables or aisles.
- Prices are nearly always negotiable. It's considered standard procedure to make an offer below the marked price and haggle from there. You'll do better if you're not insulting and don't act like a know-it-all. You'll also learn more if you ask questions instead of showing off your vast knowledge.
- Bring cash. Bring more than you plan to spend in case an irresistible bargain shows up. Many vendors will not accept checks or charge cards.
- If you find something you want at a price that's reasonable, buy it. The odds are good that if you wait and come back later, it will be gone.
- On the other hand, know what you're looking for and research what a reasonable price would be ahead of time. Don't get carried away and overspend for something you could order cheaper tomorrow online.
- Hold onto a gun while you're negotiating the price on it until the deal is closed or you're ready to walk away. The moment you set it down, that guy who has been standing patiently next to you may say, "I'll take it."
- Don't interrupt a negotiation in process, and don't interrupt a dealer who is on the phone doing a background check or otherwise processing a sale. That work requires their full attention.
- Be sure you have your official I.D. and any other documents that may be required in your state to

complete a gun purchase.

- If you're bargain hunting, consider renting a table. With easy access to valuation information online, the days of dramatically underpriced merchandise at gun shows have pretty much passed. However, any items that are marked at bargain rates are usually snatched up by table-holders during Friday dealer-only set-up before the public is admitted Saturday morning. You'll also get better parking and get in early with other dealers, avoiding the lines. If you do want to bargain hunt without renting a table, be at the front door before opening on Saturday. Or, make the final rounds before load-out Sunday afternoon when a dealer may want to just get something sold so he doesn't have to pack it out and knows he won't get a better offer before the end of the show.
- If you've brought a gun to sell, or to research the value or learn more about, look for folks with similar items on their table. They will probably be the most knowledgeable about that particular type of firearm. Compare prices for similar items. Realize that if they're there as dealers, they'll want to buy low enough to make a profit on resale and may try to buy at 50% to 75% of what they think they can re-sell for. If they're a collector, they may want your variation for their collection and be able to offer closer to full value. Either way, they probably know about the type of gun that they're displaying, so ask questions and listen to the answers. Of course, bear in mind that some skeezy folk will bad-mouth a gun to try to take advantage of an unknowledgeable seller.
- Keep the classic gun collector platitudes in mind. Buy the gun, not the story. For every gun you buy, buy a book. Look a gun over carefully before making an offer, and use a flashlight or cell phone light for close inspection. Keep a dose of skepticism. Ask yourself, "Why is this gun for sale?" Nearly all gun show sales are "as is, where is, right now." You can't bring it back for a refund next Monday.

- If you bring your kids, that's great! We need the next generation to appreciate firearms. That said, be sure they're enjoying themselves, and be especially sure that they mind the No. 1 rule—don't touch the guns, and keep your hands in your pockets.
- Wear comfortable shoes. Bring a notepad to remember table locations. If permitted, bring water or another beverage and snacks in a backpack. If you're with a friend, let them know what you're looking for so they can help you check out the tables. Ask questions and learn stuff. Indulge in buying something that catches your fancy. And gun shows are one of the best venues ever for people-watching but do be subtle.

Legal Matters

This isn't legal advice but a general layperson's summary of some of the regulations on gun sales at gun shows. At the time of this writing, the ATF has proposed some new regulations on private sales of guns and the definition of what constitutes being engaged in the business of selling firearms. Do your own research or seek legal counsel before relying on this information.

Some of the table-holders are full-time professional FFL-holding firearms dealers, while others are hobbyists and collectors. Despite what ill-informed (or intentionally deceptive) media and anti-gun politicians would have you believe, all firearms laws apply to sales of guns at gun shows. There is no "gun show loophole." Representatives of BATF often attend shows and are even sometimes provided their own tables.

An FFL (Federal Firearms License) dealer selling post-1898 firearms at a gun show in their home state must follow the same procedures they would at their shop, including background check and completing the form 4473. The gun show location is considered an extension of their licensed premises. Out-of-state dealers can't sell directly to private individuals at gun shows.

Private individuals who don't have federal dealer licenses, whether table-holders or attendees, must follow all applicable laws and regulations. Under federal law, a non-FFL individual can sell a personally owned firearm to an appropriate FFL licensee or to another private individual who is legally eligible to own the gun in question. For handguns, both the buyer and the seller must be legal residents of the state where the gun show is located. Careful private sellers will require identification from their buyers and assurance that the buyer is legally eligible to own the gun in question. Also, all state and local laws must be followed. Almost half of the states require a background check for private sales of handguns.

Transfers between private individuals or sales by out-of-state FFL's to individuals can be processed by in-state FFL dealers at the show, in the same way that internet sales are facilitated. Most shows keep a list of attending in-state dealers who are willing to handle such transfers for a fee.

Table-holders who don't have a dealer's Federal Firearms License need to be aware that it is illegal to be "engaged in the business of dealing in firearms" without an FFL. Generally, an FFL is not required for occasional sales of personal guns or to liquidate a personally owned collection. However, if you're someone who is buying at shows with the intention of reselling at a profit or who, in the words of BATF, *devotes time, attention and labor to dealing in firearms as a regular course of trade or business with the principal objective of livelihood and profit through the repetitive purchase and resale of firearms,* do yourself a favor and get a Dealer FFL.

In addition to Dealer FFLs, the BATF also issues Collector FFLs, sometimes called C&R FFLs. These are not licenses for selling guns for profit. They do allow licensed collectors to buy guns defined as "Curios and Relics" (C&Rs) directly from dealers, distributors, or other persons without having to go through a licensed dealer.

To be a C&R, such a gun must fit one of three categories.

a) At least fifty years old, or

b) Certified by the curator of a government museum as of museum interest, or

c) Derive its value substantially from its novelty, rarity, oddity, or historical attribution.

The first two classes are fairly self-evident. The "novelty/rarity/oddity" class is open to interpretation. On request, the ATF will determine whether a particular gun is a C&R on that basis. The list of C&Rs approved by this process is available online. It looks as if most commemorative guns are usually approved as C&Rs, for one example.

C&R FFLs are required to keep records, but the process is less rigorous than for a dealer, and they are not required to turn in their records on expiration of the FFL. A C&R FFL may be a good idea for an active collector seeking to build their personal collection, but remember—the C&R FFL is not a license to engage in the firearms business.

Types of Gun Shows

Each gun show is unique, but they tend to fall into general classes.

a) **General collector gun shows.** These are sponsored by state or regional gun collector clubs and tend to attract more antique, collectible, rare, and unusual firearms. They will often include a display competition for collectors to show educational exhibits of arms from their collections, with trophies and/or cash awards for the best displays. If you have an interest in guns that extends at all beyond Glocks and ARs, these are usually the most rewarding shows to attend.

b) **Specialty collector gun shows.** These are staged by collector clubs that specialize in a specific brand or type of firearm such as Colt, Winchester, or Smith & Wesson. They nearly always include a display competition and often include talks, seminars, banquets or other special events for the membership. Many are open only to members of the club and special approved guests and draw a national audience. Most only happen once a year. If you want to see the best and rarest of that particular manufacturer, you'll see better examples at these shows than at nearly any museum.

Sometimes a specialty collecting club will have their annual meeting and exhibit competition in conjunction with a large general gun show.

c) **Commercial promoter gun shows.** These are by far the most common type of gun show and are produced by promoters who are in the gun show business. The same promoter usually has multiple shows throughout the year, sometimes at different locations. Most tend to attract table-holders from the area of the show and feature current or recent production guns and related items, with fewer antique, classic and unusual firearms. They also tend to have more non-gun flea market-type tables.

d) **Local shows.** These are a bit of a vanishing breed, sometimes conducted by a fraternal organization or other similar local group as an event/fundraiser rather than an ongoing commercial production. They can be small, sometimes with fewer than 100 tables, but tend to be relaxed and friendly and sometimes entice a few locally owned personal guns from years past out of the woodwork.

e) **National convention-style events.** These are not your traditional gun show with tables by collectors and small dealers, but rather huge national events with elaborate professional displays by major manufacturers and others in the firearms industry. Some are targeted specifically at selling to distributors and dealers while others are open to the general public. Rather than 8-ft. tables, the displays range from 10x10-ft. booths to massive exhibits. Generally, only current production arms are on exhibit, and those with the aim of getting orders from dealers, introducing new models, and promoting their brand to the gunnish public. They are splendid affairs, but in most cases, there are no older or used guns and no gun sales to the public (although there's lots of other stuff you can buy).

The Best Gun Shows

First off, there ain't no such thing as a bad gun show. They're all interesting, and you never know where you'll find that special treasure or amazing bargain. That said, some events are generally recognized as standing out from the crowd, with an emphasis on general collector shows.

- **Wanenmacher's Tulsa Arms Show.** The world's largest gun show has to be listed first. Over 4,000 tables with 11 acres under one roof and three miles of aisles! Originally sponsored by Indian Territory Arms Collectors, this show still features a display competition and often hosts specialty collector clubs such as the Ruger Collectors. Guns of all types and eras are on sale from ARs to flintlocks. If you can't find something you like here, you're too damn picky. April 6–7 and Nov. 9–10, 2024. *tulsaarmsshow.com*
- **Las Vegas Antique Arms Show.** All types of collectible arms. Hosts the NRA National Gun Collectors Display competition, attracting exhibits of the finest collections. 1,000 tables. Jan. 26–27, 2024. *antiquearmsshow.com*
- **Colorado Gun Collectors Association**. Some refer to this Greeley, CO show as the World Series of gun collector displays. 800 tables. May 18–19, 2024. *cgca.com*
- **Baltimore Antique Arms Show**. Sponsored by the Maryland Arms Collectors Assoc., this show is to the East what the CGCA show is to the West, with outstanding exhibits and sales tables. Restricted to antique and classic firearms, with only pre-1899 handguns allowed. 1,000 tables. March 16–17, 2024. *baltimoreshow.com*
- **Ohio Gun Collectors Association.** Seven meetings a year in Wilmington and Cleveland, you must be a member or the invited guest of a member to attend. Recognized nationwide. *ogca.com*
- **MVACA Kansas City National Summer Arms Show.** The Missouri Valley Arms Collectors Association hosts this show the last weekend of July each year, with an outstanding display competition. 750 tables, July 27–28, 2024. *mvaca.org*
- **Texas Gun Collectors Association.** You know Texas has got to have great gun shows. The 2024 TGCA shows are April 26-28 in Waco and Oct. 18–20 in Denton. Also worthwhile are the Dallas Arms Collectors Association show Sept. 23 & 24 and the Houston Gun Collectors Association Shows in Feb. & Sept. *tgca.org*
- **Winchester Arms Collectors Association Cody Show.** WACA's annual display show in Cody, WY, hosts all sorts of guns in addition to Winchesters. 300 tables, July 12–14, 2024. Be sure to check out the spectacular Cody Firearms Museum and visit Yellowstone Park while you're there. *winchestercollector.org/cody-show/*
- **National Gun Day.** This Louisville, KY, event is a commercial show with no display competition but one of the largest with 1,250 tables, attracting vendors from throughout the country. Feb.

24–25 and Oct. 5–6, 2024. *nationalgunday.com*

- **The Nation's Gun Show.** Chantilly, VA, multiple shows each year, 1,300 tables. A large well-attended commercial gun show near the nation's capital. The outstanding NRA National Firearms Museum at NRA Headquarters in Fairfax VA is an easy visit while in the area. *thenationsgunshow.com*

Members only:

- **Smith & Wesson Collectors Association Symposium**—Five-day annual event at a different location each year with display competition, sales tables, lectures, social events and fundraising auction. *theswca.org*
- **Colt Collectors Association**—Four-day annual event at a different location each year. Display competition, sales tables, social events and fund-raising auction. *coltcollectors.com*

Other folks have recommended these shows:

- Oaks Gun Show near King of Prussia PA, commercial show, 1,500 tables.
- Claude Hall's Oklahoma City, OKC Gun Show, monthly commercial show.
- Indian Territory Antique & Collector Arms Show, Shawnee, OK, 230 tables.
- Oregon Arms Collectors, two-day show in August in Hillsboro, OR, and monthly one-day shows.
- Lakeland Rifle & Pistol Club, Lakeland, FL.
- Yankee Lake Gun Shows, Brookfield, OH.

Firearms Conventions

- **NRA Annual Meeting.** May 16–19, 2024, Dallas. The annual meeting of members includes seminars, social events, political rallies, auctions, and a massive convention-style exhibit hall featuring impressive displays by firearms manufacturers and related companies. There is also a national gun collector display competition which brings out the finest collections in the world. The NRA Gun Collectors Committee and NRA Museums Division also sponsor a national collectors' display competition each year at a traditional gun show in 2024 at the Vegas show, as mentioned previously. *nraam.org*
- **SHOT Show.** Jan. 23–26, 2024, Las Vegas. The Shooting, Hunting, and Outdoors Trade Show is a gathering for the firearms industry, featuring impressive commercial displays and booths similar to the NRA Annual Meeting exhibits. It is open to FFL dealers and members of the firearms industry only. *shotshow.org*
- **Dallas Safari Club** and **Safari Club International.** The DSC Convention and Expo is Jan. 11–14, 2024, and the SCI Convention is Jan. 31–Feb. 3, 2024 in Nashville. Both feature elaborate displays of high-end hunting firearms, safari outfitters, and other goods and services of interest to elite hunters, along with spectacular taxidermy. There are also booths of high-end jewelry, furs, and handbags, which are usually occupied by browsing safari wives obviously thinking *So HOW much did hubby spend on that last expedition? biggame.org and safariclub.org*
- **NRA Great American Outdoor Show.** Feb. 3–11, 2024, Harrisburg PA. Like a gun show on steroids, combined with hunting, fishing, archery and general outdoor pursuits. Open to the public, with convention-style displays and sales booths along with speakers and seminars. *greatamericanoutdoorshow.org*

In Conclusion

Do a gun show. Enjoy yourself. Bring a friend with you and make new ones. Gun shows aren't just about the Second Amendment right to keep and bear. They're also a celebration of the First Amendment freedom of speech and the right of the people to peaceably assemble. With cool guns!

As Two-bit Cowboy noted in the smith-wesson.com online forum, *I can think of no other single type event that attracts as many like-minded folks as a gun show, and those are exactly the folks I want to socialize with.*

Speaking of the NRA ...

I get a lot of questions about the current state of affairs at the National Rifle Association.

The NRA has gone through a rough few years. This has mainly resulted from the exposure of some bad management decisions and business practices. Most of the publicity has come from the politically motivated lawsuit by New York Attorney General Letitia James and smear campaigns by TheTrace.org, funded by Everytown for Gun Safety and anti-gun billionaire Michael Bloomberg. These have been eagerly picked up and spread by a smirking mainstream media.

The anti-gunners were clever to do this. When a powerful, multi-million-member organization is the most effective force blocking attempts to whittle away at and eventually destroy Second Amendment rights, the obvious solution is to gut that association. They did a pretty good job.

But here's the deal.

Warts and all, the NRA is the only reason you can still own an AR, attend a gun show or carry a personal defense handgun. There are other great gun rights groups out there—Gun Owners of America, the Second Amendment Foundation, the National Association for Gun Rights and the Citizens Committee for the Right to Keep and Bear Arms, to name a few. All are doing important work. By all means, join and support them. However, none of them have the influence, power and reach to fill NRA's shoes nor the potential to be able to do so in the foreseeable future.

And the NRA is far more than the leading protector of the Second Amendment. A sampling of other programs include:

- Firearms education, training about a million gun owners each year.
- Child gun safety programs, with the Eddie Eagle program reaching 28 million preschool through 4th grade kids since 1988.
- Law enforcement training, with 13,000 NRA-certified police firearms instructors nationwide.
- Leading promotor and sponsor of competitive shooting programs with 11,000 tournaments and 50 national championships annually.
- Hunter education and training and protection of hunting rights.

While working for the NRA, I was continually impressed by the dedication and commitment of NRA staffers—their ability and competence. They are working diligently despite the turmoil and attacks and are doing a great job.

Yeah, some dirty laundry has been aired in public. However, you can find as bad or worse carryings-on in both major political parties, many large religions and charitable organizations, and various government agencies and businesses. Work within the organization to fix the problems; if you disagree with the leadership, work to change it. However, don't throw the baby out with the bathwater.

The NRA has protected and served American gun owners for over 150 years. Today, it needs your support.

You're just not pulling your weight if you're a gun owner and not an NRA member. *membership.nra.org*

A

2A ARMAMENT
Boise, Idaho

2A Armament is a subsidiary of 2A Machine, a CNC, ISO 9001 and AS 9100 certified advanced-manufacturing machining shop for the aerospace, medical, prosthetic, motorsports, semiconductor and outdoor recreation markets. Established 2009.

BLR-16 GEN 2 Rifle

Calibers: 5.56 NATO/.223 Rem., 16-in. barrels. 2A Armament is a subsidiary of 2A Machine, a CNC, ISO 9001 and AS 9100 certified advanced-manufacturing machining shop for the aerospace, medical, prosthetic, motorsports, semiconductor and outdoor recreation markets. Established 2009. Based in Boise, Idaho. BLR-16 Gen 2 is company's lightest rifle at 5.0 lbs. No magazine included. BLR Gen 2 Carbon has Proof Research carbon-fiber barrel, Timney 2-stage trigger, MAGPUL CTR stock, and "2A-GRAY" Cerakote finish. Palouse-Lite Rifle has forged U/L receiver. Weight: 5.3 lbs.

NIB	Exc.	V.G.	Good	Fair	Poor
3590	3300	3100	2900	—	—

BLR-16 Kuiu Vias 2.0

NIB	Exc.	V.G.	Good	Fair	Poor
2570	2190	1860	1580	1340	—

BLR-16 GEN 2 Carbon Rifle

NIB	Exc.	V.G.	Good	Fair	Poor
3420	2900	2470	2000	1780	—

XLR-18 Rifle

Calibers: .308 Win. Barrels: 18 in. Xanthos Lite fully assembled rifle is Cerakoted in Cobalt Grey and weighs in at 6.75 lbs. Introduced 2020. Key features include Straight Cut Xanthos Lite rail, tension lock design for attachment with an M-LOK mounting solution. Titanium parts include gas block, takedown pins, and X4 brake. Lower receiver is CNC machined 7075-T6 billet with flared mag-well, type III class 2 anodized finish, rear tensioning screw, rear takedown spring retainer, and screw-in bolt catch pin. Upper receiver has retained port door rod, M4-style feed ramps, machined T numbers in Picatinny rail. Bolt and carrier (full mass) are 8620 machined body with QPQ process, 9310 machined bolt, cryogenically treated, MPT, QPQ process. Barrel is a lightweight contour .308 profile, 4150 gun barrel steel with QPQ Nitride, black oxide extension, rifle-length gas system, .308 Match chamber, 1 in 10 twist. Other features: .750 diameter titanium gas block; titanium .308 X4 brake; BCM MOD 0 grip, BCM SOPMOD stock; Timney 2-stage, flat trigger; through-drilled titanium takedown pins.

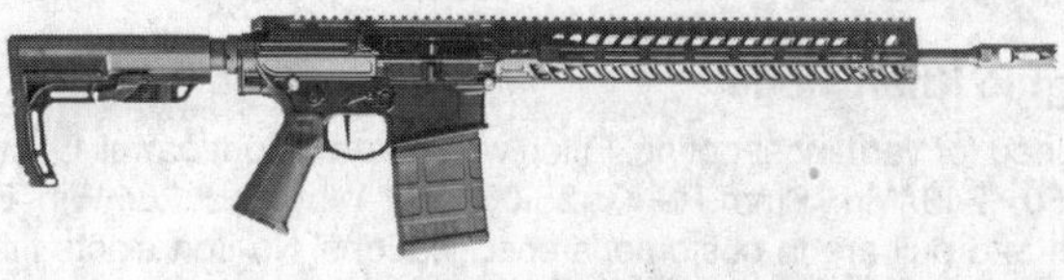

NIB	Exc.	V.G.	Good	Fair	Poor
2460	2260	1920	1630	1390	—

XLR-20 Rifle

Calibers: 6.5 Creedmoor. Barrels: 20 in. Similar configuration to XLR-18 rifles. Xanthos Lite XLR-20 weight, 6.85 lbs. Barrel is 2A contour lightweight profile, 4150 barrel steel with QPQ Nitride, black oxide extension, rifle-length gas system, 6.5mm Creedmoor SAAMI Chamber, 1:8 twist.

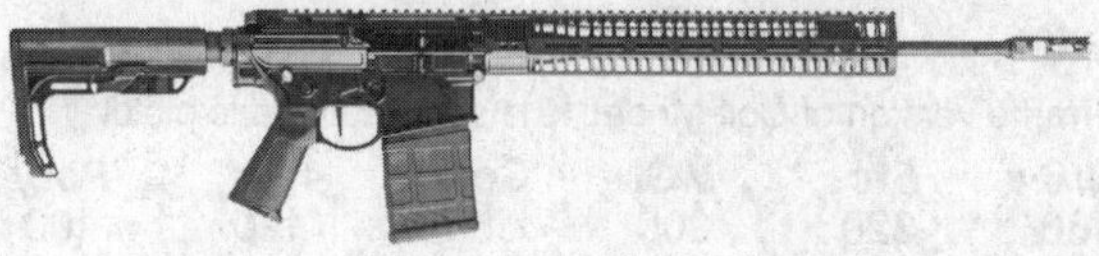

NIB	Exc.	V.G.	Good	Fair	Poor
2540	2140	1820	1550	1320	—

A. J. ORDNANCE

This company developed one of the first double-action only semi-automatic pistols, the Thomas .45. Limited production of less than 1,000 guns in 1977. Delayed blowback action that is unique, in every shot was double-action. Pistol was chambered for .45 ACP cartridge and had a 3.5" stainless steel barrel, with fixed sights and plastic grips. Detachable magazine held 6 shots. Standard finish was matte blue. Chrome plating was available and would add approximately 15 percent to values listed.

NIB	Exc.	V.G.	Good	Fair	Poor
1250	800	600	400	250	180

A-SQUARE

Previously located in Bedford, Kentucky and Chamberlain, South Dakota. Prices shown are for these models. Current models are custom made to order by Broadsword Group in Glenrock, Wyoming. Add slight premium for Kentucky-built rifles and .577 T-Rex caliber.

Hannibal Grade

Using P-17 Enfield action, with 22" to 26" barrel. Rifle chambered for 32 calibers from 7mm Rem. Magnum up to and including .500 A-Square Magnum and .577 Tyrannosaur. Blued, with checkered walnut pistol grip stock. Introduced in 1986. Weights range from 9 to 13.25 lbs., depending on caliber.

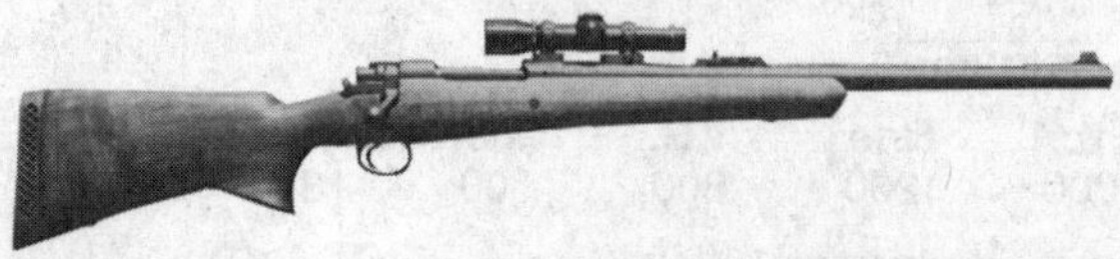

NIB	Exc.	V.G.	Good	Fair	Poor
3400	2900	2200	1500	600	350

Caesar Grade

Utilizing Remington Model 700 action. Chambered for same cartridges as above, with exception that A-Square proprietary cartridges are not available. Also made in left-hand version. Introduced in 1986. Weight 8.5 to 11 lb. range.

NIB	Exc.	V.G.	Good	Fair	Poor
3400	2900	2200	1500	600	350

Hamilcar Grade

Smaller and lighter version of Hannibal Grade. Designed to be chambered for .30-06 cartridges. Weight 8 to 8.5 lbs. Introduced in 1994.

NIB	Exc.	V.G.	Good	Fair	Poor
3400	2900	2200	1500	600	350

Genghis Khan Model

Designed for varmint shooting. Fitted with heavyweight barrel. Offered in .22-250, .243 Win., 6mm Rem., .25-06, .257 Wby. and .264 Win. Barrel length and pull are to customer's specifications. No iron sights fitted to this model. Weight about 11 lbs.

NIB	Exc.	V.G.	Good	Fair	Poor
3400	2900	2200	1500	600	350

A & R SALES SOUTH
El Monte, California

A&R Sales South also made frames for custom 1911 builds.

45 Auto

Alloy-frame version of Colt Model 1911 semi-automatic pistol.

NIB	Exc.	V.G.	Good	Fair	Poor
480	320	200	150	120	100

Mark IV Sporter

Semi-automatic copy of M-14 military rifle. Manufactured in .308-caliber (7.65mm NATO) only.

NIB	Exc.	V.G.	Good	Fair	Poor
950	650	500	380	200	100

ABADIE
Liege, Belgium

Made by L. Soleil et fils.

Abadie Model 1878 Antique

9.1mm double-action revolver, with 6-shot cylinder, octagonal barrel and integral ejector rod, some military usage.

Exc.	Fine	V.G.	Good	Fair	Poor
700	500	400	300	200	100

Abadie Model 1886 Antique

Similar to Model 1878, 9.1mm, standard-issue sidearm for Portugal.

Exc.	Fine	V.G.	Good	Fair	Poor
700	500	400	300	200	100

ABBEY, F.J. & CO.
Chicago, Illinois

Abbey Brothers produced a variety of percussion rifles and shotguns, which are all individual design. Prices listed represent what a plain F.J. Abbey & Company firearm might realize.

Rifle Antique

Exc.	Fine	V.G.	Good	Fair	Poor
2000	1200	800	500	300	200

Shotgun Antique

Exc.	Fine	V.G.	Good	Fair	Poor
2000	1250	910	580	150	100

ABBEY, GEORGE T.
Utica, New York, and Chicago, Illinois

George T. Abbey originally worked in Utica, New York from 1845 to 1852. He moved to Chicago in 1852 and was in business until 1874. He manufactured a wide variety of percussion and cartridge firearms primarily from imported actions and barrels. Values listed represent those of his most common products.

Single-Barrel Shotgun Antique

Exc.	Fine	V.G.	Good	Fair	Poor
1500	850	700	550	200	140

Side-by-Side Shotgun Antique

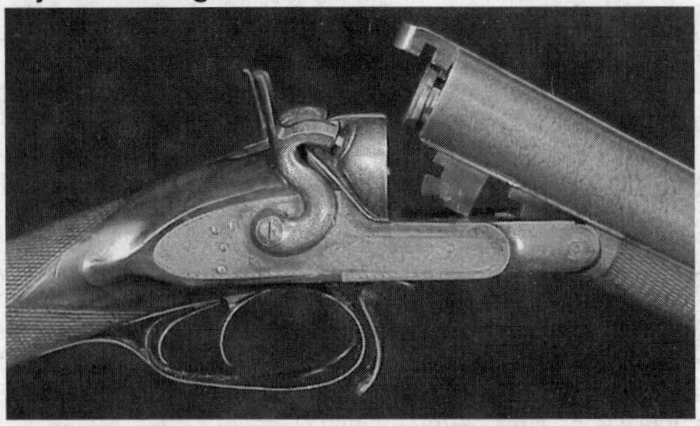

Exc.	Fine	V.G.	Good	Fair	Poor
2300	1200	940	680	250	170

Over/Under Shotgun Antique

Exc.	Fine	V.G.	Good	Fair	Poor
2500	1300	1140	980	250	170

ABESSER & MERKEL
Suhl, Germany

Crown Grade

Single-barrel trap gun, with Greener cross bolt-action and two underbolt locks. Offered in 12-gauge, with barrel lengths from 28" to 34". Ventilated rib standard. Skip line checkering. Pistol- or straight-grip stock. Weight between 7 and 7.5 lbs. Engraved receiver with game scenes.

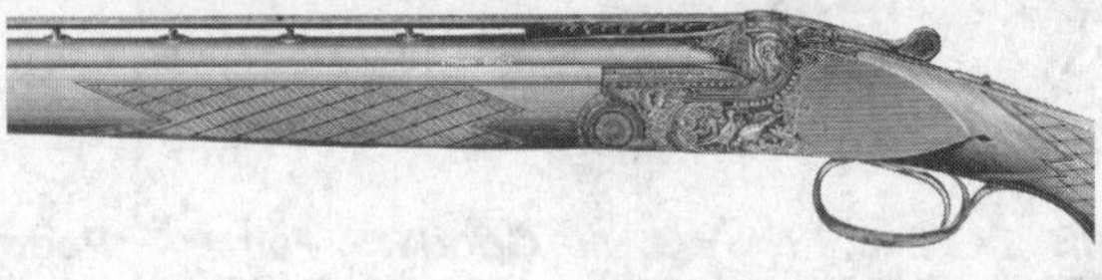

Courtesy Dan Sheil

NIB	Exc.	V.G.	Good	Fair	Poor
—	5750	4500	3500	900	—

Diamond Grade

Side-by-side shotgun offered in 12-, 16-, 20-, 28-gauge and .410 bore. Auto ejectors, double triggers and full coverage engraving. Artistic stock carving behind frame. Skip line checkering. Many extras offered on this grade will affect price. Barrel lengths from 25" to 32". Weight from 6.5 to 7 lbs. Prices are for standard gun with no extras. Note: Add 50 percent for 20-gauge; 100 percent for 28-gauge or .410 bore.

Courtesy Dan Sheil

NIB	Exc.	V.G.	Good	Fair	Poor
—	11000	8750	6000	2750	700

Empire Grade

Side-by-side shotgun, with Anson-Deeley action. Receiver is fully engraved, with game birds and fine scroll. Stock is carved behind action. Checkering is fine skip line-style. Auto ejectors. Pistol- or straight-grip stock, with or without Monte Carlo and cheekpiece. Prices listed are for pre-war guns, with fluid steel barrels. Note: Add 50 percent for 20-gauge; 100 percent for 28-gauge or .410 bore.

Courtesy Dan Sheil

NIB	Exc.	V.G.	Good	Fair	Poor
—	12750	10000	8500	2000	700

Excelsior Grade

Side-by-side shotgun fitted with engraved side plates. Anson-Deeley action with double triggers. Fine line checkering. Figured walnut stock. All gauges offered from 12- to 28-gauge and .410 bore. Barrel lengths from 25" to 32". Many extra cost options available. Note: Add 50 percent for 20-gauge; 100 percent for 28-gauge or .410 bore.

Courtesy Dan Sheil

NIB	Exc.	V.G.	Good	Fair	Poor
—	8750	7000	6000	2500	700

Diana Grade

Over/under combination gun, with Greener cross bolt-action. Safety located on side of pistol grip. Iron sights. Set trigger for rifle barrel. Wide variety of centerfire calibers offered, with barrel lengths from 26" to 30".

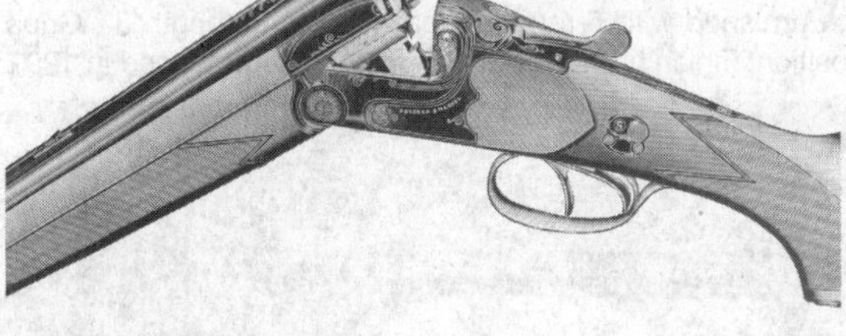

Courtesy Dan Sheil

NIB	Exc.	V.G.	Good	Fair	Poor
—	9000	7500	5500	3000	700

Vandalia Grade

Over/under gun chambered for 2.75" 12-gauge shells. Barrel lengths from 28" to 32". Walnut stock, with pistol- or straight-grip. Skip line checkering. Double triggers with extractors. Premium for factory multi-barrel combinations.

Courtesy Dan Sheil

NIB	Exc.	V.G.	Good	Fair	Poor
—	7000	5500	4250	3000	700

Nimrod

This is a drilling, with Greener cross bolt-action and double under bolt. Safety located on side of grip. Top two barrels may be 12-, 16- or 20-gauge. Bottom barrel offered in a variety of centerfire calibers. Iron sights. Pistol- or straight-grip stock. Receiver engraved with game scenes. Note: Add 50 percent for 20-gauge.

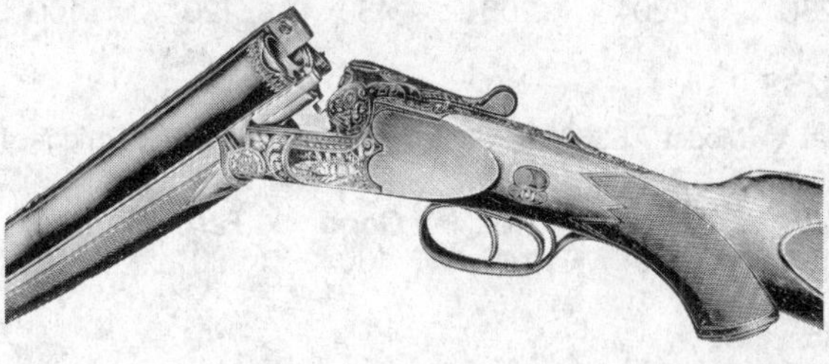

Courtesy Dan Sheil

NIB	Exc.	V.G.	Good	Fair	Poor
—	12000	9500	5750	4500	700

Magazine Rifle

Bolt-action rifle offered in a wide variety of calibers. Barrel lengths from 24" to 30". Calibers from 6.5mm to .404 Rimless. This model may have Zeiss scope or other special order features that will affect price. Note: Add $2000 for Magnum actions.

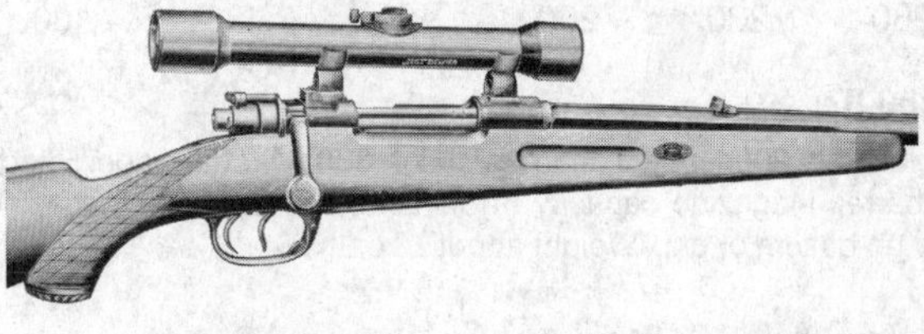

Courtesy Dan Sheil

NIB	Exc.	V.G.	Good	Fair	Poor
—	4750	4950	3000	1100	700

ACCU-MATCH
Mesa, Arizona

Accu-Match Custom Pistol

Competition pistol built on Colt 1911 design. Chambered for .45 ACP. Fitted with 5.5-in. match-grade stainless steel barrel, slide and frame, with extended slide release and safety. Fitted with beavertail grip safety and wrap-around finger groove rubber grips. Pistol has threaded three port compensator and dual-action recoil spring system, with three-dot sight system. Reportedly made only in 1995 and fewer than 200 produced.

NIB	Exc.	V.G.	Good	Fair	Poor
1050	800	630	450	380	330

ACCU-TEK
Chino, California

AT-380SS

Introduced in 1991. Semi-automatic pistol chambered for .380 ACP cartridge. Fitted with 2.75" barrel, with adjustable rear sight for windage. Black composition grips. Stainless steel construction. Furnished with 5-round magazine. Weight about 20 oz.

NIB	Exc.	V.G.	Good	Fair	Poor
250	220	200	150	120	100

AT-32SS

Similar to Model AT-380SS. Chambered for .32 ACP cartridge. Introduced in 1991.

NIB	Exc.	V.G.	Good	Fair	Poor
190	160	140	130	80	40

AT-25

Similar to AT-32SS and AT-380SS. Chambered for .25 ACP cartridge.

NIB	Exc.	V.G.	Good	Fair	Poor
150	130	120	100	70	60

AT-9/40/45SS Series

Double-action only compact stainless steel model in 9mm, .40 S&W or .45 ACP. Features 3-dot sights, 6- or 7-shot capacity, 3.2" barrel. Weight 28 oz.

NIB	Exc.	V.G.	Good	Fair	Poor
260	230	200	180	120	100

AT-380 II

Introduced in 2004. Pistol chambered for .380 ACP cartridge. Fitted with 2.8" barrel. Magazine capacity 6 rounds. Stainless steel. Magazine release on bottom of grip. Weight about 23 oz.

NIB	Exc.	V.G.	Good	Fair	Poor
260	220	190	180	120	100

CP-9SS

Semi-automatic double-action-only stainless steel pistol. Chambered for 9mm cartridge. Fitted with 3.2" barrel, with adjustable rear sight for windage. Magazine capacity 8 rounds. Grips black checkered nylon. Weight about 28 oz. Introduced in 1992.

NIB	Exc.	V.G.	Good	Fair	Poor
240	200	170	150	100	80

CP-45SS

Similar to Model CP-9SS. Chambered for .45 ACP cartridge. Furnished with 6-round magazine. Introduced in 1996.

NIB	Exc.	V.G.	Good	Fair	Poor
220	200	170	150	100	80

CP-40SS

Introduced in 1992. Similar to CP-9SS. Chambered for .40 S&W cartridge. Furnished with 7-round magazine.

NIB	Exc.	V.G.	Good	Fair	Poor
220	200	170	150	100	80

BL-9

Semi-automatic double-action-only pistol. Chambered for 9mm cartridge. Furnished with 5-round magazine. Barrel length 3". Grips black composition. Finish black. Weight about 22 oz. Introduced in 1997.

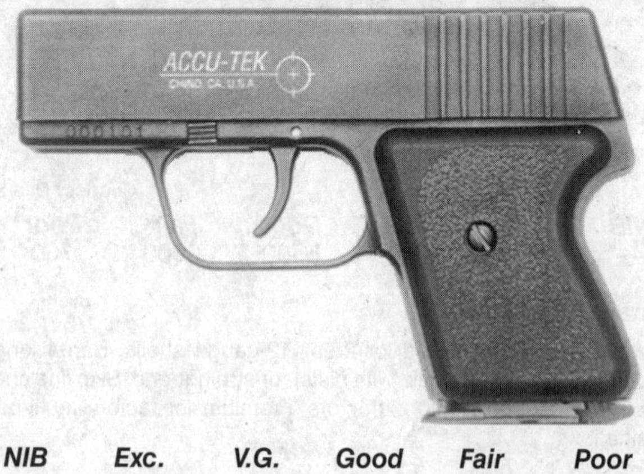

NIB	Exc.	V.G.	Good	Fair	Poor
240	200	150	140	90	70

BL-380

Similar to Model BL-9. Chambered for .380 ACP cartridge. Introduced in 1997.

NIB	Exc.	V.G.	Good	Fair	Poor
170	150	130	120	80	60

HC-380SS

Semi-automatic pistol chambered for .380 ACP cartridge, with 2.75" barrel. Stainless steel finish. Furnished with 10-round magazine. Weight about 28 oz. Introduced in 1993.

NIB	Exc.	V.G.	Good	Fair	Poor
280	260	200	190	120	100

LT-380

Single-action semi-automatic pistol in .380 ACP, with 6-shot magazine and 2.8" barrel. Blued or two-tone stainless slide, with aluminum frame. Black, pink, purple or OD green grips. Introduced in 2012.

NIB	Exc.	V.G.	Good	Fair	Poor
280	260	200	180	120	100

ACCURACY INTERNATIONAL

Portsmouth, England

Manufacturer of a series of competition rifles as well as tactical rifles for law enforcement and the military. Many options and variations have been made from 1978 to the present.

Palmamaster

This bolt-action rifle was designed for competition shooting with a laminated stock in NRA Prone or UIT style. Chambered in .308 Winchester. Discontinued in 2002.

NIB	Exc.	V.G.	Good	Fair	Poor
2750	2400	2000	1500	1000	800

Cismmaster

Target rifle chambered in .22 BR, 6mm BR, .243 Winchester, 6.5x55, 7.5x55, .308 Winchester. Made from late 1990s until 2002.

NIB	Exc.	V.G.	Good	Fair	Poor
3200	2800	2200	1550	1300	900

AE

Competition rifle chambered in .243 Winchester, .260 Remington, 6.5 Creedmoor or .308 Winchester.

NIB	Exc.	V.G.	Good	Fair	Poor
3300	2850	2400	1700	1400	1000

AT

Tactical rifle chambered in .308 Winchester. Fixed stock with adjustable cheekpiece, buttpad spacers, pistol grip, 24" quick-change barrel. Introduced in 2014.

NIB	Exc.	V.G.	Good	Fair	Poor
3300	2850	2400	1700	1400	1000

AW

Tactical rifle chambered in .243 Winchester, .260 Remington, 6.5 Creedmoor, .308 Winchester, .300 Winchester Magnum, .338 Lapua. Features a green synthetic stock with thumbhole grip.

NIB	Exc.	V.G.	Good	Fair	Poor
5000	4400	3700	3000	2000	1200

AX

Designed primarily as a sniper rifle for law enforcement and the military. Chambered in .243, .260, 6.5 Creedmoor, .308, .300 Win. Magnum, .338 Lapua. Note: Add $1,000 for .300 Win. or .338 Lapua.

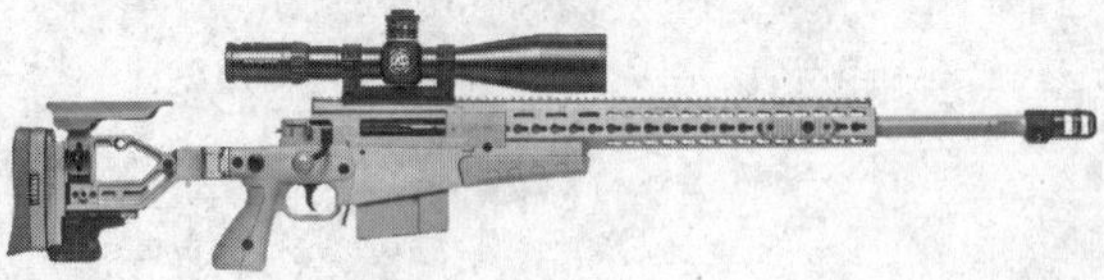

NIB	Exc.	V.G.	Good	Fair	Poor
6500	5700	4700	3500	2200	1400

AXMC

Multi-caliber variation of AX in .308, .300 Win. Magnum or .338 Lapua Magnum. Caliber can be changed in the field by switching barrel, bolt and magazine insert. Note: Add $1,000 for each additional caliber.

NIB	Exc.	V.G.	Good	Fair	Poor
7500	6750	6000	5000	—	—

AX50

The AX50 model is similar to the AX, but chambered in .50 BMG.

NIB	Exc.	V.G.	Good	Fair	Poor
9800	8500	7000	5000	3000	2000

ACHA

Domingo Acha
Vizcaya, Spain

Atlas

6.35mm semi-automatic pistol, manufactured during 1920s, in Model 1906 Browning style. Grips are plain checkered hard rubber. Some grips had ACHA trademark of Count's head. Name "Atlas" appears on slide. Later models incorporated a grip safety.

Courtesy James Rankin

NIB	*Exc.*	*V.G.*	*Good*	*Fair*	*Poor*
—	260	180	130	90	50

Looking Glass (Ruby-Style)

7.65mm semi-automatic pistol in Ruby-style. Pistols furnished with 7-, 9- or 12-round magazine.

Courtesy James Rankin

NIB	*Exc.*	*V.G.*	*Good*	*Fair*	*Poor*
—	350	200	150	100	50

Looking Glass

6.35mm or 7.65mm caliber semi-automatic pistol. Various markings seen on these pistols and their grips. They were sold in both France and Spain by different distributors. Pistol pictured has two trademarks: "Domingo Acha" on grips and "Fabrique D'Arms de Guerre De Grande Presision" on slide.

Courtesy James Rankin

NIB	*Exc.*	*V.G.*	*Good*	*Fair*	*Poor*
—	330	200	150	100	50

ACME

See—DAVENPORT ARMS CO., MALTBY HENLEY & CO., MERWIN & HULBERT & CO., DUMOULIN & CO., F., HOPKINS & ALLEN

ACME ARMS

New York, New York

A trade name found on .22-, .32-caliber revolvers and 12-gauge shotguns. Marketed by Cornwall Hardware Company.

.22 Revolver

7-shot single-action revolver.

NIB	*Exc.*	*V.G.*	*Good*	*Fair*	*Poor*
—	380	280	180	120	80

.32 Revolver

5-shot single-action revolver.

NIB	*Exc.*	*V.G.*	*Good*	*Fair*	*Poor*
—	400	300	200	150	100

Shotgun

12-gauge double-barrel shotgun, with external hammers.

NIB	*Exc.*	*V.G.*	*Good*	*Fair*	*Poor*
—	400	280	180	120	80

ACME HAMMERLESS

Made by Hopkins & Allen
Norwich, Connecticut

Acme Hammerless

.32- or .38-caliber, 5-shot revolver. Exposed or enclosed hammer. Sometimes known as "Forehand 1891".

NIB	*Exc.*	*V.G.*	*Good*	*Fair*	*Poor*
—	300	220	180	50	20

ACTION ARMS LTD.

Philadelphia, Pennsylvania

AT-84, AT-88

Pistol is Swiss version of CZ-75. Built at ITM, Solothurn, Switzerland. AT-84 chambered for 9mm cartridge; AT-88 for .41 Action Express. Both have 4.75" barrel. 9mm has magazine capacity of 15 rounds; .41 AE has 10 rounds. Finish blue or chrome. Walnut grips.

Courtesy James Rankin

NIB	Exc.	V.G.	Good	Fair	Poor
650	500	450	380	300	150

AT-84P, AT-88P

As above, with 3.7" barrel and smaller frame.

NIB	Exc.	V.G.	Good	Fair	Poor
650	500	450	380	300	150

AT-84H, AT-88H

As above, with 3.4" barrel and smaller frame.

NIB	Exc.	V.G.	Good	Fair	Poor
650	500	450	380	300	150

Timber Wolf Carbine

Introduced in 1989. Slide-action carbine features 18.5" barrel. Adjustable rear sight and blade front sight. Chambered for .357 Magnum or .44 Magnum cartridges. Offered in blue or hard chrome finish. Weight about 5.5 lbs. Built in Israel by Israel Military Industries. Note: Add 20 percent for .44 Magnum.

NIB	Exc.	V.G.	Good	Fair	Poor
750	580	400	300	200	130

Action Arms/IMI Uzi Carbine Models A and B

See Israel Weapon Industries / Israel Military Industries.

ADAMS ARMS
Brooksville, Florida

Adams Arms' proprietary gas-piston operating systems mechanically actuate the bolt carrier external of the receiver.

PZ Rifle

11.5- and 16-in. barrels in 5.56; 16 in. .308 Win.

NIB	Exc.	V.G.	Good	Fair	Poor
770	650	550	470	—	—

P-SERIES RIFLES

Proprietary gas-piston operating systems mechanically actuate the bolt carrier external to the receiver. The P1 model features ergonomic mid-length handguards, a standard Picatinny adjustable block piston system, tactical stock and grip with QD mounts, and an enhanced triggerguard. Barrel lengths and chamberings: 16 in. (5.56). The P2 model includes an ergonomic free-float rail, and the P-Series Micro Block piston system. P2 barrel lengths and chamberings: 16" (5.56); 16" (.300 BLK). P3 line features Proof Research carbon-fiber-wrapped barrel, jet comp, ergonomic free-float rail, and P-Series Micro Block piston system. SEE POLITICAL PANIC PRICING.

P1 Rifle

Adams Arms' proprietary gas-piston operating systems mechanically actuate the bolt carrier external of the receiver. P1 model features ergonomic mid-length handguards, standard Picatinny adjustable block piston system, tactical stock and grip with QD mounts, enhanced triggerguard. Barrel lengths and chamberings: 16 in. (5.56). P2 model includes ergonomic free float rail, P-Series Micro Block piston system. P2 barrel lengths and chamberings: 16 in. (5.56); 16 in. (300 BLK). P3 line features Proof Research carbon-fiber-wrapped barrel, jet comp, ergonomic free float rail, and P-Series Micro Block piston system. Other features include CMC Flat Bow trigger, a rubber ergonomic grip, adjustable stock with cheek riser. P3 barrel lengths and chamberings: 16 in. (.223 Wylde), 20 in. (.224 Valkyrie).

NIB	Exc.	V.G.	Good	Fair	Poor
710	680	600	500	—	—

P2 Rifle

Ergonomic free float rail. 7.5, 11.5, and 16-in. barrels in 5.56; 8 and 16 in. in .300 BLK; 12.5 and 16 in. in .308., and 18 in. in 6.5 Creedmoor.

NIB	Exc.	V.G.	Good	Fair	Poor
1240	1200	1140	970	—	—

P3 Rifle

Proof Research carbon-fiber-wrapped barrel, jet comp, free float rail. 16-in. barrel in .223 Wylde, 12.5 in. in .300 BLK, 20 in. in .224 Valkyrie, 17 in. in .308., and 24 in. in 6.5 Creedmoor.

NIB	Exc.	V.G.	Good	Fair	Poor
2550	2450	2370	2100	—	—

PCC Model

9mm. Free-float rail, flip-up sights, PCC flash hider.

NIB	Exc.	V.G.	Good	Fair	Poor
1400	1200	1010	860	—	—

ADAMY GEBRUDER

Suhl, Germany

Over/Under Shotgun

12- or 16-gauge double-barrel over/under shotgun, with 26" to 30" barrels. Double triggers. Walnut stock. Cape guns, custom guns and drillings may bring substantially more.

NIB	Exc.	V.G.	Good	Fair	Poor
—	2100	1700	1250	750	400

ADCO ARMS

This company imported several shotguns from Turkey about 2001 to 2012 under the Diamond brand. It currently imports parts for AR-style and other tactical firearms.

Diamond Double Over/Under

Available in 12- or 20-gauge, with 26" or 28" barrels, choke tubes, checkered walnut stock, selective trigger and automatic ejectors. Imperial grade has a higher-grade wood.

Field Grade

NIB	Exc.	V.G.	Good	Fair	Poor
400	350	300	250	200	150

Imperial Grade

NIB	Exc.	V.G.	Good	Fair	Poor
600	500	380	300	250	200

Double Side-by-Side

NIB	Exc.	V.G.	Good	Fair	Poor
700	600	480	400	350	250

Imperial Semi-Automatic

NIB	Exc.	V.G.	Good	Fair	Poor
400	350	300	220	180	120

Imperial Pump

NIB	Exc.	V.G.	Good	Fair	Poor
380	320	280	200	150	100

ADCOR DEFENSE

Baltimore, Maryland

Elite Rifles

Caliber: 5.56 NATO/.223 Rem. ADCOR's rifles use a ringless, gas-driven piston built into the top of the forward rail system. Adjustable cyclic rate, no carrier tilt, and a free-floating barrel. Forward ambi charging handle is non-reciprocating. Barrel lengths: 10.5, 14.5, 16 in. for 5.56. Rifle-length gas-system barrel lengths of 18 and 20 in. 1:7 twist chrome-lined barrels. Weight: 7 lbs.

NIB	Exc.	V.G.	Good	Fair	Poor
2200	—	—	—	—	—

ADIRONDACK ARMS CO. / A.S. BABBITT CO.

Plattsburgh, New York 1870-1874
Sold to Winchester in 1874

Orvil M. Robinson Patent Rifle

Robinson tube-fed repeating rifle was made in New York, between 1870 and 1874. Early models 1870-1872 marked "A.S. Babbitt"; later models 1872-1874 "Adirondack Arms Co.". Company was sold to Winchester in 1874, but they never produced Robinson after that date. Rifle has been found in two styles: first with small fingers on hammer to cock and operate mechanism; second with buttons on receiver to retract bolt and cock hammer. Rifle made in .44-caliber, with octagonal barrel usually found in 26" or 28" length. Frames predominantly brass. Some iron frames have been noted and will bring a premium of approximately 25 percent. Barrel and magazine tube have blued finish. Fewer than 600 made.

Courtesy Buffalo Bill Historical Center, Cody, Wyoming

First Model Antique

Exc.	Fine	V.G.	Good	Fair	Poor
6000	3000	2250	1500	800	560

Second Model Antique

Exc.	Fine	V.G.	Good	Fair	Poor
6000	3000	2250	1500	800	560

ADLER

Engelbrecht & Wolff
Blasii, Germany

Extremely rare and unusually designed semi-automatic pistol. Adapted for 7.25mm Adler cartridge. Striker-fired blowback pistol, with 3.4" barrel. Single-column magazine has 8-round capacity. Weight about 24 oz. Produced in a very limited number. Probably only a few hundred between 1906 and 1907. Value is speculative due to rarity. Few known sales.

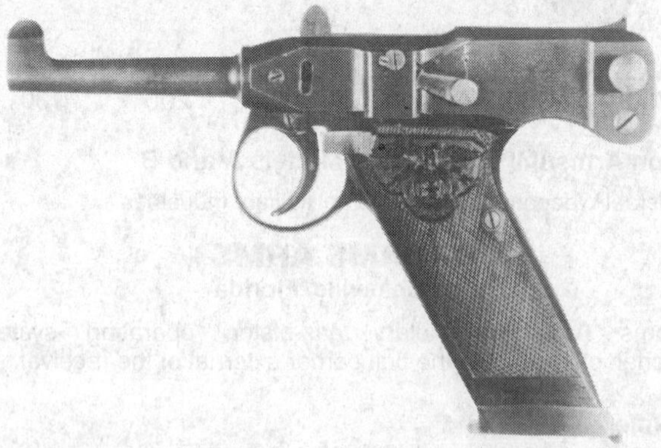

NIB	Exc.	V.G.	Good	Fair	Poor
—	10000	7000	5000	2500	1250

ADVANCED SMALL ARMS INDUSTRIES

Solothurn, Switzerland

One Pro .45

Introduced in 1997. Built in Switzerland by ASAI. Pistol features 3-in. barrel chambered for .45 ACP cartridge. Based on short-recoil operation. Available in double-action or double-action-only. Also available is a kit (purchased separately) to convert pistol to .400 CorBon caliber. Pistol weight about 24 oz. empty.

NIB	Exc.	V.G.	Good	Fair	Poor
1000	600	490	420	310	280

ADVANTAGE ARMS U.S.A., INC.

Distributed by Wildfire Sports
St. Paul, Minnesota

Model 422

.22- or .22-caliber Magnum four-barrel derringer, with 2.5" barrels. Entirely made of aluminum alloy. Finished in blue or nickel-plate. Manufactured in 1986 and 1987.

NIB	Exc.	V.G.	Good	Fair	Poor
400	280	200	150	110	50

AERO

Guernica, Spain

Model 1914 (Aero)

7.65mm caliber semi-automatic pistol, with 3.25" barrel in Ruby design. "Aero" name on slide along with an airplane. Magazine capacity 7 rounds. Weight about 23 oz.

Courtesy James Rankin

NIB	Exc.	V.G.	Good	Fair	Poor
—	350	200	150	100	50

AERO PRECISION

Tacoma, Washington

Aero Precision Inc. specializes in manufacturing aerospace parts, firearms components, mil-spec parts, and it supplies OEM products for other firearms makers. Aero Precision offers scope mounts, lower receivers, upper receivers and firearms. aeroprecisionusa.com

AC-15 Rifles

Caliber: 5.56 NATO/.223 Rem., .223 Wylde, .300 Blackout. Barrel lengths: 16 and 18 in. in 5.56 and .223 Wylde chambers and 16 in. in 300 BLK. 6.3 lbs.

NIB	Exc.	V.G.	Good	Fair	Poor
1000	850	720	610	520	440

AR15 M4E1 Rifles

Chambering: .223 Wylde for .223 Rem. or 5.56 NATO. Built on Enhanced Series Upper Receiver, which has an integrated upper receiver and handguard system that's free-floated. Barrel: 16" .223 Wylde, mid-length, 1:8" twist, 416 stainless steel, bead blasted. Handguard: Gen 2 Enhanced Series. Gas System: Low profile gas block and mid-length gas tube. Bolt Carrier Group: M16 Cut, 8620 steel, phosphate finish, staked. Muzzle Device: Standard A2 flash hider. Stock: Magpul STR. Grip: Magpul MOE. Magazine: Magpul 30-round PMAG. Weight: approx. 7 pounds. SEE POLITICAL PANIC PRICING.

NIB	Exc.	V.G.	Good	Fair	Poor
990	900	800	700	—	—

AETNA ARMS CO.

New York

.22-caliber spur trigger revolver, with octagonal barrel and 7-shot cylinder. Barrel marked "Aetna Arms Co. New York". Manufactured approximately 1870 to 1880. Copy of S&W No. 1.

Antique

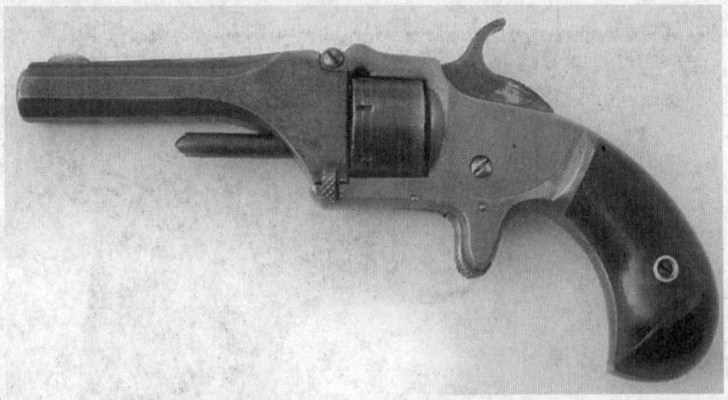

Exc.	Fine	V.G.	Good	Fair	Poor
550	380	260	150	100	70

AFFERBACH, W. A.
Philadelphia, Pennsylvania

Maker known to have produced copies of Henry Deringer percussion pocket pistols. Though uncommon, their values would be approximately as listed.

Antique

Exc.	Fine	V.G.	Good	Fair	Poor
2750	1800	1350	900	300	210

AGNER (SAXHOJ PRODUCTS, INC.)
Copenhagen, Denmark

Model M 80

.22-caliber single-shot stainless steel target pistol, with 5.9" barrel, adjustable sights and walnut grips. Pistol fitted with dry fire mechanism. The safety is a removeable key. Also available in left-hand version. Imported from 1981 to 1986.

Courtesy James Rankin

NIB	Exc.	V.G.	Good	Fair	Poor
—	1250	880	600	450	200

AGUIRRE
Eibar, Spain

Spanish manufacturer of pistols prior to World War II.

Basculant

6.35mm semi-automatic pistol. Marked on slide "Cal. 6.35 Automatic Pistol Basculant".

NIB	Exc.	V.G.	Good	Fair	Poor
—	230	180	130	90	50

LeDragon

As above, with slide marked "Cal. 6.35 Automatic Pistol LeDragon". Patterned after Browning Model 1906. Stylized dragon molded into grips.

Courtesy James Rankin

NIB	Exc.	V.G.	Good	Fair	Poor
—	230	180	130	90	50

AGUIRRE Y ARANZABAL (AyA)
Eibar, Spain

SIDE-BY-SIDES

Matador

12-, 16-, 20-, 28-gauge or .410 bore boxlock double-barrel shotgun, with 26", 28" or 30" barrels. Single-selective trigger and automatic ejectors. Blued, with walnut stock. Manufactured from 1955 to 1963. Note: Add 100 percent for 28-gauge; 200 percent for .410 bore.

NIB	Exc.	V.G.	Good	Fair	Poor
—	550	420	350	300	200

Matador II

As above in 12- or 20-gauge, with ventilated rib.

NIB	Exc.	V.G.	Good	Fair	Poor
—	580	420	380	300	200

Matador III

As above, with 3" chambers. Note: Add 20 percent for 20-gauge.

NIB	Exc.	V.G.	Good	Fair	Poor
800	700	600	400	320	200

Bolero

As above, with non-selective single trigger and extractors. Manufactured until 1984.

NIB	Exc.	V.G.	Good	Fair	Poor
—	500	380	320	300	200

Iberia

12- or 20-gauge Magnum boxlock double-barrel shotgun, with 26", 28" or 30" barrels. Double triggers and extractors. Blued, with walnut stock.

NIB	Exc.	V.G.	Good	Fair	Poor
—	600	450	400	320	200

Iberia II

Similar to above in 12- or 16-gauge, with 28" barrels and 2.75" chambers.

NIB	Exc.	V.G.	Good	Fair	Poor
—	620	500	420	320	250

Model 106

12-, 16- or 20-gauge boxlock double-barrel shotgun, with 28" barrels. Double triggers and extractors. Blued, with walnut stock. Manufactured until 1985.

NIB	Exc.	V.G.	Good	Fair	Poor
—	600	500	400	300	250

Model 107-LI

As above, with receiver lightly engraved and English-style stock. In 12- or 16-gauge only.

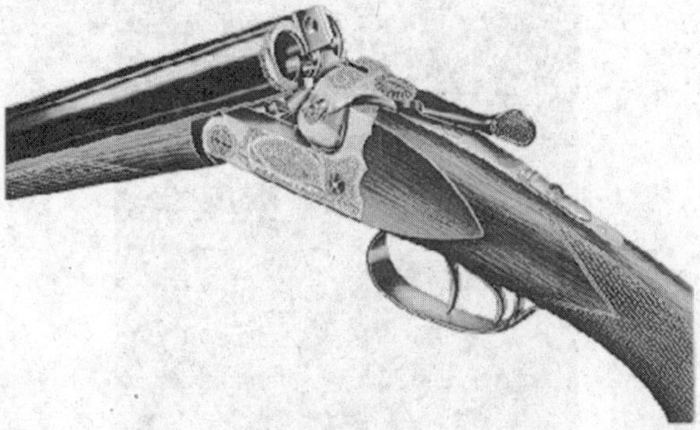

NIB	Exc.	V.G.	Good	Fair	Poor
—	680	580	500	320	280

Model 116

12-, 16- or 20-gauge sidelock double-barrel shotgun, with 27" to 30" barrels. Double triggers and ejectors. Engraved, blued, with walnut stock. Manufactured until 1985.

NIB	Exc.	V.G.	Good	Fair	Poor
—	1100	980	800	500	350

Model 117

As above, with 3" chambers.

NIB	Exc.	V.G.	Good	Fair	Poor
—	1150	1000	850	600	400

Model 117 "Quail Unlimited"

As above in 12-gauge only, with 26" barrels. Receiver engraved "Quail Unlimited of North America". Forty-two were manufactured.

NIB	Exc.	V.G.	Good	Fair	Poor
—	1500	1200	880	650	420

Model 210

Exposed hammer 12- or 16-gauge boxlock shotgun, with 26" to 28" barrels. Double triggers. Blued, with walnut stock. Manufactured until 1985.

NIB	Exc.	V.G.	Good	Fair	Poor
—	800	680	550	400	320

Model 711 Boxlock

12-gauge boxlock double-barrel shotgun, with 28" or 30" barrels. Ventilated ribs. Single-selective trigger and automatic ejectors. Manufactured until 1984.

NIB	Exc.	V.G.	Good	Fair	Poor
—	900	800	700	500	350

Model 711 Sidelock

As above, with sidelocks. Manufactured in 1985 only.

NIB	Exc.	V.G.	Good	Fair	Poor
—	1200	1000	750	500	400

Senior

Custom order 12-gauge double-barrel sidelock shotgun. Gold inlaid and engraved. Made strictly to individual customer's specifications.

NIB	Exc.	V.G.	Good	Fair	Poor
17000	13750	9750	7000	4500	2250

OVER/UNDERS

Model 79 "A"

12-gauge boxlock over/under double-barrel shotgun, with 26", 28" or 30" barrels. Single-selective trigger and automatic ejectors. Blued, with walnut stock. Manufactured until 1985.

NIB	Exc.	V.G.	Good	Fair	Poor
—	1250	1050	920	750	500

Model 79 "B"

As above, with moderate amount of engraving.

NIB	Exc.	V.G.	Good	Fair	Poor
—	1350	1150	950	800	580

Model 79 "C"

As above, with extensive engraving.

NIB	Exc.	V.G.	Good	Fair	Poor
—	2000	1800	1500	1150	680

Model 77

As above, patterned after Merkel shotgun.

NIB	Exc.	V.G.	Good	Fair	Poor
—	3000	2700	2000	1500	1000

Coral "A"

12- or 16-gauge over/under boxlock double-barrel shotgun, with 26" or 28" barrels. Ventilated ribs, double triggers and automatic ejectors. Fitted with Kersten cross bolt. Manufactured until 1985.

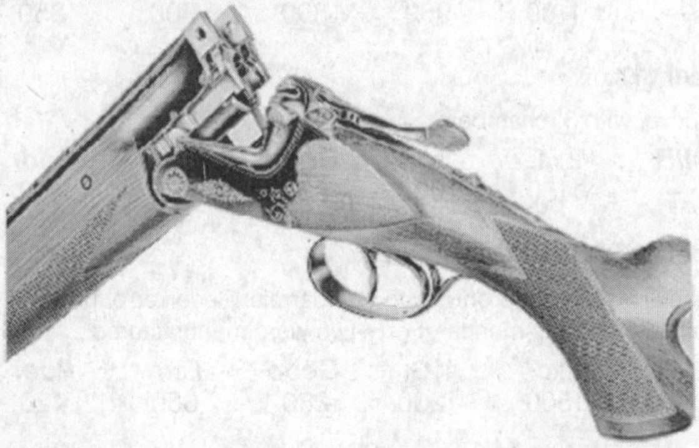

NIB	Exc.	V.G.	Good	Fair	Poor
—	1250	900	700	500	300

Coral "B"

As above, with engraved French case-hardened receiver.

NIB	Exc.	V.G.	Good	Fair	Poor
—	1400	1100	750	600	350

AyA sidelock shotguns use Holland & Holland system. Features double triggers, articulated front trigger, cocking indicators, bushed firing pins, replaceable firing pins, replaceable hinge pins and chopper lump barrels. Frame and sidelocks case colored. Weight between 5 and 7 lbs., depending on gauge and barrel length. Barrel lengths offered in 26", 27", 28" and 29" depending on gauge. All stocks are figured walnut, with hand checkering and oil finish. Available with several extra cost options that may affect price. Also influencing price of new guns is fluctuating dollar in relation to Spanish currency.

RECENTLY IMPORTED SHOTGUNS

SIDELOCK SIDE-BY-SIDES

Model No. 1

Offered in 12-, 16-, 20-, 28-gauge or .410 bore, with special English scroll engraving. Fitted with automatic ejectors and straight-grip stock. Exhibition quality wood.

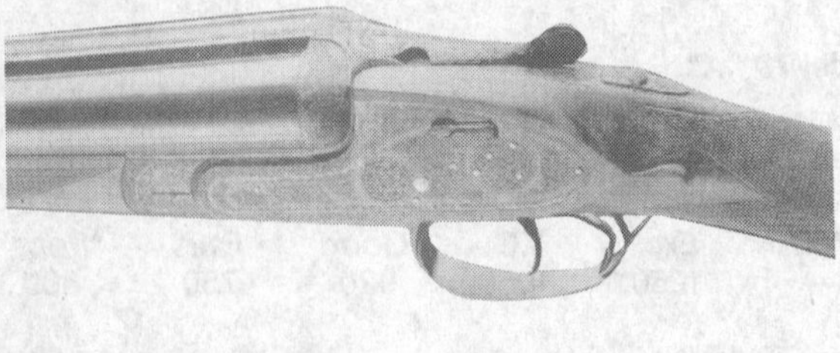

NIB	Exc.	V.G.	Good	Fair	Poor
11000	10000	8000	4750	2300	700

Model No. 1 Round Body

As above, with round body action.

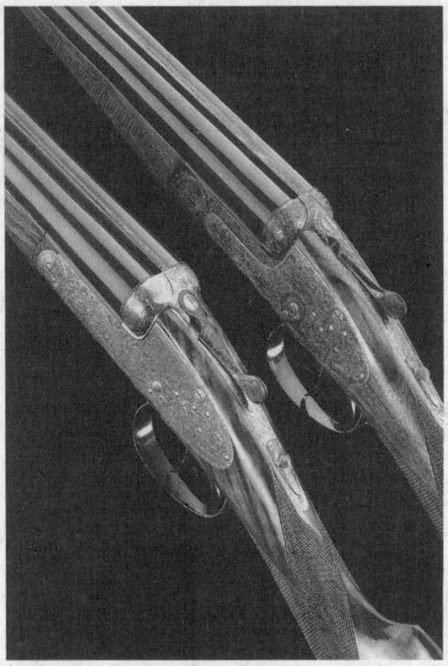

NIB	Exc.	V.G.	Good	Fair	Poor
12000	11000	9000	5250	—	—

Model No. 1 Deluxe

Deluxe version of No. 1, with finer wood and engraving. Note: Add $350 for round body.

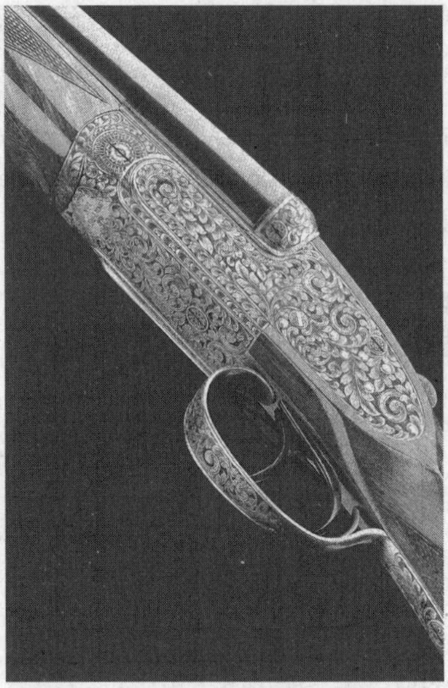

NIB	Exc.	V.G.	Good	Fair	Poor
15000	12500	9000	5250	2400	700

Model No. 2

Offered in 12-, 16-, 20-, 28-gauge and .410 bore. Has automatic ejectors, straight-grip and select walnut stock.

NIB	Exc.	V.G.	Good	Fair	Poor
—	5000	4000	2500	1850	700

Model No. 2 Round Body

As above, with round body action.

NIB	Exc.	V.G.	Good	Fair	Poor
—	5200	4250	2750	1950	700

Model No. 53

Chambered for 12-, 16- and 20-gauge. Features three locking lugs, side clips, automatic ejectors and straight-grip stock.

NIB	Exc.	V.G.	Good	Fair	Poor
7500	6000	4000	2750	1000	700

Model No. 56

Available in 12-gauge only. Features three locking lugs, side clips, special wide action body and raised matted rib. Select walnut straight-grip stock.

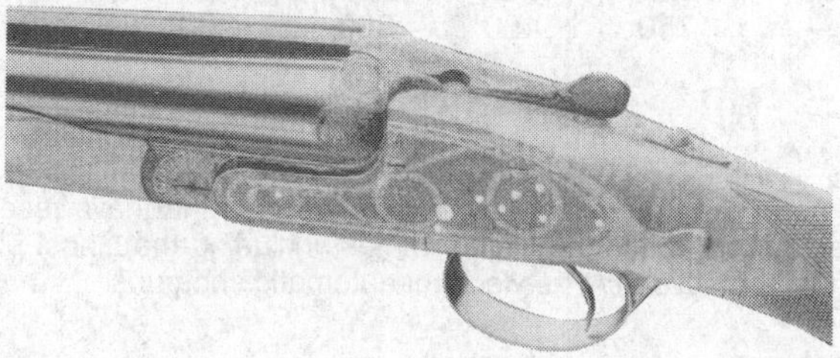

NIB	Exc.	V.G.	Good	Fair	Poor
12500	9250	7250	5400	2000	1000

Model XXV Sidelock

Offered in all gauges. Fitted with Churchill-type rib. Automatic ejectors, select straight-grip and walnut stock standard.

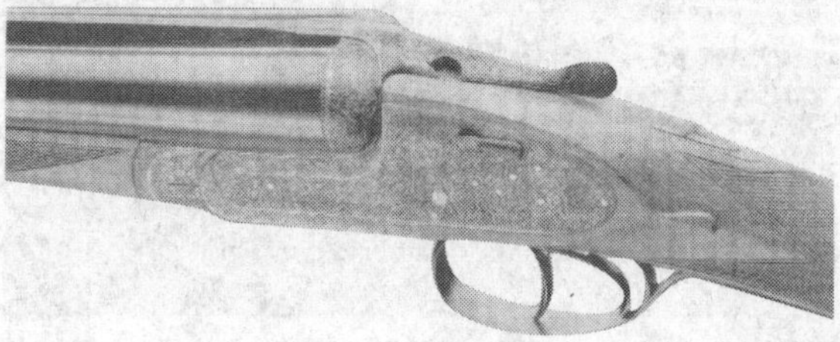

NIB	Exc.	V.G.	Good	Fair	Poor
5900	5250	4250	3200	1750	1000

These AyA guns utilize Anson & Deeley system. Double locking lugs, detachable cross pin and separate trigger plate that gives access to firing mechanism. Frame case colored. Barrels are chopper lump. Firing pins bushed. Automatic safety and ejectors standard. Barrels offered in 26", 27" and 28", depending on gauge. Weight between 5 and 7 lbs., depending on gauge.

BOXLOCK SIDE-BY-SIDES

Adarra

Offered in all major gauges, with the option of double non-selective or selective single triggers. Grade 2 walnut stock has a hand rubbed oil finish, cut checkering, straight-grip and a splinter forend. Receiver has a bold foliate engraving pattern, with choice of color case-hardened old silver or white finish. Introduced in 2013.

NIB	Exc.	V.G.	Good	Fair	Poor
4250	3800	3000	2450	1500	500

Model XXV Boxlock

Available in 12- and 20-gauge only. Hand-checkered select walnut stock, with straight-grip stock.

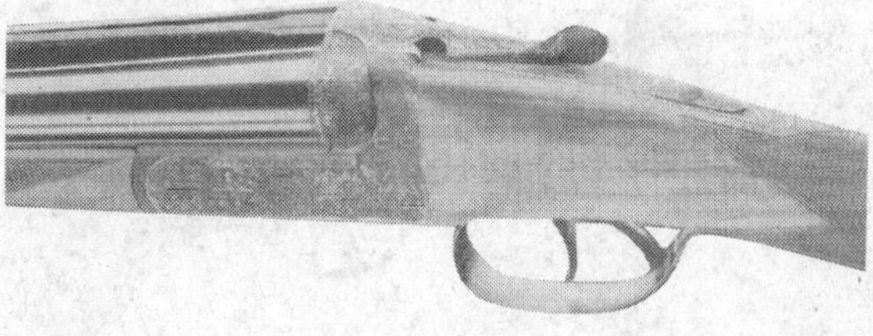

NIB	Exc.	V.G.	Good	Fair	Poor
—	3500	2250	800	600	350

Model No. 4

Available in 12-, 16-, 20-, 28-gauge and .410 bore. Hand-checkered select walnut stock, with straight-grip. Light scroll engraving. Note: Add 75 percent for 28-gauge and .410 bore.

NIB	Exc.	V.G.	Good	Fair	Poor
—	3000	2650	1250	—	—

Model No. 4 Deluxe

Same as above, with select walnut stock and slightly more engraving coverage. Note: Add 75 percent for 28-gauge and .410 bore.

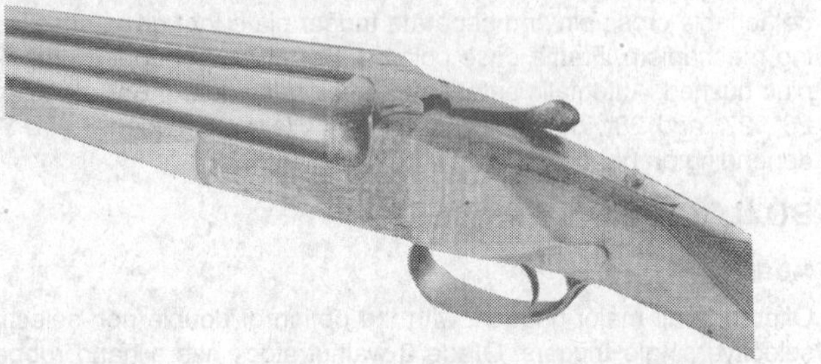

NIB	Exc.	V.G.	Good	Fair	Poor
—	5000	4000	1500	1000	550

These AyA shotguns are similar in design and appearance to Gebruder Merkel over/under sidelocks, with three-part forend, Kersten cross bolt and double under locking lugs.

OVER/UNDERS

Model No. 37 Super

Available in 12-, 16- or 20-gauge. Ventilated rib, automatic ejectors, internally gold-plated sidelocks. Offered with three different types of engraving patterns; ducks, scroll or deep cut engraving. Very few of this model imported into U.S.

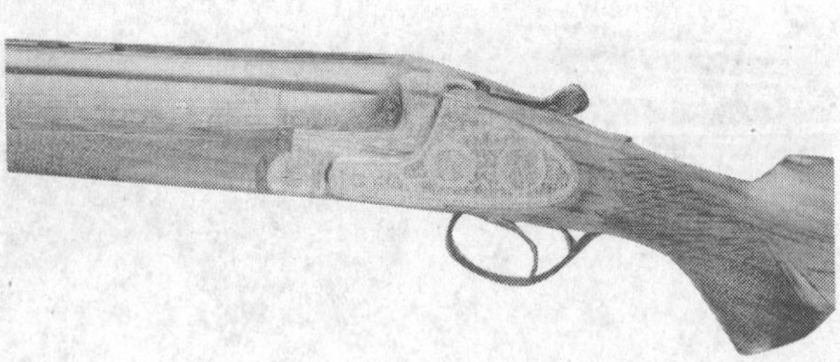

NIB	Exc.	V.G.	Good	Fair	Poor
—	12000	9500	5000	3500	2000

Model Augusta

Top-of-the-line AyA model offered in 12-gauge only. Features presentation wood and deep cut scroll engraving. Very few imported into U.S.

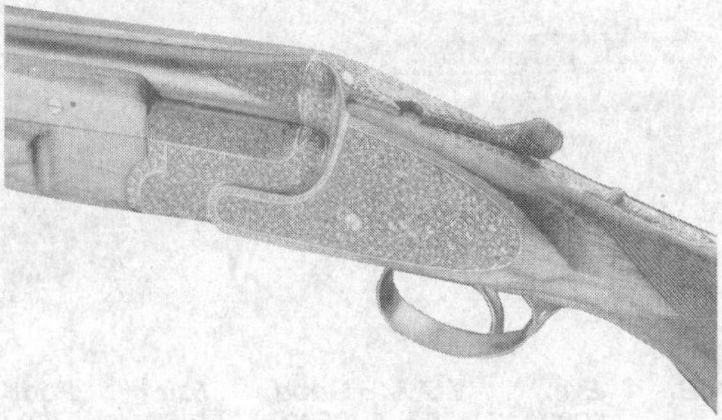

NIB	Exc.	V.G.	Good	Fair	Poor
—	18000	8000	4500	3500	1500

AIR MATCH
Paris, Kentucky

Air Match 500

.22-caliber single-shot target pistol, with 10.5" barrel. Adjustable sights and front-mounted counterweights. Blued, with walnut grips. Imported from 1984 to 1986.

NIB	Exc.	V.G.	Good	Fair	Poor
780	600	420	300	250	120

AJAX ARMY

Brand name use by Iver Johnson & Meachem.

Single-Action

Spur-trigger single-action solid-frame revolver. Chambered for .44 rimfire cartridge. Had 7" barrel. Blued, with walnut grips. Manufactured in 1880s.

NIB	Exc.	V.G.	Good	Fair	Poor
—	750	450	360	280	200

AKDAL
Istanbul, Turkey

This company manufactures several firearms that have recently been imported into the United States, including the Ghost pistol series and several AR-style semi-automatic shotguns.

Ghost

A 9mm striker-fired polymer-frame pistol, with features similar to the Glock. Has a 15-round magazine and interchangeable grip backstraps of different sizes. 1990-present.

NIB	Exc.	V.G.	Good	Fair	Poor
400	320	280	200	150	100

MKA 1919

A 12-gauge shotgun built on an AR-15 type frame. Features include a detachable 5-round magazine and three interchangeable choke tubes. Used by Turkish land forces. Introduced 2007.

NIB	Exc.	V.G.	Good	Fair	Poor
600	500	350	290	230	150

ALAMO RANGER
Spain

Double-action Spanish copy of Colt SAA. Chambered for .38 Long Colt or .38 Special. Cylinder held 6 shots. Finish blued and grips checkered hard rubber. Maker of this pistol unknown.

NIB	Exc.	V.G.	Good	Fair	Poor
—	350	220	120	80	40

ALASKA
Norwich, Connecticut

See—HOOD FIREARMS CO.

ALASKA MAGNUM
Fairbanks, Alaska

Manufacturer of high-grade AR-style rifles designed for hunting large game. Features include stainless steel barrels, nickel plated bolt carrier groups, free float handguards, synthetic or laminate stocks. Chamberings include .300 Ruger, .338 Ruger, .450 Bushmaster and proprietary calibers 6.9AR Short, .375 GrizzinatAR and .460 GrizzinatAR.

Kodiak or Grizzly Model

NIB	Exc.	V.G.	Good	Fair	Poor
3400	2850	2000	1700	—	—

Wolverine Model

NIB	Exc.	V.G.	Good	Fair	Poor
2500	2000	1600	1200	—	—

ALCHEMY CUSTOM WEAPONRY
Genesco, Illinois

Manufacturer of custom 1911 pistols since 2011. Extensive list of custom options available.

Anomaly

1911 style. Steel frame. 4.25-in. barrel. Chambered in 9mm, .38 Super or .45 ACP. 8-shot magazine. Blued or hard chrome finish. Checkered wood or G10 grips. Introduced 2018.

NIB	Exc.	V.G.	Good	Fair	Poor
3000	2560	2210	1410	1160	910

Brimstone

1911 style. CCO sized frame. 4.25-in. barrel. Chambered in 9mm or .45 ACP. 7-shot magazine. Blued or hard chrome finish. Checkered wood grips. Introduced 2018.

NIB	Exc.	V.G.	Good	Fair	Poor
2800	2410	2110	1610	1060	900

Classic Carry

1911 style. Commander sized frame. 4.25-in. barrel. Ring hammer. Chambered in 9mm, .38 Super or .45 ACP. 8-shot magazine. Blued or hard chrome finish. Checkered wood grips. Introduced 2019.

NIB	Exc.	V.G.	Good	Fair	Poor
2600	2210	1660	1210	1010	760

Prime

1911 style. Full sized frame. 5-in. barrel. Skeletonized hammer. Chambered in 9mm, .38 Super or .45 ACP. 8-shot magazine. Blued or hard chrome finish. Checkered wood grips. Introduced 2018.

NIB	Exc.	V.G.	Good	Fair	Poor
2600	2210	1660	1210	1010	760

Prime Elite

1911 style. Full sized frame. 5-in. barrel. Skeletonized hammer. Chambered in 9mm, .38 Super or .45 ACP. 8-shot magazine. Hand polished blued or brushed hard chrome finish. Checkered wood grips. Introduced 2019.

NIB	Exc.	V.G.	Good	Fair	Poor
3000	2560	1910	1410	1160	910

ALDAZABAL
Eibar, Spain

See—ALDAZABAL, LETURIONDO & CIA

Model 1919 (Reims, or Model 1914)

Vest pocket semi-automatic pistol. Copied from FN Browning Model 1906. Caliber 6.35mm.

Courtesy James Rankin

NIB	Exc.	V.G.	Good	Fair	Poor
—	230	180	130	90	50

Modelo 1919

Ruby-style 7.65mm semi-automatic pistol, with 9-round magazine capacity. Trademark of knight's head over three As is on side of slide and grips. Very similar to M1916 made by both Jose Aldazabal and Aldabazal Leturiondo y Cia for French and Allied military use. Military markings such as "AL" bring a slight premium.

Courtesy James Rankin

NIB	Exc.	V.G.	Good	Fair	Poor
—	330	180	150	100	50

Military Model

Semi-automatic pistol in Ruby-style. Caliber 7.65mm, with 9-round magazine.

Courtesy James Rankin

NIB	Exc.	V.G.	Good	Fair	Poor
—	350	200	150	100	50

Aldazabal

Another typical low-quality Ruby-type semi-automatic. Browning blowback copy. Chambered for 7.65mm cartridge. Had 7-shot detachable magazine, blued finish, with checkered wood grips. Company ceased production before Spanish Civil War.

NIB	Exc.	V.G.	Good	Fair	Poor
—	300	160	120	60	40

ALERT
Norwich, Connecticut

See—HOOD FIREARMS CO.

ALEXANDER ARMS
Radford, Virginia

This manufacturer of AR-style rifles and carbines is probably best known for developing the .50 Beowulf and 6.5 Grendel cartridges. In addition to those chamberings, rifles have been made in 5.56 NATO, .300 AAC, .338 Lapua Magnum and .17 HMR in most standard AR models and variations. Barrels are 16", 18", 20" or 24". Models are available for consumer, law enforcement and military markets. Depending on the specific model, features include forged flattop receiver with Picatinny rail, button-rifled stainless steel barrels, composite free-floating handguard, A2 flash hider, M4 collapsible stock, gas piston operating system. Listed below is a sampling of the company's many recent and current models.

AR SERIES

Calibers: .17 HMR, 5.56 NATO, 6.5 Grendel, .300 AAC, .50 Beowulf. Produces a range of AR-15-type rifles and carbines. Barrels: 16", 18", 20" or 24". Depending on the model, features include a forged flattop receiver with Picatinny rail, button-rifled stainless-steel barrels, composite free-floating handguard, A2 flash hider, M4 collapsible stock, and gas-piston operating system. SEE POLITICAL PANIC PRICING.

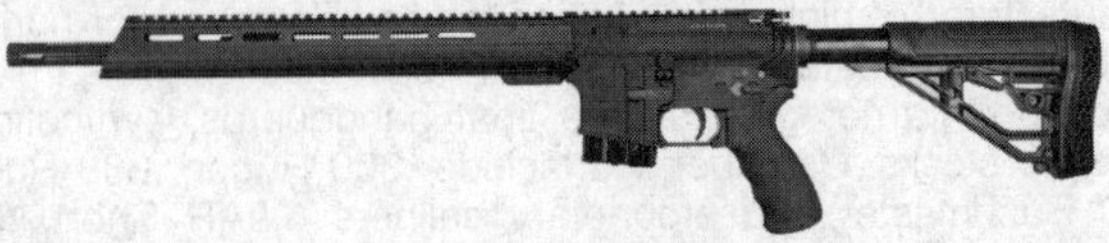

NIB	Exc.	V.G.	Good	Fair	Poor
1530	—	—	—	—	—

R-BEOPREC .50 Beowulf Precision Rifle

NIB	Exc.	V.G.	Good	Fair	Poor
1400	1200	1000	—	—	—

R-BEOENTRY .50 Beowulf Entry

NIB	Exc.	V.G.	Good	Fair	Poor
1200	1000	850	—	—	—

R-50 .50 Beowulf Hunter

NIB	Exc.	V.G.	Good	Fair	Poor
1500	1250	1000	—	—	—

R-65 HUNT 6.5 Grendel

NIB	Exc.	V.G.	Good	Fair	Poor
1600	1350	1100	—	—	—

R-GSR 6.5 Grendel Sniper Rifle

NIB	Exc.	V.G.	Good	Fair	Poor
3000	2400	2000	—	—	—

R-338 Ulfbehrt .338 Lapua

Caliber: .338 Lapua Mag. Custom-designed adjustable gas-piston operating system. Barrel: 27.5" chrome moly with three-prong flash hider. Stock: Magpul PRS. Length: 41.25" (folded), 50" (extended stock). Weight: 19.8 lbs.

NIB	Exc.	V.G.	Good	Fair	Poor
7030	4200	3200	—	—	—

R-556 5.56 NATO Incursion

NIB	Exc.	V.G.	Good	Fair	Poor
1100	950	800	—	—	—

R-300 16ST .300 AAC

NIB	Exc.	V.G.	Good	Fair	Poor
1100	950	800	—	—	—

R-17 .17 HMR

NIB	Exc.	V.G.	Good	Fair	Poor
1370	1100	950	—	—	—

Highlander Pistol

AR-15 pistol platform. Calibers offered include .17 HMR, 6.5 Grendel, .300 AAC, and .50 Beowulf. Barrels are 11.5" to 12" depending on caliber; threaded. Manticore Arms 9" Transformer handguard. Standard trigger. SB Tactical SBA3 brace and Ergo Grip. Direct Impingement Operating System except for .17 HMR (blowback system). Various Cerakote finishes. 10-rnd. magazine.

NIB	Exc.	V.G.	Good	Fair	Poor
1740	1600	1470	—	—	—

ALPHA PROJ

SEE CZECHPOINT, INC.

ALEX PRO FIREARMS

Alexandria, Minnesota

Alex Pro Firearms (APF) was established in May 2013. Firearms come in several lines, including Carbines, DMR Rifles, Varmint, Target, Hunter, and MLR (Magnum Long Rifle). Specializes in making nickel-boron bolt-carrier group and hunting-caliber AR-style rifles in both AR-15 and AR-10 sizes. Carbine chamberings: 5.56 NATO/.223 Rem., 223 Wylde, 300 Blackout, .308 Win., 9mm Luger, 450 Bushmaster. DMR chamberings: 22 Nosler, 6mm ARC, .223 Wylde, 6.5 Grendel. Varmint chamberings: .204 Ruger, 22 Nosler, .22-250 Rem., 223 Wylde, .243 Win. Target chamberings: .204 Ruger, 223 Wylde, .22-250 Rem., .243 Win., 6.5 CM, .308 Win. Hunter chamberings: 6.5 CM, 6.8 SPC, .308 Win., 450 Bushmaster. MLR chamberings: 26 Nosler, 28 Nosler, 30 Nosler, 33 Nosler, 7mm Rem. Mag, .300 Win. Mag.

AR-15 RIFLE SERIES

Calibers: .204 Ruger, 22 Nosler, 5.56 NATO/, 6mm ARC, 6.5 Grendel, 6.8 SPC, .300 BLK, .350 Legend, .450 Bushmaster, 9mm Luger. Specializes in making nickel-boron bolt-carrier groups and hunting-caliber AR-style rifles in both AR-15 and AR-10 sizes. Established 2013. SEE POLITICAL PANIC PRICING.

Carbine Slim Tactical 5.56

NIB	Exc.	V.G.	Good	Fair	Poor
730	—	—	—	—	—

AR-15 Alpha .300 BLK

NIB	Exc.	V.G.	Good	Fair	Poor
850	—	—	—	—	—

Carbine Sidecharging 9mm

NIB	Exc.	V.G.	Good	Fair	Poor
690	—	—	—	—	—

DMR 6ARC Carbon-Fiber Proof Research Barrel

NIB	Exc.	V.G.	Good	Fair	Poor
1750	—	—	—	—	—

AR-10 RIFLE SERIES

Calibers: .22-250 Rem., .243 Win. 6mm CM, 6.5 CM, .308 Win. SEE POLITICAL PANIC PRICING.

AR-10 Target

NIB	Exc.	V.G.	Good	Fair	Poor
1690	—	—	—	—	—

MLR RIFLE SERIES

Calibers: 28 Nosler, 7mm Rem. Mag., .300 PRC, .300 Win. Mag. SEE POLITICAL PANIC PRICING.

MLR .300 Win. Mag. SST

NIB	Exc.	V.G.	Good	Fair	Poor
2550	—	—	—	—	—

ALFA

Eibar, Spain

See—ARMERO ESPECIALISTAS REUNIDES

Alfa

"Alfa" was a trademark given a number of revolvers based upon both Colt and Smith & Wesson designs. In calibers ranging from .22- to .44-calibers. Note: Add 50 percent for S&W N-frame copies.

NIB	Exc.	V.G.	Good	Fair	Poor
—	250	200	100	80	50

Omega

Semi-automatic 6.35 or 7.65mm pistol marked "Omega" on slide and grips.

NIB	Exc.	V.G.	Good	Fair	Poor
—	220	180	100	80	50

ALKARTASUNA FABRICA DE ARMAS

Guernica, Spain

Company began production during World War I, to help Gabilondo y Urresti supply sidearms to the French. After hostilities ceased, they continued to produce firearms under their own name. They produced a number of variations in both 6.35mm and 7.65mm marked "Alkar". Collector interest is very thin. Factory burned down in 1920 and by 1922 business had totally ceased.

Alkar

6.35mm semi-automatic pistol, with cartridge counter in grip plates. One variation of many. Built in 6.35mm or 7.65mm.

Courtesy James Rankin

NIB	Exc.	V.G.	Good	Fair	Poor
—	230	180	130	90	50

Alkar (Ruby-Style)

7.65mm semi-automatic pistol built in Ruby-style. Pistol supplied to French government during World War I.

Courtesy James Rankin

NIB	Exc.	V.G.	Good	Fair	Poor
—	350	200	150	100	50

ALL RIGHT FIREARMS CO.

Lawrence, Massachusetts

Little All Right Palm Pistol Antique

Squeezer-type pocket pistol, invented by E. Boardman and A. Peavy in 1876. Made in .22-caliber. Had 5-shot cylinder, with 1.625" or 2.375" barrel. Barrel octagonal, with tube on top which houses sliding trigger. Finish nickel. Black hard rubber grips have "Little All Right" & "All Right Firearms Co., Manufacturers Lawrence, Mass. U.S.A." molded into them. Several hundred produced in late 1870s.

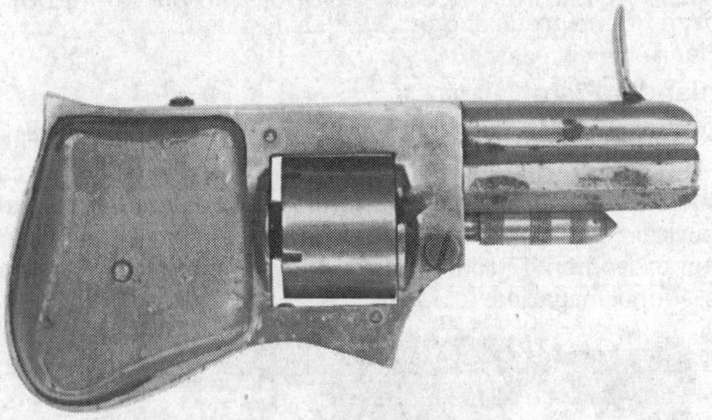

Courtesy Milwaukee Public Museum, Milwaukee, Wisconsin

Exc.	Fine	V.G.	Good	Fair	Poor
3250	2950	2000	1050	500	350

ALLEN, ETHAN

Grafton, Massachusetts

Founded by Ethan Allen in early 1800s. It became a prolific gun-making firm that evolved from Ethan Allen to Allen & Thurber (A&T), as well as Allen & Wheelock Company (A&W). It was located in Norwich, Connecticut and Worchester, Massachusetts, as well as Grafton. Eventually it became the Forehand & Wadsworth Company in 1871, after the death of Ethan Allen. There were many and varied firearms produced under all headings described above. If one desires to collect Ethan Allen firearms, it would be advisable to educate oneself, as there are a number of fine publications available on the subject. Basic models and their values are listed.

Allen First Model Pocket Rifle Antique

Manufactured by Ethan Allen in Grafton, Massachusetts. Percussion single-shot pistol with saw-handle grip, chambered for .31 percussion. Larger caliber versions have also been noted. Barrel lengths from 5" to 9" that were part-octagon in configuration. Iron mountings. Blued, with walnut grips. Barrel marked, "E. Allen/ Grafton/Mass." as well as "Pocket Rifle/Cast Steel/Warranted". Approximately 2,000 manufactured from 1831 to 1842.

Exc.	Fine	V.G.	Good	Fair	Poor
2500	1650	1200	750	200	140

Allen Second Model Pocket Rifle Antique

Rounded frame big-type grip version of First Model.

Exc.	Fine	V.G.	Good	Fair	Poor
—	1550	1100	650	200	140

Allen & Thurber Bar Hammer Pistol Antique

Double-action pistol, with top-mounted bar hammer. Chambered for .28- to .36-caliber percussion. Half-octagon barrels from 2" to 10" in length. They screwed out of the frame so it was possible to breech load them. Finish blued. Rounded walnut grips. They were marked, "Allen & Thurber/Grafton Mass.". Approximately 2,000 manufactured between early 1830s and 1860. Internal note - prices reduced

Exc.	Fine	V.G.	Good	Fair	Poor
1200	900	700	400	250	150

Allen & Thurber Tube Hammer Pistol Antique

Version similar to Bar Hammer. Curved hammer without spur. Few hundred manufactured between early 1830s and 1840s.

Exc.	Fine	V.G.	Good	Fair	Poor
—	2900	2100	1300	400	280

Allen & Thurber Sidehammer Pistol Antique

Single-shot target-type pistol. Chambered for .34-, .41- and .45-caliber percussion. Part-octagon barrel from 6" to 10" in length. Wooden ramrod mounted under barrel. Hood quality rear sight that was adjustable. Ornate triggerguard had a graceful spur at its rear. Finish blued. Rounded walnut grip. Barrel marked, "Allen & Thurber, Worchester". Approximately 300 manufactured in late 1840s and early 1850s.

Exc.	Fine	V.G.	Good	Fair	Poor
2500	1400	1020	650	200	140

Allen & Thurber Center Hammer Pistol (Antique)

Single-action chambered for .34-, .36- or .44-caliber percussion. Half-octagon barrel from 4" to 12" in length. Centrally mounted hammer that was offset to right side to allow for sighting the pistol. Finish blued, with walnut grips. Marked, "Allen & Thurber, Allen Thurber & Company". Some specimens marked, "Allen & Wheelock". Several thousand manufactured between late 1840s and 1860.

Exc.	Fine	V.G.	Good	Fair	Poor
2000	1200	750	450	200	150

Allen & Thurber Double-Barrel Single Trigger Pistol (Antique)

Side-by-side double-barrel pistol, with single trigger. Chambered for .36-caliber percussion, with 3" to 6" round barrels. Finish blued, with walnut grips. Examples with ramrod mounted under barrel have been noted. Flute between barrels was marked, "Allen & Thurber", "Allen Thurber & Company" or "Allen & Wheelock". Approximately 1,000 manufactured in 1850s.

Exc.	Fine	V.G.	Good	Fair	Poor
2000	1250	920	600	150	100

Allen & Wheelock Center Hammer Pistol (Antique)

Single-action pocket pistol, chambered for .31- to .38-caliber percussion. Octagon barrels from 3" to 6" in length. Finish blued. Square butt walnut grips. Barrel marked, "Allen & Wheelock". Approximately 500 manufactured between 1858 and 1865.

Exc.	Fine	V.G.	Good	Fair	Poor
1800	1100	820	550	100	70

Allen Thurber & Company Target Pistol (Antique)

Deluxe single-action target pistol. Chambered for .31- or .36-caliber percussion. Had heavy octagon barrel from 11" to 16" in length. Wooden ramrod mounted underneath barrel. Mountings were German silver. Detachable walnut stock. Deluxe engraved patchbox. Weapon was engraved and barrel marked, "Allen Thurber & Co./Worchester/Cast Steel". Firearm furnished in fitted case, with stock, false muzzle and various accessories. Considered to be a very high grade target pistol in its era. Very few manufactured in 1850s. Note: Values listed are for pistol only. Triple to quadruple value for complete cased set with detachable shoulder stock and accessories.

Exc.	Fine	V.G.	Good	Fair	Poor
3500	2500	1500	750	400	250

Allen Pepperboxes (Antique)

The pepperbox was the first widely successful repeating handgun. During the period from early 1830s to 1860s, company manufactured over 50 different variations of revolving pepperbox-type pistol. They were commercially quite successful and actually competed successfully with Colt revolving handguns for more than a decade. Widely used throughout United States, as well as Mexico and during our Civil War. They are widely collectible, because of the number of variations that exist. Potential collector should avail himself of information available on the subject.

Most Allen pepperboxes are double-action only, where a cluster of barrels rotates for a new shot each time the trigger is pulled. They will be found marked Allen, Thurber & Co.; Allen & Thurber; and Allen & Wheelock. The bar-hammer models usually have "Allen's Patent" marked on the hammer, and some of these will be found with distributor markings and no other Allen markings. There are many variations, all of which will effect value. Some include:

Location of manufacture, marked on barrel with company name:
- Grafton, Mass., 1830s-1842, worth premium
- Norwich, C-T, 1842-1847
- Worcester, Mass., 1847-1865

Trigger type:
- Traditional trigger and triggerguard
- Ring-trigger

Hammer system:
- Bar-hammer, double-action only
- Hammerless (concealed-hammer) double-action only
- There is one single-action model with a shotgun-style hammer

Size – Variations in caliber, number of shots, and barrel length are known:
- Dainty -.28 cal. 6-shot, Grafton only, 2.75" to 3" barrels, worth premium
- Small or Pocket - .25, .28, .31 or .34 cal.; four- five- or six-shots depending on caliber, 2.5" to 5" barrels
- Standard or Medium – usually .31 or .32 cal., five or six-shot, 3" to 5" barrels
- Dragoon - .36 cal. 6-shot, large frame, 5.5" to 6" barrels, worth premium
- With or without nipple shield

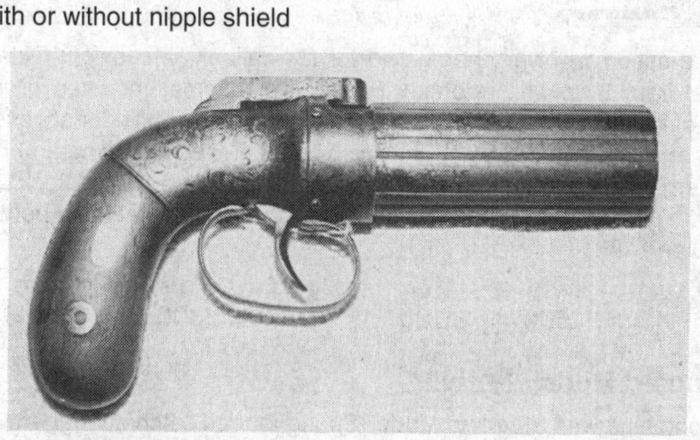

Small or Pocket Allen Pepperbox. Common variations: (Antique)

Exc.	Fine	V.G.	Good	Fair	Poor
1750	1300	850	500	300	175

Medium or Standard Allen Pepperbox. Common variations: (Antique)

Exc.	Fine	V.G.	Good	Fair	Poor
2000	1550	1100	700	500	350

Dragoon-Size Allen Pepperbox. Common variations: (Antique)

Exc.	Fine	V.G.	Good	Fair	Poor
5000	3000	2000	1250	750	500

Allen & Wheelock Large Frame Pocket Revolver (Antique)

Double-action pocket revolver chambered for .34-caliber percussion. Octagon barrel from 3" to 5" in length. No sights. The 5-shot unfluted cylinder was game scene engraved. Finish blued. Rounded walnut grips. Bar-type hammer. First conventional revolver manufactured by this company. Directly influenced by pepperbox pistol, for which Ethan Allen had become famous. Marked, "Allen & Wheelock" as well as "Patented April 16, 1845". Approximately 1,500 manufactured between 1857 and 1860.

Courtesy Milwaukee Public Museum, Milwaukee, Wisconsin

Exc.	Fine	V.G.	Good	Fair	Poor
2000	1250	900	600	150	100

Allen & Wheelock Small Frame Pocket Revolver Antique

Version similar to Large Frame Pocket Revolver, except chambered for .31-caliber percussion. Octagon barrel length "2 to 3.5". Slightly smaller in size, but finished and marked the same. Approximately 1,000 made between 1858 and 1860.

Exc.	Fine	V.G.	Good	Fair	Poor
—	1400	1050	700	350	240

Allen & Wheelock Sidehammer Belt RevolverEarly Production Antique

Single-action revolver chambered for .34-caliber percussion. Octagon barrel from 3" to 7.5" in length. Featured a hammer mounted on right side of frame and 5-shot engraved unfluted cylinder. Cylinder access pin is inserted from rear of weapon. Finish blued. Case colored hammer and triggerguard. Flared butt walnut grips. Marked, "Allen & Wheelock". Two basic types. Values for early model, of which 100 manufactured between 1858 and 1861.

Exc.	Fine	V.G.	Good	Fair	Poor
—	1500	1120	750	300	210

Standard Model Antique

Second type was Standard Model. Spring-loaded catch on triggerguard, as opposed to friction catch on early model. Approximately 1,000 manufactured between 1858 and 1861.

Exc.	Fine	V.G.	Good	Fair	Poor
—	1200	900	600	200	140

Allen & Wheelock Sidehammer Pocket Revolver Antique

Version chambered for .28-caliber percussion. Had 2" to 5" octagon barrel. Frame slightly smaller than belt model.

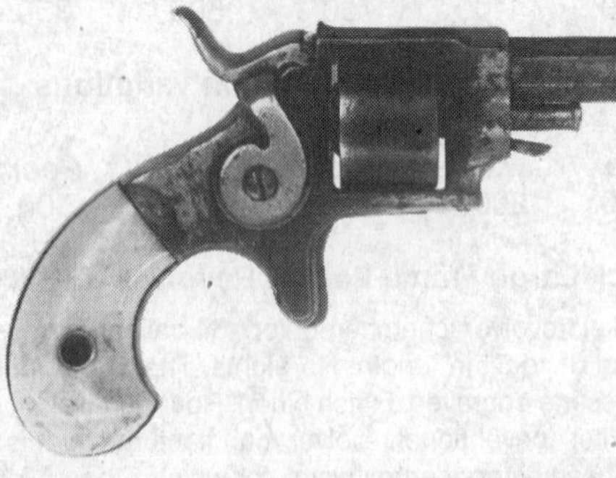

Courtesy Milwaukee Public Museum, Milwaukee, Wisconsin

Sidehammer Pocket RevolverEarly Production Antique

100 manufactured.

Exc.	Fine	V.G.	Good	Fair	Poor
—	1300	1010	720	250	170

Standard Production Antique

1,000 manufactured.

Exc.	Fine	V.G.	Good	Fair	Poor
2100	980	690	400	220	150

Allen & Wheelock Sidehammer Navy Revolver Antique

Large-frame military-type revolver. Similar to Side Hammer Belt Model. Chambered for .36-caliber percussion. Features octagon 5.5" to 8" barrel, with 6-shot engraved cylinder. Early production guns have friction style catch to secure triggerguard/loading lever on the left sideplate. Approximately 100 manufactured between 1858 and 1861.

Sidehammer Navy RevolverEarly Production Antique

Exc.	Fine	V.G.	Good	Fair	Poor
—	4300	3140	1980	580	400

Side Hammer Navy RevolverStandard Model Antique

Has a spring-loaded catch on rear of the triggerguard. 1,000 manufactured.

Exc.	Fine	V.G.	Good	Fair	Poor
5000	3700	2700	1700	480	330

Allen & Wheelock Center Hammer Army Revolver Antique

Large military-type single-action revolver chambered for .44-caliber percussion. Had 7.5" half-octagon barrel and 6-shot unfluted cylinder. Hammer mounted in center of frame. Finish blued. Case colored hammer and triggerguard. Walnut grips. Barrel marked, "Allen & Wheelock. Worchester, Mass. U.S./Allen's Pt's. Jan. 13, 1857. Dec. 15, 1857, Sept. 7, 1858". Approximately 700 manufactured between 1861 and 1862.

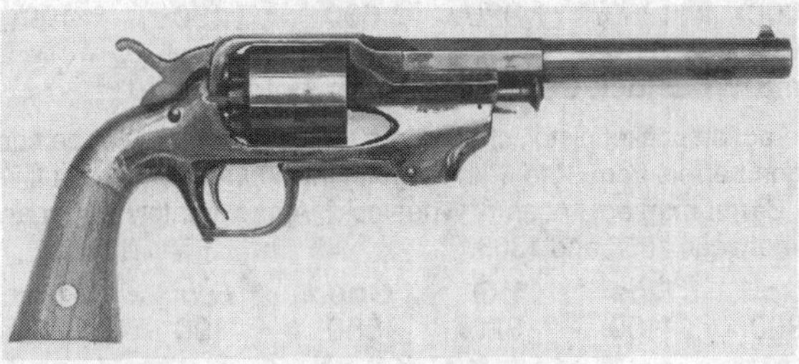

Exc.	Fine	V.G.	Good	Fair	Poor
6000	3500	2000	1600	1000	500

Center Hammer Navy Revolver Antique

Similar to Army Revolver. Chambered for .36-caliber percussion, with 7.5" full-octagon barrel. Examples have been noted with 5", 6" or 8" barrels. prices reduced

Exc.	Fine	V.G.	Good	Fair	Poor
4500	2800	1800	1000	600	350

Allen & Wheelock Center Hammer Percussion Revolver Antique

Single-action revolver chambered for .36-caliber percussion. Octagonal 3" or 4" barrel, with 6-shot unfluted cylinder. Finish blued, with walnut grips. Model supposedly was made for Providence, Rhode Island, Police Department and has become commonly referred to as "Providence Police Model". Approximately 700 manufactured between 1858 and 1862.

Exc.	Fine	V.G.	Good	Fair	Poor
2500	1750	1250	750	200	140

Allen & Wheelock Lipfire Army Revolver Antique

Large military-type single-action revolver. Chambered for .44 lipfire cartridge. Had 7.5" half-octagon barrel, with 6-shot unfluted cylinder that had notches at its rear for cartridge lips. Finish blued. Case colored hammer and triggerguard. Square butt walnut grips. Barrel marked, "Allen & Wheelock, Worchester, Mass." Resembled Center Hammer Percussion Army Revolver. Two basic variations. Total of 250 Lipfire Army Revolvers manufactured in early 1860s. Early model with top hinged loading gate, add 10% premium

Exc.	Fine	V.G.	Good	Fair	Poor
6000	3000	2000	1500	900	350

Allen & Wheelock Lipfire Navy Revolver Antique

Similar to Army model. Chambered for .36 lipfire cartridge, with octagonal 4", 5", 6", 7.5" or 8" barrel. Approximately 500 manufactured in 1860s.

Exc.	Fine	V.G.	Good	Fair	Poor
5000	3300	2300	1300	400	280

Allen & Wheelock Lipfire Pocket Revolver Antique

Smaller version chambered for .32 lipfire cartridge, with octagonal 4", 5" or 6" barrel. Approximately 200 manufactured in early 1860s.

Exc.	Fine	V.G.	Good	Fair	Poor
3500	2200	1570	950	250	170

Allen & Wheelock .32 Sidehammer Rimfire Revolver Antique

Single-action spur-trigger pocket revolver chambered for .32-caliber rimfire cartridge. Octagonal barrels from 3" to 5" in length. Finish blued. Flared-butt and walnut grips. Marked, "Allen & Wheelock Worchester, Mass.". Three variations, with a total of approximately 1,000 manufactured between 1859 and 1862.

.32 Sidehammer Rimfire RevolverFirst Model Antique

Rounded top strap.

Exc.	Fine	V.G.	Good	Fair	Poor
1120	800	620	450	150	100

Second Model Antique

Marked on frame July 3, 1860

Exc.	Fine	V.G.	Good	Fair	Poor
1100	800	610	420	150	100

Third Model Antique

Patent dates 1858 and 1861.

Exc.	Fine	V.G.	Good	Fair	Poor
1050	780	590	400	120	80

Allen & Wheelock .22 Sidehammer Rimfire Revolver Antique

Smaller version of .32 revolver chambered for .22 rimfire cartridge. Octagonal barrels from 2.25" to 4" in length. Has 7-shot unfluted cylinder. Many variations. Approximately 1,500 manufactured between 1858 and 1862.

.22 Sidehammer Rimfire RevolverEarly Model First Issue Antique

Access pin enters from rear.

Exc.	Fine	V.G.	Good	Fair	Poor
1300	850	660	480	100	70

Second Issue Antique

Access pin enters from front.

Exc.	Fine	V.G.	Good	Fair	Poor
1300	850	660	480	100	70

Third Issue Antique

Separate rear sight.

Exc.	Fine	V.G.	Good	Fair	Poor
1420	1250	920	600	150	100

Fourth to Eighth Issue Antique

Very similar, values the same.

Exc.	Fine	V.G.	Good	Fair	Poor
900	750	520	300	100	70

Allen & Wheelock/Ethan Allen Single-Shot Center Hammer Antique

Single-shot derringer-type pistol. Chambered for .22-caliber rimfire cartridge. Had part-octagon barrels from 2" to 5.5" in length that swung to right side for loading. Some had automatic ejectors, others did not. Frame brass or iron, with bird's-head or squared butt walnut grips. Marked, "Allen & Wheelock" or "E. Allen & Co.". Very few manufactured in early 1860s.

Single-Shot Center HammerEarly Issue Antique

Full-length octagon barrel. Round iron frame. Rarely encountered.

Exc.	Fine	V.G.	Good	Fair	Poor
1280	1150	770	400	100	70

Standard Issue Antique

Squared butt or bird's-head.

Exc.	Fine	V.G.	Good	Fair	Poor
1180	1050	670	300	100	70

Allen & Wheelock .32 Single-Shot Center Hammer Antique

Larger-frame pocket pistol chambered for .32 rimfire cartridge. Has part- or full-octagon barrel 4" or 5" in length. Swung to right side for loading. Otherwise similar to .22-caliber version.

Exc.	Fine	V.G.	Good	Fair	Poor
1180	1050	670	300	100	70

Ethan Allen Vest Pocket Derringer Antique

Small pocket pistol chambered for .22 rimfire cartridge. Had 2" part-octagon barrel that swung to right for loading. Cartridges were manually extracted. Featured brass frame. Blued or plated barrel and walnut bird's-head grips. Barrel marked, "Allen & Co. Makers". Extremely small firearm. Approximately 200 manufactured between 1869 and 1871.

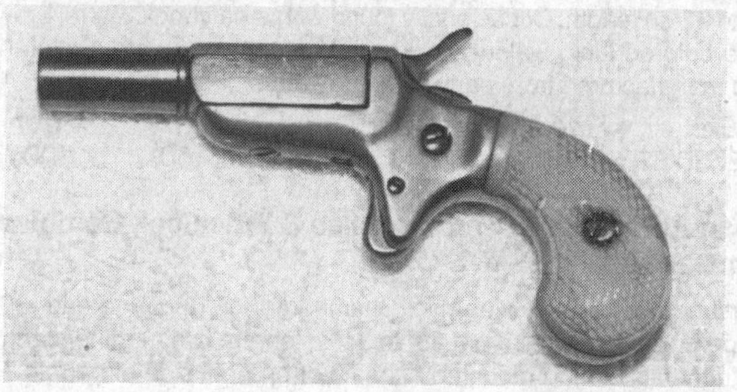

Exc.	Fine	V.G.	Good	Fair	Poor
1600	980	700	420	100	70

Ethan Allen .32 Derringer Antique

Similar to Vest Pocket version. Larger in size and chambered for .32 rimfire cartridge. Had part-octagon barrel from 2" to 4" in length that swung to right for loading. Version featured automatic extractor. Barrel marked, "E. Allen & Co. Worchester, Mass.". Very rare firearm. Made between 1865 and 1871.

Exc.	Fine	V.G.	Good	Fair	Poor
1500	880	640	400	100	70

Ethan Allen .41 Derringer Antique

Same size and configuration as .32-caliber model, except chambered for .41 rimfire cartridge. Barrel lengths of 2.5" to 2.75". Markings the same. Approximately 100 manufactured, between 1865 and 1871.

Exc.	Fine	V.G.	Good	Fair	Poor
2200	950	650	350	100	70

Allen & Wheelock Center Hammer Muzzleloading Rifle (Antique)

Single-shot rifle chambered for .44-caliber percussion. Had 36" round barrel, with octagonal breech. Center-mounted hammer offset to right for sighting. Iron mountings. Finish browned. Case colored lock. Ramrod mounted under barrel. Walnut buttstock, with crescent buttplate and no forearm. Approximately 100 manufactured in 1850s.

Exc.	Fine	V.G.	Good	Fair	Poor
1850	600	420	250	120	80

Allen & Thurber/Allen & Wheelock Sidehammer Muzzleloading Rifle (Antique)

Similar to Center Hammer model, with hammer mounted on right side of lock. Chambered for .38-caliber percussion, with octagon barrel from 28" to 32" in length. Occasionally found with a patchbox. Barrel browned. Case colored lock, walnut stock with crescent butt-plate. Several hundred manufactured from early 1840s to 1860s.

Exc.	Fine	V.G.	Good	Fair	Poor
2750	900	620	350	150	100

Ethan Allen/Allen & Thurber/Allen & Wheelock Combination Gun (Antique)

Over/under or side-by-side rifle. Chambered for 12-gauge and .38-caliber percussion. Barrels from 28" to 34" in length. Two hammers and double triggers. Ramrod mounted beneath or on right side of barrels. Finish browned, with walnut stock. Examples with patchbox have been noted. Production was very limited. Over/under versions worth approximately 20 percent more than side-by-side values given. Manufactured between 1840s and 1860s.

Exc.	Fine	V.G.	Good	Fair	Poor
6000	4350	3050	1750	600	420

Allen & Wheelock Sidehammer Breechloading Rifle (Antique)

Unique rifle chambered for .36- to .50-caliber percussion. Offered with various lengths and part-octagon barrels. Unusual breech mechanism that was activated by a rotating lever, which resembled a water faucet. Barrel browned. Case colored lock and walnut stock. Marked, "Allen & Wheelock/ Allen's Patent July 3, 1855". Approximately 500 manufactured between 1855 and 1860.

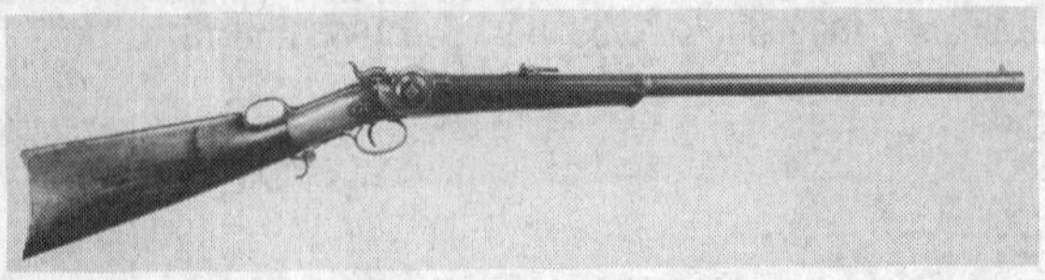

Courtesy Buffalo Bill Historical Center, Cody, Wyoming

Exc.	Fine	V.G.	Good	Fair	Poor
3550	1600	1050	500	350	240

Allen & Wheelock Drop Breech Rifle (Antique)

Single-shot rifle chambered for .22- through .44 rimfire cartridges. Part-octagon barrel from 23" to 28" in length. Breech activated by combination triggerguard action lever. Opening breech automatically ejected empty cartridge. External hammer manually cocked. Featured an adjustable sight. Barrel blued. Case colored frame and walnut stock. Marked, "Allen & Wheelock/ Allen's Pat. Sept. 18, 1860". Approximately 2,000 manufactured between 1860 and 1871.

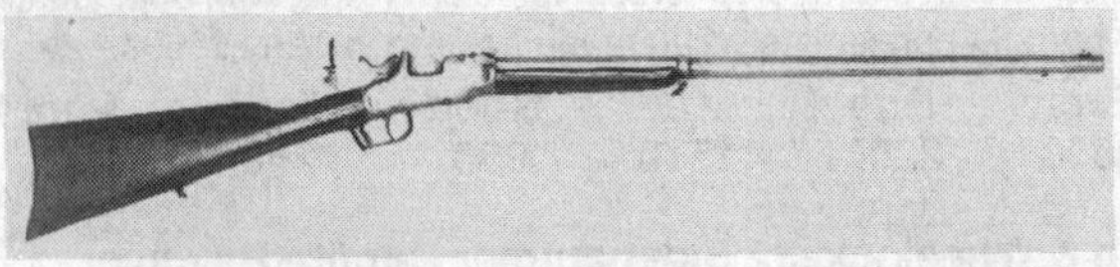

Courtesy Milwaukee Public Museum, Milwaukee, Wisconsin

Exc.	Fine	V.G.	Good	Fair	Poor
1550	600	400	200	100	70

Lipfire Revolving Rifle (Antique)

A 6-shot cylinder-type rifle chambered for .44-caliber lipfire cartridge. Unfluted cylinder, with slots at its rear to allow for cartridge lips. Round barrels were 26" to 28" in length, with octagon breech. Finish blued. Case colored frame and walnut buttstock. Not marked with maker's name. Approximately 100 manufactured between 1861 and 1863.

Courtesy Buffalo Bill Historical Center, Cody, Wyoming

Exc.	Fine	V.G.	Good	Fair	Poor
18500	7000	4500	2000	780	540

Allen & Thurber Double-Barrel Shotgun (Antique)

Side-by-side shotgun chambered for 10- or 12-gauge. Barrel length 28". Loaded by means of trapdoor-type breech that had a lever handle. Finish blued, with checkered walnut stock. Few hundred manufactured between 1865 and 1871.

Exc.	Fine	V.G.	Good	Fair	Poor
1800	800	520	250	120	80

ALLEN & THURBER

See—ALLEN, ETHAN

ALLEN & WHEELOCK

See—ALLEN, ETHAN

ALLEN FIREARMS

Santa Fe, New Mexico

See—ALDO UBERTI

ALPHA ARMS CO.

Flower Mound, Texas

Alpha Arms Co. produced high-grade bolt-action rifles, on a semi-custom basis. Manufactured a number of standard models, but offered many options at additional cost. Some of these options were custom sights, finishes and octagonal barrels. These extra features would add value to models listed. Company operated from 1983 until 1987.

Jaguar Grade I

Built on Mauser-type action, with barrel lengths from 20" to 24". Chambered for most calibers between .222 Rem. and .338 Win. Magnum. Stock made from a synthetic laminated material the company called "Alphawood". Introduced in 1987 and only produced that year.

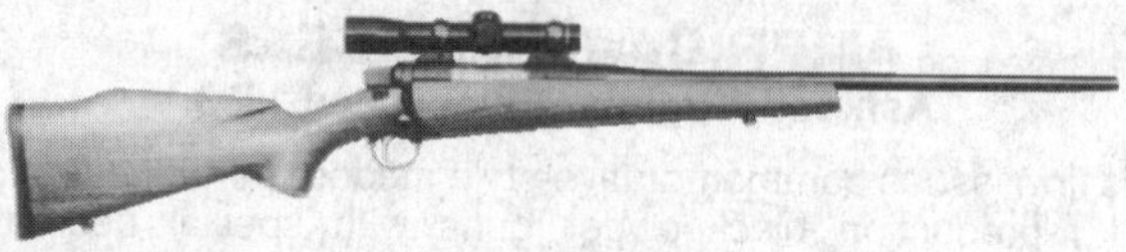

NIB	Exc.	V.G.	Good	Fair	Poor
1700	1100	750	500	300	200

Jaguar Grade II

Similar to Grade I, with Douglas Premium barrel.

NIB	Exc.	V.G.	Good	Fair	Poor
1820	1280	800	500	400	250

Jaguar Grade III

Has Douglas barrel plus hand-honed trigger and action. Three-position safety like Winchester Model 70.

NIB	Exc.	V.G.	Good	Fair	Poor
1950	1500	1050	700	400	200

Jaguar Grade IV

Has all features of Grade III, with specially lightened action and sling-swivel studs.

NIB	Exc.	V.G.	Good	Fair	Poor
2000	1750	1200	900	500	250

Alpha Big-Five

Similar to Jaguar Grade IV. Chambered for .300 Win. Magnum, .375 H&H Magnum and .458 Win. Magnum. Reinforced through-bolt stock to accommodate recoil of larger caliber cartridges for which it was chambered. Had decelerator recoil pad. Manufactured in 1987 only. Note: Add 20 percent for .458.

NIB	Exc.	V.G.	Good	Fair	Poor
2200	1850	1500	950	600	300

Alpha Grand Slam

Features same high quality as Jaguar models. Available in left-hand model. Has fluted bolt, laminated stock and matte blue finish. Note: Deduct 10 percent for left-hand version.

NIB	Exc.	V.G.	Good	Fair	Poor
1700	1500	1250	700	450	250

Alpha Custom

Similar to Grand Slam, with select grade stock.

NIB	Exc.	V.G.	Good	Fair	Poor
1700	1500	1250	750	500	250

Alpha Alaskan

Similar to Grand Slam. Chambered for .308 Win., .350 Rem. Magnum, .358 Win. and .458 Win. Magnum. Features all stainless steel construction. Note: Add 20 percent for .458.

NIB	Exc.	V.G.	Good	Fair	Poor
2000	1750	1450	850	500	250

ALSOP, C.R.
Middletown, Connecticut

This firearms manufacturer made revolvers during 1862 and 1863. They made two basic models: Navy and Pocket. Some collectors consider Alsop to be a secondary U.S. martial handgun, but no verifying government contracts are known to exist.

First Model Navy Revolver Antique

.36-caliber revolver, with 3.5", 4.5", 5.5" or 6.5" barrel length and 5-shot cylinder. Has blued finish, wood grips and peculiar hump in its backstrap. First model has a safety device, which blocks the spur trigger. This device is found on serial numbers 1-100. Markings are: "C.R. Alsop Middletown, Conn. 1860 & 1861" on barrel; cylinder, "C.R. Alsop" & "Nov. 26th, 1861"; side plate, "Patented Jan. 21st, 1862".

Exc.	Fine	V.G.	Good	Fair	Poor
7500	5000	3000	1500	700	400

Standard Model Navy Revolver Antique

Exactly the same as First Model, without safety device. Serial numbered 101 to 300.

Exc.	Fine	V.G.	Good	Fair	Poor
6000	4000	2500	1000	600	400

Pocket Model Revolver Antique

.31-caliber 5-shot revolver, with spur trigger, 4" round barrel, blued finish and wood grips. Very similar in appearance to Navy model, but smaller in size. Marked: "C.R. Alsop Middletown, Conn. 1860 & 1861" on barrel; cylinder, "C.R. Alsop Nov. 26th, 1861". Serial numbered 1-300.

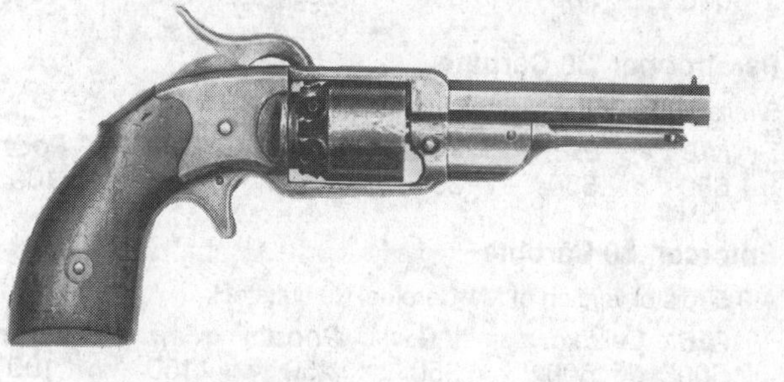

Courtesy Milwaukee Public Museum, Milwaukee, Wisconsin

Exc.	Fine	V.G.	Good	Fair	Poor
3800	1750	900	500	350	200

AMAC
American Military Arms Corporation
(formerly Iver Johnson)
Jacksonville, Arkansas

Iver Johnson Arms Co. was founded in 1871 in Fitchsburg, Massachusetts. One of the oldest and most successful of old-line arms companies, on which our modern era has taken its toll. In 1984 company moved to Jacksonville, Arkansas; in 1987 it was purchased by American Military Arms Corporation. This company has released some of the older designs as well as some new models. In 1993, company went out of business. Original Iver Johnson line is listed under its own heading.

U.S. Carbine .22

Semi-automatic military-style carbine patterned after M1 of WWII fame. Chambered for .22 LR cartridge. Has 18.5" barrel. Features military-style peep sights and 15-shot detachable magazine.

NIB	Exc.	V.G.	Good	Fair	Poor
380	300	250	200	150	50

Wagonmaster Lever-Action Rifle

Chambered for .22 rimfire cartridge. Styled after Win. 94. Has an 18.5" barrel, straight-grip stock and a forend barrel band. Adjustable sights. Tubular magazine holds 15 LR cartridges.

NIB	Exc.	V.G.	Good	Fair	Poor
300	220	150	100	80	50

Wagonmaster .22 Magnum

Same as Wagonmaster. Chambered for .22 rimfire Magnum.

NIB	Exc.	V.G.	Good	Fair	Poor
320	250	180	120	100	50

Targetmaster Pump-Action Rifle

A slide- or pump-action chambered for .22 rimfire cartridge. Has 18.5" barrel, with adjustable sights and straight-grip stock. Holds 12 LR cartridges.

NIB	Exc.	V.G.	Good	Fair	Poor
320	180	140	120	80	50

Li'L Champ Bolt-Action Rifle

A scaled-down single-shot chambered for .22 rimfire cartridge. Has 16.25" barrel, adjustable sights, molded stock and nickel-plated bolt. Overall length 33". Designed to be an ideal first rifle for a young shooter.

NIB	Exc.	V.G.	Good	Fair	Poor
180	120	80	40	40	20

M .30 Cal. Carbine

Military-style carbine styled after M1 of WWII fame. Chambered for .30 Carbine cartridge. Has 18" barrel, with military-style sights and hardwood stock. Detachable 5-, 15- and 30-round magazines available.

NIB	Exc.	V.G.	Good	Fair	Poor
600	500	350	250	150	100

Paratrooper .30 Carbine

Similar to M1 model, with folding stock.

NIB	Exc.	V.G.	Good	Fair	Poor
650	550	380	280	180	100

Enforcer .30 Carbine

A 9.5" pistol version of M1 Carbine. No buttstock.

NIB	Exc.	V.G.	Good	Fair	Poor
600	500	350	250	150	100

Long Range Rifle System/AMAC Model 5100

Specialized long-range bolt-action rifle. Chambered for .50-caliber Browning Machine gun cartridge. Has 33" barrel and special muzzle brake system. Custom order version in .338- or .416-caliber also available.

NIB	Exc.	V.G.	Good	Fair	Poor
4100	3550	2900	2000	900	450

TP-22 and TP-25

Compact double-action pocket automatic styled after Walther TP series. Chambered for .22 rimfire or .25 centerfire cartridges. Has 2.75" barrel, fixed sights and black plastic grips. Detachable magazine holds 7 shots. Finish blue or nickel-plated. Note: Nickel-plated version worth 10 percent more than blue.

NIB	Exc.	V.G.	Good	Fair	Poor
260	200	150	100	80	50

AMAC 22 Compact or 25 Compact

Compact single-action semi-automatic pocket pistol. Chambered for .22 rimfire or .25 ACP cartridge. Has 2" barrel, 5-shot magazine, plastic grips and blue or nickel finish. Note: Add 10 percent for nickel.

NIB	Exc.	V.G.	Good	Fair	Poor
260	200	150	100	80	50

AMERICA REMEMBERS

Ashland, Virginia. Established 1993.

This firm issues commemorative-style modern cartridge firearms and reproduction blackpowder guns with special decoration usually memorializing an individual, event, organization, or concept. The guns themselves are manufactured by other firms and are marketed by direct advertisement to end buyer rather than through distributors. The entire list of over 175 variations can be found at americaremembers.com and range from an Aaron Tippon Tribute Colt .45 Pistol to a Zorro Tribute revolver. Unlike most commemoratives issued directly by firearms manufacturers, there is usually not a pre-set limit on the number produced.

The American Historical Foundation produced and marketed decorated firearms in a similar manner and was acquired by America Remembers in 2005. A separate firm, Franklin Mint, sold non-firing replica guns with a similar approach.

There is not a strong secondary collector market for these. Resale values will generally start at where an undecorated example of the same firearm in the same condition would sell. A buyer with a strong fondness for the event, organization, or person commemorated may pay an additional premium for the decoration.

See additional comments on this general type of gun under the COLT COMMEMORATIVES section.

A separate firm, Franklin Mint, sold non-firing replica guns with a similar approach.

AMERICAN ARMS

Garden Grove, California

Eagle .380

Pistol was a stainless steel copy of Walther PPKS. Semi-automatic blowback chambered for .380 ACP. Double-action, 3.25" barrel and 6-shot detachable magazine. Optional feature a black Teflon finish, that would increase value by 10 percent. Company ceased production in 1985.

NIB	Exc.	V.G.	Good	Fair	Poor
—	320	250	200	150	100

AMERICAN ARMS CO.

Boston, Massachusetts

History of American Arms is rather sketchy. It appears the company was formed in 1853 as G. H. Fox Co., then became American Tool & Machine Co. in 1865. In 1870, they formed a new corporation called American Arms Company, with George Fox as principle stockholder. This corporation was dissolved in 1873; a second American Arms Co. was incorporated in 1877 and a third in 1890. It is unclear if these corporations had essentially the same owners, but George H. Fox appears as a principle owner in two of the three. One could assume that financial problems forced them to bankrupt one corporation and reorganize under another. American Arms manufactured firearms in Boston, Massachusetts, from 1866 until 1893. In 1893 they moved to Bluffton, Alabama and manufactured guns until 1901.

Fox Model "Swing Out" Hammer Double (Antique)

Manufactured from 1870 to 1884. Designed by George H. Fox, not to be confused with A.H. Fox. Model unusual, in that barrel swings to right for loading and barrel release is located on tang. Comes in 10- and 12-gauge, 26", 28", 30" and 32" with twist Damascus or laminated barrels. Early production models have conventional soldered together barrels. Later variations after 1878, feature a unique design in that barrels are dovetailed together. Guns could be ordered with several options and choices of finish. These would add premium value to a particular gun.

Exc.	Fine	V.G.	Good	Fair	Poor
2000	950	670	400	150	100

Semi-Hammerless Double (Antique)

Manufactured from 1892 to 1901. Features cocking lever that cocks an internal firing pin. Comes in 12-gauge, with 30" twist barrels.

Exc.	Fine	V.G.	Good	Fair	Poor
1500	750	550	350	150	100

Whitmore Model Hammerless Double (Antique)

Manufactured from 1890 to 1901. Comes in 10-, 12- and 16-gauge, with 28", 30" or 32" twist laminated or Damascus barrels. Marked "Whitmore's Patent".

Courtesy Nick Niles, Paul Goodwin photo

Exc.	Fine	V.G.	Good	Fair	Poor
1500	780	580	380	150	100

Semi-Hammerless Single-Barrel (Antique)

Manufactured from 1882 to 1901. Comes in 10-, 12- and 16-gauge, with 28", 30" or 32" twist or Damascus barrel.

Exc.	Fine	V.G.	Good	Fair	Poor
1500	750	520	300	100	70

TOP-BREAK REVOLVERS

(Antique)

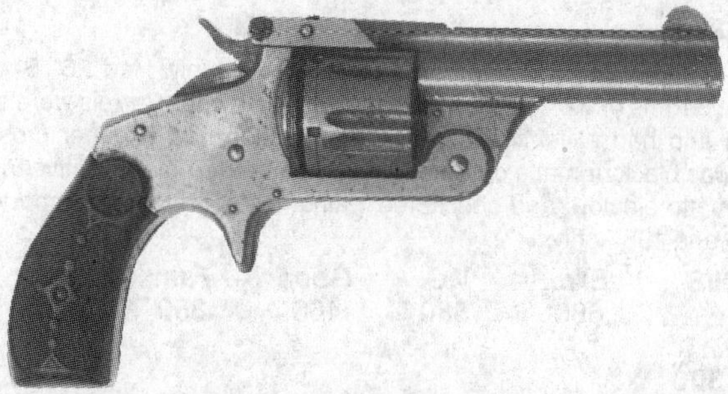

Courtesy Milwaukee Public Museum, Milwaukee, Wisconsin

Spur Trigger Single-Action Five-Shot Revolver (Antique)

Revolvers made between 1883 and 1887 in .38 S&W only. Feature an unusual manual ring extractor and double-fluted cylinder. Nickel plated, with hard rubber grips. Marked "American Arms Company Boston Mass.".

Exc.	Fine	V.G.	Good	Fair	Poor
400	275	200	150	85	50

Standard Trigger Double-Action Model 1886 Revolver (Antique)

Standard trigger and triggerguard. Comes in .32 short and .38 S&W, with 3.5" barrel. Blue or nickel finish. Early models equipped with ring extractor and double-fluted cylinder. Later variations have standard star extractor and single-fluted cylinder.

Exc.	Fine	V.G.	Good	Fair	Poor
375	250	175	125	75	50

Hammerless Model 1890 Double-Action (Antique)

Manufactured from 1890 to 1901. Has adjustable single- or double-stage trigger pull and several unusual safety devices. Comes in .32 and .38 S&W, with 3.25" ribbed barrel, fluted cylinder, nickel finish, hard rubber grips with logo and ivory or mother of pearl grips. Marked "American Arms Co. Boston/Pat. May 25, 1886". Top strap marked "Pat. Pending" on early models and "Pat's May 25'86/Mar 11'89/June 17'90" on later models.

Exc.	Fine	V.G.	Good	Fair	Poor
300	100	90	80	20	10

DOUBLE-BARREL DERRINGERS

(Antique)

American Arms Co. manufactured a two-barrel derringer-style pocket pistol. Barrels were manually rotated to load and fire the weapon. Pistol had nickel-plated brass frame, blued barrels and walnut grips. Markings were: "American Arms Co. Boston, Mass." on one barrel and "Pat. Oct. 31, 1865" on other barrel. Approximately 2,000-3,000 produced between 1866 and 1878. Beware of fakes! Most common is a combination of one barrel in .22 rimfire and the other in .32 rimfire. Also made with both barrels in .32 rimfire or both in .41 rimfire. Very few, around 50, were made with both barrels in .22 rimfire, too rare to value. Both barrels in .38 rimfire have been reported, but it's unclear whether that variation was actually produced.

Combination .22 caliber R.F. and .32 caliber R.F. (Antique)

Two-caliber combination, with 3" barrel and square butt only. Most common variation.

Exc.	Fine	V.G.	Good	Fair	Poor
1500	1000	600	350	250	125

.32 caliber R.F., Both Barrels (Antique)

3" barrel, with square butt.

Courtesy Milwaukee Public Museum, Milwaukee, Wisconsin

Exc.	Fine	V.G.	Good	Fair	Poor
1050	500	350	200	120	80

.41 caliber R.F., Both Barrels (Antique)

2.625" barrel, with square-butt only.

Exc.	Fine	V.G.	Good	Fair	Poor
1850	900	550	200	100	70

AMERICAN ARMS, INC.

North Kansas City, Missouri

SIDE-BY-SIDE SHOTGUNS

York/Gentry

These two designations cover the same model. Prior to 1988, this model was called York. In 1988, receiver was case colored and designation changed to Gentry. Model chambered for 12-, 20-, 28-gauge and .410 bore. Had chrome-lined barrels from 26" to 30" in length, double triggers,

3" chambers and automatic ejectors. Boxlock action featured scroll engraving. Walnut stock was hand checkered. Introduced in 1986.

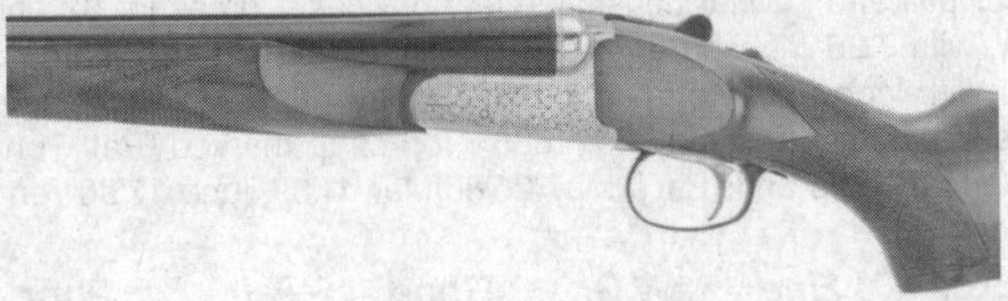

NIB	Exc.	V.G.	Good	Fair	Poor
—	1200	450	370	200	150

10 Gauge Magnum Shotgun

10-gauge, with 3.5" chambers and 32" barrels. Featured scroll-engraved chromed boxlock action and double triggers. Imported from Spain in 1986 only.

NIB	Exc.	V.G.	Good	Fair	Poor
850	750	550	350	250	150

12 Gauge Magnum Shotgun

As above, chambered for 12-gauge 3.5" Magnum shell.

NIB	Exc.	V.G.	Good	Fair	Poor
800	700	500	300	200	150

Brittany

Chambered for 12- and 20-gauge, with 25" or 27" barrels and screw-in choke tubes. Had solid matted rib and case colored engraved boxlock action. Automatic ejectors, single-selective trigger, hand checkered walnut straight-grip stock, with semi-beavertail forend, were standard on this model. Introduced in 1989.

NIB	Exc.	V.G.	Good	Fair	Poor
850	750	600	450	380	200

Turkey Special

Utilitarian model designed to be an effective turkey hunting tool. Chambered for Magnum 10- and 12-gauges. Has 26" barrels. Finish Parkerized. Stock finished in non-glare matte. Sling-swivel studs and recoil pad are standard. Introduced in 1987.

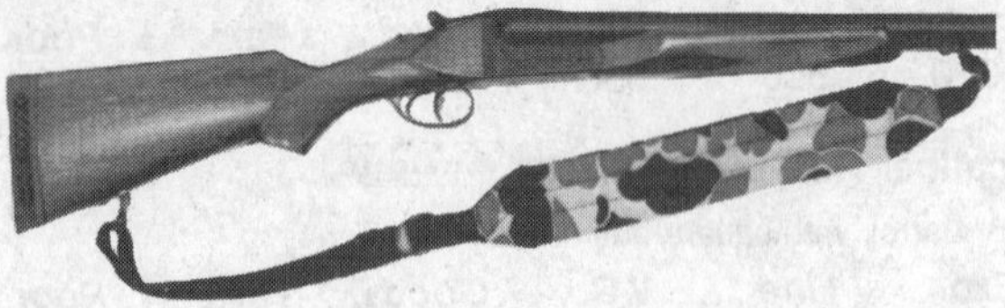

NIB	Exc.	V.G.	Good	Fair	Poor
—	800	450	350	250	150

Waterfowl Special

Similar to Turkey Special. Chambered for 10-gauge only. Furnished with camouflaged sling. Introduced in 1987.

NIB	Exc.	V.G.	Good	Fair	Poor
—	800	550	350	250	150

Specialty Model

Similar to Turkey Special. Offered in 12-gauge 3.5" Magnum.

NIB	Exc.	V.G.	Good	Fair	Poor
880	750	500	300	200	150

Derby

Chambered for 12-, 20-, 28-gauge and .410 bore. Has 26" or 28" barrels, with 3" chambers and automatic ejectors. Double- or single-selective triggers offered. Sidelock action is scroll engraved and chromed. Checkered straight-grip stock and forearm are oil-finished. Introduced in 1986. No longer imported. Note: Add 10 percent for 28 gauge or .410 bore; 50 percent for two-gauge sets.

NIB	Exc.	V.G.	Good	Fair	Poor
—	1250	850	650	450	300

Grulla #2

Top-of-the-line model. Chambered for 12-, 20-, 28-gauge and .410 bore. Barrels are 26" or 28", with concave rib. Hand-fitted full sidelock action is extensively engraved and case colored. Various chokes, double triggers and automatic ejectors. Select walnut straight-grip stock. Splinter forend is hand-checkered and has a hand-rubbed oil finish. Introduced in 1989. No longer imported.

NIB	Exc.	V.G.	Good	Fair	Poor
2500	1750	1250	900	500	250

OVER/UNDER SHOTGUNS

F.S. 200

Trap or skeet model chambered for 12-gauge only. Had 26" Skeet & Skeet barrels or 32" Full choke barrels on trap model. Barrels were separated and had a ventilated rib. Boxlock action had Greener crossbolt and was black or matte chrome-plated. Featured single-selective trigger, automatic ejectors and checkered walnut pistol grip stock. Imported in 1986 and 1987 only.

NIB	Exc.	V.G.	Good	Fair	Poor
—	680	580	460	350	150

F.S. 300

Similar to F.S. 200, with lightly engraved side plates and 30" barrel. Offered in trap grade. Imported in 1986 only.

NIB	Exc.	V.G.	Good	Fair	Poor
—	800	680	560	450	250

F.S. 400

Similar to F.S. 300, with engraved matte chrome-plated receiver. Imported in 1986 only.

NIB	Exc.	V.G.	Good	Fair	Poor
—	1100	950	800	650	350

F.S. 500

Similar to F.S. 400, with same general specifications. Not imported after 1985.

NIB	Exc.	V.G.	Good	Fair	Poor
—	1150	1000	850	700	350

Waterfowl Special

Chambered for 12-gauge Magnum, with 3.5" chambers. Has 28" barrels, with screw-in choke tubes. Automatic ejectors and single-selective trigger. Finish Parkerized, with matte finished stock, sling swivels and camouflaged sling and recoil pad. Introduced in 1987.

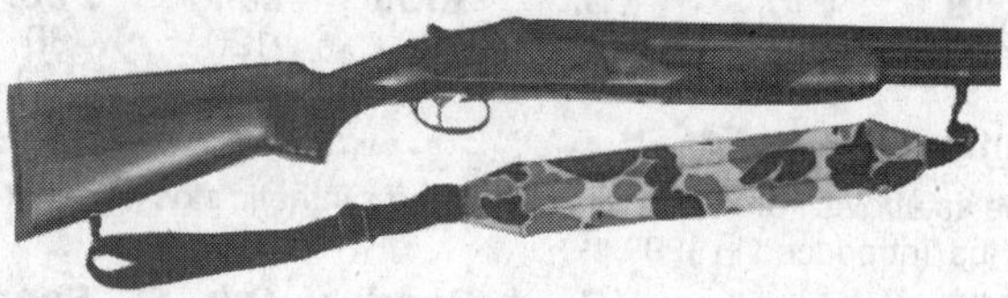

NIB	Exc.	V.G.	Good	Fair	Poor
880	700	500	350	300	150

Waterfowl 10 Gauge

Same as Waterfowl Special. Chambered for 10-gauge Magnum, with double triggers.

NIB	Exc.	V.G.	Good	Fair	Poor
—	550	450	400	300	200

Turkey Special

Similar to Waterfowl Special in 10-gauge, with 26" barrel and screw-in choke tubes.

NIB	Exc.	V.G.	Good	Fair	Poor
980	850	600	350	300	200

Lince

Chambered for 12- and 20-gauge. Has 26" or 28" barrels, with 3" chambers and various chokes. Boxlock action has Greener crossbolt blued or polished and chrome-plated. Barrels blued, with ventilated rib. Single-selective trigger and automatic ejectors. Imported in 1986 only.

NIB	Exc.	V.G.	Good	Fair	Poor
—	500	420	350	300	200

Silver Model

Similar to Lince. Plain un-engraved brushed-chrome-finished receiver. Imported in 1986 and 1987.

NIB	Exc.	V.G.	Good	Fair	Poor
—	500	420	350	300	200

Silver I

Similar to Silver. Available in 12-, 20-, 28-gauge and .410 bore. Has single-selective trigger, fixed chokes, extractors and recoil pad. Introduced in 1987. Note: Add $25 for 28-gauge and .410 bore guns.

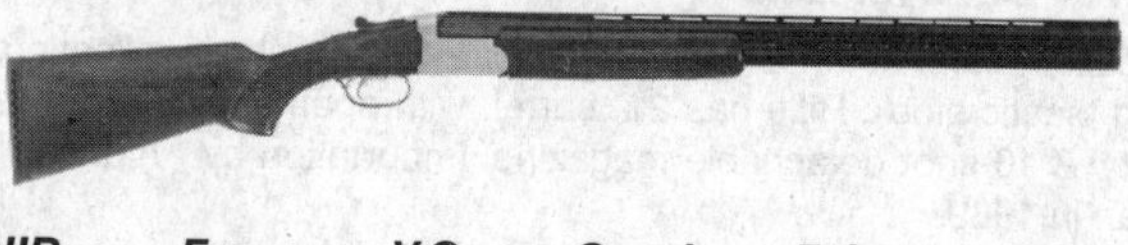

NIB	Exc.	V.G.	Good	Fair	Poor
800	550	320	280	200	180

Silver II

Similar to Silver I, with screw-in choke tubes, automatic ejectors and select walnut. Introduced in 1987. Note: Add $25 for 28-gauge and .410 bore guns.

NIB	Exc.	V.G.	Good	Fair	Poor
—	550	500	350	300	150

Silver II Lite

Introduced in 1994. Designed as an upland game gun. Offered in 12-, 20- and 28-gauge, with 26" barrels. Chambered for both 2.75" and 3" shells. Frame made from a lightweight steel alloy. No longer imported.

NIB	Exc.	V.G.	Good	Fair	Poor
880	780	550	400	300	150

Silver Competition/Sporting

Offered in 12-gauge, with choice of 28" or 30" barrels which are made from chrome moly. Barrels have elongated forcing cones, chromed bores and are ported to help reduce recoil. Comes with interchangeable choke tubes. Single-selective trigger is mechanical. Weight about 7.5 lbs. In 1996 a 20-gauge model was added, with 28" barrel and 3" chambers.

NIB	Exc.	V.G.	Good	Fair	Poor
950	800	600	400	300	150

Silver Hunter

Introduced in 1999. Offered in 12- and 20-gauge, with 26" and 28" barrels. Single-selective trigger with extractors. Choke tubes standard. Weight about 7 lbs.

NIB	Exc.	V.G.	Good	Fair	Poor
620	500	400	300	200	100

Bristol/Sterling

Chambered for 12- and 20-gauge. Various barrel lengths, with ventilated rib and screw-in choke tubes. Chambers are 3". Chrome-finished action is boxlock, with Greener crossbolt and game scene engraved on side plates. Automatic ejectors and single-selective trigger. Introduced in 1986. In 1989, designation was changed to Sterling. No longer imported.

NIB	Exc.	V.G.	Good	Fair	Poor
820	750	680	500	400	200

Sir

Chambered for 12- and 20-gauge, with 3" chambers, various barrel lengths, chokes and ventilated rib. Chrome-finished sidelock action has Greener crossbolt and engraved with a game scene. Automatic ejectors and single-selective trigger. Imported in 1986. No longer imported.

NIB	Exc.	V.G.	Good	Fair	Poor
—	880	750	620	500	250

Royal

Chambered for 12- and 20-gauge. Manufactured in various barrel lengths and chokes, with ventilated rib and 3" chambers. Chrome-finished sidelock action has Greener crossbolt and profusely scroll-engraved. Automatic ejectors and single-selective trigger. Select pistol grip walnut stock is hand-checkered and oil-finished. Imported in 1986 and 1987. No longer imported.

NIB	Exc.	V.G.	Good	Fair	Poor
—	1500	1280	1000	800	400

Excelsior

Similar to Royal, with extensive deep relief engraving and gold inlays. Imported in 1986 and 1987. No longer imported.

NIB	Exc.	V.G.	Good	Fair	Poor
—	1750	1500	1200	880	450

SINGLE-BARREL SHOTGUNS

AASB

Standard single-barrel break-open hammerless shotgun. Chambered for 12-, 20-gauge and .410 bore. Has 26" barrel, with various chokes and 3" chambers. Pistol grip stock and matte finish. Introduced in 1988. No longer imported.

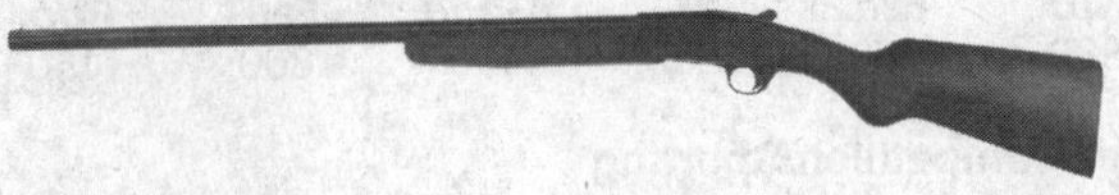

NIB	Exc.	V.G.	Good	Fair	Poor
—	100	80	60	40	20

Campers Special

Similar to standard model, with 21" barrel and folding stock. Introduced in 1988. No longer imported.

NIB	Exc.	V.G.	Good	Fair	Poor
110	100	80	70	50	40

Youth Model

Chambered for 20-gauge and .410 bore. Has 12.5" stock, with recoil pad. Introduced in 1989. No longer imported.

NIB	Exc.	V.G.	Good	Fair	Poor
120	100	80	60	50	40

Slugger

Version has 24" barrel, with rifle sights. Chambered for 12- and 20-gauge, with recoil pad. No longer imported.

NIB	Exc.	V.G.	Good	Fair	Poor
120	100	80	60	50	40

10 Gauge Model

Chambered for 10-gauge 3.5" Magnum. Has 32" Full choke barrel and recoil pad. Introduced in 1988. No longer imported.

NIB	Exc.	V.G.	Good	Fair	Poor
180	140	100	80	60	40

Combo Model

Similar in appearance to other single-barrel models. Offered in interchangeable-barreled rifle/shotgun combination—28" barreled .22 Hornet and 12-gauge; or 26" barreled .22 LR and 20-gauge. Furnished with fitted hard case to hold interchangeable barrels. Introduced in 1989. No longer imported.

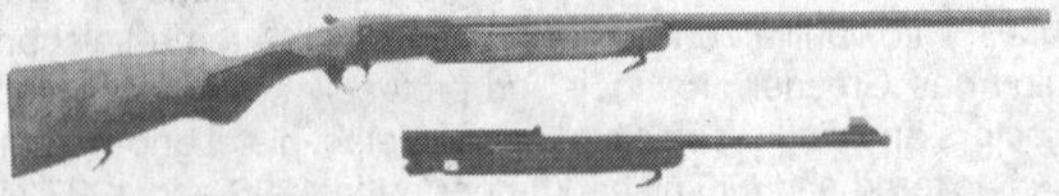

NIB	Exc.	V.G.	Good	Fair	Poor
250	200	180	140	110	80

SEMI-AUTO SHOTGUNS

Phantom Field

Chambered for 12-gauge and fitted with choice of 24", 26" or 28" barrels. Fitted with 3" chamber. Gas operated action. Choke tubes standard. Five-round magazine. Checkered walnut stock. Weight about 7 lbs. Introduced in 1999.

NIB	Exc.	V.G.	Good	Fair	Poor
400	350	300	220	120	80

Phantom Synthetic

Same as above. Furnished with checkered synthetic stock. Weight about 6.75 lbs. Introduced in 1999.

NIB	Exc.	V.G.	Good	Fair	Poor
400	350	300	220	120	80

Phantom HP

Features 19" threaded barrel for external choke tubes. Five-round magazine. Weight about 6.75 lbs. Introduced in 1999.

NIB	Exc.	V.G.	Good	Fair	Poor
400	380	320	300	150	100

RIFLES

ZCY.308

An AK-47 type design and chambered in .308 Winchester. Imported in 1988 only.

NIB	Exc.	V.G.	Good	Fair	Poor
700	600	480	380	300	200

AKY39

Semi-automatic version of Soviet AK-47. Manufactured by Yugoslavia. Offered with folding tritium night sights and wooden fixed stock. Imported in 1988.

NIB	Exc.	V.G.	Good	Fair	Poor
—	600	480	390	300	200

AKF39

Same rifle as AKY39, with metal folding stock.

NIB	Exc.	V.G.	Good	Fair	Poor
—	620	550	480	300	200

AKC47

Basically same rifle as AKY39, without tritium night sights.

NIB	Exc.	V.G.	Good	Fair	Poor
—	580	450	380	300	200

AKF47

Same rifle as AKC47, with metal folding stock.

NIB	Exc.	V.G.	Good	Fair	Poor
—	620	550	480	300	200

EXP-64 Survival Rifle

.22-caliber semi-automatic take-down rifle. Self-storing in a floating oversized plastic stock. Rifle has 21" barrel, with open sights and crossbolt safety. A 10-shot detachable magazine. Importation by American Arms began in 1989.

NIB	Exc.	V.G.	Good	Fair	Poor
160	150	120	100	80	50

SM-64 TD Sporter

.22 LR semi-automatic, with take-down 21" barrel. Adjustable sights, checkered hardwood stock and forend. Importation began in 1989.

NIB	Exc.	V.G.	Good	Fair	Poor
200	160	110	80	60	40

1860 Henry

Replica of lever action Henry rifle. Brass frame. Steel half-octagon barrel, with tube magazine. Chambered for .44-40 or .45 Long Colt. Offered in 18.5" or 24" barrels. Weight with 24" barrel about 9.25 lbs. Built by Uberti.

NIB	Exc.	V.G.	Good	Fair	Poor
950	800	650	400	300	200

1866 Winchester

Replica of Winchester 1866. Offered in .44-40 or .45 Long Colt. Barrel lengths 19" or 24". Brass frame. Weight about 8.25 lbs. for 24" barrel model. Built by Uberti.

NIB	Exc.	V.G.	Good	Fair	Poor
820	700	500	300	200	100

1873 Winchester

Replica of Winchester Model 1873. Offered with choice of 24" or 30" barrels. Chambered for .44-40 or .45 Long Colt. Case-hardened steel frame. Weight about 8.25 lbs. for 24" model. Built by Uberti. Note: Add $80 for 30" barrel.

NIB	Exc.	V.G.	Good	Fair	Poor
850	720	550	320	220	120

1885 Single-Shot High Wall

Chambered for .45-70 cartridge. Winchester replica fitted with 28" round barrel. Weight about 8.75 lbs. Built by Uberti.

NIB	Exc.	V.G.	Good	Fair	Poor
850	700	550	350	200	100

Sharps Cavalry Carbine

Sharps replica fitted with 22" round barrel. Chambered for .45-70 cartridge. Adjustable rear sight. Weight about 8 lbs.

NIB	Exc.	V.G.	Good	Fair	Poor
700	600	420	350	200	100

Sharps Frontier Carbine

Similar to Cavalry carbine, with 22" octagonal barrel and double-set triggers. Weight about 7.75 lbs.

NIB	Exc.	V.G.	Good	Fair	Poor
780	620	480	380	220	120

Sharps Sporting Rifle

Features 28" octagonal barrel. Chambered for .45-70 or .45-120 cartridge. Double-set triggers. Adjustable rear sight. Checkered walnut stock. Weight about 9 lbs.

NIB	Exc.	V.G.	Good	Fair	Poor
780	620	480	380	220	120

Sharps 1874 Deluxe Sporting Rifle

Similar to above, with browned barrels.

NIB	Exc.	V.G.	Good	Fair	Poor
800	650	500	400	250	150

HANDGUNS

Model EP-.380

High-quality stainless steel pocket pistol. Chambered for .380 ACP cartridge. Double-action semi-automatic that holds 7 shots and has a 3.5" barrel. Grips are checkered walnut. Imported from West Germany beginning in1988.

NIB	Exc.	V.G.	Good	Fair	Poor
420	360	320	280	220	100

Model PK-22

Domestic semi-automatic chambered for .22 LR. Double-action with 3.5" barrel and 8-shot finger extension magazine. Made of stainless steel and has black plastic grips. Manufactured in U.S.A. by American Arms.

NIB	Exc.	V.G.	Good	Fair	Poor
240	200	150	120	100	80

Model CX-22

Compact version of PK-22, with 2.75" barrel and 7-shot magazine. Manufacture began in 1989.

NIB	Exc.	V.G.	Good	Fair	Poor
220	200	160	120	100	80

Model TT Tokarev

Yugoslavian version of Soviet Tokarev. Chambered for 9mm Parabellum, with safety added to make importation legal. Has 4.5" barrel, 9-shot magazine and blued finish. Checkered plastic grips. Importation began in 1988.

NIB	Exc.	V.G.	Good	Fair	Poor
350	220	180	150	120	100

Model ZC-.380

Scaled-down version of Tokarev. Chambered for .380 ACP. Has 3.5" barrel and holds 8 shots. Finish and grips are same as on full-sized version. Importation from Yugoslavia began in 1988.

NIB	Exc.	V.G.	Good	Fair	Poor
300	220	180	150	120	100

Aussie Model

Introduced in 1996. Australian-designed semi-automatic pistol made in Spain. Chambered for 9mm or .40 S&W cartridge. Polymer frame, with nickeled steel slide. Sold with 10-shot magazine. Barrel length 4.75"; weight 23 oz.

NIB	Exc.	V.G.	Good	Fair	Poor
400	350	300	250	200	100

Regulator

Built by Uberti. Single-action revolver has case-hardened frame, polished brass triggerguard and backstrap. Barrel and cylinder are blued. One piece walnut grips. Choice of chambers in .44-40, .45 LC or .357 Magnum. Barrel lengths 4.75", 5.5" to 7.5". Weight about 34 oz., with 5.75" barrel.

NIB	Exc.	V.G.	Good	Fair	Poor
400	320	280	180	—	—

Regulator Deluxe

Same as above, with steel triggerguard and backstrap. Chambered in .45 Long Colt only.

NIB	Exc.	V.G.	Good	Fair	Poor
380	300	250	150	—	—

AMERICAN BARLOCK WONDER

See—CRESCENT ARMS CO.

AMERICAN CLASSIC

(Eagle Imports)
Wanamassa, NJ

American Classic 1911-A1

Full-size 1911-A1 style semi-automatic chambered in .45 ACP. Series 70 lockwork, 8-round magazine with bumper pad, lowered ejection port, throated barrel, checkered wood grips, military-style sights, matte blue or hard chrome finish and 5" barrel. Weight 39 oz. American Classic II has additional features including Novak-style sights, combat trigger and hammer, extended safety and slide stop front slide serrations, deep blue or hard chrome finish. Note: Add $35 for Classic II; $50 for hard chrome finish.

NIB	Exc.	V.G.	Good	Fair	Poor
500	400	350	320	250	200

American Classic 1911-A1 II

Calibers: .45 ACP, 9mm, .38 Super. Capacity: 8-round magazine. Barrel: 5 in. Grips: Checkered walnut. Sights: Novak-style rear, fixed front. Finish: Blue or hard chromed. Other variations include Trophy model with checkered mainspring housing, fiber-optic front sight, hard-chrome finish.

NIB	Exc.	V.G.	Good	Fair	Poor
620	550	450	350	—	—

American Classic Commander/Amigo

Same features as American Classic II, except 4.25" barrel, weight 35 oz. Amigo model is Officer's Model style, with 3.5" barrel, 7-round magazine. Note: Add $50 for hard chrome finish; $35 for Amigo model.

NIB	Exc.	V.G.	Good	Fair	Poor
520	450	400	340	260	200

American Classic Compact Commander

Caliber: .45 ACP. Capacity: 7-round magazine. Barrel: 4.25 in. Grips: Textured hardwood. Sights: Fixed Novak style. Finish: Blue, hard chrome, two-tone.

NIB	Exc.	V.G.	Good	Fair	Poor
700	—	—	—	—	—

American Classic Trophy Model

Caliber: .45 ACP. Capacity: 8-round magazine. Barrel: 5 in. Grips: Textured hardwood. Sights: Fixed, fiber-optic front/Novak rear. Finish: Hard chrome. Features: Front slide serrations, ambidextrous thumb safety.

NIB	Exc.	V.G.	Good	Fair	Poor
720	600	550	500	400	300

American Classic .22 Model

Full-size alloy-frame 1911-style pistol. Chambered for .22 LR. Same dimensions as American Classic, with military-type sights, checkered wood grips, matte blue finish and two 10-round magazines.

NIB	Exc.	V.G.	Good	Fair	Poor
300	280	230	200	160	100

American Classic XB

Full-size 1911 with features similar to American Classic 1911-A1, except has a high capacity magazine with 14 - 17 rounds. Available in .38 Super, 9mm, .40 S&W or ,45 ACP. New in 2018.

NIB	Exc.	V.G.	Good	Fair	Poor
700	620	550	500	400	300

American Classic BX

Calibers: .45 ACP, 9mm. Capacity: 14- or 17-round magazine. Barrel: 5 in. Grips: Checkered aluminum. Sights: Mil-Spec style. Finish: Blue.

NIB	Exc.	V.G.	Good	Fair	Poor
700	620	550	500	—	—

AMERICAN DERRINGER CORP.

Waco, Texas

Model 1 Derringer

Fashioned after Remington over/under derringer. High quality rugged pistol. Built from high tensile strength stainless steel. Over 60 different rifle and pistol calibers to choose from, on special order. Upper barrel can be chambered different from lower barrel, on request. Available in high polish finish or satin finish. Offered with rosewood, bacote, walnut or blackwood grips. Ivory, bonded ivory, stag or pearl are available at extra cost. Overall length 4.8"; barrel length 3"; width across frame .9"; width across grip 1.2". Typical weight 15 oz. in .45-caliber. All guns furnished with French fitted leatherette case. Prices determined by caliber. Note: Premium for rifle cartridges.

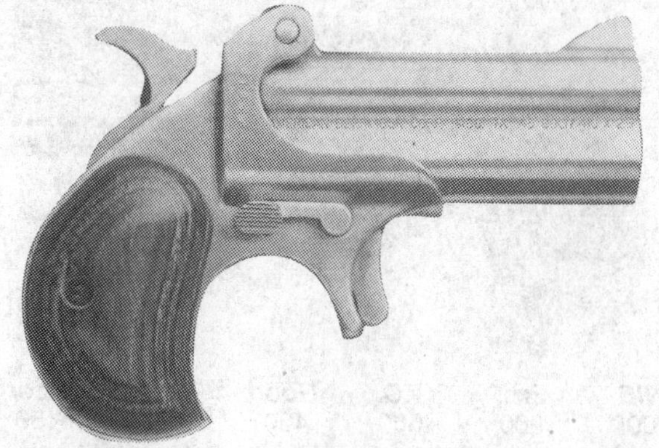

Caliber: .22 Long Rifle through .357 Magnum and .45 ACP

NIB	Exc.	V.G.	Good	Fair	Poor
550	450	350	280	220	150

Calibers: .41 Mag., .44-40, .44 Special, .44 Mag., .45 Long Colt, .410 Bore, .22 Hornet, .223 Rem., 30-30, and .45-70 Gov't.

NIB	Exc.	V.G.	Good	Fair	Poor
600	520	450	350	250	150

Model 1 Lady Derringer

Similar to Model 1. Chambered for .38 Special, .32 Magnum, .45 Colt or .357 Magnum. Offered in two grades. Note: Add $75 for .45 Colt and .45/.410; $50 for .357 Magnum.

Deluxe

High polished stainless steel. Scrimshawed ivory grips, with cameo or rose design.

NIB	Exc.	V.G.	Good	Fair	Poor
700	600	500	300	220	150

Deluxe Engraved

Same as above. Hand engraved in 1880s style.

NIB	Exc.	V.G.	Good	Fair	Poor
750	600	500	400	250	150

Model 1 NRA 500 Series

Limited edition of 500. Available in gold and blue finishes over stainless steel.

NIB	Exc.	V.G.	Good	Fair	Poor
600	450	300	150	120	100

Model 1 Texas Commemorative

Built with solid brass frame and stainless steel barrel. Dimensions same as Model 1. Grips are stag or rosewood and offered in .45 Colt, .44-40 or .38 Special. Barrels marked "Made in the 150th Year of Texas Freedom". Limited to 500 pistols in each caliber.

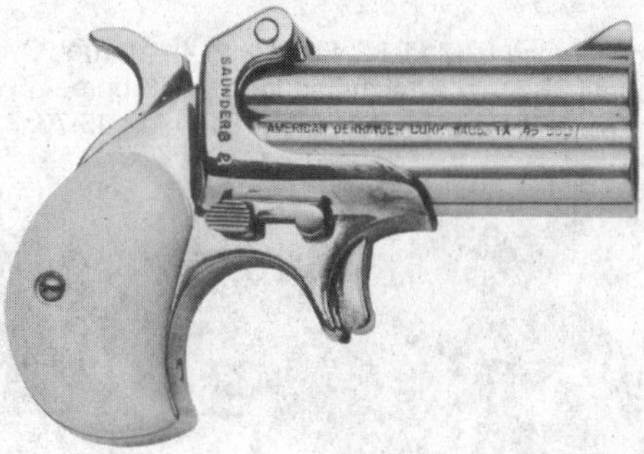

Caliber: .38 Special

NIB	Exc.	V.G.	Good	Fair	Poor
420	350	250	150	100	80

Calibers: .45 Colt and .44-40

NIB	Exc.	V.G.	Good	Fair	Poor
600	450	300	200	120	100

Deluxe Engraved

Special serial number engraved on backstrap.

NIB	Exc.	V.G.	Good	Fair	Poor
700	550	400	350	180	120

Model 1 125th Anniversary Commemorative

Built to commemorate 125th Anniversary of derringer, 1866 to 1991. Similar to Model 1. Marked with patent date "December 12, 1865". Brass frame and stainless steel barrel. Chambered for .44-40, .45 Colt or .38 Special.

NIB	Exc.	V.G.	Good	Fair	Poor
420	350	250	150	100	60

Deluxe Engraved

NIB	Exc.	V.G.	Good	Fair	Poor
650	480	380	250	180	100

Model 2 Pen Pistol

Introduced in 1993. Legal pistol that cannot be fired from its pen position. Requires it be pulled apart and bent 80 degrees to fire. Made from stainless steel. Offered in .22 LR, .25 ACP and .32 ACP. Length in pen form 5.6"; pistol form 4.2". Barrel length 2". Diameter varies from .500" to .625". Weight 5 oz. No longer in production.

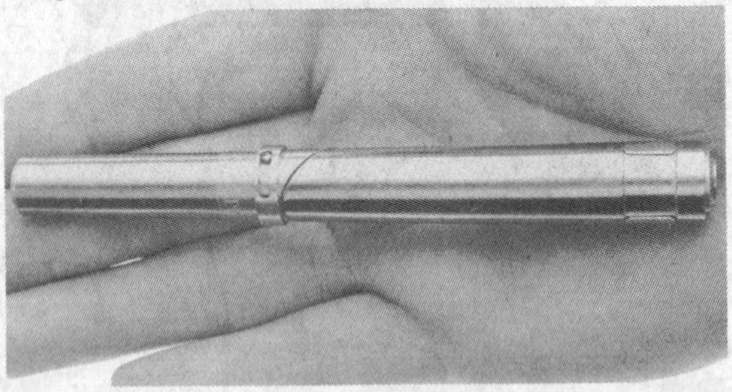

NIB	Exc.	V.G.	Good	Fair	Poor
1250	900	750	600	—	—

Model 3

Single-barrel derringer. Barrel length 2.5" and swings down to load. Frame and barrel stainless steel. Offered in .38 Special or .32 Magnum. Weight about 8 oz. Discontinued.

NIB	Exc.	V.G.	Good	Fair	Poor
200	180	120	80	60	50

Model 4

Similar in appearance to Model 3. Fitted with 4.1" barrel. Overall length 6"; weight about 16.5 oz. Chambered for 3" .410 bore, .45 Long Colt, .44 Magnum or .357 Magnum. Note: Add $150 for .45-70; $100 for .44 Magnum.

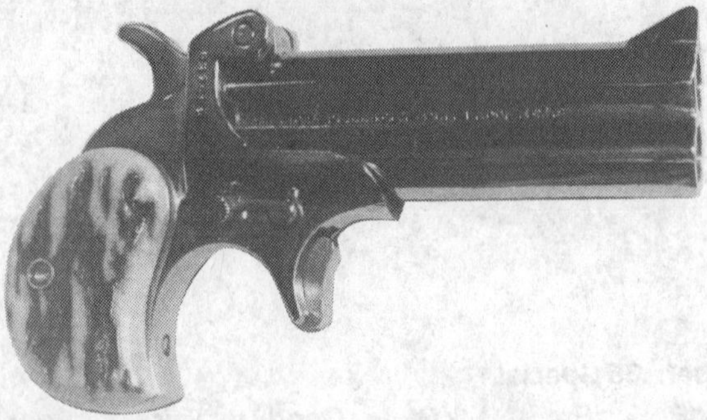

NIB	Exc.	V.G.	Good	Fair	Poor
500	420	350	250	100	80

Engraved

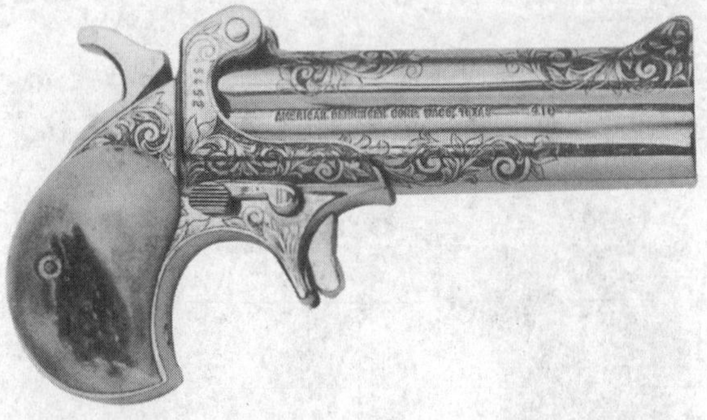

NIB	Exc.	V.G.	Good	Fair	Poor
1000	900	600	400	280	150

Alaskan Survival Model

Similar to Model 4, with upper barrel chambered for .45-70 and lower barrel for .45 LC or .410. Both barrels can also be chambered for .44 Magnum or .45-70. Comes with over-sized rosewood grips.

NIB	Exc.	V.G.	Good	Fair	Poor
700	620	400	250	180	100

Model 6

Double-barrel derringer fitted with 6" barrel chambered for .45 LC or .410 bore. Weight about 21 oz. Rosewood grips are standard. Optional calibers .357 Magnum or .45 ACP. Note: Oversize grips optional and add about $35 to value.

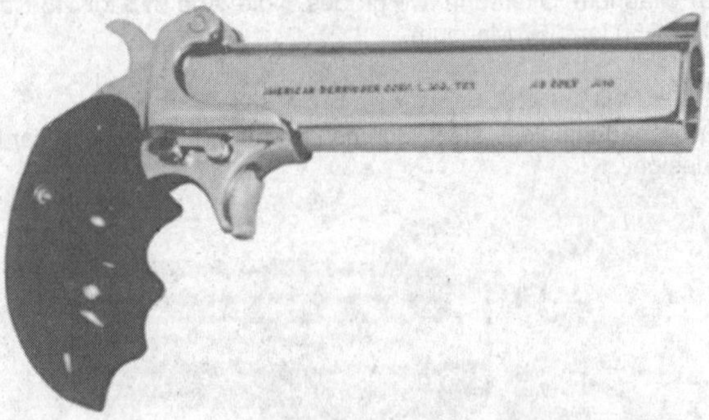

NIB	Exc.	V.G.	Good	Fair	Poor
750	600	450	300	150	100

Engraved

NIB	Exc.	V.G.	Good	Fair	Poor
1000	900	700	450	280	150

Double-Action Derringer

High Standard-type double-barrel double-action derringer. Chambered for .22 LR or .22 Magnum. Barrel length 3.5"; overall length 5.125". Weight about 11 oz. Finish blue with black grips.

NIB	Exc.	V.G.	Good	Fair	Poor
300	240	180	100	80	80

DA 38 Double-Action Derringer

Similar to above. Chambered for .38 Special, .357 Magnum, 9mm Luger and .40 S&W. Finish satin stainless. Grip made from aluminum. Grips are rosewood or walnut. Note: Add $40 for .40 S&W.

NIB	Exc.	V.G.	Good	Fair	Poor
500	400	300	200	150	100

Mini Cop 4-Shot

Four-barrel derringer chambered for .22 Magnum rimfire cartridge.

NIB	Exc.	V.G.	Good	Fair	Poor
600	400	300	220	100	80

Cop 4-Shot

Same as above. Chambered for .357 Magnum cartridge.

NIB	Exc.	V.G.	Good	Fair	Poor
1000	900	500	320	180	100

Model 7 Derringer--Lightweight

Manufactured as a backup gun for police officers. Frame and barrels made of aircraft aluminum alloy; other parts are stainless steel. Weight 7.5 oz. Appearance and function are similar to Model 1. Finish is a gray matte, with thin matte-finished grips of rosewood or bacote. Chambered for and priced as listed.

.32 S&W Long / .32 Magnum

NIB	Exc.	V.G.	Good	Fair	Poor
500	400	250	120	100	80

.38 S&W and .380 ACP

NIB	Exc.	V.G.	Good	Fair	Poor
500	400	250	120	100	80

.22 LR and .38 Special

NIB	Exc.	V.G.	Good	Fair	Poor
500	400	250	120	100	80

.44 Special

NIB	Exc.	V.G.	Good	Fair	Poor
650	520	400	300	250	150

Model 8

Single-action two-shot target pistol, with manually operated hammer block safety. Safety automatically disengages when hammer is cocked. Barrel length 8". Chambered for .45 Colt and .410 shotshell. Weight 24 oz.

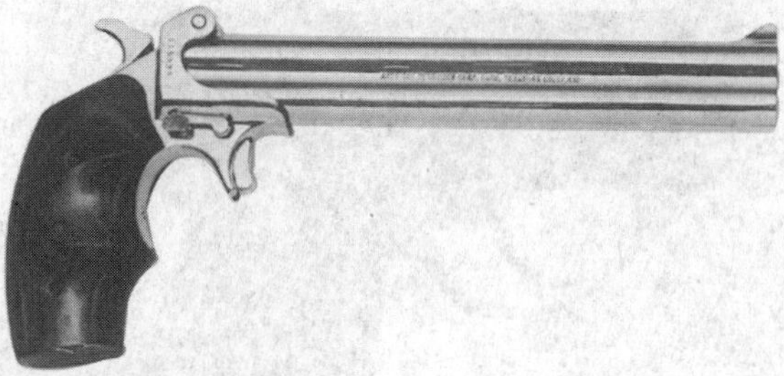

NIB	Exc.	V.G.	Good	Fair	Poor
700	600	480	350	180	100

Engraved

NIB	Exc.	V.G.	Good	Fair	Poor
1500	1000	680	450	300	120

Model 10 Derringer

Similar to Model 1, with frame of aluminum alloy. All other parts including barrels, stainless steel. Has a gray matte finish and thin grips of rosewood or bacote. Weight 10 oz. Chambered for .38 Special, .45 ACP or .45 Colt. Note: Add $75 for .45 Colt.

NIB	Exc.	V.G.	Good	Fair	Poor
500	380	250	120	100	80

Model 11 Derringer

Stainless steel barrel and all other parts aluminum. Weight 11 oz. Chambered for .38 Special, .380 Auto, .32 Magnum, .22 LR and .22 Magnum. Grips and finish are the same as on Model 10.

NIB	Exc.	V.G.	Good	Fair	Poor
500	380	250	120	100	80

Semmerling LM-4

LM-4 was designed as ultimate police backup/defense weapon. Manually operated 5-shot repeater only 5.2" long, 3.7" high and 1" wide. Chambered for .45 ACP. Undoubtedly smallest 5-shot .45 ever produced. LM-4 made of a special tool steel. Blued or at extra cost hard chrome-plated. Stainless steel version also available. LM-4 is not a semi-automatic, although it physically resembles one. Slide is flicked forward and back after each double-action squeeze of the trigger. This weapon is virtually handbuilt. Features high visibility sights and smooth trigger. Note: Add $200 for hard chrome; 35 percent for stainless steel.

NIB	Exc.	V.G.	Good	Fair	Poor
3500	3000	2000	1500	600	200

LM-5

Built of stainless steel. Semi-automatic chambered for .32 or .25 Auto. Barrel length 2.25"; overall length 4"; height 3". Wooden grips standard. Offered in limited quantities. Weight about 15 oz. Discontinued.

NIB	Exc.	V.G.	Good	Fair	Poor
550	450	300	150	100	50

Millennium Series 2000

Chambered for .38 Special, .45 Colt or .44-40. Single-action. Fitted with scrimshaw grips, with Yellow Rose of Texas on left side and Lone Star flag on right side. Weight about 15 oz. Supplied with red velvet box with silver inlay. Introduced in 1999.

NIB	Exc.	V.G.	Good	Fair	Poor
500	320	200	150	100	80

Gambler Millennium 2000

Similar to Millennium Series. Fitted with rosewood grips, with etched Lone Star of Texas. Supplied with brown leatherette box, with copper logo inlay.

NIB	Exc.	V.G.	Good	Fair	Poor
700	600	500	350	200	100

Women of Texas Series

Same features as Millennium Series 2000. Stamped "Women of Texas Series 2000".

NIB	Exc.	V.G.	Good	Fair	Poor
700	600	500	350	200	100

Cowboy Series 2000

Same features as Gambler Millennium 2000. Stamped on barrel "Cowboy Series 2000".

NIB	Exc.	V.G.	Good	Fair	Poor
700	600	500	350	200	100

AMERICAN FIRE ARMS MFG. CO., INC.

San Antonio, Texas

Company operated between 1972 and 1974, producing .25 ACP pocket pistol and stainless steel .38 Special derringer. A .380 Auto was produced on an extremely limited basis.

American .38 Special Derringer

Well-made stainless steel over/under derringer. Similar in appearance and function to old Remington over/under. Had 3" barrels that pivoted upward for loading. Single-action that had an automatic selector and spur trigger. Smooth grips were of walnut. Approximately 3,500 manufactured between 1972 and 1974.

NIB	Exc.	V.G.	Good	Fair	Poor
350	300	220	150	120	90

American .25 Automatic

Small blowback semi-automatic pocket pistol. Chambered for .25 ACP cartridge. Had 2" barrel. Made of stainless steel or blued carbon steel. Grips were plain uncheckered walnut. Detachable magazine held 7 shots. Manufactured until 1974. Note: Add 20 percent for stainless steel.

Courtesy J.B. Wood

NIB	Exc.	V.G.	Good	Fair	Poor
330	280	200	120	100	80

American .380 Automatic

Similar to .25 except larger. Barrel was 3.5". Made in stainless steel only. Grips were smooth walnut and held 8 shots. Only 10 of these .380s manufactured between 1972 and 1974. Extremely rare, but there is little collector base for this company's products. Value is difficult to estimate.

NIB	Exc.	V.G.	Good	Fair	Poor
—	600	550	480	380	200

AMERICAN FRONTIER FIREARMS
Aguanga, California

1871, 72 Open Top Standard Model

Offered in .38- or .44-caliber, with non-rebated cylinder. Barrel lengths 7.5" or 8" in round. Blued finish except silver backstrap and triggerguard. Walnut grips.

NIB	Exc.	V.G.	Good	Fair	Poor
800	620	500	400	220	100

Richards & Mason Conversion 1851 Navy Standard Model

Offered in .38- and .44-calibers, with Mason ejector assembly and non-rebated cylinder. Choice of octagon barrels in 4.75", 5.5" or 7.5". Blued finish, with blued backstrap and triggerguard. Walnut grips.

NIB	Exc.	V.G.	Good	Fair	Poor
800	620	500	400	220	100

1860 Richards Army Model

Chambered for .44 Colt and .38-caliber. Rebated cylinder with-/without ejector assembly. Barrel length 7.5". High polish blue finish, with silver triggerguard and case-hardened frame. Note: Guns shipped without ejector assembly will be supplied with a ramrod and plunger, typical of the period.

NIB	Exc.	V.G.	Good	Fair	Poor
800	620	500	400	220	100

AMERICAN GUN CO., NEW YORK
Norwich, Connecticut
Maker—Crescent Firearms Co.

Side-by-Side Shotgun

Typical trade gun made around turn of the century, by Crescent Firearms Co., to be distributed by H. & D. Folsom. These are sometimes known as "Hardware Store Guns", as that is where many were sold. This particular gun chambered for 12-, 16- or 20-gauge and produced with-/without external hammers. Length of barrels varied as did chokes. Some produced with Damascus barrels; some with fluid steel. Latter are worth approximately 25 percent more. Note: Full listing of most variations of Crescent Arms Co. and shotguns marked with American Gun Co., see "Crescent F.A. Co.".

Knickerbocker Pistol

See—KNICKERBOCKER

AMERICAN HISTORICAL FOUNDATION
Ashland, Virginia

See—AMERICA REMEMBERS

AMERICAN INDUSTRIES
Cleveland, Ohio
aka CALICO LIGHT WEAPONS SYSTEMS
Cornelius, Oregon - (previously Sparks, Nevada)

Calico M-100

Semi-automatic carbine. Has 16.1" barrel, with flash suppressor. Chambered for .22 LR. Features folding stock, full shrouding handguards, 100-round capacity, helical feed, detachable magazine, ambidextrous safety, pistol grip storage compartment, black finished alloy frame and adjustable sights. Introduced in 1986.

NIB	Exc.	V.G.	Good	Fair	Poor
600	500	400	300	200	—

Calico M-100P/M-110

Similar to M-100. .22 rimfire, with 6" barrel, muzzle brake and no shoulder stock.

NIB	Exc.	V.G.	Good	Fair	Poor
600	500	400	300	200	—

Calico M-100S Sporter/M-105

Similar to Model 100, with futuristically styled walnut buttstock and forearm.

NIB	Exc.	V.G.	Good	Fair	Poor
600	500	400	300	200	—

Calico M-101 Solid Stock Carbine

Introduced in 1994. Features 100-round magazine and composite buttstock that is removable.

NIB	Exc.	V.G.	Good	Fair	Poor
650	530	400	300	200	—

Calico M-900

Black polymer-stocked rifle similar to M-100S. Chambered for 9mm Parabellum. Has delayed blowback action. Features stainless steel bolt and alloy receiver. Cocking handle is non-reciprocating. Rear sight is fixed, with adjustable front. A 50-round magazine standard; 100-round model optional. Introduced in 1989.

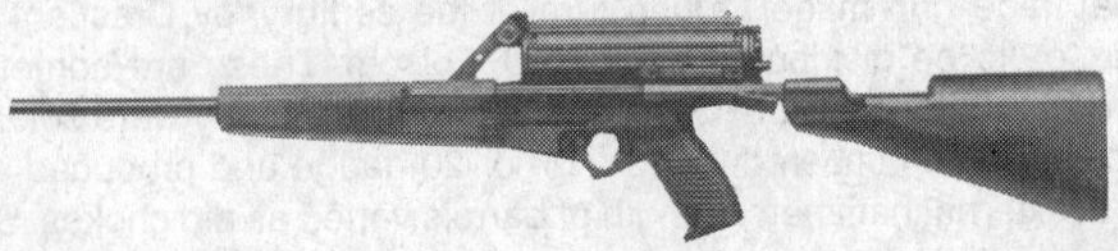

NIB	Exc.	V.G.	Good	Fair	Poor
850	700	550	400	300	—

Calico M-950 Pistol

Similar to Model 900 rifle, with 6" barrel. No shoulder stock.

NIB	Exc.	V.G.	Good	Fair	Poor
850	700	550	400	300	—

Calico M-951

M-951 is a tactical carbine, with sliding buttstock. Barrel 6" in length; weight about 7 lbs.

NIB	Exc.	V.G.	Good	Fair	Poor
850	700	550	400	300	—

Calico M-951S

Same as above. Furnished with more conventional buttstock. Referred to as light tactical carbine. Weight about 7.25 lbs.

NIB	Exc.	V.G.	Good	Fair	Poor
850	700	550	400	300	—

AMERICAN INTERNATIONAL

Salt Lake City, Utah
aka American Research & Development

180 Carbine (SAM-180)

Firearm imported from Austria. Semi-automatic 16.5" barreled carbine. Chambered for .22 LR. Sights are adjustable and stock made of high-impact plastic. Unique horizontally mounted drum magazine holds 177 rounds and affixed to top of receiver. A select-fire version available for law enforcement agencies only, and optional laser lock sight system. Later manufactured by Feather Industries in Boulder, Colorado. Now known as SAM-180.

NIB	Exc.	V.G.	Good	Fair	Poor
1400	1200	650	400	200	100

AMERICAN LONGRIFLE

Also known as the Pennsylvania Rifle or the Kentucky Rifle, the American Longrifle is not a specific model by a specific manufacturer, but rather a type of gun made by numerous individual gunsmiths. It is considered the first indigenous American firearms design, created by German immigrant gunsmiths in the early 1700s. It was developed from the German Jaeger short barrel large-caliber flintlock muzzleloading hunting rifle. Functional changes included decreasing the caliber to save scarce lead and lengthening the barrel to increase velocity to compensate for the smaller projectile. Defining characteristics of the American Longrifle include a long rifled barrel typically 34 to 48 inches or more, with most common calibers being in the .36 to .52 range, along with a full-length one-piece stock extending almost to the muzzle. The classic longrifle stock has a graceful droop to the buttstock and is often made of maple or curly maple. Although the style originated in Pennsylvania, the term "Kentucky Rifle" came into widespread common usage through a popular song of 1815 called "The Hunters of Kentucky" which celebrated Andrew Jackson's victory over the British at the Battle of New Orleans:

But Jackson he was wide awake,
And was not scar'd at trifles,
For well he knew what aim we take,
With our Kentucky rifles.

The general pattern was in fairly wide use by 1740, and the "Golden Age of Kentucky Rifles" is generally considered to be roughly 1776 to 1815. During this era ornate decoration was widely popular including carved stocks and decorative stock brass or silver inlays, along with highly ornate patchboxes. The longrifle pattern continued to be made into the percussion era. Original flintlock longrifles were often converted to percussion ignition. Longrifle production continued into the 20th century, and they are still being hand-made today. Over 1,000 makers of longrifles from the 18th and 19th century have been identified. The maker's name may be marked on the barrel, although many are unmarked. Some gunsmiths purchased their locks from lock manufacturers, many of them British, and a name on a lockplate is more likely to identify the lock maker than the gunsmith who made the gun.

Most gunsmiths who made longrifles also made other muzzleloaders including muskets, pistols, fowlers, and target or match rifles. Most of these types will bring less than the longrifle configuration. An over/under or swivel barrel double barrel longrifle or longrifle-style combination gun will bring a premium.

The values shown are for pre-1880 longrifles and are simplistic generalizations, since each longrifle is an individual hand-made piece. Higher values are paid for ornate decoration, original flintlock configuration, and noted gunsmiths. Factors that decrease values include conversion to percussion or modern reconversion to flintlock, or later production undecorated rifles, sometimes called "Southern rifles" or "plain rifles" (which is different than "plains rifles", q.v.)

Golden Age Original (Antique)

Flintlock, ornate decoration. Values vary wildly.

Exc.	Fine	V.G.	Good	Fair	Poor
—	100000	—	20000	—	2000

Plain Original Flintlock (Antique)

Original percussion, period conversion to percussion, or recoversion to flintlock.

Exc.	Fine	V.G.	Good	Fair	Poor
—	10000	5000	2500	1000	500

AMERICAN TACTICAL IMPORTS

Summerville, So. Carolina

AT CS/FS Series

These SA/DA pistols in 9mm, .40 S&W and .45 ACP were made in Turkey. Imported into U.S. in 2010 and 2011. Model designations were CS9, CS40, C45; and FS9, FS40. Features include a high-capacity magazine, ported slide and polymer frame.

NIB	Exc.	V.G.	Good	Fair	Poor
350	300	250	200	150	100

AT MS380

Similar to Beretta Cheetah design. This .380 model was imported from Turkey in 2010.

NIB	Exc.	V.G.	Good	Fair	Poor
320	280	220	180	140	100

Milsport

R-15-style platform chambered in .223/556 or 9mm with either 5.5-(9mm), 7.5- or 8.5-in. barrel. MLOK handguard. Add $230 for 9mm model.

NIB	Exc.	V.G.	Good	Fair	Poor
590	430	330	280	260	210

GSG-522

Semi-automatic tactical rifle chambered in .22 LR. Features include 16.25" barrel, black finish overall, polymer forend and buttstock, backup iron sights, receiver-mounted Picatinny rail, 10-round magazine. Several other rifle and carbine versions available. This model is part of ATI's German Sporting Gun Series.

NIB	Exc.	V.G.	Good	Fair	Poor
420	360	320	250	200	100

GSG-AK

Part of the German Sporting Gun Series, this model is patterned after the AK-47. Offered in several variations and stock designs. Note: Add 25 percent for hardwood stock and gold receiver; 20 percent for adjustable polymer stock.

NIB	Exc.	V.G.	Good	Fair	Poor
320	280	220	180	140	100

GSG-16

German Sport Gun .22LR semi-auto carbine, 16.25" barrel, collapsible stock, 22-round mag., 5.84 lbs, polymer receiver.

NIB	Exc.	V.G.	Good	Fair	Poor
330	280	230	—	—	—

German Sport Guns GSG-MP40P

Reproduction semi-automatic version of the WWII MP-40 machine pistol chambered in 9mm with 25-rnd. magazine. constructed go alloy and polymer with 7-in. barrel.

NIB	Exc.	V.G.	Good	Fair	Poor
590	430	330	280	260	210

FXH Series

Similar to the FX series but with polymer frame with finger grooves. Chambered in 9mm or .45 ACP. Offered in various barrel lengths. Introduced 2015. Variations include FXH-45, FXH45C compact model, FXH-45D subcompact model; 9mm models include FXH-9 and FXH-9C. Add $20 for 9mm models. Add $30 for ported and treaded barrel models.

NIB	Exc.	V.G.	Good	Fair	Poor
600	530	420	380	300	250

Galeo

Galil-style platform operated by a Kalashnikov-pattern gas-driven piston system. Built with IMI Galil kits and new US parts. Chambered in .223/556 13-in. barrel.

NIB	Exc.	V.G.	Good	Fair	Poor
1300	1110	860	660	560	430

ATI GSG 1911

Caliber .22 Long Rifle. Full sized 1911-style pistol chambered for .22 LR. Features include zinc alloy frame, walnut grips, 10-round magazine, ambidextrous thumb safety and extended grip safety. Target model has adjustable sights, target grips and accessory rail. Note: Add $30 for Target model.

NIB	Exc.	V.G.	Good	Fair	Poor
280	250	220	200	180	150

SX Cavalry Shotgun

This over/under series of shotguns is made in Turkey. Offered in 12-, 20-, 28-gauge and .410 bore. Features include Turkish walnut stock, five choke tubes, single-selective trigger, extractors and alloy receiver with light engraving.

NIB	Exc.	V.G.	Good	Fair	Poor
420	380	320	280	220	200

Cavalry Road Agent

Side-by-side double-barrel shotgun in 12-, 20-gauge or .410 bore. Barrel 18.5" and comes with five choke tubes. Features include double triggers, external hammers with decocker and Turkish walnut stock. New in 2017.

NIB	Exc.	V.G.	Good	Fair	Poor
520	450	400	350	300	280

TAC-P, TAC-S Shotgun Series

This duo of tactical shotguns consists of a slide-action (TAC-P) and semi-automatic (TAC-S), with similar features. In 12-gauge only. Barrel length 18.5", with a cylinder bore. Synthetic stock has a pistol grip. Both models available with an interchangeable 28" barrel, with three choke tubes. Note: Add $100 for this option.

TAC-P

NIB	Exc.	V.G.	Good	Fair	Poor
220	200	160	120	100	80

TAC-S

NIB	Exc.	V.G.	Good	Fair	Poor
320	280	220	180	140	100

Crusader Field

Gauges: 12 ga., 3 in., 20 ga., 3 in., 28 ga., 2.75 in, .410 bore, 3 in. Barrels: 26 in., 28 in., 30 in., ventilated rib. Weight: 6.0-6.5 lbs. Stock: Turkish walnut with oil finish. Features: ATI's new O/U line has both Field and Sport models. Made from 7075 aluminum with laser engraving on the receiver. Single selective trigger, fiber-optic front sight, extractors, chrome-moly steel barrel. Ships with five chokes: flush on the Field, extended on the Sport.

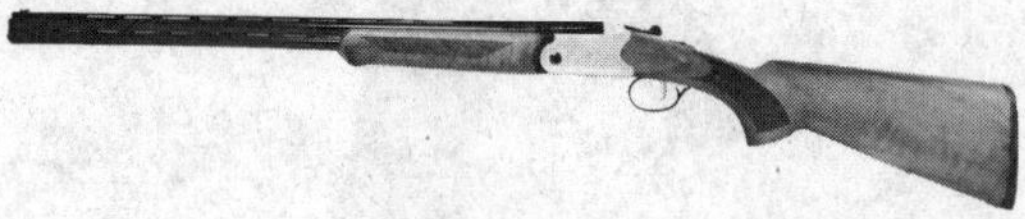

NIB	Exc.	V.G.	Good	Fair	Poor
430	380	300	250	—	—

Crusader Sport

NIB	Exc.	V.G.	Good	Fair	Poor
490	430	320	250	—	—

Milsport

AR-type semi-auto rifle, 5.56, .300Blackout, 9mm, 6.5 Grendel. 16" barrel, 6-position stock, 6.5 lbs. Numerous variations include calibers, colors, stock, and finishes — some of which impact price.

NIB	Exc.	V.G.	Good	Fair	Poor
600	530	480	380	—	—

Milsport Shotgun

AR type semi-auto .410 shotgun, 18.5" barrel, 5-round mag.

NIB	Exc.	V.G.	Good	Fair	Poor
680	580	480	380	—	—

OMNI SERIES

Calibers: 5.56/.223 Rem.; .22 LR, .300 BLK, 9mm Luger. American Tactical, Inc. is a firearms manufacturer and importer based out of Summerville, SC. Built on forged aluminum Mil-Sport upper and polymer hybrid Omni lower receiver. Barrels: M4 profile, 1:7" button-cut rifling, black-nitride coated. Carbine-length gas system with rail-height Picatinny-topped gas block, six-position adjustable Roger's Superstock, and A2-style compensator. AR-15 pattern, Mil-Spec lower parts kit. Maxx line comes with high-strength-fiberglass composite polymer upper and lower receiver with strengthened metal inserts and one magazine. Mil-Sport AR-15 pattern rifle is built on an M16A3-pattern forged aluminum upper and AR-15 Mil-Sport pattern lower receiver. 9mm Milsport Carbines feature a billet aluminum receiver, 31-round ETS Glock-style magazines. Limited Lifetime Warranty.

NIB	Exc.	V.G.	Good	Fair	Poor
800	—	—	—	—	—

Omni Hybrid Maxx

AR-type semi-auto rifle with metal-reinforced polymer upper and lower receivers. 5.56, .300 Blackout, .22 LR. 16" barrel, six-position stock, 6.25 lbs. Numerous variations include calibers, colors, stock, and finishes — some of which impact price. Values are for basic models. Deduct $150 for .22 LR caliber.

NIB	Exc.	V.G.	Good	Fair	Poor
480	430	380	330	—	—

Omni Hybrid Maxx Pistol

AR-style pistol with 7.5" or 10.5" barrel in 5.56 NATO. Free-floating Key-Mod quad rail.

NIB	Exc.	V.G.	Good	Fair	Poor
580	500	420	350	280	200

ATI Omni Hybrid Quad Rail 16" 5.56

NIB	Exc.	V.G.	Good	Fair	Poor
450	—	—	—	—	—

Omni Hybrid Shotgun

AR-type semi-auto .410 shotgun, 18.5" barrel, five-round mag.

NIB	Exc.	V.G.	Good	Fair	Poor
600	530	480	—	—	—

Bulldog

Gauge: 12 ga. 3", 20 ga. 3". Barrel: 16" and 18.5" with ported shroud. Length: 23.5"–26". Weight: 4.5 lbs. Stock: Black synthetic with fixed bullpup style with adjustable cheek riser. Features: Gas-operated tactical bullpup shotgun with AR-style charging handle, adjustable cheek rest, and both Picatinny and M-LOK rails. Housing for spare five-round magazine. Extra magazine can also be attached to the bottom rail and used as a foregrip. Includes quick acquisition flip-up sights and three choke tubes.

NIB	Exc.	V.G.	Good	Fair	Poor
300	—	—	—	—	—

AMERICAN WESTERN ARMS INC. (AWA)

Delray Beach, Florida

Lightning Rifle LE

Copy of Colt Lightning slide-action rifle. Chambered for .32-20, .38 Special, .38-40, .44-40 or .45 Colt cartridge. Choice of round barrel lengths in 20" or 24". Engraved AWA logo and stag scene on receiver. Limited edition to 500 guns.

NIB	Exc.	V.G.	Good	Fair	Poor
1200	950	780	500	300	180

Lightning Rifle

Slide-action rifle chambered for those cartridges above. Choice of 24" round or octagon barrel. Blued finish. Note: Add $40 for octagon barrel.

NIB	Exc.	V.G.	Good	Fair	Poor
800	680	500	400	300	180

Lightning Carbine

As above, with 20" round or octagon barrel. Note: Add $40 for octagon barrel.

NIB	Exc.	V.G.	Good	Fair	Poor
800	680	500	400	300	180

Lightningbolt

Handgun version of Lightning rifle, with 12" barrel and variety of finishes. Chambered in .45 Colt. Values shown are for blued version.

NIB	Exc.	V.G.	Good	Fair	Poor
1000	800	680	500	400	200

Model 1892 Lever Action

Reproduction of Winchester 1892 carbine/rifle in .357 Magnum, .44-40, .45 Colt. Carbine model has 20" octagon barrel; rifle 24" round barrel.

NIB	Exc.	V.G.	Good	Fair	Poor
750	650	500	400	300	200

Peacekeeper

Single-action revolver assembled in U.S.A. from parts made in Italy (circa 2000 - 2003). Based on Colt Single Action Army and offered in standard barrel lengths associated with that design. Calibers are .32-20, .38-40, .357 Magnum, .44-40, .44 Special and .45 Colt. Blue, case-hardened or nickel finish and hard rubber grips. Engraved versions were available in various grades based on amount of coverage — add $1500 to $2000. Nickel finish would command a $150 to $200 premium.

NIB	Exc.	V.G.	Good	Fair	Poor
750	600	500	400	300	200

Longhorn

An economy variation of Peacekeeper.

NIB	Exc.	V.G.	Good	Fair	Poor
450	400	320	300	220	200

AMES, N.P. PISTOLS
Springfield, Massachusetts

Overall length 11.625"; barrel length 6"; caliber .54. Markings: on lockplate forward of hammer "N.P. AMES/SPRINGFIELD/MASS"; on tail either "USN" or "USR" over date; on barrel standard U.S. Navy inspection marks. N. P. Ames of Springfield, Mass. received a contract from the U.S. Navy in September 1842, for delivery of 2,000 single-shot muzzleloading percussion pistols. All are distinguished by having a lock mechanism that lies flush with right side of stock. On first 300 Ames pistols, this lock terminates in a point; balance produced made with locks with a rounded tail. This "boxlock" had been devised by Henry Nock in England and was adapted to U.S. Navy for percussion pistols they ordered from Ames and Derringer. In addition to the 2,000 pistols for Navy, U.S. Revenue Cutter Service purchased 144 (distinguished by "U S R" marks) for the forerunner of U.S. Coast Guard. Latter commands triple price over "U S N" marked pistols, while Navy pistols with pointed tails quadruple value.

Model 1842 US Navy Pistol (Antique)

"Deringer" marked pistols worth modest premium.

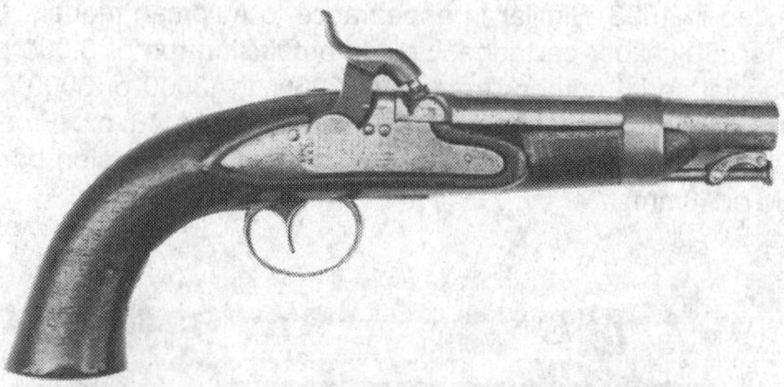

Exc.	Fine	V.G.	Good	Fair	Poor
3000	1500	1000	700	500	300

AMES SWORD CO.
Chicopee Falls, Massachusetts

Turbiaux Le Protector (Antique)

Ames Sword Co., became one of three U.S. companies that produced this unique French palm-squeezer pistol. Design consists of a round disk, with protruding barrel on one side and lever on the other. Disk contains a cylinder that holds seven 8mm rimfire or ten 6mm rimfire cartridges. Barrel protrudes between fingers and lever trigger is squeezed to fire the weapon. Design was patented in 1883 and sold successfully in France into 1890s. In 1892, Peter Finnegan bought the patents and brought them to Ames Sword. He contracted with them to produce 25,000 pistols for Minneapolis Firearms Company. After approximately 1,500 were delivered, Finnegan declared insolvency and after litigation, Ames secured full patent rights. Ames Company produced Protector Revolvers until at least 1917. (See Chicago Firearms Co. and Minneapolis Firearms Co.)

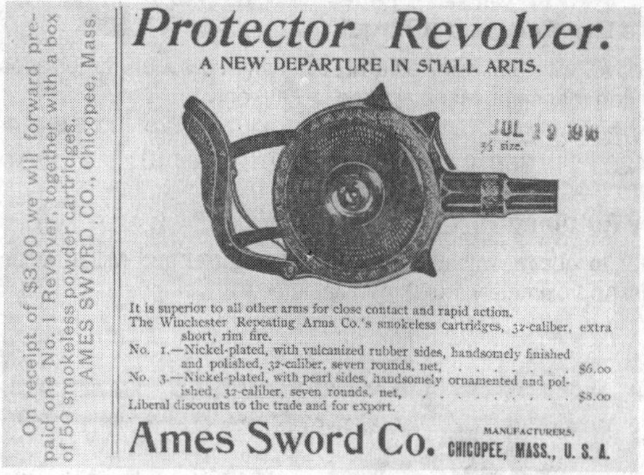

Exc.	Fine	V.G.	Good	Fair	Poor
3500	1800	1350	900	550	380

AMT
Formerly ARCADIA MACHINE AND TOOL
Irwindale, California
See—GALENA INDUSTRIES INC. & AUTO-MAG

AMT is one of several companies that succeeded Auto Mag Corp. Original manufacturer of Auto Mag pistols operated from approximately 1984 to 1998. Prices in this section are for these earlier AMT-built guns only. In 1998, Galena Ind., of Sturgis, South Dakota, purchased the rights to produce most of the AMT-developed firearms and manufactured several models from 1999 to 2001. In 2005, the rights to several AMT models were acquired by Crusader Gun Co. of Houston, parent company of High Standard Mfg. Co. Also see listing for Auto Mag.

HANDGUNS

Lightning

Single-action semi-automatic .22-caliber pistol. Available with barrel lengths of 5" (Bull only), 6.5", 8.5", 10.5" and 12.5" (either Bull or tapered). Adjustable sights as well as trigger. Grips are checkered black rubber. Manufactured between 1984 and 1987.

Courtesy John J. Stimson, Jr.

NIB	*Exc.*	*V.G.*	*Good*	*Fair*	*Poor*
—	360	250	210	100	80

Bull's Eye Regulation Target

As above, with 6.5" ventilated rib bull barrel, wooden target grips and extended rear sight. Manufactured in 1986 only.

NIB	*Exc.*	*V.G.*	*Good*	*Fair*	*Poor*
420	360	290	230	140	130

Baby Automag

Similar to above, with 8.5" ventilated rib barrel and Millett adjustable sights. Approximately 1,000 manufactured.

Courtesy J.B. Wood

NIB	*Exc.*	*V.G.*	*Good*	*Fair*	*Poor*
750	660	560	460	340	290

Automag II

Stainless steel semi-automatic .22 Magnum pistol. Available with 3.375", 4.5" and 6" barrel lengths. Millett adjustable sights and grips of black grooved plastic. First manufactured in 1987. Discontinued 2001. Reintroduced in 2005 by Crusader Gun Co. Values shown are for original models made by AMT. Note: Deduct 10 percent for Crusader models.

Courtesy J.B. Wood

NIB	*Exc.*	*V.G.*	*Good*	*Fair*	*Poor*
780	680	580	480	360	300

Automag III

Semi-automatic pistol chambered for .30 Carbine and 9mm Win. Magnum cartridge. Barrel length 6.37"; overall length 10.5". Magazine capacity 8 rounds. Fitted with Millett adjustable rear sight and carbon fiber grips. Stainless steel finish. Weight 43 oz. Discontinued 2001. Reintroduced in 2005 by Crusader Gun Co. Values shown are for original models made by AMT. Note: Deduct 10 percent for Crusader models.

NIB	*Exc.*	*V.G.*	*Good*	*Fair*	*Poor*
540	450	340	270	200	160

Automag IV

Similar in appearance to Automag III. Chambered for .45 Win. Magnum. Magazine capacity 7 rounds. Weight 46 oz. Discontinued 2001. Reintroduced in 2005 by Crusader gun Co. Values shown are for original models made by AMT. **NOTE** Deduct 10 percent for Crusader models.

NIB	*Exc.*	*V.G.*	*Good*	*Fair*	*Poor*
540	450	340	270	200	160

Automag V

Introduced in 1993. Similar in appearance to Automag models. Chambered for .50-caliber cartridge. Limited production run of 3,000 pistols, with special serial number from "1 of 3000" to "3000 of 3000". Barrel length 6.5". Magazine capacity 5 rounds. Weight 46 oz. Production stopped in 1995. Note: Add $300 each for extra conversion barrels in .45 WM or 10mm.

Courtesy J.B. Wood

NIB	*Exc.*	*V.G.*	*Good*	*Fair*	*Poor*
820	700	630	520	380	330

Javelina

Produced in 1992. Chambered for 10mm cartridge. Fitted with 7" barrel, with adjustable sights. Rubber wrap-around grips. Adjustable trigger. Magazine is 8 rounds. Weight about 47 oz.

Courtesy J.B. Wood

NIB	Exc.	V.G.	Good	Fair	Poor
560	460	360	290	220	190

Back Up Pistol .22/.380

Small semi-automatic pocket pistol. Chambered for .22 LR or .380 ACP cartridges. Fitted with 2.5" barrel. Offered with black plastic or walnut grips. Weight 18 oz. Magazine capacity 5 rounds. Originally manufactured by TDE, then Irwindale Arms Inc. and then by AMT.

NIB	Exc.	V.G.	Good	Fair	Poor
450	380	300	260	180	160

Back Up Pistol.45 ACP, .40 S&W, 9mm

Courtesy J.B. Wood

NIB	Exc.	V.G.	Good	Fair	Poor
560	480	430	380	250	200

.38 Super, .357 SIG, .400 CorBon

Note: Prices for current production by High Standard Mfg. Co. Note: Add $100 for .400 CorBon

NIB	Exc.	V.G.	Good	Fair	Poor
560	480	430	380	250	200

9mm, .38 Super, .40 S&W, .45 ACP

NIB	Exc.	V.G.	Good	Fair	Poor
560	480	430	380	250	200

.380 Back Up II

Introduced in 1993. Similar to Back Up model. Addition of double safety extended finger grip on magazine and single-action-only. Special order pistol only.

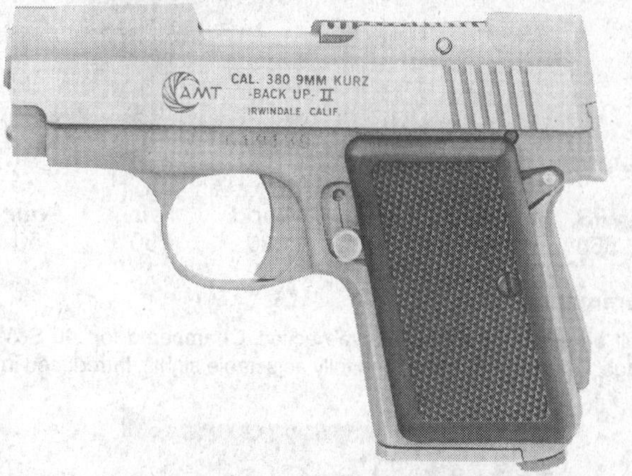

NIB	Exc.	V.G.	Good	Fair	Poor
300	230	160	120	100	80

Hardballer/Government Model

Similar to Colt Gold Cup .45 ACP. Offered in two versions: first has fixed sights and rounded slide top; second has adjustable Millett sights and matte rib. Magazine capacity 7 rounds. Wrap-around rubber grips are standard. Long grip safety, beveled magazine well and adjustable trigger common to both variations. Weight 38 oz.

Hardballer

Adjustable sights.

Courtesy J.B. Wood

NIB	Exc.	V.G.	Good	Fair	Poor
480	410	330	260	170	140

Government Model

Fixed sights.

NIB	Exc.	V.G.	Good	Fair	Poor
460	380	330	280	180	140

Longslide

Similar to Hardballer Model. Fitted with 7" barrel. Magazine capacity 7 rounds. Weight 46 oz.

NIB	Exc.	V.G.	Good	Fair	Poor
500	430	320	260	170	140

.400 Accelerator

Similar to models above. Chambered for .400 CorBon cartridge. Fitted with 7" barrel. Fully adjustable sights. Introduced in 1997.

NIB	Exc.	V.G.	Good	Fair	Poor
560	550	400	320	250	150

Commando

Built on Government model-type action. Chambered for .40 S&W cartridge. Fitted with 5" barrel and fully adjustable sights. Introduced in 1997.

NIB	Exc.	V.G.	Good	Fair	Poor
460	400	330	260	170	140

On Duty

Semi-automatic pistol. Features double-action-only trigger action or double-action with decocker. Chambered for 9mm, .40 S&W or .45 ACP calibers. Barrel length 4.5"; overall length 7.75". Finish black anodized matte. Carbon fiber grips are standard. Furnished with 3-dot sights. Weight 32 oz.

NIB	Exc.	V.G.	Good	Fair	Poor
660	410	300	260	170	140

Skipper

Identical to Hardballer, with 1" shorter barrel and slide. Discontinued in 1984.

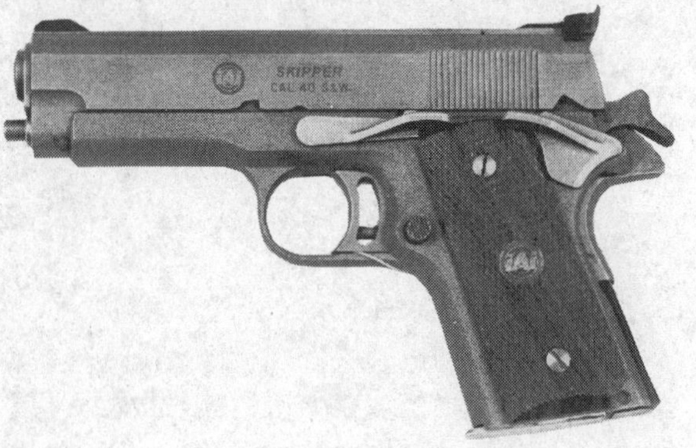

NIB	Exc.	V.G.	Good	Fair	Poor
460	410	350	290	200	160

Combat Skipper

Similar to Colt Commander. Discontinued in 1984.

NIB	Exc.	V.G.	Good	Fair	Poor
480	440	380	320	220	180

RIFLES

Lightning

Patterned after Ruger 10/22. Said to have been discontinued for that reason. Rifle has 22" barrel and 25-round detachable magazine, with folding stock. Introduced in 1986.

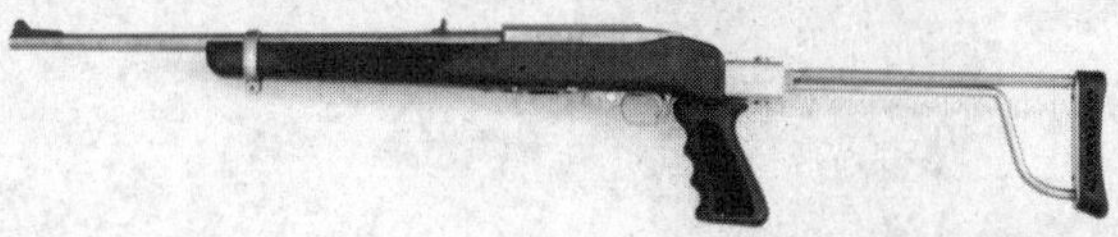

Courtesy J.B. Wood

NIB	Exc.	V.G.	Good	Fair	Poor
380	250	180	120	80	50

Small Game Hunter

As above, with full stock and 10-round magazine. Introduced in 1986.

NIB	Exc.	V.G.	Good	Fair	Poor
350	220	180	150	120	100

Small Game Hunter II

Semi-automatic rifle chambered for .22 LR cartridge. Stock is checkered black matte nylon. Fitted with removable recoil pad for ammo, cleaning rod and knife. Rotary magazine holds 10 rounds. Stainless steel barrel and action. Barrel is a heavy weight target type, 22" long. Weight 6 lbs.

NIB	Exc.	V.G.	Good	Fair	Poor
350	220	180	150	120	100

Hunter

Semi-automatic rifle chambered for .22 Rimfire Magnum cartridge. Stock is checkered black matte nylon. Other features similar to Small Game Hunter II, including weight.

NIB	Exc.	V.G.	Good	Fair	Poor
380	250	200	150	120	100

Magnum Hunter

Similar to above. Chambered for .22 Rimfire Magnum cartridge. Fitted with 22" accurized barrel. Barrel and action are stainless steel. Comes standard with 5-round magazine and composite stock. Laminated stock was available at an extra cost, as is a 10-round magazine.

NIB	Exc.	V.G.	Good	Fair	Poor
520	400	350	250	200	150

Target Model

Semi-automatic rifle chambered for .22 LR cartridge. Fitted with 20" target barrel. Weight about 7.5 lbs. Choice of Fajen or Hogue stock. Note: Hogue stock deduct $50.

NIB	Exc.	V.G.	Good	Fair	Poor
600	500	450	300	200	—

Challenge Edition

Custom ordered .22-caliber semi-automatic rifle. Built on Ruger 10/22-like receiver. Offered in 18" or 22" barrel lengths, with all stainless steel construction. McMillan fiberglass stock. Weaver-style scope mounts.

NIB	Exc.	V.G.	Good	Fair	Poor
1050	800	550	400	300	180

Single-Shot Standard

Custom-built rifle, with choice of barrel length, composite stock, adjustable trigger, post '64 Winchester action, all in stainless and chrome moly steel. Chambered for all standard calibers. First offered in 1996.

NIB	Exc.	V.G.	Good	Fair	Poor
880	680	500	350	200	180

Single-Shot Deluxe

Custom-built rifle on Mauser-type action, with choice of match-grade barrel lengths and custom Kevlar stock. Built from stainless and chrome moly steel. Chambered for all standard calibers. First offered in 1996.

NIB	Exc.	V.G.	Good	Fair	Poor
1800	1400	950	650	400	220

Bolt-Action Repeating--Standard

Similar in construction and features to Standard Single-Shot rifle.

NIB	Exc.	V.G.	Good	Fair	Poor
840	680	500	350	200	180

Bolt-Action Repeating--Deluxe

Similar in construction and features to Deluxe Single-Shot rifle.

NIB	Exc.	V.G.	Good	Fair	Poor
1800	1400	950	650	400	220

ANCION MARX
Liege, Belgium

Company began production in 1860s, with a variety of cheaply made pinfire revolvers. They later switched to solid-frame centerfire "Velo-Dog"-type revolvers, chambered for 5.5mm or 6.35mm. They were marketed in various countries under many different trade names. See Oury, D.D. Quality of these revolvers is quite poor and collector interest, almost non-existent. Values do not usually vary because of trade names.

Antique

Exc.	Fine	V.G.	Good	Fair	Poor
200	140	110	80	40	20

ANDERSON
Anderson, Texas

Underhammer Pistol **Antique**

Unmarked under hammer percussion pistol. Chambered for .45-caliber. Had 5" half-round/half-octagonal barrel, with all steel saw handle-shaped frame, flared butt with walnut grips. Finish blued. Little information on this pistol. Found with no maker's mark; there is considerable doubt that these were actually made in Anderson Texas. It's more likely that they were made by Blunt & Syms.

Exc.	Fine	V.G.	Good	Fair	Poor
900	700	500	300	250	150

ANDERSON MANUFACTURING
Hebron, Kentucky

AM-15 RIFLE SERIES

Calibers: 5.56 NATO, 6.5 Grendel, .300 BLK, 7.62x39. Produces a range of AR-15-type rifles and carbines. Barrels: 16", 18", 24". Builds include CNC-machined 7075 T6 aluminum forgings for uppers and lowers, machined to military specifications and marked "Multi-Cal" to be used with multiple calibers on the AR-15 platform. Proprietary RF85 metal treatment on some rifles. SEE POLITICAL PANIC PRICING.

NIB	Exc.	V.G.	Good	Fair	Poor
530	—	—	—	—	—

AM-15 M4 Optic Ready 5.56

NIB	Exc.	V.G.	Good	Fair	Poor
530	500	450	—	—	—

AM-15 M4 Optic Ready 5.56 RF85

NIB	Exc.	V.G.	Good	Fair	Poor
800	700	600	—	—	—

AM-15 M4 Optic Ready 7.62x39

NIB	Exc.	V.G.	Good	Fair	Poor
700	630	550	—	—	—

AM-15 M4 Optic Ready 7.62x39 RF85

NIB	Exc.	V.G.	Good	Fair	Poor
860	750	650	—	—	—

AM-10 GEN 2 RIFLE SERIES

Calibers: .308 Win., Barrels: 16", 18", 24". Features common to all AM-10 Gen 2 rifles include Forged 7075-T6 aluminum upper and lower receivers with Type-3 hard anodizing; 8620 steel nitrided bolt carrier; 9310 steel bolt; 4150 chrome-moly vanadium barrels, 1:10" twist rifling; standard charging handles, six-position receiver extensions, enhanced flared magwells. Models include Ranger, Battle Rifle, and Marksman XL. Introduced June 2022. SEE POLITICAL PANIC PRICING.

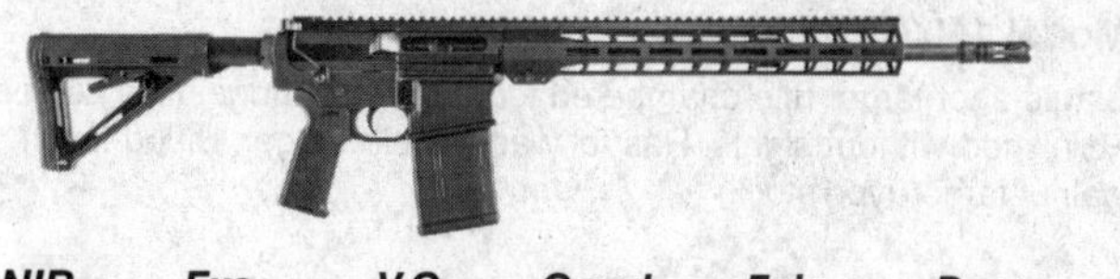

NIB	Exc.	V.G.	Good	Fair	Poor
850	—	—	—	—	—

AM-10 EXTSP-RT2 .308 Win.

NIB	Exc.	V.G.	Good	Fair	Poor
1100	1000	880	—	—	—

AM-10 EXTSP-RT2 6.5 Creedmoor

NIB	Exc.	V.G.	Good	Fair	Poor
1200	1050	900	—	—	—

Ranger .308 Win., 18"

NIB	Exc.	V.G.	Good	Fair	Poor
900	—	—	—	—	—

AM-9 PISTOL CALIBER CARBINE SERIES

Caliber: 9mm Para. Barrel: 16" 4150 Chrome Moly Vanadium, 1:10" twist, 1/2-36 tpi muzzle threads. Anderson Knight Stalker Flash Hider, 15-in. Anderson M-LOK Handguard w/upper-height top Picatinny rail. Magpul furniture, K2 Grip and Black MOE stock, and PMAG 27 GL9 magazine (27 rd). Introduced 2018. SEE POLITICAL PANIC PRICING.

NIB	Exc.	V.G.	Good	Fair	Poor
790	—	—	—	—	—

AM-9 PCC

NIB	Exc.	V.G.	Good	Fair	Poor
790	—	—	—	—	—

ANDRUS & OSBORN

Canton, Connecticut

Underhammer Pistol (Antique)

Pistol of percussion type. Chambered for .25-caliber. Part-round/part-octagonal barrel is 6" long. Features small silver star inlays along its length. Barrel marked "Andrus & Osborn/Canton Conn.", with an eagle stamped beside it. Marked "Cast Steel" near breech. Grips walnut. Finish browned. Active 1863 to 1867.

Exc.	Fine	V.G.	Good	Fair	Poor
1400	750	550	350	250	150

ANSCHUTZ, J.G. GmbH

Ulm, Germany

Originally founded in 1856, by Julius and Lusie Anschutz. Company was originally called J.G. Anschutz and manufactured a wide variety of firearms. In 1950 in Ulm, the new company was founded: J.G. Anschutz GmbH. Values for new guns fluctuate according to currency variations.

RIMFIRE

Mark 10 Target

Single-shot bolt-action rifle. Chambered for .22 LR cartridge. Has 26" heavy barrel, with adjustable target-type sights. Finish blued. Walnut target stock had an adjustable palm rest. Manufactured between 1963 and 1981.

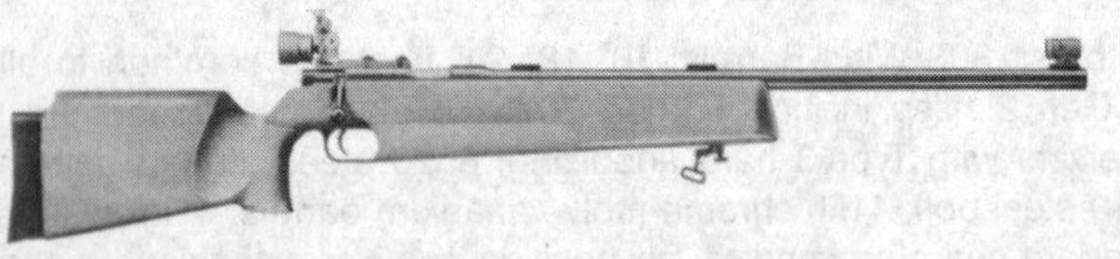

NIB	Exc.	V.G.	Good	Fair	Poor
500	420	350	210	150	100

Model 1403D

Single-shot target rifle chambered for .22 LR cartridge. Has 26" barrel. Furnished without sights. Has fully adjustable trigger. Blued finish, with walnut target-type stock.

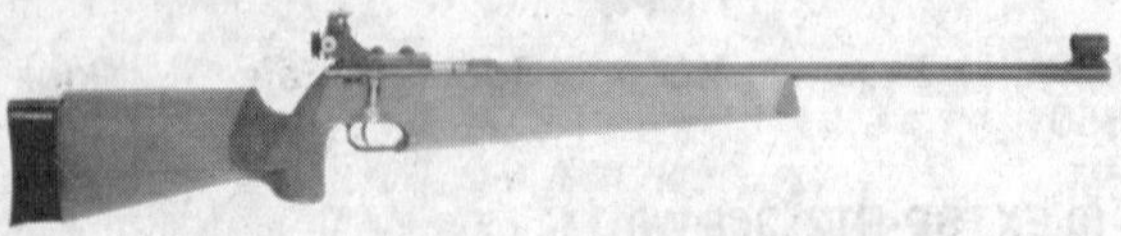

NIB	Exc.	V.G.	Good	Fair	Poor
850	780	680	500	380	250

Model 1407

Similar to Mark 10. Furnished without sights. Known as "I.S.U." model. Discontinued in 1981.

NIB	Exc.	V.G.	Good	Fair	Poor
520	450	380	240	180	100

Model 1408

Heavier-barreled version of Model 1407.

NIB	Exc.	V.G.	Good	Fair	Poor
520	450	380	240	180	100

Model 1411

Designed specifically to be fired from prone position.

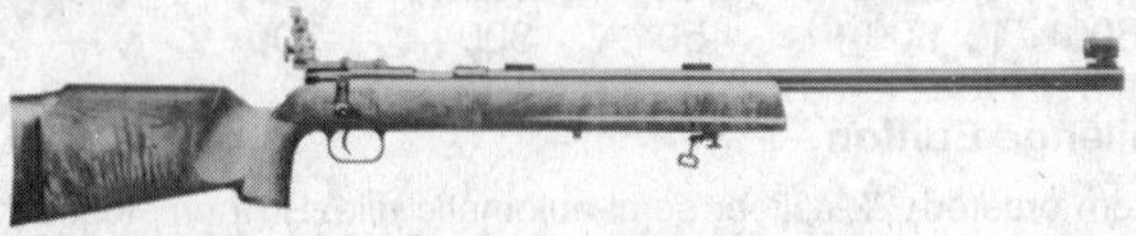

NIB	Exc.	V.G.	Good	Fair	Poor
750	650	450	210	150	100

Model 1413 Match

High-grade competition version, with heavy target barrel. Furnished without sights; optional sights extra. Walnut stock has adjustable cheekpiece.

NIB	Exc.	V.G.	Good	Fair	Poor
780	680	550	400	280	150

Model 1416D HB Classic

Chambered for .22 LR cartridge. Magazine capacity 5 rounds. Fitted with match-grade trigger and target grade barrel. Checkered walnut stock. Built on the 64 action.

NIB	Exc.	V.G.	Good	Fair	Poor
900	720	600	400	220	120

Model 1416D KL Classic

Sporting rifle chambered for .22 LR cartridge. Fitted with American-style stock of European walnut or hardwood. Built on Anschutz Match 64 action. Left-handed model also offered.

NIB	Exc.	V.G.	Good	Fair	Poor
900	720	600	300	200	100

Model 1416D Custom

Chambered for .22 LR cartridge. Features European-style stock, with Monte Carlo cheekpiece and schnabel forend.

NIB	Exc.	V.G.	Good	Fair	Poor
880	650	550	300	200	100

Model 1418D KL Mannlicher

Hunting rifle, with full-length Mannlicher-type stock. Made with hand-checkered walnut. Chambered for .22 LR, with 5-round magazine. Open iron sights. Weight about 5.5 lbs.

NIB	Exc.	V.G.	Good	Fair	Poor
1200	950	700	450	200	150

Model 1418/19

Lower-priced sporter model. Formerly imported by Savage Arms.

NIB	Exc.	V.G.	Good	Fair	Poor
700	650	420	200	120	80

Model 1433D

Centerfire version of Model 54 target rifle. Chambered for .22 Hornet. Special-order item. Features set trigger and 4-round detachable magazine. Finish blued, with full-length Mannlicher stock. Discontinued in 1986.

NIB	Exc.	V.G.	Good	Fair	Poor
1500	950	700	400	200	100

Model 1533

Similar to Model 1433D, except chambered for .222 Remington cartridge. This model has a Mannlicher-style stock. Discontinued in mid 1990s.

NIB	Exc.	V.G.	Good	Fair	Poor
1200	1050	900	750	600	300

Model 1449D Youth

Bolt-action rifle chambered for .22 LR cartridge. Fitted with 16" barrel and adjustable rear sight. Stock is European hardwood, with 12.25" length of pull. Magazine capacity 5 rounds. No longer imported.

NIB	Exc.	V.G.	Good	Fair	Poor
450	300	250	100	80	60

Model Woodchucker

Sold by distributor RSR. Bolt-action .22-caliber. Similar to Model 1449D Youth.

NIB	Exc.	V.G.	Good	Fair	Poor
450	300	250	100	80	60

Model 1451E Target

Single-shot .22-caliber target rifle. Fitted with 22" barrel. Can be fitted with micrometer iron sights or telescope sights. Checkered pistol grip and adjustable buttplate. Weight about 6.25 lbs.

NIB	Exc.	V.G.	Good	Fair	Poor
620	500	400	200	120	80

Model 1451R Sporter Target

Bolt-action target rifle chambered for .22 LR cartridge. Fitted with target-style stock and 22" heavy barrel. Furnished with no open sights. Two-stage target trigger is standard. Weight about 6.5 lbs.

NIB	Exc.	V.G.	Good	Fair	Poor
650	520	420	220	180	100

Model 1451D Custom

Similar to above. Fitted with checkered walnut sporting stock, with Monte Carlo comb and cheekpiece. Barrel length 22.75", with open sights. Weight about 5 lbs.

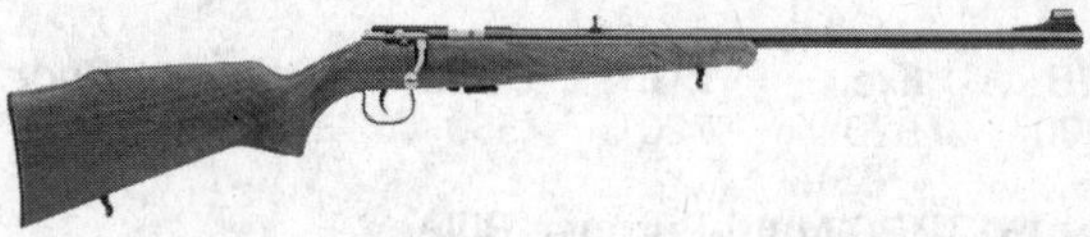

NIB	Exc.	V.G.	Good	Fair	Poor
680	550	450	250	150	100

Model 1451D Classic

Similar to Model 1451 Custom, with straight walnut stock. Weight about 5 lbs.

NIB	Exc.	V.G.	Good	Fair	Poor
700	600	500	300	150	100

Model 1516D KL Classic

Same as above. Chambered for .22 Magnum cartridge.

NIB	Exc.	V.G.	Good	Fair	Poor
780	600	500	300	200	100

Model 1516D KL Custom

Same as above. Chambered for .22 Magnum cartridge.

NIB	Exc.	V.G.	Good	Fair	Poor
850	650	550	450	250	100

Model 1517

Bolt action rifles chambered for .17 HRM rimfire cartridge. Stainless steel barrels were only manufactured 2007-2008.

Model 1517D Classic

Based on the 64 action. Bolt-action rifle chambered for .17 HMR cartridge. Fitted with 23" barrel. Checkered walnut stock. Magazine capacity 4 rounds. Weight about 5.5 lbs. Introduced in 2003.

NIB	Exc.	V.G.	Good	Fair	Poor
980	800	700	550	400	300

Model 1517D HB Classic

Similar to Model 1516D. Fitted with a heavy barrel without sights. Weight about 6.2 lbs. Introduced in 2003.

NIB	Exc.	V.G.	Good	Fair	Poor
1050	850	750	550	400	300

Model 1517D Monte Carlo

Chambered for .17 HMR cartridge. Fitted with 23" barrel. Checkered walnut stock, with schnabel forend and Monte Carlo comb. Weight about 5.5 lbs. Introduced in 2003.

NIB	Exc.	V.G.	Good	Fair	Poor
1000	820	720	550	400	300

Model 1517MPR Multi-Purpose Rifle

Introduced in 2003. Features 25.5" heavy barrel without sights, two-stage trigger, hardwood stock with beavertail forend. Chambered for .17 HMR cartridge. Weight about 9 lbs. Note: Available with a number of extra cost options.

NIB	Exc.	V.G.	Good	Fair	Poor
1100	920	800	600	450	350

Model 1517 Thumbhole Stock

Thumbhole stock version of 1517 series with 18" standard barrel or 23" heavy barrel. Walnut or multi-colored laminate stock. Note: Add $100 for laminate stock.

NIB	Exc.	V.G.	Good	Fair	Poor
1450	1250	1000	750	500	300

Model 1517 AV

Features 18" threaded barrel and Manners walnut or laminate stock. Also available with Manners MT6 stock, with adjustable buttplate and camo finish. New in 2017. Note: Add $100 for MT6 stock.

NIB	Exc.	V.G.	Good	Fair	Poor
1600	1450	1250	900	500	300

Model 1518D Mannlicher

Same as above. Chambered for .22 Magnum.

NIB	Exc.	V.G.	Good	Fair	Poor
1200	950	700	350	220	120

Model 184

High-grade bolt-action sporting rifle chambered for .22 LR cartridge. Has 21.5" barrel, with folding-leaf sight. Finish blued, with checkered walnut Monte Carlo stock and schnabel forend. Manufactured between 1963 and 1981.

NIB	Exc.	V.G.	Good	Fair	Poor
580	420	320	220	150	100

Model 54 Sporter

High-grade bolt-action sporting rifle chambered for .22 LR cartridge. Has 24" tapered round barrel and 5-shot detachable magazine. Features folding leaf-type rear sight. Finish blued, with checkered walnut Monte Carlo stock. Manufactured between 1963 and 1981.

NIB	Exc.	V.G.	Good	Fair	Poor
750	680	600	350	250	120

Model 54M

Version chambered for .22 Rimfire Magnum cartridge.

NIB	Exc.	V.G.	Good	Fair	Poor
800	700	620	380	280	120

Model 141

Bolt-action sporter chambered for .22 LR cartridge. Has 23" round barrel, with blued finish and walnut Monte Carlo stock. Manufactured between 1963 and 1981.

NIB	Exc.	V.G.	Good	Fair	Poor
800	650	450	200	150	100

Model 141M

Chambered for .22 Rimfire Magnum cartridge.

NIB	Exc.	V.G.	Good	Fair	Poor
820	680	480	220	180	100

Model 164

Bolt-action rifle. Fitted with 23" round barrel. Chambered for .22 LR cartridge. Has Monte Carlo stock with open sights. Magazine holds 5 rounds.

NIB	Exc.	V.G.	Good	Fair	Poor
700	620	480	320	180	100

Model 164M

Same as above. Chambered for .22 Win. Magnum cartridge.

NIB	Exc.	V.G.	Good	Fair	Poor
720	650	500	220	180	100

Model 153

Bolt-action sporting rifle chambered for .222 Remington cartridge. Has 24" barrel, with folding-leaf rear sight. Finish blued, with checkered French walnut stock. Featuring rosewood forend tip and pistol grip cap. Manufactured between 1963 and 1981.

NIB	Exc.	V.G.	Good	Fair	Poor
900	750	580	300	220	150

Model 153-S

Version offered with double-set triggers.

NIB	Exc.	V.G.	Good	Fair	Poor
950	780	620	350	280	150

Model 64

Single-shot bolt-action rifle. Chambered for .22 LR cartridge. Has 26" round barrel. Furnished without sights. Finish blued. Walnut target-type stock featured beavertail forearm and adjustable buttplate. Manufactured between 1963 and 1981.

NIB	Exc.	V.G.	Good	Fair	Poor
600	450	350	200	150	100

Model 64MS

Version designed for silhouette shooting. Has 21.25" barrel, blued finish and target-type walnut stock with stippled pistol grip.

NIB	Exc.	V.G.	Good	Fair	Poor
950	850	620	400	300	200

Model 64 MPR

Multi-purpose target repeater. Chambered for .22 LR cartridge. Fitted with 25.5" heavy barrel. Offered with optional sights. Choice of stainless steel barrel, with beavertail or beavertail with swivel rail. Weight about 9 lbs.

NIB	Exc.	V.G.	Good	Fair	Poor
1100	850	700	400	300	200

Model RX22

An AR-style semi-automatic rifle chambered for .22 LR cartridge. Features are similar to most AR-type rimfire rifles, including 16.5" barrel, Picatinny accessory rail, 10-shot magazine, folding iron backup sights, fixed or folding adjustable stock with pistol grip and choice of black or desert tan finish. Also available with skeletonized wood stock. Made in Germany and imported by Steyr.

NIB	Exc.	V.G.	Good	Fair	Poor
850	720	600	450	300	150

Model 54.18MS

High-grade silhouette rifle chambered for .22 LR cartridge. Has 22" barrel. Match-grade action, with fully adjustable trigger. Furnished without sights. Finish blued, with target-type walnut stock.

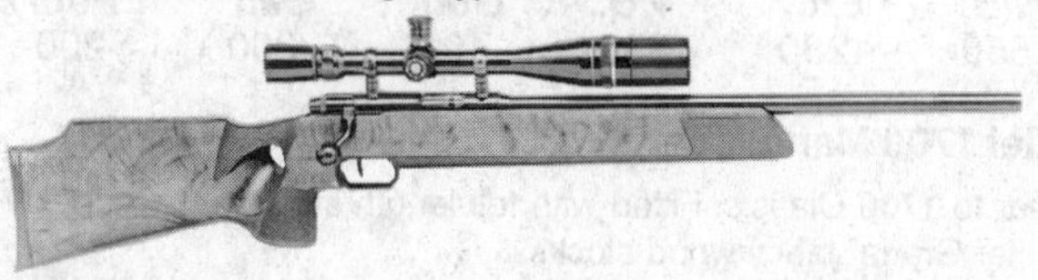

NIB	Exc.	V.G.	Good	Fair	Poor
2150	1500	1000	500	300	200

Model 54.MS REP

Repeating rifle, with 5-shot detachable magazine. Thumbhole stock, with ventilated forearm.

NIB	Exc.	V.G.	Good	Fair	Poor
2100	1600	1050	500	300	200

Model 520/61

Blowback-operated semi-automatic rifle. Chambered for .22 LR cartridge. Has 24" barrel and 10-round detachable magazine. Finish blued, with checkered walnut stock. Discontinued in 1983.

NIB	Exc.	V.G.	Good	Fair	Poor
680	550	300	200	100	80

Model 525 Sporter

Semi-automatic rifle chambered for .22 LR cartridge. Has 24" barrel, with adjustable sights and 10-round detachable magazine. Finish blued, with checkered Monte Carlo-type stock. Introduced in 1984. Carbine version with 20" barrel was originally offered, but discontinued in 1986.

NIB	Exc.	V.G.	Good	Fair	Poor
720	600	450	250	180	100

Model 2000 MK

Single-shot rifle chambered for .22 LR cartridge. Has 26" round barrel, with target-type sights. Finish blued, with walnut stock. Not imported after 1988.

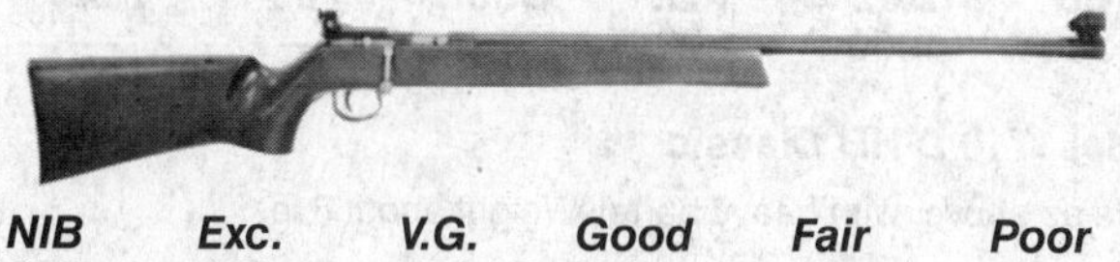

NIB	Exc.	V.G.	Good	Fair	Poor
650	600	450	200	150	100

Model 2007 Supermatch

Introduced in 1993. Target rifle chambered for .22 LR cartridge. Has 19.75" barrel fitted to Match 54 action. Trigger is a two-stage. Stock is standard ISU configuration, with adjustable cheekpiece. Weight about 10.8 lbs. Offered in left-hand model.

NIB	Exc.	V.G.	Good	Fair	Poor
2350	1850	1350	750	350	200

Model 2013 Supermatch

Similar to above. Fitted with International stock, with palm rest and buttstock hook. Weight about 12.5 lbs.

NIB	Exc.	V.G.	Good	Fair	Poor
3200	2600	1850	1250	600	300

Model 1903D

Designed for advanced junior shooter. Target rifle has 25.5" barrel on Match 64 action, with single stage trigger. Walnut stock is fully adjustable. Weight about 9.5 lbs. Offered in left-hand model.

NIB	Exc.	V.G.	Good	Fair	Poor
950	800	700	400	300	200

Model 1803D

High-grade target rifle chambered for .22 LR cartridge. Has 25.5" heavy barrel, with adjustable target sights. Features adjustable trigger. Finish blued, with light-colored wood stock. Dark stippling on pistol grip and forearm. Stock features adjustable cheekpiece and buttplate. Introduced in 1987.

NIB	Exc.	V.G.	Good	Fair	Poor
1200	1000	780	600	450	200

Model 1808D RT Super

Single-shot running-boar type rifle. Chambered for .22 LR cartridge. Has 32.5" barrel furnished without sights. Finish blued, with heavy target-type walnut stock with thumbhole. Furnished with barrel weights. Weight about 9.4 lbs. Available in left-hand version.

NIB	Exc.	V.G.	Good	Fair	Poor
1500	1300	1150	750	450	250

Model 1907ISU Standard Match

Chambered for .22 LR cartridge. Designed for both prone and position shooting. Weight 11.2 lbs. Built on Match 54 action. Fitted with 26" barrel. Two-stage trigger. Removable cheekpiece and adjustable buttstock.

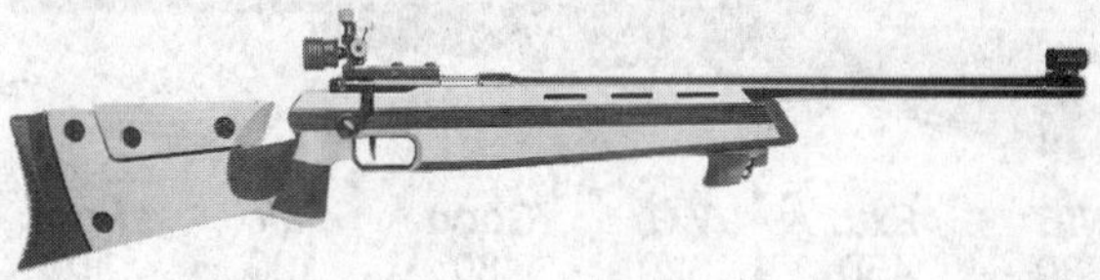

NIB	Exc.	V.G.	Good	Fair	Poor
1600	1350	1000	450	300	200

Model 1910 Super Match II

High-grade single-shot target rifle chambered for .22 LR cartridge. Has 27.25" barrel. Furnished with diopter-type target sights. Finish blued, with adjustable cheekpiece and buttplate. Walnut thumbhole stock. Hand and palm rest are not included.

NIB	Exc.	V.G.	Good	Fair	Poor
2300	1850	1400	900	500	250

Model 1911 Prone Match

Version has stock designed specifically for firing from prone position.

NIB	Exc.	V.G.	Good	Fair	Poor
1850	1550	1050	650	400	250

Model 1913 Super Match

Virtually hand-built match target rifle. Chambered for .22 LR cartridge. Features single-shot action. Has adjustable diopter-type sights on 27.25" heavy barrel. Custom-made gun. Features every target option conceivable. Finish blued, with fully adjustable walnut stock.

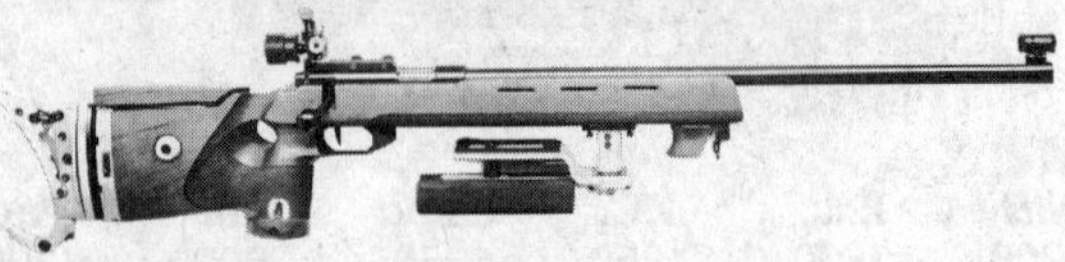

NIB	Exc.	V.G.	Good	Fair	Poor
2700	2100	1600	1000	500	250

Model 1827B Biathlon

Repeating bolt-action target rifle chambered for .22 LR cartridge. Specially designed for biathlon competition. Production is quite limited and on a custom basis.

NIB	Exc.	V.G.	Good	Fair	Poor
1850	1500	1150	800	400	250

Model 1827BT Biathlon

Similar to above. Features straight-pull Fortner bolt system. Available in left-hand model.

NIB	Exc.	V.G.	Good	Fair	Poor
2900	2350	1750	1000	500	250

Achiever

Introduced in 1993. Target rifle chambered for .22 LR cartridge. Designed for beginner shooter. Furnished with 5-shot clip, but can be converted to single-shot with an adapter. Barrel length 19.5". Action is Mark 2000, with two-stage trigger. Stock pull is adjustable from 12" to 13". Weight about 5 lbs.

NIB	Exc.	V.G.	Good	Fair	Poor
520	400	300	150	120	100

Achiever Super Target

Designed for advanced junior shooter. Has 22" barrel. Weight about 6.5 lbs.

NIB	Exc.	V.G.	Good	Fair	Poor
580	450	320	180	120	100

Bavarian 1700

Classic-style sporting rifle chambered for .22 LR, .22 Rimfire Magnum, .22 Hornet and .222 Remington cartridges. Features 24" barrel, with adjustable sights. Has detachable magazine. Blued finish. Checkered walnut European-style Monte Carlo stock, with cheekpiece. Introduced in 1988. Values shown are for centerfire.

NIB	Exc.	V.G.	Good	Fair	Poor
1300	950	600	400	300	200

Classic 1700

Similar in appearance to Bavarian. Furnished with American-style stock, with fluted comb. Same calibers as Bavarian. Weight 6.75 lbs. Note: Add $175 for "Meister Grade" fancy wood stocks.

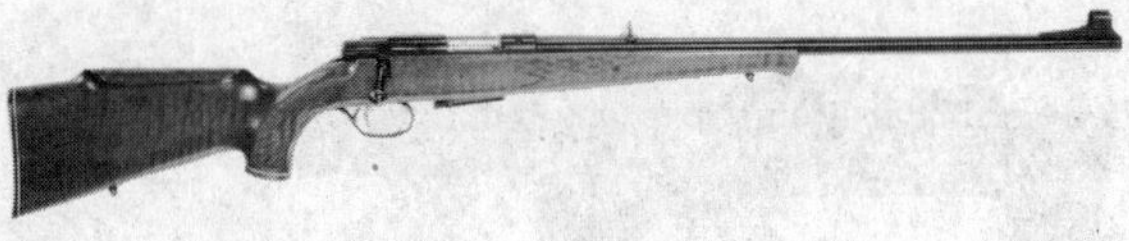

NIB	Exc.	V.G.	Good	Fair	Poor
1300	950	600	400	300	200

Custom 1700

Similar to Bavarian and Classic in caliber offerings, but offered with fancy European walnut stock, with roll-over cheekpiece with Monte Carlo. Pistol grip has palm swell. Fitted with a white lined rosewood grip cap, with white diamond insert. Forend is schnabel type and stock checkered in ship line pattern. Note: Add $175 for "Meister Grade" fancy wood stocks.

NIB	Exc.	V.G.	Good	Fair	Poor
1650	1280	750	400	300	200

Model 1700 Mannlicher

Similar to 1700 Classic. Fitted with full-length stock. Note: Add $175 for "Meister Grade" fancy wood stocks.

NIB	Exc.	V.G.	Good	Fair	Poor
1550	1200	850	550	350	200

Model 1700 FWT

Same specifications as 1700 Custom. Fitted with McMillan laminated fiberglass stock. Weight about 6.25 lbs.

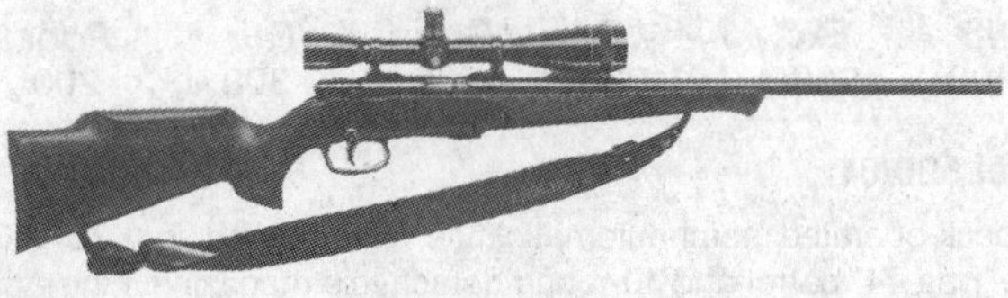

NIB	Exc.	V.G.	Good	Fair	Poor
1220	900	700	500	300	200

Model 1700 FWT Deluxe

Same as above. Fitted with laminated wood grain stock.

NIB	Exc.	V.G.	Good	Fair	Poor
1120	900	800	550	300	200

Model 1710 D Classic

Bolt-action .22-caliber rifle, with 23.6" barrel and no sights. Walnut stock checkered. Magazine capacity 5 rounds. Weight about 7.3 lbs.

NIB	Exc.	V.G.	Good	Fair	Poor
1300	1050	800	—	—	—

Model 1710 D HB Classic

Same as above, with heavy barrel. Weight about 8 lbs.

NIB	Exc.	V.G.	Good	Fair	Poor
1350	1050	750	480	300	150

Model 1710 D KL Monte Carlo

Same as Classic, with Monte Carlo stock. Folding leaf rear sight, with hooded front sight. Weight about 7.5 lbs.

NIB	Exc.	V.G.	Good	Fair	Poor
1300	1000	780	420	320	180

Model 1710 D HB Classic 150 Years Anniversary Version

Similar to Model 1710 D HB Classic, with heavy stainless barrel. Stock laser-engraved, with 150th Anniversary and 1901 "Germania" logos. Introduced in 2007. Only 150 units were produced.

NIB	Exc.	V.G.	Good	Fair	Poor
2100	1700	1200	700	400	200

Model 1712 Silhouette Sporter

Chambered in .22 LR. Features include two-stage trigger, deluxe walnut stock, 21.6" blued sightless barrel and 5-shot magazine.

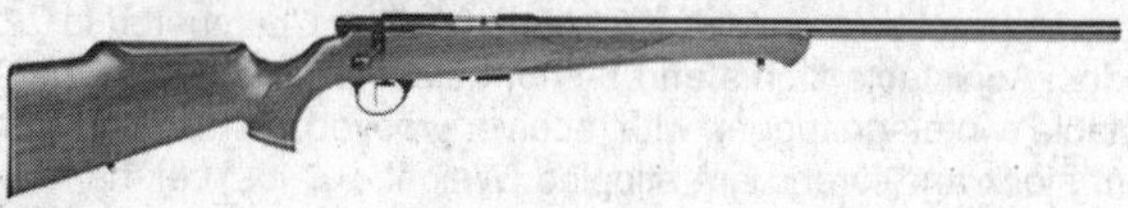

NIB	Exc.	V.G.	Good	Fair	Poor
1150	920	680	420	200	100

Model 1702 D HB Classic

Chambered in .17 Mach 2. Features include finely-tuned double-stage trigger, walnut stock, 23" blued heavy sightless barrel and 5-shot magazine.

NIB	Exc.	V.G.	Good	Fair	Poor
1300	1150	700	450	250	120

Model 1502 D HB Classic

Similar to Model 1702 D HB, with single-stage trigger and fewer refinements. Note: Add 10 percent for beavertail forend.

NIB	Exc.	V.G.	Good	Fair	Poor
600	400	300	200	100	50

Model 1907 Club

Single-shot economy target rifle chambered in .22 LR. Features include target trigger, short lock time, 26" blued barrel, micrometer rear peep and hood front sights. Ambidextrous removable cheekpiece and walnut buttstock, with rubber buttplate and stock spacers. Weight 9.7 lbs.

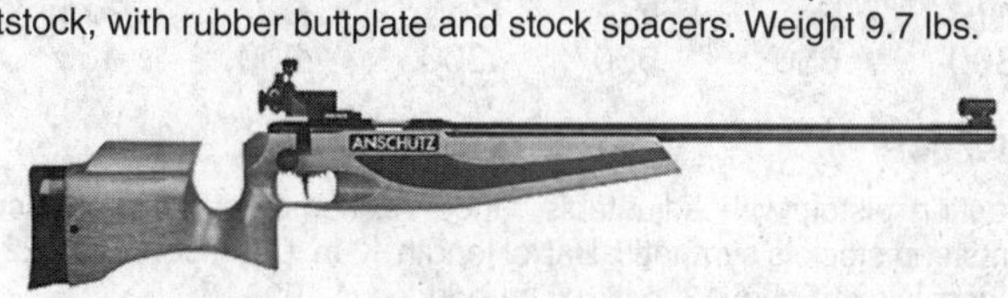

NIB	Exc.	V.G.	Good	Fair	Poor
1800	1500	1200	900	—	—

Model 1717 D Classic

Bolt-action model chambered for .17 HMR cartridge. Fitted with 23.6" barrel, with no sights. Checkered walnut stock. Weight about 7.3 lbs.

NIB	Exc.	V.G.	Good	Fair	Poor
1380	1000	680	480	300	150

Model 1717 D HB Classic

Same as above, with heavy barrel. Weight about 8 lbs.

NIB	Exc.	V.G.	Good	Fair	Poor
1480	1200	700	500	320	180

Model 1727

Straight-pull action repeater based on Biathlon type action, with very fast lock time. Chambered for .22 Hornady Magnum Rimfire cartridge. German walnut stock, with cheekpiece and schnabel forend. Match-grade 22" barrel. Introduced in 2014. Fortner straight-pull action. Numerous variations. .22 LR, .17 HMR, .17 Mach2.

NIB	Exc.	V.G.	Good	Fair	Poor
3400	2800	2100	1450	800	350

CENTERFIRE

Model 1730 D Classic

Bolt-action rifle chambered for .22 Hornet cartridge. Fitted with 23.6" barrel. Magazine capacity 5 rounds. Checkered walnut stock. No sights. Weight about 7.3 lbs.

NIB	Exc.	V.G.	Good	Fair	Poor
1620	1320	750	520	350	220

Model 1730 D HB Classic

Same as above, with heavy barrel. Weight about 8 lbs.

NIB	Exc.	V.G.	Good	Fair	Poor
1550	1250	700	500	320	180

Model 1730 D KL Monte Carlo

Model has Monte Carlo stock and folding leaf rear sight, with hooded front sight. Weight about 7.5 lbs.

NIB	Exc.	V.G.	Good	Fair	Poor
1620	1320	750	520	350	220

Model 1733D KL Mannlicher

Introduced in 1993. Features Mannlicher stock built on a Match 54 action. Stock has rosewood schnabel tip. Checkering is done in a skip-line pattern. Chambered for .22 Hornet. Weight about 6.25 lbs.

NIB	Exc.	V.G.	Good	Fair	Poor
1450	1150	680	480	300	180

Model 1740 D Classic

Bolt-action model chambered for .222 Remington cartridge. Checkered walnut stock, with no sights. Magazine capacity 3 rounds. Weight about 7.3 lbs.

NIB	Exc.	V.G.	Good	Fair	Poor
1620	1320	750	520	350	220

Model 1743D

Chambered for classic .222 Remington cartridge. Features a full-length Mannlicher stock. Other features similar to 1740D series.

NIB	Exc.	V.G.	Good	Fair	Poor
1350	1150	900	700	500	250

Model 1740 D HB Classic

Same as above, with heavy barrel. Weight about 7.3 lbs.

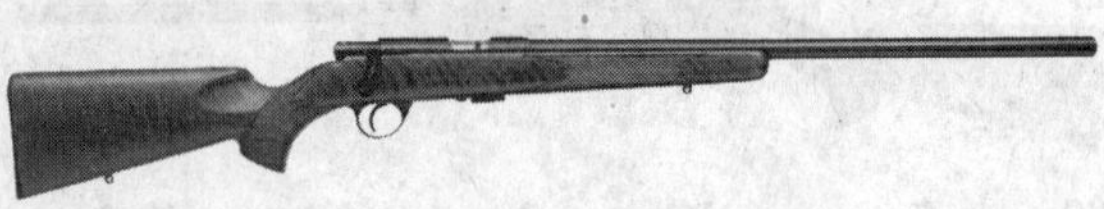

NIB	Exc.	V.G.	Good	Fair	Poor
1550	1250	700	500	320	180

Model 1740 D KL Monte Carlo

Fitted with Monte Carlo stock. Folding leaf rear sight and hooded front sight. Weight about 7.3 lbs.

NIB	Exc.	V.G.	Good	Fair	Poor
1620	1320	750	520	350	220

Model 1770D

Built on an action designed specifically for centerfire cartridges. Chambered for .223 Remington round. Model has a medium weight 22" barrel, detachable 3-round magazine and large bolt handle. Choice of classic Monte Carlo or German-style walnut stock. Introduced in 2009.

NIB	Exc.	V.G.	Good	Fair	Poor
2100	1700	1200	900	650	300

Model 1771

Series of centerfire bolt-action rifles, current production as of 2020. Calibers include .17 Hornet, 4.6x30, .22 Hornet, .204 Ruger, .222 Rem., and .300 Blackout. Base models include 1771 two-stage trigger, 1771G two-stage trigger, 1771 E Single Shot, and 1771 D. Models available at premium prices include 1771 E DJV Single Shot (add $175), 1771 DJV (add $275), and Anschutz Anniversary edition (add $1500). Calibers include .17 Hornet, 4.6x30, .22 Hornet, .204 Ruger, .222 Rem., and .300 Blackout.

NIB	Exc.	V.G.	Good	Fair	Poor
2250	2000	1750	—	—	—

Model 1780D

A centerfire rifle chambered for .30-06 or .308 Winchester. Features include a 21" barrel, 5-round detachable magazine and choice of a classic sporter walnut thumbhole or camo finished stock.

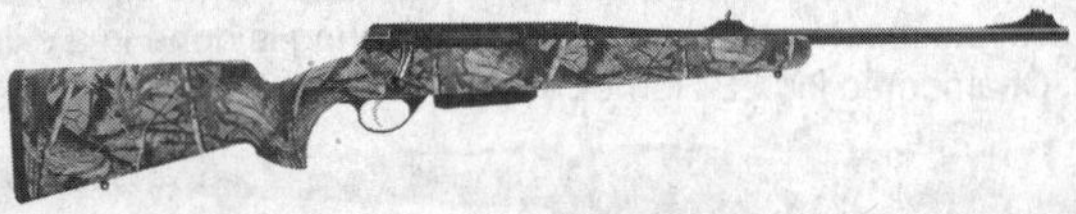

NIB	Exc.	V.G.	Good	Fair	Poor
1200	1050	900	750	600	300

Model 1781

Centerfire bolt-action rifles, current production as of 2020, 6.5 Creedmoor, 20.5" barrel. Trigger adjustable from single-stage to two-stage. Picatinny rail. Available as Classic Stock Model or German Stock Model. For the Anschutz Anniversary Edition add $1500.

NIB	Exc.	V.G.	Good	Fair	Poor
2750	2500	2250	—	—	—

Model 1782

Centerfire bolt-action rifles, current production as of 2020, 6.5 Creedmoor, 22.8" barrel. Trigger adjustable from single-stage to two-stage. Picatinny rail. Available as Classic Stock Model or German Stock Model.

NIB	Exc.	V.G.	Good	Fair	Poor
2650	2400	2150	—	—	—

PISTOLS

One source reports that a two-letter code on the rear of the barrel indicates the year of production, with A=0, B=1, C=2, D=3, E=4, F=5, G=6, H=7, I or J=8, K=9. For example, KD would be 1993 production. Additional model and pricing information on Anschutz bolt action pistols is invited.

Exemplar (1416P/1451P)

Bolt-action pistol built on Model 64 Match Action. Chambered for .22 LR cartridge. Adjustable sights and 5-shot detachable magazine. Features adjustable two-stage trigger, with receiver grooved for attaching a scope. Walnut stock and forend are stippled. Weight: 3.5 lbs. Left-hand action (for right-handers). Finish: blued finish. Barrel: 6.92-in. or 10-in.. Action single shot (Model1451P), or repeater with 5-shot mag, (Model 1416P). Left-hand version available. Add $15 for single shot (Model 1451P) Add $100 for right-hand action (for left-handers). Introduced in 1987, discontinued in 1997.

NIB	Exc.	V.G.	Good	Fair	Poor
500	410	360	300	250	200

Exemplar XIV

Similar to standard Exemplar, with 14" barrel. Introduced in 1988.

NIB	Exc.	V.G.	Good	Fair	Poor
600	500	400	250	200	100

Exemplar Hornet

Chambered for .22 Hornet cartridge. Introduced in 1988.

NIB	Exc.	V.G.	Good	Fair	Poor
800	650	580	300	200	100

Model 64P

Bolt-action pistol, with adjustable trigger. Action is grooved for scope mounts and stock is synthetic. Barrel length 10 in. Chambered for .22 LR cartridge. Weight about 3 lb. 8 oz. Introduced in 1998.

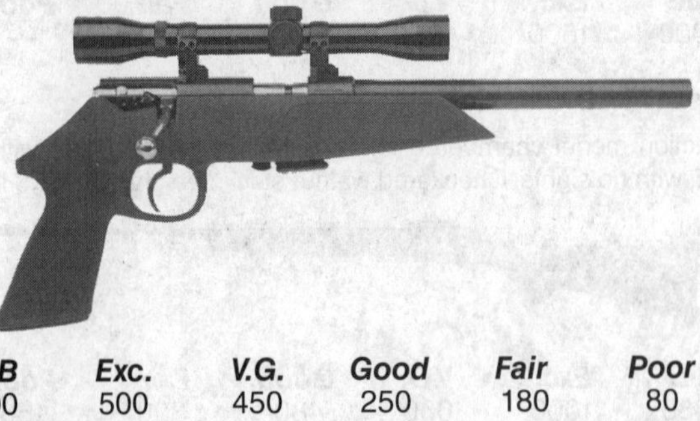

NIB	Exc.	V.G.	Good	Fair	Poor
600	500	450	250	180	80

Model 64P Mag

Same as above. Chambered for .22 WMR cartridge.

NIB	Exc.	V.G.	Good	Fair	Poor
650	530	480	360	220	110

Model 210 Free Pistol

Single-shot .22-caliber target pistol using Martini-falling-block-action. Barrel length 11", set trigger and adjustable sights. Blued finish, with checkered walnut grips and forend. Manufactured during 1930s.

NIB	Exc.	V.G.	Good	Fair	Poor
—	1500	1200	1000	820	400

Model 210A

As above, with a lightweight alloy frame.

NIB	Exc.	V.G.	Good	Fair	Poor
—	1420	1120	980	780	350

Model 200 Free Pistol

As above, without a set trigger.

NIB	Exc.	V.G.	Good	Fair	Poor
—	1120	1050	880	550	300

Model 17LP

Rimfire pistol. Caliber: .17 HMR. 4-shot magazine. Like the Model 64LP. Imported 2003-2004

NIB	Exc.	V.G.	Good	Fair	Poor
550	470	410	370	300	230

Model 1730 MSPE Field

Rimfire pistol. Caliber: .22 Hornet. Barrel: 9.3 in. Action: single-shot with a target-style stock and ventilated forend. This pistol sports ergonomic grips and a left-hand bolt (for righties) on a 54 Match action. Action is drilled and tapped for optics.

NIB	Exc.	V.G.	Good	Fair	Poor
1160	1000	800	650	550	490

ANTI GARROTTER

England

Percussion belt pistol marked "Balls Pat. Steel". Oval is 7" long and barrel protrudes 1.5"; approximately .45-caliber. A cord runs from lock up and through sleeve and is fired by pulling the cord. Beware of modern fakes. Intended to be worn on back of belt to defend against "garrotting" attacks from behind.

Antique

Reproductions have been reported.

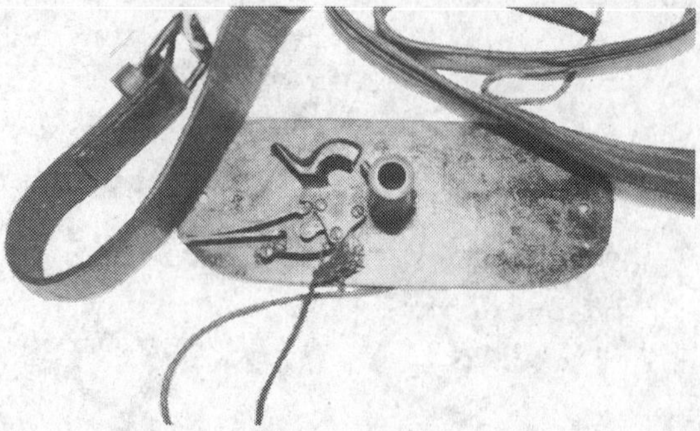

Exc.	Fine	V.G.	Good	Fair	Poor
5000	2500	2000	1200	600	420

ANZIO IRON WORKS

St. Petersburg, Florida

This manufacturer specializes in large caliber rifles for ultra long range shooting.

Takedown Competition

Caliber .338 Lapua or .50 BMG. Five-shot detachable magazine. Many options.

.338 Lapua

Barrel lengths 26" or 29".

NIB	Exc.	V.G.	Good	Fair	Poor
4200	3800	3000	2200	1400	900

.50 BMG

Barrel length 30".

NIB	Exc.	V.G.	Good	Fair	Poor
3600	3100	2400	1750	1100	800

20/50 Rifle

Caliber 20mm or .50 BMG. Single-shot or magazine fed repeater. Barrel length 40" or 45". Note: Add $1000 for repeating model.

NIB	Exc.	V.G.	Good	Fair	Poor
7000	6000	5000	3800	2500	1000

APACHE

Eibar, Spain

See—Ojanguren Y Vidosa

Various makers including L. Dolne, Liege, Belgium; J. Delhaxhe, France; possibly others.

Knuckleduster Antique

Combination weapon incorporating a 5mm or 7mm pinfire revolver with brass knuckles and usually a folding dagger blade. Several variations exist, most of which feature a folding design where the revolver cylinder is held inside the clenched fist when the knucks are worn on the fingers. Most have folding triggers as well. The "Apache" nickname reportedly comes from the Les Apaches French street gangs of the turn of the 20th century. Believed to have been made from late 1860s to early 20th century.

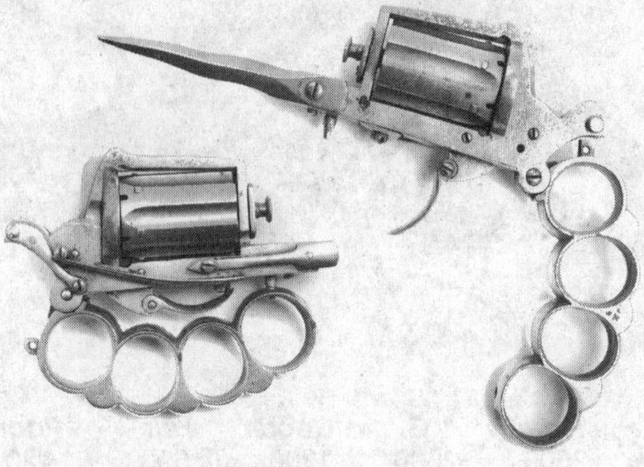

Photo courtesy of NRA Museums

Exc.	Fine	V.G.	Good	Fair	Poor
6500	4750	3500	2500	1750	700

APALOZO HERMANOS
Zumorraga, Spain

Spanish manufacturer from approximately 1920 to 1936. Trademark, dove-like bird normally found impressed into grips.

Apaloza

Copy of Colt Police Positive revolver.

NIB	Exc.	V.G.	Good	Fair	Poor
—	280	150	100	70	50

Paramount

Copy of Model 1906 Browning. Chambered for 6.35mm. "Paramount" stamped on slide and top of each grip plate.

Courtesy James Rankin

NIB	Exc.	V.G.	Good	Fair	Poor
—	230	180	130	90	50

Triomphe

Copy of Browning Model 1906 in caliber 6.35mm. Slide inscribed "Pistolet Automatique Triomphe Acier Comprime". "Cal. 6.35mm" stamped on each grip plate along with dove logo.

Courtesy James Rankin

NIB	Exc.	V.G.	Good	Fair	Poor
—	280	180	100	50	30

AR-7 INDUSTRIES
Meriden, Connecticut

AR-7 Explorer

Semi-automatic .22-caliber take-down rifle. Fitted with 16" barrel and 8-round magazine. Adjustable rear peep sight. Weight 2.5 lbs.

NIB	Exc.	V.G.	Good	Fair	Poor
200	150	90	60	50	20

AR-7C Explorer

Same as above, with camo stock.

NIB	Exc.	V.G.	Good	Fair	Poor
220	180	100	60	50	20

AR-7 Sporter

Similar to standard AR-7, with metal skeleton stock. Aluminum ventilated shrouded barrel. Weight about 3.8 lbs.

NIB	Exc.	V.G.	Good	Fair	Poor
250	150	120	80	60	40

AR-7 Target

Features tubular stock, with cantilever 3-9x40mm scope. Fitted with 16" bull barrel. Weight about 5.7 lbs.

NIB	Exc.	V.G.	Good	Fair	Poor
300	200	150	80	60	40

AR-7 Bolt-Action

Similar in all respects to standard semi-automatic AR-7, with bolt-action.

NIB	Exc.	V.G.	Good	Fair	Poor
220	120	90	60	50	20

ARCUS
Bulgaria

Arcus-94

Introduced in 1998. Semi-automatic pistol chambered for 9mm cartridge. Fitted with ambidextrous safety and 10-round magazine. Imported from Bulgaria.

NIB	Exc.	V.G.	Good	Fair	Poor
420	320	280	200	150	100

AREX
Ljubijana, Slovenia

Arex Rex

Series of semi-automatic pistols imported from Slovenia by FIME Group of Las Vegas, Nevada. Offered in three sizes—standard, combat and compact—chambered in .32 Auto, 9mm, 9x19 and .40 S&W. Barrel lengths 3.85" to 4.25"; weight 25 to 29 oz. Browning short-recoil operating system, except for .32 Auto which is blowback. Classic double/single-action design with manual safety, slide stop/decocker, steel frame and slide. Black or Flat Dark Earth finish. Sights are contrasting white dots. Introduced in 2016. Note: Add 10 percent for FDE finish.

NIB	Exc.	V.G.	Good	Fair	Poor
550	480	400	300	250	200

Rex Alpha

Similar to Arex Rex but with 5-in. barrel and chambered in 9mm. Equipped with adjustable sights.

NIB	Exc.	V.G.	Good	Fair	Poor
1100	1000	760	560	460	350

Rex Delta

Striker-fired 9mm with 4-in. barrel and polymer frame. Steel sights. Introduced in 2019.

NIB	Exc.	V.G.	Good	Fair	Poor
480	430	330	230	210	160

ARIZAGA, G.
Eibar, Spain

Spanish manufacturer prior to World War II.

Arizaga (Model 1915)

7.65mm semi-automatic pistol. Patterned after Ruby-style military pistols. Magazine capacity 9 or 12 rounds. Wood grips.

NIB	Exc.	V.G.	Good	Fair	Poor
—	350	180	130	90	50

Mondial

Similar design to Astra pistol in 100 series. Chambered for 6.35mm cartridge. Has Owl and Mondial on each grip plate.

NIB	Exc.	V.G.	Good	Fair	Poor
—	300	190	140	80	40

Pinkerton

Arizaga's standard model known to exist, with cartridge counter. Slide marked "Pinkerton Automatic 6.35".

NIB	Exc.	V.G.	Good	Fair	Poor
—	300	180	100	80	40

Warwick

Same design as Mondial in caliber 7.65mm. "Warwick" appears on each grip plate.

NIB	Exc.	V.G.	Good	Fair	Poor
—	300	190	140	80	40

ARIZMENDI, ZULAICA
Eibar, Spain

Cebra Pistol

Semi-automatic 7.65mm pistol. Patterned after Ruby-style of Spanish automatics. Slide marked "Pistolet Automatique Cebra Zulaica Eibar", together with letters "A.Z." in an oval. Generally found with checkered wood grips.

Courtesy James Rankin

NIB	Exc.	V.G.	Good	Fair	Poor
—	350	200	150	100	50

Cebra Revolver

Copy of a Colt Police Positive revolver marked "Made in Spain". Word "Cebra" cast in grips.

NIB	Exc.	V.G.	Good	Fair	Poor
—	250	150	120	80	50

ARLINGTON ORDNANCE
Westport, Connecticut

This company imported rebuilt M1 Garand and M1 Carbine rifles from Korea in the 1990s.

M1 Garand

Caliber .30-06 or .308 Winchester. New barrels, inspected components, rebuilt gas-operating systems.

NIB	Exc.	V.G.	Good	Fair	Poor
—	880	800	700	500	400

M1 Carbne

Caliber .30 carbine. Used models with import stamp and upgraded wood stock.

NIB	Exc.	V.G.	Good	Fair	Poor
—	800	700	600	450	300

ARIZMENDI, FRANCISCO

Eibar, Spain

Originally founded in 1890s. Reformed in 1914. Manufactured semi-automatic pistols.

Singer

Singer was manufactured in a number of different variations and in calibers 6.35mm and 7.65mm. Earlier called Victor. 6.35mm model resembled Browning 1906; 7.65mm model a Browning Model 1910.

6.35mm

Courtesy James Rankin

NIB	Exc.	V.G.	Good	Fair	Poor
—	230	180	130	90	50

7.65mm

Courtesy James Rankin

NIB	Exc.	V.G.	Good	Fair	Poor
—	200	150	100	80	40

Teuf Teuf

Teuf Teuf was chambered in calibers 6.35mm and 7.65mm. The 7.65mm was only slightly larger than 6.35mm model. Pistol copied its name from Browning Model 1906 and from Belgium Teuf Teuf. Pistol shown is a cartridge indicator model.

Courtesy James Rankin

6.35mm

NIB	Exc.	V.G.	Good	Fair	Poor
—	230	180	100	50	40

7.65mm

NIB	Exc.	V.G.	Good	Fair	Poor
—	230	180	100	50	40

Walman

Walman was manufactured in a number of variations and in calibers 6.35mm, 7.65mm and .380. Earliest semi-automatic production was in 1908 through 1926. Certain variations were called American Model. Model in .380-caliber had a squeeze grip safety.

6.35mm

Courtesy James Rankin

NIB	Exc.	V.G.	Good	Fair	Poor
—	220	200	100	50	40

7.65mm

Courtesy James Rankin

NIB	Exc.	V.G.	Good	Fair	Poor
—	250	200	120	60	40

.380

Courtesy James Rankin

NIB	Exc.	V.G.	Good	Fair	Poor
—	260	220	140	60	40

Arizmendi

Solid-frame folding-trigger revolver chambered for 7.65mm or .32-caliber. Normal markings are trademark "FA" and a circled five-pointed star.

NIB	Exc.	V.G.	Good	Fair	Poor
—	200	150	80	50	20

Boltun—1st Variation

Bolton semi-automatic pistol was made in both calibers 6.35mm and 7.65mm. Almost an exact copy of Belgian Pieper. 7.65mm model was only slightly larger than 6.35mm model.

6.35mm

NIB	Exc.	V.G.	Good	Fair	Poor
—	250	200	120	60	40

7.65mm

NIB	Exc.	V.G.	Good	Fair	Poor
—	250	200	120	60	40

Boltun—2nd Variation

Boltun 2nd variation chambered for 7.65mm cartridge. Almost an exact copy of Browning Model 1910. Made into 1930s.

NIB	Exc.	V.G.	Good	Fair	Poor
—	250	200	120	90	50

Roland

Chambered for 6.35 and 7.65mm cartridges. Manufactured during 1920s. The 7.65mm was only slightly larger than 6.35mm model.

Courtesy James Rankin

6.35mm

NIB	Exc.	V.G.	Good	Fair	Poor
—	250	180	130	80	40

7.65mm

NIB	Exc.	V.G.	Good	Fair	Poor
—	250	180	130	80	40

Puppy

Variation of "Velo-Dog" revolver. Barrel stamped "Puppy". Frame bearing "FA" trademark.

NIB	Exc.	V.G.	Good	Fair	Poor
—	250	200	120	60	40

Pistolet Automatique

Normal markings include "FA" trademark.

NIB	Exc.	V.G.	Good	Fair	Poor
—	250	200	120	60	40

Kaba Spezial

6.35mm semi-automatic pistol. Patterned after Browning Model 1906. Kaba Spezial was originally made by August Menz of Suhl, Germany and sold by Karl Bauer of Berlin, Germany. Name "Kaba" was derived from first two initials of Karl Bauer. These two pistols do not look alike.

Courtesy James Rankin

NIB	Exc.	V.G.	Good	Fair	Poor
—	280	150	100	50	40

Ydeal

Ydeal was made in four variations and in calibers 6.35mm, 7.65mm and .380. All four variations resemble Browning Model 1906, with 7.65mm and .380-caliber being slightly larger.

Courtesy James Rankin

6.35mm

NIB	Exc.	V.G.	Good	Fair	Poor
—	230	180	130	90	50

7.65mm

NIB	Exc.	V.G.	Good	Fair	Poor
—	230	180	130	90	50

.380

NIB	Exc.	V.G.	Good	Fair	Poor
—	230	180	130	90	50

ARMALITE, INC.

Costa Mesa, California
Geneseo, Illinois (current production)

In 1995, Eagle Arms purchased Armalite trademark and certain other assets. New companies are organized under Armalite name. Original company formed in mid 1950s, developed AR-10, which in turn led to the development of M-16 series of service rifles, still in use today. All current models are produced at Geneseo, Illinois, facility. SEE POLITICAL PANIC PRICING.

AR-24 Pistol

15-shot, 9mm, double-action, semi-automatic pistol. Steel frame, fixed or adjustable sights. Compact version available. Introduced 2006. Pricing is for full-size pistol, with adjustable sights. Note: Deduct 15 percent for fixed sight versions.

NIB	Exc.	V.G.	Good	Fair	Poor
600	450	320	280	200	120

AR-24 Tactical Custom

Similar to above, with tactical refinements including stippled front and back straps, 3-dot luminous sights, etc. Also available in compact version (shown).

NIB	Exc.	V.G.	Good	Fair	Poor
630	480	350	300	220	150

AR-17 Shotgun

Gas-operated semi-automatic 12-gauge shotgun, with 24-in. barrel and interchangeable choke tubes. Receiver and barrel are made of an aluminum alloy, with an anodized black or gold finish. Stock and forearm are of plastic. Approximately 2,000 manufactured during 1964 and 1965. Note: Add 10 percent for gold finish. Extraordinarily lightweight at 5.5 lbs., two-shot capacity.

NIB	Exc.	V.G.	Good	Fair	Poor
1000	800	650	450	350	150

AR-7 Explorer Rifle

.22 LR semi-automatic carbine, with 16-in. barrel. Receiver and barrel partially made of an alloy. Most noteworthy feature of this model is it can be disassembled and component parts stored in the plastic stock. Manufactured between 1959 and 1973. Reintroduced in 1999.

NIB	Exc.	V.G.	Good	Fair	Poor
380	300	200	150	100	80

AR-7 Custom

As above, with walnut cheekpiece stock. Manufactured between 1964 and 1970.

NIB	Exc.	V.G.	Good	Fair	Poor
480	400	300	250	200	180

AR-180

Gas-operated semi-automatic rifle chambered for .223 or 5.56mm cartridge. AR-180 is civilian version of AR18, which is fully automatic. Simple and efficient rifle that was tested by various governments and found to have potential. Rifle was also manufactured by Howa Machinery Ltd. and Sterling Armament Co. of England. Most common version is manufactured by Sterling. Those built by Armalite and Howa bring a small premium. ArmaLite Costa Mesa production.

Armalite Costa Mesa

NIB	Exc.	V.G.	Good	Fair	Poor
—	2700	2200	1850	1200	—

AR-180Howa

NIB	Exc.	V.G.	Good	Fair	Poor
—	2700	2200	1850	1200	1100

Sterling

NIB	Exc.	V.G.	Good	Fair	Poor
—	2300	1850	1500	900	—

AR-180B

Similar to original AR-180. Chambered for .223 cartridge. Fitted with 19.8" barrel and integral muzzle brake. Lower receiver is polymer while upper receiver is sheet steel. Trigger group is standard M15. Accepts standard M15 magazines. Weight about 6 lbs.

NIB	Exc.	V.G.	Good	Fair	Poor
—	2300	1870	1590	1350	—

AR-10A4 Rifle

Introduced in 1995. Features 20" stainless steel heavy barrel. Chambered for .308 Win. or .243 Win. cartridge. Has a flattop receiver, optional two-stage trigger, detachable carry handle and scope mount. Equipped with two 10-round magazines. Weight about 9.6 lbs. Note: Add $100 for stainless steel barrel.

NIB	Exc.	V.G.	Good	Fair	Poor
1500	1250	980	830	—	—

AR-10A4 Carbine

Similar to above. Chambered for .308 Win. cartridge. Fitted with 16" barrel. Flattop receiver. Sold with two 10-round magazines. Weight about 9 lbs. Note: Add $100 for stainless steel barrel.

NIB	Exc.	V.G.	Good	Fair	Poor
1500	1250	960	820	—	—

AR-10A2 Rifle

Model has 20" heavy barrel. Chambered for .308 cartridge, without removable carry handle. Weight about 9.8 lbs. Note: Add $100 for stainless steel barrel.

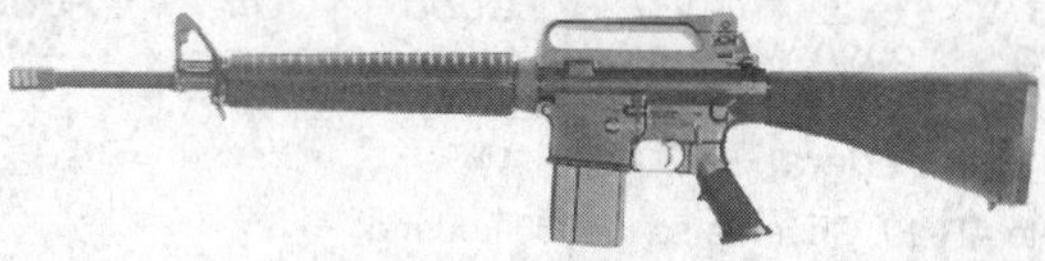

NIB	Exc.	V.G.	Good	Fair	Poor
1460	1240	1060	900	760	650

AR-10A2 Carbine 10A2CB

Similar to above, with 16" barrel. Weight about 9 lbs. Note: Add $100 for stainless steel barrel.

NIB	Exc.	V.G.	Good	Fair	Poor
—	2000	1700	1440	—	—

AR-10B

Chambered for .308 cartridge. Fitted with 20" barrel. Trigger is single-stage or optional two-stage match type. Model has several early M16 features such as tapered handguard, pistol grips and short buttstock in original brown color. Fitted with early charging handle. Limited production. Weight about 9.5 lbs. Introduced in 1999.

NIB	Exc.	V.G.	Good	Fair	Poor
—	1430	1210	1030	—	—

AR-10(T) Rifle

Features 24" heavy barrel, with two-stage trigger. Front sight and carry handle are removable. Handguard is fiberglass. Weight about 10.4 lbs.

NIB	Exc.	V.G.	Good	Fair	Poor
—	1620	1380	1170	—	—

AR-10(T) Carbine

Similar to AR-10T, with 16.25" target weight barrel. Weight about 8.5 lbs.

NIB	Exc.	V.G.	Good	Fair	Poor
—	1700	1450	1230	—	—

AR-10(T) Ultra

Chambered for .300 Remington Ultra Short Action Magnum cartridge. Barrel length 24". Two-stage National Match trigger. Offered in choice of green or black stock. Sold with 5-round magazine.

NIB	Exc.	V.G.	Good	Fair	Poor
—	1500	1280	1080	—	—

AR-10 SOF

Introduced in 2003. Features M4-style fixed stock. Flattop receiver. Chambered for .308 cartridge. Offered in both A2 and A4 configurations.

NIB	Exc.	V.G.	Good	Fair	Poor
—	1330	1130	960	—	—

AR-10 A-Series SuperSASS Gen II A10SBF

Caliber: 7.62x51. SuperSASS (Semi-Automatic Sniper System) civilian model has a 15" Armalite Gen II M-LOK free-float handguard, Magpul PRS Gen II adjustable stock, an adjustable gas system for suppressed and un-suppressed fire. Barrel: 20" stainless, 1:10" RH twist. 11.4 lbs.

SEE POLITICAL PANIC PRICING.

NIB	Exc.	V.G.	Good	Fair	Poor
3070	2980	2900	2800	—	—

AR-10 .338 Federal

Similar to AR-10. Chambered in .338 Federal.

NIB	Exc.	V.G.	Good	Fair	Poor
—	1520	1290	1100	—	—

AR-10 Tactical Rifle

Calibers: .308 Win. Slim handguard with octagonal profile, full-length MIL-STD 1913 12 o'clock rail. Adjustable gas block, Magpul MBUS flip-up sights. Non-NFA models come in barrel lengths of 16", 18", and 20". SEE POLITICAL PANIC PRICING.

NIB	Exc.	V.G.	Good	Fair	Poor
1990	1850	1700	1600	—	—

AR10 TAC 6.5

Caliber: 6.5 Creedmoor. Capacity: 25 rounds, windowed PMAG. Barrel: 22 in. med-heavy 1:8 stainless steel, black nitride finish. Stock: Magpul PRS with adjustable length-of-pull and comb height. Sights: Magpul MBUS front and rear. Weight: 10 lbs. Overall Length: 44 in. Features: ArmaLite Two-Stage Trigger, AR10 15 in. tactical handguard, ATB762 muzzle brake. New 6.5 CM chambering is superbly accurate for match shooting. Introduced 2020.

NIB	Exc.	V.G.	Good	Fair	Poor
2200	1870	1590	1350	—	—

AR-10 3-Gun (3GN13/3GN18)

Caliber: 7.62x51/.308 Win. Capacity: 25 rounds, windowed PMAG. Barrel: 13.5 in., pinned and welded, or 18 in. stainless steel, 1:10 twist. Stock: MBA-1 Light Weight Precision with adjustable length-of-pull and comb height. Sights: Mil-Std 1913 top rail. Weight: 8.8-9.9 lbs. Overall lengths: 36.25, 40.25, 41.25 in. Features: Timney 4-lb. single-stage trigger, ArmaLite Tunable Competition Muzzle Brake, ambidextrous safety and Raptor charging handle, 12 in. free-floating, tactical Key-Mod handguard, ERGO wide grip. Introduced 2020.

NIB	Exc.	V.G.	Good	Fair	Poor
2270	1930	1640	1400	—	—

AR-10 Pistol

Introduced in 2015. Features 13.9-in. stainless steel barrel. Chambered for .308 Win. cartridge. 12-in. KeyMod handguard raptor Bambi chagrin handle. Weight about 8.8 lbs.

NIB	Exc.	V.G.	Good	Fair	Poor
2800	2430	1880	1430	—	—

AR-10 Competition Rifle

Calibers: .308 Win. Built for 3-Gun and practical rifle competition. Timney 4-lb. single-stage trigger, Ergo wide grip MBA-1 buttstock with adjustable cheek piece and length-of-pull. Factory ambidextrous safety and Raptor charging handle, adjustable gas block. SEE POLITICAL PANIC PRICING.

NIB	Exc.	V.G.	Good	Fair	Poor
1900	—	—	—	—	—

AR-10 Defensive Sporting Rifle

Caliber: .308 Win. Weight: 6.1 lbs. Forged flat-top receiver with MIL-STD 1913 rail. Optics-ready and pinned Mil-spec A2 front sight base models. SEE POLITICAL PANIC PRICING.

NIB	Exc.	V.G.	Good	Fair	Poor
950	900	800	700	—	—

M15A2 National Match

Chambered for .223 cartridge. Variation features 20" stainless steel match barrel, with two-stage trigger, A2-style forward assist and hard coated anodized receiver. Equipped with 10-round magazine. Weight about 9 lbs.

NIB	Exc.	V.G.	Good	Fair	Poor
1300	1110	940	800	—	—

M15 SOF

Chambered for .223 cartridge. Fitted with flattop receiver and M4-style fixed stock. Introduced in 2003. Offered in both A2 and A4 configurations.

NIB	Exc.	V.G.	Good	Fair	Poor
—	940	800	680	—	—

M15A2 HBAR

Introduced in 1995. Features 20" heavy barrel chambered for .223 cartridge. A2-style forward assist, recoil check brake. Formerly sold with 10-round magazine. Weight about 8.2 lbs.

NIB	Exc.	V.G.	Good	Fair	Poor
—	980	830	700	—	—

M15A2-M4A1C Carbine

Similar to M15A2 heavy barrel, with 16" heavy barrel. Flattop receiver, with detachable carry handle. Introduced in 1995. Note: Add $100 for Match trigger.

NIB	Exc.	V.G.	Good	Fair	Poor
—	1000	850	720	—	—

M15A2-M4C Carbine

Similar to M4A1C Carbine, with flattop receiver and detachable carry handle.

NIB	Exc.	V.G.	Good	Fair	Poor
—	950	810	690	—	—

M15A4T Eagle Eye

Chambered for .223 cartridge. Fitted with 24" stainless steel heavy weight barrel. Has National Match two-stage trigger, Picatinny rail and NM fiberglass handguard tube. Sold with 7-round magazine and 4-section cleaning rod with brass tip, sling, owner's manual and lifetime warranty.

NIB	Exc.	V.G.	Good	Fair	Poor
1200	1020	870	740	—	—

Eagle-15 Versatile Sporting Rifle – 15EAVSR

Eagle-15 Versatile Sporting Rifle – 15EAVSR Caliber: .223 Rem., 5.56x45 (.223 Wylde chamber). Capacity: one 30-round Magpul PMAG. Barrel: 16 in. HB, chrome moly, 1:8 RH twist, flash suppressor. Stock: 6-position collapsible stock. Sights: Mil-Std 1913 rail section. Weight: 6.6 lbs. Overall Length: 31.1 in. collapsed, 34.5 in. extended. Features: Carbine length gas system, 15 in. Versatile Sporting Rifle Key-Mod handguard, forged flat top with Mil-Std 1913 rail, 7075-T6 aluminum upper receiver, forged 7075-T6 aluminum lower receiver.

NIB	Exc.	V.G.	Good	Fair	Poor
820	700	600	—	—	—

M15A4 Special Purpose Rifle (SPR)

Fitted with 20" heavy barrel, detachable front sight and carry handle, NM sights and Picatinny rail. Weight about 7.8 lbs.

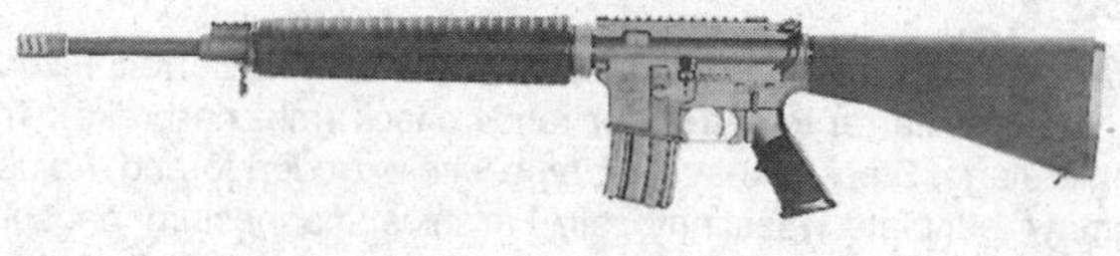

NIB	Exc.	V.G.	Good	Fair	Poor
—	1000	850	720	—	—

M15A4 Action Master

Variation features 20" stainless steel heavy barrel, with two-stage trigger, Picatinny rail and fiberglass handguard tube. Weight about 9 lbs.

NIB	Exc.	V.G.	Good	Fair	Poor
1030	950	810	690	580	500

PRE-BAN MODELS

M15A4 Eagle Spirit

Similar to Action Master above, with 16" stainless steel barrel. Weight about 7.6 lbs.

NIB	Exc.	V.G.	Good	Fair	Poor
1300	1110	940	800	680	580

M15A4 Carbine 6.8 & 7.62x39

Shorty carbine version of AR-15. Chambered in 6.8 Remington and 7.62x39. 16" chrome-lined barrel with flash suppressor, front and rear Picatinny rails for mounting optics and two-stage tactical trigger. Ten-round magazine. Anodized aluminum/phosphate finish. Overall length 36.6"; weight: 7 lbs.

NIB	Exc.	V.G.	Good	Fair	Poor
950	810	690	580	500	420

M15 Battalion Rifle BAT15

Caliber: 5.56 NATO. Weight: 6.3 lbs. Forged flat-top receiver, MIL-STD 1913 rail, gas block w/MIL-STD 1913 rail.

NIB	Exc.	V.G.	Good	Fair	Poor
1400	640	540	460	390	330

M-15 Competition Rifle

Calibers: .223 Wylde. Built for 3-Gun and practical rifle competition. Timney 4-lb. single-stage trigger, Ergo wide grip MBA-1 buttstock with adjustable cheek piece and length-of-pull. Factory ambidextrous safety and Raptor charging handle, adjustable gas block. On the 13.5" .223 Wylde model, a tunable proprietary Armalite muzzle brake is pinned and welded to create an overall length of 16". SEE POLITICAL PANIC PRICING.

NIB	Exc.	V.G.	Good	Fair	Poor
1450	1350	1230	1040	890	750

M-15 Defensive Sporting Rifle

Caliber: 5.56 NATO. Weight: 6.1 lbs. Forged flat-top receiver with MIL-STD 1913 rail. Optics-ready and pinned Mil-spec A2 front sight base models. SEE POLITICAL PANIC PRICING.

NIB	Exc.	V.G.	Good	Fair	Poor
700	600	580	490	420	360

M-15 Light Tactical Carbine

Caliber: 5.56 NATO. Armalite free-floating tactical M-LOK handguard, low-profile gas block. Weight: 6 lbs.

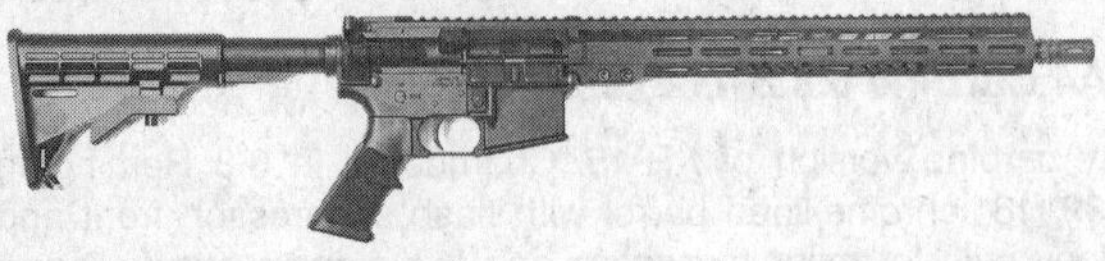

NIB	Exc.	V.G.	Good	Fair	Poor
900	850	720	610	520	440

M-15 Tactical Rifle

Calibers: 5.56 NATO/.223 Rem. Slim handguard with octagonal profile, full-length MIL-STD 1913 12 o'clock rail. Adjustable gas block, Magpul MBUS flip-up sights. Non-NFA models come in barrel lengths of 14.5", 16". SEE POLITICAL PANIC PRICING.

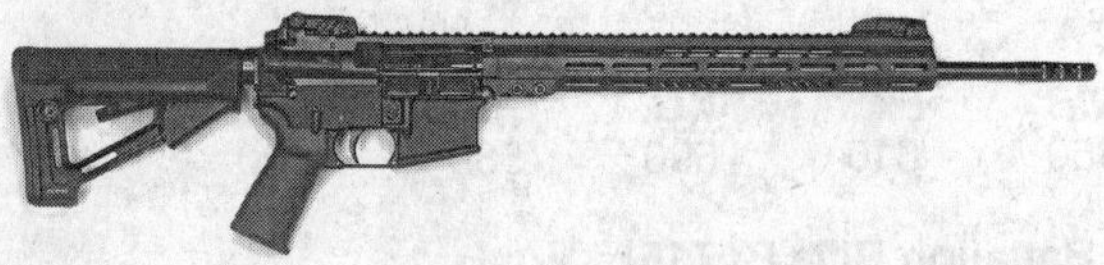

NIB	Exc.	V.G.	Good	Fair	Poor
1590	1500	1400	1250	1100	900

M-15 Pistol

Introduced in 2015. Features 6- or 11.5-in. steel barrel. Chambered for .223 Rem./5.56 NATO cartridge. 12-in. KeyMod handguard raptor Bambi chagrin handle. Weight about 6 lbs.

NIB	Exc.	V.G.	Good	Fair	Poor
2100	1880	1460	1130	910	730

Golden Eagle

Fitted with 20" stainless extra-heavy barrel, with NM two-stage trigger and NM sights. Sold with 30-round magazine. Weight about 9.4 lbs.

NIB	Exc.	V.G.	Good	Fair	Poor
—	1180	1000	850	720	610

HBAR

Pre-ban rifle has 20" heavy barrel, 30-round magazine and sling. Weight about 8 lbs.

NIB	Exc.	V.G.	Good	Fair	Poor
1300	1110	940	800	680	580

M4C Carbine

Pre-ban variation fitted with 16" heavy barrel, collapsible stock and fixed flash suppressor. Weight about 6.2 lbs.

NIB	Exc.	V.G.	Good	Fair	Poor
—	790	670	570	480	410

BOLT GUNS

AR-30A1 Standard

Introduced in 2013. This is an upgraded version of bolt-action AR-30M. Improvements include better ergonomics and versatility. Chambered in .300 Win. Magnum or .338 Lapua. Note: Add $125 for .338 Lapua caliber; $200 for target version with an adjustable fixed stock.

NIB	Exc.	V.G.	Good	Fair	Poor
3000	2400	1800	1250	—	—

AR-30M

Chambered for .338 Lapua, .300 Win. Magnum or .308 Winchester cartridges. Barrel length 26 in. with muzzle brake. Adjustable buttstock. Weight about 12 lbs. Reduced version of AR-50. Note: Add $150 for .338 Lapua.

NIB	Exc.	V.G.	Good	Fair	Poor
2000	1700	1300	1000	—	—

AR-31

This target model in .308 Winchester has an 18- or 24-in. barrel, stock that's adjustable for length-of-pull and comb height, bipod, muzzle brake and single-stage trigger. It accepts Armalite AR-10B double-stack magazines up to 25-round capacity.

NIB	Exc.	V.G.	Good	Fair	Poor
3200	2600	2000	1500	—	—

AR-50

Introduced in 2000. Chambered for .50 BMG or .416 Barrett. Fitted with 31-in. tapered barrel threaded for recoil check (muzzle brake). Trigger is single-stage. Stock is 3-section type with extruded forend. Adjustable Pachmayr buttplate. Picatinny rail. Finish is magnesium phosphated steel and hard anodized aluminum. Bipod. Single shot. Weight about 33 lbs. Note: Add $400 for National Match Model.

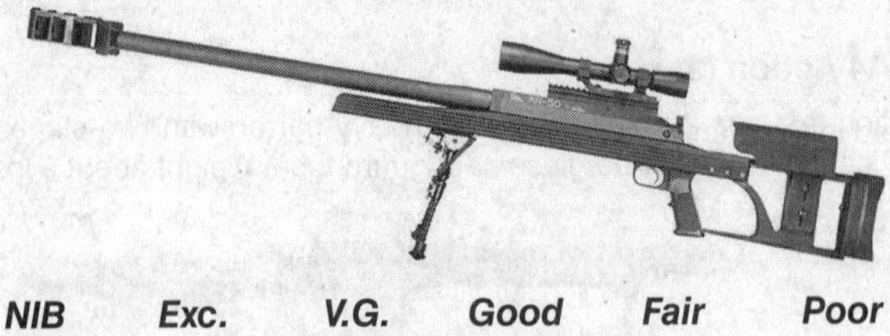

NIB	Exc.	V.G.	Good	Fair	Poor
3400	2650	2000	1500	—	—

ARMAS DE FUEGO

Guernica, Spain

See—ALKARTASUNA FABRICA DE ARMAS

ARMERO ESPECIALISTAS
Eibar, Spain

See—ALFA

ARMES DE CHASSE
Chadds Ford, Pennsylvania

Importer of firearms manufactured by Franchi, P. Beretta and other arms manufactured in Germany.

Model EJ

Over/under Anson & Deeley action 12-gauge shotgun, with double triggers as well as automatic ejectors. Blued barrels, silver finished receiver and checkered walnut stock. Manufactured in Germany. Introduced in 1989.

NIB	*Exc.*	*V.G.*	*Good*	*Fair*	*Poor*
1500	1250	900	650	500	250

Model EU

As above, with ventilated rib barrel. Non-selective single trigger. Introduced in 1989.

NIB	*Exc.*	*V.G.*	*Good*	*Fair*	*Poor*
1600	1300	850	650	500	250

Highlander

Side-by-side double-barrel 20-gauge shotgun, with boxlock action. Available in various barrel lengths and choke combinations, with double triggers and manual extractors. Blued, with checkered walnut stock. Manufactured in Italy. Introduced in 1989.

NIB	*Exc.*	*V.G.*	*Good*	*Fair*	*Poor*
1350	800	650	350	250	120

Chesapeake

As above chambered for 3.5" 12-gauge shell. Bores are chrome-lined and suitable for steel shot. Fitted with automatic ejectors and double triggers. Manufactured in Italy. Introduced in 1989.

NIB	*Exc.*	*V.G.*	*Good*	*Fair*	*Poor*
1450	1000	700	480	400	200

Balmoral

English-style straight-grip 12-, 16- or 20-gauge boxlock shotgun. Fitted with false side plates. Receiver and side plates case-hardened. Barrels blued. Fitted with single trigger and automatic ejectors. Manufactured in Italy. Introduced in 1989.

NIB	*Exc.*	*V.G.*	*Good*	*Fair*	*Poor*
1200	920	720	500	400	200

Model 70E

A 12-, 16- or 20-gauge side-by-side shotgun. Fitted with 27" or 28" barrels. Action based upon Anson & Deeley design, with Greener crossbolt. Receiver case-hardened. Barrels blued. Walnut stock checkered. Manufactured in Germany. Introduced in 1989.

NIB	*Exc.*	*V.G.*	*Good*	*Fair*	*Poor*
1220	920	720	500	400	200

Model 74E

As above, with game scene engraving. More fully figured walnut stock. Introduced in 1989.

NIB	*Exc.*	*V.G.*	*Good*	*Fair*	*Poor*
1480	1050	900	650	500	250

Model 76E

As above, with engraved false side plates. Fully figured walnut stock. Introduced in 1989.

NIB	*Exc.*	*V.G.*	*Good*	*Fair*	*Poor*
2000	1500	1100	750	600	300

ARMINEX LTD.
Scottsdale, Arizona

Tri-Fire

Semi-automatic pistol chambered for 9mm, .38 Super or .45 ACP cartridges. Fitted with 5", 6" or 7" stainless steel barrels. Presentation cases were available at an extra cost of $48. Approximately 250 manufactured from 1981 to 1985. Note: Available with conversion units that add approximately $130 if in excellent condition.

Courtesy James Rankin

NIB	*Exc.*	*V.G.*	*Good*	*Fair*	*Poor*
950	800	600	300	180	100

Target Model

As above, with 6" or 7" barrel.

Courtesy James Rankin

NIB	*Exc.*	*V.G.*	*Good*	*Fair*	*Poor*
1000	850	650	350	220	100

ARMINUS

See—FREIDRICH PICKERT
See—HERMANN WEIRAUCH
See—F. I. E.

ARMITAGE INTERNATIONAL, LTD.
Seneca, South Carolina

Scarab Skorpion

Blowback-operated semi-automatic pistol. Patterned after Czechoslovakian Scorpion sub-machine gun. Chambered for 9mm cartridge, with

4.6" barrel having military-type sights. Fitted with 32-round detachable box magazine. Standard finish is matte black. Grips are plastic.

NIB	Exc.	V.G.	Good	Fair	Poor
750	600	500	350	250	—

ARMSCO FIREARMS CORP.

Ankara, Turkey
U.S.A.—Des Plaines, Illinois

Built by Huglu Hunting Firearms Corporation in Turkey, which was established in 1927. Armsco is U.S. representative. First year of business in U.S. was 2002.

SINGLE-SHOT

Model 301A

Single-shot model offered in 12-, 16-, 20-, 28-gauge and .410 bore. Barrel lengths from 22" to 32" depending on gauge. Checkered walnut stock. Weight varies from 5- to 5.5 lbs. depending on gauge.

NIB	Exc.	V.G.	Good	Fair	Poor
200	150	80	50	40	20

SIDE-BY-SIDES

Model 202B

Boxlock shotgun offered in 12-, 16-, 20-, 28-gauge and .410 bore. Barrel lengths from 22" to 32" depending on gauge. Double triggers. Hand engraved about 50 percent coverage. Fixed chokes or choke tubes. Checkered walnut stock with cheekpiece. Weight about 6.4- to 7.3 lbs. depending on gauge.

NIB	Exc.	V.G.	Good	Fair	Poor
550	420	320	200	120	50

Model 202A

Same as above. Offered with standard buttstock.

NIB	Exc.	V.G.	Good	Fair	Poor
780	620	450	300	180	80

Model 201A

Offered in gauges from 12-gauge to .410 bore. Sideplates with 50 percent hand engraving. Choice of single or double triggers.

NIB	Exc.	V.G.	Good	Fair	Poor
700	520	450	300	180	80

Model 200A

Boxlock in gauges 12-gauge to .410 bore, with single trigger. Hand engraved 50 percent coverage.

NIB	Exc.	V.G.	Good	Fair	Poor
750	580	450	300	180	80

Model 205A

Offered in 12-gauge to .410 bore, with barrel lengths 22" to 32" depending on gauge. Boxlock frame with 60 percent hand engraved coverage. Single trigger. Checkered walnut stock. Weights are 6.1- to 6.8 lbs. depending on gauge.

NIB	Exc.	V.G.	Good	Fair	Poor
990	750	600	420	200	100

Model 210AE

Offered in 12-, 16- and 20-gauge, with single trigger and automatic ejectors. Boxlock frame is 60 percent hand engraved. Optional fixed or choke tubes.

NIB	Exc.	V.G.	Good	Fair	Poor
1250	950	700	450	300	200

Model 210BE

Same as above, with double triggers.

NIB	Exc.	V.G.	Good	Fair	Poor
1150	850	680	450	300	200

OVER/UNDERS

Model 104A

Chambered for 12-gauge through .410 bore, with double triggers. Barrel lengths from 22" to 32" depending on gauge. Ventilated rib. Checkered walnut stock. Fixed or choke tubes. Weight from 6.6- to 7.3 lbs. depending on gauge. Receiver is 15 percent hand engraved.

NIB	Exc.	V.G.	Good	Fair	Poor
420	300	250	200	120	80

Model 103D

Same as above, with single trigger and schnabel forearm.

NIB	Exc.	V.G.	Good	Fair	Poor
600	480	380	320	180	80

Model 103DE

Same as above, with automatic ejectors.

NIB	Exc.	V.G.	Good	Fair	Poor
750	580	520	420	200	80

Model 103C

Similar to Model 103D, with blued receiver, gold inlaid birds and 40 percent engraving coverage.

NIB	Exc.	V.G.	Good	Fair	Poor
720	550	520	420	200	80

Model 103CE

Same as above, with automatic ejectors.

NIB	Exc.	V.G.	Good	Fair	Poor
870	650	580	480	220	100

Model 103F

Similar to Model 103D, with 80 to 100 percent hand engraved side plates.

NIB	Exc.	V.G.	Good	Fair	Poor
850	620	550	450	220	100

Model 103FE

Same as above, with automatic ejectors.

NIB	Exc.	V.G.	Good	Fair	Poor
970	750	600	480	250	120

Model 101SE

Offered in 12-gauge only. Barrel lengths 28", 30" or 32" with ventilated rib. Single trigger and automatic ejectors. Hand engraved receiver. Checkered walnut stock. Weight from 6.6- to 7.3 lbs. depending on barrel length.

NIB	Exc.	V.G.	Good	Fair	Poor
1320	980	750	450	280	120

Model 101BE

Same as above, with adjustable comb.

NIB	Exc.	V.G.	Good	Fair	Poor
1320	980	750	450	280	120

SEMI-AUTOMATICS

Model 401A

Semi-automatic shotgun. Uses short-recoil inertia-operated system. Chambered for 12-gauge shell up to 3". Barrel lengths from 22" to 32". Ventilated rib. Plastic or walnut stock. Fixed or choke tubes. Fully engraved receiver. Weight from 6.9- to 7.2 lbs. depending on barrel length. Magazine capacity 6 rounds.

NIB	Exc.	V.G.	Good	Fair	Poor
420	350	280	220	120	80

Model 401B

Same as above, with 4-round magazine capacity.

NIB	Exc.	V.G.	Good	Fair	Poor
420	350	280	220	120	80

Model 501GA

Gas-operated shotgun chambered for 3" 12-gauge shell. Barrel lengths from 22" to 32". Black receiver with 15 percent hand engraved coverage. Magazine capacity 7 rounds. Walnut or plastic stock. Weight from 6.8- to 7.3 lbs. depending on barrel length.

NIB	Exc.	V.G.	Good	Fair	Poor
420	350	280	220	120	80

Model 501GB

Same as above, with 4-round magazine.

NIB	Exc.	V.G.	Good	Fair	Poor
420	350	280	220	120	80

Model 601GB

Same as Model 501GB, with full coverage engraved silver receiver.

NIB	Exc.	V.G.	Good	Fair	Poor
450	380	300	250	120	80

Model 601GA

Same as Model 501GA, with 7-round magazine capacity.

NIB	Exc.	V.G.	Good	Fair	Poor
450	380	300	250	120	80

Model 701GA

Chambered for 20-gauge 3" shell. Fitted with barrel lengths from 22" to 32". Ventilated rib. Walnut stock. Fixed or choke tubes. Magazine capacity 7 rounds. Weight 6- to 6.4 lbs. depending on barrel length.

NIB	Exc.	V.G.	Good	Fair	Poor
450	380	300	220	120	80

Model 701GB

Same as above, with 4-round magazine.

NIB	Exc.	V.G.	Good	Fair	Poor
450	380	300	220	120	80

PUMP-ACTIONS

Model 801A

Slide-action 12-gauge shotgun, with plastic stock. Barrel length from 22" to 32". Fixed or choke tubes. Magazine capacity 7 rounds. Weight about 7 lbs.

NIB	Exc.	V.G.	Good	Fair	Poor
300	280	250	180	100	50

Model 801B

Same as above, with 4-round magazine.

NIB	Exc.	V.G.	Good	Fair	Poor
300	280	250	180	100	50

ARMSCOR PRECISION INTERNATIONAL

Pahrump, Nevada

Armscor Precision International imports firearms made by Arms Corporation of the Philippines. Also see Rock Island Armory.

RIFLES

M14R

Civilian version of U.S. M14 rifle chambered in .308 Win.. Manufactured from new and surplus parts. Introduced in 1986, discontinued in 2006. Note: Deduct 30 percent for Norinco parts.

NIB	Exc.	V.G.	Good	Fair	Poor
1800	1500	1100	650	400	200

M14 National Match

As above. Built to A.M.T.U. MIL specifications. Introduced in 1987.

NIB	Exc.	V.G.	Good	Fair	Poor
2000	1700	1300	900	500	250

FAL

Civilian version of FN FAL rifle. Assembled from new and Argentine surplus parts. Introduced in 1987.

NIB	Exc.	V.G.	Good	Fair	Poor
1600	1250	800	400	300	150

M36 Israeli Sniper Rifle

Specialized weapon built upon Armscorp M14 receiver in Bullpup style. Barrel length 22" of free floating design for accuracy. Chambered for .308 cartridge. There is an integral flash suppressor and a bipod. Furnished with 20-shot detachable magazine. This civilian version first offered for sale in 1989.

NIB	Exc.	V.G.	Good	Fair	Poor
3200	2650	2000	1500	850	400

Expert Model

.22-caliber semi-automatic rifle, with 21" barrel, open sights and 10-shot magazine. Introduced in 1989.

NIB	Exc.	V.G.	Good	Fair	Poor
220	200	180	140	100	80

Model M14P

.22-caliber bolt-action rifle. Fitted with 23" barrel, open sights and 5-shot detachable magazine. Mahogany stock.

NIB	Exc.	V.G.	Good	Fair	Poor
150	90	80	50	40	20

Model M14D

As above, with adjustable rear sight and checkered stock. Manufactured in 1987 only.

NIB	Exc.	V.G.	Good	Fair	Poor
160	100	80	60	40	20

Model 14Y

Bolt-action rifle chambered for .22 LR cartridge. Fitted with 18" barrel and 10-round magazine. Weight about 5.2 lbs.

NIB	Exc.	V.G.	Good	Fair	Poor
150	120	100	80	50	20

Model 12Y

Bolt-action rifle is a single-shot. Chambered for .22 LR. Fitted with 18" barrel. Weight about 5 lbs.

NIB	Exc.	V.G.	Good	Fair	Poor
120	100	80	50	40	20

Model 1400

Bolt-action rifle chambered for .22 LR cartridge. Fitted with 22.5" barrel and 10-round magazine. Weight about 6.5 lbs.

NIB	Exc.	V.G.	Good	Fair	Poor
220	200	150	120	100	80

Model M1500

.22 Magnum bolt-action rifle. Fitted with 22.5" barrel, open sights, 5-shot magazine and checkered mahogany stock. Weight about 6.5 lbs.

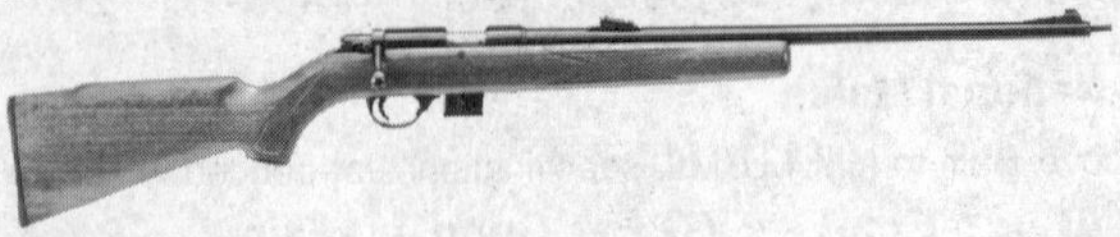

NIB	Exc.	V.G.	Good	Fair	Poor
250	200	150	120	100	80

Model M1600

.22-caliber copy of U.S. M16 rifle, with 18" barrel and detachable 15-round magazine. Weight about 6.2 lbs.

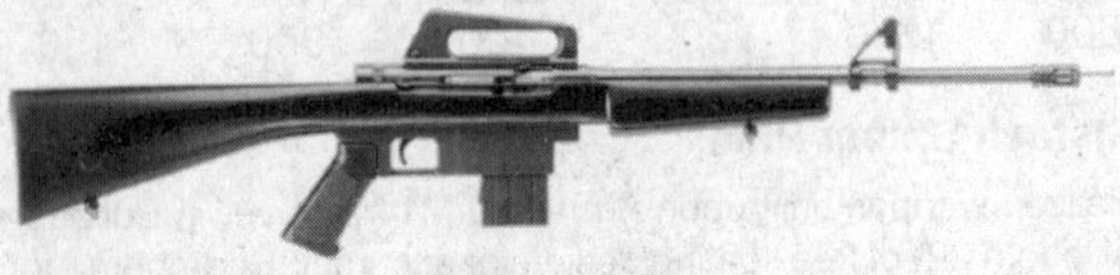

NIB	Exc.	V.G.	Good	Fair	Poor
300	200	120	100	80	50

Model M1600R

As above, with stainless steel collapsible stock and shrouded barrel. No longer in production.

NIB	Exc.	V.G.	Good	Fair	Poor
320	220	150	120	100	80

Model M1600C

As above, with 20" barrel and fiberglass stock. No longer in production.

NIB	Exc.	V.G.	Good	Fair	Poor
300	200	120	100	80	50

Model M1600W

As above, with mahogany stock. No longer in production.

NIB	Exc.	V.G.	Good	Fair	Poor
300	200	120	100	80	50

Model M1800

.22 Hornet bolt-action rifle. Fitted with 22.5" barrel, 5-shot magazine and mahogany Monte Carlo-style stock. Weight about 6.6 lbs.

NIB	Exc.	V.G.	Good	Fair	Poor
250	200	150	80	50	40

Model 20C

Chambered for .22 LR, with 15-round magazine and 18.25" barrel. Weight about 6.2 lbs.

NIB	Exc.	V.G.	Good	Fair	Poor
180	150	90	70	50	40

Model M20P

.22-caliber 15-shot semi-automatic rifle. Fitted with 20.75" barrel, open sights and plain mahogany stock. Weight about 6.3 lbs.

NIB	Exc.	V.G.	Good	Fair	Poor
180	150	90	70	50	40

Model M2000

As above, with adjustable sights and checkered stock. Weight about 6.4 lbs.

NIB	Exc.	V.G.	Good	Fair	Poor
180	150	90	70	50	40

Model AK22S

.22-caliber semi-automatic rifle resembling Russian AKA47. Barrel length 18.5", 15-round magazine and mahogany stock. Weight about 7.5 lbs.

NIB	Exc.	V.G.	Good	Fair	Poor
280	220	200	120	80	50

Model AK22F

As above, with folding stock. No longer in production.

NIB	Exc.	V.G.	Good	Fair	Poor
280	220	200	120	80	50

HANDGUNS

Hi-Power

Argentine-made version of Browning semi-automatic pistol. Chambered for 9mm, with 4.75" barrel. Matte finish, with checkered synthetic grips. Introduced in 1989.

NIB	Exc.	V.G.	Good	Fair	Poor
450	350	300	250	200	100

Detective HP—Compact

As above, with 3.5" barrel.

NIB	Exc.	V.G.	Good	Fair	Poor
480	380	350	280	200	100

P22

Copy of Colt Woodsman .22-caliber semi-automatic pistol. Available with 4" or 6" barrels and 10-shot magazine. Finish blued, grips of checkered hardwood. Introduced in 1989.

NIB	Exc.	V.G.	Good	Fair	Poor
250	150	120	100	80	50

SD9

Israeli-made 9mm double-action semi-automatic pistol, with 3" barrel. Assembled extensively from sheet metal stampings. Loaded chamber indicator and 6-round magazine. This model also known as Sirkus SD9. Manufactured by Sirkus Industries in Israel. Introduced in 1989.

Courtesy Jim Rankin

NIB	Exc.	V.G.	Good	Fair	Poor
300	250	200	150	100	80

Armscor 1911A1-45 FS GI

1911-style semi-automatic pistol. Chambered in .45 ACP (8 rounds), 9mm Parabellum, .38 Super (9 rounds). Features include checkered plastic or hardwood grips, 5" barrel, Parkerized steel frame and slide, drift adjustable sights. Note: Add $50 for Commander or Officer's model.

NIB	Exc.	V.G.	Good	Fair	Poor
400	350	300	250	200	100

Model M100

Double-action swing-out cylinder revolver. Chambered for .22, .22 Magnum and .38 Special cartridges. Has 4" ventilated rib barrel. Six-shot cylinder and adjustable sights. Blued, with checkered mahogany grips. No longer in production.

NIB	Exc.	V.G.	Good	Fair	Poor
200	180	150	110	80	50

Model 200P

Introduced in 1990. This 6-shot revolver chambered for .38 Special cartridge. Fitted with 4" barrel, fixed sights and wood or rubber grips. Weight about 26 oz.

NIB	Exc.	V.G.	Good	Fair	Poor
180	150	120	100	80	60

Model 200TC

Introduced in 1990. Similar to above. Fitted with adjustable sights and checkered wood grips. Weight about 28 oz.

NIB	Exc.	V.G.	Good	Fair	Poor
200	180	150	120	100	80

Model 200DC

Similar to Model 200P, with 2.5" barrel. Weight about 22 oz.

NIB	Exc.	V.G.	Good	Fair	Poor
180	150	120	100	80	60

Model 201S

Similar to Model 200P in stainless steel.

NIB	Exc.	V.G.	Good	Fair	Poor
200	180	150	120	100	80

Model 202

Chambered for 38 Special cartridge. This 6-shot revolver fitted with 4" barrel and fixed sights. Blued finish. Weight about 27 oz.

NIB	Exc.	V.G.	Good	Fair	Poor
150	120	100	80	50	20

Model 206

Similar to Model 202, with 2.88" barrel. Weight about 25 oz.

NIB	Exc.	V.G.	Good	Fair	Poor
180	140	110	80	50	20

Model 210

Same as Model 202, with adjustable sights. Weight about 27 oz.

NIB	Exc.	V.G.	Good	Fair	Poor
200	150	120	80	50	20

MAP1 FS

Single-/double-action 9mm semi-automatic, with 16+1 capacity. Fixed sights, 4.45" barrel, weight 40.5 oz. Nickel alloy steel frame and slide. (Shorter, lighter MS model has 3.66" barrel.) Introduced 2006.

NIB	Exc.	V.G.	Good	Fair	Poor
—	350	300	200	120	80

MAPP1 FS

Single-/double-action 9mm semi-automatic, with 16+1 capacity. Fixed sights, 4.45" barrel, weight 40.5 oz. Polymer frame with integrated accessory rail and nickel alloy steel slide. (Shorter, lighter MS model has 3.66" barrel.) Introduced 2006.

NIB	Exc.	V.G.	Good	Fair	Poor
—	350	300	200	180	80

Model 1911-A1

Semi-automatic pistol similar in design to Colt Model 1911 pistol. Chambered for .45 ACP cartridge. Fitted with 5" barrel. Blued finish. Magazine capacity 8 rounds. Weight about 39 oz. Also sold under Charles Daly name.

NIB	Exc.	V.G.	Good	Fair	Poor
500	400	300	200	150	80

Model 1911-A2

Same as above, with double column magazine and 13 round capacity. Weight about 43 oz. Note: Add $100 for two-tone finish; $130 for chrome finish.

NIB	Exc.	V.G.	Good	Fair	Poor
600	500	380	250	200	110

SHOTGUNS

Model 30D

Slide-action 12-gauge shotgun. Fitted with 28" or 30" barrels and various chokes. Magazine holds 6 cartridges. Weight about 7.6 lbs.

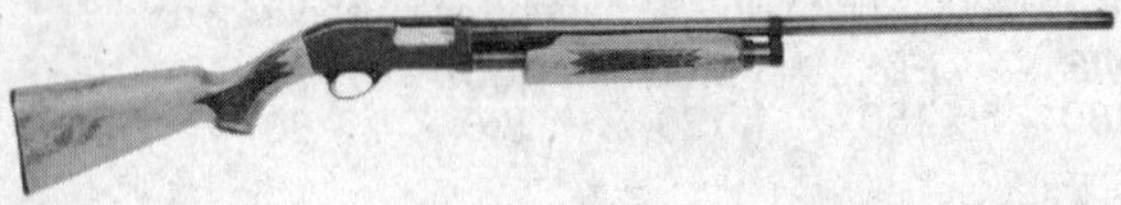

NIB	Exc.	V.G.	Good	Fair	Poor
200	180	150	120	100	80

Model 30DG

As above, with 20" barrel, fitted rifle sights and 7-shot magazine. Weight about 7.2 lbs.

NIB	Exc.	V.G.	Good	Fair	Poor
180	150	120	100	80	70

Model 30R

As above, with shotgun bead sights, 18.5" or 20" barrel. Weight between 7- and 7.2 lbs. depending on barrel length.

NIB	Exc.	V.G.	Good	Fair	Poor
180	150	120	100	80	70

Model 30RP

As above, with auxiliary black composition pistol grip and 18.5" barrel.

NIB	Exc.	V.G.	Good	Fair	Poor
180	150	120	100	80	70

Model 30 SAS1

Slide-action 12-gauge, with 20" barrel and heat shield. Chambered for 3" shell. Open cylinder choke. Parkerized finish. Weight about 8 lbs.

NIB	Exc.	V.G.	Good	Fair	Poor
200	150	100	80	50	20

ARNOLD ARMS
Arlington, Washington

A survey of Arnold Arms over the last few months at Gunbroker and Guns Int. shows no appreciable increase in used values.

Varminter I

Features heavy match-grade barrel, with straight taper. Lengths from 24" to 26". Calibers from .222 Rem. to .257 Arnold Magnum. Choice of McMillian Varmint stock in various finishes. Pacific Research Varmint stock in flat black. Weight from 9- to 11 lbs. depending on caliber and configuration.

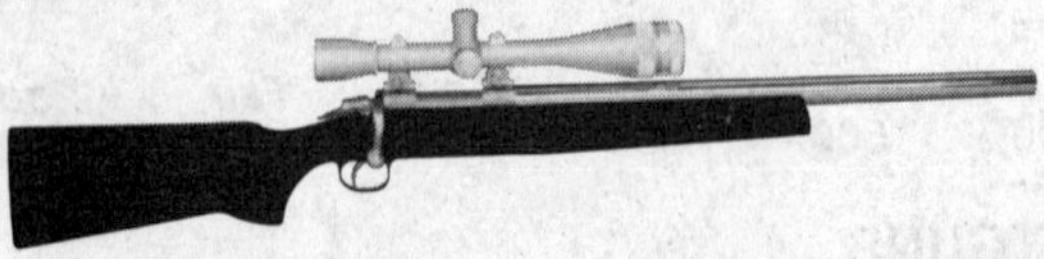

NIB	Exc.	V.G.	Good	Fair	Poor
2600	2000	1450	1050	700	200

Varminter II

Variation features 24" to 26" medium weight match barrel, with choice of McMillan or Pacific Research sporter stocks. Choice of triggers. Weight 7.5- to 9 lbs. depending on configuration. Calibers from .223 Rem. to .257 Arnold Magnum.

NIB	Exc.	V.G.	Good	Fair	Poor
2600	2000	1450	1050	700	200

Alaskan

Bolt-action rifle chambered for calibers .223 to .338 Win. Magnum. Barrel lengths 22" to 26" depending on caliber. Stocks are synthetic in black woodland or arctic camo. Sights optional. Rifle drilled and tapped for scope mounts. Trigger fully adjustable. Choice of chrome moly steel or stainless steel. Introduced in 1996.

NIB	Exc.	V.G.	Good	Fair	Poor
2600	2000	1450	1050	700	200

Alaskan Trophy

Similar to Alaskan Rifle. Chambered for .300 Magnum to .458 Win. Magnum. Barrel lengths 24" to 26" depending on caliber. Choice of walnut, synthetic or fibergrain stock. Fitted with iron sights. Choice of stainless or chrome moly steel. Introduced in 1996.

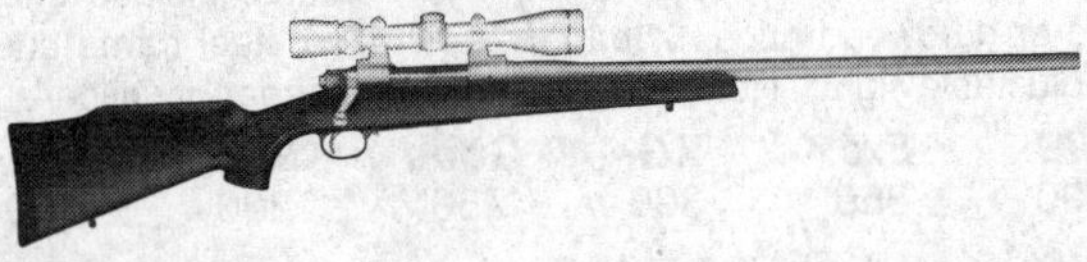

NIB	Exc.	V.G.	Good	Fair	Poor
3100	2500	1450	1050	700	200

Alaskan Guide

Offered in choice of calibers .257 to .338 Magnum. Barrel lengths 22" to 26" depending on caliber. Buyer has choice of "A" English walnut stock or deluxe synthetic stock. No open sights.

Synthetic Stock

NIB	Exc.	V.G.	Good	Fair	Poor
3700	2900	2200	1400	650	300

Walnut Stock

NIB	Exc.	V.G.	Good	Fair	Poor
4300	3400	2500	1480	700	320

Grand Alaskan

Version fitted with AAA fancy select or exhibition wood. Built in calibers .300 Magnum to .458 Win. Magnum.

"AAA" English Walnut

NIB	Exc.	V.G.	Good	Fair	Poor
6000	5000	3750	2500	1500	450

"Exhibition" Grade Walnut

NIB	Exc.	V.G.	Good	Fair	Poor
7400	6000	5000	3900	1650	320

Safari

Introduced in 1996. Features calibers .223 to .458 Win. Magnum. Barrel lengths 22" to 26" depending on caliber. Apollo is a controlled or push feed type, with one-piece cone-head bolt. Fully adjustable trigger, with chrome moly or stainless steel construction. Sights are optional. Rifle drilled and tapped for scope mounts. Choice of A fancy English or AA fancy English walnut.

"A" Fancy English Walnut

NIB	Exc.	V.G.	Good	Fair	Poor
4300	3500	2700	1650	800	300

"AA" Fancy English Walnut

NIB	Exc.	V.G.	Good	Fair	Poor
4400	3500	2700	1650	800	300

African Trophy

Similar to Safari Rifle. Stocked in AAA fancy walnut, with wrap-around checkering.

NIB	Exc.	V.G.	Good	Fair	Poor
6300	5000	3250	2500	1750	300

Grand African

Similar to Safari rifle, with addition of Exhibition Grade wood. Calibers .338 to .458 Magnum.

NIB	Exc.	V.G.	Good	Fair	Poor
7600	6100	5000	3900	1650	320

Serengeti Synthetic

Similar to Safari rifle, with fiber-grain stock in classic or Monte Carlo style. Checkering or stipple finish. Calibers .243 to .300 Magnum. Introduced in 1996.

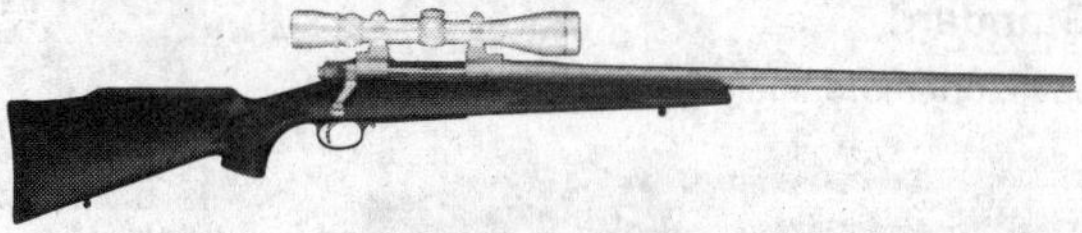

NIB	Exc.	V.G.	Good	Fair	Poor
2600	2100	1600	1150	700	220

African Synthetic

Similar to Safari rifle, with fiber-grain stock, checkering or stipple finish. Calibers .338 to .458 Magnum.

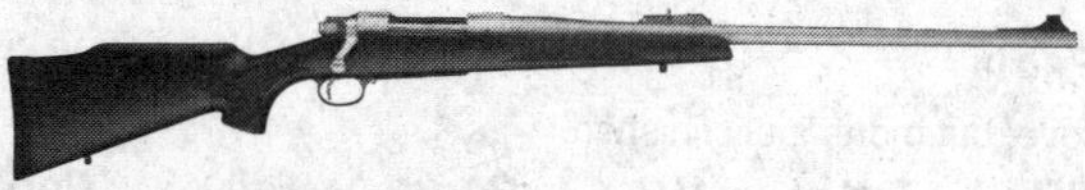

NIB	Exc.	V.G.	Good	Fair	Poor
3300	2600	1800	1400	750	250

Neutralizer Mark I

Built on Remington 700 or Winchester action. Bolt-action rifle chambered in choice of calibers from .223 to .300 Win. Magnum. Barrel length 24" to 26" depending on caliber, with Magnum barrels up to 28". A fiberglass tactical stock, with adjustable cheekpiece and buttplate is standard in various finishes. Note: Deduct $400 for Winchester action.

NIB	Exc.	V.G.	Good	Fair	Poor
2900	2300	1700	1300	700	280

Neutralizer Mark II

Same as above, with Apollo action.

NIB	Exc.	V.G.	Good	Fair	Poor
4000	3200	2250	1700	900	320

Benchrest Rifles

Custom built. Unable to price individual rifles.

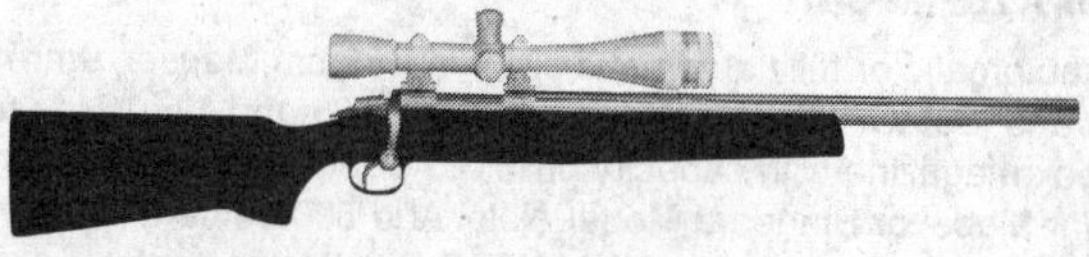

Prone Rifles

Custom built. Unable to price individual rifles.

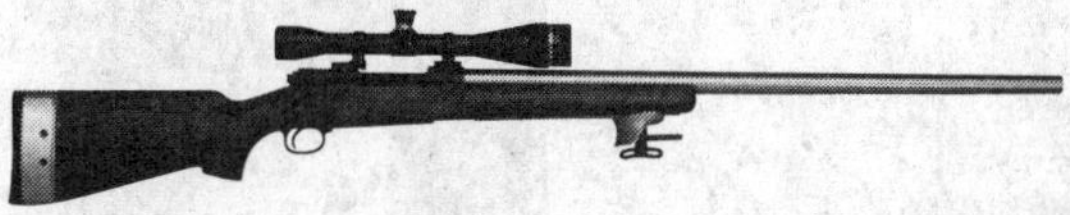

X-Course Rifles

Custom built. Unable to price individual rifles.

1,000 Yard Match Rifles

Custom built. Unable to price individual rifles.

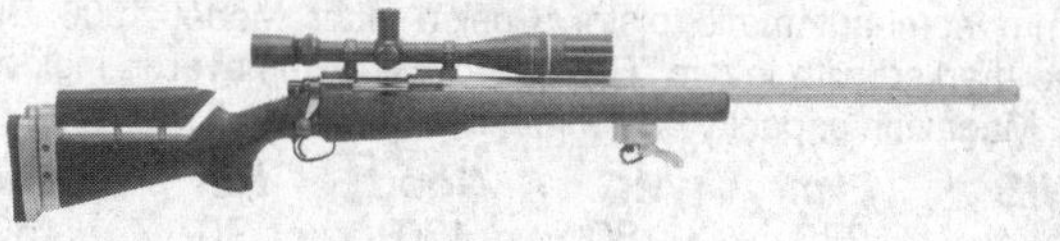

Fully Accurized Production Rifles

Rifles offered in standard blue or stainless steel, with walnut or synthetic stock. Chambered from .223 to .338 Win. Magnum. Built on Remington, Ruger or Winchester actions.

NIB	Exc.	V.G.	Good	Fair	Poor
1250	1100	750	600	400	200

AROSTEGUI, EULOGIO

Eibar, Spain

Azul Royal (Model 31)

Semi-automatic or fully automatic pistol in calibers 7.63 Mauser, 9mm Bergmann or .38 ACP. Manufactured between 1935 and 1940. Fitted with 10-round integral magazine. Note: Add 300 percent for fully automatic machine pistol version. NFA/BATFE regulations apply.

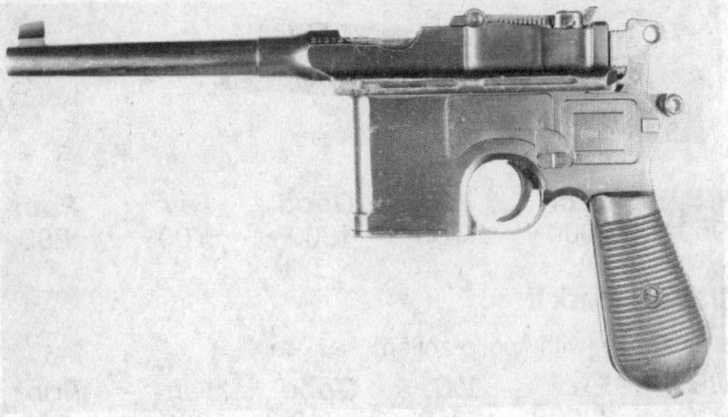

Courtesy James Rankin

NIB	Exc.	V.G.	Good	Fair	Poor
—	3000	2500	1000	500	300

Super Azul (M-34)

Semi-automatic or fully automatic pistol in 7.63mm Mauser, 9mm Bergmann and .38 ACP. Manufactured between 1935 and 1940. Has removable box magazine with capacity of 10, 20 or 30 rounds. Also known as the War Model or Standard Model. Note: Add 300 percent for fully automatic machine pistol version. NFA/BATFE regulations apply.

Courtesy James Rankin

NIB	Exc.	V.G.	Good	Fair	Poor
—	3000	2500	1000	500	300

Azul 6.35mm

6.35mm semi-automatic pistol. Copied after Model 1906 Browning. Frame marked with letters "EA" in a circle. A retriever is molded in the grips. Magazine capacity 6 or 9 rounds.

NIB	Exc.	V.G.	Good	Fair	Poor
—	230	180	130	90	50

Azul 7.65mm

7.65mm semi-automatic pistol. Copied after Model 1910 FN. Magazine capacity 7 or 9 rounds.

NIB	Exc.	V.G.	Good	Fair	Poor
—	250	200	150	100	80

Velo-Dog

Folding trigger 5.5mm or 6.35mm revolver bearing trademark "EA" on grips.

NIB	Exc.	V.G.	Good	Fair	Poor
—	350	150	90	50	30

ARRIETA S.L.

Elgoibar, Spain

Company produces a wide variety of double-barrel shotguns. Price range from $450 to more than $10,000. It is recommended that highly engraved examples, as well as small bore arms, be individually appraised. Note: For 20- or 28-gauge and .410 bore, add 10 percent to values shown.

490 Eder

Double-barrel boxlock shotgun, with double triggers and extractors. Discontinued in 1986.

NIB	Exc.	V.G.	Good	Fair	Poor
—	550	420	320	250	100

500 Titan

Holland & Holland-style sidelock double-barrel shotgun, with French case-hardened and engraved locks. Double triggers on extractors. No longer imported after 1986.

NIB	Exc.	V.G.	Good	Fair	Poor
—	680	500	400	300	150

501 Palomara

As above, but more finely finished. Discontinued in 1986.

NIB	Exc.	V.G.	Good	Fair	Poor
—	800	600	500	400	200

505 Alaska

As above, but more intricately engraved. Discontinued in 1986.

NIB	Exc.	V.G.	Good	Fair	Poor
—	900	750	600	500	250

510 Montana

Holland & Holland-style sidelock double-barrel shotgun, with internal parts gold-plated.

NIB	Exc.	V.G.	Good	Fair	Poor
3800	3000	1800	950	600	350

550 Field

As above, without internal parts gold-plated.

NIB	Exc.	V.G.	Good	Fair	Poor
3200	2750	1250	850	500	250

557 Standard

As above, but more finely finished.

NIB	Exc.	V.G.	Good	Fair	Poor
5900	5000	3800	2700	1500	800

558 Patria

As above, but more finely finished.

NIB	Exc.	V.G.	Good	Fair	Poor
3650	3150	1750	1250	800	400

560 Cumbre

As above, but featuring intricate engraving.

NIB	Exc.	V.G.	Good	Fair	Poor
3800	3200	1800	1200	800	400

570 Lieja

NIB	Exc.	V.G.	Good	Fair	Poor
6200	5500	4200	3000	2000	1000

575 Sport

NIB	Exc.	V.G.	Good	Fair	Poor
6750	6000	5000	3750	2400	1100

578 Victoria

Engraved in the English manner, with floral bouquets.

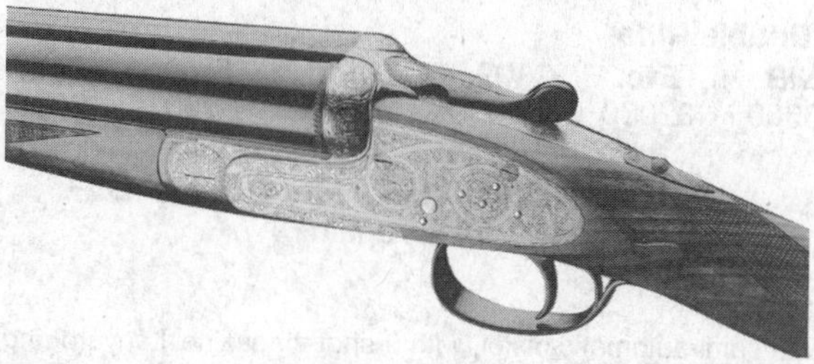

NIB	Exc.	V.G.	Good	Fair	Poor
10000	8500	7000	5000	2800	1200

585 Liria

As above, but more finely finished.

NIB	Exc.	V.G.	Good	Fair	Poor
11000	9500	8000	6000	3000	1500

588 Cima

NIB	Exc.	V.G.	Good	Fair	Poor
4800	4000	2250	1500	900	400

590 Regina

NIB	Exc.	V.G.	Good	Fair	Poor
4250	3500	2700	1750	1000	500

595 Principe

As above, but engraved with relief-cut hunting scenes.

NIB	Exc.	V.G.	Good	Fair	Poor
7500	6000	4000	3000	2000	1000

600 Imperial

Double-barrel shotgun has a self-opening action.

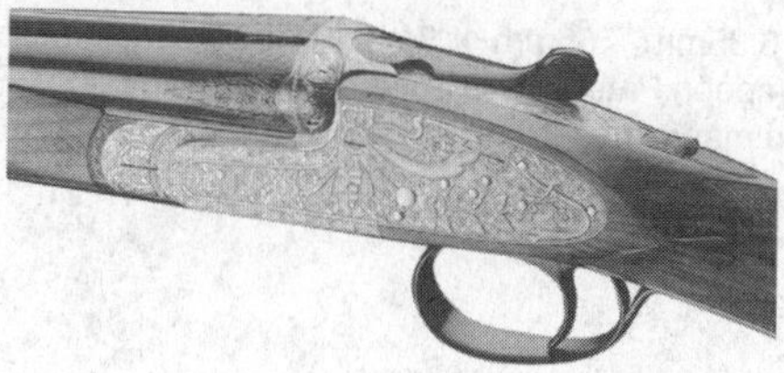

NIB	Exc.	V.G.	Good	Fair	Poor
10000	8500	7000	4500	3200	2100

601 Imperial Tiro

As above, but nickel-plated. Fitted with self-opening action.

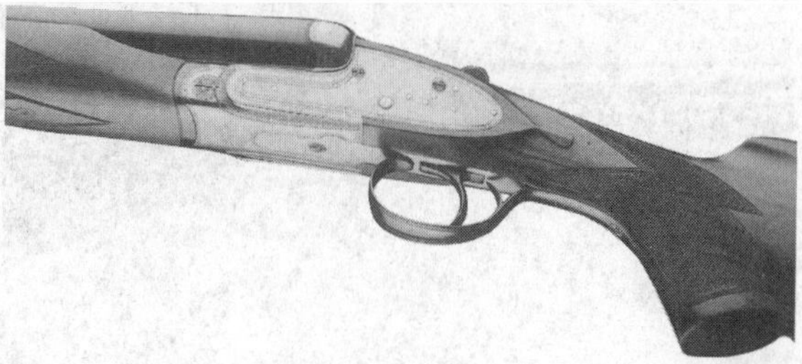

NIB	Exc.	V.G.	Good	Fair	Poor
11000	9500	8000	5200	3800	2200

801

Detachable sidelock self-opening action double-barrel shotgun. Engraved in manner of Churchill.

NIB	Exc.	V.G.	Good	Fair	Poor
12000	10200	7500	5000	3000	2000

802

As above, with Holland & Holland-style engraving.

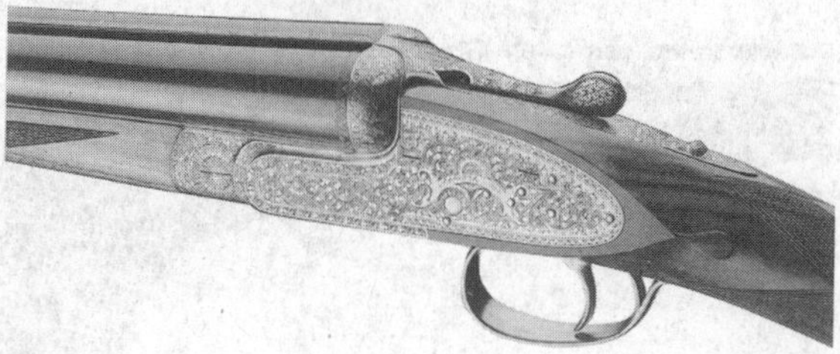

NIB	Exc.	V.G.	Good	Fair	Poor
12500	11000	8000	6000	4000	2000

803

As above, with Purdey-style engraving.

NIB	Exc.	V.G.	Good	Fair	Poor
14000	12000	8500	5000	4000	2000

871

Features hand detachable sidelocks, with Holland ejectors. Scroll engraving.

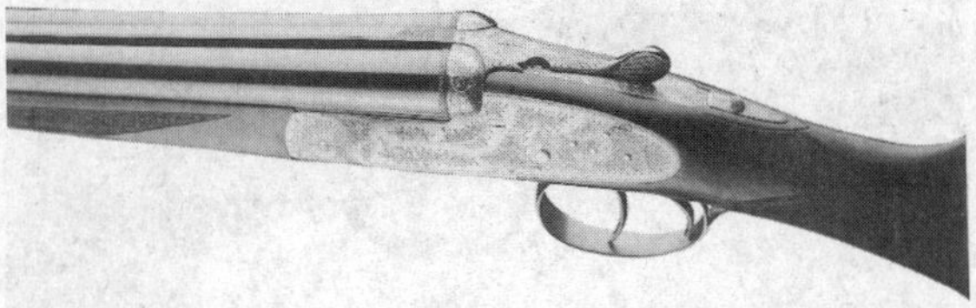

NIB	Exc.	V.G.	Good	Fair	Poor
5300	4400	2500	1500	1000	750

872

Same features as Model 871, with addition of more engraving coverage using a tighter scroll.

NIB	Exc.	V.G.	Good	Fair	Poor
14000	12500	10000	7000	5000	2000

873

Features hand detachable sidelocks and game scene engraving.

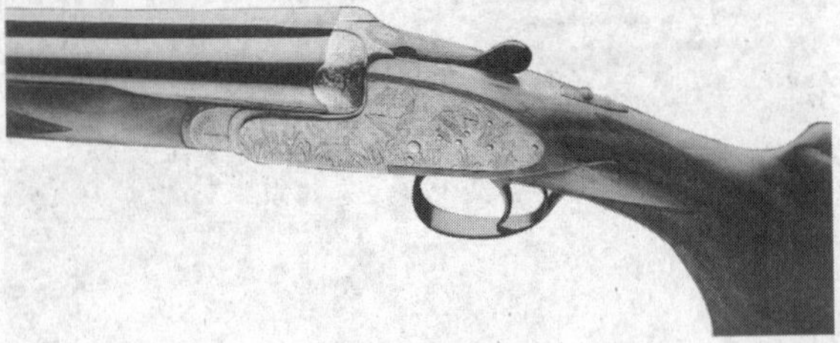

NIB	Exc.	V.G.	Good	Fair	Poor
15000	13500	11000	7000	5000	2000

874

Same features as above, with addition of blued frame and gold outlines.

NIB	Exc.	V.G.	Good	Fair	Poor
11000	9000	8000	6000	4000	2000

875

Custom manufactured sidelock double-barrel shotgun. Built solely to customer's specifications.

NIB	Exc.	V.G.	Good	Fair	Poor
17000	15000	12500	7000	5000	2000

R-1 Double Rifle

NIB	Exc.	V.G.	Good	Fair	Poor
18000	16000	12500	8000	3000	1000

R-2 Double Rifle

NIB	Exc.	V.G.	Good	Fair	Poor
40000	32000	20000	12000	5000	2000

ARRIZABALAGA, HIJOS de C.

Eibar, Spain

Arrizabalaga

7.65mm semi-automatic pistol, with 9-shot magazine. Lanyard ring fitted to butt. Checkered wood grips. "ARRIZABALAGA" on slide.

Courtesy James Rankin

NIB	Exc.	V.G.	Good	Fair	Poor
—	300	200	130	90	50

Campeon

Model 1919 6.35mm, 7.65mm or 9mm Kurtz semi-automatic pistol. Slide marked "Campeon Patent 1919"; plastic grips "Campeon". Supplied with 6- or 8-round magazines. Note: Add 25 percent for 9mm Kurtz.

Courtesy James Rankin

NIB	Exc.	V.G.	Good	Fair	Poor
—	300	230	150	90	50

Jo Lo Ar

Model 1924 semi-automatic pistol, with tip-up barrel, cocking lever and no triggerguard. Jo Lo Ar was built in five calibers: 6.35mm, 7.65mm, 9mm Kurtz, 9mm Largo and .45 ACP. "Jo-Lo-Ar" appears on slide and grips. Premium for larger calibers. Note: Add 400 percent for .45.

Courtesy James Rankin

NIB	Exc.	V.G.	Good	Fair	Poor
—	1100	920	800	450	200

Sharpshooter

6.35mm, 7.65mm or 9mm Corto (short) semi-automatic pistol. Fitted with a cocking lever. Barrel tips up for cleaning or when using as a single-shot. "SHARPSHOOTER" appears on slide.

Courtesy James Rankin

NIB	Exc.	V.G.	Good	Fair	Poor
—	400	300	220	150	100

ARSENAL, INC.

Las Vegas, Nevada

SA M-7

Semi-automatic rifles manufactured in U.S. Similar to AK-47 in appearance. Chambered for 7.62x39 cartridge. Fitted with 16" barrel. Black polymer stock.

NIB	Exc.	V.G.	Good	Fair	Poor
1700	1200	900	700	—	—

SA M-7 Classic

As above, with blonde wood stock.

NIB	Exc.	V.G.	Good	Fair	Poor
1750	1250	950	700	—	—

SA M-7S

Similar to SA M-7, with scope rail added.

NIB	Exc.	V.G.	Good	Fair	Poor
1730	1200	900	700	—	—

SA RPK-5

Similar to SA M-7. Chambered for 5.56 NATO. Has 23.5" heavy barrel, with folding tripod and muzzle threads.

NIB	Exc.	V.G.	Good	Fair	Poor
1800	1400	950	700	—	—

SA RPK-7

Chambered for 7.62x39 cartridge. Rifle similar to RPK. Fitted with 23" barrel with bipod. Solid blonde wood stock, with trap in stock for cleaning kit.

NIB	Exc.	V.G.	Good	Fair	Poor
1700	1200	900	700	—	—

SAS M-7

Based on the Bulgarian ARM1F, with under-folding stock. Chambered for 7.62x39mm. Made from 2004 to 2007.

NIB	Exc.	V.G.	Good	Fair	Poor
1700	1200	900	700	—	—

SAS M-7 Classic

Based on Russian AKS-47, with heavy barrel, blonde wood and under-folding stock. Introduced in 2007.

NIB	Exc.	V.G.	Good	Fair	Poor
1800	1500	1200	900	—	—

SLR-104

Chambered for 5.45x39.5 cartridge, with Bulgarian-made receiver and barrel. Other parts made in U.S.A. Mil-spec polymer stock, with folding buttstock. Introduced in 2003.

NIB	Exc.	V.G.	Good	Fair	Poor
1200	1000	800	600	—	—

SLR-106

Chambered for 5.56 NATO/.223 round, with Bulgarian stamped receiver, original Bulgarian chrome lined hammer-forged barrel. U.S. made polmer stock, with left-side folding buttstock. Other features include pistol grip, removable muzzle brake, black or desert sand color and Picatinny rails.

NIB	Exc.	V.G.	Good	Fair	Poor
1200	1000	800	600	—	—

SLR-107

Chambered for 7.62x39 caliber. General features are similar to SLR-106 model.

NIB	Exc.	V.G.	Good	Fair	Poor
1200	1000	800	600	—	—

ASCASO
Cataluna, Spain

Spanish Rebublican Government

Copy of Astra Model 400. Chambered for 9mm Largo cartridge. Barrel marked "F. Ascaso Tarrassa" in an oval. Built by the Spanish government during Spanish Civil War. Very few were made.

Courtesy James Rankin

NIB	Exc.	V.G.	Good	Fair	Poor
—	850	750	550	300	200

ASHEVILLE ARMORY
Asheville, North Carolina

Confederate Enfield-Type Rifle (Antique)

.58-caliber percussion rifle, with 32.5" barrel and full stock secured by two iron barrel bands. Finished in white brass, triggerguard and buttplate on walnut stock. Lockplate marked "Asheville, N.C." Approximately 300 made in 1862 and 1863. As with many confederate arms, values are speculative due to extreme rarity. Expert consultation advised.

Courtesy Milwaukee Public Museum, Milwaukee, Wisconsin

Exc.	Fine	V.G.	Good	Fair	Poor
42000	19200	12100	5000	3250	2270

ASHTON, PETER & WILLIAM
Middletown, Connecticut

Underhammer Pistol (Antique)

.28- to .38-caliber single-shot percussion revolver, with 4" or 5" half-octagonal barrels marked "P.H. Ashton" or "W. Ashton". Blued or browned, with walnut grips. Active 1850s.

Exc.	Fine	V.G.	Good	Fair	Poor
1500	850	500	350	250	150

ASTON, H./H. ASTON & CO. PISTOLS
Middleton, Connecticut

U.S. Model 1842 Percussion Pistol (Antique)

Overall length 14"; barrel length 8.5"; caliber .54. Markings: on lockplate forward of hammer "U S/H. ASTON" or "U S/H. ASTON & CO.", on tail "MIDDTN/CONN/(date)"; on barrel, standard government inspection marks. Henry Aston of Middleton, Connecticut received a contract from U.S. War Department in February 1845, for 30,000 single-shot percussion pistols. These were delivered between 1846 and 1852, after which Ira N. Johnston continued production under a separate contract. Three thousand of these pistols were purchased for Navy usage. Many of these were subsequently marked with a small anchor on barrel near breech. These Navy purchases will command a slight premium.

Courtesy Milwaukee Public Museum, Milwaukee, Wisconsin

Exc.	Fine	V.G.	Good	Fair	Poor
3500	2000	1200	900	700	350

ASTRA-UNCETA SA
Guernica, Spain

Astra is a brand name placed on guns built by Esperanza y Unceta and then Unceta y Cia. This Spanish company has now incorporated its trade name into its corporate name and is now know as Astra-Unceta SA. Firm under direction of Don Pedron Unceta and Don Juan Esperanza began business in Eibar on July 17, 1908 and moved to Guernica in 1913. Astra trademark was adopted on November 25, 1914. Esperanza began production of the Spanish Army's Campo Giro pistol in 1913. Model 1921 was marketed commercially as Astra 400. After Spanish Civil War, Unceta was one of only four handgun companies permitted to resume manufacturing operations. An interesting and informative side note is that pistols with 1000 to 5000 model numbers were made after 1945. Astra merged with Star before going out of business in 2006.

Victoria

6.35mm semi-automatic pistol, with 2.5" barrel. Blued, with black plastic grips. Manufactured prior to 1913.

NIB	Exc.	V.G.	Good	Fair	Poor
—	300	250	200	130	80

Astra 1911

6.35mm and 7.65mm semi-automatic pistol. External hammer. Checkered hard rubber grips. 7.65mm model was manufactured before 6.35mm model.

Courtesy James Rankin

NIB	Exc.	V.G.	Good	Fair	Poor
—	430	380	200	170	160

Astra 1924

6.35mm semi-automatic pistol, with 2.5" barrel. Slide marked "Esperanza y Unceta Guernica Spain Astra Cal 6.35 .25". Blued, with black plastic grips.

NIB	Exc.	V.G.	Good	Fair	Poor
—	300	200	120	100	80

Astra 100 (Old Model)

Semi-automatic pistol in caliber 7.65mm. Checkered hard rubber grips. Magazine capacity 12 rounds. Introduced after WWII.

Courtesy James Rankin

NIB	Exc.	V.G.	Good	Fair	Poor
—	550	400	300	200	100

Astra 200

6.35mm semi-automatic pistol, with 2.5" barrel and 6-shot magazine. Fitted with grip safety. Also known as "Firecat" in United States. Manufactured from 1920 to 1966. Note: Add 25 percent for factory engraving.

Courtesy James Rankin

NIB	Exc.	V.G.	Good	Fair	Poor
—	300	200	120	100	80

Astra 400 or Model 1921

9x23 Bergman (9mm Largo) caliber semi-automatic pistol, with 6" barrel. Blued, with black plastic grips. Adopted for use by the Spanish Army. Approximately 106,000 made prior to 1946. Recent importation has depressed the price of these guns. Note: Any with Nazi proofs marks are worth a 100 percent premium, but caution is advised.

NIB	Exc.	V.G.	Good	Fair	Poor
—	710	410	260	210	160

Astra 300

As above in 7.65mm or 9mm short. Those used during WWII by German forces bear Waffenamt marks. Approximately 171,000 manufactured prior to 1947. Note: Add 100% for Nazi-proofed.

Courtesy Orvel Reichert

NIB	Exc.	V.G.	Good	Fair	Poor
—	910	510	310	210	160

Astra 600

Similar to Model 400 in 9mm Parabellum. In 1943 and 1944 approximately 10,500 manufactured. Some of these WWII guns will have Nazi proof stamp and bring a premium. A further 49,000 were made in 1946 and commercially sold.

NIB	Exc.	V.G.	Good	Fair	Poor
—	580	380	280	180	100

Astra 700

Single-action semi-automatic pistol in caliber 7.65mm. Magazine capacity 9 rounds. Introduced in 1926.

Courtesy James Rankin

NIB	Exc.	V.G.	Good	Fair	Poor
—	500	400	300	150	100

Astra 800

Similar to Model 600, with external hammer and loaded chamber indicator. Blued, with plastic grips having trade name "Condor" cast in them. Approximately 11,400 made from 1958 to 1969.

NIB	Exc.	V.G.	Good	Fair	Poor
—	1940	1760	1260	810	710

Astra 900

Modified copy of Mauser Model C96 semi-automatic pistol. Blued, with walnut grips. Note: Early examples with small Bolo grip marked "Hope" on chamber will bring a 20 percent premium. Serial numbers 32,788 through 33,774 were used by German Army in WWII and bring a 50 percent premium. Add 50 percent for matching Astra-made stock.

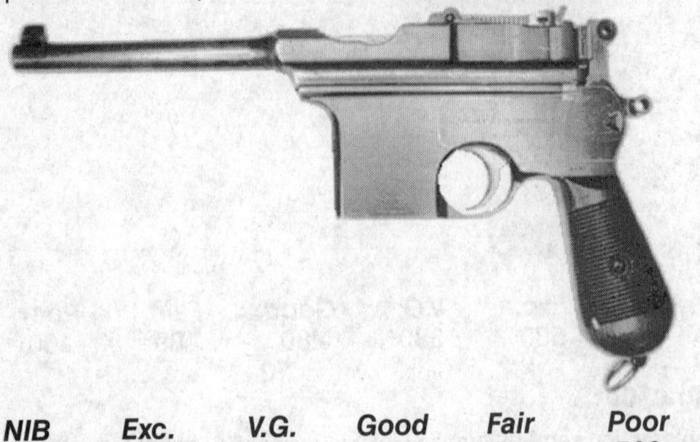

NIB	Exc.	V.G.	Good	Fair	Poor
—	4000	2260	1010	650	500

Astra 1000

Single-action semi-automatic pistol in caliber 7.65mm. Magazine capacity 12 rounds. Introduced after WWII.

Courtesy James Rankin

NIB	Exc.	V.G.	Good	Fair	Poor
—	750	600	450	200	100

Astra 2000 (Or Cub)

Single-action semi-automatic pistol in .22- or 6.35mm caliber. No grip safety. With external hammer. Blued, with plastic grips.

NIB	Exc.	V.G.	Good	Fair	Poor
—	330	230	180	150	80

Astra 3000

Model 300 in 7.65mm or 9mm short, with 6- or 7-shot magazine. Loaded chamber indicator. Manufactured from 1948 to 1956.

Paul Goodwin photo

NIB	Exc.	V.G.	Good	Fair	Poor
—	600	500	320	200	100

Astra 4000 Falcon

Semi-automatic pistol known later as "Falcon". Calibers were .22 LR, 7.65mm and 9mmK. Magazine capacity 7, 8 and 10 rounds. Manufactured beginning 1955.

Courtesy James Rankin

NIB	Exc.	V.G.	Good	Fair	Poor
—	580	480	320	200	100

Astra 5000 Constable

.22, 7.65mm or 9mm short semi-automatic pistol (resembling Walther PP pistol), with 3.5" barrel. Blued, chrome-plated or stainless steel, with plastic grips. Also available with 6" barrel as a sport model. Introduced in 1965. Note: Add 15 percent for Constable Sport version with 6" barrel and adjustable sight.

NIB	Exc.	V.G.	Good	Fair	Poor
—	400	300	250	200	100

Astra 7000

Enlarged version of Model 2000 in .22-caliber.

NIB	Exc.	V.G.	Good	Fair	Poor
—	580	480	320	200	100

Astra A-80

.38 Super, 9mm or .45-caliber double-action semi-automatic pistol, with 3.75" barrel. Magazine capacity 9- or 15-shot, depending on caliber. Blued or chrome-plated, with plastic grips. Introduced in 1982.

Courtesy James Rankin

NIB	Exc.	V.G.	Good	Fair	Poor
400	350	300	250	200	100

Astra A-90

As above in 9mm or .45-caliber only. Introduced in 1986.

NIB	Exc.	V.G.	Good	Fair	Poor
450	350	300	250	200	100

Constable A-60

.380-caliber double-action semi-automatic pistol, with 3.5" barrel, adjustable sights and 13-shot magazine. Blued, with plastic grips. Introduced in 1986.

NIB	Exc.	V.G.	Good	Fair	Poor
400	300	200	150	100	80

Astra Cadix

.22- or .38 Special double-action revolver, with 4" or 6" barrel. Swing-out cylinder holds 5- or 9-shots. Blued, with plastic grips. Manufactured from 1960 to 1968.

NIB	Exc.	V.G.	Good	Fair	Poor
—	220	180	120	90	70

.357 Double-Action Revolver

Similar to Cadix in .357 Magnum caliber, with 3", 4", 6" or 8.5" barrel. Adjustable sights and 6-shot cylinder. Blued or stainless steel, with walnut grips. Manufactured from 1972 to 1988. Note: Add 10 percent for stainless steel.

NIB	Exc.	V.G.	Good	Fair	Poor
300	250	180	120	100	80

.44/.45 Double-Action Revolver

As above in .41-, .44 Magnum or .45 ACP caliber, with 6" or 8.5" barrels and 6-shot cylinder. Blued or stainless steel, with walnut grips. Manufactured from 1980 to 1987. Note: Add 25 percent for stainless steel.

NIB	Exc.	V.G.	Good	Fair	Poor
—	380	320	250	200	100

Terminator

As above in .44 Special or .44 Magnum, with 2.75" barrel. Adjustable sights and 6-shot cylinder. Blued or stainless steel, with rubber grips. Note: Add 10 percent for stainless steel.

NIB	Exc.	V.G.	Good	Fair	Poor
—	380	330	260	200	100

Convertible Revolver

Similar to .357 D/A revolver. Accompanied by a cylinder chambered for 9mm Parabellum. Barrel length 3". Blued, with walnut grips. Introduced in 1986.

NIB	Exc.	V.G.	Good	Fair	Poor
—	400	320	280	150	100

RECENTLY IMPORTED PISTOLS

Model A-70

Lightweight semi-automatic pistol chambered for 9mm or .40 S&W cartridge. Fitted with 3-dot combat sights. Barrel 3.5" long. Magazine capacity 8 rounds for 9mm; 7 rounds for .40 S&W. Black plastic grips. Blue finish standard. Weight 29 oz. Note: Add $35 for nickel finish.

NIB	Exc.	V.G.	Good	Fair	Poor
380	260	220	180	150	100

Model A-75

Introduced in 1993. All standard features of Model 70 plus selective double-/single trigger action and decocking lever. Chambered for 9mm, .40 S&W or .45 ACP. Offered in blue or nickel finish, with steel or alloy frame in 9mm only. Weight: steel frame in 9mm and .40 S&W is 31 oz.; .45 ACP is 34.4 oz.; featherweight 9mm is 23.5 oz. Note: Add $35 for nickel finish.

NIB	Exc.	V.G.	Good	Fair	Poor
380	320	250	200	150	100

Model A-100

Semi-automatic service pistol. Chambered for 9mm Parabellum, .40 S&W or .45 ACP cartridges. Trigger is double-action for first shot, single-action for follow-up shots. Equipped with decocking lever. Barrel 3.8" long; overall length 7.5". Magazine capacity: 9mm is 17 rounds; .40 S&W is 13 rounds; .45 is 9 rounds. Blue or nickel finish standard. Weight about 34 oz. Also available in featherweight model 9mm at 26.5 oz. Note: Add $35 for nickel finish.

NIB	Exc.	V.G.	Good	Fair	Poor
400	350	300	250	200	100

Model A-100 Carry Comp

Similar to Model A-100, with 4.25" barrel and 1" compensator. Blue finish only. Weight about 38 oz. Magazine capacity: 9mm is 17 rounds; .40 S&W and .45 ACP is 10 rounds.

NIB	Exc.	V.G.	Good	Fair	Poor
480	380	300	250	200	100

ATCSA
Armas de Tiro y Casa
Eibar, Spain

Colt Police Positive Copy

.38-caliber 6-shot revolver resembling Colt Police Positive.

NIB	Exc.	V.G.	Good	Fair	Poor
—	250	120	100	60	40

Target Pistol

.22-caliber single-shot target pistol utilizing a revolver frame.

NIB	Exc.	V.G.	Good	Fair	Poor
—	300	180	120	100	60

AUBREY, A.J.
Meriden, Connecticut

Double-Barrel Shotguns

Good quality doubles made for Sears. Value depends on condition, grade and model. Prices range between $100 and $1500.

AUER, B.
Louisville, Kentucky

Pocket Pistol (Antique)

.60-caliber percussion pocket pistol, with 4" octagonal barrel. Long tang extending well back along grip. Browned silver furniture. Checkered walnut stock. Lock marked "B. Auer". Produced during 1850s. Few sales recorded. Values are speculative.

Exc.	Fine	V.G.	Good	Fair	Poor
2700	1400	1000	650	400	150

AUGUSTA MACHINE WORKS
Augusta, Georgia

1851 Colt Navy Copy

.36-caliber percussion revolver, with 8" barrel and 6-shot cylinder. Unmarked except for serial numbers. Stop cylinder slots 6 or 12. Blued, with walnut grips. Very rare revolver. Only 100 made. Surviving examples rarely come available for sale, and might bring $10,000-$20,000. Beware of fakes.

AUSTIN & HALLECK, INC.
Weston, Missouri; later Provo, Utah

Model 320 LR BLU

Inline percussion bolt-action rifle. Fitted with 26" half octagon/half round barrel in .50-caliber. Receiver and barrel blue. Adjustable trigger. Receiver drilled and tapped for scope mount. Stock is black synthetic, with checkering. Weight about 7.87 lbs.

NIB	*Exc.*	*V.G.*	*Good*	*Fair*	*Poor*
450	380	300	250	200	100

Model 320 S/S

Similar to above, with stainless steel barrel and action.

NIB	*Exc.*	*V.G.*	*Good*	*Fair*	*Poor*
500	400	300	250	200	100

Model 420 LR Classic

Similar to Model 320 series. Standard lightly figured Maple stock in classic configuration. Available in blue or stainless steel. Premium for fancy wood.

NIB	*Exc.*	*V.G.*	*Good*	*Fair*	*Poor*
500	420	300	250	200	100

Model 420 LR Monte Carlo

Same as classic series, with Monte Carlo stock and cheekpiece. Premium for fancy wood.

NIB	*Exc.*	*V.G.*	*Good*	*Fair*	*Poor*
500	420	300	250	200	100

Mountain Rifle

.50-caliber percussion or flintlock rifle, with double-set triggers, 32" octagonal barrel, buckhorn sights, curly Maple stock and crescent steel buttplate. Weight about 7.5 lbs. Premium for fancy wood.

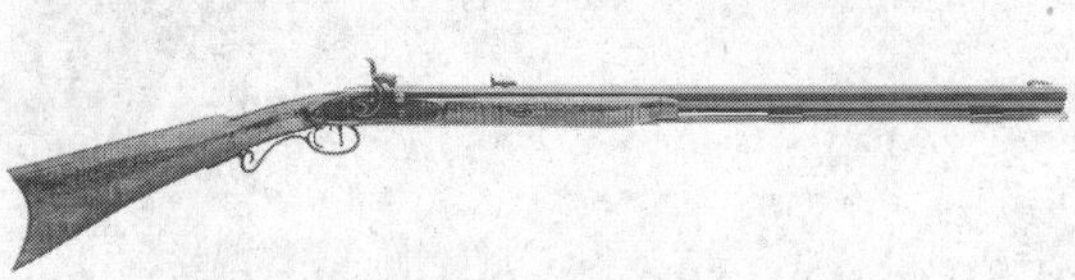

NIB	*Exc.*	*V.G.*	*Good*	*Fair*	*Poor*
500	400	300	250	200	100

ATKIN GRANT & LANG
London

Also see Lang, J.

Three makers of high end British double guns who merged over the years. The first was established 1821 by Joseph Lang, joined in 1925 by Stephen Grant (est. 1866), and then in 1960 by Henry Atkin (est. 1875). The firm currently offers guns under each of those three individual names – Joseph Land side by side double rifles, Stephen Grant over under shotguns, and Joseph Lang side by side and over under shotguns. As with many of the makers of finest British sporting arms, each gun in individually made and must be evaluated on its own. Recent sales and offerings have ranged from under $2,000 to over $30,000.

AUSTRALIAN AUTOMATIC ARMS LTD.
Tasmania, Australia

SAR

5.56mm semi-automatic rifle, with 16.25" or 20" barrel, 5- or 20-shot magazine, black plastic stock and forend. Imported from 1986 to 1989.

NIB	*Exc.*	*V.G.*	*Good*	*Fair*	*Poor*
1200	950	650	350	250	120

SAP

10.5" barreled pistol version of above. Imported from 1986 to 1989.

NIB	*Exc.*	*V.G.*	*Good*	*Fair*	*Poor*
1150	900	600	320	250	120

SP

Sporting rifle version of SAR, with wood stock and 5-shot magazine. Introduced in 1989.

NIB	*Exc.*	*V.G.*	*Good*	*Fair*	*Poor*
980	850	580	300	250	120

AUTAUGA ARMS INC.
Prattville, Alabama

MK II

.32 ACP semi-automatic blowback pistol, with double-action trigger. Barrel length 2.25". Fixed sights. Overall length 4.25". Weight about 13.5 oz. Magazine capacity 6 rounds. Introduced in 1999.

NIB	*Exc.*	*V.G.*	*Good*	*Fair*	*Poor*
320	280	220	200	150	100

AUTO MAG
Various Manufacturers

High Powered stainless steel semi-automatic pistol. Developed by Sanford Arms Company of Pasadena, California, in 1960s. Chambered for a special cartridge known as .44 AMP, which had a 240-grain .44-caliber bullet. Production of this arm has been carried out by a number of companies over the past 47 years, beginning in 1971. Believed that fewer than 9,000 have been produced by eight manufacturers involved. See also Galena Industries, Inc. and AMT.

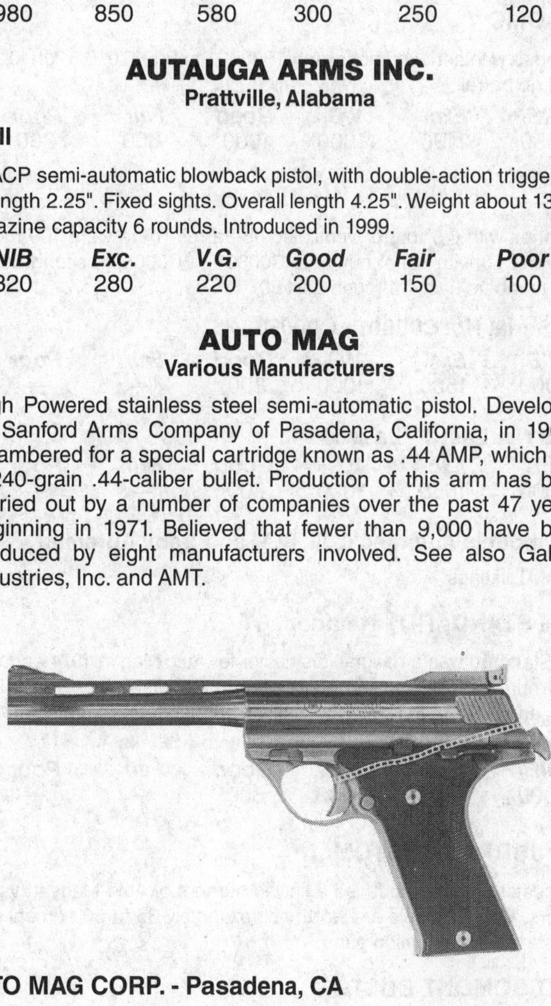

AUTO MAG CORP. - Pasadena, CA

Serial number range A0001 through A3300. Made in .44 AMP only, with 6.5" ventilated rib barrel. This model is generally considered the best quality of the Auto Mag series.

NIB	Exc.	V.G.	Good	Fair	Poor
4000	3000	2000	1500	—	—

TDE CORP. - North Hollywood, CA

Serial number range A3400 to A05015.

.44 AMP

NIB	Exc.	V.G.	Good	Fair	Poor
3000	2500	2000	1500	—	—

.357 AMP

NIB	Exc.	V.G.	Good	Fair	Poor
2700	2000	1500	950	—	—

TDE CORP. - El Monte, CA

Serial number range A05016 to A08300. 6.5", 8" or 10" ventilated rib barrel. .

.44 AMP

NIB	Exc.	V.G.	Good	Fair	Poor
2500	1900	1400	900	—	—

.357 AMP

NIB	Exc.	V.G.	Good	Fair	Poor
2000	1500	1000	600	—	—

TDE-OMC

"B" series with serial number range B00001 to B00370. 6.5" or 10" ventilated rib barrel.

NIB	Exc.	V.G.	Good	Fair	Poor
2550	2100	1600	1000	600	300

AMT

"C" series with 6.5" or 10" ventilated rib barrel. There were 100 models sold. First 50 with serial numbers C00001 to C00050; second 50 with serial numbers Last 1 through Last 50.

AMTSerial No. C00001 - C00050

NIB	Exc.	V.G.	Good	Fair	Poor
2000	1500	1000	800	—	—

Serial No. Last 1 - Last 50

NIB	Exc.	V.G.	Good	Fair	Poor
2000	1650	1000	800	—	—

AMT models Automag II, III, IV, V, and Baby Automag

See AMT listings.

HIGH STANDARD - Hamden, CT

High Standard was a national distributor for Auto Mag in 1974 and 1975. Serial numbers with an "H" prefix were interspersed between H1 and H198, and H17219 to H17222. A total of 134 handguns were sold: 108 in .44 AMP; 26 in .357 AMP.

NIB	Exc.	V.G.	Good	Fair	Poor
2000	1500	1000	800	—	—

L. E. JURRAS CUSTOM

This custom maker produced a limited number of Auto Mags in various calibers. These models are worth approximately 35 to 50 percent more than standard production guns.

KENT LOMONT CUSTOM

All pistols made by this gunmaker are prototypes. Potential purchasers are advised to secure a qualified appraisal.

Harry Sanford Commemorative

Approximately 300 models were made by Galena Industries in 1999 and 2000, to commemorate the founder of the Auto Mag company. All have a "STURGIS, SD" address and Harry Sanford signature on the barrel. Potential purchasers are advised to secure a qualified appraisal.

NIB	Exc.	V.G.	Good	Fair	Poor
4500	4000	3500	3000	—	—

AUTO MAG LTD. CORP.

Loris, SC

Current manufacturer of Auto Mag pistols since 2015.

93 Founder's Edition .44

NIB	Exc.	V.G.	Good	Fair	Poor
4000	3400	—	—	—	—

Auto Mag Classic .44

NIB	Exc.	V.G.	Good	Fair	Poor
3500	2980	—	—	—	—

AUTO ORDNANCE CORP.

Auto Ordnance makes reproductions of 1911 Government Model pistol, Thompson sub-machine gun (semi-automatic only) and M-1 Carbine. Variations of 1911 are marketed under both Auto Ordnance and Thompson brand names. In 1999, the company was bought by Kahr Arms and moved from West Hurley, New York to Worcester, Massachusetts.

Auto Ordnance 1911A1

Standard model in .45 ACP with 5" barrel, Parkerized finish, fixed sights, plastic or checkered walnut grips. Also offered in 9mm, .38 Super, 10mm (all discontinued in 1996) and .40 S&W (discontinued in 1993). Blue, satin nickel and two-tone finish were optional until 2005. In 2011 a 100th Anniversary Model was introduced, with appropriate roll marks. Note: Add $35 for nickel, two-tone finish or 100th Anniversary Model.

NIB	Exc.	V.G.	Good	Fair	Poor
560	520	480	400	300	200

Thompson Model 1911TC

.45 ACP semi-automatic, with fixed sights and 7+1 capacity. Stainless frame and slide. 5" barrel, weight 39 oz. Laminate grips.

NIB	Exc.	V.G.	Good	Fair	Poor
650	520	400	300	200	100

Thompson Model 1911CAF

.45 ACP semi-automatic, with fixed sights and 7+1 capacity. Aluminum frame and stainless slide. 5" barrel, weight 31.5 oz. Laminate grips.

NIB	Exc.	V.G.	Good	Fair	Poor
650	520	400	300	200	100

Thompson 1911 A1—Standard

9mm, .38 Super or .45-caliber copy of Colt Model 1911 A1. Weight 39 oz. Note: Add $20 for 9mm and .38 Super (both discontinued in 1997).

NIB	Exc.	V.G.	Good	Fair	Poor
480	320	280	200	150	100

Thompson 1911 A1—Parkerized

NIB	Exc.	V.G.	Good	Fair	Poor
480	320	280	200	150	100

Thompson 1911 A1—Deluxe

Same as above in Hi-profile white 3-dot sight system. Black textured rubber wrap-around grips.

NIB	Exc.	V.G.	Good	Fair	Poor
800	650	500	300	150	100

Thompson 1911 A1—Custom High Polish

Introduced in 1997. Features special high polish blued finish, with numerous special options. Stocks rosewood, with medallion. Fitted with 5" barrel. Chambered for .45 ACP. Weight about 39 oz.

NIB	Exc.	V.G.	Good	Fair	Poor
580	480	—	—	—	—

Thompson 1911 A1—10mm

Same as above. Chambered for 10mm cartridge. Magazine capacity 8 rounds. Discontinued in 1997.

NIB	Exc.	V.G.	Good	Fair	Poor
700	550	400	250	180	100

Thompson 1911 A1—Duo Tone

Chambered for .45 ACP. Slide blued. Frame satin nickel. Discontinued in 1997.

NIB	Exc.	V.G.	Good	Fair	Poor
500	420	350	220	150	100

Thompson 1911 A1—Satin Nickel

Chambered for .45 ACP or .38 Super. Finish satin nickel on both frame and slide. Blade front sight. Black checkered plastic grips. Discontinued in 1997.

NIB	Exc.	V.G.	Good	Fair	Poor
500	420	350	220	150	100

Trump Commemorative 1911

NIB	Exc.	V.G.	Good	Fair	Poor
1350	—	—	—	—	—

Thompson 1911 A1—Competition

Chambered for .45 ACP or .38 Super. Fitted with 5" barrel, compensator and other competition features. Such as, custom Commander hammer, flat mainspring housing, beavertail grip safety, full-length recoil guide rod, extended ejector, slide stop and thumb safety. Weight 42 oz.; 10" overall. Discontinued in 1997. Note: Add $10 for .38 Super.

NIB	Exc.	V.G.	Good	Fair	Poor
700	620	500	350	300	150

Thompson 1911 A1—Pit Bull

Chambered for .45 ACP. Fitted with 3.5" barrel. High profile sights. Black textured rubber wrap-around grips. Magazine capacity 7 rounds. Weight 36 oz.

NIB	Exc.	V.G.	Good	Fair	Poor
500	420	350	220	150	100

Thompson 1911 A1—General

Commander-size pistol, with 4.5" barrel. High profile sights. Chambered for .45 ACP or .38 Super. Weight 37 oz. Discontinued in 1997.

NIB	Exc.	V.G.	Good	Fair	Poor
500	420	350	220	150	100

ZG-51 "Pit Bull"

Same as above, with 3.5" barrel in .45-caliber. Introduced in 1988. In 1994 renamed "PIT BULL". Discontinued.

NIB	Exc.	V.G.	Good	Fair	Poor
500	420	350	220	150	100

GI Spec 1911A1

Auto-Ord now produces an accurate Mil-Spec copy of the WWII US-issued 1911 with "US" logo wood or plain, brown plastic grips, matte black or Parkerized finished in .45 ACP or 9mm Luger.

NIB	Exc.	V.G.	Good	Fair	Poor
640	540	460	390	240	140

1911 Special Editions

Auto-Ordnance has released several special commemorative models featuring engraving and special finishes including 75th Anniversary Iwo Jima, Bootlegger, Fly Girls of WWII, Liberty Special, Promises Kept, Revolution Special, Squadron Special, Trump 2020, and Victory Girls WWII. Retails vary between $1,215 and $1,277. Values are about the same for all models.

NIB	Exc.	V.G.	Good	Fair	Poor
1060	900	800	—	—	—

1911 Case Hardened

A Mil-Spec 1911 with a case-hardened finish, .45 Cal., 5" barrel, Wood Grips with "US" logo. The casehardened finish has a clear protective coat.

NIB	Exc.	V.G.	Good	Fair	Poor
1150	980	840	710	430	250

Auto-Ordnance Thompson Semi-Automatic Model 1927 Series

First generation Auto-Ordnance Thompson Model 1927 manufactured by Colt Patent Firearms from 1927 to 1936. They were modified from original 15,000 Model 1921 Sub-Machineguns into a semi-automatic-only configuration. By removing the full-automatic rocker pivot assembly and converting the selector paddle into "single-fire" only position, allowing fire control assembly to be used as a semi-automatic only firearm. An estimated 50 such Model 1927 Semi-Automatic Carbines are believed to have been assembled and sold. Since these fire from an open bolt as the fully automatic Model 1921 and are (or can be readily converted to) full automatic, these first generation Model 1927 Thompson guns are considered to be machine guns by BATFE and must be transferred through a Class III dealer. Due to the scarcity of these firearms, a list of values would be very speculative. A base price of $35,000 is a good place to start. Note: Many thanks to George Layman for his assistance in contributing to this section. — Editor.

Second Generation Auto Ordnance Thompson Model 1927

Produced from 1975-1997 by Numrich Arms, West Hurley, N.Y. Approved for sale as a legal to own semi-automatic by BATFE on March 20, 1975. Serial numbers 1 to 29,585.

1927 A1 Deluxe Model

Features include adjustable sights, cooling fins, Cutts Compensator, 16.5" barrel, with one 20- or 30-shot box magazine. Available with choice of horizontal or vertical grip. Original price in 1980 was $489.95. Numrich Auto Ordnance guns, with all accessories including FBI reproduction hard case should add $650 to values listed.

NIB	Exc.	V.G.	Good	Fair	Poor
1850	1700	1500	1100	900	700

1927 A1 Deluxe Model (First 932 Carbines)

First 932 Thompson Model 1927 A1 Deluxe Semi-Automatic Carbines were equipped with numerous original Auto Ordnance surplus parts produced in Bridgeport, CT. in early 1940s. Genuine Lyman-manufactured adjustable rear sights and original Cutts Compensators were supplied on this first year batch of West Hurley, NY-made Thompson Deluxe Carbines.

NIB	Exc.	V.G.	Good	Fair	Poor
2800	2000	1700	1500	1350	1150

1927 A1 Standard Model

Plain barrel, banded front sight, horizontal forearm, WWII stamped steel "L" style, non-adjustable rear sight. Original 1980 price $469.95. Note: Fewer of these were manufactured than Deluxe Model and are considered scarce, thus priced accordingly.

NIB	Exc.	V.G.	Good	Fair	Poor
2200	1900	1580	1200	1000	800

1927 A3

This is a .22-caliber variation of Model 1927 A1, with 16" barrel and aluminum alloy receiver. Discontinued in 1994. Note: Add $500 for drum magazine.

NIB	Exc.	V.G.	Good	Fair	Poor
1350	900	680	550	420	250

1927 A5 .45 ACP Caliber Auto Ordnance Semi-Automatic Pistol

A 13" barrel version of M1927A1 Deluxe Carbine. Classified as a pistol and manufactured without buttstock. Original style Thompson 1927 "A" banded type front sight. Production terminated in 1995, as a result of the 1994 Assault Weapons Ban, due to certain physical characteristics, primarily the vertical fore-grip. All were grandfathered in after production had terminated. Not commonly encountered.

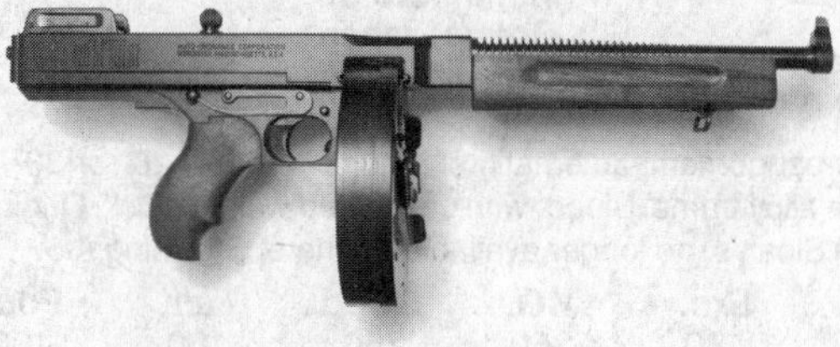

NIB	Exc.	V.G.	Good	Fair	Poor
2500	1900	1600	1400	1100	950

M-1 Semi-Automatic Carbine

Numrich/AO introduced this copy of WWII M-1 Thompson in 1980. Identical to simplified war-time version introduced in 1942. Features 16.5" barrel, side-mounted M-1 style bolt and frame, non-adjustable rear sight with "V" ears and horizontal front-grip. Milled from solid steel. Scarce.

NIB	Exc.	V.G.	Good	Fair	Poor
2100	1800	1500	1400	1200	1000

Third Generation Auto Ordnance Thompson Model 1927 Semi-Automatic Carbine

Successor to West Hurley, NY-made Thompson Model 1927. Kahr Arms, Worcester, MA is owner of Auto Ordnance trademark from 1999 to present.

TA5100D

Semi-Automatic Deluxe version of Thompson 1927 A1. Has aluminum receiver, 10.5" barrel, 100-round drum, cooling fins, Cutts Compensator and adjustable rear sights.

NIB	Exc.	V.G.	Good	Fair	Poor
1400	1200	1000	800	600	400

T1B

1927 A1 Deluxe Model, with finned 16.5" barrel, adjustable rear sights, detachable buttstock and Cutts Compensator.

NIB	Exc.	V.G.	Good	Fair	Poor
1800	1600	1400	1100	900	700

T150D

1927 A1 Deluxe Model, with finned barrel, adjustable rear sights, fixed buttstock, Cutts Compensator and 50-round drum.

NIB	Exc.	V.G.	Good	Fair	Poor
1550	1400	1250	1000	850	500

T5

Lightweight Deluxe Model, with 16.5" finned barrel, aluminum receiver, walnut stock, horizontal forearm, black nylon sling and 30-round magazine.

NIB	Exc.	V.G.	Good	Fair	Poor
1150	950	750	500	400	280

TA510D

1927-style pistol, which was the first of its type, reintroduced since discontinued Numrich 1927 A5 in 1995. Features 10.5" finned barrel, adjustable rear sights, 10-round drum to conform with states requiring 10-round magazine and aluminum receiver.

NIB	Exc.	V.G.	Good	Fair	Poor
1200	1000	800	550	400	300

T1SB

1927 A1 with 10.5" Short Barrel. Detachable or non-detachable buttstock. Requires Class 3 transfer. As close to original made in 1927 as possible. Note: Deduct 20 percent for non-detachable buttstock.

NIB	Exc.	V.G.	Good	Fair	Poor
2000	1700	1400	1000	700	450

M1SB

Short-barreled (10.5" finned and compensated) variant of semi-automatic M1. Does not accept drum magazines. Requires Form 3.

NIB	Exc.	V.G.	Good	Fair	Poor
1500	1150	700	400	300	150

1927A-1C Lightweight Deluxe 9mm

All the classic details of the time honored original are reproduced in today's semi-auto Thompson. The frame and receiver are machined from aluminum and weight is only 9.5 lbs, compared to the steel version's 13 lbs. The wood is American walnut, and calibers are 9mm Luger or .45 caliber both with a 16 1/2" finned barrel and compensator. Add $30 for .45 ACP model.

NIB	Exc.	V.G.	Good	Fair	Poor
1160	990	840	720	430	250

M1927A-1 Case Hardened

A deluxe Thompson 1927A-1 semi-auto with a case-hardened finish with clear protective coat in .45 ACP with 16.5" barrel.

NIB	Exc.	V.G.	Good	Fair	Poor
1530	1300	1100	940	560	340

M1927A-1 Deluxe Chrome or Gold Plated

A variety of deluxe Thompson 1927A-1 semi-autos are available with striking finishes such as titanium gold or chrome plating. Many ship with a 50-round drum magazine and 20-round stick magazine. Add $400 for models with Tiger Stripe.

NIB	Exc.	V.G.	Good	Fair	Poor
2900	2480	2100	1790	1080	650

M1927A-1 "US"

A .45 ACP semi-automatic version of the Thompson M1 from WWII with the frame and receiver milled from solid steel or aluminum, the wood is American walnut and Cerakoted in Army O.D. green as part of Auto-Ordnance's commemoration of WWII.

NIB	Exc.	V.G.	Good	Fair	Poor
1490	1270	1080	920	550	330

Auto Ordnance 1927A-1 Deluxe Pistol

Semi-automatic. A 10-in. barrel version of M1927A1 Deluxe Carbine. Original-style Thompson 1927 "A" banded type front sight. Horizontal foregrip. 10-, 50- or 100-rnd. drum magazine. Introduced 2008.

NIB	Exc.	V.G.	Good	Fair	Poor
1500	1300	910	660	560	430

M1 Carbine

Newly manufactured replica of military M1 carbine. Chambered in .30 Carbine. Introduced 2005. Birch stock, Parkerized finish. Note: Add 5 percent for walnut stock.

NIB	Exc.	V.G.	Good	Fair	Poor
950	800	650	500	300	120

M1 Carbine Paratrooper

Standard M1 Carbine action in a paratrooper folding stock with walnut folding stock, wood handguard and 15-round magazine.

NIB	Exc.	V.G.	Good	Fair	Poor
1020	860	740	630	380	230

M1 Carbine Special Editions

A variety of M1 Carbine Special Editions are made with full or folding stock and laser engraved to commemorate actions during WWII including Iwo Jima, WWII Vengeance and Airborne. Add about $150 for the folding stock versions.

NIB	Exc.	V.G.	Good	Fair	Poor
1180	1000	850	730	440	260

AUTO POINTER

Yamamoto Co.
Tokyo, Japan

Auto Pointer Shotgun

12- or 20-gauge semi-automatic shotgun, with 26", 28" or 30" barrels. Aluminum alloy frame. Blued, with checkered walnut stock. Originally imported by Sloan's, no longer available. Clone of Browning A-5.

NIB	Exc.	V.G.	Good	Fair	Poor
—	480	350	250	180	100

AXTELL RIFLE CO.

Riflesmith, Inc.
Sheridan, Montana

#1 Long Range Creedmore

Single-shot rifle. Chambered for .40-50BN, .40-70SS, .40-70BN, .40-90, .45-70, .45-90 and .45-100. Weight about 10 lbs. Numerous options will affect price.

NIB	Exc.	V.G.	Good	Fair	Poor
4700	3750	3000	2200	1400	300

New Model Sharps 1877

Chambered for .45-90, .45-100 and .45-70 cartridges. Fitted with choice of 30" to 34" half round/half octagon barrel, with double-set triggers.

NIB	Exc.	V.G.	Good	Fair	Poor
5200	4000	3250	2500	1500	250

#2 Long Range

Long Range #2 rifle. Chambered for all the same calibers as #1 Long Range Creedmore. Weight about 10 lbs.

NIB	Exc.	V.G.	Good	Fair	Poor
3900	3000	1900	900	550	300

Lower Sporting Rifle

Chambered for same calibers as above. Weight between 9 and 12 lbs. depending on barrel options.

NIB	Exc.	V.G.	Good	Fair	Poor
2600	2000	1380	700	400	200

Business Rifle

Same calibers as above. Weight about 8.5 lbs.

NIB	Exc.	V.G.	Good	Fair	Poor
2400	1800	1280	700	400	200

Overbaugh Schuetzen

Chambered for .40-50BN and .40-50 straight. Weight 11 to 14 lbs. depending on barrel options.

NIB	Exc.	V.G.	Good	Fair	Poor
4400	3500	3000	2200	1400	300

AYA

For AyA shotguns, see entry under Aguirre y Aranzabal.

AZANZA & ARRIZABALAGA

Eibar, Spain

M1916

Ruby-style 7.65mm semi-auto blowback. "A.A" is marked on pistols used by France in World War I.

Courtesy James Rankin

NIB	Exc.	V.G.	Good	Fair	Poor
—	350	200	150	100	50

Reims

6.35mm or 7.65mm caliber semi-automatic pistol, with 6- or 8-round magazine capacity. Most pistols have their slides marked: 1914 Model Automatic Pistol "Reims" Patent.

Courtesy James Rankin

NIB	Exc.	V.G.	Good	Fair	Poor
—	230	180	130	90	50

AZPIRI

Eibar, Spain

Spanish manufacturer of pistols prior to World War II.

Avion

6.35mm semi-automatic pistol. Copied after Model 1906 Browning. Marked "Pistolet Automatique Avion Brevete" on slide as well as on each side of grip plate along with an airplane logo. Manufactured from 1914 to 1918.

Courtesy James Rankin

NIB	Exc.	V.G.	Good	Fair	Poor
—	230	180	130	90	50

Colon

As above in 6.35mm caliber. Marked "Automatic Pistol Colon".

NIB	Exc.	V.G.	Good	Fair	Poor
—	230	180	130	90	50

B

B.R.F.
South Africa

B.R.F.

.25-caliber semi-automatic pistol. Similar to P.A.F., with 2" barrel and 6-shot magazine. "U-SA" means Union of South Africa. Little is known about manufacturer of this pistol, its origin or dates of manufacture.

NIB	Exc.	V.G.	Good	Fair	Poor
—	300	200	120	100	70

BABBIT, A. S.
Plattsburgh, New York
See—ADIRONDACK ARMS

BABCOCK, MOSES
Charlestown, Massachusetts

Babcock Underhammer Cane Gun (Antique)

.52-caliber percussion cane gun, with 27" barrel. Overall length about 33". Folding trigger under hammer, with wood handle. Hammer marked "Moses Babcock/Charlestown". Active 1850s and 1860s.

Exc.	Fine	V.G.	Good	Fair	Poor
3000	2000	850	600	350	200

Baby Hammerless

See KOLB

BACON
Norwich, Connecticut

Three firearms manufacturing firms were headed by Thomas K. Bacon between the late 1840s and the late 1860s: Bacon & Co., Bacon Mfg. Co., and Bacon Arms Company. Bacon Arms Company continued manufacturing spur-trigger revolvers after Bacon's death in 1873 through 1888.

(Antique)

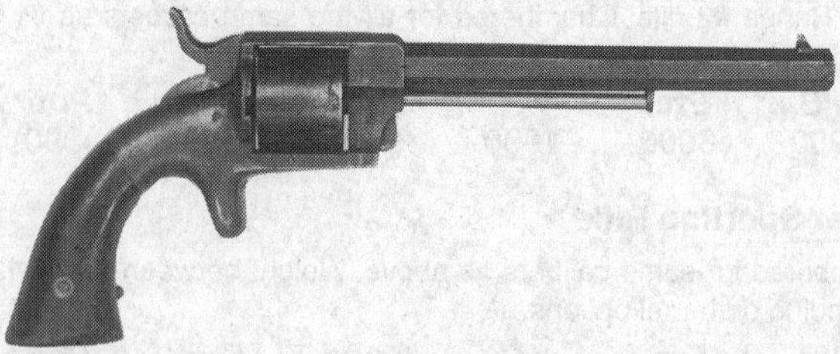

Courtesy Milwaukee Public Museum, Milwaukee, Wisconsin

Thomas K. Bacon Underhammer Pepperbox (Antique)

.31 cal. six-shot single-action percussion pepperboxes, most with 4" barrels, but 3" and 5" also produced (rare, worth premium). The hammer on the underside of the frame has a curved rearward extension to aid in cocking. Made with ribbed barrels or fluted barrels (worth slight premium.)

Exc.	Fine	V.G.	Good	Fair	Poor
1700	1100	850	600	350	240

Bacon & Co. Single-Shot Percussion Pistols

Several variations made in .31 to .36 caliber with 2" to 6" barrels. Different configurations include underhammer traditional trigger traditional hammer single-action, ring-trigger traditional hammer single-action, same with all-metal construction and bar hammer double-action.

NIB	Exc.	V.G.	Good	Fair	Poor
900	600	470	350	180	120

Bacon Arms Co. Topstrap Pocket Revolver, 1st Model, 1st Model

.31 cal. five-shot percussion revolver with topstrap over cylinder. Cylinder release is a button on left side of frame.

NIB	Exc.	V.G.	Good	Fair	Poor
3000	1800	1300	800	400	280

Bacon Arms Co. Topstrap Pocket Revolver, 2nd Model

As above, except cylinder is retained by a cross screw. "Union Arms" marking worth slight premium.

NIB	Exc.	V.G.	Good	Fair	Poor
2750	1600	1170	750	350	240

Bacon Mfg. Co. Open-Top Pocket Revolver, 1st Model

.31 cal. five-shot percussion revolver, with open-top like Colt Model 1849 or Manhattan Pocket Model. Unfluted cylinder with panel scenes and octagonal barrel.

NIB	Exc.	V.G.	Good	Fair	Poor
2750	1600	1170	750	350	240

Bacon Mfg. Co. Open-Top Pocket Revolver, 2nd Model

As above except fluted cylinder and round barrel. Numerous distributor markings observed, some of which will bring a small premium, including Fitch & Waldo, Hart & Bro., Tomes Son & Melvin, Union Arms, and Western Arms

NIB	Exc.	V.G.	Good	Fair	Poor
2750	1600	1170	750	350	240

Bacon Mfg. Co. Open-Top Pocket Revolver, 3rd Model

As above, except unfluted cylinder and round barrel. Hopkins & Allen continued production of this model with both round and octagonal barrels and will bring a slight premium.

NIB	Exc.	V.G.	Good	Fair	Poor
2500	1500	1100	700	300	210

Bacon Mfg. Co. Navy Model Revolver (Antique)

.38 rimfire, six-shot, 7.5" barrel solid-frame spur-trigger revolver. First Type has cylinder that is removed by withdrawing a hinged lever under the barrel, with a variant that uses a removable knurled disc. Second Type has a swing-out cylinder, opened by removing the under-barrel rod. Values are similar for all types.

Exc.	Fine	V.G.	Good	Fair	Poor
2500	1500	1100	700	300	210

Bacon Mfg. Co. Swing-Out Cylinder Revolver

.32 rimfire six-shot, 4" barrel solid-frame spur-trigger revolver. There is an ejector rod under the barrel, and the cylinder swings out to the right for loading and unloading. May have "Western Arms" or "Union Arms" markings.

NIB	Exc.	V.G.	Good	Fair	Poor
3000	2250	1500	850	500	250

Bacon Mfg. Co. Removable Triggerguard Pocket Revolver

.32 rimfire six-shot 4" barrel open-top revolver with traditional triggerguard shape, offered in two different frame sizes for .32 RF Short and .32 RF Long cartridges. Triggerguard unscrews to release cylinder pin and remove cylinder. A few were made in .22 rimfire with 2.5" barrel and will bring a premium.

NIB	Exc.	V.G.	Good	Fair	Poor
1000	700	500	325	200	150

Bacon Pocket Cartridge Revolvers, 1860s production (Antique)

Spur-trigger solid-frame revolvers, usually .32 rimfire, 5- or 6-shot, most are square butt but some birdshead butt. Shorter cylinder than later production Bacon Arms Pocket Models. Scarce.There are several variations and models, but most will bring similar values. A rare small frame variation in .22 or .25 rimfire will bring about double.

Exc.	Fine	V.G.	Good	Fair	Poor
450	300	260	230	130	90

Bacon Arms Co. Spur-trigger Revolvers, 1870s & 1880s production (Antique)

Small solid-frame single-action spur-trigger revolvers, usually with birdshead butt, various calibers, and various configurations. Longer cylinder than earlier production Bacon Mfg. Pocket Models. May not have Bacon markings, but instead various colorful trade names, likely including Big Bonanza, Conqueror, Daisy, Express, Guardian, Little Giant, Penetrator, and Reliable.

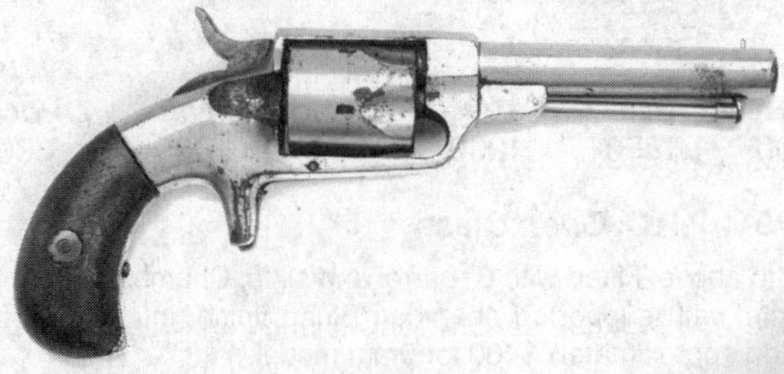

Photo courtesy of NRA Museums

Exc.	Fine	V.G.	Good	Fair	Poor
280	200	170	150	80	50

Bacon Single-Shot Rimfire Derringer

Most are .22 rimfire;.30 rimfire also reported. Also marketed by Merwin & Bray under their company name, and others such as H.C. Lombard & Co.

NIB	Exc.	V.G.	Good	Fair	Poor
600	450	350	275	200	100

BAER CUSTOM, LES

Le Claire, Iowa

Long-standing 1911 pistolsmith is now producing custom quality 1911 pistols on a semi-production basis. Each pistol features a large number of custom characteristics such as forged steel frame, full slide recoil rod, double-serrated slide, beveled magazine well, checkered front strap, beavertail safety, extended magazine release button, Bo-Mar sights and many others, depending on specific model. Representative sampling of these fine Baer pistols appears below.

COMPETITION PISTOLS

Baer 1911 Ultimate Master Combat Pistol-Compensated

Chambered for .38 Super or .45 ACP. Fitted with triple-port tapered cone compensator. Note: Add $100 for .38 Super.

NIB	Exc.	V.G.	Good	Fair	Poor
3240	2710	2080	1580	1360	1000

Baer 1911 Ultimate Master Steel Special

Designed for steel targets and Bianchi-style competition. Similar to above, but designed for light loads. Chambered for .38 Super. Hard chrome finish.

NIB	Exc.	V.G.	Good	Fair	Poor
2900	2250	1500	950	750	350

Baer 1911 Ultimate Master Combat Pistol

Similar to other Baer Master series pistols. Offered in .45 ACP, .400 Cor-Bon and .38 Super. Fitted with a large number of special features. Offered in 5" or 6" version. The 5" version also offered in 9x23 caliber.

6-Inch Model

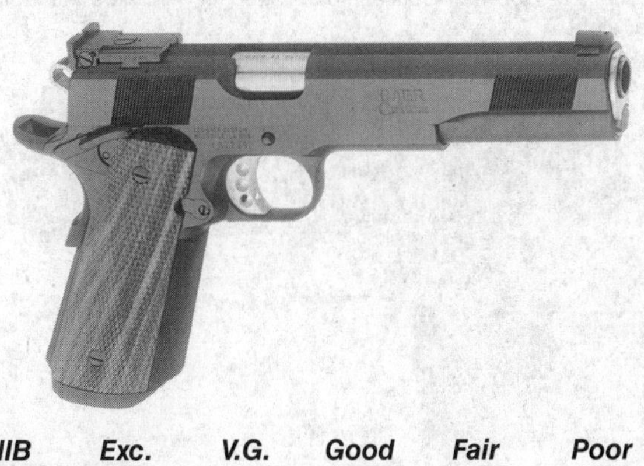

NIB	Exc.	V.G.	Good	Fair	Poor
3360	3030	2280	1670	1380	1110

5-Inch Model

NIB	Exc.	V.G.	Good	Fair	Poor
3230	2910	2180	1610	1310	1080

Baer 1911 Ultimate Master Para

Designed for IPSC competition. Offered in Unlimited version with compensator and scope; Limited version with iron sights and no compensator.

Unlimited Model

.45 ACP, .38 Super, 9x23.

NIB	Exc.	V.G.	Good	Fair	Poor
3400	2700	1750	1200	850	400

Limited Model

NIB	Exc.	V.G.	Good	Fair	Poor
2900	2000	1500	900	650	300

Baer 1911 Bullseye Wadcutter Pistol

Designed for use with wadcutter loads only. Chambered for .45 ACP. Note: Add $125 for Baer Optical mount; $200 for 6-in. slide with LoMount BoMar sight.

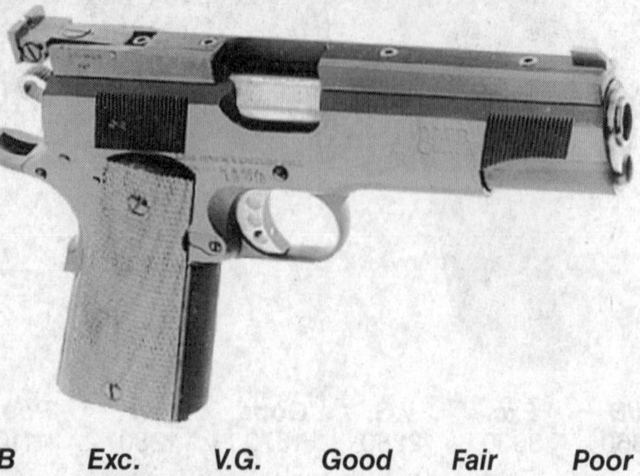

NIB	Exc.	V.G.	Good	Fair	Poor
2540	2290	1720	1260	1030	830

Baer 1911 National Match Hardball Pistol

Designed for DCM matches. Chambered for .45 ACP.

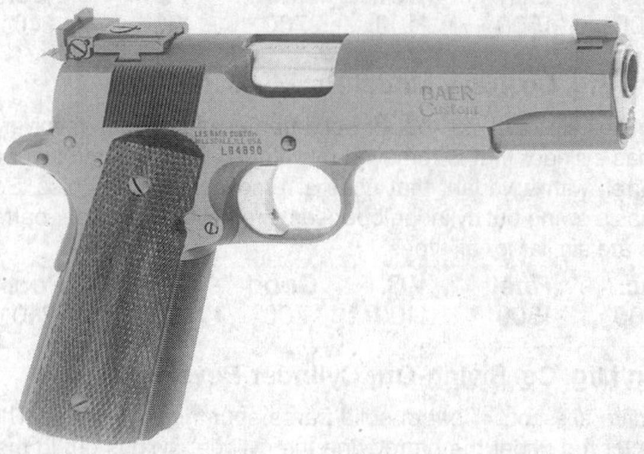

NIB	Exc.	V.G.	Good	Fair	Poor
2400	2100	1800	1550	900	300

Baer 1911 Target Master

Designed for NRA centerfire matches. Chambered for .45 ACP.

NIB	Exc.	V.G.	Good	Fair	Poor
1450	1150	750	550	450	250

Baer 1911 IPSC Action Pistol

Chambered for .45 ACP, with blued slide and frame.

NIB	Exc.	V.G.	Good	Fair	Poor
1700	1350	850	600	450	300

Baer 1911 P.P.C. Distinguished Match

Introduced in 1999. Features 5" barrel, with adjustable Aristrocrat rear sight. Many, many special features such as double serrated slide, lowered and flared ejection port, extended ambi safety, checkered front strap, etc. Offered in .45 ACP and 9mm, with supported chamber. Blued finish and one magazine. Note: Add approximately $400 for 9mm model.

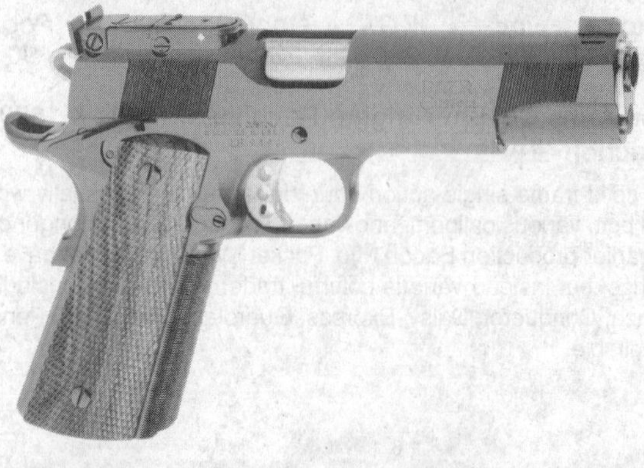

NIB	Exc.	V.G.	Good	Fair	Poor
2400	1850	1200	650	480	300

Baer 1911 P.P.C. Open Class

Similar to above. Fitted with 6" barrel and slide. Chambered for .45 ACP and 9mm, with supported chamber. Blued finish. Introduced in 1999. Note: Add approximately $400 for 9mm model.

NIB	Exc.	V.G.	Good	Fair	Poor
2600	1950	1300	700	500	350

DUTY & DEFENSE PISTOLS

Baer 1911 Premier II

Designed as a duty or defense pistol. Chambered for .45 ACP, .400 CorBon, 9mm (Parabellum), .38 Super, .40 S&W and 9x23 cartridges. Fitted with 5" slide. Note: Add $150 for stainless steel version; $100 for .400 CorBon; $250 for 9x23.

NIB	Exc.	V.G.	Good	Fair	Poor
2320	2090	1570	1160	940	760

Baer 1911 Premier II—6-Inch Barrel

Same as above. Fitted with 6" match-grade barrel. Chambered for 9mm, .38 Super, .40 S&W, .400 CorBon, 10 mm. Note: Add $100 for .400 CorBon; $300 for .38 Super. 9x23 not offered with 6" slide.

NIB	Exc.	V.G.	Good	Fair	Poor
2570	2310	1730	1270	1040	860

Baer 1911 Premier II—Light Weight (LW1)

Same features as standard Premier II, with reduced weight aluminum frame. Furnished with low mount LCB adjustable rear sight. Offered in .45 ACP only.

NIB	Exc.	V.G.	Good	Fair	Poor
1900	1400	1000	800	500	350

Baer 1911 Premier II—Hunter

Same as above. Fitted with 6" match-grade barrel. Chambered for 10mm. Fiber-optic front sight. Introduced 2017.

NIB	Exc.	V.G.	Good	Fair	Poor
2200	1600	1250	800	550	400

Baer 1911 Premier II—Light Weight (LW2)

Same as above, with fixed combat-style rear sight.

NIB	Exc.	V.G.	Good	Fair	Poor
1900	1550	1100	900	700	350

Baer 1911 Premier II—Super-Tac

Similar to standard Premier II models, with low mount adjustable rear night sight and front sight. Special BEAR COAT finish. Offered in .45 ACP, .40 S&W, .400 CorBon, 9mm, .38 Super. Note: Add $200 for dual caliber .45 ACP/.400 CorBon combo.

NIB	Exc.	V.G.	Good	Fair	Poor
2700	2100	1500	1100	700	400

Baer 1911 Prowler III

Similar to Premier II, with tapered cone stub weight, full-length guide rod and reverse plug. Special order only.

NIB	Exc.	V.G.	Good	Fair	Poor
2580	1700	1200	950	700	350

Baer 1911 Prowler IV

Chambered for .45 ACP or .38 Super. Built on Para-Ordnance oversize frame. Fitted with 5" slide. Special order only. Note: Add $300 for optional 6" barrel and slide.

NIB	Exc.	V.G.	Good	Fair	Poor
2580	1900	1250	900	650	300

Baer 1911 Custom Carry—Commanche Length

Chambered for .45 ACP and 9mm. Has several options including 4.5" barrel, stainless steel slide and frame, lightweight aluminum frame with blued steel slide. As of 2000, furnished with night sights. Note: Add $40 for stainless steel; $130 for lightweight frame.

NIB	Exc.	V.G.	Good	Fair	Poor
1850	1400	950	600	450	250

Baer 1911 Custom Carry—5"

Same as above. Chambered for .45 ACP, 9mm, .38 Super. Offered with 5" slide. Not offered in aluminum frame. Note: Add $40 for stainless steel.

NIB	Exc.	V.G.	Good	Fair	Poor
2120	1700	950	600	450	250

Baer 1911 Thunder Ranch Special

Features steel frame and slide, with front and rear serrations. Deluxe fixed rear sight, with tritium insert. Checkered front strap. Numerous special features. Slim line grips, with Thunder Ranch logo. Seven-round magazine standard. Special serial numbers with "TR" prefix. Offered in .45 ACP. Note: Add 5 percent for home defense model; 10 percent for Commanche length; 20 percent for 25th Anniversary Special Edition.

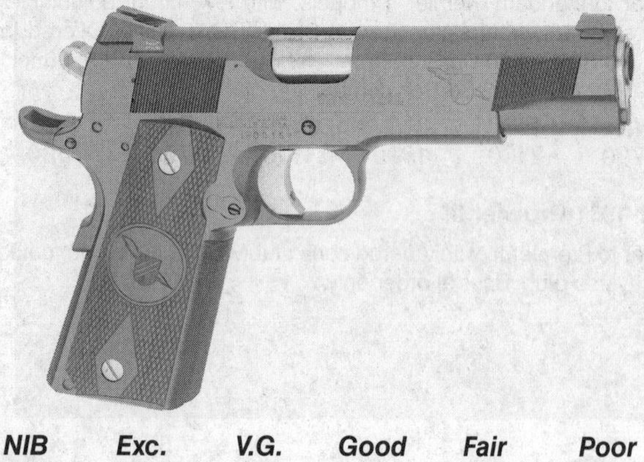

NIB	Exc.	V.G.	Good	Fair	Poor
1990	1500	950	600	450	250

Baer 1911 Thunder Ranch Special Engraved Model

Like the Baer 1911 Thunder Ranch Special, with engraved frame and slide. Ivory grips.

NIB	Exc.	V.G.	Good	Fair	Poor
6600	4750	2500	1500	1150	650

Baer S.R.P. (Swift Response Pistol)

Chambered for .45 ACP. Built on Para-Ordnance frame. This unit similar to one supplied to FBI. Supplied with wooden presentation box. Note: Deduct $300 from NIB through Fair prices for S.R.P. models built on Baer frame or shorter 4."5 frame.

NIB	Exc.	V.G.	Good	Fair	Poor
2920	2560	2240	1410	1150	900

Baer 1911 Monolith

Introduced in 1999. Features 5" barrel and slide with extra long dust cover. Chambered in .45 ACP, .400 CorBon, .40 S&W, 9x23, 9mm, or .38 Super all with supported chamber. Many special features such as BoMar sights, Commander-style hammer, speed trigger, etc. Blued finish with one magazine. Weight about 37 oz. Note: Add $250 for all other supported calibers.

NIB	Exc.	V.G.	Good	Fair	Poor
2420	2100	1850	1580	950	740

Baer 1911 Monolith Heavyweight

Introduced in 1999. Similar to Monolith, with addition of heavier frame that adds 3.5 oz. Same calibers as available on Monolith. Weight about 40 oz. Note: Add $200 for all other supported calibers.

NIB	Exc.	V.G.	Good	Fair	Poor
2470	2160	1890	1620	980	760

Baer 1911 Monolith Tactical Illuminator

Introduced in 1999. Same features as Monolith Heavyweight, with addition of light mounted under dust cover. Offered in .45 ACP and .40 S&W with supported chamber. Weight with light about 44 oz. Note: Add $275 for all other supported calibers.

NIB	Exc.	V.G.	Good	Fair	Poor
1850	1500	1050	800	420	250

Baer 1911 Monolith Commanche

Fitted with 4.25" slide and dust cover covering length of slide. Has all features of standard Monolith. Comes with night sights and deluxe fixed rear sight. Edges rounded for tactical carry. Chambered in .45 ACP, 9mm, .38 Super. Introduced in 2001.

NIB	Exc.	V.G.	Good	Fair	Poor
2480	2160	1890	1620	980	760

Baer 1911 Monolith Commanche Heavyweight

Exactly as above, with thicker dust cover to add an additional 2 oz. of weight. Introduced in 2001.

NIB	Exc.	V.G.	Good	Fair	Poor
2520	2190	1920	1650	990	770

Baer 1911 Stinger

Features shorter Officer's grip frame and Commanche slide and barrel. Many special features. Offered in .45 ACP. Choice of aluminum frame with blued slide; aluminum frame with stainless steel slide; stainless steel frame and slide. Weight in aluminum about 28 oz.; stainless steel about 34 oz. Introduced in 1999. Note: Add $300 for aluminum frame and blued slide with supported calibers; $340 for aluminum frame with stainless slide and supported chamber; $140 for stainless frame and slide with supported chamber.

NIB	Exc.	V.G.	Good	Fair	Poor
2300	2000	1760	1500	900	700

Baer 1911 Stinger Stainless

Same as above, with stainless steel frame and slide. Introduced in 2001.

NIB	Exc.	V.G.	Good	Fair	Poor
2380	2060	1800	1550	930	760

Baer 1911 .38 Super Stinger

Same as above, with blue or chrome finish.

NIB	Exc.	V.G.	Good	Fair	Poor
2840	2500	2180	1630	1100	900

Black Baer 1911

Caliber 9mm. DuPont S coating on entire pistol for complete corrosion resistance. Black recon grips. Compact size with 4.25" barrel. All corners rounded for concealed carry. Many special features including slide fitted to frame, Baer speed trigger with crisp 4-lb. pull, tactical extended combat safety, beveled magazine well, polished feed ramp, throated barrel, checkered slide stop, lowered and flared ejection port, checkered front strap at 30 lpi, flat checkered mainspring housing at 20 lpi. Tuned for total reliability. Comes with two 9-round magazines. Introduced in 2016.

NIB	Exc.	V.G.	Good	Fair	Poor
2980	2600	1950	1430	1180	900

Baer Boss

Same as Premier II series except .45 ACP only with tactical features package.

NIB	Exc.	V.G.	Good	Fair	Poor
2630	2300	1730	1270	1040	800

Baer Hemi 572

Inspired by Chrysler Hemi muscle car with tactical features package.

NIB	Exc.	V.G.	Good	Fair	Poor
2770	2430	1830	1340	1100	860

Baer 1911 Gunsite Pistol

Caliber .45 ACP. Full size with 5" barrel. Fixed combat sights. Blued finish. Gunsite logo engraved on slide and grips. Introduced 2019.

NIB	Exc.	V.G.	Good	Fair	Poor
2250	1960	1470	1080	890	690

Baer 1911 Kenai Special

Caliber 10mm. Full size with 5" barrel. Fiber-optic front sight, adjustable rear sight. Hard chrome finish. Bear claw engraving on slide. Introduced 2019.

NIB	Exc.	V.G.	Good	Fair	Poor
3630	3160	2370	1740	1430	1100

Baer Shooting USA Custom Pistol

Same as Premier II series except .45 ACP only with Shooting USA logo engraved on slide.

NIB	Exc.	V.G.	Good	Fair	Poor
2250	1960	1470	1320	890	690

NEW CONCEPT PISTOLS

Line of 1911 pistols offering custom features at slightly lower cost. Each succeeding grade offers a few more features.

Baer 1911 Concept I

Chambered for .45 ACP. Fitted with BoMar sights.

NIB	Exc.	V.G.	Good	Fair	Poor
2140	1930	1460	1070	880	710

Baer 1911 Concept II

Same as above. Fitted with Baer adjustable sights.

NIB	Exc.	V.G.	Good	Fair	Poor
2140	1930	1460	1070	880	710

Baer 1911 Concept III

Same as above, with stainless steel frame. Blued steel slide. BoMar sights.

NIB	Exc.	V.G.	Good	Fair	Poor
2400	2160	1620	1190	980	760

Baer 1911 Concept IV

Same as above, with Baer adjustable sights.

NIB	Exc.	V.G.	Good	Fair	Poor
2400	2160	1620	1190	980	760

Baer 1911 Concept V

Model has both stainless steel slide and frame. BoMar sights.

NIB	Exc.	V.G.	Good	Fair	Poor
2370	2150	1610	1180	980	760

Baer 1911 Concept V 6"

Identical to Concept V, with addition of 6" barrel and slide. Introduced in 1999.

NIB	Exc.	V.G.	Good	Fair	Poor
2050	1990	1080	900	650	350

Baer 1911 Concept VI

Same as above. Fitted with Baer adjustable sights.

NIB	Exc.	V.G.	Good	Fair	Poor
2430	2190	1650	1210	990	780

Baer 1911 Concept VI L.W.

Same as above. Built on aluminum frame, with supported chamber. National Match barrel.

NIB	Exc.	V.G.	Good	Fair	Poor
2050	1990	1080	900	650	350

Baer 1911 Concept VII

Features all blued 4.5-in. steel frame and slide. Baer fixed night sights.

NIB	Exc.	V.G.	Good	Fair	Poor
2370	2130	1600	1180	960	780

Baer 1911 Concept VIII

Same as above, with stainless steel slide and frame. Fixed combat night sights standard.

NIB	Exc.	V.G.	Good	Fair	Poor
2420	2180	1630	1200	990	810

Baer 1911 Concept IX

Version has lightweight aluminum frame, with 4.5" steel slide.

NIB	Exc.	V.G.	Good	Fair	Poor
2100	1850	1500	1250	700	300

Baer 1911 Concept X

Features 4.5" stainless steel slide. Lightweight aluminum frame.

NIB	Exc.	V.G.	Good	Fair	Poor
2100	1850	1500	1250	700	300

Baer Lightweight .22-caliber 1911 Models

4.5" Model with fixed sights

NIB	Exc.	V.G.	Good	Fair	Poor
1520	1400	950	800	550	300

5" Model with fixed sights

NIB	Exc.	V.G.	Good	Fair	Poor
1620	1400	950	800	550	300

5" Model with Bo-Mar sights

NIB	Exc.	V.G.	Good	Fair	Poor
1700	1480	1000	850	600	300

Baer Limited Edition Presentation Grade 1911

Fully hand-engraved Baer 1911, with special bluing in presentation wooden box.

NIB	Exc.	V.G.	Good	Fair	Poor
7350	6760	5500	4000	3260	2500

Model 1911 Twenty-Fifth Anniversary

Custom-engraved limited collector edition .45 ACP semi-automatic. Built on fully functional equipped Baer Premier II. Hand-engraved both sides of slide and frame. Les Baer signature. Inlaid with white gold. Ivory grips. Deep blue finish. Presentation box. Introduced 2006.

NIB	Exc.	V.G.	Good	Fair	Poor
7000	6000	5000	4000	1150	500

Ultimate Recon

Semi-automatic with integral Picatinny rail, 5" barrel, .45 ACP. Blue or chrome. Comes with SureFire X-200 light. Fixed sights. 4-lb. trigger. Two 8-round magazines. Cocobolo grips. Note: Add $500 for hard chrome.

NIB	Exc.	V.G.	Good	Fair	Poor
3070	2590	1650	1100	780	450

RIFLES

In 2019, Les Baer Custom listed no AR-15 rifles on its website or in its printed catalog.

AR Super Varmint

Chambered in .223, .204 Ruger, 6x45 LBC, .264 LBC. Fitted with choice of 18", 20" or 24" heavy barrels, with 1-in-12 twist. Flat top rail. Choice of single-/two-stage trigger. Aluminum free-floating handguard. Bear Coat finish. Introduced in 2000. Note: Add $230 for .204 Ruger in V.G. or better condition.

NIB	Exc.	V.G.	Good	Fair	Poor
3500	2430	2060	1750	—	—

AR Super Match

Introduced in 2002. Chambered in .223, .204 Ruger, 6x45 LBC, .264 LBC. Wide number of custom features, with barrel lengths from 18" to 24". Special match carrier with integral rail system. Note: Add $230 for .204 Ruger in V.G. or better condition.

NIB	Exc.	V.G.	Good	Fair	Poor
—	2480	2100	1790	—	—

AR .223 M4-A2 Flattop

Features flattop rail, match bolt and carrier. 16" barrel has integral compensator. Single-stage trigger. Knights Armament Systems rail adapter. Bear Coat finish. Introduced in 2000.

NIB	Exc.	V.G.	Good	Fair	Poor
—	2500	2130	1810	1540	1310

AR .223 IPSC Action Model

Similar to above, with 18" Super Match heavy barrel. Integral compensator. Introduced in 2000.

NIB	Exc.	V.G.	Good	Fair	Poor
—	2650	2250	1920	1630	1390

AR .223 NRA Match Rifle

Numerous custom features. Fitted with 30" barrel. Special front and rear sights. Note: Add $750 for special sight package.

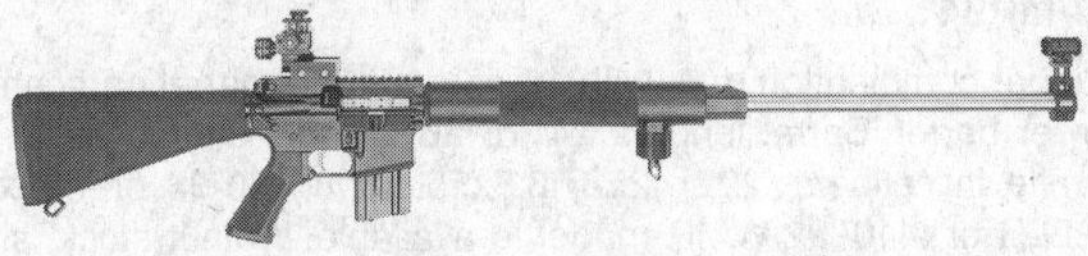

NIB	Exc.	V.G.	Good	Fair	Poor
—	2650	2250	1920	—	—

Bullpup Muzzleloader

.50-caliber muzzleloader. Fitted with 28" stainless steel barrel, Williams front sight and M16 National Match rear sight. Maple or synthetic stock. Internal ignition system. Discontinued. Note: Add $30 for maple stock and stainless steel.

NIB	Exc.	V.G.	Good	Fair	Poor
750	580	400	300	230	—

Thunder Ranch Rifle

.223 model fitted with bench-rest 16" barrel. Upper receiver has carry handle and top rail. Free-floating handguard, jewel two-stage trigger, floating front sight and many other custom features. "Thunder Ranch" logo stamped on lower receiver. Weight about 7.5 lbs. Introduced in 2004.

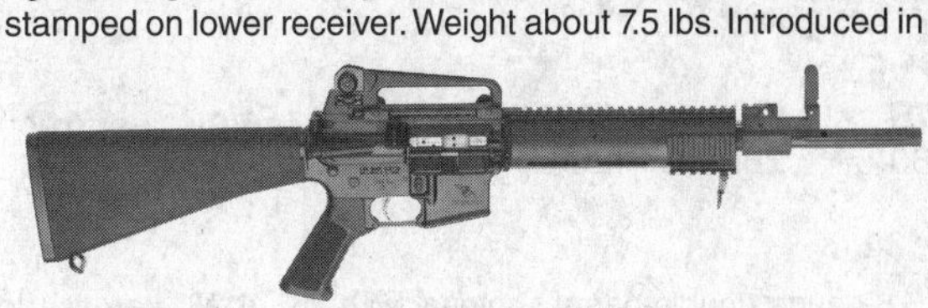

NIB	Exc.	V.G.	Good	Fair	Poor
—	2680	2270	1930	—	—

LBC Semi-Auto Match Rifle

Chambered in .308 Win. or 6.5 Creedmoor. Comes with choice of 18", 20" or 24" LBC Bench rest stainless steel barrel, Picatinny Flat Top rail, precision machined free-float handguard and Harris bipod. Optional Magpul stock.

NIB	Exc.	V.G.	Good	Fair	Poor
—	3100	2640	2240	1900	1620

.308 Monolith S.W.A.T.

Military type match sniper rifle. Chambered in .308 Winchester. Solid full-length Picatinny rail for scope mounting. DuPont S coating on barrel, two-stage trigger group with choice of 18", 20" (standard) or 24" barrel. Two magazines and soft case included. Introduced in 2011.

NIB	Exc.	V.G.	Good	Fair	Poor
—	4000	3400	2890	—	—

BAFORD ARMS, INC.

Bristol, Tennessee

Thunder Derringer

.410 bore/.45 Colt or .44 Special single-shot pistol, with 3" interchangeable barrels and spur trigger. Additional interchangeable barrels are chambered in calibers from .22 to 9mm. Also available with scope. Blued, with walnut grip. Introduced in 1988. Note: Add $50 for interchangeable barrel.

NIB	Exc.	V.G.	Good	Fair	Poor
200	150	100	80	70	40

Fire Power Model 35

9mm semi-automatic pistol, with 4.75" barrel, Millett adjustable sights and 14-shot magazine. Fitted with combat safety hammer and Pachmayr grips. Stainless steel. Introduced in 1988.

NIB	Exc.	V.G.	Good	Fair	Poor
550	450	360	300	250	120

BAIKAL

Izhevsk, Russia

Baikal is a Russian firearms manufacturer. A history that goes back to World War II when it made military weapons like Tokarev pistols for the old Soviet Union. After the war, company expanded into sporting firearms, mainly shotguns.

IJ-27E1C

12- or 20-gauge Magnum over/under shotgun, with 26" Skeet-Skeet or 28" Modified-Full ventilated rib barrels, single-selective trigger and extractors. Blued, with walnut stock.

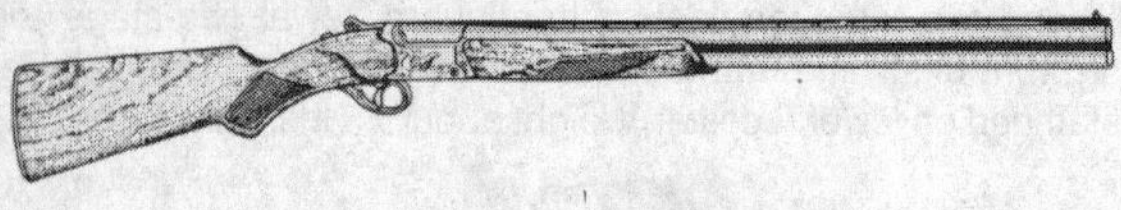

NIB	Exc.	V.G.	Good	Fair	Poor
380	280	200	150	100	80

TOZ - 34

12- or 28-gauge double-barrel shotgun, with 26" or 28" barrels, double triggers, cocking indicators and extractors. Blued, with checkered walnut stock. Also available with silver-plated receiver.

NIB	Exc.	V.G.	Good	Fair	Poor
400	300	250	200	100	80

Model MC-8-0

12-gauge double-barrel shotgun, with 26" Skeet-Skeet or 28" Full-Modified barrels, hand fitted action and engraved receiver.

NIB	Exc.	V.G.	Good	Fair	Poor
2000	1250	950	700	500	250

Model MC-5-105

Model TOZ-34, with engraved receiver.

NIB	Exc.	V.G.	Good	Fair	Poor
1200	850	700	500	300	150

Model MC-7

As above, with relief engraved receiver.

NIB	Exc.	V.G.	Good	Fair	Poor
2250	1750	1200	800	550	250

IZH18/MP18

Single-barrel shotgun chambered for 12-, 20-gauge or .410 bore. Choice of 26.5" or 29.5" barrels. Hardwood stock and ejectors. Introduced in 1999.

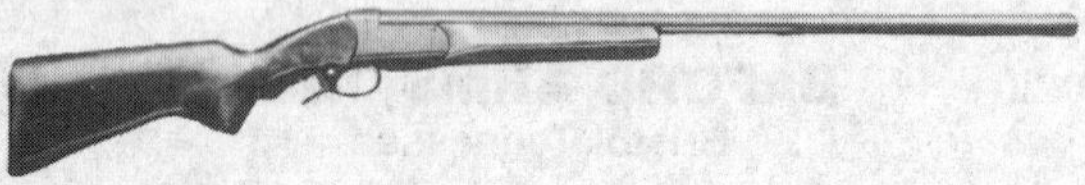

NIB	Exc.	V.G.	Good	Fair	Poor
100	80	50	40	20	10

IZK18MAX

Similar to above, with polished nickel receiver, ventilated rib, walnut stock, screw-in chokes and ejectors. Offered in 12-, 20-gauge and .410 bore.

NIB	Exc.	V.G.	Good	Fair	Poor
170	120	100	80	50	20

IZH43

Side-by-side available in 12-, 16-, 20-, 28-gauge or .410 bore. Barrel lengths 20" to 28" depending on gauge. Internal hammers. Single-selective trigger, ejectors. Walnut stock. Note: Add $80 for 28-gauge and .410 bore.

NIB	Exc.	V.G.	Good	Fair	Poor
350	280	200	150	100	80

IZH43K

Introduced in 1999. A 12- or 20-gauge, 3" side-by-side external hammer shotgun. Barrel lengths 18.5", 20", 24", 26" and 28". Single-selective or double trigger. Engraved side plates. Walnut stock with pistol grip. Weight about 7.3 lbs. Note: Deduct $40 for double triggers.

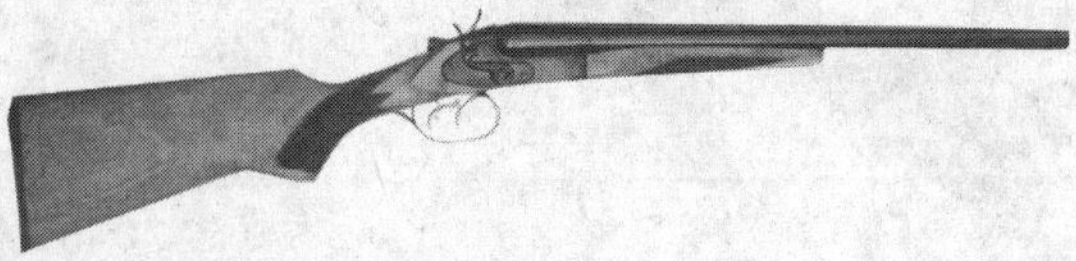

NIB	Exc.	V.G.	Good	Fair	Poor
380	300	250	180	120	100

MP213 Coach Gun

Similar to above, with internal hammers. Single-/double triggers. Weight about 7 lbs. Barrel inserts for .45-70 were offered. Note: Add 25 percent for .45-70 inserts.

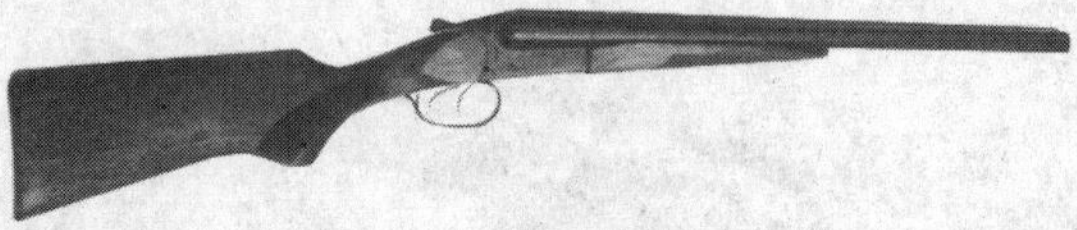

NIB	Exc.	V.G.	Good	Fair	Poor
650	500	400	350	100	80

IZH27

Over/under gun chambered for 12-, 20-, 28-gauge and .410 bore. Choice of 26.5" or 28.5" barrels. Walnut stock. Single trigger with ejectors. Fixed chokes. Note: Add $35 for screw-in chokes; $85 for 28-gauge and .410 bore.

NIB	Exc.	V.G.	Good	Fair	Poor
350	280	200	150	100	80

MP233

Over/under gun chambered for 12-gauge 3" shell, with choice of 26", 28" or 30" barrels. Walnut checkered stock. Single-/double triggers. Screw-in chokes. Removable trigger assembly. Weight about 7.3 lbs. Introduced in 1999.

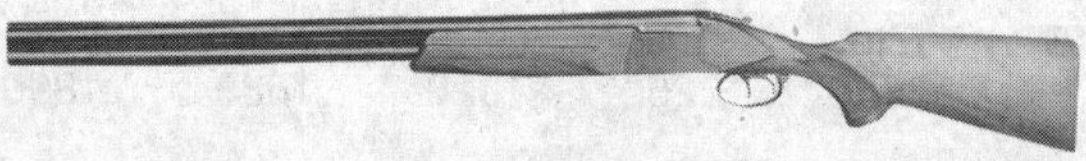

NIB	Exc.	V.G.	Good	Fair	Poor
700	600	500	400	180	100

IZH94/MP94

Over/under combination gun, with 12-gauge upper barrel and centerfire rifle lower barrel. Barrel lengths 24" or 26". Model offered as an over/under rifle in calibers .222, .223, 6.5x55, .308, .30-06 or 7.62x39. A .410/.22LR or .410/.22 WMR model is available. Walnut stock, single-/double trigger. Weight about 8 - 10 lbs. Open sights. Note: Deduct 40 percent for .410.

NIB	Exc.	V.G.	Good	Fair	Poor
520	480	420	350	300	180

IZH81

Pump-action shotgun chambered for 12-gauge 3" shells. Barrel lengths

20", 26" or 28". Five-round detachable magazine. Walnut stock. Note: Add $60 for ventilated rib.

NIB	Exc.	V.G.	Good	Fair	Poor
300	220	160	120	100	50

MP131K

Pump-action shotgun, with choice of two different feeding sources: tubular magazine or detachable 3- or 5-round box magazine.

NIB	Exc.	V.G.	Good	Fair	Poor
300	220	160	120	100	50

MP133

Slide-action shotgun chambered for 12-gauge 3.5" shell. Available barrel lengths 20", 24", 26" or 28". Ventilated rib on all barrel lengths except 20". Walnut stock. Choke tubes for all barrel lengths except 20" (Cylinder choke). Introduced in 2001.

NIB	Exc.	V.G.	Good	Fair	Poor
300	220	160	120	100	50

MP153

Semi-automatic shotgun chambered for 12-gauge 3" shell. Barrels 26" or 28". Walnut or black synthetic stock. Weight about 7.8 lbs. Screw-in chokes. Introduced in 1999.

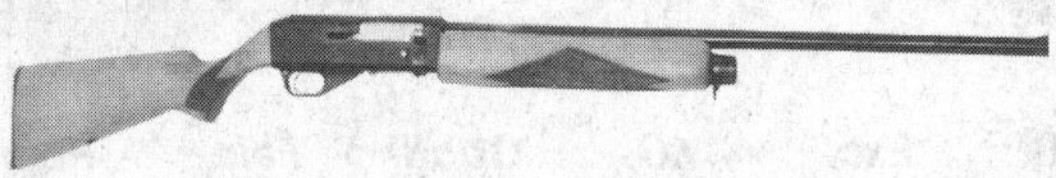

NIB	Exc.	V.G.	Good	Fair	Poor
400	320	250	200	100	60

IZH35

Semi-automatic pistol chambered for .22 LR cartridge. Fully adjustable target-grip, adjustable trigger assembly, cocking indicator, detachable scope. Fitted with 6" barrel. Introduced in 2000.

NIB	Exc.	V.G.	Good	Fair	Poor
500	400	350	200	160	100

MP310

Originally imported as Model IZH2. Over/under now marketed as MP310. Offered in 12-, 20-gauge or .410 bore, with 26" or 28" barrels. Hammer forged barrels, machined steel receiver. Monoblock checkered walnut two-piece stock. Hard chrome-lined barrels, ventilated rib, ejectors, auto safety and single selective trigger. Note: Add $100 for Sporting Clays model.

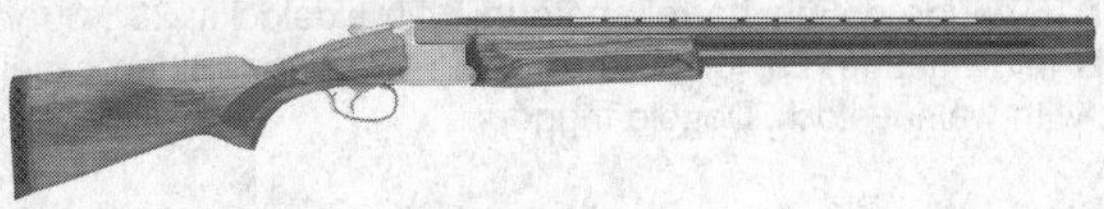

NIB	Exc.	V.G.	Good	Fair	Poor
580	500	400	300	250	200

MP220

Side-by-side field gun has single selective trigger, ejectors, machined steel boxlock receiver, checkered walnut stock with recoil pad, splinter forend, automatic tang safety and screw-in chokes. In 12-, 16-, 20-, 28-gauge and .410 bore. Weight 8 to 10 lbs.

NIB	Exc.	V.G.	Good	Fair	Poor
300	250	200	180	150	100

CURRENTLY IMPORTED BAIKAL SHOTGUNS

Importer—EUROPEAN AMERICAN ARMORY

A custom-made over/under shotgun with detachable sidelocks. Produced in limited quantities and most often to the purchaser's specifications.

BAILONS GUNMAKERS, LTD.

Birmingham, England

Most products of this company **were** produced strictly on custom order. No longer in business.

Hunting Rifle

Bolt-action sporting rifle. Produced in a variety of calibers with 24" barrel, open sights, double-set triggers and 3- or 4-shot magazine. Blued, with well-figured walnut stock. Values listed for standard grade rifle.

NIB	Exc.	V.G.	Good	Fair	Poor
3500	2950	2450	1900	680	320

BAKER

London, England

Gas Seal Percussion Revolver (Antique)

.577-caliber percussion revolver, with 6.5" octagonal barrel and 6-shot cylinder. When hammer is cocked, cylinder is forced forward tightly against barrel breech, thus creating a gas seal. Blued case-hardened, with walnut grips. Rarely seen. Values are speculative. Sales are rare. The value shown below was for a cased gun with accessories.

Exc.	Fine	V.G.	Good	Fair	Poor
—	3500	—	—	—	—

BAKER GUN & FORGING CO.

Batavia, New York

Baker Gun & Forging Company founded in early 1890, by Elias Baker, brother of William Baker. Made from drop forged parts, Baker single-/double barrel shotguns quickly gained a reputation for strength and reliability among shooters of the period. Offered in a wide variety of grades, from plain utilitarian to heavily embellished models. Baker shotguns have in recent years become highly collectible. Company was sold on December 24, 1919, to H. & D. Folsom Arms Company of Norwich, Connecticut. Folsom Company had, for almost 20 years, been Baker Company's sole New York City agent and had marketed at least one Baker model that was only made for them. From 1919 to approximately 1923, Folsom continued to assemble and make Baker shotguns. Late model Bakers were made by Crescent Firearms Company and have serial numbers with an "F" suffix. Baker Gun & Forging Company was the first American arms manufacturer to: 1. Make a single barrel trap shotgun.2. Make a single barrel trap shotgun with ventilated rib. 3. Make arms with an intercepting firing pin block safety. 4. Make a double barrel shotgun, with hammers directly behind the firing pins. 5. Use a long swinging sear, that once adjusted, gave consistent trigger pull throughout the working life of an arm. Baker shotguns manufactured between 1913 and 1923, that were engraved by Rudolph J. Kornbrath, command substantial price premiums over values listed.

Baker Trap Gun

12-gauge single-barrel boxlock shotgun, with 30" or 32" barrel. Blued case-hardened, with walnut stock.

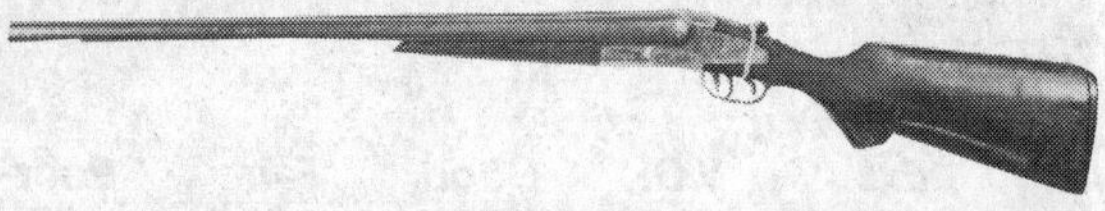

NIB	Exc.	V.G.	Good	Fair	Poor
—	1800	1450	1050	500	250

Elite Grade

Standard scrollwork. Simple game scenes engraved on receiver.

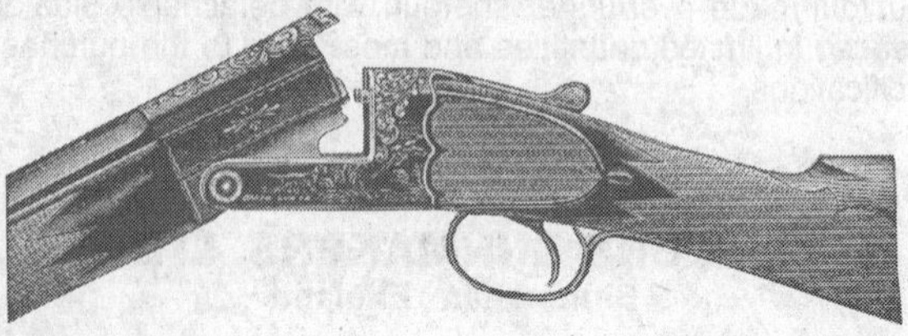

NIB	Exc.	V.G.	Good	Fair	Poor
—	3200	2750	2000	1000	600

Superba

Heavily engraved on receiver and sides of barrel breech.

NIB	Exc.	V.G.	Good	Fair	Poor
—	5500	4650	3500	2400	1200

Expert Grade Double Shotgun

Highest grade shotgun manufactured by Baker Gun & Forging Company. General specifications as above. Stock of imported English or French walnut. Engraving full coverage type and partially chiselled. Automatic ejectors and single trigger, if requested. Built on special order only.

NIB	Exc.	V.G.	Good	Fair	Poor
—	7000	5500	4000	1800	750

Deluxe Grade Double Shotgun

Designation given those Expert Grade shotguns produced by H. & D. Folsom from 1919 to 1923. Characteristics identical to those listed for Baker Expert Grade Double Shotgun. Note: Add 80 percent for this model. Very rare.

Black Beauty Double Shotgun

Made solely for H. & D. Folsom Arms Company. A 12- or 16-gauge double barrel shotgun, with sidelocks; 26", 28", 30" or 32" barrels in 12-gauge; 26", 28" or 30" barrels in 16-gauge. Barrels blued, receiver case-hardened, sideplates finished with black oxide, stock is walnut. Automatic ejectors and single trigger are extra cost options.

NIB	Exc.	V.G.	Good	Fair	Poor
—	1150	1000	850	700	250

Grade S Double Shotgun

As above, with simple engraving.

NIB	Exc.	V.G.	Good	Fair	Poor
—	2400	2000	1100	500	250

Grade R Double Shotgun

As above, with case-hardened sideplates. Engraved with simple scrollwork and game scenes.

NIB	Exc.	V.G.	Good	Fair	Poor
—	3200	2600	1700	1100	500

Paragon Grade Shotgun

As above, with finely cut scrollwork and detailed game scenes engraved on sideplates. Stock of finely figured walnut.

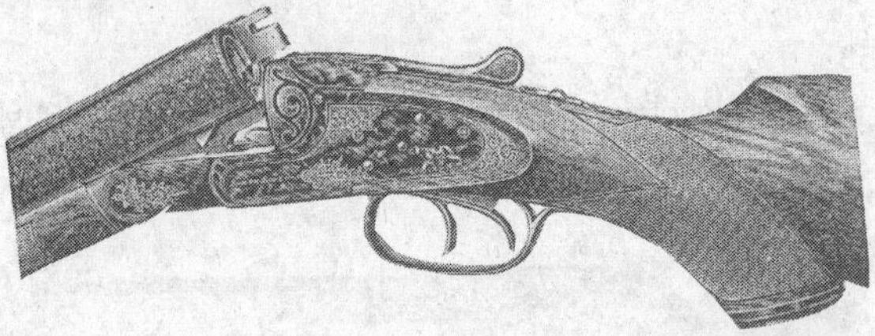

NIB	Exc.	V.G.	Good	Fair	Poor
—	5000	4000	3000	2000	800

Paragon Grade—Model NN

As above, but more finely engraved. Built on special order only. Automatic ejectors.

NIB	Exc.	V.G.	Good	Fair	Poor
—	4500	3500	2700	2000	800

Batavia Special

12- or 16-gauge double-barrel shotgun, with sidelocks; 28", 30" or 32" barrels in 12-gauge; 28" or 30" barrels in 16-gauge. Blued case-hardened, with walnut stock. Double triggers.

NIB	Exc.	V.G.	Good	Fair	Poor
—	850	550	450	220	180

Batavia Brush Gun

12- or 16-gauge double-barrel shotgun, with sidelocks and 26" barrels. Blued case-hardened, with walnut stock. Sling rings and swivels optional.

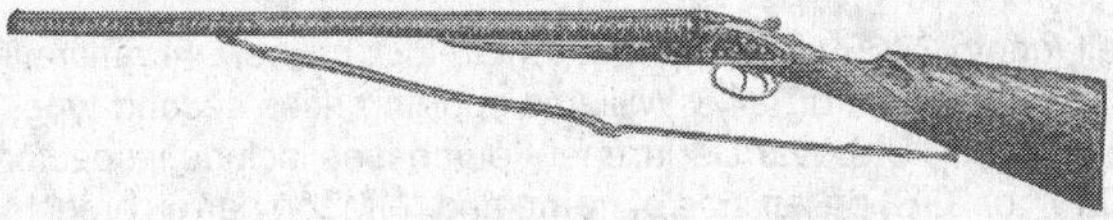

NIB	Exc.	V.G.	Good	Fair	Poor
—	750	600	550	220	180

Batavia Leader

12- or 16-gauge double-barrel shotgun, with sidelocks; 26", 28", 30" or 32" barrels in 12-gauge; 26", 28" or 30" barrels in 16-gauge. Blued case-hardened, with walnut stock. Double triggers.

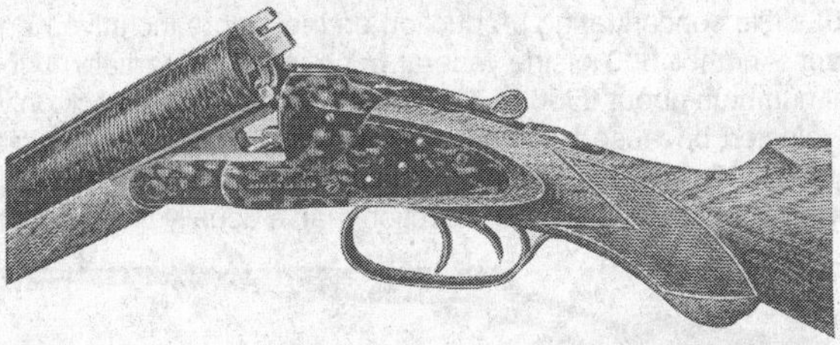

NIB	Exc.	V.G.	Good	Fair	Poor
—	1500	1000	600	400	200

Batavia Damascus

As above, with Damascus barrels.

NIB	Exc.	V.G.	Good	Fair	Poor
—	1750	1200	600	220	180

Baker Hammer Gun

10-, 12- or 16-gauge double-barrel shotgun, with sidehammers. 30" and 32" barrels in 10-gauge; 26" to 32" barrels in 12-gauge; 26" to 30" barrels in 16-gauge. Browned case-hardened, with walnut stock. Double triggers.

NIB	Exc.	V.G.	Good	Fair	Poor
—	450	350	280	200	100

Batavia Automatic Rifle

.22-caliber semi-automatic rifle, with 2"4 round barrel. Detachable 7-shot magazine. Blued, with walnut stock.

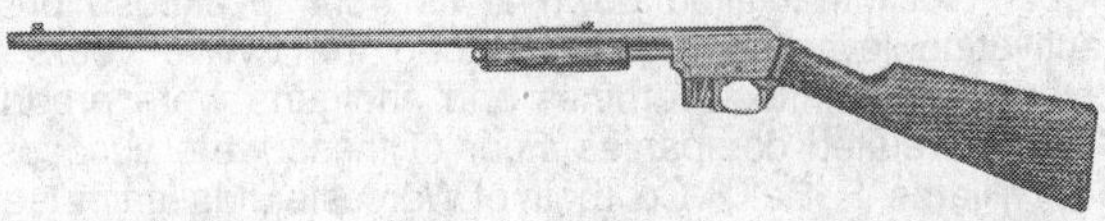

NIB	Exc.	V.G.	Good	Fair	Poor
—	620	550	300	160	70

BAKER, M.A.

Fayetteville, North Carolina

In business from 1857 through 1862. Baker produced sporting arms prior to Civil War. During Civil War, Baker altered muskets and "common rifles". In addition, it is thought, Baker made rifles for State of North Carolina with lockplates stamped "M.A. Baker/ Fayetteville/N.C.". These rifles resembled U.S. Model 1841 rifle and had these characteristics: overall length 51.5"; barrel length 35.125"; caliber .50.

Confederate Conversion (Antique)

Sporting rifle values depend on configuration, decoration & condition. A near-excellent ornate rifle recently sold for more than $8500. The confederate conversion value range shown below is highly speculative due to extreme rarity. Fakes exist.

Exc.	Fine	V.G.	Good	Fair	Poor
25000	—	—	—	—	1000

BAKER, THOMAS

Baker shotguns and rifles were extensively imported into United States during nineteenth and early twentieth centuries.

BAKER, WILLIAM

Marathon, Syracuse and Ithaca, New York

William Baker designed and built double barrel shotguns from approximately 1869 until his death in 1889. His hammerless designs were used by Baker Gun & Forging Company of Batavia, New York, which was established by his brother Elias in early 1890.

BALL REPEATING CARBINE

Lamson & Co.
Windsor, Vermont

Ball Repeating Carbine (Antique)

.50-caliber lever-action repeating carbine, with 20.5" round barrel and 7-shot magazine. Receiver marked "E.G. Lamson & Co./Windsor, Vt./ U.S./Ball's Patent/June 23, 1863/Mar. 15, 1864". Blued case-hardened, with walnut stock. Late production examples of this carbine have been noted with browned or bright barrels. In excess of 1,500 made between

1864 and 1867.

Courtesy Milwaukee Public Museum, Milwaukee, Wisconsin

Exc.	Fine	V.G.	Good	Fair	Poor
6000	4000	2000	1200	800	400

BALLARD PATENT ARMS

(until 1873; after 1875, see MARLIN)

On Nov. 5, 1861 C.H. Ballard, of Worcester, Massachusetts, received a patent for a breech-loading mechanism that would remain in production for nearly thirty years. Ballard patented a breech-block that tilted down at its front to expose breech by activating lever/triggerguard. During the twelve years that followed, Ballard rifles, carbines and shotguns were produced by five interrelated companies. Four of these were successive: Ball & Williams, R. Ball & Co. (both of Worcester, Massachusetts), Merrimack Arms & Manufacturing Co. and Brown Manufacturing Company (both of Newburyport, Massachusetts). These four companies produced Ballard arms in a successive serial range (1 through approximately 22,000), all marked on top of frame and barrel where it joins the frame. In 1863 another company, Dwight, Chapin & Company of Bridgeport, Connecticut, also produced Ballard rifles and carbines in a larger frame size, but in a different serial range (1 through about 1,900), usually marked on left side of frame below agents' mark. Large frame carbines and rifles were produced to fulfill a U.S. War Department contract initially for 10,000 of each, subsequently reduced to 1,000 of each, issued to Merwin & Bray sole agents for Ballard Patent Arms between 1862 and 1866. Most production during this period concentrated on military contracts, either for U.S. War Department or state of Kentucky, although state of New York also purchased 500 for its state militia.

Ballard (Ball & Williams) Sporting Rifles, First Type (Serial numbers 1-100) Antique

Barrel length 24"; caliber .38 rimfire. Markings: "BALL & WILLIAMS/ Worcester, Mass." and "BALLARD'S PATENT/Nov. 5, 1861" on octagonal barrel. Distinctive feature of earliest production of Ballard rifles is presence of internal extractor conforming to patent specifications. After approximately 100 rifles, this feature was dropped in favor of a manual extractor located under the barrel.

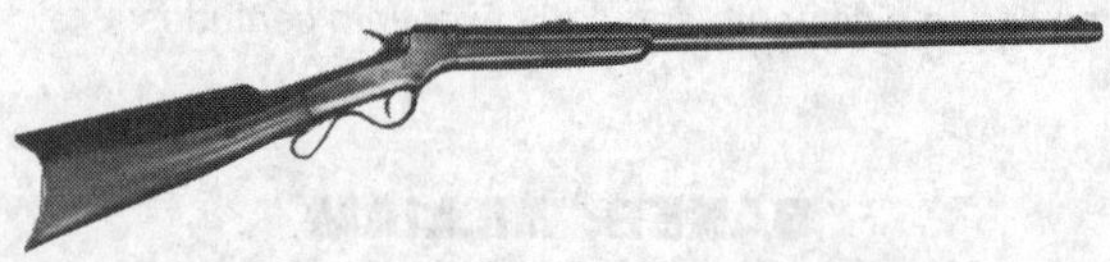

Courtesy Milwaukee Public Museum, Milwaukee, Wisconsin

Exc.	Fine	V.G.	Good	Fair	Poor
5000	3000	2120	1250	500	350

Ballard (Ball & Williams) Sporting Rifles, Second Type (Serial numbers 200-1600, and 1600-14,000, interspersed with martial production) Antique

Barrel length 24", 28" or 30" usually octagonal, but part round/part octagonal as well; calibers .32, .38 and .44 rimfire. Markings: "BALL & WILLIAMS/Worcester, Mass.", "BALLARD'S PATENT/Nov. 5, 1861" and "MERWIN & BRAY, AGT'S/ NEW YORK", on facets of barrel until about serial no. 9000. Thereafter, patent name and date on right side of frame and manufacturer and agents on left side of frame. On early production (200 to 1500), extractor knob is smaller and crescent shaped. Early production (prior to about serial no. 10,000) have solid breech-blocks; after that number breech-blocks are made in two halves. A few of these arms were made with bronze frames to facilitate engraving and plating. These should command a higher premium.

Exc.	Fine	V.G.	Good	Fair	Poor
2800	1750	1200	700	300	200

Ballard (Ball & Williams) Sporting Rifles, Third Type (Serial numbers 14,000-15,000) Antique

These arms essentially the same as second type in characteristics, but have Merwin & Bray's alternate percussion mechanism built into breechblock. Hammer is accordingly marked on left side "PATENTED JAN. 5, 1864".

Exc.	Fine	V.G.	Good	Fair	Poor
1400	1100	820	550	220	150

Ballard (Ball & Williams) Military Carbines (Serial numbers 1500-7500, and 8500-10500) Antique

Overall length 37.25"; barrel (bore) length 22"; caliber .44 rimfire. Markings: same as Ballard/Ball & Williams sporting rifles second type. Additional marks on U.S. War Department purchases include inspector's initials "MM" or "GH" on left side of frame and "MM" on barrel, breechblock, buttplate and on left side of buttstock in script within an oval cartouche. Three thousand of earlier production (serial numbers 1700 through about 5000) of these carbines were sold to state of Kentucky under an August 1862 contract, extended in April 1863. In November 1863, Kentucky contracted for an additional 1,000 carbines. In the interim, state of New York purchased 500 for distribution to its militia. U.S. War Department ordered 5,000 under a contract signed in January of 1864, but Ball & Williams delivered only 1,500 (serial numbers noted in range of 9800 through 10600) while concentrating production on their more lucrative Kentucky contract. Another 600 of the federal contract were partially inspected (serial numbers about 6500 to 7100-MM in cartouche in stock only), but were rejected because barrels had been rifled prior to proofing; these were sold to Kentucky in September 1864 on an open market purchase. Carbines marked with federal inspection marks usually bring a premium.

Courtesy Milwaukee Public Museum, Milwaukee, Wisconsin

Exc.	Fine	V.G.	Good	Fair	Poor
5000	3500	1800	1000	600	200

Ballard (Ball & Williams) "Kentucky" Half-Stock Rifles Antique

Overall length 45.375"; barrel (bore) length 30"; caliber .44 rimfire. These half-stock rifles bear standard Ball & Williams markings upon their barrels. In addition they have state ownership mark "KENTUCKY" on barrel forward of rear sights. Total of 1,000 (serial numbers about 7100 through 8550) were contracted by Kentucky in November 1863 and delivered between January and April 1864.

Courtesy Milwaukee Public Museum, Milwaukee, Wisconsin

Exc.	Fine	V.G.	Good	Fair	Poor
3700	2200	1350	800	400	250

Ball & Williams Ballard Military Rifle Antique

There is not enough known about these rifles and probably never will be. Chambered most frequently for .44 and .54 rimfire cartridges and feature outside tangs and extractors. Offered with 30" round barrel and full-length forearm. There are three barrel bands and sling swivels. Government ordered only 35 of these for use in Civil War; if one was to be definitely authenticated as a genuine martial specimen, it would be quite valuable. Many of these rifles were marked "Kentucky" on top of receiver, because militia of that state armed its men with Ballard rifles and carbines. This marking was a sales aid used by the company and does not indicate militia ownership. Number manufactured is not known. Barrel markings are as on First Model.

Exc.	Fine	V.G.	Good	Fair	Poor
5000	2850	2050	1250	300	210

Ball & Williams Ballard Civil War Military Carbine Antique

This model has a 22" part-round, part-octagonal barrel. Chambered for .44 rimfire cartridge. Has outside tang and extractor. Stock and forearm are walnut, with a barrel band sling swivel. Buttstock bears an oval cartouche surrounding inspector's marks "MM". These letters also appear stamped on major metal parts. Government ordered 1,509 for use in Civil War. Barrel was marked same as rifle.

Exc.	Fine	V.G.	Good	Fair	Poor
5500	3750	2620	1500	500	350

Ballard (Ball & Williams) "Kentucky" Full-Stock Rifles Antique

Overall length 45.25"; barrel (bore) length 30"; caliber .46 rimfire. Marked on frame with standard Ball & Williams manufacturer (left), agent (left) and patent (right) markings. Rifles are additionally distinguished by state ownership mark "KENTUCKY" stamped into top of frame near breech. Kentucky contracted for 3,000 of these arms in November 1863, initially in .56-caliber. However, by mutual consent of state and contractors, in February 1864 caliber of arms was changed to .46. All deliveries were made in this caliber, beginning in July 1864 and continuing until March 1865 (serial numbers 10,400 to 14,500).

Courtesy Milwaukee Public Museum, Milwaukee, Wisconsin

Exc.	Fine	V.G.	Good	Fair	Poor
3500	2000	1200	700	400	250

Ballard (Dwight, Chapin & Co.) Carbines Antique

Overall length 37.75"; barrel (bore) length 22"; caliber .56 rimfire. Markings: on left side of round-topped frame "BALLARD'S PATENT/NOV. 5 1861"; on right side of frame "DWIGHT, CHAPIN & CO./BRIDGEPORT CONN." (through serial no. about 125, deleted after that number) over "MERWIN & BRAY/AGT'S N.Y." over serial no. Inspection letters "D" frequently appear on carbines with Dwight, Chapin, & Co. markings, indicative of preliminary inspection by E. M. Dustin, of U.S. Ordnance Department. Often mistaken as early Ballard production from a fictitious Fall River, Massachusetts, factory, these carbines and their complementing rifles were in fact not placed into production until 1863, as evident by split, two-piece breechblocks. Both carbines and rifles originated from a contract entered into between U.S. War Department and Merwin & Bray in October 1862 for 10,000 of each arm, subsequently reduced to 1,000 of each by Commission on Ordnance and Ordnance Stores. Because Ball & Williams facilities were tied up with Kentucky contracts, Merwin & Bray turned to small parts maker of Dwight, Chapin & Co. in Bridgeport, Connecticut. Although they tooled for production, they fell short of scheduled delivery dates and although about 100 carbines had been inspected, no deliveries were accepted (due to caliber problems) by U.S. government, effectively bankrupting Dwight, Chapin & Co. Completed carbines and unfinished parts were sent to Worcester and assembled by Ball & Williams. Merwin & Bray sold all 1,000 carbines in Kentucky in April 1864 on an open market purchase.

Courtesy Milwaukee Public Museum, Milwaukee, Wisconsin

Exc.	Fine	V.G.	Good	Fair	Poor
3000	2250	1800	900	500	250

Ballard (Dwight, Chapin & Co.) Full-Stock Rifles Antique

Overall length 53"; barrel (bore) length 30"; caliber .56 rimfire. Markings: same as Dwight, Chapin & Co. carbines, but none found with "DWIGHT, CHAPIN & CO./BRIDGEPORT, CONN." stamping above agents marks. History of these rifles same as .56-caliber carbines, with serial numbers interspersed in production of carbines (1 through 1850). Evidently only about 650 rifles were completed of the 1,000 set up. Of these, 35 were sold to a U.S. agent in Florida in February 1864 and 600 to Kentucky in April 1864 with the 1,000 carbines.

Exc.	Fine	V.G.	Good	Fair	Poor
2450	2000	1410	820	350	240

Ballard (R. Ball & Co.) Sporting Rifles Antique

Overall length varies according to barrel length; barrel (bore) length usually 24", 28" and 30"; calibers .32, .38, .44 and .46 rimfire. Markings: frame markings of R. Ball & Co. rifles are similar to Ball & Williams production, only eliminating Ball & Williams marking on left side. Cartridge size, e.g. "No. 44", usually also stamped on top of barrel or frame. Merwin & Bray's patented alternate ignition device usually present with left side of hammer usually marked "PATENTED JAN. 5, 1864". Serial numbers (which follow in sequence with Ball & Williams production. i.e. after no. about 15,800) appear on top of barrel and frame. After William Williams withdrew from Ball & Williams partnership in mid-1865, business continued under name of R. Ball & Co., with Richard Ball's son-in-law, E.J. Halstead, in charge after the former's paralytic stroke in the fall of 1865.

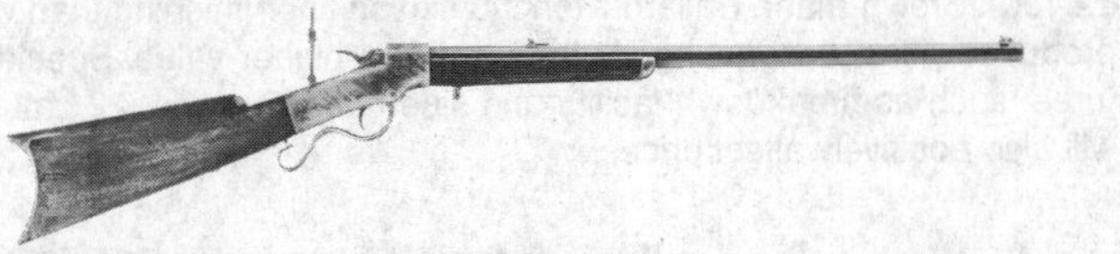

Courtesy Rock Island Auction Company

Exc.	Fine	V.G.	Good	Fair	Poor
2650	2200	1590	980	400	280

Ballard (R. Ball & Co.) Carbines Antique

Overall length 37.25"; barrel (bore) length 22"; caliber .44 rimfire. Markings: same as R. Ball & Co. sporting rifles; "No. 44" on top of frame near breech. Although firm evidence is elusive, approximately 1,000 of these carbines were manufactured in anticipation of a Canadian contract, which never came to fruition. Serial numbers are interspersed with sporting rifles, in 16,400 through 17,700 range. All are equipped with Merwin & Bray dual ignition block.

Exc.	Fine	V.G.	Good	Fair	Poor
3000	2250	1800	900	500	250

Ballard (Merrimack Arms & Manufacturing Co.) Sporting Rifles Antique

Overall length varies with barrel length; usual barrel lengths 24", 28", 30"; calibers .22, .32, .44, .46, .50 rimfire. Markings: left side of frame marked with both manufacturing and patent marks, "MERRIMACK ARMS & MFG. CO./NEWBURYPORT, MASS." over "BALLARD'S PATENT/ NOV. 5, 1861". Caliber usually marked on top of barrel or frame, e.g. "No. 38" together with serial no. Left side of hammer marked "PATENTED JAN. 5, 1864" if breech fitted with Merwin & Bray's alternate ignition device. In spring of 1866 Edward Bray of Brooklyn, New York, former partner of Joseph Merwin, purchased Ballard machinery from R. Ball & Co. and set up a new plant in Newburyport, Massachusetts, primarily for production of sporting rifles. Glut of surplus arms on the market following American Civil War, however, forced him into bankruptcy in early 1869, after producing only about 2,000 Ballard rifles, carbines and a limited number of 20-gauge shotguns. Serial numbers continue in sequence of Ball & Williams/R. Ball & Co. production (serial numbers about 18,000 through 20,300). Prices of these rifles will vary considerably depending on degree of finish or engraving.

Exc.	Fine	V.G.	Good	Fair	Poor
2200	1900	1340	780	350	240

Ballard (Merrimack Arms & Manufacturing Co.) Carbines Antique

Overall length 37.25"; barrel (bore) length 22"; caliber .44 rimfire. Markings: same as Merrimack Arms & Mfg. Co. sporting rifles. In March 1866, state of New York purchased 100 Ballard carbines (serial numbers about 18,500 to 18,600) for use by its prison guards. In January 1870, an additional 70 (serial numbers 19,400 to 19,500) were purchased from New York City arms merchants Merwin, Hulbert & Co. to arm guards at Sing Sing Prison. Between these two purchases Merrimack Arms & Mfg. Co. had shortened its new "tangless" frames by .125", prime distinction between the two purchases. Despite rarity of both types of carbines, they do not command high prices.

Exc.	Fine	V.G.	Good	Fair	Poor
3500	2500	2000	1000	600	300

Ballard (Brown Mfg. Co.) Sporting Rifles Antique

Dimensions: same as Merrimack Arms & Mfg. Co. sporting rifles. Markings: left side of frame marked with manufacturer, "BROWN MFG. CO. NEWBURYPORT, MASS.". Over patent, "BALLARD'S PATENT/ NOV. 5, 1861". Serial no. on top of barrel and frame. Upon the failure of Merrimack Arms & Manufacturing Company in early 1869, plant was purchased by John Hamilton Brown, who continued producing Ballard patent rifles until 1873 in a serial range consecutive with that of its three predecessors (Ball & Williams, R. Ball & Co. and Merrimack Arms & Mfg. Co.). Approximately 2,000 Ballard arms were produced during period of Brown's manufacture of Ballard (serial numbers about 20,325 through 22,100). Brown-made Ballards' tend to exhibit finer finishing than earlier produced rifles, accounting for their average higher value. Special features, such as breakdown facility and side extractors (on .22 cal. rifles) will also positively affect prices.

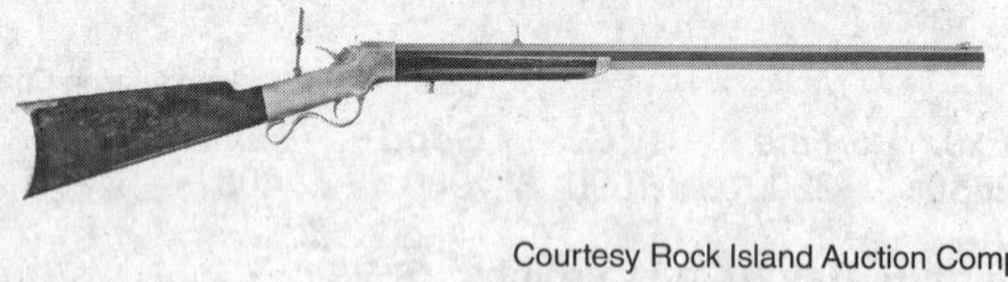

Courtesy Rock Island Auction Company

Exc.	Fine	V.G.	Good	Fair	Poor
2200	1820	1250	680	350	240

Ballard (Brown Mfg. Co.) Full-Stock Military Rifles Antique

Overall length 52.5"; barrel (bore) length 30"; caliber .46 rimfire. Markings: same as Brown Mfg. Co. sporting rifles, with addition of caliber marking, "No. 46", on top of barrel forward of rear sight. Cause for production of Ballard/Brown military rifle has yet to be determined, but it has been speculated that they were possibly manufactured in anticipation of a sale to France during Franco-Prussian War. In any event, sale was not culminated and many, if not most, of estimated 1,000 produced were "sporterized" by shortening fore-stock and sold by commercial dealers in United States. Serial numbers concentrate in 20,500 through 21,600 range, with sporting rifles interspersed in the sequence. Rifles that have not been sporterized command a premium.

Exc.	Fine	V.G.	Good	Fair	Poor
2350	1950	1370	800	350	240

BALLARD RIFLE AND CARTRIDGE CO.

Onsted, Michigan

All models feature American black walnut stocks, case-hardoning and rust blued barrels. There are a number of special order features that are available with these rifles.

No. 1-1/2 Hunter's Rifle

Features 30" round barrel, single trigger, S lever, plain forend and rifle buttstock. Blade front sight and Rocky Mountain rear sight are standard. Calibers from .32-40 to .50-70. Weight about 10.5 lbs.

NIB	Exc.	V.G.	Good	Fair	Poor
3000	2350	1950	1200	700	300

No. 1-3/4 Far West Rifle

Offered with 30" round barrel in standard or heavy weight. Single-/double-set triggers, S lever, ring-style lever, blade front sight and Rocky Mountain rear sight. Offered in calibers from .32-40 to .50-90. Weight with standard 30" barrel about 10.5 lbs.; heavyweight barrel 11.75 lbs.

NIB	Exc.	V.G.	Good	Fair	Poor
2900	2400	1900	1200	700	300

No. 2 Sporting Model

Stock in plain walnut, with crescent butt. Offered in 24", 26", 28" or 30" octagon barrel, with blade front and Rocky Mountain rear sights. Straight-grip action with S lever, in calibers .38-40, .44-40 and .45 Colt. Discontinued.

NIB	Exc.	V.G.	Good	Fair	Poor
2050	1650	1300	1220	700	300

No. 3 Gallery Rifle

Chambered for .22-caliber rimfire cartridge. Features 24", 26" or 30" lightweight octagon barrel. Rifle-style buttstock, with steel crescent buttplate, S lever, blade and Rocky Mountain sights. Weight with standard 26" barrel about 7.5 lbs.

NIB	Exc.	V.G.	Good	Fair	Poor
3000	2650	2300	1200	700	300

No. 3F Fine Gallery Rifle

Same as above, with fancy checkered walnut stock, pistol grip, single-/double-set triggers, full-loop lever, light Schuetzen buttstock, globe front and tang rear sight. Weight with standard 26" barrel about 7.75 lbs.

NIB	Exc.	V.G.	Good	Fair	Poor
3500	3000	2400	1500	750	300

No. 4 Perfection Model

Features plain walnut stock, with rifle or shotgun butt. Offered in 28", 30" or 32" octagon barrel, with blade front sight and Rocky Mountain rear sight. Straight-grip action, with single-/double-set triggers. S lever or ring lever. Calibers from .32-40 to .50-90.

NIB	Exc.	V.G.	Good	Fair	Poor
3400	2900	2300	1200	700	300

No. 4-1/2 Mid-Range Model

Features checkered fancy walnut stock. Standard or heavy weight half octagon barrel 30" or 32", with single-/double-set triggers. Pistol grip hard rubber or steel shotgun butt, horn forend cap, full-loop lever and globe front sight. Offered in calibers from .32-40 to .40-70. Weight with standard barrel 10.75 lbs.; heavy barrel 11.5 lbs.

NIB	Exc.	V.G.	Good	Fair	Poor
3200	2650	2100	1100	600	250

No. 5 Pacific Model

Features 30" or 32" octagon barrel in standard or heavy weight. Stocks in rifle or shotgun configuration, double-set triggers, ring lever, blade front sight and Rocky Mountain rear sight. Calibers from .38-55 to .50-90. Weight with standard 30" barrel 10.75 lbs.; heavyweight barrel 12 lbs.

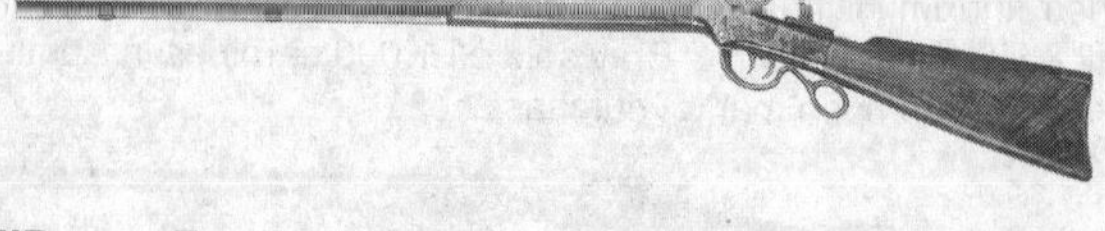

NIB	Exc.	V.G.	Good	Fair	Poor
3350	2600	2250	1200	700	300

No. 5-1/2 Montana Model

Model has fancy walnut stock, double-set triggers and ring lever. Shotgun steel butt. Barrels 28", 30" or 32" extra heavy octagon, in calibers .45-70, .45-110 and .50-90. Under barrel wiping rod. Weight about 14.5 lbs.

NIB	Exc.	V.G.	Good	Fair	Poor
3300	2600	2000	110	600	220

No. 6 Off-Hand Rifle Model (Schuetzen)

Features fancy walnut checkered stock, with hand rubbed finish. Heavy Schuetzen buttplate. Horn insert on forend. Choice of 30", 32" or 34" half-octagon barrel, with globe front sight. Straight-grip action with double-set triggers, Schuetzen ball, spur lever and deluxe rust bluing. Offered in .22 LR, .32-40, .38-55, .40-65 and .40-70 calibers.

NIB	Exc.	V.G.	Good	Fair	Poor
3300	2700	2100	1100	600	250

No. 7 Long Range Model

Features fancy walnut checkered stock, with 32" or 34" standard or heavy weight half octagon barrel. Pistol grip stock, with rubber or steel shotgun butt, single-/double-set triggers, full-loop lever, horn forend cap and globe front sight. Calibers from .32-40 to .45-110. Weight with standard 32" barrel 11.75 lbs.; heavyweight barrel 12.25 lbs.

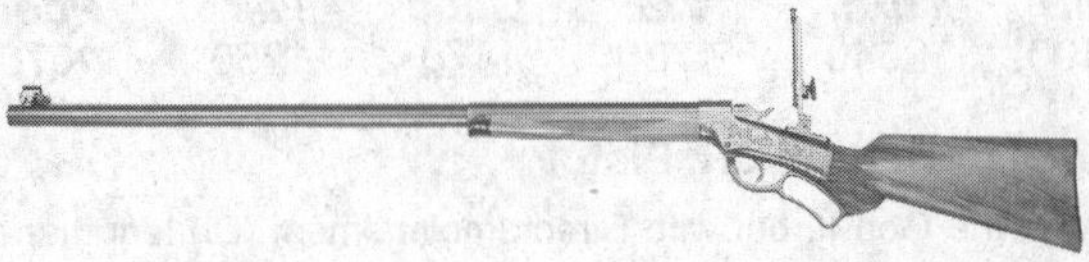

NIB	Exc.	V.G.	Good	Fair	Poor
3100	2550	2200	1100	600	250

No. 8 Union Hill Model

Features 30" or 32" half-octagon standard or heavy barrel, single-/double-set triggers, pistol grip stock with cheekpiece, full-loop lever, hook Schuetzen buttplate and fancy walnut checkered stock. Offered in calibers from .22 LR to .40-70. Weight with standard barrel in .32-caliber 10.5 lbs.; heavyweight barrel in .40-caliber 11.5 lbs. Not furnished with sights.

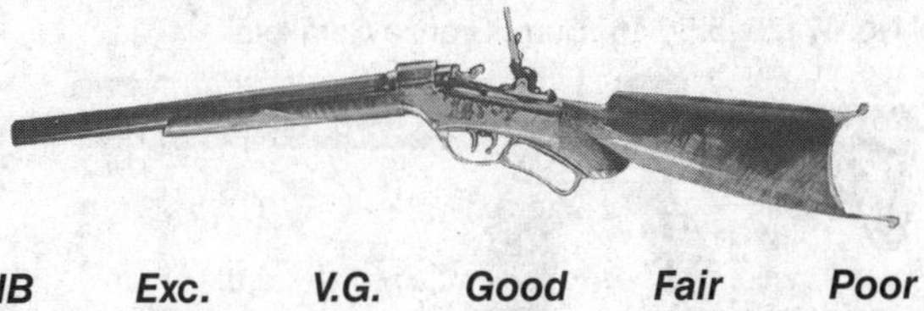

NIB	Exc.	V.G.	Good	Fair	Poor
3600	2000	1700	900	450	200

Model 1885 High Wall

Single-shot rifle. Chambered for a wide variety of calibers from .18 Bee to .577 Express. Barrel lengths to 34". American walnut stock. Many options to choose from that will affect price. Introduced in 2000.

NIB	Exc.	V.G.	Good	Fair	Poor
3050	2500	2000	1180	650	280

BALLESTER—MOLINA

See—HAFDASA

BALLARD, C. H.

Worcester, Massachusetts

Single-Shot Derringer (Antique)

.41-caliber rimfire spur trigger single-shot pistol, with 2.75" barrel marked "Ballard's". Blued, with silver-plated frame. Walnut grips. Manufactured during 1870s. Note: Add 20 percent for iron frame model.

Exc.	Fine	V.G.	Good	Fair	Poor
1500	800	600	400	250	150

BARRETT, F.A. MFG. CO.

Murfreesboro, Tennessee

Scopes pictured are not included in values. SEE POLITICAL PANIC PRICING.

Barrett MRAD

Chambered in .338 Lapua Magnum, with user-changeable barrel system. Match-grade trigger. Thumb-operated safety can be configured to right or left. Folding stock has adjustable cheekpiece and length of pull. Finished in Barrett's Multi-Role Brown. Introduced in 2011.

NIB	Exc.	V.G.	Good	Fair	Poor
6500	4500	4000	3500	—	—

Model 82 Rifle

.50-caliber BMG semi-automatic rifle, with 37" barrel and 11-shot magazine. Barrel fitted with muzzle brake. Receiver with telescope. Parkerized. Weight about 35 lbs. Manufactured from 1985 to 1987. Model No. 13318 .50 BMG/ 20"/Black.

NIB	Exc.	V.G.	Good	Fair	Poor
8000	7000	5500	4700	—	—

Model 82A1

As above, with 20" or 29" barrel without sights. 10-round magazine. 10X telescope and iron sights optional. Comes with hard carrying case. Weight 28.5 lbs. Model number 14030 is for .50 BMG/20"/ Tan Cerakote Finish.

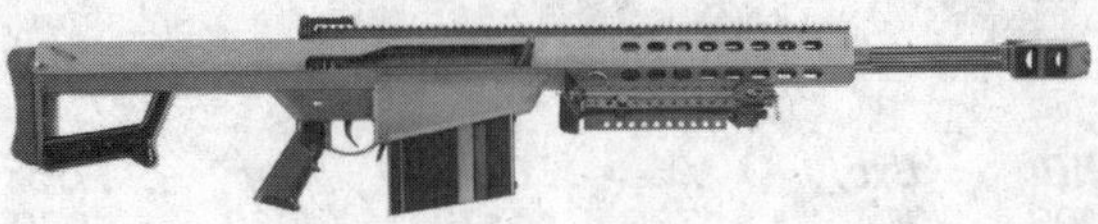

NIB	Exc.	V.G.	Good	Fair	Poor
12000	9000	6000	5000	—	—

Model 95M

Introduced in 1995. .50-caliber BMG bolt-action rifle. Features 29" barrel and 5-round magazine. Scope optional. Weight 22 lbs.

NIB	Exc.	V.G.	Good	Fair	Poor
6200	5700	5200	4500	—	—

Model 99

Single-shot bolt-action rifle. Chambered for .50 BMG or .416 Barrett. Standard barrel length 32". Optional barrel lengths 25" or 29". Weight about 25 lbs. with 32" barrel. Note: Add $200 for fluted barrel.

NIB	Exc.	V.G.	Good	Fair	Poor
4500	3800	3000	2500	—	—

Model 107

Chambered for .50-caliber cartridge. Semi-automatic rifle fitted with 29" barrel and muzzle brake. Bipod detachable and adjustable. M1913 accessory rail. Supplied with two 10-round magazines. Weight about 32 lbs.

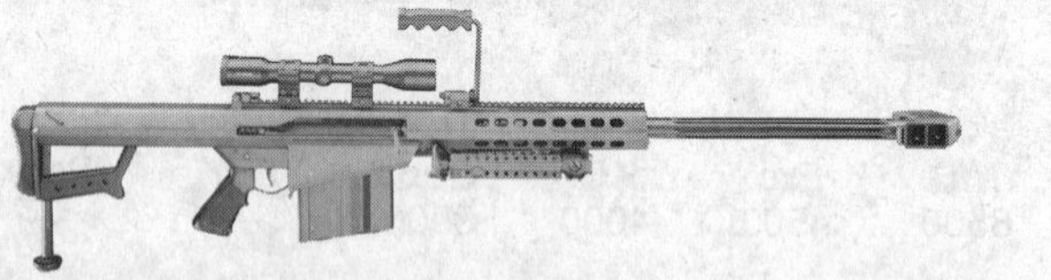

NIB	Exc.	V.G.	Good	Fair	Poor
10050	8540	7260	6170	5250	4460

M107A1

4-lbs. weight reduction from Model 107. Comes in 29" and 20" fluted barrels. Pricing is for model number 18065 50 BMG/29"/FDE Cerakote.

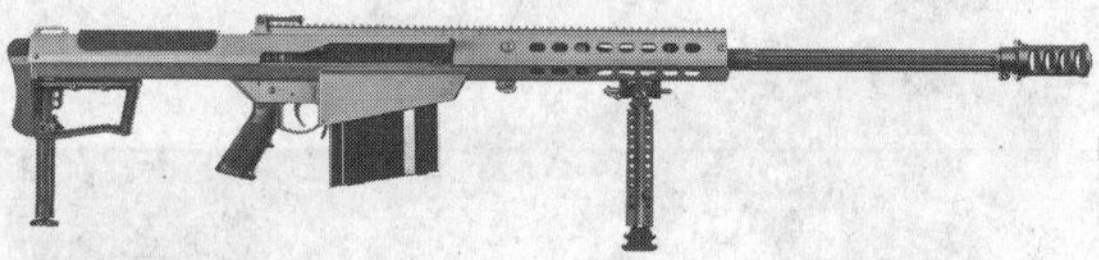

NIB	Exc.	V.G.	Good	Fair	Poor
13000	10250	8750	7250	—	—

Model 468

Built on semi-automatic AR-15-style lower receiver. Features 16" barrel, with muzzle brake. Chambered for 6.8 SPC cartridge. Folding front and rear sight. Integrated Rail system. Weight about 7.3 lbs.

NIB	Exc.	V.G.	Good	Fair	Poor
2400	2040	1730	1470	1250	1070

REC7

NIB	Exc.	V.G.	Good	Fair	Poor
1700	1450	1230	1040	890	750

REC7 Gen II

This piston-driven AR-style model was introduced in 2008. Chambered in 5.56 NATO or 6.8 SPC. Mag-pull MOE pistol grip stock, 16" barrel, Barrett handguard with KeyMod rail attachment. Other features are flash suppressor, flip-up iron sights and 30-shot magazine. Offered in black, gray, Flat Dark Earth or OD green finish. Note: Deduct $400 for 2008-2013 first generation production.

NIB	Exc.	V.G.	Good	Fair	Poor
2400	2040	1730	1470	1250	1070

REC7 DI Carbine, SBR, Pistol

Similar to the Gen II, but with Direct Impingement (DI) lengthened gas system for reliability with or without a suppressor. Available in 5.56 NATO, 6.8 SPC, and 300 BLK. Receivers are 7075-T6 aluminum coated in Type 3 Class 2 hardcoat anodizing, then finished with Cerakote. Magpul furniture, custom Radian Raptor ambidextrous charging handle, Geissele or ALG Defense trigger, and extended slimline Barrett handguard with Magpul M-LOK accessory mounting slots. 16" Carbine rifling twist rates are 1:7 for 5.56 NATO; 1:10 for 6.8 SPC; and 1:7 for 300 Blackout. Weight, about 6.2 pounds. OAL is 36". SBR and Pistol have 10.25" barrels with 1:7 twist in 5.56 NATO and 300 BLK. OAL length for both is 26.2"; weigh about 5.5 lbs.

REC7 DI Carbine

Model No. 17125, 5.56/16"/Burnt Bronze Cerakote.

NIB	Exc.	V.G.	Good	Fair	Poor
2000	1500	1250	1000	—	—

REC7 DI DMR

Caliber: 5.56 NATO. Capacity: 20. DMR line has an 18" 1:7.7" barrel. Overall length: 35.3". Weight: 7.9 lbs.

NIB	Exc.	V.G.	Good	Fair	Poor
2600	2500	2400	2200	—	—

REC10 Carbine

Caliber: .308 Win. Capacity: 20. Direct impingement gas system. DMR model has 16 in. barrel, 1:10 twist. Overall length: 34.5 in. Weight: 9.0 lbs. LR model has 20 in. barrel, 1:10 twist. Overall length: 41.5 in. Weight: 11.1 lbs.

NIB	Exc.	V.G.	Good	Fair	Poor
2570	2230	1900	1610	1370	1170

Barrett Sovereign Shotgun

This series of over/under and side-by-side shotguns are chambered in 12-, 20- and 28-gauge. Featuring round body steel boxlock receivers, with ornamental sideplates, scroll engraving, coin finish, AAA-grade Turkish walnut stocks with classic checkering, single selective trigger, automatic ejectors and interchangeable choke tubes. Albany is an over/under, with a slightly open Prince of Wales grip: Beltrami is a side-by-side, with a straight-grip stock (shown in photo). These classic-style shotguns are made by Fausti Stefano of Italy. Introduced in 2016. Note: Add $400 for 28-gauge.

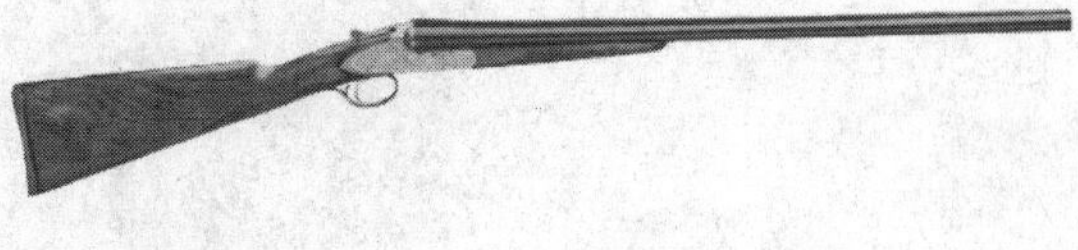

Albany O/U

NIB	*Exc.*	*V.G.*	*Good*	*Fair*	*Poor*
5200	4300	3500	—	—	—

Beltrami SxS

NIB	*Exc.*	*V.G.*	*Good*	*Fair*	*Poor*
5700	4800	4000	—	—	—

BARRETT, J. B. and A.B. & CO.

Wytheville, Virginia

Barrett Muskets and Rifled Muskets Antique

Overall length 57.75"; barrel length 41.5" to 42"; caliber .69. Markings: although Barretts placed no marks of their own, on their alterations most were effected on Virginia Manufactory muskets, whose lockplates are marked "VIRGINIA/Manufactory" forward of hammer and "RICHMOND/(date)" on tail. For many years collectors considered adaptations of Hall rifles and carbines from breech-loaders to muzzleloaders to be the product of J.B. Barrett & Co. of Wytheville. Recent evidence, however, confirms that those adaptations were actually effected in Danville, Virginia, by another firm (see READ & WATSON). Nevertheless, Barretts of Wytheville did adapt arms during early years of American Civil War. Adaptation effected almost exclusively upon Virginia Manufactory flintlock muskets, consisted of percussioning by means of cone-in-barrel and rifling of barrels with seven narrow grooves. In 1861 and 1862, Barretts percussioned a total of 1250 muskets, of which 744 were rifled. Expert authentication recommended. Values are speculative.

Courtesy Milwaukee Public Museum, Milwaukee, Wisconsin

Exc.	*Fine*	*V.G.*	*Good*	*Fair*	*Poor*
—	16500	10000	6000	2200	1000

BAR-STO PRECISION MACHINE

Burbank, California

Bar-Sto 25

.25-caliber semi-automatic pistol, with brushed stainless steel receiver and slide. Walnut grips. Produced in 1974.

NIB	*Exc.*	*V.G.*	*Good*	*Fair*	*Poor*
—	320	280	180	120	100

BASCARAN, MARTIN A.

Eibar, Spain

Spanish manufacturer of pistols prior to World War II.

Martian 6.35mm

6.35mm semi-automatic pistol. Slide marked "Automatic Pistol Martian". Blued, with black plastic grips having monogram "MAB" cast in them.

NIB	*Exc.*	*V.G.*	*Good*	*Fair*	*Poor*
—	280	200	140	100	80

Martian 7.65mm

Semi-automatic pistol patterned after Ruby military pistols. "Martian" stamped on slide. Wood grips and lanyard loop.

Courtesy James Rankin

NIB	*Exc.*	*V.G.*	*Good*	*Fair*	*Poor*
—	280	200	140	100	80

Thunder

Semi-automatic pistol in caliber 6.35mm. Almost a duplicate of Martian. "Thunder" stamped on slide and each grip plate.

Courtesy James Rankin

NIB	*Exc.*	*V.G.*	*Good*	*Fair*	*Poor*
—	280	200	140	100	50

BAUER, F. A. CORP.

Fraser, Michigan

The Rabbit

.22-caliber over .410 bore combination rifle/shotgun, with tubular metal stock. Manufactured between 1982 and 1984. Similar to Garcia Bronco.

NIB	*Exc.*	*V.G.*	*Good*	*Fair*	*Poor*
—	320	300	220	120	80

Bauer 25 Automatic

.25-caliber semi-automatic pistol. Made of stainless steel, with 2.5" barrel and 6-shot magazine. Walnut or imitation pearl grips. Manufactured from 1972 to 1984. After 1984, this pistol was produced under the name of Fraser for a few years. Note: Add 15 percent for NIB.

Courtesy James Rankin

NIB	Exc.	V.G.	Good	Fair	Poor
300	250	200	160	120	80

BAYARD
Herstal, Belgium

See—PIEPER, H. & N. & BERGMANN

BAYONNE, MANUFACTURE D'ARMES
aka MAB
Bayonne, France

Model A

Manufactured in 1921. Chambered for 6.35mm cartridge. Patterned after Browning Model 1906. Squeeze grip safety, with 6-round magazine.

Courtesy James Rankin

NIB	Exc.	V.G.	Good	Fair	Poor
—	300	180	120	80	50

Model B

Manufactured in 1932. Chambered for 6.35mm cartridge. Exposed hammer, no grip safety and 6-round magazine.

Courtesy James Rankin

NIB	Exc.	V.G.	Good	Fair	Poor
—	280	160	90	80	50

Model C

Manufactured in 1933. Chambered for 7.65mm and .380 cartridge. Patterned after Browning Model 1910. Seven-round magazine.

Courtesy James Rankin

NIB	Exc.	V.G.	Good	Fair	Poor
—	320	220	200	120	90

Model D

Manufactured in 1933. Chambered for 7.65mm and .380 cartridge. Basically a Model C, with longer barrel and 9-round magazine. Note: Add 100 percent for Nazi-marked pistols.

Courtesy James Rankin

NIB	Exc.	V.G.	Good	Fair	Poor
—	400	300	250	120	100

Model E

Manufactured in 1949. Chambered for 6.35mm cartridge. Patterned after Model D, with streamlined grips and 10-round magazine.

NIB	Exc.	V.G.	Good	Fair	Poor
—	420	320	300	150	120

Model F

Manufactured in 1950. Chambered for .22 LR cartridge. Interchangeable barrel lengths, target grips and 10-round magazine.

Courtesy James Rankin

NIB	Exc.	V.G.	Good	Fair	Poor
—	420	320	200	150	120

Model G

Manufactured in 1951. Chambered for .22 LR and 7.65mm cartridge. Some with Dural frâmes. Magazine capacity: 10 rounds .22 LR; 8 rounds 7.65mm.

Courtesy James Rankin

NIB	Exc.	V.G.	Good	Fair	Poor
—	450	350	220	150	120

Model GZ

Manufactured in calibers .22 LR, 6.35mm, 7.65mm and .380. Almost identical to Model G. Dural frames and two-tone finishes on some variations.

NIB	Exc.	V.G.	Good	Fair	Poor
—	450	350	280	150	120

Model P-8 & P-15

In 1966 MAB manufactured Model P-8 and Model P-15 in 9mm Parabellum, with 8- and 15-round magazines. Basically the same gun, with different magazine capacities. Model P-15 went to French military as well as some commercial sales.

Courtesy James Rankin

NIB	Exc.	V.G.	Good	Fair	Poor
—	480	350	300	250	180

Model P-15 M1 Target

MAB Model P-15 was manufactured for target shooting using 9mm Parabellum cartridge. Most M1 Target MABs were purchased by French military for their target teams.

Courtesy James Rankin

NIB	Exc.	V.G.	Good	Fair	Poor
—	880	750	500	350	180

Model R

Manufactured in caliber 7.65mm Long in 1951. Model R similar to Model D. Model R's later produced in several calibers: .22 LR furnished with 10-round magazine and two different barrel lengths; 7.65mm had 9-round magazine; .380 and 9mm Parabellum fitted with 8-round magazines. Note: Deduct 15 percent for 7.65 Long.

.22 Long Rifle

NIB	Exc.	V.G.	Good	Fair	Poor
—	350	250	220	150	120

7.65mm & 7.65mm Long & .380

NIB	Exc.	V.G.	Good	Fair	Poor
—	350	250	220	150	120

9mm Parabellum

NIB	Exc.	V.G.	Good	Fair	Poor
—	800	500	360	310	260

Model R PARA Experimental

In late 1950's, MAB began experimenting with Model R in caliber 9mm Parabellum. There were many of these experimental-type pistols. The 8-round, rotating barrel Model R shown, led directly to Model P-15 series.

Courtesy James Rankin

NIB	Exc.	V.G.	Good	Fair	Poor
—	1500	1250	1000	500	250

Model "Le Chasseur"

Manufactured in 1953. "Le Chasseur" was a target model in .22 LR. Had a 9-round magazine, external hammer, target sights and grips. Note: MAB pistols sold in U.S.A. were retailed by Winfield Arms Company of Los Angeles, California. Marked "Made in France for WAC". This does not affect value.

NIB	Exc.	V.G.	Good	Fair	Poor
—	300	200	150	120	90

BEATTIE, J.

London, England

Beattie produced a variety of revolvers during percussion period, some of which were imported into United States. During the period this firm was in business, it was located at these London addresses:

43 Upper Marylebone Street	1835-1838
52 Upper Marylebone Street	1838-1842
52 Upper Marylebone Street & 223 Regent Street	1842-1846
205 Regent Street	1851-1882
104 Queen Victoria Street	1882-1894

Beattie Gas Seal Revolver (Antique)

.42-caliber single-action percussion revolver, with 6.25" octagonal barrel. When hammer is cocked, cylinder is forced forward against barrel breech, thus effecting a gas seal. Blued case-hardened, with walnut grips.

Exc.	Fine	V.G.	Good	Fair	Poor
5100	3500	2850	2200	1100	770

BEAUMONT

Maastrict, Netherlands

1873 Dutch Service Revolver, Old Model (Antique)

9.4mm double-action 6-shot revolver. Weight 2 lbs. 12 oz.

Exc.	Fine	V.G.	Good	Fair	Poor
700	400	300	200	100	70

1873 Dutch Service Revolver, New Model (Antique)

As above, with 6-shot cylinder.

Exc.	Fine	V.G.	Good	Fair	Poor
700	400	300	200	100	70

1873 KIM, Small Model (Antique)

As above, with octagonal barrel. 5-shot cylinder.

Exc.	Fine	V.G.	Good	Fair	Poor
780	500	370	250	120	80

M1871 Beaumont Rifle (Antique)

Early bolt-action single-shot Dutch military rifle.

Exc.	Fine	V.G.	Good	Fair	Poor
950	650	500	350	150	100

M1871-88 Beaumont Vitali Rifle (Antique)

Similar to the M1871 Beaumont rifle with the addition of a fixed box magazine.

Exc.	Fine	V.G.	Good	Fair	Poor
700	450	350	250	125	70

BEAUMONT, ADAMS

See—DEANE, ADAMS & DEANE

BECKER AND HOLLANDER

Suhl, Germany

Beholla

Semi-automatic pistol in caliber 7.65mm. Introduced in 1908 in Germany. Manufactured by Becker & Hollander until 1920. After that date three different companies produced Beholla under names of Stenda, Menta and Leonhardt.

Courtesy James Rankin

NIB	Exc.	V.G.	Good	Fair	Poor
—	500	350	220	180	100

BEEMAN PRECISION ARMS, INC.

Santa Rosa, California

Although primarily known as an importer and retailer of airguns, Beeman Precision Arms, Inc., has marketed several firearms.

MP-08

.380-caliber semi-automatic pistol, with 3.5" barrel and 6-shot magazine. Resembling German Luger. Blued. Introduced in 1968.

NIB	Exc.	V.G.	Good	Fair	Poor
480	380	280	220	200	120

P-08

As above in .22-caliber, with 8-shot magazine. Walnut grips. Introduced in 1969.

NIB	Exc.	V.G.	Good	Fair	Poor
480	380	280	220	200	120

SP Standard

.22-caliber single-shot target pistol, with 8" to 15" barrels. Fitted with adjustable sights and walnut grips. Imported in 1985 and 1986.

NIB	Exc.	V.G.	Good	Fair	Poor
320	220	200	180	150	100

SP Deluxe

As above, with walnut forend.

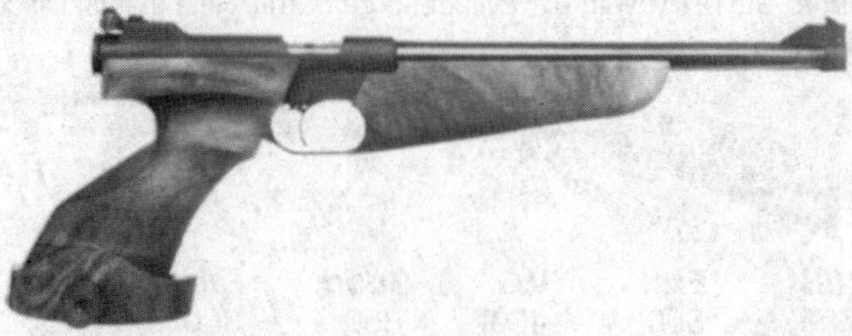

NIB	Exc.	V.G.	Good	Fair	Poor
350	250	220	200	150	100

BEERSTECHER, FREDERICK

Philadelphia, Pennsylvania (1846-1856)
Lewisburg, Pennsylvania (1857-1868)

Superposed Load Pocket Pistol (Antique)

.41-caliber superposed load percussion pistol, with an average barrel length of 3 in. German silver mounts. Walnut stock. Hammer fitted with movable twin striker head so the first charge in barrel can be fired and then second fired. Lock normally marked "F. Beerstecher's/Patent 1855". Prospective purchasers are advised to secure a qualified appraisal prior to acquisition. Rare. Values are speculative.

Exc.	Fine	V.G.	Good	Fair	Poor
15000	—	—	5000	—	—

1855 Superposed Percussion Rifle (Antique)

Very few made. Single-hammer rifle with two percussion nipples for superposed loads in the same barrel. Known configurations include .38 & .54 cal., with 33.5- to 35.5-in. oct. barrel, patchbox. Values are speculative.

Exc.	Fine	V.G.	Good	Fair	Poor
15000	—	—	5000	—	—

BEHOLLA

See—BECKER AND HOLLANDER

BEISTEGUI, HERMANOS

Eibar, Spain

See—GRAND PRECISION

BENELLI

Italy

SHOTGUNS

SL SERIES

Model SL-121 V

Semi-automatic 12-gauge, with 3" chambers and various barrel lengths and chokes. Black anodized alloy receiver. Discontinued in 1985.

NIB	Exc.	V.G.	Good	Fair	Poor
650	500	400	350	300	150

Model SL-121 Slug

Similar to SL-121 V, with 21" cylinder-bore barrel. Rifle sights. Discontinued in 1985.

NIB	Exc.	V.G.	Good	Fair	Poor
700	550	400	350	300	150

Model SL-123 V

Model has improved fast third-generation action. Otherwise resembles earlier SL-121.

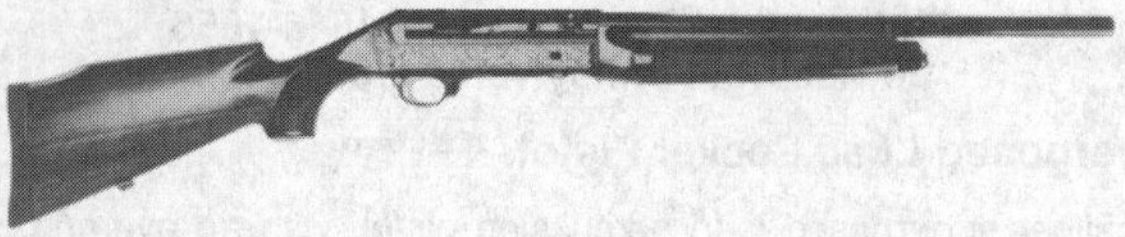

NIB	Exc.	V.G.	Good	Fair	Poor
750	600	500	400	350	200

Model SL-201

20-gauge, with 26" Improved Cylinder barrel. Similar in appearance to SL-123.

NIB	Exc.	V.G.	Good	Fair	Poor
500	480	420	350	300	150

M SERIES

M3 Super 90

Improved version of Benelli pump-action and semi-automatic inertia recoil system. Shotgun can be converted from pump to semi-automatic, by turning a spring-loaded ring located at end of forearm. Has rotating bolt system. Chambered for 12-gauge, with 3" chamber. Has 19.75" barrel, with cylinder bore, rifle sights and 7-round tubular magazine. Matte black finish, black fiberglass pistol grip stock and forearm. Introduced in 1986. Note: Add $50 for open rifle sights.

NIB	Exc.	V.G.	Good	Fair	Poor
1500	1300	950	700	450	300

M3 Super 90 Folding Stock

Same as above. Furnished with folding tubular steel stock.

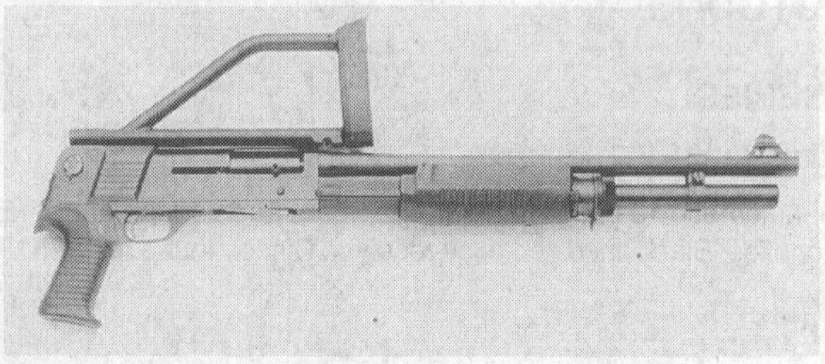

NIB	Exc.	V.G.	Good	Fair	Poor
1500	1350	1150	850	600	300

M4

Adopted by U.S. Marine Corps, this 12-gauge shotgun features a choice of three modular buttstock and two barrel configurations. Top-mounted Picatinny rail. Barrel length 18.5". Magazine capacity 6 rounds. Ghost ring sights. Weight about 8.4 lbs. Matte black finish. Introduced in 2003. Civilian version does not have collapsible buttstock.

M4 with skeleton stock with cheekpiece

M4 with standard stock

NIB	Exc.	V.G.	Good	Fair	Poor
1900	1400	1000	720	500	200

M1014 Limited Edition

Introduced in 2003. Version of M4. Fitted with skeleton buttstock. Special U.S. flag engraving on receiver. Fitted with 18.5" barrel and Picatinny rail, with ghost ring sights. Limited to 2,500 shotguns.

NIB	Exc.	V.G.	Good	Fair	Poor
2000	1500	1000	750	550	250

M1 Practical

Designed for IPSC events. Features over sized safety, speed loader, larger bolt handle, muzzle brake, adjustable ghost ring sight and optics rail. Offered with extended magazine tube and 26" barrel. Weight about 7.6 lbs.

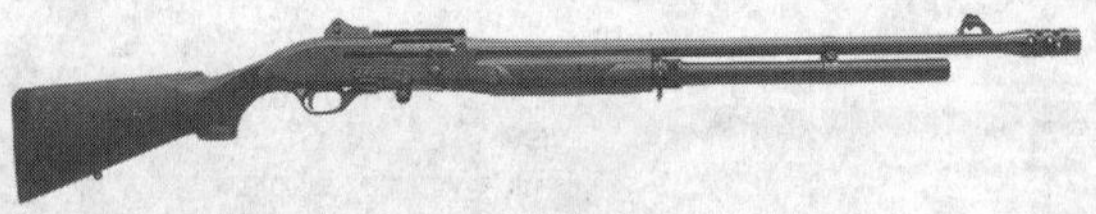

NIB	Exc.	V.G.	Good	Fair	Poor
1200	1000	750	500	280	120

M1 Super 90 Tactical

Semi-automatic 12-gauge shotgun, with inertia recoil system. Features 18.5" plain barrel. Three screw-in choke tubes. Available in standard polymer or pistol grip stock. Ghost ring sights standard. Weight 6.5 lbs. Introduced in 1993.

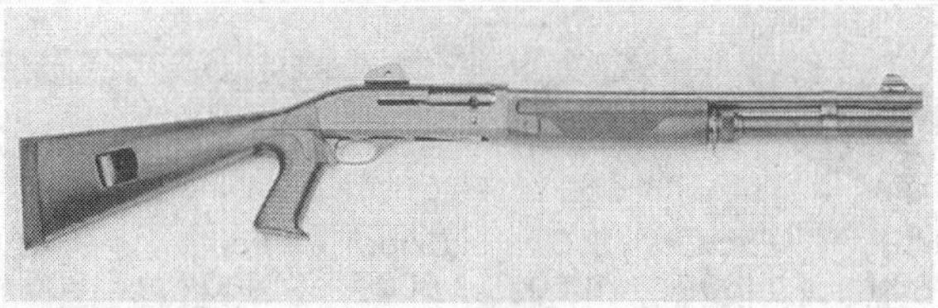

NIB	Exc.	V.G.	Good	Fair	Poor
1000	850	700	500	450	250

M1 Super 90 Slug Gun

Equipped with standard black polymer stock and 19.75" plain barrel. Fitted with 7-shot magazine. Ghost ring sights are an option. Weight 6.7 lbs. Camo model introduced in 2000. Note: Add $100 for Camo model.

NIB	Exc.	V.G.	Good	Fair	Poor
1000	750	550	450	350	250

M1 Super 90 Entry Gun

Fitted with black polymer pistol grip stock and 14" plain barrel. Magazine holds 5 shells. Plain or ghost ring sights available. CAUTION: NFA Weapon, Restricted sale, Class III Transfer required.

M1 Super 90 Defense Gun

Comes standard with polymer pistol grip stock, 19.75" barrel, plain or ghost ring sights. Offered in 12-gauge only. Weight 7.1 lbs.

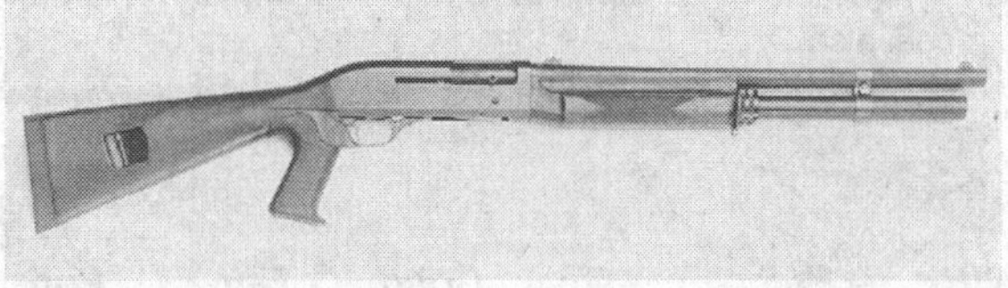

NIB	Exc.	V.G.	Good	Fair	Poor
900	700	600	500	450	250

M1 Super 90 Field

Similar to other Super 90 series guns, with 21", 24", 26" or 28" ventilated rib barrel and screw-in choke tubes. In 1998 this model was available with 24" rifled bore and matte rib. Add $80 for this barrel. Left-hand model added in 2000. In 2001 this model was offered in 20-gauge as well.

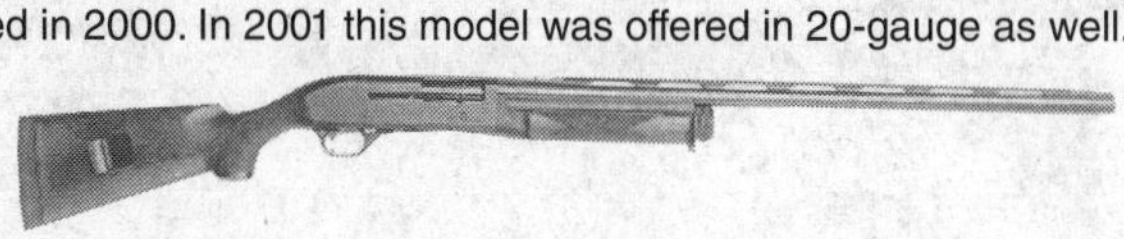

NIB	Exc.	V.G.	Good	Fair	Poor
900	650	600	550	450	200

M1 Super 90 Camo Field

Same as above, with camouflage receiver barrel, buttstock and forearm. Offered in 24", 26" and 28" ventilated rib barrels. Introduced in 1997. In 1998 this model also offered with 21" ventilated rib barrel. Left-hand model added in 2000. In 2001 this model offered in 20-gauge as well. Note:Add $50 for 20-gauge.

NIB	Exc.	V.G.	Good	Fair	Poor
700	600	500	380	300	200

M1 Field Steady Grip

Introduced in 2003. Features vertical pistol grip, drilled and tapped receiver. Extra Full choke tube. Barrel length 24". Weight about 7.3 lbs.

NIB	Exc.	V.G.	Good	Fair	Poor
1180	900	600	320	180	100

M1 Super 90 Sporting Special

Introduced in 1993. This 12-gauge shotgun similar to Super 90, with addition of non-reflective surfaces, 18.5" plain barrel and 3 choke tubes (IC, Mod, Full). Gun fitted with ghost ring sights.

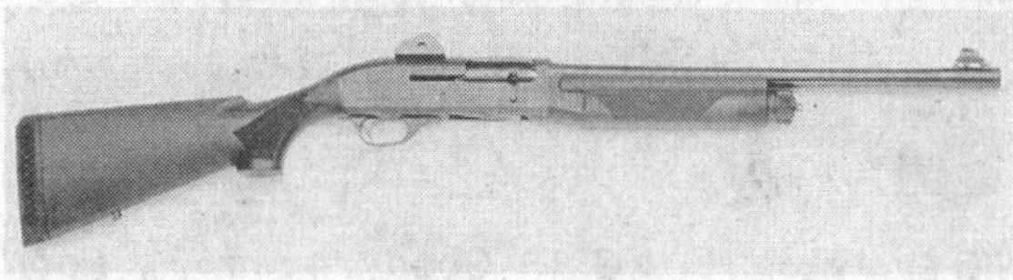

NIB	Exc.	V.G.	Good	Fair	Poor
720	600	500	400	350	200

M2 Practical with ComforTech

Introduced in 2005. Chambered for 12-gauge 3" shell. Fitted with 25" plain barrel, with compensator and ghost ring rear sight. Receiver fitted with Picatinny rail. Magazine capacity 8 rounds. Weight about 7.6 lbs.

NIB	Exc.	V.G.	Good	Fair	Poor
1200	1000	750	600	400	280

M2 Tactical

12-gauge 3" gun fitted with 18.5" barrel, with choke tubes and choice of rifle or ghost ring sights. Pistol grip or extended pistol grip. Black synthetic stock. Magazine capacity 5 rounds. Weight about 7 lbs. Note: Add $70 for ComforTech version; $65 for ghost ring sights.

NIB	Exc.	V.G.	Good	Fair	Poor
1250	1050	850	600	400	280

M2 Field with ComforTech

12-gauge model offered with 21", 24", 26" or 28" barrel. Black matte synthetic finish or Max-5, Shadow Grass Blades (SGB), or APG camo. 20-gauge has 24", 26", or 28" barrel in black, Max-5, SGB, Timber. Average 12-gauge weight 7 lbs.; 20 gauge 5.8 lbs. Note: Add $75 for camo.

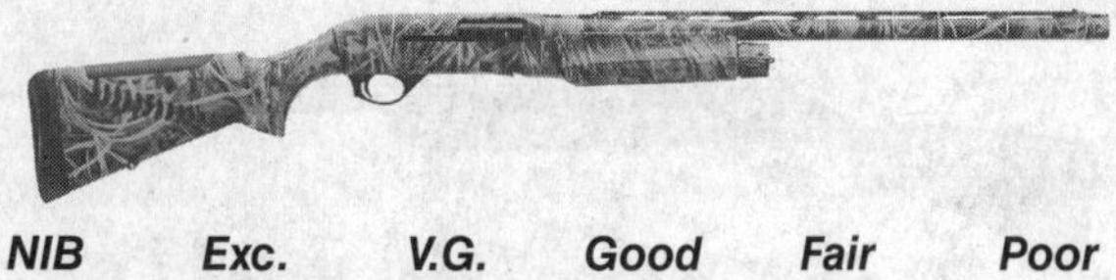

NIB	Exc.	V.G.	Good	Fair	Poor
1400	1200	1000	800	600	400

M2 Field without ComforTech

Same features as above, without ComforTech features. Available only in satin walnut, with 26" or 28" barrel.

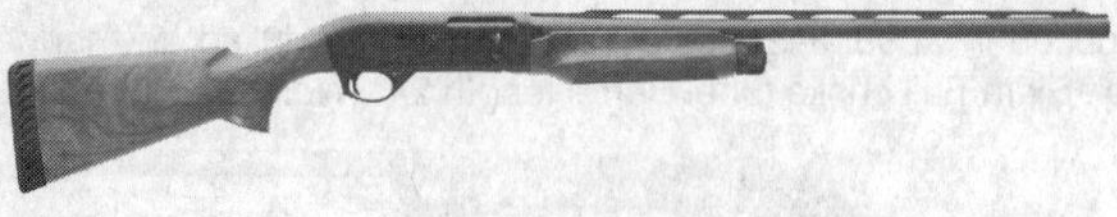

NIB	Exc.	V.G.	Good	Fair	Poor
1080	820	550	520	300	200

M2 Turkey Edition

From the Benelli Performance Shop. Offered in 12- or 20-gauge. Barrel 24", 3" chamber, ComforTech stock with Realtree APG or Mossy Oak Bottomland camo finish. Pistol grip stock is optional. A Burris FastFire II sight included. Custom work and features include honed and polished action, custom-tuned trigger group, three Rob Roberts Triple Threat choke tubes, lengthened and polished forcing cone, HiViz Comp front sight, oversized bolt handle and enlarged bolt release.

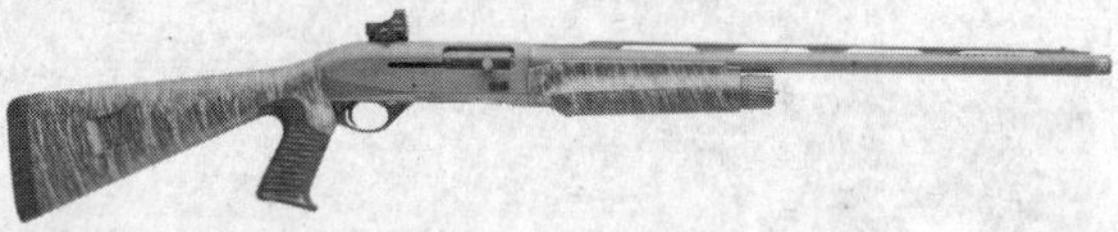

NIB	Exc.	V.G.	Good	Fair	Poor
2100	1700	1350	900	600	400

M2 Waterfowl Edition

From the Benelli Performance Shop. Similar to Turkey Edition except with 28" barrel, Optifade stock (12-ga.), Realtree Max-5 or ComforTech (20-ga.). Custom work and features include honed and polished action, custom-tuned trigger group, three Rob Roberts Triple Threat choke tubes, lengthened and polished forcing cone, HiViz Comp front sight, oversized bolt handle, enlarged bolt release and a paracord survival sling.

NIB	Exc.	V.G.	Good	Fair	Poor
1800	1400	1000	600	400	300

M2 Field 2023 Redesign

Gauges: 12 ga., 20 ga. Barrel: 24", 26", and 28" Crio treated. Stock: Black synthetic, Mossy Oak Bottomland, Gore Optifade, Realtree Max-7. Features: The workhorse Field line gets a full redesign for 2023, including sleeker stock dimensions, a longer forend grip surface, an oversized bolt release button, and a new MicroCell recoil unit. A revised bolt touts improved smoothness of cycling with Benelli's Inertia Drive system. Ships with Crio chokes. Available in both standard and compact models.

NIB	Exc.	V.G.	Good	Fair	Poor
1280	1050	—	—	—	—

M4 Tactical

Operates with an Auto Regulating Gas Operated (A.R.G.O.) semi-automatic system. Barrel length 18.5". Features include a Picatinny rail, fully adjustable ghost ring sight, windage adjustable front sight and black synthetic stock with optional pistol grip. Several other camo finishes have been offered including Desert Cerakote (shown). Titanium Cerakote finish on metal surfaces.

NIB	Exc.	V.G.	Good	Fair	Poor
1800	1400	1000	600	400	300

M4 H20

Introduced 2017. M4 H2O Tactical has Titanium Cerakote finish added to the barrel, receiver and magazine tube. Bolt is a black Cerakote finish, enhancing corrosion resistance and durability. Black synthetic pistol grip or black synthetic tactical stock. 7.8 lbs., OAL of 40 inches, sling attachments, standard Modified choke.

NIB	Exc.	V.G.	Good	Fair	Poor
2000	1800	1600	1400	1200	1000

MONTEFELTRO SERIES

Now updated with Benelli's Inertia-Drive bolt system. 12 and 20 ga. Barrel: 24", 26", 28". Three Crio chokes. Satin Walnut stocks. Red fiber-optic front sight. Standard and compact versions are available.

NIB	Exc.	V.G.	Good	Fair	Poor
1380	1190	1000	—	—	—

Montefeltro Super 90

Introduced in 1987. Similar to Super 90 Field. Checkered walnut stock and forearm, with gloss finish. Offered with 21", 24", 26" or 28" ventilated rib barrel. Available in 12-gauge only, with 3" chambers. Offered in left-hand model also.

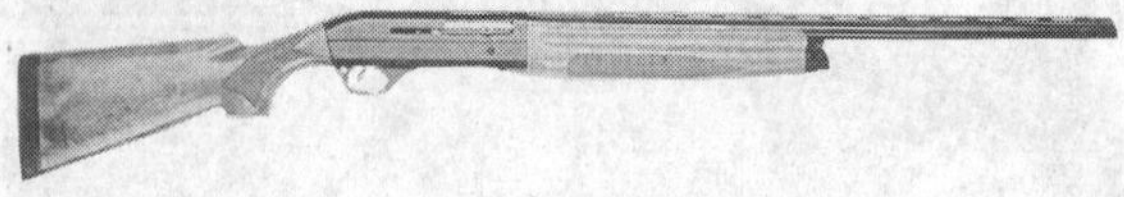

NIB	Exc.	V.G.	Good	Fair	Poor
900	700	600	500	450	350

Montefeltro 20 Gauge

Introduced in 1993. Features walnut checkered stock, with 26" ventilated rib barrel. In 1995 a 24" ventilated rib barrel offered. Weight 5.75 lbs. Note: Add $75 for short stock model.

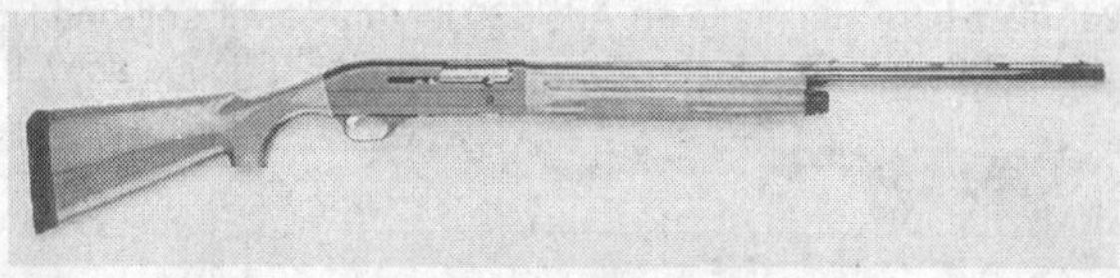

NIB	Exc.	V.G.	Good	Fair	Poor
900	700	600	500	450	350

Montefeltro 20 Gauge Camo

Same as above, with Realtree Camo finish. Offered with 26" ventilated rib barrel. Introduced in 1998.

NIB	Exc.	V.G.	Good	Fair	Poor
950	750	700	600	500	400

Montefeltro 20 Gauge Limited

Introduced in 1995. Features finely etched nickel plate receiver, with scroll and game scenes highlighted in gold. Stock is select grade walnut.

Fitted with 26" ventilated rib barrel.

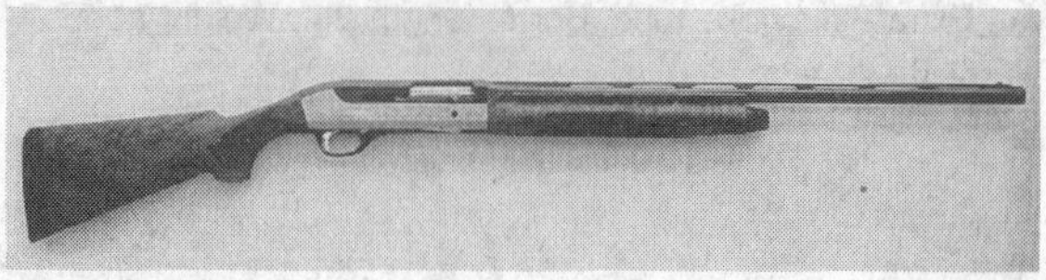

NIB	Exc.	V.G.	Good	Fair	Poor
1750	1250	800	500	400	350

Montefeltro Silver

Same features as the standard Montefeltro model, but with bright nickel-plated alloy receiver and AA-grade walnut stock. Receiver features a pair of gold flushing quail on the right side and a gold pointing setter on the left.

NIB	Exc.	V.G.	Good	Fair	Poor
1600	1400	1200	1000	800	600

Montefeltro Silver Featherweight

Introduced 2019. Has elements of Ultra Light and Montefeltro Silver shotguns to make light, quick-handling model. Satin walnut stocks with WeatherCoat, engraved nickel receivers, blued barrels in 12 and 20 gauge, 3" chambers. 26" barrel for 12 gauge; 24" for 20. Five Extended Crio chokes. Shim kit for drop and cast. Comes with hard case. Red-bar front sight.

NIB	Exc.	V.G.	Good	Fair	Poor
1800	1600	—	—	—	—

Montefeltro (2005)

Updated version of Montefeltro series. Slight change in receiver, different trigger, upgraded wood and name "Montefeltro" in gold on receiver. Offered in 12- or 20-gauge, with 3" chambers. Checkered select walnut stock, with pistol grip. Choice of 24", 26" or 28" ventilated rib barrel, with choke tubes. Red bar front sight. Weight for 12-gauge about 6.9 lbs.; 20-gauge about 5.6 lbs.

NIB	Exc.	V.G.	Good	Fair	Poor
1300	1000	950	700	500	350

Montefeltro Compact

In 20-gauge only. This model has a 24" or 26" barrel, shorter length-of-pull and satin finish stock. Introduced in 2012.

NIB	Exc.	V.G.	Good	Fair	Poor
1000	850	600	450	300	200

Montefeltro Synthetic

Model was introduced in 2013 in 12-gauge only, with a black synthetic stock and 26" or 28" barrel.

NIB	Exc.	V.G.	Good	Fair	Poor
1000	850	600	450	300	200

Montefeltro Sporting

Chambered for 3" magnum in 12 gauge, the Montefeltro can switch from field loads to magnums with no adjustments and total reliability. Satin-finished walnut stock, 30" barrel. Red bar front sight, metal mid-bead.

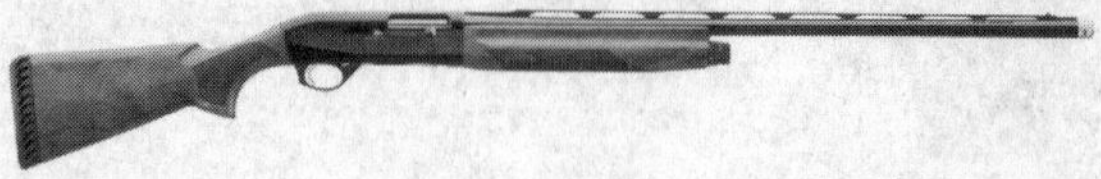

NIB	Exc.	V.G.	Good	Fair	Poor
1200	1000	800	600	400	—

BLACK EAGLE SERIES

Black Eagle Competition Gun

Offered in 12-gauge only. Fitted with etched receiver, mid rib bead, competition stock and 5 screw-in choke tubes. Available in 26" or 28" ventilated rib barrel. Upper receiver steel while lower receiver is lightweight alloy. Weight 7.3 lbs.

NIB	Exc.	V.G.	Good	Fair	Poor
1300	800	750	700	400	280

Black Eagle

Similar to Black Eagle Competition Model, with standard grade wood. Matte black finish on receiver. Introduced in 1997.

NIB	Exc.	V.G.	Good	Fair	Poor
900	600	480	320	220	150

Black Eagle Executive Series

Offered in 12-gauge only. Special order only shotgun. Offered with 21", 24", 26", 28" ventilated rib barrels. Each grade or level of gun engraved with increasing levels of coverage. Stock is fancy walnut.

Grade I

NIB	Exc.	V.G.	Good	Fair	Poor
6200	5000	3500	2500	1500	700

Grade II

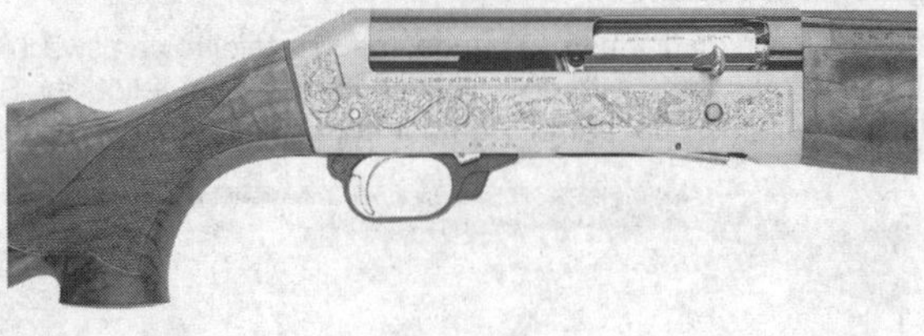

NIB	Exc.	V.G.	Good	Fair	Poor
7000	5500	4000	3000	1600	800

Grade III

NIB	Exc.	V.G.	Good	Fair	Poor
8500	6500	4750	3200	1800	900

SUPER BLACK EAGLE SERIES

Super Black Eagle

Similar to Montefeltro Super 90 Hunter, with polymer or walnut stock and forearm. Offered with 24", 26" or 28" ventilated rib barrel and 5 screw-in choke tubes. Chambered for 12-gauge from 2.75" to 3.5". Introduced in 1989. The 24" barrel introduced in 1993.

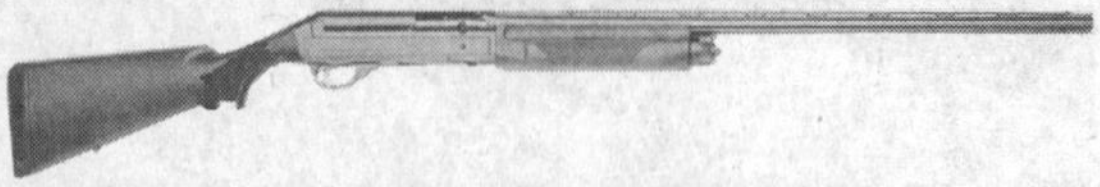

NIB	Exc.	V.G.	Good	Fair	Poor
1500	1100	850	600	300	200

Super Black Eagle Left-Hand

Introduced in 1999. Same as Black Eagle in left-hand version. Camo version also available.

NIB	Exc.	V.G.	Good	Fair	Poor
1500	1100	850	600	300	200

Super Black Eagle Custom Slug Gun

12-gauge model has 24" rifled barrel, with 3" chamber. Comes standard with matte metal finish. Weight 7.6 lbs.

NIB	Exc.	V.G.	Good	Fair	Poor
1500	1100	850	600	500	350

Super Black Eagle Camo Gun

Introduced in 1997. Features 24", 26" or 28' ventilated rib barrels chambered for 12-gauge shells. Has Realtree Xtra Brown Camo finish. Stock is camo polymer as is forearm.

NIB	Exc.	V.G.	Good	Fair	Poor
1600	1200	850	600	500	400

Super Black Eagle Steady Grip

Similar to above. Equipped with vertical pistol grip. Drilled and tapped receiver. Extra Full choke tube. Barrel length 24". Weight about 7.3 lbs. Introduced in 2003.

NIB	Exc.	V.G.	Good	Fair	Poor
1460	1100	650	580	320	220

Super Black Eagle Limited Edition

Introduced in 1997. Features 26" ventilated rib barrel, matte metal finish and satin select grade wood stock. Nickel plated receiver is finely etched with scroll and game scenes. Limited to 1,000 guns.

NIB	Exc.	V.G.	Good	Fair	Poor
2000	1500	1050	750	520	380

SUPER BLACK EAGLE 2 SERIES

Series of guns introduced in 2005. Major features are new butt pad, grip and cryogenically treated barrels for which specially designed longer choke tubes are required. Benelli offers this series with or without "ComforTech" features. This system reduces recoil up to 48 percent and muzzle climb by 15 percent.

Super Black Eagle 2 with ComforTech

Offered in 12-gauge, with 3.5" chambers. Barrel lengths 24", 26" or 28", with choke tubes and red bar front sight. Available in synthetic or various camo finishes. Magazine capacity 3 rounds. Weight about 7.2 lbs. with 26" barrel.

NIB	Exc.	V.G.	Good	Fair	Poor
1460	1100	700	600	360	250

Super Black Eagle 2 without ComforTech

Model without ComforTech. Same options as above, with addition of walnut stock. Note: Add $60 for walnut stock; $110 for camo models.

NIB	Exc.	V.G.	Good	Fair	Poor
1360	1000	650	580	320	220

Super Black Eagle 2 Rifled Slug with ComforTech

12-gauge 3" chamber gun, with 24" rifled barrel and adjustable sights. Available with synthetic stock or Timber HD camo stock. Weight about 7.4 lbs. Note: Add $120 for Camo version.

NIB	Exc.	V.G.	Good	Fair	Poor
1540	1150	650	580	320	220

Super Black Eagle 2 Turkey Gun

12-gauge 3" chamber shotgun (3.5" chambers on non-ComforTech guns). Fitted with 24" smooth bore barrels and choke tubes. Red bar front sight. Weight about 7.1 lbs. Available with Timber HD camo stock, with or without ComforTech. Note: Add $130 for ComforTech version.

NIB	Exc.	V.G.	Good	Fair	Poor
1460	1050	700	600	360	250

Super Black Eagle 2 Steady Grip

12-gauge 3.5" chamber gun. Fitted with 24" barrel and red bar front sight. Choke tubes. Stock is camo, with steadygrip pistol grip. Weight about 7.3 lbs. Model comes without ComforTech.

NIB	Exc.	V.G.	Good	Fair	Poor
1200	950	650	500	300	200

SUPER BLACK EAGLE 3 SERIES

Similar to Black Eagle 2 series. Additional features include a red bar front sight, metal bead middle sight and ComforTech II black synthetic stock with cheek piece. Choice of Realtree Max 5, Gore Sitka Optifade Waterfowl Timber or Mossy Oak Bottomland camo coverage. Has oversized operating controls and triggerguard for shooter's wearing gloves. Stock is adjustable for drop and cast with series of shims. Easy locking breech closing system provides smoother functioning operation when closing action on a shotshell. Introduced in 2017. Left-hand models introduced in 2018. Realtree Max-7 camo is available across the line on both right- and left-hand models. 28-Gauge additions: 3" chambers now available in variants with black synthetic and all camos. 26" or 28" barrels.

NIB	Exc.	V.G.	Good	Fair	Poor
1700	1550	1390	1130	960	—

Super Black Eagle 3 26" or 28" Black Synthetic

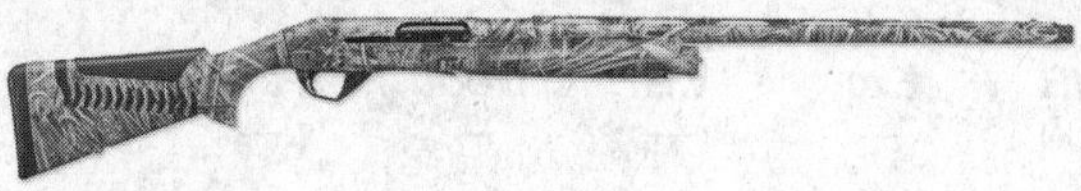

NIB	Exc.	V.G.	Good	Fair	Poor
1700	1500	1350	1200	1100	1000

Super Black Eagle 3 26" or 28" GORE OPTIFADE Timber

NIB	Exc.	V.G.	Good	Fair	Poor
1800	1700	1500	1350	1200	1100

Super Black Eagle 3 26" or 28" Mossy Oak Bottomland

NIB	Exc.	V.G.	Good	Fair	Poor
1800	1700	1500	1350	1200	1100

Super Black Eagle 3 26" or 28" Shadow Grass Blades

NIB	Exc.	V.G.	Good	Fair	Poor
1800	1700	1500	1350	1200	1100

Super Black Eagle 3 28" Satin walnut

NIB	Exc.	V.G.	Good	Fair	Poor
1700	1500	1350	1200	1100	1000

Super Black Eagle 3 24" Black Synthetic

NIB	Exc.	V.G.	Good	Fair	Poor
1800	1700	1500	1350	1200	1100

Super Black Eagle 3 26" or 28" Left-Handed Black Synthetic

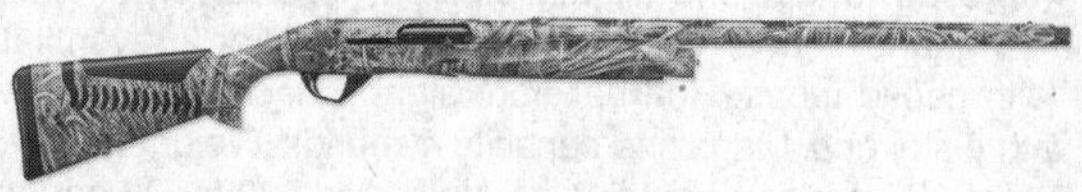

NIB	Exc.	V.G.	Good	Fair	Poor
1700	1600	1450	1300	1200	1100

Super Black Eagle 3 28" Left-Handed Realtree Max-5

NIB	Exc.	V.G.	Good	Fair	Poor
1800	1700	1500	1350	1200	1100

Super Black Eagle 3 Turkey Performance Shop

NIB	Exc.	V.G.	Good	Fair	Poor
2780	—	—	—	—	—

Super Black Eagle 3 Waterfowl Performance Shop

NIB	Exc.	V.G.	Good	Fair	Poor
2950	—	—	—	—	—

Super Black Eagle 3 BE.S.T.

Benelli expands its SBE III line with the new BE.S.T. model, so named for the Benelli Surface Treatment, a proprietary coating that protects steel from rust and corrosion and was tested over several months in saltwater with no signs of corrosion. Parts treated with BE.S.T. are backed with a 25-year warranty against rust and corrosion. The BE.S.T. package will be available on select SBE III models.

NIB	Exc.	V.G.	Good	Fair	Poor
1900	1770	1500	1290	1000	—

LEGACY SERIES

Legacy

Features coin finished alloy receiver. Introduced in 1998. Chambered for 12-gauge 2.75" or 3" shell. Fitted with 26" or 28" ventilated rib barrel. Mid and front sights. Weight about 7.5 lbs. Buttstock and forearm are select walnut. 20-gauge added in 1990 with 24" or 26" ventilated rib barrels. Weight 6 lbs.

NIB	Exc.	V.G.	Good	Fair	Poor
1300	800	750	700	400	280

Legacy Limited Edition

Offered in both 12- and 20-gauge. Features select walnut stock and etched game scenes with gold filled accents. 12-gauge features waterfowl scenes and fitted with a 28" barrel; 20-gauge has upland game scenes and a 26" barrel. Introduced in 2000. Limited to 250 guns in each gauge.

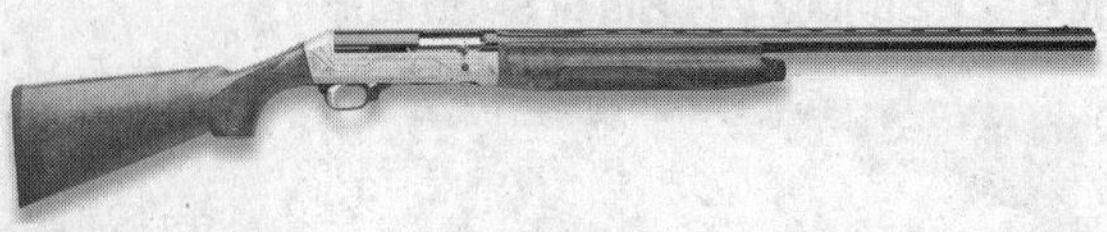

NIB	Exc.	V.G.	Good	Fair	Poor
1600	1200	900	550	380	300

Legacy (2005)

Updated version of Legacy. Changes are in engraving pattern, upgraded wood, improved trigger and slightly different receiver style. Offered in 12- and 20-gauge, with 3" chambers. Choice of 26" or 28" ventilated rib barrel, with choke tubes. Red bar front sight. Checkered select walnut stock, with pistol grip. Magazine capacity 4 rounds. Weight for 12-gauge about 7.4 lbs.; 20-gauge about 5.8 lbs. Note: Add $30 for 20-gauge.

NIB	Exc.	V.G.	Good	Fair	Poor
1440	1050	900	580	320	220

NOVA SERIES

Nova

"Slide-action series" introduced in 1999. Features polymer molded frame, with steel cage chambered for 3.5" shells. Choice of 24", 26" or 28" ventilated rib barrels. A 18.5" slug barrel also offered. Two- or four-shot magazine extensions offered as well. Weight with 28" barrel 8 lbs. Choice of camo or black synthetic pistol grip stock. In 2001 offered in 20-gauge.

NIB	Exc.	V.G.	Good	Fair	Poor
350	280	220	180	150	80

Nova Slug

12-gauge shotgun has 18.5" cylinder bored barrel, with open rifle or ghost ring sights. Black synthetic stock. Chambered for 2.75" or 3" shells. Magazine capacity 4 rounds. Weight about 7.2 lbs. Introduced in 2000. Note: Add $40 for ghost ring sights.

NIB	Exc.	V.G.	Good	Fair	Poor
350	280	220	200	150	100

Nova Rifled Slug

Introduced in 2000. This 12-gauge features 24" rifled barrel, with open rifle sights. Black synthetic or Timber HD camo stock. Chambered for 2.75" or 3" shells. Magazine capacity 4 rounds. Weight about 8 lbs. Note: Add $75 for Camo version.

NIB	Exc.	V.G.	Good	Fair	Poor
520	420	350	250	180	120

Nova Field Slug Combo

12-gauge 3" gun equipped with 24" and 26" barrel. 26" barrel fitted with ventilated rib and choke tube; 24" barrel is rifled and fitted with cantilever scope mount. Black synthetic stock.

NIB	Exc.	V.G.	Good	Fair	Poor
540	420	320	250	180	120

Nova H2O Pump

Introduced in 2003. Features a largely polymer exterior, with corrosion-resistant finish. Barrel, magazine tube, magazine cap, trigger group and other internal parts are nickel plated. Chambered for 12-gauge. Fitted with 18.5" barrel. Black synthetic stock. Magazine capacity 4 rounds. Open rifle sights. Weight about 7.2 lbs.

NIB	Exc.	V.G.	Good	Fair	Poor
600	500	400	250	150	100

Nova Turkey

Gauge: 20 ga. 3 in. Barrel: 24 in. with ventilated rib. Length: 45.5 in. Weight: 6.5 lbs. Stock: Synthetic with full Mossy Oak Bottomland camouflage. Features: Benelli's new addition to the Nova family targets run-and-gun hunters seeking a lighter-built and -recoiling turkey gun. Ergonomic forend. Red bar fiber-optic front sight. Magazine cutoff button. Ships with three chokes (IC, M, F).

NIB	Exc.	V.G.	Good	Fair	Poor
500	—	—	—	—	—

Supernova

Introduced in 2006. Supernova incorporates Benelli's ComforTech stock system into Nova pump shotgun. Available in 24", 26" and 28" barrel lengths in matte black synthetic; 24" and 26" barrel lengths in Advantage Timber camo; 26" and 28" barrel lengths in Max-4 camo. Weight about 8 lbs. with 28" barrel. All versions chambered for 3.5" shells. Three choke tubes. Note: Add 15 percent for camo versions.

NIB	Exc.	V.G.	Good	Fair	Poor
480	380	250	180	150	80

Supernova SteadyGrip

As above, with extended pistol grip in 24" barrel only. Matte black synthetic or Advantage Timber stock. Note: Add 15 percent for camo model.

NIB	Exc.	V.G.	Good	Fair	Poor
460	380	250	180	150	80

Supernova Tactical

Matte black synthetic stock, with 18" barrel. Available with ComforTech or pistol grip stock. Fixed cylinder bore. Open rifle sights. Ghost ring sights optional.

NIB	Exc.	V.G.	Good	Fair	Poor
400	320	220	150	120	80

SPORT SERIES

Sport Model

Introduced in 1997. First shotgun with removable interchangeable carbon fiber ventilated ribs. Offered in 12-gauge only with choice of 26" or 28" barrels; 20-gauge with 28" barrel. Butt pad adjustable. Weight: 7 lbs. for 26" models; 7.3 lbs. for 28" models.

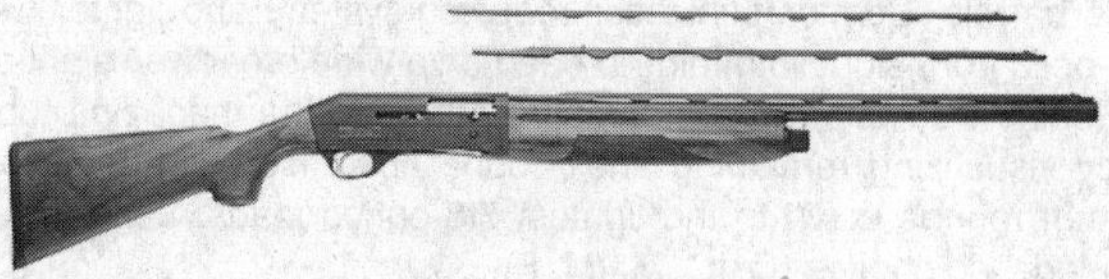

NIB	Exc.	V.G.	Good	Fair	Poor
1300	1000	650	400	250	100

SuperSport with ComforTech

Introduced in 2005. Offered in 12 and 20 gauge with 3" chambers. 12 gauge has 28" or 30" ported barrel with carbon-fiber finish, Extended Crio Chokes (Chrome) in C, IC, M, IM, F, and red-bar front sight. 20-gauge has 28" barrel. Weight about 7.25 lbs.

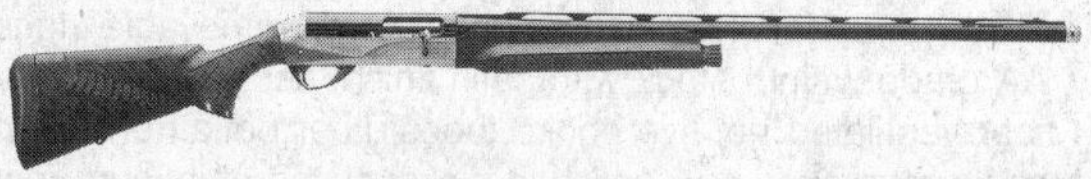

NIB	Exc.	V.G.	Good	Fair	Poor
2000	1800	1600	1400	1200	1000

Sport II Model

Introduced in 2003. Features cryogenically treated barrels and extra-long choke tubes. Chambered for 12-gauge shell in 2.75" or 3", with 28" or 30" barrel; 20-gauge with 28" barrel. Ventilated rib and choke tubes. Magazine capacity 4 rounds. Red bar front sight. Weight about 7.9 lbs.

NIB	Exc.	V.G.	Good	Fair	Poor
1470	1100	700	480	320	150

Cordoba

Introduced in 2005. Chambered for 12-gauge 3" shell. Fitted with cryogencially treated ported barrels in 28" or 30" lengths, with extended choke tubes. Ventilated rib is 10mm width. Synthetic stock, with adjustable length butt pads. Red bar front sight. Weight about 7.25 lbs.

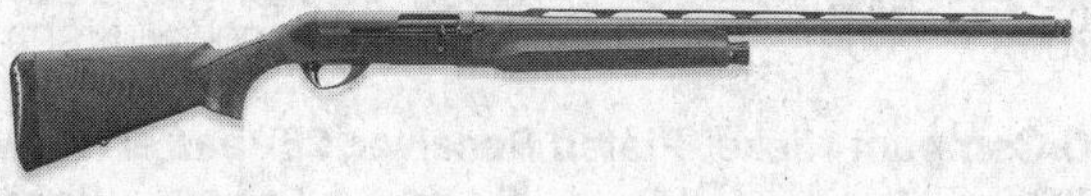

NIB	Exc.	V.G.	Good	Fair	Poor
1800	1530	1200	850	380	300

Vinci

Gas-operated 12-gauge semi-automatic shotgun chambered for 2.75" and 3". Features include modular disassembly; interchangeable choke tubes; 26" to 28" ribbed barrel; black, Max-5 finish; synthetic contoured stocks; optional Steady-Grip model. Weight 6.7 to 6.9 lbs. Note: Add $100 for camo finish.

NIB	Exc.	V.G.	Good	Fair	Poor
1200	1000	850	600	400	300

Super Vinci

Unlike Vinci, Super Vinci fires 12-gauge 2.75", 3" and 3.5" Magnum ammunition interchangeably. Barrel lengths 26", 28" and 30". Features Crio chokes, red bar front sight, metal bead mid-sight. Receiver drilled and tapped for scope mounting. Weight about 7 lbs. Available in black synthetic, Realtree MAX-5, Gore Optifade Waterfowl Marsh, and Shadow Grass Blades. New in 2011. Note: Add $100 for camo finish.

NIB	Exc.	V.G.	Good	Fair	Poor
1400	1150	900	650	450	350

Ultra Light

Inertia-driven 12-, 20-, and 28-gauge semi-automatic. Features alloy receiver, carbon fiber rib and small proportions to bring weight down to about 6 lbs. for 12 gauge, 5.2 lbs. for 20, and 5.0 lbs. for 28. Walnut stock, with Weathercoat finish. Chambered for 3" shells. Offered in 24" or 26" barrel only, with 3 Crio chokes, C,IC,M. Introduced 2006. 28-gauge introduced 2012.

NIB	Exc.	V.G.	Good	Fair	Poor
1440	1050	900	580	320	220

EXECUTIVE SERIES

Limited edition 12-gauge semi-automatic, with engraved gray lower receiver, highly polished blue barrel and upper receiver. Extra select grade walnut stock. Made in three grades, Type 1, Type 2 and Type 3, with increasing levels of engraving and wood. Limited importation.

Executive SeriesType 1

NIB	Exc.	V.G.	Good	Fair	Poor
6250	5000	4000	3000	—	—

Type 2

NIB	Exc.	V.G.	Good	Fair	Poor
7250	6000	5000	4000	—	—

Type 3

NIB	Exc.	V.G.	Good	Fair	Poor
8500	7200	6200	5000	—	—

RAFFAELLO SERIES

Limited production 12-gauge semi-automatic, available only through Benelli World Class dealers. Offered in three grades, Standard, Deluxe and Deluxe Legacy. Deluxe grade has scroll engraving and coin finished receiver. Deluxe Legacy has gold inlaid wildlife, high-grade walnut stock and also made in 20-gauge. Note: Add 25 percent for Deluxe grade; 50 percent for Deluxe Legacy.

NIB	Exc.	V.G.	Good	Fair	Poor
1600	1450	1150	800	600	400

ETHOS SERIES

Ethos features a recoil reduction system advertised as reducing felt recoil by 42 percent. The Benelli inertia-driven operating system cycles all loads. Introduced in 2014 a 12-gauge, with 20-, 28-gauge added in 2016. Barrel lengths 26" or 28", with five choke tubes and interchangeable fiber optic red, yellow and green front sights. Other features include a totally new receiver design, a two-part carrier latch for easy loading, AA-grade checkered walnut stock, and choice of engraved nickel-plated or anodized receiver. Note: Add $200 for engraved/nickel receiver. The Ethos Sport line was introduced in 2018. The Sport line has a larger recoil-reducing cheek comb pad, a raised, wide sporting rib, and ported barrel. Available in 12-, 20-, and 28-gauge models. Cycles light target loads, such as 7/8 oz. in 12 gauge.

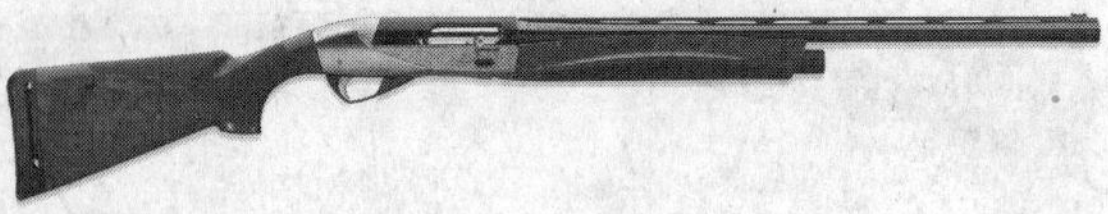

NIB	Exc.	V.G.	Good	Fair	Poor
1800	1550	1200	850	400	200

Benelli Ethos Black Anodized Receiver 26", 28" barrels.

NIB	Exc.	V.G.	Good	Fair	Poor
1800	1700	1500	1350	1200	1100

Benelli Ethos Sport

Ethos Sport Engraved Nickel-Plated Receiver; 28", 30" barrels.

NIB	Exc.	V.G.	Good	Fair	Poor
2000	1750	1500	—	—	—

Ethos Small Gauge

Nickel-Plated Receiver; 26", 28" barrels; 20, 28 ga.

NIB	Exc.	V.G.	Good	Fair	Poor
1950	1800	1600	—	—	—

Ethos BE.S.T.

Benelli expands its Ethos line with the new BE.S.T. model, so named for the Benelli Surface Treatment, a proprietary coating that protects steel from rust and corrosion and was tested over several months in saltwater with no signs of corrosion. Parts treated with BE.S.T. are backed with a 25-year warranty against rust and corrosion.

NIB	Exc.	V.G.	Good	Fair	Poor
1990	—	—	—	—	—

Ethos Super Sport

Gauge: 12 ga. 3in., 20ga. 3in. Barrel: 26 in. or 28 in. ventilated wide rib. Length: 49.5–51.5 in. Weight: 5.4–7.0 lbs. Stock: Carbon-fiber finish composite stock and forend. Features: Benelli expands their Ethos semi-automatic line with the Super Sport competition-ready model. Light-weight, weather-resistant carbon-fiber finish furniture. Inertia-Driven semi-automatic with ComforTech recoil-reducing system. Ported Crio barrel. Fiber optic front sight and mid-barrel bead. Nickel-plated receiver. Capacity of 4+1 rounds. Ships with five extended Crio chokes (C, IC, M, IM, F).

NIB	Exc.	V.G.	Good	Fair	Poor
2010	—	—	—	—	—

Ethos Cordoba BE.S.T.

Gauge: 12 ga. 3in., 20ga. 3in, 28ga. 3in. Barrel: 28 in. or 30 in. ventilated wide rib. Length: 49.5–51.5 in. Weight: 5.4–7.0 lbs. Stock: Black Synthetic. Features: Benelli expands their Ethos line of Inertia-Driven semi-autos with the new BE.S.T. (Benelli Surface Treatment). This Cordoba version is designed for high-volume shooting like that of dove hunting in Argentina — the gun's namesake location. Specialty features include ported barrels, ComforTech recoil-reducing system, and lighter weight. Fiber-optic front sight with mid-rib bead on a wide broadway sight channel. Shell View system places small windows in the magazine tube for quickly visualizing remaining shell count. Advertised to handle 3-inch magnum rounds down to the lightest 7/8-ounce loads. Ships with five extended Crio chokes (C, IC, M, IM, F).

NIB	Exc.	V.G.	Good	Fair	Poor
2060	—	—	—	—	—

828 U SERIES

Benelli's first over/under shotgun. Features include removable trigger assembly, AA grade walnut stock with satin finish, separated barrels with carbon fiber ventilated rib, five choke tubes, fiber optic front sight and matte black or engraved and polished nickel-plated aluminum receiver. Introduced in 2015 in 12-gauge only. Left-handed and compact models added 2017. Sport model added 2019. 828U Sport has steel locking system; adjustment for balance, adjustable trigger position, carbon-fiber rib with integrated sight channel, anti-glare barrels.

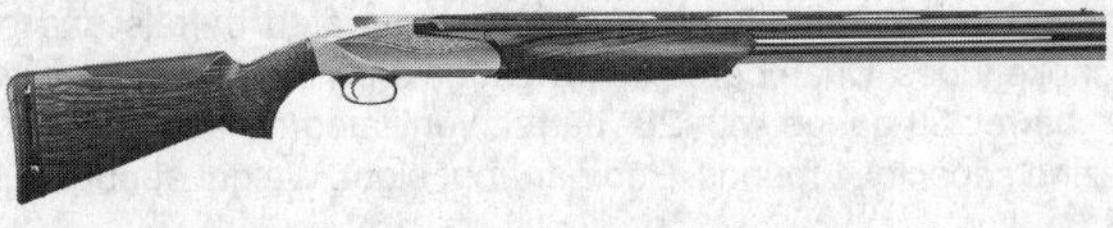

NIB	Exc.	V.G.	Good	Fair	Poor
2100	1850	1500	1100	900	500

828 U Black Anodized Receiver, 26", 28", 30" barrels

NIB	Exc.	V.G.	Good	Fair	Poor
2400	2200	2000	1800	1600	1200

828 U Nickel-Plated Receiver

NIB	Exc.	V.G.	Good	Fair	Poor
2800	2600	2400	2200	2000	1800

828 U LH Nickel-Plated Receiver, 26", 28" barrels

NIB	Exc.	V.G.	Good	Fair	Poor
2800	2600	2400	2200	2000	1800

828 U Compact Nickel-Plated Receiver, 26" barrel

NIB	Exc.	V.G.	Good	Fair	Poor
2800	2600	2400	2200	2000	1800

828 U Sport, Matte-Blued Steel Receiver, 30" barrel

NIB	Exc.	V.G.	Good	Fair	Poor
4000	3800	3600	3400	3200	3000

828 U Performance Shop

Added in 2019 with bronze anodized receiver and 24" barrels. Optimized for fast handling with slightly shorter length of pull. Lengthened forcing cones and Triple Threat chokes produce tighter patterns over longer ranges. 6.5 lbs. Shells are partially extracted, not ejected. Carbon-fiber stepped rib, fiber-optic front sight. Shims allow dozens of adjustments for custom fit. Eight chokes.

NIB	Exc.	V.G.	Good	Fair	Poor
3500	—	—	—	—	—

828 U 20-Gauge Nickel

NIB	Exc.	V.G.	Good	Fair	Poor
2980	—	—	—	—	—

828 U Limited Edition

With nickel-plated steel frame, elegant engraved and gold inlayed game scene, and AA-grade Walnut. This 12 ga. with 28-in. barrel shows metalwork finished in B.E.S.T. coating. Limited to 200 units.

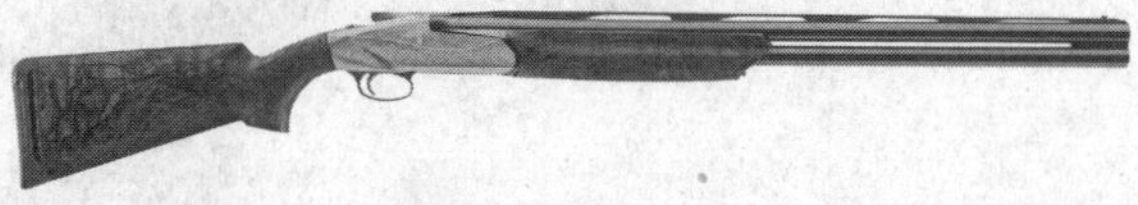

NIB	Exc.	V.G.	Good	Fair	Poor
6400	—	—	—	—	—

828U Steel BE.S.T.

Gauges: 12 ga., 20 ga. Barrels: 26", 28", 30". Stock: AA-grade satin walnut with Progressive Comfort system. Features: Sleek steel receiver that is slightly heavier yet balanced for a smooth swing. Red fiber-optic front sight. Progressive comfort stock system. Gloss-blued barrel finish with satin BE.S.T steel corrosion-resistant treatment. Dual ejectors. Has 3" chambers. Ships with five Crio chokes. 6.85 to 7.65 lbs.

NIB	Exc.	V.G.	Good	Fair	Poor
3230	3000	—	—	—	—

RIFLES

Model R1 Rifle

Introduced in 2003. Chambered for .30-06, .300 Win. Magnum, .270 WSM, .300 WSM, .338 Win. Magnum. Barrels cryogenically treated. Action is gas operated. Interchangeable barrel offered in 20" and 22" in .30-06; 20" and 24" in .300 Win. Magnum. Walnut stock. Detachable magazine has 4-round capacity. Weight about 7 to 7.2 lbs. depending on caliber and barrel length.

NIB	Exc.	V.G.	Good	Fair	Poor
900	650	500	400	300	220

R1 Limited Edition Rifle

High-grade version available from about 2010 to 2013. AAA-grade walnut stock and forend. Coin finished receiver, with engraving of game scenes including gold inlays and adjustable sights. In .30-06 only.

NIB	Exc.	V.G.	Good	Fair	Poor
2500	2000	1500	1100	800	500

Model R1 Carbine

As above, with 20" barrel chambered for .30-06 or .300 Win. Magnum calibers. Weight about 7 lbs.

NIB	Exc.	V.G.	Good	Fair	Poor
950	700	500	400	300	220

Model R1 ComforTech Rifle

Similar to Model R1, with ComforTech recoil-absorbing stock. Introduced 2006. Note: Add 10 percent for Realtree camo and adjustable comb.

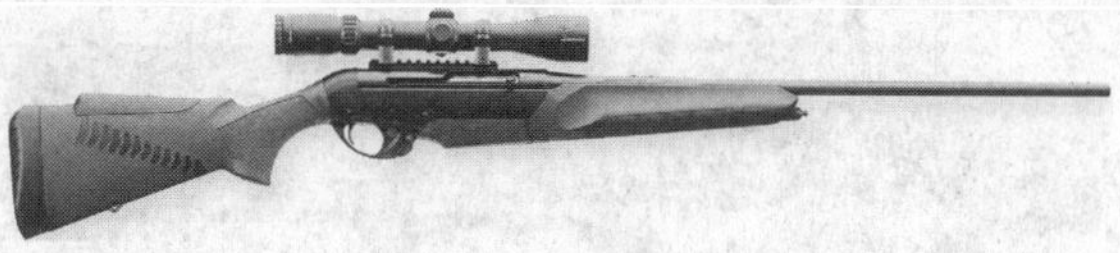

NIB	Exc.	V.G.	Good	Fair	Poor
950	700	500	400	300	220

Model MR1 Rifle

Gas-operated semi-automatic rifle chambered in 5.56 NATO. Features include 16" 1:9 hard chrome-lined barrel, synthetic stock with pistol grip, rotating bolt, military-style aperture sights with Picatinny rail. Comes equipped with 5-round detachable magazine but accepts M16 magazines.

NIB	Exc.	V.G.	Good	Fair	Poor
1140	960	800	550	350	250

Lupo

Calibers: .30-06, .300 WSM, .270 Win. Capacity: 5. Barrel: 22 to 24 in., Crio-treated, free-floating attached to a hardened steel extension. Stock: Synthetic. Sights: None, drilled and tapped. Weight: 7 lbs. Features: Shims allow the stock to be set in 36 different positions, progressive comfort system.

NIB	Exc.	V.G.	Good	Fair	Poor
2030	1900	1800	—	—	—

Lupo Wood B.E.S.T.

Calibers: 6.5 Creedmoor, .308 Win., .300 Win. Mag. Capacity: 4–5 round box magazine. Barrel: 22- and 24-in. Crio-treated, free-floating, threaded barrel with thread cover. Length: 44.225–46.625 in. Stock: AA-grade satin Walnut. Sights: Two-piece Picatinny bases. No iron sights. Weight: 7.1 lbs. Features: The new model Lupo replaces synthetic furniture with Walnut but keeps most other features. Also adds B.E.S.T. surface treatment to metal surfaces for added durability. Trigger reach spacers. Ambidextrous safety. Progressive comfort recoil reduction system. Sub-MOA guarantee.

NIB	Exc.	V.G.	Good	Fair	Poor
1780	—	—	—	—	—

HANDGUNS

Model B-76

All-steel double-action semi-automatic chambered for 9mm Parabellum. Has 4.25-in. barrel, fixed sights and 8-round detachable magazine.

NIB	Exc.	V.G.	Good	Fair	Poor
1110	810	610	410	360	300

Model B-76S

Target version of B-76. Has 5.5-in. barrel, adjustable sights and target-grips.

NIB	Exc.	V.G.	Good	Fair	Poor
1580	1230	930	710	610	510

Model B-77

Similar to B-76 except chambered for .32 ACP.

NIB	Exc.	V.G.	Good	Fair	Poor
420	300	250	200	150	100

Model B-80

Similar to B-76 except chambered for .30 Luger cartridge.

NIB	Exc.	V.G.	Good	Fair	Poor
520	400	300	200	150	100

Model B-80S

Target version of B-80, with 5.5" barrel and adjustable sights. Features target-grips.

NIB	Exc.	V.G.	Good	Fair	Poor
580	480	400	300	200	100

Model MP90S Match (World Cup)

Semi-automatic single-action pistol. Chambered for .22 Short, .22 LR or .32 S&W Wadcutter. Fitted with 4.375" barrel, with walnut match style fully adjustable grips, blade front sight and fully adjustable rear sight. Barrel has adjustable weights below. Magazine capacity 5 rounds. Weight about 39 oz. Previously imported by European American Armory, now imported by Benelli USA. Note: Add 10 percent for .32 S&W.

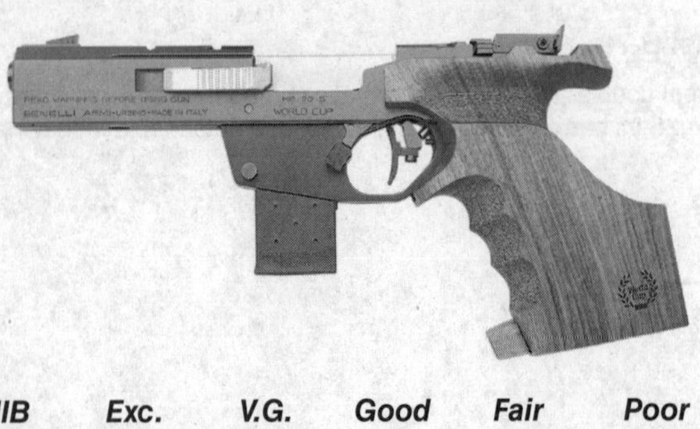

NIB	Exc.	V.G.	Good	Fair	Poor
1450	1250	950	700	400	200

Model MP95E Match (Atlanta)

Similar to above, with anatomically shaped grips. Choice of blue or chrome finish. Previously imported by European American Armory, now imported by Benelli U.S.A. Note: Add $60 for chrome finish.

NIB	Exc.	V.G.	Good	Fair	Poor
1020	880	760	630	530	460

BENTLEY, DAVID
Birmingham, England

Bentley was a prolific maker of both percussion and cartridge arms between 1845 and 1883.

BENTLEY, JOSEPH
Birmingham and Liverpool, England

Best known for his transitional and later patented percussion revolvers, years 1829-1862.

Bentley Revolver (Antique)

.44-caliber double-action percussion revolver, with 7" barrel and 5-shot cylinder. Blued case-hardened, with walnut grips. Found with Webley made frames.

Exc.	Fine	V.G.	Good	Fair	Poor
4500	2750	2370	2000	750	520

BERETTA, DR. FRANCO
Brescia, Italy

This series of shotguns made by Beretta company in Brescia, Italy and imported under Dr. Franco Beretta name in 1980s.

Black Diamond Field Model

Over/under series offered in all standard gauges. Walnut stock, coin-finished receiver, fixed chokes, SST and auto ejectors. Note: Four embellished grades were offered, Grades One through Four, with increasing levels of scrollwork, engraving and higher grades of French walnut stocks.

NIB	Exc.	V.G.	Good	Fair	Poor
800	650	500	400	300	200

Grade One

NIB	Exc.	V.G.	Good	Fair	Poor
1400	1200	1000	850	400	200

Grade Two

NIB	Exc.	V.G.	Good	Fair	Poor
1600	1400	1200	1000	500	300

Grade Three

NIB	Exc.	V.G.	Good	Fair	Poor
2200	1900	1650	1400	600	300

Grade Four

NIB	Exc.	V.G.	Good	Fair	Poor
3500	2800	2250	1750	700	350

Gamma Standard

12-, 16- or 20-gauge boxlock over/under shotgun, with 26" or 28" barrels, single trigger and automatic ejectors. Blued French case-hardened, with walnut stock. Imported from 1984 to 1988.

NIB	Exc.	V.G.	Good	Fair	Poor
900	780	600	420	250	100

Gamma Deluxe

As above, but more finely finished.

NIB	Exc.	V.G.	Good	Fair	Poor
1200	980	800	600	350	120

Gamma Target

As above in trap or skeet version. Imported from 1986 to 1988.

NIB	Exc.	V.G.	Good	Fair	Poor
1200	980	800	600	350	120

America Standard

.410 bore boxlock over/under shotgun, with 26" or 28" barrels. Blued French case-hardened, with walnut stock. Imported from 1984 to 1988.

NIB	Exc.	V.G.	Good	Fair	Poor
650	480	320	280	200	100

America Deluxe

As above, but more finely finished.

NIB	Exc.	V.G.	Good	Fair	Poor
700	520	380	300	220	100

Europa

As above, with 26" barrel and engraved action. Imported from 1984 to 1988.

NIB	Exc.	V.G.	Good	Fair	Poor
800	720	580	420	280	100

Europa Deluxe

As above, but more finely finished.

NIB	Exc.	V.G.	Good	Fair	Poor
850	780	620	480	300	1000

Francia Standard

.410 bore boxlock double-barrel shotgun, with varying barrel lengths, double triggers and manual extractors. Blued, with walnut stock. Imported from 1986 to 1988.

NIB	Exc.	V.G.	Good	Fair	Poor
600	500	380	250	120	100

Alpha Three

12-, 16- or 20-gauge boxlock double-barrel shotgun, with 26" or 28" barrels, single triggers and automatic ejectors. Blued French case-hardened, with walnut stock. Imported from 1984 to 1988.

NIB	Exc.	V.G.	Good	Fair	Poor
750	650	500	320	150	100

Beta Three

Single-barrel break-open field-grade gun. Chambered for all gauges and offered with ventilated rib barrel from 24" to 32" in length. Receiver is chrome-plated and stock of walnut. Imported from 1985 to 1988.

NIB	Exc.	V.G.	Good	Fair	Poor
320	220	200	180	120	40

BERETTA, PIETRO

Brescia, Italy

PISTOLS

Model 1915

7.65mm and 9mm Glisenti caliber semi-automatic pistol, with 3.5-in. barrel, fixed sights and 8-shot magazine. Blued, with walnut grips. The 7.65mm pistol has single-line inscription while 9mm Glisenti has double line. Various styles of wood grips on this model. Manufactured between 1915 and 1922. Replaced by Model 1915/19.

Courtesy James Rankin

Model 1915 in 9mm Glisenti

NIB	Exc.	V.G.	Good	Fair	Poor
—	1510	1260	1010	500	400

Model 1915/1917

Improved version of above pistol. Chambered for 7.65mm cartridge. Also incorporates a new barrel-mounting method and longer cutout in top of slide. Note: Add 100 percent for Navy Model.

Courtesy Orvel Reichert

NIB	Exc.	V.G.	Good	Fair	Poor
—	760	610	280	230	180

Model 1919

Similar to Model 1915 in 6.35mm caliber. Manufactured with minor variations. Different names between 1919 and 1940s.

Courtesy James Rankin

NIB	Exc.	V.G.	Good	Fair	Poor
—	550	450	350	300	150

Model 1923

9mm Glisenti caliber semi-automatic pistol, with 4" barrel and 8-shot magazine. Blued with steel grips. Slide marked, "Brev 1915-1919 Mlo 1923". Manufactured from 1923 to 1935. Add $400 to $500 if slotted for shoulder stock and VG or EXC condition.

NIB	Exc.	V.G.	Good	Fair	Poor
—	2000	1500	800	400	200

Model 1931

7.65mm caliber semi-automatic pistol, with 3.5" barrel and open-top slide. Blued, with walnut grips. Marked "RM" separated by an anchor.

NIB	Exc.	V.G.	Good	Fair	Poor
—	500	420	320	250	180

Model 1934

As above with 9mm short (.380 ACP) caliber. Slide marked "P. Beretta Cal. 9 Corto-Mo 1934 Brevet Gardone VT." This inscription is followed by date of manufacture that was given numerically, followed by a Roman numeral that denoted year of manufacture on Fascist calendar, which began in 1922. Examples are marked "RM" (Navy), "RE" (Army), "RA" (Air Force) and "PS" (Police). Manufactured between 1934 and 1959. This was a main service pistol for Italian Armed Forces during WWII.

Courtesy Orvel Reichert

NIB	Exc.	V.G.	Good	Fair	Poor
—	650	550	400	180	100

Air Force "RA" marked

NIB	Exc.	V.G.	Good	Fair	Poor
—	800	650	500	250	180

Navy "RM" marked

NIB	Exc.	V.G.	Good	Fair	Poor
—	850	700	550	280	200

Model 1934 Romanian Contract

Identical to Model 1934, except slide marked "9mm Scurt" instead of 9mm Corto.

NIB	Exc.	V.G.	Good	Fair	Poor
—	700	600	450	280	180

Model 1935

As above in 7.65mm caliber. Post-war versions are known. Manufactured from 1935 to 1959.

Courtesy Orvel Reichert

NIB	Exc.	V.G.	Good	Fair	Poor
—	400	380	250	180	120

Model 318

Improved version of old Model 1919, with butt reshaped to afford a better grip. Chambered for .25 ACP cartridge. Has 2.5" barrel. Variety of finishes with plastic grips. In U.S. known as "Panthe". Manufactured between 1935 and 1946.

NIB	Exc.	V.G.	Good	Fair	Poor
—	350	280	250	180	120

Model 418

As above, with rounded grip and cocking indicator. Known as "Bantam" in U.S. Introduced in 1947.

NIB	Exc.	V.G.	Good	Fair	Poor
—	280	220	180	120	90

Model 420

Engraved and chrome-plated Model 418.

NIB	Exc.	V.G.	Good	Fair	Poor
—	350	300	280	200	150

Model 421

Engraved gold-plated Model 418, with tortoise-shell grips.

NIB	Exc.	V.G.	Good	Fair	Poor
—	480	420	320	250	150

Model 948

.22 LR version of Model 1934. Either 3.5" or 6" barrel.

NIB	Exc.	V.G.	Good	Fair	Poor
—	350	300	200	120	90

Model 949 Olympic Target

.22-caliber semi-automatic pistol, with 8.75" barrel, adjustable sights and muzzle brake. Blued, with checkered walnut grips. Manufactured from 1959 to 1964.

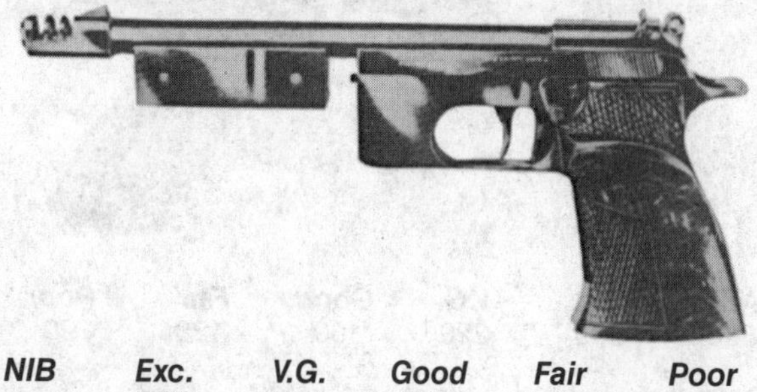

NIB	Exc.	V.G.	Good	Fair	Poor
—	750	600	500	400	200

U22 Neos 4.5/6.0

Semi-automatic .22-caliber pistol. Introduced in 2002. Chambered for .22 LR cartridge. Fitted with 4.5" or 6" barrel, with integral scope rail. Magazine capacity 10 rounds. Weight about 32- to 36 oz. depending on barrel length.

NIB	Exc.	V.G.	Good	Fair	Poor
250	200	160	120	100	80

U22 Neos 4.5 Inox/6.0 Inox

Same as above, with special two-tone finish.

NIB	Exc.	V.G.	Good	Fair	Poor
300	250	200	150	100	80

U22 Neos 6.0/7.5 DLX

Introduced in 2003. Features 6" or 7.5" barrel, with target sights and polymer grips with inlays. Adjustable trigger and interchangeable sights. Laser-engraved slide. Weight about 36 oz.

NIB	Exc.	V.G.	Good	Fair	Poor
340	280	200	150	100	80

U22 Neos 6.0/7.5 Inox DLX

As above, with Inox finish.

NIB	Exc.	V.G.	Good	Fair	Poor
380	300	220	160	120	90

BERETTA 70 SERIES

These pistols began production in 1958 replacing Models 1934, 1935, 948 and 949. During late 1960s, several of these models briefly utilized a 100 series designation for U.S. market. During latter part of 1970s, a magazine safety was added to 70 series and pistols became known as Model 70S. The 70S designation replaced model designations 70 through 75 making these older model numbers obsolete. Only Model 76 designation continued.

The 70 Series design included a cross bolt safety, sear block safety, slide hold-open device and push-button magazine release. Shortly after its introduction, cross bolt safety pushbutton was replaced with lever-type sear block safety located in the same place.

Note: Above information was supplied by contributing editor John Stimson, Jr.

Model 70 (Model 100)

Model 948 with cross bolt safety, hold-open device and push-button magazine release. Fixed sights. There are a number of sub-variations available chambered for .22 LR, .32 ACP and .380 ACP cartridges. Available with 3.5" or 5.9" barrel. Has a detachable magazine. Also known as "Puma" when marketed in U.S. by J.L. Galef & Sons. Introduced in 1958. Discontinued in 1985.

NIB	Exc.	V.G.	Good	Fair	Poor
520	450	350	280	120	80

Model 70S

Improved Model 70. Chambered for 7.65 (.32 ACP), 9mm Corto (.380 ACP) and .22 LR cartridge. Magazine capacity 7, 8 and 9 rounds respectively.

NIB	Exc.	V.G.	Good	Fair	Poor
550	480	380	300	120	80

Model 71/Jaguar (Model 101)

Similar to above. Chambered for .22 LR cartridge. Magazine capacity 10 rounds. Frame is alloy. Fitted with 5.9" barrel. Models imported into U.S. prior to 1968 were fitted with 3.5" barrels.

NIB	Exc.	V.G.	Good	Fair	Poor
420	380	300	220	120	80

Model 72

Essentially a Model 71. Sold with two sets of barrels; 3.5" and 5.9". Fixed sights.

NIB	Exc.	V.G.	Good	Fair	Poor
450	400	320	250	150	120

Model 76 (102)

A .22 LR target pistol. Barrel shrouded with an aluminum sleeve. Rear part of sleeve extended above slide to hold an adjustable rear sight.

Marketed in U.S. as "Sable". Magazine capacity 10 rounds. Briefly after 1968, imported into U.S. as Model 102 "New Sable".

Courtesy John J. Stimson, Jr.

NIB	Exc.	V.G.	Good	Fair	Poor
800	730	660	580	460	390

Model 950/Minx

.22-caliber semi-automatic pistol, with 2.25" barrel hinged at front. This could be pivoted forward for cleaning or loading, making this a semi-automatic or single-shot pistol. Blued, with plastic grips. Introduced in 1955. A 4" barrel version also available. Known as "Minx" in U.S.

NIB	Exc.	V.G.	Good	Fair	Poor
320	250	220	140	100	50

Model 950B/Jetfire

As above in .25-caliber. Known as "Jetfire" in U.S.

NIB	Exc.	V.G.	Good	Fair	Poor
320	250	220	140	100	50

Model 950 Jetfire Inox

Same as Model 950 Jetfire, with stainless steel finish. Introduced in 2000.

NIB	Exc.	V.G.	Good	Fair	Poor
340	250	180	140	80	50

Model 3032 Tomcat

Double-action semi-automatic pistol. Similar in appearance to Model 950. Chambered for .32 ACP cartridge. Barrel length 2.45"; overall length 5". Fixed blade front sight and drift adjustable rear sight. Plastic grips. Seven-round magazine. Blued or matte black finish. Weight 14.5 oz. Note: Add $30 for blued finish.

NIB	Exc.	V.G.	Good	Fair	Poor
380	320	250	200	1350	80

Model 3032 Tomcat Inox

Same as above, with stainless steel finish. Introduced in 2000.

NIB	Exc.	V.G.	Good	Fair	Poor
400	320	250	200	120	80

Model 3032 Tomcat Titanium

Same as above, with titanium finish and plastic grips. Weight about 16 oz. Introduced in 2001.

NIB	Exc.	V.G.	Good	Fair	Poor
580	450	350	290	210	150

Alley Cat

Introduced in 2001. Special limited run promotion pistol. Chambered for .32 ACP cartridge. Model is a Tomcat, with special features such as AO Big Dot night sights. Supplied with an Alcantara inside-the-pants holster.

NIB	Exc.	V.G.	Good	Fair	Poor
580	450	350	290	210	150

Model 951

9mm caliber semi-automatic pistol, with 4.5" barrel and fixed sights. Blued, with plastic grips. Known as "Brigadier" at one time. Introduced 1952.

NIB	Exc.	V.G.	Good	Fair	Poor
—	450	380	280	150	100

Model 20

.25 ACP double-action pistol, with 2.5" barrel and 9-shot magazine. Blued, with walnut or plastic grips. Discontinued in 1985.

NIB	Exc.	V.G.	Good	Fair	Poor
300	250	200	150	90	80

Model 21 Bobcat

Small frame semi-automatic pistol. Chambered for .22 LR or .25 ACP cartridge. Features 2.4" tip-up barrel with fixed sights. Magazine capacity of 8 rounds (.25 ACP) or 7 rounds (.22 LR). Comes with plastic or walnut grips. Deluxe version with gold line engraving. Weight about 11 to 11.8 oz. depending on caliber.

Standard Model

NIB	Exc.	V.G.	Good	Fair	Poor
320	280	250	220	180	100

Model 21EL

Gold engraved model.

NIB	Exc.	V.G.	Good	Fair	Poor
400	350	320	280	200	110

Model 21 Inox

Stainless steel.

NIB	Exc.	V.G.	Good	Fair	Poor
320	250	200	140	100	80

Model 90

Double-action semi-automatic .32 auto pocket pistol, with 3.5" barrel and 8-round magazine. Manufactured from 1969 to 1983.

NIB	Exc.	V.G.	Good	Fair	Poor
—	400	350	300	200	120

92 SERIES

Model 92

9mm caliber double-action semi-automatic pistol, with 5" barrel, fixed sights and 16-round double-stack magazine. Blued, with plastic grips. Introduced in 1976. Now discontinued.

NIB	Exc.	V.G.	Good	Fair	Poor
860	730	630	500	320	270

Model 92SB-P

As above, with polished finish. Manufactured from 1980 to 1985.

NIB	Exc.	V.G.	Good	Fair	Poor
620	480	400	320	250	200

Model 92SB Compact

As above, with 4.3" barrel and shortened grip frame that holds a 14-shot magazine. Blued or nickel-plated, with wood or plastic grips. Introduced in 1980. Discontinued in 1985. Note: Add $20 for wood grips; 15 percent for nickel version.

NIB	Exc.	V.G.	Good	Fair	Poor
500	420	380	320	250	200

Model 92FS

Current production Model 92 chambered for 9mm Parabellum cartridge. Barrel length 4.9". Rear sight is 3-dot combat drift adjustable. Magazine capacity 15 rounds. Semi-automatic pistol features double-/single-action operation. Safety is manual type. Frame is light alloy sandblasted and anodized black. Barrel slide is steel. Grips are plastic checkered, with black matte finish. Equipped with spare magazine cleaning rod and hard carrying case. Weight 34.4 oz. empty.

NIB	Exc.	V.G.	Good	Fair	Poor
600	500	460	390	310	280

Model 92FS Inox

Introduced in 2001. Chambered for 9mm cartridge. Fitted with 4.9" barrel. Slide is black stainless steel, with lightweight frame and combat-style triggerguard, reversible magazine release and ambidextrous safety. Gray wrap-around grips. Weight about 34 oz.

NIB	Exc.	V.G.	Good	Fair	Poor
700	580	420	350	220	180

Model 96

Identical to Model 92FS. Fitted with 10-round magazine. Chambered for .40 S&W. Introduced in 1992.

NIB	Exc.	V.G.	Good	Fair	Poor
600	500	460	390	310	280

Model 96 Combat

Introduced in 1997. Single-action-only, with competition tuned trigger. Developed for practical shooting competition. Barrel length 5.9". Supplied with weight as standard. Rear sight is adjustable target type. Tool kit included as standard. Weight 40 oz.

NIB	Exc.	V.G.	Good	Fair	Poor
1360	1060	910	780	560	500

Model 96 Stock

Similar to Model 96 in double-/single-action, with half-cock notch for cocked and locked carry. Fitted with 4.9" barrel with fixed sights. Three interchangeable front sights are supplied as standard. Weight 35 oz. Introduced in 1997. No longer in U.S. product line.

NIB	Exc.	V.G.	Good	Fair	Poor
1200	990	860	730	550	490

Model 96A1

An evolution of the M9 service pistol for military and law enforcement. Chambered in .40 S&W, this model comes with three 12-round magazines. Features include an integral Picatinny accessory rail, improved recoil buffer and Bruniton finish.

NIB	Exc.	V.G.	Good	Fair	Poor
660	580	490	440	300	280

Model 92A1

Chambered for 9mm. Other features identical to Model 96A1.

NIB	Exc.	V.G.	Good	Fair	Poor
680	580	480	380	250	150

Model 92/96FS Inox

Same as above except barrel, slide, trigger, extractor and other components are made of stainless steel. Frame made of lightweight anodized aluminum alloy. Model 96FS discontinued in 1993.

NIB	Exc.	V.G.	Good	Fair	Poor
680	550	450	350	300	280

Model 92/96FS Centurion

Chambered for 9mm or .40 S&W (Model 96). Features 4.3" barrel, but retains full grip to accommodate 15-round magazine (9mm); 10 rounds (.40 S&W). Weight about 33.2 oz. Introduced in 1993. Black sandblasted finish.

NIB	Exc.	V.G.	Good	Fair	Poor
550	450	400	300	200	150

Model 92FS/96 Brigadier

Same as 92FS and 96, with heavier slide to reduce felt recoil. Removable front sight. Weight about 35 oz.

NIB	Exc.	V.G.	Good	Fair	Poor
660	550	400	300	150	80

Model 92FS/96 Brigadier Inox

Same as above, with stainless steel finish. Introduced in 2000.

NIB	Exc.	V.G.	Good	Fair	Poor
700	600	480	320	180	100

Model 92G-SD/96G-SD

Introduced in 2003. Features a decock mechanism built around single-/double-action trigger system. In addition, pistol has an integral accessory rail on frame. Fitted with 9mm or .40 S&W, 4.9" barrel, with heavy slide and 3-dot tritium sights. Weight about 35 oz.

NIB	Exc.	V.G.	Good	Fair	Poor
1000	750	500	350	200	120

Model 92F

9mm Parabellum caliber double-action semi-automatic pistol, with 4.9" barrel, fixed sights and 15-shot double-stack magazine and an extended base. Matte blued finish, with walnut or plastic grips. Introduced in 1984. No longer in production.

NIB	Exc.	V.G.	Good	Fair	Poor
600	500	450	380	300	280

Model 92F U.S. Marked Slide

A special limited edition of 100 pistols made for the Armed Forces Reserves, with BER prefix serial numbers and U.S. M9 markings on frame and slide.

NIB	Exc.	V.G.	Good	Fair	Poor
1700	1500	1250	900	—	—

Model 92F Compact

As above, with 4.3" barrel and 13-shot magazine. No longer in production.

NIB	Exc.	V.G.	Good	Fair	Poor
550	460	400	380	300	280

Model 92/96 Compact "Type M"

Essentially same as Model 92FS Compact, with the exception of a single column magazine that holds 8 rounds and reduces grip thickness of pistol. Weight 30.9 oz. Discontinued in 1993, reintroduced in 1998. Model 96 version (.40 S&W) introduced in 2000. Note: Add $90 for Tritium night sights.

NIB	Exc.	V.G.	Good	Fair	Poor
700	550	350	300	200	150

Model 92/96M Compact Inox

Same as above, with stainless steel slide and frame. Introduced in 2000.

NIB	Exc.	V.G.	Good	Fair	Poor
700	550	450	350	300	200

Model 92D Compact "Type M"

Same as above, with double-action-only trigger function. Note: Add $90 for Tritium night sights.

NIB	Exc.	V.G.	Good	Fair	Poor
550	450	350	300	200	150

Model 92FS Deluxe

Identical dimensions to full size Model 92FS. Addition of gold-plated engraved frame and gold-plated extra magazine. In fitted leather presentation hard case. Grips walnut briar, with gold initial plate. Introduced in 1993.

NIB	Exc.	V.G.	Good	Fair	Poor
5500	4500	3000	2000	1500	1000

Model 92FS "470th Anniversary" Limited Edition

Limited to only 470 pistols worldwide. Features high polish finish, with stainless steel gold-filled engravings, walnut grips, Anniversary logo on top of slide and on back of chrome plated magazine. Supplied with walnut case.

NIB	Exc.	V.G.	Good	Fair	Poor
2080	1300	800	600	380	200

Model 92/96D

Same specifications as standard Model 92 and Model 96. Variation has no visible hammer. Double-action-only. No manual safety. Weight 33.8 oz.

NIB	Exc.	V.G.	Good	Fair	Poor
420	380	320	280	200	150

Model 92/96DS

Same as above, with same manual safety as found on 92FS pistol. Introduced in 1994.

NIB	Exc.	V.G.	Good	Fair	Poor
420	380	320	280	200	150

Model 92G/96G

Designed for French Gendarmerie. This model has now been adopted for French Air Force as well as other government agencies. Features hammer drop lever that does not function as safety when lever is released, but lowers hammer and returns to ready to fire position automatically. Offered to law enforcement agencies only.

NIB	Exc.	V.G.	Good	Fair	Poor
650	550	480	400	250	100

Model 92/96 Vertec

Introduced in 2002. Chambered for 9mm or .40 S&W cartridges. Fitted with 4.7" barrel. Double-/single-action trigger. Features a new vertical grip design, with shorter trigger reach and thin grip panels. Removable front sight and integral accessory rail on frame. Magazine capacity 10 rounds. Weight about 32 oz.

NIB	Exc.	V.G.	Good	Fair	Poor
700	580	420	300	220	160

Model 92 Competition Conversion Kit

Kit includes 7.3" barrel, with counterweight and elevated front sight, semi-automatic, walnut grips and fully adjustable rear sight. Comes in special carrying case, with basic pistol. Note: Kit Price Only.

NIB	Exc.	V.G.	Good	Fair	Poor
500	350	300	200	150	100

Model 92/96 Combo

Features specially designed Model 96 pistol, with extra 92FS slide and barrel assembly. Barrel lengths are 4.66". Sold with one 10-round magazine in both 9mm and .40 S&W.

NIB	Exc.	V.G.	Good	Fair	Poor
850	720	600	420	280	200

Model M9 Limited Edition

Introduced in 1995 to commemorate 10th Anniversary of U.S. military's official sidearm. This 9mm pistol limited to 10,000 units. Special engraving on slide with special serial numbers. Slide stamped "U.S. 9mm M9-BERETTA U.S.A.-65490".

Standard Model

NIB	*Exc.*	*V.G.*	*Good*	*Fair*	*Poor*
820	700	450	300	200	100

Deluxe Model

Walnut grips, with gold plated hammer and grip screws.

NIB	*Exc.*	*V.G.*	*Good*	*Fair*	*Poor*
880	750	500	350	200	100

Model 92 Billennium

Introduced in 2001. Limited production pistol of 2,000 units world wide. Chambered for 9mm cartridge. Steel frame, with checkered front and backstrap. Nickel alloy finish, with unique engraving. Carbon fiber grips. Interchangeable sights, with adjustable rear sight. Carry case standard. Single action.

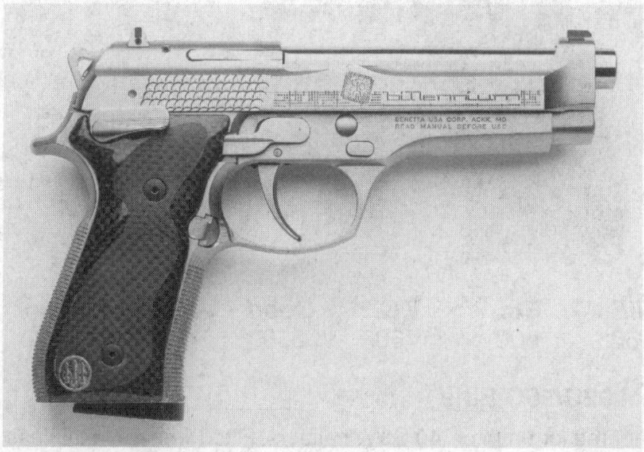

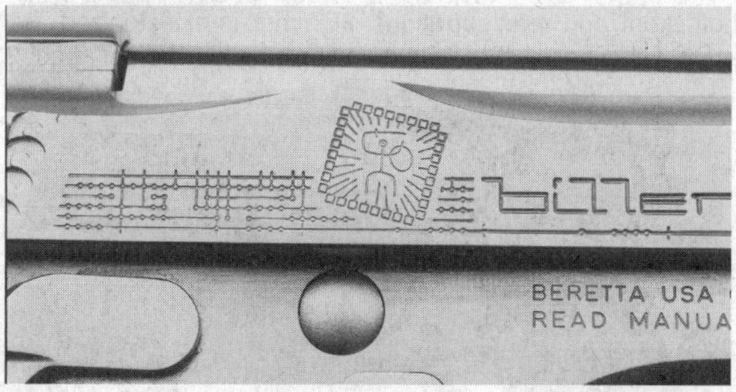

NIB	*Exc.*	*V.G.*	*Good*	*Fair*	*Poor*
1760	1460	1110	900	660	580

92 Steel-I

Steel-frame semi-automatic in 9mm or .40 S&W. Single- or single-/double-action. 15+1 capacity, 4.7" barrel, weight 42.3 oz. IDPA certified. Fixed 3-dot sights. Introduced 2006.

NIB	*Exc.*	*V.G.*	*Good*	*Fair*	*Poor*
1350	1000	700	480	300	150

M9A1

Semi-automatic single-/double-action in 9mm developed for U.S. Marine Corps. Capacity 10+1 or 15+1. Fixed sights. Introduced 2006.

NIB	*Exc.*	*V.G.*	*Good*	*Fair*	*Poor*
820	650	450	300	200	120

M9A3

Upgraded M9 chambered in 9mm. Can be converted from safety/decocker. Has 4.9" threaded barrel, two-tone Flat Dark Earth/Gray finish, Picatinny rail, removable front sight and Vertec straight-grip with wrap-around backstrap.

NIB	*Exc.*	*V.G.*	*Good*	*Fair*	*Poor*
1000	900	800	710	560	500

92X SERIES

The latest iteration of the Model 92 line, 92X series includes straight backstrap, wrap-around high-texture thin grips, combat sights, extended magazine release, convertible from safety-decocker to decocker only, beveled mag well, DA/SA, 9mm.

Model 92X Full Size

9mm, Picatinny rail. 15-, 17-, or 10-round mags, 4.7" barrel. 33.3 oz.

NIB	*Exc.*	*V.G.*	*Good*	*Fair*	*Poor*
680	600	580	—	—	—

Model 92X Compact

9mm. Models available with or without rail. 10- or 13-round mags, 4.25" barrel. 27.2 oz.

NIB	Exc.	V.G.	Good	Fair	Poor
680	600	580	—	—	—

Model 92X Centurion

9mm, Picatinny rail. 15-, 17-, or 10-round mags. 4.25" barrel. 28.5 oz. Introduced 2020.

Model 92X Performance

Similar to Model 92 series but for competition. Chambered for 9mm cartridge. Barrel length 4.9". Adjustable rear sight, fiber-optic front. Magazine capacity 15 rounds. Semi-automatic pistol features double-/single-action operation with Extreme-S trigger mechanism. Safety is manual type on frame. Frame is Vertec-style made of steel with beaver tail. Slide is Brigadier style. Grips are texture polymer, with matte stainless finish. Weight 47.61 oz. empty.

NIB	Exc.	V.G.	Good	Fair	Poor
1400	1300	1250	1200	1000	800

ELITE TEAM SERIES

In 1999, Beretta introduced a new series of pistols based on company's M92/96 pistol. Each of these pistols has specific features for specific shooting requirements.

Model 92/96 Custom Carry

Fitted with 4.3" barrel, shortened grip and low profile control levers. Safety lever is left side only. Magazine capacity 10 rounds. "CUSTOM CARRY" engraved on slide. Chambered for 9mm or .40 S&W calibers.

NIB	Exc.	V.G.	Good	Fair	Poor
620	500	400	300	200	100

Model 92/96 Border Marshall

Commercial version of pistol built for Immigration and Naturalization Service. Fitted with heavy-duty steel slide and short 4.7" I.N.S. style barrel. Rubber grips and night sights are standard. "BORDER MARSHALL" engraved on slide. Offered in 9mm or .40 S&W calibers.

NIB	Exc.	V.G.	Good	Fair	Poor
750	600	480	350	220	150

Model 92G/96G Elite

Chambered for 9mm or .40 S&W calibers. Fitted with 4.7" stainless steel barrel and heavy-duty Brigadier-style slide. Action is decock only. Slide has both front and rear serrations. Hammer is skeletonized. Beveled magazine well. Special "ELITE" engraving on slide. Weight about 35 oz.

NIB	Exc.	V.G.	Good	Fair	Poor
820	650	450	380	250	160

Model 92G Elite II

Version of Elite was developed for competition shooter. Fitted with 4.7" barrel and heavy slide. Has skeletonized hammer. Beveled magazine well and extended release. Checkered front and backstrap grip. Weight about 35 oz.

NIB	Exc.	V.G.	Good	Fair	Poor
920	720	550	400	280	150

Model 92G Elite LTT

Version of Elite developed with Langdon Tactical. Fitted with 4.7" barrel, M9A1 frame, Vertec slide with front cocking serrations. Has skeletonized hammer. Beveled magazine well and extended release. Checkered front and backstrap grip. Weight 35 oz.

NIB	Exc.	V.G.	Good	Fair	Poor
1100	1000	900	880	500	480

Model 92FS Inox Tactical

Model has satin matte finish on its stainless steel slide. Frame is anodized aluminum. Black rubber grips and night sights are standard. Offered in 9mm only.

NIB	Exc.	V.G.	Good	Fair	Poor
780	620	500	350	220	100

COUGAR SERIES

Model 8000/8040/8045 Cougar

Compact size pistol using a short recoil rotating barrel. Features a firing pin lock, chrome lined barrel, anodized aluminum alloy frame, with Bruniton finish. Overall length 7"; barrel length 3.6"; overall height 5.5"; unloaded weight 33.5 oz. Offered in double-/single-action as well as double-action-only. Magazine holds 10 rounds. Available in 9mm or .40 S&W. In 1998 Beretta added .45 ACP caliber. Note: Add $50 for .45 ACP and Inox stainless finish.

NIB	Exc.	V.G.	Good	Fair	Poor
620	520	400	350	250	150

Model 8000/8040/8045 Mini Cougar

Introduced in 1997. Similar in design to full size model. Offered in 9mm, .40 S&W or .45 ACP. Fitted with 3.6" barrel (3.7" on .45 ACP). Empty weight 27 oz. Offered in double-/single-action or double-action-only. Magazine capacity: 10 rounds for 9mm; 8 rounds for .40 S&W. Weight between 27 oz. and 30 oz. depending on caliber. Note: Add $50 for .45 ACP and Inox stainless finish.

NIB	Exc.	V.G.	Good	Fair	Poor
500	450	350	220	120	80

Model 8000F—Cougar L

Similar to above. Fitted with a shortened grip frame. Chambered for 9mm cartridge. Fitted with a 3.6" barrel. Overall height as been reduced by .4". Weight about 28 oz. Introduced in 2003.

NIB	Exc.	V.G.	Good	Fair	Poor
600	500	400	300	180	100

Model 9000F

Introduced in 2000. Chambered for 9mm or .40 S&W cartridge. Fitted with 3.4" barrel. Has polymer frame. "F" type has single-/double-action trigger. Fixed sights. Magazine capacity 10 rounds. Weight about 27 oz.; overall length 6.6"; overall height 4.8". External hammer and black finish.

NIB	*Exc.*	*V.G.*	*Good*	*Fair*	*Poor*
550	450	350	200	120	80

Model 9000D

Same as above, with double-action-only trigger.

NIB	*Exc.*	*V.G.*	*Good*	*Fair*	*Poor*
550	450	350	280	150	100

Model 9000S

Chambered for 9mm or .40 S&W cartridges. Magazine capacity 10 rounds. Optional spacer Model 92/96 magazines can also be used. Three-dot sight system. Accessory magazine bottom that extends when griped, but retracts when holstered is standard. Steel alloy frame and slide. Weight about 27 oz. Introduced in 2001.

NIB	*Exc.*	*V.G.*	*Good*	*Fair*	*Poor*
550	450	350	200	120	80

CHEETAH SERIES

Model 84/Cheetah

Small semi-automatic pistol chambered for .380 cartridge. Double-column magazine that holds 13 rounds. Offered in blue or nickel finish. Grips are checkered black plastic or checkered wood.

NIB	*Exc.*	*V.G.*	*Good*	*Fair*	*Poor*
590	460	370	320	210	190

Model 84BB

Similar to Model 84, but incorporates different features such as a firing pin blocking device and loaded chamber indicator. Single-column magazine holds 8 rounds of .380 shells. Discontinued in 1993.

NIB	*Exc.*	*V.G.*	*Good*	*Fair*	*Poor*
420	380	320	280	200	150

Model 85/Cheetah

Similar in appearance to Model 84. Features single-column magazine, with capacity of 8 rounds. Available in blue or nickel finish. Grips are checkered black plastic. Weight 22 oz.

NIB	*Exc.*	*V.G.*	*Good*	*Fair*	*Poor*
700	580	480	400	300	260

Model 86/Cheetah

.380 ACP semi-automatic pistol has 4.4" tip-up barrel. Magazine capacity 8 rounds. Furnished with checkered wood grips. Weight 23 oz.

NIB	*Exc.*	*V.G.*	*Good*	*Fair*	*Poor*
680	500	300	250	200	150

Model 87/Cheetah

.22-caliber double-action semi-automatic target pistol, with 3.8" or 6" barrel, adjustable sights and 7-shot magazine. Blued, with checkered walnut grips. Introduced in 1986.

NIB	*Exc.*	*V.G.*	*Good*	*Fair*	*Poor*
830	730	660	580	380	280

Model 87 Target

.22-caliber single-action target pistol. Features adjustable rear sight, integral scope base and external hammer. Anodized aluminum frame. Weight about 41 oz. Introduced in 2000.

NIB	*Exc.*	*V.G.*	*Good*	*Fair*	*Poor*
930	800	680	600	400	300

Model 89/Gold Standard

.22-caliber semi-automatic target pistol, with adjustable sights and 10-shot detachable magazine. Matte finish, with hand-fitting walnut grips. Introduced in 1988.

NIB	*Exc.*	*V.G.*	*Good*	*Fair*	*Poor*
900	720	550	400	300	150

Model APX

A striker-fired polymer-frame pistol series chambered in 9mm or .40 S&W. Barrel is 4.25" and magazine capacity 10 rounds (where required), 14 (.40) or 17 (9mm), Safety features include a striker deactivation button, trigger safety and firing-pin block safety. Weight 29 oz. Combat model has threaded barrel; RDO model a cut-out section for optics. Grip frame housing has interchangeable insert available in OD Green, FDE or Wolf Gray finish. Introduced in 2017/2018. Note: Add $150 for Combat model; $75 for RDO

NIB	*Exc.*	*V.G.*	*Good*	*Fair*	*Poor*
480	400	320	250	200	150

APX Centurion

Similar to APX but mid-size version. Barrel is 3.7" and magazine capacity is 10 (where required), 13 (40) or 15 (9mm). Weight: 27 oz. Available in matte black finish. Introduced 2018.

NIB	*Exc.*	*V.G.*	*Good*	*Fair*	*Poor*
480	400	320	250	200	150

APX Carry

Similar to APX but sub-compact version. Barrel is 3" and magazine capacity is 6 (9mm). Weight: 19.8 oz. Grip frame housing has interchangeable insert available in OD Green, FDE or Wolf Gray finish. Introduced 2018.

NIB	Exc.	V.G.	Good	Fair	Poor
480	400	320	250	200	150

Model PX4 Storm Pistol

Introduced in 2005. Features single-/double action trigger, with decocker and chambered for 9mm, .45 ACP or .40 S&W cartridges. Fitted with 4" barrel. Interchangeable grip backstraps. Reversible magazine release button. Picatinny rail. Fixed sights. Magazine capacity: 14 rounds .40 S&W, 17 rounds 9mm. Weight about 27.5 lbs. Compact model has 3.2" barrel and smaller grip frame. Magazine capacity reduced by two rounds.

NIB	Exc.	V.G.	Good	Fair	Poor
500	450	380	250	200	120

Model PX4 Storm Inox

Same features as PX4 Storm, except for stainless steel slide. Introduced in 2015.

NIB	Exc.	V.G.	Good	Fair	Poor
580	500	400	—	—	—

Model PX4 Storm Compact Carry

Same features as PX4 Storm, except Compact Carry size. Introduced in 2018.

NIB	Exc.	V.G.	Good	Fair	Poor
900	800	780	700	500	400

Model PX4 Storm Subcompact

Similar to above, with smaller dimensions and chambered in 9mm and .40 S&W only. Round capacity: 10- (.40) or 13- (9mm). Overall length 6.2". Weight: 26.1 oz.

NIB	Exc.	V.G.	Good	Fair	Poor
500	450	380	250	200	120

Model PX4 Storm SD (Special Duty)

Similar to PX4 Storm in .45 ACP only. Matte black slide and OD polymer frame, 9- or 10-round magazine. Overall length 8.2". Weight 28.6 oz.

NIB	Exc.	V.G.	Good	Fair	Poor
900	750	580	450	300	150

90-Two

Wrap-around polymer grip standard or slim. Single-/double-action semi-automatic in 9mm (10+1, 15+1 or 17+1 capacity) or .40 S&W (10+1 or 12+1 capacity). Types D, F or G. Fixed sights. 4.9" barrel, 32.5 oz. Introduced 2006. Note: Add 10 percent for luminous sights.

NIB	Exc.	V.G.	Good	Fair	Poor
600	480	350	290	210	150

BU9 Nano

Micro-compact DA-only 9mm, with 6+1 round capacity, 3" barrel, polymer frame, adjustable sights. Weight 17 oz. Introduced 2011.

NIB	Exc.	V.G.	Good	Fair	Poor
420	380	300	220	150	100

Pico

Similar to Nano, except chambered in .380 ACP with a more compact design. Double-action-only firing system, with 2.7" barrel. Width .725", weight 11.5 oz. Adjustable sights, ambidextrous slide release and comes with two 6+1 magazines. Introduced in 2013.

NIB	Exc.	V.G.	Good	Fair	Poor
350	320	250	200	150	100

Stampede

Introduced in 2003. Single-action revolver chambered for .45 Colt, .44-40 or .357 Magnum cartridge. Choice of 4.75", 5.5" or 7.5" barrel. Blued, with Beretta case color and black polymer grips. Weight about 2.3 lbs. depending on barrel length. Discontinued in 2013.

NIB	Exc.	V.G.	Good	Fair	Poor
520	400	280	200	120	80

Stampede Buntline

.45 Colt with 18" barrel, satin-finish grips and gold Beretta medallion. Other features similar to Stampede Blue model.

NIB	Exc.	V.G.	Good	Fair	Poor
800	700	550	480	350	250

Stampede Nickel

Similar to Stampede Blue, with brushed nickel finish and walnut grips.

NIB	Exc.	V.G.	Good	Fair	Poor
500	400	300	200	120	80

Stampede Deluxe

As above, with charcoal blue finish and Beretta case color. Select walnut grips.

NIB	Exc.	V.G.	Good	Fair	Poor
620	500	380	250	200	120

Stampede Patton Model

Similar to Deluxe model, with light engraving on case color frame, light gold inlays and faux ivory grips.

NIB	Exc.	V.G.	Good	Fair	Poor
900	800	700	600	450	350

Stampede Bisley

Single-action 6-shot Bisley. Replica revolver in .45 Colt or .357 Magnum. Blued, with 4.75", 5.5" or 7.5" barrel. Introduced 2006. Note: Add 10 percent for nickel.

NIB	Exc.	V.G.	Good	Fair	Poor
620	500	380	250	200	120

Laramie

Break-open single-action revolver. Reminiscent of S&W #3. Chambered for.45 LC or .38 Special. Six-shot cylinder. Adjustable rear sight. 5" or 6.5" barrels. Introduced 2006. Discontinued 2008. Made by Beretta subsidiary Uberti. Note: Add 10 percent for nickel finish.

NIB	Exc.	V.G.	Good	Fair	Poor
1000	880	600	380	220	140

RIFLES

1873 Renegade Short Lever-Action Rifle

Lever-action rifle chambered in .45 Colt, .357 Magnum. Patterned after 1873 Winchester. Features include 20" round barrel, blued finish, checkered walnut buttstock and forend, adjustable rear sight and fixed blade front. Ten-round tubular magazine.

NIB	Exc.	V.G.	Good	Fair	Poor
1400	1050	880	600	380	220

Gold Rush Slide-Action Rifle and Carbine

External replica of old Colt Lightning Magazine Rifle. Chambered in .357 Magnum and .45 Colt. Features include 20" round or 24.5" octagonal barrel, case-hardened receiver, walnut buttstock and forend, crescent buttplate, 13-round (rifle) or 10-round (carbine) magazine. Available as Standard Carbine, Standard Rifle or Deluxe Rifle.

NIB	Exc.	V.G.	Good	Fair	Poor
1200	1050	880	600	380	220

Cx4 Storm

Introduced in 2003. Semi-automatic carbine has 16.6" barrel. Chambered for 9mm, .40 S&W or .45 ACP cartridge. Synthetic stock, with rubber recoil pad that has adjustable stock spacers. Ghost ring rear sight, with adjustable post front sight. Forward accessory rail. Magazine capacity: 10 rounds .40 S&W or 9mm; 8 rounds .45 ACP. Weight about 5.75 lbs.

NIB	Exc.	V.G.	Good	Fair	Poor
800	650	500	350	200	100

AR-70

.223-caliber semi-automatic rifle, with 17.7" barrel, adjustable diopter sights and 8- or 30-shot magazine. Black epoxy finish, with synthetic stock. Weight about 8.3 lbs. No longer imported into U.S.

NIB	Exc.	V.G.	Good	Fair	Poor
2100	1900	1500	1000	750	400

ARX 100

Tactical semi-automatic rifle that is a civilian version of ARX-160 select-fire military rifle developed for the Italian Armed Forces. (This is not to be confused with ARX-160 .22 rimfire rifle.) Modular design allows easy maintenance. Standard configuration with four Picatinny rails. All controls are ambidextrous. Chambered for 5.56 NATO. Introduced in 2013.

NIB	Exc.	V.G.	Good	Fair	Poor
1400	1100	900	700	550	250

ARX 160

Similar in appearance and operation to ARX 100 design, but chambered in .22 Long Rifle.

NIB	Exc.	V.G.	Good	Fair	Poor
500	420	350	250	150	100

BM-59 Garand

Gas-operated semi-automatic rifle, with detachable box magazine. Chambered for .308 cartridge. Walnut stock. Barrel length 19.3" with muzzle brake. Magazine capacity 5, 10 or 20 rounds. Weight about 9.5 lbs.

NIB	Exc.	V.G.	Good	Fair	Poor
3000	2700	2100	1500	400	200

Model 500 Custom

Bolt-action rifle in three action lengths, 24" barrel, open sights. Chambered in .222 Rem., .223 Rem., .243 Win., .270 Win., .308 Win., .30-06. Blued finish and checkered walnut stock. Offered in several grades.

NIB	Exc.	V.G.	Good	Fair	Poor
—	600	520	400	320	280

Model 500S

NIB	Exc.	V.G.	Good	Fair	Poor
—	620	550	420	350	300

Model 500DL

NIB	Exc.	V.G.	Good	Fair	Poor
—	1400	1250	1000	780	650

Model 500DEELL

NIB	Exc.	V.G.	Good	Fair	Poor
—	1600	1450	1200	980	800

Model 500DEELLS

NIB	Exc.	V.G.	Good	Fair	Poor
—	1620	1480	1220	1000	820

Model 501

.243- or .308-caliber bolt-action rifle, with 23" barrel, furnished without sights and 6-shot magazine. Blued, with checkered walnut stock. Discontinued in 1986. Offered in same variations as Model 500 series-501S, 501DL, 501DLS, 501EELL and 501EELLS. Values for this series are same as for 500 series rifles.

Model 502

.270, 7mm Rem. Magnum and .30-06 caliber bolt-action rifle, with 24" barrel (without sights) and 5-shot magazine. Blued, with checkered walnut stock. Discontinued in 1986. Available in same variations as Model 500 and Model 501. Valued approximately 10 percent higher in each variation.

Mato Standard

Bolt-action rifles built on Mauser 98 type action, with controlled-round feed, three-position safety, adjustable trigger. Chambered in .270 Win., .280 Rem., .30-06, .300 Win. Magnum, .338 Win. Magnum. Composite stock.

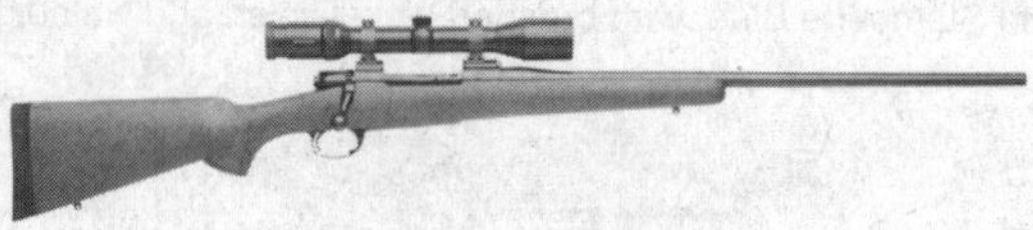

NIB	Exc.	V.G.	Good	Fair	Poor
1200	1000	800	600	300	180

Mato Deluxe

Bolt-action rifle introduced into Beretta product line in 1997. Stock is XXX Claro walnut, with hand-rubbed oil-finish and black forend tip. Chambered for .270 Win., .280, .30-06, 7mm Magnum, .300 Magnum, .338 Magnum and .375 H&H. Weight about 8 lbs.

NIB	Exc.	V.G.	Good	Fair	Poor
2000	1500	1000	750	350	200

Beretta 1873 Renegade

Lever-action rifle based on Winchester 1873 design. Chambered in .357 Magnum or .45 Colt. Barrel length 20", with octagonal profile. Straight-grip walnut stock.

NIB	Exc.	V.G.	Good	Fair	Poor
1200	1000	750	600	300	200

Beretta 1876

Lever-action rifle based on Winchester 1876 design. In .45-75 chambering, with 28" octagonal barrel and full-length tubular magazine.

NIB	Exc.	V.G.	Good	Fair	Poor
1450	1200	850	700	350	250

PREMIUM RIFLES

Model S689 Sable

9.3x74R or .30-06 caliber over/under rifle, with boxlock action, 23" ribbed barrels and express-type sights. Blued case-hardened or nickel-plated, with checkered walnut stock. Double triggers and automatic ejectors. Offered in three grades. Note: Add $1,200 extra 20-gauge barrel with forearm; $2,000 scope with claw mounts.

Silver Sable

NIB	Exc.	V.G.	Good	Fair	Poor
4000	3200	2500	1750	1200	300

Gold Sable

NIB	Exc.	V.G.	Good	Fair	Poor
8000	6500	4500	3000	1500	350

Diamond Sable

NIB	Exc.	V.G.	Good	Fair	Poor
12000	11000	7500	5500	2000	1000

SSO Express

.375 H&H and .458 Win. Magnum caliber over/under double-barrel rifle, with 23" barrels, folding express sights, double triggers and automatic ejectors. Furnished with fitted case. Available on custom order basis. Should be individually appraised.

NIB	Exc.	V.G.	Good	Fair	Poor
18000	13000	9500	6000	3500	2500

SSO5 Express

More finely finished version of above.

NIB	Exc.	V.G.	Good	Fair	Poor
20000	15000	11000	8000	5000	3000

SSO6

Premium grade sidelock over/under express rifle. Equipped with double triggers. Offered in 9.3x74R, .375 H&H Magnum and .458 Win. Magnum. Fitted with 24" barrel, with express sights. Claw mounts for Zeiss scopes are available from factory. Receiver is case colored, with light scroll engraving. Special select walnut used in stock and forearm, with fine line checkering. Stock comes with cheekpiece and rubber recoil pad. Furnished with leather case. Weight about 11 lbs. Made to customer's specifications. Discontinued 2014.

NIB	Exc.	V.G.	Good	Fair	Poor
67500	54000	40000	28000	12000	3000

SSO6 EELL

Offered in same calibers as above. Furnished with hand-engraved game scenes, with gold inlays. Walnut stock is special select briar, with fine diamond line checkering.

NIB	Exc.	V.G.	Good	Fair	Poor
110000	90000	70000	40000	18000	10000

Model 455

Premium grade side-by-side express rifle, with slide locks. Available in these calibers: .375 H&H Magnum, .458 Win. Magnum, .470 Nitro Express, .500 Nitro Express and .416 Rigby. Receiver is case colored, without engraving. Walnut stock highly figured, with fine line checkering. Comes supplied with express sights. Claw mounts and Zeiss scope offered at customer's request only on .375, .458 and .416. Weight about 11 lbs.

NIB	Exc.	V.G.	Good	Fair	Poor
80000	70000	55000	40000	20000	5000

Model 455 EELL

Same as above. Furnished with case colored game scene engraving, with gold inlays. Walnut briar stock, with fine diamond line checkering. Supplied with leather case and accessories.

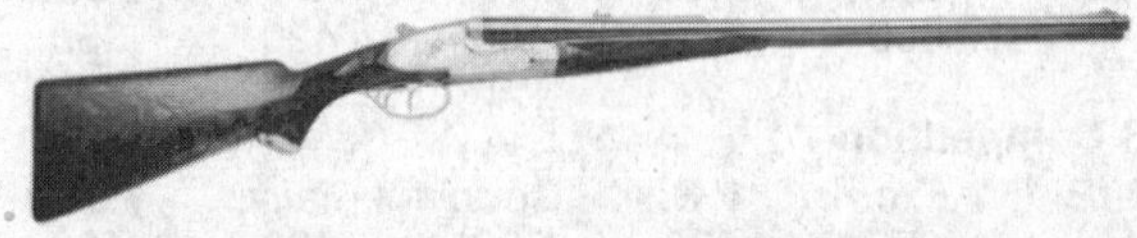

NIB	Exc.	V.G.	Good	Fair	Poor
110000	85000	60000	45000	25000	10000

SHOTGUNS

Beretta shotguns are marked with a symbol or "0" stamping to indicate type of fixed choke in barrel or barrels. Usually this stamping is on side of barrel in rear, near receiver on semi-automatics and near ejectors on double-barrel shotguns. Beretta shotguns with screw-in Mobilchoke tubes will have notches cut in them to indicate amount of choke placed in tube.

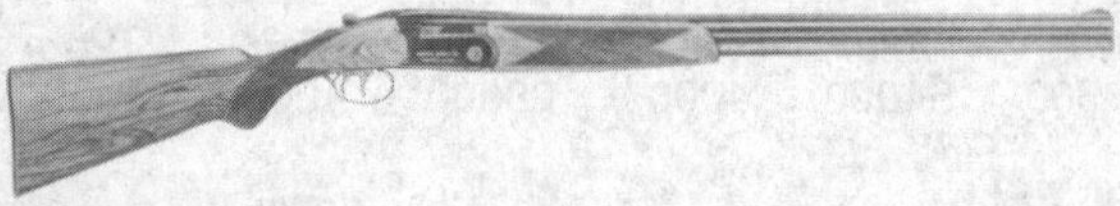

BL SERIES

BL series of over/under shotguns were manufactured between 1968 and 1973. Chambered for 12-, 20- or 28-gauge. Offered with 26", 28" or 30" ventilated rib barrels, with various choke combinations. They feature boxlock actions and offered with single-/double triggers and manual extractors or automatic ejectors. Finish blued, with checkered walnut stocks. Configurations differ basically in quality of materials, workmanship and degree of ornamentation. Note: Add 50 percent for 20-gauge; 75 percent for 28-gauge.

BL-1

NIB	*Exc.*	*V.G.*	*Good*	*Fair*	*Poor*
—	500	450	350	220	150

BL-2

NIB	*Exc.*	*V.G.*	*Good*	*Fair*	*Poor*
—	420	380	300	250	200

BL-2/S (Speed Trigger)

NIB	*Exc.*	*V.G.*	*Good*	*Fair*	*Poor*
—	450	400	320	280	220

BL-2 Stakeout

18" barrel.

NIB	*Exc.*	*V.G.*	*Good*	*Fair*	*Poor*
—	400	350	280	220	180

BL-3

NIB	*Exc.*	*V.G.*	*Good*	*Fair*	*Poor*
—	600	550	480	420	350

BL-3 Competition

NIB	*Exc.*	*V.G.*	*Good*	*Fair*	*Poor*
—	650	600	520	480	400

BL-4

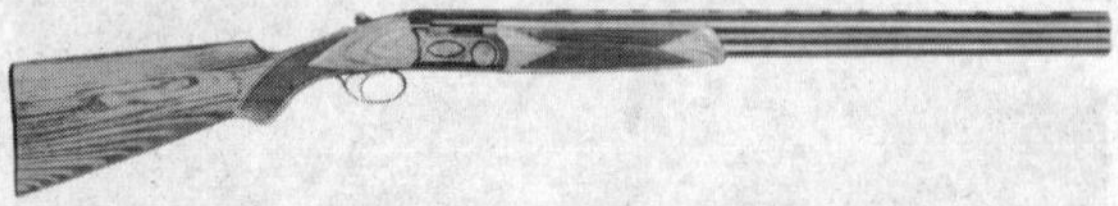

NIB	*Exc.*	*V.G.*	*Good*	*Fair*	*Poor*
—	800	750	650	520	420

BL-4 Competition

NIB	*Exc.*	*V.G.*	*Good*	*Fair*	*Poor*
—	850	800	700	580	450

BL-5

NIB	*Exc.*	*V.G.*	*Good*	*Fair*	*Poor*
—	900	850	720	580	450

BL-5 Competition

NIB	*Exc.*	*V.G.*	*Good*	*Fair*	*Poor*
—	950	900	780	600	480

BL-6

Sidelock.

NIB	*Exc.*	*V.G.*	*Good*	*Fair*	*Poor*
—	1250	1150	1000	850	680

BL-6 Competition

NIB	*Exc.*	*V.G.*	*Good*	*Fair*	*Poor*
—	1300	1200	1050	900	720

Model S55 B

12- or 20-gauge over/under shotgun, with 26", 28" or 30" ventilated rib barrels, various choke combinations and boxlock action with single-selective trigger and extractors. Blued, with checkered walnut stock.

NIB	*Exc.*	*V.G.*	*Good*	*Fair*	*Poor*
—	550	500	400	320	280

Model S56 E

As above more finely finished.

NIB	*Exc.*	*V.G.*	*Good*	*Fair*	*Poor*
—	600	550	450	380	320

Model S58 Competition

As above, with 26" or 30" barrels, wide ventilated ribs. Competition-type stocks.

NIB	*Exc.*	*V.G.*	*Good*	*Fair*	*Poor*
—	700	650	550	480	400

Silver Snipe

12-,20-, 28-gauge over/under shotgun, with 26", 28" or 30" barrels. Boxlock action, with double trigger and extractors. Blued, with checkered walnut stock. Manufactured from 1955 through 1967. Single-selective trigger version, with ventilated rib and automatic ejectors would be worth approximately an additional 50 percent. Note: Add 50 percent for 20-gauge; 80 percent for 28-gauge.

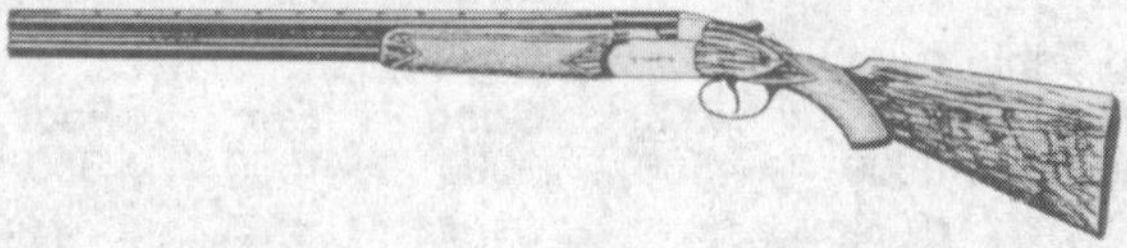

NIB	*Exc.*	*V.G.*	*Good*	*Fair*	*Poor*
—	700	600	500	350	200

Golden Snipe

As above, with ventilated rib and automatic ejectors. Note: Add 10 percent for single-selective trigger; 50 percent for 20-gauge; 80 percent for 28-gauge.

NIB	*Exc.*	*V.G.*	*Good*	*Fair*	*Poor*
—	850	700	500	350	200

Model 57 E

As above more finely finished. Manufactured between 1955 and 1967.

NIB	*Exc.*	*V.G.*	*Good*	*Fair*	*Poor*
—	950	800	600	480	250

ASEL Model

12- or 20-gauge over/under shotgun, with 26", 28" or 30" ventilated rib barrel and various choke combinations. Single-selective trigger and automatic ejectors. Blued, with checkered pistol grip stock. Manufactured between 1947 and 1964. Prices listed for 20-gauge. Note: Add 30 percent for EELL grade; deduct $1000 from Exc. condition for 12-gauge.

NIB	*Exc.*	*V.G.*	*Good*	*Fair*	*Poor*
—	4250	2500	1200	750	400

Model 409 PB

12-, 16-, 20- and 28-gauge boxlock double-barrel shotgun, with 27", 28" or 30" barrels, double triggers and extractors. Various choke combinations. Blued, with checkered walnut stock. Manufactured between 1934 and 1964. Note: Add 50 percent for 20-gauge; 100 percent for 28-gauge.

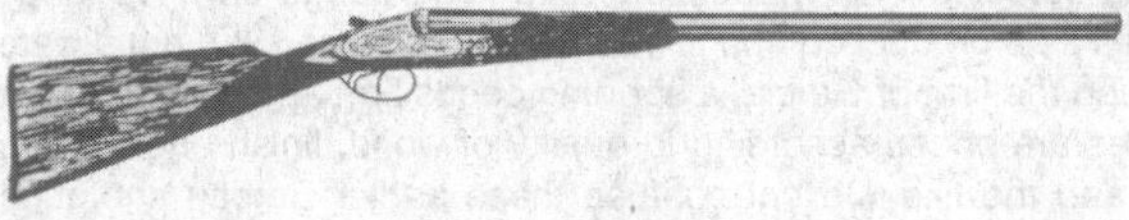

NIB	Exc.	V.G.	Good	Fair	Poor
1400	1100	850	620	500	250

Model 410

As above, with 32" Full-choke barrel. Blued, with checkered walnut stock. Introduced in 1934, 10-gauge only.

NIB	Exc.	V.G.	Good	Fair	Poor
2000	1400	1200	800	600	300

Model 410 E

More finely finished version of 409PB.

NIB	Exc.	V.G.	Good	Fair	Poor
2100	1600	1350	1000	750	400

Model 411 E

Model 410, with false sideplates and more heavily engraved. Manufactured between 1934 and 1964. Note: Add 25 percent for 20-gauge; 100 percent for 28 gauge.

NIB	Exc.	V.G.	Good	Fair	Poor
2400	2100	1750	1250	800	420

Model 424

12- and 20-gauge boxlock shotgun, with 26" or 28" barrels, double triggers, various choke combinations and extractors. Blued, with checkered walnut stock. In 20-gauge designated Model 426 and worth an additional 50 percent.

NIB	Exc.	V.G.	Good	Fair	Poor
1500	1200	950	680	500	220

Model 426 E

As above, with silver inlays and heavier engraving, single-selective trigger and automatic ejectors. Not imported after 1983.

NIB	Exc.	V.G.	Good	Fair	Poor
1750	1400	1150	880	700	350

Model 625

12- or 20-gauge boxlock double-barrel shotgun, with 26", 28" or 30" barrels, various choke combinations, double triggers and extractors. Moderately engraved. Blued, with checkered walnut grip. Imported between 1984 and 1986. Note: Add 50 percent for 20 gauge.

NIB	Exc.	V.G.	Good	Fair	Poor
1200	900	750	600	500	250

Model 626 Field Grade

12- or 20-gauge boxlock double-barrel shotgun, with 26" or 28" barrel, various choke combinations, single trigger and automatic ejectors. Engraved, blued with checkered walnut stock. Imported between 1984 and 1988.

NIB	Exc.	V.G.	Good	Fair	Poor
1400	1000	820	700	580	480

Model 626 Onyx

Boxlock side-by-side shotgun offered in 12- and 20-gauge. Choice of 26" or 28" solid rib barrels, with screw-in chokes. Double triggers are standard, but single trigger available on request. Receiver anti-glare black matte finish. Stock walnut, with hand checkering and pistol grip. Weight: 12-gauge 6 lbs. 13 oz.; 20-gauge 6 lbs. 13 oz.

NIB	Exc.	V.G.	Good	Fair	Poor
1600	1250	850	750	500	400

Model 627 EL

Offered in 12-gauge only, with choice of 26" or 28" solid rib barrels. Walnut is highly figured and fine cut checkered. Receiver silver, with side plates engraved with scroll. Comes with hard case.

NIB	Exc.	V.G.	Good	Fair	Poor
2600	2000	1750	1500	1250	650

Model 627 EELL

Same as above. Fitted with scroll engraved side plates and game scenes. Walnut highly figured, with fine line checkering. Straight-grip stock also offered. Comes with hard case.

NIB	Exc.	V.G.	Good	Fair	Poor
3850	3500	3000	2500	1500	1000

GR Series

Moderately priced series of side-by-side boxlock double shotguns. Imported from 1968 to about 1976. Offered in 12- or 20-gauge, with Fixed chokes. GR-2 has double triggers with folding front trigger, extractors. GR-3 has single selective trigger, better wood. GR-4 has automatic ejectors, higher grade wood. Prices shown are for 12-gauge models. Note: Add 50 percent for 20-gauge.

GR-1

NIB	Exc.	V.G.	Good	Fair	Poor
1000	850	700	600	500	350

GR-2

NIB	Exc.	V.G.	Good	Fair	Poor
1150	950	800	700	600	400

GR-3

NIB	Exc.	V.G.	Good	Fair	Poor
1250	1050	900	800	700	500

Silver Hawk

10- or 12-gauge boxlock double-barrel shotgun, with 30" barrels, double triggers and extractors. Blued, with silver-finished receiver and checkered walnut stock. 10-gauge version worth an additional 20 percent. Discontinued in 1967.

NIB	Exc.	V.G.	Good	Fair	Poor
—	700	500	380	250	150

Silver Hawk Featherweight

Similar to above. Made in 12-, 16-, 20- and 28-gauge, with 26", 28", 30" or 32" barrels. Standard choices of Fixed chokes. Single-/double triggers. Automatic ejectors. Note: Add 10 percent for single trigger; 50 percent for

20-gauge; 80 percent for 28-gauge.

NIB	Exc.	V.G.	Good	Fair	Poor
1000	880	750	600	450	300

Model 470 Silver Hawk

Introduced in 1997 to commemorate Beretta's 470 years in the gunmaking business. Offered in 12- or 20-gauge configurations. Receiver silver chrome with engraving. Top lever checkered, with gold inlaid hawk's head. Fitted with straight-grip stock, splinter forearm of select walnut with oil-finish. Choice of 26" or 28" barrels, with auto ejection or manual extraction. Weight: 12-gauge about 6.5 lbs.; 20-gauge about 6 lbs.

NIB	Exc.	V.G.	Good	Fair	Poor
2400	2000	1500	—	—	—

Model 470 Silver Hawk EL

Introduced in 2002. Features color case-hardened frame and side plates, with gold filled game scene engraving. Offered in 12- or 20-gauge, with choice of 26" or 28" barrels. Weight: 5.9 lbs. for 20-gauge; 6.5 lbs. for 12-gauge.

NIB	Exc.	V.G.	Good	Fair	Poor
4800	4000	3000	—	—	—

Model 471 Silver Hawk

Introduced in 2003. Side-by-side shotgun has boxlock receiver. Offered in 12- and 20-gauge. Choice of 26" or 28" barrels, pistol grip with beavertail forend or straight-grip stock with splinter forend. Straight-grip stock, with case color receiver is available at a premium. Select walnut stock with oil-finish. Single-selective trigger. Weight: about 6.5 lbs. in 12-gauge; 5.9 lbs. in 20-gauge. Note: Add $350 for straight-grip stock, with case color receiver.

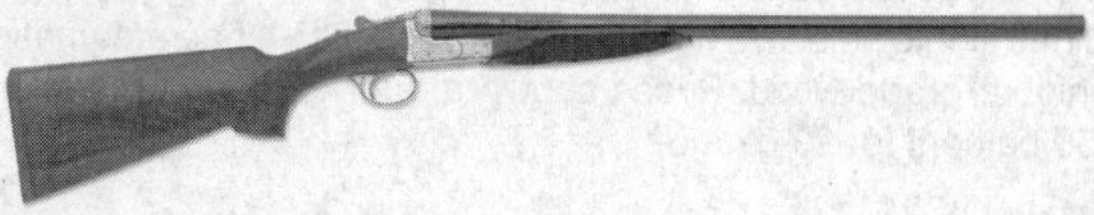

NIB	Exc.	V.G.	Good	Fair	Poor
3000	2500	2000	1500	900	400

Model 471 EL

High-grade variation of above. Has satin-finished Turkish walnut stock and coin-finished receiver with gold accents.

NIB	Exc.	V.G.	Good	Fair	Poor
7600	6400	4800	3500	1700	500

Model 486 Parallelo

Side-by-side model introduced in 2014. Chambered in 12-gauge only, with a round action decorated with English style scroll engraving and scalloped coin-finish. Checkered walnut stock has a straight-grip, with splinter forend. Other features include single selective trigger, choice of automatic ejectors or manual extractors and choke tubes or fixed chokes.

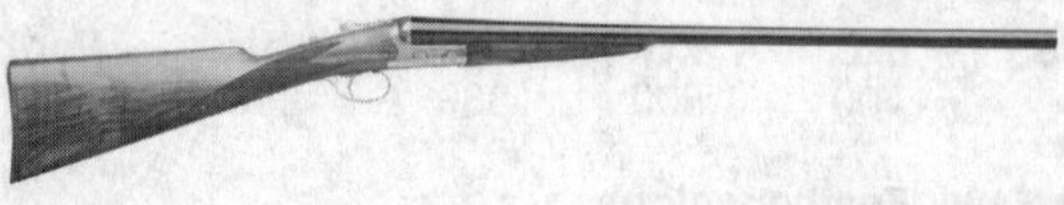

NIB	Exc.	V.G.	Good	Fair	Poor
4600	3700	2900	2200	1200	500

BERETTA "SO" SERIES & OTHER PREMIUM SHOTGUNS

Over/under shotguns fitted with side-locks, automatic ejectors, single-/double triggers. Barrel lengths from 26" to 30", with a wide variety of choke combinations. Introduced 1948 in 12-gauge only. No longer imported as a production gun in 1986. Many of these "SO" guns were sold through the firm of Garcia, a sporting goods firm and distributor. Various grades are priced according to quality of wood, finish engraving coverage and the like. Do not confuse these earlier Beretta shotguns with present line of premium grade Berettas now being imported into U.S.

SO-1

NIB	Exc.	V.G.	Good	Fair	Poor
—	4000	2400	1500	800	400

SO-2

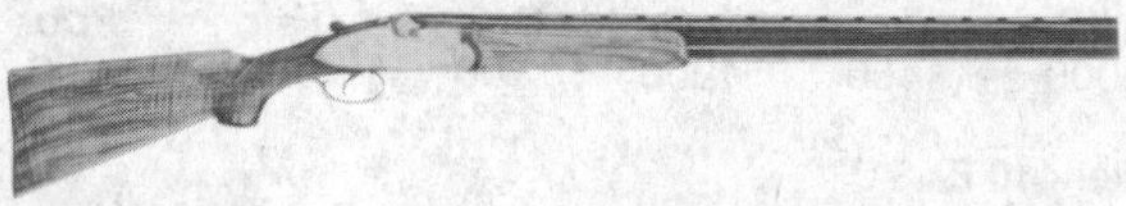

NIB	Exc.	V.G.	Good	Fair	Poor
—	6000	4500	2000	900	500

SO-3

Note: Add 15 percent for SO-3 EL, 25 percent for SO-3 EELL

NIB	Exc.	V.G.	Good	Fair	Poor
10000	8500	6500	4000	1500	1000

SO-4

NIB	Exc.	V.G.	Good	Fair	Poor
8000	7000	5500	3500	2000	1500

SO-5 (Garcia SO-3 EELL)

NIB	Exc.	V.G.	Good	Fair	Poor
—	—	7900	5900	3500	2500

SO-6 (450 or 451 EL) Side-by-Side

Fitted with Holland & Holland-style sidelocks and third fastener.

NIB	Exc.	V.G.	Good	Fair	Poor
—	7500	6500	5500	3500	2500

SO-7 (451 EELL) Side-by-Side

NIB	Exc.	V.G.	Good	Fair	Poor
—	8900	7900	5900	4000	3000

SO-5 Trap

Premium grade Beretta over/under shotgun. Built for competition trap shooting. Available in 12-gauge, with 30" ventilated rib barrels standard. Barrels in 28" and 32" may be special ordered. Receiver silver with light scroll engraving. Stock is select highly figured walnut, with pistol grip. Offered in International or Monte Carlo dimensions. Special trap rubber recoil pad is furnished. Weight 8 lbs. 2 oz. Furnished with leather case and tools.

NIB	Exc.	V.G.	Good	Fair	Poor
22500	18000	12000	6500	3000	600

SO-5 Trap 2 Barrel Set

NIB	Exc.	V.G.	Good	Fair	Poor
28000	20000	13000	6500	3000	600

SO-5 Sporting Clays

Offered in 12-gauge only, with 28", 30" or 32" barrels; 26" on special order. Sporting clay dimension walnut stock, with pistol grip and rubber recoil pad. Weight 7 lbs. 8 oz.

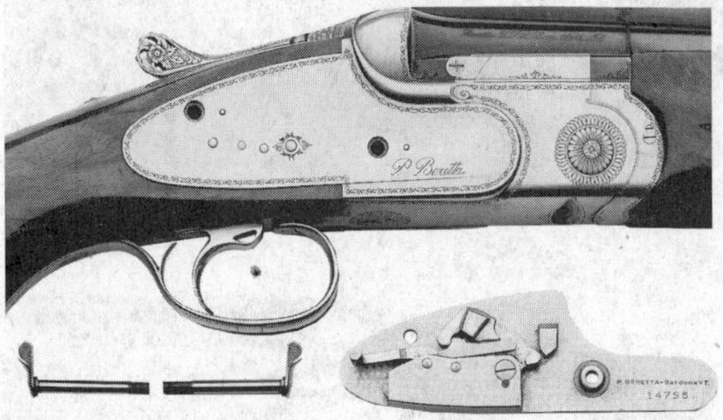

SO-5 sidelocks

NIB	Exc.	V.G.	Good	Fair	Poor
20500	10000	7500	5000	2750	500

SO-5 Skeet

Same general specifications as SO-5 Trap. Furnished to skeet dimensions. Offered in 12-gauge only, with 26" or 28" ventilated rib barrels choked skeet. Weight 7 lbs. 8 oz.

NIB	Exc.	V.G.	Good	Fair	Poor
20500	16000	7500	5000	2750	500

SO-6 EL

Premium grade Beretta available in several different configurations. Similar to SO-5. Available in 12-gauge only. Features true side-lock action, single-selective or non-selective trigger, Fixed or screw-in choke tubes. Receiver offered in silver finish or case-hardened, without engraving. Highly select walnut, with fine line checkering. Choice of pistol- or straight-grip. Supplied with leather fitted hard case. Weight about 7 lbs. 4 oz. depending on barrel length.

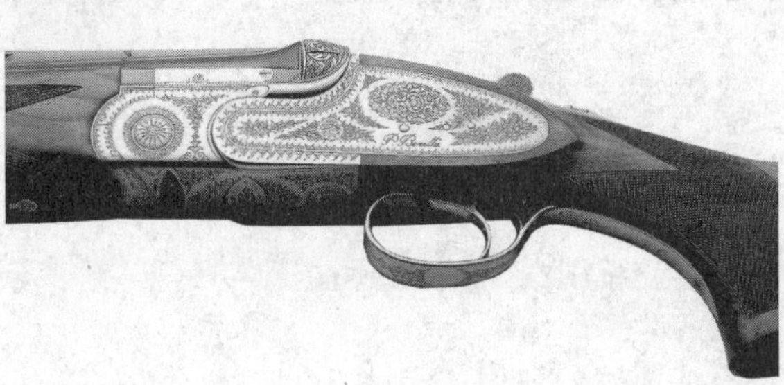

SO-6 receiver

SO-6 Trap

NIB	Exc.	V.G.	Good	Fair	Poor
26500	13000	8500	5000	1700	500

SO-6 Skeet

NIB	Exc.	V.G.	Good	Fair	Poor
26500	13000	8500	5000	1700	500

SO-6 Sporting Clays

NIB	Exc.	V.G.	Good	Fair	Poor
26500	13000	8500	5000	1700	500

SO-6 EELL

Higher grade in SO-6 series. Features silver receiver, custom engraving with scroll or game scenes. Gold inlays are available on request. Choice of barrel lengths from 26" to 30". Choice of pistol-/straight-grip. All the same features of SO-6, with higher fit and finish. Offered in 12-gauge only.

NIB	Exc.	V.G.	Good	Fair	Poor
65000	50000	38000	20000	12000	600

SO-6 EESS

Same specifications as SO-6 EELL grade. Ruby, sapphire or emerald side plates, with diamond brilliants.

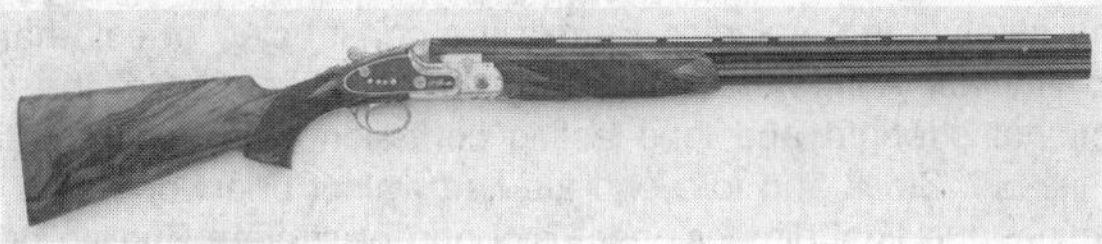

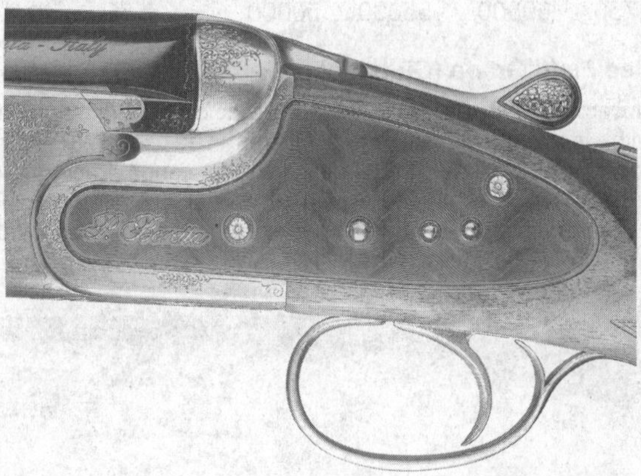

NIB	Exc.	V.G.	Good	Fair	Poor
95000	80000	60000	30000	—	—

SO-7

One of Beretta's best-grade sidelock double-barrel shotgun. Elaborately engraved. Has highest grade walnut stock. No longer in production.

NIB	Exc.	V.G.	Good	Fair	Poor
—	10500	8850	7250	5500	4500

SO-9

Model over/under is Beretta's highest grade. Offered in 12-, 20-, 28-gauge and .410 bore. True side lock (removable) receiver is highly engraved, with scroll or game scenes by Italy's finest craftsmen. Barrel lengths 26" to 30", with solid hand filed rib. Walnut stock is finest available. Either pistol-/straight-grip. Stock dimensions to customers request. A custom fitted leather case, with accessories is supplied with gun. Custom order gun. Independent appraisal is strongly suggested prior to sale.

NIB	Exc.	V.G.	Good	Fair	Poor
38000	30000	22000	15000	7500	2000

SO-10

Beretta's custom-made highest grade over/under sidelock. In 12-, 20-, 28-gauge or .410 bore. Receiver machined from a solid block of tri-alloy steel. Polishing of surfaces all done by hand. Highest grade walnut stock made to owner's specifications. Numerous engraving patterns. Introduced in 2003.

NIB	Exc.	V.G.	Good	Fair	Poor
85000	78000	65000	50000	—	—

SO Sparviere

Sparviere (Italian for "hawk") is a premium sidelock over-under shotgun for the upland hunter and shooter wanting a heirloom-quality work of art. The action features upward of 100 hours of engraving. The action of the SO Sparviere features an exclusive system for opening the two sideplates and gaining access to the inside firing mechanism. The classic Beretta sidelocks can be easily and rapidly opened to the side by actioning the safety/barrel selector. Barrels are constructed of cold-hammer forged Boehler Antinit steel, ensuring perfect alignment of the tubes, exceptional strength and long-lasting corrosion resistance. Ventilated rib is file-cut. Stock and fore end are fine walnut briarwood. The client determines the final dimensions. Pistol grip or straight English grip. 12 gauge, 26–32" barrels.

NIB	Exc.	V.G.	Good	Fair	Poor
62750	60000	55000	50000	—	—

Jubilee Field Grade (Giubileo)

Introduced in 1998. Beretta's finest boxlock over/under shotgun. Fitted with sideplates without screws. Offered in 12-, 20-, 28-gauge and .410 bore, with 26" to 30" barrel depending on gauge. Each gun richly engraved with fine scroll and signed by master engravers. Highly figured walnut, with pistol-/straight-grip. Weights range from about 7 lbs. in 12-gauge to 5.5 lbs. in .410 bore.

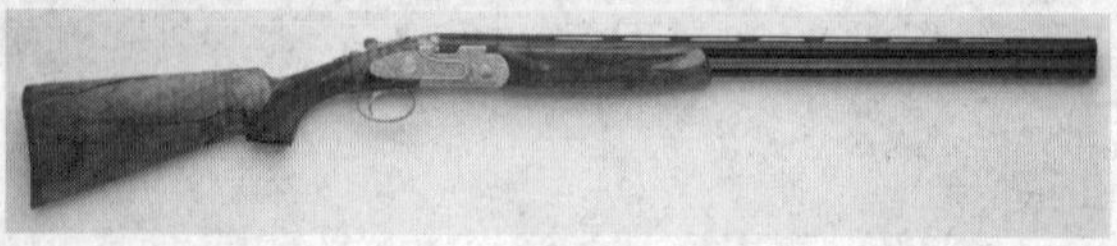

SO-9 with close-ups of engraving patterns

Single Gun

NIB	Exc.	V.G.	Good	Fair	Poor
14750	12000	8250	4500	2200	600

Matched Pair

NIB	Exc.	V.G.	Good	Fair	Poor
32650	—	—	—	—	—

Jubilee Sporting Grade

Similar to above model in terms of finish. Offered in 12-gauge only. Choice of 30" or 32" barrels. Pistol grip standard. Note: Add $1,500 for two barrel combination, with 20-gauge barrel and extended chokes.

NIB	Exc.	V.G.	Good	Fair	Poor
14750	12000	8250	4500	2200	600

Jubilee II (Giublio)

Side-by-side model offered in 12- or 20-gauge only, with straight-grip stocks. Choice of 26" or 28" barrels. Full coverage scroll engraving and highly figured walnut. Double triggers by special order only. Weight about: 12-gauge 6.5 lbs.; 20-gauge 6 lbs.

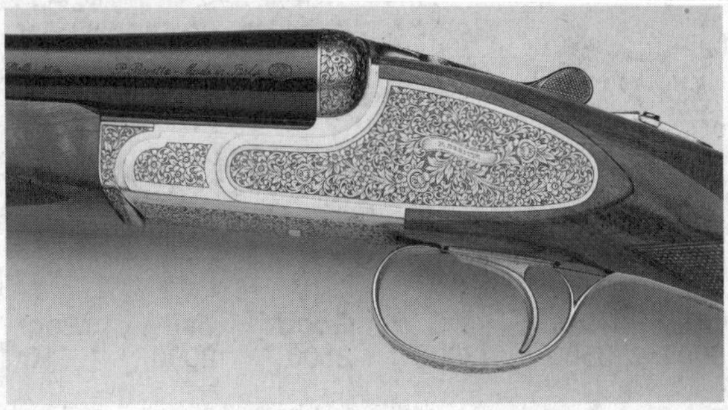

Single Gun

NIB	*Exc.*	*V.G.*	*Good*	*Fair*	*Poor*
14750	12000	8250	4500	2200	600

Matched Pair

NIB	*Exc.*	*V.G.*	*Good*	*Fair*	*Poor*
32650	26000	17000	9200	4000	900

ASE Deluxe Sporting

Boxlock over/under gun offered in 12-gauge only, with choice of 28" or 30" barrels. Classic European scroll engraving. Offered in both field and competition configuration. Weight about 7.5 lbs. for 12-gauge.

NIB	*Exc.*	*V.G.*	*Good*	*Fair*	*Poor*
25000	18500	12000	900	700	400

Model 687 EELL Gallery Special

Special version of this model. Especially engraved guns, with upgraded wood that are only made for Beretta Galleries. Offered in 12-, 20-, 28-gauge and .410 bore.

Single Gun

NIB	*Exc.*	*V.G.*	*Good*	*Fair*	*Poor*
8500	7300	5900	4500	3300	500

Special Combo—20/28 Gauge

NIB	*Exc.*	*V.G.*	*Good*	*Fair*	*Poor*
9500	8600	6700	5800	4000	600

Matched Pair

NIB	*Exc.*	*V.G.*	*Good*	*Fair*	*Poor*
17100	15500	11500	8000	4750	700

Imperiale Montecarlo

Side-by-side gun chambered for 12-, 20-, 28-gauge shell. True sidelock action. Choice of 26", 27" or 28" barrels, with Fixed chokes. Other lengths by special request. Weight about: 7.3 lbs. for 12-gauge; 6.5 lbs. for 20-gauge; 6.2 lbs. for 28-gauge. Master engraved and signed. Beretta's top-of-the-line series built to customer's specifications. Seek qualified appraisal. MSRP from $150,000.

Diana

Side-by-side gun chambered for 12- or 20-gauge, with choice of barrel lengths. Action is true sidelock, with exposed hammers. Weight about: 12-gauge 7.2 lbs.; 20-gauge 6.4 lbs. Master engraved and signed. Hand made to customer's specifications. Seek qualified appraisal. MSRP from $170,000.

Model 451 Series

Custom order sidelock shotgun. Prospective purchasers are advised to secure a qualified appraisal prior to acquisition.

NIB	*Exc.*	*V.G.*	*Good*	*Fair*	*Poor*
8000	6900	5000	4000	2000	700

Model 450 Series

Model same as 451 series, with exception of being a Holland & Holland sidelock design. Prospective purchasers are advised to secure a qualified appraisal prior to acquisition.

NIB	*Exc.*	*V.G.*	*Good*	*Fair*	*Poor*
9000	7500	5800	4500	2500	1000

Model 452

Premium grade side-by-side shotgun fitted with sidelocks (removable). Offered in 12-gauge only. 26", 28" or 30" solid rib barrels. Receiver highly polished silver finish, without engraving. Triggers may be double-/single-selective or single non-selective. Stock and forearm special select walnut, with fine line checkering. Choice of pistol-/straight-grip. Comes with leather hard case. Weight about 6 lbs. 13 oz.

NIB	*Exc.*	*V.G.*	*Good*	*Fair*	*Poor*
24000	19000	14500	8500	4500	2500

Model 452 EELL

Same as above. Furnished with fine scroll or game scene engraving. Highest grade walnut furnished for stock and forearm. Leather case with accessories furnished.

NIB	*Exc.*	*V.G.*	*Good*	*Fair*	*Poor*
31000	27500	19500	11000	7000	600

BERETTA ONYX SERIES

Series designation first used in 2003 to simplify product line. Instead of using numeric model references, company now refers to these guns and others by series name.

Onyx

Over/under gun offered in 12-, 20- and 28-gauge. Choice of 26" or 28" barrels. Features boxlock action, with select checkered walnut stock, single-selective trigger, schnabel forend and auto safety. Black rubber recoil pad. Blued barrels and action. Weight about 6.8 lbs. for 12-gauge.

NIB	*Exc.*	*V.G.*	*Good*	*Fair*	*Poor*
1680	1350	950	650	480	200

Onyx Waterfowler 3.5

As above in 12-gauge, with 3.5" chamber. Matte black finish.

NIB	*Exc.*	*V.G.*	*Good*	*Fair*	*Poor*
1750	1400	1050	700	500	250

White Onyx

Introduced in 2003. Features receiver machined in a jeweled pattern, with satin nickel alloy. Offered in 12-, 20- and 28-gauge, with choice of 26" or 28" barrels. Select checkered walnut stock, with schnabel forend. Weight about 6.8 lbs. for 12-gauge.

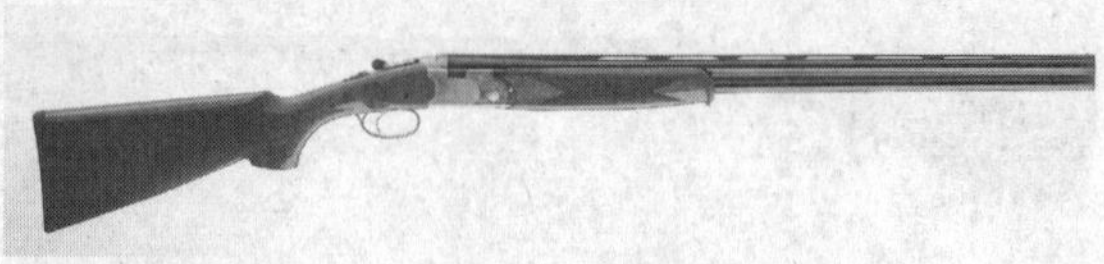

NIB	*Exc.*	*V.G.*	*Good*	*Fair*	*Poor*
1780	1420	1250	700	500	250

Onyx Pro

Introduced in 2003. Over/under shotgun offered in 12-, 20- and 28-gauge. Choice of 26" or 28" ventilated rib barrels, with choke tubes. Single-selective trigger. Checkered X-Tra wood stock. Gel-Tek recoil pad. Supplied with plastic carry case. Weight about 6.8 lbs.

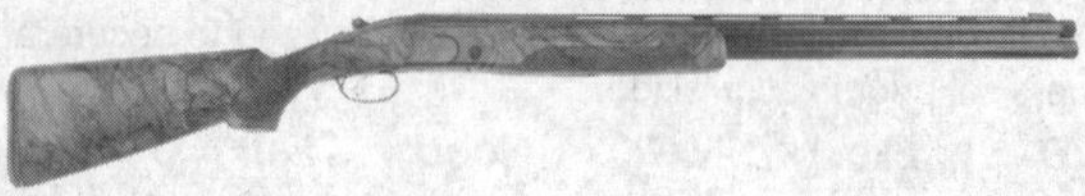

NIB	*Exc.*	*V.G.*	*Good*	*Fair*	*Poor*
1700	1300	1000	600	400	200

Onyx Pro 3.5

As above in 12-gauge, with 3.5" chamber. Weight about 6.9 lbs. Introduced in 2003.

NIB	*Exc.*	*V.G.*	*Good*	*Fair*	*Poor*
1700	1300	1000	600	400	200

BERETTA 682 SERIES

682/682 Gold

High-grade quality-built over/under shotgun. Offered in 12- and 20-gauge. Also available in some configurations in 28-gauge and .410 bore, with barrel lengths from 26" to 34" depending on type of shooting required. Fitted with single-selective trigger and automatic ejectors. Barrels fitted with ventilated rib and various fixed or screw-in choke combinations. Stock is high-grade walnut, with fine checkering in stock dimensions to fit function of gun. Frame is silver, with light scroll borders on most models. This model covers a wide variety of applications. These are listed by grade and/or function: Note: Beretta Competition Series shotguns are also referred to as 682 Gold Competition Series guns, such as Model 682 Gold Trap or Model 682 Gold X Trap Combo and so forth.

682 Super Skeet

Model offered in 12-gauge only, with 28" ventilated rib barrels choked skeet and skeet. Single-selective trigger and auto ejectors standard. This Super Skeet features ported barrels and adjustable length of pull and drop. Fitted hard case standard. Weight 7 lbs. 8 oz.

NIB	*Exc.*	*V.G.*	*Good*	*Fair*	*Poor*
1800	1400	1100	850	650	300

682 Gold Skeet

Standard 12-gauge skeet. Features choice of 26" or 28" ventilated rib barrels, choked Skeet and Skeet. Walnut stock of International dimensions, with special skeet rubber recoil pad. Gun supplied with hard case. Weight 7 lbs. 8 oz.

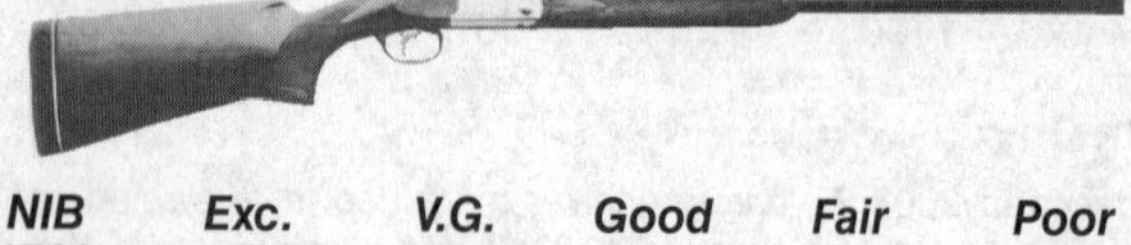

NIB	*Exc.*	*V.G.*	*Good*	*Fair*	*Poor*
1700	1300	1000	800	650	300

682 Four Barrel Set

Skeet gun fitted with four barrels in 12-, 20-, 28-gauge and .410 bore. Each barrel is 28", choked Skeet and Skeet. Fitted with ventilated rib.

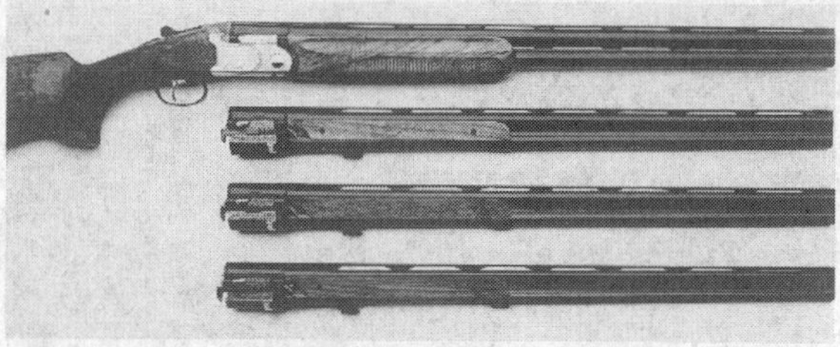

NIB	*Exc.*	*V.G.*	*Good*	*Fair*	*Poor*
4000	3500	3000	2500	2000	650

682 Super Sporting/682 Gold Sporting Ported

Built for sporting clays. This 12- or 20-gauge model features ported barrel, adjustable length of pull and drop. Fitted with 28" or 30" ventilated barrel, with screw-in chokes; Fixed chokes on special order. Checkered walnut stock, with pistol grip and recoil pad. Supplied with case. Introduced in 1993. Weight: 12-gauge 7 lbs. 8 oz.; 20-gauge 6 lbs. 3 oz.

NIB	*Exc.*	*V.G.*	*Good*	*Fair*	*Poor*
2400	2000	1600	1100	700	350

682 Gold Sporting

Standard version of 12- or 20-gauge Super Sporting. Choice of 28" or 30" ventilated rib barrel, with screw-in chokes. Checkered walnut stock, with recoil pad. Introduced in 1993.

NIB	*Exc.*	*V.G.*	*Good*	*Fair*	*Poor*
2000	1650	1400	1250	950	350

682 Sporting Combo

Similar to 682 Sporting, with addition of two 12-gauge 28" and 30" barrels, fitted with screw-in chokes. Supplied with hard case.

NIB	*Exc.*	*V.G.*	*Good*	*Fair*	*Poor*
3200	2700	2250	1750	1250	650

682 Super Trap

12-gauge trap model (20-gauge set of barrels is available on special order) features ported 30" or 32" ventilated rib barrels, with Fixed or screw-in chokes. Automatic ejectors, single non-selective trigger, standard. Checkered walnut stock can be adjusted for length of pull and drop of comb. Offered in Monte Carlo or International dimensions. Weight about 8 lbs. 6 oz.

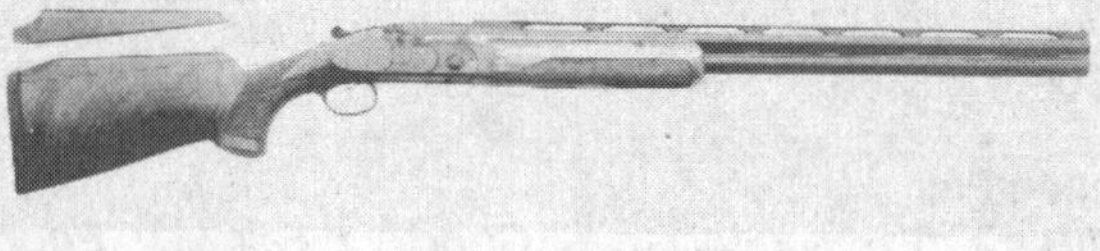

NIB	*Exc.*	*V.G.*	*Good*	*Fair*	*Poor*
2300	2000	1700	1250	950	500

682 Top Single Super Trap

Same as Super Trap. Available in single-barrel configuration of 32" or 34".

NIB	*Exc.*	*V.G.*	*Good*	*Fair*	*Poor*
2600	2150	1700	1350	950	500

682 Top Combo Super Trap

This configuration features single-barrel and over/under barrel, both interchangeable. Combinations are: 30"/32" and 30"/34".

NIB	Exc.	V.G.	Good	Fair	Poor
3300	2980	2350	1750	1250	650

682 Trap

Standard variation of Beretta trap gun. This 12-gauge comes standard with 30" ventilated rib barrels. However, 28" and 32" barrels can be special ordered. Fixed or screw-in chokes available. Three-position sliding trigger allows for adjustable length of pull. Checkered walnut stock, with recoil pad standard. Stock available in Monte Carlo or International dimensions. Customer has choice of silver or black receiver. Comes cased.

NIB	Exc.	V.G.	Good	Fair	Poor
2300	1950	1700	1250	900	450

682 Top Single Trap

12-gauge single-barrel trap gun available in 32" or 34" ventilated rib barrel.

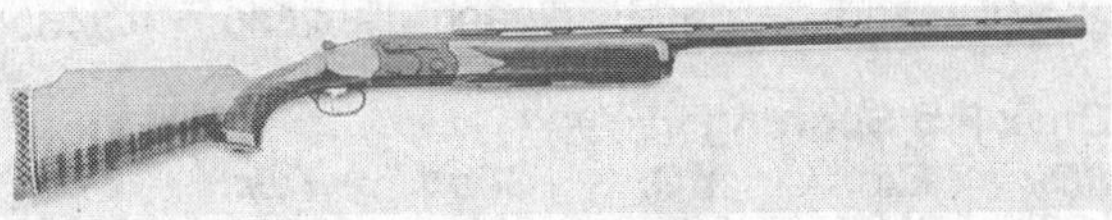

NIB	Exc.	V.G.	Good	Fair	Poor
2000	1600	1200	1000	600	450

682 Mono Combo Trap

Special configuration features single-barrel, with ventilated rib set to place single-barrel in bottom position of what would normally be an over/under setup. Second barrel is an over/under also provided as part of the set. Single-barrel is 34" and over/under set is 32" in length.

NIB	Exc.	V.G.	Good	Fair	Poor
2500	2100	1500	1200	750	500

682 Top Combo

Trap combination features standard placement single-barrel, with interchangeable over/under barrel. Barrel sets available in 30"/32", 30"/34" and 32"/34". Barrels fitted with ventilated rib.

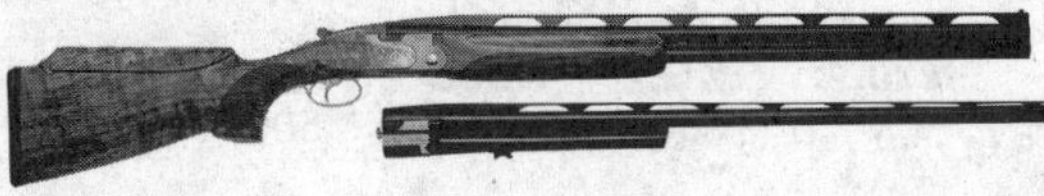

NIB	Exc.	V.G.	Good	Fair	Poor
2500	2000	1500	1000	950	500

682 Gold Trap with Adjustable Stock

Introduced in 1998. Over/under features choice of 30" or 32" barrels, with Monte Carlo stock and adjustable drop, cast and comb. Trigger adjustable for length of pull. Selected walnut stock, with oil-finish. Black rubber recoil pad standard. Weight about 8.8 lbs. Note: Add $800 for Top Combo set.

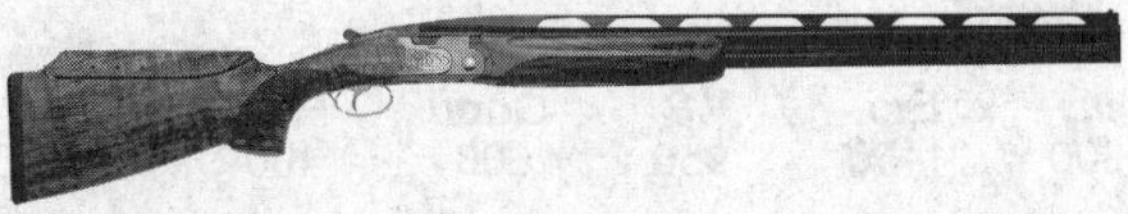

NIB	Exc.	V.G.	Good	Fair	Poor
2200	1800	1500	—	—	—

682 Gold Skeet with Adjustable Stock

Introduced in 1999. This 12-gauge features skeet stock with adjustable comb. Stock drop and cast may also be adjusted. Graystone receiver. Comes with case. Offered in choice of 28" or 30" barrels. Single-selective trigger adjustable for length of pull. Black rubber recoil pad standard. Weight about 7.5 lbs.

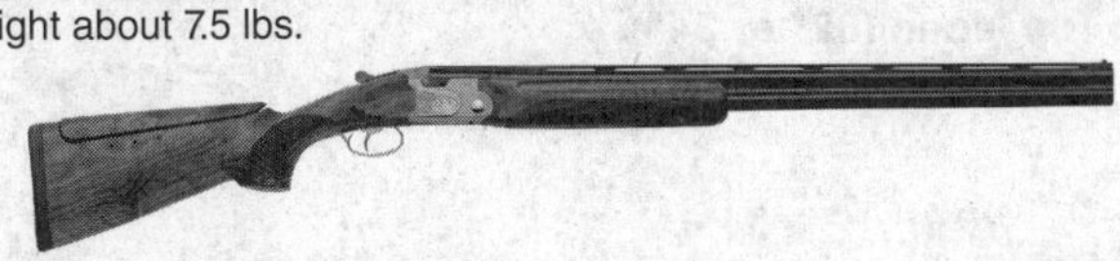

NIB	Exc.	V.G.	Good	Fair	Poor
2000	1700	1500	1200	900	600

682 Gold "Live Bird"

Introduced in 1995. Has gray receiver, with select walnut stock. Single-selective trigger is adjustable for length of pull. Offered in 12-gauge only, with 30" barrels. Average weight 8.8 lbs.

NIB	Exc.	V.G.	Good	Fair	Poor
2550	1950	1600	1150	850	400

S682 Gold E Trap

Chambered for 12-gauge 3", with choice of 30" or 32" barrels overbored and choke tubes. Highly select walnut stock, with black rubber pad. Single-selective trigger, with adjustable length of pull. Beavertail forend. Adjustable Monte Carlo stock. Front white bead with mid bead sight. Carry case standard. Weight about 8.8 lbs. Introduced in 2001.

NIB	Exc.	V.G.	Good	Fair	Poor
3900	3300	2750	1800	900	450

S682 Gold E Trap Combo

Offers same features as Trap model, with interchangeable over/under barrels. Top single-barrel with under rib. Introduced in 2001.

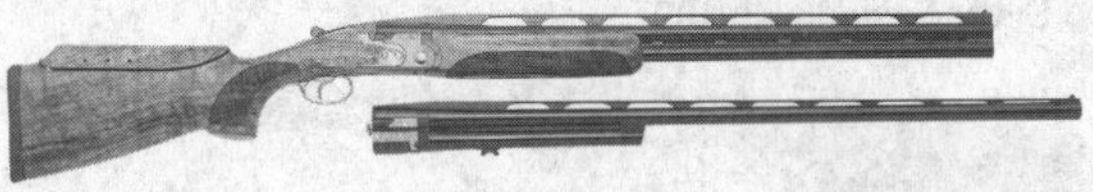

NIB	Exc.	V.G.	Good	Fair	Poor
5600	4400	3100	1700	800	350

S682 Gold E Skeet

12-gauge skeet gun features special skeet-style stock, with beavertail forend. Adjustable stock. Barrel lengths 28" or 30". Single-selective trigger. Weight about 7.5 lbs. Introduced in 2001.

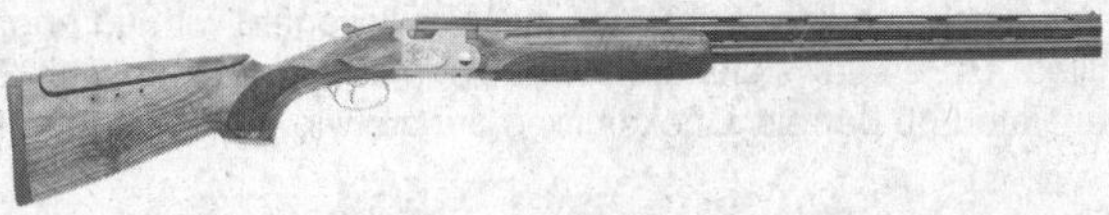

NIB	Exc.	V.G.	Good	Fair	Poor
4000	3600	2750	1500	620	350

S682 Gold E Sporting

12-gauge model. Choice of 28", 30" or 32" barrels, with extended choke tubes and tapered top rib. White front sight and mid bead. Sporting clay-style stock of select walnut. Weight about 7.6 lbs. Introduced in 2001.

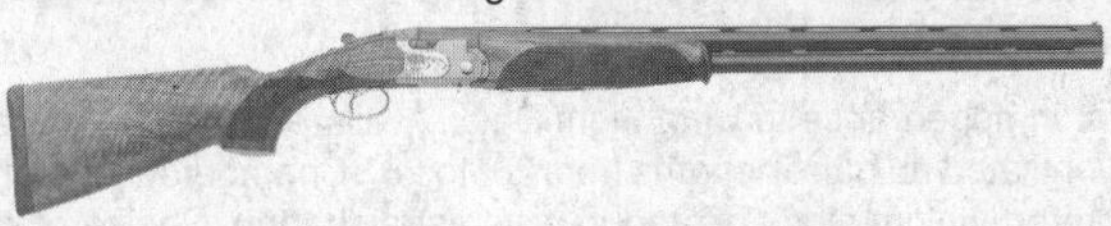

NIB	Exc.	V.G.	Good	Fair	Poor
4150	3200	2350	1200	480	300

BERETTA 685 SERIES

Model 685

Lower priced over/under chambered for 12- or 20-gauge, with 3" chambers. Satin-chromed boxlock action, with single trigger and extractors. Not imported after 1986.

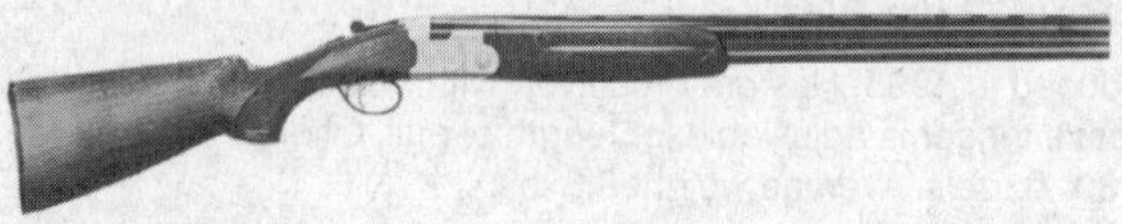

NIB	Exc.	V.G.	Good	Fair	Poor
—	750	680	550	380	200

BERETTA 686 SERIES

686/686 Silver Perdiz Sporting

Beretta over/under shotgun available in a number of different configurations. This basic model features ventilated rib barrels from 24" to 30"; 30" is a special order. Screw-in chokes or Fixed chokes are available. All configurations offered in 12- and 20-gauge, with 28-gauge and .410 bore available on special order only. Fitted with checkered American walnut stock, with black rubber recoil pad and special grip cap. Some models have silver receiver, with scroll engraving and others have black receivers with gold-filled contours. This 686 series was renamed in 1994.

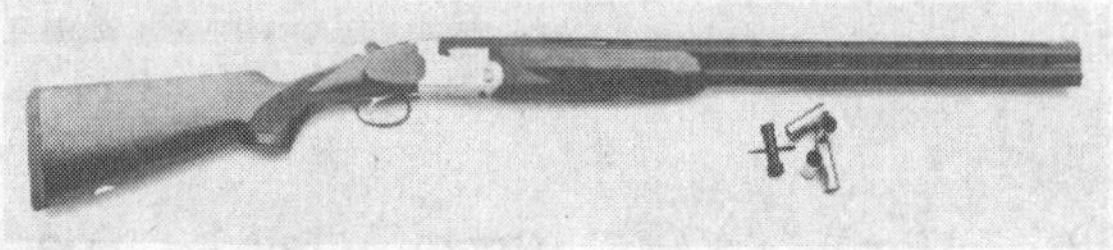

686 Essential/Silver Essential

Introduced in 1994. This 686 model designed to be an entry level 686. Offers all mechanical features of 686 series, without any frills. Offered in 12-gauge only, with 26" or 28" barrels with open-side rib. Plain walnut stock, with checkering and plain blue receiver. Weight about 6.7 lbs. Renamed Silver Essential in 1997.

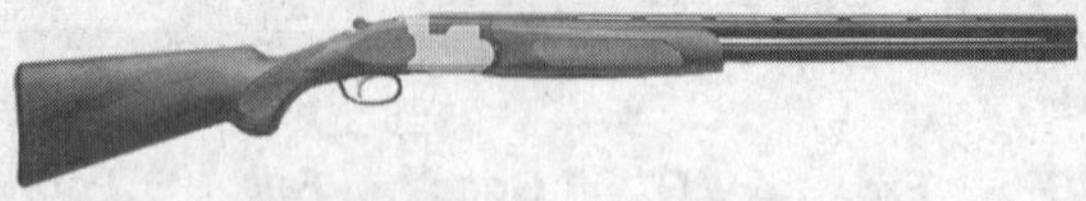

Beretta 686 Silver Essential

NIB	Exc.	V.G.	Good	Fair	Poor
900	750	600	450	350	200

686 Ultra Light Onyx

Features black anodized light alloy receiver accented with an engraved gold-filled "P. Beretta" signature. Available in 12-gauge only, with 26" or 28" ventilated rib barrels. Chokes fixed or screw-in type. Weight 5 lbs. 1 oz.

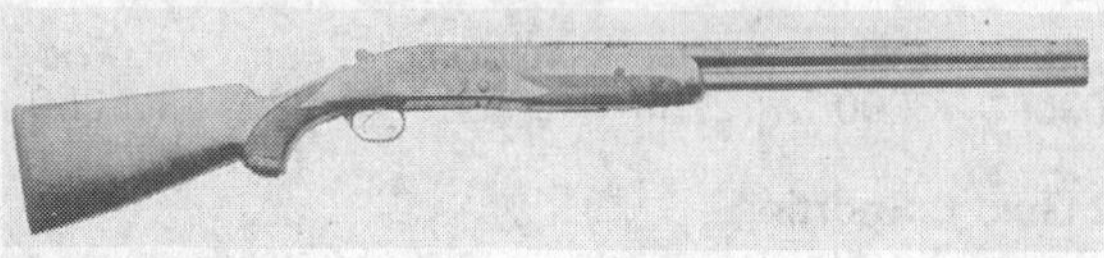

NIB	Exc.	V.G.	Good	Fair	Poor
1050	850	750	600	500	400

686 Onyx

Similar in appearance to Ultra Light Onyx. Available in 12- or 20-gauge, with ventilated rib barrel lengths from 26" to 28". Chambers are 3" or 3.5". Checkered walnut stock offered in pistol-/straight-grip. Choice of choke types. Weight: 12-gauge 6 lbs.13 oz.; 20-gauge 6 lbs. 3 oz. A 12-gauge version with 3.5" chambers and 28" barrel offered (new in 1999) with matte wood finish, matte black receiver, beavertail forend with fingerwells and silver finish trigger.

NIB	Exc.	V.G.	Good	Fair	Poor
1800	1350	950	650	500	400

686 Onyx 2 Barrel Set

Same as above. Supplied with 20-gauge 28" ventilated rib barrel; 28-gauge 26" ventilated rib barrel.

NIB	Exc.	V.G.	Good	Fair	Poor
2100	1650	1500	800	650	500

686 Onyx Pro

NIB	Exc.	V.G.	Good	Fair	Poor
3000	2800	2650	2400	2200	2000

686 Onyx Pro Field 20 & 28 Gauge Combo

NIB	Exc.	V.G.	Good	Fair	Poor
3900	3800	3650	3400	3200	3000

686 Onyx Pro Trap

NIB	Exc.	V.G.	Good	Fair	Poor
3250	3100	2950	2800	2600	2450

686 Onyx Pro Sporting

NIB	Exc.	V.G.	Good	Fair	Poor
3360	3200	3050	2900	2700	2650

686 Silver Receiver

Model is basic 686. Features plain semi-matte silver receiver. Available in 12- or 20-gauge; 28-gauge available on special order. Ventilated rib barrels offered in lengths from 24" to 30", with Fixed chokes or choke tubes.

NIB	Exc.	V.G.	Good	Fair	Poor
1200	900	780	650	500	400

686 L/686 Silver Perdiz

Same as above. Furnished with scroll engraved silver receiver. Offered in 28-gauge, with 26" or 28" ventilated rib barrels. Weight 5 lbs. 5 oz.

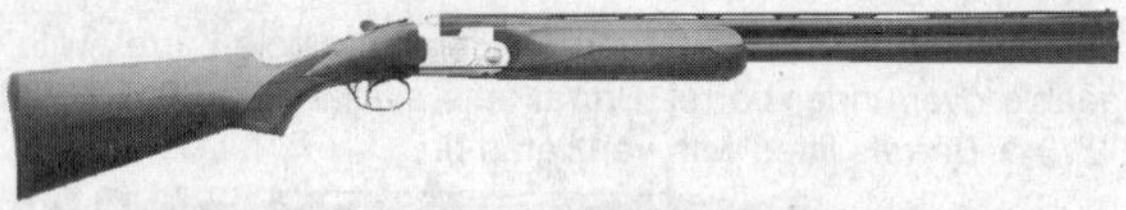

NIB	Exc.	V.G.	Good	Fair	Poor
1200	950	750	650	500	400

686 Silver Pigeon

Introduced in 1996. Replaces Silver Perdiz. Has electroless nickel finish on scroll engraved receiver. Offered in 12-, 20- and 28-gauge, with 26" or 28" barrels. Average weight 6.8 lbs. New variation introduced in 1999. Features 20-gauge gun with 28" barrels, straight-grip stock and matte nickel receiver.

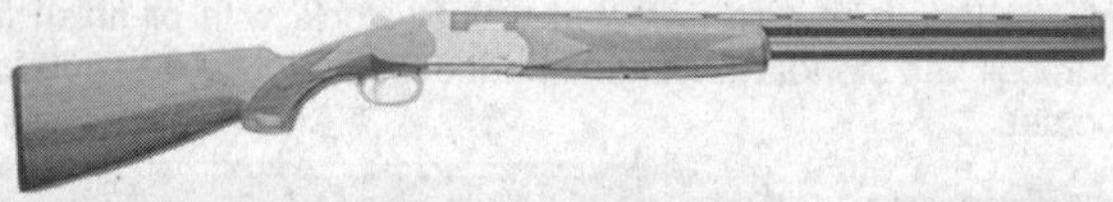

NIB	Exc.	V.G.	Good	Fair	Poor
1800	1450	950	600	400	200

Sporting

NIB	Exc.	V.G.	Good	Fair	Poor
1500	1050	750	600	400	200

Trap (30")

NIB	Exc.	V.G.	Good	Fair	Poor
1400	1000	700	500	400	300

Trap Top Mono (32" or 34")

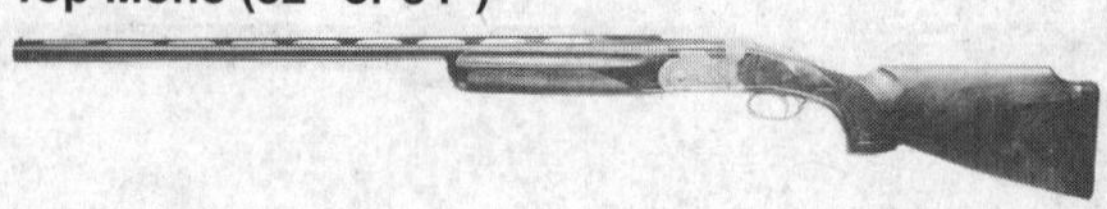

NIB	Exc.	V.G.	Good	Fair	Poor
1300	900	600	500	400	300

686 Silver Pigeon S

Essentially same as Silver Pigeon models. Packaged with carrying case that includes five choke tubes, accessory recoil pad and sling swivels. A .410-bore offering on a proportionally smaller receiver was added in 2006. Note: Add $700 for two barrel 20/28-gauge set.

NIB	Exc.	V.G.	Good	Fair	Poor
2000	1600	1280	820	580	350

686 Silver Pigeon 1

Gauges: 12 ga., 3 in., 20 ga., 3 in., 28 ga., 2.75 in., .410 bore. Barrels: 26 in., 28 in, 30 in., with 6x6 rib. Weight: 6.2-7.25 lbs. Stock: Selected walnut in either left- or right-handed versions with a choice of Schnabel or rounded forend. Features: The improved version of the Silver Pigeon features upgraded Steelium Optima HP barrels, deeper laser engraving of floral motifs, and oil-finished stocks. MicroCore recoil pad, dual conical locking lugs, tang safety and barrel selector, single gold-plated trigger. Includes five interchangeable Mobil chokes and a fitted hard carrying case. Available in both Field and Sporting models.

NIB	Exc.	V.G.	Good	Fair	Poor
2100	1950	1900	1850	1800	1600

686 Silver Pigeon 1 Sporting

NIB	Exc.	V.G.	Good	Fair	Poor
2000	1950	1900	1850	1800	1600

686E Sporting

Offered in 12- or 20-gauge, with choice of 28" or 30" barrels. Five Beretta screw-in chokes. Modern ellipsis receiver engraving. Special carrying case. Introduced with new styling in 2001.

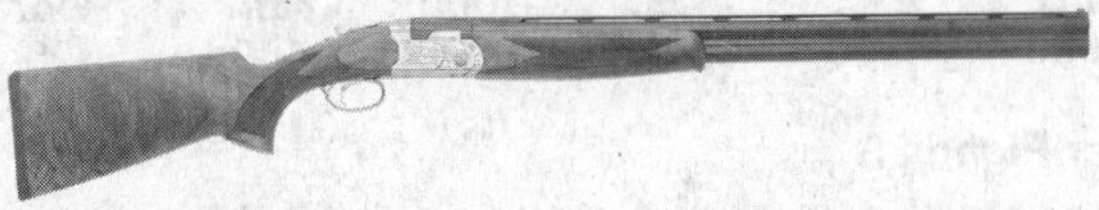

NIB	Exc.	V.G.	Good	Fair	Poor
2100	1700	1350	820	580	350

686 EL/Gold Perdiz

Model available in 12- or 20-gauge, with 26" or 28" ventilated rib barrels. Receiver silver, with scroll engraving fitted with side plates. Fitted hard case comes with gun.

NIB	Exc.	V.G.	Good	Fair	Poor
1900	1350	1100	800	700	350

686 Hunter Sport

Sporting clay 12- or 20-gauge shotgun. Features silver receiver, with scroll engraving. Wide 12.5mm target rib. Radius recoil pad. Offered in 26" or 28" ventilated rib barrels, with screw-in chokes. Offered first time in 1993.

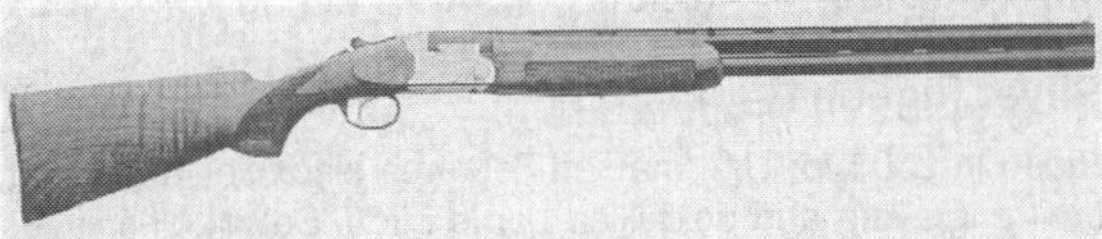

NIB	Exc.	V.G.	Good	Fair	Poor
1200	950	750	600	500	250

686 Onyx Hunter Sport

Same as above. Offered in 12-gauge only, with matte black finish on receiver and barrels. Weight 6 lbs.13 oz. Introduced in 1993.

NIB	Exc.	V.G.	Good	Fair	Poor
1100	850	650	600	500	250

BERETTA WING SERIES

686 Whitewing

Introduced in fall of 1998. Over/under shotgun chambered for 12-gauge shell. Fitted with 26" or 28" barrels, with Beretta's choke system. Receiver polished nickel, with engraved game scenes and gold-plated trigger. Walnut pistol grip stock, with gloss finish.

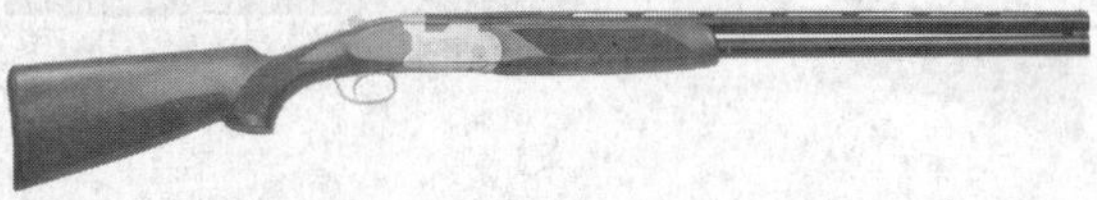

NIB	Exc.	V.G.	Good	Fair	Poor
1350	1020	800	550	380	250

686 Blackwing

Introduced in 2002. Similar to Whitewing, with exception of blued receiver and schnabel forend.

NIB	Exc.	V.G.	Good	Fair	Poor
1450	1100	900	600	420	300

686 Sporting Combo

Same specifications as Hunter Sport, with addition of interchangeable 30" 12-gauge barrel.

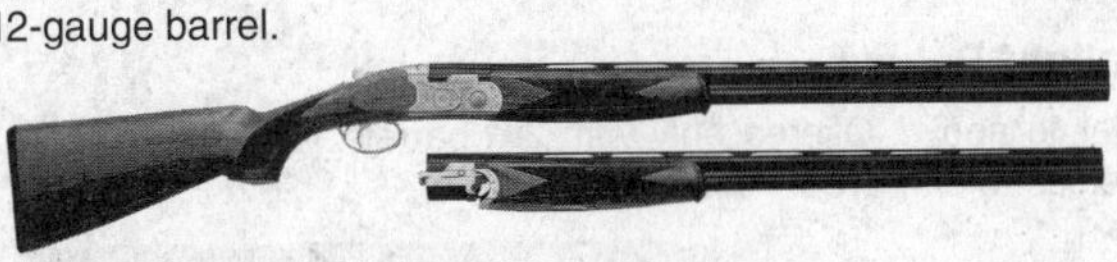

NIB	Exc.	V.G.	Good	Fair	Poor
1900	1600	1250	1000	700	320

686 Collection Trap

Introduced in 1996. Features special multi-colored stock and forend. Offered in 12-gauge only, with 30" barrels. Factory recoil pad standard. Average weight 7.7 lbs.

NIB	Exc.	V.G.	Good	Fair	Poor
1500	1000	750	500	400	300

686 Collection Sport

Similar to above. Offered with 28" barrels.

NIB	Exc.	V.G.	Good	Fair	Poor
1500	980	750	500	400	300

686 Quail Unlimited 2002 Covey Limited Edition

Offered in 20- or 28-gauge, with 26" or 28" ventilated rib barrels. Choke tubes. Engraved receiver with gold quail inlays. Weight about 6.8 lbs.

NIB	Exc.	V.G.	Good	Fair	Poor
1950	1550	1250	1000	700	320

686 Ringneck Pheasants Forever

Introduced in 2003. Chambered for 12- or 20-gauge. Fitted with 26" or 28" ventilated rib barrels. Checkered walnut stock, with pistol grip. Single-selective trigger. Gel-Tek recoil pad. Schnabel forend. Weight about 6.8 lbs. on 12-gauge.

NIB	Exc.	V.G.	Good	Fair	Poor
2020	1550	1100	750	450	280

BERETTA ULTRALIGHT SERIES

Ultralight

Over/under chambered for 12-gauge 2.75" shells. Fitted with choice of 26" or 28" barrels. Receiver is light aluminum alloy nickel finish, with game scene engraving. Black rubber recoil pad standard. Single-selective trigger, pistol grip and schnabel forearm. Weight about 5.75 lbs.

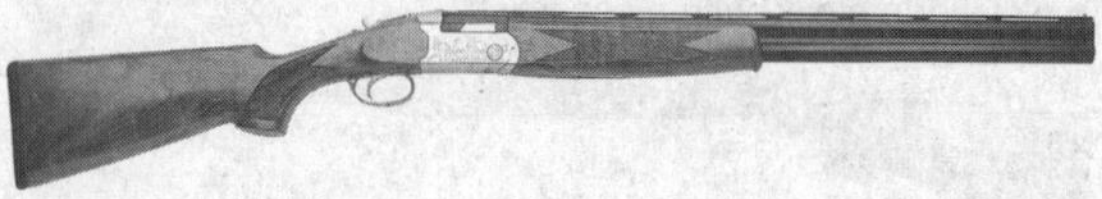

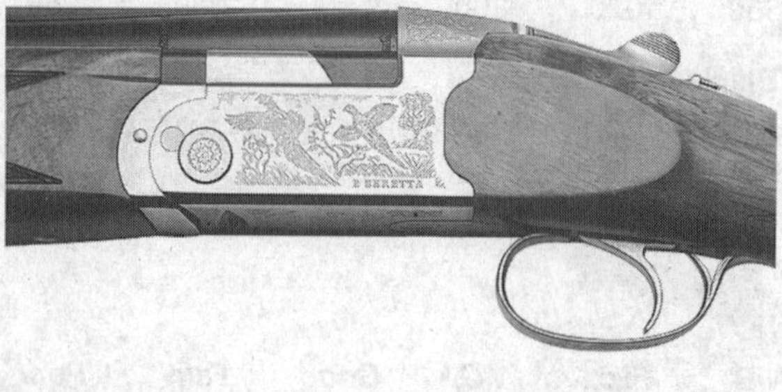

Ultralight receiver

NIB	*Exc.*	*V.G.*	*Good*	*Fair*	*Poor*
1900	1500	900	600	380	180

Ultralight Deluxe

Similar to above. Offered only with 28" barrels. Nickel receiver is gold game scene engraved. First offered in 1998.

NIB	*Exc.*	*V.G.*	*Good*	*Fair*	*Poor*
2400	2000	1600	1100	700	350

BERETTA 687/PIGEON SERIES

687/687 Silver Pigeon Sporting

Similar to Model 686. Slightly more ornate version. This series renamed in 1994.

687 L/Silver Pigeon

Offered in 12- or 20-gauge, with 26" or 28" ventilated rib barrels. Boxlock receiver scroll engraved with game scenes. Auto ejectors and double-/single triggers offered.

NIB	*Exc.*	*V.G.*	*Good*	*Fair*	*Poor*
1800	1100	950	800	650	300

687 Silver Pigeon II

Introduced in 1999. Features deep relief game scene engraving on silver receiver. Select walnut stock, with oil-finish. Available in 12-gauge only. Choice of 26" or 28" ventilated rib barrels. Single-selective trigger. Weight about 6.8 lbs.

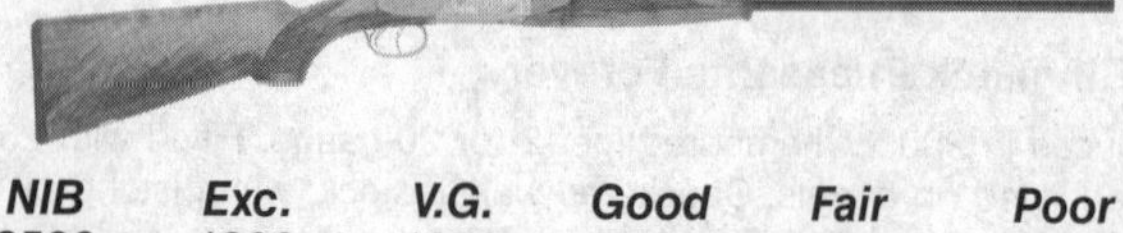

NIB	*Exc.*	*V.G.*	*Good*	*Fair*	*Poor*
2500	1900	1250	700	420	300

687 Silver Pigeon III

Gauge: 12 ga. 3 in., 20 ga. 3 in., 28 ga. 2.75 in., .410 bore, 3 in. Barrels: 26, 28, 30 in. with 6x6 windowed rib. Stock: Class 2.5 Walnut with gloss finish. Features: The 687 Silver Pigeon III stems from the 680 series design. Trapezoid shoulders and dual conical locking lugs. Fine engraving with game scenes and floral motif done with 5-axis laser. MicroCore 20mm buttpad. The 28-gauge and .410-bore doubles are built on a smaller frame. Gold-colored single selective trigger. Tang safety selector. Steelium barrels. The 12, 20, and 28 gauges use 70mm Optima HP choke tubes while the .410 is equipped with 50mm Mobil Chokes.

NIB	*Exc.*	*V.G.*	*Good*	*Fair*	*Poor*
2750	2200	1600	1100	700	350

687 Silver Pigeon Sporting

Sporting clays version available in 12- or 20-gauge, with 28" or 30" barrels.

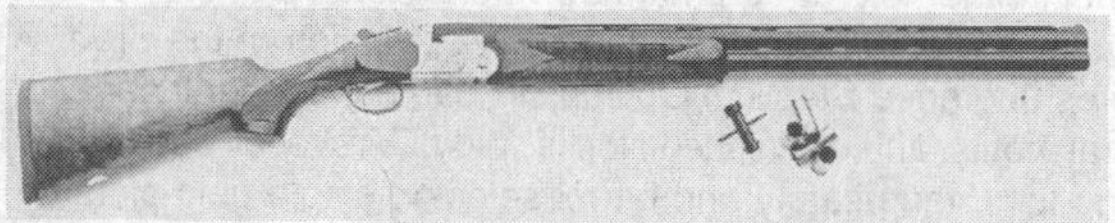

NIB	*Exc.*	*V.G.*	*Good*	*Fair*	*Poor*
1900	1400	1000	700	420	300

687 Silver Pigeon II Sporting

Introduced in 1999. Features deep relief engraving, with oil-finished select walnut stock. Schnabel forend. Single-selective trigger. Offered in 12-gauge only. Choice of 28" or 30" barrels. Black rubber recoil pad. Weight about 7.7 lbs.

NIB	*Exc.*	*V.G.*	*Good*	*Fair*	*Poor*
2500	1900	1250	800	480	320

Silver Pigeon S

New in 2007. Silver Pigeon S Series features scroll and floral engraving on satin nickel-alloy finished receiver. Available in 12-, 20- and 28-gauge, with 26" or 28" barrels. .410 bore with 28" barrels. All come with five chokes. Weight about 6.8 lbs.

NIB	*Exc.*	*V.G.*	*Good*	*Fair*	*Poor*
1800	1480	900	600	380	280

Silver Pigeon S Combo

Combo model comes with 26" 20-gauge barrels; 28" 28-gauge barrels.

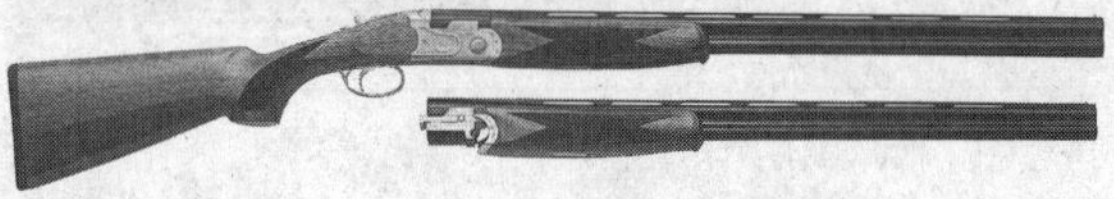

NIB	*Exc.*	*V.G.*	*Good*	*Fair*	*Poor*
2200	1880	1100	900	600	300

687 Sporting Combo

Offered in 12-gauge only, with two sets of 12-gauge interchangeable ventilated rib barrels in 28" and 30".

NIB	*Exc.*	*V.G.*	*Good*	*Fair*	*Poor*
2500	2100	1850	1500	750	400

687 Silver Pigeon IV

Introduced in 2003 for U.S. market. Features black finish receiver, with full scroll engraving and gold-filled game birds. Select oil-finished walnut stock, with Gel-Tek recoil pad. Offered in 12-, 20- or 28-gauge, with 26" or 28" barrels. Single-selective trigger, with fluted beavertail forend. Weight about 6.8 lbs. in 12-gauge.

NIB	Exc.	V.G.	Good	Fair	Poor
2660	1950	1850	1500	750	400

687 Silver Pigeon V

Top-of-the-line model in Silver Pigeon Series. Available in 12-, 20- and 28-gauge, with 26" and 28" barrels and .410 bore (added in 2006). Pistol grip stock of richly figured walnut, with oil-finish. Color case-hardened receiver, with gold-filled game bird inlays. English stocked versions of 20-, 28-gauge and .410 bore added in 2006.

NIB	Exc.	V.G.	Good	Fair	Poor
3600	2400	1700	1250	750	380

687 EL/687 Gold Pigeon

Model offered with scroll engraved gold inlaid game animals. Fitted with side plates. Stock highly figured walnut, with fine line checkering. Available in 12-, 20-, 28-gauge or .410 bore in 26" or 28" ventilated rib barrels, with screw-in chokes. Comes with fitted hard case. Weight: 12-gauge 6 lbs. 13 oz.; 20-gauge 6 lbs. 3 oz.; 28-gauge/.410 bore 5 lbs. 5 oz. Series renamed in 1994. In 2001, Beretta enhanced engraving on Model 687EL Gold Pigeon.

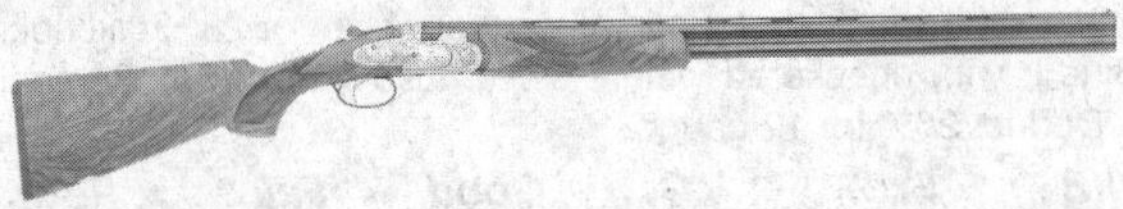

12 and 20 gauge

NIB	Exc.	V.G.	Good	Fair	Poor
3400	2450	1800	1200	750	350

28 gauge and .410 bore

NIB	Exc.	V.G.	Good	Fair	Poor
3450	2500	1850	1250	800	400

687 EL Gold Pigeon Sporting

Sporting clays model chambered for 12-gauge. Fitted with 28" or 30" ventilated rib barrels. Offered new in 1993. Comes with fitted hard case.

NIB	Exc.	V.G.	Good	Fair	Poor
3400	2450	1750	1250	900	450

687 EELL/Diamond Pigeon

Same as above including gauge and barrel offerings. Furnished with more fully figured walnut and finer checkering. Fitted with side plates that are scroll engraved with fine cut game scenes. This grade also available in straight-grip English stock version in 20-gauge as well as combo set of 20-gauge and 28-gauge interchangeable 26" barrels. All 687 EELL models fitted with hard case. Series renamed in 1994.

12 and 20 gauge

NIB	Exc.	V.G.	Good	Fair	Poor
6500	5200	4500	3000	1500	700

28 gauge and .410 bore

NIB	Exc.	V.G.	Good	Fair	Poor
7000	5500	4500	3000	1500	700

Combo

NIB	Exc.	V.G.	Good	Fair	Poor
8000	6800	5000	3500	1300	500

687 EELL Diamond Pigeon Skeet

Same as above. Addition of skeet configuration. A 12-gauge version offered with 28" ventilated rib barrels choked skeet and skeet. Weight about 7 lbs. 8 oz. A 4 barrel set also offered with interchangeable 12-, 20-, 28-gauge and .410 bore barrels choked skeet and skeet.

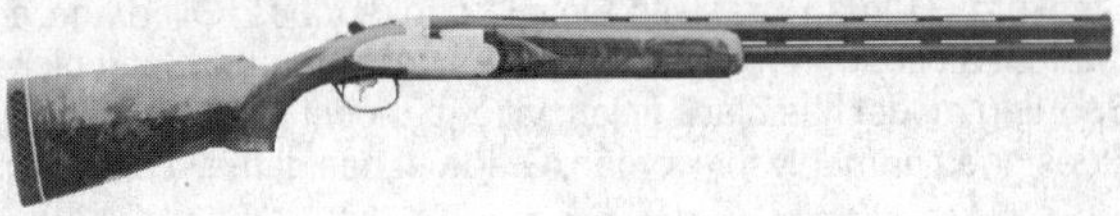

12 gauge

NIB	Exc.	V.G.	Good	Fair	Poor
3500	3000	2500	1750	1450	480

4 Barrel Set

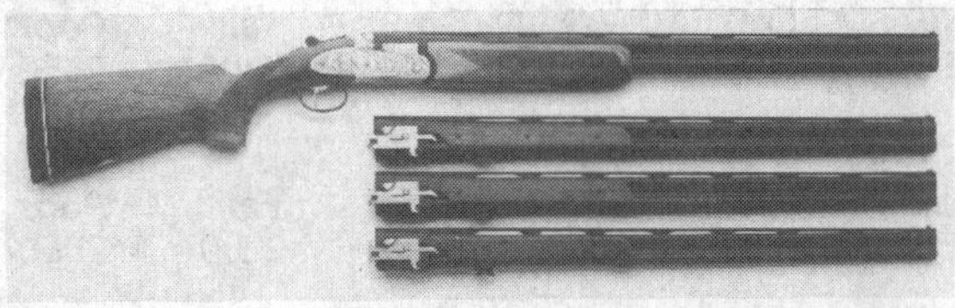

NIB	Exc.	V.G.	Good	Fair	Poor
6400	5000	4500	3750	2500	1500

With Adjustable Stock

Same as Skeet version above, with adjustable comb, drop and cast. Introduced in 1999.

NIB	Exc.	V.G.	Good	Fair	Poor
5000	4000	3200	2500	1500	500

687 EELL Diamond Pigeon Sporting

Sporting clays version of 687 EELL. In 12-gauge only, with 28" ventilated rib barrels fitted with screw-in chokes.

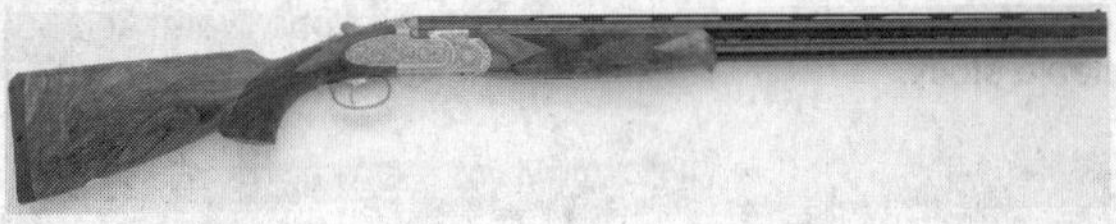

NIB	Exc.	V.G.	Good	Fair	Poor
6000	4750	3500	2500	1750	1200

687 EELL Trap

Fitted with International or Monte Carlo trap stock dimensions. Offered in 12-gauge, with 30" ventilated rib barrels. Fixed or screw-in choke tubes. Weight about 8 lbs. 6 oz.

NIB	Exc.	V.G.	Good	Fair	Poor
4000	3000	2500	2000	1500	1000

687 EELL Top Combo

Single-barrel trap gun. Choice of one single-barrel set and one over/under steel rod barrel. In 30"/32" or 32"/34".

NIB	Exc.	V.G.	Good	Fair	Poor
4700	3500	3000	2250	2000	1000

687 EELL King Ranch

Similar to Silver Pigeon Grade IV, with special cowboy and western engraving. In 20- or 28-gauge only. Introduced 2006. Discontinued 2009.

NIB	Exc.	V.G.	Good	Fair	Poor
3300	2750	2200	1700	1250	800

BERETTA 690 SERIES

Over/under chambered for 12-, 20-, 28-gauge and .410 bore. Barrels are 28" Steelium Optima Bore, with Optima choke tubes. Oiled and checkered walnut stock, with rounded semi-beavertail forend. Satin nickel finish. Sporting model has black finish; Vittoria model in 20-gauge only has stock designed primarily for women; Grade III has game scene roll mark.

Model 690 SeriesField Grade I, Vittoria

NIB	Exc.	V.G.	Good	Fair	Poor
2300	2200	2050	1900	1800	1600

Field Grade III

NIB	Exc.	V.G.	Good	Fair	Poor
2900	2800	2750	2500	2400	2250

Sporting

NIB	Exc.	V.G.	Good	Fair	Poor
2800	2700	2550	2400	2200	2050

Model 691 Sporting Vittoria

Introduced 2019. First Beretta shotgun specifically designed for women. Made of grade 2.5 oiled walnut, the length of pull is reduced and the comb features a semi-Monte Carlo design with a slight drop and additional "toe-out" cast. The checkering on both the stock and the forend are extra fine.

NIB	Exc.	V.G.	Good	Fair	Poor
2800	2700	2550	2400	—	—

Model 692

Introduced in 2014. Replaces 682 series with some features from that series and others from the high-grade DT10 Trident. It has a 1.6" wide receiver for improved balance and weight distribution. In 12-gauge only. Features include 30" or 32" barrels, extra long forcing cones, adjustable trigger and ejectors/extractors, and an optional adjustable comb that can be set to the shooter's drop and cast needs. Gun's balance can also be adjusted by way of weights in the buttstock. This competition-level gun is offered in Sporting, Trap and Skeet configurations. Note: Add $500 for adjustable stock.

Sporting

NIB	Exc.	V.G.	Good	Fair	Poor
4000	3500	3000	2500	—	—

Trap

NIB	Exc.	V.G.	Good	Fair	Poor
3800	3300	2800	2200	—	—

Skeet

NIB	Exc.	V.G.	Good	Fair	Poor
4400	3700	3200	2800	—	—

Model 693

Introduced in July 2014, the 693 over-under blends the best of Beretta's 686/687 series with a few structural and cosmetic innovations. The 693 comes equipped with Steelium barrels and with the OptimaChoke HP system. 3" chamber. The 693 is lighter than the previous generation 687s. With a 26" barrel, about 7 lbs. Rib Type: 6x6mm, flat vented. Sight: Front bead. Chokes: Optima HP Flush: F-IM-M-IC-C. Hand-rubbed-oil Grade 2.5+ walnut.

NIB	Exc.	V.G.	Good	Fair	Poor
2900	2500	2100	1775	—	—

Model 694

Gauge: 12 ga., 3 in. Barrels: 28 in., 30 in., 32 in., with either 10x8 or 10x10 ventilated rib. Weight: 7.8-8.1 lbs. Stock: Walnut with 35/50 and 35/55 B-Fast options. Features: Designed specifically for competition shooting, the 694 has a slim, modern design. Steelium Plus barrels for dense, uniform patterns. Forend iron system with adjustable opening. MicroCore 18mm recoil pad, single centrally positioned adjustable trigger, 1.5 pitch checkering, 2.5-plus grade wood. Matte gray Nistan finish with blue inlay trim. Balance weights of 20g and 40g available separately. Both Sporting and Trap models available.

NIB	Exc.	V.G.	Good	Fair	Poor
4250	3600	3100	—	—	—

Model FS-1

Single-barrel boxlock shotgun in all gauges. A 26" or 28" Full choke barrel. Blued, with checkered walnut stock. Also known as "Companion". Note: Deduct 25% for 12-gauge.

NIB	Exc.	V.G.	Good	Fair	Poor
—	300	220	180	120	90

TR-1 Trap

12-gauge single-barrel boxlock trap gun, with 32" ventilated rib Full choke barrel. Blued, with checkered Monte Carlo stock. Manufactured between 1968 and 1971.

NIB	Exc.	V.G.	Good	Fair	Poor
—	380	250	200	150	100

TR-2 Trap

As above, with high competition-type ventilated rib. Manufactured between 1969 and 1973.

NIB	Exc.	V.G.	Good	Fair	Poor
—	400	280	220	180	120

Mark II Trap

12-gauge boxlock single-barrel trap shotgun, with 32" or 34" Full-choke barrel, competition-type rib and automatic ejector. Blued, with checkered Monte Carlo type walnut stock. Manufactured between 1972 and 1976.

NIB	Exc.	V.G.	Good	Fair	Poor
—	800	620	520	450	280

MODEL ASE 90/GOLD SERIES

Competition trap model over/under shotgun. Features trigger lock assembly that is removable in the field so a spare can be used in event of failure. Single non-selective trigger has three-way adjustment. Ventilated rib is wide and side ribs are also ventilated. Walnut stock and forearms are interchangeable. Special trap recoil pad standard. Receiver silver, with gold inlays or blued on special order. ASE 90 weight about 8 lbs. 6 oz.

ASE 90 Pigeon

Equipped with 28" barrels choked Improved-Modified and Full.

NIB	Exc.	V.G.	Good	Fair	Poor
6750	5250	3750	2750	1200	500

ASE 90 Trap

Comes standard with 30" ventilated rib barrels.

NIB	Exc.	V.G.	Good	Fair	Poor
5950	5250	3750	2750	1200	500

ASE 90 Gold X Trap Combo

Introduced in 1993. Set features single-barrel and interchangeable over/under barrels in 30"/32" and 30"/34" combinations.

NIB	Exc.	V.G.	Good	Fair	Poor
6950	2500	1750	1200	700	350

ASE 90 Skeet

Skeet version of ASE 90 series. Features same basic specifications as trap model. Configured for competition skeet. Offered in 12-gauge only, with 28" Skeet and Skeet chokes. Weight about 7 lbs. 11 oz.

NIB	Exc.	V.G.	Good	Fair	Poor
5950	2500	1750	1200	700	350

ASE 90 Sporting Clay

Configured for sporting clays competition. Offered in 12-gauge only, with 28" or 30" ventilated rib barrels.

NIB	Exc.	V.G.	Good	Fair	Poor
6950	5200	4000	3000	1500	1000

Model SL-2

12-gauge slide-action shotgun, with 26", 28" or 30" ventilated rib barrels. Various chokes. Blued, with checkered walnut stock. Manufactured between 1968 and 1971.

NIB	Exc.	V.G.	Good	Fair	Poor
—	350	300	250	200	150

BERETTA PIGEON SERIES

As above in three grades.

Pigeon SeriesSilver Pigeon

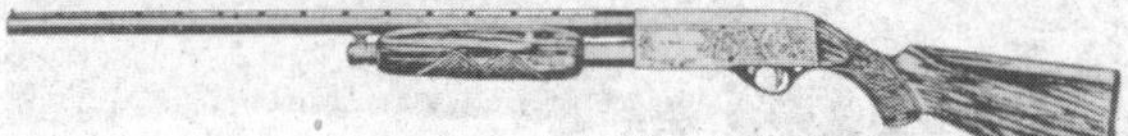

NIB	Exc.	V.G.	Good	Fair	Poor
—	300	250	200	150	110

Gold Pigeon

NIB	Exc.	V.G.	Good	Fair	Poor
—	450	400	300	250	200

Ruby Pigeon

NIB	Exc.	V.G.	Good	Fair	Poor
—	600	550	450	380	280

Silver Pigeon 1

Introduced 2019. Derived from the 680 series. The pistol grip stock and forend of the 686 Silver Pigeon I are manufactured from selected, oil-finished walnut and are finely checkered. Forend is available in Schnabel or rounded version. Microcore recoil pad. Locking system has trapezoidal shoulders and dual conical locking lugs. 5-axis laser engravings in floral motif. Gold-colored single selective trigger with selector located on top of the safety tang. 680 platform ejection system. Steelium Optima Bore HP barrels in tri-alloy Beretta steel on the 12- and 20-gauge hunting version, 26", 28" and 30". 80mm double forcing cone, 70mm Optima Choke HP chokes. The 28-gauge and .410 versions are fitted with the traditional Beretta barrels with 50mm Mobil Chokes. 6x6 vented top rib with non-reflective checkering and traditional steel front bead. Sporting version features a 10x8 rib and ventilated side ribs.

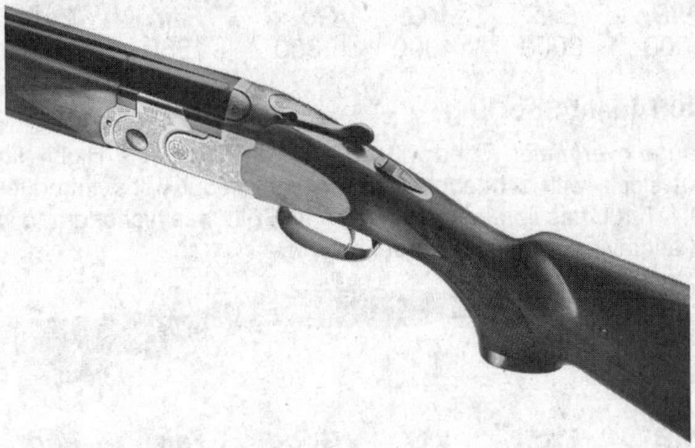

NIB	Exc.	V.G.	Good	Fair	Poor
2000	1800	1600	1400	1200	1050

DT 10 TRIDENT SERIES

These shotguns feature removable trigger mechanism, overbored barrels and special choke tubes.

DT 10 Trident Trap

12-gauge over/under, with a number of options. Barrel is 30" or 32". Highly select walnut stock fitted with Monte Carlo comb. Stock also adjustable. Rib type is .375" with progressive step. Full black rubber recoil pad. Weight about 8.8 lbs. Top single model also offered with 34" barrel. Introduced in 2000. Discontinued 2009.

NIB	Exc.	V.G.	Good	Fair	Poor
7000	5000	4000	2750	1600	500

DT 10 Trident Trap Combo Top

Same as above, with both over/under barrels and single-barrel combo.

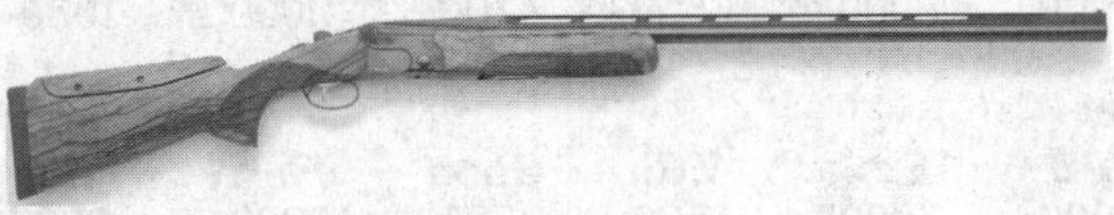

NIB	Exc.	V.G.	Good	Fair	Poor
9000	7500	6500	4700	3000	500

DT 10 Trident Trap Bottom Single

Introduced in 2001. Features choice of 30"/34" or 32"/34" barrel combo. Select walnut stock. Fitted with adjustable point-of-impact rib. Weight about 8.8 lbs.

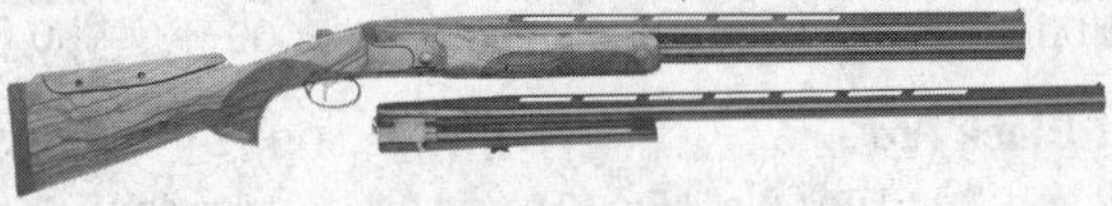

NIB	Exc.	V.G.	Good	Fair	Poor
10500	8500	7500	4700	3000	500

DT 10 Trident Skeet

12-gauge skeet model. Fitted with 28" or 30" barrel. Walnut stock is adjustable. Weight about 8 lbs. Introduced in 2000.

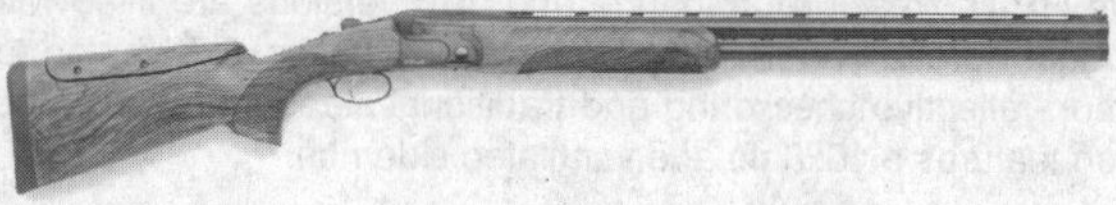

NIB	Exc.	V.G.	Good	Fair	Poor
7000	6000	4000	2850	1880	400

DT 10 Trident Sporting

12-gauge over/under. Fitted with 28", 30" or 32" barrels. Highly figured walnut stock, with schnabel forend. Weight about 8 lbs. Introduced in 2000. DT 10L has floral engraving; DT 10 EELL has higher grade wood, hand engraving and special order only.

NIB	Exc.	V.G.	Good	Fair	Poor
7000	6000	4000	2850	1880	400

DT 10L

NIB	Exc.	V.G.	Good	Fair	Poor
8500	7000	5000	3000	1500	500

DT 10 Trident sportingDT 10 EELL

NIB	Exc.	V.G.	Good	Fair	Poor
13000	11000	8600	6000	3000	800

DT 11 SERIES

DT 11

Top of the line Beretta competition over/under model. Upgraded from DT10 series, with an even wider frame, high-grade hand-checkered walnut stock made to customer's specifications, redesigned top lever and safety selector. In 12-gauge only. Barrel choices are 29.5", 30" or 32", with choke tubes or Fixed Modified and Full chokes, and 2.750" chambers. Variations include Sporting, Skeet, Trap and International Trap, and several sub-categories. Values shown are for the base models in each category.

Sporting

NIB	Exc.	V.G.	Good	Fair	Poor
9900	8000	6500	4700	2000	1000

Skeet

NIB	Exc.	V.G.	Good	Fair	Poor
9000	7000	5500	4500	2000	900

Trap

NIB	Exc.	V.G.	Good	Fair	Poor
9900	8000	6500	4800	2000	1000

International Trap

NIB	Exc.	V.G.	Good	Fair	Poor
7400	6400	5300	4300	2000	900

DT11 Black Pro

Introduced 2018. DT11 Black Pro 12 gauge has an adjustable TSK stock and 30" barrels. 5 OBHP extended chokes included. Beretta by TSK stock has adjustable the comb, cast, length-of-pull, and pitch and two removable muzzle weights. Cross-bolt action is 3mm wider than DT10. Steelium Pro barrels with 480mm forcing cone, barrel bridges are internally hollowed, windowed side ribs. 3" chamber. Sporting and Skeet models.

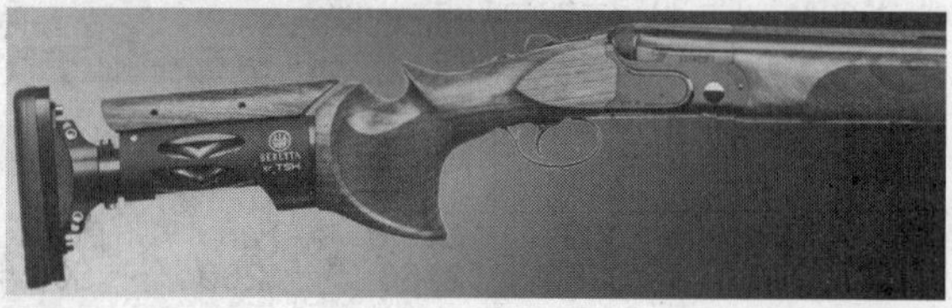

NIB	Exc.	V.G.	Good	Fair	Poor
11700	—	—	—	—	—

DT 11 EELL

NIB	Exc.	V.G.	Good	Fair	Poor
15900	—	—	—	—	—

Ultraleggero

Gauges: 12 ga. Barrels: 26", 28". Steelium Optima-Bore HP with 6x6 rib. Weight: 6.4 to 6.6 pounds. Stock: Wood with Schnabel forend. Features: Built to be the lightest steel receiver shotgun on the market, using techno-polymer receiver inserts. Extralight recoil pad. Single mechanical trigger. Includes ABS hard case and OCHP choke tubes.

NIB	Exc.	V.G.	Good	Fair	Poor
2860	2790	—	—	—	—

SV10 Perennia

New in 2008. Perennia over/under is a 3" 12-gauge shotgun. Featuring oil-finished select walnut stock and laser-engraved nickel high-phosphorous-based finish on receiver. Barrels are 26" or 28". Features Optimachoke HP system introduced in 2008. User-selectable automatic or mechanical shell extraction. Beretta's Kick-Off recoil reduction system available on 28" Perennia. Includes five choke tubes and plastic carrying case. Note: Add $400 for Kick-Off version.

NIB	Exc.	V.G.	Good	Fair	Poor
3250	2000	1450	800	600	300

SL3

Introduced 2018. Designed as a slimmed-down, modernized field-grade iteration of the high-end SO10. Barrels in 26", 28", 30". Boxlock with barrels anchored at hinge pins, lower hooks, and locking pins. Hammer leaf spring trigger from competition shotguns. Newly designed ejectors, Optima Bore HP barrels, rounded receiver.

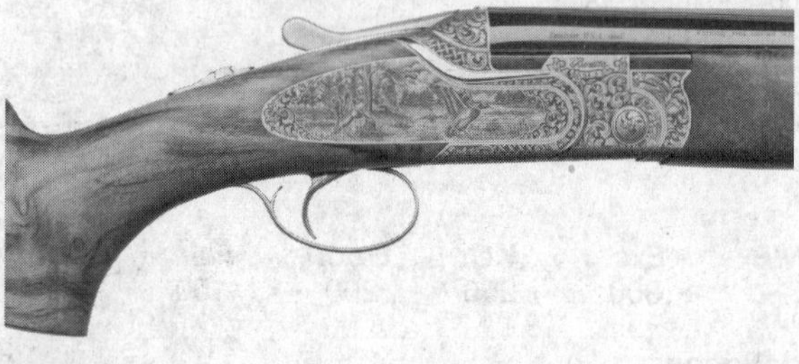

NIB	Exc.	V.G.	Good	Fair	Poor
20000	—	—	—	—	—

SEMI-AUTOMATIC SHOTGUNS

AL SERIES

A 12- or 20-gauge semi-automatic shotgun, with 26", 28" or 30" barrels. Various choke combinations. Blued, with checkered walnut stock. Manufactured between 1969 and 1976.

AL-1

NIB	Exc.	V.G.	Good	Fair	Poor
—	400	380	300	220	150

AL-2

NIB	Exc.	V.G.	Good	Fair	Poor
—	350	300	250	180	120

AL-2 Competition

NIB	Exc.	V.G.	Good	Fair	Poor
—	400	350	300	220	180

AL-2 Magnum

NIB	Exc.	V.G.	Good	Fair	Poor
—	420	380	320	250	200

AL-3

NIB	Exc.	V.G.	Good	Fair	Poor
—	400	350	300	220	180

AL-3 Deluxe Trap

NIB	Exc.	V.G.	Good	Fair	Poor
—	780	700	600	500	420

Model 301

Improved version of AL Series. Manufactured between 1977 and 1982. Also available as slug gun, with 22" barrel and rifle sights.

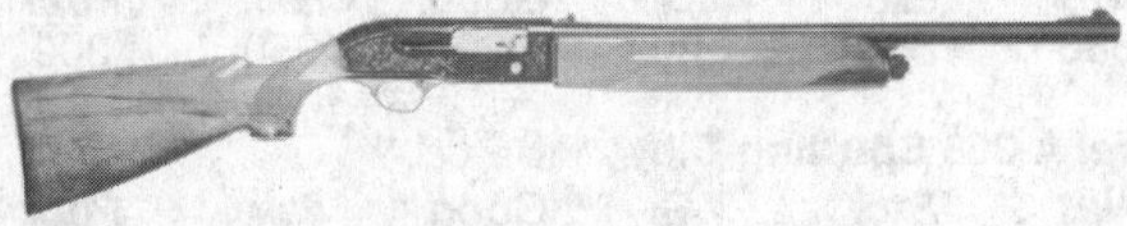

NIB	Exc.	V.G.	Good	Fair	Poor
—	400	350	300	220	180

Model 1200 Field Grade

12-gauge semi-automatic shotgun, with 28" ventilated rib barrel, screw-in choke tubes and 4-round tubular magazine. Matte blued, with checkered walnut or black synthetic stock. Introduced in 1984.

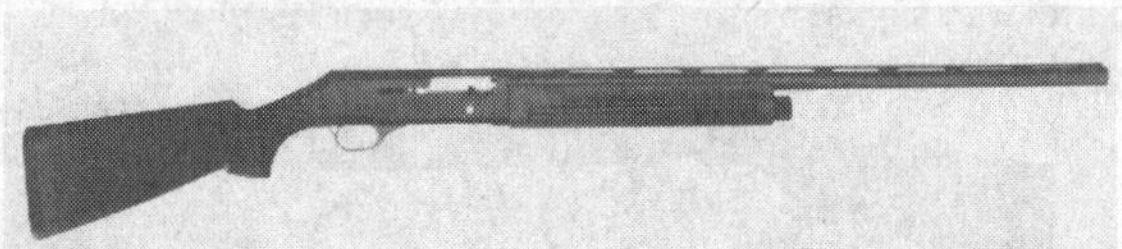

NIB	Exc.	V.G.	Good	Fair	Poor
450	400	300	250	200	150

Model 1200 Magnum

3" chamber.

NIB	Exc.	V.G.	Good	Fair	Poor
580	520	420	320	250	200

Model 1200 Riot

20" cylinder bore barrel.

NIB	Exc.	V.G.	Good	Fair	Poor
580	520	420	320	250	200

Model 1201

This 12-gauge semi-automatic shotgun, has a short recoil system. Features synthetic stock, with matte black finish and lightweight alloy receiver. Available in two basic configurations: Field Grade choice of 24", 26" and 28" ventilated rib barrel with screw-in chokes; Riot Model with 18" plain cylinder choked barrel and full or pistol grip-only stock (introduced in 1993). Weight: Field Grade about 6 lbs. 12 oz.; Riot Model about 6 lbs. 5 oz. Note: Add $40 for Riot Model with pistol grip; $75 for Riot Model with Tritium sights; $100 for ghost ring sights.

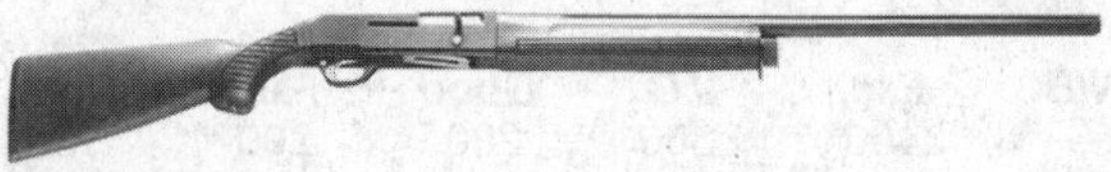

Field Grade

NIB	Exc.	V.G.	Good	Fair	Poor
450	400	350	300	200	150

Riot Model

NIB	Exc.	V.G.	Good	Fair	Poor
650	500	400	350	250	180

Model 1301 Comp

Designed for tactical competition. Choice of 21" or 24" barrel drilled and tapped for rail installation, Optimabore choke system, fiber optic front sight with middle bead and Blink operating system. In 12-gauge only, with 3" chamber. Tactical model is similar, but with 18.5" barrel, oversized operating controls, ghost ring sight and adjustable buttstock. Introduced in 2014.

NIB	Exc.	V.G.	Good	Fair	Poor
1150	1050	950	850	700	550

1301 Viper

NIB	Exc.	V.G.	Good	Fair	Poor
780	650	550	450	400	350

1301 Tactical Marine

Introduced 2019. 37.25" long and weighs 6.4 lbs. 18.5" barrel that comes with both a flush-fitting and extended Beretta Optima HP-compatible Cylinder choke tube. Blink gas-operating system as found on the A400 platform. Stock's LOP is 13.1", with two spacers and a set of shims to adjust drop and cast. Oversized controls for handling with gloves. Ghost-ring rear sight and blade front. Rear sight is adjustable for elevation and windage and has tritium dots. Front blade also has a tritium dot and is protected by two wings. Comes with 3.1" section of aluminum Picatinny rail top mounted on the receiver. Aluminum receiver and steel barrel are coated with silver Aqua-Tech marine finish.

NIB	Exc.	V.G.	Good	Fair	Poor
1000	900	800	700	600	500

1301 Comp Pro

Introduced 2019. Pro version has oversized cocking handle and bolt-release lever, polymeric stock with the Kick-Off Plus system. Rubber Comfort Grip improves sensitivity and pistol grip. MicroCore recoil plate. Blue anodized Ergal aluminum alloy receiver; gas system has rotating head B-Link closure system, 3" chamber with an oversized 3.5" ejection opening. Loading gate is enlarged. Drilled and tapped for a Picatinny rail. Beretta Steelium barrels topped by a 10x8 stepped rib with fiber-optic sight and mid-bead sight.

NIB	Exc.	V.G.	Good	Fair	Poor
1680	1550	1450	1350	1200	1100

Model 302

12- or 20-gauge semi-automatic shotgun. Using 2.75" or 3" shells interchangeably, various barrel lengths and screw-in choke tubes. Blued, with checkered walnut stock. Manufactured between 1982 and 1987.

NIB	Exc.	V.G.	Good	Fair	Poor
—	400	350	280	200	150

Model 302 Super Lusso

As above, with heavily engraved receiver and gold-plated contrasting parts. Presentation grade walnut used for hand-checkered stock. Discontinued in 1986.

NIB	Exc.	V.G.	Good	Fair	Poor
—	2150	2000	1600	1050	850

Model Vittoria/Pintail

Semi-automatic 12-gauge shotgun. Introduced to Beretta product line in 1993. Has short recoil operation. Offered with 24" or 26" ventilated rib barrel, with screw-in chokes. A 24" rifled choke tube version for slugs is also available. Non-reflective matte finish is put on all wood and metal surfaces. Equipped with sling swivels and walnut stock. Weight about 7 lbs. Renamed in 1994.

NIB	Exc.	V.G.	Good	Fair	Poor
600	500	420	350	250	200

ES100 Pintail Synthetic

Introduced in 1999. Essentially same as Pintail above. Addition of black synthetic stock and choice of 24", 26" or 28" ventilated rib barrels, with screw-in chokes. Weight about 7 lbs.

NIB	Exc.	V.G.	Good	Fair	Poor
550	450	380	320	250	200

ES100 Pintail Rifled Slug

Introduced in 1997. Features 24" fully rifled barrel, with adjustable rear sight and removable blade front sight. Receiver is drilled and tapped for scope mount. Hardwood stock with matte finish. Anodized aluminum alloy receiver. Weight about 7 lbs. Fitted with 3" chambers.

NIB	Exc.	V.G.	Good	Fair	Poor
650	550	450	400	250	200

ES100 Rifled Slug

Variation same as Pintail Rifled Slug. Addition of black synthetic stock. Introduced in 1999.

NIB	Exc.	V.G.	Good	Fair	Poor
600	500	420	350	250	200

ES100 Rifled Slug Combo

Same as above, with addition of 28" smooth bored barrel.

NIB	Exc.	V.G.	Good	Fair	Poor
700	600	520	450	350	250

ES100 NWTF Special Camo

12-gauge fitted with 24" barrel and 3" chambers. Stock Mossy Oak camo. Metal black matte finish. Weight about 7.3 lbs. Introduced in 1999.

NIB	Exc.	V.G.	Good	Fair	Poor
980	750	550	380	210	150

A-303 SERIES

12- or 20-gauge semi-automatic shotgun, with 26", 28", 30" or 32" ventilated rib barrels and screw-in choke tubes. Blued, with checkered walnut stock. Introduced in 1987. Various models differ slightly in configuration and/or quality of materials.

Model A-303

NIB	Exc.	V.G.	Good	Fair	Poor
650	600	480	380	300	250

Model A-303 Upland

24" barrel.

NIB	Exc.	V.G.	Good	Fair	Poor
680	650	520	420	350	300

Model A-303 Sporting Clay

NIB	Exc.	V.G.	Good	Fair	Poor
740	700	580	480	400	350

Model A-303 Competition (Trap or Skeet)

NIB	Exc.	V.G.	Good	Fair	Poor
680	650	530	420	350	300

Model A-303 Slug Gun

22" barrel with sights.

NIB	Exc.	V.G.	Good	Fair	Poor
680	650	520	420	350	300

Model A-303 Youth Gun

Version of Model 303. Available in 20-gauge, with shorter length of pull 13.5", than standard. Fitted with rubber recoil pad, screw-in choke tubes and checkered walnut stock.

NIB	Exc.	V.G.	Good	Fair	Poor
500	450	400	300	250	200

Model A-303 Ducks Unlimited

Commemorative version of Model 303. Chambered for 12- or 20-gauge. Manufactured: 5,500 in 12-gauge (1986 and 1987); 3,500 in 20-gauge (1987 and 1988). Commemorative firearms are collectible when NIB, with all furnished materials.

12 Gauge

NIB	Exc.	V.G.	Good	Fair	Poor
580	500	420	320	280	220

20 Gauge

NIB	Exc.	V.G.	Good	Fair	Poor
680	600	520	420	380	320

MODEL AL390/MALLARD SERIES

Series of 12-gauge semi-automatic shotguns. Features self-compensating gas-operating recoil system. All loads from target to 3 Magnums can be used in same gun. Field Model features anodized light alloy receiver, with scroll engraving and matte black receiver top. Magazine capacity 3 rounds. Checkered walnut stock, with recoil pad. Available in ventilated rib barrel lengths from 24" to 30", with 32" on special request. A 22" or 24" slug plain barrel also available. Chokes are fixed or screw-in at customer's option. Shotgun weight about 7 lbs. Beginning in 1996 Beretta offered Silver Mallard shotguns chambered for 20-gauge shell and available with 24", 26 or 28" barrels. Average weight for these 20-gauge guns is 6.4 lbs.

Field Grade

NIB	Exc.	V.G.	Good	Fair	Poor
800	600	450	350	300	200

Slug Gun

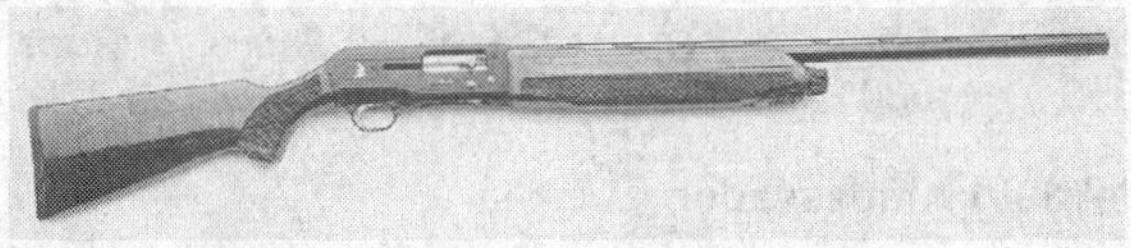

NIB	Exc.	V.G.	Good	Fair	Poor
800	600	450	350	300	200

Synthetic Stock

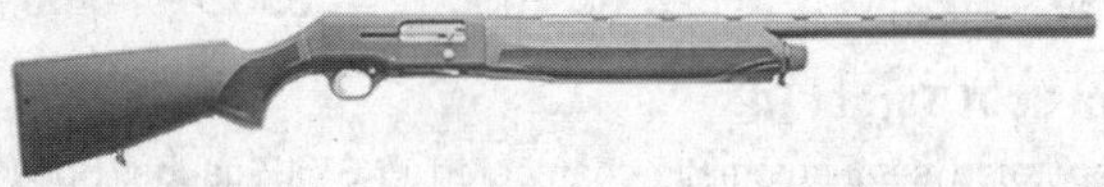

NIB	Exc.	V.G.	Good	Fair	Poor
800	600	450	350	300	200

Camouflage

NIB	Exc.	V.G.	Good	Fair	Poor
800	600	450	350	300	200

Deluxe Grade/Gold Mallard

Gold-filled game animals and select walnut stock.

NIB	Exc.	V.G.	Good	Fair	Poor
700	650	500	350	300	200

AL390 Trap

NIB	Exc.	V.G.	Good	Fair	Poor
680	600	500	400	300	200

AL390 Super Trap

Features ported barrels in 30" or 32", adjustable length of pull and comb.

NIB	Exc.	V.G.	Good	Fair	Poor
800	700	600	500	300	200

AL390 Skeet

NIB	Exc.	V.G.	Good	Fair	Poor
620	550	450	350	250	200

AL390 Super Skeet

Features ported barrel, adjustable cast and length of pull, with adjustable drop. 12-gauge only.

NIB	Exc.	V.G.	Good	Fair	Poor
1000	800	600	500	300	200

AL390 Sporting

NIB	Exc.	V.G.	Good	Fair	Poor
700	550	450	350	250	200

20 gauge

Same as above in 20-gauge. Introduced in 1997. Weight about 6.8 lbs.

NIB	Exc.	V.G.	Good	Fair	Poor
800	600	450	350	250	200

Ported

NIB	Exc.	V.G.	Good	Fair	Poor
720	650	550	400	300	200

AL390 Sport Gold Sporting

Introduced in 1997. Similar to above models, with silver sided receiver and gold engraving. Select walnut stock. 12-gauge only, with choice of 28" or 30" ventilated rib barrels. Weight about 7.6 lbs.

NIB	Exc.	V.G.	Good	Fair	Poor
1100	900	700	450	300	180

AL390 Sport Sporting Youth

Semi-automatic shotgun. Offered in 20-gauge only, with 26" ventilated rib barrel. Length of pull 13.5", with adjustable drop and cast on buttstock. Introduced in 1997. Weight about 6.7 lbs.

NIB	Exc.	V.G.	Good	Fair	Poor
820	680	500	350	200	180

AL390 NWTF Special Youth

Introduced in 1999. Features shortened walnut stock, with 24" 20-gauge ventilated rib barrel. Black matte finish. Weight about 6.4 lbs.

NIB	Exc.	V.G.	Good	Fair	Poor
900	700	520	380	220	180

AL390 Sport Sporting Youth Collection

Same as above, with multi-colored stock and forearm. Introduced in 1997.

NIB	Exc.	V.G.	Good	Fair	Poor
900	750	520	380	220	180

AL390 Sport Diamond Sporting

Introduced in 1998. Features silver sided receiver, with gold engraving. Select walnut stock, with oil-finish and adjustable for drop and cast. Available in 12-gauge, with 28" or 30" barrels. Sold with spare trigger group and orange front sight beads. Weight about 7.6 lbs.

NIB	Exc.	V.G.	Good	Fair	Poor
3000	2600	1950	1300	600	300

AL390 Camo

12-gauge shotgun offered with 24" or 28" ventilated rib barrel. Barrel, receiver, stock and forearm have woodland camo finish. Weight about 7.5 lbs. Offered first time in 1997.

NIB	Exc.	V.G.	Good	Fair	Poor
1000	780	600	450	300	150

AL390 Waterfowl/Turkey Model

Matte finish.

NIB	Exc.	V.G.	Good	Fair	Poor
550	500	450	350	300	250

AL390 NWTF Special Camo

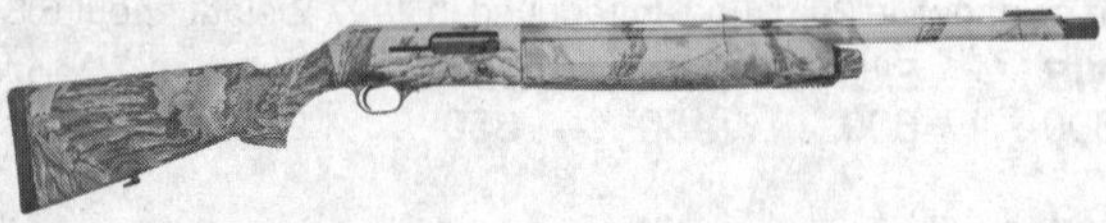

NIB	Exc.	V.G.	Good	Fair	Poor
1100	880	620	500	320	150

AL390 NWTF Special Synthetic

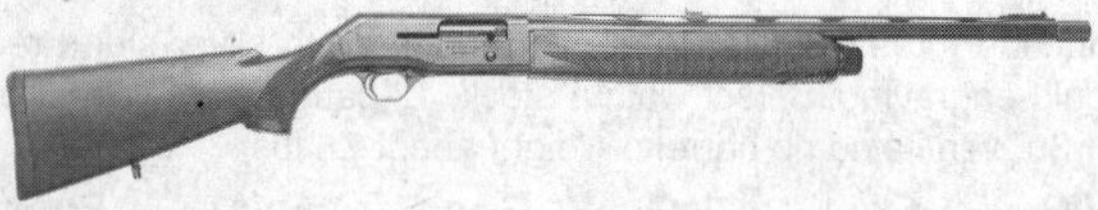

NIB	Exc.	V.G.	Good	Fair	Poor
920	750	600	450	300	150

Super Trap

Ported barrels, adjustable comb and length of pull.

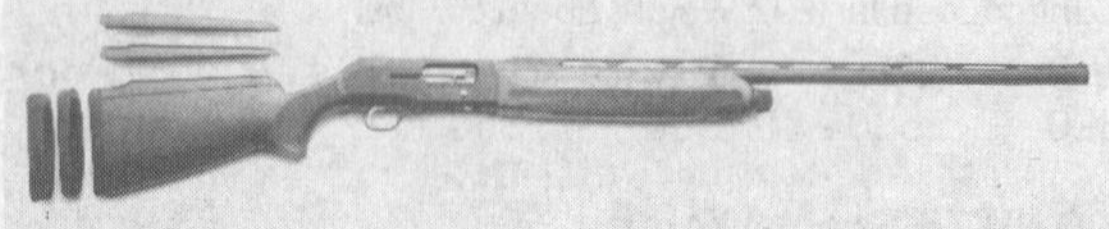

NIB	Exc.	V.G.	Good	Fair	Poor
980	800	650	500	320	180

Super Skeet

Ported barrels, adjustable comb and length of pull.

NIB	Exc.	V.G.	Good	Fair	Poor
950	800	650	500	320	180

3901 SERIES

Series introduced in 2005. Built around A390 shotgun. The 3901 guns feature gas operating system, choke tubes and removable trigger group.

Model 3901

Introduced in 2003. Semi-automatic shotgun offered in 12-gauge, with 26" or 28" barrel. Charcoal gray synthetic stock. Black rubber recoil pad. Non-reflective black finish. Weight about 7.5 lbs.

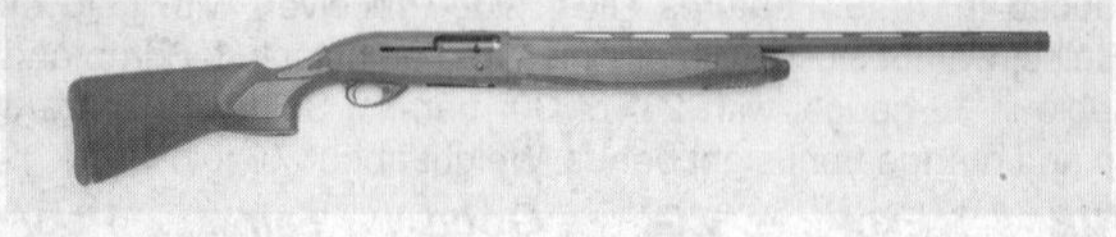

NIB	Exc.	V.G.	Good	Fair	Poor
730	580	450	300	220	180

Model 3901 RL

As above in 20-gauge, with reduced-length buttstock. Introduced in 2003.

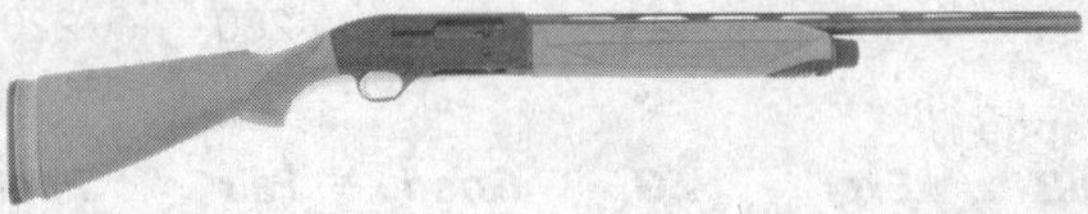

NIB	Exc.	V.G.	Good	Fair	Poor
730	580	450	300	220	180

Model 3901 Camo

12-gauge offered in Mossy Oak Shadowgrass camo stock. Choice of 24" or 26" barrel. Introduced in 2003.

NIB	Exc.	V.G.	Good	Fair	Poor
840	650	480	350	250	180

Model 3901 Citizen

Offered in 12- or 20-gauge, with 26" or 28" ventilated rib barrels and choke tubes. Black synthetic stock. Rubber recoil pad. Weight about: 7.6 lbs. 12-gauge; 7 lbs. 20-gauge.

NIB	Exc.	V.G.	Good	Fair	Poor
750	600	450	300	220	180

Model 3901 Statesman

As above, with checkered walnut stock.

NIB	Exc.	V.G.	Good	Fair	Poor
850	680	480	320	250	180

Model 3901 Ambassador

Model has all features of Statesman. Fitted with select checkered X-tra wood stock, with Gel-Tek recoil pad. Weight about: 7.2 lbs. 12-gauge; 6.6 lbs. 20-gauge.

NIB	Exc.	V.G.	Good	Fair	Poor
950	750	520	450	350	200

Model 3901 Target RL

Gas-operated semi-automatic chambered in 3" 12-gauge. Specifically designed for smaller-stature shooters, with adjustable length of pull from 12" to 13". Stock adjustable for cast on or cast off. Adjustable comb and Sporting style flat rib. Available in 12-gauge only, with 26" or 28" barrel.

NIB	Exc.	V.G.	Good	Fair	Poor
900	700	550	400	300	180

AL 391 URIKA SERIES

Urika

Introduced in 2000. Semi-automatic shotgun offered in 12- and 20-gauge. Choice of barrels from 24" to 30" depending on gauge. Stock walnut, with checkered grip and forend. Rubber recoil pad. Gold trigger. Choke tubes. Weight about: 7.3 lbs. 12-gauge; 6 lbs. 20-gauge.

NIB	Exc.	V.G.	Good	Fair	Poor
850	750	600	450	300	180

Urika Synthetic

Same as above. Fitted with black synthetic stock and gripping inserts. Offered in 12-gauge only. Introduced in 2000.

NIB	Exc.	V.G.	Good	Fair	Poor
950	750	620	520	320	200

Urika Camo

12-gauge offered with Realtree Hardwoods camo or Advantage Wetlands camo. In 24" or 26" barrels. Weight about 7.3 lbs. First introduced in 2000.

NIB	Exc.	V.G.	Good	Fair	Poor
1050	800	650	550	300	180

Urika Gold

Features 26" or 28" barrel, with choke tubes. Black receiver model offered in both 12- and 20-gauge. Weight about 7.3 lbs. Silver receiver model (lightweight) available in 12- gauge only. Weight about 6.6 lbs. Both configurations fitted with highly figured walnut stock. Gold trigger. Introduced in 2000.

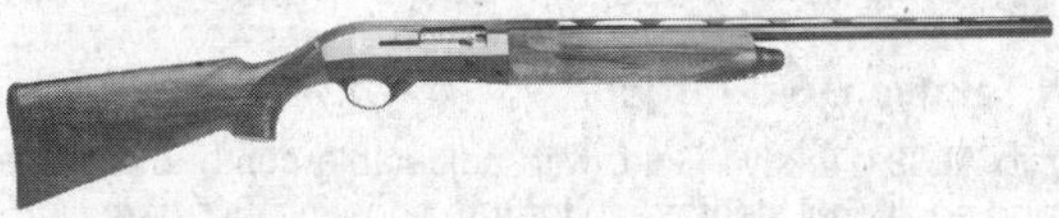

NIB	Exc.	V.G.	Good	Fair	Poor
900	820	750	680	320	200

Urika Youth

20-gauge features walnut stock, with shorter length of pull than standard and 24" barrel. Weight about 6 lbs. Introduced in 2000.

NIB	Exc.	V.G.	Good	Fair	Poor
900	800	600	450	280	200

Urika Sporting

Offered in 12- and 20-gauge. Fitted with 28" or 30" barrels. Select walnut checkered stock. Gold trigger. Chambered for 3" shells. Weight about: 7.3 lbs. 12-gauge; 6 lbs. 20-gauge. Introduced in 2000.

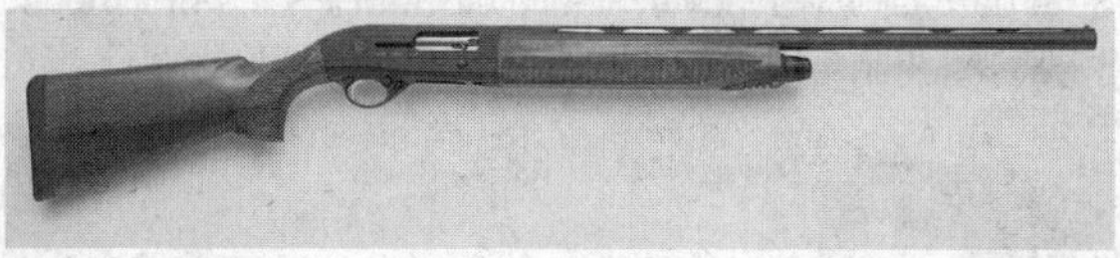

NIB	Exc.	V.G.	Good	Fair	Poor
1100	750	600	500	350	180

Urika Gold Sporting

Offered in 12-gauge, with black or silver receiver. The 20-gauge offered with black receiver only. Fitted with 28" or 30" barrels. Highly select checkered walnut stock. Chambered for 3" shells. Introduced in 2000. Note: Add $30 for 12-gauge silver receiver.

NIB	Exc.	V.G.	Good	Fair	Poor
1300	950	700	600	450	180

Urika Trap

12-gauge fitted with 30" or 32" barrels. Select checkered walnut stock, with Monte Carlo comb. Chambered for 3" shells. Weight about 7.2 lbs. Introduced in 2000.

NIB	Exc.	V.G.	Good	Fair	Poor
1000	750	600	500	350	180

Urika Gold Trap

Similar to standard Urika Trap, with highly selected checkered walnut stock and black receiver.

NIB	Exc.	V.G.	Good	Fair	Poor
1300	950	700	600	450	180

Urika Parallel Target RL/SL

This is a 12-gauge competition model, fitted with 28" or 30" barrels and select walnut Monte Carlo stock. The "RL" has standard stock configurations, while the "SL" has a shorter length of pull.

NIB	Exc.	V.G.	Good	Fair	Poor
1100	750	600	500	350	200

URIKA OPTIMA SERIES

First offered in 2003, these shotguns are similar to standard Urika model. Feature Beretta's Optima-Bore overbored barrels, with flush Optima-Choke Plus tubes.

Urika Optima

Offered in 12-gauge, with 26" or 28" ventilated rib barrel. Checkered select walnut stock. Gold trigger. Chamber is 3". Weight about 7.3 lbs.

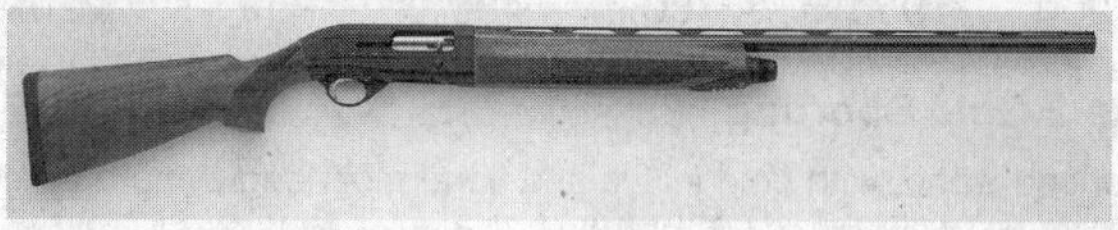

NIB	Exc.	V.G.	Good	Fair	Poor
1500	1180	820	650	450	300

Urika Synthetic Optima

As above, with synthetic stock and rubber inserts. Weight about 7.4 lbs.

NIB	Exc.	V.G.	Good	Fair	Poor
1300	1100	750	580	400	320

Urika Optima Camo

As above, with camo stock.

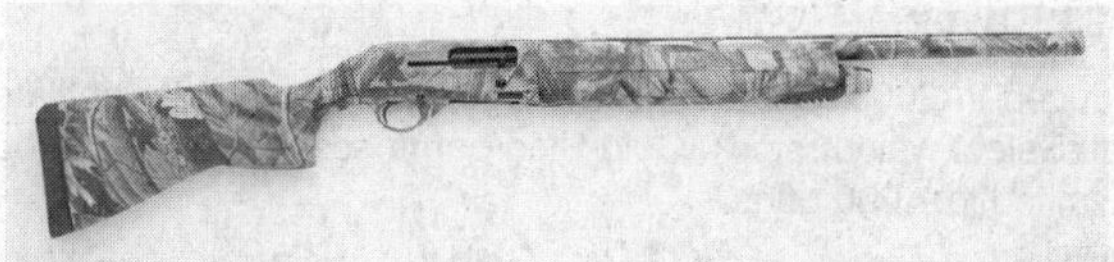

NIB	Exc.	V.G.	Good	Fair	Poor
1350	1200	950	620	450	250

URIKA 2 SERIES

Introduced in 2007. Urika 2 is an enhanced version of original AL391 Urika. Improvements include addition of spinning self-cleaning action for faster cycling and longer functioning periods between cleanings.

Urika 2 X-Tra Grain

Series features Beretta's wood-enhancement treatment to highlight color contrast of wood. Offered in 3", 12- and 20-gauge, with 26" and 28" barrels. A 20-gauge youth model, with shorter stock and 24" barrel also offered.

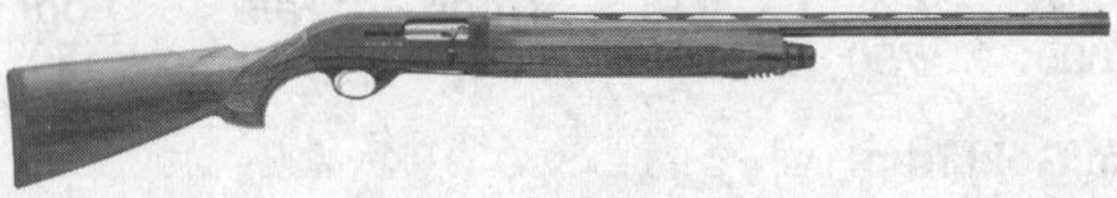

NIB	Exc.	V.G.	Good	Fair	Poor
1000	900	720	580	400	250

Urika 2 Gold

Select oil-finished wood stock and forend, with gold-filled game bird inlays on receiver. 12-gauge 28" barrel; 20-gauge 26" barrel.

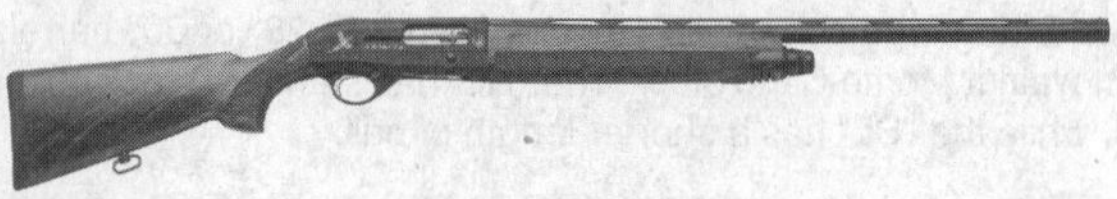

NIB	Exc.	V.G.	Good	Fair	Poor
1350	1080	720	500	380	250

Urika 2 Kick-Off

Waterfowl models feature Beretta's Kick-Off recoil reduction system. Matte black synthetic, Max-4 or Realtree AP finish, with 26" or 28" barrel. Note: Add 10% for camo finish; deduct 30 percent for models without Kick-Off.

NIB	Exc.	V.G.	Good	Fair	Poor
1200	950	700	480	350	220

Urika 2 Sporting X-Tra Grain

Sporting clay model in 12- and 20-gauge, with 28" or 30" barrel.

NIB	Exc.	V.G.	Good	Fair	Poor
1200	950	700	480	350	220

Urika 2 Gold Sporting

Enhanced wood, with gold inlays and floral motif engraving on receiver. In 12-gauge, with 28" or 30" barrel.

NIB	Exc.	V.G.	Good	Fair	Poor
1300	1020	780	520	380	280

Urika 2 Parallel Target X-Tra Grain

Target model in 12-gauge, with 28", 30" or 32" barrel.

NIB	Exc.	V.G.	Good	Fair	Poor
1250	980	750	520	380	300

Urika 2 Gold Parallel Target

Enhanced wood, with gold inlays and floral motif engraving on receiver. In 12-gauge, with 30" or 32" barrel.

NIB	Exc.	V.G.	Good	Fair	Poor
1400	1080	750	520	400	260

AL391 Covey

Introduced in 2003. Offered in 20-gauge, with 26" or 28" ventilated rib barrel. Select walnut stock. Gold-filled game scenes. Weight about 5.9 lbs. Limited to 1,000 guns.

NIB	Exc.	V.G.	Good	Fair	Poor
1350	1080	720	500	380	250

AL391 Ringneck

As above, with gold-filled pheasants. In 12-gauge only. Weight about 7.3 lbs. Limited to 1,000 guns. Introduced in 2003.

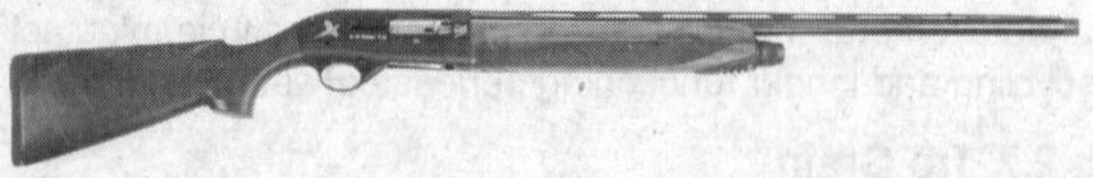

NIB	Exc.	V.G.	Good	Fair	Poor
1360	1080	800	550	400	300

AL391 Teknys

Features nickel receiver, with polished sides and anti-glare top. Offered in 12- or 20-gauge, with 26" or 28" ventilated rib barrel. Xtra-wood stock with Gel-Tek recoil. Weight about: 7.2 lbs. 12-gauge; 5.9 lbs. 20-gauge. Introduced in 2003.

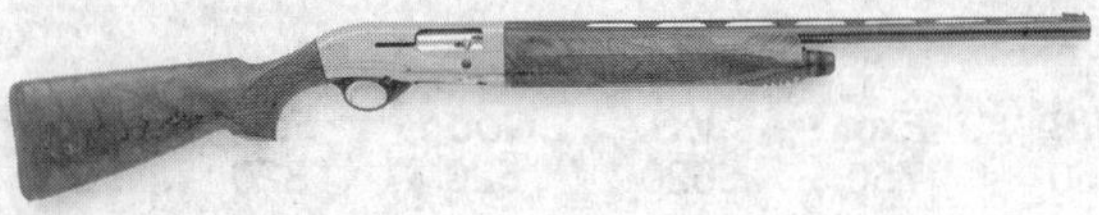

NIB	Exc.	V.G.	Good	Fair	Poor
1150	900	750	500	350	250

AL391 Teknys Gold

As above, with engraved hunting scene on receiver, gold plated trigger, jeweled breech bolt and carrier. Select walnut checkered stock, with oil-finish. Introduced in 2003.

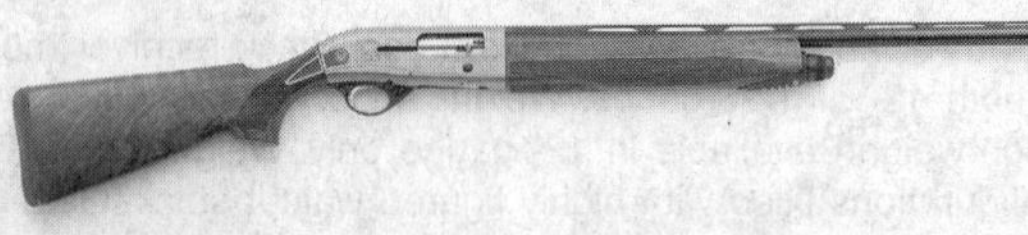

NIB	Exc.	V.G.	Good	Fair	Poor
1460	1100	850	580	420	320

AL391 Teknys Gold Target

Similar to AL391 Teknys Gold, with adjustable comb, 8.5 oz. recoil reducer and additional stepped rib for trap shooting. 30" barrel.

NIB	Exc.	V.G.	Good	Fair	Poor
1660	1300	980	600	450	350

AL391 Teknys King Ranch

Introduced in 2005.

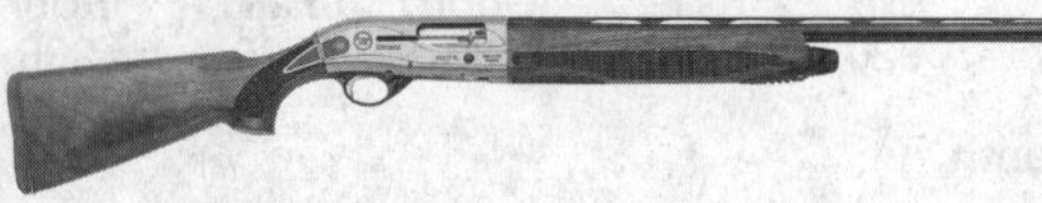

NIB	Exc.	V.G.	Good	Fair	Poor
1650	1300	1000	720	620	380

AL391 XTREMA SERIES

AL391 Xtrema 3.5

Introduced in 2002. This model is a Urika overbuilt to handle 12-gauge 3.5" Super Magnum loads. Offered with choice of 24", 26" or 28" ventilated rib barrels, with black synthetic stock or choice of various camo stocks. Weight about 7.8 lbs. Note: Add $100 for camo finish.

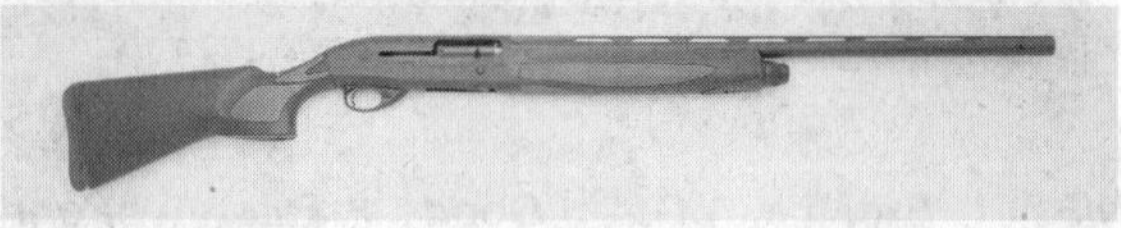

NIB	Exc.	V.G.	Good	Fair	Poor
1150	900	750	500	350	250

AL391 Xtrema2

Upgraded version of Xtrema. Additional recoil-reducing features introduced in 2005. Available with 24", 26" or 28" barrels, with black Max-4 HD or Hardwoods HD synthetic stock. Optima-Bore five choke system. Optional Kick Off recoil reduction feature available. Note: Add 10 percent for camo finish; 30 percent for Kick Off option.

NIB	Exc.	V.G.	Good	Fair	Poor
1300	950	800	650	400	300

AL391 Xtrema2 Slug Gun

24" rifled barrel version of Xtrema2. Introduced in 2006. Black synthetic only. Note: Add 10 percent for Kick Off option.

NIB	Exc.	V.G.	Good	Fair	Poor
1200	920	800	650	400	300

UGB25 XCEL

Introduced in 2005. Semi-automatic break-open competition trap gun. Chambered for 12-gauge 2.75" shell. Gun is fed from side with bottom ejection. Choice of 30" or 32" barrel, with high trap-style interchangeable rib. Choke tubes. Checkered walnut stock has adjustable comb and length of pull. Weight about 7.7 to 9 lbs. depending on barrel length and rib.

NIB	Exc.	V.G.	Good	Fair	Poor
3600	2800	2150	1680	850	450

A300 Outlander Sporting

Introduced 2018. Optimized to run lighter loads, the gas system also includes a valve system that decreases the pressure of more powerful shells. Additionally, the A300 Sporting's larger, heavier walnut stock dampens kick. 30-inch barrel, widened rib, front and mid beads, palm swell on the grip, and extended chokes. Three-inch-chamber 12-gauge comes with three MobilChoke Victory tubes (IC, M and F).

NIB	Exc.	V.G.	Good	Fair	Poor
950	800	650	500	—	—

A300 Outlander Camo Turkey

NIB	Exc.	V.G.	Good	Fair	Poor
800	650	500	—	—	—

A300 Outlander Turkey Xtra Green Camo

NIB	Exc.	V.G.	Good	Fair	Poor
1000	850	750	650	550	450

A300 Outlander Trident

NIB	Exc.	V.G.	Good	Fair	Poor
900	750	600	500	400	350

A300 Ultima Turkey

Gauges: 12 ga., 20 ga. Barrels: 24". Stock: Synthetic in Realtree Edge or Mossy Oak DNA. Features: New turkey hunting-specific addition to the A300 Ultima family of semi-autos. Low-profile receiver with oversized loading port. Enlarged controls. Picatinny top rail. Mid bead and fiber-optic front sight. KickOff recoil system comes standard. Extended Mobil choke.

NIB	Exc.	V.G.	Good	Fair	Poor
920	850	—	—	—	—

A300 Ultima Patrol

Gauges: 12 ga., 20 ga. Barrel: 19.1" Stock: Synthetic. Features: New defense-style addition to the A300 Ultima family of semi-autos. Low-profile receiver with oversized loading port. Enlarged controls. Wide 7x7 stepped rib with a mid-bead. KickOff recoil system included as standard configuration on most models. Tactical sights with fiber optic front. Thinner forend with M-LOK and QD points. 7+1-round extended magazine tube secured with barrel clamp. Add 8% for the tiger stripe finish.

NIB	Exc.	V.G.	Good	Fair	Poor
980	—	—	—	—	—

A350 Xtrema

3.5" waterfowl gun. Self-cleaning piston and cross tube magazine. 28" forged barrel made from Steelium; uses Optima HP choke system. Micro Core recoil pad. Length-of-pull adjustments and drop/cast shims provided. Introduced 2016.

NIB	Exc.	V.G.	Good	Fair	Poor
1000	850	700	550	400	—

A400 Xplor Unico

Self-regulation gas-operated shotgun. Chambered to shoot all 12-gauge loads from 2.75" to 3.5". Features include Kick-Off hydraulic damper; 26" or 28" "Steelium" barrel, with interchangeable choke tubes; anodized aluminum receiver; sculpted, checkered walnut buttstock and forend. Note: Add $100 for Kick-Off Recoil reduction system.

NIB	Exc.	V.G.	Good	Fair	Poor
1500	1250	1050	800	550	300

A400 Xcel Sporting

Similar to Xplor Unico, except designed for Sporting Clays competition. 12-gauge, 3" chambers, with 28" 30" and 32" barrels. Blue aluminum receiver, optional Kick-Off recoil reduction system. Gun Pod optional system available, with digital readout of temperature, ammo pressure and other information. Note: Add $100 for Kick-Off Recoil reduction system or Gun Pod.

NIB	Exc.	V.G.	Good	Fair	Poor
1600	1300	1050	800	550	300

A400 Extreme KO

Uses Beretta's Blink gas-operating system. Said to be able to handle all 12-gauge loads from 2.750" to 3.500". Includes Kick-Off recoil reduction system. Synthetic stock offered in black or camo, with non-slip rubber gripping sections.

NIB	Exc.	V.G.	Good	Fair	Poor
1500	1250	1000	800	600	350

A400 Extreme Plus

Introduced 2018. Building on the company's A400 Xtreme Unico model, the A400 Xtreme Plus combines the advanced barrel technologies used in clay shooting with the needs of the waterfowler. The Steelium Plus barrel design features a 14" forcing cone. The 7x7 stepped rib has a fiber-optic front sight and an integral mid-bead. Enlarged loading port, extended charging handle and bolt release, Kick-Off Mega system and Soft-Comb stock. Available in Realtree Max-5, Mossy Oak Bottomland,

DRT, Black Synthetic, and Optifade finishes. 26", 28", and 30" barrels. 3.5" chamber. Receiver is drilled and tapped to attach a Picatinny rail (rail not included). Hard polymer case. Five Black Edition chokes. RL (Reduced Length) version introduced 2019.

NIB	Exc.	V.G.	Good	Fair	Poor
1650	1400	1250	1100	950	800

A400 Xcel Multi Target

This model has a quick-adjustable rib and comb to allow multi-competition use for skeet, trap and sporting clays. In 12-gauge only, with 30" or 32" barrel and four Optima HP choke tubes. Stock available with a Micro-Core recoil pad or internal Kick-Off system. Note:Add $100 for Kick-Off.

NIB	Exc.	V.G.	Good	Fair	Poor
2500	2000	1300	900	450	300

A400 Upland

Introduced 2018. First Beretta wood stock with Kick-Off Plus technology that reduces recoil up to 50%. Nickel-plated receiver with game-scene engraving. New pistol grip and forend. Available in 12-gauge only with a 3" chamber. Comes with 24", 26", 28" and 30" Steelium barrels and a 6x6 sighting rib. OCHP (Optima Choke High Performance) choke system. Receiver accepts mounting rings for red dot or optical sights.

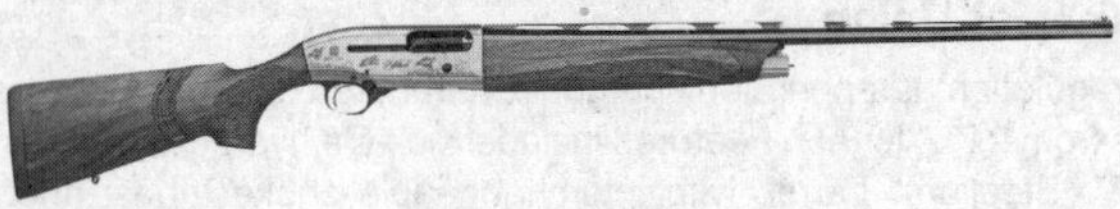

NIB	Exc.	V.G.	Good	Fair	Poor
1500	1400	1300	1200	—	—

A400 Upland 28

Gauges: 28 ga. Barrels: 28" with 5x5 top rib. Stock: Wood, pistol grip style. Features: Latest addition to the A400 Upland family of gas-operated semi-autos. Nickel-plated receiver with unique "28" gauge-specific receiver engraving. Magnum, 3" chamber. Field strip without tools. Extra-light recoil pad. Ships with three OPHC flush chokes.

Beretta's Upland 28 was unveiled at SHOT Show 2023 to much fanfare. Photo: Corey Graff

NIB	Exc.	V.G.	Good	Fair	Poor
1710	1620	—	—	—	—

A400 Lite Max-5

Introduced 2018. 12-gauge and 20-gauge variants, 3" chamber, 26" or 28" Steelium tri-alloy steel barrels. Realtree MAX-5 camo finish, Kick-Off Plus shock absorption and GunPod 2 monitoring system. The GunPod 2 is a built-in monitoring system within the grip that keeps track of shots fired in total and per each individual session. Interfaces with mobile app to allow the user to keep track of the path and distance covered on a map per each hunting trip.

NIB	Exc.	V.G.	Good	Fair	Poor
1500	1400	1300	1200	—	—

A400 Xcel Parallel Target

NIB	Exc.	V.G.	Good	Fair	Poor
1700	1600	1500	1350	1200	1000

TX4 Storm

Gas-operated semi-automatic shotgun. Chambered for 3" 12-gauge shells. Features include 18" barrel, with interchangeable choke tubes; adjustable ghost ring rear sight, with military-style front sight; adjustable length of pull; integral Picatinny rail on receiver; 5+1 capacity; soft rubber grip inlays in buttstock and forend.

NIB	Exc.	V.G.	Good	Fair	Poor
1200	1000	750	500	350	250

PUMP SHOTGUNS

RS202 Pump Shotguns

Pump action 12 ga., introduced in the 1980s. RS202P has a traditional wooden stock. RS202M1 & RS202M2 have a folding stock, with the M2 adding a ventilated barrel shield handguard and other features. Pricing for these models and pump shotgun Models RS151, RS200, SL2, and the Pigeon series, along with semi-auto/pump Model M3P to be provided in future editions. Reader input is invited.

BERGARA
Bergara, Spain

This Spanish barrel maker began making sporting and tactical rifles for the U.S. market in 2013.

B-14 Timber and Woodsman

NIB	Exc.	V.G.	Good	Fair	Poor
800	680	580	350	250	150

B-14 Hunter

A bolt-action hunting rifle in two synthetic-stocked models with hinged floorplate (Hunter with No. 4 profile barrel, Ridge with No. 5 barrel and muzzle threaded 5/8x24). Barrel lengths can include 18", 22" and 24" depending on caliber. Calibers include .22-250, .243, 6.5 Creedmoor, .270 Win, 7-08, 7mm Rem Mag, .308 Win, .30-06 and .300 Win Mag. Introduced in 2013 as the B-14 Hunter model. Note: Add $40 for Ridge.

NIB	Exc.	V.G.	Good	Fair	Poor
700	600	500	300	180	120

B-14 HMR

This Hunting Match rifle has a heavy barrel No. 5.5 or 6, threaded muzzle and AICS-style magazines. Features include fully adjustable carbon-fiber stock, sliding plate extractor, plunger ejector, two-position safety, adjustable trigger and Cerakote Gray finish. Calibers include .22-250, 6mm C, 6.5 C, 7mm Rem Mag, .308, .300 Win Mag, .450 Bushmaster. Introduced in 2017. Note: Add $30 for left-hand action.

NIB	Exc.	V.G.	Good	Fair	Poor
980	830	700	420	250	150

B-14 BMP

The Bergara Match Precision rifle is currently chambered in 6.5 Creedmoor (No. 6 profile barrel 24") or.308 Winchester (No. 6, 20") with 5-shot AICS-style detachable magazine. Fully adjustable BMP Chassis stock.

NIB	Exc.	V.G.	Good	Fair	Poor
1450	1220	1050	620	380	200

B-14R Rimfire

Caliber: .22 LR. Capacity: 10. Barrel: 18 in., 4140 Bergara. Stock: HMR composite. Sights: None. Weight: 9.25 lbs. Features: Threaded muzzle, B-14R action, Remington 700 accessories compatible.

NIB	Exc.	V.G.	Good	Fair	Poor
1000	900	—	—	—	—

B-14 Squared Crest

Calibers: 6.5 Creedmoor, 6.5 PRC, .308 Win., .300 Win. Mag. Barrel: 20", (22 in. .300 WM) round steel. Weights: from 6.8–7.2 lbs. Stock: 100% carbon fiber with carbon spine. Features: Addition to the B-14 bolt action family. Sniper Gray Cerakote metalwork. Sub-MOA guarantee. Threaded muzzle with Omni brake. M5 AICS-style magazine.

NIB	Exc.	V.G.	Good	Fair	Poor
1850	—	—	—	—	—

BCR-13 Sport Hunter

Bolt-action rifle has a pillar-bedded McMillan Hunter stock, with olive/black/tan finish. Shilen or Timney trigger. 22" barrel, with Weaver style two-piece scope base. Chambered in .270 Win., .308 Win., .30-06. Discontinued.

NIB	Exc.	V.G.	Good	Fair	Poor
3000	2500	2000	1800	1000	500

BC-15 Long Range Hunter

Similar to BCR-13. Has McMillan A3 Sporter stock, with olive/black/tan finish. Chambered in .300 Win. Magnum or .300 Rem. Ultra Magnum, with 24" barrel. Discontinued.

NIB	Exc.	V.G.	Good	Fair	Poor
3600	3000	2400	2000	1200	500

BX-11 Takedown Hunter

Chambered in .243 Win., .270 Win., .308 Win., .30-06 or .300 Win. Magnum, with black synthetic or walnut stock featuring rubber grip panels. Can be broken down for easy carry or storage. Discontinued.

NIB	Exc.	V.G.	Good	Fair	Poor
1600	1450	1200	900	540	320

BCR-19 Tactical Rifle

Features OD Green McMillan A4 stock, with adjustable butt and comb, pillar-bedding, Timney or Shilen trigger and 26" nitride finished stainless steel barrel. Chambered in .308 Win. or .300 Win. Magnum. Discontinued.

NIB	Exc.	V.G.	Good	Fair	Poor
3900	3400	3000	2500	1500	900

BCR-17 Medium Tactical

Similar to BCR-19, with 22" barrel. McMillan A3 stock, with olive/black/tan finish. Chambered only in .308 Win. Discontinued.

NIB	Exc.	V.G.	Good	Fair	Poor
3600	3000	2200	1900	1000	500

Mountain Hunter

Features a Bergara custom action, lightweight fiberglass stock, 20" stainless No. 2 contour barrel, pillar-bedded action and Timney trigger. Chambered in .243 Win., .270 Win., 7mm-08 Rem., .308 Win., .30-06 or .300 Win. Magnum. Weight less than 5.9 lbs. Discontinued.

NIB	Exc.	V.G.	Good	Fair	Poor
2700	2300	1800	1080	650	250

Mountain 2.0

Calibers: 6.5 Creedmoor, 6.5 PRC, .308 Win., 28 Nosler, .300 Win. Mag., .300 PRC. Capacity: 2 to 4. Barrel: 22 to 24-in., No. 3 stainless steel. Stock: Carbon fiber. Sights: None, drilled and tapped. Features: Trigger tech trigger, two-lug action, Cerakote finished metal.

NIB	Exc.	V.G.	Good	Fair	Poor
2150	—	—	—	—	—

Premier Series Classic

This series of rifles is advertised as being as close to custom as it can get. Custom features include a choice of high-grade hand-rubbed oil-finish Grade 5 Monte Carlo walnut or hand-laid fiberglass stock, both featuring an aluminum bedding block. Premier action has a separate floating bolt head, two-positioned safety that allows bolt to operate while on safe, Timney trigger and hinged floor plate. Premier Classic chambered in 6.5 C, .270, .280 Ackley Imp, .308, .30-06 and .300 Win Mag. Introduced in 2016. Discontinued.

NIB	Exc.	V.G.	Good	Fair	Poor
2000	1600	1250	1060	640	380

Premier Long Range

Available in 6mm Creedmoor, 6.5mm Creedmoor, .270 Win., .280 Ackley Imp., .308 Win., .300 Win. Magnum. Barrel lengths 20", 24" or 26". Adjustable carbon-fiber stock. Other features similar to other Premier series. models. Introduced in 2017. Discontinued.

NIB	Exc.	V.G.	Good	Fair	Poor
2300	2000	1650	1400	840	500

PREMIER SERIES

Barrel and bolt action of 416 stainless steel, Cerakote finished metal, its one-piece bolt has two locking lugs with floating bolt head, two-position safety, TriggerTech trigger and 1-MOA accuracy guarantee. These features are common on the new models added in 2019 below.

Ridgeback

As PSR above with weight about 10 lbs. with medium Palma-taper barrel, lengths of 20", 24" or 26" depending on caliber, adjustable fiberglass stock, AICS-style detachable magazine and threaded muzzle. Calibers include: 6mm Creedmoor, 6.5 Creedmoor, 6.5 PRC, .308 Win., .300 Win. Mag., .300 PRC. New for 2019.

NIB	Exc.	V.G.	Good	Fair	Poor
1800	1600	—	—	—	—

Highlander

As PSR above, with average weight of 7.4 lbs, fiberglass stock, hinged floorplate No. 5 profile barrel chambered in 6.5 C, 6.5 PRC, .270 Win, 7-08, .280 Ackley Imp, 7mm Rem Mag, .308, .30-06, .300 Win Mag, .300 PRC. New for 2019.

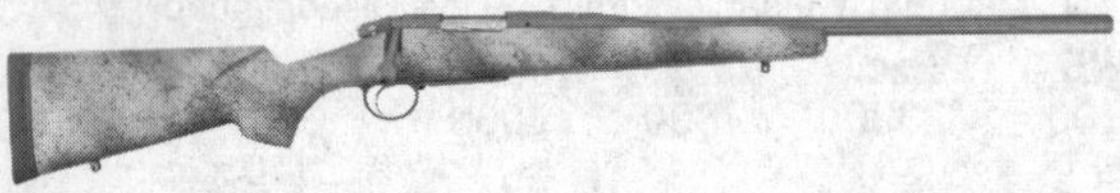

NIB	Exc.	V.G.	Good	Fair	Poor
1600	1350	—	—	—	—

Mountain

As PSR above with weight about 6.3 lbs, carbon fiber stock, hinged floor plate and No. 3 barrel profile of 22"-24" chambered in 6.5 C, .270 Win, .280 Ackley Imp, .308, .30-06, .300 Win Mag.

NIB	Exc.	V.G.	Good	Fair	Poor
1850	1580	1350	800	480	300

Approach

As PSR above with weight about 8.4 lbs, fiberglass stock, No. 5.5 barrel taper, lengths of 20"-26", AICS-style detachable magazine and threaded muzzle. Calibers include .22-250, 6mm C, 6.5 C, 6.5 PRC, 7-08, 7mm Rem Mag, .308, .300 Win Mag, .300 PRC, .450 Bushmaster.

NIB	Exc.	V.G.	Good	Fair	Poor
1680	1400	1200	720	450	300

HMR PRO

As PSR above with weight about 9.6 lbs, AICS-style detachable magazine, threaded muzzle, fully adjustable buttstock with mini-chassis and free-floated barrel of No. 5.5 or 6 taper, 20"-26". Calibers include 6mm Creedmoor, 6.5 Creedmoor, 6.5 PRC, 7mm-08, 7mm Rem. Mag., .308, .300 Win. Mag., .300 PRC, .450 Bushmaster.

NIB	Exc.	V.G.	Good	Fair	Poor
1450	1250	1050	620	380	300

LRP

As PSR above with weight about 9.6 lbs, AICS-style detachable magazine, threaded muzzle, fully adjustable XLR Element chassis stock, No. 5.5 taper barrel in 20"-26". Calibers include 6mm Creedmoor, 6.5 Creedmoor, .308 Win. and .300 Win Mag.

NIB	Exc.	V.G.	Good	Fair	Poor
1700	1450	1250	900	500	300

Premier Canyon

Calibers: 6.5 Creedmoor, 6.5 PRC, .308 Win., 28 Nosler, .300 Win. Mag., 300 PRC, .375 H&H. Capacity: AICS-style detachable 3-round mag. provided, 5-round long action. 375 uses hinged floorplate with 3-round capacity. Barrel: 20–22 in. No. 4 taper, fluted stainless steel. Weight: 6.2–6.5 lbs. Length: 41–44 in. Stock: AG Composite 100% carbon fiber. Sights: Drilled and tapped for Remington 700 bases with 8-40 screws. Features: Classic style hunting rifle. Bolt uses a non-rotating gas shield, coned bolt nose, and sliding plate extractor. TriggerTech frictionless release trigger with two-position safety. Threaded muzzle with Omni Muzzle Brake. Sniper Grey Cerakote. Guaranteed MOA accuracy.

NIB	Exc.	V.G.	Good	Fair	Poor
2250	—	—	—	—	—

Premier Divide

Calibers: 6.5 Creedmoor, 6.5 PRC, .308 Win., .300 Win. Mag. Capacity: AICS-style detachable, 5 standard, 3 magnum. Barrel: 22 in., 24 in. No. 6 CURE carbon fiber. Weight: 7.2–7.4 lbs. Length: 43–46 in. Stock: AG Composite 100% carbon fiber. Sights: Drilled and tapped for Remington 700 bases with 8-40 screws. Features: Built to bridge the divide between tactical and hunting rifles. Bolt uses a non-rotating gas shield, coned bolt nose, and sliding plate extractor. TriggerTech frictionless release trigger with two-position safety. Threaded muzzle with Omni Muzzle Brake. Patriot Brown Cerakote finish. Guaranteed MOA accuracy.

NIB	Exc.	V.G.	Good	Fair	Poor
2630	—	—	—	—	—

Premier MG Lite

Calibers: 6.5 Creedmoor, 6.5 PRC, .308 Win., .300 Win Mag. Capacity: 5 standard, 3 magnum. Barrel: 22 in. or 24 in. fully free-floated, proprietary CURE carbon fiber. Weight: 6.7–6.8 lbs. Length: 43–45 in. Stock: Ultralightweight XLR Element 4.0 magnesium chassis with folding buttstock. Sights: Drilled and tapped for Remington 700 bases with 8-40 screws. Features: Precision bolt-action hunting rifle with a non-rotating gas shield, coned bolt nose, and sliding plate extractor. TriggerTech frictionless release trigger with two-position safety. Threaded muzzle with Omni Muzzle Brake. Graphite Black Cerakote. Guaranteed MOA accuracy.

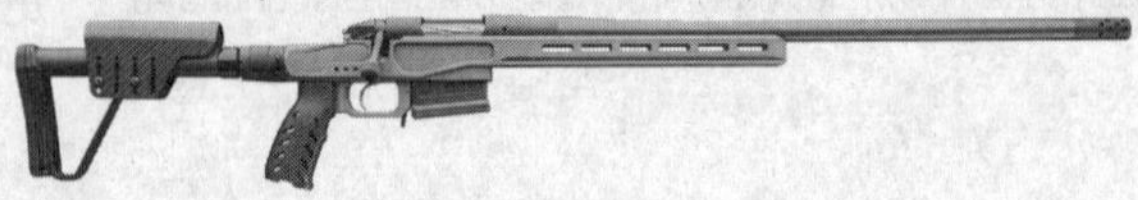

NIB	Exc.	V.G.	Good	Fair	Poor
3100	—	—	—	—	—

BERGER, JEAN MARIUS

St. Etienne, France

Berger (Antique)

Berger was a magazine-fed repeating pistol in 7.65mm. Self loader and cocker. Had all characteristics of semi-automatic except for recoil operating system.

Courtesy James Rankin

Exc.	Fine	V.G.	Good	Fair	Poor
6500	4500	3750	2000	1250	900

BERGMANN, THEODOR

Gaggenau, Germany

Theodor Bergmann was a successful industrialist, designer and sometimes inventor, with a deep interest in firearms. Based in Gaggenau, Germany, his first automatic pistol patent dates from 1892. By 1894, he had prototype pistols refined with the help of Louis Schmeisser, being evaluated by various governments. When his designs went into commercial production in 1896, however, they were actually manufactured by the firm of V. Charles Schilling in Suhl, the heart of German arms manufacture. Later he licensed manufacture of his "Mars" pistol to Anciens Establishment Pieper ("Bayard"). After WWI, affiliated with Lignose firm producing a line of .25-caliber pocket pistols first under Bergmann name, but later marketed as Lignose. Still later, several pistol designs from August Menz firm were marketed under "Bergmann Erben" trademark, though it's doubtful if Bergmann's firm actually had much part in their production or sale.

Model 1894 Bergmann Schmeisser

Made in prototype form only. Few examples surviving. Known serial numbers no higher than mid teens. Most are large framed. Chambered for 8mm Bergmann-Schmeisser cartridge. At least one was made in 7.5mm Swiss revolver for Swiss army testing. A few very compact versions, with a unique folding trigger for 5mm Bergmann. Early Bergmann pistols had no extractor, counting on gas pressure to blow the fired (rimless-grooveless) cartridge from chamber. Too rare to price.

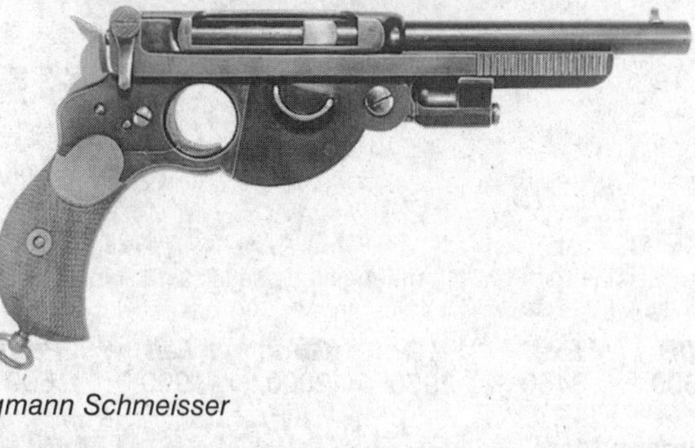

Bergmann Schmeisser

Model 1896 Number 2

1896 Number 2 pistols were quite compact. Chambered for 5mm Bergmann cartridge. Early Number 2s also featured a folding trigger and no extractor. After serial 500 or so reverted to a more conventional in-the-frame trigger and an extractor was added. About 2000 of later model were produced. Cased sets are known. Add about 50 percent to value.

Folding Trigger

Courtesy James Rankin

NIB	Exc.	V.G.	Good	Fair	Poor
9000	8000	5000	3250	1500	800

Conventional Trigger

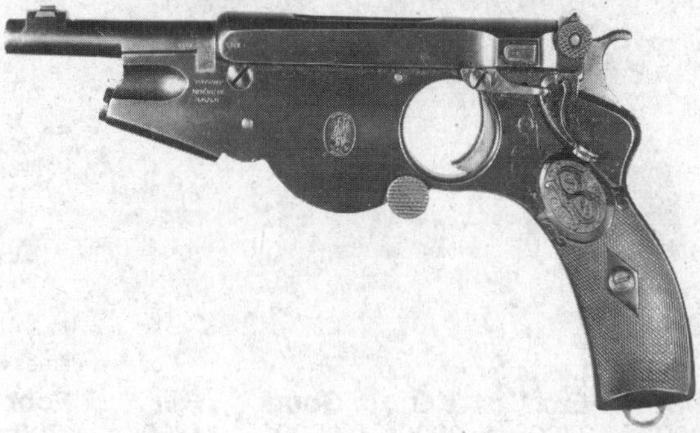

Courtesy James Rankin

NIB	Exc.	V.G.	Good	Fair	Poor
—	6000	3500	2250	1000	600

Model 1896 Number 3

Number 3 was a larger version of Number 2. Chambered for 6.5mm Bergmann cartridge. Early examples had a slim grip frame. Up to about serial 800 were made without extractors like early Number 2s. These bring about 20 percent premium over later examples. Number 3 serials range to a little over 4000. Add about 20 percent for dealer markings (usually English) and 50 percent for cased sets. A few target models, with long barrel, adjustable sights and set triggers are known. Will bring about three times the price of a standard Number 3.

First Variation

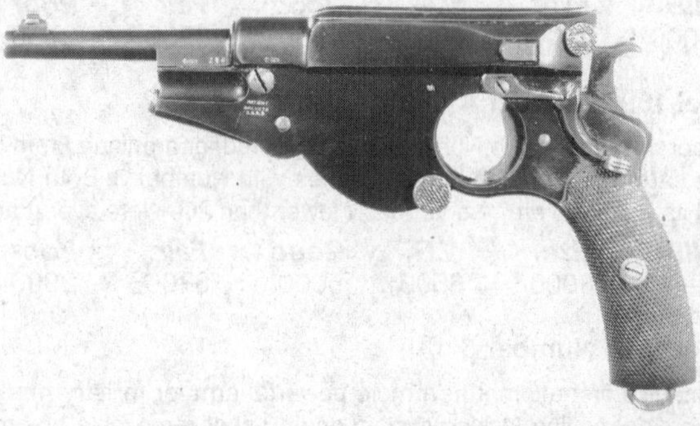

Courtesy James Rankin

NIB	Exc.	V.G.	Good	Fair	Poor
5000	4050	3500	2750	1650	800

Second Variation

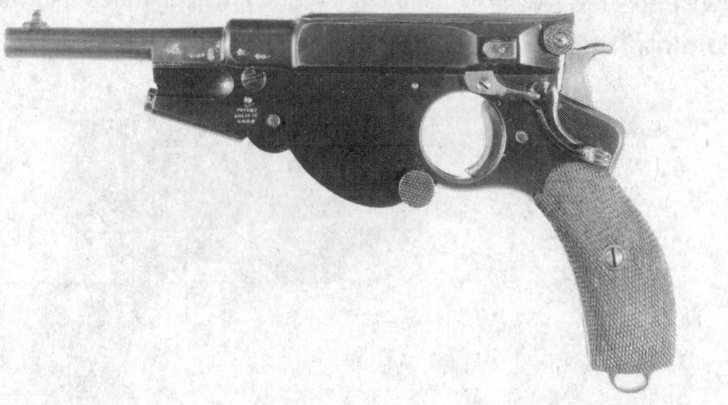

Courtesy James Rankin

NIB	Exc.	V.G.	Good	Fair	Poor
4200	3500	3200	2500	1650	800

Third Variation

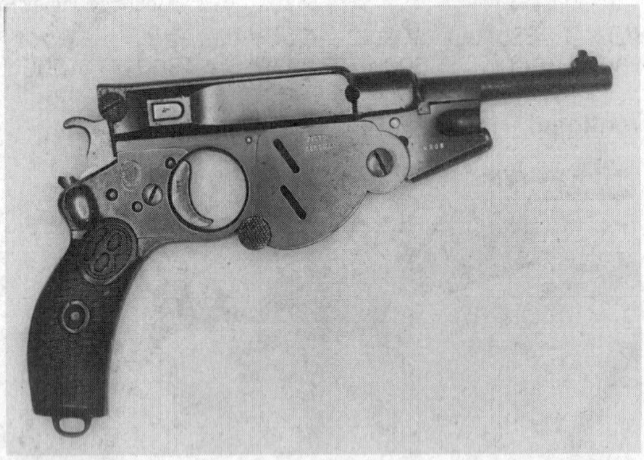

Courtesy James Rankin

NIB	Exc.	V.G.	Good	Fair	Poor
4000	3700	3200	2500	1650	800

Holster and Stock Model

Courtesy James Rankin

NIB	Exc.	V.G.	Good	Fair	Poor
12000	9000	6000	4950	3250	2750

Model 1896 Number 4

Number 4 is identical to Number 3. Chambered for a unique 8mm Bergmann cartridge. Serialed in same series with Number 3. Both Number 4 and its cartridge are rare; probably fewer than 200 were ever made.

NIB	Exc.	V.G.	Good	Fair	Poor
—	8000	6500	5000	3700	2900

Model 1897 Number 5

Bergmann's first attempt at a more powerful arm for military market. A unique side-moving locking system and 10-shot removable box magazine. 7.8mm cartridge resembled 7.63mm Mauser, with a longer neck. Note: Add 60 percent for original metal framed leather holster-stock.

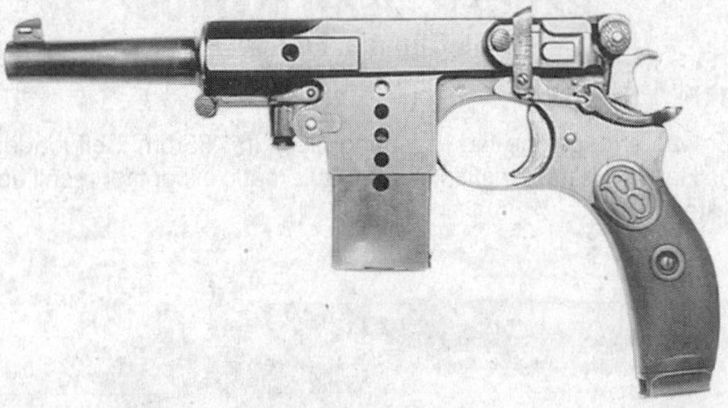

NIB	Exc.	V.G.	Good	Fair	Poor
11000	9500	7500	4950	3000	2250

Model 1897 Number 5 Carbine

Limited number of approximately 1000 Bergmann Model 5s were made, with 12" barrel. Solid wood detachable buttstock and marked "Karabiner Bergmann" on action cover. Very few were made with full-length Mannlicher-type stock and sold as Bergmann Model 1897/07 Sporting Carbine; these are worth about 50 percent more than long barreled pistol, with detachable stock.

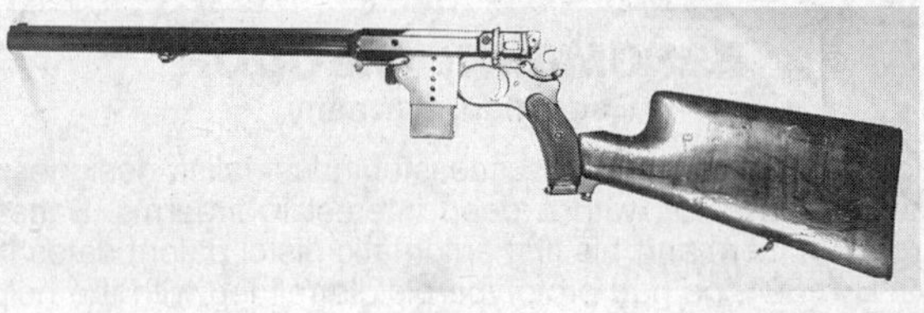

Courtesy Joe Schroeder

NIB	Exc.	V.G.	Good	Fair	Poor
18500	16000	11500	7000	3000	2000

Bergmann Simplex

Simplex combined some features of 1896 pistols. Improvements developed from "Mars", resulting in a reasonable compact pocket pistol that came on the market in early 1900s. Chambered for unique Bergmann-Simplex 8mm cartridge, however, competition from better Browning and other designs doomed it to a short production life. Very early examples had checkered wood grips and bring a premium, as do very late examples (above serial 3000) that have magazine release behind magazine instead of on front of frame.

NIB	Exc.	V.G.	Good	Fair	Poor
4500	3450	2950	2000	900	600

Bergmann Mars

Mars was Bergmann's first really successful pistol aimed at military market. Early examples, about 100 of total 1000 or so Mars pistols made, were chambered for 7.63mm Mauser cartridge. Later Mars pistols identified by a large "9mm" on chamber, were chambered for special 9mm cartridge that later became known as 9mm Bergmann-Bayard. Mars was adopted by Spanish government in 1905 as their first military automatic pistol, but none were ever delivered by Bergmann. At least two Mars pistols were also made in .45-caliber for U.S. Army trials in 1906, but did not perform well and were dropped from the trials; these are too rare to price. Note: Add 25 percent for low serial number guns chambered for 7.63mm Mauser; 50 percent for original Bergmann Mars holster stock.

NIB	Exc.	V.G.	Good	Fair	Poor
9000	7000	5300	3850	2500	1650

Bergmann Bayard Model 1908

Shortly after receiving Spanish contract for Mars pistol, Bergmann's arrangement with Schilling to produce Bergmann pistols ended. However, he negotiated an arrangement with Anciens Establishment Pieper (Bayard) to produce Mars and after some minor modifications, AEP filled the Spanish contract. They also marketed the gun commercially and later secured a production contract from Danish Army as Model 1910. Spanish contract (proofed with a small circle divided into three segments) and very early commercial pistols have hard rubber grips that proved very fragile in service; these bring a premium as do original unmodified Danish contract guns (with a contract number and Danish letter D proof). A few Model 1908 Bergmann Bayards were equipped with leather and wood holster stocks; a complete rig is worth at least twice the price of an unslotted pistol.

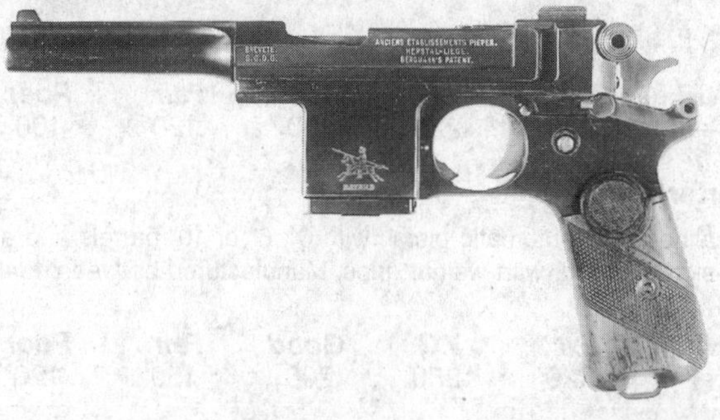

Courtesy James Rankin

NIB	Exc.	V.G.	Good	Fair	Poor
4250	3500	2700	1600	780	550

Bergmann Post War Pistols

Shortly after WWI ended, Bergmann came on the market with a line of .25-caliber pocket pistols; the 2 and 3 were conventional vest pocket designs with a short and long grip frame respectively; the 2a and 3a were identical except for an "Einhand" (one-hand) feature that enabled user to cycle slide by pulling front of triggerguard with his trigger finger. This enhanced feature will approximately double the values listed here. Soon into production (at about serial 8000) Bergmann affiliated with Lignose firm and later Model 2 and 3 pistols were marketed under Lignose name.

Model 2

Courtesy Joe Schroeder

NIB	Exc.	V.G.	Good	Fair	Poor
—	320	280	200	150	100

Model 3a

Courtesy Joe Schroeder

NIB	Exc.	V.G.	Good	Fair	Poor
—	400	380	320	280	150

Bergmann Erben Pistols

Bergmann Erben pistols appear to be an attempt by Bergmann family to keep Bergmann name associated with firearms, without actually investing any design or production effort. Bergmann Erben pistols were all August Menz designs and were undoubtedly made by Menz as well. Most noteworthy was "Spezial" model, a very sophisticated double-action .32 pocket pistol that could be cocked for single-action fire by pulling and then releasing trigger. Also noteworthy were several compact vest pocket .25s that also bore Bergmann Erben name.

Bergmann Erben Spezial

NIB	Exc.	V.G.	Good	Fair	Poor
—	1650	1350	900	650	400

Bergmann Erben Model II Pistol

Courtesy James Rankin

NIB	Exc.	V.G.	Good	Fair	Poor
—	550	500	330	220	120

BERGMANN, EINHAND

See—LIGNOSE

BERNARDELLI, VINCENZO

Brescia, Italy

Established in 1721, this company originally manufactured military arms. Entered commercial sporting arms market in 1928.

HANDGUNS

Vest Pocket Model

Similar to Walther Model 9. In 6.35mm caliber semi-automatic pistol, with 2.25" barrel and 5-shot magazine. An extended 8-shot version also available. Blued, with plastic grips. Manufactured between 1945 and 1948.

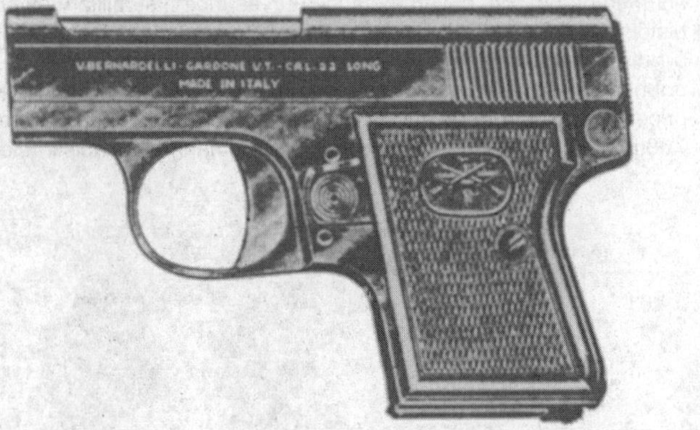

NIB	Exc.	V.G.	Good	Fair	Poor
—	350	250	180	120	100

Pocket Model

As above in 7.65mm caliber. Also offered with extended barrels that protruded beyond end of slide. Introduced in 1947.

NIB	Exc.	V.G.	Good	Fair	Poor
—	300	220	200	150	100

Baby Model

As above in .22 short or LR. Manufactured between 1949 and 1968.

NIB	Exc.	V.G.	Good	Fair	Poor
—	300	220	180	120	100

Sporter Model

.22-caliber semi-automatic pistol, with 6", 8" or 10" barrels and adjustable sights. Blued, with walnut grips. Manufactured between 1949 and 1968.

NIB	Exc.	V.G.	Good	Fair	Poor
—	320	250	200	150	120

Revolvers

.22 rimfire and .32-caliber double-action revolver, with 1.5", 2" or 5" barrels. A .22-caliber 7" barrel version, with adjustable sights also available. Manufactured between 1950 and 1962.

NIB	Exc.	V.G.	Good	Fair	Poor
—	250	180	150	120	100

Model 60

.22, .32 ACP or .380 ACP caliber semi-automatic pistol, with 3.5" barrel and fixed sights. Blued, with plastic grips. Manufactured since 1959.

NIB	Exc.	V.G.	Good	Fair	Poor
—	280	200	180	150	120

Model 68

.22 rimfire caliber or .25 ACP semi-automatic pistol, with 2" barrel and 5-shot magazine. Blued, with plastic grips. No longer imported into U.S.

NIB	Exc.	V.G.	Good	Fair	Poor
—	300	180	150	100	80

Model 80

.22 or .380 ACP caliber semi-automatic pistol, with 3.5" barrel and adjustable sights. Blued, with plastic grips. Imported between 1968 and 1988.

NIB	Exc.	V.G.	Good	Fair	Poor
350	280	200	150	130	100

Model AMR

As above, with 6" barrel.

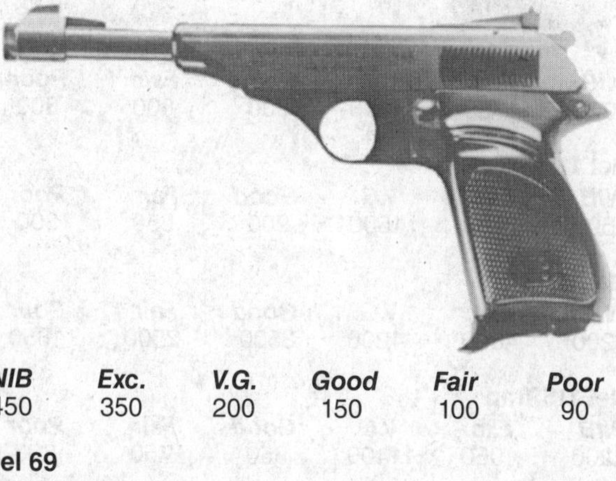

NIB	Exc.	V.G.	Good	Fair	Poor
450	350	200	150	100	90

Model 69

.22-caliber semi-automatic target pistol, with 6" heavy barrel and 10-shot magazine. Blued, with checkered walnut grips.

NIB	Exc.	V.G.	Good	Fair	Poor
450	380	300	220	150	100

Model PO10

.22-caliber single-action semi-automatic target pistol, with 6" barrel, adjustable target sights, barrel weights and adjustable trigger. Matte-black finish, with stippled walnut grips. Introduced in 1989. Weight 40 oz. Sold with special hard case.

NIB	Exc.	V.G.	Good	Fair	Poor
800	700	500	300	200	100

Model PO18

7.65mm or 9mm Parabellum caliber double-action semi-automatic pistol, with 4.75" barrel and 16-shot double stack detachable magazine. All-steel construction. Blued, with plastic grips. Walnut grips available for an additional $40. Introduced in 1985.

NIB	Exc.	V.G.	Good	Fair	Poor
550	450	300	280	200	100

Model PO18 Compact

As above, with 4" barrel and shorter grip frame. 14-shot double-column magazine. Introduced in 1989.

NIB	*Exc.*	*V.G.*	*Good*	*Fair*	*Poor*
550	450	300	280	200	100

Model P. One

Full-size semi-automatic pistol. Chambered for 9mm or .40 S&W calibers. Fitted with 4.8" barrel. Can be fired double-/single-action. Ten-shot magazine. Weight 2.14 lbs. Available in black or chrome finish. Note: Add $50 for chrome finish.

NIB	*Exc.*	*V.G.*	*Good*	*Fair*	*Poor*
620	520	400	280	200	100

Model P. One-Compact

Same as above, with 4" barrel. Offered in .380-caliber, 9mm and .40 S&W. Weight 1.96 lbs.

NIB	*Exc.*	*V.G.*	*Good*	*Fair*	*Poor*
650	550	400	280	200	100

Practical VB Target

Designed for Practical shooting. This 9mm pistol has 6" barrel, with choice of 2 or 4 port compensator. Fitted with numerous extra features. Weight 2.2 lbs.

NIB	*Exc.*	*V.G.*	*Good*	*Fair*	*Poor*
1500	1200	850	600	400	200

Practical VB Custom

As above, but designed for IPSC rules.

NIB	*Exc.*	*V.G.*	*Good*	*Fair*	*Poor*
2250	1900	1400	900	600	300

Model USA

.22, .32 ACP or .380 ACP caliber semi-automatic pistol, with 3.5" barrel, adjustable sights, steel frame and loaded chamber indicator. Blued, with plastic grips.

NIB	*Exc.*	*V.G.*	*Good*	*Fair*	*Poor*
450	350	200	150	100	90

SHOTGUNS

MODEL 115 SERIES

12-gauge over/under boxlock double-barrel shotgun, with various barrel lengths and choke combinations. Single triggers and automatic ejectors.

Model 115

NIB	*Exc.*	*V.G.*	*Good*	*Fair*	*Poor*
1520	1250	900	700	550	300

Model 115S

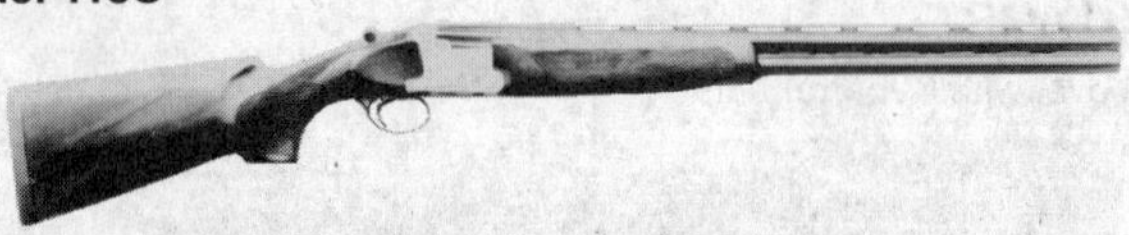

NIB	*Exc.*	*V.G.*	*Good*	*Fair*	*Poor*
2000	1750	1200	800	600	300

Model 115L

NIB	*Exc.*	*V.G.*	*Good*	*Fair*	*Poor*
2500	2000	1500	900	650	300

Model 115E

NIB	*Exc.*	*V.G.*	*Good*	*Fair*	*Poor*
5200	4800	4200	3500	2500	1850

Model 115 Trap

NIB	*Exc.*	*V.G.*	*Good*	*Fair*	*Poor*
2200	1950	1400	950	750	600

Model 115S Trap

NIB	*Exc.*	*V.G.*	*Good*	*Fair*	*Poor*
2700	2450	1900	1450	1150	900

Model 115E Trap

NIB	*Exc.*	*V.G.*	*Good*	*Fair*	*Poor*
5250	4800	4200	3500	2500	1850

MODEL 190 SERIES

12-gauge over/under shotgun, with various barrel lengths and choke combinations. Single-selective trigger and automatic ejectors. Engraved and silver-finished, with checkered walnut stock. Introduced in 1986. Various versions differ in degree of ornamentation and quality of materials utilized in construction.

Model 190

NIB	Exc.	V.G.	Good	Fair	Poor
1050	950	750	600	480	400

Model 190MC

NIB	Exc.	V.G.	Good	Fair	Poor
1150	1050	850	700	580	500

Model 190 Special

NIB	Exc.	V.G.	Good	Fair	Poor
1350	1150	950	800	680	600

Model 190 Combo Gun

.243-, .308-, .30-06 caliber and 12-, 16-, 20-gauge combination over/under rifle/shotgun, with boxlock action, double triggers and automatic ejectors. Blued, with checkered walnut stock. Introduced in 1989.

NIB	Exc.	V.G.	Good	Fair	Poor
1620	1420	920	780	650	580

ORIONE SERIES

12-gauge boxlock over/under shotgun, with various barrel lengths and choke combinations. Finishes and triggers optional, as were extractors or automatic ejectors.

Orione

NIB	Exc.	V.G.	Good	Fair	Poor
1150	900	700	500	400	200

Orione S

NIB	Exc.	V.G.	Good	Fair	Poor
1150	900	700	500	400	200

Orione L

NIB	Exc.	V.G.	Good	Fair	Poor
1250	1000	800	600	500	250

Orione E

NIB	Exc.	V.G.	Good	Fair	Poor
1350	1150	850	600	500	250

S. Uberto I Gamecock

12-, 16-, 20- or 28-gauge boxlock side-by-side shotgun, with 25.75" or 27.5" barrels, various chokes, double triggers and extractors. Automatic ejectors were available and would be worth a 20 percent premium. Blued, with checkered stock.

NIB	Exc.	V.G.	Good	Fair	Poor
—	950	700	500	350	250

Brescia

12-, 16- or 20-gauge sidelock double-barrel shotgun, with exposed hammers, various barrel lengths, choke combinations, sidelock action, double triggers and manual extractors. Blued, with English-style checkered walnut stock.

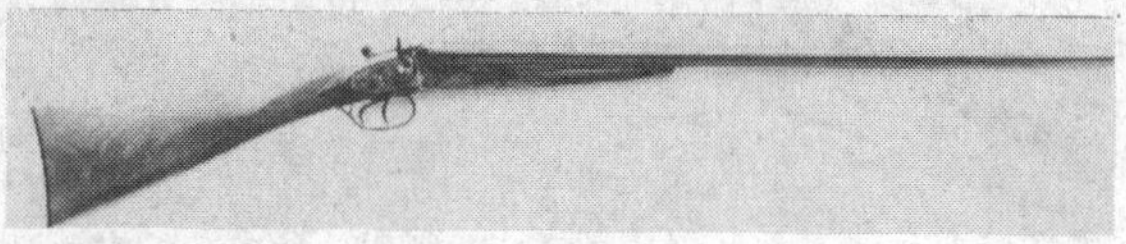

NIB	Exc.	V.G.	Good	Fair	Poor
1850	900	700	450	350	220

Italia

Higher grade version of Brescia.

NIB	Exc.	V.G.	Good	Fair	Poor
2250	1250	750	600	400	250

Italia Extra

Highest grade hammer gun Bernardelli produces.

NIB	Exc.	V.G.	Good	Fair	Poor
5900	2750	1500	1000	750	300

UBERTO SERIES

12-, 16-, 20- or 28-gauge Anson & Deeley boxlock double-barrel shotgun, with various barrel lengths and choke combinations. Increased value of various models depends on degree of engraving options and quality of materials and workmanship utilized in their construction.

S. Uberto 1

NIB	Exc.	V.G.	Good	Fair	Poor
1000	800	650	480	350	250

S. Uberto 1E

NIB	Exc.	V.G.	Good	Fair	Poor
1100	900	700	500	350	250

S. Uberto 2

NIB	Exc.	V.G.	Good	Fair	Poor
1500	1100	800	500	350	250

S. Uberto 2E

NIB	Exc.	V.G.	Good	Fair	Poor
1750	1350	950	600	400	250

S. Uberto F.S.

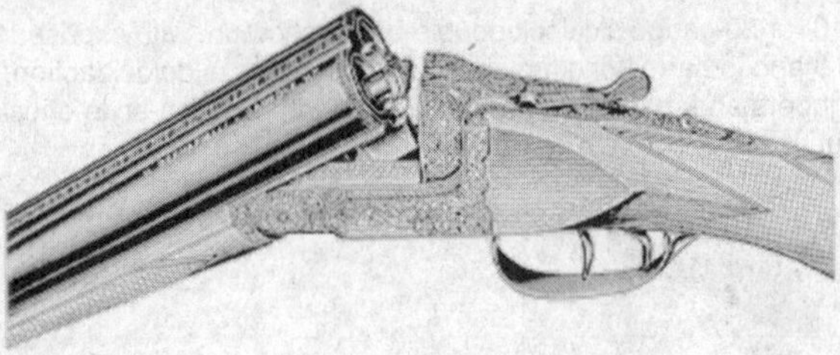

NIB	Exc.	V.G.	Good	Fair	Poor
2000	1500	1100	800	400	250

S. Uberto F.S.E.

NIB	Exc.	V.G.	Good	Fair	Poor
2250	1750	1200	800	400	250

ROMA SERIES

Similar to S. Uberto Series, with false sideplates. Values of respective variations result from degree of ornamentation and quality of materials and workmanship utilized in construction.

Roma 3

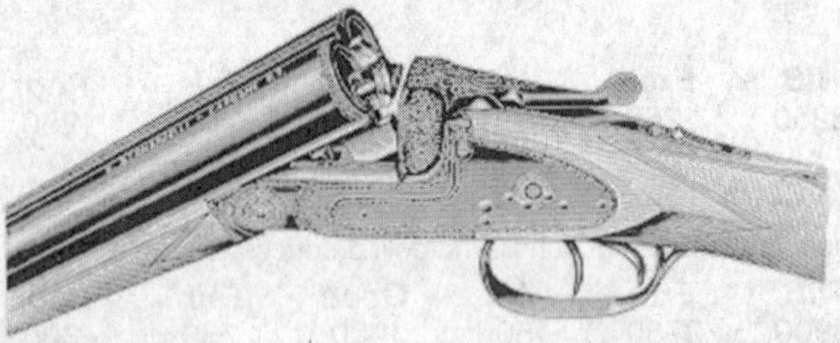

NIB	Exc.	V.G.	Good	Fair	Poor
1550	1200	800	600	300	200

Roma 3E

NIB	Exc.	V.G.	Good	Fair	Poor
1750	1300	900	650	300	200

Roma 4

NIB	Exc.	V.G.	Good	Fair	Poor
1950	1400	1100	750	400	250

Roma 4E

NIB	Exc.	V.G.	Good	Fair	Poor
2000	1500	1200	750	400	250

Roma 6

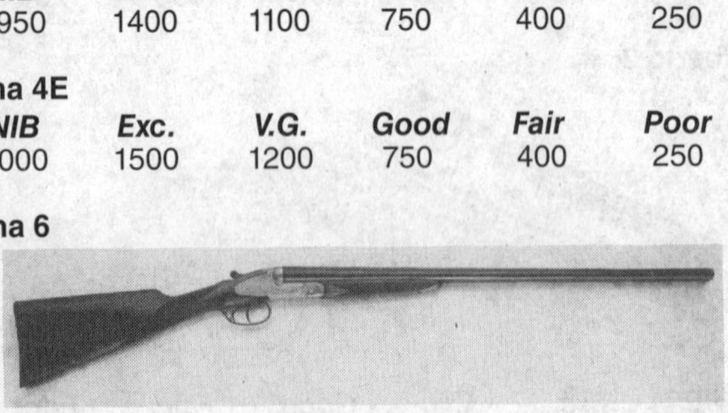

NIB	Exc.	V.G.	Good	Fair	Poor
2100	1750	1400	850	500	250

Roma 6E

NIB	Exc.	V.G.	Good	Fair	Poor
2200	1800	1400	850	500	250

Roma 7

NIB	Exc.	V.G.	Good	Fair	Poor
2900	2500	1800	1200	700	350

Roma 8

NIB	Exc.	V.G.	Good	Fair	Poor
3500	3000	2250	1550	850	400

Roma 9

NIB	Exc.	V.G.	Good	Fair	Poor
4000	3500	2750	1700	950	450

Elio

12-gauge boxlock double-barrel shotgun, with various barrel lengths and choke combinations, lightweight frame, double triggers and extractors. Scroll-engraved, silver-finished receiver, blued barrels and select checkered walnut stock.

NIB	Exc.	V.G.	Good	Fair	Poor
1000	800	600	500	350	250

Elio E

As above, with automatic ejectors.

NIB	Exc.	V.G.	Good	Fair	Poor
1100	900	700	550	350	250

Hemingway

As above, with coin finished receiver engraved with hunting scenes, 23.5" barrels, double-/single trigger and select checkered walnut stock. Available in 12-, 20- and 28-gauge.

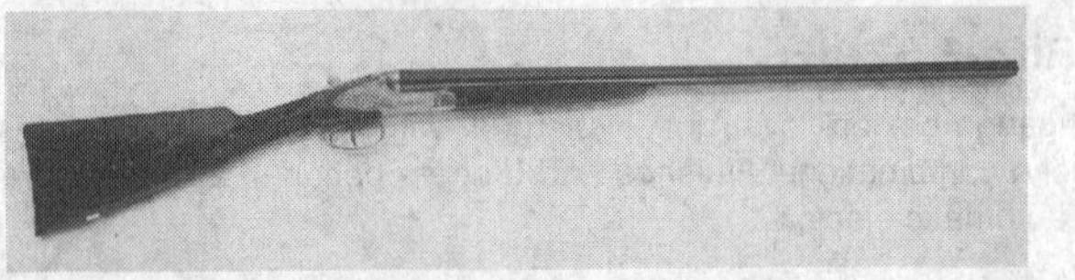

NIB	Exc.	V.G.	Good	Fair	Poor
1750	1350	900	700	400	250

Hemingway Deluxe

Same as above fitted with full side plates.

NIB	Exc.	V.G.	Good	Fair	Poor
2250	1750	1200	800	400	250

Las Palomas Pigeon Model

Live pigeon gun in 12-gauge, with single trigger.

NIB	Exc.	V.G.	Good	Fair	Poor
3800	3250	2500	2000	1500	750

HOLLAND V.B. SERIES

12- or 20-gauge sidelock shotgun, with various barrel lengths, detachable Holland & Holland-type locks, single triggers and automatic ejectors. Models listed vary in amount of engraving and quality of their wood. Prospective purchasers are advised to secure a qualified appraisal prior to acquisition.

Holland V.B. Liscio

NIB	Exc.	V.G.	Good	Fair	Poor
8000	5500	4000	3000	2000	1000

Holland V.B. Inciso

NIB	Exc.	V.G.	Good	Fair	Poor
10250	7500	5250	4000	2500	1250

Holland V.B. Lusso

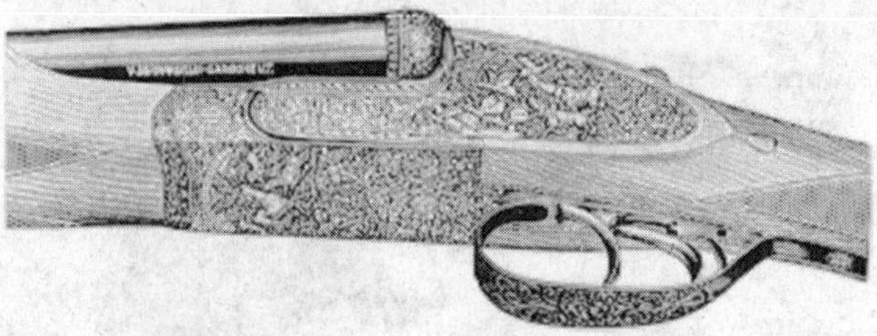

NIB	Exc.	V.G.	Good	Fair	Poor
11000	8000	6000	4500	2500	1250

Holland V.B. Extra

NIB	Exc.	V.G.	Good	Fair	Poor
13000	10000	7500	5500	3000	1500

Holland V.B. Gold

NIB	Exc.	V.G.	Good	Fair	Poor
45000	30000	22500	15000	7500	3000

Luck

Over/under shotgun, with single-selective trigger or double triggers and automatic ejectors. Choice of fixed chokes or choke tubes. Available in 12-gauge. Blued or coin finish receiver.

NIB	Exc.	V.G.	Good	Fair	Poor
1400	1100	850	600	400	200

Giardino/Garden Gun (9mm Rimfire)

Semi-automatic shotgun chambered for 9mm shot cartridge. Fitted with 4-round magazine. Weight 5 lbs.

NIB	Exc.	V.G.	Good	Fair	Poor
850	600	420	300	250	100

RIFLES

Carbina VB Target

Semi-automatic carbine chambered for .22 LR cartridge. Barrel is 20.8". Magazine capacity 10 rounds.

NIB	Exc.	V.G.	Good	Fair	Poor
650	550	400	300	200	100

Comb 2000

Rifle/shotgun combination in 12- or 16-gauge, with variety of centerfire calibers to choose from. Barrels are 23.5" long. Set trigger, special rib for scope mount and cheekpiece stock, with pistol grip. Weight 6.75 lbs.

NIB	Exc.	V.G.	Good	Fair	Poor
2900	2100	1200	800	400	250

Express 2000

Over/under double rifle chambered for variety of European calibers. Fitted with automatic ejectors, double-set triggers or single trigger, muzzle adjustment device. Barrel length 23.5".

NIB	Exc.	V.G.	Good	Fair	Poor
3350	2550	1700	1200	600	300

Express VB

Side-by-side double rifle, chambered for variety of European calibers up to .375 H&H. Double-/single trigger, auto ejectors and finely engraved receiver with beavertail forearm. Cheekpiece stock with pistol grip.

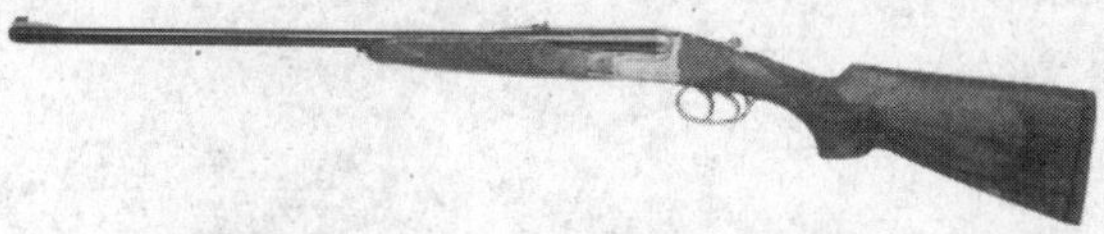

NIB	Exc.	V.G.	Good	Fair	Poor
5900	4900	3750	2000	1000	750

Express VB Deluxe

Same as above, with side plates and select walnut stock finely checkered.

NIB	Exc.	V.G.	Good	Fair	Poor
6300	5200	4000	2000	1000	750

Minerva

Side-by-side double rifle, with exposed hammers chambered for 9.3x74R cartridge. Fitted with fancy walnut stock, double triggers, hand-cut rib and other high-quality features.

NIB	Exc.	V.G.	Good	Fair	Poor
6700	5900	4550	2500	1200	750

BERNARDON MARTIN

St. Etienne, France

Small firm active between 1906 and 1912. Gun designer was Martin and money man was Bernadon.

1907/8 Model

7.65mm caliber semi-automatic pistol. Left side of slide marked "Cal. 7.65mm St. Etienne". Trademark "BM" molded into grips. Sometimes found with 32-round horseshoe magazine. Occasionally Bernardon Martin pistol will be noted with word "Hermetic" stamped on slide in letters that do not match other markings on weapon. This was but another name for Model 1907/8. Guns with this stamping were most likely assembled after company ceased operations. Note: Add 50 percent for horseshoe magazine.

Courtesy James Rankin

NIB	Exc.	V.G.	Good	Fair	Poor
—	1100	880	700	450	280

1908/9 Model

Introduced late in 1908. Similar to Model 1907/8, with addition of grip safety.

NIB	Exc.	V.G.	Good	Fair	Poor
—	920	780	600	380	220

BERNEDO, VINCENZO

Eibar, Spain

B C

B C in caliber 6.35mm and most of barrel exposed. Recoil spring is housed in rear of receiver. B C closely resembles Tanque pistol.

Courtesy James Rankin

NIB	Exc.	V.G.	Good	Fair	Poor
—	320	220	200	180	150

Bernado

Model 7.65mm is in Spanish style of Ruby automatic pistols.

Courtesy James Rankin

NIB	Exc.	V.G.	Good	Fair	Poor
—	220	150	120	80	50

BERSA

Ramos Mejia, Argentina

Model 644

A blowback pocket pistol chambered for .22 LR. Trigger system single-action. Barrel length 3.5"; overall length 6.57"; weight empty about 28 oz. This is basic Bersa model from which its other models derive their design and function.

NIB	Exc.	V.G.	Good	Fair	Poor
280	180	150	120	100	80

Model 622

Similar to Model 644, with slightly longer barrel.

NIB	Exc.	V.G.	Good	Fair	Poor
280	180	150	120	100	80

Model 97

Slightly larger version of Model 644. Chambered for 9mm Short.

NIB	Exc.	V.G.	Good	Fair	Poor
360	320	270	240	160	130

Model 23

.22 rimfire caliber double-action semi-automatic pistol, with 3.5" barrel and 10-shot detachable magazine. Blued or satin nickel-plated, with checkered walnut grips.

NIB	Exc.	V.G.	Good	Fair	Poor
300	200	150	120	100	80

Model 223

As above, with squared triggerguard and nylon grips. Imported after 1988.

NIB	Exc.	V.G.	Good	Fair	Poor
—	280	180	120	100	80

Model 224

As above, with 4" barrel. Imported after 1988.

NIB	Exc.	V.G.	Good	Fair	Poor
—	280	180	120	100	80

Model 225

As above, with 5" barrel. Discontinued in 1986.

NIB	Exc.	V.G.	Good	Fair	Poor
—	280	180	120	100	80

Model 226

As above, with 6" barrel. Discontinued in 1988.

Courtesy John J. Stimson, Jr.

NIB	Exc.	V.G.	Good	Fair	Poor
—	280	180	120	100	80

Model 323

.32 ACP caliber single-action semi-automatic pistol, with 3.5" barrel, fixed sights and 7-shot detachable magazine. Blued, with molded plastic grips. Not imported after 1986.

NIB	Exc.	V.G.	Good	Fair	Poor
—	220	120	100	80	50

Model 383

As above in .380-caliber. Discontinued in 1988.

NIB	Exc.	V.G.	Good	Fair	Poor
—	250	150	120	90	80

Model 383A

.380 ACP caliber double-action semi-automatic pistol, with 3.5" barrel, fixed sights and 7-shot magazine. Blued, with checkered walnut grips. Overall length 6.6"; weight about 24 oz. Available in blue or nickel finish.

NIB	Exc.	V.G.	Good	Fair	Poor
300	200	150	120	100	80

Model 83

Similar to above model, with double-action operating system. Weight about 26 oz. Introduced in 1988.

NIB	Exc.	V.G.	Good	Fair	Poor
300	200	150	120	100	80

Model 85

As above, with double-column magazine. Introduced in 1988.

NIB	Exc.	V.G.	Good	Fair	Poor
350	250	200	150	100	80

Model 86

Similar to Model 85 in .380-caliber. Features matte blue or satin nickel finish, wrap-around rubber grips and three-dot sight. Magazine capacity 13 rounds

NIB	Exc.	V.G.	Good	Fair	Poor
350	250	220	200	150	100

Thunder 9

Introduced in 1993. A double-action 9mm pistol that features ambidextrous safety, reversible extended magazine release, ambidextrous slide release, adjustable trigger stop, combat-style hammer, three-dot sights and matte blue finish. Magazine capacity 15 rounds.

NIB	Exc.	V.G.	Good	Fair	Poor
400	350	300	280	180	140

Series 95/Thunder 380

Semi-automatic double-action pistol chambered for .380 cartridge. Choice of matte blue or nickel finish. Barrel length 3.5". Fixed sights. Magazine capacity 7 rounds. Weight about 23 oz. Note: Add $50 for nickel.

NIB	Exc.	V.G.	Good	Fair	Poor
260	200	150	100	80	50

BPCC Series

Semi-automatic striker-fire pistol chambered for .380 ACP, 9mm, or .40 S&W cartridge. Polymer frame, ambidextrous controls. Choice of matte black, FDE, urban grey, OD, turquolse or duo-tome finish. Barrel length 3.3". Fixed 3-dot sights. Magazine capacity 8 rounds. Weight about 21.5 oz. Introduced 2014.

NIB	Exc.	V.G.	Good	Fair	Poor
300	200	150	100	80	50

Thunder 380 Matte Plus

Semi-automatic double-action blued pistol in .380, with 15-round magazine. Fixed sights and polymer grips. Introduced 2006.

NIB	Exc.	V.G.	Good	Fair	Poor
350	280	250	200	150	100

Thunder Pro Ultra Compact

Pro Ultra Compact Series features DA/SA operation, skeletonized hammer, loaded chamber indicator, checkered black polymer grips and choice of matte black, nickel, two-tone or stainless finish. Chambered in 9mm, .40 S&W or .45 ACP. Barrel lengths 3.25" for 9mm and .40; 3.50" for .45. Note: Add $40 for nickel or stainless finish.

NIB	Exc.	V.G.	Good	Fair	Poor
440	380	320	300	200	150

Thunder 9/40 High Capacity Series

Double-action semi-automatic available chambered for 9mm or .40 S&W. Matte blued or satin nickel-plate. Fixed sights and polymer grips. LOA 7.5", Barrel length 4.25". Weight 26 oz. Introduced 2006.

NIB	Exc.	V.G.	Good	Fair	Poor
440	380	320	300	200	150

Thunder Deluxe

Semi-automatic double-action pistol. Chambered for .380 cartridge. Blued finish. Fixed sights. Barrel length 3.5". Weight about 23 oz. Magazine capacity 9 rounds.

NIB	Exc.	V.G.	Good	Fair	Poor
320	220	180	100	80	50

Thunder 22

Double-action semi-automatic, with 3.5" barrel and 10-shot magazine. Matte black, satin nickel or two-tone finish.

NIB	Exc.	V.G.	Good	Fair	Poor
300	250	200	150	100	80

BERTRAND, JULES

Liege, Belgium

See—OURY, D.D.

Le Novo

See—OURY

Lincoln

7.65mm caliber.

NIB	Exc.	V.G.	Good	Fair	Poor
—	300	220	180	100	50

Le Rapide

6.35mm caliber semi-automatic pistol. Jules Bertrand logo on slide as well as Le Rapide. Both are on each side of grip plates.

Courtesy James Rankin

NIB	Exc.	V.G.	Good	Fair	Poor
—	350	280	200	120	50

BERTUZZI
Brescia, Italy

This maker of best quality sidelock over/under and side-by-side shotguns closed its doors in 2009, after more than 100 years in business. Values shown are approximate retail prices in recent years, depending on the wide range of optional features.

OVER/UNDER SHOTGUNS

Zeus

12-, 16-, 20- or 28-gauge sidelock shotgun, with automatic ejectors, single-selective trigger and deluxe checkered walnut stock. Custom order in various barrel lengths and chokes. Engraved. Rarely seen on used gun market. From $18,000 to $39,000

Zeus Extra Lusso

As above, with best wood and engraving. Cased. From $35,000 to $79,000.

Zeus Boss System

Chambered for 12-, 16-, 20- or 28-gauge. Fitted with Boss locking system and ejectors. One-of-a-kind gun with best quality wood and engraving. From $65,000 to $135,000.

Gull Wing

Burtuzzi's best gun, with unique sidelock design mounted on a center plate. Release located on top of safety to allow sidelock access. These shotguns usually take about three years to build. Consult distributor about options and availability. From $125,000 to $240,000.

Ariete Extra Lusso

Best quality hammer gun in all gauges from 12 to 28. Limited quantities. From $65,000 to $135,000.

SIDE-BY-SIDE SHOTGUNS

Orione

12-, 16-, 20- or 28-gauge boxlock shotgun, with Anson & Deeley through bolt. In various barrel lengths and chokes, single-selective trigger and automatic ejectors. Hand checkered walnut stock, with semi-beavertail forearm. Engraving. From $25,000 to $40,000.

Venere

Best quality sidelock gun, with traditional or round frame. Special order to customer specifications. Engraved guns bring a premium. From $30,000 to $70,000.

Ariete

Best quality hammer gun, with or without self cocking hammers and ejectors. Offered in 12-gauge through .410 bore. Many options. From $25,000 to $55,000.

Gull Wing

One-of-a-kind custom built gun, with quick release sidelocks. Delivery time about three years. Contact distributor for more information. From $85,000 to $150,000.

BIGELOW, BENJAMIN
Marysville, California

Pill Lock Revolving Rifle (Antique)

— SEE BILLINGHURST, WILLIAM

BIG HORN ARMORY
Cody, Wyoming 2007-present

Big Horn Armory Model 89 Rifle and Carbine

Lever-action rifle or carbine chambered for .500 S&W Magnum. Features include walnut or maple stocks with pistol grip; aperture rear and blade front sights; recoil pad; sling swivels; enlarged lever loop; magazine capacity 5 (rifle) or 7 (carbine) rounds. Guns may be made to order, with additional cost for additional features. Trapper 16" barrel and rifle 22" barrel bring premium over standard carbine 18" barrel.

NIB	Exc.	V.G.	Good	Fair	Poor
2300	1800	1500	900	700	500

Model 89 Black Thunder

Calibers: .500 S&W Magnum. Capacity: 6-round tubular magazine. Barrel: 16.25 in. steel. Weight: 7 lbs. 6 oz. Length: 36 in. Stock: Black laminate with M-LOK rail on the front of the forend. Sights: Skinner iron sights and factory-installed scout rail. Features: Expansion of the Model 89 lever-action line built as a carbine with a shorter barrel, ideal for hunting, home defense, and survival. Robust stainless steel construction, heat-treated, and coated with a black nitride finish. Bighorn Armory rifles built in Cody, WY.

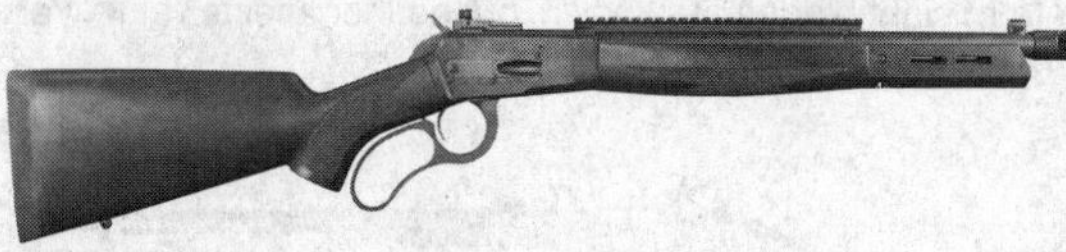

NIB	Exc.	V.G.	Good	Fair	Poor
1190	—	—	—	—	—

Big Horn Armory Models 90, 90A, & 90B

As above, except 90 is chambered for .460 S&W Magnum, 90A for .454 Casull or .500 Linebaugh, and 90B for .45 Colt or .475 Linebaugh. Values are slightly higher than the Model 89.

Big Horn Armory 500 Auto Max

AR pattern rifle chambered for .500 Auto Max, a rimless version of the .500 S&W, and is promoted as the most powerful rifle on the AR platform.

NIB	Exc.	V.G.	Good	Fair	Poor
2000	1700	1400	900	—	—

Big Horn Armory 500 Auto Max Pistol

AR-style pistol with 10" barrel and blade pistol stock chambered for 500 Auto Max, introduced 2020. Values will probably be like the 500 Auto Max rifle.

BIGHORN ARMS CO.
Watertown, South Dakota

Target Pistol

.22-caliber single-shot pistol resembling semi-automatic. Ventilated rib barrel 6" in length. Stock of molded plastic.

NIB	Exc.	V.G.	Good	Fair	Poor
—	280	180	100	80	60

Shotgun

Single-shot 12-gauge shotgun, with 26" barrel blued. Plastic stock.

NIB	Exc.	V.G.	Good	Fair	Poor
—	200	120	60	50	30

BIGHORN RIFLE CO.
Orem, Utah

Bighorn Rifle

A former custom rifle manufacturer located in Orem, Utah. These made-to-order rifles were available in any caliber, with various options. Values are speculative.

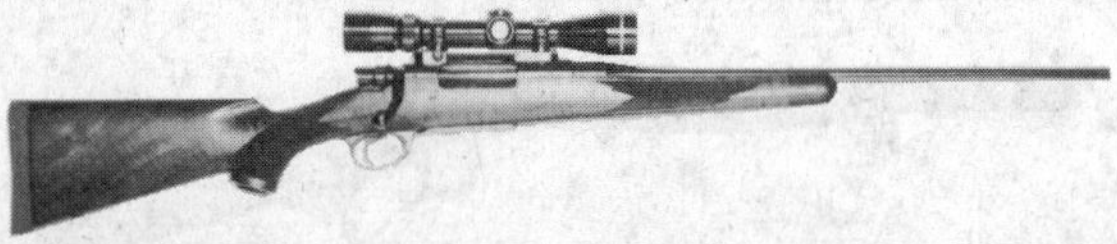

NIB	Exc.	V.G.	Good	Fair	Poor
2000	1650	1200	850	650	300

BILHARZ, HALL & CO.
Location Unknown

Breechloading ("Rising Breech") Carbine (Antique)

Overall length 40"; barrel length 21"; caliber 54. Markings: either "P" or "P/CS" on upper left side of barrel and top of rising breech. Peculiar feature of this carbine is manner in which breech-block exposes chamber. A box-like chamber at rear of barrel rises vertically to expose chamber for a paper cartridge by activating lever/trigger-guard mechanism. Only 100 of this type were delivered to Confederacy in September 1862. Two types of front sight blades are known, but neither affects value. Very rare confederate arm. Values are speculative.

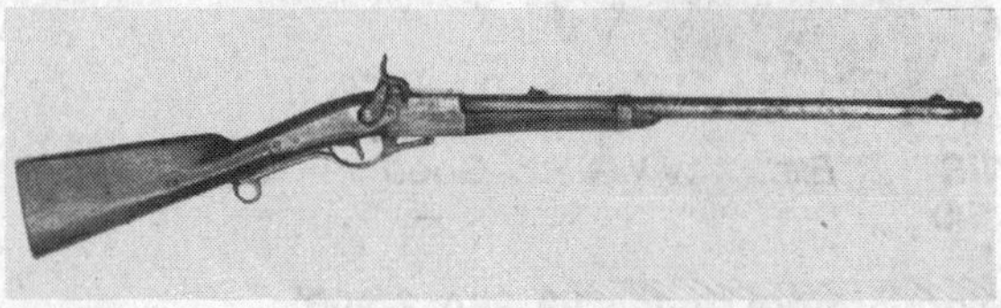

Courtesy Milwaukee Public Museum, Milwaukee, Wisconsin

Exc.	Fine	V.G.	Good	Fair	Poor
70000	45000	30000	20000	10000	5000

Muzzleloading Carbine (Antique)

Overall length 37.5"; barrel length 22"; caliber .58. Markings: "P/CS" on upper left of barrel near breech; "CSA" on top near breech. Modeled after Springfield U.S. M1855 rifle carbine. Bilharz, Hall & Co. muzzleloading carbine has often been mistakenly identified as a product of D.C. Hodgkins & Sons of Macon, Georgia. Serial numbers (found internally) belie that identification. Instead these arms are part of deliveries made to Richmond from middle of 1863 until March 1864. Serial numbers, noted in excess of 700, suggest that about 1,000 were produced. Two basic types, earlier (through serial number 300) were made with brass nosecaps; later type (about serial number 310 through at least 710) have pewter nosecaps on short fore-stock; neither type affects value. Expert authentication recommended. Values are speculative.

Exc.	Fine	V.G.	Good	Fair	Poor
30000	20000	10000	6000	3000	1500

BILLINGHURST, WILLIAM
Rochester, New York

Billinghurst originally worked for James and John Miller of Rochester. After James Miller's death in 1837, Billinghurst established his own shop where he produced revolving rifles based upon Miller's 1829 patent. While these arms were originally made with percussion ignition systems (either pill or percussion cap), later examples using self-contained metallic cartridges are sometimes encountered. Billinghurst also established a well-deserved reputation for making extremely accurate percussion target pistols and rifles.

Underhammer Rifle (Antique)

Billinghurst also produced high-quality underhammer heavy barrel benchrest or target model percussion rifles. Often found with scopes.

Exc.	Fine	V.G.	Good	Fair	Poor
7000	5000	3000	2000	1000	500

Underhammer Pistol - ("Buggy Rifle") (Antique)

Pistol is somewhat different than most under hammers encountered. Barrels are 12" to 18" in length. Heavy octagonal construction. Chambered from .30- to .38-caliber and utilize percussion ignition system. Higher grade versions feature a part-round barrel. Important to note that no two pistols are alike. These pistols were furnished with detachable shoulder stocks and a good many were cased with telescopic sights and false muzzles. This is a high quality weapon; if encountered with optional accessories, it would definitely warrant an individual appraisal. This firearm was manufactured in 1850s and 1860s. Note: Add 50 percent for shoulder stock.

Exc.	Fine	V.G.	Good	Fair	Poor
5000	2500	1500	900	600	350

Revolving Rifle (Antique)

Calibers vary from .40 to .50 with barrels from 24" to 29"; walnut stocks. Barrels marked: "W. Billinghurst, Rochester, N.Y.", or "W. Billinghurst". Found with pill lock or percussion ignition. Over-under double barrel combination gun may bring double the single barrel model. Former Billinghurst apprentice Benjamin Bigelow produced a similar pill-lock revolving rifle in Marysville, California. Fewer than five surving Bigelow examples are known; worth premium."

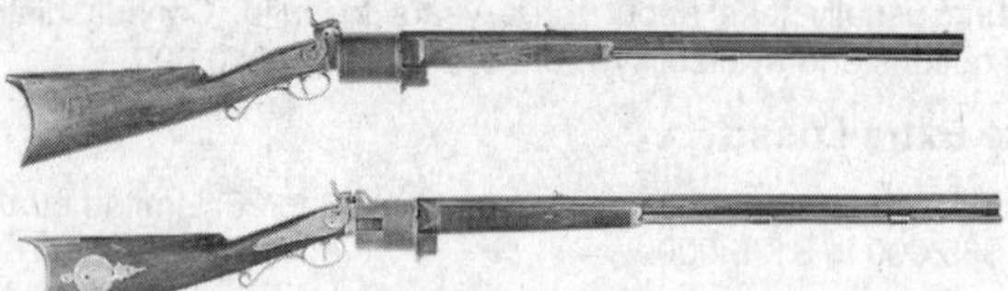

Exc.	Fine	V.G.	Good	Fair	Poor
7000	5500	4250	3000	2000	1000

BILLINGS, CHARLES E.
Hartford, Connecticut

Vest Pocket Pistol (Antique)

.32 rimfire caliber single-shot spur trigger pistol, with 2.5" round barrel. An unusually large grip. Barrel stamped "Billings Vest Pocket Pistol Pat. April 24, 1866". Blued, with walnut grips. Manufactured between 1865 and 1868.

Exc.	*Fine*	*V.G.*	*Good*	*Fair*	*Poor*
3500	1500	1020	550	200	140

BINGHAM LTD.
Norcross, Georgia

PPS 50

.22 rimfire caliber semi-automatic rifle. Patterned after Soviet PPSH submachine gun, with 16" barrel and 50-round drum magazine. Blued, walnut or beech stock with vented handguard. Manufactured between 1976 and 1985.

NIB	*Exc.*	*V.G.*	*Good*	*Fair*	*Poor*
—	580	400	280	220	100

AK-22

.22 rimfire caliber semi-automatic rifle. Patterned after Soviet AK-47, with 15- or 29-shot magazine. Walnut or beech stock. Manufactured between 1976 and 1985.

NIB	*Exc.*	*V.G.*	*Good*	*Fair*	*Poor*
—	360	220	150	100	80

Bantam

.22 rimfire or .22 rimfire Magnum caliber bolt-action rifle, with 18.5" barrel. Manufactured between 1976 and 1985.

NIB	*Exc.*	*V.G.*	*Good*	*Fair*	*Poor*
—	200	80	70	50	40

BISMARCK

Pocket Revolver (Antique)

.22-caliber spur trigger revolver, with 3" round ribbed barrel and 7-shot unfluted cylinder. Brass frame. Remainder plated with rosewood grips. Barrel marked "Bismarck". Manufactured in 1870s.

Exc.	*Fine*	*V.G.*	*Good*	*Fair*	*Poor*
550	220	150	90	50	30

BITTERLICH, FRANK J.
Nashville, Tennessee

A .41-caliber single-shot percussion pistol in a variety of octagonal barrel lengths, German silver mounts, walnut stock. Barrel and locks marked "Fr.J. Bitterlich/Nashville, Tenn." Produced between 1861 and 1867.

Percussion Pistol (Antique)

Bitterlich also made percussion shotguns.

Exc.	*Fine*	*V.G.*	*Good*	*Fair*	*Poor*
6500	5000	4000	2000	800	400

BITTNER, GUSTAV
Wieport, Bohemia

1893 Manual Repeating Pistol (Antique)

7.7mm Bittner caliber repeating pistol, with 4.5" barrel. Bolt containing firing pin rotates to lock breech. Operated by finger lever that encloses trigger. Manufactured in mid-1890s. Fewer than 500 made. Bitterlich also made percussion shotguns.

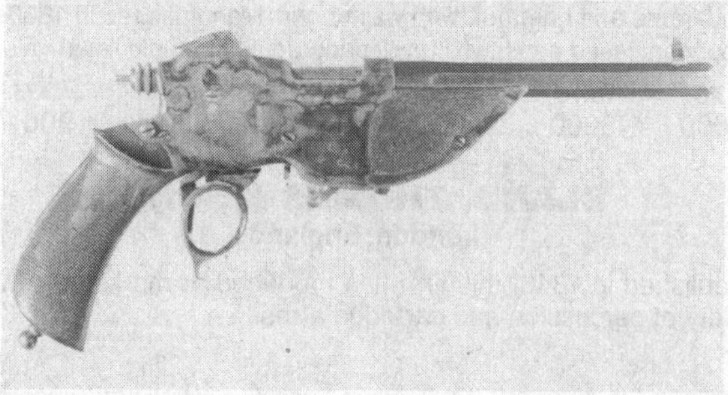

Exc.	*Fine*	*V.G.*	*Good*	*Fair*	*Poor*
16000	10000	6000	4000	2000	1000

BLACKOUT DEFENSE
Chandler, Arizona

Aerospace manufacturer that now specializes in precision tactical firearms of the AR style.

Quantum DTL

Chamber: .223 Wylde. Barrel: 13.9", 14.5", 16", mid-length gas system. Pinned and welded muzzle device to exceed 16.0 in. total overall length as needed. Heavy profile, 416-R stainless steel, gun-drilled and reamed in 5R rifling and 1:8" twist. Stress relieved, precision air gauged. Dual Taper Lock (DTL) system secures and centers the barrel. Quantum-series lower receivers use patented Presslock technology with linear compression pad for a tight, rattle-free fitment, no carrier tilt. Handguard: 7-side M-LOK compatible. Stryker ambidextrous charging handle. Weight: 6.875 lbs. Black anodized is standard receiver color; several other colors are $50-$75 upcharges. Many options for gas block, charging handle, triggers, etc. SEE POLITICAL PANIC PRICING.

NIB	*Exc.*	*V.G.*	*Good*	*Fair*	*Poor*
2000	—	—	—	—	—

BLAKE, J. H.
New York, New York

Blake Bolt-Action Rifle

.30-40 Krag caliber bolt-action rifle, with 30" barrel and 7-shot magazine. Stock secured by three barrel bands. Blued, with walnut stock. Manufactured between 1892 and 1910.

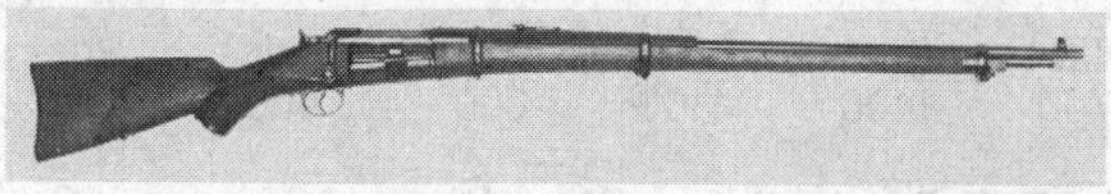

Courtesy Milwaukee Public Museum, Milwaukee, Wisconsin

NIB	*Exc.*	*V.G.*	*Good*	*Fair*	*Poor*
—	—	3500	1700	680	200

BLANCH, JOHN
London, England

London, est. 1809. In addition to standard configuration percussion pistols listed here, Blanch also produced Adams patent and Tranter patent double action percussion revolvers (see Adams and Tranter listings), double barrel percussion shotguns, and screwbarrel percussion pocket pistols (values about half those of standard pistols).

Blanch Percussion Pistol (Antique)

.69-caliber single-shot percussion pistol, with 5" Damascus barrel. Engraved frame and hammer, with walnut grip. Manufactured in 1830s. Often found in cased pairs, which will bring double to triple listed values.

Exc.	Fine	V.G.	Good	Fair	Poor
5000	3000	1000	750	500	300

BLAND, THOMAS & SONS
London, England

Established in 1840, this firm has produced or marketed a wide variety of percussion and cartridge arms.

BLASER JAGDWAFFEN
Germany

RIFLES

Model K77

Single-shot rifle chambered in a variety of calibers. A 24" barrel and silver-plated engraved receiver. Walnut stock. Introduced in 1988. Discontinued in 1990. Note: Add $750 per barrel for extra barrels.

NIB	Exc.	V.G.	Good	Fair	Poor
2400	1850	1200	850	650	300

Model R-84

Bolt-action sporting rifle. Chambered in a variety of calibers, with 23" or 24" barrel. Interchangeable barrels available for this model. Walnut stock. Imported beginning in 1988.

NIB	Exc.	V.G.	Good	Fair	Poor
2500	2000	1400	950	700	300

Model R-93 LX

A straight-pull-back bolt-action rifle, with interchangeable barrels. In calibers from .22-250 to .416 Rem. Magnum. Barrel length for standard calibers is 22" and Magnum calibers 26". Magazine capacity 3 rounds. Receiver is drilled and tapped for Blaser scope mounts. Weight about 7 lbs. Two-piece walnut stock. Introduced by SIGARMS into U.S. in 1998. Note: Add $200 for left-hand rifles; $800 for .416 Rem. Magnum.

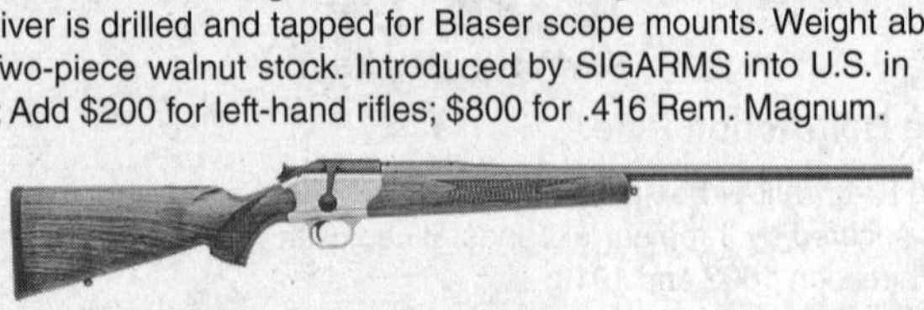

NIB	Exc.	V.G.	Good	Fair	Poor
1700	1400	1100	800	600	300

Model R-93 Prestige

Updated and upgraded standard model, with all features of R-93 LX. Light scroll engraving on receiver.

NIB	Exc.	V.G.	Good	Fair	Poor
3280	2750	1800	1300	700	350

Model R-93 Classic

Similar to above. Choice of calibers and barrel lengths. Addition of highly figured walnut stock and game scene engraved receiver. Note: Add $200 for left-hand rifles; $800 for .416 Rem. Magnum.

NIB	Exc.	V.G.	Good	Fair	Poor
2900	2400	1750	1250	900	300

Model R-93 Luxus

Updated and upgraded model of R-93 Classic. Features high grade Turkish walnut stock, with ebony forend. Side plates engraved with game scenes.

NIB	Exc.	V.G.	Good	Fair	Poor
5000	4000	3000	2000	1000	500

Model R-93 Synthetic

Also available in same wide range of interchangeable barrels and calibers. Features one-piece black synthetic stock. Note: Add $200 for left-hand rifles; $800 for .416 Rem. Magnum.

NIB	Exc.	V.G.	Good	Fair	Poor
1800	1500	1000	850	600	400

Model R-93 Attache

Features custom made stock of highly figured walnut, with cheekpiece, leather covered buttplate, silver pistol grip cap, ebony forend tip and custom checkering. Sold with leather carrying case. Note: Add $200 for left-hand rifles.

NIB	Exc.	V.G.	Good	Fair	Poor
5500	4650	3300	2450	1650	500

Model R-93 Safari Synthetic

Chambered for .416 Rem. Magnum cartridge. Fitted with 24" heavy barrel, with open sights. Weight 9.5 lbs. Black synthetic stock. Other Blaser barrels will interchange on this model.

NIB	Exc.	V.G.	Good	Fair	Poor
2100	1700	1250	880	500	280

Model R-93 Safari LX

Same as R-93 Safari Synthetic, with exception of two-piece walnut stock.

NIB	Exc.	V.G.	Good	Fair	Poor
2500	2000	1550	1000	750	350

Model R-93 Safari Classic

Features engraved receiver and fancy walnut stock.

NIB	Exc.	V.G.	Good	Fair	Poor
2500	2000	1550	1000	750	350

Model R-93 Safari Attache

Top-of-the-line version of R-93 series. Features engraved receiver, fancy walnut stock and other custom options found on R-93 Attache model.

NIB	Exc.	V.G.	Good	Fair	Poor
6000	5000	3950	2900	1500	400

Model R-93 Grand Luxe

Offered in same wide range of calibers as other Blaser models. Addition of high grade walnut stock, fully hand engraved receiver and matching scroll sideplates. Introduced in 1999. Note: Add $200 for left-hand rifles.

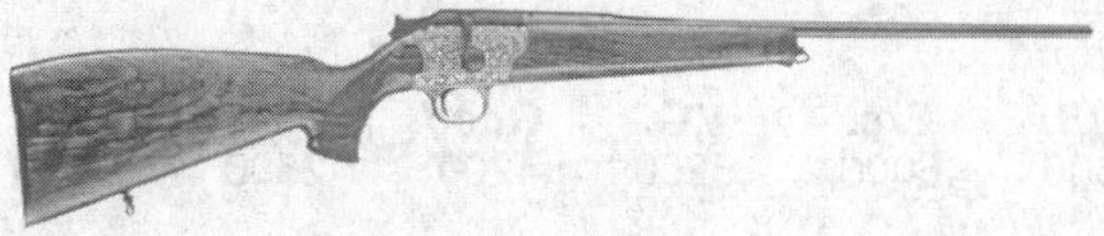

NIB	Exc.	V.G.	Good	Fair	Poor
6000	5000	4000	2000	1000	400

Model R-93 Long Range Sporter

Introduced in 1998. Bolt-action rifle chambered for most popular cartridges. Barrel length 24" without muzzle brake. Removable box magazine holds 10 rounds. Stock is aluminum and fully adjustable. Weight about 10.4 lbs. No longer in production.

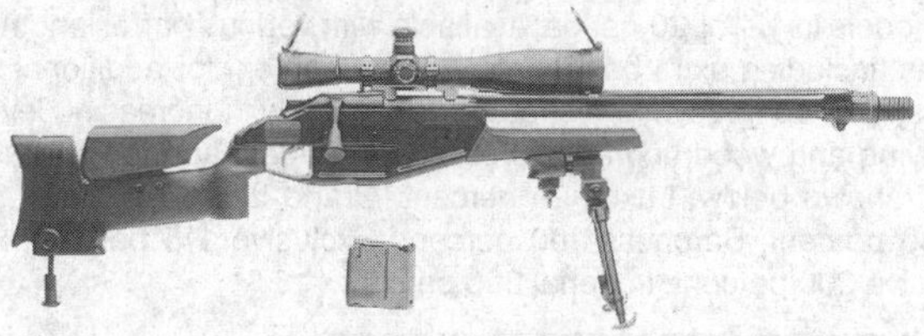

NIB	Exc.	V.G.	Good	Fair	Poor
2200	1780	1250	880	500	280

Model R-93 Long Range Sporter 2

Introduced in 2000. A second-generation version of Long Range Sporter model above. Chambered for .300 Win. Magnum and .308, both of which are interchangeable. Also chambered for .338 Lapua cartridge which does not interchange with other calibers. Cheekpiece improved. New front rail has been added to this model. Barrel length 24" without muzzle brake. Weight about 10.4 lbs. Note: Add $350 for .338 Lapua.

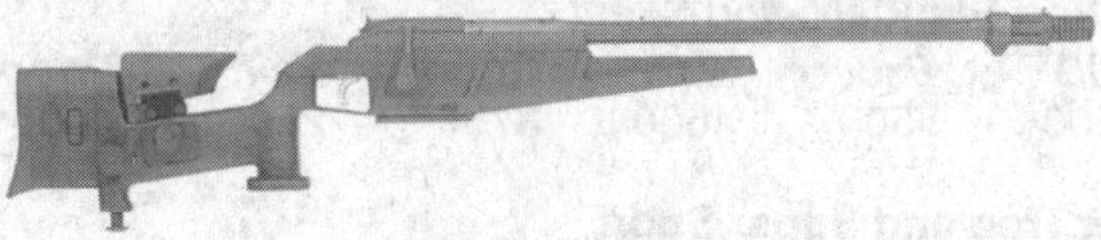

NIB	Exc.	V.G.	Good	Fair	Poor
3480	2700	1900	1280	800	380

CURRENT RIFLE PRODUCTION

Model R8 Ultimate

The new R8 Ultimate bolt-action rifle is available in the R8 Ultimate and R8 Ultimate Leather. Both have an ergonomic synthetic thumbhole stock with an adjustable comb, adjustable recoil pad and adjustable recoil absorption system. The R8 can be configured in 43 calibers. Note: Price shown for R8 Ultimate. Add about 20 percent for the Ultimate Leather. Introduced 2019.

NIB	Exc.	V.G.	Good	Fair	Poor
3850	3250	2780	—	—	—

R8 Ultimate Carbon

Calibers: Available in a wide range of calibers from .22 LR to .500 Jeffery, now including 6.5 Creedmoor and 6.5 PRC. Barrel: 20.5, 23, or 25.75 in. Stock: Hand-laid 100% carbon-fiber thumbhole stock with Elastomer grip inserts. An Ultimate Carbon Leather variant is available with dark brown weather-proof leather inserts. Sights: Drilled and tapped. Features: Straight-pull bolt-action hunting rifle with interchangeable barrels and bolt heads. Ultimate Carbon variant designed for max performance and minimum weight. Blaser Precision trigger. Thumb-activated safety slide/cocking mechanism. Optional upgrades include an adjustable comb and recoil absorption system or adjustable recoil pad. Imported from Germany by Blaser Group.

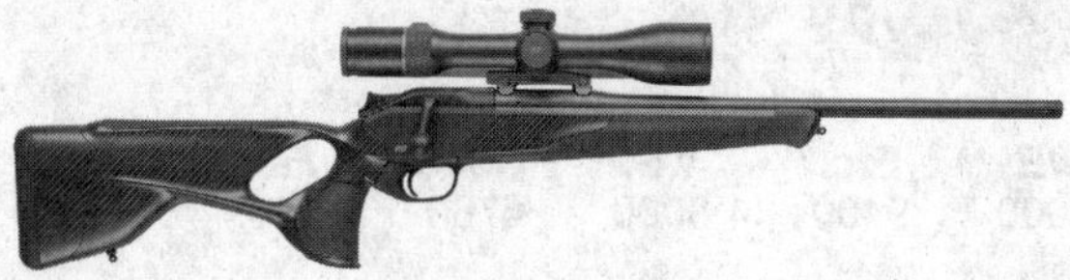

NIB	Exc.	V.G.	Good	Fair	Poor
11230	—	—	—	—	—

Model R-8 Professional

Improved variation of R-93 action, with detachable magazine. Offered in many calibers from .222 Rem. to 10.3x60R. Offered in several high-grade models similar to those in R-93 series. Prices shown are for the basic model, with synthetic stock. Note: Add 15% to 300% for high-grade versions.

NIB	Exc.	V.G.	Good	Fair	Poor
3350	2850	2400	1450	850	400

Model R8 Professional Success

Similar to R-8 Professional model, except with synthetic thumbhole stock in Dark Brown or Dark Green color. Leather inlays are optional. Introduced in 2013.

NIB	Exc.	V.G.	Good	Fair	Poor
3850	3250	2780	1680	1000	450

Model R8 Professional Hunter

Chambered in most popular dangerous-game calibers. Has high-grade wood, all steel receiver, with several stock and finish options.

NIB	Exc.	V.G.	Good	Fair	Poor
7200	6000	5100	3000	1800	500

Blaser R8 Jaeger

Higher grade versions of R8 series. Stock is Grade 3 walnut with Bavarian cheekpiece, black forend tip, rubber recoil pad. Many options available. Prices shown are for the mid-level Jaeger model. Higher grades available.

NIB	Exc.	V.G.	Good	Fair	Poor
3880	2300	1980	1180	700	300

Model K-95 Jaeger

Single-shot model, with break-open action. Receiver is aluminum, with engraving on side plates. Barrel length 23.6" for standard calibers and 25.6" for Magnum calibers. Oil-finish Turkish walnut stock. Interchangeable barrels in calibers from .243 to .300 Wby. Magnum. Weight about 5.5 lbs. Introduced in 2001.

NIB	Exc.	V.G.	Good	Fair	Poor
4450	3780	3200	1900	1150	500

Model R8 Ruthenium

A high-grade R8 featuring Grade 8 walnut stock with Bavarian cheekpiece with double rabbet, and a forearm with an ebony forend tip. Receiver, fluted barrel and trigger given Blaser's black, high-gloss "Diamond Like Carbon" finish.

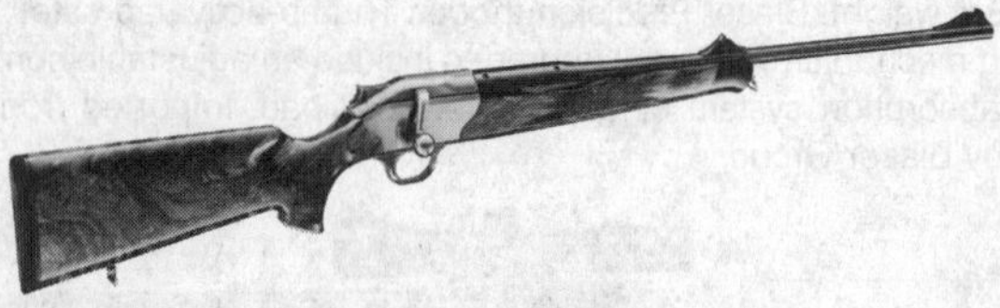

NIB	Exc.	V.G.	Good	Fair	Poor
11000	9400	8000	6780	—	—

Model K-95 Custom I

Same as above, with fancy Turkish walnut stock. Hand engraving on receiver and side plates with choice of engraving motif. MSRP from $13,721.

Model K-95 Stutzen Luxus

Introduced in 2003. Break-action single-shot rifle offered in 23 calibers. Fancy walnut Mannlicher-style two-piece stock. Interchangeable barrels.

NIB	Exc.	V.G.	Good	Fair	Poor
8000	7000	6000	5000	4000	900

Model R8 Baronesse

Ultra-high grade with Grade 8 wood, fully engraved receiver, gold-colored trigger and titanium-nitride bolt head, wooden bolt knob, fluted barrel, rifle case and leather sling.

NIB	Exc.	V.G.	Good	Fair	Poor
16000	13500	11550	9850	—	—

R8 Stradivari

Standard with the high-grade wood grade 10, receiver, fluted octagonal barrel and trigger given Blaser's black, high-gloss "Diamond Like Carbon" finish.

NIB	Exc.	V.G.	Good	Fair	Poor
17500	15000	12650	10750	—	—

Ultimate Bolt-Action

Unique bolt-action design imported into the U.S. in the 1980s. Chambered in most popular calibers from .22-250 to .375 H&H. Features include interchangeable barrels and bolt heads, single-set trigger, and exposed hammer. Left-hand models at no additional cost. Available in several high-grade models. The prices shown are for the standard model. Note: Add a premium of 15% to 200% for higher-grade engraving and wood.

NIB	Exc.	V.G.	Good	Fair	Poor
1400	1200	1000	800	550	300

Blaser S2 Double Rifle

Series of side-by-side double rifles offered in two different models, Standard and Safari. Standard calibers range from .22 Hornet to 9.3x74R, including several European rimmed cartridges. Safari model chamberings for .375 H&H, .470 NE, .500/416 NE and 500 NE. Both series available in standard or five higher grades offering increasing levels of wood and engraving. Higher grade models are in order: Luxus, Super Luxus, Exclusive, Super Exclusive and Imperial. Prices shown are for basic standard models. Extra sets of barrels in different calibers offered, including shotgun barrels. Barrel sets are not interchangeable between Standard and Safari models. Note: Add 15 to 200 percent or more for higher grades.

Standard

NIB	Exc.	V.G.	Good	Fair	Poor
6800	6000	5200	4200	2500	1000

Safari

NIB	Exc.	V.G.	Good	Fair	Poor
9500	8500	7000	5800	3500	1500

SHOTGUNS

F3 SERIES

Over/under series of shotguns. Offered in standard, sporting, skeet and trap models in 12- or 20-gauge. Available with various barrel lengths and options, including extra barrel sets. Add 40 percent for additional set of barrels. Offered in several higher grades, each with increasing levels of engraving and wood upgrades. For higher grades, add the following to prices shown below: Luxus 20 percent; Grand Lux 60 percent; Super Lux 80 percent; Baroness 100 percent; Exclusive 115 percent; Super Exclusive 200 percent; Imperial 300 percent.

NIB	Exc.	V.G.	Good	Fair	Poor
—					

F3 SeriesGame Standard

NIB	Exc.	V.G.	Good	Fair	Poor
5500	4700	3900	3000	2000	1000

Sporting Standard and Skeet

NIB	Exc.	V.G.	Good	Fair	Poor
6500	5500	4600	3750	2500	1000

Super Trap and Super Sport

NIB	Exc.	V.G.	Good	Fair	Poor
7500	6750	5900	4500	3000	1000

HANDGUNS

Blaser HHS

Single-shot pistol has R93 receiver. Fitted with 14" barrel and pistol grip fancy Turkish walnut stock. All R93 calibers are offered in both right-/left-hand models. Introduced in 2003. Note: Add $100 for left-hand models.

NIB	Exc.	V.G.	Good	Fair	Poor
4250	3250	2000	1300	70	400

BLISS, F. D.

New Haven, Connecticut

Bliss Pocket Revolver (Antique)

.25-caliber spur trigger revolver, with 3.25" octagon barrel, 6-shot magazine and square butt. Blued, with hard rubber or walnut grips. Barrel stamped "F.D. Bliss New Haven, Ct.". There was an all-brass framed version made early in production. This model would be worth approximately 50 percent more than values listed here for standard model. Approximately 3,000 manufactured circa 1860 to 1863.

Exc.	Fine	V.G.	Good	Fair	Poor
1000	700	500	350	200	100

BLUNDERBUSS

Blunderbuss refers to a type of firearm, not a specific maker or model. It is a short-barrel shoulder arm, usually flintlock, with a large-diameter bore and distinctive flared muzzle. Most barrels were 14 to 24 inches, with a bore diameter of usually 16 to 10 gauge, flaring to around 2 to 3 inches at the muzzle. Barrel may be brass or steel; muzzle flare may be "duckbill" oval rather than round. They were loaded with shot or round balls and used for close-range defense, potentially against multiple assailants, with main applications being naval anti-boarding weapons and coach guns. The flared muzzle was not necessarily to spread the shot pattern, but rather to serve as a loading funnel, especially on a moving platform such as a ship's deck or a rolling coach. They were more common in Europe, especially England, than America. They are often lack a maker's name on the barrel, although the lock may have a lockmaker's name. Most are flintlock, although earlier types such as snaphaunce or miquelet were also made in blunderbuss configuration and some made later for percussion ignition. Blunderbuss pistols and wall-mounted swivel guns were also produced. Flared muzzle guns were also made in the Mideast and Asia, and they usually bring substanially less than European and American examples, and may be low-value non-functional recent production examples made for the tourist trade. Values shown are generalizations for flintlock European or American shoulder-fired blunderbusses. Premium for naval-issue arms or spring-opening bayonets or prominent known maker. Swivel guns may bring similar values, pistols a bit less, boxlock pistols substantially less. Percussion specimens or Turkish/ Ottoman antique flintlocks may bring about half.

Common Models Antique

Photo courtesy Uploadalt

A flintlock blunderbuss, built for Tippu Sultan.

Exc.	*Fine*	*V.G.*	*Good*	*Fair*	*Poor*
—	4000	2750	2000	1200	500

BLISS & GOODYEAR

New Haven, Connecticut

In addition to percussion revolvers, Bliss & Goodyear later produced inexpensive spurtrigger cartridge pocket revolvers under trade names including "Prairie King"

Pocket Model Revolver Antique

.28-caliber 6-shot percussion revolver, with 3" octagonal barrel, unfluted cylinder. Solid frame, with removable side plate. Blued, with brass frame and walnut grips. Approximately 3,000 manufactured in 1860.

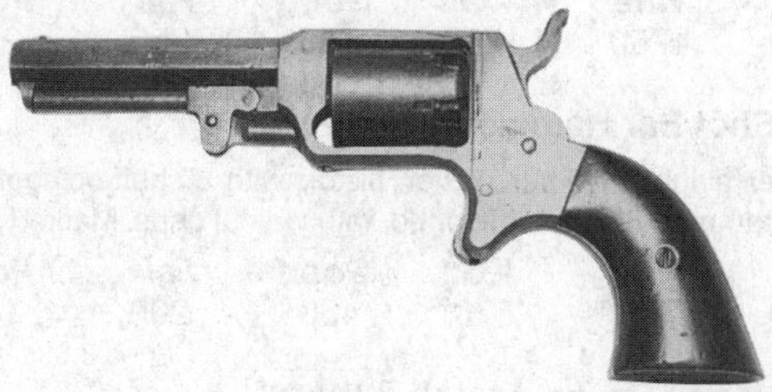

Exc.	*Fine*	*V.G.*	*Good*	*Fair*	*Poor*
1800	1200	800	600	300	150

BLUNT & SYMS

New York, New York

Under Hammer Pepperbox Antique

Pepperboxes produced by Blunt & Syms are noteworthy for the fact they incorporate a ring trigger cocking/revolving mechanism and a concealed under hammer. They were produced in a variety of calibers and standard finish was blued. Normally these pistols are found marked simply "A-C" on face of barrel group. Some examples though are marked "Blunt & Syms New York". This firm was in business from approximately 1837 to 1855.

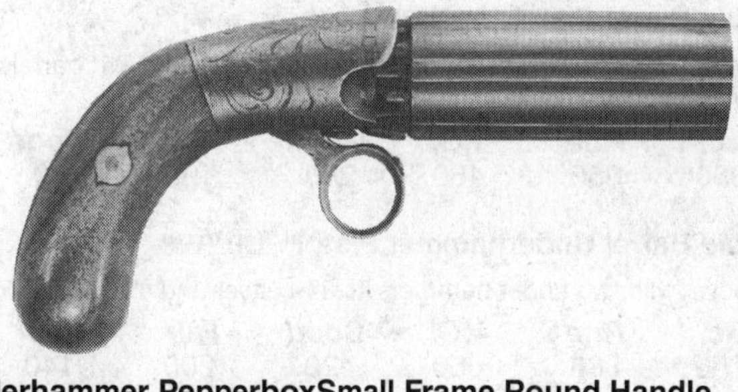

Underhammer PepperboxSmall Frame Round Handle .25-.28-Caliber Antique

Exc.	*Fine*	*V.G.*	*Good*	*Fair*	*Poor*
1750	1000	600	400	200	150

Medium Frame Round Handle .31-Caliber Antique

Premium for unfluted/ribbed barrels (barrel cluster appears to be a cylinder). Approx. double value for deep fluted barrels (appearing to be full round individual barrels).

Exc.	*Fine*	*V.G.*	*Good*	*Fair*	*Poor*
1750	1000	600	400	200	150

Round Handle Dragoon .36-Caliber Antique

Exc.	*Fine*	*V.G.*	*Good*	*Fair*	*Poor*
3000	1600	1000	600	400	200

Medium Frame Saw Handle .31-Caliber Antique

Exc.	*Fine*	*V.G.*	*Good*	*Fair*	*Poor*
2000	1200	650	450	225	150

Under Hammer PepperboxSaw Handle Dragoon .36-Caliber Antique

Exc.	*Fine*	*V.G.*	*Good*	*Fair*	*Poor*
3200	1700	1100	750	300	200

Dueling Pistol Antique

.52-caliber percussion single-shot pistol, with octagonal barrel normally of 9" length. Steel furniture, with walnut stock. Barrel marked "B&S New York/Cast Steel".

Exc.	Fine	V.G.	Good	Fair	Poor
3000	1750	1230	750	350	230

Single-Shot Bar Hammer Antique

.36-caliber single-shot percussion pistol, with 6" half-octagonal barrel and bar hammer. Blued or browned, with walnut grips. Marked as above.

Exc.	Fine	V.G.	Good	Fair	Poor
1200	700	570	450	200	140

Side Hammer Pocket Pistol Antique

.31- or .35-caliber single-shot percussion pistol, with 2.5" to 6" octagonal barrel. Blued, with walnut grips.

Exc.	Fine	V.G.	Good	Fair	Poor
1250	650	530	420	200	140

Side Hammer Belt Pistol Antique

As above in calibers ranging from .36 to .44, with barrel lengths of 4" or 6".

Exc.	Fine	V.G.	Good	Fair	Poor
1400	750	560	380	150	100

Ring Trigger Pistol Antique

.36-caliber percussion single-shot pistol, with 3" to 5" half-octagonal barrel and ring trigger. Blued, with walnut grips.

Exc.	Fine	V.G.	Good	Fair	Poor
1020	650	510	380	150	100

Double Barrel Pistol Antique

.36- to .44-caliber percussion double-barrel pistol, with 7.5" barrels and walnut grips. Ring trigger variation of this model is known.

Exc.	Fine	V.G.	Good	Fair	Poor
1350	650	460	280	120	80

Double Barrel Underhammer Pistol Antique

As above, with two under hammers in .34-caliber and 4" barrels.

Exc.	Fine	V.G.	Good	Fair	Poor
1750	880	650	420	200	140

Derringer Style Pistol Antique

.50-caliber single-shot percussion pistol, with 3" barrel, German silver mounts and walnut stock. Lock marked "Blunt & Syms/New York".

Exc.	Fine	V.G.	Good	Fair	Poor
1800	680	540	400	200	140

BOBERG ARMS CORP.

White Bear Lake, Minnesota 2011-2016

Founded in 2011 and sold to Bond Arms in 2016.

XR9

Semi-automatic chambered in 9mm, with 3.35-in. (XR9-S) or 4.2-in. (XR9-L) barrel. Striker-fired with locked-breech action, rotating barrel, stainless steel slide, aluminum frame. Magazine capacity 7-rounds. Fixed low-profile 3-dot sights. Patented new design lifts cartridges straight into chamber, eliminating need for feed ramp and allowing for a longer barrel than other subcompact pistols. Introduced in 2013. Note: Add $350 for platinum or onyx finish. Currently produced by Bond Arms as the Bullpup 9.

NIB	Exc.	V.G.	Good	Fair	Poor
980	860	660	560	460	350

XR45

Similar to XR9. Chambered for .45 ACP cartridge. Magazine capacity 6 rounds. Barrel length 3.75-in. Aluminum frame, with stainless steel slide and polymer grip panels. Two-tone satin silver slide and black frame. Introduced in 2014. Note: Add $100 for Tritium night sights.

NIB	Exc.	V.G.	Good	Fair	Poor
1050	960	810	560	470	370

BODEO

Italian Service Revolver Antique

System Bodeo Modello 1889 (Enlisted Model) Antique

Double action with folding trigger

Exc.	Fine	V.G.	Good	Fair	Poor
700	500	400	300	150	70

Modello 1889 (Officer's Model) Antique

Double action with standard round triggerguard.

Exc.	Fine	V.G.	Good	Fair	Poor
550	400	320	250	100	70

BOLUMBURO, G.

Eibar, Spain

Bristol

Semi-automatic pistol in caliber 7.65mm. Made in style of Ruby military pistols. "Bristol" stamped on slide. Wood grips.

Courtesy James Rankin

NIB	Exc.	V.G.	Good	Fair	Poor
—	300	180	150	90	40

Marina 6.35mm

Semi-automatic pistol in caliber 6.35mm. "Marina" stamped on each grip's plate.

Courtesy James Rankin

NIB	Exc.	V.G.	Good	Fair	Poor
—	300	200	150	90	40

Marina 7.65mm

As above in 7.65mm, with "Marina" stamped on slide. Wood grips and lanyard loop.

Courtesy James Rankin

NIB	Exc.	V.G.	Good	Fair	Poor
—	280	200	150	90	40

Rex

Semi-automatic pistol in caliber 7.65mm. "Rex" stamped on slide. Wood grips and lanyard loop.

Courtesy James Rankin

NIB	Exc.	V.G.	Good	Fair	Poor
—	280	200	150	90	40

BOND ARMS INC.

Grandbury, Texas

Bond Arms makes a wide variety of over-under double-barrel derringers based on the classic Remington design with the addition of a triggerguard. Various calibers, barrel lengths, finishes, and types of decoration are available. The models listed here are representative of their product line.

Texas Defender

Stainless steel over/under derringer. Chambered for a variety of calibers such as .45 Colt/.410, .357 Magnum, 9mm, .45 ACP and .44 Magnum. Removable triggerguard. Barrels are interchangeable. Grips are laminated black ash or rosewood. Barrel length 3", with blade front sight and fixed rear sight. Weight about 21 oz. Introduced in 1997. Note: Add 300 percent for full factory engraved model.

NIB	Exc.	V.G.	Good	Fair	Poor
—	400	300	200	150	100

Bullpup 9

Compact 9mm pistol previously produced as the Boberg Arms XR9. See that listing for full description and values.

Bond Patriot

Features an American flag and bald eagle laser engraved on grips. Chambered for .45 Colt/.410 shotshell or .357 Magnum/.38 Special. Standard Bond features include rebounding hammer, retracting firing pins, crossbolt safety and spring-loaded cammed locking lever. Weight 22 oz.; barrel length 3". Introduced in 2015.

NIB	Exc.	V.G.	Good	Fair	Poor
500	420	380	320	250	200

PT2A

Model is the Protect The 2nd Amendment derringer. It has a 4.25" barrel in .357 Magnum/.38 Special or .45 Colt/.410 shotgun. Barrels are engraved on one side with the Second Amendment to the U.S. Constitution and In God We Trust on the other. Grips are extended and checkered rosewood. Weight 23.5 oz. Comes with Bond premium leather holster. Introduced in 2017.

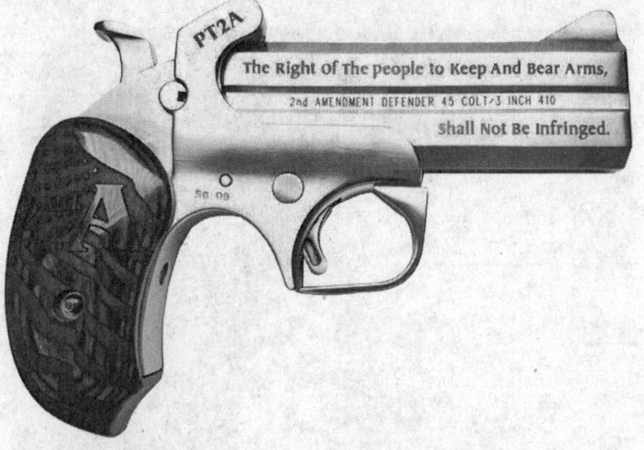

NIB	Exc.	V.G.	Good	Fair	Poor
750	600	500	—	—	—

Snake Slayer IV

Modern variation of Remington over/under derringer. Interchangeable 4.5" barrel assemblies, rosewood grip panels, stainless finish, fixed sights. Chambered for .410-bore shotshell/.45 LC, 9mm, 10mm, .40 S&W, .45 ACP. Weight 23 oz.

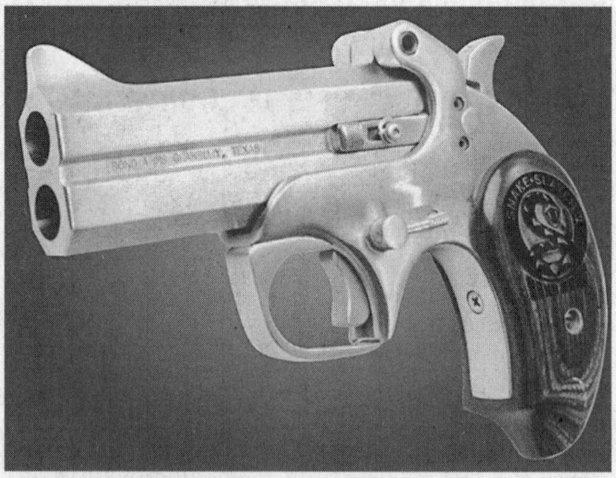

NIB	Exc.	V.G.	Good	Fair	Poor
—	400	300	200	150	100

Bullpup

Similar to Boberg pistol. Semi-automatic with DAO trigger chambered in 9mm. Equipped with 3.35-in. barrel. Engraved rosewood grips. Introduced 2017.

NIB	Exc.	V.G.	Good	Fair	Poor
1100	960	830	660	430	380

Snake Slayer

3.5" barrels; weight 22 oz. Interchangeable barrel assemblies, rosewood grip panels, stainless fixed sights. Chambered for .410-bore shotshell/.45 LC, 9mm, 10mm, .40 S&W, .45 ACP.

NIB	Exc.	V.G.	Good	Fair	Poor
—	400	300	200	150	100

Cowboy Defender

Derringer with 3" barrels. Weight 19 oz. Interchangeable barrels, rosewood grip panels, stainless fixed sights. Variety of chambering options such as .410-bore, .45 LC, .357 Magnum, .38 Special, .45 ACP, .44 Special, .44-40 Win, .40 S&W, 10mm, etc. No triggerguard. Automatic extractor (except for 9mm, 10mm, .40 S&W, .45 ACP).

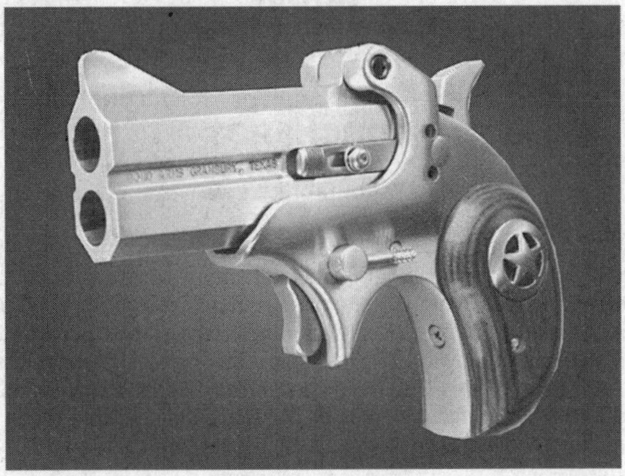

NIB	Exc.	V.G.	Good	Fair	Poor
400	350	300	220	150	80

Century 2000

Similar to Cowboy Defender, with 3.5" barrels to allow use of .410 Magnum shotshells, .357/.38 Special, .45 ACP, .44 Special, .44-40 Win, .40 S&W, 10mm, etc. Automatic extractor (except for 9mm, 10mm, .40 S&W, .45 ACP).

NIB	Exc.	V.G.	Good	Fair	Poor
420	380	300	220	150	80

Grizzly

Caliber: .45 Colt/.410 bore. Capacity: 2 rounds. Barrel: 3 in. Grip: Rosewood. Sights: Fixed front and rear. Features: Similar to other Bond Arms derringers, this model is chambered in .45 Colt and 2.5-inch, .410-bore shotshells. Vibrant rosewood grips with grizzly-bear artwork adorn the Grizzly. It includes a matching leather holster embossed with a grizzly bear.

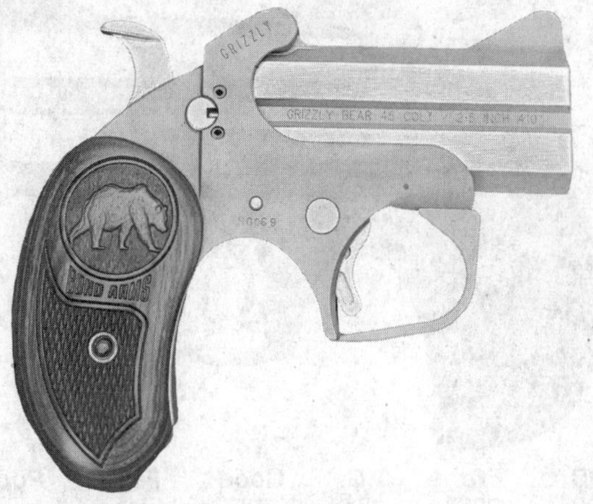

NIB	Exc.	V.G.	Good	Fair	Poor
370	300	250	—	—	—

Roughneck

Caliber: 9mm, .357 Magnum, .45 ACP. Capacity: 2 rounds. Barrel: 2.5 in. Grip: Textured rubber. Sights: Fixed front and rear. Weight: 22 oz. Features: A member of the new Bond Arms Rough series of derringers that includes the premium features found in all Bond guns, including stainless steel barrel, cross-bolt safety, retracting firing pin, spring-loaded, cam-lock lever and rebounding hammer. Each gun of the new series undergoes a quick clean up and deburring and then is bead-blasted, giving it a rough finish. This lightweight tips the scales at 22 ounces.

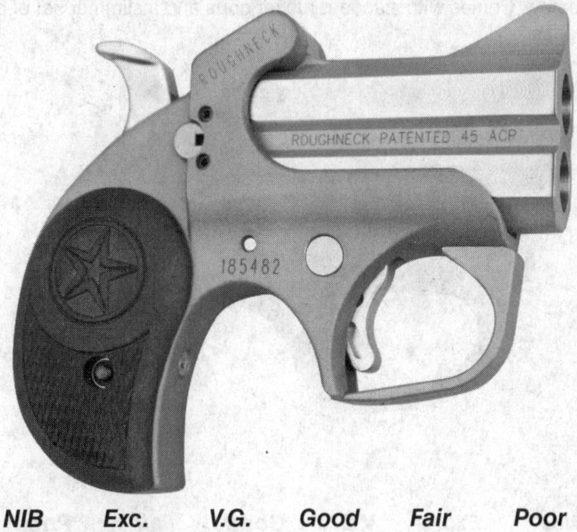

NIB	Exc.	V.G.	Good	Fair	Poor
275	220	175	—	—	—

Rough N Rowdy

Caliber: .45 Colt/.410 bore. Capacity: 2 rounds. Barrel: 3 in. Grip: Black rubber. Sights: Fixed front and rear. Features: Similar to Bond Arms Roughneck, this model is chambered in .45 Colt and 2.5-inch, .410 bore shotshells.

NIB	Exc.	V.G.	Good	Fair	Poor
300	225	175	—	—	—

Rowdy XL

Caliber: .45 Colt/.410. Barrel: 3.5" Extended grip size. Length: 5.75" Weight 22 oz. Grip: B6 Resin.

NIB	Exc.	V.G.	Good	Fair	Poor
260	—	—	—	—	—

Stinger

Calibers: 9mm, .380 ACP. The all-new Stinger has the same quality as Bond Arms' regular models but has half the weight and a slimmer profile. Features: Stainless steel matte barrel, 7075 anodized aluminum frame. Total weight: 12 oz. Rebounding hammer, retracting firing pins, cross-bolt safety. Comes with standard rubber grips and a slimmer set of polymer grips.

NIB	Exc.	V.G.	Good	Fair	Poor
280	250	230	—	—	—

Stubby

Caliber: .22 LR, .380 ACP, 9mm. Barrel: 2.2" Thin nylon grip. Fixed sight. Length: 4.5" Height: 3.75" Weight: 13.3 oz. Trigger pull: 7 lbs. Width: 5/16".

NIB	Exc.	V.G.	Good	Fair	Poor
220	—	—	—	—	—

Cyclops

Caliber: .45-70 Govt. Barrel: 4.25" Length: 6.75" Grip: B6 Nylon. Weight: 28 oz. Extended grip. Trigger pull: 7 lbs.

NIB	Exc.	V.G.	Good	Fair	Poor
520	—	—	—	—	—

BOOM
Hatfield, Massachusetts
See—SHATTUCK, C.S.

BORCHARDT
Berlin, Germany
Waffenfabrik Lowe

Borchardt (Antique)

Forerunner of German Luger. Borchardt was a semi-automatic pistol. Chambered for 7.65mm Borchardt cartridge. Fitted with 6.5" barrel. Magazine held 8 rounds. Pistol was designed by Hugo Borchardt and manufactured by Ludwig Lowe of Berlin. Later models manufactured by DWM, Deutsch Waffen Und Munitionsfabriken, Berlin. Many Borchardts come with a case which holds shoulder stock, holster, extra magazines and numerous other accessories.

Courtesy James Rankin

Pistol Only (Antique)

Exc.	Fine	V.G.	Good	Fair	Poor
15000	8000	6000	4000	2000	1400

Pistol with Case and Accessories (Antique)

Exc.	Fine	V.G.	Good	Fair	Poor
20000	12000	9750	7500	4000	2800

BORSIG
East Germany

See—MAKAROV

BOSIS, LUCIANO

Brescia, Italy

Bosis is a maker of high-grade sidelock over/under and side-by-side guns in gauges 12, 20, 28 and .410. These guns are made on custom-order basis.

Over/Under

Values for used guns in excellent condition begin at $30,000. Secure an expert appraisal prior to sale.

Side-by-Side

Values for used guns in excellent condition begin at $20,000. Secure an expert appraisal prior to sale. Note: Small gauge guns will bring a premium of 20 percent.

BOSS & CO.

London, England

Thomas Boss worked for great British gunmaker Joseph Manton, before becoming a pieceworker to the London trade. In 1891, John Robertson was taken in as a partner and under his control the firm was established as one of London's best gunmakers, rivaled only by James Purdey. Current Boss shotgun prices (2019) begin at about 88,000 British pounds for O/U and 68,000 for SxS. Double rifles are very limited in production and prices begin at about 100,000 pounds. Used values are shown in U.S. dollars. Boss values will vary greatly depending on vintage, configuration and engraving. These values should be considered to be generalizations.

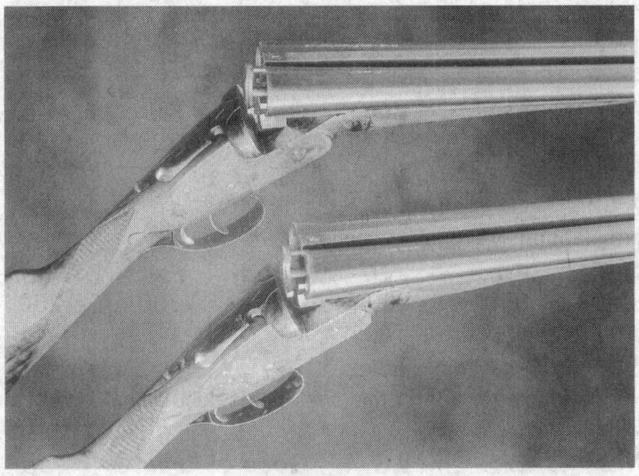

A cased pair of Boss & Co. sidelock shotguns

SXS Shotgun

NIB	*Exc.*	*V.G.*	*Good*	*Fair*	*Poor*
70000	60000	50000	40000	—	—

O/U Shotgun

NIB	*Exc.*	*V.G.*	*Good*	*Fair*	*Poor*
90000	80000	70000	60000	—	—

O/U Rifle

NIB	*Exc.*	*V.G.*	*Good*	*Fair*	*Poor*
150000	140000	130000	—	—	—

SXS Rifle

NIB	*Exc.*	*V.G.*	*Good*	*Fair*	*Poor*
80000	70000	60000	50000	—	—

BOSWELL, CHARLES

London, England

One of England's more established makers of best-quality rifles and shotguns. In 1988, company was purchased by an American consortium and Cape Horn Outfitters of Charlotte, North Carolina was appointed their sole agent. In 2004, South Carolina shooting instructor Chris Batha became the agent for Charles Boswell rifles and shotguns.

Double Rifle, Boxlock

.300 H&H, .375 H&H or .458 Win. Magnum double-barrel boxlock rifle, with double triggers and walnut stock. Other features were made to customer's specifications. A .600 Nitro Express version was also available. Note: Add 50 percent for .600 Nitro Express.

NIB	*Exc.*	*V.G.*	*Good*	*Fair*	*Poor*
—	47000	39500	29500	19950	600

Double Rifle, Sidelock

As above, with Holland & Holland-style sidelocks. Note: Add 50 percent for .600 Nitro Express.

NIB	*Exc.*	*V.G.*	*Good*	*Fair*	*Poor*
—	63000	47500	35000	22000	600

Shotgun, Boxlock

Side-by-side made to order model prior to 1996. Produced in 12-, 20-, 28-gauge and .410 bore. Select European walnut stock, single trigger and engraved game scenes on receiver. Note: Current side-by-side or over/under in boxlock and sidelock designs are priced from $85,500.

NIB	*Exc.*	*V.G.*	*Good*	*Fair*	*Poor*
6000	5000	3800	3000	1500	700

BOSWORTH, B. M.

Warren, Pennsylvania

Underhammer Pistol (Antique)

.38-caliber single-shot percussion pistol, with under hammer and 6" half-octagonal barrel. Frame marked "BM Bosworth". Browned, with brass grips forming part of frame. Made circa 1850 to 1860.

Exc.	*Fine*	*V.G.*	*Good*	*Fair*	*Poor*
1850	800	550	300	120	80

BRAENDLIN ARMOURY

London, England

.450-caliber 8-barrel pistol, with hinged barrels, rotating firing pin and double-action lock. Manufactured during 1880s.

(Antique)

Exc.	*Fine*	*V.G.*	*Good*	*Fair*	*Poor*
8550	5500	4500	3500	1850	1290

BRAND

New York

Maker—E. Robinson

Brand Breech Loading Carbine (Antique)

.50 rimfire caliber carbine, with 22" barrel secured by one barrel band. Frame marked "Brand's Patent July 29,1862/E. Robinson Manfr/New York". Carbine was produced in limited numbers, primarily for trial purposes.

BRAVO COMPANY USA, INC.

Hartland, Wisconsin

Founded in 2003, produces a wide array of AR-15 and AR-10 rifles, carbines and parts.

M4 Carbine Mod 0

Caliber: 5.56mm NATO. Capacity: 30 rounds. Barrel: 16", standard government profile, 1:7" twist, M4 feed ramp barrel extension. USGI chrome-lined bore and chamber. Mil-spec 11595E barrel steel, manganese phosphate finish. Stock: BCM Gunfighter. Sights: Flat-top rail, post front. Weight: 6.3 lbs. Overall Length: 32.5" to 35.5". MOD 0 has BCM PKMR Handguard. 6.3 pounds.

NIB	Exc.	V.G.	Good	Fair	Poor
1110	1050	950	800	—	—

M4 Carbine Mod 2

Caliber: 5.56mm NATO. Capacity: 30 rounds. Barrel: 16", standard government profile, 1:7" twist, M4 feed ramp barrel extension. USGI chrome-lined bore and chamber. Mil-Spec 11595E barrel steel, manganese phosphate finish. Stock: BCM Gunfighter. Sights: Flat-top rail, post front. Weight: 6.3 lbs. Overall Length: 32.5" to 35.5". MOD 2 has BCM QRF Handguard. 6.5 lbs.

NIB	Exc.	V.G.	Good	Fair	Poor
1400	1310	1250	1100	950	—

RECCE-16 KMR-A Carbine

Caliber: 5.56mm NATO. Capacity: 30 rounds. Barrels: 14.5", 16", 1:7" twist, M4 feed ramp barrel extension. USGI chrome-lined bore and chamber. Mil-spec 11595E barrel steel, manganese phosphate finish. Stock: BCM. Sights: M4 feed ramp flat-top with laser T-markings. Mid-length gas systems. Five models in the RECCE-14 line: KMR-A and KMR-A LW, MCMR and MCMR LW, and QRF. Four additional models in the RECCE-16 line: KMR-A Precision, MCMR Precision, and 300 BLK KMR-A and 300 BLK MCMR.

NIB	Exc.	V.G.	Good	Fair	Poor
1680	1600	1500	1350	—	—

MID16 MOD 0

Caliber: 5.56mm NATO. Mid-length gas systems. MOD 0 has PKMR handguard. MOD 2 has QRF Handguard.

NIB	Exc.	V.G.	Good	Fair	Poor
1130	—	—	—	—	—

MK12 MOD-A5 Marksman Rifle

Caliber: 5.56mm NATO. Based on the U.S. Navy MK12 Mod 0 Special Purpose Rifle (SPR), the BCM MK12 is a heavily modified DMR-type weapon. 18" barrels, various contours. Also includes RECCE-18 rifles. Weights: 7-9 lbs. SEE POLITICAL PANIC PRICING.

NIB	Exc.	V.G.	Good	Fair	Poor
4200	4000	3900	3750	—	—

BREDA, ERNESTO
Milan, Italy

Andromeda Special

12-gauge boxlock shotgun, with various barrel lengths and chokes, single-selective triggers and automatic ejectors. Engraved satin-finished, with checkered walnut stock.

NIB	Exc.	V.G.	Good	Fair	Poor
—	1150	780	600	420	300

Vega Special

12-gauge boxlock over/under shotgun, with 26" or 28" barrels, various choke combinations, single-selective trigger and automatic ejectors. Engraved and blued, with checkered walnut stock.

NIB	Exc.	V.G.	Good	Fair	Poor
—	850	700	600	380	280

Vega Special Trap

As above, with competition-styled stock, 30" or 32" barrels and full chokes.

NIB	Exc.	V.G.	Good	Fair	Poor
—	1350	1050	850	500	350

Sirio Standard

Similar to Vega, with extensive engraving and higher degree of finishing. There is a 28" barreled skeet version available in this model.

NIB	Exc.	V.G.	Good	Fair	Poor
—	2750	2000	1950	1350	650

Standard Semi-Automatic

12-gauge semi-automatic shotgun, with 25" or 27" ventilated rib barrels, screw-in choke tubes, engraved receiver and checkered walnut stock.

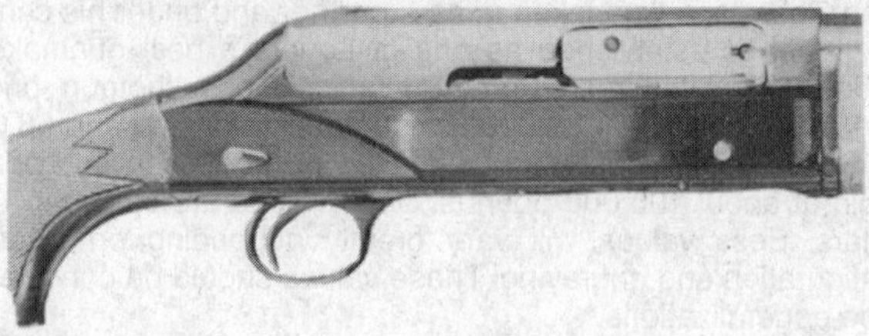

NIB	Exc.	V.G.	Good	Fair	Poor
—	380	280	220	180	120

Grade I

As above, with more engraving and finer wood.

NIB	Exc.	V.G.	Good	Fair	Poor
—	650	480	320	220	180

Grade II

A more elaborately engraved version of the Grade I.

NIB	Exc.	V.G.	Good	Fair	Poor
—	850	600	450	380	250

Grade III

The most deluxe version in this line, with select walnut and extensive engraving.

NIB	Exc.	V.G.	Good	Fair	Poor
—	1050	800	650	580	250

Magnum Model

Same as standard in 12-gauge Magnum.

NIB	Exc.	V.G.	Good	Fair	Poor
—	440	320	250	180	80

Gold Series Antares Standard

12-gauge semi-automatic shotgun, with 25" or 27" ventilated rib barrel and screw-in choke tubes. Blued, with checkered walnut stock.

NIB	Exc.	V.G.	Good	Fair	Poor
—	650	420	350	280	220

Gold Series Argus

As above, with alloy frame.

NIB	Exc.	V.G.	Good	Fair	Poor
—	650	480	380	300	250

Gold Series Aries

As above in 12-gauge Magnum.

NIB	Exc.	V.G.	Good	Fair	Poor
—	700	500	400	320	280

M1 Garand

Virtual duplicate of US M1 Garand. Chambered in .30-06. Made in mid-1950s by Breda under contract for Denmark. Values shown are for correct, non-import marked specimens. Note: Deduct up to 50 percent for built-up parts guns or non-matching guns.

NIB	Exc.	V.G.	Good	Fair	Poor
—	2200	1600	800	400	250

BREN 10

Huntington Beach, California

See—DORNAUS & DIXON INC.

Manufactured from 1983 until 1986. Deduct 15 percent for aftermarket magazines.

BRETTON

Ste. Etienne, France

Baby Standard

12- or 20-gauge over/under shotgun, with various barrel lengths, choke combinations and double triggers. Blued, checkered walnut stock.

NIB	Exc.	V.G.	Good	Fair	Poor
1350	980	720	550	400	320

Deluxe Grade

12-, 16- and 20-gauge over/under shotgun. Engraved coin-finished receiver, with walnut stock.

NIB	Exc.	V.G.	Good	Fair	Poor
2150	1880	1400	800	500	320

BRIGGS, H. A.

Norwich, Connecticut

Briggs Single-Shot Pistol

.22-caliber single-shot spur trigger pistol, with 4" part-round/part-octagonal barrel and downward rotating breechblock. Blued, with walnut grips. Frame marked "H.A. Briggs/Norwich, Ct." Manufactured in 1850s and 1860s.

NIB	Exc.	V.G.	Good	Fair	Poor
—	—	2950	1250	450	200

BRILEY MANUFACTURING INC.

Houston, Texas

El Presidente Model—Unlimited

1911-style pistol can be built on a Caspian Arms STI or SVI frame. Includes scope mount, compensator, match barrel, cocking sight, lowered and flared ejection port, front and rear serrations, aluminum guide rod and numerous other custom features. Offered in most calibers. Blued finish.

NIB	Exc.	V.G.	Good	Fair	Poor
2400	2000	1450	1000	700	350

Versatility Plus Model—Limited

Built on a 1911 frame, with BoMar sight, checkered mainspring housing and checkered front strap. Many other custom features. Available in .45 ACP, .40 S&W and 9mm.

NIB	Exc.	V.G.	Good	Fair	Poor
1950	1650	1200	800	400	220

Versatility Model—Limited

Similar to above model, without several features such as checkered front strap. Available in .45 ACP, .40 S&W, 9mm.

NIB	Exc.	V.G.	Good	Fair	Poor
1480	1150	800	580	260	200

Lightning Model—Action Pistol

Built on a 1911 frame. Features many custom components including titanium compensator. Weight no more than 40 oz. Available in 9mm and .38 Super only.

NIB	Exc.	V.G.	Good	Fair	Poor
2450	1950	1300	850	420	200

Carry Comp Model—Defense

Built on a 1911 frame. Features dual port cone compensator, with many custom features. Barrel length about 5". Offered in .45 ACP only.

NIB	Exc.	V.G.	Good	Fair	Poor
2450	2000	1550	1000	500	250

BRIXIA
Brescia, Italy

Model 12

Commercial version of Model 1910 Glisenti in 9mm Glisenti caliber. Brixia was a simplified Glisenti and was made to replace Glisenti for military market. Italian military did not accept them and only a few were made for commercial market. Only markings are monogram eagle holding a shield cast in grips.

Courtesy James Rankin

NIB	Exc.	V.G.	Good	Fair	Poor
—	1300	950	7850	450	320

BRNO ARMS
Uhersky Brod, Czech Republic

Brno firearms have been manufactured since 1918 in what was once known as Czechosolvakia, now the Czech Republic. Various Brno rifles, pistols, shotguns and combination guns have been brought into U.S. since late 1940s by several importers including Continental Arms, Magnum Research, Bohemia Arms, EAA and others. There has been a close association between Brno and CZ (Ceska Zbrojovka) for many years. CZ-USA of Kansas City, Kansas, is current importer of both brands. Only Brno models currently being imported are single-shot and over/under rifles and over/under combination rifle/shotguns.

ZG-47

Bolt-action rifle based on Mauser system. Chambered for .270, 7x57, 7x64, .30-06, 8x57, 8x60, 8x64S, 9.3x62 and on special order 10.75x68. Barrel length 23.6". Adjustable trigger. Hinged floorplate. Weight about 7.7 lbs.

Standard

NIB	Exc.	V.G.	Good	Fair	Poor
—	1000	900	800	650	400

Deluxe

NIB	Exc.	V.G.	Good	Fair	Poor
—	1100	950	850	600	450

ZH-SERIES

Double-barrel over/under boxlock series of shotguns. Interchangeable barrels in shotgun and rifle configurations, of various lengths, double triggers and automatic ejectors. Models listed represent different gauges and/or calibers offered. Note: Add $75 for ZH models with set triggers and cheekpiece; $300 to $400 for interchangeable barrels depending on gauge and caliber.

ZH-300

NIB	Exc.	V.G.	Good	Fair	Poor
—	680	580	400	320	250

ZH-301

12-gauge/12-gauge.

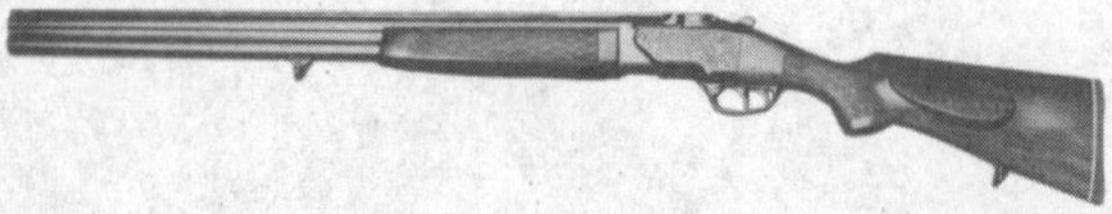

NIB	Exc.	V.G.	Good	Fair	Poor
—	600	500	400	350	200

ZH-302

12-gauge/12-gauge Skeet.

NIB	Exc.	V.G.	Good	Fair	Poor
—	600	550	450	400	250

ZH-303 12

12-gauge/12-gauge Trap.

NIB	Exc.	V.G.	Good	Fair	Poor
—	600	550	450	400	250

ZH-304

12-gauge/7x57R.

NIB	Exc.	V.G.	Good	Fair	Poor
—	1000	800	500	400	250

ZH-305

12-gauge/6x52R.

NIB	Exc.	V.G.	Good	Fair	Poor
—	900	700	500	400	220

ZH-306

12-gauge/6x50R Magnum.

NIB	Exc.	V.G.	Good	Fair	Poor
—	850	650	450	350	200

ZH-308

12-gauge/7x65R.

NIB	Exc.	V.G.	Good	Fair	Poor
—	850	700	500	400	220

ZH-309

12-gauge/8x57 JRS.

NIB	Exc.	V.G.	Good	Fair	Poor
—	850	700	500	400	220

ZH-321

16-gauge/16-gauge.

NIB	Exc.	V.G.	Good	Fair	Poor
—	750	620	450	400	220

ZH-324

16-gauge/7x57R.

NIB	Exc.	V.G.	Good	Fair	Poor
—	880	700	500	400	220

ZH-328

16-gauge/7x65R.

NIB	Exc.	V.G.	Good	Fair	Poor
—	850	700	500	400	220

Model 300 Combo

Model ZH-300, with 8 interchangeable barrels in a fitted case. Introduced in 1986.

NIB	Exc.	V.G.	Good	Fair	Poor
5000	4000	3000	2750	2000	1500

Model 500

Model ZH-300, with acid-etched decoration, automatic ejectors and 12-gauge.

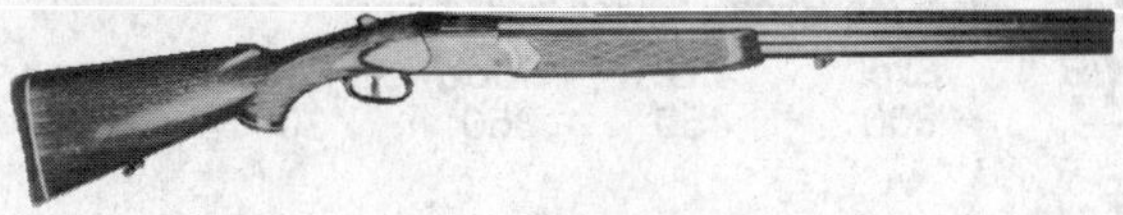

NIB	Exc.	V.G.	Good	Fair	Poor
—	800	600	420	350	280

ZP-49

12-gauge sidelock double-barrel shotgun, with double triggers and automatic ejectors. Blued, with walnut stock. Imported in 1986 only.

NIB	Exc.	V.G.	Good	Fair	Poor
—	1050	800	650	450	320

ZP-149

As above, without engraving.

NIB	Exc.	V.G.	Good	Fair	Poor
—	600	500	400	300	200

ZP-349

As above, with buttstock having cheekpiece and beavertail forearm.

NIB	Exc.	V.G.	Good	Fair	Poor
—	800	650	500	350	250

ZBK-100

Single-barrel shotgun in 12- or 20-gauge, with 27" barrel and walnut stock. Weight about 5.5 lbs.

NIB	Exc.	V.G.	Good	Fair	Poor
250	200	150	120	100	80

RIFLES

ZKW-465 (Hornet Sporter)

.22 Hornet caliber bolt-action rifle, with 23" barrel, express sights and double-set triggers. Blued, with walnut stock.

NIB	Exc.	V.G.	Good	Fair	Poor
—	1500	1100	950	800	550

Model 21H

6.5x57mm, 7x57mm or 8x57mm caliber bolt-action sporting rifle, with 23.625" barrel, express sights and double-set triggers. Blued, with walnut stock.

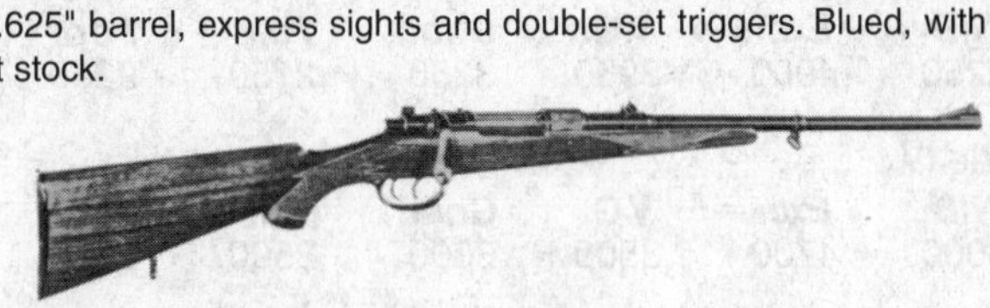

NIB	Exc.	V.G.	Good	Fair	Poor
—	1250	1050	900	750	600

Model 22F

As above, with Mannlicher-style stock. Barrel length 20.5".

NIB	Exc.	V.G.	Good	Fair	Poor
—	1300	1100	900	650	500

Model I

.22-caliber bolt-action rifle, with 22.75" barrel having folding leaf rear sights. Blued, with walnut stock.

NIB	Exc.	V.G.	Good	Fair	Poor
—	550	400	300	250	200

Model II

As above, with a more finely figured walnut stock.

NIB	Exc.	V.G.	Good	Fair	Poor
—	600	450	350	300	220

ZKM 611

Semi-automatic rifle chambered for .17 HMR or .22 WRM cartridge. Fitted with 20" barrel. Magazine capacity 6 rounds. Weight about 6.2 lbs.

NIB	Exc.	V.G.	Good	Fair	Poor
700	620	520	300	180	120

ZKM 451

Semi-automatic rifle chambered for .22 LR cartridge. Fitted with 22" barrel. Magazine capacity 7 rounds. Weight about 5.25 lbs.

NIB	Exc.	V.G.	Good	Fair	Poor
450	300	250	120	100	80

ZKM 451 LUX

Same as above, with select walnut stock.

NIB	Exc.	V.G.	Good	Fair	Poor
500	350	250	150	120	100

ZBK 680

.22 Hornet or .222-caliber bolt-action rifle, with 23.5" barrel, double-set triggers and 5-shot magazine. Blued, with walnut stock.

NIB	Exc.	V.G.	Good	Fair	Poor
920	750	550	400	320	220

Super Express Rifle

Over/under sidelock double-barrel rifle, with 23.5" barrels, double triggers and automatic ejectors. Engraved, blued with walnut stock. Available in 6 grades:

Standard Model

NIB	Exc.	V.G.	Good	Fair	Poor
5500	4150	3000	2500	1750	1250

Grade I

NIB	Exc.	V.G.	Good	Fair	Poor
7500	5900	4750	4500	3600	3250

Grade II

NIB	Exc.	V.G.	Good	Fair	Poor
6500	5150	4000	3500	2750	2250

Grade III

NIB	Exc.	V.G.	Good	Fair	Poor
6250	4900	3950	3250	2750	2250

Grade IV

NIB	Exc.	V.G.	Good	Fair	Poor
6000	4700	3500	3000	2500	2250

Grade V

NIB	Exc.	V.G.	Good	Fair	Poor
5750	3950	3250	2750	2250	1750

Grade VI

NIB	Exc.	V.G.	Good	Fair	Poor
4900	4250	3100	2600	1950	1500

ZH-344/348/349

Over/under rifle chambered for 7x57R, 7x65R, or 8x57JRS.

NIB	Exc.	V.G.	Good	Fair	Poor
1500	980	700	550	400	280

Model 98 Standard

Bolt-action rifle chambered for a variety of calibers from 7x64 to 9.3x62. Fitted with 23" barrel, figured walnut stock, buttplate and open sights. Weight about 7.25 lbs. Note: Add $100 for set trigger.

NIB	Exc.	V.G.	Good	Fair	Poor
800	650	400	300	200	150

Model 98 Full Stock

Same as above, with full one-piece stock and set trigger.

NIB	Exc.	V.G.	Good	Fair	Poor
1000	700	500	400	350	200

ZK 99

Tip-up centerfire rifle chambered for a wide variety of calibers from 6.5x57R to .30-06. Barrel length 23". Weight about 5.75 lbs.

NIB	Exc.	V.G.	Good	Fair	Poor
1000	750	550	400	200	150

ZBK 110

Single-shot tip-open rifle chambered for .22 Hornet, .222 Rem., 5.6x50R Magnum and 5.6x52R. Barrel length 23.5". Open sights. Walnut stock without checkering. Weight about 6 lbs.

NIB	Exc.	V.G.	Good	Fair	Poor
450	350	250	200	150	80

ZBK 110 LUX

Same as above, with select walnut stock and checkering. Open sights.

NIB	Exc.	V.G.	Good	Fair	Poor
440	350	250	200	150	80

ZBK 110 Super Lux

Same as above, with fancy walnut stock and checkering. Open sights.

NIB	Exc.	V.G.	Good	Fair	Poor
650	520	400	300	150	80

HANDGUNS

ZKR 551

Double-/single-action revolver, with 6-round cylinder. Adjustable rear sight. Walnut grips. Fitted with 6" barrel. Chambered for .38, .32 S&W Long and .22 LR. Weight about 35 oz.

NIB	Exc.	V.G.	Good	Fair	Poor
1800	1350	900	700	500	280

BROLIN ARMS

La Verne, California

Brolin Arms was in business from approximately 1995 to 2000. Imported handguns from Hungary, Mauser military rifles from Europe and shotguns from China. Company also manufactured a series of 1911-pattern pistols

LEGEND SERIES—1911 AUTO PISTOL

L45—Standard Auto Pistol

Standard model, with 5" barrel chambered for .45 ACP. Fitted with throated match barrel, polished feed ramp, lowered ejection port, beveled magazine well and fixed sights. Other custom features as well. Finish matte blue, with 7-round magazine. Weight about 36 oz.

NIB	Exc.	V.G.	Good	Fair	Poor
550	400	300	200	120	80

L45C—Compact Auto Pistol

Similar to standard model, with 4.5" barrel. Weight about 32 oz.

NIB	Exc.	V.G.	Good	Fair	Poor
600	550	320	220	150	100

L45T

Version of L45 series. Introduced in 1997. Fitted with compact slide on full-size frame. Weight 36 oz. Note: Add $50 for Novak sights.

NIB	Exc.	V.G.	Good	Fair	Poor
600	550	320	200	120	80

PATRIOT SERIES—DPC CARRY-COMP PISTOLS

P45 Comp—Standard Carry Comp

Features 4" barrel, with integral compensator cut into slide. Other features are custom beavertail grip safety, adjustable aluminum trigger, flat-top slide and checkered wood grips. Weight about 37 oz.

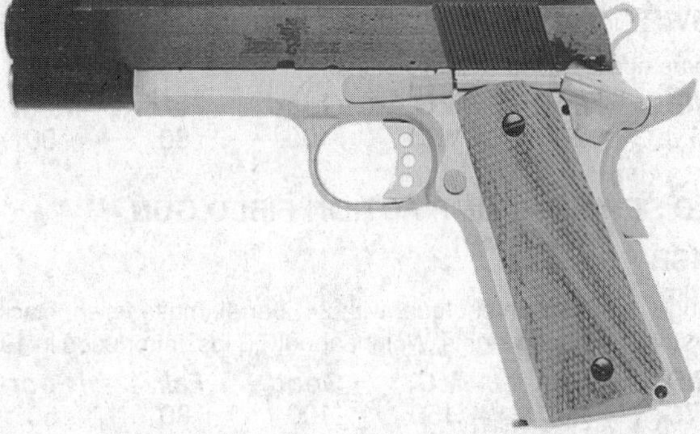

NIB	Exc.	V.G.	Good	Fair	Poor
600	550	380	220	110	100

P45C Comp—Compact Carry Comp

Similar to above. Fitted with 3.25" barrel. Weight about 33 oz. Note: Add $20 for two-tone finish.

NIB	Exc.	V.G.	Good	Fair	Poor
600	550	380	220	110	100

P45T

Addition to Patriot Series introduced in 1997. Has all features of Patriot pistols. Fitted with compact slide and full size frame. Weight about 35 oz. Available in two-tone finish for additional $20. Note: Add $50 for Novak sights.

NIB	Exc.	V.G.	Good	Fair	Poor
600	550	380	220	110	100

TAC SERIES—TACTICAL 1911 PISTOLS

TAC-11

Series and model introduced in 1997. Has all features of L45 series. Additions of special 5" conical match barrel, Novak Low Profile sights, black rubber contour grips, "iron claw" extractor and optional night sights. Chambered for .45 ACP. Supplied with 8-round magazine. Weight about 37 oz. Note: Add $90 for Tritium night sights.

NIB	Exc.	V.G.	Good	Fair	Poor
650	580	400	250	150	100

TAC SERIES—DOUBLE-ACTION PISTOLS

MS45

Full-size double-action pistol chambered for .45 ACP cartridge. Fitted with 8-round magazine and low- profile 3-dot sights. Standard finish matte blue. Note: Add $20 for royal blue finish.

NIB	Exc.	V.G.	Good	Fair	Poor
650	580	400	250	150	100

M45

Similar to above, with longer barrel. Chambered for .45 ACP and 8-round magazine. Note: Add $20 for royal blue finish.

NIB	Exc.	V.G.	Good	Fair	Poor
550	480	300	250	150	100

M40

Same as M45. Chambered for .40 S&W cartridge. Magazine capacity 10 rounds. Note: Add $50 for Novak sights.

NIB	Exc.	V.G.	Good	Fair	Poor
500	400	280	250	150	100

M90

Same as M45. Chambered for 9mm cartridge. Magazine capacity 10 rounds. Note: Add $20 for royal blue finish.

NIB	Exc.	V.G.	Good	Fair	Poor
500	400	300	250	150	100

MC40

Compact version of full-size double-action models. Fitted with full-size frame, but shorter slide. Chambered for .40 S&W cartridge. Magazine capacity 10 rounds. Note: Add $20 for royal blue finish.

NIB	Exc.	V.G.	Good	Fair	Poor
600	500	300	250	150	100

MC90

Same as above chambered for 9mm cartridge.

NIB	Exc.	V.G.	Good	Fair	Poor
500	400	280	250	150	100

MB40

Super-compact double-action pistol. Features concealed hammer. Chambered for .40 S&W cartridge. Magazine capacity 6 rounds. Note: Add $20 for royal blue finish.

NIB	Exc.	V.G.	Good	Fair	Poor
550	450	300	250	150	100

MB90

Same as above chambered for 9mm cartridge.

NIB	Exc.	V.G.	Good	Fair	Poor
550	450	300	250	150	100

PRO SERIES—COMPETITION PISTOL

Pro-Stock—Competition Pistol

Chambered for .45 ACP. Designed for competition shooter. Many special features standard such as full-length recoil guide, front strap high relief cut, serrated flat mainspring housing, ambidextrous thumb safety and fully adjustable rear sight. Barrel length 5". Weight about 37 oz. Note: Add $20 for two-tone finish.

NIB	Exc.	V.G.	Good	Fair	Poor
700	600	500	350	180	100

Pro-Comp—Competition Pistol

Similar to competition model above. Fitted with integral compensator and 4" barrel. Weight about 37 oz. Note: Add $20 for two-tone finish.

NIB	Exc.	V.G.	Good	Fair	Poor
750	650	500	380	200	100

SHOTGUNS

LAWMAN SERIES—PERSONAL SECURITY SHOTGUN

HL18SB

Pump-action 12-gauge shotgun, with 18.5" barrel, black synthetic stock and bead sights. Weight about 7 lbs. Introduced in 1997. Copy of Remington Model 870.

NIB	Exc.	V.G.	Good	Fair	Poor
300	250	200	150	100	50

HL18SR

Same as above. Fitted with rifle sights.

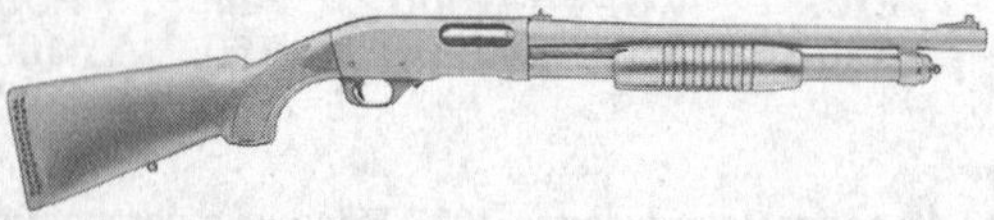

NIB	Exc.	V.G.	Good	Fair	Poor
320	280	220	180	120	60

HL18SBN

Same as above, with nickel finish.

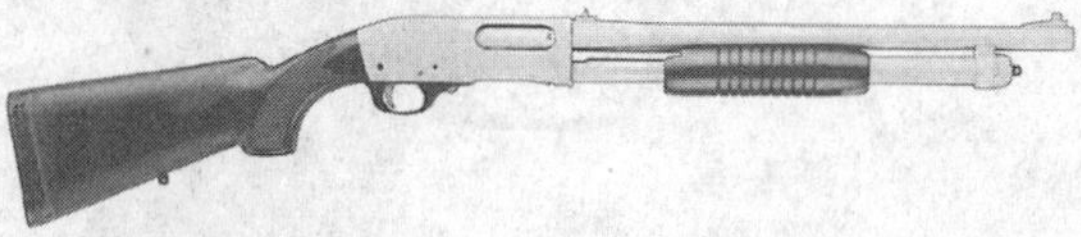

NIB	Exc.	V.G.	Good	Fair	Poor
270	200	150	100	80	50

HL18WB

This version has wood stock and bead sights.

NIB	Exc.	V.G.	Good	Fair	Poor
300	250	200	150	100	50

HL18WR

Same as above. Fitted with rifle sights.

NIB	Exc.	V.G.	Good	Fair	Poor
270	200	150	100	80	50

FIELD SERIES—PUMP ACTION FIELD GUN

HF24SB

12-gauge pump action shotgun, with 24" barrel, matte finish, black synthetic stock and bead sights. Weight about 7.3 lbs. Introduced in 1997.

NIB	Exc.	V.G.	Good	Fair	Poor
270	200	150	100	80	50

HF28SB

Same as above. Fitted with 28" barrel. Weight 7.4 lbs.

NIB	Exc.	V.G.	Good	Fair	Poor
270	200	150	100	80	50

HF24WB

Features 24" barrel, with wood stock.

NIB	Exc.	V.G.	Good	Fair	Poor
270	200	150	100	80	50

HF28WB

Same as above, with 24" barrel.

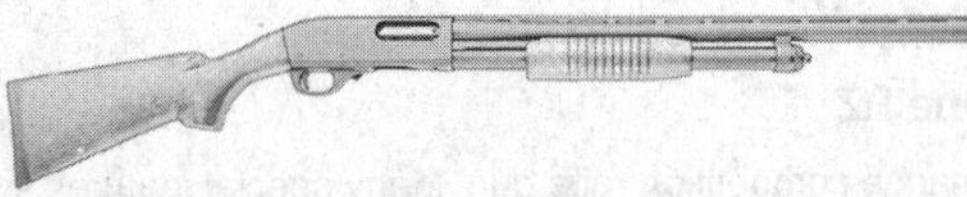

NIB	Exc.	V.G.	Good	Fair	Poor
270	200	150	100	80	50

Slug Special

Slide-action shotgun chambered for 3" 12-gauge shell. Choice of 18.5" or 22" barrel, with rifle or ghost ring sights, fixed improved cylinder choke, 4" extended rifled choke or fully rifled barrel. Wood or synthetic stock.

NIB	Exc.	V.G.	Good	Fair	Poor
270	200	150	100	80	50

Turkey Special

12-gauge 3" model. Fitted with 22" extra full choke ventilated rib barrel. Wood or synthetic stock.

NIB	Exc.	V.G.	Good	Fair	Poor
270	200	150	100	80	50

FIELD COMBO—TWO BARREL COMBO SET

HC28SB

Set consists of 18.5" and 28" barrel, synthetic stock, pistol grip, bead sight.

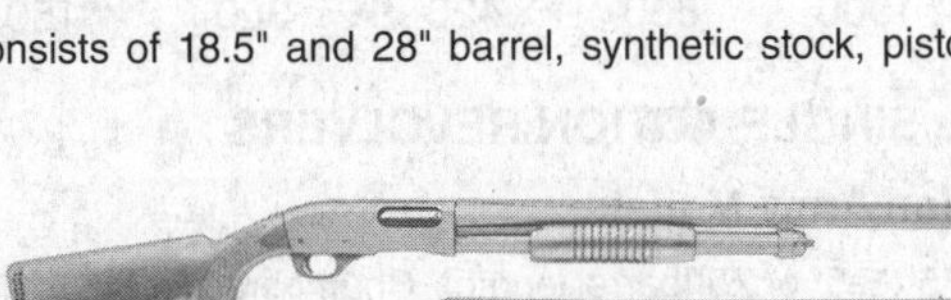

NIB	Exc.	V.G.	Good	Fair	Poor
300	250	200	120	80	50

HC28SR

Same as above, with rifle and bead sight.

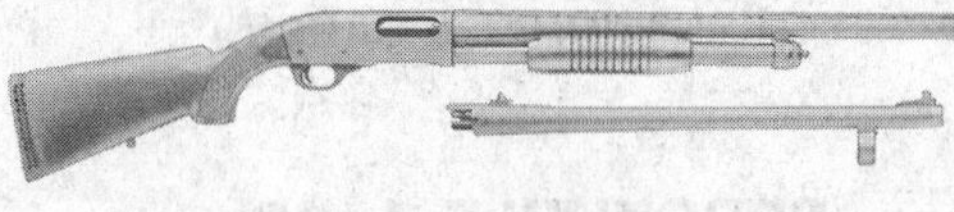

NIB	Exc.	V.G.	Good	Fair	Poor
320	250	200	120	80	50

HC28WB

Features wood stock, pistol grip and bead sight.

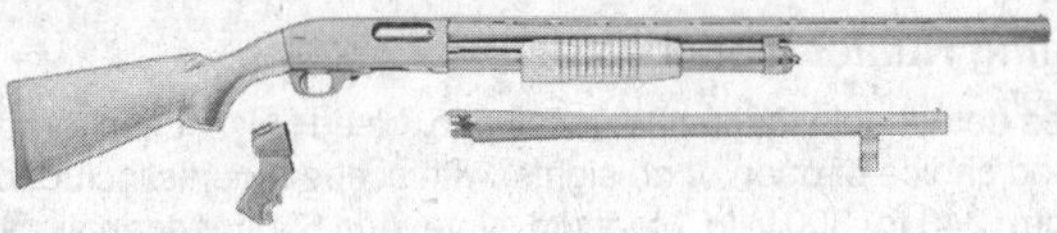

NIB	Exc.	V.G.	Good	Fair	Poor
300	250	200	120	80	50

HC28WR

Same as above, with wood stock. Rifle and bead sight.

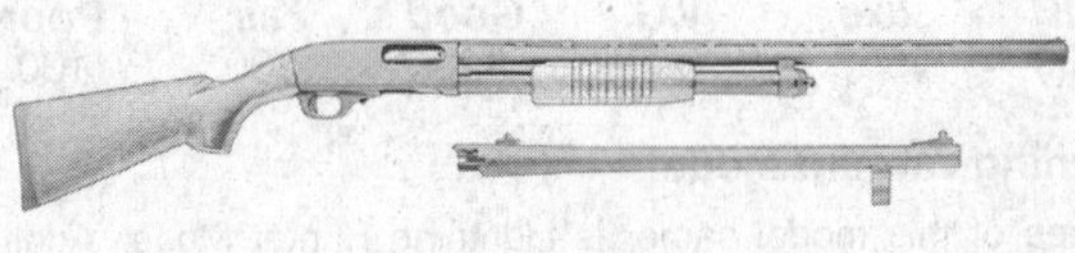

NIB	Exc.	V.G.	Good	Fair	Poor
320	250	200	120	80	50

SEMI-AUTOMATIC SHOTGUNS

BL-12 Security

12-gauge shotgun has 3" chamber and 5-round magazine. Fitted with 18.5" ventilated rib barrel. Synthetic stock standard.

NIB	Exc.	V.G.	Good	Fair	Poor
350	320	300	200	150	80

BL-12 Field

Similar to above, with 28" ventilated rib barrel. Wood or synthetic stock.

NIB	Exc.	V.G.	Good	Fair	Poor
350	320	300	200	150	80

SAS-12 Security

12-gauge shotgun chambered for 2.75" 12-gauge shells. Fitted with 24" ventilated rib or rifle sight barrel. Detachable box magazine; 3 round standard, 5 round optional. Synthetic stock.

NIB	Exc.	V.G.	Good	Fair	Poor
350	320	300	200	150	80

RIFLES

Legacy

.50-caliber muzzleloader, with inline ignition system. Walnut stain hardwood stock and recoil pad. Finish blue or chrome. Note: Add $20 for chrome finish.

NIB	Exc.	V.G.	Good	Fair	Poor
180	150	100	80	50	20

Mitchell PPS-50

Semi-automatic rifle chambered for .22 LR cartridge. Detachable 10-round magazine. Copy of Russian PPSh machine gun used in WWII.

NIB	Exc.	V.G.	Good	Fair	Poor
400	320	280	220	180	100

MAUSER RIFLES

All of these Mauser rifles introduced in 1998, to Brolin product line.

Lightning Model

Features sliding bolt that locks directly into barrel. Chambered for 7.62x39mm cartridge and .308 Win. Blue finish. Choice of colored synthetic stocks. Open sights standard.

NIB	Exc.	V.G.	Good	Fair	Poor
550	450	350	320	200	100

Lightning Hunter Model

Features detachable magazine, recoil pad, blued finish, checkered wood stock and choice of open or no sights, with scope mounts included. Calibers from .243 to .300 Win. Magnum. Note: Add $50 for open sights; $50 for stainless steel.

NIB	Exc.	V.G.	Good	Fair	Poor
650	500	350	320	200	100

Lightning Hunter All Weather Model

Same as above, with black synthetic stock.

NIB	Exc.	V.G.	Good	Fair	Poor
700	550	350	320	200	100

Lightning Varmint Model

Features of this model same as Lightning Hunter Model. Addition of heavy fluted barrel, with special varmint wood or synthetic stock. Chambered for .22-250 and .243 cartridges.

NIB	Exc.	V.G.	Good	Fair	Poor
900	700	550	450	300	120

Lightning Sniper

Features heavy fluted barrel, with detachable magazine. Choice of special wood or synthetic stock. Built-in bi-pod rail. Offered in .308 or .300 Win. Magnum calibers.

NIB	Exc.	V.G.	Good	Fair	Poor
1000	800	600	450	300	120

Lightning Professional

Model has heavy fluted barrel, no sights and recoil compensator. Tuned trigger system standard. All-weather adjustable stock, with pistol grip. Available in .308 or .300 Win. Magnum calibers.

NIB	Exc.	V.G.	Good	Fair	Poor
900	700	550	400	300	120

2000 Classic

2000 Classic features interchangeable caliber system for cartridges in same action length. Detachable magazine. High-grade walnut stock, with cut checkering and rosewood forend. Single-set trigger standard. Offered in .270, .308, .30-06, 7mm Rem. Magnum and .300 Win. Magnum.

NIB	Exc.	V.G.	Good	Fair	Poor
1500	1250	800	500	300	120

2000 Varmint

Features heavy fluted barrel, with special varmint wood stock and accessory rail. Offered in .22-250 and .243-calibers. Standard without sights.

NIB	Exc.	V.G.	Good	Fair	Poor
2200	1700	1200	800	400	200

2000 Sniper

Features interchangeable caliber system, heavy fluted barrel, no sights, single-set trigger, all-weather stock, with built-in bi-pod rail. Offered in .308 and .300 Win. Magnum calibers.

NIB	Exc.	V.G.	Good	Fair	Poor
2200	1750	1250	800	400	200

2000 Professional

Has all features of Sniper rifle. Addition of recoil compensator and special all-weather pistol grip stock. Each rifle custom built.

NIB	Exc.	V.G.	Good	Fair	Poor
3500	2750	1700	90	550	250

20/22

High-quality .22 bolt-action rifle. Chambered for .22 LR or .22 Magnum cartridge. Available in both standard and deluxe configuration. Note: Add $100 for deluxe version.

NIB	Exc.	V.G.	Good	Fair	Poor
750	580	480	400	300	120

1898 Commemorative

Celebrates 100 year Anniversary of '98 Mauser. Chambered for 8mm Mauser cartridge. Limited edition rifle.

NIB	Exc.	V.G.	Good	Fair	Poor
2300	1750	1400	1000	680	300

98

Original Mauser action built to Safari calibers. Chambered for .375 H&H or .416 Rigby.

NIB	Exc.	V.G.	Good	Fair	Poor
10000	8000	6250	5000	1500	400

CUSTOM SHOP

Formula One RZ

High-performance competition race gun. Many special features such as supported barrel chamber, 6-port compensator, tuned trigger, extended magazine release and many other options as standard. Chambered for .38 Super, .40 S&W cartridges. Blue finish. Note: Add $400 for double-action.

NIB	Exc.	V.G.	Good	Fair	Poor
2500	2000	1400	1050	700	350

Formula One RS

Designed as Limited Class competition gun, with 5" barrel. Chambered for .38 Super, .40 S&W or .45 ACP calibers. Features adjustable rear sight, tuned trigger, checkered front strap, mainspring housing and other special features. Note: Add $300 for double-action.

NIB	Exc.	V.G.	Good	Fair	Poor
2000	1600	1250	880	500	350

Formula Z

Custom-built combat pistol. Chambered for .40 S&W, .400 CorBon or .45 ACP calibers. Fitted with 4" or 5" barrel. Features many extra-cost features as standard.

NIB	Exc.	V.G.	Good	Fair	Poor
1300	1000	650	420	300	150

MITCHELL SINGLE-ACTION REVOLVERS

Single-Action Army Model

Offered in 4.75", 5.5" or 7.5" barrel lengths. Chambered for .45 Long Colt, .357 Magnum or .44-40 calibers. Offered in blue finish, with case-hardened frame or nickel finish. Available with dual cylinders, i.e. .45 LC/.45 ACP. Note: Add $50 for nickel finish; $150 for dual cylinder models.

NIB	Exc.	V.G.	Good	Fair	Poor
400	350	280	180	120	80

BRONCO

Eibar, Spain

See—ECHAVE & ARIZMENDI (FIREARMS INTERNATIONAL & GARCIA)

BROOKLYN F. A. CO.

Brooklyn, New York

Slocum Pocket Revolver (Antique)

.32-caliber spur-trigger revolver, with 3" round barrel. Frame silver-plated brass and scroll engraved; remainder blued or plated, with walnut grips. Barrel marked "B.A. Co. Patented April 14, 1863". Approximately 10,000 manufactured in 1863 and 1864. Cylinder has five individual tubes that slide forward to open for loading and then ejecting spent cartridges, as a way to circumvent STW's Rollin White patent on a cylinder bored through end-to-end.

Exc.	Fine	V.G.	Good	Fair	Poor
1250	750	500	350	200	100

Slocum Unfluted Cylinder Pocket Revolver (Antique)

As above in .22- or .32-caliber, with 5- or 7-shot cylinder. Approximately 250 manufactured in .32 rimfire; 100 in .22 rimfire. Note: Add 25 percent for .22-caliber.

Exc.	Fine	V.G.	Good	Fair	Poor
1300	800	550	350	225	100

BROWN PRODUCTS, ED
Perry, Missouri

There are a number of extra options available on Ed Brown handguns and rifles that may affect values. In August of 2010, Ed Brown announced he would no longer be accepting orders for new rifles, and for an indefinite period of time, would be focusing on his core business of handguns. Rifle parts and limited services remain available.

Alpha Elite

Similar to Alpha Carry but with 5" barrel. Produced 2016–17.

NIB	Exc.	V.G.	Good	Fair	Poor
2430	2110	1760	1530	1100	900

Alpha Carry

Bobtail frame. Features 4.25" barrel. Chambered for .45 ACP cartridge. Chainlink texture of grip straps. Produced 2016–17.

NIB	Exc.	V.G.	Good	Fair	Poor
2430	2110	1760	1530	1100	900

CCO

4.25" commander model 9mm, .38 Super or .45 ACP. Weight 34 oz. Snakeskin texture on grip straps. Introduced 2018. CCO Lightweight with aluminum frame add 15%.

NIB	Exc.	V.G.	Good	Fair	Poor
2830	2480	2130	1930	1280	1000

Commander Bobtail

Features 4.25" barrel. Chambered for .45 ACP, .400 CorBon, .40 S&W, .38 Super, 9x23 or 9mm Luger cartridge. Modified Hogue grips from exotic wood standard. Completely handmade and built to customer's specifications. Many available options.

NIB	Exc.	V.G.	Good	Fair	Poor
2200	1700	1200	700	500	300

Classic Custom

Chambered for .45 ACP cartridge. Custom built pistol, with many extra features such as Videki trigger, Ed Brown wide thumb safety, stainless steel thumb safety, extended safety, adjustable rear sight, etc. All hand-fitted parts.

NIB	Exc.	V.G.	Good	Fair	Poor
3700	3330	2500	1830	1490	1210

Class A Limited

Custom-built pistol offered in a number of different calibers from .45 ACP to 9mm Luger. Fitted with 4.25" Commander length slide. Many special features. Price listed for basic pistol.

NIB	Exc.	V.G.	Good	Fair	Poor
2450	1750	1300	800	500	320

EVO-KC9

Bobtail frame, 4.25" commander model 9mm, eternal extractor. Weight 34 oz. Snakeskin texture on grip straps. Introduced 2018.

NIB	Exc.	V.G.	Good	Fair	Poor
1710	1500	1280	1160	800	600

EVO-E9

1911 platform with full-size frame chambered in 9mm with 4-in. bull barrel.

NIB	Exc.	V.G.	Good	Fair	Poor
2300	2060	1800	1400	930	730

Executive Commander

4.25" commander model 9mm or .45 ACP. Weight 35 oz. Introduced 2017.

NIB	Exc.	V.G.	Good	Fair	Poor
3000	2580	2160	1830	1210	1060

Kobra Custom .45

Introduced in 2002. Features a snakeskin treatment on fore-strap, mainspring housing and slide. Novak night sights and Hogue checkered wood grips standard. Many other custom features.

NIB	Exc.	V.G.	Good	Fair	Poor
2500	2000	1400	1100	500	300

Kobra Carry .45

Same as above, with shorter grip frame and barrel.

NIB	Exc.	V.G.	Good	Fair	Poor
2500	2000	1400	1100	500	300

Executive Target

1911 Executive Elite modified for target/range, with adjustable BoMar rear sight, ambidextrous safety. Weight 38 oz. Barrel 5". Chambered for .45 ACP. Magazine 7-rounds.

NIB	Exc.	V.G.	Good	Fair	Poor
2700	2200	1550	1200	600	300

Executive Elite

Government model 5" barrel, weight 38 oz., chambered for .45 ACP, 7-round magazine. Fixed sights. Blue/blue, stainless/blue or all-stainless.

NIB	Exc.	V.G.	Good	Fair	Poor
2450	1950	1400	1000	500	300

Executive Carry

4.25" commander model .45 ACP, with Ed Brown Bobtail. Weight 38 oz., 7-round magazine, fixed sights. Blue/blue, stainless/blue or all-stainless.

NIB	Exc.	V.G.	Good	Fair	Poor
2400	1800	1300	1100	500	300

FX1/FX1 RMR

4.25" model, 9mm, .38 Super, or .45 ACP. Optic mount. Snakeskin texture. Introduced 2017.

NIB	Exc.	V.G.	Good	Fair	Poor
3500	2960	1760	1680	1480	1280

Special Forces

Blue/blue 1911 semi-automatic, with 5" barrel and fixed 3-dot night sights. Chambered for .45 ACP. Weight 38 oz., 7-round magazine. Cocobolo grips.

NIB	Exc.	V.G.	Good	Fair	Poor
2500	2000	1400	1100	500	300

Special Forces SR

Similar features as Special Forces, with suppressor-ready barrel, accessory rail, Trijicon RMR optic, and front and rear slide serrations. Also available in 9mm.

NIB	Exc.	V.G.	Good	Fair	Poor
3750	3100	2300	1600	800	400

Jim Wilson Limited Edition

Ed Brown's first special edition 1911, designed in 2006 in collaboration with Jim Wilson, popular gun writer, retired Texas Sheriff and noted singer of cowboy and American West songs. Based on Executive Elite model. Added enhancements include Tru-Ivory grips, 25 lpi checkered frame, plain black Novak sights, hand polished frame and slide. Limited production in 2007.

NIB	Exc.	V.G.	Good	Fair	Poor
2700	2200	1800	—	—	—

Jeff Cooper Commemorative Limited Edition

Limited manufacture in 2008 in memory of Jeff Cooper. Dean of 1911 school of magazine writers, WWII and Korean War veteran, professor, originator of the sport of practical pistol competition, founder of IPSC (International Practical Shooting Confederation) and Gunsite Academy. Created with input from Col. Cooper's friends and family. Virtually all Ed Brown enhancements are included, plus Cooper's pen and sword logo on the exhibition grade Cocobolo grips. "DVC" on slide standing for latin phrase "Diligentia, Vis, Celeritas", meaning "Accuracy, Power, Speed", which later became the motto of IPSC.

NIB	Exc.	V.G.	Good	Fair	Poor
2700	2200	1800	—	—	—

Massad Ayoob Limited Edition

Based on Executive Carry model. Added enhancements and features suggested by renowned author, shooting champion and expert witness, Massad Ayoob. These include Ed Brown Bobtail frame, 4.25" barrel, 4.5 lb. trigger pull, 25 lpi checkering on front strap and Ayoob's signature on slide. Limited production in 2009 and 2010.

NIB	Exc.	V.G.	Good	Fair	Poor
2700	2200	1800	—	—	—

RIFLES

Savanna

Fitted with long action. Chambered for calibers from .257 Ackley to .338 Win. Magnum. Barrel lightweight 24" for standard calibers; 24" medium weight for Magnum calibers. Talley scope mounts included. Fiberglass stock, recoil pad, steel triggerguard and floorplate standard.

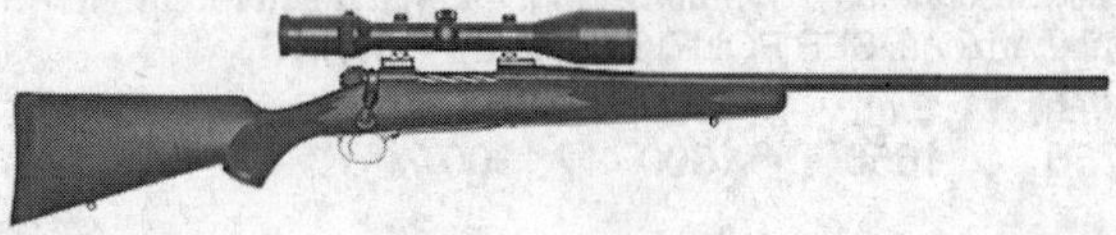

NIB	Exc.	V.G.	Good	Fair	Poor
3800	3000	2000	1500	900	400

Damara

Similar to Savanna in lightweight configuration, with natural-finish stainless barrel.

NIB	Exc.	V.G.	Good	Fair	Poor
3200	2650	2000	1300	650	400

Varmint

Custom-made rifle, with short single-shot action, 26" medium-weight or 24" heavyweight barrel. H-S Precision stock. Available in calibers from .222 to 6.5/.284.

NIB	Exc.	V.G.	Good	Fair	Poor
3500	2800	2000	1300	750	400

Bushveld

Based on a Dakota controlled feed action. Fitted with 24" medium-/heavyweight barrel. Calibers from .330 Dakota to .458 Win. Magnum. Detachable box magazine. Monte Carlo fiberglass stock, recoil pad, steel trigger and floorplate standard, as is Talley scope mounts. Weight about 8.5 lbs.

NIB	Exc.	V.G.	Good	Fair	Poor
4400	3250	2000	1500	900	400

Express

Centerfire bolt-action rifle. Chambered for a wide variety of large Africa-class calibers. Dropped box magazine, fully controlled feed, fluted bolt, McMillan stock, iron sights.

NIB	Exc.	V.G.	Good	Fair	Poor
3600	2900	2350	1600	800	400

Marine Sniper

Duplicate of Vietnam-era McMillan sniper rifle. Controlled feed, fluted bolt, hinged floorplate, woodland camo stock, blackened stainless steel barrel and receiver. Offered in .308 and .300 Win. Magnum calibers. Weight about 9.25 lbs.

NIB	Exc.	V.G.	Good	Fair	Poor
3700	2950	2350	1600	900	400

Light Tactical

Short-action rifle, with lightweight floorplate and triggerguard. Fitted with 21" medium-weight barrel. Black fiberglass stock, with aluminum bedding block. Available in calibers from .22-250 to .308.

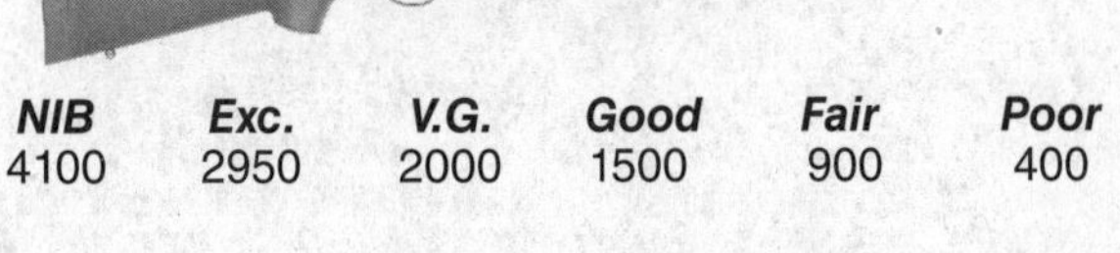

NIB	Exc.	V.G.	Good	Fair	Poor
4100	2950	2000	1500	900	400

Tactical

Similar to above. Built on long-action, with heavyweight 26" blued barrel. McMillan A-3 black tactical stock. Available in .308 and .300 Win. Magnum.

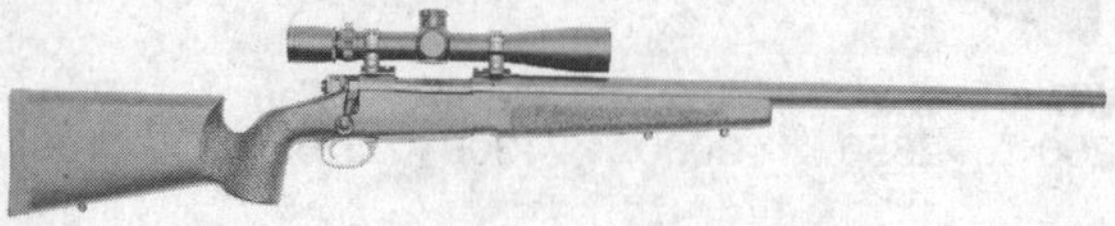

NIB	Exc.	V.G.	Good	Fair	Poor
3900	3350	2500	1600	950	400

Ozark

Rifle built on short-action, with blind magazine. A 21" lightweight barrel fitted for standard calibers; medium-weight 21" barrel for Magnum calibers. Chambered for calibers from .22-250 to .308. Talley scope mounts included as is fiberglass stock, recoil pad, steel triggerguard and floorplate.

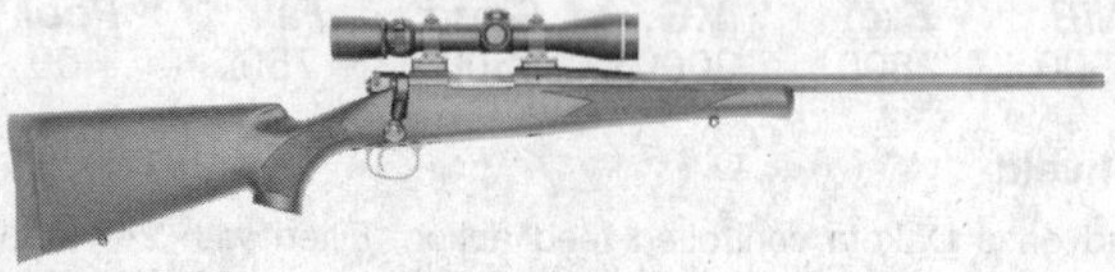

NIB	Exc.	V.G.	Good	Fair	Poor
3800	3000	2000	1500	900	400

Denali

Lighter-weight version of Ozark, with 22" super lightweight barrel. Chambered for calibers .25-06 to .300 WSM. Weight about 6.75 lbs.

NIB	Exc.	V.G.	Good	Fair	Poor
3800	3000	2000	1500	900	400

Peacekeeper

Single-shot long-action rifle. Chambered for .30-378 Wby., .338-378 Wby. or .338 Lapua caliber. Fitted with heavy 26" barrel with muzzle brake. Fiberglass tactical stock with recoil pad. Leupold Mark 4 scope mounts standard. Weight about 13 lbs.

NIB	Exc.	V.G.	Good	Fair	Poor
4500	3250	2100	1300	800	400

Fueled by Ed Brown MP

9mm pistol, Models MP-FP1, -FP2, & -FP3 have similar values.

NIB	Exc.	V.G.	Good	Fair	Poor
2000	—	—	—	—	—

BROWN MANUFACTURING CO.

Newburyport, Massachusetts
See—BALLARD PATENT ARMS

Southerner Derringer (Antique)

.41-caliber spur-trigger single-shot pocket pistol, with pivoted 2.5" or 4" octagonal barrel marked "Southerner". Silver-plated or blued, with walnut grips. Manufactured by Merrimack Arms Co. from 1867 to 1869; Brown Manufacturing Co. from 1869 to 1873.

Courtesy W. P. Hallstein III and son Chip

Brass Framed (Antique)

2.5" barrel.

Exc.	Fine	V.G.	Good	Fair	Poor
880	600	460	320	120	80

Iron Frame (Antique)

2.5" barrel (Brown Mfg. only).

Exc.	Fine	V.G.	Good	Fair	Poor
1020	800	650	500	200	140

Brass Frame 4" Barrel (Antique)

Exc.	Fine	V.G.	Good	Fair	Poor
3700	2000	1750	1500	500	350

Brown Mfg. Co./Merrill Patent Breechloading Rifles (Antique)

Overall length 54.75"; barrel (bore) length 35"; caliber .577. Markings on breechblock-bolt mechanism: "BROWN MFG. CO. NEWBURYPORT, MASS./PATANTED OCT. 17, 1871". Patent issued to George Merrill in 1871, permitted Brown Manufacturing Co. to alter probably up to 1,000 English P1853 rifle-muskets to single-shot breechloading system. Large bolt handle projecting upward at end of breech readily distinguishes these arms.

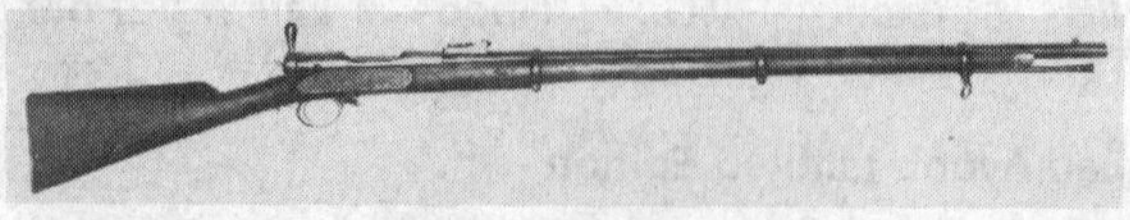

Courtesy Milwaukee Public Museum, Milwaukee, Wisconsin

Exc.	Fine	V.G.	Good	Fair	Poor
2500	1250	1020	800	300	210

BROWNELLS, INC.

Grinnell, Iowa

Established 1939 by Bob Brownell as a gunsmithing supplier, today produces its own line of ARs and optics

"What Would Stoner Do" 2020 Rifle

Caliber: 5.56 NATO or .223 Rem (.223 Wylde chamber). Capacity: 30-round Magpul P-Mag. Barrel: 14.5" with titanium flash hider for OAL of 16", 1/2-28 tpi muzzle threads. Twist rate: 1:8", Nitride finish. Upper/lower receivers: KE Arms MK3 polymer receiver. Weight: 4 lbs. Trigger: SLT-1 Sear Link Technology. Overall Length: 42". Manufactured by KE Arms of Phoenix, Arizona. SEE POLITICAL PANIC PRICING.

NIB	Exc.	V.G.	Good	Fair	Poor
1750	1650	1500	1300	—	—

BRN-10 Retro Rifle

Caliber: .308 Winchester. Capacity: one supplied 20-round Brownells aluminum magazine. Compatible with metal DPMS/SR-25 magazines. Barrel: 20 in., 1:10 RH twist, 5/8-24 tpi muzzle threads, QPQ Nitride finish, 3-prong Dutch-style flash hider, .750-in. diameter at the gas block.

Direct impingement. Upper/Lower Receivers: Machined from 7075 T6 aluminum billet. Stock: Type D, no trap door. Sights: Rear enclosed by the carry handle. A2-style horizontal thumbwheel adjusts elevation. Windage is changed by loosening a setscrew and drifting the rear peep. Standard AR-15-style front sight base. Weight: 8.6 lbs. Trigger: AR-15 style. Overall Length: 40.5 in. Features: Re-creation of Eugene Stoner's original lightweight .308 caliber battle rifle, Armalite AR-10. Slab-sided lower with straight magazine well. Serrated takedown pins, selector lever, magazine release and bolt release. No forward assist and shell deflector. "Trigger"-style charging handle located under the carry handle. Carrier has flats and two stabilizing flanges at the rear found on early carriers, and the entire bolt/carrier group is chrome plated. Bolt machined from 9310 carbon steel and magnetic particle inspected (MPI). Functional heavy fluting on the barrel under the handguard. Brown furniture. Many components are compatible with modern DPMS/SR-25 parts or AR-15 parts. The BRN-10B is inspired by later export rifles and has a closed-prong, Portuguese-type flash hider, later-style black furniture, and a lightweight barrel. Weight: 7.8 lbs. Length: 40.75 in.

BRN-10A

NIB	*Exc.*	*V.G.*	*Good*	*Fair*	*Poor*
2000	1100	900	—	—	—

BRN-10B

NIB	*Exc.*	*V.G.*	*Good*	*Fair*	*Poor*
1700	1050	900	—	—	—

BRN-605 5.56 Carbine

Caliber: 5.56 NATO. Capacity: (1) 20-round metal. Barrel: 15.5 in.; 1:12 RH twist. A1-profile, standard 3-prong "duckbill" flash hider. Upper/Lower Receivers: Machined 7075 T6 aluminum receivers. XBRN16E1 lower has partial "fence" around the magazine release. Upper has forward assist, but no shell deflector. Stock: Fixed "Type D" buttstock. Sights: Windage-adjustable A1-type rear sight drum. Weight: 7.5 lbs. Overall Length: 34 in. Features: Colt's first carbine variant of the M16 rifle. Black furniture of reinforced polymer, triangular cross-section handguard. As of 2022, only available as a build kit, not as a complete rifle.

NIB	*Exc.*	*V.G.*	*Good*	*Fair*	*Poor*
1060	850	700	—	—	—

BRN-PROTO 5.56

Caliber: 5.56 NATO. Faithful replica of Eugene Stoner's very first AR-15 prototype. Features: Trigger-like charging handle under the carry handle, "slick-side" upper receiver, and stock, handguard, and pistol grip of brown reinforced polymer that replicates the look of original fiberglass furniture. Round cross-section handguard, matte-gray, anodized receiver, skinny A1-profile barrel, three-prong "duckbill" flash suppressor. Capacity: (1) 25-round steel bodied magazine replica. Barrel, 20 in. with 1:12 rifling. Rifle-length gas tube. Internal dimensions conform to modern "mil-spec" standards. As of 2022, only available as a build kit, not as a complete rifle.

NIB	*Exc.*	*V.G.*	*Good*	*Fair*	*Poor*
880	—	—	—	—	—

BRN-601

Caliber: 5.56 NATO. Faithful reproduction of the first-ever AR-15 issued to the U.S. Military during the early 1960s. Based on iconic Model 601 rifle, which entered military service with the U.S. Air Force and other military units in SE Asia during the early years of the 1960s. The rifle is constructed from all-new parts and features green furniture and slab-side receivers that are close to the original design envisioned by Eugene Stoner. Triangle-shaped charging handle, three-prong flash hider, and a slick-side bolt-carrier group. Length: 40 in. Weight: 6.7 lbs. As of 2022, only available as a build kit, not as a complete rifle.

NIB	*Exc.*	*V.G.*	*Good*	*Fair*	*Poor*
1000	—	—	—	—	—

XBRN16E1 Rifle

XBRN16E1 — Rifle

Caliber: 5.56 NATO. Detailed reproduction of the first AR-style rifle issued to ground troops during the early years of the Vietnam War. With forward assist, black triangle handguard, and three-prong flash hider. The gun is constructed with all new-production parts. Length: 40 in. Weight: 6.8 lbs. A1-style sights, 1:12 rate of twist, gray-anodized receiver. As of 2022, only available as a build kit, not as a complete rifle.

NIB	*Exc.*	*V.G.*	*Good*	*Fair*	*Poor*
1280	—	—	—	—	—

XBRN177E2 Carbine

Caliber: 5.56 NATO. The XBRN177E2 Carbine reproduction is based on the AR platform that was commonly issued to Special Operations forces during the Vietnam war. All-new parts, polymer CAR buttstock, XM177 flash hider, phosphate bolt-carrier group. Gray-anodized receiver, 12.7-in. barrel with a pinned and welded muzzle device that meets BATFE regulations. Overall length: 34 in. Weight: 5.8 lbs. As of 2022, only available as a build kit, not as a complete rifle.

NIB	*Exc.*	*V.G.*	*Good*	*Fair*	*Poor*
1330	—	—	—	—	—

BROWN PRECISION, INC.

Los Molinos, California

This company pioneered manufacture of fiberglass gunstocks in 1960s. Since 1975 has been making custom rifles on various Winchester, Remington and Ruger actions. Calibers available include virtually any popular chambering available in original action. Company offers many optional features, which will affect values. Values shown are for base models of current and recent production. Deduct $1,000 for rifles made on customer-supplied action.

Custom High Country

Note: Add $900 for take-down model.

NIB	*Exc.*	*V.G.*	*Good*	*Fair*	*Poor*
4250	3500	2750	1800	1000	600

Pro Hunter

NIB	*Exc.*	*V.G.*	*Good*	*Fair*	*Poor*
4800	4000	3000	2000	1400	1000

Pro Hunter Elite

Note: Add $900 for take-down model.

NIB	*Exc.*	*V.G.*	*Good*	*Fair*	*Poor*
6000	5200	4200	3000	2000	1200

Pro Varminter/Light Varminter

NIB	*Exc.*	*V.G.*	*Good*	*Fair*	*Poor*
3500	2750	2000	1200	800	500

Tactical Elite

NIB	*Exc.*	*V.G.*	*Good*	*Fair*	*Poor*
4250	3500	2750	1800	1000	600

EARLY PRODUCTION

Open Country Varmint Rifle (disc. 1992)

NIB	Exc.	V.G.	Good	Fair	Poor
1200	900	700	600	400	250

Law Enforcement Model (disc. 1992)

NIB	Exc.	V.G.	Good	Fair	Poor
1200	900	700	600	400	250

Blaser Action Model (disc. 1989)

NIB	Exc.	V.G.	Good	Fair	Poor
1600	1200	800	650	500	350

BROWN, E.A. MANUFACTURING CO.

Garfield, Minnesota

Brown BF Classic Single-Shot Pistol

Falling block single-shot pistol, with 15" Match-grade barrel. Chambered for calibers from .17 Ackley to .45-70 Government. Walnut thumbrest grips. Hand-fitted. Introduced in 1998.

NIB	Exc.	V.G.	Good	Fair	Poor
1200	1000	750	600	400	200

Brown Model 97D Single-Shot Rifle

Single-shot falling block rifle. Chambered for calibers from .17 Ackley to .45-70 Government. Barrel lengths up to 26". Sporter-style stock with pistol grip, cheekpiece and schnabel forend. Blue/black finish. Weight about 6 lbs. No sights.

NIB	Exc.	V.G.	Good	Fair	Poor
1500	1250	1000	750	500	300

BROWNING ARMS CO.

Morgan, Utah

Early Semi-Automatic Pistols

In the period between 1900 and the development of Model 1935 Hi-Power Pistol, Browning had a number of semi-automatic pistols manufactured by Fabrique Nationale of Herstal, Belgium. They were Models 1900, 1903, 1905, 1910, 1922, Baby and 1935 Model Hi-Power. These firearms will be listed in more detail, with their respective values in Fabrique Nationale section of this text.

Hi-Power Modern Production

This version of FN Model 1935 is quite similar in appearance to original described in FN section. Chambered for 9mm Parabellum cartridge. Has 4.75" barrel. Available with 10- or 13-round double-column detachable magazine. Blued, with checkered walnut grips. Has fixed sights and been produced in its present configuration since 1954. Matte-nickel version offered between 1980 and 1984 was also available and would be worth approximately 15 percent additional. From 1994 to 2010 available in .40 S&W. Production of all Browning Hi-Power models were discontinued in 2018. Note: Add $100 for adjustable sights; $500 for internal extractor (pre-1962).

Spur Hammer Version

NIB	Exc.	V.G.	Good	Fair	Poor
1100	900	600	500	300	150

Round Hammer Version

NIB	Exc.	V.G.	Good	Fair	Poor
1350	1100	900	700	450	200

Hi-Power—.30 Luger

Version similar to standard Hi-Power, except chambered for .30 Luger cartridge. Approximately 1,500 imported between 1986 and 1989. Slide marked "FN". Note: Browning-marked versions are quite rare and worth approximately 30 percent additional.

NIB	Exc.	V.G.	Good	Fair	Poor
1000	900	720	450	300	200

Tangent Sight Model

Version similar to standard Hi-Power, with addition of adjustable rear sight calibrated to 500 meters. Approximately 7,000 imported between 1965 and 1978. Note: If grip frame is slotted to accept a detachable shoulder stock add approximately 20 percent to value; but be wary of fakes. Add an additional 10 percent for "T" series serial numbers.

NIB	Exc.	V.G.	Good	Fair	Poor
1450	1250	1000	650	450	200

Renaissance Hi-Power

Heavily engraved version, with matte-silver finish. Features synthetic-pearl grips and gold-plated trigger. Import ended in 1979. Note: Add $500 for internal extractor.

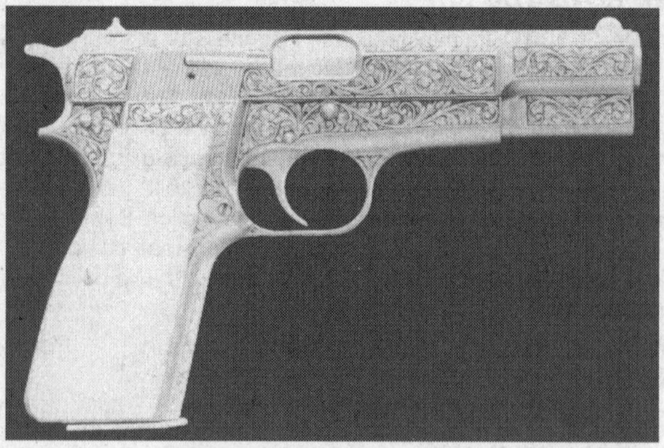

Spur Hammer Model

NIB	Exc.	V.G.	Good	Fair	Poor
3360	2900	2100	1750	1000	600

Ring Hammer Model

NIB	Exc.	V.G.	Good	Fair	Poor
3900	3400	3000	2000	1500	900

Adjustable Sight Spur Hammer Model

NIB	Exc.	V.G.	Good	Fair	Poor
3300	3000	2100	1750	1000	600

Renaissance .25-Caliber

NIB	Exc.	V.G.	Good	Fair	Poor
2400	2100	1700	1500	1000	600

Renaissance .380-Caliber

With pearl grips.

NIB	Exc.	V.G.	Good	Fair	Poor
2700	2400	2000	1600	1000	600

Renaissance .380-Caliber (Model 1971)

With wood grips and adjustable sights.

NIB	Exc.	V.G.	Good	Fair	Poor
2300	2000	1700	1500	900	500

Cased Renaissance Set

Features one example of fully engraved and silver-finished .25 ACP "Baby", .380 ACP pistol and Hi-Power. Set furnished in a fitted walnut case or black leatherette. Imported between 1955 and 1969. Note: Add 30 percent for early coin finish.

Courtesy Rock Island Auction Company

NIB	Exc.	V.G.	Good	Fair	Poor
9600	8400	6600	3800	—	—

Louis XVI Model

Heavily engraved Hi-Power pistol. Features leaf-and-scroll pattern, satin-finished, checkered walnut grips. Furnished in fitted walnut case. To realize its true potential, this pistol must be NIB. Imported between 1980 and 1984.

Diamond Grip Model

NIB	Exc.	V.G.	Good	Fair	Poor
3150	2500	2000	800	400	300

Medallion Grip Model

NIB	Exc.	V.G.	Good	Fair	Poor
1950	1750	1600	800	400	300

Hi-Power Centennial Model

Version similar to standard fixed-sight Hi-Power. Chrome-plated, with inscription "Browning Centennial/1878-1978" engraved on slide. Furnished with fitted case. There were 3,500 manufactured in 1978. As with all commemorative pistols, in order to realize its collector potential, this model should be NIB with all supplied material. Prices for pistols built in Belgium

NIB	Exc.	V.G.	Good	Fair	Poor
1600	1300	1000	800	400	300

Hi-Power Capitan

Fitted with tangent sights. Introduced in 1993. Furnished with walnut grips. Weight about 32 oz. Assembled in Portugal.

NIB	Exc.	V.G.	Good	Fair	Poor
980	900	760	510	360	300

Hi-Power Practical

First introduced in 1993. Furnished with blued slide and chrome frame. Has Pachmayr wrap-around rubber grips, round-style serrated hammer and removable front sight. Available with adjustable sights. Weight 36 oz. Assembled in Portugal.

NIB	*Exc.*	*V.G.*	*Good*	*Fair*	*Poor*
960	880	710	460	400	380

Hi-Power Silver Chrome Model

Furnished in hard chrome. Fitted with wrap-around Pachmayr rubber grips. Assembled in Portugal. Weight 36 oz. Introduced in 1981. Dropped from Browning product line in 1984. Reintroduced in 1991. Note: Add 10 percent for models with all Belgian markings.

NIB	*Exc.*	*V.G.*	*Good*	*Fair*	*Poor*
1460	1200	910	660	410	380

Hi-Power .40 S&W

Introduced in 1994. New version of Hi-Power furnished with adjustable sights, molded grips, 5" barrel and 10-round magazine. Weight about 35 oz. Discontinued 2010.

NIB	*Exc.*	*V.G.*	*Good*	*Fair*	*Poor*
800	600	450	300	200	150

Hi-Power Mark III

Introduced in 1991. Matte blued or green finish, low-profile fixed sights and two-piece molded grips, with thumbrest. Weight 32 oz.

NIB	*Exc.*	*V.G.*	*Good*	*Fair*	*Poor*
900	700	500	300	200	180

Hi-Power Gold Classic

Limited edition model introduced in 1984. Planned production of 500, but less than 350 were made. Elaborate engraving with five gold inlays, silver/gray finish, carved and checkered wood grips.

NIB	*Exc.*	*V.G.*	*Good*	*Fair*	*Poor*
4500	3850	3000	2000	—	—

Hi-Power Classic

As above, except with less engraving and no gold inlays.

NIB	*Exc.*	*V.G.*	*Good*	*Fair*	*Poor*
2200	1650	1100	800	600	400

Baby Browning

.25-caliber semi-automatic is same as FN Baby Model. Made by Fabrique Nationale in Belgium from 1931 until 1983. Many were imported into U.S., with Browning rollmark from 1954 to 1968. See "Baby" Model under Fabrique Nationale section for more details. Prices shown for Browning-marked model.

NIB	*Exc.*	*V.G.*	*Good*	*Fair*	*Poor*
750	600	500	450	350	200

Browning Model 1955

Semi-automatic pistol same as FN Model 1910. From 1912 to 1983 in .32 ACP and .380 ACP. See Fabrique Nationale section for more information. Imported into U.S. by Browning from 1954 to 1968. Prices shown for Browning-marked pistols. Note: Add $200 for .32 ACP

NIB	*Exc.*	*V.G.*	*Good*	*Fair*	*Poor*
800	700	550	450	350	200

Pro-9/Pro-40

9mm or .40 S&W double-action pistol fitted with 4" barrel. Stainless steel slide. Grips are composite, with interchangeable backstrap inserts. Magazine capacity 16 rounds 9mm; 14 rounds .40 S&W. Weight about 30 oz.

NIB	*Exc.*	*V.G.*	*Good*	*Fair*	*Poor*
600	500	380	—	—	—

BDA-380

Double-action semi-automatic pistol. Chambered for .380 ACP cartridge. Features 3.75" barrel, with 14-round double-stack detachable magazine. Finish blued or nickel-plated, with smooth walnut grips. Manufactured in Italy by Beretta. Introduced in 1977. Note: Add 10 percent for nickel finish.

NIB	*Exc.*	*V.G.*	*Good*	*Fair*	*Poor*
730	560	480	400	280	220

BDA

Double-action semi-automatic pistol. Manufactured between 1977 and 1980 for Browning by SIG-Sauer of Germany. Identical to SIG-Sauer Model 220. Chambered for 9mm Parabellum, .38 Super and .45 ACP cartridges. Note: Add 30 percent for .38 Super.

NIB	*Exc.*	*V.G.*	*Good*	*Fair*	*Poor*
900	670	550	440	300	250

BDM Pistol

Double-action semi-automatic pistol. Chambered for 9mm cartridge. Fitted with selector switch that allows shooter to choose between single-/double-action model. Features 4.75" barrel, with adjustable rear sight. Magazine capacity 15 rounds. Weight 31 oz. First introduced in 1991.

NIB	*Exc.*	*V.G.*	*Good*	*Fair*	*Poor*
600	450	350	250	200	150

BDM Silver Chrome

Variation of BDM introduced in 1997. Features silver chrome finish on slide and frame, balance in contrasting matte blue finish.

NIB	*Exc.*	*V.G.*	*Good*	*Fair*	*Poor*
660	500	400	300	250	200

BDM Practical

Introduced in 1997. Same as above, with silver chrome on frame only.

NIB	*Exc.*	*V.G.*	*Good*	*Fair*	*Poor*
600	450	350	250	200	150

BPM-D

Introduced in 1997. New version of BDM (Browning Pistol Model Decocker) features double-action pistol, with first shot fired double-action and subsequent shots fired single-action. No manual safety. Decock lever also releases slide.

NIB	*Exc.*	*V.G.*	*Good*	*Fair*	*Poor*
600	450	350	250	200	150

BRM-DAO

9mm pistol is a redesigned version of Model BDM. Initials stand for "Browning Revolver Model Double-Action-Only". Has finger support triggerguard for two-handed control. All other features same as BPM-D pistol. Weight about 31 oz.

NIB	*Exc.*	*V.G.*	*Good*	*Fair*	*Poor*
600	450	350	250	200	150

Nomad

Blowback-operated semi-automatic pistol. Chambered for .22 LR cartridge. Offered with 4.5" or 6.75" barrel. Has 10-round detachable magazine, with adjustable sights and all-steel construction. Finish blued, with black plastic grips. Manufactured between 1962 and 1974 by FN.

NIB	Exc.	V.G.	Good	Fair	Poor
600	530	400	300	200	180

Challenger

More deluxe target pistol. Chambered for .22 LR cartridge. Offered with 4.5" or 6.75" barrel. Has 10-round magazine. Constructed entirely of steel. Adjustable sights. Finish blued, with gold-plated trigger. Checkered wrap-around walnut grips. Manufactured between 1962 and 1974 by FN.

Courtesy John J. Stimson, Jr.

NIB	Exc.	V.G.	Good	Fair	Poor
790	680	610	500	400	360

Renaissance Challenger

Version fully engraved, satin-nickel finish. Furnished with fleece-lined pouch.

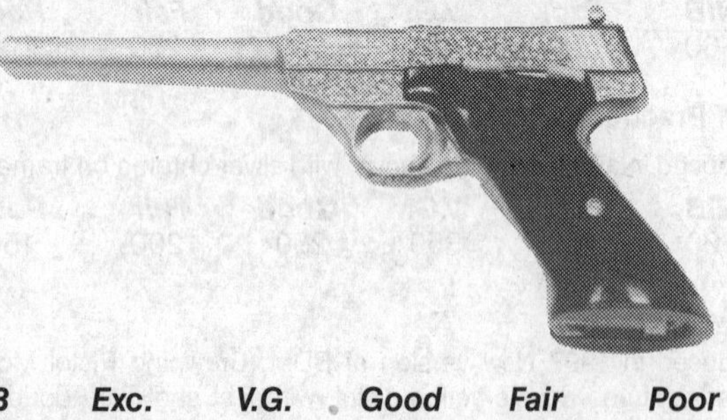

NIB	Exc.	V.G.	Good	Fair	Poor
3400	2550	1910	800	550	400

Gold Line Challenger

Version blued and has gold-inlaid line around outer edges of pistol. It was cased in fleece-lined pouch. Built in Belgium.

NIB	Exc.	V.G.	Good	Fair	Poor
3500	2800	1900	1000	500	350

Challenger II

Blowback-operated semi-automatic pistol. Chambered for .22 LR cartridge. Has 6.75" barrel, with alloy frame. Finish blued, with phenolic impregnated hardwood grips. Manufactured between 1976 and 1982 in Salt Lake City, Utah.

NIB	Exc.	V.G.	Good	Fair	Poor
480	430	380	260	180	160

Challenger III

Version features 5.5" bull barrel, with adjustable sights. Manufactured between 1982 and 1984 in Salt Lake City, Utah. A 6.75" tapered-barrel version was available and known as Sporter.

NIB	Exc.	V.G.	Good	Fair	Poor
430	400	300	150	120	90

Browning Collector's Association Edition

Fully engraved. 100 manufactured. Fitted with two-piece grip.

NIB	Exc.	V.G.	Good	Fair	Poor
2950	2250	1650	1200	800	400

Medalist

High-grade semi-automatic target pistol. Chambered for .22 LR cartridge. Has 6.75" ventilated rib barrel, with adjustable target sights. Supplied with three barrel weights and dry-fire-practice mechanism. Finish blued, with target type thumbrest walnut grips. Manufactured between 1962 and 1974 by FN. Four additional high-grade versions of this pistol that differed in degree of ornamentation.

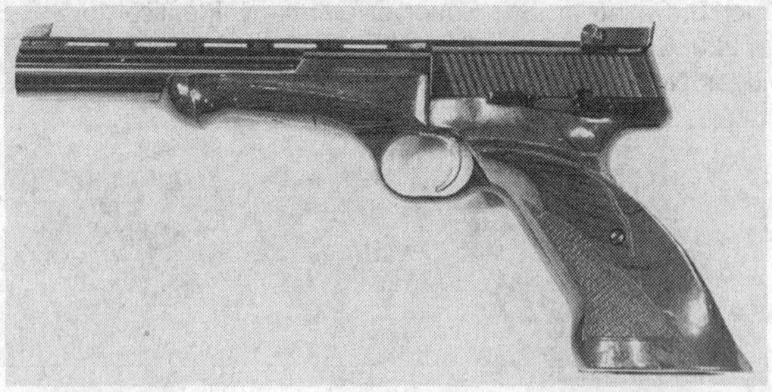

NIB	Exc.	V.G.	Good	Fair	Poor
1800	1400	950	680	380	250

International Medalist

About 700 sold in U.S. from 1977 to 1980. Barrels were 5.875" long. Built in Belgium.

Courtesy John J. Stimson, Jr.

NIB	Exc.	V.G.	Good	Fair	Poor
1300	900	600	450	300	150

Second Model International Medalist

Same as above, with flat-sided barrel, dull finish and adjustable palm rest. Built in Belgium.

Courtesy John J. Stimson, Jr.

NIB	Exc.	V.G.	Good	Fair	Poor
1100	720	450	300	200	150

Gold Line Medalist

Introduced in 1962. Discontinued in 1974. Estimated 400 guns produced.

NIB	Exc.	V.G.	Good	Fair	Poor
4000	3500	2250	1000	750	500

Renaissance Medalist

Model built entirely in Belgium from 1970 to 1974, with one-piece grip.

NIB	Exc.	V.G.	Good	Fair	Poor
5000	4500	3000	1500	900	700

BUCK MARK SERIES

Buck Mark

Blowback-operated semi-automatic pistol. Chambered for .22 LR cartridge. Has 5.5" bull barrel, with adjustable sights; 11-round detachable magazine; matte blued, with skip-line checkered synthetic grips. Introduced in 1985. Produced in U.S. Note: Add $25 for stainless steel version, introduced in 2005.

NIB	Exc.	V.G.	Good	Fair	Poor
400	340	310	280	180	160

Buck Mark Plus

Version similar to standard, with plain wood grips. Introduced in 1987. Produced in U.S. Note: Add $35 for nickel finish. Introduced in 1991.

NIB	Exc.	V.G.	Good	Fair	Poor
480	430	380	330	230	180

Buck Mark Varmint

Version has 9.75" bull barrel, with full-length ramp to allow scope mounting. No sights. Introduced in 1987. Produced in U.S.

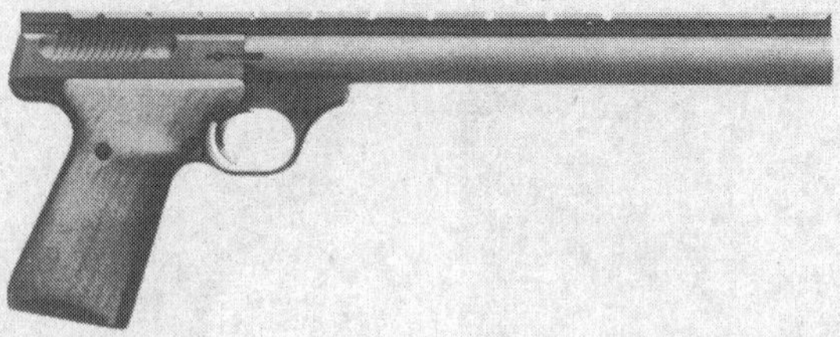

NIB	Exc.	V.G.	Good	Fair	Poor
400	300	250	200	180	120

Buck Mark Silhouette

Version features 9.75" bull barrel, with adjustable sights. Introduced in 1987.

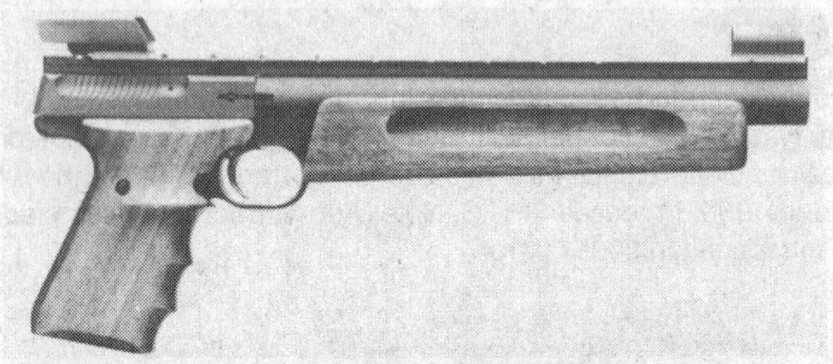

NIB	Exc.	V.G.	Good	Fair	Poor
450	350	280	220	180	140

Buck Mark 22 Micro

Version of Buck Mark 22. Fitted with 4" bull barrel. Available in blue, matte blue or nickel finish. Also in Micro Plus variation, with walnut grips. Weight 32 oz. Introduced in 1992. Note: Add $75 for nickel finish. Introduced in 1996; $25 for stainless steel version. Introduced in 2005.

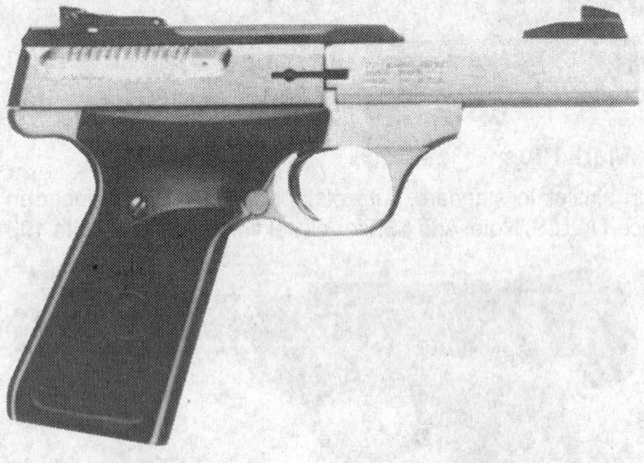

NIB	Exc.	V.G.	Good	Fair	Poor
380	300	260	200	160	140

Micro Plus

NIB	Exc.	V.G.	Good	Fair	Poor
330	280	230	200	140	130

Buck Mark 5.5

.22-caliber pistol has 5.5" heavy bull barrel fitted with target sights. Offered in three separate models:

Blued Target

Version has blued finish, contoured walnut grips, target sights. Weight 35.5 oz. Introduced in 1990.

NIB	Exc.	V.G.	Good	Fair	Poor
480	400	250	150	100	100

Blued Target (2005)

Introduced in 2005. Features new target-style Cocabolo grips, full length scope mount. Hooded target sights. Weight 35 oz.

NIB	Exc.	V.G.	Good	Fair	Poor
520	420	300	200	150	100

Gold Target

Same as above. Has gold anodized frame and top rib. Slide blue. Walnut grips. Introduced in 1991.

NIB	Exc.	V.G.	Good	Fair	Poor
550	420	300	200	150	120

Field

Same action and barrel as Target Model, with hoodless adjustable field sights. Slide and barrel blued; rib and frame anodized blue. Grips are walnut. Introduced in 1991.

NIB	Exc.	V.G.	Good	Fair	Poor
450	340	220	150	100	100

Field (2005)

Features new target-style grips and full-length scope rail. Weight about 35 oz.

NIB	*Exc.*	*V.G.*	*Good*	*Fair*	*Poor*
520	420	300	220	160	100

Buck Field Plus

.22-caliber pistol has 5.5" barrel, with Truglo/Marbles' front sight. Grips laminated rosewood. Barrel polished blue. Weight about 24 oz.

NIB	*Exc.*	*V.G.*	*Good*	*Fair*	*Poor*
420	320	220	200	150	80

Buck Mark Bullseye

Introduced in 1996. Designed for metallic silhouette competition. Fluted barrel 7.25" long. Adjustable trigger pull and rear sight, removable barrel are some of the features. Weight about 36 oz. Choice of laminated wood or rubber grips. Note: Add $90 for rosewood target grips; $150 for stainless.

NIB	*Exc.*	*V.G.*	*Good*	*Fair*	*Poor*
550	420	280	180	120	80

Buck Mark Unlimited Match

Fitted with 14" barrel and top rib. Front sight hood slightly rearward of muzzle for maximum sight radius of 15". All other features same as Silhouette model. Weight 64 oz.

NIB	*Exc.*	*V.G.*	*Good*	*Fair*	*Poor*
700	520	380	220	180	120

Buck Mark Challenge

Introduced in 1999. Features lightweight 5.5" barrel, with adjustable rear sight. Smaller grip diameter. Matte blue finish. Magazine capacity 10-rounds. Weight about 25 oz. Buck Mark Challenge Rosewood model has laminated rosewood grips, TruGlo fiber optic front sight, gold-plated trigger. Note: Add $85 for this model.

NIB	*Exc.*	*V.G.*	*Good*	*Fair*	*Poor*
350	250	200	180	120	100

Buck Mark Camper

Fitted with heavy 5.5" barrel. Matte blue finish. Magazine capacity 10-rounds. Weight about 34 oz. Introduced in 1999. Note: Add $60 for stainless steel version.

NIB	*Exc.*	*V.G.*	*Good*	*Fair*	*Poor*
300	220	150	120	100	80

Buck Mark Camper Cocobola UDX

Similar to above, with Cocobolo Ultra DX grips and TruGlo front sight. Introduced 2008.

NIB	*Exc.*	*V.G.*	*Good*	*Fair*	*Poor*
380	300	240	150	100	80

Buck Mark Camper Stainless UFX

Features tapered bull 5.5" barrel, overmolded FX ambidextrous grips, with checkered panels, Pro-Target adjustable sights and gold-plated trigger.

NIB	Exc.	V.G.	Good	Fair	Poor
360	320	280	260	170	140

Buck Mark Camper UFX Suppressor-Ready

Similar to Buck Mark Camper UFX except with threaded muzzle. Introduced in 2019.

NIB	Exc.	V.G.	Good	Fair	Poor
500	480	430	400	380	200

Buck Mark Practical URX Fiber Optic

Matte gray finish, 5.5" tapered bull barrel, Ultra-grip RX ambidextrous grips, adjustable ProTarget rear sight, with TruGlo fiber-optic front sight. Introduced 2008.

NIB	Exc.	V.G.	Good	Fair	Poor
350	300	200	150	100	80

Buck Mark Hunter

.22 LR pistol features 7.25" heavy round barrel, with TruGlo/Marbles front sights, adjustable rear sight and integrated scope base. Grips Cocabolo target-style. Weight about 38 oz. Introduced in 2005.

NIB	Exc.	V.G.	Good	Fair	Poor
420	380	330	280	180	160

Buck Mark Limited Edition 25th Anniversary

Limited to 1,000 pistols. Features 6.75" barrel, with matte blued finish and scrimshaw etched ivory grips. Pistol rug furnished as standard equipment.

NIB	Exc.	V.G.	Good	Fair	Poor
500	350	300	220	150	120

Buck Mark Bullseye Target

Blowback single-action .22 LR semi-automatic. Matte blued, heavy 7.25" round and fluted stainless bull barrel. Laminated rosewood grip, adjustable sights. Introduced 2006.

NIB	Exc.	V.G.	Good	Fair	Poor
700	450	300	220	150	180

Buck Mark Bullseye Target URX

Blowback single-action semi-automatic in .22 LR. Matte blued, heavy 7.25" round and fluted bull barrel. Grooved rubberized grip. Weight 39 oz. Adjustable sights. Introduced 2006.

NIB	Exc.	V.G.	Good	Fair	Poor
480	400	320	220	150	180

Buck Mark Contour 5.5 URX

Blowback single-action .222 semi-automatic. Matte blued, contoured 5.5" barrel. Full-length scope base. Weight 36 oz. Adjustable sights. Multiple barrel lengths and options. Introduced 2006.

NIB	Exc.	V.G.	Good	Fair	Poor
480	430	380	330	220	180

Buck Mark Contour Lite 5.5 URX

.22 LR blowback single-action semi-automatic. Matte blued, contoured 5.5" barrel. Full-length scope base. Weight 28 oz. Adjustable sights. Multiple barrel lengths and options. Introduced 2006.

NIB	Exc.	V.G.	Good	Fair	Poor
530	480	430	380	270	220

Buck Mark FLD Plus Rosewood UDX

.22 LR blowback single-action semi-automatic. "FLD" sculpted grip, with rosewood panels. Blued, contoured 5.5" barrel. Weight 34 oz. Adjustable rear and fiber optic front sight. Multiple barrel lengths and options. Introduced 2006.

NIB	Exc.	V.G.	Good	Fair	Poor
480	400	320	280	220	150

Buck Mark Lite Splash 5.5 URX

Blowback single-action semi-automatic. Matte blued finish, gold splash anodizing. Chambered for .22 LR, 5.5" barrel. Rubberized ambidextrous grip. Adjustable sights; fiber optic front sight. Weight 28 oz. Available with 7.5" barrel. Introduced 2006.

NIB	Exc.	V.G.	Good	Fair	Poor
450	380	320	280	220	150

Buck Mark Micro Standard Stainless URX

With 4" stainless barrel in .22 LR. Weight 32 oz. Ambidextrous rubberized grip. Adjustable sights. Available in alloy steel. Introduced 2006.

NIB	Exc.	V.G.	Good	Fair	Poor
400	350	320	280	220	150

Buck Mark Micro Bull

4" stainless bull barrel; .22 LR; weight 33 oz. Plastic grip panels. Adjustable sights. Introduced 2006.

NIB	Exc.	V.G.	Good	Fair	Poor
350	280	220	180	120	100

Buck Mark Plus Stainless Black Laminated UDX

Similar to Buck Mark Standard. Stainless UDX, with ambidextrous grips. Introduced 2007.

NIB	Exc.	V.G.	Good	Fair	Poor
500	380	300	220	150	120

Buck Mark Plus UDX

Similar to Buck Mark FLD Plus, with ambidextrous walnut grips. Introduced 2007.

NIB	Exc.	V.G.	Good	Fair	Poor
480	430	380	330	230	180

Full Line Dealer Buck Mark Plus Rosewood UDX

Similar to Buck Mark Plus UDX, with ambidextrous rosewood grips. Available only to full-line and Medallion-level Browning dealers. Introduced 2007.

NIB	Exc.	V.G.	Good	Fair	Poor
420	350	300	220	150	120

Buck Mark Plus Stainless UDX

.22 LR semi-automatic, with finger-grooved wood grips. Barrel 5.5". Weight 34 oz. Adjustable sights, fiber-optic front sight. Available blued alloy steel. Introduced 2006.

NIB	Exc.	V.G.	Good	Fair	Poor
530	460	400	360	260	200

Buck Mark Standard Stainless URX

.22 LR semi-automatic. Stainless bull barrel 5.5". Weight 34 oz. Ambidextrous rubberized grip. Adjustable sights. Available in alloy steel. Introduced 2006.

NIB	Exc.	V.G.	Good	Fair	Poor
400	320	280	200	120	100

Buck Mark Plus Vision Americana Suppressor-Ready

Caliber: .22 LR. Capacity: 10-round magazine. Barrel: 5.875-in. Grip: UFX rubber overmolded grips. Sights: Optics-ready, adjustable Pro-Target with fiber-optic front sight. Length: 9.9 in. overall. Weight: 27 oz. unloaded. Finish: anodized red, white and blue. Features: Blowback operating system, aluminum barrel sleeve with lightening cuts, removable muzzle brake.

NIB	Exc.	V.G.	Good	Fair	Poor
800	750	700	—	—	—

Buck Mark Plus Vision Black/Gold Suppressor-Ready

Caliber: .22 LR. Capacity: 10-round magazine. Barrel: 5.875 in. Grip: UFX rubber overmolded grips. Sights: Optics-ready, adjustable Pro-Target with fiber-optic front sight. Length: 9.9 in. overall. Weight: 27 oz. unloaded. Finish: anodized black and gold. Features: Blowback operating system, aluminum barrel sleeve with lightening cuts, removable muzzle brake.

NIB	Exc.	V.G.	Good	Fair	Poor
720	640	590	—	—	—

Browning 1911-22

Scaled-down version of 1911A1. Chambered in .22 LR. Aluminum slide, alloy frame, blowback operated, with single-action trigger. Controls are standard 1911 including thumb and grip safeties. Other features include 10-round magazine, brown composite grips, matte blue finish. Weight 16 oz. Barrel length 4.25". Introduced in 2011. Compact model has 3.625" barrel. Note: Add $400 for Anniversary Edition.

NIB	Exc.	V.G.	Good	Fair	Poor
500	450	400	350	300	200

Browning 1911-22 A1 Polymer Frame w/Rail

Polymer frame variation with 4.25" or 3.625" barrel. Extended grip safety, stipled black laminate grip, accessory rail, skelton trigger and hammer. Weight from 13 to 14 oz. Other features are similar to standard 1911-22. Compact model has 3.625" barrel.

NIB	Exc.	V.G.	Good	Fair	Poor
580	500	450	400	300	200

Browning 1911-22 Polymer Desert Tan

This polymer variation has a two-tone Desert Tan/Black finish. Also offered with bright pink composite grips. Other features are similar to standard 1911-22. Compact model has 3.625" barrel.

NIB	Exc.	V.G.	Good	Fair	Poor
500	420	380	350	320	180

Browning 1911-22 Black Label

Polymer frame with black laminated and stippled grips, checkered front strap, matte black finish, commander-style hammer, combat sights, optional Picatinny rail, suppressor ready. Also offered with suppressor-ready extended barrel and G-10 black/gray grips. Compact model has 3.625" barrel and available with Picatinny rail and suppressor-ready feature. Note: Add $100 for suppressor-ready and rail models.

NIB	Exc.	V.G.	Good	Fair	Poor
560	500	400	300	250	200

Browning 1911-380 Medallion Pro

Similar to 1911-22 Black Label Pro series except with two-tone finish and rosewood grips. Introduced in 2017.

NIB	Exc.	V.G.	Good	Fair	Poor
580	540	460	420	320	270

Browning 1911-380

Similar to 1911-22 models, except chambered for .380 ACP and slide is made of steel instead of an alloy as in the .22 version. Extended and ambidextrous thumb safety, extended slide release and grip safety. Introduced in 2015.

NIB	Exc.	V.G.	Good	Fair	Poor
580	480	400	320	250	200

Browning 1911-380 Black Label Pro Series

Pro model features choice of night sights or 3-dot combat sights, G10 composite grips, black slide finish and Picatinny rail. Pro Stainless has same features plus stainless slide, satin silver finish. Medallion Pro has checkered rosewood grips with gold Buckmark logo, blackened stainless finish and two magazines. Pro compact versions have same features and a 3.625" barrel.

NIB	Exc.	V.G.	Good	Fair	Poor
680	600	520	450	350	250

Browning 1911-380 Black Label

Has a polymer frame, with features similar to 1911-22 Black Label. Pro model (shown) has rail, night sights and G-10 black/gray grips. Compact model offered, with limited production.

NIB	Exc.	V.G.	Good	Fair	Poor
560	500	460	370	300	280

SHOTGUNS

SUPERPOSED SHOTGUNS

Series of over/under double-barrel shotguns. Chambered for 12-, 20-, 28-gauge and .410 bore. Offered with ventilated rib barrels from 26.5" to 32" in length. Features various choke combinations. Shotgun built on boxlock action. Features double-/single-selective triggers. Automatic ejectors. A number of versions offered that differ in amount of ornamentation and quality of materials and workmanship utilized in manufacture. Values for small-bore models are generally higher. Series introduced in 1930. Manufactured by Fabrique Nationale in Belgium. Factory restored guns or very fine non-factory restorations Superposed guns will bring close to factory original prices. Note: Extra factory installed barrels add $1000 to $2500 depending on grade of gun.

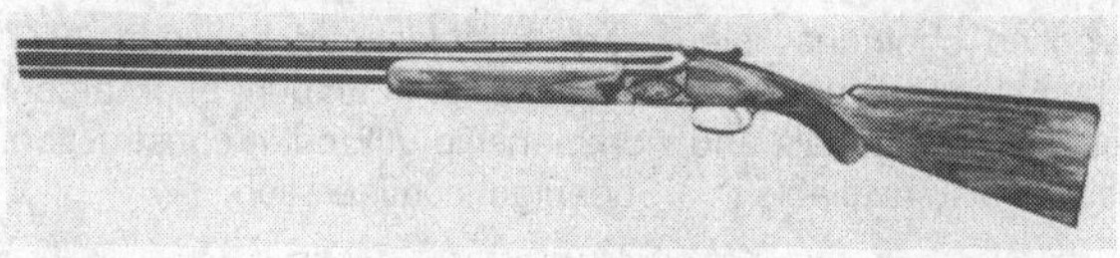

PRE-WAR SUPERPOSED, 1930-1940

Browning Superposed shotgun prices are divided into three different categories. First category for pre-war guns built from 1930 to 1940. These pre-war Superposed guns manufactured in 12-gauge only from serial number 1 to around 17,000. These shotguns were offered in four different grades: Grade I, Pigeon, Diana and Midas. Note: Add 15 percent for twin-single triggers; 10 percent for ventilated rib. Deduct 25 percent for recoil pads or shorter than standard stocks.

Grade I

Rock Island Auction Company, August, 2004

NIB	Exc.	V.G.	Good	Fair	Poor
—	2800	2500	1500	700	400

Pigeon

NIB	Exc.	V.G.	Good	Fair	Poor
—	6000	4800	3000	1500	800

Diana

NIB	Exc.	V.G.	Good	Fair	Poor
—	8500	7200	4750	2000	900

Midas

NIB	Exc.	V.G.	Good	Fair	Poor
—	12500	9500	5000	2500	1000

SUPERPOSED FROM 1947-1959

Second category of Superposed produced and sold from 1947 to 1959. Built in 12- and 20-gauge; as well as 28-gauge and .410 bore which were introduced in 1959. These shotguns were graded using a Roman numeral system instead of names. They are: Grade I, Grade II, Grade III, Grade IV, Grade V and Grade VI. Values listed are for 12-gauge. Add premium or deductions as listed. Number of 28-gauge and .410 bore guns sold in late 1959 number less than 100; Grade VI sold in North America unknown, but most likely very small. This is a very rare grade. Proceed with caution. Note: Add 60 percent for 20-gauge; 100 percent for 28-gauge and .410 (1959 only). Deduct 40 percent for trap; 10 percent for standard weight 12-gauge Grade I.

Grade I

NIB	Exc.	V.G.	Good	Fair	Poor
3700	2500	1400	900	300	250

Grade II

NIB	Exc.	V.G.	Good	Fair	Poor
6500	4500	2500	1200	600	380

Grade III

NIB	Exc.	V.G.	Good	Fair	Poor
7000	6000	3900	2200	750	450

Grade IV

NIB	Exc.	V.G.	Good	Fair	Poor
10000	8500	4500	2400	1200	550

Grade V

NIB	Exc.	V.G.	Good	Fair	Poor
10000	7500	4000	2400	1200	650

Grade VI

NIB	Exc.	V.G.	Good	Fair	Poor
17000	15000	8500	4000	2200	850

SUPERPOSED FROM 1960-1976

Browning Superposed shotguns built from 1960 to 1976 revert back to older grade names. They are Grade I, Pigeon, Pointer, Diana and Midas. These shotguns were available in 12-, 20-, 28-gauge and .410 bore. This last production period is a little more complicated due to manufacturing changes that some collectors consider important, such as round knobs and long tangs.

Prices listed reflect Superposed field guns produced from 1960 to 1965 in round pistol grip knob, with long triggerguard tang in 12-gauge. All other variations during this period one should consider:

Salt wood damage deduct a minimum of 60 percent; round knob short tang (circa 1966-1969) deduct 50 percent; flat knob short tang (circa 1969-1971) deduct 50 percent; flat knob long tang (circa 1971-1976) deduct 25 percent; New Style Skeet and Lightning Trap (recoil pad, flat knob, full beavertail forearm) with long triggerguard tang (1971-1976) deduct 35 percent; with short triggerguard tang deduct 40 percent; Broadway rib deduct an additional 10 percent; skeet chokes on field guns deduct 5 percent; recoil pads on 2.75" chambered field guns deduct 20 percent; Master engraver signed guns (Funken, Watrin, Vrancken) add 10 percent; shorter than standard stock length deduct 25 percent; barrel lengths of 32" add 10 percent; 20-gauge add 50 percent; 28-gauge add 100 percent; .410 bore add 60 percent. Note: These premiums could double for higher grade models in NIB or Excellent condition.

Grade I Standard Weight

NIB	Exc.	V.G.	Good	Fair	Poor
3000	2000	1500	700	500	250

Grade I Lightweight

NIB	Exc.	V.G.	Good	Fair	Poor
3200	2200	1600	800	600	300

Pigeon Grade

NIB	Exc.	V.G.	Good	Fair	Poor
6500	5500	3800	2000	1000	600

Pointer Grade—(Rare)

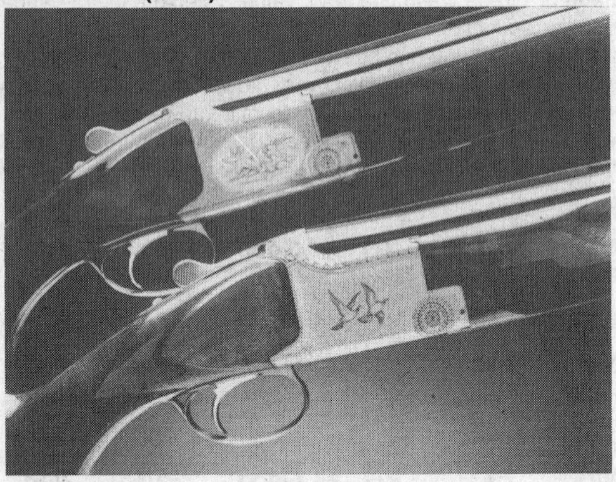

NIB	Exc.	V.G.	Good	Fair	Poor
10500	8050	5600	3000	2000	1000

Diana Grade

NIB	Exc.	V.G.	Good	Fair	Poor
11000	8250	5700	3000	2000	1000

Midas Grade

FN also built Exhibition Grades that were sold in this country under Browning name. Collectors consider a true Exhibition Grade as one not having a "C" prefix in serial number. These particular guns are considered quite desirable and should be appraised on an individual basis. Superposed in this category can range in price from $10,000 to $20,000 depending on gauge, engraving coverage and options.

Second type of Exhibition Grade known as "C" type that was first sold in U.S. from about 1973 to 1977 and is so called because of "C" prefix in serial number. There were about 225 of these guns sold in U.S. They came in quite a few grades and some were specially ordered. Although lower grades are not considered by some to be true exhibitions (pre-C series) highest "C" series grades are a match to the best of older exhibitions. In 2000, an all option Superlight 2 barrel set with sideplates engraved by Vranken sold for $22,000. Generally depending on gun, prices will range between $6,000 and $25,000. These "C" grade guns should also be appraised individually.

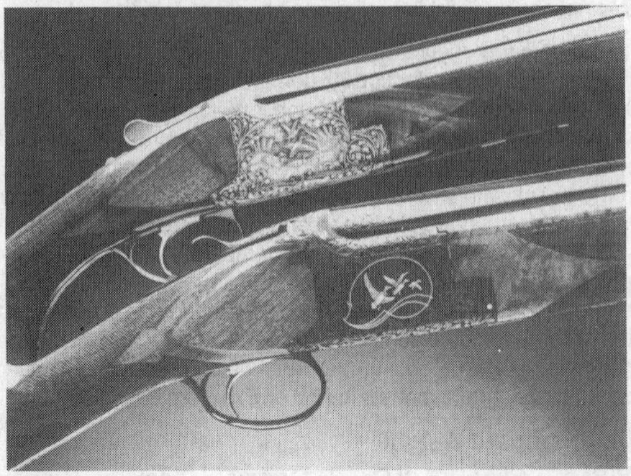

NIB	Exc.	V.G.	Good	Fair	Poor
15000	12000	9000	7000	5000	4000

Superposed Superlight

First introduced in 1967 in 12-gauge; 1969 in 20-gauge. Special order 28-gauge and .410 bore are also seen. Offered in 26.5" barrel lengths, with 27.5" barrels in 12-gauge and 28" barrels in smaller bores available on special order. Features rounded frame and straight-grip stock, with tapered, solid or ventilated rib barrels. Regular production on Superlight ended in 1976 for grades listed. Production did continue for Superlight in P-series beginning in 1977. Note: Add 50 percent premium for 20-gauge; 100 percent premium for 28-gauge; 30 percent premium for .410 bore.

Grade I

NIB	Exc.	V.G.	Good	Fair	Poor
4500	3750	1800	700	500	250

Pigeon Grade

NIB	Exc.	V.G.	Good	Fair	Poor
7000	5900	4000	2500	1000	800

Pointer Grade—(Rare)

NIB	Exc.	V.G.	Good	Fair	Poor
11000	9000	6000	3500	2000	1000

Diana Grade

NIB	Exc.	V.G.	Good	Fair	Poor
11000	8500	6500	3500	2000	1000

Midas Grade

NIB	Exc.	V.G.	Good	Fair	Poor
15500	12000	9000	7000	5000	4000

SUPERPOSED PRESENTATION GRADE SERIES

Superposed shotguns listed were manufactured between 1977 and 1984 by FN in Belgium. Models listed differ in amount of ornamentation and quality of materials and workmanship utilized in construction. This series was also available in a Superlight configuration.

Note: Due to the tremendous variation of P-Series guns, prices here reflect Superlight configuration. An all option Superlight with checkered butt, oil-finish and three-piece forend will bring 25-30 percent more. For all other variations one should consider: Trap guns deduct 35 percent; new style skeet deduct 30 percent; skeet choked field guns deduct 5 percent; recoil pads on field guns deduct 30 percent; flat knob long tang hunting guns with no options deduct 35 percent; flat knob long tang hunting guns with all options add 25 percent; guns signed by J. Baerten add 5 percent; P-4V guns with no gold deduct 20 percent; hand filed ventilated rib add 5 percent; Presentation Grade guns with extra sets of barrels add approximately $1,500 to $2,500 depending on gauge and combination.

P1, P2, and P3 grades add premium listed:
20-gauge guns—55 percent.
28-gauge guns—100 percent.
.410 bore—30 percent.
P4 grade add premium listed:
20-gauge guns—55 percent.
28-gauge guns—100 percent.
.410 bore—40 percent.

Presentation 1 (without gold inlays)

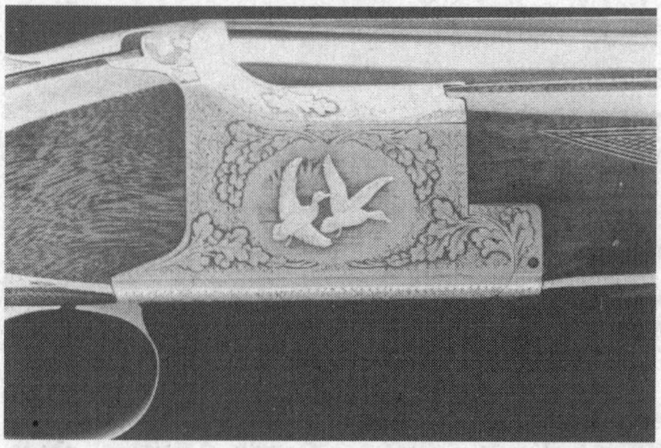

NIB	Exc.	V.G.	Good	Fair	Poor
4500	3700	1900	1000	600	500

Presentation 1 Gold-inlaid

NIB	Exc.	V.G.	Good	Fair	Poor
7500	6000	3250	1400	700	500

Presentation 2 (without gold inlays)

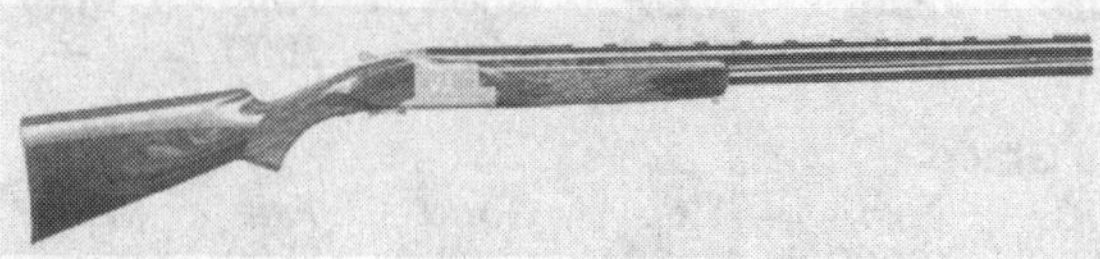

NIB	Exc.	V.G.	Good	Fair	Poor
6250	5250	3700	1800	1000	600

Presentation 2 Gold-inlaid

NIB	Exc.	V.G.	Good	Fair	Poor
10000	8500	4950	2500	1500	1000

Presentation 3 Gold-inlaid

Note: Early hand-engraved P3 models (approximately 25 produced) add 40 percent. These early guns are rare, proceed with caution.

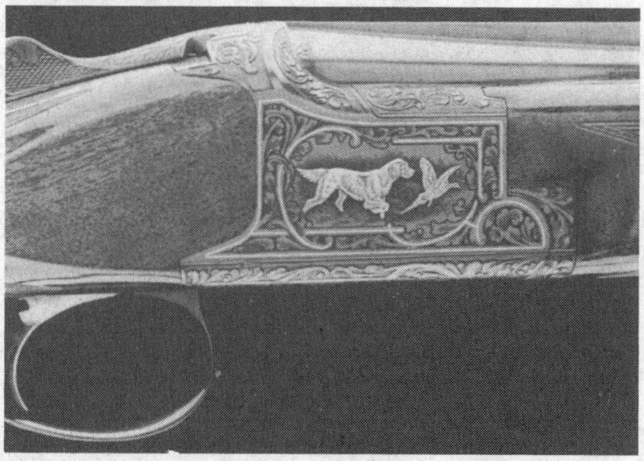

NIB	Exc.	V.G.	Good	Fair	Poor
12000	9500	5500	4000	2000	1300

Presentation 4 Gold-inlaid

Note: P4 Grade guns with no gold, deduct approximately 20 percent.

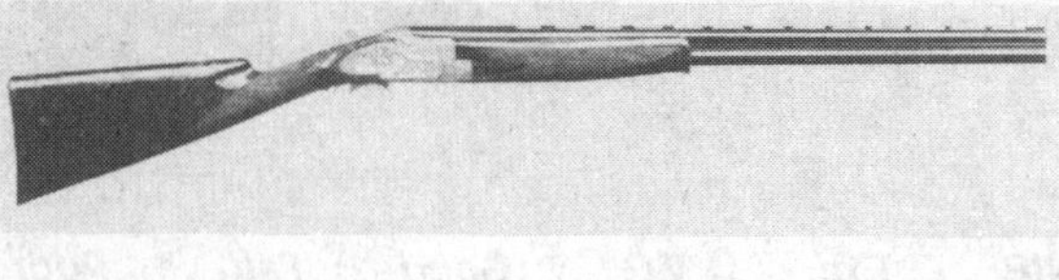

NIB	Exc.	V.G.	Good	Fair	Poor
17500	15000	9800	6750	5000	3500

SUPERPOSED WATERFOWL LIMITED EDITION SERIES

Model issued in three different versions: Mallard, Pintail and Black Duck. Each edition was limited to 500 guns, all in 12-gauge.

1981 Mallard Issue

NIB	Exc.	V.G.	Good	Fair	Poor
9500	7000	4900	3300	1900	1100

1982 Pintail Issue

NIB	Exc.	V.G.	Good	Fair	Poor
9500	7000	4900	3300	1900	1100

1983 Black Duck Issue

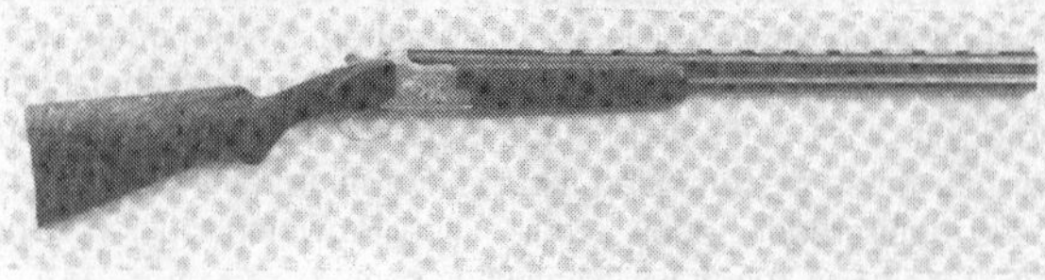

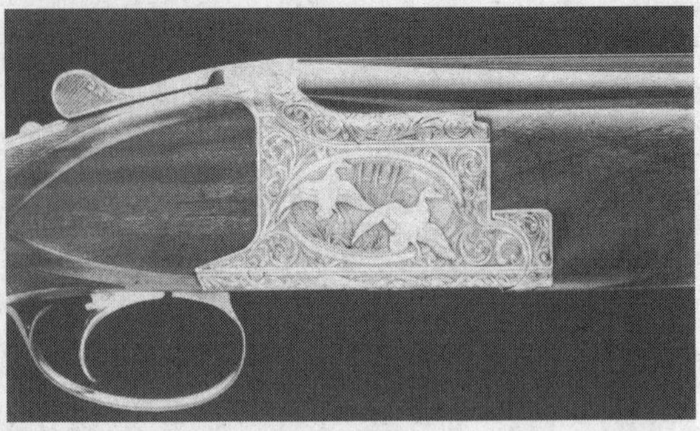

NIB	Exc.	V.G.	Good	Fair	Poor
10000	7000	4900	3300	1900	1100

Bicentennial Model

Produced in 1976 to commemorate 200 year Anniversary of America. Total of 53 guns built in this special edition. All of these Superposed were 12-gauge, with 28" barrels. Each was numbered for one of fifty states plus District of Columbia. Two additional guns were built for Smithsonian Institution and Liege Firearms Museum. All were fitted with side plates, with gold inlays. To reflect their true value, guns must be in unfired condition, in their original case and with all papers.

NIB	Exc.	V.G.	Good	Fair	Poor
15000	9000	5950	2750	1500	1000

FN/BROWNING SUPERPOSED

Number of FN Browning Superposed B-25 shotguns were imported into this country by Browning in various grades. These Superposed were intended originally for FN's European market. There are a large number of variations and grades. It is strongly suggested that an expert appraisal be sought prior to sale. These guns are marked with both Browning and FN barrel address.

Classic

Produced about 2,500 guns in 1986. Offered in 20-gauge, with 26" barrels. Silver gray receiver, with engraving.

NIB	Exc.	V.G.	Good	Fair	Poor
4000	3200	2650	2000	800	300

Gold Classic

Similar to above. More finely finished. Engraved with gold inlays. About 350 built in 1986.

NIB	Exc.	V.G.	Good	Fair	Poor
9000	7500	5000	2450	1750	400

Custom Shop B25 & B125 Superposed

These special order Superposed models were available from the Browning Custom Shop from mid 1980s through 1990s for Model B25 and until 2004 for B125. Several grades were offered with different levels of engraving and wood quality, all in 12- or 20-gauge. B125 models were assembled in Belgium, with components manufactured in other countries to hold down costs. B25s were made entirely in Belgium. Values shown here are for these discontinued models. For information on current Superposed high-grade models, contact the Browning Custom Shop at 801-876-2711 or on line at www.browning.com.

B-125 Hunting or Sporting Clays Model

A-Style Engraving

NIB	Exc.	V.G.	Good	Fair	Poor
3800	3200	2700	2000	1500	700

B-Style Engraving

NIB	Exc.	V.G.	Good	Fair	Poor
4100	3500	3000	2450	1800	800

C-Style Engraving

NIB	Exc.	V.G.	Good	Fair	Poor
4500	3800	3300	2750	2000	900

B-125 Trap Model

C-Style Engraving

NIB	Exc.	V.G.	Good	Fair	Poor
4800	4000	3500	2950	2000	900

B-25

Grade 1

NIB	Exc.	V.G.	Good	Fair	Poor
10000	8000	6200	4500	2500	—

Pigeon Grade

NIB	Exc.	V.G.	Good	Fair	Poor
14000	11800	8500	6700	2500	—

Pointer Grade

NIB	Exc.	V.G.	Good	Fair	Poor
15500	12000	9800	7500	3000	—

Diana Grade

NIB	Exc.	V.G.	Good	Fair	Poor
16500	13000	10800	8400	3500	—

Midas Grade

NIB	Exc.	V.G.	Good	Fair	Poor
17500	13800	11300	9000	3500	—

Custom Shop BSL

Side-by-side equipped with Browning sidelock barrel, Holland & Holland-type locks, with double trigger and automatic ejectors. Assembled and finished by Labeau-Courally. Offered in 12- and 20-gauge. Engraved grayed or case colored receiver. Introduced into Browning product line in 2001.

Case Colored Receiver (BSL Grade LC1)

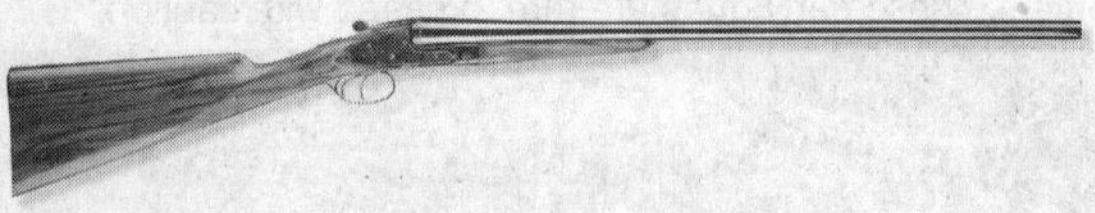

NIB	Exc.	V.G.	Good	Fair	Poor
15000	12500	9000	—	—	—

Engraved Gray Receiver (BSL Grade LC2)

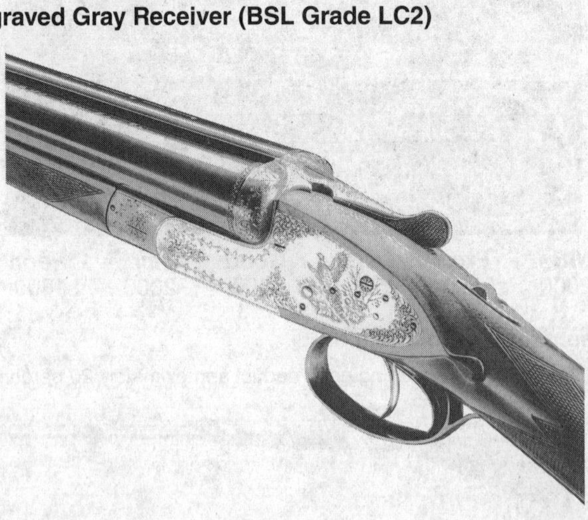

NIB	Exc.	V.G.	Good	Fair	Poor
18000	16000	12500	—	—	—

Liege

Over/under shotgun chambered for 12-gauge. Offered with 26.5", 28" or 30" ventilated rib barrels and various choke combinations. Features boxlock action, with non-selective single trigger and automatic ejectors. Finish blued, with checkered walnut stock. Approximately 10,000 manufactured between 1973 and 1975. U.S. versions marked Browning Arms Company on barrel.

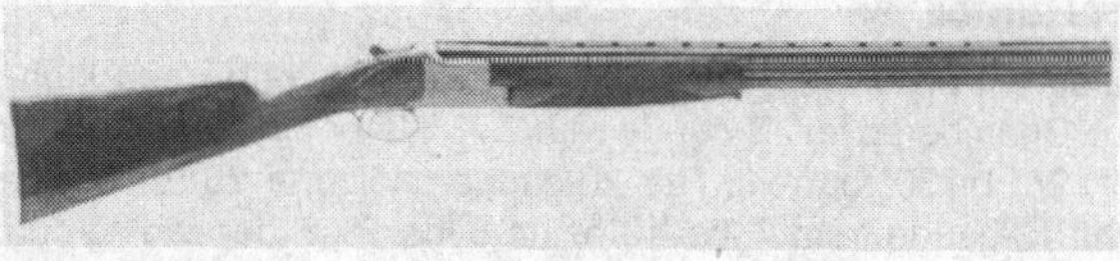

NIB	Exc.	V.G.	Good	Fair	Poor
1500	850	650	450	300	200

B27

Improved version of Liege. Was imported into U.S., some without Browning Arms Company markings and only FN barrel address. Others may have both barrel addresses. Offered in a number of variations that differed in amount of ornamentation and quality of materials and workmanship utilized. Features same action as Liege over/under gun.

Standard

NIB	Exc.	V.G.	Good	Fair	Poor
1200	950	650	350	250	200

Deluxe

NIB	Exc.	V.G.	Good	Fair	Poor
1600	1200	850	500	350	250

Deluxe Trap

NIB	Exc.	V.G.	Good	Fair	Poor
1600	1200	850	450	300	250

Deluxe Skeet

NIB	Exc.	V.G.	Good	Fair	Poor
1600	1200	850	450	300	250

Grand Deluxe

NIB	Exc.	V.G.	Good	Fair	Poor
2000	1500	1000	650	500	400

City of Liege Commemorative

250 manufactured.

NIB	Exc.	V.G.	Good	Fair	Poor
2500	1650	1000	600	450	300

ST-100

Over/under trap gun. Features separated barrels, with adjustable point of impact. Chambered for 12-gauge. Has 30" or 32" barrel, with full choke and floating ventilated rib. Features single trigger and automatic ejectors. Finish blued, with checkered walnut stock. Manufactured by FN between 1979 and 1981.

NIB	Exc.	V.G.	Good	Fair	Poor
3750	2700	1800	1000	700	400

CITORI SERIES

Over/under double-barrel shotgun chambered for all gauges. Offered with ventilated rib barrels of 26" through 30" in length. Has boxlock action, with single-selective trigger and automatic ejectors. Various grades differ in amount of ornamentation and quality of materials and workmanship utilized in construction. Series is manufactured in Japan by B.C. Miroku. Introduced in 1973. Note: All Citori models, add 15-20 percent premium for 28-gauge and .410; 30 percent for 16-gauge.

Grade I

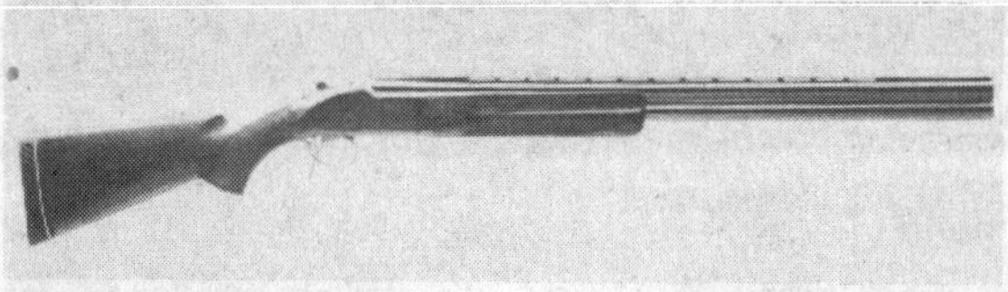

NIB	Exc.	V.G.	Good	Fair	Poor
1200	900	720	550	420	300

Upland Special—Grade I

Offered with straight-grip stock and 24" rib barrels. Available in 12- or 20-gauge. Weight 6 lbs. 11 oz. in 12-gauge; 6 lbs. in 20-gauge. Introduced in 1984.

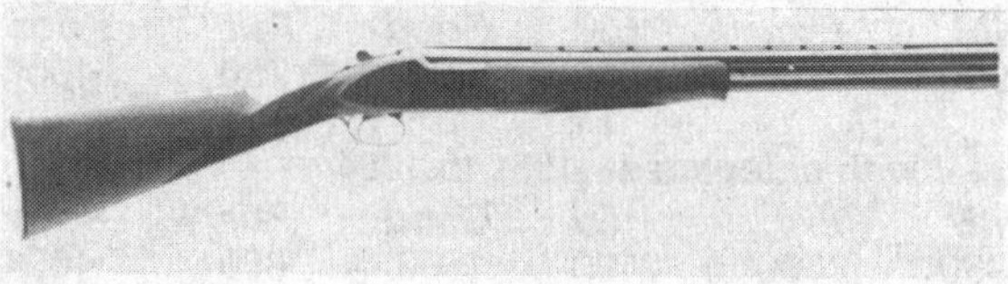

NIB	Exc.	V.G.	Good	Fair	Poor
1350	950	700	600	400	300

Grade II—1978 to 1983

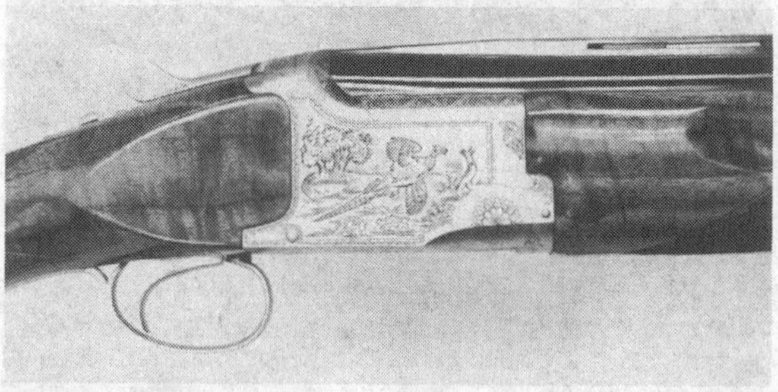

NIB	Exc.	V.G.	Good	Fair	Poor
—	1500	1300	1000	650	400

Grade II—Choke Tubes

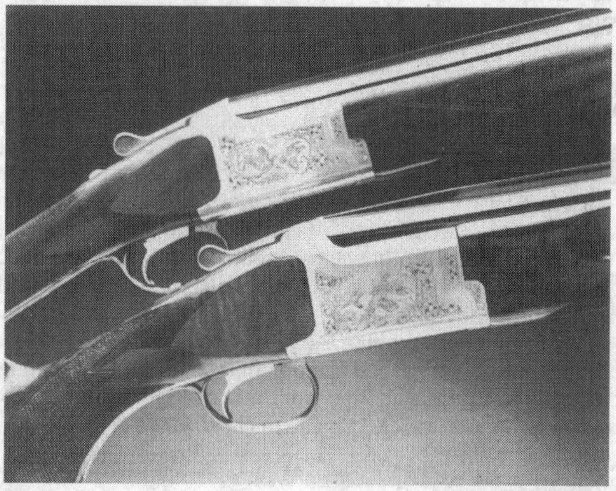

NIB	Exc.	V.G.	Good	Fair	Poor
1600	1400	1000	780	650	400

Grade V—1978 to 1984

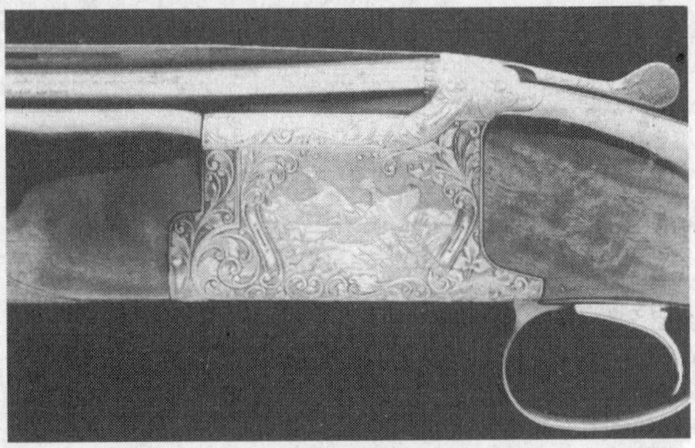

NIB	Exc.	V.G.	Good	Fair	Poor
2900	2300	1600	950	750	400

Grade V with sideplates—1981 to 1984

NIB	Exc.	V.G.	Good	Fair	Poor
2950	2500	2100	1500	800	400

Grade VI—Choke Tubes

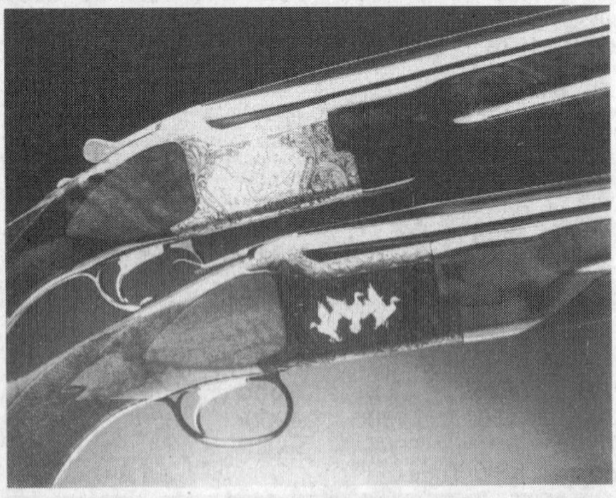

NIB	Exc.	V.G.	Good	Fair	Poor
1950	1650	1200	1000	750	500

Citori Field Sporting Grade VII

Gauge: 12 ga. 3 in., 20 ga. 3 in., 28 ga. 2.75 in., .410 bore 3 in. Barrels: 30 or 32 in., steel with ventilated rib. Weight: 7 lbs. 7oz.–8 lbs. 2 oz. Length: 47.5–49.5 in. Stock: Grade VI / VII Black Walnut with gloss oil finish and nameplate inlay for owner's initials. Features: Browning expands its high-end O/U with the addition of sub-gauge offerings. This shotgun comes from the Browning High Grade Program and shows silver bird and dog engraving. Triple Trigger System with three trigger shoes and gold-plated trigger, and triggerguard engraving. Silver Nitride receiver finish. Cut checkering at 20 LPI. Polished blued barrels with chrome plated chambers. Hi-Viz Pro Comp sight and ivory mid bead. Inflex recoil pad. Includes five extended Black Midas Grade choke tubes (F, IM, M, IC, SK).

NIB	Exc.	V.G.	Good	Fair	Poor
5490	—	—	—	—	—

Citori Trap Max

Gauge: 12 ga., 2.75 in. Barrels: 30 in., 32 in., ported with 5/16 to 7/16 adjustable ventilated rib. Weight: 9.0-9.2 lbs. Length: 47.75-49.75 in. Stock: Grade V/VI black walnut with gloss-oil finish. Features: Graco adjustable Monte Carlo comb. Buttplate adjusts for location and angle. Gra-Coil recoil reduction system increases comfort and offers length-of-pull adjustment. Adjustable rib allows for 50/50 or 90/10 POI. Semi-beavertail forearm with finger grooves, Pachmayr Decelerator XLT recoil pad. Close radius grip and palm swell. Triple Trigger System with three trigger shoes, gold-plated trigger, Hi-Viz Pro Comp sight, ivory mid-bead, polished blue barrels, Silver-Nitride receiver, chrome-plated chamber. Five Invector DS Extended choke tubes ideal for trap (F, LF, M, IM, IM).

NIB	Exc.	V.G.	Good	Fair	Poor
5350	—	—	—	—	—

Citori Hunter

Features full pistol grip stock, with beavertail forearm and high-gloss walnut. Chambered for 12-gauge with 2.75", 3" or 3.5" chambers. Choice of 26", 28" or 30" barrels. The 20-gauge choice of 26" or 28" barrels. Weight: 12-gauge from 7 lbs. 13 oz. to 8 lbs. 9 oz. depending on barrel length; 20-gauge about 6.75 lbs. Note: Add $75 for 3.5" models.

NIB	Exc.	V.G.	Good	Fair	Poor
1500	1100	850	650	550	450

Citori Sporting Hunter

Same features as Hunter, with exception of stock configuration. Sporting Hunter has Sporting model buttstock and Superposed-style forearm. Fitted with contoured sporting recoil pad. Introduced in 1998. Note: Add $75 for 3.5" models.

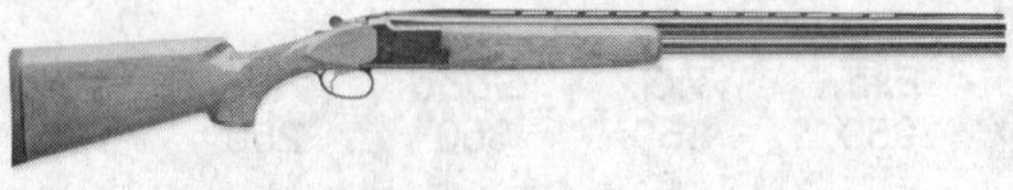

NIB	Exc.	V.G.	Good	Fair	Poor
1550	1400	1050	750	550	450

Citori Satin Hunter

Chambered for 12-gauge shells. Hunting-style stock. Choice of 26" or 28" barrels. Special satin wood finish, with matte black receiver and barrels. Offered in Grade I only. Weight about 8 lbs. Introduced in 1999. Note: Add $100 for 3.5" chamber.

NIB	Exc.	V.G.	Good	Fair	Poor
1250	1000	820	700	500	380

Citori Satin Hunter Micro Midas

Budget-priced Citori, with same features and handling qualities that have made other Citoris so popular. Available in 12- or 20-gauge, with 24" or 26" barrels. Satin-finished walnut stock, with 13" length of pull. Vector-Pro lengthened forcing cones. Weight: 6 lbs. 3 oz. to 6 lbs. 10 oz. New in 2011.

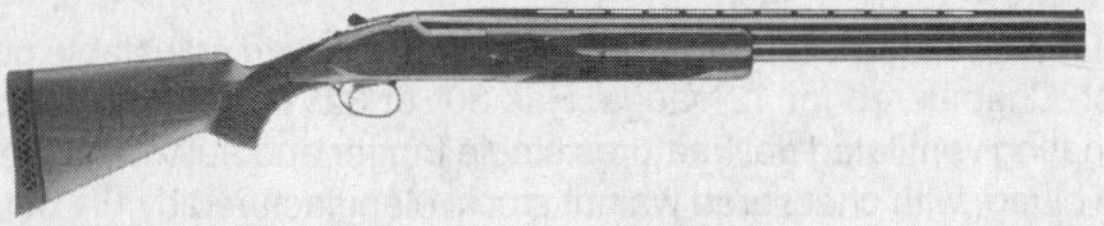

NIB	Exc.	V.G.	Good	Fair	Poor
1300	1050	900	800	500	300

Citori Lightning

Lightweight version that features a slimmer profile. Has checkered round-knob pistol grip stock. Offered in all gauges. Same barrel lengths as standard Citori. Features screw-in choke tubes known as Invectors. Introduced in 1988. Offered in 12-, 16-, 20-, 28-gauge and .410 bore. Weights are 6.5 lbs. to 8 lbs. depending on gauge and barrel length. Models differ in amount of ornamentation and quality of materials and workmanship utilized. Note: Add $300 for 28-gauge and .410 bore; $150 for 16-gauge.

Grade I

NIB	Exc.	V.G.	Good	Fair	Poor
1650	1200	900	600	450	380

Grade III

NIB	Exc.	V.G.	Good	Fair	Poor
2450	1900	1400	980	600	450

Grade IV

NIB	Exc.	V.G.	Good	Fair	Poor
2610	1950	1450	1020	650	500

Grade VI

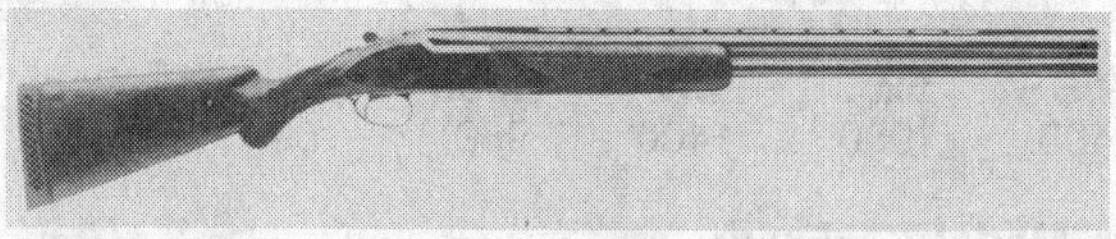

NIB	Exc.	V.G.	Good	Fair	Poor
3800	3000	2250	1500	700	550

Grade VII

NIB	Exc.	V.G.	Good	Fair	Poor
4800	4000	3000	2300	1900	1500

Citori Lightning Feather

Introduced in 1999. Features a lightweight alloy receiver. Offered in 12-gauge Grade I only, with choice of 26" or 28" barrels. Weight with 28" barrels about 7 lbs. 11 oz. In 2000, this model offered in 20-gauge, with 26" or 28" barrels and 3" chambers. Weight of 20-gauge about 6.5 lbs.

NIB	Exc.	V.G.	Good	Fair	Poor
1870	1400	980	600	400	300

Citori Lightning Feather Combo

Features 20- and 28-gauge, with 27" barrel. The 20-gauge with 3" chambers; 28-gauge with 2.75" chambers. Pistol grip stock. Weight about 6.25 lbs. Supplied with Browning luggage case. Introduced in 2000.

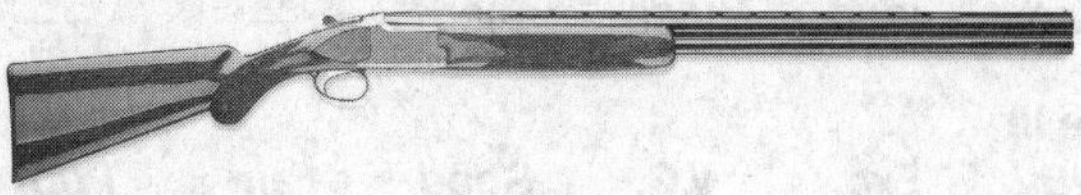

NIB	Exc.	V.G.	Good	Fair	Poor
3200	2400	2000	1500	1000	500

Citori Feather XS

Offered in 12-, 20-, 28-gauge and .410 bore. Has lightweight alloy receiver. Fitted with walnut stock, pistol grip, black recoil pad and schnabel forearm. Triple trigger system. Hi-Viz Comp sight system standard. Weight about 7 lbs. 12-gauge; 6.5 lbs. 20-gauge; 6 lbs. 28-gauge and .410 bore. Introduced in 2000.

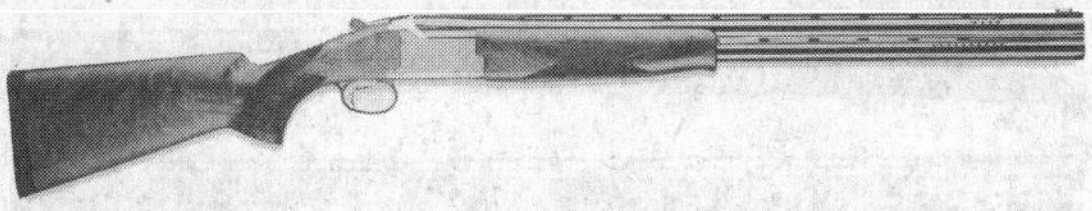

NIB	Exc.	V.G.	Good	Fair	Poor
2000	1500	1200	900	600	400

Citori Superlight Feather

Chambered for 12- or 20-gauge, with straight-grip stock and schnabel forearm. Has alloy receiver. Checkered walnut stock. Offered with 26" barrels. Weight about 6 lbs. Introduced in 2002.

NIB	Exc.	V.G.	Good	Fair	Poor
1940	1450	1100	800	550	350

Citori Super Lightning Grade I

Introduced in 2005. This 12- or 20-gauge features blued receiver, with gold line border. Checkered satin finished select walnut stock, with pistol grip and schnabel forearm. Barrels are 26" or 28", with choke tubes. Recoil pad on 12-gauge. Weight about 8 lbs. 12-gauge; 6.75 lbs. 20-gauge.

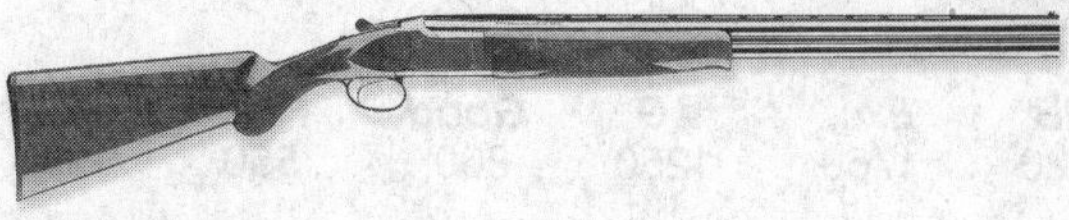

NIB	Exc.	V.G.	Good	Fair	Poor
1860	1400	1050	750	500	300

Citori Classic Lightning Grade I

Offered in 12- or 20-gauge, with choice of 26" or 28" ventilated rib barrels and choke tubes. Receiver scroll engraved on silver nitride finish. Checkered select walnut stock, with oil-finish. Forearm is Lightning style. Recoil pad on 12-gauge. Weight about 8 lbs. 12-gauge; 6.75 lbs. 20-gauge. Introduced in 2005.

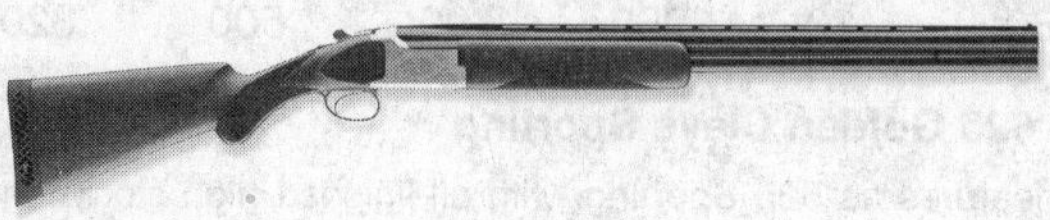

NIB	Exc.	V.G.	Good	Fair	Poor
1890	1420	1080	780	520	320

Citori Classic Lightning Feather Grade I

Introduced in 2005. Features high relief engraved alloy receiver. Chambered for 12- or 20-gauge. Fitted with 26" or 28" ventilated rib barrels and choke tubes. Checkered select stock, with schnabel forearm. Recoil pad on 12-gauge. Weight about 7 lbs. 12-gauge; 6.25 lbs. 20-gauge.

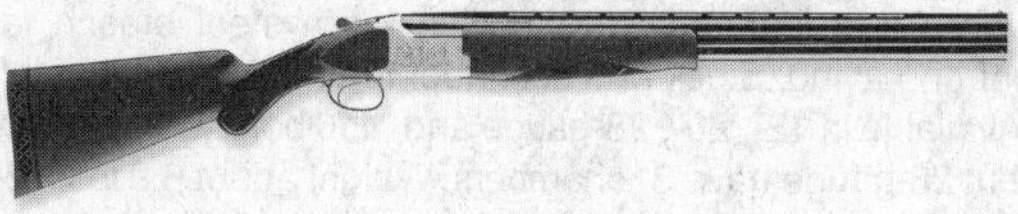

NIB	Exc.	V.G.	Good	Fair	Poor
1950	1450	1100	780	520	320

Citori High-Grade Side Plate Four Gauge Combo

Introduced 2019. Four-barrel sets in 12, 20, 28 gauge and .410 bore, full-coverage engraved side plates, gloss oil finish Grade VI/VIII walnut.

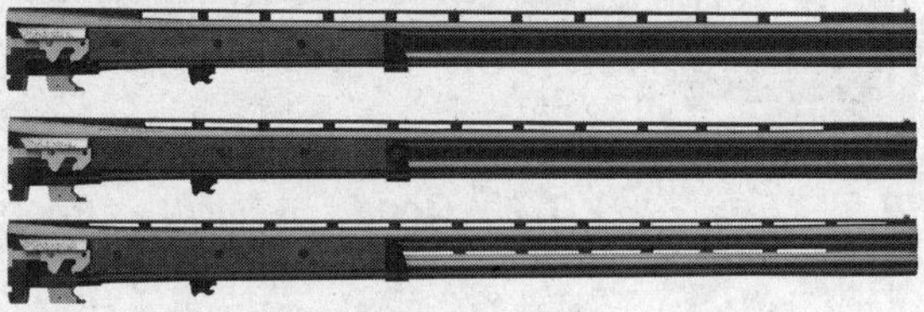

NIB	Exc.	V.G.	Good	Fair	Poor
10000	—	—	—	—	—

Citori 525 Sporting

Introduced in 2002. Chambered for 12- or 20-gauge. Fitted with choice of 28" or 30" ventilated rib ported barrels. Stock redesigned with Euro checkering pattern and more pronounced palm swell. Weight about 8 lbs. 12-gauge; 7 lbs. 20-gauge. In 2003 offered in both 28-gauge and .410 bore. Note: Add $275 for adjustable comb.

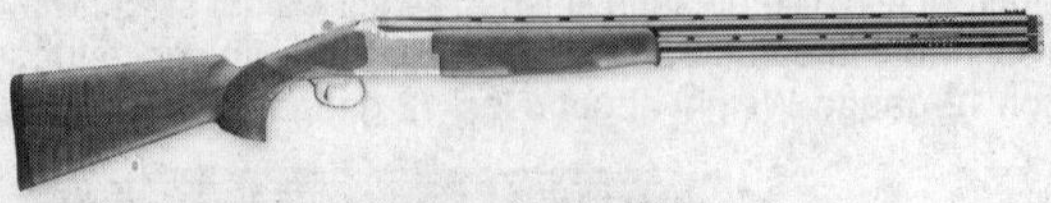

NIB	Exc.	V.G.	Good	Fair	Poor
2320	1750	1250	800	550	350

Citori 525 Field

As above, with choice of 26" or 28" barrels. Barrels are unported. Ventilated recoil pad. Introduced in 2002. In 2003 offered in both 28-gauge and .410 bore.

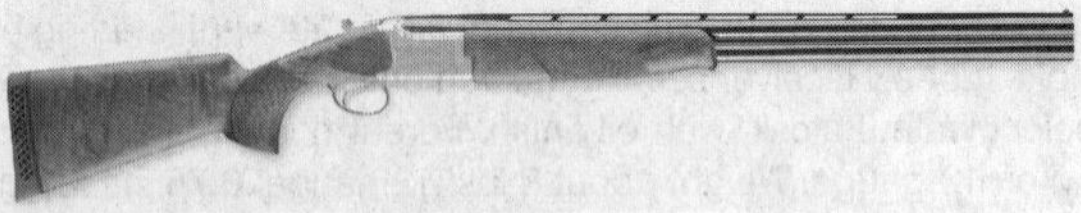

NIB	Exc.	V.G.	Good	Fair	Poor
1980	1480	950	700	500	320

Citori 525 Golden Clays Sporting

Same features as 525 Sporting, with oil-finished high stock, engraved receiver and gold inlays. In 2003 offered in both 28-gauge and .410 bore.

NIB	Exc.	V.G.	Good	Fair	Poor
4450	3250	2600	1950	1200	550

Citori 525 Feather

Lightweight Citori features alloy receiver, with steel breech face and high-relief engraving. Stock and schnabel forend Grade II/III oil-finished walnut. Available in 12-, 20-, 28-gauge and .410 bore, with 26" or 28" barrels. All but 28-gauge have 3" chambers. Weight about 6.9 lbs. 12-gauge; 5.5 to 5.7 lbs. in others. Three choke tubes.

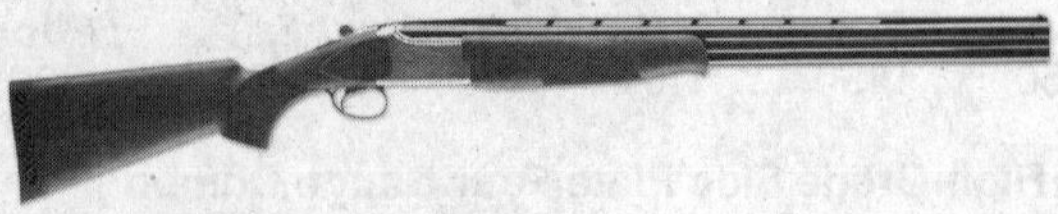

NIB	Exc.	V.G.	Good	Fair	Poor
2300	1750	1250	800	550	350

Citori 625 Sporting

Introduced in 2008. This 2.75" 12-gauge has 28", 30" or 32" ported barrels. Browning's Vector Pro lengthened forcing cones system. Stock and schnabel forend Grade III/IV walnut. Steel receiver has silver nitride finish, with high-relief engraving and gold embellishment. Five choke tubes included. Weight 7.9 to 8.2 lbs. Note: Add 5 percent for adjustable comb stock.

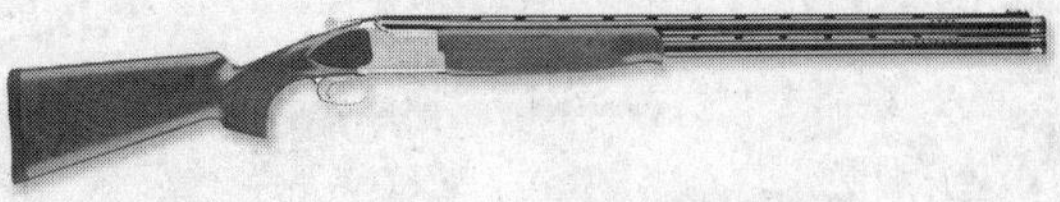

NIB	Exc.	V.G.	Good	Fair	Poor
3500	2700	1980	1200	850	550

Citori 625 Sporting Left-Hand

As above, but configured for left-hand shooters.

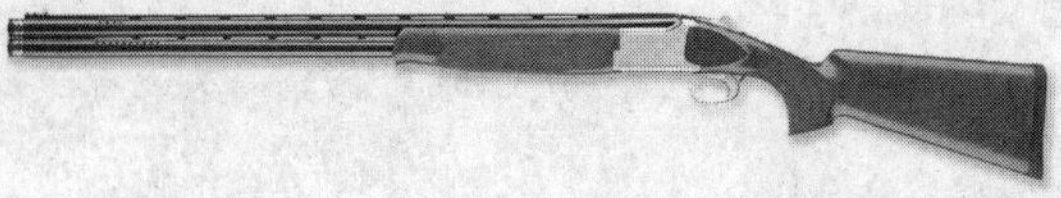

NIB	Exc.	V.G.	Good	Fair	Poor
3500	2700	1980	1200	850	550

Citori 625 Field

26" or 28" barrels, gloss oil-finish Grade II/III walnut stock and schnabel forend. Steel receiver, with silver nitride finish and high-relief engraving. Three choke tubes. Chambered for 12-, 20-, 28-gauge and .410. Weight: 7 lbs. 14 oz. to 6 lbs. 12 oz.

NIB	Exc.	V.G.	Good	Fair	Poor
2400	1900	1400	980	600	450

Citori Model 725 Field

Over/under in 12 or 20 gauge, with 28 gauge and .410 bore added in 2015, with 26", 28", and 30" barrels and Invector DS choke tubes. New action design has lower profile than other Citori models. Single-selective mechanical trigger, automatic ejectors, checkered Grade II/III walnut stock, with gloss finish and recoil pad. Silver nitride finish, with high relief engraving. Introduced in 2012. Higher grade models available with more engraving and higher grade wood. Weights range from 6.6 lbs. (20) to 7.5 lbs. (12-gauge, 30" barrel). All have 3" chambers except for 28 gauge at 2.75". Several variants are no longer in production, including 725 Sporting Grade V; 725 Sporting Long Length of Pull; 725 Sporting Long Length of Pull, Adjustable Comb; 725 Sporting Non-Ported; 725 Western Rose Sporting Clays — Limited Series; 725 Ol' West Sporting Clays — Limited Series; 725 Sporting Non-Ported, Adjustable Comb; 725 Sporting Grade VII; 725 Citori 725 Grade VII Small Gauge; 725 High Grade Trap — Grade V; 725 High Grade Trap — Grade VII; 725 Black Gold High Grade Edition — Sporting; 725 Skeet; 725 Skeet with Adjustable Comb; 725 S3 Sporting; 725 High Rib Sporting Left Hand; 725 High Rib Sporting Adjustable Left Hand; 725 Trap Left-Hand Adjustable Comb.

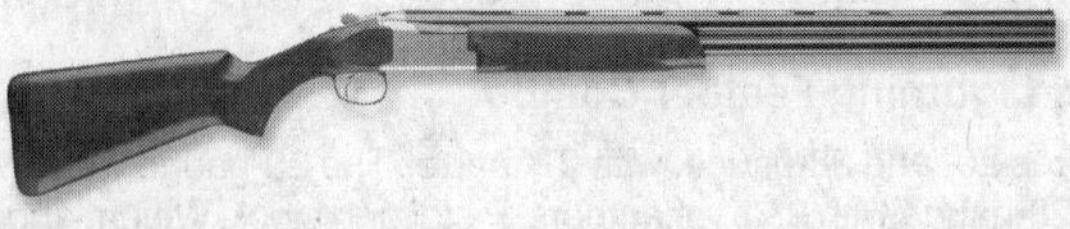

NIB	Exc.	V.G.	Good	Fair	Poor
2150	1750	1550	1400	—	—

Grade III

NIB	Exc.	V.G.	Good	Fair	Poor
3300	2750	—	—	—	—

Grade V

NIB	Exc.	V.G.	Good	Fair	Poor
5000	4600	—	—	—	—

Grade VI

NIB	Exc.	V.G.	Good	Fair	Poor
5350	4600	—	—	—	—

Grade VII Small Gauge

NIB	Exc.	V.G.	Good	Fair	Poor
5600	4900	—	—	—	—

725 Feather

Gauges: 12 ga., 3 in., 20 ga., 3 in. Barrels: 26 in., 28 in., with 0.25-in. ventilated rib. Weight: 5 lbs., 12 oz.-6 lbs., 9 oz. Length: 43.75-45.75 in. Stock: Grade II/III walnut with gloss-oil finish. Features: Lightweight aluminum-alloy receiver with steel breech face and hinge pin, Silver-Nitride finish. New accented engraving. Inflex recoil pad, ivory bead sight, gold-plated trigger. Ideal for hunting and sporting clays. Includes three Invector DS flush-mount choke tubes (F, M, IC).

NIB	Exc.	V.G.	Good	Fair	Poor
2480	2000	1900	1750	1600	—

Citori Model 725 Field - 725 Feather Superlight

Introduced 2019. Low-profile alloy receiver with steel breech face and hinge pin, engraved silver nitride finish, mechanical trigger system, straight grip stock with Schnabel forearm, oil finish Grade II/III walnut. Weighs 6.125 lbs. for 12-gauge model, 5.5 lbs. for 20 gauge.

NIB	Exc.	V.G.	Good	Fair	Poor
2350	2200	2000	1900	1750	1600

Citori Model 725 Field725 Skeet

NIB	Exc.	V.G.	Good	Fair	Poor
2800	2500	2000	1500	1000	700

Citori Model 725 Field - 725 Skeet w/adjustable comb

NIB	Exc.	V.G.	Good	Fair	Poor
3100	2800	2200	1600	1100	800

Citori Model 725 Sporting

NIB	Exc.	V.G.	Good	Fair	Poor
2800	2500	2000	1500	1000	700

Citori Model 725 Field - 725 Sporting Left Hand (2019)

NIB	Exc.	V.G.	Good	Fair	Poor
2700	2500	2100	1800	—	—

Citori Model 725 Sporting w/adjustable comb

NIB	Exc.	V.G.	Good	Fair	Poor
3100	2800	2200	1600	1100	800

Citori Model 725 Field - 725 Sporting Left Hand w/adjustable comb (2019)

NIB	Exc.	V.G.	Good	Fair	Poor
3100	2800	2200	1600	1100	800

Citori Model 725 Field - 725 High Rib Sporting

NIB	Exc.	V.G.	Good	Fair	Poor
3150	3000	—	—	—	—

Citori Model 725 Golden Clays

NIB	Exc.	V.G.	Good	Fair	Poor
4600	4000	3000	2200	1000	500

Citori Model 725 Field725 Trap

NIB	Exc.	V.G.	Good	Fair	Poor
3000	2700	2200	1750	1200	900

Citori Model 725 Field - 725 Pro Trap

NIB	Exc.	V.G.	Good	Fair	Poor
3500	3300	3100	2900	—	—

Citori Model 725 Field - 725 Pro Sporting

NIB	Exc.	V.G.	Good	Fair	Poor
3500	3300	3100	2900	—	—

Citori Model 725 Trap Grade VII

NIB	Exc.	V.G.	Good	Fair	Poor
5600	5000	4200	3500	2000	900

Citori Model 725 Sporting Medallion High Grade

Gauge: 12 ga. 3 in. Barrels: 30 or 32 in., steel with floating 5/16 to 7/16-in. rib. Weight: 7 lbs. 8 oz.–7 lbs. 10 oz. Length: 48–50 in. Stock: Grade IV Turkish Walnut with gloss oil finish. Features: Browning expands the higher end of the Citori family. Extensive receiver engraving with gold enhancement. Cut checkering at 20 LPI and right-hand palm swell. HiViz Pro-Comp front sight. Chrome-plated chamber. Tapered locking bolt and full-width hinge pin. Triple trigger system with three included shoes. Blued receiver finish and polished blued barrels. Inflex recoil pad. Gold-plated trigger. Name plate inlay for owner's initials. Includes five Invector DS extended choke tubes (F, IM, M, IC, SK) and Negrini locking hard case.

NIB	Exc.	V.G.	Good	Fair	Poor
6830	—	—	—	—	—

Citori CX

Introduced 2019. Crossover design with lightweight barrels, vented high post rib and side ribs, Vector Pro forcing cones. Triple Trigger System offers three optional trigger shoe profiles, one supplied. Steel receiver with high-polished blue finish, new Citori CX logo on sides of receiver in gold. 60/40 point of impact, 3" chromed chamber. Grade II American walnut stock, gloss finish; Inflex recoil pad. Vector Pro lengthened forcing cones; three Midas grade extended Invector-Plus choke tubes (F, M, IC); ivory front and mid bead sights. 28", 30", 32" barrels.

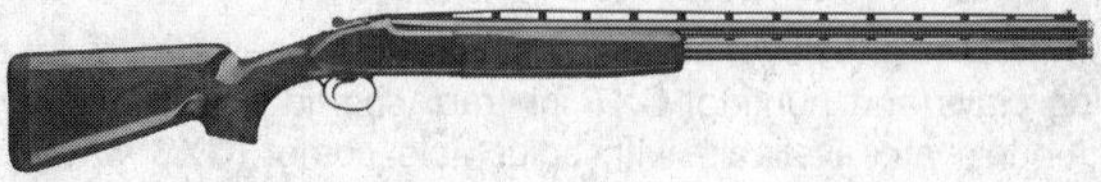

NIB	Exc.	V.G.	Good	Fair	Poor
1820	1650	1480	1250	—	—

Citori CX with Adjustable Comb

Introduced 2019. Crossover design with lightweight barrels, vented high post rib and side ribs, Vector Pro forcing cones and adjustable comb.

NIB	Exc.	V.G.	Good	Fair	Poor
2250	1950	1800	1550	—	—

Citori CXS Micro

Introduced 2019. Crossover design with lightweight profile barrels, compact 13" length of pull, flat point of impact, vented rib and side ribs, Vector Pro forcing cones and more.

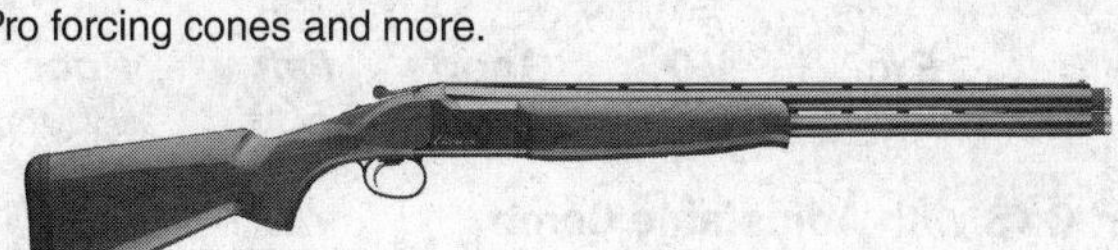

NIB	Exc.	V.G.	Good	Fair	Poor
1800	—	—	—	—	—

Citori White Lightning — New Production

Introduced 2019. Steel receiver "in the white" with intricate engraving, polished blued barrels, oil finish grade III/IV walnut, extended black band Invector-Plus choke tubes. For .410 bore and 28 ga., NIB: 2400

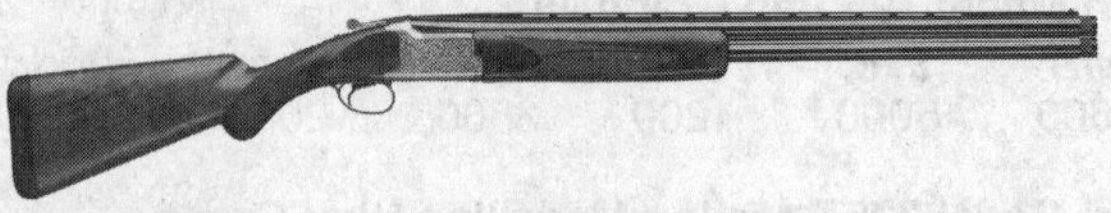

NIB	Exc.	V.G.	Good	Fair	Poor
2050	1700	1580	1400	—	—

Citori Gran Lightning — New Production

Introduced 2019. Lightning style Grade V/VI satin finish walnut stock, high polish blued barrel and high relief engraved receiver, ivory front and mid-bead, Midas grade Invector-Plus extended black band chokes.

NIB	Exc.	V.G.	Good	Fair	Poor
2900	—	—	—	—	—

Citori Feather Lightning — New Production

Introduced 2019. High-strength and lightweight alloy receiver with steel breech face and hinge pin, intricate engraving, polished blued barrels, oil finish grade III/IV walnut, extended black band Invector-Plus choke tubes.

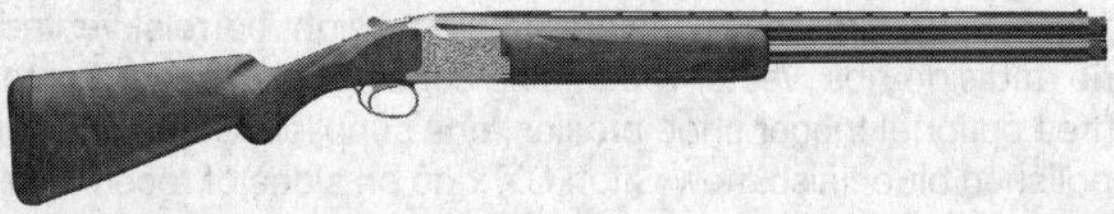

NIB	Exc.	V.G.	Good	Fair	Poor
2500	—	—	—	—	—

Citori CXS, CXT

Crossover design to cover several shooting disciplines. CXS is for skeet, sporting clays and hunting. CXT for trap, sporting clays and hunting. Both models are available with adjustable comb. (CXS w/adjustable comb is shown). Features include Grade II American walnut stock, semi-beavertail forend with finger grooves and Inflex recoil pad. All CX models have 32" barrels with lengthened forcing cones, three Invector-Plus Midas Grade choke tubes, ventilated top and side ribs, ivory front and middle bead sights. CXT barrels are ported. New in 2018. Note: Add $350 for adjustable comb.

Citori CXS

Crossover design with lightweight profile barrels, flat point of impact, vented rib and side ribs, Vector Pro forcing cones.

NIB	Exc.	V.G.	Good	Fair	Poor
1850	1450	1150	900	500	300

Citori CXS with Adjustable Comb

NIB	Exc.	V.G.	Good	Fair	Poor
2200	1900	1750	1500	—	—

Citori CXS, CXTCXT

High-rib trap model.

NIB	Exc.	V.G.	Good	Fair	Poor
1880	1500	1200	950	500	300

Citori CXS 20/28 Ga. Combo

NIB	Exc.	V.G.	Good	Fair	Poor
3620	—	—	—	—	—

Citori CXT with Adjustable Comb

NIB	Exc.	V.G.	Good	Fair	Poor
2300	—	—	—	—	—

Citori Esprit

Introduced in 2002. Features removable decorative sideplates, schnabel forearm and high-grade walnut stock. Offered in 12-gauge only, with 28" ventilated rib barrels. Weight about 8.25 lbs.

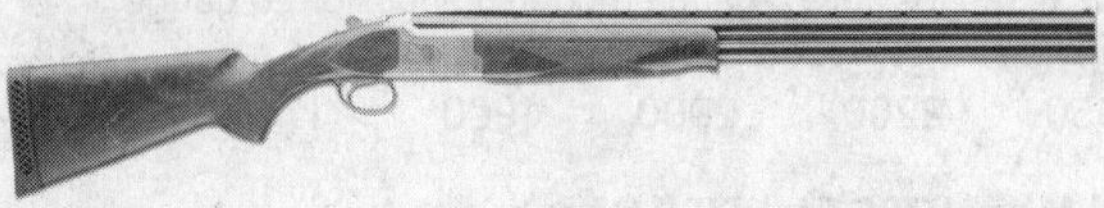

NIB	Exc.	V.G.	Good	Fair	Poor
2450	1980	1400	980	600	450

Citori Sporting Clays

Specifically designed for sporting clay shooting. Offered in 12-gauge only. Each model is back-bored, ported and fitted with Invector-Plus choke tubes. Barrels are chrome-plated. Receiver blued, with gold inscription. Pigeon Grade has gold detailing and high grade gloss walnut stock. Signature Grade features red and black print on stock, with gold decals. Trigger is adjustable to three length of pull positions. Comes with three interchangeable trigger shoes. Each model fitted with rubber recoil pad.

NIB	Exc.	V.G.	Good	Fair	Poor
2450	1980	1400	980	600	450

Citori Lightning Sporting

Features rounded pistol grip and Lightning forearm, with choice of high or low ventilated rib. Chambered for 3" shells. Offered in 28" or 30" barrels. Weight about 8.5 lbs. Introduced in 1989.

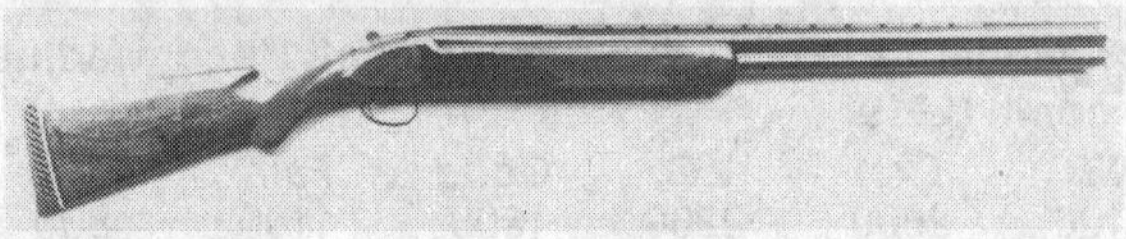

NIB	Exc.	V.G.	Good	Fair	Poor
1400	1000	800	600	450	300

Pigeon Grade

NIB	Exc.	V.G.	Good	Fair	Poor
1450	1100	900	650	450	300

Golden Clays

First introduced in 1994.

NIB	Exc.	V.G.	Good	Fair	Poor
2800	2250	1650	900	450	300

Citori Privilege

High-grade model features game scene engraved sideplates, unique checkering pattern oil-finish high-grade walnut stock, with pistol grip. Offered in 12-gauge only. Choice of 26" or 28" barrels. Weight about 8 lbs. Introduced in 2000. In 2001 a 20-gauge version, with 26" or 28" barrels was introduced. Discontinued in 2003.

Citori Privilege left side.

NIB	Exc.	V.G.	Good	Fair	Poor
4600	4000	3000	2500	1500	1000

Citori XS Sporting Clays

Introduced in 1999. Features silver nitride receiver, gold accents and European-style stock, with schnabel forend. Available in 12- or 20-gauge. Choice of 28", 30" or 32" barrels. Weight varies: 8 lbs. 12-gauge to 7 lbs. 20-gauge.

NIB	Exc.	V.G.	Good	Fair	Poor
2600	2050	1450	1000	620	480

Citori Ultra XS Skeet

Offered in 12-gauge only. Choice of 28" or 30" ported barrels. Chambered for 2.75" shells. Semi-beavertail forearm. Triple trigger system standard. Adjustable comb optional. Walnut stock, with pistol grip. Black recoil pad. Weight about 7.75 lbs. Introduced in 2000. In 2001 a 20-gauge version with 28" or 30" barrels was introduced. Note: Add $275 for adjustable comb.

NIB	Exc.	V.G.	Good	Fair	Poor
2540	1900	1380	950	600	450

Citori XS Special

12-gauge 2.75" chamber gun. Choice of 30" or 32" ventilated rib barrels, porting and extended choke tubes. Checkered walnut stock, with adjustable comb and pistol grip. Semi-beavertail forearm. Silver engraved receiver. Weight about 8.7 lbs.

NIB	Exc.	V.G.	Good	Fair	Poor
2820	2100	1550	1100	680	480

Citori Plus

Features adjustable point of impact from 3" to 12" above point of aim. Receiver on Grade I blued, with scroll engraving. Walnut stock is adjustable. Forearm is a modified beavertail style. Available in 30" or 32" barrels that are back-bored and ported. Non-ported barrels are optional. Weight about 9 lbs. 6 oz. Introduced in 1989.

Grade I

NIB	Exc.	V.G.	Good	Fair	Poor
1300	1080	750	500	400	300

Pigeon Grade

NIB	Exc.	V.G.	Good	Fair	Poor
1850	1500	950	700	500	300

Signature Grade

NIB	Exc.	V.G.	Good	Fair	Poor
1750	1450	950	700	500	300

Golden Clays

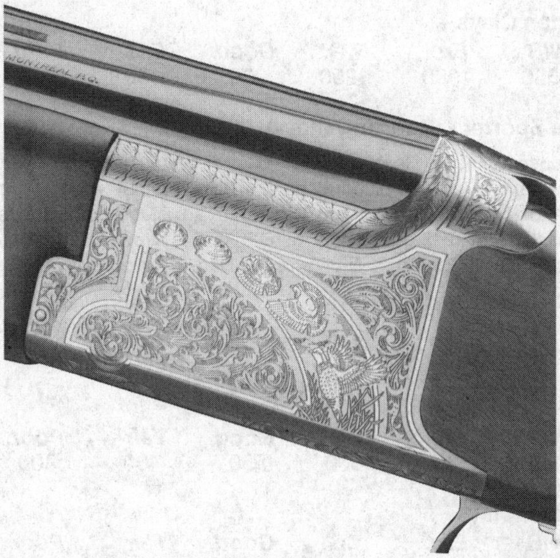

NIB	Exc.	V.G.	Good	Fair	Poor
2850	2300	1500	900	450	300

Citori Trap Combination Set

Version offered in Grade I only. Features 34" single-barrel and 32" set of over/under barrels. Furnished in fitted case. Discontinued.

NIB	Exc.	V.G.	Good	Fair	Poor
—	1950	1350	950	800	700

Citori CX White

NIB	Exc.	V.G.	Good	Fair	Poor
2150	—	—	—	—	—

Citori CX White Adjustable

NIB	Exc.	V.G.	Good	Fair	Poor
2650	—	—	—	—	—

Citori CX Micro

NIB	Exc.	V.G.	Good	Fair	Poor
2250	—	—	—	—	—

Citori CXS White

NIB	Exc.	V.G.	Good	Fair	Poor
2190	—	—	—	—	—

Citori CXT White

NIB	Exc.	V.G.	Good	Fair	Poor
2250	—	—	—	—	—

GTI Model

Features 13mm wide rib ventilated side ribs, pistol grip stock, semi-beavertail forearm. Offered in 28" or 30" barrel. Weight about 8 lbs. Not offered in Pigeon Grade. Introduced in 1989.

Grade I

NIB	Exc.	V.G.	Good	Fair	Poor
1200	980	750	600	450	300

Signature Grade

NIB	Exc.	V.G.	Good	Fair	Poor
1200	980	750	600	450	300

Golden Clays

NIB	Exc.	V.G.	Good	Fair	Poor
2580	1980	1250	900	450	300

Ultra Sporter - (Sporting Clays)

Introduced in 1995. Replaces GTI model. Features 10mm to 13mm tapered rib. Offered with blued or gray receiver. Walnut stock, with pistol grip and semi-beavertail forearm. Fitted with adjustable comb and length of pull. Offered in 12-gauge only, with 28" or 30" barrels. Average weight 8 lbs. Note: Add $200 to NIB price for Ultra Sporters with adjustable comb.

NIB	Exc.	V.G.	Good	Fair	Poor
1550	1200	800	550	400	300

Golden Clays

NIB	Exc.	V.G.	Good	Fair	Poor
2900	2300	1600	1100	750	400

Citori Superlight

Lighter-weight version of Citori. Chambered for all gauges. Offered with same features as Lightning Series. Grades differ in amount of ornamentation, quality of materials and workmanship utilized. Series introduced in 1983.

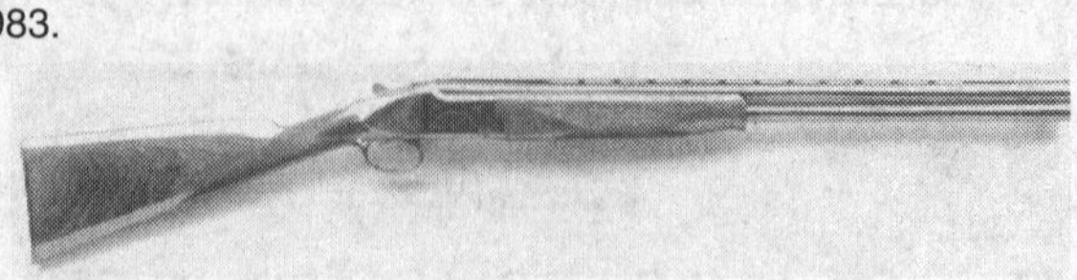

NIB	Exc.	V.G.	Good	Fair	Poor
5600	4900	—	—	—	—

Citori Superlight Feather

Introduced in 1999. Features straight-grip stock, with schnabel forend. Lightweight alloy receiver. Offered in 12-gauge Grade I only. Choice of 26" or 28" barrels. Weight with 28" barrels about 6 lbs. 6 oz.

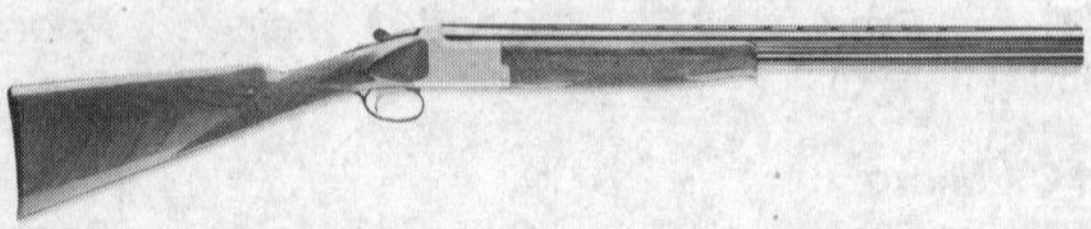

NIB	Exc.	V.G.	Good	Fair	Poor
1700	1250	900	600	480	350

Micro Lightning

Offered in 20-gauge only. Has reduced dimensions for smaller shooters. Available with 24" ventilated rib barrels. Weight 6 lbs. 3 oz. Introduced in 1991.

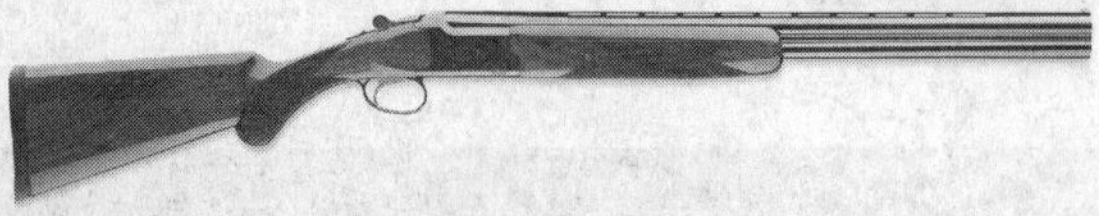

NIB	Exc.	V.G.	Good	Fair	Poor
1100	900	700	600	400	300

Gran Lightning

Essentially a Grade I Lightning, with high grade select walnut stock and satin finish. Receiver and barrels blued. Offered in 12- and 20-gauge. Choice of 26" or 28" ventilated rib barrels. Choke tubes standard. Weight about 8 lbs. 12-gauge; 6 lbs. 11 oz. 20-gauge. Introduced in 1990. In 2004, 28-gauge and .410 bore were added. Discontinued in 2005.

NIB	Exc.	V.G.	Good	Fair	Poor
2000	1600	1200	1000	750	600

Gran Lightning 16 Gauge

This model was reintroduced in 2015, only in 16-gauge. Has Grade V/VI wood and high relief engraved receiver

NIB	Exc.	V.G.	Good	Fair	Poor
2400	2100	—	—	—	—

Citori White Lightning

Introduced in 1998. Features silver nitride scroll engraved receiver. Offered in 3" 12- and 20-gauge. Choice of 26" or 28" barrels. In 2004 available in 28-gauge and .410 bore. Weight about 8 lbs. 12-gauge; 6.8 lbs. 20-gauge. Invector-Plus chokes standard. Lightning-style stock. Note: Add $75 for 28-gauge and .410 models.

NIB	Exc.	V.G.	Good	Fair	Poor
1500	1200	950	700	600	380

Citori White Upland Special

Introduced in 2000. Features shortened straight-grip stock, schnabel forearm and 24" barrel. Fitted with 2.75" barrel. Chambered for 12- and 20-gauge only. Weight about 6.75 lbs.

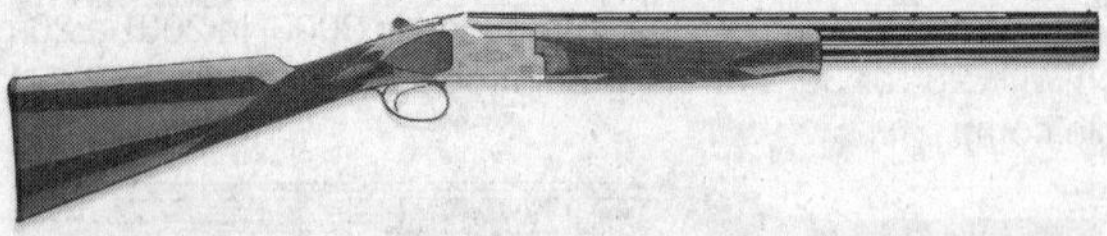

NIB	Exc.	V.G.	Good	Fair	Poor
1650	1200	980	720	620	400

Citori Skeet

Series of guns chambered for all gauges. Designed for competition skeet shooting. Similar to standard Citori, with high-post target rib and 26" or 28" barrels. Versions differ in amount of engraving, quality of materials and workmanship utilized.

Grade I

NIB	Exc.	V.G.	Good	Fair	Poor
1000	920	750	550	420	350

Grade II

Discontinued 1983.

NIB	Exc.	V.G.	Good	Fair	Poor
—	1000	900	750	450	300

Grade III

NIB	Exc.	V.G.	Good	Fair	Poor
1500	1200	900	750	450	300

Grade V

Discontinued 1984.

NIB	Exc.	V.G.	Good	Fair	Poor
1600	1200	900	750	450	300

Grade VI

NIB	Exc.	V.G.	Good	Fair	Poor
2000	1750	1200	900	450	300

Golden Clays

First introduced in 1994.

NIB	Exc.	V.G.	Good	Fair	Poor
2400	2000	1500	900	450	300

3 Gauge Sets

Consists of 20-, 28-gauge and .410 bore. Interchangeable 28" ventilated rib barrels. Introduced in 1987.

Grade I

NIB	Exc.	V.G.	Good	Fair	Poor
2600	2100	1500	1250	1000	800

Grade III

NIB	Exc.	V.G.	Good	Fair	Poor
3400	2900	2300	1750	1300	1000

Grade VI

NIB	Exc.	V.G.	Good	Fair	Poor
3500	3000	2500	2000	1500	1100

4 Gauge Sets

Set has 12-, 20-, 28-gauge and .410 bore. Interchangeable ventilated rib barrels in 26" or 28" lengths. Introduced in 1981.

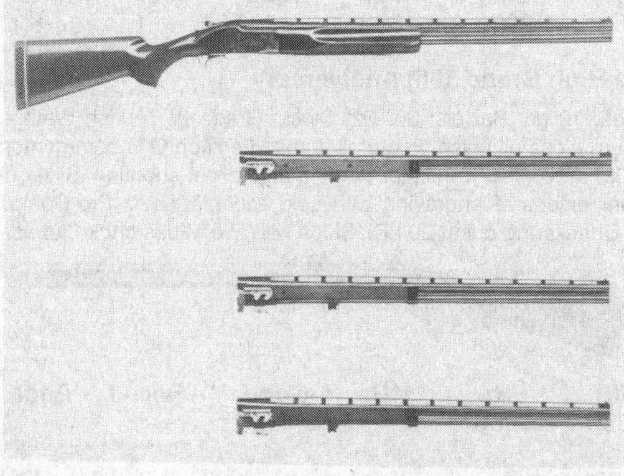

Grade I

NIB	Exc.	V.G.	Good	Fair	Poor
3400	2750	2250	1700	1250	900

Grade III

NIB	Exc.	V.G.	Good	Fair	Poor
3500	2900	2500	1900	1350	900

Grade VI

NIB	Exc.	V.G.	Good	Fair	Poor
3900	3300	2900	2250	1400	950

Citori Trap

Version similar to standard Citori. Offered in 12-gauge only, with 30" or 32" barrels. Features high rib, Monte Carlo-type stock, with recoil pad. Versions differ in amount of ornamentation, quality of materials and workmanship utilized.

Grade I

NIB	Exc.	V.G.	Good	Fair	Poor
1200	980	750	550	420	350

Plus Trap

Adjustable rib and stock. Introduced in 1989.

NIB	Exc.	V.G.	Good	Fair	Poor
1700	1450	1000	750	600	500

Grade II

Discontinued 1983.

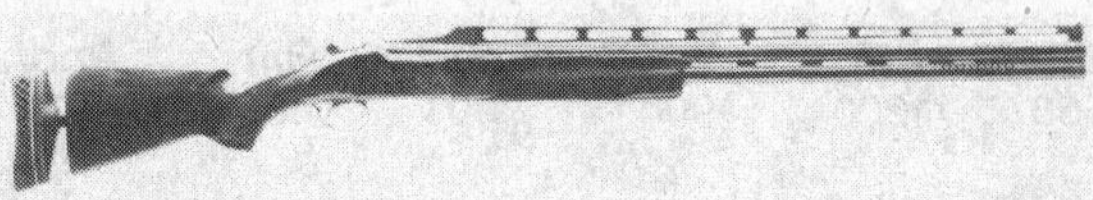

NIB	Exc.	V.G.	Good	Fair	Poor
—	1200	1000	680	450	350

Grade III

NIB	Exc.	V.G.	Good	Fair	Poor
1600	1450	1000	750	600	500

Grade V

Discontinued 1984.

NIB	Exc.	V.G.	Good	Fair	Poor
—	1500	1350	900	650	450

Grade VI

NIB	Exc.	V.G.	Good	Fair	Poor
2200	1900	1550	1250	1000	800

Citori XT Trap

Introduced in 1999. Fitted with contoured beavertail Monte Carlo stock, with or without adjustable comb. Grayed receiver highlighted in gold, with light scroll work. Choice of 30" or 32" barrels. Weight about 8 lbs. 11 oz. Note: Add $275 for adjustable comb.

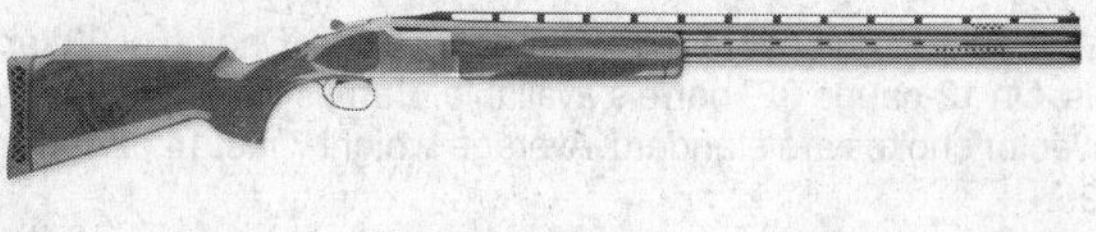

NIB	Exc.	V.G.	Good	Fair	Poor
2500	1700	1200	900	650	400

Golden Clays

First introduced in 1994.

NIB	Exc.	V.G.	Good	Fair	Poor
2950	2250	1500	900	450	300

Signature Grade

NIB	Exc.	V.G.	Good	Fair	Poor
2150	1750	900	600	450	300

Citori XT Trap Gold

Introduced in 2005. Features gold game scene engraving pattern on silver receiver. Choice of 30" or 32" ventilated rib ported barrels, with choke tubes. Checkered select walnut stock, with adjustable comb and semi-beavertail forearm. Stock also has adjustable length of pull and recoil reduction system. Weight about 9 lbs.

NIB	Exc.	V.G.	Good	Fair	Poor
4520	3300	2900	2250	1400	650

Model 325 Sporting Clays

Introduced in 1993. Has European design featuring scroll-engraved grayed receiver, schnabel forearm, 10mm wide ventilated rib, three interchangeable and adjustable trigger shoes. Back-bore barrels are ported. Fitted with choke tubes. Available in 12- and 20-gauge. 12-gauge offered with 28", 30" or 32" barrels; 20-gauge 28" or 30" barrels fitted with conventional chokes. Weight about: 12-gauge 7 lbs. 14 oz.; 20-gauge 6 lbs. 12 oz.

NIB	Exc.	V.G.	Good	Fair	Poor
1550	1200	900	700	450	300

Special Sporting

Similar to Sporting model. Fitted with 2.75" chamber. Choice of 28", 30" or 32" ported barrels. Fitted with high post rib. Stock has full pistol grip. Optional adjustable comb. Weight about 8.3 lbs. depending on barrel length.

Grade I

NIB	Exc.	V.G.	Good	Fair	Poor
1350	980	750	600	450	300

Signature Grade

NIB	Exc.	V.G.	Good	Fair	Poor
1350	1000	750	600	450	300

Pigeon Grade

NIB	Exc.	V.G.	Good	Fair	Poor
1500	1300	850	600	450	300

Golden Clays

NIB	Exc.	V.G.	Good	Fair	Poor
2600	1980	1250	900	450	300

Model 425 Sporting Clays

Citori over/under gun offered in 12- and 20-gauge. Choice of 28" and 30" barrels. On 12-gauge 32" barrels available. Barrels fitted with 10mm wide rib. Invector chokes are standard. Average weight 7 lbs. 14 oz. Introduced in 1995.

NIB	Exc.	V.G.	Good	Fair	Poor
1650	1200	850	600	450	300

Model 425 Golden Clays

Same as above, with high-grade wood. Engraved receiver. Note: Add $200 to NIB price for Model 425 with adjustable comb.

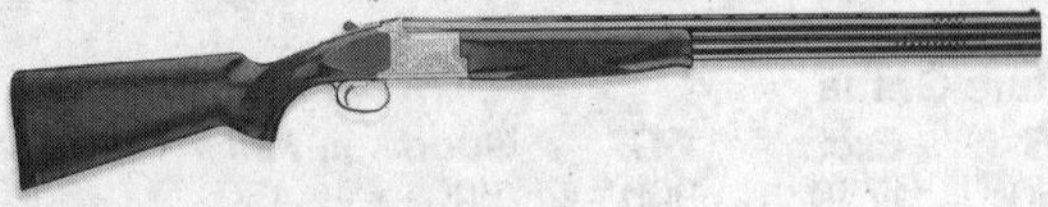

NIB	Exc.	V.G.	Good	Fair	Poor
3000	2450	1650	1100	600	300

Light Sporting 802ES (Extended Swing)

Introduced in 1996. Features 28" ventilated rib barrel, with 2" stainless steel extension tubes for extended swing of 30". Additional 4" extension also included. Thus barrel can be 28", 30" or 32" according to needs. Chambered for 12-gauge, with adjustable length of pull. Walnut stock, pistol grip and schnabel forearm. Weight about 7.5 lbs.

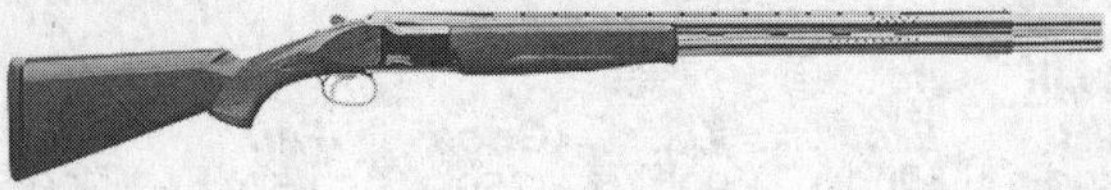

NIB	Exc.	V.G.	Good	Fair	Poor
—	1500	900	700	500	250

Citori Plus Combo

Features single-barrel trap and interchangeable over/under set of barrels. Other features similar to Citori Plus Grade 1. Barrel combinations: 32" over/under with 34" single-barrel; 30" over/under with 32" or 34" single-barrel. Introduced in 1989.

NIB	Exc.	V.G.	Good	Fair	Poor
2500	2100	1750	1100	700	450

Citori Ultra XS Prestige

New in 2008. This 12-gauge sporting clays model features adjustable comb. Grade III/IV walnut stock, with right-hand palm swell. Ported barrels are 28", 30" or 32". Gold accented high relief Ultra XS Special engraving on steel/silver nitride finish receiver. Weight about 8 lbs.

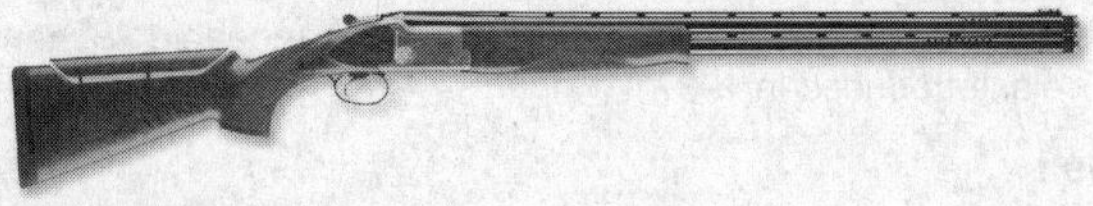

NIB	Exc.	V.G.	Good	Fair	Poor
4500	3300	2900	2250	1400	600

Citori Composite

Gauges: 12 ga. Barrels: 26", 28", 30". Stock: Black composite with adjustable comb. Features: Synthetic stocked addition to the Citori O/U family. Has 3" chambers. Polished blue metalwork with non-glare stock finish. Ivory front bead. Inflex 2 recoil pad. Overmolded grip panels. Gold-plated trigger. Ships with three InvectorPlus flush choke tubes.

NIB	Exc.	V.G.	Good	Fair	Poor
B	2000	1890	—	—	—

Citori High Grade 50th Anniversary

Gauges: 12 ga. Barrels: 30", 32". Stock: Grade IV Turkish Walnut with premium gloss oil finish. Features: Limited edition O/U commemorating the 50th anniversary. Built for hunting and target shooting. Silver nitride receiver extensive engraving with gold accents. HiViz Pro-Comp front sight. Checkering cut at 20 LPI. Ships with five Midas choke tubes.

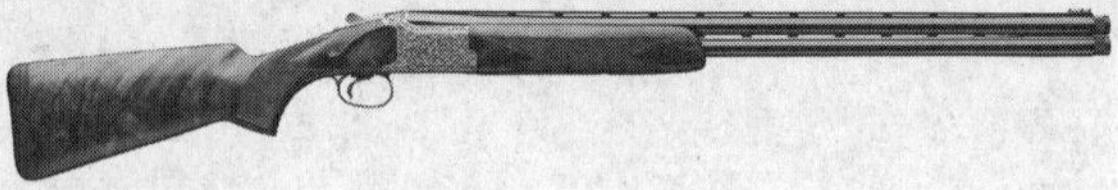

NIB	Exc.	V.G.	Good	Fair	Poor
8350	7250	—	—	—	—

BT-99 SERIES

BT-99

Break-open single-barrel trap gun. Chambered for 12-gauge only. Offered with 32" or 34" ventilated rib barrel, with screw-in choke tubes. Features boxlock action, with automatic ejectors. Finish blued, with checkered walnut stock and beavertail forearm. Introduced in 1968 by B.C. Miroku.

NIB	Exc.	V.G.	Good	Fair	Poor
1000	850	750	500	400	350

BT-99 Stainless

First introduced in 1993.

NIB	Exc.	V.G.	Good	Fair	Poor
1680	1250	900	700	550	350

BT-99 Signature Grade I

First introduced in 1993.

NIB	Exc.	V.G.	Good	Fair	Poor
1300	1050	700	600	500	300

BT-99 Pigeon Grade

First introduced in 1993.

NIB	Exc.	V.G.	Good	Fair	Poor
1600	1250	800	650	500	300

BT-99 Golden Clays

First introduced in 1994. In 2003 offered with adjustable comb. Weight about 9 lbs. Available with 32" or 34" barrel.

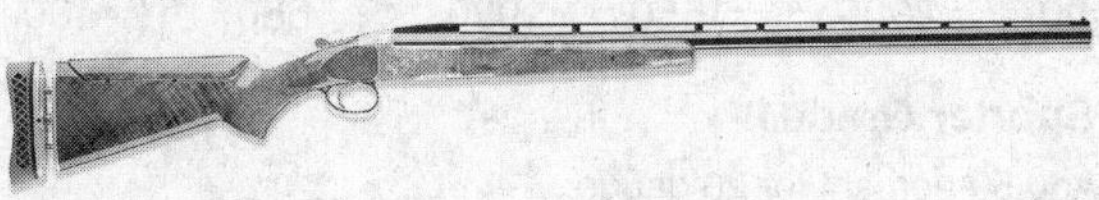

NIB	Exc.	V.G.	Good	Fair	Poor
3700	2500	1750	1100	500	300

BT-99 with Adjustable Buttplate and Comb

Customized-fit single shot, break-action trap shotgun. Graco Pro Fit adjustable comb and buttpad plate. High-post ventilated floating rib. Beavertail forearm.

NIB	Exc.	V.G.	Good	Fair	Poor
1600	1250	800	650	500	300

BT-99 Plus

Version features adjustable ventilated rib and recoil reduction system. Has adjustable stock, recoil pad and back-bored barrel. Introduced in 1989.

NIB	Exc.	V.G.	Good	Fair	Poor
1350	1200	900	700	500	300

BT-99 Plus With Ejector

NIB	Exc.	V.G.	Good	Fair	Poor
2500	2050	1400	800	600	400

BT-99 Plus—Pigeon Grade

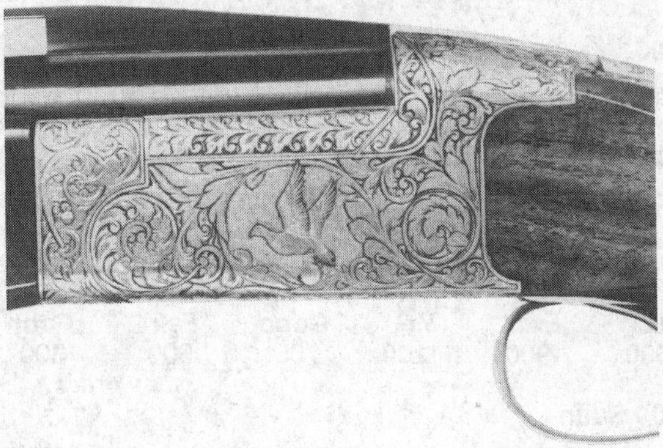

NIB	Exc.	V.G.	Good	Fair	Poor
1700	1300	900	800	550	350

BT-99 Plus—Signature Grade

NIB	Exc.	V.G.	Good	Fair	Poor
1600	1200	850	700	500	300

BT-99 Plus Stainless—Grade I

Same as standard version. Offered in stainless steel. First introduced in 1993. Available in 32" and 34" barrels. Weight about 8 lbs. 11 oz.

NIB	Exc.	V.G.	Good	Fair	Poor
1700	1350	900	700	500	350

BT-99 Plus—Golden Clays

First introduced in 1994.

NIB	Exc.	V.G.	Good	Fair	Poor
2700	2250	1750	900	450	300

BT-99 Micro with Adjustable Buttplate and Comb

Youth/Smaller framed shooter fit-customized single shot, break action, trap shotgun. Graco Pro Fit adjustable comb and buttpad plate. High-post ventilated floating rib. Beavertail forearm.

NIB	Exc.	V.G.	Good	Fair	Poor
1550	1150	800	650	450	300

BT-99 Plus Micro

Slightly reduced dimensions. Offered in barrel lengths from 28" to 34". Weight about 8 lbs. 6 oz. Introduced in 1991.

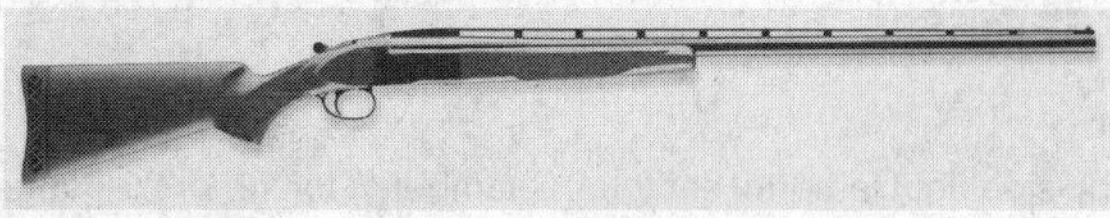

NIB	Exc.	V.G.	Good	Fair	Poor
1350	1100	900	700	500	300

BT-99 Grade III

New in 2008. BT-99 features gloss finish Monte Carlo Grade III/IV walnut stock. Gold accented high relief engraving on receiver. Note: Add 10 percent for adjustable comb stock.

NIB	Exc.	V.G.	Good	Fair	Poor
2400	1950	1250	750	550	350

BT-99 Max High Grade

Introduced 2018. Adjustable high-post rib, Graco adjustable comb, length-of-pull adjustable GraCoil Recoil Reduction System, angle/location adjustable Graco buttpad plate, gloss oil finish Grade V/VI walnut stock, hull ejector, Pachmayr Decelerator XLT recoil pad, Midas Grade choke tubes, universal BT Trap fitted case included.

NIB	Exc.	V.G.	Good	Fair	Poor
4650	4000	3250	2500	—	—

BT-100 SERIES

BT-100

First introduced in 1995. Single-barrel trap features adjustable trigger and length of pull. Stock Monte Carlo or adjustable comb. Barrel 32" or 34". Choice blue or stainless finish. Weight about 8.9 lbs.

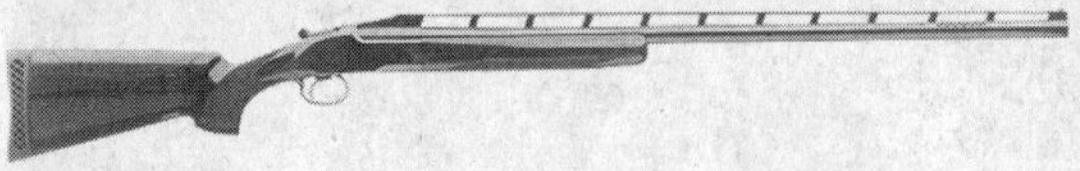

NIB	Exc.	V.G.	Good	Fair	Poor
2500	1900	1200	700	500	300

BT-100 Satin

Introduced in 1999. Features matte black receiver. Available in 32" or 34" barrels, without ejector selector. Grade I only.

NIB	Exc.	V.G.	Good	Fair	Poor
1950	1300	1050	600	400	200

BT-100 Thumbhole

Same as standard BT-100, with additional feature of thumbhole stock. Offered in blue and stainless.

NIB	Exc.	V.G.	Good	Fair	Poor
2580	2000	1350	1000	600	400

Recoilless Trap

First introduced in 1993. Features advanced design that eliminates recoil up to 72 percent. Receiver a special bolt-action single-shot and black anodized. Fitted with adjustable ventilated rib so point of impact can be moved. Adjustable length of pull. Standard Model a 12-gauge with 30" barrel. Micro Model fitted with 27" barrels. Choke tubes supplied. Weight: Standard Model 9 lbs. 1 oz.; Micro Model 8 lbs. 10 oz.

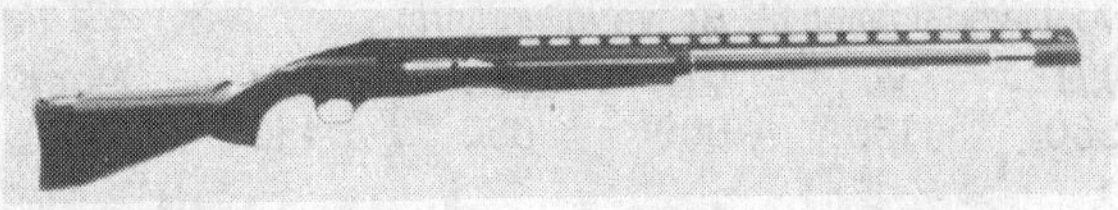

NIB	Exc.	V.G.	Good	Fair	Poor
1250	1100	900	700	500	350

BSS SERIES

BSS

Side-by-side double-barrel shotgun. Chambered for 12- or 20-gauge. Offered with 26", 28" or 30" barrel. Various choke combinations. Features boxlock action. Automatic ejectors. Early guns had non-selective single trigger; late production selective trigger. Finish blued, with checkered walnut stock and beavertail forearm. Manufactured between 1978 and 1987 by B.C. Miroku. Note: Add 20 percent single-selective trigger; 50 percent 20-gauge.

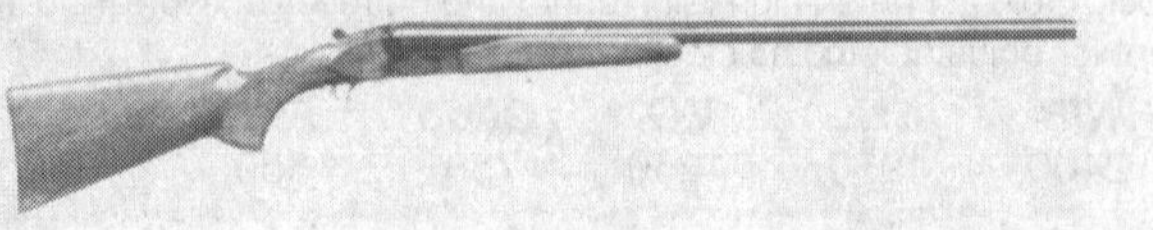

NIB	Exc.	V.G.	Good	Fair	Poor
1350	1100	900	750	550	400

BSS Grade II

Version features game scene engraving and satin coin finished receiver. Discontinued in 1984. Note: Add 50 percent for 20-gauge.

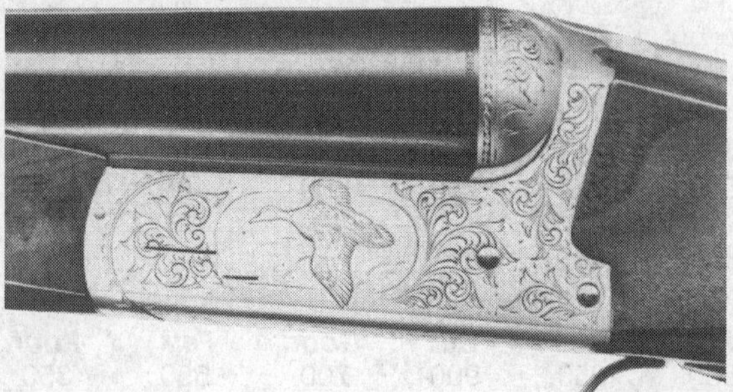

NIB	Exc.	V.G.	Good	Fair	Poor
3200	2800	2000	1400	1100	800

BSS Sporter

Version features English-style straight-grip stock and splinter forearm. Stock was oil-finished. Offered with 26" or 28" barrel. Note: Add 25 percent for 20-gauge.

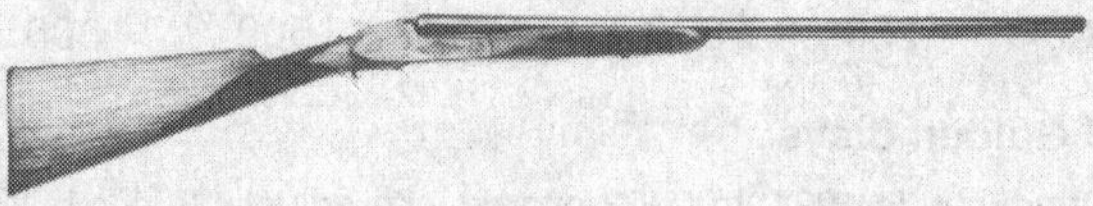

NIB	Exc.	V.G.	Good	Fair	Poor
2400	2000	1550	980	650	400

BSS Sporter Grade II

Note: Add 50 percent for 20 gauge.

NIB	Exc.	V.G.	Good	Fair	Poor
3100	2700	1950	1400	1000	800

BSS Sidelock

Version features engraved sidelock action. Offered in 12- or 20-gauge, with 26" or 28" barrel. Has straight-grip stock and splintered forearm. Manufactured in Korea between 1983 and 1987. Last few dozen 12-gauge sidelocks produced were an uncatalogued version of earlier guns. These guns had very finely engraved game scenes, with English scroll. Add 30 percent premium for this variation. Note:Add 50 percent for 20 gauge

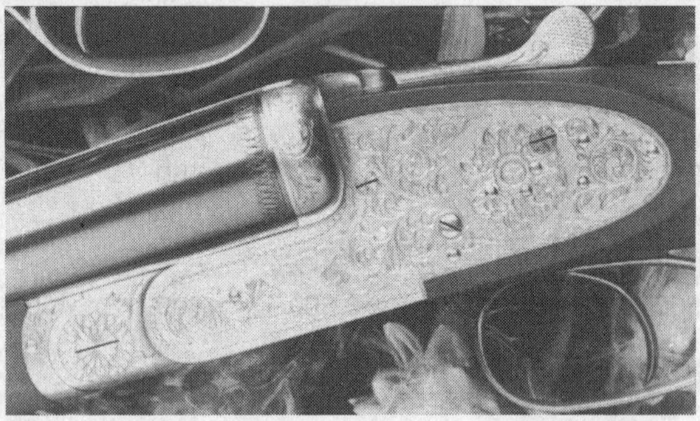

NIB	Exc.	V.G.	Good	Fair	Poor
4100	3600	2400	1750	800	500

CYNERGY SERIES

Series introduced in 2004. Browning calls it third generation over/under gun. Cynergy has a number of new design features such as monolock hinge system for lower profile, inflex recoil pad, new mechanical trigger system, adjustable comb, back-bored barrels and impact ejectors.

Cynergy Field

12-gauge 3" model features checkered walnut stock and forearm. Silver nitrate receiver with engraving. Choice of 26" or 28" ventilated rib barrels, with choke tubes. Weight about 7.75 lbs. Synthetic stock with adjustable comb offered. Note: Add $400 for Grade II/III oil-finished stock and engraved game birds on guns produced 2010 - 2014. Deduct $40 for synthetic stock.

NIB	Exc.	V.G.	Good	Fair	Poor
1600	1250	1000	800	700	600

Cynergy Classic Field

More traditionally styled 12-gauge was added to Cynergy line in 2006. Features steel receiver, with silver nitride finish and game bird scenes on each side. Satin finish walnut stock and schnabel style forend. Three choke tubes. Available in barrel lengths of 26" and 28". Average weight 7.75 lbs.

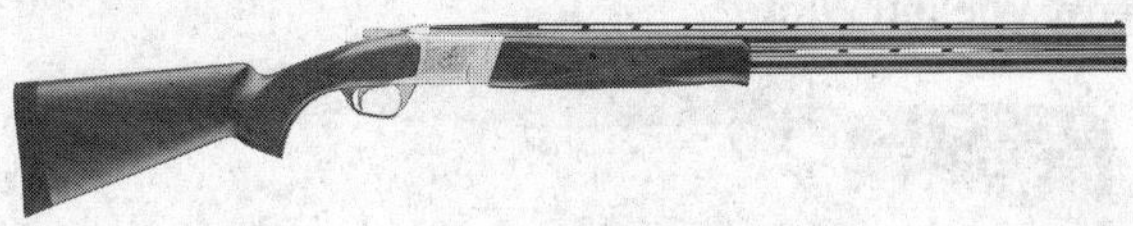

NIB	Exc.	V.G.	Good	Fair	Poor
2150	1850	1400	1000	580	320

Cynergy Field Small Gauge

Introduced in 2005. Chambered for 20-, 28-gauge and .410 bore. Choice of 26" or 28" ventilated rib barrels. Weight about 6.25 lbs.

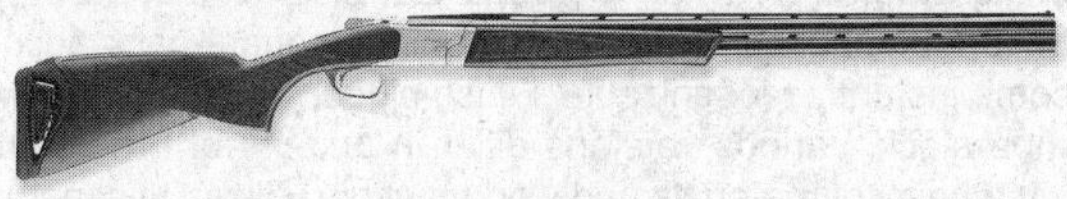

NIB	Exc.	V.G.	Good	Fair	Poor
2100	1850	1450	1050	580	320

Cynergy Sporting

As above, with higher grade walnut stock. Choice of 28", 30" or 32" ventilated rib barrels, with choke tubes. Ported barrels. Hi-Viz front sight. Weight about 8 lbs. Synthetic stock with adjustable comb offered. Note: Deduct $40 for synthetic stock.

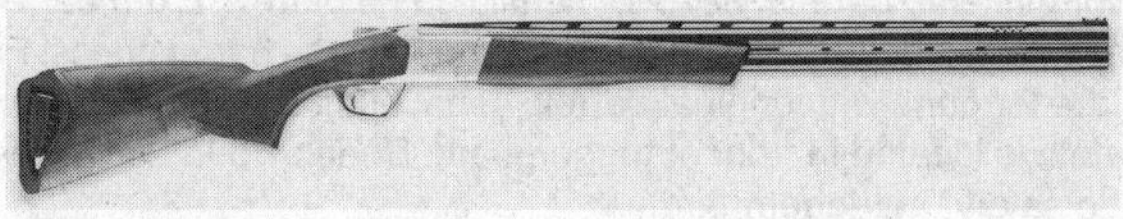

NIB	Exc.	V.G.	Good	Fair	Poor
2000	1600	1200	900	500	300

Cynergy Classic Sporting

New for 2006. Traditionally styled version of Cynergy Sporting. Available in 12-gauge, with 28", 30" or 32" ported barrels. Oil-finish walnut stock, with schnabel forend. Browning logo on steel receiver, with silver nitride finish. Three Invector-Plus Midas Grade choke tubes. Average weight 7.75 lbs.

NIB	Exc.	V.G.	Good	Fair	Poor
2750	2200	1800	900	500	300

Cynergy Classic Field Grade III

Similar to Classic Cynergy Field, with full coverage high-relief engraving on receiver and top lever. Gloss finish Grade III/IV walnut.

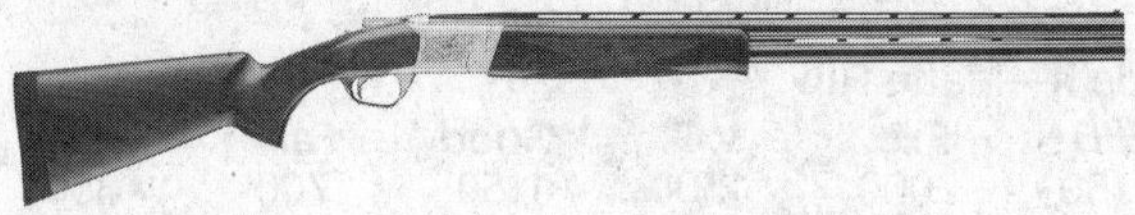

NIB	Exc.	V.G.	Good	Fair	Poor
3400	2600	2000	1650	950	550

Cynergy Classic Field Grade VI

Similar to Cynergy Classic Field Grade III, with more extensive gold high-lighted engraving.

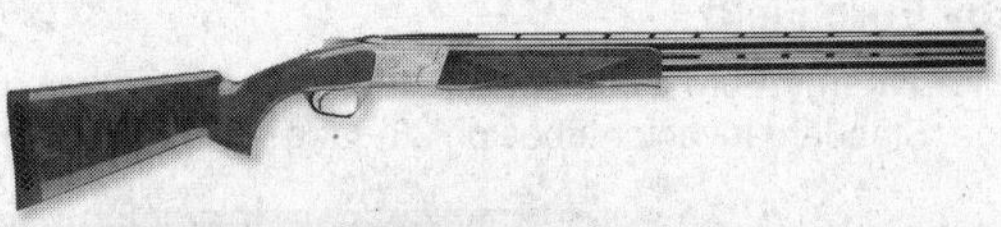

20 GA.

12 GA.

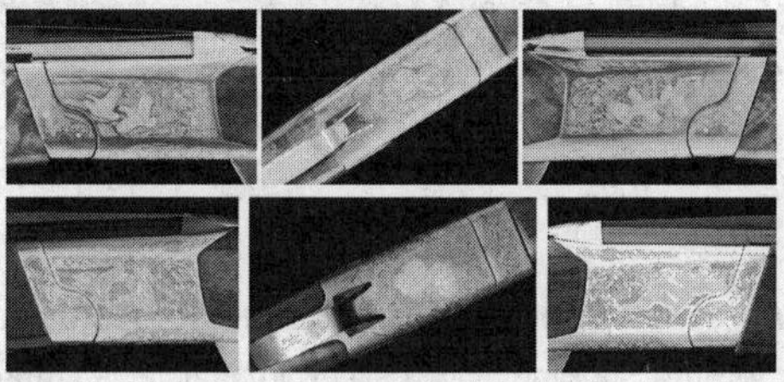

NIB	Exc.	V.G.	Good	Fair	Poor
5100	4200	3450	2300	1400	600

Cynergy Sporting Adjustable Comb

Similar to Cynergy Sporting, with comb adjustable for cast and drop. Average weight 8.2 lbs. Introduced 2006.

NIB	Exc.	V.G.	Good	Fair	Poor
2900	2000	1480	1050	750	450

Cynergy Sporting Small Gauge

As above in 20- or 28-gauge. Choice of 28", 30" or 32" ported barrels in 20-gauge; 28" or 30" ported barrels in 28-gauge. Weight about 6.25 to 6.5 lbs. depending on barrel length. Introduced in 2005.

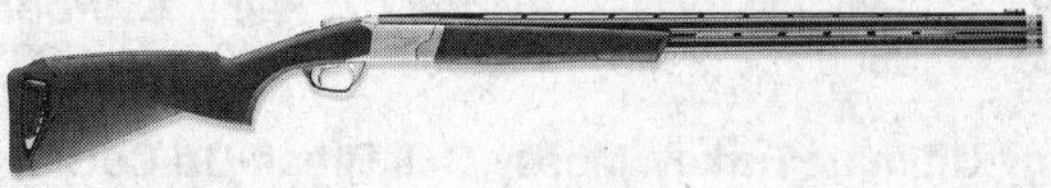

NIB	Exc.	V.G.	Good	Fair	Poor
2300	1750	1200	850	620	400

Cynergy Feather

Lightweight Cynergy 12-gauge introduced in 2006; followed by 20-, 28-gauge and .410 bore versions in 2008. Satin finish walnut stock. Weight about 6.5 lbs. 12-gauge; 5 lbs. in others.

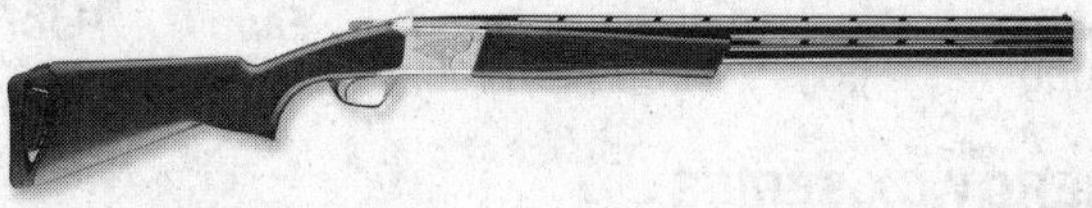

NIB	Exc.	V.G.	Good	Fair	Poor
2050	1800	1300	950	680	450

Cynergy Feather Composite

As above, with synthetic stock and forend. 12-gauge only.

NIB	Exc.	V.G.	Good	Fair	Poor
2300	1700	1200	950	680	450

Cynergy Euro Sporting

Sporting clays and skeet versions come in 2.75" 12- and 20-gauge, with 28", 30" or 32" barrels. Stock oil-finish Grade III/IV walnut. Three choke tubes. Weight about 8 lbs. 12-gauge; 6.5 lbs. 20-gauge.

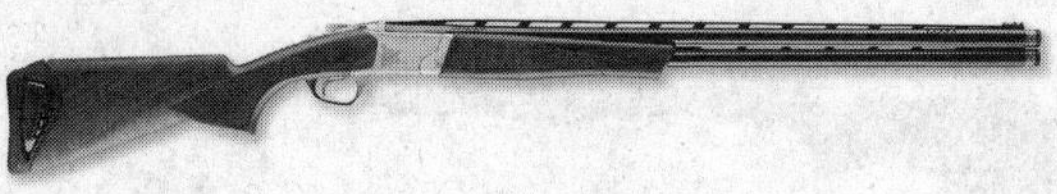

NIB	Exc.	V.G.	Good	Fair	Poor
3500	2800	2200	1650	950	550

Cynergy Euro Field

Similar to Cynergy Euro Sporting. Has Invenctor Plus tubes in 12- and 20-gauge. Standard Invector tubes on 28-gauge and .410 bore.

NIB	Exc.	V.G.	Good	Fair	Poor
2500	1900	1200	700	500	300

Cynergy Euro Sporting Composite with Adjustable Comb

Similar to Euro Sporting Composite, with adjustable comb.

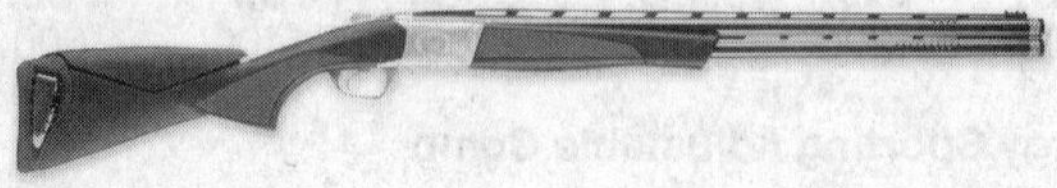

NIB	Exc.	V.G.	Good	Fair	Poor
3800	3000	2000	1650	950	550

Cynergy Classic Trap Unsingle Combo

Trap shotgun in 12-gauge. Comes with double-barrel set in 32/34", 32/32", 30/34" or 30/32". Gloss finish Monte Carlo Grade III/IV walnut stock, with right-hand palm swell. Adjustable comb. Weight about 8.9 lbs. Four choke tubes. Aluminum fitted carrying case.

NIB	Exc.	V.G.	Good	Fair	Poor
4800	3800	2900	2250	1400	600

Cynergy Ultimate Turkey, Mossy Oak Break-Up Country

Short Picatinny rail designed for red-dot optic. Marble Arms Bullseye rear sight and fiber-optic front sight. Five Invector-Plus choke tubes, including extended Ultimate Full Turkey, Spreader, and flush fit full, modified and improved cylinder. Camo composite stock.

NIB	Exc.	V.G.	Good	Fair	Poor
2000	1800	1600	1400	—	—

CYNERGY CX SERIES

Introduced 2017. Crossover barrel design with a 60/40 point of impact, ventilated top and side ribs, satin finish Grade I walnut stock, three Invector-Plus Midas Grade choke tubes included, ivory front and mid-bead sights. MonoLock Hinge creates o/u with an ultra-low profile steel receiver with silver nitride finish. Reverse Striker ignition system; mechanical trigger. Impact ejectors, top-tang barrel selector/safety, Grade I walnut stock with Inflex recoil pad. Vector Pro lengthened forcing cones, three Invector-Plus Midas Grade choke tubes, adjustable length-of-pull trigger, 1/4" stock spacers to adjust length of pull. Ivory front and mid-bead sights.

Cynergy CX Composite

Charcoal gray composite stock with black rubber overmolding in grip areas.

NIB	Exc.	V.G.	Good	Fair	Poor
1450	1300	1150	1000	—	—

Cynergy CX

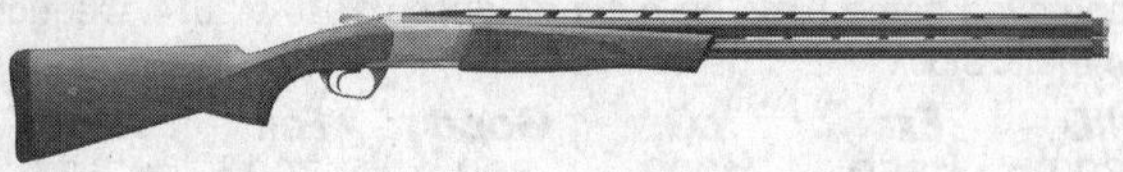

NIB	Exc.	V.G.	Good	Fair	Poor
3150	3000	2800	2400	—	—

Cynergy Micro Midas

NIB	Exc.	V.G.	Good	Fair	Poor
1700	1500	1250	—	—	—

Cynergy Wicked Wing

NIB	Exc.	V.G.	Good	Fair	Poor
2100	1750	1500	—	—	—

EARLY PRODUCTION AUTO-5

Series of recoil-operated semi-automatic shotguns. Designed by John M. Browning. Offered in 12- or 16-gauge. Barrel lengths 26", 28", 30" or 32", with various chokes and ribs. Has unique square-back action that has become instantly recognizable. Finish blued, with checkered walnut round-knob stock. Various versions differ in amount of ornamentation, type of rib, quality of materials and workmanship utilized in construction. Series manufactured in Belgium by FN between 1903 and 1939. First example appeared in U.S. in 1923. Pre-WWI 16-gauge guns introduced in 1936, had 2.5625" chambers; early models should be inspected by qualified gunsmith before firing.

Note: 16-gauge not converted to 2.75" chamber deduct 30 percent. Grade III or Grade IV prices are not nearly as affected by chamber length because of their rarity. Original pre-war barrels were serial numbered to gun. Extra barrels serial numbered to gun add $100 for plain barrels, $200 for matte rib barrels, $275 for ventilated rib barrels. Extra barrels on Grade IV guns add an additional 30 percent to these barrel prices. Prices given are for guns with original barrels serial numbered to gun. Remember safety is located in front of triggerguard. Deduct 10 to 25 percent for "suicide safety" in triggerguard.

Grade I—Plain Barrel

NIB	Exc.	V.G.	Good	Fair	Poor
950	850	750	600	400	280

Grade I—Matte Rib

NIB	Exc.	V.G.	Good	Fair	Poor
1200	1100	980	800	550	350

Grade I—Vent Rib

NIB	Exc.	V.G.	Good	Fair	Poor
1100	1000	900	720	520	320

Grade II—Plain Barrel

NIB	Exc.	V.G.	Good	Fair	Poor
1600	1500	1200	1000	600	350

Grade II—Matte Rib

NIB	Exc.	V.G.	Good	Fair	Poor
2150	2000	1500	1150	700	350

Grade II—Vent Rib

NIB	Exc.	V.G.	Good	Fair	Poor
2050	1900	1400	1050	500	350

Grade III—Plain Barrel

NIB	Exc.	V.G.	Good	Fair	Poor
3000	2800	1900	1350	780	380

Grade III—Matte Rib

NIB	Exc.	V.G.	Good	Fair	Poor
3800	3600	3000	2000	900	450

Grade III—Vent Rib

NIB	Exc.	V.G.	Good	Fair	Poor
3700	3500	2900	1850	800	400

Grade IV—Plain Barrel

NIB	Exc.	V.G.	Good	Fair	Poor
4400	4000	3500	2500	1000	500

Grade IV—Matte Rib

NIB	Exc.	V.G.	Good	Fair	Poor
5000	4500	3800	2850	1200	700

Grade IV—Vent Rib

NIB	Exc.	V.G.	Good	Fair	Poor
4900	4400	3700	2750	1100	600

American Browning Auto-5

Recoil-operated semi-automatic shotgun was another variation of early production Auto-5. Chambered for 12-, 16- or 20-gauge. Manufactured by Remington Company for Browning. Quite similar to Remington's Model 11 shotgun. Features Browning logo and different type of engraving. Approximately 45,000 manufactured between 1940 and 1942. Note: Add 20 percent for ventilated rib; 10 percent for 20-gauge.

NIB	Exc.	V.G.	Good	Fair	Poor
—	680	580	450	380	200

MID-PRODUCTION AUTO-5—FN MANUFACTURE STANDARD WEIGHT

Version of recoil-operated semi-automatic Auto-5 shotguns. Manufactured by FN in Belgium between 1952 and 1976. Offered in 12- or 16-gauge, with 26" through 32" barrels. Various chokes. Finish blued, with checkered walnut stock. Black buttplate marked "Browning Automatic" with "FN" in center oval. Guns made prior to 1967 will be found with round-knob pistol grips. Flatbottom variation introduced in 1967. Note: Add 25 percent for guns with round-knob pistol grip; 35 percent for straight-grip stock; 20 percent for 16-gauge guns NIB or excellent condition.

Plain Barrel

NIB	Exc.	V.G.	Good	Fair	Poor
1100	900	800	650	400	300

Matte Rib

NIB	Exc.	V.G.	Good	Fair	Poor
1400	1100	900	700	500	350

Vent Rib

NIB	Exc.	V.G.	Good	Fair	Poor
1300	1000	850	650	450	320

Auto-5 Lightweight

Version chambered for 12- or 20-gauge. Featured lighter-weight scroll-engraved receiver. Manufactured between 1952 and 1976 by FN. 20-gauge introduced in 1958. Note: Add 15 percent for ventilated rib; 50 percent for 20-gauge.

NIB	Exc.	V.G.	Good	Fair	Poor
1200	900	650	550	450	350

Auto-5 Magnum

Version featured 3" chambers. Offered with 26" through 32" full-choke barrels. Manufactured between 1958 and 1976 by FN. 12-gauge introduced in 1958; 20-gauge in 1967. Note: Add 20 percent for ventilated rib; 50 percent for 20-gauge.

NIB	Exc.	V.G.	Good	Fair	Poor
1100	850	600	500	400	300

Auto-5 Skeet

Version similar to Lightweight Model. Chambered for 12- or 20-gauge, with 26" or 28" ventilated rib Skeet-choked barrel. Note: Add 50 percent for 20-gauge.

NIB	Exc.	V.G.	Good	Fair	Poor
1250	1000	700	600	450	350

Auto-5 Trap Model

Version similar to standard-weight model, except chambered for 12-gauge only, with 30" ventilated rib Full-choke barrel. Manufactured by FN until 1971.

NIB	Exc.	V.G.	Good	Fair	Poor
1200	900	650	550	450	350

Sweet Sixteen

Version similar to standard-weight. Chambered for 16-gauge only. Has gold-plated trigger. Manufactured by FN between 1936 and 1976. Not all A-5 16-gauges are Sweet Sixteens. Look for gold-plated trigger "Sweet Sixteen" script and lack of a suicide safety. Note: Add 50 percent for matte or ventilated rib in NIB or excellent condition; 25 percent for others.

NIB	Exc.	V.G.	Good	Fair	Poor
1650	1500	1100	900	550	400

Buck Special

Version features 24" cylinder-bore barrel, with adjustable rifle sights. Produced in 12- and 20-gauge 2.75" and 3" Magnum chambers; 16-gauge with 2.75" chambers. Manufactured by FN between 1963 and 1976. Prices for 12-gauge guns. Note: Add 50 percent for 16- or 20-gauge.

NIB	Exc.	V.G.	Good	Fair	Poor
1250	1000	800	650	450	350

Two Millionth Commemorative

Version commemorated Two Millionth Auto-5 shotgun produced by FN. Engraved with special high-polish blue finish. High-grade checkered walnut stock. Furnished in a black fitted case along with a book on Browning Company. There were 2,500 manufactured between 1971 and 1974. As with all commemoratives, it must be NIB to realize its top potential.

NIB	Exc.	V.G.	Good	Fair	Poor
3200	1850	950	620	480	300

LATE PRODUCTION AUTO-5—B.C. MIROKU MANUFACTURE

In 1976 production of Auto-5 shotgun was begun by B.C. Miroku in Japan. This move was accomplished after approximately 2,750,000 Auto-5 shotguns were manufactured by FN in Belgium between 1903 and 1976. Japanese-manufactured guns, in the opinion of many knowledgeable people, show no less quality or functionality but are simply not as desirable from a collector's standpoint. In 1999 Browning discontinued production of Auto-5 shotgun. Note: Since discontinuance of Auto-5, values for Japanese examples have risen, approaching those of Belgian guns.

Auto-5 Light 12

Version chambered for 12-gauge 2.75" chamber only. Offered with lightweight receiver. Barrel has ventilated rib and choke tubes. Introduced in 1975.

NIB	*Exc.*	*V.G.*	*Good*	*Fair*	*Poor*
950	800	680	500	400	350

Auto-5 Light 20

Version similar to Light 12. Chambered for 20-gauge only.

NIB	*Exc.*	*V.G.*	*Good*	*Fair*	*Poor*
1200	1000	850	700	500	400

Auto-5 Magnum

Version features 3" chambers. Offered with 26", 28", 30" or 32" barrels. Introduced in 1976 by Miroku. Discontinued in 1996.

NIB	*Exc.*	*V.G.*	*Good*	*Fair*	*Poor*
1000	800	600	450	350	300

Auto-5 Buck Special

Version has 24" barrel cylinder-bored with adjustable sights. Introduced by Miroku in 1976.

NIB	*Exc.*	*V.G.*	*Good*	*Fair*	*Poor*
1000	800	600	450	350	300

Auto-5 Skeet

Competition model features 26" or 28" Skeet-bored barrels, with ventilated rib. Manufactured between 1976 and 1983 by Miroku.

NIB	*Exc.*	*V.G.*	*Good*	*Fair*	*Poor*
820	550	450	350	—	200

Sweet Sixteen

Version similar to Belgian-produced Sweet Sixteen. Offered standard with ventilated rib and screw-in Invector choke tubes. Introduced in 1988 by Miroku. Discontinued in 1992.

NIB	*Exc.*	*V.G.*	*Good*	*Fair*	*Poor*
1350	1100	750	550	380	220

A-5 DU 50th Anniversary

High-grade version of Auto-5. Produced to commemorate 50th Anniversary of Ducks Unlimited. Highly engraved. Features high-gloss bluing and fancy checkered walnut stock. Approximately 5,500 manufactured by Miroku in 1987. Auctioned by Ducks Unlimited chapters to raise money for their organization. Because of this fact, it is difficult to furnish an accurate value. Commemorative firearms must be NIB with all furnished materials to command premium collector value. We furnish what we feel is a general value.

NIB	*Exc.*	*V.G.*	*Good*	*Fair*	*Poor*
3000	2000	800	600	450	300

A-5 DU Sweet Sixteen

Special version of Miroku-manufactured Sweet Sixteen. Auctioned by Ducks Unlimited chapters in 1988. There were 5,500 produced. All specifications and cautions that were furnished for 50th Anniversary gun also apply here.

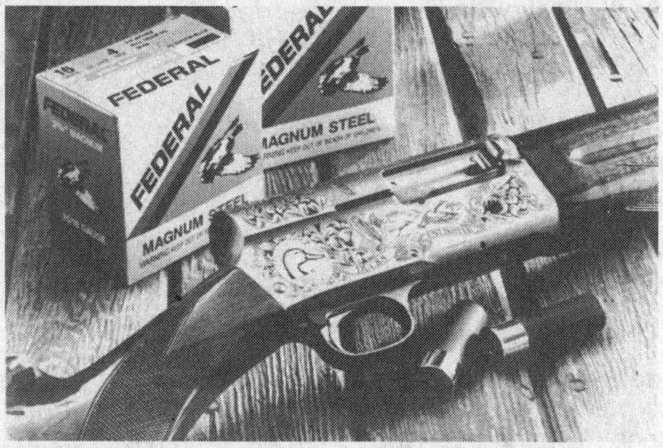

NIB	*Exc.*	*V.G.*	*Good*	*Fair*	*Poor*
2500	1500	850	600	400	300

Auto-5 Classic

Special limited edition series of A-5 shotguns built in 12-gauge only. Classic is photo-etched with game scenes on silver gray receiver. 5,000 of these guns were manufactured in 1984. Gold Classic similar in appearance, but features gold inlays and limited to 500 guns.

Classic

NIB	*Exc.*	*V.G.*	*Good*	*Fair*	*Poor*
2000	1680	1200	750	520	300

Gold Classic

Produced by FN.

NIB	*Exc.*	*V.G.*	*Good*	*Fair*	*Poor*
10000	8500	7000	6000	—	—

Auto-5 Light Buck Special

Lightweight version of Buck Special. Chambered for 2.75" shell. Fitted with 24" ventilated rib barrel. Conventional choked for slug or buckshot. Barrel has adjustable rear sight and ramp front sight. Weight 8 lbs.

NIB	*Exc.*	*V.G.*	*Good*	*Fair*	*Poor*
850	650	550	450	380	220

Auto-5 Stalker

New for 1992. Available in lightweight or Magnum version. Light Stalker available in 12-gauge, with 26" or 28" barrel and choke tubes. Magnum Stalker offered in 12-gauge (3" chamber), with 28" or 30" barrel and choke tubes. Weight: Light Stalker 8 lbs. 4 oz.; Magnum Stalker 8 lbs. 11 oz.

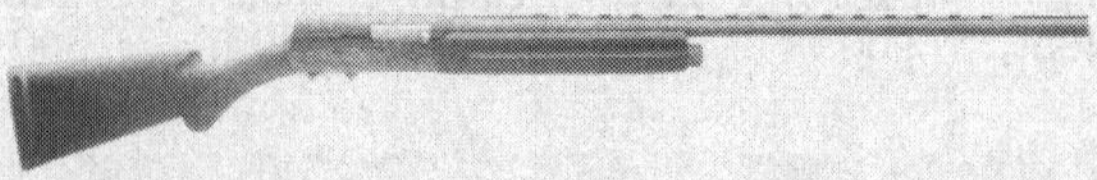

Light Stalker

NIB	*Exc.*	*V.G.*	*Good*	*Fair*	*Poor*
780	600	550	400	300	220

Magnum Stalker

NIB	*Exc.*	*V.G.*	*Good*	*Fair*	*Poor*
800	650	600	380	280	250

Auto-5 Final Tribute Limited Edition

Introduced in 1999. Commemorative A-5 limited to 1,000 shotguns. Represents final production of this model. Chambered for 12-gauge shell. Fitted with 28" ventilated rib barrel. Has special engraved receiver.

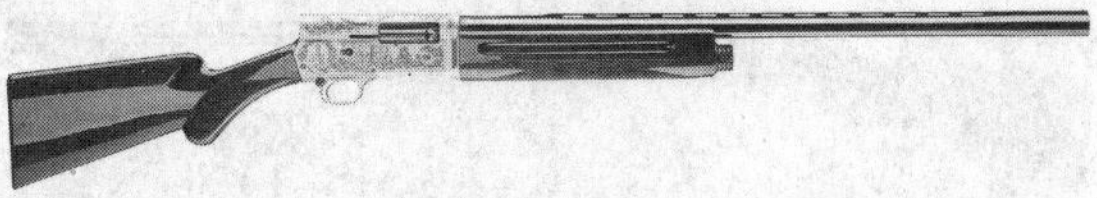

NIB	Exc.	V.G.	Good	Fair	Poor
5000	3750	2500	2000	1300	500

Browning A5

With squared "hump-back" receiver, A5 similar in appearance to Classic Auto-5. Totally different semi-automatic shotgun. Operates with Browning's short-recoil Kinematic action. In 12-gauge only, with 3" or 3.5" chamber. A5 designed to function with a wide range of 2.75", 3", and 3.5" loads. Barrel length 26", 28" or 30", with ventilated rib. Brass bead front, ivory bead middle sights and three Invector-DS Flush choke tubes (F, M, IC). A5 Hunter model has checkered walnut stock. Also offered with black composite stock (A5 Stalker) or Mossy Oak Duck Blind or Break-Up Infinity camo finish or with black composite stock. All are shim adjustable for cast and drop. Introduced in 2012. Note: Deduct $100 for Stalker model. Note: Add $50 for 3.5"-chamber models.

NIB	Exc.	V.G.	Good	Fair	Poor
1750	1200	950	700	350	250

Browning A5 Hunter High Grade

Same features as standard A5, plus engraving of pheasants and mallards, with intricate scrollwork. Grade 2.5 walnut stock. Introduced in 2017.

NIB	Exc.	V.G.	Good	Fair	Poor
1650	1400	1200	1000	900	800

Browning A5 Ultimate

Higher-trade variation with brushed satin finish. Engraved receiver, with intricate scroll pheasants and mallards. Other features include: oil-finished Grade III walnut stock, ivory middle bead, fiber optic front sight and Vector Pro lengthened forcing cone.

NIB	Exc.	V.G.	Good	Fair	Poor
1750	1500	1100	900	—	—

Browning A5 Wicked Wing

Same features as Ultimate model, except has Cerakote Burnt Bronze finish on receiver and barrel. Mossy Oak Shadow Grass blades camo on stock and forearm, with textured gripping surfaces. Introduced in 2017.

NIB	Exc.	V.G.	Good	Fair	Poor
2000	1500	1100	900	—	—

Browning A5 Sweet Sixteen

Same features as standard A5, except chambered for 16-gauge. Offered with 26" or 28" barrel, with 2.75" chamber and bi-tone receiver. 16-gauge only. 28" barrel, 2.75" chamber. 5.8 lbs.

NIB	Exc.	V.G.	Good	Fair	Poor
1550	1300	1000	700	400	250

Double Automatic Shotgun

Short recoil-operated semi-automatic shotgun. Chambered for 12-gauge only. Offered with 26", 28" or 30" barrels plain or ventilated rib. Has various chokes. Receiver steel. Finish blued or silver, with checkered walnut stock. Tubular magazine holds only two shots—hence its name. Manufactured between 1954 and 1972. Note: Add 25 percent for ventilated rib.

NIB	Exc.	V.G.	Good	Fair	Poor
1000	800	650	550	400	250

Twelvette Double Auto

Similar to Double Automatic, except has aircraft aluminum alloy frame color-anodized in blue, silver, green, brown or black. Red-, gold- or royal blue-colored receivers were rarest colors and would command approximately 50 to 75 percent premium. Offered with plain or ventilated rib barrel. Approximately 65,000 produced between 1954 and 1972. Note: Add 25 percent for ventilated rib.

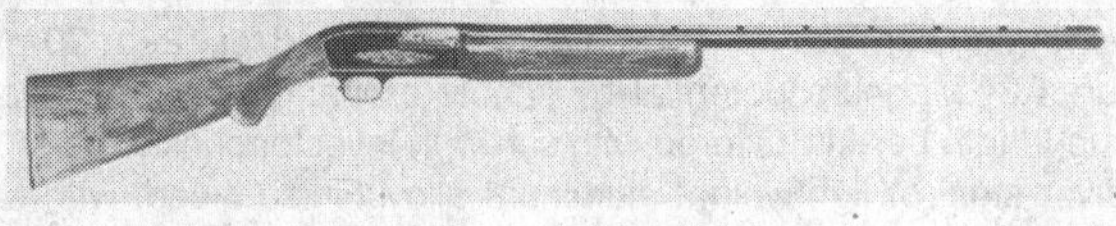

NIB	Exc.	V.G.	Good	Fair	Poor
1050	850	720	600	450	300

Twentyweight Double Auto

Similar in all respects to Twelvette, except .75 lb. lighter. Offered with 26.5" barrel. Manufactured between 1952 and 1971. Note: Add 25 percent for ventilated rib.

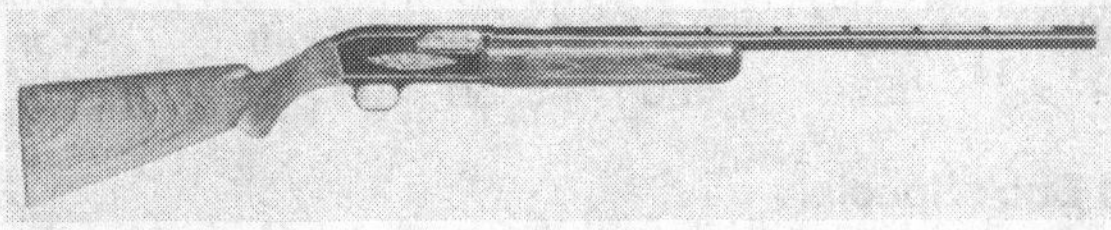

NIB	Exc.	V.G.	Good	Fair	Poor
1100	900	800	700	500	350

2000 SERIES

B-2000

Gas-operated semi-automatic shotgun. Chambered for 12- or 20-gauge. Offered with 26", 28" or 30" ventilated rib barrel and various chokes. Finish blued, with checkered walnut stock. Assembled in Portugal from parts manufactured by FN in Belgium. Approximately 115,000 imported between 1974 and 1981.

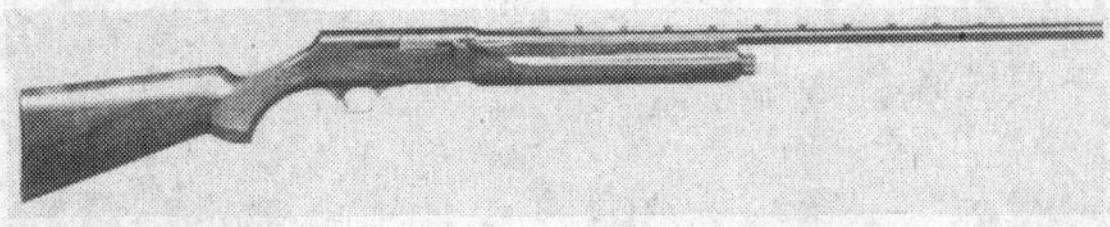

NIB	Exc.	V.G.	Good	Fair	Poor
620	550	480	300	220	180

B-2000 Magnum

Features barrel with 3" chambers. Offered standard with recoil pad.

NIB	Exc.	V.G.	Good	Fair	Poor
780	580	500	300	220	180

B-2000 Buck Special

Version has 24" cylinder-bored barrel, with rifle sights.

NIB	Exc.	V.G.	Good	Fair	Poor
620	480	420	280	220	180

B-2000 Trap

Has 30" Full-choke barrel, with floating rib. Monte Carlo-type trap stock.

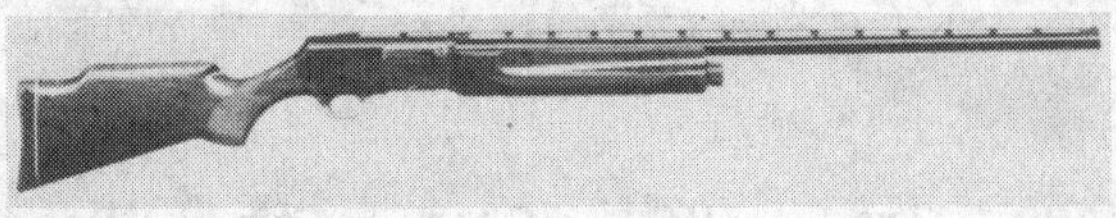

NIB	Exc.	V.G.	Good	Fair	Poor
600	480	420	280	220	180

B-2000 Skeet

Features 26" skeet-bored barrel, with floating ventilated rib. Skeet-type stock. Note: Add 20 percent for 20-gauge gun.

NIB	Exc.	V.G.	Good	Fair	Poor
—	600	450	380	280	200

80 SERIES

B-80

Gas-operated semi-automatic shotgun. Chambered for 12- or 20-gauge. Features 3" Magnum potential by simply exchanging barrel. Features various-length barrels. Offered with screw-in Invector chokes as of 1985. Receiver steel or lightweight aluminum alloy. Finish blued, with checkered walnut stock. Assembled in Portugal from parts manufactured by Beretta in Italy. Manufactured between 1981 and 1988. Note: Add 20 percent for 20-gauge gun.

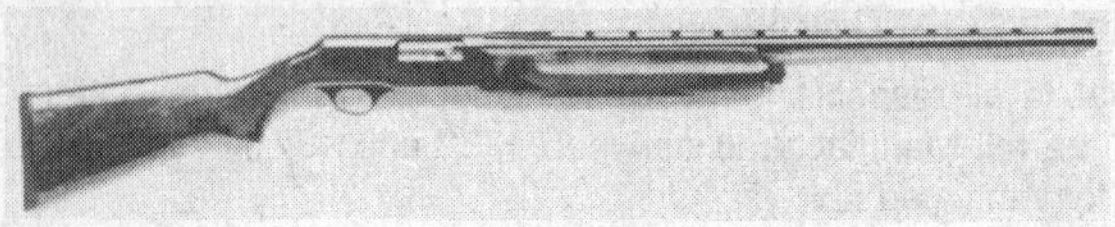

NIB	Exc.	V.G.	Good	Fair	Poor
—	550	450	380	320	220

B-80 Buck Special

Features 24" cylinder-bored barrel, with rifle sights. Discontinued in 1984.

NIB	Exc.	V.G.	Good	Fair	Poor
—	500	400	350	300	200

B-80 DU Commemorative

Produced to be auctioned by American Ducks Unlimited chapters. In order to realize collector potential, it must be NIB with all supplied materials. Values supplied are general.

NIB	Exc.	V.G.	Good	Fair	Poor
950	650	550	420	320	280

GOLD SERIES

Gold 10

First introduced in 1993. Gas-operated 5-shot semi-automatic shotgun. Chambered for 10-gauge shell. Offered with 26", 28" or 30" ventilated rib barrel. Standard model has walnut stock, blued receiver and barrel. Stalker Model fitted with graphite composite stock, non-glare finish on receiver and barrel. Both models fitted with choke tubes. Weight about 10 lbs. 10 oz.

NIB	Exc.	V.G.	Good	Fair	Poor
950	700	550	450	300	150

Gold Evolve

Introduced in 2004. Updated version of original Gold gun. Features newly designed receiver, magazine cap, ventilated rib design, checkering pattern and Hi-Viz sights. Offered in 12-gauge 3" chamber. Choice of 26", 28" or 30" barrel, with choke tubes. Weight about 7 lbs. for 28" model.

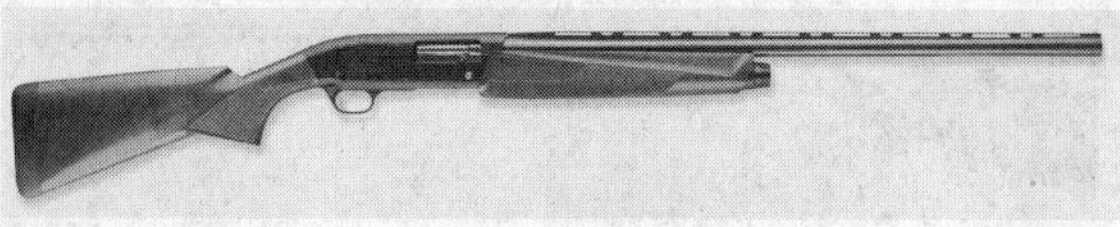

NIB	Exc.	V.G.	Good	Fair	Poor
1200	880	700	520	400	220

Gold Light 10 Gauge Camo

10-gauge offered with 26" or 28" barrels and Mossy Oak or Shadow Grass camo. Lightweight alloy receiver reduces weight to 9 lb. 10 oz. Introduced in 2001.

NIB	Exc.	V.G.	Good	Fair	Poor
1280	980	780	600	450	250

Gold 10 Gauge Combo

10-gauge has choice of two ventilated rib barrels in lengths of 24"/26" or 24"/28". Walnut stock, with black ventilated recoil pad. Weight with 28" barrels about 10 lbs. 10 oz.

NIB	Exc.	V.G.	Good	Fair	Poor
1150	800	680	500	380	250

Gold Stalker

NIB	Exc.	V.G.	Good	Fair	Poor
1020	720	550	450	300	150

Gold Classic Stalker

Introduced in 1999. Features classic Browning squared receiver and shim-adjustable stock. Chambered for 12-gauge shells. Choice of 26" or 28" ventilated rib barrels. Has 3" chambers. Black synthetic stock. Weight about 7 lbs. 3 oz.

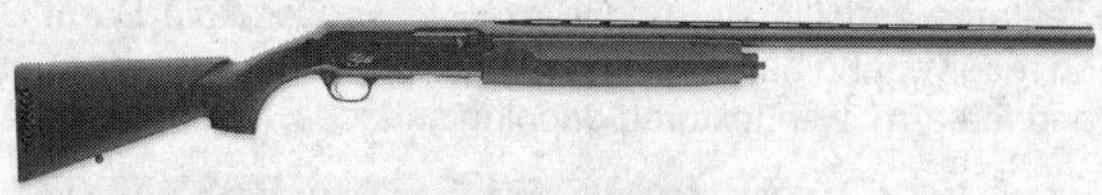

NIB	Exc.	V.G.	Good	Fair	Poor
850	680	550	400	280	120

Gold 3-1/2" 12 Gauge

Introduced in 1997. Features 3.5 chamber. Can operate 2.75" or 3" shells as well. Choice of barrel lengths from 26" to 30". Invector-Plus chokes. Magazine capacity: 4/2.75" shells; 3/3" shells; or 3/3.5" shells. Weight about 7 lbs. 10 oz.

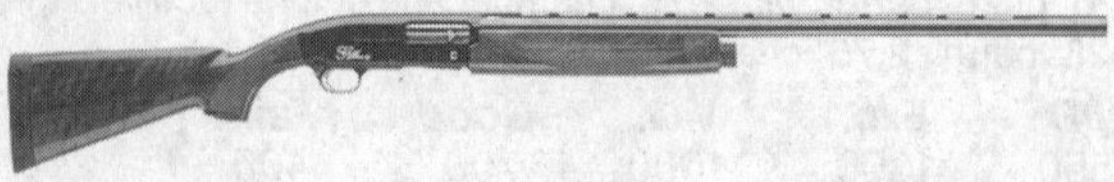

NIB	Exc.	V.G.	Good	Fair	Poor
1000	800	600	450	200	150

Gold 12 Gauge Hunter

Introduced in 1994. Semi-automatic shotgun built on same gas operating system as Gold 10. Offered with 26", 28" or 30" barrel. Magazine capacity: 4/3" shells. Walnut stock has full checkered pistol grip, with black rubber recoil pad. Invector-Plus choke tubes supplied. Weight about 7.5 lbs. Available (1998) in Stalker version, with non-glare matte metal parts and stocks.

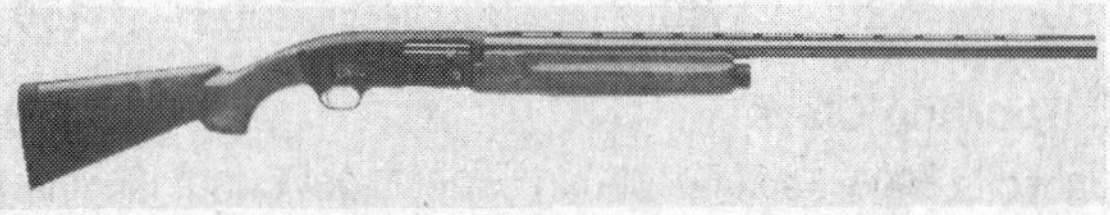

NIB	*Exc.*	*V.G.*	*Good*	*Fair*	*Poor*
750	520	400	300	200	150

Gold Classic Hunter

Introduced in 1999. Features squared receiver, fully adjustable selected walnut stock and deep blued barrels. Choice of 26", 28" or 30" ventilated rib barrel. Offered with 3" chamber 12-gauge only.

NIB	*Exc.*	*V.G.*	*Good*	*Fair*	*Poor*
850	600	500	400	280	220

Gold Classic 20 Gauge

Offered with 26" or 28" ventilated rib barrels and select walnut stock. Shim-adjustable. Squared receiver. Weight about 6 lbs. 12 oz. Introduced in 1999.

NIB	*Exc.*	*V.G.*	*Good*	*Fair*	*Poor*
800	600	500	400	280	220

Gold Classic High Grade

Introduced in 1999. Features traditional square receiver, with engraved silver/gray finish. Offered in 12-gauge only, with 3" chambers and 28" ventilated rib barrel. Select walnut stock. Weight about 7 lbs. 6 oz.

NIB	*Exc.*	*V.G.*	*Good*	*Fair*	*Poor*
1500	1200	780	500	220	160

Gold Deer Hunter

Introduced in 1997. Features choice of fully rifled or smooth bore barrel and Invector choke system. Both versions come with cantilever scope mount. Stock and forearm select walnut. Receiver has non-glare black finish. Barrel satin finish. Barrel length 22" on both barrels. Weight about 7 lbs. 12 oz. Price listed for smoothbore barrel. Note: Add $40 for fully rifled version.

NIB	*Exc.*	*V.G.*	*Good*	*Fair*	*Poor*
880	650	500	400	200	150

Gold Deer Hunter 20 Gauge

Same as above. Chambered for 20-gauge 3" shell. Furnished with fully rifled 22" barrel. Cantilever scope mount. Introduced in 2001.

NIB	*Exc.*	*V.G.*	*Good*	*Fair*	*Poor*
1020	900	620	500	300	200

Gold Deer Stalker

Introduced in 1999. Same as above. Fitted with black synthetic stock.

NIB	*Exc.*	*V.G.*	*Good*	*Fair*	*Poor*
950	700	600	500	300	150

Gold Deer Mossy Oak

Introduced in 1999. Camo finish.

NIB	*Exc.*	*V.G.*	*Good*	*Fair*	*Poor*
820	680	580	450	200	120

Gold Waterfowl Mossy Oak Shadow Grass

Introduced in 1999. Camo finish.

NIB	*Exc.*	*V.G.*	*Good*	*Fair*	*Poor*
950	700	600	500	200	120

Gold Waterfowl Mossy Oak Breakup

Introduced in 2000. Camo finish.

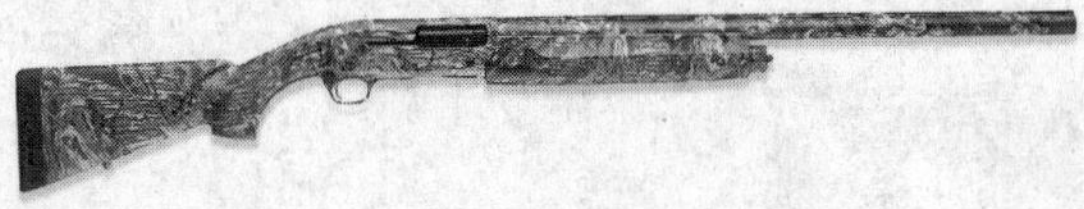

NIB	*Exc.*	*V.G.*	*Good*	*Fair*	*Poor*
950	700	580	450	200	120

Gold Turkey/Waterfowl Mossy Oak

Introduced in 1999. Camo finish.

NIB	*Exc.*	*V.G.*	*Good*	*Fair*	*Poor*
950	700	580	450	200	120

Gold Turkey/Waterfowl Stalker

Introduced in 1999. Features black synthetic stock, 24" barrel, Hi-Viz sight and 3" or 3.5" chambers. Weight about 7 lbs. 4 oz.

NIB	*Exc.*	*V.G.*	*Good*	*Fair*	*Poor*
900	650	580	450	200	120

Gold Turkey/Waterfowl Hunter

12-gauge 3" or 3.5" chambered gun. Offered with 24" ventilated rib barrel. Select walnut stock, with black ventilated recoil pad. Weight about 7 lbs. Introduced in 1999.

NIB	Exc.	V.G.	Good	Fair	Poor
880	620	550	450	200	120

Gold NWTF Series

Finished in Mossy Oak Breakup pattern. Bears "NWTF" logo on buttstock. Fitted with 24" barrel, Hi-Viz front sight, X-full extended Turkey choke. Offered in configurations listed.

Gold Light 10 Gauge

NIB	Exc.	V.G.	Good	Fair	Poor
1350	950	780	600	420	180

Gold 10-Gauge Field

Gauge: 10 ga. 3.5 in. Barrel: 26 in. or 28 in. with ventilated rib. Weight: 9 lbs. 9 oz.–9 lbs. 10 oz. Length: 48.0–50.0 in. Stock: Composite with camouflage coverage in either Mossy Oak Shadow Grass Habitat or Mossy Oak Break-Up Country. Features: Browning's autoloading Gold Light 10-gauge shotgun is redesigned as the Gold 10 Gauge Field. The new style composite stock and forearm wear textured gripping surfaces with the buttstock able to be trimmed up to ¾-inch to shorten LOP. Added Inflex recoil pad. Silver bead front sight. Integral sling swivel studs. Capacity of 4+1 magnum shells. Standard Invector-style flush-mount interchangeable choke tubes with three included (F, M, IC).

NIB	Exc.	V.G.	Good	Fair	Poor
1630	—	—	—	—	—

Gold 12 Gauge

3.5" Chamber, Shadow Grass

NIB	Exc.	V.G.	Good	Fair	Poor
1280	900	720	550	380	150

3" Chamber

NIB	Exc.	V.G.	Good	Fair	Poor
1100	780	650	580	380	150

3.5" Chamber Ultimate Turkey Gun

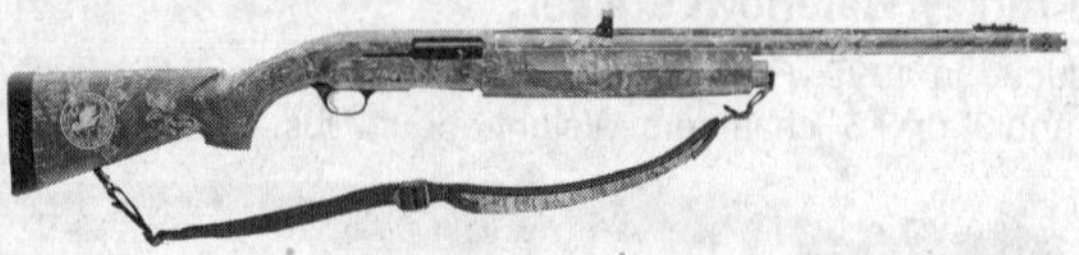

NIB	Exc.	V.G.	Good	Fair	Poor
1280	1000	900	720	380	200

Gold Hunter

Chambered for 12- and 20-gauge. Offered in 26" or 28" barrel lengths. Weight about 6.8 lbs.

NIB	Exc.	V.G.	Good	Fair	Poor
750	620	400	300	200	150

Gold Sporting Clays

Introduced in 1996. Features ported barrel in 28" or 30" lengths. Recoil pad standard. Weight about 7.5 lbs.

NIB	Exc.	V.G.	Good	Fair	Poor
800	680	480	380	200	150

Gold Ladies/Youth Sporting Clays

Offered in 12-gauge only, with 2.75" chambers. Features 28" ventilated rib barrel. Overall dimensions have been adjusted to fit women. Black solid recoil pad. Weight about 7 lbs. 6 oz. Introduced in 1999.

NIB	Exc.	V.G.	Good	Fair	Poor
1200	900	620	450	300	120

Gold "Golden Clays" Ladies Sporting Clays

Introduced in 2005. 12-gauge 2.75 chambered gun. Fitted with 28" ventilated rib ported barrel, with 4 choke tubes. Silver receiver engraved with gold enhancements. Weight about 7.75 lbs.

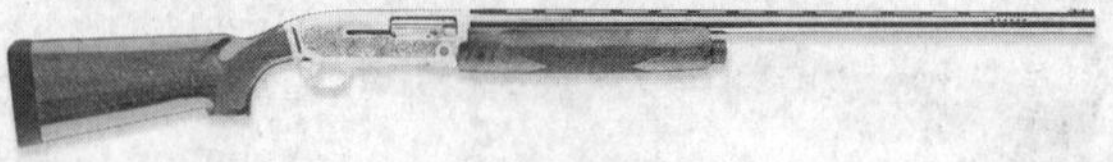

NIB	Exc.	V.G.	Good	Fair	Poor
1500	1380	1050	800	580	300

Gold "Golden Clays" Sporting Clays

As above, with standard stock dimensions. Choice of 28 or 30" barrels. Introduced in 2005.

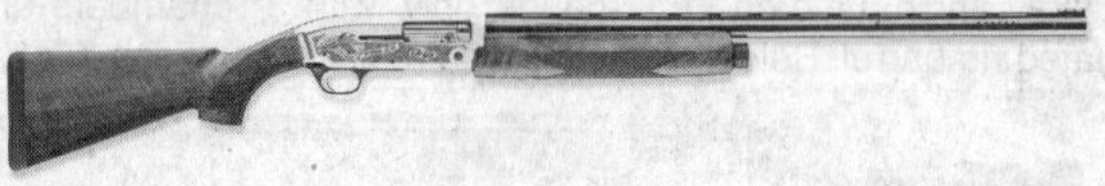

NIB	Exc.	V.G.	Good	Fair	Poor
1800	1300	1050	800	580	300

Gold Micro

Introduced in 2001. Features 20-gauge gun, with 26" barrel, smaller pistol grip, shorter length of pull. Back-bored barrel, with choke tubes. Weight about 6 lb. 10 oz.

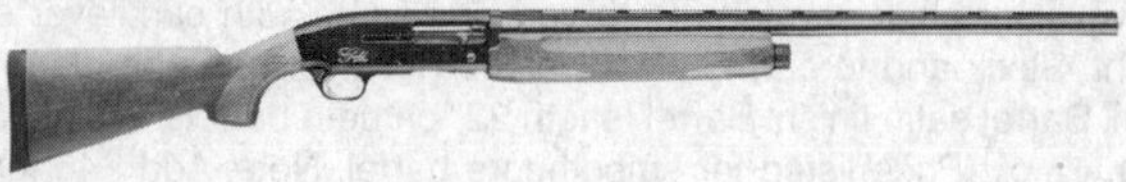

NIB	Exc.	V.G.	Good	Fair	Poor
920	650	580	480	300	120

Gold Upland

Offered in 12- or 20-gauge. Barrel lengths: 12-gauge 24"; 20-gauge 26". Straight-grip stock with 3" chamber. Weight: 12-gauge 7 lbs.; 20-gauge 6.75 lbs. Introduced in 2001.

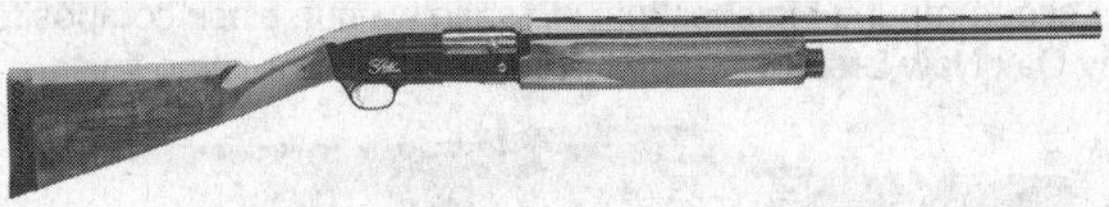

NIB	Exc.	V.G.	Good	Fair	Poor
950	700	600	480	300	120

Gold Fusion

Features a new style ventilated rib, adjustable comb pro-comp sight and five choke tubes. Offered in 12-gauge, 3" chambers with 26" or 28" barrels. Introduced in 2001. In 2002 offered in 20-gauge as well as 12-gauge, with choice of 26" or 28" ventilated rib barrel. Weight about: 12-gauge 7 lbs.; 20-gauge 6.5 lbs.

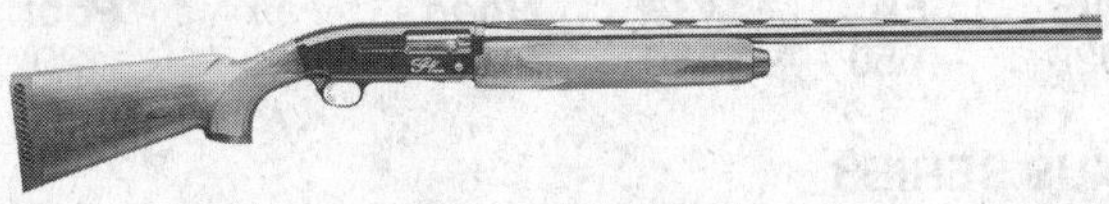

NIB	Exc.	V.G.	Good	Fair	Poor
900	720	650	500	300	120

Gold Fusion High Grade

Similar to Gold Fusion. Addition of high grade Turkish walnut stock, silver nitride receiver with game scene in gold. Five choke tubes and hard case standard. Introduced in 2005.

NIB	Exc.	V.G.	Good	Fair	Poor
1600	1250	900	620	450	300

Golden Clays

Introduced in 1999. Chambered for 12-gauge shell with 2.74" chamber. Choice of 28" or 30" ventilated rib ported barrels. Engraved silver/gray receiver. Select walnut stock. Weight about 7 lbs. 3 oz.

NIB	Exc.	V.G.	Good	Fair	Poor
1250	1000	820	680	420	300

Gold Superlite Hunter

Introduced in 2006. Uses an aluminum alloy receiver and alloy magazine tube to reduce weight to about 7 lbs. in 12-gauge. Gloss finish walnut stock. Available with 3" or 3.5" chamber and 26" or 28" barrel. Magazine cut-off feature on 3.5" model. A 6.5 lb. 20-gauge with 3" chamber and 26" or 28" barrel also offered. Three choke tubes. Note: Add 15% for 3.5" chamber.

NIB	Exc.	V.G.	Good	Fair	Poor
900	650	580	480	300	120

Gold Superlite FLD Hunter

Similar to Gold Superlite Hunter, with semi-humpback style receiver, satin finish walnut stock and 3" chamber only. Magazine cut-off on 12-gauge models. Adjustable shim system and three choke tubes.

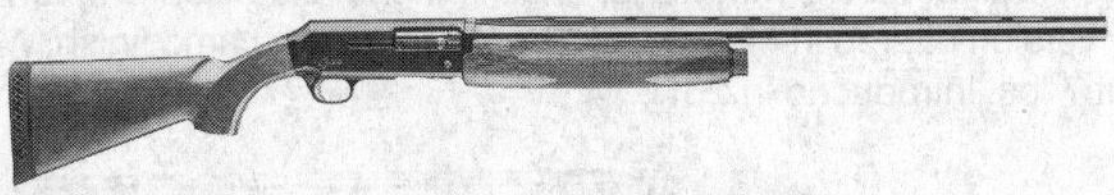

NIB	Exc.	V.G.	Good	Fair	Poor
920	650	580	480	300	120

Gold Superlite Micro

Similar to Gold Superlite Hunter, with compact dimensions for smaller shooters. Only in 20-gauge, with 26" barrel. Weight about 6.25 lbs. Three choke tubes.

NIB	Exc.	V.G.	Good	Fair	Poor
920	650	580	480	300	120

500 SERIES

A-500G/A-500R

Self-adjusting gas-operated semi-automatic shotgun. Chambered for 12-gauge only. Offered with 26", 28" or 30" barrels, with ventilated rib and screw-in Invector choke tubes. Has 3" chambers. Can fire any load interchangeably. Finish blued, with checkered walnut stock and recoil pad. Features light engraving. Introduced in 1987. The 2008 recoil version (A-500R) has a slightly better reputation for functioning than gas-operated A-500G. Values are roughly similar.

NIB	Exc.	V.G.	Good	Fair	Poor
580	490	420	350	280	220

A-500G Sporting Clays

Gas-operated version designed for sporting clays. Features choice of 28" or 30" ventilated rib barrel, with semi-gloss finish and gold lettering "Sporting Clays". Ventilated recoil pad standard. Weight about 8 lbs.

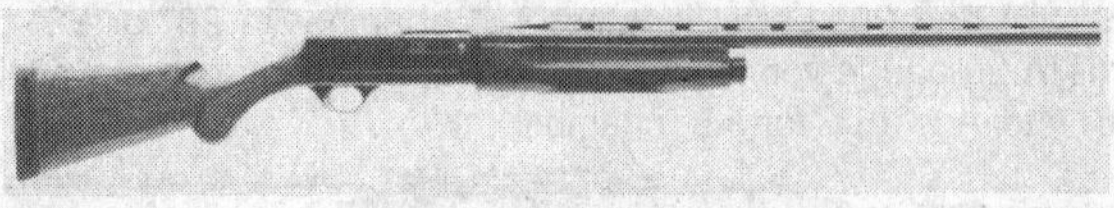

NIB	Exc.	V.G.	Good	Fair	Poor
550	420	350	300	200	150

A-500R Hunting Model

Similar in appearance to A-500G, except this model operates on a short recoil design. Buttstock features full pistol grip. Available with 26", 28" or 30" ventilated rib barrels. Choke tubes standard. Weight about 7 lbs. 13 oz.

NIB	Exc.	V.G.	Good	Fair	Poor
480	380	300	250	200	150

A-500R Buck Special

Same as Hunting Model, with addition of adjustable rear sight, contoured front ramp sight and gold bead. Choke tubes standard, as is 24" barrel. Weight 7 lbs. 11 oz.

NIB	Exc.	V.G.	Good	Fair	Poor
500	420	350	300	220	150

SILVER SERIES

Value-priced series of gas-operated autoloaders. Introduced in 2006. All models feature semi-humpback design and aluminum alloy receiver. Weights vary from 7.25 to 7.5 lbs. depending on barrel length and stock material. Three choke tubes provided with all models. Discontinued models in the Silver line include: Lightning Full Line Dealer, Micro Midas Buckthorn Pink, Silver Deer Mossy Oak Tree Stand, Hunter with TopCote, Micro, Mossy Oak Break-Up Infinity; NWTF Mossy Oak Break-Up Infinity, Rifled Deer Mossy Oak Break-Up Infinity, Rifled Deer Satin, Stalker, Mossy Oak Duck Blind, Mossy Oak New Break-Up, Mossy Oak New Shadow Grass, Sporting Micro, Sporting, Rifled Deer Stalker, Mossy Oak Break-Up Country, Stalker, Sporting Micro Adjustable, NWTF Mossy Oak Break-Up Country, Mossy Oak Shadow Grass Blades, Hunter Micro Midas, Hunter, Rifled Deer Satin, and Field A-TACS AU.

Silver Field Composite

NIB	Exc.	V.G.	Good	Fair	Poor
840	750	650	550	—	—

Silver Field, Mossy Oak Shadow Grass Blades

NIB	Exc.	V.G.	Good	Fair	Poor
980	800	650	550	—	—

Silver Black Lightning

NIB	Exc.	V.G.	Good	Fair	Poor
980	800	650	550	—	—

Silver Field

NIB	Exc.	V.G.	Good	Fair	Poor
900	750	600	500	—	—

Silver Field Micro Midas

NIB	Exc.	V.G.	Good	Fair	Poor
1000	850	700	600	—	—

Silver Rifled Deer, Mossy Oak Break-Up Country

NIB	Exc.	V.G.	Good	Fair	Poor
1000	850	700	600	—	—

Silver Rifled Deer Matte

NIB	Exc.	V.G.	Good	Fair	Poor
1050	950	800	650	—	—

Silver Hunter

Features satin finish walnut stock and forend. Available with 3" chambers in 26", 28" and 30" barrel lengths; 3.5" chamber in 26" or 28" barrel lengths. A 20-gauge version with 26" or 28" barrels became available in 2008. Note: Add 15% for 3.5" chamber.

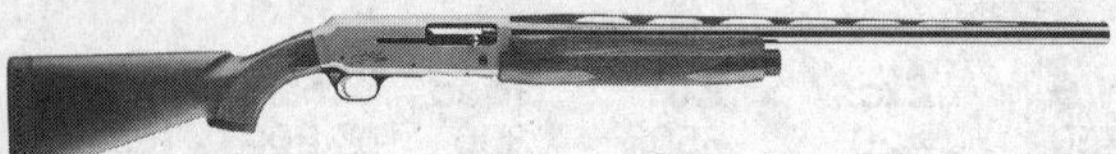

NIB	Exc.	V.G.	Good	Fair	Poor
1000	850	700	500	400	250

Silver Stalker

Similar to Silver Hunter, with matte black composite stock and forend. Sling swivel studs. 3.5" chamber only.

NIB	Exc.	V.G.	Good	Fair	Poor
820	680	550	380	280	180

Silver Micro

20-gauge, with 26" barrel. Shorter stock dimensions for smaller shooters.

NIB	Exc.	V.G.	Good	Fair	Poor
820	700	550	380	280	180

Silver Sporting Micro

This 2.75" 12-gauge includes adjustment spacers for changing stock length. Barrel is 28". Three choke tubes included. Weight about 7 lbs.

NIB	Exc.	V.G.	Good	Fair	Poor
1150	900	720	600	380	250

Silver NWTF

New in 2008. This 3" 12-gauge turkey gun is fully camouflaged with Mossy Oak's New Break-Up pattern. Barrel 24" outfitted with fiber-optic rifle sights. Weight about 7 lbs. Note: Add 10 percent for 3.5" chamber.

NIB	Exc.	V.G.	Good	Fair	Poor
1100	900	720	600	380	250

Silver Rifled Deer

New in 2008. This 3" 12-gauge slug gun features rifled barrel, with cantilever scope mount. Finishes include satin walnut, black composite and Mossy Oak New Break-Up camo. Note: Add 10% for camo finish.

NIB	Exc.	V.G.	Good	Fair	Poor
1100	900	720	600	380	250

Silver–Mossy Oak

Similar to Silver Stalker. Choice of Mossy Oak New Break-Up with 26" barrel or Mossy Oak New Shadow Grass with 26" or 28" barrel.

NIB	Exc.	V.G.	Good	Fair	Poor
920	650	580	480	300	120

MAXUS SERIES

Introduced in 2009. Replacement for Gold line.

Maxus

Autoloading shotgun chambered for 3" or 3.5" shells. Aluminum receiver, lightweight profi le 26" or 28" barrel with ventilated rib, composite stock, Vector Pro lengthened forcing cone, DuraTouch Armor Coating overall. Weight 6.875 lbs. Discontinued Maxus shotguns include: Sporting Golden Clays Maple; Rifled Deer, Mossy Oak Break-Up Infinity; Realtree Max-4; Mossy Oak Duck Blind; Hunter Maple; All-Purpose, Mossy Oak Break-Up Infinity; Maxus Sporting Golden Clays Maple; Rifled Deer - Mossy Oak Break-Up Country; Rifled Deer Stalker; A-TACS AU (Arid/Urban); All Purpose Hunter A-TACS FG (Foliage/Green).

Maxus Stalker

Matte black finish overall. Note: Add $150 for 3.5" chamber.

NIB	Exc.	V.G.	Good	Fair	Poor
1200	980	800	620	480	300

Maxus Mossy Oak Duck Blind

Mossy Oak Duck Blind finish overall. Note: Add $150 for 3.5" chamber.

NIB	Exc.	V.G.	Good	Fair	Poor
1300	980	800	620	480	300

Maxus Hunter

Gas-operated autoloader available with 3" or 3.5" Magnum chambers. Barrel lengths: 26", 28", 30" (22" for rifled version). Lengthened forcing cone. Stock is shim-adjustable for length of pull, cast and drop. Glossy-finished walnut stock, with 22 lpi checkering. Maxus Hunter and Rifled Deer version offered in Mossy Oak Break-Up Infinity camo finish. Weight about 7 lbs. Introduced in 2011.

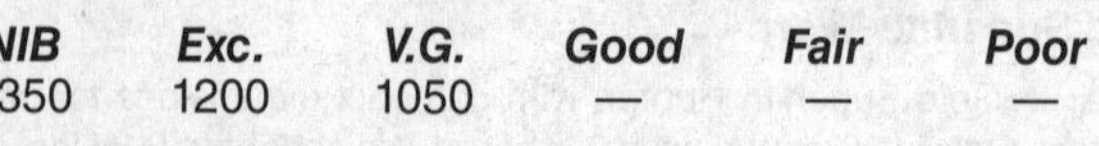

NIB	Exc.	V.G.	Good	Fair	Poor
1350	1200	1050	—	—	—

Maxus Sporting Carbon

Gas-operated 12-gauge autoloader, with 3" chamber. Aluminum alloy receiver has satin nickel finish, laser engraving. Barrel lengths 28" or 30". Gloss-finished high-grade walnut stock. Available with carbon fiber stock and Rifled Deer Stalker version with cantilevered scope base and

22" barrel. New 2011. Note: Deduct 15 percent for Deer Stalker/Carbon

NIB	Exc.	V.G.	Good	Fair	Poor
1550	1450	1350	1200	—	—

Maxus II

Gauge: 12 ga. Choice of 3 or 3.5-in. models. Barrel: 26, 28, or 30 in. Weight: 7.0 lbs.–7.3 lbs. Stock: Dependent on model, but current listings include black synthetic and camouflaged variants. Features: Builds on Browning's Power Drive gas-operated Maxus autoloader in a II version with enhancements. Chrome chamber and bore. Ramped triggerguard for easier loading. Composite stock can be trimmed and is shim adjustable for cast, drop, and LOP. Rubber overmolding on the stock, including SoftFlex cheek pad and Inflex recoil pad. Oversized controls. New screw-on magazine cap design. Includes Invector-Plus choke tubes, extended on most models, as well as an ABS hard case.

NIB	Exc.	V.G.	Good	Fair	Poor
1910	1500	1250	1000	—	—

Maxus Sporting Golden Clays

Top of the Maxus line, with satin nickel finished receiver, gold enhanced engraving, Grade III walnut stock and forend. Features include a High Viz fiber optic front sight, extra fast trigger lock time, stock adjustable for length of pull, cast and comb height.

NIB	Exc.	V.G.	Good	Fair	Poor
1850	1750	1550	1300	—	—

Maxus Ultimate

Features intricately laser-engraved satin nickel finish receiver, with pheasants on right side and mallards on left. Barrels are 26", with three Invector choke tubes. Grade III gloss Turkish walnut stock, with cut checkering at 22 lpi and Inflex recoil pad.

NIB	Exc.	V.G.	Good	Fair	Poor
1700	1550	1300	1100	—	—

Maxus Wicked Wing - Mossy Oak Shadow Grass Blades

NIB	Exc.	V.G.	Good	Fair	Poor
1600	1450	1200	—	—	—

BPS SERIES

Slide-action shotgun chambered for 10, 12 or 20 gauge. Offered with various length ventilated rib barrels, with screw-in Invector chokes. Features 3" Magnum chambers, bottom-ejection system that effectively makes it ambidextrous. Has double slide bars and 5-shot tubular magazine. Constructed of all steel. Introduced by B.C. Miroku in 1977. In 2019, the line was redesigned with a larger triggerguard, a new satin-finished walnut stock, a matte-blued barrel with a ventilated rib, an Inflex recoil pad three Invector-Plus choke tubes, and a silver bead front sight. In 2019, the 10 gauge was no longer offered. Barrel lengths were 26" and 28" with 3" chambers. 12 gauges weigh around 7.6 lbs. 20 gauges come in at 7.1 lbs.

BPS Field (Walnut) 2019

NIB	Exc.	V.G.	Good	Fair	Poor
590	500	430	—	—	—

BPS Field Composite

NIB	Exc.	V.G.	Good	Fair	Poor
620	530	450	—	—	—

BPS Field Composite 2019

NIB	Exc.	V.G.	Good	Fair	Poor
540	430	400	—	—	—

BPS Field Composite Camo

NIB	Exc.	V.G.	Good	Fair	Poor
720	620	530	—	—	—

BPS Field Waterfowl 2019

NIB	Exc.	V.G.	Good	Fair	Poor
620	530	450	—	—	—

BPS Field Grade

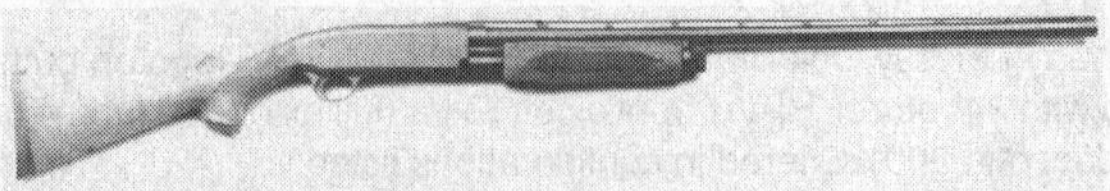

NIB	Exc.	V.G.	Good	Fair	Poor
350	300	280	200	200	150

28 Gauge

Introduced in 1994. Weight approximately 7 lbs.

NIB	Exc.	V.G.	Good	Fair	Poor
420	320	300	220	210	150

BPS Magnum

10- or 12-gauge, 3.5" chambers.

NIB	Exc.	V.G.	Good	Fair	Poor
510	400	350	300	250	150

BPS Waterfowl 12 Gauge Camo

Introduced in 1999.

NIB	Exc.	V.G.	Good	Fair	Poor
520	420	350	300	250	150

BPS Waterfowl 12 Gauge Mossy Oak Break-Up

NIB	Exc.	V.G.	Good	Fair	Poor
580	480	380	320	250	150

BPS Mossy Oak New Break-up

Similar to BPS Hunter, with Mossy Oak New Break-up camo finish overall; chambers 3" and 3.5"; 12-gauge only.

NIB	Exc.	V.G.	Good	Fair	Poor
750	620	400	300	200	150

BPS Mossy Oak Duck Blind

Similar to above, with Mossy Oak Duck Blind finish overall.

NIB	Exc.	V.G.	Good	Fair	Poor
750	620	400	300	200	150

BPS Rifled Deer Mossy Oak New Break-up

Similar to BPS Rifled Deer Hunter, with Mossy Oak New Break-up camo finish overall.

NIB	Exc.	V.G.	Good	Fair	Poor
750	620	400	300	200	150

BPS NWTF Series

Finished in Mossy Oak Breakup pattern. Bears NWTF logo on buttstock. Fitted with 24" barrel, Hi-Viz front sight, Extra Full extended turkey choke. Introduced in 2001. Offered in configurations listed.

10 Gauge

NIB	Exc.	V.G.	Good	Fair	Poor
620	480	400	320	200	120

12 Gauge 3.5" Chamber

NIB	Exc.	V.G.	Good	Fair	Poor
620	480	400	320	200	120

12 Gauge 3" Chamber

NIB	Exc.	V.G.	Good	Fair	Poor
550	450	380	320	200	120

BPS Stalker

Matte finish black stock.

NIB	Exc.	V.G.	Good	Fair	Poor
440	390	320	280	200	150

BPS Stalker—Combo

Combination of 28" ventilated rib barrel and choice of 22" fully rifle barrel or 20.5" Invector barrel, with Extra Full turkey choke. Introduced in 2000.

NIB	Exc.	V.G.	Good	Fair	Poor
650	520	480	320	200	120

BPS Game Gun

These models are designed for turkey and deer hunting. Introduced in 1992 in 12-gauge only, with 20.5" barrel. Turkey Special has Fixed Extra-Full choke barrel, while Deer Special originally came with 5" rifled tube. In 1998, a fully rifled barrel became an option for Deer Special. In 2007, a 20-gauge version was introduced. Turkey Special is drilled and tapped for scope mounts. Deer Special has cantilever mounting system plus iron sights. Note: Deduct 15% for Deer Special without a fully rifled barrel.

Game Gun Deer Special (shown above)

NIB	Exc.	V.G.	Good	Fair	Poor
600	500	420	380	320	250

Game Gun Turkey Special

NIB	Exc.	V.G.	Good	Fair	Poor
400	380	350	320	300	250

BPS 10 Gauge Mossy Oak Shadow Grass Camo

Introduced in 1999.

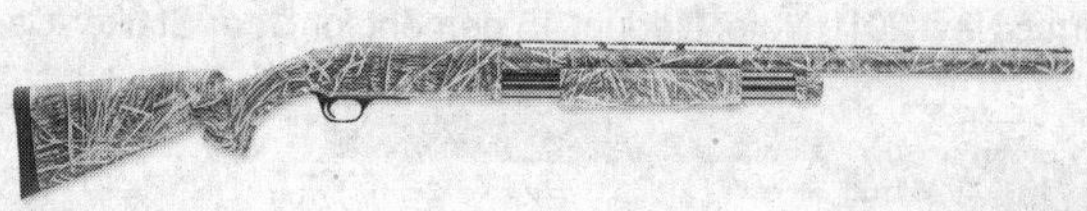

NIB	Exc.	V.G.	Good	Fair	Poor
580	480	380	320	180	120

BPS 10 Gauge Turkey

Fitted with 24" ventilated rib barrel, black synthetic stock and black solid recoil pad. Introduced in 1999. Weight about 9 lbs. 2 oz.

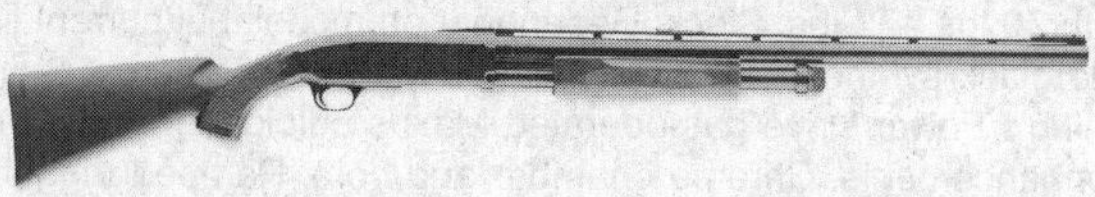

NIB	Exc.	V.G.	Good	Fair	Poor
520	420	380	320	200	120

BPS Micro 20 Gauge

Features 22" ventilated rib barrel, shorter pistol grip stock and lighter-weight. Weight about 6.75 lbs. Introduced in 2001.

NIB	Exc.	V.G.	Good	Fair	Poor
450	350	300	250	200	120

BPS Upland Special

Chambered for 20-gauge shell. Fitted with 22" ventilated rib barrel. Walnut stock is straight-grip. Weight about 6.5 lbs. Available in 12- or 20-gauge, with 22" barrel. A 16-gauge version, with 24" or 26" barrel introduced in 2008. A very beautiful little pump.

NIB	Exc.	V.G.	Good	Fair	Poor
550	380	300	280	200	120

BPS Small Gauge

Introduced in 2000. Chambered for 28-gauge and .410 bore. The 28-gauge offered with choice of 26" or 28" ventilated rib barrel and Invector chokes. The .410 available with 26" ventilated rib barrel and Invector chokes. Weight about 6.75 lbs. each.

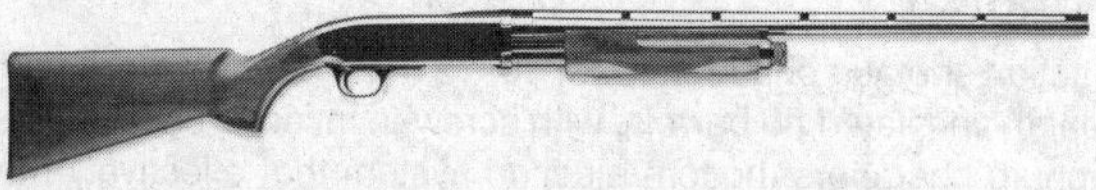

NIB	Exc.	V.G.	Good	Fair	Poor
520	450	320	280	200	120

BPS Pigeon Grade

Furnished in 12-gauge only, with high grade walnut stock and gold trimmed receiver.

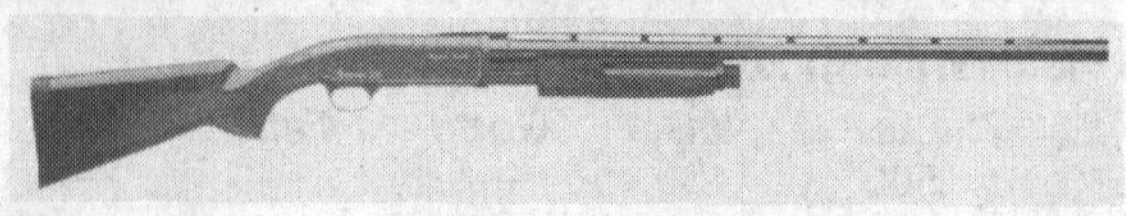

NIB	Exc.	V.G.	Good	Fair	Poor
500	400	300	220	180	120

BPS Buck Special

24" barrel with sights.

NIB	Exc.	V.G.	Good	Fair	Poor
450	400	350	300	220	180

BPS Trap Model

NIB	Exc.	V.G.	Good	Fair	Poor
—	380	320	280	200	150

BPS Micro Trap

Similar to BPS Trap Model, with compact dimensions (13.75" length of pull, 48.25" overall length). 12-gauge only. CAUTION: Do not interchange Invector choke tubes with Invector-Plus choke tubes. May cause personal injury.

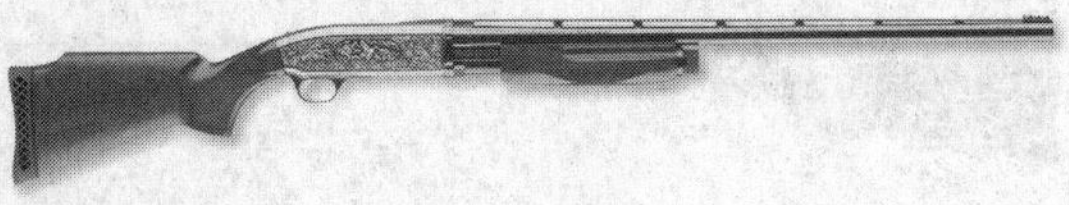

NIB	Exc.	V.G.	Good	Fair	Poor
700	—	—	—	—	—

BPS Youth Model

Short stock, 22" barrel.

NIB	Exc.	V.G.	Good	Fair	Poor
440	390	320	280	200	150

BPS Waterfowl Deluxe

Chambered for 12-gauge 3" chamber. Features etched receiver, with gold-plated trigger. Otherwise, similar to standard BPS.

NIB	Exc.	V.G.	Good	Fair	Poor
—	600	520	420	320	250

BPS Ducks Unlimited Versions

Limited-edition guns produced to be auctioned by Ducks Unlimited. Furnished with a case. Must be NIB with furnished materials to realize their collector potential.

NIB	Exc.	V.G.	Good	Fair	Poor
650	520	420	320	250	180

MODEL 12

Grade I

Slide-action shotgun chambered for 20- and 28-gauge, with 26" Modified choke and ventilated rib barrel. Reproduction of Winchester Model 12 shotgun. Has 5-round tubular magazine, with floating high-post rib and take-down feature. Blued, with walnut stock. Introduced in 1991. Total production limited to 7,000 guns.

NIB	Exc.	V.G.	Good	Fair	Poor
820	620	420	300	250	200

Grade V

Extensively engraved version of Grade I Model 12. Features select walnut stock, with deluxe checkering and high-gloss finish. Gold inlays. Introduced in 1991. Production limited to 5,000 guns. Discontinued 1992. Note: Add 30 percent for 28-gauge.

NIB	Exc.	V.G.	Good	Fair	Poor
1300	950	700	450	—	—

LIMITED EDITION MODEL 42

New version of .410 bore pump shotgun. Last produced by Winchester in 1963. Available in two grades, both fitted with 26" ventilated rib barrels. Grade I features plain blued receiver, with walnut stock. Grade V features blued receiver, with scroll engraving and gold inlays. Both models choked Full. Weight 6 lbs. 4 oz.

Grade I

NIB	Exc.	V.G.	Good	Fair	Poor
900	600	500	400	—	—

Grade V

NIB	Exc.	V.G.	Good	Fair	Poor
1450	1000	700	500	—	—

A-BOLT SHOTGUN

Introduced in 1995. Bolt-action shotgun offered in 12-gauge, with 3" chamber. Rifled barrel version 22" long, while Invector barrel version 23" long, with 5" rifle tube installed. Has 2-shot detachable magazine. Average weight about 7 lbs. Considered "Rolls Royce" of bolt shotguns and becoming quite desirable. Manufacture ceased in 1998. Note: Deduct $50 for Invector rifled choke tube model.

Hunter Version

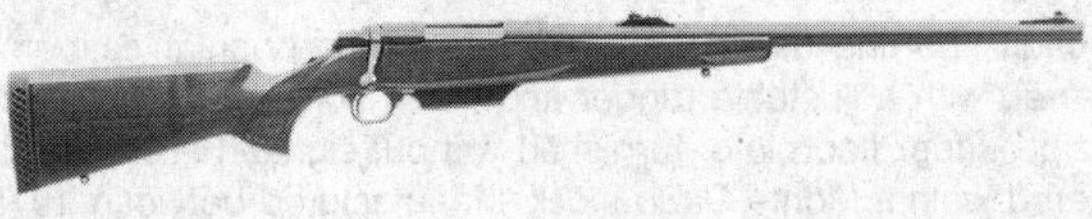

NIB	Exc.	V.G.	Good	Fair	Poor
1000	850	750	500	300	100

Stalker Version

NIB	Exc.	V.G.	Good	Fair	Poor
900	750	650	400	200	100

RIFLES

High-Power Bolt-Action Rifle

High-grade bolt-action sporting rifle manufactured by FN in Belgium (from 1959 to 1975) or Sako of Finland (from 1961 to 1975). Built on Mauser or Sako action. Chambered for a number of popular calibers from .222 Remington up to .458 Winchester Magnum. Three basic grades that differed in amount of ornamentation, quality of materials and workmanship utilized. Certain calibers are considered to be rare and will bring a premium from collectors of this firearm. We recommend securing a qualified appraisal on these rifles if a transaction is contemplated. We furnish general values only.

Note: From 1959 through 1966, FN Mauser actions with long extractors were featured. These Mauser actions will bring a premium depending on caliber. From 1967 on, FN Supreme actions with short extractors were used. Only .30-06 and .270-calibers continued with long extractor Mauser actions.

CAUTION: Buyer and seller alike, some rare calibers may be worth as much as 100 percent or more over prices listed for rare calibers such as .284 Win., .257 Roberts, .300 H&H and .308 Norma Magnum. High-Power bolt-action rifles seemed to be particularly hard hit by salt wood. That is why short extractor rifles bring less than long extractor guns. No factory replacement stocks are known to still be available. Deduct 20-25 percent for short extractor rifles. Proceed with caution.

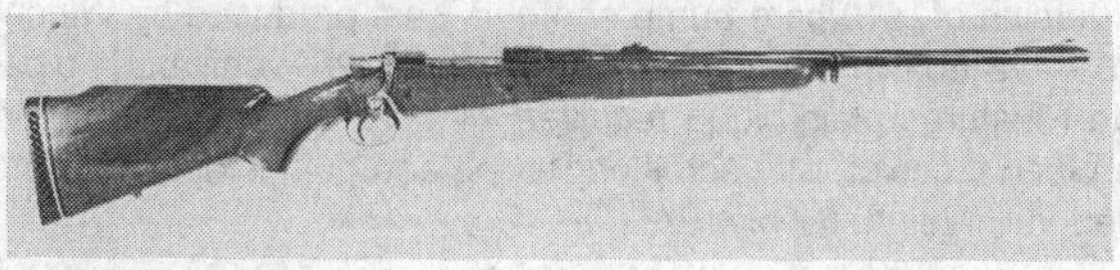

Safari Grade

Standard model and calibers.

NIB	Exc.	V.G.	Good	Fair	Poor
1600	1350	1100	850	400	300

Medallion Grade

Scroll engraved, standard calibers.

NIB	Exc.	V.G.	Good	Fair	Poor
3200	2500	1900	1400	750	400

Olympian Grade

Extensive game scene engraving, standard calibers.

NIB	Exc.	V.G.	Good	Fair	Poor
8500	6300	5250	4250	2500	1500

Model BBR

Bolt-action sporting rifle chambered for various popular calibers. Has 24" barrel, with adjustable trigger and fluted bolt. Features detachable magazine under floorplate, furnished without sights. Finish blued, with checkered walnut Monte Carlo stock. Manufactured between 1978 and 1984 by Miroku.

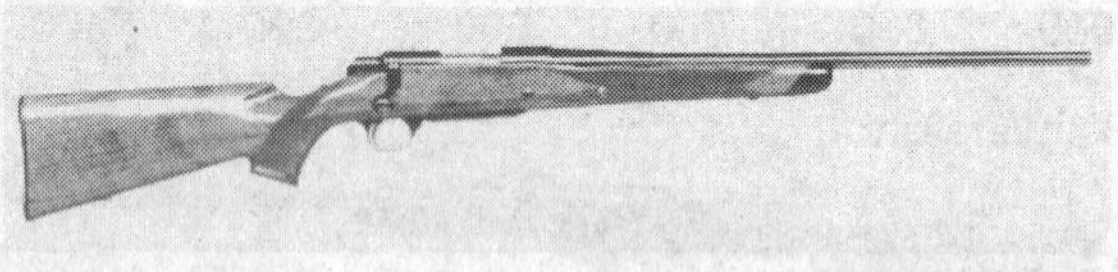

NIB	Exc.	V.G.	Good	Fair	Poor
680	580	400	350	280	200

BOSS™ SYSTEM

Introduced by Browning in 1994. New accuracy system allows shooter to fine-tune his Browning rifle to particular load he is using. Consists of a tube on end of rifle-muzzle that allows shooter to select best setting for ammunition type. System also reduces recoil. BOSS stands for "Ballistic Optimizing Shooting System". This option will add approximately $80 to value of particular Browning rifle on which it is fitted.

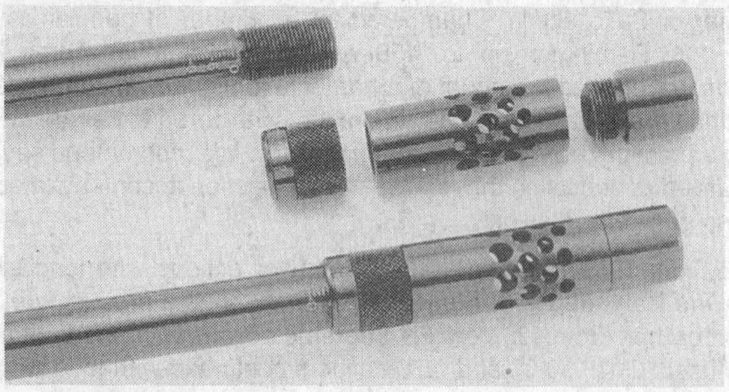

X-BOLT SERIES

Introduced in 2008. X-Bolt series of rifle features adjustable three-position Feather Trigger system, newly-designed bolt release, improved scope mounting system, tang safety. Generally slimmer sleeker profile.

X-Bolt Composite Stalker

Features include steel receiver, matte blue finish, free-floating crowned barrel, matte black composite stock with palm swell, Inflex recoil pad. Various barrel lengths depending on chambering, which include both medium and long cartridges ranging from .243 Winchester to .338 Winchester Magnum. Introduced in 2008.

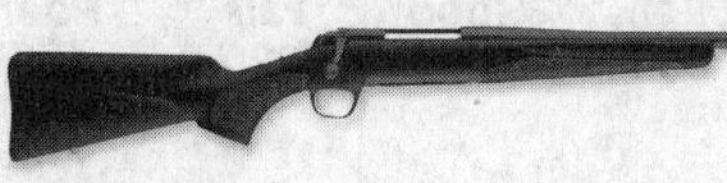

NIB	Exc.	V.G.	Good	Fair	Poor
850	700	600	500	350	200

X-Bolt Stainless Stalker

Similar to above, with stainless steel receiver and barrel. Various barrel lengths depending on chambering, which include both medium and long cartridges ranging from .243 Winchester to .375 H&H Magnum. Introduced in 2008.

NIB	Exc.	V.G.	Good	Fair	Poor
850	700	600	500	350	200

X-Bolt Hunter

Similar to above, with sculpted satin-finished walnut stock and cut checkering. Low-luster blued barrel and receiver. Various barrel lengths depending on chambering, which include both medium and long cartridges ranging from .243 Winchester to .338 Winchester Magnum. Left-hand model available.

NIB	Exc.	V.G.	Good	Fair	Poor
850	700	600	500	350	200

X-Bolt Hunter Long Range

Calibers: 6.5 Creedmoor, 6.5 PRC, .308 Win., .270 Win., .30-06, 7MM Rem. Mag., .300 Win. Mag. Capacity: 3 to 4. Barrel: 22 to 26 in., blued sporter, heavy. Stock: Satin finish checkered walnut. Sights: None, drilled and tapped. Weight: 7.6 to 8 lbs. Features: Ambidextrous adjustable comb, muzzle brake with suppressor threads.

NIB	Exc.	V.G.	Good	Fair	Poor
1140	980	830	—	—	—

X-Bolt Max Long Range

Calibers: 6mm Creedmoor, 6.5 Creedmoor, .308 Win., .300 WSM, 7MM Rem. Mag., 28 Nosler, .300 Win. Mag, .300 RUM, 6.5 PRC, 30 Nosler, .300 PRC. Capacity: 3 to 4. Barrel: 26 in., satin gray stainless steel sporter, heavy. Stock: Composite black, gray splatter. Sights: None, drilled and tapped. Weight: 8.2 to 8.6 lbs. Features: Adjustable comb, extended bolt handle, three swivel studs for sling and bipod use.

NIB	Exc.	V.G.	Good	Fair	Poor
1200	1000	850	—	—	—

X-Bolt Medallion

Similar to above, with high-gloss finish. Engraved blued barrel and receiver. Various barrel lengths depending on chambering, which include both medium and long cartridges ranging from .243 Winchester to .375 H&H Magnum. Introduced in 2008. Available in left-hand version.

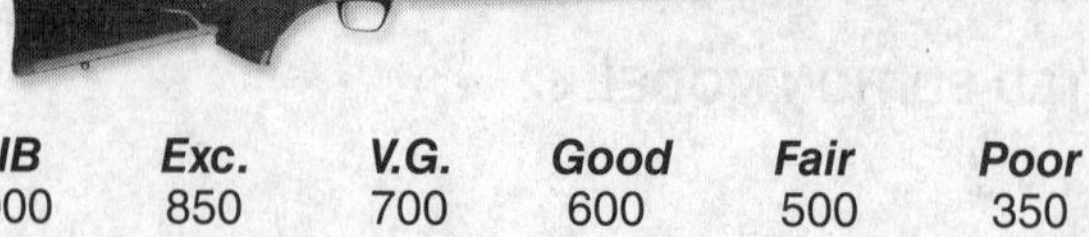

NIB	Exc.	V.G.	Good	Fair	Poor
1000	850	700	600	500	350

X-Bolt Micro Hunter

Similar to Browning X-Bolt Hunter, with compact dimensions (13.3125" length of pull, 41.25" overall length). Left-hand available.

NIB	Exc.	V.G.	Good	Fair	Poor
800	700	600	500	350	200

X-Bolt Eclipse Hunter

Features laminated gray satin finished thumbhole stock, with Monte Carlo cheekpiece and grooved forend. Same calibers and other features of standard X-Bolt Hunter models.

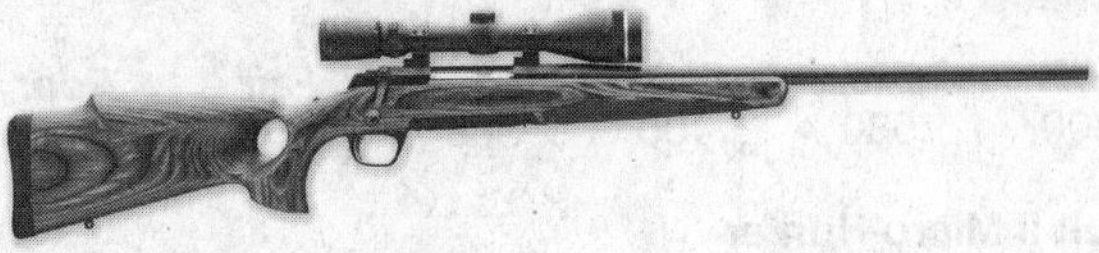

NIB	Exc.	V.G.	Good	Fair	Poor
900	800	680	500	350	250

X-Bolt Varmint Stalker

Similar to X-Bolt Stalker, with medium-heavy free-floated barrel, target crown, composite stock. Cartridges .223, .22-250, .243 Winchester and .308 Winchester only.

NIB	Exc.	V.G.	Good	Fair	Poor
1000	850	700	600	500	350

X-Bolt RMEF White Gold

Similar to X-Bolt Medallion, with gold-engraved matte stainless finish. Rocky Mountain Elk Foundation grip cap. Chambered in .325 WSM only.

NIB	Exc.	V.G.	Good	Fair	Poor
1300	1000	850	650	550	380

X-Bolt RMEF Special Hunter

Similar to above. Matte blued finish, without gold highlights.

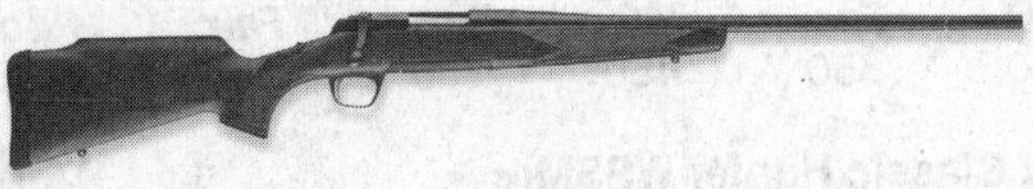

NIB	Exc.	V.G.	Good	Fair	Poor
900	700	600	500	350	200

X-Bolt Hell's Canyon

Chambered in popular calibers from .243 to .300 Win. Magnum, including .26 Nosler. Free floating and fluted barrel has muzzle brake. Stock has A-TACS AU camo, with palm swell and textured grip Finish is Cerakote Burnt Bronze.

NIB	Exc.	V.G.	Good	Fair	Poor
1050	880	650	500	350	250

X-Bolt Hells Canyon Max Long Range

Calibers: 6.5 Creed, 6.5 PRC, 7mm Rem. Mag., 28 Nosler, .280 Ackley Improved, .300 Win. Mag., 30 Nosler, .300 Rem. Ultra Mag., .300 PRC, 6.8 Western. Capacity: 3- or 4-round box magazine. Barrel: 26-in. heavy sporter. Weight: 8–8 lbs. 7oz. Length: 46-3/4 in. Stock: Composite Max in either A-TACS AU or OVIX camo with adjustable comb, LOP spacers, and vertical pistol grip. Features: Long-range bolt-action platform with steel receiver. Cerakote Burnt Bronze finish. Removeable Browning Recoil Hawg muzzle brake. Top tang thumb safety. Extended bolt handle. Three swivel studs. FeatherTrigger, InFlex recoil pad. Gold-plated trigger and branding detail.

NIB	Exc.	V.G.	Good	Fair	Poor
1440	—	—	—	—	—

X-Bolt Max Varmint/Target

Calibers: .204 Ruger, .223 Rem., .22-250 Rem., 6.5 Creedmoor, .308 Win., 28 Nosler, .300 Win. Mag. Capacity: 3 to 5. Barrel: 26 in., stainless steel heavy bull, fluted. Stock: Composite. Sights: None, drilled and tapped. Weight: 9 to 9.5 lbs. Features: Quarter-inch and two-thirds-inch LOP spacers, extended bolt handle, gray textured stock, suppressor ready.

NIB	Exc.	V.G.	Good	Fair	Poor
1300	—	—	—	—	—

X-Bolt Western Hunter

Calibers: 6.5 Creed, 6.5 PRC, 7mm Rem. Mag., 28 Nosler, .280 Ackley Improved, .300 Win. Mag., 30 Nosler, .300 Rem. Ultra Mag, .300 PRC, 6.8 Western. Capacity: 3- or 4-round removeable rotary magazine. Barrel: 22, 24, or 26-in. sporter contour. Length: 42 3/4–46 3/5 in. Weight: 6 lbs. 5 oz.–7 lbs. 7oz. Stock: Composite with A-TACS AU camouflage and textured grip panels. Features: Bolt action X-Bolt platform with removeable muzzle brake. New adjustable comb system. Ergonomic bolt handle. Top tang thumb safety. Feather Trigger, InFlex recoil pad. Sling studs. Bolt unlock button. X-Lock scope mount system. Gold-plated trigger and branding detail.

NIB	Exc.	V.G.	Good	Fair	Poor
990	—	—	—	—	—

X-Bolt Western Hunter Long Range

Calibers: 6.5 Creed, 6.5 PRC, 7mm Rem. Mag., 28 Nosler, .280 Ackley Improved, .300 Win. Mag., 30 Nosler, .300 Rem. Ultra Mag, .300 PRC, 6.8 Western. Capacity: 3- or 4-round removeable rotary magazine. Barrel: 26-in. heavy sporter contour with removeable muzzle brake. Length: 46–46.75 in. Weight: 7 lb. 7 oz.–7 lb. 12 oz. Stock: Composite with new adjustable comb system. Choice of A-TACS AU or OVIX camo finish. Textured grip panels. Features: Radial muzzle brake. Top tang thumb safety. Extended bolt handle. Feather Trigger, InFlex recoil pad. X-Lock scope mount system. Gold-plated trigger. Sling studs.

NIB	Exc.	V.G.	Good	Fair	Poor
1030	—	—	—	—	—

X-Bolt Mountain Pro

Caliber: 6.5 Creedmoor, 6.5 PRC, 6.8 Western, .300 WSM, .30-06 Spfld., 7mm Rem. Mag., 28 Nosler, .300 Win. Mag., 30 Nosler, .300 PRC, .300 Rem. UM. Capacity: 3- or 4-round box magazine. Barrel: 22, 23, 24, or 26 in. sporter weight, threaded, with Recoil Hawg muzzle brake. Length: 42–46.75 in. Weight: 5 lbs. 14 oz.–6 lbs. 6 oz. Stock: Carbon fiber filled with noise-dampening foam and finished with accent graphics. Features: Choice of either Burnt Bronze or Tungsten models. Big game bolt-action semi-custom hunting rifle. New proprietary lapping process for easier bore cleaning and avoiding break-in. Cerakote finish on stainless steel barrel and action. Spiral fluted bolt and barrel. Quarter-pound weight reduction over previous models. Removeable Picatinny accessory rail. Swivel studs. Feather trigger. X-Lock optics mounting system. InFlex recoil pad. Gold-plated trigger and brand detail. Thread protector included. Mountain Pro SPR in either Burnt Bronze or Tungsten w/ 18", 20", and 22" threaded barrels with Recoil Hawg brake.

NIB	Exc.	V.G.	Good	Fair	Poor
2460	2300	2200	—	—	—

X-Bolt Speed

Calibers: .243 Win., 6.5 Creed, 6.5 PRC, 7mm-08 Rem., .308 Win., .270 Win., .270 WSM, .300 WSM, 7mm Rem. Mag., 28 Nosler, .280 Ackley Improved, .30-06, .300 Win. Mag., .300 Rem. Ultra Mag., .300 PRC, 6.8 Western. Capacity: 3- or 4-round removeable rotary magazine. Barrel: 22, 24, or 26-in. sporter contour. Length: 42 3/4–46 3/5 in. Weight: 6 lbs. 5 oz.–6 lbs. 13 oz. Stock: Composite with either A-TACS AU or OVIX camouflage and textured grip panels. Features: Bolt-action X-Bolt platform with removeable muzzle brake. Smoked Bronze Cerakote finish. Ergonomic bolt handle. Top tang thumb safety. Feather Trigger, InFlex recoil pad. Sling studs. Bolt unlock button. X-Lock scope mount system. Gold-plated trigger and branding detail.

NIB	Exc.	V.G.	Good	Fair	Poor
1220	—	—	—	—	—

X-Bolt Pro Series

NIB	Exc.	V.G.	Good	Fair	Poor
2660	—	—	—	—	—

X-Bolt Target Max Competition

Caliber: 6mm Creed, 6mm GT, 6.5 Creedmoor, .308 Win. Barrel: 26" heavy stainless bull (Heavy model), 22" fluted sporter weight (Lite model). Weights: 9 to 12 lbs. Stock: Nylon-filled MAX with vertical grip and adjustable comb. Features: Specialized bolt-action target rifles aimed at competitions. Built on stiffer, heavier receivers. Factory ARCA/Swiss rail. Threaded barrel with Recoil Hawg brake. Textured grip panels. Gold-plated trigger. Extra capacity magazine.

NIB	Exc.	V.G.	Good	Fair	Poor
1550	—	—	—	—	—

A-BOLT SERIES

Note: In 2004, new calibers were offered for A-Bolt series depending on model. They are .25 WSSM and .223 Rem. All A-Bolt II Descriptions: "II" designation dropped from A-Bolt name in 2006.

A-Bolt Hunter

Current bolt-action rifle manufactured by B.C. Miroku. Chambered for various popular calibers. Offered with 22", 24" or 26" barrel. Has short-/long-action. Adjustable trigger. Detachable box magazine mounted under floorplate. Furnished without sights. Blued, with checkered walnut stock. Introduced in 1985.

NIB	Exc.	V.G.	Good	Fair	Poor
580	400	350	300	250	200

A-Bolt II Hunter

Introduced in 1994. New model features newly designed anti-bind bolt and improved trigger system. In 2001, .300 Winchester Short Magnum cartridge offered for this model. In 2003, a left-hand model introduced.

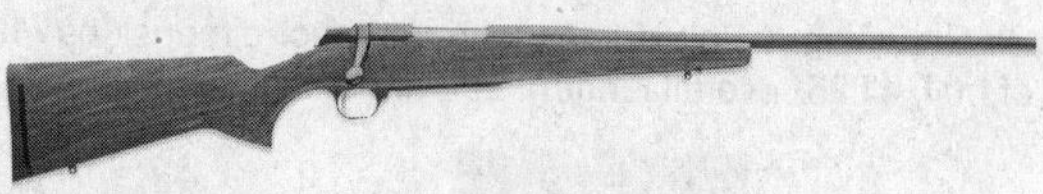

NIB	Exc.	V.G.	Good	Fair	Poor
800	580	400	300	250	200

A-Bolt II Hunter WSSM

Similar to A-Bolt Hunter. Chambered for .223 WSSM and .243 WSSM cartridges. Stock design different, with addition of longer pistol grip and thicker forearm. Weight about 6.25 lbs. Introduced in 2003.

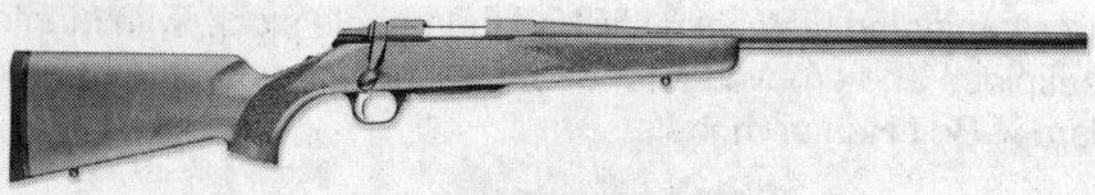

NIB	Exc.	V.G.	Good	Fair	Poor
800	580	400	300	250	200

A-Bolt II Micro Hunter

Introduced in 1999. Features shorter length of pull and shorter barrel length than Hunter model. Offered in .22 Hornet, .22-250, 7mm-08, .308, .243 and .260 calibers. Weight about 6 lbs. In 2003, .270 WSM, 7mm WSM and .300 WSM calibers were added for this model as well as left-hand version. Note: Add $30 for left-hand; $30 for WSM calibers.

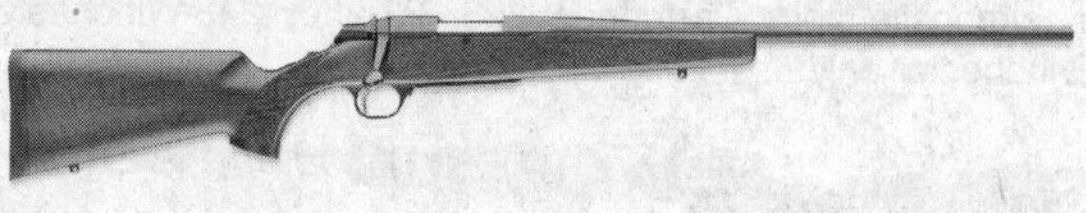

NIB	Exc.	V.G.	Good	Fair	Poor
650	520	350	250	200	150

A-Bolt II Classic Hunter

Features Monte Carlo stock, low luster bluing, select walnut and double bordered checkering. Offered in .30-06, .270, 7mm Rem. Magnum and .300 Win. Magnum. No sights. Weight about 7 lbs. Introduced in 1999.

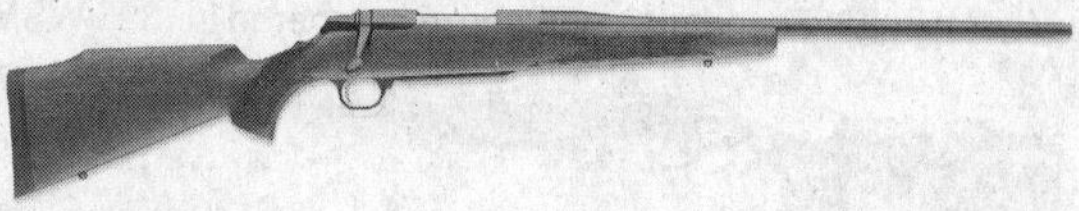

NIB	Exc.	V.G.	Good	Fair	Poor
680	500	400	250	200	150

A-Bolt Stainless Hunter

Features black composite stock, stainless steel receiver and barrel, no sights. Chamberings range from .243 Winchester to .300 WSM. Weight about 6.5 lbs. Introduced in 2008.

NIB	Exc.	V.G.	Good	Fair	Poor
800	650	450	300	250	200

A-Bolt Classic Hunter WSSM

As above, but chambered for .223 WSSM and .243 WSSM cartridges. Weight about 6.25 lbs. Introduced in 2003.

NIB	Exc.	V.G.	Good	Fair	Poor
800	650	450	300	250	200

A-Bolt Mountain Ti

Features lightweight stainless steel 23" barrel, titanium receiver and lightweight fiberglass stock. Chambered for .270 WSM, 7mm WSM and .300 WSM cartridges. Weight about 5.5 lbs. Calibers: .243, 7mm-08,

.308, .325 WSM. Introduced in 2004.

NIB	Exc.	V.G.	Good	Fair	Poor
1700	1300	1050	800	580	350

A-Bolt Composite Stalker

Supplied with composite stock and matte finish bluing. Offered in .338 Win. Magnum, .300 Win. Magnum, 7mm Rem. Magnum, .25-06, .270, .280, .30-06. Introduced in 1988. In 2001, .300 Winchester Short Magnum cartridge was offered for this model. Calibers: .223 WSSM, .243 WSSM, .25 WSSM, .223, .243, .7mm-08, .270 WSM, 7mm WSM, .300 WSM, .325 WSM, .25-06, .270, .280, .30-06, 7mm RM, .300 WM, .338 WM. Note: Add 10% for BOSS or left-hand version.

NIB	Exc.	V.G.	Good	Fair	Poor
550	350	300	250	200	150

A-Bolt II Composite Stalker

Same as above, with 1994 improvements. Note: Add $80 for BOSS system.

NIB	Exc.	V.G.	Good	Fair	Poor
670	520	400	300	250	200

A-Bolt Composite Stalker WSSM

As above, but chambered for .223 WSSM or .243 WSSM cartridge. Weight about 6 lbs. Introduced in 2003.

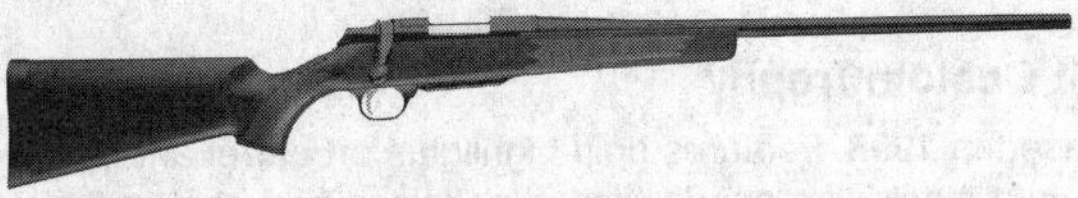

NIB	Exc.	V.G.	Good	Fair	Poor
700	550	400	300	250	200

A-Bolt Stainless Stalker

Bolt-action rifle. Calibers: .223 WSSM, .243 WSSM, .25 WSSM, .223, .243, .7mm-08, .270 WSM, 7mm WSM, .300 WSM, .325 WSM, .25-06, .270, .280, .30-06, 7mm RM, .300 WM, .338 WM, .375 H&H. Barrel: 22", 23", 24", 26" stainless steel, sightless (except for .375 H&H). Magazine: detachable box. Stock: black composite. Note: Add $30 for .300 and .338 calibers; 10 percent for BOSS system and left-hand version.

NIB	Exc.	V.G.	Good	Fair	Poor
600	450	400	350	300	250

A-Bolt II Composite Stainless Stalker

Same as above, with 1994 improvements. Note: Add $30 for Magnum calibers; $110 for BOSS system.

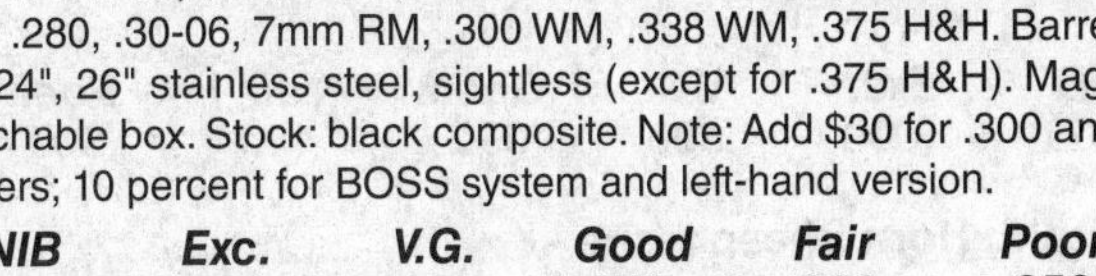

NIB	Exc.	V.G.	Good	Fair	Poor
850	650	550	400	300	250

A-Bolt Stainless Stalker WSSM

As above, but chambered for .223 WSSM and .243 WSSM calibers. Stock design slightly different from standard A-Bolt Stalker. Weight about 6 lbs. Introduced in 2003.

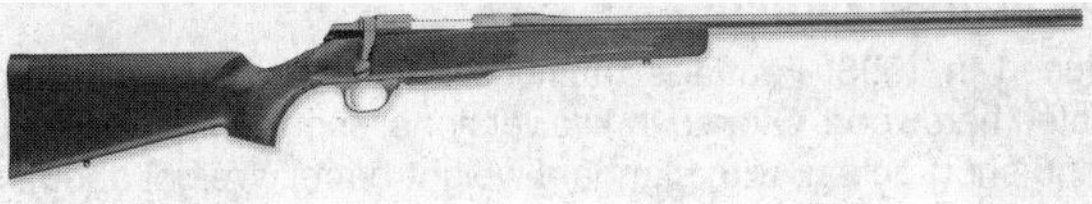

NIB	Exc.	V.G.	Good	Fair	Poor
880	680	550	400	300	250

A-Bolt Carbon Fiber Stainless Stalker

Features a Christensen Arms patent carbon barrel. Chambered for .22-250 or .300 Win. Magnum. Weight about: 6.25 lbs. short action; 7 lbs. long action. Introduced in 2000. In 2001, .300 Winchester Short Magnum cartridge offered for this model.

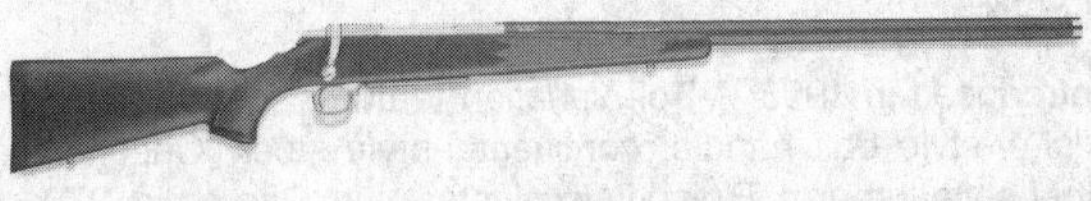

NIB	Exc.	V.G.	Good	Fair	Poor
1400	1200	1000	900	700	350

A-Bolt II Heavy Barrel Varmint

Introduced in 1994. Features all A-Bolt II improvements in a heavy barrel varmint rifle. Offered in .22-250 and .223 Rem. calibers, with 22" barrel. Equipped with black laminated wood stock.

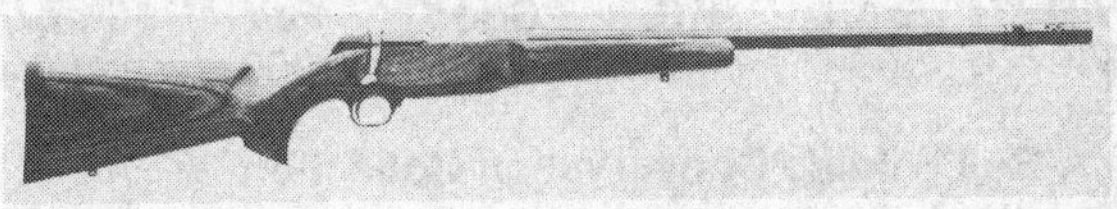

NIB	Exc.	V.G.	Good	Fair	Poor
680	600	520	420	320	250

A-Bolt Varmint Stalker

Introduced in 2002. Features new armor coated synthetic stock. Matte blue metal finish. Chambered for .223 Rem. and .22-250 Rem. cartridges. Fitted with 24" barrel on .223 and 26" barrel on .22-250. Weight about 8 lbs.

NIB	Exc.	V.G.	Good	Fair	Poor
790	650	520	420	320	250

A-Bolt Varmint Stalker WSSM

As above, but chambered for .223 WSSM and .243 WSSM cartridges. Weight about 7.75 lbs. Introduced in 2003.

NIB	Exc.	V.G.	Good	Fair	Poor
820	650	520	420	320	250

A-Bolt Eclipse M-1000

Thumbhole stock. Calibers: .270, .30-06, 7mm RM, .22-250, .308, .270 WSM, .7mm WSM, .300 WSM. Fitted with 26" barrel with BOSS system. Stock laminated hardwood, with gray/black finish. Forearm benchrest style. Weight about 9 lbs. 13 oz. Note: Add 10% for BOSS.

NIB	Exc.	V.G.	Good	Fair	Poor
1140	700	620	450	350	250

A-Bolt Eclipse M-1000 WSM & Stainless

Introduced in 2004. Offered in all WSM calibers. M-1000 blued with heavy barrel; stainless fitted with heavy bull barrel. Barrel length 26". Weight 9.85 lbs. No sights. Note: Add $200 for stainless model.

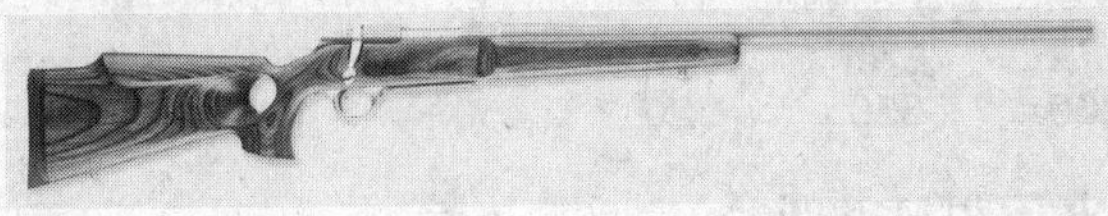

NIB	Exc.	V.G.	Good	Fair	Poor
1050	820	680	500	350	200

A-Bolt Eclipse Varmint

Introduced in 1996. Features thumbhole stock made from gray/black laminated hardwood. Offered in two versions: short-action, heavy-barrel; long and short action, with standard-weight barrel. Weight about: 9 lbs.; standard-barrel 7.5 lbs. depending on caliber.

NIB	Exc.	V.G.	Good	Fair	Poor
950	800	600	500	400	250

Euro-Bolt

First introduced in 1993. A-Bolt variation features rounded bolt shroud, Mannlicher-style bolt handle, continental-style stock. Cheekpiece and schnabel-style forearm. Finish is low-luster blue. Offered in .270, .30-06 and 7mm Rem. Magnum calibers. Weight about 7 lbs.

NIB	Exc.	V.G.	Good	Fair	Poor
650	500	450	350	250	150

A-Bolt II Euro Bolt

Same as above, with 1994 improvements.

NIB	Exc.	V.G.	Good	Fair	Poor
850	500	450	350	250	150

NRA A-Bolt Wildlife Conservation Collection

Commemorates NRA's Environment Conservation and Hunting Outreach Program. Caliber: .243 Win. Barrel: 22" blued sightless. Stock satin-finish walnut. NRA Heritage logo lasered on buttstock. MSRP: $797.

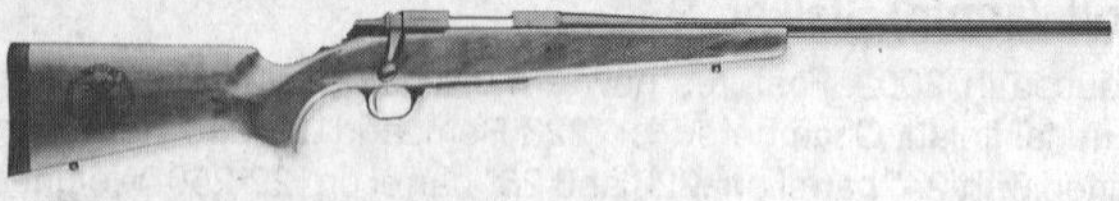

A-Bolt Medallion Model

Calibers: .223 WSSM, .243 WSSM, .25 WSSM, .223, .243, .7mm-08, .270 WSM, 7mm WSM, .300 WSM, .325 WSM, .25-06, .270, .280, .30-06, 7mm RM, .300 WM, .338 WM. Note: Add $35 for .300 and .338 calibers; 10 percent for BOSS or left-hand version.

NIB	Exc.	V.G.	Good	Fair	Poor
800	600	500	400	300	250

A-Bolt II Medallion

Same as above, with 1994 improvements. In 2003, offered in left-hand version.

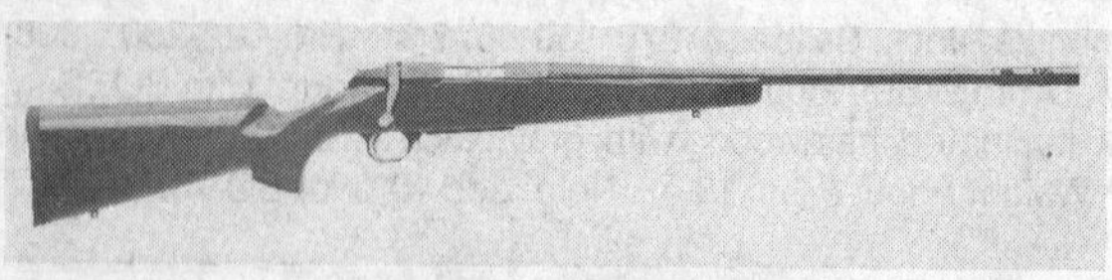

NIB	Exc.	V.G.	Good	Fair	Poor
760	600	450	350	300	250

A-Bolt II Medallion WSSM

As above chambered for .223 WSSM or .243 WSSM cartridge. Weight about 6.25 lbs. Introduced in 2003.

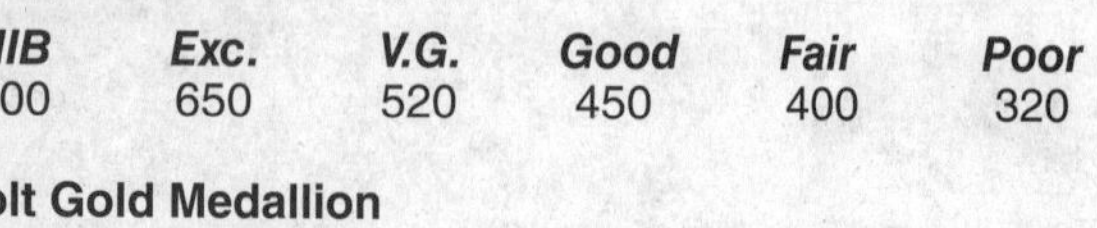

NIB	Exc.	V.G.	Good	Fair	Poor
800	650	520	450	400	320

A-Bolt Gold Medallion

Version has fancy grade walnut stock with cheekpiece. Lightly engraved. Gold-inlaid letters. Introduced in 1988.

NIB	Exc.	V.G.	Good	Fair	Poor
690	620	550	450	400	320

A-Bolt II Gold Medallion

Same as above, with 1994 improvements.

NIB	Exc.	V.G.	Good	Fair	Poor
690	620	550	450	400	320

A-Bolt II White Gold Medallion

Features gold engraved stainless receiver and barrel, select walnut stock, with brass spacers and rosewood caps. European-style cheekpiece. No sights. Introduced in 1999. Offered in .30-06, .270, 7mm Rem. Magnum and .300 Win. Magnum. Weight about 7 lbs. 8 oz.

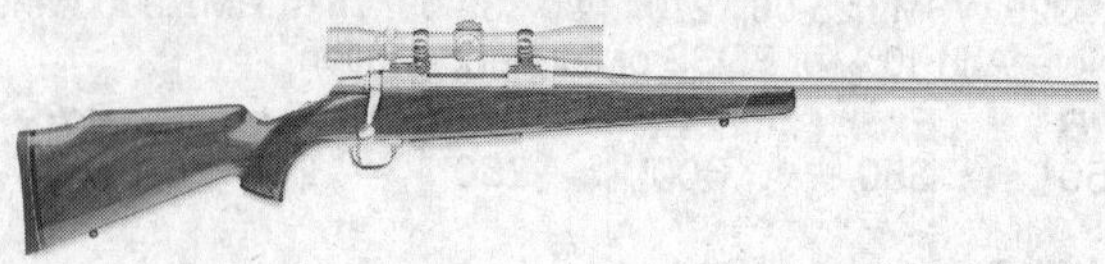

NIB	Exc.	V.G.	Good	Fair	Poor
1100	800	650	500	420	350

A-Bolt White Gold Medallion RMEF

Introduced in 2003. Special edition for Rocky Mountain Elk Foundation. Chambered for 7mm Rem. Magnum. Fitted with 26" barrel. Both action and barrel stainless steel. Special RMEF logo on grip cap. Weight about 7.75 lbs. Note: Add 5% for WSM calibers.

NIB	Exc.	V.G.	Good	Fair	Poor
1200	950	750	600	450	320

A-Bolt Custom Trophy

Introduced in 1998. Features gold highlights on barrel and receiver, select walnut stock with shadowline cheekpiece and skeleton pistol grip. Barrel octagonal. Chambered for .270 and .30-06 with 24" barrel and 7mm Rem. Magnum and .300 Win. Magnum with 26" barrel. Weight varies from 7 lbs. 11 oz. to 7 lbs. 3 oz. depending on caliber.

NIB	Exc.	V.G.	Good	Fair	Poor
1300	1000	800	650	420	300

A-Bolt Big Horn Sheep Issue

High-grade version of A-Bolt. Chambered for .270 cartridge. Features deluxe skipline checkered walnut stock, with heavily engraved receiver and floorplate. Two gold sheep inlays. There were 600 manufactured in 1986 and 1987.

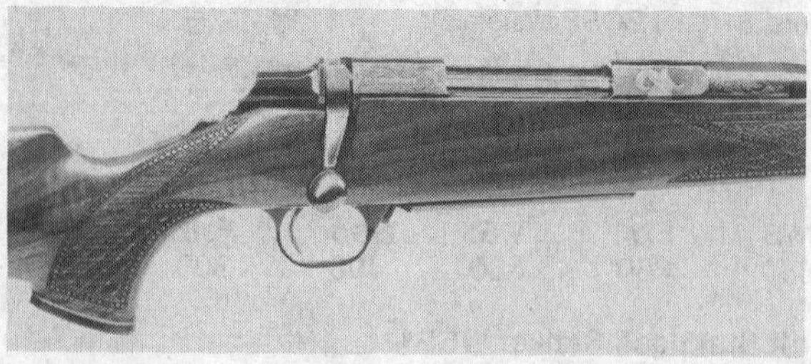

NIB	Exc.	V.G.	Good	Fair	Poor
1050	800	600	450	400	320

A-Bolt Micro-Medallion

Smaller version of A-Bolt Hunter. Chambered for popular cartridges that fit short action. Has 20" barrel without sights and 3-round magazine. Introduced in 1988.

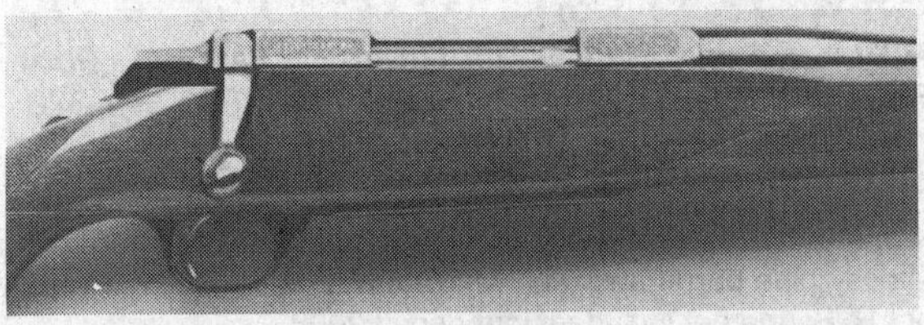

NIB	Exc.	V.G.	Good	Fair	Poor
520	480	400	350	300	250

A-Bolt II Micro-Medallion

Same as above, with 1994 improvements.

NIB	Exc.	V.G.	Good	Fair	Poor
520	480	400	350	300	250

A-Bolt Pronghorn Issue

Deluxe version of A-Bolt. Chambered for .243 cartridge. Heavily engraved and gold inlaid. Features presentation-grade walnut stock, with skipline checkering and pearl-inlaid borders. There were 500 manufactured in 1987.

NIB	Exc.	V.G.	Good	Fair	Poor
1300	1000	750	500	400	320

A-Bolt Special Hunter RMEF

Similar to A-Bolt Hunter. Honors Rocky Mountain Elk Foundation. Chambered in .325 WSM. Satin finish. Introduced 2007.

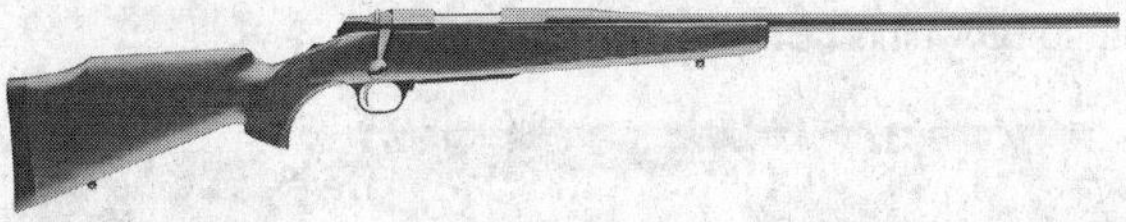

NIB	Exc.	V.G.	Good	Fair	Poor
800	600	500	400	300	250

A-Bolt White Gold RMEF

Similar to A-Bolt Special Hunter RMEF, with stainless barrel, receiver and glossy finish. Introduced 2007.

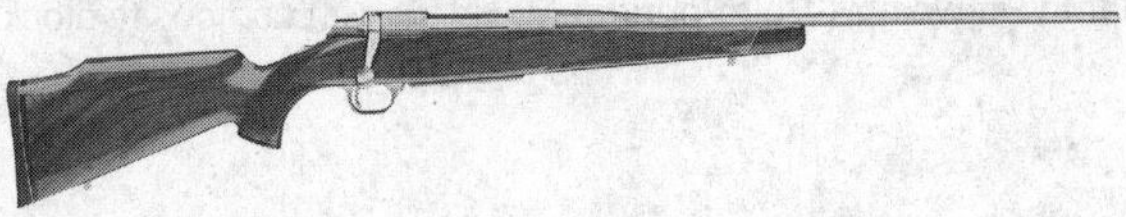

NIB	Exc.	V.G.	Good	Fair	Poor
1100	780	600	480	320	200

A-Bolt Target

Similar to A-Bolt, with 28" heavy bull blued barrel and receiver. Satin finish gray laminated stock, with adjustable comb and semi-beavertail forend. Chambered in .223, .308 Winchester and .300 WSM.

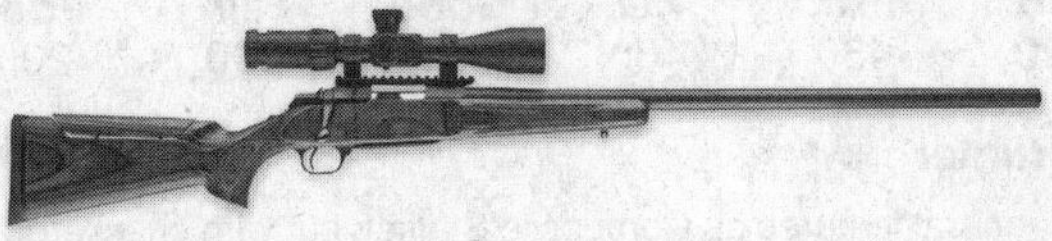

NIB	Exc.	V.G.	Good	Fair	Poor
1280	1000	800	650	420	300

A-Bolt Target Stainless

Similar to above, with stainless receiver and barrel.

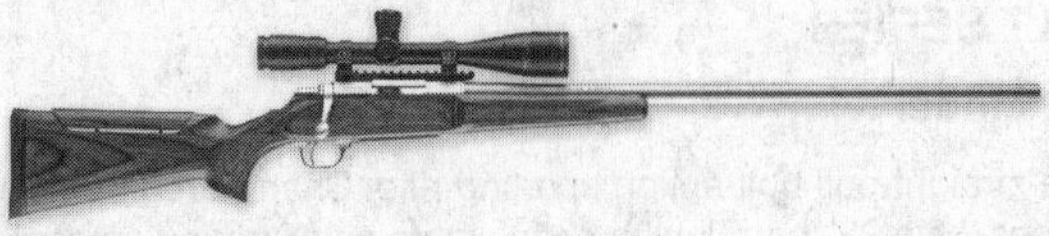

NIB	Exc.	V.G.	Good	Fair	Poor
1500	1280	1000	800	650	420

A-Bolt .22 Grade I

Bolt-action sporting rifle. Chambered for .22 LR or .22 Magnum cartridges. Features 60-degree bolt and 22" barrel. Available with or without open sights. Has 5-round detachable magazine. Adjustable trigger. Finish blued, with checkered walnut stock. Introduced in 1986. Note: Add 15 percent for .22 Magnum.

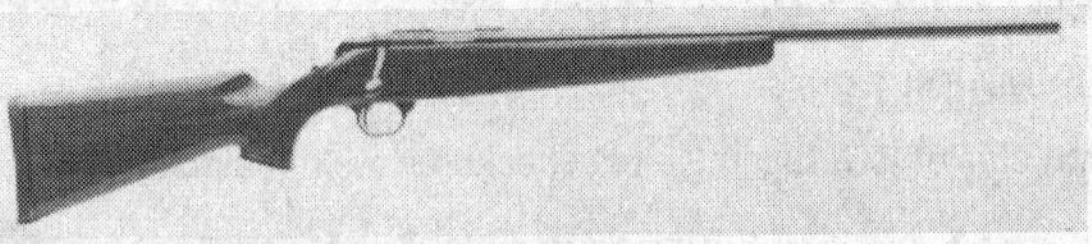

NIB	Exc.	V.G.	Good	Fair	Poor
340	280	210	150	120	100

A-Bolt .22 Gold Medallion

Deluxe high-grade version features select stock, with rosewood pistol grip cap and forend tip. Lightly engraved. Gold-filled letters. Introduced in 1988.

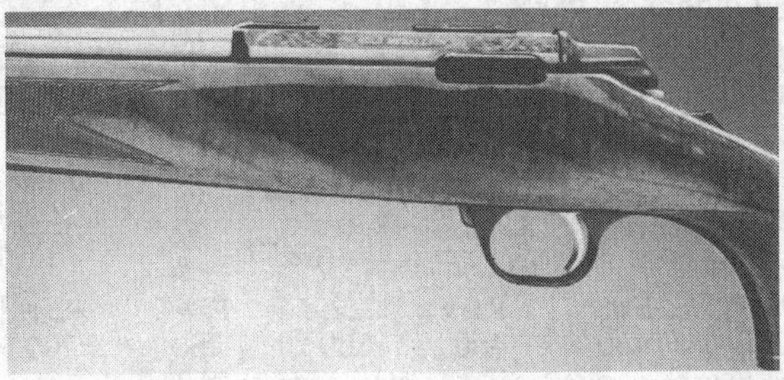

NIB	Exc.	V.G.	Good	Fair	Poor
450	400	350	300	220	180

AB3 Composite Stalker

Made on an A-Bolt action, with synthetic stock, matte blue finish and free-floating barrel. Stock has textured grip panels and polymer recoil pad. Picatinny rail scope mount included. The 3-round magazine is detachable. Offered in: .243 Win., 6.5 Creedmoor, .270 Win., .270 WSM, 7mm-08 Rem., 7mm Rem. Magnum, .308 Win., .30-06, .300 Win. Magnum, .300 WSM. Micro Stalker has 13" length of pull, Pachmayr Decelerator recoil pad. Offered in .243 Win., 6.5 Creedmoor, 7mm-08 Rem., .308 Win.

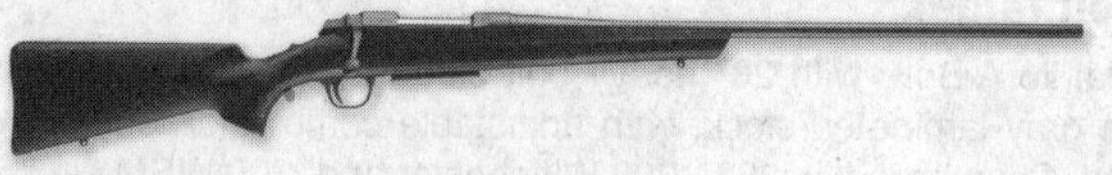

NIB	Exc.	V.G.	Good	Fair	Poor
520	450	400	350	300	200

AB3 Hunter

Same general features as Composite Stalker, but with checkered walnut stock. Chambered in .243 Win., 6.5 Creedmoor, .270 Win., .270 WSM, 7mm-08 Rem., 7mm Rem. Magnum, .308 Win., .30-06, .300 Win. Magnum, .300 WSM

NIB	Exc.	V.G.	Good	Fair	Poor
580	500	420	350	300	200

T-BOLT SERIES

T-Bolt Model T-1

Unique straight-pull bolt-action sporting rifle. Chambered for .22-caliber cartridges. Has 22" barrel, with open sights and 5-round magazine. Finish blued, with plain walnut stock. Manufactured between 1965 and 1974 by FN. Many T-Bolt rifles affected by salt wood. Proceed with caution. Reintroduced in 2006 with rotary magazine.

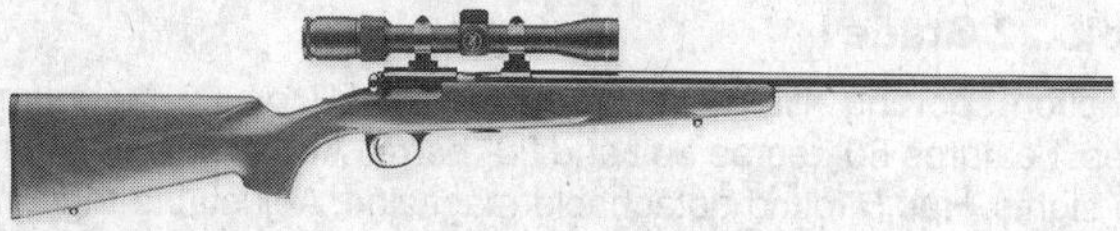

NIB	Exc.	V.G.	Good	Fair	Poor
—	550	400	350	150	100

T-Bolt Model T-2

Version similar to T-1, with select checkered walnut stock and 24" barrel.

NIB	Exc.	V.G.	Good	Fair	Poor
800	600	450	380	250	200

T-Bolt (2006)

Reintroduction of classic and collectible T-bolt straight-pull .22 rifle. Introduced in 2006. Chambered for .17 HMR, .22 WMR or .22 LR.

NIB	Exc.	V.G.	Good	Fair	Poor
600	480	450	380	250	200

T-Bolt Target/Varmint

Similar to reintroduced T-Bolt, with floating heavy target barrel and other accurizing refinements. Introduced 2007.

NIB	Exc.	V.G.	Good	Fair	Poor
650	520	500	420	300	250

T-Bolt Target/Varmint Stainless

Similar to above, with stainless steel receiver and barrel. Introduced 2008.

NIB	Exc.	V.G.	Good	Fair	Poor
850	720	650	520	350	320

T-Bolt Composite Hunter

Sporter version of new T-Bolt, with black composite Monte Carlo stock and glossy blue barrel and receiver. Chambered in .17 HMR, .22 WMR or .22 LR. Scope not included. Introduced 2008.

NIB	Exc.	V.G.	Good	Fair	Poor
680	520	500	420	300	250

T-Bolt Composite Target/Varmint

Sporter version of new T-Bolt Target/Varmint, with black composite Monte Carlo stock and glossy blue barrel and receiver. Chambered in .17 HMR, .22 WMR or .22 LR. Scope not included. Introduced 2008.

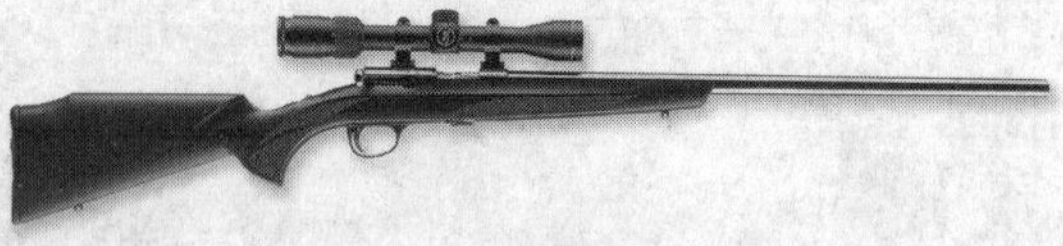

NIB	Exc.	V.G.	Good	Fair	Poor
700	550	520	450	320	280

T-Bolt Composite Target/Varmint Left-Hand

Similar to T-Bolt Composite Target/Varmint in left-hand version.

NIB	Exc.	V.G.	Good	Fair	Poor
720	550	520	450	320	280

T-Bolt Sporter

Sporter version of new T-Bolt, with satin walnut stock and bright blue barrel and receiver. Scope not included. Introduced 2008.

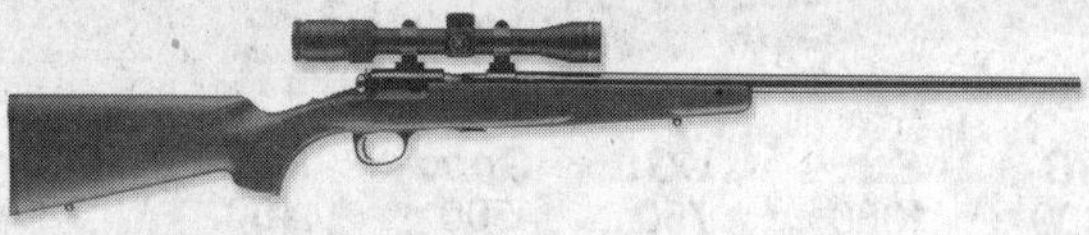

NIB	Exc.	V.G.	Good	Fair	Poor
700	550	520	450	320	280

T-Bolt Sporter Left-Hand

Similar to Browning T-Bolt Sporter in left-hand version.

NIB	Exc.	V.G.	Good	Fair	Poor
700	550	520	450	320	280

T-Bolt Composite Sporter Left-Hand

Similar to Browning T-Bolt Sporter Left-Hand, with composite stock.

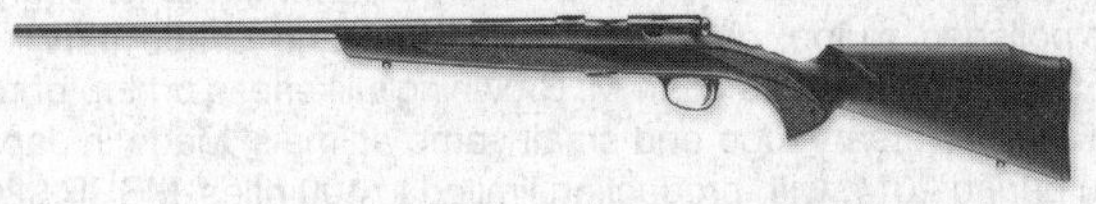

NIB	Exc.	V.G.	Good	Fair	Poor
700	550	520	450	320	280

T-Bolt Maple

Caliber: .22 LR. Barrel: 20" threaded (Target SR); 22" sporter weight (Sporter). Weight: 4 lbs., 14 oz. (Sporter) 6 lbs., 2 oz. (Target SR). Stock: AAA-Grade Maple with a gloss finish and cut checkering at 20 LPI. Features: Straight-pull bolt action operation in special maple furniture. Double helix 10-round magazine. Adjustable trigger. Polished chamber. Polymer buttplate. Swivel studs. Receiver drilled and tapped.

NIB	Exc.	V.G.	Good	Fair	Poor
830	—	—	—	—	—

Acera Straight Pull Rifle

Introduced in 1999. Features straight-action bolt system. Chambered for .30-06 with 22" barrel; .300 Win. Magnum with 24" barrel. Open sights optional as is BOSS system. Detachable box magazine. Checkered walnut stock. Prices listed for .30-06, with no sights and no BOSS. Note: Add $100 for .300 Win. Magnum with no sights and no BOSS.

NIB	Exc.	V.G.	Good	Fair	Poor
1100	780	600	480	320	200

Model 52 Limited Edition

Based on design of original Winchester Model 52 .22-caliber bolt-action rifle. Fitted with 24" barrel and oil-finished walnut stock. Metal pistol grip cap and rosewood forend tip. Drilled and tapped for scope. Five-round detachable magazine. Blued finish. Weight about 7 lbs. From 1991 to 1992, 5,000 Model 52s were built.

NIB	Exc.	V.G.	Good	Fair	Poor
1000	880	700	600	—	—

BPR-22

Short-stroke slide action rifle. Chambered for .22 LR and Magnum cartridges. Has 20.25" barrel, with open sights and 11-round tubular magazine. Finish blued, with checkered walnut stock. Manufactured between 1977 and 1982. Note: Add $100 for .22 Magnum models.

NIB	Exc.	V.G.	Good	Fair	Poor
—	500	350	220	120	100

BPR-22 Grade II

Version engraved. Select walnut stock. Note: Add 20% for .22 Magnum models.

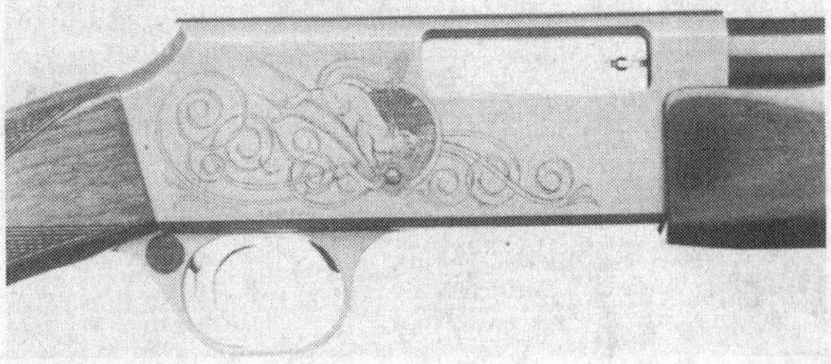

NIB	Exc.	V.G.	Good	Fair	Poor
—	600	400	280	220	150

Trombone Model

Slide-action rifle chambered for .22 LR cartridge. Has 24" barrel, with open sights and take-down design. Tubular magazine and hammerless action. Approximately 150,000 manufactured by FN between 1922 and 1974. Approximately 3,200 were imported by Browning in 1960s. Marked with FN barrel address or Browning Arms address. Browning-marked guns worth approximately 40% additional. Values given for FN-marked guns.

NIB	Exc.	V.G.	Good	Fair	Poor
1300	1000	800	700	450	320

Semi-Automatic .22 (SA-22)

Blowback-operated semi-automatic rifle. Chambered for .22 Long Rifle or Short cartridge. Features take-down barrel design, with 19.25" barrel and 11-round tubular magazine inside buttstock. Loaded through a hole in middle of buttstock. Finish blued, with checkered walnut stock and beavertail forearm. Lightweight compact firearm manufactured by FN between 1956 and 1974 for U.S. marked guns. A number of versions that differ in amount of ornamentation, quality of materials and workmanship.

NIB	Exc.	V.G.	Good	Fair	Poor
880	—	—	—	—	—

Grade I

Note: Add 50 percent for Grade I .22 Short; 20 percent for Early Wheel Sight manufactured 1959-1960.

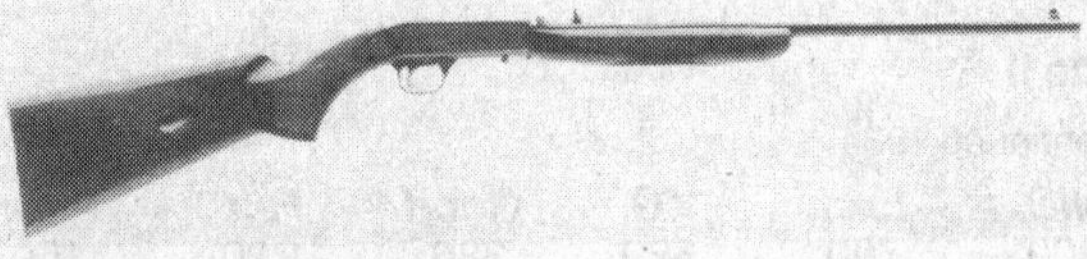

NIB	Exc.	V.G.	Good	Fair	Poor
850	700	600	500	400	350

Grade II

French grayed receiver. Note: Add 300 percent for Grade II short.

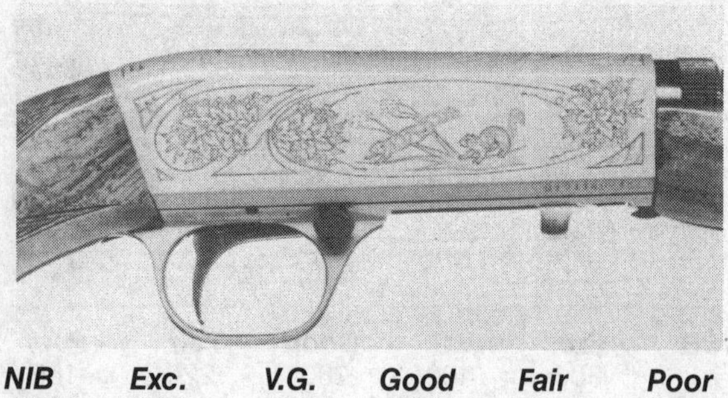

NIB	Exc.	V.G.	Good	Fair	Poor
1600	1200	900	700	300	200

Grade III

French grayed receiver. Note: Premium engravers: add 40 percent to Grade III; 800 percent to Grade III short. Deduct 20 percent for unsigned Grade III, 1956-1960.

NIB	Exc.	V.G.	Good	Fair	Poor
3250	2700	1900	1200	700	400

Semi-Auto .22 (SA-22, Miroku Mfg.)

Similar to Belgian FN, except produced as of 1976 by B.C. Miroku in Japan. Collector interest not as high as in FN version.

Grade I

NIB	Exc.	V.G.	Good	Fair	Poor
600	500	400	280	120	100

Grade II

Discontinued 1984.

NIB	Exc.	V.G.	Good	Fair	Poor
900	700	520	380	220	150

Grade III

Discontinued 1983.

NIB	Exc.	V.G.	Good	Fair	Poor
1300	1000	750	500	300	200

Grade VI

Gold plated animals.

NIB	Exc.	V.G.	Good	Fair	Poor
1200	950	750	520	320	280

Semi-Auto .22 High Grade 100th Anniversary

A limited production model, with octagon barrel, high relief engraving, highly polished bluing, gold bead front sight and Grade III/IV walnut stock. Engraving features John M. Browning's likeness on top of receiver, 100th Anniversary logo and small game animals. Made in Japan by Miroku during 2014, with production limited to 100 rifles. MSRP $2000.

NIB	Exc.	V.G.	Good	Fair	Poor
1800	1650	—	—	—	—

BAR-22

Blowback-operated semi-automatic rifle. Chambered for .22 LR cartridge. Has 20.25" barrel, with open sights and 15-round tubular magazine. Features polished lightweight alloy receiver. Finished blue, with checkered walnut stock. Manufactured between 1977 and 1985 by Miroku.

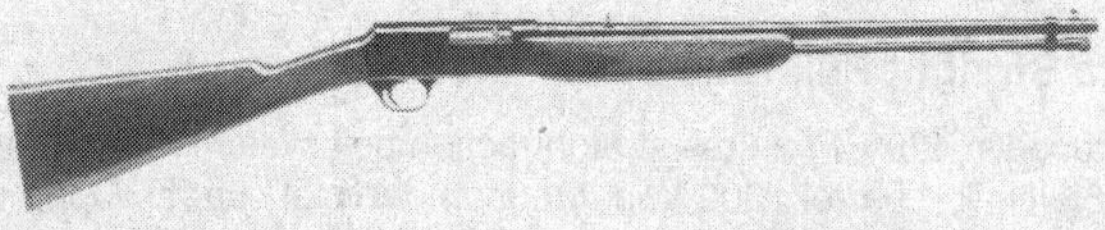

NIB	Exc.	V.G.	Good	Fair	Poor
—	600	520	290	160	120

BAR-22 Grade II

Deluxe version, with engraved silver-finished receiver. Select walnut stock. Discontinued in 1985.

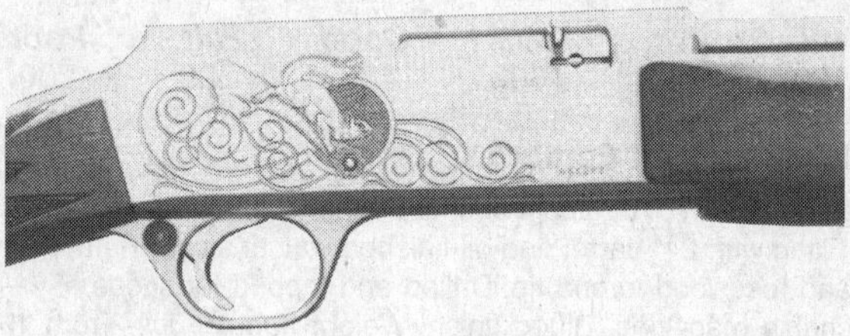

NIB	Exc.	V.G.	Good	Fair	Poor
—	700	580	380	180	150

Buck Mark Rifle

Model uses same design as Buck Mark pistol. Fitted with 18" barrel (heavy on target model) and thumbhole pistol grip. Magazine capacity 10 rounds. Integral rail scope mount. Introduced in 2001. Weight about: 4.25 lbs. Sporter; 5.5 lbs. Target model.

Target Model

NIB	Exc.	V.G.	Good	Fair	Poor
600	460	320	250	200	120

Sporter Model

NIB	Exc.	V.G.	Good	Fair	Poor
590	450	320	250	200	120

Buck Mark Field Target Gray Laminate

Introduced in 2003. Features light-weight carbon composite barrel, gray laminate stock and integral scope rail. Chambered for .22 cartridge. Fitted with 18" barrel. Weight: 5.5 lbs. standard; 3.75 lbs. Lite model.

NIB	Exc.	V.G.	Good	Fair	Poor
650	520	400	320	250	180

Patent 1900 High Power

Semi-automatic sporting rifle. Chambered for .35 Remington cartridge. Similar in configuration to Remington Model 8 rifle. Has 22" barrel, with open sights and 5-round integral magazine. Finish blued, with plain walnut stock. Approximately 5,000 manufactured between 1910 and 1931. Deluxe model, with ribbed barrel and checkered walnut stock available. Worth approximately 15 percent additional. Very rare in USA.

NIB	Exc.	V.G.	Good	Fair	Poor
—	1500	1000	700	480	300

BAR SERIES

Bar High Power Rifle

Gas-operated semi-automatic sporting rifle. Chambered for various popular calibers from .243 up to .338 Magnum cartridges. Offered with 22" or 24" barrel, with folding leaf sight until 1980. Finish blued, with checkered walnut stock. Various grades offered, differed in amount of ornamentation, quality of materials and workmanship utilized. Earlier models manufactured in Belgium by FN; these guns would be worth approximately 15 percent additional over guns assembled in Portugal from parts manufactured by FN. Early .338 Magnum model rarely encountered and would be worth approximately 25 percent additional. Grade I values furnished are for Portuguese-assembled guns from 1977 until introduction of BAR Mark II in 1993. This model introduced in 1967; discontinued in 1977.

NIB	Exc.	V.G.	Good	Fair	Poor
1300	—	—	—	—	—

Grade I

NIB	Exc.	V.G.	Good	Fair	Poor
1000	720	650	480	220	100

Grade I Magnum

NIB	Exc.	V.G.	Good	Fair	Poor
1150	750	680	400	250	120

Grade II Deluxe

1967-1974.

NIB	Exc.	V.G.	Good	Fair	Poor
1200	900	820	480	300	180

Grade II Deluxe Magnum

1968-1974.

NIB	Exc.	V.G.	Good	Fair	Poor
1280	950	850	500	320	200

Grade III

Discontinued 1984. Note: Grade III offered in two variations. First was hand-engraved and produced in Belgium. Second was photo-etched and built in Belgium and assembled in Portugal. Second variation will not be as valuable as first.

NIB	Exc.	V.G.	Good	Fair	Poor
1700	1450	1100	800	400	250

Grade III Magnum

Discontinued 1984. Note: Prices indicated are for 1970 through 1974 production. Guns assembled in Portugal deduct 30 percent. .338 Win. Magnum caliber rare in Grade III add 75 percent premium.

NIB	Exc.	V.G.	Good	Fair	Poor
1800	1550	1150	850	400	250

Grade IV

Game scene engraved. Hand-engraved from 1970 through 1976, then etched thereafter. Grade IV rifles discontinued in 1984. Note: Add 40 percent for pre-1977 rifles; 10 percent for premium engraving.

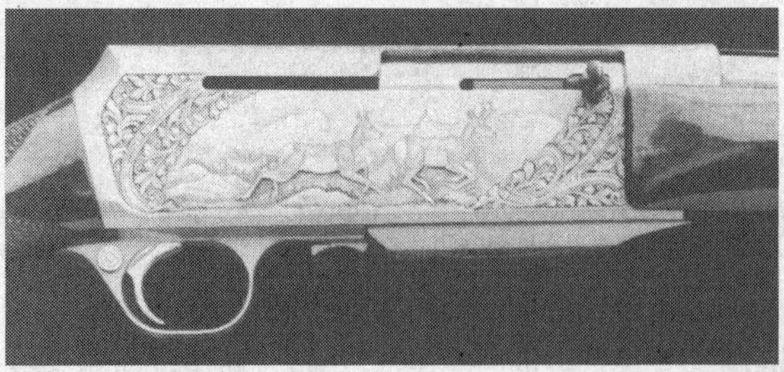

NIB	Exc.	V.G.	Good	Fair	Poor
2600	2200	1500	1000	500	400

Grade IV Magnum

NIB	Exc.	V.G.	Good	Fair	Poor
2800	2400	1600	1100	500	450

Grade V

Gold Inlaid: 1971-1974.

NIB	Exc.	V.G.	Good	Fair	Poor
6500	5800	4500	3200	1400	700

Grade V Magnum

1971-1974. Note: Add up to 100 percent for special order variations on Grade V rifles.

NIB	Exc.	V.G.	Good	Fair	Poor
6750	6000	4600	3300	1500	750

North American Deer Rifle Issue

Deluxe version of BAR. Chambered for .30-06 only. Features photo-etched silver-finished receiver and deluxe checkered walnut stock. Produced and furnished 600 with walnut case and accessories. Discontinued in 1983. As with all commemorative's, it must be NIB to command premium values.

NIB	Exc.	V.G.	Good	Fair	Poor
4000	3600	2400	1800	450	250

BAR Mark II Safari Rifle

Improved version of BAR. First introduced by Browning in 1967. Announced in 1993, this Mark II design uses a new gas system, with newly designed buffering system to improve reliability. Has new bolt release lever, new easily removable trigger assembly. Available with- or with-out sights. Walnut stock, with full pistol grip and recoil pad on Magnum gun are standard. Receiver blued, with scroll engraving. Rifles with Magnum calibers have 24" barrel; standard calibers fitted with 22" barrel. Available in .243, .308, .270, .30-06, 7mm Rem. Magnum, .300 Win. Magnum, .338 Win. Magnum. Weight: Standard calibers 7 lbs. 9 oz.; Magnum calibers 8 lbs. 6 oz. Scope not included. Note: Add 30 percent for .270 Wby. Magnum, which was made for one year only.

NIB	Exc.	V.G.	Good	Fair	Poor
950	800	600	450	250	150

BAR Mark II Lightweight

Version of Mark II. Introduced in 1997. Features light-weight alloy receiver and shortened 20" barrel. Offered in .30-06, .270 Win., .308 Win. and .243 Win. calibers. Not offered with BOSS system. Weight about 7 lbs. 2 oz.

NIB	Exc.	V.G.	Good	Fair	Poor
750	600	500	420	180	120

BAR Mark III

Offered in .243 Win., 7mm-08 Rem., 7mm Rem. Magnum, .270 Win., .270 WSM, .30-30 Win., .308 Win., .300 Win. Magnum. Satin nickel finish receiver, with high relief engraving. Barrel lengths 22", 23" or 24" depending on caliber. Checkered Grade II walnut stock, shim adjustable. Introduced in 2016.

NIB	Exc.	V.G.	Good	Fair	Poor
1050	850	700	550	400	300

BAR Composite Stalker

Introduced in 2001. Features composite buttstock and forend, with removable magazine. Offered in short action (.243 and .308) with sights; standard action (.270 and .30-06) with no sights; Magnum calibers (7mm, .330 Win., and .338) with no sights and with BOSS system. Note: Add $75 for Magnum calibers; $140 for BOSS.

NIB	Exc.	V.G.	Good	Fair	Poor
900	720	550	420	180	120

BAR High Grade Models

Models will feature high grade walnut stock, with highly polished blued barrel. Receivers will be grayed with game animals: mule deer and whitetail on standard calibers (.270 and .30-06); elk and moose on Magnum calibers (7mm Magnum and .300 Win. Magnum).

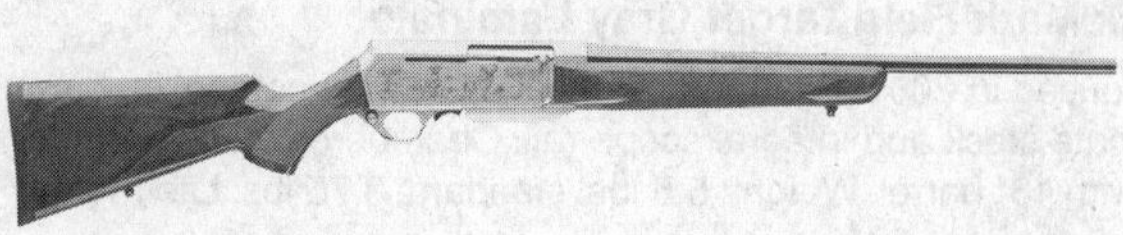

NIB	Exc.	V.G.	Good	Fair	Poor
1820	1450	1100	800	550	400

BAR ShortTrac

Introduced in 2004. Features ability to chamber Magnum cartridges. Offered in .270 WSM, 7mm WSM, .325 WSM, .300 WSM, .243 and .308. Fitted with 23" barrel in Magnum calibers; 22" barrel in non-Magnum. Receiver alloy steel. Redesigned stock adjustable for length of pull. Weight about: 7.25 lbs. Magnum calibers; 6.75 lbs. others. Note: Add 10% for camo finish.

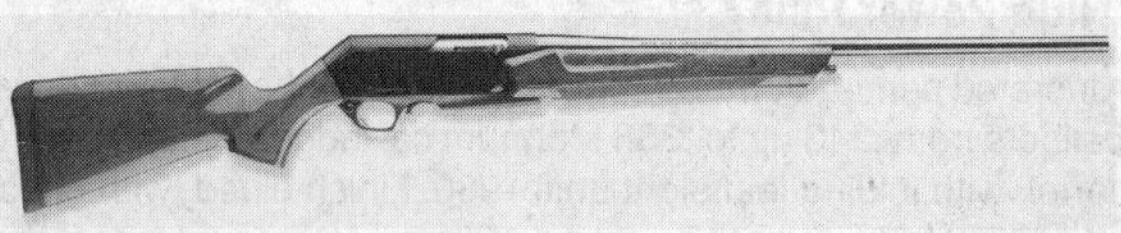

NIB	Exc.	V.G.	Good	Fair	Poor
950	650	450	350	250	200

BAR ShortTrac Stalker

Similar to BAR ShortTrac, with matte blue barrel. Composite stock. Introduced 2006.

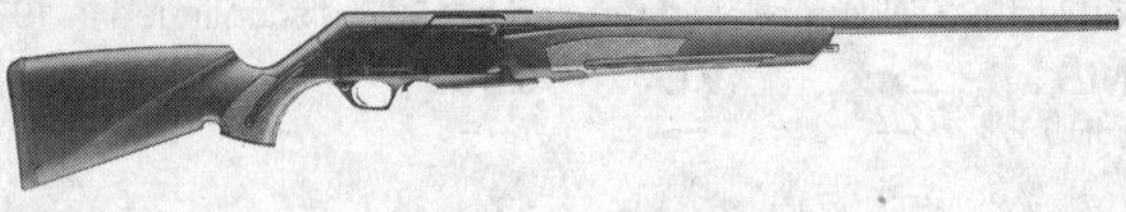

NIB	Exc.	V.G.	Good	Fair	Poor
850	670	550	450	350	250

BAR ShortTrac Left-Hand

Similar to BAR ShortTrac in left-hand. Introduced 2007.

NIB	Exc.	V.G.	Good	Fair	Poor
950	650	450	350	250	200

BAR ShortTrac Mossy Oak New Break-up

Similar to BAR ShortTrac, with Mossy Oak Break-up finish overall.

NIB	Exc.	V.G.	Good	Fair	Poor
1280	1000	750	600	480	350

BAR ShortTrac Digital Green

Similar to above, with Digital Green camo finish overall.

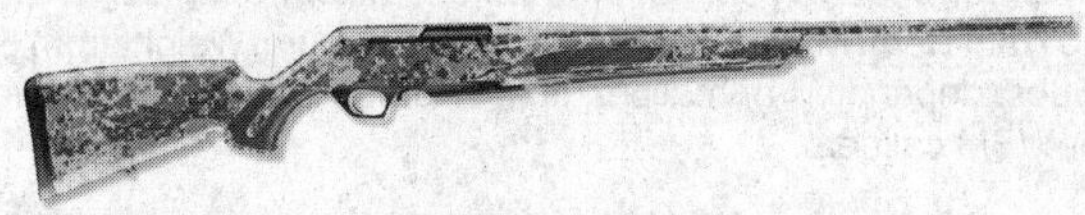

NIB	Exc.	V.G.	Good	Fair	Poor
1280	1000	750	600	480	350

BAR LongTrac

Similar to above. Made for long action calibers such as .270, .30-06, 7mm Rem. Magnum and .300 Win. Magnum. Barrel length 22" for .270 and .30-06; 24" for other two calibers. Weight about: 7 lbs. .270 and .30-06; 7.5 lbs. 7mm and .300. Introduced in 2004. Note: Add $75 for Magnum calibers; 10 percent for camo finish.

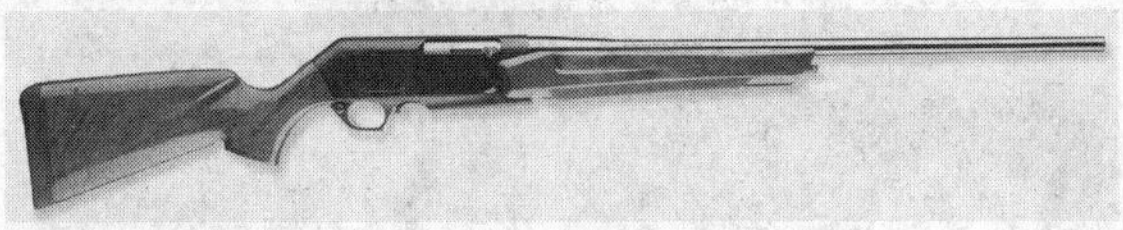

NIB	Exc.	V.G.	Good	Fair	Poor
950	650	450	350	250	200

BAR LongTrac Stalker

Long-action version of BAR ShortTrac Stalker.

NIB	Exc.	V.G.	Good	Fair	Poor
850	670	550	450	350	250

BAR LongTrac Left-Hand

Similar to BAR LongTrac in left-hand. Introduced 2007.

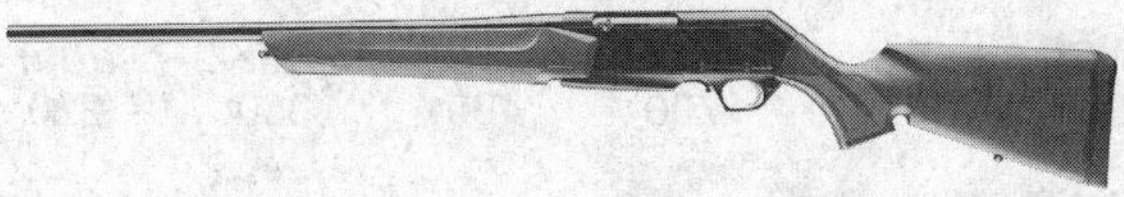

NIB	Exc.	V.G.	Good	Fair	Poor
950	1000	750	600	480	350

BAR LongTrac Mossy Oak New Break-up

Similar to BAR LongTrac, with Mossy Oak Break-up finish overall.

NIB	Exc.	V.G.	Good	Fair	Poor
1280	1000	750	600	480	350

Model BPR

Initials "BPR" stands for Browning Pump Rifle. Introduced in 1997. Similar in appearance to BAR. Offered in both long-/short-action calibers, with barrel lengths from 22" to 24". Short action calibers: .243 Win. and .308 Win. Long action calibers: .270 Win., .30-06, 7mm Rem. Magnum and .300 Win. Magnum. Weight about 7 lbs. 3 oz. Discontinued 2003.

NIB	Exc.	V.G.	Good	Fair	Poor
800	680	520	400	300	200

BL SERIES

BL-22 Grade I

Lever-action rifle chambered for .22 rimfire cartridge. Has 18" barrel, with tubular magazine and folding leaf rear sight. Western-style firearm that features an exposed hammer. Finish blued, with walnut stock. Introduced in 1970 by Miroku.

NIB	Exc.	V.G.	Good	Fair	Poor
450	350	200	150	120	100

BL-22 Grade II

Similar to above, with scroll-engraved receiver. Checkered select walnut stock.

NIB	Exc.	V.G.	Good	Fair	Poor
480	350	220	180	150	120

BL-22 Field Series Grade I

Introduced in 2005. Features satin nickel receiver, walnut stock with no checkering. Blued trigger. Magazine capacity 16 rounds. Weight about 5 lbs.

NIB	Exc.	V.G.	Good	Fair	Poor
500	380	350	200	150	100

BL-17 Field Series Grade I

As above chambered for .17 Mach 2 cartridge. Weight about 5.2 lbs.

NIB	Exc.	V.G.	Good	Fair	Poor
650	580	400	200	150	100

BL-22 Field Series Grade II

As above, with checkered stock, gold trigger. Scroll engraving on receiver.

NIB	Exc.	V.G.	Good	Fair	Poor
560	420	350	200	150	120

BL-17 Field Series Grade II

As above chambered for .17 Mach 2 cartridge.

NIB	Exc.	V.G.	Good	Fair	Poor
700	600	450	250	150	120

BL-22 Grade II Octagon

Introduced in 2005. Has 24" octagon barrel chambered for .22 Long and Long Rifle cartridges. Receiver silver nitride, with scroll engraving and gold trigger. Magazine capacity 16 rounds. Gold bead front sight. Weight about 5.25 lbs.

NIB	Exc.	V.G.	Good	Fair	Poor
720	550	380	280	200	150

BL-17 Grade II Octagon

As above, but chambered for .17 Mach 2 cartridge. Magazine capacity 16 rounds. Weight about 5.35 lbs. Introduced in 2005.

NIB	Exc.	V.G.	Good	Fair	Poor
750	580	380	280	200	150

BL-22 Classic

Introduced in 1999. Same features as BL-22 Grade I.

NIB	Exc.	V.G.	Good	Fair	Poor
420	380	280	200	180	120

BL-22 NRA Grade 1

Similar to BL-22 Grade 1, with "NRA" logo lasered on buttstock.

NIB	Exc.	V.G.	Good	Fair	Poor
500	450	350	300	—	—

BL-22 Gray Laminate Stainless

Similar to BL-22, with gray laminated stock, nickeled receiver and stainless steel barrel. Introduced 2006.

NIB	Exc.	V.G.	Good	Fair	Poor
720	550	380	280	200	150

BL-22 Micro Midas

Chambered for .22 LR. Designed for younger shooter, with 12" length of pull. Lever action, with short 33-degree throw. Full-length tubular magazine, American walnut stock, gloss finish, straight-grip. Receiver steel, with blued finish. Grooved for scope mounts. New 2011.

NIB	Exc.	V.G.	Good	Fair	Poor
400	350	300	250	200	150

Model 81 BLR

Contemporarily designed lever-action sporting rifle. Chambered for various popular calibers from .22-250 up to .358 Winchester. Has 20" barrel, with adjustable sights. Features 4-round detachable magazine and rotary locking bolt. Finish blued, with checkered walnut stock and recoil pad. Introduced in 1971. Manufactured that year in Belgium. In 1972, manufacture moved to Miroku in Japan. In 2003, straight-grip stock introduced and WSM calibers added from .270 to .300. Weight about 6.5 lbs. Note: Add 20 percent for Belgian manufactured version.

NIB	Exc.	V.G.	Good	Fair	Poor
900	680	500	300	200	150

BLR Lightning (Lightweight)

Introduced in 1996. Features lightweight aluminum receiver, with walnut stock and checkered pistol grip. Offered in both long-/short-action calibers from .223 Rem. to 7mm Rem. Magnum. Barrel length 20" for short-action; 22" to 24" for long-action. Open sights standard. Weight about 7 lbs. depending on caliber. In 2003 a straight-grip stock introduced.

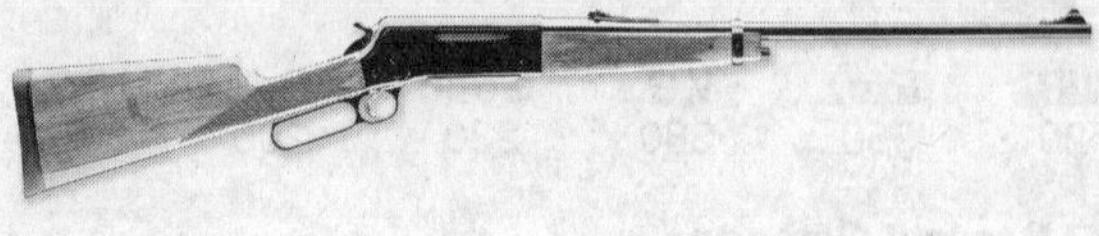

NIB	Exc.	V.G.	Good	Fair	Poor
740	600	450	300	200	150

BLR Lightweight '81

Features straight-grip checkered walnut stock. Fitted with 20" or 22" barrel; magazine capacity 4 or 5 rounds, depending on caliber. Chambered for calibers .22-25-, .243, 7mm-08, .308, .358, .450 Marlin, .270 WSM, .300 WSM and .325 WSM. Offered in long-action chambered for .270, .30-06, 7mm Rem. Magnum and .300 Win. Magnum. Weight from 6.5 lbs. to 7.75 lbs. depending on caliber. Note: Add 20 percent for long-action; $70 for WSM calibers.

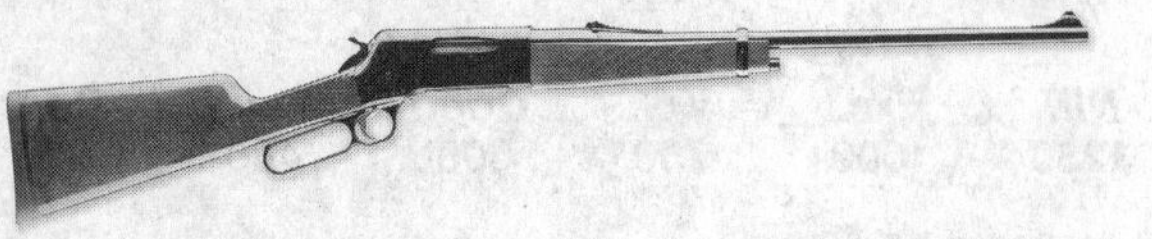

NIB	Exc.	V.G.	Good	Fair	Poor
730	550	420	320	220	120

BLR Lightweight Takedown

Similar to BLR Lightweight, with take-down feature. Introduced 2007.

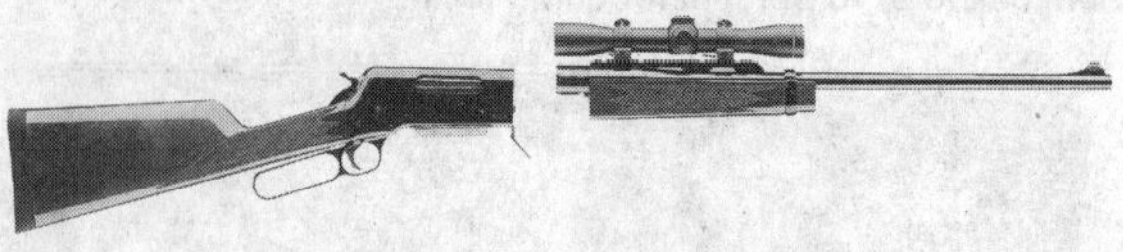

NIB	Exc.	V.G.	Good	Fair	Poor
780	650	580	380	200	150

BLR Lightweight '81 Stainless Takedown

Similar to above, with stainless steel barrel and receiver. Introduced 2008.

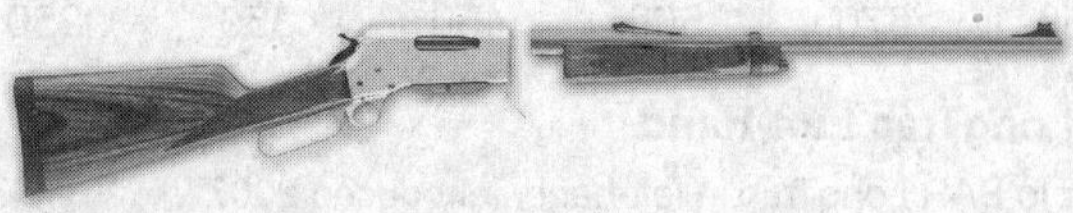

NIB	Exc.	V.G.	Good	Fair	Poor
980	850	700	480	350	220

Model B-78

Introduced in 1973. Single-shot lever-action falling block. Offered in several calibers from .22-250 to .45-70. Barrel lengths from 24" to 26" in round or octagonal shape. No sights except .45-70. Checkered walnut stock. First built in 1973. Discontinued in 1983. Note: Add 15 percent for .45-70 caliber.

NIB	Exc.	V.G.	Good	Fair	Poor
1400	1100	850	600	350	250

Model 53

Offered in 1990. Reproduction of Winchester Model 53. Like original, chambered for .32-20 cartridge. Limited edition offering confined to 5,000 rifles. Features hand-cut checkering, high-grade walnut stock, full pistol grip and semi-beavertail forend. Pistol grip fitted with metal grip cap. Barrel length 22". Finish blue.

NIB	Exc.	V.G.	Good	Fair	Poor
900	800	650	500	320	200

Model 65 Grade I

Limited-edition lever-action rifle. Chambered for .218 Bee cartridge. Has tapered round 24" barrel, with open sights. Patterned after Winchester Model 65. Has 7-round tubular magazine. Finish blued, with plain walnut stock. Metal buttplate. Manufactured 3,500 in 1989.

NIB	Exc.	V.G.	Good	Fair	Poor
850	680	500	300	200	150

Model 65 High Grade

Deluxe version features silver-finished scroll engraved receiver, with gold animal inlays and gold-plated trigger, select checkered walnut stock. Manufactured 1,500 in 1989.

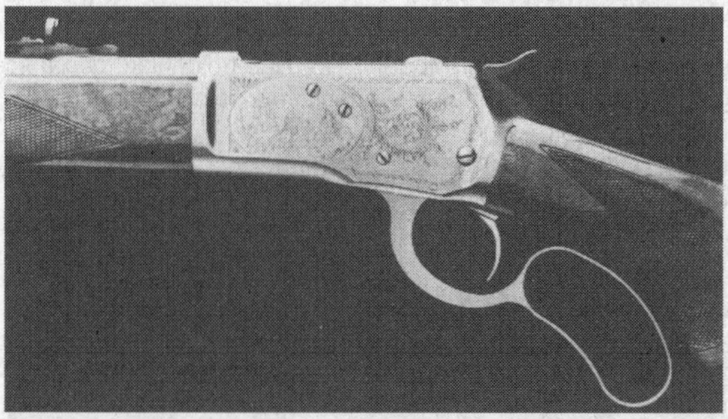

NIB	Exc.	V.G.	Good	Fair	Poor
1650	1200	820	500	—	—

Model 71 Grade I

Reproduction of Winchester Model 71. Chambered for .348 cartridge. Has 20" or 24" barrel, with open sights and 4-round tubular magazine. Finish blued, with plain walnut stock. Manufactured 4,000 20" carbines; 3,000 24" rifles, in 1986 and 1987.

NIB	Exc.	V.G.	Good	Fair	Poor
—	950	750	600	400	250

Model 71 High Grade

Version similar to Grade I. Scroll engraved grayed receiver, with gold-plated trigger and gold inlays. Manufactured 3,000 each of carbines and rifles in 1986 and 1987.

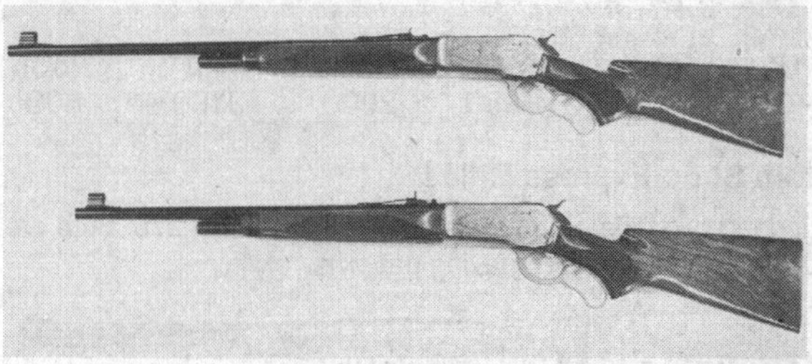

NIB	Exc.	V.G.	Good	Fair	Poor
—	1400	950	750	500	320

Jonathan Browning Centennial Mountain Rifle

Limited edition blackpowder rifle. Chambered for .50 ball. Fitted with 30" octagon barrel and single-set trigger. Figured walnut stock and engraved lock plate. Cased, with powder horn. Limited to 1,000 rifles in 1978.

NIB	Exc.	V.G.	Good	Fair	Poor
1250	750	600	450	350	250

Jonathan Browning Mountain Rifle

Same as above, without fancy wood case or engraving. Chambered for .45- or .54-caliber.

NIB	Exc.	V.G.	Good	Fair	Poor
800	500	400	300	200	180

Model 1878 (Original)

Based on John M. Browning's first patent. Single-shot rifle. Only firearm manufactured by Browning brothers. Offered in several calibers. Only a few hundred probably exist with Ogden, Utah barrel address. Design later sold to Winchester. Sold under Winchester name as Model 1885 High Wall.

NIB	Exc.	V.G.	Good	Fair	Poor
—	50000	40000	30000	15000	5000

Model 1885 High Wall

Single-shot rifle, with falling block action and octagonal free-floating barrel. Similar to Model 78. Introduced in 1985. Stock is high grade walnut, with straight-grip and recoil pad. Furnished with 28" barrel. Offered in these calibers: .223, .22-250, .270, .30-06, 7mm Rem. Magnum, .45-70 Gov't. Weight about 8 lbs. 12 oz.

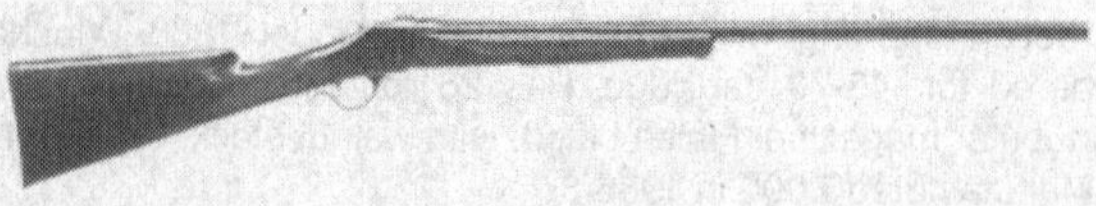

NIB	Exc.	V.G.	Good	Fair	Poor
1280	950	650	500	200	100

Model 1885 Low Wall

Introduced in 1995. Similar to above in a more accurate version of original Low Wall. Thin octagon barrel 24" in length. Trigger pull adjustable. Walnut stock fitted with pistol grip and schnabel forearm. Offered in .22 Hornet, .223 Rem. and .243 Win. calibers. Weight about 6.4 lbs.

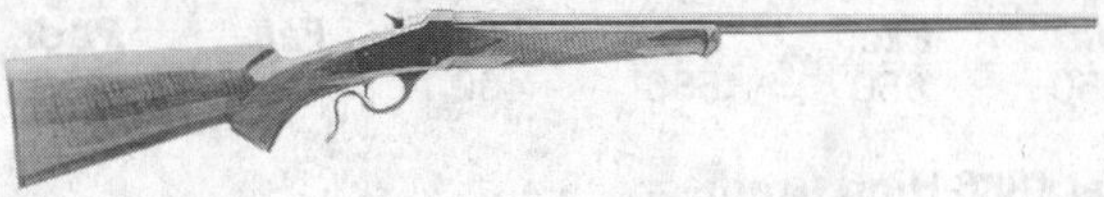

NIB	Exc.	V.G.	Good	Fair	Poor
1150	850	550	400	300	150

Model 1885 Low Wall Traditional Hunter

Introduced in 1998. Similar to Low Wall, with half-octagon half-round 24" barrel. Chambered for .357 Magnum, .44 Magnum and .45 Colt cartridges. Case colored receiver and crescent butt, with tang sight also featured. Weight about 6.5 lbs.

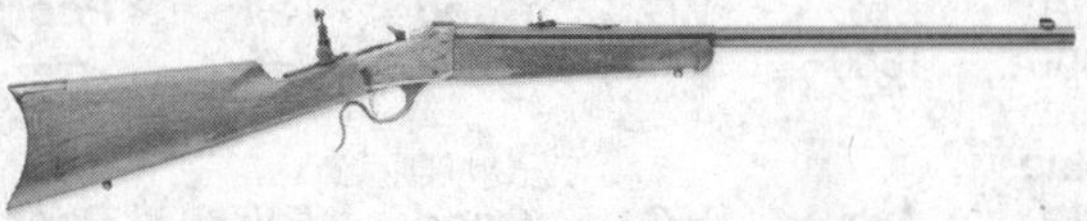

NIB	Exc.	V.G.	Good	Fair	Poor
1150	850	550	400	300	150

Model 1885 BPCR (Black Powder Cartridge Rifle)

Introduced in 1996 for BPCR metallic silhouette shoots. Chambered for .45-70 or .40-60 caliber. Receiver case colored, 28" round barrel fitted with vernier sight with level. Walnut stock has checkered pistol grip. Fitted with tang sight. Weight about 11 lbs.

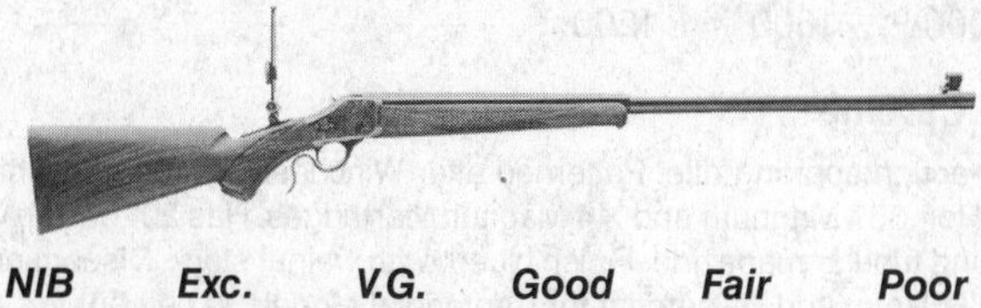

NIB	Exc.	V.G.	Good	Fair	Poor
1600	1300	800	400	300	150

Model 1885 BPCR Creedmoor Type

Introduced in 1998. Chambered for .45-90 cartridge. Features 34" heavy half-round barrel, with long range tang sight and wind gauge front sight. Weight about 11 lbs. 13 oz.

NIB	Exc.	V.G.	Good	Fair	Poor
1800	1500	1150	900	500	300

Model 1885 High Wall Traditional Hunter

Variation of Model 1885 series. Introduced in 1997. Fitted with an oil-finish walnut stock and crescent buttplate. Barrel octagonal and 28" in length. Rear sight buckhorn. Fitted with tang-mounted peep sight. Front sight gold bead classic style. Chambered for .30-30, .38-55 and .45-70 cartridges. Weight about 9 lbs. In 1998, .454 Casull caliber added.

NIB	Exc.	V.G.	Good	Fair	Poor
1200	950	700	580	400	280

Model 1886 Grade I

Lever action sporting rifle. Patterned after Model 1886 Winchester. Chambered for .45-70 cartridge. Has 26" octagonal barrel, with full-length tubular magazine. Finish blued, with walnut stock. Crescent buttplate. Manufactured 7,000 in 1986.

NIB	Exc.	V.G.	Good	Fair	Poor
1350	950	720	600	450	300

Carbine

NIB	Exc.	V.G.	Good	Fair	Poor
950	650	550	400	320	250

Model 1886 High Grade

Deluxe version of Model 1886. Features game scene engraving, with gold accents and checkered select walnut stock. "1 of 3,000" engraved on top of barrel. Manufactured 3,000 in 1986.

NIB	Exc.	V.G.	Good	Fair	Poor
1900	1600	1000	700	—	—

Carbine

NIB	Exc.	V.G.	Good	Fair	Poor
1600	1100	900	600	—	—

Model 1886 Montana Centennial

Similar to High Grade, with different engraving pattern. Designed to commemorate Centennial of State of Montana. There were 2,000 manufactured in 1986. All commemorative's must be NIB with all supplied materials to command collector interest.

NIB	Exc.	V.G.	Good	Fair	Poor
2000	1600	1200	—	—	—

B-92 Carbine

Lever-action sporting rifle. Patterned after Winchester Model 92. Chambered for .357 Magnum and .44 Magnum cartridges. Has 20" barrel, with 11-round tubular magazine. Finish blued, with walnut stock. Discontinued in 1986. Note: Add 10 percent for Centennial Model; 30 percent for .357 Magnum.

NIB	Exc.	V.G.	Good	Fair	Poor
—	700	620	400	250	120

Model 1895 Grade I

Lever-action sporting rifle. Chambered in .30-40 Krag and .30-06 cartridge. Patterned after Model 1895 Winchester. Has 24" barrel and 4-round integral box magazine. Buckhorn rear sight and blade front. Finish blued, with walnut stock. Manufactured 6,000 in .30-06 and 2,000 chambered for .30-40 Krag, in 1984.

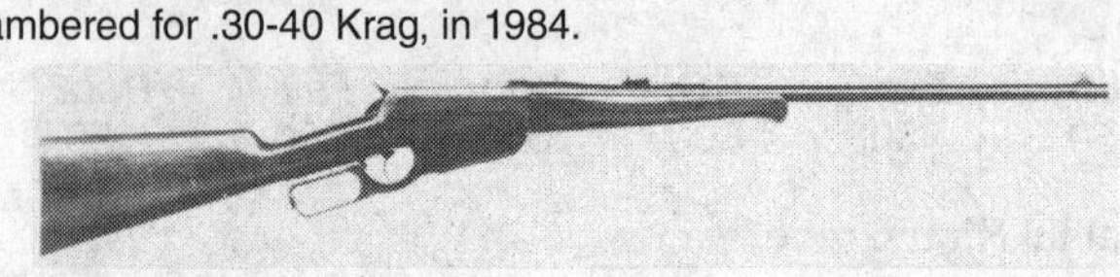

NIB	Exc.	V.G.	Good	Fair	Poor
—	950	680	480	380	280

Model 1895 High Grade

Deluxe engraved version of Model 1895. Has gold-inlaid game scenes and gold-plated trigger. Features checkered select walnut stock. Produced 2,000 in 1984—1,000 in each caliber.

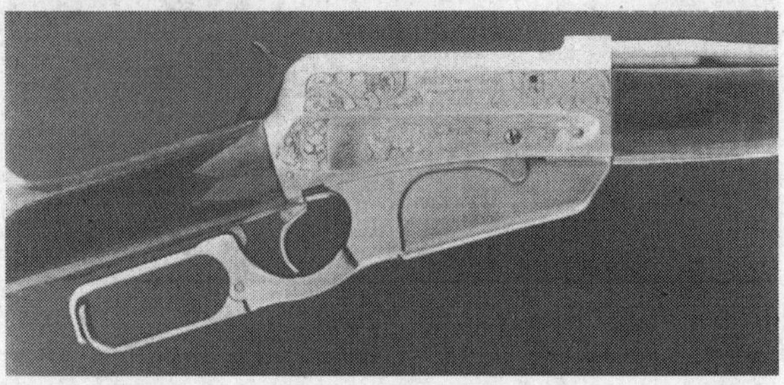

NIB	Exc.	V.G.	Good	Fair	Poor
—	1500	1250	900	700	400

Express Rifle

Over/under superposed rifle. Chambered for .270 Winchester or .30-06 cartridges. Has 24" barrels, with folding express sights and automatic ejectors. Features a single trigger. Receiver engraved. Finish blue, with deluxe checkered walnut stock. Introduced in 1980. Discontinued in 1986.

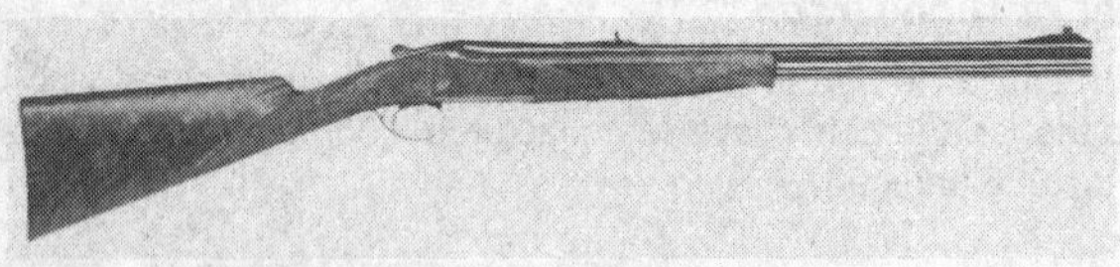

NIB	Exc.	V.G.	Good	Fair	Poor
—	6500	3950	2000	1100	800

Custom Shop Express Rifles

Produced in two different models, Herstall and CCS 375. Both are custom-built, with choice of engraving patterns.

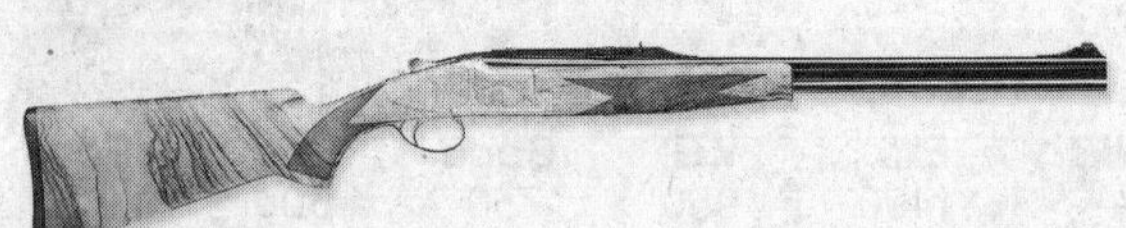

Herstal Express Rifle

NIB	Exc.	V.G.	Good	Fair	Poor
—	23000	17500	12000	5500	700

Continental Set

Consists of Express Rifle chambered for .30-06 cartridge. Furnished with an extra set of 20-gauge over/under barrels. Shotgun barrels are 26.5" in length. Single trigger, automatic ejectors and heavily engraved receiver. Select walnut stock hand checkered and oil-finished. Furnished with a fitted case. Manufactured 500 between 1978 and 1986.

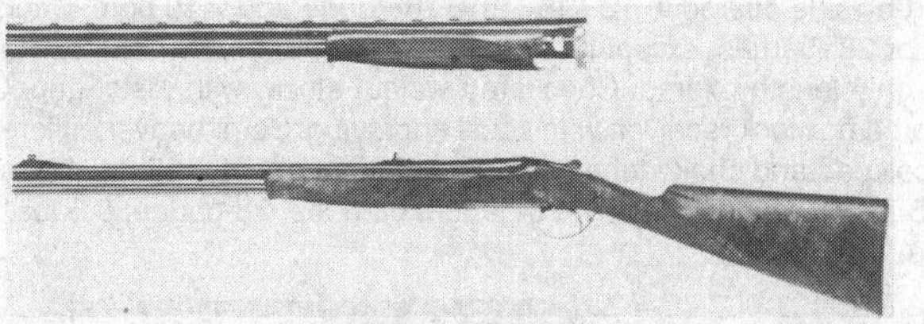

NIB	Exc.	V.G.	Good	Fair	Poor
10000	9250	8000	4500	2000	1000

BRUCE & DAVIS
Webster, Massachusetts

Double-Barreled Pistol (Antique)

.36-caliber double-barrel percussion pistol, with 3" to 6" round barrels. Barrel rib marked "Bruce & Davis". Blued, with walnut grips. Manufactured during 1840s.

Exc.	Fine	V.G.	Good	Fair	Poor
950	650	500	300	150	75

BRUCHET
Ste. Etienne, France

Model A Shotgun

12-gauge or .410 bore side-by-side shotgun, with double triggers and automatic ejectors. Barrel lengths and chokes to customer specifications. Produced on limited basis (50 per year) since 1982. Base price listed.

NIB	Exc.	V.G.	Good	Fair	Poor
3600	2750	1900	1450	1000	500

Model B

As above, with finer finish and spring-assisted action opener. Imported since 1982.

NIB	Exc.	V.G.	Good	Fair	Poor
6950	5250	4000	3000	2250	1250

BRUFF, R.P.
New York, New York

Pocket Pistol (Antique)

.41-caliber single-shot percussion pistol, with 2.5" to 3" barrels. Marked "R.P. Bruff NY" in an arch and "Cast Steel". German silver, with checkered walnut stock. Manufactured between 1861 and 1870.

Exc.	Fine	V.G.	Good	Fair	Poor
1900	820	520	220	100	70

BRYCO ARMS
Carson City, Nevada
See—JENNINGS

BSA GUNS LTD.
Birmingham, England

Established in 1861, this firm has produced a wide variety of firearms over the years. Most common of these arms that are currently available in United States are listed.

SINGLE-SHOT

No. 12 Cadet Martini

.310-caliber single-shot Martini action rifle, with 29" barrel, adjustable sights and straight-grip walnut stock. Manufactured approximately 80,000 from 1911 to 1913. Many of those imported into U.S. were altered to .22-caliber.

NIB	Exc.	V.G.	Good	Fair	Poor
—	750	500	300	150	100

Centurian Match Rifle

As above in .22-caliber, with 24" barrel, adjustable sights. Pistol grip walnut stock.

NIB	Exc.	V.G.	Good	Fair	Poor
—	600	450	300	200	100

Model 13 Sporter

As above in .22 Hornet, with hunting sights.

NIB	Exc.	V.G.	Good	Fair	Poor
—	650	420	300	220	100

Martini International Match

As above, with heavy match barrel, ISU-style sights and match stock. Manufactured from 1950 to 1953.

NIB	Exc.	V.G.	Good	Fair	Poor
—	750	580	320	250	120

Martini International Light

As above, with 26" lighterweight barrel.

NIB	Exc.	V.G.	Good	Fair	Poor
—	750	580	320	250	120

Martini International ISU

As above meeting ISU specifications, with 28" barrel. Manufactured from 1968 to 1976.

NIB	Exc.	V.G.	Good	Fair	Poor
—	850	680	400	320	200

BOLT-ACTIONS

Royal

Bolt-action sporting rifle. Manufactured in a variety of calibers. 24" barrel, with checkered French walnut stock.

NIB	Exc.	V.G.	Good	Fair	Poor
—	550	500	250	200	100

Majestic Deluxe

.22 Hornet, .222, .243, 7x57mm, .308 or .30-06 bolt-action sporting rifle, with 22" barrel. Folding rear sight, checkered walnut stock, with schnabel forend tip. Imported from 1959 to 1965. Note: Add 60 percent for .22 Hornet.

NIB	Exc.	V.G.	Good	Fair	Poor
—	550	350	250	200	100

Majestic Deluxe Featherweight

As above in .270 or .458 Magnum, with thinner barrel. Note: Add 25 percent for .458; 75 percent for .458.

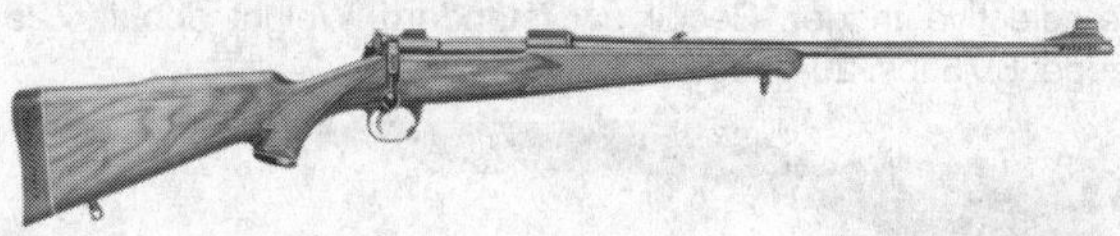

NIB	Exc.	V.G.	Good	Fair	Poor
—	550	350	250	200	100

Monarch Deluxe

As above drilled and tapped for telescopic sight. Available in heavy barreled varmint version in .222- or .243-caliber. Imported from 1966 to 1974.

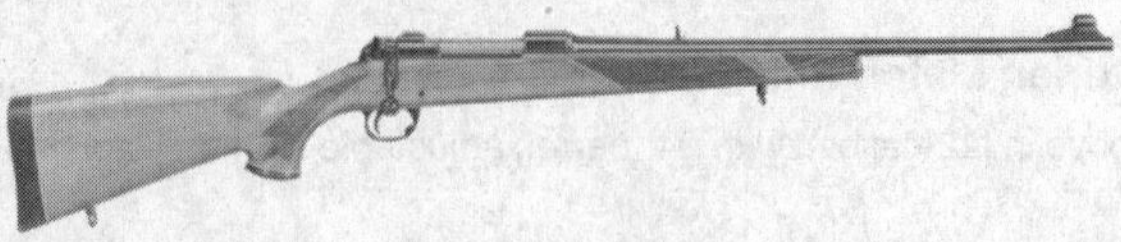

NIB	Exc.	V.G.	Good	Fair	Poor
—	550	380	280	220	100

HERTERS U9

Firm of Herters, Inc. of Waseca, Minnesota, imported BSA rifle actions beginning in 1965 that were used for custom-made rifles. Commencing in 1986, BSA began production of a new line of bolt-action sporting rifles on Model CF-2 action. Standard production models listed.

Sporter/Classic

Hunting rifle available in a variety of calibers, with checkered walnut stock. Introduced in 1986.

NIB	Exc.	V.G.	Good	Fair	Poor
—	450	320	280	200	100

Varminter

As above, with matte-finished heavy barrel in .222-, .22-250- or .243-caliber. Introduced in 1986.

NIB	Exc.	V.G.	Good	Fair	Poor
—	350	280	220	180	100

Stutzen Rifle

As above, with 20.5" barrel. Mannlicher-style stock.

NIB	Exc.	V.G.	Good	Fair	Poor
—	480	350	280	220	100

Regal Custom

As above, with engraved receiver, checkered walnut stock and ebony forend. Imported only in 1986.

NIB	Exc.	V.G.	Good	Fair	Poor
—	920	750	600	500	250

CFT Target Rifle

.308-caliber single-shot version of above, with 26.5" barrel and adjustable sights. Imported only in 1987.

NIB	Exc.	V.G.	Good	Fair	Poor
—	750	600	550	400	200

SHOTGUNS

Royal

Side-by-side chambered for 12- or 20-gauge 3" shells. Choice of 26" or 28" barrels, with multi-chokes. Checkered select walnut stock, with straight-grip. Splinter forearm. Case colored receiver, with side plates. Single-selective trigger. Recoil pad standard. Weight about: 7.25 lbs. 12-gauge; 6.75 lbs. 20-gauge.

NIB	Exc.	V.G.	Good	Fair	Poor
1500	1150	900	680	—	—

Classic

Side-by-side offered in 12-, 16-, 20-, 28-gauge and .410 bore. Choice of 26" or 28" barrels, except for 28-gauge and .410 bore where 26" barrels are only length offered. Checkered walnut stock, with pistol grip. Case colored box lock receiver, with scroll engraving. Semi-beavertail forearm. Recoil pad and choke tubes standard. Weight about: 7.25 lbs. 12-gauge; 6.75 lbs. 16-gauge; 6.6 lbs. 20-gauge; 6.25 lbs. 28-gauge; 6.5 lbs. .410 bore.

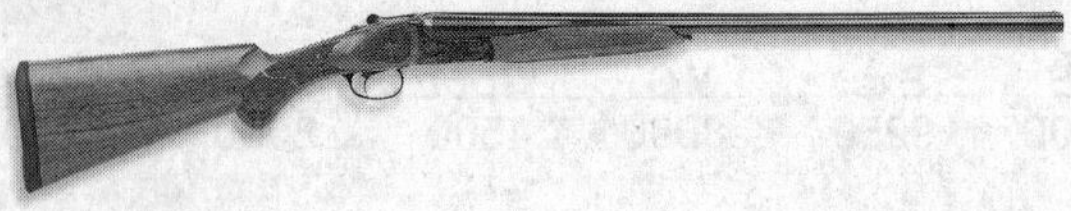

NIB	Exc.	V.G.	Good	Fair	Poor
1300	980	800	600	400	200

Falcon

Over/under in 12- or 20-gauge with 3" chambers. Choice of 26" or 28" barrels, with ventilated rib and choke tubes. Checkered walnut stock, with pistol grip. Case colored scroll engraved receiver. Single-selective trigger. Automatic ejectors. Recoil pad standard. Weight about: 7.25 lbs. 12-gauge; 7 lbs. 20-gauge.

NIB	Exc.	V.G.	Good	Fair	Poor
1200	900	880	500	300	150

Falcon Sporting

Similar to Falcon. Offered only in 12-gauge, with 2.75" chambers. Choice of 28" or 30" ventilated rib barrels, with 5 choke tubes. Barrels ported. Checkered walnut stock, with schnabel forearm. Weight about 7.7 lbs.

NIB	Exc.	V.G.	Good	Fair	Poor
1250	950	780	480	280	120

Silver Eagle

Over/under chambered for 12- or 20-gauge 3" shell. Fitted with 26" or 28" ventilated rib barrels, with choke tubes. Checkered walnut stock, with pistol grip. Single-selective trigger. Blued boxlock receiver. Recoil pad standard. Weight about: 7.2 lbs. 12-gauge; 6.75 lbs. 20-gauge.

NIB	Exc.	V.G.	Good	Fair	Poor
490	380	300	250	200	120

Silver Eagle II

Similar to Silver Eagle above. Addition of automatic ejectors.

NIB	Exc.	V.G.	Good	Fair	Poor
590	420	280	220	180	100

200 Series

Series of semi-automatic shotguns. Chambered for 12-, 16-, 20-, 28-gauge and .410 bore. Offered with 26" or 28" ventilated rib barrels, with choke tubes in 12-, 16- and 20-gauge; 28-gauge and .410 bore in 26" barrels only.. All gauges offered with walnut or synthetic stocks. 20-gauge offered in a youth model, with shortened stock. All gauges have 3" chambers except for 28-gauge, with 2.75" chambers. Weights range from 7.4 lbs. to 6.5 lbs. Note: Add $70 for walnut stock.

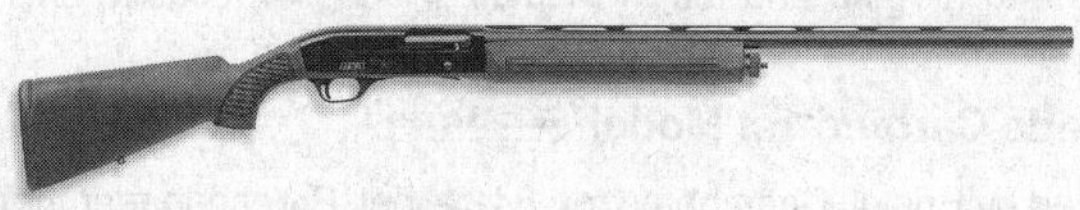

NIB	Exc.	V.G.	Good	Fair	Poor
390	290	220	200	100	80

300 SM Series

Semi-automatic series offered in 12-gauge only, with 3.5" chambers. Choice of 24", 26" or 28" ventilated rib barrels, with choke tubes. Synthetic stock. Weight about 7.3 lbs.

NIB	Exc.	V.G.	Good	Fair	Poor
420	320	250	220	180	100

BUCO
Germany

Buco Gas Pistol

Odd firearm looks more like a telescope than pistol. Chambered for 10.55mm gas cartridge. Single-shot. Overall approximately 5.5" long in its open or cocked position. Barrel is smoothbore and 3.75" in length. No sights or safety—one simply pulls inner tube back much like extending a telescope, unscrews end cap, inserts round and screws cap back into place. When needed, a thumbnail is used to depress sear and fire pistol. Marked on end cap "Buco DRGM". No more information available as to quantity or year of manufacture.

NIB	Exc.	V.G.	Good	Fair	Poor
—	—	650	500	350	150

BUDISCHOWSKY
Norton Armament Corp.
Mt. Clemens, Michigan

TP-70

.22 or .25 ACP caliber semi-automatic pistol, with 2.5" barrel, fixed sights and 6-shot magazine. Stainless steel, with plastic grips. Manufactured between 1973 and 1977.

Note: German-designed Budischowsky was originally made in Michigan by Norton Armament Corp. Michigan-made Budischowsky's are considered better quality than later examples made in Florida and Utah. Deduct 15% for non-Michigan manufacture.

.22 Rimfire Caliber

NIB	Exc.	V.G.	Good	Fair	Poor
550	420	350	300	220	150

.25 ACP Caliber

NIB	Exc.	V.G.	Good	Fair	Poor
520	400	320	280	180	120

BUL TRANSMARK LTD.
Tel-Aviv, Israel

Model M5

This model was brought into the USA from 1996 to 2010 by several importers, including ISA, KBI, EAA and others. Semi-automatic bears a resemblance to Model 1911. Frame polymer, slide stainless steel. Available in 9mm, .38 Super, .40 S&W and .45 ACP. Magazine limited to 10 rounds. Note: Add 40 to 60 percent for IPSC competition models.

NIB	Exc.	V.G.	Good	Fair	Poor
750	600	450	350	200	100

BULLARD REPEATING ARMS CO.
Springfield, Massachusetts

Designed by James H. Bullard. Rifles listed were manufactured in competition with those produced by Whitney Arms Company and Winchester Repeating Arms Company. Approximately 12,000 made between 1886 and 1890.

Small Frame (Antique)

.32-40 and .38-45 caliber-lever action rifle, with 26" octagonal barrel. Half or full length magazine tube. Blued or case-hardened, with walnut stock. Receiver stamped "Bullard Repeating Arms Company/Springfield, Mass., U.S.A. Pat. Aug. 16, 1881". Caliber marked on top of frame.

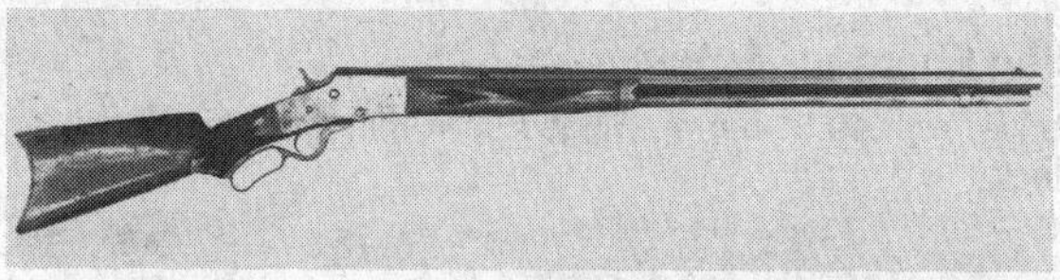

Courtesy Milwaukee Public Museum, Milwaukee, Wisconsin

Exc.	Fine	V.G.	Good	Fair	Poor
6000	3000	2000	1500	500	300

Large Frame (Antique)

.40-75 through .45-85 caliber lever-action rifle, with 28" octagonal barrel. Other features and markings as above. Can be custom ordered in .50-95 and .50-115.

Exc.	Fine	V.G.	Good	Fair	Poor
7000	4000	3000	2000	750	300

Carbine (Antique)

.45-70 caliber lever-action rifle, with 22" round barrel. Sliding dust cover on receiver. Marking and finish as above.

Exc.	Fine	V.G.	Good	Fair	Poor
9500	6000	4000	2750	1200	500

Musket (Antique)

.45-70 caliber lever-action rifle, with 30" round barrel. Full-length stock secured by two barrel bands. Rod under barrel, military sights and same sliding cover on receiver as found on Carbine. Examples noted without manufacturer's markings.

Exc.	Fine	V.G.	Good	Fair	Poor
8500	5000	3500	2500	1000	500

BULLDOG SINGLE-SHOT PISTOL
Connecticut Arms & Manufacturing Co.
Naubuc, Connecticut

Bulldog (Antique)

.44- or .50-caliber single-shot spur trigger pistol, with 4" or 6" barrels. Pivoting breech-block that moves to left for loading. Blued, case-hardened and stamped "Connecticut Arms & Manf. Co. Naubuc Conn. Patented Oct. 25, 1864". Only a few hundred manufactured. Produced between 1866 and 1868. Note: Add 40 percent for .50-caliber 6" barreled versions.

Exc.	Fine	V.G.	Good	Fair	Poor
1650	680	480	280	150	100

BURGESS GUN CO.

Buffalo, New York
See—COLT and WHITNEY

One of the most prolific 19th century designers was Andrew Burgess, who established his own company in 1892. Burgess Gun Company manufactured slide action shotguns and rifles, operated by a unique pistol grip prior to their being purchased by Winchester Repeating Arms Company in 1899. Arms based on Burgess' patents were manufactured by a variety of American gun makers. Serial numbers for all Burgess shotguns begin at 1000.

12 Gauge Slide Action Shotgun

12-gauge slide-action shotgun, with 28" or 30" barrel. Blued, with walnut stock. Available with 6 grades of engraving. Values listed are for standard plain model.

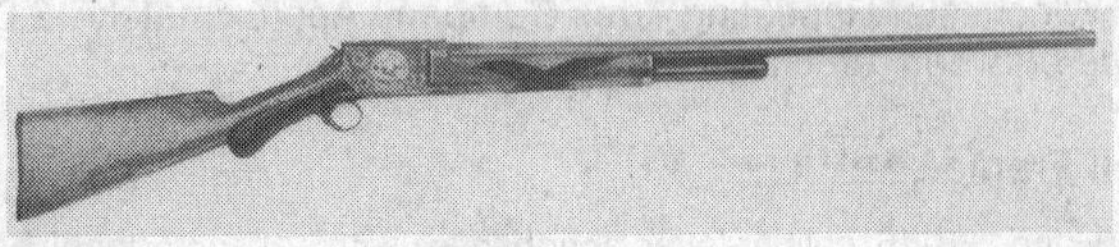

Antique

Exc.	*Fine*	*V.G.*	*Good*	*Fair*	*Poor*
2500	1500	1000	600	200	100

Folding Shotgun Antique

As above, with 19.5" barrel. Hinged so it may be folded back against buttstock.

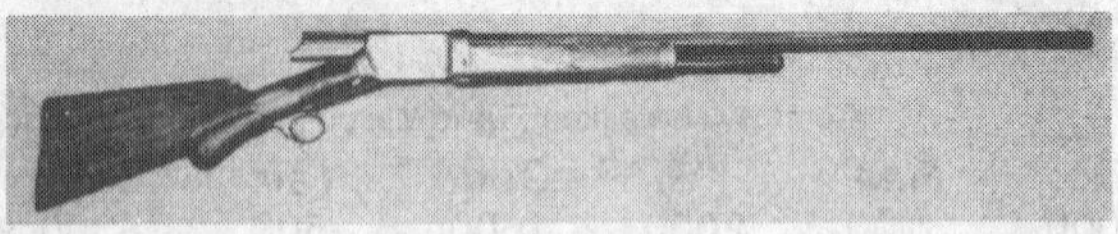

Exc.	*Fine*	*V.G.*	*Good*	*Fair*	*Poor*
12000	7000	3000	1500	750	400

Slide Action Rifle Antique

Extremely rare rifle based upon shotgun design described above. Manufactured in at least three calibers, with varying barrel lengths. Blued, with walnut stock. Burgess-made rifle values are speculative.

Exc.	*Fine*	*V.G.*	*Good*	*Fair*	*Poor*
—	6000	—	1500	—	—

BURGSMULLER, K.

Krelensen, Germany

Burgo

Rohm RG10 under another name. It is a poor quality inexpensive .38-caliber revolver. Examples marketed by Burgsmuller are so marked. Virtually worthless.

Regent

Regent is a .22-caliber revolver that resembles Colt Police Positive in appearance. Higher quality than Burgo. Manufacturer not known.

NIB	*Exc.*	*V.G.*	*Good*	*Fair*	*Poor*
—	160	120	80	50	0

BURNSIDE RIFLE CO.

Bristol Firearms Co.
Bristol & Providence, Rhode Island

Bristol, Rhode Island Antique

Historically desirable firearm for Civil War collectors. Designer, Ambrose E. Burnside, was to become a well- known Union general. Rifle, of which there were four distinct models, was used quite extensively in Civil War. This carbine was manufactured first by Bristol Firearms Co., which made entire production of first model and also some of second model. In 1862 Burnside Firearms Co. was formed. They produced remainder of second models and all third and fourth models. Production ceased entirely in 1865.

Burnside Carbine 1st Model Antique

Produced by Bristol. Chambered for .54-caliber. Breech-loader that uses percussion ignition system, but features a cartridge of sorts made of copper and a tape priming device that was located inside frame. Has 22" round barrel, with no forend, walnut stock and inspector's cartouche. Finish blued and case colored. Frame stamped "Burnside's /Patent/March 25th/1856". Approximately 250 1st Models manufactured.

Exc.	*Fine*	*V.G.*	*Good*	*Fair*	*Poor*
15000	6000	3750	1500	500	350

2nd Model Antique

2nd Model features an improved breech-block opening mechanism located inside triggerguard. Barrel is 21" long. Other features similar to 1st Model. Marked "Bristol Firearm Co." or "Burnside Rifle Co./Providence-R.I.". Barrel marked "Cast Steel 1861" and some breech-block devices marked "G.P. Foster Pat./April 10th 1860". Approximately 1,500 2nd Models manufactured in 1861 and 1862.

Courtesy Milwaukee Public Museum, Milwaukee, Wisconsin

Exc.	*Fine*	*V.G.*	*Good*	*Fair*	*Poor*
5500	2500	1620	750	300	210

3rd Model Antique

Differs from 2nd Model in it has a forend, with a barrel band and slightly modified hammer. Markings same as Burnside-manufactured 2nd Models. Approximately 2,000 produced in 1862.

Exc.	*Fine*	*V.G.*	*Good*	*Fair*	*Poor*
3500	1250	870	500	250	170

4th Model Antique

Differs from others in it features a hinged breech that permits simpler loading of odd-shaped Burnside percussion cartridge. Frame marked "Burnside's Patent/Model of 1864". Other features similar to 3rd Model. Approximately 50,000 manufactured between 1862 and 1865. Some references also list a 5th Model. Similar to the 4th Model, with the addition of a guide screw in the right center of the frame. Both 4th & 5th Models are valued here as 4th Models.

Courtesy Milwaukee Public Museum, Milwaukee, Wisconsin

Exc.	*Fine*	*V.G.*	*Good*	*Fair*	*Poor*
4000	2000	1400	800	400	280

BUSHMASTER FIREARMS INTERNATIONAL

Huntsville, Alabama

In 2006, Bushmaster was purchased by Freedom Group, parent company of Remington, Marlin/H&R, DPMS, Para USA and Dakota Arms. In 2011, Bushmaster plant in Maine was closed and production moved to Remington facility in Ilion, New York and later to Huntsville, Alabama. Parent Remington Outdoor Company announced it would no longer produce Bushmaster products in January 2020. In September 2020, Remington itself declared bankruptcy in 2020 and its assets were dispersed to various competitors. The Bushmaster trademarks were sold to Crotalus Holdings Inc. of Minden, Nevada. SEE POLITICAL PANIC PRICING.

ACR Basic (Adaptive Combat Rifle)

Series of modular AR-15 pattern rifles in 5.56 NATO/.223 Rem., with all major components configurable to user preference, including barrel, stock and handguard. Features include adjustable gas piston-driven system, ambidextrous controls, 16.5-in. barrel, A2 birdcage flash hider and 30-round magazine. Made in several variations beginning in 2010. Coyote is number 90847. Prices shown are for basic folder configuration with black stock 90958. (Model no. 90838. 5.56/.223/16.5 in. barrel.)

NIB	Exc.	V.G.	Good	Fair	Poor
1770	1510	1280	1090	920	790

ACR Enhanced

Semi-automatic Adaptive Combat Rifle chambered in 5.56 NATO, 6.8 SPC, .300 Blackout, .450 Bushmaster. Barrel is quickly interchangeable and available in 10.5, 14.5, 16.5 and 18.5 in. AAC Blackout 51T flash hider, 3-rail enhanced handguard, with 7-position folding/telescoping stock. A-TACs model has fixed A-frame composite camo stock, with rubber butt pad and sling mounts. Introduced in 2013. Prices shown are for 5.56/16.5 in. 90704. (Model no. 90705. 5.56/16.5 in. Coyote Brown. Gas piston.)

NIB	Exc.	V.G.	Good	Fair	Poor
1950	1660	1410	1200	1020	870

ACR DMR

Chambered in 5.56 NATO with 18.5-in. barrel, Geissele trigger, Magpul PRS or PRS2 stock (current model). Modular design on current production model for quick and easy caliber change. Designated Marksman Rifle. Model no. 90958. 5.56/18.5 in. 51T AAC flash hider. Prices shown are for 18.5-in./5.56mm model 90958.

NIB	Exc.	V.G.	Good	Fair	Poor
2300	1960	1660	1410	1200	1020

ACR Pistol

Similar to Air series but with 10.5-in. barrel, AAC SquareDrop handguard. Weight is 6.5 pounds. Introduced 2019.

NIB	Exc.	V.G.	Good	Fair	Poor
2150	1610	1160	1010	960	810

XM-10 Standard

Chambered in .308 Win. 16-in. heavy profile barrel with mid-length gas system and A2 birdcage flash hider. Receiver-length Picatinny optics rail with two 1.25-in. optics risers. Milled gas block, 6-position telescoping stock, one 20-round magazine. Price shown for model number 90702.

NIB	Exc.	V.G.	Good	Fair	Poor
1000	850	720	610	520	440

XM15-E2S Target Model

Furnished with 20-in. heavy barrel and A-2 stock. Weight 8.35 lbs. Note: Add $10 for 24-in. barrel; $20 for 26-in. barrel; $75 for A3 carry handle.

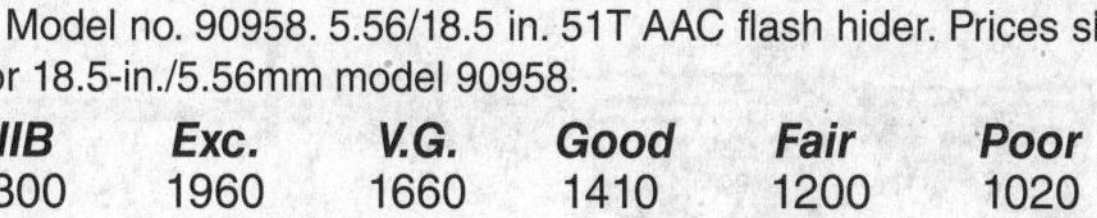

NIB	Exc.	V.G.	Good	Fair	Poor
—	750	640	540	460	390

XM15-E2S V-Match Competition Rifle

Specially designed competition rifle, with 20-, 24- or 26-in. barrel lengths. Fitted with black anodized aluminum handguard. Weight about 8.1 lbs. Note: Add $75 for A3 carry handle.

NIB	Exc.	V.G.	Good	Fair	Poor
—	850	720	610	520	440

XM15-E2S V-Match Carbine

As above, with 16-in. barrel. Weight about 6.9 lbs. Note: Add $75 for A3 carry handle.

NIB	Exc.	V.G.	Good	Fair	Poor
—	850	720	610	520	440

XM15 3-Gun Enhanced Carbine

Designed for 3-Gun competition, with crimson anodized upper and lower receiver, 16-in. mid-length stainless barrel, 15-in. carbon-fiber free-float tube, Rolling Thunder compensator and Timney trigger. Other features include Boron nitride bolt carrier group, Bravo Company charging handle, ambidextrous selector switch, Magpul MIAD grip and MOE stock. Introduced in 2014.

NIB	Exc.	V.G.	Good	Fair	Poor
—	1400	1190	1010	860	730

XM15 Patrolman's Carbine

NIB	Exc.	V.G.	Good	Fair	Poor
—	750	640	540	460	390

XM15-E2S Shorty Carbine

This "post-ban" model M16 is a gas-operated semi-automatic rifle. Chambered for .223 Remington cartridge. Fitted with heavy 16-in. barrel and 30-round magazine. Overall length 35 in.; empty weight 6.72 lbs. Note: Add $50 for fluted barrel; $75 for A3-type carry handle.

NIB	Exc.	V.G.	Good	Fair	Poor
—	750	640	540	460	390

XM15-E2S Dissipator

Similar to above model, with 16-in. barrel. Fitted with longer plastic handguard to give a longer sight radius. Weight 7.2 lbs. Note: Add $75 for A3 carry handle.

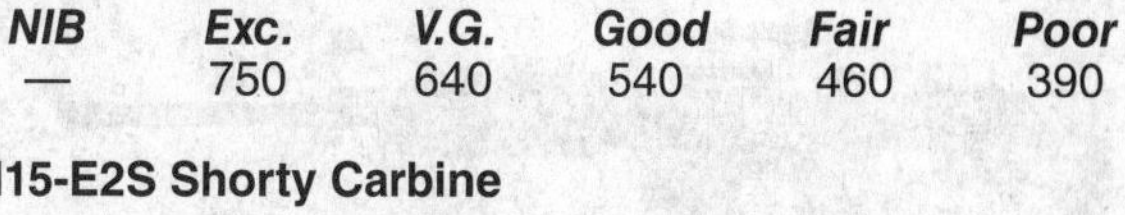

NIB	Exc.	V.G.	Good	Fair	Poor
—	1000	850	720	610	520

M4 Post-Ban Carbine

Introduced in 2001. Features 14.5-in. barrel, with permanently attached Mini Y Comp muzzle brake (total length 16 in.) and pinned fixed-length Tele-style stock. Chambered for .223-caliber. M16A2 rear sight. Supplied with 10-round magazine. Weight about 6.6 lbs.

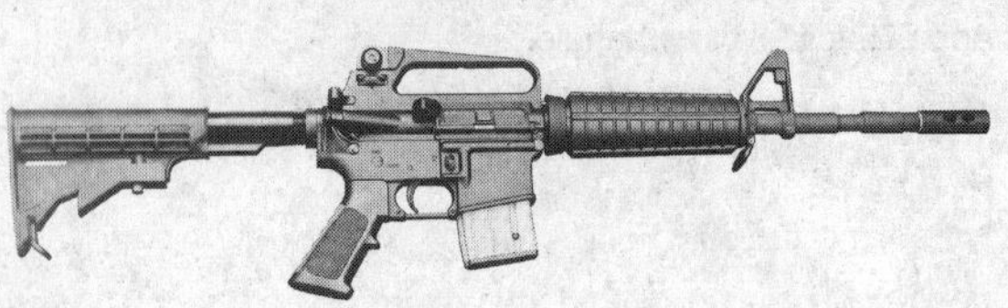

NIB	Exc.	V.G.	Good	Fair	Poor
—	950	810	690	580	500

M4A3 Post-Ban Carbine

Same as above, with removable carry handle. Introduced in 2001.

NIB	Exc.	V.G.	Good	Fair	Poor
—	1030	870	740	630	540

MOE Series

Features Magpul Original Equipment (MOE) accessories, including rifle-length handguard, adjustable stock, grip and 30-shot magazine. Chambered for .223 (5.56) or .308. Note: Add $400 for .308.

NIB	Exc.	V.G.	Good	Fair	Poor
—	550	470	400	340	290

M4 Patrolman's MOE Rifle

The M4 Patrolman's MOE rifle is the company's staple, with upgraded features, including Magpul furniture, a 16" barrel made from 4150 CMV, with a salt bath nitride finish, and a 1:7" twist rate. It comes with Magpul MOE SL handguard, CTR stock, and MOE grip in ODG. The rifle also features a Mil-spec trigger, a detachable carry handle, and an F-Marked A2 front sight. It uses PMAG Gen M2 30-round black magazines and an A2 flash hider. Made in the USA. Weight w/o magazine: 6.9 lbs. Length: 32.5" to 35.5". SEE POLITICAL PANIC PRICING.

NIB	Exc.	V.G.	Good	Fair	Poor
740	—	—	—	—	—

DCM Competition Rifle

Features 20-in. extra heavy barrel, with free floating forend. Competition sights and trigger. Supplied with buttstock weight, 10-round magazine and hard carrying case.

NIB	Exc.	V.G.	Good	Fair	Poor
1230	1040	890	750	640	540

XM-15 Standard Heavy-Barrel Carbine

5.56/.223. Features include chrome-lined HBAR heavy-profile 16-in. vanadium steel barrel, fixed or removable carry handle, six-position telestock. Overall length 32.5 in. Weight 6.93 lbs. to 7.28 lbs. Price shown for model 90212.

NIB	Exc.	V.G.	Good	Fair	Poor
—	680	570	490	420	350

XM15-E2S Minimalist Series

Introduced 2017. Chambered in 5.56/.223, .300 BLK, and .450 BM. Includes rifle-length AAC SquareDrop handguard, allowing fast, solid attachment of accessories at seven different angles. Mission First Tactical Minimalist Stock, 16-in. 1:8 4150 lightweight contour barrel with Melonite (FNC) finish. A3 flattop upper receiver, AAC 51T flash hider, ALG Defense Advanced Combat Trigger, Mission First Tactical grip and magazine. Weight, 6.0 lbs for 5.56. Overall length, 35 in. Price shown for model 91056 in 5.56/16 in. M-Lok variants available in 5.56 (90178) with a 1:8 twist rate and 300 BLK (90179) with a 1:9 twist rate.

NIB	Exc.	V.G.	Good	Fair	Poor
—	760	650	550	470	400

M4A3 Gas Piston Rifle

Semi-automatic AR-style rifle chambered in .223. Features include 16-in. barrel, telescoping stock, carry handle, 30-round magazine and piston assembly rather than direct gas impingement. Overall length 32.5 in. Weight 7.46 lbs.

NIB	Exc.	V.G.	Good	Fair	Poor
—	1500	1280	1080	920	780

6.8 SPC Carbine

AR-style semi-automatic rifle chambered in 6.8 SPC. Features include 16-in. M4 profile barrel, with Izzy muzzle brake, 26-round magazine, six-position telestock. Available in A2 (fixed carry handle) or A3 (removable carry handle) configuration. Overall length 32.75 in. Weight 6.57 lbs. Also chambered in 7.62x39mm. Price shown for model BCWA2F16M468.

NIB	Exc.	V.G.	Good	Fair	Poor
—	1200	1020	870	740	630

Carbon 15 9mm Carbine

Semi-automatic carbine chambered in 9mm Parabellum. Carbon fiber frame, 16-in. steel barrel, six-position telescoping stock, 30-round detachable magazine. Introduced 2006.

NIB	Exc.	V.G.	Good	Fair	Poor
830	700	600	510	430	370

Carbon 15 Top Loading Rifle

Semi-automatic rifle chambered in .223. Carbon fiber frame, 16-in. steel barrel, retractable stock, Picatinny rail, 10-round fixed magazine. Based on AR-15. Introduced 2006.

NIB	Exc.	V.G.	Good	Fair	Poor
930	790	670	570	480	410

Predator

Semi-automatic rifle chambered in .223. 20-in. DCM-type barrel, fixed composite buttstock, 2-stage competition trigger, Picatinny rail, .500-in. scope risers. Based on AR-15. Introduced 2006. Price is for model number 90629.

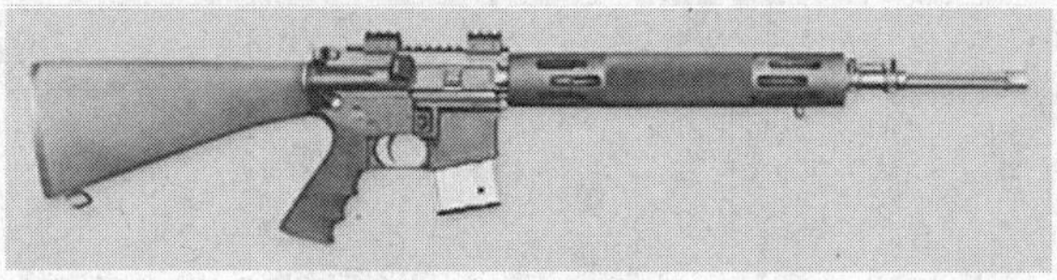

NIB	Exc.	V.G.	Good	Fair	Poor
900	770	650	550	470	400

Varminter

Chambered in 5.56 NATO/.223 Rem. with lined 24-in. fluted heavy or stainless barrel. Magpul MOE stock has pistol grip; adjustable on stainless model. Two-stage trigger. Price is for model number 90641.

NIB	Exc.	V.G.	Good	Fair	Poor
900	770	650	550	470	400

.308 Hunter

Designed for the hunter. Chambered in .308 Winchester, with 20-in. heavy-fluted barrel. Chrome lined bore and chamber. Features include 5-round magazine, mid-length gas system, two .75-in. mini risers for optics mounting, Hogue rubberized pistol grip, standard A2 stock. Vista Hunter has A2 grip. Weight about 8.5 lbs. Note: Add $100 for Vista Hunter if NIB.

NIB	Exc.	V.G.	Good	Fair	Poor
1400	1190	1010	860	730	620

ORC Series

Optics Ready Carbine series for shooters who wish to add various optical holograph, red dot or scope sights. Chambered in .223/5.56, with magazine capacity of 30 rounds or .308 with 20-round magazine. Gas piston system taps gas from barrel much like AK and FAL designs. Provides a cleaner operation with less recoil. Detented plug in gas block allows for easy cleaning. Barrel length 16 in.; weight 6.6 lbs. (.223) to 7.75 lbs. (.308). Note: Add $200 for .308 chambering. Price is for model number M4 5.56/16 in. 90391.

NIB	Exc.	V.G.	Good	Fair	Poor
—	950	810	690	580	500

Quick Response Carbine

This model equipped with detachable red dot sight, 16-in. barrel, 10-shot magazine and six-position collapsible stock. Price is for model number 91046.

NIB	Exc.	V.G.	Good	Fair	Poor
—	580	490	420	360	300

.450 Carbine

Chambered for .450 Bushmaster cartridge providing big-bore power in AR platform. Developed with Hornady Mfg., cartridge propels a 250-grain bullet at 2200 fps, ideal for most North American big game. Barrel length 16 or 20 in., A3 flattop receiver with Picatinny rail. Weight about 8.5 lbs.

NIB	Exc.	V.G.	Good	Fair	Poor
—	880	740	630	540	460

450 Bushmaster 20

Caliber: .450 Bushmaster. Snake Charmer muzzle brake, 20” barrel, 14” BFI free-float handguard, DM2S two-stage trigger, five-round aluminum magazine, fixed A2-style shoulder stock.

NIB	Exc.	V.G.	Good	Fair	Poor
1010	—	—	—	—	—

Bushmaster AK Carbine

AR-type rifle, with AK-type muzzle brake and permanently pinned suppressor. 5.56 NATO caliber.

NIB	Exc.	V.G.	Good	Fair	Poor
—	1030	870	740	630	540

Bushmaster .300 AAC Blackout

AR-type rifle chambered for .300 AAC cartridge. Developed by Advanced Armament Corporation, which is now part of Freedom Group that owns Bushmaster. Round's ballistics are similar to 7.62x39 and .300 Whisper wildcat. .300 AAC is factory loaded by Remington, including a sub-sonic load. Compatible with AR-15 magazines.

NIB	Exc.	V.G.	Good	Fair	Poor
—	730	620	530	450	380

BA50 .50 BMG Rifle and Carbine

Bolt-action 10-round repeater intended for long-range target shooting. 30-in. barrel, muzzle brake. Carbine has 20-in. barrel.

NIB	Exc.	V.G.	Good	Fair	Poor
4950	4210	3580	3040	2580	2200

Carbon 15 .223 Pistol

AR-style semi-automatic pistol chambered in 5.56/.223. Features include 7.5-in. stainless steel barrel, carbon composite receiver, shortened handguard, full-length optics rail, A2-type front sight with dual-aperture flip-up rear. 30-round magazine. Overall length 20 in. Weight 2.88 lbs.

NIB	Exc.	V.G.	Good	Fair	Poor
750	640	540	460	390	330

Carbon 15 9mm Pistol

Operating controls similar to AR-type rifles, 30-round capacity. Weight with loaded magazine 5.5 lbs. Carbon-fiber receiver, forend and grip, with Chrome Moly steel barrel. Full-length Picatinny rail.

NIB	Exc.	V.G.	Good	Fair	Poor
750	640	540	460	390	330

Carbon 15 Type 97 Pistol

Similar to above, without handguard.

NIB	Exc.	V.G.	Good	Fair	Poor
700	600	510	430	360	310

BUTLER, WM. S.

Rocky Hill, Connecticut

Butler Single-Shot Pistol (Antique)

.36-caliber single-shot percussion pocket pistol, with 2.5" barrel. Frame and grip made in one piece. Frame marked "Wm. S. Butler's Patent/ Patented Feb.3, 1857".

Exc.	Fine	V.G.	Good	Fair	Poor
1000	700	500	350	200	100

BUTTERFIELD, JESSE

Philadelphia, Pennsylvania

Butterfield Army Revolver (Antique)

.41-caliber revolver, with 7" octagonal barrel and unfluted 5-shot cylinder. Features a special priming device disk that was loaded in front of triggerguard. Brass frame blued, with walnut grips. Frame stamped "Butterfield's Patent Dec. 11, 1855/Phila.". Approximately 650 manufactured in 1861 and 1862.

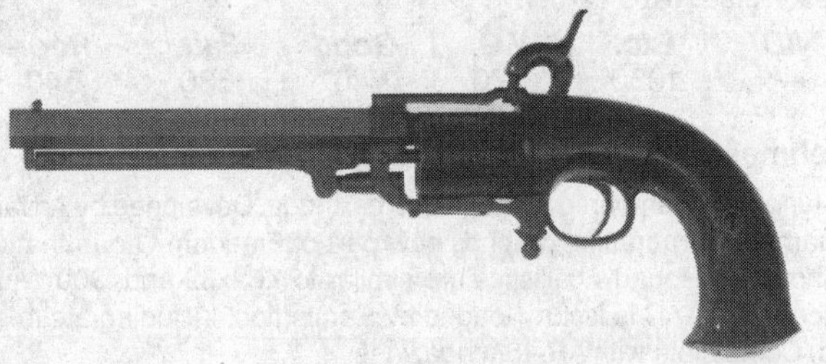

Courtesy Milwaukee Public Museum, Milwaukee, Wisconsin

Exc.	Fine	V.G.	Good	Fair	Poor
8000	6500	4000	2500	1200	750

Butterfield Pocket Pistol Antique

Manufactured in 1850s. .41-caliber single-shot percussion pistol, with 2" to 3.5" barrel. German silver, with walnut stocks. Lock marked "Butterfield's/Patent Dec 11, 1855". Tube holds primers and advances one over the nipple each time the hammer is cocked. Extremely rare. Values are very speculative

Exc.	Fine	V.G.	Good	Fair	Poor
9000	4250	2950	1650	1000	700

C

CABANAS, INDUSTRIAS S.A.

Aguilas, Mexico

This company manufactures a variety of bolt-action single-shot rifles that utilize .22-caliber blanks to propel a .177-caliber pellet. Scarce, but not especially valuable.

Mini-82 Youth

NIB	Exc.	V.G.	Good	Fair	Poor
80	60	50	40	30	20

R-83 Larger Youth

NIB	Exc.	V.G.	Good	Fair	Poor
80	80	60	50	40	30

Safari A

NIB	Exc.	V.G.	Good	Fair	Poor
100	90	80	50	40	30

Varmint

NIB	Exc.	V.G.	Good	Fair	Poor
120	110	90	80	—	40

Espronceda IV

NIB	Exc.	V.G.	Good	Fair	Poor
120	110	90	80	50	40

Leyre

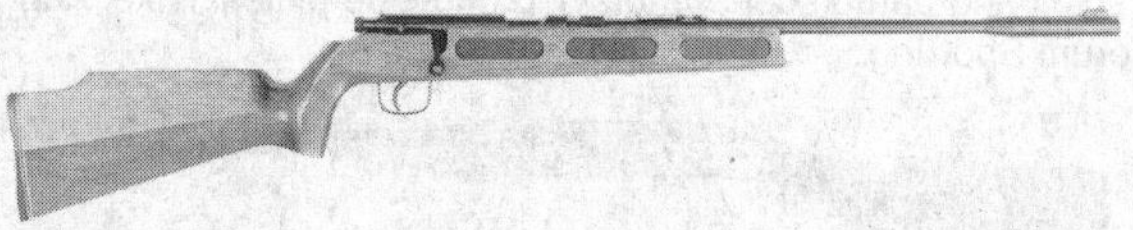

NIB	Exc.	V.G.	Good	Fair	Poor
140	120	100	80	60	50

Master

NIB	Exc.	V.G.	Good	Fair	Poor
150	130	110	100	80	60

CABOT GUN COMPANY

Cabot, PA

Manufacturer of custom 1911 platform pistols with limited production runs. Typically in VG or better condition. Values range from $6,995 NIB, $6,200 Exc. and $5,500 VG.

CADEX DEFENCE

Saint-Jean-sur-Richelieu, Quebec

Canadian manufacturer of high-end bolt guns, rifle chassis and tactical firearm accessories.

CDX-R7 CRBN SERIES

Calibers: 6.5 Creedmoor, 6.5 PRC, .308 Win., .300 WSM, .300 PRC, .338 Lapua Mag. Capacity: Varies by box magazine. Barrel: 24 or 26 in. Proof Research carbon fiber threaded. Weight: 8.2–8.3 lbs. Length: 45.25–48.06 in. Stock: Lightweight Tundra Strike chassis with aluminum bedding blocks available in 14 color combinations. Cadex recoil pad, neoprene cheek pad, and rubberized grip panel. Sights: None. 0 MOA Picatinny rail standard, 20 or 30 MOA rails available. Features: Bolt-action rifle designed with backcountry hunters in mind. Hunting style muzzle brake and bolt knob. Spiral fluted bolt. Cerakote metalwork. DX2 Evo single-/two-stage selectable trigger. Oversized triggerguard and mag release. Hard case included.

NIB	Exc.	V.G.	Good	Fair	Poor
3160	—	—	—	—	—

CDX-R7 SPTR SERIES

Calibers: 6.5 Creedmoor, 6.5 PRC, .308 Win., .300 WSM, .300 PRC, 338 Lapua Mag. Capacity: varies by box magazine. Barrel: 24 or 26 in. sporter profile stainless, fluted and threaded. Weight: 8.2–8.5 lbs. Length: 45.25–48.06 in. Stock: Lightweight Tundra Strike chassis with aluminum bedding blocks available in 14 color combinations. Cadex recoil pad, neoprene cheek pad, and rubberized grip panel. Sights: None. 0 MOA Picatinny rail standard, 20 or 30 MOA rails available. Features: Bolt-action rifle similar to the CRBN series, but without the carbon-fiber barrel. Hunting-style muzzle brake and bolt knob. Spiral fluted bolt. DX2 Evo single-/two-stage selectable trigger. Oversized triggerguard and mag release. Hard case included.

NIB	Exc.	V.G.	Good	Fair	Poor
2570	—	—	—	—	—

CDX-R7 CPS SERIES

Calibers: 6.5 Creedmoor, .308 Win. Capacity: Multiple magazine sleeves to fit most mags on the market. Barrel: 16.5-in. Bartlein heavy, straight-taper, fluted, threaded. Weight: 10.49 lbs. Length: 33.5 in. Stock: Lightweight with small contour forend tube and rail placement at 3, 6, and 9 o'clock. Takedown QD skeleton buttstock. Available in 14 color combinations. Cadex recoil pad, neoprene cheek pad, and rubberized grip panel. Sights: None. 0 MOA Picatinny rail standard, 20 or 30 MOA rails available. Features: Military-quality bolt-action platform for the civilian market. Spiral-fluted bolt. DX2 Evo single-/two-stage selectable trigger. Optional MX2 muzzle brake. Hard case included.

NIB	Exc.	V.G.	Good	Fair	Poor
4330	—	—	—	—	—

CAESAR GUERINI
Italy

This manufacturer makes a series of high-quality over/under shotguns for field use and clay target sports. Shown here is a sampling of the many different models. Many options are available, including custom stock dimensions, wood upgrades and extra barrels. Imported by Caesar Guerini USA, Cambridge, MD.

Flyway

Over/under 12-gauge 3" gun offered with 28" or 30" ventilated rib barrels, with choke tubes. Checkered walnut stock with pistol grip. Trap-style forearm with finger grooves. Single-selective trigger and ejectors. Weight about 8 lbs. depending on barrel length.

NIB	Exc.	V.G.	Good	Fair	Poor
2000	1600	1350	1200	900	500

Woodlander

This field gun available in 12-, 20-, 28-gauge and .410 bore, with 26", 28" or 30" barrels and five flush fitting choke tubes. Features include an oil-finished stock of Turkish walnut, with cut checkering and a rounded Prince of Wales or straight-grip. Receiver is color case-hardened, with a gold ruffed grouse on the bottom. Choice of manual or automatic safety.

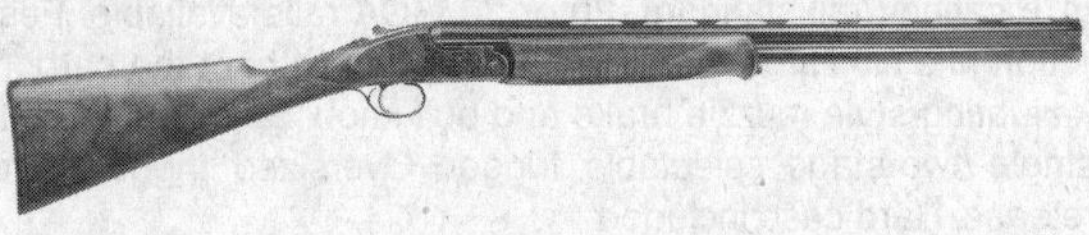

NIB	Exc.	V.G.	Good	Fair	Poor
3200	2600	1750	1300	900	500

Magnus Light

Offered in 12-, 20- or 28-gauge, with choice of 26" or 28" ventilated rib barrels and choke tubes. Alloy frame with Tinaloy finish and side plates. Scroll engraved with gold game birds. Checkered walnut stock with Prince of Wales-style pistol grip. Weight about: 6 lbs. 12-gauge; 5.4 lbs. 20-gauge; 5.25 lbs. 28-gauge.

NIB	Exc.	V.G.	Good	Fair	Poor
4000	3100	2000	1500	1000	500

Magnus

Similar to Magnus Light, with case-hardened steel receiver. Weight about: 6.75 lbs. 12-gauge; 6.5 lbs. 20-gauge; 6.25 lbs. 28-gauge.

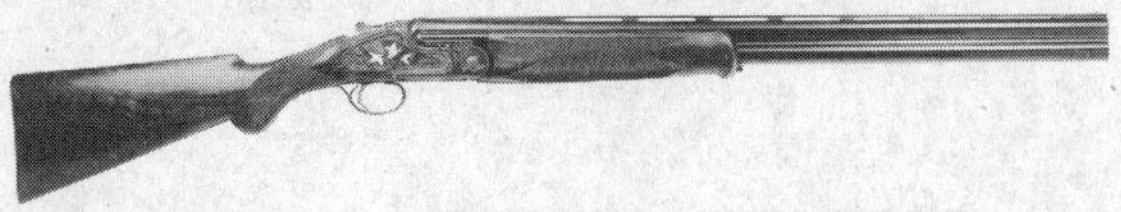

NIB	Exc.	V.G.	Good	Fair	Poor
4000	3100	2000	1500	1000	500

Magnus Sporting

Similar to Summit, with upgraded wood and sidelock-style receiver. Scroll engraving and gold game birds.

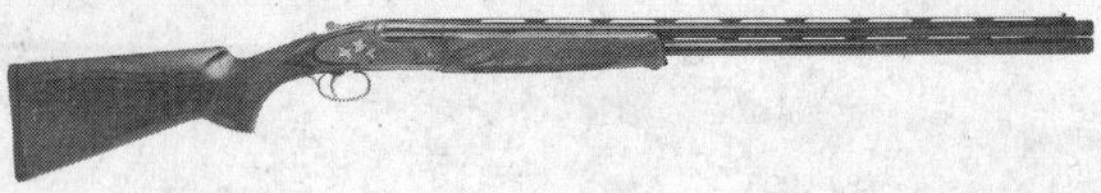

NIB	Exc.	V.G.	Good	Fair	Poor
4600	3600	2800	1800	1000	500

Maxum

Offered in 12-, 20- and 28-gauge, with hand-polished coin-finish receiver, hand-rubbed oil walnut stock, deep relief floral scroll hand-finished engraving on receiver, side plates and forend assembly. Comes with velvet-lined lockable hard case and five choke tubes.

NIB	Exc.	V.G.	Good	Fair	Poor
5400	4500	3200	2400	1200	600

Tempio

Over/under gun offered in 12-, 20- and 28-gauge, with choice of 26" or 28" barrels and choke tubes. Checkered Circassian walnut stock, with Prince of Wales-style pistol grip. Alloy receiver is a gray finish of Tinaloy. Engraved with scroll and gold game birds. Single-selective trigger with ejectors. Weight about: 6.8 lbs. 12-gauge; 6.4 lbs. 20-gauge; 6.25 lbs. 28-gauge.

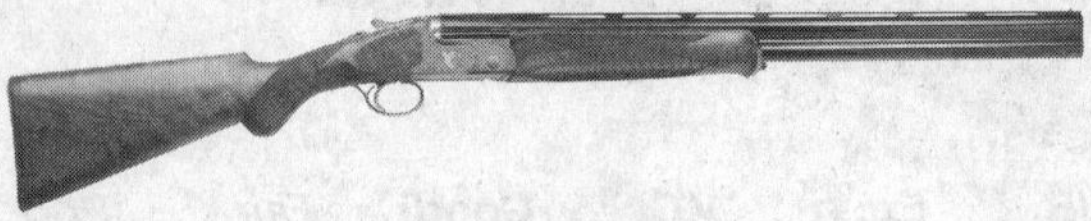

NIB	Exc.	V.G.	Good	Fair	Poor
3500	2700	1800	1500	800	400

Forum/Forum Sporting

Offered in 12-, 20- and 28-gauge, with choice of 26" or 28" barrels on Forum. Forum Sporting has 30", 32" or 34" barrels. Gun has silver receiver, with scroll and game scene engraving and side plates. Note: Add $700 for Forum Sporting.

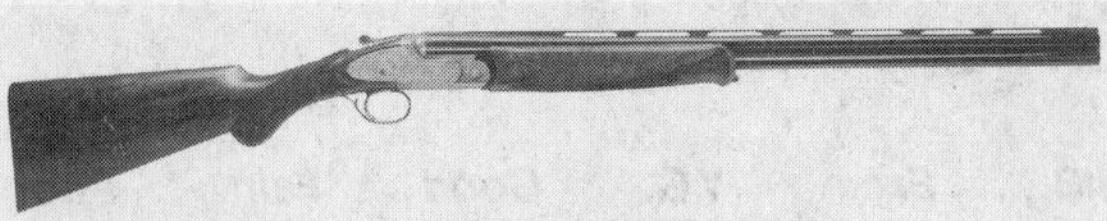

NIB	Exc.	V.G.	Good	Fair	Poor
9000	7000	4750	3250	1600	700

Summit Sporting/Summit Limited

Offered in 12-, 20- or 28-gauge, with choice of 30" or 32" ventilated rib barrels and extended choke tubes. Alloy receiver with engraving. Single-selective trigger adjustable for length of pull. Ejectors. Checkered walnut stock, with pistol grip. Weight about: 8 lbs. 12-gauge; 7.5 lbs. 20-gauge; 7.45 lbs. 28-gauge. Note: Add $500 for Summit Limited.

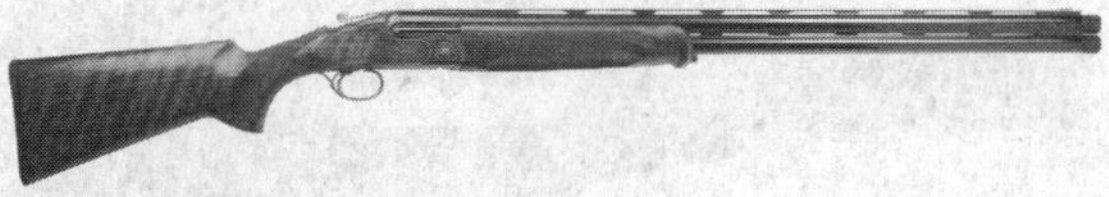

NIB	Exc.	V.G.	Good	Fair	Poor
3300	2500	1650	1200	750	300

Summit Ascent Sporting

Sporting Clays model with a high tapered 10mm rib to allow upright shooting position for better target visabilty. In 12-gauge, with 30" or 32" barrels and six Maxis competition choke tubes. Stock has adjustable comb, hand-rubbed oil finish and cut checkering at 26 lpi.

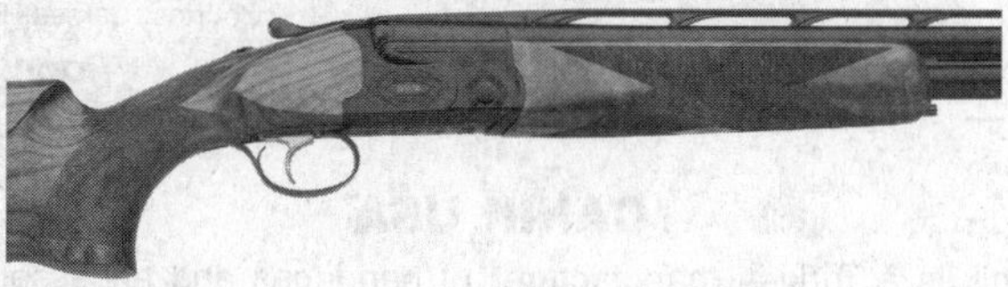

NIB	Exc.	V.G.	Good	Fair	Poor
4120	3300	2700	2000	1000	600

Essex

Over/under with oil-finished stock and coin-finished receiver. Scroll engraving. Available in 12-, 20-, 28-gauge and .410 bore all with 3" chambers. New in 2006.

NIB	Exc.	V.G.	Good	Fair	Poor
4250	3500	2300	1650	1000	500

Ellipse Evo

Rounded action in 12-, 20- or 28-gauge, with coin-finished receiver, hand-rubbed oil-finished stock with rounded grip, choke tubes and 28" barrels. Choice of selective or non-selective trigger, manual or automatic safety. Also offered in 12-gauge sporting (Evolution) and Limited versions. Note: Add $1800 for Evolution; deduct $1500 for Limited.

NIB	Exc.	V.G.	Good	Fair	Poor
5500	4200	3400	2700	1500	700

Ellipse Curve Gold

NIB	Exc.	V.G.	Good	Fair	Poor
8650	8590	8400	8170	—	—

Apex

This over/under series is offered in 12-, 20-, 28-gauge and .410 bore, with coin-finished scroll-engraved receiver and hand-rubbed oil-finished walnut stock. Barrels are currently only 28", but early models were made with 26" and 30". Five choke tubes are included. A Sporting Clays model is available, with 32" barrels in 12-gauge only, with high-grade walnut stock. Note: Add $500 for Sporting Clays model if excellent or better condition.

NIB	Exc.	V.G.	Good	Fair	Poor
6900	5800	4900	3500	2250	900

Invictus I Sporting

12-gauge Sporting Clays model with 30" or 32" barrels. Ventilated rib, hand-rubbed oil-finished walnut stock and forend, coin-finished receiver and some light scroll engraving. Introduced in 2014. Note: Add $1500 for Invictus V Sporting, with high-grade hand engraving.

NIB	Exc.	V.G.	Good	Fair	Poor
6200	4900	3700	—	—	—

Invictus I Trap

In 12-gauge with 32" barrels, 12mm tapered adjustable rib with 25mm height, three Maxis competition choke tubes. 5" long DuoCon forcing cones. Monte Carlo stock, with 4-way adjustable comb, ventilated rubber recoil pad, semi-beavertail forend with finger grooves. Receiver has hand-polished coil finish. Weight 8 lbs. 15 oz. Also offered in Unsingle model with 34" barrel or in combo configuration.

NIB	Exc.	V.G.	Good	Fair	Poor
7800	6300	5000	4000	2000	800

Revenant

Addition of a new combo set to the high-grade 2019 Revenant O/U with a tapered, solid rib and highly engraved maple leaf and branch design receiver. Now with a 20/28-gauge combo barrel set.

NIB	Exc.	V.G.	Good	Fair	Poor
13000	10000	7500	—	—	—

Revenent Sporting

Gauge: 20 ga. 3 in., 28 ga. 2.75 in. Barrels: 28 or 30 in. with non-ventilated center rib, tapered from 8–6mm. Weight: 6 lbs. 6 oz.–6 lbs. 11 oz. Stock: Extra-deluxe wood grade with hand-rubbed oil finish. Left-hand stock option available by special order. Features: Fine-grade over-under Sporting version of the Revenant. Hand-polished coin finish with Invisalloy protective finish. Long-tang triggerguard. Anson rod forend escutcheon. Intricate engraving and gold inlay that takes over 40-hours to produce each Revenant action. Wood butt plate. Silver front bead. Checkered at 26 LPI. Premium Revenant gun case included. Ships with five nickel-plated flush-fitting chokes.

NIB	Exc.	V.G.	Good	Fair	Poor
13000	10000	7500	—	—	—

Syren Julia Sporting

Gauge: 12 ga. 2.75 in. Barrels: 30 in. ventilated rib tapered from 10–8mm. Weight: 7 lbs. 15 oz. Stock: Deluxe Turkish Walnut with hand-rubbed, semi-gloss oil finish. Left-hand stock option and adjustable comb (RH) available by special order Features: Named after Julia, daughter of Julius Caesar, as a top-tier, competition-grade target gun in the Syren line of shotguns for women. Fantasy-style receiver engraving depicting a woman's face evolving from floral scrollwork. Rich case color hardened finish. Checking cut at 26 LPI. Black rubber recoil pad. DuoCon forcing cones. White Bradley style front sight and silver center bead. DTS trigger system with take-up, over-travel, and LOP adjustments. Manual safety. Includes six MAXIS competition chokes as well as plastic hard case, combination locks, and velvet sleeves.

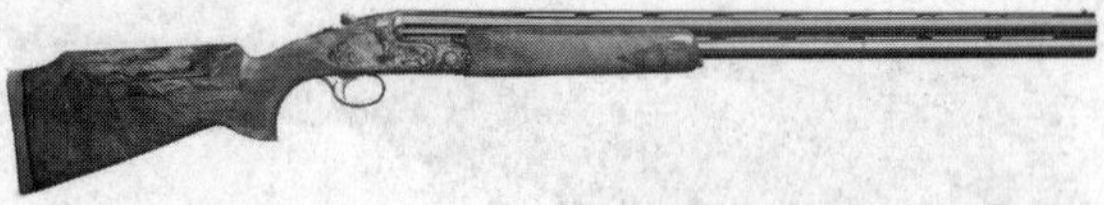

NIB	Exc.	V.G.	Good	Fair	Poor
6000	5100	4350	—	—	—

CALICO

Cleveland, Ohio

See—AMERICAN INDUSTRIES, INC.

CAMEX-BLASER USA, INC.

Ft. Worth, Texas

See—BLASER JAGDWAFFEN

CAMPO GIRO

Eibar, Spain

Esperanza y Unceta Model 1904

Designed by Lt. Col. Venancio Aguirre. Produced in limited numbers.

NIB	Exc.	V.G.	Good	Fair	Poor
—	3000	2000	1500	1000	800

Model 1910

Similar to above in 9mm Largo. Tested, but not adopted by Spanish army.

NIB	Exc.	V.G.	Good	Fair	Poor
—	2000	1500	1000	800	600

Model 1913

An improved version of above. About 1,300 made.

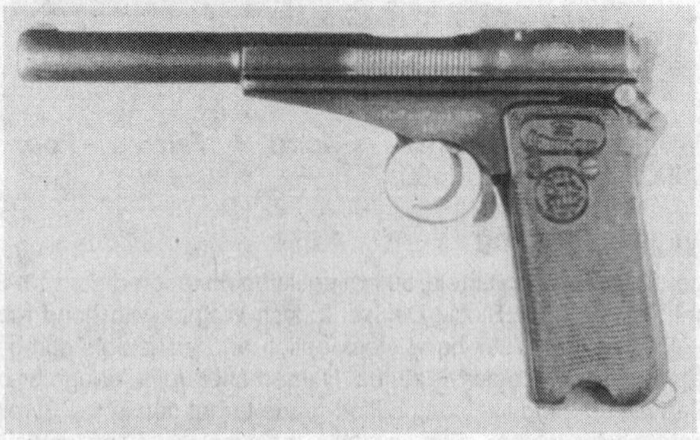

Courtesy James Rankin

NIB	Exc.	V.G.	Good	Fair	Poor
—	1500	1250	850	600	500

Model 1913/16

An improved version of above. About 13,000 built.

Courtesy James Rankin

NIB	Exc.	V.G.	Good	Fair	Poor
—	2000	1550	1000	600	350

CANIK USA

Canik is a Turkish manufacturer of handguns and accessories used around the world and imported to the U.S. exclusively by Century Arms.

CANIK TP9 SERIES

Caliber: 9mm. Capacity: 18-round magazine. Barrel: 4.07-in. Grip: Textured polymer, modular backstraps. Sights: White dot front, u-notch rear. Length: 7.1 in. overall. Weight: 27.8 oz. unloaded. Finish: Matte black, FDE. Features: DA/SA trigger with decocker.

NIB	Exc.	V.G.	Good	Fair	Poor
380	330	300	200	140	—

CANIK TP9 SERIES

TP9SA Mod.2

NIB	Exc.	V.G.	Good	Fair	Poor
350	300	280	250	200	—

TP9SF

NIB	Exc.	V.G.	Good	Fair	Poor
380	370	350	330	230	—

TP9SF Elite

NIB	Exc.	V.G.	Good	Fair	Poor
420	390	360	340	250	—

TP9SFx

NIB	Exc.	V.G.	Good	Fair	Poor
500	420	410	360	310	—

TP9 Elite Combat

NIB	Exc.	V.G.	Good	Fair	Poor
720	600	530	480	370	—

CANIK METE SERIES

Caliber: 9mm. Capacity: 18- and 20-round magazine. Barrel: 4.46-in. Grip: Textured polymer, modular backstraps. Sights: White dot 3-dot, optics-ready. Length: 7.56 in. overall. Weight: 27.8 oz. unloaded. Finish: Matte black, FDE. Features: Striker fire.

NIB	Exc.	V.G.	Good	Fair	Poor
480	430	400	350	260	—

Mete SFX

NIB	Exc.	V.G.	Good	Fair	Poor
560	520	500	430	380	—

CANIK RIVAL SERIES

Caliber: 9mm. Capacity: 18-round magazine. Barrel: 5-in. Grip: Textured polymer, modular backstraps. Sights: Fiber-optic front, adj. rear, optics-ready. Length: 8.1 in. overall. Weight: 29.5 oz. unloaded. Finish: Matte black, black with gold accents. Features: Striker fire.

NIB	Exc.	V.G.	Good	Fair	Poor
1000	990	950	900	880	—

Mete SFX Rival

NIB	Exc.	V.G.	Good	Fair	Poor
630	610	550	450	420	—

CARACAL

Caracal-F

Chambered for 9mm Parabellum. Caracal has a DAO trigger and is striker-fired. Features include a polymer frame, steel slide, ambidextrous magazine release and 18-round magazine. Weight 26.5 oz. Barrel length 4.1". Finish matte blue. Caracal-C is compact variation, with 3.5" barrel. Weight 24.7 oz. Made in United Arab Emirates. Introduced in 2011.

NIB	Exc.	V.G.	Good	Fair	Poor
540	460	400	300	200	100

CARD, S. W.

Underhammer Pistol (Antique)

A .34-caliber single-shot percussion pocket pistol, with 7.75" half octagonal barrel marked "S.W. Card" and "Cast Steel". Blued, with walnut grips.

Exc.	Fine	V.G.	Good	Fair	Poor
1500	450	300	150	100	50

CARLTON, M.
Haverhill, New Hampshire

Underhammer Pistol (Antique)

A .34-caliber percussion under hammer single-shot pistol, with 3.5" to 7.75" half-octagonal barrel marked "M. Carleton & Co.". Browned, with walnut grips. Active 1830s and 1840s.

Exc.	Fine	V.G.	Good	Fair	Poor
1800	600	400	200	150	100

CASARTELLI, CARLO
Brescia, Italy

Sidelock Shotgun

Custom order sidelock shotgun. Available in any gauge, barrel length, choke, automatic ejectors, single-selective trigger and choice of engraving style.

NIB	Exc.	V.G.	Good	Fair	Poor
16000	14500	10500	8250	6000	4000

Kenya Double Rifle

Custom order full sidelock rifle that is available in all standard and Magnum calibers.

NIB	Exc.	V.G.	Good	Fair	Poor
33000	29000	24000	18900	13000	9000

Africa Model

Bolt-action rifle built on a square-bridge Magnum Mauser action. Chambered for heavy Magnum calibers and can be taken down for transport. Other features on a custom order basis.

NIB	Exc.	V.G.	Good	Fair	Poor
9750	8800	7500	5750	4750	3750

Safari Model

Built on a standard Mauser bolt-action. Chambered for non-Magnum calibers.

NIB	Exc.	V.G.	Good	Fair	Poor
8000	7200	5800	4500	3250	2500

CASE WILLARD & CO.
New Hartford, Connecticut

Underhammer Pistol (Antique)

A .31-caliber single-shot percussion pistol, with 3" half-octagonal barrel marked "Case Willard & Co./New Hartford Conn.". Blued brass frame, with walnut grips.

Exc.	Fine	V.G.	Good	Fair	Poor
1400	550	370	200	150	100

CASPIAN ARMS, LTD.
Hardwick, Vermont

This company is primarily a 1911 component manufacturer.

Vietnam Commemorative

Government Model engraved by J.J. Adams and nickel-plated. Walnut grips have a branch service medallion inlaid. Gold plating was available for an additional $350. There were 1,000 manufactured in 1986.

Courtesy James Rankin

NIB	Exc.	V.G.	Good	Fair	Poor
1800	1350	950	650	480	300

CASULL ARMS, INC.

Afton, Wyoming

CA 2000

Chambered for .22 LR cartridge. This stainless steel palm sized revolver has a 5-round cylinder, with fold-up trigger. Double-action-only. Most recently produced "Velo-Dog". Discontinued.

NIB	Exc.	V.G.	Good	Fair	Poor
550	420	350	250	200	180

CA 3800

Chambered for .38 Casull cartridge (124 gr. 1800+fps). Fitted with 6" match barrel, magazine capacity of 8 rounds and full-length two-piece guide rod. Checkering on front strap and mainspring housing is 20 lpi. Match trigger and numerous other special features. Weight about 40 oz. Introduced in 2000. Discontinued. Note: Add $300 for extra .45 ACP barrel.

NIB	Exc.	V.G.	Good	Fair	Poor
2600	2050	1700	1200	650	300

CENTURY GUN COMPANY

Evansville, Knightstown & Greenfield, Indiana

Former manufacturer of large-caliber revolvers made in Evansville or Knightstown, Indiana between 1973 and 2001 or Greenfield, Indiana between 2002 and 2004.

Model 100

Single-action revolver, with 6-round capacity. Chambered originally for .45-70 Government, later for .30-30 Win., .375 Win., .444 Marlin, .50-70 and .50-110. Barrel lengths from 6.5" to 12", weight from 5.5- to 6 lbs. Adjustable sights, crossbolt safety. Prices shown are for .45-70 caliber. Note: Add 100 percent for .50-110 caliber; 20 percent for other calibers; 100 to 200 percent if in excellent condition for early production .45-70 guns marked Evansville, Indiana.

NIB	Exc.	V.G.	Good	Fair	Poor
1200	1100	900	750	400	200

CENTURY INTERNATIONAL ARMS CO.

Delray Beach, Florida

Century International Arms is a leading importer of military firearms. It was founded in 1961 in Albans, Vermont, moved to Boca Raton, Century's focus is on self-loading rifles currently, since the surplus supply of bolt-actions for sporterizing has dried up. There are no appreciable increases in used values.

Centurion 39 AK Pistol

This current production AK-47 style pistol has a 11.4" barrel, black polymer stock and pistol grip. Other features include four Picatinny rails and M-16 type birdcage muzzle brake.

NIB	Exc.	V.G.	Good	Fair	Poor
820	700	550	400	300	200

Centurion UC-9 Carbine

Based on UZI submachine gun in semi-automatic. Chambered in 9mm, with folding stock, 16" barrel and two 32-round magazines.

NIB	Exc.	V.G.	Good	Fair	Poor
900	750	600	500	400	250

Centurion Over/Under Shotgun

New shotgun in 12-, 20-, 28-gauge and.410 bore, with 2.75" chambers. Checkered walnut stock. Receiver is blue. Offered in 28" ventilated rib barrels in Full and Modified chokes. Weight about 7.35 lbs. for 12-gauge; 5.3 lbs. for .410 bore.

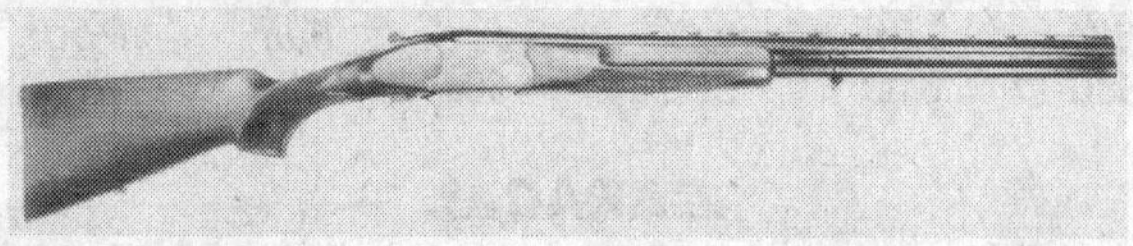

NIB	Exc.	V.G.	Good	Fair	Poor
—	380	320	220	180	120

Centurion 98 Sporter

Refinished and rebuilt on a surplus German Mauser 98 action, with new commercial 22" barrel. No sights. Synthetic stock, with recoil pad is standard. Chambered for .270 or .30-06. Weight about 7 lbs. 13 oz.

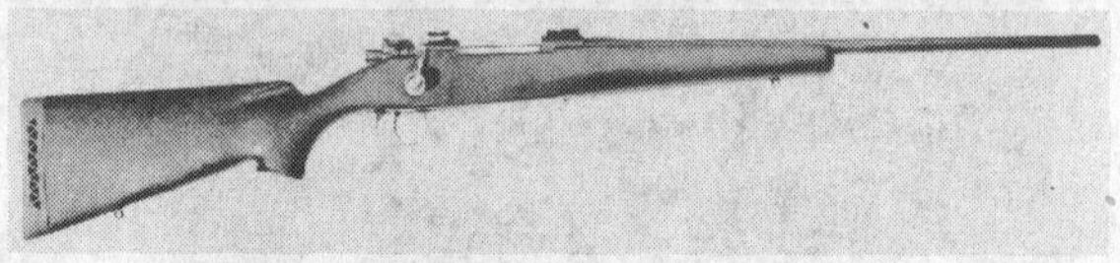

NIB	Exc.	V.G.	Good	Fair	Poor
—	300	250	180	150	100

Century Centurion 14

Bolt-action rifle uses an Enfield Pattern 14 action. Drilled and tapped for scope mount. Barrel is 24". Chambered for 7mm Rem. Magnum. Walnut stock checkered, with pistol grip and Monte Carlo comb. No sights.

NIB	Exc.	V.G.	Good	Fair	Poor
350	300	250	180	150	100

C93 Pistol

Based on Hecker & Koch MP-5 in semi-automatic. Chambered in 5.56 NATO or 7.63x39mm. Barrel 8.5", with flash suppressor and two 40-round magazines.

NIB	Exc.	V.G.	Good	Fair	Poor
900	750	600	500	400	250

CZ 999 / CZ 40

Based on CZ 9 and CZ 40 pistols in 9mm or .40 S&W. Barrels 3.5" or 4.24", with 15-round double-stack magazines. Current model made by Zastava in Serbia.

NIB	Exc.	V.G.	Good	Fair	Poor
450	400	350	300	200	150

Enfield Sporter No. I Mark III

Refinished rifle has a cut down Sporter-style stock. Action and sights are original. Caliber is .303.

NIB	Exc.	V.G.	Good	Fair	Poor
—	250	200	150	100	50

Enfield Sporter No. 4 Mark I

With new walnut stock.

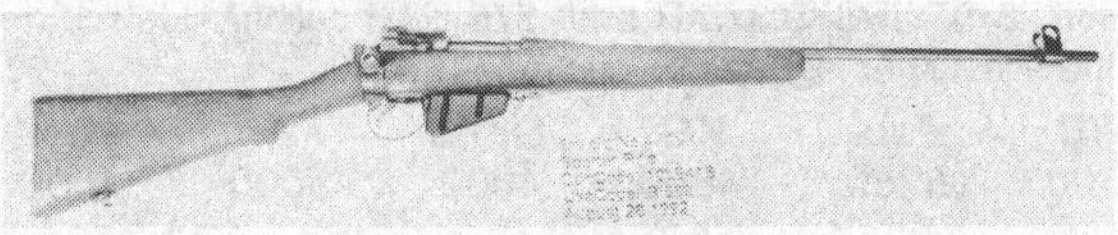

NIB	Exc.	V.G.	Good	Fair	Poor
—	260	210	150	100	50

TOZ-17

An original Russian rifle chambered for .22 LR. Has 21" barrel, 5-round magazine, checkered stock and iron sights. Weight about 5.4 lbs.

NIB	Exc.	V.G.	Good	Fair	Poor
—	180	140	110	50	40

TOZ-17-1

Same as above, with hooded front sight and tangent rear sight. Receiver grooved for scope mount.

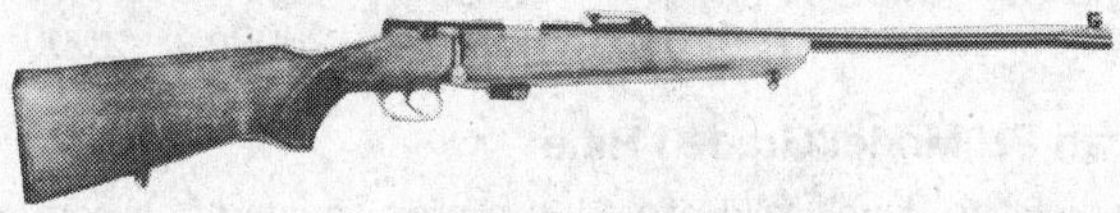

NIB	Exc.	V.G.	Good	Fair	Poor
—	180	140	120	60	50

Mexican Mauser Model 1910 Sporter

Converted from military rifle to sporter by cutting down the stock. Metal refinished, barrel re-bored and re-chambered for .30-06 cartridge. Box magazine holds 5 rounds. Barrel 23"; weight about 8 lbs.

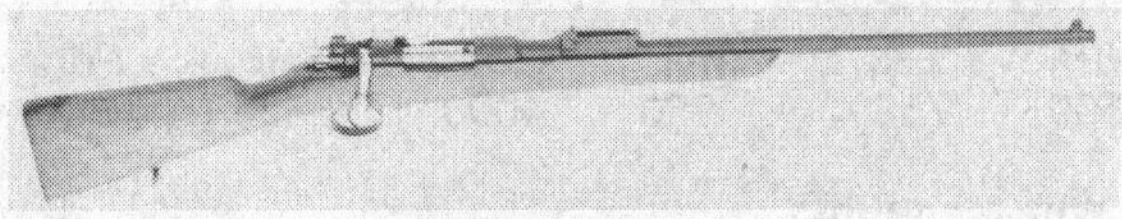

NIB	Exc.	V.G.	Good	Fair	Poor
—	180	140	120	60	50

FAL Sporter

Refinished FAL receiver and barrel installed on a synthetic thumbhole stock. Flash suppressor and bayonet lug have been removed. Barrel 20.75"; weight about 10 lbs.

NIB	Exc.	V.G.	Good	Fair	Poor
1250	1000	800	550	400	250

M-14 Rifle

Imported from China by Century International. Features 22" barrel chambered for .308 Win. cartridge. Stock walnut, with rubber pad. Parkerized finish. Weight about 8.25 lbs.

NIB	Exc.	V.G.	Good	Fair	Poor
750	650	550	300	150	100

M85 Mini Mauser

Bolt action rifle in .22 Hornet, .223 Rem., or 7.62x39mm. Offered with standard Monte Carlo or full-length Mannlicher-style stock. Barrel lengths 18", 20" or 22". Current production model made in Serbia by Zastava.

NIB	Exc.	V.G.	Good	Fair	Poor
500	400	320	250	200	150

Tiger Dragunov Rifle

Shortened version of Russian SVD sniper rifle. Fitted with 20.8" barrel. Chambered for 7.62x54R cartridge. Sells with 5-round magazine and 4x range finding scope. Imported from Russia. Weight about 8.5 lbs.

NIB	Exc.	V.G.	Good	Fair	Poor
2500	1750	1200	700	—	—

GP WASR 10 Rifle

AK-47 design in 7.62x39mm caliber. Comes with two double-stack 30-round magazines. Available with 5- or 10-round fixed magazine. New, made by Romarm in Romania.

NIB	Exc.	V.G.	Good	Fair	Poor
500	400	320	280	200	100

Pietta SAA Millenium

Patterned after Colt Single Action Army Model of 1873. Chambered in .22 LR, .357 Magnum, .44-40 Win. or .45 Colt, with 4.75", 5.5" or 7.5" barrel, hardwood walnut-stained grips and case colored frame. Made in Italy by Pietta

NIB	Exc.	V.G.	Good	Fair	Poor
400	350	300	250	200	150

Pietta Semi-Auto Shotgun

Made in 20-gauge only, with 28" ventilated rib barrel and four choke tubes. Stock is black polymer. Metal finish is matte black, dark nickel or bright nickel. Inertia operating system is similar to that of Benelli line.

NIB	Exc.	V.G.	Good	Fair	Poor
750	680	600	500	350	200

PW 87

Lever-action shotgun patterned after Winchester Model 1887. Made in 12-gauge only, with 19" barrel, Modified choke and hardwood stock. New production model imported from China.

NIB	Exc.	V.G.	Good	Fair	Poor
350	300	250	200	150	100

Shooter's Arms 1911 Pistol

Standard 1911-A .45 ACP design in full-size version with 5" barrel or

Commodore model with 4.25" barrel. Magazine capacity 8 shots. New, manufactured in Philippines.

NIB	Exc.	V.G.	Good	Fair	Poor
450	380	320	280	200	100

Saiga Semi-auto Shotgun

A 12-gauge shotgun based on AK-47 design. Five-round capacity. Weight 7.9 lbs. Has a 19" barrel, black synthetic stock, sight rail. Made in Russia.

NIB	Exc.	V.G.	Good	Fair	Poor
600	500	420	380	200	100

S.A.R. Series

AK-47 style semi-automatic rifle, with wood stock and forearm. Capacity 10 or 30 rounds. Chambered for 7.62x39mm, 5.45x39mm or .223. Made in Romania by Romarm.

NIB	Exc.	V.G.	Good	Fair	Poor
800	650	500	350	200	100

CETME
Madrid, Spain

Cetme Autoloading Rifle

A .308-caliber semi-automatic rifle, with fluted chamber, 17.74" barrel, aperture rear sight and 20-round detachable magazine. Black with military-style wood stock. Identical in appearance to H&K 91 assault rifle.

NIB	Exc.	V.G.	Good	Fair	Poor
1500	1100	800	600	350	200

CHAMPLIN FIREARMS
Enid, Oklahoma

Champlin Firearms Company manufactures custom order rifles built to customer's specifications. Prospective purchasers are advised to secure a qualified appraisal prior to purchase.

Bolt-Action Rifle

These arms featured round or octagonal barrels, set triggers, a variety of sights and well figured walnut stocks.

NIB	Exc.	V.G.	Good	Fair	Poor
5500	4500	3500	2900	2200	1500

CHAPMAN, CHARLES
Chattanooga, Tennessee

Chapman produced a limited number of percussion carbines and rifles during the Civil War. Carbines had an overall length of 39.5" and .54-caliber barrels 24" in length. Their furniture was of brass. Chapman rifles resembled the U.S. Model 1841 rifle, but did not have patch boxes. Overall length 48.5", barrel length 33", caliber .58. Chapman rifles and carbines are marked "C. CHAPMAN" on the lockplates. Prospective purchasers are strongly advised to secure an expert appraisal prior to acquisition.

Confederate Percussion Long Guns (Antique)

Very rare; values are speculative.

Courtesy Milwaukee Public Museum, Milwaukee, Wisconsin

Exc.	Fine	V.G.	Good	Fair	Poor
—	35000	17500	9000	6000	2000

CHAPMAN, G. & J.
Philadelphia, Pennsylvania

Chapman Pocket Revolver (Antique)

A .32-caliber revolver, with 4" round barrel and 7-shot cylinder. Frame made of brass, while barrel and cylinder are steel. Barrel marked "G. &J. Chapman/Philada/Patent Applied For/1861". Manufactured during 1860s.

Exc.	Fine	V.G.	Good	Fair	Poor
2550	1050	800	550	280	190

CHAPUIS ARMES
St. Bonnet Le Chateau, France

Manufacturer of double rifles and shotguns imported by William Larkin Moore of Scottsdale, Arizona.

RG Express Model 89 Rifle

A 7x65R, 8x57 JRS, 9.3x74R and .375 H&H caliber sidelock double-barreled rifle. Other features on customer's order.

NIB	Exc.	V.G.	Good	Fair	Poor
6500	5750	4800	4000	3000	1500

Utility Grade Express Model Rifle

Side-by-side boxlock-action double rifle, with case colored or coin finish receiver. Offered in a variety of calibers: 9.3x74R, 8x57JRS, 7x65R, 8x75RS and .30-06. Checkered walnut stock with pistol grip.

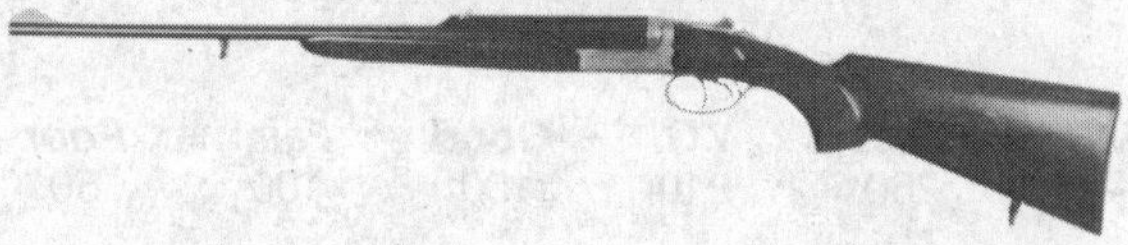

NIB	Exc.	V.G.	Good	Fair	Poor
6000	4800	4000	3000	1500	750

Super Orion Rifle Series

This series of over/under rifles was offered in a wide range of European calibers plus, .30-06 and .300 Win. Magnum. Several grades were available. Prices shown are for C-15 model, which was imported in the 1990s. These rifles also were offered with a set of shotgun barrels. Currently imported by William Larkin Moore in Scottsdale, Arizona.

NIB	Exc.	V.G.	Good	Fair	Poor
8000	7000	5200	4000	2000	1000

African PH Model Grade I Rifle

Boxlock-action double rifle offered in a wide variety of calibers which determines retail price. Hand engraved case colored receiver. Pistol grip stock, with European-style cheekpiece.

.470 Nitro & .416 Rigby

NIB	Exc.	V.G.	Good	Fair	Poor
12500	9500	8500	6000	3750	700

.375 H&H

NIB	Exc.	V.G.	Good	Fair	Poor
9500	7500	6250	4000	2500	600

.300 Win. Magnum

NIB	Exc.	V.G.	Good	Fair	Poor
8500	6500	5250	3000	1750	500

.30-06, 9.3x74R

NIB	Exc.	V.G.	Good	Fair	Poor
8000	6000	5000	3000	1750	500

African PH Model Grade II

Same as above, with master engraving and game scenes. Note: Add 20 to 25 percent to above NIB prices.

Rols

Calibers: .30-06 Spfld., .300 Win. Mag., .375 H&H (6.5 Creed & .308 Win. available on Carbon only). Barrel: 24," 25.5" Weights: 5.3-5.5 lbs.

(Carbon); 6.6-7.2 lbs. (Classic & Deluxe) Stock: High-grade Circassian Walnut, pistol grip-style with Schnabel forend on Classic and Deluxe. Carbon-fiber black on Carbon model. Features: Straight-pull bolt action rifle. Sub-MOA accuracy guarantee. Action and locking system tested for up to 123,000 PSI. Manual decocker. Single trigger. Manual safety. Open rifle sights with slots for Recknagel scope mounts. Quick detach rotary magazine. Ready to accept barrels in different calibers. Ships with prestige-grade custom hard case.

NIB	Exc.	V.G.	Good	Fair	Poor
5600	—	—	—	—	—

X4 Double Rifle

Caliber: 9.3x74R, .30-06 Spfld. Barrel: 22". Weight: 6 lbs. Stock: AAA-grade Circassian Walnut with English-style cheekpiece. Features: The double can be re-regulated for new loads. Built on a Progress 28-gauge scalloped receiver. Intricate engraving. Double triggers and ejectors. Adjustable rear and ramp front sights. Machined for Recknagel scope mounts.

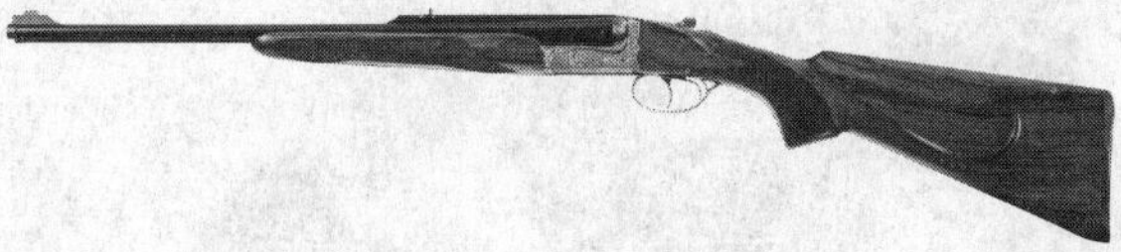

NIB	Exc.	V.G.	Good	Fair	Poor
7080	—	—	—	—	—

RGP Shotgun

A 16- or 20-gauge boxlock shotgun. Most options available on order.

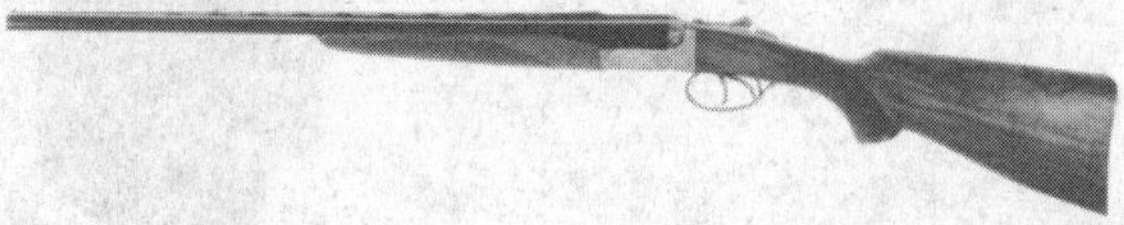

NIB	Exc.	V.G.	Good	Fair	Poor
3000	2500	2000	1800	1250	900

St. Bonnet Model Shotgun

Side-by-side shotgun, with sideplates on a boxlock action. Scroll-engraved case-colored receiver. Straight-grip stock and double triggers. Offered in 12, 16, or 20 gauge.

NIB	Exc.	V.G.	Good	Fair	Poor
4000	3250	2000	1250	800	500

Faisan Classic

Gauges: 12 ga., 20 ga., 28 ga., (.410 bore on Classic only). Barrels: 28" with ventilated rib. Weight: 5.5 to 6.2 pounds. Stock: Grade-3 Walnut (Classic), Grade-5 Circassian Walnut (Artisan). Features: Fine over-under line built on an all-steel action. "Faisan" is French for "pheasant." Receivers scaled to gauges. The low profile keeps barrels closer to the supporting hand to make pointing intuitive. Round action. Single trigger. Automatic safety and auto ejectors. Brass front bead. Pistol grip-style buttstock. The Classic receiver is laser engraved with a coin finish and game scenes. Ships with five choke tubes and a custom hard case. Add 5% for 20 ga., 21% for 28 ga., and 15% for .410 bore.

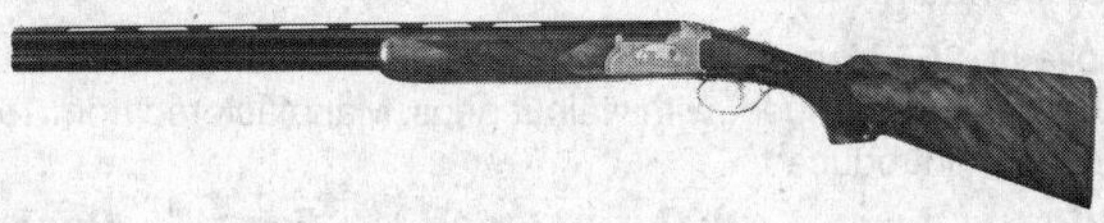

NIB	Exc.	V.G.	Good	Fair	Poor
5100	4500	—	—	—	—

Faisan Artisan

Gauges: 12 ga., 20 ga., 28 ga., (.410 bore on Classic only). Barrels: 28" with ventilated rib. Weight: 5.5 to 6.2 pounds. Stock: Grade-3 Walnut (Classic), Grade-5 Circassian Walnut (Artisan). Features: Fine over-under line built on an all-steel action. "Faisan" is French for "pheasant." Receivers scaled to gauges. The low profile keeps barrels closer to the supporting hand to make pointing intuitive. Round action. Single trigger. Automatic safety and auto ejectors. Brass front bead. Pistol grip-style buttstock. The Artisan is hand-engraved with coin finish and game scenes. Ships with five choke tubes and a custom hard case. Add 2% for 20 ga., 11% for 28 ga.

NIB	Exc.	V.G.	Good	Fair	Poor
10550	10000	9750	—	—	—

Chasseur Classic

Gauges: 12 ga., 20 ga., 28 ga. Barrels: 28" with wide solid rib. Weight: 5.5 to 6.2 pounds. Stock: AAA-Grade Walnut (Classic), Grade-5 Circassian Walnut (Artisan). Features: Fine side-by-side built on a scalloped boxlock action. Extensive receiver engraving of game scenes and acanthus scrolls. Laser engraving on the Classic with straight grip stock style. Automatic safety. Double triggers. Auto ejectors. Brass front bead. Snag-free checkered wood buttplate. Ships with five choke tubes and a custom hard case. Add 4% for 20 gauge; 11% for 28 gauge.

NIB	Exc.	V.G.	Good	Fair	Poor
5230	5000	4760	—	—	—

Chasseur Artisan

Gauges: 12 ga., 20 ga., 28 ga. Barrels: 28" with wide solid rib. Weight: 5.5 to 6.2 pounds. Stock: AAA-Grade Walnut (Classic), Grade-5 Circassian Walnut (Artisan). Features: Fine side-by-side built on a scalloped boxlock action. Extensive receiver engraving of game scenes and acanthus scrolls. Hand engraving on Artisan. Classic straight grip stock style. Automatic safety. Double triggers. Auto ejectors. Brass front bead. Snag-free checkered wood buttplate. Ships with five choke tubes and a custom hard case. Add 4% for 20 gauge; 11% for 28 gauge.

NIB	Exc.	V.G.	Good	Fair	Poor
10550	10000	9670	—	—	—

CHARTER ARMS CORP.

Ansonia, Connecticut/Shelton, Connecticut

Founded in 1962, Charter Arms has had several name and location changes. Original production was in Stratford, Connecticut until 1991 and in Ansonia, Connecticut from 1992 to 1996. From 1998 to 2005 the company name was Charter 2000. It was located in Shelton, Connecticut, where the current company, again known as Charter Arms is headquartered. Note: Several current production models are available with scratch-resistant hardened Blacknitride finish for approximately $100 more.

Undercover

Chambered for .38 Special cartridge. Fitted with 2" barrel. Stainless steel or blued frame, with 5-round cylinder. Round butt. Weight about 20 oz. Note: Add $20 for stainless steel.

NIB	Exc.	V.G.	Good	Fair	Poor
280	230	180	150	100	80

Undercover Stainless Steel

As above in stainless steel.

NIB	Exc.	V.G.	Good	Fair	Poor
390	330	230	180	130	100

Police Undercover

Chambered for .38 Special or .32 Magnum. Fitted with 2" barrel in blue or stainless steel finish. Offered with walnut or rubber grips. Overall length 6.25". Weight between 16- and 19 oz., depending on grips and finish.

NIB	Exc.	V.G.	Good	Fair	Poor
350	300	180	150	100	80

Undercover Lite

Similar to Undercover, with lightweight aluminum alloy frame. Frame finishes: black/stainless, red/stainless and red/black.

NIB	Exc.	V.G.	Good	Fair	Poor
390	330	230	180	130	100

Off Duty

Chambered for .38 Special or .22 LR and fitted with 2" barrel. Offered with walnut or rubber grips, blue or stainless steel finish and choice of spur or pocket hammer. Weight: .38 Special between 17- and 23 oz. depending on grip and finish; .22 LR between 19- and 22 oz. Overall length 4.75". Nickel finish with rubber grips also offered.

NIB	Exc.	V.G.	Good	Fair	Poor
330	280	230	180	130	100

Off Duty (Hammerless)

New Off Duty model. Double-action-only with hammer enclosed in frame. Aluminum frame, stainless barrel and cylinder. 12 oz., .38 Special 5 shot, 2" barrel. Finish variation available.

NIB	Exc.	V.G.	Good	Fair	Poor
390	300	250	—	—	—

On Duty

Similar to above, except with semi-concealed hammer. Hammer spur is partially exposed to allow cocking for single-action fire.

NIB	Exc.	V.G.	Good	Fair	Poor
390	300	250	—	—	—

Undercoverette

As above, with a thinner grip in .32 S&W.

NIB	Exc.	V.G.	Good	Fair	Poor
350	300	250	130	100	80

Bulldog

Similar to Undercover model in .44 Special caliber, with 2.5" or 3" barrel and 5-shot cylinder. Discontinued; replaced by Target and Pug models.

NIB	Exc.	V.G.	Good	Fair	Poor
330	280	230	180	130	100

Stainless Steel Bulldog

As above in stainless steel.

NIB	Exc.	V.G.	Good	Fair	Poor
350	300	250	200	150	130

Target Bulldog

As above in .357 Magnum or .44 Special, with 4" barrel. Fitted with adjustable rear sights. Blued, with walnut grips. Manufactured from 1986 to 1988. Later reintroduced.

NIB	Exc.	V.G.	Good	Fair	Poor
350	300	250	200	150	130

Heller Commemorative Bulldog

Fully engraved model in .44 Special, with wood presentation case and engraved knife. Commemorating U.S. Supreme Court Heller case of

2011, affirming Second Amendment rights. Only 250 made.

NIB	Exc.	V.G.	Good	Fair	Poor
1400	1200	1000	—	—	—

Bulldog Pug

Chambered for .44 Special cartridge. Fitted with 2.5" barrel. Available with walnut or neoprene grips in blue or stainless steel finish. Choice of spur or pocket hammer. Cylinder holds 5 rounds. Overall length 7"; weight between 20- and 25 oz., depending on grip and finish.

NIB	Exc.	V.G.	Good	Fair	Poor
350	300	250	200	150	130

Stainless Steel Bulldog Pug

As above in stainless steel.

NIB	Exc.	V.G.	Good	Fair	Poor
380	330	280	230	180	130

Bulldog Tracker

As above, with 2.5", 4" or 6" barrel. In .357 Magnum only.

NIB	Exc.	V.G.	Good	Fair	Poor
380	330	280	230	180	130

Police Bulldog

As above, with 3.5" or 4" barrel. In .32 H&R Magnum, .38 Special or .44 Special.

NIB	Exc.	V.G.	Good	Fair	Poor
350	300	250	200	150	130

Stainless Steel Police Bulldog

As above in stainless steel. Available in .357 Magnum.

NIB	Exc.	V.G.	Good	Fair	Poor
350	300	250	200	150	130

Pit Bull

9mm Federal, .38 Special or .357 Magnum caliber double-action revolver, with 2.5", 3.5" or 4" barrel. Blued, with rubber grips.

NIB	Exc.	V.G.	Good	Fair	Poor
400	350	250	180	130	90

Pitbull Rimless

Improved version of above, with dual coil-spring extractor system. Design does not require use of moon clips. Chambered in 9mm (6-round capacity) or .40 S&W (5 rounds). Barrel is 2.2", stainless glass beaded finish. Black rubber grips and fixed sights.

NIB	Exc.	V.G.	Good	Fair	Poor
400	350	300	280	230	180

Pitbull .45

Similar to 9mm Pitbull Rimless, except chambered for .45 ACP. Barrel length 2.5"; weight 22 oz. Introduced in 2016.

NIB	Exc.	V.G.	Good	Fair	Poor
430	350	300	250	230	200

The Mag Pug

A 5-shot revolver chambered for .357 Magnum. Stainless or blue. Ported 2.2" barrel. Weight 23 oz. Fixed sights, rubber grips.

NIB	Exc.	V.G.	Good	Fair	Poor
350	300	250	200	150	130

Patriot

Built on Bulldog frame. Chambered in .327 Federal Magnum (six-shot). Rubber grips, 2.2" or 4" barrel. Comes with Kershaw "327" knife.

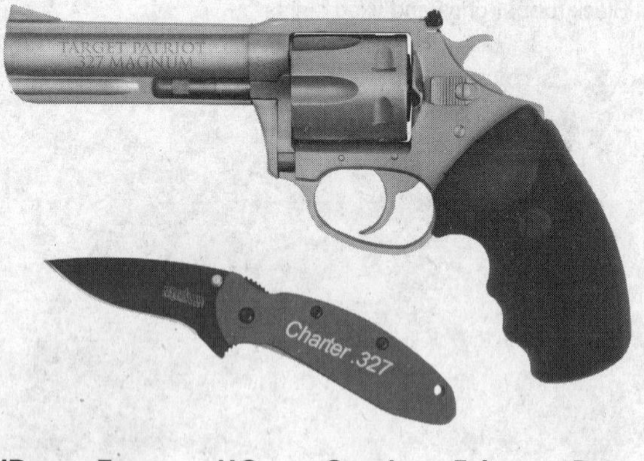

NIB	Exc.	V.G.	Good	Fair	Poor
430	300	230	180	150	100

Boomer

A five-shot .44 Special, with 2" ported barrel, rubber grips, stainless or Nitride finish. Introduced in 2016.

NIB	Exc.	V.G.	Good	Fair	Poor
390	300	250	230	200	100

Southpaw

Snubnose revolver chambered in .38 Special or +P. Five-shot cylinder, 2" barrel, matte black aluminum alloy frame, with stainless steel cylinder. Cylinder latch and crane assembly are on right side of frame for convenience of left-hand shooters. Rubber Pachmayr-style grips. Weight 12 oz.

NIB	Exc.	V.G.	Good	Fair	Poor
400	350	250	180	130	90

Pink Lady

Similar to Undercover Lite, with pink anodized frame. .38 Special only. Available as Chic Lady, with high polish pink finish and pink faux alligator case. DAO version also available. Note: Add $50 for Chic Lady.

NIB	Exc.	V.G.	Good	Fair	Poor
380	330	280	230	180	130

Goldfinger

Similar to Undercover Lite, with gold anodized frame. .38 Special only.

NIB	Exc.	V.G.	Good	Fair	Poor
380	330	280	230	180	130

Pathfinder

Similar to above in .22 LR or .22 Magnum caliber, with 2", 3" or 6" barrel. Adjustable sights.

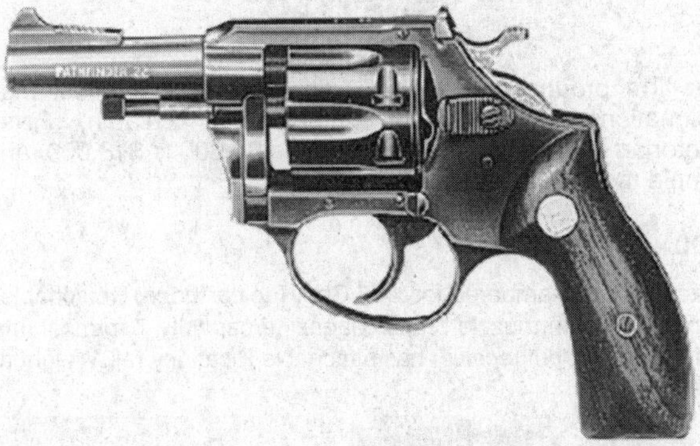

NIB	Exc.	V.G.	Good	Fair	Poor
350	300	250	200	150	130

Pathfinder Stainless Steel

As above in stainless steel.

NIB	Exc.	V.G.	Good	Fair	Poor
360	310	260	210	160	140

Dixie Derringer, Current Production

Stainless mini-revolver chambered for .22 LR (5 oz.) or .22 Magnum (6 oz.). 5-shot, 1.175" barrel.

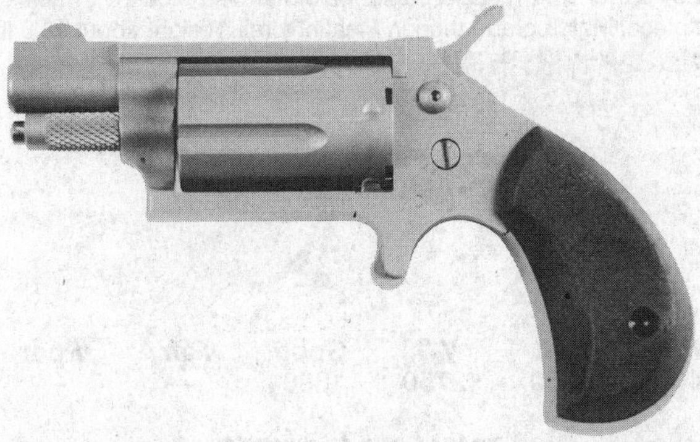

NIB	Exc.	V.G.	Good	Fair	Poor
180	140	100	80	50	30

Model 40

A .22-caliber double-action semi-automatic pistol, with 3.5" barrel and 8-shot magazine. Stainless steel with plastic grips. Manufactured from 1984 to 1986.

NIB	Exc.	V.G.	Good	Fair	Poor
—	280	230	200	150	100

Model 79K

A .32- or .380-caliber double-action semi-automatic pistol, with 3.5" barrel and 7-shot magazine. Stainless steel with plastic grips. Manufactured from 1986 to 1988.

NIB	Exc.	V.G.	Good	Fair	Poor
—	350	300	250	180	130

Model 42T

A .22-caliber semi-automatic pistol, with 6" barrel and adjustable sights. Blued, with walnut grips. Manufactured in 1984 and 1985.

NIB	Exc.	V.G.	Good	Fair	Poor
500	450	400	330	270	200

Explorer II Pistol

A .22-caliber semi-automatic pistol, with 6", 8" or 10" barrels. Available with camo, black, silver or gold finish and plastic grips. Discontinued in 1986. Based on the Explorer AR7 Rifle with detachable barrel.

NIB	Exc.	V.G.	Good	Fair	Poor
230	180	130	70	50	30

AR-7 Explorer Rifle

A .22-caliber semi-automatic rifle, with 16" barrel, 8-shot magazine and hollow plastic stock which can house the barrel when detached.

NIB	Exc.	V.G.	Good	Fair	Poor
180	130	80	60	40	30

Field King Rifle

Available with blue or stainless steel finish. Chambered for .25-06, .270, .30-06 or .308, with 22" barrel. Magazine capacity 4 rounds. Checkered fiberglass stock with cheekpiece. Weight about 8 lbs.

NIB	Exc.	V.G.	Good	Fair	Poor
300	230	180	130	80	50

Field King Carbine

Same as above, with 18" barrel compensator (20" total). Chambered for .308.

NIB	Exc.	V.G.	Good	Fair	Poor
350	250	200	150	80	50

Target Magnum

Caliber: .357 Magnum. Capacity: 6 rounds. Barrel: 6 in. Grip: Full. Sights: Fully adjustable rear, fixed front. Features: This revolver of the Mag Pug series is built on Charter's XL frame. The 6-inch barrel and fully adjustable sights make this a great target piece that can also be used for hunting. Like all Charters, this one is made in the USA.

NIB	Exc.	V.G.	Good	Fair	Poor
400	340	290	250	—	—

Professional II

Caliber: .357 Magnum. Capacity: 6 rounds. Barrel: 3 in. Grip: Wood. Sights: Fixed rear, LitePipe front. Features: Built on Charter's large frame, the PROFESSIONAL II is a member of the PROFESSIONAL series of revolvers that is finished in a tough and attractive Blacknitride finish.

NIB	Exc.	V.G.	Good	Fair	Poor
430	360	—	—	—	—

Professional III

Caliber: .357 Magnum. Capacity: 6 rounds. Barrel: 4.2 in. Grip: Wood. Sights: Fixed rear, LitePipe front. Features: The PROFESSIONAL III is also a member of the PROFESSIONAL series of American-made revolvers from Charter Arms. This one, however, is built on Charter's XL frame, with a wood grip and a Blacknitride finish.

NIB	*Exc.*	*V.G.*	*Good*	*Fair*	*Poor*
450	380	—	—	—	—

Professional IV

Caliber: .32 Magnum. Capacity: 7 rounds. Barrel: 3 in. Grip: Wood. Sights: Fixed rear, LitePipe front. Features: A member of the PROFESSIONAL series, the PROFESSIONAL IV is manufactured on the large frame and features a 7-shot cylinder chambered in .32 Magnum. The finish is stainless steel.

NIB	*Exc.*	*V.G.*	*Good*	*Fair*	*Poor*
450	380	—	—	—	—

Professional V

Caliber: .357 Magnum. Capacity: 6 rounds. Barrel: 3 in. Grip: Wood. Sights: Fixed rear, LitePipe front. Features: A member of the PROFESSIONAL series, the PROFESSIONAL V is manufactured on the large frame and features a 6-shot cylinder chambered in .357 Magnum. The finish is stainless steel.

NIB	*Exc.*	*V.G.*	*Good*	*Fair*	*Poor*
400	360	—	—	—	—

Professional VI

Caliber: .357 Magnum. Capacity: 6 rounds. Barrel: 4.2 in. Grip: Wood. Sights: Fixed rear, LitePipe front. Features: The final model in the PROFESSIONAL series, the PROFESSIONAL VI is manufactured on Charter Arms' XL frame and features a 6-shot cylinder. The finish is stainless steel.

NIB	*Exc.*	*V.G.*	*Good*	*Fair*	*Poor*
450	380	—	—	—	—

CHEYTAC

Arco, Idaho

This firm produces bolt action sniper / tactical rifles. Model designations include M200 Intervention, Paladin, Perses, Praetorian M300 with retail prices in the $4,000 to $13,000 range. Sample models listed below.

M-200

Bolt-action rifle chambered for .408 CheyTac cartridge. Detachable barrel length 30" with muzzle brake. Magazine capacity 7 rounds. Integral bipod. No sights, but receiver has attachable Picatinny rail. Weight about 27 lbs.

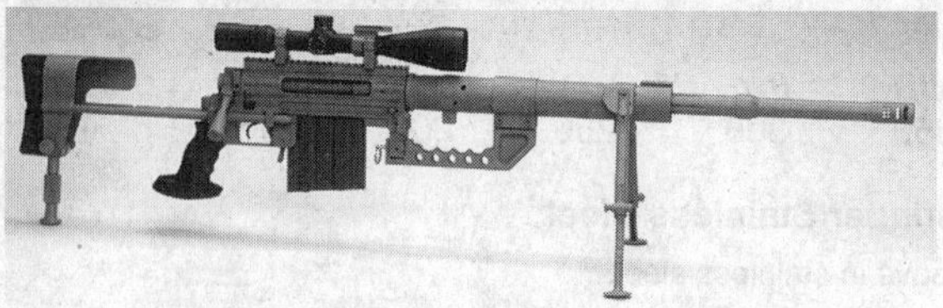

NIB	*Exc.*	*V.G.*	*Good*	*Fair*	*Poor*
11000	8250	6900	5400	—	—

M-310

Single-shot bolt-action rifle chambered for .408 CheyTac cartridge. Fitted with 25" barrel with muzzle brake. McMillian A-5 stock with adjustable cheekpiece. Match grade trigger. Picatinny rail. Weight about 16.5 lbs.

NIB	*Exc.*	*V.G.*	*Good*	*Fair*	*Poor*
4400	3250	2750	1880	—	—

CHIAPPA ARMS

Dayton, Ohio

1911-22

1911-style semi-automatic pistol chambered in .22 LR. Features include: alloy frame; steel barrel; matte blue-black or bright nickel finish; walnut-like grips; two 10-round magazines; fixed sights; straight blowback action. Note: Add $25 for target model with adjustable sights, $25 for OD or tan finish, $100 for Tactical Model, with fiber-optic sight, threaded muzzle.

NIB	*Exc.*	*V.G.*	*Good*	*Fair*	*Poor*
260	220	200	150	100	80

M9

Replica of Beretta M9 pistol in 9mm or .40 S&W. Barrel length 4.9" or 4.3" (Compact model).

NIB	*Exc.*	*V.G.*	*Good*	*Fair*	*Poor*
500	420	380	300	220	180

M9-22

Replica of Beretta M9 9mm military pistol. Chambered for .22 Long Rifle, with checkered black plastic or checkered wooden grips. Operating features are identical to 9mm version. Tactical model has threaded barrel. Note: Add $25 for this variation.

NIB	*Exc.*	*V.G.*	*Good*	*Fair*	*Poor*
320	280	220	200	150	100

MC14

Double/single-action .380, with 13-round magazine. Black finish, 3.8" barrel. Original Chiappa design.

NIB	Exc.	V.G.	Good	Fair	Poor
450	380	320	250	200	150

Rhino

Unique revolver chambered in 9x19, 9x21, .357 Magnum and .40 S&W. Features include 2", 4", 5" or 6" barrel; fixed or adjustable sights; visible hammer or hammerless design. Weight 24 to 33 oz. Walnut or synthetic grips with black frame; hexagonal-shaped cylinder. Unique design fires from bottom chamber of cylinder. Note: Add $75 for wood grips; $100 for brushed nickel finish (White Rhino model); $300 for gold finish (Rhino 60DS). Deduct $200 for polymer frame model.

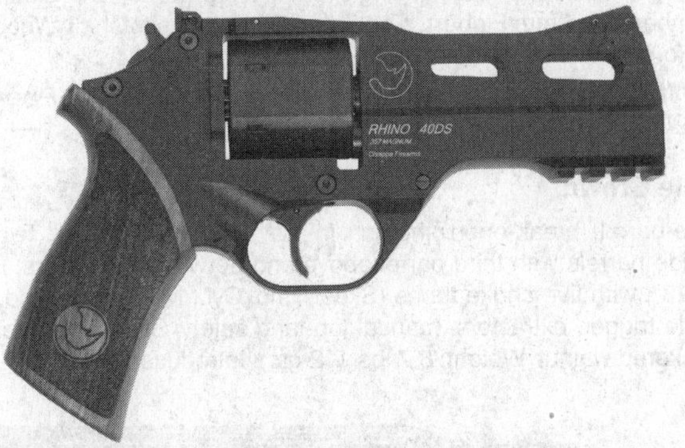

NIB	Exc.	V.G.	Good	Fair	Poor
950	800	600	500	400	300

Rhino 30DS Nebula .357 MAG/3-Inch

Type of Gun: Revolver, Caliber: .357 Magnum, Action: Single/Double, Barrel Length: 3 in. (76mm) Capacity: 6. Feed In: manual, Trigger System: Single. Grips: Blue laminate medium. Front Sight: Fixed red fiber optic. Rear Sight: Adjustable elevation and windage green fiber optic, Safety: Internal, Weight: 1.7 lbs. Length: 7.5 in. (190 mm) Material: Machined 7075-T6 alloy frame/steel cylinder and barrel finish: Muti-Color PVD. Extraction: Manual. Notes: Includes three moon clips, removal tool, gun lock and black leather holster

NIB	Exc.	V.G.	Good	Fair	Poor
1430	—	—	—	—	—

PAK-9

AK-style design 9mm pistol, with 6.3" barrel. Introduced in 2016. Note: Add $27 for converter that allows use of Beretta or Glock magazines.

NIB	Exc.	V.G.	Good	Fair	Poor
500	420	350	300	220	150

SAA 1873

Based on Colt Single-Action Army design in .22 LR caliber. Offered in several variations, with 4.75", 5.5" or 7.5" barrels (and 12" Buntline model). Six or 10-shot cylinder. Some models come with interchangeable .22 Magnum cylinder. Fixed or adjustable sights. Note: Add $40 for extra cylinder; $100 for 12" barrel; $25 for 10-shot model.

NIB	Exc.	V.G.	Good	Fair	Poor
180	150	120	100	80	70

1873-22

Replica of Colt Single Action Army revolver. Chambered in .22 Long Rifle, with 6-round cylinder. Introduced in 2011 and discontinued in 2012. Available with extra cylinder in .22 WMR. Note: Add $50 for extra cylinder; $40 for target model.

NIB	Exc.	V.G.	Good	Fair	Poor
180	150	120	100	80	60

1873-22-10

Same features as above, with 10-round cylinder. Available with extra cylinder in .22 WMR. Also offered in .17 HMR caliber, with adjustable sights. Note: Add $50 for .22 WMR extra cylinder; $30 for .17 HMR model.

NIB	Exc.	V.G.	Good	Fair	Poor
200	180	150	120	90	80

Model 1886 Kodiak Rifle

Lever-action rifle chambered for .45-70 Government cartridge. Replica of Winchester 1886, with 18.5" half-octagon barrel, express sights, black synthetic stock and hard-chrome matte gray finish. Standard model has 4-round half-length tubular magazine. Trapper model 6-shot magazine, blue finish and walnut stock. Note: Deduct $150 for Trapper model.

NIB	Exc.	V.G.	Good	Fair	Poor
1500	1200	900	700	500	400

Model 1886 Rifle

Similar features as Kodiak Rifle, except has 26" octagon barrel with full-length tubular magazine, walnut stock and forend with crescent buttplate.

NIB	Exc.	V.G.	Good	Fair	Poor
1350	1150	900	650	400	300

Model 1892 Rifle

Replica of Winchester model 1892 lever-action rifle. Chambered for .38 Special, .357 Magnum, .38-40 WCF, .44-40 WCF, .44 Magnum, .45 Colt. Offered in several variations, with barrel lengths from 16" to 24" with different sighting options. Take-down model with octagonal barrel available. Note: Add $200 for take-down model; $100 for buckhorn rear/interchangeable blade front sights.

NIB	Exc.	V.G.	Good	Fair	Poor
900	750	600	500	400	250

1886 Lever-Action Wildlands

Caliber: .45-70. Capacity: 4. Barrel: 18.5-in., stainless steel, Cerakote dark gray finish, heavy, threaded. Stock: Laminate. Sights: Fixed fiber-optic front, skinner peep rear. Weight: 9.5 lbs. Features: Take-down style, 38.3 in. overall length.

NIB	Exc.	V.G.	Good	Fair	Poor
1980	—	—	—	—	—

1892 Lever-Action Wildlands

Caliber: .44 Mag. Capacity: 5. Barrel: 16.5 in., stainless steel, Cerakote dark gray or color case finish, heavy. Stock: Wood laminate or hand-oiled walnut. Sights: Fixed fiber-optic front, Skinner peep rear. Weight: 6.3 lbs. Features: Takedown and solid-frame configurations, mag tube fed.

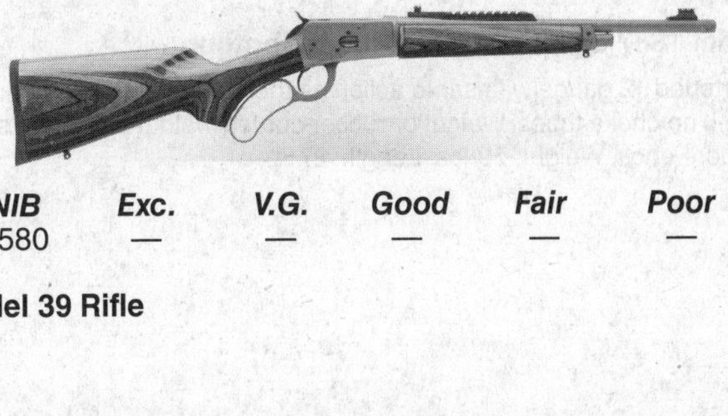

NIB	Exc.	V.G.	Good	Fair	Poor
1580	—	—	—	—	—

Model 39 Rifle

Replica of Marlin Model 39 rifle. Chambered for .22 Short, Long and Long Rifle. Has 18.5" barrel, hardwood or synthetic stock and forend. Take-down model.

NIB	Exc.	V.G.	Good	Fair	Poor
350	280	220	200	180	150

Model LA322 Rifle

Similar to Model 39 Rifle, with internal changes and improvements. Lever action, with 15-shot tubular magazine. Blue or case colored finish. Deluxe model available with oil-finished walnut stock, color case-hardened or black chrome finish. Kodiak Cub has matte chrome finish, straight-grip stock. Note: Add $150 for Deluxe model; $200 for Kodiak Cub.

NIB	Exc.	V.G.	Good	Fair	Poor
400	350	300	250	200	180

Little Sharps Rifle

Replica of Sharps single-shot rifle has been made in several rimfire and centerfire chamberings. Including .17 HMR, .17 Hornet, .22 LR, .22 WMR, .22 Hornet, .30-30, .38-55 and .45 Colt. Features include 24" or 26" octagon barrel with tang sight, walnut stock and forend. Target model in .17 Hornet only has heavy barrel, with spirit level front sight. Hunter model has no sights, half round and half octagon barrel and also made only in .17 Hornet. Note: Deduct $150 for Target .17 Hornet; $250 for Hunter .17 Hornet.

NIB	Exc.	V.G.	Good	Fair	Poor
1200	1000	850	600	400	200

Little Badger

Caliber: .22 LR. Barrel: 16.5" blued steel. Weight: 2.9 lbs. Stock: Folding steel rod system. Features: Ultralight, minimalist, folding Take Down Xteme (TDX) version of the skeletonized break-action rimfire. Single shot with shell holder and quad Picatinny forend. OAL of 31". Alloy frame. Barrel threaded at 1/2x28. Fixed M1 military-style front sight and adjustable rear. Half cock hammer safety. Picatinny rail behind triggerguard. Ships with polymer tube for storage.

NIB	Exc.	V.G.	Good	Fair	Poor
240	—	—	—	—	—

Sharps Down Under

Replica of Sharps Model 1874 single-shot rifle. Chambered in .38-55 WCF, .45-70, .45-90, .45-110, .45-120 or .50-90. Full octagon 34" barrel, double-set triggers, walnut stock and color case-hardened finish.

NIB	Exc.	V.G.	Good	Fair	Poor
1800	1550	1200	850	600	400

Model 1887 Lever-Action Shotgun

Replica of Model 1887 Winchester 12 gauge, with 5-shot tubular magazine, 22" or 28" barrel and choke tubes. 2.75" chamber, 3 Beretta/Benelli Mobile Choke Thread MC-3 tubes (IC, M, F). Walnut stocks, blued-steel barrels, color case-finished receivers. Weight: 9.3 lbs. Length: 45".

NIB	Exc.	V.G.	Good	Fair	Poor
1000	900	750	600	400	250

Model 1887 Lever-Action T-Model Shotgun

Shortened 12 gauge with same action as the Model 1887 shotgun. 18.5" barrel, no choke tubes. Walnut or rubber-coated-walnut pistol grip stocks and fore ends. Weight: 7.9 lbs. Length: 27.5".

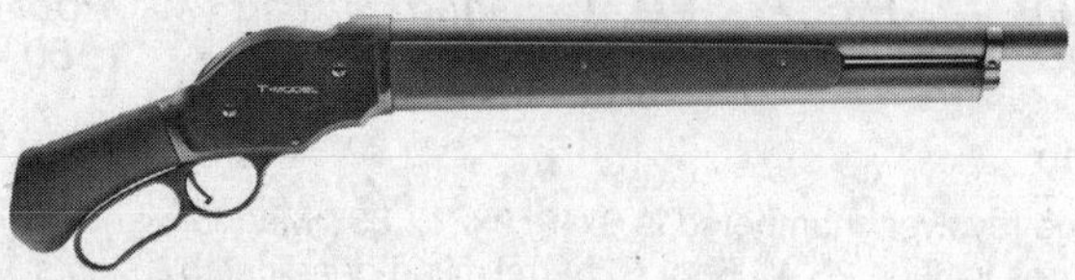

NIB	Exc.	V.G.	Good	Fair	Poor
1000	900	750	600	400	250

Little Badger Deluxe Shotgun

Folding break-open action, single shot, alloy frame, 24" steel barrel chambered in 9mm Flobert, a common European shotshell. Wood stock and forend. 3.6 lbs. Length: 38.5".

NIB	Exc.	V.G.	Good	Fair	Poor
200	100	50	—	—	—

Triple Crown

Triple-barrel, break-open shotgun in 12-, 20- or 28-gauge. Two side-by-side barrels with third barrel above and between the others. Barrels are 28", with five choke tubes (Skeet, Imp. Cyl., Mod., Imp. Mod., Full). Single trigger, extractors, manual top-tang safety. Stock and forend are checkered walnut. Weight: 8.7 lbs. (12-ga.). Introduced in 2017.

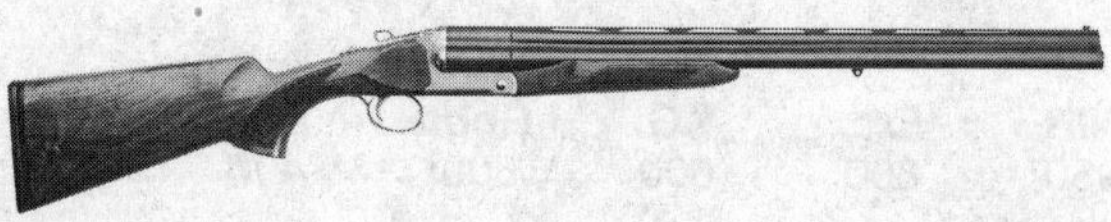

NIB	Exc.	V.G.	Good	Fair	Poor
1650	1350	1000	—	—	—

204/214 Series

Over/under models in 20- or 12-gauge. Model 204X: a 20-gauge, with 26" barrels with extractors. Model 214E: a 12-gauge, with 28" barrels and automatic ejectors. Both models have five choke tubes, selective single trigger, checkered walnut stock and forend. Note: Add $25 for camo stock.

NIB	Exc.	V.G.	Good	Fair	Poor
700	620	520	380	300	250

CHICAGO FIREARMS CO.

Chicago, Illinois

Protector Palm Pistol (Antique)

A .32-caliber radial cylinder revolver. Designed to fit in the palm of your hand. Operated by a hinged lever mounted to rear of the circular frame. Sideplates are marked "Chicago Firearms Co., Chicago, Ill." and "The Protector". Blued, with hard rubber grip panels or nickel-plated, with pearl grip panels. Manufactured by Ames Manufacturing Company. Note: Add 25 percent for pearl grip panels without cracks or chips; 50 percent for blued finish.

Photo by Stoney Roberts

Exc.	Fine	V.G.	Good	Fair	Poor
3000	2000	1500	1000	750	520

CHIPMUNK RIFLES

Lewiston, Idaho

See—KEYSTONE

CHRISTENSEN ARMS

Gunnison, Utah

There are a number of custom options offered by this company for its rifles. Many of these options may affect price. Prices listed are for standard models with standard features.

Carbon One

Bolt-action rifle, with Remington 700 action. Chambered for .17- through .243-caliber. Fitted with a custom trigger, match-grade stainless steel barrel and black synthetic stock. Weight about 6 lbs.

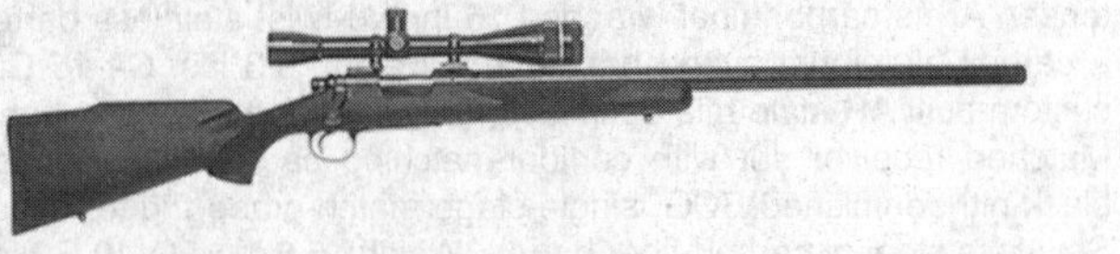

NIB	Exc.	V.G.	Good	Fair	Poor
3900	2750	1900	1200	700	500

Carbon Lite

Similar to above. Weight about 5 lbs.

NIB	Exc.	V.G.	Good	Fair	Poor
3900	2750	1900	1200	700	500

Carbon King

This model utilizes a Remington 700 BDL long action. Chambered for .25-caliber through .30-06. Stainless steel barrel, custom trigger and black synthetic stock are standard. Weight about 6.5 lbs.

NIB	Exc.	V.G.	Good	Fair	Poor
3900	2750	1900	1200	700	500

Carbon Cannon

Similar to above. Chambered for belted Magnum calibers. Weight about 7 lbs.

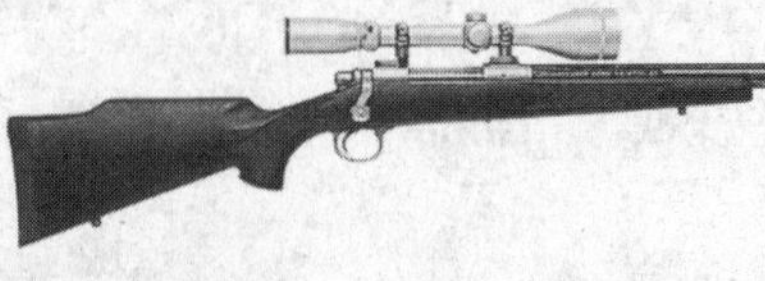

NIB	Exc.	V.G.	Good	Fair	Poor
3900	2750	1900	1200	700	500

Carbon Challenge I

Built on a Ruger 10/22 action. Fitted with a Volquartsen trigger, stainless steel bull barrel and black synthetic stock. Weight about 3.5 lbs. Note: Add 20 percent for .17-caliber.

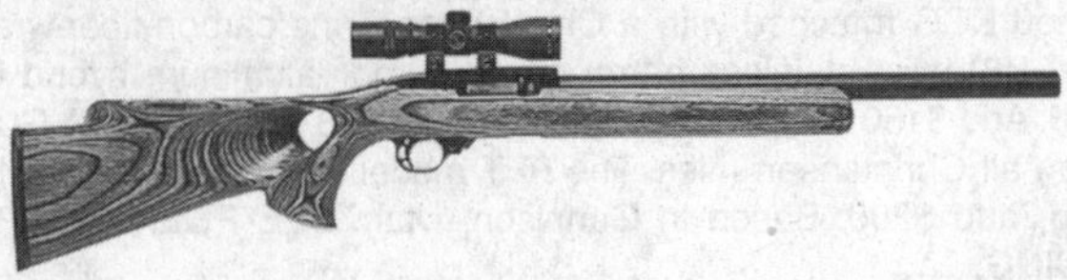

NIB	Exc.	V.G.	Good	Fair	Poor
1800	1300	880	600	400	180

Carbon Challenge II

Similar to above. Fitted with an AMT action and trigger. Weight about 4.5 lbs. Discontinued.

NIB	Exc.	V.G.	Good	Fair	Poor
1300	1000	700	550	320	120

Carbon Tactical

Bolt-action model uses Remington 700 BDL action. Available in most any caliber. Fitted with custom trigger, match-grade stainless steel barrel and black synthetic stock. Weight about 7 lbs.

NIB	Exc.	V.G.	Good	Fair	Poor
3900	2750	1900	1200	700	500

Carbon Conquest

Chambered for .50-caliber BMG cartridge. Built on McMillan stainless steel bolt action. Magazine capacity 5 rounds. Barrel length 32" with muzzle brake. Composite stock. Weight about 20 lbs. Note: Deduct $1,000 for single-shot model.

NIB	Exc.	V.G.	Good	Fair	Poor
6250	4000	3250	1700	880	400

Carbon One Hunter

Semi-custom bolt-action rifle built around choice of receivers; steel barrel encased in carbon alloy shroud; synthetic stock. All popular calibers. Weight 6.5- to 7 lbs.

NIB	Exc.	V.G.	Good	Fair	Poor
1500	1300	880	550	380	120

Carbon Ranger Repeater

Semi-custom bolt-action rifle chambered in .50 BMG. Five-shot magazine; steel Pac-Nor barrel encased in carbon alloy. Muzzle brake. Weight 20 lbs.

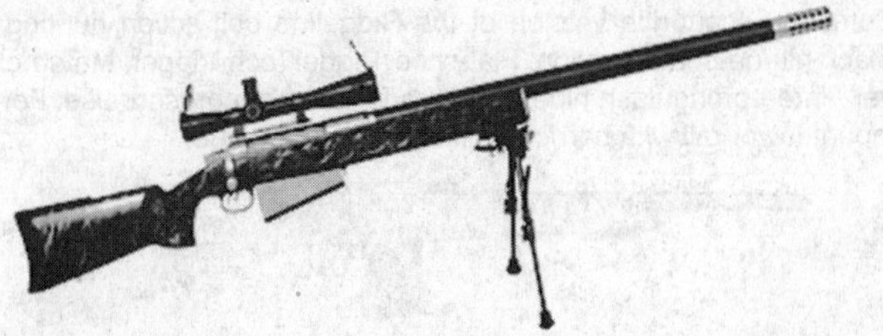

NIB	Exc.	V.G.	Good	Fair	Poor
8000	7000	5500	4000	2000	1000

Carbon Ranger Single Shot

Similar to Repeater but single-shot.

NIB	Exc.	V.G.	Good	Fair	Poor
6500	5000	3000	2000	1100	500

Summit Carbon

Bolt-action model with carbon fiber barrel, adjustable trigger, carbon stock in standard or thumbhole style. Offered in most popular calibers from .223 Rem. to .338 Lapua. Also made with steel barrel. Introduced in 2014.

NIB	Exc.	V.G.	Good	Fair	Poor
5000	4200	3700	2700	—	—

Summit Steel

NIB	Exc.	V.G.	Good	Fair	Poor
4000	3200	2700	2000	—	—

Mesa Titanium Edition

Calibers: 6.5 Creedmoor, 6.5 PRC, .308 Win., .300 Win. Mag. Capacity: 3 to 4 Barrel: 22 to 24 in., 416R stainless steel, threaded. Stock: Carbon-fiber composite, sporter style. Sights: None, drilled and tapped. Weight: 6.1 lbs. Features: LimbSaver recoil pad, nitride-treated bolt, match-grade trigger.

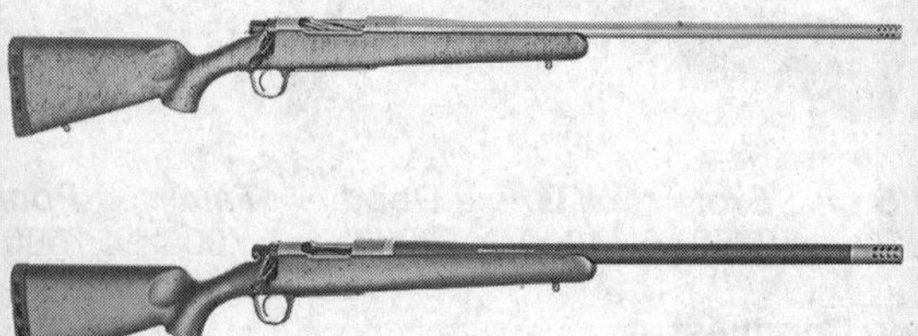

NIB	Exc.	V.G.	Good	Fair	Poor
1700	1600	1400	—	—	—

Ridgeline Titanium Edition

Calibers: 6.5 Creedmoor, 6.5 PRC, .308 Win., .300 Win. Mag. Capacity: 3 to 4. Barrel: 22 to 24 in., 416R stainless steel, carbon-fiber wrapped. Stock: Carbon-fiber composite, sporter style. Sights: Picatinny rail. Weight: 5.8 lbs. Features: Titanium radial brake, M16-style extractor, LimbSaver recoil pad.

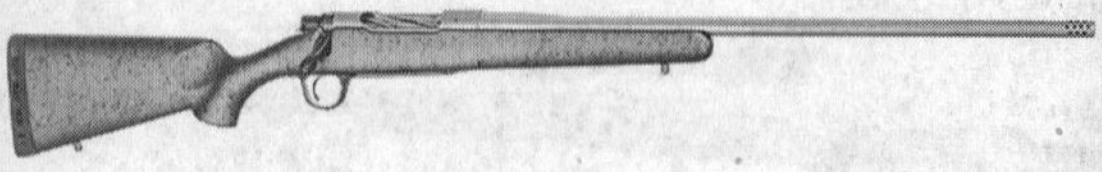

NIB	Exc.	V.G.	Good	Fair	Poor
2400	2000	1750	—	—	—

Ridgeline Scout

Calibers: .223 Rem, 6mm ARC, 6.5 Creed, .308 Win., .300 Blackout. Capacity: 10-round AICS box magazine. Barrel: 16-in. carbon-fiber wrapped stainless, button rifled, free-floating. Weight: From 5.9 lbs. Stock: Carbon-fiber composite, sporter style with stainless steel bedding pillars. Tan with black webbing. Sights: No iron sights. 0 MOA rail. Features: Compact, scout-rifle version of the Ridgeline bolt-action hunting rifle. Black nitride-coated action. Flat-shoe TriggerTech trigger. Match chamber. Three-prong flash hider removes for easy suppressor use. Forward mount lower rail with barricade stop. MOA guarantee.

NIB	Exc.	V.G.	Good	Fair	Poor
2000	—	—	—	—	—

Ridgeline FFT

Calibers: .450 Bushmaster, .22-250 Rem., .243 Rem, 6.5 Creed, 6.5 PRC, 6.5-284, 26 Nosler, .270 Win., 7mm-08, .280 Ackley, 28 Nosler, 7mm Rem. Mag., .308 Win., .30-06, 30 Nosler, .300 WSM, .300 Win. Mag., .300 PRC, .300 RUM. Capacity: FFT hinged floor plate with internal magazine. 4-round standard, 3-round magnum. Barrel: 20 or 22-in. carbon-fiber wrapped stainless, button-rifled, hand-lapped, free-floating. Weight: From 5.3 lbs. Stock: Proprietary Flash Forged Technology (FFT) carbon-fiber sporter style with stainless steel bedding pillars. Choice of black with gray webbing, green with black and tan webbing, Sitka Subalpine camo, or Sitka Elevated II camo. Sights: No iron sights. Drilled and tapped at 6-48 for Remington 700 bases. Features: Upgraded version of the Ridgeline uses the latest in carbon-fiber technology to build the rifle a full pound lighter. New side-baffle brake and stylish paint scheme distinguish the upgraded model. Choice of natural stainless or Burnt Bronze Cerakote metalwork. Enlarged ejection port. Billet aluminum bottom metal. Sub-MOA guarantee, excluding .450 Bushmaster. Multiple calibers available in a left-hand rifle.

NIB	Exc.	V.G.	Good	Fair	Poor
2200	—	—	—	—	—

Modern Sporting Rifles

Chamber: .223 Wylde. The CA5five6 build features a forged aluminum receiver set and a black nitride-finished BCG matched with a Christensen Arms carbon-fiber-wrapped 16 in. 1:8-twist stainless barrel and a carbon-aluminum hybrid handguard. Weight: 6.3 lbs. CA-15 G2 is a custom-built AR-style rifle optimized for weight and accuracy. Features: Matched receiver set with contour-matching carbon-fiber handguard, black nitride-finished BCG, single-stage match-grade trigger assembly. Stainless steel or carbon-fiber barrels. Weight: 5.8 lbs. CA-10 G2 in .308 Win. (18 in. barrel, 1:10 twist) and 6.5 CM (20 in. barrel 1:8 twist) is designed for larger calibers and longer shots. Features: Aerospace-grade carbon-fiber free-floating handguard, billet aluminum receiver set, M-Lok or KeyMod fitments. Similar barrel finishes and triggers to CA-15 G2. Weight: 7.2 lbs. CA-10 DMR is a long-range rifle with an aluminum receiver set, proprietary barrel nut, and aerospace-grade carbon fiber handguard assembly. Comes with Christensen Arms carbon-fiber-wrapped barrel options in 6.5 CM (20 and 22 in., 1:8 twist) and .308 Win. (18 and 20 in., 1:10 twist). Titanium side baffle brake, ⊠x24 threaded muzzle. Weight: 7.8 lbs.

Modern Hunting Rifle (MHR)

Calibers: 6.5 Creed, 6.5 PRC, 6.8 Western, .308 Win., 7mm PRC, 7mm Rem. Mag., .300 Win. Mag., .300 PRC. Barrel: 22", 24" carbon-fiber-wrapped stainless steel. Weight: 7.4 lbs. Stock: Aluminum mini chassis with FFT carbon-fiber stock. Features: Modular bolt-action design blending chassis rifle design with hunting features. Sub-MOA accuracy guarantee. Removeable side-baffle brake. V-Block bedding. Toolless adjustable comb. Forward Picatinny and M-LOK points. Match chamber. Hand-lapped button-rifled free-floating barrel design. Black nitride action finish. Multiple stock finishes are available. TriggerTech trigger. Internal magazine with AICS drop-box compatibility.

NIB	Exc.	V.G.	Good	Fair	Poor
3250	—	—	—	—	—

CA5five6

Black anodized. Caliber: 5.56

NIB	Exc.	V.G.	Good	Fair	Poor
1900	—	—	—	—	—

CA5five6 Black Anodized 5.56

Chamber: .223 Wylde. Forged aluminum receiver set and a black nitride-finished BCG matched with a Christensen Arms carbon-fiber-wrapped 16-in. 1:8" twist stainless barrel and a carbon-aluminum hybrid handguard. Add $150 for Cerakote finish. Weight: 6.3 lbs. Sub-MOA Guarantee on all Christensen rifles. The FFT model has a carbon-fiber handguard, add $200. Based in Gunnison, Utah. SEE POLITICAL PANIC PRICING.

NIB	Exc.	V.G.	Good	Fair	Poor
1500	—	—	—	—	—

CA-15

AR-15 type semi-automatic rifle in .223 Rem., with forged aluminum upper and lower receivers. Most standard features of AR-15 style models including full Picatinny rail, Timney trigger, ambidextrous charging handle, 30-round magazine. Made in several variations. Note: Add $500 for Recon model, with 16" or 20" carbon fiber match grade barrel, titanium "birdcage" suppressor, several camo finishes. Chambered in .204 Ruger, 6.5 Grendel, 6.8 SPC, .300 Blackout.

NIB	Exc.	V.G.	Good	Fair	Poor
2400	2000	1500	1000	750	400

CA-15 G2

Caliber: 5.56

NIB	Exc.	V.G.	Good	Fair	Poor
2520	—	—	—	—	—

CA-15 G2 5.56 Carbon-Fiber Barrel

Chamberings: .223 Wylde, 6mm ARC. Custom-built AR-style rifle optimized for weight and accuracy. Features: Matched receiver set with contour-matching carbon-fiber handguard, black nitride-finished BCG, single-stage match-grade trigger assembly. 16-in. stainless-steel barrel, 1:8" twist. Add $400 for the 16" carbon-fiber barrel, 1:7.5" twist. Weight: 5.8 lbs.

NIB	Exc.	V.G.	Good	Fair	Poor
2300	—	—	—	—	—

CA-10 DMR

Chambering: .308 Win. (18" barrel, 1:10" twist). Long-range rifle with an aluminum receiver set, proprietary barrel nut, and aerospace-grade carbon fiber handguard assembly. Comes with Christensen Arms carbon-fiber-wrapped barrel. Titanium side baffle brake, 5/8X24 threaded muzzle. Weight: 7.8 lbs.

NIB	Exc.	V.G.	Good	Fair	Poor
3300	—	—	—	—	—

Ranger 22

Caliber: .22 LR. Capacity: 10. Barrel: 18 in., carbon-fiber tension. Stock: Carbon-fiber composite, ambidextrous grip. Sights: Picatinny rail. Weight: 5.1 lbs. Features: Sub-MOA guarantee, Trigger Tech Remington 700 trigger, dual opposing locking lugs.

NIB	Exc.	V.G.	Good	Fair	Poor
700	600	500	—	—	—

CA-10 G2

Chamberings: .308 Win. (18" barrel, 1:10" twist) and 6.5 CM (20" barrel 1:8" twist) is designed for larger calibers and longer shots. Features: Aerospace-grade carbon-fiber free-floating handguard, billet aluminum receiver set, M-LOK or KeyMod fitments. Carbon-fiber barrel only. Weight: 7.2 lbs. SEE POLITICAL PANIC PRICING.

NIB	Exc.	V.G.	Good	Fair	Poor
3100	—	—	—	—	—

1911 G5

Based on full-size 1911A1 design in 9mm or .45 ACP. Barrel length 5" (4" on G4 model). Many enhanced features including checkered mainspring housing and front strap, VZ G10 grips, skeletonized hammer and trigger, full-length guide rod, night sights, several choices of finishes.

NIB	Exc.	V.G.	Good	Fair	Poor
2500	2000	1750	1400	900	400

1911 C4

Commander size variation of G5, with 4.25" barrel. Other features similar to 1911 G5. Also available with Titanium frame.

NIB	Exc.	V.G.	Good	Fair	Poor
2400	1950	1500	1200	600	400

with Titanium Frame

Same as above, with Titanium frame.

NIB	Exc.	V.G.	Good	Fair	Poor
4200	3500	2600	2000	900	600

1911 A4/A5

Standard 1911A1 configuration in 9mm or .45 ACP, with 4" barrel (G4) or 5" barrel (G5), Aluminum frame, with stainless steel slide for polished black finish for two-tone appearance. Features include skeletonized hammer and trigger, G10 grips, night sights, checkered mainspring housing and front strap. Introduced in 2017.

NIB	Exc.	V.G.	Good	Fair	Poor
1800	1500	1200	1000	—	—

1911 Officer

Christensen makes a series of 1911-type pistols in .45 ACP caliber. These are offered in full-size, Commander and Officers sizes (shown) in both standard and lightweight variants. Features include stainless steel slide, aerospace aluminum mainspring housing, adjustable trigger, tritium night sights, Cerakote finish, carbon-fiber grips and ambidextrous safety. Note: Add $800 for titanium frame.

NIB	Exc.	V.G.	Good	Fair	Poor
2100	1800	1400	1000	750	600

1911 Damascus

Full-size model with damascus-pattern finish, 5" barrel, titanium frame, Novak trijicon sights, skeletonized hammer and trigger, full-length guide rod with no bushing. Introduced in 2013.

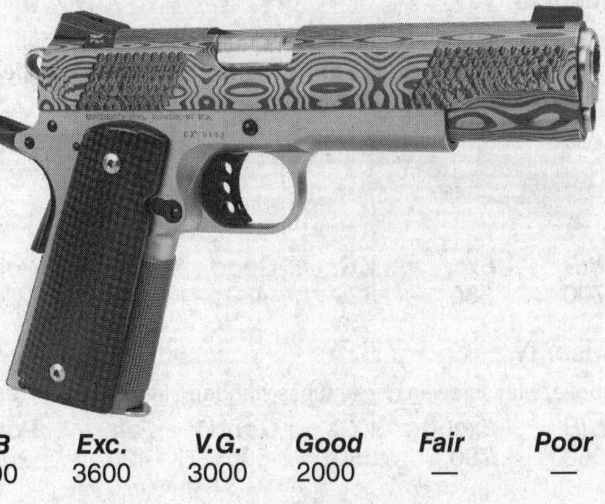

NIB	Exc.	V.G.	Good	Fair	Poor
4200	3600	3000	2000	—	—

CHURCHILL

Various European Manufacturers and Importers

SIDE-BY-SIDE SHOTGUNS

Windsor I

A 10-, 12-, 16-, 20-, 28-gauge and .410 bore Anson & Deeley double-barrel boxlock shotgun. Barrel lengths from 23" through 32", various choke combinations, double triggers and extractors. Scroll-engraved silver-finished, with checkered walnut pistol grip and forend.

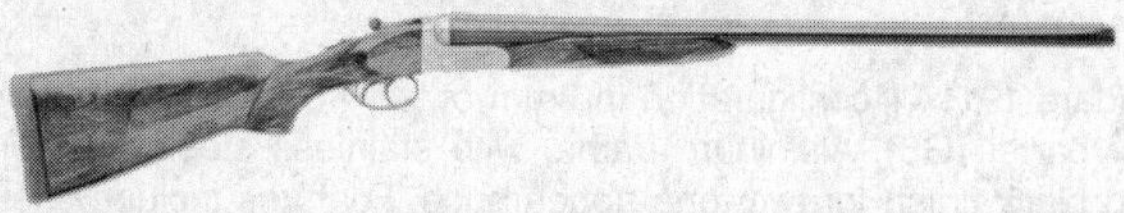

NIB	Exc.	V.G.	Good	Fair	Poor
800	600	500	400	300	200

Windsor II

As above in 10-, 12- and 20-gauge only, with automatic ejectors. Not imported after 1987.

NIB	Exc.	V.G.	Good	Fair	Poor
800	600	550	450	350	250

Windsor VI

As above with sidelocks. Chambered for 12- and 20-gauge only, with automatic ejectors. Not imported after 1987.

NIB	Exc.	V.G.	Good	Fair	Poor
1100	800	750	650	500	350

Royal

A 12-, 20-, 28-gauge and .410 bore boxlock double-barrel shotgun, with various barrel lengths and chokes, double triggers and extractors. Case-hardened, with checkered walnut stock. Introduced in 1988.

NIB	Exc.	V.G.	Good	Fair	Poor
650	500	420	350	280	120

OVER/UNDER SHOTGUNS

Monarch

A 12-, 20-, 28-gauge or .410 bore over/under shotgun, with a boxlock-action, 25", 26" or 28" ventilated rib barrels. Double- or single-selective trigger extractors. Checkered walnut stock.

NIB	Exc.	V.G.	Good	Fair	Poor
600	480	420	380	300	150

Windsor III

A 12-, 20-gauge and .410 bore boxlock double-barrel shotgun, with 27" or 30" ventilated rib barrels, extractors, single-selective trigger, scroll-engraved, silver finished and checkered walnut stock.

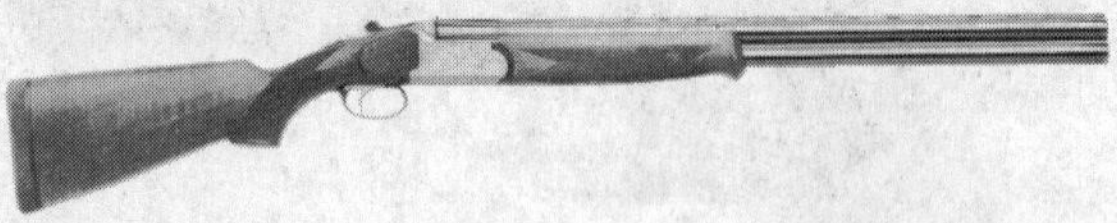

NIB	Exc.	V.G.	Good	Fair	Poor
700	580	520	480	400	200

Windsor IV

As above, with screw-in choke tubes standard. Introduced in 1989.

NIB	Exc.	V.G.	Good	Fair	Poor
980	780	650	500	420	200

Regent

As above in 12- and 20-gauge, with 27" ventilated rib barrels, screw-in choke tubes, scroll-engraved false sideplates, automatic ejectors, single-selective trigger and checkered walnut stock. Not imported after 1986.

NIB	Exc.	V.G.	Good	Fair	Poor
950	750	650	550	450	250

Regent II

As above, with finer overall finishing.

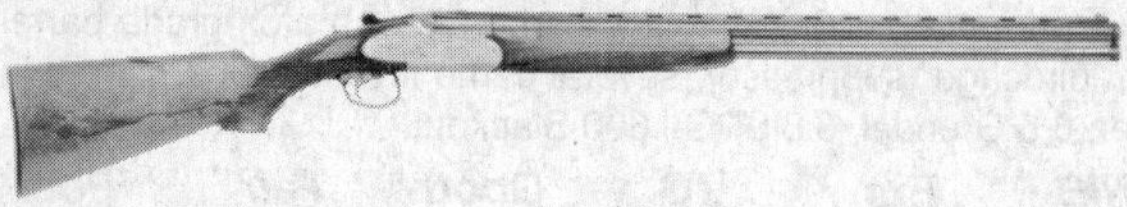

NIB	Exc.	V.G.	Good	Fair	Poor
1250	1000	850	750	500	250

Regent Shotgun/Rifle Combination

A .222, .223, .243, .270, .308 or .30-06 caliber/12-gauge over/under rifle/shotgun, with 25" ventilated rib, automatic ejectors and single-selective trigger. Silver finished, scroll engraved and checkered walnut stock.

NIB	Exc.	V.G.	Good	Fair	Poor
1050	820	720	600	450	250

Windsor Grade Semi-Automatic

A 12-gauge semi-automatic shotgun, with 26", 28" or 30" ventilated rib barrels and screw-in choke tubes. An etched and anodized alloy receiver, with checkered walnut stock.

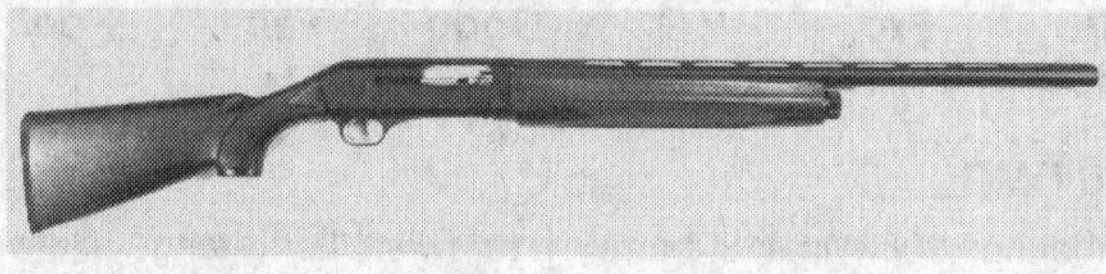

NIB	Exc.	V.G.	Good	Fair	Poor
500	380	320	280	220	180

Regent Grade Semi-Automatic

Chambered for 12-gauge, with choice of 26", 28" or 30" barrels. Standard chokes or choke tubes. Walnut stock with pistol grip. Introduced in 1984; discontinued in 1986. Weight about 7.5 lbs.

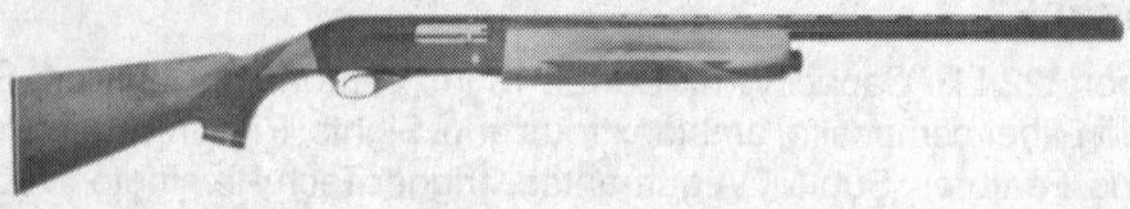

NIB	Exc.	V.G.	Good	Fair	Poor
500	380	320	280	220	180

Windsor Grade Slide-Action

A 12-gauge slide-action shotgun, with 26" through 30" ventilated rib barrel, various chokes, double slide rails and an anodized alloy receiver. Checkered walnut stock. Discontinued in 1986.

NIB	Exc.	V.G.	Good	Fair	Poor
—	500	380	300	250	180

RIFLES

Highlander

A .25-06 through .300-caliber Win. Magnum bolt-action rifle, with 22" barrel with or without sights, 3-shot magazine and checkered walnut stock.

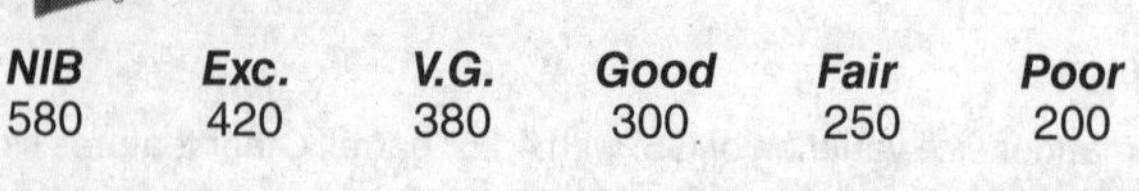

NIB	Exc.	V.G.	Good	Fair	Poor
580	420	380	300	250	200

Regent

As above, with Monte Carlo-style comb and cheekpiece. Discontinued in 1988.

NIB	Exc.	V.G.	Good	Fair	Poor
—	650	500	420	350	280

CHURCHILL, E. J. LTD.
London, England

One of One Thousand Rifle

A .270 to .458 Magnum caliber bolt-action rifle, with 24" barrel and select French walnut stock, trap pistol grip cap and recoil pad. Only 100 actually produced for 20th Anniversary of Interarms in 1973.

NIB	Exc.	V.G.	Good	Fair	Poor
—	1750	1050	850	700	550

Premier Over/Under

Sidelock ejector gun available in 12-, 20- or 28-gauge. Single or double trigger with choice of finish. Barrel lengths built to order. Deluxe Turkish walnut with choice of grip. Fine scroll engraving. Weight about: 12-gauge 7 lbs.; 20-gauge 6.75 lbs. Many extra cost options available. Note: Add $3,000 for 28-gauge guns.

NIB	Exc.	V.G.	Good	Fair	Poor
47000	36500	26000	20000	10000	800

Premier Side-by-Side

Similar to over/under gun, with side-by-side barrels. Offered in 16-gauge as well as 12-, 20- and 28-gauge. Weight about: 6.5 lbs. 12-gauge; 6 lbs. 16-gauge; 5.8 lbs. 20-gauge. Many extra options are available. Note: Add $3,000 for 28-gauge guns.

NIB	Exc.	V.G.	Good	Fair	Poor
38000	30000	20000	16500	7000	600

Premier Double Rifle

Similar in construction to side-by-side shotgun. Rifle chambered for .300 H&H, .375 H&H or .500 Nitro Express. Weight: 9.5 lbs. .300; 9.75 lbs. .375; 12.5 lbs. .500. Many extra-cost options. Note: Add $3,000 for .500 N.E. guns.

NIB	Exc.	V.G.	Good	Fair	Poor
55000	45000	35000	20000	13000	800

Baronet Magazine Rifle

This rifle uses standard Mauser 98 action, with fully adjustable trigger, 3 position safety and box release floor plate. Barrel length is custom to order. Border engraving. Chambered for .30-06 or .375 H&H. Weight about: 8.5 lbs. .30-06; 9 lbs. .375. Many extra-cost options offered. Seek an expert opinion prior to a sale.

NIB	Exc.	V.G.	Good	Fair	Poor
13000	9750	7000	45000	2750	580

CHYLEWSKI, WITOLD
Switzerland

A 6.35mm caliber semi-automatic pistol, with 6-round magazine marked "Brevete Chylewski" and bears the name "Neuhausen" on left side of pistol. Approximately 1,000 made between 1910 and 1918. Pistol was designed to be cocked with one hand.

NIB	Exc.	V.G.	Good	Fair	Poor
—	—	1250	850	550	280

CIMARRON, F. A. CO.
Fredericksburg, Texas 1993-Present

Houston, Texas 1984-1993

In business since 1984, this company imports quality firearms from Uberti, Armi San Marco, Pedersoli and others. Cimarron also sells Uberti-manufactured blackpowder Colt reproductions, from Patterson to Model 1862 Pocket. For prices and specifications on these models see Uberti section.

PERCUSSION REVOLVERS

Texas Ranger Walker Model of 1847

This model is a replica of the famous blackpowder pistol that played a big role in the Mexican-American war and the history of Texas. Ranger Captain Samuel Walker collaborated with Samuel Colt to design a revolver powerful enough to take down an enemy or his horse. The huge six-round weapon had a 9-inch .44-caliber barrel and has often been described as the gun that put Colt on the map. Introduced in 2018, this model is to be manufactured only for five years, commemorating the 200th Anniversary of the Texas Rangers in 2023. A portion of Cimarron's revenue from the sale of these Walker models will be donated to the Former Texas Ranger Foundation, founded in 1971 to serve current and former Texas Rangers and their families. Model No. CA020 with standard blue, charcoal blue (+$91), and original finish ($130).

NIB	Exc.	V.G.	Good	Fair	Poor
580	490	—	—	—	—

Dragoon Revolvers

1st Model Dragoon .44, 7 1/2"

6-shot, .44 caliber. With the 1847 Walker's military success, Colt immediately began improving his revolver by making needed changes. First in his line of his improved "revolving horse pistols" was the 1st Model Dragoon. Improvements included a loading lever catch under the barrel, which was also shortened from 9" to 7" inches, and the Dragoon's cylinder was reduced by 1/4", bringing the sixgun's overall weight from 4 pounds 9 ounces, down to 4 pounds 2 ounces. Cimarron's 1st Model Dragoon has oval cylinder stop notches, square-back brass triggerguard and backstrap, German silver blade front sight and notched hammer lip rear sight, the "Ranger and Indian" scene roll engraved on the blued cylinder and the oiled walnut one-piece Walker-style grip. The part round/part octagonal barrel is also blued while the loading lever assembly, frame and hammer are color casehardened, and Cimarron's Dragoon uses the improved flat main spring. Model No. CA080 with standard blue, charcoal blue (+$70), and original finish ($100).

NIB	Exc.	V.G.	Good	Fair	Poor
480	400	—	—	—	—

2nd Model Dragoon .44, 7 1/2"

6-shot, .44 caliber. Externally distinguishable from the 1st Model by its rectangular cylinder stop notches with bullet-shaped guide grooves, six locking pins at the breech, and the 2nd's grip is not as flared at the bottom as the earlier Colts. Improved flat main spring with a roller bearing added to the hammer where it engages the spring. Maintains the same 7.5" part-octagon/part-round barrel with the German silver blade front sight and the rear sight cut into the hammer lip. Blued barrel and roll engraved cylinder with the "Ranger and Indian" scene, the color casehardened frame, lever and hammer, brass backstrap and triggerguard and one-piece oiled walnut grip. Originals fetch five and six-figure prices. Model No. CA081 with standard blue, charcoal blue (+$70), and original finish ($100).

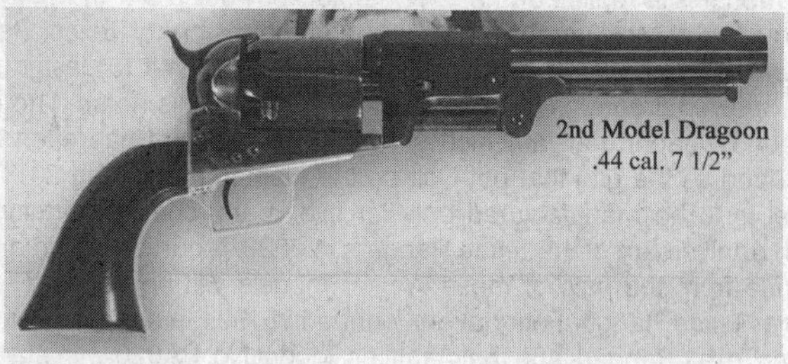
2nd Model Dragoon
.44 cal. 7 1/2"

NIB	Exc.	V.G.	Good	Fair	Poor
470	400	—	—	—	—

3rd Model Dragoon Civilian .44, 7 1/2

6-shot, .44 caliber. Final version of the Dragoon revolver series. 3rd Model is recognizable by its oval triggerguard, rather than the square back versions of former models. Blued trigger, part octagon/part round barrel; cylinder continues the Dragoon's "Ranger and Indian" roll-engraved cylinder scene. German silver blade front sight and notched hammer rear sight, color cased frame, hammer and loading lever. Model No. CA086 with standard blue, charcoal blue (+$70), and original finish ($100).

3rd Model Dragoon
.44 cal. 7 1/2"

NIB	Exc.	V.G.	Good	Fair	Poor
470	400	—	—	—	—

Whitneyville Dragoon

6-shot, .44 caliber. The Whitneyville was the first revolver manufactured in Hartford, Connecticut by Sam Colt. Original, turned out in late 1847, featured several improvements over the Walker model, such as a shortened cylinder, the barrel wedge entered from the left side of the shortened barrel lug, and a loading lever latch was added. Has early Walker-style flared bottomed, oiled walnut grip and square back brass triggerguard and backstrap that's cut for attaching a shoulder stock. Model No. CA083 with standard blue, charcoal blue (+$70), and original finish ($100).

Whitneyville Dragoon
.44 cal. 7 1/2"

NIB	Exc.	V.G.	Good	Fair	Poor
480	400	—	—	—	—

1851 Navy Laser Engraved .36 Cal.

6-shot, .36 caliber. Replica of the most famous cap-and-ball six-shooter. Casehardened frame, brass backstrap and brass triggerguard, old silver frame, standard blue finish. One-piece diamond-checkered walnut grip. 2.72 lbs. No. PP51LSR36.

NIB	Exc.	V.G.	Good	Fair	Poor
430	360	—	—	—	—

1851 Navy Oval Triggerguard

6-shot, .36 caliber. 1851 Oval Navy has authentic oval triggerguard, blue and color casehardened finish or Cimarron's "Original Finish." Roll-engraved naval battle scene depicted on the unfluted cylinder, 7 1/2" octagon barrel, varnished one-piece walnut stocks. Period bead front sight and notched hammer rear sight. No. CA000.

NIB	Exc.	V.G.	Good	Fair	Poor
350	300	—	—	—	—

1851 Navy London

6-shot, .36 caliber. The '51 London Model Navy is unique from its American cousin in that it features a color casehardened backstrap, and oval triggerguard, rather than the American model's brass version. Wears traditional blued, roll-engraved cylinder with the naval battle scene depicting Texas' navy's victory over the Mexican navy, 7 1/-inch octagon barrel and trigger, traditional color cased loading lever and hammer. Brass bead front sight and notched hammer rear sight, varnished one-piece walnut grips. No. CA005.

1851 Navy London (steel grip frame)
.36 cal. 7 1/2"

NIB	Exc.	V.G.	Good	Fair	Poor
380	320	—	—	—	—

Leech & Rigdon 7.5" .36 CSA Battle Flag Inlay

Part of company's The Blue and The Gray series. Detailed replica of handguns originally used by officers and soldiers during the Civil War, this one designed by Thomas Leech and Charles Rigdon in Columbus, Mississippi for the Confederate Government. Flag inlay hand carved from micarta knife handle material by legendary grip carver and maker, Paul Persinger of El Paso, Texas. Fredericksburg (Texas) jeweler Champe Jennings casts the inlays from silver. No. CA003C00M16.

NIB	Exc.	V.G.	Good	Fair	Poor
750	640	540	—	—	—

1860 Army Cut For Stock

6-shot, .44 caliber. Replica of the early 1860 military models with the brass backstrap and triggerguard, Standard Blue, Charcoal Blue, or Cimarron's Original Finish. Resembles military version with 4-screw frame, cutout recoil shield to allow fitting attachable shoulder stock, 2.7 lbs. Rounded contours, 8" round barrel, "creeping" (rack-and-pinion style) lever. No. CA040.

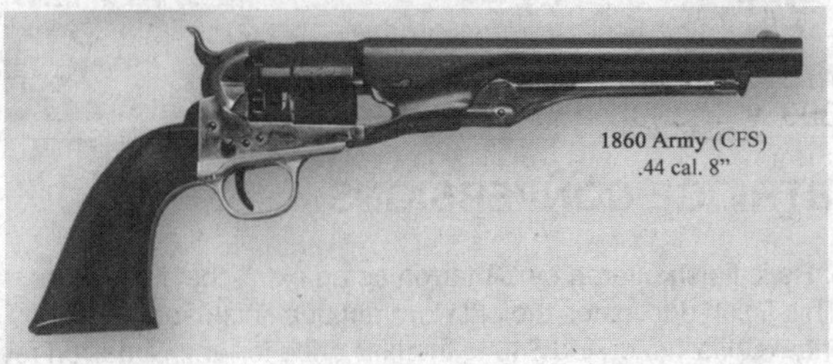

NIB	Exc.	V.G.	Good	Fair	Poor
380	320	—	—	—	—

1860 Army Civilian .44 cal., 8", Blue Steel Frame

6-shot, .44 caliber. Offered in the 3-screw civilian-style color casehardened frame, loading lever and hammer, with an 8" round barrel in standard blue and charcoal blue. It's also available in original finish. The '60 civilian sports a brass triggerguard and backstrap, one-piece walnut stocks. No. CA047. Charcoal blue (+$70) and original finish (+$100). Casehardened frame color is No. CA048.

NIB	Exc.	V.G.	Good	Fair	Poor
380	320	—	—	—	—

1860 Army Fluted Cylinder .44 cal., 8"

6-shot, .44 caliber. Replica produced like the standard 1860 Army revolver with the full round rebated cylinder, except this version has a full fluted cylinder, without the engraved naval battle cylinder scene. Replica is made with four-screw color casehardened frame, blued steel backstrap and brass triggerguard, with either Standard Blue or the Charcoal Blue finish (+$70). No. CA041.

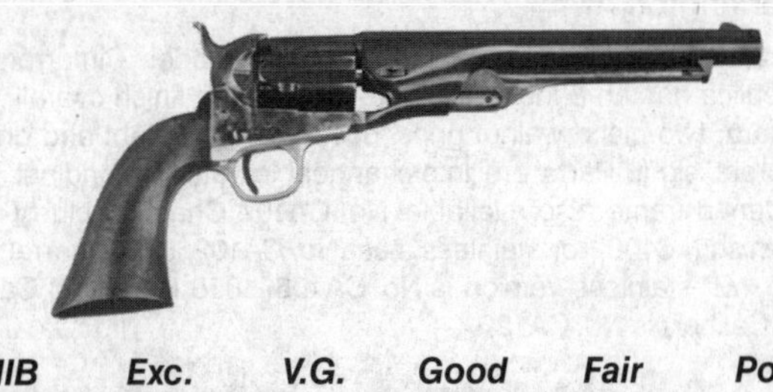

NIB	Exc.	V.G.	Good	Fair	Poor
380	320	—	—	—	—

McCulloch Colt

6-shot, .44 caliber. Replica is offered in the Original Finish, as one might find a genuine McCulloch Colt. This 8" barreled, .44 caliber percussion six-shooter has full-fluted cylinder and the military-type four-screw frame. No. CA041A00.

NIB	Exc.	V.G.	Good	Fair	Poor
480	410	—	—	—	—

1861 Navy Military Cut For Stock .36 cal., 7 1/2"

NIB	Exc.	V.G.	Good	Fair	Poor
380	320	—	—	—	—

1861 Navy Civilian .36 cal., 7 1/2"

'61 Navy civilian model has brass backstrap. No. CA063.

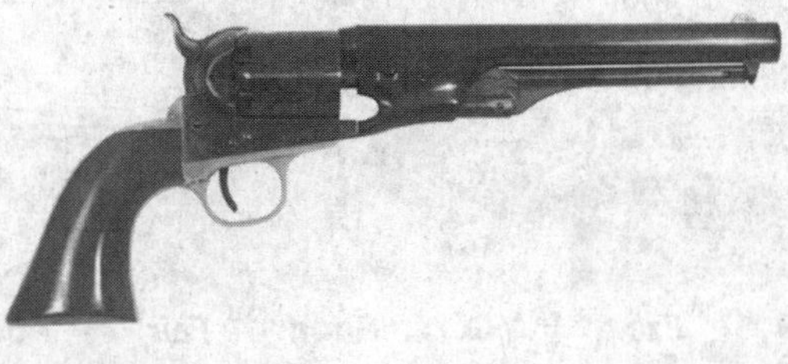

NIB	Exc.	V.G.	Good	Fair	Poor
380	320	—	—	—	—

1858 Navy

6-shot, .36 caliber. Original manufactured from 1863–1878. Reproduction has topstrap design that gave the handgun, 7 1/2" octagon barrel, blued overall except for the brass triggerguard, blued post-type blade front sight, grooved topstrap rear sight, and authentic two-piece walnut grips. Like Cimarron's 1858 Army model, the parts of this Remington lookalike are interchangeable with the original. Charcoal blue (+$70) or original finish (+$100). No. CA112.

NIB	Exc.	V.G.	Good	Fair	Poor
400	340	—	—	—	—

1858 Remington Army

6-shot, .44 caliber. Like the mid-19th century model, Cimarron's .44 caliber replica has an 8-inch octagonal barrel, blue finish overall, brass triggerguard, two-piece walnut grips, post-type front sight and grooved topstrap rear sight. Parts are interchangeable with the original. Color casehardened frame also available. No. CA107. Charcoal blue (+$70), original finish (+$100), or stainless steel No. CA102. 5 1/2" barrel is No. CA108; 5 1/2" stainless version is No. CA106. 1858 Revolving Carbine, (18", .44 Caliber) is No. CA120.

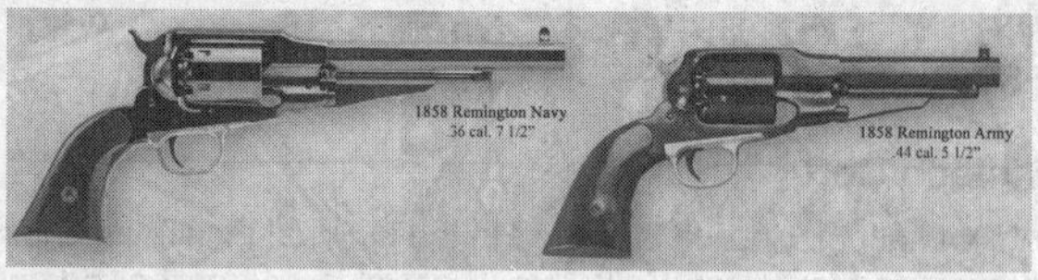

NIB	Exc.	V.G.	Good	Fair	Poor
400	340	—	—	—	—

1858 Remington Army 5 1/2"

NIB	Exc.	V.G.	Good	Fair	Poor
400	340	—	—	—	—

1858 Remington Army Stainless 8"

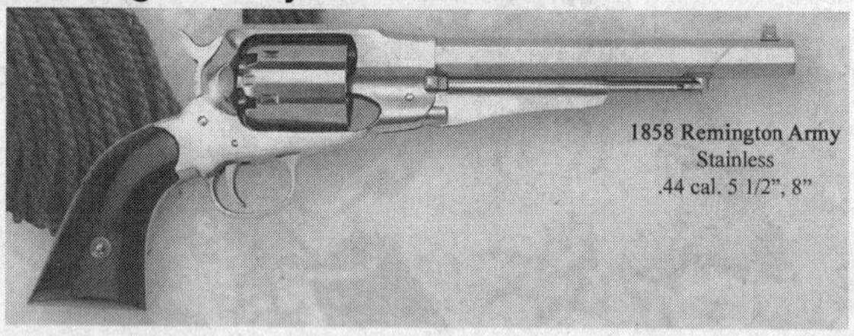

NIB	Exc.	V.G.	Good	Fair	Poor
480	400	—	—	—	—

1858 Remington Army Stainless 5 1/2"

NIB	Exc.	V.G.	Good	Fair	Poor
480	400	—	—	—	—

1858 Remington Army Revolving Carbine

NIB	Exc.	V.G.	Good	Fair	Poor
600	510	—	—	—	—

1848 Model Baby Dragoon

5-shot .31 caliber. The "Baby Dragoon" was made without a loading lever. 4-inch octagon-barreled, .31 caliber, pocket pistol with color case hardening, one-piece walnut stock, and brass backstrap and triggerguard. Standard blue finish. Charcoal blue (+$70), original finish (+$100). No. CA031.

NIB	Exc.	V.G.	Good	Fair	Poor
370	320	—	—	—	—

1849 Wells Fargo

5-shot, .31 cal., 4" barrel. Casehardened brass frame, one-piece walnut grip, standard blue/charcoal blue/original finish. No. CA038.

NIB	Exc.	V.G.	Good	Fair	Poor
370	320	—	—	—	—

1849 Colt's Pocket Model

5-shot, .31 caliber. Smaller version of 1851 Navy. With about 340,000 produced between 1850 and 1873, more '49 Pockets were manufactured than any other Colt percussion firearm. Cimarron's copy has 4-inch barrel, the most popular of several barrel lengths of the original. Color casehardened frame, loading lever and hammer; brass backstrap and triggerguard, one-piece walnut stocks. Standard blue finish. Charcoal blue (+$70), original finish (+$100). No. CA035.

NIB	Exc.	V.G.	Good	Fair	Poor
380	320	—	—	—	—

1862 Colt Police Pocket

5-shot, .36 caliber. Original manufactured from 1861 until approximately 1873. Color casehardened frame, hammer and loading lever; brass backstrap and triggerguard, one-piece walnut stocks and half-fluted cylinder. Offered in barrel lengths of 4 1/2" (CA072), 5 1/2" (CA071), and 6 1/2" (CA070). Charcoal blue (+$70), original finish (+$100).

NIB	Exc.	V.G.	Good	Fair	Poor
390	330	—	—	—	—

CARTRIDGE CONVERSIONS

Note: Relic finish offered by Cimarron as an extra cost item on its revolvers. This finish duplicates the old worn antique finish seen on many used historical Colts. Note: Add $40 to the NIB price for any Cimarron revolver with this finish.

Model 1851 Conversion

Chambered for .38 Special, .38 Colt and .44 Colt. Fitted with 5" or 7" barrels.

NIB	Exc.	V.G.	Good	Fair	Poor
550	450	330	230	150	100

Model 1860 Conversion

Chambered for .38 Special, .38 Colt and .44 Colt. Fitted with 5" or 7.5" barrels.

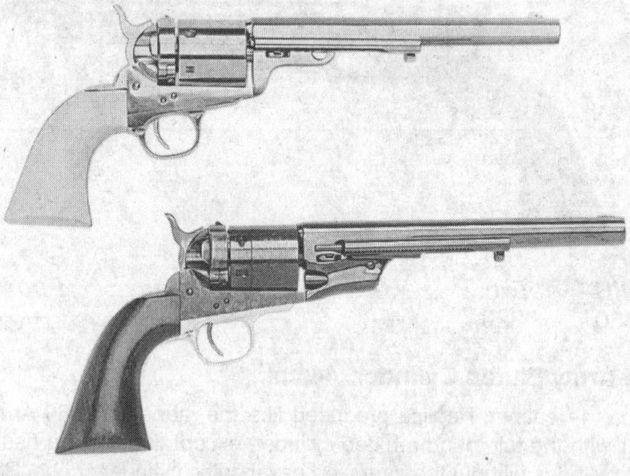

NIB	Exc.	V.G.	Good	Fair	Poor
550	450	330	230	150	100

Model 1861 Conversion

Chambered for .38 Special, .38 Colt and .44 Colt. Fitted with 5" or 7" barrels.

NIB	Exc.	V.G.	Good	Fair	Poor
550	450	330	230	150	100

Bad Boy

Modern classic single action design, .44 Mag or 10mm, 6" octagon barrel.

NIB	Exc.	V.G.	Good	Fair	Poor
700	630	550	450	—	—

'62 Pocket Navy Conversion

Copy of Colt Pocket Navy conversion; .380ACP; 6" barrel.

NIB	Exc.	V.G.	Good	Fair	Poor
530	450	380	330	—	—

Model 1872 Open Top

This revolver offered in a number of different calibers and configurations. Chambered for .44 SP, .44 Colt, .44 Russian, .45 Schofield, .38 Colt, .38 Special. Can be fitted with Army or Navy grips. Barrel lengths are 4.75", 5.5" or 7.5". Offered in regular blued finish, charcoal blue finish or original finish. Note: Add $40 for charcoal finish; $50 for original finish; $25 for silver-plated back strap and triggerguard.

NIB	Exc.	V.G.	Good	Fair	Poor
450	400	350	300	200	100

COLT SINGLE-ACTION ARMY COPIES

Cimarron Arms reproduction of 1873 Colt Single-Action Army revolver comes in two basic configurations. First is "Old Model", with black powder frame, screw-in cylinder pin retainer and circular bull's eye ejector head. Second is "pre-war Model" style frame, with spring loaded cross-pin cylinder retainer and half moon ejector head. Old Model revolvers are available in authentic old style charcoal blue finish at an extra charge. Unless otherwise stated, all of these Colt reproductions are produced by Uberti of Italy. Plain walnut grips are standard unless noted. Note: Relic finish offered by Cimarron as an extra cost item on its revolvers. This finish duplicates the old worn antique finish seen on many used historical Colts. Add $40 to NIB price for any Cimarron revolver with this finish.

General Custer 7th Cavalry Model

Has U.S. military markings and fitted with 7.5" barrel on an Old Model frame. Offered in .45 LC only.

NIB	Exc.	V.G.	Good	Fair	Poor
530	450	350	300	200	100

Rough Rider U.S. Artillery Model

This version of Old Model fitted with 5.5" barrel and chambered for .45 LC.

NIB	Exc.	V.G.	Good	Fair	Poor
550	450	350	300	200	100

Frontier Six Shooter

This revolver offered with choice of 4.75", 5.5" or 7.5" barrel. Chambered for .38 WCF, .357 Magnum, .44 WCF, .45 LC or .45 LC with extra .45 ACP cylinder. Note: Add $40 to NIB price for charcoal blue finish; $30 for extra .45 ACP cylinder; $50 for stainless steel.

NIB	Exc.	V.G.	Good	Fair	Poor
450	350	300	280	180	80

Sheriff's Model No Ejector

Fitted with 3" barrel. Chambered in .44 WCF or .45 LC. Built on an Old Model frame.

NIB	Exc.	V.G.	Good	Fair	Poor
450	350	300	280	180	80

New Sheriff's Model w/ejector

This variation fitted with 3.5" barrel with ejector. Available in .357 Magnum, .44 WCF, .44 Special and .45 LC. Note: Add $35 for checkered walnut grips.

NIB	Exc.	V.G.	Good	Fair	Poor
500	400	330	280	180	80

Wyatt Earp Buntline

Limited edition model fitted with 10" barrel. Chambered for .45 LC cartridge. Model P frame. Silver shield inlaid in grip.

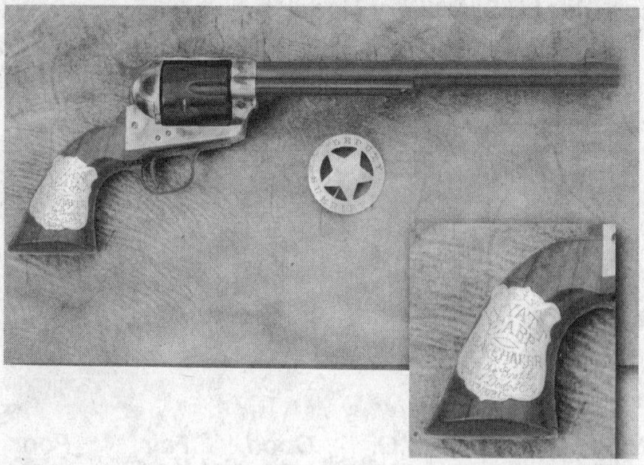

NIB	Exc.	V.G.	Good	Fair	Poor
780	600	500	430	300	130

New Thunderer

Frame based on Old Model fitted with bird's-head grip. Choice of plain or checkered walnut grips. Originally offered in 3.5" or 4.75" barrel lengths; in 1997 5.5" barrels were offered. Chambered for .357 Magnum, .44 WCF, .44 Special or .45 LC/.45 ACP. Note: Add $35 for checkered grips.

NIB	Exc.	V.G.	Good	Fair	Poor
580	450	330	280	180	80

Thunderer Long Tom

Same as New Thunderer, except for barrel length of 7.5".

NIB	Exc.	V.G.	Good	Fair	Poor
550	430	350	280	180	80

Thunderstorm

Single-action revolver in blue or stainless finish, with checkered wood grips. Chambered in .357 Magnum or .45 Colt, with 3.5" or 4.75" barrel. Wide target sights with action smoothed for competition. Note: Add $100 for stainless finish.

NIB	Exc.	V.G.	Good	Fair	Poor
880	780	700	500	400	300

Lightning

Similar to Thunderer, with a smaller grip frame. Chambered for .38 Special cartridge or .22 LR. Fitted with 3.5", 4.75" or 5.5" barrel. Finish is blue, with case-hardened frame.

NIB	Exc.	V.G.	Good	Fair	Poor
480	380	320	250	150	70

Lightning .32s

Features two cylinders chambered for .32-20 and .32 H&R cartridges. Choice of 3.5", 4.75" or 5.5" barrel. Introduced in 2004.

NIB	Exc.	V.G.	Good	Fair	Poor
550	400	350	280	180	80

New Model P

Offered in Old Model or Pre-War styles. Choice of 4.75", 5.5" or 7.5" barrel. Chambered for .32 WCF, .38 WCF, .44 WCF, .44 Special or .45 LC.

NIB	Exc.	V.G.	Good	Fair	Poor
480	400	330	280	180	80

Stainless Frontier Model P

Model P in stainless steel. Chambered for .357 Magnum or .45 LC cartridge. Barrels are 4.75", 5.5" or 7.5". Introduced in 2004.

NIB	Exc.	V.G.	Good	Fair	Poor
550	450	400	300	200	100

A.P. Casey Model P U.S. Cavalry

Fitted with a 7.5" barrel. Chambered for .45 LC. Revolver has U.S. markings (APC) on an Old Model frame.

NIB	Exc.	V.G.	Good	Fair	Poor
550	380	330	250	150	80

Rinaldo A. Carr Model P U.S. Artillery

Model P built on an Old Model frame. Chambered for .45 LC. Fitted with 5.5" barrel. U.S. markings (RAC).

NIB	Exc.	V.G.	Good	Fair	Poor
550	430	380	280	180	100

Evil Roy Model

Features a Model P frame, with wide square-notch rear sight and wide-width front sight. Slim grips checkered or smooth. Tuned action with lightened trigger. Chambered for .357 Magnum, .45 LC or .44-40 cartridge. Barrel lengths 4.75" or 5.5". Introduced in 2004.

NIB	Exc.	V.G.	Good	Fair	Poor
630	550	480	380	250	130

Model P Jr.

Similar to Model P, but sized 20 percent smaller. Chambered for .38 Special cartridge. Fitted with 3.5" or 4.75" barrel. Blue, with case-hardened frame.

NIB	Exc.	V.G.	Good	Fair	Poor
480	400	330	250	150	80

Model P Jr. .32s

Introduced in 2004. Features two cylinders chambered for .32-20 and .32 H&R cartridges. Choice of 3.5", 4.75" or 5.5" barrel.

NIB	Exc.	V.G.	Good	Fair	Poor
550	400	350	250	150	80

Cimarron 1880 Frontier Flat Top

Introduced in 1998. Target version of Colt Single-Action Army. Rear sight adjustable for windage and front adjustable for elevation. Offered with choice of 4.75", 5.5" or 7.5" barrel. Chambered for .45 LC, .45 Schofield, .44 WCF and .357 Magnum. Choice of Model P frame or Pre-War frame.

NIB	Exc.	V.G.	Good	Fair	Poor
550	450	330	230	150	100

Cimarron Bisley

Exact copy of Colt Bisley, with case-hardened frame. Choice of 4.75", 5.5" or 7.5" barrels. Calibers from .45 LC, .45 Schofield, .44 WCF to .357 Magnum. Introduced in 1998.

NIB	Exc.	V.G.	Good	Fair	Poor
550	450	330	230	150	100

Cimarron Bisley Flat Top

Offered in same barrel lengths and calibers as standard Bisley, with the addition of a windage adjustable rear sight and elevation adjustable front sight. Introduced in 1998.

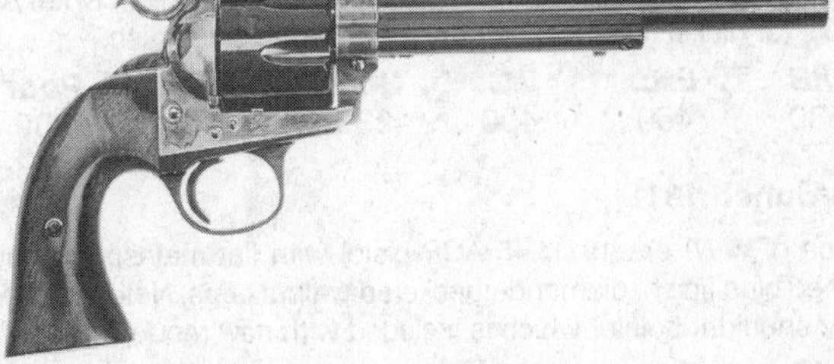

NIB	Exc.	V.G.	Good	Fair	Poor
550	450	330	230	150	100

El Pistolero

Budget-priced revolver introduced in 1997. Features a brass backstrap and triggerguard, with plain walnut grips. Offered in 4.75", 5.5" and 7.5" barrel lengths. Chambered for .45 LC or .357 Magnum.

NIB	Exc.	V.G.	Good	Fair	Poor
350	250	200	130	80	50

Doc Holliday Thunderer

Nickel-plated SAA in .45 LC. Has a 3.5" barrel and Cimarron Tru Ivory grips. Comes with a matching numbered dagger and a shoulder holster designed to carry both items.

NIB	Exc.	V.G.	Good	Fair	Poor
1300	1000	800	650	450	300

Rooster Shooter SAA

Replica of SAA used by John Wayne in many movies. Chambered in .357 Magnum, .44-40 or .45 LC. Antique gray finish and artificial ivory grips. Introduced in 2010.

NIB	Exc.	V.G.	Good	Fair	Poor
800	700	530	400	300	250

Man With No Name Conversion

Replica of 1851 Navy Cartridge Conversion used by Clint Eastwood in several "spaghetti westerns". In .38 Colt or .38 Special, 7.5" barrel, cased colored finish. A special edition with rattlesnake inlay on grip worth $150 premium.

NIB	Exc.	V.G.	Good	Fair	Poor
600	530	450	390	300	200

SMITH & WESSON COPIES

Model 3 Schofield

Based on original model of 1875 designed by Army Ordnance officer Col. George Schofield of the 10th Cavalry. Top-break action, with rapid ejection system. Original was chambered for proprietary .45 Schofield cartridge. This new model offered in .38 Special, 44-40 or .45 Colt. The .45 Colt models will also fire .45 Schofield ammo. Barrel lengths are: 7" cavalry length in all calibers, 5" in .38 or .45; 3.5" in .45 Colt only.

NIB	Exc.	V.G.	Good	Fair	Poor
1000	800	600	500	400	250

Model No. 3 Russian

Copy of the S&W 3rd Model Russian Model, 6 ½" barrel, .44 Russian or .45 Colt.

NIB	Exc.	V.G.	Good	Fair	Poor
1000	800	600	500	400	250

Model No. 3 American

Copy of the S&W American model, announced in 2020. Values anticipated to be similar to the Schofield and Russian Models

OTHER CARTRIDGE HANDGUNS

Model 1911A1

Manufactured by Chiappa. Standard full-size replica of Colt .45 ACP Government Model in blue, polished blue or nickel finish. Note: Add 40 percent for nickel finish; 30 percent for polished blue finish.

NIB	Exc.	V.G.	Good	Fair	Poor
530	450	400	330	250	200

Wild Bunch 1911

Replica of WWI era 1911 .45 ACP pistol with flat mainspring housing, polished blue finish, diamond-checkered walnut grips. Note: Add $100 for tanker shoulder holster which is included with new model.

NIB	Exc.	V.G.	Good	Fair	Poor
650	600	500	400	350	300

Titan Derringer

An over/under, two-shot derringer. Chambered in 9mm or .45 Colt/.410 shotshell. Made by Cobra Enterprises.

NIB	Exc.	V.G.	Good	Fair	Poor
350	300	250	200	150	100

Diablo Derringer

Chambered in .22 LR, .22 WMR, .32 H&R Magnum or .38 Special.

NIB	Exc.	V.G.	Good	Fair	Poor
200	180	150	130	100	80

LONG GUNS

RIFLES

Model 1865 Spencer

Chambered for .56-50 centerfire cartridge.

NIB	Exc.	V.G.	Good	Fair	Poor
1350	980	780	650	380	250

Henry Civil War Model

Offered in .44 WCF or .45 LC, with 24.25" barrel. Note: Add $80 for charcoal blue or white finish.

NIB	Exc.	V.G.	Good	Fair	Poor
1400	1200	1000	630	350	200

Henry Civilian Model

Same as above, without military markings.

NIB	Exc.	V.G.	Good	Fair	Poor
1200	930	750	630	350	200

Model 1866 Yellowboy Carbine

Reproduction of Winchester Model 1866. Fitted with 19" barrel. Chambered for .38 Special, .44 WCF or .45 LC. Note: Add $20 for charcoal blue.

NIB	Exc.	V.G.	Good	Fair	Poor
1000	850	600	530	300	150

Model 1866 Yellowboy Rifle

Same as above, fitted with a 24.25" barrel. Note: Add $40 for charcoal blue.

NIB	Exc.	V.G.	Good	Fair	Poor
1100	900	600	530	300	150

Model 1866 Yellowboy Trapper

As above, with 16" barrel.

NIB	Exc.	V.G.	Good	Fair	Poor
950	730	600	530	300	150

Model 1873 Winchester Rifle

Lever-action rifle offered in .357 Magnum, .44 WCF or .45 LC. Fitted with a 24.25" barrel. Note: Add $40 for charcoal blue; $140 for pistol grip option.

NIB	Exc.	V.G.	Good	Fair	Poor
1150	930	750	680	400	200

Model 1873 Long Range Rifle

Similar to Model 1873, but fitted with a 30" barrel. Note: Add $140 for pistol grip option; $1,250 for 1 of 1000 engraving option.

NIB	Exc.	V.G.	Good	Fair	Poor
1180	950	780	680	400	200

Model 1873 Carbine

Same as standard Model 1873, but fitted with a 19" barrel. Note: Add $40 for charcoal blue.

NIB	Exc.	V.G.	Good	Fair	Poor
1150	930	750	680	400	200

Model 1873 Short Rifle

Fitted with a 20" barrel. Production ceased in 1998. Note: Add $40 for charcoal blue.

NIB	Exc.	V.G.	Good	Fair	Poor
1150	930	750	680	400	200

Model 1873 Trapper

As above, with 16" barrel.

NIB	Exc.	V.G.	Good	Fair	Poor
1150	930	750	680	400	200

Model 1873 Deluxe Sporting Rifle

Fitted with 24" barrel, checkered walnut stock and pistol grip.

NIB	Exc.	V.G.	Good	Fair	Poor
1220	930	850	730	400	200

Model 1873 Evil Roy Rifle

Chambered for .357 or .45 Colt cartridge. Fitted with 20" barrel.

NIB	Exc.	V.G.	Good	Fair	Poor
1450	1200	950	700	400	200

Model 1873 Larry Crow Signature Series Rifle

Chambered for .357 Magnum or .45 Colt cartridge. Fitted with 20" barrel.

NIB	Exc.	V.G.	Good	Fair	Poor
1550	1300	1050	800	400	200

Model 1892 Solid Frame Rifle

Offered with 20" or 24" octagon barrels. Chambered for .357 Magnum, .44WCF or .45 Colt cartridges.

NIB	Exc.	V.G.	Good	Fair	Poor
850	680	580	450	300	150

Model 1892 Takedown Rifle

As above, with take-down feature.

NIB	Exc.	V.G.	Good	Fair	Poor
980	780	680	530	380	200

1894 Rifle

Based on the Winchester 1894 lever action rifle, 20" or 26" barrel in .38-55 or .30-30.

NIB	Exc.	V.G.	Good	Fair	Poor
1200	980	850	750	—	—

Model 1886

Replica of Winchester 1886. Caliber .45-70 Government.

NIB	Exc.	V.G.	Good	Fair	Poor
1400	1250	900	750	400	250

Billy Dixon Model 1874 Sharps

Reproduction of Model 1874 Sharps rifle. Chambered for .45-70 cartridge. Fitted with 32" tapered octagon barrel. Stock is hand-checkered, with oil-finish walnut. Double-set triggers standard.

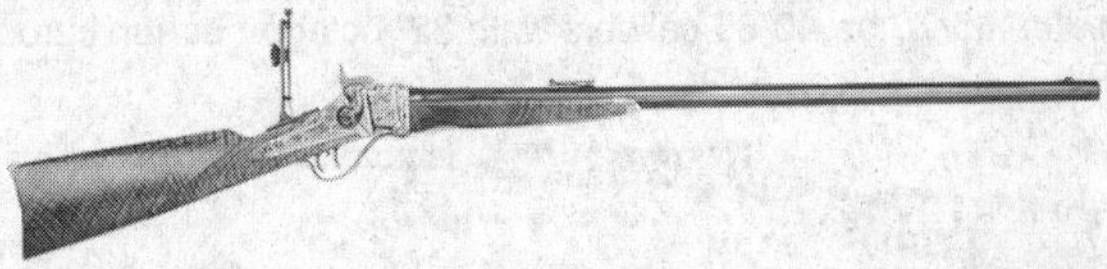

NIB	Exc.	V.G.	Good	Fair	Poor
1650	1230	1100	700	500	250

Remington Rolling Block

Remington reproduction was introduced to Cimarron in 1997. Represents Rolling Block Sporting rifle, with 30" tapered octagon barrel. Chambered for .45-70 cartridge. Hand-checkered satin-finished walnut stock.

NIB	Exc.	V.G.	Good	Fair	Poor
1300	1000	900	550	300	180

Adobe Walls Rolling Block

Chambered for .45-70 cartridge. Fitted with 30" octagon barrel. Hand-checkered walnut stock, with hand finishing. Case colored receiver and German silver nose cap. Weight about 10- to 13 lbs. Introduced in 2004.

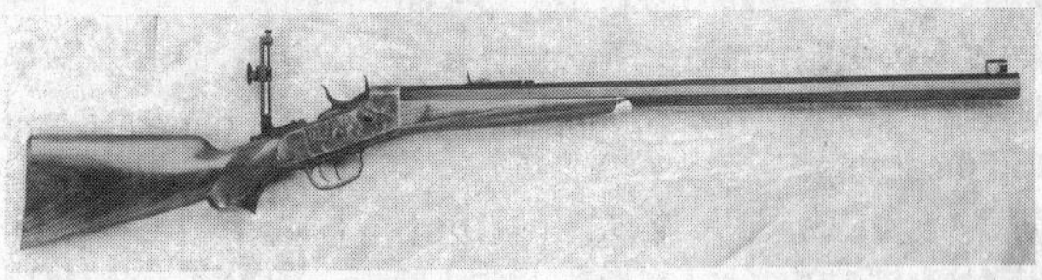

NIB	Exc.	V.G.	Good	Fair	Poor
1430	1050	950	600	350	230

Model 1885 High Wall

Reproduction of Winchester Model 1885. Chambered for .45-70, .45-90, .45-120, .40-65, .348 Win., .30-40 Krag or .38-55 cartridges. Fitted with 30" barrel. Walnut stock and case colored receiver.

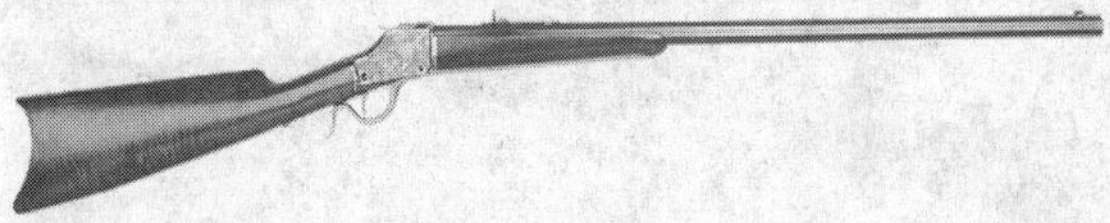

NIB	Exc.	V.G.	Good	Fair	Poor
1000	800	650	500	300	130

Model 1885 Deluxe High Wall

As above, with checkered walnut stock and pistol grip.

NIB	Exc.	V.G.	Good	Fair	Poor
1180	880	700	550	300	130

Model 1885 Low Wall

Introduced in 2004. chambered for .22 LR, .22 Hornet, .30-30, .32-20, .38-40, .357 Magnum, .44-40 and .44 Magnum cartridges. Hand checkered walnut stock, with pistol grip. Octagon barrel 30" long. Single-/double-set trigger.

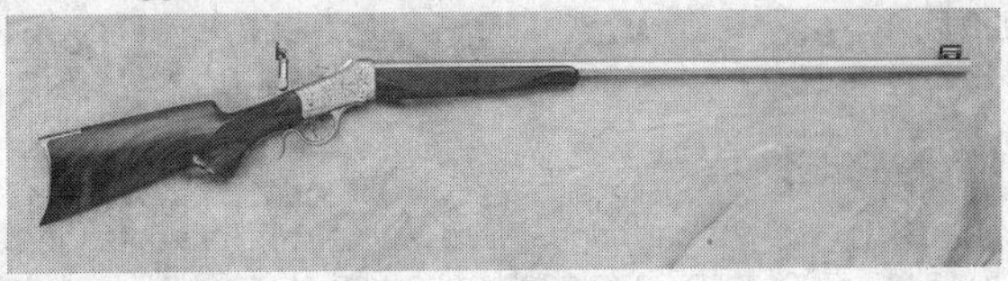

NIB	Exc.	V.G.	Good	Fair	Poor
1180	850	700	550	300	130

Texas Ranger Carbine

Copy of Sharps Model 1859 Military Carbine. Round barrel 22" long. Receiver case colored. Stock American black walnut. Chambered for .45-70 cartridge. Marked "T*S" on barrel. Introduced in 2004.

NIB	Exc.	V.G.	Good	Fair	Poor
1200	900	730	600	350	150

Sharps Silhouette

Offered in .45-70 or .40-65 calibers, with 32" octagon barrel. Introduced in 1998.

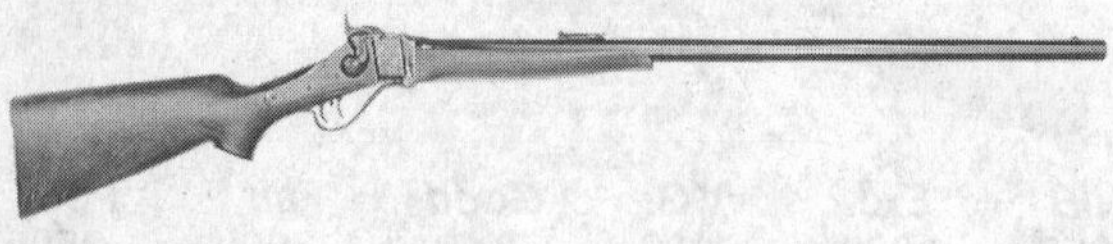

NIB	Exc.	V.G.	Good	Fair	Poor
1100	850	700	600	350	150

Quigley Sharps Sporting Rifle

Chambered for .45-70 or .45-120 caliber. Fitted with heavy 34" octagon barrel. Introduced in 1998.

NIB	Exc.	V.G.	Good	Fair	Poor
1730	1350	1180	700	450	280

Sharp's No. 1 Sporting Rifle

Plain walnut stock with pistol grip. Fitted with a 32" barrel. Chambered for .45-70 cartridge.

NIB	Exc.	V.G.	Good	Fair	Poor
1350	1050	900	500	300	150

Pride of the Plains Model

Based on Sharps Model 1874 Sporting Rifle. Chambered for .45-70 cartridge. Features a 32" octagon barrel, hand-checkered walnut stock with pistol grip, coin nickel receiver, Creedmore tang sight and target front sight with inserts. Introduced in 2004.

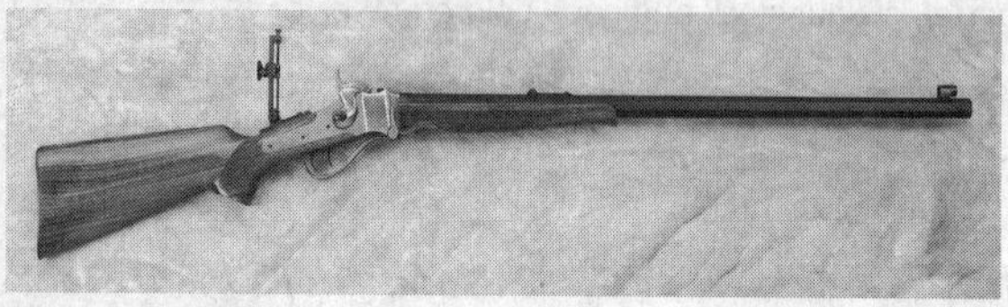

NIB	Exc.	V.G.	Good	Fair	Poor
1620	1200	930	500	300	150

Professional Hunter Model

Basic Sharps Model 1874. Chambered for .45-70 cartridge. Fitted with a 32" barrel, case colored receiver, walnut stock with shotgun butt and double-set triggers. Introduced in 2004.

NIB	Exc.	V.G.	Good	Fair	Poor
1160	850	730	500	300	150

Big Fifty Model

Chambered for .50-90 cartridge. Fitted with a 34" half-octagon barrel. Fancy walnut stock with hand checkering and pistol grip. Case colored receiver, German silver nose cap and Hartford-style Soule Creedmore sights, with spirit level and globe front sight. Weight about 11 lbs. Introduced in 2004.

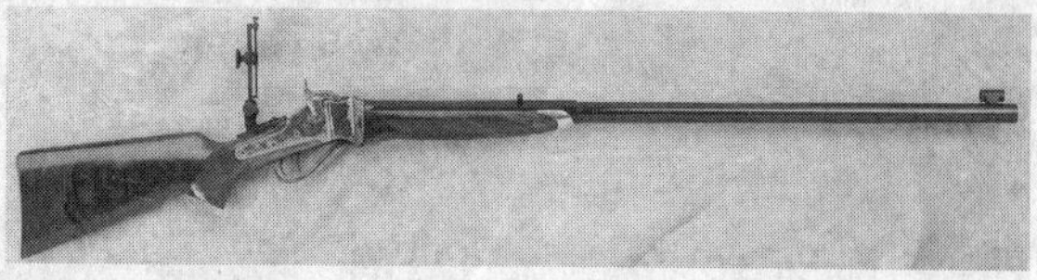

NIB	Exc.	V.G.	Good	Fair	Poor
1890	1400	1150	700	450	280

Springfield Trapdoor Carbine

Based on the famous Springfield design. Chambered for .45-70.

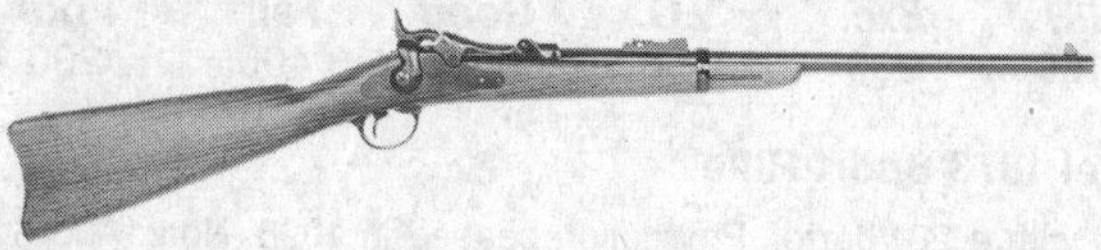

NIB	Exc.	V.G.	Good	Fair	Poor
1250	1000	800	500	300	150

Springfield Trapdoor Officer's Model

Officer's version of Springfield Trapdoor model. Chambered for .45-70.

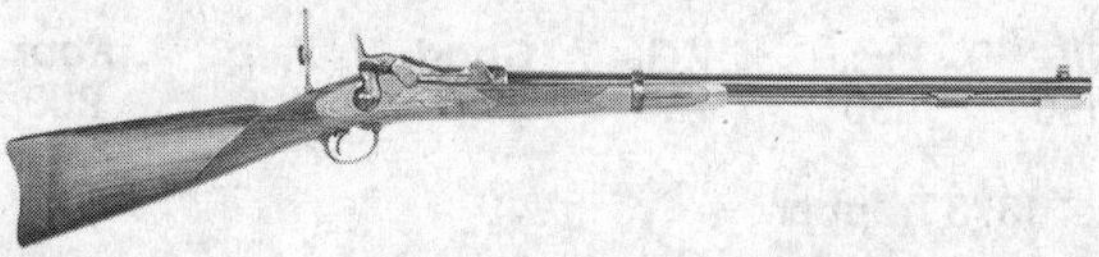

NIB	Exc.	V.G.	Good	Fair	Poor
1150	900	780	500	280	150

U.S. Shooting Team Creedmoor Sharps

Chambered in .45-70, with 34" round barrel, hand-checkered European walnut stock with hand-rubbed oil-finish and color case-hardened frame. Sales of this model (a percentage) was used to win the first organized shooting event in the United States, will be donated by Cimarron to the USA Shooting Team in support of their efforts in international shooting sports. Made in Italy by Chiappa and imported by Cimarron.

NIB	Exc.	V.G.	Good	Fair	Poor
1400	1150	900	700	400	200

SHOTGUNS

1878 Coach Gun

Side-by-side double-barrel 12-gauge, with hammers, double triggers, 22" or 26" barrels. Standard or polished blue "U.S.A." finish. Note: Add $100 for U.S.A. finish.

NIB	Exc.	V.G.	Good	Fair	Poor
500	430	380	300	250	200

1881 Coach Gun

Side-by-side double-barrel in 12- or 20-gauge, with 22", 26", 28" or 30" barrels. Hammerless design. Interchangeable choke tubes. Walnut stock with straight-/pistol grip.

NIB	Exc.	V.G.	Good	Fair	Poor
600	500	400	330	280	230

Model 1887 Shotgun

Lever-action limited edition replica of Model 1887 Winchester 12-gauge, with 5-shot magazine, 20", 22", 24" or 28" barrel. Color case-hardened frame.

NIB	Exc.	V.G.	Good	Fair	Poor
1150	980	750	600	400	250

Model 1897 Shotgun

Replica of Winchester 12-gauge pump-action model. Exposed hammer, semi-pistol grip walnut stock, choke tubes.

NIB	Exc.	V.G.	Good	Fair	Poor
500	400	350	300	200	150

MUZZLELOADERS

Santa Fe Hawken .50 cal, 30" Octagon Barrel

Original produced from the early 1800s through the 1870s, the Hawken plains rifle was the best known of the breed. Cimarron .50 caliber Santa Fe Hawken wears a color casehardened lock and hammer, fancy maple stock, a custom, shallow groove, fast 1-in-24-inch twist rifling, and a 30-inch, browned octagon, Sharps-style barrel with a buckhorn rear and a German silver blade front sight. No. SH801.

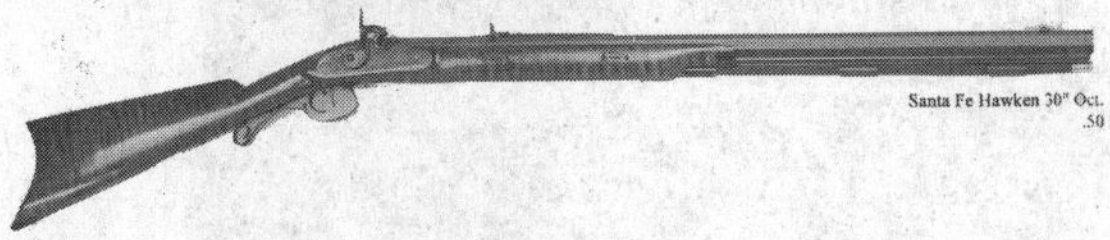

NIB	Exc.	V.G.	Good	Fair	Poor
1450	1230	1050	—	—	—

CITADEL
Reno, NV

Trademark of Legacy Sports International. Imported 1911-style platform. Models include full-size Government-style frame, Commander frame and Officer-style frame. Values are consistent across frame sizes. Introduced 2009.

M-1911 Government

1911-style platform with 5-in. barrel, chambered in 9mm, .38 Super or .45 ACP. Various finishes including matte black, nickel, polished nickel, and Cerakote. Introduced 2019.

NIB	Exc.	V.G.	Good	Fair	Poor
600	520	450	370	330	280

CLAPP, HOFFMAN & CO. CLAPP, GATES & CO. RIFLES
Alamance, North Carolina

Maker of Confederate Civil War rifles, 1862 - 1864. Overall length: Types I, II, & III 51.25" to 52", Type IV varies between 46.5" and 51"; barrel length: Types I, II, & III 35.25" to 36", Type IV varies between 31.25" and 35.875"; caliber: Types I, II, & III .50, Type IV .577; markings: none. Despite the absence of makers marks, the Clapp, Gates & Co. products are readily distinguished by their part-round, part-octagonal (octagonal section on Types I to III, about 4" long, 4.75" to 5.5" on Type IV rifles) barrels having only a slightly raised bolster projecting from the upper right quarter. This small bolster accommodates the boxlock that distinguished the first 100 rifles produced. This gave way to a standard percussion lock on subsequent production, which required that the hammer bend sharply to the left to strike the cone. Type I and Type II rifles were adapted to a "footprint" saber bayonet lug on the right side of the barrel; Types III and IV also had a saber bayonet lug on the right side of the barrel but of the standard pattern. Types III and IV are distinguished by their caliber, the former being .50, the latter .577. Prices reflect Type II through IV production; Type I (while extant) has never been offered for sale and would presumably bring a significantly higher premium.

Confederate Rifle (Antique)

Very rare; values are speculative.

Exc.	Fine	V.G.	Good	Fair	Poor
39500	19500	11700	3900	2000	1000

CLARK, F. H.
Memphis, Tennessee

Pocket Pistol (Antique)

A .41-caliber single-shot percussion pistol, with 3.5" to 5" barrel, German silver mounts and end cap. Barrel stamped "F.H. Clark & Co./Memphis". Manufactured in 1850s and 1860s. London made R.S. Clark pocket pistols bring less.

Exc.	Fine	V.G.	Good	Fair	Poor
5350	1900	1220	550	200	140

CLARK SHERRARD
See—TUCKER SHERRARD

CLASSIC DOUBLES
Tochigi City, Japan

Importer of Japanese shotguns, formerly imported by Winchester as the Model 101 and Model 23. These models were discontinued by Winchester in 1987 and imported by Classic Doubles until 1990.

Model 201 Classic

A 12- or 20-gauge boxlock side-by-side double-barrel shotgun, with 26" ventilated rib barrels, screw-in choke tubes single-selective trigger and automatic ejectors. Blued, with checkered walnut stock and beavertail forearm.

NIB	Exc.	V.G.	Good	Fair	Poor
2400	1950	1700	1500	1250	900

Model 201 Small Bore Set

As above, with a smaller receiver and two sets of barrels. Chambered for 28-gauge and .410 bore. Barrels are 28" in length.

NIB	Exc.	V.G.	Good	Fair	Poor
4100	3500	2950	2250	1750	1250

Model 101 Classic Field Grade I

A 12- or 20-gauge over/under shotgun, with 25.5" or 28" ventilated rib barrels, screw-in choke tubes, automatic ejectors and a single-selective trigger. Engraved, blued with checkered walnut stock.

NIB	Exc.	V.G.	Good	Fair	Poor
2000	1750	1500	1250	1000	700

Classic Field Grade II

As above, in 28-gauge and .410 bore. Highly engraved, with a coin-finished receiver and deluxe walnut stock. A round knob pistol grip and fleur-de-lis checkering.

NIB	Exc.	V.G.	Good	Fair	Poor
2500	2000	1750	1500	1250	900

Classic Sporter

As above in 12-gauge only, with 28" or 30" barrels, ventilated rib and screw-in choke tubes. Frame is coin-finished, with light engraving and a matted upper surface to reduce glare. Stock is select walnut. Designed for sporting clays.

NIB	Exc.	V.G.	Good	Fair	Poor
2250	1800	1500	1250	1000	700

Waterfowl Model

As above with 30" barrels, 3" chambers, ventilated rib and screw-in choke tubes. Overall finish is a subdued matte with light engraving.

NIB	Exc.	V.G.	Good	Fair	Poor
1650	1350	1000	850	650	500

Classic Trap Over/Under

Designed for competition trap shooting, with 30" or 32" barrels, a ventilated center and top rib, automatic ejectors, screw-in choke tubes and a single trigger. Blued, with light engraving and a walnut stock in straight or Monte Carlo style.

NIB	Exc.	V.G.	Good	Fair	Poor
2250	1750	1500	1250	1000	700

Classic Trap Single

As above, with a single 32" or 34" barrel.

NIB	Exc.	V.G.	Good	Fair	Poor
2250	1800	1500	1250	1000	700

Classic Trap Combo

As above, with a single barrel and a set of over/under barrels.

NIB	Exc.	V.G.	Good	Fair	Poor
3000	2500	2000	1750	1250	1000

Classic Skeet

As above, with 27.5" barrels.

NIB	Exc.	V.G.	Good	Fair	Poor
2250	1750	1500	1250	1000	700

Classic Skeet 4 Gauge Set

As above, furnished with four sets of barrels chambered for 12-, 20-, 28-gauge, and .410 bore.

NIB	Exc.	V.G.	Good	Fair	Poor
4150	3750	3000	2500	1850	1500

CLEMENT, CHAS.

Liege, Belgium

Model 1903

A 5.5mm Glisenti caliber semi-automatic pistol. Barrel raises at muzzle to begin the loading procedure.

Courtesy James Rankin

NIB	Exc.	V.G.	Good	Fair	Poor
—	580	480	350	220	110

Model 1907

As above, in 6.35mm and 7.65mm caliber.

Courtesy Orvel Reichert

NIB	Exc.	V.G.	Good	Fair	Poor
—	480	400	320	200	100

Model 1908

Similar to Model 1907, with magazine release at the bottom of frame. Fitted with a larger grip.

Courtesy J.B. Wood

NIB	Exc.	V.G.	Good	Fair	Poor
—	580	450	300	200	120

Model 1909

Semi-automatic pistol in 6.35mm and 7.65mm calibers. Similar to Model 1908, with barrel and chamber housing in one piece.

Courtesy James Rankin

NIB	Exc.	V.G.	Good	Fair	Poor
—	580	450	300	220	100

Model 1910

Redesigned version of above, with barrel and housing all one piece. This unit is held in position by the triggerguard.

Courtesy Orvel Reichert

NIB	Exc.	V.G.	Good	Fair	Poor
—	580	480	400	350	280

Model 1912

A 6.35mm caliber semi-automatic pistol marked "Clement's Patent"; others, "Model 1912 Brevet 243839". This model is quite different from earlier Clement models.

Courtesy James Rankin

NIB	Exc.	V.G.	Good	Fair	Poor
—	420	300	250	200	100

American Model

Revolver copy of Colt Police Positive. Chambered for .38-caliber.

NIB	Exc.	V.G.	Good	Fair	Poor
—	420	300	250	150	90

CLERKE PRODUCTS

Santa Monica, California

Hi-Wall

Copy of Winchester Model 1885 High Wall rifle, with the action activated by a lever. Receiver is case colored. Chambered for almost all modern calibers. Features 26" barrel, walnut stock with a pistol grip and schnabel forend. Manufactured between 1972 and 1974.

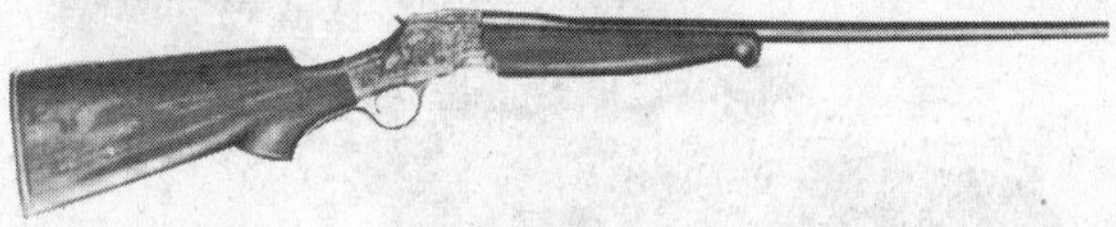

NIB	Exc.	V.G.	Good	Fair	Poor
980	850	650	420	300	200

Deluxe Hi-Wall

As above, with half-round/half-octagonal barrel, select walnut stock and recoil pad. Manufactured between 1972 and 1974.

NIB	Exc.	V.G.	Good	Fair	Poor
1100	980	750	520	400	250

CMMG, INC.

Boonville, Missouri

CMMG was established in 2002. It manufactures high-quality and affordable AR-15s, .22 LR AR-15 conversion kits and accessories. Numerous Variations exist.

Banshee 100 MK10

Caliber: 10mm. Capacity: 30-round magazine. Barrel: 8 in. Grips: AR15 A2 style. Sights: Optic-ready, Picatinny-style rail. Length: 23.9 in. overall. Weight: 5.1 lbs. unloaded. Finish: Black or various Cerakote finishes. Features: Radial Delayed Blowback operating system to significantly reduce felt recoil. M4-type upper receiver and forged 7075-T6 lower. Furniture includes an M-LOK handguard and A2-style grip. Made in the USA.

NIB	Exc.	V.G.	Good	Fair	Poor
1160	980	850	700	—	—

Banshee 200 MK10

Caliber: 10mm. Capacity: 30-round magazine. Barrel: 8 in. Grips: Magpul MOE. Sights: Optic-ready, Picatinny-style rail. Length: 24.3 in. overall, brace collapsed. Weight: 5.5 lbs. unloaded. Finish: Black or various Cerakote finishes. Features: Radial Delayed Blowback operating system to reduce felt recoil. M4-type upper receiver and forged 7075-T6 lower. Furniture includes an M-LOK handguard and CMMG Standard RipBrace with 6-position enhanced receiver extension and ambi sling plate. Available in various Cerakote colors. Made in the USA.

NIB	Exc.	V.G.	Good	Fair	Poor
1290	1000	900	750	—	—

Banshee 300 MK10

Caliber: 10mm. Capacity: 30-round magazine. Barrel: 8 in. Grips: AR15 A2 style. Sights: Optic-ready, Picatinny-style rail. Length: 23.9 in. overall.

Weight: 5.1 lbs. unloaded. Finish: Black or various Cerakote finishes. Features: Radial Delayed Blowback operating system to reduce felt recoil. M4-type upper receiver and forged 7075-T6 lower. Furniture includes an M-LOK handguard and CMMG Standard RipBrace with 6-position enhanced receiver extension and ambi sling plate. CMMG Oversized Ambi charging handle and ambi safety selector. Available in various Cerakote colors. Made in the USA.

NIB	Exc.	V.G.	Good	Fair	Poor
1250	1100	950	800	—	—

Resolute 100 Rifles and Carbines

Calibers: 5.7x28mm (Conversion), 9mm (Conversion), .350 Legend, .458 SOCOM, .22 LR, .300 Blackout, .308 Win., .40 S&W, .45 ACP, 5.56x45mm, 5.7x28mm (FN), 6.5 Grendel, 7.62x39mm, 9mm (Colt), 9mm (Glock). Capacity: 30-round Magpul PMAG (5.56). Barrel: 16.1, 16.6, or 17 in. (varies by chambering), 1:7 twist, medium taper, 4140CM, SBN (5.56). Stock: CMMG M4 with 6-position receiver extension. Sights: Flat-top rail. Weight: 6.3 lbs. Overall Length: 32.5 to 35.5 in. Features: Forged 7075-T6 AL M4-type upper, AR-15-type lower, Type III hard-coat anodize finish, CMMG single-stage Mil-Spec trigger, integrated or CMMG triggerguard, Mil-Spec charging handle, A2-style pistol grip, CMMG RML15 M-LOK free-floating handguard, M4-style buttstock, salt bath nitride barrel finish, M4 Mil-Spec receiver end plate, A2 Comp, threaded 1/2-28, standard safety selector.

NIB	Exc.	V.G.	Good	Fair	Poor
1500	1280	1050	930	—	—

Resolute 200 Rifles and Carbines

Calibers: 5.7x28mm (Conversion), 9mm (Conversion), .350 Legend, .458 SOCOM, .22 LR, .300 Blackout, .308 Win., .40 S&W, .45 ACP, 5.56x45mm, 5.7x28mm (FN), 6.5 Grendel, 7.62x39mm, 9mm (Colt), 9mm (Glock). Capacity: 30-round Magpul PMAG (5.56). Barrel: 16.1, 16.6, or 17 in. (varies by chambering), 1:7 twist, medium taper, 4140CM, SBN (5.56). Stock: CMMG Ripstock. Sights: Flat-top rail. Weight: 6.3 lbs. Overall Length: 32.5 to 35.5 in. Features: Forged 7075-T6 AL M4-type upper, AR-15-type lower, Type III hard-coat anodize finish, CMMG single-stage Mil-Spec trigger, integrated or Magpul MOE triggerguard, Mil-Spec charging handle, Magpul MOE pistol grip, CMMG RML15 M-LOK free-floating handguard, M4-style buttstock, salt bath nitride barrel finish, M4 Mil-Spec receiver end plate, CMMG SV muzzle device threaded 1/2-28, standard safety selector.

NIB	Exc.	V.G.	Good	Fair	Poor
1600	1350	1150	975	—	—

Resolute 300 Rifles and Carbines Mk4 5.56

Calibers: 5.7x28mm (Conversion), 9mm (Conversion), .350 Legend, .458 SOCOM, .22 LR, .300 Blackout, .308 Win., .40 S&W, .45 ACP, 5.56x45mm, 5.7x28mm (FN), 6.5 Grendel, 7.62x39mm, 9mm (Colt), 9mm (Glock). Capacity: 30-round Magpul PMAG (5.56). Barrel: 16.1, 16.6, or 17 in. (varies by chambering), 1:7 twist, medium taper, 4140CM, SBN (5.56). Stock: CMMG Ripstock. Sights: Flat-top rail. Weight: 6.3 lbs. Overall Length: 32.5 to 35.5 in. Features: Forged 7075-T6 AL M4-type upper, AR-15-type lower, laser-engraved "Resolute" on lower receiver. Premier Cerakote finish (10 color options), Geissele SSA two-stage trigger, integrated or Magpul MOE triggerguard, CMMG ambidextrous charging handle, Magpul MOE pistol grip, CMMG RML15 M-LOK free-floating handguard, M4-style buttstock, salt bath nitride barrel finish, M4 Mil-Spec receiver end plate, CMMG SV muzzle device threaded 1/2-28, CMMG ambidextrous safety selector.

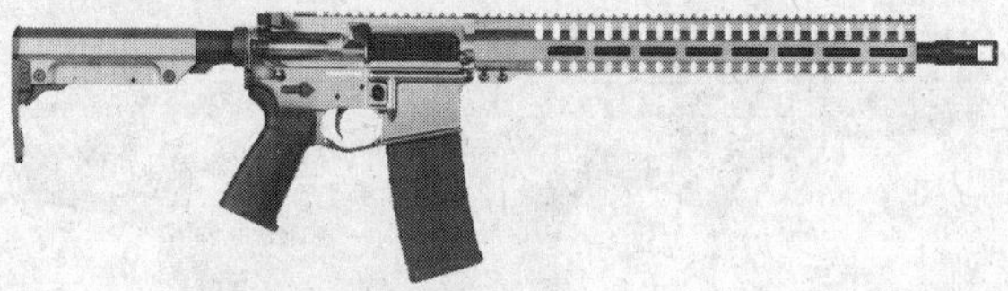

NIB	Exc.	V.G.	Good	Fair	Poor
1700	1450	1230	1000	—	—

Resolute MK4

Calibers: .22 LR, 5.56 NATO, 5.7x28mm, 6mm ARC, 6.5 Grendel, .300 Blackout, .308 Win., 7.62x39mm, .350 Legend, 9mm Luger, .40 S&W, .45 ACP. The Mk4 is the carbine-length AR-15 direct-impingement platform. The Mk3 platform (AR-10) is based on the LR-308/DPMS Gen 1 high-pattern design. Pistol-caliber-carbine designations include MkG, MkGs, Mk9, Mk17, and Mk57. The Mk47 designation is for the 7.62x39mm chambering. Weight for the 5.56 MK4 is 6.4 lbs; length is 32.5" Add $150 for 5.7x28mm, 9mm; add $175 for Mk9 9mm with Colt-style SMG magazines. SEE POLITICAL PANIC PRICING.

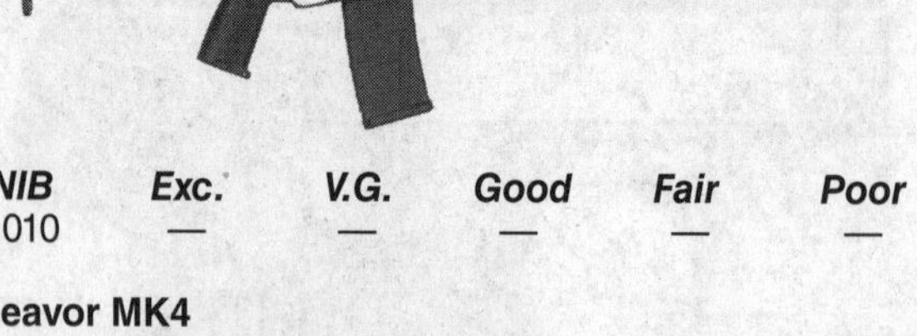

NIB	Exc.	V.G.	Good	Fair	Poor
1010	—	—	—	—	—

Endeavor MK4

Calibers: 5.56x45mm, 6.5 Creedmoor, .308 Win. Longer and heavier (18", 20", 24") stainless barrels compared to the Resolute line. Platforms: Mk3, Mk4. Lengths start at 37.8" for the 18" barrel length, weight 7 lbs. Add $600 for the 20" barrel; add $650 for 24" barrel. SEE POLITICAL PANIC PRICING.

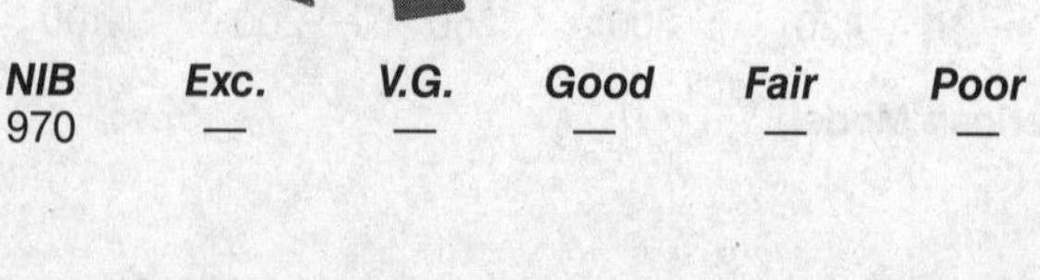

NIB	Exc.	V.G.	Good	Fair	Poor
970	—	—	—	—	—

COBRA ENTERPRISES, INC.

Salt Lake City, Utah

DERRINGERS

Standard Series

Offered chambered in .22 LR, .22 WMR, .25 ACP and .32 ACP. Over/under barrels are 2.4". Pearl or laminate wood grips. Weight about 9.5 oz. Introduced in 2002.

NIB	Exc.	V.G.	Good	Fair	Poor
250	200	160	120	100	80

Long Bore Series

Chambered for .22 WMR, .38 Special or 9mm cartridge. Fitted with a 3.5" barrel. Black synthetic, laminate oak or laminate rosewood grips. Chrome or black finish. Weight about 16 oz.

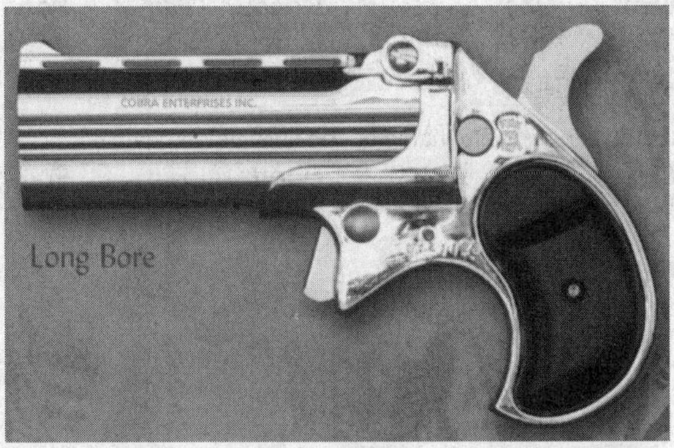

NIB	Exc.	V.G.	Good	Fair	Poor
250	200	160	120	100	80

Big Bore Series

Chambered for .22 WMR, .32 H&R Magnum and .38 Special. Barrel length 2.75". Choice of black synthetic, laminate oak or laminate rosewood grips. Chrome or black finish. Weight about 14 oz.

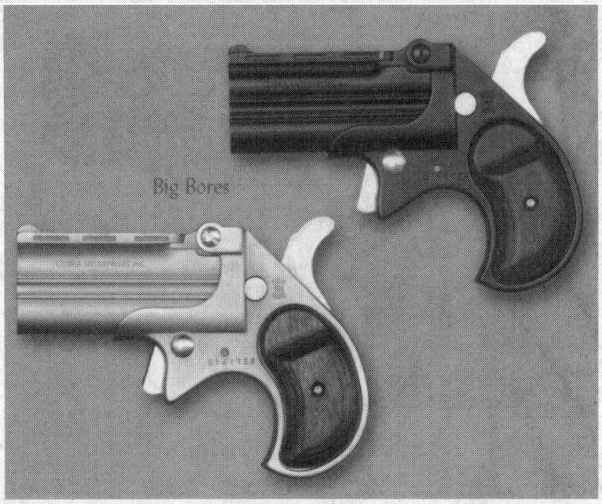

NIB	Exc.	V.G.	Good	Fair	Poor
250	200	160	120	100	80

SEMI-AUTOMATIC PISTOLS

C-32/C-380

Chambered for .32 ACP or .380 cartridges. Fitted with 2.8" barrel. Chrome or black finish. Magazine capacity 5 rounds for .380; 6 rounds for .32 ACP. Weight about 22 oz.

NIB	Exc.	V.G.	Good	Fair	Poor
180	120	80	60	40	20

C-9mm

Double-action-only pistol chambered for 9mm cartridge. Fitted with 3.3" barrel. Magazine capacity 10 rounds. Load indicator. Polymer grips. Weight about 21 oz.

NIB	Exc.	V.G.	Good	Fair	Poor
280	220	150	120	80	40

Patriot .45

Double-action-only pistol chambered for .45 ACP cartridge. Barrel length 3". Frame is black polymer. Slide is stainless steel. Magazine capacity 6 rounds. Weight about 20 oz.

NIB	Exc.	V.G.	Good	Fair	Poor
350	220	150	120	80	40

COBRAY INDUSTRIES

S.W.D., Inc.
Atlanta, Georgia

M-11 Pistol

A 9mm caliber semi-automatic pistol. Fires from the closed bolt. Made of steel stampings, with a parkerized finish. Patterned after, though a good deal smaller than, Ingram Mac 10. Note: Add $70 for stainless steel; $150 for pre-ban models.

NIB	Exc.	V.G.	Good	Fair	Poor
480	400	360	300	280	260

M-12

Same as above, but chambered for .380 ACP cartridge. Note: Add $150 for pre-ban models.

NIB	Exc.	V.G.	Good	Fair	Poor
480	400	360	300	280	260

TM-11 Carbine

As above in 9mm caliber, with 16.25" shrouded barrel and telescoping metal shoulder stock.

NIB	Exc.	V.G.	Good	Fair	Poor
—	450	350	220	150	100

TM-12 Carbine

As above, but chambered for .380 ACP cartridge.

NIB	Exc.	V.G.	Good	Fair	Poor
—	450	350	220	150	100

Terminator Shotgun

Single-shot 12- or 20-gauge shotgun that fires from an open bolt position. The cocked bolt is released to slam home on the shell when trigger is pulled. The 18" barrel is cylinder bored. There is a telescoping wire stock and finish is Parkerized. We have seen many of these advertised at sky-high prices, but junk is junk.

NIB	Exc.	V.G.	Good	Fair	Poor
—	180	120	80	60	40

COCHRAN TURRET

C. B. Allen
Springfield, Massachusetts

Underhammer Turret Rifle (Antique)

A .36- or .40-caliber percussion radial cylinder rifle, with 31" or 32" octagonal barrels and walnut stocks. Barrel marked "Cochrans/Many/Chambered/&/Non Recoil/Rifle" and top strap "C.B. Allen / Springfield". These rifles were produced in variations listed. Manufactured during late 1830s and 1840s.

1st Type (Antique)

Fitted with a circular top strap secured by two screws. Serial numbered from 1 to approximately 30.

Exc.	Fine	V.G.	Good	Fair	Poor
—	18000	12250	6500	2150	1500

2nd Type (Antique)

Fitted with a rectangular hinged top strap, the locking catch of which serves as the rear sight. Serial numbered from approximately 31 to 155.

Exc.	Fine	V.G.	Good	Fair	Poor
29500	15000	10050	5100	1800	1260

3rd Type (Antique)

As above, with a smaller hammer and plain triggerguard.

Exc.	Fine	V.G.	Good	Fair	Poor
18000	15000	10050	5100	1800	1260

Pistol (Antique)

Action similar to above with 4" to 7" barrels.

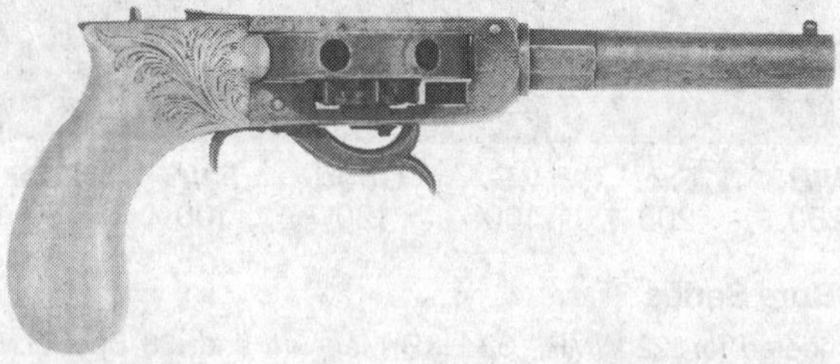

Exc.	Fine	V.G.	Good	Fair	Poor
26500	21000	15350	9700	3000	2100

CODY, MICHAEL & SONS

Nashville, Tennessee

Received a contract with the State of Tennessee for "Mississippi" rifles with brass patchboxes in late 1861. Barrel length 36"; caliber .54. Cody often used reworked Model 1817 rifle barrels and sporting pattern single screw lockplates. Rifles are unmarked except for large engraved serial number on top of breech plug tang.

Confederate Model 1841 Type Rifle (Antique)

Very rare; values are speculative.

Exc.	Fine	V.G.	Good	Fair	Poor
29500	13000	7570	2150	780	540

COFER, T. W.
Portsmouth, Virginia

Cofer Navy Revolver (Antique)

A .36-caliber spur trigger percussion revolver, with 7.5" octagonal barrel and 6-shot cylinder. Top strap marked "T.W. Cofer's/Patent" and barrel "Portsmouth, Va." Manufactured in limited quantities during the Civil War. Sources report there are only about 16 known surviving Cofer revolvers in at least two variations. Recent sales of three different specimens appearing to be in very good to fine condition are reported sold in the $70,000 to $130,000 each range. Estimates have been as high as $350,000. Listed values are speculative.

Exc.	Fine	V.G.	Good	Fair	Poor
—	13000	70000	—	—	—

COGSWELL
London, England

Cogswell Pepperbox Pistol (Antique)

A .47-caliber 6-shot percussion pepperbox, with case-hardened barrels, German silver frame and walnut grips. Normally marked "B. Cogswell, 224 Strand, London" and "Improved Revolving Pistol". Cogswell also made single and double barrel percussion pistols and Tranter/Adams style double action percussion pistols.

Exc.	Fine	V.G.	Good	Fair	Poor
4400	1950	1460	980	550	380

COLTON MANUFACTURING CO.
Toledo, Ohio

Colton Manufacturing Co. provided Sears with its first American-made hammerless house brand double. Sears advertised their sidelock hammerless gun as "the equal of any gun made, regardless of price" in their 1900 Fall catalog No. 110. There were four models: three sideplated boxlock-types and a unique unitized coil spring driven striker assembly version. All these, especially the latter, were designed to be mass produced. Many of the distinctive sidelock-within-a-sideplated model were produced but they are seldom seen today either because they were used-up or did not hold up well and were scrapped. Sears replaced Colton with the more traditional design Fryberg gun in 1902. Values depend on grade. There appears to be at least two levels of quality and condition ranging from $300 to $1,500. Colton-marked guns are scarce.

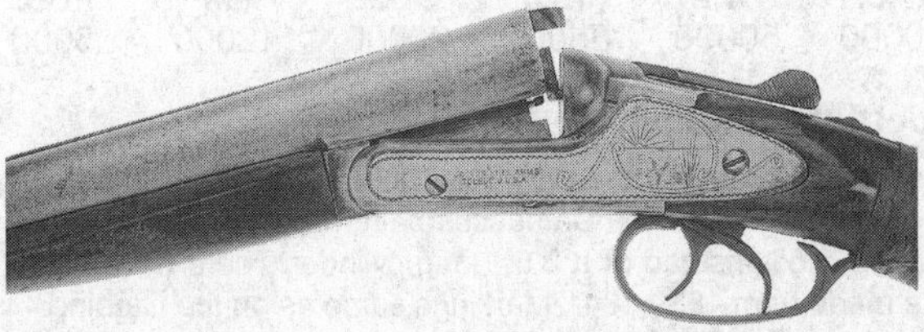

Courtesy Nick Niles, Paul Goodwin photo

COLT'S PATENT FIRE ARMS MANUFACTURING COMPANY
Hartford, Connecticut

Any factory or period engraved antique Colt, or a historic piece with solid documentation, will increase the value substantially. Such guns are valued more as a work of art or a historic artifact. Any early pre-1849 antique or military issued antique Colt in Antique Excellent condition with 80% or more original finish is rare. As original finish approaches 98%, the Antique Excellent value may increase dramatically. High condition percussion Colts in their original wood cases with original accessories will add substantially to the value. Later-added improvised period or modern-made cases and repro accessories add only modestly to the value.

COLT PATERSON MODELS

(Antique)

Colt Patersons are widely considered to be the first successful repeating handgun design, even though they were produced in limited numbers for a brief period of time and were initially a commercial failure.They take their nickname from the manufacturing location, Paterson NJ, and all are single action revolvers with folding triggers.Surviving examples are rare, highly desireable, and seldom offered for sale. Values are speculative.

Pocket or Baby Paterson Model No. 1 (Antique)

Paterson was the first production revolver manufactured by Colt. First made in 1837. Model 1 or Pocket Model is most diminutive of Paterson line. Revolver is serial numbered in its own range, #1 through #500. Numbers are not visible without dismantling revolver. Barrel lengths run from 1.75" to 4.75". Standard model has no attached loading lever. Chambering is .28-caliber percussion and holds 5-shots. Finish is all blued. Grips are varnished walnut. It has a roll-engraved cylinder scene and barrel stamped "Patent Arms Mfg. Co. Paterson N.J. Colt's Pt." Cased examples in Very Good or better condition can bring upwards of $200,000. In 2019 an Excellent+ Baby Paterson, cased with accessories, sold at Rock Island Auction for $644,000

Exc.	Fine	V.G.	Good	Fair	Poor
120000	70000	50000	35000	15000	10500

Belt Model Paterson No. 2 (Antique)

Belt Model Paterson is a larger revolver, with a straight-grip and octagonal barrel that is 2.5" to 5.5" in length. Chambered for .31-caliber percussion and holds 5-shots. Finish all blued, with varnished walnut grips and no attached loading lever. It has a roll-engraved cylinder scene and barrel stamped "Patent Arms Mfg. Co. Paterson N.J. Colt's Pt." Serial number range is #1-#850 and shared with #3 Belt Model. Made from 1837-1840. An excellent cased example was auctioned by Rock Island Auction in 2007 for $414,000.

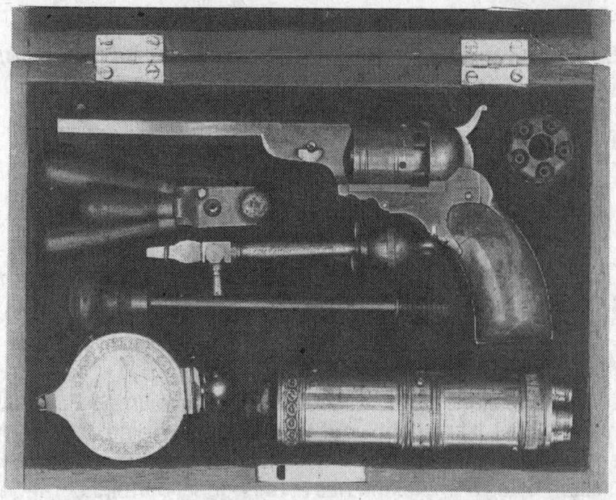

Courtesy Buffalo Bill Historical Center, Cody, Wyoming

Exc.	Fine	V.G.	Good	Fair	Poor
140000	70000	47500	25000	12000	8400

Belt Model Paterson No. 3 (Antique)

This revolver is quite similar to Model #2, except grips are curved outward at the bottom to form a more hand-filling configuration. They are serial numbered in the same #1-#850 range. Some attached loading levers have been noted on this model, but they are extremely rare and would add approximately 35 percent to value.

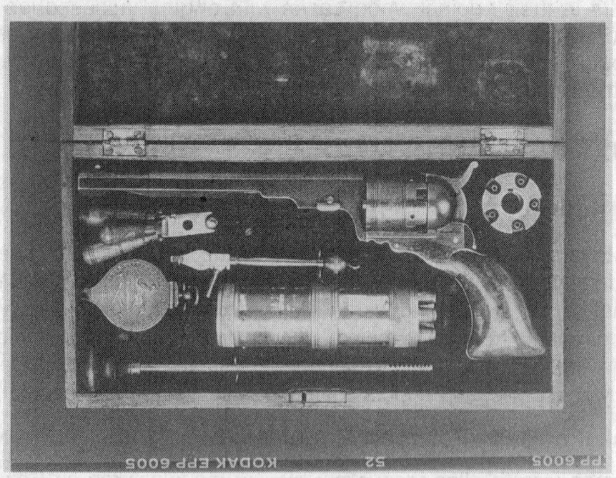

Exc.	Fine	V.G.	Good	Fair	Poor
155000	70000	57500	45000	20000	14000

Ehlers Model Pocket Paterson (Antique)

John Ehlers was a major stockholder and treasurer of Patent Arms Mfg. Co. when it went bankrupt. He seized the assets and inventory. These revolvers were Pocket Model Patersons that were not finished at the time. Ehlers had them finished and marketed them. They had an attached loading lever and abbreviation "Mfg Co." was deleted from barrel stamping. There were 500 revolvers involved in Ehlers variation totally. They were produced from 1840-1843.

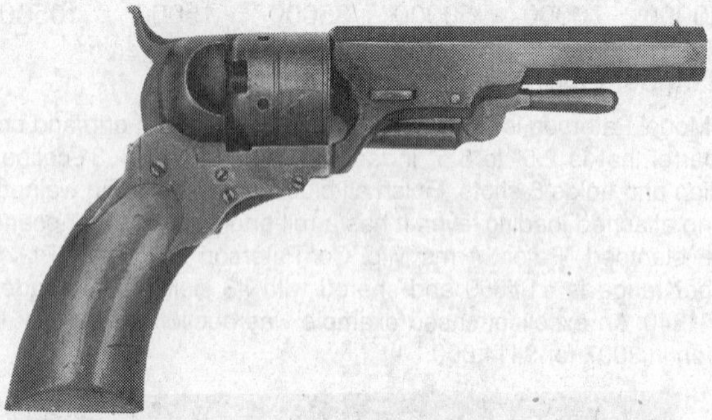

Exc.	Fine	V.G.	Good	Fair	Poor
120000	60000	50000	40000	15000	10500

Ehlers Belt Model Paterson (Antique)

Same specifications apply to this larger revolver as they do to Ehlers Pocket Model. It falls within the same 500 revolver involvement and is rare.

Exc.	Fine	V.G.	Good	Fair	Poor
120000	60000	50000	40000	12000	8400

Texas Paterson Model No. 5 (Antique)

This is the largest and most sought after of Paterson models, also known as Holster Model. It has been verified as actually seeing use by both military and civilians on the American frontier. It is chambered for .36-caliber percussion, holds 5-shots and has an octagonal barrel that ranges from 4" to 12" in length. It has been observed with and without the attached loading lever, but those with it are rare. Finish is blued, with a case colored hammer. Grips are varnished walnut. Cylinder is roll-engraved; barrel stamped "Patent Arms Mfg. Co. Paterson, N.J. Colts Pt." Most Texas Patersons are well used and have a worn appearance. One in excellent or V.G. condition would be highly prized. A verified military model would be worth a great deal more than standard, so a qualified appraisal would be essential. Serial number range is #1-#1000. Manufactured from 1838-1840. Attached loading lever brings approximately a 25 percent premium.

An 1836 Colt Paterson Revolver sold in September, 2011, for $977,500 at a Heritage Auction in Dallas, Texas. (Price includes a 15% buyer's premium.) This is believed to be a world record for the sale of a single American firearm. The very rare No. 5 Holster Model with a 9" barrel, ivory grips, attached loading lever and accessories in a box, is the finest known surviving example of Samuel Colt's first revolver. Two other Colt percussion revolvers were sold at the same auction for more than $800,000. (See Third Model Dragoon and Model 1861 Navy listings.) Such prices are extreme exceptions to the values of typical models. In 2011 an Excellent+ Texas Paterson, cased with accessories, reported as the finest known, sold at Heritage Auction for $977,500

Exc.	Fine	V.G.	Good	Fair	Poor
150000	120000	100000	80000	25000	17500

COLT REVOLVING LONG GUNS 1837-1847

First Model Ring Lever Rifle (Antique)

This was actually the first firearm manufactured by Colt; first revolver appeared a short time later. There were 200 of First Models made in 1837 and 1838. Octagonal barrel of First Model is 32" long and browned, while rest of the finish is blued. Stock is varnished walnut with a cheekpiece inlaid with Colt's trademark. Ring lever located in front of frame is pulled to rotate the 8-shot cylinder and cock the hammer. Rifle is chambered for .34-, .36-, .38-, .40- and .44-caliber percussion. Cylinder is roll-engraved and barrel is stamped "Colt's Patent/Patent Arms Mfg. Co., Paterson, N. Jersey". This model has a top strap over the cylinder. They were made both with and without an attached loading lever. Latter is worth approximately 10 percent more.

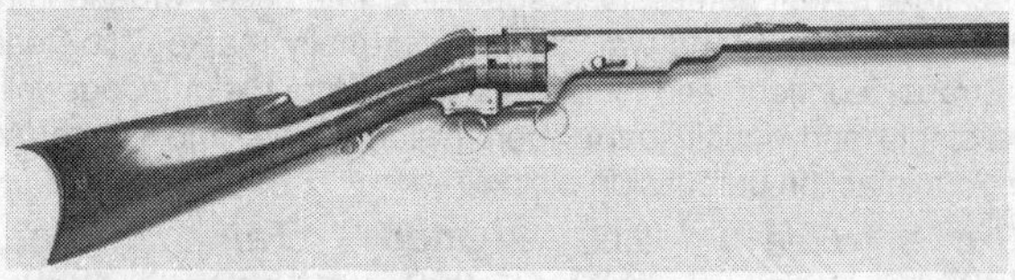

Courtesy Bonhams & Butterfields, San Francisco, California

Exc.	Fine	V.G.	Good	Fair	Poor
80000	60000	40000	25000	15000	5500

Second Model Ring Lever Rifle (Antique)

Quite similar in appearance to First Model. Its function is identical. Major difference is absence of top strap over the cylinder. It had no trademark stamped on the cheekpiece. Second Model offered with 28" and 32" octagonal barrel. Chambered for .44-caliber percussion, holding 8-shots. There were approximately 500 produced from 1838-1841. Presence of an attached cheekpiece would add approximately 10 percent to value.

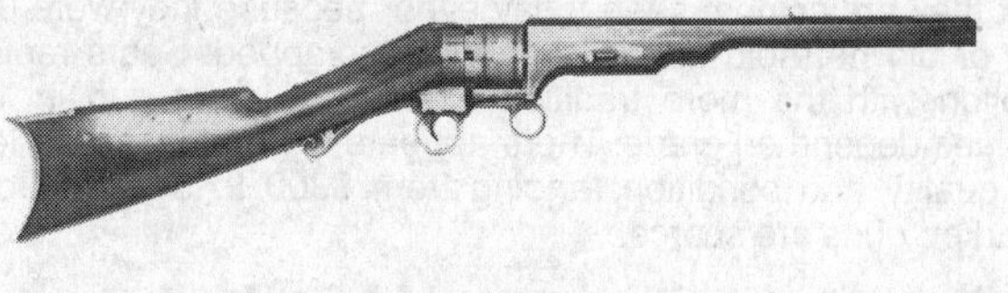

Courtesy Bonhams & Butterfields, San Francisco, California

Exc.	Fine	V.G.	Good	Fair	Poor
70000	50000	35000	20000	12000	5000

Model 1839 Shotgun (Antique)

Quite similar in appearance to 1839 Carbine. Chambered for 16-gauge and holds 6-shots. Has a Damascus pattern barrel. Most notable difference is a 3.5" (instead of a 2.5") long cylinder. There were only 225 of these made from 1839-1841. Markings same as on the Carbine.

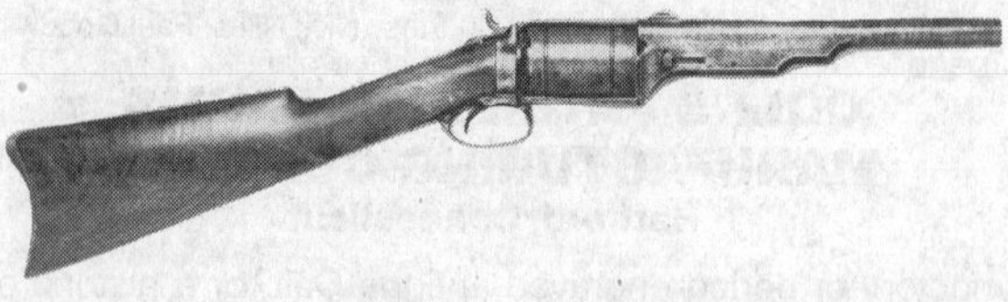

Courtesy Bonhams & Butterfields, San Francisco, California

Exc.	Fine	V.G.	Good	Fair	Poor
39000	23500	18500	13500	8000	5600

Model 1839 Carbine (Antique)

This model has no ring, but features an exposed hammer for cocking and rotating the 6-shot cylinder. Chambered for .525 smoothbore and comes standard with a 24" round barrel. Other barrel lengths have been noted. Finish is blued, with a browned barrel and varnished walnut stock. Cylinder is roll-engraved and barrel stamped "Patent Arms Mfg. Co. Paterson, N.J.-Colt's Pt." There were 950 manufactured from 1838-1841. Later variations of this model are found with the attached loading lever standard. Earlier models without one would bring approximately 25 percent additional. There were 360 purchased by the military and stamped "WAT" on the stock. These would be worth twice what a standard model would bring.

Courtesy Bonhams & Butterfields, San Francisco, California

Exc.	Fine	V.G.	Good	Fair	Poor
33000	20000	16000	12000	6000	4200

Model 1839/1848 Carbine Antique

In 1848, Colt acquired a number of Model 1839 Carbines (approximately 40) from the state of Rhode Island. In an effort to make them marketable they were refinished and the majority fitted with plain cylinders (brightly polished) having integral ratchets around the arbor hole. Barrel length 24"; caliber .525; barrel browned; cylinder polished; frame blued; furniture case-hardened; walnut stock varnished.

Exc.	Fine	V.G.	Good	Fair	Poor
34000	26000	21500	17000	10000	7000

Model 1854 Russian Contract Musket Antique

In 1854, Colt purchased a large number of U.S. Model 1822 flintlock muskets that the company altered to percussion cap ignition and rifled. The reworked muskets are dated 1854 on barrel tang and at rear of the lockplate. In most instances the original manufactory marks, such as Springfield or Harpers Ferry at rear of the lockplate, have been removed, while U.S. and eagle between hammer and bolster remain. Percussion nipple bolster is marked COLT'S PATENT. Some examples have been noted with date 1858. Barrel length 42"; caliber .69; lock and furniture burnished bright; walnut stock oil-finished.

Exc.	Fine	V.G.	Good	Fair	Poor
14000	12000	10000	8000	4000	2800

COLT WALKER-DRAGOON MODELS

Walker Model Revolver Antique

Walker is a massive revolver. Weight 4 lbs., 9 oz. and has a 9" part-round/part-octagonal barrel. Cylinder holds 6-shots and chambered for .44-caliber percussion. There were 1,000 Walker Colts manufactured in 1847 and nearly all of them saw extremely hard use. Originally this model had a roll-engraved cylinder, military inspection marks and barrel stamping that read "Address Saml. Colt-New York City". Practically all examples noted have had these markings worn or rusted beyond recognition. Because the Walker is perhaps the most desirable and sought-after Colt from a collector's standpoint and because of the extremely high value of a Walker in any condition, qualified appraisal is definitely recommended. These revolvers were serial numbered A, B, C, D Company 1-220 and E Company 1-120. An Excellent example was auctioned by James D. Julia in 2008 for $920,000. A military Walker with about half of the original finish remaining sold at Rock Island Auction in 2019 for $1,035,000. The finest known civilian model in original factory case sold at Rock Island Auction in 2018 for $1,840,000.

Courtesy Buffalo Bill Historical Center, Cody, Wyoming

Exc.	Fine	V.G.	Good	Fair	Poor
500000	280000	225000	170000	60000	25000

Civilian Walker Revolver Antique

Identical to military model, but has no martial markings. They are found serial numbered 1001 through 1100.

Exc.	Fine	V.G.	Good	Fair	Poor
—	500000	225000	170000	60000	25000

Whitneyville Hartford Dragoon Antique

Similar in appearance to Walker colt. Revolver fitted with 7.5" barrel and silver plated iron backstrap and triggerguard. Limited edition, with a total of 2,400 guns built. Serial numbers between 1100 through 1340.

Exc.	Fine	V.G.	Good	Fair	Poor
70000	60000	50000	40000	2500	12000

Walker Replacement Dragoon Antique

Extremely rare Colt (300 produced) is sometimes referred to as "Fluck", in memory of the gentleman who first identified it as a distinct and separate model. Produced by Colt as replacements to the military for Walkers that were no longer fit for service due to mechanical failures. They were large 6-shot .44-caliber percussion revolvers, with 7.5" part-round/part-octagonal barrels. Serial numbers ran from 2216 to 2515. The frame, hammer and loading lever are case colored; remainder blued. Grips, which are longer than other Dragoons and similar to Walkers, are of varnished walnut and bear inspectors mark "WAT" inside an oval cartouche on one side and letters "JH" on the other. Frame is stamped "Colt's/Patent/U.S." Letter "P" appears on various parts of the gun.

Exc.	Fine	V.G.	Good	Fair	Poor
50000	35000	20000	10000	7500	5000

First Model Dragoon Antique

Another large 6-shot .44-caliber percussion revolver. Has a 7.5\ part-round/part-octagonal barrel. Frame, hammer and loading lever are case colored; remainder blued, with a brass grip frame and square backed triggerguard. Triggerguard is silver-plated on the Civilian Model only. Another distinguishing feature on First Model is the oval cylinder stop notches. Serial number range is 1341-8000. There were approximately 7,000 made. Cylinder is roll-engraved; barrel stampings read \"Address Saml. Colt, New York City.\" \"Colt\'s Patent\" appears on the frame. Military Models, letters \"U.S.\" also appear on the frame."

Exc.	Fine	V.G.	Good	Fair	Poor
—	—	0	—	—	0

Military Model Antique

Exc.	Fine	V.G.	Good	Fair	Poor
45000	30000	17000	10000	8000	4000

Civilian Model Antique

Exc.	Fine	V.G.	Good	Fair	Poor
40000	25000	15000	10000	8000	4000

Second Model Dragoon

Most of the improvements that distinguish this model from First Model are internal and not readily apparent. Most obvious external change is the rectangular cylinder-stop notches. This model is serial numbered from 8000-10700. Total production of approximately 2,700 revolvers manufactured in 1850 and 1851. There is a Civilian Model, Military Model and an extremely rare variation that was issued to the militias of New Hampshire and Massachusetts (marked \MS.\")."

Civilian Model Antique

Exc.	Fine	V.G.	Good	Fair	Poor
40000	17000	8000	6000	4000	2000

Military Model Antique

Exc.	Fine	V.G.	Good	Fair	Poor
45000	18000	9000	7000	4500	2000

Militia Model Antique

Exc.	Fine	V.G.	Good	Fair	Poor
40000	20000	15000	15000	5000	2500

Third Model Dragoon

Most common of all large Colt percussion revolvers. Approximately 10,500 were manufactured from 1851 through 1861. Quite similar in appearance to Second Model. Obvious external difference is the round triggerguard. Third Model Dragoon was first Colt revolver available with a detachable shoulder stock. There are three basic types of stocks and all are quite rare as only 1,250 were produced. There are two other major variations we will note—\C.L.\" Dragoon, which was a militia-issued model and is rare; late-issue model with an 8\" barrel. These are found over serial number 18000 and only 50 were produced.

A historic cased Gustave Young-engraved ivory-gripped Colt Third Model Dragoon was sold for $805,000 at a Texas auction in 2011. Revolver was inscribed \"Colonel P.M. Milliken\". Milliken was an officer of the 1st Ohio volunteer calvary and killed leading a charge against the Confederate Army at Stone River, Tennessee in 1862. Two other Colt percussion revolvers were sold at the same auction for more than $800,000. (See Texas Paterson No. 5 and Model 1861 Navy listings.) Such prices are extreme exceptions to values of typical models."

Courtesy Buffalo Bill Historical Center, Cody, Wyoming

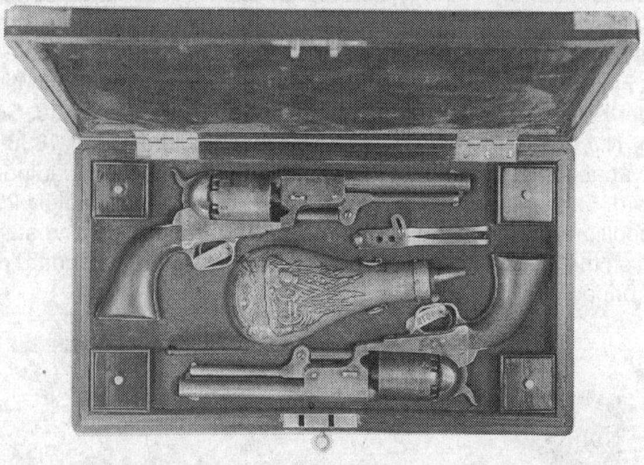

Courtesy Buffalo Bill Historical Center, Cody, Wyoming

Civilian Model Antique

Exc.	Fine	V.G.	Good	Fair	Poor
38000	16000	7000	4000	3000	2000

Military Model Antique

Exc.	Fine	V.G.	Good	Fair	Poor
37000	15000	6500	3500	3000	2000

Shoulder Stock Cut Revolvers Antique

Exc.	Fine	V.G.	Good	Fair	Poor
37000	15000	6500	3500	3000	2000

Shoulder Stocks Antique

Exc.	Fine	V.G.	Good	Fair	Poor
15000	9000	7500	6000	3000	2000

C.L. Dragoons Antique

Hand engraved, not stamped. Engraved "C.L. Dragoons" reportedly for "Crocheron Light Dragoons." These Third Models are believed to be the only Colts that were sold to a Confederate unit. Expert authentication is essential.

Exc.	Fine	V.G.	Good	Fair	Poor
—	35000	25000	15000	8000	4000

8" Barrel Late Issue Antique

Exc.	Fine	V.G.	Good	Fair	Poor
37000	15000	6500	35000	3000	2000

Hartford English Dragoon Antique

A variation of Third Model Dragoon. Only notable differences are British proof-marks and distinct #1-#700 serial number range. Other than these two features, description given for Third Model would apply. These revolvers were manufactured in Hartford, but were finished at Colt's London factory from 1853-1857. Some bear the hand-engraved barrel marking "Col. Colt London". Many English Dragoons were elaborately engraved and individual appraisal would be a must. Two hundred revolvers came back to America in 1861 to be used in the Civil War.

Exc.	Fine	V.G.	Good	Fair	Poor
30000	12000	5000	3000	2500	1500

Model 1848 Baby Dragoon

A small 5-shot .31-caliber percussion revolver. An octagonal barrel in lengths of 3", 4", 5" and 6". Most were made without an attached loading lever, although some with loading levers have been noted. Frame, hammer and loading lever (when present) are case colored; barrel and cylinder blued. Grip frame and triggerguard are silver-plated brass. Approximately 15,500 manufactured between 1847 and 1850. Serial range is between 1-15500. Barrels are stamped "Address Saml. Colt/New York City". Some have been noted with the barrel address inside brackets. Frame is marked "Colt's/Patent". First 10,000 revolvers have Texas Ranger/Indian roll-engraved cylinder scene; later guns stagecoach holdup scene. This is a popular model and many fakes have been noted. Note: Add 15 percent for attached loading lever.

Texas Ranger/Indian Scene Antique

Courtesy Bonhams & Butterfields, San Francisco, California

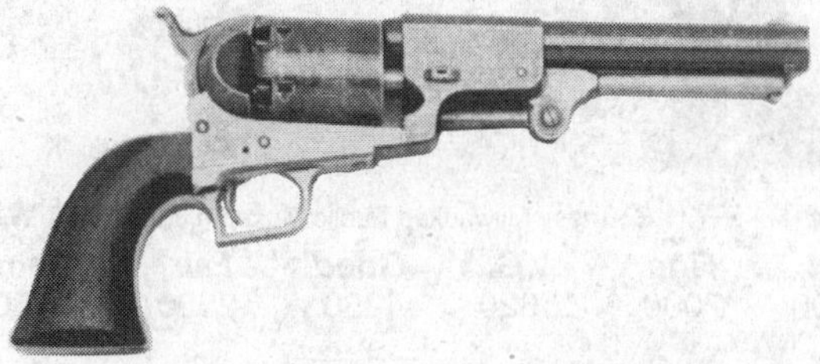

Courtesy Bonhams & Butterfields, San Francisco, California

Exc.	Fine	V.G.	Good	Fair	Poor
16000	10000	7000	4500	1500	750

Stagecoach Holdup Scene Antique

Exc.	Fine	V.G.	Good	Fair	Poor
15000	9000	5500	3750	1500	750

Model 1849 Pocket Revolver Antique

A small 5- or 6-shot .31-caliber percussion revolver. An octagonal barrel of 3", 4", 5" or 6" in length. Most had loading gates, but some did not. Frame, hammer and loading lever are case colored; cylinder and barrel are blued. Grip frame and round triggerguard are made of brass and are silver plated. Both large and small triggerguard variations noted. Most plentiful of all Colt percussion revolvers, with approximately 325,000 manufactured over a 23-year period, 1850-1873. There are over 200 variations of this model and one should consult an expert for individual appraisals. There are many fine publications specializing in the field of Colt percussion revolvers that would be helpful in identification of the variations. Values represented here are for standard model. Examples of variations include: slight premium for 6" barrel; slight premium for crowned muzzle; US martial marked worth 4X to 5X standard value; original 3" barrel (incorrectly called "Wells Fargo Model") worth double.

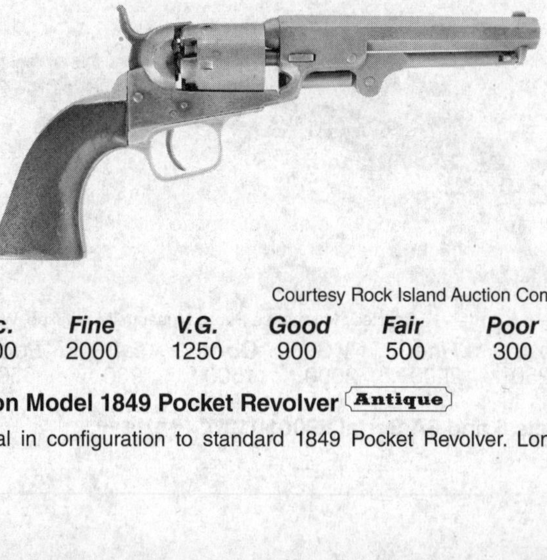

Courtesy Rock Island Auction Company

Exc.	Fine	V.G.	Good	Fair	Poor
3000	2000	1250	900	500	300

London Model 1849 Pocket Revolver Antique

Identical in configuration to standard 1849 Pocket Revolver. London-made models have a higher quality finish and their own serial number range, 1-11000. Manufactured from 1853 through 1857. Feature a roll-engraved cylinder scene. Barrels are stamped "Address Col. Colt/London". First 265 revolvers, known as early models, have brass grip frames and small round triggerguards. They are quite rare and worth approximately 50 percent more than standard model that has a steel grip frame and large oval triggerguard. Found cased more often than most models. Original casing with accessories may double value in lower conditions and up to quadruple value in excellent condition.

Exc.	Fine	V.G.	Good	Fair	Poor
2750	1800	1200	700	500	300

Model 1851 Navy Revolver

Undoubtedly, the most popular revolver Colt produced in the medium size and power range. It is a 6-shot .36-caliber percussion revolver, with 7.5\ octagonal barrel. Has an attached loading lever. Basic model has a case colored frame hammer and loading lever, with silver-plated brass grip frame and triggerguard. Grips are varnished walnut. Colt manufactured approximately 215,000 of these fine revolvers between 1850 and 1873. Basic Navy features a roll-engraved cylinder scene of a battle between the navies of Texas and Mexico. There are three distinct barrel stampings—serial number 1-74000, \"Address Saml. Colt New York City\"; serial number 74001-101000 \"Address Saml. Colt. Hartford, Ct.\"; and serial number 101001-215000 \"Address Saml. Colt New York U.S. America\". Left side of frame is stamped \"Colt\'s/Patent\" on all variations. This model also available with a detached shoulder stock. Values for shoulder stocks today are nearly as high as for the revolver itself. Careful appraisal should be secured before purchase. The number of variations within 1851 Navy model designation makes it necessary to read specialized text available on the subject."

Square Back Triggerguard, 1st Model, Serial #1-1000 Antique

Courtesy Rock Island Auction Company

Exc.	Fine	V.G.	Good	Fair	Poor
35000	25000	12000	8000	5000	3000

Square Back Triggerguard, 2nd Model, Serial #1001-4200 Antique

Exc.	Fine	V.G.	Good	Fair	Poor
30000	20000	10000	7000	4000	2000

Small Round Triggerguard, 3rd Model, Serial #4201-85000 Antique

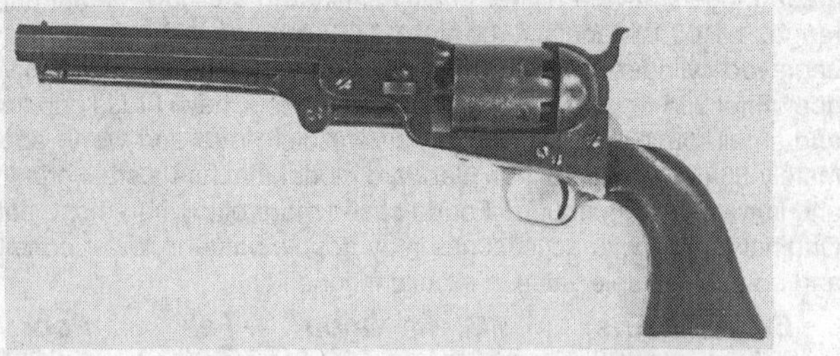

Courtesy Milwaukee Public Museum, Milwaukee, Wisconsin

Exc.	Fine	V.G.	Good	Fair	Poor
8000	5000	3000	2000	1000	500

Large Round Triggerguard, 4th Model, Serial #85001-215000 Antique

Original iron grip frame (as opposed to standard brass gripstrap) adds around 10% to the value. Note that steel backstraps are standard on 2nd Model London 1851 Navy Models, and do not bring a premium on those guns.

Exc.	Fine	V.G.	Good	Fair	Poor
8000	5000	3000	2000	1000	500

Martial Model Antique

"U.S." stamped on left side of frame; inspector's marks and cartouche on grips.

Exc.	Fine	V.G.	Good	Fair	Poor
15000	8000	5000	3500	1500	900

Shoulder Stock Variations

Revolvers cut for shoulder stocks will bring a premium. A revolver with a detachable should stock may bring 150% of what the gun alone will bring. Canteen shoulder stock will bring more. Fakes and reproductions abound, buyer beware.

London Model 1851 Navy Revolver

These revolvers are physically similar to U.S.-made model. Exception, barrel address reads "Address Col. Colt. London" and British proof-marks stamped on barrel and cylinder. There were 42,000 made between 1853 and 1857. They have their own serial number range #1-#42,000. There are two major variations of London Navy. Again, a serious purchaser would be well advised to seek qualified appraisal as fakes have been noted.

1st Model Antique

Serial #1-#2,000, with a small round brass triggerguard and grip frame. Squareback guard worth a 40 percent premium.

Exc.	Fine	V.G.	Good	Fair	Poor
15750	7600	5170	2750	1500	1050

2nd Model Antique

Serial #2,001-#42,000, steel grip frame and large round triggerguard. Martial variations that bring premiums include British War Department (W.D. marked with broad arrow), Austrian Kriegs Marine (K.M. marked) and Upper Canada or Lower Canada (UC or LC marked).

Exc.	Fine	V.G.	Good	Fair	Poor
7500	4500	3250	2000	700	480

Hartford Manufactured Variation Antique

Serial numbers in 42,000 range.

Exc.	Fine	V.G.	Good	Fair	Poor
14000	8500	6750	5000	3000	2100

COLT SIDE HAMMER MODELS

Model 1855 Side Hammer "Root" Pocket Revolver

"Root", as it's popularly known, was the only solid-frame revolver Colt ever made. It has a spur trigger, walnut grips and hammer mounted on right side of frame. Standard finish is a case colored frame, hammer and loading lever, with barrel and cylinder blued. Chambered for both .28-caliber and .31-caliber percussion. Each caliber has its own serial number range—1-30000 for .28-caliber; 1-14000 for .31-caliber. Model consists of seven basic variations. Serious student should avail himself of the fine publications dealing with this model in depth. Colt produced Side Hammer Root from 1855-1870.

Model 1 and 1A Serial #1-384 Antique

3.5 octagonal barrel, .28-caliber roll-engraved cylinder. Hartford barrel address without pointing hand.

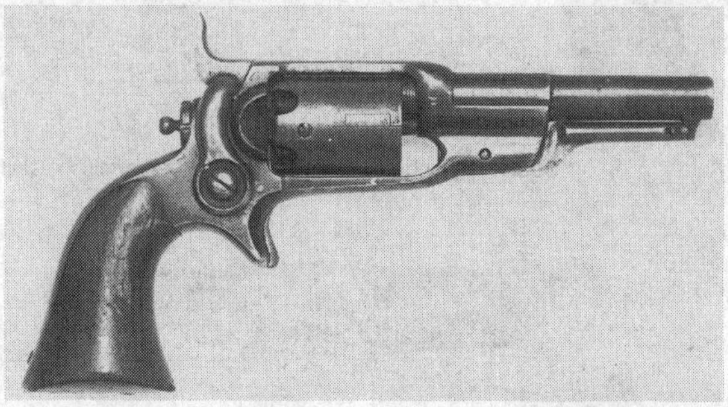

Courtesy Milwaukee Public Museum, Milwaukee, Wisconsin

Exc.	Fine	V.G.	Good	Fair	Poor
12000	7000	5620	4250	2500	1750

Model 2 Serial #476-25000 Antique

Same as Model 1, with pointing hand barrel address.

Exc.	Fine	V.G.	Good	Fair	Poor
3300	2000	1600	1200	700	480

Model 3 Serial #25001-30000 Antique

Same as Model 2, with a full fluted cylinder.

Exc.	Fine	V.G.	Good	Fair	Poor
4000	2400	1920	1450	980	680

Model 3A and 4 Serial #1-2400 Antique

.31-caliber, 3.5 barrel, Hartford address, full fluted cylinder.

Exc.	Fine	V.G.	Good	Fair	Poor
3300	2000	1600	1200	700	480

Model 5 Serial #2401-8000 Antique

.31-caliber, 3.5 round barrel, address "Col. Colt New York".

Exc.	Fine	V.G.	Good	Fair	Poor
4250	2500	2000	1500	930	650

Model 5A Serial #2401-8000 Antique

Same as Model 5, with a 4.5" barrel.

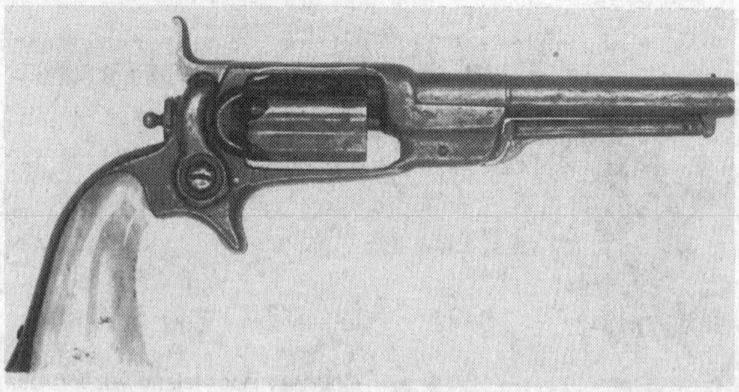

Courtesy Milwaukee Public Museum, Milwaukee, Wisconsin

Exc.	Fine	V.G.	Good	Fair	Poor
4250	2500	2000	1500	930	650

Models 6 and 6A Serial #8001-11074 Antique

Same as Model 5 and 5A, with roll-engraved cylinder scene.

Exc.	Fine	V.G.	Good	Fair	Poor
4250	2500	2000	1500	930	650

Models 7 and 7A Serial #11075-14000 Antique

Same as Models 6 and 6A, with a screw holding in cylinder pin.

Exc.	Fine	V.G.	Good	Fair	Poor
4750	2850	2270	1700	1000	700

COLT SIDE HAMMER LONG GUNS

Model 1855 Sporting Rifle, 1st Model

A 6-shot revolving rifle, chambered for .36-caliber percussion. Comes with 21", 24", 27" or 30" round barrel that is part octagonal where it joins the frame. Stock is walnut, with an oil- or varnish-finish. Frame, hammer and loading lever are case colored; rest of the metal blued. Hammer is on right side of frame. 1st Model has no forend and an oiling device is attached to the barrel underlug. Triggerguard has two spur-like projections in front and back of bow. Roll-engraved cylinder scene depicts a hunter shooting at five deer and is found only on this model. Standard stampings are "Colt's Pt./1856" and "Address S. Colt Hartford, Ct. U.S.A.".

Early Model Antique

Low serial numbers, with hand-engraved barrel marking "Address S. Colt Hartford, U.S.A."

Exc.	Fine	V.G.	Good	Fair	Poor
15200	12000	10750	9500	7500	5250

Production Model Antique

Exc.	Fine	V.G.	Good	Fair	Poor
13250	11500	10000	8500	6750	4720

Model 1855 1st Model Carbine Antique

Identical to 1st Model Rifle. Offered with 15" and 18" barrel.

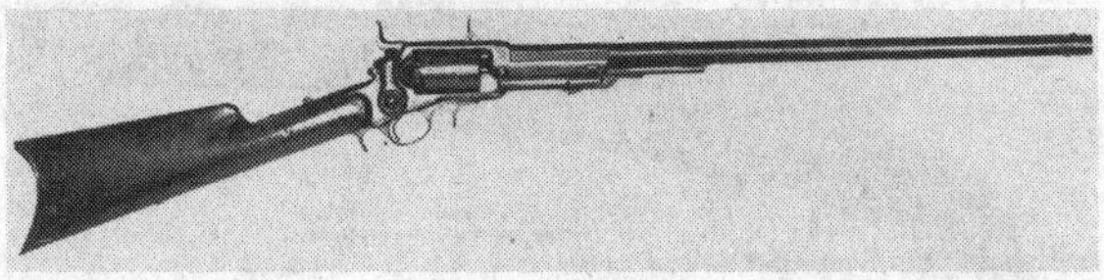

Courtesy Milwaukee Public Museum, Milwaukee, Wisconsin

Exc.	Fine	V.G.	Good	Fair	Poor
16000	13000	11500	10000	7500	5250

Model 1855 Half Stock Sporting Rifle Antique

Although this rifle is quite similar in appearance and finish to 1st Model, there are some notable differences. Features a walnut forend that protrudes halfway down the barrel. Two types of triggerguards—a short projectionless one or a long model, with a graceful scroll. There is a 6-shot model chambered for .36- or .44-caliber or 5-shot model chambered for .56-caliber. Cylinder is fully fluted. Markings are "Colt's Pt/1856" and "Address Col. Colt/Hartford Ct. U.S.A." Approximately 1,500 manufactured between 1857 and 1864.

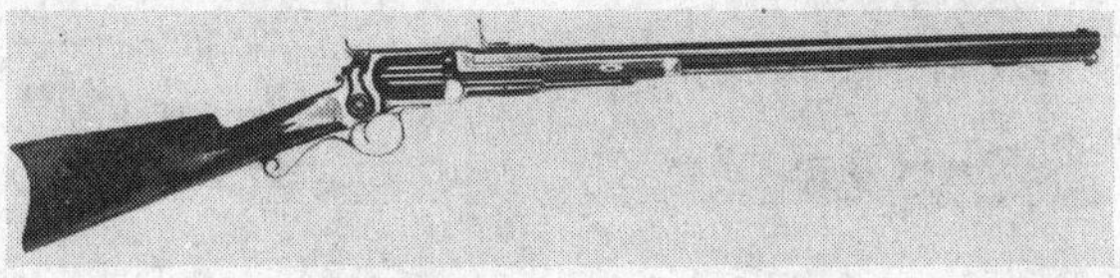

Courtesy Milwaukee Public Museum, Milwaukee, Wisconsin

Exc.	Fine	V.G.	Good	Fair	Poor
11500	9100	8170	7250	5750	4020

Model 1855 Full Stock Military Rifle Antique

Holds 6-shots in its .44-caliber chambering and 5-shots when chambered for .56-caliber. A rare .64 caliber version was also made with total production fewer than 25, worth substantial premium. Another side hammer revolving rifle that resembles Half Stock model. Barrels are round and part-octagonal where they join the frame. Come in lengths of 21", 24", 27", 31" and 37". Hammer and loading lever are case colored; rest of metal parts blued. Walnut buttstock and full length forend are oil-finished with sling swivels. Cylinder is fully fluted. Military models have provisions for affixing a bayonet, military-style sights and bear "U.S." martial mark on examples that were actually issued to the military. Standard stampings found on this model are "Colt's Pt/1856" and "Address Col. Colt Hartford, Ct. U.S.A." An estimated 9,300 manufactured between 1856 and 1864.

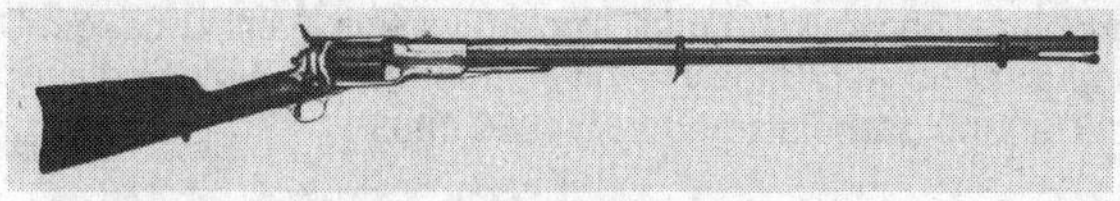

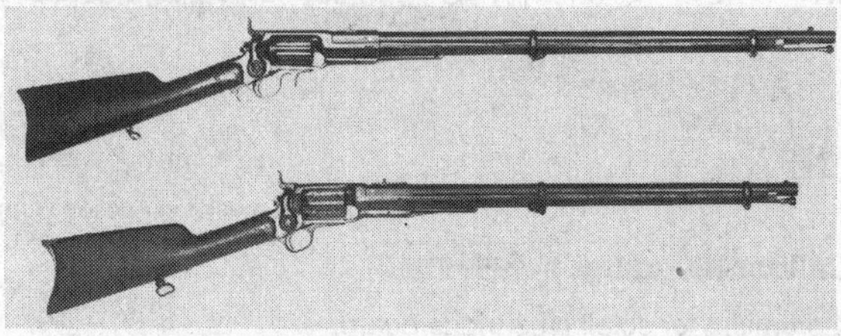

Courtesy Milwaukee Public Museum, Milwaukee, Wisconsin

Exc.	Fine	V.G.	Good	Fair	Poor
18000	14400	12960	11520	9220	6450

Martially Marked Models Antique

Exc.	Fine	V.G.	Good	Fair	Poor
40000	23000	16870	10750	6000	4200

Without Martial Markings Antique

Exc.	Fine	V.G.	Good	Fair	Poor
17000	13500	11250	9000	5000	3500

Model 1855 Full Stock Sporting Rifle Antique

Similar in appearance to Military model, with these notable exceptions. No provision for attaching a bayonet, sling swivels and it has sporting-style sights. Buttplate is crescent shaped. This model has been noted chambered for .56-caliber in 5-shot version and chambered for .36-, .40-, .44- and .50-caliber in 6-shot variation. Quite scarce in .40- and .50-caliber and will bring a 10 percent premium. Standard markings are "Colt's Pt/1856" and "Address Col. Colt/Hartford Ct. U.S.A." Production on this model was quite limited (several hundred at most) between 1856 and 1864.

Exc.	Fine	V.G.	Good	Fair	Poor
13500	10500	9500	8500	4000	2800

Model 1855 Revolving Carbine Antique

Similar in appearance to 1855 Military Rifle. Barrel lengths of 15", 18" and 21", plus absence of a forend make the standard Carbine Model readily identifiable. Markings are the same. Approximately 4,400 manufactured between 1856 and 1864.

Exc.	Fine	V.G.	Good	Fair	Poor
17000	14000	12000	10000	6000	4200

Model 1855 Artillery Carbine Antique

Identical to standard carbine. Chambered for .56-caliber only. Has a 24" barrel, full-length walnut forend and bayonet lug.

Exc.	Fine	V.G.	Good	Fair	Poor
19000	15000	13500	12000	6500	4550

Model 1855 British Carbine Antique

British-proofed version, with barrel lengths up to 30". Brass triggerguard, buttplate and chambered for .56-caliber only. This variation usually found in 10000-12000 serial number range.

Exc.	Fine	V.G.	Good	Fair	Poor
18000	14500	12750	11000	6000	4200

Model 1855 Revolving Shotgun

Very much resembles Half Stock Sporting Rifle. Made with 27", 30", 33" and 36" smoothbore barrel. Has a 5-shot cylinder chambered for .60- or .75-caliber (20- or 10-gauge). Case colored hammer and loading lever; rest of metal blued, with an occasional browned barrel noted. Buttstock and forend are oil- or varnish-finished walnut. No rear sight and small triggerguard, with the caliber stamped on it. Some have been noted with the large scroll triggerguard; these would add 10 percent to value. Rarest shotgun variation would be a full stocked version in either gauge. Qualified appraisal would be highly recommended. Serial numbered in its own range #1-#1100. Manufactured from 1860-1863.

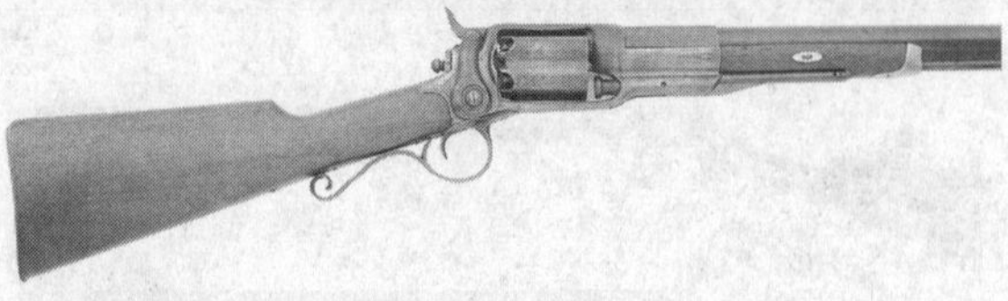

Courtesy Amoskeag Auction Company

.60 Caliber (20 gauge) Antique

Slight premium for scroll type triggerguard.

Exc.	Fine	V.G.	Good	Fair	Poor
15000	8000	6000	3000	2000	1000

.75 Caliber (10 gauge) Antique

Substantial premium for deluxe models.

Exc.	Fine	V.G.	Good	Fair	Poor
15000	8000	6000	3000	2000	1000

Model 1861 Single-Shot Rifled Musket

With the advent of Civil War, Union army seriously needed military arms. Colt was given a contract to supply 112,500 1861-pattern percussion single-shot muskets. Between 1861 and 1865, 75,000 were delivered. They have 40" rifled barrels chambered for .58-caliber. Musket is equipped with military sights, sling swivels and bayonet lug. Metal finish is bright steel. Stock is oil-finished walnut. Military inspector marks are found on all major parts. "VP" over an eagle is stamped on breech along with a date. Colt address and a date are stamped on lockplate. A large number of these rifles were altered to Snyder breech loading system for Bey of Egypt.

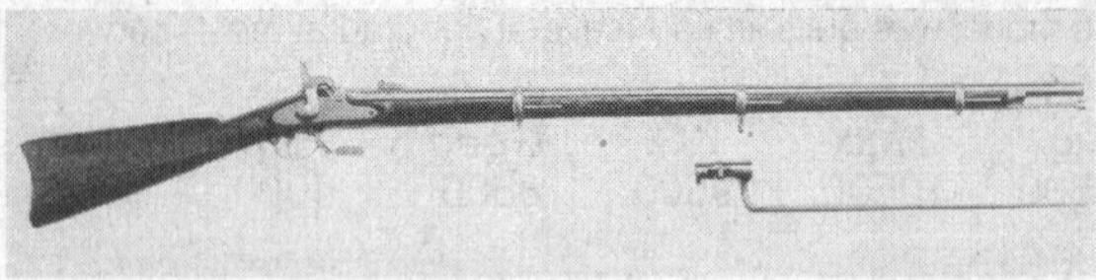

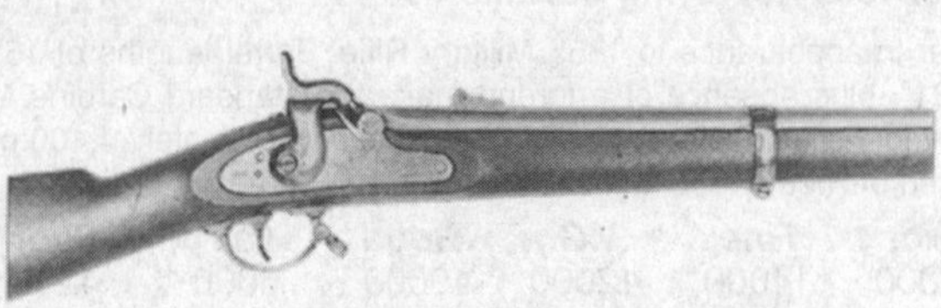

Courtesy Milwaukee Public Museum, Milwaukee, Wisconsin

Production Model Antique

Exc.	Fine	V.G.	Good	Fair	Poor
6000	4500	3500	2500	1500	850

COLT PERCUSSION REVOLVERS

Model 1860 Army Revolver

Third most produced of Colt percussion handguns. Primary revolver used by Union Army during Civil War. Colt delivered 127,156 of these revolvers to be used during those hostilities. It is a 6-shot .44-caliber percussion revolver. Either 7.5" or 8" round barrel, with an attached loading lever. Frame, hammer and loading lever are case colored; barrel and cylinder blued. Triggerguard, front strap are brass; back-strap blued steel. Grips are one-piece walnut. Early models have barrels stamped "Address Saml. Colt Hartford Ct.". Later models stamped "Address Col. Saml. Colt New-York U.S. America". "Colt's/Patent" stamped on left side of frame; ".44 Cal." on triggerguard. Cylinder is roll engraved with naval battle scene. Between 1860 and 1873, Colt manufactured 200,500 of these 1860 Army Revolvers. London marked 1860 Army revolvers bring similar prices to standard production.

Martial Marked Model Antique

In 2019 Rock Island Auction sold the "Finest known" US 1860 Army, 98%+ , for $184,000.

Exc.	Fine	V.G.	Good	Fair	Poor
13000	8000	6250	4500	2000	1400

Civilian Model Antique

Found in 3- or 4-screw variations. May or may not be cut for a shoulder stock. Civilian models are usually better finished.

Courtesy Milwaukee Public Museum, Milwaukee, Wisconsin

Exc.	Fine	V.G.	Good	Fair	Poor
11500	6500	5250	3000	1500	1000

Full Fluted Cylinder Model Antique

Approximately 4,000 Army's were made, with full fluted cylinders. They appear in first 8,000 serial numbers.

Courtesy Milwaukee Public Museum, Milwaukee, Wisconsin

Exc.	Fine	V.G.	Good	Fair	Poor
15000	1000	7000	5000	2500	1500

Shoulder Stock for 1860 Army

Revolvers cut for shoulder stocks will bring a premium. A revolver with a detachable shoulder stock may bring 150% of what the gun alone will bring. Fakes and reproductions abound, buyer beware.

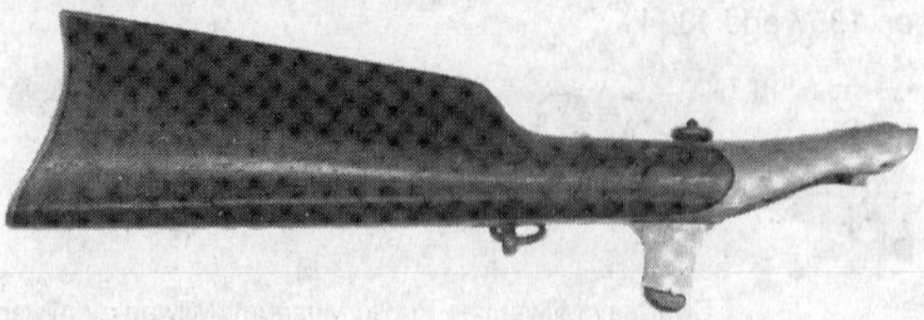

Courtesy Milwaukee Public Museum, Milwaukee, Wisconsin

Model 1861 Navy Revolver

A 6-shot 7.5" round-barreled .36-caliber percussion revolver. Frame, hammer and attached loading lever are case colored. Barrel and cylinder are blued. Grip frame and triggerguard are silver-plated brass. Grips are one-piece walnut. Cylinder has roll-engraved naval battle scene and barrel stamping "Address Col. Saml. Colt New-York U.S. America". Frame is stamped "Colts/Patent" with "36 Cal." on triggerguard. Not many variations within 1861 Navy model designation. Less than 39,000 were made between 1861 and 1873.

A very exceptional cased and engraved presentation-grade Model 1861 Navy was sold at auction in 2011 for $805,000. Three Colt percussion revolvers sold for over $800,000 at auction. (See Texas Paterson No. 5 and Third Model Dragoon listings.) Such prices are extreme exceptions to values of typical models.

Courtesy Rock Island Auction Company

Fluted Cylinder Model (Antique)

Approximately first 100 made with full fluted cylinders.

Exc.	Fine	V.G.	Good	Fair	Poor
23000	14000	11120	8250	4750	3320

Military Model (Antique)

Marked "U.S." on frame, inspector's cartouche on grip. 650 marked "U.S.N." on butt.

Exc.	Fine	V.G.	Good	Fair	Poor
20000	12000	9500	7000	4000	2800

Cut for stock (Antique)

Only 100 3rd-type stocks made. Appear between serial #11000- #14000. These are very rare revolvers.

Exc.	Fine	V.G.	Good	Fair	Poor
10000	7000	5500	4000	2000	1250

Revolver (Antique)

Exc.	Fine	V.G.	Good	Fair	Poor
14000	8500	6750	5000	2500	1750

Stock (Antique)

Seldom sold; values are speculative.

Exc.	Fine	V.G.	Good	Fair	Poor
—	10000	8120	6250	3750	2620

Civilian Model (Antique)

Exc.	Fine	V.G.	Good	Fair	Poor
15000	8000	5000	3500	1500	1000

Model 1862 Pocket Navy Revolver

A smaller 5-shot .36-caliber percussion revolver. Resembles configuration of 1851 Navy. Has 4.5", 5.5" or 6.5" octagonal barrel, with attached loading lever. Frame, hammer and loading lever case colored; barrel and cylinder blued. Grip frame and triggerguard silver-plated brass; one-piece grips of varnished walnut. Stagecoach holdup scene is roll-engraved on cylinder. Frame stamped "Colt's/Patent"; barrel "Address Col. Saml. Colt New-York U.S. America". Approximately 19,000 manufactured between 1861 and 1873. Serial numbered in same range as Model 1862 Police. Because a great many were used for metallic cartridge conversions, they are quite scarce today. Note: London Address Model, with blued steel grip frame would be worth more than standard model. Add 50 percent. Longer barrels will bring a premium over 4.5" length.

Standard Production Model (Antique)

Premium for London barrel address.

Exc.	Fine	V.G.	Good	Fair	Poor
8000	2700	1600	1100	750	500

Model 1862 Police Revolver

A slim attractively designed revolver. Some consider it the most aesthetically pleasing of all Colt percussion designs. Has a 5-shot half-fluted cylinder chambered for .36-caliber. Offered with 3.5", 4.5", 5.5" or 6.5" round barrel. Frame, hammer and loading lever case colored; barrel and cylinder blued. Grip frame silver-plated brass; one-piece grips varnished walnut. Barrel stamped "Address Col. Saml Colt New-York U.S. America"; frame "Colt's/Patent" on left side. One of the cylinder flutes marked "Pat Sept. 10th 1850". Approximately 28,000 manufactured between 1861 and 1873. Many were converted to metallic cartridge use, so they are quite scarce on today's market. Note: London Address Model would be worth approximately twice the value of standard model. Longer barrels will bring a premium over 3.5" or 4.5" length.

Courtesy Milwaukee Public Museum, Milwaukee, Wisconsin

Standard Production Model (Antique)

Premium for London barrel address.

Exc.	Fine	V.G.	Good	Fair	Poor
7500	2500	1500	1000	750	500

COLT METALLIC CARTRIDGE CONVERSIONS

Thuer Conversion Revolver

Although quite simplistic and not commercially successful, Thuer Conversion was the first attempt by Colt to convert percussion revolvers to the new metallic cartridge system. This conversion was designed around the tapered Thuer cartridge. Consists of a ring that replaced the back part of cylinder, which had been milled off. This ring stamped "Pat. Sep./15, 1868". Ejection position is marked with letter "E". These conversions have rebounding firing pins and are milled to allow loading from the front of revolver. This conversion was undertaken on six different models listed; all other specifications, finishes, markings, etc., not directly affected by the conversion would be the same as previously described. From a collectible and investment standpoint, Thuer Conversion is very desirable. Competent appraisal should be secured if acquisition is contemplated. Note: Blued models will bring higher prices than nickel models in the same condition.

Model 1849 Pocket (Antique)

Exc.	Fine	V.G.	Good	Fair	Poor
35000	15500	9750	4000	2000	1400

Model 1851 Navy (Antique)

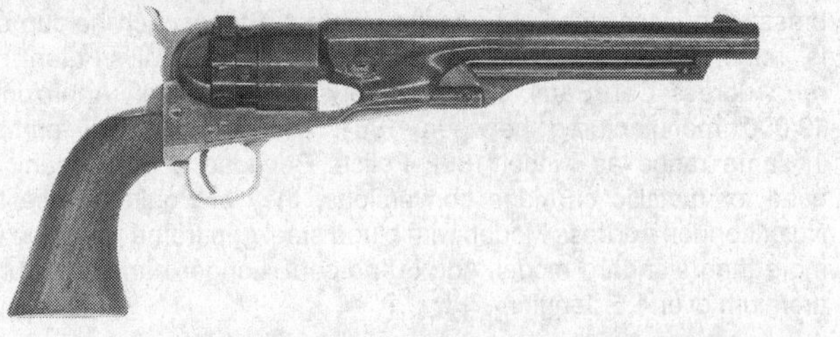

Courtesy Milwaukee Public Museum, Milwaukee, Wisconsin

Exc.	Fine	V.G.	Good	Fair	Poor
28000	18000	11500	5000	2000	1400

Model 1860 Army (Antique)

Exc.	Fine	V.G.	Good	Fair	Poor
30000	19500	12750	6000	2000	1400

Model 1861 Navy (Antique)

Exc.	Fine	V.G.	Good	Fair	Poor
30000	19500	12750	6000	2000	1400

Model 1862 Police (Antique)

Exc.	Fine	V.G.	Good	Fair	Poor
20000	13500	8500	3500	1500	1000

Model 1862 Pocket Navy (Antique)

Exc.	Fine	V.G.	Good	Fair	Poor
25000	16000	9750	3500	1500	1000

Richards Conversion, 1860 Army Revolver

Colt's second attempt at metallic cartridge conversion. It met with quite a bit more success than the first. Richards Conversion was designed for .44 Colt cartridge. Has a 6-shot cylinder and an integral ejector rod to replace the loading lever that had been removed. Other specifications pertaining to 1860 Army Revolver remain as previously described, if they are not directly altered by the conversion. Richards Conversion adds a breechplate, with a firing pin and its own rear sight. Approximately 9,000 of these Conversions manufactured between 1873 and 1878. Note: Blued models will bring higher prices than nickel models in the same condition.

Civilian Model (Antique)

Premium for early cylinder with 12 cylinder stop slots.

Exc.	Fine	V.G.	Good	Fair	Poor
12000	7000	3500	1500	1000	500

Martially Marked (Antique)

This variation found with mixed serial numbers and a second set of conversion serial numbers. "U.S." stamped on left side of barrel lug. Inspector's cartouche appears on grip. Very rare Colt revolver.

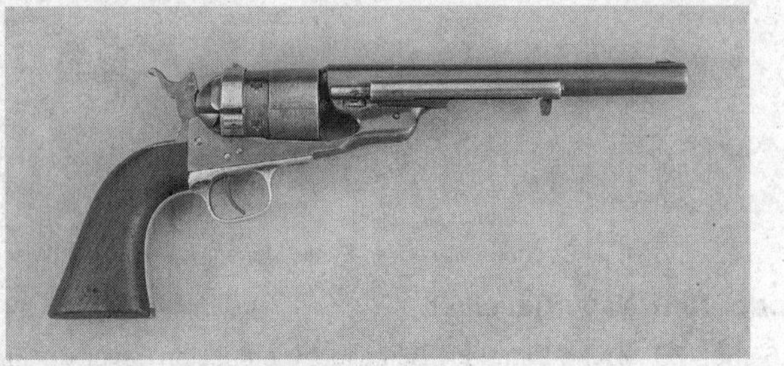

Courtesy Little John's Auction Service, Inc., Paul Goodwin photo

Exc.	Fine	V.G.	Good	Fair	Poor
25000	15000	5000	3000	1500	1000

Transition Richards Model (Antique)

Variation marked by presence of a firing pin hammer.

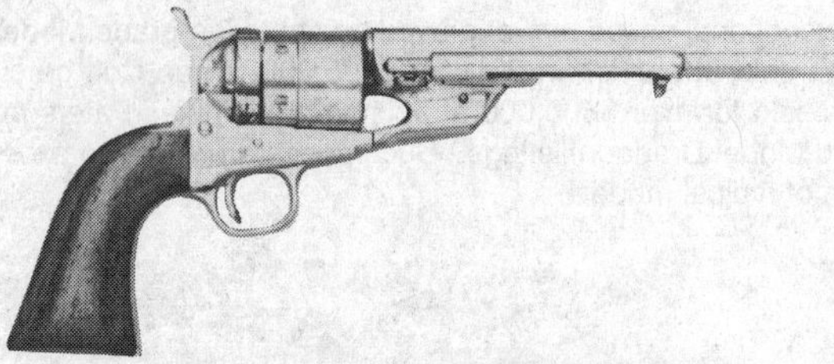

Courtesy Bonhams & Butterfields, San Francisco, California

Exc.	Fine	V.G.	Good	Fair	Poor
18000	11000	4000	2000	1200	600

Richards-Mason Conversion, 1860 Army Revolver (Antique)

This conversion is different from Richards Conversion, in a number of readily apparent aspects. Barrel was manufactured with a small lug, much different in appearance than seen on standard 1860 Army. Breechplate does not have its own rear sight. There is a milled area to allow hammer to contact base of the cartridge. These Conversions were also chambered for .44 Colt cartridge. Cylinder holds 6-shots. There is an integral ejector rod in place of the loading lever. Barrels on some are stamped "Address Col. Saml. Colt New-York U.S. America" or "Colt's Pt. F.A. Mfg. Co. Hartford, Ct." Patent dates 1871 and 1872 stamped on left side of frame. Finish of these revolvers and grips, were for the most part, same as on unconverted Armies; for the first time, nickel-plated guns are found. Approximately 2,100 of these Conversions produced in 1877 and 1878. Note: Blued models will bring higher prices than nickel models in same condition.

Exc.	Fine	V.G.	Good	Fair	Poor
17000	8000	4000	2500	1000	500

Richards-Mason Conversions 1851 Navy Revolver

These revolvers were converted in the same way as 1860 Army previously described. Major difference being .38-caliber rimfire or centerfire. Finishes are mostly the same as on unconverted revolvers, but nickel-plated guns are not rare. Note: Blued models will bring higher prices than nickel models in same condition.

Production Model Serial #1-3800 (Antique)

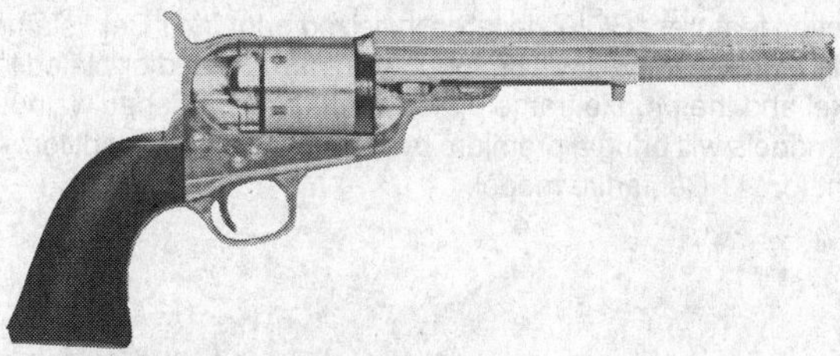

Courtesy Bonhams & Butterfields, San Francisco, California

Exc.	Fine	V.G.	Good	Fair	Poor
11000	5500	3750	2000	800	560

U.S. Navy Model Serial #41000-91000 Antique

"USN" stamped on butt; steel grip frame.

Exc.	Fine	V.G.	Good	Fair	Poor
16000	9500	6250	3000	1000	700

Richards-Mason Conversion 1861 Navy Revolver

Specifications for this model same as 1851 Navy Conversion described above, with base revolver being different. There were 2,200 manufactured in 1870s. Note: Blued models will bring higher prices than nickel models in same condition.

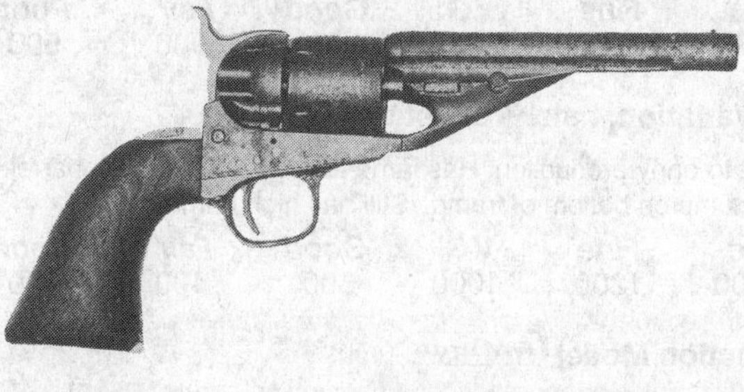

Courtesy Wallis & Wallis, Lewes, Sussex, England

Standard Production Model Serial #100-3300 Antique

Exc.	Fine	V.G.	Good	Fair	Poor
7500	5000	3500	1750	900	500

U.S. Navy Model Serial #1000-9999 Antique

Exc.	Fine	V.G.	Good	Fair	Poor
15000	7500	5500	3500	1000	700

Model 1862 Police and Pocket Navy Conversions

Conversion of these two revolver models is the most difficult to catalog of all Colt variations. Approximately 24,000 of these produced between 1873 and 1880. There are five basic variations, with a number of subvariations. Confusion is usually caused by different ways in which these were marked. Depending upon what parts were utilized, caliber markings could be particularly confusing. One must also consider the fact that many of these conversion revolvers found their way into secondary markets, such as Mexico, Central and South America. They were either destroyed or received sufficient abuse to obliterate most identifying markings. Five basic variations are all chambered for .38 rimfire or centerfire cartridge. All held 5-shots. Most were found with round roll-engraved stagecoach holdup scene. Half-fluted cylinder from 1862 Police is quite rare on the conversion revolver and not found at all on some of the variations. Finishes on these guns were pretty much the same as they were before conversion, but not unusual to find nickel-plated specimens. Basic variations are listed. Note: Blued models will bring higher prices than nickel models in same condition. Half-fluted cylinder add 20 percent.

Round Barrel Pocket Navy with Ejector Antique

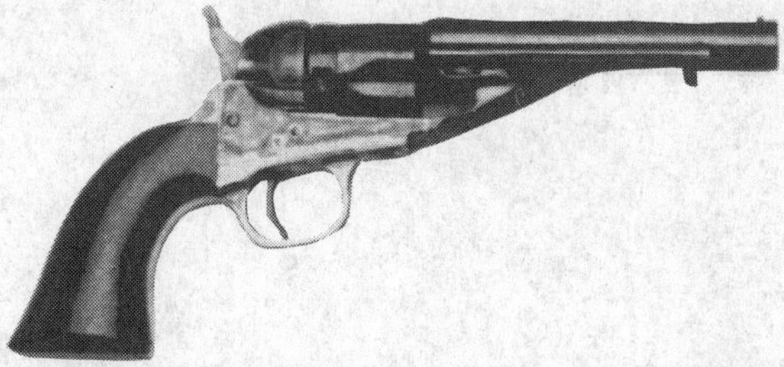

Exc.	Fine	V.G.	Good	Fair	Poor
3500	2500	1850	1000	700	300

3.5" Round Barrel Without Ejector Antique

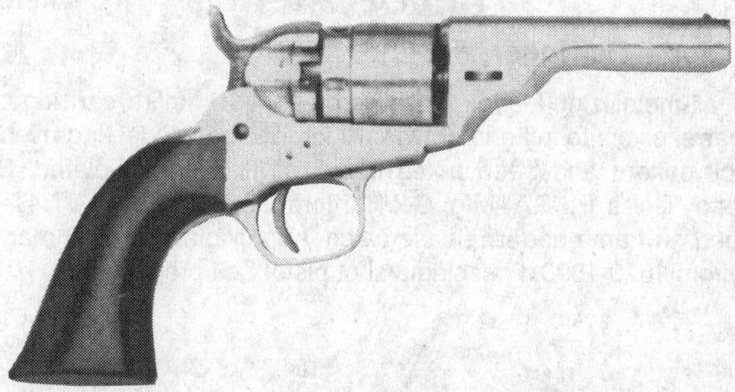

Exc.	Fine	V.G.	Good	Fair	Poor
3000	2250	1750	900	600	300

4.5" Octagonal Barrel Without Ejector Antique

Premium for rare 3" barrel.

Exc.	Fine	V.G.	Good	Fair	Poor
3250	2350	1800	950	650	300

Model 1862 Pocket Navy Octagon Barrel with Ejector Antique

Exc.	Fine	V.G.	Good	Fair	Poor
3500	2500	1850	1000	700	300

Model 1862 Police Round Barrel with Ejector Antique

Exc.	Fine	V.G.	Good	Fair	Poor
3500	2500	1850	1000	700	300

Model 1871-1872 Open Top Revolver

First revolver Colt manufactured especially for a metallic cartridge. It was not a conversion. Frame, 7.5" or 8" round barrel and 6-shot cylinder were produced for .44 rimfire metallic cartridge. Grip frame and some internal parts were taken from 1860 Army and 1851 Navy. Although this model was not commercially successful and not accepted by U.S. Ordinance Department, it did pave the way for Single-Action Army that came out shortly thereafter, and was an immediate success. Model is all blued, with case colored hammer. There are some with silver-plated brass grip frames, but most are blued steel. One-piece grips are of varnished walnut. Cylinder is roll-engraved with naval battle scene. Barrel stamped "Address Col. Saml. Colt New-York U.S. America". Later production revolvers are barrel stamped "Colt's Pt. F.A. Mfg. Co. Hartford, Ct. U.S.A." First 1,000 revolvers were stamped "Colt's/Patent". After that, 1871 and 1872 patent dates appeared on the frame. There were 7,000 revolvers manufactured in 1872 and 1873.

1860 Army Grip Frame Antique

Exc.	Fine	V.G.	Good	Fair	Poor
20000	12500	5000	3000	1500	750

1851 Navy Grip Frame Antique

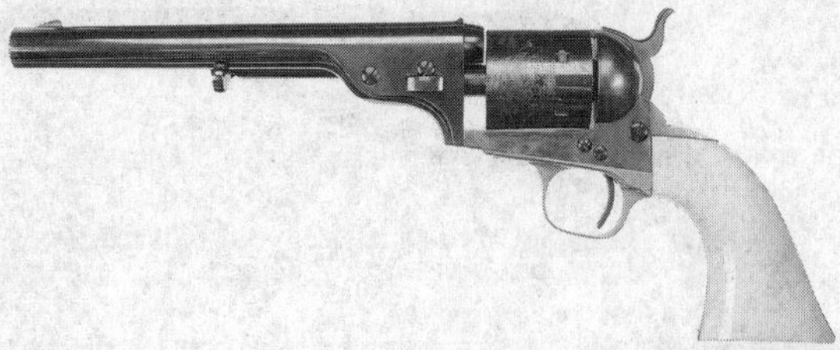

Exc.	Fine	V.G.	Good	Fair	Poor
25000	15000	8000	4000	1750	1000

COLT DERRINGERS AND POCKET REVOLVERS

First Model Derringer Antique

Small all-metal single-shot. Chambered for .41 rimfire cartridge. The 2.5" barrel pivots to left and downward for loading. Model engraved with a scroll pattern and been noted blued, silver or nickel-plated. Barrel stamped "Colt's Pt. F.A. Mfg. Co./Hartford Ct. U.S.A/ No.1". ".41 Cal." stamped on frame under release catch. Approximately 6,500 manufactured from 1870-1890. First single-shot pistol Colt produced.

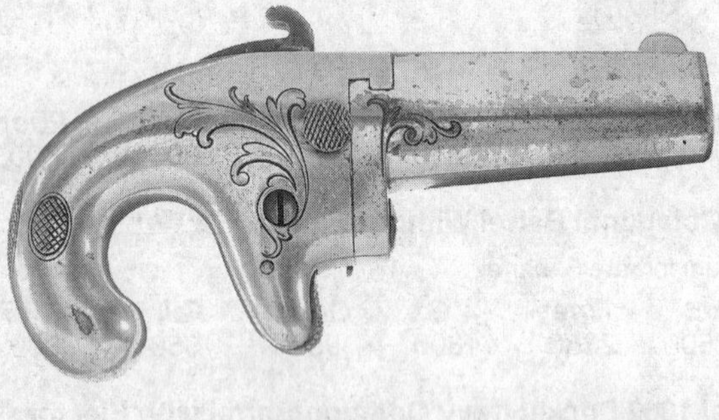

Courtesy Rock Island Auction Company

Exc.	Fine	V.G.	Good	Fair	Poor
5000	2250	1400	900	600	400

Second Model Derringer Antique

Although this model has the same odd shape as First Model, it is readily identifiable by checkered varnished walnut grips and "No 2" on barrel after address. A .41 rimfire with 2.5" barrel that pivots in the same manner as First Model. Approximately 9,000 manufactured between 1870 and 1890. Note: Add 100 percent for .41 Centerfire model.

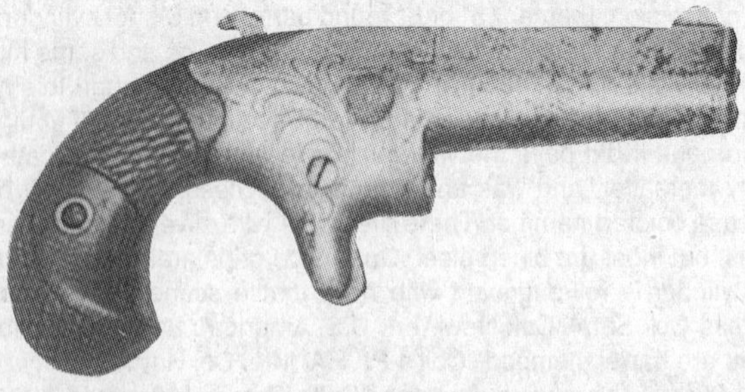

Courtesy Wallis & Wallis, Lewes, Sussex, England

Exc.	Fine	V.G.	Good	Fair	Poor
2500	1500	900	400	250	170

Third Model Derringer

Designed by Alexander Thuer, who was also responsible for Colt's first metallic cartridge conversion. Often referred to as "Thuer Model" for this reason. Chambered for .41 rimfire cartridge, has a 2.5" barrel that pivots to the right (but not down) for loading. Third Model has a more balanced appearance than its predecessors and its commercial success (45,000 produced between 1875 and 1910) reflects this. Barrel on this model stamped "Colt" in small block letters on first 2,000 guns. Remainder of production features "COLT" in large italicized print. ".41 Cal." stamped on left side of frame. Model will be found with barrel blued or plated in silver or nickel and the bronze frame plated. Grips are varnished walnut. Note: Blued models will bring a premium over nickel in same condition. Add 25 percent for .41 Centerfire model.

Jim Supica photo

First Variation, Early Production Antique

Has a raised area ("pregnant frame") on underside of frame through which barrel screw passes. Spur is not angled. Small block "Colt" lettering on barrel.

Exc.	Fine	V.G.	Good	Fair	Poor
4000	2500	2000	1500	900	500

First Variation, Late Production Antique

Similar to early production. Has large italicized "COLT" on barrel. Eliminated bump on bottom of frame. Still has high hammer.

Exc.	Fine	V.G.	Good	Fair	Poor
2000	1200	1000	800	400	280

Production Model Antique

Hammer angled back. Slight premium for early production with tight grip curl of previous variation.

Exc.	Fine	V.G.	Good	Fair	Poor
1500	1000	600	400	250	170

House Model Revolver

There are two basic versions of this model. Both chambered for .41 rimfire cartridge. 4-shot version is known as "Cloverleaf" due to shape of the cylinder when viewed from front. Approximately 7,500 of nearly 10,000 House revolvers were 4-shot configuration. Offered with 1.5" or 3" barrel. The 1.5" length is quite rare. Some octagonal barrels in this length have been noted. 5-shot round-cylinder version accounts for the rest of production. Found with serial numbers over 6100 and offered with 2.875" length barrel only. Model stamped on top strap "Pat. Sept. 19, 1871". Has brass frames that were sometimes nickel-plated. Barrels are found blued or plated. Grips are varnished walnut or rosewood. Slightly fewer than 10,000 of both variations manufactured from 1871-1876. Note: Blued models will bring a premium over nickel in same condition.

Cloverleaf with 1.5" Round Barrel Antique

Exc.	Fine	V.G.	Good	Fair	Poor
6000	4000	2000	1500	900	500

Cloverleaf with 3" Barrel Antique

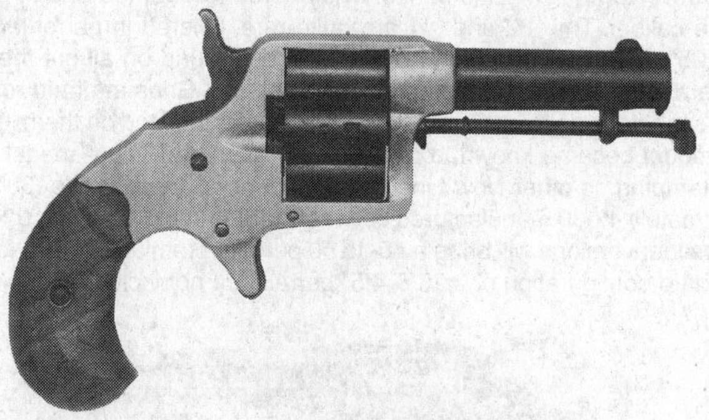

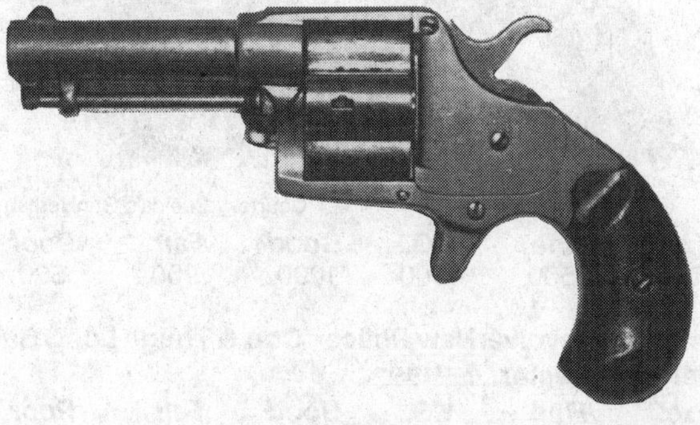

Courtesy Buffalo Bill Historical Center, Cody, Wyoming

Exc.	Fine	V.G.	Good	Fair	Poor
2000	1500	1000	500	200	140

House Pistol with 5-Shot Round Cylinder Antique

Exc.	Fine	V.G.	Good	Fair	Poor
1550	1300	900	500	200	140

Open Top Pocket Revolver

A .22-caliber rimfire 7-shot revolver offered with 2.375" or 2.875" barrel. Model was a commercial success, with over 114,000 manufactured between 1871 and 1877. Would undoubtedly been a great deal more sold had not the cheap copies begun to flood the market at that time, forcing Colt to drop this model from the line. Revolver has a silver or nickel-plated brass frame and nickel-plated or blued barrel and cylinder. Grips are varnished walnut. Cylinder bolt slots are found toward the front on this model. "Colt's Pt. F.A. Mfg. Co./Hartford, Ct. U.S.A." stamped on barrel; ".22 Cal." on left side of frame. Note: Blued models will bring a premium over nickel in same condition.

Early Model with Ejector Rod Antique

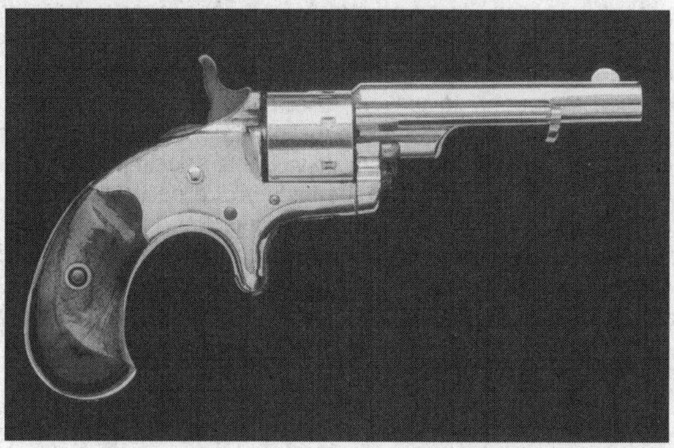

Courtesy Bonhams & Butterfields

Exc.	Fine	V.G.	Good	Fair	Poor
2000	1750	1270	800	400	280

Production Model without Ejector Rod Antique

Exc.	Fine	V.G.	Good	Fair	Poor
1250	600	450	300	150	100

New Line Revolver .22

This was smallest framed version of five distinct New Line Revolvers. A 7-shot cylinder and 2.25" octagonal barrel. Frame is nickel-plated and balance of revolver nickel-plated or blued. Grips are of rosewood. Approximately 55,000 of these made from 1873-1877. Colt also stopped production of New Lines rather than try to compete with "Suicide Specials". "Colt New .22" is found on barrel; ".22 Cal." on frame. Barrel also stamped "Colt's Pt. F.A. Mfg.Co./Hartford, Ct. U.S.A." Note: Blued models will bring higher prices than nickel models in same condition.

1st Model Antique

Short cylinder flutes.

Exc.	Fine	V.G.	Good	Fair	Poor
1300	600	450	300	150	100

2nd Model Antique

Long cylinder flutes. Premium for rare Kittridge "Little Colt" marking on right side of barrel.

Exc.	Fine	V.G.	Good	Fair	Poor
750	500	370	250	120	80

New Line Revolver .30 Antique

Larger version of .22 New Line. Basic difference is size, caliber, caliber markings and offering of a blued version with case colored frame. Approximately 11,000 manufactured from 1874-1876. Note: Prices are for nickel finish. Blued models will bring a premium of 100 percent. Premium for rare Kittridge "Little Pony" marking on right side of barrel.

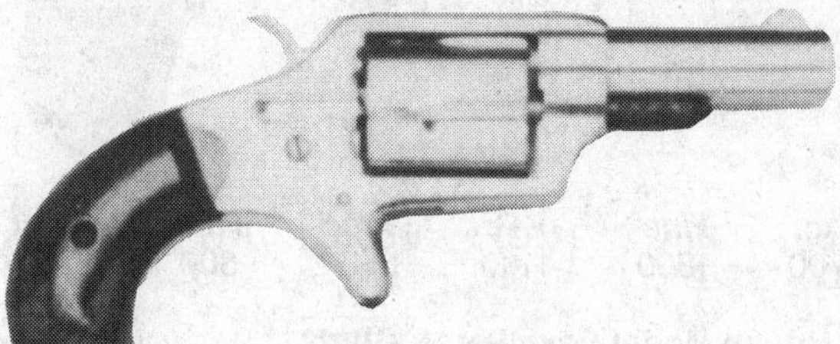

Courtesy Wallis & Wallis, Lewes, Sussex, England

Exc.	Fine	V.G.	Good	Fair	Poor
1000	750	520	300	150	100

New Line Revolver .32 Antique

Same basic revolver as .30-caliber, except chambered for .32-caliber rimfire or centerfire and is so marked. There were 22,000 manufactured from 1873-1884. Model was offered with rare 4" barrel. This variation would be worth nearly twice the value of a standard model. Note: Prices are for nickel finish. Blued models will bring a premium of 100 percent.

Exc.	Fine	V.G.	Good	Fair	Poor
1550	850	570	300	150	100

New Line Revolver .38 Antique

Approximately 5,500 manufactured between 1874 and 1880. Chambered for .38-caliber rimfire or centerfire and is so marked. This model in a 4" barrel would also bring twice the value. Note: Prices are for nickel finish. Blued models will bring a premium of 100 percent.

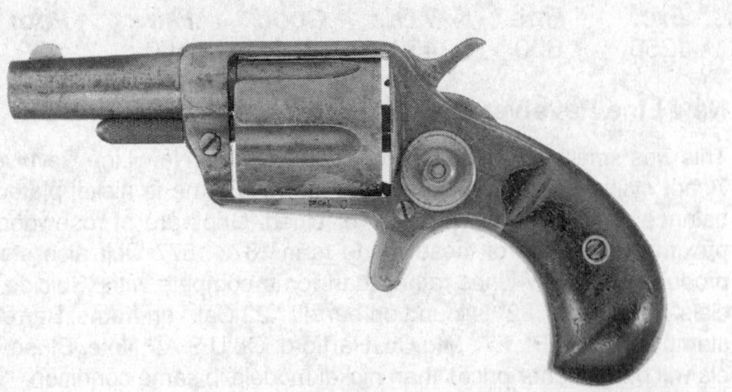

Courtesy Rock Island Auction Company

Exc.	Fine	V.G.	Good	Fair	Poor
1500	800	600	400	200	140

New Line Revolver .41 Antique

The "Big Colt", as it was sometimes known in advertising of its era. Chambered for .41-caliber rimfire or centerfire and is so marked. Large caliber of this variation makes this the most desirable of New Lines to collectors. Approximately 7,000 manufactured from 1874-1879. A 4" barrel version would again be worth a 100 percent premium. Note: Prices are for nickel finish. Blued models will bring a premium of 100 percent.

Exc.	Fine	V.G.	Good	Fair	Poor
2700	1800	1100	650	300	210

New House Model Revolver Antique

Revolver similar to other New Lines. Features a square-butt instead of bird's-head configuration, 2.25" round barrel without ejector rod and a thin loading gate. Chambered for .32 (rare), .38 and .41 centerfire cartridges. Finish was full nickel-plated or blued, with case colored frame. Grips are walnut, rosewood or (for the first time on a Colt revolver) checkered hard rubber, with an oval around the word "Colt". Barrel address is same as on other New Lines. Frame marked "New House" with caliber. Approximately 4,000 manufactured between 1880-1886. .32-caliber model would bring a 10 percent premium. Note: Prices are for nickel finish. Blued models will bring a premium of 100 percent.

Courtesy Milwaukee Public Museum, Milwaukee, Wisconsin

Exc.	Fine	V.G.	Good	Fair	Poor
1500	1000	720	450	250	170

New Police "Cop & Thug" Revolver Antique

Final revolver in New Line series. Chambered for .32, .38 and .41 centerfire caliber. The .32 and .41 are quite rare. Offered in barrel lengths of 2.25", 4.5", 5.5" and 6.5". An ejector rod is found on all but the 2.5" barrel. Finish is nickel or blued and case colored. Grips are hard rubber, with scene of a policeman arresting a criminal embossed on them; thusly the model became known to collectors as "Cop and Thug" model. Barrel stamping as other New Lines; frame stamped "New Police .38". Approximately 4,000 manufactured between 1882-1886. Note: The .32- and .41-caliber versions will bring a 40- to 50 percent premium. Values for the standard configuration of 2.25 & 4.5" barrels are not included.

Courtesy Supica's GunHeritage.com

Exc.	Fine	V.G.	Good	Fair	Poor
4000	2500	1500	1000	900	500

New Police RevolverNew Police "Cop & Thug" Long Barrel Model with Ejector Antique

Exc.	Fine	V.G.	Good	Fair	Poor
—	4500	2320	1400	950	500

COLT SINGLE-ACTION ARMY REVOLVERS ("SAA")

Antique

Colt Single Action Army ("SAA") or Peacemaker or Model 1873. Few interruptions or changes in design, it has been manufactured from 1873 until the present. Variations in this model are myriad. Produced in 30 different calibers; barrel lengths from 2.5" to 16", with 4.75", 5.5" and 7.5" standard. The standard finish is blued, with case colored frame. Many are nickel-plated. Examples have been found silver-/gold-plated, with combinations thereof. Finest engravers in the world have used SAA as a canvas to display their artistry. Standard grips from 1873-1883 were walnut, either oil-stained or varnished. From 1883 to approximately 1897 standard grips were hard rubber, with eagle and shield. After this date, at serial number 165000, hard rubber grips featured Rampant Colt. Many special-order grips were available, notably pearl and ivory, which were often checkered or carved in ornate fashion. Variables involved in establishing values on this model are extreme. Added to this, one must also consider historical significance, since SAA played a big part in formative years of the American West. Fortunately for those among us interested in SAA, there are a number of fine publications available dealing exclusively with this model. It is my strongest recommendation that they be acquired and studied thoroughly to prevent extremely expensive mistakes. Colt factory records are nearly complete for this model and research should be done before acquisition of rare or valuable specimens. Colt factory will provide a letter documenting the history of a particular model for a fee of $100, as of 2014. For historically significant, factory engraved or celebrity owned guns, fees may be higher. Archive department's address is: Colt Archive Properties, P. O. Box 1868, Hartford, CT 06144. Some research data can be obtained by telephone: 800-962-2658 ext. 1343.

For our purposes we will break down Single-Action Army production as follows:

Antique or Black Powder, 1873-1898, serial number 1-175000 Cylinder axis pin is retained by a screw in front of frame.

Pre-war, 1899-1940, serial number 175001-357859 Cylinder axis pin is retained by a spring-loaded button through side of frame. This method is utilized on the following models, as well.

Post-war 2nd Generation, 1956-1978, serial number 0001SA-99999SA

3rd Generation, 1978-Present, serial #SA1001. Breakdown of production by caliber will follow the chapter. It is important to note that the rarer calibers and larger calibers bring higher values in this variation. As a rule of thumb, nickel guns will bring a deduction of 20- to 30 percent. Revolvers with 4.75" barrels add 10- to 15 percent. Checkered grips add 20 percent.

Note: U.S. Military SAAs: Collectors call specimens with original 7-1/2" barrels "Cavalry models" and those with barrels shortened by the government to 5-1/2" "Artillery models," which generally bring less than the Cavalry models. A Cavalry model with its barrel cut after military use, or an Artillery model with its barrel "stretched" back to 7-1/2" will bring less than an Artillery model.

Premium for rare calibers. Generally .32-20 and .41 Colt will bring a little less than other calibers.

Antique

"SAA 1st Year Production Pinched Frame" 1873 Only"" Antique

It is necessary to categorize this variation on its own. This is one of the rarest and most interesting of all SAAs—not to mention that it is the first. On this model, top strap is pinched or constricted approximately .5 up from hammer to form the rear sight. Highest surviving serial number having this feature is #156, lowest #1. From these numbers it is safe to assume that the first run of SAAs were all pinched-frame models; but there is no way to tell how many there were, since Colt did not serial number the frames in the order that they were manufactured. An educated guess would be there were between 50 and 150 pinched frame guns in all and that they were all made before mid-July 1873. Reason for change came about on the recommendation of Capt. J.R. Edie, a government inspector who thought that the full fluted top strap would be a big improvement in sighting capabilities of the weapon. Barrel length of first model is 7.5"; standard caliber .45 Colt; proper grips were of walnut. Front sight blade is German silver. Needless to say, this model will rarely be encountered, and if it is, it should never be purchased without competent appraisal. Very rare. Values are speculative.

Exc.	Fine	V.G.	Good	Fair	Poor
—	150000	80000	60000	25000	10000

SAA Early Military Cavalry Model 1873-1877 Antique

Serial number range on this first run of military contract revolvers extends to #24000. Barrel address is in early script style, with # symbol preceding and following. Frame bears martial marking "US" and walnut grips have inspector's cartouche stamped on them. Front sight is steel as on all military models; barrel length 7.5"; caliber .45 Colt; ejector rod head is bull's-eye or donut style, with a hole in the center of it. Finish features military polish and case colored frame, with remainder blued. Authenticate any potential purchase; many spurious examples have been noted. Rarely found in higher condition grade, values are speculative. In 2020, Rock Island sold the "Finest known Ainsworth inspected" SAA for $207,000.

Exc.	Fine	V.G.	Good	Fair	Poor
50000	25000	20000	15000	7000	3500

SAA Early Civilian Model 1873-1877 Antique

Identical to Early Military Model, but has no military acceptance markings or cartouches. Some could have German silver front sight blade. Early bull's-eye ejector rod head is used on this model. Civilian Model has a higher degree of polish than is found on military models. Finish on these early models could be plated or blued, with case colored frame. Has a script barrel address. Grips are standard one-piece walnut. Ivory-grip models are worth a premium.

Exc.	Fine	V.G.	Good	Fair	Poor
20000	15000	7500	3500	2000	1000

SAA .44 Rimfire Model 1875-1880 Antique

Model made to fire .44 Henry Rimfire cartridge. It was to be used as a compatible companion sidearm to Henry and Winchester 1866 rifles, that were used extensively during this era. However, this was not the case; and .44 Rimfire was doomed to economic failure as soon as it appeared on the market. By that time, it had already been established that large-caliber centerfire cartridges were a good deal more efficient than their rimfire counterparts. Large-caliber rimfires were deemed obsolete before this Colt ever hit the market. The result of this was that Colt's sales representatives sold most of the production to obscure banana republics in South and Central America, where this model received much abuse. Most had original 7.5" barrels cut down; nearly all were denied even the most basic maintenance, making the survival rate of this model quite low. All this adds to its desirability as a collector's item and makes the risk of acquiring a fake that much greater. This model is unique in that it was the only SAA variation to have its own serial number range, starting with #1 and continuing to #1892, the latest known surviving specimen. Block style barrel markings were introduced during this production run. At least 90 of these revolvers were converted by the factory to .22 rimfire and one was shipped chambered for .32 rimfire.

Exc.	Fine	V.G.	Good	Fair	Poor
50000	25000	15000	10000	7000	3000

SAA Late Military Cavalry Model 1878-1891 Antique

Later Military Models are serial numbered to approximately #136000. They bear block-style barrel address without the # prefix and suffix. Frames are marked "US"; grips have inspector's cartouche. Finish is military-style polish, case colored frame and remainder blued. Grips are oil-stained walnut. On military marked Colts, it is imperative that potential purchases be authenticated as many fakes have been noted. Note: Revolvers produced from 1878 to 1885 will command a premium. Seek an expert appraisal prior to sale. In original 7.5" barrel configuration, US military SAAs are called "Cavalry Models," to differntiate them from the government altered 5.5" barrel "Artillery Models." Year of production and government inspector initials can impact value. High condition guns are very rare. In 2019 Rock Island Auction sold the "Finest known 1880 Production Colt Cavalry Model" in unfired As New condition for $403,500.

Exc.	Fine	V.G.	Good	Fair	Poor
35000	12500	7500	4000	2500	1750

SAA Artillery Model 1895-1903 Antique

A number of "US" marked SAAs were returned either to the Colt factory or to the Springfield Armory, where they were altered and refinished. These revolvers have 5.5" barrels and any combination of mixed serial numbers. They were remarked by inspectors of the era. They have case colored frame, blued cylinder and barrel. Some have been noted all blued within this variation. This model, as with other military marked Colts, should definitely be authenticated before purchase. Some of these revolvers fall outside the 1898 antique cutoff date that has been established by the government. In our experience are not quite as desirable to investors. They are generally worth approximately 20 percent less. Add a 50 percent premium for specimens marked "New York State Militia". These have 7.5" barrels and only 800 are documented in Colt records. Be sure to obtain documentation from the factory for these models. Premium for rare artillery models with matching serial numbers.

Exc.	Fine	V.G.	Good	Fair	Poor
11000	7500	4500	2500	1700	1200

SAA London Model Antique

These SAAs were manufactured to be sold through Colt's London Agency. Barrel stamped "Colt's Pt. F.A. Mfg. Co. Hartford, Ct. U.S.A. Depot 14 Pall Mall London". This model is available in various barrel lengths. They are generally chambered for .45 Colt, .450 Boxer, .450 Eley, .455 Eley and rarely .476 Eley, largest of the SAA chamberings. A good many of these London Models were cased and embellished and should be individually appraised. This model should be authenticated as many spurious examples have been noted.

Exc.	Fine	V.G.	Good	Fair	Poor
9000	5000	3500	2250	1400	1000

SAA Frontier Six-Shooter with Etched Barrel 1878-1882

Antique

Several thousand SAAs were made with the legend "Colt's Frontier Six Shooter" acid-etched into left side of barrel instead of being stamped. This etching is not deep and today collectors will become ecstatic if they discover a specimen with mere vestiges of the etched panel remaining. These acid-etched SAAs are serial numbered #45000-#65000. They have various barrel lengths and finishes, but all are chambered for .44-40 caliber. After 1882, FRONTIER SIXSHOOTER was stamped on the barrel of .44-40 models rather than etched. These stamp-marked models are valued under SAA Standard Civilian Production.

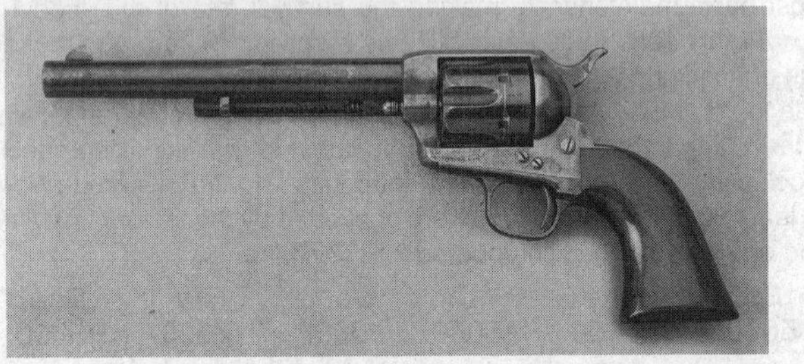

Courtesy Little John's Auction Service, Inc., Paul Goodwin photo

Exc.	Fine	V.G.	Good	Fair	Poor
18000	12500	9050	5600	3000	2000

SAA Sheriff's or Storekeeper's Model 1882-1898 Antique

Made in several barrel lengths: 2.5", 3", 3.5", 4", 4.75" and 7.5". The 2.5" and 7.5" guns are very rare and can bring premiums of 25 to 50 percent, depending on condition. Most have 4" barrels. Features no ejector rod or housing and frame is made without the hole in right forward section to accommodate ejector assembly. Sheriff's or Storekeeper's Model is numbered above serial #73000. Manufactured with various finishes and chambered for numerous calibers. This model continued after 1898 into smokeless or modern era. Examples with smokeless-powder frame made after 1898 are worth approximately 20 percent less. Although faking this model is quite difficult, it has been successfully attempted. Note: Nickel models will command a premium.

Courtesy Little John's Auction Service, Inc., Paul Goodwin photo

Exc.	Fine	V.G.	Good	Fair	Poor
45000	20000	12000	8500	4000	2500

SAA Flattop Target Model 1888-1896 Antique

Model highly regarded and sought after by collectors. It is not only rare (only 925 manufactured), but an extremely attractive and well-finished variation. Chambered for 22 different calibers from .22 rimfire to .476 Eley. The .22 rimfire, .38 Colt, .41 and .45 Colt are the most predominant chamberings. The 7.5" barrel length is most commonly encountered. Serial number range between #127000-#162000. Some have been noted in higher ranges. Finish is all blued, with case colored hammer. Checkered grips are hard rubber or walnut. Most identifying feature of flattop is lack of a groove in the top strap and sight blade dovetailed into the flattop. Front sight has a removable blade insert. Values given are for a standard production model chambered for calibers previously mentioned as being the most common. It is important to have other calibers individually appraised, as variance in values can be quite extreme.

Exc.	Fine	V.G.	Good	Fair	Poor
18000	13500	10000	6500	3250	2270

Bisley Model 1894-1915

Named for target range in Great Britain where their National Target Matches were held, since the nineteenth century. Designed as a target revolver, with an odd humped-back grip that was supposed to better fill the hand while target shooting. Easily identified by wide low profile hammer spur, wide trigger and name "Bisley" stamped on barrel. Bisley production fell within serial number range #165000-#331916. There were 44,350 made. Offered in 16 different chamberings from .32 Colt to .455 Eley. Most common calibers were .32-20, .38-40, .41, .44-40 and .45 Colt. Barrel lengths 4.75", 5.5" and 7.5". Frame and hammer are case colored; remainder blued. Smokeless-powder models produced after 1899 utilized push-button cylinder pin retainer. Grips are checkered hard rubber. This model was actually designed with English sales in mind; though it did sell well over there, American sales accounted for most of Bisley production. Values we provide here cover the standard calibers and barrel lengths. Rare calibers and/or other notable variations can bring greatly fluctuating values.

NIB	Exc.	V.G.	Good	Fair	Poor
—	8000	5750	4000	2000	950

Bisley Model Flattop Target 1894-1913

Model quite similar to Standard Bisley, with flattop frame and dovetailed rear sight feature. Has removable front sight insert, all blued finish with case colored hammer only. Available with 7.5" barrel. Smokeless-powder models produced after 1899 utilized push-button cylinder pin retainer. Calibers same as standard Bisley. Colt manufactured 976 of these revolvers. Advice regarding appraisal would also apply.

NIB	Exc.	V.G.	Good	Fair	Poor
—	22500	14000	8500	2750	1450

SAA Standard Civilian Production Models 1876-1898

Antique

Final designated category for black powder or antique SAAs includes all revolvers not previously categorized. Barrel lengths 4.75", 5.5" and 7.5" are chambered for any one of 30 different calibers. Finishes could be blued, blued and case colored or plated in nickel, silver, gold or combinations thereof. Grips could be walnut, hard rubber, ivory, pearl, stag or bone. Possibilities are endless. Values given here are for basic model and we again strongly advise securing qualified appraisal when not completely sure of any model variation. Note: Add 20 percent premium for serial numbers between 54000 and 130000; 40 percent for serial numbers between 22000 and 54000; 20 to 30 percent for original box, depending on condition; 10 percent for 4.75" barrel. Caliber affects price. .44 -40 models stamped "Frontier Six-Shooter" and .45 Colt models bring a bit more; .41 Colt and .32-20 brings a bit less. Rare calibers can bring a substantial premium.

Exc.	Fine	V.G.	Good	Fair	Poor
10000	6000	4000	2500	1500	1000

COLT PRE-WAR SINGLE ACTION ARMY REVOLVER 1899-1940

Standard Production Pre-war Models (1899-1940)

The 1899 cutoff has been thoroughly discussed, but it is interesting to note that the actual beginning production date for smokeless models was 1900. Pre-war Colts, all in all, are quite similar to the antiques—finishes, barrel lengths, grips, etc. Calibers are also similar, with the exception of obsolete ones being dropped and new discoveries added. Most apparent physical difference between smokeless-powder and blackpowder models is previously discussed method of retaining the cylinder axis pin. Pre-war Colts utilized the spring-loaded button through side of the frame. Blackpowder models utilized a screw in front of the frame. Values we furnish for this model designation are for these standard models only. Serial number range on pre-war SAAs is 175001-357859. Any variation can have marked effects on value fluctuations. Qualified appraisal should be secured. Note: Scarce chamberings command 30 percent to 100 percent premium. Early production guns can also bring a premium. Add 10- to 25 percent for original box, depending on condition; 25 percent for original ivory, pearl or checkered wood grips; 35 percent for stag grips.

1896-1899, Serial numbers 165000-182000

NIB	Exc.	V.G.	Good	Fair	Poor
—	25000	15750	10800	4000	2000

1899-1908, Serial numbers 182000-300000

NIB	Exc.	V.G.	Good	Fair	Poor
—	20000	13500	9000	2800	1600

1908-1914, Serial numbers 300000-328000

NIB	Exc.	V.G.	Good	Fair	Poor
—	18000	9000	7250	2400	1600

1914-1920, Serial numbers 328000-339000

NIB	Exc.	V.G.	Good	Fair	Poor
—	16000	8000	6250	2400	1500

1920-1940, Serial numbers 339000-357000

NIB	Exc.	V.G.	Good	Fair	Poor
—	11000	6750	5500	2400	1500

Long Fluted Cylinder Model (1913-1915)

Strange as it may seem, Colt Company has an apparent credo they followed to never throw anything away. That credo was never more evident than with this model. These Long Flute Cylinders were actually left over from model 1878 Double-Action Army Revolvers. Someone in the hierarchy at Colt had an inspiration that drove gunsmiths on the payroll slightly mad: to make these cylinders fit SAA frames. There were 1,478 of these Long Flutes manufactured. Chambered for .45 Colt, .38-40, .32-20, .41 Colt and .44 Smith & Wesson Special. Offered in three standard barrel lengths and were especially well-polished, having what has been described as Colt's "Fire Blue" on the barrel and cylinder. Frame and hammer are case colored. Fitted with checkered hard rubber grips. Particularly fine examples of Colt's craft. Rare.

NIB	Exc.	V.G.	Good	Fair	Poor
—	22500	13500	5500	2500	1600

COLT POST-WAR SINGLE ACTION ARMY REVOLVER (AKA SECOND GENERATION)

Standard Post-war Model (1956-1975)

In 1956, shooting and gun-collecting fraternity succeeded in convincing Colt there was a market for a re-introduced SAA. Revolver was brought back in the same external configuration. Only changes were internal. Basic specifications as to barrel length and finish availability were the same. Calibers available were .38 Special, .357 Magnum, .44 Special and .45 Colt. Serial number range of re-introduced 2nd Generation Colt is #000ISA-73000SA. Values are established by four basic factors: caliber (popularity and scarcity), barrel length, finish and condition. The .38 Special is rarest caliber; .45 Colt and .44 Special are more sought after than .357 Magnum. Special feature revolvers such as 350 factory-engraved guns produced during this period, must be individually appraised. Ivory situation in the world today has become quite a factor, as ivory grips are found on many SAAs. Remember as always, when in doubt secure a qualified appraisal. Note: Values shown are for 5.5" barrel models. Add 15 percent for 4.75"; 10 percent for 7.5"; 20 percent for nickel finish; $250 for ivory grips.

.38 Special

NIB	Exc.	V.G.	Good	Fair	Poor
3250	2750	1850	1200	900	700

.357 Magnum

NIB	Exc.	V.G.	Good	Fair	Poor
2750	2250	1330	1000	850	700

.44 Special

NIB	Exc.	V.G.	Good	Fair	Poor
3500	2850	2000	1200	1100	850

.45 Colt

NIB	Exc.	V.G.	Good	Fair	Poor
3750	3200	2200	1650	1100	850

Sheriff's Model (1960-1975)

Between 1960 and 1975, approximately 500 Sheriff's Models manufactured. First of these were marketed by Centennial Arms. They have 3" barrels and no ejector rod assemblies. Frames were made without the hole for ejector rod to pass through. Blued, with case colored frames; 25 revolvers were nickel-plated and would bring a sizable premium if authenticated. Barrels marked "Colt Sheriff's Model". Serial number has an "SM" suffix. Chambered for .45 Colt cartridge. Note: Add 100 percent for nickel finish.

NIB	Exc.	V.G.	Good	Fair	Poor
2750	2200	1650	1100	830	650

Buntline Special (1957-1975)

"Buntline Special" was named after a dime novelist named Ned Buntline, who supposedly gave this special long barrel revolver to Wyatt Earp. Story is suspected to be purely legend as no Colt records exist to lend it credence. Be that as it may, Colt factory decided to take advantage of the market and produced 12" barreled SAA from 1957-1974. Approximately 3,900 were manufactured. Chambered for .45 Colt cartridge. Offered in blued and case colored finish. Only 65 Buntlines are nickel-plated, making this an extremely rare variation that definitely should be authenticated before purchase. Walnut grips are most commonly noted. Also offered with checkered hard rubber grips. Barrels marked on left side "Colt Buntline Special .45". Note: Add 100 percent for nickel finish.

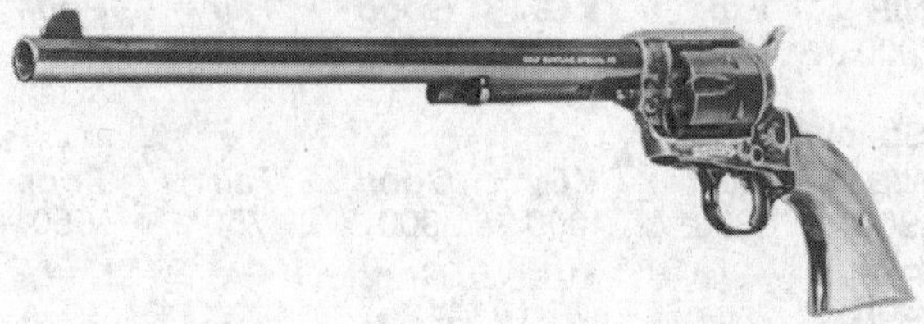

NIB	Exc.	V.G.	Good	Fair	Poor
2700	1750	1400	950	700	600

New Frontier (1961-1975)

New Frontier is readily identified by its flattop frame and adjustable sight. Has a high front sight. Colt manufactured approximately 4,200 of them. Chambered for .357 Magnum, .45 Colt, .44 Special (255 produced) and rarely (only 49 produced) in .38 Special. A few were chambered for .44-40 cartridge. The 7.5" barrel length is by far the most common, but 4.75" and 5.5" barrels are also offered. Standard finish is case colored and blued. Nickel-plating and full blue are offered, but are rarely encountered. Standard grips are walnut. Barrel stamped on left side "Colt New Frontier S.A.A.". Serial number has "NF" suffix. Note: Add 25 percent for 4.75" barrel; 20 percent for 5.5" barrel; 50 percent for full blue and .38 Special; 30 percent for .44 Special and .44-40.

NIB	Exc.	V.G.	Good	Fair	Poor
2750	2250	1350	900	700	550

New Frontier Buntline Special (1962-1967)

Rare model, as Colt only manufactured 70 during this five-year period. Similar to standard Buntline, with 12" barrel. Chambered for .45 Colt only.

NIB	Exc.	V.G.	Good	Fair	Poor
3750	3000	2200	1650	1100	800

COLT THIRD GENERATION SINGLE ACTION ARMY 1976-1981

Colt made some internal changes in 1976 to the SAA. External configuration was not altered. Serial number range began in 1976 with #80000SA and in 1978 #99999SA was reached. At this time the suffix became a prefix. New serial range began with #SA01001. Value is determined, in much the same manner, as described in section on 2nd Generation SAAs. Caliber, barrel length, finish and condition are once again the four main determining factors. Prevalence of special-order guns was greater during this period and many more factory-engraved SAAs were produced. Colt's Custom Shop was quite active during this period. Custom guns are valued according to the prevailing market. Note: Add 10 percent for 4.75" barrel and nickel plated; $250 for ivory grips.

.38 Special

NIB	Exc.	V.G.	Good	Fair	Poor
2150	1650	1150	950	750	600

.357 Magnum

NIB	Exc.	V.G.	Good	Fair	Poor
1900	1350	900	800	700	600

.44-40

NIB	Exc.	V.G.	Good	Fair	Poor
2000	1500	1000	830	700	600

.44-40 Black Powder Frame (Screw Retaining Cylinder Pin)

NIB	Exc.	V.G.	Good	Fair	Poor
2000	1500	1050	850	730	630

.44 Special

NIB	Exc.	V.G.	Good	Fair	Poor
1900	1350	1000	900	750	650

.45 Colt

NIB	Exc.	V.G.	Good	Fair	Poor
2000	1500	1100	900	750	650

Sheriff's Model 3rd Generation

Similar to 2nd Generation Sheriff's Model. Serial number and the fact this model is also chambered for .44-40, are the only external differences. Colt offered this model with interchangeable cylinders—.45 Colt/.45 ACP or .44-40/.44 Special—available in 3" barrel, blued and case colored finish standard. Note: Add 30 percent for interchangeable cylinders; 10 percent for nickel finish; $250 for ivory grips.

NIB	Exc.	V.G.	Good	Fair	Poor
1500	1200	1000	830	700	600

Buntline Special 3rd Generation

Same basic configuration as 2nd Generation, with 12" barrel. Standard finish blued and case colored. Chambered for .45 Colt, with checkered hard rubber grips. Note: Add 20 percent for nickel finish.

NIB	Exc.	V.G.	Good	Fair	Poor
1650	1400	1100	1000	800	700

New Frontier 3rd Generation

Similar in appearance to 2nd Generation guns. 3rd Generation New Frontiers have five-digit serial numbers; 2nd Generation guns four-digit numbers. That and calibers offered are basically the only differences. 3rd Generations are chambered for .44 Special and .45 Colt and rarely found in .44-40. Barrel lengths 7.5" standard, with 4.75" and 5.5" rarely encountered. Note: Add 20 percent for .44-40; 35 percent for 4.75" barrel; 25 percent for 5.5" barrel.

NIB	Exc.	V.G.	Good	Fair	Poor
1800	1350	850	680	530	450

COLT RECENT PRODUCTION SINGLE ACTION ARMY 1982-PRESENT

Standard Single-Action Army

Basic SAA model offered during this time frame in .45 Colt, .44 Special or .357 Magnum, with standard barrel lengths: 4.75", 5.50" or 7.50". Limited production of calibers other than .45 Colt. As of mid 2018, the Colt Custom Shop was temporarily not taking orders for engraving or other optional features on the SAA, but these services may be offered in the future. Note: Add $200 for nickel finish in Very Good or better condition.

NIB	Exc.	V.G.	Good	Fair	Poor
1650	1450	1200	1000	800	600

Colt Cowboy (CB1850)

Introduced in 1998, this model is a replica of Single Action Army. Features a modern transfer bar safety system. Made in USA using some Canadian-built parts. Offered with 5.5" barrel. Chambered for .45 Colt. Sights are fixed, with walnut grips. Blued barrel with case colored frame. Discontinued in 2003.

NIB	Exc.	V.G.	Good	Fair	Poor
850	650	500	400	300	200

"Colt Single-Action Army Legend Rodeo"""

A limited-edition revolver built to commemorate Colt's official PRCA sponsorship. Limited to 1,000. Chambered for .45 LC. Fitted with a 5.5 barrel. Nickel finish Buffalo horn grips, with gold medallions. Machine engraved and washed in gold. Discontinued 1998.

NIB	Exc.	V.G.	Good	Fair	Poor
2750	2250	—	—	—	—

Frontier Six Shooter (2008)

New re-introduction of classic .44-40 Peacemaker. Black powder-style frame and 4.75", 5.5" and 7.5" barrel lengths. Blued finish, with color case-hardened frame or nickel. Discontinued 2010.

NIB	Exc.	V.G.	Good	Fair	Poor
1550	1100	750	600	400	200

Sheriff's and Storekeeper's Model (2008)

New re-introduction of classic Sheriff's (4" barrel) and Storekeeper's Model (3" barrel), without ejector assembly. Black powder-style frame. Blued finish, with color case-hardened frame or nickel. .45 Colt or .44-40. Discontinued 2010.

NIB	Exc.	V.G.	Good	Fair	Poor
1550	1100	750	600	400	200

175th Anniversary SAA Limited Edition

From Colt Custom Shop to celebrate 175th Anniversary of the Colt Company. Introduced in 2011, with production limited to 175 units in each of three standard barrel lengths; 4.75", 5.5" and 7.5". In .45 Colt only features include a black powder frame, Royal Blue finish, 24 karat Gold plated scroll on the frame, cylinder and barrel depicting Rampant Colt icon, Colt Dome, Serpentine Colt, Sam Colt signature and a banner with the text "1836 — 175th Anniversary — 2011".

NIB	Exc.	V.G.	Good	Fair	Poor
2500	1500	1200	1000	700	400

New Frontier Third Generation, Current Production

Re-introduction of adjustable-sighted, flattop-frame version of Single Action Army, last made in 1983. Chambered in .357 Magnum, .44 Special or .45 Colt in all three standard barrel lengths. Rear sight is adjustable for windage and elevation. There is a ramp style front sight. Finish is Colt's Royal Blue on both barrel and cylinder, with color case-hardened frame. Two-piece walnut grips are decorated with a gold medallion. Introduced in 2011.

NIB	Exc.	V.G.	Good	Fair	Poor
1500	1220	900	700	600	500

COLT SCOUT MODEL

A surprising number of Colt pistols are still found in their original boxes, even older models. This can add 100 percent value to the pistol. My thanks to Bruce Buckner, Jr., for his suggestions for and corrections to this section. Anyone wishing to procure a factory letter authenticating a Single Action Army should do so by writing to: COLT HISTORIAN, P.O. BOX 1868, HARTFORD, CT 06144. There is a charge of $75 per serial number for this service. If Colt cannot provide the desired information, $10 will be refunded. Enclose the Colt model name, serial number and your name and address, along with the check.

Frontier Scout (1957-1971)

Scaled-down version of SAA. Chambered for .22 LR with an interchangeable .22 Magnum cylinder. Offered with 4.75" or 9.5" barrel. Frame is alloy. First year production frames were duotone, with frame left in white and balance of revolver blued. All blue models and wood grips became available in 1958. In 1961 duotone model was dropped from production. All Q series guns were offered in duotone finish; F series guns were made in duotone and full blue. A .22 Magnum model was first offered in 1959. In 1964 dual cylinders were introduced. These revolvers have "Q" or "F" serial number suffixes. In 1960 the "K" series Scout was introduced and featured a heavier frame, nickel plating and wood grips. Majority of commemorative revolvers are of this type. This series was discontinued in 1970. Prices are about 15 percent higher than for "Q" and "F" series guns. Note: Add 50 percent for 9.5" Buntline; 10 percent for extra cylinder.

NIB	Exc.	V.G.	Good	Fair	Poor
480	350	230	200	180	100

Peacemaker & New Frontier .22

Similar to Frontier Scout, with a steel case colored or blued frame. Fitted with old style black plastic eagle grips. Peacemaker .22 and New Frontier .22 revolvers were initially offered with 4.75", 6" and 7.5" barrels (Buntline). After about one year of production 4.75" barrel was discontinued and a 4.4" barrel was offered in each model. Also has an interchangeable .22 Magnum cylinder.

Peacemaker .22 was only available with a steel receiver and color case-hardened finish. Grip frames were alloy. Same is true of New Frontier .22 revolvers except that (as noted in the book), New Frontier .22 GS series was available with color case-hardened or blue receivers. Both Peacemaker .22 and New Frontier .22 revolvers were available in single caliber (.22 LR only) and dual caliber (.22 LR and .22 Magnum) models. The factory had separate model numbers for these variations. Also, the factory offered "P" series or "62" model Frontier Scouts and Buntline Scouts. This was a significant model variation. Most of these revolvers had a "G" suffix although some built in 1974 had a "L" suffix. In 1982 through 1986 a New Frontier model with cross-bolt safety was offered. This model is often referred to as "GS" series. This revolver was offered with adjustable sights only. No Peacemakers were offered in this series.

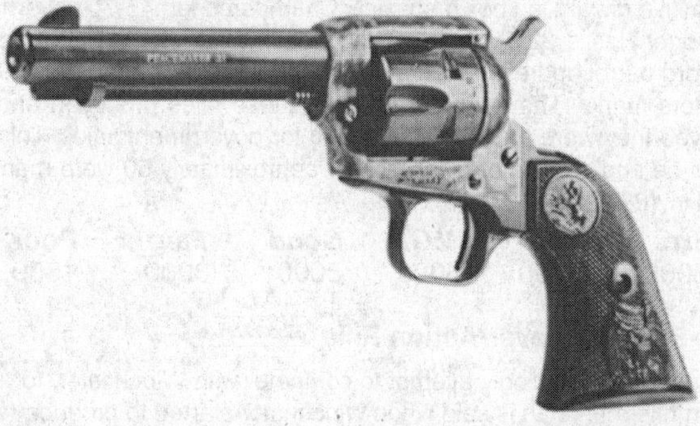

NIB	Exc.	V.G.	Good	Fair	Poor
580	500	330	230	150	100

Scout Model SAA (1962-1971)

Basically a scaled-down version of SAA. Chambered for .22 LR cartridge. Offered with 4.75", 6" or 7" barrel. Earlier production has case colored frames with remainder blued; later production is all blued. Grips are checkered hard rubber. Discontinued in 1986.

NIB	Exc.	V.G.	Good	Fair	Poor
430	330	230	160	110	80

COLT ANTIQUE LONG ARMS

Berdan Single-Shot Rifle

A scarce rifle on today's market. Approximately 30,200 manufactured, but nearly 30,000 were sent to Russia. Produced from 1866-1870. A trapdoor-type action chambered for .42 centerfire. Standard model has 32.5" barrel; carbine 18.25". Finish blued, with walnut stock. Rifle was designed and patent held by Hiram Berdan, Commander of Civil War "Sharpshooters" Regiment. This was actually Colt's first cartridge arm. The 30,000 rifles and 25 half-stocked carbines that were sent to Russia were in Russian Cyrillic letters. Few examples made for American sales have Colt's name and Hartford address on the barrel.

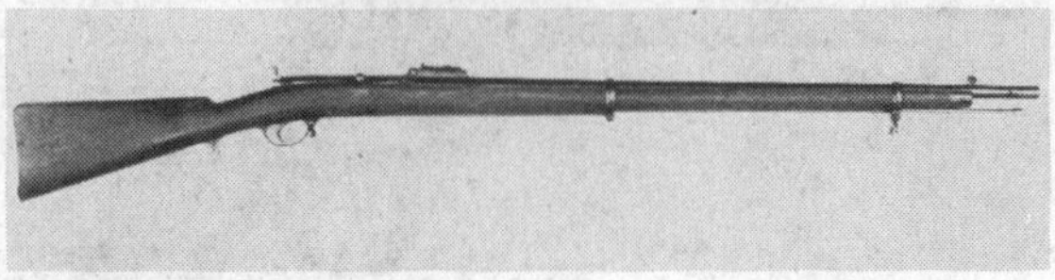

Courtesy Milwaukee Public Museum, Milwaukee, Wisconsin

Berdan Russian Order Antique

30,000 manufactured.

Exc.	Fine	V.G.	Good	Fair	Poor
10000	5000	3250	1500	750	520

Berdan Carbine Russian Order Antique

25 manufactured.

Exc.	Fine	V.G.	Good	Fair	Poor
12500	6500	4150	1800	750	520

Berdan U.S. Sales Antique

100 manufactured.

Exc.	Fine	V.G.	Good	Fair	Poor
10000	5000	3250	1500	750	520

Berdan Carbine U.S. Sales Antique

25 manufactured.

Exc.	Fine	V.G.	Good	Fair	Poor
12500	6500	4150	1800	750	520

Colt-Franklin Military Rifle Antique

Rifle was not a successful venture for Colt. Patents were held by William B. Franklin, a vice-president of the company. Bolt-action rifle, with a primitive gravity-fed box magazine. Chambered for .45-70 government cartridge. Has a 32.5" barrel. Blued, with walnut stock. Rifle has Colt Hartford barrel address and stamped with an eagle's head and U.S. inspectors marks. There were only 50 of these rifles produced and it is believed they were prototypes intended for government sales. This was not to be and production ceased after approximately 50 were manufactured in 1887 and 1888.

Exc.	Fine	V.G.	Good	Fair	Poor
18000	12000	8000	5000	3000	1500

Colt-Burgess Lever-Action Rifle Antique

Represented Colt's only attempt to compete, with Winchester, for lever-action rifle market. It is said when Winchester started to produce revolving handguns for prospective marketing, Colt dropped the Burgess from its line. Chambered for .44-40. Has 25.5" barrel and 15-shot tubular magazine. Carbine version has 20.5" barrel and 12-shot magazine. Finish blued, with case colored hammer and lever. Stock is walnut, with an oil-finish. Colt Hartford address is on barrel and "Burgess Patents" stamped on bottom of lever. There were 3,775 rifles manufactured—1,219 with round barrels and 2,556 with octagonal barrels. Also, 2,593 Carbines. Burgess was produced from 1883-1885.

Courtesy Buffalo Bill Historical Center, Cody, Wyoming

Burgess Rifle - Octagonal Barrel Antique

Exc.	Fine	V.G.	Good	Fair	Poor
12500	10000	7500	5000	2000	1400

Burgess Rifle - Round Barrel Antique

Exc.	Fine	V.G.	Good	Fair	Poor
12000	9500	7100	4700	1800	1260

Burgess Carbine Antique

Exc.	Fine	V.G.	Good	Fair	Poor
17500	13000	9750	6500	2500	1750

Burgess Baby Carbine Antique

Lighter frame and barrel (RARE).

Exc.	Fine	V.G.	Good	Fair	Poor
20000	15000	11250	7500	3000	2100

Lightning Slide-Action, Medium-Frame

First slide-action rifle Colt produced. Chambered for .32-20, .38-40 and .44-40. Intended to be a companion piece to SAAs in same calibers. Has a 26" barrel with 15-shot tube magazine; carbine 20" barrel with 12-shot magazine. Finish blued, with case colored hammer; walnut stock is oil-finished; forend usually checkered. Colt name and Hartford address stamped on barrel along with patent dates. Approximately 89,777 manufactured between 1884 and 1902.

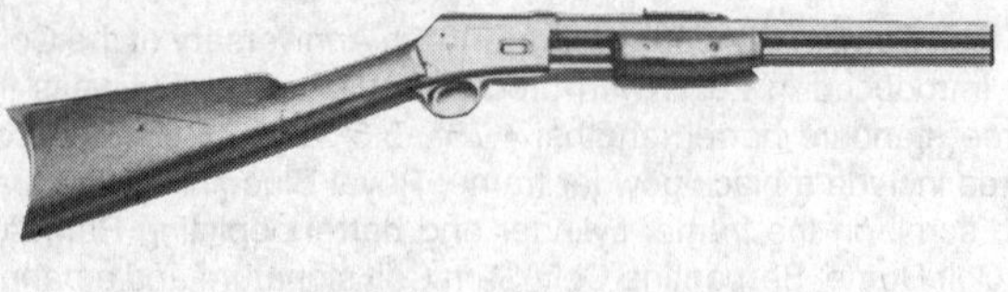

Courtesy Bonhams & Butterfields, San Francisco, California

Lightning Rifle Antique

Exc.	Fine	V.G.	Good	Fair	Poor
5500	3500	2750	2000	1000	700

Lightning Carbine Antique

Exc.	Fine	V.G.	Good	Fair	Poor
7500	4000	3250	2500	1500	1050

Military Rifle or Carbine Antique

.44-40 caliber, short magazine tube, bayonet lug and sling swivels.

Exc.	Fine	V.G.	Good	Fair	Poor
7000	4000	3000	2000	1500	1050

Baby Carbine Antique

1 lb., lighter version of standard carbine.

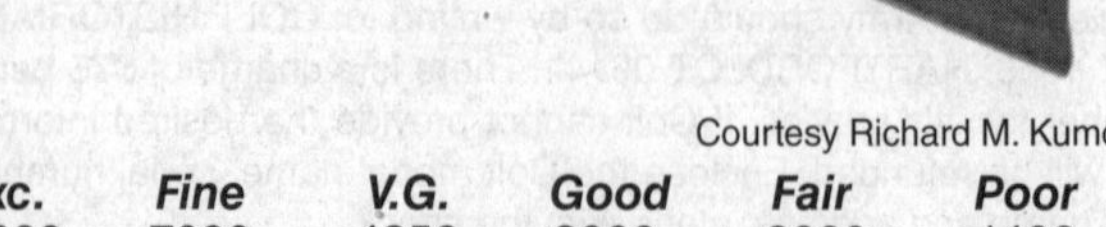

Courtesy Richard M. Kumor Sr.

Exc.	Fine	V.G.	Good	Fair	Poor
10000	7000	4250	3000	2000	1400

San Francisco Police Rifle Antique

.44-40 caliber, #SFP 1-SFP401 on bottom tang.

Exc.	Fine	V.G.	Good	Fair	Poor
9000	6000	4500	3000	2000	1400

Lightning Slide-Action Small-Frame (Antique)

Well-made rifle and first of its type Colt manufactured. Chambered for .22 Short and Long. Standard barrel length 24"; finish blued with case colored hammer. Stock walnut; some checkered, some not. Barrel stamped with Colt name, Hartford address and patent dates. There were 89,912 manufactured between 1887 and 1904.

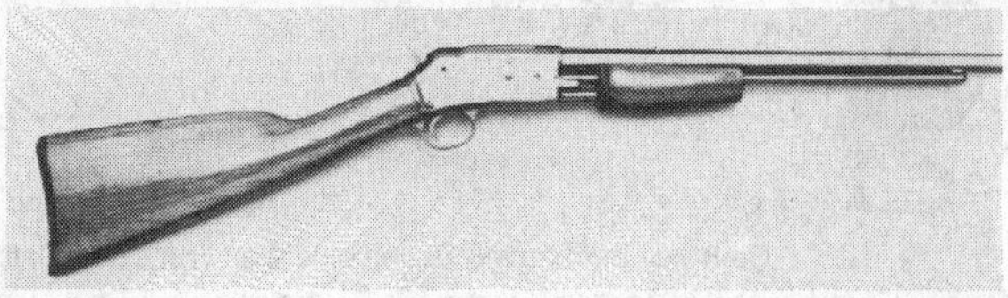

Courtesy Bonhams & Butterfields, San Francisco, California

Exc.	Fine	V.G.	Good	Fair	Poor
4000	2500	1700	1200	700	350

Lightning Slide-Action, Large-Frame (Large Lightning Express)

Similar in appearance to medium-frame Lightning, though larger in size. Chambered in larger rifle calibers of the era, from .38-56 up to .50-95 Express. Larger calibers are more desirable from a collector's standpoint. Has a 28" barrel; carbine a 22" barrel. Finish blued, with case colored hammer. Stock is oiled walnut; forend checkered. Colt name and Hartford address stamped on barrel along with patent dates. Rifle is quite large and has come to be known as "Express Model". Colt manufactured 6,496 between 1887 and 1894.

Lightning Slide-Action, Large-Frame (Express)Rifle - Octagonal Barrel (Antique)

Exc.	Fine	V.G.	Good	Fair	Poor
10500	5500	3750	2000	1000	700

Large Lightning Rifle - Round Barrel (Antique)

Exc.	Fine	V.G.	Good	Fair	Poor
10500	5500	3750	2000	1000	700

Large Lightning Carbine (Antique)

22" barrel.

Exc.	Fine	V.G.	Good	Fair	Poor
12500	6500	4500	2500	1000	700

Large Lightning Baby Carbine (Antique)

22" barrel 1 lb. lighter.

Exc.	Fine	V.G.	Good	Fair	Poor
14000	7000	5000	4000	1500	850

Model 1878 Double-Barrel Shotgun (Antique)

Chambered in 10- or 12-gauge. Has 28", 30" or 32" barrel. It is a sidelock double trigger hammer gun, with case colored locks and breech. Barrels are browned Damacus-patterned. Checkered walnut stock is varnished or oil-finished. Colt's Hartford address stamped on barrel rib; Colt's name on lock. This has been regarded as one of the finest shotguns made in America, although Colt had difficulty competing with the less expensive European imports of the day. Production ceased after only 22,690 were manufactured between 1878 and 1889. Note: Add 300 percent for fully engraved model. Higher grades bring higher values.

Exc.	Fine	V.G.	Good	Fair	Poor
4500	2250	1500	750	300	210

Model 1883 Double-Barrel Shotgun (Antique)

A hammerless boxlock, chambered for 8-, 10- or 12-gauge. Barrels are 28", 30" or 32"; features double triggers. Frame and furniture are case colored; barrels browned with Damascus pattern. Checkered walnut stock is varnished or oil-finished. Colt's Hartford address stamped on barrel rib. "Colt" stamped on each side of frame. Again, as in Model 1878, this is rated as one of the finest of all American-made shotguns. There were many special orders and they require individual appraisal. Colt manufactured 7,366 of these guns between 1883 and 1895. Note: Add 300 percent for fully engraved model; 200 percent for 8-gauge. Higher grades bring higher values.

Exc.	Fine	V.G.	Good	Fair	Poor
6000	3500	2000	1000	500	300

Double-Barrel Rifle (Antique)

One of the rarest of all Colt firearms. A prize for the Colt collector. Only 35 of these guns manufactured. They were said to be the special interest of Caldwell Hart Colt, Samuel Colt's son, who was an avid arms collector. It is said that most of the 35 guns produced wound up in his collection or those of his friends. Chambered for .45-70 or one of the larger variations thereof. It is an exposed hammer sidelock with double triggers. Locks, breech and furniture are case colored; barrels browned or blued. Barrels are 28" in length and checkered stock was oil-finished or varnished walnut. Barrel rib stamped with Colt name and Hartford address. Locks are also stamped "Colt". One must exercise extreme caution in dealing with this model as there have been Model 1878 shotguns converted into double rifles. Colt manufactured 35 guns from 1879-1885. Values are speculative.

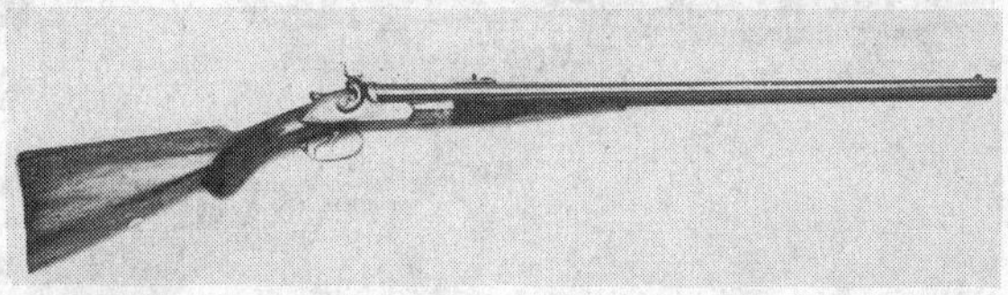

Courtesy Bonhams & Butterfields, San Francisco, California

Exc.	Fine	V.G.	Good	Fair	Poor
75000	35500	17750	10000	6000	3000

COLT DOUBLE-ACTION REVOLVERS

Model 1877 "Lightning" and "Thunderer"

Model 1877 was Colt's first attempt at manufacturing a double-action revolver. Shows a striking resemblance to Single Action Army. Sales on this model were brisk, with over 166,000 produced between 1877 and 1909. Chambered for two different cartridges; .38 Colt known as Lightning" and .41 Colt as "Thunderer". (Also about 300 to 350 made in .32 caliber as the "Rainmaker".) Standard finishes are blued, with case colored frame and nickel plate. Bird's-head grips are of checkered rosewood on early guns and hard rubber on majority of the production run. Barrel lengths most often encountered are 2.5" and 3.5" without an ejector rod and 4.5" and 6" with rod. Other barrel lengths from 1.5" through 10" were offered. Model 1877 holds 6-shots in either caliber. There were quite a few different variations found within this model designation. Values furnished are for standard variations. Antiques made before 1898 would be more desirable from an investment standpoint. These revolvers have a reputation as "watchmaker's nightmares" and non-functioning examples command substantially reduced prices. Note: Add 25 percent premium for blued guns; 50 percent premium for shorter than 2.5"; 10 percent for .41-caliber "Thunderer"; 50 percent for over 6" barrel; 20 percent for London barrel address; 50 percent for .32-caliber; 10 percent for rosewood grips.

Model 1877 DA "Lightning" and "Thunderer"Without Ejector, 2.5" and 3.5" Barrel (Antique)

Premiums for etched barrel marking, 2.5" barrel, and "Metropolitan Police Dept. D.C." marking. Substantial premium for rare .32 caliber Rainmaker model.

Exc.	Fine	V.G.	Good	Fair	Poor
3000	1200	650	500	350	240

With Ejector, 4.5" and 6" Barrel (Antique)

Exc.	Fine	V.G.	Good	Fair	Poor
2500	1200	770	750	450	310

Model 1878 "Frontier"

A large and somewhat ungainly looking revolver. Solid frame with removable triggerguard. Cylinder does not swing out and there is a thin loading gate. Bird's-head grips made of checkered hard rubber; walnut would be found on early models. Finish blued and case colored or nickel-plated. Model 1878 holds 6-shots and standard barrel lengths are 4.75, 5.5" and 7.5", with an ejector assembly and 3", 3.5" and 4" without. Standard chamberings for Model 1878 are .32-20, .38-40, .41 Colt, .44-40 and .45 Colt. This model was fairly well received because it is chambered for large calibers that were popular in that era. Colt manufactured 51,210 between 1878 and 1905. Antique models made before 1898 would be more desirable from an investment standpoint. Note: Add 15 percent premium for blued revolvers; 10- to 50 percent premium for calibers other than .44-40 or .45.

1878 DA Standard (Antique)

Premium for "R.M." marked Mexican military purchase.

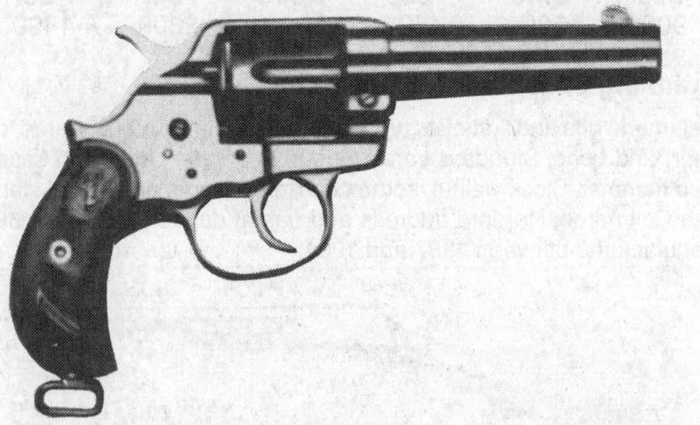

Courtesy Bonhams & Butterfields, San Francisco, California

Exc.	Fine	V.G.	Good	Fair	Poor
4000	2000	1200	800	400	280

1878 DA Omnipotent (Antique)

Special order version of above, with name Omnipotent" stamped on barrel. Very rare. Values are speculative.

Exc.	Fine	V.G.	Good	Fair	Poor
7000	6000	4500	3000	1000	700

1878 DA Sheriff's Model (Antique)

Chambered for .44-40 or .45 Colt. Barrel lengths 3.5 or 4".

Exc.	Fine	V.G.	Good	Fair	Poor
5000	2500	1500	1000	800	560

Model 1902 (Philippine or Alaskan Model)

U.S. Ordnance contract Model 1878. Has a 6" barrel and chambered for .45 Colt. Finish blued and there is a lanyard swivel on the butt. Model bears U.S. inspector's marks. Sometimes referred to as Philippine or Alaskan model. Triggerguard is quite a bit larger than standard.

Courtesy Bonhams & Butterfields

NIB	Exc.	V.G.	Good	Fair	Poor
—	5500	3500	1800	1000	600

Model 1889 Navy—Civilian Model (Antique)

1889 Navy is an important model from a historical standpoint. It was the first double-action revolver Colt manufactured, with a swing-out cylinder. They produced 31,000 of them between 1889 and 1894. Chambered for .38 Colt and .41 Colt cartridges. Cylinder holds 6-shots. Offered with 3", 4.5" or 6" barrel; finish was blued or nickel-plated. Grips are checkered hard rubber, with "Rampant Colt" in an oval molded into them. Patent dates 1884 and 1888 appear in the barrel marking and serial numbers stamped on the butt. Note: Add premium for blued models; 20 percent for 3" barrel

Exc.	Fine	V.G.	Good	Fair	Poor
1500	1000	800	600	300	210

Model 1889 U.S. Navy—Martial Model (Antique)

This variation has a 6" barrel, chambered for .38 Colt and offered in blued finish only. "U.S.N." stamped on the butt. Most Navy models were altered at the Colt factory to add Model 1895 improvements. Note: Original unaltered specimen would be worth as much as 50 percent premium over altered values listed.

Courtesy Bonhams & Butterfields, San Francisco, California

Exc.	Fine	V.G.	Good	Fair	Poor
7000	4000	2000	1000	500	350

Model 1892 New Army and Navy —Civilian Model

Similar in appearance to 1889 Navy. Main differences are improvements to lock-work function. Has double bolt stop notches, double cylinder locking bolt and shorter flutes on the cylinder. The .38 Smith & Wesson and .32-20 were added to .38 Colt and .41 Colt chamberings. Checkered hard rubber grips are standard, with plain walnut grips found on some contract series guns. Barrel lengths and finishes are the same as described for Model 1889. Patent dates 1895 and 1901 appear stamped on later models. Colt manufactured 291,000 of these revolvers between 1892 and 1907. Antiques before 1898 are more desirable from an investment standpoint. Note: Add 20 percent for 3 barrel.

NIB	Exc.	V.G.	Good	Fair	Poor
—	1500	800	500	200	100

Model 1892 "New Army and Navy" —Civilian ModelModel 1892 U.S. Navy—Martial Model

NIB	Exc.	V.G.	Good	Fair	Poor
—	2500	2000	800	600	400

Model 1892 "New Army and Navy" —Civilian Martial Model

NIB	Exc.	V.G.	Good	Fair	Poor
—	2500	2000	800	600	400

Model 1892 "New Army and Navy" —Civilian ModelModel 1894/1896 Army

NIB	Exc.	V.G.	Good	Fair	Poor
—	2400	2200	900	650	400

Model 1905 Marine Corps

Variation of New Army and Navy Model. Derived from late production, with its own serial range #10001-10926. Only 926 produced between 1905 and 1909. Quite rare on today's market and is eagerly sought after by Colt Double-Action collectors. Chambered for .38 Colt and .38 Smith & Wesson Special cartridges. Holds 6-shots, has a 6" barrel and offered in blued finish only. Grips are checkered walnut and quite different than those found on previous models. "U.S.M.C." stamped on the butt; patent dates of 1884, 1888 and 1895 stamped on barrel. Of these revolvers 125 were earmarked for civilian sales and do not have Marine Corps markings; these will generally be found in better condition. Values are similar.

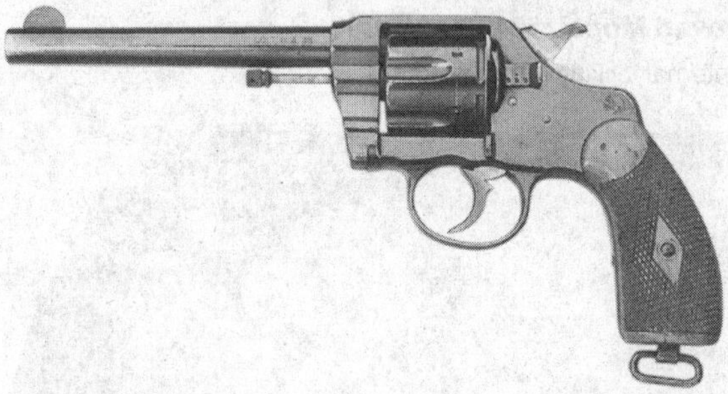

Courtesy Faintich Auction Services, Inc., Paul Goodwin photo

NIB	Exc.	V.G.	Good	Fair	Poor
—	3500	2750	2250	1700	800

New Service Model

This model was in continual production from 1898 through 1944. Chambered for 11 different calibers: .38 Special, .357 Magnum, .38-40, .44 Russian, .44 Special, .44-40, .45 ACP, .45 Colt, .450 Eley, .455 Eley and .476 Eley. Offered in barrel lengths from 2" to 7.5", blued or nickel-plated. Checkered hard rubber grips were standard until 1928. Then checkered walnut grips were used, with an inset Colt medallion. This was the largest swing-out cylinder double-action revolver that Colt ever produced. Approximately 356,000 were manufactured over the 46 years they were made. There are many different variations of this revolver and one should consult a book dealing strictly with Colt for a thorough breakdown and description. Note: Add 30 percent for nickel finish; 40 percent for factory ivory or pearl grips.

Courtesy Cherry's Collector Firearms Auction, Paul Goodwin photo

Early Model, #1-21000

NIB	Exc.	V.G.	Good	Fair	Poor
—	2750	2000	1400	650	400

Early Model Target, #6000-15000

Checkered walnut grips, flattop-frame, 7.5" barrel.

Courtesy Faintich Auction Services, Inc., Paul Goodwin photo

NIB	Exc.	V.G.	Good	Fair	Poor
—	3500	1700	1400	650	400

Improved Model, #21000-325000

Has internal locking improvements.

Courtesy Faintich Auction Services, Inc., Paul Goodwin photo

NIB	Exc.	V.G.	Good	Fair	Poor
—	2200	1600	900	450	300

Improved Target Model, #21000-325000

Courtesy Faintich Auction Services, Inc., Paul Goodwin photo

NIB	Exc.	V.G.	Good	Fair	Poor
—	2600	1650	650	400	300

U.S. Army Model 1909, #30000-50000

5.5" barrel, .45 Colt, walnut grips, "U.S. Army Model 1909" on butt.

NIB	Exc.	V.G.	Good	Fair	Poor
—	2750	2000	1600	800	400

U.S. Navy Model 1909, #50000-52000

Same as above with "U.S.N." on butt.

NIB	Exc.	V.G.	Good	Fair	Poor
—	3500	2700	1900	1000	550

U.S. Marine Corps Model 1909, #21000-23000

Checkered walnut grips, "U.S.M.C." on butt.

NIB	Exc.	V.G.	Good	Fair	Poor
—	4250	3250	2300	1700	700

U.S. Army Model 1917, #150000-301000

Smooth walnut grips, 5.5" barrel, .45 ACP. Model designation stamped on butt.

Courtesy Faintich Auction Services, Inc., Paul Goodwin photo

NIB	Exc.	V.G.	Good	Fair	Poor
—	1500	1000	700	400	300

Model 1917 Civilian, #335000-336000

Approximately 1,000 made in .45 ACP only, from Army parts overrun. No military markings.

NIB	Exc.	V.G.	Good	Fair	Poor
—	1700	1000	700	400	300

Late Model New Service, #325000-356000

Checkered walnut grips and internal improvements.

NIB	Exc.	V.G.	Good	Fair	Poor
—	1700	1000	700	400	300

Shooting Master, #333000-350000

Round-butt, checkered walnut grips with Colt medallion, 6" barrel, "Colt Shooting Master" on barrel, flattop-frame with target sights. Chambered for .38 Special cartridge. Note: Add 100 percent premium for .44 Special, .45 ACP and .45 Colt.

Courtesy Faintich Auction Services, Inc., Paul Goodwin photo

NIB	Exc.	V.G.	Good	Fair	Poor
—	2250	1400	900	400	300

Magnum Model New Service, Over #340000

Chambered for .357 Magnum, .38 Special.

NIB	Exc.	V.G.	Good	Fair	Poor
—	2700	2250	1100	600	350

New Pocket Model

First swing-out cylinder, double-action pocket revolver made by Colt. Chambered for .32 Colt and .32 Smith & Wesson. Holds 6-shots and offered with barrel lengths of 2.5", 3.5", 5" and 6". Finish blued or nickel-plated. Grips are checkered hard rubber, with oval Colt molded into them. "Colt's New Pocket" stamped on frame. Patent dates 1884 and 1888 stamped on barrel of later-production guns. Approximately 30,000 of these manufactured between 1893 and 1905. Antiques made before 1898 are more desirable. Note: Add 25 percent for early production without patent dates; 10 percent for 5" barrel.

NIB	*Exc.*	*V.G.*	*Good*	*Fair*	*Poor*
1300	1000	750	600	400	200

Pocket Positive

Externally, same revolver as New Pocket, but has positive lock feature. Manufactured between 1905 and 1940.

NIB	*Exc.*	*V.G.*	*Good*	*Fair*	*Poor*
1400	900	700	550	350	200

Army Special Model

Heavier-framed improved version of New Army and Navy revolver. Chambered for .32-20, .38 Colt, .38 Smith & Wesson and .41 Colt. Offered with 4", 4.5", 5" and 6" barrel. Finish blued or nickel-plated. Grips checkered hard rubber. Serial number range #291000-#540000. Manufactured between 1908-1927.

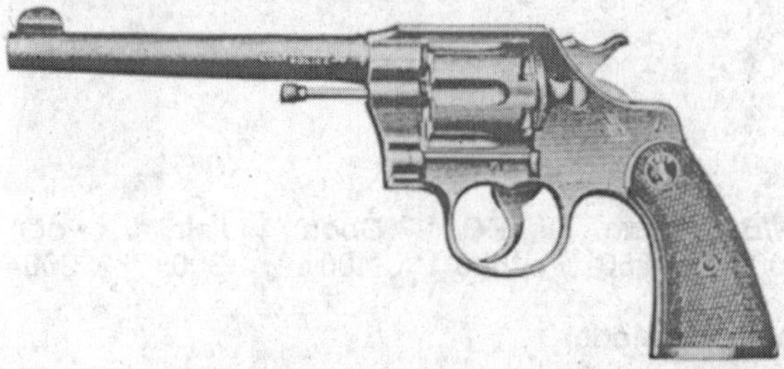

NIB	*Exc.*	*V.G.*	*Good*	*Fair*	*Poor*
1200	850	650	500	350	200

New Police Model

Appears similar to New Pocket Model. Frame stamped "New Police". Chambered for .32 Colt, .32 Colt New Police and .32 Smith & Wesson cartridges. Barrel lengths 2.5", 4" and 6". Finishes blued or nickel-plated. Colt manufactured 49,500 of this model from 1896-1907. New York City Police Department purchased 4,500 of these revolvers and backstraps are so marked. Also, a target model of 5,000 were produced. Features 6" barrel, with flattop-frame and target sights. Note: Add 30 percent for New York Police marked; 20 percent for target model.

NIB	*Exc.*	*V.G.*	*Good*	*Fair*	*Poor*
1250	900	700	550	350	200

Police Positive

Externally same as New Police. Additions of positive lock feature and two new chamberings—.38 New Police and .38 Smith & Wesson. Manufactured from 1905-1947.

NIB	*Exc.*	*V.G.*	*Good*	*Fair*	*Poor*
1200	700	480	250	200	150

Police Positive Target

Basically same as New Police Target, with positive lock feature. Chambered in .22 LR, .22 WRF as well as other cartridges offered in earlier model. Note: Deduct 20 percent for WRF. A .22-caliber Police Positive chambered for .22 Short and Long cartridge may be seen with British proofs. Several such revolvers were sold to London Armory in this configuration during the late 1920s. A NIB example recently sold for $1,200.

NIB	*Exc.*	*V.G.*	*Good*	*Fair*	*Poor*
1250	800	600	300	180	100

Police Positive Special

Similar to Police Positive. Has a slightly larger frame to accept longer cylinder needed to chamber more powerful cartridges such as .38 Special, in addition to original chamberings. Manufactured from 1907-1973.

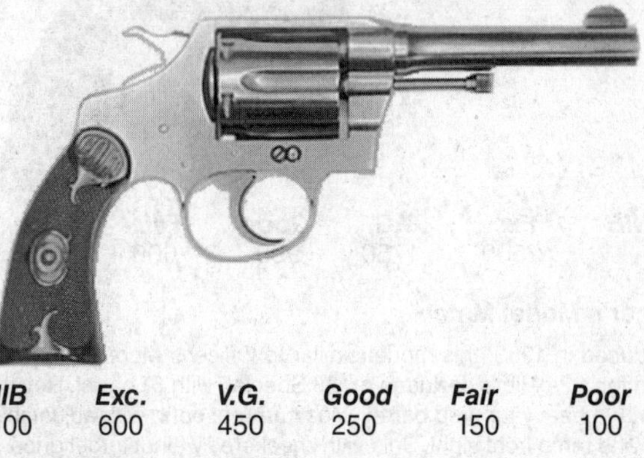

NIB	*Exc.*	*V.G.*	*Good*	*Fair*	*Poor*
1100	600	450	250	150	100

Police Positive Special Mark V

Introduced in 1994, this is an updated version of Police Positive Special. Features an underlug 4" barrel, with rubber grips and fixed sights. Butt is rounded. Revolver is rated to fire .38-caliber +P rounds. Overall length 9". Weight about 30 oz.

NIB	Exc.	V.G.	Good	Fair	Poor
550	400	300	150	100	80

Officer's Model Target 1st Issue

Chambered for .38 Special cartridge. Has a blued 6" barrel. Flattop-frame with adjustable target sights. Colt manufactured this model from 1904-1908.

NIB	Exc.	V.G.	Good	Fair	Poor
2000	1450	1000	800	500	250

Officer's Model Target 2nd Issue

Similar to 1st Issue, but offered in .22 LR, .32 Police Positive caliber and .38 Special. Furnished with 4", 4.5", 5", 6" and 7.5" barrel in .38 Special only. Checkered walnut grips. Colt manufactured this model between 1908 and 1940.

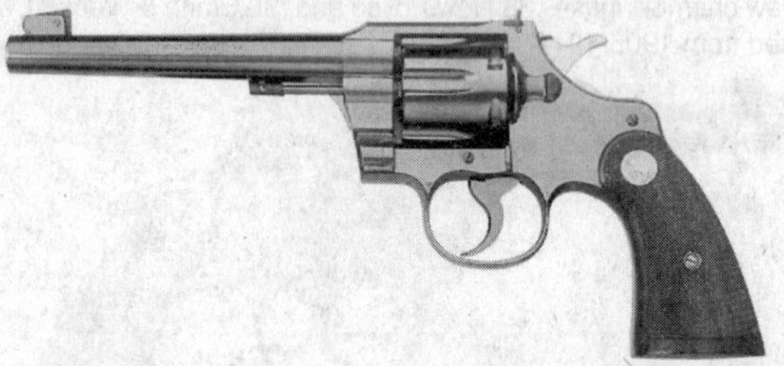

Courtesy Faintich Auction Services, Inc., Paul Goodwin photo

NIB	Exc.	V.G.	Good	Fair	Poor
1900	1350	950	700	400	220

Camp Perry Single-Shot

Created by modifying an Officer's Model frame to accept a special flat single-shot "cylinder". This flat chamber pivots to the left side and downward for loading. Chambered for .22 LR and offered with an 8" (early production) or 10" (late production) barrel. Finish blued, with checkered walnut grips. Name "Camp Perry Model" stamped on left side of chamber; caliber on the barrel. Colt named this model after the site of U.S. Target Competition held annually at Camp Perry, Ohio. Colt manufactured 2,525 of these between 1920 and 1941. Note: This gun serial numbered 101-2525 with 2488 produced from 1926-1941. In 1934 standard barrel length was reduced from 10" to 8" at approximately serial number 2150. Add 100 percent premium for 10" barrel; 50 percent premium for original box.

NIB	Exc.	V.G.	Good	Fair	Poor
—	2500	1750	950	600	400

Officer's Model Match

Introduced in 1953, this model similar to Officer's Model Target. Chambered for .22-caliber cartridge or .38 Special, with 6" barrel. Revolver fitted with a heavy tapered barrel, wide hammer spur, with adjustable rear sight and ramp front sight. Sold with checkered walnut target grips. Blued finish is standard. Discontinued in 1970. Standard of long action could be fired both double- or single-action. The .22-caliber version prices are listed. Officer's Model Match in .38-caliber will bring approximately 20 percent less. Note: This model also produced in .22 Magnum. Rather a rare gun in this caliber, with approximately 800 produced.

NIB	Exc.	V.G.	Good	Fair	Poor
—	750	600	450	350	250

.22 Caliber in Short Action—Single-Action-Only

NIB	Exc.	V.G.	Good	Fair	Poor
—	1000	750	600	500	350

Official Police

Popular revolver in Colt line for many years. Manufactured from 1927 to 1969. Chambered for .32-20 and .41 Colt. These calibers were discontinued in 1942 and 1930, respectively. The .38 Special was chambered throughout the entire production run and .22 LR was added in 1930. Holds 6-shots, has a square-butt and offered with 2", 4", 5" and 6" barrel lengths. Grips are checkered walnut. Finish blued or nickel-plated. Note: Add 10 percent for nickel-plated; 20 percent for .22 LR; 80- to 100 percent for rare round-butt model. Deduct 10 percent for 1947-1969 production. These barrels have no patent dates.

NIB	Exc.	V.G.	Good	Fair	Poor
1000	850	600	400	300	200

Commando Model

This model, for all intents and purposes, is an Official Police. Chambered for .38 Special, with 2", 4" or 6" barrel. Parkerized and stamped "Colt Commando" on the barrel. Approximately 50,000 manufactured between 1942-1945 for use in World War II. Note: Add 30 percent for 2" barrel.

Courtesy Richard M. Kumor, Sr.

NIB	Exc.	V.G.	Good	Fair	Poor
—	1600	1000	750	500	300

Marshal Model

Official Police marked "Colt Marshal" on barrel and an "M" suffix in the serial number. Has 2" or 4" barrel and round butt. Finish is blued. Approximately 2,500 manufactured between 1954 and 1956.

NIB	Exc.	V.G.	Good	Fair	Poor
1950	1500	1000	800	500	250

Colt .38 SF-VI

Introduced in 1995, this model is essentially a Detective Special in stainless steel, with a new internal mechanism. Has a transfer bar safety mechanism. Fitted with 2" barrel and cylinder holds 6 rounds of .38 Special. A 4" barrel in bright stainless steel also available. Weight 21 oz.; overall length 7".

NIB	Exc.	V.G.	Good	Fair	Poor
650	480	350	220	150	100

Colt .38 SF-VI Special Lady

Introduced in 1996, this 2" barrel version similar to above model. Addition of a bright finish and bobbed hammer. Weight 21 oz.

NIB	Exc.	V.G.	Good	Fair	Poor
650	450	300	200	150	100

Detective Special 1st Issue / 2nd Issue

Actually a Police Positive Special, with 2" barrel. Originally chambered for .32 New Police, .38 New Police (which were discontinued) and .38 Special, which continued until end of production run. Finish blued or nickel and offered with wood or plastic grips. Over 400,000 manufactured between 1926 and 1972. A few 2nd issue (post WWII) units came with 3" barrels. Note: Add 50 percent for pre-war 1st issue (serial number 331000 - 490000); 25 percent for nickel finish; 30 percent for 3" barrel.

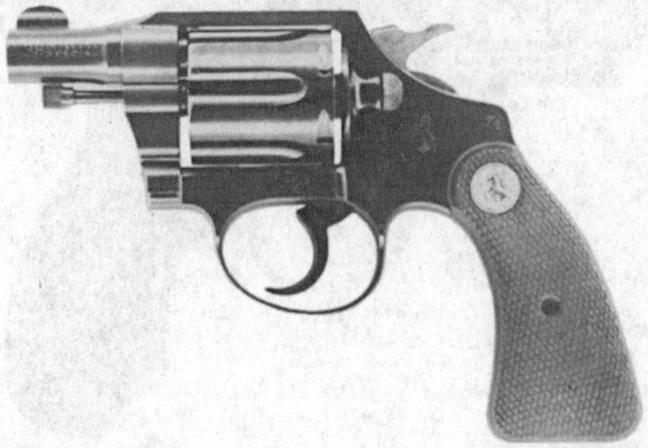

NIB	Exc.	V.G.	Good	Fair	Poor
1800	1100	800	700	450	220

Detective Special 3rd Issue

Basically a modernized, streamlined version. Features 2" or 3" barrel, shrouded ejector rod, wrap-around checkered walnut grips and chambered for .38 Special. Finished in blue or nickel plate. Made from 1973 to 1986 and 1993 to 1995. Note: Add $50 for nickel finish.

NIB	Exc.	V.G.	Good	Fair	Poor
950	800	700	600	500	250

Detective Special II (DS-II)

Introduced in 1997, this version of Detective special, features new internal lock work and a transfer bar safety mechanism. Fitted with 2" barrel, capacity of 6 rounds and chambered for .38 Special. In 1998 this model was offered chambered for .357 Magnum cartridge as well. Rubber combat style grips are standard. Stainless steel finish. Weight about 21 oz.

NIB	Exc.	V.G.	Good	Fair	Poor
650	480	300	220	—	—

Colt Magnum Carry

Introduced in 1999, this model is essentially a renamed Detective Special II. Stainless steel finish. Weight 21 oz.

NIB	Exc.	V.G.	Good	Fair	Poor
650	480	300	250	—	—

Banker's Special

Bankers Special is a 2" barreled, easily concealed revolver. Designed with bank employees in mind. Chambered in .38 Colt New Police or .22 LR. U.S. Postal Service equipped its railway mail clerks with this model. Approximately 35,000 manufactured between 1926 and 1943. Note: Nickel models will command a premium. .22-caliber will command a premium of up to 50 percent.

NIB	Exc.	V.G.	Good	Fair	Poor
2300	1500	980	500	250	150

Cobra 1st Issue

Cobra 1st Issue is simply an alloy-framed lightweight version of Detective Special. Weight only 15 oz. Chambered for .32, .38 Special and .22 LR. Available in round- or square-butt version, with 4" barrel only. Manufactured between 1950 and 1973.

NIB	Exc.	V.G.	Good	Fair	Poor
1200	850	650	520	200	100

Cobra 2nd Issue

Same as Cobra 1st Issue in .38 Special only. Streamlined with wraparound walnut grips and shrouded ejector rod. Note: Add 30 percent for nickel.

NIB	Exc.	V.G.	Good	Fair	Poor
900	800	600	450	350	250

Cobra (Current Production)

Marks Colt's return to double-action revolver market. Completely new and different design from earlier model. A 6-shot .38 Special +P, with all steel construction. Has a 2" barrel, with red fiber optic front sight, frame trench rear, Hogue rubber grips, matte stainless finish. Introduced in 2017.

NIB	Exc.	V.G.	Good	Fair	Poor
600	520	450	—	—	—

Agent 1st Issue

Basically same as Cobra 1st Issue, with shortened grip frame. This was done to make Agent more concealable. Colt manufactured Agent 1st Issue from 1955-1973.

NIB	Exc.	V.G.	Good	Fair	Poor
900	800	600	450	350	250

Border Patrol

Model is quite rare, as Colt manufactured only 400 of them in 1952. Basically a Police Special, with heavy 4" barrel. Chambered for .38 Special and built to be strong. Finish is blued. Serial numbered in 610000 range.

NIB	Exc.	V.G.	Good	Fair	Poor
3750	3500	2800	2000	1000	500

Agent L.W. 2nd Issue

Streamlined version, with shrouded ejector rod. Last four years of its production was matte finished. Manufactured between 1973 and 1986.

NIB	Exc.	V.G.	Good	Fair	Poor
—	550	400	280	180	150

Aircrewman Special

Especially fabricated for the Air Force, to be carried by their pilots for protection. Extremely lightweight at 11 oz. Frame and cylinder are made of aluminum alloy. Has 2" barrel and chambered for .38 Special. Finish was blued, with checkered walnut grips. Approximately 1,200 manufactured in 1951 and marked "U.S." or "A.F".

NIB	Exc.	V.G.	Good	Fair	Poor
4500	3500	3000	1500	800	400

Courier

.22 LR revolver. 3,000 made from 1953-1956.

NIB	Exc.	V.G.	Good	Fair	Poor
1500	750	600	500	350	150

Trooper

Designed specifically by Colt to fill the need for a large heavy-duty powerful revolver, that was accurate. Trooper filled that need. Offered with 4" or 6" barrel, blued or nickel finishes and checkered walnut grips. Trooper chambered for .38 Special, .357 Magnum and there is a .22 rimfire version for target shooters. Manufactured between 1953 and 1969. Note: Add 10 percent for .357 or .22.

NIB	Exc.	V.G.	Good	Fair	Poor
850	600	480	300	150	100

Colt .357 Magnum

Deluxe version of Trooper. Offered with a special target, wide hammer and large target-type grips. Sights are same as Accro target model. Features 4" or 6" barrel and blued finish. Manufactured between 1953 and 1961. Fewer than 15,000 produced.

NIB	Exc.	V.G.	Good	Fair	Poor
850	680	500	300	200	150

Diamondback

Medium-frame, duty-type weapon suitable for target work. Has a short frame of Detective Special, with ventilated rib 2.5", 4" or 6" barrel. Chambered for .38 Special and .22 rimfire for target shooters. Finish blued or nickel-plated, with checkered walnut grips. Diamondback features adjustable target sights, wide target hammer and steel frame. Manufactured between 1966 and 1986. Very few Diamondbacks were chambered for .22 WMR. Another premium should be added for these models. Since fakes exist, a factory letter documenting this chambering is strongly advised. Note: Premium of 100 percent for 2.5" barrel or nickel finish in .22 LR caliber; 20 percent in .38 Special.

.38 Special

NIB	Exc.	V.G.	Good	Fair	Poor
1200	1000	650	550	400	250

.22 Long Rifle

NIB	Exc.	V.G.	Good	Fair	Poor
1800	1500	1000	750	500	300

Viper

Alloy-framed revolver chambered for .38 Special. Has a 4" barrel. Manufactured between 1977 and 1984. Viper is essentially a lightweight version of Police Positive.

NIB	Exc.	V.G.	Good	Fair	Poor
1000	750	500	200	120	100

Python

Python was often described as the Cadillac of Colt double-action revolver line. Originally designed to be a large-frame .38 Special target revolver, but shortly before Python was introduced in 1955, Colt management decided to chamber it for .357 Magnum. (A .38 Special 8" barrel variation was made in early 1980s. See separate listing.) Python was offered in barrel lengths of 2.5", 3" (very rare), 4", 6" and 8". Features included a ventilated rib, full lug barrel and adjustable rear sight. Finish choices were Royal Blue, nickel plated, matte stainless and high polished "Ultimate" stainless. Python remained in the catalog as a regular production item until 1996. The following year Colt Custom Shop started making Python on a special-order-only basis. Known as Python Elite, it was produced by the Custom Shop until 2006. In recent years, values of Colt "snake guns" have increased significantly. Combinations of rare features, high condition, and special history bring premium prices. In 2017 and 2018, Rock Island Auction Company sold four Pythons in the $20,000 to $26,000 range. An engraved specimen featured on the cover of Standard Catalog of Firearms sold for nearly $55,000, and Elvis Presley's engraved Python brought $175,500. A new version was introduced by Colt in 2020.

Blue or Royal Blue Finish

Note: Add 10- to 15 percent for early production from 1955 to 1969 with checkered wood grips (serial number 1 — 99999); 50 percent for rare 3" barrel.

NIB	Exc.	V.G.	Good	Fair	Poor
3500	3200	2500	1600	900	600

Polished Nickel Finish

Note: Add 30 percent for satin nickel instead of polished nickel; 25 percent for 2.5" or 8" barrel; 200- to 250 percent for 3" barrel. A Colt Archive Letter is recommended for 3" model.

NIB	Exc.	V.G.	Good	Fair	Poor
3400	3100	2400	1500	800	500

Matte Stainless Steel

Note: Add 100 percent for 2.5" barrel; 10 percent for 8".

NIB	Exc.	V.G.	Good	Fair	Poor
3500	3200	2500	1600	900	600

Ultimate Bright Stainless

Note: Add 30 percent for 2.5" barrel; 10 percent for 8".

NIB	Exc.	V.G.	Good	Fair	Poor
3500	3000	2200	1600	900	600

Python Elite

Custom Shop model features stainless steel satin finish or blued. Adjustable red ramp front sight. Custom wood grips. Choice of 4" or 6" barrel. Note: Value estimates shown are for Royal Blue finish. Deduct 20 percent for more common stainless Elite model.

NIB	Exc.	V.G.	Good	Fair	Poor
3900	3500	2800	2200	1200	800

Python .38 Special

An 8" barreled Python chambered for .38 Special only. Limited-production venture was not a success. Offered in blue only. Note: Add 40- to 50 percent for nickel finish.

NIB	Exc.	V.G.	Good	Fair	Poor
2900	2400	2000	1600	900	600

Python Hunter

Hunter was a special 8" .357 Magnum Python, with an extended eye relief Leupold 2X scope. Grips are neoprene, with gold Colt medallions. Revolver with mounted scope and accessories. Fitted into a Halliburton extruded aluminum case. Hunter was manufactured in 1981 only.

NIB	*Exc.*	*V.G.*	*Good*	*Fair*	*Poor*
4200	3750	2800	2000	1350	700

Python Silhouette

In .357-caliber, with 8" barrel. Similar to Python Hunter, except for Silhouette barrel markings. As with Hunter, Leupold 2x scope is included.

NIB	*Exc.*	*V.G.*	*Good*	*Fair*	*Poor*
4300	3850	2900	2050	1400	750

Python Ten Pointer

Similar to Hunter model, except it came from the factory with a 3x Burris scope and two sets of grips, wood and composite.

NIB	*Exc.*	*V.G.*	*Good*	*Fair*	*Poor*
4200	3750	2800	2200	1200	800

Python Grizzly

Hybrid limited edition from Colt Custom Shop in mid '90s. Only 999 were made. Featured a Python Magna-Ported barrel and Colt King Cobra frame.

NIB	*Exc.*	*V.G.*	*Good*	*Fair*	*Poor*
4300	3850	2900	2400	1500	800

Python 2020 Reintroduction

Stainless steel, chambered .357 Magnum. 6" or 4.25" barrel.

NIB	*Exc.*	*V.G.*	*Good*	*Fair*	*Poor*
1500	1250	—	—	—	—

Python 3-inch Barrel

Caliber: .357 Magnum. Capacity: 6-round cylinder. Barrels: 3 in. Grips: Walnut. Sights: Fully adjustable rear, fixed red ramp interchangeable front. Features: New and improved and available only in stainless steel. Has recessed target crown and user-interchangeable front sight.

NIB	*Exc.*	*V.G.*	*Good*	*Fair*	*Poor*
1120	—	—	—	—	—

Lipsey's Exclusive Colt Python (Tyler Gun Works)

Caliber: .357 Magnum/.38 Special, 3" barrel. Tyler Gun Works Premier Grade-Engraved with stag grips.

NIB	*Exc.*	*V.G.*	*Good*	*Fair*	*Poor*
1800	—	—	—	—	—

Metropolitan MK III

Basically a heavier-duty version of Official Police. Chambered for .38 Special. Fitted with 4" heavy barrel. Finished in blue only. Manufactured from 1969-1972.

NIB	*Exc.*	*V.G.*	*Good*	*Fair*	*Poor*
750	520	350	250	100	80

Lawman MK III

Offered chambered for .357 Magnum, with 2" or 4" barrel. Checkered walnut grips. Blued or nickel-plated. Manufactured Lawman between 1969 and 1983.

NIB	*Exc.*	*V.G.*	*Good*	*Fair*	*Poor*
750	550	400	300	200	100

Lawman MK V

Improved version of MK III. Entailed a re-designed grip, shorter lock time and improved double-action. Manufactured 1982-1985.

NIB	Exc.	V.G.	Good	Fair	Poor
850	700	600	400	250	150

Trooper MK III

Revolver intended to be target-grade version of MK III series. Offered with 4", 6" or 8" ventilated rib barrel, with a shrouded ejector rod similar in appearance to Python. Chambered for .22 LR, .22 Magnum and .357 Magnum. Features adjustable target sights, checkered walnut target grips and blued or nickel-plated. Manufactured between 1969 and 1983. Note: Add $100 for .22 LR; $200 for .22 WMR.

NIB	Exc.	V.G.	Good	Fair	Poor
750	400	320	200	150	100

Trooper MK V

Improved version of MK III. Manufactured between 1982 - 1985.

NIB	Exc.	V.G.	Good	Fair	Poor
820	550	380	200	150	100

Boa

Basically a deluxe version of Trooper MK V. Has all the same features plus high polished blue found on Python. Manufactured 1,200 of these revolvers in 1985. Entire production was purchased and marketed by Lew Horton Distributing Company in Southboro, Massachusetts.

NIB	Exc.	V.G.	Good	Fair	Poor
9500	8500	6500	5000	4000	2000

Peacekeeper

Designed as a duty-type weapon, with target capabilities. Offered with 4" or 6" barrel chambered for .357 Magnum. Features adjustable sights and neoprene combat-style grips. Matte blued finish. Manufactured between 1985 - 1987.

NIB	Exc.	V.G.	Good	Fair	Poor
1000	850	650	500	350	250

King Cobra

King Cobra has a forged steel frame, barrel and full length ejector rod housing. Barrel fitted with a solid rib. Model equipped with an adjustable white outline rear sight and red insert front sight. Colt black neoprene combat style grips are standard. Discontinued. Note: In 1998 all King Cobras were drilled and tapped for scope mounts. Add 20 percent for 2.5" barrel.

Blued

NIB	Exc.	V.G.	Good	Fair	Poor
1800	1500	1100	900	700	500

Stainless Steel

Offered in 4" or 6" barrel lengths. In 1997, introduced with optional barrel porting. No longer in production.

NIB	Exc.	V.G.	Good	Fair	Poor
2000	1700	1250	1000	800	600

High Polish Stainless Steel

NIB	Exc.	V.G.	Good	Fair	Poor
2900	2300	1700	1200	900	700

King Cobra Target

.357 Magnum, 4.25-in. barrel, stainless steel, adjustable rear & elevated fiber-optic front sight, wood medallion grips, enlarged triggerguard. Introduced 2020.

NIB	Exc.	V.G.	Good	Fair	Poor
1050	900	—	—	—	—

Anaconda

Double-action .44 Magnum revolver introduced in 1990. Offered with 4", 6" or 8" barrel lengths. Weight: 4" model 47 oz.; 6" model 63 oz.; 8" model 59 oz. Anaconda holds 6 rounds and available with matte stainless steel finish. For 1993, a new chambering in .45 Colt was offered with 6" or 8" barrel in matte stainless steel finish. Revolver chambered for .44 Remington Magnum cartridge. Constructed of matte-finished stainless steel and black neoprene finger groove grips, with gold Colt medallions. In 1996, Realtree model was offered with 8" barrel. Chambered for .44 Magnum cartridge. Furnished with adjustable rear and ramp front sights or with Redfield 2.5-7x scope. No longer in production. Re-introduced in 2001, in .44 Magnum with 4", 6" or 8" barrel. Once again, discontinued. Note: In 1998, Anaconda was drilled and tapped for scope mounts and buyers had the option of barrel porting. Add $1000 for Anaconda First Edition model, with Ultimate Stainless finish, aluminum case. Total of 1,000 made in 1990 only.

.44 Magnum

NIB	Exc.	V.G.	Good	Fair	Poor
2200	1600	1200	1000	700	400

.45 Colt

NIB	Exc.	V.G.	Good	Fair	Poor
2500	1900	1450	1200	800	500

Realtree Camo Model—Adjustable Sights

NIB	Exc.	V.G.	Good	Fair	Poor
2400	1800	1300	1100	750	450

Realtree Camo Model—Scope Mounts

NIB	Exc.	V.G.	Good	Fair	Poor
2450	1850	1400	1200	800	500

COLT SEMI-AUTOMATIC PISTOLS

Colt Firearms Co. was the first of American gun manufacturers to take advent of the semi-automatic pistol seriously. This pistol design was becoming popular among European gun makers in late 1880s and early 1900s. In the United States, however, the revolver was firmly ensconced as the accepted design. Colt realized that if the semi-automatic could be made to function reliably, it would soon catch on. Powers that be at Colt were able to negotiate with some of the noted inventors of the day, including Browning, to secure or lease the rights to manufacture their designs. Colt also encouraged creativity of their employees, with bonuses and incentives. Through this innovative thinking, Colt soon became the leader in semi-automatic pistol sales—a position that they have never really relinquished to any other American gun maker. Colt semi-automatic pistols represent an interesting field for the collector of Colt handguns. There were many variations with high enough production to make it worthwhile to seek them out. There are a number of fine books on Colt semi-automatics and anyone wishing to do so will be able to learn a great deal about them. Collector interest is high in this field and values are definitely on the rise.

Model 1900

First of Colt automatic pistols. Actually a developmental model, with only 3,500 being produced. Model 1900 was not really a successful design. Quite clumsy and out of balance in the hand, however, it was reliable in function during Army trials. Chambered for .38 rimless smokeless cartridge. A detachable magazine that holds seven cartridges. Barrel length 6". Finish blued, with case colored hammer and safety/sight combination. Grips are plain walnut, checkered walnut or hard rubber. Pistol is a Browning design and left side of slide stamped "Browning's Patent" with 1897 patent date. Colt sold 200 pistols to the Navy and 200 to the Army for field trials and evaluation. Remaining 3,300 were sold on the civilian market. Manufactured from 1900-1903. Note: Many of the original 1900 pistols had the original sight/safety converted to Model 1902 configuration. These are worth about 50 percent less than unconverted pistols.

Standard Civilian Production

NIB	Exc.	V.G.	Good	Fair	Poor
—	15000	12000	5000	2500	1000

U.S. Navy Military Model

NIB	Exc.	V.G.	Good	Fair	Poor
—	25000	20000	8500	4200	1650

U.S. Army Military Model—1st Contract

NIB	Exc.	V.G.	Good	Fair	Poor
—	32500	24000	10000	4500	1800

U.S. Army Military Model—2nd Contract

NIB	Exc.	V.G.	Good	Fair	Poor
—	24000	18500	7500	4000	1500

Model 1902 Sporting Pistol

Chambered for .38 ACP cartridge. Has a 7-round detachable magazine, 6" barrel and blued. Checkered hard rubber grips featuring "Rampant Colt" molded into them. Most notable features of 1902 Sporting Model are rounded butt, rounded hammer spur, dovetailed rear sight and 1897-1902 patent dates. Manufactured approximately 7,500 of these pistols between 1903 and 1908.

Paul Goodwin photo

NIB	Exc.	V.G.	Good	Fair	Poor
—	5760	4260	3260	1760	900

Model 1902 Military Pistol

Early Model with Front of Slide Serrated

NIB	Exc.	V.G.	Good	Fair	Poor
—	6000	5000	4000	1500	750

Standard Model with Rear of Slide Serrated

NIB	Exc.	V.G.	Good	Fair	Poor
—	5000	4000	3000	1000	400

U.S. Army Marked, #15001-15200 with Front Serrations

NIB	Exc.	V.G.	Good	Fair	Poor
—	18000	15000	10000	5000	2000

Model 1903 Pocket Hammer Pistol

First automatic pocket pistol Colt produced. Essentially identical to 1902 Sporting Model, with a shorter slide. Barrel length 4.5". Chambered for .38 ACP cartridge. Blued, with case colored hammer. Checkered hard rubber grips have "Rampant Colt" molded into them. Detachable magazine holds 7 rounds. Approximately 26,000 manufactured between 1903 - 1929.

Paul Goodwin photo

NIB	Exc.	V.G.	Good	Fair	Poor
—	5000	4000	2760	900	750

Model 1903 Hammerless, .32 Pocket Pistol (Model M)

Second pocket automatic Colt manufactured. Another of John Browning's designs, it developed into one of Colt's most successful pistols. Chambered for .32 ACP cartridge. Initially barrel length was 4", then shortened to 3.75". Detachable magazine holds 8 rounds. Standard finish blue, with quite a few nickel plated. Early model grips are checkered hard rubber, with "Rampant Colt" molded into them. Many of the nickel plated pistols had pearl grips. In 1924 grips were changed to checkered walnut, with Colt medallions. Name of this model can be misleading as it is not a true hammerless, but a concealed hammer design. Features a slide stop and grip safety. Manufactured 572,215 civilian versions of this pistol and approximately 200,000 more for military contracts. Manufactured between 1903 and 1945. Note: Add 40 percent for Early Model 1897 patent date; $100 for nickel-plated with pearl grips; 20 percent for 4" barrel to #72,000.

Courtesy Richard M. Kumor, Sr.

Courtesy Orvel Reichert

NIB	Exc.	V.G.	Good	Fair	Poor
2000	1500	1000	650	400	300

U.S. Military Model

Serial prefix M, marked "U.S. Property" on frame, Parkerized finish. Note: Premium of 50 percent for pistols issued to General Officers.

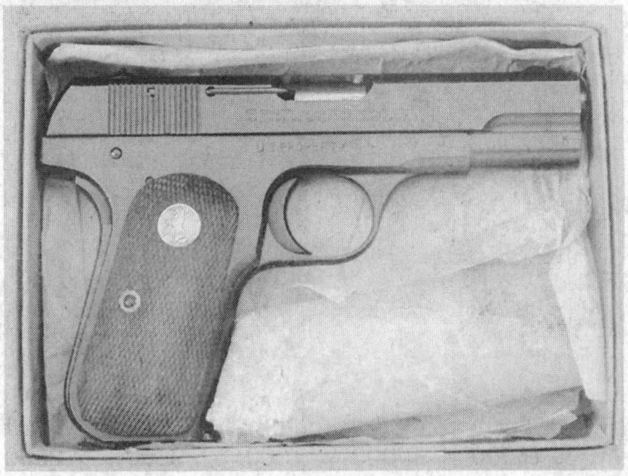

NIB	Exc.	V.G.	Good	Fair	Poor
3200	2000	1500	1000	750	400

Model 1908 Hammerless .380 Pocket Pistol

Essentially same as .32 Pocket Pistol. Chambered for more potent .380 ACP, also known as 9mm Browning short. Other specifications are the same. Manufactured approximately 138,000 in this caliber for civilian sales. An unknown number were sold to the military. Note: Add $100 for nickel with pearl grips.

Standard Civilian Model

NIB	Exc.	V.G.	Good	Fair	Poor
2500	1900	1500	900	700	500

Military Model

Serial prefix M, marked "U.S. Property" on frame, blue finish. Note: Add 50 percent for General Officer's pistol.

NIB	Exc.	V.G.	Good	Fair	Poor
—	4000	3000	2000	800	400

Model 1908 Hammerless .25 Vest Pocket Model

Smallest automatic Colt made. Chambered for .25 ACP cartridge. Has 2" barrel and is 4.5" long overall. Weight a mere 13 oz. A true pocket pistol. Detachable magazine holds 6-shots. Offered in blue or nickel-plate, with grips of checkered hard rubber and checkered walnut on later versions. Has a grip safety, slide lock and magazine disconnect safety. Another Browning design. Fabrique Nationale manufactured this pistol in Belgium before Colt picked up the rights to make it in the U.S. A commercial success by Colt's standards, with approximately 409,000 manufactured between 1908 and 1941. Note: Add 30 percent for nickel finish; 50 percent for factory pearl grips.

Courtesy Orvel Reichert

Civilian Model

NIB	Exc.	V.G.	Good	Fair	Poor
1350	1000	600	400	300	150

Military Model

"U.S. Property" marked on right frame. Very rare.

NIB	Exc.	V.G.	Good	Fair	Poor
4500	3500	2500	1350	450	300

Model 1905 .45 Automatic Pistol

Spanish American War and experiences with the Moros in Philippine campaign, taught a lesson about stopping power or lack of it. United States Army was convinced they needed a more powerful handgun cartridge. This led Colt to the development of a .45-caliber cartridge suitable for the semi-automatic pistol. Model 1905 and .45 rimless round were the result. In actuality, this cartridge was not nearly powerful enough to satisfy the need, but it led to the development of .45 ACP. Colt believed this pistol/cartridge combination would be a success and was geared up for mass production. Army actually bought only 200 of them and total production was approximately 6,300 from 1905 to 1911. Has a 5" barrel and detachable 7-shot magazine. Blued, with case colored hammer. Grips are checkered walnut. Hammer was rounded on first 3,600 pistols and changed to a spur hammer on later models. Right side of slide stamped "Automatic Colt / Caliber 45 Rimless Smokeless". Not a commercial success for Colt—possibly because it has no safety, whatsoever, except for the floating inertia firing pin. The 200 military models have grip safeties only. A small number (believed to be less than 500) were grooved to accept a shoulder stock. Stocks were made of leather and steel, and double as a holster. These pistols have been classified "Curios and Relics" under the provisions of the Gun Control Act of 1968.

NIB	Exc.	V.G.	Good	Fair	Poor
—	7500	5000	3000	1500	800

Civilian Model

NIB	Exc.	V.G.	Good	Fair	Poor
—	7000	5000	3000	1500	800

Military Model, Serial #1-201

NIB	Exc.	V.G.	Good	Fair	Poor
—	15000	12000	8000	4000	1000

COLT 1911/1911A1

Soon after the first Military 1911 pistol was shipped, in Jan. 1912, first Commercial equivalent pistol called "GOVERNMENT MODEL" was also shipped. Strictly speaking, "GOVERNMENT MODEL" is not a "MODEL OF 1911" and "MODEL OF 1911" is not a "GOVERNMENT MODEL". Yet between these two models, most parts will interchange. Main differences are finish and markings.

Colt Government (Commercial) models all had VP (Verified Proof) mark on triggerguard bow. Colt-made 1911 Military pistols did not have verified proof mark, unless pistol was returned to Colt for repair where they replaced barrel and re-proofed (fired) the pistol. Colt-made 1911A1 pistols (with exception of 1924 Transition contract) all had the verified proof mark.

Collectors of Commercial Government Model pistols, usually have a different perspective regarding pistols that they wish to collect than do collectors of Military "MODEL OF 1911". Since military pistols have been presumed to have gone through a war, most examples that one sees are usually in considerably worse condition than contemporary commercial pistols. Indeed, the commercial collector usually expects to see typical examples that are in far better condition than typical military examples. Many commercial collectors purchase only "Near New" or "New in Box" examples.

Prices listed for commercial Government Models have the same condition categories as do military pistols, but NIB, Exc. and V.G. are the only ones that have much collector interest, as Good, Fair and Poor categories are often relegated as "Shooters without any significant collector interest". Reality is, pistols in these three later categories are often very difficult to sell, except at a shooter price, despite the numbers quoted in this guide. Commercial collectors are often as fixated about originality as with condition, to the point that a whole cottage industry has grown up that specializes in creating reproduction boxes that are represented as ORIGINAL boxes.

Yet, the beginning collector has few tools to determine if pistol is original or has original finish. Black and white photos in books are of little use in showing what original finish looks like. Only by looking at original pistols can one's eyes become calibrated as to what original finish looks like. Until then, the beginner collector will be at the mercy of fakers and counterfeiters. Buy the best books and read them. Look at as many pistols as you can manage. — Karl Karash

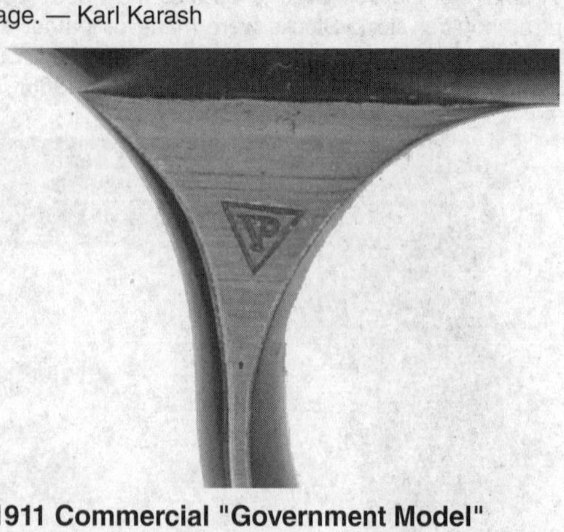

Early Colt 1911 Commercial "Government Model"

Serial numbers through about C4500. High polish on all parts and fire-blue finish on trigger, slide stop, thumb safety, hammer pins, ejector and stock screws. Pistols in latter part of serial range did not have fire-blued stock screws. Pistols through about serial C350 had the dimpled magazine catch. Main spring housing pin was rounded on both ends in pistols through about serial C2000. Keyhole (punch and sawcut) magazines were shipped on pistols through serial C3500. Note: Add 30 percent for three-digit serial number; 60 percent for two-digit serial number; 50- to 100 percent for finish 99-100 percent.

Courtesy Karl Karash

NIB	Exc.	V.G.	Good	Fair	Poor
—	15000	10000	7500	3500	2000

Standard Colt 1911 "Commercial Model" with Un-numbered Slide

From about serial #C4500 to about serial #C127300 with un-numbered slide. No fire-blue. Polished finished but not mirror finish. Loop magazine until about C90000. Note: Add 20- to 50 percent for finish 99-100 percent.

NIB	Exc.	V.G.	Good	Fair	Poor
8000	5000	2500	1500	1100	850

Standard Colt 1911 Commercial "Government Model" with Numbered Slide

Colt started to number the slide, with receiver's serial number at about #C127300. This practice continued for commercial production through WWII. All 1911 commercial pistols after about serial C127300 to about C136000 (when 1911A1 production changes were phased in). First numbered slide pistols (in the C127xxx range) had the slide numbered on the bottom of slide rail. This only lasted a short time and numbering was moved to behind firing pin stop plate by serial C128000. Deduct 20 percent for a mismatched slide number. Changes between 1911 Commercial Government Model and 1911A1 Commercial Government were phased in during this period. A number of variations within these serial number ranges are of specific interest and are listed separately below. Note: Add 20- to 50 percent for finish 99-100 percent.

NIB	Exc.	V.G.	Good	Fair	Poor
8500	5300	2700	1600	1200	950

FOREIGN CONTRACTS

Colt 1911 Commercial "Government Model" Argentine Contracts

Multiple contracts were awarded by Argentina between 1914 and 1948 to supply .45-caliber pistols to their armed forces, police and government agencies. These contracts totaled 21,616 pistols, of which 2,151 were 1911 model. Pistols differ from Standard Government Model in that they are usually marked with an Argentine crest as well as normal Colt commercial markings including C prefix serial number. Colt also supplied Argentina 1911A1 model modelo 1927" that had its own serial number range of #1 to #10000 with no C prefix. Most of these pistols are well used, re-blued, had mixed parts and have import markings. Prices listed are for completely original pistols. Re-blue=Fair/Poor. Note: Add 20- to 100 percent for finish 99-100 percent.

NIB	Exc.	V.G.	Good	Fair	Poor
2400	1500	1100	750	500	400

Colt 1911 Commercial "Government Model" Russian Order

This variation chambered for .45 ACP and has Russian version of Anglo Zakazivat" stamped on frame. About 51,000 of these blued pistols manufactured in 1915-1916. Found between serial numbers C21000 and C89000. Rarely encountered today, but a few have recently been imported and advertised. One should be extremely cautious and verify authenticity if contemplating a purchase, as fakes have been noted. Despite market uncertainties, demand for original pistols is high. (Re-blue=Fair/Poor)

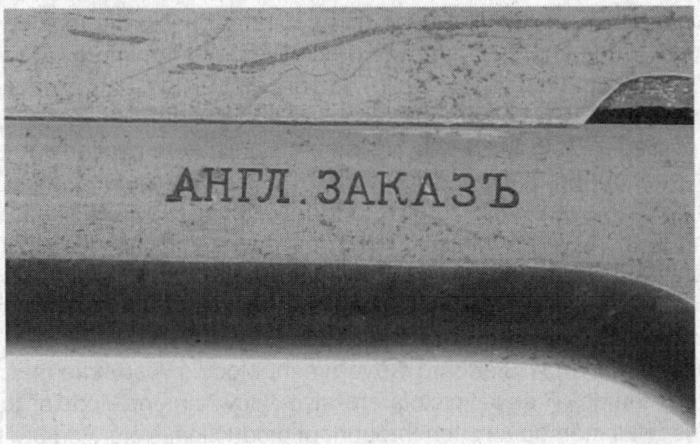

NIB	Exc.	V.G.	Good	Fair	Poor
—	15000	11000	7500	5000	2000

Colt 1911 Commercial "Government Model" Canadian Contract

This group of 5,099 pistols, serial numbered between about C3077 and C13500, were purchased by the Canadian Government in 1914. Most observed pistols appear to be unmarked and can be identified only by a Colt factory letter. Others have been observed with Canadian Broad Arrow property mark, as well as unit markings. Often these unit markings are applied in a very rudimentary manner that detracts considerably from the appearance. (Any applied markings done crudely, deduct 10-50 percent.) Due to the nature of these markings, a Colt factory letter is probably a requirement to authenticate these pistols. Re-finish=Fair/Poor. Note: Add 20- to 50 percent for finish. 99-100 percent.

NIB	Exc.	V.G.	Good	Fair	Poor
—	5100	3500	2200	1750	1200

Colt 1911 Commercial "Government Model" British Contract

Chambered for British .455 cartridge. Marked on right side of slide British Broad Arrow" proofmark will often be found. Pistols were made in 1915-1919 and follow same numeric serial number sequence as normal Government models, except "C" prefix was replaced with a "W". They are commercial series pistols. Magazine well of these .455 pistols is slightly larger than a standard Cal. .45 Auto pistol and will accept a Cal. .45 magazine, but a standard Cal. .45 will not accept a Cal. .455 magazine. All pistols in W19001 to W19200 range, as well as some in W29000 range, are believed to be JJ marked above left triggerguard bow. Add 25 percent for JJ marked. Some pistols in C101000 to about C109000 range have RAF marks as well as a welded ring in the lanyard loop. Most RAF pistols have been re-finished and many have been converted to .45-cal. by changing barrels. Re-finish=Fair/Poor. Note: Add 20- to 50 percent for finish 99-100 percent; 25 percent for RAF. Deduct 35 percent for wrong barrel.

NIB	Exc.	V.G.	Good	Fair	Poor
—	7000	5000	3500	2300	1750

Norwegian Kongsberg Vapenfabrikk Pistol Model 1912 (Extremely Rare)

Serial number 1-96. Note: Pistols are so rare that almost any price would not be out of order for an original pistol. Add 20- to 30 percent for finish 99-100 percent.

NIB	Exc.	V.G.	Good	Fair	Poor
—	10000	6500	4400	3200	2500

Norwegian Kongsberg Vapenfabrikk Pistol Model 1914

Serial number 97-32854. Note: Add 20- to 50 percent for finish 99-100 percent.

NIB	Exc.	V.G.	Good	Fair	Poor
—	2000	1500	1200	1000	800

Norwegian Kongsberg Vapenfabrikk Model 1914 (Copy)

Serial number 29615 to 30535. Waffenamt marked on slide and barrel. CAUTION: Fakes have been reported. Any Waffenamt marked pistol outside this serial range is probably counterfeit. Note: Add 20- 30 percent for finish 99-100 percent.

NIB	Exc.	V.G.	Good	Fair	Poor
—	9000	6000	4000	2800	1900

MODEL 1911 U.S. MILITARY SERIES

For a complete look at the many variations of Colt Model 1911 that were made for U.S. Military forces, see *Standard Catalog of Military Firearms, 8th Edition*. This publication covers history, technical data, photos and values of the world's military arms and accessories. Following is a brief summary of estimated values for Model 1911 pistols manufactured for U.S. forces between 1912 and 1919.

Colt 1912

Serial number range 1-17250.

NIB	Exc.	V.G.	Good	Fair	Poor
—	12500	8500	5500	3000	1500

Colt 1913-1915

Serial number ranges 17251-72570, 83856-102596, 107597-113496, 120567-125566, 133187-137400.

NIB	Exc.	V.G.	Good	Fair	Poor
—	7500	6000	4000	2000	1400

Colt 1917-1918

Serial number range 137401-594000.

NIB	Exc.	V.G.	Good	Fair	Poor
—	4500	3000	2000	1000	500

Springfield Armory 1914-1916

Serial number ranges 72751-83855, 102597-107596, 113497-120566, 125567-133186.

NIB	Exc.	V.G.	Good	Fair	Poor
—	9000	6000	4500	2750	1600

Remington-UMC 1918-1919

Serial number range 1-21676.

NIB	Exc.	V.G.	Good	Fair	Poor
—	7500	4750	3500	2000	1300

North American Arms 1918

Less than 100 manufactured in Canada, but none delivered to U.S. government. One of the most rare 1911 models, so beware of fakes. Get an expert appraisal before buying or selling.

NIB	Exc.	V.G.	Good	Fair	Poor
—	110000	55000	40000	25000	10000

"PRE AND POST WWII COLT 1911A1 COMMERCIAL GOVERNMENT MODEL"""

Commercial Government Models" made by Colt between the wars may be the best pistols Colt ever produced. Civilian configurations of 1911 and 1911A1 were known as "Government Models". Identical to military models, with exception of fit, finish and markings. However, commercial production of 1911A1 pistols stopped when WWII started. Therefore, production changes of 1911A1 pistols were not carried over to contemporary commercial pistols, because there was no contemporary commercial production. "C" serial number prefix designated commercial series until 1950, when it was changed to a "C" suffix. "Government Model" pistols were polished and blued until about serial number C230,000, when top, bottom and rear were matte finished. Words "Government Model" as well as "Verified Proof" mark were stamped on all but about the first 500 pistols, when post-war production commenced at C220,000. Some of these first 500 also lacked verified proof mark. First post-war pistols used some leftover military parts such as triggers and stocks. Pre-war pistols all had checkered walnut grips. Post-war pistols generally had plastic grips until "midrange" serial when wood grips returned. There were a number of different commercial models manufactured. They are individually listed.

Manufactured by Colt from 1925-1942 from about serial number C136000 to about serial number C215000. Only a few pistols from serial #C202000 to C215000 were shipped domestically, as most were shipped to Brazil or renumbered into military models. See Model 1911A1 commercial to military conversions.

Standard Colt 1911A1 "Commercial Government Model" Domestic Sales

These pistols have numbered slides. NO foreign markings, NO Swartz safeties or additions. Note: Add 30- to 60 percent for finish 99-100 percent.

NIB	Exc.	V.G.	Good	Fair	Poor
—	4500	3500	2500	1000	500

Standard Colt 1911A1 "Commercial Government Model" Export Sales

Usually with foreign crest or foreign inscription of a county such as Argentina or Brazil. Pistol has a numbered slide. Some variations with foreign markings are more rare than standard domestic pistols. Argentine pistols do not have collector interest that others or Standard" domestic pistols have, because the market has been flooded with Argentine imports in recent years.

Argentine Colt-made 1911A1 model pistols without Swartz safeties

Note: Add 20- to 30 percent for finish 99-100 percent.

NIB	Exc.	V.G.	Good	Fair	Poor
—	2000	1450	850	650	550

Brazilian, Mexican, and other South American (except Argentina)

Colt-made "1911A1 Commercial Government Model" pistols. Note: Add 20- to 100 percent for finish 99-100 percent.

NIB	Exc.	V.G.	Good	Fair	Poor
—	6500	4500	2800	1700	1000

Colt National Match Caliber .45, Pre-WWII, .45 (without Swartz safeties)

A National Match Commercial pistol, was introduced by Colt at the 1930 National Matches at Camp Perry. Production began in 1932. Right side of slide marked "NATIONAL MATCH" and mainspring housing had no lanyard loop. National Match modifications to standard pistol, as described in Colt literature included: Tighter barrel, better sights and a hand-polished action. Tighter barrel probably amounted to a tighter fit between barrel bushing and barrel. Hand-polishing of action probably produced a greatly improved trigger pull, but overall, barrel slide lockup was probably only superficially improved. Colt also advertised a "Selected Match Grade" barrel. Colt advertising indicated that scores using National Match pistols improved greatly and probably did to a degree, but most of the improvement was probably due to the improved (wider) sights and improved trigger pull. The very first pistols had fixed sights, but by about SN C177,000 the "Stevens Adjustable Rear Target Sight" was available. Both fixed and adjustable sights were available thereafter throughout production. Total number of National Match pistols, with each type of sight is not known, but one author (Kevin Williams, Collecting Colt's National Match Pistols) estimates that the percentage of adjustable sight equipped National Match pistols may have been only 20 percent. Note that the Colt National Match pistol is not referred to here as a "1911A1", because this pistol lacks the military lanyard loop that is present in all Standard Government Models. Also note that "Colt National Match" Pre-war pistols are also "Government Models" as the receiver was marked as such throughout production. Note: Add 30- to 60 cercent for finish 99-100 percent.

With Adjustable Sights

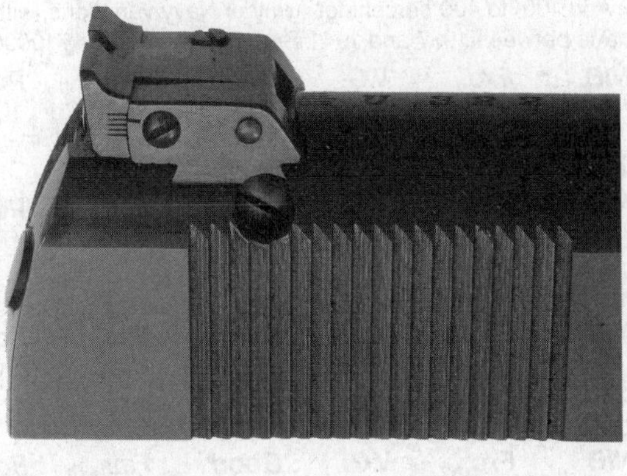

NIB	Exc.	V.G.	Good	Fair	Poor
—	12000	7500	4500	2500	900

Fixed Sights

NIB	Exc.	V.G.	Good	Fair	Poor
—	9000	6000	3000	1750	750

Swartz Safeties, Pre-WWII, Firing Pin and Hammer/Sear

The "Swartz Safeties" are a pair of devices that Colt installed in 1911A1 commercial "Government Models" and 1911A1 Commercial National Match pistols in the late 1930s and early 1940s. First device, a firing pin block that was actuated by the grip safety, prevented the firing pin from moving forward unless the grip safety was squeezed. Second, Swartz Safety Device the Hammer/Sear safety prevented a possible unsafe half cock position. Swartz firing pin block safety can be observed by pulling the slide back all the way and looking at the top of the frame. A Swartz-safety-equipped 1911A1 pistol will have a second pin protruding up next to the conventional disconnect pin. A second Swartz safety (the Swartz Sear Safety), is usually built into pistols equipped with the Swartz firing pin block safety. The sear safety can sometimes be detected by the drag marks of the notched sear on the round portion of the hammer that the sear rides on. Pulling the hammer all the way back will expose these drag marks if they are visible. Presence of the drag marks, however, does not ensure that the Swartz-modified sear safety parts are all present. Disassembly may be required to verify the correct parts are all present.

The Swartz Safeties are referred to in Colt Factory letters as the "NSD" (New Safety Device). (From SN C162,000 to C215,000 about 3,000 total National Match pistols were made with and without Swartz safeties.) The number of National Match pistols having the Swartz safeties is unknown. However, only a few pistols below serial C190000 had the safeties installed and of the pistols made after C190000, most were Standard Models shipped to Brazil and Argentina. Brazilian pistols were without the safeties or the cutouts. Argentine pistols were shipped in two batches of 250 pistols each. Both of these Argentine batches appear to have had the safeties installed as a number of them have recently been imported into the U.S.A. Probably much less than half of the total Colt made National Match pistols had the Swartz safeties. Total number of pistols (both Standard Government Model and National Match) shipped with Swartz safeties may be less than 3,000. And, probably much less than half of the total Colt made National Match pistols had the Swartz safeties. Swartz safeties were also installed in late Super .38 and Super Match .38 pistols.

Standard Colt 1911A1 Commercial "GOVERNMENT MODEL" Marked Pistol with Numbered Slide and "Swartz Safeties"

No foreign markings. Fixed sights only, no additions whatsoever. Rare, seldom seen. Note: Add 20- 50 percent for finish 99-100 percent.

NIB	Exc.	V.G.	Good	Fair	Poor
—	7500	4500	3000	1500	1000

Colt National Match Caliber Pre-WWII, .45. Pre-WWII (with "Swartz Safeties")

Serial number C186,000-C215,000 probably less than 1,500 pistols. Colt would re-work fixed sights equipped pistols on a repair order, with Stevens adjustable sight. Therefore, a Colt letter showing that the pistol was originally shipped with adjustable sights is in order for any adjustable sight-equipped pistol. Note: Add 30- to 60 percent for finish 99-100 percent.

Stevens Adjustable Sights

NIB	Exc.	V.G.	Good	Fair	Poor
—	15000	11000	7000	4000	2200

Fixed Sights

NIB	Exc.	V.G.	Good	Fair	Poor
—	12000	9000	6000	3750	1500

Standard 1911A1 Pre-WWII, "GOVERNMENT MODEL" Export Sales

With Swartz Safeties" and usually a foreign crest or foreign inscription mainly from Argentina. Vast majority of Swartz equipped foreign contract pistols were shipped to Argentina, but Argentine pistols do not have the collector interest that others or the plain domestic pistols have, because the market has been flooded with Argentine imports in recent years.

The few Argentine Swartz equipped pistols that remain in original and excellent or better condition, usually sell for less than their "plain Jane" domestic counterparts and for much less than the much rarer Brazilian and Mexican pistols. Perhaps these depressed prices represent a bargin for collectors, with an eye to the future when the supply of these extremely rare pistols dries up. Re-blue = Fair/Poor. Note: Add 20- to 30 percent for finish 99-100 percent.

NIB	Exc.	V.G.	Good	Fair	Poor
—	2000	1500	1200	900	750

Normal Brazilian and Mexican Pistols

These pistols do not have Swartz safeties. Most examples seen are refinished = Fair/Poor. Note: Add 20- 30 percent for finish 99-100 percent.

NIB	Exc.	V.G.	Good	Fair	Poor
—	7500	5000	3500	2750	1750

Argentine Contract Pistols "Modelo Argentino 1927, Calibre .45"

These pistols delivered to Argentina in 1927. Right side of slide marked with the two-line inscription Ejercito Argentino Colt Cal .45 Mod. 1927". Also the Argentine National Seal and "Rampant Colt". SN 1-10,000. Verified proof, Assembler's mark and Final inspectors mark under left stock by upper bushing. None had Swartz Safeties. Most of these pistols were re-blued. Re-blued = Fair/Poor. Note: Abundance of these and other refinished Argentine pistols has depressed the prices of all original finish Argentine pistols. Add 20- to 50 percent for finish 99-100 percent.

NIB	Exc.	V.G.	Good	Fair	Poor
—	1800	1350	950	700	600

Military to Commercial Conversions

Some 1911 Military pistols that were brought home by GIs, were subsequently returned to the Colt factory by their owners for repair or refinishing. If the repair included a new barrel, the pistol would have been proof fired and a normal Verified proof mark affixed to the triggerguard bow in the normal commercial practice. If the pistol was re-finished between about 1920 and 1942, the slide would probably be numbered to the frame again in the normal commercial practice. These pistols are really re-manufactured Colt pistols of limited production and should be valued at least that of a contemporary 1911A1 commercial pistol, but usually sell for less. Only pistols marked with identifiable Colt markings should be included in this category. Very seldom seen. Since Colt rework records are lost, re-worked and re-finished pistols without identifiable Colt applied markings are probably not verifiable as Colt re-works and should be considered re-finished pistols of unknown pedigree. Note:

Finish 99-100 percent add 30 percent.

NIB	Exc.	V.G.	Good	Fair	Poor
—	2800	1900	1500	1000	880

Super .38 1929 Model, Pre-WWII

Pistol is identical in outward physical configuration to .45 ACP Colt Commercial. Chambered for .38 Super cartridge. Magazine holds 9 rounds. Right side of slide marked "Colt Super .38 Automatic" in two lines, followed by "Rampant Colt". Last few thousand pre-war Super .38 pistols made, had Swartz Safety parts installed. Some pistols were assembled post-war, with leftover parts. Post-war-assembled pistols did not have Swartz safeties installed but most (possibly all) had the cutouts. In 1945, 400 pistols were purchased by the U.S. Government. These 400 pistols bear the G.H.D. acceptance mark as well as Ordnance crossed cannons. (G.H.D. and Ordnance marked add 30-50 percent. A factory letter is probably necessary here.) Some collectors feel that post-war assembly and post-war chemical tank bluing adds a premium, others feel that it requires a deduction. Note: Add 33 percent for finish 99-100 percent; 20 percent for Swartz Safeties; 50 percent for nickel finish.

NIB	Exc.	V.G.	Good	Fair	Poor
10000	7000	5000	3000	2000	1000

Super Match .38 1935 Model, Pre-WWII

Only 5,000 of these specially fit and finished target-grade pistols were manufactured. Have fixed sights or Stevens adjustable sights. Top surfaces are matte-finished to reduce glare. Twelve hundred pistols were purchased and sent to Britain in 1939, at the then-costly rate of $50 per unit. Last few thousand pre-war Super .38 pistols made had Swartz safety parts installed, but some pistols were assembled post-war with leftover parts. Post-war-assembled pistols did not have Swartz safeties installed, but most (possibly all) had the cutouts. In 1945, 400 pistols were purchased by the U.S. Government. These 400 pistols bear the G.H.D. acceptance mark as well as Ordnance crossed cannons. G.H.D. and Ordnance marked add 30-50 percent. A factory letter is probably necessary here. Swartz Safeties add 20 percent. Some collectors feel that post-war assembly and post-war chemical tank bluing adds a premium, others feel that it requires a deduction. Note: Add 20- 75 percent for both models for finish 99-100 percent.

Adjustable Sights

NIB	Exc.	V.G.	Good	Fair	Poor
—	11500	8000	5000	3000	2000

Fixed Sights

NIB	Exc.	V.G.	Good	Fair	Poor
—	10000	6500	4000	2000	1250

MODEL 1911A1 U.S. MILITARY SERIES

A complete look at the many variations of Colt Model 1911A1 that were made for U.S. Military forces, *see Standard Catalog of Military Firearms, 8th Edition*. This publication covers history, technical data, photos and values of the world's military arms and accessories. Following is a summary of estimated values for Model 1911A1 pistols manufactured for U.S. forces between 1924 and end of WWII in 1945.

Colt

Note: Add 100- to 400 percent for Army or Navy variations, with blue finish made between 1937 and 1941. Serial number range 710000-734xxx.

NIB	Exc.	V.G.	Good	Fair	Poor
—	4500	3800	2900	2200	1000

Ithaca

NIB	Exc.	V.G.	Good	Fair	Poor
—	2500	1800	1200	900	600

Remington Rand

NIB	Exc.	V.G.	Good	Fair	Poor
—	2550	2260	2000	1000	900

Union Switch & Signal

NIB	Exc.	V.G.	Good	Fair	Poor
—	7000	4800	3800	3000	2000

Singer Mfg. Co.

Note: Highly collectible model and fakes are known to exist. 500 of these guns were made, with serial numbers from S800001 to S800500. An appraisal from a recognized Colt expert is strongly suggested, whether buying or selling. Deduct 50 percent for unserialed or presentation pistols.

NIB	Exc.	V.G.	Good	Fair	Poor
—	100000	70000	50000	29000	15000

COLT 1911A1 POST WWII COMMERCIAL PRODUCED, DOMESTIC SALES, 1946-1969

SN C220,000 to about C220,500

No "GOVERNMENT MODEL" marking. Few have no verified proof. Many parts are leftover military. Note: Add 20- to 50 percent for finish 99-100 percent.

NIB	Exc.	V.G.	Good	Fair	Poor
8500	6000	4000	2500	1500	1000

SN C220,500 to about C249,000 verified proof and "GOVERNMENT MODEL" marking

Many parts are leftover military in first few thousand pistols. No foreign markings. Note: Add 20- to 30 percent for finish 99-100 percent. Deduct 30 percent for foreign markings.

NIB	Exc.	V.G.	Good	Fair	Poor
4500	3500	2500	1500	1000	750

SN 255,000-C to about 258,000-C Slide Factory Roll Marked "PROPERTY OF THE STATE OF NEW YORK", verified proof, and "GOVERNMENT MODEL" marking (250 pistols total)

Few leftover military parts are still used. Few pairs of pistols remain as consecutive pairs. Note: Add 20- to 50 percent for finish 99-100 percent; 10 percent for consecutive pairs.

Courtesy Karl Karash

NIB	Exc.	V.G.	Good	Fair	Poor
—	4000	2500	1600	1100	800

"SN 249,500-C to about 335,000-C, verified proof and GOVERNMENT MODEL" marking""

No foreign markings. Note: Add 20- to 30 percent for finish 99-100 percent. Deduct 30 percent for foreign markings.

NIB	Exc.	V.G.	Good	Fair	Poor
—	2200	1500	1000	500	400

SN 334,500-C to about 336,169-C, BB (Barrel Bushing) marked

About 1000 pistols. Verified proof and "GOVERNMENT MODEL" marking. Note: Add 20- to 50 percent for finish 99-100 percent.

NIB	Exc.	V.G.	Good	Fair	Poor
3300	2200	1750	1350	1000	750

ACE and SERVICE MODEL ACE

Ace Model .22 Pistol

Starting on June 21, 1913, U.S. Military along with "Springfield Armory" and "Colt Patented Firearms Manufacturing Co." attempted to develop a .22-cal. rimfire pistol that could be used for training purposes. By 1927, the military became convinced that a pistol identical to standard "Service Pistol", but in .22-cal. rimfire was impractical and dropped the idea. In 1930 Colt purchased advertising that, in effect, requested the shooting public to let the company know if they would be interested in a .22 rimfire pistol built similar to "Government Model". The response must have been positive, because in 1931 Colt Ace appeared on the market. Ace uses a frame similar to the frame of "Government Model", with a highly modified slide and heavy barrel. Chambered for .22 LR cartridge only. Size is the same as larger-caliber version and weight is 36 oz. Operation is straight blowback. Ace has a 10-round detachable magazine and features "Improved Ace Adjustable Target Sight". Markings on left side of slide are the same as on "Government Model"; right side reads "Colt Ace 22 Long Rifle". The Army purchased a few pistols (totaling 206) through 1936. The Army concluded that the function of Ace was less than perfect, as they concluded the .22 rimfire lacked the power to consistently and reliably operate the slide. Approximately 11,000 Ace pistols were manufactured and in 1941 they were discontinued. Many owners today find that although ACE is somewhat selective to ammunition, with full power loads it is a highly reliable pistol that does not require the constant cleaning needed by the "Service Model Ace". Note: Add 33 percent for finish 99-100 percent.

NIB	Exc.	V.G.	Good	Fair	Poor
7000	4500	3000	1800	950	700

Pre-1945 Service Model Ace .22 R. F. Pistol

In 1937, Colt introduced this improved version of the Ace Pistol. It utilizes a floating chamber, invented by David "Carbine" Williams the firearm's designer who invented the "Short Stroke Gas Piston", that is the basis of the MI carbine, while serving time on a Southern chain gang. Colt advertised that this pistol, with its floating chamber would give the Service Model Ace the reliability and "feel" of a .45 Auto. Today, owners of Service Model ACE pistols find they require regular maintenance and cleaning in order to keep the close-fitting floating chamber from binding. Furthermore, fouling appears to be much worse with some brands and types of ammunition. Most owners feel that although the perceived recoil of Service Model ACE is noticeably greater than that of ACE, it falls far short of a .45 Auto's recoil. Serial number is prefixed by letters "SM". External configuration is the same as Ace. Slide is marked "Colt Service Model Ace .22 Long Rifle". Most were sold to the Army and some on a commercial basis. There were a total of 13,803 manufactured before production ceased in 1945. Note: Add 20- to 30 percent for both models for finish 99-100 percent; 35 percent for "US Property" marking on blued pistols.

Blued pistols (before about SN SM 3840)

NIB	Exc.	V.G.	Good	Fair	Poor
—	11000	7500	4000	1500	1000

Parkerized pistols (after about SN SM 3840)

NIB	Exc.	V.G.	Good	Fair	Poor
—	5000	3000	1800	950	700

Service Model Ace-Post-War

Introduced in 1978. Similar to pre-war model. Production ceased in 1982. Note: Add 20- to 30 percent for finish 99-100 percent.

NIB	Exc.	V.G.	Good	Fair	Poor
—	1400	1050	950	700	600

Conversion Units .22-.45, .45-.22

In 1938, Colt released a .22-caliber conversion unit. With this kit, one who already owned a "Government Model" could simply switch the top half and fire inexpensive .22 rimfire ammunition. Unit consists of a slide marked "Service Model Ace" barrel, with floating chamber, ejector, slide lock, bushing, recoil spring, 10-shot magazine and box. Conversion Units feature the Stevens adjustable rear sight. Later that same year a kit to convert Service Model Ace to .45 ACP was offered. In 1942 production of these units ceased. The .22 kit was re-introduced in 1947; .45 kit was not brought back. Be alert, as sometimes a conversion unit is found on a Service Model ACE receiver and a Service model Ace upper is sold as a "Conversion Unit". Conversion Units are ALWAYS marked "Conversion Unit". "Service Model ACE" pistols lack the "Conversion Unit" marking. Note: Finish 99-100 percent add 20-30 percent. Deduct 20 percent if box is missing.

Pre-war and Post-war "U" numbered Service Model Ace Conversion Unit, .22-.45 (to convert .45 cal. to .22 cal.)

Pre-war conversion units were serial numbered U1-U2000.

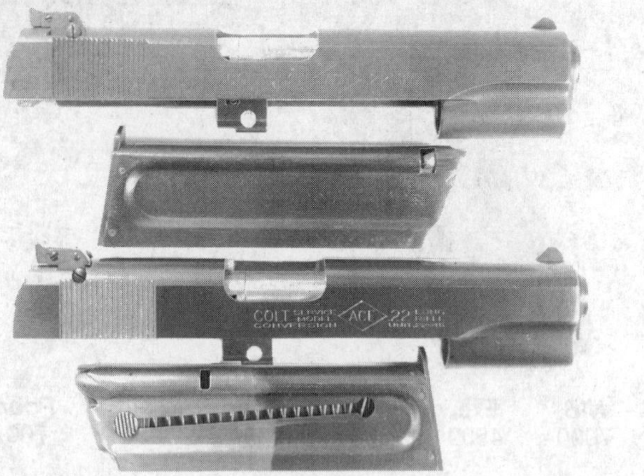

Courtesy Karl Karash

NIB	Exc.	V.G.	Good	Fair	Poor
2000	1500	1000	550	500	450

Post-war Conversion Units

These were serial numbered U2001-U2670.

NIB	Exc.	V.G.	Good	Fair	Poor
1200	800	550	500	450	420

Pre-war Service Model Ace (Re-) Conversion Unit, .45-22

To convert SMA .22 Cal. to .45 Cal. SN 1-SN 112. Watch out for fakes.

NIB	Exc.	V.G.	Good	Fair	Poor
5000	3500	2500	1500	750	550

Post-war .22 Conversion Unit Unnumbered

30 percent premium for Stevens adjustable sights, 1946 only.

NIB	Exc.	V.G.	Good	Fair	Poor
600	400	350	250	220	180

Military National Match .45 Pistols

Re-built from service pistols at Springfield Armory, between 1955 and about 1967 and Rock Island in 1968. Pistols were built and re-built each year, with a portion being sold to competitors by the NRA. Each year improvements were added to the re-build program. Four articles in "National Rifleman" document these pistols well: August 1959, April 1963, June 1966 and July 1966. Many parts for these pistols have been available and many "Look Alike" pistols have been built by basement armorers. Pistols generally came with a numbered box and shipping papers. Prices listed are for pistols with numbered box or papers. Less box and papers deduct 30 percent. When well-worn, these pistols will offer little over a standard pistol. Early pistols are much less commonly seen, but seem to be less sought after since they look largely like normal issue pistols. Note: Add 20- to 30 percent for finish 99-100 percent.

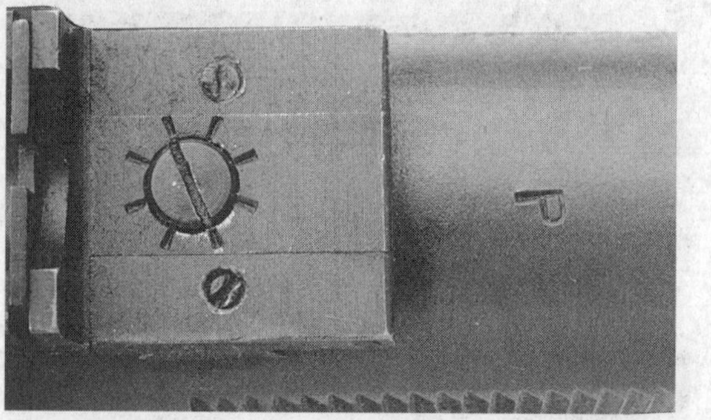

Paul Goodwin photo

NIB	Exc.	V.G.	Good	Fair	Poor
2500	2000	1300	1100	700	480

Military National Match Pistols (Drake Slide)

In 1964, Springfield Armory used some of these specially machined and hardened slides to build the Military National Match pistols that year. This year's pistol are perhaps the most identifiable NM pistol due to the unique slide marking. However, Drake was the only supplier of slides that year. Colt supplied slides in the following year (1965). Note: Add 20- to 30 percent for finish 99-100 percent.

Courtesy Karl Karash

NIB	Exc.	V.G.	Good	Fair	Poor
2700	2100	1300	1100	700	480

Gold Cup National Match (pre-Series 70)

Chambered for .45 ACP. Features flat mainspring housing of 1911. Has a match-grade barrel and bushing. Parts were hand-fitted and slide has an enlarged ejection port. Trigger is the long version, with an adjustable trigger stop and sights are adjustable target-type. Finish blued, with checkered walnut grips and gold medallions. Slide marked "Gold Cup National Match". Serial number is prefixed by letters "NM". Pistol manufactured from 1957 to 1970. Note: Add 20- to 30 percent for finish 99-100 percent.

NIB	Exc.	V.G.	Good	Fair	Poor
1750	1400	1000	700	500	400

Gold Cup MKIII National Match

Pistol is identical to Gold Cup .45, except chambered for .38 Mid-Range Wad Cutter round. Manufactured from 1961 until 1974. Note: Add 20- to 30 percent for finish 99-100 percent.

Courtesy John J. Stimpson

NIB	Exc.	V.G.	Good	Fair	Poor
1800	1500	1000	600	450	350

Colt 1911A1 AMU (Army Marksmanship Unit)

Note: Deduct 70 percent for Army modified pistols.

NIB	Exc.	V.G.	Good	Fair	Poor
—	2700	2250	1450	900	400

COLT LICENSED AND UNLICENSED FOREIGN-MADE 1911A1 AND VARIATIONS

Argentine D.G.F.M.

[[Direccion General de Fabricaciones Militares made at the F.M.A.P. (Fabrica Militar de Arms Portatiles [Military Factory of Small Arms]). Licensed copies SN 24,000 to 112,494. Parts are generally interchangeable with Colt-made 1911A1 type pistols. Most pistols were marked "D.G.F.M. - (F.M.A.P.)". Late pistols marked FM within a cartouche on right side of slide. Pistols are found both with and without import markings, often in excellent condition, currently more often in re-finished condition and with a seemingly endless variety of slide markings. None of these variations have yet achieved any particular collector status or distinction, unless new in box. In fact, many of these fine pistols have and continue to be used as platforms for the highly customized competition and target pistols that are currently popular. Re-finished=Fair/Poor. Note: Add 10- to 30 percent for finish 99-100 percent-NIB.

]]

Courtesy Karl Karash

NIB	Exc.	V.G.	Good	Fair	Poor
2000	1400	900	680	520	480

Argentine-Made Ballester Molina

Un-licensed Argentine re-designed versions. (Parts are NOT interchangeable with Colt except for barrel and magazine.) These pistols are found both with and without import markings. Pistols without import markings usually have a B prefix number stamped on left rear part of the mainspring housing and are often in excellent to new original condition. Vast majority of currently available pistols are found in excellent but re-finished condition. Only pistols with no import markings that are in excellent-to-new original condition have achieved any particular collector status. Most of these pistols that are being sold today are being carried and shot rather than being collected. Re-finished = Fair/Poor. Note: Add 10- to 30 percent for finish 99-100 percent-NIB.

Courtesy Karl Karash

NIB	Exc.	V.G.	Good	Fair	Poor
800	600	380	300	220	190

Brazilian Models 1911A1

Made by "Fabrica de Itajuba" in Itajuba, Brazil. The Imbel Model 973, made by "Industriade Material Belico do Brazil" in Sao Paulo, Brazil. The Itajuba is a true copy of Colt 1911A1 and the Imbel is also believed to be a true copy. However, an Imbel has yet to be examined by the author. Too rarely seen in U.S.A. to establish a meaningful price.

COLT MODEL 1911A1 1970 - CURRENT

Model 1911A1 was manufactured by Colt until 1971, when the Series 70 Government Model superseded it. Modifications in the new model were slightly heavier slide and slotted collet barrel bushing. In 1983, Colt introduced Series 80 models, which had an additional passive firing pin safety lock. Half-cock notch was also re-designed. Beginning of 1992 another change was made to Model 1911A1 in the form of an enhanced pistol. Included were Government models, Commander, Officer's, Gold Cup and Combat Elite. These modifications are the result of Colt's desire to meet the shooters demand for a more "customized" pistol. Colt chose some of the most popular modifications to perform on their new enhanced models. They include beavertail safety grip, slotted Commander-style hammer, relief cut under the triggerguard, beveled magazine well, slightly longer trigger, flat top rib and angled slide serrations. Model 1911A1 may be the most modified handgun in the world.

MKIV Series 70 Government Model

Essentially a newer version of 1911A1. Has prefix "70G" from 1970-1976, "G70" from 1976-1980 and "70B" from 1980-1983, when production ceased. Offered in blue or nickel plate. Checkered walnut grips, with Colt medallion. Chambered for .45 ACP, .38 Super, 9mm and 9mm Steyr (foreign export only). Note: Add 35 percent for bright nickel finish; 10 percent for satin nickel; 10 percent for .38 Super, 9mm Parabellum or 9mm Steyr.

NIB	Exc.	V.G.	Good	Fair	Poor
1500	1000	800	600	500	400

MKIV Series 70 Gold Cup National Match

Newer version of 1957 National Match. Features a slightly heavier slide and Colt Elliason sights. Chambering is .45 ACP only. Accurizer barrel and bushing was introduced on this model. Manufactured from 1970-1983.

NIB	Exc.	V.G.	Good	Fair	Poor
2200	1750	1500	1100	750	500

Series 70 Gunsite Pistol

Features 5" barrel, thin rosewood grips, Gold Cup serrations, Heinie front sight and Novak rear sight, plus several other special features. Available in blue or stainless steel. Introduced in 2004.

NIB	Exc.	V.G.	Good	Fair	Poor
1200	1050	820	600	400	200

Series 70 Gunsite Pistol Commander

As above, with 4.25" barrel.

NIB	Exc.	V.G.	Good	Fair	Poor
1200	1050	820	600	400	200

COLT ENHANCED GOVERNMENT MODELS

In 1992, Colt introduced a new set of features for its Model 1911A1 series pistols. New features include: a flattop slide, angled rear slide serrations, scalloped ejection port, combat style hammer, beavertail grip safety, relief cut-under triggerguard and long trigger. Models that are affected by this new upgrade are: Delta Elite, Combat Elite, Government Model, Combat Commander, Lightweight Commander, Officer's ACP, Officer's ACP Lightweight.

COMMANDER SERIES

A shortened version of Government model. Has a 4.25" barrel, lightweight alloy frame and rounded spur hammer. Total weight of the Commander is 27.5 oz. Serial number has suffix "LW". Chambered for .45 ACP, 9mm, .38 Super and some for 7.65 Parabellum for export only. Introduced in 1949.

Pre-70 Series (1949-1969)

Note: Deduct 20 percent for 9mm.

NIB	Exc.	V.G.	Good	Fair	Poor
1500	1250	1000	800	600	400

Series 70 (1970-1983)

NIB	Exc.	V.G.	Good	Fair	Poor
1200	1000	850	700	600	300

Series 80 (1983-1996)

NIB	Exc.	V.G.	Good	Fair	Poor
900	750	600	500	400	300

Combat Commander

Combat Commander was produced in response to complaints from some quarters about the excessive recoil and rapid wear of the alloy-framed Commander. This model is simply a Commander, with a steel frame. Combat Commander weight 32 oz. and offered in blue or satin nickel, with walnut grips. No longer in production. Note: Add 40 percent for Series 70 model

NIB	Exc.	V.G.	Good	Fair	Poor
850	550	480	380	300	200

MK IV Series 80 Government Model

Introduced in 1983. It is, for all purposes, externally the same as Series 70. Basic difference is the addition of the new firing pin safety on this model. No longer in production.

NIB	Exc.	V.G.	Good	Fair	Poor
980	830	680	600	530	460

Blued

NIB	Exc.	V.G.	Good	Fair	Poor
850	720	600	500	400	250

Nickel Plated

NIB	Exc.	V.G.	Good	Fair	Poor
1000	800	650	500	400	250

Stainless Steel

NIB	Exc.	V.G.	Good	Fair	Poor
950	800	650	500	400	250

Polished Stainless Steel

NIB	Exc.	V.G.	Good	Fair	Poor
1000	800	700	500	400	250

Colt 1991A1

The 1991 Series is a direct descendant of original Model 1911. The long trigger, flat mainspring housing and recoil spring system are like the original design. Upgrades include high profile white dot sights and lowered ejection port. Based on Series 80 MKIV Colt design, it was introduced in 1992. Early models were offered in 9mm. Standard model in .45 ACP, with a 7+1 capacity. A .38 Super version is available. See separate listing.

NIB	Exc.	V.G.	Good	Fair	Poor
750	680	550	350	150	120

M1991A1 Commander

Chambered for .45 ACP, this model has all the same features as standard M1991A1, with a slightly shorter 4.25" barrel. Re-introduced in 2004. Note: In 1997, Colt offered this model in stainless steel, with fixed white dot sights. Add $100 to NIB price.

NIB	Exc.	V.G.	Good	Fair	Poor
800	550	400	300	220	120

M1991A1 Compact

Chambered for .45 ACP, this model has a 3.25" barrel. It is 1.5" shorter than standard M1991A1 model and .375" shorter in height. Magazine holds 6 rounds. No longer in production. Note: In 1997, Colt offered this model in stainless steel, with fixed white dot sights. Add $50 to NIB price.

NIB	Exc.	V.G.	Good	Fair	Poor
850	600	420	300	150	120

M1991A1 .38 Super

Has the same features as .45 ACP M1991A1 Government Model, except chambered for .38 Super cartridge. Magazine capacity is 9 + 1. Available only with bright stainless steel finish.

NIB	Exc.	V.G.	Good	Fair	Poor
900	800	650	500	380	300

MK IV Series 80 Gold Cup National Match

Externally same as Series 70 Gold Cup, with new firing pin safety.

Blued

NIB	Exc.	V.G.	Good	Fair	Poor
1200	900	680	500	350	250

Stainless Steel

NIB	Exc.	V.G.	Good	Fair	Poor
1200	900	680	500	350	250

Polished Stainless Steel

NIB	Exc.	V.G.	Good	Fair	Poor
1200	900	680	500	350	250

Officer's ACP

Shortened version of Government Model. Barrel 3.5"; weight 37 oz. Chambered for .45 ACP only, with checkered walnut grips. Officer's ACP introduced in 1985. No longer in production.

Blued

NIB	Exc.	V.G.	Good	Fair	Poor
1000	700	520	320	250	200

Matte Blued

NIB	Exc.	V.G.	Good	Fair	Poor
1000	700	520	320	250	200

Satin Nickel

Discontinued 1985.

NIB	Exc.	V.G.	Good	Fair	Poor
1050	750	580	380	300	200

Stainless Steel

NIB	Exc.	V.G.	Good	Fair	Poor
1100	800	620	420	340	200

Lightweight Officer's ACP

An alloy-framed version. Weight 24 oz. Introduced in 1986. No longer in production.

NIB	Exc.	V.G.	Good	Fair	Poor
1000	700	520	320	250	200

Concealed Carry Officer's Model

Features a lightweight aluminum frame, with stainless steel Commander slide. Barrel length 4.25". Chambered for .45 ACP cartridge. Fitted with lightweight trigger, combat style hammer and Hogue grips. Weight about 34 oz. Introduced in 1998. No longer in production.

NIB	Exc.	V.G.	Good	Fair	Poor
1200	1000	810	710	460	430

Delta Gold Cup

Introduced in 1992. Chambered for 10mm. Features 5-in. barrel, stainless steel finish, adjustable Accro sights, special trigger and black rubber wrap-around grips. Features all of the new "Enhanced" model features. No longer in production.

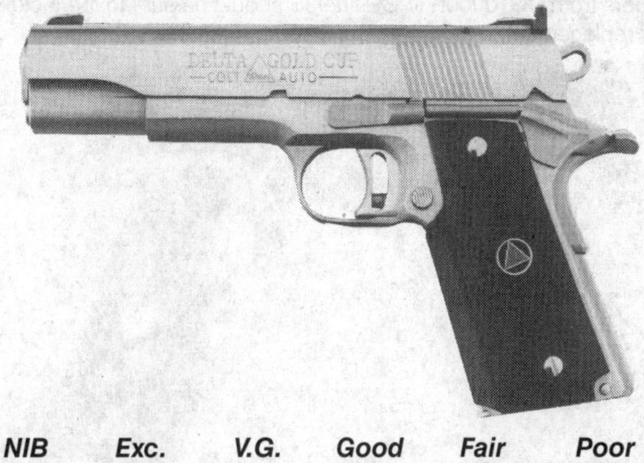

NIB	Exc.	V.G.	Good	Fair	Poor
1560	1210	900	660	580	530

Delta Elite

Chambered for 10mm Norma cartridge. Offered in blue or stainless steel. Grips are black neoprene, with the Delta medallion. Features a high-profile three-dot combat sight system. Delta Elite introduced in 1987; discontinued in 1996; re-introduced in 2008. Note: Deduct 20 percent for current production model.

Blued

NIB	Exc.	V.G.	Good	Fair	Poor
1200	920	650	420	300	250

Stainless Steel

NIB	Exc.	V.G.	Good	Fair	Poor
1250	950	680	400	300	250

Polished Stainless Steel

NIB	Exc.	V.G.	Good	Fair	Poor
1250	950	680	400	300	250

Combat Elite

Specialized Government model. Has a 5" barrel and adjustable Accro sights. Chambered in .45 ACP or .38 Super. Weight 38 oz. Has an 8-round magazine for .45 ACP; 9-round magazine for .38 Super. Finish blue or matte stainless steel. No longer in production. (Colt issued a recall notice for the safety on this model in June 2009. Pistols with serial numbers from CG10000E to CG11293E should be sent to the factory for parts replacement.)

NIB	Exc.	V.G.	Good	Fair	Poor
1200	1060	930	830	630	530

Combat Target Model

Introduced in 1996, this 5" barrel 1911 model features a fitted barrel, Gold Cup-style trigger, tuned action, flattop slide, relieved ejection port, skeletonized hammer, wide grip safety, high cut triggerguard, beveled magazine well, and adjustable sights. Weight 39 oz. Offered in both blue and stainless steel. Chambered for the new 9x23 cartridge as well as .45 ACP and .38 Super. No longer in production. In 1997, Colt expanded Target Model to include a number of different variations. They are listed. Note: Add $50 for stainless steel version.

NIB	Exc.	V.G.	Good	Fair	Poor
1050	880	700	600	400	200

Combat Target Commander

Barrel length 4.25". Chambered for .45 ACP. Stainless steel finish. Weight 36 oz. Has all other Combat Target features. No longer in production.

NIB	Exc.	V.G.	Good	Fair	Poor
1050	880	700	600	400	200

Combat Target Officer's ACP

Fitted with a 3.5" barrel and chambered for .45 ACP. Stainless steel finish. Weight about 34 oz. Has all other Combat Target features. No longer in production.

NIB	Exc.	V.G.	Good	Fair	Poor
1050	880	700	600	400	200

Special Combat Government

Pistol features a 5" barrel, double diamond rosewood grips, extended ambidextrous thumb safety. Steel checkered mainspring housing, with extended magazine well. Chambered for .45 ACP or .38 Super cartridges. Adjustable Bomar rear sight. Magazine capacity 8 rounds. Choice of hard chrome or blue/satin nickel finish.

NIB	Exc.	V.G.	Good	Fair	Poor
2000	1700	1500	1200	800	400

Special Combat Government Carry Model

1911-style semi-automatic pistol, chambered in .45 ACP (8+1) or .38 Super (9+1). Semi-custom features include Novak front and rear night sights, skeletonized three-hole trigger, slotted hammer, black/silver synthetic grips, Smith & Alexander upswept beavertail grip, palm swell safety and extended magazine well. Wilson tactical ambidextrous safety. 5" barrel. Available blued, hard chrome, or blue/satin nickel finish depending on chambering.

NIB	Exc.	V.G.	Good	Fair	Poor
1780	1460	1130	960	680	580

Close Quarters Battle (CQB) Pistol

From Colt Custom Shop, this .45 ACP model was designed for and is primarily manufactured for U.S. Marine Corps. Features a Desert Tan Cerakoted receiver and slide, 5" National Match barrel with accessory rail and a flat, serrated mainspring housing with extended grip safety and lanyard loop. Grips are G-10 composite and sights are Novak 3-Dot Night Sights.

NIB	Exc.	V.G.	Good	Fair	Poor
1850	1700	1500	1200	800	400

XSE SERIES MODEL O PISTOLS

Introduced in 1999, these models are an enhanced version of Colt 1911. Features front slide serrations, checkered double diamond rosewood grips, adjustable McCormick trigger, three-dot dovetail rear sights, ambidextrous safety, enhanced tolerances, aluminum frame and stainless steel slide. Chambered for .45 ACP cartridge.

XSE Model O Government (01070XS)

Fitted with 5" barrel and 8-round magazine.

NIB	Exc.	V.G.	Good	Fair	Poor
950	800	600	480	350	200

XSE Model O Concealed Carry Officer's (09850XS)

Fitted with 4.25" barrel and 7-round magazine.

NIB	Exc.	V.G.	Good	Fair	Poor
1000	850	620	480	350	200

XSE Model O Commander (04012XS)

Fitted with 4.25" barrel and 8-round magazine.

NIB	Exc.	V.G.	Good	Fair	Poor
950	800	600	480	350	200

XSE Model O Lightweight Commander (04860XS)

Fitted with 4.25" barrel and 8-round magazine. Weight about 26 oz.

NIB	Exc.	V.G.	Good	Fair	Poor
950	800	600	480	350	200

Colt Defender

Single-action pistol introduced in 1998. Features a lightweight aluminum alloy frame and stainless steel slide. Chambered for .45 ACP or .40 S&W cartridge. Fitted with a 3" barrel. Magazine capacity 7 rounds. Rubber wrap-around grips. Weight about 23 oz.; overall length 6.75".

NIB	Exc.	V.G.	Good	Fair	Poor
850	650	480	300	250	200

Colt Defender Model O (07000D)

Takes the place of Defender. Introduced in 2000. Brushed stainless finish, with 3" barrel. Skeletonized composite trigger, beveled magazine well, extended thumb safety and upswept beavertail, with palm swell. Chambered for .45 ACP only. (Colt issued a recall notice for the guide pad on this model in June 2009. Pistols with serial numbers from DR33036 to DR35948 should be sent to the factory for parts replacement.)

NIB	Exc.	V.G.	Good	Fair	Poor
950	700	520	350	200	140

1911 – WWI Replica

Single-action semi-automatic, chambered in .45 ACP. Faithful external re-production of WWI-era service pistol, with original-style roll marks grips, sights, carbonia blue finish, etc. Series 70 lockwork. Made from 2003 - 2009.

NIB	Exc.	V.G.	Good	Fair	Poor
1020	850	620	580	400	200

1911 - WWI 1918 Replica

Based on military model made in 1918. Black finish and WWI roll marks. Offered in a Presentation Grade, with blue or nickel finish and Colt Custom Shop "A" engraving. Excellent or new condition could add a premium of 100 percent. Made in 2008 and 2009. (Colt issued a recall notice for the safety on this model in June of 2009. Pistols with serial numbers from 1001WWI to 3431WWI should be sent to the factory for parts replacement.)

NIB	Exc.	V.G.	Good	Fair	Poor
1400	1080	850	700	500	400

1911A1 - WWII Replica

Replica of U.S. Military sidearm of WWII. Parkerized finish, WWII-ear roll marks, lanyard loop, original style composite grips and packaging. Made in .45 ACP only, by Colt Custom Shop from 2001 to 2004. Series 70 lockwork. (Colt issued a recall notice for the safety on this model in June 2009. Pistols with serial numbers from 4597WMK to 5414WMK should be sent to the factory for parts replacement.)

NIB	Exc.	V.G.	Good	Fair	Poor
1080	950	700	580	400	200

Colt New Agent Double Action Only

Similar to New Agent single-action, except has double-action-only operating system. Spur-less hammer design, with second-strike capability and no manual safety. Double-diamond slim fit grips, snag free trench sighting system, 7-shot magazine. In .45 ACP only. (Colt issued a recall notice for the safety and guide pad on this model in June of 2009. Pistols with serial numbers from GT01001 to GT04505 should be sent to the factory for parts replacement.)

NIB	Exc.	V.G.	Good	Fair	Poor
850	750	600	500	400	200

Colt Model 1991 DAO

Double-action-only version of Lightweight Government Model. Spur-less hammer design, with second-strike capability and no manual safety. Double-diamond slim fit grips, 7-shot magazine. In .45 ACP only. Introduced in 2011.

NIB	Exc.	V.G.	Good	Fair	Poor
950	800	700	550	400	250

Colt Model 1911 100th Anniversary Series

These two limited edition Model 1911s, were introduced in 2011 to commemorate 100th Anniversary of the legendary pistol. Model 1911ANVIII is based on 1918 configuration, with custom roll marks on receiver relating to 100th Anniversary. Higher grade version, Model 1911ANVII, features scroll engraving and historic Colt symbols high-lighted in 24 karat gold. Comes in a glass-topped walnut display case. Production was limited to 750 units. Higher grade variants limited to 100 units, with A, B, C or D levels of engraving scheduled at prices ranging from $2640 to $6528.

1911ANVII

NIB	Exc.	V.G.	Good	Fair	Poor
2150	1800	1500	—	—	—

1911ANVIII

NIB	Exc.	V.G.	Good	Fair	Poor
1080	900	750	—	—	—

Gunsite Model 1911

Made from 2003 to 2005 to commemorate Gunsite Shooting Academy. Special features include: Heinie front and Novak rear sights, Chip McCormick hammer and sear, checkered rosewood grips and flat serrated mainspring housing. Chambered in .45 ACP, with two 8-shot magazines.

NIB	Exc.	V.G.	Good	Fair	Poor
1350	1050	900	800	650	350

Colt Government Model 1911 .22 LR Series

Licensed re-production of 1911A1 in .22 LR, manufactured by Umarex USA. Blow-back action, with 12-shot magazine. Other standard 1911 specifications including 5" barrel, thumb and grip safeties, diamond checkered wood grips, blue finish and drift-adjustable rear sight. (Gold Cup has fully adjustable sight.) Weight about 33 oz. Offered in three variants: standard model, Rail Gun and Gold Cup. Introduced in 2011. Prices below are for standard model.

NIB	Exc.	V.G.	Good	Fair	Poor
350	300	280	220	180	100

Colt Concealed Carry

Chopped lightweight 1911-style semi-automatic, chambered in .45 ACP. Weight 25 oz. unloaded; overall length 6.75"; 7+1 capacity; Series 80 lockwork; black anodized aluminum frame, with double-diamond wood grips. Introduced 2007.

NIB	Exc.	V.G.	Good	Fair	Poor
950	700	520	350	200	150

New Agent

7+1 .45 ACP semi-automatic, with aluminum frame, fixed sights, Series 80 action, slim-fit grips and 6.75" overall length. Introduced 2007.

NIB	Exc.	V.G.	Good	Fair	Poor
950	700	520	350	200	150

Colt Rail Gun

1911-style semi-automatic pistol, chambered in .45 ACP. Stainless steel frame and slide, front and rear slide serrations, skeletonized trigger, integral accessory rail, Smith & Alexander upswept beavertail grip, palm swell safety, white dot front sight and Novak rear. Rosewood double diamond grips, tactical thumb safety, National Match barrel. Capacity 8+1. Note: Add $300 for Cerakote Desert Tan finish.

NIB	Exc.	V.G.	Good	Fair	Poor
950	700	520	350	200	150

Competition Pistol

Full-size 1911A1 Government Model in .45 ACP, 9mm or .38 Super, with competition enhanced features including National Match barrel, Novak adjustable rear and fiber optic front sights, extended grip safety. Introduced in 2016. Note: Add $100 for .38 Super; $100 for stainless steel.

NIB	Exc.	V.G.	Good	Fair	Poor
800	700	600	400	—	—

Gold Cup Trophy

Newest variation of classic Gold Cup series. In .45 ACP or 9mm, with 5 National Match barrel, wide target trigger, 25 lpi checkering on front and backstrap, G10 grips, fully adjustable Bomar rear sight and fiber optic front sight.

NIB	Exc.	V.G.	Good	Fair	Poor
1550	1250	1000	800	600	500

Wiley Clapp Series

Various 1911 pistol frame sizes offered by Talo. Models include a CCO, Government 1911, Lightweight Commander, Stainless Commander. Introduced 2017. Values are similar across all models.

NIB	Exc.	V.G.	Good	Fair	Poor
1125	1030	960	840	630	500

Double Eagle

Chambered for 9mm, .38 Super, 10mm Auto and .45 ACP cartridges. Has 5" barrel and 8-round detachable box magazine. Constructed of stainless steel and checkered black synthetic grips. Sights are fixed and utilize the three-dot system. Manufactured from 1990 to 1996. Note: Add 20 percent for 9mm, .38 Super or 10mm.

NIB	Exc.	V.G.	Good	Fair	Poor
1000	800	650	500	400	300

Double Eagle Officer's Model

Compact version of double-action Double Eagle pistol. Chambered for .45 ACP only. No longer in production.

NIB	Exc.	V.G.	Good	Fair	Poor
1020	850	620	580	400	200

Double Eagle Combat Commander

Based on standard Double Eagle design, with a slightly shorter 4.25" barrel. Double Eagle Combat Commander fits between standard model and smaller Officer's Model. Available in .45 ACP and .40 S&W (1993). Weight 36 oz., holds 8 rounds, has white dot sights and checkered Xenoy grips. Finish is matte stainless steel. No longer in production.

NIB	Exc.	V.G.	Good	Fair	Poor
1020	850	620	580	350	200

Double Eagle First Edition

This version of double-action Double Eagle pistol is chambered for 10mm Auto. Furnished with Cordura holster, double-magazine pouch, three magazines and zippered black Cordura case.

NIB	Exc.	V.G.	Good	Fair	Poor
1100	880	650	500	380	300

Pocket Nine

Double-action semi-automatic pistol, chambered for 9mm cartridge. Frame is aluminum alloy and slide stainless steel. Barrel length 2.75". Magazine capacity 6 rounds. Wrap-around rubber grips standard. Overall length 5.5". Weight about 17 oz. No longer in production.

NIB	Exc.	V.G.	Good	Fair	Poor
950	700	520	350	250	180

Tac Nine

Introduced in 1999. This double-action-only semi-automatic pistol is chambered for 9mm cartridge. Has 2.75" barrel, with an aluminum alloy frame and stainless steel slide. Tritium night sights. Wrap-around rubber grips are standard. Finish is black oxide. Enhanced tolerances. Weight about 17 oz. No longer in production.

NIB	Exc.	V.G.	Good	Fair	Poor
980	720	550	380	250	180

Mustang

More compact version of .380 Government Model. Has 2.75" barrel and 5-round detachable magazine. No longer in production. Note: Add 10 percent for nickel finish and stainless steel.

NIB	Exc.	V.G.	Good	Fair	Poor
850	650	480	300	250	200

Mustang PocketLite

Lightweight version of Mustang. Features an aluminum alloy receiver.

Finish is blued only and has synthetic grips. Introduced in 1987; discontinued 1999; re-introduced 2012. Note: Deduct 20 percent for 2012 model.

NIB	Exc.	V.G.	Good	Fair	Poor
800	600	480	300	250	200

Mustang Lite

Similar to Pocket Lite, except has black polymer frame with ribbed grips, matte black stainless slide.

NIB	Exc.	V.G.	Good	Fair	Poor
450	400	360	320	280	250

Government Pocketlite LW

Similar to Mustang, but fitted with a 3.25" barrel and 7-round magazine. Has an aluminum frame and stainless steel slide. Fixed sights. Black composition grips. Weight about 15 oz. No longer in production.

NIB	Exc.	V.G.	Good	Fair	Poor
850	650	480	300	250	200

Mustang Pocketlite XSP

Similar in design and operation to standard Mustang Pocketlite model, except it has a polymer receiver, black finish and squared triggerguard. Introduced in 2013.

NIB	Exc.	V.G.	Good	Fair	Poor
580	480	430	300	260	230

Mustang Plus II

This version of Mustang pistol features 2.75" barrel, with longer grip frame that accommodates a 7-round magazine. Introduced in 1988. Offered in blue and stainless steel. No longer in production. Note: Add 10 percent for stainless steel.

NIB	Exc.	V.G.	Good	Fair	Poor
850	650	480	300	250	200

Colt Pony

Introduced in 1997. Semi-automatic pistol chambered for .380 ACP. Fitted with a 2.75" barrel and bobbed hammer. Double-action-only. Grips are black composition. Sights are ramp front with fixed rear. Finish is Teflon and stainless steel. Magazine capacity 6 rounds. Overall length 5.5". Weight 19 oz. No longer in production.

NIB	Exc.	V.G.	Good	Fair	Poor
850	650	480	300	250	200

Colt Pony PocketLite

Same as above, with aluminum and stainless steel frame. Weight about 13 oz. No longer in production.

NIB	Exc.	V.G.	Good	Fair	Poor
850	650	480	300	250	200

.380 Series 80 Government Model

Single-action blowback-operated semi-automatic pistol, chambered for .380 ACP cartridge. Has a 3.25" barrel and 7-round magazine. Sights are fixed. Available blued, nickel plated or stainless steel. Synthetic grips. Introduced in 1985. No longer in production. Note: Add 10 percent for nickel finish and stainless steel.

NIB	Exc.	V.G.	Good	Fair	Poor
880	680	500	320	280	200

Colt CZ40

Introduced in 1998, this double-action .40 S&W pistol was built for Colt by CZ in Czech Republic. Fitted with a 4-in. barrel and black polymer grips. Frame is alloy, with carbon steel slide and blue finish. Magazine capacity 10 rounds. Weight about 34 oz. No longer in production.

NIB	Exc.	V.G.	Good	Fair	Poor
1060	910	760	610	530	510

Colt Model 2000

Introduced in 1992, Model 2000 was a new departure for Colt from its traditional service style semi-automatic pistols. Chambered for 9mm double-action-only pistol, with 4.5" barrel and choice between polymer or aluminum alloy frame. Weight: polymer frame 29 oz.; aluminum alloy frame 33 oz. Grips are black composition and sights are white dot. Dropped from Colt line in 1994.

NIB	Exc.	V.G.	Good	Fair	Poor
760	660	530	460	330	280

COLT .22 RIMFIRE SEMI-AUTOMATIC PISTOLS

For Colt Ace, see Model 1911 section.

COLT WOODSMAN

Text and photos by Bob Rayburn

The original Colt .22 Target Model was designed by John Moses Browning and improved by engineers at Colt Firearms prior to the start of production in 1915. Major design updates were made in 1947 and again in 1955. Those three designs constitute what collectors call the three series of Woodsman pistols. First Series refers to all those built on the frame used prior to and during WWII. Second Series includes all versions built on the second frame design from 1947 until 1955 and Third Series means the third frame design as used from 1955 to the end of production in 1977.

Each series had a Target Model, Sport Model and Match Target Model. All models are very similar: Sport Model for example, is merely a Target Model with a short barrel and in some cases different sights or grips. Match Target is nearly the same as Sport or Target Model, but with a heavier slab-sided barrel, squared-off frame at the front of receiver to mate with the heavy barrel and improved sights. In the post-war years there were also three very similar economy models: First the Challenger, then Huntsman and finally Targetsman. The actions of these economy models are identical to higher-end models of the same period internally; they lack only some of the refinements.

These guns were not assembled in strict numerical sequence. Furthermore, even when changes were made, old parts were used up at the same time new parts were being introduced. As a result, there is no hard and fast serial number dividing line for any particular feature and serial number overlaps of several thousand are common.

All models of the Woodsman line, in all three series, are discussed here, but there are numerous variations in details that are primarily of interest to specialized collectors. For more details see Bob Rayburn's Colt Woodsman Pocket Guide, a 96-page pocket-sized guide to the Colt Woodsman line, available for $11 (including shipping) from:

Bob Rayburn
PO Box 97104
Lakewood, WA 98497 or online at www.colt22.com or www.coltwoodsman.com

Except for NIB, values listed here are for the pistol only, without extras, for guns in the middle of each condition range. These are guidelines to the prevailing retail values for collector or shooter who is buying it as the end user, not what one might expect to receive from a gun dealer who is buying it to resell. Furthermore, within the Excellent and Very Good condition categories, there is a considerable spread in value, especially for the older and more collectible versions. Excellent, for example, means 98 percent or more original blue, but a very nice pre-Woodsman with 100 percent of the original blue would likely be worth twice as much to a serious collector as one with only 98 percent. At the other end of the condition scale, in the Fair and Poor categories, the individual values of component parts become significant, and effectively set a floor value. A poor condition, rusty, pitted pre-Woodsman or First Series Match Target would still have good value if it included the original magazine and grips in nice condition, for example. In addition, there are sometimes rare variations within the broad categories that can significantly enhance the value. Include the original crisp condition box, instructions, and tools, and the value goes up more, especially for high condition early guns. On the other hand, rust, pitting (even very minor), re-bluing, or other non-factory modifications will significantly reduce the values from those listed in the Very Good category or better.

FIRST SERIES

In 1915, intended market was the target shooter and there was only one model: Colt .22 LR Automatic Target Pistol. That model, however, proved to be very popular not only with target shooters, but also with hunters, trappers, campers and other outdoorsmen. Management at Colt noticed this, of course, and decided to give the pistol a new name that more closely reflected its widespread use. THE WOODSMAN, was name chosen and that roll mark was added to side of receiver in 1927, at approximately serial number 54000. To further satisfy the broader market, Colt introduced the Sport Model in 1933 and Match Target Model in 1938. Compact and beautifully balanced Sport Model was a near perfect "kit gun" for the outdoorsman. Match Target was designed for special needs of the serious target shooters. Approximately 54,000 pre-Woodsmans (all with 6.625" barrels) and a combined total of approximately 110,000 Woodsman marked Sport and Target Models were produced in the first series. Sport Model and Target Model were serial numbered together after Sport Model was added to the line in 1933. It was not possible to easily determine how many of each were manufactured. Safe to say Target Model far outnumbered Sport Model. During the war years of 1942-45, Match Target was the only Woodsman model built. Virtually the entire production was for the US military.

Pre-Woodsman

Model made from 1915-1927. Has a 10-round magazine, blue finish, checkered walnut grips and 6.625" barrel. Designed for .22 LR standard velocity ammunition. Rear sight adjustable for windage, front sight for elevation. Up until approximately serial number 31000 the barrel was a very thin, so-called "pencil barrel". Barrel weight and diameter were increased slightly in 1922, to what collectors now call the "medium weight barrel". Also numerous small changes in grips, magazines and markings over the years. Approximately 54,000 were made in all variations.

An early pre-Woodsman

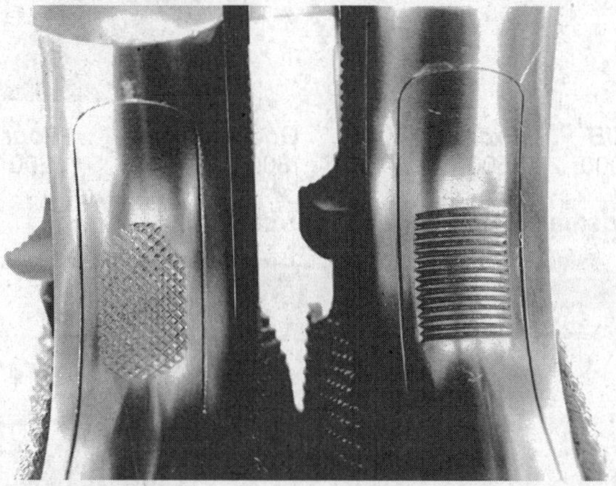

A checkered pattern in an oval on the mainspring housing (left) indicates a pre-Woodsman or First Series Woodsman Target model that was designed for standard velocity .22 Long Rifle ammunition only. A series of horizontal parallel lin

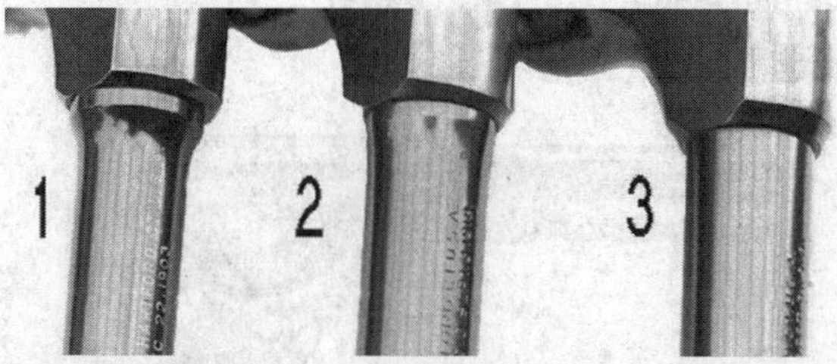

The three barrel profiles used with the Colt pre-Woodsman and First Series Target Model: from left to right, in order used, the pencil barrel, medium weight barrel and straight taper barrel.

NIB	Exc.	V.G.	Good	Fair	Poor
2800	2200	1400	850	350	200

Woodsman Target

Initially, this was exactly the same as late pre-Woodsman, with the exception of THE WOODSMAN marking on side of receiver. Later there were small changes in sights, trigger and markings. In 1934, barrel profile was again modified to a larger diameter, heavier barrel. This third and final pre-WWII barrel profile lacked the fillet or step-down, as was present on earlier pencil barrel and medium barrel, therefore commonly called the "straight taper" barrel. A significant modification occurred in 1932, when a new heat-treated mainspring housing and stiffer recoil spring were phased in to allow use of increasingly popular high velocity .22 LR ammunition. While this change had widely reported to have taken place at serial number 83790, it was actually phased in over a period of time and a range of serial numbers, spanning at least 81000-86000, within which range both standard and high speed versions can be found. Fortunately, Colt changed the marking on back of mainspring housing (see photo) to allow visual differentiation. Colt also sold a conversion kit to modify older guns for use with high velocity ammunition. Kit consisted of a new style mainspring housing, stiffer recoil spring and coil type magazine spring for use in the very early guns that had a Z type magazine spring.

NIB	Exc.	V.G.	Good	Fair	Poor
2500	1700	1100	500	250	200

Woodsman Sport

THE WOODSMAN, proving to be increasingly popular with outdoorsmen of all types, Colt decided to market a Woodsman better suited for "take along" gun for hiking, camping, etc. This was accomplished in 1933, by merely shortening the barrel from 6.625" to 4.5" and announcing the new Sport Model. Other than barrel length, the only difference between Target Model and Sport Model was an adjustable front sight on Target Model and fixed front sight on Sport Model. Later, a front sight adjustable for elevation would be an available option for Sport Model. Colt called this arrangement "Target Sights". Indeed, it was the same front sight used on Target Model. First Series Sport Model, with adjustable front sight will command a premium of approximately 25 percent over values listed.

NIB	Exc.	V.G.	Good	Fair	Poor
2600	1800	1300	600	250	200

Woodsman Match Target

Colt introduced Match Target Woodsman in 1938, with its own serial number series beginning at MT1 and continuing until 1944 with serial number MT16611. New features included larger grips, heavier barrel (6.625") and rear sight fully adjustable for both windage and elevation. To signify its intended market, a Bullseye Target pattern was placed on side of barrel. That led to its nickname "Bullseye Match Target". Elongated one-piece wrap-around walnut grips also picked up a nickname due to their unusual shape. Unfortunately, the so-called "Elephant Ear" grips are somewhat fragile and often broken. In addition, many serious target shooters of the day replaced them with custom grips with thumb rest and palm swell. Original grips were set aside and eventually lost or discarded. For those reasons, original grips are often missing and that severely affects value. Values listed assume original one-piece walnut wrap-around Elephant Ear grips, no cracks, repairs or modifications and a correct Match Target marked magazine. Values listed for Fair and Poor condition are primarily salvage value and reflect the high value of original "Elephant Ear" grips and Match Target marked magazines for spare parts. Approximately 11,000 produced for civilian market from 1938-1942.

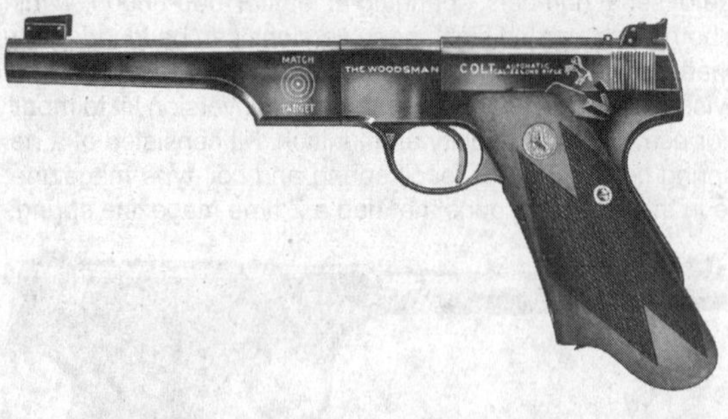

NIB	Exc.	V.G.	Good	Fair	Poor
4000	3500	2200	1500	700	600

Military Woodsman Match Target

After U.S. entered WWII at the end of 1941, civilian production at Colt stopped and total effort was devoted to U.S. military. Slightly more than 4000 First Series Match Target Woodsman's were delivered on U.S. Government contract from 1942-1944. Most of them, but not all, had serial numbers above MT12000. With possible rare exceptions, they all had U.S. Property or U.S. military markings, standard blue finish, 6.625" barrel and extended length plastic stocks. Plastic stocks are sometimes erroneously called elephant ear stocks. Military plastic stocks are still relatively easy to find and inexpensive. Since they will fit any First Series Colt Woodsman, they are often used as replacement grips on non-military guns. Since military guns had plastic grips, rather than costly and desirable "Elephant Ear" grips, salvage value in Fair and Poor condition range is less than that for civilian model.

NIB	Exc.	V.G.	Good	Fair	Poor
4400	3500	2000	1100	500	400

SECOND SERIES

After WWII, Colt entered a lengthy period of clearing up government contracts and re-tooling for the civilian market. Woodsman line was extensively revised and modernized. Second Series guns began appearing near the end of 1947, although no appreciable numbers were shipped until 1948. Second Series Woodsman had essentially same action and many of the same internals as First Series guns, but larger, heavier and a longer grip frame. New features included a magazine safety, automatic slide stop when magazine was emptied, fully adjustable rear sight, heavier barrels and 6" barrel length on Target and Match Target Models, rather than 6.625" as on First Series. Other new features included a push button magazine release just aft of triggerguard like that on large frame Government Model semi-automatics, lanyard ring concealed in butt and provision for attaching a plastic grip adapter to the backstrap, thereby accommodating different sized hands. Elevation adjustment was incorporated into rear sight of all Woodsman models and adjustable front sight replaced with a fixed blade. Serial numbers restarted at 1-S and are intermixed for all three models. Approximately 146,000 of the three models were produced.

In 1950, Colt added Challenger to Second Series pistols, first of the economy models. Internally, Challenger is nearly identical to Woodsman pistols of same era, but externally lacks most of the refinements introduced with Second Series Woodsman. Has no magazine safety, automatic slide stop, adjustable sights, push button magazine release, lanyard ring or grip adapters. Available with 4.5" or 6" barrel and had its own serial number series beginning with 1-C. Approximately 77,000 were produced.

Woodsman Target 6" barrel

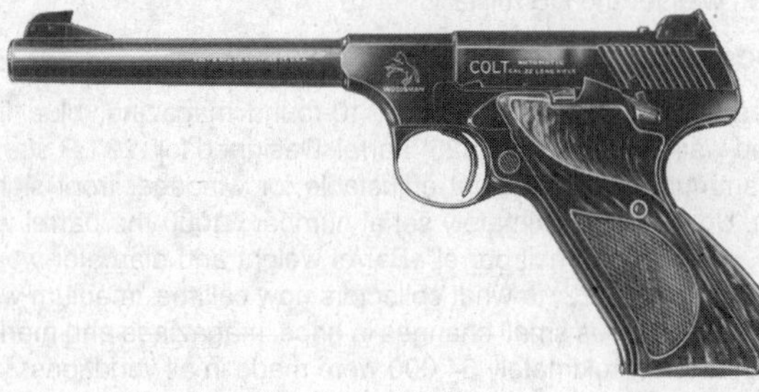

NIB	Exc.	V.G.	Good	Fair	Poor
1800	1400	1000	750	350	200

Woodsman Sport 4.5" barrel

NIB	Exc.	V.G.	Good	Fair	Poor
2000	1500	1050	800	350	200

Woodsman Match Target 6" barrel

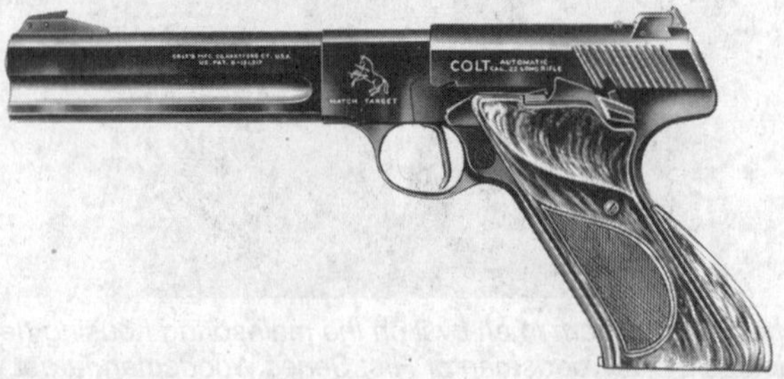

NIB	Exc.	V.G.	Good	Fair	Poor
2200	1700	1400	950	600	350

Woodsman Match Target 4.5" barrel

Introduced in 1950.

"Second Series Match Target Model with 4.5 barrel.""

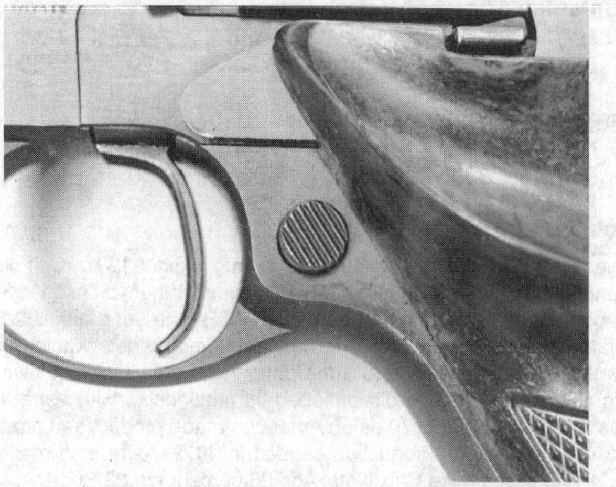

NIB	Exc.	V.G.	Good	Fair	Poor
2500	1800	1500	1100	650	400

Challenger 4.5" barrel

NIB	Exc.	V.G.	Good	Fair	Poor
1050	900	600	450	300	200

Challenger 6" barrel

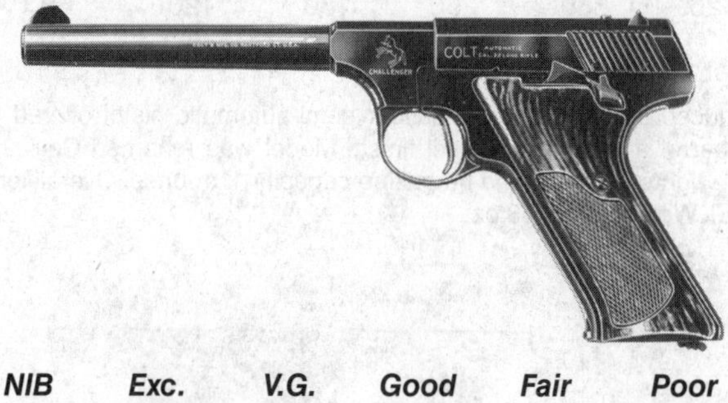

NIB	Exc.	V.G.	Good	Fair	Poor
950	800	500	400	250	200

THIRD SERIES

In 1955, Colt again re-designed the Woodsman line. Most obvious change was location of magazine release, which was again placed at heel of butt, just like First Series guns. Other changes made over time in markings, grips, sights and trigger. Sport, Target and Match Target models continued. Challenger was replaced by very similar Huntsman, with 4.5" or 6" barrel. In 1959, Targetsman was added to line. Targetsman differs from Huntsman only in having an adjustable rear sight and thumbrest on left grip panel. Available with 6" barrel only. All Third Series models had black plastic grips until 1960 and checkered walnut grips thereafter. Huntsman has no thumbrest on grips. All other Third Series models have a thumbrest on left grip panel.

It is difficult to impossible to determine how many of each model was produced in Third Series, due to a very complex serial numbering scheme. Approximately 1000 Third Series Sport, Target and Match Target Models were numbered at the end of Second Series serial number range, from 146138-S to 147138-S. Numbers were then restarted at 160001-S, so there are no post-WWII Woodsmans with numbers in 148xxx-S to 159xxx-S range. Challenger serial numbers, meantime, had reached approximately 77143-C prior to Challenger being replaced by Huntsman (note C suffix, for Challenger). Huntsman initially continued in Challenger serial number series, although numbers skipped forward to 90000-C before re-starting. Targetsman, when added to the line early in 1959, joined Huntsman in using -C suffix serial numbers, which were by then up to 129300-C. Then in 1969, when Woodsman serial numbers had reached 241811-S and -C numbers had reached 194040-C, Colt decided to integrate the serial numbers for all versions of Woodsman, Huntsman and Targetsman and re-start numbering again. This time they started with 001001S. That worked fine until numbers reached 099999S and rolled over to 100000S. Numbers used in 1951-52 were then being inadvertently duplicated, with one small exception: earlier guns had -S suffix while later ones had only an S (no hyphen before the S). Apparently that was not enough of a distinction to satisfy federal regulations, so when Colt discovered the error after approximately 1,330 had already been numbered, the existing "double headers" were hand stamped with an S prefix, in addition to S suffix, in order to salvage them. Serial numbers were then re-started yet again, this time at 300000S, and continued to 317736S, when production ended.

Woodsman Target 6" barrel

NIB	Exc.	V.G.	Good	Fair	Poor
1200	1000	700	450	280	180

Woodsman Sport 4.5" barrel

NIB	Exc.	V.G.	Good	Fair	Poor
1400	1100	750	500	300	200

Woodsman Match Target 6" barrel

NIB	Exc.	V.G.	Good	Fair	Poor
1900	1600	950	720	500	300

Woodsman Match Target 4.5" barrel

Added to line in 1950.

With the introduction of Third Series guns, Colt moved the magazine catch back to the heel of the butt, where it had been on the First Series.

NIB	Exc.	V.G.	Good	Fair	Poor
2100	1800	1050	800	550	350

Huntsman 6" or 4.5" barrel

NIB	Exc.	V.G.	Good	Fair	Poor
850	750	500	360	220	180

Targetsman 6" barrel

NIB	Exc.	V.G.	Good	Fair	Poor
950	800	550	400	250	200

Colt Junior Pocket Model

This diminutive unit is only 4.5" long overall; weight 12 oz. Colt did not manufacture this pistol, but rather had it made for them by Astra in Spain. Introduced in 1958. Chambered for .25 ACP. One year later .22 Short version appeared. Both had external hammers and detachable 6-round magazines. Passage of 1968 Gun Control Act, made import of a weapon this size illegal, so Colt discontinued its relationship with Astra. Pistol was re-introduced in 1970 as an American-made product and produced for two more years. Production ceased in 1972. Astra also made this pistol and called it the Cub. Note: Add 25 percent for .22 Short.

NIB	Exc.	V.G.	Good	Fair	Poor
520	380	250	180	120	80

Cadet / Colt .22

Introduced in 1994, this .22-caliber semi-automatic pistol offered with 4.5" barrel and stainless steel finish. Model was renamed Colt .22 in 1995. Sights are fixed and magazine capacity 11 rounds. Overall length 8.625". Weight about 33 oz.

NIB	Exc.	V.G.	Good	Fair	Poor
350	300	260	220	120	50

Colt .22 Target

Introduced in 1995. Features 6" bull barrel, removable front sight and adjustable rear sight. Black composite monogrip stock. Stainless steel finish. Weight 40.5 oz.

NIB	Exc.	V.G.	Good	Fair	Poor
480	320	300	250	150	80

COLT MODERN LONG ARMS

Colteer I-22

Single-shot bolt-action rifle, chambered for .22 LR or .22 Magnum. Plain uncheckered walnut stock, 20" barrel and adjustable sights. Approximately 50,000 manufactured between 1957 and 1966.

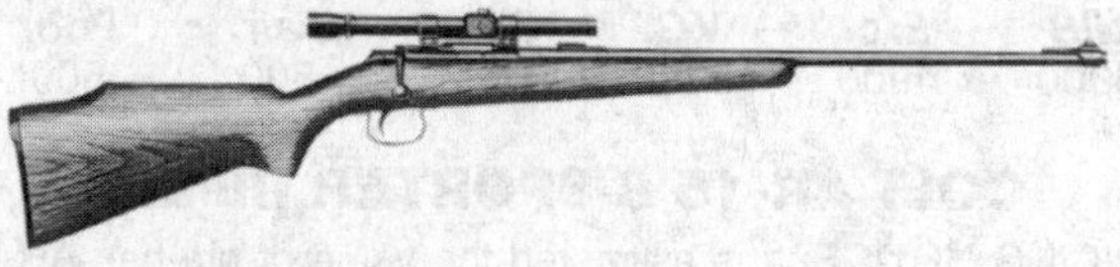

NIB	Exc.	V.G.	Good	Fair	Poor
350	300	180	120	90	20

Stagecoach

Semi-automatic saddle ring carbine. Chambered for .22 LR, 16.5" barrel and 13-shot tubular magazine. Stock is fancy walnut and receiver has stagecoach holdup scene roll-engraved on it. Approximately 25,000 manufactured between 1965 and 1975.

NIB	Exc.	V.G.	Good	Fair	Poor
450	400	350	200	150	100

Courier

Similar to Stagecoach, with pistol grip stock and beavertail forearm. Manufactured between 1970 and 1975.

NIB	Exc.	V.G.	Good	Fair	Poor
420	400	300	200	120	90

Colteer

Less-expensive version of Stagecoach. Features 19.5" barrel, 15-shot tubular magazine. Stock in a plainer grade walnut. No roll engraving. Approximately 25,000 manufactured between 1965 and 1975. Note: Add 50 percent for .22 rimfire Magnum.

NIB	Exc.	V.G.	Good	Fair	Poor
420	400	300	180	100	90

Colt 57 "Bolt-Action" Rifle

Rifle manufactured for Colt by Jefferson Mfg. Co of New Haven, Connecticut. Utilizes a Fabrique Nationale Mauser action. Checkered American walnut stock, with Monte Carlo comb. Offered with adjustable sights. Chambered for .243 or .30-06. Also, a deluxe version features higher-grade wood. Approximately 5,000 manufactured in 1957. Note: Add 20 percent for deluxe version.

NIB	Exc.	V.G.	Good	Fair	Poor
680	550	450	350	300	220

Coltsman Bolt-Action Rifle

Coltsman was manufactured for Colt by Kodiak Arms. Utilizes Mauser or Sako action. Offered in .243, .308, .30-06 and .300 Winchester Magnum. Barrel length of 22" or 24" in the Magnum chambering. Stock is checkered American walnut. Approximately 10,000 manufactured between 1958 and 1966. Deluxe version features a higher-grade skipline-checkered walnut stock and rosewood forend tip; called "The Coltsman Custom". Note: Add 50 percent for Coltsman Custom.

NIB	Exc.	V.G.	Good	Fair	Poor
700	650	550	450	350	250

Coltsman Pump Shotgun

Manufactured by Jefferson Arms, utilizing an aluminum alloy frame made by Franchi. Chambered for 12-, 16- and 20-gauge. Has 26" or 28" plain barrel. Approximately 2,000 manufactured between 1961 and 1965.

NIB	Exc.	V.G.	Good	Fair	Poor
380	350	300	280	200	150

Semi-Automatic Shotgun

Manufactured for Colt by the firm of Luigi Franchi in Italy. Features an aluminum alloy receiver and chambered for 12- or 20-gauge. Barrel length 26", 28", 30" or 32"—ventilated rib or plain. Deluxe version "The Custom Auto" features a fancy walnut stock and hand-engraved receiver. Approximately 5,300 manufactured between 1962 and 1966. Note: Add 25 percent for Custom Auto.

NIB	Exc.	V.G.	Good	Fair	Poor
400	380	320	300	220	180

Double-Barrel Shotgun

During 1961 and 1962, Colt had approximately 50 side-by-side shotguns made for them by a French gun manufacturer. They have the Colt name on breech area of barrels and are in 467000-469000 serial range. There is little information available on this gun. Colt never went past the test-market stage.

NIB	Exc.	V.G.	Good	Fair	Poor
—	1200	950	650	500	400

Colt Light Rifle

Introduced in 1999, this bolt-action rifle offered in both long and short action calibers from .243 to .300 Win. Magnum. Fitted with 24" barrel and adjustable trigger. Stock is black synthetic. Action and barrel are matte black. Long action calibers. Weight about 6 lbs., with short action rifle about 5.4 lbs. Adjustable trigger. No sights.

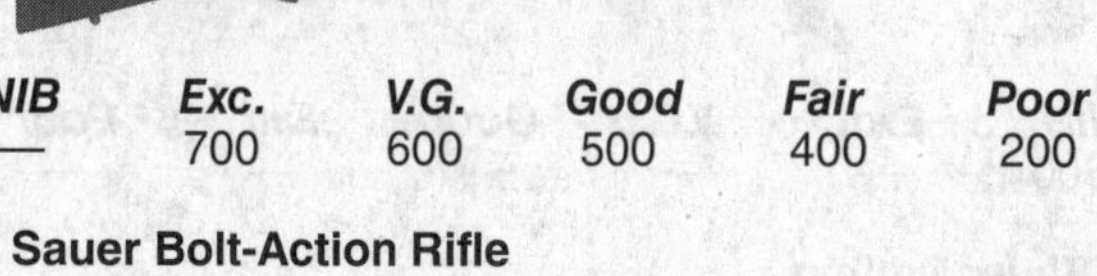

NIB	Exc.	V.G.	Good	Fair	Poor
—	700	600	500	400	200

Colt Sauer Bolt-Action Rifle

High quality and unique rifle, manufactured for Colt by J.P. Sauer & Son of Germany. Rifle features a non-rotating bolt, that makes Colt Sauer action smoother functioning than most. Has 24" barrel, skipline-checkered walnut stock, rosewood forend tip, pistol grip cap and recoil pad. There are five basic configurations: Standard Action chambered for .25-06, .270 Winchester and .30-06; Short Action chambered for .22-250, .243 Winchester and .308 Winchester; Magnum Action chambered for .7mm Remington Magnum, .300 Winchester Magnum and .300 Weatherby Magnum; "Grand Alaskan" and "Grand African" heavier versions chambered for .375 H&H Magnum and .458 Winchester Magnum, respectively. All discontinued by Colt in 1985.

Colt Sauer Short Action

Note: Add $50 for Standard Action; 20 percent for Magnum Action; 50 percent for "Grand Alaskan"; 75 percent for "Grand African".

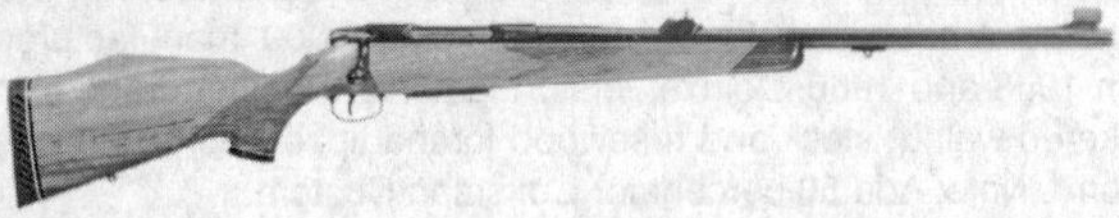

NIB	*Exc.*	*V.G.*	*Good*	*Fair*	*Poor*
2000	1950	1850	1500	800	500

Colt Model 2012 SA308

This precision rifle series is offered in several configurations. The 2012 SA308 is a tactical model in .308 Winchester, with 22" spiral fluted heavy stainless steel match-grade barrel with muzzle brake. Other fetures are an aluminum stock with pistol grip, aluminum handguard with 2/3-length Picatinny rail and an ajustable Timney single stage trigger. Weight about 13 lbs. The 2012 MT308T model has similar features, with a custom Manners composite stock in Coyote Tan finish. Weight 10.25 lbs. The 2012 LT available in .308 or 260 Remington, with gray laminate stock, medium heavy 22" barrel. Weight 8.5 lbs. These rifles are a joint effort, with Colt Custom Shop and Cooper Firearms of Montana.

SA308

NIB	*Exc.*	*V.G.*	*Good*	*Fair*	*Poor*
3250	2750	2200	1750	900	400

MT308T

NIB	*Exc.*	*V.G.*	*Good*	*Fair*	*Poor*
2800	2350	1850	1400	600	300

LT

NIB	*Exc.*	*V.G.*	*Good*	*Fair*	*Poor*
2400	1950	1450	1000	500	250

CBX

Caliber: 6.5 Creedmoor, .308 Win. Barrel: 24" (.308), 26" (6.5) Weight: 10.75 lbs. Stock: Aluminum chassis with adjustable LOP and cheek riser. Features: Precision bolt-action chassis rifle system. Flat bottom receiver. AICS magazine compatible. User-adjustable trigger. Extended forend with ARCA rail and M-LOK slots. Picatinny rail. 60-degree bolt throw. Black nitride barrel finish. Pistol grip with thumb shelf and ambidextrous magazine latch.

NIB	*Exc.*	*V.G.*	*Good*	*Fair*	*Poor*
1600	—	—	—	—	—

Colt Sauer Drilling

Rather unique firearm. One which many American enthusiasts are not familiar—a 3-barreled gun. Features side-by-side shotgun in 12-gauge, over a .30-06 or .243 rifle barrel. Name based on German word for three, as this is where the concept was developed. Quite popular in Europe where game preserve style of hunting is prevalent, but has little use in America where our hunting seasons don't often overlap. Drilling has 25" barrels and pop-up sights for rifle barrel and nicely engraved. Discontinued by Colt in 1985.

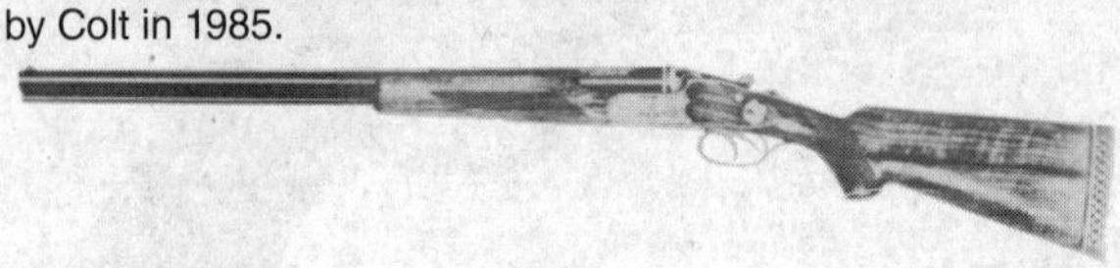

NIB	*Exc.*	*V.G.*	*Good*	*Fair*	*Poor*
4500	4000	3000	2000	1500	1100

Colt-Sharps Rifle

Introduced in 1970 as the last word in sporting rifles. Colt-Sharps is a falling-block action that was advertised as a modern Sharps-Borchardt. Undertaking was first-class all the way. Finish is high polish blue, with deluxe-grade hand-checkered walnut stock and forend. Chambered for .17 Remington, .22-250, .243, .25-06, 7mm Remington Magnum, .30-06 and .375 H&H Magnum. Offered cased with accessories. Manufactured between 1970 and 1977. Note: Add 25 percent for .375.

NIB	*Exc.*	*V.G.*	*Good*	*Fair*	*Poor*
6000	4900	3200	1550	800	500

COLT AR-15 & SPORTER RIFLES

PRICING NOTICE: It is estimated the value of pre-ban AR-15s declined 10-15 percent, since 1994-2004 Assault Weapons ban has lapsed, but market has once again spiked due to demand. Pricing status of AR-15 is still volatile. SEE POLITICAL PANIC PRICING.

COLT AR-15 PRE-BAN PRODUCTION 1964 TO 1989

AR-15 Sporter (Model #6000)

Semi-automatic rifle firing from a closed bolt. Introduced into Colt product line in 1964. Similar in appearance and function to military version M-16. Chambered for .223 cartridge. Fitted with standard 20" barrel, no forward assist, no case deflector, but with a bayonet lug. Weight about 7.5 lbs. Dropped from production in 1985.

NIB	*Exc.*	*V.G.*	*Good*	*Fair*	*Poor*
—	2500	2130	1810	1540	—

AR-15 Sporter w/Collapsible Stock (Model #6001)

Same as above, fitted with 16" barrel and folding stock. Weight about 5.8 lbs. Introduced in 1978; discontinued in 1985.

NIB	*Exc.*	*V.G.*	*Good*	*Fair*	*Poor*
—	3050	2590	2200	1870	—

AR-15 Carbine (Model #6420)

Introduced in 1985. Has 16" standard weight barrel. All other features same as previous discontinued AR-15 models. Version dropped from Colt product line in 1987.

NIB	*Exc.*	*V.G.*	*Good*	*Fair*	*Poor*
—	2500	2120	1800	1530	—

AR-15 9mm Carbine (Model #6450)

Same as above. Chambered for 9mm cartridge. Weight 6.3 lbs.

NIB	*Exc.*	*V.G.*	*Good*	*Fair*	*Poor*
—	2600	2210	1880	1600	—

AR-15A2 Sporter II (Model #6500)

Introduced in 1984. An updated version, with heavier barrel and forward assist. AR sight still utilized. Weight about 7.8 lbs.

NIB	Exc.	V.G.	Good	Fair	Poor
—	1830	1550	1320	1120	—

AR-15A2 Government Model Carbine (Model #6520)

Added to Colt line in 1988, this 16" standard barrel carbine featured for the first time a case deflector and improved A2 rear sight. Fitted with 4-position telescoping buttstock. Weight about 5.8 lbs.

NIB	Exc.	V.G.	Good	Fair	Poor
—	2300	1960	1960	1410	—

AR-15A2 Government Model (Model #6550)

Introduced in 1988. Rifle equivalent to the Carbine. Features 20" A2 barrel, forward assist, case deflector, but still retains the bayonet lug. Weight about 7.5 lbs. Discontinued in 1990. USMC model.

NIB	Exc.	V.G.	Good	Fair	Poor
—	2200	1870	1590	1350	—

AR-15A2 H-BAR (Model #6600)

Introduced in 1986. This version features special 20" heavy barrel. All other features the same as A2 series of AR15s. Discontinued in 1991. Weight about 8 lbs.

NIB	Exc.	V.G.	Good	Fair	Poor
—	2200	1870	1590	1350	—

AR-15A2 Delta H-BAR (Model #6600DH)

Same as above. Fitted with 3x9 scope and detachable cheekpiece. Dropped from Colt line in 1990. Weight about 10 lbs.

NIB	Exc.	V.G.	Good	Fair	Poor
—	2550	2170	1840	1570	—

COLT AR-15 PRE-BAN PRODUCTION 1989 TO 1994

Sporter Lightweight Rifle

Lightweight model has 16" barrel and finished in matte black. Available in: .223 Rem. caliber (Model #6530) weight 6.7 lbs.; 9mm caliber (Model #6430) weight 7.1 lbs.; 7.65x39mm (Model #6830) weight 7.3 lbs. All furnished with two 5-round box magazines. Cleaning kit and sling are also supplied with each new rifle. Buttstock and pistol grip are made of durable nylon. Handguard is reinforced fiberglass and aluminum lined. Rear sight is adjustable for windage and elevation. Newer models are referred to simply as Sporters. Not fitted with a bayonet lug and receiver block. Has different size pins. Note: Model 6830 will bring about $25 less than these prices.

NIB	Exc.	V.G.	Good	Fair	Poor
—	2200	1870	1590	1350	—

Sporter Target Model Rifle (Model #6551)

This 1991 model is a full size version of Lightweight Rifle. Weight 7.5 lbs. Has a 20" barrel. Offered in .223 Rem. caliber only, with target sights adjustable to 800 meters. New rifles furnished with two 5-round box magazines, sling and cleaning kit. Note: Deduct 30 percent for post-9/94 guns.

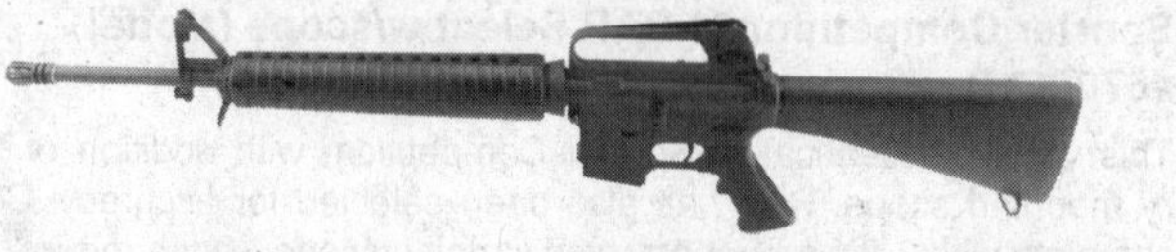

NIB	Exc.	V.G.	Good	Fair	Poor
—	1850	1570	1340	1140	—

Sporter Match H-BAR (Model #6601)

This 1991 variation of AR-15 is similar to Target Model. Has 20" heavy barrel, target type sights adjustable out to 800 meters and chambered for .223-caliber. Supplied with two 5-round box magazines, sling and cleaning kit. Weight 8 lbs.

NIB	Exc.	V.G.	Good	Fair	Poor
—	1850	1570	1340	1140	—

AR-15 (XM16E1)

Rifle made upon request for foreign contracts. Very rare. Proceed with caution. Variation will command a premium price over standard AR-15 rifle. Secure an appraisal before purchase.

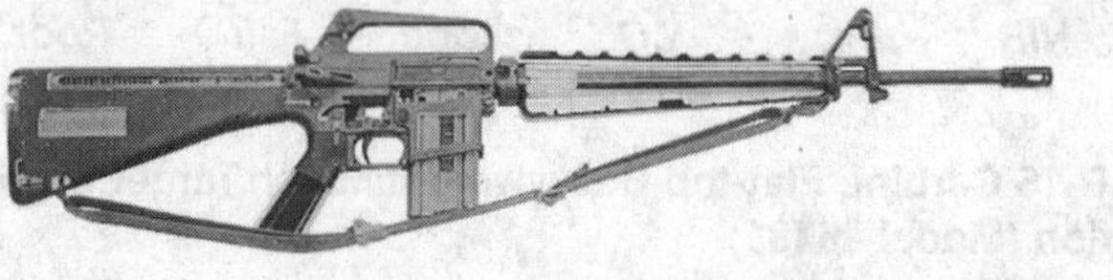

Courtesy Richard M. Kumor, Sr.

NIB	Exc.	V.G.	Good	Fair	Poor
—	2550	2170	1840	1570	—

Sporter Match Delta H-BAR (Model #6601 DH)

Same as above, but supplied with a 3x9 scope. Weight about 10 lbs. Discontinued in 1992.

NIB	Exc.	V.G.	Good	Fair	Poor
—	2550	2170	1840	1570	—

Match Target H-BAR Compensated (Model #6601C)

Same as regular Sporter H-BAR, with addition of a compensator.

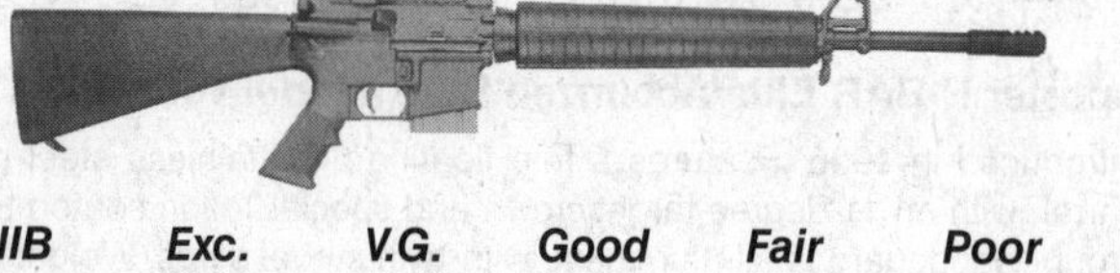

NIB	Exc.	V.G.	Good	Fair	Poor
—	2250	1910	1630	1380	—

Colt Match Target M4

Similar to above, with carbine-length barrel.

NIB	Exc.	V.G.	Good	Fair	Poor
—	2200	1870	1590	1350	—

Sporter Competition H-BAR (Model #6700)

Introduced in 1992. Competition H-BAR available in .223-caliber, with 20" heavy barrel counterbored for accuracy. Carry handle is detachable, with target sights. With carry handle removed the upper receiver is dovetailed and grooved for Weaver-style scope rings. New rifles furnished with two 5-round box magazines, sling and cleaning kit. Weight abut 8.5 lbs. Note: Deduct 35 percent for post-9/94 guns.

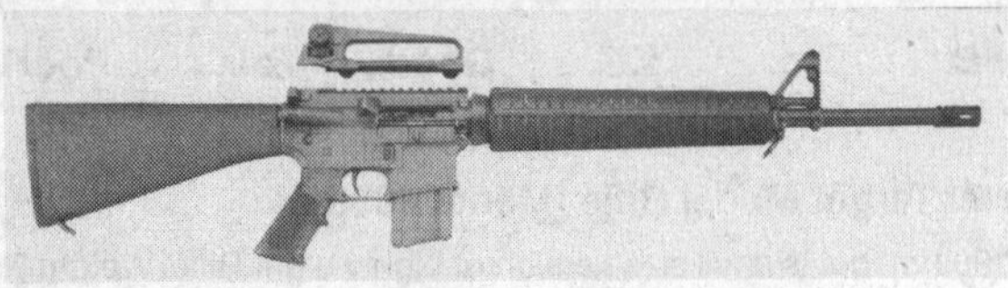

NIB	Exc.	V.G.	Good	Fair	Poor
—	1930	1640	1390	1180	—

Sporter Competition H-BAR Select w/scope (Model #6700CH)

This variation identical to Sporter Competition, with addition of factory mounted scope. Rifle has also been selected for accuracy. Comes complete with 3-9X rubber armored variable scope, scope mount, carry handle with iron sights and nylon carrying case.

NIB	Exc.	V.G.	Good	Fair	Poor
—	2250	1910	1630	1380	—

Match Target Competition H-BAR Compensated (Model #6700C)

Same as Match Target, with compensator.

NIB	Exc.	V.G.	Good	Fair	Poor
—	2000	1700	1450	1230	—

AR-15 Carbine Flat-top Heavyweight/Match Target Competition (Model #6731)

This variation in Sporter series features heavyweight 16" barrel, with flat-top receiver. Chambered for .223 cartridge. Equipped with a fixed buttstock. Weight about 7.1 lbs.

NIB	Exc.	V.G.	Good	Fair	Poor
—	1400	1190	1010	860	—

AR-15 Tactical Carbine (Model #6721)

Similar to above model, with exception of buttstock which is telescoping and adjusts to 4 positions. Chambered for .223 cartridge. Weight about 7 lbs. Majority of these guns were for law enforcement only. Only 134 rifles are pre-ban. Note: Add 100 percent premium if serial number is below BD000135.

NIB	Exc.	V.G.	Good	Fair	Poor
—	2200	1870	1590	1350	—

Sporter H-BAR Elite/Accurized Rifle (Model #6724)

Introduced in 1996. Features a free floating 24" stainless steel match barrel, with an 11 degree target crown and special Teflon coated trigger group. Handguard is all-aluminum, with twin swivel studs. Weight about 9.26 lbs.

NIB	Exc.	V.G.	Good	Fair	Poor
—	1550	1320	1120	950	—

COLT AR-15 POST-BAN PRODUCTION 1994 TO PRESENT

Colt SP6920

Sporter version of classic Colt M4 carbine. Chambered for .223 Remington. Chrome-lined bore with 6 grooves, 1" to 7" right hand twist. Four-position collapsible stock. Flattop receiver with removable carry handle. Matte black finish. Introduced in 2011. Discontinued.

NIB	Exc.	V.G.	Good	Fair	Poor
1100	940	800	680	570	—

Colt SP6940

Same gun as SP6920, with one-piece upper receiver. Fully floated barrel, which allows easier mounting of optical, laser or light accessories. No carry handle. Matte black finish. Introduced in 2011. Discontinued.

NIB	Exc.	V.G.	Good	Fair	Poor
1380	1170	990	840	720	—

Match Target Competition H-BAR (Model 6700)

This 5.56 NATO model has a flattop upper receiver grooved for Weaver scope mounts, 20" heavy barrel, detachable carry handle with 600 meter rear sight system. Weight 8.5 lbs. Introduced in 1992; discontinued 2013.

NIB	Exc.	V.G.	Good	Fair	Poor
1150	980	830	710	600	—

Match Target Lightweight (Model MT6530)

Chambered in 5.56 NATO, 7.62x39 or 9mm. Has 16" barrel and handguard, with adjustable rear sight. Weight 7 lbs.

NIB	Exc.	V.G.	Good	Fair	Poor
1130	960	810	690	590	—

Match Target M4 Carbine (Model MT6400)

Chambered in 5.56 NATO/.223 Rem., with 16.1" barrel, fixed tube buttstock and detachable carrying handle. This model is a semi-automatic version of the one currently issued to U.S. armed forces. Introduced in 2002; discontinued 2013.

NIB	Exc.	V.G.	Good	Fair	Poor
1150	980	830	710	600	—

Match Target H-BAR Rifle (Model MT6601)

Similar to Match Target M4 Carbine, but with 20" heavy barrel. Introduced in 1986; discontinued 2010.

NIB	Exc.	V.G.	Good	Fair	Poor
1130	960	810	800	590	—

Colt 9mm Carbine (Model AR6951)

Chambered in 9mm with 32-shot magazine, 16.1" barrel with flash suppressor. Muddy Girl or matte black finish. Note: Deduct $300 for matte black finish.

NIB	Exc.	V.G.	Good	Fair	Poor
1130	960	810	690	590	—

M.A.R.C. 901LE901-16S

NIB	Exc.	V.G.	Good	Fair	Poor
2300	1960	1660	1410	1200	—

LE6920 M4 Carbine

Caliber: 5.56 NATO. Barrel: 16.1-in. chrome lined. Sights: Adjustable. Based on military M4. Direct gas/locking bolt operating system. Magpul MOE handguard, carbine stock, pistol grip, vertical grip. Add 12 percent for Magpul version.

NIB	Exc.	V.G.	Good	Fair	Poor
1100	1000	950	880	—	—

LE6940

Similar to LE6920 with free floating barrel, fixed four-position rail system, 30-round magazine, MBUS Gen 2 rear sight. Introduced in 2015.

NIB	Exc.	V.G.	Good	Fair	Poor
1300	1110	940	800	680	—

LE6960

This model also known as the Combat Unit Carbine. Has 16" barrel, direct gas impingement system, Magpul MOE SL buttstock and pistol grip. Optics ready. Mid length gas system. Black anodized finish. Introduced 2017.

NIB	Exc.	V.G.	Good	Fair	Poor
1130	960	810	690	590	—

Expanse M4

Entry-level AR-15 style rifle, with standard features including a 16" barrel chambered for .223/5.56 NATO. Mil Spec grip, trigger and collapsible stock, direct impingement gas operation and 30-round magazine. Introduced in 2016.

NIB	Exc.	V.G.	Good	Fair	Poor
680	570	490	420	350	—

Modular Carbine CM762

Caliber: .308 Win. (7.62×51 NATO). Barrel Length: 16.1", chrome-lined, 1:12" RH twist. Rail: 15" M-LOK. Length: 36.75" (stock extended). Weight: 8.8 lbs. Magazine: 20 rds. SEE POLITICAL PANIC PRICING.

NIB	Exc.	V.G.	Good	Fair	Poor
2600	2450	2200	2000	—	—

Modular Carbine CM65

Introduced 2018. 6.5 Creedmoor chambering with 18" barrel, 1-in-8" twist.

NIB	Exc.	V.G.	Good	Fair	Poor
1400	1190	1010	860	730	—

AR-15 MILITARY CLASSICS

Colt periodically reissues rifles of current production, but with older model names.

M4A1SOCOM

Reissued 2018. Closely replicates the markings and configuration of the M4A1 SOCOM Carbine. The lower receiver features PROPERTY OF THE US GOVT, M4A1 CARBINE, and CAL. 5.56 MM. The barrel is a true SOCOM 14.5" heavy barrel with the iconic M203 flats under the Knights Armament Rail System. Extended flash hider has been pinned and welded to achieve a non-NFA length of 16.1". Includes the side-sling swivel at the gas block and an ambidextrous safety selector.

NIB	Exc.	V.G.	Good	Fair	Poor
1480	1250	1070	910	770	—

M16A1 Retro Reissue

Caliber: 5.56 NATO. Classic design, unique triangular handguard, 20" pencil-profile chrome-lined barrel with a 1:12" twist, and recognizable carrying handle. SEE POLITICAL PANIC PRICING.

NIB	Exc.	V.G.	Good	Fair	Poor
2600	2550	2400	2250	—	—

XM177E2 Retro Carbine

Caliber: 5.56 NATO. Built to the Original Colt Model 629 specifications from the 1960s. 11.5-in. barrel with extended flash hider, vinyl-acetate coated aluminum buttstock reproduction, and U.S. Property-marked roll-marks.

NIB	Exc.	V.G.	Good	Fair	Poor
2550	1930	1640	1400	1190	—

M4 CARBINES

M4 Trooper Patrol Carbine

NIB	Exc.	V.G.	Good	Fair	Poor
780	660	560	480	410	—

M4 Carbine OEM1

Handguards, buttstock, triggerguard, magazine, and rear sight omitted. Accepts most aftermarket drop-in-style handguards that utilize the factory barrel nut and retaining ring. Also available with low profile gas block and without handguard retaining ring.

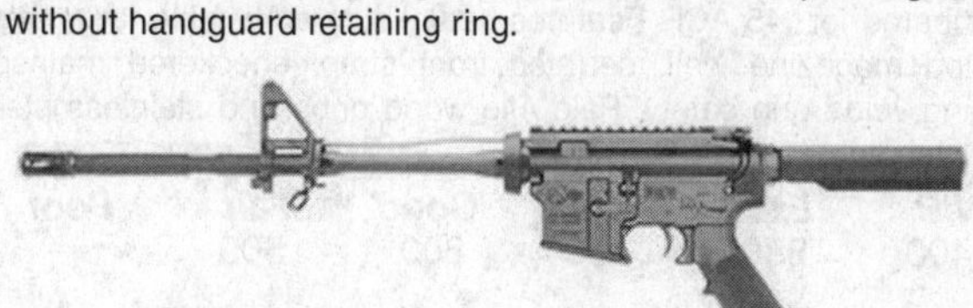

NIB	Exc.	V.G.	Good	Fair	Poor
950	810	690	580	500	—

M4 Carbine MPS

16.1" chrome-lined barrel with 1-in-7" twist. Magpul MOE SL handguards, MOE SL carbine stock, MOE SL pistol grip, MOE vertical grip, and a Magpul Back-up Sight.

NIB	Exc.	V.G.	Good	Fair	Poor
1080	910	780	660	560	—

M4 Carbine Magpul

NIB	Exc.	V.G.	Good	Fair	Poor
1140	—	—	—	—	—

COLT CUSTOM SHOP

Colt Custom Shop offers various customizing, upgrading and engraving services on current catalog models For information, contact Colt at www.colt.com or 800-962-2658. Shown here is a sampling of previously customized models.

Colt 1911 Black Army

Caliber: .45 ACP. Capacity: 7-round magazine. Barrel: 5 in. Grips: Double diamond checkered rosewood. Sights: Fixed, round front/retro rear. Finish: Matte blue. Features: Series 70 firing system, lanyard loop, reproduction of WWI U.S. Military model.

NIB	Exc.	V.G.	Good	Fair	Poor
900	750	—	—	—	—

Special Combat Government Model (Competition)

Competition ready model. Chambered for .45 ACP. Fitted with skeletonized trigger, upswept grip safety, custom tuned action, polished feed ramp, throated barrel, flared ejection port, cutout commander hammer, two 8-round magazines, hard chromed slide and receiver, extended thumb safety, Bomar rear sight, Clark dovetail front sight and flared magazine funnel. Pistol has been accurized and shipped with a certified target.

NIB	Exc.	V.G.	Good	Fair	Poor
1750	1200	800	500	300	—

Special Combat Government Model (Carry)

Has all the same features as competition model, except it has a royal blue finish, special bar-dot night sights, ambidextrous safety. Also been accurized and shipped with a certified target.

NIB	Exc.	V.G.	Good	Fair	Poor
1550	1000	700	400	300	—

Gold Cup Commander

Chambered for .45 ACP. Features heavy-duty adjustable target sights, beveled magazine well, serrated front strap, checkered mainspring housing, wide grip safety, Palo Alto wood grips and stainless steel or royal blue finish.

NIB	Exc.	V.G.	Good	Fair	Poor
1400	880	650	600	500	—

U.S. Shooting Team Gold Cup

Limited edition Gold Cup .45 ACP, with special blue, sights, grips. U.S. Shooting Team logo rolled on the slide. Limited to 500 pistols and built for Lew Horton.

NIB	Exc.	V.G.	Good	Fair	Poor
1400	880	650	600	500	—

Gold Cup Trophy

Newest variation of classic Gold Cup series. In .45 ACP or 9mm, with 5" National Match barrel, wide target trigger, 25 lpi checkering on front and backstrap, G10 grips, fully adjustable Bomar rear sight and fiber optic front sight.

NIB	Exc.	V.G.	Good	Fair	Poor
1000	900	680	620	520	—

McCormick Commander

Limited edition pistol made for Lew Horton in 1995. Limited to 100 pistols. Has many special features. Slide is engraved and there is a gold rampant colt on the slide.

NIB	Exc.	V.G.	Good	Fair	Poor
1600	1000	750	600	500	380

McCormick Officer

Lew Horton exclusive pistol, has factory installed McCormick parts and hard chrome finish. Total of 500 guns built in 1995.

NIB	Exc.	V.G.	Good	Fair	Poor
1500	880	650	600	500	380

McCormick Factory Racer

Limited edition pistol from Lew Horton. Full size government model, with hard chrome finish, special barrel, trigger safety and other custom features. Each gun roll marked "McCormick Factory Racer" on the slide. Special serial numbers from MFR001 to MFR500.

NIB	Exc.	V.G.	Good	Fair	Poor
1300	780	650	600	500	380

Colt Classic .45 Special Edition

Lew Horton model limited to 400 pistols. Features a royal blue polish with special "Classic .45" gold etched on the slide. Pearlite grips.

NIB	Exc.	V.G.	Good	Fair	Poor
1300	780	650	600	500	380

125th Anniversary Edition Peacemaker

Introduced in 1998. Features a V-shaped rear sight, with two-line patent date. Barrel is 4.75" and chambered for .45 Colt cartridge. Cylinder is second generation type and hammer is knurled. Frame and hammer are case colored, with blue barrel. Grips are two piece walnut, with oil-finish. Special serial number range SA74000 to SA75999.

NIB	Exc.	V.G.	Good	Fair	Poor
1950	1350	950	600	500	380

Custom Anaconda

Custom-tuned action, Magnaported barrel, with Elliason rear sight. Contoured trigger is polished smooth. Comes with Pachmayr grips and brushed stainless steel finish.

NIB	Exc.	V.G.	Good	Fair	Poor
1950	1280	800	600	300	200

Ultimate Python

Custom tuned action, with both Elliason and Accro sighting systems. Both rubber and walnut grips are included. Bright stainless steel or royal blue finish. Available only with 6" barrel. Note: Add 10 percent for Ultimate Stainless finish.

NIB	Exc.	V.G.	Good	Fair	Poor
4500	4000	3000	2200	1000	500

Anaconda Hunter

Comes with a Leupold 2X scope, heavy-duty mounts, cleaning accessories, both walnut and rubber grips, in a hard case. Furnished only with an 8" barrel.

NIB	Exc.	V.G.	Good	Fair	Poor
1800	1280	800	600	300	200

Bobbed Detective Special

First offered in 1994. Features bobbed hammer, front sight with night sight and honed action. Available in chrome or blue finish.

NIB	Exc.	V.G.	Good	Fair	Poor
780	600	450	300	150	100

Limited Class .45 ACP

1911 auto. Designed for tactical competition. Supplied with a parkerized matte finish, lightweight composite trigger, extended ambidextrous safety, upswept grip safety, beveled magazine well. Accurized and shipped with a signed target. Introduced in 1993.

NIB	Exc.	V.G.	Good	Fair	Poor
1450	1050	650	450	300	200

Compensated Model .45 ACP

Competition pistol has a hard chrome receiver, bumper on magazine, extended ambidextrous safety, blue slide with full profile BAT compensator, Bomar rear sight and flared funnel magazine well. Introduced in 1993.

NIB	Exc.	V.G.	Good	Fair	Poor
1450	1050	650	450	300	200

Compensated .45 ACP Commander

Introduced in 1998 and limited to 500 pistols. Fitted with a full-length guide rod, extended beavertail safety, skeletonized hammer, Novak-style sights and checkered walnut double-diamond grips.

NIB	Exc.	V.G.	Good	Fair	Poor
1350	980	580	400	300	200

Nite Lite .380

Supplied with a bar-dot night sight, special foil mark on barrel slide, Teflon-coated alloy receiver, stainless slide, high-capacity grip-extension magazine and standard magazine. Shipped with a soft carrying case. Introduced in 1993.

NIB	Exc.	V.G.	Good	Fair	Poor
1350	980	580	400	300	200

Standard Tactical Model

Built for 20th Anniversary of IPSC competition shooting in 1996. Built on Colt Government model, with round top slide and chambered for .45 ACP. Many special features and serial numbers. Limited to 1,500 pistols.

NIB	Exc.	V.G.	Good	Fair	Poor
1450	880	600	450	300	200

Superior Tactical Model

Same as above. Built on an enhanced frame, with many custom features. Special serial numbers limited to 500 pistols.

NIB	Exc.	V.G.	Good	Fair	Poor
1550	980	700	550	400	200

Deluxe Tactical Model

Same as above, with added features. Limited to 250 pistols.

NIB	Exc.	V.G.	Good	Fair	Poor
1650	1080	800	650	500	300

COLT COMMEMORATIVES

Beginning in the 1961, Colt began producing various limited edition "Commemorative" firearms. Most were based on the Single Action Army or reproduction percussion revolvers. These guns would have special decoration which celebrated an historic event or individual or organization, often associated with the Old West. Nearly two hundred different commemorative models were introduced through the early 1990s. In those years they found a market with some collectors, and the value of these guns tended to increase after production ended. Their popularity waned in more recent decades. Commemoratives that are As New in Box will still generally bring a premium over plain versions of the same model. The premium usually depends on how many were made (the fewer, the more value) and the quality and elaborateness of the decoration. However, once a commemorative begins to show use or wear, the value drops rapidly towards the value of a plain model. Some non-firearms manufacturers such as America Remembers and Franklin Mint bought plain Colts or Colt copies and decorated them as commemoratives. These tend to bring significantly less than factory-made commemoratives.

COLT'S MANUFACTURING COMPANY 2nd GENERATION PERCUSSION REVOLVERS

From 1971 to 1982 Colt produced a line of reproduction percussion revolvers based on the original 19th century models. Generally the appearance and configuration of a reproduction will be similar to the original — refer to photos in the Colt Percussion Revolver section. Parts were manufactured in both Italy and America and during this time were assembled by Colt in the U.S. These are called 2nd Generation Colts. Colt continued to produce limited edition revolvers from 2nd Generation parts through the early 1990s. See section on Colt Commemoratives above for comments on values of commemorative and limited edition Colt 2nd & 3rd generation revolvers.

Walker

This .44-caliber large-frame revolver fitted with 9" barrel.

(Above, top right) In 1953, the Woodsman rear sight was changed from the Coltmaster (bottom) to the Accro (top).

NIB	Exc.	V.G.	Good	Fair	Poor
950	750	500	430	350	—

Walker Heritage Model

NIB	Exc.	V.G.	Good	Fair	Poor
1000	850	600	—	—	—

First Model Dragoon

Made from 1980 to 1982; serial numbers 24100-34500.

NIB	Exc.	V.G.	Good	Fair	Poor
600	400	300	—	—	—

Second Model Dragoon

Made from 1980 to 1982; serial numbers as above.

NIB	Exc.	V.G.	Good	Fair	Poor
600	400	300	—	—	—

Third Model Dragoon

Made from 1980 to 1982; serial numbers as above.

NIB	Exc.	V.G.	Good	Fair	Poor
600	400	300	—	—	—

Model 1848 Pocket Pistol

Made in 1981; serial numbers 16000-17851.

NIB	Exc.	V.G.	Good	Fair	Poor
600	420	320	—	—	—

Model 1851 Navy Revolver

Made from 1971 to 1978; serial numbers 4201-25100 and 24900-29150.

NIB	Exc.	V.G.	Good	Fair	Poor
600	400	300	—	—	—

Model 1860 Army Revolver

Made from 1978 to 1982; serial numbers 201000-212835.

NIB	Exc.	V.G.	Good	Fair	Poor
600	400	300	—	—	—

Model 1861 Navy Revolver

Made during 1980 and 1981; serial numbers 40000-43165.

NIB	Exc.	V.G.	Good	Fair	Poor
600	400	300	—	—	—

Model 1862 Pocket Pistol

Made from 1979 to 1984; serial numbers 8000-58850.

NIB	Exc.	V.G.	Good	Fair	Poor
600	400	300	—	—	—

Model 1862 Police Revolver

Made from 1979 to 1984; serial numbers in above range.

NIB	Exc.	V.G.	Good	Fair	Poor
600	400	300	—	—	—

COLT BLACKPOWDER ARMS CO. 3rd GENERATION SIGNATURE SERIES

Brooklyn, New York

These were manufactured from 1994 to 2002 in Brooklyn, New York, under license from Colt Firearms using Italian cast parts. Most have the Sam Colt signature on the backstrap and are called Signature or 3rd Generation models. Production was divided into two eras — the C Series with bright Royal Blue finish and the F Series with darker Colt Blue finish. While there were a number of variations, commemoratives, and limited editions, the main models are listed below. Also see comments on Colt Commemoratives above.

1842 Paterson Colt No. 5 Holster Model

A copy of No. 5 Holster model. Chambered for .36-caliber ball. Fitted with 7.5" octagon barrel. Hand-engraved. Special order revolver.

Special order Paterson Colt No. 5 Holster Model

NIB	Exc.	V.G.	Good	Fair	Poor
1900	1200	900	600	450	200

Walker

This .44-caliber large-frame revolver fitted with 9 barrel.

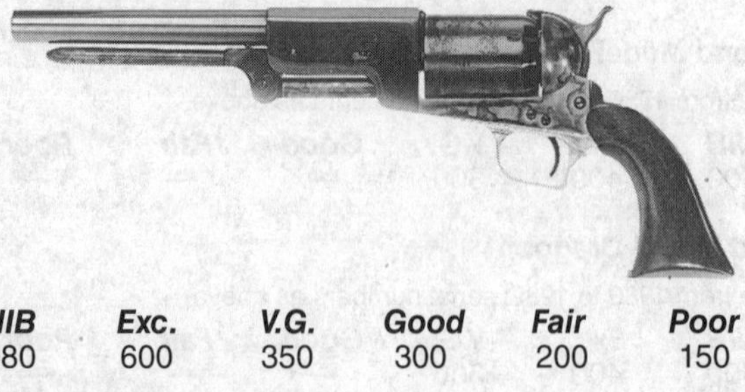

NIB	Exc.	V.G.	Good	Fair	Poor
980	600	350	300	200	150

Walker 150th Anniversary Model

Marked "A Company No. 1" in gold. Introduced 1997.

NIB	Exc.	V.G.	Good	Fair	Poor
980	600	350	300	200	150

Whitneyville Hartford Dragoon

Similar in appearance to Walker colt. Revolver fitted with 7.5 barrel and silver plated iron backstrap and triggerguard. Limited edition, with a total of 2,400 guns built. Serial numbers between 1100 through 1340.

NIB	Exc.	V.G.	Good	Fair	Poor
1080	700	450	30	220	200

Marine Dragoon

Special limited edition presentation grade in honor of U.S. Marine Corps.

NIB	Exc.	V.G.	Good	Fair	Poor
1100	720	450	30	220	200

3rd Model Dragoon

Another large-frame revolver, with 7.5" barrel, brass backstrap, 3-screw frame and unfluted cylinder.

NIB	Exc.	V.G.	Good	Fair	Poor
680	500	350	300	200	150

Steel Backstrap

NIB	Exc.	V.G.	Good	Fair	Poor
600	420	380	320	200	150

Fluted Cylinder

NIB	Exc.	V.G.	Good	Fair	Poor
610	440	380	320	200	150

Cochise Dragoon

Commemorative issue Third Model, with gold inlay frame and barrel with special grips.

NIB	Exc.	V.G.	Good	Fair	Poor
980	600	350	300	200	150

Colt 1849 Model Pocket

Small-frame revolver chambered in .31-caliber, with 4" barrel. Fitted with one-piece walnut grips.

NIB	Exc.	V.G.	Good	Fair	Poor
580	480	320	280	200	150

Colt 1851 Model Navy

Medium-frame revolver chambered in .36-caliber, with 7.5" barrel. Walnut grips and case color frame.

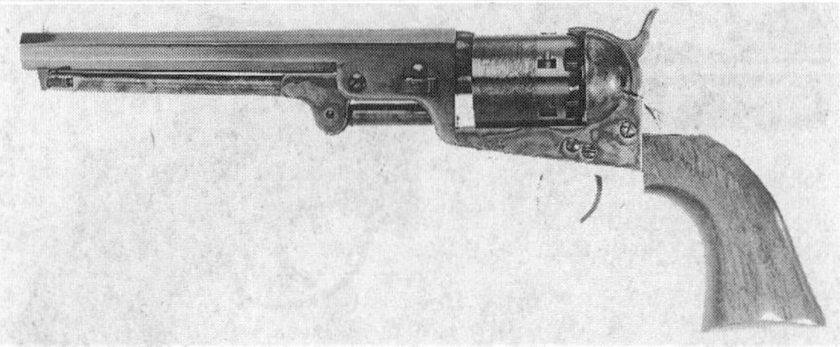

NIB	Exc.	V.G.	Good	Fair	Poor
640	580	400	300	200	120

Dual Cylinder

NIB	Exc.	V.G.	Good	Fair	Poor
680	600	400	300	200	120

Colt Model 1860 Army

Model chambered in .44-caliber, with roll engraved cylinder and one piece walnut grips. Barrel length 8".

NIB	Exc.	V.G.	Good	Fair	Poor
680	580	400	300	200	120

Dual Cylinder

NIB	Exc.	V.G.	Good	Fair	Poor
700	600	450	350	220	150

Colt 1860 Officer's Model

Deluxe version of standard 1860. Special blued finish and gold crossed sabres. This is a 4-screw frame, with 8" barrel and 6-shot rebated cylinder.

NIB	Exc.	V.G.	Good	Fair	Poor
680	580	450	380	250	150

Colt Model 1860 Army Gold U.S. Cavalry

Features a gold engraved cylinder and gold barrel bands.

NIB	Exc.	V.G.	Good	Fair	Poor
650	580	450	380	250	150

Stainless Steel

NIB	Exc.	V.G.	Good	Fair	Poor
580	400	350	300	200	150

Colt 1860 Heirloom Edition

Elaborately engraved revolver done in Tiffany-style. Fitted with Tiffany-style grips.

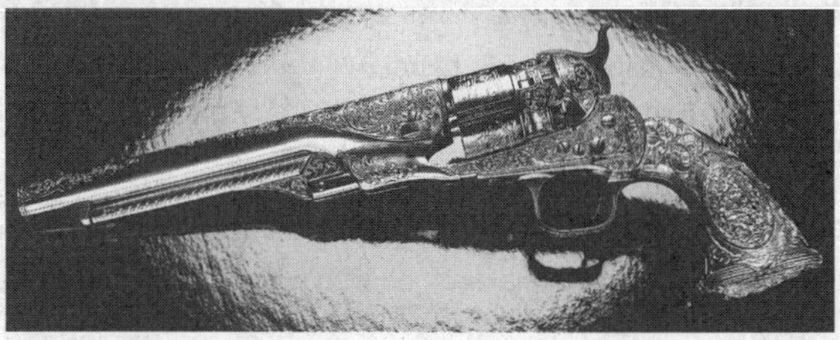

NIB	Exc.	V.G.	Good	Fair	Poor
4100	3000	2180	1400	850	450

Colt Model 1861 Navy

This .36-caliber revolver features 7.5" barrel, with engraved cylinder, case colored frame and one piece walnut grips.

NIB	Exc.	V.G.	Good	Fair	Poor
700	550	350	300	200	150

General Custer

Same as above, with engraved frame and cylinder.

NIB	Exc.	V.G.	Good	Fair	Poor
980	850	700	500	300	200

Colt Model 1862 Pocket Navy

Small-frame revolver. Fitted with round engraved cylinder, 5" octagon barrel and hinged loading lever. Chambered for .36-caliber.

NIB	Exc.	V.G.	Good	Fair	Poor
550	480	320	280	200	150

Colt Model 1862 Trapper-Pocket Police

Small-frame revolver. Fitted with 3.5" barrel, silver backstrap and trigger-guard. Cylinder is semi-fluted. Chambered in .36-caliber.

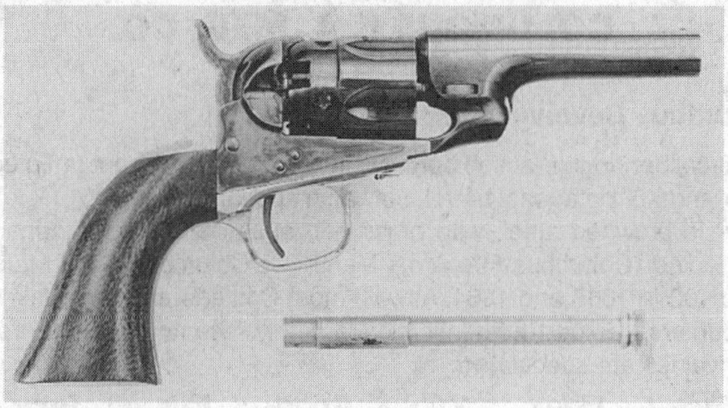

NIB	Exc.	V.G.	Good	Fair	Poor
600	480	320	280	200	150

Colt 1861 Musket

Civil War musket chambered in .58-caliber. Lockplate, hammer, buttplate, three barrel bands and 40" barrel are finished bright. Stock is a one-piece oil-finish affair. Bayonet and accessories are extra.

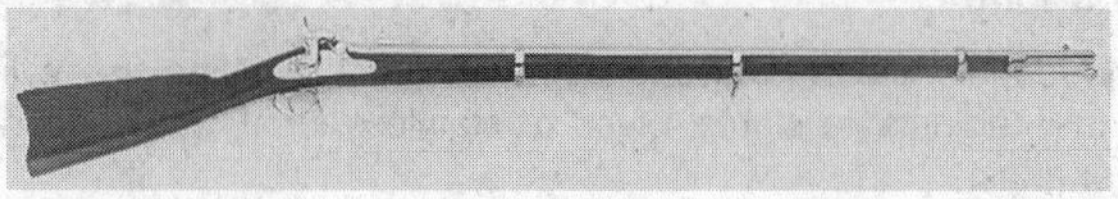

NIB	Exc.	V.G.	Good	Fair	Poor
800	650	500	320	280	150

Artillery Model

Same as above, fitted with 31.5" barrel.

NIB	Exc.	V.G.	Good	Fair	Poor
800	650	500	320	280	150

Presentation 1 of 1000

Limited to 1,000 guns. Special finished with a high polish and Colt's signature in gold on triggerguard. Sold with special custom wooden case.

NIB	Exc.	V.G.	Good	Fair	Poor
1650	1300	750	600	450	300

Presentation 1 of 1000 - Artillery Model

Same as above, with 31.5" barrel.

NIB	Exc.	V.G.	Good	Fair	Poor
1650	1300	750	600	450	300

Colt Gamemaster .50

Introduced in 1997. Rifle similar to above in general outline and in .50-caliber. Fitted with 31.5" barrel. Weight about 13 lbs.

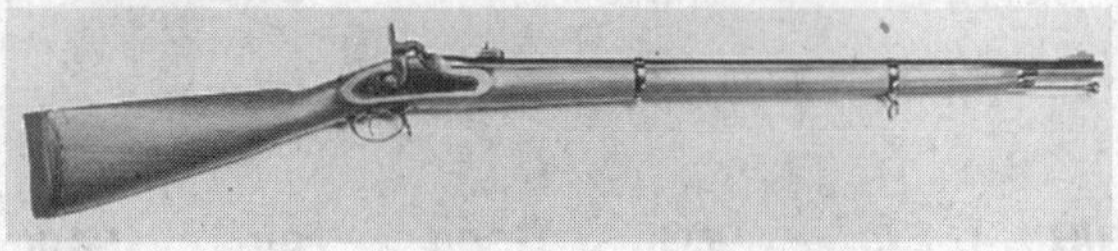

NIB	Exc.	V.G.	Good	Fair	Poor
800	650	480	300	220	120

COLUMBIA ARMORY

Columbia, Tennessee

Columbia Armory was a trade name reportedly used on some revolvers by Maltby Henley & Co., Crescent Firearms Company, and Foehl & Weeks. The name has also been observed on a Sedgely/Kolb large frame Baby Hammerless model. See listings at those manufactures.

Antique

Columbia Armory was a trade name reportedly used on some revolvers by Maltby Henley & Co., Crescent Firearms Company, and Foehl & Weeks. The name has also been observed on a Sedgely/Kolb large frame Baby Hammerless model. See listings at those manufacturers.

COLUMBUS F. A. MFG. CO.

Columbus, Georgia

Columbus Revolver **Antique**

A .36-caliber double-action percussion revolver, with 6-shot unfluted cylinder and 7.5" octagonal barrel. Similar in appearance to 1851 Colt Navy. Pistol is browned steel, with brass grip straps and walnut grips. Barrel marked "Columbus Fire Arms Manuf. Co/Columbus Ga.". Manufactured 100 in 1863 and 1864. As with most Confederate arms, fakes are encountered. Expert authentication is highly recommended. Extremely rare, values are speculative.

Exc.	Fine	V.G.	Good	Fair	Poor
—	150000	—	75000	—	—

COMANCHE

Buenos Aires, Argentina

See—FIRESTORM

Comanche I

Single-/double-action revolver chambered in .22 LR. Nine-shot cylinder, 6" barrel, adjustable sights, blued or stainless steel construction with rubber grips.

NIB	Exc.	V.G.	Good	Fair	Poor
220	150	100	60	40	20

Comanche II

Similar to above in .38 Special, with 2", 3" or 4" barrel.

NIB	Exc.	V.G.	Good	Fair	Poor
220	150	100	60	40	20

Comanche III

Similar to above in .357 Magnum. Additional 6" barrel option.

NIB	Exc.	V.G.	Good	Fair	Poor
250	150	100	60	40	20

Super Comanche

Single-shot break-action pistol chambered in .410/.45 Colt. Matte black finish, rubber grips.

NIB	Exc.	V.G.	Good	Fair	Poor
200	150	120	80	50	20

COMMANDO ARMS

Knoxville, Tennessee

Formerly known as Volunteer Enterprises. Name change took place in 1978. General configuration appears similar to the Thompson.

Mark III Carbine

A .45 ACP caliber semi-automatic rifle, with 16.5" barrel, peep rear sight and vertical fore-grip. Manufactured between 1969 and 1976.

NIB	Exc.	V.G.	Good	Fair	Poor
680	550	380	300	220	150

Mark 9 Carbine

As above in 9mm caliber.

NIB	Exc.	V.G.	Good	Fair	Poor
680	550	380	300	220	150

Mark .45

New designation for Mark III after the company changed its name.

NIB	Exc.	V.G.	Good	Fair	Poor
680	550	380	300	220	150

COMPETITOR CORP.

New Ipswich, New Hampshire

Competitor Single-Shot

Single-shot pistol chambered for calibers from .22 LR to .50 Action Express. Choice of barrel lengths from 10.5", 14" and 16". Ramp front sight. Adjustable single stage trigger. Interchangeable barrels. Matte blue finish. Weight about 59 oz. depending on barrel length. Introduced in 1988.

NIB	Exc.	V.G.	Good	Fair	Poor
460	320	280	220	180	120

CONNECTICUT ARMS & MFG. CO.

Norfolk, Connecticut

Naubuc, Connecticut 1866-late 1880s

Pocket Revolver (Antique)

A .28-caliber spur trigger revolver, with 3" octagonal barrel, 6-shot unfluted cylinder, using a cup-primed cartridge and loads from front of the cylinder. There is a hinged hook on side of the frame under the cylinder that acts as the extractor. Silver-plated brass blued, with walnut grips. Barrel marked "Conn. Arms Co. Norfolk, Conn." Approximately 2,700 manufactured in 1860s.

Exc.	Fine	V.G.	Good	Fair	Poor
950	750	520	300	100	70

Hammond Bulldog Single Shot Derringer (Antique)

Large .44 rimfire single shot; 4" octagon barrel. Rare variations worth premium include 6" barrel, .50 rimfire or Bull Dozer marking.

Exc.	Fine	V.G.	Good	Fair	Poor
3000	1700	1350	1000	700	480

CONNECTICUT SHOTGUN MANUFACTURING COMPANY

New Britain, Connecticut

This firm produces a wide variety of fine double-barrel shotguns with a wide range of grades, features, and levels of engraving. Retail prices range from the $2,000 to $100,000 range. Model designations include: A. Galazan, A10, Christian Hunter, AH Fox, Model 21, Inverness, RBL, Revelation. Their current website lists 650 model variations. Some of these are listed below.

RBL Side-By-Side Shotgun

Round-action SXS shotguns made in the USA. Chambered in 12-, 16-, 20-, 28-gauge and .410 bore with scaled frames. Barrel lengths 26", 28", 30" and 32", with five TruLock choke tubes. Deluxe fancy-grade walnut buttstock and forend, Quick Change recoil pad in two lengths. Various dimensions and options available depending on gauge. Values shown are for 12-gauge. Note: Add 20 percent for 20-gauge; 30 percent for 28-gauge; 75 percent for .410 bore.

NIB	Exc.	V.G.	Good	Fair	Poor
4000	2950	2000	1280	800	400

A-10 American

Sidelock design in 12-, 20- or 28-gauge with XX grade walnut stock and light scroll engraving. Offered in standard barrel lengths from 26" to 32". Options include higher-grade wood and engraving. Prices shown are for standard model. Introduced in 2010

NIB	Exc.	V.G.	Good	Fair	Poor
7500	6000	4500	3500	—	—

Model 21

A faithful rendition of famous Winchester side-by-side shotgun that was in production from 1931 to 1959. On custom-order from 1960 to 1993. Made in all gauges and standard barrel lengths, with many options. Each gun is custom made to order. Introduced in 2002. Prices are for standard 12-, 16- and 20-gauge models. Note: Add $3000 for 28-gauge or .410 bore, plus $10,000 if made on optional small frame.

NIB	Exc.	V.G.	Good	Fair	Poor
15000	12000	9500	7000	3500	—

Model 21 Grand American

As above with high-grade gold-inlayed engraving, AAA-grade walnut stock, with elaborate checkering and carving patterns. Comes with two sets of barrels. Note: Add $3000 for 28-gauge or .410 bore, plus $10,000 if made on optional small frame.

NIB	Exc.	V.G.	Good	Fair	Poor
25000	20000	17500	15000	8000	—

Model 21 Over/Under

An over/under model patterned after classic Winchester side-by-side. Made on the same machining and tooling, with the same manufacturing techniques as SXS model, resulting in virtually the same balance, feel and appearance. Features include automatic ejectors, single-selective trigger, American walnut stock with straight- or pistol grip. Made only in 20-gauge, with 26", 28", 30" or 32" barrels that are steel-shot compatible. Comes with five choke tubes. Wood upgrades are available at prices up to $900.

NIB	Exc.	V.G.	Good	Fair	Poor
3400	2900	2450	1900	1350	750

Model 21 Side-By-Side Rifle

In .22 Long Rifle caliber, this very unique double rifle is built on a frame even smaller than the .410 frame. Each gun is custom made, with many upgrades and engraving options available. Higher grades have a MRSP from $30,000 to $34,000. Note: A few custom made-to-order models in various centerfire calibers have been built in the past, with very limited production. Values are estimated to be approximately 50 percent higher than the rimfire model.

NIB	Exc.	V.G.	Good	Fair	Poor
22500	18000	14000	—	—	—

A.H. Fox

Conn. Shotgun Co. also makes high-grade side-by-side shotguns, based on classic A.H. Fox models of early 20th century. These are CE and DE grades, with many available options and upgrades. Prices shown are for base CE model.

NIB	Exc.	V.G.	Good	Fair	Poor
16500	12000	9500	—	—	—

CONNECTICUT VALLEY ARMS CO.

Lawrenceville, Georgia

RIFLES

Express Rifle

A .50-caliber double-barrel percussion rifle, with 28" barrels. Blued, with walnut stock. Note: Add 25 percent for deluxe version.

NIB	Exc.	V.G.	Good	Fair	Poor
220	190	160	140	120	100

Over/Under Rifle

A .50-caliber double-barrel over/under rifle, with 26" barrels. Blued, with walnut stock.

NIB	Exc.	V.G.	Good	Fair	Poor
400	320	260	200	160	130

Hawken Rifle

A .50-caliber with 28" octagonal barrel, double-set triggers and walnut stock.

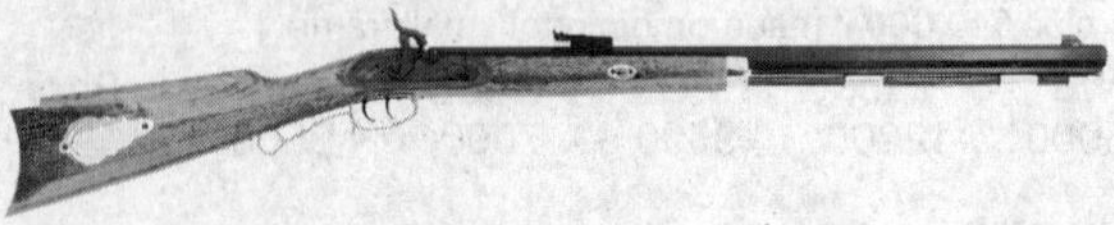

NIB	Exc.	V.G.	Good	Fair	Poor
250	200	160	130	100	80

Presentation Grade Hawken

As above, with engraved lock, patchbox and finely figured stock.

NIB	Exc.	V.G.	Good	Fair	Poor
300	240	190	150	120	100

Pennsylvania Long Rifle

A .50-caliber flintlock rifle, with 40" octagonal barrel, double-set triggers and walnut stock.

NIB	Exc.	V.G.	Good	Fair	Poor
—	350	280	220	180	140

Kentucky Rifle

A .45-caliber percussion rifle, with 33.5" octagonal barrel and walnut stock.

NIB	Exc.	V.G.	Good	Fair	Poor
—	210	170	130	110	90

Mountain Rifle

A .50- or .54-caliber percussion half-stock rifle.

NIB	Exc.	V.G.	Good	Fair	Poor
—	200	160	130	100	80

Blazer Rifle

A .50-caliber percussion rifle, with 28" octagonal barrel and walnut stock.

NIB	Exc.	V.G.	Good	Fair	Poor
—	120	90	70	60	50

Apollo Shadow SS

Introduced in 1993. Rifle features an inline stainless steel bolt spring-action. A 24" blued round barrel with octagonal one piece receiver drilled and tapped. Stock is black hardwood-textured with Dura Grip. Pistol grip and recoil pad. Offered in .50- or .54-caliber. Weight about 9 lbs.

NIB	Exc.	V.G.	Good	Fair	Poor
—	150	120	100	80	60

Apollo Classic

Similar to above Apollo, with dark brown stained laminated hardwood stock. Pistol grip, raised comb and recoil pad. Weight about 8.5 lbs.

NIB	Exc.	V.G.	Good	Fair	Poor
—	170	140	110	90	70

Apollo Carbelite

Offered in .50-caliber, with percussion bolt and 27" blued round taper barrel. Octagonal receiver drilled and tapped. Fitted with Carbelite composite stock with Monte Carlo and cheekpiece with pistol grip. Weight about 7.5 lbs.

NIB	Exc.	V.G.	Good	Fair	Poor
—	200	160	130	100	80

Apollo Starfire

Chambered for .50-caliber bullet. Rifle is an inline type, with 24" stainless steel barrel. Synthetic stock, checkered pistol grip, raised comb and cheekpiece. Weight about 6.5 lbs.

NIB	Exc.	V.G.	Good	Fair	Poor
—	160	130	110	80	70

Apollo Eclipse Rifle

Offered in .50- or .54-caliber, with 24" round barrel and blued steel receiver. Synthetic stock, with checkered pistol, raised comb and cheekpiece. Weight about 6.5 lbs.

NIB	Exc.	V.G.	Good	Fair	Poor
—	150	120	100	80	60

Apollo Dominator

Fitted with a synthetic thumbhole stock and 24" round barrel. Chambered for .50-caliber bullet. Introduced in 1996. Weight about 8.5 lbs.

NIB	Exc.	V.G.	Good	Fair	Poor
—	200	160	130	100	80

Apollo Brown Bear

This .50-caliber rifle fitted with a hardwood stock, pistol grip, raised comb and cheekpiece. Round 24" barrel. Introduced in 1996. Weight about 6.5

lbs.

NIB	Exc.	V.G.	Good	Fair	Poor
—	160	130	110	80	70

Frontier Carbine

Fitted with 24" blued barrel, Offered in .50-caliber percussion or flintlock. Case-hardened lock, with hardwood stock. Weight about 6.75 lbs.

NIB	Exc.	V.G.	Good	Fair	Poor
150	120	100	80	80	50

Plainsman Rifle

This .50-caliber percussion rifle has 26" octagonal barrel, with case-hardened lock and hardwood stock. Weight about 6.5 lbs.

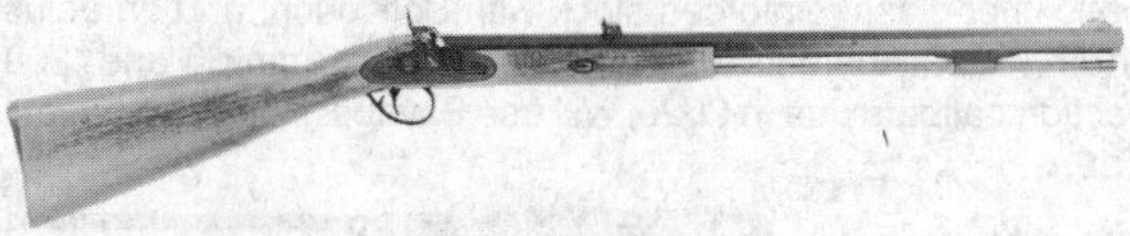

NIB	Exc.	V.G.	Good	Fair	Poor
—	180	140	120	90	70

Panther Carbine

Percussion rifle available in .50- or .54-caliber. Fitted with 24" blued octagonal barrel and Hawken-style case-hardened lock. Stock is textured black Dura Grip over hardwood, with Monte Carlo comb, cheekpiece and pistol grip. Weight about 7.5 lbs.

NIB	Exc.	V.G.	Good	Fair	Poor
—	120	100	80	60	50

Bushwacker Rifle

This .50-caliber percussion rifle fitted with 26" octagonal barrel. Case-hardened engraved lock, brown stained hardwood stock and rounded nose. Weight about 7.5 lbs.

NIB	Exc.	V.G.	Good	Fair	Poor
—	120	90	70	60	50

Trophy Carbine

Fitted with 24" half-round/half-octagon barrel and Hawken-style lock. Stock is walnut with Monte Carlo comb, cheekpiece and pistol grip. Offered in .50- or .54-caliber percussion. Weight about 6.75 lbs.

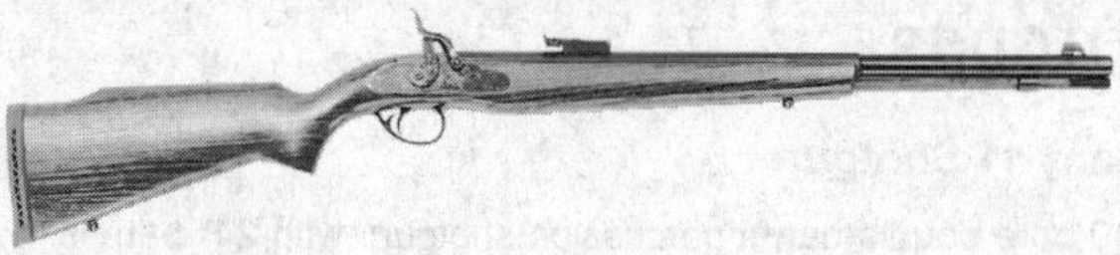

NIB	Exc.	V.G.	Good	Fair	Poor
—	140	110	90	70	60

Varmint Rifle

Lightweight percussion rifle in .32-caliber, with 24" octagon barrel and case colored lock. Stock is hardwood. Weight about 6.75 lbs.

NIB	Exc.	V.G.	Good	Fair	Poor
—	140	110	90	70	60

Woodsman Rifle LS

Introduced in 1994. Features 26" blued octagon barrel, with dark brown stained laminated hardwood stock. Offered in .50- or .54-caliber percussion. Weight about 6.5 lbs.

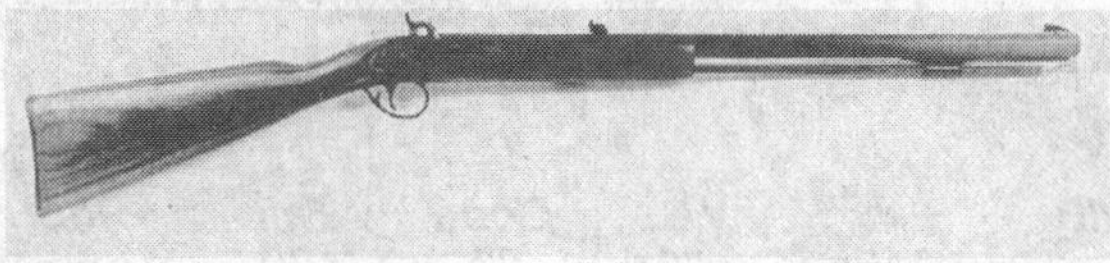

NIB	Exc.	V.G.	Good	Fair	Poor
—	120	100	80	60	50

Frontier Hunter Carbine

Offered in .50- or .54-caliber, this percussion rifle fitted with 24" blued octagon barrel. Case-hardened 45° offset hammer. Stock is dark stained laminated hardwood. Weight about 7.5 lbs.

NIB	Exc.	V.G.	Good	Fair	Poor
—	120	100	80	60	50

Grey Wolf Rifle

Offered in .50- or .54-caliber, this percussion rifle fitted with 26" matte blue octagon barrel. Case-hardened engraved lock. Stock is matte gray composite, with raised comb, checkered pistol grip and buttplate. Weight about 6.5 lbs.

NIB	Exc.	V.G.	Good	Fair	Poor
—	120	100	80	60	50

Lone Grey Wolf Rifle

Introduced in 1994. This .50-caliber percussion rifle features 26" matte blued octagon barrel. Triggerguard is oversized. Composite stock is black and has a raised comb, checkered pistol grip and recoil pad. Weight about 6.5 lbs.

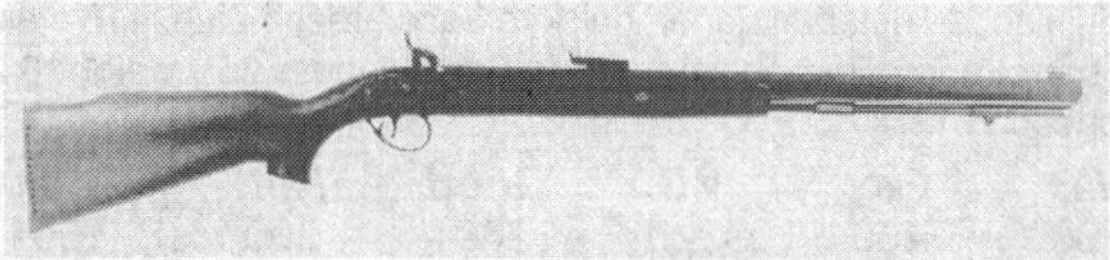

NIB	Exc.	V.G.	Good	Fair	Poor
—	140	110	90	70	60

Timber Wolf Rifle

Introduced in 1994. Similar to above model, but furnished with Realtree composite stock. Raised comb, checkered pistol grip and buttplate. Weight about 6.5 lbs.

NIB	Exc.	V.G.	Good	Fair	Poor
—	140	120	90	70	60

Tracker Carbine LS

Introduced in 1994. Fitted with 21" blued half-round/half-octagon barrel. Hawken-style lock. Stock is laminated dark brown with matte finish and straight-grip. Chambered for .50-caliber percussion. Weight about 6.5 lbs.

NIB	Exc.	V.G.	Good	Fair	Poor
—	140	120	90	70	60

Stag Horn

Introduced in 1996. This inline rifle chambered for .50- or .54-caliber bullet. Round barrel is 24", with blued finish. Stock isynthetic, with checkered pistol grip, raised comb and cheekpiece. Weight about 6.5 lbs.

NIB	Exc.	V.G.	Good	Fair	Poor
—	140	110	90	70	60

Electra

A .50-caliber inline muzzleloader that uses electronic-arc ignition rather than caps or primers. Powered by common 9v battery. Finishes include stainless/camo, stainless/black composite and blued/black composite. Introduced in 2007. Price given for stainless/camo version.

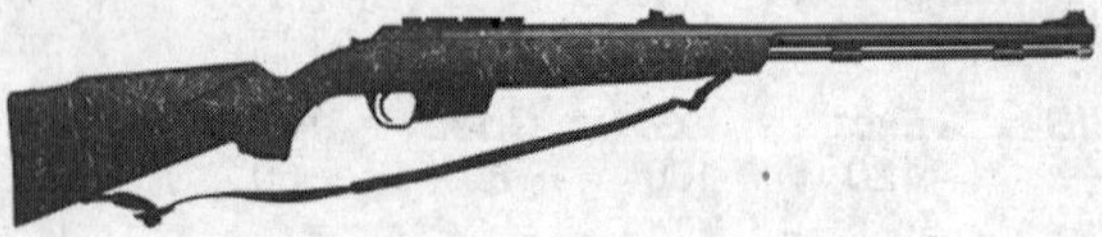

NIB	Exc.	V.G.	Good	Fair	Poor
500	400	320	260	200	160

Accura MR

Break-action .50-caliber inline ignition muzzleloading rifle, with weather guard finish, adjustable trigger, quick release breech plug, 416 stainless steel barrel and camo polymer stock. Barrel length 25", weight 6.2 lbs. Introduced 2012.

NIB	Exc.	V.G.	Good	Fair	Poor
500	400	320	260	200	160

Accura PR Nitride/Blk .50 ISM

28" nitride-treated 416 grade stainless steel barrel, quick-release breech plug, Quake Claw sling, DuraSight Dead-On one-piece scope mount, soft-touch stock with rubber grip panels, PalmSaver solid aluminum ramrod, CrushZone recoil pad. With scope, add $150. With scope and case, add $200.

NIB	Exc.	V.G.	Good	Fair	Poor
500	400	320	260	200	160

Accura LR

Caliber: .45, .50. Barrel: 30 in., Nitride-treated, 416 stainless steel Bergara. Stock: Ambidextrous thumbhole camo. Sights: DuraSight Dead-On one-piece scope mount, scope not included. Weight: 6.75 lbs. Features: Reversible hammer spur, CrushZone recoil pad, quick-release breech plug.

NIB	Exc.	V.G.	Good	Fair	Poor
600	—	—	—	—	—

Optima V2

Break-action .50-caliber inline ignition muzzleloading rifle, with black or camo finishes, quick-release breech plug, 416 stainless-steel barrel and polymer standard or thumb-hole stock. Barrel length 26", weight 6.7 lbs. Note: Add $25.00 for thumbhole stock. Outfit (+$40 BPI-PR2020SVP) adds Durasight Fiber Optic Sights, Cleaning Patches, Magnum Speed Loaders, Wonder Gel Cleaning Solvent, Anti-Seize stick, Breech Brush, Powerbelt Bullets, and Muzzleloading Basics DVD. Scope Package (BPI-PR2020SSC) add $100.

NIB	Exc.	V.G.	Good	Fair	Poor
300	240	190	150	120	100

Cascade

CVA's first venture into a bolt-action centerfire rifle features a 22" 4140 carbon steel barrel, threaded muzzle, 70-degree bolt throw, two-position safety and 4-round, flush fit, detachable magazine in a charcoal gray, synthetic fiber-glass reinforced stock with SoftTouch, and an adjustable length of pull. Calibers include 6.5 Creedmoor, 7mm-08 and .308 with long-action calibers due in 2020. Will use Savage 110 scope bases. New for 2019.

NIB	Exc.	V.G.	Good	Fair	Poor
650	550	480	—	—	—

Wolf .50-Cal Muzzleloaders

Entry-level line with black ambidextrous stocks, Quick-Release Breech Plug, break-action breech, blued carbon steel or 416 grade stainless steel, DuraSight fiber-optic sights. CVA's solid aluminum PalmSaver ramrod standard on all Wolf models. 24" barrel, reversible hammer spur, CrushZone recoil pad. 14" length of pull, 39" overall length, 6.25 lbs. No. BPI-PR2110. Scope and case (BPI-PR2110SC), add $90. With scope, case, and camo stock (BPI-PR2115NSC), add $200.

NIB	Exc.	V.G.	Good	Fair	Poor
200	160	130	100	80	70

Cascade XT

Calibers: 6.5 Creedmoor, .308 Win., .450 Bushmaster, .350 Legend, 6.5 PRC, 7mm Rem. Mag., .300 Win. Mag. Barrel: 22", 24", 26" #5 Taper fluted, threaded. Stock: Synthetic with Realtree Excape camo and SoftTouch finish. Features: Precision-oriented version of the Cascade bolt action. Heavier barrel with radial muzzle brake. Tactical-style bolt knob. Two-position safety. Dual front swivel studs. Graphite black Cerakote metalwork. MOA guarantee. Flush-fit, dropbox magazine.

NIB	Exc.	V.G.	Good	Fair	Poor
670	—	—	—	—	—

SHOTGUNS

Brittany 11 Shotgun

A .410 bore double-barrel percussion shotgun, with 24" barrels, double triggers and walnut stock.

NIB	Exc.	V.G.	Good	Fair	Poor
300	240	190	150	120	100

Trapper Shotgun #1

A 12-gauge percussion single-barrel shotgun, with 28" barrel threaded for choke tubes and walnut stock.

NIB	Exc.	V.G.	Good	Fair	Poor
220	180	140	120	90	70

Classic Turkey Double-Barrel Shotgun

A 12-gauge percussion breech-loading shotgun, with 28" barrel. Checkered stock is European walnut with straight-grip. Weight about 9 lbs.

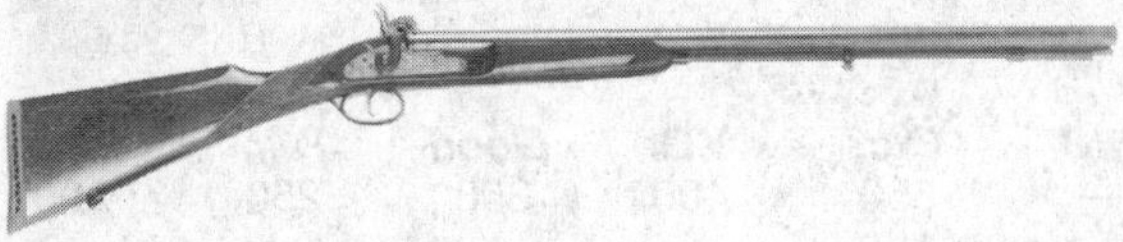

NIB	Exc.	V.G.	Good	Fair	Poor
280	220	180	140	110	90

Trapper Shotgun #2

A single-barrel 12-gauge shotgun, with 28" barrel. Stock is straight-grip hardwood with checkering. Supplied with three interchangeable chokes. Weight about 6 lbs.

NIB	Exc.	V.G.	Good	Fair	Poor
250	200	160	130	100	80

PISTOLS

Made by Pedersoli, Uberti and other Italian makers.

Siber

A .45-caliber percussion pistol patterned after Swiss Siber. Made by Pedersoli, Uberti and other Italian makers.

NIB	Exc.	V.G.	Good	Fair	Poor
380	300	240	190	150	120

Kentucky

A .45-caliber single-shot percussion pistol, with 10" barrel and walnut stock.

NIB	Exc.	V.G.	Good	Fair	Poor
—	120	100	80	60	50

Philadelphia Derringer

A .45-caliber single-shot percussion pistol, with 3.25" barrel and walnut stock.

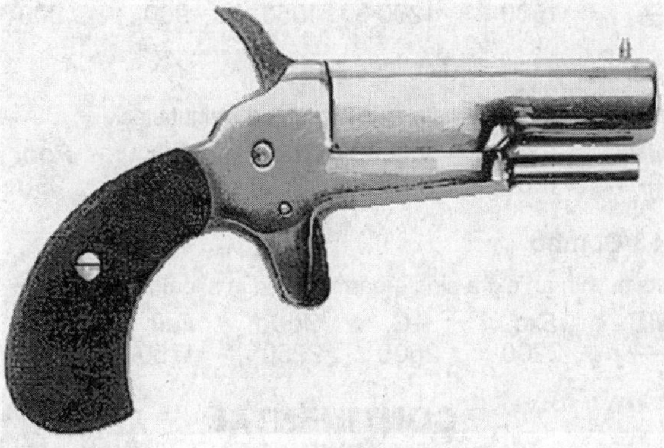

NIB	Exc.	V.G.	Good	Fair	Poor
—	100	80	60	50	40

Sheriff's Model

A .36-caliber percussion revolver, nickel-plated with walnut grips.

NIB	Exc.	V.G.	Good	Fair	Poor
—	200	160	130	100	80

3rd Model Dragoon

NIB	Exc.	V.G.	Good	Fair	Poor
—	200	160	130	100	80

Colt Walker Replica

NIB	Exc.	V.G.	Good	Fair	Poor
300	240	190	150	120	100

Remington Bison

NIB	Exc.	V.G.	Good	Fair	Poor
—	220	190	160	140	120

Pocket Police

NIB	Exc.	V.G.	Good	Fair	Poor
—	100	80	60	50	40

Pocket Revolver

Chambered for .31-caliber. Fitted with 4" octagon barrel. Cylinder holds five bullets. Solid brass frame. Weight about 15 oz.

NIB	Exc.	V.G.	Good	Fair	Poor
150	140	120	110	100	90

Wells Fargo

NIB	Exc.	V.G.	Good	Fair	Poor
150	120	100	80	60	50

1851 Navy

NIB	Exc.	V.G.	Good	Fair	Poor
220	190	160	140	120	100

1861 Navy

NIB	Exc.	V.G.	Good	Fair	Poor
220	190	160	140	120	100

1860 Army

NIB	Exc.	V.G.	Good	Fair	Poor
220	190	160	140	120	100

1858 Remington

NIB	Exc.	V.G.	Good	Fair	Poor
220	190	160	140	120	100

1858 Remington Target

As above, but fitted with adjustable sights.

NIB	Exc.	V.G.	Good	Fair	Poor
220	190	160	140	120	100

Bison

A 6-shot .44-caliber revolver, with 10.25" octagonal barrel. Solid brass frame. Weight about 48 oz.

NIB	Exc.	V.G.	Good	Fair	Poor
200	160	130	100	80	70

Hawken Pistol

A .50-caliber percussion pistol, with 9.75" octagon barrel. Stock is hardwood. Weight about 50 oz.

NIB	Exc.	V.G.	Good	Fair	Poor
200	160	130	100	80	70

NEW PRODUCTION

Plains Rifle

Caliber: .50. Barrel: 28 in., Nitride, fluted, stainless steel Bergara. Stock: Ambidextrous composite Realtree MAX-1 XT. Sights: DuraSight Dead-On one-piece scope mount, scope not included. Weight: 7.2 lbs. Features: Solid aluminum PalmSaver ramrod, reversible cocking spur, Quake Claw sling.

NIB	*Exc.*	*V.G.*	*Good*	*Fair*	*Poor*
550	—	—	—	—	—

Paramount Pro

Caliber: .45, magnum. Barrel: Fluted Bergara free-floating, Cerakote/Nitride stainless steel/camo. Stock: Grayboe fiberglass. Sights: Threaded 3/4x20, scope not included. Weight: 8.75 lbs. Features: TriggerTech trigger, VariFlame breech plug, accessory trap door, self-deploying ramrod.

NIB	*Exc.*	*V.G.*	*Good*	*Fair*	*Poor*
1600	—	—	—	—	—

Paramount Pro Colorado

Caliber: .50, magnum. Barrel: Fluted Bergara free-floating, Cerakote/Nitride stainless steel/camo. Stock: Grayboe fiberglass. Sights: Williams peep sight. Weight: 8.75 lbs. Features: TriggerTech trigger, VariFlame breech plug, accessory trap door, self-deploying ramrod.

NIB	*Exc.*	*V.G.*	*Good*	*Fair*	*Poor*
1600	—	—	—	—	—

CONSTABLE, R.
Philadelphia, Pennsylvania

Pocket Pistol (Antique)

Single-shot percussion pistol, with 3" round or octagonal barrel. German-silver mounts and walnut stock. Pistols are marked "R. Constable Philadelphia". Manufactured during late 1840s and 1850s. Richard Constable also made a variety of other muzzleloading arms.

Exc.	*Fine*	*V.G.*	*Good*	*Fair*	*Poor*
2200	1100	820	550	200	140

CONTENTO/VENTUR

SIDE-BY-SIDES

Model 51

A 12-, 16-, 20-, 28-gauge and .410 bore boxlock double-barrel shotgun, with 26", 28", 30" and 32" barrels. Various chokes, extractors and double triggers. Checkered walnut stock. Introduced in 1980, discontinued 1985.

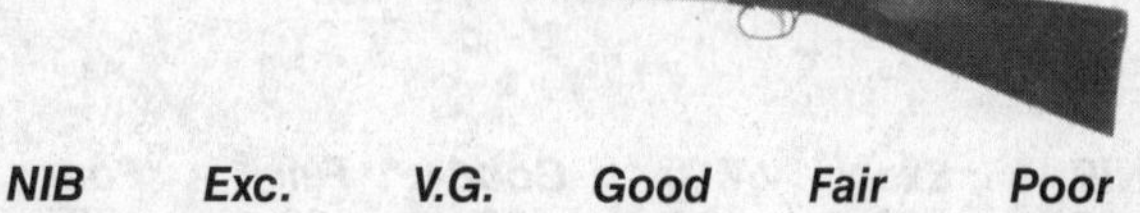

NIB	*Exc.*	*V.G.*	*Good*	*Fair*	*Poor*
—	500	350	300	220	150

Model 52

As above in 10-gauge.

NIB	*Exc.*	*V.G.*	*Good*	*Fair*	*Poor*
—	500	350	300	220	150

Model 53

As above, with scalloped receiver, automatic ejectors and available with single-selective trigger. Discontinued in 1985. Note: Add 25 percent for single-selective trigger.

NIB	*Exc.*	*V.G.*	*Good*	*Fair*	*Poor*
—	550	400	350	250	200

Model 62

A 12-, 20- or 28-gauge H&H sidelock shotgun, with various barrel lengths and chokes. Automatic ejectors, cocking indicators, floral engraved receiver and checkered walnut stock. Discontinued in 1982.

NIB	*Exc.*	*V.G.*	*Good*	*Fair*	*Poor*
—	1150	800	750	600	450

Model 64

As above, but more finely finished. No longer in production.

NIB	*Exc.*	*V.G.*	*Good*	*Fair*	*Poor*
—	1250	900	850	700	550

OVER/UNDERS

Over/Under

A 12-gauge over/under shotgun, with 32" barrels, screw-in choke tubes, high ventilated rib, automatic ejectors and standard single-selective trigger. Checkered with Monte Carlo walnut stock.

NIB	*Exc.*	*V.G.*	*Good*	*Fair*	*Poor*
—	1250	900	750	600	500

Mark 2

As above, with an extra single-barrel. Fitted in a leather case.

NIB	*Exc.*	*V.G.*	*Good*	*Fair*	*Poor*
—	1500	1200	1050	900	800

Mark 3

As above, but engraved with a finely figured walnut stock.

NIB	*Exc.*	*V.G.*	*Good*	*Fair*	*Poor*
—	1850	1500	1250	1100	950

Mark 3 Combo

As above, with an extra single-barrel. Fitted in a leather case.

NIB	*Exc.*	*V.G.*	*Good*	*Fair*	*Poor*
—	3200	2600	2250	1750	1300

CONTINENTAL
RWM
Cologne, Germany

Continental Pocket Pistol (6.35mm)

A 6.35mm caliber semi-automatic pistol, with 2" barrel, internal hammer and 7-shot detachable magazine. Blued, with plastic grips and slide marked "Continental Kal. 6.35". Produced during 1920s. Note: Pistol may have been manufactured in Spain and carried German proof marks, because it was sold by RWM in Germany.

NIB	Exc.	V.G.	Good	Fair	Poor
—	300	150	120	100	80

Continental Pocket Pistol (7.65mm)

German-made pistol chambered for 7.65mm cartridge. Fitted with 3.9" barrel. Rear sight is a U-notch in slide. Magazine capacity 8 rounds. Weight about 20 oz. Made prior to 1914.

NIB	Exc.	V.G.	Good	Fair	Poor
—	500	300	220	150	100

CONTINENTAL ARMS CO.

Norwich, Connecticut

Pepperbox (Antique)

.22-caliber 5-barrel pepperbox, with spur trigger and 2.5" barrels marked "Continental Arms Co. Norwich Ct. Patented Aug. 28, 1866". Some examples found marked "Ladies Companion".

Courtesy Milwaukee Public Museum, Milwaukee, Wisconsin

Exc.	Fine	V.G.	Good	Fair	Poor
2250	1000	670	350	250	170

CONTINENTAL ARMS CO.

Leige, Belgium

Double Rifle

A .270, .303, .30-40, .30-06, .348, 375 H&H, .400 Jeffreys, .465, .475, .500 and .600 Nitro Express caliber Anson & Deeley boxlock double-barreled rifle, with 24" or 26" barrels. Double triggers and checkered walnut stock.

NIB	Exc.	V.G.	Good	Fair	Poor
—	6500	4500	3750	3000	2250

COOK & BROTHER RIFLES AND CARBINES

New Orleans, Louisiana

In early 1861, Ferdinand W.C. Cook and his brother Francis L. Cook, both English emigres, joined to form Cook & Brother in New Orleans to manufacture rifles and carbines following the English P1853 series for the newly seceded state of Louisiana and its neighbors. Between June 1861 and the federal occupation of New Orleans in April 1862, this firm produced about 200 cavalry and artillery carbines and about 1000 rifles. Having successfully moved the armory's machinery before federal occupation, the firm continued manufacture of rifles in Selma, Alabama during 1862, probably completing another 1,000 rifles with the New Orleans lock markings from the parts brought with them. Re-established in Athens, Georgia in early 1863, the firm continued to build both carbines and rifles, manufacturing more than 5,500 above the New Orleans production through 1864. The firm's products were clearly among the best small arms made within the Confederacy. As with all Confederate arms, beware of fakes. Expert evaluation recommended.

Cook & Brother Rifles (New Orleans & Selma production) (Antique)

Overall length 48.75"; barrel length 33"; caliber .58. Markings: representation of a Confederate flag ("Stars & Bars") and "COOK & BROTHER/ N.O./1861 (or) 1862" on lock; same usually on barrel together with serial number and "PROVED" near breech. Rifles in the early production have long range rear sights and unusual two piece block and blade front sights as well as an integral bayonet lug with guide on right side of barrel. Later production utilizes a brass clamping ring for the bayonet, a block open rear sight and a simple block and blade front sight. Earlier production will claim a premium if in good condition.

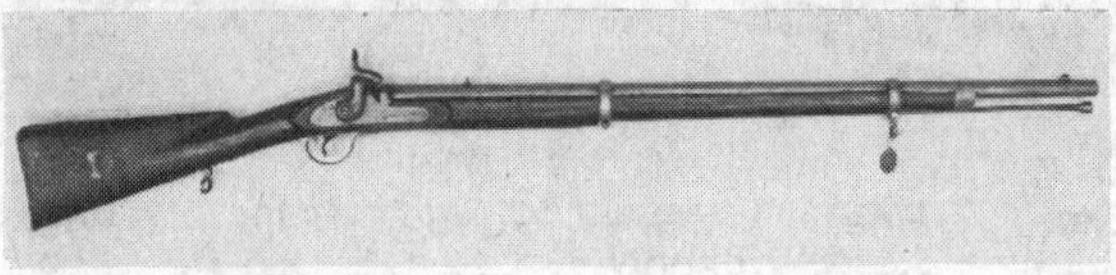

Courtesy Milwaukee Public Museum, Milwaukee, Wisconsin

Exc.	Fine	V.G.	Good	Fair	Poor
—	—	30000	—	—	—

Cook & Brother Carbines (New Orleans production) (Antique)

Overall length 40" (artillery), 37" (cavalry); barrel length 24" (artillery), 21" to 21.5" (cavalry); caliber .58. Markings: As on Cook & Brother rifles (New Orleans production) artillery and cavalry carbines were produced in New Orleans in a separate serial range from the rifles. Total production is thought not to have exceeded 225, divided evenly between 1861 and 1862 dates. In addition to the overall and barrel lengths, the main difference between the artillery and cavalry carbines is the manner in which they were carried. The former bears standard sling rings on the upper band and the triggerguard strap, the latter has a bar with a ring on the left side of the stock. Both are exceedingly rare.

Exc.	Fine	V.G.	Good	Fair	Poor
—	—	25000	—	—	—

Cook & Brother Rifles (Athens production) (Antique)

Overall length 49"; barrel length 33"; caliber .58. Markings: representation of a Confederate flag ("Stars & Bars") and "COOK & BROTHER/ ATHENS GA./date (1863 or 1864) and serial number on lock; "PROVED" on barrel near breech; serial number on various metal parts. After reestablishing their plant at Athens, Georgia, in the spring of 1863, Cook & Brother continued to manufacture rifles in a consecutive serial range after their New Orleans/Selma production (beginning about serial number 2000) and continued to make arms well into 1864 (through at least serial number 7650) until Sherman's army threatened the plant and necessitated the employment of its workforce in a military capacity as the 23rd Battalion Georgia State Guard.

Courtesy Milwaukee Public Museum, Milwaukee, Wisconsin

Exc.	Fine	V.G.	Good	Fair	Poor
—	—	25000	—	—	—

Cook & Brother Carbines (Athens production) (Antique)

Overall length 40" (artillery) or 37" (cavalry); barrel lengths 24" (artillery) or 21" to 21.5" (cavalry); caliber .58. Markings: same as on Athens production rifles. Artillery and cavalry carbines were manufactured in the same serial range as the Athens production rifles (about 2000 through 7650). As in New Orleans production, the artillery and cavalry carbines are distinguished from one another by their respective lengths. Unlike New Orleans/Selma production, however, some of the cavalry carbines are mounted with sling swivels of the artillery style, while others bear the sling ring on the left side and additionally have a swivel ring to secure the ramrod.

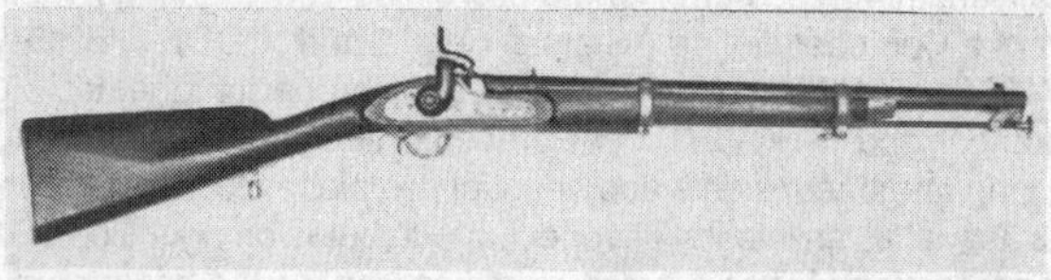

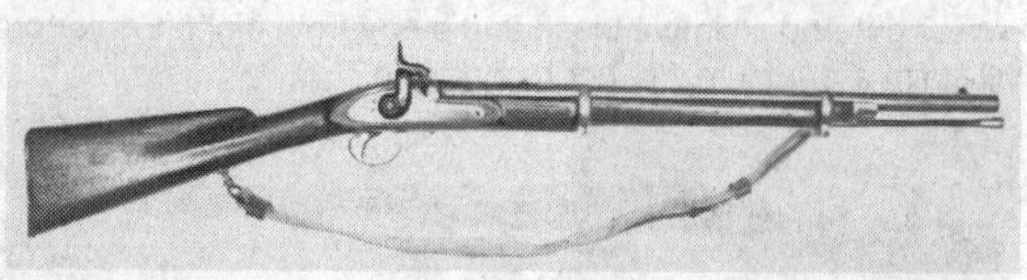

Exc.	Fine	V.G.	Good	Fair	Poor
—	—	25000	—	—	—

COONAN ARMS/COONAN INC.

Blaine, Minnesota

Original Coonan Arms was based in St. Paul, Minnesota from 1983 to 1994 and in Maplewood, Minnesota from 1994 to 1998. That company ceased operations in 1998. Current manufacturer was established as Coonan Inc. in 2009 and is located in Blaine, Minnesota. Note: Add $40 for 6" barrel; $130 for Bomar adjustable sights; $40 for .38 Special conversion; $40 for checkered walnut grips; $100 with Teflon slide; $100 with Teflon frame.

Model A

A .357 Magnum semi-automatic pistol, with 5" barrel, 7-shot detachable magazine and fixed sights. Stainless steel with walnut grips. Introduced in 1981; discontinued 1984.

NIB	Exc.	V.G.	Good	Fair	Poor
1200	1000	880	500	350	280

Model B

An improved version of Model A, with a linkless barrel system, extended grip safety, enclosed trigger bar and more contoured grip. A 6" barrel is available, as are adjustable sights, as extra cost options. A .38 Special conversion is also available. Introduced in 1985. A number of other options are also available that will affect value.

NIB	Exc.	V.G.	Good	Fair	Poor
1300	1180	920	680	500	300

Comp I

As above, with 6" barrel, attached compensator and stippled front grip strap. Introduced in 1989.

NIB	Exc.	V.G.	Good	Fair	Poor
1600	1250	1000	700	550	350

Comp I Deluxe

As above, with blued stainless steel slide, checkered grip straps and finer finishing.

NIB	Exc.	V.G.	Good	Fair	Poor
1650	1300	1050	750	600	400

Classic (Current Production)

Features an integrated compensator, with 5-in. barrel. Supplied with checkered walnut grips, Millett adjustable rear sight and two-tone Teflon finish. Magazine capacity 7 rounds; weight 42 oz.; overall length 8.3 in.

NIB	Exc.	V.G.	Good	Fair	Poor
1310	1150	1030	880	750	580

Cadet

Chambered for .357 Magnum cartridge, Has 3.9" barrel, with smooth walnut grips and fixed rear sight. Magazine capacity 6 rounds; weight about 39 oz.; overall length 7.8"; height 5.3". Coonan Arms refers to this model as "Short Grip".

NIB	Exc.	V.G.	Good	Fair	Poor
1150	880	680	500	400	400

Cadet II

Same as above, with standard grip. Magazine capacity 7 rounds.

NIB	Exc.	V.G.	Good	Fair	Poor
1150	880	680	500	400	200

Coonan .45 ACP

A 1911-style pistol similar to Coonan .357 models, except chambered in .45 ACP. Features 5" linkless barrel, pivoting trigger, external extractor, Novak style sights, smooth walnut grips and stainless finish. Introduced in 2016.

NIB	Exc.	V.G.	Good	Fair	Poor
1300	1050	900	—	—	—

Coonan MOT

A 1911 style pistol in .45 ACP. Features include a brushed stainless finish, link-less barrel, external extractor and pivoting trigger. Introduced in late 2017.

NIB	Exc.	V.G.	Good	Fair	Poor
1200	900	700	—	—	—

COOPER, J. M. & CO.

Philadelphia, Pennsylvania

Pocket Revolver (Antique)

A .31-caliber percussion double-action revolver, with 4", 5" or 6" octagonal barrel and 6-shot unfluted cylinder. Blued, with walnut grips. During first two years of production they were made in Pittsburgh, Pennsylvania and were so marked. Approximately 15,000 manufactured between 1864 and 1869. Note: Add 20 percent for Pittsburgh-marked models.

Courtesy Milwaukee Public Museum, Milwaukee, Wisconsin

Exc.	Fine	V.G.	Good	Fair	Poor
1850	780	490	200	100	70

COOPER FIREARMS

Stevensville, Montana

Cooper Firearms, long known for small-caliber varminters, now makes hunting rifles for big game as well in seven actions including single-shots and repeaters (including muzzleloaders), in 23 models and about 50 standard American, European, and some wildcat calibers. Options include upgrades for the wood stocks, and synthetic stocks.

Synthetic Hunting Rifles

There is a synthetic-stocked model available in any of the action sizes with fixed or detachable magazines, in blue or stainless steel. Calibers and options vary considerably, and only the base price is shown.

Backcountry

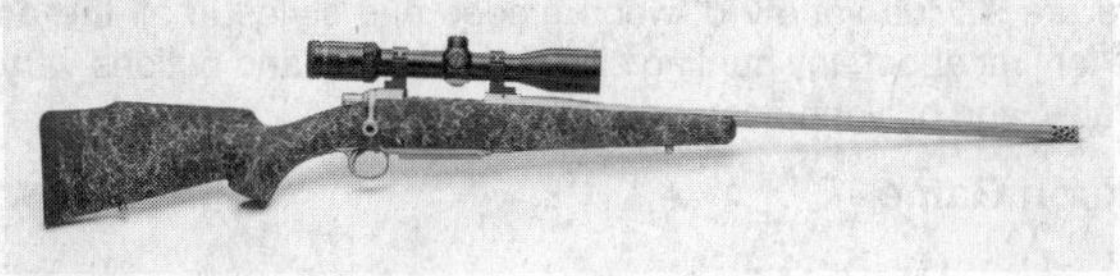

NIB	Exc.	V.G.	Good	Fair	Poor
3000	2550	2150	1850	—	—

Timberline

NIB	Exc.	V.G.	Good	Fair	Poor
2600	2200	1880	1600	—	—

Open Country LR

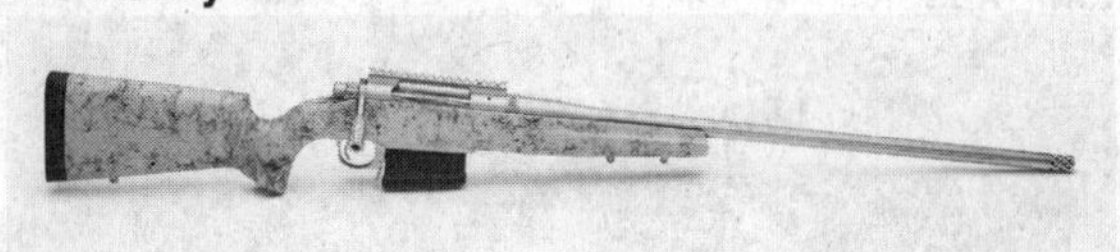

NIB	Exc.	V.G.	Good	Fair	Poor
2800	2250	1900	1600	—	—

Jackson Hunter

NIB	Exc.	V.G.	Good	Fair	Poor
2600	2200	1880	1600	—	—

Excalibur

NIB	Exc.	V.G.	Good	Fair	Poor
2600	2200	1880	1600	—	—

Open Country LR Lightweight

NIB	Exc.	V.G.	Good	Fair	Poor
3800	3220	2750	2350	—	—

Raptor

NIB	Exc.	V.G.	Good	Fair	Poor
2760	2350	2000	1700	—	—

Synthetic Hunting Rifles

Phoenix

NIB	Exc.	V.G.	Good	Fair	Poor
2500	2120	1800	1550	—	—

Synthetic Hunting Rifle

TRP3

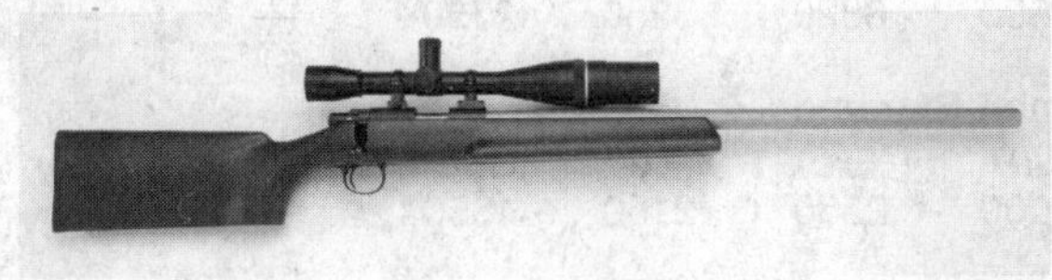

NIB	Exc.	V.G.	Good	Fair	Poor
2760	2350	2000	1700	—	—

Synthetic Hunting Rifles

Muzzleloader Synthetic

NIB	Exc.	V.G.	Good	Fair	Poor
2000	1700	1450	1220	—	—

Wood-Stocked Hunting Rifles

There are a wide variety of wood grades and styles in all the actions sizes for just about any hunting situation. Calibers and options vary considerably, and only the base price is shown.

Jackson Game

NIB	Exc.	V.G.	Good	Fair	Poor
2600	2200	1880	1600	—	—

Classic

NIB	Exc.	V.G.	Good	Fair	Poor
2600	2200	1880	1600	—	—

Custom Classic

NIB	Exc.	V.G.	Good	Fair	Poor
3500	2980	2550	2150	—	—

Varminter

NIB	Exc.	V.G.	Good	Fair	Poor
2500	2120	1800	1550	—	—

Montana Varminter

NIB	Exc.	V.G.	Good	Fair	Poor
2600	2200	1880	1600	—	—

Schnabel

NIB	Exc.	V.G.	Good	Fair	Poor
2600	2200	1880	1600	—	—

Mannlicher

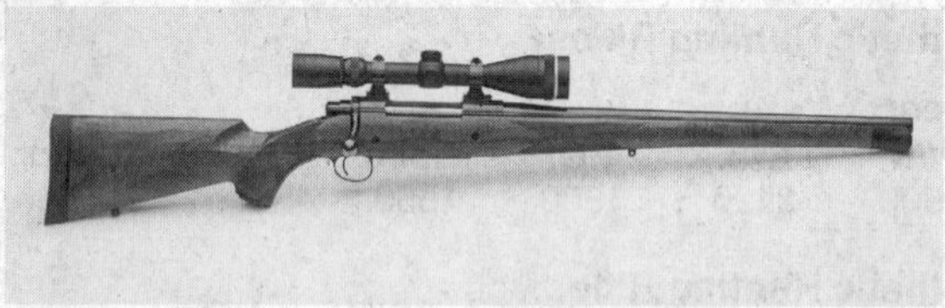

NIB	Exc.	V.G.	Good	Fair	Poor
4500	3820	3250	2750	—	—

Varmint Extreme

NIB	Exc.	V.G.	Good	Fair	Poor
3000	2550	2150	1850	—	—

Jackson Squirrel

NIB	Exc.	V.G.	Good	Fair	Poor
2600	2200	1880	1600	—	—

Var-Tac

NIB	Exc.	V.G.	Good	Fair	Poor
2600	2200	1880	1600	—	—

Muzzleloader Wood

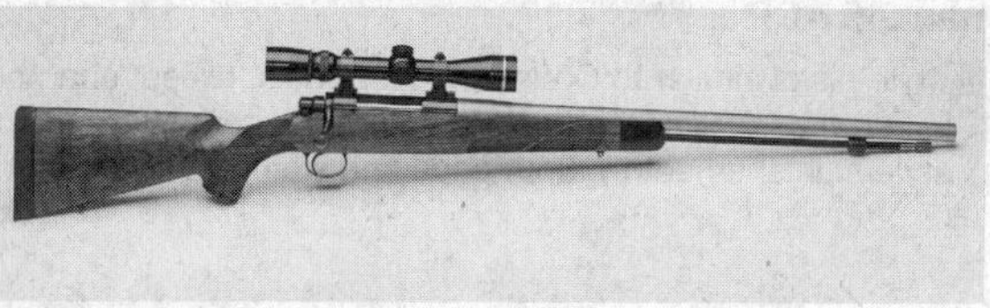

NIB	Exc.	V.G.	Good	Fair	Poor
3560	3000	2550	2050	—	—

Model 38; Model 40

Bolt-action rifle chambered for .17 AK Hornet, .22 K Hornet or .22 Hornet. Made as a repeater in early '90s, single-shot from 1997 to present. Model 40 has a 3-lug bolt and some Anschutz parts.

Model 36 Marksman

Premium bolt-action repeating rifle chambered for .22 LR cartridge. In Centerfire calibers .17 CCM and .22 Hornet. The 23" Shilen barrel is mated to a solid bar stock receiver. High grade walnut used in stocks that are fine-lined checkered. Manufactured from 1992 to 1999.

Model 36 Marksman Standard

NIB	Exc.	V.G.	Good	Fair	Poor
1100	900	700	500	300	200

Model 36 Marksman Classic

NIB	Exc.	V.G.	Good	Fair	Poor
1800	1200	800	600	400	200

Model 36 Marksman Custom Classic

NIB	Exc.	V.G.	Good	Fair	Poor
2000	1650	1150	850	600	300

Model 36 Marksman Western Classic

NIB	Exc.	V.G.	Good	Fair	Poor
4000	3400	2900	2450	—	—

Model 36 Marksman BR-50 w/Jewell Trigger

NIB	Exc.	V.G.	Good	Fair	Poor
1800	1450	1100	800	600	300

Model 36 Marksman IR-50-50 w/Jewell Trigger

NIB	Exc.	V.G.	Good	Fair	Poor
1800	1450	1100	800	600	300

Model 36 Marksman Featherweight w/Jewell Trigger

NIB	Exc.	V.G.	Good	Fair	Poor
1800	1450	1100	800	600	300

Model 38; Model 40 Classic

NIB	Exc.	V.G.	Good	Fair	Poor
1800	1500	1100	800	600	300

Model 38; Model 40 Custom Classic

NIB	Exc.	V.G.	Good	Fair	Poor
2000	1750	1250	850	600	300

Model 38: Model 40 Western Classic (octagon barrel)

NIB	Exc.	V.G.	Good	Fair	Poor
2900	2300	1750	1300	700	350

Model 38; Model 40 Mannlicher Model

Bolt-action rifle chambered for .17 AK Hornet, .22 K Hornet or .22 Hornet. Made as a repeater in early '90s, single-shot from 1997 to its being discontinued. Model 40 has a 3-lug bolt and some Anschutz parts.

NIB	Exc.	V.G.	Good	Fair	Poor
3650	3000	2450	1850	800	450

COOPERATIVA OBRERA
Eibar, Spain

Longines

A 7.65mm caliber semi-automatic pistol. Slide marked "Cal. 7.65 Automatic Pistol Longines".

NIB	Exc.	V.G.	Good	Fair	Poor
—	280	180	150	110	80

COPELAND, FRANK
Worcester, Massachusetts

Copeland Pocket Revolver .22

A .22 cartridge spur trigger revolver, with 2.5" barrel, 7-shot magazine, unfluted cylinder and lock notches on front. Frame is brass blued, walnut or rosewood grips. Barrel marked "F. Copeland, Worcester, Mass." Manufactured in 1860s.

NIB	Exc.	V.G.	Good	Fair	Poor
—	—	700	300	120	100

Copeland .32 Revolver

A .32-caliber spur trigger revolver, with 5-shot fluted cylinder and iron frame. Nickel-plated. Barrel marked "F. Copeland, Sterling, Mass." Manufactured in 1860s.

NIB	Exc.	V.G.	Good	Fair	Poor
—	—	700	300	150	80

COSMI, A. & F.
Torrette, Italy

Semi-Automatic

A 12- and 20-gauge top-break semi-automatic shotgun, with various barrel lengths and chokes. An 8-shot magazine and ventilated rib. Basically a custom-built made-to-order gun. There is a standard and deluxe model, with differences in degree of embellishment.

Standard Model

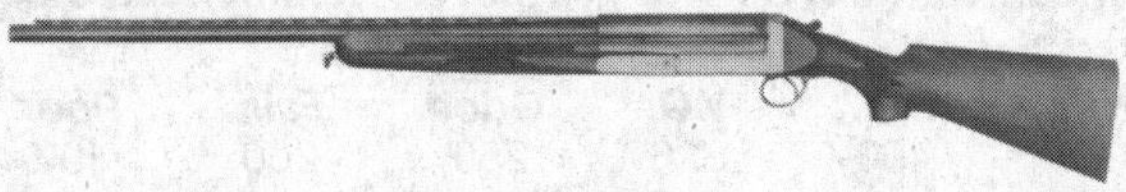

NIB	Exc.	V.G.	Good	Fair	Poor
14000	8500	4750	3250	2200	1500

Deluxe Model

NIB	Exc.	V.G.	Good	Fair	Poor
15500	9500	6000	4250	3250	1750

COSMOPOLITAN ARMS CO.
Hamilton, Ohio

Breech Loading Rifle

A .52-caliber single-shot percussion rifle, with 31" round barrel. Frame marked "Cosmopolitan Arms Co. Hamilton 0. U.S./Gross Patent". Blued, with walnut buttstock. Approximately 100 made between 1859 and 1862.

NIB	Exc.	V.G.	Good	Fair	Poor
—	—	7000	2750	780	450

COWLES & SON
Chicopee, Massachusetts

Single-Shot Antique

A .22- or .30-caliber single-shot spur trigger pistol, with 3.25" round barrel. Silver-plated brass frame blued, with walnut grip. Approximately 200 manufactured in 1865.

Courtesy Richard M. Kumor Sr.

Exc.	Fine	V.G.	Good	Fair	Poor
1500	780	510	250	100	70

CPA RIFLES
Dingman's Ferry, Pennsylvania 2000-Present; Schwenksville, Pennsylvania 1993-2000; Maple Glen, Pennsylvania 1987-1993

This company builds rifles based on Stevens Model 44-1/2. Several different configurations are offered, which are listed. Note: There are a number of special order options and custom features available at extra charge that will affect value.

Schuetzen Rifle

This model is usually built to order as to stock style, caliber, barrel size, shape and length. Many calibers are available from .22 Short to .40-65 Winchester. Sights are extra.

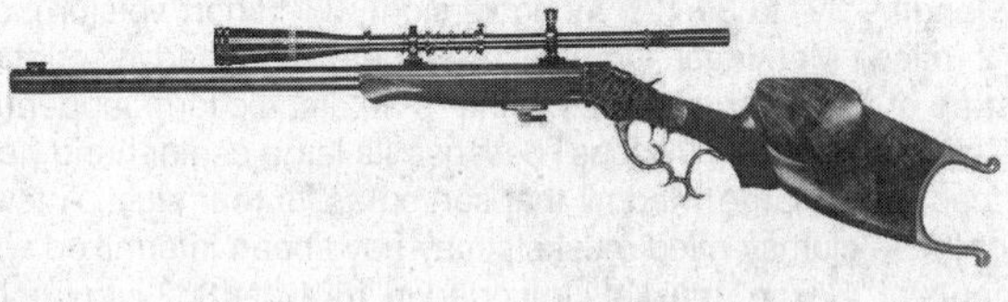

NIB	Exc.	V.G.	Good	Fair	Poor
2900	2250	1600	980	600	300

Silhouette Rifle

This model as produced is approved for BPCR competition by NRA. Has sporting-style stock with low comb or Model 52 style with more drop. Calibers are from .38-55 to .45-110, with other calibers available. Standard barrel #4 part octagon 30" in length. Sights are extra.

NIB	Exc.	V.G.	Good	Fair	Poor
2550	1900	1350	700	550	250

Sporting Rifle

This model uses a sporting-style stock, with standard forearm and schnabel tip. Offered in rimmed calibers including .222, .225, .22 Hornet and others. Standard barrels are round or part octagon, with weights from #1 to #5 and up to 28" in length. Sights are extra.

NIB	Exc.	V.G.	Good	Fair	Poor
2480	1900	1350	700	550	250

Varmint Rifle

As above, with a semi-beavertail forearm.

NIB	Exc.	V.G.	Good	Fair	Poor
2480	1900	1350	700	550	250

CRAUSE, CARL PHILLIP
Herzberg, Germany

Carl Phillip Crause (who signed his products only with his last name) operated a gun manufactory in Herzberg on the Harz in northwestern German kingdom of Hannover from the close of Napoleonic Wars until 1857. Main production of his factory was devoted to military arms for Hannover and surrounding principalities. Weapons of his manufacture included Brunswick

M1835 and M1848 rifles, Hannovarian M1850 and M1854 rifle-muskets and yager rifles, and M1840 and M1849 rifle-muskets of Hanseatic League (a coalition of north German states of Oldenberg, Hamburg, Bremen, and Lubeck). Latter two arms were subsequently altered to accept the elongated projectiles popular during 1850s. A few thousand evidently were imported into the United States and saw service during American Civil War.

Hanseatic League M1840 Rifled Musket (Antique)

Overall length 55.5"; barrel length 40.25"; caliber .70. Markings: on lockplate forward of hammer, "Crause in Herzberg" in script, the "s" in the archaic form, appearing as an "f". Of the 6,000 muskets of this type made, approximately half were sent to the United States in 1861 during the arms crisis that accompanied the outbreak of the American Civil War. A total of 2,680 of these were issued to Ohio and at least one regiment (the 56th Ohio) was armed with these rifled muskets. These arms were mistakenly identified during the period as being Saxon due to the similarity of the large squared off foresection of the lockplate.

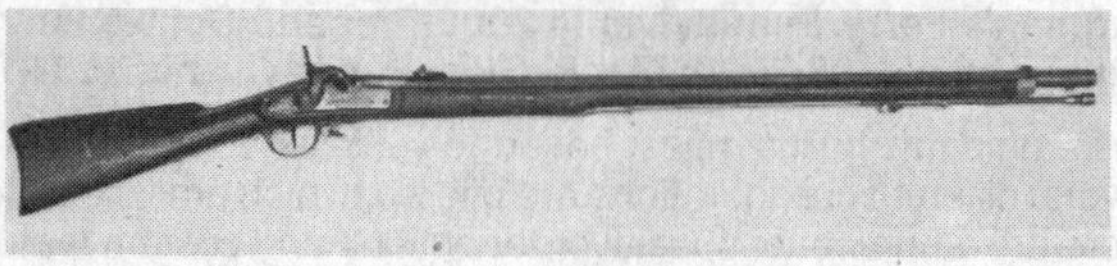

Courtesy Milwaukee Public Museum, Milwaukee, Wisconsin

Exc.	Fine	V.G.	Good	Fair	Poor
1700	800	590	380	200	140

Oldenberg M1849 Rifled Musket (Antique)

Overall lengths 55.5" to 56.625" (long version), 49.5" (short version); barrel lengths 39" to 39.125" (long version), 33" (short version); caliber .69-.72 (rifled). Markings: "Crause in Herzberg" inscribed in script on the backstrap of the hammer housing, the "s" in archaic form, appearing as an "f". Nicknamed the "Cyclops" because its large center-hung hammer is pierced with a large window that served as its rear sight. A few hundred of these clumsy rifled muskets may have been intermixed with the shipments of "Saxon" muskets imported in 1861 or 1862 into the United States during the American Civil War.

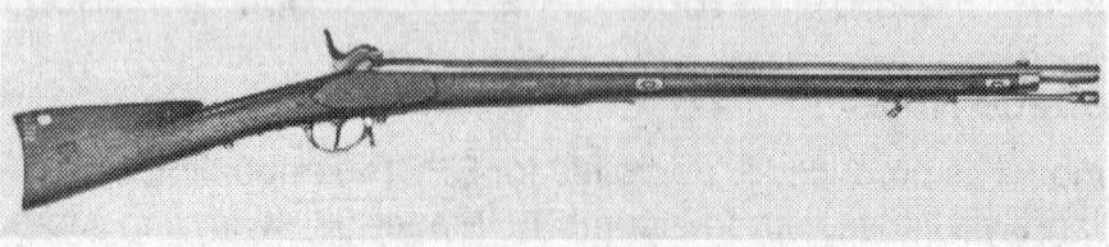

Courtesy Milwaukee Public Museum, Milwaukee, Wisconsin

Exc.	Fine	V.G.	Good	Fair	Poor
1980	850	620	400	250	170

CRESCENT F. A. CO.

Norwich, Connecticut

Company made good quality inexpensive single- and double-barrel shotguns at its Norwich works, beginning about 1892. It was bought by H&D Folsom of New York City, large importers and distributors of firearms and sporting goods, so they could add an American-made sidelock hammer side-by-side to their extensive range of imported guns. Crescent guns were offered in 12-, 16-, 20- and 28-gauges and later, 44XL shot caliber with Damascus twist laminated or Armory steel barrels depending on the shooter's wants. In 1898 VL&D said these were the best American hammer guns in the market for the money.

Huge quantities of these "Hardware Guns" were produced in a profusion of private brands as well as in Folsom's house brand "American Gun Co. of NY". In 1922 Crescent brand replaced "American Gun Co. of NY" and can be found on many thousands of doubles. In 1905 Crescent's first hammerless sidelock was introduced as the American Gun Co. "Knickerbocker" Model No. 6. This very popular model became the Crescent "Peerless" No. 6 in 1922. In 1928 it became the Crescent "Empire" No. 60 and in 1931 the Crescent-Davis "New Empire" No. 88, "New Empire" No. 9 and "Empire" No. 9.

Crescent was bought by J. Stevens Arms Co., Division of Savage Arms Corp. about 1930. It was merged with Davis-Warner Arms Corp. successors to N.R. Davis & Sons Co. and became Crescent-Davis Arms Corp. In 1932 the operation was moved to the Stevens plant at Springfield, Mass. where some sidelock doubles were assembled. Crescent-Davis brand guns remained in Steven's full line catalog until 1941, but from 1937 to 1941 the doubles sold in the C-D brand were on either Stevens or Davis boxlock frames.

DOUBLES

Triumph—Hammerless Boxlock

NIB	Exc.	V.G.	Good	Fair	Poor
—	800	650	420	300	200

Model 2655—Laminated Barrels Hammer Sidelock

NIB	Exc.	V.G.	Good	Fair	Poor
—	580	450	320	200	150

Model 2665—Damascus Barrels Hammer Sidelock

NIB	Exc.	V.G.	Good	Fair	Poor
—	580	450	320	200	150

Crescent American Hammer Gun No. 0—Hammer Sidelock

NIB	Exc.	V.G.	Good	Fair	Poor
—	400	320	250	200	100

American Machine Made 2641—Hammer Sidelock

NIB	Exc.	V.G.	Good	Fair	Poor
—	450	350	300	250	200

American Machine Made 2650—Hammer Sidelock

NIB	Exc.	V.G.	Good	Fair	Poor
—	580	450	320	200	150

American Machine Made 2660—Damascus Barrels Hammer Sidelock

NIB	Exc.	V.G.	Good	Fair	Poor
—	700	550	400	280	180

American Gun Co. NY No. 1 Armory—Hammerless Sidelock

NIB	Exc.	V.G.	Good	Fair	Poor
—	450	320	250	200	100

American Gun Co. NY No. 2—Hammerless Sidelock

NIB	Exc.	V.G.	Good	Fair	Poor
—	580	450	300	250	200

American Gun Co. No. 3—Damascus Barrels Hammer Sidelock

NIB	Exc.	V.G.	Good	Fair	Poor
—	700	550	420	300	250

American Gun Co. No. 4—Hammer Sidelock

NIB	Exc.	V.G.	Good	Fair	Poor
—	800	650	520	400	300

American Gun Co. No. 5—Damascus Barrels Hammer Sidelock

NIB	Exc.	V.G.	Good	Fair	Poor
—	920	800	650	450	350

Folsom Arms Co. No. 0 Armory—Hammer Sidelock

NIB	Exc.	V.G.	Good	Fair	Poor
—	450	320	250	200	100

Folsom Arms Co. No. 2—Hammer Sidelock

NIB	Exc.	V.G.	Good	Fair	Poor
—	580	450	300	200	150

Folsom Arms Co. No. 3—Damascus Barrel

NIB	Exc.	V.G.	Good	Fair	Poor
—	700	550	420	300	200

Knickerbocker No. 6 Armory—Hammerless Sidelock

Courtesy Nick Niles, Paul Goodwin photo

NIB	Exc.	V.G.	Good	Fair	Poor
—	450	320	250	200	100

Knickerbocker No. 7—Hammerless Sidelock

NIB	Exc.	V.G.	Good	Fair	Poor
—	450	320	250	200	100

Knickerbocker No. 8—Damascus Barrels Hammerless Sidelock

NIB	Exc.	V.G.	Good	Fair	Poor
—	580	450	300	250	200

New Knickerbocker Armory—Hammerless Sidelock

NIB	Exc.	V.G.	Good	Fair	Poor
—	450	320	250	200	100

New Knickerbocker WT—Hammerless Sidelock

Courtesy Nick Niles, Paul Goodwin photo

NIB	Exc.	V.G.	Good	Fair	Poor
—	500	380	250	200	150

New Knickerbocker Damascus Barrels—Hammerless Sidelock

NIB	Exc.	V.G.	Good	Fair	Poor
—	580	450	300	250	200

American Gun Co. Small Bore No. 28—Straight Stock Hammer Sidelock

NIB	Exc.	V.G.	Good	Fair	Poor
—	920	780	650	400	300

American Gun Co. Small Bore No. 44—Straight Stock Hammer Sidelock

NIB	Exc.	V.G.	Good	Fair	Poor
—	1020	820	700	480	350

American Gun Co. No. 0—Armory Straight Stock—Hammer Sidelock

Courtesy Nick Niles, Paul Goodwin photo

NIB	Exc.	V.G.	Good	Fair	Poor
—	400	300	250	200	100

American Gun Co. No. 28—Nitro Straight Stock—Hammer Sidelock

NIB	Exc.	V.G.	Good	Fair	Poor
—	920	780	650	400	300

American Gun Co. No. 44—Nitro Straight Stock—Hammer Sidelock

NIB	Exc.	V.G.	Good	Fair	Poor
—	1020	820	700	480	350

American Gun Co. Midget Field No. 28—Hammer Sidelock

NIB	Exc.	V.G.	Good	Fair	Poor
—	920	780	650	400	300

American Gun Co. Midget Field No. 44—Hammer Sidelock

Courtesy Nick Niles, Paul Goodwin photo

NIB	Exc.	V.G.	Good	Fair	Poor
—	1020	820	700	500	350

Crescent 1922 Model No. 66—Quail—Hammerless Sidelock

NIB	Exc.	V.G.	Good	Fair	Poor
—	700	550	400	280	180

Crescent Firearms Co. No. 0—Hammer Sidelock

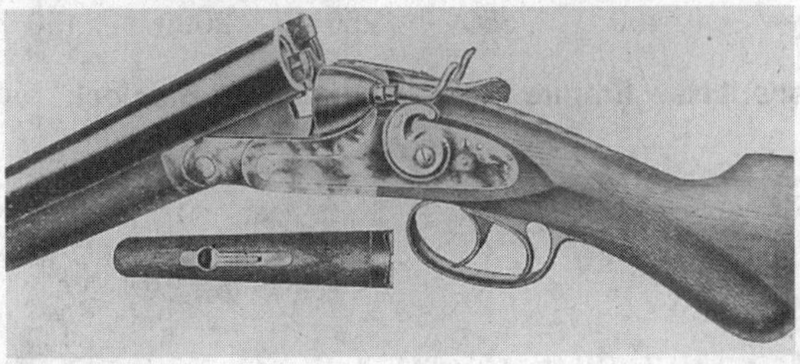

NIB	Exc.	V.G.	Good	Fair	Poor
—	450	350	250	200	150

Crescent Firearms Co. No. 0—Nickel—Hammer Sidelock

NIB	Exc.	V.G.	Good	Fair	Poor
—	600	450	350	250	200

Crescent Firearms Co. No. 6—Peerless—Hammerless Sidelock

NIB	Exc.	V.G.	Good	Fair	Poor
—	450	350	250	200	150

Crescent Firearms Co. No. 6E—Peerless Engraved—Hammerless Sidelock

NIB	Exc.	V.G.	Good	Fair	Poor
—	700	550	400	280	180

Crescent Firearms Co. No. 66—Quail—Hammerless Sidelock

NIB	Exc.	V.G.	Good	Fair	Poor
—	750	550	420	300	200

Crescent Firearms Co. No. 60—Empire—Hammerless Sidelock

Courtesy Nick Niles, Paul Goodwin photo

NIB	Exc.	V.G.	Good	Fair	Poor
—	500	400	350	300	200

Crescent Firearms Co. No. 6—Peerless—Hammerless Sidelock

Courtesy Nick Niles, Paul Goodwin photo

NIB	Exc.	V.G.	Good	Fair	Poor
—	450	350	300	200	150

Crescent Firearms Co. No. 44—Improved—Hammer Sidelock

NIB	Exc.	V.G.	Good	Fair	Poor
—	800	600	500	400	300

Crescent Empire No. 60—Hammerless Sidelock

NIB	Exc.	V.G.	Good	Fair	Poor
—	400	300	250	200	100

New Crescent Empire Red Butt—Hammerless Sidelock

NIB	Exc.	V.G.	Good	Fair	Poor
—	450	350	250	200	150

Crescent New Empire No. 88—Hammerless Sidelock

NIB	Exc.	V.G.	Good	Fair	Poor
—	450	350	250	200	150

Crescent New Empire No. 9—Hammerless Sidelock

Courtesy Nick Niles, Paul Goodwin photo

NIB	Exc.	V.G.	Good	Fair	Poor
—	400	300	250	200	100

Crescent Certified Empire No. 60—Hammerless Sidelock

NIB	Exc.	V.G.	Good	Fair	Poor
—	450	300	250	200	150

Crescent Certified Empire No. 9—Hammerless Sidelock

NIB	Exc.	V.G.	Good	Fair	Poor
—	500	380	300	250	200

Crescent Certified Empire No. 88—Hammerless Sidelock

Courtesy Nick Niles, Paul Goodwin photo

NIB	Exc.	V.G.	Good	Fair	Poor
—	580	450	400	350	300

Crescent Davis No. 600—Hammerless Boxlock

Courtesy Nick Niles, Paul Goodwin photo

NIB	Exc.	V.G.	Good	Fair	Poor
—	450	350	300	250	200

Crescent Davis No. 900—Hammerless Boxlock

NIB	Exc.	V.G.	Good	Fair	Poor
—	580	450	400	350	300

Single-Shot

Made in 12-, 16-, 20-, 28-gauge and .410. Barrel lengths were 26", 28", 30" and 32", with various chokes. Had an exposed hammer, fluid steel barrel and walnut pistol grip stock.

NIB	Exc.	V.G.	Good	Fair	Poor
—	200	120	100	80	50

Revolver

Typical S&W copy made by Crescent in Norwich, Connecticut. A top-break double-action, that was found blued or nickel-plated, with checkered black hard rubber grips. Cylinder held 5 shots. Chambered for .32 S&W cartridge.

NIB	Exc.	V.G.	Good	Fair	Poor
—	250	150	120	80	40

Crescent Certified Shotgun NFA, Curio or Relic

Crescent Certified Shotgun is a .410 smooth bore pistol with 12.25" barrel. Manufactured from approximately 1930 to 1932 by Crescent-Davis Arms Corp., Norwich, Connecticut, and possibly thereafter until 1934 by J. Stevens Arms Co., which purchased the company. In various distributor catalogs, it is termed "Ever-Ready" Model 200 and advertised with a blued frame. Specimens have been observed with "tiger-stripe" (like an H&R Handy-Gun) or Colt SAA or Winchester-type case-hardening. Total production is unknown but serial numbers ranging from 1305 to 3262 have been observed, suggesting it may have been fewer than 4,000. Treasury Department ruled .410 Crescent to be a "firearm" in the "any other weapon" category under NFA in 1934, when its retail price was about $11.

Barrel is marked proof tested .410 gauge on top and 2-1/2 IN SHELLS on the middle left side. Receiver's left side is stamped crescent certified shotgun/crescent-davis arms corporation/norwich, conn., u.s.a. Earliest guns also have .410 stamped at the top of the left side of the receiver near the breech, but this marking does not appear on later guns. It is a rather heavy (57 oz. unloaded) handgun. Note: Add $100 to $300 for original cardboard box. IMPORTANT! This gun is considered a Class III firearm by the Federal Government. This means that it is illegal to possess unless it has been previously registered with the BATFE. Any transfer must be registered with the BATFE. There is currently no way to legally register an unregistered Class III firearm.

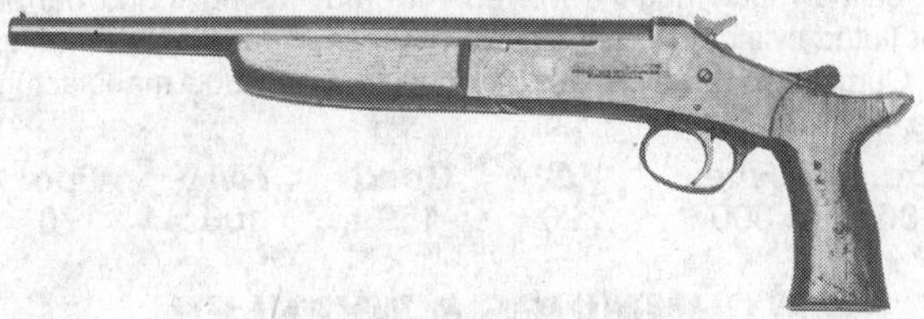

NIB	Exc.	V.G.	Good	Fair	Poor
—	980	720	550	350	250

Brand Names Used by Crescent Arms

American Bar Lock Wonder made for Sears, Roebuck & Co. American Boy made for Townley Metal & Hardware Co. American Gun Co. (H & D Folsom house brand) American Gun Company of New York. American Nitro Armory Gun Co., Baker Gun Co. (if no foreign proof marks) T. Barker New York — if a sidelock hammerless double without proofs. Bellmore Gun Co. Berkshire No. 3000 made for Shapleigh Hardware Co. of St. Louis, MO. Black Beauty — hammerless doubles. Bluefield ClipperBluegrass Arms Co. made for Belknap Hardware Co. of Louisville, KY. Blue WhistlerBridge Black Prince. Bridge Gun Co. Bridge Gun Works Bridgeport Arms Co. (if no foreign proof marks). Bright Arms Co. Canadian Belle Carolina Arms Co. made for Smith Wadsworth Hardware Co. of Charlotte, NC. Caroline Arms Central Arm Co. made for Shapleigh Hardware Co. of St. Louis, MO. Chatham Arms Co. Cherokee Arms Co. made for C. M. McClung Co. of Knoxville, TN. Chesapeake Gun Co. Chicago Long Range Wonder 1908-1918 made for Sears, Roebuck & Co. of Chicago, IL. Colonial Columbian New York Arms Co. Compeer made for Van Camp Hardware & Iron Co. of Indianapolis, IN. Connecticut Arms Co. Cumberland Arms Co. Crescent Fire Arms Co. Creve Cour (if no foreign proof marks) made for Isaac Walker Hardware Co. of Peoria, IL. Cruso-Daniel Boone Gun Co. made for Belknap Hardware Co. of Louisville, KY. Delphian Arms Co. (some models without foreign proof marks) made for Supplee-Biddle Hardware Co. of Philadelphia, PA. Delphian Manufacturing Co. (some models), Diamond Arms Co. (some models) made for Shapleigh Hardware Co. of St. Louis, MO. Dunlap Special made for Dunlap Hardware Co. of Macon, GA. E.C. Mac made for E.C. Meacham Arms Co. of St. Louis, MO. Elgin Arms Co. made for Strauss & Schram and Fred Biffar & Co. both of Chicago, IL. Elmira Arms Co. Empire Arms Co. made for Sears, Roebuck & Co. of Chicago, IL. Empire State Arms Co. Enders Oakleaf made for Shapleigh Hardware Co. of St. Louis, MO. Enders Special Service made for Shapleigh Hardware Co. Enders Royal Service made for Shapleigh Hardware Co. Essex made for Belknap Hardware Co. of Louisville, KY. Excel made for Montgomery Ward & Co. of Chicago, IL. Farwell Arms Co. made for Farwell, Ozmun & Kirk of St. Paul, MN. Faultless made for John M. Smythe Co. of Chicago, IL. Faultless Goose Gun made for John M. Smyth Co. of Chicago, IL. The Field after 1894: Folsom Arms Co. (also used by H & D Folsom on Belgian imports) F.F. Forbes (H & D Folsom house brand) Fort Pitt Arms Co. Fremont Arms Co. (also used on Belgian imports) Gold Medal Wonder-Greenfield (some models) made for Hibbard, Spencer, Bartlett & Co. of Chicago, ILH.B.C. (some models) made for Hudson's Bay Co. of Canada H.S.B. & Co. (some models) made for Hibbard, Spencer, Bartlett & Co. of Chicago, IL. Hanover Arms Co. (if no foreign proof marks) S.H. Harrington (if no foreign proof marks) Hartford Arms Co. made for both Simmons Hardware and Shapleigh Hardware Co. of St. Louis, MO. Harvard (H & D Folsom house brand)Hermitage (some models) made for Grey-Dusley Hardware Co. of Nashville, TN Hip Spe Bar (some models) made for Hibbard, Spencer, Bartlett & Co. of Chicago, IL. Hibbard (some models) made for Hibbard, Spencer, Bartlett & Co. of Chicago, IL. Howard Arms Co. made for Fred Biffar & Co. of Chicago, IL. Hudson (some models) made for Hibbard, Spencer, Bartlett & Co. of Chicago, IL. Hunter made for Belknap Hardware Co. Louisville, KY. Interstate Arms Co. made for Townley Metal & Hardware Co. of Kansas City, MO. Jackson Arms Co. made for C.M. McClung & Co. of Knoxville, TN. Joseph Arms Co. Norwich, Conn.K K and Keen Kufter (some models) made for Shapleigh Hardware Co. of St. Louis, MO. Kingsland Special and Kingsland 10 Star made for Geller, Ward & Hasner of St. Louis, MO. Kirk Gun Co. made for Farwell, Ozmun & Kirk of St. Paul, MN. Knickerbocker (up to 1915, H & D Folsom house brand), Knockabout (before 1925) made for Montgomery Ward & Co. of Chicago, IL. Knoxall (only hammerless doubles) Laclede Gun Co.Lakeside made for Montgomery Ward & Co. of Chicago, IL. Leader Gun Co. made for Charles Williams Stores of New York, NY Lee's Special and Lee's Munner Special made for Lee Hardware Co. of Salina, KS. Long Range Marvel, Long Range Winner, and Long Range Wonder made between 1893 to 1909 for Sears, Roebuck & Co. of Chicago, IL. F.A. Loomis Marshwood Massachusetts Arms Co. made before 1920 for Blish, Mizet and Silliman Hardware Co. of Atchison, KS. Mears (if no foreign proof marks) Metropolitan made for Siegal-Cooper Co. of New York, NY. Minnesota Arms Co. made for Farwell, Ozmun, Kirk & Co. of St. Paul, MN. Mississippi Arms Co. St. Louis (some models) made for Shepleigh Hardware Co. of St. Louis, MO. Mississippi Valley Arms Co. (some models) made for Shapleigh Hardware Co. of St. Louis, MO. Mohawk made for Glish, Mizet and Lilliman Hardware Co. of Atchinson, KS. Monitor R. Murdock, National Firearms Co. (some models) National Arms Co. hammer doubles (without foreign proof marks) and hammerless doubles made for May Hardware Co. of Washington, D.C. and Moskowitz and Herbach Co. of Philadelphia, PA. New Britain Arms Co.'s Monarch New Elgin Arms Co. New Empire New England (some models after 1914) made for Sears, Roebuck & Co.New England Arms Co. (some models) Newport Model CN made for Hibbard, Spencer, Bartlett and Co. of Chicago. Newport Model WN (some models) made for Hibbard, Spencer, Bartlett and Co. of Chicago. New Rival made for Van Camp Hardware and Iron Co. of Indianapolis, IN. New York Arms Co. made for Garnet Carter Co. of Chattanooga, TN. New York Machine Made (some models) New York Match Gun (some models) New York Nitro Hammerless, Nitro Bird made for Conover Hardware Co. of Kansas City, MO. Nitro Hunter made for Belknap Hardware Co. of Louisville, KY. Nitro King 1908 to 1917 made for Sears, Roebuck & Co. of Chicago, IL. Norwich Arms Co. Not-Noc Manufacturing Co. made for Belknap Hardware Co. of Louisville, KY and Canton Hardware Co. of Canton, OH. Osprey made for Lou J. Eppinger, Detroit, MI. Oxford made for Belknap Hardware Co. of Louisville, KY. Peerless (H & D Folsom house brand) Perfection made for H. G. Lipscomb & Co. of Nashville, TN. Piedmont made for Piedmont Hardware Co. of Danville, PA. Piedmont Arms Co. Pioneer Arms (if no foreign proof marks) made for Kruse and Baklmann Hardware Co. of Cincinnati, OH. Quail (H & D Folsom house brand) Queen City made for Elmira Arms Co. of Elmira, NY. Red Chieftan (model 60) made for Supplee Biddle Hardware Co. of Philadelphia, PARev-O-Noc (some models) made for Hibbard, Spencer, Bartlett & Co. of Chicago, IL. Rich-Con made for Richardson & Conover Hardware Co. Charles Richter (some models) made for New York Sporting Goods Co. of New York, NY. Rickard Arms Co. made for J. A. Rickard Co. of Schenectady, NY. Rival (some models) made for Van Camp Hardware and Iron Co. of Indianapolis, IN. Rocket Special Royal Service made for Shapleigh Hardware Co. of St. Louis, MO. Rummel Arms Co. made for A. J. Rummel Arms Co. of Toledo, OH. Ruso (if no foreign proof marks)St. Louis Arms Co. (sidelock hammerless doubles) made for Shapleigh Hardware Co. of St. Louis, MO. Seminole (hammerless) unknown Shue's Special made for Ira M. Shue of Hanover, PA. Smithsonian (some models) John M. Smythe & Co. made for John M. Smythe Hardware Co. of Chicago, IL. Southern Arms Co. (some models)Special Service made for Shapleigh Hardware Co. of St. Louis, MO. Spencer Gun Co. made for Hibbard, Spencer, Bartlett & Co. of Chicago, IL. Sportsman (some models) made for W. Bingham & Co. of Cleveland, OH. Springfield Arms Co. used until 1930. (H & D Folsom house brand). This brand was also used by Stevens and James Warner guns. Square Deal made for Stratton, Warren Hardware Co. of Memphis, TN. Star Leader (some models) State Arms Co. made for J.H. Lau & Co. of New York, NY. Sterling Arms Co. Sullivan Arms Co. made for Sullivan Hardware Co. of Anderson, SC. Superior (some models) made for Paxton & Gallagher Co. of Omaha, NE. Syco (some models) made for Wyeth Hardware Co. of St. Joseph, MO. Ten Star & Ten Star Heavy Duty (if no foreign proof marks) made for Geller, Ward & Hasner Co. of St. Louis, MO. Tiger (if no foreign proof marks) made for J.H. Hall & Co. of Nashville, TN. Townley's Pal and Townley's American Boy made for Townley Metal & Hardware Co. of Kansas City, MO. Trap's Best made for Watkins, Cottrell Co. of Richmond, VA. Triumph (some models) made for Sears, Roebuck & Co. of Chicago, IL. Tryon Special (some models) made for Edward K. Tryon Co.

of Philadelphia, PA. U.S. Arms Co. (if no foreign proof marks) made for Supplee-Biddle Hardware Co. of Philadelphia, PA. U.S. Field Utica Firearms Co. (some models) made for Simmons Hardware Co. of St. Louis, MO. Victor & Victor Special made for Hibbard, Spencer, Bartlett & Co. of Chicago, IL. Virginia Arms Co. made for Virginia-Carolina Co. of Richmond, VA. Volunteer (some models) made for Belknap Hardware Co. of Louisville, KY. Vulcan Arms Co. made for Edward K. Tryon Co. of Philadelphia, PA. Warren Arms Co. (if no foreign proof marks) Washington Arms Co. (some models) Wauregan (some models) Wautauga (some models) made for Wallace Hardware Co. Morristown, TN. Wildwood made for Sears, Roebuck & Co. of Chicago, IL. Wilkinson Arms Co. (if no foreign proof marks) made for Richmond Hardware Co. of Richmond, VA. Wilshire Arms Co. made for Stauffer, Eshleman & Co. of New Orleans, LA. Winfield Arms Co. (H & D Folsom house brand) Winoca Arms Co. made for Jacobi Hardware Co. of Philadelphia, PA. Witte Hardware Co. (some models) made for Witte Hardware Co. of St. Louis, MO. Wolverine Arms Co. made for Fletcher Hardware Co. of Wilmington, NC. Worthington Arms Co. made for George Worthington Co. of Cleveland, OH

CRISPIN, SILAS
New York, New York

Crispin Revolver (Antique)

A .32 Crispin caliber 5- or 6-shot revolver produced in limited quantities. Some are marked "Smith Arms Co., New York City. Crispin's Pat. Oct. 3, 1865". Most noteworthy feature of these revolvers is the cylinder is constructed in two pieces so that the belted Crispin cartridge can be used. It is believed that these revolvers were only made on an experimental basis, between 1865 and 1867.

Exc.	Fine	V.G.	Good	Fair	Poor
19000	7500	5000	2500	1000	700

CROSSFIRE
LaGrange, Georgia

This combination rifle/shotgun is manufactured by Saco Defense, Inc. for Crossfire. It is the first production firearm to combine the shotgun and rifle into a pump action multi-shot weapon.

MK-1

Designed to fire both .223 Rem. cartridge and 12-gauge 3" shotgun shell from two different barrels. A dual action long gun operated with a pump action. Overall length 38". Shotgun has 4-round detachable magazine; rifle has AR-15 type 5-round magazine. Shotgun barrel furnished with choke tubes. Offered in black oxide finish or camo finish. Weight about 8.6 lbs. Introduced in 1999. Note: Add $100 for camo finish.

NIB	Exc.	V.G.	Good	Fair	Poor
1200	1000	850	730	—	—

CRUCELEGUI, HERMANOS
Eibar, Spain

A 5mm, 6.35mm, 7.65mm and 8mm caliber double-action revolver. Trade names used were; Puppy, Velo-Mith, Le-Brong, Bron-Sport, C.H. and Brong-Petit.

NIB	Exc.	V.G.	Good	Fair	Poor
—	250	150	80	60	40

CUMMINGS, O. S.
Lowell, Massachusetts

Cummings Pocket Revolver (Antique)

A .22-caliber spur trigger revolver, with 3.5" ribbed round barrel and 7-shot fluted cylinder. Nickel-plated with rosewood grip. Barrel stamped "O.S. Cummings Lowell, Mass." Approximately 1,000 manufactured in 1870s.

Exc.	Fine	V.G.	Good	Fair	Poor
680	300	220	150	100	70

CUMMINGS & WHEELER
Lowell, Massachusetts

Pocket Revolver (Antique)

Similar to Cummings Pocket Revolver, with subtle differences: such as length of flutes on cylinder; size and shape of grip. Barrel slightly longer and marked "Cummings & Wheeler, Lowell, Mass.".

Exc.	Fine	V.G.	Good	Fair	Poor
750	350	250	150	100	70

CUSTOM GUN GUILD
Doraville, Georgia

Wood Model IV

Falling block single-shot rifle produced in a number of popular calibers. Barrel lengths from 22" to 28". Stock of select checkered walnut. Lightweight, about 5.5 lbs. Manufactured in 1984 only. Not often encountered on today's market.

NIB	Exc.	V.G.	Good	Fair	Poor
—	3750	2750	2500	1750	1000

CZ
(Ceska Zbrojovka)
Uhersky Brod, Czech Republic

Established by Karel Bubla and Alois Tomiska in 1919. This company later merged with Hubertus Engineering Company. In 1949, company was nationalized. CZ regularly exports 90 percent of its production to over 80 countries.

Note: As of 1998, CZ firearms have been imported exclusively by CZ-USA, a wholly-owned distribution subsidiary of Ceska Zbrojovka a.s. Uhersky Brod, (CZUB) of the Czech Republic.

Fox

A 6.35mm caliber semi-automatic pistol, with 2.125" barrel, tubular slide, folding trigger and no triggerguard. Fox and CZ are inscribed on slide. CZ logo on each grip plate. Blued, with plastic grips. Manufactured between 1919 and 1936.

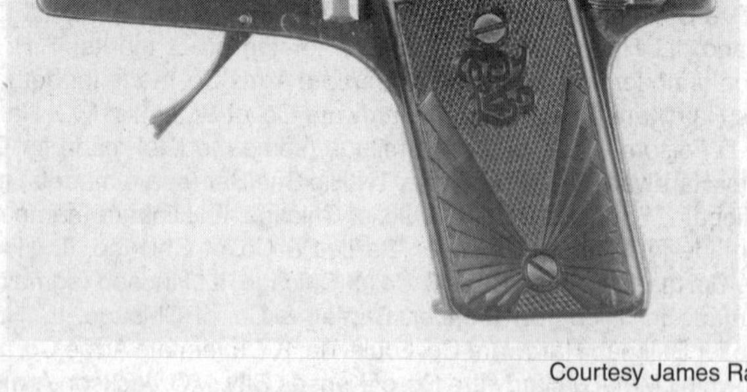

Courtesy James Rankin

NIB	Exc.	V.G.	Good	Fair	Poor
—	900	750	600	400	200

CZ 1921 Praga

Semi-automatic pistol in 7.65mm caliber. First service pistol manufactured in Czechoslovakia. Production began in 1920. Praga stamped on slide and on each grip plate for commercial models. Service models fitted with wood grips.

Courtesy James Rankin

NIB	Exc.	V.G.	Good	Fair	Poor
—	650	550	480	350	200

Army Pistol 1922 (Nickl-Pistole)

Designed by Josef Nickl of Mauser. First approved by Army in 1921. Chambered for .380 ACP (9mmKurtz/9x17mm) cartridge. Plagued by design problems. Produced only in 1922 and 1923. Fewer than 22,000 built.

NIB	Exc.	V.G.	Good	Fair	Poor
—	650	500	350	200	150

CZ 1922

Semi-automatic pistol in 6.35mm caliber. Very similar to Fox above. Has no sights but fitted with a conventional triggerguard. CZ stamped on slide and CZ logo on each grip plate. Grips are plastic or wood. Manufactured between 1922 and 1936.

Courtesy James Rankin

NIB	Exc.	V.G.	Good	Fair	Poor
—	550	450	350	300	200

CZ 1924

First large-production military pistol produced by CZ. Chambered for 9mmK cartridge. First of CZ models with wrap-around grips of both wood and plastic. CZ logo seen on plastic grips. Lanyard loop attached to base of butt. Manufactured from 1925 to 1932.

Courtesy James Rankin

NIB	Exc.	V.G.	Good	Fair	Poor
—	650	500	400	300	200

CZ 1927

Semi-automatic pistol chambered for 7.65mm cartridge. Marked same as CZ 1924, but cocking grooves on slide are cut vertically instead of sloped as on earlier model. This model was blued, with checkered wrap-around plastic grips. These early guns were beautifully made and marked, "Ceska Zbrojovka AS v Praze". After the war, these pistols continued in production until 1951. More than 500,000 manufactured.

Note: Some of these pistols were made with an extended barrel for the use of a silencer. This variation brings a large premium. Fewer than 10 CZ27s were made in .22-caliber. An expert opinion is suggested if a sale is contemplated. Note: Add 50 percent for Nazi-proofed.

NIB	Exc.	V.G.	Good	Fair	Poor
—	650	480	300	200	160

CZ 1936

A 6.35mm caliber semi-automatic pistol, with 2.5" barrel and double-action-only lockwork. Has plastic wrap-around grips, with CZ logo on each side. Replaced Model 1922 in 1936. Discontinued in 1940, because of wartime production.

Courtesy James Rankin

NIB	Exc.	V.G.	Good	Fair	Poor
—	450	350	300	200	100

CZ 1938

Semi-automatic double-action pistol in 9mmK caliber. Manufactured for Czechoslovakian military from 1938 to 1940. Barrel length 4.7"; weight about 32 oz.; magazine capacity 8 rounds. Wrap-around plastic grips, with CZ logo on each side.

Courtesy James Rankin

NIB	Exc.	V.G.	Good	Fair	Poor
—	550	500	400	300	200

CZ 1945

A small .25-caliber (6.35mm) pocket pistol that is double-action-only. Produced and sold after World War II. Modified version of CZ 1936. Approximately 60,000 built between 1945 and 1949.

Courtesy James Rankin

NIB	Exc.	V.G.	Good	Fair	Poor
—	350	300	250	180	120

CZ 1950

Blowback-operated semi-automatic double-action pistol chambered for 7.65mm cartridge. Patterned after Walther Model PP, with a few differences. Safety catch is located on frame instead of slide; triggerguard is not hinged as on Walther. Dismantled by means of a catch on side of the frame. Intended to be a military pistol designed by Kratochvil brothers, it proved to be underpowered and was adopted by the police. Few were released on the commercial market.

Courtesy James Rankin

NIB	Exc.	V.G.	Good	Fair	Poor
—	250	150	120	100	50

CZ 52

This 8-shot semi-automatic pistol was the Czech answer to the already obsolete Russian Tokarev design. From 1952 to 1954, 200,000 CZ 52 pistols were manufactured at two different locations in Czechoslovakia. The Czech-designed Model 52 with its phosphate finish and unique roller cam locking action was designed to handle high pressure 7.62x25mm Tokarev ammunition intended for sub-machine guns, logistically precluding the need to supply two different varieties of ammunition. Retained in service until 1982, the CZ 52 underwent several re-furbishing programs in the 1970s and 1980s. These pistols may be identified by a VOZ or VOP cartouche and two digits depending on the year. Such pistols indicate a high degree of usage and should be reduced by 10 percent versus unmarked variations. This model was replaced by the CZ 82 9mm Makarov in 1983.

NIB	Exc.	V.G.	Good	Fair	Poor
—	480	420	350	300	200

Model 1970

This model was an attempt to correct dependability problems with Model

50. There is little difference to see externally between the two except for markings and grip pattern. Production began during 1960s, ended in 1983.

Courtesy Rock Island Auction Company

NIB	Exc.	V.G.	Good	Fair	Poor
—	250	200	150	100	80

RIFLES

Model 52 (7.62 x 45) Carbine

NIB	Exc.	V.G.	Good	Fair	Poor
—	450	300	250	200	120

Model 52/57 (7.62 x 39)

NIB	Exc.	V.G.	Good	Fair	Poor
—	520	320	280	220	150

CZ-USA - Kansas City, Kansas

CZ first entered U.S. market in 1990 through various distributors. In January 1998, CZ-USA opened its office in Kansas City, Kansas. This office includes full sales and warranty service as well as an on-site gunsmith.

CZ Model 3

Bolt-action rifle introduced in 2004. Produced in U.S.A. Offered in both right- and left-hand configurations. Chambered for Winchester Short Magnums: .270, 7mm and .300. Walnut stock, with choice of stainless steel or blue finish. Fitted with 24" barrel. No sights. Magazine capacity 3 rounds; weight about 7.5 lbs. Note: Add $30 for stainless steel.

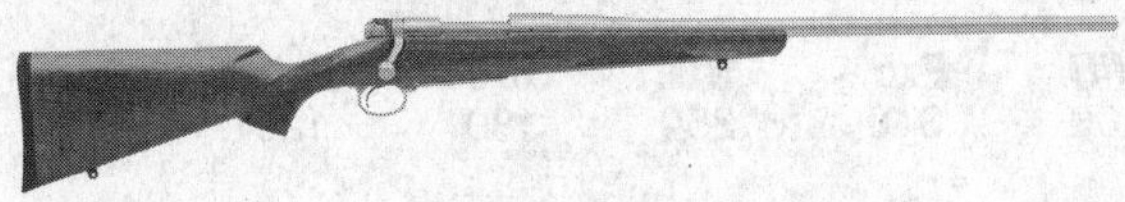

NIB	Exc.	V.G.	Good	Fair	Poor
970	680	580	400	200	100

CZ 452-2E LUX

Bolt-action rifle chambered for .22 LR or .22 Win. Magnum cartridge. Fitted with 24.8" barrel. Hooded front and adjustable rear sight. Trigger adjustable for pull. Pistol grip stock is a European-style Turkish walnut. Supplied with a 5-round magazine. Blued finish. Weight about 6.6 lbs. Note: Add $40 for .22 WMR.

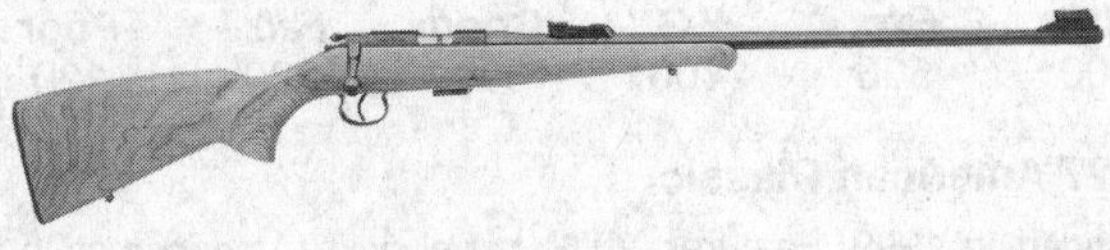

NIB	Exc.	V.G.	Good	Fair	Poor
490	350	220	150	120	100

CZ ZKM-452D

As above, with walnut Monte Carlo-style stock.

NIB	Exc.	V.G.	Good	Fair	Poor
—	420	300	220	150	100

CZ 452-2E ZKM Style

Similar to above, but chambered for .22 LR only. Fitted with black synthetic stock, matte nickel finish and 22.5" barrel. Weight about 6 lbs.

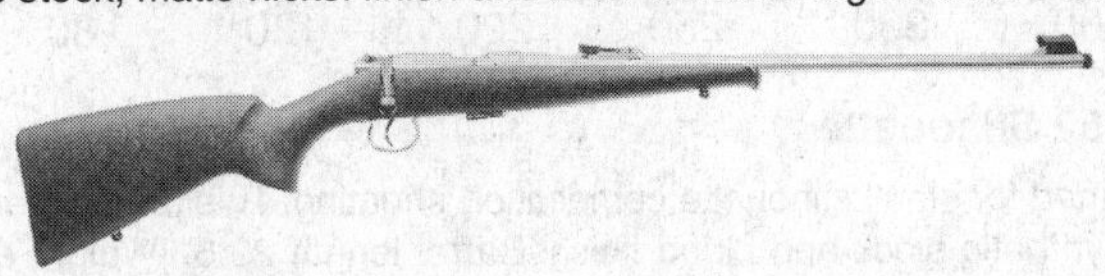

NIB	Exc.	V.G.	Good	Fair	Poor
480	320	220	180	120	100

CZ 452 Training Rifle

Chambered for .22 LR cartridge and fitted with 24.8" barrel. Detachable magazine has 5-round capacity. Beechwood stock. Adjustable sights. Weight about 5.4 lbs.

NIB	Exc.	V.G.	Good	Fair	Poor
380	280	180	150	120	100

CZ 452 American Classic

Chambered for .22 LR and .22 Win. Magnum cartridge. Features American-style Circassian walnut stock, with 18 lpi checkering. Fitted with 21" barrel, with recessed target crown. Supplied with a 5-round magazine. Blued finish. Weight about 6.5 lbs. Introduced in 1999. In 2005 .17 Mach 2 caliber was offered. Note: Add $40 for .22 WMR. or .17 HMR.

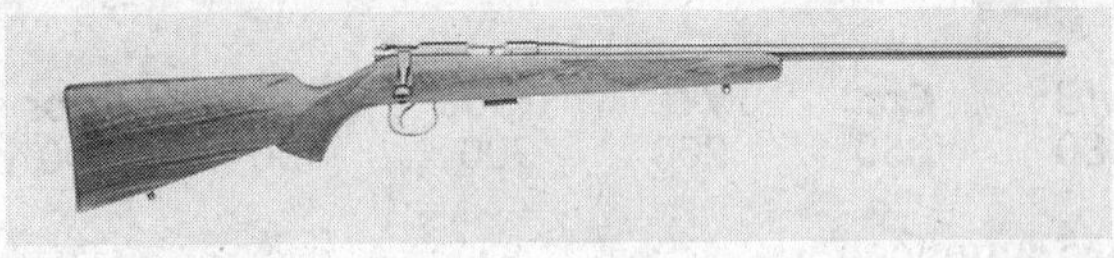

NIB	Exc.	V.G.	Good	Fair	Poor
460	350	250	150	10	100

CZ 452 Varmint

Bolt-action rifle chambered for .22 LR cartridge and fitted with 20" barrel. American-style Turkish walnut stock. Blued finish. Weight about 7.5 lbs. In 2005 .17 Mach 2 was offered. Note: Add $20 for .17 Mach 2 caliber.

NIB	Exc.	V.G.	Good	Fair	Poor
420	300	250	200	150	120

CZ 452 Scout

Designed for the younger shooter. Features shortened buttstock, 16.2" barrel and reduced weight receiver. Chambered for .22 LR cartridge. Open adjustable sights. Weight 3.9 lbs. Introduced in 2000.

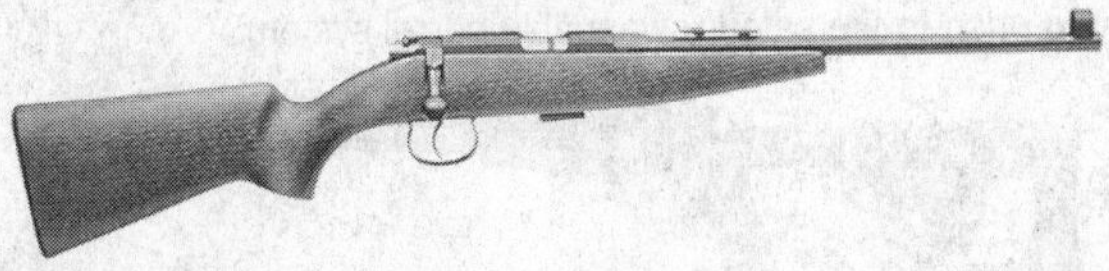

NIB	Exc.	V.G.	Good	Fair	Poor
280	200	150	120	100	80

CZ 452 Style

Chambered for .22 LR cartridge and fitted with 22.5" barrel. Features synthetic stock, with matte nickel finish. Magazine capacity 5 or 10 rounds. Weight about 5.3 lbs.

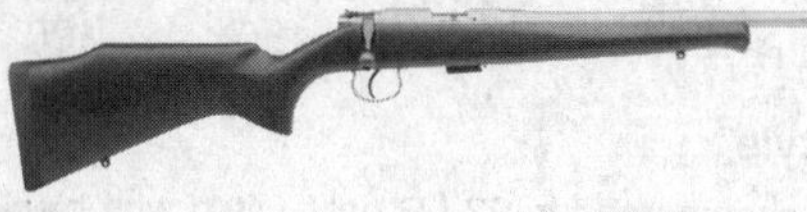

NIB	Exc.	V.G.	Good	Fair	Poor
400	300	250	220	120	80

CZ 452 Silhouette

Designed for small silhouette competition shooting. This .22-caliber rifle has synthetic stock and blued finish. Barrel length 22.5". Weight about 5.3 lbs.

NIB	Exc.	V.G.	Good	Fair	Poor
400	300	250	220	120	80

CZ 452 FS

Introduced in 2004. Chambered for .22 LR or .22 WMR cartridge. Fitted with full-length Turkish walnut stock. Barrel length 20.5". Adjustable sights. Weight about 6.5 lbs.

NIB	Exc.	V.G.	Good	Fair	Poor
480	350	260	200	150	100

CZ 455 American

Updated version of popular CZ 452. Action forged from steel billets. Walnut stock, cut checkering, oil-finish. No sights furnished, 20.5" barrel. Trigger adjustable for weight and pull. Detachable magazine. Available with CZ Switch Barrel Set in .22 LR and .17 HMR. Single-barrel guns chambered for .22LR, .22 WMR or .17 HMR. Thumbhole Varmint Model available, with thumbhole camo stock, single-set trigger, fluted barrel. Note: Add $150 Thumbhole Varmint Model; $100 Switch Barrel set.

NIB	Exc.	V.G.	Good	Fair	Poor
350	300	250	220	170	100

Model 457 Varmint Precision Chassis

Caliber: .22 LR. Capacity: 5. Barrel: 16.5 or 24 in., suppressor ready, cold hammer-forged, heavy. Stock: Aluminum chassis. Sights: None, integral 11mm dovetail. Weight: 7 lbs. Features: Fully adjustable trigger, receiver mounted push-to-fire safety, swappable barrel system.

NIB	Exc.	V.G.	Good	Fair	Poor
1100	900	775	—	—	—

CZ 457 Varmint Precision Trainer MTR

Caliber: .22 LR. Capacity: 5-round detachable box magazine. Barrel: 16.2-in. cold hammer forged Varmint weight. Sights: No iron sights, integral 11mm Dovetail. Length: 33.5 in. Weight: 7.1 lbs. Stock: Manners carbon-fiber stock with colored highlights. Forearm is recessed, drilled, and threaded for ARCA rail. Features: The upgraded Varmint Precision Trainer makes use of a barrel borrowed from the Match Target Rifle (MTR). Match chamber. Heavy barrel threaded at 1/2x28. Designed to provide the same look and feel as a full-size tactical rifle but with more economical training. American-style, two position, push-to-fire safety. 60-degree bolt rotation. Fully adjustable trigger. Same swappable barrel system as the Model 455. Competition-grade rimfire rifle.

NIB	Exc.	V.G.	Good	Fair	Poor
1450	—	—	—	—	—

CZ 512

Rimfire semi-automatic rifle. Dual guide rods for smooth operation. Hammer forged barrel, adjustable sights. Receiver machined for 11mm dovetail mounts. Field stripping via a coin modular design for simple takedown. Aluminum upper receiver with polymer lower. Beechwood stock. Chambered for .22LR and .22 WMR.

NIB	Exc.	V.G.	Good	Fair	Poor
400	350	300	220	180	120

CZ 513 Basic

Simplified version of CZ 452. Features plain beechwood stock, with no checkering. Iron sights. Chambered for .22 LR cartridge. Barrel length 21". Weight about 5.4 lbs. Introduced in 2004.

NIB	Exc.	V.G.	Good	Fair	Poor
280	200	170	120	100	80

CZ 511

Semi-automatic rifle chambered for .22 LR cartridge. Fitted with 22" barrel. Two-position rear sight. Supplied with an 8-round magazine. Cross bolt safety. Turkish walnut stock. Blued finish. Weight about 5.4 lbs.

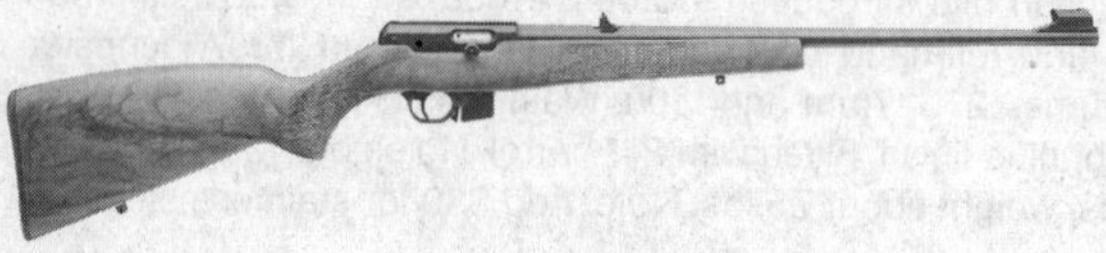

NIB	Exc.	V.G.	Good	Fair	Poor
400	340	250	180	120	80

CZ 527

Bolt-action chambered for .22 Hornet, .222 Rem. and .223 Rem. Rear sight adjustable. Checkered walnut stock. Barrel length 23.6"; magazine capacity 5 rounds; weight about 6.2 lbs.

NIB	Exc.	V.G.	Good	Fair	Poor
600	500	400	300	220	120

CZ 527 American Classic

Introduced in 1999. Features 20.5" barrel, with American-style Turkish walnut stock. Weight about 7.6 lbs. Blued finish. In 2005, this model chambered for .204 Ruger cartridge with 22" barrel. Note: Add $170 for English walnut stock; $200 for fancy American walnut; $30 for maple; $30 for laminate stock.

NIB	Exc.	V.G.	Good	Fair	Poor
600	500	400	300	200	100

CZ 527 Lux

Bolt-action center fire rifle. Chambered for .22 Hornet, .222 Rem. or .223 Rem. cartridge. Fitted with 23.6" barrel, with hooded front sight and fixed rear sight. Trigger is an adjustable single-set type. Turkish walnut stock in Bavarian-style. Blued finish. Supplied with a 5-round magazine. Weight about 6.6 lbs.

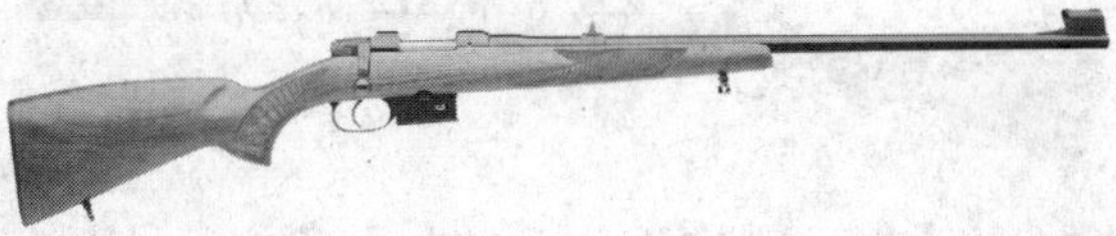

NIB	Exc.	V.G.	Good	Fair	Poor
600	480	350	250	150	100

CZ 527 Premium (Lux)

Introduced in 2000. Features hand fitted actions, fancy walnut stock, 18 lpi checkering and satin finish. Offered in .22 Hornet and .223 Rem. Barrel length 22". Magazine capacity 5 rounds. Weight about 6.2 lbs.

NIB	Exc.	V.G.	Good	Fair	Poor
650	520	400	300	180	120

CZ 527 FS

Similar to above model, but fitted with 20.5" barrel and Mannlicher-style stock. Blued finish. Weight about 6 lbs.

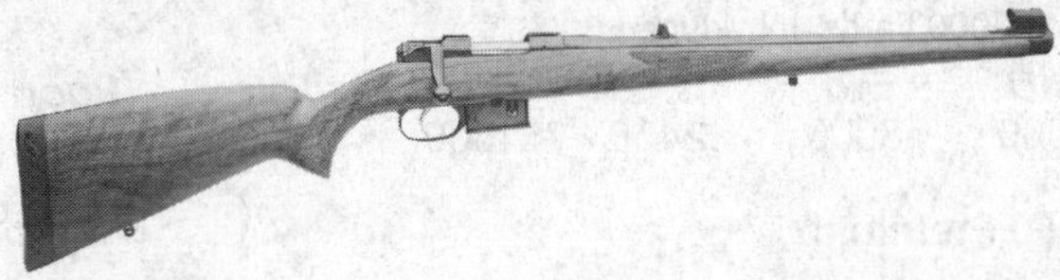

NIB	Exc.	V.G.	Good	Fair	Poor
690	520	400	300	180	120

CZ 527 Varmint

Chambered for .17 Hornet, .17 Remington, .204 Ruger, .222 Remington and .223 Remington cartridges. Fitted with 24" heavy barrel. Checkered Turkish walnut, gray laminate or black H-S Precision Kevlar stock. No sights. Detachable magazine. Weight about 7.2 lbs. Note: Add $50 for laminate; $150 for Kevlar stock.

NIB	Exc.	V.G.	Good	Fair	Poor
600	480	350	180	120	100

CZ 527 Carbine

Introduced in 2000. Chambered for 7.62x39 cartridge. Fitted with 18.5" barrel. Detachable magazine capacity 5 rounds. Open sights. Weight about 6 lbs.

NIB	Exc.	V.G.	Good	Fair	Poor
600	480	350	220	180	100

CZ 527 Prestige

Upgraded CZ 527 American, with jeweled bolt. Semi-fancy Turkish walnut, with hand-rubbed finish. Chambered for .22 Hornet or .223 Remington cartridges. Barrel length 21.9". Weight about 6.2 lbs. Introduced in 2001.

NIB	Exc.	V.G.	Good	Fair	Poor
880	680	600	480	280	150

CZ 537

Bolt-action rifle chambered for .270, .308 and .30-06 cartridges. Rear sight is adjustable. Stock checkered walnut. Barrel length 23.6". Magazine capacity 5 rounds. Weight about 7.9 lbs. Discontinued.

NIB	Exc.	V.G.	Good	Fair	Poor
600	480	380	250	200	100

CZ 550 American Classic

Similar to Model CZ 550. Chambered for .243, .308, .270 and .30-06 cartridges. Fitted with 20.5" barrel. American-style Turkish walnut stock. No sights. Supplied with 5-round internal magazine. Blued finish. Weight about 7.6 lbs. Introduced in 1999.

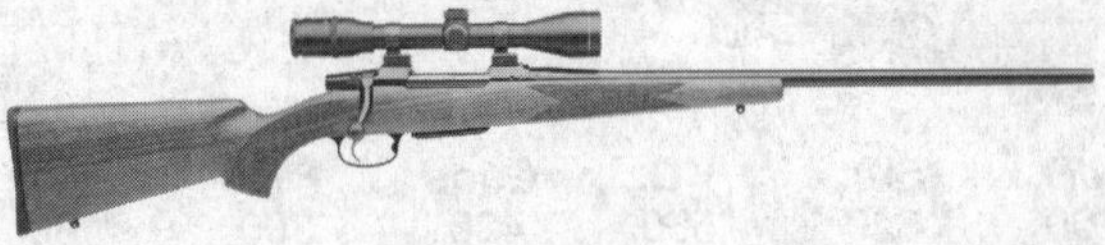

NIB	Exc.	V.G.	Good	Fair	Poor
620	500	400	300	200	100

CZ 550

Chambered for .243, .270, .30 and .30-06 cartridges. Bolt-action features 24" barrel and high comb walnut stock. No open sights. Weight about 7.25 lbs.

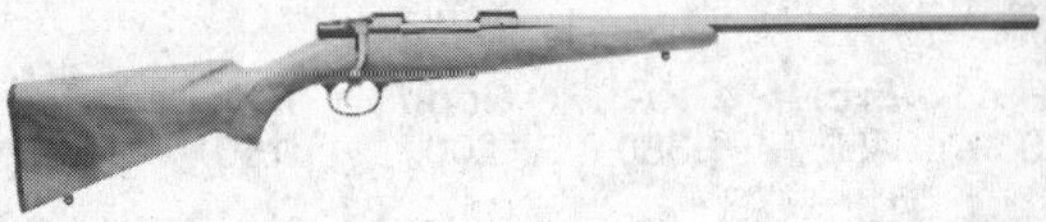

NIB	Exc.	V.G.	Good	Fair	Poor
700	520	400	300	200	100

CZ 550 Battue Lux

Chambered for .30-06 cartridge. Ramp rear sight. Barrel length 20.25". Checkered walnut stock. Weight about 7.25 lbs.

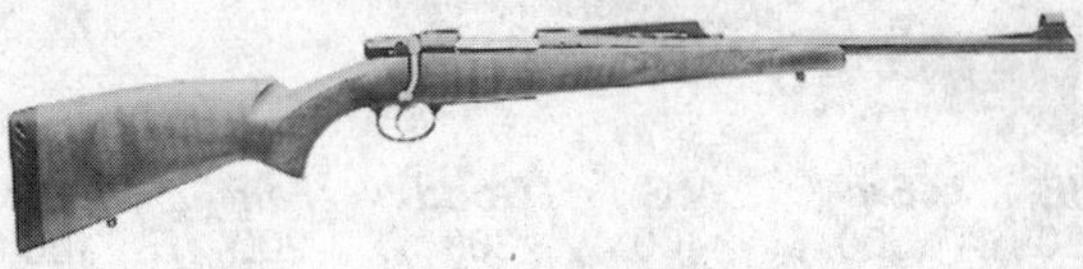

NIB	Exc.	V.G.	Good	Fair	Poor
700	520	400	300	200	100

CZ 550 FS Battue

Same as above, with full-length stock.

NIB	Exc.	V.G.	Good	Fair	Poor
750	600	500	380	200	100

CZ 550 Minnesota

Chambered for .270 Win. and .30-06 calibers. Barrel length 23.5". No sights. Supplied with recoil pad. Weight about 7.25 lbs.

NIB	Exc.	V.G.	Good	Fair	Poor
650	550	450	320	220	120

CZ 550 Minnesota DM

Same as above, with detachable magazine. Calibers .270 Win. and .308.

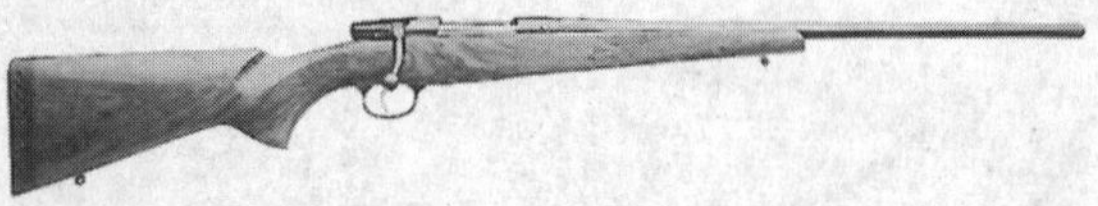

NIB	Exc.	V.G.	Good	Fair	Poor
720	580	480	350	220	120

CZ 550 Prestige

Similar to CZ 550 American. Added features of jeweled bolt, semi-fancy walnut and hand-rubbed finish. Chambered for .270 or .30-06 cartridges, with 23.6" barrel. Weight about 7.3 lbs. Introduced in 2001.

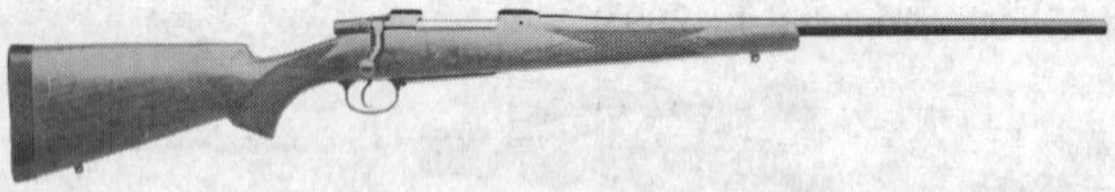

NIB	Exc.	V.G.	Good	Fair	Poor
700	620	550	420	300	180

CZ 550 Lux

Chambered for 7x57, 6.5x55 SE and 9.3x62 cartridges. Barrel length 23.6". Fixed magazine capacity 5 rounds. Bavarian-style stock, with Turkish walnut. Open sights. Weight about 7.3 lbs.

NIB	Exc.	V.G.	Good	Fair	Poor
580	450	380	200	150	80

CZ 550 Varmint

Chambered for .308 Win. cartridge. Fitted with 25.6" heavy barrel. No sights. Checkered walnut varmint-style stock. Ventilated recoil pad. Single-set trigger. Detachable magazine holds 4 rounds. Weight about 9.3 lbs. In 2004 an HS Precision Kevlar stock was also offered. Note: Add $200 for Kevlar stock.

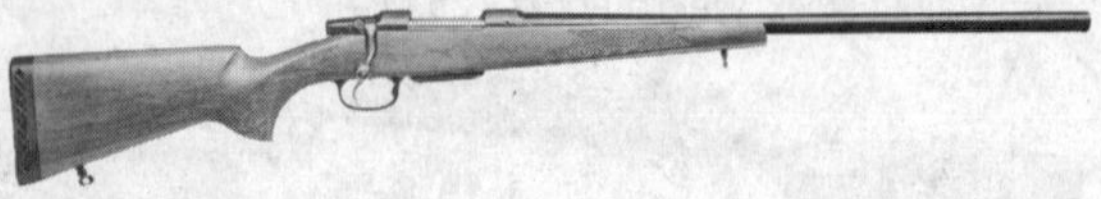

NIB	Exc.	V.G.	Good	Fair	Poor
650	500	400	300	200	100

CZ 550 Varmint Laminate

As above, with gray laminate stock. Offered in .22-250. Introduced in 2002.

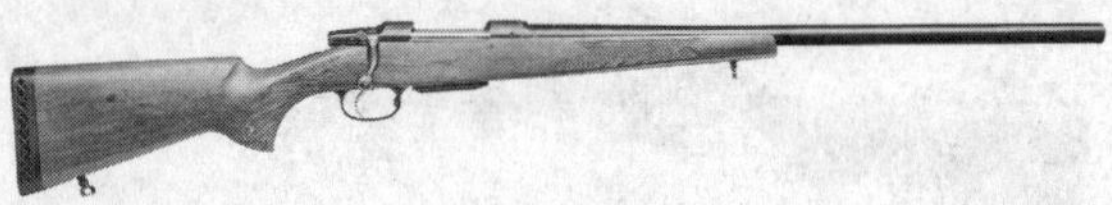

NIB	Exc.	V.G.	Good	Fair	Poor
750	600	450	350	200	120

CZ 550 Safari Magnum

Chambered for .300 Win. Magnum, .375 H&H, .458 Win. Magnum and .416 Rigby cartridges. Bolt-action rifle fitted with 25" barrel and 5-round internal magazine. Sights are one standing and two folding express rear, with hooded front sight. Blued finish. Bavarian-style Turkish walnut stock. Weight about 9.2 lbs.

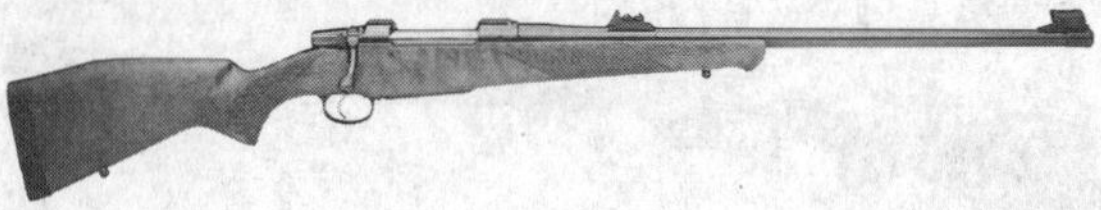

NIB	Exc.	V.G.	Good	Fair	Poor
920	750	500	400	300	200

CZ 550 American Safari Magnum

Introduced in 2004. Similar to Safari Magnum above, with American pattern stock. Offered with American walnut, brown laminate or camo laminate and fancy American walnut stock. Note: Add $200 for laminate stock; $600 for fancy wood stock.

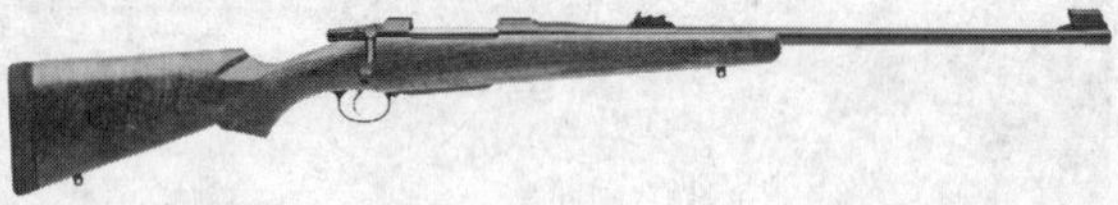

NIB	Exc.	V.G.	Good	Fair	Poor
920	750	500	400	300	200

CZ 550 Ultimate Hunting Rifle

Similar to CZ 550 Safari Magnum, but chambered for .300 Win. Magnum only. Custom select wood and 23.6" barrel. Accuracy guaranteed at one MOA to 1000 yards. Introduced 2006.

NIB	Exc.	V.G.	Good	Fair	Poor
3600	3000	2450	1500	680	300

CZ 550 Premium

Introduced in 2000. Features hand-fitted action, fancy walnut stock and 18 lpi checkering. Chambered for .30-06 and .270 Win. cartridges. Barrel length 23.6". Weight about 7.3 lbs.

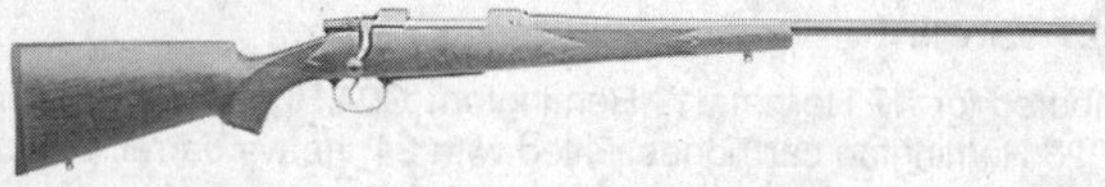

NIB	Exc.	V.G.	Good	Fair	Poor
920	750	500	400	300	200

CZ 550 Medium Magnum

Designed around a mid-sized Magnum action. Fitted with 23.6" barrel. Fixed magazine capacity of 5 rounds. Chambered for .300 Win. Magnum or 7mm Rem. Magnum. Single-set trigger and adjustable rear sight. Weight about 7.3 lbs. Introduced in 2001.

NIB	Exc.	V.G.	Good	Fair	Poor
700	580	420	300	200	100

CZ 550 Safari Classic Custom

Chambered for .404 Jeffery, .450 Rigby or .505 Gibbs. Fancy grade checkered walnut stock. Single-set trigger. Express sights. Note: Add $100 for .505 Gibbs.

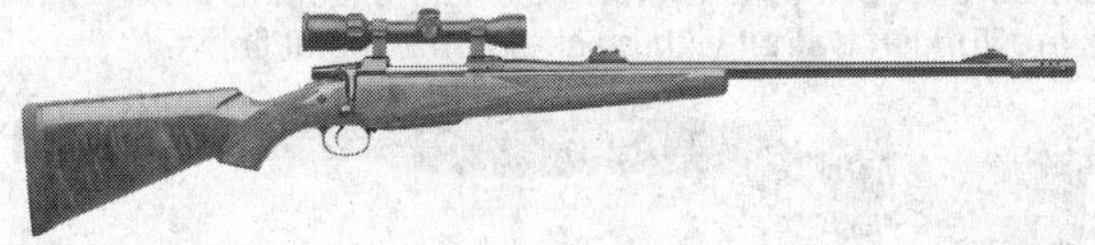

NIB	Exc.	V.G.	Good	Fair	Poor
2400	2000	1400	750	400	300

CZ 557

Bolt-action carbine with 20.5" barrel, steel receiver with integral scope rails. Oil-finished walnut or synthetic stock with cheekpiece. Adjustable rear and fiber optic front sights. Chambered in .243 Win., 6.5x55, .270 Win., .308 Win., .30-06. Introduced in 2014.

NIB	Exc.	V.G.	Good	Fair	Poor
700	600	520	420	350	300

CZ 584

Combination 12-gauge/7x57Rmm, .222- or .308-caliber over/under combination rifle/shotgun. Automatic ejectors, 24.5" ventilated rib barrels and single triggers. Blued, with walnut stock.

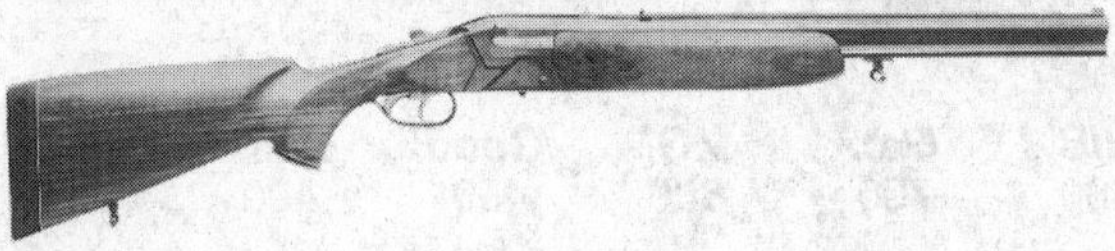

NIB	Exc.	V.G.	Good	Fair	Poor
1000	780	600	500	400	200

CZ ZKK 600

Offered in 7x57mm, 7x64mm, .270 or .30-06. Features Mauser-type bolt-action, with controlled feed, non-rotating extractor and dovetailed receiver in three action lengths. Note: Add $100 for pop-up receiver sight that was discontinued in 1977.

NIB	Exc.	V.G.	Good	Fair	Poor
750	620	500	420	320	180

CZ ZKK 601

As above, in .243- or .308-caliber.

NIB	Exc.	V.G.	Good	Fair	Poor
700	600	500	420	320	180

CZ ZKK 602

As above, in .300 H&H, .375 H&H, .458 Win. Magnum.

NIB	Exc.	V.G.	Good	Fair	Poor
800	700	600	500	400	200

CZ 700 Sniper M1

Introduced in 2001. Chambered for .308 Winchester cartridge. Fitted with 25.6" heavy barrel. Receiver has permanently attached Weaver rail. Laminated stock has adjustable cheekpiece and buttplate, with adjustable trigger. Magazine capacity 10 rounds. Weight about 12 lbs.

NIB	Exc.	V.G.	Good	Fair	Poor
2350	1800	1300	700	400	200

CZ 750 Sniper

Bolt-action rifle; .308 Win., 10-shot detachable magazine, 26" blued barrel, two scope mount systems, polymer stock, weight 12 lbs. Introduced 2006.

NIB	Exc.	V.G.	Good	Fair	Poor
2000	1750	1550	1050	600	320

CZ 550 Urban Sniper

Compact profile in a modern sniper rifle. Free floating 16" barrel, with target crown. Surefire muzzle brake, with suppressor compatibility. Bell & Carlson fiberglass stock, aluminum bedding block, oversized bolt handle and single-stage trigger. Available with 5- or 10-round magazine. Chambered for .308 Winchester, with other calibers on request.

NIB	Exc.	V.G.	Good	Fair	Poor
2000	1720	1400	950	500	300

CZ 600 Alpha

Calibers: .223 Rem, .224 Valkyrie, 6mm Creed, 6.5 Creed, .308 Win., 6.5 PRC, 7.62x39, .30-06, .300 Win. Mag. Capacity: 3 or 5 rounds depending on caliber, detachable locking magazine. Barrel: 18-, 20-, or 22-in. semi-heavy, cold hammer forged. Weight: 6.6–7.5 lbs. Length: 40.7–43.1 in. Stock: Black polymer with serrated grip zones. Sights: No iron sights. Integral, two-piece bases. Features: CZ's new 600 family of bolt-action rifles. The Alpha is essentially the base model. Threaded, suppressor ready. Adjustable, single-stage trigger. Sling studs. Sub-MOA guarantee.

NIB	Exc.	V.G.	Good	Fair	Poor
680	—	—	—	—	—

CZ 600 Lux

Calibers: .223 Rem, .308 Win., .30-06, .300 Win. Mag. Capacity: 3 or 5 rounds depending on caliber, detachable locking magazine. Barrel: 20 or 24 in. light cold-hammer forged, threaded. Weight: 6.8–8.6 lbs. Length: 41–44 in. Stock: Oil-finished, select-grade Walnut, Bavarian-style with fish-scale checkering. Sights: Rear adjustable iron sights with fiber-optic front. Drilled and tapped for Remington 700 mounts. Features: CZ's new 600 family of bolt-action rifles. The Lux fits a steel receiver to a European-style Walnut stock. Matching wooden bolt knob. Adjustable, single-stage trigger. Vertical, two-position tang safety. Sling studs. Sub-MOA guarantee.

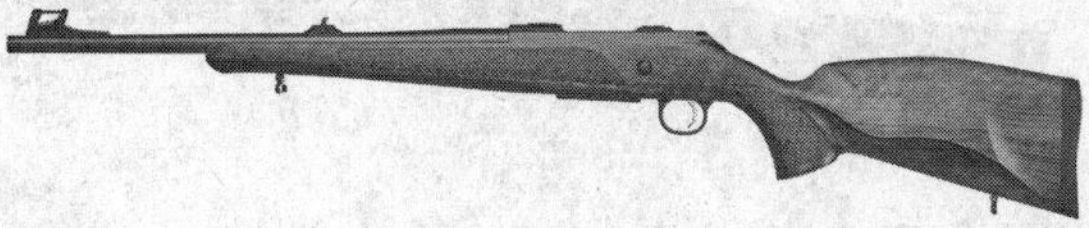

NIB	Exc.	V.G.	Good	Fair	Poor
800	—	—	—	—	—

CZ 600 Range

CZ 600 Range
Calibers: 6mm Creedmoor, .308 Win. Capacity: 5-round detachable magazine. Barrel: 24 in. heavy, cold hammer forged, threaded. Weight: 10 lbs. Length: 44.9 in. Stock: Laminate Precision with tool-less adjustable comb. Sights: None. Drilled and tapped for Remington 700 mounts. Features: CZ's new 600 family of bolt-action rifles. The Range is designed as the precision shooting and varmint hunting model. Adjustable, single-stage trigger. Vertical two-position safety. Suppressor ready. Dual forend sling studs. QD studs beneath the forend and sockets on each side. Five-shot Sub-3/4 MOA guarantee at 100 meters.

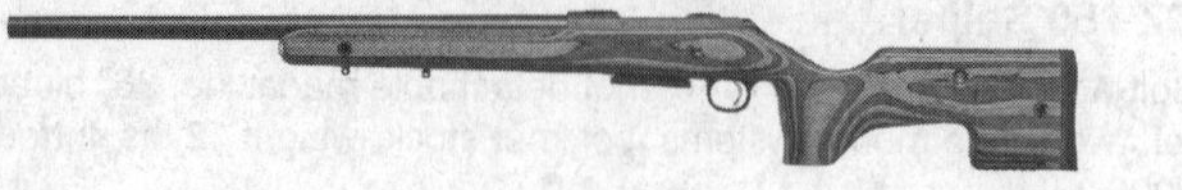

NIB	*Exc.*	*V.G.*	*Good*	*Fair*	*Poor*
1080	—	—	—	—	—

CZ 600 Trail

Calibers: .223 Rem, 7.62x39. Capacity: 10-round detachable magazine. The .223 Rem. uses AR-style mags; 7.62 uses CZ Bren 2 mags. Barrel: 16.2-in. semi-heavy, cold hammer forged, threaded. Weight: 6.1 lbs. Length: Adjustable from 27.2–35 in. Stock: Polymer black PDW-style, four-position adjustable; Aluminum forend with M-LOK slots. Sights: None. Picatinny rail. Features: CZ's new 600 family of bolt-action rifles. The Trail is designed as a light, compact that will feel familiar to those accustomed to AR-platforms. Built on an aluminum action with a polymer chassis. Adjustable, two-stage trigger. Suppressor ready. Ambidextrous mag release and AR-style safety.

NIB	*Exc.*	*V.G.*	*Good*	*Fair*	*Poor*
1080	—	—	—	—	—

SHOTGUNS

OVER-UNDERS

All-American

Introduced 2017. CNC-cut throughout. Buttstock has a 4-way comb combined with adjustable buttplate hardware (cast, toe, LOP). Lower bore axis of the bottom barrel, which fires first. 30" or 32" barrels, lengthened forcing cones, factory ported. Extended chokes (mid-thread pattern), a black chrome-finish action, select wood. C, IC, LM, M, and IM chokes.

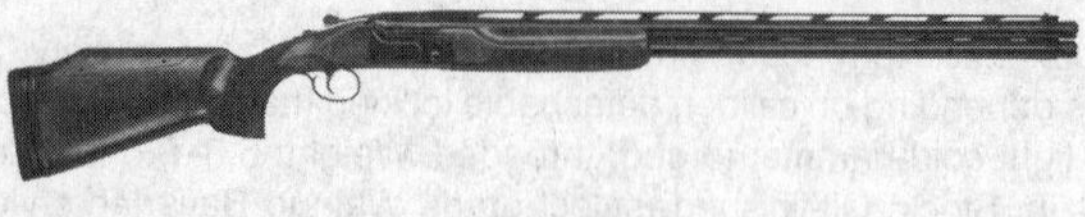

NIB	*Exc.*	*V.G.*	*Good*	*Fair*	*Poor*
2250	2150	1950	1750	1550	—

Drake

NIB	*Exc.*	*V.G.*	*Good*	*Fair*	*Poor*
600	500	400	300	—	—

Quail

Pheasants Forever 2019 Youth Gun of the Year. Nearly identical to the CZ Drake, with the Quail having a slightly shorter length of pull. Chambered in 20 gauge with 28" barrels, single extractor, five choke tubes. Stocks are Turkish walnut with black-chrome metal finish.

NIB	*Exc.*	*V.G.*	*Good*	*Fair*	*Poor*
550	450	350	250	—	—

Reaper

NIB	*Exc.*	*V.G.*	*Good*	*Fair*	*Poor*
850	750	650	550	450	—

CZ 581

A 12-gauge over/under double-barrel boxlock shotgun, with 28" ventilated rib barrels, single trigger and automatic ejectors. Blued, with walnut stock.

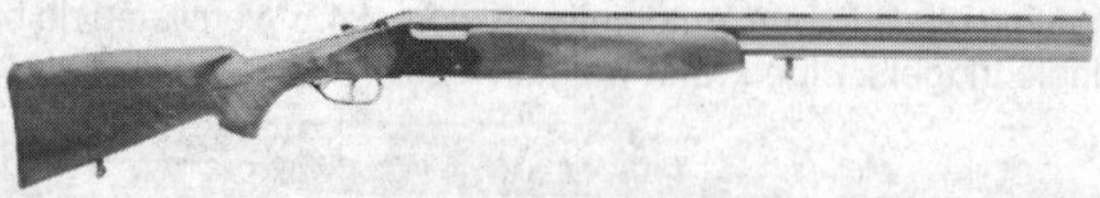

NIB	*Exc.*	*V.G.*	*Good*	*Fair*	*Poor*
880	700	600	450	400	200

Model 206

NIB	*Exc.*	*V.G.*	*Good*	*Fair*	*Poor*
1450	1350	1250	1050	850	—

Redhead

This over/under available in 12, 20 or 28 gauge, with choke tubes and .410 bore with fixed chokes. Barrel lengths 26" or 28". Single-selective trigger with extractors on 28 gauge and .410 bore. Checkered walnut stock with pistol grip. Receiver finish is silver. Weight from 6 lbs. to 8 lbs., depending on gauge. Premier Reduced Length has a shorter length of pull (13" instead of 14.5") as well as shorter 24" barrels. Only available in 20 gauge.

NIB	*Exc.*	*V.G.*	*Good*	*Fair*	*Poor*
1250	1100	980	800	—	—

Redhead Premier Target

Comes fitted with a special Monte Carlo stock with a right-hand palm swell. Has 30" barrels and a 10mm stepped rib designed for rising trap targets. 5 extended choke tubes (C, IC, M, IM, Full).

NIB	*Exc.*	*V.G.*	*Good*	*Fair*	*Poor*
1350	1250	1150	1000	900	—

CZ Sporter

This dedicated sporting clays over/under is a 12-gauge, with adjustable comb stock and forend of #3 Circassian walnut. Features chrome-lined barrels back-bored to .736 and automatic ejectors. Barrels are 30" or 32". Five choke tubes included. Weight about 9 lbs.

NIB	Exc.	V.G.	Good	Fair	Poor
1250	1100	980	800	—	—

Redhead Premier 16 Gauge

28-in. barrel.

NIB	Exc.	V.G.	Good	Fair	Poor
920	—	—	—	—	—

Redhead Premier Project Upland

Gauge: 12, 20, 28 ga. Barrel: 28 in. with 8mm flat vent rib. Length: 43.75 in. Weight: 6.9–7.7 lbs. Stock: Grade III Turkish Walnut. Features: Project Upland hunting O/U with silver satin chrome receiver finish. One piece CNC'd action, 3-in. chamber. Gloss black chrome barrel finish. Brass front bead. Single mechanical trigger selectable for barrels. Manual tang safety. Patent pending magnetic chambers. Includes five chokes (F, IM, M, IC, C).

NIB	Exc.	V.G.	Good	Fair	Poor
1390	—	—	—	—	—

Canvasback

Over/under offered in 12- or 20-gauge. Fitted with 26" or 28" barrels, with choke tubes. Single-selective trigger with extractors. Black receiver finish. Weight about 7.5 lbs.

NIB	Exc.	V.G.	Good	Fair	Poor
650	550	450	350	200	—

Mallard

This 12- or 20-gauge over/under gun fitted with double triggers and extractors. Barrel length 28". Checkered walnut stock with pistol grip. Coin finish receiver.

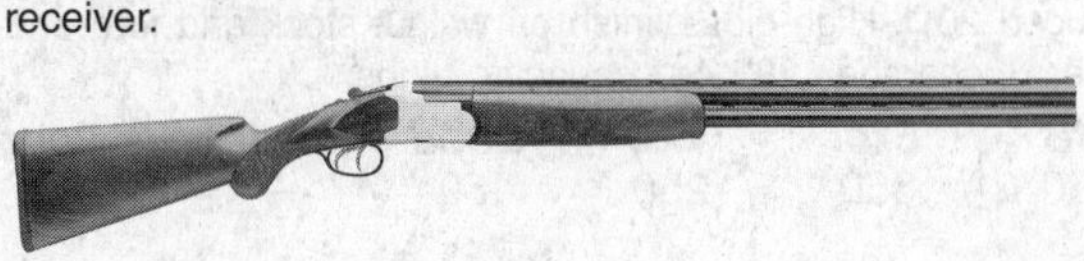

NIB	Exc.	V.G.	Good	Fair	Poor
500	400	300	200	—	—

Sterling

Versions include SCTP, Upland, Upland Sterling Southpaw, Lady. SCTP has 4-way adjustable comb and increased pitch (around 8 degrees) to make it more comfortable to shoulder. This classy shotgun is built on the Upland Sterling receiver and is chambered in 12 gauge with 28" barrels.

NIB	Exc.	V.G.	Good	Fair	Poor
900	800	700	600	500	400

Upland

Versions include Ultralight and Ultralight. 6 lbs. available in 26" and 28" models. CNC-cut aluminum alloy frame. Lacks mid-rib between the barrels to save weight.

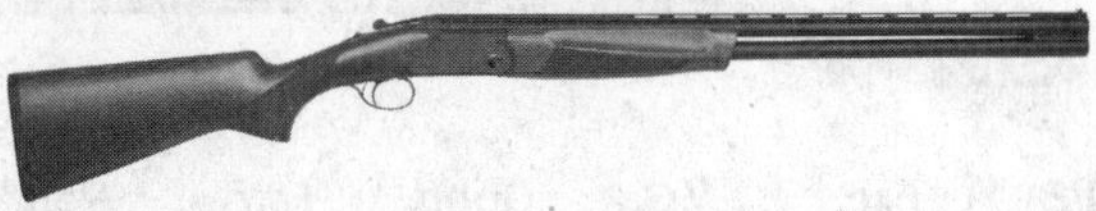

NIB	Exc.	V.G.	Good	Fair	Poor
700	600	500	400	—	—

Wingshooter Elite

Replaced Wingshooter model in 2014.

NIB	Exc.	V.G.	Good	Fair	Poor
950	850	750	650	550	450

Woodcock

Available in 12-, 20-, 28-gauge and .410 bore, with 26" or 28" barrel, choke tubes except for fixed chokes on .410 bore. Single-selective trigger with ejectors except 12- and 20-gauge. Receiver case colored with sideplate. Checkered walnut stock with pistol grip. Note: Add $75 for 28-gauge and .410 bore.

NIB	Exc.	V.G.	Good	Fair	Poor
1100	1000	900	800	700	600

Woodcock Custom Grade

Similar to Woodcock, but stocked with Grade IV walnut. Offered only in 20-gauge with 28" barrels.

NIB	Exc.	V.G.	Good	Fair	Poor
1500	1250	980	600	400	200

Upland Ultralight All-Terrain

Gauges: 12 ga., 3 in., 20 ga., 3 in. Barrels: 28 in., 30 in. Stock: Walnut, various styles. Features: CZ's new All-Terrain series encompasses five existing shotgun models. The new package includes upgraded wood, OD Green Cerakote finish on all metalwork, as well as a set of rare earth magnets added to the extractor/ejectors of the SxS and O/U models to keep shells from dropping out while handling a dog or working in the blind.

NIB	Exc.	V.G.	Good	Fair	Poor
820	—	—	—	—	—

Redhead Premier All-Terrain

NIB	Exc.	V.G.	Good	Fair	Poor
1040	—	—	—	—	—

Drake All-Terrain

NIB	Exc.	V.G.	Good	Fair	Poor
700	—	—	—	—	—

SEMI-AUTO SHOTGUNS

CZ 1012

Gauge: 12 ga., 3 in. Capacity: 4+1. Barrel: 28 in., 8mm flat ventilated rib. Weight: 6.5-6.9 lbs. Length: 47 in. Stock: Options in either Turkish walnut or black synthetic. Features: The company's first gas-less, inertia-driven semi-automatic wears a gloss-black chrome barrel finish along with a choice of three receiver finishes: standard blued, bronze or gray. Oversized controls ideal for use when wearing gloves. Cross-bolt safety located at front of triggerguard. Includes five chokes (F, IM, M, IC, C). Addition of 26-inch barreled models to the existing 1012 inertia-driven repeater lineup. Includes two camouflaged synthetic stock options as well as checkered Walnut, consistent with the existing 1012 family.

NIB	Exc.	V.G.	Good	Fair	Poor
560	450	350	250	—	—

1012 All Terrain

Gauge: 12 ga., 3 in. Capacity: 4+1. Barrel: 28 in., 8mm flat ventilated rib. Weight: 6.5 lbs. Length: 47 in. Stock: Turkish walnut with checkering. Features: The company's first gas-less, inertia-driven semi-automatic joins the All-Terrain family, which means it includes OD Green Cerakote on all exterior metalwork. Includes installed magazine plug. Oversized controls ideal for use when wearing gloves, sling studs, rubber recoil pad. Cross-bolt safety located at front of triggerguard. Includes five extended black chokes (F, IM, M, IC, C) and ships in a hard case.

NIB	Exc.	V.G.	Good	Fair	Poor
1100	850	700	600	—	—

1012 Bottomlands

Gauge: 12 ga., 3 in. Capacity: 4+1. Barrel: 28 in., 8mm flat ventilated rib. Weight: 6.5 lbs. Length: 47 in. Stock: Synthetic with full Mossy Oak Bottomland camouflage. Features: The company's first gas-less, inertia-driven semi-automatic is now dressed for hunting with full camouflage coverage on furniture, receiver and barrels. Oversized controls, sling studs, rubber recoil pad. Cross-bolt safety located at front of triggerguard. Includes five extended chokes (F, IM, M, IC, C).

NIB	Exc.	V.G.	Good	Fair	Poor
680	580	480	400	—	—

CZ 712

Gas-operated semi-automatic 12-gauge 3" chamber shotgun, built on a light-weight alloy receiver. Offered with 26" or 28" ventilated rib barrels. Magazine is 4 rounds. Checkered walnut stock, with blued finish. Weight about 7 lbs. Introduced in 2004.

NIB	Exc.	V.G.	Good	Fair	Poor
420	320	280	200	150	100

CZ 712 3-Gun

Semi-automatic 12-gauge designed for 3-gun competition. Black synthetic stock, matte black chrome finish, 22" barrel with 9-shot magazine extension and three choke tubes. Introduced in 2016.

NIB	Exc.	V.G.	Good	Fair	Poor
580	500	420	380	—	—

CZ 712 G2

Fit with a Turkish walnut stock, the G2 version adds laser-engraved checkering, right-hand palmswell as well as a barrel lock ring to make assembly easier. Target G2 has 30-inch barrel and a larger target-style stock.

NIB	Exc.	V.G.	Good	Fair	Poor
450	350	250	150	—	—

CZ 712 G3

Gauges: 12 ga. Barrels: 20", 26", 28" with 7mm flat-vent rib. Stock: Turkish Walnut, synthetic camo Terra. Features: Redesign third-generation gas-operated gun chambering 2.75" or 3" shells. Two interchangeable pistons are included for light and heavy loads. Chrome-lined barrel. Ships with five extra-long Active-Choke tubes.

NIB	Exc.	V.G.	Good	Fair	Poor
500	450	—	—	—	—

CZ 720

Introduced in 2004. Discontinued, replaced with the CZ 720 G2. Gas-operated semi-automatic 20 gauge 3" chamber shotgun, built on a light-weight alloy receiver. Offered with 26" or 28" ventilated rib barrels. Magazine is 4 rounds. Checkered walnut stock, with blued finish. Weight about 7 lbs.

NIB	Exc.	V.G.	Good	Fair	Poor
420	320	280	200	150	100

CZ 912

Introduced 2011. High-gloss finish on walnut stock and fore end, alloy receiver. 3" chamber, 28", 4+1 capacity. 7.4 lbs.

NIB	Exc.	V.G.	Good	Fair	Poor
450	350	250	150	—	—

CZ 920

Introduced 2013. Smaller-frame 20-gauge version of 12-gauge 912.

NIB	Exc.	V.G.	Good	Fair	Poor
480	380	280	180	—	—

PUMP ACTIONS

CZ 612/620/628

Slide-action shotguns in 12-gauge (CZ 612). Offered in Field, Home Defense, Turkey, Waterfowl, Trap, Target, Big Game and Youth models. Note: Add $50 for 3.5"-chamber Magnum Turkey and Magnum Waterfowl; $100 for Trap. CZ 620 and CZ 628 are 20- and 28-gauge versions of CZ 612.

NIB	Exc.	V.G.	Good	Fair	Poor
480	400	300	200	—	—

Durango

Side-by-side gun offered in 12 or 20 gauge, with 20" barrels and choke tubes. Extractors. Case colored receiver. Single trigger. Checkered walnut with pistol grip.

NIB	Exc.	V.G.	Good	Fair	Poor
700	600	500	400	300	—

Amarillo

Boxlock side-by-side offered in 12 or 20 gauge, with 20" barrels and choke tubes. Extractors. Case-colored receiver. Double triggers. Checkered walnut with pistol grip. Imported as late as 2006.

NIB	Exc.	V.G.	Good	Fair	Poor
600	500	400	300	200	—

Grouse

New in 2008, the Grouse is a single trigger side-by-side in 12-, 20-, 28-gauge and .410 bore, with 3" chambers (2.75" in 28-gauge). White chrome-plated receiver with scroll engraving. Prince of Wales grip and semi-beavertail schnabel forend. Barrels are 28" in 12- and 20-gauge; 26" in 28-gauge and .410 bore. Includes five choke tubes (.410 is choked IC/MOD). Note: Add 20 percent for 28-gauge and .410 bore.

NIB	Exc.	V.G.	Good	Fair	Poor
850	750	650	550	450	350

SIDE-BY-SIDES

Hammer Coach

Introduced 2006. 12-gauge 3" cowboy gun, with double triggers, color case-hardened receiver, external rebounding hammers and Turkish walnut pistol grip stock and splinter forend. Fixed C/C in 20" barrels. 8mm flat rib. Gloss black chrome metal finish. Extractor. Manual tang safety.

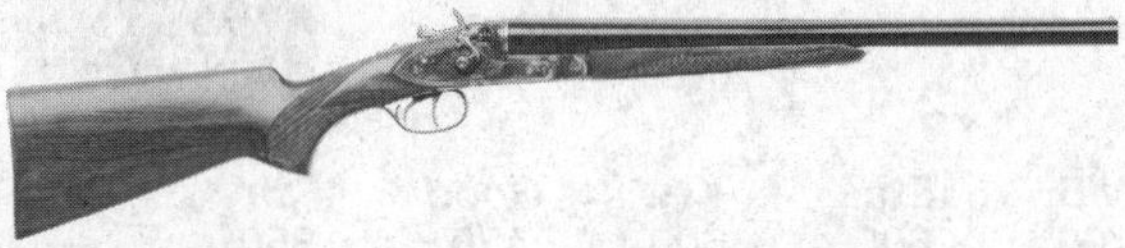

NIB	Exc.	V.G.	Good	Fair	Poor
850	750	650	550	450	350

Hammer Classic

30" barrels, 5 chokes (F, IM, M, IC, C). Introduced 2010.

NIB	Exc.	V.G.	Good	Fair	Poor
950	850	750	650	550	450

Partridge

New in 2008, this side-by-side is available in 12-, 20-, 28-gauge and .410 bore, with 3" chambers (2.75" in 28-gauge), each with a frame scaled to its bore size. White chrome-plated receiver with scroll engraving. Boxlock action and double triggers. Straight-grip stock and splinter forend. Barrels are 28" in 12- and 20-gauge; 26" in 28-gauge and .410 bore. Includes five choke tubes (.410 bore is choked IC/MOD). Note: Add 20 percent for 28-gauge and .410 bore.

NIB	Exc.	V.G.	Good	Fair	Poor
570	470	370	270	170	—

Ringneck

Discontinued 2015, replaced with the Sharp-Tail. Side-by-side chambered for 12, 16, 20, 28 gauge and .410 bore, with 26" or 28" barrels and choke tubes. Case-colored receiver with side plates. Single-selective trigger with extractors. Checkered walnut stock with pistol grip. Note: Add $100 for 16 gauge; $175 for 28 gauge and .410 bore.

NIB	Exc.	V.G.	Good	Fair	Poor
—	900	800	700	600	500

Ringneck Custom Grade

Select Grade IV walnut used in manufacture of this 20-gauge, with 28" barrels.

NIB	Exc.	V.G.	Good	Fair	Poor
1200	1000	700	450	300	200

Sharp-Tail

Based on Ringneck, but with much smaller one-piece CNC-cut receiver with independent floating firing pins, coil spring operated hammers and newly designed sears. Color case-hardened finish on receiver. Single-selectable mechanical trigger, pistol grip buttstock. Available in 12, 16, 20, 28, and .410 with 28-inch barrels. Turkish walnut stocks, single extractor and 5 flush choke tubes (except 16 and .410, which have fixed IC/Mod). Comes in plastic case. Note: +$200 for 28 gauge and .410.

NIB	Exc.	V.G.	Good	Fair	Poor
950	850	750	650	550	—

Bobwhite

Straight-grip stock and double triggers.

NIB	Exc.	V.G.	Good	Fair	Poor
800	620	550	400	300	200

Bobwhite G2

Reintroduced in 2019 in 12, 20 and 28 gauges, with black-chrome finish. Weight 7.3 lbs. with 28" barrel.

NIB	Exc.	V.G.	Good	Fair	Poor
600	500	400	—	—	—

Bobwhite G2 All-Terrain

Gauges: 12 ga., 3 in., 20 ga., 3 in. Barrels: 28 in., 30 in. Stock: Walnut, various styles. Features: CZ's new All-Terrain series encompasses five existing shotgun models. The new package includes upgraded wood, OD Green Cerakote finish on all metalwork, as well as a set of rare earth magnets added to the extractor/ejectors of the SxS and O/U models to keep shells from dropping out while handling a dog or working in the blind.

NIB	Exc.	V.G.	Good	Fair	Poor
760	—	—	—	—	—

Bobwhite G2 Project Upland

Gauge: 12, 20, 28 ga. Barrel: 28 in. with 8mm flat rib.Weight: 6.25–7.15 lbs. Stock: English-style straight grip with Grade III Turkish Walnut. Features: Project Upland hunting SxS designed with crowd-sourced input. Lovely color casehardened receiver finish, dual extractors, and gloss black chrome barrel finish. Splinter forend. Dual triggers and manual tang safety. Hand-engraving borrowed from Sharp Tail model. Includes five chokes (F, IM, M, IC, C).

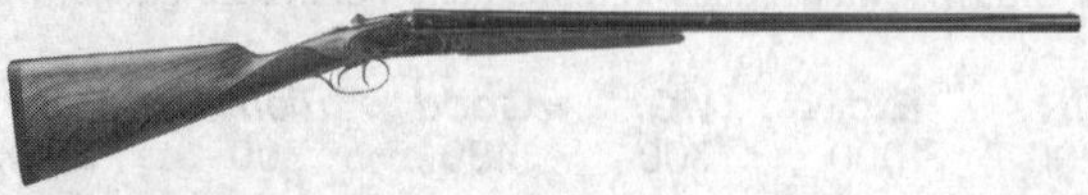

NIB	Exc.	V.G.	Good	Fair	Poor
1310	—	—	—	—	—

Bobwhite G2 Intermediate

Built on the Bobwhite G2 but with more compact dimensions for smaller-framed shooters. The 26-in. barrel is 2 in. shorter than standard. Length of pull is also shorter at 14 in. even. Available only in 20 ga. Built for teens/smaller-stature shooters, as well as handling in tight spaces. All other features remain the same.

NIB	Exc.	V.G.	Good	Fair	Poor
680	—	—	—	—	—

Bobwhite G2 Southpaw

Built on the Bobwhite G2 but the stock is "cast-on," or built in the opposite direction so it properly fits when brought up to the left shoulder. All other features remain, with the Southpaw using 28-in. barrels and available in 12 or 20 ga.

NIB	Exc.	V.G.	Good	Fair	Poor
680	—	—	—	—	—

SINGLE-BARREL MODELS

CZ All-American Single Trap

Introduced in 2019, this dedicated singles 12 gauge 3" trap gun has a 4-way adjustable comb and adjustable butt plate hardware (cast, toe, LOP). Adjustable reach to trigger. 30", 32" or 34" barrels with lengthened forcing cone and porting. Extended chokes in C, IC, LM, M, and IM constrictions. Heavy beavertail forend style, manual tang safety. Gloss blue barrel and receiver finish. Length 48", weight 8.5 lbs.

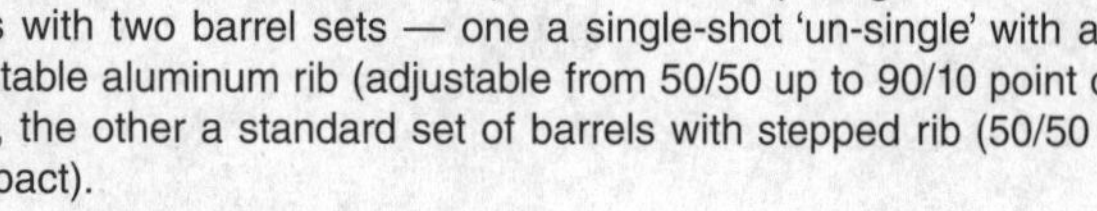

NIB	Exc.	V.G.	Good	Fair	Poor
2250	2150	1950	1750	1550	—

All-American Trap Combo

Built for ATA shooters who compete in both trap singles and doubles. Ships with two barrel sets — one a single-shot 'un-single' with a dial-adjustable aluminum rib (adjustable from 50/50 up to 90/10 point of impact), the other a standard set of barrels with stepped rib (50/50 point of impact).

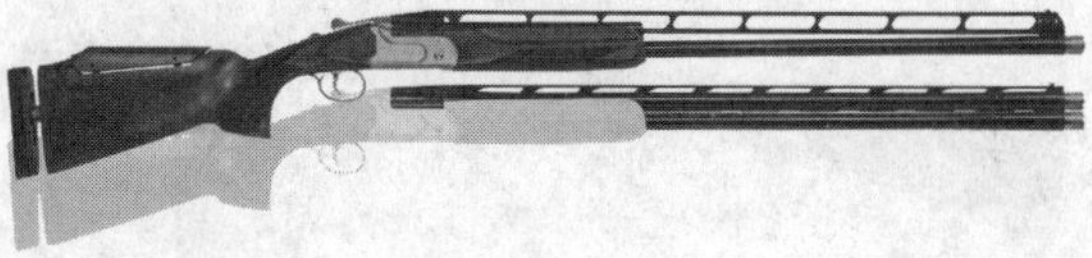

NIB	Exc.	V.G.	Good	Fair	Poor
3000	2800	2600	2400	2200	—

PISTOLS

All currently imported CZ pistols can be ordered with tritium night sights with the exception of models CZ 97B and CZ 100. Add $80 for this option. Note: Substantial premium for factory-engraved examples.

CZ 75

CZ 75

Designed by Koucky brothers in 1975, this model bears little resemblance to previous CZ pistols. Considered by many, including the late Jeff Cooper, to be the best pistol ever to come from Czech Republic. One of the finest semi-automatics in the world. Chambered for 9mm Parabellum cartridge, it is copied in many countries. Has a breech-lock system utilizing a Browning-style cam. Slide rides on inside of the slide rails. Magazine capacity 15 rounds; barrel length 4.72"; overall length 8". Empty pistol weight 34.5 oz. Offered in black paint, matte or polished blue finish.

NIB	Exc.	V.G.	Good	Fair	Poor
700	600	500	430	350	—

CZ 75 B

Introduced in 1994. An updated version of original CZ 75. Features pinned front sight, commander hammer, non-glare ribbed barrel and squared triggerguard. Also offered in .40 S&W chamber. Note: Add $20 for glossy blue; $25 for dual tone finish; $25 for nickel; $80 for tritium night sights; $30 for .40 S&W.

NIB	Exc.	V.G.	Good	Fair	Poor
700	600	500	430	350	—

CZ 75 30th Anniversary

Introduced in 2005. Features special 30th Anniversary engraving, gold inlays, gold plated controls, high gloss blue finish, engraved blonde finished birch grips. Magazine capacity 15 rounds. Limited to 1,000 pistols.

NIB	Exc.	V.G.	Good	Fair	Poor
850	680	500	400	300	200

CZ 75 Compact

Introduced in 1992. Compact version of CZ 75. Offered in black paint, matte or polished blue finish. Traditional single-/double-action. Barrel length 3.9"; overall length 7.3"; weight about 32 oz. In 2005, offered with accessory rail and ambidextrous manual safety. Add $50 to prices. Note: Add $20 for glossy blue; $25 for dual tone finish; $25 for nickel; $80 for tritium night sights; $30 for .40 S&W.

NIB	Exc.	V.G.	Good	Fair	Poor
700	600	500	430	350	—

CZ 75 Compact D

Essentially same as CZ 75 Compact, with decocking double-action system and lightweight alloy frame. Weight about 25 oz. Note: Only 20 of these pistols imported into U.S. No longer in production. Expert appraisal suggested prior to sale.

NIB	Exc.	V.G.	Good	Fair	Poor
560	450	300	220	150	100

CZ 75 B Tactical

Chambered for 9mm Luger cartridge. Fitted with 4.7" barrel. Has a single-/double-action trigger. Fixed sights. Rubber grips. Slide is black polycoat. Frame a military green finish. Weight about 35 oz. Note: Add 10% for night sights.

NIB	Exc.	V.G.	Good	Fair	Poor
480	400	320	250	180	120

CZ 75 Tactical Sport

Large steel frame CZ 75 variant in 9mm or .40 S&W, with 5.3" barrel, checkered wood grips and fixed sights. Weight 45 oz. Introduced in 2016.

NIB	Exc.	V.G.	Good	Fair	Poor
1100	900	800	680	500	—

CZ 75 BD

Has all the same features as Model 75 B, with addition of a decocking double-action. Black polycoat finish.

NIB	Exc.	V.G.	Good	Fair	Poor
450	400	300	220	150	100

CZ BD Compact

Introduced in 2001. Features 3.9" barrel, with decocking lever. Chambered for .40 S&W cartridge. Blued finish. Magazine capacity 10 rounds. Weight about 32 oz. All other features same as CZ 75 B Compact.

NIB	Exc.	V.G.	Good	Fair	Poor
400	350	300	220	150	100

CZ BD Compact Carry

Same as above, with rounded edges including triggerguard.

NIB	Exc.	V.G.	Good	Fair	Poor
420	380	300	220	150	100

CZ 75 B SA

Introduced in 2000. Features single-action trigger designed for competitive shooting that can be carried in condition one. Fitted with straight trigger and manual safety. Chambered for 9mm cartridge. Weight about 35 oz.

NIB	Exc.	V.G.	Good	Fair	Poor
520	400	320	220	150	100

CZ 75 Semi-Compact

Introduced in 1994. Same barrel length as Compact (3.9"), but same full-size grip as CZ 75. Magazine capacity 15 rounds of 9mm. Overall length 7.3".

NIB	Exc.	V.G.	Good	Fair	Poor
500	350	300	250	180	100

CZ 75 D PCR Compact

Introduced in 2000. Chambered for 9mm cartridge. Features light alloy frame and 3.9" barrel. Trigger both single-/double-action with a decocking lever. Low-profile sights. Serrated front and rear backstrap. Designed for the Czech national police force. Magazine capacity 10 rounds. Weight about 27 oz.

NIB	Exc.	V.G.	Good	Fair	Poor
520	420	350	220	150	100

CZ 75 Champion

Chambered for .40 S&W, 9mm and 9x21 cartridges. Single-action-only trigger with straight trigger. Fitted with 4.5" barrel, low profile adjustable sights and three port compensator. Furnished with blue slide and nickel frame. Hand fitted. Weight about 36 oz.

NIB	Exc.	V.G.	Good	Fair	Poor
1480	1150	980	680	500	—

CZ 75 DAO

Similar to CZ 75, with double-action-only trigger, no safety lever and spurless hammer. Offered in 9mm and .40 S&W. Barrel length 4.7". Weight about 35 oz. Introduced in 2000.

NIB	Exc.	V.G.	Good	Fair	Poor
700	600	500	430	350	—

CZ 75 Standard IPSC (ST)

Designed and built for IPSC competition. Chambered for .40 S&W and fitted with 5.4" barrel. Single-action-only trigger. Special high-profile sights. Weight about 45 oz.

NIB	Exc.	V.G.	Good	Fair	Poor
1000	850	780	620	—	—

CZ 75 M IPSC

Similar to CZ 75 Standard IPSC, with the addition of a two-port compensator and blast shield to protect frame-mounted optics. Slide racker standard. Red-dot optics. Barrel length 3.9". Weight about 45 oz. Introduced in 2001.

NIB	Exc.	V.G.	Good	Fair	Poor
1350	1200	1050	680	—	—

CZ 75 Silver Anniversary

Commemorates 25th Anniversary of CZ Model 75 pistol. Features high polish nickel finish, with walnut grips. Number "25" inlaid in grips. Total of 1000 pistols will be produced, with about 500 allocated for U.S. market.

NIB	Exc.	V.G.	Good	Fair	Poor
850	700	600	500	400	220

CZ 75 Stainless

All-steel construction, double-stack magazines, three-dot fixed sights. Chambered for 9mm., 16+1 or 10+1 capacity, and 4.72" barrel. First stainless from CZ. Introduced 2006.

NIB	Exc.	V.G.	Good	Fair	Poor
750	650	550	450	—	—

CZ 75 Phantom

Similar to the CZ 75 SP-01 Shadow but with further refinements for competition use. Introduced 2019.

NIB	Exc.	V.G.	Good	Fair	Poor
750	650	550	450	—	—

CZ 75 SP-01 Shadow

Chambered 9mm for IPSC "Production" Division competition. 19+1 capacity, 4.72" barrel., weight 41 oz., wood grip. Introduced 2006.

NIB	Exc.	V.G.	Good	Fair	Poor
1100	600	500	400	300	180

CZ 75 Shadow 2 Orange

Similar to the CZ 75 SP-01 but with polymer frame. Introduced 2009–13 and 2017.

NIB	Exc.	V.G.	Good	Fair	Poor
1000	930	800	680	—	—

CZ 75 SP-01 Shadow Custom

Chambered in 9mm Parabellum. Steel slide and frame, CZ Custom Shop trigger job. Cold hammer-forged barrel, fiber-optic front sight, aluminum grips and 19-round magazine. Weight 36 oz., 4.7" barrel and dual-tone finish. Customized for IPSC Production division. Introduced in 2011.

NIB	Exc.	V.G.	Good	Fair	Poor
1000	930	800	680	—	—

CZ 75 Shadow 2 SA

Caliber: 9mm. Capacity: 17-round magazine. Barrel: 4.89 in. Grips: Textured blue aluminum. Sights: Fiber-optic front, HAJO rear. Length: 8.53 in. overall. Weight: 46.5 oz. unloaded. Finish: Nitride black. Features: Single-action-only trigger. Swappable magazine release with adjustable, extended button with three settings. Ambidextrous manual thumb safety.

NIB	Exc.	V.G.	Good	Fair	Poor
1250	1050	900	750	—	—

CZ 75 TS 2

Caliber: 9mm or 40 S&W. Capacity: 20-round magazine. Barrel: 5.28 in. Grip: Thin textured aluminum. Sights: Serrated fiber-optic front, serrated fixed rear. Length: 8.86 in. overall. Weight: 48.5 oz. unloaded. Finish: Blued. Features: Full dust cover, competition-ready, improved ergonomics.

NIB	Exc.	V.G.	Good	Fair	Poor
1400	1130	1050	1000	980	—

CZ 75 TS Czechmate

Comes with all parts necessary to compete in IPSC Open or Limited divisions. Chambered in 9mm Parabellum. Steel slide and frame, single-action grips. Comes with a compensator and C-More red-dot sight installed and an ambidextrous slide racker. Includes front-sight adapter that replaces compensator, rear sight, ambidextrous safeties, aluminum grips, magazine well, one 26- and three 20-round magazines. Weight 48 oz., 5.4" barrel, matte blue finish. Introduced in 2011.

NIB	Exc.	V.G.	Good	Fair	Poor
2900	2500	2000	1500	—	—

CZ 75 TS 2 Racing Green

Caliber: 9mm. Capacity: 20-round magazine. Barrel: 5.28". Grip: Thin textured green anodized aluminum. Sights: Serrated fiber-optic front, serrated fixed rear. Length: 8.86". overall. Weight: 48.5 oz. unloaded. Finish: Blued. Features: Full dust cover, competition-ready, improved ergonomics.

NIB	Exc.	V.G.	Good	Fair	Poor
1700	—	—	—	—	—

CZ 75 Tactical Sport

Large steel frame CZ 75 variant in 9mm or .40 S&W, with 5.3" barrel, checkered wood grips and fixed sights. Weight 45 oz. Introduced in 2016.

NIB	Exc.	V.G.	Good	Fair	Poor
1100	900	680	500	400	200

CZ 75B 45th Anniversary

Caliber: 9mm. Capacity: 16-round magazine. Barrel: 4.6". Grips: Engraved wood. Sights: Fixed, three-dot tritium. Length: 8.1". overall. Weight: 35.2 oz. unloaded. Finish: Blued. Features: Limited edition pistol, only 1,000 produced. Engraved frame and slide.

NIB	Exc.	V.G.	Good	Fair	Poor
1720	—	—	—	—	—

CZ 75 Kadet Conversion

A separate conversion kit for CZ 75/85 series. Converts these pistols to .22 LR. Adjustable rear sight. Supplied with 10-round magazine.

NIB	Exc.	V.G.	Good	Fair	Poor
300	220	200	150	100	50

CZ 85

CZ 85 B

Similar in appearance to CZ 75. Offers some new features such as ambidextrous safety and slide stop levers, squared triggerguard, adjustable sight and ribbed slide. Caliber, magazine capacity and weight same as CZ 75. Note: Add $20 for glossy blue; $25 for dual tone and nickel finish; $30 for .40 S&W.

NIB	*Exc.*	*V.G.*	*Good*	*Fair*	*Poor*
650	550	470	400	—	—

CZ 85 Combat

Similar to CZ 85, with addition of adjustable sights, walnut grips, round hammer and free dropping magazine. Note: Add $20 for glossy blue; $25 for dual tone and nickel finish; $30 for .40 S&W.

NIB	*Exc.*	*V.G.*	*Good*	*Fair*	*Poor*
600	500	430	350	—	—

CZ 40B

Introduced in 2002 and similar to CZ 75. Features an alloy frame similar in shape to Colt Model 1911. A single-/double-action design. Barrel length 4.7". Magazine capacity 10 rounds. Chambered for .40 S&W cartridge. Weight about 35 oz.

NIB	*Exc.*	*V.G.*	*Good*	*Fair*	*Poor*
620	500	400	300	200	120

CZ Kadet

Chambered for .22 LR cartridge. Fitted with 4.7" barrel. A fixed barrel blowback semi-automatic pistol. Adjustable sights and blue finish. Weight about 36 oz.

NIB	*Exc.*	*V.G.*	*Good*	*Fair*	*Poor*
750	690	540	460	—	—

CZ 2075 RAMI

Introduced in 2004, this 9mm or .40 S&W pistol fitted with 3" barrel. Has single-/double-action trigger. Design based on CZ 75. Magazine capacity: 10 rounds 9mm; 8 rounds .40 S&W. Weight about 25 oz.

NIB	*Exc.*	*V.G.*	*Good*	*Fair*	*Poor*
600	500	430	370	—	—

CZ 83

Fixed-barrel .380-caliber pistol. Features ambidextrous safety and magazine catch behind triggerguard. Stripped by means of a hinged triggerguard. Barrel length 3.8"; overall length 6.8"; weight about 23 oz. Note: Add $5 for nickel finish. In 1993, Special Editions of this pistol were introduced. These Special Editions consist of special finishes for then-currently imported CZ pistols. They are high polish blue, nickel, chrome, gold and combination of these finishes. These Special Edition finishes may affect price; they add between $100 and $250 to cost of the pistol when new.

NIB	Exc.	V.G.	Good	Fair	Poor
480	320	200	180	150	120

CZ 97 B

Planned for production in summer of 1997. Chambered for .45 ACP cartridge. Fitted with 4.8" barrel. Has single-/double-action mode. Magazine capacity 10 rounds. Wood grips with blue finish. Weight about 40 oz.

NIB	Exc.	V.G.	Good	Fair	Poor
750	640	550	460	—	—

CZ 100

Semi-automatic pistol introduced in 1996. Chambered for 9mm or .40 S&W cartridge. Has plastic frame and steel slide. Barrel length 3.75". Weight about 24 oz. U.S. magazine capacity 10 rounds.

NIB	Exc.	V.G.	Good	Fair	Poor
520	450	320	2000	150	100

CZ 1911 A1

Classic full-size 1911 A1 in .45 ACP, with 5" barrel, steel slide and frame with black oxide finish. Checkered walnut grips and fixed sights. Made in U.S.A. Introduced in 2015.

NIB	Exc.	V.G.	Good	Fair	Poor
750	700	650	—	—	—

CZ Scorpion Evo

Blowback-operated 9mm semi-automatic, with 7.75" barrel. Imported as a pistol, it's a civilian version of CZ Scorpion EVO 3-A1 sub-gun. Low-profile sights, with four aperture sizes on an 11" Picatinny rail. Features include ambidextrous controls, an arm brace adapter which adds an AR-style pistol buffer tube to rear of the action. Introduced in 2015.

NIB	Exc.	V.G.	Good	Fair	Poor
1100	930	800	680	—	—

CZ 805 Bren S1

Imported as a pistol. AR style model, with 16.2" threaded barrel in 5.56 NATO or .300 Blackout. Magazine capacity 30 rounds. Folding adjustable stock, top and bottom accessory Picatinny rails, black or Flat Dead Earth finish. Introduced in 2016.

NIB	Exc.	V.G.	Good	Fair	Poor
2000	1700	1500	1200	—	—

CZ Bren 2 Ms

Similar to e CZ 805 Bren S1 but with polymer frame and chambered in either 5.56 NATO or 7.62x39mm. Introduced in 2018.

NIB	Exc.	V.G.	Good	Fair	Poor
1700	1450	1230	1000	—	—

P SERIES

CZ P-01

Introduced in 2002, this pistol replaced CZ 75 with Czech National Police. Features forged aluminum alloy frame and 3.8" barrel. Decocker single-/double-action. Fixed sights. Fitted with M3 accessory rail. Rubber grips and 14-round magazine. Black polycoat finish. Weight 29 oz.

NIB	Exc.	V.G.	Good	Fair	Poor
700	600	500	430	—	—

CZ P-06

The .40 S&W version of the P-01. Magazine capacity 10 rounds.

NIB	Exc.	V.G.	Good	Fair	Poor
730	630	500	430	350	300

P-07 Series

Polymer frame SA/DA trigger. Chambered in 9mm or .40 S&W. Equipped with a 3.8" barrel, fixed sights, and decocking lever. Imported 2009–2013.

NIB	Exc.	V.G.	Good	Fair	Poor
550	480	400	340	—	—

CZ P-09 Duty

Full-size high-capacity variation of P-01/P-06 series. Chambered in 9mm (19-round magazine) or .40 S&W (15-rounds). Low-profile sights, Picatinny rail, black polymer frame and black steel slide. P-07 model is a single-stack variation.

NIB	Exc.	V.G.	Good	Fair	Poor
680	580	480	400	—	—

CZ P-10 C

NIB	Exc.	V.G.	Good	Fair	Poor
400	390	340	320	240	—

CZ P-10 C

NIB	Exc.	V.G.	Good	Fair	Poor
400	390	340	320	240	—

P-10 C Urban Grey

Striker fired 9mm pistol built for suppressor use. Has threaded barrel, high visibility night sights and fiber reinforced polymer frame, with two-tone Urban Grey finish. Polymer grips with interchangeable backstraps. Compact size with 4.6" barrel, 15-round capacity. Weight 26 oz. Introduced in 2018.

NIB	Exc.	V.G.	Good	Fair	Poor
500	430	350	300	—	—

CZ P-10 F

Caliber: 9mm. Capacity: 19-round magazine. Barrel: 4.5 in. Weight: 26 oz. Length: 8 in. overall. Grips: Textured polymer. Sights: Fixed, 3-dot. Features: Striker-fire.

NIB	Exc.	V.G.	Good	Fair	Poor
540	500	450	340	320	—

CZ P-10 F Competition-Ready

Caliber: 9mm. Capacity: 19-round magazine. Barrel: 5 in. Grip: Thin textured polymer. Sights: Fiber-optic front, serrated fixed rear; optic ready. Length: 8.5 in. overall. Weight: 30 oz. unloaded. Finish: Matte black, gold accents. Features: Striker-firer, competition ready, Apex Tactical extended magazine catch and extended slide stop, and HB Industries trigger.

NIB	Exc.	V.G.	Good	Fair	Poor
900	800	770	700	600	—

CZ P-10 C

NIB	Exc.	V.G.	Good	Fair	Poor
300	290	270	260	240	—

CZ P-10 S

NIB	Exc.	V.G.	Good	Fair	Poor
370	360	330	310	270	—

CZ - Strakonice

Strakonice, Czech Republic

This firm is a separate company from the one located in Uhershy Brod. Prior to the collapse of the Soviet Union both companies were owned and operated by the state.

Model TT 40/45/9

Semi-automatic pistol chambered for .40 S&W, .45 ACP or 9mm cartridges. Fitted with 3.8" barrel. Trigger is single-/double-action or double-action-only. Magazine capacity 10 rounds. Weight about 26 oz.

NIB	Exc.	V.G.	Good	Fair	Poor
580	420	300	200	120	100

D

D. W. M.
Berlin, Germany

See—LUGER & BORCHARDT

Model 22

A 7.65mm caliber semi-automatic pistol, with 3.5" barrel. Blued with walnut grips; later changed to plastic grips. Approximately 40,000 manufactured between 1921 and 1931.

NIB	*Exc.*	*V.G.*	*Good*	*Fair*	*Poor*
—	950	780	500	400	250

DAEWOO
Pusan, Korea

DH-40

Semi-automatic pistol chambered for .40 S&W cartridge. Barrel 4.13"; magazine capacity 11 rounds. Weight about 32 oz.

NIB	*Exc.*	*V.G.*	*Good*	*Fair*	*Poor*
500	380	300	250	180	100

DP-51B

Semi-automatic pistol chambered for 9mm cartridge. Fitted with 4.13" barrel. Magazine capacity 13 rounds; overall length 7.5"; weight about 28 oz.

NIB	*Exc.*	*V.G.*	*Good*	*Fair*	*Poor*
400	320	280	220	180	100

DP-51SB

More compact design, with 3.6" barrel and 10-round magazine. Weight 27 oz. Stainless steel finish.

NIB	*Exc.*	*V.G.*	*Good*	*Fair*	*Poor*
450	400	280	220	180	100

DP-51CB

Same as above, fitted with a 3.6" barrel. Magazine capacity 10 rounds. Weight about 26 oz.

NIB	*Exc.*	*V.G.*	*Good*	*Fair*	*Poor*
450	380	300	250	180	100

DP-52

Semi-automatic pistol chambered for .22 LR cartridge. Has 3.82" barrel; magazine capacity 10 rounds. Operates in double/single-action modes. Overall length 6.7"; weight about 23 oz.

NIB	*Exc.*	*V.G.*	*Good*	*Fair*	*Poor*
400	320	250	200	150	100

DH380

Introduced in 1996. Semi-automatic pistol chambered for .380 ACP cartridge. Fitted with 3.8" barrel; magazine capacity 8 rounds. Firing is double/single-action. Weight about 24 oz.

NIB	Exc.	V.G.	Good	Fair	Poor
420	380	280	220	150	100

DR200

Introduced in 1996. Post-ban semi-automatic rifle chambered for .223 Rem. cartridge. Features black matte finish, with synthetic thumbhole stock. Barrel length 18.3". Uses AR-15 magazines, not included with rifle. Weight about 9 lbs.

NIB	Exc.	V.G.	Good	Fair	Poor
1000	900	700	500	—	—

K-2/AR-100 (Max I)

A 5.56mm caliber pre-ban semi-automatic rifle, with 18" barrel. Gas-operated rotary bolt-action, magazines interchangeable with those from M-16. Black. Introduced in 1985. No longer imported.

NIB	Exc.	V.G.	Good	Fair	Poor
2000	1700	1450	1000	—	—

K1A1 (Max II)

Rifle is quite similar to K-2/AR-100, with a folding composite stock.

NIB	Exc.	V.G.	Good	Fair	Poor
2000	1700	1450	1000	—	—

DAISY
Rogers, Arkansas

VL Rifle

A .22 combustible cartridge single-shot rifle, with 18" barrel and plastic stock. Cartridge ignited by compressed air. Manufactured during 1968 and 1969. Believed fewer than 20,000 made. Add considerable premium if large quantity of VL ammunition is present.

NIB	Exc.	V.G.	Good	Fair	Poor
280	100	80	80	50	20

VL Presentation Model

As above, with walnut stock. Approximately 4,000 made in 1968 and 1969.

NIB	Exc.	V.G.	Good	Fair	Poor
280	150	120	100	80	50

VL Cased Presentation Model

As above, with gold plaque inlaid in the stock. Fitted case containing 300 VL cartridges.

NIB	Exc.	V.G.	Good	Fair	Poor
320	200	180	120	100	80

Model 2201/2211

Bolt-action single-shot rifle chambered for .22 LR cartridge. Fitted with a 19" barrel and octagon shroud. Ramp blade front sight, with adjustable notch rear sight. Synthetic stock Model 2211; walnut stock Model 2201. Trigger is adjustable. Weight about 6.5 lbs.

NIB	Exc.	V.G.	Good	Fair	Poor
200	150	100	60	50	20

Model 2202/2212

Similar to above in appearance, but fitted with 10-round rotary magazine. Synthetic stock Model 2212; walnut stock Model 2202. Weight about 6.5 lbs.

NIB	Exc.	V.G.	Good	Fair	Poor
200	150	100	60	50	20

Model 2203/2213

Semi-automatic rifle chambered for .22 LR cartridge. Has 7-round magazine and 19" barrel. Synthetic stock Model 2213; walnut stock Model 2203. Weight about 6.5 lbs.

NIB	Exc.	V.G.	Good	Fair	Poor
220	180	120	80	80	50

DAKIN GUN CO.
San Francisco, California

Model 100

A 12- and 20-gauge boxlock double-barrel shotgun, with 26" or 28" barrels, various chokes, extractors and double triggers. Engraved, blued, with a checkered walnut stock. Manufactured in the 1960s.

NIB	Exc.	V.G.	Good	Fair	Poor
—	480	320	280	200	100

Model 147

As above, with ventilated rib barrels.

NIB	Exc.	V.G.	Good	Fair	Poor
—	450	380	250	200	100

Model 160

As above, with single-selective trigger.

NIB	Exc.	V.G.	Good	Fair	Poor
—	700	600	450	250	150

Model 215

As above, but more finely finished.

NIB	Exc.	V.G.	Good	Fair	Poor
—	1800	1600	1100	500	250

Model 170

A 12-, 16- and 20-gauge over/under shotgun, with 26" or 28" ventilated rib barrels, various chokes and double triggers. Blued and lightly engraved. Discontinued in the 1960s.

NIB	Exc.	V.G.	Good	Fair	Poor
—	500	420	350	280	150

DAKOTA ARMS, INC.

Sturgis, South Dakota

Master gunsmiths Don Allen and Pete Grisell formed Dakota Arms in 1986. The company offers four basic models, with an array of options. Remington Arms Co. purchased the company in 2009. Note: All prices are base prices. Dakota's many extra cost options greatly affect the new price and used value of its arms. Shotguns are no longer offered through Dakota Arms.

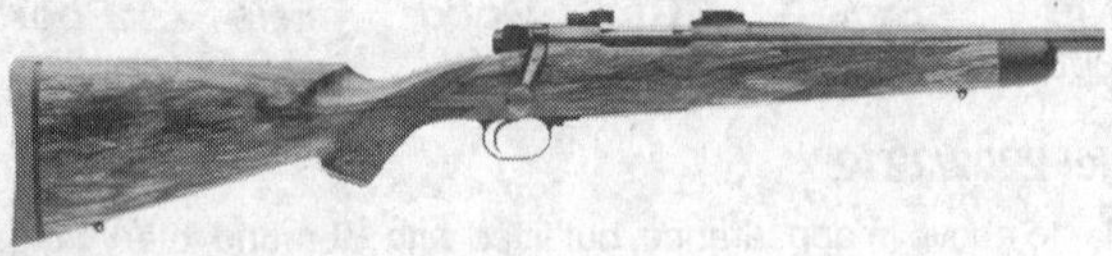

RIFLES

Dakota 76 Classic

The flagship of the Dakota line, the Model 76 Classic has been made for more than 30 years. Standard features include a flat-bottom action with integral recoil lug, Mauser controlled-round-feed action in one of five sizes including Short, Short Magnum, Standard, Standard Magnum and Long Magnum, actions drilled and tapped for 8-40 screws, right- or left-hand configurations, 3-position safety, 1-piece bolt and mechanical ejector. Available in chamberings from .22-250 to .416 Remington (see 76 Safari for larger African chamberings), with 23" barrel, matte blue metal. The English walnut stock is checkered and the action pillar and fully bedded.

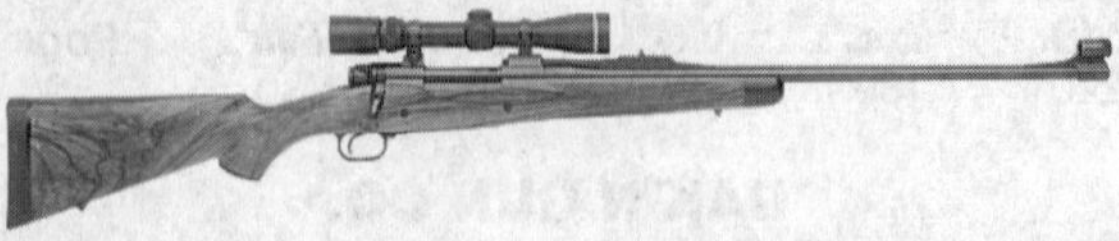

NIB	Exc.	V.G.	Good	Fair	Poor
5500	5100	4350	3680	2200	1350

Dakota 76 Deluxe

As above with the addition of a color-case receiver, triggerguard, crossbolt and buttplate (optional). Slim, exhibition-grade English walnut.

NIB	Exc.	V.G.	Good	Fair	Poor
7300	6500	5700	4500	—	—

Dakota 76 Alpine

As above, in calibers .22-250 to .30-06, 22" featherweight barrel, no sights, English walnut. Add $1800 for Alpine Deluxe.

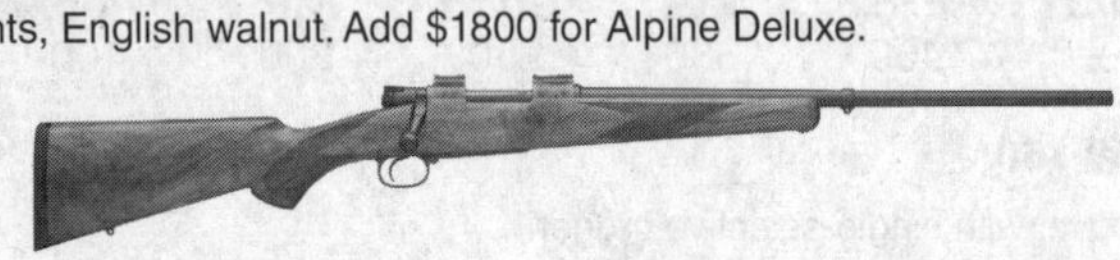

NIB	Exc.	V.G.	Good	Fair	Poor
5700	4600	4000	3200	2200	1320

Dakota 76 Mannlicher

As above, in calibers from .22-250 to .30-06, 20" barrel, color case receiver, iron sights, Talley scope bases, full-length English walnut Mannlicher stock.

NIB	Exc.	V.G.	Good	Fair	Poor
7000	6250	5500	4650	—	—

Dakota 76 Safari

As above, in calibers from 7mm Rem Mag to .458 Lott, XXX grade walnut, shadowline cheeckpiece, ebony forend tip, right- or left-hand action.

NIB	Exc.	V.G.	Good	Fair	Poor
7200	6400	5700	4900	—	—

Dakota 76 African

As above, in calibers from 7mm Rem Mag to .458 Lott (including .404 Jeffrey, .416 Rigby and .450 Dakota), XXX grade walnut, shadowline cheeckpiece, ebony forend tip, two cross bolts with ebony plugs, straddle floorplate with inside release, drop-belly magazine with 4-round capacity, (most calibers), mercury recoil reducer in stock forend, quarter rib with one fixed-blade and banded/hooded front sight. Right- or left-hand action.

NIB	Exc.	V.G.	Good	Fair	Poor
8000	7250	6500	5000	—	—

Dakota 76 Professional Hunter

Available as Safari or African in pillar-bedded fiberglass stock with cheekpiece, 14" LOP, 23" Douglas premium stainless barrel in calibers .375 H&H, .404 Jeffery, .416 Remington, .416 Rigby, .450 Dakota, .450 Rigby or .458 Lott., single-island fixed-blade rear and ramp front sight, black Cerakote metal. Introduced in 2013.

NIB	Exc.	V.G.	Good	Fair	Poor
7500	6500	5000	4000	2200	1320

Dakota 76 Traveler

As above in a threadless takedown model available in four action sizes (Standard, Magnum, Long Magnum and Rigby), limited to 2-barrel sets with XXX English walnut stock, 24" premium barrel in matte blue. Chamberings from 6.5x55 to .450 Dakota, weight of 9.5 to 10 lbs. Note: Add $1500 for Safari grade; add $2500 for African grade.

NIB	Exc.	V.G.	Good	Fair	Poor
7220	6150	5200	4000	—	—

Dakota 76 Varmint Grade

Introduced in 1996. Chambered for a variety of cartridges from .17 Rem. to 6mm PPC. Single-shot bolt-action design available in right-/left-hand versions. Barrel length 24". Varmint-style stock is semi-fancy walnut, with oil-finish and no checkering. Many extra cost options offered for this model. Discontinued.

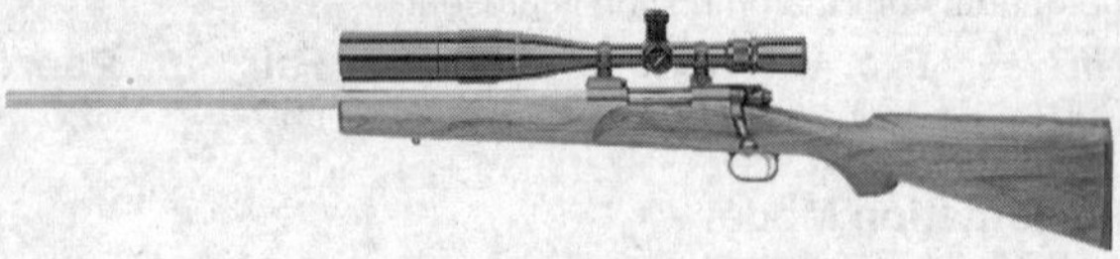

NIB	Exc.	V.G.	Good	Fair	Poor
2500	2000	1500	1100	800	400

Limited Edition .30-06 Model 76

Ultra-decked-out version of Model 76; commemorates 100th Anniversary of .30-06 cartridge; production limited to 101 units. Introduced 2006.

NIB	Exc.	V.G.	Good	Fair	Poor
8000	5500	4000	2650	1700	500

Dakota 97 Classic

The 97 features a lighter, round-body action, controlled-round feed, match-grade barrel and adjustable Model 76 trigger. Chrome moly action drilled and tapped for 8-40 screws, 24" (short action) or 26" barrel (long action), calibers from .22-250 to .375 H&H, no sights, synthetic stock, right- or left-hand action. Add $500 for stainless steel barrel and action.

NIB	Exc.	V.G.	Good	Fair	Poor
3500	2980	2520	2150	1300	780

Dakota 97 Outfitter

As above, with stainless steel barrel and action, Cerakote metal and synthetic stock in matching colors (many color options available), iron sights. Takedown action.

NIB	Exc.	V.G.	Good	Fair	Poor
4600	4000	3200	2500	1850	1100

Model 97 Varmint Hunter

Built on Model 97 action. Standard features are fiberglass stock, round-action, single-shot, adjustable trigger and black recoil pad. Barrel length 24". Offered in calibers from .220 Swift to .308 Winchester. Weight about 8 lbs. Introduced in 1999. Discontinued.

NIB	Exc.	V.G.	Good	Fair	Poor
2200	1750	1000	750	600	300

Model 97 Long Range Hunter

Introduced in 1997. Bolt-action rifle offered in 13 calibers: .250-6, .257 Roberts, .270 Win., .280 Rem., 7mm Rem. Magnum, 7mm Dakota Magnum, .30-06, .300 Win. Magnum, .300 Dakota Magnum, .338 Win. Magnum, .330 Dakota Magnum, .375 H&H and .375 Dakota Magnum. Barrel length depends on caliber, but are 24" or 26". Trigger is fully adjustable. Many other special features. Stock is black synthetic, with one-piece bedding. Black recoil pad standard. Weight about 7.7 lbs. Discontinued.

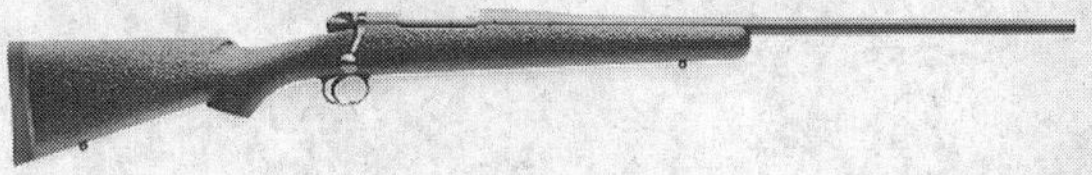

NIB	Exc.	V.G.	Good	Fair	Poor
2800	2400	2200	1500	800	380

Dakota Varminter

Single-shot, small, round stainless steel bolt action with 1-piece bolt, plunger ejector, and box-style match trigger. Match grade 24" stainless sporter barrel in a wide variety of varmint and benchrest calibers. Weight about 7 lbs. Guaranteed 1/2 MOA accuracy. Note: Deluxe in XX Claro Walnut (add $800).

NIB	Exc.	V.G.	Good	Fair	Poor
2000	1700	1450	1220	750	450

Dakota Varminter Heavy Barrel

As above but with varmint contour barrel and wide-forend walnut or synthetic stock.

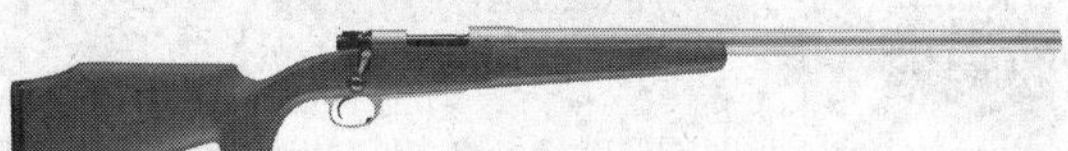

NIB	Exc.	V.G.	Good	Fair	Poor
2400	2000	1750	1480	900	520

Model 10 Single Shot Deluxe

Same as above, with exhibition grade English walnut.

NIB	Exc.	V.G.	Good	Fair	Poor
6000	5400	4700	4000	—	—

Sharps Rifle

With proportions reduced in size by 20% from the 1874 Sharps, the Dakota Sharps has a 25" octagon or 1/2 octagon, 1/2 round barrel, straight- or pistol grip stock with XX walnut, with and color case action and steel buttplate. Offered for rimmed cartridges from .17 HMR to .444 Marlin with sight options from tang sight to Malcom-style scope. Weight around 8 lbs. Introduced in 2003.

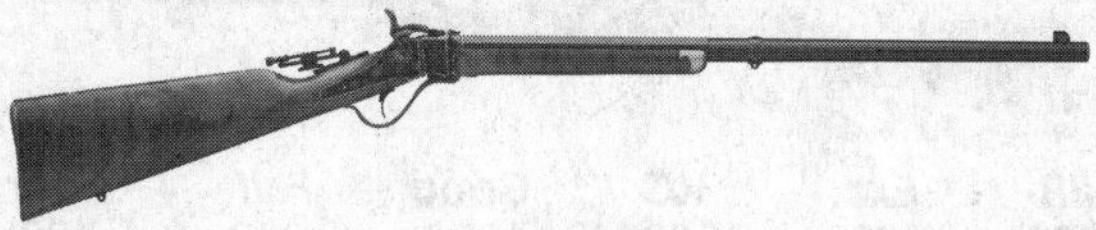

NIB	Exc.	V.G.	Good	Fair	Poor
4000	3600	3250	2750	—	—

Model 10 Single Shot

Built on a single-shot falling action. Features 23" barrel and choice of XX grade wood with oil-finish. Fine line checkering, steel grip cap and .5" recoil pad are also standard. Weight about 5.5 lbs.

NIB	Exc.	V.G.	Good	Fair	Poor
4500	4000	2750	1550	900	400

Limited Edition .30-06 Model 10

Ultra-decked-out version of Model 10; commemorates 100th Anniversary of .30-06 cartridge; production limited to 101 units. Available 2006–2007.

NIB	Exc.	V.G.	Good	Fair	Poor
8000	5500	4000	2650	1700	500

Dakota .22 Long Rifle Sporter

Fitted with 22" barrel, X grade oil-finish walnut, with fine line checkering and steel grip cap. A .5" black recoil pad standard. Weight about 6.5 lbs. Ceased production in 1998.

NIB	Exc.	V.G.	Good	Fair	Poor
1750	1300	800	650	500	280

Dakota .22 Long Rifle Sporter (New Model)

Re-introduction (2003) of Dakota .22 rifle. Discontinued.

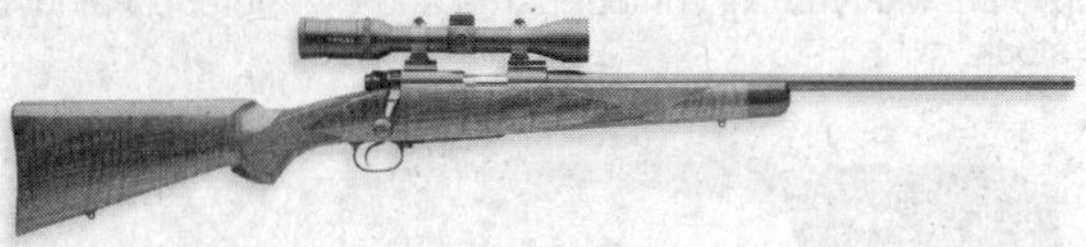

NIB	Exc.	V.G.	Good	Fair	Poor
2800	2500	2000	1350	700	350

Model 97 Lightweight Hunter

Introduced in 1998. Features barrel lengths from 22" to 24" in both short-/long-actions. Special lightweight composite stock is used. Calibers offered range from .22-250 to .330 Dakota Magnum. Weight between 6.15 to 6.5 lbs., depending on caliber and barrel length. Note: Add 50 to 70 percent for Deluxe with AAA grade wood. Discontinued.

NIB	Exc.	V.G.	Good	Fair	Poor
2000	1500	1100	800	500	380

Model T-76 Longbow Tactical Rifle

Long range tactical bolt-action rifle available in 3 calibers: .338 Lapua, .300 Dakota Magnum and .330 Dakota Magnum. Fiberglass stock is an A-2 McMillan in black or olive green. Adjustable length of pull, with bipod spike in forearm. The 28" stainless steel barrel is .950 diameter at the muzzle, with muzzle brake. Rifle sold with a number of accessories; case with bipod, tool kit and tool box. Weight about 13.7 lbs. Discontinued.

NIB	Exc.	V.G.	Good	Fair	Poor
4600	4250	3000	1650	800	400

Classic Predator

Bolt-action rifle chambered for .17 VarTarg, .17 Rem., .17 Tactical, .20 VarTarg, .20 Tactical, .20 PPC, .204 Ruger, .221 Rem. Fireball, .222 Rem., .222 Rem. Magnum, .223 Rem., .22 BR, 6 PPC and 6 BR. Fitted with a 22" stainless steel barrel, checkered special select Claro walnut stock, with cheekpiece. Discontinued.

NIB	Exc.	V.G.	Good	Fair	Poor
3800	3000	2200	1700	800	380

Serious Predator

As above, with AAA Claro walnut stock. Discontinued.

NIB	Exc.	V.G.	Good	Fair	Poor
3000	2250	2000	1650	800	400

All-Weather Predator

As above, with varmint style composite stock. Discontinued.

NIB	Exc.	V.G.	Good	Fair	Poor
2500	2000	1600	1000	500	300

Double Rifle

Available in most common calibers. Fitted with exhibition walnut, with pistol grip. Barrel is 25". Round-action with selective ejectors, recoil pad and hard case. Prices listed for guns without engraving. Offered from 2001–2005. Discontinued.

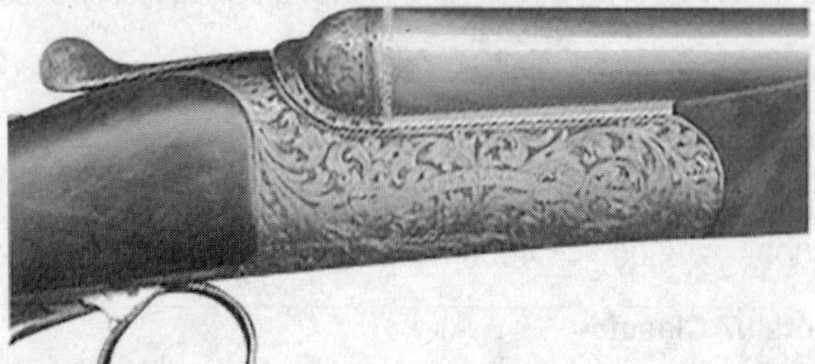

NIB	Exc.	V.G.	Good	Fair	Poor
30000	24000	18000	10000	3500	800

SHOTGUNS

Classic Grade

Grade features case colored round-action, with straight-grip and fancy walnut oil-finish stock. Forearm is splinter type. Double trigger standard, with choice of chokes. No longer in production.

NIB	Exc.	V.G.	Good	Fair	Poor
7950	5200	4400	3000	2000	600

Premier Grade

Grade features case colored round-action, with 50 percent engraving coverage. Exhibition grade English walnut stock, with straight-grip and splinter forearm. Oil rubbed finish. Double triggers are standard, with choice of chokes. Note: Add 10 percent for 28-gauge and .410 bore.

NIB	Exc.	V.G.	Good	Fair	Poor
13950	9500	7000	4750	2900	500

Dakota American Legend

Introduced in 1996. Side-by-side shotgun offered in 12-, 20-, 28-gauge and .410 bore. Concave rib, splinter forearm, double triggers, straight-grip stock, 27" barrels and full scroll engraving on frame. Many additional extra cost options are offered that can greatly affect price. Base price listed.

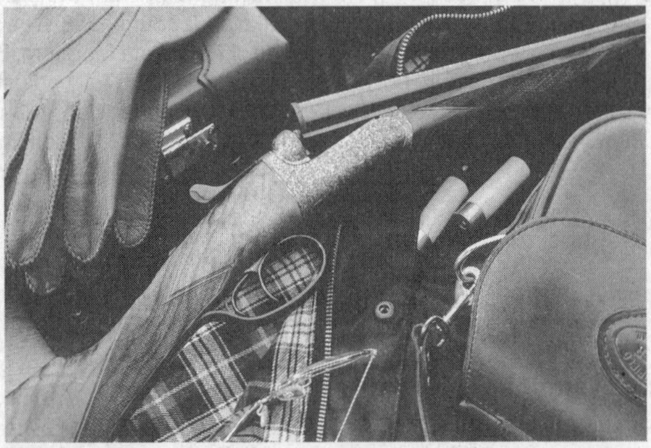

NIB	Exc.	V.G.	Good	Fair	Poor
18000	14000	11500	7900	5000	600

Dakota Shotgun

Similar to American Legend. Offered in two grades of finish. New grades first offered in 1997.

DAKOTA ARMS INC.—FERLIB SHOTGUNS

In 2000, Dakota Arms Inc. became the exclusive importer of Ferlib shotguns in the U.S. Models listed are imported and sold by Dakota Arms Inc.

Model 7

NIB	Exc.	V.G.	Good	Fair	Poor
10950	8000	6500	5000	4000	700

Prince Model

NIB	Exc.	V.G.	Good	Fair	Poor
11950	9000	7500	6000	4500	700

Prince Model Side-Lever

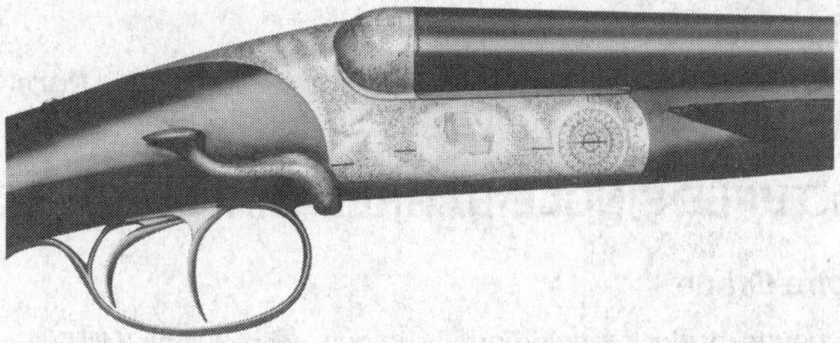

NIB	Exc.	V.G.	Good	Fair	Poor
14500	10500	8500	7000	5500	700

Rex

NIB	Exc.	V.G.	Good	Fair	Poor
14950	11000	8500	7000	5500	700

Premier

NIB	Exc.	V.G.	Good	Fair	Poor
16950	12500	10000	7200	5500	600

Sideplate Model

NIB	Exc.	V.G.	Good	Fair	Poor
14400	10500	8500	7000	5500	700

Sideplate Model with Gold

NIB	Exc.	V.G.	Good	Fair	Poor
15100	11250	10000	7200	5500	600

Sideplate with Scroll

NIB	Exc.	V.G.	Good	Fair	Poor
14000	10500	8500	7000	5500	700

Hammer Gun

NIB	Exc.	V.G.	Good	Fair	Poor
19000	14000	12000	10000	5000	700

H.H. Model—no engraving

NIB	Exc.	V.G.	Good	Fair	Poor
20000	15000	13000	11000	570	680

Esposizione

NIB	Exc.	V.G.	Good	Fair	Poor
25500	18000	13000	10000	7000	700

L'Inglesina

NIB	Exc.	V.G.	Good	Fair	Poor
25500	18000	13000	10000	7000	700

Model E "Fantasy"

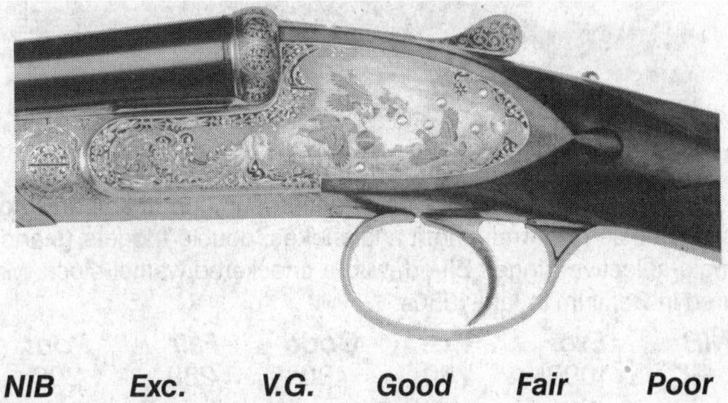

NIB	Exc.	V.G.	Good	Fair	Poor
39500	27500	22000	15500	11000	700

Boss—no engraving

NIB	Exc.	V.G.	Good	Fair	Poor
29500	20000	15000	10000	7000	750

DAKOTA ARMS INC.—SIACE SHOTGUNS

Imported from Italy in 2004 and called Dakota SuperLight. Shotguns are side-by-sides, with boxlock actions.

Field

Available in 12-, 16-, 20-, 24-, 28- and 32-gauge as well as .410 bore. Case colored receiver with select Turkish walnut. Checkering is 24 lpi. Double triggers. Border engraving. Weight about 5.5 lbs. for 20-gauge. Note: Add $600 for 16-, 32-gauge and .410 bore.

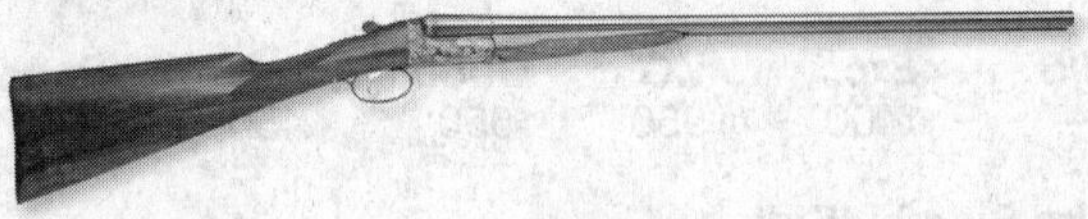

NIB	Exc.	V.G.	Good	Fair	Poor
4500	3500	2400	1780	1100	500

Grade II

As above, with 65 percent coverage of English scroll. Note: Add $700 for 16-, 32-gauge and .410 bore.

NIB	Exc.	V.G.	Good	Fair	Poor
5500	4250	3200	1600	800	400

Grade III

NIB	Exc.	V.G.	Good	Fair	Poor
6500	5000	4000	3000	1650	400

DALY, CHARLES

Charles Daly was co-founder of Schoverling & Daly sporting goods company in New York City in 1865. The company imported some of the better-made shotguns from Europe and Charles Daly was used as the brand name. Daly trademark was sold several times over the years, with various owners importing guns from Belgium, Germany, Japan, Italy and other countries.

Model 500

Gauge: .410 bore, 3 in. Barrel: 28 in. Length: 43.25 in. Weight: 4.4 lbs. Stock: Checkered walnut English-style buttstock. Features: Charles Daly's new pair of baby-bore SxS Model 500 includes two versions, both steel, one with a black engraved receiver and the other black engraved with gold accents. Double triggers, extractors, manual safety, brass front bead. Includes five Mobil style chokes (SK, IC, M, IM, F).

NIB	Exc.	V.G.	Good	Fair	Poor
800	—	—	—	—	—

EARLY PRUSSIAN GUNS

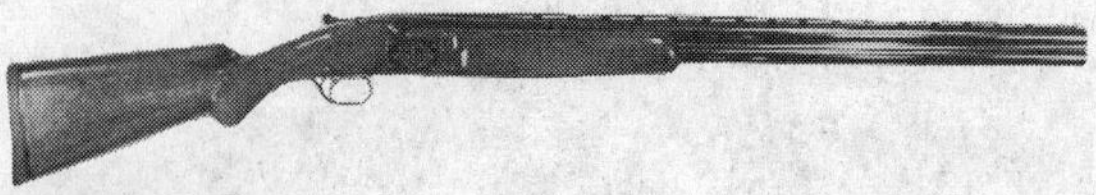

Commander Over/Under Model 100

Boxlock over/under Anson & Deeley action shotgun chambered for all gauges. Choice of barrel length and chokes, double triggers (standard) or single-selective trigger. Blued, with a checkered walnut stock. Manufactured in Belgium in late 1930s.

NIB	Exc.	V.G.	Good	Fair	Poor
—	1000	750	480	280	200

Commander Over/Under Model 200

As above, with a better-grade walnut stock.

NIB	Exc.	V.G.	Good	Fair	Poor
—	1100	850	550	300	200

Superior Side-by-Side

As above, with an Anson & Deeley boxlock action and double triggers. Blued, with a walnut stock. Not manufactured after 1933. Note: Add $600 for 20-gauge; $1000 for 10-gauge.

NIB	Exc.	V.G.	Good	Fair	Poor
—	1400	950	650	450	250

Empire Side-by-Side

As above, but engraved with a better grade of walnut.

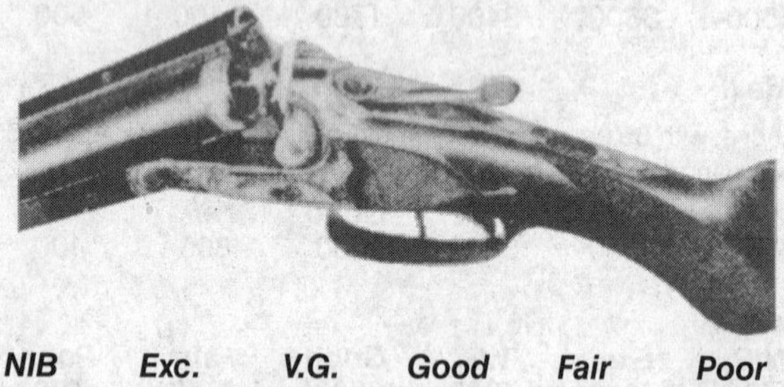

NIB	Exc.	V.G.	Good	Fair	Poor
—	3750	3000	2250	1250	600

Note: Prices shown for Empire and Diamond grade models are for those manufactured by Sauer. Add 20 to 30 percent for Linder manufacture.

Diamond Grade Side-by-Side

A deluxe version of above.

NIB	Exc.	V.G.	Good	Fair	Poor
—	5750	4500	3750	3000	1200

Regent Diamond Grade Side-by-Side

Custom order version of above.

NIB	Exc.	V.G.	Good	Fair	Poor
—	11500	8500	7000	5500	2500

Empire Over/Under

A 12-, 16- and 20-gauge Anson & Deeley boxlock shotgun. Choice of barrel length and choke, double triggers and automatic ejectors. Engraved with fine quality scrollwork and walnut stock. Discontinued in 1933.

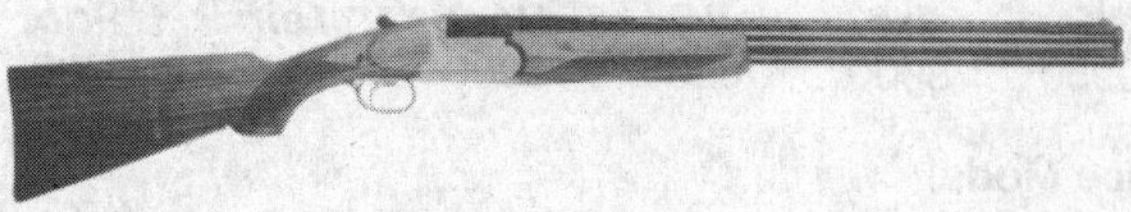

NIB	Exc.	V.G.	Good	Fair	Poor
—	3500	2750	2000	1150	500

Diamond Grade Over/Under

As above, but more finely finished.

NIB	Exc.	V.G.	Good	Fair	Poor
—	5500	3750	3250	2500	1250

SEXTUPLE SINGLE-BARREL TRAP

Empire Grade

A 12-gauge boxlock single-barrel shotgun, with 30" or 34" Full choke barrels, ventilated rib and automatic ejectors. Strong action features six locking lugs. Engraved with a walnut stock. Manufactured after 1933.

NIB	Exc.	V.G.	Good	Fair	Poor
—	2950	2450	1850	1500	750

Regent Diamond Grade

As above, with more engraving and better grade walnut stock.

NIB	Exc.	V.G.	Good	Fair	Poor
—	7500	6300	5500	4500	2000

DRILLINGS

Superior Grade

A 12-, 16- and 20-gauge over/under rifle/shotgun, with a rifle barrel in .25-20, .25-35 or .30-30. Engraved with a walnut stock. Not manufactured after 1933.

NIB	Exc.	V.G.	Good	Fair	Poor
—	3700	2450	1800	1450	800

Diamond Grade

As above, with more engraving and better grade walnut stock.

NIB	Exc.	V.G.	Good	Fair	Poor
—	5250	4500	3750	3000	1500

Regent Diamond Grade

As above, with elaborate engraving and highest quality walnut stock.

NIB	Exc.	V.G.	Good	Fair	Poor
—	12500	9500	7200	5800	3000

B.C. MIROKU GUNS

Empire Grade Side-by-Side

A 12-, 16- and 20-gauge Anson and Deeley boxlock shotgun, with 26", 28" and 30" barrels, various chokes, extractors and a single trigger. Blued, with a checkered walnut stock. Manufactured between 1968 and 1971. Note: Add 10 percent for ventilated rib barrels and/or 20-gauge.

NIB	Exc.	V.G.	Good	Fair	Poor
—	750	550	380	200	100

Superior Grade Single Barrel Trap

A 12-gauge boxlock shotgun, with 32" or 34" ventilated rib barrels, Full choke and automatic ejector. Blued, with Monte Carlo walnut stock. Manufactured between 1968 and 1976.

NIB	Exc.	V.G.	Good	Fair	Poor
—	680	520	450	350	200

Over/Unders

A 12-, 20-, 28-gauge and .410 bore boxlock shotgun, with 26", 28" and 30" barrels and ventilated ribs. Various choke combinations were offered, with single-selective triggers and automatic ejectors. Blued, with checkered walnut stocks. Differences between grades are degree and quality of engraving and grade of walnut used for stock. Smaller-bore guns bring a premium as listed. Manufactured between 1963 and 1976 by B.C. Miroku. Note: Add 10 percent 20-gauge; 20 percent 28-gauge; 30 percent .410.

Venture Grade

NIB	Exc.	V.G.	Good	Fair	Poor
—	900	680	500	380	200

Venture Grade Skeet or Trap

Offered with 26" Skeet & Skeet or 30" Full choke.

NIB	Exc.	V.G.	Good	Fair	Poor
—	800	550	480	380	200

Field Grade

Chambered for 12- and 20-gauge only.

NIB	Exc.	V.G.	Good	Fair	Poor
—	900	700	500	420	200

Superior Grade

NIB	Exc.	V.G.	Good	Fair	Poor
—	1200	900	600	520	200

Superior Grade Trap

NIB	Exc.	V.G.	Good	Fair	Poor
—	800	600	520	420	200

Diamond Grade

NIB	Exc.	V.G.	Good	Fair	Poor
—	1800	1400	980	650	300

Diamond Grade Trap or Skeet

With 26" Skeet & Skeet or 30" Full choke barrels and Monte Carlo stocks. Note: Add 5 percent for wide rib.

NIB	Exc.	V.G.	Good	Fair	Poor
—	1500	1100	800	650	350

ITALIAN MANUFACTURE SEMI-AUTOMATIC SHOTGUNS

Manufactured by the firm Breda in Milan, Italy. Semi-automatic "Novamatic" produced in 1968. All other models began Italian production in 1976. Imported by KBI, Inc. until 2010.

Novamatic Lightweight

A 12-gauge semi-automatic shotgun, with 26" or 28" ventilated rib barrel and screw-in choke tubes. Receiver is alloy, with checkered walnut stock. Imported under the Daly name in 1968 only.

NIB	Exc.	V.G.	Good	Fair	Poor
—	400	320	280	180	120

Novamatic Trap

As above, with Monte Carlo stock and 30" Full choke barrel.

NIB	Exc.	V.G.	Good	Fair	Poor
—	420	340	290	200	150

Charles Daly Automatic

A 12-gauge Magnum semi-automatic shotgun, with 26" or 28" ventilated rib barrels, screw-in choke tubes and 5-shot magazine. A slug gun is available, with rifle sights. Checkered walnut grip in two versions—pistol grip and English-style straight-grip. Note: Choke-tube model would be worth a 10 percent premium.

NIB	Exc.	V.G.	Good	Fair	Poor
—	480	400	300	220	150

Field Grade

Introduced in 1999, this model has several variations all in 12-gauge. Standard gun choice of 24", 26", 28" or 30" barrels, with screw-in chokes and synthetic stocks. Slug gun offered with 22" barrel in blue or nickel finish. A full coverage camo model offered in same configurations as field grade. Note: Add $30 for nickel slug gun; $100 for camo gun.

NIB	Exc.	V.G.	Good	Fair	Poor
420	360	260	200	150	100

Superior Grade Hunter

Offered in 12-gauge, with choice of 26", 28" or 30" ventilated rib barrels. Walnut stock, with hand checkering. Gold trigger and highlights. Introduced in 1999.

NIB	Exc.	V.G.	Good	Fair	Poor
550	420	360	240	160	100

Superior Grade Sporting

Same as above, with 28" or 30" ported barrel and select walnut stock.

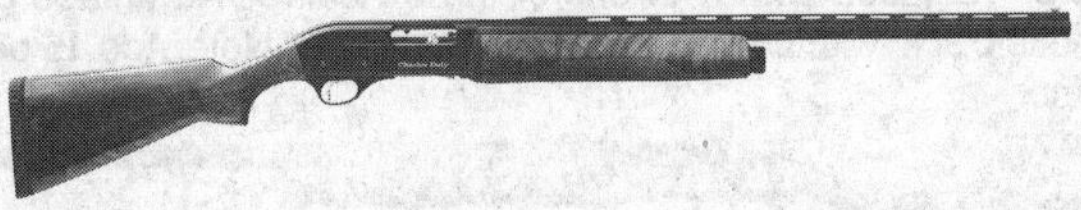

NIB	Exc.	V.G.	Good	Fair	Poor
570	450	360	240	160	100

Superior Grade Trap

This 12-gauge offered with a choice of 30" or 32" ventilated rib barrel. Walnut stock with hand checkering. Introduced in 1999.

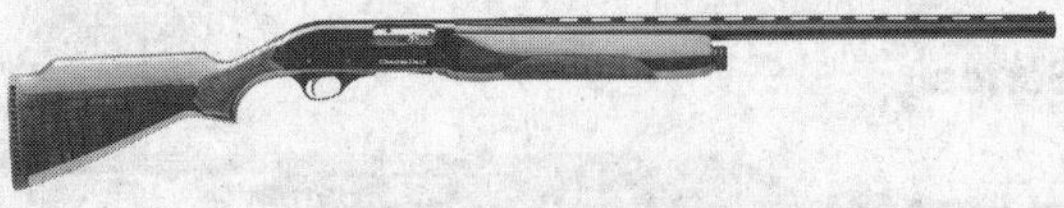

NIB	Exc.	V.G.	Good	Fair	Poor
620	480	390	270	180	100

Field Hunter VR-MC

This series of 3" semi-automatic 12-gauges is finished in one of four Realtree/Advantage camo patterns or matte black. Barrels are 24", 26" or 28". Advantage Timber model available in 20-gauge and black matte available in 20- and 28-gauge. Note: Add 15 percent for camo.

NIB	Exc.	V.G.	Good	Fair	Poor
420	360	260	200	150	100

Field Hunter VR-MC Youth

As above, with 1.6" shorter stock and 22" barrel. 20-gauge only.

NIB	Exc.	V.G.	Good	Fair	Poor
400	340	230	160	120	100

Superior II

New in 2007, Superior II line of semi-automatics features oil-finished Turkish walnut stocks and three chokes.

NIB	Exc.	V.G.	Good	Fair	Poor
600	520	400	280	200	100

Hunter

Available in 12- and 20-gauge, with 26" or 28" barrel. 28-gauge with 26" barrel.

NIB	Exc.	V.G.	Good	Fair	Poor
600	520	400	280	200	100

Sport

In 12-gauge only, with 28" or 30" ported barrel and wide rib.

NIB	Exc.	V.G.	Good	Fair	Poor
600	520	400	280	200	100

Trap

In 12-gauge 30" ported barrel only, with Monte Carlo comb and wide rib.

NIB	Exc.	V.G.	Good	Fair	Poor
650	550	420	280	200	100

Field Hunter Maxi-Mag VR-MC Semi-Auto

This 3.5" 12-gauge comes in one of three Realtree/Advantage camos and matte black, with 24", 26" or 28" ported barrel. Note: Add 15 percent for camo.

NIB	Exc.	V.G.	Good	Fair	Poor
420	360	260	200	150	100

CURRENT SEMI-AUTO SHOTGUNS

600 Series

Model 600

Gas operating system, chrome-lined chambers and bores, aluminum receiver and synthetic stocks in 12, 20, and 28 gauge, in 26" or 28" barrels. Rem Choke Thread MC-3 with IC, M, and F chokes. Fiber-Optic front sight. About 6.8 lbs., lengths vary from 47.6" to 49.6".

NIB	Exc.	V.G.	Good	Fair	Poor
400	300	200	100	—	—

Model 601 Field

NIB	Exc.	V.G.	Good	Fair	Poor
250	150	80	—	—	—

Model 635

12-gauge 3.5" magnum chrome-lined chamber and bore along with aluminum receivers and synthetic stocks in the popular Realtree camo patterns. Interchangeable Rem threaded choke tubes (SK, IC, M, IM, F).

NIB	Exc.	V.G.	Good	Fair	Poor
520	450	380	300	200	100

Model CA612

Inertia-driven rotary bolt system. 12-gauge in 22", 24", 28" barrels. Tactical version has a pistol grip stock.

NIB	Exc.	V.G.	Good	Fair	Poor
520	450	380	300	200	100

N4S Bullpup Semi-Auto Shotgun

The CD Defense N4S Bullpup Shotgun features a 19.75" barrel with a Modified Beretta/Benelli Mobil Choke, chambered in 3" 12 gauge. It has adjustable front and rear flip-up sights and comes with a 5-round magazine. 9.3 lbs., 29.25" long. Aluminum receiver, synthetic stock and forend.

NIB	Exc.	V.G.	Good	Fair	Poor
480	380	300	200	100	—

AR-12S SEMI-AUTO SHOTGUN

Daly's tactical subsidiary, CD Defense, makes this AR-pattern 3" 12-gauge with an adjustable comb, carry handle, adjustable rear sight, and standard front sight. Comes with a 5-round magazine.

NIB	Exc.	V.G.	Good	Fair	Poor
380	300	250	200	100	—

Honcho Tactical Semi-Auto

Introduced 2019. 12-gauge 3-inch, 14" barrel. 4+1 tubular magazine. Rubber-coated walnut pistol grip and forend. 5.3 lbs. Cylinder bore choke. Black synthetic bird's head grip. 27" long.

NIB	Exc.	V.G.	Good	Fair	Poor
980	850	750	650	550	450

AR .410 Upper

Gauge: .410 bore 2.5 in. Barrel: 19 in. Length: 26.75 in. Weight: 4.9 lbs. Stock: Upper only with quad Picatinny rail forend. Features: Charles Daly enters the AR market with a .410 bore shotgun upper. Built of black anodized aluminum. Auto-ejection, gas-operated system. Windage-adjustable rear sight and elevation adjustable rear flip-up sights. Ships with a five-round magazine but compatible with 10 and 15 rounders. This upper must be used with a Mil-Spec lower and carbine-length buffer tube.

NIB	Exc.	V.G.	Good	Fair	Poor
360	—	—	—	—	—

TURKISH SHOTGUNS

Model 105

This 3" 12-gauge over/under features an engraved nickel-plated steel receiver, double triggers and extractors. Chokes are fixed Modified and Full with 28" barrels; or Modified and Improved Cylinder with 26" barrels.

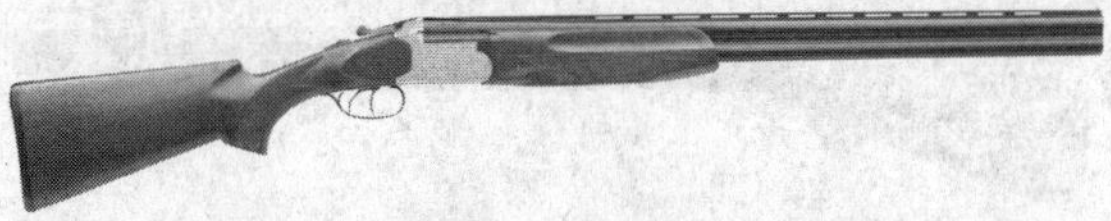

NIB	Exc.	V.G.	Good	Fair	Poor
600	450	400	300	180	100

Model 106/206

Similar to Model 105, but in 12-, 20- and 28-gauge and .410 bore. Model 106 has a blued receiver, with raised gold ducks and rounded pistol grip. All but the .410 include three screw-in chokes. Barrels are 26" or 28" in 12- and 20-gauge and 26" in 28-gauge and .410. Frames are scaled to gauge. Note: Add $50 for 28-gauge and .410 bore; $50 for model 206 with SST ejectors.

NIB	Exc.	V.G.	Good	Fair	Poor
650	500	400	300	180	100

Model 306

This 3" side-by-side is offered in 12- and 20-gauge, with 26" or 28" barrels. Turkish walnut stock, gold-plated single selective trigger and extractors. Three choke tubes.

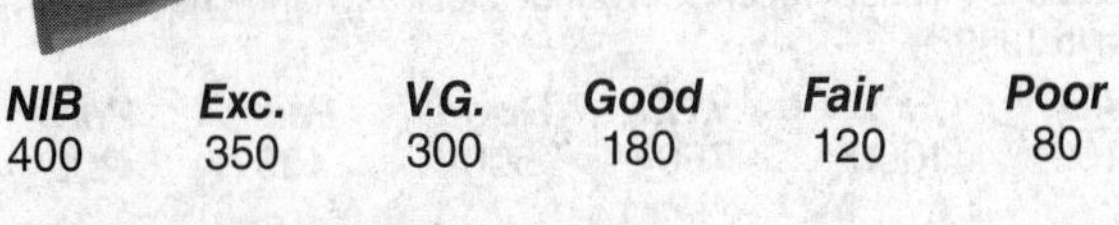

NIB	Exc.	V.G.	Good	Fair	Poor
400	350	300	180	120	80

PUMP SHOTGUNS

300 SERIES

Model 300

12- and 20-gauge pump guns. 28" barrels for 12s; 22" and 26" barrels for 20s. Dual pump-action bars. Interchangeable Rem threaded choke tubes (IC, M, F). 6.4 lbs., 47" long.

NIB	Exc.	V.G.	Good	Fair	Poor
260	200	150	100	—	—

Model 301

NIB	Exc.	V.G.	Good	Fair	Poor
250	200	150	100	—	—

Model 335

Drilled and tapped for provided Picatinny rail and chambered in the 3.5" 12 gauge. Features Realtree camo with a fiber-optic front sight. Adjustable folding synthetic Realtree buttstock.6.9 lbs. 41.28"-44.5" long. 24" barrel, 3 Rem Chokes (XXF, M, F).

NIB	Exc.	V.G.	Good	Fair	Poor
350	300	250	200	100	—

Honcho Pump

Introduced 2019. 12-gauge 3-inch, 14" barrel. Rubber-coated walnut pistol grip and forend. 5.7 lbs. Cylinder bore choke. Black synthetic bird's head grip. 27.25" long. One version is mag-fed.

NIB	Exc.	V.G.	Good	Fair	Poor
980	850	750	650	550	450

Field Grade

This 12-gauge pump gun offered with 24", 26", 28" or 30" barrels. Fixed chokes. A slug gun offered with 18.5" barrels, with blue or nickel finish. Camo version also offered. First introduced in 1999. Also offered in 20-gauge in both full size and youth. Note: Add $10 for nickel gun; $80 for full camo gun.

NIB	Exc.	V.G.	Good	Fair	Poor
300	220	160	120	100	60

Field Tactical

This pump gun chambered for the 12-gauge shell. Fitted with an 18.5" barrel and fixed blade front sight. An 18.5" slug barrel with adjustable sights is also offered. Black synthetic stock. Blued or nickel finish. Note: Add $30 for nickel finish.

NIB	Exc.	V.G.	Good	Fair	Poor
350	280	190	150	120	80

Field Hunter MM (Maxi-Mag)

This 12-gauge pump gun chambered for 3.5" Magnum shell. Offered with choice of 24", 26" or 28" ventilated rib ported barrels. Black synthetic stock, with camo stock also available. Weight about 6.75 lbs. Note: Add $50 for camo finish.

NIB	Exc.	V.G.	Good	Fair	Poor
280	220	150	120	100	60

Field Hunter Maxi-Mag VR-MC Pump

Newer versions of Maxi-Mag are recognized by an updated forend and availability in Timber or Hardwoods camo or matte black. All are 3.5"

12-gauge, with a 24", 26" or 28" ported barrel. Note: Add 15 percent for camo.

NIB	Exc.	V.G.	Good	Fair	Poor
350	300	260	200	150	100

OVER/UNDER GUNS

Model 202

Gauges: 12 ga., 3 in., 20 ga., 3 in., .410 bore, 3 in. Barrels: 26 in., 28 in., ventilated rib. Length: 43-45 in. Weight: 6.2-7.3 lbs. Stock: Checkered walnut. Features: The new Charles Daly 202 line of O/U shotguns are built of aluminum alloy. Silver receivers are engraved with a dog scene. Single selective mechanical reset trigger, fixed fiber-optic front sight, extractors, rubber buttpad. Includes five extended Mobil style chokes (SK, IC, M, IM, F).

NIB	Exc.	V.G.	Good	Fair	Poor
420	400	350	300	200	—

Model 204X

Break-open 12- and 20-gauges for wing shooters, trap shooters or sporting clays enthusiasts. 12-gauges come in 24", 26", and 28" barrels with extractors, 3" chambers, and hand-oiled checkered-walnut furniture. 20-gauges come in 20" and 26" barrels. Comes with 5 Rem Chokes (SK, IC, M, IM, F), and the trigger is a single-selective mechanical reset and manual safety. Front sight is a fixed fiber optic. Weight: about 6.8 lbs. Length: 45". Finish: Blued receiver, blued steel barrels.

NIB	Exc.	V.G.	Good	Fair	Poor
600	500	400	300	200	100

206 Field Grade

An over/under series including field, sporting and trap models, all in 12-gauge only. Features include 28", 30" and 32" barrels, automatic ejectors, single selective trigger, choke tubes, ventilated rib, checkered oil-finished walnut stock and forend. Made in Turkey by Akkar Silah Sanayi.

NIB	Exc.	V.G.	Good	Fair	Poor
650	550	480	400	300	200

Model 206— 206S Sporting Model

NIB	Exc.	V.G.	Good	Fair	Poor
1100	1000	800	650	550	450

Model 206206T Trap Model

NIB	Exc.	V.G.	Good	Fair	Poor
1200	1050	900	750	650	500

Model 206 Post 2013 Current Production206 Field Grade

NIB	Exc.	V.G.	Good	Fair	Poor
900	800	650	550	480	400

Model 214E

Break-open 12 and 20 gauges for wing shooters, trap shooters or sporting clays enthusiasts. 12-gauges come with 26", 28", and 30" barrels with extractors, 3" chambers, and hand-oiled checkered-walnut stock and forend. 20 gauge comes with 26" barrels. Comes with 5 Rem Chokes (SK, IC, M, IM, F), and the trigger is a single-selective mechanical reset and manual safety. Front fiber-optic sight. Weight: about 7.3 lbs. Length: 45". Finish: Blued receiver and barrels. Sporting Clays model features select wood, extended chokes, an inertial reset trigger, secondary fiber-optic sights, an adjustable stock, and 30" barrels.

NIB	Exc.	V.G.	Good	Fair	Poor
620	520	420	320	200	100

Model 214E Over/Under Sporting Clays

NIB	Exc.	V.G.	Good	Fair	Poor
1130	1000	900	800	600	400

Country Squire Over/Under Folding

Features a folding stock, with over/under ventilated rib barrels 25.5" in length. Gold double triggers and walnut stock. Chokes are Full and Full.

NIB	Exc.	V.G.	Good	Fair	Poor
550	450	320	250	180	120

Field II Hunter

A 12-, 20-, 28-gauge and .410 bore over/under shotgun, with 26" or 28" chrome-lined ventilated rib barrels. Crossbolt boxlock-action, single-selective trigger and extractors. Blued, with a stamped checkered walnut stock. Introduced in 1989. Weight: 12-gauge about 7 lbs.; 28-gauge and .410 bore about 6.75 lbs. Note: Add $150 for ejectors.

NIB	Exc.	V.G.	Good	Fair	Poor
900	780	580	400	250	200

Field Ultra Light

Introduced in 1999. Offered in 12- or 20-gauge, with 26" barrel choked Improved Cylinder/Modified. Receiver is aluminum alloy. Walnut stock, with pistol grip and slim forend. Weight about 5.5 lbs.

NIB	Exc.	V.G.	Good	Fair	Poor
950	850	650	450	—	—

Field III

An economy level model in 12- or 20-gauge, imported from Turkey in the 1980s.

NIB	Exc.	V.G.	Good	Fair	Poor
400	350	300	250	200	150

Empire

Similar to Field II Hunter, with automatic ejectors, screw-in choke tubes and a silver-finished receiver. Walnut stock is hand-checkered. Introduced in 1989.

NIB	Exc.	V.G.	Good	Fair	Poor
1150	1000	750	500	400	200

Empire II EDL Hunter

Offered in 12-, 20-, 28-gauge and .410 bore. Features 26" or 28" ventilated rib barrels (26" only on 28-gauge or .410). Choke tubes on 12- and 20-gauge and Fixed chokes on 28-gauge and .410 guns. Receiver has game scene engraving, with nine gold inlays. Weight 6.25 to 7.25 lbs.

depending on gauge.

NIB	Exc.	V.G.	Good	Fair	Poor
2000	1500	1100	700	380	200

Empire Sporting

Offered in 12-gauge, with choice of 28" or 30" barrels. Fitted with a Monte Carlo stock and automatic ejectors.

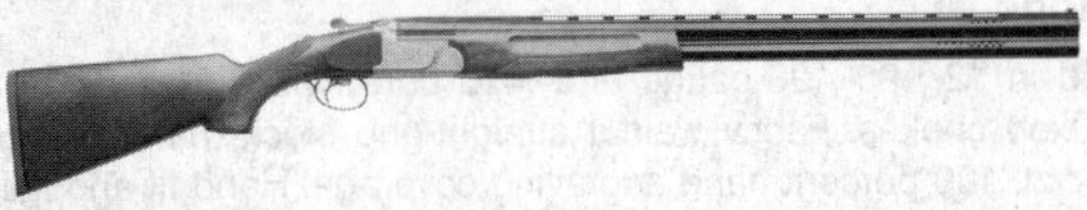

NIB	Exc.	V.G.	Good	Fair	Poor
1850	1420	1000	600	380	200

Empire Grade Combination

An over/under, with 12-gauge top barrel and rifle lower barrel. Rifle calibers are .22 Hornet, .223 Rem., .22-250, .243, .270, .308 and .30-06. Barrel length 23.5". Weight about 7.25 lbs.

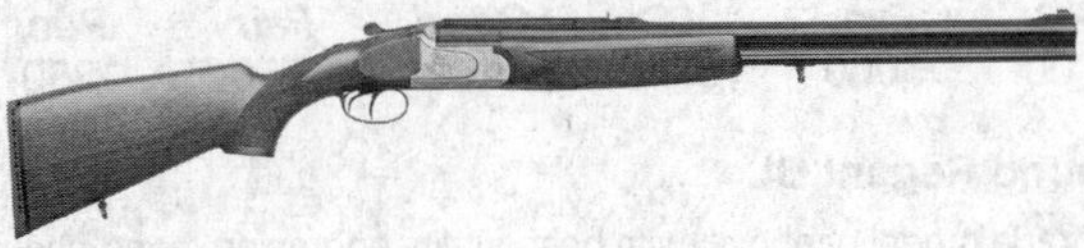

NIB	Exc.	V.G.	Good	Fair	Poor
2190	1600	1150	800	380	200

Empire Trap

This 12-gauge features Monte Carlo stock with 30" barrels.

NIB	Exc.	V.G.	Good	Fair	Poor
2250	1650	1200	750	320	150

Empire Grade Trap Combo

Features 30" over/under barrel, with an additional 32" single barrel. Buttstock has fully adjustable comb. Introduced in 1999. Note: Deduct $600 for non-adjustable stock.

NIB	Exc.	V.G.	Good	Fair	Poor
4000	3000	2000	1450	680	380

Diamond GTX DL Hunter

As above in 12- and 20-gauge Magnum. Various barrel lengths and screw-in choke tubes, single trigger, automatic ejectors and select walnut stock. Extra fancy walnut stock and hand engraved frame.

NIB	Exc.	V.G.	Good	Fair	Poor
9000	8000	6000	5000	2000	1000

Diamond GTX Sporting

This 12-gauge features a choice of 28" or 30" barrels, with automatic ejectors and Monte Carlo stock.

NIB	Exc.	V.G.	Good	Fair	Poor
5900	4500	2750	1250	900	450

Diamond GTX Trap or Skeet

As above, with 26" or 30" barrels. Available in 1989. Note: Add 5 percent for wide rib.

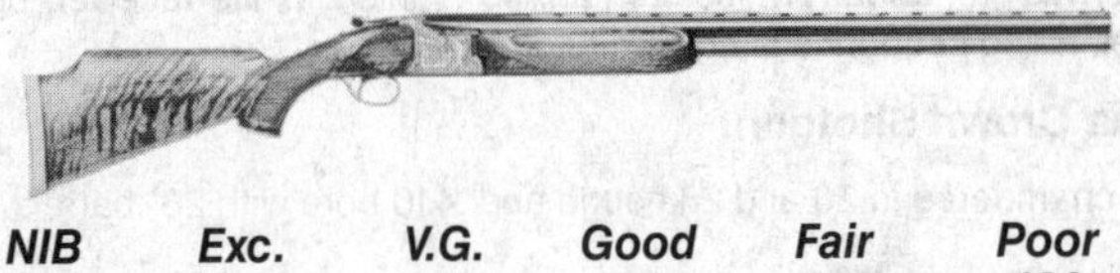

NIB	Exc.	V.G.	Good	Fair	Poor
5900	4500	2750	1250	900	400

Diamond GTX Trap Combo

This model has a fully adjustable stock. Choice of 30" over/under barrels and 32" single barrel.

NIB	Exc.	V.G.	Good	Fair	Poor
7500	5700	4250	2650	1000	450

Presentation Grade

As above, with a Purdey-type boxlock action and engraved false sideplates. Stock of deluxe French walnut. Discontinued in 1986.

NIB	Exc.	V.G.	Good	Fair	Poor
—	5500	3750	1650	900	450

Superior II

A 12-, 20-, 28-gauge and .410 bore over/under shotgun, with 26" or 28" ventilated rib barrels. Various chokes, single trigger and automatic ejectors. Engraved blued, with walnut stock. Weight: 12- and 20-gauge about 7 lbs.; 28-gauge and .410 about 6.75 lbs.

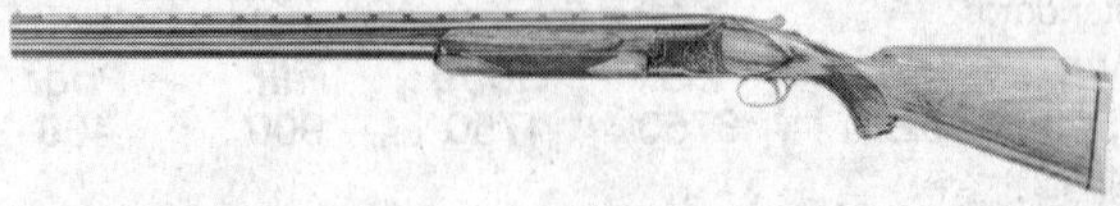

NIB	Exc.	V.G.	Good	Fair	Poor
620	550	350	300	200	150

Superior II Sporting

This 12-gauge fitted with choice of 28" or 30" barrels, Monte Carlo stock and automatic ejectors.

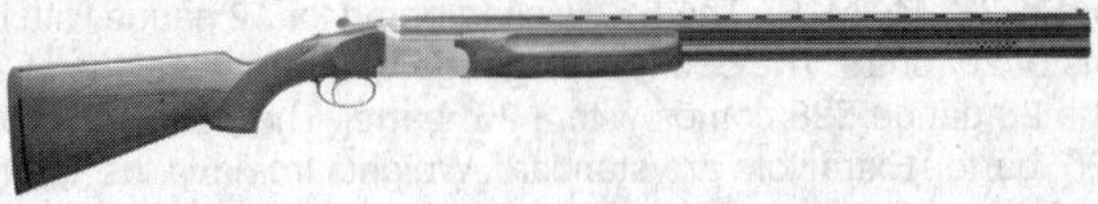

NIB	Exc.	V.G.	Good	Fair	Poor
650	580	380	320	220	160

Superior Grade Trap

This 12-gauge fitted with 30" barrels, Monte Carlo stock and automatic ejectors.

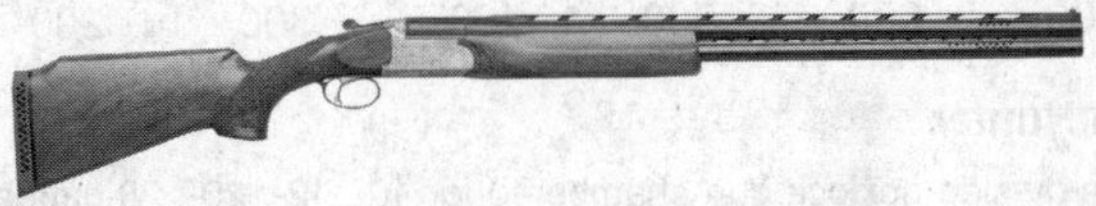

NIB	Exc.	V.G.	Good	Fair	Poor
1700	1250	900	620	420	200

Superior Grade Combination

This is an over/under, with 12-gauge top barrel and rifle lower barrel. Rifle calibers are .22 Hornet, .223 Rem. and .30-06. Barrel length 23.5". Weight about 7.25 lbs.

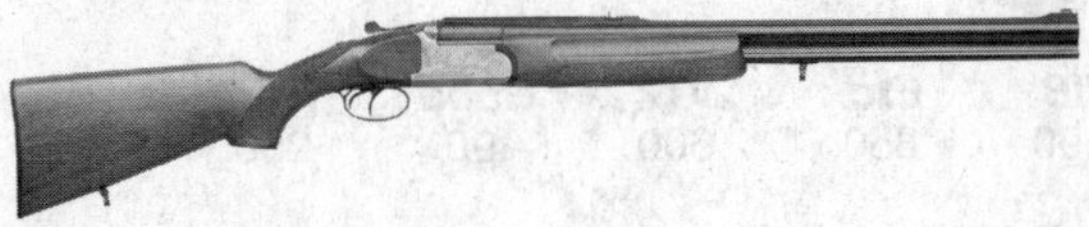

NIB	Exc.	V.G.	Good	Fair	Poor
1480	1100	800	550	350	180

SINGLE-BARREL SHOTGUNS

Model 101

Gauges: 12 ga., 3 in., 20 ga., 3in., .410 bore. Barrels: 26 in., 28 in. Weight: 5.0-8.1 lbs. Length: 41.75-43.75 in. Stock: Choice of either checkered walnut or black synthetic stocks. Features: These updated break-action single shots have become more affordable than ever. Though built of steel, they're still quite light. Brass front bead, manual safety, single trigger, extractor, rubber butt pad. Includes a Modified Beretta/Benelli Mobil choke tube.

NIB	Exc.	V.G.	Good	Fair	Poor
120	100	50	—	—	—

Empire Trap Mono

Single-barrel trap gun, with choice of 30" or 32" barrels. Automatic ejectors and Monte Carlo fully adjustable stock. Note: Deduct $600 for non-adjustable stock.

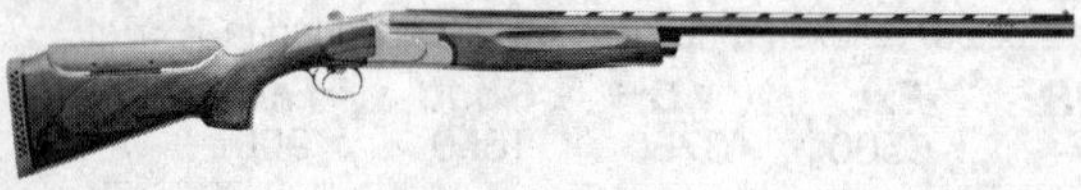

NIB	Exc.	V.G.	Good	Fair	Poor
2450	1800	1250	900	380	180

Diamond GTX Mono

Model has fully adjustable stock. Barrel choice 30". Automatic ejectors are standard.

NIB	Exc.	V.G.	Good	Fair	Poor
6500	5250	3750	1750	900	400

SIDE-BY-SIDE GUNS

Models 512 & 520

The 500-Series double-barrel break-action shotguns are in the classic side-by-side configuration with barrels firing right to left with single reset-ting trigger. Barrels have interchangeable Rem MC-5 threaded choke tubes (SK, IC, M, IM, F). The 512 is chambered for 12 gauge with barrel lengths of 20" or 28". The 520 is a 20 gauge with barrel lengths of 20" or 26". The 28 gauge 528 comes with a 26" barrel. The 536 is a .410 bore with 26" barrel. Extractors are standard. Weights from 5.4 lbs. to 5.6 lbs. "T" models are Coach-style models.

NIB	Exc.	V.G.	Good	Fair	Poor
700	600	500	400	300	200

Field Hunter

A side-by-side boxlock gun chambered for 10-, 12-, 20-, 28-gauge and .410 bore. Barrel length from 26" to 32" depending on gauge. Extractors are standard. Weight from 6.75 lbs. to 8.75 lbs. depending on gauge. Nickel receiver, with game scene engraving. Note: Add $40 for 28-gauge and .410 guns; $100 for automatic ejectors.

NIB	Exc.	V.G.	Good	Fair	Poor
1190	850	600	400	250	100

Superior Hunter

A 12-, 20-, 28-gauge and .410 bore boxlock double-barrel shotgun, with 26" or 28" barrels, various chokes, boxlock action and single trigger. Blued, with walnut stock. In 2002, offered in 10-gauge with 28" barrels. Note: Add $50 for 28-gauge and .410 guns.

NIB	Exc.	V.G.	Good	Fair	Poor
1660	1200	850	600	350	150

Empire Hunter

Offered in 12- and 20-gauge, with 26" or 28" barrels. Chokes are Fixed. Weight about 7 lbs. Silver receiver with game scene engraving, straight stock, splinter forearm, automatic ejectors.

NIB	Exc.	V.G.	Good	Fair	Poor
2120	1500	1100	700	400	200

Diamond DL

Offered in 12-, 20-, 28-gauge and .410 bore, with 26" or 28" barrels and Fixed chokes. Fancy walnut straight-grip stock, hand detachable sidelocks, 100 percent hand engraving coverage. Hand fit and finished. Weight: 12- and 20-gauge about 6.75 lbs.; 28-gauge and .410 about 5.75 lbs. Model generally made on special order only. Note: Add $450 for 28-gauge and .410 bore.

NIB	Exc.	V.G.	Good	Fair	Poor
6700	5000	3500	1500	750	350

Diamond Regent DL

High grade model of above, with best quality engraving, hand-checkered AAA-grade walnut stock, fixed chokes. Limited importation in 1997.

NIB	Exc.	V.G.	Good	Fair	Poor
18000	16000	12500	—	—	—

Country Squire Side-by-Side Folding

Features a folding stock, with 25.5" barrels, gold double triggers and walnut stock. Chokes are Full and Full.

NIB	Exc.	V.G.	Good	Fair	Poor
480	380	280	200	140	100

Model 306

In 12- or 20-gauge, with 26" or 28" barrels, choke tubes, single trigger and extractors. Imported from Turkey from 2006 to 2008.

NIB	Exc.	V.G.	Good	Fair	Poor
600	520	450	300	200	150

Classic Coach

Same features as Model 306 above, except with 20" barrels and 12-gauge only.

NIB	Exc.	V.G.	Good	Fair	Poor
650	580	500	350	200	150

TRIPLE-BARREL SHOTGUNS

The Charles Daly Triple-Barrel Shotguns are mainly 12 gauge 3"-chamber over/unders with interchangeable choke tubes using Rem choke threads. These break-open actions have 28" barrels with extractors and hand-oiled checkered-walnut furniture, with an LOP of 14.5", drop at heel of 2.125", and a drop at comb of 1.125". Five Rem Chokes are supplied (SK, IC, M, IM, F), and the trigger is a single-non-selective mechanical reset and manual safety. The front sight is a fixed fiber optic blade. Weight: about 8.7 lbs. Length: 45". Finish: White receiver, blued barrel. Firing sequence is right, left, top.

Triple Crown Shotgun

Also chambered in 20 and 28 gauge and .410 bore with 26" barrels.

NIB	Exc.	V.G.	Good	Fair	Poor
1400	1200	1000	800	600	400

Triple Magnum Shotgun

Gauges: 12 ga. Barrels: 28". Stock: Addition of True Timber DRT or Prairie camouflage synthetic. Features: Triple-barreled break-action shotgun with full camo coverage of barrels and stocks. Set of five Interchangeable MC-5 Rem chokes. Distributed by Chiappa Firearms. Magnum 3.5" chambers. Single non-selective mechanical trigger with right, left, top firing sequence.

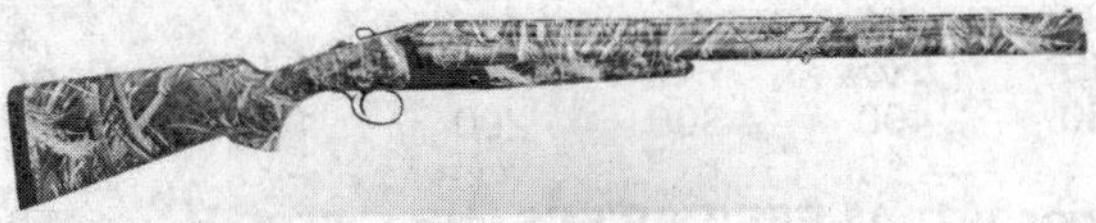

NIB	Exc.	V.G.	Good	Fair	Poor
1930	1820	1680	1490	—	—

Triple Threat Shotgun

Has compact 18.5" barrels and a removable buttstock for easy storage or use as a pistol grip. 8.2 lbs. and overall length of 35.5" with buttstock in place.

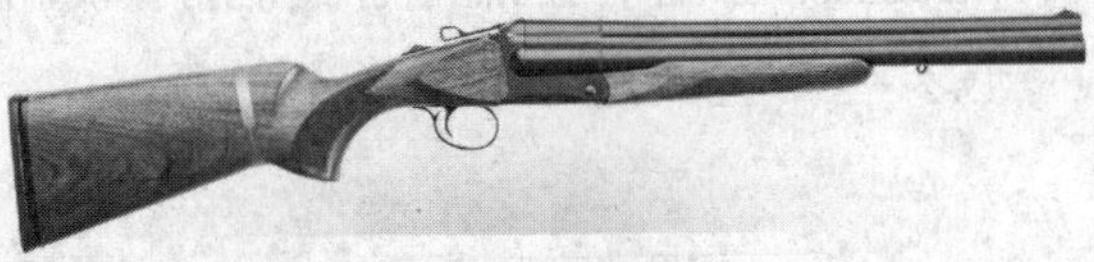

NIB	Exc.	V.G.	Good	Fair	Poor
1450	1250	1050	850	650	450

Honcho Tactical Triple

Introduced 2019. 12-gauge 3-inch and .410 bore. 18.5" barrel and 27" overall length. Rubber-coated walnut pistol grip and forend. Brass front bead. 6 lbs. Cylinder-bore choke.

NIB	Exc.	V.G.	Good	Fair	Poor
1300	1100	950	750	—	—

RIFLES

Field Grade Mauser 98

Bolt-action rifle offered in a wide variety of calibers from .243 Win. to .458 Win. Magnum. Barrel length 23" for all calibers. Stock is black synthetic. Open sights. Note: Add $175 for .375 H&H and .458 Win. Magnum; $50 for stainless steel.

NIB	Exc.	V.G.	Good	Fair	Poor
460	350	300	220	150	100

Field Grade Mini-Mauser 98

Version chambered for short cartridges such as .22 Hornet, .223, .22-250 and 7.62x39mm. Barrel length 19.25". Magazine capacity 5 rounds.

NIB	Exc.	V.G.	Good	Fair	Poor
600	480	350	250	180	120

Superior Grade Mauser 98

Similar to Field Grade Mauser, with addition of hand-checkered walnut stock.

NIB	Exc.	V.G.	Good	Fair	Poor
600	420	320	220	160	100

Superior Grade Mini-Mauser 98

Same as Field Grade Mini-Mauser, with addition of hand-checkered walnut stock.

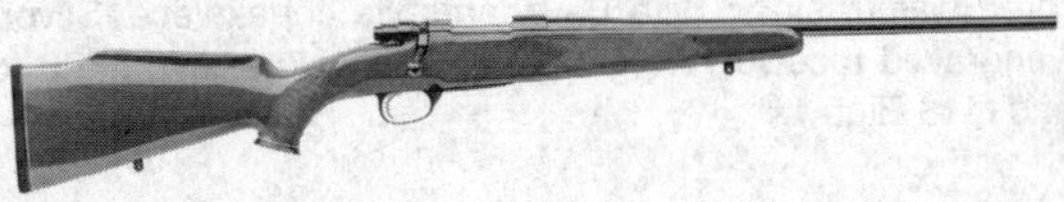

NIB	Exc.	V.G.	Good	Fair	Poor
600	450	320	250	150	100

Field Grade Rimfires

Chambered for .22 LR cartridge. Fitted with a 22" barrel bolt-action version; 20" barrel in semi-automatic or 17.5" barrel in bolt-action. True Youth model 16.25" barrel in bolt-action single-shot. Note: Add $25 for True Youth model.

NIB	Exc.	V.G.	Good	Fair	Poor
120	100	80	50	20	10

Superior Grade Rimfires

Chambered for .22, .22 Magnum or .22 Hornet in bolt-action or .22 LR semi-automatic. Walnut stock with checkering. Open sights. Note: Add $20 for .22 Magnum; $170 for .22 Hornet.

NIB	Exc.	V.G.	Good	Fair	Poor
180	120	100	80	50	20

Superior II Grade Rimfire

Introduced in 2005. Chambered for .22 LR, .22 WMR or .17 HMR cartridges. Fitted with a 22" barrel. Open sights on .22 LR. Drilled and tapped for scope mounts on .22 WMR and .17 HMR. Oiled walnut stocks with checkering. Note: Add $40 for .22 Magnum; $75 for .17 HMR.

NIB	Exc.	V.G.	Good	Fair	Poor
260	200	180	150	120	100

Empire Grade Rimfires

Empire Grade has select walnut stock, with 24 lpi hand-cut checkering. Grip and forearm caps highly polished and blued metal finish. Same configurations as Superior Grade rifles. Note: Add $20 for .22 Magnum; $100 for .22 Hornet.

NIB	Exc.	V.G.	Good	Fair	Poor
340	280	220	180	120	100

Superior Grade Express

Chambered for .30-06 cartridge and fitted with 23.5" barrel. Open sights, with dovetail receiver for scope mounting. Silver receiver with game scene engraving. Checkered walnut stock with sling swivels. Weight about 7.75 lbs.

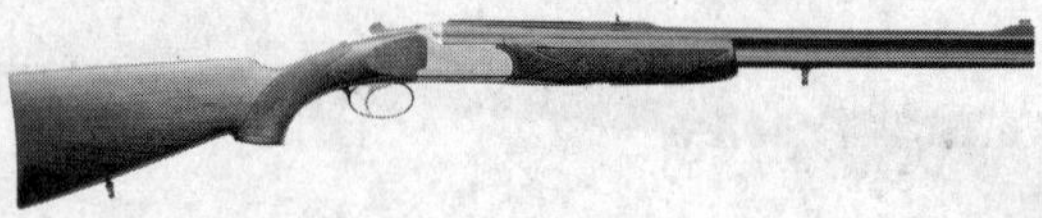

NIB	Exc.	V.G.	Good	Fair	Poor
3250	2700	1800	1480	1000	500

Empire Express

Chambered for .30-06, .375 H&H or .416 Rigby cartridge, with open sights and dovetail receiver for scope mounting. Barrel length 23.5". Checkered walnut stock, with Bavarian-style cheekpiece. Silver game scene engraved receiver. Weight about 8 lbs. Note: Add $700 for .375 H&H and .416 Rigby.

NIB	Exc.	V.G.	Good	Fair	Poor
3600	3000	2300	1780	1250	600

DM-4 Series

This series of rifles and carbines were manufactured in 2008 and 2009, with forged aluminum alloy receivers, manganese phosphate or stainless barrels, forward assist and other features typically found on quality made AR-type models. All were chambered in 5.56 NATO. Many of the popular AR configurations were offered with 16" or 20" barrels, sighting and grip options, mounting rails, finishes and other regular features found in the AR family. Prices shown are for standard DM-4 Carbine. Many available options can double these values.

NIB	Exc.	V.G.	Good	Fair	Poor
950	820	700	500	—	—

HANDGUNS

Daly ZDA

Introduced in 2005. Chambered for 9mm or .40 S&W cartridge. Fitted with 4.5" ramped barrel. Ambidextrous slide release/decocker/lock as well as magazine release. Loaded chamber indicator. Magazine capacity: 15 rounds 9mm; 12 rounds .40 S&W.

NIB	Exc.	V.G.	Good	Fair	Poor
590	450	380	300	180	100

Field 1911-A1 FS/MS/CS

Chambered for .45 ACP, with choice of 5" (FS), 4" (MS) or 3.5" (CS) barrel. Various special features such as front and rear slide serrations, extended beavertail safety and lightweight trigger. Magazine capacity 8 rounds. Overall length 8.75".

NIB	Exc.	V.G.	Good	Fair	Poor
580	400	300	200	180	120

Superior 1911-A1 EFS/EMS/ECS

Same as Field Grade described above, with blued frame and stainless steel slide. Introduced in 1999.

NIB	Exc.	V.G.	Good	Fair	Poor
550	450	350	200	180	120

Empire 1911-A1 EFS

Same as Field Grade. Full stainless, with both stainless steel slide and frame. Introduced in 1999.

NIB	Exc.	V.G.	Good	Fair	Poor
630	480	350	220	200	120

Field 1911-A2P

Same as above, with 10-round magazine.

NIB	Exc.	V.G.	Good	Fair	Poor
570	450	350	220	200	120

.22 Caliber Conversion Kit

Offered with adjustable sights for models with 5" barrel only. First offered in 1999.

NIB	Exc.	V.G.	Good	Fair	Poor
200	150	100	60	40	20

Field 1911-A1 PC

Fitted with 4" barrel and slide. Polymer frame. Produced under license from STI. Introduced in 1999.

NIB	Exc.	V.G.	Good	Fair	Poor
580	400	300	200	180	120

Superior 1911-A1 PC

Same as model above, with stainless steel slide and black polymer frame. Introduced in 1999.

NIB	Exc.	V.G.	Good	Fair	Poor
600	420	320	220	200	120

Field 1911 Target EFST

Fitted with 5" barrel. Chambered for .45 ACP cartridge. Eight-round magazine. Blued finish. Fully adjustable rear sight, with dovetail front sight. Weight about 40 oz.

NIB	Exc.	V.G.	Good	Fair	Poor
620	480	350	240	200	120

Empire 1911 Target EFST

As above, with stainless steel finish.

NIB	Exc.	V.G.	Good	Fair	Poor
790	600	480	350	240	120

Empire Custom Match Target

Same as Empire Target, with hand-polished stainless steel finish and 20 lpi checkered front strap.

NIB	Exc.	V.G.	Good	Fair	Poor
800	600	500	380	260	140

Daly HP

Introduced in 2003. This U.S.-made 9mm pistol is similar to the famous Browning Hi-Power. Fitted with 5" barrel. XS sighting system. Weight about 35 oz.

NIB	Exc.	V.G.	Good	Fair	Poor
550	400	350	220	200	120

Daly M-5 Government

Polymer frame pistol chambered for 9mm, .40 S&W or .45 ACP cartridge. Fitted with 5" barrel, high rise beavertail and ambidextrous safety. Low profile sights. Weight about 34 oz. Made in Israel by BUL. Introduced in 2003.

NIB	Exc.	V.G.	Good	Fair	Poor
720	580	400	280	220	100

Daly M-5 Commander

Same as above. Fitted with 4.375" barrel. Weight about 30 oz.

NIB	Exc.	V.G.	Good	Fair	Poor
720	580	400	280	220	100

Daly M-5 Ultra-X

An ultra compact model.

NIB	Exc.	V.G.	Good	Fair	Poor
720	580	400	280	220	100

Daly M-5 IPSC

Has a 5" barrel. Fitted with a stainless steel slide and adjustable sights. Flared and lowered ejection port. Extended magazine release. Weight about 34 oz.

NIB	Exc.	V.G.	Good	Fair	Poor
1500	1150	720	600	320	120

Daly Classic 1873 Single-Action Revolver

Chambered for .45 Colt or .357 Magnum. Revolver offered with 4.75", 5.5" or 7.5" barrel. Choice of walnut or simulated ivory grips. Stainless steel, blue or case colored finish. Introduced in 2005. Imported from Italy. Note: Add $30 for steel backstrap and triggerguard; $200 for stainless steel.

NIB	Exc.	V.G.	Good	Fair	Poor
450	350	280	250	200	150

DAN ARMS OF AMERICA
Allentown, Pennsylvania

These are Italian-made shotguns. Manufactured by Silma and imported by Dan Arms of America. Production ceased in 1988.

SIDE-BY-SIDES

Field Grade

Boxlock shotgun chambered for all gauges, with 26" or 28" barrels. Various choke combinations, double triggers and extractors. Blued, with walnut stock.

NIB	Exc.	V.G.	Good	Fair	Poor
—	320	260	220	150	120

Deluxe Field Grade

As above, with single trigger and automatic ejectors.

NIB	Exc.	V.G.	Good	Fair	Poor
—	460	400	320	250	200

OVER/UNDERS

Lux Grade I

12- and 20-gauge over/under shotgun, with 26", 28" or 30" ventilated rib barrels, double triggers and extractors. Blued finish, with walnut stock.

NIB	Exc.	V.G.	Good	Fair	Poor
—	320	260	200	150	100

Lux Grade II

As above in 12-gauge only, with single trigger.

NIB	Exc.	V.G.	Good	Fair	Poor
—	350	300	250	200	150

Lux Grade III

As above in 20-gauge only, with automatic ejectors.

NIB	Exc.	V.G.	Good	Fair	Poor
—	400	320	280	220	180

Lux Grade IV

As above in 12-gauge only, with screw-in choke tubes.

NIB	Exc.	V.G.	Good	Fair	Poor
—	450	380	320	280	200

Silver Snipe

Shotgun in 12- or 20-gauge. Manufactured to custom order, with engraved false sideplates and select walnut stock.

NIB	Exc.	V.G.	Good	Fair	Poor
—	1250	1000	800	600	350

DANCE & BROTHERS
Columbia, Texas

J.H., G.P. and D.E. Dance began production of percussion revolvers for the Confederate States of America in Columbia, Texas, in mid-1862, moving to Anderson, Texas in early 1864. Based on surviving serial numbers, combined output at both places did not exceed 350 pistols. Most of these were in the "Army" (.44-caliber) size but a limited number of "Navy" (.36-caliber) were also manufactured. Nearly all are distinguished by the absence of a "recoil shield" on the frame behind the cylinders. As Colt M1851 "Navy" revolvers closely resemble the Dance Navy revolvers, great care must be exercised in examining revolvers purported to be Dance Navies. Expert evaluation recommended.

.36 Caliber (Antique)

As with most confederate arms, sales are rare and values are speculative.

Courtesy Milwaukee Public Museum, Milwaukee, Wisconsin

Exc.	Fine	V.G.	Good	Fair	Poor
85000	67500	43750	20000	7000	4900

.44 Caliber (Antique)

Exc.	Fine	V.G.	Good	Fair	Poor
150000	—	50000	—	—	—

DANIEL DEFENSE

Savannah, Georgia
2001-present

SEE POLITICAL PANIC PRICING.

DDM4 MODELS

This series of AR-type carbine comes in several variations. Different receiver and stock configurations, and rail/sight systems. See model descriptions below for details.

DDM4V1

The original Daniel Defense rifle, 5.56/16" M4-profile barrel, carbine gas system. DDM4 Rail 12.0 FSP, Daniel Defense buttstock and pistol grip.

NIB	Exc.	V.G.	Good	Fair	Poor
2100	1800	1550	1250	—	—

DDM4V4S SBR

Short-barreled rifle (SBR) in 5.56/11.5". DDM4 rail 10.0, carbine length gas system, low-profile gas block. Daniel Defense rail panels, Daniel Defense buttstock and pistol grip. DDM4V7S (02-128-07344-047) has M-LOK attachment handguard. DDM4300S (02-122-17026-047) chambered in 300 BLK. NFA items.

NIB	Exc.	V.G.	Good	Fair	Poor
2000	1700	1450	1100	—	—

DDM4V7

Caliber: 5.56 NATO/.223. Non-NFA Barrels: 16". Weight: 7.4 lbs. Lengths: 34.75" to 37.85" overall. Stock: Glass-filled polymer with SoftTouch overmolding. Sights: None. Features: The lower receiver is mil-spec with an enhanced, flared magazine well and QD swivel attachment point. The upper receiver has M4 feed ramps. Lower and upper CNC machined of 7075-T6 aluminum, hard coat anodized. Add $190 for Cerakote finishes added in 2023. SEE POLITICAL PANIC PRICING.

NIB	Exc.	V.G.	Good	Fair	Poor
2360	1660	1410	1240	1100	—

DDM4V7 LW

First rifle in the DDM4 lineup to feature the M-LOK attachment technology with the Daniel Defense MFR 15.0 rail. 5.56/16" lightweight profile barrel, mid-length gas system, free-floating MFR 15.0 handguard.

NIB	Exc.	V.G.	Good	Fair	Poor
1750	1500	1250	1100	—	—

DDM4 V7 SLW

6 lbs., 5.56/14.5" Lightweight profile barrel, Extended Flash Suppressor pinned and welded to reach the NFA required 16" minimum barrel length.

NIB	Exc.	V.G.	Good	Fair	Poor
1750	1500	1250	1100	—	—

DDM4V7 Pro

5.56/18" model with MFR XS 15.0 M-LOK rail.

NIB	Exc.	V.G.	Good	Fair	Poor
2180	1700	1450	1200	—	—

DDM4V7 Pro Rattlecan

NIB	Exc.	V.G.	Good	Fair	Poor
2200	—	—	—	—	—

DDM4V9

15" DDM4 quad rail over a 5.56/16" Government-profile barrel. Mid-length gas system.

NIB	Exc.	V.G.	Good	Fair	Poor
1980	1700	1450	1200	—	—

DDM4V11

V11 designates KeyMod attachment handguard series. This is the 5.56/16" model.

NIB	Exc.	V.G.	Good	Fair	Poor
1750	1500	1250	1100	—	—

DDM4V11 Pro

Competition model with 5.56/18" and Slim Rail 15.0 with uninterrupted Picatinny rail on top and KeyMod attachment at 3, 6, and 9 o'clock. BCM Gunfighter charging handle, Muzzle Climb Mitigator brake, Geissele Automatics Super Dynamic 3-Gun trigger.

NIB	Exc.	V.G.	Good	Fair	Poor
2100	1750	1500	1250	—	—

DDM4V11 300 MIL SPEC+

NIB	Exc.	V.G.	Good	Fair	Poor
2100	1800	1550	1250	—	—

DDM4 Ambush

Hunting rifle line in hydro-dipped Kryptek Highlander camo pattern. Mid-length gas system, Daniel Defense MFR 15.0 free-floating handguard. Continuous Picatinny rail on top, M-Lok attachment on the sides and bottom, muzzle threaded 1/2x28 tpi with knurled thread protector. Geissele

Super Semi-Automatic 2-stage trigger, ambidextrous safety selector, BCM Gunfighter charging handle, Daniel Defense Enhanced Pistol Grip and 6-position adjustable buttstock. Pricing is for 02-110-02095 5.56/18" barrel.

NIB	Exc.	V.G.	Good	Fair	Poor
1730	1500	1230	1100	—	—

DDM4 Ambush 6.8

6.8mm SPC/18", 5⁄8x24 muzzle thread.

NIB	Exc.	V.G.	Good	Fair	Poor
1950	1650	1400	1200	—	—

DDM4 PDW

AR-type pistol. 7" barrel.

NIB	Exc.	V.G.	Good	Fair	Poor
2100	1750	1500	—	—	—

MK12

New in 2014, this model is in 5.56 NATO caliber, with 20-round Magpul magazine, 18" barrel, glass-filled polymer stock, with Soft Touch overmolding and pistol grip.

NIB	Exc.	V.G.	Good	Fair	Poor
2340	1650	1400	1200	—	—

M4A1

Classic M4-style AR, with 16" barrel (muzzle brake), pin and welded DD flash suppressor and RIS II rail. Introduced in 2017.

NIB	Exc.	V.G.	Good	Fair	Poor
1970	1900	1750	1600	—	—

M4A1 RIII Rifle

Caliber: 5.56 NATO/.223. Similar to DD4 RIII but with a 14.5" M4 barrel and pinned and welded Daniel Defense flash suppressor. Comes in FDE and black colors. Weight: 6.39 lbs. Length: 31.5" to 34.75".

NIB	Exc.	V.G.	Good	Fair	Poor
2150	—	—	—	—	—

DD5V1

AR-15 style rifle in .308 Win. Offered with all standard AR features and many available options. These include DD Superior suppressor device, Geissele trigger, 15" Picatinny rail, pistol grip stock, KeyMod handguard, flared mag well and ambidextrous safety. 7.62x51mm/16" model. 8.3 lbs., KeyMod handguard.

NIB	Exc.	V.G.	Good	Fair	Poor
2700	2300	1950	1660	—	—

DD5V2

Introduced 2017. 7.62x51mm/18" model with a 4-bolt connection system, optimized upper receiver, improved bolt carrier group, ambidextrous controls, a configurable modular charging handle, Geissele SSA two-stage trigger, DD Superior Suppression Device, 15" Picatinny top rail. Weighs 8.6 lbs. Additional DD5 models recently introduced similar rifles in other calibers. DD5 features include ambidextrous controls. Values similar to above: DD5V3 – 7.62mm, 16" barrel; DD5V4 – 7.62mm or 6.5 Creedmoor, 18" barrel; DD5V5 – 6.5 Creedmoor or .260 Rem, 20" barrel.

NIB	Exc.	V.G.	Good	Fair	Poor
2700	2300	1950	1660	—	—

DD5V3

Calibers: 7.62x51mm/.308 Win. Capacity: 20-round Magpul PMAG. Barrel: 16 in., 5/8x24 tpi muzzle thread, S2W barrel profile, 1:11 twist. Stock: Daniel Defense Buttstock. Sights: Full-length top rail. Trigger: Daniel Defense Mil-Spec. Handguard: Daniel Defense DD5 Rail 15.0, 6061-T6 aluminum, M-LOK. Weight: 8.3 lbs. Overall Length: 33.375 to 37 in. Features: Intermediate gas system, two-position adjustable gas block, DLC-coated bolt carrier group, cold hammer chrome-lined forged barrel, Mil-Spec heavy phosphate coated. 4-Bolt Connection System, ambidextrous controls (bolt catch, magazine release, safety selector, furniture, GRIP-N-RIP charging handle). Lower Receiver: Enhanced flared magazine well and rear receiver QD swivel attachment point. CNC machined of 7075-T6 aluminum, Type III hard-coat anodized. Upper Receiver: CNC machined of 7075-T6 aluminum, Type III hard-coat anodized. Daniel Defense Superior Suppression Device, 6-position Mil-Spec 7075-T6 aluminum receiver extension. Daniel Defense Pistol Grip, accepts all SR-25 magazines.

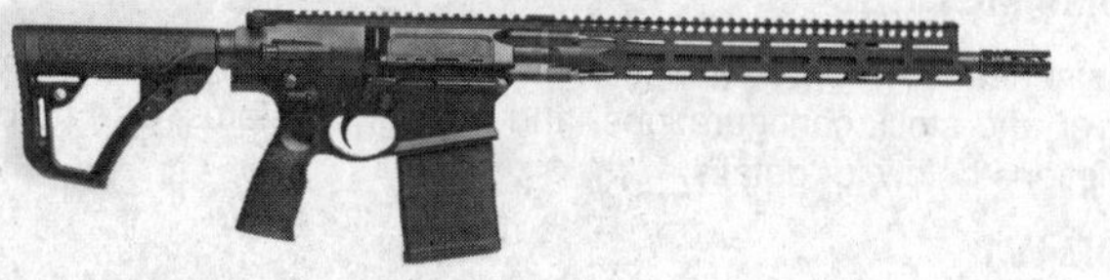

NIB	Exc.	V.G.	Good	Fair	Poor
2600	2500	2350	2100	—	—

DD5V4

7.62mm, 6.5 CM. 18-in. barrel.

NIB	Exc.	V.G.	Good	Fair	Poor
2610	2200	1800	1500	—	—

DD5V5

6.5 CM, .260 Rem. 20-in. barrel.

NIB	Exc.	V.G.	Good	Fair	Poor
2390	2200	1800	1500	—	—

DD4 RIII Rifle

Caliber: 5.56 NATO/.223. New ambidextrous DD4 lower and 12.5" RIS III M-LOK rail system rather than Picatinny quad rail. Includes six-bolt lock-up found on the RIS II but with less weight. Ambidextrous GRIP-N-RIP Charging Handle. 16" cold-hammer-forged Government Profile barrel, mid-length gas system, CMV-steel, 1:7" twist. Daniel Defense Flash Suppressor, 17-4 PH stainless steel, salt bath nitride finished. Bolt Carrier Group: M16 Profile, Mil-spec MP tested, chrome lined, properly staked gas key. Daniel Defense buttstock and pistol grip. Weight: 6.52 lbs. Length: 32 1/4" to 35 7/8". Introduced: Spring 2022, available 2023. Made in the USA. SEE POLITICAL PANIC PRICING.

NIB	Exc.	V.G.	Good	Fair	Poor
2150	—	—	—	—	—

Delta 5

Bolt-action rifle with synthetic stock. 6.5 Creedmoor with 24" barrel or .308 Winchester with 20" barrel.

NIB	Exc.	V.G.	Good	Fair	Poor
2300	2000	1650	—	—	—

MK18 Pistol

MK18 system features 10.3-in. barrel. Chambered in 5.56 NATO. Features SB Tactical SBA3 brace.

NIB	Exc.	V.G.	Good	Fair	Poor
1800	1600	1350	—	—	—

M4300 Pistol

10.3-in. barrel. Chambered in .300 BLK.

NIB	Exc.	V.G.	Good	Fair	Poor
1750	1550	1330	—	—	—

M4 PDW Pistol

7-in. barrel. Chambered in .300 BLK. Features Maxim Defense CQB brace.

NIB	Exc.	V.G.	Good	Fair	Poor
2100	1800	1500	1300	—	—

M4V7P Pistol

10.3-in. barrel. Chambered in .300 BLK. Features SOB brace.

NIB	Exc.	V.G.	Good	Fair	Poor
2000	1700	1400	1200	—	—

DANSK REKYLRIFFEL SYNDIKAT

Copenhagen, Denmark

This firm was founded in 1896. In 1936 it became known as Madsen, makers of the famous Madsen light machine gun. Schouboe pistols were designed by Jens Schouboe, chief engineer for Dansk. They were developed in 1900-1902. First year of manufacture was in 1902.

Schouboe Model 1902

A 7.65mm caliber semi-automatic pistol, with conventional blowback design. Production began in 1903 and ended in 1908, with fewer than 1,000 manufactured.

Courtesy James Rankin

NIB	Exc.	V.G.	Good	Fair	Poor
—	15500	12000	8200	5000	3000

Schouboe Model 1904

A semi-automatic pistol in caliber 11.35mm. Model 1904 was an enlarged Model 1902. Name Dansk Rekylriffel is stamped on the slide.

Courtesy James Rankin

NIB	Exc.	V.G.	Good	Fair	Poor
—	24500	20500	16500	11000	5000

Schouboe Model 1907

An 11.35mm caliber semi-automatic pistol. Designed to fire a 55-grain, copper-aluminum-and-wood projectile at a velocity of 1625 fps. Pistol has the name Dansk Rekylriffel and Schouboe stamped on slide. Some of these pistols had grip frames slotted for stocks. Five hundred were manufactured before production stopped in 1917. Note: Combination holster/shoulder stocks were made for this model, but are extremely rare. If present with a pistol, they would add approximately $5,000 to the value.

Courtesy James Rankin

NIB	Exc.	V.G.	Good	Fair	Poor
—	24000	20000	16000	10500	5000

Schouboe Model 1907 9mm

As above, chambered for 9mm cartridge. Very few of these pistols were built.

Courtesy James Rankin

NIB	Exc.	V.G.	Good	Fair	Poor
—	14000	11000	8250	5500	3000

Schouboe Model 1910/12

Chambered for 11.35mm cartridge. Involved in U.S. military tests in 1912.

Courtesy James Rankin

NIB	Exc.	V.G.	Good	Fair	Poor
—	24500	21500	16500	11000	5000

Schouboe Model 1916

Also chambered for 11.35mm cartridge. Fitted with a very large slide release and safety lever on left side of pistol. Name of manufacturer stamped on slide.

Courtesy James Rankin

NIB	Exc.	V.G.	Good	Fair	Poor
—	24000	21050	16500	11000	5000

DARDICK CORP.
Hamden, Connecticut

Perhaps one of the most unusual firearms to have been designed and marketed in the United States during the 20th century. It utilizes a "tround" which is a triangular plastic case enclosing a cartridge. Action of these arms consists of a revolving carrier that brings the trounds from the magazine into line with the barrel. Discontinued in 1962. Values below are for boxed examples, with a supply of tround ammunition. Deduct 50 to 75 percent for unboxed loose examples, without ammunition.

Series 110

3" barrel. Chambered in .38 Dardick only.

NIB	Exc.	V.G.	Good	Fair	Poor
—	2500	1650	1500	1100	500

Series 1500

6" barrel. Chambered for .22, .30 and .38 Dardick. Note: Carbine conversion kit consisting of a long barrel and shoulder stock was available and would bring a premium of $750 to $1400 depending on the condition.

NIB	Exc.	V.G.	Good	Fair	Poor
—	5000	3000	1750	1500	900

DARLING, B. & B. M.
Belingham, Massachusetts

Pepperbox Pistol (Antique)

A .30-caliber percussion 6-shot pepperbox, with 3.25" length barrels. Blued, with walnut grips. One of the rarest American pepperboxes and copies are known to have been made. Consequently, prospective purchasers are advised to secure a qualified appraisal prior to acquisition. Manufactured during the late 1830s.

Exc.	Fine	V.G.	Good	Fair	Poor
17000	—	—	5000	—	—

DARNE, S. A.
St. Etienne, France

SIDE-BY-SIDE SHOTGUNS

A 12-, 16-, 20- or 28-gauge sliding breech double-barrel shotgun. Manufactured in a variety of barrel lengths and numerous optional features. Manufactured from 1881 to 1979. Note: Darnes have been undergoing a surge in popularity the last few years, because of their unique design. Depending on circumstances and amount of factory engraving and ornamentation present, individual examples may bring considerably in excess of values listed below. Deduct 25 percent for 2.5" chambers.

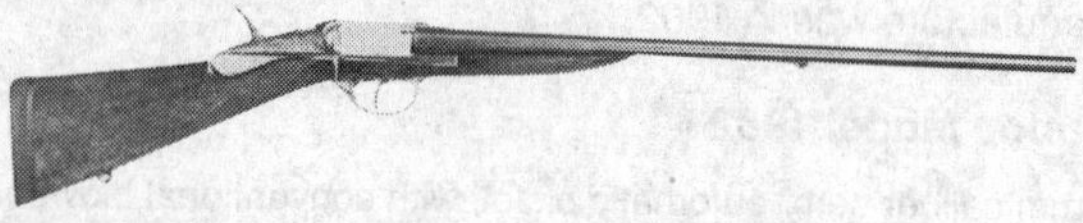

Model R11

NIB	Exc.	V.G.	Good	Fair	Poor
—	2500	2000	1200	800	550

Model R13

NIB	Exc.	V.G.	Good	Fair	Poor
—	3000	2600	2250	1100	750

Model R15

NIB	Exc.	V.G.	Good	Fair	Poor
—	4000	3000	2450	1500	750

Model V19

NIB	Exc.	V.G.	Good	Fair	Poor
—	4500	3600	2950	2050	1250

Model V22

NIB	Exc.	V.G.	Good	Fair	Poor
—	5000	4100	3500	2500	1700

Model V Hors Series No. I

NIB	Exc.	V.G.	Good	Fair	Poor
—	7500	5500	4050	3250	1500

DAVENPORT FIREARMS CO.

Providence, Rhode Island
Norwich, Connecticut

Double-Barrel Shotguns

Text and prices by Nick Niles. William Hastings Davenport's company, also made and marked double-barrel, visible hammer guns in Providence, R.I. on Orange St., 1880-1882 and in Norwich, Conn. ca. 1890-1909. All are monbloc designs of which there were four models. 1st model: made at Providence, ca. 1881, had hammers rising out of the boxlock frame. 2nd model: made in Norwich, Conn. about 1898, is a typical boxlock. 3rd model: made in Norwich, Conn., ca. 1909, has small sidelocks set in larger boxlock frames. Its barrels have un-notched extensions and notched under-lugs. 4th model: also from Norwich, possibly made after the 1901 takeover by Hopkins & Allen, also has sidelocks set in boxlock frames, but the barrels have half moon lugs and notched barrel extensions. Few Davenport doubles are seen, although single-barrel guns are often found.

1st Model Antique

Exc.	Fine	V.G.	Good	Fair	Poor
880	500	450	400	300	210

2nd Model

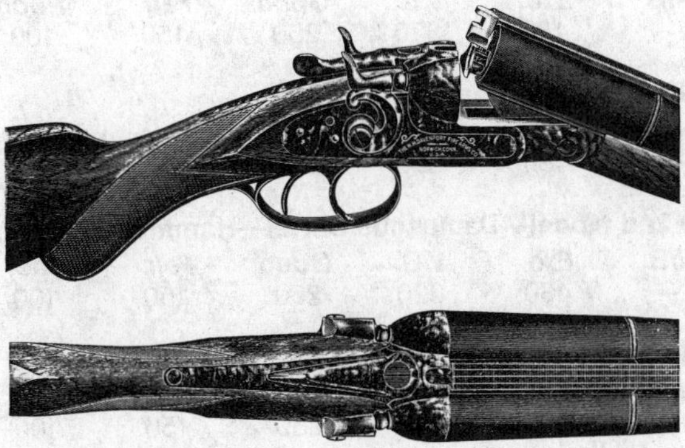

NIB	Exc.	V.G.	Good	Fair	Poor
—	700	450	300	200	150

3rd Model

NIB	Exc.	V.G.	Good	Fair	Poor
—	1200	880	500	400	300

4th Model

NIB	Exc.	V.G.	Good	Fair	Poor
—	900	450	300	250	200

Single-Barrel Shotgun

A 10-, 12-, 16- or 20-gauge side-hammer single-barrel shotgun, with 26" to 36" barrels and extractors. Blued, case-hardened, with walnut stock. Manufactured from approximately 1880 to 1915.

NIB	Exc.	V.G.	Good	Fair	Poor
—	—	450	300	150	80

8 Gauge Goose Gun

As above in 8-gauge.

NIB	Exc.	V.G.	Good	Fair	Poor
—	—	550	250	180	100

Falling Block Single-Shot Rifle

A .22, .25 or .32 rimfire single-shot rifle, with 24" round barrel and exposed hammer. Blued, with walnut stock. Barrel marked "The W.H. Davenport Fire Arms Co. Norwich, Conn. U.S.A. Patented Dec. 15, 1891". Manufactured between 1891 and 1910.

NIB	Exc.	V.G.	Good	Fair	Poor
—	—	680	420	320	200

DAVIDSON, F.A.

Eibar, Spain

Arms bearing this name were manufactured in Spain by Fabrica De Armas.

Model 63B

A 12-, 16-, 20-, 28-gauge or .410 bore double-barrel boxlock shotgun, with 25" to 30" barrels. Engraved, nickel-plated with a walnut stock. Made from 1963 to 1976.

NIB	Exc.	V.G.	Good	Fair	Poor
—	350	220	200	150	100

Model 69 SL

A 12- or 20-gauge sidelock double-barrel shotgun, with 26" or 28" barrels and finished as above.

NIB	Exc.	V.G.	Good	Fair	Poor
—	420	350	300	220	120

Stagecoach Model 73

A 12- or 20-gauge Magnum sidelock double-barrel shotgun, with 20" barrels and exposed hammers.

NIB	Exc.	V.G.	Good	Fair	Poor
—	300	250	180	150	100

DAVIS, A. JR.

Stafford, Connecticut

UnderHammer Pistol Antique

A .31-caliber single-shot under hammer percussion pistol, with 7.5" half octagonal barrel and brass frame. Grips are maple and formed with a bottom tip. Top strap marked "A. Davis Jr./Stafford Conn.".

Exc.	Fine	V.G.	Good	Fair	Poor
2500	2000	1500	750	400	200

DAVIS, N.R. & CO./DAVIS, N.R. & SONS

(See also Davis-Warner Arms Corporation)

Manufacturer of percussion and later cartridge shotguns, from 1853 to 1919. Cartridge shotguns embodied Nathan R. Davis' patented improvements of 1879, 1884 and 1886. Though only made in plain serviceable grades, Davis shotguns were extremely well made and lived up to the company's motto "As Good as the Best".

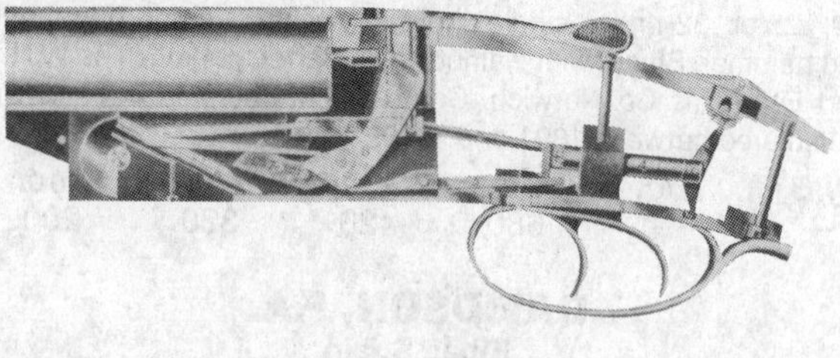

Grade A and B Hammerless Shotguns
Made in 12- or 16-gauge, with 28", 30" or 32" barrels.

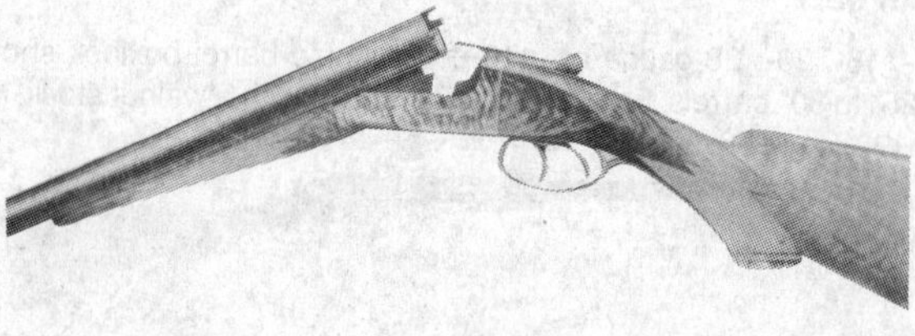

NIB	*Exc.*	*V.G.*	*Good*	*Fair*	*Poor*
—	900	680	400	200	100

Grade C Hammerless Shotgun
Made in 10-gauge, with 30" or 32" barrels.

NIB	*Exc.*	*V.G.*	*Good*	*Fair*	*Poor*
—	900	680	400	200	100

Grade D and DS Hammer Shotguns
Made in 12- or 16-gauge, with 28", 30" or 32" barrels.

NIB	*Exc.*	*V.G.*	*Good*	*Fair*	*Poor*
—	880	680	420	200	100

Grade E and F Single-Barrel Shotguns
Made in 12- or 16-gauge, with 30" or 32" barrels.

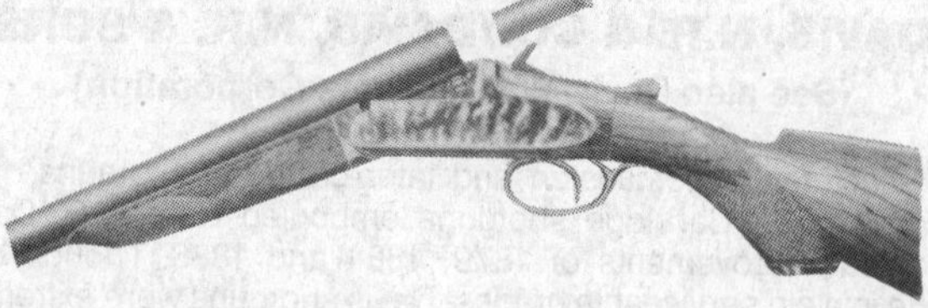

NIB	*Exc.*	*V.G.*	*Good*	*Fair*	*Poor*
—	350	250	120	80	50

N.R. DAVIS BRANDS

1st Button Opener—Hammer Boxlock

NIB	*Exc.*	*V.G.*	*Good*	*Fair*	*Poor*
—	480	320	250	150	100

1st Sidelever—Hammer Boxlock

NIB	*Exc.*	*V.G.*	*Good*	*Fair*	*Poor*
—	480	320	250	150	100

2nd Sidelever—Hammer Boxlock

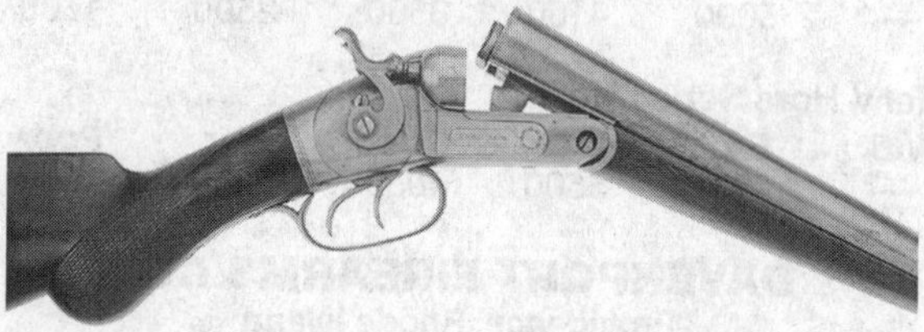

Courtesy Nick Niles, Paul Goodwin photo

NIB	*Exc.*	*V.G.*	*Good*	*Fair*	*Poor*
—	480	320	250	150	100

1st Toplever—Hammer Boxlock

Courtesy Nick Niles, Paul Goodwin photo

NIB	*Exc.*	*V.G.*	*Good*	*Fair*	*Poor*
—	480	320	250	150	100

2nd Toplever—Hammer Boxlock

NIB	*Exc.*	*V.G.*	*Good*	*Fair*	*Poor*
—	480	320	250	150	100

3rd Toplever—Hammer Boxlock

NIB	*Exc.*	*V.G.*	*Good*	*Fair*	*Poor*
—	480	320	250	150	100

1879 1st Model—Hammer Boxlock

NIB	*Exc.*	*V.G.*	*Good*	*Fair*	*Poor*
—	480	320	250	150	100

1879 2nd Model—Damascus Barrel—Hammer Boxlock

NIB	*Exc.*	*V.G.*	*Good*	*Fair*	*Poor*
—	480	320	250	150	100

1885—Hammerless Boxlock

NIB	*Exc.*	*V.G.*	*Good*	*Fair*	*Poor*
—	480	320	250	150	100

1886 Rival—Hammerless Boxlock

NIB	*Exc.*	*V.G.*	*Good*	*Fair*	*Poor*
—	350	280	200	150	100

1886 Rival Improved—Hammerless Boxlock

NIB	*Exc.*	*V.G.*	*Good*	*Fair*	*Poor*
—	350	280	200	150	100

1897 "G" —Hammer Sidelock

NIB	*Exc.*	*V.G.*	*Good*	*Fair*	*Poor*
—	350	280	200	150	100

N.R. DAVIS & SONS BRAND

Hammerless 1900—Boxlock

NIB	*Exc.*	*V.G.*	*Good*	*Fair*	*Poor*
—	350	280	200	150	100

Hammerless A—Damascus Barrel—Boxlock

NIB	*Exc.*	*V.G.*	*Good*	*Fair*	*Poor*
—	350	280	200	150	100

Hammerless B—Boxlock

NIB	Exc.	V.G.	Good	Fair	Poor
—	350	280	200	150	100

Hammerless C—Engraved Damascus Barrel—Boxlock

NIB	Exc.	V.G.	Good	Fair	Poor
—	400	320	250	150	100

Hammerless D—Engraved—Boxlock

NIB	Exc.	V.G.	Good	Fair	Poor
—	480	380	300	250	200

New Model—Hammerless Boxlock

NIB	Exc.	V.G.	Good	Fair	Poor
—	350	280	200	150	100

"D.S." Straight Stock—Engraved—Hammerless Boxlock

NIB	Exc.	V.G.	Good	Fair	Poor
—	350	280	200	150	100

Davis Special—Hammerless Boxlock

NIB	Exc.	V.G.	Good	Fair	Poor
—	920	650	500	400	250

Davis "B" Manga Steel—Hammerless Boxlock

NIB	Exc.	V.G.	Good	Fair	Poor
—	920	650	500	400	250

CRESCENT-DAVIS BRANDS

Model No. 600—Hammerless Boxlock

NIB	Exc.	V.G.	Good	Fair	Poor
—	700	550	300	200	100

Model No. 900—Hammerless Boxlock

NIB	Exc.	V.G.	Good	Fair	Poor
—	700	550	300	200	100

DAVIS & BOZEMAN

Central, Alabama

Pattern 1841 Rifle Antique

A .58-caliber single-shot percussion rifle, with 33" round barrel, full walnut stock, two barrel bands, brass furniture and an iron ramrod. Lock marked "D. & B. Ala." as well as serial number and date of manufacture.

Exc.	Fine	V.G.	Good	Fair	Poor
—	35000	17500	9000	6000	2000

DAVIS INDUSTRIES

Mira Loma, California

This company was founded in 1987 by Jim Davis in Chino, California. Company ceased operations in 2001. Remaining stocks and production machinery purchased by Cobra Enterprises, 1960 S. Milestone Drive, Suite F, Salt Lake City, UT 84104.

D-Series Deringer

A .22 LR, .22 WMR, .25 ACP and .32 ACP caliber double-barrel over/under derringer, with 2.4" barrels. Black Teflon or chrome-plated finish, with laminated wood grips. Weight about 9.5 oz.

NIB	Exc.	V.G.	Good	Fair	Poor
150	80	40	30	20	20

Big Bore D-Series

Similar to above, but chambered for .38 Special and .32 H&R Magnum. Barrel length 2.75". Weight about 11.5 oz.

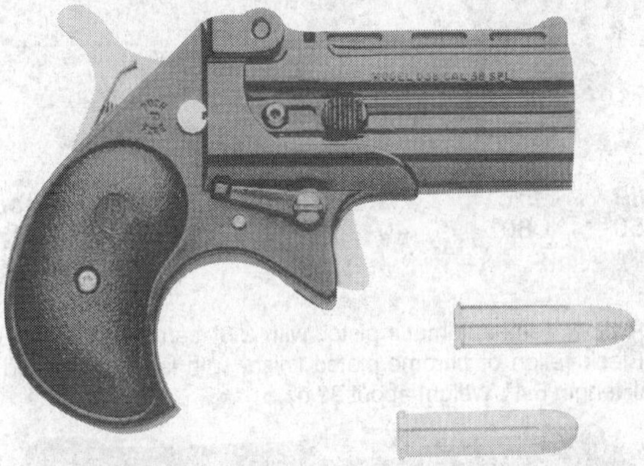

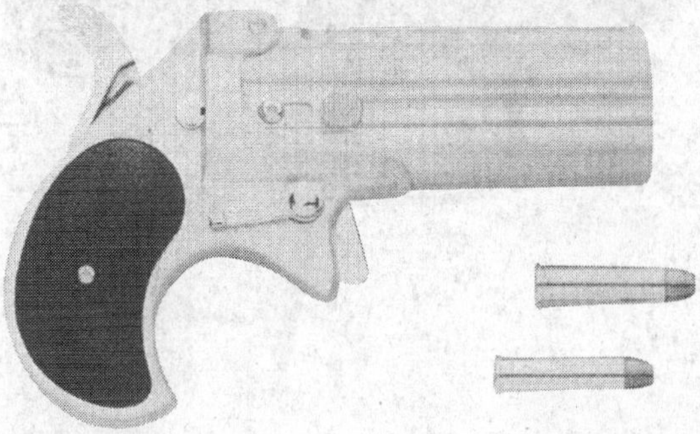

NIB	Exc.	V.G.	Good	Fair	Poor
150	80	40	30	20	20

Long Bore D-Series

Introduced in 1994. This two-shot pistol chambered for .22 LR , .22 WMR, .32 ACP, .32 H&R Magnum, .380 ACP, 9mm and .38 Special cartridges. Barrel length 3.75"; overall length 5.65"; weight about 13 oz.

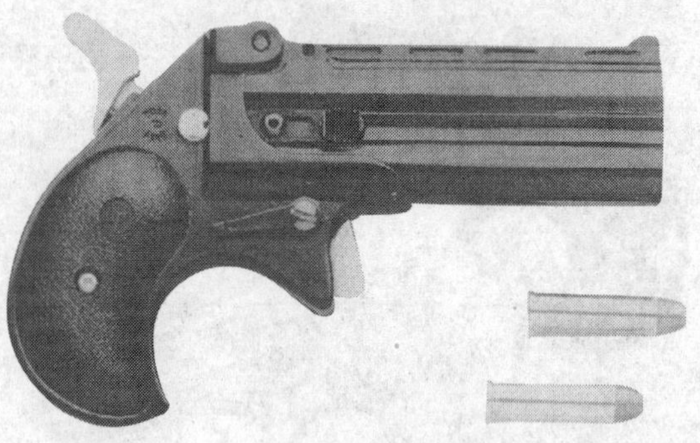

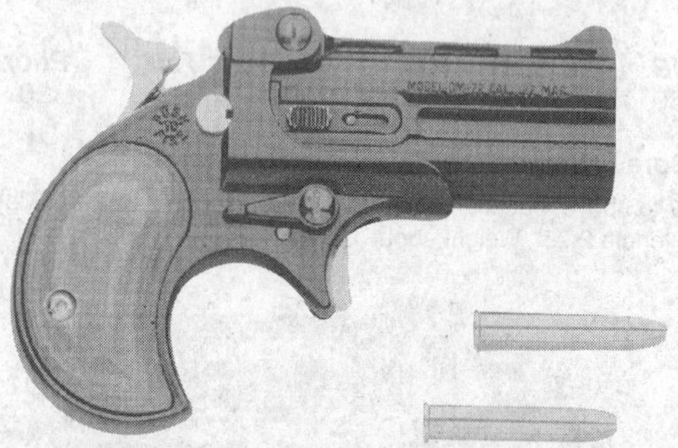

NIB	Exc.	V.G.	Good	Fair	Poor
150	80	40	30	20	20

P-32

A .32-caliber semi-automatic pistol, with 2.8" barrel and 6-shot magazine. Black Teflon or chrome-plated finish, with laminated wood grips. Overall length 5.4". Weight about 22 oz.

NIB	Exc.	V.G.	Good	Fair	Poor
150	80	40	30	20	20

P-380

As above, in .380-caliber.

NIB	Exc.	V.G.	Good	Fair	Poor
180	80	60	50	40	30

DAVIS-WARNER ARMS CORPORATION

Norwich, Connecticut

Established in 1917, when N.R. Davis & Sons purchased the Warner Arms Company. Manufactured shotguns, as well as revolvers and semi-automatic pistols. Ceased operations in 1930. Crescent Arms Company purchased the proprietary rights to the name and briefly assembled shotguns under the name (probably from parts acquired in the purchase), until Crescent was in turn purchased by J.C. Stevens. Initially, Davis-Warner shotguns were identical to those made by Davis, but they subsequently made a Davis Grade B.S. Hammerless, Davis-Warner Expert and Davis Grade D.S. Pistols made by the company included .32-caliber revolvers and two Browning Patent semi-automatics made in Belgium for the company.

Davis Grade B.S. Hammerless Shotgun

Made in 12-, 16- or 20-gauge, with 28", 30" or 32" barrels.

Courtesy William Hammond

NIB	Exc.	V.G.	Good	Fair	Poor
—	880	650	400	200	100

Davis-Warner Expert Hammerless

Made in 12-, 16- or 20-gauge, with 26", 28", 30" or 32" barrels.

Courtesy Nick Niles, Paul Goodwin photo

NIB	Exc.	V.G.	Good	Fair	Poor
—	880	650	400	200	100

"BS"—Hammerless Boxlock

NIB	Exc.	V.G.	Good	Fair	Poor
—	350	280	200	150	100

"Maximin"—Hammerless Boxlock

Courtesy Nick Niles, Paul Goodwin photo

NIB	Exc.	V.G.	Good	Fair	Poor
—	480	320	250	200	150

"DS"—Hammerless Boxlock

NIB	Exc.	V.G.	Good	Fair	Poor
—	350	280	200	150	100

Deluxe—Hammerless Boxlock

NIB	Exc.	V.G.	Good	Fair	Poor
—	350	280	200	150	100

Premier—Hammerless Boxlock

NIB	Exc.	V.G.	Good	Fair	Poor
—	350	280	200	150	100

Peerless Ejector—Hammerless Boxlock

Courtesy Nick Niles, Paul Goodwin photo

NIB	Exc.	V.G.	Good	Fair	Poor
—	480	320	250	200	150

Hypower—Hammerless Boxlock

NIB	Exc.	V.G.	Good	Fair	Poor
—	480	320	250	200	150

Ajax (Model 800)

Courtesy Nick Niles, Paul Goodwin photo

NIB	Exc.	V.G.	Good	Fair	Poor
—	480	320	250	150	100

Ajax—Hammerless Boxlock

Courtesy Nick Niles, Paul Goodwin photo

NIB	Exc.	V.G.	Good	Fair	Poor
—	350	280	200	150	100

Certified (Savage)

Courtesy Nick Niles, Paul Goodwin photo

NIB	Exc.	V.G.	Good	Fair	Poor
—	480	320	250	150	100

Deluxe Special (Model 805)

Automatic ejectors.

NIB	Exc.	V.G.	Good	Fair	Poor
—	580	450	300	200	150

Premier Special (Model 802)

NIB	Exc.	V.G.	Good	Fair	Poor
—	580	450	300	200	150

Premier (Model 801)

NIB	Exc.	V.G.	Good	Fair	Poor
—	480	320	250	150	100

Warner Infallible Semi-Automatic Pistol

Fyrberg Patent .32 ACP. Not a particularly robust design.

NIB	Exc.	V.G.	Good	Fair	Poor
—	350	280	180	120	80

Davis-Warner Swing-Out Revolver

Double-action .32-caliber revolver, with 5" or 6" barrel.

NIB	Exc.	V.G.	Good	Fair	Poor
—	200	150	120	80	50

Davis-Warner Semi-Automatic Pistols

Browning Patent .25 ACP, .32 ACP or .380-caliber pistols.

NIB	Exc.	V.G.	Good	Fair	Poor
—	350	280	180	120	80

DAW, G. H.
London, England

Daw Revolver Antique

A .38-caliber double-action percussion revolver, with 5.5" barrel marked "George H. Daw, 57 Threadneedle St. London, Patent No. 112". Blued, with walnut grips. Manufactured in the 1860s. The revolver pictured and priced is a Pryce and Cashmore Patent type revolver. Daw also made Bulldog pattern revolvers that sell for lower prices.

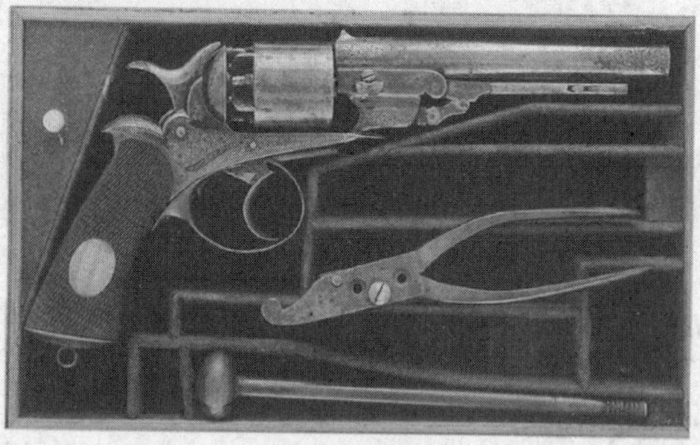

Exc.	Fine	V.G.	Good	Fair	Poor
5750	3500	2740	1980	1000	700

DEANE, ADAMS & DEANE

See—ADAMS

Adams Model 1851 Self-Cocking Revolver (Antique)

.436-caliber double-action percussion revolver, with 7.5" octagonal barrel and 5-shot cylinder. Barrel and frame blued. Cylinder case-hardened. Grips walnut. Top strap marked "Deane, Adams and Deane 30 King William St. London Bridge". Revolver does not have hammer spur and functions only as double-action.

Exc.	Fine	V.G.	Good	Fair	Poor
2980	1480	1130	780	400	280

Adams Pocket Revolver (Antique)

As above in .31-caliber, with 4.5" barrel.

Exc.	Fine	V.G.	Good	Fair	Poor
2350	1300	950	600	400	280

Beaumont-Adams Revolver (Antique)

As above, with Tranter Patent loading lever. Hammer made with a spur.

Exc.	Fine	V.G.	Good	Fair	Poor
3000	1500	1000	800	400	300

DEANE-HARDING

London, England

Revolver (Antique)

A .44-caliber percussion revolver, with 5.25" barrel and 5-shot cylinder. Blued case-hardened, with walnut grips. Manufactured during late 1850s.

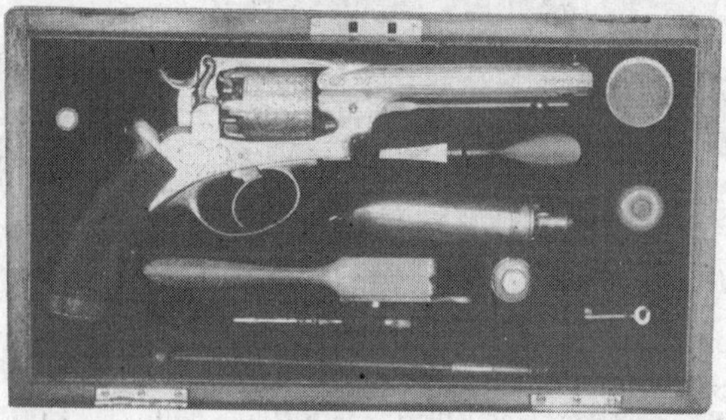

Courtesy Bonhams & Butterfields, San Francisco, California

Exc.	Fine	V.G.	Good	Fair	Poor
4000	2500	1500	1100	850	500

DECKER, WILHELM

Zella St. Blasii, Germany

A 6.35mm double-action revolver, with 6-shot cylinder and concealed hammer. Unusual bar-type trigger design. Blued, with plastic grips. Manufactured prior to 1914. Very few of these revolvers were produced.

Revolver

NIB	Exc.	V.G.	Good	Fair	Poor
—	2100	1500	750	320	100

DEL HAXHE

See—APACHE

DEL-TON, INC.

Elizabethtown, North Carolina

Del-Ton offers a complete line of AR-15 style modern sporting rifles. Hundreds of variations and options are available.

AR-15 SERIES

Chamberings: 5.56 NATO, .223 Wylde, 7.62x39. Del-Ton offers a complete line of AR-15-style modern sporting rifles. Dozens of variations and options. Product lines include Alpha, DT Scout, DT Sport Mod 2, Echo, Sierra, and SXT. Based in Elizabethtown, North Carolina. SEE POLITICAL PANIC PRICING.

NIB	Exc.	V.G.	Good	Fair	Poor
600	—	—	—	—	—

DTI Sierra 3G

Caliber: .223 Wylde, 16" barrel

NIB	Exc.	V.G.	Good	Fair	Poor
1300	—	—	—	—	—

AR-10 SERIES

Chambering: .308 Win. Echo optics-ready and Alpha sighted models. Upper and lower receivers: Forged 7075 T6 aluminum, integral triggerguard, 18" CMV 1x10 barrel, Magpul M-LOK standard length handguard, ERGO Sure Ambi grip, Magpul 20-rd. P-Mag. SEE POLITICAL PANIC PRICING.

Alpha 308 M-LOK Rifle

Chambering: .308 Win. Echo optics-ready and Alpha sighted models.

Upper and lower receivers: Forged 7075 T6 aluminum, integral triggerguard, 18" CMV 1x10 barrel, Magpul M-LOK standard-length handguard, ERGO Sure Ambi grip, Magpul 20-round P-Mag.

NIB	Exc.	V.G.	Good	Fair	Poor
990	900	850	700	—	—

DEMIRETT, J.
Montpelier, Vermont

Under-Hammer Pistol Antique

A .27-caliber single-shot percussion pistol, with 3" to 8" barrels and an under hammer. Barrel marked "J. Demerrit / Montpelier / Vermont". Blued, with maple, walnut or stag horn grips. Active from 1866 to mid-1880s.

Exc.	Fine	V.G.	Good	Fair	Poor
2700	820	580	350	200	140

DEMRO
Manchester, Connecticut

XF-7 Wasp Carbine

A 9mm or .45-caliber semi-automatic carbine, with 16.5" barrel and folding stock. Fires from open bolt.

NIB	Exc.	V.G.	Good	Fair	Poor
—	750	600	450	300	150

T.A.C. Model 1

As above, with fixed stock.

NIB	Exc.	V.G.	Good	Fair	Poor
—	750	600	450	300	150

DERINGER REVOLVER AND PISTOL CO.
Philadelphia, Pennsylvania

After Henry Deringer's death, his name was used by I.J. Clark, who manufactured rimfire revolvers on Charles Foehl's patents between 1870 and 1879.

Deringer Model I Antique

A .22-caliber spur trigger revolver, with hinged octagonal barrel and 7-shot cylinder. Manufactured circa 1873.

Exc.	Fine	V.G.	Good	Fair	Poor
—	650	460	280	150	100

Deringer Model II Antique

As above, with round barrel and also available in .32-caliber.

Exc.	Fine	V.G.	Good	Fair	Poor
—	420	310	200	100	70

Centennial 1876 Antique

A .22-, .32- or .38-caliber solid frame revolver.

Exc.	Fine	V.G.	Good	Fair	Poor
—	900	670	450	200	140

DERINGER RIFLES AND PISTOLS, HENRY
Philadelphia, Pennsylvania

Henry Deringer Sr. and his son, Henry Jr., were well established in Philadelphia by the close of the War of 1812, having made both sporting and military rifles at that place since the turn of the century. Henry Jr. continued in the gun trade until the outbreak of the American Civil War, primarily producing flintlock and percussion military rifles. At least 2,500 "Northwest guns" and 1,200 rifles for the Indian trade, a few percussion martial pistols, but most importantly the percussion pocket pistols that became so popular they took on his misspelled name as a generic term, the "derringers".

Deringer U.S. M1814 Military Rifle Antique

Overall length 48.5"; barrel length 32.75"; caliber .54. Markings: on lockplate, "US/H. DERINGER/PHILADA"; on top flat of barrel, "H. DERINGER/PHILADA" and standard U.S. proofmarks. U.S. M1814 rifle is distinguished by its part octagonal barrel, whose bands were secured by wedge-shaped spring bands and distinctive finger ridges on triggerguard strap. Henry Deringer Sr. received a contract for 2,000 of these rifles in 1814, but delivered only 50 that year, devoting his resources instead to a more lucrative Pennsylvania state contract for rifles.

Exc.	Fine	V.G.	Good	Fair	Poor
9000	2950	2220	1500	850	590

Deringer U.S. M1817 Military Rifle (Types I & II)

Overall length 51.25"; barrel length 36"; caliber .54. Markings: on lockplate, "US/H. DERINGER/PHILADA" forward of cock, date on tail; standard U.S. proofmarks on barrel. U.S. M1817 "common" rifle followed much the same design elements as its predecessor, U.S. M1814 rifle; however, barrel is fully round, with its bands secured by full band springs and on earlier production, finger ridges on triggerguard strap were eliminated in favor of a plain strap formed into a hand-grip. On the 6,000 rifles manufactured under his 1840 contract, Deringer eliminated the "pistol grip" in favor of a plain strap, distinguishing Type II production from Type I. As one of four major contractors for the U.S. M1817 rifle, Deringer produced a total of 111,000 rifles for the U.S. War Department. Many of the rifles from the first two contracts (2,000 in 1821, 3,000 in 1823) were distributed to Southern states under the 1808 Militia Act. Accordingly, Deringer M1817 rifles altered to percussion by traditional Southern methods may generate a premium.

In Flintlock Antique

Exc.	Fine	V.G.	Good	Fair	Poor
8000	3500	2620	1750	800	560

Altered to Percussion Antique

Exc.	Fine	V.G.	Good	Fair	Poor
4000	1250	920	600	400	280

Deringer Original Percussion Martial Rifles (Types I & II) Antique

Overall length 51.25"; barrel length 36"; caliber .54. Markings: Type I-on lockplate forward of hammer "DERINGER/PHILA"; also known to exist with standard U.S. M1817 lock markings and barrel marks; Type II-on lockplate forward of hammer "US/DERINGER/PHILADELA" or "DERINGER/PHILADELA" and same on top of barrel. Although Type I rifle of this series appears at first glance to be a late contract rifle altered to percussion by means of the cone-in barrel method, in fact, it is an original percussion rifle made by Deringer from modified spare parts that remained after the completion of his 1840 contract. Type II rifle also evidences having been made from modified parts; however, its cone is set in an elongated bolster brazed to the right side of barrel. Speculation concerning these rifles is rampant; however, available evidence indicates that Deringer produced about 600 of these, most likely produced at the beginning of American Civil War.

Courtesy Milwaukee Public Museum, Milwaukee, Wisconsin

Exc.	Fine	V.G.	Good	Fair	Poor
4750	1550	1170	800	450	310

Deringer Original Percussion Rifle-Muskets Antique

Overall length 57.75"; barrel length 42"; caliber .69. Markings: on lock forward of hammer, "US/DERINGER/PHILADELA". Just as original percussion rifle appears to be an altered arm, the rare Deringer rifle muskets at first appear to have been flintlocks. However, these arms are original percussion, having been made from spare or rejected parts from the U.S. M1816 muskets. Brazed bolsters are identical in style to that of Type II original percussion rifles made by Deringer. Barrels are rifled with seven grooves and barrels accordingly bear a rear sight. Deringer probably assembled a hundred of these rifles in 1861 to arm some company of Pennsylvania's early war regiments.

Courtesy Milwaukee Public Museum, Milwaukee, Wisconsin

Exc.	Fine	V.G.	Good	Fair	Poor
4000	1300	1010	720	450	310

Deringer U.S. Navy Contract "Boxlock" Pistols (Antique)

Overall length 11.625; barrel length 6"; caliber .54. Markings: on lockplate, "US/DERINGER/ PHILADELIA" or merely "DERINGER/PHILADEL\" in the center; tail either plain or marked "U.S.N./(date)"; barrels sometimes marked with U.S. Navy inspection marks. Deringer was granted a contract with the U.S. Navy in 1845 for 1,200 of the new "boxlock" percussion pistols also made by Ames. All of these appear to have been delivered. From the extra parts, Deringer is thought to have assembled several hundred extra pistols, some of which he rifled. The latter bring a premium, even though quantities remain enigmatic.

Exc.	Fine	V.G.	Good	Fair	Poor
4050	1550	1380	1220	750	520

Deringer Percussion Pocket Pistols (Antique)

The most famous of Henry Deringer's products, an estimated 15,000 were produced between the Mexican War through the Civil War, usually in pairs. Popularity of the pistol is attested in large number of imitations and nickname "Derringer" applied to them, even when clearly not Deringer's products. Prices can fluctuate widely based on agent marks occasionally found on barrel. Care is advised in purchasing purported "true" derringers. Beware of fakes! Deringer Percussion Pocket Pistols Caliber varied, usually .41 or larger. They were usually sold in pairs, and a cased pair will bring a premium. Collectors divide these into three sizes – Small Pocket Size with 1 ½" to 3" barrels (the very smallest ones will bring a slight premium), no ramrods. Medium Pocket Size with 3 ½" to 6" barrels. Larger ones have ramrods. Duelling Size with 7" to 9" barrels, with ramrods. Rare, worth premium.

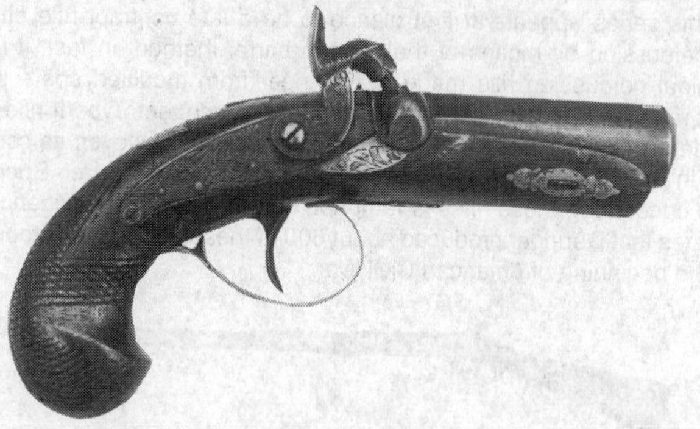

Courtesy Milwaukee Public Museum, Milwaukee, Wisconsin

Exc.	Fine	V.G.	Good	Fair	Poor
7000	2250	1920	1600	800	560

Principal Makers of Deringer-Style Pocket Pistols

William AFFLERBACH, Philadelphia, PA
Balthaser AUER, Louisville, KY
Frederick BEERSTECHER, Philadelphia and Lewisburg, PA
Franz J. BITTERLICH, Nashville, TN
BLUNT & SYMS, New York, NY
Richard P. BRUFF, New York, NY
Jesse S. BUTTERFIELD, Philadelphia, PA
Daniel CLARK, Philadelphia, PA
Richard CONSTABLE, Philadelphia, PA
DELONG & SON, Chattanooga, TN
MOSES DICKSON, Louisville, KY
Horace E. DIMICK, St. Louis, MO
Gustau ERICHSON, Houston, TX
B.J. EUSTACE & Company, St. Louis, MO
James E. EVANS, Philadelphia, PA
W.S. EVANS, Philadelphia, PA
FIELD, LANGSTROTH & Company, Philadelphia, PA
Daniel FISH, New York, NY
FOLSOM BROTHERS & Company, New Orleans, LA
August G. GENEZ, New York, NY
George D. H. GILLESPIE, New York, NY
Frederick G. GLASSICK, Memphis, TN
James GOLCHER, Philadelphia, PA
Joseph GRUBB & Company, Philadelphia, PA
John H. HAPPOLDT, Charlestown, SC
John M. HAPPOLDT, Columbus, GA & Charlestown, SC
HAWS & WAGGONER, Columbia, SC
HODGKINS & SONS, Macon, GA
Louis HOFFMAN, Vicksburg, MS
HYDE & GOODRICH, New Orleans, LA
Joseph JACOB, Philadelphia, PA
William W. KAYE, Philadelphia, PA
Benjamin KITTERIDGE, Cincinnati, OH
Peter W. KRAFT, Columbia, SC
John KRIDER, Philadelphia, PA
Jacob KUNTZ, Philadelphia, PA
Martille La FITTE, Natchitoches, LA
A. Frederich LINS, Philadelphia, PA
C. LOHNER, Philadelphia, PA
John P. LOWER, Denver, CO
A.R. MENDENHALL, Des Arc, AK
John MEUNIER, Milwaukee, WI
William D. MILLER, New York, NY
MURPHY & O'CONNELL, New York, NY
—— NEWCOMB, Natchez, MS
Charles A. OBERTEUFFER, Philadelphia, PA
Stephen O'DELL, Natchez, MS
Henry C. PALMER, St. Louis, MO
R. PATRICK, New York, NY
REID & TRACY, New York, NY
William ROBERTSON, Philadelphia, PA
ROBINSON & KRIDER, Philadelphia, PA
Ernst SCHMIDT & Company, Houston, TX
SCHNEIDER & GLASSICK, Memphis, TN
W.A. SEAVER, New York, NY
Paul J. SIMPSON, New York, NY
SLOTTER & Company, Philadelphia, PA
Patrick SMITH, Buffalo, NY
SPRANG & WALLACE, Philadelphia, PA
Adam W. SPIES, New York, NY
Casper SUTER, Selma, AL
Jacob F. TRUMPLER, Little Rock, AK
Edward TRYON, Jr., Philadelphia, PA
George K. TRYON, Philadelphia, PA
TUFTS & COLLEY, New York, NY
WOLF, DASH & FISHER, New York, NY
Alfred WOODHAM, New York, NY
Andrew WURFFLEIN, Philadelphia, PA
John WURFFLEIN, Philadelphia, PA

Agent Names Found On Deringer Pocket Pistols

W.C. ALLEN, San Francisco, CA
W.H. CALHOUN, Nashville, TN
CANFIELD & BROTHERS, Baltimore, MD
F. H. CLARK & CO., Memphis, TN
COLEMAN & DUKE, Cahaba, AL
M.W. GALT & BROTHER, Washington, DC

J.B. GILMORE, Shreveport, LA
A.B. GRISWOLD & CO., New Orleans, LA
HYDE & GOODRICH, New Orleans, LA
LULLMAN & VIENNA, Memphis, TN
A.J. MILLSPAUGH, Shreveport, LA
H.G. NEWCOMB, Natchez, MS
A.J. PLATE, San Francisco, CA
J.A. SCHAFER, Vicksburg, MS
S.L. SWETT, Vicksburg, MS
A.J. TAYLOR, San Francisco, CA
WOLF & DURRINGER, Louisville, KY

DESENZANI, LABORATORIES ARMI
Brescia, Italy

Over/Under
These custom made guns are all unique. Used guns in excellent condition will bring $35,000. Values increase depending on the small gauges, amount and coverage of engraving.

Side-By-Side
These custom made guns are all unique. Used guns in excellent condition will bring $25,000. Values increase depending on the small gauges, amount and coverage of engraving.

DESERT EAGLE
See—MAGNUM RESEARCH, INC.

DESERT INDUSTRIES
Las Vegas, Nevada

See—STEEL CITY ARMS

DESTROYER CARBINE
Spain

Destroyer Carbine
A 9mm Bayard/Large caliber bolt-action rifle, with 20" barrel and 7-shot magazine. Full length stock, with two barrel bands.

NIB	Exc.	V.G.	Good	Fair	Poor
—	500	400	200	100	40

DETONICS FIREARMS INDUSTRIES / NEW DETONICS / DECTONICS USA LLC
Bellevue, Washington / Phoenix, Arizona / Pendergrass, Georgia

This series of compact 1911-type pistols, was first manufactured by Detonics Firearms Industries in Bellvue, WA from 1976 to 1988. That firm was sold to New Detonics Mfg. Corp. of Phoenix, AZ, which operated from 1989 to 1992. In 2004, the brand was resurrected and returned to production by Detonics USA in Pendergrass, GA. Then in 2007, Detonics USA and all if its predecessors was sold to a group of investors who established the current company, known only as Detonics, in Millstadt, IL. The company name was changed in 2013 to Detonics Defense Technologies.

Mark I
A .45-caliber semi-automatic pistol, with 3.25" barrel and 6-shot magazine. Matte blued with walnut grips. Discontinued in 1981.

NIB	Exc.	V.G.	Good	Fair	Poor
—	550	450	400	300	200

Mark II
As above, with satin nickel-plated finish. Discontinued in 1979.

NIB	Exc.	V.G.	Good	Fair	Poor
—	550	450	400	300	200

Mark III
As above, with hard chrome plating. Discontinued in 1979.

NIB	Exc.	V.G.	Good	Fair	Poor
—	600	500	450	350	250

Mark IV
As above, with polished blue finish. Discontinued in 1981.

NIB	Exc.	V.G.	Good	Fair	Poor
—	550	450	400	300	200

Combat Master
The Mark I in 9mm, .38 Super or .45-caliber.

NIB	Exc.	V.G.	Good	Fair	Poor
980	800	600	500	400	250

Combat Master Mark V
As above, in stainless steel with a matte finish. Discontinued in 1985.

NIB	Exc.	V.G.	Good	Fair	Poor
980	800	600	500	400	250

Combat Master Mark VI
As above, with adjustable sights. Sides of slide are polished. 1,000 were made in .451 Detonics Magnum caliber. Note: Add 40 percent for .451 Detonics Magnum.

NIB	Exc.	V.G.	Good	Fair	Poor
900	750	600	500	400	250

Combat Master Mark VII
As above, without sights. Note: Add 40 percent for .451 Detonics Mag-

num.

NIB	Exc.	V.G.	Good	Fair	Poor
900	750	600	500	400	250

Military Combat MC2

As above, in 9mm, .38 Super or .45-caliber. Fixed sights, dull finish and Pachmayr grips. Discontinued in 1984.

NIB	Exc.	V.G.	Good	Fair	Poor
680	600	500	420	300	200

Scoremaster

As above, in .45- or .451 Detonics Magnum, with 5" or 6" barrel, Millet sights and grip safety.

NIB	Exc.	V.G.	Good	Fair	Poor
1250	1000	800	600	400	250

Janus Competition Scoremaster

As above, in .45-caliber with compensated barrel. Introduced in 1988.

NIB	Exc.	V.G.	Good	Fair	Poor
1750	1450	1250	850	650	300

Servicemaster

As above, with a 4.25" barrel, interchangeable sights and matte finish. Discontinued in 1986.

NIB	Exc.	V.G.	Good	Fair	Poor
—	1000	800	600	400	200

Pocket 9

A 9mm double-action semi-automatic pistol, with 3" barrel and 6-shot magazine. Matte finish stainless steel. Discontinued in 1986.

NIB	Exc.	V.G.	Good	Fair	Poor
—	500	400	300	220	180

Combat Master

Fitted with a 3.5" barrel chambered for the .45 ACP, .40 S&W, .357 SIG, .38 Super or the 9mm Para cartridges. Checkered rosewood grips. Low profile fixed sights. Magazine capacity 6 rounds. Height of pistol 4.75". Overall length 7". Weight about 34 oz. All stainless steel including springs. Introduced in 2005, by Detonics USA.

NIB	Exc.	V.G.	Good	Fair	Poor
1300	1050	650	420	300	180

Street Master

Chambered for .45 ACP cartridge and fitted with a 5" barrel. Checkered rosewood grips. All stainless steel including springs. Height 4.75". Overall length 8.5". Weight about 39 oz. Magazine capacity 6 rounds. Fixed sights. Introduced in 2005, by Detonics USA.

NIB	Exc.	V.G.	Good	Fair	Poor
1200	950	680	450	320	200

Model 9-11-01

Introduced in 2005, by Detonics USA. Chambered for .45 ACP cartridge and fitted with a 5" barrel. All stainless steel construction. Checkered rosewood grips. Height about 5.5". Overall length 8.625". Weight about 43 oz. Magazine capacity 7 rounds. Fixed sights.

NIB	Exc.	V.G.	Good	Fair	Poor
1200	950	680	450	320	200

DETONICS DEFENSE TECHNOLOGIES

Millstadt, Illinois

Most recent manufacturer of Detonics 1911-style pistols. As of mid 2016, all models listed below are no longer in production.

Combat Master

Latest version of very first compact 1911 developed in the 1970s by original Detonics company. In .45 ACP, with 3.5" octagonal barrel, two-tone finish, aluminum/Dymondwood grips, 6+1 capacity, stainless steel frame and slide. Weight 30 oz. Introduced in 2010.

NIB	Exc.	V.G.	Good	Fair	Poor
850	780	700	550	—	—

Nemesis HT

Full-size with 5" barrel, chambered in .40 S&W. Weight 38 oz., capacity 9+1. Other features same as above. Introduced in 2011.

NIB	Exc.	V.G.	Good	Fair	Poor
1950	1800	1500	1100	—	—

DTX

Polymer frame double-action-only pistol. Chambered in 9mm or .40 S&W. Barrel 4.25"; weight 25 oz.; capacity 16+1 (9mm), 14+1 (.40). Introduced in 2011.

NIB	Exc.	V.G.	Good	Fair	Poor
980	900	780	620	450	250

DEUTSCHE WERKE

Erfurt, Germany

Ortgies

Semi-automatic pistol in 6.35mm and 7.65mm. The 6.35mm pistol manufactured in 1921 and 7.65mm model in 1922 by Ortgies Company. Pistols had "HO" logo for Heinrich Ortgies on each grip. Later, Ortgies Company was bought by Deutsche Werke. Grip logo was "D". Over the period Ortgies were manufactured with four different slide legends.

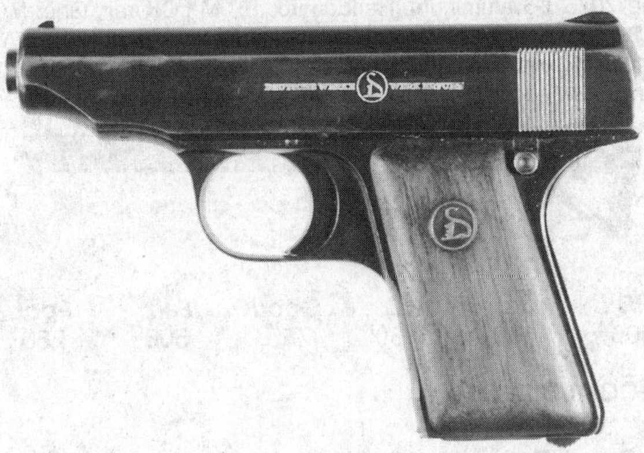

Courtesy James Rankin

NIB	Exc.	V.G.	Good	Fair	Poor
—	450	320	280	200	100

Ortgies 9mm

As above, with addition of a hold-open button on left side of slide. Caliber is 9mmK, aka .380 ACP.

Courtesy James Rankin

NIB	Exc.	V.G.	Good	Fair	Poor
—	450	380	250	180	100

DEVISME, F. P.

Paris, France

One of the more popular French gunsmiths of the mid-19th century. F.P. Devisme manufactured a wide variety of firearms, including single-shot percussion pistols, double-barrel percussion rifles and shotguns, percussion revolvers and cane guns. After 1858, this maker manufactured cartridge weapons of the same style as his percussion arms. Quality of all his products is uniformly high and impossible to provide a generalized price guide.

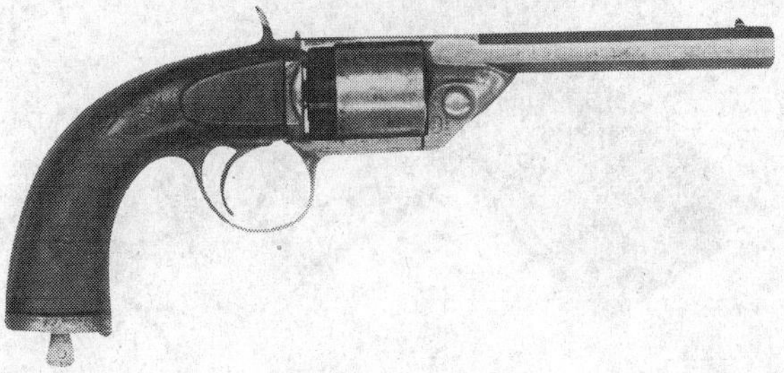

DIAMOND

Turkey

Gold Series Semi-Automatic Shotgun

Chambered for 12-gauge shell, with 3" chamber. Barrel length 28". Turkish walnut stock or synthetic stock. Black receiver, with gold-filled engraving. Also available with 24" slug barrel with sights. Note: Add $50 for walnut stock.

NIB	Exc.	V.G.	Good	Fair	Poor
350	300	200	150	100	80

Gold Series Pump-Action Shotgun

Offered with same features as semi-automatic Gold gun, with slide-action. Note: Add $25 for walnut stock.

NIB	Exc.	V.G.	Good	Fair	Poor
300	250	180	120	100	80

Silver Series Mariner Semi-Automatic Shotgun

A 12-gauge stainless steel and anodized alloy semi-automatic gun, with 3" chambers. Fitted with 22" ventilated rib barrel and synthetic stock.

NIB	Exc.	V.G.	Good	Fair	Poor
420	350	280	200	150	100

Silver Series Mariner Pump-Action Shotgun

A 12-gauge pump gun, with 20" slug barrel and synthetic stock. Stainless steel and alloy.

NIB	Exc.	V.G.	Good	Fair	Poor
350	280	200	150	100	80

Diamond Elite Semi-Automatic Shotgun

A 12-gauge 3" chamber shotgun. Offered with 22" to 28" barrels, with 3 choke tubes. Engraved receiver.

NIB	Exc.	V.G.	Good	Fair	Poor
320	280	200	150	100	80

Diamond Panther Pump-Action Shotgun

As above, in a slide-action configuration.

NIB	Exc.	V.G.	Good	Fair	Poor
250	200	200	150	100	80

Diamond Panther Semi-Automatic Shotgun

A 12-gauge gun, with 3" chambers and 20" or 28" ventilated rib barrel. Furnished with 3 choke tubes. Synthetic stock.

NIB	Exc.	V.G.	Good	Fair	Poor
320	280	200	150	100	80

Diamond Elite Pump-Action Shotgun

As above, with slide-action. Offered with 18.5" slug barrel.

NIB	Exc.	V.G.	Good	Fair	Poor
300	250	180	120	100	80

DIAMONDBACK FIREARMS

Cocoa, Florida

DB380

Small variation of DB9. Chambered for .380. Barrel length 2.8"; weight 8.8 oz. Introduced in 2011. Note: Add $200 for Crimson Trace laser grip.

NIB	Exc.	V.G.	Good	Fair	Poor
380	320	280	250	—	—

DB9 SERIES

DB9

Polymer-frame striker-fired mini-compact 9mm, with 6+1 capacity. Weight 11 oz. Very compact design, with 3" barrel, overall length 5.6", height 4" and width .80". Available in several sight and finish options including black, stainless, pink, orange and teal. Introduced in 2011. Note: Add $200 for Crimson Trace laser grip.

NIB	Exc.	V.G.	Good	Fair	Poor
360	340	300	250	200	120

DB9 FS

Full-size variation of DB9, with 4.75" barrel and 15-round magazine. Weight 21.5 oz.

NIB	Exc.	V.G.	Good	Fair	Poor
380	350	300	250	200	120

DB15 SERIES

Caliber: 5.56 NATO. Barrel: Diamondback Barrels 5.56, 16", Medium, 4150 CrMov, Black Nitride, 1:8 RH. Gas System: Carbine-Length. BCG: Shot-Peened, Magnetic Particle Inspected mil-spec 8620 Carrier. Upper: A3 Flattop Forged 7075 T-6 Aluminum, T-Marked. Lower: 7075 T-6 Aluminum (DB-15 Carbon Lower). Handguard: 15" M-LOK Rail. Grip: MOE. Stock/Brace: MOE Carbine Stock. Magazine: Gen3 PMAG 30 Round. Sights: N/A. Muzzle Device: A2 Flash Hider (1/2x28). Trigger: Mil-spec. Weight: 6.6 lbs. Overall Length: 32.5" to 35.75". Introduced 2012. SEE POLITICAL PANIC PRICING.

NIB	Exc.	V.G.	Good	Fair	Poor
510	470	400	320	—	—

DB15 NB

Upgraded model of DB15, with nickel boron coated barrel, upper and lower receivers. Magpul six-position stock and pistol grip. Variety of finish and sight options.

NIB	Exc.	V.G.	Good	Fair	Poor
1050	900	700	550	400	200

DB10 SERIES

[[Caliber: 6.5 Creedmoor, .308 Win. Barrel: Diamondback Barrels mid-length 16", light, 4150 CrMov, black nitride, 1:10" RH twist: Gas System: Mid-length. BCG: Shot-peened, Magnetic Particle Inspected mil-spec 8620 Carrier. Upper: A3 flattop forged 7075 T-6 aluminum. Lower: Forged 7075 T-6 aluminum. Handguard: 15" M-LOK rail. Grip: MOE K Grip. Stock/Brace: MOE Carbine Stock. Magazine: Gen M3 PMAG 20 Rd. Muzzle Device: A2 .30 Cal Flash Hider [5/8x24]. Weight: 8.2 lbs. Length 31-1/8" to 33-3/4". SEE POLITICAL PANIC PRICING.

]] NIB	Exc.	V.G.	Good	Fair	Poor
1600	1400	1150	750	500	250

DB10CCMLB .308 Win.

NIB	Exc.	V.G.	Good	Fair	Poor
800	—	—	—	—	—

DB1065CBGB 6.5 CM

NIB	Exc.	V.G.	Good	Fair	Poor
1250	—	—	—	—	—

DBX

Caliber: 5.7x28mm. Capacity: 20-round magazine. Barrel: 8". Grips: Magpul MOE-K. Sights: Optics-ready, Picatinny rail. Length: 16.9" overall, brace folded. Weight: 3 lbs. unloaded. Finish: Black hardcoat anodized. Features: DBX muzzle brake, compatible with FN Five-seveN, side-folding brace. Uses an AR-15 mil-spec trigger.

NIB	Exc.	V.G.	Good	Fair	Poor
1100	900	750	—	—	—

DBAM29

Caliber: 9mm. Capacity: 12- or 17-round magazine. Barrel: 3.5 in. Grips: Textured grip. Sights: Fixed, 3-dot. Length: 6.6 in. overall. Weight: 21 oz. unloaded. Finish: Black.

NIB	Exc.	V.G.	Good	Fair	Poor
300	—	—	—	—	—

Sidekick

Caliber: .22 LR/.22 Mag. Convertible. Action: Single & Double Grips: Checkered glass filled Nylon. Capacity: 9 rounds., Front Sight: Blade., Rear Sight: Integral., Barrel length: 4.5 inch. Overall length: 9.875 in. Frame and handle material: Zinc, frame and handle finish: Black Cerakote. Weight: 32.5 oz., Twist: 1:16 RH. Grooves: 6. The Sidekick is chambered in both .22 LR and .22 Mag with 9-shot cylinders. It has a 9-round capacity and weighs 32.5 ounces. Swing-out cylinders allow the user to switch between .22 LR and .22 Mag in seconds.

NIB	Exc.	V.G.	Good	Fair	Poor
240	—	—	—	—	—

DICKINSON, E. L. & J.
Springfield, Massachusetts

Ranger

A .32-caliber spur trigger revolver, with 6-shot cylinder.

NIB	Exc.	V.G.	Good	Fair	Poor
—	—	520	450	200	100

Single-Shot

A .32-caliber single-shot pistol, with 3.75" hinged barrel, silver plated brass frame, blued barrel and walnut grips.

NIB	Exc.	V.G.	Good	Fair	Poor
—	—	780	650	250	100

DICKSON, NELSON & CO.
Dawson, Georgia

Rifle (Antique)

A .58-caliber single-shot percussion rifle, with 34" barrel, full stock secured by two barrel bands, brass furniture and iron loading rod. Lock marked "Dickson/Nelson & Co./C.S." as well as "Ala." and date of manufacture. Prospective purchasers are advised to secure a qualified appraisal prior to acquisition. Carbine version of this arm known and has a 24" barrel.

Exc.	Fine	V.G.	Good	Fair	Poor
39500	14000	8500	3000	2000	1400

DIMICK, H.E.
St. Louis, Missouri

See PLAINS RIFLE

Percussion Pistol (Antique)

This maker primarily known for half stock Plains Rifles. He also manufactured a limited number of percussion pistols. These vary in length, caliber, stock form and type of furniture. Values listed should only be used as a rough guide. Prospective purchasers should secure a qualified appraisal prior to acquisition. Active 1849 to 1873.

Exc.	Fine	V.G.	Good	Fair	Poor
—	7500	5120	2750	900	630

DOLNE, L.

See—APACHE

DOMINGO ACHA

See—ACHA

DOMINO
Brescia, Italy

Model OP 601 Match Pistol

A .22-caliber short semi-automatic pistol, with 5.6" ventilated barrel, target sights, adjustable and removable trigger. Blued, with adjustable walnut grips.

NIB	Exc.	V.G.	Good	Fair	Poor
1700	1200	800	550	300	180

Model SP 602 Match Pistol

As above, in .22 LR caliber.

Courtesy John J. Stimsom, Jr.

NIB	Exc.	V.G.	Good	Fair	Poor
1700	1200	800	550	300	180

DORNAUS & DIXON ENTERPRISES, INC.
Huntington Beach, California

Standard Bren 10

10mm caliber double-action semi-automatic pistol, with 5-in. barrel and 10-shot magazine. Stainless frame and satin-blued slide. Manufactured between 1983 and 1986. Value includes original factory magazine.

NIB	Exc.	V.G.	Good	Fair	Poor
3260	2510	1960	1500	760	560

M & P Model

As above, with matte black finish.

NIB	Exc.	V.G.	Good	Fair	Poor
4000	3010	2560	2000	1000	960

Special Forces Model

Chambered for 10mm cartridge. Similar to M&P model. Offered in two models: Model D has a dark finish; Model L has a light finish. Prices listed are for Model D. Note: Add 25 percent for Model L.

NIB	Exc.	V.G.	Good	Fair	Poor
3810	3010	2410	1900	1000	800

Dual-Master Presentation Model

As above, with .45-caliber extra barrel slide. Fitted walnut case.

NIB	Exc.	V.G.	Good	Fair	Poor
6120	4380	2190	1220	880	500

Marksman Model

Similar to Standard Model in .45-caliber. There were 250 manufactured for "Marksman Shop" in Chicago, Illinois.

NIB	Exc.	V.G.	Good	Fair	Poor
1960	1610	1510	960	760	530

Jeff Cooper Commemorative

Suppose to be 2,000 manufactured in 1986, but no one knows how many were actually produced. Some estimates are less than 10. Chambered for 10mm. High-gloss blue finish, with 22kt. gold-plated details. Grips are laser engraved. Whole affair furnished in a walnut display case. Very rare and value ranges from 7,550 to 150,000 depending on condition.

Bren 10 (2010 Series)

Several Bren 10 models were manufactured by Vltor in Tucson, Arizona from 2010 to 2011. Limited production of approximately 2000 guns. Specifications similar to original Standard and Marksman models with choice of 4" or 5" barrels, 10mm or .45 ACP chambering, stainless or two-tone finish.

NIB	Exc.	V.G.	Good	Fair	Poor
1100	1000	850	700	500	300

DORNHEIM, G.C.
Suhl, Germany

Gecado Model 11

A 6.35mm semi-automatic pistol, bearing the name "Gecado" on the slide. Fitted with a 2.2" barrel. Magazine capacity 6 rounds. Weight about 15 oz. Marketed by G.C. Dornheim. Copy of FN Browning Model 1906.

Courtesy James Rankin

NIB	Exc.	V.G.	Good	Fair	Poor
—	300	220	120	80	50

Gecado 7.65mm

A 7.65mm semi-automatic pistol bearing the name "Gecado" on the slide. Fitted with 2.6" barrel. Magazine capacity 7 rounds. Weight about 21 oz. Marketed by G.C. Dornheim.

NIB	Exc.	V.G.	Good	Fair	Poor
—	280	150	120	80	50

DOUBLESTAR CORP.
Winchester, Kentucky

SEE POLITICAL PANIC PRICING.

Star EM-4

Chambered for .223 cartridge. Fitted with 16" barrel. Rifle supplied with A-2 or flattop upper and Colt M-4 handguard.

NIB	Exc.	V.G.	Good	Fair	Poor
920	750	600	500	280	120

Star-15

Has 20" barrel, A-2 buttstock and handguard. Supplied with A-2 or flattop upper. In .223 or 7.62x39 calibers.

NIB	Exc.	V.G.	Good	Fair	Poor
780	620	580	450	220	100

Star Lightweight Tactical Rifle

Fitted with 15" fluted barrel, permanently attached muzzle brake and short tactical buttstock. Supplied with A-2 or flattop upper.

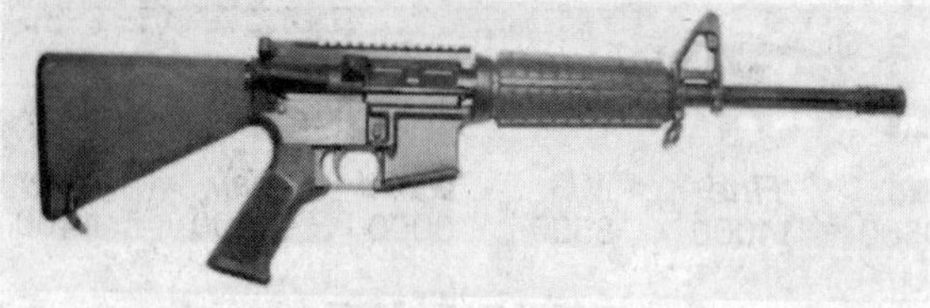

NIB	Exc.	V.G.	Good	Fair	Poor
880	700	580	450	220	100

Star Carbine

Has 16" match grade barrel. Supplied with A-2 or non-collapsing CAR buttstock. Upper receiver A-2 style or flattop. In .223 or 7.62x39 calibers.

NIB	Exc.	V.G.	Good	Fair	Poor
780	620	580	450	220	100

Star DS-4 Carbine

Features 16" M-4 barrel, with 6-position buttstock, oval handguard and A-2 flash hider. Weight about 6.75 lbs. Choice of A-2 or flattop upper receiver.

NIB	Exc.	V.G.	Good	Fair	Poor
880	700	580	450	220	100

Star Super Match Rifle

Choice of match grade barrel lengths; 16", 20", 22" or 24". Supplied with flattop upper or tactical Hi-Rise upper. Note: Add $50 for .204 Ruger or 6.8 SPC; $100 for 6.5 Grendel, all discontinued.

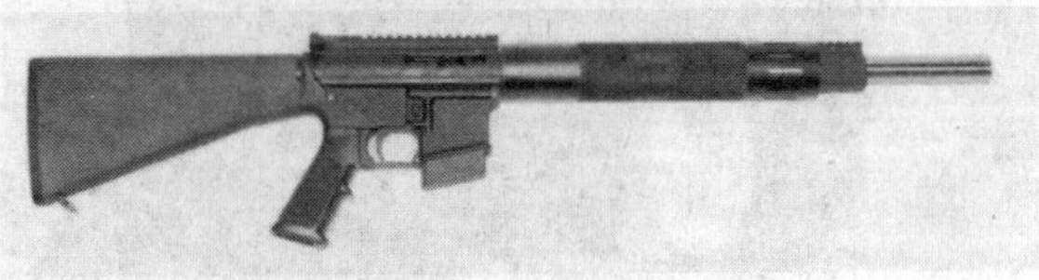

NIB	Exc.	V.G.	Good	Fair	Poor
950	800	680	450	220	100

Star Critterslayer

Fitted with 24" fluted super match barrel, with flattop upper and free floating handguard. Match 2 stage trigger. Fitted with Harris LMS swivel bipod and Ergo grip, with palm swell.

NIB	Exc.	V.G.	Good	Fair	Poor
1300	1000	750	600	400	180

STAR10

Series of AR-10 .308-size firearms includes Star10-B .308 rifle, Star10-BX .260 Rem rifle, Star10-P .308 pistol (brings $200-$250 less than rifles.)

NIB	Exc.	V.G.	Good	Fair	Poor
2500	2250	—	—	—	—

STARCAR

Basic AR-15 type, 16" heavy barrel, adjustable stock, 5.56 NATO.

NIB	Exc.	V.G.	Good	Fair	Poor
930	830	—	—	—	—

DSC Expedition Rifle

Offered with 16" or 20" lightweight barrel and integral muzzle brake. Stock sights and receiver are A-2 configuration.

NIB	Exc.	V.G.	Good	Fair	Poor
820	650	580	450	220	100

DSC Star-15 CMP Service Rifle

Fitted with 20" chrome lined heavy match barrel. National Match front and rear sights. CMP free float handguard. National Match trigger. A-2 upper receiver.

NIB	Exc.	V.G.	Good	Fair	Poor
1000	750	650	580	450	220

DSC Star CMP Improved Service Rifle

Similar to above model, with 20" Wilson Arms premium grade heavy match barrel. McCormick single- or two-stage Match trigger and Tippie Competition rear sight.

NIB	Exc.	V.G.	Good	Fair	Poor
1300	980	820	650	580	300

DSC Star 15 Lightweight Tactical

Fitted with 16" fluted heavy barrel and tactical "shorty" A-2 buttstock.

NIB	Exc.	V.G.	Good	Fair	Poor
880	700	580	450	220	100

DSC Star Dissipator

Features 16" barrel, with full length handguard. Available with A-2 or flattop upper receiver.

NIB	Exc.	V.G.	Good	Fair	Poor
880	700	580	450	220	100

DSC Star 15 9mm Carbine

Chambered for 9mm cartridge. Fitted with 16" heavy barrel. A-2 or flattop upper receiver. Available with A-2 or CAR buttstock.

NIB	Exc.	V.G.	Good	Fair	Poor
1000	750	650	580	450	220

C2S 1911 pistol

Compact version. Add $100 for Bobtail version with curved lower backstrap.

NIB	Exc.	V.G.	Good	Fair	Poor
2000	1800	—	—	—	—

PhD 1911 pistol

"Personal Home Defense" .45 ACP, Cylinder & Slide internals.

NIB	Exc.	V.G.	Good	Fair	Poor
1350	1200	—	—	—	—

DSC .300 Blackout AR Pistol

AR-style pistol in .300 AAC caliber, with 7.5" or 9" barrel. A2 muzzle brake, free-float aluminum handguard and pistol grip.

NIB	Exc.	V.G.	Good	Fair	Poor
1200	1000	750	600	450	300

3GR Rifles

This series is offered as 3-Gun competition rifles. AR-type 5.56 NATO. Variations include 3GR with 18" fluted barrel, 3GR 2.0 with 16" barrel, and 3GR 2.0 Go-Fast Red with 16" barrel. Values are similar for all three, slight premium for the 18" barrel.

NIB	Exc.	V.G.	Good	Fair	Poor
1450	1300	—	—	—	—

Always Ready

AR-type carbine, 16" barrel, flattop. 5.56 NATO, and slight premium for .300 Blackout

NIB	Exc.	V.G.	Good	Fair	Poor
1350	1200	—	—	—	—

APR7

AR-pattern pistol, 7.5" barrel. 5.56 NATO, and slight premium for .300 Blackout or 9mm.

NIB	Exc.	V.G.	Good	Fair	Poor
1300	1150	—	—	—	—

C3 Constant Carry Carbine

AR type. 16" lightweight barrel, 5.9 lb. overall weight, 5.56 NATO. Add $100-$150 for sights.

NIB	Exc.	V.G.	Good	Fair	Poor
1100	900	—	—	—	—

Covert Dragon

AR type. 16" quick change barrel, 6-position stock, 5.56 NATO.

NIB	Exc.	V.G.	Good	Fair	Poor
1350	1200	—	—	—	—

Midnight Dragon

AR type. 24" spiral fluted barrel, skeleton stock, two-stage trigger, 5.56 NATO.

NIB	Exc.	V.G.	Good	Fair	Poor
1300	1150	—	—	—	—

Mini Dragon

AR-type pistol. 7.5, 9, 10.5, or 11.5" barrel, pistol grip with buffer tube at rear, 5.56 NATO or .300 Blackout.

NIB	Exc.	V.G.	Good	Fair	Poor
900	780	—	—	—	—

MSD Mil Spec Dragon

M4-pattern AR. 16" barrel, 6 position stock.

NIB	Exc.	V.G.	Good	Fair	Poor
1100	930	—	—	—	—

DS4 carbine

AR type. 16" barrel, adjustable stock, 5.56 NATO.

NIB	Exc.	V.G.	Good	Fair	Poor
950	830	—	—	—	—

MDM (Modern Designated Marksman)

AR type. 16" free floating heavy barrel, 5.56 NATO.

NIB	Exc.	V.G.	Good	Fair	Poor
1550	1350	—	—	—	—

1911 Combat Pistol

Full-size Government Model .45 ACP, with 5" barrel, stainless slide, forged frame, black finish. Novak white-dot LoMount sights, Picatinny rail, 8-shot magazine, checkered wood grips. Introduced 2010.

NIB	Exc.	V.G.	Good	Fair	Poor
1600	1350	1100	800	500	300

C2 1911

Commander size .45 ACP, with 4.25" barrel, round butt or bobtail grip, black or gray Ion Bond finish, Novak 3-dot sights and 8-round magazine. Note: Add $150 for bobtail grip.

NIB	Exc.	V.G.	Good	Fair	Poor
1900	1700	1300	1000	—	—

C2G 1911

Upgraded full size 1911 .45, with features of 1911 C2. Plus 5" hand-fitted match barrel, with optional Picatinny rail. Also available in 10mm. Note: Add $200 for 10mm.

NIB	Exc.	V.G.	Good	Fair	Poor
1900	1700	1300	1000	—	—

DOUBLETAP DEFENSE

St. Louis, Missouri

Doubletap

An over/under model, with tip-up action double-action trigger. Chambered in 9mm or .45 ACP. Grip has space to carry two extra rounds. Weight 12 to 14 oz. Note: Add $100 for ported barrels; $200 for titanium frame.

NIB	Exc.	V.G.	Good	Fair	Poor
420	350	300	250	200	160

DOUG TURNBULL MANUFACTURING CO.

Bloomfield, New York

Company began operation in 1983 as a one-man shop. Today the company numbers 14 people and does finish work for most major firearms manufacturers. Company also installs Miller single triggers. Models listed are a series of special run firearms produced by Turnbull.

DT COLT

A current Colt SAA re-worked to look like the pre-1920 SAA. Assigned serial numbers beginning with 001DT. Revolvers are offered in .45 Colt, .44-40 and .38-40 calibers. Barrel lengths 4.75", 5.5" and 7.5". Standard DT has color case-hardened frame, rest of gun charcoal blue. Cylinder flutes are enlarged and front of cylinder is beveled. Many special options offered which will affect cost. Prices listed are for standard revolvers. Values for these very special guns is strictly what the market will bear.

Year Offered—1998

NIB	Exc.	V.G.	Good	Fair	Poor
1800	—	—	—	—	—

Year Offered—1999

NIB	Exc.	V.G.	Good	Fair	Poor
2250	—	—	—	—	—

Year Offered—2000

NIB	Exc.	V.G.	Good	Fair	Poor
2500	—	—	—	—	—

EHBM Colt

A Colt SAA current production revolver, limited to 50 guns. Chambered for .45 Colt. Fitted with 5.5" barrel. Special features. Serial numbers EHBM01 to EHBM50. First offered in 2000.

NIB	Exc.	V.G.	Good	Fair	Poor
2650	2300	—	—	—	—

Smith & Wesson No. 3 Schofield

Introduced in 2002, a special new production S&W Schofield. Special serial numbers with "DTR" prefix starting with serial number 0001. Frame, barrel and cylinder are charcoal blued. Trigger, triggerguard and barrel latch are bone color case-hardened. Factory wood grips are standard. Engraving is optional.

NIB	Exc.	V.G.	Good	Fair	Poor
2300	2450	—	—	—	—

Colt/Winchester Cased Set

Cased set, with Colt Model 1873 engraved revolver and Winchester Model 1894. Colt chambered for .45 Colt cartridge, fitted with 7.5" barrel, engraving "B" coverage; Model 1894 chambered for .45 Colt cartridge, in saddle ring configuration, engraving pattern #9 with deer. Checkered walnut stock. Limited to five sets total. Serial numbers 160DT to 164DT.

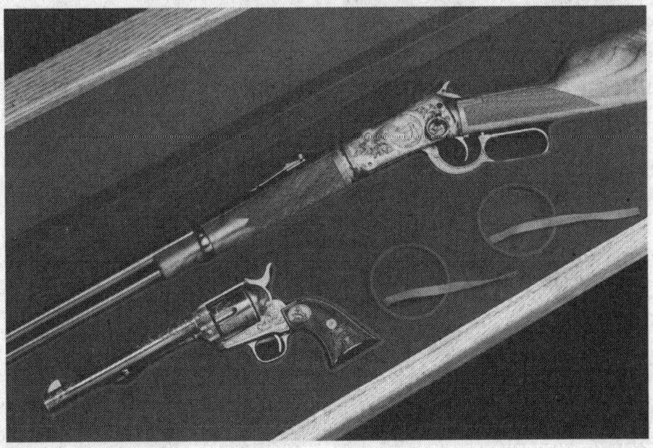

NIB	Exc.	V.G.	Good	Fair	Poor
5750	4300	—	—	—	—

General Patton Colt

Limited run of engraved Colt Model 1873 Single Action Army revolvers. Helfricht-style full-coverage engraving. Chambered for .45 Colt cartridge, fitted with 4.75" barrel and ivory grips. Silver-plated finish. Limited to 10 revolvers total. Serial numbers GP01 to GP10.

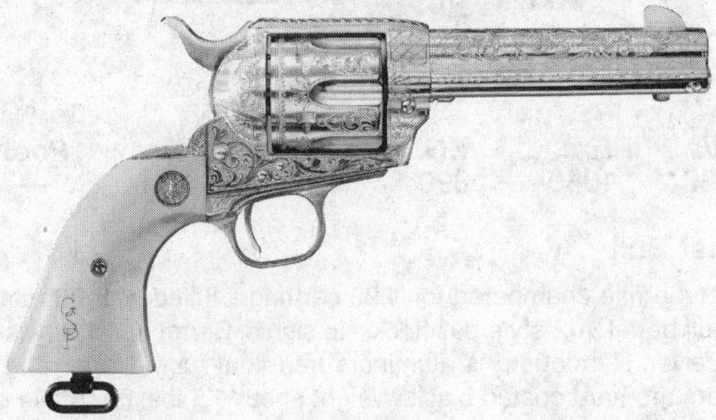

NIB	Exc.	V.G.	Good	Fair	Poor
5250	4000	—	—	—	—

Theodore Roosevelt Colt

Colt SAA revolver features carved ivory grips, Nimschke-style full-coverage engraving, with gold cylinder, hammer and ejector rod. Chambered for .44-40 cartridge, fitted with 7.5" barrel. Balance of gun silver plated. Supplied with fitted case. Limited to 25 revolvers total. Serial numbers TR01 to TR25.

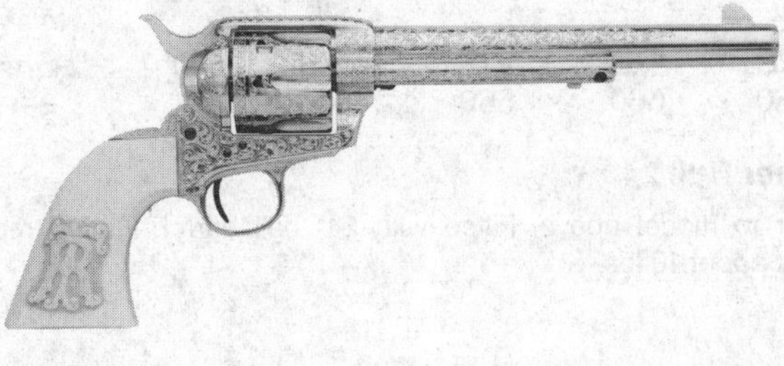

NIB	Exc.	V.G.	Good	Fair	Poor
7750	6000	—	—	—	—

Theodore Roosevelt Winchester Model 1876

Custom rifle limited to 25 units. Serial numbered from TR01 to TR-25. Each rifle engraved and checkered in style of original. Chambered for .45-70 cartridge. Fitted with 28" half-round barrel. Gold inlaid stock oval. Portion of the proceeds of each rifle goes to benefit Doug Turnbull Conservation Laboratory at the National Firearms Museum.

NIB	Exc.	V.G.	Good	Fair	Poor
29000	—	—	—	—	—

Cowboy Classic

Custom-tuned and authentically finished USFA 1873-style single-action revolver. Chambered in virtually all historically-correct centerfire cartridges. Barrel: 4.75", 5.5" and 7.5". Black hard rubber grips standard. Bone charcoal case-hardened and charcoal blue finish. Introduced 2006.

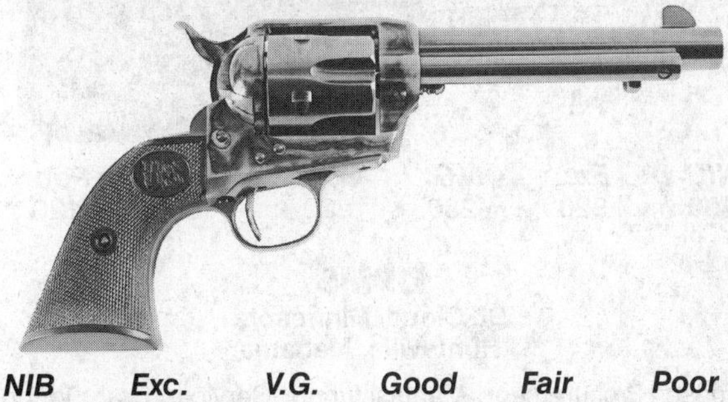

NIB	Exc.	V.G.	Good	Fair	Poor
1650	1300	—	—	—	—

Model 1911 Heritage

Made-to-order re-production of original design in the year 1911, to have the look and feel of pistols made during WWI. Chambered in .45 ACP. Features include hand-checkered American black walnut double-diamond grips, color case-hardened frame and hammer, a short and wide checkered spur hammer and two two-tone magazines. Several other variants are offered including Commander size and engraved models

NIB	Exc.	V.G.	Good	Fair	Poor
2080	1750	—	—	—	—

DOWNSIZER CORPORATION
Santee, California

Model WSP

Introduced in 1999. Billed as world's smallest pistol by manufacturer. Single-/double-action-only pistol, with tip-up barrel. Chambered for .22 Magnum, .32 Magnum, .357 Magnum, 9mm, .40 S&W and .45 ACP cartridges. Barrel length 2.1"; overall length 3.25"; height 2.25"; thickness .9"; weight about 11 oz. Built from stainless steel.

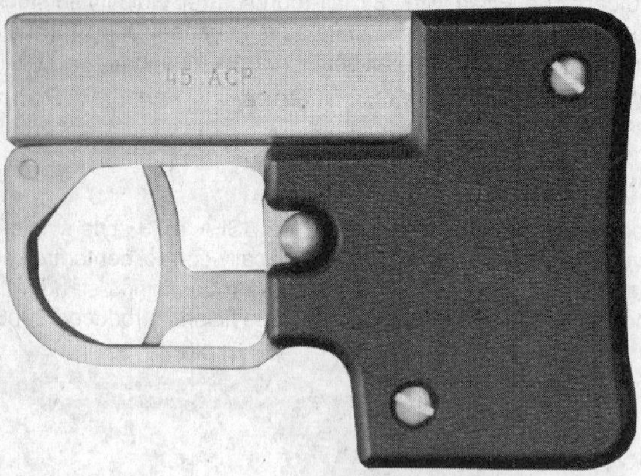

NIB	Exc.	V.G.	Good	Fair	Poor
400	320	280	220	180	120

DPMS

St. Cloud, Minnesota
Huntsville, Alabama

Defense Procurement Manufacturing Services was founded in 1985 manufacturing firearms parts and years later started manufacturing AR-style rifles. DPMS Panther was acquired by Cerebrus / Freedom Group in 2007, and eventually by Remington Outdoor Company. DPMS rifles are no longer being produced. Note: Values listed do not include the scopes or other optics shown in the pictures. SEE POLITICAL PANIC PRICING.

GII AP4

Chambered in .308 Win., with 16" lightweight chrome-lined barrel. M4 6-position collapsible stock, A2 pistol grip, carbine-length Glacier Guard handguard, Magpul Gen 2 rear sight, anodized and Teflon-coated upper and lower receivers.

NIB	Exc.	V.G.	Good	Fair	Poor
1080	910	780	660	—	—

GII MOE

NIB	Exc.	V.G.	Good	Fair	Poor
1100	940	800	680	—	—

GII Bull

NIB	Exc.	V.G.	Good	Fair	Poor
950	810	690	580	—	—

GII SASS

NIB	Exc.	V.G.	Good	Fair	Poor
1750	1490	1260	1080	—	—

GII Recon

NIB	Exc.	V.G.	Good	Fair	Poor
1200	1020	870	740	—	—

GII Hunter

Chambered in .243 Win., .260 Rem., .308 Win. or .338 Federal. Has 20" stainless steel barrel with no sights, Magpul MOE stock with pistol grip and a free-float tube handguard. Compact model identical except with 18" barrel. Introduced in 2014.

NIB	Exc.	V.G.	Good	Fair	Poor
1230	1040	890	750	—	—

Panther Bull

AR-15 type rifle chambered for .223 cartridge. Fitted with 20" stainless steel bull barrel. A-2 style buttstock. No sights. Barrel has 1:9 twist. Flattop receiver. Handguard is aluminum free float tube. Upper and lower receivers are hard coated black. Weight about 9.5 lbs. Each rifle comes standard with two 7-round magazines, sling and cleaning kit.

NIB	Exc.	V.G.	Good	Fair	Poor
780	660	560	480	—	—

Panther Bull 24

Similar to model above. Fitted with 24" bull barrel. Flattop receiver. Weight about 10 lbs.

NIB	Exc.	V.G.	Good	Fair	Poor
830	700	600	510	—	—

Panther Deluxe Bull 24 Special

Fitted with 24" stainless steel fluted bull barrel. Adjustable A-2 style buttstock. Flattop receiver. Adjustable sniper pistol grip. Weight about 10 lbs.

NIB	Exc.	V.G.	Good	Fair	Poor
980	830	700	600	—	—

Panther Extreme Super Bull 24

Fitted with 24" stainless steel extra heavy bull barrel (1.150" dia.). Skeletonized stock. Flattop receiver. Weight about 11.75 lbs.

NIB	Exc.	V.G.	Good	Fair	Poor
980	830	700	600	—	—

Panther Bulldog

Fitted with 20" stainless steel fluted bull barrel. Black synthetic A-2-style buttstock. Flattop receiver. Adjustable trigger. Weight about 10 lbs.

NIB	Exc.	V.G.	Good	Fair	Poor
980	830	700	600	—	—

Panther Bull Sweet 16

Fitted with 16" stainless steel bull barrel. Flattop receiver. Weight about 7.75 lbs.

NIB	Exc.	V.G.	Good	Fair	Poor
750	640	540	460	—	—

Panther Bull SST 16

Similar to model above, with stainless steel lower receiver. Weight about 9 lbs.

NIB	Exc.	V.G.	Good	Fair	Poor
1150	980	830	710	—	—

Panther Bull Classic

Fitted with 20" 4150 steel bull barrel. Square front post sight, adjustable A-2 rear sight. Weight about 9.75 lbs.

NIB	Exc.	V.G.	Good	Fair	Poor
780	660	560	480	—	—

Panther Arctic

Similar to Bull Classic, with 20" fluted bull barrel and flattop receiver. Black A-2 style buttstock, with white coat finish on receiver and handguard. Black Teflon finish on barrel. Weight about 8.25 lbs.

NIB	Exc.	V.G.	Good	Fair	Poor
900	770	650	550	—	—

Panther Classic

Fitted with 20" 4150 steel heavy barrel. Square front post sight and A-2 rear sight. A-2 round handguard. Weight about 9.5 lbs.

NIB	Exc.	V.G.	Good	Fair	Poor
750	640	540	460	—	—

Panther DCM

Similar to model above, with 20" stainless steel heavy barrel and NM rear sight. DCM free-float handguard. Adjustable trigger. Weight about 9.5 lbs.

NIB	Exc.	V.G.	Good	Fair	Poor
900	770	650	550	—	—

Panther Classic 16 Post Ban

Fitted with 1" 4150 steel heavy barrel. A-2 style sights. Round handguard. Weight about 7.25 lbs.

NIB	Exc.	V.G.	Good	Fair	Poor
750	640	540	460	—	—

Panther Free Float 16 Post Ban

Similar to model above, with 16" barrel. Fitted with ventilated free-floated barrel and tube handguard. Weight about 7.25 lbs.

NIB	Exc.	V.G.	Good	Fair	Poor
800	680	580	490	—	—

Panther Southpaw Post Ban

Fitted with 20" 4150 steel heavy barrel. A-2 style sights. Upper receiver modified for left-hand ejection. Weight about 9.5 lbs.

NIB	Exc.	V.G.	Good	Fair	Poor
830	700	600	510	—	—

Panther Race Gun

Similar to Panther Bull, with 24" fluted bull barrel. Sights: JP Micro adjustable rear, JP front sight adjustable for height. Includes Lyman globe and Shaver inserts.

NIB	Exc.	V.G.	Good	Fair	Poor
1380	1170	1000	850	—	—

Panther Tuber

Similar to Panther Bull 24, with 16" barrel and cylindrical aluminum shroud.

NIB	Exc.	V.G.	Good	Fair	Poor
680	570	490	420	—	—

Panther Single Shot Rifle

AR-15 style single-shot rifle, with manually-operated bolt. No magazine.

NIB	Exc.	V.G.	Good	Fair	Poor
680	570	490	420	—	—

Panther Pardus

Similar to Panther Post Ban, with 16" bull barrel, telescoping buttstock and tan Teflon finish. Introduced 2006.

NIB	Exc.	V.G.	Good	Fair	Poor
1300	1110	940	800	—	—

Panther 20th Anniversary Rifle

Similar to Panther Post-ban, with 20" bull barrel and engraved chrome-plated lower receiver. Introduced 2006.

NIB	Exc.	V.G.	Good	Fair	Poor
1600	1360	1160	990	840	710

Panther 6.8 Rifle

Similar to Panther DCM, with 20" chrome-moly barrel. Chambered for 6.8x43 Remington SPC. Introduced 2006.

NIB	Exc.	V.G.	Good	Fair	Poor
880	740	630	540	—	—

Panther Mark 12

Similar to other Panthers, with flash hider and other refinements. Introduced 2007.

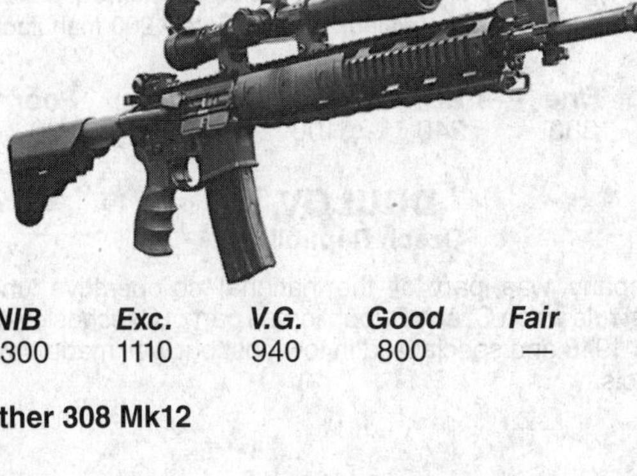

NIB	Exc.	V.G.	Good	Fair	Poor
1300	1110	940	800	—	—

Panther 308 Mk12

Semi-automatic AR-style rifle chambered in .308 Win./7.62 NATO. Features include 16" 4140 chrome-moly heavy 1:10 barrel; phosphated steel bolt; 4-rail free-floated handguard; flip-up front and rear sights; aluminum lower; two 19-round magazines; matte black finish overall; Magpul CTR adjustable stock.

NIB	Exc.	V.G.	Good	Fair	Poor
1450	1230	1050	890	—	—

Panther SDM-R

Similar to other Panthers, with stainless steel barrel and Harris bipod. Introduced 2007.

NIB	Exc.	V.G.	Good	Fair	Poor
1150	980	830	710	—	—

Panther Arms 5.56 Oracle

Semi-automatic AR-style rifle chambered in 5.56 NATO. Features include 16" 4140 chrome-moly 1:9 barrel; phosphated steel bolt; oval Glacier Guard handguard; flattop upper with Picatinny rail; aluminum lower; two 30-round magazines; Pardus 6-position telescoping stock. Also available on larger platform in .308 Winchester/7.62 NATO.

NIB	Exc.	V.G.	Good	Fair	Poor
480	400	340	290	—	—

Panther 3G1

Semi-automatic AR-style rifle chambered in 5.56 NATO. Features include 18" 416 stainless 1:9 barrel; phosphated steel bolt; VTAC modular handguard; flattop upper with Picatinny rail; aluminum lower; two 30-round magazines; Magpul CTR adjustable stock.

NIB	Exc.	V.G.	Good	Fair	Poor
1080	910	780	660	—	—

Prairie Panther

Semi-automatic AR-style rifle chambered in 5.56 NATO. Features include 20" 416 stainless fluted heavy 1:8 barrel; phosphated steel bolt; free-floated carbon fiber handguard; flattop upper with Picatinny rail; aluminum lower; two 30-round magazines; skeletonized Zytel stock; finished in King Desert Shadow camo overall.

NIB	Exc.	V.G.	Good	Fair	Poor
800	680	580	490	—	—

Panther RAPTR

Semi-automatic AR-style rifle chambered in 5.56 NATO. Features include 16" 4140 chrome-moly 1:9 barrel; phosphated steel bolt; ERGO Z-Rail 4-rail handguard; front vertical grip; standard A-2 sights; aluminum lower; four 30-round magazines. Discontinued 2012.

NIB	Exc.	V.G.	Good	Fair	Poor
1330	1130	1000	810	—	—

Panther A-15 Pump Pistol

Same as above. Fitted with 10.5" barrel. Weight about 5 lbs.

NIB	Exc.	V.G.	Good	Fair	Poor
1450	1100	750	580	—	—

Panther REPR

Semi-automatic AR-style rifle chambered in .308 Win./7.62 NATO. Features include 18" 416 stainless steel 1:10 barrel; phosphated steel bolt; 4-rail free-floated handguard; no sights; aluminum lower; two 19-round magazines; Coyote Brown camo finish overall.

NIB	Exc.	V.G.	Good	Fair	Poor
2030	1720	1460	1240	1060	900

Panther A-15 Pump Rifle

Model has 20" 4150 steel heavy barrel, with A-2 style sights. Fitted with A-2 compensator and modified to slide-action. Weight about 8.5 lbs.

NIB	Exc.	V.G.	Good	Fair	Poor
1380	1170	1000	840	—	—

Panther DCM .22 LR

Rimfire version of Panther series, with 20" fluted stainless H-Bar barrel, A-2 upper receiver, National Match sights. Also available with 16" barrel (Panther AP4) and flattop receiver. Note: Deduct $75 for AP4 model

NIB	Exc.	V.G.	Good	Fair	Poor
830	700	600	510	—	—

Panther Lite 308/338

Chambered for .308 Win. or .338 Federal. A-3 flattop design, with 20" free-floated barrel and handguard. Various options offered.

NIB	Exc.	V.G.	Good	Fair	Poor
1230	1040	890	750	—	—

Panther 6.5

Basic Panther model chambered for 6.5 Creedmoor. Stainless steel free-floated 24" barrel, A-3 flattop upper, mil-spec stock.

NIB	Exc.	V.G.	Good	Fair	Poor
1030	870	740	630	—	—

TAC 2/TAC 20

This model in 5.56 NATO, with 16" barrel, Magpul ACS stock with MOE pistol grip and A2 front and rear sights. Weight about 8.5 lbs. TAC 20 model similar, but in .308 Winchester with 20" heavy barrel. Introduced in 2012.

NIB	Exc.	V.G.	Good	Fair	Poor
950	810	690	580	—	—

LRT-SASS

Semi-automatic rifle based on AR-15 design. Chambered in .308 Win., 18" stainless steel barrel with flash hider. Collapsible Vitor Clubfoot carbine stock and 19-round detachable magazine. Introduced 2006. Mini-SASS chambered in 5.56 NATO. Note: Deduct $150 for Mini-SASS.

NIB	Exc.	V.G.	Good	Fair	Poor
1680	1420	1210	1030	—	—

LR-260

Similar to LRT-SASS, with 24" stainless steel barrel. Chambered in .260 Remington. Also available with 20" chrome-moly barrel as LR-260H. Introduced 2006.

NIB	Exc.	V.G.	Good	Fair	Poor
1000	850	720	610	—	—

LR-243

Similar to LR-260, with 20" chrome-moly barrel. Chambered in .243 Win. Introduced 2006.

NIB	Exc.	V.G.	Good	Fair	Poor
1200	1020	870	740	—	—

LR-204

Similar to LRT-260. Chambered in .204 Ruger. Introduced 2006.

NIB	Exc.	V.G.	Good	Fair	Poor
980	830	700	600	—	—

6.8 SPCII Hunter

Chambered for Remington 6.8 SPC cartridge, with 18" barrel and Miculek compensator. A-3 flattop design with forward assist. Skeletonized stock.

NIB	Exc.	V.G.	Good	Fair	Poor
1050	890	760	650	—	—

300 AAC Blackout

Chambered for .300 AAC cartridge. Chrome-lined 16" heavy barrel comes with Blackout suppressor adapter. AP4 stock, free-float handguard.

NIB	Exc.	V.G.	Good	Fair	Poor
880	740	630	540	—	—

308 Recon

Similar to 300 AAC Blackout model, except chambered for .308 Winchester. Standard weight, 16" barrel with Blackout suppressor adapter. A-3 flattop upper receiver, Magpul MOE stock with 4-Rail handguard.

NIB	Exc.	V.G.	Good	Fair	Poor
930	790	670	570	—	—

DREYSE

See—RHEINMETALL

DRISCOLL, J.B.

Springfield, Massachusetts

Single-Shot Pocket Pistol Antique

Small pistol chambered for .22 rimfire. Has 3.5" octagonal barrel that pivots downward for loading after trigger-like hook under breech is pulled. Spur trigger, silver-plated brass frame and blued barrel. Square butt is flared at bottom and grips are walnut. Approximately 200 manufactured in late 1860s.

Exc.	Fine	V.G.	Good	Fair	Poor
1000	380	240	100	50	30

DRULOV

Czech Republic

This Company was part of the national co-operative under communist rule when Czech Republic was part of Czechoslovakia. Formed in 1948 and specialized in low-cost but well made rimfire target pistols.

Model 70 Standard

A bolt-action single-shot pistol chambered for .22 LR. Knob at rear of frame opened the bolt. When bolt is closed firing pin is cocked. Barrel 9.75" long, with an adjustable front sight for windage. Rear sight is adjustable for elevation. Wooden wrap-around grips with thumb rest are standard. Weight about 44 oz.

NIB	*Exc.*	*V.G.*	*Good*	*Fair*	*Poor*
—	300	200	180	100	80

Model 70 Special

Same as above, with addition of set trigger.

NIB	*Exc.*	*V.G.*	*Good*	*Fair*	*Poor*
—	350	250	200	150	100

Model 75

Features set trigger, better sights and grip. Rear sight is fully adjustable.

NIB	*Exc.*	*V.G.*	*Good*	*Fair*	*Poor*
—	400	300	250	200	150

Pav

Target pistol introduced between WWI and WW II. Inexpensive pistol, with fixed front sight and notch for rear sight. Also a single-shot chambered for .22 LR cartridge. Barrel is 10.25"; weight about 35 oz.

Courtesy Orvel Reichert

NIB	*Exc.*	*V.G.*	*Good*	*Fair*	*Poor*
—	180	150	100	80	50

DS ARMS, INC.

Barrington, Illinois

DS Arms, Inc. began selling its rifles to the public in 1996. Based on actual blueprints of famous FN/FAL rifle, SA58 rifles are made in the U.S. All SA58 rifles are fitted with fully adjustable gas system, Type I, II or III forged receiver, hand-lapped barrel, muzzle brake, elevation adjustable post front sight, windage adjustable rear peep sight with 5 settings from 200 to 600 meters, detachable metric magazine, adjustable sling and hard case. It also manufactures a series of AR-15 type rifles and carbines. Virtually all parts are made by DS Arms, Inc. SEE POLITICAL PANIC PRICING.

SA58

SA58 24" Bull

Fitted with 24 stainless steel barrel and .308 match chamber. Overall length 44.5". Weight about 11.5 lbs.

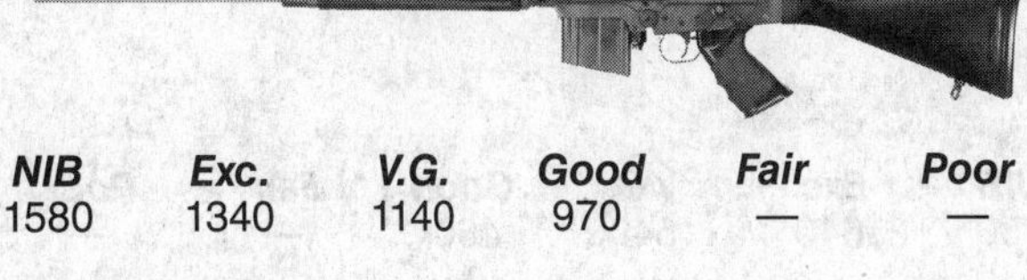

NIB	*Exc.*	*V.G.*	*Good*	*Fair*	*Poor*
1580	1340	1140	970	—	—

SA58 21" Bull

Same as above. Fitted with 21 stainless steel barrel. Weight about 11.1 lbs.

NIB	*Exc.*	*V.G.*	*Good*	*Fair*	*Poor*
1580	1340	1140	970	—	—

SA58 Medium Contour

Offered with 21" barrel in stainless or blued steel. Weight about 10.5 lbs. Note: Add $250 for stainless steel.

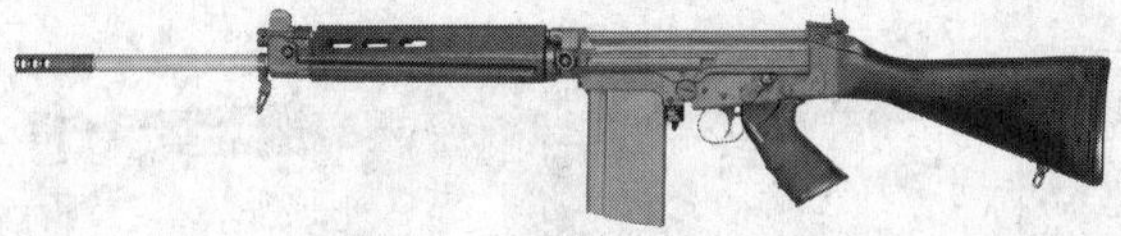

NIB	*Exc.*	*V.G.*	*Good*	*Fair*	*Poor*
1600	1360	1160	980	—	—

SA58 Carbine

Fitted with 16.25" barrel cut for factory light bipod. Blued finish. Stainless steel version also available. Overall length 37.5". Weight about 8.35 lbs. Note: Add $250 for stainless steel.

NIB	*Exc.*	*V.G.*	*Good*	*Fair*	*Poor*
1400	1190	1010	860	—	—

SA58 Standard

Model has 21" barrel cut for factory light bipod. Weight about 8.75 lbs. Blued finish.

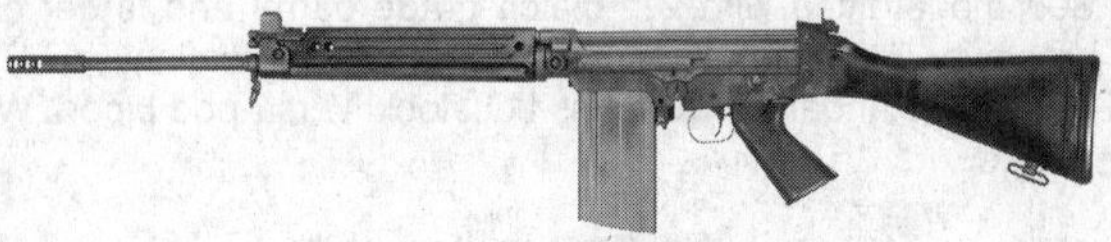

NIB	*Exc.*	*V.G.*	*Good*	*Fair*	*Poor*
1400	1190	1010	860	—	—

SA58 Tactical

Fitted with 16.25" fluted barrel, black synthetic stock, Type I receiver, adjustable sights and detachable magazine. Blued finish. Weight about 8.25 lbs.

NIB	*Exc.*	*V.G.*	*Good*	*Fair*	*Poor*
1400	1190	1010	860	—	—

SA58 Congo

This .308 model features 18" bipod-cut barrel, with short Belgian-style flash hider. Type I receiver with carry handle. Synthetic buttstock and pistol grip. Aluminum lower. Detachable magazine. Adjustable sights. Weight about 8.6 lbs.

NIB	Exc.	V.G.	Good	Fair	Poor
1580	1340	1140	970	—	—

SA58 Para Congo Edition

Fitted with Type II receiver, carry handle and 18" bipod-cut barrel. Short Belgian-style flash hider. Steel lower. Folding steel Para stock. Adjustable sights. Weight about 9.85 lbs.

NIB	Exc.	V.G.	Good	Fair	Poor
1980	1680	1430	1210	—	—

SA58 Predator

Offered in .308, .260 Rem. or .243. Has Type I receiver, 16" or 19" medium carbine barrel with target crown. Green furniture. Aluminum lower. Picatinny rail. Weight about 9 lbs. with 16" barrel.

NIB	Exc.	V.G.	Good	Fair	Poor
1550	1320	1120	950	—	—

SA58 Gray Wolf

This .308 model fitted with 21" match grade barrel and target crown. Type I receiver. Aluminum lower. Extended safety. Picatinny rail. Target pistol grip with standard or X-series buttstock. Versa-pod bipod. Weight about 13 lbs.

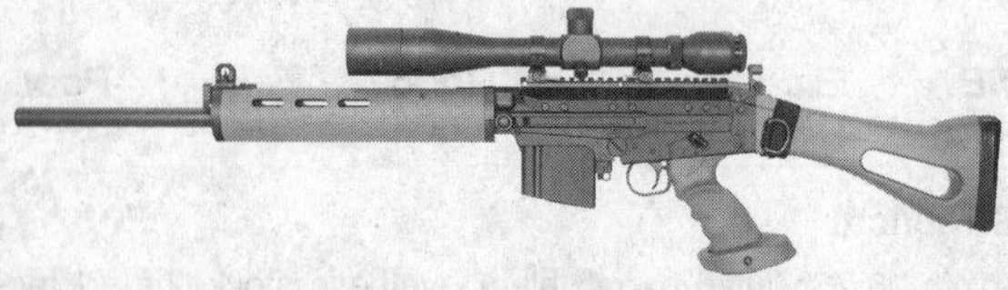

NIB	Exc.	V.G.	Good	Fair	Poor
1750	1490	1260	1080	—	—

SA58 T48 Replica

Chambered for .308 cartridge and fitted with 21" barrel. Replica Browning flash hider. Supplied with 10- or 20-round fixed magazine and stripper clip top cover. Wooden stock. Weight about 9.7 lbs.

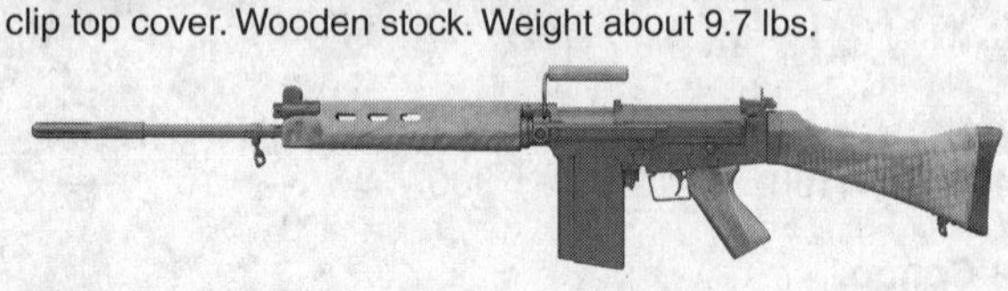

NIB	Exc.	V.G.	Good	Fair	Poor
1580	1340	1140	970	—	—

SA58 Cold Warrior Rifle

Patterned after one of the last contract FAL's that FN produced, for the country of Bolivia. Holland-style rear sight, 50.63 PARA-style folding cocking handle, Type 3 receiver, cut for carry handle. The receiver as well as the top cover feature a matte black DuraCoat finish. This rifle is fully compatible and interchangeable with all metric pattern parts & accessories.

NIB	Exc.	V.G.	Good	Fair	Poor
1450	1230	1050	890	—	—

SA58 Improved Battle Rifle

Introduced 2019 and chambered in 7.62x51mm NATO. Available with several different barrel lengths, adjustable gas-piston-operated. All I Series models come with Battle Rifle buttstock that allows the rifle to fire while folded. The stock features side folding and L.O.P. adjustment buttons. Cheek-piece adjusts for height and tilt/angle.

NIB	Exc.	V.G.	Good	Fair	Poor
2250	1910	1620	1380	—	—

SA58 Improved Battle Carbine

Introduced 2019 and chambered in 7.62x51mm NATO. 16" Fluted Tactical Barrel.

NIB	Exc.	V.G.	Good	Fair	Poor
2250	1910	1620	1380	—	—

SA58 Improved Battle Weapon

Introduced 2019 and chambered in 7.62x51mm NATO. 11" medium-contour barrel SBR. NFA item.

NIB	Exc.	V.G.	Good	Fair	Poor
2250	1910	1620	1380	—	—

SA58 Improved Battle Pistol

Introduced 2019 and chambered in 7.62x51mm NATO. 11" pistol barrel and folding arm brace and M-LOK handguard included.

NIB	Exc.	V.G.	Good	Fair	Poor
1780	1530	1300	—	—	—

SA58 Improved Battle Pistol 8.25"

Introduced 2019 and chambered in 7.62x51mm NATO. 8.25" pistol barrel, folding arm brace, and M-LOK handguard included.

NIB	Exc.	V.G.	Good	Fair	Poor
2000	1700	1450	—	—	—

DS-AR

S1 Rifle

Introduced in 2004, this 5.56-caliber rifle features 20" or 24" bull barrel. Picatinny gas black sight base. Flattop receiver. Free-floating aluminum handguard. A-2 stock. Ten-round magazine. Discontinued.

NIB	Exc.	V.G.	Good	Fair	Poor
1000	850	720	610	—	—

CVI Carbine

Similar to model above, with 16" barrel, forged front sight base and integral muzzle brake. D-4 handguard. Fixed CAR buttstock. Ten-round magazine. Discontinued.

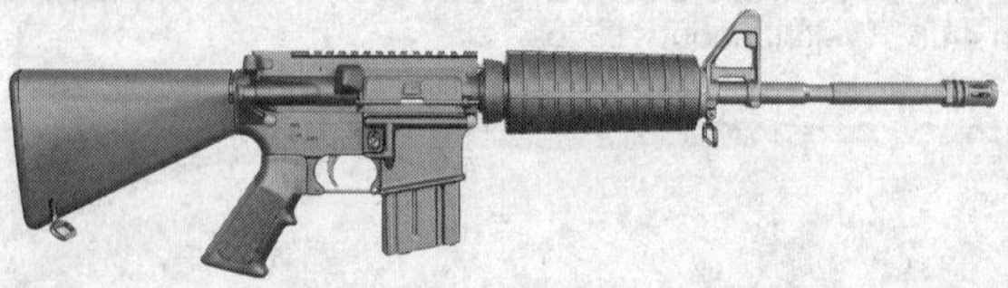

NIB	Exc.	V.G.	Good	Fair	Poor
750	640	540	460	—	—

LE4 Carbine

As above, with pre-ban features. For law enforcement only. Discontinued.

NIB	Exc.	V.G.	Good	Fair	Poor
1180	1000	850	720	—	—

DS-AR S Series Rifle

Introduced in 2005. Chambered for .223 cartridge. Fitted with choice of 16", 20" or 24" stainless steel match grade bull barrel. A-2 stock with free-floating handguard. Flattop receiver, National Match 2 stage trigger. Magazine capacity 10, 20 or 30 rounds.

NIB	Exc.	V.G.	Good	Fair	Poor
1350	1150	980	830	—	—

AR-15 Service Series

Caliber: 5.56 NATO. Capacity: ASC 30-round gray alloy magazine. Barrel: 14.5". with permanently affixed A2 bird cage flash hider for 16" barrel O.A.L., or 20" A2 government profile rifle-length barrel. M4-profile, chrome-lined chamber and bore, 4150 - 11595E mil-spec barrel steel, 1:7" twist. Stock: Mil-spec. M4 style, six-position mil-spec buffer tube. Sights: Top rail segments. Forged front sight tower (F-Marked). Weight: 6.9 lbs. Features: Carbine-length gas system, M4 feed ramps on both barrel extension and upper receiver. Stainless-steel carbine-length gas tube, Knight's Armament Co. M4 RAS carbine-length handguard assembly. Knight's forward vertical grip. DSArms-forged A3M4 mil-spec upper receiver, DSArms-forged lower receiver, both are hardcoat anodized per MIL-A-8625F, Type-3, Class-2 finish. Mil-spec M16 complete bolt carrier group. Mil-spec A2-style pistol grip. SEE POLITICAL PANIC PRICING.

NIB	Exc.	V.G.	Good	Fair	Poor
1100	1010	900	790	—	—

DS-AR Carbine

Chambered for .223 cartridge. Fitted with 16" D4 barrel and flash hider. Choice of: fixed or collapsible stock; forged flattop or A-2 upper receiver. Magazine capacity 10, 20 or 30 rounds. Introduced in 2005.

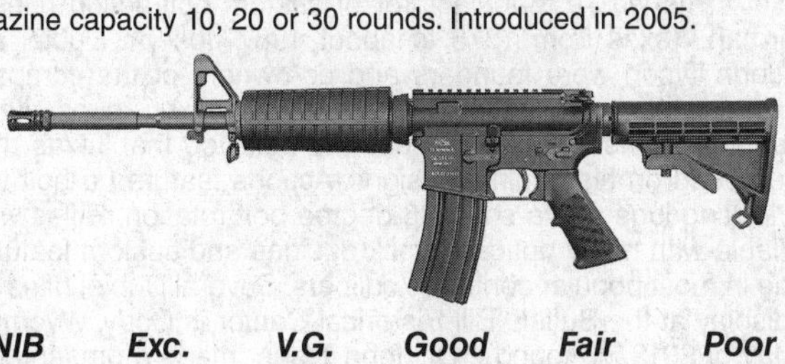

NIB	Exc.	V.G.	Good	Fair	Poor
1350	1150	980	830	—	—

DS-AR Rifle

As above, with 20" heavy barrel, flash hider and fixed stock. Introduced in 2005.

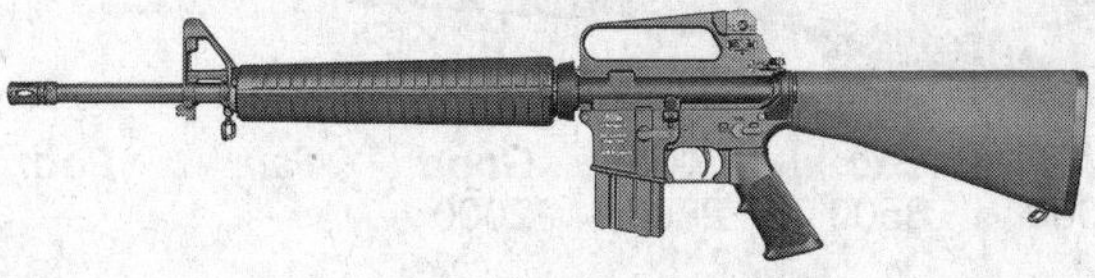

NIB	Exc.	V.G.	Good	Fair	Poor
1380	1170	1000	840	—	—

DS-AR DCM Rifle

Chambered for .223 cartridge with Wylde chamber. Fitted with 20" match grade Badger barrel. DCM free-float handguard system. National Match two-stage trigger. National Match rear sight. A-2 upper receiver. Introduced in 2005.

NIB	Exc.	V.G.	Good	Fair	Poor
1550	1320	1120	950	—	—

DS-AR CQB MRP

Introduced in 2005. Features 16" chrome lined barrel and A-2 flash hider. Collapsible stock with MRP quad rail. Monolithic rail platform upper. Flattop or A-2 upper receiver. Supplied with 30-round magazine.

NIB	Exc.	V.G.	Good	Fair	Poor
2380	2020	1720	1460	—	—

DSA Z4 Gas Trap Carbine (GTC)

Introduced in 2005. Fitted with 16" chrome lined barrel, M4 profile fluted and Vortec flash hider. Collapsible 6-position stock, with free float tactical rail. Gas trap system. Flattop upper receiver. Magazine capacity 10, 20 or 30 rounds.

NIB	Exc.	V.G.	Good	Fair	Poor
1650	1400	1190	1010	—	—

ZM-4 SERIES

Caliber: 5.56 NATO. Capacity: Magpul Custom G2 MOE 30-round magazine, black with flat dark earth ribs. Barrels: 14.7", 16", and 20", lightweight mid-length. 1:8" twist, M4 feed ramps on both barrel extension and upper receiver. Stock: B5 Systems Custom SOPMOD Stock. Weight: 6.9 lbs. Trigger: ALG Defense Advanced Combat Trigger. Overall Length: 33" to 35". Features: Premium match barrel machined from either 416-R stainless steel or 4150-11595 Mil-spec material, 5.56 match chamber. Enhanced A3M4 upper receiver, upgraded fire control group, ambidextrous selector switch and WarZ triggerguard, bolt catch and charging handle. Midwest Industries 15". Combat Series M-LOK free float handguard. Magpul Custom MIAD Modular Pistol Grip, flat dark earth with black two-tone. DSArms Enhanced FDE alloy triggerguard, SureFire Pro Comp (1/2x28 tpi). SEE POLITICAL PANIC PRICING.

NIB	Exc.	V.G.	Good	Fair	Poor
780	660	560	480	—	—

ZM-4 Gas Piston CQB

NIB	Exc.	V.G.	Good	Fair	Poor
2550	2170	1840	1570	—	—

ZM-4 War Z M4

Caliber: 5.56 NATO. Capacity: Magpul Custom G2 MOE 30-round magazine, black with Flat Dark Earth ribs. Barrel: 16", lightweight mid-length, 1:8 twist, M4 feed ramps on both barrel extension and upper receiver. Stock: B5 Systems Custom SOPMOD Stock, Flat Dark Earth, B5 Systems QD end plate. Sights: Full-length top rail. Weight: 6.9 lbs. Trigger: ALG Defense Advanced Combat Trigger. Overall Length: 33" to 35". Features: Premium match barrel machined from either 416-R Stainless Steel or 4150-11595 mil-spec material, 5.56 match chamber. Enhanced A3M4 upper receiver, upgraded fire control group, ambidextrous selector switch and WarZ triggerguard, bolt catch and charging handle. Low-mass sand-cut bolt carrier group with nitride finish. DuraCoat finish in Flat Dark Earth over the hard-coat anodized lower receiver, upper receiver and handguard. 4140-steel MK12-style low-profile, set-screw gas block, stainless steel mid-length gas tube. Midwest Industries 15". Combat Series M-LOK free-float handguard. Magpul Custom MIAD Modular Pistol Grip, Flat Dark Earth with black two-tone. DSArms Enhanced FDE alloy triggerguard, SureFire Pro Comp (1/2x28 tpi).

NIB	Exc.	V.G.	Good	Fair	Poor
1330	1130	960	810	—	—

ZM-4 Combat Companion

NIB	Exc.	V.G.	Good	Fair	Poor
860	740	630	530	—	—

ZM-4 A3 M4 Flat Top Carbine

NIB	Exc.	V.G.	Good	Fair	Poor
600	550	500	400	300	—

ZM-4 Custom FDE

NIB	Exc.	V.G.	Good	Fair	Poor
1150	980	830	710	—	—

ZM-4 Titanium V2 Edition

NIB	Exc.	V.G.	Good	Fair	Poor
1150	980	830	710	—	—

ZM-4 Stainless Steel Slim Series

NIB	Exc.	V.G.	Good	Fair	Poor
600	510	430	370	—	—

RPD Traditional Rifle

Chambered for 7.62x39 cartridge, this belt-fed semi-automatic rifle comes with two 100-round belt and drum sets. Barrel length 20.5". Stock is wood. Weight about 17 lbs. Introduced in 2013.

NIB	Exc.	V.G.	Good	Fair	Poor
1850	1570	1340	1140	—	—

RPD Carbine

Similar to Traditional Rifle, with 17.5" fluted barrel, fully adjustable AR-style stock with SAW-style pistol grip and lighter-weight alloy frame. Weight about 14 lbs. Introduced in 2013.

NIB	Exc.	V.G.	Good	Fair	Poor
2330	1980	1680	1430	—	—

BOLT-ACTION RIFLES

DS-MP1

Bolt-action rifle chambered for .308 cartridge. Built on custom Remington 700 action. Fitted with 21" Badger barrel, with target crown. Black McMillan A5 stock. Matte black finish. Introduced in 2004.

NIB	Exc.	V.G.	Good	Fair	Poor
2800	2100	1680	1050	—	—

HANDGUNS

B&T TP9 Tactical Pistol

Swiss made recoil-operated rotating-bolt semi-automatic. Chambered in 9mm Parabellum. Semi-automatic civilian-legal version of B&T TP9SF select-fire sub-machine gun. Imported from Switzerland by DSA from 2008 to 2011.

NIB	Exc.	V.G.	Good	Fair	Poor
1100	950	780	600	—	—

SA58TAC

Based on FAL design with 8" barrel. Chambered in 7.62x39. This is considered a pistol. Features include a 20-shot magazine, alloy lower receiver, SAW pistol grip, Para extended scope mount and black nylon stock. Introduced in 2013.

NIB	Exc.	V.G.	Good	Fair	Poor
1500	1200	1000	750	—	—

Patriot FDR-15

Caliber: 5.56 NATO. Mil-Spec base model rifle with enhanced tolerances. 7075-T6511 lower, upper, and handrail with a match-grade barrel together capable of sub-MOA accuracy. Barrel: 16-in. medium contour, 1:8 twist.

NIB	Exc.	V.G.	Good	Fair	Poor
1300	—	—	—	—	—

Fu King F15 Forged

Caliber: 5.56 NATO. FU KING F15 forged receiver set, 13-in. M-LOK free-float handguard, 16-in. 1:8 twist stainless barrel. Black nitride bolt-carrier group, MIL-SPEC stock, grip, and charging handle. A2 flash hider.

NIB	Exc.	V.G.	Good	Fair	Poor
850	—	—	—	—	—

DUBIEL ARMS CO.

Sherman, Texas

Dubiel Arms was a manufacturer of custom bolt-action rifles in Sherman, Texas from 1975 to about 1987. Joseph Dubiel and Dr. John Tyson were founders and co-owners of the company. Dubiel's father was John Dubiel, a well-known gunsmith in Oklahoma in the 1920s and '30s. It is believed that Texas rifles were based on his original designs. Actions featured a bolt with five locking lugs and a short 36-degree bolt rotation. Rifles were available with many options, stock designs and custom features. Made in most popular centerfire calibers. Several Dubiel rifles are on display at the Buffalo Bill Historical Center in Cody, Wyoming. In May of 2012, co-founder Dr. John Tyson, made a presentation of nine rifles to the NRA National Firearms Museum in Fairfax, Virginia. Prices shown are estimated values of basic models. Various options would increase these values significantly.

NIB	Exc.	V.G.	Good	Fair	Poor
5000	3500	2800	2000	—	—

DUMOULIN

Herstal, Belgium

Guns produced by Ernest Dumoulin are essentially handmade to customer's order. They are of highest quality, both in materials and workmanship. There are many options available that have a tremendous impact on value fluctuations. Models and values listed here are base prices.

SHOTGUNS

Europa Model

Side-by-side double-barrel chambered for 12-, 20-, 28-gauge and .410 bore. Available in any length barrel and choke combination. Anson & Deeley boxlock action and automatic ejectors. One has the option of double- or single-selective triggers and choice of six different moderate engraving patterns. Select walnut stock is oil-finished. Introduced in 1989.

NIB	*Exc.*	*V.G.*	*Good*	*Fair*	*Poor*
3500	2750	1950	1250	800	400

Leige Model

Side-by-side double-barrel chambered for 12-, 16-, 20- and 28-gauge. Similar to Europa, with greater degree of finish and more engraving. Walnut is of a higher grade. Introduced in 1986.

NIB	*Exc.*	*V.G.*	*Good*	*Fair*	*Poor*
5750	4200	2750	1500	950	420

Continental Model

Side-by-side chambered for 12-, 20-, 28-gauge and .410 bore. Barrel lengths and chokes are on custom-order basis. A true sidelock action, with automatic ejectors and choice of triggers. Six different engraving patterns. Stock is made of high grade hand-checkered oil-finished walnut. Introduced in 1989.

NIB	*Exc.*	*V.G.*	*Good*	*Fair*	*Poor*
7500	6000	4500	3000	1500	400

Etendart Model

Side-by-side chambered for 12-, 20- and 28-gauge. Best grade side-by-side built on purely made-to-order basis. Profusely engraved and uses exhibition grade walnut in its stock. There are 12 different engraving patterns from which to choose. Cost is according to embellishments chosen. Values given here are for basic model.

NIB	*Exc.*	*V.G.*	*Good*	*Fair*	*Poor*
14500	11000	8500	4000	3000	700

Superposed Express International

An over/under chambered for 20-gauge. Furnished with a set of rifle barrels. Customer's choice of seven calibers. Walnut is a deluxe grade and engraving available at extra cost. Made-to-order gun. Value here for the most basic model. Discontinued in 1985

NIB	*Exc.*	*V.G.*	*Good*	*Fair*	*Poor*
—	2500	2000	1250	750	400

Boss Royal Model

Best grade over/under chambered for 12-, 20- and 28-gauge. Full sidelock gun made to customer's specifications, using finest materials and workmanship available. Introduced in 1987.

NIB	*Exc.*	*V.G.*	*Good*	*Fair*	*Poor*
18500	15000	12000	8000	4500	700

Eagle Model Combination Gun

This model has a rifle or shotgun barrel that is chambered for 12- or 20-gauge. Rifle calibers available are .22 Hornet, .222 Remington, .222 Remington Magnum, 6mm, .243, .25-06, .30-06, 6.5 x 57R, 7 x 57R, 8 x 57JRS and 9.3 x 74R. Action is boxlock, with automatic ejectors. Other specifications are on custom-order basis. Introduced in 1989.

NIB	*Exc.*	*V.G.*	*Good*	*Fair*	*Poor*
2750	2250	1500	950	750	400

DOUBLE RIFLES

Europa I

Made-to-order over/under double-barreled rifle. Available in same calibers as Eagle Combination gun. Has Anson & Deeley boxlock. All other options to customer's specifications.

NIB	*Exc.*	*V.G.*	*Good*	*Fair*	*Poor*
6000	4700	3500	4000	1250	500

Continental I Model

More deluxe over/under rifle, with true sidelock-action. Calibers the same as Europa. Specifications are to customer's order, with 12 engraving patterns to choose from at extra cost. Introduced in 1989.

NIB	*Exc.*	*V.G.*	*Good*	*Fair*	*Poor*
9000	7150	5500	4000	2000	600

Pionnier Express Rifle

Side-by-side double rifle chambered for .22 Hornet through .600 Nitro Express. Anson & Deeley boxlock-action and quite deluxe throughout. Specifications are to customer's order. There are basically 12 models available (P-1 through P-XII). Differences among these models are in degree of ornamentation and quality of walnut used for the stock. Values range from approximately $10,000 to $15,000 for basic models.

Aristocrat Model

Low-profile single-shot chambered for all calibers up to .375 H&H. Deluxe made-to-order rifle, with exhibition-grade walnut and 12 engraving patterns available.

NIB	*Exc.*	*V.G.*	*Good*	*Fair*	*Poor*
—	9500	7500	5800	3000	700

BOLT-ACTION RIFLES

Centurion Model

Custom-order rifle built on Mauser or Sako action. Chambered for all calibers from .270 to .458 Winchester Magnum. Barrel lengths available were 21.5", 24" and 25.5"; many engraving options from which to choose. Stock of deluxe French walnut, with rosewood forend tip and pistol grip cap. Discontinued in 1986.

NIB	*Exc.*	*V.G.*	*Good*	*Fair*	*Poor*
7500	6000	5000	4000	—	—

Centurion Classic

Similar to Mauser-actioned Centurion. Chambered for non-Magnum calibers only. Walnut used for stock is a better grade.

NIB	*Exc.*	*V.G.*	*Good*	*Fair*	*Poor*
1280	950	750	600	500	400

Diane

More deluxe version of Centurion Classic.

NIB	*Exc.*	*V.G.*	*Good*	*Fair*	*Poor*
1800	1550	1250	900	650	500

Amazone

A 20" barreled full-length stocked upgraded version of Diane.

NIB	*Exc.*	*V.G.*	*Good*	*Fair*	*Poor*
2100	1750	1400	950	700	500

Bavaria Deluxe

Similar to Centurion, with same barrel lengths and calibers available. Engraving styles available are more deluxe. Discontinued in 1985.

NIB	*Exc.*	*V.G.*	*Good*	*Fair*	*Poor*
2350	1800	1400	950	700	500

Safari Model

Similar to Bavaria Deluxe. Chambered for heavy Magnum calibers only.

NIB	Exc.	V.G.	Good	Fair	Poor
3280	2700	1900	1450	900	500

Safari Sportsman

Built on a Magnum Mauser action. Chambered for .375 H&H, .404 Jeffreys, .416 Rigby and .505 Gibbs. A true big game rifle. Made available in 1986.

NIB	Exc.	V.G.	Good	Fair	Poor
4500	3650	2400	1550	1100	—

African Pro

More deluxe version of Safari Sportsman. Folding leaf rear sight, hooded front sight and ebony or buffalo horn forend tip.

NIB	Exc.	V.G.	Good	Fair	Poor
5200	3950	2700	1700	1300	750

DUMOULIN & CO., F.

Liege, Belgium 1894-1915

ACME Arms

Trade name used on double-barrel shotguns.

NIB	Exc.	V.G.	Good	Fair	Poor
—	400	280	180	130	80

DUSEK, F.

Opocno, Czech Republic

Dusek commenced business in mid-1920s and continued to make firearms through WWII. They manufactured pistols for Nazi Germany under the contract code "aek". After the war, the communists took over and Dusek's designs were re-delegated to the CZ factory.

Perla

This 6.35mm pistol has a fixed barrel and open-topped slide. Resembles a Walther design and is striker-fired. Slide is marked "Automat Pistole Perla 6.35mm"; grips "Perla 6.35". Dusek made this model from early 1930s until WWII.

NIB	Exc.	V.G.	Good	Fair	Poor
—	340	220	160	100	80

Duo

DAK-5 replace with DAK-6-7. Note: Nazi-marked examples will bring a 25 percent premium.

Courtesy J.B. Wood

NIB	Exc.	V.G.	Good	Fair	Poor
—	380	250	200	100	80

E

EAA

See—EUROPEAN AMERICAN ARMORY

E.M.F. CO., INC.

Santa Ana, California

See—UBERTI, ALDO

An importer and distributor of quality Italian-made reproduction firearms by makers such as Pietta, Pedersoli, and Uberti. Most of its offerings are listed in the section dealing with Aldo Uberti firearms. E.M.F. also markets a line of 1911 pistols made in the Philippines.

HANDGUNS

Hartford Bisley

Single-action revolver fitted with Colt Bisley grip. Chambered for .45 Long Colt as well as .32-20, .357 Magnum, .38-40 and .44-40 calibers. Barrel lengths 4.75", 5.5 and 7.5". Plain walnut grips.

NIB	*Exc.*	*V.G.*	*Good*	*Fair*	*Poor*
520	420	300	220	140	100

Hartford Express

Single-action Colt SAA frame and barrel, with Colt Lightning-style grip. Chambered for .45 Long Colt in 4.75", 5.5" or 7.5" barrel lengths.

NIB	*Exc.*	*V.G.*	*Good*	*Fair*	*Poor*
520	420	300	220	140	100

Hartford Pinkerton

Features 4" barrel, with ejector and bird's-head grip. Chambered for 45 Long Colt, .32-20, .357 Magnum, .38-40, .44-40 and .44 Special.

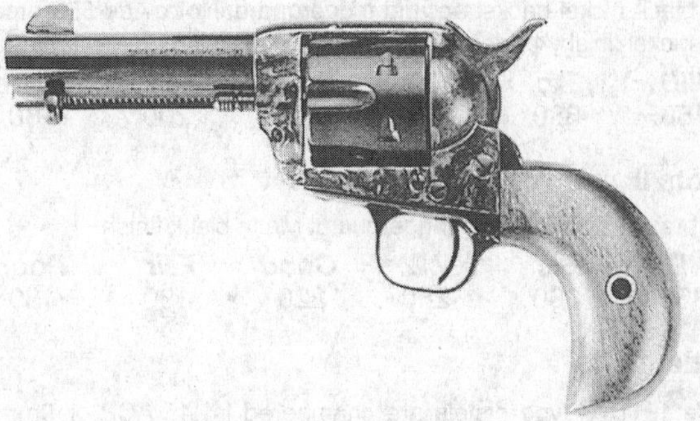

NIB	*Exc.*	*V.G.*	*Good*	*Fair*	*Poor*
520	420	300	220	140	100

Russian Model 1875

Top-break action in .44 Russian or .45 Colt, with various barrel lengths. Imported from 2006 to 2008.

NIB	*Exc.*	*V.G.*	*Good*	*Fair*	*Poor*
750	650	500	400	300	200

Remington Model 1875 Army Frontier

Offered in .357 Magnum, .44-40 or .45 Colt, with 5.5" or 7.5" barrel. Imported from 2003 to 2013. **Note:** Add $200 to $250 for engraved models or nickel finish.

NIB	*Exc.*	*V.G.*	*Good*	*Fair*	*Poor*
450	380	320	280	200	150

Schofield Model

Replica of Smith & Wesson Schofield in .45 Colt. Made by Uberti and imported from 2000 to 2003.

NIB	*Exc.*	*V.G.*	*Good*	*Fair*	*Poor*
600	500	450	350	280	200

EMF-Pietta Great Western II

Caliber 9mm. Barrel lengths: Gunfighter (3.5" and 4.75"). Liberty and Posse (3.5"). The Californian is 4.75" These revolvers offer various options from laser engraving, brass or steel grip frames and grip materials.

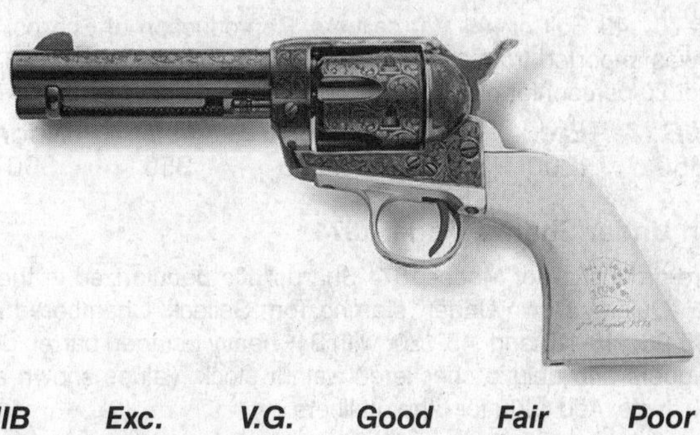

NIB	*Exc.*	*V.G.*	*Good*	*Fair*	*Poor*
440	—	—	—	—	—

DAKOTA SAA SERIES

E.M.F. has imported this brand of Colt-style single-action revolvers made by several Italian manufacturers since the 1970s. Made in standard SAA calibers and barrel lengths.

Dakota Old Model

With brass backstrap and triggerguard. Note: Add 50 to 75 percent for engraved models.

NIB	Exc.	V.G.	Good	Fair	Poor
420	350	300	250	200	180

Dakota New Model

With black nickel backstrap and triggerguard. Note: Add 35 percent for satin nickel finish; 45 percent for bright nickel finish.

NIB	Exc.	V.G.	Good	Fair	Poor
450	380	300	250	200	180

Dakota II

With brass backstrap and triggerguard. Matte black finish.

NIB	Exc.	V.G.	Good	Fair	Poor
350	300	280	220	180	150

Citadel 1911

These 1911 A1-type pistols are chambered in .45 ACP or 9mm, with 3.5" or 5" barrels. Matte black, satin nickel, bright nickel finish. Optional Hogue green, black or sand grips. Note: Add $50 for Hogue grips.

NIB	Exc.	V.G.	Good	Fair	Poor
500	420	350	300	250	200

RIFLES

Lightning Standard

This replica of Colt Lightning slide-action rifle was chambered in .357 Magnun, .44-40 Win., or .45 Colt. Choice of 20", 24" or 26" round or octagon barrel. Straight-grip walnut stock and forend, semi-buckhorn rear sight. Deluxe model has color case-hardened finish, checkered stock. Super Deluxe has coin-finished frame with engraving and high grade checkered walnut. Made by Pedersoli and imported from 2008 to 2013. Note: Add $150 for Deluxe; $250 for Super Deluxe.

NIB	Exc.	V.G.	Good	Fair	Poor
1250	1050	800	620	500	400

Rolling Block

Replica of Remington Rolling Block rifle in .45-70 caliber, with 26" (carbine) or 30" octagon barrel. Target Deluxe model has checkered grip, case-hardened finish, silver forend cap. Made by Pedersoli and imported from 1991 to 2013. Note: Add $300 for Target Deluxe.

NIB	Exc.	V.G.	Good	Fair	Poor
850	750	600	400	320	250

1874 Sharps Sporting or Militay Rifle

In .45-70, .45 Colt or .45-120 calibers. Reproduction of Sharps Single Shot was imported from 1999 to 2008 and re-introduced in 2013. Note: Deduct 20 percent for older model.

NIB	Exc.	V.G.	Good	Fair	Poor
1350	1200	850	700	350	300

Down Under Sharps Model 1874

This re-production of Model 1874 Sharps rifle popularized in the 1990 movie "Quigley Down Under" starring Tom Selleck. Chambered in .45-70, .45-90, .45-110 and .45-120, with 34" heavy octagon barrel, double-set triggers and deluxe checkered walnut stock. Values shown are for .45-70. Note: Add $100 for other calibers.

NIB	Exc.	V.G.	Good	Fair	Poor
2000	1700	1350	1000	400	300

Winchester Lever Actions

E.M.F. has imported re-productions of several famous Winchester lever-action rifles and carbines since 1987. Among these are: Model 1860 in .44-40 or .45 Colt; 1866 Yellow Boy in .22 LR and WMR, .32-20, .38-40, .38 Special, .44-40 and .45 Colt; 1873 in .22 WMR, .32-20, .38-40, .44 Special, .44-40 and .45 Colt; 1886/71 in .45-70; and Model 1892 in .357 Magnum, .44 Magnum and .45 Colt.

Model 1860

NIB	Exc.	V.G.	Good	Fair	Poor
900	750	550	400	300	200

Model 1866

NIB	Exc.	V.G.	Good	Fair	Poor
750	620	500	350	250	200

Model 1873

NIB	Exc.	V.G.	Good	Fair	Poor
900	750	550	400	300	200

Model 1886/71

NIB	Exc.	V.G.	Good	Fair	Poor
1700	1500	1350	1000	400	300

Model 1892

NIB	Exc.	V.G.	Good	Fair	Poor
450	400	350	300	200	150

EAGLE ARMS, DIVISION OF ARMALITE

Geneseo, Illinois

See—BERSA, AMERICAN CLASSICS

Previous manufacturer of AR-15 type rifles from 1990 to 2005. From 1995 to 2002, a division of ArmaLite, Inc.

PRE-BAN MODELS

Golden Eagle

Identical in design to AR-15. Fitted with 20" stainless steel extra-heavy barrel. National Match sights and two-stage trigger. Weight about 9.4 lbs.

NIB	Exc.	V.G.	Good	Fair	Poor
1250	1000	900	750	650	—

HBAR

Similar to above, with heavy 20" barrel. Weight about 8 lbs.

NIB	Exc.	V.G.	Good	Fair	Poor
1450	1150	1000	800	600	—

SPR

Similar to above, with exception of detachable carry handle. Weight about 7.6 lbs.

NIB	Exc.	V.G.	Good	Fair	Poor
1450	1150	1000	800	600	—

M4C Carbine

Features 16" barrel, with 4.33" flash suppressor. Retractable stock. Weight about 6.2 lbs.

NIB	Exc.	V.G.	Good	Fair	Poor
1450	1150	1000	800	600	—

M4A1C Carbine

Similar to above, with detachable carry handle. Weight about 6 lbs.

NIB	Exc.	V.G.	Good	Fair	Poor
1450	1150	1000	800	600	—

POST-BAN MODELS

Golden Eagle

Re-introduction of earlier model. Limited production in 2002.

NIB	Exc.	V.G.	Good	Fair	Poor
1200	950	800	700	—	—

AR-10 Match Rifle

Chambered for .308 Win., with 20" or 24" chrome-moly barrel. Features include flattop upper receiver, black stock and forearm, 10-round magazine.

NIB	Exc.	V.G.	Good	Fair	Poor
1200	900	800	650	—	—

Model M15 Series

Chambered for .223 or .308 in various AR-15 type configurations. Manufactured from 2002 to 2005. Note: Add $200 for .308-caliber; $150 for Eagle Spirit model with National Match accessories.

Eagle-15 Pistol

AR-15 style platform with 6- or 11-in. barrel. Chambered in .223 Rem./5.56 NATO. Equipped with either 5- or 10-in. KeyMod handguard and SIG brace.

NIB	Exc.	V.G.	Good	Fair	Poor
900	700	580	450	—	—

ECHAVE & ARIZMENDI
Eibar, Spain

Basque, Echasa, Dickson, or Dickson Special Agent

These four pistols are the same semi-automatic pistols. Chambered in .22 LR, 6.35mm, 7.65mm and 9mmK respectively. Magazine capacities are 10, 9, 7 and 6 rounds. Manufactured with alloy frames and various finish combinations. Specific model names are stamped on slides and grip plates.

Courtesy James Rankin

NIB	Exc.	V.G.	Good	Fair	Poor
—	300	180	120	90	50

Bronco Model 1913

Semi-automatic pistol in caliber 6.35mm. Patterned after Browning Model 1906, with squeeze grip safety. "Bronco" stamped on slide and each side of grip plate.

Courtesy James Rankin

NIB	Exc.	V.G.	Good	Fair	Poor
—	300	180	120	90	50

Bronco Model 1918

Semi-automatic pistol chambered for 6.35mm or 7.65mm. Both are patterned after Browning Model 1906, with squeeze grip safety. The 7.65mm pistol approximately .5" longer and higher than 6.35mm. Magazine capacity: 7.65mm 7 rounds; 6.35mm 6 rounds.

Courtesy James Rankin

NIB	Exc.	V.G.	Good	Fair	Poor
—	300	180	120	90	50

Echasa

Similar to 6.35mm Bronco, without grip safety. Marked "Model 1916".

NIB	Exc.	V.G.	Good	Fair	Poor
—	300	180	120	90	50

Lightning

Re-named version of Bronco in 6.35mm.

NIB	Exc.	V.G.	Good	Fair	Poor
—	300	180	120	90	50

Lur Panzer

Copy of Luger toggle-lock-action chambered for .22 rimfire. Almost an exact copy, except for different trigger assembly and less robust mainspring. Marked "Lur Cal.22 LR Made in Spain". Plastic grips have "Panzer" molded into them.

NIB	Exc.	V.G.	Good	Fair	Poor
—	260	220	150	120	100

Pathfinder

Semi-automatic pistol similar to above Bronco. In calibers 6.35mm and 7.65mm. Sold in U.S. by Stoeger. The 7.65mm Pathfinder holds 12 rounds. Values listed are for both pistol models.

NIB	Exc.	V.G.	Good	Fair	Poor
—	300	180	120	90	50

Protector Model 1915 and 1918

Semi-automatic pistol in caliber 6.35mm. Similar to Echasa model. "Protector" stamped on slide while grip plates have various logos of firms that marketed the pistol.

Courtesy James Rankin

NIB	Exc.	V.G.	Good	Fair	Poor
—	280	180	100	70	40

Selecta Model 1918

Semi-automatic pistol chambered for 7.65mm cartridge. Patterned after Protector, but chambered for 7.65mm. "Selecta" stamped on slide and Echave Arizmendi logo on each of grip plates.

Courtesy James Rankin

NIB	Exc.	V.G.	Good	Fair	Poor
—	300	180	120	90	50

ECHEVERRIA, STAR-BONIFACIO SA (STAR)

Eibar, Spain

An old-line Spanish company that survived Spanish Civil War. Founded in 1908 by Jean Echeverria, but early records of the company were lost during the civil war. Early pistols the company produced were patterned after Mannlicher designs and trade name Star was the closest thing to Steyr that could be used. After the close of WWI, the company began production of open-topped slide Star for which they have become known. They also produced a large 1911-type pistol that was successful. During the civil war, the plant was damaged and company records destroyed; but after cessation of hostilities, they were one of only three gun companies that were allowed to remain in business. Company is now defunct.

Star Model 1908

First pistol produced under Star banner. A Mannlicher copy chambered for 6.35mm, 3" fixed barrel and open-topped slide. Detachable magazine holds 8 shots. Finish blued, grips are checkered plastic. Slide marked "Automatic Pistol Star Patent".

Courtesy James Rankin

NIB	Exc.	V.G.	Good	Fair	Poor
—	350	280	200	150	100

Star Model 1914

Similar to Model 1908, with 5" barrel and larger grips that have Star name molded into them. Model was first to have six-pointed star surrounded by rays of light (that became Star trademark) stamped on its slide.

Courtesy James Rankin

NIB	Exc.	V.G.	Good	Fair	Poor
—	350	280	200	150	100

Star Model 1919

Copy of Mannlicher design. Differs from its predecessors chiefly in the way pistol is disassembled. Has a spring catch at top of triggerguard, a small spur on hammer and magazine release was relocated to a button behind the triggerguard instead of a catch at bottom of butt. Chambered for 6.35mm, 7.65mm and 9mm short, with various barrel lengths offered. Maker's name, as well as Star trademark stamped into slide. Produced until 1929.

Courtesy James Rankin

NIB	Exc.	V.G.	Good	Fair	Poor
—	350	280	200	150	100

Star Model 1919 New Variation

Same as above, with full spur hammer.

Courtesy James Rankin

NIB	Exc.	V.G.	Good	Fair	Poor
—	350	280	200	150	100

Modelo Militar

Represents the first pistol Star produced that was not a Mannlicher design. Copied from Colt 1911. Chambered initially for 9mm Largo in hopes of securing a military contract. When this contract was awarded to Astra, Star chambered Model 1919 for .38 Super, .45 ACP and put it on the commercial market. Model like Colt 1911—has a Browning-type swinging link and same type of lock-up. However, there is no grip safety and thumb safety functions differently. Note: Add 30 percent for guns marked .38 Super.

NIB	Exc.	V.G.	Good	Fair	Poor
—	420	320	240	180	120

Star Model A

Modification of Model 1919. Chambered for 7.65mm, 7.63mm Mauser, 9mm Largo and .45 ACP cartridge. Slide similar in appearance to 1911 Colt. Spur hammer has a small hole in it. Early models had no grip safety, but later production added this feature. Some models slotted for addition of shoulder stock.

NIB	Exc.	V.G.	Good	Fair	Poor
—	420	320	240	180	120

Star Model B

Similar to Model A, except almost an exact copy of Colt 1911. Chambered for 9mm Parabellum. Has a spur hammer with no hole. Introduced in 1928.

Courtesy Orvel Reichert

NIB	Exc.	V.G.	Good	Fair	Poor
470	390	350	260	200	170

Star Model C

Model B chambered for 9mm Browning Long cartridge. Manufactured in 1920s.

NIB	Exc.	V.G.	Good	Fair	Poor
—	350	260	180	120	90

Star Model CO

Pocket pistol similar to early open-topped Star pistols. Chambered for 6.35mm cartridge. Finish blued, with checkered plastic grips that bear Star name and logo. Manufactured between 1930 and 1957.

Courtesy James Rankin

NIB	Exc.	V.G.	Good	Fair	Poor
—	280	200	120	100	80

Star Model D

Medium-sized pistol similar in appearance to smaller Model A. Chambered for 9mm Short cartridge. Called "Police and Pocket Model" after it was adopted by the Spanish police. Manufactured between 1930 and 1941.

NIB	Exc.	V.G.	Good	Fair	Poor
—	500	400	300	200	100

Star Model DK Starfire

Single-action .380, with 3.125" barrel, fixed sights, brown plastic grips. Imported from 1957 until 1968. Alloy frame available in blue finish or various colors. Note: Add $100 for colored frame.

Courtesy James Rankin

NIB	Exc.	V.G.	Good	Fair	Poor
550	420	400	350	300	150

Star Model E

Pocket pistol chambered for 6.35mm cartridge. A 2.5" barrel and external hammer. Detachable magazine holds 5 rounds. Finish blued, with checkered plastic grips. Manufactured between 1932 and 1941.

NIB	Exc.	V.G.	Good	Fair	Poor
—	250	200	160	110	80

Star Model F

First of .22-caliber Star pistols. Has a 4" barrel, 10-shot magazine and fixed sights. Finish blued and plastic grips checkered. Manufactured between 1942 and 1967.

NIB	Exc.	V.G.	Good	Fair	Poor
—	300	260	200	110	80

Star Model F Target

Similar to Model F, with 6" barrel.

NIB	Exc.	V.G.	Good	Fair	Poor
—	320	280	210	120	100

Star Model F Sport

Has a 5" barrel. Manufactured between 1962 and 1967.

NIB	Exc.	V.G.	Good	Fair	Poor
—	320	280	210	120	100

Star Model F Olympic

Has a 6" barrel and adjustable sights. Furnished with muzzle brake and barrel weights. Manufactured between 1942 and 1967.

Courtesy James Rankin

NIB	Exc.	V.G.	Good	Fair	Poor
—	350	260	180	120	90

Star Model F Olympic Rapid Fire

Similar to Olympic. Chambered for .22 Short only.

NIB	Exc.	V.G.	Good	Fair	Poor
—	380	300	180	150	120

Star Model FR

Has an adjustable sight and a slide stop. The 4" barrel is heavier with flattened sides. Manufactured between 1967 and 1972.

NIB	Exc.	V.G.	Good	Fair	Poor
—	320	280	210	120	100

Star Model FRS

Similar to Model FR, with 6" barrel. Also available chrome-plated, with white checkered plastic grips. Introduced in 1967.

NIB	Exc.	V.G.	Good	Fair	Poor
—	300	220	180	120	100

Star Model FM

Heavier-framed version of Model FRS. Has a 4.5" barrel. Available in blue or chrome-plated. Introduced in 1972.

NIB	Exc.	V.G.	Good	Fair	Poor
—	320	280	210	120	100

Star Model H

Similar to old Model CO—only larger in size. Chambered for 7.65mm cartridge. Manufactured between 1932 and 1941.

NIB	*Exc.*	*V.G.*	*Good*	*Fair*	*Poor*
360	310	270	200	170	130

Star Model HK

Pocket-sized version of Model F. Chambered for .22 Short. Has a 2.5" barrel. Quite scarce on today's market.

NIB	*Exc.*	*V.G.*	*Good*	*Fair*	*Poor*
—	320	280	210	120	100

Star Model HN

Simply Model H chambered for 9mm Short cartridge. Manufactured and discontinued same time as Model H was.

NIB	*Exc.*	*V.G.*	*Good*	*Fair*	*Poor*
380	340	290	210	180	140

Star Model I

Improved version of Model H, with 4-in. barrel and re-contoured grip. Chambered for 7.65mm and produced until 1941. After the war it was resumed and survived until mid-1950s. Replaced by modernized Model IR that would be valued approximately the same.

NIB	*Exc.*	*V.G.*	*Good*	*Fair*	*Poor*
360	310	270	200	170	130

Star Model M

Similar to Model B. Chambered for .38 Auto (NOT .38 Super) cartridge.

NIB	*Exc.*	*V.G.*	*Good*	*Fair*	*Poor*
—	380	300	180	150	120

Star Model P

Post-war version of Model B. Fitted with 5" barrel. Chambered for .45 ACP cartridge. Checkered walnut grips and blued finish.

NIB	*Exc.*	*V.G.*	*Good*	*Fair*	*Poor*
—	400	350	260	200	120

Star Model CU "Starlet"

Similar to Model CO, with an alloy frame that was anodized in black, blue, gray, green or gold. A steel slide that is blued or chrome-plated. Checkered white plastic grips. Chambered for .25 ACP cartridge. Has a 2.5 barrel, fixed sights and 5-shot magazine. Introduced in 1975 and not imported after 1986.

NIB	*Exc.*	*V.G.*	*Good*	*Fair*	*Poor*
—	250	180	140	100	80

Star Model 1941 S

Add 100 percent to prices listed for pistols issued to Spanish Air Force, with box cleaning rod, instruction sheet and two numbered magazines.

Courtesy Richard M. Kumor Sr.

NIB	*Exc.*	*V.G.*	*Good*	*Fair*	*Poor*
—	250	210	180	120	80

Star Model BKS "Starlight"

Smallest locked-breech automatic chambered for 9mm cartridge at the time. Has an alloy frame and 4.25 barrel. Similar in appearance to scaled-down Colt 1911, without grip safety. Has an 8-shot magazine. Blued or chrome-plated, with checkered plastic grips. Manufactured between 1970 and 1981.

NIB	*Exc.*	*V.G.*	*Good*	*Fair*	*Poor*
—	320	280	210	120	100

Star Model PD

Chambered for .45 ACP cartridge. Has a 4-in. barrel, alloy frame, 6-shot magazine, adjustable sights. Blued, with checkered walnut grips. Introduced in 1975.

NIB	*Exc.*	*V.G.*	*Good*	*Fair*	*Poor*
460	380	310	230	200	180

Star Model BM

Steel-framed 9mm styled after Colt 1911. Has an 8-shot magazine and 4" barrel. Available blued or chrome-plated.

NIB	Exc.	V.G.	Good	Fair	Poor
350	300	250	200	150	120

Star Model BKM

Similar to Model BM, with alloy frame.

NIB	Exc.	V.G.	Good	Fair	Poor
380	320	280	220	180	120

Star Model 28

First of Star's Super 9s. Double-action semi-automatic chambered for 9mm Parabellum cartridge. Has a 4.25-in. barrel and steel frame. Magazine holds 15 shots. Construction of this pistol was totally modular and has no screws in its design. Blued, with checkered synthetic grips. Manufactured in 1983 and 1984.

NIB	Exc.	V.G.	Good	Fair	Poor
460	410	360	260	200	160

Star Model 30M

Improved version of Model 28, that is quite similar in appearance. Introduced in 1985.

NIB	Exc.	V.G.	Good	Fair	Poor
450	350	300	250	200	120

Star Model 30/PK

Similar to Models 28 and 30M, with lightweight alloy frame.

NIB	Exc.	V.G.	Good	Fair	Poor
450	350	300	250	200	120

Megastar

Double-action semi-automatic pistol chambered for 10mm or .45 ACP cartridge. Features a three-position ambidextrous selective decocking lever, rubber grips, combat-style triggerguard, slotted hammer and checkered mainspring housing. Barrel length 4.6"; magazine capacity 12 rounds. Available in blue or Starvel (brushed chrome). Weight 47.6 oz.

NIB	Exc.	V.G.	Good	Fair	Poor
500	450	350	250	200	100

Firestar M43, M40, and M45

Compact large caliber semi-automatic pistol offered in: M43 9mm; M45 .45 ACP; M40 .40 S&W. Features an ambidextrous safety, steel frame and slide, checkered rubber grips. Barrel: 3.4" on M43 and M40; 3.6" on M45. Choice of blue or Starvel (brushed chrome) finish. Finger rest magazine optional. Weight: M43 and M40 30 oz.; M45 35 oz. Introduced in 1990.

NIB	Exc.	V.G.	Good	Fair	Poor
400	300	250	200	150	100

Starfire Model 31P

Evolved from Models 28 and 30. Chambered for 9mm Parabellum or .40 S&W. Trigger action is double-/single-action. Barrel length 3.9". Fitted with two-position safety/decocking lever. Magazine capacity: 9mm 15 rounds; .40 S&W 11 rounds. Weight 39 oz.

NIB	Exc.	V.G.	Good	Fair	Poor
420	350	300	250	200	100

Starfire Model 31PK

Similar to Model 31P. Built on an alloy frame. Chambered for 9mm only, with 15-round magazine capacity. Weight 30 oz.

NIB	Exc.	V.G.	Good	Fair	Poor
400	320	280	220	200	100

Ultrastar

Introduced in 1994. Compact 9mm or .40 S&W semi-automatic pistol. Polymer frame features 3.57" barrel, 9-round magazine, blued finish and overall length of 7". Weight about 26 oz. Has a double-action operating system, windage adjustable rear sight and ambidextrous two-position safety.

NIB	Exc.	V.G.	Good	Fair	Poor
400	360	300	280	200	100

ECLIPSE

Enterprise Gun Works
Pittsburgh, Pennsylvania

Single-Shot Derringer

Pocket pistol made by the firm of James Bown & Son, doing business as Enterprise Gun Works. Chambered for .22- or .32-caliber rimfire cartridges. A few in .25 rimfire have been noted and would add approximately 25 percent to values listed. Barrel 2.5" in length and part-round/part-octagonal. Pivots sideways for loading. Spur trigger and bird's-head grip. Barrel stamped "Eclipse". Made of nickel-plated iron, with walnut grips. Approximately 10,000 manufactured between 1870 and 1890.

NIB	Exc.	V.G.	Good	Fair	Poor
—	—	650	250	100	80

84 GUN CO.

Eighty Four, Pennsylvania

In business for a brief time in early 1970s. Company produced three basic bolt-action rifles—each in four grades that differ in amounts of embellishment and grades of wood. There is little known about this company and its products. Basic models are listed and values are approximate.

Classic Rifle

Grade 1 - Grade 4 available. $650—$1800

Lobo Rifle

Grade 1 - Grade 4 available. $625—$2700

Pennsylvania Rifle

Grade 1 - Grade 4 available. $625—$2800

EL DORADO ARMS

See—UNITED SPORTING ARMS, INC.

ELGIN CUTLASS

(C.B. Allen / Merrill, Mossman and Blair)
Springfield and Amherst, Massachusetts

Manufactured by two companies—C.B. Allen of Springfield, Massachusetts and Morill, Mosman and Blair of Amherst, Massachusetts. A unique pistol that has an integral knife attachment affixed to the gun barrel. Designed and patented by George Elgin and simultaneously produced by the two companies. Inspiration for this weapon was supposedly Jim Bowie, who at that time had made a name as a knife fighter with his large "Bowie" knife. Blades for these pistols were supplied by N.P. Ames of the famed Ames Sword Co. These pistols are much sought after and one must exercise caution as fraudulent examples have been noted.

C. B. ALLEN-MADE PISTOLS

U.S. Navy Elgin Cutlass Pistol (Antique)

Chambered for .54-caliber percussion. Has a 5" octagonal smooth-bore barrel. Bowie-style blade is 11" long by 2" wide. Forged together with triggerguard and knuckle guard that protects the grip. Handle is walnut. Pistol issued to U.S. Navy's Wilkes-South Sea Exploration Expedition. Markings are "C.B. Allen / Springfield / Mass." "Elgin's Patent" and letters "CB", "CBA" along with date 1837. If the sheath that was issued with this knife pistol is included and in sound condition, it would add approximately $700 to value. There were 150 manufactured for U.S. Navy in 1838.

Exc.	Fine	V.G.	Good	Fair	Poor
—	35500	14000	10750	4750	3325

Civilian Model (Antique)

Chambered for .35- or .41-caliber percussion. Has a 4" octagonal barrel, with 7.5"-10" knife blade, round triggerguard, but does not have knuckle bow across the grip, as found on military model. Marked "C.B. Allen Springfield, Mass." Blades marked "N.P. Ames" have been noted. Approximately 100 manufactured in 1837.

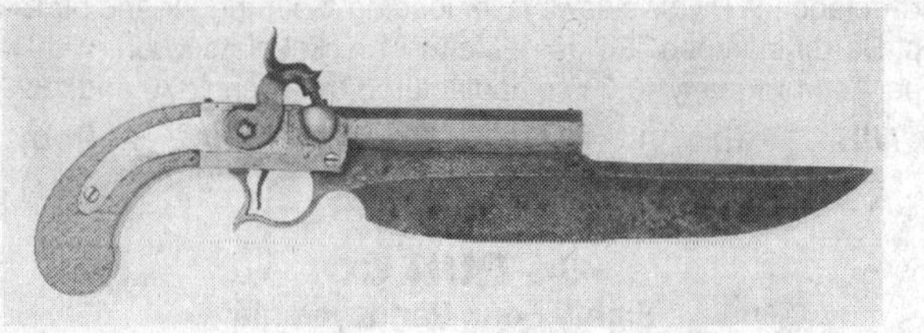

Exc.	Fine	V.G.	Good	Fair	Poor
33500	13000	9620	6250	3250	2270

MORILL, MOSMAN AND BLAIR-MADE PISTOLS

Small Model (Antique)

Main difference in pistols of the two makers is; this model has a round barrel and square-back triggerguard, that comes to a point at the rear. This version chambered for .32-caliber percussion and has 2.75" barrel. Knife blade is 7.5" in length and screwed to frame. Model is unmarked except for a serial number. Number produced is unknown. Manufactured in 1837.

Exc.	Fine	V.G.	Good	Fair	Poor
33500	13000	9620	6250	3250	2270

Large Model (Antique)

Chambered for .36-caliber percussion. Has 4" round barrel and 9" knife blade. Pistol usually marked "Cast Steel" and serial numbered. Blade etched with an American eagle, stars and urn with flowers. "Elgin Patent" etched in center. Manufactured in 1837.

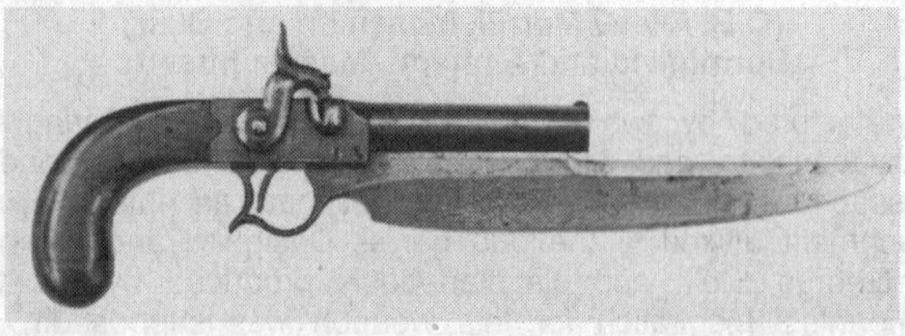

Courtesy Milwaukee Public Museum, Milwaukee, Wisconsin

Exc.	Fine	V.G.	Good	Fair	Poor
37000	14500	10750	7000	3900	2730

ELLS, JOSIAH

Pittsburgh, Pennsylvania

POCKET REVOLVER

Three distinct variations of this percussion revolver. Chambered for .28- and .31-caliber; have 6-shot unfluted cylinders; have been noted with 2.5", 3" and 3.75" octagonal barrels.

Model 1 (Antique)

Have an open-topped frame. Chambered for .28-caliber. Cylinder holds 5- or 6-shots. Hammer is of the bar type. Offered with 2.5" or 3" barrel. Markings are "J. Ells; Patent; 1854". Approximately 625 manufactured between 1857 and 1859.

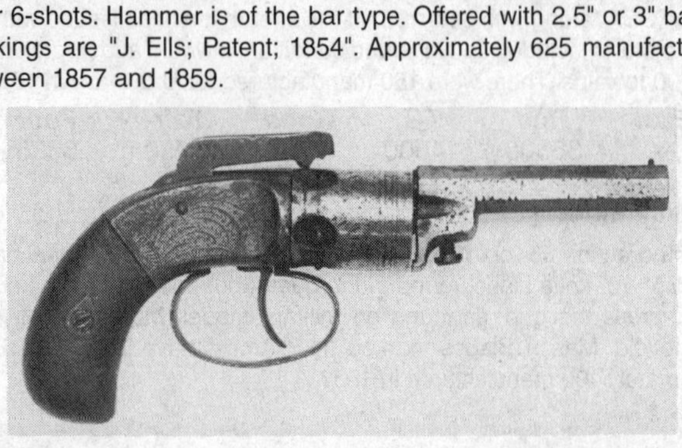

Courtesy Milwaukee Public Museum, Milwaukee, Wisconsin

Exc.	Fine	V.G.	Good	Fair	Poor
1700	880	630	380	200	140

Model 2 (Antique)

Similar to first, with solid-topped frame. Has 5-shot cylinder and 3.75" long barrels. Approximately 550 manufactured

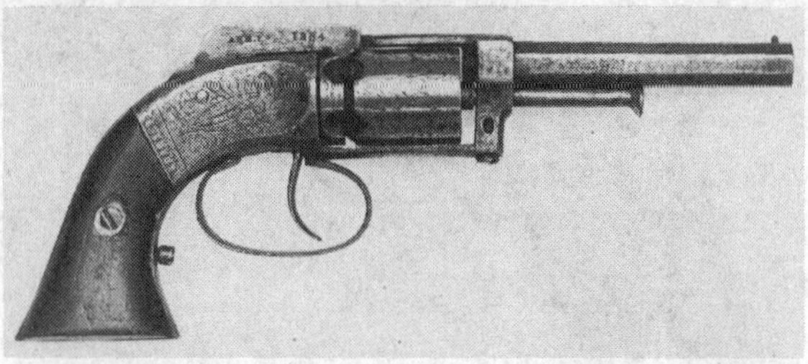

Courtesy Milwaukee Public Museum, Milwaukee, Wisconsin

Exc.	Fine	V.G.	Good	Fair	Poor
1750	750	550	360	200	140

Model 3 (Antique)

Radically different from its forerunners. Closed-top frame and conventional spur-type hammer that strikes from right side. Functions as a double-/single-action. Chambered for .28-caliber, 5-shot cylinder and 3.75" barrel. About 200 manufactured between 1857 and 1859.

Exc.	Fine	V.G.	Good	Fair	Poor
1850	1000	710	420	200	140

ENDERS, CARL

Suhl, Germany

Side-by-Side Shotgun (Antique)

Percussion damascus double-barrel side-by-side in 12-gauge. Ornate checkering, with cheekpiece and engraved metal work. This firm made high-quality firearms, mostly side-by-side guns. Gun pictured was made circa 1850-1860. Firm in business about 1835 to approximately 1890.

Courtesy Jim Cate

Exc.	Fine	V.G.	Good	Fair	Poor
1250	550	420	300	150	100

ENFIELD AMERICAN, INC.

Atlanta, Georgia

MP-45

Blowback-operated semi-automatic assault pistol. Chambered for .45 ACP cartridge. Offered barrel lengths 4.5" through 18.5". Long barrel features a shroud. Finish is Parkerized. Four different magazines available in 10, 20, 30 and 50 round capacities. Manufactured in 1985 only.

NIB	Exc.	V.G.	Good	Fair	Poor
—	580	480	300	180	120

ENTREPRISE ARMS, INC.

Irwindale, California

ELITE SERIES

Basic model with stainless steel barrels, fixed sights, squared triggerguard, adjustable match trigger, checkered slide release, high ride grip safety, flat mainspring housing and a number of other special features. Magazine capacity 10 rounds.

Elite P500

Chambered for .45 ACP. Fitted with 5" barrel. Weight about 40 oz.

NIB	Exc.	V.G.	Good	Fair	Poor
600	500	400	350	200	100

Elite P425

Has 4.25" barrel. Weight about 38 oz.

NIB	Exc.	V.G.	Good	Fair	Poor
600	500	400	350	200	100

Elite P325

Has 3.25" barrel. Weight 36 oz.

NIB	Exc.	V.G.	Good	Fair	Poor
600	500	400	350	200	100

TACTICAL SERIES

Models have ambidextrous thumb lock, lightweight match hammer and matching sear. National match barrel with match extractor, full length one-piece guide rod, Novak sights, dovetail front sight, matte black finish and host of other features. Magazine capacity 10 rounds.

Tactical P500

Chambered for .45 ACP cartridge. Barrel 5". Weight about 40 oz.

NIB	Exc.	V.G.	Good	Fair	Poor
900	800	600	500	350	100

Tactical P425

Fitted with 4.25" barrel. Weight about 38 oz.

NIB	Exc.	V.G.	Good	Fair	Poor
900	800	600	500	350	100

Tactical P325

Fitted with 3.25" barrel. Weight 36 oz.

NIB	Exc.	V.G.	Good	Fair	Poor
900	800	600	500	350	100

Tactical P325 Plus

Features 3.25" barrel. Fitted to full size Government model frame. Weight about 37 oz.

NIB	Exc.	V.G.	Good	Fair	Poor
950	800	620	500	360	100

TITLEIST NATIONAL MATCH SERIES

Model chambered for .45 ACP or .40 S&W cartridge. Has all features of Elite Series. Adjustable rear sight and dovetail Patridge front sight. Many other special features.

Titleist P500

Fitted with 5" barrel. Weight about 40 oz. Note: Add $20 for .40 S&W chambering.

NIB	Exc.	V.G.	Good	Fair	Poor
900	800	600	500	350	100

Boxer Model

Chambered for .45 ACP cartridge. Fitted with 5" barrel. Features a ramped bull barrel, wide ambidextrous safety and high-mass chiseled slide. Weight about 44 oz.

NIB	Exc.	V.G.	Good	Fair	Poor
1200	980	750	600	380	120

TOURNAMENT SERIES

These are top-of-the-line models. They have all features of Elite Series, plus over-sized magazine release button, checkered front strap and flared extended magazine well.

TSM I

Limited class competition pistol. All models are hand crafted. Fitted with 5" barrel and choice of calibers. Weight about 40 oz.

NIB	Exc.	V.G.	Good	Fair	Poor
1900	1750	1380	900	680	300

TSM II

Long slide model, with cocking serrations on front and rear of slide. Barrel 6"; weight about 44 oz.

NIB	Exc.	V.G.	Good	Fair	Poor
2300	1750	1380	900	680	300

TSM III

Open class pistol designed for scope mount. Fitted with 7-port compensator. Many other custom features. Barrel 5.5"; weight about 44 oz.

NIB	Exc.	V.G.	Good	Fair	Poor
2500	2000	1520	1050	700	310

FN Rifle

Entreprise also made receivers for the .308 FN FAL pattern semi-auto rifles. FN FAL types assembled on an Entreprise receiver typically bring $500 to $900 depending on condition.

ERA
Brazil

ERA Side-by-Side Shotgun

Inexpensive shotgun chambered for 12-, 20-gauge and.410 bore. Offered with 26", 28" or 30" barrels and various choke combinations. Double triggers and extractors, with checkered hardwood pistol grip stock. Also available as Quail model, with 20" barrel; Riot model with 18" barrel. These two models not offered in .410 bore.

NIB	Exc.	V.G.	Good	Fair	Poor
—	200	150	120	100	80

ERA Over/Under Shotgun

Chambered for 12- or 20-gauge, with 28" ventilated rib barrels that were choked Full and Modified. Boxlock with double triggers, extractors and hardwood stock. Also offered in trap and skeet model, chambered for 12-gauge only and appropriately choked. Note: Latter two models would be worth 10 percent premium over values listed.

NIB	Exc.	V.G.	Good	Fair	Poor
—	320	280	250	200	150

ERICHSON, G.
Houston, Texas

Pocket Pistol (Antique)

Close copy of Philadelphia-style Henry Deringer. Chambered for .45-caliber percussion. Has 3.25" barrel. Mountings are German silver and not engraved. Stock is walnut. Hammer is deeply fluted and forend carved. Barrel marked "G. Erichson / Houston, Texas". Number produced unknown, but examples are scarce. Manufactured in 1850s and 1860s.

Exc.	Fine	V.G.	Good	Fair	Poor
6500	3000	2000	1000	400	280

ERMA WERKE WAFFENFABRIK
Erfurt, Germany
Post-war Dachau, Germany

Known primarily as a manufacturer of sub-machine guns, they are also in the handgun and rifle business. In 1933, they answered the German army's need for an inexpensive practice weapon by producing a .22 rimfire conversion unit for the Luger pistol. This was marketed commercially and available for many years. Success of this unit led the company to produce other inexpensive target and plinking pistols. After the war, they were re-organized in the western sector and resumed sub-machine gun production. In 1964, they returned to the sporting firearms business, with the introduction of their .22 rimfire Luger-lookalike pistol. Since then, they have produced many like-quality firearms. They were imported by Excam of Hialeah, Florida. This association is now terminated and they are currently imported by Beeman Precision in Santa Rosa, California and Mandell Shooting Supplies in Scottsdale, Arizona.

PISTOLS

Erma .22 Luger Conversion Unit

Produced for the German army in 1933 and then became a successful commercial item. It would turn a standard 9mm or 7.65mm Luger into an inexpensive-to-shoot .22 rimfire. Unit consists of barrel insert, breech-block and toggle unit, with its own lightened recoil spring and .22 magazine. Unit was furnished with a wooden box. There were many different sized units to fit various caliber and barrel-length Lugers, but all used the same parts and concept. These units have become desirable to Luger collectors.

NIB	Exc.	V.G.	Good	Fair	Poor
—	500	420	350	280	200

.22 Target Pistol (Old Model)

Semi-automatic target pistol in caliber .22 LR. Offered with 4", 6" or 8" barrels. Frame made from cast zinc alloy and there is an external hammer. Adjustable sights and balance weights were available. Magazine capacity 10 rounds. Weight about 35 oz. Manufactured in 1936 and 1937.

Courtesy James Rankin

NIB	Exc.	V.G.	Good	Fair	Poor
—	800	720	500	350	100

.22 Target Pistol (New Model) Master Model

Improved version of old model. Features new grip angle, magazine and take-down device like that of the Luger. There were interchangeable barrels and three basic models — "Sport", "Hunter" and "Master". Difference was length of barrels — 4", 8" and 12" respectively. Magazine capacity 10 rounds. Weight about 39 oz. Manufactured between 1937 and 1940. Discontinued due to Erma's involvement in the war effort.

Courtesy James Rankin

NIB	Exc.	V.G.	Good	Fair	Poor
—	850	700	500	400	120

KGP SERIES

Made to resemble the Luger quite closely. They utilized mechanical features of the .22 conversion unit and developed a pistol around it. Many different versions of this pistol chambered for .22 rimfire, .32 ACP and .380 ACP. Original designation was KGP-68; but the Gun Control Act of 1968 required that a magazine safety be added and model was redesignated KGP-68A. Last designations for the three calibers are KGP-22, KGP-32 and KGP-38. Manufactured between 1964 - 1986 and their values listed.

KGP-68

A 4" barrel and chambered for .32 ACP and .380 ACP cartridges. Has a 6-shot magazine and anodized alloy receiver. Weight about 23 oz. Model also known as Beeman MP-08.

NIB	*Exc.*	*V.G.*	*Good*	*Fair*	*Poor*
—	450	400	300	200	100

KGP-69

A .22 rimfire version of this series, with 8-shot magazine capacity. Weight about 30 oz. Also known as Beeman P-08.

NIB	*Exc.*	*V.G.*	*Good*	*Fair*	*Poor*
—	340	280	140	120	100

KGP-22

Later version of KGP-69 chambered for .22 rimfire.

NIB	*Exc.*	*V.G.*	*Good*	*Fair*	*Poor*
—	350	300	250	200	120

KGP-32 & KGP-38

Two designations are later versions of KGP-68 and 68A.

NIB	*Exc.*	*V.G.*	*Good*	*Fair*	*Poor*
—	350	300	250	200	120

ET-22 "Navy Luger" Long-Barreled Pistol

A rare firearm. According to some estimates only 375 were produced. Features a 11.75 barrel and chambered for .22 rimfire cartridge. Artillery Luger-type rear sight and checkered walnut grips, with a smooth walnut forend. Pistol furnished with a red-felt-lined black leatherette case.

NIB	*Exc.*	*V.G.*	*Good*	*Fair*	*Poor*
—	900	680	400	250	150

ESP 85A

High-quality target pistol imported by Mandall Shooting Supply. Features an interchangeable barrel system that converts chambering from .22 rimfire to .32 S&W long wad cutter. Barrels are both 6" in length. Adjustable and interchangeable sights and 5- or 8-shot detachable magazine. Weight about 41 oz. Finish blued and grips are stippled target types. Gun furnished in padded hard case, with two extra magazines and take-down tools. Introduced in 1989.

NIB	*Exc.*	*V.G.*	*Good*	*Fair*	*Poor*
1100	1000	850	700	550	450

EP-25

Semi-automatic pistol in caliber 6.35mm. Fitted with 2.75" barrel. Weight about 18 oz. Mostly marketed outside of Germany. Polished blue finish and wood grips. Erma stamped on slide and on each grip plate.

Courtesy James Rankin

NIB	*Exc.*	*V.G.*	*Good*	*Fair*	*Poor*
—	280	200	150	100	80

RX-22 and PX-22

Semi-automatic .22 rimfire copy of Walther PPK. Has a 7-round magazine. Assembled in U.S., with parts from Germany by various companies that marketed the pistol in U.S. Black plastic wrap-around grips, with Erma logo on each side.

Courtesy James Rankin

NIB	*Exc.*	*V.G.*	*Good*	*Fair*	*Poor*
—	240	180	150	100	80

REVOLVERS

ER-772 Match

Target revolver chambered for .22 rimfire. Has 6" shrouded barrel with solid rib. Swing-out cylinder holds 6-shots and sights are adjustable. Finish blued, with stippled target grips. Introduced in 1989.

NIB	*Exc.*	*V.G.*	*Good*	*Fair*	*Poor*
1000	800	600	350	250	200

ER-773 Match

Similar to ER-772, except chambered for .32 S&W long cartridge.

NIB	*Exc.*	*V.G.*	*Good*	*Fair*	*Poor*
900	750	500	380	250	200

ER-777

Basically similar revolver to ER-773, except has 4.5" or 5" barrel and chambered for .357 Magnum cartridge. Revolver is larger and has standard sport grips. Introduced in 1989.

NIB	*Exc.*	*V.G.*	*Good*	*Fair*	*Poor*
800	600	450	350	250	200

RIFLES

EM1.22

Semi-automatic .22 rimfire version of M1 Carbine. Has an 18" barrel and 15-round magazine. Manufactured between 1966 and 1976.

NIB	*Exc.*	*V.G.*	*Good*	*Fair*	*Poor*
—	350	220	150	120	100

EG-72, EG-722

A 15-shot slide-action carbine chambered for .22 rimfire. A 18.5" barrel and open sights. Finish is blued. Manufactured between 1970 and 1985.

NIB	*Exc.*	*V.G.*	*Good*	*Fair*	*Poor*
—	250	160	100	80	50

EG-712, EG-73

Lever copy of Winchester 94 Carbine. Chambered for .22 rimfire or .22 rimfire Magnum (EG-73). Has an 18.5" barrel and holds 15-shots in a tubular magazine. Manufactured between 1973 and 1985.

NIB	*Exc.*	*V.G.*	*Good*	*Fair*	*Poor*
—	250	180	150	120	100

SR-100

Long-range precision bolt-action rifle, chambered for .308 Win., .300 Win. Magnum or .338 Lapua calibers. Barrel length on .308 Win. is 25.25", other calibers 29.25". All barrels fitted with muzzle brake. Trigger is adjustable. Stock laminated, with thumbhole and adjustable recoil pad and cheekpiece. Weight about 15 lbs.

NIB	*Exc.*	*V.G.*	*Good*	*Fair*	*Poor*
8800	7000	5000	2750	1300	600

ERQUIAGA
Eibar, Spain

Another Spanish company that commenced business during WWI, as a subcontractor on the French "Ruby" contract. They manufactured the usual poor quality, 7.65mm Eibar-type pistol.

Fiel

Trade name found on Ruby subcontract pistol described above. Marked "Erquiaga y Cia Eibar Cal. 7.65 Fiel".

Courtesy James Rankin

NIB	*Exc.*	*V.G.*	*Good*	*Fair*	*Poor*
—	200	150	120	100	80

Fiel 6.35

After the end of WWI, a 1906 Browning copy was made. Chambered for 6.35mm cartridge. Markings are "Automatic Pistol 6.35 Fiel No. 1". Later models had "EMC" molded into grip.

NIB	*Exc.*	*V.G.*	*Good*	*Fair*	*Poor*
—	200	140	100	80	50

Marte

Another poor-quality "Eibar" -type pistol. Chambered for 6.35mm. Made in early 1920s.

NIB	*Exc.*	*V.G.*	*Good*	*Fair*	*Poor*
—	200	140	100	80	50

ERRASTI, A.
Eibar, Spain

Errasti manufactured a variety of inexpensive yet serviceable pistols, from early 1900s until the Spanish Civil War.

Velo Dog

Usual cheap solid-frame folding-trigger revolvers one associates with model designation. Chambered in 5.5mm and 6.35mm. Made in early 1900s.

NIB	Exc.	V.G.	Good	Fair	Poor
—	250	150	100	80	50

M1889

In 1915-1916 Errasti produced the 10.4mm Italian army service revolver. Quality was reasonably good. Marked "Errasti Eiber" on the right side of frame.

NIB	Exc.	V.G.	Good	Fair	Poor
—	400	300	200	120	80

Errasti

Two "Eibar"-type Browning copies were made under this trade name. One chambered for 6.35mm the other 7.65mm. Both marked "Automatic Pistol Errasti".

Courtesy James Rankin

NIB	Exc.	V.G.	Good	Fair	Poor
—	200	140	110	80	50

Errasti Oscillante

Manufactured in the 1920s, these revolvers were copied from Smith & Wesson Military & Police design. Chambered for .32-, .38- and .44-calibers, with .38 being most frequently encountered. Note: Add 30 percent for .44-caliber.

NIB	Exc.	V.G.	Good	Fair	Poor
—	250	200	120	100	50

Dreadnaught, Goliath and Smith Americano

These three trade names found on a group of poor quality nickel-plated revolvers. Made from 1905 through 1920. Obvious copies of Iver Johnson design. They had break-open actions, ribbed barrel and chambered for .32-, .38- and .44-calibers. They are scarce today, as most have long since fallen apart. Note: Add 30 percent for .44-caliber.

NIB	Exc.	V.G.	Good	Fair	Poor
—	220	180	100	80	50

ESCODIN, M.
Eibar, Spain

This company made a Smith & Wesson revolver copy from 1924 through 1931. Chambered for .32 and .38 Special. Only marking is a coat of arms stamped on left side of frame.

NIB	Exc.	V.G.	Good	Fair	Poor
—	180	120	100	80	50

ESCORT
Turkey

SEMI-AUTOMATIC SHOTGUNS

Model AS

This 12-gauge 3" model fitted with 28" ventilated rib barrel and choke tubes. Walnut stock. Black finish. Magazine capacity 4 rounds. Weight about 7 lbs.

NIB	Exc.	V.G.	Good	Fair	Poor
450	360	240	200	150	100

Model PS

This 12-gauge 3" model similar to above, with black polymer stock and finish. Also offered in Shadow Grass camo or Mossy Oak Break-Up camo. Choice of Spark or TriViz front sights. Barrel length 28" except for TriViz variation with 24" barrel. Weight about 7 lbs. Note: Add $100 for camo coverage; $45 for TriViz model.

NIB	Exc.	V.G.	Good	Fair	Poor
500	400	300	200	150	100

Model PS AimGuard

This 12-gauge 3" model is fitted with 20" Fixed choke barrel in Cylinder bore. Black polymer stock and finish. Magazine capacity 5 rounds. Weight about 6.4 lbs.

NIB	Exc.	V.G.	Good	Fair	Poor
400	300	200	120	100	80

Combo Model

This 12-gauge 3" model is offered with two sets of barrels: one 28" with Full choke tube; the other 24" with Turkey choke tube. Polymer stock with Mossy Oak Break-Up. Receiver is fitted with a dovetail mount. Weight about 7 lbs.

NIB	Exc.	V.G.	Good	Fair	Poor
580	420	360	300	200	100

Escort Semi-Auto Slug Gun

Slug gun available in 12- or 20-gauge. Rifled barrel 22" long with 1:26 twist. Self-regulating gas piston. Has Hi-Viz sights and equipped with a cantilevered scope base. Black synthetic stock. Overall length, 42". Weight: 6.3 lbs. (20-gauge); 7 lbs. (12-gauge).

NIB	Exc.	V.G.	Good	Fair	Poor
530	480	380	300	250	200

Escort Extreme Series

Available for 12-gauge 3" or 3.5" Magnum, with 28" barrel, Hi-Viz sights and choke tubes. Several camo patterns for turkey or waterfowl hunting. Extreme Waterfowl Youth model available in 20-gauge with 22" barrel.

Extreme 3.5

NIB	Exc.	V.G.	Good	Fair	Poor
800	680	500	400	300	200

Extreme 3

NIB	Exc.	V.G.	Good	Fair	Poor
700	600	450	400	300	150

Extreme Waterfowl Youth

NIB	Exc.	V.G.	Good	Fair	Poor
600	520	400	350	300	150

PUMP-ACTION SHOTGUNS

Field Hunter

This 12-gauge 3" model fitted with 28" ventilated rib barrel and choke tubes. Offered with black polymer stock of Mossy Oak Break-Up or Shadow Grass camo pattern. A 24" barrel with TriViz also offered. Magazine capacity 4 rounds. Weight about 7 lbs. Note: Add $50 for camo finish; $100 for TriViz sights.

NIB	Exc.	V.G.	Good	Fair	Poor
320	220	160	140	100	80

FieldHunter Turkey

Gauges: 12 ga., 3 in., 20 ga., 3 in, .410 bore, 3 in. Capacity: 4+1. Barrels: 22 in., 24 in., 26 in., ventilated rib. Length: 42-46 in. Weight: 6.0-6.9 lbs. Stock: Synthetic with camo finish. Features: The pump-action Turkey model addition to the FieldHunter family is built of aircraft alloy with a black chrome-finished steel barrel that is camo coated. Cantilever Weaver optics rail, fully adjustable green rear fiber-optic sight with windage-adjustable front red fiber-optic sight. Cross-bolt safety, rubber butt pad, sling studs. Includes three chokes (Ext Turkey, F, IM).

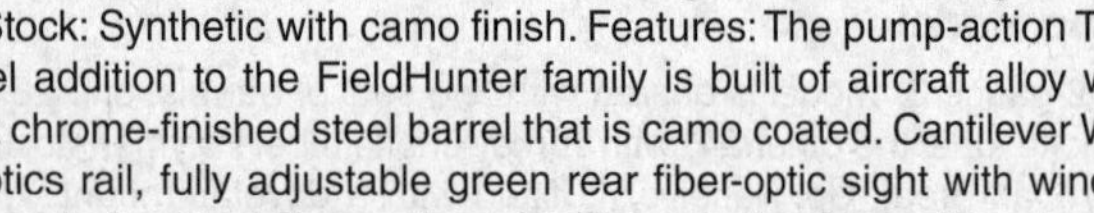

NIB	Exc.	V.G.	Good	Fair	Poor
330	—	—	—	—	—

AimGuard

This 12-gauge 3" model fitted with 20" barrel and Fixed Cylinder bore choke. Black polymer stock. Magazine capacity 5 rounds. Weight about 6.4 lbs. Note: Add 10 percent for 18" barrel and nickel finish.

NIB	Exc.	V.G.	Good	Fair	Poor
320	220	160	140	100	80

Escort Pump Slug Gun

Same specifications as semi-automatic except slide-action. Weight: 6 lbs. (20-gauge); 6.7 lbs. (12-gauge).

NIB	Exc.	V.G.	Good	Fair	Poor
430	380	290	250	200	150

Slugger

Gauge: 12 ga., 3 in. Capacity: 5+1. Barrels: 26 in., 28 in., ventilated rib. Length: 38 in. Weight: 6.4-6.5 lbs. Stock: Black synthetic. Slugger Tactical has pistol grip. Features: The pump-action Slugger is built of black-anodized aircraft alloy with a black chrome-finished steel barrel. Fixed cylinder bore choke, cross-bolt safety, fiber-optic front sight, rubber butt pad, sling studs.

NIB	Exc.	V.G.	Good	Fair	Poor
230	150	130	—	—	—

RIMFIRE RIFLES

22LR Rifle

Caliber: .22 LR. Capacity: 10. Barrel: 25 in., blued, chrome plated. Stock: Synthetic or Turkish walnut. Sights: Fiber optic. Weight: 6.4 lbs. Features: Checkered grip and forearm, extremely affordable.

NIB	Exc.	V.G.	Good	Fair	Poor
220	180	130	—	—	—

ESPIRIN, HERMANOS

Eibar, Spain

Euskaro

Poor-quality often unsafe revolver. Manufactured from 1906 until WWI. They are copies of Iver Johnson design break-open actions. Chambered for .32-, .38- and .44-calibers. Product epitomizes the worst Eibar had to offer during pre-Civil War era. Note: Add 30 percent for .44-caliber.

NIB	Exc.	V.G.	Good	Fair	Poor
—	200	120	80	50	20

EUROARMS OF AMERICA

Winchester, Virginia

An importer of blackpowder muzzleloading firearms, primarily replicas of early American weapons.

REVOLVERS

1851 Navy

Replica of Colt revolver chambered for .36- or .44-caliber percussion. Has a square-back silver-plated triggerguard and 7.5" barrel.

NIB	Exc.	V.G.	Good	Fair	Poor
280	220	170	110	80	40

1851 Navy Police Model

Chambered for .36-caliber, with 5-shot fluted cylinder and 5.5" barrel.

NIB	Exc.	V.G.	Good	Fair	Poor
280	220	170	110	80	40

1851 Navy Sheriff's Model

A 5" barreled version of Navy Model.

NIB	Exc.	V.G.	Good	Fair	Poor
280	220	170	110	80	40

1851 "Schneider & Glassick" Navy

Replica of Confederate revolver chambered for .36- or .44-caliber percussion.

NIB	Exc.	V.G.	Good	Fair	Poor
150	100	80	60	50	40

1851 "Griswold & Gunnison" Navy

Replica of Confederate revolver chambered for .36- or .44-caliber percussion.

NIB	Exc.	V.G.	Good	Fair	Poor
280	240	170	110	80	40

1862 Police

Replica of Colt Model 1862 chambered for .36-caliber percussion, with 7.5" barrel and steel frame.

NIB	Exc.	V.G.	Good	Fair	Poor
280	220	170	110	80	40

1860 Army

Replica of Colt revolver chambered for .44-caliber percussion. Offered with 5" or 8" barrel.

NIB	Exc.	V.G.	Good	Fair	Poor
280	220	170	110	80	40

1861 Navy

Replica of Colt revolver chambered for .36-caliber percussion.

NIB	Exc.	V.G.	Good	Fair	Poor
280	220	170	110	80	40

1858 Remington Army or Navy

Replicas of Remington percussion revolvers chambered for .36- or .44-caliber.

NIB	Exc.	V.G.	Good	Fair	Poor
280	220	170	110	80	40

RIFLES

Rifles listed are modern replicas of early American and British firearms. They are good quality and quite serviceable.

Cook & Brother Carbine

NIB	Exc.	V.G.	Good	Fair	Poor
600	500	380	250	200	100

1863 J.P. Murray

NIB	Exc.	V.G.	Good	Fair	Poor
600	500	380	250	200	100

1853 Enfield Rifled Musket

NIB	Exc.	V.G.	Good	Fair	Poor
610	520	380	250	200	100

1858 Enfield Rifled Musket

NIB	Exc.	V.G.	Good	Fair	Poor
610	520	380	250	200	100

1861 Enfield Musketoon

NIB	Exc.	V.G.	Good	Fair	Poor
500	380	250	200	100	60

1803 Harper's Ferry

NIB	Exc.	V.G.	Good	Fair	Poor
600	500	380	250	200	100

1841 Mississippi Rifle

NIB	Exc.	V.G.	Good	Fair	Poor
600	500	380	250	200	100

Pennsylvania Rifle

NIB	Exc.	V.G.	Good	Fair	Poor
400	350	280	220	150	100

Hawken Rifle

NIB	Exc.	V.G.	Good	Fair	Poor
400	350	280	220	150	100

Cape Gun

NIB	Exc.	V.G.	Good	Fair	Poor
450	400	320	280	200	150

Buffalo Carbine

NIB	Exc.	V.G.	Good	Fair	Poor
450	400	320	280	200	150

1862 Remington Rifle

NIB	Exc.	V.G.	Good	Fair	Poor
450	400	320	280	200	150

Zouave Rifle

NIB	Exc.	V.G.	Good	Fair	Poor
450	400	320	280	200	150

SHOTGUNS

Duck Gun

Single-barreled percussion fowling piece chambered for 8-, 10- or 12-gauge. Has a 33" smoothbore barrel and case colored hammer and lock. Stock is walnut with brass mountings. Introduced in 1989. Note: Add 20 percent for 8-gauge.

NIB	Exc.	V.G.	Good	Fair	Poor
450	400	320	280	200	150

Standard Side-by-Side

Side-by-side chambered for 12-gauge percussion. Has 28" barrels, with engraved locks and walnut stock.

NIB	Exc.	V.G.	Good	Fair	Poor
480	400	350	300	200	120

EUROPEAN AMERICAN ARMORY CORP./U.S. SPORTING GOODS, INC.

Rockledge, Florida

EAA WITNESS PISTOLS

EAA Witness P-Series Full Size

Introduced in 1998, P-Series is a polymer-frame variation of original steel-frame Witness DA/SA pistols. Chambered for 9mm, .40 S&W, .45 ACP, .38 Super and 10mm cartridges. Barrel length 4.55". Overall length 8.5" with an empty weight of 31 oz. Rear sight adjustable for windage. Magazine capacity: 9mm 28 rounds; .40 S&W 15 rounds; .45 ACP 10 rounds; 10mm 15 rounds. Note: Add $30 for ported barrel.

NIB	Exc.	V.G.	Good	Fair	Poor
520	420	320	220	180	100

EAA Witness P-Series Carry-Comp

Fitted with a 4.25" ported barrel. Chambered for .45 ACP.

NIB	Exc.	V.G.	Good	Fair	Poor
470	380	280	200	150	100

EAA Witness P-Series Compact

Similar to above, with barrel length of 3.55". Weight about 26 oz. Note: Add $30 for ported barrel.

NIB	Exc.	V.G.	Good	Fair	Poor
450	350	250	200	150	100

EAA Witness P-S Series

Built on a different frame size from P-Series pistols. Chambered for .22 LR, 9mm or .40 S&W cartridges. Barrel length 4.55". Weight about 31 oz.

NIB	Exc.	V.G.	Good	Fair	Poor
400	320	280	200	150	100

SAR B6P

Similar to other polymer-frame Witness models. In 9mm only, with 4.5" or 3.8" barrel. Magazine capacity 13 or 16 rounds. Made by Sarsilmaz. Note: Add $50 for Pavona Compact Lady model offered in several different color frame finishes.

NIB	Exc.	V.G.	Good	Fair	Poor
350	300	250	220	180	150

EAA Witness Carry Comp

Offered in 9mm, .41 AE, .40 S&W and .45 ACP. Features 1" steel compensator. Barrel 4.1" long. Overall length same as standard model as is magazine capacity. Offered in blue or blue chrome finish. Weight 34 oz. Note: Add 15 percent for.45 ACP.

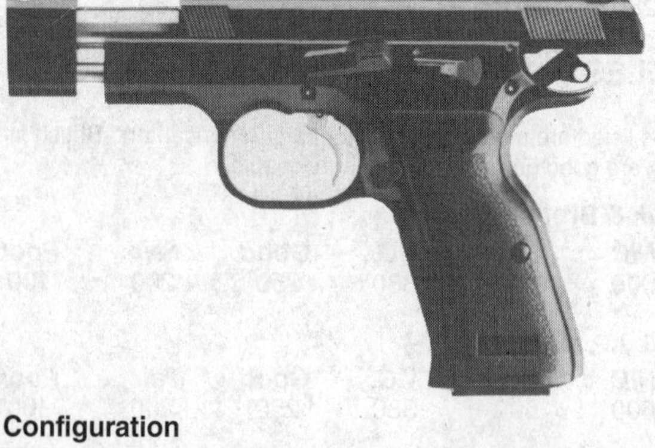

New Configuration

NIB	Exc.	V.G.	Good	Fair	Poor
500	450	380	320	250	180

EAA Witness Standard

This is the original Witness model with a steel frame. Based on CZ-75 design. Made by Tanfoglio in Italy, it has been imported by EAA since 1990. Available in 9mm, .41 AE, .40 S&W and .45 ACP, with 4.5" barrel. Magazine capacity: 9mm 16 rounds; .41 AE 11 rounds; .40 S&W 12 rounds; .45 ACP 10 rounds. Offered in blue, chrome, two-tone and stainless steel. Weight about 33 oz. Note: Add 5 percent for chrome, two-tone and stainless steel.

New Configuration

NIB	*Exc.*	*V.G.*	*Good*	*Fair*	*Poor*
500	380	300	220	180	120

EAA Witness Subcompact

Offered in same calibers as standard model. Fitted with 3.66" barrel and shorter grip. Magazine capacity: 9mm 13 rounds; .41 AE 9 rounds; .40 S&W 9 rounds; .45 ACP 8 rounds. Weight about 30 oz. Offered in blue, chrome, two-tone and stainless steel. Note: Add 5 percent for chrome, two-tone and stainless steel.

New Configuration

NIB	*Exc.*	*V.G.*	*Good*	*Fair*	*Poor*
460	350	280	220	180	120

EAA Witness Sport L/S

Features longer slide for its 4.75" barrel. Offered in 9mm, .41 AE, .40 S&W and .45 ACP. Magazine capacity: 9mm 19 rounds; .41 AE 13 rounds; .40 S&W 14 rounds; .45 ACP 11 rounds. Also fitted with adjustable rear sight and extended safety. Available in two-tone finish. Weight about 34.5 oz. A ported barrel offered as an option. Note: Add 10 percent for .45 ACP.

New Configuration

NIB	*Exc.*	*V.G.*	*Good*	*Fair*	*Poor*
620	550	500	400	300	200

EAA Witness Combo 9/40

Offers a 9mm and .40 S&W conversion kit. Kits consist of a slide, barrel, recoil spring, guide and magazine. Available in standard or subcompact size in blue, chrome or two-tone finish. Note: Add 5 percent for chrome or two-tone finish.

NIB	*Exc.*	*V.G.*	*Good*	*Fair*	*Poor*
600	500	420	350	280	180

EAA Witness Silver Team Match

Designed as a competition pistol. Fitted with 5.25" barrel. Features dual chamber compensator, single-action trigger, extended safety, competition hammer, paddle magazine release, checkered walnut grips and adjustable rear sight or drilled and tapped for scope mount. Offered in: 9mm 19 rounds; .40 S&W 14 rounds; .41 AE 13 rounds; .45 ACP 11 rounds and 9 x 21. Finish is blue. Weight about 34 oz.

NIB	Exc.	V.G.	Good	Fair	Poor
900	800	700	600	450	300

EAA Witness Sport

Built on standard Witness frame. Addition of an adjustable rear sight and extended safety. Offered in 9mm, .41 AE, .40 S&W, .45 ACP in standard model magazine capacity. Weight 33 oz. Available in two-tone finish. Note: Add 10 percent for .45 ACP.

New Configuration

NIB	Exc.	V.G.	Good	Fair	Poor
550	480	400	300	200	150

EAA Witness Hunter

Features camo finish with 6" barrel. Chambered for .45 ACP or 10mm cartridge. Drilled and tapped for scope mount and adjustable sights. Magazine capacity 10 rounds. Weight about 41 oz. Also available with blued finish.

NIB	Exc.	V.G.	Good	Fair	Poor
1100	900	680	500	250	150

EAA Witness Gold Team Match

This is a full race competition pistol. Features triple chamber compensator, beaver tail grip safety, beveled magazine well, adjustable rear sight or drilled and tapped for scope mount, extended safety and magazine release, competition hammer, square triggerguard, checkered front and backstrap, competition grips and hard chrome finish. Same barrel length, magazine capacity and calibers as Silver Team Match. Weight 38 oz.

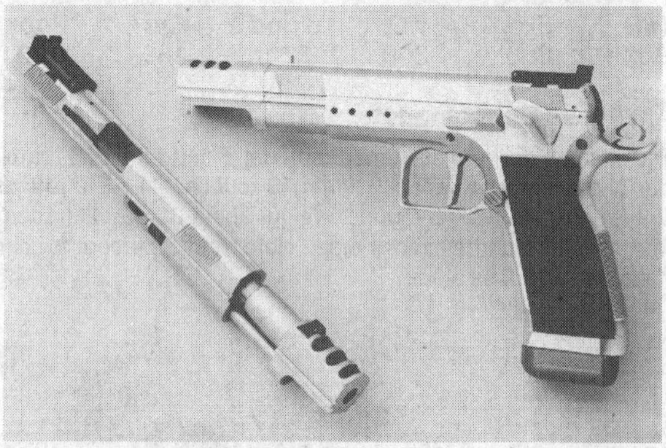

NIB	Exc.	V.G.	Good	Fair	Poor
1800	1400	1000	750	600	400

EAA Witness Limited Class Pistol

Built on Witness Match frame. Features competition grips, high-capacity magazine, extended safety and magazine release, single-action trigger, long slide with adjustable rear sight and match grade barrel. Offered in 9mm, .40 S&W, .38 Super and .45 ACP, with blue finish.

NIB	Exc.	V.G.	Good	Fair	Poor
1200	980	720	550	400	300

EAA Witness Stock

Introduced in 2005 Features 4.5" tapered cone barrel chambered for 9mm, .40S&W, .45ACP or .10mm cartridge. Hard chrome finish, extended safety, wood checkered grips and fully adjustable sights. Weight about 33 oz.

NIB	Exc.	V.G.	Good	Fair	Poor
820	700	600	400	200	100

EAA Witness Multi Class Pistol Package

This package consists of one Witness Limited Class pistol, with a complete unlimited class top half. Top half is made up of standard length slide with super sight, recoil guide and spring, match grade competition barrel (threaded for compensator) and a dual chamber compensator. Available in 9mm, .40 S&W, 9 x 21, .45 ACP, 9 x 23 and .38 Super. Finish is blue.

NIB	Exc.	V.G.	Good	Fair	Poor
1700	1350	850	600	300	200

EAA Witness Elite Match

Single-action semi-automatic featuring 4.5" polygonal rifled steel barrel, adjustable rear sights, rubber grips. Two-tone finish. Chambered for 9 mm (18+1), 10 mm (15+1), 38 Super (15+1), .40 S&W (15+1) and .45 ACP (10+1). Weight 33 oz. Introduced 2006.

NIB	Exc.	V.G.	Good	Fair	Poor
720	600	450	300	200	100

EAA Witness 1911

Made by Tanfoglio in Italy. This is a standard size 1911 in .45 ACP. Made in two variations, one with a steel frame (shown) and the other is polymer. Operating controls are standard 1911, with added features like an accessory rail, flat mainspring housing, skeleton hammer and trigger, extended grip safety and ambidextrous manual safety. Introduced in 2014. Values shown are for polymer model. Note: Add $250 for steel frame.

NIB	Exc.	V.G.	Good	Fair	Poor
520	440	350	280	200	150

Zastava EZ Pistol

CZ-75 clone. Single-/double-action pistol, with 4" (Full Size) or 3.5" (Compact) barrel and polymer frame. Chambered in 9mm, .40 S&W or .45 ACP. Magazine capacity varies from 7 rounds (.45 ACP) to 15 (9mm).

NIB	Exc.	V.G.	Good	Fair	Poor
450	400	320	280	160	100

Thor

Single-shot pistol chambered for .223 Rem., .270 Win., .30-06, .300 Win., .308, .375 Win., .44 Magnum, .45-70, .50 S&W, .7mm-08 or .7mm Rem. Magnum. Fitted with 14" barrel. Receiver has an integral top rail for scope mount. Weight about 5 lbs.

NIB	Exc.	V.G.	Good	Fair	Poor
1150	850	680	500	360	140

Witness Pavona Series

Similar to P-Series with polymer frame but with 3.8-in. barrel. Chambered in .380 ACP, 9mm or .40 S&W. Equipped with 9- or 13-rnd. magazine. Finish available in a variety of colors.

NIB	Exc.	V.G.	Good	Fair	Poor
430	380	330	230	210	160

OTHER EAA IMPORTED FIREARMS

EAA GIRSAN PISTOLS

Turkish manufacturer imported by EAA

EAA Girsan MC1911 Match Elite

All-steel competition grade 1911 pattern pistol, .45 ACP

NIB	Exc.	V.G.	Good	Fair	Poor
800	700	600	—	—	—

EAA GIRSAN PISTOLS

EAA Girsan MC288SA-TV

Striker-fired recoil-operated 9mm semi-auto pistol, red-dot optic, 15-round mag., adjustable grips.

NIB	Exc.	V.G.	Good	Fair	Poor
440	350	300	—	—	—

BUL 1911 SERIES

BUL Government

Chambered for .45 ACP cartridge. Fitted with 4.8" barrel, polymer frame, tactical rear sight, with dovetail front sight, fully checkered grip. Black or stainless steel slide. Weight about 24 oz. Magazine capacity 10 rounds. Introduced in 2002. Note: Add $50 for stainless steel slide.

NIB	Exc.	V.G.	Good	Fair	Poor
550	450	300	200	120	80

Commander

Same as above. Fitted with 3.8" barrel.

NIB	Exc.	V.G.	Good	Fair	Poor
550	450	300	200	120	80

Stinger

This model has a 3" barrel.

NIB	Exc.	V.G.	Good	Fair	Poor
550	450	300	200	120	80

EAA Big Bore Bounty Hunter

Single-action revolver made in Germany. Features three-position hammer, forged barrel and walnut grips. Offered in .357 Magnum, .45 Long Colt and .44 Magnum. Barrel lengths 4.5", 5.5" or 7.5". Choice of finish includes blue or case colored frame, chrome, gold or blue and gold. Note: Add 20 percent for chrome, gold or blue and gold finish.

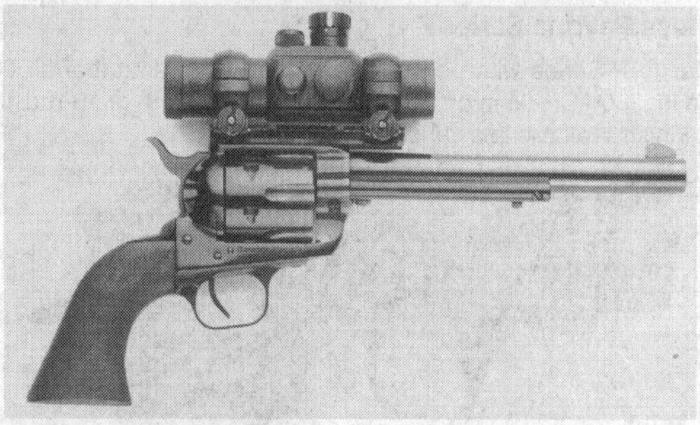

NIB	Exc.	V.G.	Good	Fair	Poor
400	300	220	180	150	120

EAA Small Bore Bounty Hunter

Single-action .22-caliber revolver. Wood grips and available in blue or blue and brass finish. Barrel lengths 4.75", 6" and 9". Chambered for .22 LR or .22 Winchester Rimfire Magnum.

NIB	Exc.	V.G.	Good	Fair	Poor
280	200	140	120	80	60

EAA Bounty Hunter Shotgun—External Hammers

Side-by-side shotgun with external hammers. Chambered for 10-, 12-, 16-, 20-, 28-gauge and .410 bore. Offered in barrel lengths of 20", 24" and 26".

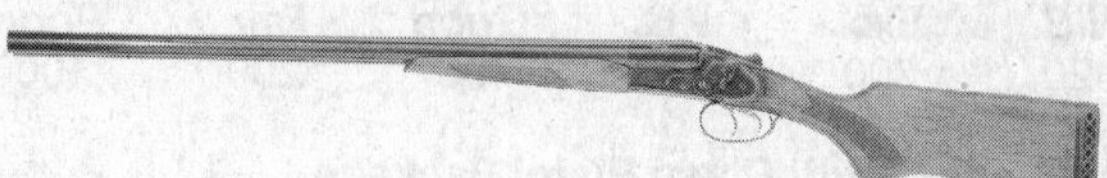

NIB	Exc.	V.G.	Good	Fair	Poor
380	300	250	180	150	120

EAA Bounty Hunter Shotgun—Traditional

Same as above, with internal hammers. Offered in 12- or 20-gauge.

NIB	Exc.	V.G.	Good	Fair	Poor
300	250	200	150	100	80

MC312 Gobbler

Gauge: 12 ga., 3.5 in. Barrel: 24 in., with ventilated turkey rib. Length: 50 in. Stock: Synthetic camouflage with either straight or pistol grip options. Features: The MC312 inertia-driven semi-auto produced by Girsan gets a turkey upgrade with a shorter barrel, mid-bead, Picatinny rail cut into the receiver, Cerakote finish receiver and barrel, cross-bolt safety, sling studs, rubber buttpad, fiber-optic front sight, and field-tested reflex optic. Includes flush mount choke tubes.

NIB	Exc.	V.G.	Good	Fair	Poor
540	—	—	—	—	—

Girsan MC312

Gauge: 12 ga. Barrel: 28 in. vent rib. Length: 50 in. Weight: 6.95 lbs. Stock: Polymer in choice of either black or camo. Features: Inertia-driven single-action hunting autoloader. Lightweight aircraft aluminum receiver 5+1 round capacity. Fiber-optic front sight. Passed EAA's 5,000-round test with no cleaning and 10,000-round test with no parts replacement.

NIB	Exc.	V.G.	Good	Fair	Poor
400	—	—	—	—	—

Girsan MC312 Goose

Gauge: 12 ga. Barrel: 30-in. vent rib. Length: 52 in. Weight: 6.75 lbs. Stock: Black polymer. Features: Goose variant of the inertia-driven MC312 line. Lightweight aircraft aluminum receiver with machined integral accessory rail for the included red-dot optic. Fiber-optic front sight. Ships with five extended choke tubes. Same 5+1 capacity as the standard MC312.

NIB	Exc.	V.G.	Good	Fair	Poor
580	—	—	—	—	—

Akkar Churchill 220

Gauge: 20 ga. Barrel: 18.5 in. Length: 37.5 in. Weight: 5.0 lbs. Stock: Black synthetic pistol grip style. Features: This Turkish-made semi-automatic springs from the Churchill 220 series of gas-driven repeaters is now re-vamped for home defense and tactical use. Optics rail machined into receiver for easy target acquisition with included red-dot optic on quick-release mount. Semi-enhanced loading port. Accessible controls. 5+1 round capacity. Checkered pistol grip stock. Black rubber recoil pad, sling swivels. Door-breaching choke tube and shrouded red fiber-optic front sight.

NIB	Exc.	V.G.	Good	Fair	Poor
430	350	280	—	—	—

EAA F.A.B. 92 Pistol

Semi-automatic pistol similar to Witness. Fitted with hammer drop safety and slide mounted safety, that is both double-/single-action. Available in full size (33 oz.) or compact size (30 oz.). Full size version has 4.5" barrel; compact fitted with 3.66" barrel. Offered in 9mm or .40 S&W in blue, two-tone or chrome finish.

NIB	Exc.	V.G.	Good	Fair	Poor
400	300	220	180	120	100

EAA European Standard Pistol

Single-action semi-automatic pistol, with external hammer, slide grip serrations, wood grips and single column magazine. Barrel length 3.2" and overall length 6.5". Chambered for .22 LR, 380 ACP and .32 ACP. Magazine capacity: 10 rounds .22 LR; 7 rounds .380 and .32. Offered in blue, blue/chrome, chrome, blue/gold. Weight 26 oz.

NIB	Exc.	V.G.	Good	Fair	Poor
200	160	110	100	80	50

EAA European Target Pistol

Features adjustable rear sight, external hammer, single-action trigger, walnut target grips and adjustable weight system. Chambered for .22 LR. Offered in blue finish. Weight 40 oz.

NIB	Exc.	V.G.	Good	Fair	Poor
360	300	220	180	150	100

EAA Windicator Standard Grade

German-built model is a double-action revolver chambered for .22 LR, .22 Winchester Rimfire Magnum, .32 H&R and .38 Special. Offered in 2", 4" and 6" barrel lengths. Cylinder capacity: .22 LR/.22 WRM 8 rounds; .32 H&R 7 rounds; .38 Special 6 rounds. Cylinder is unfluted, finish blue.

NIB	Exc.	V.G.	Good	Fair	Poor
280	160	140	110	80	60

EAA Windicator Basic Grade

Chambered for .38 Special or .357 Magnum, with 2" barrel. Fluted cylinder holds 6 rounds. Finish is blue.

NIB	Exc.	V.G.	Good	Fair	Poor
280	160	140	110	80	60

EAA Windicator Tactical Grade

Similar in appearance to standard grade. Chambered for .38 Special, with 2" or 4" barrel. The 4" barrel has an integral compensator. Finish is blue.

2" Barrel

NIB	Exc.	V.G.	Good	Fair	Poor
190	150	120	100	80	60

4" Barrel

NIB	Exc.	V.G.	Good	Fair	Poor
250	200	150	120	100	80

EAA Windicator Target Grade

Model has these special features: adjustable trigger pull, walnut grips, adjustable rear sight, drilled and tapped for scope mount, target hammer, adjustable trigger stop. Fitted with 6" target barrel. Chambered for .22 LR, .38 Special, .357 Magnum. Blue finish.

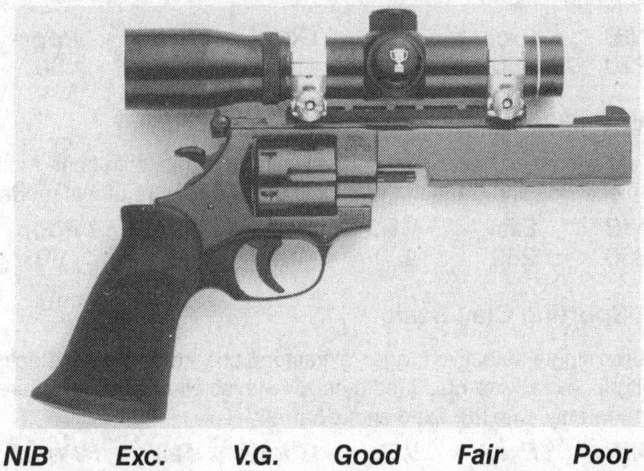

NIB	Exc.	V.G.	Good	Fair	Poor
350	280	220	200	150	100

EAA PM2 Shotgun

Pump-action 12-gauge shotgun, with 6-round box magazine. Barrel length 20". Finish blue or chrome. Stock is black composite. Weight 6.8 lbs. Discontinued in 1993. Note: Add $100 for optional night sights.

NIB	Exc.	V.G.	Good	Fair	Poor
450	350	300	250	200	150

EAA HW 60 Rifle

German-made target rifle chambered for .22 LR. Features an adjustable trigger and other target and match grade components. Barrel length 26.8", stock stippled walnut and finish blue. Weight about 10.8 lbs.

Target Grade

NIB	Exc.	V.G.	Good	Fair	Poor
700	600	500	400	300	200

Match Grade

NIB	Exc.	V.G.	Good	Fair	Poor
800	680	550	450	350	250

EAA SABATTI

These firearms are made by Sabatti firm in Gardone, Italy. It is an old line company, having been in the firearms business since 1674. Company also produces and supplies component parts to many of Italy's premier gun makers. These shotguns and rifles are manufactured for the cost-conscious buyer.

EAA Sabatti Falcon

Field grade over/under shotgun, with checkered walnut stock and pistol grip, boxlock action, double triggers and extractors. Offered in 12- or 20-gauge with 3" chambers. Also available in 28-gauge and .410 bore with 26" or 28" barrels. Barrel lengths are available in 26", 28" or 30". Chokes are Fixed.

12/20 Gauge

NIB	Exc.	V.G.	Good	Fair	Poor
580	420	400	350	300	250

28/.410

NIB	Exc.	V.G.	Good	Fair	Poor
620	480	420	380	320	280

EAA SP 1822

Sabatti rifle chambered for .22 LR. Semi-automatic carbine, with two-piece adjustable stock.

NIB	Exc.	V.G.	Good	Fair	Poor
220	180	120	100	80	60

EAA SP 1822H

Heavy barrel version of above model without sights. Receiver fitted with scope mount base.

NIB	Exc.	V.G.	Good	Fair	Poor
220	180	120	100	80	60

EAA SP 1822TH

This variation also has a heavy barrel without sights, with base mounts. One-piece Bell and Carlson thumbhole stock is feature of this model.

NIB	Exc.	V.G.	Good	Fair	Poor
350	260	220	180	120	90

EAA Sporting Clay Basic

Features single-selective trigger, extractors, checkered walnut stock and pistol grip, extra wide rib. Flued receiver with scroll engraving. Offered in 12-gauge only, with 28" fixed choke barrel.

NIB	Exc.	V.G.	Good	Fair	Poor
350	280	250	200	150	100

EAA Sporting Clay Pro

Similar to basic sporting clay. Addition of a select walnut stock, screw-in choke tubes, automatic ejectors, recoil pad. Comes with hard shell case.

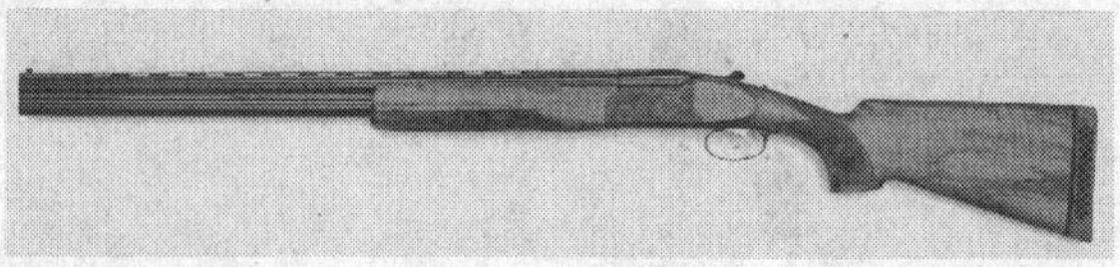

NIB	Exc.	V.G.	Good	Fair	Poor
950	720	650	550	450	300

EAA Sporting Clay Pro Gold

Same as above, with gold inlay receiver.

NIB	Exc.	V.G.	Good	Fair	Poor
1000	750	650	550	450	300

Churchill 812 Field

Gauges: 12 ga., 3 in., 20 ga., 3 in., 28 ga., .410 bore. Barrels: 26 in., 28 in., with ventilated rib. Length: 45.2-47.2 in. Stock: Select Turkish walnut. Features: These Turkish made Akkar O/Us have silver-finish receiver, rubberized buttpad, checkered stock, single selective trigger, Nitride-silver receiver, gold-plated trigger, red fiber-optic front sight, tang safety selector, chrome-lined barrels, auto ejectors. Ships with three choke tubes.

NIB	Exc.	V.G.	Good	Fair	Poor
850	700	600	—	—	—

Churchill 812 Sporting

Gauge: 12 ga., 3 in. Barrels: 28 in., 30 in., with 10mm ventilated rib. Length: 47.2-49.2 in. Stock: Select-grade Turkish walnut. Features: These Turkish made Akkar O/Us have a case-color finish engraved receiver, adjustable comb, hand-rubbed oil finish, hammer-forged back-bored barrels, fiber-optic front sight, rubber buttpad, checkered stock, single selective trigger, gold-plated trigger, red fiber-optic front sight, tang safety selector, chrome-lined barrels, auto ejectors. Ships with three choke tubes.

NIB	Exc.	V.G.	Good	Fair	Poor
1500	1200	850	—	—	—

Churchill 512

Gauges: 12 ga., 3in., 20 ga., 3 in., 28 ga., 3 in., .410 bore. Barrels: 26 in., 28 in. Length: 45-47 in. Stock: Standard Turkish walnut. Features: These Turkish made Akkar side-by-sides have a Nitride-silver receiver, rubber buttpad, checkered stock, single selective gold-plated trigger, front bead, manual safety, chrome-lined barrels, extractors. Ships with three choke tubes.

NIB	Exc.	V.G.	Good	Fair	Poor
900	750	600	—	—	—

Akkar Churchill 620

Gauge: 20 ga. Barrel: 18.5 in. Length: 37.5 in. Weight: 5.0 lbs. Stock: Black Synthetic pistol grip style. Features: This Turkish-made pump builds on the Churchill 620 series of slide actions now re-vamped for home defense and tactical use. Optics rail machined into receiver for easy target acquisition with included red-dot optic on quick-release mount. Semi-enhanced loading port. Accessible controls. Checkered pistol grip stock. Black rubber recoil pad, sling swivels. Door-breaching choke tube and shrouded red fiber-optic front sight.

NIB	Exc.	V.G.	Good	Fair	Poor
370	270	200	—	—	—

EAA Saba

A side-by-side shotgun. Features an engraved silver boxlock receiver, double-/single triggers, selective ejectors, solid raised matted rib and select European walnut checkered stock. Offered in 12-, 20-, 28-gauge and .410 bore. Barrel length 26" or 28" with Fixed chokes.

NIB	Exc.	V.G.	Good	Fair	Poor
780	600	500	400	300	250

EAA/Saiga Shotgun

Semi-automatic shotgun based on AK-47 design. Chambered for 12-, 20-gauge and .410 bore. Barrel lengths 20", 24", 26" or 28". Blued finish with optional camo finish. Detachable 5-round box magazine. Introduced in 1999. Note: Deduct $175 for .410 variation.

NIB	Exc.	V.G.	Good	Fair	Poor
600	520	450	350	200	120

EAA/Saiga Rifle

Same as above, but chambered for 7.62x39 or .308 cartridge. Fitted with 20" barrel. Choice of wood or synthetic stock. Introduced in 1999. Note: Add $100 for .308 caliber.

NIB	Exc.	V.G.	Good	Fair	Poor
550	450	300	200	120	80

EAA Rover 870

High-quality bolt-action rifle. Walnut stock is checkered, with rubber recoil pad. Adjustable rear sight and receiver is drilled and tapped for scope mount. Barrel length 22". Chambered for these cartridges: .22-250, .243, .25-06, .270, .308, .30-06, 7mm Rem. Magnum, .300 and .338 Win. Magnum.

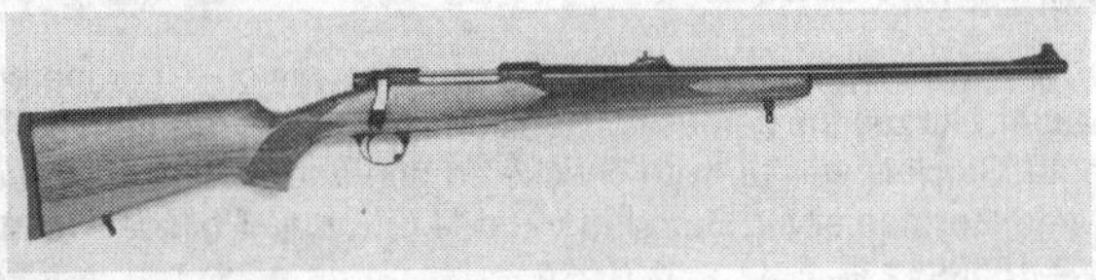

NIB	Exc.	V.G.	Good	Fair	Poor
580	440	380	300	200	120

EAA Benelli Silhouette Pistol

Specialized competition pistol, with a semi-automatic action. Stocks are match-type walnut with stippling. Palm shelf is adjustable. Barrel 4.3" long. Fully adjustable sights. Chambered for .22 LR, .22 Short and .32 WC. Supplied with loading tool and cleaning rod. The .22-caliber version weight 38.5 oz. Overall length 11.7".

NIB	Exc.	V.G.	Good	Fair	Poor
2000	1350	1000	750	600	400

MP94 Combo Gun

An over/under combination model, with a 12-gauge shotgun barrel atop a rifle barrel. Chambered for .223 or .308. A .410/22 LR version is also available. Barrels are 20". Stock checkered walnut. Sights are an adjustable rear and ramp front with bead. Other features include double triggers, Picatinny scope rail and four choke tubes for the shotgun barrel.

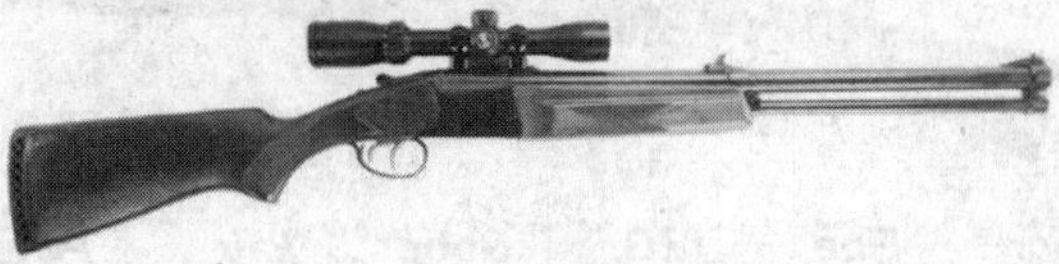

NIB	Exc.	V.G.	Good	Fair	Poor
680	520	400	300	250	120

Model .410/22 LR

NIB	Exc.	V.G.	Good	Fair	Poor
480	400	320	250	200	120

Model 221 Double Rifle

An affordable side-by-side double rifle in .30-06 or .45-70, with 23.5" barrels, checkered walnut stock, double triggers and extractors. Sights are an adjustable rear and ramp front with bead, plus a Picatinny or 11mm scope rail.

NIB	Exc.	V.G.	Good	Fair	Poor
1000	850	650	500	400	350

EVANS REPEATING RIFLE CO.

Mechanic Falls, Maine

Incorporated in 1873, this firm produced repeating rifles based upon patents issued to Warren R. Evans (1868-1871) and later George F. Evans (1877, 1878 and 1879). Most distinctive feature of these arms is they used a butt magazine operating on the principle of an Archimedean screw. Distributed by Merwin, Hulbert & Company, as well as Schuyler, Hartley & Graham, Evans rifles met with some success. One of their earliest advocates was William F. Cody (Buffalo Bill). Company ceased operations in 1879, after approximately 15,000 arms had been made.

LEVER-ACTION RIFLES

Rifle is totally unique for a number of reasons. Holds the most rounds of any repeating rifle that did not have a detachable magazine, with capacities up to 38 rounds on some models. Rifle was chambered for its own cartridge—the .44 Evans of which there were two versions: a 1" cartridge in the "Old Model" and "Transition Model" and a 1.5" cartridge in "New Model". Finish on these rifles is blued, with nickel-plated levers and buttplates noted on some examples. Stocks are walnut. Approximately 12,250 models manufactured between 1873 and 1879.

Old Model

This variation chambered for 1" .44 Evans cartridge. Has a butt stock that covers only the top half of revolving 34-shot magazine located in butt of rifle. Buttplate appears as if it is reversed and markings on the "Old Model" are "Evans Repeating Rifle/Pat. Dec. 8, 1868 & Sept. 16, 1871". There are three versions of Old Model listed. Manufactured between 1874 and 1876 and serial numbered 1-500.

Military Musket (Antique)

This version has 30" barrel, with two barrel bands and provisions for a bayonet. Only 50 estimated manufactured.

Exc.	Fine	V.G.	Good	Fair	Poor
8000	4500	3000	2000	800	560

Sporting Rifle (Antique)

Approximately 300 of this model produced, with 26", 28" or 30" octagonal barrel.

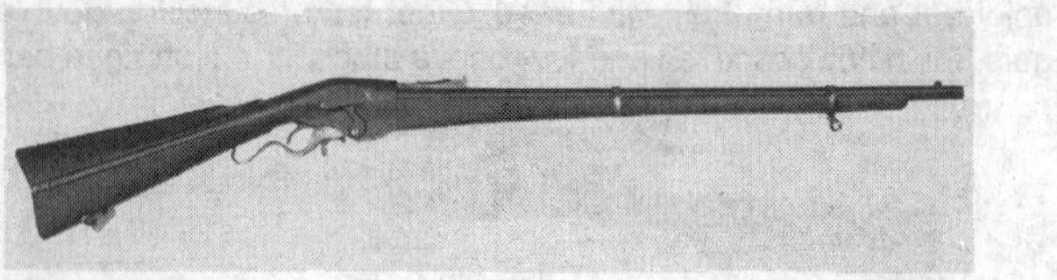

Exc.	Fine	V.G.	Good	Fair	Poor
5700	2500	1750	1500	700	480

Carbine Antique

This variation has 22" barrel, with one barrel band and sling swivel. There were 150 produced.

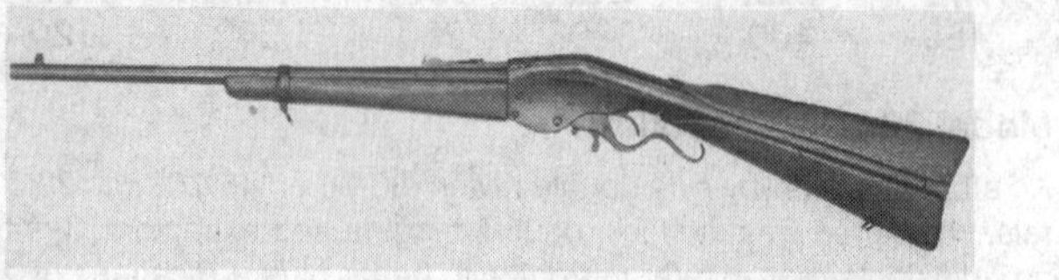

Exc.	Fine	V.G.	Good	Fair	Poor
5800	2700	1850	1200	500	350

Transitional Model

Has a buttstock that covers both top and bottom of rotary magazine, with an exposed portion in middle of the butt. Buttplate does not have backward appearance and barrel marked "Evans Repeating Rifle Mechanic Falls Me./Pat Dec. 8, 1868 & Sept. 16, 1871". This version manufactured in 1876 and 1877. Serial numbered between 500-2185, for a total of approximately 1,650 manufactured.

Military Musket Antique

Has a 30" barrel and two barrel bands. 150 were produced.

Exc.	Fine	V.G.	Good	Fair	Poor
5800	2700	1870	1250	500	350

Carbine Antique

Produced 450, with 22" barrel and one barrel band.

Exc.	Fine	V.G.	Good	Fair	Poor
5800	2700	1870	1250	500	350

Sporting Rifle Antique

Has 26", 28" or 30" barrel. There were 1,050 produced.

Exc.	Fine	V.G.	Good	Fair	Poor
5200	2600	1500	1000	500	350

Montreal Carbine Antique

Special issue marked Montreal", sold by R.H. Kilby, Evans' Canadian sales agent. Between 50 and 100 produced.

Exc.	Fine	V.G.	Good	Fair	Poor
5800	2700	1870	1250	500	350

New Model

Approximately 10,000 New Model were produced. Chambered for 1.5" .44 Evans cartridge, with magazine capacity reduced to 28. Frame was re-designed and rounded at top and forend fit flush to receiver. Lever and hammer are streamlined and a dust cover over loading gate. Markings are same as on Transitional Model, with "U.S.A." added to last line. This version was not serial numbered and any numbers found are assembly numbers only

Military Musket Antique

3,000 produced, with 30" barrel and two barrel bands.

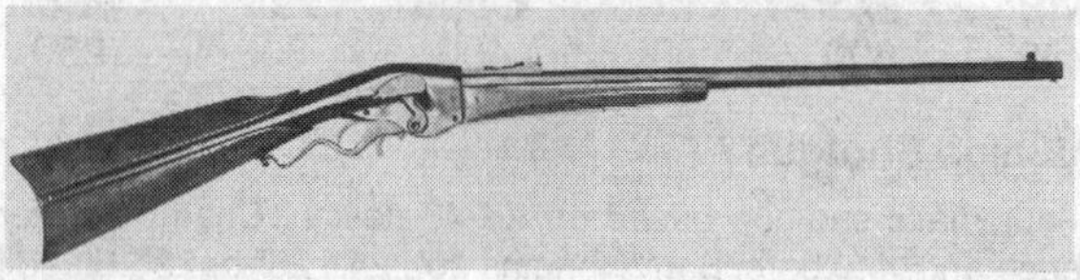

Courtesy Bonhams & Butterfields, San Francisco, California

Exc.	Fine	V.G.	Good	Fair	Poor
4000	2500	1870	1250	500	350

Carbine Antique

4,000 produced, with 22" barrel, one barrel band and sling swivel.

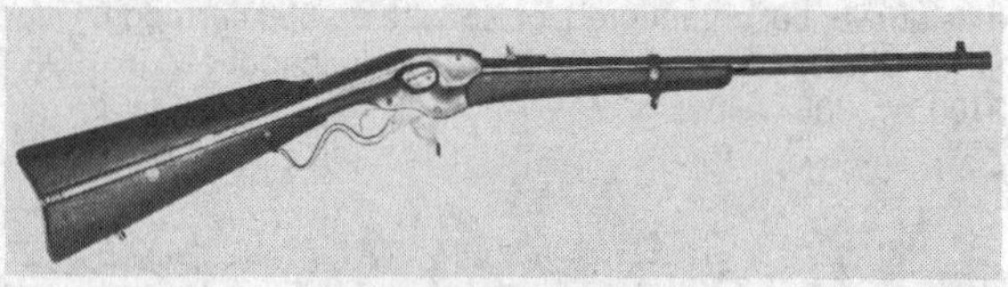

Courtesy Buffalo Bill Historical Center, Cody, Wyoming

Exc.	Fine	V.G.	Good	Fair	Poor
3500	1800	1350	900	400	280

Sporting Rifle Antique

3,000 produced, with 26", 28" or 30" octagonal barrels.

Exc.	Fine	V.G.	Good	Fair	Poor
5000	2500	1350	900	400	280

EVANS, J. E.
Philadelphia, Pennsylvania

Pocket Pistol Antique

Copy of Philadelphia-made Henry Deringer pistol. Chambered for .41-caliber. Utilizes the percussion ignition system. Barrels from 2.5" to 3" in length. Stock is walnut, with checkered grip and mountings are scroll engraved German silver. Barrel marked "J.E. Evans Philada." Manufactured in 1850s.

Exc.	Fine	V.G.	Good	Fair	Poor
2500	1850	1310	780	350	240

EXCAM
Hialeah, Florida

An importer of firearms, not a manufacturer. Erma and Uberti products imported by this company are under their own heading in this book. Other products that they imported are listed here. No longer in business.

TA 76

Patterned after Colt Single Action Army and chambered for .22 rimfire cartridge. Has a 4.75", 6" or 9" barrel and blue finish, with wood grips. Offered with brass triggerguard and backstrap. Also offered chrome-plated. A combo model with an extra .22 Magnum cylinder is available and would add 10 percent to listed values.

NIB	Exc.	V.G.	Good	Fair	Poor
—	150	100	70	40	30

TA 38 Over/Under Derringer

Two-shot derringer patterned after Remington derringer. Chambered for .38 Special cartridge. Has 3" barrels that pivot upward for loading. Blued, with checkered nylon grips. Discontinued in 1985.

NIB	Exc.	V.G.	Good	Fair	Poor
—	130	90	70	40	30

TA 90

Double-action semi-automatic copy of CZ-75, that some experts rate as the finest combat handgun in the world. Chambered for 9mm Parabellum and has a 4.75" barrel. Constructed of steel and finished with matte blue or chrome. Checkered wood or rubber grips. Detachable magazine holds 15 rounds.

NIB	Exc.	V.G.	Good	Fair	Poor
420	380	320	280	200	150

BTA-90B

Compact version of TA 90. Has a 3.5" barrel and 12-round detachable magazine. Similar in all other respects to standard model. Rubber grips only.

NIB	Exc.	V.G.	Good	Fair	Poor
420	380	320	280	200	150

TA 90 SS

Competition version of TA 90. Similar to standard model, except it is compensated and features adjustable sights. Offered blued or chrome-plated. Introduced in 1989.

NIB	Exc.	V.G.	Good	Fair	Poor
650	580	500	400	320	220

TA 41, 41C, and 41 SS

Series of pistols identical to TA 90 series, except they are chambered for .41 Action Express cartridge. Values are about 10 percent higher than 9mm versions. Introduced in 1989.

Warrior Model W 722

Double-action revolver chambered for .22 rimfire and .22 rimfire Magnum, with an interchangeable cylinder. Has a 6" barrel, adjustable sights and 8-shot cylinder capacity. Blued, with checkered plastic grips. Model not imported after 1986.

NIB	Exc.	V.G.	Good	Fair	Poor
—	150	90	50	40	20

Model W384

Double-action revolver chambered for .38 Special cartridge, with 4" or 6" ventilated rib barrel. Blued finish and plastic grips. Discontinued in 1986.

NIB	Exc.	V.G.	Good	Fair	Poor
—	180	120	100	80	50

Model W357

Similar to W384, except chambered for .357 Magnum cartridge. Discontinued in 1986.

NIB	Exc.	V.G.	Good	Fair	Poor
—	200	150	120	100	80

Targa GT 26

A blowback-operated semi-automatic pistol, chambered for .25 ACP cartridge. Has a 2.5" barrel and 6-shot detachable magazine. Finished in blue or matte chrome, with choice of alloy or steel frame. Grips are wood.

Steel Frame Version

NIB	Exc.	V.G.	Good	Fair	Poor
120	90	80	50	40	30

Alloy Frame Version

NIB	Exc.	V.G.	Good	Fair	Poor
100	80	50	40	30	20

GT 22

Semi-automatic pistol, chambered for .22 LR cartridge. Has a 4" barrel, fixed sights and 10-round magazine. Available blued or matte chrome-plated, with wooden grips.

NIB	Exc.	V.G.	Good	Fair	Poor
200	180	150	120	90	70

GT 22T

Similar to GT 22, with 6" barrel and adjustable target-type sights.

NIB	Exc.	V.G.	Good	Fair	Poor
220	200	180	150	100	80

GT 32

Blowback-operated semi-automatic pistol, chambered for .32 ACP cartridge. Has a 7-round magazine. Blued or matte chrome-plated, with wood grips.

NIB	Exc.	V.G.	Good	Fair	Poor
200	180	150	120	90	80

GT 380

Similar to GT 32, except chambered for .380 ACP cartridge.

NIB	Exc.	V.G.	Good	Fair	Poor
220	180	150	120	100	80

GT 380XE

Similar to GT 380, with 11-shot high-capacity detachable magazine.

NIB	Exc.	V.G.	Good	Fair	Poor
220	200	180	150	120	100

EXCEL INDUSTRIES

Ontario, California

Accelerator Pistol

Semi-automatic pistol currently available in .22 WMR or 5.7x28mm. Previously chambered for .22 LR, .17 HMR and .17 Mach 2. Barrel length 6.5" or 8.5" and diameter .875". Stainless steel with polymer grip. Barrel fitted with an aluminum rib, target sights and Weaver base. Magazine capacity 9 rounds. Weight about 54 oz. Introduced in 2004. Note: Add $50 to $75 for red dot optical sight or factory-mounted scope; $100 for 5.7x28mm chambering.

NIB	Exc.	V.G.	Good	Fair	Poor
420	320	250	160	120	80

Accelerator Rifle

As above, with 18" fluted stainless steel barrel and black polymer pistol grip stock. Fully adjustable removable sights on a Weaver rail. Weight about 8 lbs. Introduced in 2004.

NIB	Exc.	V.G.	Good	Fair	Poor
460	350	280	200	150	100

X-22

Blow-back semi-automatic in .22 LR, with 10- or 25-round magazine. Barrel is 4.375-in., overall length 12 in. Sights are fully adjustable. Frame is CNC-machined aluminum, with accessory rail. Rifle variation with 18-in. barrel is also available, with comparable values.

NIB	Exc.	V.G.	Good	Fair	Poor
410	340	300	230	200	180

X-57 / X-30

Centerfire series of AR-type pistols, chambered in 5.7x28mm or .30 Carbine. Magazine capacity: 25-rounds 5.7; 20-rounds .30 Carbine; 10-rounds where required by law. Features are similar to X-22 model, except barrel length is 8.5", overall length 16". Rifle variation with 18" barrel is also available, with comparable values.

NIB	Exc.	V.G.	Good	Fair	Poor
600	520	420	350	250	150

F

F-1 FIREARMS
Spring, Texas

Texas-based F-1 Firearms is a manufacturer of primarily semi-automatic AR-15-style rifles and carbines.

BDRX-15 Skeletonized Rifle

Caliber: .223 Wylde chamber for 5.56 NATO or .223 Rem., .224 Valkyrie, .300 AAC, 7.62x39mm. Modular build; user selects options on almost all components. Barrel: 16" (standard) or 18", light, medium, fluted contours, 1:8" twist. 1:10" twist on 7.62x39mm, stainless and black-nitride finishes. Upper/Lower Receivers: 7075-T6511 BDRx-15 billet receiver matched set, skeletonized. Weight: 8 lbs. Introduced 2019. 60-degree beveled magwell. SEE POLITICAL PANIC PRICING.

NIB	Exc.	V.G.	Good	Fair	Poor
1700	1600	1500	1300	—	—

BDRX-15 Special Edition Steampunk

Similar to BDRX-15, but with specific feature set. Barrel: 16-in., .223 Wylde Proof Research carbon-fiber barrel, Slay-AR brake in rose gold. F-1 Firearms grip and foregrip, minimalist stock, Hiperfire EDT2 trigger, ambi charging handle. Discontinued.

NIB	Exc.	V.G.	Good	Fair	Poor
3400	—	—	—	—	—

BDRX-10 Skeletonized Rifle

Calibers: .308 Win., 6.5 Creedmoor. Similar to the BDRX-15 line. Barrels: 16", 18", 20", 1:10" twist, medium contour (.308, 416 stainless steel), 22" Criterion (6.5 CM). Add $250 for a Proof Research carbon-fiber barrel. Large-frame DPMS high-profile compatible. Accepts all mil-spec (DPMS) patterned parts as well as SR25-pattern mags.

NIB	Exc.	V.G.	Good	Fair	Poor
2200	2100	2000	1800	1600	—

BDRX-10 Special Edition Steampunk

Similar to BDRX-10, but with specific feature set. Barrel: 16-in., Proof Research, Slay-AR brake in black DLC. F-1 Firearms grip and foregrip, Magpul CTR stock, Hiperfire EDT2 trigger, ambi charging handle. Discontinued.

NIB	Exc.	V.G.	Good	Fair	Poor
4300	—	—	—	—	—

FDR-15 Rifle

Caliber: 5.56 NATO. Mil-spec base model rifle with enhanced tolerances. 7075-T6511 lower, upper, and handrail with a match-grade barrel. Barrel: 16" medium contour, 1:8" twist.

NIB	Exc.	V.G.	Good	Fair	Poor
800	—	—	—	—	—

Fu King F15 Forged Rifle

Caliber: 5.56 NATO. FU KING F15 forged receiver set, 13" M-LOK free-float handguard, 16" 1:8" twist stainless barrel. Black nitride bolt-carrier group, mil-spec stock, grip, and charging handle. A2 flash hider.

NIB	Exc.	V.G.	Good	Fair	Poor
800	—	—	—	—	—

F.A.S.
Italy

Model 601

High-grade competition target pistol, chambered for .22 Short cartridge. Semi-automatic, with 5.5" barrel and adjustable target sights. Detachable magazine holds 5 rounds. Finish is blued, with wrap-around target grips. Discontinued in 1988.

NIB	Exc.	V.G.	Good	Fair	Poor
—	1450	1150	780	550	300

Model 602

Similar to Model 601, except chambered for .22 LR. Discontinued in 1987.

NIB	Exc.	V.G.	Good	Fair	Poor
—	1250	980	720	500	250

Model 603

Chambered for .32 S&W Wadcutter cartridge. Features adjustable grips. Discontinued in 1987.

NIB	Exc.	V.G.	Good	Fair	Poor
—	1350	1080	780	500	250

F.I.E.

Hialeah, Florida

Firearms Import and Export engaged in the business of importing Franchi shotgun (which is listed under its own heading) and Arminius revolver (which is made in Germany). They were also distributors for Titan semi-automatic pistols, which are manufactured in U.S.A. They were also importing a series of 9mm pistols from Italy, that are produced by Tanfoglio and known as TZ series. F.I.E. no longer in business as of 1990.

HANDGUNS

TZ 75

Copy of CZ 75 Czechoslovakian combat pistol, produced by Tanfoglio in Italy. A 9mm double-action semi-automatic, with 4.75" barrel, all-steel construction, fixed sights and 15-shot magazine. Offered blued or matte chrome plated, with wood or rubber grips.

NIB	Exc.	V.G.	Good	Fair	Poor
450	350	300	250	200	150

TZ 75 Series 88

Improved version that is also chambered for .41 Action Express cartridge. Has a firing pin safety and can be carried cocked and locked. Few other minor changes. Introduced in 1988.

NIB	Exc.	V.G.	Good	Fair	Poor
500	380	320	250	200	150

KG-99

Blowback-operated semi-automatic assault pistol, chambered for 9mm Parabellum cartridge. Has a 36-round magazine. Discontinued in 1984.

NIB	Exc.	V.G.	Good	Fair	Poor
550	450	350	250	200	150

Spectre Assault Pistol

Assault-type semi-automatic pistol, chambered for 9mm Parabellum. Has a 30- or 50-round magazine available. Introduced in 1989.

NIB	Exc.	V.G.	Good	Fair	Poor
800	680	580	400	300	200

Titan II .22

Semi-automatic pistol chambered for .22 LR. Has a 10-shot magazine and blued finish, with walnut grips. Made in the U.S.A.

NIB	Exc.	V.G.	Good	Fair	Poor
280	150	100	80	50	20

Titan E32

Single-action blowback-operated semi-automatic pistol, that was chambered for .32 ACP and now chambered for .380 ACP cartridge. Finish is blue or chrome-plated. Grips are walnut.

NIB	Exc.	V.G.	Good	Fair	Poor
300	180	150	120	100	80

Super Titan 11

Similar to Titan, except it has a 12-round high-capacity magazine.

NIB	Exc.	V.G.	Good	Fair	Poor
320	200	180	150	100	80

Titan 25

Smaller version of Titan Series, chambered for .25 ACP cartridge. Blued or chrome-plated.

NIB	Exc.	V.G.	Good	Fair	Poor
200	80	50	40	30	20

Titan Tigress

Similar to Titan 25, except gold-plated and cased.

NIB	Exc.	V.G.	Good	Fair	Poor
220	120	90	80	50	30

D38 Derringer

Two-shot over/under Remington-style derringer. Chambered for .38 Special cartridge and chrome-plated. Dropped from line in 1985.

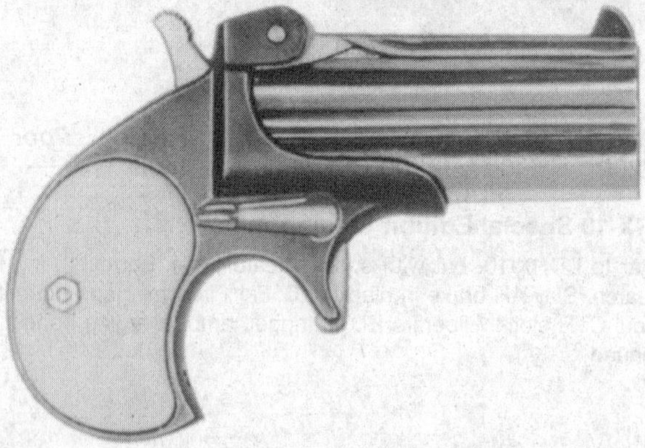

NIB	Exc.	V.G.	Good	Fair	Poor
140	80	40	40	20	20

D86 Derringer

Single-shot derringer with 3" barrel. Chambered for .38 Special cartridge and chrome-plated. An ammunition storage compartment in butt and transfer bar safety makes it safer to carry. Introduced in 1986.

NIB	Exc.	V.G.	Good	Fair	Poor
150	80	60	50	40	20

SINGLE ACTION ARMY REPLICA REVOLVERS

There is a series of single-action .22-caliber revolvers, that were patterned after Colt Single Action Army. Manufactured in U.S.A. or Brescia, Italy. They are inexpensive and of fair quality. Differences between these models are basically barrel lengths, type of sights and finish. All are chambered for .22 LR and have interchangeable .22 Magnum cylinders. We list them for reference purposes.

Cowboy

NIB	Exc.	V.G.	Good	Fair	Poor
250	120	100	80	80	50

Gold Rush

NIB	Exc.	V.G.	Good	Fair	Poor
250	120	100	80	80	50

Texas Ranger

NIB	Exc.	V.G.	Good	Fair	Poor
200	80	80	50	40	20

Buffalo Scout

Note: Add 50 percent for faux "gold" -plated Yellow Rose of Texas variant.

NIB	Exc.	V.G.	Good	Fair	Poor
180	80	70	50	40	20

Legend S.A.A.

NIB	Exc.	V.G.	Good	Fair	Poor
250	120	100	80	80	50

ARMINIUS REVOLVERS

Hombre

Single-action made in Germany by Arminius. Patterned after Colt Single Action Army revolver. Hombre chambered for .357 Magnum, .44 Magnum and .45 Colt cartridges. Offered with 5.5", 6" or 7.5" barrel. Case colored frame, blued barrel and cylinder, with smooth walnut grips. Backstrap and triggerguard offered in brass will bring a 10 percent premium.

NIB	Exc.	V.G.	Good	Fair	Poor
320	220	180	120	100	80

Model 522TB

Swing-out cylinder double-action revolver, chambered for .22 rimfire cartridge. Has a 4" barrel and blued, with wood grips.

NIB	Exc.	V.G.	Good	Fair	Poor
250	120	100	80	50	30

722

Similar to 522, with an 8-shot cylinder and 6" barrel. Available with chrome finish.

NIB	Exc.	V.G.	Good	Fair	Poor
250	120	100	80	50	30

532TB

A 7-shot double-action revolver, chambered for .32 S&W cartridge. Has a 4" barrel, adjustable sights and finished in blue or chrome.

NIB	Exc.	V.G.	Good	Fair	Poor
250	130	110	80	60	40

732B

Similar to 532TB, with 6" barrel and fixed sights. Discontinued in 1988.

NIB	Exc.	V.G.	Good	Fair	Poor
220	100	80	60	50	40

Standard Revolver

Double-action swing-out cylinder revolver. Chambered for .32 Magnum or .38 Special. Has a 4" or 6" barrel. Fixed sights and blued, with wood grips. Model made in U.S.A. Introduced in 1989.

NIB	Exc.	V.G.	Good	Fair	Poor
220	100	80	50	40	20

Models 384TB and 386TB

These two models are double-action. Chambered for .38 Special cartridge. The 384 has a 4" barrel; 386 a 6" barrel. Available in blue or chrome plate. Both discontinued in 1985.

NIB	Exc.	V.G.	Good	Fair	Poor
250	120	100	80	60	50

Model 357TB

Similar to 384TB, except chambered for .357 Magnum cartridge. Offered with 3", 4" or 6" barrel.

NIB	Exc.	V.G.	Good	Fair	Poor
250	120	100	80	60	50

222, 232, and 382TB

These models are double-action swing-out cylinder revolvers. Chambered for .22 rimfire, .32 S&W and .38 Special. They are 2"-barreled snub-nosed revolvers, with blued or chrome-plated finishes. Discontinued in 1985.

NIB	Exc.	V.G.	Good	Fair	Poor
200	100	80	50	40	20

Model 3572

Similar revolver to 382TB, except chambered for .357 Magnum cartridge. Discontinued in 1984.

NIB	Exc.	V.G.	Good	Fair	Poor
250	120	100	80	60	50

SHOTGUNS AND RIFLES

Model 122

Bolt-action rifle chambered for .22 rimfire, with 21" barrel and adjustable sights. Has a 10-shot magazine and walnut Monte Carlo stock. Introduced in 1986.

NIB	Exc.	V.G.	Good	Fair	Poor
200	100	80	50	40	20

Single-Shot

Brazilian made chambered for 12- or 20-gauge and .410 bore. Single-barrel break-open, with 25" through 30" barrel lengths. Various chokes. Blued, with a wood stock. Introduced in 1985.

NIB	Exc.	V.G.	Good	Fair	Poor
150	100	60	40	40	20

S.O.B.

Similar to single-shot, with 18.5" barrel and pistol grip instead of standard stock. Discontinued in 1984.

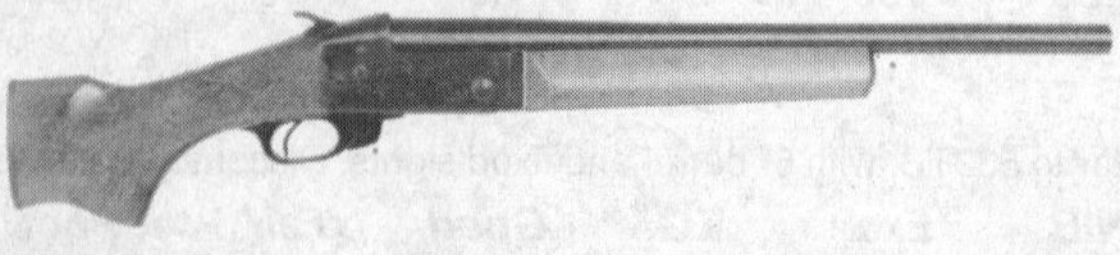

NIB	Exc.	V.G.	Good	Fair	Poor
160	110	60	40	40	20

Sturdy Over/Under

Chambered for 12- and 20-gauge. Has 3" chambers and 28" ventilated rib barrels, with various chokes. An over/under with double triggers and extractors. Frame is engraved and silver finished. Manufactured in Italy by Maroccini and imported between 1985 and 1988.

NIB	Exc.	V.G.	Good	Fair	Poor
400	300	220	180	150	100

Brute

Side-by-side chambered for 12- or 20-gauge and .410 bore. Has 19" barrels, double triggers and extractors, with a wood stock. Dropped from line in 1984.

NIB	Exc.	V.G.	Good	Fair	Poor
300	200	120	100	80	50

SPAS-12

A unique shotgun in that it can function as a pump or automatic, with the touch of a button. A paramilitary-type shotgun. Chambered for 12-gauge, with 21.5" barrel and 9-shot tube magazine. Has an alloy receiver and optional folding stock. Finish is all black. Manufactured by Franchi in Italy. Note: Some early models had detachable wood stocks. These are rarely encountered. Seek a qualified appraiser for evaluations.

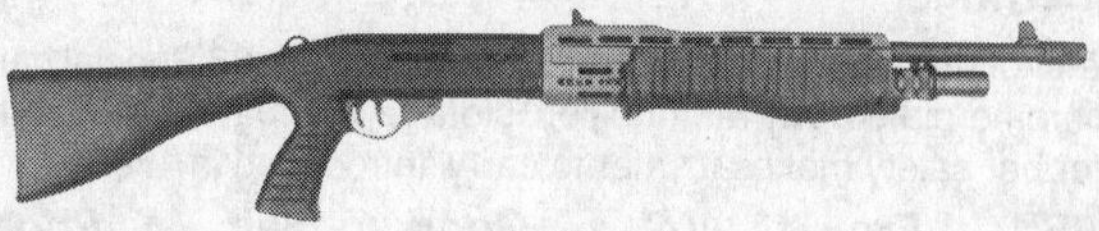

NIB	Exc.	V.G.	Good	Fair	Poor
1500	1100	900	700	400	300

LAW-12

A paramilitary-type 12-gauge semi-automatic shotgun, that is gas-operated. Has a 9-shot tube magazine. Barrel is 21.5" in length and choked Cylinder Bore. Has a military special black finish and black synthetic stock.

NIB	Exc.	V.G.	Good	Fair	Poor
850	650	400	300	200	100

SAS-12

A paramilitary-type slide-action shotgun, chambered for 12-gauge. Has a 21.5" barrel and choked Cylinder Bore. Finish is similar to LAW-12. Manufactured by Franchi in Italy.

NIB	Exc.	V.G.	Good	Fair	Poor
850	650	500	400	300	200

FABARM

Brescia, Italy

In 1998, H&K took over importation of Fabarm shotgun line in U.S. Imported by Tristar and Sig Arms from 2005 - 2009. Currently imported by Fabarm USA.

SEMI-AUTOMATIC SHOTGUNS

Ellegi Standard

Gas-operated semi-automatic shotgun, chambered for 12-gauge. Has a 28" ventilated rib barrel, with choice of choke. Receiver is blue anodized alloy, with a photo-etched game scene. Stock and forearm are checkered walnut. Introduced in 1989. Ellegi Model available in six other configurations. Differences are in barrel length and choke, type of choke tubes and finish. Basically the guns are quite similar to standard model. These variations are listed.

NIB	Exc.	V.G.	Good	Fair	Poor
700	620	520	450	350	250

Ellegi Multichoke

NIB	Exc.	V.G.	Good	Fair	Poor
700	620	520	450	350	250

Ellegi Innerchoke

NIB	Exc.	V.G.	Good	Fair	Poor
720	650	550	480	380	280

Ellegi Magnum

NIB	Exc.	V.G.	Good	Fair	Poor
720	650	550	480	380	280

Ellegi Super Goose

NIB	Exc.	V.G.	Good	Fair	Poor
800	720	620	550	450	350

Ellegi Slug

NIB	Exc.	V.G.	Good	Fair	Poor
780	700	600	520	420	320

Ellegi Police

NIB	Exc.	V.G.	Good	Fair	Poor
580	500	450	400	300	220

XLR5 Velocity

Semi-automatic 12-gauge shotgun, designed for clay target shooting. With 2.75" chamber, Turkish walnut stock, adjustable comb and rib, 30" or 32" barrel and five choke tubes. Also available in left-hand configuration. Velocity Silver model has titanium receiver. Note: Add $150 for left-hand model; $300 for Velocity Silver.

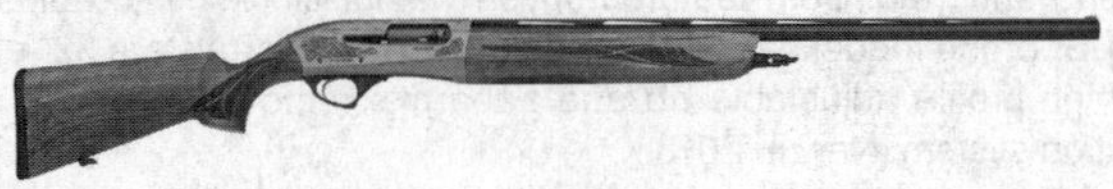

NIB	Exc.	V.G.	Good	Fair	Poor
1750	1600	1200	900	750	400

XLR Chesapeake

Gauge: 12 ga. 3 in. Barrel: 28 or 30 in. with flat rib. Stock: All-Terrain camouflage composite with soft-touch finish. Both right- and left-handed option available for each model. Features: The Italian-made, gas-operated, semi-automatic XLR Chesapeake springs from Fabarm's XLR5 family of repeaters and is built for hunters. Pulse Pistol system acts as a brake, eliminating the valve system to cycle varying ammo types. Cerakote Midnight Bronze finish on action and barrel. Red fiber-optic bar front sight. Soft comb insert and rubberized buttpad. TriBore XP barrel with tapered bore for improved patterns and lower recoil. Inner HP extended choke tubes come standard.

NIB	Exc.	V.G.	Good	Fair	Poor
1640	1400	—	—	—	—

XLR5 VelocityLR (Long Rib)

NIB	Exc.	V.G.	Good	Fair	Poor
1900	1750	1300	1000	750	400

AR (Adjustable Rib)

NIB	Exc.	V.G.	Good	Fair	Poor
2350	2050	1700	1200	750	400

L4S Initial Hunter

Semi-automatic shotgun in 12-gauge, with 26" or 28" barrel, black anodized frame and Turkish walnut stock with hand-oiled finish. Innovative feature allowing removal of forend to clean the action without removing barrel. Grey Hunter and Deluxe Hunter models feature engraved receivers and higher-grades of wood. Note: Add $400 for Grey Hunter; $700 for Deluxe Hunter.

NIB	Exc.	V.G.	Good	Fair	Poor
1050	850	650	500	400	300

L4S Grey Sporting

Designed for sporting clays in 12-gauge, with 2.75" chamber, 28" or 30" barrel with 5 Exis HP choke tubes, Tribore tapered bore and tapered rib. Extended competition style controls. Frame has titanium finish.

NIB	Exc.	V.G.	Good	Fair	Poor
1900	1550	1300	950	600	300

SLIDE-ACTION SHOTGUNS

Model S.D.A.S.S.

Chambered for 12-gauge with 3" chamber. Offered with 20" or 24.5" barrel, threaded for external choke tubes. Has 8-shot tube magazine, twin action bars, alloy receiver and matte black finish. Defensive-type shotgun and imported since 1989. Special Police and Martial Model are variations of basic slide-action. Differ in barrel length and choke. Police Model has a shrouded barrel.

NIB	Exc.	V.G.	Good	Fair	Poor
350	280	200	150	100	80

Special Police

NIB	Exc.	V.G.	Good	Fair	Poor
520	480	420	350	280	200

Martial Model

NIB	Exc.	V.G.	Good	Fair	Poor
480	420	380	300	220	180

SINGLE-SHOT SHOTGUNS

Omega Standard

Has an alloy receiver chambered for 12- or 20-gauge and .410 bore. Has 26" or 28" barrels, with various chokes. Finish is black, with a beech stock. Introduced in 1989.

NIB	Exc.	V.G.	Good	Fair	Poor
150	120	100	80	50	40

Omega Goose Gun

Chambered for 12-gauge only, with 35.5" full-choke barrel.

NIB	Exc.	V.G.	Good	Fair	Poor
200	140	120	100	80	50

SIDE-BY-SIDE SHOTGUNS

Beta Model

Double-barrel is chambered for 12-gauge only, with choice of barrel length and choke. Boxlock action, with false side plates, single trigger and automatic ejectors. Finish is blued, with checkered select walnut stock. Introduced in 1989.

NIB	Exc.	V.G.	Good	Fair	Poor
920	850	750	600	450	300

Beta Europe

Deluxe version features single-selective triggers. A game scene engraved coin-finished receiver. Stock is straight English style, with a splinter forend. Introduced in 1989.

NIB	Exc.	V.G.	Good	Fair	Poor
1750	1500	1250	1000	750	500

OVER/UNDER SHOTGUNS

Field Model

Chambered for 12-gauge. Has 29" ventilated rib barrels, with various chokes. Receiver is coin-finished and stock checkered walnut. Discontinued in 1985.

NIB	Exc.	V.G.	Good	Fair	Poor
900	700	600	500	400	300

Gamma Field

Chambered for 12- or 20-gauge. Offered with 26", 28" or 29" ventilated rib barrels and various choke combinations. Screw-in choke tubes are available and would be worth a 10 percent premium. Has a boxlock coin-finished receiver that is moderately engraved and checkered walnut stock.

NIB	Exc.	V.G.	Good	Fair	Poor
920	850	780	650	500	350

Gamma Paradox Gun

Chambered for 12-gauge only. Top barrel is rifled for accurate placement of slugs. Barrels are 25" long, with ventilated rib. Bottom barrel has three screw-in choke tubes. Has a single-selective trigger and automatic ejectors. Finish is similar to Field Model. Introduced in 1989.

NIB	Exc.	V.G.	Good	Fair	Poor
1000	900	820	750	600	450

Gamma Trap or Skeet

Competition-grade guns, with 27.5" barrel and five screw-in choke tubes on skeet model, or 29" barrel with screw-in trap chokes. Both models feature single-selective triggers and automatic ejectors; trap model has Monte Carlo stock. Moderately engraved and coin-finished boxlock actions. Introduced in 1989.

NIB	Exc.	V.G.	Good	Fair	Poor
1000	900	820	750	600	450

Gamma Sporting Competition Model

Designed for Sporting Clays and chambered for 12-gauge only. The 29" barrel has a wide rib and furnished with five screw-in choke tubes. It has single-selective trigger, automatic ejectors and checkered walnut stock, with a competition recoil pad. Finished like skeet and trap models. Introduced in 1989.

NIB	Exc.	V.G.	Good	Fair	Poor
1000	900	820	750	600	450

Elos

Over/under offered only in 20- or 28-gauge, with round action, 28" barrels, 5 choke tubes, steel or aluminum alloy frame, with case colored or titanium finish. Stock and forend are checkered Turkish walnut, with hand-rubbed oil-finish. Deluxe model features game scene engraving and premium grade Turkish walnut. Values shown are for standard 20-gauge. New in 2013. Note: Add $150 for 28-gauge; $500 for Deluxe model.

NIB	Exc.	V.G.	Good	Fair	Poor
2050	1750	1420	1100	850	450

Elos N2 Sporting

Sporting clays model with 30" or 32" barrels, 12-gauge only. Tribore tapered bore, 4 Exis HP choke tubes and adjustable trigger. Turkish walnut stock, with adjustable comb. Introduced in 2018.

NIB	Exc.	V.G.	Good	Fair	Poor
2400	2100	—	—	—	—

ELOS 2 Elite

Gauge: 12 ga. 3 in., 20 ga. 3 in. Barrels: 28 in. ventilated rib. Stock: Deluxe-grade European Walnut with matte oil finish and pistol grip design. Features: Left-handed stock option available by special order. Rich case-colored action with gold inlay of sporting birds. Hand-cut checkering. Brass front bead. Single gold-plated trigger. TriBore HP barrel and Inner HP flush-fitting chokes. Ships with Integrale case.

NIB	Exc.	V.G.	Good	Fair	Poor
2900	—	—	—	—	—

ELOS N2 Allsport Combo

Gauge: 12 ga. Barrels: 30 in. O/U with 34 in. Unsingle combo; 32 in. O/U with 34 in. Unsingle combo. Stock: Turkish Walnut with TriWood enhanced finish. Available with left-hand stock option or Modified Compact Stock with shorter LOP. Features: The Elos N2 Allsport Type T Combo is built for competition shooting. Microcell 22mm recoil pad. Quick Release Rib (QRR) rib on O/U barrels. Adjustable competition trigger. Adjustable comb. TriBore HP barrel. Hand-cut checkering. Single trigger. Includes five EXIS HP Competition extended choke tubes. Ships with hard case.

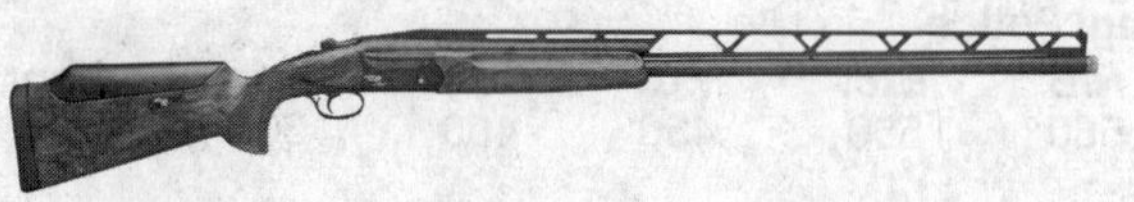

NIB	Exc.	V.G.	Good	Fair	Poor
2910	2500	—	—	—	—

Axis Competition

Competition-grade over/under in 12-gauge only. Two variants are offered: Sporting and Trap. Both feature Turkish walnut stocks, with adjustable comb. Sporting model has 30" or 32" barrels; Trap barrels are 32" or 34", with high-profile adjustable rib and Fabarm's removable Kinetik recoil reduction system. New in 2013.

Sporting

NIB	Exc.	V.G.	Good	Fair	Poor
2600	2200	1800	1250	900	450

Trap

NIB	Exc.	V.G.	Good	Fair	Poor
3700	3000	2500	1850	1100	550

H&K 1997-2004 IMPORTED SHOTGUNS

Camo Lion

Introduced in 1999, this 12-gauge model features a ported barrel system in 24", 26" or 28" lengths. Wetlands camo finish. Five choke tubes and hard plastic case included. Weight about 7 lbs.

NIB	Exc.	V.G.	Good	Fair	Poor
800	650	450	300	180	100

Red Lion

A 12-gauge semi-automatic, with 3" chambers. Has a three-shot magazine, matte finish and walnut stock. Rubber ventilated recoil pad, with leather cover and set of five choke tubes. Available with 24", 26" or 28" ventilated rib barrel. Weight about 7 lbs.

NIB	Exc.	V.G.	Good	Fair	Poor
800	650	450	300	180	100

Red Lion Ducks Unlimited 2001

Offered only through Ducks Unlimited banquet program. This is a 12-gauge, 28" barrel, with select walnut stock. Oil-finish. Unique serial numbers from 0001DU2001 to 3600DU2001. Receiver engraved with waterfowl scene and DU logo. Comes with lockable case. Limited to 3,600 shotguns.

NIB	*Exc.*	*V.G.*	*Good*	*Fair*	*Poor*
980	780	620	500	320	200

Gold Lion

Has many features of Red Lion model, with addition of high-grade oil-finished walnut stock and olive wood pistol grip cap. Trigger is gold plated.

NIB	*Exc.*	*V.G.*	*Good*	*Fair*	*Poor*
800	650	450	300	180	100

Gold Lion Mark III

Semi-automatic model is an improved version of Gold Lion. Addition of enhanced walnut stock, lightweight receiver with scroll engraving and gold inlays. Fitted with 28" TriBore barrel and chambered for 3", 12-gauge shell. Supplied with five choke tubes. Weight about 7.2 lbs.

NIB	*Exc.*	*V.G.*	*Good*	*Fair*	*Poor*
980	780	620	500	320	200

Sporting Clays Lion

Introduced in 1999. Features a ported barrel and special "TriBore" system. Offered in 12-gauge with 28" barrel. Walnut stock with rubber recoil pad, gold-plated trigger, matte blue finish, red front sight bar, 10mm channeled rib, two extra front sights (green and white) and set of five choke tubes. Weight about 7.2 lbs.

NIB	*Exc.*	*V.G.*	*Good*	*Fair*	*Poor*
980	780	620	500	320	200

Rex Lion

Introduced in 2002. Features 12-gauge, with 3" chambers and 26" or 28" ventilated rib barrel. Choke tubes. High-grade walnut stock, with olive wood grip cap. Silver and black frame, with scroll engraving and gold inlay. Weight about 7 lbs. Limited edition.

NIB	*Exc.*	*V.G.*	*Good*	*Fair*	*Poor*
1050	800	650	450	300	180

Sporting Clays Extra

Introduced in 2000. Features 28" or 30" ventilated rib barrel, with carbon fiber finish on both barrel and receiver. Also supplied with eight competition choke tubes and fitted luggage case. Stock is adjustable. Weight about 7.3 lbs.

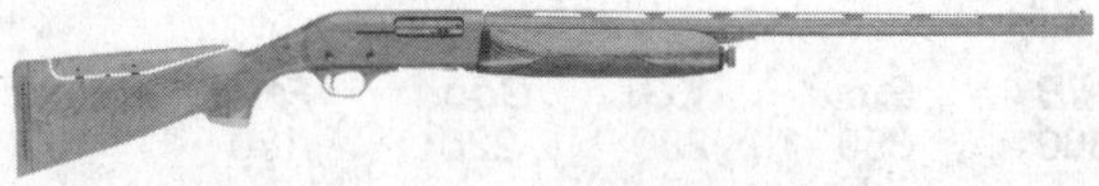

NIB	*Exc.*	*V.G.*	*Good*	*Fair*	*Poor*
850	680	450	300	180	100

Tactical Semi-Auto

A 12-gauge semi-automatic shotgun, fitted with 20" barrel threaded for chokes. Receiver-mounted Picatinny rail. Flip-up front sight. Optional magazine extension has 7-round capacity. Optional pistol grip. Weight about 6.6 lbs. Introduced in 2001.

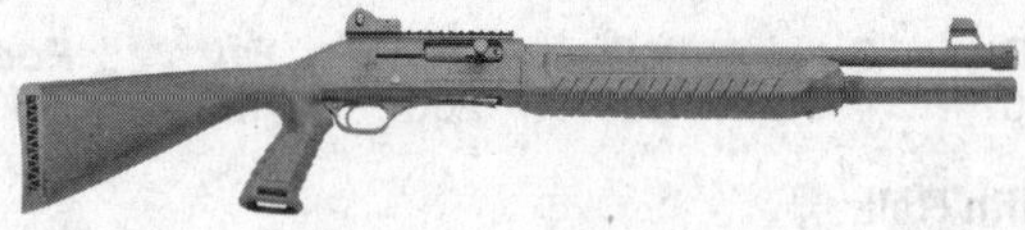

NIB	*Exc.*	*V.G.*	*Good*	*Fair*	*Poor*
650	550	400	260	150	100

Home Security HD

Semi-automatic shotgun chambered for 12-gauge 3" shell. Fitted with 20" plain barrel, with cylinder screw-in choke. Matte black finish. Black polymer stock. Magazine capacity 5 rounds. Weight about 7.5 lbs.

NIB	*Exc.*	*V.G.*	*Good*	*Fair*	*Poor*
600	480	300	220	150	100

H368

This 12-gauge 3" model, features 28" TriBore ventilated rib barrel, matte black synthetic stock or Realtree camo stock. Light-weight alloy matte black receiver. Magazine capacity 2 rounds. Weight about 7.2 lbs. Introduced in 2003. Available in a left-hand model. Note: Add $60 for camo stock; $90 for left-hand model.

NIB	*Exc.*	*V.G.*	*Good*	*Fair*	*Poor*
650	550	400	260	150	100

FP6 Field Pump

Introduced in 2001. Features black alloy receiver with screw-in chokes. Chambered for 12-gauge with 28" barrel. Black synthetic stock. Optional 24" rifled barrel. Weight about 7 lbs. Available in Mossy Oak Break-up Camo.

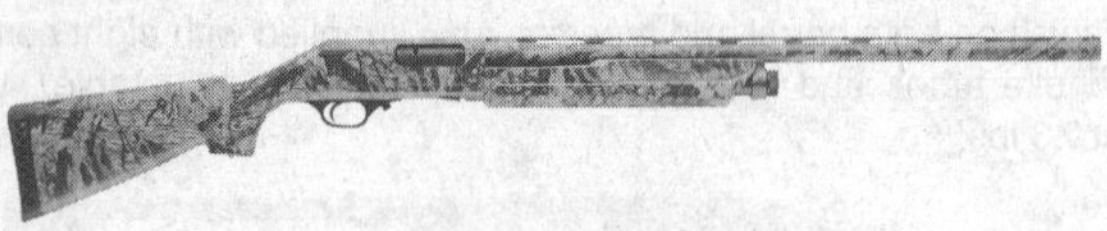

NIB	Exc.	V.G.	Good	Fair	Poor
380	350	280	220	180	100

FP6

A 12-gauge slide-action shotgun, with 3" chamber, 20" barrel, heat shield black polymer stock and threaded barrel for exterior chokes. Weight about 6.6 lbs. Available with carbon fiber finish.

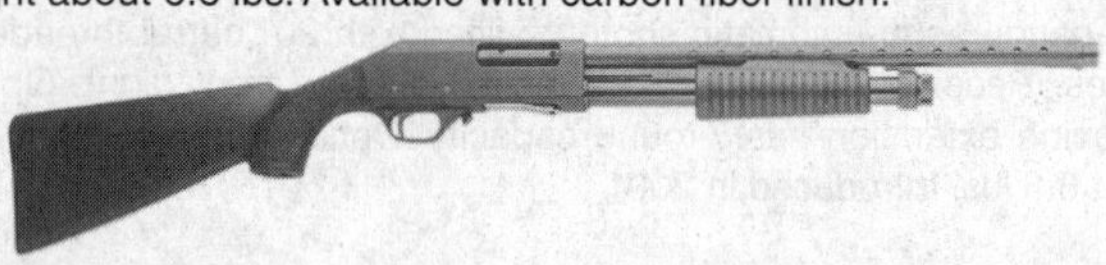

NIB	Exc.	V.G.	Good	Fair	Poor
500	400	300	200	120	100

FP6 with Rail

Introduced in 1999. Similar to standard FP6, with addition of Picatinny rail mounted on top of receiver. Also fitted with flip-up front sight. In 2003 this model offered with 20" TriBore barrel, with barrel threaded choke, new style front sight and ghost ring rear sight. Note: Available with 14" barrel. Requires BATF tax and all NFA rules apply to purchase and sale of this restricted shotgun. Accessory wire stock and pistol grip available for an additional $150.

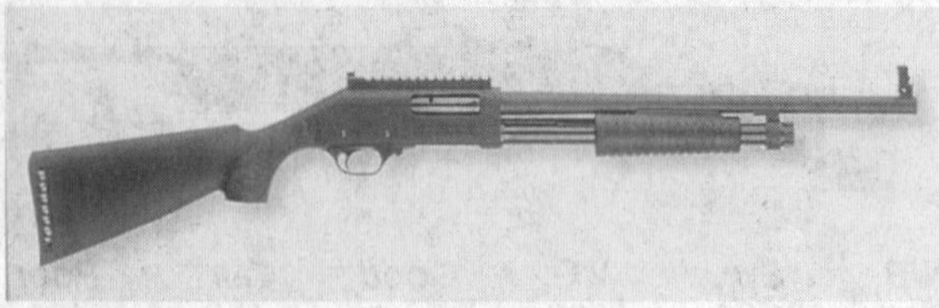

NIB	Exc.	V.G.	Good	Fair	Poor
510	410	300	200	120	100

Max Lion

This over/under gun chambered for 12- or 20-gauge, 3" shell. Fitted with single-selective trigger, auto ejectors, high grade walnut stock, leather covered recoil pad, set of five choke tubes and fitted luggage-style case. Choice of 26", 28" or 30" barrels on 12-gauge; 26" or 28" on 20-gauge. Weight about 7.5 lbs. for 12-gauge; 7 lbs. for 20-gauge. Note: In 1999 Max Lion was offered with TriBore barrel system. Models with this system add $70 to NIB price.

NIB	Exc.	V.G.	Good	Fair	Poor
1200	900	700	550	300	180

Max Lion Light

Introduced in 2000. Features 24" barrels in both 12- and 20-gauge. Receiver has gold game bird inlay. Single trigger, automatic ejectors and select walnut stock. Weight about 7 lbs.

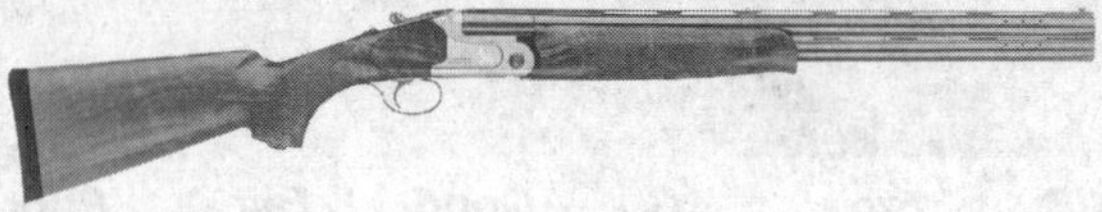

NIB	Exc.	V.G.	Good	Fair	Poor
1200	900	700	550	300	180

Max Lion Paradox

Introduced in 2002. Features 12-gauge 3" gun, with 24" barrels. Bottom barrel is rifled. Case-hardened receiver, with checkered walnut stock. Weight about 7.6 lbs.

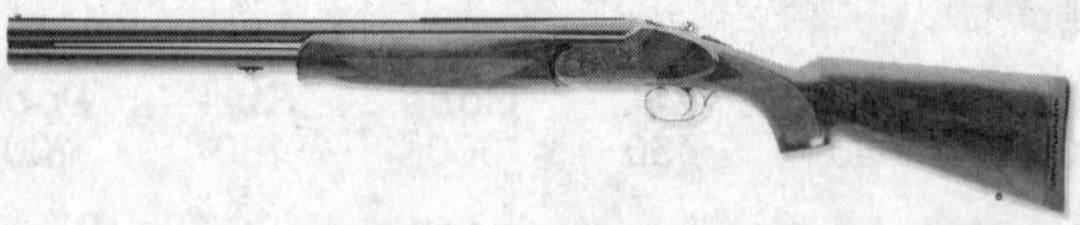

NIB	Exc.	V.G.	Good	Fair	Poor
1420	1180	900	700	550	300

Sporting Clays Competition Lion

Available in 12- or 20-gauge, with 28" 10mm channeled rib barrels. Single-selective trigger and automatic ejectors. Recoil reducer installed in buttstock. Ported barrels. Set of 5 choke tubes standard. Leather covered recoil pad. High grade walnut stock. Introduced in 1999.

NIB	Exc.	V.G.	Good	Fair	Poor
920	820	600	500	300	150

Sporting Clays Max Lion

Chambered for 12-gauge 3" shell and fitted with 32" TriBore ventilated rib barrel. Select walnut stock with hand checkering, adjustable trigger and leather covered recoil pad. Engraved gold inlay receiver is case colored. Supplied with eight choke tubes. Weight about 7.9 lbs. Introduced in 2003.

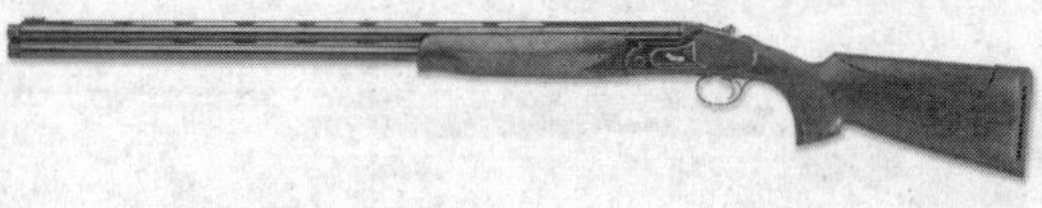

NIB	Exc.	V.G.	Good	Fair	Poor
920	820	600	500	300	150

Sporting Clays Competition Extra

This 12-gauge model features a choice of 28" or 30" barrels. Walnut stock adjustable. Finish carbon fiber. Gun supplied with set of eight choke tubes. Introduced in 2000. Weight about 7.8 lbs.

NIB	Exc.	V.G.	Good	Fair	Poor
1000	780	620	500	400	150

Black Lion Competition

Similar to Max Lion. Choice of gauges, barrel lengths and features. Less figured walnut stock and black receiver finish.

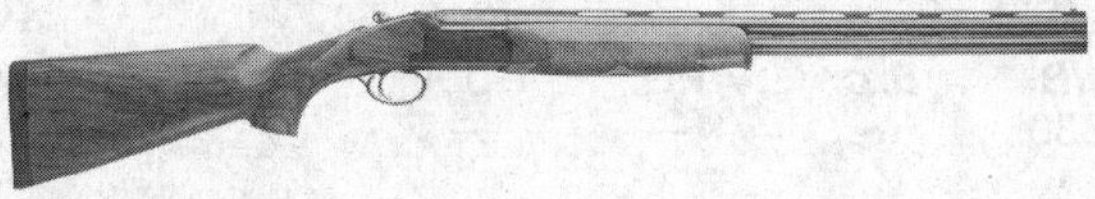

NIB	Exc.	V.G.	Good	Fair	Poor
1050	800	650	520	420	180

Monotrap

Single-barrel trap gun, with 30" ventilated rib barrel. Forearm has built-in recoil reduction system. Single-selective trigger and automatic ejectors. Adjustable comb. Shotgun is 12-gauge built on 20-gauge receiver. Weight about 6 lbs. Introduced in 2000.

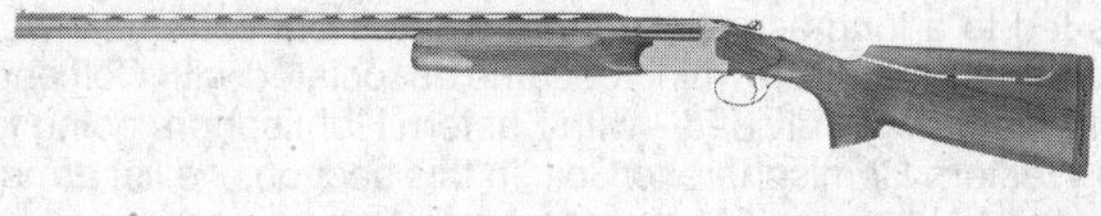

NIB	Exc.	V.G.	Good	Fair	Poor
1800	1350	1100	750	600	500

Silver Lion

Available in both 12- and 20-gauge, with 26" or 28" barrel. 30" barrels in 12-gauge. Silver finish receiver etched and stock high quality walnut, with leather covered pad. Scalable forearm standard. Single-selective trigger and auto ejectors. Five chokes tubes are included. Weight about: 7.5 lbs. 12-gauge; 7 lbs. 20-gauge.

NIB	Exc.	V.G.	Good	Fair	Poor
920	820	600	500	300	150

Silver Lion Youth

This 20-gauge over/under features shortened buttstock and 24" ported barrels. Single-selective trigger and automatic ejectors standard. Walnut stock. Rubber recoil pad. Silver steel receiver. Weight about 6 lbs. Introduced in 1999.

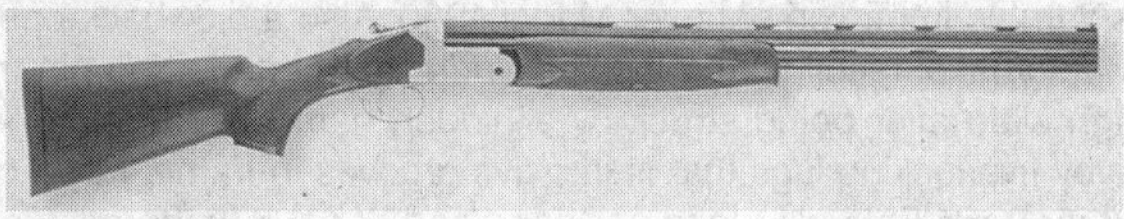

NIB	Exc.	V.G.	Good	Fair	Poor
800	780	680	500	320	150

Super Light Lion Youth

Similar to Silver Lion Youth model, but chambered for 12-gauge shells. Aluminum receiver and 24" ported barrels. Introduced in 1999. Weight about 6.5 lbs.

NIB	Exc.	V.G.	Good	Fair	Poor
800	780	680	500	320	150

Ultra Mag Lion

This model is a 12-gauge, with 3.5" chambers, black receiver, single-selective trigger, auto ejectors, blackened walnut stock, leather covered recoil pad and set of five choke tubes. Barrel length 28". Weight 7.9 lbs.

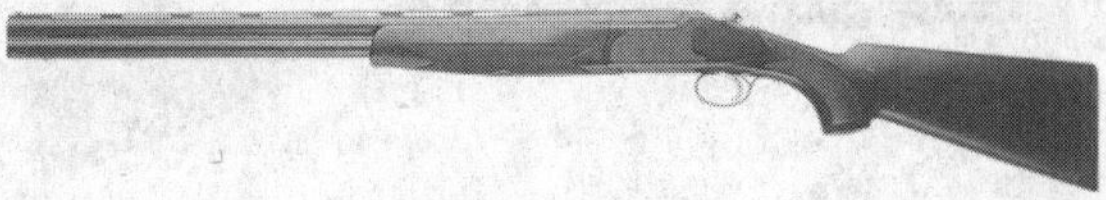

NIB	Exc.	V.G.	Good	Fair	Poor
800	780	680	500	320	150

Super Light Lion

Features lightweight alloy receiver, with 12 gauge 24" barrels, single-selective trigger, non-auto ejectors, walnut stock, five choke tubes and leather covered recoil pad. Weight about 6.5 lbs. Note: Add $125 for Tri-Bore system.

NIB	Exc.	V.G.	Good	Fair	Poor
800	780	680	500	320	150

Camo Turkey Mag

Introduced in 1999. Features unported TriBore 20" barrel. Receiver has Picatinny rail on top. Full extra brown camo finish. Chambered for 12-gauge with 3.5" chambers. Weight about 7.5 lbs.

NIB	Exc.	V.G.	Good	Fair	Poor
920	820	600	500	300	150

Ultra Camo Mag Lion

This 12-gauge 3.5" model fitted with 28" barrels. Wetlands camo pattern finish. Non-automatic ejectors. Weight about 8 lbs. Introduced in 1999. Standard with steel screw-in chokes and regular screw-in chokes.

NIB	Exc.	V.G.	Good	Fair	Poor
920	820	600	500	300	150

Classic Lion Grade I

Offered in 12-gauge with 3" chambers. Single-selective trigger, auto-ejectors, walnut stock and buttplate. Fitted with 26" barrels. Weight about 7 lbs.

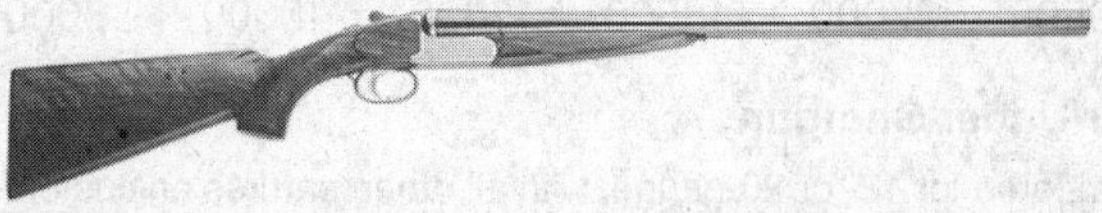

NIB	Exc.	V.G.	Good	Fair	Poor
1200	920	820	600	500	300

Classic Lion Grade II

Similar to Grade I, with addition of oil-finished stock and removable side-plates. Game scene engraving. Weight 7.2 lbs.

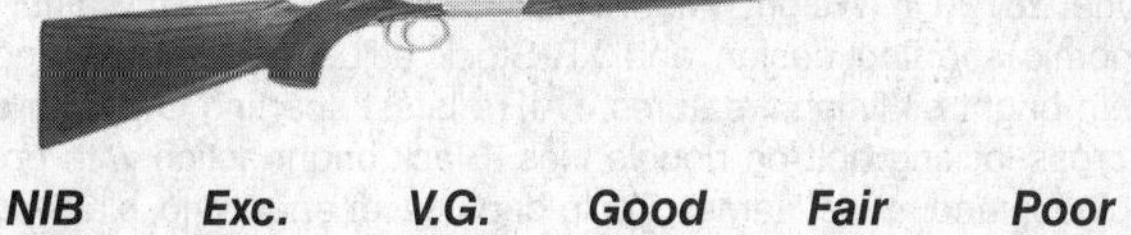

NIB	Exc.	V.G.	Good	Fair	Poor
1200	920	820	600	500	300

Classic Lion Elite

Introduced in 2002, this 12-gauge model features 26" or 28" barrels. Case colored receiver and straight-grip stock. Fixed chokes. Weight about 7 lbs.

NIB	Exc.	V.G.	Good	Fair	Poor
1300	1020	850	650	520	320

Autumn

Gauge: 20 ga. 3 in. Barrels: 28 or 30 in. with textured top rib. Weight: 5 lbs. 9 oz.–6 lbs. 2 oz. Stock: Deluxe Turkish Walnut with hand-oiled matte finish. Available in either English-style straight stock or standard pistol grip style. Left-hand option available by special order. Features: Fine grade side-by-side built in Italy. Color casehardened receiver finish with ornamental scroll engraving. Four lug locking system. Monolithic action design machined from steel forging. Splinter forend with English stock or Semi-beavertail with pistol grip stock. Hand-fit walnut buttplate. Single trigger, tang-mounted safety/selector, auto-ejectors. Ships with Integrale case. Includes five INNER HP long choke tubes.

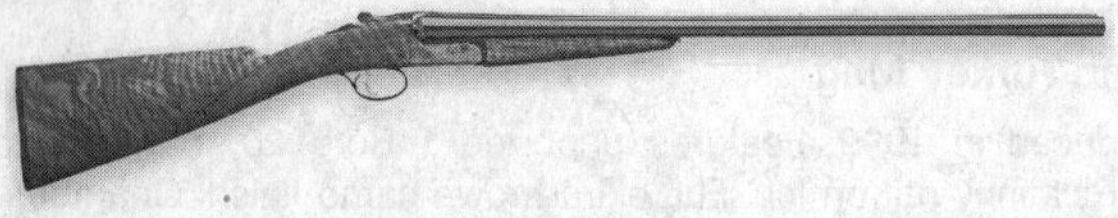

NIB	Exc.	V.G.	Good	Fair	Poor
4000	3400	—	—	—	—

FABBRI, ARMI

Gardone V.T., Italy

Fabbri Armi currently manufactures one of the best shotguns in the world. Available as a custom made-to-order item and are not often seen in the used gun market. Values for guns of this nature and quality are impossible to accurately establish in a book of this nature. There are so many options and conditions that make prices fluctuate greatly. We give an estimated figure, as a base starting point. See Karl Lippard's book Fabbri Shotguns, Colorado Springs, Colorado, VM Publications 1998, for more value details.

Side-by-Side Shotgun

Chambered for 12- or 20-gauge, with all other features on custom-order basis. Model no longer in production. Note: Deduct $10,000 for Type One Model.

NIB	Exc.	V.G.	Good	Fair	Poor
39500	27000	18500	15000	10000	8000

Over/Under Shotgun

Chambered for 12- or 20-gauge, with all other features on custom-order basis. Prices listed are for Boehler barrels. Note: Add 50 percent for vacuum arc remelted steel barrels. Deduct 50 percent for Phoenix barrels.

NIB	Exc.	V.G.	Good	Fair	Poor
41500	26000	18500	15000	10000	8000

F.A.I.R. Carrera One

Gauge: 12 ga. 3 in. Barrels: 30 in. chrome-lined with flat 11mm vent rib. Optional 28, 30 in. Weight: 7 lbs. Stock: Selected European Walnut with ergonomic sporting design and XR-Stock adjustment system (comb/heel) in bright oil finish. Features: FAIR's latest sporting O/U with oversize cross-locking bolt on double lugs. Black bright action with golden clay pigeon and model names. Triple-depth laser engraving, black selective single trigger, top tang manual safety. Long-stroke automatic ejectors. Oil-resistant ventilated rubber recoil pad. Fine-pitch laser checkering. Red fiber-optic front sight. Technichoke XP70 system with 5 tubes. Packed in V500SP case.

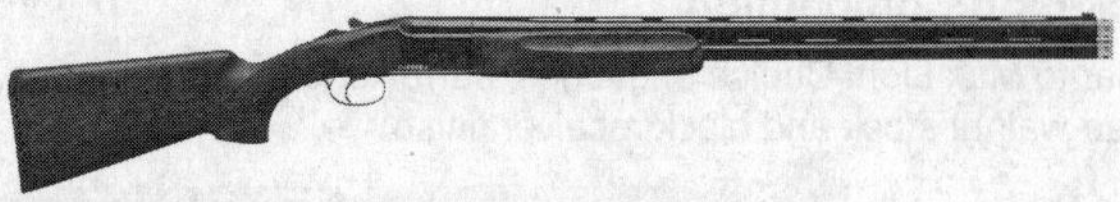

NIB	Exc.	V.G.	Good	Fair	Poor
1830	—	—	—	—	—

FABRIQUE NATIONALE

Herstal, Belgium

In 1889, Fabrique Nationale (or FN) was founded by a group of Belgian investors for the purpose of manufacturing Mauser rifles for Belgian army. This was to be accomplished under the license from Mauser, with technical assistance of Ludwig Loewe of Berlin. A few years later, in late 1890s, John Browning arrived in Europe seeking a manufacturer for his semi-automatic shotgun. He had severed his ties with Winchester, after a disagreement. This led to a long association that worked out extremely well for both parties. Later Browning became associated with Colt and the world market was divided—with Eastern Hemisphere going to FN and Western Hemisphere to Colt. In this section, we list arms that bear the FN banner. FN-manufactured firearms produced under the Browning banner, are listed in Browning section of this book.

PISTOLS

Model 1900

Blowback-operated semi-automatic pistol, chambered for 7.65mm cartridge. Has 4-in. barrel and fixed sights. Blued, with molded plastic grips. Manufactured between 1899 and 1910. Model referred to as "Old Model". Note: Add premium of 30 to 50 percent for factory nickel finish.

NIB	Exc.	V.G.	Good	Fair	Poor
—	1800	1500	1000	600	360

Model 1903

Considerable improvement over Model 1900. Also a blowback-operated semi-automatic; recoil spring located under barrel and firing pin travels through slide after being struck by a hidden hammer. Barrel is held in place by five locking lugs that fit into five grooves in frame. Pistol chambered for 9mm Browning long cartridge and has a 5-in. barrel. Finish is blued, with molded plastic grips. Detachable magazine holds 7 rounds. There is a detachable shoulder stock/holster along with a 10-round magazine that was available for this model. Accessories are extremely rare and if present, would make the package worth approximately five times that of the pistol alone. Approximately 58,000 manufactured between 1903 and 1939. Note: Add premium of 30 to 50 percent for factory nickel finish.

NIB	Exc.	V.G.	Good	Fair	Poor
—	3500	2960	2500	1500	780

Model 1905

A smaller version of Model 1903. Designed to be a pocket pistol. Chambered for 6.35mm cartridge. Became known as "Vest Pocket" and was also basis for many Eibar copies. Has 2.5" barrel and produced in two distinct variations. First variation had no safety lever or slide lock and relied on grip safety. Second variation, that occurred at approximately serial number 150,000, added this safety lever and slide lock, which helped simplify dismantling of pistol. Available blued or nickel-plated. Plated models would bring 30 to 50 percent premium. Approximately 1,086,100 manufactured between 1906 and 1959. Known in U.S. as Model 1905 and in Europe as Model 1906.

1st Variation, Under Approx. Serial Number 150,000

NIB	Exc.	V.G.	Good	Fair	Poor
750	650	500	350	200	120

2nd Variation, Over Approx. Serial Number 150,000

NIB	Exc.	V.G.	Good	Fair	Poor
650	550	400	300	180	100

Model 1910

Chambered for 7.65mm and 9mm short. Has a 3.5-in. barrel, blued and molded plastic grips. Principal difference between this model and its predecessors, is the recoil spring on Model 1910 is wrapped around the barrel. This gives the slide a more graceful tubular appearance, instead of old slab-sided look. Has triple safety features of 1906 Model, 2nd variation. This model adopted by police forces around the world. Manufactured between 1912 and 1954. Note: Add $100 for .380 (9mm Short) chambering.

Courtesy Orvel Reichert

NIB	Exc.	V.G.	Good	Fair	Poor
810	660	510	310	240	190

Model 1922

Variation of Model 1910. Made for military and police use in several European countries, between 1922 and 1944. Note: Add 75 percent if Nazi marked with original magazine; 100 percent for "WaA613" marking.

NIB	Exc.	V.G.	Good	Fair	Poor
550	400	300	200	150	120

"Baby" Model

Smaller and lighter version of Model 1906. Chambered for 6.35mm cartridge. Has 2 barrel. No grip safety or slide lock on this model. Appears to be more square in shape than Model 1906. Offered in blue, with molded plastic grips. Early models have word "Baby" molded into grips; post-1945 versions do not. Also a nickel-plated version with pearl grips. Over 500,000 of these manufactured between 1931 and 1983. Late-production specimens command a slight premium.

NIB	Exc.	V.G.	Good	Fair	Poor
800	650	500	300	220	150

MODEL 1935/HI-POWER/GP

Last design from John Browning developed between 1925 and 1935. Pistol known as Model 1935, P-35, Hi-Power or HP and also GP (which stood for "Grand Puissance") and referred to by all those names at one time or another. HP is essentially an improved version of Colt 1911 design. Swinging link replaced with fixed cam, which was less prone to wear. Chambered for 9mm Parabellum and has a 13-round detachable magazine. Only drawback to the design, that the trigger pull is not as fine as that of the 1911, as there is a transfer bar instead of stirrup arrangement. This is necessary, due to increased magazine capacity resulting in thicker grip. Barrel is 4.75" in length. External hammer with manual and magazine safety. Available with various finishes and sight options. Furnished with shoulder stock. Model 1935 used by many countries as their service pistol, as there are many variations. We list these versions and their approximate values.

Pre-War Commercial Model

Found with sliding tangent rear sight and slotted for detachable shoulder stock. Manufactured from 1935 until 1940.

Tangent Sight Version

Note: Add 50 percent for Wood holster stock..

NIB	Exc.	V.G.	Good	Fair	Poor
2800	2000	1800	1500	1000	400

Pre-War Military Contract

Model 1935 adopted by many countries as a service pistol. Following, is a list:

Belgium

NIB	Exc.	V.G.	Good	Fair	Poor
—	3000	2600	2000	600	380

Canada and China

NIB	Exc.	V.G.	Good	Fair	Poor
—	2500	2000	950	650	400

Great Britain

NIB	Exc.	V.G.	Good	Fair	Poor
—	2500	1700	1000	550	320

Estonia

NIB	Exc.	V.G.	Good	Fair	Poor
—	3750	3100	2000	600	380

Holland

NIB	Exc.	V.G.	Good	Fair	Poor
—	3000	2600	2000	650	400

Latvia

NIB	Exc.	V.G.	Good	Fair	Poor
—	3000	2600	2000	780	500

Lithuania

NIB	Exc.	V.G.	Good	Fair	Poor
—	3600	2500	1200	650	400

Romania

NIB	Exc.	V.G.	Good	Fair	Poor
—	3000	2600	2000	780	500

German Military Pistole Model 640(b)

In 1940, Germany occupied Belgium and took over the FN plant. Production of Model 1935 continued, with Germany taking the output. FN plant was assigned production code "ch" and many thousands were produced. Finish on these Nazi guns runs from as fine as Pre-war Commercial series to downright crude. Possible to see how war was progressing for Germany by finish on their weapons. One must be cautious with some of these guns as there have been fakes noted, with their backstraps cut for shoulder stocks, producing what would appear to be a more expensive variation. Individual appraisal should be secured if any doubt exists.

Fixed Sight Model

NIB	Exc.	V.G.	Good	Fair	Poor
—	1000	750	400	300	250

Tangent Sight Model

50,000 manufactured.

Courtesy Orvel Reichert

NIB	Exc.	V.G.	Good	Fair	Poor
—	2200	1600	1000	550	400

Captured Pre-war Commercial Model

These pistols were taken over when plant was occupied. Slotted for stocks and have tangent sights. Few produced between serial number 48,000 and 52,000. All noted have WA613 Nazi proof mark. Beware of fakes!

NIB	Exc.	V.G.	Good	Fair	Poor
—	1700	1400	1150	750	500

Post-War Military Contract

Manufactured from 1946, they embody some design changes—such as improved heat treating and barrel locking. Pistols produced after 1950 do not have barrels that can interchange with earlier models. Earliest models have an "A" prefix on serial number and do not have the magazine safety. Pistols were produced for many countries and there were many thousands manufactured.

Fixed Sight

NIB	Exc.	V.G.	Good	Fair	Poor
—	750	420	380	300	250

Tangent Sight

NIB	Exc.	V.G.	Good	Fair	Poor
—	1000	680	580	400	300

Slotted and Tangent Sight

NIB	Exc.	V.G.	Good	Fair	Poor
—	1500	1050	750	500	400

Post-War Commercial Model

Introduced in 1950 and 1954. Those imported into U.S.A. are marked Browning Arms Co. These pistols have commercial polished finish.

Fixed Sight

NIB	Exc.	V.G.	Good	Fair	Poor
—	850	500	350	300	250

Tangent Sight

NIB	Exc.	V.G.	Good	Fair	Poor
—	1000	650	500	400	350

Slotted and Tangent Sight

NIB	Exc.	V.G.	Good	Fair	Poor
—	1500	1100	800	550	450

RIFLES

Model 1889

NIB	Exc.	V.G.	Good	Fair	Poor
—	350	250	200	120	100

Model 1949 or SAFN 49

NIB	Exc.	V.G.	Good	Fair	Poor
—	600	500	300	220	150

Model 30-11 Sniper Rifle

NIB	Exc.	V.G.	Good	Fair	Poor
—	5000	4500	3500	2750	2000

FN-FAL

50.00—21" Rifle Model

NIB	Exc.	V.G.	Good	Fair	Poor
3000	2750	2250	2000	1850	1000

50.63—18" Paratrooper Model

NIB	Exc.	V.G.	Good	Fair	Poor
3800	3350	2950	2750	2450	1100

50.64—21" Paratrooper Model

NIB	Exc.	V.G.	Good	Fair	Poor
3300	3000	2700	2200	1900	1000

50.41—Synthetic Butt H-Bar

NIB	Exc.	V.G.	Good	Fair	Poor
2800	2400	2000	1800	1200	1000

50.42—Wood Butt H-Bar

NIB	Exc.	V.G.	Good	Fair	Poor
2800	2400	2000	1800	1200	1000

FN-FAL "G" Series (Type I Receiver)

Standard

NIB	Exc.	V.G.	Good	Fair	Poor
6500	5000	4000	3000	2000	1000

Lightweight

NIB	Exc.	V.G.	Good	Fair	Poor
6500	5000	4000	3000	2000	1000

FN CAL

NIB	Exc.	V.G.	Good	Fair	Poor
7000	6500	5000	3000	1500	1000

FNC

Note: Prices are for Belgian-made guns only.

Standard

Fixed stock, 16" or 18" barrel.

NIB	Exc.	V.G.	Good	Fair	Poor
3000	2800	2500	2000	1500	1000

Paratrooper Model

Folding stock, 16" or 18" barrel.

NIB	Exc.	V.G.	Good	Fair	Poor
3000	2800	2500	2000	1500	1000

Musketeer Sporting Rifles

Bolt-action rifle built on Mauser-action. Chambered for various popular cartridges. Has a 24" barrel and blued, with checkered walnut stock. Manufactured between 1947 and 1963.

NIB	Exc.	V.G.	Good	Fair	Poor
—	450	350	300	250	200

Deluxe Sporter

Higher-grade version of Musketeer, with same general specifications. Manufactured between 1947 and 1963.

NIB	Exc.	V.G.	Good	Fair	Poor
—	550	450	400	280	200

FN Supreme

Chambered for popular standard calibers. Has a 24" barrel, with an aperture sight and checkered walnut stock. Manufactured between 1957 and 1975.

NIB	Exc.	V.G.	Good	Fair	Poor
—	800	650	500	450	400

Supreme Magnum Model

Similar to standard Supreme, except chambered for .264 Win. Magnum, 7mm Rem. Magnum and .300 Win. Magnum. Furnished with recoil pad. Manufactured between same years as standard model.

NIB	Exc.	V.G.	Good	Fair	Poor
—	800	650	500	400	400

FAIRBANKS, A. B.

Boston, Massachusetts

Fairbanks All Metal Pistol (Antique)

Odd pistol was produced of all metal. A one-piece cast brass frame, handle, an iron barrel and lock system. Chambered for .33-caliber and utilizes percussion ignition system. Barrel lengths noted are 3" to 10". Barrels are marked "Fairbanks Boston. Cast Steel". Manufactured between 1838 and 1841.

Exc.	Fine	V.G.	Good	Fair	Poor
1500	1200	950	500	300	200

FALCON FIREARMS

Northridge, California

Portsider

Copy of Colt 1911. Built for left-handed individual. Constructed of stainless steel and similar in all other respects to Colt. Introduced in 1986. A scarce 1911.

NIB	Exc.	V.G.	Good	Fair	Poor
700	580	450	380	300	220

Portsider Set

Matching serial numbered pair. Consisting of left- and right-handed version, in a case. Only 100 manufactured in 1986 and 1987.

NIB	Exc.	V.G.	Good	Fair	Poor
1400	1250	1000	750	600	480

Gold Falcon

Frame machined from solid 17-karat gold. Slide is stainless steel and sights have diamond inlays. Engraved to customer's order. Only 50 manufactured.

NIB	Exc.	V.G.	Good	Fair	Poor
50000	30000	—	—	—	—

FAMARS, A. & S.

Brescia, Italy

A. Famars shotgun is one of the world's finest and was available on a custom order basis. This makes it quite difficult to accurately establish values in a book of this nature. We list them and give an estimated value in their basic form only. The company ceased production in 2012.

Engraving Pattern Descriptions (Older Discontinued Patterns)

S2—Traditional fully engraved fine English scroll, with coverage highlighting selected areas of receiver and forend metal. Wood grade AA.

S3—Traditional hand-engraved scroll, with some open areas around scroll coverage on receiver and forend metal. Wood grade AAA.

S4—Traditional full coverage, intricate and high in detail. Patterns may be English, German or game scene. Wood grade AAAA.

S5—Grade S4 patterns with animals inlaid in 24k gold. Wood grade AAAA.

S4E—Extremely high detail scenes and elaborate ornamental work, where subject matter is selected by customer. Wood grade AAAAA.

S5E—Similar to S4E level, but with raised or flush gold inlay work. Wood grade AAAAA.

SXO—Best work by world's best engravers. Museum quality. Wood grade AAAAAA.

Zeus

Engraved side-by-side boxlock in 12-, 20-, 28-gauge and .410 bore. Note: Add 10 percent for smaller gauges.

In the white

NIB	Exc.	V.G.	Good	Fair	Poor
19000	12000	9000	6500	4750	750

D2 pattern

NIB	Exc.	V.G.	Good	Fair	Poor
20000	12000	9000	6500	4750	750

S3 pattern

NIB	Exc.	V.G.	Good	Fair	Poor
22000	20000	12000	9000	6500	900

Tribute

Engraved side-by-side droplock, offered in 12- or 20-gauge.

In the white

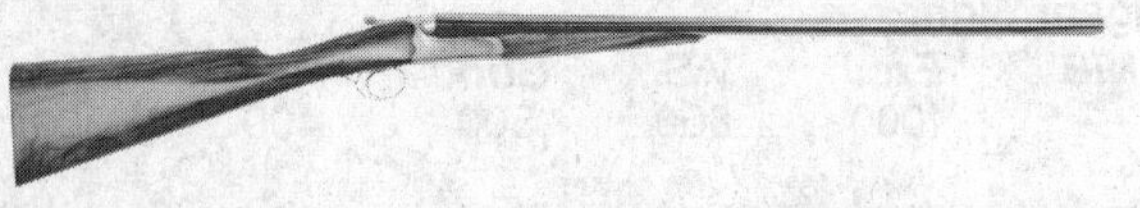

NIB	Exc.	V.G.	Good	Fair	Poor
21400	20800	12000	9000	6500	900

D2 pattern

NIB	Exc.	V.G.	Good	Fair	Poor
22600	20500	12000	9000	6500	900

S3 pattern

NIB	Exc.	V.G.	Good	Fair	Poor
24300	22000	12000	9000	6500	900

Venus

Side-by-side sidelock shotgun, with choice of engraving patterns and coverage. Offered in 12-, 20-, 28-gauge or .410 bore.

In the white

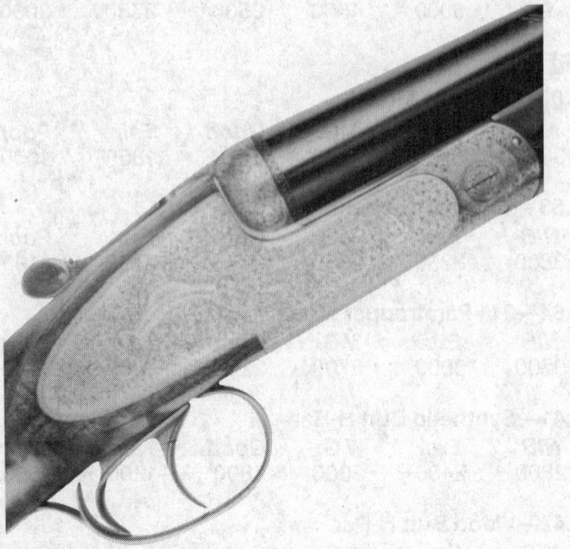

NIB	Exc.	V.G.	Good	Fair	Poor
32700	30500	20000	12000	9000	900

D2 pattern

NIB	Exc.	V.G.	Good	Fair	Poor
33900	31500	—	—	—	—

D3 pattern

NIB	Exc.	V.G.	Good	Fair	Poor
37000	10500	—	—	—	—

D4 pattern

NIB	Exc.	V.G.	Good	Fair	Poor
42800	39000	—	—	—	—

D5 pattern

NIB	Exc.	V.G.	Good	Fair	Poor
48200	42000	—	—	—	—

D4E pattern

NIB	Exc.	V.G.	Good	Fair	Poor
53500	47500	—	—	—	—

D5E pattern

NIB	Exc.	V.G.	Good	Fair	Poor
58500	51500	—	—	—	—

DXO pattern

NIB	Exc.	V.G.	Good	Fair	Poor
85000	55000	—	—	—	—

Veneri

Side-by-side sidelock shotgun.

NIB	Exc.	V.G.	Good	Fair	Poor
32000	30000	—	—	—	—

D2 pattern

NIB	Exc.	V.G.	Good	Fair	Poor
32700	30500	—	—	—	—

Jorema Royal

An over/under shotgun with sidelocks. Offered in 12-, 20-, 28-gauge and .410 bore. Note: Add 15 percent for smaller gauges.

In the white

NIB	Exc.	V.G.	Good	Fair	Poor
32700	26000	—	—	—	—

S2 pattern

NIB	Exc.	V.G.	Good	Fair	Poor
33900	20000	—	—	—	—

S3 pattern

NIB	Exc.	V.G.	Good	Fair	Poor
37300	29500	—	—	—	—

S4 pattern

NIB	Exc.	V.G.	Good	Fair	Poor
42900	33500	—	—	—	—

S5 pattern

NIB	Exc.	V.G.	Good	Fair	Poor
48200	29500	—	—	—	—

S4E pattern

NIB	Exc.	V.G.	Good	Fair	Poor
53500	42500	—	—	—	—

S5E pattern

NIB	Exc.	V.G.	Good	Fair	Poor
53500	42500	—	—	—	—

SXO pattern

NIB	Exc.	V.G.	Good	Fair	Poor
85000	66500	—	—	—	—

Excaliber BL

An over/under shotgun, with single trigger and removable trigger group. Offered in 12-, 20-, 28-gauge and .410 bore.

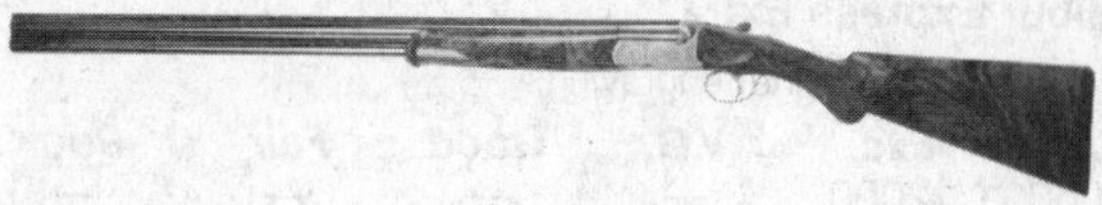

NIB	Exc.	V.G.	Good	Fair	Poor
11800	6500	—	—	—	—

Excalibur BL Extra

Finer engraving than standard.

NIB	Exc.	V.G.	Good	Fair	Poor
15460	8900	—	—	—	—

Excalibur BL Prestige

Finer engraving than BL Extra.

NIB	Exc.	V.G.	Good	Fair	Poor
17820	10750	—	—	—	—

Excalibur BLX

Over/under shotgun with sideplates.

NIB	Exc.	V.G.	Good	Fair	Poor
11150	9000	—	—	—	—

Excalibur BLX Extra

Same as above, with finer engraving.

NIB	Exc.	V.G.	Good	Fair	Poor
16760	14000	—	—	—	—

Excalibur BLX Prestige

Finer engraving than BLX Extra.

NIB	Exc.	V.G.	Good	Fair	Poor
16900	13750	—	—	—	—

Excalibur SL

Over/under shotgun with sidelocks.

NIB	Exc.	V.G.	Good	Fair	Poor
26120	14800	—	—	—	—

Excalibur SL Extra

Same as above, with finer engraving.

NIB	Exc.	V.G.	Good	Fair	Poor
30000	16000	—	—	—	—

Excalibur SL Prestige

Finer engraving than SL Extra.

NIB	Exc.	V.G.	Good	Fair	Poor
33000	18000	—	—	—	—

Excalibur Express

An over/under double rifle in calibers from 7x65R to .375 H&H.

NIB	Exc.	V.G.	Good	Fair	Poor
20200	11500	—	—	—	—

Excalibur Express Extra

Same as above, with finer engraving.

NIB	Exc.	V.G.	Good	Fair	Poor
27060	12000	—	—	—	—

Excalibur Express Prestige

Finer engraving than Express Extra.

NIB	Exc.	V.G.	Good	Fair	Poor
32060	15250	—	—	—	—

African Express

Side-by-side boxlock double rifle. Calibers from .22 Long Rifle to .600 NE.

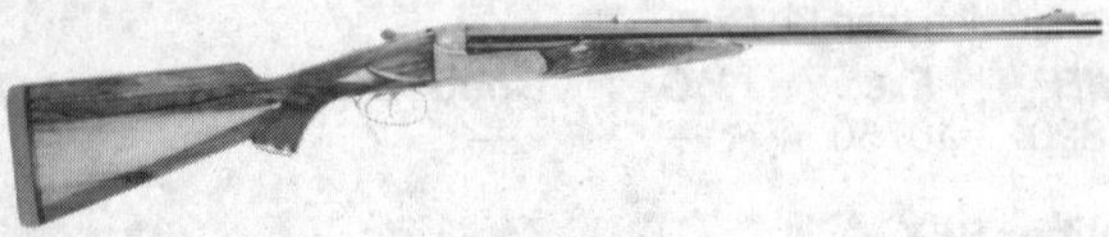

NIB	Exc.	V.G.	Good	Fair	Poor
34000	17500	—	—	—	—

Venus Express Professional

Side-by-side double rifle with sidelocks.

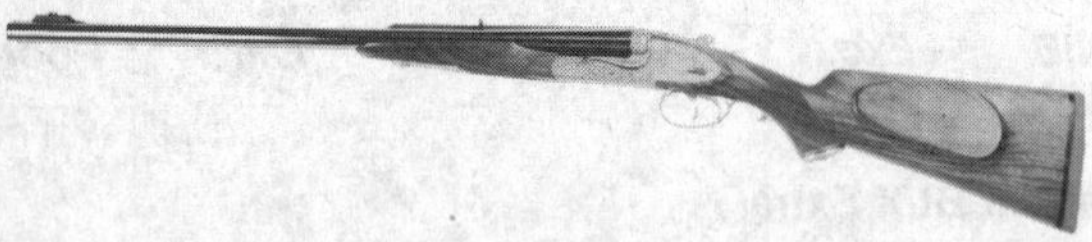

NIB	Exc.	V.G.	Good	Fair	Poor
45000	34500	—	—	—	—

Venus Express Extra

Side-by-side double rifle with sidelocks. Calibers from .375 H&H to .500 NE.

NIB	Exc.	V.G.	Good	Fair	Poor
95750	50000	—	—	—	—

FARROW ARMS CO.

Holyoke, Massachusetts
Mason, Tennessee

Farrow Falling Block Rifle

Designed by W.M. Farrow, a target shooter, who had worked on Ballard rifles for Marlin Company. Farrow rifles are chambered for various calibers and have barrel lengths from 28"- 36" of octagonal configuration. Feature tang sights and are all blued or have a nickel-plated receiver. Stocks are walnut. Two grades offered, that varied according to grade of wood used. Rifles are quite scarce on today's market. Number manufactured between 1885 and 1900 is unknown.

No. 1 Model (Antique)

Fancy walnut with checkering and Schutzen buttplate.

Exc.	Fine	V.G.	Good	Fair	Poor
13500	4500	3220	1950	750	520

No. 2 Model (Antique)

Plainer wood and no checkering.

Exc.	Fine	V.G.	Good	Fair	Poor
11000	3300	2450	1600	500	350

FAUSTI, STEFANO

Italy

Fausti has been manufacturing quality over/under and side-by-side shotguns in Italy, for the European market since 1948. In 2009, the company established an office in Fredericksburg, Virginia and now imports a wide range of models

OVER/UNDER SHOTGUNS

Low-profile boxlock design scaled to various gauges. All standard barrel lengths with five choke tubes (.410 has fixed M/F). Offered in 12-, 16-, 20-, 28-gauge and .410 bore in four grades: Caledon (shown), Caledon SL, Class and Class SL, each with increased level of walnut, laser engraving and inlays. Features include automatic ejectors, single-selective trigger, rounded pistol grip. SL models have false side plates. Prices shown are for 12- and 20-gauge models. Note: Add $500 for 16-, 28-gauge or .410 bore.

Caledon

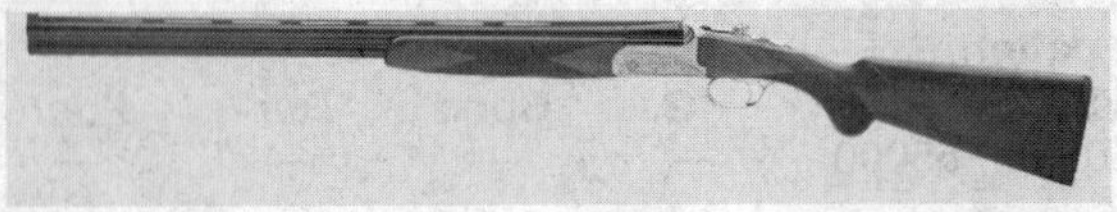

NIB	Exc.	V.G.	Good	Fair	Poor
1800	1450	1200	950	600	400

Caledon SL

NIB	Exc.	V.G.	Good	Fair	Poor
2500	2000	1600	1350	900	500

Class

NIB	Exc.	V.G.	Good	Fair	Poor
2200	1750	1400	1100	750	500

Class SL

NIB	Exc.	V.G.	Good	Fair	Poor
2900	2250	1700	1450	1000	500

Class Express

Calibers: .243 Win., 6.5x55, 6.5x57R, 7x57R, .308 Win., .270 Win., .30-06, .30R Blaser, .45-70, .444 Marlin, 9.3x74, 8x57 JRS. Barrel: 24 in. Weight: 7.6 lbs. average. Stock: A-Grade Walnut with oil finish. Pistol grip style. Sights: Fiber-optic sight on ramp, adjustable for elevation. Features: O/U double rifle in a wide range of chamberings. LOP of 14.49 in. Choice of single or double triggers, no selector. Automatic ejectors. Includes VL151 gun case.

NIB	Exc.	V.G.	Good	Fair	Poor
4750	—	—	—	—	—

Round Body

Similar to other over/under models, except built on Fausti-designed rounded receiver. AAA grade oil-finished walnut stock. Not available in 12-gauge. Prices shown are for 20-gauge. Note: Add $500 for 16-, 28-gauge or .410 bore.

NIB	Exc.	V.G.	Good	Fair	Poor
3750	3200	2600	2000	1200	500

MAGNIFICENT SERIES

Higher grade series with AAA+ walnut stock and deep-sculpted engraving. Offered in a field version and sporting clays model (shown). Prices shown are for 12- or 20-gauge. Note: Add $500 for 16-, 28-gauge or .410 bore.

Magnificent Field

NIB	Exc.	V.G.	Good	Fair	Poor
4500	3600	3000	2400	1600	700

Magnificent Sporting

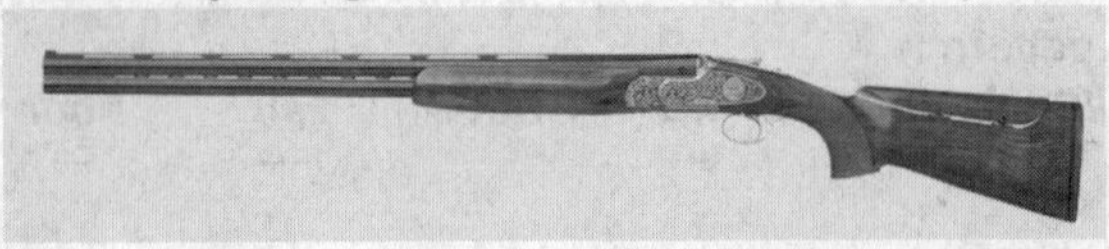

NIB	Exc.	V.G.	Good	Fair	Poor
5400	4500	3750	3000	2000	900

SIDE-BY-SIDE SHOTGUNS

Model DEA

Built on a low boxlock action, with modified Anson & Deeley mechanism. Straight-grip AAA-grade oil-finished walnut stock. Automatic ejectors, non-selective single trigger. Made in 12-, 16-, 20-, 28-gauge and .410 bore. Also offered as Duetto model, with interchangeable 28-gauge and .410 bore barrel sets. Prices shown are for 12- or 20-gauge. Note: Add $500 for other gauges; $1800 for Duetto model.

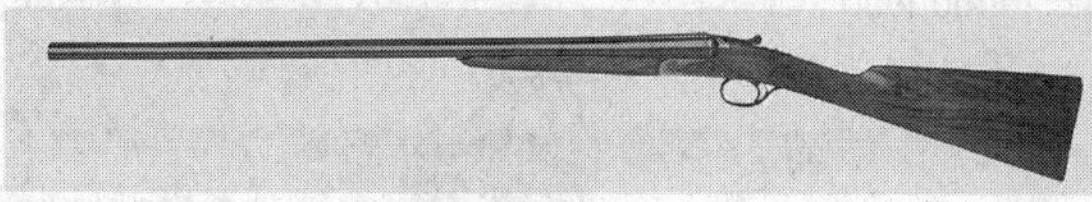

NIB	Exc.	V.G.	Good	Fair	Poor
3000	2500	2000	1600	1000	500

DEA Express

Calibers: .243 Win., 7x57R, .308 Win., .270 Win., .30-06, .30R Blaser, .45-70, .444 Marlin, 9.3x74, 8x57 JRS. Barrel: 24 in. Weight: 7 lbs. average. Stock: A-Grade Walnut with oil finish. Pistol grip style. Sights: Fiber-optic sight on ramp, adjustable for elevation. Features: SxS double rifle in a wide range of chamberings. LOP of 14.49 in. Choice of single or double triggers, no selector. Automatic ejectors. Includes VL151 gun case.

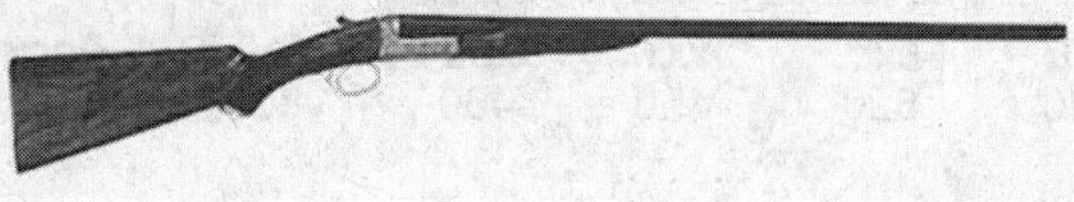

NIB	Exc.	V.G.	Good	Fair	Poor
6550	—	—	—	—	—

RIFLES

Classic Express Rifle

Over/under design, with oil-finished walnut stock, automatic ejectors and choice of double or single trigger. Calibers are .30-06, .444 Marlin, .45-70, 30R Blaser, 8x57 JRS and 9.3x74R. Barrels are 24" with adjustable fiber optic sight.

NIB	Exc.	V.G.	Good	Fair	Poor
4500	3600	3000	2400	1600	700

FAYETTEVILLE ARMORY

Fayetteville, North Carolina

In 1861, U.S. Arsenal at Fayetteville, North Carolina, was seized by officials of that state and later turned over to the government of Confederate States of America. While still controlled by the state of North Carolina, a number of inferior flintlock arms were altered at the arsenal from flint to percussion, including a number of U.S. M1836 pistols and U.S. M1819 Hall rifles (latter also shortened and re-modeled into cavalry carbines). In accordance with an agreement between the governors of Virginia and North Carolina, rifle machinery seized at the former U.S. Armory at Harpers Ferry, Virginia, was also sent to Fayetteville, where in 1862 the Confederacy began construction of rifles modeled after U.S. M1855 rifle. Production continued until 1865, when the advance of Sherman's armies necessitated evacuation of the armory.

Fayetteville Armory Percussion Pistols (U.S. M1836 Pistols, Altered) Antique

Overall length 13.25"; barrel length 8.5"; caliber .54. Markings: same as U.S. M1836 contact pistols, i.e. the locks marked with eagle head over "A. WATERS/MILBURY MS./(date)" or "US/R. JOHNSON/MIDDN CONN./(date)" and various barrel proofmarks; also occasionally marked "N. CAROLINA".

Fayetteville Armory altered approximately 900 U.S. M1836 pistols from flintlock to percussion. These arms were altered by enlarging the flint touchhole and screwing in a cylindrical drum in place of the pan and frizzen. Distinguishing feature of Fayetteville alteration is the clean-out screw at face of cylinder and "S" shaped hammer, not unlike that used on post-1862 dated rifles. No recent sales observed. Values are very speculative.

Courtesy Milwaukee Public Museum, Milwaukee, Wisconsin

Exc.	Fine	V.G.	Good	Fair	Poor
3250	1350	1150	950	400	280

Fayetteville Armory Rifles (Types I through IV) Antique

Overall length 49.125"; barrel length 33"; caliber .58. Markings: on barrel, an eagle over "C.S.A./FAYETTEVILLE" forward of the hammer and date on rounded tail. "CSA" also found on buttplates; date on top of barrel; proofmarks (eagle head, "V" and "P") on left quarter of barrel near breech.

From 1862 to early 1865, Fayetteville Armory produced four variants of old U.S. M1855 rifle on machinery that had been lent to North Carolina by Virginia, after its capture in April 1861. Earliest 1862 production (Type I) utilized unmilled lockplates captured at Harpers Ferry and distinguished by having a "hump" (where the Maynard primer would have been milled) that extends to arc of hammer. Type II production utilized newly made locks received from Richmond during balance of 1862; they had a relatively low "hump" whose upper surface matched contour of stock. By end of 1862, Fayetteville was producing its own lock, the plate of which resembled U.S. M1861 rifle musket, but with a distinctive "S" shaped hammer. This lock distinguishes both Type III and Type IV production. All rifles made through 1863 continued to bear a saber bayonet lug on right side of barrel. In 1864, however, this was eliminated in favor of a triangular socket bayonet. Absence of the saber bayonet lug and remodeled front sight distinguishes Type IV production. Because the barrel machinery went to Richmond, production at Fayetteville was continually hindered, seldom reaching more than 300 per month in three years that Fayetteville rifle was manufactured. (Note: Rarity of Type I production will usually generate a premium for that variant.)

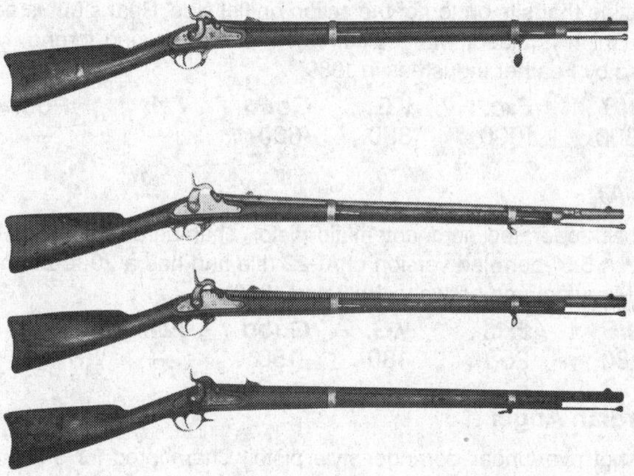

Courtesy Milwaukee Public Museum, Milwaukee, Wisconsin

Exc.	Fine	V.G.	Good	Fair	Poor
50000	25000	15000	7000	2000	600

FEATHER INDUSTRIES, INC.
Trinidad, Colorado

In 1998, Feather centerfire carbines design was changed to use Uzi magazines. In 2008, it was changed again to use Glock magazines.

AT-22

Blowback-operated semi-automatic chambered for .22 LR cartridge. Removable shrouded 17" barrel and folding metal stock. Adjustable sights and finish is black. Detachable 20-round magazine. Introduced in 1986.

NIB	Exc.	V.G.	Good	Fair	Poor
450	200	180	150	—	—

AT-9

Similar to AT-22, except chambered for 9mm Parabellum cartridge. Has a 16" barrel and 32-round magazine. Introduced in 1988.

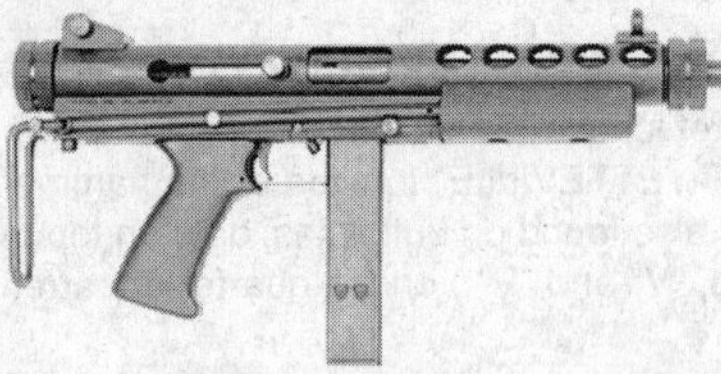

NIB	Exc.	V.G.	Good	Fair	Poor
800	680	300	250	—	—

KG-9

A 9mm semi-automatic assault rifle. Introduced in 1989.

NIB	Exc.	V.G.	Good	Fair	Poor
720	500	420	380	—	—

KG-22

Similar in appearance to KG-9, except chambered for .22 LR. Has a 20-round detachable magazine. Introduced in 1989.

NIB	Exc.	V.G.	Good	Fair	Poor
400	280	220	180	—	—

SAR-180

Current incarnation of old American 180, which was manufactured in Austria a number of years ago. Chambered for .22 LR and has a 17.5" barrel. Blowback-operated semi-automatic, that has a 165-round drum magazine that sits on top of the action on flat side. Rear sight is adjustable. Finish is blued, with walnut stock, pistol grip and forend. Model revived by Feather Industries in 1989.

NIB	Exc.	V.G.	Good	Fair	Poor
1200	1000	850	600	—	—

Mini-AT

Blowback-operated semi-automatic pistol, chambered for .22 LR cartridge. A 5.5"-barreled version of AT-22 rifle and has a 20-round magazine. Manufactured between 1986 and 1989.

NIB	Exc.	V.G.	Good	Fair	Poor
380	250	180	150	—	—

Guardian Angel

Two-shot over/under derringer-style pistol. Chambered for 9mm Parabellum. Can be converted to fire .38 Super cartridge. Constructed of stainless steel and has an internal hammer and fully enclosed trigger. Introduced in 1988.

NIB	Exc.	V.G.	Good	Fair	Poor
220	120	100	80	—	—

FEDERAL ENGINEERING CORP.
Chicago, Illinois

XC-220

Blowback-operated semi-automatic rifle, chambered for .22 LR cartridge. Has a 16.5" barrel and steel receiver that is blued. Stock is black synthetic. Introduced in 1984.

NIB	Exc.	V.G.	Good	Fair	Poor
650	450	380	220	180	120

XC-450

Similar in appearance to XC-220, except chambered for .45 ACP cartridge. Has a 30-round detachable magazine.

NIB	Exc.	V.G.	Good	Fair	Poor
750	520	450	400	300	250

XC-900

A 9mm Parabellum version of same basic firearm. Has a 32-round magazine. Introduced in 1984.

NIB	Exc.	V.G.	Good	Fair	Poor
750	520	450	400	300	250

FEDERAL ORDNANCE, INC.
South El Monte, California

An importer, as well as a manufacturer, that basically fabricates new and custom firearms out of existing older military parts. Firearms they import are military surplus weapons. Firearms covered here are of Federal Ordnance manufacture.

M-14 Semi-Automatic

Semi-automatic version of M-14 service rifle. Constructed of a newly manufactured receiver, that has no selector and select surplus G.I. parts. Re-finished to original specifications. Furnished with 20-round magazine. Has wood or fiberglass stock. Introduced in 1986. Although this model is a battle rifle and falls into the category affected by, wild price fluctuations, we have been experiencing prices for this gun staying fairly stable due to a fairly constant supply. Manufactured since 1986.

NIB	Exc.	V.G.	Good	Fair	Poor
1200	900	700	600	450	380

Model 714 Broomhandle Mauser

Re-manufactured C96-type pistol, chambered for 7.63mm or 9mm Parabellum. Utilizes a new manufactured frame and surplus parts. Features a 10-round detachable magazine, adjustable sights and walnut grips. Manufactured 1986 to 1991. Bolo Model, with a smaller grip, produced in 1988 only.

NIB	Exc.	V.G.	Good	Fair	Poor
650	500	400	300	250	100

Model 713 Mauser Carbine

A 16"-barreled version of Mauser, with fixed walnut stock. Standard magazine. Chambered for 7.63mm or 9mm Parabellum. Re-finished. Introduced in 1987.

NIB	Exc.	V.G.	Good	Fair	Poor
—	1250	1000	900	700	580

Model 713 Deluxe

Chambered for 7.63mm. Has 16" barrel, with detachable shoulder stock made of deluxe walnut. Modified to accept detachable magazines. Furnished with two 20-shot units. Has 1000-meter adjustable sight. Furnished in a fitted leather case. Only 1,500 manufactured in 1986.

NIB	*Exc.*	*V.G.*	*Good*	*Fair*	*Poor*
2000	1750	1500	1250	1000	800

Standard Broomhandle

Re-furbished surplus C-96 Mauser pistol, with new 7.63mm or 9mm barrel. All springs are replaced and entire gun re-finished. Furnished with shoulder stock/holster of Chinese manufacture.

NIB	*Exc.*	*V.G.*	*Good*	*Fair*	*Poor*
800	650	520	450	350	280

Ranger 1911A1

Federal Ordnance's version of 1911A1 Colt service pistol. Made of all steel, chambered for .45 ACP, has checkered walnut grips and phiosphate-style finish. Introduced in 1988.

NIB	*Exc.*	*V.G.*	*Good*	*Fair*	*Poor*
500	380	320	280	220	150

FEG (FEGYVER ES GAZKESZULEKGYAR)

Budapest, Hungary

Rudolf Frommer, was a first-class engineer, who became associated with Fegyvergyar in 1896. In 1900, he became manager and held that position until his retirement in 1935. He died one year later in 1936. His designs were successful and prolific. They were used militarily and sold on the commercial market as well.

PISTOLS

Model 1901

An odd pistol that was not successful at all. Chambered for 8mm cartridge, that was the forerunner of 8mm Roth Steyr. Has long slender barrel, which was actually a collar with the barrel within. A rotary bolt, external hammer and is recoil-operated. There is a 10-round integral magazine and is loaded from top via a stripper clip. Manufactured from 1903 to 1905.

Courtesy James Rankin

NIB	*Exc.*	*V.G.*	*Good*	*Fair*	*Poor*
—	2450	1800	1000	700	350

Model 1906

Improved version of 1901, chambered for 7.65mm Roth-Sauer cartridge. For all intents and purposes, the same action; on later models a detachable 10-round magazine was adopted. Manufactured between 1906 and 1910 in small quantities.

NIB	*Exc.*	*V.G.*	*Good*	*Fair*	*Poor*
—	2300	1750	1000	700	350

Model 1910

Final version in this series of pistols, with the addition of grip safety. Chambered for 7.65mm Browning.

NIB	*Exc.*	*V.G.*	*Good*	*Fair*	*Poor*
—	2600	1950	1100	700	350

Frommer Stop Model 1912

Semi-automatic pistol in caliber 7.65mm or 9mmK. Unusual, in that it operates on a long recoil system. Frommer is stamped on the slide, as well as Frommer Stop logo on each side of wood or plastic grip plates.

Courtesy James Rankin

NIB	*Exc.*	*V.G.*	*Good*	*Fair*	*Poor*
—	450	300	220	150	50

Frommer Baby Model

Smaller version of Stop Model 1912. Designed as a pocket pistol, with 2" barrel and chambered for same calibers. Manufactured at the same time as Stop Model.

Courtesy James Rankin

NIB	Exc.	V.G.	Good	Fair	Poor
—	380	250	200	120	80

Frommer Lilliput

Pocket pistol chambered for 6.35mm and outwardly resembles Baby. Actually a simple blowback-operated semi-automatic pistol. A good deal less complex to produce. Introduced in 1921.

Courtesy James Rankin

NIB	Exc.	V.G.	Good	Fair	Poor
—	350	220	180	120	80

Model 1929

Semi-automatic pistol in 9mmK. Based on Browning designed blowback-action. Pistol replaced earlier models. Few made in .22 LR.

Courtesy James Rankin

NIB	Exc.	V.G.	Good	Fair	Poor
—	450	350	220	180	100

.22 Caliber

NIB	Exc.	V.G.	Good	Fair	Poor
—	980	820	720	450	250

Model 1937

Semi-automatic pistol in caliber 7.65mm or 9mmK. Pistol was designed by Frommer and manufactured by Femaru. Also known as Model 1937.

Courtesy James Rankin

Nazi Proofed 7.65mm Version

NIB	Exc.	V.G.	Good	Fair	Poor
—	450	350	220	180	100

9mm Short Hungarian Military Version

NIB	Exc.	V.G.	Good	Fair	Poor
—	420	320	200	180	100

Model R-9

Copy of Browning Hi-Power semi-automatic pistol. Chambered for 9mm Parabellum and has a 4.75" barrel. Frame is steel and finish is blued, with checkered wood grips. Detachable magazine holds 13 shots and sights are fixed. Imported in 1986 and 1987 only.

NIB	Exc.	V.G.	Good	Fair	Poor
—	380	250	220	180	100

Model AP-9

Pistol has been manufactured in Hungary, under a number of different names. Known as AP-9, Walam 48, AP-66 and Attila. Semi-automatic pistol in calibers 7.65mm and 9mmK. Similar to Walther Model PP. Has a 7-round magazine and alloy frame. Various styles of grip plates.

Courtesy James Rankin

NIB	Exc.	V.G.	Good	Fair	Poor
—	320	200	150	100	50

Model PPH

Copy of Walther PP, chambered for .380 ACP cartridge. Double-action semi-automatic, with 3" barrel. Alloy frame, blued finish, with thumb rest checkered plastic grips. Imported in 1986 and 1987 only.

NIB	Exc.	V.G.	Good	Fair	Poor
—	350	200	180	100	80

Model B9R

Semi-automatic pistol, chambered for .380 ACP cartridge. Fitted with a 4" barrel. Features double-/single-action trigger operation. Frame is alloy. Weight about 25 oz. Magazine capacity 15 rounds.

NIB	Exc.	V.G.	Good	Fair	Poor
380	220	200	180	120	80

RK 59

Hungary's first domestically produced military and police semi-automatic blowback pistol in 9mm Makarov caliber, to replace older M48 Tokarev-style pistol in 7.62x25mm. The RK 59 has an aluminum frame that was found to be an economically attractive move, however, it was soon learned that the frame was prone to accelerated wear due to the soft nature of aluminum coupled with the 9mm Makarov cartridge. It lasted in service but two years, only to be replaced by the R 61. Blue steel slide, with markings of RK 59, caliber and Communist Kadar crest. Less than 1,900 were imported from 1993 to 1996. Scarce.

NIB	Exc.	V.G.	Good	Fair	Poor
—	700	550	450	380	280

R 61

This improved version of RK 59 was identical with its two-tone appearance, however, Hungary's engineers at FEG learned that a one percent mix of Titanium sufficiently hardened the aluminum frame to withstand the stress of the somewhat high velocity 9mm Makarov cartridge. The seven-shot pistol was officially replaced for the military upon introduction of the PA 63 in 1964. Production continued into the 1970s and it was used mainly by police organizations during that time. Imported primarily in the 1990s by the now defunct KBI of Harrisburg, PA, some R 61 pistols were re-chambered to use the .380 ACP cartridge with most marked as such on the exposed chamber. Deduct 20 percent for such conversions. As with the RK 59, it is comparable in size to the Walther PPK.

NIB	Exc.	V.G.	Good	Fair	Poor
—	480	400	350	250	200

Model PA-63

Same as above, but chambered for 9mm Makarov (9x18mm) cartridge.

NIB	Exc.	V.G.	Good	Fair	Poor
—	280	180	120	100	50

Model FP-9

Copy of Browning Hi-Power pistol. Chambered for 9mm Luger cartridge. Features walnut checkered grip, with blue finish. Barrel 5" and overall length 8". Top of slide features full-length ventilated rib, with fixed sights. Weight 35 oz. Magazine capacity 14 rounds.

NIB	Exc.	V.G.	Good	Fair	Poor
300	180	150	120	90	70

Model P9R

Similar to model above and follows Browning Hi-Power lines, with exception of ventilated rib. Barrel length 4.66". Pistol offered in blue or chrome finish. Magazine capacity 15 rounds.

Blue

NIB	Exc.	V.G.	Good	Fair	Poor
450	400	320	250	200	150

Chrome

NIB	Exc.	V.G.	Good	Fair	Poor
480	420	350	280	240	160

Model P9RK

Similar to model above. Fitted with 4.12" barrel and 7.5" overall length. Finger grooves on front and backstrap are serrated. Weight about 34 oz.

NIB	Exc.	V.G.	Good	Fair	Poor
300	200	150	120	90	70

RIFLES

SA-2000-M

Introduced in 1999. A semi-automatic rifle chambered for 7.62x39mm or .223 cartridge. Fitted with detachable 10-round magazine, synthetic stock and muzzle brake.

NIB	Exc.	V.G.	Good	Fair	Poor
580	450	350	250	150	100

AMD-65 AK47

Hungarian AK-47 clone, chambered in 7.62xc39. Fixed or folding-stock versions are available.

NIB	Exc.	V.G.	Good	Fair	Poor
650	500	380	280	180	120

FEINWERKBAU

Oberndorf, Germany

Known predominately for production of high quality, extremely accurate air rifles and pistols. They also produce some of the most accurate target .22-caliber firearms in the world today. These firearms are listed:

Model 2000 Universal

Single-shot bolt-action target rifle, chambered for .22 rimfire cartridge. Has a 26.5" barrel, with adjustable aperture sights and fully adjustable trigger. There were four different stock configurations offered, with stippled pistol grips and forearms. An electronic trigger was available as a $450 option. Discontinued in 1988.

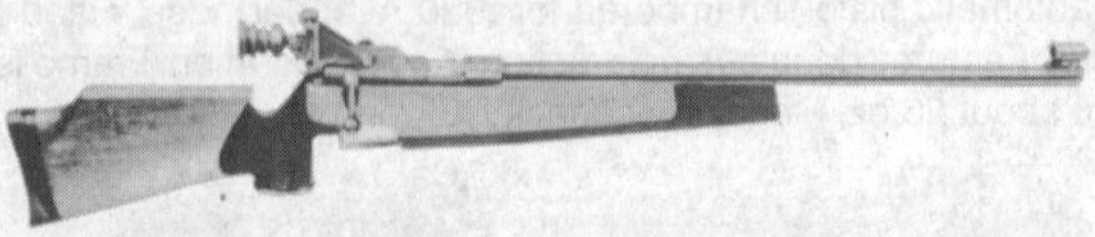

NIB	Exc.	V.G.	Good	Fair	Poor
—	1800	1250	950	650	550

Mini 2000

Has a 22" barrel. Electronic trigger available at additional cost.

NIB	Exc.	V.G.	Good	Fair	Poor
—	1550	1050	850	550	450

Running Boar Rifle

Has a thumbhole stock, with an adjustable cheekpiece. Furnished without sights. Specially designed for offhand Running Boar Competitions.

NIB	Exc.	V.G.	Good	Fair	Poor
—	1800	1250	950	650	550

Match Rifle

Has 26.75" barrel and adjustable cheekpiece stock.

NIB	Exc.	V.G.	Good	Fair	Poor
—	1650	1100	850	550	450

Model 2600 Ultra Match Free Rifle

Similar to Model 2000, with laminated thumbhole stock. Heavy 26" barrel, fully adjustable sights and trigger. Offered with electronic trigger for an additional $400. Introduced in 1986.

NIB	Exc.	V.G.	Good	Fair	Poor
1950	1400	1150	850	650	550

FEMARU

Budapest, Hungary

Hungary became a communist satellite in the mid-1950s. At this time, Femaru company was designated to replace the firm of Fegyvergyar, as the official Hungarian arms manufacturer. The products are of good quality.

Model 37

Semi-automatic pistol built in both 7.65mm and 9mm Short calibers. Well designed pistol of quality construction. Fitted with a grip safety and exposed hammer. Hungarian military adopted the pistol in 1937. Produced until late 1940s. Early guns were marked "Femaru Fegyver es Gepgyar RT Budapest". During the war, Nazi code for these guns was "jhv". The 9mm have a 7-round magazine; 7.65mm an 8-round. During World War II the Germans designed this pistol the "Pistol Mod 37 Kal 7.65 (Ung)". Note: Add 75 percent for Nazi proofed examples.

Courtesy Richard M. Kumor, Sr.

NIB	Exc.	V.G.	Good	Fair	Poor
—	350	280	220	150	100

Hege

Complete copy of Walther PP. Chambered for 7.65mm. Manufactured to be sold by Hegewaffen of Germany. Slide is so marked along with Pegasus in a circle. Designation "AP 66 Cal.7.65" also appears. Pistol intended for export sales in U.S. and other western countries.

NIB	Exc.	V.G.	Good	Fair	Poor
—	350	220	180	120	100

Tokagypt

15,000 of these pistols built in 1958, under contract for the Egyptian army. Modified version of Soviet TT-33 Tokarev, chambered for 9mm Parabellum, with a safety added. Balance were sold commercially, some under trademark "Firebird".

NIB	Exc.	V.G.	Good	Fair	Poor
—	480	350	280	200	120

Walam

Another Walther PP copy of excellent quality. Chambered for 9mm short or .380 ACP. Pistols sold on commercial market—some designated Model 48.

NIB	Exc.	V.G.	Good	Fair	Poor
—	350	220	180	120	100

FERLIB
Gardone V.T., Italy

From 2000 to 2005, Dakota Arms Inc. was the importer and distributor of Ferlib shotguns into the United States. See Dakota Arms Inc. listing in this edition for more information on models distributed by Dakota Arms.

Model F.VI

High-grade side-by-side shotgun. Chambered for all gauges and essentially custom-ordered. Available in various barrel lengths and chokes. Anson and Deeley boxlock-action, double triggers and automatic ejectors. Action is case colored and stock is hand-checkered select walnut. Single-selective triggers are available for an additional $375. Note: Add 10 percent for 28-gauge and .410 bore.

NIB	Exc.	V.G.	Good	Fair	Poor
4750	3600	—	—	—	—

Model F.VII

Has scroll-engraved coin-finished frame, but otherwise similar to Model F.VI. Single trigger option and small gauge premium are same.

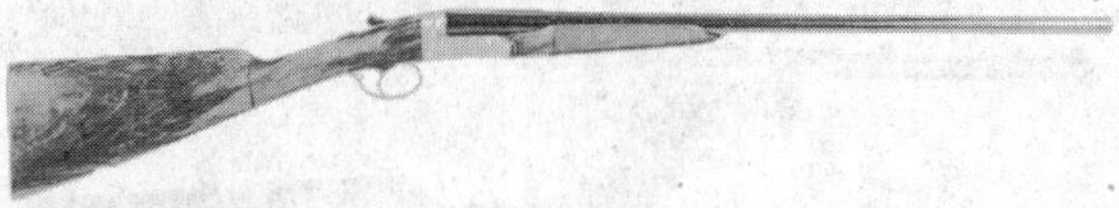

NIB	Exc.	V.G.	Good	Fair	Poor
12000	8500	—	—	—	—

Model F.VII/SC

More deluxe version, with gold inlays and game scene-engraved receiver. Options and premium are same.

NIB	Exc.	V.G.	Good	Fair	Poor
13000	9500	—	—	—	—

Model F.VII Sideplate

Features false sideplates that are completely covered with game scene engraving. Model is standard, with single-selective trigger. Small gauge premium is applicable.

NIB	Exc.	V.G.	Good	Fair	Poor
15000	10500	—	—	—	—

Model F.VII/SC Sideplate

False sideplate model, with gold inlays accenting the full coverage engraving. Note: Add 10 percent for 28-gauge and .410.

NIB	Exc.	V.G.	Good	Fair	Poor
16000	11500	—	—	—	—

Hammer Gun

Features boxlock action with external hammers. Other features are custom ordered to purchaser's specifications.

NIB	Exc.	V.G.	Good	Fair	Poor
20000	14500	—	—	—	—

FERRY, ANDREWS & CO.
Stafford, Connecticut

Underhammer Pistol (Antique)

Boot pistol chambered for .36-caliber percussion. Has 3" part-round, part-octagonal barrel. Similar to other under hammer pistols that were produced in Connecticut and Massachusetts. Top strap marked "Andrews Ferry & Co." Number manufactured unknown. Produced in 1850s.

Exc.	Fine	V.G.	Good	Fair	Poor
1550	700	550	400	120	80

FIALA ARMS COMPANY
New Haven, Connecticut

Fiala Repeating Target Pistol

Different type of pistol than what is commonly encountered. Outwardly it resembles a semi-automatic Colt Woodsman; in actuality it is a manually operated firearm that must be cycled by hand after every shot. Chambered for .22 rimfire and offered with interchangeable barrels in lengths of 3", 7.5" and 20". Also offered a detachable buttstock. Finish is blued and grips are found in both smooth and ribbed walnut. Rear sight is a square-notched blade that tips up into an elevation-adjustable peep sight. Marked "Fiala Arms and Equipment Co. Inc. / New Haven Conn. / Patents Pending" on right side of frame behind grip and Model 1920/ Made in U.S.A. on right side of frame above triggerguard. Left side of frame marked "FIALA ARMS" above image of polar bear with "TRADE MARK" below polar bear in area above triggerguard. Pistol furnished in one of three variations of cases that were optionally available: canvas case, black leatherette case velvet-lined and fitted with a lock and key, and tan leather version of leatherette case. A fixed 7.5" barrel variation was also produced. A 7.5" smoothbore barrel was cataloged as a silencer. Some 20" smoothbore barrels were produced. Some pistols bear the names "Columbia Arms Company" and "Botwinik Brothers". Government has classified this pistol with its stock as a "Curio or Relic" and in its complete state a very desirable collectible. Note: See also Schall & Co.

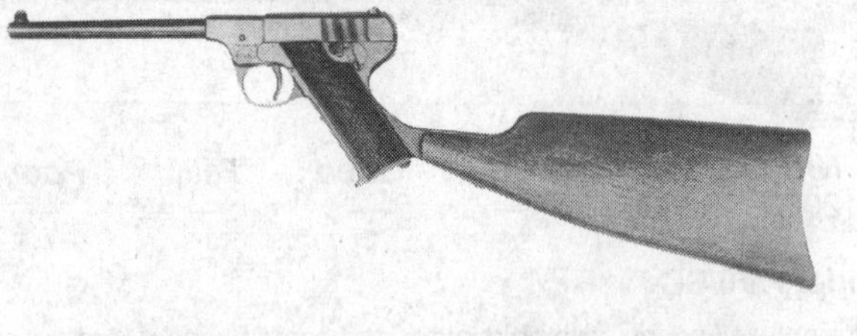

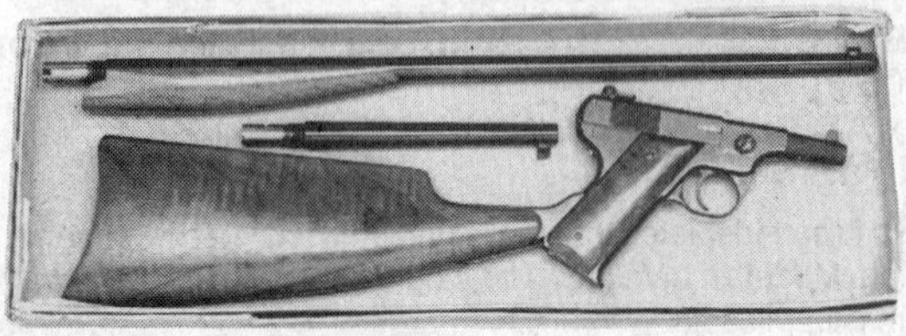

Courtesy Butterfield & Butterfield, San Francisco, California

Complete, Three Barrels, Stock, Tools, and Case

NIB	Exc.	V.G.	Good	Fair	Poor
—	2500	2100	1250	680	550

Gun Only

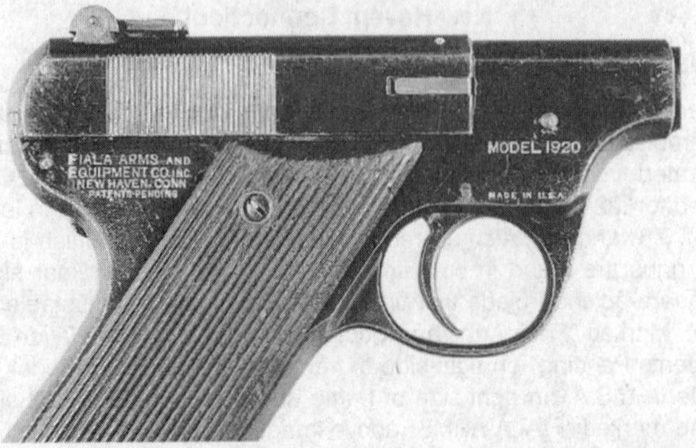

Courtesy Dr. Jon Miller

NIB	Exc.	V.G.	Good	Fair	Poor
—	800	700	450	280	180

FIERCE FIREARMS

Redmond, Utah

A Utah-based firearm maker specializing in custom long-range rifles. Also produces AR-15 style rifles and carbines, and muzzleloaders.

Carbon Fury

Calibers: .300 PRC, 6.5 Creedmoor, 6.5 PRC, 7MM Rem. Mag, .300 Win. Mag, .300 RUM, .300 WSM, 28 Nosler. Capacity: 4 to 5. Barrel: 24 to 26 in., stainless steel liner, carbon-fiber overlay. Stock: Carbon-fiber Monte Carlo. Sights: None, drilled and tapped. Weight: 6.6 lbs. Features: Guaranteed half-inch three-shot group at 100 yards; target crown for accuracy.

NIB	Exc.	V.G.	Good	Fair	Poor
2700	—	—	—	—	—

Rival

Calibers: 6.5 Creedmoor, 6.5 PRC, 7mm Rem., 28 Nosler, .300 Win., .300 PRC, .300 RUM. Capacity: 4 to 5. Barrel: 20 to 26 in., spiral-fluted, match-grade stainless steel or carbon fiber. Stock: Fierce Tech C3 carbon fiber. Sights: None, drilled and tapped. Weight: 6.4 to 7 lbs. Features: Cerakote finish, Trigger Tech trigger, built-in bipod rail.

NIB	Exc.	V.G.	Good	Fair	Poor
2200	—	—	—	—	—

MTN Reaper

Calibers: 6.5 Creed, 6.5 PRC, 7mm PRC, 7mm Rem. Mag., .308 Win., .300 Win. Mag., .300 PRC. Barrel: 18" or 20" (short action), 20" or 22" (long action) C3 carbon fiber. Weight: 5.8-6.6 lbs. Stock: Ultralite magnesium chassis with push button carbon-fiber fold and lock stock. Features: Precision machined two-lug bolt action. 70-degree bolt throw with tactical knob. Bix'nAndy trigger. AccurateMag box magazine. NIX muzzle brake. Limbsaver buttpad. Spiral fluted bolt. 0-MOA scope rail. Guaranteed 1/2 MOA accuracy.

NIB	Exc.	V.G.	Good	Fair	Poor
3180	—	—	—	—	—

FINNISH LION

Valmet, Sweden

ISU Target Rifle

Single-shot bolt-action rifle, chambered for .22 rimfire cartridge. Has a 27" heavy barrel and target stock with accessories. Features target adjustable sights. Manufactured between 1966 and 1977.

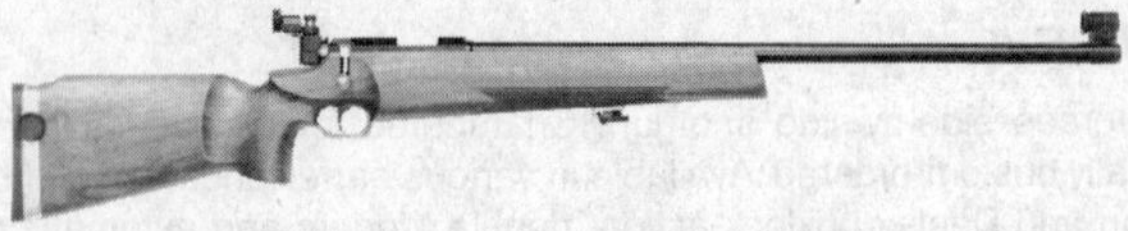

NIB	Exc.	V.G.	Good	Fair	Poor
—	480	320	280	200	120

Champion Free Rifle

Has a 29" heavy barrel and double-set triggers. Otherwise similar to ISU model. Manufactured between 1965 and 1972.

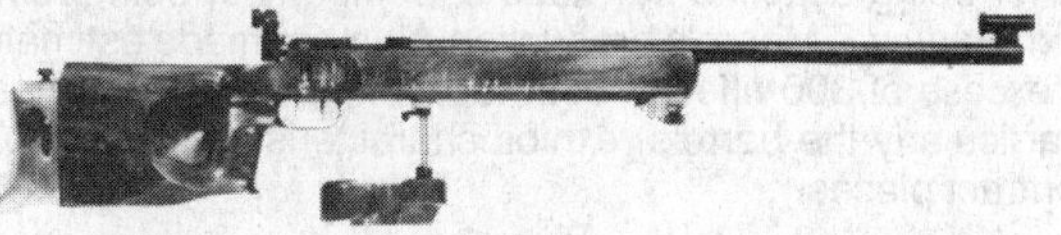

NIB	Exc.	V.G.	Good	Fair	Poor
—	900	750	600	380	280

Match Rifle

Similar to Champion rifle, with thumbhole stock and adjustable buttplate. Manufactured between 1937 and 1972.

NIB	Exc.	V.G.	Good	Fair	Poor
—	900	750	600	380	280

FIOCCHI OF AMERICA, INC.

Ozark, Missouri

See—PARDINI AND A. ZOLI

Imports above firearms. They are listed in their own respective sections.

FIREARMS INTERNATIONAL

Washington, D.C.

See—STAR AND GARCIA

Once importer of Star Model D, as it was sold in U.S.A. They also imported various other .25-caliber Colt copies, that are not considered collectible and would be valued in the $150-and-under range. For the .22/.410 Bronco, see "Garcia".

FIRESTORM

Argentina

Firestorm .22 LR

Semi-automatic pistol, chambered for .22 LR cartridge. Ten-round magazine capacity. Matte blue finish or duotone.

NIB	Exc.	V.G.	Good	Fair	Poor
250	180	140	100	80	40

Firestorm .32

Double-action semi-automatic chambered for .32 with 10+1 capacity. Blued, 3.5" barrel, weight 23 oz. Fixed sights and rubber grips. Introduced 2006.

NIB	Exc.	V.G.	Good	Fair	Poor
280	220	160	120	100	50

Firestorm .380

Semi-automatic double-action pistol. Chambered for .380 ACP cartridge and fitted with 3.5" barrel. Fixed three-dot combat sights. Matte blue or duotone finish. Magazine capacity 7 rounds. Weight about 23 oz.

NIB	Exc.	V.G.	Good	Fair	Poor
300	220	200	150	100	50

Mini Firestorm 9mm

This 9mm semi-automatic double-action pistol, fitted with 3.5" barrel. White outline drift adjustable target sights. Matte blue finish. Polymer grips. Magazine capacity 10 rounds. Weight about 25 oz.

NIB	Exc.	V.G.	Good	Fair	Poor
350	280	220	160	120	80

Mini Firestorm .40 S&W

As above, but chambered for .40 S&W cartridge.

NIB	Exc.	V.G.	Good	Fair	Poor
350	280	220	160	120	80

Firestorm .45 Government

Single-action semi-automatic pistol, chambered for .45 ACP cartridge. Fitted with 5.125" barrel and 3 dot fixed combat sights. Magazine capacity 7 rounds. Black rubber grips. Matte blue, nickel or duotone finish. Weight about 36 oz.

NIB	Exc.	V.G.	Good	Fair	Poor
350	280	220	160	120	80

Compact Firestorm .45 Government

As above, with 4.25" barrel. Weight about 34 oz.

NIB	Exc.	V.G.	Good	Fair	Poor
350	280	220	160	120	80

Mini Firestorm .45 Government

As above, with 3.14" barrel. Black polymer grips. Magazine capacity 10 rounds. Weight about 31 oz.

NIB	Exc.	V.G.	Good	Fair	Poor
350	280	220	160	120	80

1911 Mil-Spec Standard Government

1911A1-style single-action semi-automatic. Chambered in .45 ACP; 5.125" barrel, steel frame, 7- or 8-round magazine. Plastic or wood grips, matte blue or deluxe polished blue finish.

NIB	Exc.	V.G.	Good	Fair	Poor
350	280	220	160	120	80

FLETCHER BIDWELL, LLC
Viroqua, Wisconsin

Spencer 1860 Military Carbine

Introduced in 2001, this is a faithful re-production of original Spencer Carbine. Chambered for .56-50 blackpowder cartridge but in centerfire. Fitted with blued, 22" round barrel. Magazine capacity 7 rounds in butt tube. Bone charcoal case-hardened receiver. Walnut stock. Blade front sight with ladder rear sight, adjustable to 800 yards. Weight about 9 lbs. Built in U.S.

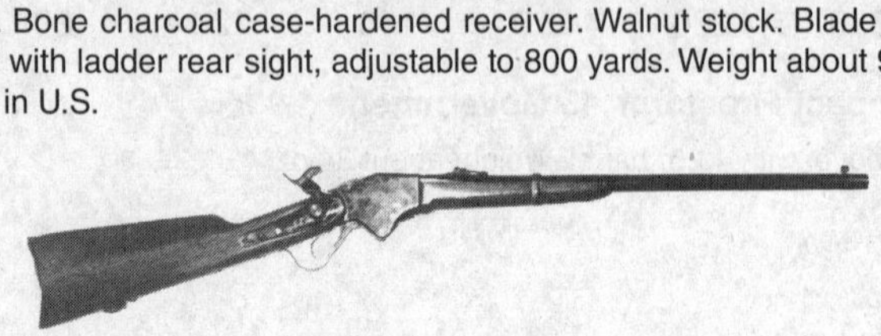

NIB	Exc.	V.G.	Good	Fair	Poor
2750	1950	1500	900	620	400

FLORENCE ARMORY
Florence, Guilford County, North Carolina

Founded in 1862, as a repair facility to alter sporting arms for military use. Majority of work done by H.C. Lamb & Company. In 1862, Captain Z. Coffin ordered stocks, barrels and locks to assemble newly made rifles. Furniture of these arms varied, either being supplied by Glaze & Company or being remainders from Searcy & Moore's production. Number made estimated to be in excess of 300 rifles in both .50- and .54-calibers. These arms (particularly the barrels) exhibit characteristics of North Carolina contract pieces.

Confederate Rifle (Antique)

No recent sales observed. Values are very speculative.

Exc.	Fine	V.G.	Good	Fair	Poor
29500	12500	8250	4000	1450	1010

FN AMERICA, LLC
McLean, Virginia

Company is a subsidiary of FN Herstal in Belgium. Essentially the sales and marketing arm for FN in U.S. market. SEE POLITICAL PANIC PRICING.

PISTOLS

Model Forty-Nine

Pistol built by FN Manufacturing, Inc. in Columbia, S.C. Has a polymer frame and stainless steel slide. Chambered for 9mm or .40 S&W cartridge. Barrel length 4.25". Magazine capacity: 16 rounds for law enforcement; 10 rounds for commercial sales. Features a repeatable secure striker trigger system. Offered in stainless steel or black coated slide. Weight about 26 oz. Offered primarily for sale to law enforcement agencies. Introduced in 2000.

NIB	Exc.	V.G.	Good	Fair	Poor
470	380	300	250	220	140

Model FNP-9/FNP-40

Introduced in 2003, this pistol chambered for 9mm or .40 S&W cartridge. Fitted with 4" barrel and featuring a polymer frame. Action is double-/single-action design, with ambidextrous manual decocking lever. Fixed sights. Ten-round magazine capacity. Weight about 33 oz.

NIB	*Exc.*	*V.G.*	*Good*	*Fair*	*Poor*
550	420	380	300	250	120

FNP-45

Longer-frame version of FNP-9, chambered for .45 ACP. Barrel length 4.5" and weight 33.3 oz. Ambidextrous mag release and decocker/safety, forward slide serrations. Magazine capacity: 10 or 15 rounds. Black or Flat Dark Earth finish. Interchangeable backstrap inserts.

NIB	*Exc.*	*V.G.*	*Good*	*Fair*	*Poor*
700	620	500	380	250	150

FNP-45 Tactical

Developed for U.S. Joint Combat Pistol Program, this .45 ACP tactical model has 5.3" threaded barrel for a suppressor or other accessories. High-profile combat sights, two mounting bases for optional red dot sights, MIL-STD 1913 rail. Black or Flat Dark Earth finish. Weight 33.6 oz.

NIB	*Exc.*	*V.G.*	*Good*	*Fair*	*Poor*
1250	1050	850	620	350	250

FNP-45 Competition

Designed as a major caliber competition pistol. Same overall features as FNP-45, plus fiber optic front sight and Picatinny rail. Introduced in 2011.

NIB	*Exc.*	*V.G.*	*Good*	*Fair*	*Poor*
1050	850	700	500	300	250

FNX-9, FNX-40

Chambered in 9mm or .40 S&W. Magazine capacity: 17 (9mm), 14 (.40). Weight 22 to 24 oz. Stainless steel slide has front and rear cocking serrations. Other features include ambidextrous operating controls. Four interchangeable backstrap inserts.

NIB	*Exc.*	*V.G.*	*Good*	*Fair*	*Poor*
600	540	450	320	250	150

FNX-45

.45 ACP variation of FNX series. Magazine capacity 15-rounds. Note: Add $100 for night sights; $300 Competition model; $400 Tactical model.

NIB	*Exc.*	*V.G.*	*Good*	*Fair*	*Poor*
700	620	550	500	450	350

FNS-9

Striker-fired polymer-frame full-size pistol. Chambered in 9mm or .40 S&W (FNS-40). Capacity: 18 rounds (9mm), 15 (.40). Black or matte silver slide, black polymer frame, ambidextrous safety, magazine release and slide lock. Fixed 3-dot sights. Night sights optional.

NIB	*Exc.*	*V.G.*	*Good*	*Fair*	*Poor*
600	520	450	400	350	300

FNH Five-seveN

Single-action design chambered for 5.7x28mm round. Magazine capacity 10 or 20 rounds. Matte black, olive drab green or Flat Dark Earth finish. Ambidextrous safety and accessory mounting rail. Barrel length 4", weight 21 oz. Three-dot combat sights, adjustable rear.

NIB	Exc.	V.G.	Good	Fair	Poor
1100	980	800	580	250	150

Model HP-SA

Famous John Browning design Hi-Power pistol. Chambered for 9mm or .40 S&W cartridge. Barrel length 4.6". Magazine capacity 10 rounds. Weight about 32 oz. Blued finish.

NIB	Exc.	V.G.	Good	Fair	Poor
900	750	600	400	200	120

Model HP-SA-SFS

Introduced in 2003. This variant of Hi-Power pistol features single-/double-action mechanism, that allows cocked-and-locked carry, with hammer and slide locked. When safety is pushed off hammer, is set in cocked position and fired single action.

NIB	Exc.	V.G.	Good	Fair	Poor
900	750	600	400	200	120

Model HP-DA/HP-DAO

Model offered in two different configurations. First with double-/single-action trigger; second is double-action-only. Chambered for 9mm cartridge. Fitted with fixed sights. Magazine capacity: 15 rounds for law enforcement; 10 rounds for commercial sales. Weight about 31 oz. Intended primarily for law enforcement sales. Introduced in 2000.

NIB	Exc.	V.G.	Good	Fair	Poor
900	750	600	400	200	120

Model HP-DA/HP-DAO Compact

As above in smaller and lighter package.

NIB	Exc.	V.G.	Good	Fair	Poor
900	750	600	400	200	120

Model BDA/BDAO Compact

Short recoil compact pistol, chambered for 9mm Parabellum cartridge. Fitted with double-/single-action trigger or double-action-only trigger. Each configuration has 10-round magazine capacity. Weight about 28 oz. Corrosion-resistant finish. Fixed sights.

NIB	Exc.	V.G.	Good	Fair	Poor
800	650	500	400	200	120

FN 502 Tactical

Caliber: .22 LR. Capacity: 10- and 15-round magazine. Barrel: 4.6" threaded. Grip: Textured polymer. Sights: Suppressor height, fixed front and rear sights. Length: 7.6" overall. Weight: 23.7 oz. unloaded. Finish: Matte black or FDE. Features: Hammer-fire, accessory rail.

NIB	Exc.	V.G.	Good	Fair	Poor
540	500	410	370	360	—

FN 509

Similar to FN 509 Compact MRD but with 4- or 4.5-in. barrel. Chambered in 9mm. Equipped with 10- or 17-rnd. magazine and 3-dot night sights. Finish available in FDE or black.

NIB	Exc.	V.G.	Good	Fair	Poor
600	530	460	380	290	270

FN 509 Compact MRD

Caliber: 9mm. Capacity: 10-, 12- or 15-round magazine. Barrel: 3.7 in. Grips: Textured grip, interchangeable backstraps. Sights: Fixed, tall co-witness; FN Low Profile Optics Mounting System. Length: 6.8 in. overall. Weight: 25.5 oz. unloaded. Finish: Black or FDE.

NIB	Exc.	V.G.	Good	Fair	Poor
700	580	—	—	—	—

FN High Power

Caliber: 9mm. Capacity: 17-round magazine. Barrel: 4.7". Grip: Textured G10. Sights: Steel. Fixed front and rear. Length: 8" overall. Weight: 40 oz. unloaded. Finish: Stainless, matte black, or FDE. Features: Hammer-fire, based on the classic High Power pistol.

NIB	Exc.	V.G.	Good	Fair	Poor
1230	1200	1100	1000	900	—

RIFLES

Rifles produced at FN manufacturing in U.S.

SPECIAL POLICE RIFLES (FN SPR)

FNAR

Semi-automatic chambered in .308 Winchester. Cold hammer-forged 16" standard or 20" heavy barrel. Magazine capacity 5 or 10 rounds. Weight 8.5 to 10 lbs. Receiver-mounted optical rail, with additional rails on forend. Matte black synthetic stock, with fully adjustable comb and length of pull via interchangeable inserts. Match-grade model available.

NIB	Exc.	V.G.	Good	Fair	Poor
1520	1300	1100	940	800	680

FNAR Competition 308 DBM

Barrel .308 Win./20" fluted. Gas, rotating bolt autoloading rifle. 10-round DBM magazines. 8.9 lbs. Blue/gray laminated stock with checkered gripping surfaces. Adjustable for cheekpiece height, cast and length of pull. Premium non-slip recoil pad. One-piece MIL-STD-1913 optics rail, hard-anodized blue receiver with Team FNH USA markings.

NIB	Exc.	V.G.	Good	Fair	Poor
1570	1340	1140	960	820	700

FN A1 SPR

Chambered for .308 and 7.62x51mm cartridge. Bolt-action. Fitted with 24" heavy barrel and no sights. Choice of hinged floorplate or detachable box magazine. Stock is McMillan A3 tactical. Weight about 10.75 lbs. Discontinued.

NIB	Exc.	V.G.	Good	Fair	Poor
1600	1350	1180	900	720	380

FN A1a SPR

Similar to above model. Fitted with 20" heavy fluted barrel. McMillan A3 tactical stock. Weight about 9.75 lbs. Discontinued.

NIB	Exc.	V.G.	Good	Fair	Poor
1600	1350	1180	900	—	—

FN A2 SPR

Fitted with 24" heavy barrel. McMillan A4 tactical stock. Badger Ordinance scope base. Weight about 10.75 lbs. Discontinued.

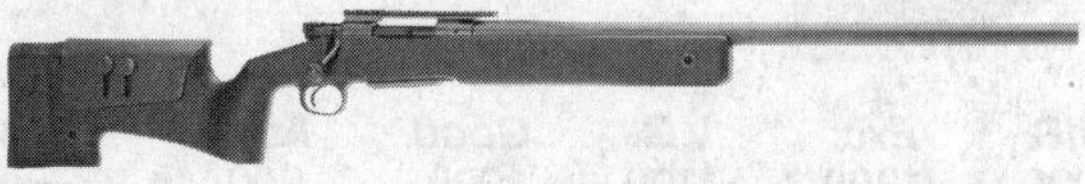

NIB	Exc.	V.G.	Good	Fair	Poor
2190	1750	1550	1280	—	—

FN A3 SPR

Model has 24" heavy barrel, with McMillan A4 adjustable stock. Badger Ordinance scope base and Badger Ordinance or FN scope rings. Supplied with FNH Parker-Hale type or Harris bipod. Weight about 10.75 lbs. Discontinued.

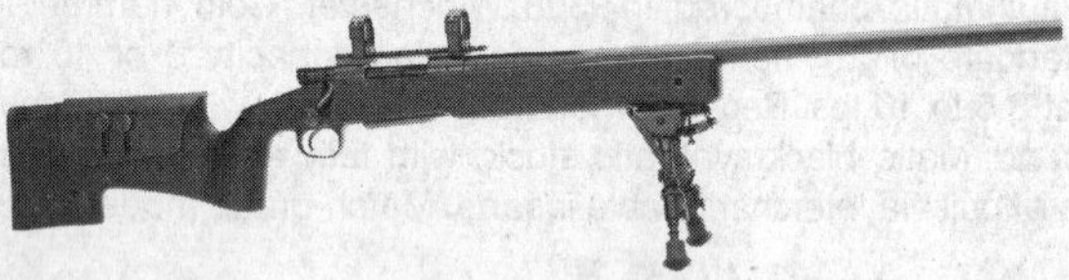

NIB	Exc.	V.G.	Good	Fair	Poor
2450	1950	1650	1380	—	—

FN A4 SPR

Fitted with 24" heavy barrel. McMillan A4 adjustable tactical stock. Scope base and rings standard. Choice of several tactical scopes. Bipod, sling, drag bag, kill flash, tool kit, cleaning kit, hard case. Weight about 10.75 lbs. Discontinued.

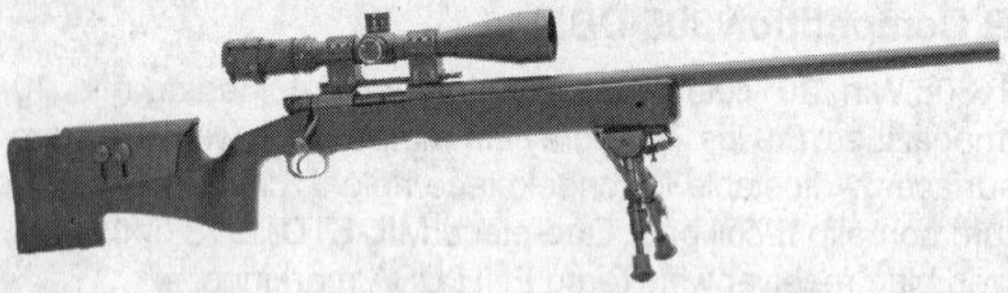

NIB	Exc.	V.G.	Good	Fair	Poor
5000	4250	3500	2800	—	—

FN A5 SPR

Model has 20" heavy fluted barrel threaded for a suppressor. Special McMillan tactical stock. Rest of features same as FN A4 model.

NIB	Exc.	V.G.	Good	Fair	Poor
6500	5750	4500	3700	—	—

FN A5M

Similar to FN A5 SPR, with McMillan fiberglass tactical stock, standard optics rail. Chambered in .300 WSM or .308 Win. Barrel length 20" to 24", standard or fluted. Discontinued.

NIB	Exc.	V.G.	Good	Fair	Poor
3000	2600	2200	1800	—	—

FNH-USA Ballista

Modular multi-caliber bolt-action tactical rifle. Chambered for .308 Win., .300 Win. Magnum or .338 Lapua. Accessory conversion kits available for each caliber. Aluminum alloy receiver, adjustable trigger, fluted 24" or 25" barrel. Ambidextrous folding stock adjustable for length of pull, comb height, buttplate height, cast-on and cast-off. New in 2012; current in 2019.

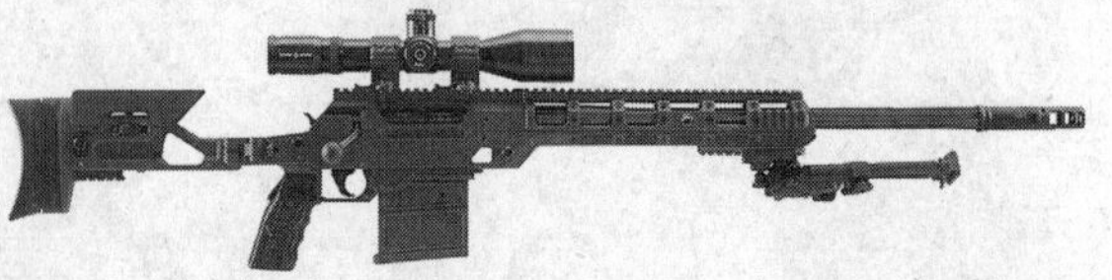

NIB	Exc.	V.G.	Good	Fair	Poor
6800	5800	4900	3600	—	—

FN SPR A5M XP

Similar to FN A5M above. Featuring a forged receiver and integral recoil lug, threaded cold hammer-forged and chrome-lined barrel in .308 in 20" or 24". Tactical box magazines of 5 and 10 rounds. Introduced 2013.

NIB	Exc.	V.G.	Good	Fair	Poor
2380	2030	1700	—	—	—

FN A5a SPR

Model has 20" heavy fluted barrel threaded for a suppressor. Special SPR McMillan adjustable tactical stock. Weight about 9.75 lbs. Discontinued.

NIB	Exc.	V.G.	Good	Fair	Poor
2460	1980	1650	1380	950	450

FN PBR (Patrol Bolt Rifle)

Introduced in 2004. Rifle chambered for .308 or .300 WSM. Offered with four different barrel lengths: 18", 20", 22" or 24". Fitted with two-piece MIL spec M1913 rail. Black Hogue stock. Magazine capacity 4 rounds. Weight about 9 lbs. Discontinued.

NIB	Exc.	V.G.	Good	Fair	Poor
1000	950	900	800	—	—

PGM PRECISION RIFLES

Rifles made by PGM Precision, a subsidary of FN, in Poisy Cedex, France.

Ultima Ratio Intervention

Bolt-action rifle, chambered for .308 and 7.62x51mm cartridge. Fitted with 23.6" ribbed barrel and integral muzzle brake. Folding bipod. Stock trigger group and action are fixed to a rigid metal girder. Stock is adjustable. No sights. Magazine capacity 5 or 10 rounds. Weight about 13.25 lbs., depending on configuration. Discontinued.

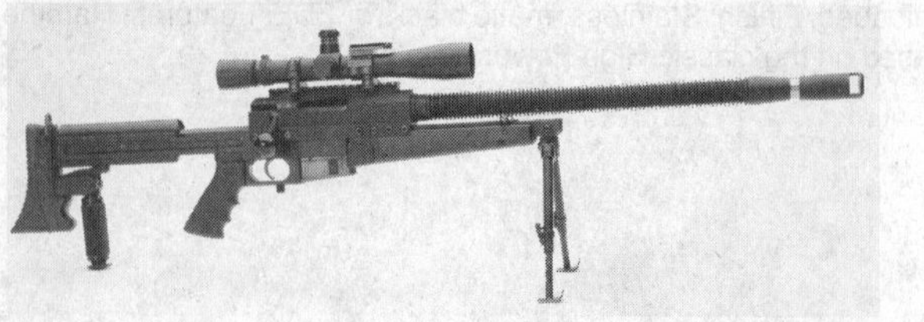

NIB	Exc.	V.G.	Good	Fair	Poor
9000	8000	6000	3250	—	—

Ultima Ratio Commando I

Similar to above model, with 18.5" fluted barrel and muzzle brake. Weight about 12 lbs. Discontinued.

NIB	Exc.	V.G.	Good	Fair	Poor
9100	8050	6100	3250	1800	—

Ultima Ratio Commando II

Similar to Commando I, with folding stock. Discontinued.

NIB	Exc.	V.G.	Good	Fair	Poor
8320	—	—	—	—	—

FN-Mini-Hecate

Chambered for .308 cartridge. Bolt-action rifle features free-loading interchangeable 18.5", 19.7", 21.7" or 23.6" match-grade barrel. Collapsible buttstock. Magazine capacity 10 rounds. Weight about 14 lbs. Introduced in 2001. Discontinued.

NIB	Exc.	V.G.	Good	Fair	Poor
9100	8050	6100	3250	—	—

.338 Lapua

Similar to Mini-Hecate, but chambered for .33 Lapua cartridge. Fitted with 27.2" barrel and integral muzzle brake. Collapsible buttstock. Weight about 15 lbs. Magazine capacity 10 rounds. Discontinued.

NIB	Exc.	V.G.	Good	Fair	Poor
10500	9000	7750	6000	—	—

FS 2000

Semi-automatic bullpup-style carbine, chambered in 5.56 NATO/.223 Rem. Features include gas-operated action with rotating bolt lockup, 17.4" barrel with muzzle brake, and fully ambidextrous polymer stock. Fired cases are ejected forward, away from shooter. A civilian version of selective fire model used by military and law enforcement. Introduced in 2006.

NIB	Exc.	V.G.	Good	Fair	Poor
3000	2500	2200	1800	—	—

FN PS90

Semi-automatic bullpup model chambered for 5.7x28mm caliber, with 10- or 30-round magazine. Barrel is 16", with integrated muzzle brake. Design features downward ejection, three M1913 accessory rails.

NIB	Exc.	V.G.	Good	Fair	Poor
1700	1450	1250	1050	—	—

SCAR SERIES

Semi-automatic tactical rifle chambered for .223 (16S) or .308 Win. (17S and 20S), with 10- or 30-round magazines. Black or FDE finish, hard-anodized aluminum receiver, telescoping side-folding polymer stock, integrated optics rail. Barrel lengths 16.25" and 20". Add 9% for 17S; 20% for 20S.

NIB	Exc.	V.G.	Good	Fair	Poor
3200	2700	2300	1950	—	—

FNH-USA SCAR 16S 5.56/20"

NIB	Exc.	V.G.	Good	Fair	Poor
3400	3300	3200	2900	2600	—

FNH-USA SCAR 17S

NIB	Exc.	V.G.	Good	Fair	Poor
3750	3650	3500	3250	3000	—

FNH-USA SCAR 20S

.308 Win. or 6.5 Creedmoor.

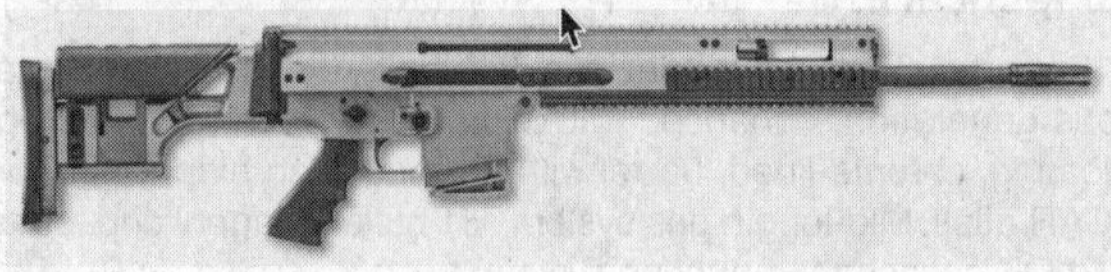

NIB	Exc.	V.G.	Good	Fair	Poor
4500	4300	4200	4000	—	—

FN 15 SERIES

FN-15

AR-style series in rifle, carbine, competition and other models. Chambered in 5.56 NATO, with 30-round magazine, 16" or 18" floating barrel. Direct impingement operation. All standard AR stock configurations. Also offered in .300 BLK. Prices shown are for basic rifle/carbine model. Note: Add $250 for Competition Model; $150 for DMR; $100 for .300 BLK.

NIB	Exc.	V.G.	Good	Fair	Poor
1100	950	800	680	—	—

FN 15 Pistol 5.56

5.56/10.5" barrel. 5.2 lbs. Chrome-lined barrel, 1:7 twist, carbine-length gas system. 9-inch M-LOK rail, SBX-K pistol stabilizing brace.

NIB	Exc.	V.G.	Good	Fair	Poor
1350	1150	980	830	710	600

FN 15 Pistol .300 BLK

300 BLK/12" barrel. 5.65 lbs.

NIB	Exc.	V.G.	Good	Fair	Poor
1330	1130	960	810	690	590

FN 15 Tactical Carbine FDE P-LOK

5.56/16". 7.2 lbs. Flat Dark Earth coloration. P-LOK handguard with M-LOK attachment.

NIB	Exc.	V.G.	Good	Fair	Poor
1350	1150	980	830	710	600

FN 15 MD Heavy Barrel Rifle

5.56/20". 10-round magazine, 8.7 lbs. Free-floated, chrome-lined heavy profile barrel and 15-inch rail. FN combat-grade trigger weighted at 4.75–7.75 lbs., fixed low-profile gas block, muzzle thread protector.

NIB	Exc.	V.G.	Good	Fair	Poor
1250	1060	900	770	650	560

FN 15 MD Heavy Barrel Carbine

5.56/16". 7.1 lbs. Free-float Midwest Industry 12" M-LOK rail.

NIB	Exc.	V.G.	Good	Fair	Poor
1250	1060	900	770	650	560

FN 15 Tactical II CA

5.56/16". 7 lbs. Meets requirements for sale in California.

NIB	Exc.	V.G.	Good	Fair	Poor
1400	1190	1010	860	730	620

FN 15 DMR II CA

5.56/18". Meets requirements for sale in California. Featureless HERA CQR stock, M-LOK accessory mounting system, MIL-SPEC H-type buffer assembly and tube.

NIB	Exc.	V.G.	Good	Fair	Poor
1900	1620	1370	1170	990	840

FN 15 Tactical II

5.56/16" barrel. 30-round magazines, 6.7 lbs. Adds FN's Rail System to previous generation, enhanced MIL-SPEC lower receiver, match-grade free floating, chrome-lined, barrel with 3-prong flash hider found on the FN SCAR rifles. Mid-length gas system, H1 buffer, Magpul grip, buttstock and M-LOK accessory mounting system.

NIB	Exc.	V.G.	Good	Fair	Poor
1400	1190	1010	860	730	620

FN 15 Tactical .300 BLK II

300 BLK, 16". 6.91 lbs.

NIB	Exc.	V.G.	Good	Fair	Poor
1430	1210	1030	880	740	630

FN 15 Tactical Carbine II

5.56/16" barrel. 6.0 lbs.

NIB	Exc.	V.G.	Good	Fair	Poor
1400	1190	1010	860	730	620

FN 15 DMR II

5.56/18". 30-round magazines. 7.03 lbs. Re-engineered with new FN Rail System with M-LOK. Barrel is a match-grade 1:7 twist with a SureFire ProComp muzzle device. Match-grade Timney trigger, Magpul MOE grip and buttstock, MIL-SPEC H-type buffer assembly and tube.

NIB	Exc.	V.G.	Good	Fair	Poor
1800	1530	1300	1110	940	800

FN 15 DMR3 Rifle

Caliber: 5.56 NATO. The Designated Marksman Rifle (DMR) includes an 18" barrel, SureFire ProComp muzzle brake, and Geissele two-stage trigger in matte black anodize, flat dark earth (FDE) or tungsten gray Cerakote colors. Barrel: Hybrid profile, cold hammer-forged, chrome-lined, 1:8" twist. Made from FN's proprietary machine-gun-barrel steel. Rifle-length direct-impingement gas system with a pinned low-profile gas block. Hodge Defense 14 5/8" aluminum handguard free-float barrel. Continuous MIL-STD Picatinny rail at 12 o'clock, multiple M-LOK attachment slots. Mil-spec lower receiver, M16-style bolt carrier group. Ergonomic pistol grip, six-position collapsible carbine stock, 30-rd. magazine, Radian Raptor-LT ambidextrous charging handle and Radian Talon ambidextrous safety selector. Length: 35.2" to 38.5". Weight: 7.4 lbs. Introduced May 2022. SEE POLITICAL PANIC PRICING.

NIB	Exc.	V.G.	Good	Fair	Poor
2210	—	—	—	—	—

FN 15 Competition

5.56/18". 10- or 30-round magazines. 8.1 lbs. Alloy-steel chrome-lined match-grade barrel with SureFire ProComp-556 muzzle brake. Mega Arms 16-inch rail system with M-LOK, Magpul MOE furniture and Timney Competition single-stage trigger.

NIB	Exc.	V.G.	Good	Fair	Poor
2000	1700	1450	1230	1040	890

FN 15 Military Collector M4

5.56/16". 6.6 lbs. Military replica rifle made to FN's and the U.S. military's specifications. 1:7" RH twist barrel, button-broached, and chrome-lined. UID-labeled lower receiver is equipped with an ambidextrous selector switch, just like the select-fire M4A1. LE-only M4 model number is 36318-02. Similar Military Collector M16 36320 has a 20" barrel, Knights Armament M5RAS Adapter rail w/ rail adapter covers. 8.2 lbs. Consumer model number 36320, LE is 36320-02.

NIB	Exc.	V.G.	Good	Fair	Poor
1790	1680	1550	1300	1150	—

FN 15 M16 Military Collector

NIB	Exc.	V.G.	Good	Fair	Poor
1790	1680	1550	1300	1150	—

FN 15 Sporting

.223/18" match-grade chrome-lined barrel, SureFire ProComp 556 muzzle brake. Timney competition trigger, Magpul grip and buttstock, and 15" Samson Evolution handguard.

NIB	Exc.	V.G.	Good	Fair	Poor
1580	1340	1140	970	820	700

FN M249S Military Collector BLK

5.56/18.5". Semi-automatic version of the M249 SAW light machine gun. Originally developed by FN Herstal as the FN MINIMI and adopted by the U.S. military in 1988. The rifle features the signature 18.5-inch FN chrome-lined barrel and operates from a closed-bolt position. Accepts both magazine and linked ammunition belt. FDE coloration is model number 56501.

NIB	Exc.	V.G.	Good	Fair	Poor
8000	6800	5780	4910	4180	3550

FN M249S PARA FDE

5.56/16.1". Part of the Military Collector Series, a semi-auto version of the currently contracted FN M249 PARA. Accepts 200-round belt or 30-round mags. Formed steel frame, folding steel bipod, folding carry handle, flip-up feed tray cover and feed mechanism, top-cover integrated MIL-STD-1913 rail systems for optics. Collapsible buttstock. Black version is model number 56509. Introduced 2017.

NIB	Exc.	V.G.	Good	Fair	Poor
9000	7650	6500	5530	4700	3990

FN 15 SRP G2

Caliber: 5.56 NATO. Capacity: One 30-round magazine. Barrel: 11.5" and 16", 1:7" RH twist, alloy steel, button-broached, chrome-plated, A2-style flash hider. Stock: 6-position, collapsible. Sights: Low-profile, folding metal front and rear sights. Full-length 12 o'clock Picatinny rail with five built-in QD points. Weight: 5.6 lbs. (11.5"); 6.25 lbs. (16"). Trigger: FN Combat Trigger, 4.75-7.75 lbs. Overall Length: 27.5-30.75 in. (11.5"); 31.9-35.2" (16") Features: Law enforcement models have a lightweight design, extended handguards and sight-ready configuration. Multiple M-LOK and quick-detach (QD) points, chrome-lined barrel with pinned low-profile gas block, MPI-inspected and marked M16-style bolt carrier. Free-floated handguard (10.5" long with 11.5" barrel, or 15" long with 16" barrel.)

NIB	Exc.	V.G.	Good	Fair	Poor
1360	1200	1100	970	—	—

TAC3 16"

NIB	Exc.	V.G.	Good	Fair	Poor
1630	1560	1450	1280	1000	—

TAC3 Duty 16"

NIB	Exc.	V.G.	Good	Fair	Poor
1530	1450	1400	1250	1000	—

SHOTGUNS

FNH-USA SC1

Over/under shotgun designed for competition. 12-gauge only, with 28" or 30" ported and back-bored barrels, Invector-Plus choke tubes, ventilated rib and mid-bead. Checkered wood, laminate wood or blue stock adjustable for comb height, cast and length of pull. Weight 8 to 8.2 lbs.

NIB	Exc.	V.G.	Good	Fair	Poor
2000	1700	1450	1100	900	500

FN Police Shotgun

Slide-action 12-gauge shotgun, chambered for 3" 12-gauge shell. Barrel length 18". Magazine capacity 7 rounds. Black synthetic stock. Corrosion-resistant finish. Weight about 6.5 lbs.

NIB	Exc.	V.G.	Good	Fair	Poor
350	280	200	150	120	—

FN Tactical Police

Similar to standard model, with ported barrel, collapsible stock and pistol grip. Weight about 6.5 lbs.

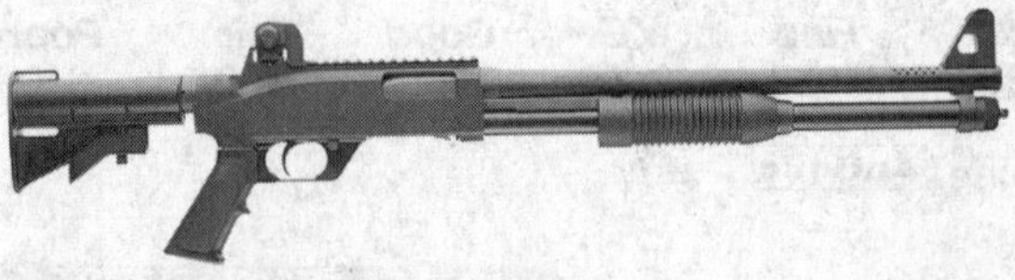

NIB	Exc.	V.G.	Good	Fair	Poor
550	480	400	300	200	—

FN Self-Loading Police

Gas-operated semi-automatic shotgun. Fitted with Picatinny rail and short stock. Chambered for 12-gauge shell. Magazine capacity 6 rounds. Weight about 7.75 lbs.

NIB	Exc.	V.G.	Good	Fair	Poor
1000	800	600	400	300	—

FOEHL & WEEKS

Philadelphia PA 1890-1894

Columbian (Antique)

A .32- or .38-caliber revolver, marked with patent date "20 January 1891".

Exc.	Fine	V.G.	Good	Fair	Poor
350	275	200	150	100	50

Columbian Automatic (Antique)

A .38-caliber revolver, with hinged barrel and cylinder assembly.

Exc.	Fine	V.G.	Good	Fair	Poor
375	275	200	150	100	50

Perfect (Antique)

As above, with concealed hammer. Also in .32-caliber.

Exc.	Fine	V.G.	Good	Fair	Poor
400	300	225	170	125	70

FOEHL, C.
Philadelphia, Pennsylvania

Derringer (Antique)

A .41-caliber percussion single-shot pistol, with 2" barrel, German silver mounts and walnut stock. Lock marked "C. Foehl".

Exc.	Fine	V.G.	Good	Fair	Poor
1950	750	520	300	110	70

FOGARTY
American Repeating Rifle Co.
Boston, Massachusetts

Fogarty Repeating Rifle and Carbine

Limited number of repeating rifles and carbines, based upon Valentine Fogarty's patents. Produced between 1866 and 1867. Calibers of these arms varies. Normal barrel lengths are 20" and 28". Blued, case-hardened, with walnut stocks. American Repeating Rifle Company purchased by Winchester Repeating Arms Company in 1869.

Rifle (Antique)

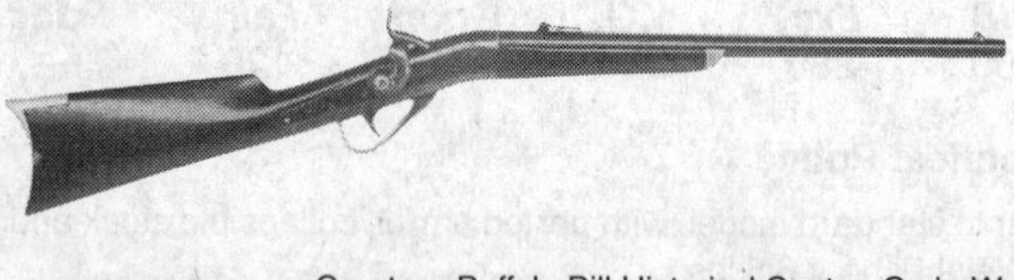

Courtesy Buffalo Bill Historical Center, Cody, Wyoming

Exc.	Fine	V.G.	Good	Fair	Poor
9500	4050	2650	1250	450	310

Carbine (Antique)

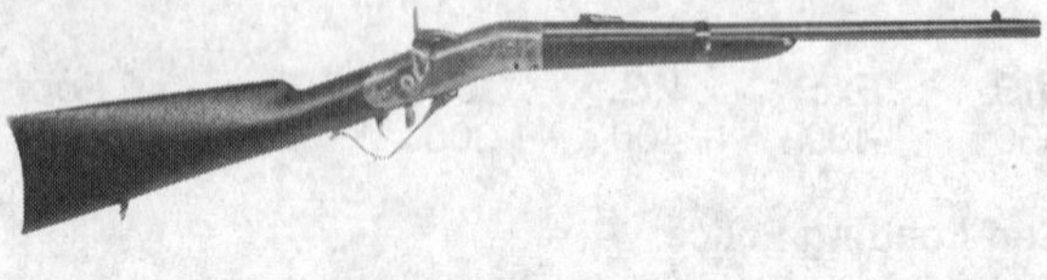

Courtesy Buffalo Bill Historical Center, Cody, Wyoming

Exc.	Fine	V.G.	Good	Fair	Poor
9500	4050	2650	1250	450	310

FOLSOM, H.
St. Louis, Missouri

Derringer

A .41-caliber single-shot percussion pocket pistol, with 2.5" barrel. German silver mounts and walnut stock. Barrel marked "H. Folsom".

NIB	Exc.	V.G.	Good	Fair	Poor
—	—	1150	800	350	280

FOLDAR
Henderson, Texas

Maker of foldable, concealable AR-style firearms.

MOBETTA B-SERIES

Caliber: 5.56 NATO, .223 Wylde chamber. Lower Receiver: FoldAR FLDR15. FoldAR's patented folding upper offers concealability and easy carry and transport. Folded length: 17 5/8". Folded width: 4 1/4". Quick-change barrel system, modular M-LOK handguard of three different lengths. Barrel: 16", 4150 alloy steel, QPQ Melonite black nitride finish, 1:7" twist, A2 compensator, muzzle threaded 1/2-28. Mil-spec components: BCG, grip, trigger, carbine stock, and non-adjustable gas block (.750 diameter). Overall Length: 32 7/8". Weight: 6.15 lbs. Introduced 2023. SEE POLITICAL PANIC PRICING.

MoBetta B-Series Rifle 16"

NIB	Exc.	V.G.	Good	Fair	Poor
1500	—	—	—	—	—

MOBETTA A-SERIES

Caliber: 5.56 NATO, .223 Wylde chamber. 300 Blackout, 6.5 Grendel. SEE POLITICAL PANIC PRICING.

MoBetta A-Series Rifle 16"

NIB	Exc.	V.G.	Good	Fair	Poor
2000	—	—	—	—	—

FOLSOM, H&D ARMS CO.

Large distributor of double-/single-barrel shotguns, produced by Crescent Firearms Co., Norwich, Connecticut. Folsom owned and later sold to Savage Arms Co. the Crescent Firearms Co., Davis Warner Co. and Baker Gun Co. around 1930. For more information see Crescent Firearms Co.

FORBES RIFLES, LLC
Westbrook, Maine

Model 24B

A production version of Model 24 made by New Ultra Light Arms Co. Chambered in .25-06, .270, 7mm Rem. Magnum, .30-06 and .300 Win. Magnum. Barrel length 24", black composite stock, no sights. Introduced 2011. Note: Add $100 for stainless and/or left-hand version.

NIB	Exc.	V.G.	Good	Fair	Poor
1300	1200	1100	900	700	350

FOREHAND & WADSWORTH
Worcester, Massachusetts

Established in 1871 and operated under the above name until 1890, when it became Forehand Arms Company. Hopkins & Allen purchased the company in 1902.

Single-Shot Derringer (Antique)

A .22-caliber single-shot pocket pistol, with 2" half-octagonal pivoted barrel. Spur trigger and nickel- or silver-plated frame. Walnut grips. Barrel marked "Forehand & Wadsworth Worcester".

Exc.	Fine	V.G.	Good	Fair	Poor
1450	600	420	250	100	70

Single-Shot .41 Derringer (Antique)

As above in .41-caliber, with 2.5" round barrel.

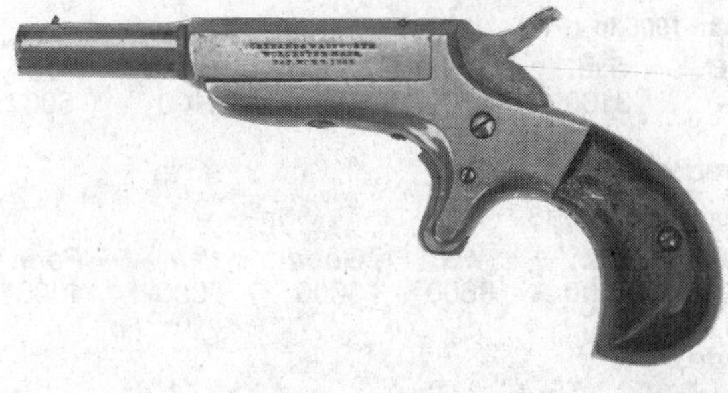

Courtesy Milwaukee Public Museum, Milwaukee, Wisconsin

Exc.	Fine	V.G.	Good	Fair	Poor
1000	850	650	450	200	140

Side-Hammer .22 Antique

A .22-caliber spur trigger revolver, with 2.25" to 4" octagonal barrel. 7-shot cylinder. Blued or nickel-plated, with walnut grips.

Exc.	Fine	V.G.	Good	Fair	Poor
680	480	340	200	100	70

Center Hammer Antique

A .32-caliber spur trigger revolver, with 3.5" octagonal barrel and 6-shot cylinder. Blued or nickel-plated, with rosewood or walnut grips. Top strap commonly found marked "Terror".

Courtesy Milwaukee Public Museum, Milwaukee, Wisconsin

Exc.	Fine	V.G.	Good	Fair	Poor
400	300	250	200	100	70

Old Model Army Single-Action Revolver Antique

A .44 Russian caliber revolver, with 7.5" round barrel and 6-shot cylinder. Barrel marked "Forehand & Wadsworth, Worchester, Mass. U.S. Patd. Oct. 22, '61, June 27, '71 Oct. 28, '73". Blued with walnut grips. Approximately 250 manufactured between 1872 and 1878.

Exc.	Fine	V.G.	Good	Fair	Poor
6000	4500	3250	2000	500	350

New Model Army Single-Action Revolver Antique

Similar to above, with 6.5" barrel and half-cock notch on hammer. Approximately 250 made between 1878 and 1882. Interesting Note: In 2008, United States Fire Arms announced plans to re-manufacture this model.

Exc.	Fine	V.G.	Good	Fair	Poor
5500	4000	2750	1500	500	350

Double-Action Revolver Antique

A .32 or .38 centerfire or rimfire caliber double-action revolver, with 3.5" barrel and 6- or 7-shot cylinder. The .32-caliber version marked "Forehand & Wadsworth Double-Action" and .38-caliber "American Bulldog". Manufactured from 1871 to 1890.

Exc.	Fine	V.G.	Good	Fair	Poor
300	200	150	100	40	20

British Bulldog Antique

A .32 or .38 centerfire solid frame double-action revolver, resembling Webley Bulldog.

Exc.	Fine	V.G.	Good	Fair	Poor
400	300	220	150	80	50

British Bulldog .44 Antique

As above in .44 Webley caliber, with 5" barrel and 5-shot cylinder.

Exc.	Fine	V.G.	Good	Fair	Poor
450	320	250	180	100	70

Swamp Angel Antique

A .41-caliber single-action revolver, with 3" barrel and 5-shot cylinder. Top strap marked "Swamp Angel".

Exc.	Fine	V.G.	Good	Fair	Poor
420	280	190	100	50	30

FOREHAND ARMS CO. 1898-1902

Perfection Automatic

A .32- or .38-caliber double-action revolver, with hinged barrel and cylinder assembly. Varying barrel lengths. Blued or nickel-plated, with hard rubber grips.

NIB	Exc.	V.G.	Good	Fair	Poor
—	280	250	100	80	50

Double-Barrel Shotguns

Good quality hammer and hammerless doubles, but few produced until taken over by Hopkins and Allen Firearms Co. Values from $100 to $1,000 depending on grade and condition.

FOWLER, B. JR.

Hartford, Connecticut

Percussion Pistol Antique

A .38-caliber single-shot percussion pistol, with 4" half octagonal barrel, iron frame and maple grips. Barrel marked "B. Fowler, Jr.". Manufactured between 1835 and 1838.

Exc.	Fine	V.G.	Good	Fair	Poor
1000	550	430	320	150	100

FOX, A. H.

Philadelphia, Pennsylvania

Ansley H. Fox established Fox Gun Company, in Baltimore, Maryland, in 1896. Subsequently, he made arms under the name Philadelphia Gun Company. As of 1905, he operated under the name A.H. Fox. In 1930, this company was purchased by Savage Arms Company, who continued manufacturing all grades of Fox shotguns. As of 1942, Savage Company only made plainer grades. Note: Fox Model B double shotguns see Savage Arms Co.

Sterlingworth

A 12-, 16- or 20-gauge boxlock double-barrel shotgun, with 26", 28" or 30" barrels. Double triggers and extractors. Automatic ejectors were also available and would add approximately 30 percent to values listed. Blued, case-hardened, with walnut stock. Manufactured from 1911 to 1946. Note: Add 50 percent for 20-gauge; 25 percent for 16-gauge.

Courtesy Nick Niles, Paul Goodwin photo

NIB	Exc.	V.G.	Good	Fair	Poor
2500	2000	1600	1000	500	280

Sterlingworth Deluxe

As above, with an ivory bead recoil pad and optional 32" barrel. Note: Add 50 percent for 20 gauge; 25 percent for 16-gauge.

NIB	Exc.	V.G.	Good	Fair	Poor
3000	2500	1900	1250	700	400

SP Grade

A 12-, 16- or 20-gauge boxlock double-barrel shotgun, with varying length barrels. Double triggers and extractors. Note: Add 35 percent for 20-gauge; 15 percent for Automatic ejectors; 25 percent for 16-gauge.

NIB	Exc.	V.G.	Good	Fair	Poor
2000	1600	1320	1050	450	220

HE Grade

Similar to early A Grade and offered in 12- and 20-gauge. Chambers were 2.25" standard, with 3" chambers available on request. Marked on the barrel "Not Warranted". This referred to pattern density, not barrel quality. Only sixty 20-gauge HE Grades appear in factory records. Manufactured from 1923 to 1942. Note: Add 20 percent for single-selective trigger; 100 percent premium for 20-gauge.

NIB	Exc.	V.G.	Good	Fair	Poor
12000	9000	6000	3200	2000	1000

High Grade Guns A-FE

Fox Company as well as Savage Arms Company, produced a variety of shotguns decorated in varying grades. Available in 12-, 16- and 20-gauge. Value depends on particular features of these arms. Prospective purchasers are advised to secure a qualified appraisal prior to acquisition. Note: A 25 percent premium should be added to grades below, for small gauge and guns with single selective trigger.

A Grade

Built from 1905 to 1942.

NIB	Exc.	V.G.	Good	Fair	Poor
3200	2600	1700	1220	600	400

AE Grade (Automatic Ejectors)

Built from 1905 to 1946.

NIB	Exc.	V.G.	Good	Fair	Poor
4000	3200	2500	1600	900	700

B Grade

Built from 1905 to 1918.

NIB	Exc.	V.G.	Good	Fair	Poor
—	3100	2700	1950	1100	500

BE Grade

Built from 1905 to 1918.

NIB	Exc.	V.G.	Good	Fair	Poor
—	4500	3600	3000	2000	1000

C Grade

Built from 1905 to 1913.

NIB	Exc.	V.G.	Good	Fair	Poor
—	3300	2700	2150	1100	550

CE Grade

Built from 1905 to 1946.

NIB	Exc.	V.G.	Good	Fair	Poor
9500	8000	5000	3750	2500	1200

XE Grade

Built from 1914 to 1945.

Courtesy William Hammond

NIB	Exc.	V.G.	Good	Fair	Poor
15000	12000	8500	6000	3000	1500

D Grade

Built from 1906 to 1913.

NIB	Exc.	V.G.	Good	Fair	Poor
12500	10000	8000	5150	2750	1000

DE Grade

Built from 1906 to 1945.

NIB	Exc.	V.G.	Good	Fair	Poor
24000	20000	15000	9000	3750	1800

F Grade

Built from 1906 to 1913.

NIB	Exc.	V.G.	Good	Fair	Poor
30000	25000	16800	9000	5700	3000

FE Grade

Built from 1906 to 1940.

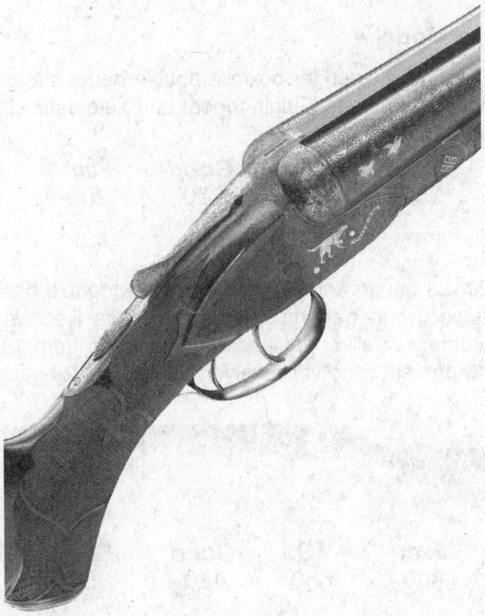

NIB	Exc.	V.G.	Good	Fair	Poor
85000	70000	55000	40000	20000	9000

Single Barrel Trap Guns

A 12-gauge single-barrel boxlock shotgun, with 30" or 32" ventilated rib barrels and automatic ejector. Approximately 571 single-barrel trap guns manufactured. Produced in four grades as listed:

J Grade

Built from 1919 to 1936.

NIB	Exc.	V.G.	Good	Fair	Poor
9500	7000	5000	4000	2000	1000

K Grade

Built from 1919 to 1931. Approximately 75 built.

NIB	Exc.	V.G.	Good	Fair	Poor
12000	9000	6500	5000	2500	1200

L Grade

Built from 1919 to 1931. Approximately 25 built.

NIB	Exc.	V.G.	Good	Fair	Poor
20000	14000	10500	8500	3000	1500

M Grade

One of the rarest, if not the rarest, Fox guns. Built from 1919 to 1932. A total of 9 guns built.

NIB	Exc.	V.G.	Good	Fair	Poor
—	30000	20000	—	—	—

RECENTLY MANUFACTURED A.H. FOX SHOTGUNS

In 1993, Connecticut Shotgun Manufacturing Company of New Britain, Connecticut, announced production of A.H. Fox shotgun in 20-gauge exclusively. Gun is hand-built and constructed to same dimensions and standards as original Fox. Gun offered in five grades, with many standard features and several optional ones as well. Each shotgun built to order. Because these guns are newly built and have no pricing history, only manufacturer's retail price for base gun will be given. Extra sets of barrels, single triggers and other extra costs options will greatly affect price.

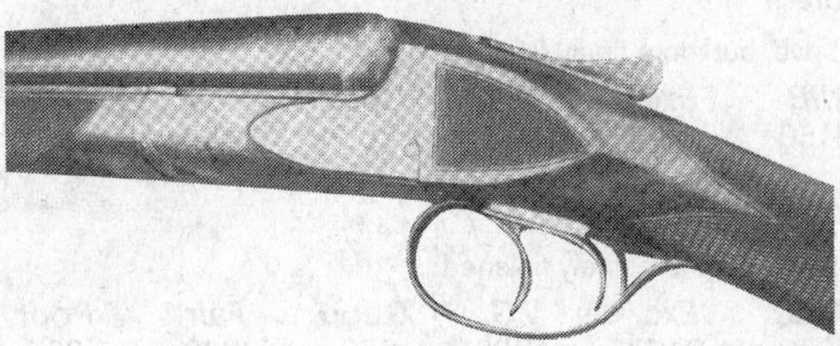

CE Grade

Retail price: $19,500

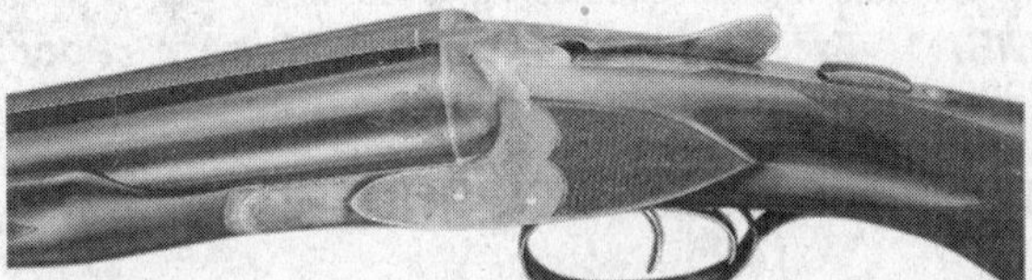

XE Grade

Retail price: $22,000

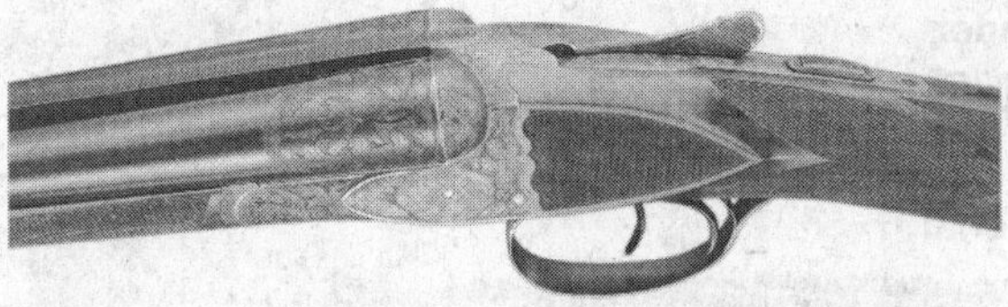

DE Grade

Retail price: $25,000

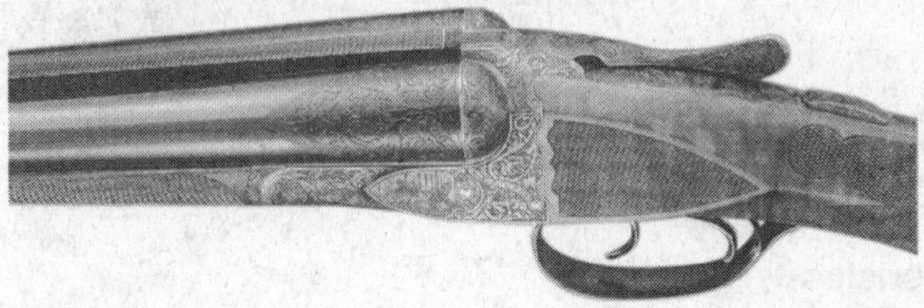

FE Grade

Retail price: $30,000

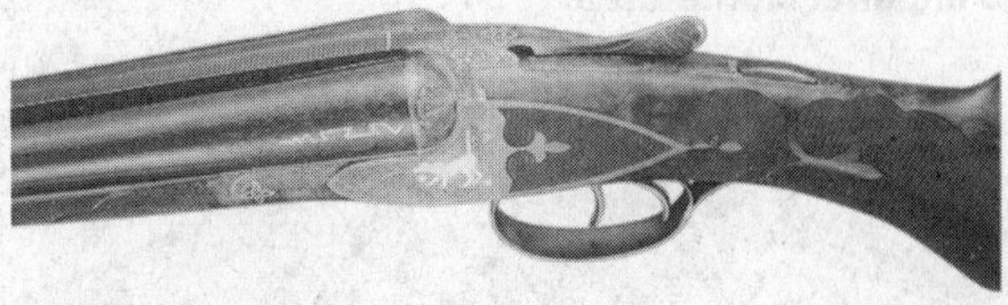

Exhibition Grade

This is the company's highest grade. Features any optional detail the customer desires, including custom engraving and exhibition quality wood. Retail price: On request from CSMC.

FRANCHI, L.

Brescia, Italy

BOXLOCK SIDE-BY-SIDE-SHOTGUNS

Astore

A 12-gauge boxlock shotgun. Manufactured in a variety of barrel lengths, with double triggers and automatic ejectors. Blued, with straight walnut stock. Manufactured from 1937 to 1960.

NIB	Exc.	V.G.	Good	Fair	Poor
2900	1600	750	500	350	200

Astore II

As above, but more finely finished.

NIB	Exc.	V.G.	Good	Fair	Poor
3150	1850	900	700	450	250

Astore 5

As above, but more finely finished.

NIB	Exc.	V.G.	Good	Fair	Poor
3350	2150	1250	950	600	300

Airone

Similar to Astore. Manufactured during 1940s.

NIB	Exc.	V.G.	Good	Fair	Poor
2900	1600	750	500	350	200

SIDELOCK SIDE-BY-SIDE SHOTGUNS

A 12-, 16-, or 20-gauge sidelock double-barrel shotgun. Manufactured in a variety of barrel lengths, with single-selective trigger and automatic ejectors. Produced in the following grades, they differ as to engraving, coverage and quality of wood.

Condor

NIB	Exc.	V.G.	Good	Fair	Poor
7500	6500	4500	3500	2500	1250

Imperial

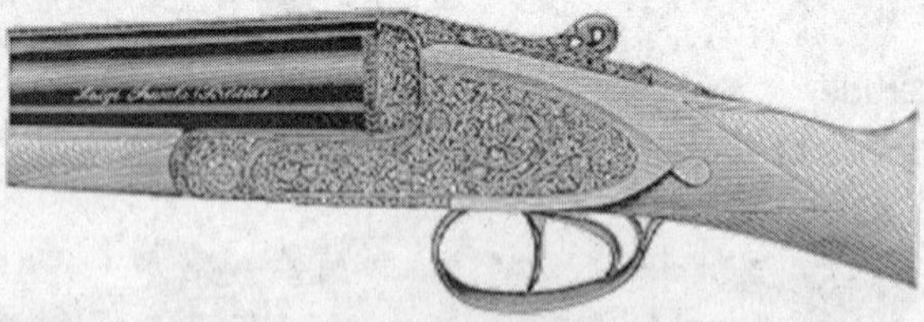

NIB	Exc.	V.G.	Good	Fair	Poor
10000	8500	6000	4500	3250	1500

Imperiales

NIB	Exc.	V.G.	Good	Fair	Poor
10500	9000	6500	5000	3500	1500

No. 5 Imperial Monte Carlo

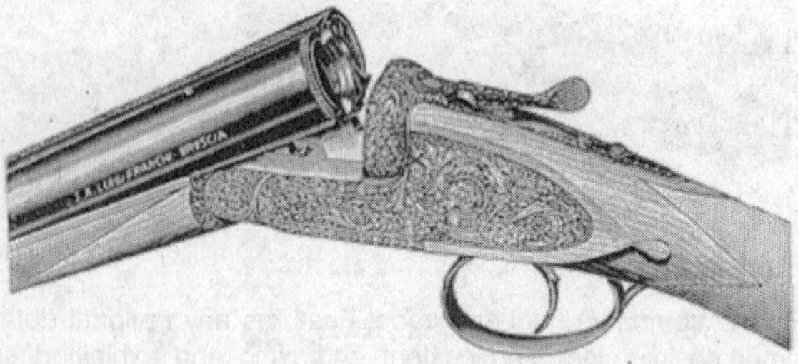

NIB	Exc.	V.G.	Good	Fair	Poor
15000	12500	9000	7500	5000	2000

No. 11 Imperial Monte Carlo

NIB	Exc.	V.G.	Good	Fair	Poor
16000	13500	10000	8000	5500	2000

Imperial Monte Carlo Extra

NIB	Exc.	V.G.	Good	Fair	Poor
20000	17500	12500	9500	7500	3500

Highlander

Introduced in 2003. Features 12, 20 or 28 gauge, fitted with 26" barrels and fixed chokes. Select walnut straight-grip stock, with splinter forend. Coin finished steel receiver. Single trigger. Weight: 6.4 lbs. 12 gauge; 5.8 lbs. 20 gauge; 5.7 lbs. 28 gauge. Note: Add $150 for 28 gauge.

NIB	Exc.	V.G.	Good	Fair	Poor
—	1300	1000	850	480	300

OVER/UNDER SHOTGUNS

Priti Deluxe Model

A 12- or 20-gauge over/under boxlock double-barrel shotgun, with 26" or 28" ventilated rib barrels. Single trigger and automatic ejectors. Introduced in 1988.

NIB	Exc.	V.G.	Good	Fair	Poor
400	350	300	250	200	150

Falconet

A 12, 16, 20, 28 gauge and .410 bore boxlock double-barrel shotgun, with single-selective trigger and automatic ejectors. Receiver was anodized in tan, ebony or silver finishes. Manufactured from 1968 to 1975. Note: Add 10 percent for silver receiver; 25 percent 28-gauge and .410 bore.

NIB	Exc.	V.G.	Good	Fair	Poor
—	800	650	420	350	250

Falconet Skeet

As above, with 26" skeet barrel. Wide rib and receiver case-hardened. Manufactured from 1970 to 1974.

NIB	Exc.	V.G.	Good	Fair	Poor
950	850	700	550	450	250

Falconet International Skeet

As above, but more finely finished.

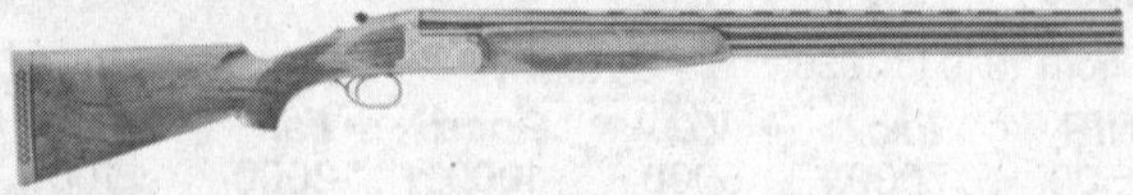

NIB	Exc.	V.G.	Good	Fair	Poor
1050	950	750	600	480	250

Falconet Trap

As above, with 30" Modified Full choke barrel and trap stock. Manufactured from 1970 to 1974.

NIB	Exc.	V.G.	Good	Fair	Poor
1000	900	700	550	450	250

Falconet International Trap

As above, but more finely finished.

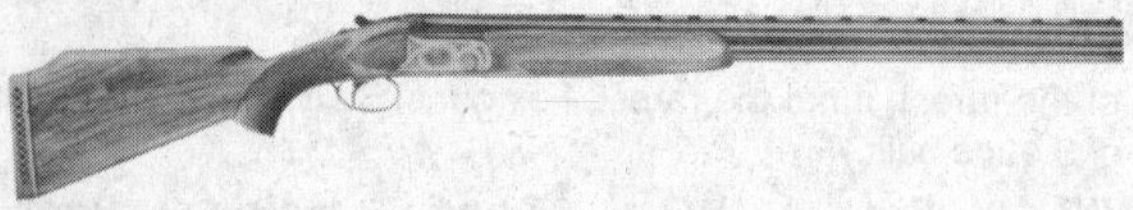

NIB	Exc.	V.G.	Good	Fair	Poor
1050	950	750	600	480	250

Peregrine Model 451

A 12-gauge boxlock double-barrel shotgun, with 26" or 28" ventilated rib barrels. Alloy receiver, single-selective trigger and automatic ejectors. Manufactured in 1975.

NIB	Exc.	V.G.	Good	Fair	Poor
800	680	500	380	280	200

Peregrine Model 400

As above, with steel frame.

NIB	Exc.	V.G.	Good	Fair	Poor
850	780	600	400	300	200

Aristocrat

Similar to above, with 26", 28" or 30" ventilated rib barrels. Manufactured from 1960 to 1969.

NIB	Exc.	V.G.	Good	Fair	Poor
850	720	600	400	300	200

Aristocrat Magnum

As above, with 3" chambers and 32" Full choke barrels.

NIB	Exc.	V.G.	Good	Fair	Poor
900	780	680	450	300	200

Aristocrat Silver King

As above, with French case-hardened receiver. Available in four grades of decoration.

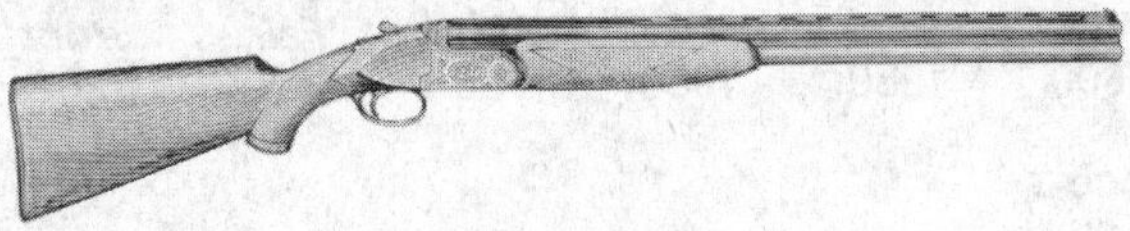

NIB	Exc.	V.G.	Good	Fair	Poor
950	880	780	480	350	200

Aristocrat Deluxe

NIB	Exc.	V.G.	Good	Fair	Poor
1250	1000	880	580	400	200

Aristocrat Supreme

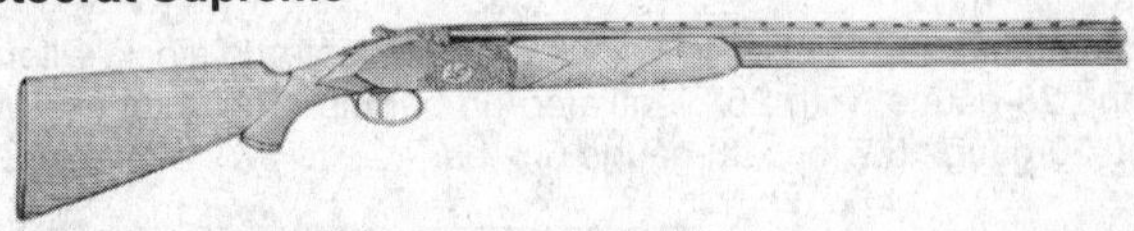

NIB	Exc.	V.G.	Good	Fair	Poor
1650	1400	950	700	580	250

Aristocrat Imperial

NIB	Exc.	V.G.	Good	Fair	Poor
2950	2450	1950	1250	950	450

Aristocrat Monte Carlo

NIB	Exc.	V.G.	Good	Fair	Poor
3750	3200	2950	2000	1500	750

Model 2003 Trap

A 12-gauge boxlock double-barrel shotgun, with 30" or 32" ventilated rib barrels. Single-selective trigger and automatic ejectors. Manufactured in 1976.

NIB	Exc.	V.G.	Good	Fair	Poor
1450	1300	900	650	500	250

Model 2004 Trap

A single-barreled version of Model 2003.

NIB	Exc.	V.G.	Good	Fair	Poor
1450	1300	900	650	500	250

Model 2005 Combination Trap

Model 2003, with both single and set of over/under barrels.

NIB	Exc.	V.G.	Good	Fair	Poor
2800	2400	1950	1200	950	450

Model 3000 "Undergun"

As above, with single-barrel fitted with high ventilated rib so it fires from lower barrel position.

NIB	Exc.	V.G.	Good	Fair	Poor
3050	2850	2200	1500	1200	600

Alcione Classic

Introduced in 2004, this 12-gauge 3" model features 26" or 28" ventilated rib barrels. Side rib ventilated. Walnut stock with schnabel forend. Optional 20-gauge barrels. Weight about 7.5 lbs.

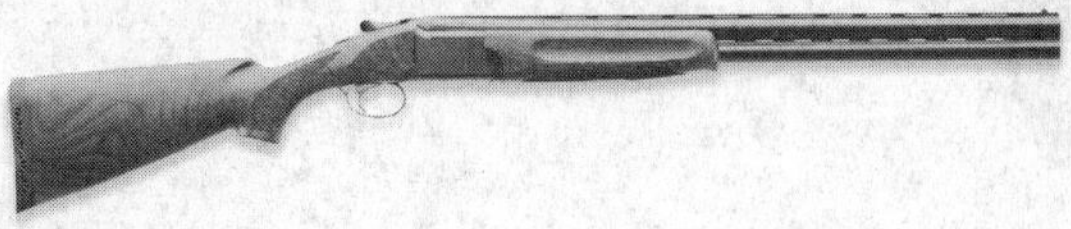

NIB	Exc.	V.G.	Good	Fair	Poor
1300	980	800	600	500	250

Alcione T (Titanium)

Introduced in 2002, this model is similar to Alcione Field. Has an aluminum alloy frame, with titanium inserts. Available in 12- and 20-gauge with 3" chambers. Choice of 26" or 28" ventilated rib barrels, with choke tubes. Weight about 6.8 lbs. for 12- and 20-gauge.

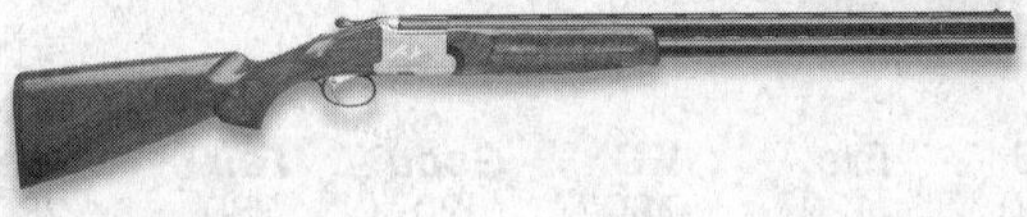

NIB	Exc.	V.G.	Good	Fair	Poor
1400	1150	950	700	600	300

Alcione T Two-Barrel Set

As above, with two-barrel set: one 12-gauge 28"; other 20-gauge 26". Introduced in 2004.

NIB	Exc.	V.G.	Good	Fair	Poor
1600	1280	1100	800	650	350

Alcione Field Model

A 12-gauge boxlock double-barrel shotgun, with 26" or 28" ventilated rib barrels. Single-selective trigger and automatic ejectors. Engraved silver receiver. Weight about 7.5 lbs.

NIB	Exc.	V.G.	Good	Fair	Poor
1200	1000	800	520	300	150

Alcione Sporting

This over/under gun designed for sporting clays competition. Fitted with mechanical triggers and ported barrels. Offered in 12-gauge only, with 30" barrels. Select walnut stock. Removable sideplates. Weight about 7.5 lbs.

NIB	Exc.	V.G.	Good	Fair	Poor
1550	1250	1000	780	400	200

Alcione LF

This 12- or 20-gauge model, features barrels of 26" in 20-gauge; 28" in 12-gauge. Both gauges are chambered for 3" shells. Walnut stock. Receiver is aluminum alloy, with etched games scenes and gold fill. Weight about 6.8 lbs.

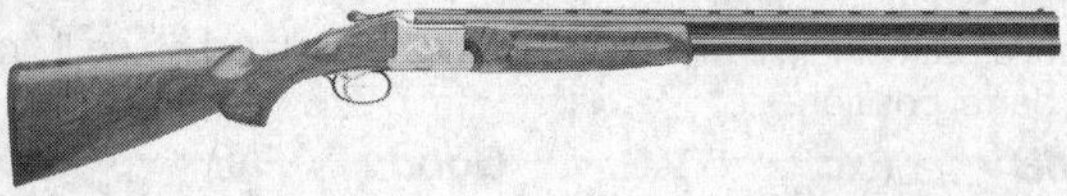

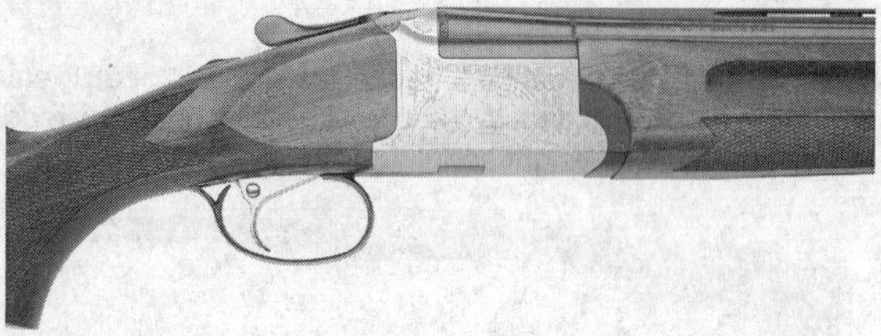

Alcione LF receiver—Right side view

NIB	Exc.	V.G.	Good	Fair	Poor
1300	1050	700	450	300	200

Alcione SL Sport

As above, but more finely finished. French case-hardened receiver.

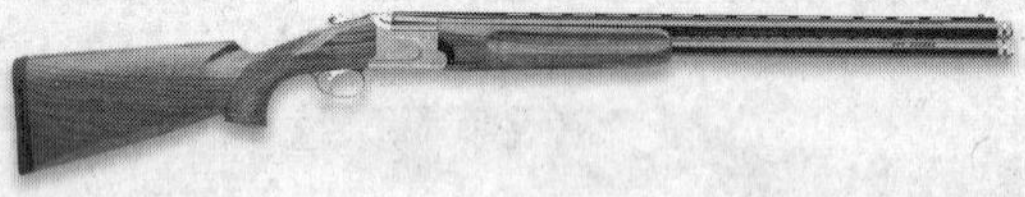

NIB	Exc.	V.G.	Good	Fair	Poor
1380	1120	780	520	380	280

Alcione SP

Chambered for 12-gauge shell and fitted with 28" ventilated rib barrels and choke tubes. Full slide lock-style side plates, with engraving of gold pheasants and mallards. Weight about 7.5 lbs. Introduced in 2003.

NIB	Exc.	V.G.	Good	Fair	Poor
1700	1450	980	700	580	340

ALCIONE SIDEPLATES

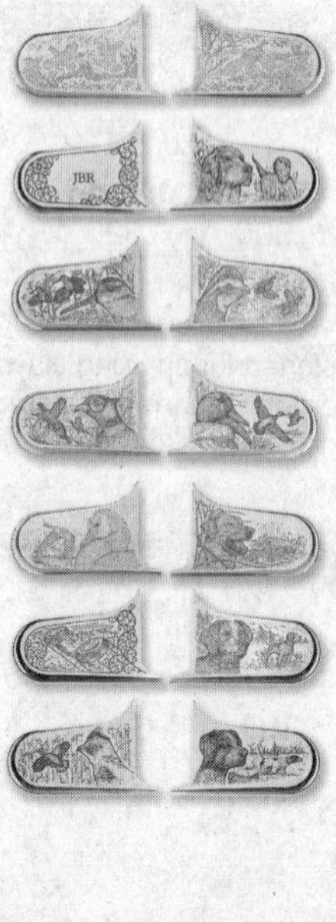

Alcione Classic SX

This 12-gauge 3" model similar to Alcione Field SX above, with blued receiver. Available with choice of 26" or 28" ventilated rib barrels. An extra 12-gauge 30" ported barrel and 20-gauge barrels are also optional. Weight about 7.5 lbs. Introduced in 2004.

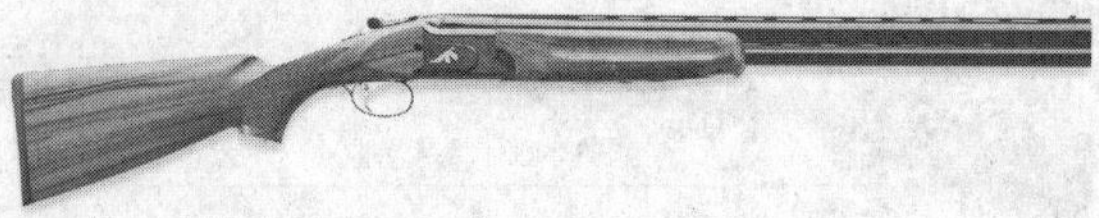

NIB	Exc.	V.G.	Good	Fair	Poor
1400	1150	950	700	600	300

Alcione Field SX

Model fitted with high grade walnut stock, fine checkering and engraved receivers. Gold filled etched side plates. Offered with 26" or 28" barrels. Weight about 7.3 lbs.

NIB	Exc.	V.G.	Good	Fair	Poor
1600	1250	1000	780	400	200

Veloce

Introduced in 2001. Chambered for 20- or 28-gauge only. Barrels: 20-gauge 28"; 28-gauge 26". Aluminum alloy receiver. Engraved side plates, with gold filled game scenes. Mechanical trigger. Select walnut stock. Weight about: 20-gauge 5.8 lbs.; 28-gauge 5.5 lbs.

NIB	Exc.	V.G.	Good	Fair	Poor
1380	1120	780	520	380	280

Veloce English Stock

Introduced in 2002. Similar to Veloce, with straight-grip stock. Offered in 20- and 28-gauge, with 26" ventilated rib barrels. Choke tubes. Weight about: 20-gauge 5.7 lbs.; 28-gauge 5.5 lbs.

NIB	Exc.	V.G.	Good	Fair	Poor
1400	1150	950	700	600	300

Veloce Grade II

This 20- or 28-gauge model, features extra-select-grade walnut stock, with gold-filled birds and scroll engraving. The 20-gauge offered with 26" or 28" ventilated rib barrel; 28-gauge fitted with 26" ventilated rib barrel. Weight about: 20-gauge 5.75 lbs.; 28-gauge 5.5 lbs.

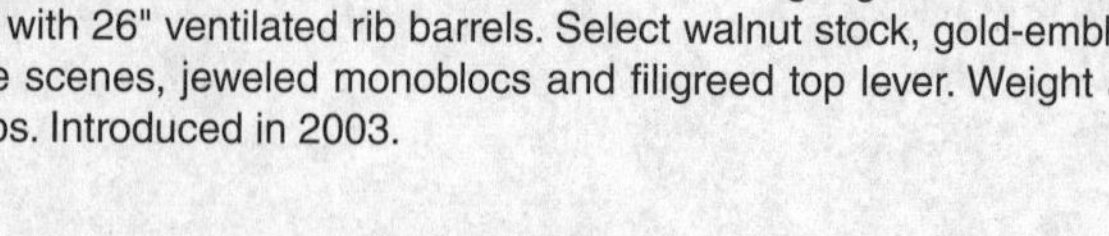

NIB	Exc.	V.G.	Good	Fair	Poor
1600	1280	1100	800	650	350

Veloce Squire Set

Model features a two-barrel set in 20- and 28-gauge. Each barrel set fitted with 26" ventilated rib barrels. Select walnut stock, gold-emblished game scenes, jeweled monoblocs and filigreed top lever. Weight about 5.5 lbs. Introduced in 2003.

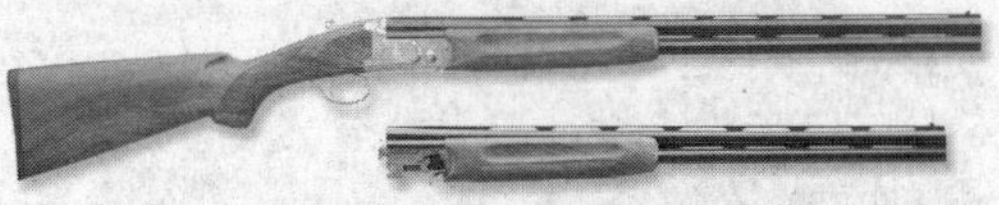

NIB	Exc.	V.G.	Good	Fair	Poor
2100	1780	1600	1200	800	400

Renaissance

Renaissance Series introduced in 2006. These over/unders feature ultra-light alloy receivers, oil-finished walnut stocks, Prince of Wales pistol grips, cut checkering and Twin Shock Absorber recoil pads with gel insert. The 3" 12- and 20-gauges have 26" or 28" barrels; 28-gauge has 26" barrel. Weights average 6.2 lbs. 12-gauge, 5.8 lbs. 20-gauge and 5.5 lbs. 28-gauge. Note: Add 5 percent to values shown for 28-gauge.

Field

Walnut stock, with engraved receiver.

NIB	Exc.	V.G.	Good	Fair	Poor
1600	1250	1000	780	400	200

Classic

A-Grade walnut, with gold inlaid receiver.

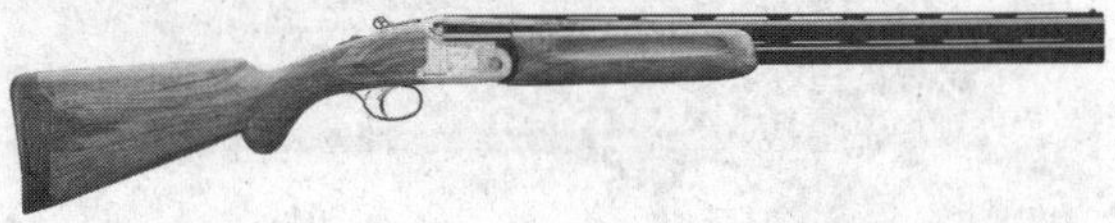

NIB	Exc.	V.G.	Good	Fair	Poor
1650	1300	1050	820	450	250

Elite

AA-Grade Walnut, with gold inlaid receiver.

NIB	Exc.	V.G.	Good	Fair	Poor
1900	1550	1300	1050	650	280

Sporting

This 3" 12-gauge model introduced in 2007. Features 30" barrel, A-Grade walnut stock, engraved receiver with gold inlay and adjustable comb. Weight about 7.9 lbs.

NIB	Exc.	V.G.	Good	Fair	Poor
1980	1620	1350	1300	820	320

Aspire

Discontinued 2015. 28 gauge and .410 bore with round-action receiver, single-selective trigger, automatic ejectors, AA-grade oil-finished walnut stock, ventilated rib and choke tubes. Barrels are 28" and weight just under 6 lbs.

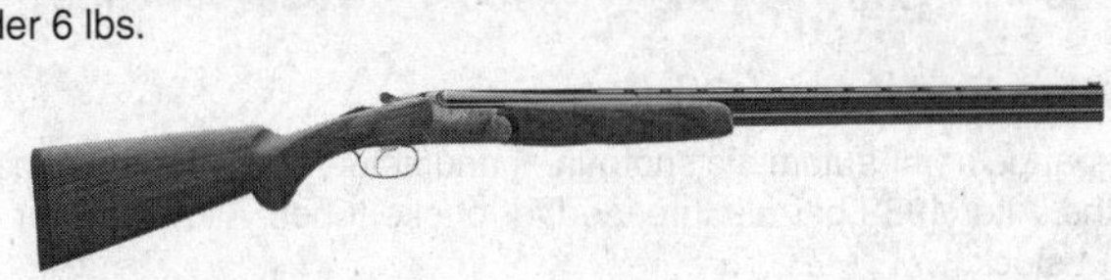

NIB	Exc.	V.G.	Good	Fair	Poor
—	1680	1420	1200	950	450

Instinct

Over/under in 12 or 20 gauge. Features 26" or 28" barrels with 3" chambers, five choke tubes, automatic ejectors, single-selective trigger, checkered A-grade walnut stock with satin finish. Available with AA-grade wood; add $200. Sporting model has 30" barrels with extended choke tubes, nickel receiver, target stock with squared pistol grip; add $350. Introduced in 2012. Sporting II introduced 2019. "L" model, chambered in 12, 20, and 28 gauge and .410 bore, has all-steel color-case receiver with the name "Instinct L" engraved in gold on the right side. Prince of Wales–style stock, satin oil-finish, 28" barrels.

NIB	Exc.	V.G.	Good	Fair	Poor
1000	850	700	550	400	300

Instinct SL

Introduced 2012 in 12 and 20 gauge. 16 gauge introduced 2018. Has polished aluminum-alloy scalloped receiver attached to 26" or 28" barrels. Red fiber-optic front sight. Stock is cut from A-grade walnut in Prince of Wales style, cut-checkering, oil-finish.

NIB	Exc.	V.G.	Good	Fair	Poor
1400	1300	1100	900	700	500

Instinct SL 28 Gauge/.410 Bore

NIB	Exc.	V.G.	Good	Fair	Poor
1600	—	—	—	—	—

Instinct LX

Introduced 2019. Upgraded Instinct model with checkered AA-Grade walnut stock and Schnabel forend. Engraved receiver with gold-inlaid highlights, vented gloss-blue barrels with 3 extended choke tubes, red fiber-optic bead, vented rib. Safety-mounted selector switch, ejectors, and a fitted hard case. In 12 or 20 gauge, 28" barrels with 3" chambers.

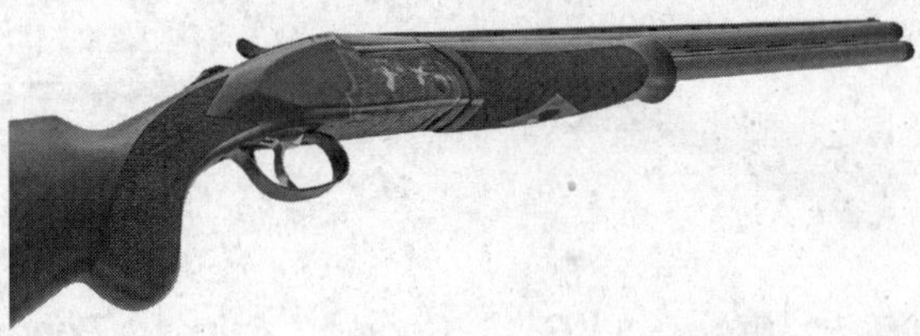

NIB	Exc.	V.G.	Good	Fair	Poor
1500	1400	1300	1200	1000	800

Instinct SLX

Gauges: 12 ga., 3 in., 16 ga., 2.75 in., 20 ga., 3 in. Barrel: 28 in., ventilated rib. Length: 46.25 in. Weight: 5.6-6.3 lbs. Stock: AA-grade walnut. Features: Similar to the SL family of O/Us, but with both reduced weight and the addition of deluxe aesthetics. Floral engraving on the receiver along with a gold trigger and inlays. Upgraded wood, Prince of Wales grip and Schnabel forend. Auto ejectors, barrel select switch, red fiber-optic front sight, gloss-blued barrels, tang safety. Includes five extended choke tubes and a hard case.

NIB	Exc.	V.G.	Good	Fair	Poor
1800	—	—	—	—	—

Instinct Sideplate

Gauges: 16 ga., 28 ga. Barrels: 28" Stock: AA-Grade Walnut with Prince of Wales grip and Schnabel forend. Features: Addition of two gauges to the upland O/U family. Three-inch chambers. Gold-inlaid game scenes and blued barrels. Auto ejectors and auto safety. Ships with five extended choke tubes and a custom-fitted hard case.

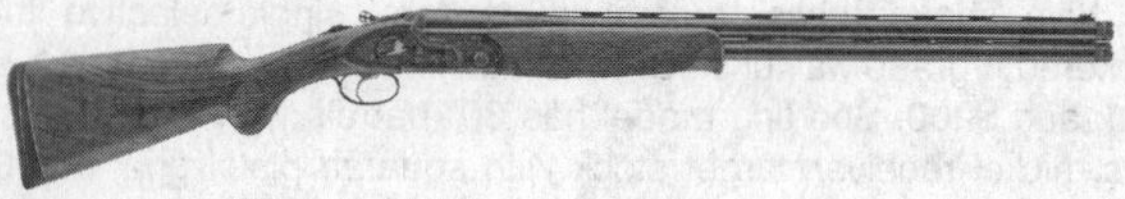

NIB	Exc.	V.G.	Good	Fair	Poor
2220	2100	1930	1700	1450	—

SEMI-AUTOMATIC SHOTGUNS

AL48

A 12- or 20-gauge semi-automatic shotgun, with 24" to 30" ventilated rib barrels (those made after 1989, threaded for choke tubes) and an alloy receiver. Walnut stock. Manufactured since 1950. Values shown are for current production. Note: Add 10 percent for Magnum Model; $75 for 28-gauge model.

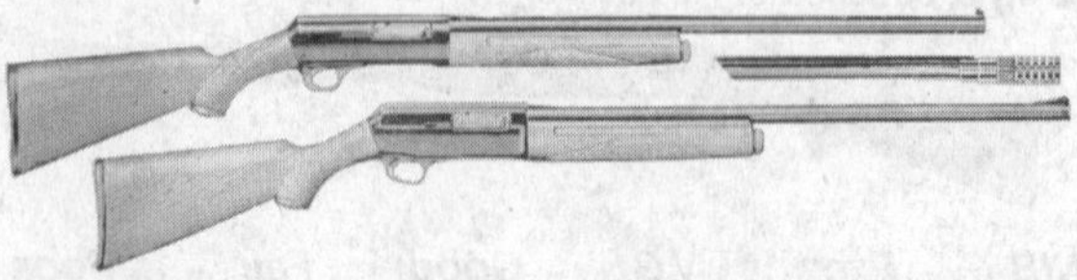

NIB	Exc.	V.G.	Good	Fair	Poor
720	550	300	250	150	100

AL 48 Short Stock (Modern)

Same as above in 20-gauge, with shorter length of pull. First imported in 2000.

NIB	Exc.	V.G.	Good	Fair	Poor
700	520	280	250	150	100

AL 48 Deluxe English Stock (Modern)

Similar to standard AL 48, with straight-grip stock. Offered in 20- and 28-gauge, with 26" ventilated rib barrel and choke tubes. Weight about 5.5 lbs. Introduced in 2002.

NIB	Exc.	V.G.	Good	Fair	Poor
800	620	380	280	180	100

Hunter Model AL48 (1950-1970)

As above, with an etched receiver and more finely figured wood. Note: Add 10 percent for Magnum model.

NIB	Exc.	V.G.	Good	Fair	Poor
550	350	300	250	200	150

Eldorado AL48 (1954-1975)

As above, but more finely finished. Manufactured from 1954 to 1975.

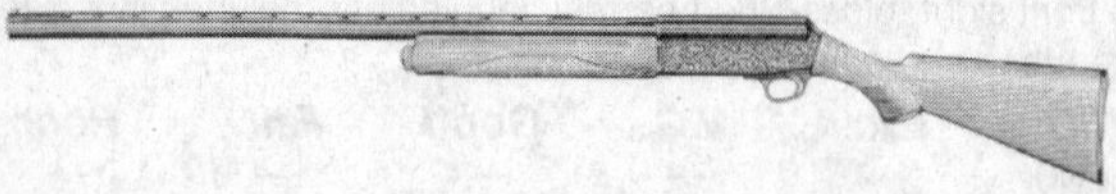

NIB	Exc.	V.G.	Good	Fair	Poor
600	420	320	250	200	150

Crown Grade

As above, with hand-done engraving and finely figured walnut stocks.

NIB	Exc.	V.G.	Good	Fair	Poor
1800	1450	1200	800	480	250

Diamond Grade

As above, with hand-done engraving and finely figured walnut stocks.

NIB	Exc.	V.G.	Good	Fair	Poor
2300	1850	1380	900	580	300

Imperial Grade

As above, with hand-done engraving and finely figured walnut stocks.

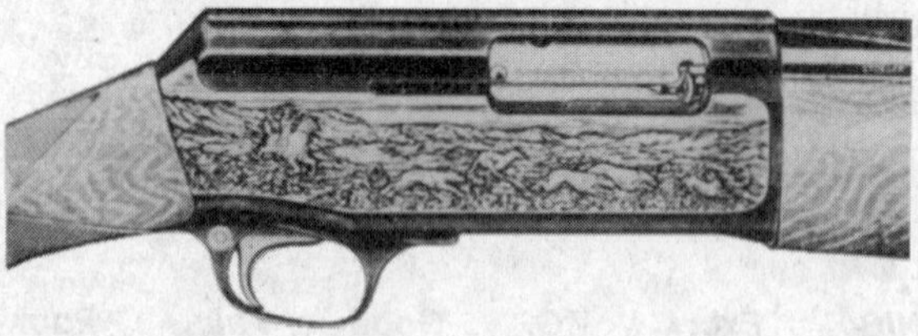

NIB	Exc.	V.G.	Good	Fair	Poor
2800	2450	1850	1250	950	450

Model 500

A 12-gauge semi-automatic shotgun, with 28" ventilated rib barrel and walnut stock. Introduced in 1976. Note: Add 10 percent for deluxe version.

NIB	Exc.	V.G.	Good	Fair	Poor
500	420	380	300	150	100

Model 520 "Eldorado Gold"

An engraved and gold-inlaid version of above.

NIB	Exc.	V.G.	Good	Fair	Poor
1250	1050	850	550	300	150

Model 530 Trap

Model 500, with 30" or 32" ventilated rib barrel and trap stock.

NIB	Exc.	V.G.	Good	Fair	Poor
680	600	500	400	300	150

Prestige Model

A 12-gauge semi-automatic shotgun, manufactured in a variety of barrel lengths. After 1989 barrels threaded for choke tubes. Alloy receiver and walnut stock.

NIB	Exc.	V.G.	Good	Fair	Poor
680	550	480	350	250	150

Elite Model

As above, with etched receiver and more finely figured stock.

NIB	Exc.	V.G.	Good	Fair	Poor
700	600	520	350	250	150

SPAS12

A 12-gauge slide-action semi-automatic shotgun, with 21.5" barrel and 9-shot magazine. Anodized black finish, with composition folding or fixed stock.

NIB	Exc.	V.G.	Good	Fair	Poor
1450	1000	800	600	480	300

Black Magic Game Model

A 12-gauge Magnum semi-automatic shotgun, with 24" to 28" ventilated rib barrels. Threaded for choke tubes, gold anodized alloy receiver, blackened barrel and walnut stock. Also available in trap or skeet configuration. Note: Add 10 percent for Skeet Model; 15 percent for Trap Model.

NIB	Exc.	V.G.	Good	Fair	Poor
750	600	520	300	250	100

Black Magic Hunter

A 12- or 20-gauge Magnum double-barrel shotgun, with 28" ventilated rib barrels. Threaded for choke tubes, single-selective triggers and automatic ejectors. Blued, with a walnut stock. Introduced in 1989.

NIB	Exc.	V.G.	Good	Fair	Poor
700	550	480	300	250	100

Black Magic Lightweight Hunter

As above, with 26" barrels and 2.75" chambers.

NIB	Exc.	V.G.	Good	Fair	Poor
980	850	650	400	300	150

Variomax 912

Introduced in 2001, this model chambered for 12-gauge 3.5" shell. Offered with choice of 24", 26", 28" or 30" barrels with ventilated rib. Black synthetic stock. Weight about 7.6 lbs. Choke tubes. In 2002 a walnut stock added as an option. Note: Add $50 for walnut stock.

NIB	Exc.	V.G.	Good	Fair	Poor
700	550	480	300	250	100

Variomax 912 Camo

Same as above, with Advantage Timber camo finish.

NIB	Exc.	V.G.	Good	Fair	Poor
750	600	520	300	250	100

Variomax 912 SteadyGrip

Introduced in 2005. Features extended pistol grip Advantage H-D camo stock, with 24" ventilated rib barrel and choke tubes. Weight about 8 lbs.

NIB	Exc.	V.G.	Good	Fair	Poor
780	620	550	320	260	100

Variopress 612 Sporting

A 12-gauge semi-automatic gas-operated shotgun, with 30" ported barrel. Extended choke tubes. Select walnut stock, with stock drop kit. Magazine capacity 5 rounds. Weight about 7 lbs. First imported in 2000.

NIB	Exc.	V.G.	Good	Fair	Poor
700	550	480	300	250	100

Variopress 612 Field

This 12-gauge model offered with barrel lengths from 24" to 28". Stock configurations are walnut, synthetic or camo. Magazine capacity 5 rounds. Weight about 7 lbs., depending on barrel length.

NIB	Exc.	V.G.	Good	Fair	Poor
700	550	480	300	250	100

Variopress 612 Defense

This 12-gauge gun fitted with 18.5" barrel and black synthetic stock. Matte black finish. Choke is cylinder. Weight about 6.5 lbs. Magazine capacity 5 rounds. First imported in 2000.

NIB	Exc.	V.G.	Good	Fair	Poor
600	500	420	350	250	150

Variopress 620 Field

Model offered in 20-gauge, with choice of walnut or camo stock. Barrel lengths from 24" to 28". Magazine capacity 5 rounds. Weight about 6 lbs. Note: Add $50 for camo stock.

NIB	Exc.	V.G.	Good	Fair	Poor
700	550	480	300	250	100

Variopress 620 Short Stock

Same as above, with 12.5" length of pull and walnut stock. First imported in 2000.

NIB	Exc.	V.G.	Good	Fair	Poor
700	550	480	300	250	100

Model 712

Semi-automatic shotgun, chambered for 12-gauge 3" shell. Choice of 24", 26" or 28" ventilated rib barrels with choke tubes. Offered in several different finishes: Weathercoat (synthetic wood), Max-4 camo and Timber HD. Choice of synthetic wood, black synthetic or camo stock. Weight about 6.8 lbs. to 7 lbs., depending on stock and barrel length. Introduced in 2004.

Weathercoat

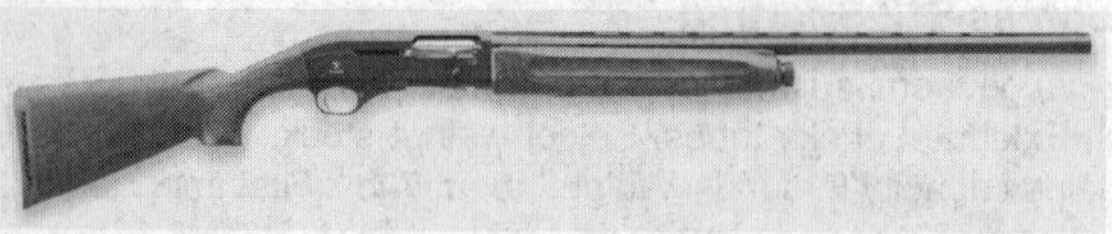

NIB	Exc.	V.G.	Good	Fair	Poor
700	600	500	380	200	100

Camo

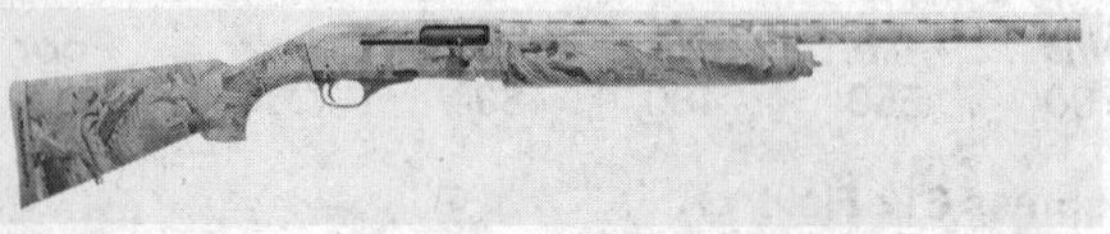

NIB	Exc.	V.G.	Good	Fair	Poor
720	620	520	400	220	120

Synthetic

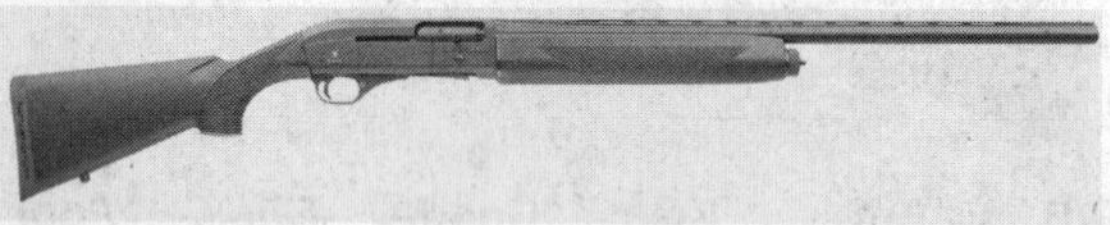

NIB	Exc.	V.G.	Good	Fair	Poor
780	650	550	420	250	150

Model 720

Similar to Model 712, but chambered for 20-gauge 3" shell. Offered with 24", 26" or 28" ventilated rib barrels. Choice of Max-4, Timber HD finish or walnut stock, with 12.5" lop. Introduced in 2004.

Camo

NIB	Exc.	V.G.	Good	Fair	Poor
750	650	550	420	250	150

Walnut Short Stock

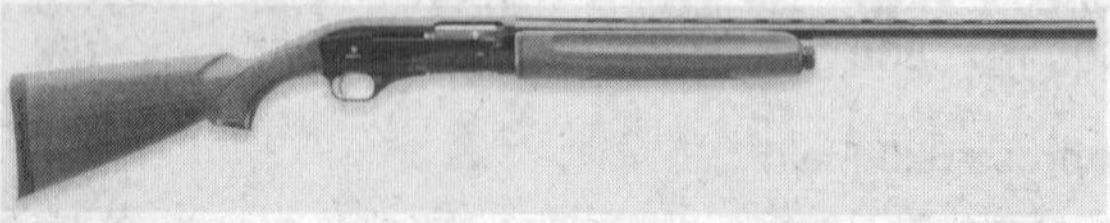

NIB	Exc.	V.G.	Good	Fair	Poor
720	620	520	400	220	120

Weathercoat

Introduced in 2005, with 28" ventilated rib barrel. Weight about 6.2 lbs.

NIB	Exc.	V.G.	Good	Fair	Poor
780	650	550	420	250	150

I-12

Introduced in 2005, this 12-gauge model offered with 3" chambers and choice of 24", 26" or 28" ventilated rib barrels. Available with synthetic, walnut, Max-4 or Timber H-D stock. Choke tubes. Weight about 7.5 lbs., depending on barrel length.

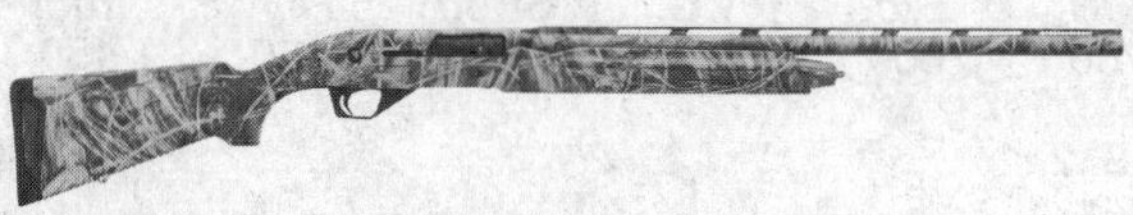

NIB	Exc.	V.G.	Good	Fair	Poor
1200	900	600	500	350	200

I-12 White Gold

Similar to Inertia I-12, with highly figured walnut stock. White gold game bird scene on a satin nickel receiver. Introduced in 2006. Available only with 28" barrel. Weight about 7.7 lbs.

NIB	Exc.	V.G.	Good	Fair	Poor
1400	1050	750	600	420	250

Fenice

Small-frame semi-automatic built on Franchi's classic recoil-operated AL-48 design. No recoil problem, however, Fenice is only in 28-gauge and .410 bore. Among the quality features are AA-grade European walnut stock, 26" or 28" barrel with ventilated rib and nickel-plated receiver with scroll engraving and inlayed game bird scene. Weight: 20-gauge 5.75 lbs.; 28-gauge 5.4 lbs.

NIB	Exc.	V.G.	Good	Fair	Poor
1150	1000	850	620	450	300

Intensity

Semi-automatic operates on Inertia Driven system, which is designed to operate with 2.75", 3" and 3.5" 12-gauge shells. Barrel lengths are 26", 28" or 30" and weight of all three length models is between 6.7 and 6.9 lbs. Synthetic stock makes it ideal for all weather conditions. Several Realtree and Mossy Oak camo designs are available. Note: Add $100 for camo models if in good or better condition.

NIB	Exc.	V.G.	Good	Fair	Poor
980	800	680	500	380	300

Affinity

Semi-automatic in 12- or 20-gauge with 3" chambers and three choke tubes. Black finish or 100 percent camo coverage. Sporting model in 12-gauge only, with 30" barrel and nickel receiver. Introduced in 2012. Note: Add $100 for camo finish; $300 for Sporting model.

NIB	Exc.	V.G.	Good	Fair	Poor
750	650	500	400	300	250

Affinity 3

Introduced in 2012. Semi-automatic in 12 or 20 gauge with 3" and 3.5" chambers and three choke tubes, 26" or 28" barrels. Satin-finish walnut, black synthetic, or camo finishes. Later models have an over-sized bolt release and charging handle, improved loading port, drilled and tapped receiver, stepped vent rib, fiber-optic front sight, Mobil choke system. Sporting model in 12 gauge only, with 30" barrel and nickel receiver. Compact model has 12.4" length-of-pull, ¼" spacers can be added as well as a full-size buttstock. Left-Hand model available in black synthetic, 28" barrel 12 gauge. Note: Add $100 for camo finish; $300 for Sporting model (2019). Catalyst model has optimized buttstock for women, with raised comb.

NIB	Exc.	V.G.	Good	Fair	Poor
980	700	600	500	400	300

Affinity 3 Companion Series

Introduced 2019. Includes detailed engravings of a Labrador Retriever on nickel-colored receiver. AA-Grade satin walnut stock and forend with cut checkering, and a gold trigger inside black triggerguard. Large bolt controls, chrome-lined barrel, vented rib and Mobil chokes. Inertia Driven action, TSA recoil pad. 12 gauge, 3" chamber, 26" and 28" barrels, IC, M, F chokes. 6.9 lbs. for 12 gauge, 6 lbs. for 20.

NIB	Exc.	V.G.	Good	Fair	Poor
1400	1300	1100	900	700	500

Affinity 3.5 Elite

Introduced 2019. Weather-resistant Cerakote finish, Franchi Precision Cones. Stocks are adjustable for drop and cast. TSA recoil pads, wide loading ports, Sure Cycle large bolt releases and oversized bolt handles. 12 gauge 3.5" chamber models come in Optifade Waterfowl Marsh/Burnt Bronze Cerakote finish or Optifade Waterfowl Timber/Cobalt Cerakote. Capacity: 4+1. Truglo dual-color fiber-optic bar front sight. 28" barrels, 49.5" OAL, 7 lbs.

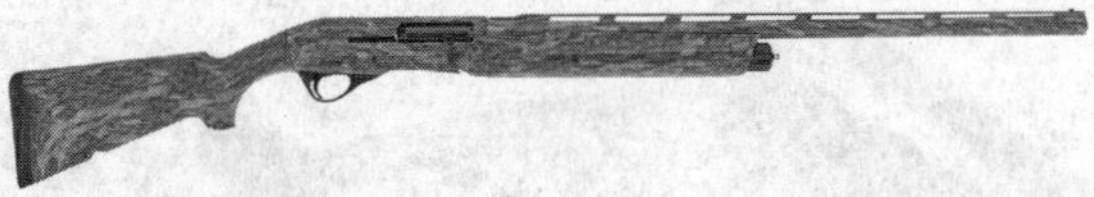

NIB	Exc.	V.G.	Good	Fair	Poor
1250	1050	850	650	450	250

Affinity 3 Elite

Introduced 2019. Similar to 3.5 Elite with 12- and 20-gauge 3" chamberings. 26" barrels in 20 gauge and 28" barrels in 12 gauge. 47.25" to 49.25" OAL, 6 to 6.9 lbs.

NIB	Exc.	V.G.	Good	Fair	Poor
1100	1000	800	600	400	200

Affinity Turkey

Gauge: 12 ga. 3.5 in, 20ga. 3in. Barrel: 24 in. ventilated rib. Length: 40.0 in. Weight: 6.7–7.5 lbs. Stock: Synthetic pistol grip style with Mossy Oak Bottomland camo. Features: Italian-made inertia-drive semi-auto for turkey hunters. Oversized controls, enlarged loading port, sling attachments. Drilled and tapped for optics mounting. Adjustable rear sight, hooded fiber-optic front sight. Capacity of 4+1 rounds. Modular trigger assembly removes quickly for cleaning. Ships with extended Turkey and Turkey XF chokes.

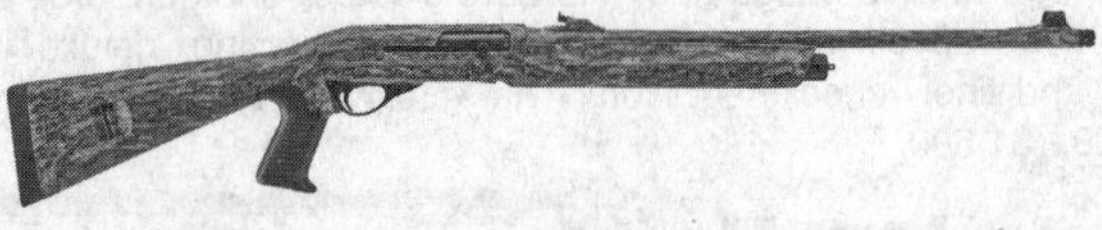

NIB	Exc.	V.G.	Good	Fair	Poor
840	550	460	—	—	—

Affinity Elite Turkey

Gauge: 12 ga. 3 in., 20 ga. 3 in. Barrel: 24 in. ventilated rib. Length: 41.0–41.4 in. Weight: 6.8– 7.7 lbs. Stock: Synthetic pistol grip style with OptiFade SubAlpine camo. Features: Built on the Affinity Italian-made Inertia-Drive semi-automatic action. Midnight Bronze Cerakote metalwork finish. Oversized controls, lengthened forcing cone. Adjustable, fiber-optic rear sight and hooded fiber-optic front. Oversized loading port, sling attachments. Picatinny rail for optics mounting. Capacity of 4+1 rounds. Ships with two gobbler-specific ported and extended chokes (Rhino Turkey and Rhino Extra-Full Turkey).

NIB	Exc.	V.G.	Good	Fair	Poor
1100	930	800	—	—	—

RIFLES

Centennial Semi-Automatic

A .22-caliber semi-automatic rifle, with 21" barrel, adjustable sights, Alloy receiver and walnut stock. Manufactured in 1968 only. Note: Add 20 percent for deluxe engraved model.

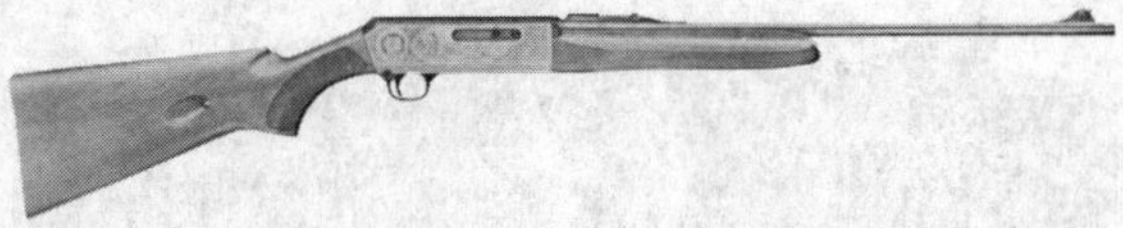

NIB	Exc.	V.G.	Good	Fair	Poor
550	380	320	250	180	120

Momentum Elite

Calibers: 6.5 Creedmoor, .308 Win., .223 Rem. Capacity: 3+1, 4+1. Barrel: 22 to 24 in., threaded, free-floating with Cerakote finish. Stock: Synthetic, ergonomic. Sights: One-piece Picatinny rail. Weight: 7.1 to 7.5 lbs. Features: TSA recoil pad, hinged floorplate, multiple camo stock options.

NIB	Exc.	V.G.	Good	Fair	Poor
780	—	—	—	—	—

Momentum Elite Varmint

Calibers: .223 Rem., .22-250 Rem., .224 Valkyrie, 6.5 Creedmoor, .308 Win. Capacity: 3–4-round flush magazines or 7–8-round extended magazines. Barrel: 24-in. free-floating, heavy, spiral-fluted, threaded. Weight: 9.0–9.4 lbs. Length: 46.75 in. Stock: Evolved EGONOM-X synthetic with removeable cheek rest and checkered-polymer grip, finished in Sitka OptiFade Subalpine camo. Sights: One-piece Picatinny rail. Features: Varmint addition to the Momentum Elite family gets caliber additions for 2022. Stock designed specifically for varmint hunting. Midnight Bronze Cerakote metalwork. RELIA-Trigger adjustable from 2–4 pounds. MOA accuracy guarantee. DEPENDA bolt with three locking lugs and 60-degree throw.

NIB	Exc.	V.G.	Good	Fair	Poor
930	—	—	—	—	—

Momentum All Terrain Elite

Caliber: .223 Rem./5.56 NATO, .308 Win./7.62 NATO. Barrel: 18" free-floating, threaded. Weight: 7.5 lbs. Stock: Synthetic in True Timber Strata. Features: Specialized version of the Momentum bolt actions. Optimized for carrying. Modular stock with a low-rise comb and M-LOK and QD points. Metalwork in Midnight Bronze Cerakote. Extended Picatinny rail. AICS 10-round magazine. Flip-up adjustable iron sights. Relia adjustable single-stage trigger and MOA guarantee. Threaded barrel with muzzle brake. TSA recoil pad.

NIB	Exc.	V.G.	Good	Fair	Poor
1350	—	—	—	—	—

FRANCOTTE, A.
Liege, Belgium

For pistols and revolvers See—AFC.

Jubilee

A 12-, 16-, 20- and 28-gauge Anson & Deeley boxlock double-barrel shotgun, with various barrel lengths and chokes. Automatic ejectors, double triggers and walnut stock.

NIB	Exc.	V.G.	Good	Fair	Poor
—	2000	1350	1100	850	450

No. 14

Courtesy William Hammond

NIB	Exc.	V.G.	Good	Fair	Poor
—	3000	2050	1700	1300	650

No. 18

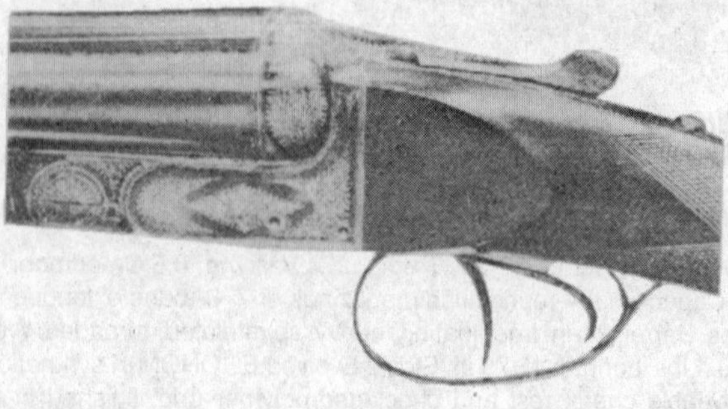

NIB	Exc.	V.G.	Good	Fair	Poor
—	3500	3000	2200	1500	750

No. 20

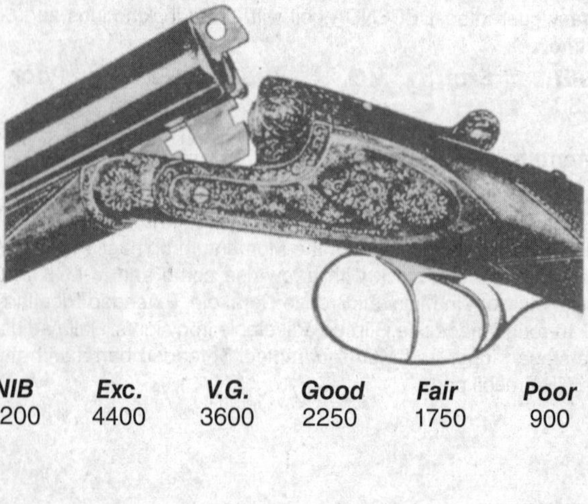

NIB	Exc.	V.G.	Good	Fair	Poor
5200	4400	3600	2250	1750	900

No. 25

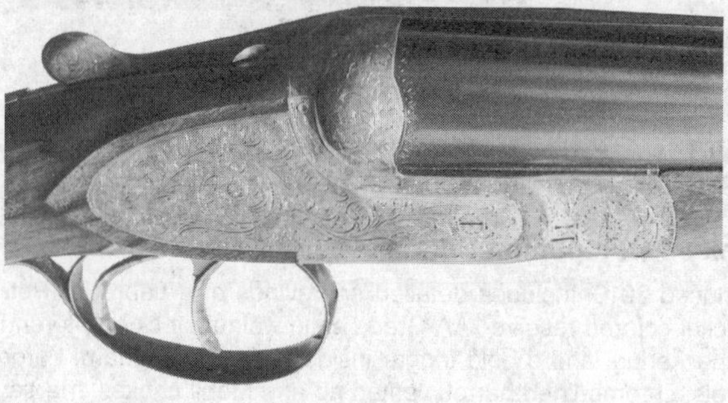

NIB	Exc.	V.G.	Good	Fair	Poor
—	6000	5200	2750	2000	1000

No. 30

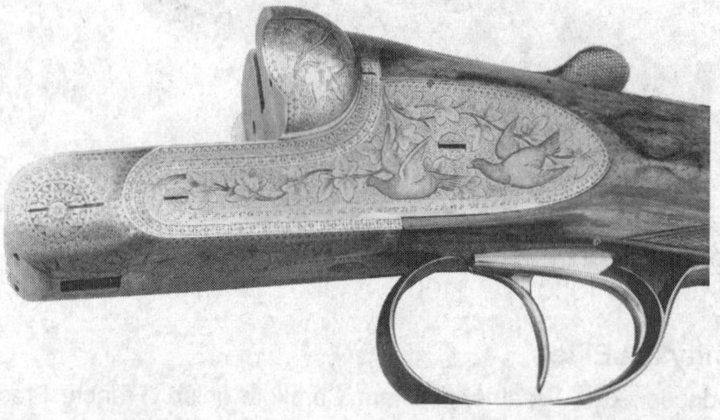

Courtesy William Hammond

NIB	Exc.	V.G.	Good	Fair	Poor
8000	6800	5000	3500	3000	1500

Eagle Grade No. 45

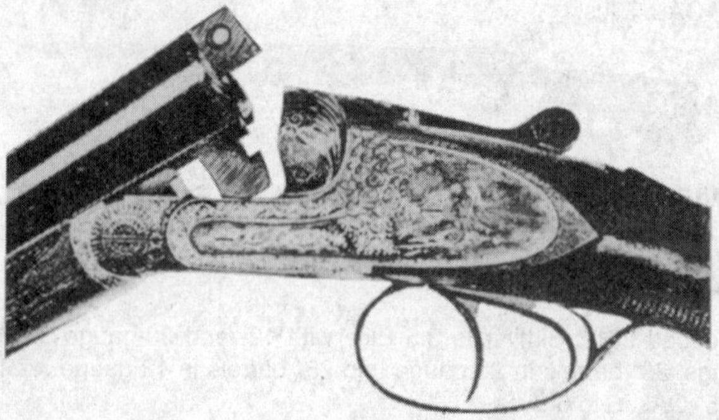

NIB	Exc.	V.G.	Good	Fair	Poor
12000	10000	8000	5000	3000	1000

Knockabout

Plain version of Jubilee Model, in 12-, 16-, 20-, 28-gauge and .410 bore. Note: Add 20 percent for 20-gauge; 30 percent for 28-gauge; 40 percent for .410 bore.

NIB	Exc.	V.G.	Good	Fair	Poor
—	2700	2000	1000	650	500

Sidelock Side-by-Side

A 12-, 16-, 20-, 28-gauge and .410 bore sidelock shotgun, ordered per customer's specifications. Extensive scroll engraving, deluxe walnut stock and finely checkered. Note: The .410 will bring a premium from $1,200 - $1,500.

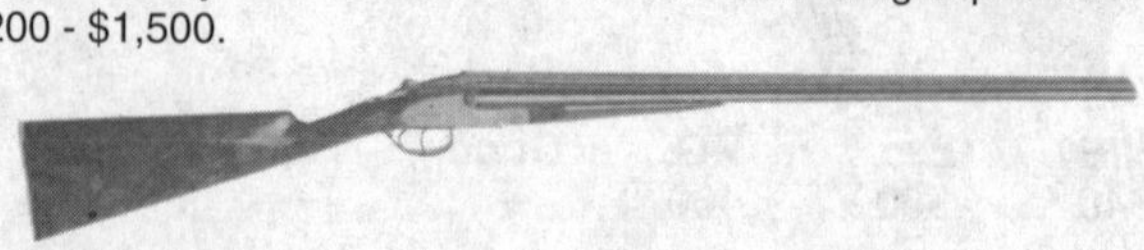

NIB	Exc.	V.G.	Good	Fair	Poor
25000	20000	12000	6500	5000	3500

Deluxe Sidelock Side-by-Side

As above, with gold-inlaid hunting scenes.

NIB	Exc.	V.G.	Good	Fair	Poor
30000	24000	16000	8000	5750	4800

CUSTOM MADE SHOTGUNS & RIFLES

These shotguns and rifles were all custom built to customer's specifications. Gauge (including 24- and 32-gauge), caliber, barrel length, engraving, wood type and style are all individually produced. No two are alike. These shotguns and rifles should be individually appraised before sale. Prices listed are subject to fluctuations in international currency.

Custom Side-by-Side Shotguns

Available in 12-, 16-, 20-, 28-gauge and .410 bore, in boxlock or sidelock actions. Barrel length, engraving, wood type and style are at customer's discretion. Retail prices range from: Basic Boxlock with 27.5" barrels and walnut stock with double triggers in 12-, 16- and 20-gauge without engraving—$18,000

Basic Boxlock in 28-gauge or .410 bore without engraving—$14,000

Basic Boxlock with 26.5" or 28" barrels and deluxe walnut stock, with scroll engraving and double triggers in 12-, 16- and 20-gauge—$23,000

Basic Boxlock in 28-gauge or .410 bore—$28,000

Prices for 24- and 32-gauge are extra. These prices do not include engraving.

Custom Double Rifles

These custom built double rifles were offered, in calibers from 9.3x74R to .470 Nitro Express, in boxlock or sidelock actions. Barrel length, engraving, wood type and style are at customer's discretion. Retail prices range from: Prices for 24- and 32-gauge are extra. These prices do not include engraving.

Boxlock in 9.3x74R, 8x57JRS and other European calibers-$14,000

Boxlock in.375 H&H and.470 NE—$19,000

Sidelock in 9.3x74R, etc.—$23,700

Sidelock in large calibers—$32,000

Custom Single-Shot Mountain Rifles

These single-shot rifles were offered in rimmed cartridges, but rimless cartridge rifles can be built on special request. Barrel length, engraving, wood type and style are at customer's discretion. Retail prices range from: Boxlock in rimmed calibers—Prices start at $13,000

Sidelock in 7x65R and 7mm Rem. Magnum—Prices start at $24,000

Custom Bolt-Action Rifles

These bolt-action rifles utilize a Mauser 98 type action, with adjustable trigger. Offered in calibers from .17 Bee to .505 Gibbs. Barrel lengths are 21" to 24.5". Engraving, wood type and style are at customers' discretion. Retail prices range from:

Standard bolt-action calibers: .270, .30-06, 7x64, 8x60S and 9.3x62—Prices start at $7,650

Short-action calibers: .222, .223—Prices start at $9,100

Magnum-action calibers: 7mm Rem. Magnum, .300 Win. Magnum, .338 Win. Magnum, .375 H&H and .458 Win. Magnum—Prices start at $8,400

African calibers: .416 Rigby, .460 Wby., .505 Gibbs—Prices start at $12,250

PLEASE Note: Prices listed are for basic models. They do not reflect the extensive list of options available on these custom firearms.

REVOLVERS AND PISTOLS

Pinfire Revolver

In the mid-19th century, Francotte was a major producer of pinfire revolvers. Developed at a time when self-contained metallic cartridges were rapidly gaining popularity over slow-loading percussion revolvers, the pinfire system competed with the rimfire, and both preceded the centerfire system. Pinfire revolvers enjoyed broad popularity in Europe for several decades. Francotte made a variety of pinfire handguns. Values here are for large caliber six-shot revolvers. High capacity revolvers, revolvers with attached folding knife bayonets, exceptionally engraved revolvers, and pinfire pepperbox revolvers may bring large premiums. Smaller-caliber revolvers will bring less. Readers with more information on Francotte pinfire revolver models, variations, and pricing are invited to submit their info to the editor for consideration in future editions. Also see listing for LeFaucheux pinfire revolvers.

NIB	Exc.	V.G.	Good	Fair	Poor
900	500	420	350	200	140

Model 1895

One of earliest Francotte pistols. Chambered for 8mm cartridge. Lever-operated repeater. Marked "A. Francotte & Co. Makers" on top of slide.

NIB	Exc.	V.G.	Good	Fair	Poor
—	7000	5500	4150	2300	1500

Trainer

Single-shot target pistol. Made for competition in .22-caliber short. "AFC" trademark on left side of frame. Model probably not made by Francotte but sold by that firm and others.

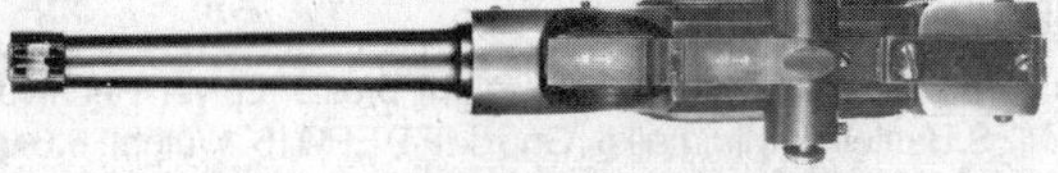

NIB	Exc.	V.G.	Good	Fair	Poor
—	3800	3150	2700	2180	1500

Semi-Auto

6.35mm, 6-shot detachable magazine pocket pistol, with blue finish. Model marked "A. Francotte A Liege" on frame.

NIB	Exc.	V.G.	Good	Fair	Poor
—	420	300	200	130	90

FRANKLIN ARMORY, INC.

Minden, Nevada

Nevada-based manufacturer of AR-15 carbines and rifles, and related parts. Also produces a popular drop-in aftermarket trigger for a variety of platforms. SEE POLITICAL PANIC PRICING.

F17-L

Caliber: .17 WSM rimfire. Capacity: One 10- or 20-round magazine. Barrel: 20" full contour, 1:9" RH twist. 11-degree target crown. Stock: Magpul MOE. Sights: Optic-ready 12 o'clock Picatinny rail. Weight: NA. Trigger: FN Combat Trigger, 4.75–7.75 lbs. Overall Length: 30.75". Features: Gas piston rimfire rifle, F17 Piston. Rotating locking bolt and piston design. Features a 12" TML M-Lok handguard/upper, .17 WSN salt bath nitride bolt carrier, Ergo Sure Grip. Libertas lower. SEE POLITICAL PANIC PRICING.

NIB	Exc.	V.G.	Good	Fair	Poor
1650	1590	1450	—	—	—

F17-SPR

Similar to F17-L. Barrel: 18-in. lightweight profile. Lower Receiver: FAI. Stock: MFS Battlelink Minimalist. Grip: MFT EPG16. Weight: 6.6 lbs.

NIB	Exc.	V.G.	Good	Fair	Poor
1610	1280	—	—	—	—

F17-M4

Similar to other F17-Series models. Barrel: 16 in. M4 Contour. Lower Receiver: FAI. Handguard/Upper: 7-in. TML M-Lok. Stock: M4. Grip: A2. Weight: 6.5 lbs.

NIB	Exc.	V.G.	Good	Fair	Poor
1530	1200	—	—	—	—

F17-VS4

Similar to other F17-Series models. Barrel: 20-in., full contour. Lower Receiver: FAI. Handguard/Upper: 12-in. TML M-LOK. Stock: A2. Grip: A2. Weight: NA. Discontinued.

NIB	Exc.	V.G.	Good	Fair	Poor
1500	1280	—	—	—	—

F17-X

Similar to other F17-Series models. Barrel: 16-in. M4 Contour. Sights: Fixed front & MBUS. Lower Receiver: FAI. Handguard/Upper: Magpul MOE SL M-Lok Gray. Stock: Magpul SL. Grip: Magpul K2. Stock: A2. Grip: A2. Weight: 6.7 lbs.

NIB	Exc.	V.G.	Good	Fair	Poor
1340	1260	1150	1000	—	—

BFS III M4

Caliber: 5.56mm/.223. Capacities: 30 rounds. AR-type rifles and carbines offered with the BFSIII Binary Trigger. Barrel: 16 in., LTW Contour, 1:7 RH twist, A2 muzzle device. Stock: M4. Sights: Optics ready, 12 o'clock full-length Picatinny rail. Weight: NA. Trigger: BFS III Binary Trigger. Overall Length: 32.5 to 35.5 in. Features: Standard charging handle, low-profile gas block, 15-in. FST Handguard/Upper, salt bath nitride bolt carrier, A2 Grip. FAI-15 lower.

NIB	Exc.	V.G.	Good	Fair	Poor
1000	900	800	700	—	—

M4-HTF R3

Caliber: .350 Legend. Capacity: One 10- or 20-round magazine. Barrel: 16" M4 contour, 1:12" RH twist, Aura XTD muzzle device. Stock: B5 Bravo. Grip: B5. Handguard: 15" FSR. Sights: Optics-ready 12 o'clock full-length Picatinny rail. Weight: NA. Trigger: BFSIII Binary Trigger or custom tuned. Features: 350 Legend was designed for use in several American states that have specific regulations for deer hunting with straight-walled centerfire cartridges. It has the same rim diameter as a 5.56 case (.378"), so it can use the same bolt. Rounds will fit in a modified AR magazine. MFT EVOLV charging handle, mid-length gas system, low-profile gas block, salt bath nitride bolt carrier, FAI-15 lower.

NIB	Exc.	V.G.	Good	Fair	Poor
1180	1100	1000	870	—	—

Libertas-L 16

Calibers: 5.56 NATO. Similar to other Franklin Armory offerings but with billet lower. Incorporates integrated ambidextrous, anti-rotational Quick Detach sling mounts. Textured Memory Index Point, enlarged and beveled magazine well, integral over-sized triggerguard. The front of the magazine well is also textured so it can be used as a grip for forward support. Carbine length, six-position collapsible stock. Barrel: 16 in. M4 Contour 1:7" RH twist. Handguard: 15" FSR. Sights: Magpul MBUS. Mid-length gas system. Stock: Magpul CTR. Grip: Ergo Ambi Sure. Add $110 for BFSIII trigger. Add $40 for 14.5" barrel with TRIUMVIR muzzle device pinned and welded.

NIB	Exc.	V.G.	Good	Fair	Poor
1600	—	—	—	—	—

FAR-15 Legacy

Caliber: 5.56 NATO or .223 Rem. Several builds make up the Fulton Armory AR lineup, six with fixed stocks, and five with front sight posts. Legacy specs include the upper receiver: M16 Slick Side, with new A1 rear sight (forged, machined, anodized). Retro 601 charging handle. Parts: GI mil-spec, GI Chrome M16/AR15 HPT/MPI Bolt with HD extractor spring, early slip ring. Barrel: 20" 1x12, "pencil" profile, match quality, chrome-lined, .223/5.56 NATO hybrid match chamber. Handguard: New M16, triangular. Gas Block/Front Sight: Forged, with bayonet lug, taper pinned. Front Sight Post: A1, round. Muzzle Device: 3-prong flash suppressor. Lower Receiver: FA, with Accu-wedge (forged, machined, anodized, & Teflon coated per mil-spec). Buttstock: Fixed, A1 with A1 buttplate. Grip: A1. Trigger: Standard military, single-stage. Included accessories: FA 10-round magazine, OD cotton web sling, and owner's manual. Precision Guarantee: 1.5 MOA with Federal Gold Medal Match Ammunition. Weight: 6.75 lbs. Length: 39".

NIB	Exc.	V.G.	Good	Fair	Poor
1500	1400	1200	1000	790	—

FAR-15 A2 Service Rifle

Similar to the FAR-15 Legacy rifle, but with 20" barrel, 1x7, A2 Government Profile, match quality, chrome lined, .223/5.56 NATO Hybrid Match Chamber and 12" round A2 handguard with heat shields. A2 weight: 8.05 lbs.

NIB	Exc.	V.G.	Good	Fair	Poor
1400	1300	1100	950	—	—

FAR-15 A4 Service Rifle

Similar to FAR-15 Legacy rifle, but with a 20" barrel, 1x7, A2 Government Profile, match quality, chrome-lined, .223/5.56 NATO Hybrid Match Chamber and 12" round A2 handguard with heat shields. The A4 lacks a carrying handle and has a top receiver Picatinny rail.

NIB	Exc.	V.G.	Good	Fair	Poor
1280	1100	1000	850	—	—

FAR-15 Peerless NM A4 Service Rifle

Similar to the FAR-15 Legacy rifle, but with a 20" 1:8" barrel, HBAR profile, match-quality, stainless steel, .223/5.56 NATO hybrid match chamber. Handguard: 12", round A2, modified for a float tube.

NIB	Exc.	V.G.	Good	Fair	Poor
1380	1200	1000	820	—	—

FRANKLIN, C. W.

Liege, Belgium

Manufacturer of utilitarian shotguns, with exposed or enclosed hammers. Circa 1900.

Single-Barrel

NIB	Exc.	V.G.	Good	Fair	Poor
—	150	80	50	40	20

Damascus Barrel Double

NIB	Exc.	V.G.	Good	Fair	Poor
—	250	150	120	100	60

Steel Barrel Double

NIB	Exc.	V.G.	Good	Fair	Poor
—	300	180	150	120	90

FRANKONIA JAGD

Favorit, Germany

Seldom seen in U.S.A. Values extremely variable, based on local market, chambering and other factors.

Favorit Standard

Chambered for various European calibers, this bolt-action rifle has 24" barrel and set triggers. Blued, with checkered walnut stock.

NIB	Exc.	V.G.	Good	Fair	Poor
—	450	300	260	180	120

Favorit Deluxe

As above, with more finely figured stock.

NIB	Exc.	V.G.	Good	Fair	Poor
—	480	320	280	200	150

Safari Model

As above, in Magnum calibers.

NIB	Exc.	V.G.	Good	Fair	Poor
—	1400	950	680	280	200

Heeren Rifle

Best quality single-shot rifle, with 26" octagonal barrel, double-set triggers and adjustable sights. Engraved with hand-checkered high-grade walnut. Blued. Produced in a variety of calibers.

NIB	Exc.	V.G.	Good	Fair	Poor
—	5000	3050	2500	1700	1250

FRASER F. A. CORP.

Fraser, Michigan

Fraser .25 cal.

A .25 ACP caliber semi-automatic pistol, with 2.25" barrel and 6-round magazine. Stainless steel with black nylon grips. There is a 24 kt. gold-plated model, that is worth approximately $100 additional. Later made under Fraser name, by a different company in 1990.

NIB	Exc.	V.G.	Good	Fair	Poor
250	180	120	100	50	40

FREEDOM ARMS

Freedom, Wyoming

Percussion Mini-Revolver

A .22-caliber spur trigger revolver, with 1", 1.75" or 3" barrel lengths, 5-shot cylinder and bird's-head grip. Stainless steel. Belt buckle available that houses pistol for additional $40.

NIB	Exc.	V.G.	Good	Fair	Poor
300	250	200	120	100	80

Bostonian (aka Boot Gun)

As above, with 3" barrel in .22 Magnum. Discontinued 1992.

NIB	Exc.	V.G.	Good	Fair	Poor
380	300	220	150	80	60

Patriot (aka Boot Gun)

As above, in .22 LR caliber. Discontinued 1992.

NIB	Exc.	V.G.	Good	Fair	Poor
380	300	220	150	80	60

Minuteman

As above, with 3" barrel. Discontinued in 1988.

NIB	Exc.	V.G.	Good	Fair	Poor
380	300	220	150	80	60

Ironsides

As above in .22 Magnum, with 1" or 1.75" barrel.

NIB	Exc.	V.G.	Good	Fair	Poor
380	300	220	150	80	60

Celebrity

As above, with belt buckle mount for .22 or .22 Magnum revolvers. Note: Add $25 for .22 Magnum model.

NIB	Exc.	V.G.	Good	Fair	Poor
400	320	280	220	150	100

PREMIER AND FIELD GRADE REVOLVERS

Both grades use the same materials and machining tolerances. Difference is in finish, standard components and warranty.

Premier Grade has a bright brushed finish, screw adjustable rear sight, laminated hardwood grips and limited lifetime warranty.

Field Grade has matte finish, adjustable rear sight for elevation only, Pachmayr rubber grips and one year warranty.

Casull Field Grade Model 83

A .454 Casull Magnum revolver, with 4.75", 6", 7.5" and 10" barrel. Standard fixed sights. Fires a 225-grain bullet. Also offered in .50 AE, .475 Linebaugh, .44 Rem. Magnum, .41 Magnum and .357 Magnum. Adjustable sights available as a $75 option. Matte stainless steel with black rubber Pachmayr grips. Introduced in 1988. Note: Add $75 for .454 Casull, .475 Linebaugh or .50 AE calibers.

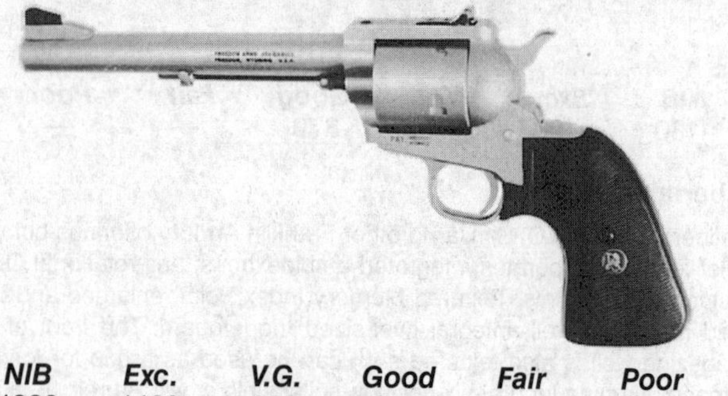

NIB	Exc.	V.G.	Good	Fair	Poor
1820	1400	800	550	—	—

Casull Premier Grade Model 83

A .454 Magnum, .44 Rem. Magnum, .45 Win. Magnum, .475 Linebaugh and .50 AE, with replaceable forcing and walnut grips. Finish is brush stainless steel. Adjustable sights are an extra cost option on this model as well. Offered in barrel lengths of 4.75", 6", 7.5" and 10" except for .475 Casull. .55 Wyoming Express added in 2006. Note: Extra cylinders are available for these models in .45 Colt, .45 Win. Magnum and .45 ACP. Add $250 to price of gun for each cylinder; $75 for .454 Casull, .475 Linebaugh or .50 AE calibers.

NIB	Exc.	V.G.	Good	Fair	Poor
2150	1800	1250	850	500	350

Model 97

Revolver chambered for .357 Magnum, .45 Colt, .44 Special and .22 LR cartridges. Available in Field or Premier grades, with choice of 4.25", 5.5" or 7.5" barrel. Optional .45 ACP cylinder of .45 Colt and .38 Special cylinder for .357 Magnum model. In 2004 this model was also offered in .17 HMR and .32 H&R Magnum calibers. Note: There are a number of extra-cost options that will affect price. Some of these options are sights, grips, Mag-Na-Port barrels, slings and trigger over-travel screws. Add $265 for extra .38 Special, .45 ACP cylinder or .22 WMR cylinder; $475 for extra fitted .22 LR match grade cylinder; $215 for match grade chambered, instead of .22 LR sport chamber.

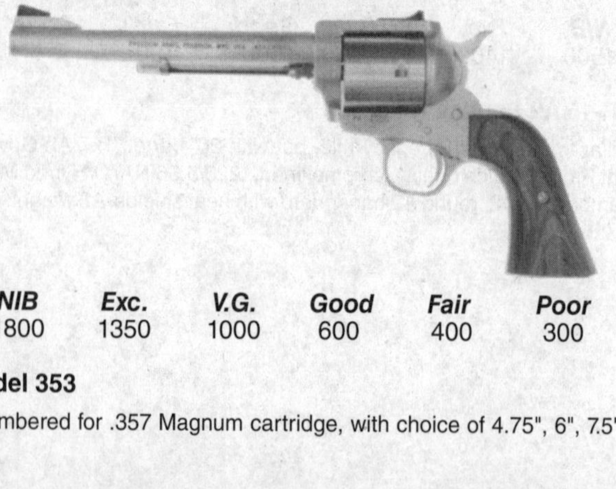

NIB	Exc.	V.G.	Good	Fair	Poor
1800	1350	1000	600	400	300

Model 353

Chambered for .357 Magnum cartridge, with choice of 4.75", 6", 7.5" or

9" barrel length. Adjustable sights. Model designation no longer used; see Model 97.

Field Grade

NIB	Exc.	V.G.	Good	Fair	Poor
1650	1300	950	550	350	250

Premier Grade

NIB	Exc.	V.G.	Good	Fair	Poor
2150	1800	1250	700	500	300

Signature Edition

As above, with highly polished finish, rosewood grips, 7.5" barrel only and fitted case. Serial numbers are DC1-DC2000. (DC represents Dick Casull, designer of firearm.) Total of 2,000 made.

NIB	Exc.	V.G.	Good	Fair	Poor
2500	1950	1300	750	550	350

Model 252

Stainless steel version of large frame revolver, chambered for .22 LR cartridge. Available in 5.12", 7.5" or 10" barrel lengths. Matte finish. Designation no longer used; see Model 97. Note: Optional .22 Magnum cylinder available for $250.

Silhouette Class

10" barrel.

NIB	Exc.	V.G.	Good	Fair	Poor
1700	1150	850	600	450	250

Varmint Class

5.12" or 7.5" barrel.

NIB	Exc.	V.G.	Good	Fair	Poor
1700	1150	850	600	450	250

Model 757

Introduced in 1999, this 5-shot revolver chambered for .475 Linebaugh cartridge. Fitted with adjustable sights. Offered in both Field and Premier grades. Choice of 4.75", 6" or 7.5" barrel lengths. Designation no longer used; see Model 83.

Field Grade

NIB	Exc.	V.G.	Good	Fair	Poor
1400	1100	750	500	400	300

Premier Grade

NIB	Exc.	V.G.	Good	Fair	Poor
1800	1450	1100	750	500	400

Model 654

This 5-shot revolver chambered for .41 Magnum cartridge. Adjustable sights. Introduced in 1999. Designation no longer used; see Model 97.

Field Grade

NIB	Exc.	V.G.	Good	Fair	Poor
1320	1050	750	500	400	300

Premier Grade

NIB	Exc.	V.G.	Good	Fair	Poor
1750	1400	1100	750	500	400

Model 83 .500 Wyoming Express

Similar to Model 83, but chambered in .500 Wyoming Express. Introduced 2007.

NIB	Exc.	V.G.	Good	Fair	Poor
2150	1800	1250	700	500	300

FREEMAN, AUSTIN T.

Hoard's Armory
Watertown, New York

Freeman Army Model Revolver (Antique)

A .44-caliber percussion revolver, with 7.5" round barrel, 6-shot unfluted cylinder with recessed nipples. Blued, walnut grips, case-hardened rammer and hammer. Frame marked "Freeman's Pat. Dec. 9, 1862/Hoard's Armory, Watertown, N.Y." Several thousand manufactured in 1863 and 1864.

Exc.	Fine	V.G.	Good	Fair	Poor
5800	2200	1500	900	600	400

FRIGON

Clay Center, Kansas
See—MAROCCHI ARMI

An importer of guns manufactured by Marocchi of Italy.

FROMMER

See—FEG (FEGYVER ES GAZKESZULEKGYAR)

FRUHWIRTH

Austria

M1872 Fruhwirth System Rifle (Antique)

An 11mm bolt-action rifle, with 25" barrel and 6-shot magazine. Blued, with full-length walnut stock.

Exc.	Fine	V.G.	Good	Fair	Poor
420	300	250	200	100	70

FUNK, CHRISTOPH

Suhl, Germany

Christoph Funk began his gun business before 1900. The vast majority of long guns were the best quality. Some collectors believe that J.P. Sauer built receivers for Funk, but this is not known for certain. Funk produced shotguns, shotgun-rifle combinations and double rifles. Some were exported to England and U.S. Most of U.S. imports are in the more common North American calibers, such as .300 Savage, 30-30, 32-20 Winchester and 12- or 16-gauge. Most are found with only a right-hand extension arm, which locks into the receiver, but some higher grades have both extension arms. Quality of these guns is extremely high. Guns were probably not made after 1940. Quality of engraving and caliber determines value. American calibers will command a higher price. Prices listed are for American calibers.

Double Rifles

Courtesy Jim Cate

NIB	*Exc.*	*V.G.*	*Good*	*Fair*	*Poor*
—	2950	2250	1450	600	400

Prewar Drilling in 16 or 12 gauge

Courtesy Jim Cate

NIB	*Exc.*	*V.G.*	*Good*	*Fair*	*Poor*
—	4500	3750	2500	1200	—

FURR ARMS

J. & G. Sale, Inc.
Prescott, Arizona

In addition to producing re-productions of various cannon, this company also manufactured one-tenth to three-quarter scale re-productions of Gatling guns. Furr products are highly desirable in some circles, with the Gatling .22 re-productions typically commanding prices in excess of $18,000 in mint, unfired condition.

FYRBERG, ANDREW

Worcester and Hopkinton, Massachusetts

Double-Barrel Shotguns

Fyrberg did work for Iver Johnson and C.S. Shattuck Co. of Hatfield, Mass. He began producing a hammerless double about 1902, a well designed boxlock with coil mainsprings. An estimated 2,000 were produced at Hopkinton and Worcester, Mass. Some have been made at Meriden, Conn. Sears cataloged the Fyrberg guns in 1902 to about 1908.

NIB	*Exc.*	*V.G.*	*Good*	*Fair*	*Poor*
—	520	420	300	200	150

Revolvers

A 3" barreled .32-caliber and 3.5" .38-caliber revolver, with round ribbed barrels and round butts. Grips bear trademark "AFCo". Model most likely made by Iver Johnson for Andrew Fyrberg.

NIB	*Exc.*	*V.G.*	*Good*	*Fair*	*Poor*
—	250	140	100	80	50

G

GABBET-FAIRFAX, H.
Birmingham, England

Mars

Designed by Hugh Gabbet-Fairfax, this semi-automatic pistol first produced on an experimental basis by Webley & Scott Revolvers in the 1890s. After Webley gave up on the idea an extremely limited number were built by Mars Automatic Pistol Syndicate, Ltd., 1897 to 1905. Pistol produced in four calibers; 8.5mm Mars, 9mm Mars, .45 Mars Short Case and .45 Mars Long Case. Most powerful handgun cartridge of its time and remained so until well after World War II. It is estimated that only about 80 of these pistols were ever produced. Note: Webley examples are worth a premium. Small "Baby" model may bring a premium.

Courtesy James Rankin

NIB	Exc.	V.G.	Good	Fair	Poor
—	45000	30500	19500	9200	6000

GABILONDO Y CIA
See—LLAMA

GABILONDO Y URRESTI
Guernica, Spain
Elgoibar, Spain
See—LLAMA

Spanish firm founded in 1904 to produce inexpensive revolvers of Velo-Dog type. Sometime around 1909 the firm began to manufacture Radium revolver. In 1914 the company produced a semi-automatic pistol distributed as Ruby. This pistol soon became the mainstay of the company, with orders of 30,000 pistols a month for the French army. End of WWI Gabilondo Y Urresti moved to Elgoeibar, Spain. Company produced a Browning 1910 replica pistol until early 1930s. It was at this point that Gabilondo began to manufacture a Colt Model 1911 copy that became known as Llama. For information of specific Llama models see Llama section. Pistols listed reflect pre-Llama period and are so marked, with the trade name of that particular model. Monogram "GC" frequently appears on grips but not on slide.

Velo-Dog Revolver

A 6.35mm double-action revolver with 1.5" barrel, folding trigger and concealed hammer. Blued, with walnut grips. Manufactured from 1904 to 1914.

NIB	Exc.	V.G.	Good	Fair	Poor
—	300	200	120	80	50

Radium

Semi-automatic pistol in caliber 7.65mm. Produced both for commercial and military market in Ruby style. "Radium" stamped on slide as well as top of each grip plate.

Courtesy James Rankin

NIB	Exc.	V.G.	Good	Fair	Poor
—	300	200	120	100	70

Ruby

A 7.65mm caliber semi-automatic pistol. Discontinued in 1930.

NIB	Exc.	V.G.	Good	Fair	Poor
—	250	180	150	100	80

Bufalo 6.35mm

Semi-automatic pistol in caliber 6.35mm. Copy of Browning Model 1906, with squeeze grip safety. Has "Bufalo" stamped on slide and Gabilondo logo along with a buffalo's head on each side of grip plates. Manufactured between 1918 and 1925. Note: Spelling of "Bufalo" as it appears on pistol.

Courtesy James Rankin

NIB	Exc.	V.G.	Good	Fair	Poor
—	280	180	150	100	80

Bufalo 7.65mm

Semi-automatic pistol in caliber 7.65mm. Patterned after Browning Model 1910, with squeeze grip safety. There were two models, with 7- or 9-round magazine. Model with 9-round magazine usually fitted with wood grips and lanyard ring. Buffalo's head is inset in each grip plate. Manufactured between 1918 and 1925.

Courtesy James Rankin

NIB	Exc.	V.G.	Good	Fair	Poor
—	280	180	120	100	80

Bufalo 9mmK

Semi-automatic pistol in caliber 9mmK. Nearly same pistol as 7.65mm model, but fitted with grip safety. "Bufalo" stamped on slide and Gabilondo logo and buffalo's head are on each grip plate. Manufactured between 1918 and 1925.

Courtesy James Rankin

NIB	Exc.	V.G.	Good	Fair	Poor
—	300	200	140	100	70

Danton 6.35mm

Semi-automatic pistol in caliber 6.35mm. Patterned after Browning Model 1906, with grip safety. "Danton" appears on slide as well as grips. Gabilondo logo on each grip plate. Manufactured between 1925 and 1931.

Courtesy James Rankin

NIB	Exc.	V.G.	Good	Fair	Poor
—	280	180	120	100	80

Danton War Model

Semi-automatic pistol in caliber 7.65mm. Similar to Bufalo above and made with-/without grip safety. Came in two models, with 9- and 20-round magazines. Fitted with lanyard ring. "Danton" stamped on slide and grips. Gabilondo logo on each side of grip plate. Manufactured between 1925 and 1931.

Courtesy James Rankin

Nine-Round Magazine

NIB	Exc.	V.G.	Good	Fair	Poor
—	280	180	120	100	80

Twenty-Round Magazine

NIB	Exc.	V.G.	Good	Fair	Poor
—	550	320	250	200	100

Perfect

Semi-automatic pistol chambered for 6.35mm and 7.65mm cartridges. Cheap low-priced pistol marketed by Mugica. Pistols usually have the word "Perfect" on grips. Slide may be stamped with the name MUGICA, but many are not.

NIB	Exc.	V.G.	Good	Fair	Poor
—	280	180	120	100	80

Plus Ultra

Pistol chambered for 7.65mm cartridge and built from 1925 to 1933. Had a 20-round magazine that gave the pistol an unusual appearance. "Plus Ultra" appears on slide and grips. Gabilondo logo on each grip plate. Equipped with lanyard ring.

Courtesy James Rankin

NIB	Exc.	V.G.	Good	Fair	Poor
—	1200	880	650	420	250

GALAND, C.F.
Liege, Belgium

Galand, Galand & Sommerville, Galand Perrin (Galand M1872) (Antique)

A 7mm, 9mm and 12mm caliber double-action revolver, with 6-shot cylinder and open frame. A unique ejection system that by means of rotating a lever downward from the triggerguard, causes barrel and cylinder to slide forward leaving ejector and spent cases behind. Circa 1872. Large-frame 11mm/12mm models bring a significant premium.

Courtesy Bonhams & Butterfields

Exc.	Fine	V.G.	Good	Fair	Poor
3000	1500	850	550	150	100

Velo-Dog

A 5.5mm Velo-Dog caliber fixed trigger and guard double-action revolver, with open-top design. Later models (.22 and 6.35mm caliber) feature folding triggers and no triggerguards.

NIB	Exc.	V.G.	Good	Fair	Poor
—	250	160	120	80	50

Le Novo

See—Oury, D.D.

Tue-Tue

A .22 short 5.5mm Velo-Dog and 6.35mm caliber double-action revolver. Concealed hammer, folding trigger and swing-out cylinder, with central extractor. Introduced in 1894.

NIB	Exc.	V.G.	Good	Fair	Poor
—	250	160	120	80	50

GALAND & SOMMERVILLE
Liege, Belgium

See—GALAND

GALEF (ZABALA)
Zabala Hermanos & Antonio Zoli
Spain

Zabala Double

A 10-, 12-, 16- and 20-gauge boxlock shotgun, with 22" to 30" barrel and various chokes. Hardwood stock. Note: Add 50 percent for 10-gauge.

NIB	Exc.	V.G.	Good	Fair	Poor
—	450	300	180	100	80

Companion

Folding 12-gauge to .410 bore single-shot underlever shotgun, with 28" or 30" barrel.

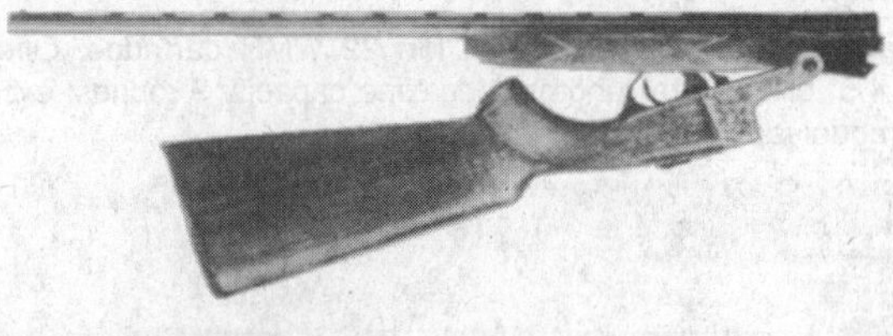

NIB	Exc.	V.G.	Good	Fair	Poor
—	200	140	100	50	20

Monte Carlo Trap

A 12-gauge underlever single-shot shotgun, with 32" ventilated rib barrel.

NIB	Exc.	V.G.	Good	Fair	Poor
—	320	280	150	100	80

Silver Snipe, Golden Snipe, and Silver Hawk

See—ANTONIO ZOLI

GALENA INDUSTRIES INC.
Sturgis, South Dakota

In 1998, Galena Industries purchased the rights to use AMT trademark and manufacturing rights to many, but not all, AMT designs. For AMT models made by AMT see that section. This company's designs have been acquired by Crusader/High Standard of Houston, Texas.

AMT Backup

Features double-action-only trigger system and offered in both stainless steel and matte black finish. Small frame .380 Backup weighs 18 oz. with its 2.5" barrel. Large frame Backups are fitted with 3" barrel and offered in 9mm, .38 Super, .357 Sig., .40 S&W, .400 CorBon and .45 ACP. Weight about 23 oz.; magazine capacity 5 to 6 rounds, depending on caliber. Note: Add $50 for .38 Super, .357 Sig, and .400 CorBon.

Galena .380 DAO Backup

NIB	Exc.	V.G.	Good	Fair	Poor
520	380	280	200	120	100

Automag II

Semi-automatic pistol chambered for .22 WMR cartridge. Offered in 3.38", 4.5" or 6" barrel lengths. Magazine capacity 9 rounds, except for 3.38" model is 7 rounds. Weight about 32 oz.

"Automag II with 4.5 barrel""

NIB	Exc.	V.G.	Good	Fair	Poor
700	550	320	220	120	100

Automag III

Pistol chambered for .30 Carbine cartridge. Barrel length 6.38". Weight about 43 oz. Stainless steel finish.

NIB	Exc.	V.G.	Good	Fair	Poor
800	680	380	250	150	100

Automag IV

Chambered for .45 Winchester Magnum cartridge. Fitted with 6.5" barrel. Magazine capacity 7 rounds. Weight about 46 oz.

NIB	Exc.	V.G.	Good	Fair	Poor
800	680	380	250	150	100

Automag .440 CorBon

Semi-automatic pistol chambered for .440 CorBon cartridge and fitted with 7.5" barrel. Magazine capacity 5 rounds. Finish matte black. Weight about 46 oz. Checkered walnut grips. Introduced in 2000. Special order only.

NIB	Exc.	V.G.	Good	Fair	Poor
1000	900	750	580	400	180

Galena Accelerator

Model has 7" barrel built on 1911 frame. Chambered for .400 CorBon. Magazine capacity 7 rounds. Weight about 46 oz. Finish stainless steel.

NIB	Exc.	V.G.	Good	Fair	Poor
850	720	550	400	300	100

Galena Hardballer

Pistol based on Colt Model 1911 design. Chambered for .45 ACP cartridge. Fitted with 5" barrel. Magazine capacity 7 rounds. Finish stainless steel. Adjustable trigger and beveled magazine well. Offered chambered for .40 S&W and .400 CorBon cartridges. Weight about 38 oz.

NIB	Exc.	V.G.	Good	Fair	Poor
1000	900	750	580	400	180

Galena Longslide

Chambered for .45 ACP cartridge and fitted with 7" barrel. Magazine capacity 7 rounds. Weight about 46 oz. Finish stainless steel.

NIB	*Exc.*	*V.G.*	*Good*	*Fair*	*Poor*
850	720	550	400	300	10

Galena Commando

Commando chambered for .40 S&W cartridge. Fitted with 4" barrel. Magazine capacity 8 rounds. Weight about 38 oz. Finish stainless steel.

NIB	*Exc.*	*V.G.*	*Good*	*Fair*	*Poor*
550	400	300	220	180	100

GALESI, INDUSTRIA ARMI

Brescia, Italy

Rino Galesi Armi, Collebeato, Italy, manufactured shotguns, revolvers and automatic pistols. Firm's name changed from Rino Galesi Armi to Industria Armi Galesi to Rigarmi di Rino Galesi. Their semi-automatic pistols were designated by model year, model number and a 500 Series. Most models named in the 500 Series came after the firm changed its name to Industria Armi Galesi.

Model 1923

A 6.35mm and 7.65mm caliber semi-automatic pistol. Has a squeeze grip safety and wood grip plates with crest. Model 1923 stamped on slide.

Courtesy James Rankin

NIB	*Exc.*	*V.G.*	*Good*	*Fair*	*Poor*
—	280	200	140	80	50

Model 1930

A 6.35mm and 7.65mm caliber semi-automatic pistol. Very few were made in 1946 in 9mm Parabellum. Based on 1910 Browning design. Blued, with plastic grips. Slide marked "Brevetto Mod. 1930".

Courtesy James Rankin

NIB	*Exc.*	*V.G.*	*Good*	*Fair*	*Poor*
—	280	200	140	80	50

9mm Parabellum

NIB	*Exc.*	*V.G.*	*Good*	*Fair*	*Poor*
—	600	500	400	300	100

Model 6

Updated Model 1930. Manufactured approximately 1938 to 1948 in calibers; 22 Short, .22 Long, .22 LR, 6.35mm, 7.65mm and 9mm Short.

Courtesy James Rankin

NIB	Exc.	V.G.	Good	Fair	Poor
—	350	180	100	80	50

Model 9

Manufactured from approximately 1947 to 1956 in calibers .22 Short, .22 Long, .22 LR, 6.35mm, 7.65mm and 9mm Short. Also listed under 500 Series. The .22 versions were marketed as "the smallest .22 pistols ever built".

Courtesy James Rankin

NIB	Exc.	V.G.	Good	Fair	Poor
—	300	180	100	80	50

GALIL
Israel

See—ISRAEL WEAPON INDUSTRIES/ISRAEL MILITARY INDUSTRIES

GALLAGER
Richardson & Overman
Philadelphia, Pennsylvania

Gallager Carbine

A .50-caliber single-shot percussion carbine, with 22.25" barrel, saddle ring and walnut stock. Blued and case-hardened. Approximately 23,000 made during Civil War.

Percussion Model (Antique)

As above, in .56-62 rimfire caliber. Approximately 5,000 made.

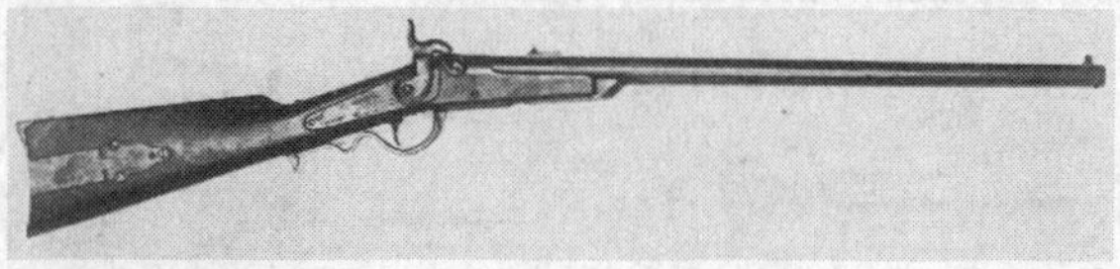

Courtesy Milwaukee Public Museum, Milwaukee, Wisconsin

Exc.	Fine	V.G.	Good	Fair	Poor
3900	2450	1970	1500	500	350

Spencer Cartridge Model (Antique)

Exc.	Fine	V.G.	Good	Fair	Poor
3420	1950	1650	1350	400	280

GAMBA, RENATO
Gardone V. T., Italy

SIDE-BY-SIDE SHOTGUNS

Hunter Super

A 12-gauge Anson & Deeley boxlock double-barrel shotgun. Variety of barrel lengths and chokes, double triggers and extractors. Engraved and silver-plated.

NIB	Exc.	V.G.	Good	Fair	Poor
1250	900	700	550	450	250

Principessa

A 12-, 20- or 28-gauge boxlock shotgun. Engraved checkered stock.

NIB	Exc.	V.G.	Good	Fair	Poor
1850	1250	900	700	500	250

Oxford 90

A 12- or 20-gauge sidelock shotgun, with various barrel lengths and chokes. Purdey locking system, double triggers and automatic ejectors. Walnut stock.

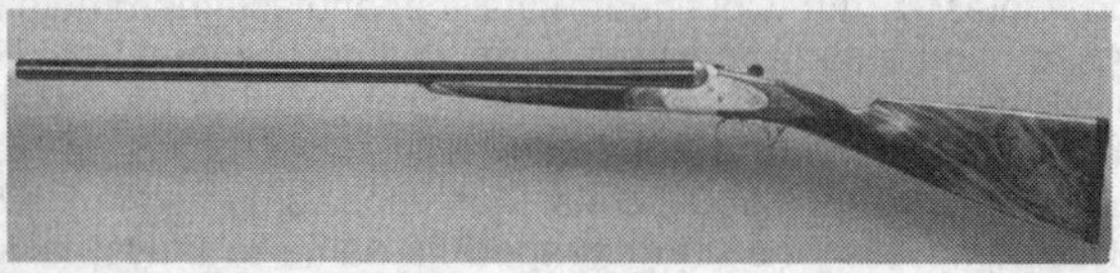

NIB	Exc.	V.G.	Good	Fair	Poor
4250	3250	1700	900	600	300

Oxford Extra

Same as above, with fine engraving.

NIB	Exc.	V.G.	Good	Fair	Poor
5200	4000	2250	1500	900	450

Gamba 624 Prince

Fitted with Wesley Richards-type frame, select walnut stock and fine hand engraving. Offered in 12-gauge with 28" barrels.

NIB	Exc.	V.G.	Good	Fair	Poor
4800	3900	2500	1500	850	400

Gamba 624 Extra

Same as above, with deep floral engraving.

NIB	Exc.	V.G.	Good	Fair	Poor
8000	5000	4500	2500	1250	600

London

A 12- or 20-gauge H&H sidelock shotgun, with various barrel lengths and chokes. Double-/single-selective trigger, automatic ejectors. Walnut stock.

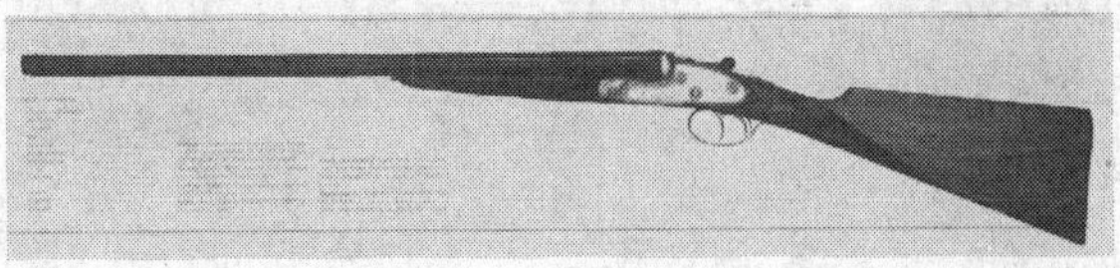

NIB	Exc.	V.G.	Good	Fair	Poor
7000	5500	4500	2500	1250	700

London Royal

As above, with engraved hunting scenes.

NIB	Exc.	V.G.	Good	Fair	Poor
8000	6500	5000	3750	2000	950

Ambassador Gold and Black

A 12- and 20-gauge H&H sidelock shotgun, with various barrel lengths and choke combinations. Single-selective trigger, automatic ejectors and a single gold line engraved on barrels and frame. Walnut stocks.

NIB	Exc.	V.G.	Good	Fair	Poor
25000	19000	13500	9500	5000	2500

Ambassador Executive

Gamba's best quality shotgun produced in 12- or 20-gauge to customer's specifications.

NIB	Exc.	V.G.	Good	Fair	Poor
28000	20000	15000	10000	5000	2500

OVER/UNDER SHOTGUNS

Country Model

A 12- and 20-gauge over/under shotgun, with 28" or 30" ventilated rib barrels, double triggers, extractors. Walnut stock.

NIB	Exc.	V.G.	Good	Fair	Poor
650	550	400	300	280	200

Grifone Model

A 12- and 20-gauge over/under shotgun, with 26", 28" or 30" ventilated rib barrels, single-selective trigger and automatic ejectors. Boxlock action silver-plated, with walnut stock. Available with screw-in chokes. This would add 10 percent to values.

NIB	Exc.	V.G.	Good	Fair	Poor
800	650	550	350	250	200

Europa 2000

A 12-gauge over/under shotgun in various barrel lengths and choke combinations. Single-selective trigger and automatic ejectors. Engraved silver-plated boxlock action, with false sideplates and walnut stock.

NIB	Exc.	V.G.	Good	Fair	Poor
1250	900	700	550	350	250

Grinta Trap and Skeet

A 12-gauge over/under shotgun, with 26" Skeet or 30" Full choke barrels, single-selective trigger, automatic ejectors and some engraving. Walnut stock.

NIB	Exc.	V.G.	Good	Fair	Poor
1350	900	700	550	350	250

Victory Trap and Skeet

As above, but more finely finished.

NIB	Exc.	V.G.	Good	Fair	Poor
1650	1150	850	600	400	250

Edinburg Match

As above, with slightly different engraving patterns.

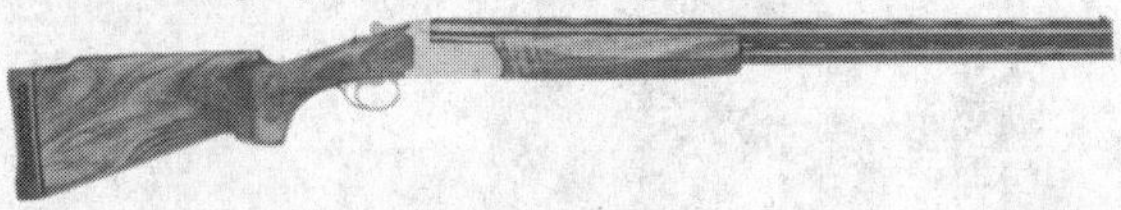

NIB	Exc.	V.G.	Good	Fair	Poor
1250	1000	800	600	400	250

Boyern 88 Combination Gun

A 12-gauge combination over/under rifle/shotgun, with double triggers and extractors. Engraved game scenes and coin-finished, with walnut stock.

NIB	Exc.	V.G.	Good	Fair	Poor
1250	900	700	500	400	250

DAYTONA SERIES

Competition shotgun first introduced into U.S. in 1986 as Type I. Type I available in different configurations, with base model selling for about $4,000 until 1991. In 1994 Gamba introduced Daytona in a wide variety of configurations and grades under a new designation called Type II. Primary difference was in location of stock bolt. Only about 80 Daytona Type II shotguns are allocated to U.S. per year. High quality shotgun with an excellent reputation. Prices listed are for 12-gauge. 20-gauge guns available on special request.

Daytona Trap

Offered in 12-gauge with 30" or 32" barrels. Select walnut stock with hand-checkering. Removable trigger group, improved Boss lock-up and boxlock receiver.

NIB	Exc.	V.G.	Good	Fair	Poor
5900	4750	3000	2250	1200	600

Daytona Sporting

Available in 12-gauge, with 30" barrel, screw-in chokes and single-selective trigger.

NIB	Exc.	V.G.	Good	Fair	Poor
4000	3250	2500	1900	1200	700

Daytona Skeet

Offered in 12-gauge, with 29" barrels and single-selective trigger.

NIB	Exc.	V.G.	Good	Fair	Poor
4000	3250	2500	1900	1200	700

Daytona America Trap

Offered in 12-gauge, with 30" or 32" barrels, high adjustable rib, adjustable stock and single trigger.

NIB	Exc.	V.G.	Good	Fair	Poor
4000	3250	2500	1900	1200	700

Daytona Game

Offered in 12-gauge, with 28" barrels and single trigger. Note: Add $300 for black frame with gold inlaid names and logo.

NIB	Exc.	V.G.	Good	Fair	Poor
3900	3500	3000	2250	1200	700

Daytona Grade 6 Engraving

Fine English scroll hand engraving, edged with gold line work.

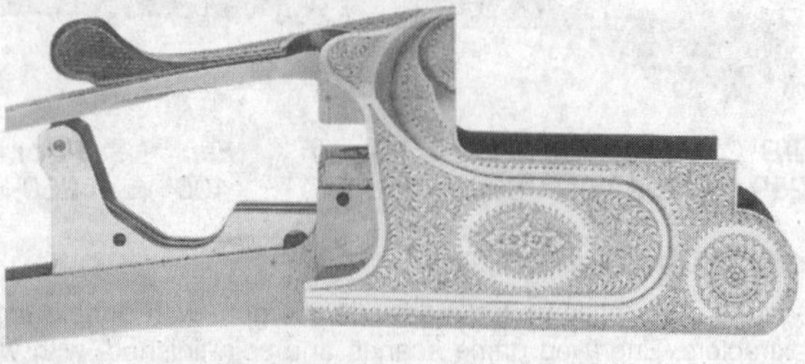

Daytona Trap and Skeet Models

NIB	Exc.	V.G.	Good	Fair	Poor
13000	5000	4000	3000	1500	700

Daytona Sporting Model

NIB	Exc.	V.G.	Good	Fair	Poor
13500	5000	4000	3000	1500	700

Daytona Grade 5 Engraving

Deep relief floral engraving, with gold inlaid griffons.

Daytona Trap and Skeet Models

NIB	Exc.	V.G.	Good	Fair	Poor
14000	9000	6500	5000	2500	1200

Daytona Sporting Model

NIB	Exc.	V.G.	Good	Fair	Poor
14500	9000	6500	5000	2500	1200

Daytona Grade 4 Engraving

Flying eagle in a landscape and very fine English scroll by master engravers.

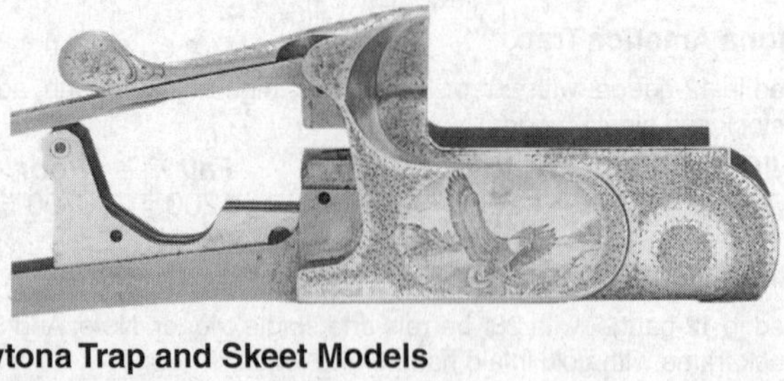

Daytona Trap and Skeet Models

NIB	Exc.	V.G.	Good	Fair	Poor
16250	10000	7500	5500	3000	1500

Daytona Sporting Model

NIB	Exc.	V.G.	Good	Fair	Poor
16750	10000	7500	5500	3000	1500

Daytona SL Grade 3 Engraving

Fitted with engraved game scene sideplates and fine English scroll by master engravers.

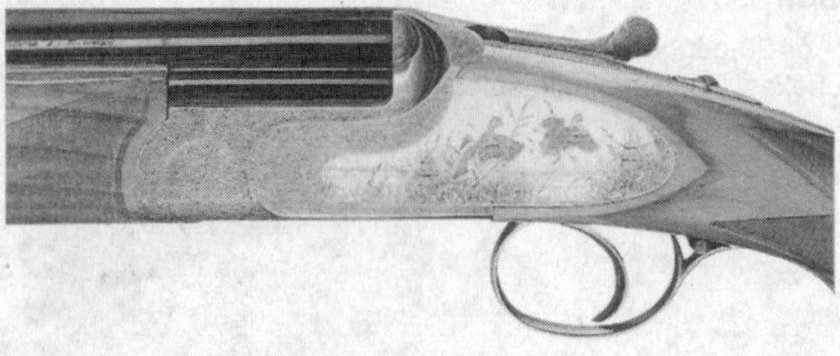

Daytona Trap and Skeet Models

NIB	Exc.	V.G.	Good	Fair	Poor
18750	15000	11000	7500	3500	1750

Daytona Sporting Model

NIB	Exc.	V.G.	Good	Fair	Poor
19250	11000	9000	6500	3500	1750

Daytona Game

NIB	Exc.	V.G.	Good	Fair	Poor
18750	11000	9000	6500	3500	1750

Daytona SLHH Grade 2 Engraving

Fitted with sideplates and Boss lock-up system, automatic ejectors, figured walnut stock. Fine game scene engraving signed by a master. Offered in 12-gauge with 28" barrels.

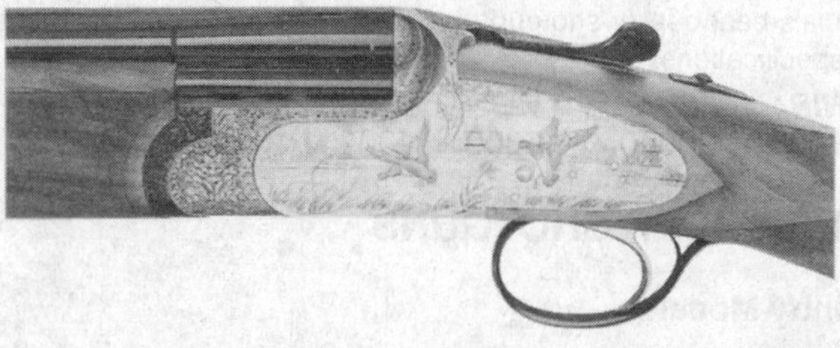

NIB	Exc.	V.G.	Good	Fair	Poor
36250	16000	12500	9500	6000	3000

Daytona SLHH Grade 1 Gold Engraving

Same as above, with gold inlaid game scenes and floral-style engraving signed by master engraver. Offered in 12-gauge with 28" barrels.

NIB	Exc.	V.G.	Good	Fair	Poor
43500	17000	13000	9500	5500	2500

Daytona SLHH "One of Thousand"

Same as above, but game scene is executed at customers direction. A totally custom ordered gun. Available in all configurations.

NIB	Exc.	V.G.	Good	Fair	Poor
125000	70000	35000	15500	7500	600

CONCORDE GAME SHOTGUNS

This over/under model offered as a slightly less expensive alternative to Daytona Series guns. Base gun available with blued or chromed action. Extra barrel are interchangeable in both 12- and 20-gauge, with 28" barrels and single triggers.

NIB	Exc.	V.G.	Good	Fair	Poor
6000	4250	3000	1500	750	450

Concorde Trap

Available in 12-gauge, with 30" or 32" barrels, single trigger.

NIB	Exc.	V.G.	Good	Fair	Poor
—	2000	1500	1000	600	450

Concorde Skeet

Available in 12-gauge, with 29" barrels and single trigger.

NIB	Exc.	V.G.	Good	Fair	Poor
6000	4250	3000	1500	750	450

Concorde Sporting

Offered in 12-gauge, with 30" barrels, screw-in chokes and single-selective trigger.

NIB	Exc.	V.G.	Good	Fair	Poor
6100	2900	2000	1500	900	500

Concorde Game Grade 7 Engraving

Game scene engraving, with fine English scroll.

NIB	Exc.	V.G.	Good	Fair	Poor
8700	4000	3250	2250	1200	600

Concorde Game Grade 8 Engraving

English scroll engraving.

NIB	Exc.	V.G.	Good	Fair	Poor
6250	3000	2500	1750	1000	500

Concorde 2nd Generation

Similar to Concorde series, with fixed trigger group. Black or chrome frame. Automatic ejectors. Select walnut stock. Choice of 12- or 20-gauge, with 28" or 30" barrels and single trigger. Introduced in 2002.

NIB	Exc.	V.G.	Good	Fair	Poor
6100	4850	3200	1950	750	300

Le Mans

Chambered for 12-gauge shell and fitted with choice of 28" or 30" barrels. Automatic ejectors. Single-selective trigger. Five choke tubes. Introduced in 2002.

NIB	Exc.	V.G.	Good	Fair	Poor
1750	1200	850	620	480	200

Hunter II

This 12-gauge model has an alloy frame, with reinforced barrel and automatic ejectors. Five choke tubes. Single-selective trigger. Barrel lengths of 26" to 27.5". Introduced in 2002.

NIB	Exc.	V.G.	Good	Fair	Poor
1600	1100	750	520	380	150

RIFLES

Safari Express

A 7x65R, 9.3x74R or .375 H&H caliber boxlock double-barrel rifle, with 25" barrels, open sights, double triggers, automatic ejectors and coin-finished scroll engraved receiver. Walnut stock.

NIB	Exc.	V.G.	Good	Fair	Poor
8500	6500	4500	1750	750	350

Mustang

A 5.6x50, 6.5x57R, 7x65R, .222 Rem., .270 Win. or .30-06 caliber sidelock single-barrel rifle, with double-set triggers, engraved sidelock action and walnut stock.

NIB	Exc.	V.G.	Good	Fair	Poor
8500	6500	4500	1750	750	350

RGZ 1000

7x64, .270 Win., 7mm Rem. Magnum and .300 Win. Magnum caliber Mauser 98 bolt-action, with 20.5" barrel. Walnut pistol grip stock and cheekpiece.

NIB	Exc.	V.G.	Good	Fair	Poor
1100	900	750	550	400	200

RGX 1000 Express

As above, with double-set triggers and 23.75" barrel.

NIB	Exc.	V.G.	Good	Fair	Poor
1250	950	750	550	400	200

PISTOLS

SAB G90

A 7.65 Parabellum or 9mm caliber double-action semi-automatic pistol, with 4.75" barrel and 15-shot magazine. Blued or chrome-plated, with walnut grips.

NIB	Exc.	V.G.	Good	Fair	Poor
580	450	350	300	250	180

SAB G91 Compact

As above, with 3.5" barrel and 12-shot magazine.

NIB	Exc.	V.G.	Good	Fair	Poor
550	400	320	280	220	150

Trident Fast Action

A .32 S&W or .38 Special caliber double-action revolver, with 2.5" or 3" barrel and 6-shot cylinder. Blued, with walnut grips.

NIB	Exc.	V.G.	Good	Fair	Poor
500	400	300	250	200	150

Trident Super

As above, with 4" ventilated rib barrel.

NIB	Exc.	V.G.	Good	Fair	Poor
550	400	320	280	220	150

Trident Match 900

As above, with 6" heavy barrel, adjustable sights. Target type walnut grips.

NIB	Exc.	V.G.	Good	Fair	Poor
850	700	550	400	350	200

GARAND
(U.S. M-1 Rifle)

ALSO SEE—ARLINGTON ORDNANCE, BERETTA, BREDA, IAI, MAUNZ, MILTECH and SPRINGFIELD ARMORY, INC.

This was the standard issue rifle for U.S. military services from 1936 to 1957. In .30-06 caliber, it is a gas-operated semi-automatic, fed by an 8-round clip that is inserted in the open action from above. Garand series was made in several variants and manufactured by many different companies over its 20 years of service. A complete history of John Garand's great rifle, see Standard Catalog of Military Firearms, published by Gun Digest Books/Krause Publications. Prices shown below are for rifles in original, unaltered condition. Many rifles seen on today's market have been re-stored or re-finished and values should be reduced from 30 to 50 percent.

Rebuilt Rifle, any manufacture

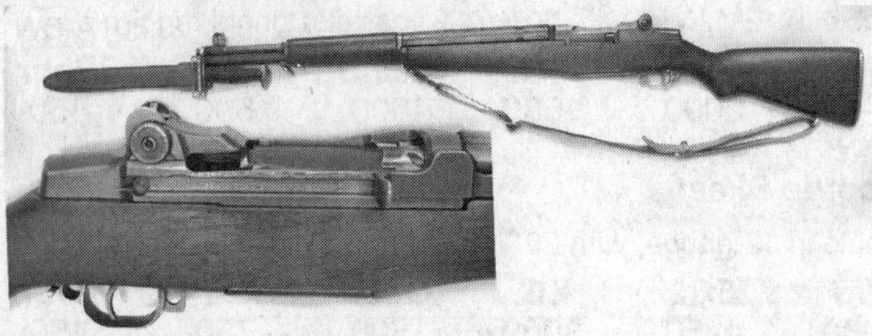

Jim Supica photo

NIB	Exc.	V.G.	Good	Fair	Poor
1200	1000	800	600	—	—

DCM Rifles

NIB	Exc.	V.G.	Good	Fair	Poor
—	850	580	450	—	—

Navy Trophy Rifles U.S.N. Crane Depot Rebuild

NIB	Exc.	V.G.	Good	Fair	Poor
—	1800	1000	900	—	—

AMF Rebuild

NIB	Exc.	V.G.	Good	Fair	Poor
—	1000	900	750	—	—

H&R Rebuild

Note: These rifles MUST be original and validated by experts.

NIB	Exc.	V.G.	Good	Fair	Poor
—	900	800	700	—	—

SPRINGFIELD ARMORY PRODUCTION

U.S. military production. For commercial guns, see Springfield Armory, Inc.

Gas trap sn: ca 81-52,000

NIB	Exc.	V.G.	Good	Fair	Poor
—	40000	35000	25000	—	—

Gas trap/modified to gas port

NIB	Exc.	V.G.	Good	Fair	Poor
—	5000	3500	2500	—	—

Pre-Dec. 7, 1941 gas port production sn: ca 410,000

NIB	Exc.	V.G.	Good	Fair	Poor
—	4000	2200	1300	900	400

WWII Production sn: ca 410,000-3,880,000

NIB	Exc.	V.G.	Good	Fair	Poor
—	1400	1100	900	750	500

Post-WWII Production sn: ca 4,200,000-6,099,361

NIB	Exc.	V.G.	Good	Fair	Poor
—	1100	850	650	500	450

Winchester Educational Contract sn: 100,000-100,500

NIB	Exc.	V.G.	Good	Fair	Poor
—	10000	6000	4500	2000	700

Winchester sn: 100,501-165,000

NIB	Exc.	V.G.	Good	Fair	Poor
—	6500	4500	3000	1100	550

Winchester sn: 1,200,00-1,380,000

NIB	Exc.	V.G.	Good	Fair	Poor
—	5500	4500	2500	750	400

Winchester sn: 2,305,850-2,536,493

NIB	Exc.	V.G.	Good	Fair	Poor
—	3500	2800	1500	500	300

Winchester sn: 1,601,150-1,640,000 "win-13"

NIB	Exc.	V.G.	Good	Fair	Poor
—	3500	2200	1800	1500	850

Harrington & Richardson Production

NIB	Exc.	V.G.	Good	Fair	Poor
—	1800	1200	900	600	300

International Harvester Production

NIB	Exc.	V.G.	Good	Fair	Poor
—	2200	1500	800	500	250

International Harvester/with Springfield Receiver (postage stamp)

NIB	Exc.	V.G.	Good	Fair	Poor
—	2800	1500	1000	—	—

International Harvester/with Springfield Receiver (arrow head)

NIB	Exc.	V.G.	Good	Fair	Poor
—	2800	1500	1000	—	—

International Harvester/with Springfield Receiver (Gap letter)

NIB	Exc.	V.G.	Good	Fair	Poor
—	2800	1500	1000	—	—

International Harvester/with Harrington & Richardson Receiver

NIB	Exc.	V.G.	Good	Fair	Poor
—	1900	1200	900	—	—

British Garands (Lend Lease)

NIB	Exc.	V.G.	Good	Fair	Poor
—	1300	1200	880	500	280

M1 Garand Cutaway

Note: Add 300 percent for examples with documentation.

NIB	Exc.	V.G.	Good	Fair	Poor
—	3000	2500	1000	600	500

SCOPED VARIANTS (SNIPER RIFLES)

Note: Sniper rifles must have sales or verification papers and original military issue scope.

M1C

NIB	Exc.	V.G.	Good	Fair	Poor
—	10000	8000	5000	—	—

M1D (USMC Issue) MC 1952

NIB	Exc.	V.G.	Good	Fair	Poor
—	3800	3000	2000	—	—

National Match

Type I

NIB	Exc.	V.G.	Good	Fair	Poor
—	4500	2500	1800	—	—

Type II

NIB	Exc.	V.G.	Good	Fair	Poor
—	3200	2200	1500	—	—

GARATE, ANITUA/G.A.C.

Eibar, Spain

Charola

A 5.5mm Clement semi-automatic pistol, with magazine located in front of trigger and exposed hammer.

Courtesy James Rankin

NIB	Exc.	V.G.	Good	Fair	Poor
—	1500	1200	750	500	400

Cosmopolite

A .38-caliber copy of Colt Police Positive. Manufactured from 1920 to 1930.

NIB	Exc.	V.G.	Good	Fair	Poor
—	280	160	120	100	80

El Lunar

Resembling Colt Police Positive in 8mm Lebel caliber. Revolver made for French government in 1915 and 1916.

NIB	Exc.	V.G.	Good	Fair	Poor
—	300	180	150	120	100

G.A.C.

Copy of Smith & Wesson Military & Police revolver. Manufactured between 1930 and 1936 in .32-20 caliber. Marked "G.A.C. Firearms Mfg. Co.".

NIB	Exc.	V.G.	Good	Fair	Poor
—	250	150	120	100	80

Modelo Militar

Close copy of Smith & Wesson Triple Lock/New Century N-frame revolver. Chambered in .44 Special. Marked "G.A.C."

NIB	Exc.	V.G.	Good	Fair	Poor
—	320	250	200	180	80

Express or Danton

A 7.65mm caliber "Eibar" semi-automatic pistol, with 9-shot magazine.

NIB	Exc.	V.G.	Good	Fair	Poor
—	280	150	100	80	50

British Service Old Pattern No.2 Mk. I Trocaola Aranzabal Military Revolver

A .455-caliber double-action break-open revolver, with 5" barrel. Adopted by Royal Army in November of 1915 and known as "Pistol OP No. 1 Mark 1".

NIB	Exc.	V.G.	Good	Fair	Poor
—	550	350	250	150	100

L'Eclair

A 5.5mm Velo-Dog caliber folding-trigger double-action revolver, with 6-shot cylinder. Manufactured from 1900 to 1914. Not to be confused with the chocolate confectionary.

NIB	Exc.	V.G.	Good	Fair	Poor
—	250	140	100	80	50

Sprinter

A 6.35mm caliber semi-automatic pistol marked "The Best Automatique Pistol Sprinter Patent 6.35mm Cartridge". Manufactured before WWI.

NIB	Exc.	V.G.	Good	Fair	Poor
—	250	140	120	80	50

La Lira

Copy of Mannlicher Model 1901 in .32 ACP caliber, with removable magazine marked "System La Lira" on breech; "Para Cartoucho Browning 7.65mm" on barrel; "G.A.C." on grips. Produced prior to WWI.

Courtesy James Rankin

NIB	Exc.	V.G.	Good	Fair	Poor
—	1200	1000	700	400	300

Triumph

Identical to La Lira model marked "Triumph Automatic Pistol".

NIB	Exc.	V.G.	Good	Fair	Poor
—	1200	1000	700	400	300

El Tigre

Copy of Winchester Model 92 lever-action rifle, .44-40.

NIB	Exc.	V.G.	Good	Fair	Poor
—	500	400	300	200	100

GARATE, HERMANOS
Ermua, Spain

Cantabria

A 6.35mm caliber folding-trigger double-action revolver, with concealed hammer, cocking spur and short barrel resembling slide on a semi-automatic. Name "Cantabria" stamped on left side.

NIB	Exc.	V.G.	Good	Fair	Poor
—	300	180	120	100	80

Velo-Stark

Double-action folding-trigger revolver, with concealed hammer.

NIB	Exc.	V.G.	Good	Fair	Poor
—	250	150	100	80	50

GARAYSAR
Fort Myers, FL

Fear 116

Gauge: 12 ga. 3 in. Barrel: 20 in. 4140 steel. Length: 39 in. Weight: 8.8 lbs. Stock: Synthetic available in a variety of colors and finishes. Features: Gas-operated semi-automatic with an aluminum receiver. Adjustable cheek rest. Front and rear flip-up sights. Ships with two five-round magazines, but also accepts 10-round mags. Includes five choke tubes (F, IM, M, IC, C), choke tube case, and hard case.

NIB	Exc.	V.G.	Good	Fair	Poor
490	—	—	—	—	—

Fear Bullpup

Gauge: 12 ga. 3 in. Barrel: 18.5 in. Length: 28.34 in. Stock: Black synthetic, with both green and FDE to follow. Features: Gas-regulated, semi-automatic bullpup-style shotgun. Built on an aluminum receiver with 4140 steel barrel. Bullpup family available in multiple model variants including 104, 105, 106, and 109, each with different options on a similar build. Ships with two five-round magazines, but also accepts 10- and 15-round mags. Adjustable cheek riser. Multiple choke options dependent on model; some fixed, others interchangeable.

NIB	Exc.	V.G.	Good	Fair	Poor
400	—	—	—	—	—

GARBI
Eibar, Spain

Model 51-B

A 12-gauge boxlock shotgun. Also available in 16- and 20-gauge, with double triggers, automatic ejectors, case-hardened or coin-finished receiver and walnut stock.

NIB	Exc.	V.G.	Good	Fair	Poor
1750	1200	850	600	—	—

Model 62-B

A 12-gauge sidelock shotgun. Also chambered for 16- and 20-gauge, with double triggers, extractors and cocking indicators. Engraved case-hardened or coin-finished receiver and walnut stock.

NIB	Exc.	V.G.	Good	Fair	Poor
1500	1050	850	650	320	180

Model 71

A 12-, 16- or 20-gauge H&H sidelock shotgun, with various barrel lengths and choke combinations. Automatic ejectors and single-selective trigger. Engraved with fine English-style scrollwork and walnut stock. Discontinued in 1988.

NIB	Exc.	V.G.	Good	Fair	Poor
2500	2000	1800	1500	700	220

Model 100

A 12-, 16- or 20-gauge H&H sidelock shotgun, with chopper-lump barrels, automatic ejectors and single trigger. Engraved in Purdey style, with walnut stock.

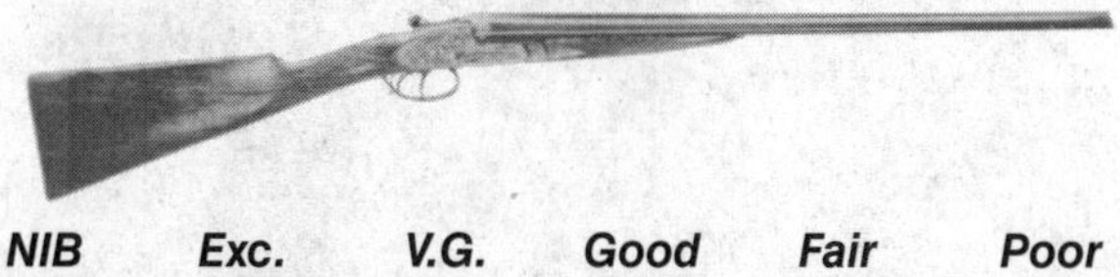

NIB	*Exc.*	*V.G.*	*Good*	*Fair*	*Poor*
4500	4000	3000	2000	900	250

Model 101

As above, with floral engraving. Discontinued in 1988 in this form, then furnished with hand-engraved Continental scroll and round body action.

NIB	*Exc.*	*V.G.*	*Good*	*Fair*	*Poor*
9500	8000	6000	4500	2000	1000

Model 102

As above, with H&H style engraving. Also in 28-gauge. Discontinued in 1988.

NIB	*Exc.*	*V.G.*	*Good*	*Fair*	*Poor*
4500	3750	3200	1600	600	250

Model 103A

Has Purdey-style engraving, with high grade wood and checkering.

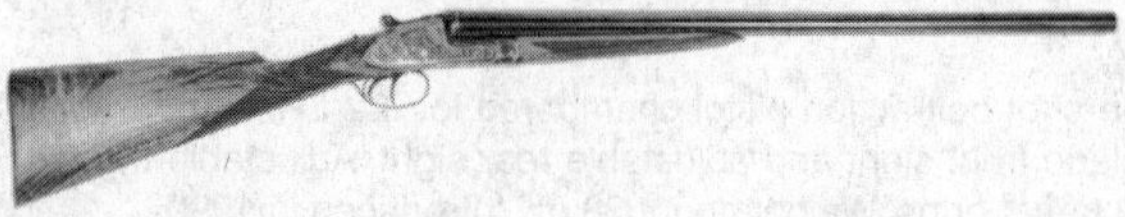

NIB	*Exc.*	*V.G.*	*Good*	*Fair*	*Poor*
17500	13000	9000	7500	2750	1000

Model 103A Royal

Same as above, with special high quality engraving, very fancy wood, hand matted rib.

NIB	*Exc.*	*V.G.*	*Good*	*Fair*	*Poor*
18500	16000	13000	8750	3750	1200

Model 103B

In 12-, 16-, 20- or 28-gauge H&H sidelock shotgun. Various barrel lengths and choke combinations. Chopper-lump barrels, H&H easy-opening mechanism, automatic ejectors, single-selective trigger and Purdey-type scroll engraving.

NIB	*Exc.*	*V.G.*	*Good*	*Fair*	*Poor*
22500	18000	14000	9500	6000	1500

Model 103B Royal

Same as above, with high quality engraving, very fancy wood, hand matted rib.

NIB	*Exc.*	*V.G.*	*Good*	*Fair*	*Poor*
25000	20000	15000	10500	4000	1500

Model 120

As above, with engraved hunting scenes. Discontinued in 1988.

NIB	*Exc.*	*V.G.*	*Good*	*Fair*	*Poor*
22500	18000	14000	9500	4000	1300

Model 200

As above, Magnum proofed double locking screws and 100 percent floral scroll engraving.

NIB	*Exc.*	*V.G.*	*Good*	*Fair*	*Poor*
20000	15000	10000	7500	3000	1300

Model Special

A special order gun. Too rare to price.

Express Rifle

Best-quality sidelock side-by-side double rifle. Stock has pistol grip and cheekpiece. Choice of English scroll or floral engraving. Calibers are 7x65R, 9.3x74R or .375 H&H.

NIB	*Exc.*	*V.G.*	*Good*	*Fair*	*Poor*
21000	15000	12000	7750	6000	1500

GARCIA
(Formerly Firearms International of Wash., D.C.)

Garcia Bronco

Single-shot .410 bore shotgun or .22 LR or .22 Magnum rifle, with swing out action. Modeled somewhat after old Hamilton No. 7. Barrel length 18.5". Stock is one-piece metal skeletonized affair. Weight about 3.5 lbs. Introduced in 1968; discontinued 1978. Built in U.S.A.

NIB	*Exc.*	*V.G.*	*Good*	*Fair*	*Poor*
350	250	220	120	90	50

Garcia Bronco .22/.410

Over/under shotgun/rifle combination. Over barrel .22 LR; under barrel chambered for .410 bore. Barrel length 18.5". One-piece metal skeletonized stock. Introduced in 1976; discontinued 1978. Weight about 4 lbs.

NIB	*Exc.*	*V.G.*	*Good*	*Fair*	*Poor*
500	380	300	200	120	80

Garcia Musketeer

Bolt-action rifle chambered for .243, .264, .270, .30-06, .307 Win. Magnum, .308 Norma, 7mm Rem. Magnum and .300 Win. Magnum. Fitted with checkered walnut stock, open sights, pistol grip, hinged floorplate and adjustable trigger. Introduced in 1970; discontinued 1972.

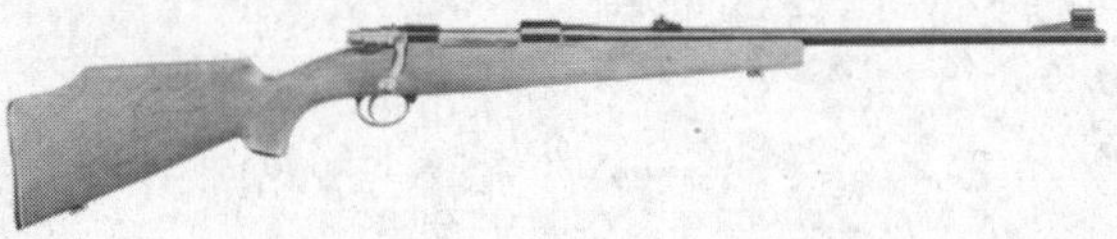

NIB	*Exc.*	*V.G.*	*Good*	*Fair*	*Poor*
600	500	350	250	200	150

GARRET, J. & F. CO.
Greensboro, North Carolina

Garrett Single-Shot Pistol (Antique)

A .54-caliber single-shot percussion pistol, with 8.5" round barrel, swivel ramrod, walnut stock and brass mounts. Marked on barrel breech "G.W." or "S.R." Approximately 500 made in 1862 and 1863.

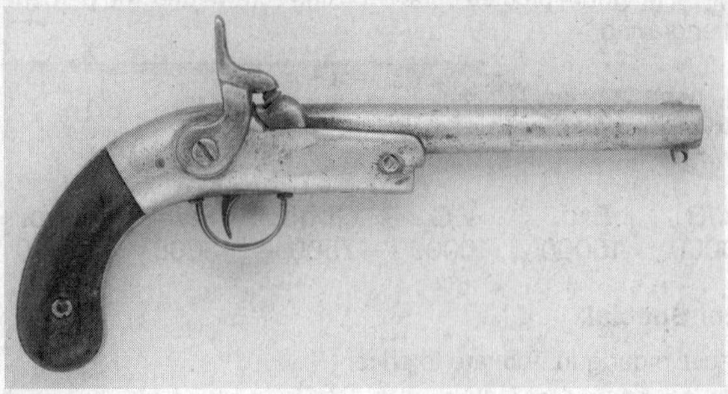

Courtesy Bonhams & Butterfields

Exc.	Fine	V.G.	Good	Fair	Poor
7000	5000	4000	3000	1500	1050

GASSER, LEOPOLD
Ottakring, Austria

M1870 (Antique)

An 11mm caliber double-action revolver, with 9.3" or 14.75" barrel and 6-shot cylinder. Marked "Gasser Patent, Guss Stahl". Bears an Austrian eagle and apple pierced by an arrow, with words "Schutz Mark".

Exc.	Fine	V.G.	Good	Fair	Poor
1800	1250	900	550	400	200

M1870/74 (Antique)

As above, with steel frame.

Exc.	Fine	V.G.	Good	Fair	Poor
1800	1250	900	550	400	200

Gasser-Kropatschek M1876 (Antique)

A 9mm caliber M1870/74. Weight 1 lb. 11 oz.

Exc.	Fine	V.G.	Good	Fair	Poor
1300	900	650	450	225	150

Montenegrin Gasser (Antique)

A 10.7mm caliber double-action revolver, with 5" or 6" barrel and 5-shot cylinder. Engraved silver and gold inlay. Ivory or bone grips. Values given are for plain, unadorned model. Embellished models will need individual appraisal.

Exc.	Fine	V.G.	Good	Fair	Poor
1200	750	550	400	200	150

Rast & Gasser M1898

A 8mm caliber double-action revolver, with 4.75" barrel, 8-shot cylinder, solid-frame with loading gate and integral ejector rod.

NIB	Exc.	V.G.	Good	Fair	Poor
—	650	420	350	180	120

GATLING ARMS CO.
Birmingham, England

See—KYNOCH

GAUCHER
France

GN 1

Single-shot bolt-action pistol chambered for .22 LR. Fitted with 10" barrel, blade front sight and adjustable rear sight. Adjustable trigger. Hardwood target grips. Weight about 38 oz. Introduced in 1990.

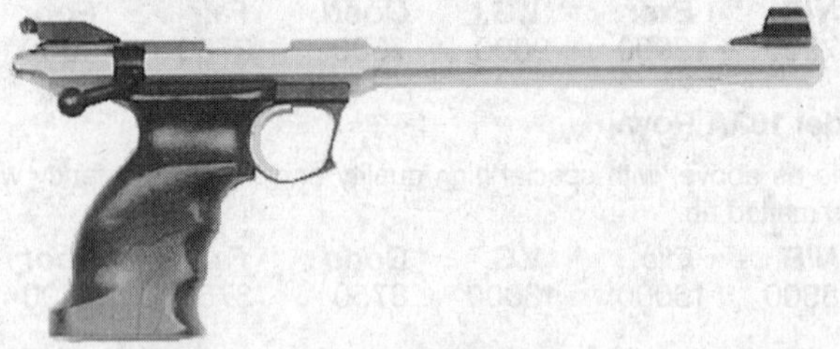

NIB	Exc.	V.G.	Good	Fair	Poor
520	420	350	220	140	100

GAULOIS
St. Etienne, France

See—LE FRANCAIS

GAVAGE, A.
Liege, Belgium

A 7.65mm caliber semi-automatic pistol, with fixed barrel and concealed hammer. Similar in appearance to Clement. Markings with "AG" molded into grips. Some have been found bearing German Waffenamts. Manufactured from 1930s to 1940s.

Courtesy James Rankin

NIB	Exc.	V.G.	Good	Fair	Poor
—	450	320	250	150	100

GAZANAGA, ISIDRO
Eibar, Spain

Destroyer M1913

A 6.35mm or 7.65mm caliber semi-automatic pistol. The 6.35mm model copied after 1906 Browning. "Destroyer" stamped on slide and Isidro logo on each side of grip plate. Produced through WWI.

Courtesy James Rankin

NIB	Exc.	V.G.	Good	Fair	Poor
—	300	200	140	80	50

Destroyer M1916

A 7.65mm caliber semi-automatic pistol, with 7- or 9-shot magazine. Ruby-style pistol manufactured by the Spanish during WWI. "Destroyer" stamped on slide. Wood grips.

Courtesy James Rankin

NIB	Exc.	V.G.	Good	Fair	Poor
—	320	220	120	80	50

Destroyer Revolver

A good quality .38-caliber copy of Colt Police Positive.

NIB	Exc.	V.G.	Good	Fair	Poor
—	300	160	160	100	80

Super Destroyer

A 7.65mm caliber copy of Walther PP. Slide stamped "Pistola Automatica 7.65 Super Destroyer".

NIB	Exc.	V.G.	Good	Fair	Poor
—	320	200	180	100	80

Surete

As above in 7.65mm caliber. Marked "Cal. 7.65 Pistolet Automatique Surete", with "IG" stamped on frame.

NIB	Exc.	V.G.	Good	Fair	Poor
—	300	160	160	100	80

GEBRUDER
See—ADAMY GEBRUDER

GECO
See—GENSCHOW, G.

GEHA
Germany

An altered Mauser 98 rifle re-barreled for use with 12-gauge shotgun shells. Barrel length 26.5", military stock shortened to half length and butt inlaid with a brass medallion marked "Geha". Manufactured from approximately 1919 to 1929.

NIB	Exc.	V.G.	Good	Fair	Poor
—	380	220	150	100	80

GEISSELE AUTOMATICS
North Wales, Pennsylvania

Maker of aftermarket triggers and AR-15 parts and accessories, Geissele Automics also produces complete firearms.

Super Duty 16".

Chamberings: 5.56 NATO. Features a Nanoweapon-coated Surefire

Closed-Tine Warcomp mounted to a 16" mag-phosphate cold hammer-forged, chrome-lined Geissele barrel. Twist: 1:7." Gas system: Geissele-length, with Geissele Super Compact Gas Block. Trigger: SSA-E X with Lightning Bow trigger, a nanocoated, two-stage unit. BCG: Machined from mil-spec 8620 steel, properly torqued and staked chrome-lined gas key. Lower: Machined from 7075-T6 aluminum with Geissele's Ultra Duty Lower Parts Kit. Ambidextrous Super Configurable safety and Ultra Precision triggerguard. Mil-spec Geissele Buffer Tube with Super-42 in H2 buffer. 15 MK16 Super Modular Rail mates to Super Duty Upper Receiver via a center aligning tab. Sights: None. Grips: Geissele Rifle Grip. Rails: 15" MK16 Super Modular. Stock: B5 Enhanced Sopmod. No magazine. Colors: Luna Black, DDC (Desert Dirt Color), ODG (OD Green). Add $225 for the 14.5" barrel with Nanocoated Surefire Closed-Tine Flash Hider, pinned and welded. SEE POLITICAL PANIC PRICING.

NIB	Exc.	V.G.	Good	Fair	Poor
2000	1890	1700	1500	—	—

GEM
Bacon Arms Company
Norwich, Connecticut

See—BACON

Gem Pocket Revolver (Antique)

A .22-caliber spur trigger revolver, with 1.25" octagonal barrel. Frame is iron, engraved nickel-plated, with walnut or ivory grips. Barrel marked "Gem". Manufactured between 1878 and 1883.

Exc.	Fine	V.G.	Good	Fair	Poor
1950	700	500	300	140	90

GEMMER, J.P.
See PLAINS RIFLE

GENEZ, A. G.
New York, New York

Located at 9 Chambers Street, Genez made a wide variety of firearms during his working life (ca. 1850 to 1875). Most commonly encountered of his arms today are single-shot percussion pistols and percussion double-barrel shotguns. More rarely seen are single-shot percussion target rifles. A number of arms he made were decorated by Louis D. Nimschke. Genez products signed by Nimschke command considerable premiums over values for standard firearms listed.

Double-Barrel Shotgun (Antique)

Most often encountered in 12-gauge. Varying barrel lengths, blued steel furniture and walnut stock.

Exc.	Fine	V.G.	Good	Fair	Poor
2800	1950	1220	500	250	170

Pocket Pistol (Antique)

A .41-caliber single-shot percussion pistol, with 3" barrel, German silver mountings and walnut stock. Manufactured in 1850s and 1860s.

Exc.	Fine	V.G.	Good	Fair	Poor
3950	1850	1170	500	180	120

GENSCHOW, G.
Hamburg, Germany

Geco

A 6.35mm, 7.65mm, .32 Long and 8mm Lebel caliber folding trigger double-action revolver.

NIB	Exc.	V.G.	Good	Fair	Poor
—	280	180	100	80	50

German Bulldog

A .32-, .38- and .45-caliber folding trigger double-action revolver, with solid frames, integral ejector rods and loading gates. Proofmarks indicate Belgian manufacture.

NIB	Exc.	V.G.	Good	Fair	Poor
—	280	180	110	80	50

GEORGIA ARMORY
Milledgeville, George

Established in 1862, this concern produced a rifle based upon U.S. Model 1855 Harper's Ferry Rifle. Nearly identical in all respects to Harpers Ferry, Georgia Armory rifle had a lockplate patterned after U.S. Model 1841 Rifle. Lock marked "G.A. ARMORY" over date (1862 or 1863). Buttplate tangs marked with serial numbers. Highest known serial number is 309. Rifles were fitted with saber bayonets. Expert authentication is highly recommended.

Confederate Rifle (Antique)

In 2019 a lock alone sold at auction for $3,250, highlighting the potential perils of only partially-authentic confederate arms assembled from mixed parts.

Exc.	Fine	V.G.	Good	Fair	Poor
65000	22000	16250	10500	3000	2100

GERING, H. M. & CO.
Arnstadt, Germany

Leonhardt

Semi-automatic pistol in caliber 7.65mm. Almost identical to Beholla pistol made by Becker. Leonhardt stamped on slide. These pistols were made for the German Army during WWI.

Courtesy James Rankin

NIB	Exc.	V.G.	Good	Fair	Poor
—	420	320	250	200	100

GERSTENBERGER & EBERWEIN
Gussenstadt, Germany

Em-Ge, G. &E., Omega & Pic

Series of poor-quality revolvers sold in U.S.A. before 1968. .22- and .32-calibers, with 2.25" barrels and 6-shot cylinder. May not be safe to shoot. Minimal value.

GEVARM
St. Etienne, France

Model A-6

This .22-caliber semi-automatic rifle fires from an open bolt. Fitted with a one-piece stock. Furnished with 8-round magazine. The E-1 20-magazine will not fit A-6 without hand fitting. Add 15 percent for higher-end A7 model. These rifles are increasingly popular on the secondary market because of their open-bolt design.

NIB	Exc.	V.G.	Good	Fair	Poor
—	800	700	480	280	160

E-1 Autoloading Rifle

A .22-caliber semi-automatic rifle, with 19" barrel, 8-shot magazine, blued with walnut grips. Two-piece stock. A 20-round magazine is an option.

NIB	Exc.	V.G.	Good	Fair	Poor
—	550	450	300	200	150

GIB
Eibar, Spain

10 Gauge Shotgun

A 10-gauge Magnum boxlock double-barrel shotgun, with 32" matte-ribbed barrels. Case-hardened, blued with walnut grips.

NIB	Exc.	V.G.	Good	Fair	Poor
—	700	500	280	150	100

GIBBS
New York, New York

Gibbs Carbine Antique

A .52-caliber single-shot percussion carbine, with sliding 22" round barrel. Blued case-hardened with walnut stock. Lock marked with American eagle and "Wm. F. Brooks/Manf New York/1863". Breech marked "L.H. Gibbs/Patd/Jany 8, 1856". Only 1,050 produced.

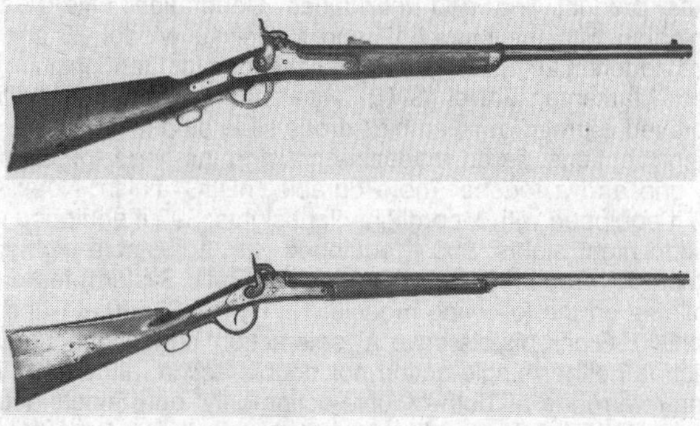

Courtesy Milwaukee Public Museum, Milwaukee, Wisconsin

Exc.	Fine	V.G.	Good	Fair	Poor
10000	7000	5000	3000	1750	750

Gibbs Pistol Antique

A caliber percussion pistol made by Hull & Thomas of Ilion, New York, in 1855 or 1856.

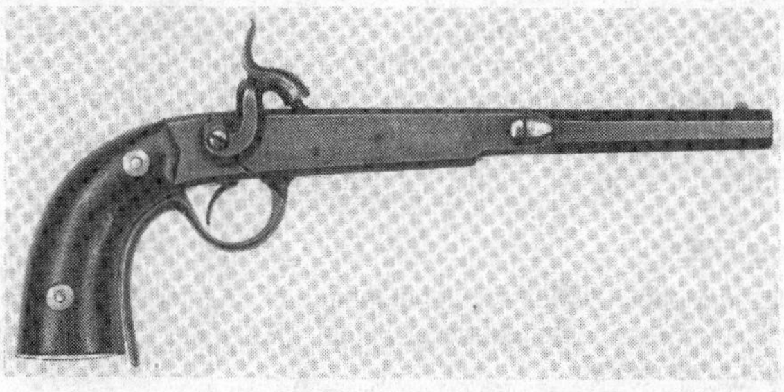

Courtesy Milwaukee Public Museum, Milwaukee, Wisconsin

Exc.	Fine	V.G.	Good	Fair	Poor
3600	2750	2000	1250	400	280

GIBBS, J. & G. / GIBBS, GEORGE
Bristol, England

Established in 1835, this concern continues in business to this day. J. & G. Gibbs 4 Redcliffe Street 1835-1842; George Gibbs 142 Thomas Street; Clare Street; 39 Corn Street. While initially known for exceptionally accurate single-shot rifles, the firm subsequently established a reputation for first quality bolt-action magazine rifles in a variety of large bore calibers. Bolt rifles by Gibbs, Rigby and others have become extremely desirable, especially in the African chamberings.

GIBBS GUNS, INC.
Greenback, Tennessee

Mark 45 Carbine

A .45 ACP caliber semi-automatic rifle, with 16.5" barrel, 5-, 15-, 30- or 90-shot magazine. Blued, with walnut buttstock and forend. Nickel-plated model available as an option. Would bring approximately $25 additional. Discontinued in 1988.

NIB	Exc.	V.G.	Good	Fair	Poor
650	480	280	200	120	100

GIBBS RIFLE COMPANY
Martinsburg, West Virginia

Gibbs Rifle Company was founded in 1991, by Val Forgett III, originally to refurbish and distribute various older military firearms. The company over the years has imported numerous black powder replicas from Europe and has also produced historical re-makes and specialty rifles.

Enfield No. 5 Jungle Carbine

Re-make of original British rifle. Chambered for .303 cartridge. Fitted with 20" barrel and flash hider. Magazine capacity 10 rounds. Weight about 7.75 lbs. New stock.

NIB	Exc.	V.G.	Good	Fair	Poor
350	300	200	150	100	50

Enfield No. 7 Jungle Carbine

Chambered for .308 Winchester cartridge. Fitted with 20" barrel and flash hider. Magazine capacity 12 rounds. Adjustable rear sight. Original wood. Weight about 8 lbs.

NIB	Exc.	V.G.	Good	Fair	Poor
650	580	480	350	250	200

Quest Extreme Carbine

An updated design of No. 5 Jungle Carbine. Chambered for .303 cartridge with 20" barrel. Nickel finish and new hardwood stock. Brass butt trap. Weight about 7.75 lbs.

NIB	Exc.	V.G.	Good	Fair	Poor
350	300	200	150	100	50

Quest II Extreme Carbine

Updated version of No. 7 Jungle Carbine, with nickel finish, see-through scope mount and hardwood stock. Chambered for .308 cartridge. Magazine capacity 12 rounds. Barrel length 20". Weight about 8 lbs.

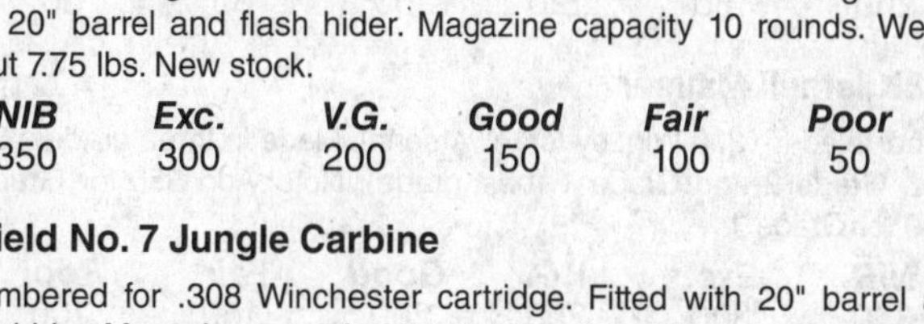

NIB	Exc.	V.G.	Good	Fair	Poor
350	300	200	150	100	50

Quest III Extreme Carbine

Similar to Quest II, with synthetic stock.

NIB	Exc.	V.G.	Good	Fair	Poor
400	320	200	150	100	50

Summit 45-70 Carbine

Bolt-action built on Enfield No. 4 action. Re-barreled to .45-70 caliber. Fitted to 21" barrel. MIL SPEC peep sight and checkered walnut stock. Weight about 8.5 lbs.

NIB	Exc.	V.G.	Good	Fair	Poor
400	320	220	180	120	80

Mauser M71/84

Chambered for 11mm Mauser cartridge and fitted with 31.5" barrel. Model has been arsenal re-conditioned, otherwise original. Weight about 10 lbs.

NIB	Exc.	V.G.	Good	Fair	Poor
300	250	180	150	100	50

Mauser M88 Commission Rifle

Fitted with 30" barrel. Chambered for 8mm cartridge. Model has been arsenal re-conditioned, otherwise original. Weight about 10 lbs.

NIB	Exc.	V.G.	Good	Fair	Poor
200	180	120	100	60	50

M98K Israeli Mauser

Re-barreled to .308 Win. by Israeli Arsenal. Made in three grades; Standard, Grade 2 and Grade 1 (best grade). Note: Add $50 for Grade 2, $100 for Grade 1.

NIB	Exc.	V.G.	Good	Fair	Poor
350	300	250	200	150	100

M1903-A4 Springfield Sniper Model

Replica of 1903-A3, with original Remington action, new barrels in .30-06, C model stock. New copy of M73B1 scope with Redfield-type rings and mounts. Parkerized finish.

NIB	Exc.	V.G.	Good	Fair	Poor
900	800	650	500	300	150

GIBBS TIFFANY & CO.
Sturbridge, Massachusetts

Underhammer Pistol (Antique)

A .28-caliber single-shot percussion pistol, with 3" to 8" barrels. Browned iron frame, walnut or maple pointed handle trimmed with brass. Top strap marked "Gibbs Tiffany & Co." Active 1820 to 1838.

Exc.	Fine	V.G.	Good	Fair	Poor
1250	650	450	250	100	70

GILLESPIE
New York, New York

Derringer Type Pocket Pistol (Antique)

A .41-caliber single-shot percussion pistol, with 2.5" barrel and walnut stock. Manufactured from 1848 to 1870.

Exc.	Fine	V.G.	Good	Fair	Poor
2950	1350	920	500	200	140

GIRSAN
See—EUROPEAN AMERICAN ARMORY

GLAZE, W. & CO.
Columbia, South Carolina

See—B. & B. M. DARLING

Glisenti Italian Military Pistol

See Standard Catalog of Military Firearms, available at GunDigestStore.com.

GLOCK
Deutsch-Wagram, Austria
Smyrna, Georgia

First imported into U.S.A. in 1985. Completely manufactured in Austria until 2004 when Glock opened its plant in Georgia to produce polymer frames. Offered in many models, but main differences are caliber, sighting systems, barrel, slide and grip length, and magazine capacity. Common features include a striker-fired action with a consistent DA-only trigger pull, trigger safety within main trigger, no grip or thumb safety, polymer frame with integral grips and steel slide. In 2010, Gen4 (fourth generation) of Glock pistols was introduced. Gen4 features include three interchangeable back-straps, reversible magazine release button, improved recoil spring assembly and rough-textured frame (RTF) to enhance grip traction. As of 2016, all new-production units of the following models had Gen4 features: M17, M19, M20, M21, M22, M23, M26, M27, M29, M30, M31, M32, M33, M34, M35, M37, M40, M41, M42, M43. In 2017, Glock continued the evolution of its product line and introduced Generation Five (Gen5) beginning with the Model 17 and Model 19. Model 26 and 34 were added in 2018. Upgrades and changes for Gen5 include the Glock Marksman Barrel (GMB), with enhanced polygonal rifling, improved barrel crown, ambidextrous slide stop levers, a variety of sight options, flared magazine housing, no finger grooves on the grip and a tougher more durable "nDLC" finish. Note: Add $70 if equipped with Meprolight night sights; $90 if equipped with Trijicon night sights; $30 if equipped with adjustable sights; 10 percent for Gen4 if NIB. MOS (Modular Optic System) feature is available on the following models: 17, 19, 34, 35, 40, 41 and 45; add $40. Glock pistols have a "safe-action" trigger mechanism, which is neither single-action nor double-action, although it has been referred to as both "double-action-only" and "single-action" in literature. The Glock safe-action trigger includes a safety lever mounted on the face of the trigger which is depressed by the shooter's trigger finger when the gun is fired. MOS (Modular Optic System) feature is available on the following models: 17, 19, 34, 35, 40, 41, 43X, 45 and 48; add $40. SEE POLITICAL PANIC PRICING.

Glock 17

Chambered for 9mm Parabellum cartridge. Has 4.49" barrel and 17-shot detachable magazine. Empty weight 21.91 oz. Note: Add $50 for Model 17 Gen4; $200 for Silver Anniversary Limited Edition; $50 for Gen5.

NIB	Exc.	V.G.	Good	Fair	Poor
550	450	350	300	—	—

Glock 17C

Similar to Model 17, with additional feature of an integral ported barrel. Specifications are same except for weight: 17C weight 21.9 oz. Available with OD green frame.

NIB	Exc.	V.G.	Good	Fair	Poor
650	550	400	300	—	—

Glock 17CC

Introduced in 1998. Compensated competition version of C variation. Fitted with extended slide stop lever, extended magazine release, adjustable sights and target trigger pull. This is a special order item only.

NIB	Exc.	V.G.	Good	Fair	Poor
650	600	500	400	—	—

Glock 17L Competition Model

Version features 6" compensated barrel and adjustable sights. Trigger is fine-tuned to provide between 5- to 8-lbs. trigger pull. Introduced in 1988. In 1990 this pistol won I.P.S.C. World Stock Gun Championship. Pistol has limited availability in U.S. Available with OD green frame.

NIB	Exc.	V.G.	Good	Fair	Poor
800	700	500	350	—	—

Glock 19

Similar in appearance to Model 17. Compact version, with 4" barrel and smaller grip that will accept 15-round or standard 17-round magazine that protrudes a bit. Weight 20.99 oz. empty. Grip straps on this model are serrated as they are on other Glock models. Introduced in 1988 and currently in production. Available with OD green frame. Note: Add $50 for Gen4; $100 for Competition model; $50 for Gen5.

NIB	Exc.	V.G.	Good	Fair	Poor
530	480	350	300	—	—

Glock 19C

Same as above, with integral ported barrel. Weight 20.7 oz. Available with OD green frame.

NIB	Exc.	V.G.	Good	Fair	Poor
650	550	280	300	—	—

Glock 19CC

Introduced in 1998, this is a compensated competition version of C variation. Fitted with extended slide stop lever, extended magazine release, adjustable sights and target trigger pull. This is special order item only.

NIB	Exc.	V.G.	Good	Fair	Poor
600	530	430	350	—	—

Glock 19X

Crossover model with Glock 17 frame and Glock 19 slide. 4.02" barrel. Gen 5 features. Coyote Tan finish. Introduced 2017.

NIB	Exc.	V.G.	Good	Fair	Poor
660	570	510	460	—	—

Glock 20 and Glock 21

Both of these models are identical in physical appearance except for caliber: Model 20 chambered for 10mm cartridge; Model 21 for .45 ACP. Barrel length on both is 4.60". Model 20 has 15-round clip, weight 26.35 oz.; Model 21 has 13-round clip, weight 25.22 oz. Available with OD green frame. Note: Add $25 for Gen4.

NIB	Exc.	V.G.	Good	Fair	Poor
550	430	350	300	—	—

Glock 20 SF Short Frame Pistol

Similar to Glock Model 20, with short-frame design. Chambered in 10mm Auto. Features include 4.61" barrel, with hexagonal rifling, fixed sights, extended sight radius. Overall length 8.07". Weight 27.51 oz.

NIB	Exc.	V.G.	Good	Fair	Poor
550	480	350	300	—	—

Glock 21 SF

Slenderized version of Model 21, with slimmer frame and ambidextrous magazine catch. Introduced 2007.

Courtesy Ken Lunde

NIB	Exc.	V.G.	Good	Fair	Poor
550	480	350	300	—	—

Glock 20C and 21C

Same as Models 20 and 21, with integral ported barrel. Available with OD green frame.

NIB	Exc.	V.G.	Good	Fair	Poor
600	480	400	330	—	—

Glock 20CC and 21CC

Introduced in 1998, this is a compensated competition version of C variation. Fitted with extended slide stop lever, extended magazine release, adjustable sights and target trigger pull. This is special order item only.

NIB	Exc.	V.G.	Good	Fair	Poor
700	600	500	350	—	—

Glock 22

Almost identical in appearance to Model 17. Model 22 chambered for .40 S&W cartridge. Standard with 15-round clip. Slightly larger and heavier slide. Weight 22.36 oz. Available with OD green frame. Note: Add $25 for Gen4.

NIB	Exc.	V.G.	Good	Fair	Poor
530	480	350	300	—	—

Glock 22C

Same as Glock 22 model, with addition of integral ported barrel. Weight 22.5 oz. Available with OD green frame.

NIB	Exc.	V.G.	Good	Fair	Poor
550	480	350	300	—	—

Glock 22CC

Introduced in 1998, this is a compensated competition version of C variation. Fitted with extended slide stop lever, extended magazine release, adjustable sights and target trigger pull. This is special order item only.

NIB	Exc.	V.G.	Good	Fair	Poor
600	500	400	330	—	—

Glock 23

Chambered for .40 S&W cartridge. Slide is slightly heavier and larger than Model 19. Weight 21.67 oz. Glock 23 magazine holds 13 rounds. Available with OD green frame. Note: Add $25 for Gen4.

NIB	Exc.	V.G.	Good	Fair	Poor
530	480	350	300	—	—

Glock 23C

Same as above, with integral ported barrel. Weight 20.9 oz. Available with OD green frame.

NIB	Exc.	V.G.	Good	Fair	Poor
550	480	350	300	—	—

Glock 23CC

Introduced in 1998, this is a compensated competition version of C variation. Fitted with extended slide stop lever, extended magazine release, adjustable sights and target trigger pull. This is special order item only.

NIB	Exc.	V.G.	Good	Fair	Poor
600	500	400	330	—	—

Glock 24

Chambered for .40 S&W cartridge. Fitted with 6" barrel. Weight 26.5 oz.

NIB	Exc.	V.G.	Good	Fair	Poor
730	630	550	430	—	—

Glock 24C

Same as above, with ported barrel.

NIB	Exc.	V.G.	Good	Fair	Poor
700	530	400	300	—	—

Glock 24CC

Introduced in 1998, this is a compensated competition version of C variation. Fitted with extended slide stop lever, extended magazine release, adjustable sights and target trigger pull. This is special order item only.

NIB	Exc.	V.G.	Good	Fair	Poor
700	600	500	350	—	—

Glock 26 and Glock 27

Both of these models are identical except for caliber. Introduced in 1995, these are subcompact versions of full-size Glocks. Model 26 chambered for 9mm cartridge; Model 27 for .40 S&W. Magazine capacity; 9mm 10 rounds; .40-caliber 9 rounds. Overall length 6.25"; barrel length 3.5"; height 4.1875"; width 1.25". Weight for both models about 20 oz. Standard are a dot front sight and white outline rear adjustable sight. Available with OD green frame. Note: Add $25 for Gen4; $50 for Gen5 MOS (Modular Optic System).

NIB	Exc.	V.G.	Good	Fair	Poor
550	480	350	300	—	—

Glock 29 and Glock 30

These two pistols were introduced in 1997. Model 29 chambered for 10mm cartridge; Model 30 for .45 ACP. Barrel length 3.78"; weight about 24 oz.; overall length 6.77". Model 29 magazine capacity 10 rounds; Model 30 has standard capacity of 10 rounds, with optional capacity of 9 rounds. Model 30 with 10-round magazine in place protrudes slightly below grip. With 9-round magazine in place fits flush with bottom of grip. Available with OD green frame. Note: Add $25 for Gen4.

NIB	Exc.	V.G.	Good	Fair	Poor
550	480	350	300	280	180

Glock 29 SF Short Frame Pistol

Similar to Glock Model 29, with short-frame design. Chambered in 10mm Auto. Features include 3.78" barrel with hexagonal rifling, fixed sights, extended sight radius. Overall length 6.97"; weight 24.52 oz.

NIB	Exc.	V.G.	Good	Fair	Poor
580	500	350	300	—	—

Glock 30

Sub-compact .45ACP, 3.78" barrel, 10-round magazine.

NIB	Exc.	V.G.	Good	Fair	Poor
580	530	450	350	—	—

Glock 31

Chambered for .357 SIG cartridge, this pistol fitted with 4.5" barrel and magazine capacity of 10 rounds (15 rounds law enforcement). Overall length 7.3", height 5.4", weight about 23.3 oz. Introduced in 1998. Available with OD green frame. Note: Add $25 for Gen4.

NIB	Exc.	V.G.	Good	Fair	Poor
550	480	350	300	280	180

Glock 31C

Same as Model 31, with integral compensator. Available with OD green frame.

NIB	Exc.	V.G.	Good	Fair	Poor
580	500	350	300	—	—

Glock 31CC

Introduced in 1998, this is a compensated competition version of C variation. Fitted with extended slide stop lever, extended magazine release, adjustable sights and target trigger pull. This is special order item only.

NIB	Exc.	V.G.	Good	Fair	Poor
700	600	500	350	—	—

Glock 32

Similar to Glock 31 except fitted with 4" barrel. Overall length 6.85"; height 5". Magazine capacity 10 rounds (13 rounds law enforcement). Weight about 21.5 oz. Introduced in 1998. Also available with OD green frame. Note: Add $25 for Gen4.

NIB	Exc.	V.G.	Good	Fair	Poor
580	500	350	300	—	—

Glock 32C

Same as above, with integral ported barrel and slide. Available with OD green frame.

NIB	Exc.	V.G.	Good	Fair	Poor
700	600	500	350	—	—

Glock 32CC

Introduced in 1998. Compensated competition version of C variation. Fitted with extended slide stop lever, extended magazine release, adjustable sights and target trigger pull. This is special order item only.

NIB	Exc.	V.G.	Good	Fair	Poor
700	600	500	350	—	—

Glock 33

This .357 SIG model has 3.5" barrel. Overall length 6.3"; height 4.2"; weight about 17.7 oz. Introduced in 1998. Available with OD green frame. Note: Add $25 for Gen4.

NIB	Exc.	V.G.	Good	Fair	Poor
580	500	350	300	—	—

Glock 34

Chambered for 9x19 cartridge. Has 5.3" barrel. Overall length 8.2". Magazine capacity 10 rounds. Empty weight about 23 oz. Available with OD green frame. Note: Add $25 for Gen4; $50 to $75 for Gen4 Competition if in excellent or better condition; $50 for Gen5 MOS (Modular Optic System).

NIB	Exc.	V.G.	Good	Fair	Poor
580	500	350	300	—	—

Glock 35

Chambered for .40 S&W cartridge. Same dimensions as Glock 34 except weight is 24.5 oz. Available with OD green frame. Note: Add $25 for Gen4; $50 to $75 for Gen4 Competition if in excellent or better condition.

NIB	Exc.	V.G.	Good	Fair	Poor
700	600	500	350	—	—

Glock 36

Introduced in 1999. Similar to Model 30. Fitted with single-column magazine capacity 6 rounds. Width .14" less than Model 30; barrel length 3.78"; weight 20 oz. Available with OD green frame.

NIB	Exc.	V.G.	Good	Fair	Poor
580	500	350	300	280	180

Glock 37

Chambered for .45 G.A.P. cartridge, which is slightly shorter than .45 ACP. Cartridge has a muzzle speed of 951 fps and muzzle energy of 405 ft. lbs. Fitted with 4.49" barrel; height 5.5"; overall length 7.3"; weight about 26 oz. Available with OD green frame. Note: Add $25 for all Gen4 variations.

NIB	Exc.	V.G.	Good	Fair	Poor
580	500	350	300	—	—

Glock 38

This .45 G.A.P. pistol fitted with 4" barrel. Height 5"; overall length 6.85". Magazine capacity 8 rounds. Weight about 24 oz. Introduced in 2005. Available with OD green frame.

NIB	Exc.	V.G.	Good	Fair	Poor
580	500	350	300	—	—

Glock 39

Introduced in 2005, this sub-compact .45 G.A.P. pistol has 3.46" barrel. Height 4.17"; overall length 6.3". Magazine capacity 8 rounds. Weight about 19.3 oz. Available with OD green frame.

NIB	Exc.	V.G.	Good	Fair	Poor
580	500	350	300	—	—

Glock 40

Similar to Glock 20 has 6.01" barrel. Introduced 2015.

NIB	Exc.	V.G.	Good	Fair	Poor
730	610	510	440	—	—

Glock 41 Sport/Service Competition

Much like Gen4 Model 21, with 5.3" barrel, RTF frame, octagonal rifling, interchangeable backstraps, dual recoil spring and new trigger system. Introduced in 2014. Chambered for .45 ACP. Model 40 is similar, except chambered in 10mm, with 6" barrel. Note: Add $50 for Model 40 in 10mm.

NIB	Exc.	V.G.	Good	Fair	Poor
650	550	420	320	—	—

Glock 42

Sub-compact model chambered in .380 ACP. Barrel 3.5" with hexagonal rifling. Has new trigger system, dual spring operating assembly and slimmest frame of any Glock, less than 1" in diameter. New in 2014.

NIB	Exc.	V.G.	Good	Fair	Poor
580	480	400	300	—	—

Glock 43

Long anticipated model from Glock is this single-stack 9mm compact. Magazine capacity 6 rounds. General features same as other Glock compacts. Barrel length 3.4"; overall length 6.26"; height 4.25"; width 1.02"; weight unloaded 17.95 oz. Introduced in 2015.

NIB	Exc.	V.G.	Good	Fair	Poor
580	480	400	300	—	—

Glock 43X

Similar to Glock 43 except with longer grip, sliver slide and 10-round magazine. Introduced 2019.

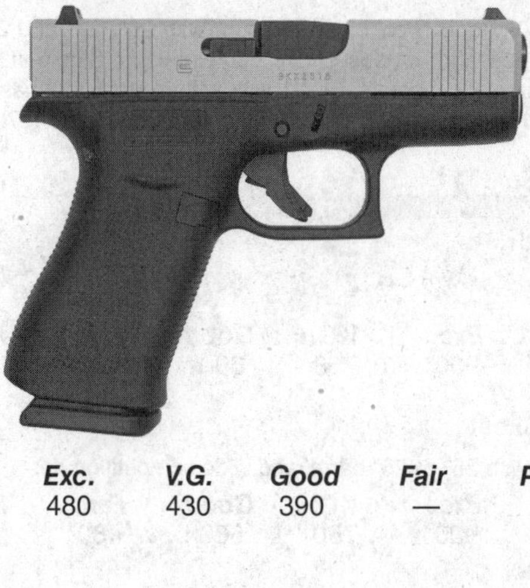

NIB	Exc.	V.G.	Good	Fair	Poor
520	480	430	390	—	—

Glock 44

Caliber: .22 LR. Capacity: 10-round magazine. Barrel: 4.02 in. Grips: Textured grip, interchangeable backstraps. Sights: Fixed, dot front/notch rear. Length: 7.28 in. overall. Weight: 14.6 oz. unloaded. Finish: Black. Features: Same size as Glock G19, hybrid slide of polymer and steel.

NIB	Exc.	V.G.	Good	Fair	Poor
400	350	300	280	—	—

Glock 45

Similar to Glock 19X except matte black, and 10- or 17-round magazine, front slide serrations. Introduced 2018.

NIB	Exc.	V.G.	Good	Fair	Poor
630	560	500	390	—	—

Glock 48

Compact 9mm, 4.17" barrel, 10-round magazine in slim-line frame.

NIB	Exc.	V.G.	Good	Fair	Poor
550	450	400	350	—	—

GODDARD

See—B. & B. M. DARLING

GOLDEN EAGLE

Nikko Limited
Tochigi, Japan

SHOTGUNS

Golden Eagle Model 5000 Grade I

A 12- or 20-gauge over/under shotgun, with 26", 28" and 30" barrels, ventilated ribs and various choke combinations. Single-selective trigger and automatic ejectors. Blued, with walnut stock that has an eagle's head inlaid into pistol grip cap. Manufactured between 1976 and early 1980s.

NIB	Exc.	V.G.	Good	Fair	Poor
1000	900	750	600	480	250

Grade I Skeet

As above, with 26" or 28" barrel and wide competition rib.

NIB	Exc.	V.G.	Good	Fair	Poor
1100	900	750	600	480	250

Grade I Trap

Similar to Skeet model, with 30" or 32" barrel.

NIB	Exc.	V.G.	Good	Fair	Poor
1200	900	750	600	480	250

Model 5000 Grade II

As above, more finely finished with a gold eagle's head inlaid in receiver.

NIB	Exc.	V.G.	Good	Fair	Poor
1100	1000	800	600	480	250

Grandee Grade III

As above, more elaborately engraved.

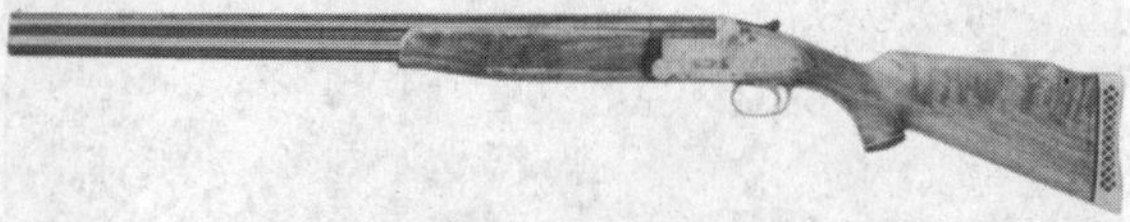

NIB	Exc.	V.G.	Good	Fair	Poor
2500	2000	1750	1400	850	500

RIFLES

Model 7000 Grade I

Mauser bolt-action rifle. Chambered for all popular American calibers, with 24" or 26" barrel, walnut stock, rosewood pistol grip cap and forend tip.

NIB	Exc.	V.G.	Good	Fair	Poor
700	600	500	380	300	200

Model 7000 African

As above in .375 H&H and .458 Win. Magnum caliber. Open sights.

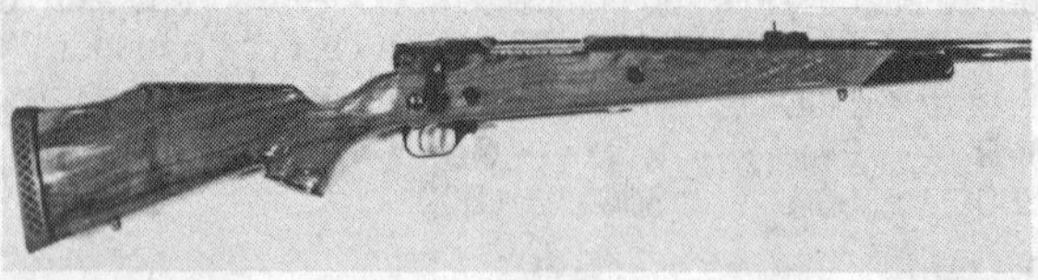

NIB	Exc.	V.G.	Good	Fair	Poor
800	650	550	400	320	250

Model 7000 Grade II

As above, but engraved.

NIB	Exc.	V.G.	Good	Fair	Poor
900	750	620	450	350	280

GONCZ CO.

Hollywood, California

GC Carbine

A 7.63mm Mauser, 9mm Parabellum, .38 Super and .45 ACP caliber semi-automatic rifle, with 16.1" barrel. Black with walnut stock. Later production models were stainless steel.

NIB	Exc.	V.G.	Good	Fair	Poor
650	500	400	280	200	120

GC Stainless

As above in stainless steel. Introduced in 1987.

NIB	Exc.	V.G.	Good	Fair	Poor
800	550	420	320	250	180

GC Collector's Edition

Limited edition with hand-polished finish.

NIB	Exc.	V.G.	Good	Fair	Poor
880	600	500	420	350	220

Halogen Carbine

GC Carbine, with powerful light source mounted under barrel. Chambered for 9mm and .45 ACP only.

NIB	Exc.	V.G.	Good	Fair	Poor
750	500	400	280	200	120

Laser Carbine

As above, with laser sighting system effective to 400 yards.

NIB	Exc.	V.G.	Good	Fair	Poor
1500	1250	1000	750	650	500

GA Pistol

GC Carbine, with 9.5" shrouded barrel and 16- or 18-shot magazine. Black with one-piece grip. Manufactured between 1985 and 1987.

NIB	Exc.	V.G.	Good	Fair	Poor
520	400	300	200	150	100

GAT-9 Pistol

As above, in 9mm caliber with adjustable trigger and hand-honed action.

NIB	Exc.	V.G.	Good	Fair	Poor
600	480	380	300	220	150

GA Collector's Edition

Hand-polished stainless steel limited production of above.

NIB	Exc.	V.G.	Good	Fair	Poor
820	680	600	500	400	300

GS Pistol

Model GA with plain 5" barrel. Made in stainless steel in 1987.

NIB	Exc.	V.G.	Good	Fair	Poor
350	280	220	180	120	80

GS Collector's Edition

Hand-polished limited-production stainless steel version of GS.

NIB	Exc.	V.G.	Good	Fair	Poor
780	620	550	480	350	250

GOUDRY, J.F.
Paris, France

Double-action 10-shot turret pistol. Marked on barrel rib J.F. Goudry Paris and Systeme A. Norl. By raising the gate on left side the turret can be removed and re-loaded or another pre-loaded turret inserted.

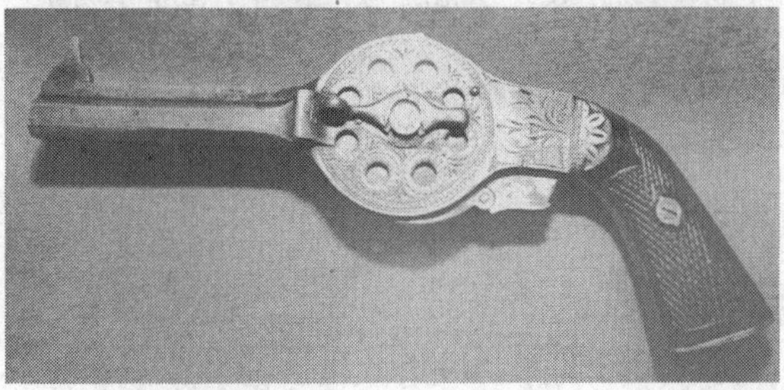

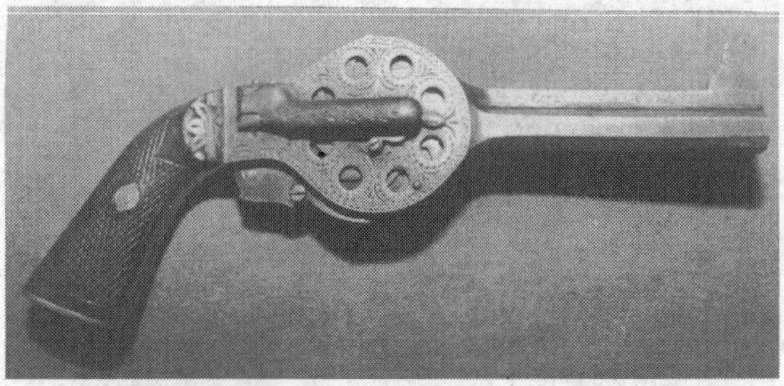

NIB	Exc.	V.G.	Good	Fair	Poor
—	—	6500	2000	1000	500

GOVERNOR
Norwich, Connecticut

Governor Pocket Revolver

A .22-caliber spur trigger revolver, with 3" barrel and 7-shot cylinder. Revolvers were made from modified Bacon pepperboxes. Top strap marked "Governor". Manufactured from approximately 1868 to 1874.

NIB	Exc.	V.G.	Good	Fair	Poor
—	—	720	650	250	100

GRABNER G.
Kolibri Rehberg, Austria

See—KOLIBRI

GRAND POWER
Lupca, Slovakia

K100 Mk12

Made in Slovakia, this is a polymer frame 9mm pistol with a steel slide and 4.25" rotating barrel. Traditional double-/single-action design, with ambidextrous controls, 15-round magazine and fixed 3-dot sights. Front sight comes with two extra inserts of different heights. Unique rotating barrel design is said to reduce felt recoil and provide better accuracy. Introduced in 2015. Imported by Eagle Imports.

NIB	Exc.	V.G.	Good	Fair	Poor
580	500	400	300	220	200

CP380D

Polymer frame, DA/SA trigger chambered in .380 ACP with 3.3-in. barrel. Equipped with 12-rnd. magazine, ambidextrous controls, picatinny rail. Finish available in black. Introduced 2016.

NIB	Exc.	V.G.	Good	Fair	Poor
420	370	300	240	190	150

K22S

Polymer frame, DA/SA trigger chambered in .22 LR with 5-in. barrel. Equipped with 10-rnd. magazine, ambidextrous controls, Picatinny rail and modular backstrap. Finish available in black. Introduced 2016.

NIB	Exc.	V.G.	Good	Fair	Poor
370	330	280	210	170	130

X-Calibur

Rotary locking mechanism. Polymer frame, DA/SA trigger chambered in 9mm with 5-in. heavy fluted barrel. Equipped with 15-rnd. magazine, ambidextrous controls, Picatinny rail, scalloped slide and modular backstrap. Finish available in black. Introduced 2016.

NIB	Exc.	V.G.	Good	Fair	Poor
820	720	560	450	370	290

GRAND PRECISION, FABRIQUE D'ARMES DE

Eibar, Spain

Bulwark Model 1913

Chambered for 6.35mm cartridge. Exact copy of Browning Model 1906. Complete with squeeze grip safety. Marketed by Beistegui Hermanos. Bulwark stamped on slide and B.H. stamped on grip plate.

Courtesy James Rankin

NIB	Exc.	V.G.	Good	Fair	Poor
—	300	200	150	80	40

Bulwark Model 1914

Chambered for 7.65mm cartridge. Style Ruby military pistols of WWI. Magazine capacity 9 rounds.

Courtesy James Rankin

NIB	Exc.	V.G.	Good	Fair	Poor
—	280	220	150	80	40

Bulwark 6.35mm

Semi-automatic pistol in caliber 6.35mm. Patterned after Browning Model 1906. Marketed by Beistegue Hermanos.

Courtesy James Rankin

NIB	Exc.	V.G.	Good	Fair	Poor
—	250	180	120	80	40

Libia 6.35mm

Also patterned after Browning Model 1906, with squeeze safety. Libia stamped on slide and each grip plate. Marketed by Beistegui Hermanos.

Courtesy James Rankin

NIB	Exc.	V.G.	Good	Fair	Poor
—	280	220	150	750	40

Libia 7.65mm

Similar to model above. Chambered for 7.65mm cartridge.

Courtesy James Rankin

NIB	Exc.	V.G.	Good	Fair	Poor
—	280	220	150	80	40

GRANGER, G.

St. Etienne, France

Side-by-Side Shotgun

Custom-order 12-, 16- and 20-gauge boxlock double-barrel shotgun. Manufactured since 1902. Because gun is imported, value of dollar frequently determines price movement.

NIB	Exc.	V.G.	Good	Fair	Poor
—	16500	13000	8500	4250	1500

GRANT, STEVEN & SON

See ATKIN GRANT & LANG.

GRAS

France

Model 1874

An 11mm caliber bolt-action rifle, with 32" barrel, walnut stock, barrel band and metal tip. Bayonet is a spike blade, with wood handle and brass butt cap.

NIB	Exc.	V.G.	Good	Fair	Poor
—	500	380	220	150	80

GRANT & LANG

See ATKIN GRANT & LANG.

GREAT WESTERN ARMS COMPANY

Los Angeles, California

Popularity of western television programs in early 1950s, spawned a renewed interest in guns that were seen in almost every episode, primarily the Single Action Army revolver. At about the same time that Bill Ruger was designing his company's first single-action, Single Six, a group of investors in the Los Angeles area, were preparing to launch Great Western Arms Company. Among this group was Dan Reeves, owner of the Los Angeles Rams professional football team, and several other prominent area businessmen. Hy Hunter's American Weapons Corp. in Burbank was chosen by the partners to be the exclusive distributor. He aggressively marketed the Frontier Six Shooter and many shooters and collectors erroneously believe, to this day, that he was the owner of the Great Western Arms. Ruger's .22 LR Single Six hit the market in 1953 and by spring of 1954, Great Western unveiled a faithful copy of the Colt Single Action Army, chambered in several centerfire calibers, including .38 Special, .357 Magnum, .357 Atomic, .44 special, .44-40, .44 Magnum, .45 Colt and .22 Long Rifle. This was the first of many Colt SAA clones. (.357 Atomic was a propriety cartridge that never got off the ground, a .357 with a slightly lengthened case. It apparently was never commercially loaded.) Standard single-action was known as Frontier Model and was made in the same barrel lengths as the original: 4.750", 5.500" and 7.500", plus a 12" Buntline Model. Grips were faux stag, with optional real stag, walnut, ivory and other materials on the handful of presentation grade engraved models. Some of the high-grade models were made for prominent political leaders and celebrities, including President Dwight D. Eisenhower, John Wayne and Elvis Presley. In addition to Frontier Model, Great Western offered several other single-action variations that are listed below, as well as a copy of Remington Double Derringer in .38 S&W or .38 Special. The company went through several ownership changes and had a tough time competing with Ruger and later Colt, which resurrected the original SAA in 1956. In 1959, the name and assets of the company were purchased by EMF (Early and Modern Firearms Co.) and in 1964 Great Western products was discontinued. The name was resurrected in 2003, when EMF imported a series of single-action revolvers, known as Great Western II 1873 SA, until about 2009. See separate listing below for these models. From a collectors perspective, interest in Great Western guns has been steadily on the increase and at the time of this writing, a dedicated following has rallied and put forth a lot of research, a book, articles and web sites. Along with other short lived modern manufacturers, Great Western Arms Co. is being afforded the same status as some obscure pre-Victorian makers now enjoy. *The editor would like to thank John Dougan for his contribution to the Great Western Arms section of Standard Catalog of Firearms.*

Centerfire Single-Action (Frontier Six Shooter)

This was Great Western's basic model and came chambered in a variety of center-fire calibers, .22 LR and .22 Magnum (WRM). Barrel lengths were offered in 4.75", 5.5", 7.5" and 12". Finishes were cyanide case colored, blued, chrome or nickel plated. The .22 / .22 WRM Convertible was listed in the catalogues after 1959. Standard grip panels were plastic imitation stag. Optional walnut, stag, pearl and ivory could be ordered. All were fitted with a Christy Gun Works firing pin mounted in the recoil shield, rather than on the hammer like the original Colts.

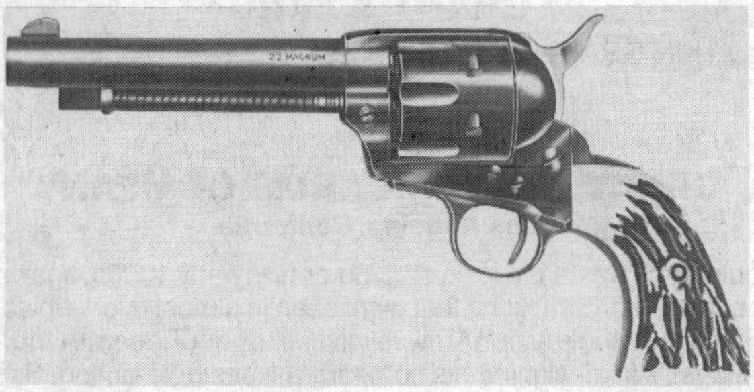

Courtesy John C. Dougan

NIB	Exc.	V.G.	Good	Fair	Poor
800	700	550	450	300	220

.22 Long Rifle Single-Action

NIB	Exc.	V.G.	Good	Fair	Poor
600	520	450	380	300	200

Target Model (.22 LR)

NIB	Exc.	V.G.	Good	Fair	Poor
700	620	500	350	300	200

Fast Draw Model

Brass backstrap and triggerguard.

NIB	Exc.	V.G.	Good	Fair	Poor
750	680	550	400	300	220

Sheriff's Model

Has a 4" barrel and no ejector rod. All were chambered in .45 Colt caliber and had serial numbers below 400. Features include nickel or blue, with case-hardened finish and faux (plastic) stag grips. There have been rumors that some of the Great Western parts were made by Colt. Sheriff's Models have been examined by experts who believe that the hammer and cylinder frame were identical to those on Colt SAA revolvers.

NIB	Exc.	V.G.	Good	Fair	Poor
1000	900	750	600	500	400

Deputy Model

Considered to be the rarest of the Great Western revolvers, it is believed that less than 100 were made, perhaps as few as 60. A 4" barrel with full length sight rib. Note: Calibers other than standard such as .22 Hornet, .32-20, .45 ACP, .22 Magnum, .30 Carbine or .357 Atomic add 10 percent premium. Factory plated pistols add 10 percent. Factory cased pistols add 20 percent. Sheriff's Model or Buntline Special add 15 percent. Factory ivory grips add $175; stag grips add $95 and pearl grips add $150. Factory-engraved guns will add $750 to $3,500 to prices depending on coverage.

NIB	Exc.	V.G.	Good	Fair	Poor
1100	1000	800	420	250	—

Derringer Models

These two-shot over/unders were based on Remington Derringer of late 19th Century. Chambered for .38 S&W or .38 Special. Some models were factory engraved and presented to Hollywood celebrities.

Engraved Model

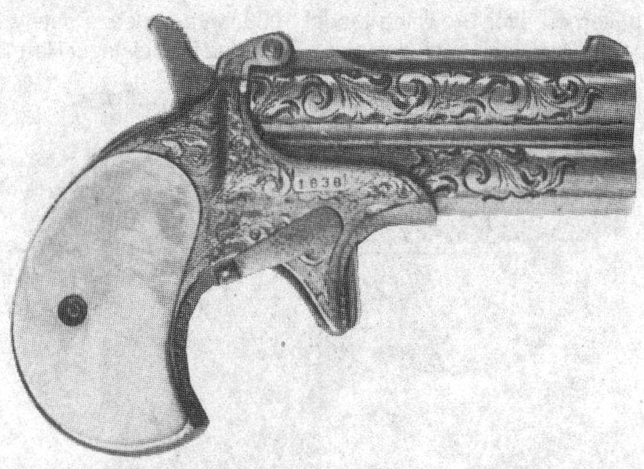

Courtesy John C. Dougan

NIB	Exc.	V.G.	Good	Fair	Poor
1300	1100	900	700	400	150

Standard Model

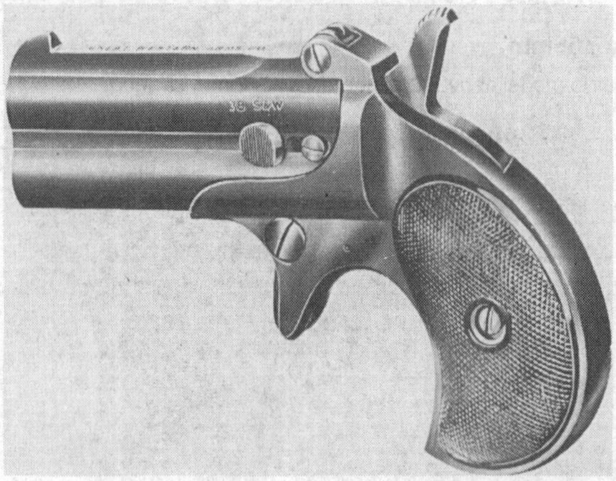

Courtesy John C. Dougan

NIB	Exc.	V.G.	Good	Fair	Poor
650	550	480	280	180	100

Production Chart

The following production schedule provides a list of Great Western serial numbers that were assigned to each year. It should be used as a general guide only.

1953.........GW1 - GW1507break;1954.........GW150 - GW4500
1955. . . . . GW4500 - GW11000
1956. . . . . GW11000 - GW11500
1957. . . . . 11500 - 15000
1958. . . . . .15000 - 17000
1959. . . . . .17000 - 18500
1960. . . . . .18500 - 20500
1961. . . . . .GW20500 - GW21500
1963.........GW21500 - GW22000

GREAT WESTERN II

Santa Ana, California

These single-action revolvers were made by Pietta in Italy. EMF, owner of the Great Western name, began importing these guns in 2003.

Custom 1873 SA

Chambered in .357, .44-40 and .45 Colt in standard SAA barrel lengths. Offered in blue, blue with color case-hardening, satin nickel or bright nickel finish. Ivory or stag grips. Engraved models were available. Imported from 2003 to 2010. Note: Add a premium of up to $100 for stag grips.

NIB	Exc.	V.G.	Good	Fair	Poor
750	620	500	400	300	200

Stainless 1873 SA

NIB	Exc.	V.G.	Good	Fair	Poor
800	650	550	450	300	200

Paladin Model

In .45 Colt, with 3.5", 5.5" or 7.5" barrel, ivory grips, blue finish. Introduced in 2013.

NIB	Exc.	V.G.	Good	Fair	Poor
480	400	320	280	200	180

Liberty Model

Similar to Paladin Model, except with laser engraving. Made in .357 Magnum and .45 Colt.

NIB	Exc.	V.G.	Good	Fair	Poor
550	480	400	350	300	200

GREEN, E.

Cheltenham, England

Green Revolver (Antique)

A .450- and .455-caliber double-action revolver. Popular with military users in late 1800s. In addition to this top-break revolver, Edwinson Green & Sons also made high quality double shotguns.

Exc.	Fine	V.G.	Good	Fair	Poor
2000	880	710	550	300	210

GREENE

Milbury, Massachusetts

Greene Breechloading Rifle (Antique)

A .53-caliber single-shot bolt-action percussion rifle, with 35" barrel, under hammer and full length walnut stock secured by three barrel bands. Marked "Greene's Patent/Nov. 17, 1857". Approximately 4,000 made by A.H. Waters Armory between 1859 and 1862.

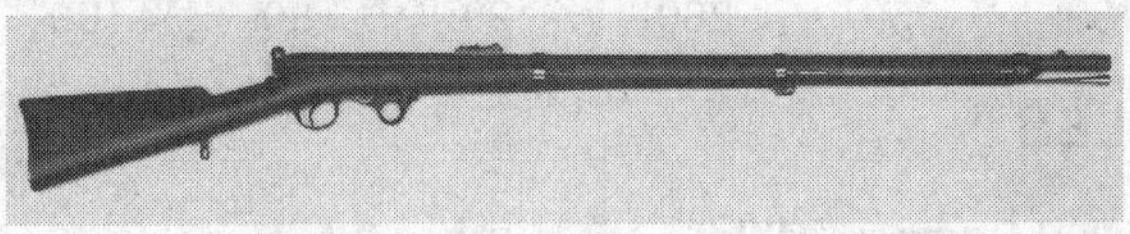

Courtesy Milwaukee Public Museum, Milwaukee, Wisconsin

Exc.	Fine	V.G.	Good	Fair	Poor
3250	1050	720	400	200	140

GREENER, W. W. LTD.

Birmingham, England

Perhaps the best known manufacturer of double-barrel shotguns in England during 19th Century. Greener was also a prolific author. His name will forever be associated with "Greener Crossbolt". Greener hammer-model shotguns were quite popular in United States during last half of 19th century. Company is still in business in Birmingham and makes a limited number of custom guns. Plain boxlock non-ejector models can start at $1,500, while high-end early guns with exceptional engraving can bring $100,000 or more. Because of the wide range of models and grades, a professional appraisal would be necessary before any transaction.

GREIFELT & CO.

Suhl, Germany

OVER/UNDER SHOTGUNS

Grade No. 1

Note: Add 25 percent for 28-gauge and .410 bore.

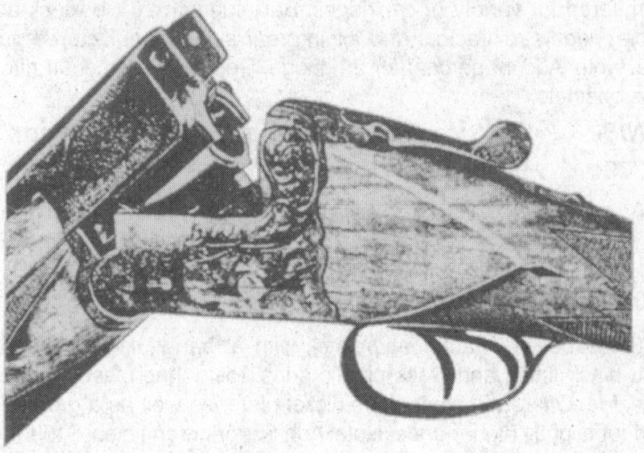

NIB	Exc.	V.G.	Good	Fair	Poor
—	3750	3250	2950	1750	1000

Grade No. 3

Similar to No. 1, with less engraving. Manufactured prior to WWII. Note: Add 25 percent for 28-gauge and .410 bore.

NIB	Exc.	V.G.	Good	Fair	Poor
—	3250	2700	1850	1250	750

Model 143E

Post-war version of No. 1. Not made in 28-gauge or .410 bore.

NIB	Exc.	V.G.	Good	Fair	Poor
—	2750	2300	1650	1200	750

Combination Gun

Combination over/under rifle/shotgun. Manufactured in all bores and variety of rifle calibers, with 24" or 26" barrels. Made prior to 1939. Note: Add 25 percent for 28-gauge and .410 bore; 10 percent for automatic ejectors. Deduct 40 percent if rifle caliber is obsolete

NIB	Exc.	V.G.	Good	Fair	Poor
—	5800	4750	3950	2500	1250

SIDE-BY-SIDE SHOTGUNS

Model 22

A 12- or 20-gauge boxlock double-barrel shotgun, with 28" or 30" barrels, sideplates, double triggers and extractors. Blued, case-hardened with walnut stock. Manufactured after 1945.

NIB	Exc.	V.G.	Good	Fair	Poor
—	2500	1950	1500	500	200

Model 22E

As above, with automatic ejectors.

NIB	Exc.	V.G.	Good	Fair	Poor
—	2750	2300	1650	550	220

Model 103

A 12- and 16-gauge boxlock shotgun, with 28" or 30" barrel, double triggers and extractors. Walnut stock, with pistol-, straight- or English-style-grip. Post-war model.

NIB	Exc.	V.G.	Good	Fair	Poor
—	2250	1800	1350	400	180

Model 103E

As above, with automatic ejectors.

NIB	Exc.	V.G.	Good	Fair	Poor
—	2500	1950	1500	500	200

Drilling

A 12-, 16- or 20-gauge double-barrel shotgun. Fitted with a rifle barrel.

Chambered for variety of cartridges. Barrel length 26", boxlock-action, double triggers, extractors and folding rear sight. Manufactured prior to 1939. Note: Add 10 percent for 20-gauge. Deduct 40 percent if rifle caliber is obsolete.

NIB	Exc.	V.G.	Good	Fair	Poor
—	3750	3200	2950	900	300

GRENDEL, INC.
Rockledge, Florida

P-10 Pistol

A .380-caliber semi-automatic pistol, with 3" barrel, 11-shot magazine, matte black finish and black plastic grips. Pistol has plastic frame and magazine. Offered in electroless nickel-plate, as well as a green Teflon finish for slightly higher price. Note: Add $5 for green finish; $15 for electroless nickel.

NIB	Exc.	V.G.	Good	Fair	Poor
300	250	200	150	120	80

P-12

Semi-automatic double-action pistol, chambered for .380 ACP cartridge. Fitted with 3" barrel, checkered polymer grips, and blued finish. Magazine capacity 10 rounds. Weight about 13 oz. Introduced in 1992.

NIB	Exc.	V.G.	Good	Fair	Poor
300	250	200	150	120	80

P-30

Introduced in 1990, this double-action semi-automatic pistol chambered for .22 WMR cartridge. Fitted with 5" or 8" barrel. Fixed sights. Magazine capacity 30 rounds. Weight about 21 oz. Discontinued in 1994.

NIB	Exc.	V.G.	Good	Fair	Poor
450	350	280	120	80	80

P-30L

Same as above, in 8" barrel only. Discontinued in 1994.

NIB	Exc.	V.G.	Good	Fair	Poor
450	350	280	120	80	80

P-30M

Similar to P-30. Fitted with removable muzzle brake.

NIB	Exc.	V.G.	Good	Fair	Poor
450	350	280	120	80	80

P-31

Semi-automatic pistol chambered for .22 WMR cartridge. Fitted with 11" barrel, muzzle brake. Black matte finish. Weight about 48 oz. Introduced in 1991. No longer in production.

NIB	Exc.	V.G.	Good	Fair	Poor
450	350	280	120	80	80

RIFLES

SRT-20F Compact Rifle

A .308-caliber bolt-action rifle, with 20" finned match grade barrel, 9-shot magazine, folding synthetic stock, integral bipod and no sights.

Courtesy Jim Supica, Old Town Station

NIB	Exc.	V.G.	Good	Fair	Poor
580	500	420	320	250	100

SRT-24

As above, with 24" barrel. Discontinued in 1988.

NIB	Exc.	V.G.	Good	Fair	Poor
600	520	450	350	280	100

R-31 Carbine

Semi-automatic carbine introduced in 1991. Chambered for .22 WMR cartridge. Fitted with 16" barrel. Muzzle brake and telescoping tubular stock. Magazine capacity 30 rounds. Weight about 4 lbs. Discontinued in 1994.

NIB	Exc.	V.G.	Good	Fair	Poor
300	250	200	150	120	100

GRIFFIN & HOWE

Andover, New Jersey

Established 1923 in New York, this firm manufactures bolt-action sporting rifles, often built on an existing model to custom specifications. Standard models such as the Hunter and Highlander are offered new in the $3,000 to $7,000 range, while custom Springfields, 70s, or 1903s may run $10,000 to $20,000. Early guns with exceptional engraving may bring much more.

GRIFFON

South Africa

Griffon 1911 A1 Combat

Semi-automatic single-action pistol, chambered for .45 ACP cartridge. Fitted with 4" ported barrel. Aluminum trigger and high-profile sights are standard. Frame is chrome and slide blued. Magazine capacity 7 rounds.

NIB	Exc.	V.G.	Good	Fair	Poor
600	500	400	300	200	120

GRISWOLD & GRIER

See—GRISWOLD & GUNNISON

GRISWOLD & GUNNISON

Griswoldville, Georgia

1851 Navy Type (Antique)

A .36-caliber percussion revolver, with 7.5" barrel and 6-shot cylinder. Frame and grip straps made of brass. Barrel and cylinder made of iron. Approximately 3,700 made between 1862 and 1864 for Confederate government. Note: This revolver sometimes referred to as Griswold and Grier. Professional authentication is highly recommended.

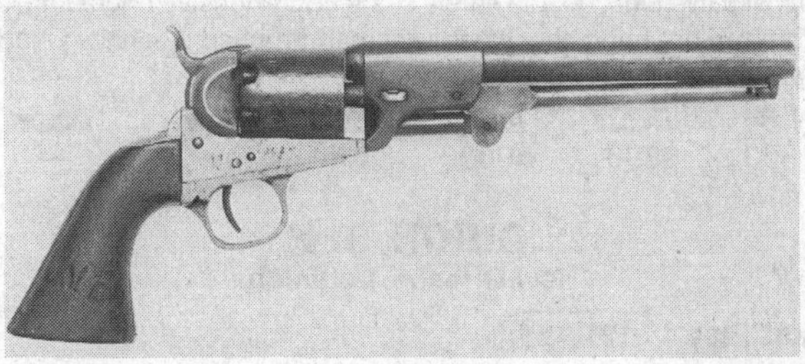

Courtesy Milwaukee Public Museum, Milwaukee, Wisconsin

Exc.	Fine	V.G.	Good	Fair	Poor
—	50000	30000	20000	1000	500

GROSS ARMS CO.

Tiffin, Ohio

Pocket Revolver (Antique)

A .25- and .30-caliber spur trigger revolver, with 6" octagonal barrel, 7-shot cylinder and marked "Gross Arms Co., Tiffin, Ohio". Blued, with walnut grips. Only a few hundred manufactured between 1864 and 1866.

Exc.	Fine	V.G.	Good	Fair	Poor
1700	600	450	300	150	100

GRUBB, J. C. & CO.

Philadelphia, Pennsylvania

Pocket Pistol (Antique)

A .41-caliber single-shot percussion pistol, with various barrel lengths. German silver walnut stock and engraved lock and triggerguard. Lock marked "J.C. Grubb". Several hundred manufactured between 1860 and 1870. Joseph C. Grubb also made or marketed double barrel percussion shotguns and double barrel percussion pistols.

Exc.	Fine	V.G.	Good	Fair	Poor
1550	800	720	650	170	110

GRULLA

Eibar, Spain

Model 216RL

Side-by-side shotgun offered in 12-, 16-, 20-, 28-gauge and .410 bore. Barrel length 28". Articulated double triggers. Action body is H&H side locks. Select walnut, with straight-grip and splinter forend. Fixed chokes. Choice of different styles of engraving. Weight range from 7.1 lbs. for 12-gauge to 6 lbs. for .410 bore. Note: Add $300 for 28-gauge and .410 bore.

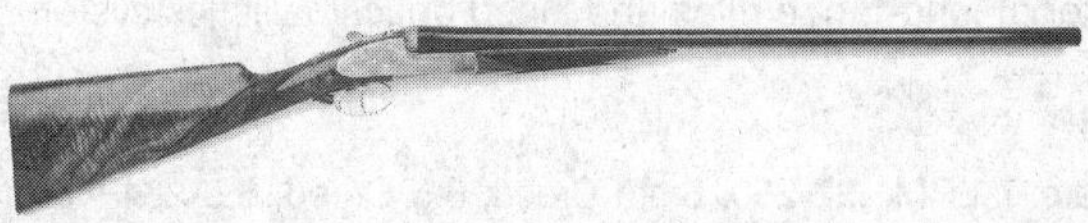

NIB	Exc.	V.G.	Good	Fair	Poor
9000	5750	3500	2000	1350	500

Royal

High-grade side-by-side series offered in all standard gauges. Featuring H&H seven-pin style sidelock and H&H, Purdey or Churchill style engraving. Custom made to buyer's specifications, with select exhibition grade walnut stock and forearm. Choice of several metal finishes. Note: Add $1000 for Purdey-style engraving; $2000 for Churchill.

NIB	Exc.	V.G.	Good	Fair	Poor
22750	19500	16000	10000	—	—

Consort

Side-by-side model, with double triggers, H&H style assisted-opening action, drop forged demi-block chopper lump barrels with concave rib and choice of old silver or case-hardened finish. This is a true sidelock action, with five pins, double safety sears and extensive engraving. Stock and forearm are hand checkered, with hand rubbed oil-finish. Chamberings are available in all standard gauges.

NIB	Exc.	V.G.	Good	Fair	Poor
11500	9800	8000	5500	—	—

GUION, T. F.
New Orleans, Louisiana

Pocket Pistol (Antique)

A .41-caliber single-shot percussion pistol, with 2.5" barrel, German silver mountings and walnut stock. Manufactured in 1850s.

Exc.	Fine	V.G.	Good	Fair	Poor
2150	1850	1200	550	280	190

GUNCRAFTER INDUSTRIES
Huntsville, Arkansas

This manufacturer of 1911-style pistols offers several different models, with typical 1911 features.

Model No. 1

Chambered in 9mm, .45 ACP and manufacturer's own proprietary .50 GI caliber. Barrel lengths include standard 5" plus 4.25" and 6". All guns are made-to-order. Note: Add 50 percent for 6" model.

NIB	Exc.	V.G.	Good	Fair	Poor
2850	2100	1500	1000	450	300

GUNWERKS
Cody, Wyoming

Maker of long-range rifles and tuned optics/ballistics systems.

Clymr

Calibers: 7 LRM, .22-250, 6mm Creed, 6.5 Creed, 6.5-284 Norma, 6.5 PRC, 28 Nosler, 7mm Rem. Mag., 7 SAUM, .300 Win. Mag., 30 Nosler, 300 PRC. Capacity: 3-round capacity in the internal mag. Option to upgrade to dropbox mags. Barrel: Carbon wrapped, threaded, 20- or 22-in. barrel come standard. Upgrade to 18 in. available. Weight: Varies by options selected. Stock: Carbon fiber in choice of ten paint finishes with negative comb and flat toe line. Sights: No sights. Drilled and tapped. Choice of multiple base, scope ring, and scope options direct from the factory. Features: Lightweight, semi-custom, bolt-action hunting rifle built for mountain hunting and available as a user-built rifle system with multiple options. Choice of standard GLR SS action or Titanium action upgrade. Add $150 for left-hand action. Eleven metal finish colors available, as well as option of directional muzzle brake or thread cap. LOP of 13.5 in. Prices increase significantly as options are added for custom factory builds.

NIB	Exc.	V.G.	Good	Fair	Poor
5250	—	—	—	—	—

HAMR 2.0

Calibers: .375 CheyTac. Barrel: 30 in. Carbon wrapped, threaded, with aggressive Cadex MX1 muzzle brake. Weight: 21.25 lbs. standard, total package. Stock: Cadex Defence Dual Strike tactical folding chassis-style with adjustable LOP. Sights: Comes standard with user option of scope (Kahles K525i, Leupold Mk 5HD, Revic PMR 428) on a 40 MOA mount. Features: Bolt-action ultra-long-range rifle built as a complete ELR system capable of shooting over two miles. The upgraded 2.0 version includes a carbon-wrapped barrel, new optic choices, and finish options. Included Elite Iron bipod encircles the centerline of the bore. Timney trigger set at 2.5 lbs. Prices increase significantly as options are added for custom factory builds. Long-range data package available.

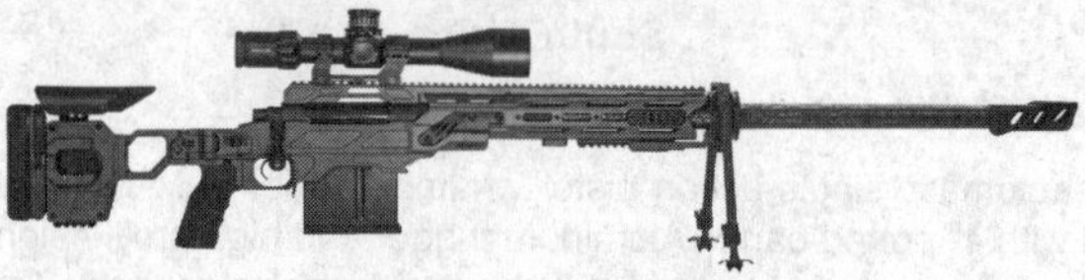

NIB	Exc.	V.G.	Good	Fair	Poor
9150	—	—	—	—	—

Werkman System

Caliber: 6.5 PRC, 7mm PRC, .300 PRC. Barrel: 22" stainless steel, cut rifled. Weight: 9.6 lbs. Stock: Gen1 Magnus carbon fiber in tan, gray, or green Fracture paint finish. Features: Bolt-action rifle system with fewer frills. GLR stainless receiver. Threaded barrel with directional brake. TriggerTech trigger. GW floorplate bottom metal. Topped with Revic Werkman RS25 rifle scope. Custom BDC turret matched to Hornady ELD Match ammunition and ballistics data for 1,000 yards. Left-hand action available for +$150.

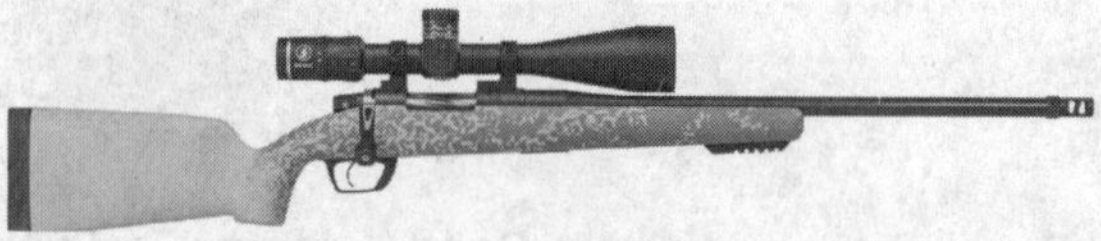

NIB	Exc.	V.G.	Good	Fair	Poor
4780	—	—	—	—	—

GUNWORKS LTD.
Buffalo, New York

Model 9 Derringer

Over/under derringer chambered in 9mm, .38 Special, .38 Super and .357 Magnum caliber. Barrels 2.5", with spur trigger and Millet sights. Nickel-plate with walnut grips. Manufacturing ceased in 1986.

NIB	Exc.	V.G.	Good	Fair	Poor
—	180	120	90	80	50

GUSTAF, CARL
Eskilstuna, Sweden

Bolt-Action Rifle

A 6.5x55, 7x64, .270, 7mm Magnum, .308, .30-06 and 9.3x62 caliber bolt-action rifle, with 24" barrel. Blued, with walnut stock in classic style or with Monte Carlo cheekpiece. Manufactured between 1970 and 1977.

NIB	Exc.	V.G.	Good	Fair	Poor
—	700	600	450	320	150

Grade II

As above, with better walnut, rosewood pistol grip cap and forend tip.

NIB	Exc.	V.G.	Good	Fair	Poor
—	850	650	480	380	180

Grade III

As above, with high-gloss finish and finely figured walnut stock.

NIB	Exc.	V.G.	Good	Fair	Poor
—	950	700	550	480	280

Deluxe Bolt-Action

As above, with engraved floorplate and triggerguard, Damascened bolt and high-grade French walnut stock. Manufactured between 1970 and 1977.

NIB	Exc.	V.G.	Good	Fair	Poor
—	1250	900	650	450	300

Varmint Model

A .222, .22-250, .243 and 6.5x55 caliber bolt-action rifle, with 27" barrel and large bolt knob made of Bakelite. Furnished without open sights. Has a heavy target-type stock. Manufactured in 1970 only.

NIB	Exc.	V.G.	Good	Fair	Poor
—	700	600	450	320	150

Grand Prix Target

A .22-caliber single-shot bolt-action rifle, with 27" barrel. Adjustable weights and butt target stock. Furnished without sights. Only manufactured in 1970.

NIB	Exc.	V.G.	Good	Fair	Poor
—	700	600	450	320	150

Model 2000

A 6.5x55, .243, .270, .308 and .30-06 caliber bolt-action rifle, with 60 percent bolt lift. Cold swagged barrel and action. Furnished with open sights. Blued, walnut stock with Monte Carlo cheekpiece. Manufactured until 1985.

NIB	Exc.	V.G.	Good	Fair	Poor
—	680	580	400	300	150

GWYN & CAMPBELL
Hamilton, Ohio

Union Carbine (Antique)

A .52-caliber single-shot breech loading percussion carbine, with round/octagonal 20" barrel marked "Gwyn & Campbell/ Patent/1862/ Hamilton,O". Blued, case-hardened with walnut stock. Approximately 8,500 made between 1862 and 1865.

Courtesy Milwaukee Public Museum, Milwaukee, Wisconsin

Exc.	Fine	V.G.	Good	Fair	Poor
6000	4000	3000	1500	800	400

H

H.J.S. INDUSTRIES, INC.
Brownsville, Texas

Frontier Four Derringer

A .22-caliber four-barreled pocket pistol, with 2.5" sliding barrels, stainless steel frame, barrel- and walnut-grips. Recalled due to risk of unintentional discharge.

NIB	Exc.	V.G.	Good	Fair	Poor
—	450	400	280	150	50

Lone Star Derringer

A .38 Special caliber single-shot spur trigger pistol, with 2.5" barrel. Stainless steel with wood grips.

NIB	Exc.	V.G.	Good	Fair	Poor
—	300	250	180	120	50

H-S PRECISION, INC.
Rapid City, South Dakota

SPR Sporter Rifle

Bolt-action rifle offered in long and short actions, with any standard SAAMI caliber. Match grade stainless steel barrel lengths are 22", 24" or 26", with optional muzzle brake available. Synthetic stock offered in various colors. Weight between 7.5 and 7.75 lbs. depending on barrel length. Magazine capacity: 4 rounds standard calibers; 3 rounds Magnum calibers.

NIB	Exc.	V.G.	Good	Fair	Poor
2380	1800	1400	900	500	250

SPL Lightweight Sporter

Introduced in 2005. Features 22", 24" or 26" fluted barrel, with choice of short or long action calibers. Detachable magazine. No sights. Pro-series synthetic stock. Weight under 7 lbs.

NIB	Exc.	V.G.	Good	Fair	Poor
2400	1820	1420	920	520	280

PHR Professional Hunter Rifle

Bolt-action rifle chambered for Magnum calibers only. Fitted with 24" or 26" stainless steel match-grade fluted barrel (except .416 Rigby). Built in recoil reduced in synthetic stock with choice of colors. Matte black finish. Weight between 7.75 lbs. and 8.25 depending on barrel length and caliber. Offered in any standard SAAMI caliber. Magazine capacity 3 rounds.

NIB	Exc.	V.G.	Good	Fair	Poor
3300	2600	1800	1050	580	300

BHR Big Game Professional Hunter Rifle

Introduced in 2005. Same features as PHR series, with addition of adjustable iron sights and specially designed stock. Weight about 7.75 to 8.25 lbs. depending on caliber and barrel length.

NIB	Exc.	V.G.	Good	Fair	Poor
3400	2700	1850	1180	620	350

PHL Professional Hunter Lightweight Rifle

Features weight of 5.75 lbs. Fitted with Pro-Series stock and choice of 20" or 22" contoured fluted stock. Matte black teflon finish. Detachable magazine. Chambered for short action calibers. Introduced in 2005.

NIB	Exc.	V.G.	Good	Fair	Poor
3100	2500	1850	1180	620	350

VAR Varmint Rifle

Offered in long or short action, with .17 Rem., 6mm PPC and .223 Rem. in single-shot. Fitted with match-grade stainless steel fluted barrel in 24" or 26" lengths. Available in a light-weight 20" barrel. Synthetic stock in choice of colors, with 20" barrel guns offered with thumbhole stocks. Black matte finish. Weight between 8 and 8.25 lbs. for standard rifles and 7.5 and 7.75 lbs. for 20" barrel guns. Available in any standard SAAMI caliber.

NIB	Exc.	V.G.	Good	Fair	Poor
3200	2500	1750	1050	580	300

Varmint Take-Down Rifle

Take-down bolt-action rifle offered in stainless steel long or short action, with 24" stainless steel match-grade fluted barrel. Matte black finish. Weight between 8.5 and 9 lbs. Note: Add $1,000 for extra barrel with same head size caliber; $1,200 for extra barrel with different head size caliber.

NIB	Exc.	V.G.	Good	Fair	Poor
3700	2900	2050	1450	600	400

Professional Hunter Take-Down Rifle

Take-down rifle offered in Magnum and Super Magnum calibers, with 24" fluted stainless steel barrel. Built in recoil reducer. Matte black finish. Weight between 8.25 and 8.75 lbs.

NIB	Exc.	V.G.	Good	Fair	Poor
4500	3200	2400	1650	750	450

Varmint Pistol

Bolt-action single-shot pistol chambered for a wide variety of calibers from .17 Rem. to 7mm BR. Fitted with heavy contour fluted stainless steel match barrel. Synthetic stock with center grip. Matte black finish. Weight about 5.25 to 5.5 lbs.

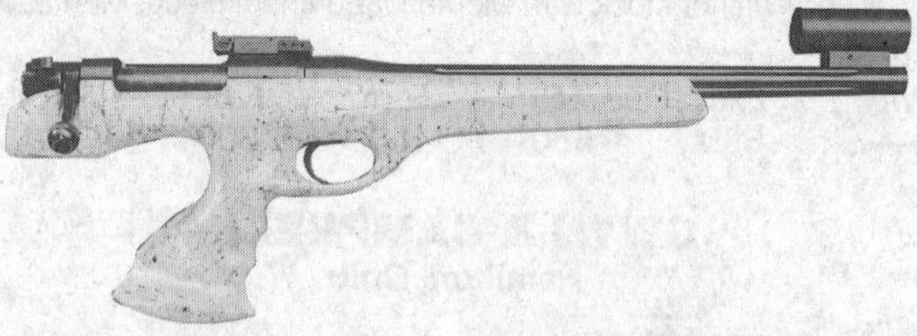

NIB	Exc.	V.G.	Good	Fair	Poor
2200	1500	950	600	400	220

Silhouette Pistol

Same as above, with sporter contoured barrel. Weight about 4.5 lbs.

NIB	Exc.	V.G.	Good	Fair	Poor
2100	1400	950	600	400	220

HTR Heavy Tactical Rifle

Bolt-action model features stainless steel long or short action, with fluted stainless steel 24" heavy barrel. Stock is synthetic, with adjustable cheekpiece and length of pull. Any standard SAAMI caliber available. Weight about 10.75 to 11.25 lbs. Matte black finish.

NIB	Exc.	V.G.	Good	Fair	Poor
3400	2700	1850	1180	620	350

Short Tactical

Chambered for .308 cartridge. Fitted with 20" fluted barrel. Matte teflon finish. Pro-Series tactical stock.

NIB	Exc.	V.G.	Good	Fair	Poor
3400	2700	1850	1180	620	350

RDR Rapid Deployment Rifle

Similar to model above, with 20" stainless steel fluted barrel and smaller stock. Thumbhole stock on request. Magazine is 4 rounds. Matte black finish. Offered in any short action SAAMI calibers. Weight between 7.5 and 7.75 lbs.

NIB	Exc.	V.G.	Good	Fair	Poor
3100	2400	1500	1180	620	350

TTD Tactical Take-Down System

Take-down rifle chambered for any standard SAAMI caliber. Fitted with 24" fluted heavy stainless steel barrel. Magazine capacity: 4 rounds standard calibers; 3 rounds Magnum calibers. Synthetic stock adjustable for length of pull and cheekpiece. Matte black finish. Weight between 11.25 and 11.75 lbs.

NIB	Exc.	V.G.	Good	Fair	Poor
5200	4400	3000	1650	750	450

HAENEL, C. G.

Suhl, Germany

Established in 1840, this company began to manufacture semi-automatic pistols after Hugo Schmeisser joined the firm in 1921 as its chief engineer.

Model 1

A 6.35mm caliber semi-automatic pistol, with 2.48" barrel, striker-fired, 6-shot magazine. Weight about 13.5 oz. Left side of slide stamped "C.G. Haenel Suhl-Schmeisser Patent". Each grip panel marked "HS" in an oval.

NIB	Exc.	V.G.	Good	Fair	Poor
—	500	400	300	200	120

Model 2

As above, but shorter (2" barrel) and lighter in weight (12 oz.). "Schmeisser" molded into grips.

Courtesy Orvel Reichert

NIB	Exc.	V.G.	Good	Fair	Poor
—	550	420	350	220	150

HAFDASA

Buenos Aires, Argentina

Ballester-Molina

Copy of Colt Model 1911 semi-automatic pistol. Differing only in absence of grip safety, smaller grip and finger grooves on slide. Slide stamped "Pistola Automatica Cal. .45 Fabricado por HAFDASA Patentes Internacional Ballester Molina Industria Argentina". Introduced in 1941.

Courtesy James Rankin

NIB	Exc.	V.G.	Good	Fair	Poor
—	480	400	300	220	100

Criolla

A .22-caliber automatic pistol similar to Ballester-Molina. Some were sold commercially under trademark "La Criolla".

NIB	Exc.	V.G.	Good	Fair	Poor
—	1000	800	650	500	250

Hafdasa

A .22-caliber semi-automatic pistol with tubular receiver. A true hammerless striker-fired, with angled grip. Markings are "HA" on butt.

NIB	Exc.	V.G.	Good	Fair	Poor
—	400	320	280	200	100

Zonda

As above marked "Zonda".

NIB	Exc.	V.G.	Good	Fair	Poor
—	400	320	280	200	100

Rigaud

A semi-automatic copy of Colt Model 1911, with no grip safety. Caliber is .45 ACP and later .22 LR. Barrel length 5". Magazine capacity 7 rounds. The .22-caliber introduced in 1940.

Courtesy James Rankin

NIB	Exc.	V.G.	Good	Fair	Poor
—	480	400	300	220	100

Campeon

Same as Ballester-Molina, with floating chamber to accommodate .22 LR cartridge. Three variations of target model: sights, trigger and barrel lengths. Pistol first introduced in 1941 until 1953.

Courtesy James Rankin

NIB	Exc.	V.G.	Good	Fair	Poor
—	750	550	400	300	200

HAHN, WILLIAM
New York, New York

Pocket Pistol (Antique)

A .41-caliber single-shot percussion pistol, with 2.5" round barrel, German silver mountings and walnut stock. Manufactured in 1860s and 1870s. Hahn also made rifles and other percussion firearms.

Exc.	Fine	V.G.	Good	Fair	Poor
1950	1050	760	480	250	170

HALE, H. J.
Bristol, Connecticut

Underhammer Pistol (Antique)

A .31-caliber single-shot under hammer percussion pistol, with 5" or 6" part-round/part-octagonal barrel. Iron frame, with pointed or round walnut butt. Markings read "H.J.Hale/Warranted/Cast Steel". Manufactured during 1850s.

Exc.	Fine	V.G.	Good	Fair	Poor
5000	3000	1200	800	400	200

HALE & TULLER
Hartford, Connecticut

Underhammer Pistol (Antique)

A .44-caliber single-shot under hammer percussion pistol, with 6" tapered round barrel and pointed walnut grip. Manufactured at Connecticut State Prison between 1837 and 1840. Values are speculative.

Exc.	Fine	V.G.	Good	Fair	Poor
4000	2500	1200	800	400	200

HALL, ALEXANDER
New York, New York

Revolving Rifle (Antique)

A .58-caliber percussion revolving rifle, with 15-shot open centered cylinder. Frame was made of brass. Barrel and cylinder of iron. Stock of walnut. Manufactured during 1850s in limited quantities. Very rare firearm.

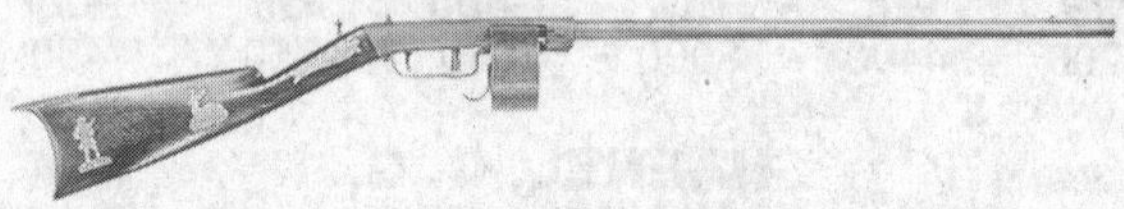

Exc.	Fine	V.G.	Good	Fair	Poor
27500	12500	8120	3750	1300	900

HALL-NORTH
Middletown, Connecticut

U.S. Military Breechloaders (Antique)

The U.S. Harpers Ferry Armory and contractor Simeon North of Middletown Connecticut manufactured Hall's patent breechloading long arms for the US military. These single-shot arms has a breechblock hinged at the rear that raised at the front for loading, and were a significant advance as the first breech-loading firearms issued by the US military. Harpers Ferry made flintlock rifle versions ca. 1817-1840 and percussion rifle and carbine models 1841-1843. North produced flintlock rifles 1830-1836 and percussion carbines 1834-1853. .52 caliber was most common, with some variations in .58 and .60 caliber. Rifle barrels were 52 5/8 inches and carbine barrels 21 to 26 inches. Most but not all carbine variations are smoothbore. Models and variations include:

HARPERS FERRY:
* 1819 Flintlock Rifle in 1st, 2nd & 3rd Types.
* 1841 Flintlock Rifle
* 1836 Percussion Carbine
* 1842 Percussion Carbine

SIMEON NORTH
* 1819 Contract Flintlock Rifle
* 1833 Percussion Carbine in .58 and .52 caliber versions.
* 1840 Percussion Carbine in 1st & 2nd Types
* 1842 Percussion Carbine
* 1843 Percussion Carbine in .52 cal. smoothbore with some converted to .58 cal. rifled.

Some of the early flintlock rifles by both makers were converted to percussion. Most of these models and variations will bring similar values, shown below. Rifles by either maker that were originally flintlock, but have been converted by the government to percussion, will bring less - about half the values shown.

There are four rare variations that will bring a premium, sometimes double or more the values listed. These include:

* Harpers Ferry 1819 Flintlock 1st Type dated 1824.
* Harpers Ferry 1842 Carbine
* North 1833 Carbines in rare .58 cal.
* North 1840 Carbines, Type I, with angular L shaped breech lever.

Photo courtesy Supica's Gunheritage.com

Exc.	*Fine*	*V.G.*	*Good*	*Fair*	*Poor*
5000	3000	2000	1250	900	500

HAMBUSH, JOSEPH

Ferlach, Austria

Boxlock Side-by-Side Shotgun

Custom-order boxlock double-barrel shotgun chambered for all gauges. Single-selective or double trigger and automatic ejectors. Features workmanship of high order. All specifications could vary with customer's wishes. Engraved with hunting scenes. Rare gun and not often encountered on today's market. Note: Pricing only estimated as not enough are traded to provide accurate values.

NIB	*Exc.*	*V.G.*	*Good*	*Fair*	*Poor*
—	1950	1100	950	580	380

Sidelock Side-by-Side Shotgun

Similar to above. Features full sidelock-action.

NIB	*Exc.*	*V.G.*	*Good*	*Fair*	*Poor*
—	3800	2500	1750	1600	1350

HAMILTON RIFLE COMPANY

Plymouth, Michigan

Manufacturer of inexpensive .22-caliber rifles. Established by Clarence J. Hamilton and his son Coello, in 1898 in Plymouth, Michigan. Company ceased production in 1945. Over 1 million rifles were produced between 1900 and 1911. Note: Despite the fact there were many Hamilton rifles sold, most of these little guns were used hard and many did not survive. Hamilton rifles in excellent condition are hardly ever encountered. No prices are quoted for rifles in this condition as few exist. Further information about these rifles is gratefully accepted by the editor.

Model 7

First rifle produced by this company. Made entirely of castings and stampings. Nickel plated. Chambered for .22 Short cartridge, with 8" brass-lined barrel that pivots for loading. Stock was metal skeleton. Production ceased in 1901. Total of 44,000 rifles produced.

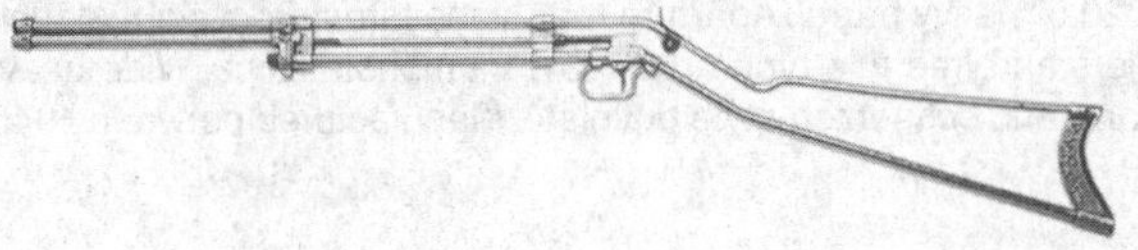

Courtesy William F. Krause

NIB	*Exc.*	*V.G.*	*Good*	*Fair*	*Poor*
—	750	500	450	300	200

Model 11

Similar to Model 7. Fitted with board-like walnut stock. Markings stamped into buttstock: "Hamilton Rifles Co., Plymouth, Mich., Pat. Pending No. 11". Produced from 1900 to 1902. Approximately 22,000 were sold.

NIB	*Exc.*	*V.G.*	*Good*	*Fair*	*Poor*
—	700	480	300	200	150

Model 15

Produced from 1901 to 1910, Chambered for .22 Short, with 8" brass lined barrel. Walnut stock. Design was an under lever single-shot, with loading port under barrel. Cocking knob located at rear of frame. Blued finish. Approximately 234,000 were sold.

NIB	*Exc.*	*V.G.*	*Good*	*Fair*	*Poor*
—	680	400	200	150	100

Model 19

Similar to Model 15, with modified loading port and 12" barrel. Few Model 19s have been seen with 13" barrels. These will bring a premium. Produced from 1903 to 1910. About 59,000 were sold.

NIB	*Exc.*	*V.G.*	*Good*	*Fair*	*Poor*
—	700	480	300	200	150

Model 23

First bolt-action rifle made by this company. Receiver is steel tube with loading port in top where barrel joins receiver. Bolt handle located at extreme rear of bolt. Cocking knob must be operated manually. Walnut stock rounded or flat. Chamberd for .22 Short and .22 Long cartridges. 15" brass lined barrel. Blued finish. Weight about 3 lbs. Produced from 1905 to 1909. About 25,000 were sold.

NIB	*Exc.*	*V.G.*	*Good*	*Fair*	*Poor*
—	700	480	300	200	150

Model 27

Single-shot tip-up .22-caliber rifle, with stamped steel receiver. Barrel length 16" brass lined or 14.875"; overall length 30". First produced in 1906.

NIB	*Exc.*	*V.G.*	*Good*	*Fair*	*Poor*
—	480	300	200	150	100

Model 027

As above with walnut stock. First produced in 1908.

NIB	*Exc.*	*V.G.*	*Good*	*Fair*	*Poor*
—	500	300	200	150	100

Model 31

Introduced in 1910. Single-shot rifle chambered for .22 Short and Long cartridge. Fitted with 15.75" barrel, with brass liner. A tip-up design. Blued finish. Weight about 2.25 lbs.

NIB	Exc.	V.G.	Good	Fair	Poor
—	720	580	400	250	200

Model 35 or Boys' Military Rifle

Single-shot .22-caliber rifle, with full-length oval walnut straight-grip stock and 15.75" brass lined barrel. Produced from 1915 to 1918. Sold with stamped steel bayonet. Few bayonets survive. Note: Add $150 for bayonet to prices.

NIB	Exc.	V.G.	Good	Fair	Poor
—	950	700	450	250	120

Model 39

Only repeating rifle built by this company. Hammerless slide-action design, with tubular magazine. Magazine capacity 15 rounds of .22 Short. Barrel length 16", with brass liner. Walnut stock, with blade front sight. Produced from 1922 to 1930. Weight about 4 lbs.

NIB	Exc.	V.G.	Good	Fair	Poor
—	580	300	200	150	100

Model 43

Bolt-action design with loading port on top of barrel. No external cocking knob, but bolt is pulled to rear when in locked position. Chambered for .22 Short and .22 Long cartridges. 15.75" brass lined barrel. Fitted with an oval walnut stock, with blade front sight and open non-adjustable rear sight. Weight about 3 lbs. Built from 1924 to 1932.

NIB	Exc.	V.G.	Good	Fair	Poor
—	580	300	200	150	100

Model 47

Bolt-action single-shot rifle, with loading port located on top of barrel. Chambered for .22 Short and Long cartridges. Cocking knob located at rear of bolt handle. Early Model 47 were built with 16" brass lined barrels. Later examples were fitted with 18.25" steel lined barrels. Early guns had an oval buttstock while later guns had a pistol grip stock. Very late guns had an all-steel barrel. Produced from 1927 to 1932.

NIB	Exc.	V.G.	Good	Fair	Poor
—	580	480	300	200	150

Model 51

Conventional type bolt-action rifle, with cocking knob located at rear of bolt. Two styles of buttstocks were used: flat style and later an oval shape. First Hamilton rifle chambered for .22 LR cartridge. Barrel was 20" steel. Finish was blue. Weight about 3.5 lbs. Produced from 1935 to 1941.

NIB	Exc.	V.G.	Good	Fair	Poor
—	550	400	250	200	150

Model 55

Bolt-action rifle chambered for .22 Short, Long and LR cartridges. Fitted with 20" steel barrel, with bead front sight and open adjustable rear sight. Walnut stock. Rarest Hamilton rifle. Only one example is known. Produced from late 1941 to early 1942.

NIB	Exc.	V.G.	Good	Fair	Poor
—	1000	—	—	—	—

HAMMERLI, SA
Lenzburg, Switzerland

RIFLES

Model 45 Smallbore Rifle

A .22-caliber bolt-action single-shot, with 27.5" heavy barrel, aperture rear and globe target front sight. Match rifle-type thumbhole stock. Manufactured between 1945 and 1957.

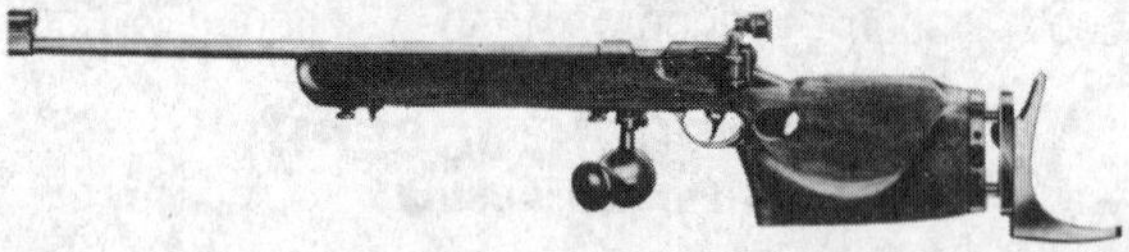

NIB	Exc.	V.G.	Good	Fair	Poor
—	820	700	600	450	250

Model 54 Smallbore Rifle

As above, with adjustable buttplate. Manufactured between 1954 and 1957.

NIB	Exc.	V.G.	Good	Fair	Poor
—	850	720	620	480	280

Model 503 Smallbore Free Rifle

Similar to Model 54, with free rifle-style stock.

NIB	Exc.	V.G.	Good	Fair	Poor
—	800	680	580	450	220

Model 506 Smallbore Match Rifle

Later version of Smallbore target series. Manufactured between 1963 and 1966.

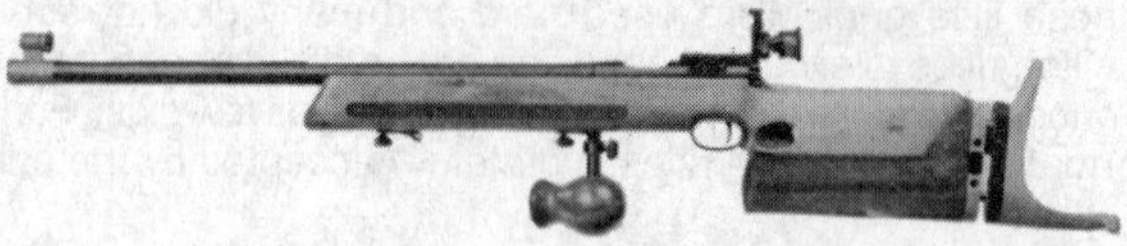

NIB	Exc.	V.G.	Good	Fair	Poor
—	850	720	620	480	280

Olympic 300 Meter

A 7x57, .30-06 or .300 H&H Magnum caliber bolt-action single-shot rifle, with 20.5" heavy barrel. Aperture rear globe target front sight, double-set triggers and free rifle-type adjustable thumbhole stock. Wide beavertail forearm and schuetzen-style buttplate. Manufactured between 1945 and 1959.

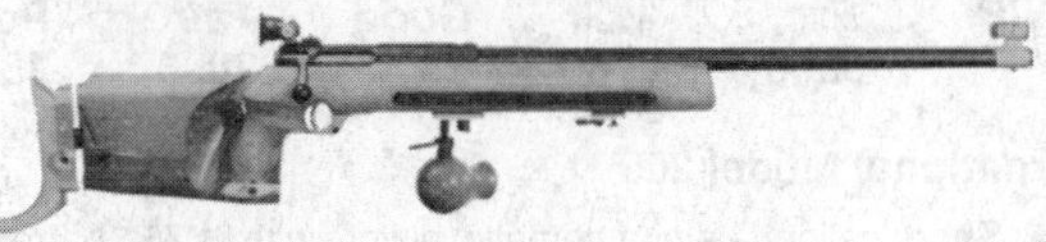

NIB	Exc.	V.G.	Good	Fair	Poor
—	1050	900	720	550	320

Sporting Rifle

Bolt-action single-shot rifle chambered for many popular calibers (American and European). Double-set triggers and classic-style stock.

NIB	Exc.	V.G.	Good	Fair	Poor
—	800	680	580	450	220

PISTOLS

Model 100 Free Pistol

A .22-caliber single-shot Martini-action target pistol, with 11.5" octagonal barrel, adjustable sights, single-set trigger and walnut stocks. Manufactured from 1933 to 1949.

NIB	Exc.	V.G.	Good	Fair	Poor
—	1000	820	700	550	320

Model 101

As above, with heavy round barrel and more sophisticated target sights. Matte-blued finish. Manufactured between 1956 and 1960.

NIB	Exc.	V.G.	Good	Fair	Poor
—	1000	820	700	550	320

Model 102

As above, with highly polished blue finish. Manufactured between 1956 and 1960.

NIB	Exc.	V.G.	Good	Fair	Poor
—	1000	820	700	550	320

Model 103

Similar to Model 101, with lighter-weight octagonal barrel, high-polished blued finish. Manufactured between 1956 and 1960.

NIB	Exc.	V.G.	Good	Fair	Poor
—	1100	920	820	650	420

Model 104

As above, with lightweight round barrel. Manufactured between 1961 and 1965.

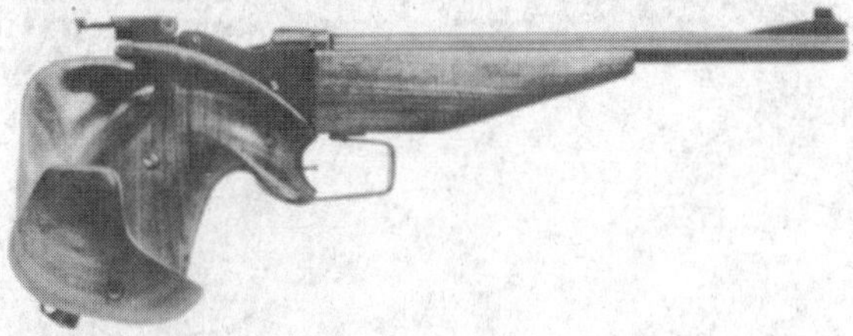

NIB	Exc.	V.G.	Good	Fair	Poor
—	950	620	550	450	300

Model 105

As above, with re-designed stock and improved action. Manufactured between 1962 and 1965.

NIB	Exc.	V.G.	Good	Fair	Poor
—	950	620	550	450	300

Model 106

As above, with improved trigger.

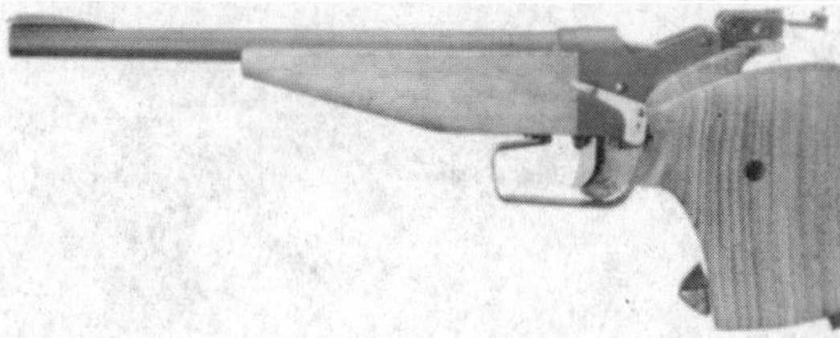

NIB	Exc.	V.G.	Good	Fair	Poor
—	950	620	550	450	300

Model 107

Variation fitted with five-level set trigger. Introduced in 1965; discontinued 1971.

NIB	Exc.	V.G.	Good	Fair	Poor
—	950	620	550	450	300

Model 107 Deluxe

As above, but engraved with carved stock.

NIB	Exc.	V.G.	Good	Fair	Poor
—	1500	1250	900	800	500

Model 120-1 Free Pistol

Bolt-action single-shot pistol in .22 LR caliber, with 9.9" barrel. Adjustable target sights activated for loading and cocking by an alloy lever on side of bolt. Blued, with checkered walnut grips

NIB	Exc.	V.G.	Good	Fair	Poor
—	1200	980	600	420	250

Model 120-2

As above, with contoured grips.

NIB	Exc.	V.G.	Good	Fair	Poor
—	1200	980	600	420	250

Model 120 Heavy Barrel

As above, with 5.7" heavy barrel.

NIB	Exc.	V.G.	Good	Fair	Poor
—	1200	980	600	420	250

Model 150

Single-shot Martini-action .22-caliber pistol, with 11.25" barrel, adjustable sights, contoured grips and single-set trigger. Blued, with walnut stocks.

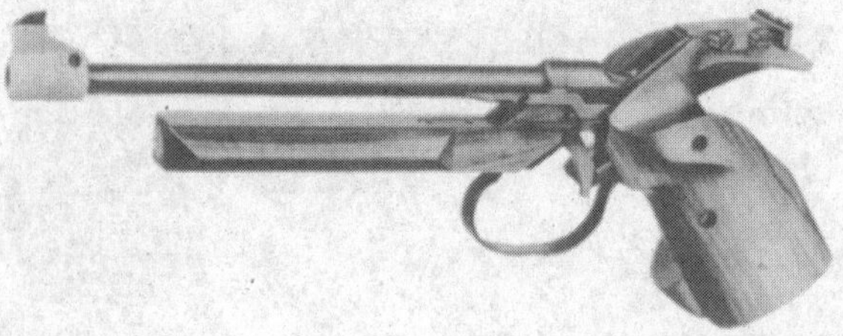

NIB	Exc.	V.G.	Good	Fair	Poor
—	1500	1100	780	500	350

Model 152

As above, with 11.25" barrel and electronic release trigger.

NIB	Exc.	V.G.	Good	Fair	Poor
—	1800	1300	1050	600	450

International Model 206

A .22-caliber semi-automatic pistol, with 7.5" barrel, integral muzzle brake, adjustable sights and walnut grips. Manufactured between 1962 and 1969.

NIB	Exc.	V.G.	Good	Fair	Poor
—	820	700	580	420	300

International Model 207

As above, with adjustable grips.

NIB	Exc.	V.G.	Good	Fair	Poor
—	850	720	600	450	320

International Model 208

A .22-caliber semi-automatic pistol, with 6" barrel, adjustable sights and 8-shot magazine. Adjustable trigger and target grips. Barrel drilled and tapped for addition of barrel weights. Manufactured between 1966 and 1988.

NIB	Exc.	V.G.	Good	Fair	Poor
—	1850	1550	1250	1000	750

International Model 208 Deluxe

As above, with engraved receiver and carved grips. Discontinued in 1988.

NIB	Exc.	V.G.	Good	Fair	Poor
—	3250	2750	2500	2000	1500

International Model 209

A .22 Short caliber semi-automatic pistol, with 4.75" barrel, muzzle brake, adjustable target sights and 5-shot magazine. Blued, with walnut grips. Manufactured between 1966 and 1970.

NIB	Exc.	V.G.	Good	Fair	Poor
—	1200	980	600	420	250

International Model 210

As above, with adjustable grips.

NIB	Exc.	V.G.	Good	Fair	Poor
—	1220	1000	620	450	280

International Model 211

As above, with non-adjustable thumb rest grips.

NIB	Exc.	V.G.	Good	Fair	Poor
—	1300	1080	700	480	300

Model 212

A .22-caliber semi-automatic pistol, with 5" barrel and adjustable sights. Blued, with walnut grips.

NIB	Exc.	V.G.	Good	Fair	Poor
—	1300	1080	700	480	300

Model 230

A .22 Short caliber semi-automatic pistol, with 6.3" barrel, 5-shot magazine, adjustable sights and walnut grip. Manufactured between 1970 and 1983.

NIB	Exc.	V.G.	Good	Fair	Poor
—	1350	1120	750	520	320

Model 232

A .22 Short caliber semi-automatic pistol, with 5" barrel, adjustable sights and 6-shot magazine. Contoured walnut grips. Introduced in 1984.

NIB	Exc.	V.G.	Good	Fair	Poor
—	1300	1080	700	480	300

Model 280

New state-of-the-art target pistol from Hammerli. Features a modular design. Frame of carbon fiber material. Has 4.6" barrel, with adjustable sights, trigger and grips. Chambered for .22 LR or .32 Wadcutter. Magazine holds 5 rounds. Introduced in 1988.

NIB	Exc.	V.G.	Good	Fair	Poor
—	1800	1500	1350	1000	600

Model SP 20

Introduced in 1998, this pistol has a very low sight line. Features a wide variety of special items such as adjustable buffer system, anatomically shaped trigger in various sizes and receiver colors. Change over caliber system from .22 LR to .32 S&W.

NIB	Exc.	V.G.	Good	Fair	Poor
1750	1320	900	800	500	—

HAMMERLI-WALTHER

Lenzburg, Switzerland

These target pistols were produced by Hammerli under license from Walther after WWII. This project continued until approximately 1963, when production ceased.

Olympia Model 200 Type 1952

A .22-caliber semi-automatic pistol, with 7.5" barrel, 10-shot magazine, adjustable target sights. Blued, with walnut grips. Manufactured between 1952 and 1958.

NIB	Exc.	V.G.	Good	Fair	Poor
—	900	780	580	480	350

Model 200 Type 1958

As above, with integral muzzle brake. Manufactured between 1958 and 1963.

NIB	Exc.	V.G.	Good	Fair	Poor
—	950	720	620	500	350

Model 201

Model 200 Type 1952, with 9.5" barrel. Manufactured between 1955 and 1957.

NIB	Exc.	V.G.	Good	Fair	Poor
—	950	720	620	500	350

Model 202

Similar to Model 201, with adjustable walnut grips. Manufactured between 1955 and 1957.

NIB	Exc.	V.G.	Good	Fair	Poor
—	950	720	620	500	350

Model 203

Similar to Model 200, with adjustable grips. Available with or without muzzle brake.

NIB	Exc.	V.G.	Good	Fair	Poor
—	950	720	620	500	350

Model 204

A .22-caliber semi-automatic pistol, with 7.5" barrel, muzzle brake and barrel weights. Manufactured between 1956 and 1963.

NIB	Exc.	V.G.	Good	Fair	Poor
—	980	750	650	520	380

Model 205

As above, with adjustable target grips. Manufactured between 1956 and 1963.

NIB	Exc.	V.G.	Good	Fair	Poor
—	1000	780	680	580	450

HAMMOND BULLDOG

Connecticut Arms & Mfg. Co.
Naubuc, Connecticut

Hammond Bulldog (Antique)

See Connecticut Arms & Manf. Co.

HAMMOND MFG. CO., GRANT

New Haven, Connecticut

Military Automatic Pistol

A .45 ACP caliber semi-automatic pistol, with 6.75" barrel and 8-shot magazine. Blued, with checkered walnut grips. Marked on right of slide "Grant Hammond Mfg. Corp. New Haven, Conn." Left side shows patent dates. Manufactured in 1917. As all known specimens of this pistol exhibit differences, it is believed they were only made as prototypes. Highest serial number known is under 20. In 1918, it was considered by the U.S. military as a possible replacement for the 1911 pistol. Automatically ejects magazine when the last round is fired. Too rare to price.

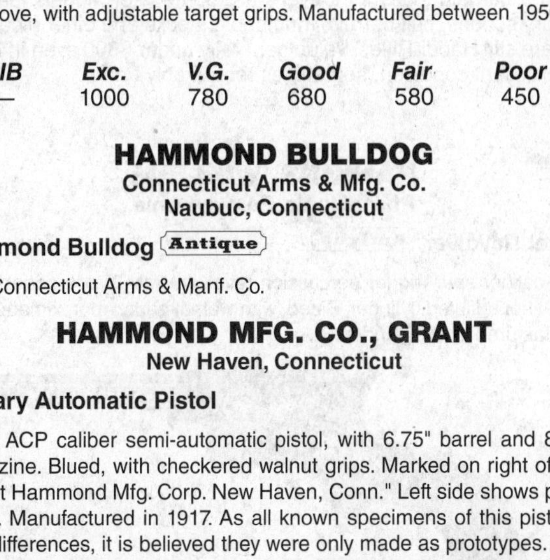

Courtesy Horst Held

Grant Hammond 7.65mm Pistol

A semi-automatic pistol in 7.65mm caliber. Has a blow-forward action and spur hammer. TOO RARE TO PRICE.

Courtesy James Rankin

H&R 1871, LLC

Gardner, Massachusetts

See—HARRINGTON & RICHARDSON

This break-action, single-shot rifle has been around in one form or another since the 1960s. Side lever release, automatic ejection, hardwood or synthetic stock, passive transfer-bar safety. Available in nearly every conceivable rimfire and centerfire chambering (except the biggest centerfires) and continued under the auspices of Marlin until the company's purchase by Remington, who discontinued the line. Nonetheless, the rifle is as good a bargain today as it ever was. Some later models feature factory scopes, bull barrels, thumbhole stocks and other niceties, but are still Handi-Rifles. Value generally under $300 even in New or Excellent condition, sometimes remarkably under.

HANKINS, WILLIAM

Philadelphia, Pennsylvania

Pocket Revolver (Antique)

A .26-caliber spur trigger percussion revolver, with 3" octagonal barrel and 5-shot unfluted cylinder. Blued, with walnut grips. Approximately 650 manufactured in 1860 and 1861.

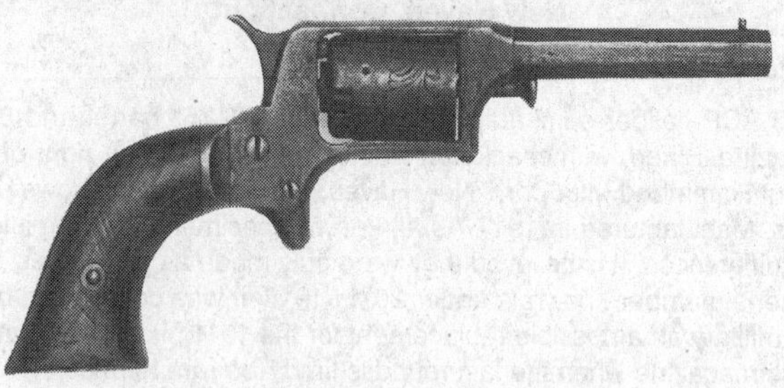

Courtesy Milwaukee Public Museum, Milwaukee, Wisconsin

Exc.	*Fine*	*V.G.*	*Good*	*Fair*	*Poor*
3250	1700	1150	600	200	140

HANUS, BILL

Newport, Oregon

Bill Hanus Classic

The late Bill Hanus, was a dealer and importer of various European shotguns until his passing in 2012. In the 1980s and 1990s, he imported his own private brand of side-by-side doubles from Ignacio Ugartechea and several other manufacturers in Italy. These guns in 16-, 20-, 28-gauge and .410 bore had double trigger ejectors and English-style stocks.

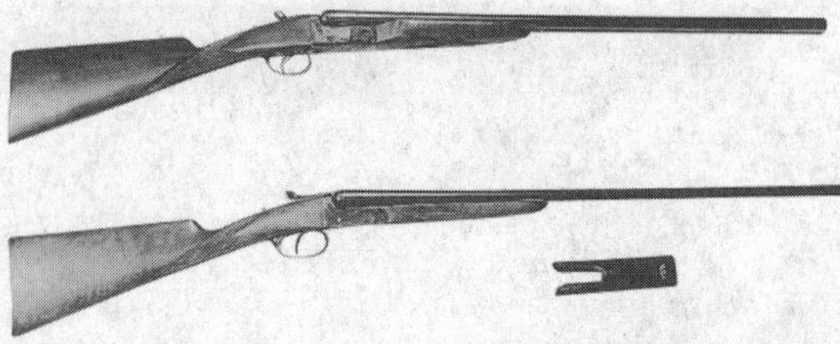

NIB	*Exc.*	*V.G.*	*Good*	*Fair*	*Poor*
2500	2000	1350	900	620	350

HARPERS FERRY

See—Standard Catalog of Military Firearms

HARRINGTON & RICHARDSON, INC.

Madison, North Carolina

One of the oldest manufacturers of firearms in the United States. Original Harrington and Richardson started in 1871 and was in existence until 1986. For all those years, the company was located in Worcester, Massachusetts. After the original company closed, in 1991 a new company, H&R 1871 was formed in Gardner, Massachusetts. In 2000, H&R 1871 was purchased by Marlin Firearms. The assets of Marlin, including H&R 1871 and its subsidiary, New England Firearms (NEF), were bought by Remington in 2007. H&R's corporate office is now located with Remington and Marlin in Madison, North Carolina, while the production facilities are at the former Remington plant in Ilion, New York. New England Firearms brand has been used for marketing some H&R products in recent years. See separate listing under New England Firearms (NEF). H&R ceased production in 2015.

Model No. 1 (Antique)

A .32- or .38-caliber spur-trigger single-action revolver, with 3" octagonal barrel, solid frame, 7- or 5-shot cylinder depending on caliber. Nickel-plated, with checkered rubber bird's-head grips. Barrel marked "Harrington & Richardson Worcester, Mass." Approximately 3,000 manufactured in 1877 and 1878.

Exc.	*Fine*	*V.G.*	*Good*	*Fair*	*Poor*
325	225	175	125	75	40

Model No. 1-1/2 (Antique)

A .32-caliber spur-trigger single-action revolver, with 2.5" octagonal barrel and 5-shot cylinder. Nickel-plated, round-butt rubber grips with an "H&R" emblem molded in. Approximately 10,000 manufactured between 1878 and 1883.

Exc.	*Fine*	*V.G.*	*Good*	*Fair*	*Poor*
300	225	175	125	75	40

Model No. 2-1/2 (Antique)

As above, with 3.25" barrel and 7-shot cylinder. Approximately 5,000 manufactured between 1878 and 1883.

Exc.	*Fine*	*V.G.*	*Good*	*Fair*	*Poor*
300	225	175	125	75	40

Model No. 3-1/2 (Antique)

Similar to Model 2-1/2 except in .38 rimfire caliber, with 3.5" barrel and 5-shot cylinder. Approximately 2,500 manufactured.

Exc.	*Fine*	*V.G.*	*Good*	*Fair*	*Poor*
300	225	175	125	75	40

Model No. 4-1/2 (Antique)

A .41 rimfire caliber spur trigger revolver, with 2.5" barrel and 5-shot cylinder. Approximately 1,000 manufactured.

Exc.	Fine	V.G.	Good	Fair	Poor
450	300	200	150	100	70

Model 1880 Antique

A .32 or .38 S&W caliber centerfire double-action revolver, with 3" round barrel, solid frame and 5- or 6-shot cylinder depending on caliber. Nickel-plated, with hard rubber grips. Marked "Harrington & Richardson Worchester, Mass." Approximately 4,000 manufactured between 1880 and 1883.

Exc.	Fine	V.G.	Good	Fair	Poor
375	275	200	125	75	50

The American Double-Action

A .32-, .38- or .44-caliber centerfire double-action revolver, with 2.5", 4.5" or 6" round or octagonal barrel, 5- or 6-shot fluted cylinder depending on caliber. Solid frame nickel-plated, with some blue models noted. Grips are hard rubber. Marked "The American Double Action." Some noted are marked "H&R Bulldog". Approximately 850,000 manufactured between 1883 and 1940. Note: Add 150 percent for .44.

NIB	Exc.	V.G.	Good	Fair	Poor
—	250	120	100	80	60

The Young America Double-Action

A .22 rimfire or .32 S&W caliber centerfire double-action revolver, with 2", 4.5" or 6" round or octagonal barrels. Solid frame and 5- or 7-shot cylinder depending on caliber. Blued or nickel-plated, with hard rubber grips. Marked "Young America Double Action" or "Young America Bulldog". Approximately 1,500,000 manufactured between 1884 and 1941.

NIB	Exc.	V.G.	Good	Fair	Poor
—	230	200	180	120	100

Hunter

A .22-caliber double-action revolver, with 10" octagonal barrel and 9-shot fluted cylinder. Blued, with checkered walnut grips.

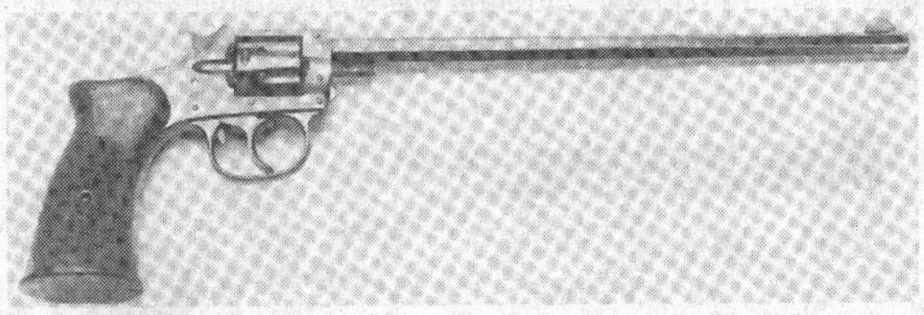

Courtesy Mike Stuckslager

NIB	Exc.	V.G.	Good	Fair	Poor
—	400	300	200	150	100

Trapper

As above, with 6" octagonal barrel and 7-shot cylinder. Otherwise similar to Hunter.

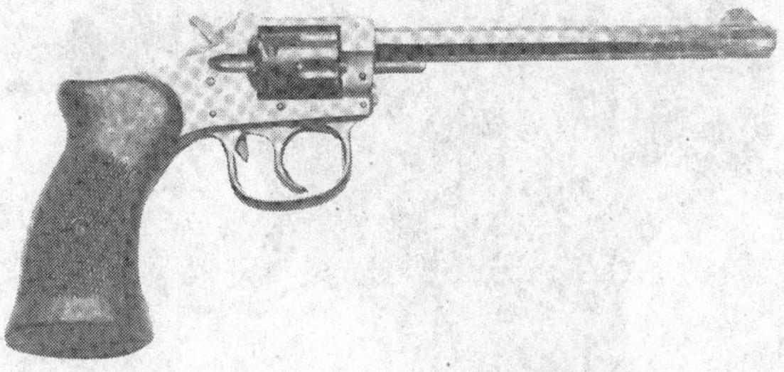

Courtesy Mike Stuckslager

NIB	Exc.	V.G.	Good	Fair	Poor
—	300	200	120	100	80

Self-Loader

A 6.35mm or 7.65mm semi-automatic pistol, with 2" or 3.5" barrel, 6- or 8-shot magazine. Similar in outline to Webley. Larger 7.65 model has a grip safety. Blued or nickel-plated, with checkered hard rubber grips that bear the H&R monogram. Slide marked "H&R Self-Loading", with 1907 or 1909 patent dates. Approximately 16,500 manufactured in 6.35mm between 1912 and 1916; 34,500 in 7.65mm between 1916 and 1924. Note: Add 10 percent for .32.

Courtesy Orvel Reichert

NIB	Exc.	V.G.	Good	Fair	Poor
—	500	400	280	200	120

First Model Hand Ejector

A .32- or .38-caliber centerfire double-action revolver, with 3.25" ribbed round barrel. Version does not feature automatic ejection found on later models. Nickel-plated, with hard rubber grips. Company name marked on barrel. Approximately 6,000 manufactured between 1886 and 1888.

NIB	Exc.	V.G.	Good	Fair	Poor
—	200	150	120	90	60

Model 1 Double-Action Revolver

A .32, .32 Long and .38 S&W caliber double-action revolver, with 3.25" ribbed round barrel and 5- or 6-shot cylinder depending on caliber. Nickel-plated, with hard rubber grips. Approximately 5,000 manufactured between 1887 and 1889.

NIB	Exc.	V.G.	Good	Fair	Poor
—	180	140	110	80	50

Model 2

Similar to Model 1, with 2.5", 3.25", 4", 5" or 6" barrels. Grips feature H&R target logo. Approximately 1,300,000 manufactured between 1889 and 1940.

NIB	Exc.	V.G.	Good	Fair	Poor
—	120	100	80	60	40

Knife Model

Model 2, with 4" ribbed round barrel having a folding 2.25" double-edged knife mounted under barrel. Blued or nickel-plated. Approximately 2,000 manufactured between 1901 and 1917.

NIB	Exc.	V.G.	Good	Fair	Poor
2000	1500	1000	700	500	150

Model 922 First Issue

A .22-caliber double-action revolver, with 2.5", 4" or 6" barrel. Blued, with checkered walnut grips.

NIB	Exc.	V.G.	Good	Fair	Poor
—	150	120	100	80	50

Target Model

A .22 LR or .22 WRF caliber double-action revolver, with 7-shot cylinder, break-open frame and 6" barrel. Fixed sights. Blued, with checkered walnut grips.

NIB	Exc.	V.G.	Good	Fair	Poor
—	150	120	100	80	50

.22 Special

A .22 LR or .22 WRF double-action break-open revolver, with 6" barrel and 7-shot cylinder. Blued, with checkered walnut grips.

NIB	Exc.	V.G.	Good	Fair	Poor
—	300	200	120	90	60

Expert

As above, with 10" barrel.

NIB	Exc.	V.G.	Good	Fair	Poor
—	400	300	200	100	50

No. 199 Sportsman

A .22-caliber single-action break-open revolver, with 6" barrel, adjustable target sights and 9-shot cylinder. Blued, with checkered walnut grips.

NIB	Exc.	V.G.	Good	Fair	Poor
—	280	200	150	100	80

Ultra Sportsman

As above, more finely finished. Special wide target hammer and improved action.

NIB	Exc.	V.G.	Good	Fair	Poor
—	320	220	180	120	90

Defender

A .38 S&W caliber double-action break-open revolver, with 4" or 6" barrel and fixed sights. Blued, with plastic grips.

NIB	Exc.	V.G.	Good	Fair	Poor
—	280	200	140	80	50

New Defender

A .22-caliber double-action break-open revolver, with 2" barrel and 9-shot cylinder. Blued, with checkered walnut round-butt grips.

NIB	Exc.	V.G.	Good	Fair	Poor
—	220	200	180	120	90

.22 U.S.R.A./Model 195 Single-Shot Match Target Pistol

Also called Model 195, this pistol underwent nearly constant modifications from its inception in 1928 until production ceased in 1941. Its development was greatly influenced by the United States Revolver Association (USRA), which established certain rules for target pistol shooting. Lack of any H&R-published model chronology for estimated 3,500 guns manufactured, makes model determination by examination complicated; further difficulty is that H&R supplied newly designed parts to owners of older variations, who would then retrofit their pistols with newer triggers, hammers, sights and triggerguards. Extracted from available literature, the parts represent approximately: 14 different stocks and virtually endless custom variations by Walter F. Roper; 5 different triggerguards; 3 different triggers; 2 different hammers; 2 different extractors; 3 barrel lengths (7", 8", 10"); and 3 barrel rib styles. From this array of potential characteristics, at least four distinct variations can be identified.

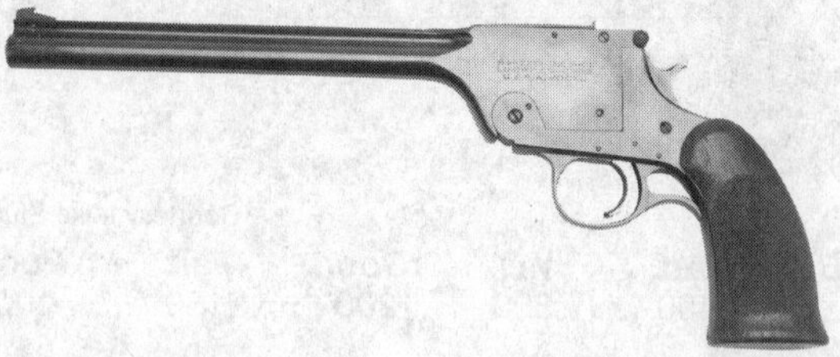

Photo Courtesy NRA Museums

.22 U.S.R.A./Model 195 Pistol, Variations 1 to 3

NIB	Exc.	V.G.	Good	Fair	Poor
—	2500	1800	1000	600	200

.22 U.S.R.A./Model 195 Pistol, Variation 4

NIB	Exc.	V.G.	Good	Fair	Poor
—	2200	1500	800	320	250

Model 504

A .32 H&R Magnum caliber double-action swing-out cylinder revolver, with 4" or 6" heavy barrel, adjustable sights and 5-shot cylinder. Blued, with black plastic or walnut grips. Smaller version manufactured with 3" or 4" barrel and round butt.

NIB	Exc.	V.G.	Good	Fair	Poor
—	350	280	150	90	60

Model 532

As above, with a cylinder that has to be removed for loading. Manufactured in 1984 and 1985.

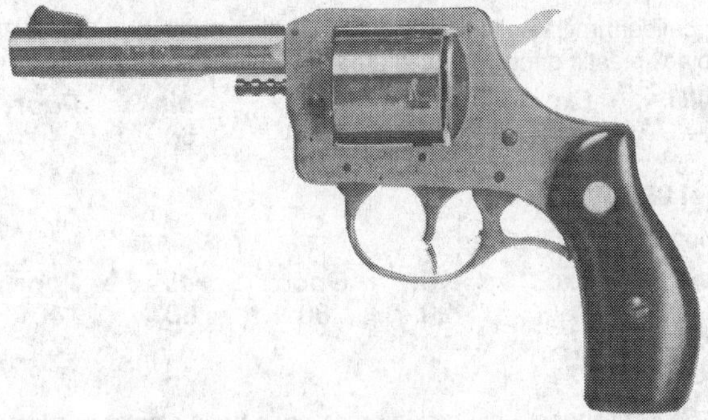

NIB	Exc.	V.G.	Good	Fair	Poor
—	280	180	120	80	50

Model 586

A .32 H&R Magnum caliber double-action revolver, with 4.5", 5.5", 7.5" or 10" barrel, adjustable sights and 5-shot cylinder. Blued, with black plastic or walnut grips.

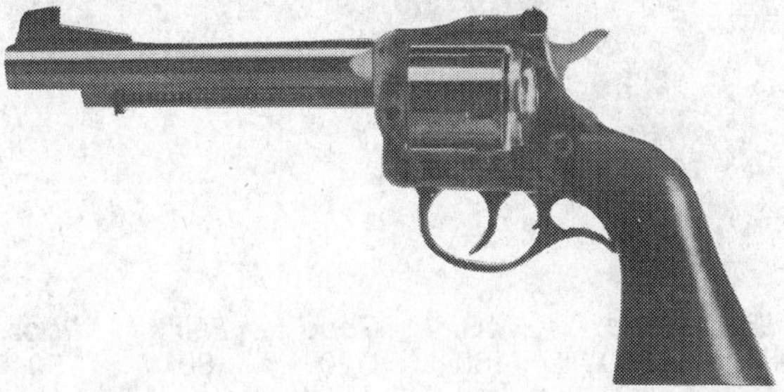

NIB	Exc.	V.G.	Good	Fair	Poor
—	320	280	180	150	100

Model 603

A .22 rimfire Magnum caliber double-action revolver, with 6" flat-sided barrel and swing-out 6-shot cylinder. Blued, with smooth walnut grips.

NIB	Exc.	V.G.	Good	Fair	Poor
—	220	160	140	110	80

Model 604

As above, with 6" ribbed heavy barrel.

NIB	Exc.	V.G.	Good	Fair	Poor
—	300	220	180	120	100

Model 622

A .22-caliber solid-frame double-action revolver, with 2.5" or 4" barrel. Blued, with round-butt plastic grips.

NIB	Exc.	V.G.	Good	Fair	Poor
—	150	100	60	50	20

Model 623

As above, but nickel-plated.

NIB	Exc.	V.G.	Good	Fair	Poor
—	160	110	80	60	40

Model 632

As above, in .32 centerfire.

NIB	Exc.	V.G.	Good	Fair	Poor
—	150	90	80	60	30

Model 642

As above, in .22 rimfire Magnum.

NIB	Exc.	V.G.	Good	Fair	Poor
—	150	80	60	50	20

Model 649

Model 622, with 5.5" or 7.5" barrel.

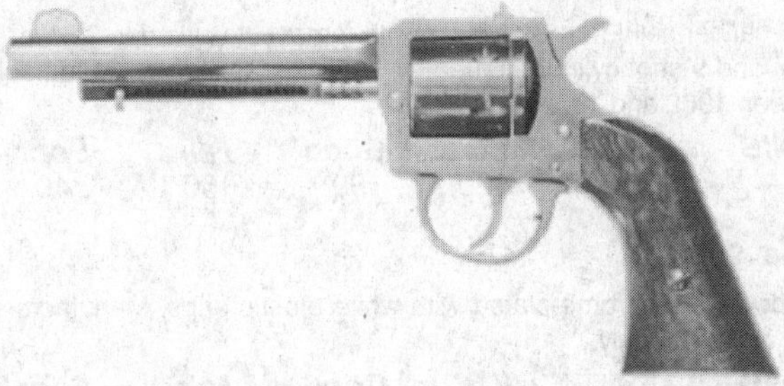

NIB	Exc.	V.G.	Good	Fair	Poor
—	150	120	100	80	50

Model 650

As above, but nickel-plated.

NIB	Exc.	V.G.	Good	Fair	Poor
—	180	150	120	80	50

Model 660

A .22-caliber solid-frame Western-style revolver, with 5.5" barrel and double-action. Blued, with walnut grips. Also known as "Gunfighter".

NIB	Exc.	V.G.	Good	Fair	Poor
—	150	120	100	50	20

Model 666

A .22 or .22 rimfire Magnum caliber double-action revolver, with 6" barrel and 6-shot cylinder. Blued, with plastic grips. Manufactured between 1976 and 1982.

NIB	Exc.	V.G.	Good	Fair	Poor
—	150	120	100	50	20

Model 676

Similar to Model 660. Blued, with case colored frame and walnut grips. Manufactured between 1976 and 1982.

NIB	Exc.	V.G.	Good	Fair	Poor
—	180	150	100	80	50

Model 686

Similar to Model 660 "Gunfighter", with 4.5", 5.5", 7.5", 10" or 12" barrel.

NIB	Exc.	V.G.	Good	Fair	Poor
—	180	150	120	100	80

Model 732

A .32-caliber double-action solid-frame revolver, with swingout cylinder, 2.5" or 4" barrel and 6-shot cylinder. Blued, with black plastic grips. Also known as "Guardsman".

NIB	Exc.	V.G.	Good	Fair	Poor
—	150	120	90	60	40

Model 733

As above, but nickel-plated and 2.5" barrel.

NIB	Exc.	V.G.	Good	Fair	Poor
—	180	150	100	80	50

Model 900

A .22-caliber solid-frame revolver, with removable cylinder, 2.5", 4" or 6" barrel and 9-shot cylinder. Blued, with black plastic grips. Manufactured between 1962 and 1973.

NIB	Exc.	V.G.	Good	Fair	Poor
—	150	120	90	60	40

Model 901

As above, but chrome-plated with white plastic grips. Manufactured in 1962 and 1963 only.

NIB	Exc.	V.G.	Good	Fair	Poor
—	150	120	90	60	40

Model 903

As above, with swing-out cylinder, flat-sided 6" barrel and 9-shot cylinder. Blued, with walnut grips.

NIB	Exc.	V.G.	Good	Fair	Poor
—	150	120	90	80	50

Model 904

As above, with ribbed heavy barrel.

NIB	Exc.	V.G.	Good	Fair	Poor
—	180	150	120	100	50

Model 905

As above, but nickel-plated.

NIB	Exc.	V.G.	Good	Fair	Poor
—	200	180	150	80	60

Model 922 Second Issue

A .22-caliber rimfire solid-frame revolver, with 2.5", 4" or 6" barrel. Blued, with black plastic grips. Manufactured between 1950 and 1982.

NIB	Exc.	V.G.	Good	Fair	Poor
—	150	90	80	60	40

Model 923

As above, but nickel-plated.

NIB	Exc.	V.G.	Good	Fair	Poor
—	160	90	80	60	40

Model 925

A .38 S&W caliber double-action break-open hand ejector revolver, with 2.5" barrel, adjustable sights and 5-shot cylinder. Blued, with one-piece wrap-around grip. Manufactured between 1964 and 1984.

NIB	Exc.	V.G.	Good	Fair	Poor
—	250	180	120	80	50

Model 935

As above, but nickel-plated.

NIB	Exc.	V.G.	Good	Fair	Poor
—	260	200	150	100	50

Model 929

A .22 rimfire solid-frame swing-out revolver, with 2.5", 4" or 6" barrel and 9-shot cylinder. Blued, with plastic grips. Also known as "Sidekick". Manufactured between 1956 and 1985.

NIB	Exc.	V.G.	Good	Fair	Poor
—	220	150	120	60	40

Model 929 Sidekick—New Model

Re-introduced in 1996. Single-/double-action revolver chambered for .22 Short, Long or LR cartridges. Cylinder holds 9 rounds. Sold with lockable storage case, nylon holster, gun oil and grease samples. Weight about 30 oz. Made from 1996 - 1999. Discontinued.

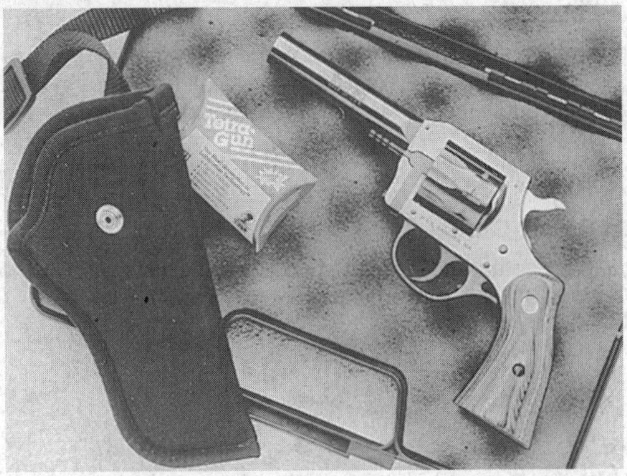

NIB	Exc.	V.G.	Good	Fair	Poor
250	180	150	100	80	50

Model 929 Sidekick Trapper Edition

As above, with gray laminate grips and special "NTA" Trapper Edition roll stamp on barrel. Made in 1996.

NIB	Exc.	V.G.	Good	Fair	Poor
280	180	150	100	80	50

Model 930

As above, but nickel-plated. Not available with 6" barrel.

NIB	Exc.	V.G.	Good	Fair	Poor
—	250	150	120	60	40

Model 939 Ultra Sidekick

As above, with ventilated rib, flat sided 6" barrel, adjustable sights, thumb rest grips. Features a safety device whereby pistol could not be fired unless it was unlocked by a furnished key. Manufactured between 1958 and 1982.

NIB	Exc.	V.G.	Good	Fair	Poor
—	220	200	150	80	50

Model 939 Premier

Similar to above models, but fitted with 6" barrel, sighting rib, adjustable rear sight, hardwood grips, high polished blued finish. Weight about 36 oz. Made from 1995 - 1999.

NIB	Exc.	V.G.	Good	Fair	Poor
250	220	200	120	80	50

Model 940

Round-barreled version of above.

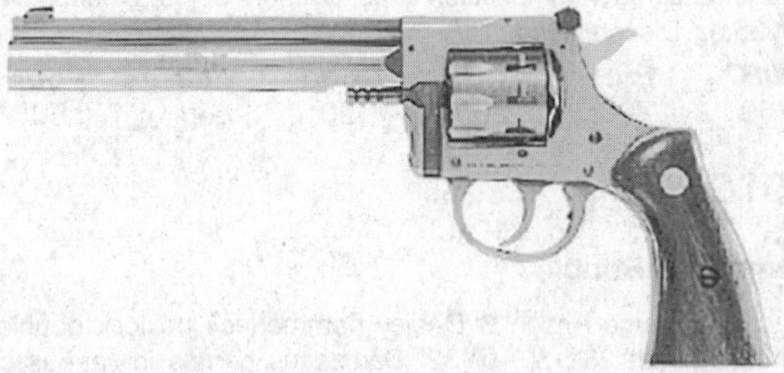

NIB	Exc.	V.G.	Good	Fair	Poor
—	220	200	120	80	50

Model 949

A .22-caliber double-action Western-type revolver, with 5.5" barrel, ejector rod, 9-shot gate-loaded cylinder and adjustable sights. Blued, with walnut grips. Manufactured between 1960 and 1985.

NIB	Exc.	V.G.	Good	Fair	Poor
—	200	180	150	80	50

Model 949 Western

Similar to above. This revolver is offered with choice of 5.5" or 7.5" barrel, adjustable rear sight, walnut grips. Case colored frame and backstrap, with blued cylinder and barrel. Weight about 36 oz.

NIB	Exc.	V.G.	Good	Fair	Poor
250	200	150	100	80	50

Model 950

As above, but nickel-plated.

NIB	Exc.	V.G.	Good	Fair	Poor
—	250	180	120	80	50

Model 976

As above, with case-hardened frame.

NIB	Exc.	V.G.	Good	Fair	Poor
—	200	150	100	80	50

Model 999 Sportsman

A .22-caliber rimfire double-action break-open self ejecting revolver, with 4" or 6" barrel ventilated rib barrel and windage adjustable sights. Blued, with walnut grips. Weight about: 30 oz. 4" barrel; 34 oz. 6" barrel.

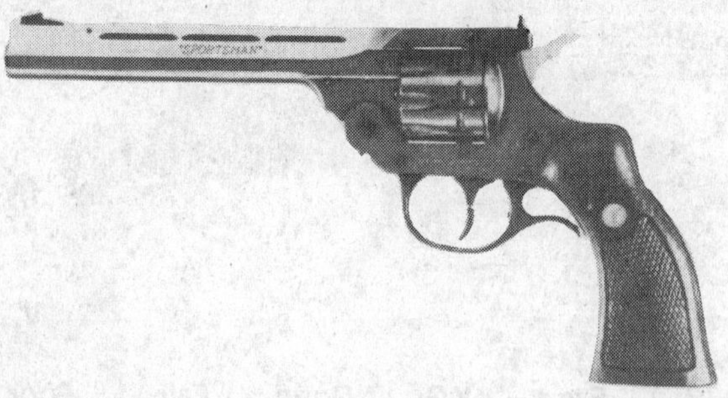

NIB	Exc.	V.G.	Good	Fair	Poor
500	420	350	300	180	100

Model 999 Engraved

As above, but engraved.

NIB	Exc.	V.G.	Good	Fair	Poor
550	450	380	300	200	120

Amtec 2000

German-designed (Erma) and American-built double-action revolver. Introduced in 1996. Offered in 2" or 3" barrel. Chambered for .38 Special cartridge. Pachmayr composition grips. Cylinder holds 5 rounds. Weight about 25 oz. Discontinued.

NIB	Exc.	V.G.	Good	Fair	Poor
250	200	200	150	80	50

SHOTGUNS

Hammerless Double

A 10- or 12-gauge Anson & Deeley hammerless boxlock double-barrel shotgun, with 28", 30" or 32" Damascus barrels in various choke combinations, double triggers and extractors. Engraved, case-hardened and walnut stock. Four grades were available. They differ in amount of engraving and quality of materials and workmanship utilized. Approximately 3,500 manufactured between 1882 and 1885.

D Grade

NIB	Exc.	V.G.	Good	Fair	Poor
—	650	550	420	300	180

C Grade

NIB	Exc.	V.G.	Good	Fair	Poor
—	750	650	500	400	280

B Grade

NIB	Exc.	V.G.	Good	Fair	Poor
—	900	750	600	500	350

A Grade

NIB	Exc.	V.G.	Good	Fair	Poor
—	2000	1750	1500	1000	550

Harrich No. 1

A 12-gauge boxlock single-barrel shotgun, with 32" or 34" ventilated rib, Full choke barrel and automatic ejector. Engraved, blued with checkered walnut stock. Imported between 1971 and 1975.

NIB	Exc.	V.G.	Good	Fair	Poor
—	1750	1500	1150	850	650

Single-Barrel Shotguns

H&R manufactured a series of single-barrel break-open shotguns, between 1908 and 1942. Chambered for various gauges, barrel lengths and chokes. Finishes were blued with walnut stocks. Little collector interest in these guns. If in sound condition are desirable as shooters only. They are Models 3, 5, 6, 7, 8, 9, as well as hinged-frame folding design.

NIB	Exc.	V.G.	Good	Fair	Poor
—	120	100	80	60	40

Turkey Mag

Single-shot break-open side release gun chambered for 12-gauge 3.5" shell, with screw-in Full choke. Hardwood stock has Mossy Oak finish. Barrel length 24", with bead front sight. Weight about 6 lbs.

NIB	Exc.	V.G.	Good	Fair	Poor
—	150	120	100	80	50

Youth Turkey Gun

Similar in appearance to Turkey Mag, but on a smaller scale. Chambered for 20-gauge 3" shell, with 22" barrel. Weight about 5.5 lbs.

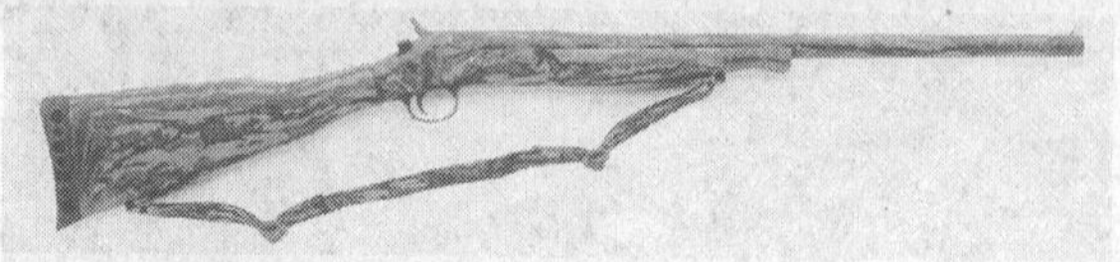

NIB	Exc.	V.G.	Good	Fair	Poor
—	140	120	90	60	40

Topper (New Production)

Break-open side release single-shot, available in 12, 20 gauge and .410 bore. The 12 gauge offered with 28" barrel while others are fitted with 26" barrel. Blued finish, with hardwood stock in black finish and semi-pistol grip. Weight about 6 lbs. Brass bead front sight, automatic ejector. Deluxe version has 3.5" chamber and screw-in choke threads, M choke supplied. 6.75 lbs., 43" OAL. Trap model has 30" barrel, vent rib with twin bead sighting system, extended IM choke, electroless nickel finish. Buttstock is checkered select-grade walnut from American Walnut Co. with Pachmayr trap recoil pad.

NIB	Exc.	V.G.	Good	Fair	Poor
—	150	100	80	60	30

Topper Deluxe

NIB	Exc.	V.G.	Good	Fair	Poor
—	120	90	70	50	40

Topper Jr. in 20 Gauge and .410 Bore Only

NIB	Exc.	V.G.	Good	Fair	Poor
—	100	80	60	40	30

Topper Jr. Classic

Similar to Topper Jr. Features black walnut stock, with butt checkering, white line spacer and black recoil pad. Weight about 7.5 lbs.

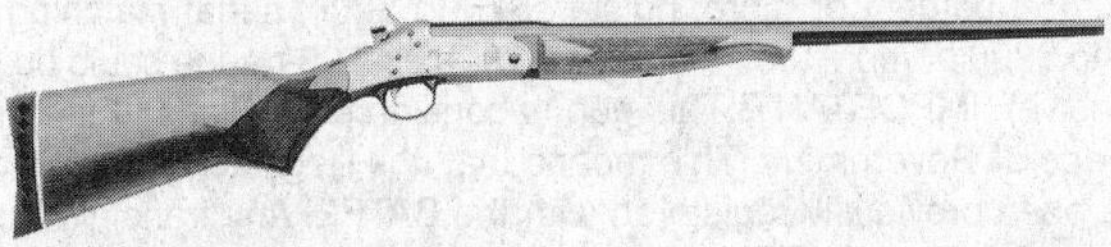

NIB	Exc.	V.G.	Good	Fair	Poor
—	100	80	60	40	30

Topper Deluxe Slug

This 12-gauge single-shot has 24" fully rifled barrel, with built-in compensator.

NIB	Exc.	V.G.	Good	Fair	Poor
—	120	90	70	50	40

Topper Deluxe Classic

Introduced in 2004. This 12-gauge 3" single-shot gun fitted with 28" ventilated rib barrel and screw-in Modified choke. American black walnut stock, with pistol grip and ventilated recoil pad. Barrel has black finish while receiver nickel finish. Weight about 5.5 lbs. In 2005, offered in 20-gauge.

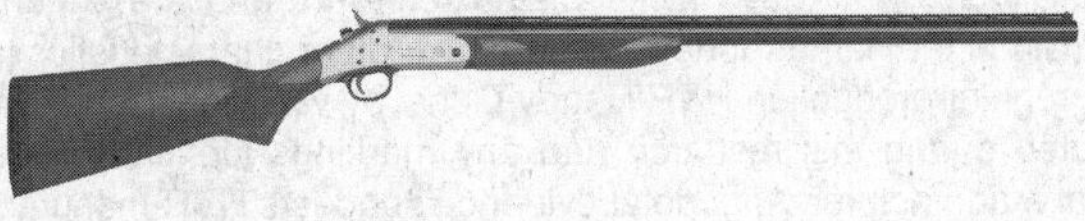

NIB	Exc.	V.G.	Good	Fair	Poor
—	200	150	100	80	50

Topper Trap Gun

Similar to above, with select checkered walnut stock, forend with fluted comb and full pistol grip; 30" barrel with two white beads and screw-in chokes (Improved Modified Extended included); deluxe Pachmayr trap recoil pad.

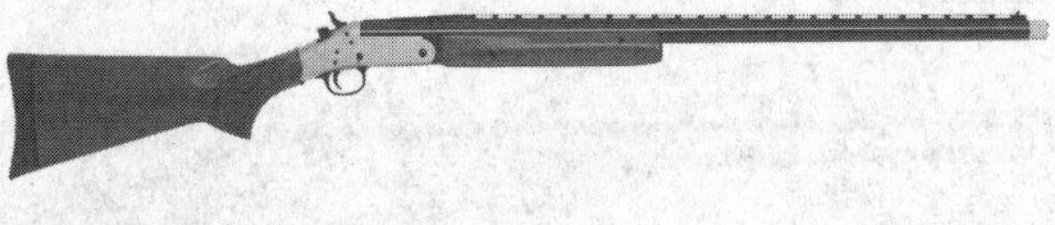

NIB	Exc.	V.G.	Good	Fair	Poor
—	280	200	160	140	80

Tamer

Single-shot survival gun chambered for 20 gauge or .410 shell with 3" chamber. Fitted with 19.5" barrel and matte nickel finish. Thumbhole/pistol grip stock is matte black polymer. Weight about 6 lbs. Fixed Full choke.

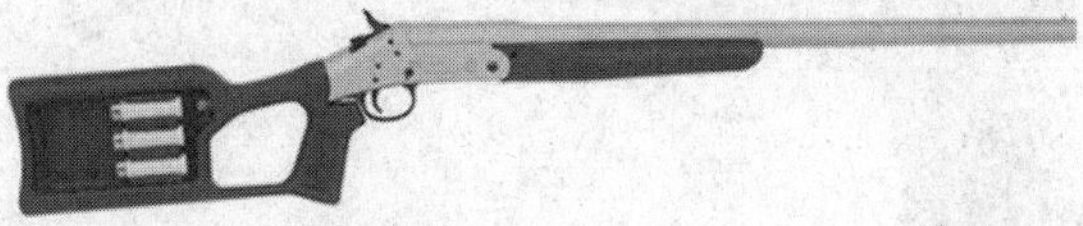

NIB	Exc.	V.G.	Good	Fair	Poor
—	120	90	60	40	30

Ultra Slug Hunter

Introduced in 1995. Uses heavy 10-gauge action fitted with 24" 12-gauge barrel. Weight about 8 lbs.

NIB	Exc.	V.G.	Good	Fair	Poor
—	120	90	70	50	40

Ultra Slug Hunter Deluxe 20 Gauge

Introduced in 1997. Chambered for 20-gauge shells. Features hand checkered camo laminated wood stock. Fitted with fully rifled heavy slug barrel 24" long.

NIB	Exc.	V.G.	Good	Fair	Poor
—	250	200	150	100	80

Ultra Slug Hunter Deluxe 12 Gauge

NIB	Exc.	V.G.	Good	Fair	Poor
—	250	200	150	100	80

Ultra Slug Youth Model

As above chambered for 20-gauge shell. Weight about 7 lbs.

NIB	Exc.	V.G.	Good	Fair	Poor
—	200	150	100	60	40

Ultra Slug Hunter Bull Barrel

As above chambered for 20-gauge.

NIB	Exc.	V.G.	Good	Fair	Poor
—	100	80	60	40	30

Ultra Slug Hunter Thumbhole Stock

Similar to above, with laminated thumbhole stock and blued or stainless steel finish. Weight 8.5 lbs. Note: Add 10 percent for stainless.

NIB	Exc.	V.G.	Good	Fair	Poor
—	280	—	—	—	—

Ultra Slug Youth Bull Barrel

Same as above, with 22" barrel.

NIB	Exc.	V.G.	Good	Fair	Poor
—	100	80	60	40	30

Ultra Lite Slug Hunter

Single-shot break-open shotgun. 12- or 20-gauge with 3" chamber; fully rifled 24" barrel; hardwood stock with walnut finish; full pistol grip; recoil pad and sling swivels. No iron sights; scope base included. Overall length 40"; weight 5.25 lbs. 20-gauge. Youth Model has 20" rifled barrel. Deluxe Model has checkered laminated stock and forend.

NIB	Exc.	V.G.	Good	Fair	Poor
—	220	150	100	80	50

Camo Laminate Turkey NWTF Edition

Introduced in 1999, this single-barrel model features a 12-gauge 3.5" chamber, 22" barrel choked Turkey Full. Polished receiver has laser engraved NWTF logo. Stock hand checkered and hardwood laminate, with green, brown and black pattern. Ventilated recoil pad and sling swivels. Camo sling are standard.

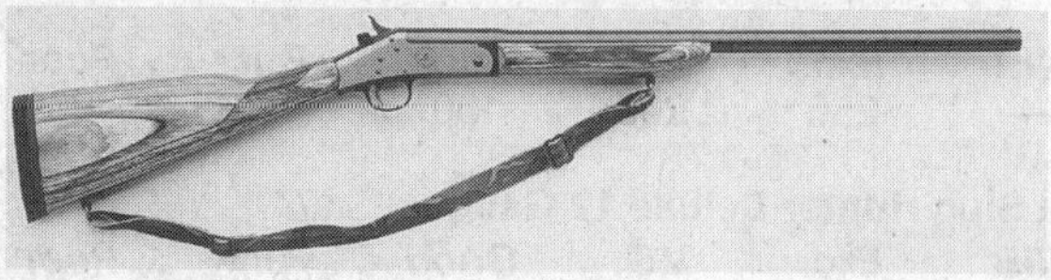

NIB	Exc.	V.G.	Good	Fair	Poor
—	200	150	100	80	50

Camo Laminate Turkey Youth NWTF Edition

Similar to Camo Turkey above, but chambered for 20-gauge with 3" chambers. Stock laminated hardwood, with special shorter dimensions.

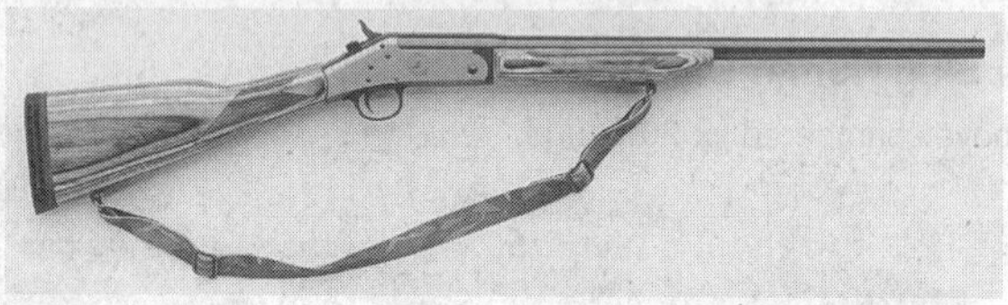

NIB	Exc.	V.G.	Good	Fair	Poor
—	200	150	100	80	50

H&R Handy-Gun (rifled barrel) Curio or Relic

Rifled-barrel H&R Handy-Guns were manufactured about 1930-34, but details of their production are not well documented. In H&R catalog #19 (copyright 1931) and #20, .22 and .32-20 are listed as available with blued frame only, 12.25" barrel, with optional ($1.50) detachable shoulder stock. Whether .22 W.R.F. version listed on page 83 of the 1932 Stoeger's Bible was manufactured is unknown. Guns that were originally factory fitted for shoulder stock (all are extremely rare) have H.&R. ARMS COMPANY/WORCESTER, MASS.U.S.A./PAT.PENDING stamped on bottom of grip in .125" letters. Production of rifled-barrel H&R Handy-Gun was halted in 1934 when the Treasury Department classified it as a "firearm" under NFA, because it was available with a shoulder stock. Any rifled-barrel H&R Handy-Gun is (and always was) exempt from NFA, if not accompanied by a shoulder stock. IMPORTANT! This gun is considered a Class III firearm by the Federal Government. This means that it is illegal to possess unless it has been previously registered with the BATFE. Any transfer must be registered with the BATFE. There is currently no way to legally register an unregistered Class III firearm.

.32-20 W.C.F. serial range mostly from 43851 (?) to 43937 (?)

NIB	Exc.	V.G.	Good	Fair	Poor
—	1600	1100	950	700	600

.22 rimfire serial range from 1 (?) to 223 (?)

NIB	Exc.	V.G.	Good	Fair	Poor
—	1400	1000	750	650	500

H&R Handy-Gun (smooth bore) NFA, Curio or Relic

The .410 bore or 28-gauge H&R Handy-Gun is a single-shot pistol, with 8" or 12.25" smoothbore barrel, made from 1921 to 1934 by Harrington & Richardson Arms Co., Worcester, Massachusetts. Shares internal parts with H&R Model 1915 (No. 5) shotgun, but Handy-Gun's shorter receiver is designed for a pistol grip, its barrels won't fit No. 5 and these firearms are serial numbered separately. About 54,000 H&R Handy-Guns were manufactured, nearly all for 2.5" shells. Production halted after government ruled H&R Handy-Gun to be a "firearm" in the "any other weapon" category under NFA, when its retail price was about $16. An H&R Handy-Gun with an 18" smoothbore barrel is subject to NFA. Note: Rare variations command premiums: 8" barrel, 25 to 50 percent; 18" barrel (rarest), 200 to 300 percent; unchoked .410, 20 to 30 percent; 28-gauge or Model 3 (only) with factory-equipped original detachable shoulder stock, 150 percent or more; holster, $75 to $200; serial matching box, $100 to $200 or more (i.e., a box for an 8" barrel 28-gauge could be quite expensive). IMPORTANT! This gun is considered a Class III firearm by the Federal Government. This means that it is illegal to possess unless it has been previously registered with the BATFE. Any transfer must be registered with the BATFE. There is currently no way to legally register an unregistered Class III firearm.

.410 bore, Model 2, Types II and III

NIB	Exc.	V.G.	Good	Fair	Poor
—	2000	1200	500	250	180

28 gauge, Model 2, Type I

NIB	Exc.	V.G.	Good	Fair	Poor
—	1500	1100	850	700	520

H&R manufactured "private-branded" or "trade-branded" H&R Handy-Guns for other distributors. One variation has ESSEX GUN WORKS on left side of receiver. Another has HIBBARD stamped on left side and MODEL W.H. stamped on right; holster with identical stampings was also available. Most have nickel-plated receivers and are serial numbered within the same ranges as, and have other characteristics identical to, regular-production H&R Handy-Guns, by variation. None of those inspected during this research had any markings identifying H&R as original manufacturer. Anecdotal evidence suggests H&R manufactured a Handy-Gun for an independent telephone company in Colorado; none were located during this research. These materials are copyright 1998 by Eric M. Larson.

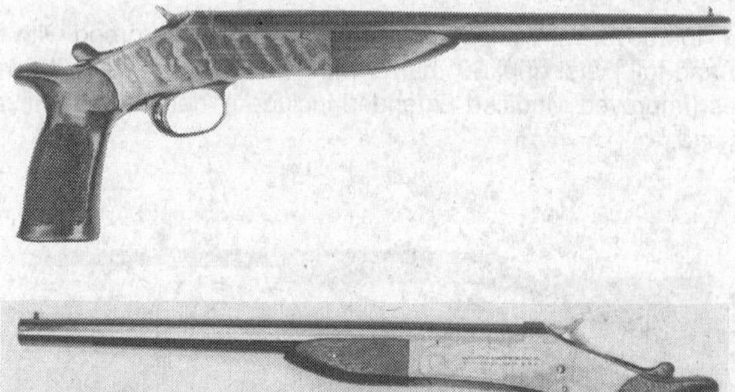

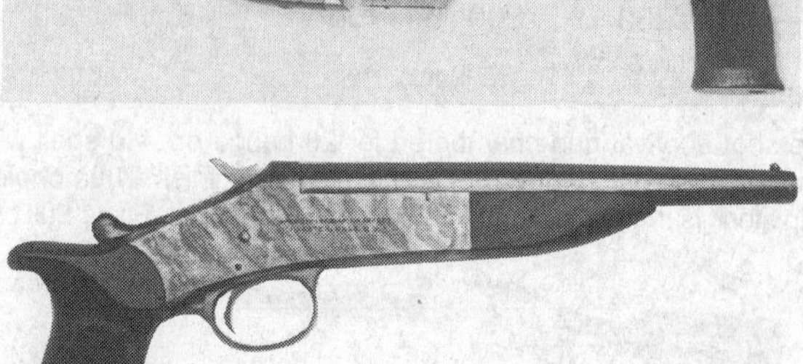

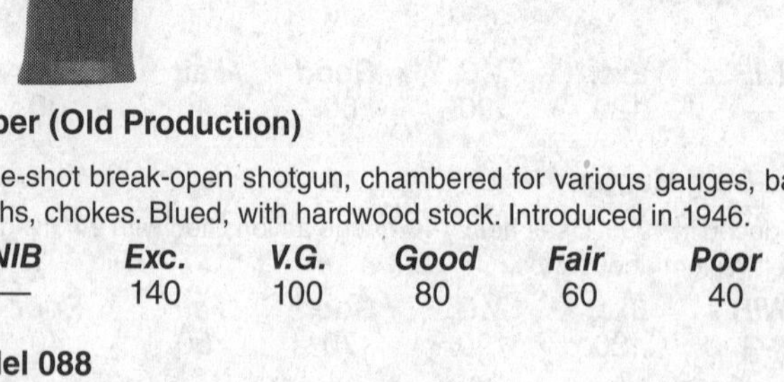

Topper (Old Production)

Single-shot break-open shotgun, chambered for various gauges, barrel lengths, chokes. Blued, with hardwood stock. Introduced in 1946.

NIB	Exc.	V.G.	Good	Fair	Poor
—	140	100	80	60	40

Model 088

An external hammer single-shot break-open shotgun chambered for all gauges. Various barrel lengths, chokes and an automatic ejector. Blued, with case colored frame and hardwood stock.

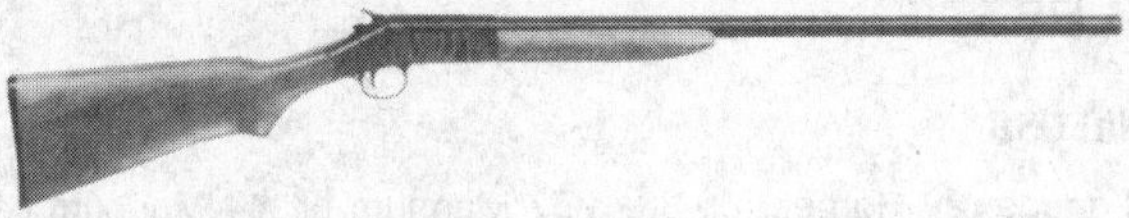

NIB	Exc.	V.G.	Good	Fair	Poor
—	80	60	50	40	30

Model 099

As above, but matte electroless nickel-plated.

NIB	Exc.	V.G.	Good	Fair	Poor
—	110	100	80	60	40

Model 162

A 12- or 20-gauge boxlock single-shot, with 24" barrel and rifle sights.

NIB	Exc.	V.G.	Good	Fair	Poor
—	120	100	80	60	40

Model 176

A 10-gauge 3.5" Magnum caliber boxlock single-barrel shotgun, with heavyweight 36" barrel and Full choke. Manufactured between 1977 and 1985.

NIB	Exc.	V.G.	Good	Fair	Poor
—	220	180	120	80	40

Model 400

A 12-, 16- or 20-gauge slide-action shotgun, with 28" Full choke barrel. Blued, with hardwood stock. Manufactured between 1955 and 1967.

NIB	Exc.	V.G.	Good	Fair	Poor
—	150	120	100	80	50

Model 401

As above, with variable choke device. Manufactured between 1956 and 1963.

NIB	Exc.	V.G.	Good	Fair	Poor
—	180	150	120	90	60

Model 402

As above, in a .410 bore. Manufactured between 1959 and 1967.

NIB	Exc.	V.G.	Good	Fair	Poor
—	180	150	120	90	60

Model 440

A 12-, 16- or 20-gauge slide-action shotgun, with 26", 28" or 30" barrel in various chokes. Blued, with hardwood stock. Manufactured between 1968 and 1973.

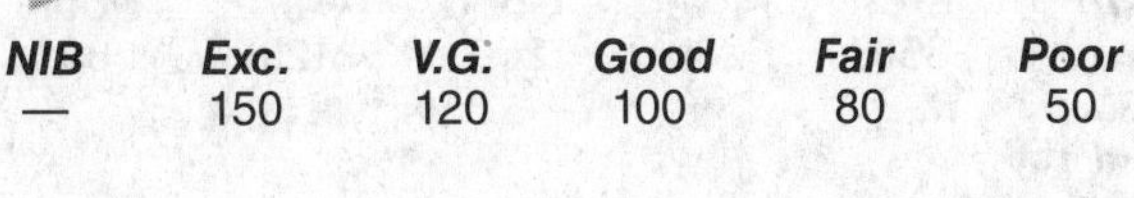

NIB	Exc.	V.G.	Good	Fair	Poor
—	150	120	100	80	50

Model 442

As above, with ventilated rib barrel and checkered stock. Manufactured between 1969 and 1973.

NIB	Exc.	V.G.	Good	Fair	Poor
—	180	150	120	90	60

Model 403

A .410 bore semi-automatic shotgun, with 26" Full choke barrel. Blued, with hardwood stock. Manufactured in 1964.

NIB	Exc.	V.G.	Good	Fair	Poor
—	300	250	180	100	80

Model 404

A 12-, 20-gauge or .410 bore boxlock double-barrel shotgun, with 26" or 28" barrels, double triggers and extractors. Blued, with walnut stock. Manufactured by Rossi in Brazil and imported between 1969 and 1972.

NIB	Exc.	V.G.	Good	Fair	Poor
—	180	150	120	90	60

Pardner Pump

Pump-action with steel receiver, double-action bars, cross-bolt safety, easy take-down. 12-gauge 28" barrel with 3" chamber and ventilated rib, screw-in Modified choke tube. Stock choices are black synthetic, walnut, or camo, with ventilated recoil pad and grooved forend. Drilled and tapped receiver top. Overall length 48.125"; weight 7.5 lbs. for 12 gauge. 20 gauge has 26" barrels. 20-gauge Compact model has 21" barrel, 13" LOP. Protector model is 12 gauge black synthetic with 18.5" barrel, swivel studs, 7.5 lbs.

NIB	Exc.	V.G.	Good	Fair	Poor
—	180	100	80	50	—

Excell

Introduced in 2005, this semi-automatic shotgun chambered for 12-gauge 3" shell. Fitted with 28" ventilated rib barrel and choke tubes. Checkered black synthetic stock. Magazine capacity 5 rounds. Weight about 7 lbs.

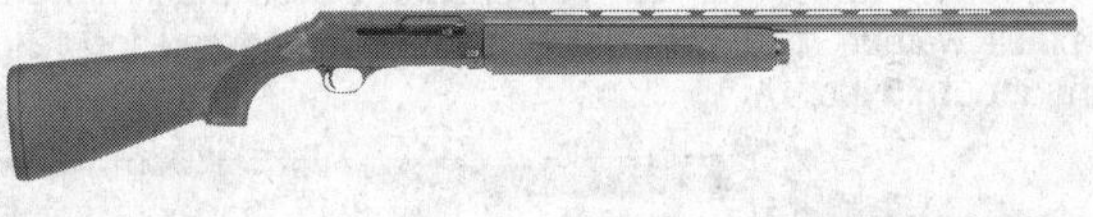

NIB	Exc.	V.G.	Good	Fair	Poor
400	360	300	200	150	100

Excell Waterfowl

As above, with Realtree Advantage Wetlands camo finish. Introduced in 2005.

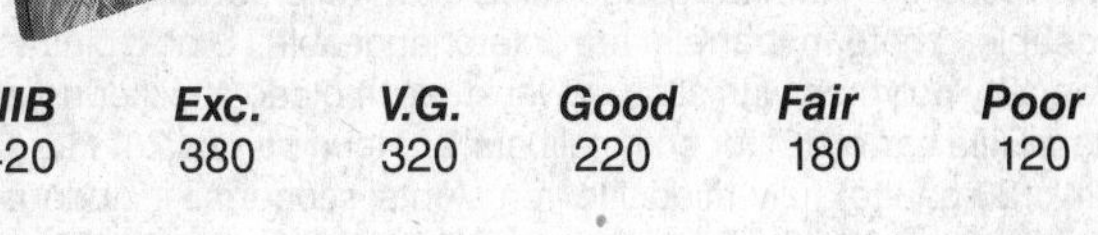

NIB	Exc.	V.G.	Good	Fair	Poor
420	380	320	220	180	120

Excell Turkey

Fitted with 22" barrel, choke tubes and fiber optic front sight. Realtree Advantage Hardwoods camo finish. Weight 7 lbs. Introduced in 2005.

NIB	Exc.	V.G.	Good	Fair	Poor
420	380	320	220	180	120

Excell Combo

Has black synthetic stock and two barrels: 28" ventilated rib with choke tubes and 24" rifled barrel. Weight about 7 lbs. depending on barrel length. Introduced in 2005.

NIB	Exc.	V.G.	Good	Fair	Poor
450	400	350	250	200	140

Pinnacle

Over/under gun chambered for 12- or 20-gauge with 3" chambers. Barrel length for 12-gauge 28"; 20-gauge 26"; both with ventilated ribs and choke tubes. Checkered walnut stock, with recoil pad and pistol grip. Weight about: 6.75 lbs. 12-gauge; 6.25 lbs. 20-gauge. Introduced in 2005.

NIB	Exc.	V.G.	Good	Fair	Poor
700	600	500	320	180	120

Model 1212

A 12-gauge over/under boxlock shotgun, with 28" ventilated rib barrels. Blued, with walnut stock. Also available with 30" barrels having 3" chambers. Manufactured by Lanber Arms of Spain and imported after 1976.

NIB	Exc.	V.G.	Good	Fair	Poor
—	450	380	320	200	120

Long Tom Classic

Introduced in 1996, this limited edition single-barrel shotgun features case-hardened frame, with 32" Full choked barrel. Stock hand-checkered black walnut, with crescent buttplate. Chambered for 12-gauge. Weight about 7.5 lbs.

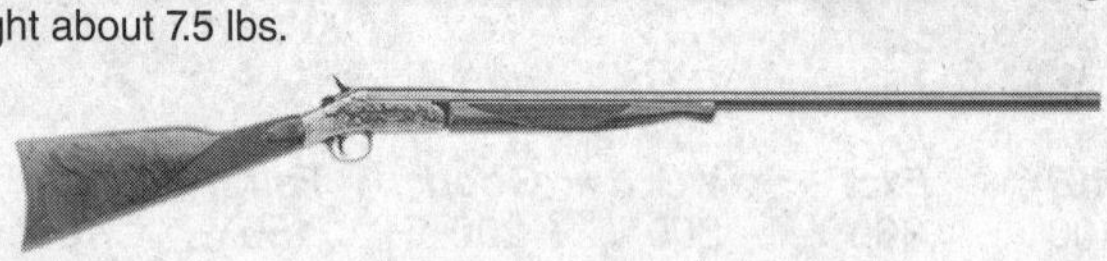

NIB	Exc.	V.G.	Good	Fair	Poor
420	400	320	250	180	120

H&R/NEF Handi-Rifle/Slug Gun Combo

Single-shot break-open rifle/shotgun combos (one rifle barrel, one shotgun barrel per combo) chambered in .44 Magnum/12-gauge rifled slug and .357 Magnum/20-gauge rifled slug. Rifle barrels are not interchangeable; shotgun barrels are interchangeable. Stock black matte high-density polymer, with sling swivel studs, molded checkering and recoil pad. Rifle barrel 22" for both calibers; shotgun barrels 28" (12-gauge) and 24" (20-gauge) fully rifled. No iron sights; scope rail included. Overall length 38" (both rifle chamberings); 42" (12-gauge); 40" (20-gauge). Weight 7 - 8 lbs.

NIB	Exc.	V.G.	Good	Fair	Poor
—	300	250	180	100	80

RIFLES

Model 058

A 20-gauge .22 Hornet, .30-30, .357 Magnum or .44 Magnum caliber rifle/shotgun outfit, with interchangeable barrels. Blued, with hardwood stock.

NIB	Exc.	V.G.	Good	Fair	Poor
—	200	150	100	80	50

Model 258

As above, with matte electroless nickel-plate finish.

NIB	Exc.	V.G.	Good	Fair	Poor
—	220	180	120	100	80

Reising Model 60

A .45 ACP caliber semi-automatic rifle, with 18.25" barrel and 12- or 20-round detachable magazine. Blued, with walnut stock. Operates on retarded blowback system and developed to be used as police weapon. Manufactured between 1944 and 1946.

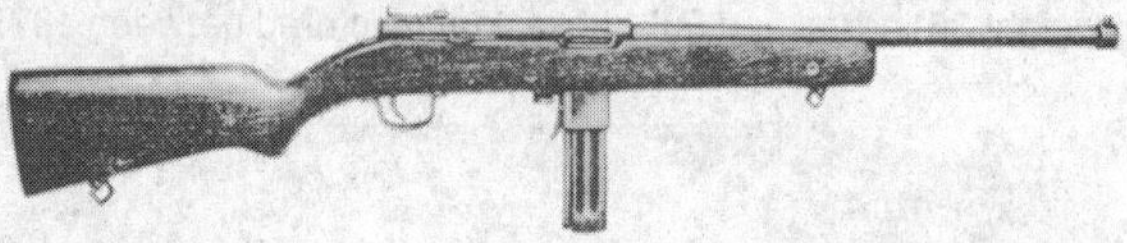

Courtesy Richard M. Kumor, Sr.

NIB	Exc.	V.G.	Good	Fair	Poor
—	2000	1600	1000	450	250

Model 65 Military (Model 58C)

A .22 LR caliber semi-automatic rifle, with 23" barrel and Redfield peep sights. Blued, with walnut stock. Manufactured between 1944 and 1956. Note: Add 100 percent if USMC marked.

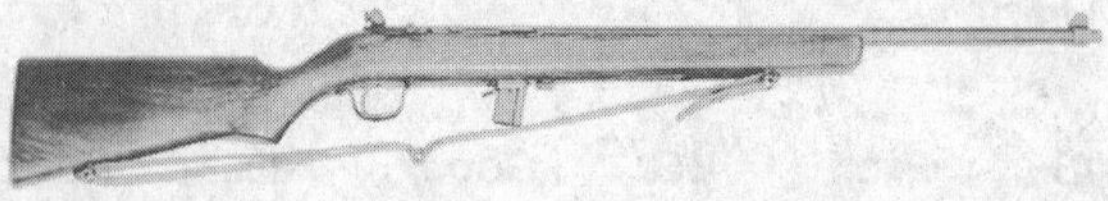

Courtesy Richard M. Kumor, Sr.

NIB	Exc.	V.G.	Good	Fair	Poor
—	500	300	200	120	90

Model 150

A .22 LR caliber semi-automatic rifle, with 20" barrel and 5-shot magazine. Blued, with walnut stock. Manufactured between 1949 and 1953.

NIB	Exc.	V.G.	Good	Fair	Poor
—	100	80	60	40	30

Model 155 (Shikari)

Single-shot break-open rifle chambered for .44 Magnum or .45-70 cartridge. Has 20" barrel with fixed sights. Finish blued, with full-length walnut stock. Introduced in 1972.

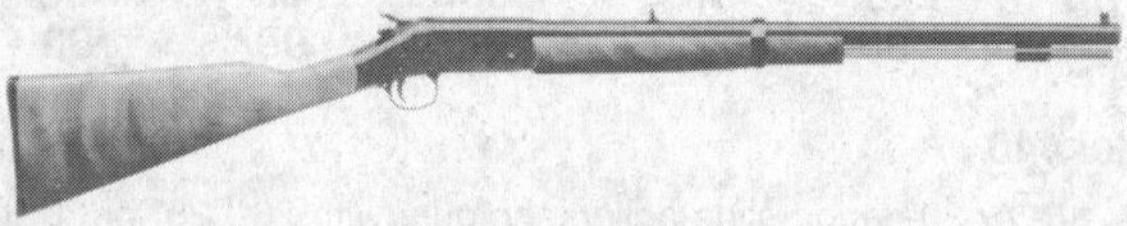

NIB	Exc.	V.G.	Good	Fair	Poor
—	380	300	220	150	100

Model 157

As above in .22 Magnum, .22 Hornet and .30-30 caliber.

NIB	Exc.	V.G.	Good	Fair	Poor
—	350	280	200	120	80

Model 158

A .357 or .44 Magnum single-shot side lever rifle, with 22" barrel. Blued case-hardened, with walnut stock. Available with interchangeable 26"

20-gauge barrel. Manufactured prior to 1986.

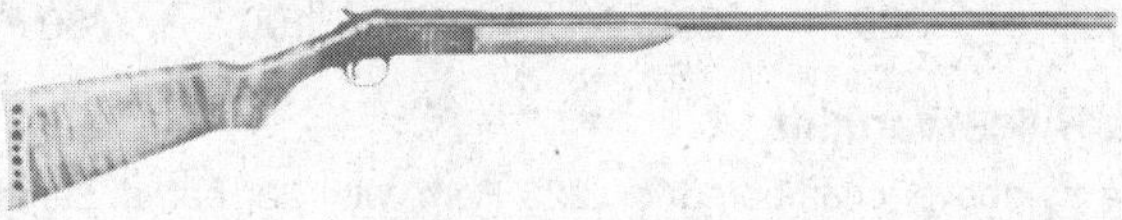

NIB	Exc.	V.G.	Good	Fair	Poor
—	350	280	200	120	80

Model 300 Ultra

A .22-250 up to .300 Winchester Magnum caliber bolt-action rifle, with 22" or 24" barrel without sights. High polished blue and checkered walnut stock. Manufactured between 1965 and 1978.

NIB	Exc.	V.G.	Good	Fair	Poor
—	450	400	350	280	180

Model 301 Carbine

As above, with 18" barrel and full-length Mannlicher-style stock.

NIB	Exc.	V.G.	Good	Fair	Poor
—	450	400	350	280	180

Model 317 Ultra Wildcat

A .17 Rem., .17-223, .222 Rem. and .223 Rem. caliber short Sako bolt-action rifle, with 20" barrel furnished without sights. Blued, with checkered walnut stock. Manufactured between 1968 and 1976.

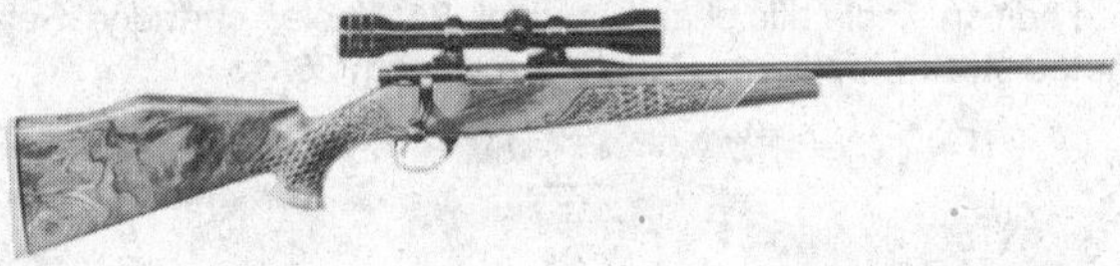

NIB	Exc.	V.G.	Good	Fair	Poor
—	550	400	350	280	180

HANDI-RIFLE SERIES

Break-action single-shot rifle, that's been around in one form or another since 1960s. Side lever release, automatic ejection, hardwood stock, transfer bar passive safety. Available in nearly every conceivable rimfire and centerfire chambering (except the biggest centerfires) and now made under auspices of Marlin. Rifle is as good a bargain today as it ever was. Some newer models feature factory scopes, bull barrels, thumbhole stocks and other niceties, but are still Handi-Rifles. Value generally under $300 even in New or Excellent condition, sometimes remarkably under.

H&R Handi-Rifle (current production)

Single-shot rifle offered in a wide range of calibers from .204 Ruger to .500 S&W. Barrel lengths from 20" to 26", with walnut-finished hardwood or synthetic stock and forend. Note: Add $25 for thumbhole stock.

NIB	Exc.	V.G.	Good	Fair	Poor
260	220	180	150	120	80

H&R Survivor

Variation of Handi-Rifle in .223 Rem., .308 Win., or .45 Colt/.410 shotshell combo. Black polymer thumbhole stock, with pistol grip, accessory rail, sling and swivels. Storage compartment in buttstock and forend.

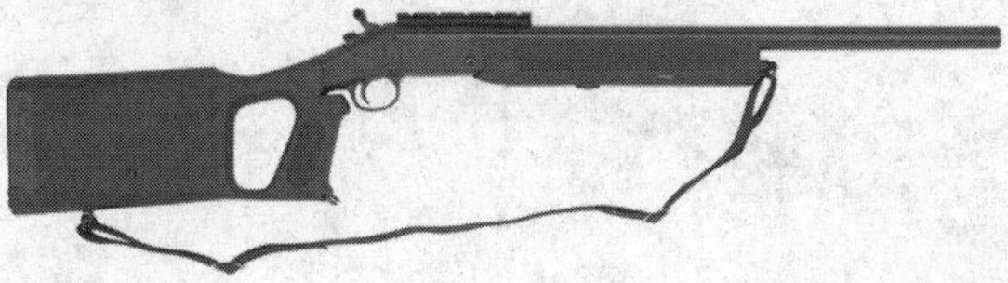

NIB	Exc.	V.G.	Good	Fair	Poor
290	250	200	180	150	100

Synthetic

Basic Handi-Rifle design, with synthetic buttstock and forend (grooved or beavertail). Available with iron sights or Picatinny rail for mounting optics.

NIB	Exc.	V.G.	Good	Fair	Poor
280	200	180	150	100	50

Stainless

Similar to above, with stainless barrel. Chambered in .223, .270 or .30-06.

NIB	Exc.	V.G.	Good	Fair	Poor
300	220	200	180	120	80

Synthetic Handi-Rifle/Slug Gun Combo

Similar to above, with extra slug barrel. Available in .44 Magnum/12-gauge and .357 Magnum/20-gauge. Introduced in 2008.

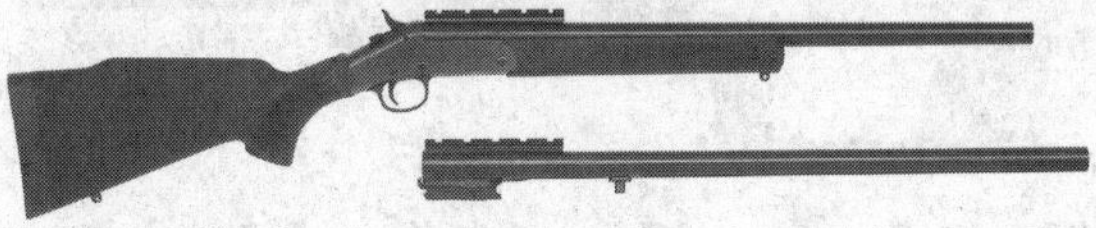

NIB	Exc.	V.G.	Good	Fair	Poor
—	320	300	220	180	100

Superlite Compact

Similar to Synthetic Handi-Rifle. Weight only 5.5 lbs. Chambered in .223 and .243. Available with optional scope.

NIB	Exc.	V.G.	Good	Fair	Poor
300	220	200	180	120	80

Ultra Varmint Rifle

Single-shot rifle chambered for .223 Rem. or .22-250 cartridge. Fitted with 22" heavy barrel. Stock hand checkered curly maple (older models) or laminated (newer models), with Monte Carlo cheekpiece. Comes with Picatinny rail for mounting optics. Weight about 7.5 lbs.

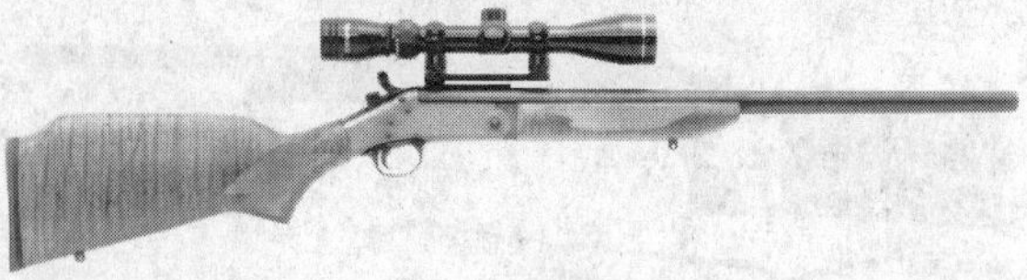

NIB	Exc.	V.G.	Good	Fair	Poor
350	300	180	120	80	50

Ultra Varmint Thumbhole

Similar to above, with laminated thumbhole stock.

NIB	Exc.	V.G.	Good	Fair	Poor
380	320	200	150	100	80

Stainless Steel Ultra Varmint Thumbhole

Similar to above, with stainless steel barrel and matte nickel receiver.

NIB	Exc.	V.G.	Good	Fair	Poor
380	320	200	150	100	80

Ultra Varmint Fluted

Introduced in 2005. Chambered for .204 Ruger, .22-250 or .223 Rem. cartridge. Fitted with 24" fluted barrel with no sights. Stock is black synthetic, with vertical adjustable knob, recoil pad and adjustable bipod mount. Weight about 7 lbs.

NIB	Exc.	V.G.	Good	Fair	Poor
350	300	180	120	80	50

Model 317P

As above, more finely finished. Manufactured between 1968 and 1976.

NIB	Exc.	V.G.	Good	Fair	Poor
—	500	480	420	380	250

Ultra Rifle—Hunting

Single-shot chambered for .25-06, .308 Win. and .357 Rem. Max. The .25-06 has 26" barrel; other two fitted with 22" barrels. Cinnamon laminated stock standard. Weight about 7 lbs. In 2001 .450 Marlin cartridge was added.

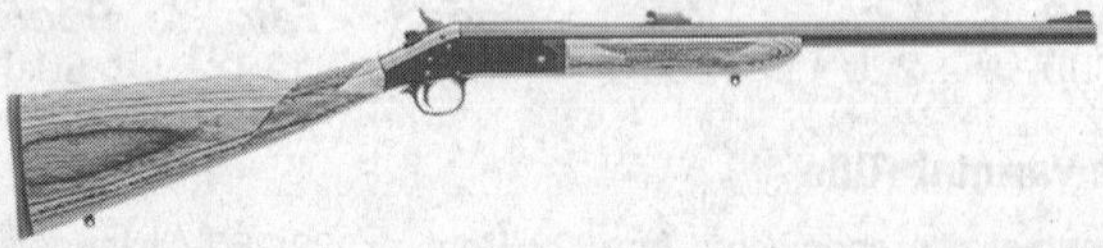

NIB	Exc.	V.G.	Good	Fair	Poor
280	200	180	150	100	50

Harrington & Richardson/New England Firearms Stainless Ultra Hunter with Thumbhole Stock

Single-shot break-open rifle chambered in .45-70 Government. 24" stainless steel barrel and receiver with scope mount rail; hammer extension; cinnamon laminate thumbhole stock. Overall length 40"; weight 8 lbs.

NIB	Exc.	V.G.	Good	Fair	Poor
380	320	200	150	100	80

Ultra Rifle—Varmint

Same as above, chambered for .223 Rem. with 22" barrel. Laminated stock, with checkered pistol grip.

NIB	Exc.	V.G.	Good	Fair	Poor
380	320	200	150	100	80

Ultra .22 Magnum Rifle

Same as above, chambered for .22 Win. Magnum. Introduced in 2001.

NIB	Exc.	V.G.	Good	Fair	Poor
300	220	200	180	120	80

Ultra Rifle—Comp

Introduced in 1997, this single-shot rifle features an integral muzzle brake on barrel end. Available in .270 Win. and .30-06 calibers, with 24" barrels. Camo laminated stock.

NIB	Exc.	V.G.	Good	Fair	Poor
300	220	200	180	120	80

Ultra Rifle Rocky Mountain Elk Foundation Commemorative

Limited edition single rifle chambered for .35 Whelen cartridge. Selected laminated stock with Monte Carlo. Barrel length 26".

NIB	Exc.	V.G.	Good	Fair	Poor
—	450	400	350	280	180

Sportster .17 HMR

A .17 HMR version of Handi-Rifle, with black polymer Monte Carlo stock and Picatinny rail for moutning optics. Overall length 38.25".

NIB	Exc.	V.G.	Good	Fair	Poor
—	250	200	150	100	50

Sportster

A .22 LR or .22 WMR version of Handi-Rifle, with black polymer stock, fluted forend and iron sights. Overall length 36.25".

NIB	Exc.	V.G.	Good	Fair	Poor
—	180	150	100	80	50

Sportster Compact

Similar to above, in .22 LR only and 2" shorter length of pull.

NIB	Exc.	V.G.	Good	Fair	Poor
—	150	120	100	80	50

Buffalo Classic

First produced in 1995. Chambered for .45-70 and .38-55 cartridges. Barrel length 32" with no sights, but dovetail front, drilled and tapped rear. Hand checkered walnut stock, with case colored crescent steel buttplate. Weight about 8 lbs. Since its introduction in 1995, about 2,000 guns produced. Factory anticipates about 1,000 rifles being built each year.

NIB	Exc.	V.G.	Good	Fair	Poor
380	320	220	180	120	50

Wesson & Harrington Brand 125th Anniversary Rifle

Introduced in 1996. Commemorates 125th Anniversary of partnership. Special rifle chambered for .45-70 Government cartridge. Receiver hand engraved. Barrel length 32". Stock American black walnut, with crescent steel butt.

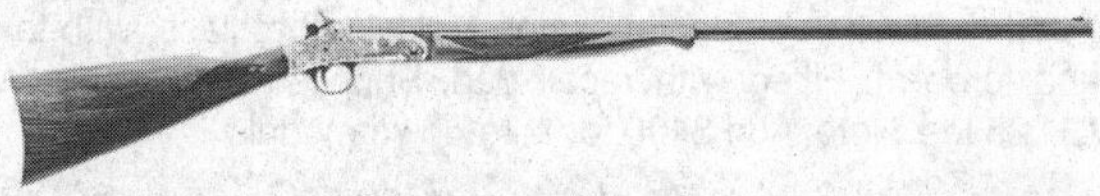

NIB	Exc.	V.G.	Good	Fair	Poor
400	320	250	200	150	80

Ultra Rifle Whitetails Unlimited 1997 Commemorative Edition

Introduced in 1997. Chambered for .45-70 Govt. cartridge. Features hand checkered black walnut stock. Special laser engraving on action and pewter finished medallion in-letted into stock. Barrel length 22".

NIB	Exc.	V.G.	Good	Fair	Poor
320	280	220	180	120	80

CR Carbine

Single-shot rifle based on Handi-Rifle design. Two-piece checkered walnut stock, with schnabel forend. Marble front and rear sights, Crescent steel buttplate. Chambered in .45 Colt. Introduced in 2007.

NIB	Exc.	V.G.	Good	Fair	Poor
380	320	220	150	100	50

Model 333

Model 300 in 7mm Magnum caliber. Manufactured in 1974.

NIB	Exc.	V.G.	Good	Fair	Poor
—	250	200	180	120	100

Model 340

A .243 to .308 Winchester caliber bolt-action rifle, with 22" barrel and 5-shot magazine. Blued, with checkered walnut stock.

NIB	Exc.	V.G.	Good	Fair	Poor
—	400	350	300	220	150

Model 360 Ultra Automatic

A .243 Win. and .308 Win. caliber semi-automatic rifle, with 22" barrel, adjustable sights and 3-shot detachable magazine. Blued, with checkered walnut stock. Manufactured between 1965 and 1978.

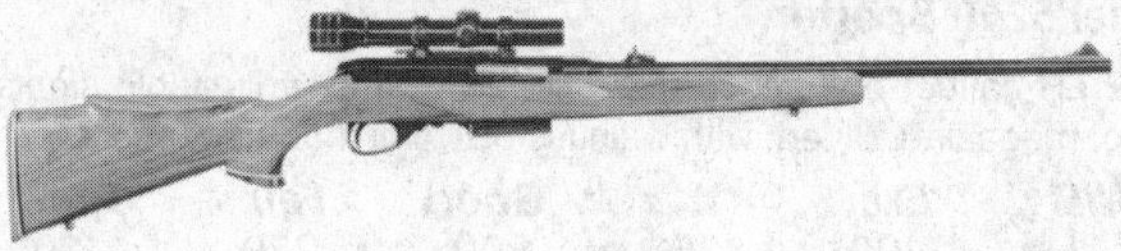

NIB	Exc.	V.G.	Good	Fair	Poor
—	420	380	280	200	100

Model 451 Medalist

A .22 LR caliber bolt-action rifle, with 26" barrel, open sights and 5-shot detachable magazine. Blued, with walnut stock. Manufactured between 1948 and 1961.

NIB	Exc.	V.G.	Good	Fair	Poor
—	180	150	120	100	80

Model 700

A .22 rimfire Magnum caliber semi-automatic rifle, with 22" barrel, adjustable sights and 5-round detachable magazine. Blued, with checkered walnut stock. Manufactured between 1977 and 1985.

NIB	Exc.	V.G.	Good	Fair	Poor
—	220	200	150	120	80

Model 700 DL

As above, with checkered walnut stock and 4X scope. Manufactured until 1985.

NIB	Exc.	V.G.	Good	Fair	Poor
—	300	250	200	150	100

Model 750

A .22 LR bolt-action single-shot rifle, with 22" barrel, sights and short stock. Blued, with hardwood stock.

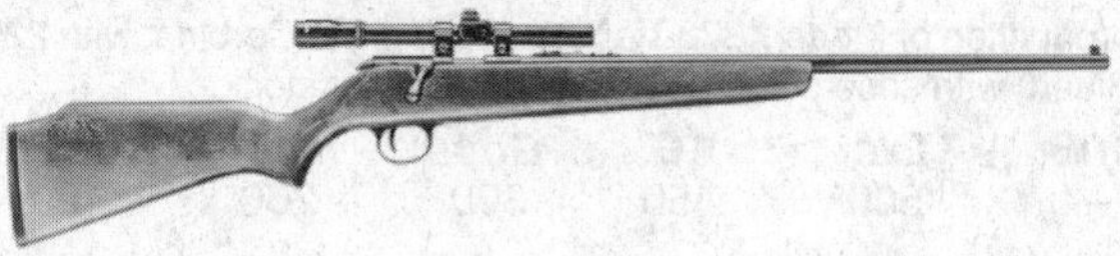

NIB	Exc.	V.G.	Good	Fair	Poor
—	100	80	60	40	20

Model 865

A .22 LR caliber bolt-action rifle, with 22" barrel, open sights and 5-shot magazine. Blued, with hardwood stock.

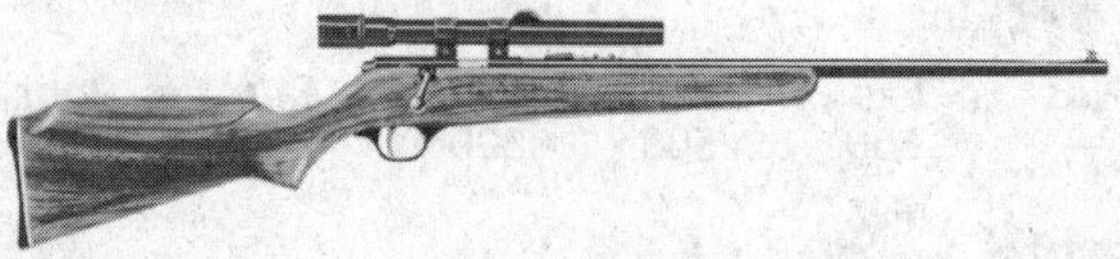

NIB	Exc.	V.G.	Good	Fair	Poor
—	100	80	60	40	20

Model 5200

A .22 LR caliber bolt-action single-shot rifle, with 28" heavy barrel without sights and adjustable trigger. Blued, with target-type walnut stock.

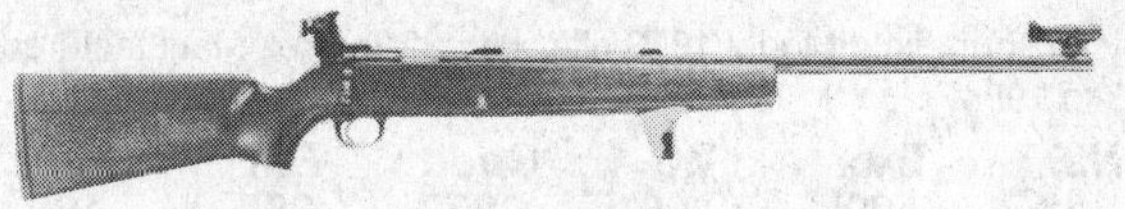

NIB	Exc.	V.G.	Good	Fair	Poor
—	400	350	300	220	120

Model 5200 Sporter

A .22 LR caliber bolt-action rifle, with 24" barrel, adjustable sights and 5-shot magazine. Blued, with walnut stock. Not manufactured after 1983.

NIB	Exc.	V.G.	Good	Fair	Poor
—	400	350	300	220	120

100th Anniversary Officer's Model

Commemorative replica of Officer's Model 1873 Trapdoor Springfield Rifle, with 26" barrel. Engraved and anniversary plaque mounted on stock. Blued, with case colored receiver and pewter forend tip. There were 10,000 manufactured in 1971. As with all commemorative's, this model most desirable when NIB with all supplied material.

NIB	Exc.	V.G.	Good	Fair	Poor
850	700	500	380	250	180

Custer Memorial Issue

Limited production issue commemorating George Armstrong Custer's Battle of Little Bighorn. Heavily engraved and gold inlaid, with high-grade checkered walnut stock. Furnished in mahogany display case, that included two books dealing with the subject. Two versions produced: Officer's Model, of which 25 were issued commemorating 25 officers that fell with Custer; another version commemorating 243 enlisted men who lost their lives at Little Bighorn. As with all commemorative's to be collectible, they must be NIB with all furnished material.

Officer's Model

25 manufactured.

NIB	Exc.	V.G.	Good	Fair	Poor
4000	3000	2000	1200	500	200

Enlisted Men's Model

243 manufactured.

NIB	Exc.	V.G.	Good	Fair	Poor
2000	1500	1000	400	250	150

Model 171

Re-production of Model 1873 Trapdoor Springfield Carbine, with 22" barrel. Blued, with case colored receiver and walnut stock.

NIB	Exc.	V.G.	Good	Fair	Poor
—	500	450	300	200	120

Model 171-DL

As above, but more finely finished.

NIB	Exc.	V.G.	Good	Fair	Poor
—	550	500	320	250	180

Model 174

Plain copy of Springfield Model 1873 Carbine in .45-70 caliber, with 22" barrel. Manufactured in 1972.

NIB	Exc.	V.G.	Good	Fair	Poor
—	520	400	320	250	180

Model 178

Copy of Springfield Model 1873 rifle, with 32" barrel. Manufactured from 1973 to 1984.

NIB	Exc.	V.G.	Good	Fair	Poor
—	520	400	320	250	180

HARRIS GUNWORKS
Phoenix, Arizona

There are a wide range of extra costs options for all Harris Gunworks models, that in many cases will dramatically affect price.

National Match Rifle

Introduced in 1989. Features bolt-action rifle chambered for 7mm-08 Rem. or .308 Win., with 5-round magazine. Fitted with 24" stainless steel match-grade barrel, with Canjar trigger. Stock is fiberglass, with adjustable buttplate. Weight about 11 lbs.

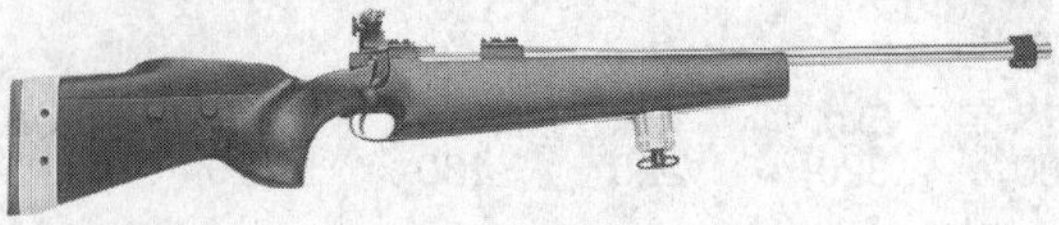

NIB	Exc.	V.G.	Good	Fair	Poor
3500	2750	1750	950	600	300

Model 86 Sniper Rifle

Chambered for .308, .30-06, .300 Win. Magnum, with 24" heavy match-grade barrel. Stock is a special design McHale fiberglass, with textured grip and forearm. Fitted with recoil pad. Supplied with bipod. Weight about 11.25 lbs. Note: Add $100 for take-down model.

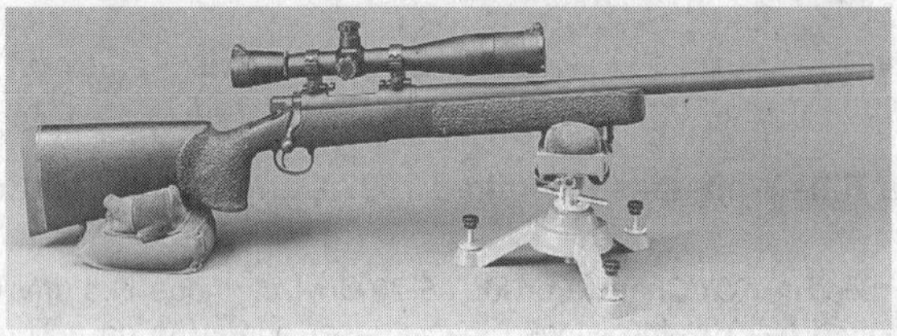

NIB	Exc.	V.G.	Good	Fair	Poor
2700	2100	1600	1000	600	350

Model 87 Series

Single-shot rifles chambered for .50 BMG. Fitted with 29" barrel and muzzle brake. Fiberglass stock. Introduced in 1987. Weight about 21.5 lbs. Note: Add $600 for Model 87R 5-shot repeater; $400 for Model 87 5-shot repeater; $300 for Model 92 Bullpup.

NIB	Exc.	V.G.	Good	Fair	Poor
4000	3500	3000	2500	1000	500

Model 88

Bolt-action .50 BMG rifles offered in two different configurations. First variation: fitted with 20" carbon graphite barrel, with add-on recoil arrestor and black teflon finish; second variation: fitted with 16.5" stainless steel barrel, with integral recoil arrestor. Both rifles weigh about 14 lbs. Titanium action available for further weight reduction.

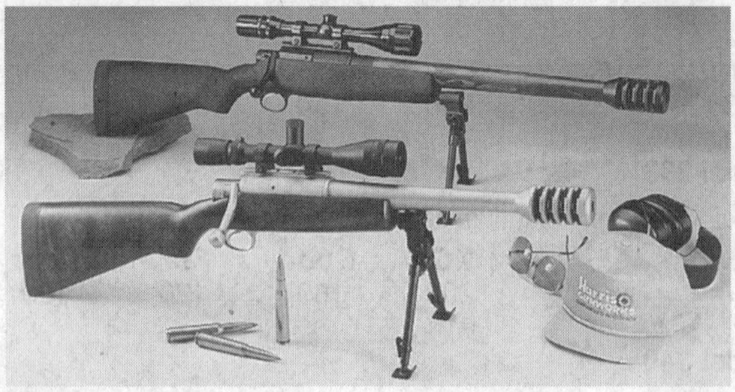

NIB	Exc.	V.G.	Good	Fair	Poor
3800	3000	2500	2000	1000	500

Model 89 Sniper Rifle

Bolt-action rifle chambered for .308 cartridge. Fitted with 28" barrel. Supplied with bipod. Stock is fiberglass, with adjustable length of pull and fitted with recoil pad. Weight about 15.25 lbs.

NIB	Exc.	V.G.	Good	Fair	Poor
2700	2100	1600	1000	600	350

Model 93

Bolt-action .50 BMG rifle, with folding hinge stock assembly. Furnished with 10- or 20-round magazine. Barrel length 29". Weight about 21 lbs.

NIB	Exc.	V.G.	Good	Fair	Poor
4000	3500	3000	2500	1000	500

Model 95

Lightweight variation of .50 BMG models featuring Titanium and graphite. Supplied with bipod. Barrel length 29". Weight about 18 lbs.

NIB	Exc.	V.G.	Good	Fair	Poor
6000	4750	3000	2000	1000	500

Model 96

Gas-operated semi-automatic .50 BMG sniper rifle. Barrel length 29". Detachable 5-round magazine. Weight about 25 lbs.

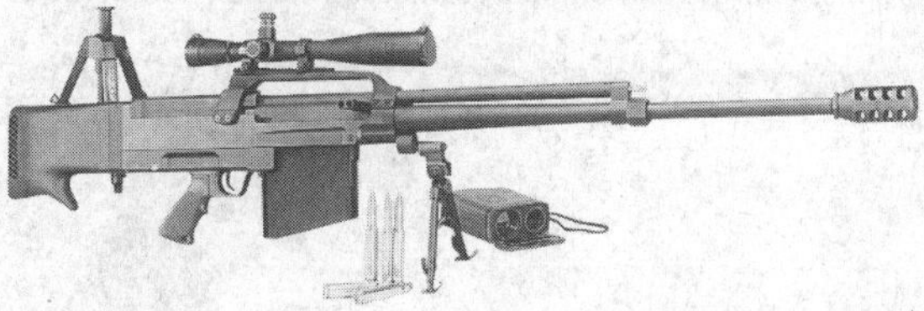

NIB	Exc.	V.G.	Good	Fair	Poor
7500	6500	4000	2500	1500	750

Long Range Rifle

Chambered for a variety of cartridges such as .300 Win. Magnum, 7mm Rem. Magnum, .300 Phoenix, .338 Lapua. Single-shot rifle fitted with 26" match-grade stainless steel barrel. Fiberglass stock, with adjustable buttplate and cheekpiece. Weight about 14 lbs.

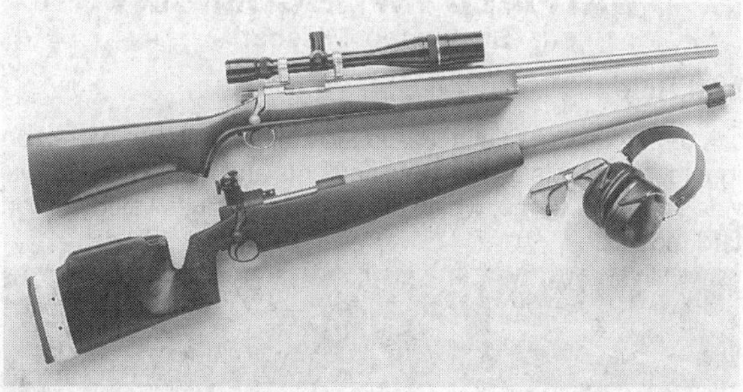

NIB	Exc.	V.G.	Good	Fair	Poor
3900	2850	1500	1000	700	350

Target/Benchrest Rifle

Offered in .243, .308, 6mm BR, 6mm PPC and 6mm Rem. Custom built for customer. Available in both left-/right-hand. Weight about 11 lbs.

NIB	Exc.	V.G.	Good	Fair	Poor
3500	2750	1750	950	600	300

Antietam Sharps Rifle

Replica of Sharps Model 1874 sidehammer, introduced in 1994. Chambered for .40-65 or .45-70. Choice of 30" or 32" octagon or round barrel. Stock fancy walnut. Straight-/pistol grip or Creedmoor, with schnabel forearm. Many optional sights offered. Weight about 11.25 lbs.

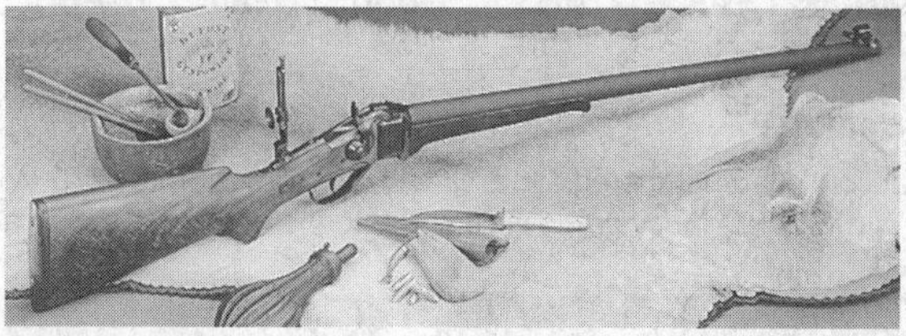

NIB	Exc.	V.G.	Good	Fair	Poor
2600	1950	1200	800	450	200

Signature Classic Sporter

Left-/right-handed bolt-action model, introduced in 1987. Choice of calibers from .22-250 to .375 H&H. Barrel lengths 22", 24" or 26" depending on caliber. Choice of fiberglass stocks in green, beige, brown or black. Wood stock optional. Weight about 7 lbs. for short action calibers.

NIB	Exc.	V.G.	Good	Fair	Poor
3150	2550	1500	1150	500	250

Signature Classic Stainless Sporter

Same as above, with barrel and action made from stainless steel. A .416 Rem. Magnum available in this variation. Available with interchangeable barrels. Note: Add $600 for interchangeable barrels.

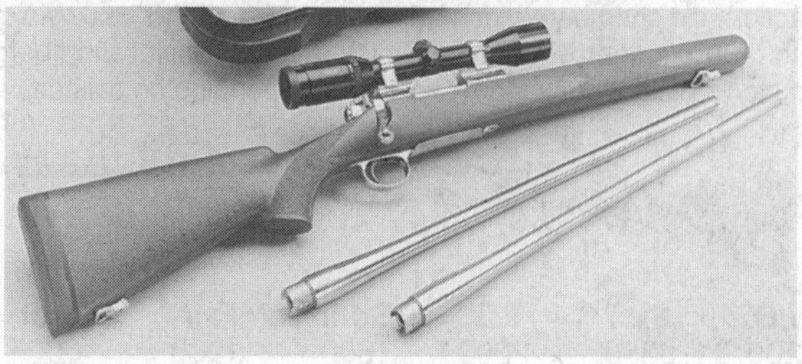

NIB	Exc.	V.G.	Good	Fair	Poor
3200	2650	1600	1250	600	300

Signature Super Varminter

Similar to Classic Sporter, except fitted with a heavy contoured barrel, adjustable trigger and special hand-bedded fiberglass stock. Chambered for .223, .22-250, .220 Swift, .243, 6mm Rem., .25-06, 7mm-08, 7mm BR, .308, .350 Rem. Introduced in 1989.

NIB	Exc.	V.G.	Good	Fair	Poor
2900	2250	1600	1050	700	350

Signature Alaskan

Similar to Classic Sporter, except fitted with match-grade barrel and single leaf rear sight. Nickel finish. Walnut Monte Carlo stock, with cheekpiece and palm swell grip. Chambered for .270 to .375 H&H. Introduced in 1989.

NIB	Exc.	V.G.	Good	Fair	Poor
3950	3200	2200	1500	700	350

Signature Titanium Mountain Rifle

Similar to Classic Sporter, except action is made of titanium alloy and barrel of chrome-moly steel. Stock is graphite reinforced fiberglass. Chambered for .270 to .300 Win. Magnum. Weight about 5.5 lbs. Introduced in 1989. Note: Add $400 for graphite steel barrel.

NIB	Exc.	V.G.	Good	Fair	Poor
3500	2750	1750	950	600	300

Sportsman 97

Bolt-action rifle chambered for a variety of calibers from .270 Win. to .338 Win. Stock is fancy grade walnut, Bastogne or English. Talon action is fitted.

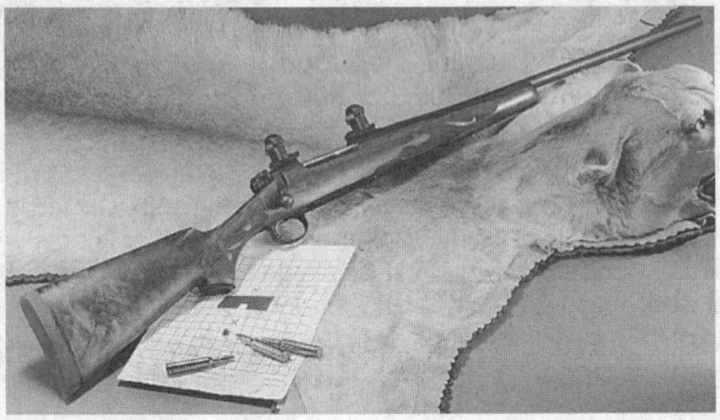

NIB	Exc.	V.G.	Good	Fair	Poor
2900	2250	1600	1050	700	350

Talon Safari Rifle

Bolt-action rifle chambered for 16 different calibers from .300 Win. Magnum to .460 Weatherby Magnum. Finish is matte black, with fiberglass Safari stock. Weight between 9 and 10 lbs. depending on caliber.

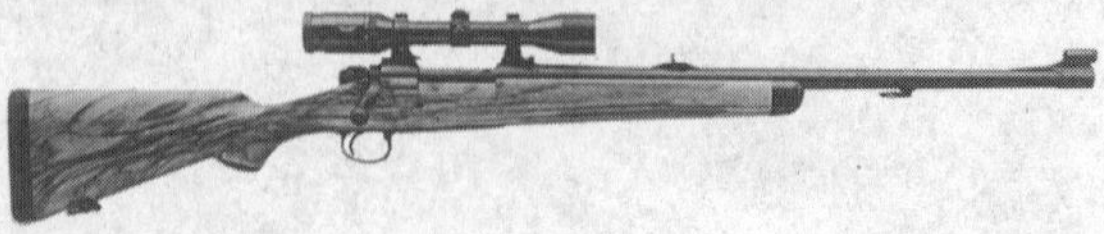

NIB	Exc.	V.G.	Good	Fair	Poor
4200	3350	2200	1600	1200	600

Talon Sporter Rifle

Bolt-action rifle, introduced in 1991. Uses a pre-64 Model 70 type action, with cone breech. Barrel and action are stainless steel. Chambered for a wide variety of calibers from .22-250 to .416 Rem. Magnum. Choice of walnut or fiberglass stock. Most barrel lengths are 24". Weight about 7.5 lbs. depending on caliber.

NIB	Exc.	V.G.	Good	Fair	Poor
3150	2550	1500	1150	500	250

Double Rifle/Shotgun

Side-by-side gun offered in .470 NE or .500 NE, as well as 12- and 20-gauge guns. Engraved receiver, AAA fancy walnut stocks and 3-leaf express sights are standard. Offered in boxlock and sidelock models.

Boxlock

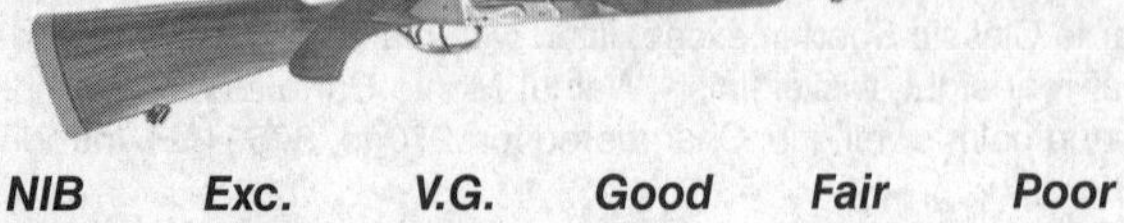

NIB	Exc.	V.G.	Good	Fair	Poor
15000	12500	9000	5000	2750	1500

Side Lock

NIB	Exc.	V.G.	Good	Fair	Poor
21000	16500	12000	7500	3100	1750

HARTFORD ARMS & EQUIPMENT CO.

Hartford, Connecticut

Established in 1925, this firm was purchased by High Standard Company in 1932.

Single-Shot Target

A .22-caliber single-shot pistol, with 6.75" round barrel, fixed sights and walnut or composition grips. Frame marked "Manfd. by the/ Hartford Arms and Equip. Co./ Hartford, Conn./ Patented .22 cal./ l.r." on left side in front of their breech. Although this pistol resembles a semi-automatic, it is in fact a single-shot manually operated pistol. Note: Add $150 premium for guns in original Hartford Arms box numbered to gun; $250 premium for guns in original High Standard box numbered to gun.

Courtesy John J. Stimson, Jr.

NIB	Exc.	V.G.	Good	Fair	Poor
—	600	450	320	250	150

Model 1925

Semi-automatic pistol chambered for .22-caliber, with 6.75" round barrel, checkered hard black rubber grips or ribbed walnut grips. Magazine capacity 10 rounds. Frame marked, "manfd. by/ the hartford arms and equip. co./ hartford, conn./ patented/ .22 cal/long rifle" on left side in front of breech. Approximately 5,000 produced from 1925 to 1932. Note: Add $150 premium for guns in original Hartford Arms box numbered to gun.

Courtesy John J. Stimson, Jr.

NIB	Exc.	V.G.	Good	Fair	Poor
—	600	480	360	220	180

HATFIELD RIFLE COMPANY

St. Joseph, Missouri

Squirrel Rifle

Flintlock or percussion rifle in .32- to .50-caliber, with 39" barrel, double-set triggers, adjustable sights, brass mounts and maple stocks. Available in a wide variety of forms, which affect values. Values listed are for plain standard models.

NIB	Exc.	V.G.	Good	Fair	Poor
550	400	350	300	220	150

SHOTGUNS

Uplander Grade I

A 20-gauge boxlock double-barrel shotgun, with 26" improved cylinder and modified barrel. Matte raised rib, single-selective trigger and automatic ejectors. Case-hardened blued, with deluxe-grade hand-checkered walnut stock. Introduced in 1987.

NIB	Exc.	V.G.	Good	Fair	Poor
1250	1050	750	600	480	200

Uplander Pigeon Grade II

As above, with scroll engraving. Fitted leather case.

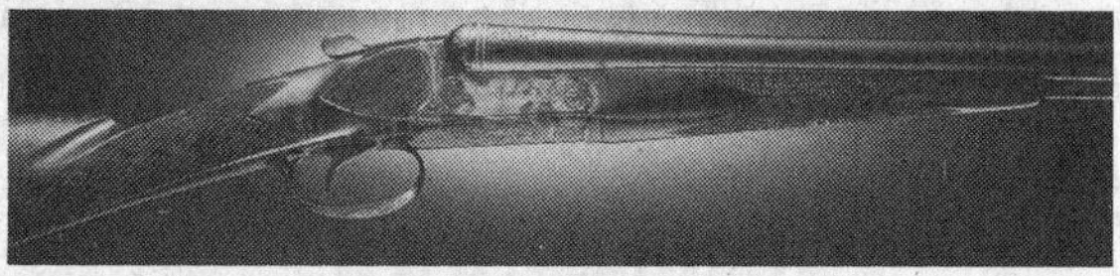

NIB	Exc.	V.G.	Good	Fair	Poor
2250	1750	1280	900	650	500

Uplander Super Pigeon Grade III

As above, with deep-relief cut engraving and leather case.

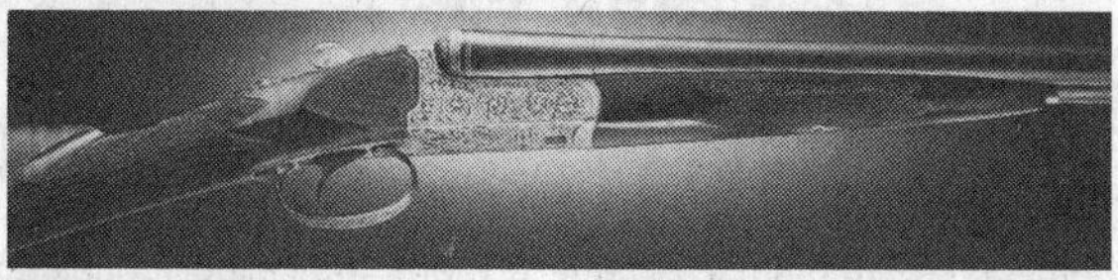

NIB	Exc.	V.G.	Good	Fair	Poor
2500	2200	1700	1400	1000	700

Uplander Golden Quail Grade IV

Gold-inlaid version of above.

NIB	Exc.	V.G.	Good	Fair	Poor
4000	3500	2750	2000	1700	1300

Uplander Woodcock Grade V

As above, with seven 24 kt. gold inlays and best quality engraving. Furnished with leather case.

NIB	Exc.	V.G.	Good	Fair	Poor
5600	5000	4250	3500	2750	2000

HAVILAND & GUNN
Ilion, New York

Gallery Pistol

A .17-caliber rimfire single-shot pistol, with 5" barrel. Barrel and frame made of one piece iron and nickel plated. No markings on these pistols whatsoever. Believed to have been made during 1870s.

NIB	Exc.	V.G.	Good	Fair	Poor
—	—	1150	550	180	100

HAWES
Los Angeles, California

Importer of handguns primarily made in Europe.

Courier

A .25-caliber blowback semi-automatic pocket pistol. Manufactured by Galesi.

NIB	Exc.	V.G.	Good	Fair	Poor
—	120	100	80	50	20

Diplomat

A .380 ACP pistol, with external hammer.

NIB	Exc.	V.G.	Good	Fair	Poor
—	150	120	100	80	50

Medallion

J.P. Sauer & Sohn manufactured revolver, with swing-out cylinder and 6" barrel. Chambered for .22 LR and .38 Special. Adjustable sights.

NIB	Exc.	V.G.	Good	Fair	Poor
—	400	300	250	120	90

Trophy

As above, with 3", 4" or 6" barrel and fixed sights.

NIB	Exc.	V.G.	Good	Fair	Poor
—	400	300	250	120	90

Tip-Up Target Pistol

Replica of Stevens Model 35 .22 LR single-shot. Globe front sight, adjustable rear.

NIB	Exc.	V.G.	Good	Fair	Poor
—	280	200	140	80	40

MARSHAL SINGLE-ACTION ARMY REVOLVERS

J. P. Sauer made a Western-styled series for Hawes. Based in appearance on Colt Single-Action Army.

Silver City

A .22 LR or .22 rimfire Magnum caliber single-action revolver, with 5.5" barrel, 6-shot cylinder and fixed sights.

NIB	Exc.	V.G.	Good	Fair	Poor
—	150	120	100	50	20

Western

A .357 Magnum, .44 Magnum, .45 Colt, .45 ACP, .44-40, 9mm, .22 LR and .22 rimfire Magnum single-action revolver, with fixed sights. Blued.

NIB	Exc.	V.G.	Good	Fair	Poor
—	350	280	200	100	80

Texas

As above, but nickel-plated.

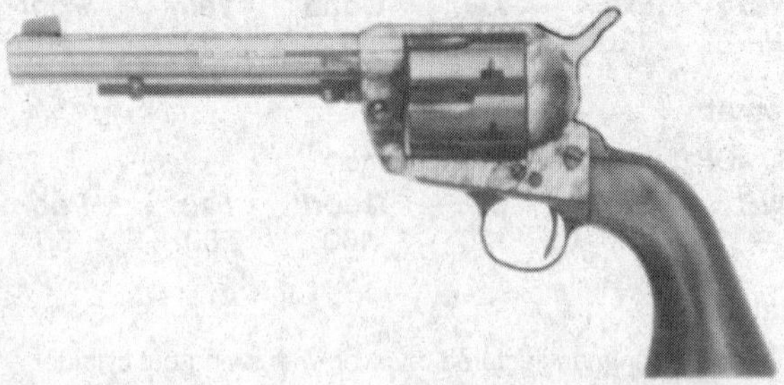

NIB	Exc.	V.G.	Good	Fair	Poor
—	350	280	200	100	80

Montana

Western Marshal, with brass backstrap and triggerguard.

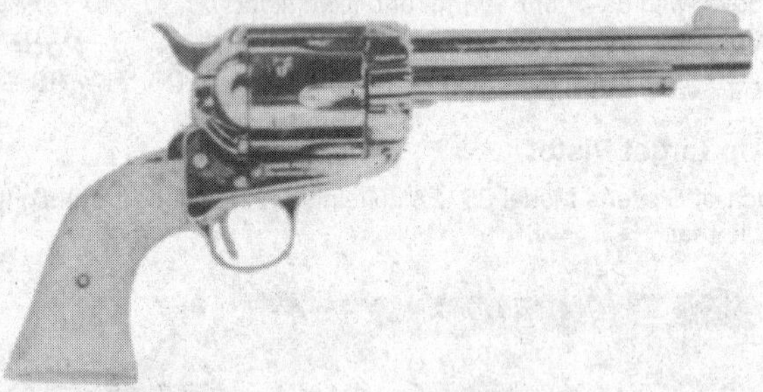

NIB	Exc.	V.G.	Good	Fair	Poor
—	350	280	200	100	80

Deputy

A .22 LR and .22 rimfire Magnum single-action revolver, with 5.5" barrel and 6-shot cylinder.

NIB	Exc.	V.G.	Good	Fair	Poor
—	150	120	100	50	20

Chief

A .357 Magnum, .44 Magnum and .45 Colt caliber revolver, with 6.5" barrel, 6-shot cylinder and adjustable sights. Blued.

NIB	Exc.	V.G.	Good	Fair	Poor
—	350	280	200	100	80

Federal

A 6-shot single-action revolver in .357 Magnum, .44 Magnum and .45 Colt caliber.

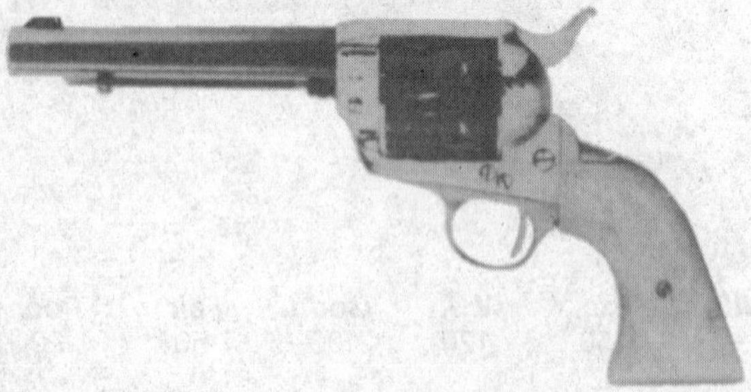

NIB	Exc.	V.G.	Good	Fair	Poor
—	350	280	200	100	80

HAWES & WAGGONER
Philadelphia, Pennsylvania

Pocket Pistol

A .41-caliber single-shot percussion pistol, with 3" barrel, German silver mountings and walnut stock. Manufactured in 1850s.

NIB	Exc.	V.G.	Good	Fair	Poor
—	—	2250	920	480	280

HAWKEN
St. Louis, Missouri

During early part of 19th century, Jacob and Samuel Hawken manufactured a variety of flintlock, percussion and cartridge rifles, shotguns and pistols. They are best known, however, for half stock Plains Rifles. Though of a plain nature, these arms were recognized for their accuracy and dependability. Early Hawken rifles will be worth a substantial premium over later examples. Some examples in very good condition may be worth as much as $50,000. Proceed with caution.

HAWKEN, J & S
See PLAINS RIFLE

HDH, SA.
Henrion, Dassy & Heuschen
Liege, Belgium

Cobold

A 9.4mm Dutch, 10.6mm German, .38- and .45-caliber double-action five-shot revolver, with solid frame, octagonal barrel and an odd safety catch that locks the cylinder.

NIB	Exc.	V.G.	Good	Fair	Poor
—	500	320	280	150	100

Puppy

A 5.5mm to 7.65mm caliber folding trigger double-action revolver. Most are "Velo-Dogs".

NIB	Exc.	V.G.	Good	Fair	Poor
—	200	150	100	80	50

Lincoln

A .22-caliber folding trigger double-action revolver, with solid frame, imitation pearl or ivory grips and engraving.

NIB	Exc.	V.G.	Good	Fair	Poor
—	200	150	100	80	50

Lincoln-Bossu

A 5.5mm or 6.35mm caliber folding trigger double-action revolver ("Velo-Dog" type), with solid-frame and hammerless.

NIB	Exc.	V.G.	Good	Fair	Poor
—	200	150	100	80	50

Left Wheeler

A Colt Police Positive copy in .32- or .38-caliber. Last revolver HDH manufactured.

NIB	Exc.	V.G.	Good	Fair	Poor
—	200	150	120	100	80

HEAVY EXPRESS INC.

Colorado Springs, Colorado

This company custom-built rifles, using its proprietary nonbelted cartridges from .260 Heavy Express Magnum to .416 Heavy Express Magnum. Company's rifles were built on Ruger Model 77 Mark II and Winchester Model 70 Classic actions. Barrels are 4140 chrome-moly blue and 416R stainless steel. Stocks include factory walnut, laminated or composite designs. Prices listed are for basic guns. Options are not included and will affect price.

Heavy Express Premier—Ruger M77 Mk II

Chambered for .260 HE Magnum, .284 HE Magnum or .300 HE Magnum. Choice of walnut, laminated or composite stocks. Note: Add $200 for stainless steel.

NIB	Exc.	V.G.	Good	Fair	Poor
1500	1150	800	600	350	180

Heavy Express Monarch—Winchester M70 Classic

Same as above. Built on Winchester M70 Classic action. Choice of stocks. Note: Add $200 for stainless steel.

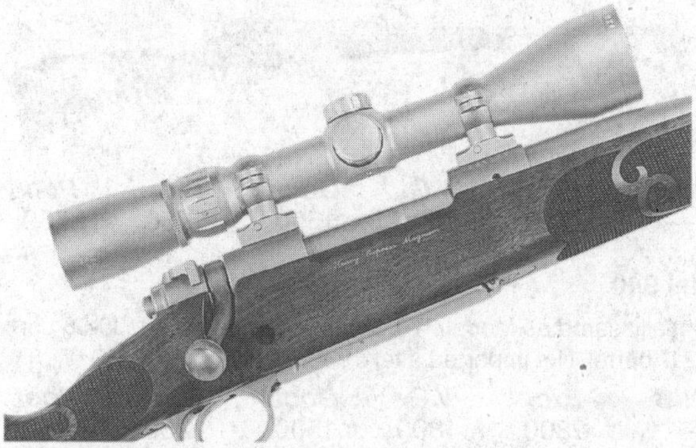

Close-up of Model 70 Classic stainless steel action.

NIB	Exc.	V.G.	Good	Fair	Poor
1780	1400	1000	750	500	250

Heavy Express Monarch—Ruger 77 MK II

Built on Ruger M77 action. Chambered for .338, .350, .375, .416 and .460 HE Magnum cartridges. Choice of stocks. Note: Add $200 for stainless steel.

NIB	Exc.	V.G.	Good	Fair	Poor
1780	1400	1000	750	500	250

Heavy Express Single-Shot—Ruger #1

Chambered in .300, .338, .350 and .416 HE Magnum cartridges. Choice of stocks. Note: Add $200 for stainless steel.

NIB	Exc.	V.G.	Good	Fair	Poor
1780	1400	1000	750	500	250

HECKLER & KOCH

Oberndorf/Neckar, Germany

End of WWII, the French dismantled Mauser factory as part of their reparations; buildings remained idle until 1949, when firearms production was again allowed in Germany. Heckler & Koch was formed as a machine tool enterprise and occupied vacant Mauser plant. In early 1950s, Edmund Heckler and Theodor Koch began to produce G3 automatic rifle based on Spanish CETME design and progressed to machine guns and sub-machine guns, eventually to production of commercial civilian rifles and pistols. In 1990, company got into financial difficulties because of a failed contract bid. In December 1990, French state consortium GIAT announced the purchase of Heckler and Koch, but a little more than a year later contract was canceled. Later in 1991, company was purchased by Royal Ordnance of Britain. In 2002, company was sold to a combined group of European investors and long-time company managers. SEE POLITICAL PANIC PRICING.

Model 91 A2

Recoil-operated rifle, with delayed-roller lock bolt. Chambered for .308 Winchester cartridge. Has 17.7" barrel, with military style aperture sights. Furnished with 20-round detachable magazine. Finished in matte black, with black plastic stock. Some areas of the country have made its ownership illegal.

NIB	Exc.	V.G.	Good	Fair	Poor
4000	3200	2500	2000	—	—

Model 91 A3

Simply Model 91, with retractable metal stock.

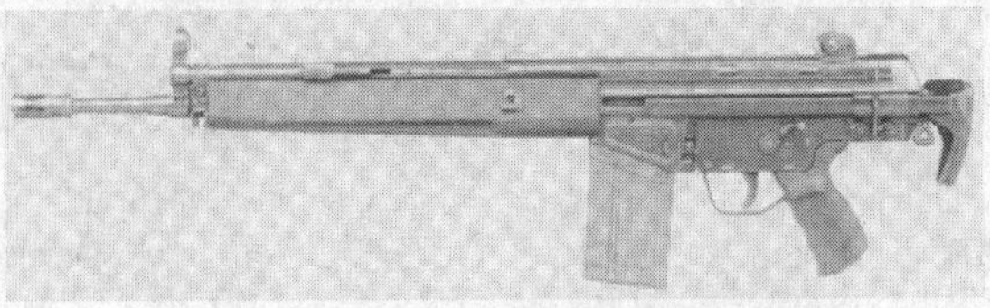

NIB	Exc.	V.G.	Good	Fair	Poor
—	4500	3500	2800	2500	—

Model 93 A2

Similar to Model 91, except chambered for .223 cartridge with 16.4" barrel. Magazine holds 25 rounds. Specifications same as Model 91.

NIB	Exc.	V.G.	Good	Fair	Poor
4000	3000	2300	1900	—	—

Model 93 A3

Model 93 with retractable metal stock.

NIB	Exc.	V.G.	Good	Fair	Poor
5000	4000	3000	2500	—	—

Model 94 A2

Carbine version chambered for 9mm Parabellum cartridge, with 16.5" barrel. Smaller-scaled weapon, with 15-shot magazine.

NIB	Exc.	V.G.	Good	Fair	Poor
3900	3300	2800	2400	—	—

Model 94 A3

Variation of Model 94, with addition of retractable metal stock.

NIB	Exc.	V.G.	Good	Fair	Poor
4100	3500	3000	2500	—	—

Model 270

Chambered for .22 LR cartridge. Sporting-styled rifle, with 16.5" barrel. Furnished with 5- or 20-round magazine. Blued, with checkered walnut stock. Discontinued in 1985.

NIB	Exc.	V.G.	Good	Fair	Poor
—	950	800	680	—	—

Model 300

Similar to Model 270, except chambered for .22 rimfire Magnum cartridge. Not imported after 1988.

NIB	Exc.	V.G.	Good	Fair	Poor
—	1450	1200	1000	700	500

Model 630

Chambered for .223. Features same roller-delayed semi-automatic action as found on paramilitary-type weapons. Sporting-style rifle with polished blue finish and checkered walnut stock. Barrel 17.7" long. Magazines offered hold 4- or 10-rounds. Importation discontinued in 1986.

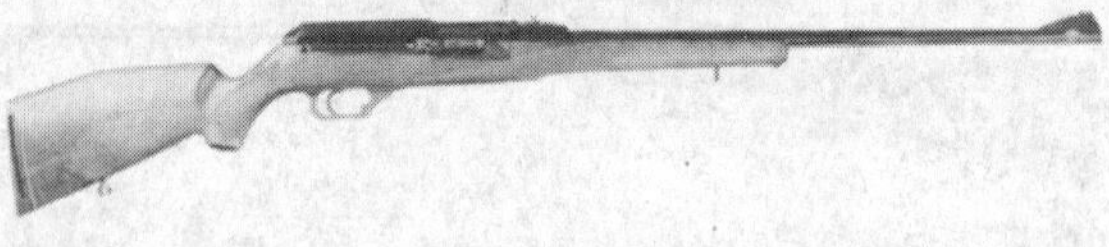

NIB	Exc.	V.G.	Good	Fair	Poor
—	1700	1450	1230	1000	750

Model 770

Similar to Model 630 except chambered for .308 Winchester cartridge and 19.7" barrel. Not imported after 1986.

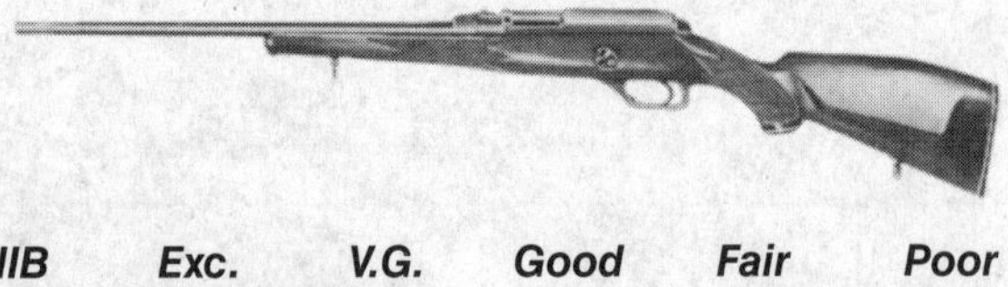

NIB	Exc.	V.G.	Good	Fair	Poor
—	2100	1800	1500	1250	750

Model 940

Essentially same as Model 770 except chambered for .30-06 cartridge, with 21" barrel. Not imported after 1986.

NIB	Exc.	V.G.	Good	Fair	Poor
—	2300	1800	1500	1250	750

Model SL6

Heckler & Koch's current sporting rifle chambered for .223 cartridge, with 17.7" barrel. Features same basic action as military versions. Matte black finish, walnut stock, with ventilated walnut handguard. Magazine holds 4 rounds.

NIB	Exc.	V.G.	Good	Fair	Poor
—	1600	1360	1150	980	750

Model SL7

Similar to SL6 except chambered for .308 Winchester cartridge and 3-round magazine.

NIB	Exc.	V.G.	Good	Fair	Poor
2500	1800	1400	1200	1000	750

Model SR9

Introduced into U.S. market after the federal government prohibited importation of H&K's other semi-automatic rifles. SR9 similar to HK91, but certified by BATF as a sporting rifle. Features special thumbhole stock made of Kevlar reinforced fiberglass. Action is a delayed-roller locked bolt semi-automatic design chambered for .308 Winchester cartridge. Barrel 19.7" in length and features adjustable rear sight, with hooded front sight. Weight 10.9 lbs.

NIB	Exc.	V.G.	Good	Fair	Poor
—	2100	1750	1500	—	—

Model SR9 (T) Target

Similar to standard model SR9, with addition of special MSG90 adjustable buttstock, PSG-1 trigger group and PSG-1 contoured hand grip. Weight 10.6 lbs.

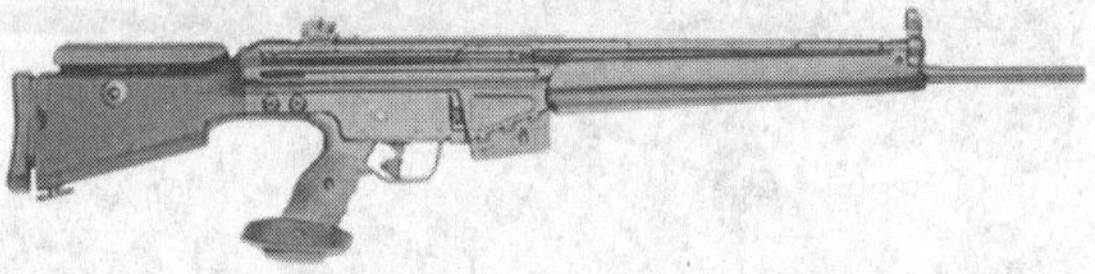

NIB	Exc.	V.G.	Good	Fair	Poor
—	2800	2380	2000	—	—

Model SR9 (TC) Target Competition

Similar to Model SR9 (T), with addition of PSG-1 adjustable buttstock. Weight 10.9 lbs.

NIB	Exc.	V.G.	Good	Fair	Poor
—	3400	2900	2500	—	—

BASR Model

Bolt-action rifle chambered for various popular calibers. Stainless steel barrel. Essentially custom built to customer's specifications. Stock is of Kevlar. Quite rare. Only 100 manufactured in 1968.

NIB	Exc.	V.G.	Good	Fair	Poor
—	4000	3600	2750	1300	800

PSG-1

High precision sniping rifle. Features delayed-roller semi-automatic action. Chambered for .308 Winchester cartridge and 5-shot magazine. Barrel length 25.6". Furnished with complete array of accessories including 6x42-power illuminated Hensoldt scope. Weight 17.8 lbs.

NIB	Exc.	V.G.	Good	Fair	Poor
—	14000	12000	10000	—	—

Model SL8-1

New generation .223 rifle modeled after military Model G36. Introduced in 2000. Built of carbon fiber polymer and gas operated. Thumbhole stock with cheekpiece. Barrel length 20.8". Magazine capacity 10 rounds. Adjustable sights. Weight about 8.6 lbs.

NIB	Exc.	V.G.	Good	Fair	Poor
1900	1650	1400	1200	—	—

SLB 2000

Introduced in 2001. Gas-operated semi-automatic rifle chambered for .30-06 cartridge. Receiver built of lightweight alloy. Barrel 16.7" in length and will accept interchangeable barrels, at some future date. Oil-finished walnut stock. Open sights, with both barrel and receiver drilled and tapped for scope mounts. Magazine capacity 2, 5 or 10 rounds. Weight about 7.25 lbs.

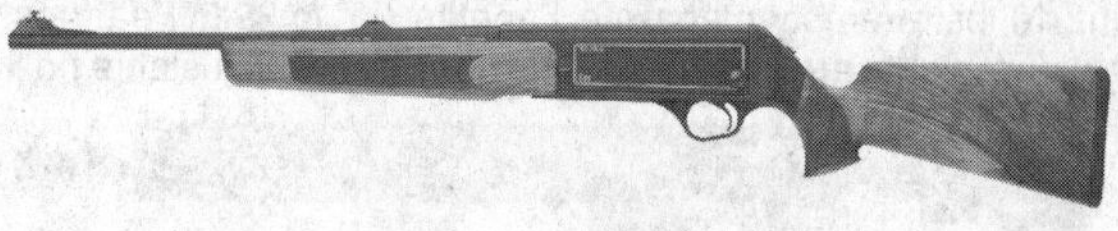

NIB	Exc.	V.G.	Good	Fair	Poor
1100	940	800	680	—	—

Model USC

Introduced in 2000. Semi-automatic blowback carbine derived from H&K's UMP sub-machine gun. Chambered for .45 ACP cartridge. Fitted with 16" barrel. Skeletonized stock. Accessory rail on top of receiver. Adjustable sights. Magazine capacity 10 rounds. Weight about 6 lbs.

NIB	Exc.	V.G.	Good	Fair	Poor
2000	1700	1400	1100	—	—

Model MP5 A5

Semi-automatic .22 LR replica of famous MP5 9mm submachine gun. Magazine capacity 25 rounds (10 were required). Barrel length 16.1", with compensator. Adjustable sights, retractable stock with pistol grip. Made by Walther and imported by Umarex.

NIB	Exc.	V.G.	Good	Fair	Poor
480	400	350	300	—	—

Model MR556A1

Caliber: .223 Remington/5.56 NATO. Capacity: 10+1. Barrel: 16.5". Weight: 8.9 lbs. Lengths: 33.9" to 37.68". Stock: Black synthetic adjustable. Features: Uses the gas piston system found on the HK 416 and G26, which does not introduce propellant gases and carbon fouling into the rifle's interior.

NIB	Exc.	V.G.	Good	Fair	Poor
2980	2800	2600	2400	—	—

MR556A1 FDE

Flat Dark Earth coloring.

NIB	Exc.	V.G.	Good	Fair	Poor
3500	2980	2530	2150	1830	1550

MR556A1 Competition Model

Introduced 2014. 5.56. Barrel: 16.5". OAL 37.68" extended; 33.90" retracted. 8.60 lbs. without magazine. Enhanced 2-stage trigger.

NIB	Exc.	V.G.	Good	Fair	Poor
2750	2340	1990	1690	1440	1220

Model MR762A1

Caliber: 7.62x51mm/.308 Win. Otherwise, similar to Model MR556A1. Weight: 10 lbs. w/empty magazine. Lengths: 36" to 39.5". Features: Various optional sights are available. The stock has five adjustable positions.

NIB	Exc.	V.G.	Good	Fair	Poor
4130	4000	3850	3630	—	—

MR762A1 Carbine

Similar to MR556A1, except 7.62x51mm chambering, 10- or 20-shot magazine, upper and lower accessory rails. Also made in LRP (Long Rifle Package), with Leupold 3-9x40mm VXR Patrol scope, LaRue Tactical BRM-6 bipod, collapsible stock with adjustable cheekpiece. Note: Add $2500 for LRP model.

NIB	Exc.	V.G.	Good	Fair	Poor
3550	3000	2600	2200	—	—

MR762A1 Long Rifle Package (LRP)

Caliber: .308 Win. Barrel: 16.5" medium -contour barrel, one 20-rd magazine. Introduced 2013.

NIB	Exc.	V.G.	Good	Fair	Poor
4000	3400	2890	—	—	—

MR762A1 Long Rifle Package II (LRP II)

Caliber: 7.62x51mm. Capacity: 10- or 20-round magazines. Barrel: 16.5" four lands and grooves, right twist, 1:11". Stock: Fully adjustable G28 buttstock. Sights: Leupold 3-9VX-R Patrol 3-9x40 mm scope, base, mounts. Weight: 10.42 lbs. Trigger: Two-stage. Overall Length: 36.5" to 40.5". Features: MR762 semi-auto rifle with LaRue/Harris bipod, new long 14.7" Modular Rail System (MRS) handguard, Blue Force Gear sling and sling mount, one 10-round and one 20-round magazine, OTIS cleaning kit, HK multi-tool, and Pelican Model 1720 case. SEE POLITICAL PANIC PRICING.

NIB	Exc.	V.G.	Good	Fair	Poor
7250	7000	6800	6150	—	—

MR762A1 Long Rifle Package III (LRP III)

Comes with Vortex Viper PSTII 3-15x44 FFP MRAD optic.

NIB	Exc.	V.G.	Good	Fair	Poor
8300	7060	6000	—	—	—

HK416 81000401

.22 LR/16.1". Semi-automatic rimfire rifle. Aluminum receiver, RIS (Rail Interface System) M-LOK. Retractable stock, pistol grip with storage compartment, adjustable flip up sights. Threaded muzzle 1/2x28. No. 81000401 comes with one 20-round magazine No. 81000402 has one 10-round magazine.

NIB	Exc.	V.G.	Good	Fair	Poor
350	300	250	220	180	160

Model MR308 A3

aliber: .308 Win. Barrel: 13, 16.5, 20 in. Weight: 9.4 lbs. Lengths: 32–35.2 in. with 13-in. barrel. Slim-line handguard with HKey mounting slots.

NIB	Exc.	V.G.	Good	Fair	Poor
5030	4280	3630	3090	2630	2230

PISTOLS

HK4

Blowback-operated semi-automatic pistol based on Mauser HSc design. Chambered for .22 LR, .25 ACP, .32 ACP and .380. These calibers easily converted by switching barrels, recoil springs and magazines. Rimfire model could be changed by rotating breechface. Conversion kits available for all calibers. Barrel 3" long; finish blued, with molded plastic thumb rest grips. Pistol sold from 1968-1973 as Harrington & Richardson HK4 and so marked. Discontinued in 1984.

.22 Caliber or .380 Caliber

NIB	Exc.	V.G.	Good	Fair	Poor
—	480	350	250	200	100

.25 Caliber or .32 Caliber

NIB	Exc.	V.G.	Good	Fair	Poor
—	350	300	250	200	100

Conversion Units

NIB	Exc.	V.G.	Good	Fair	Poor
—	150	120	90	60	30

P9

Single-action delayed-blowback semi-automatic pistol. Chambered for 9mm, 7.65mm Parabellum and .45 ACP. Action based on G-3 rifle mechanism. Barrel length 4". Pistol has internal hammer, thumb-operated hammer drop and decocking lever. Also a manual safety and loaded-chamber indicator. Finish is Parkerized. Grips are molded plastic and well contoured. Fixed sights. Manufactured between 1977 and 1984. Model rarer than P9S model.

NIB	Exc.	V.G.	Good	Fair	Poor
1000	800	650	400	300	200

P9S

Similar to Model P9 except action features double-action capability. Chambered for .45 ACP and 9mm Parabellum, with 5.5-in. barrel. Manufactured between 1977 and 1984.

NIB	Exc.	V.G.	Good	Fair	Poor
1280	1010	910	710	500	300

P9S Target Model

Similar to model P9S. Chambered for 9mm or .45 ACP cartridges. Adjustable sights and trigger. Discontinued in 1984.

NIB	Exc.	V.G.	Good	Fair	Poor
1950	1580	1210	860	760	650

P9S Competition

Similar to P9S target, with addition of barrel weights and special competition grips.

NIB	Exc.	V.G.	Good	Fair	Poor
4000	3260	2310	1960	1660	1450

VP 70Z

Blowback-operated semi-automatic chambered for 9mm Parabellum cartridge. Striker-fired and double-action-only. Barrel 4.5-in. long. Double-column magazine holds 18 rounds. Finish blued. Receiver and grip molded from plastic. Discontinued in 1984.

NIB	Exc.	V.G.	Good	Fair	Poor
750	680	610	500	460	410

P7 PSP

First of squeeze-cocked H&K pistols. Single-action semi-automatic placed in firing position by pressure on front of grip strap. This moves striker into battery; firing is then accomplished by single-action pressure on trigger, releasing grip strap cocking device and decocking mechanism. This particular model does not have extended finger guard on trigger. Does not have ambidextrous safety. Discontinued in 1984.

NIB	Exc.	V.G.	Good	Fair	Poor
3000	2500	2000	1500	800	520

P7 K3

This is "Squeeze Cocker" chambered for .380 or .22 LR caliber. Has a recoil buffer that is oil-filled and 3.8-in. barrel. Magazine holds 8 rounds. Introduced in 1988.

NIB	Exc.	V.G.	Good	Fair	Poor
5000	4000	2500	1500	880	760

.22 Caliber Conversion Kit

This unit will convert P7 K3 to fire .22 LR cartridge.

NIB	Exc.	V.G.	Good	Fair	Poor
1500	1200	650	300	150	80

.32 ACP Caliber Conversion Kit

NIB	Exc.	V.G.	Good	Fair	Poor
1000	900	400	100	80	50

P7 M8

This is an 8-shot newer version of "Squeeze Cocker". Has heat-shield finger guard, ambidextrous safety, 4-in. barrel and 3-dot sight system. Finish is matte blue or nickel, with stippled black plastic grips. No longer in production. Note: Add $100 for night sights introduced in 1993.

NIB	Exc.	V.G.	Good	Fair	Poor
3700	3000	2000	1500	880	760

P7 M10

New addition to P7 series in 1993. Variation chambered for .40 S&W cartridge. Magazine holds 10 rounds. Finish available blue or nickel. Weight 2.69 lbs. Note: Add $100 for night sights.

NIB	Exc.	V.G.	Good	Fair	Poor
4500	3500	2750	2000	1480	1250

P7 M13

Version similar to P7 M8 except it has a double column 13-shot magazine. Note: Add $100 for night sights.

NIB	Exc.	V.G.	Good	Fair	Poor
5000	3750	3000	2000	1480	1250

SP89

Introduced in early 1990s. Large frame semi-automatic pistol chambered for 9mm cartridge. Features 15-round magazine and square notch rear sight, with hooded front sight. Has 4.5" barrel; 13" overall; weight 4.4 lbs. In August 1993 no longer imported due to ban on assault pistols.

NIB	Exc.	V.G.	Good	Fair	Poor
5500	4500	3500	2500	—	—

USP SERIES

Late in 1999, H&K began shipping its USPs and Mark 23s with an internal locking system. This lock-out is installed in the grip and blocks movement of hammer, trigger and slide. Operated with two pronged key supplied with pistol. This system is in addition to traditional trigger lock that is sold with each H&K firearm. In 2001, stainless steel version of these pistols were discontinued.

In 2005, H&K offered a limited edition run of color frame variations for USP line. These colors are Desert tan, green and gray.

Gray: USP 45 and USP 40 Compact

Green: USP 45, USP 40, USP 40 Compact and USP 45

Tactical Desert Tan: USP 45, USP 40, USP 40 Compact and USP 45 Tactical and Mark 23

Retail prices are same for these color variations as standard black frame pistols

USP 40

Introduced in 1993, this new semi-automatic H&K pistol features a new design that incorporates a short recoil modified Browning action. Chambered for .40 S&W cartridge, this model has 4.13" barrel and magazine capacity of 13 rounds. Stainless steel model introduced in 1996. Weight 1.74 lbs. Available in seven different variations from traditional double-action to double-action-only and various safety locations and styles. Variants numbered by H&K are listed.

1.DA/SA with safe position and control lever on left side of frame.
2.DA/SA with safe position and control lever on right side of frame.
3.DA/SA without safe position and decocking lever on left side of frame.
4.DA/SA without safe position and decocking lever on right side of frame.
5.DA only with safe position and safety lever on left side of frame.
6.DA only with safe position and safety lever on right side of frame.
7.DA only without control lever.
9.DA/SA with safe position and safety lever on left side of frame.
10.DA/SA with safe position and safety lever on right side of frame.

Note: Add $45 for stainless steel model.

NIB	Exc.	V.G.	Good	Fair	Poor
900	800	650	300	250	120

USP 9

Same as USP 40, but chambered for 9mm cartridge. Magazine holds 16 rounds. Weight 1.66 lbs. Choice of seven variations as listed above for USP 40. New for 1993. Note: Add $45 for stainless steel.

NIB	Exc.	V.G.	Good	Fair	Poor
900	800	650	300	250	120

USP 9SD

Variation of USP 9 fitted with target sights to see over an optional sound suppressor. Barrel threaded left-hand. Does not have O-ring and does not require thread cap. Introduced in 2004.

NIB	Exc.	V.G.	Good	Fair	Poor
980	820	680	320	280	150

USP 40 Compact

Same as 9mm Compact model. Chambered for .40 S&W cartridge. Weight about 27 oz. All other dimensions the same.

NIB	Exc.	V.G.	Good	Fair	Poor
900	800	650	300	250	120

USP 45

Introduced in 1995. Slightly larger than 9mm and .40 S&W models. Barrel length 4.41"; overall 7.87"; weight 1.9 lbs. USP 45 available in same variants as other USP models. Magazine capacity 12 rounds. Note: Add $45 for stainless steel.

NIB	Exc.	V.G.	Good	Fair	Poor
1100	950	780	500	350	200

USP 9 Compact

Introduced in 1997, this 9mm model is smaller version of full size USP 9. Internal differences due to size. Barrel length .58"; overall length 6.81". Magazine capacity 10 rounds. Weight about 26 oz. Available with stainless steel slide. Note: Add $45 to NIB price.

NIB	Exc.	V.G.	Good	Fair	Poor
800	600	450	300	200	150

USP Compact LEM (Law Enforcement Modification)

Introduced in 2002. Identical to USP Compact .40 S&W Variant 7, with double-action-only trigger. Special trigger mechanism improves double-action trigger performance and reduces weight of pull between 7.5 and 8.5 lbs. Offered in blued finish.

NIB	Exc.	V.G.	Good	Fair	Poor
1150	1000	750	500	300	150

USP 45 Match

Introduced in 1997. Match grade variation of USP. Chambered for .45 ACP cartridge. Fitted with 6.02" barrel, with barrel weight assembly. Adjustable rear and target front sight. Adjustable trigger stop. Blued finish. Weight about 38 oz. Available in stainless steel version. Note: Add $60 for stainless steel.

NIB	Exc.	V.G.	Good	Fair	Poor
1500	1300	1050	800	480	280

USP 45 Compact

Introduced in 1997. Chambered for .45 ACP cartridge. Has 3.8" barrel; overall length 7.1"; weight about 28 oz. Magazine capacity 8 rounds.

NIB	Exc.	V.G.	Good	Fair	Poor
1100	950	780	500	350	200

USP 45 Compact Tactical

Blued semi-automatic .45 ACP. Double-action with 4.46" barrel, 8 round capacity. Polymer grip. Weight about 27.5 oz.

NIB	*Exc.*	*V.G.*	*Good*	*Fair*	*Poor*
1100	950	780	500	350	200

USP .357 Compact

Introduced in mid-1998. Pistol built on same frame as .40 S&W Compact. Chambered for .357 SIG cartridge. Magazine capacity 10 rounds. Weight about 28 oz. Also was made in full-size version, with 4.25" barrel. Discontinued in 2005.

NIB	*Exc.*	*V.G.*	*Good*	*Fair*	*Poor*
850	700	500	380	250	150

USP 45 Expert

Introduced in fall of 1998. This .45 ACP pistol fitted with 5.2" barrel and slide, with 10-round magazine. Overall length 8.7"; height 1.87"; weight about 30 oz. Adjustable low-profile sights. Limited availability between 1,000 and 2,500 pistols. In 2003 offered chambered for 9mm and .40 S&W cartridge. Note: H&K price reduction in 2005.

NIB	*Exc.*	*V.G.*	*Good*	*Fair*	*Poor*
1360	1200	900	600	300	150

USP 45 Tactical

Introduced in 1998. Enhanced version of USP 45. Fitted with 4.9" threaded barrel, with adjustable high profile target sights. Overall length 8.6"; weight about 36 oz. Magazine capacity 10 rounds. Availability limited to 1,000 and 2,500 pistols.

NIB	*Exc.*	*V.G.*	*Good*	*Fair*	*Poor*
1100	850	620	420	300	180

USP Elite

Introduced in 2003. Features 6.2" barrel chambered for 9mm or .45 ACP cartridge. Fitted with match trigger, adjustable trigger stop, adjustable micrometer rear target sights, extended floorplate and loaded chamber indicator. Weight about 30 oz. empty. Magazine capacity 10 rounds. Note: H&K price reduction in 2005.

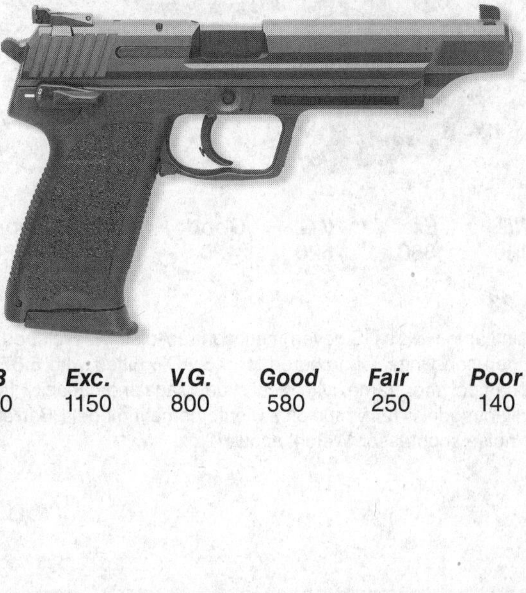

NIB	*Exc.*	*V.G.*	*Good*	*Fair*	*Poor*
1400	1150	800	580	250	140

USP 45 50th Anniversary Commemorative

Limited to 1,000 pistols. Features high polish blue with 50th Anniversary logo engraved in gold and silver. Supplied with custom-made wooden box and commemorative coin. Introduced in 2000.

NIB	Exc.	V.G.	Good	Fair	Poor
1100	850	620	420	300	180

P2000 GPM

Introduced in 2003. Similar to USP compact LEM pistol. Several modular features, such as interchangeable back straps, ambidextrous slide release and short trigger reset distance. Chambered for 9mm or .40 S&W cartridge. Fitted with 3.62" barrel. Fixed sights. Magazine capacity: 12 rounds .40 S&W and .357 SIG; 13 rounds 9mm. Weight about 22 oz. Note: Add $30 for magazine disconnect.

NIB	Exc.	V.G.	Good	Fair	Poor
880	700	500	350	250	120

P2000 SK

Semi-automatic double-action pistol is a subcompact version of P2000. Chambered for 9mm or .40 S&W cartridge as well as .357 SIG. Has 2.5" barrel; overall length 6.4". Magazine capacity: 10 rounds 9mm; 12 rounds .357 SIG; 9 rounds .40 S&W. Weight about 21 oz. Introduced in 2004.

NIB	Exc.	V.G.	Good	Fair	Poor
1100	850	620	420	300	180

Mark 23

Very similar to H&K's US government contract pistol. Developed for special Operation Units. Chambered for .45 ACP. Fitted with 5.87" barrel. Pistol has polymer frame, with steel slide. Magazine capacity 10 rounds on civilian models; 12 rounds on law enforcement models. Barrel threaded for noise suppressor. Weight about 42 oz.

NIB	Exc.	V.G.	Good	Fair	Poor
2200	1850	1200	880	500	250

HK45

Full-size autoloader chambered in .45 ACP. Features include polygonal bore, front and rear slide serrations, integrated Picatinny rail, ambi mag release levers, interchangeable backstrap panels, polymer frame, modular action design allowing for double-/single-action or double-action-only operation. Measures 7.52" overall length. 10+1 capacity.

NIB	Exc.	V.G.	Good	Fair	Poor
1100	850	620	420	300	180

HK45 Compact

Similar to above, with 8 round capacity; overall length 7.2".

NIB	Exc.	V.G.	Good	Fair	Poor
1100	850	620	420	300	180

P30

Polymer-frame 9mm autoloader. Features include loaded chamber indicator, integral Picatinny rail, oversized triggerguard, double-/single-action firing mode with decocker, "Hostile Environment" black finish, ambidextrous, oversized controls. Note: Add 10 percent for longslide variant. Deduct $200 for subcompact P30SK.

NIB	*Exc.*	*V.G.*	*Good*	*Fair*	*Poor*
950	750	600	450	250	150

VP SERIES

VP9/VP40

Calibers: 9mm, .40 S&W. Capacities: 10- or 15-round magazine. .40 S&W (10 or 13). Barrel: 4.09". Weight: 25.6 oz. Length: 7.34". overall. Sights: Fixed three-dot, drift adjustable. Features: Striker-fired system with HK-enhanced light pull trigger. Ergonomic grip design with interchangeable backstraps and side panels.

NIB	*Exc.*	*V.G.*	*Good*	*Fair*	*Poor*
800	750	650	600	520	—

VP9 Match

NIB	*Exc.*	*V.G.*	*Good*	*Fair*	*Poor*
1030	880	760	710	630	—

VP9L OR

NIB	*Exc.*	*V.G.*	*Good*	*Fair*	*Poor*
990	880	900	790	700	—

VP9SK

NIB	*Exc.*	*V.G.*	*Good*	*Fair*	*Poor*
750	730	650	580	460	—

VP9 Tactical OR

NIB	*Exc.*	*V.G.*	*Good*	*Fair*	*Poor*
1000	930	870	750	550	—

HEINZELMANN, C.E.

Plochipnam Neckar, Germany

Heim

A 6.35mm semi-automatic pistol, with 2" barrel. Detachable magazine holds 6 rounds. Weight about 11 oz. Manufactured during 1930s. Marked on frame "C.E. Heinzelmann Plochingen A.N. Patent Heim-6.35".

NIB	*Exc.*	*V.G.*	*Good*	*Fair*	*Poor*
—	800	680	550	400	200

HEIZER DEFENSE

Pevely, Missouri

PS1 Pocket Shotgun

Single-shot pistol chambered for .45 Colt/.410 shotshell rounds. Tip-up barrel with titanium frame. Choice of black, polished silver or several bright color finishes. Introduced in 2013.

NIB	*Exc.*	*V.G.*	*Good*	*Fair*	*Poor*
400	350	300	250	200	150

HELFRICHT

Zella-Mehlis, Germany

Model 3 Pocket Pistol

A 6.35mm semi-automatic pistol, with 2" barrel and 6-shot magazine. Weight about 11 oz. Blued, with checkered black plastic grips having monogram "KH" cast in them. Pistols have no external sights.

Courtesy James Rankin

NIB	*Exc.*	*V.G.*	*Good*	*Fair*	*Poor*
—	500	400	300	200	100

Model 4 Pocket Pistol

Semi-automatic pistol in caliber 6.35mm. Checkered black plastic grips, with "KH" logo on each grip.

Courtesy James Rankin

NIB	Exc.	V.G.	Good	Fair	Poor
—	400	300	200	150	100

HENRION & DASSY

Liege, Belgium

Semi-Automatic

A 6.35mm semi-automatic pistol, with 2.5" barrel and 5-shot magazine. Blued, with black plastic grips marked "H&D".

NIB	Exc.	V.G.	Good	Fair	Poor
—	600	500	450	380	280

HENRY

See—WINCHESTER

HENRY, ALEXANDER

Edinburgh, Scotland

Noted for both the rifling system he developed and falling block single-shot rifles he made.

Single-Shot Rifle (Antique)

High-grade single-shot features true falling-block action that is activated by a side lever on action. Available in popular European cartridges of the era. Barrel length varies from 22" to 28". Rifle exhibits fine quality materials and workmanship. Select-grade walnut stock and schnabel forend are hand checkered. Finish scroll-engraved and blued. Company manufactured firearms from 1869 until 1895.

Exc.	Fine	V.G.	Good	Fair	Poor
3800	1500	1100	700	400	280

Double Rifle (Antique)

Side-by-side double-barreled Express Rifle chambered for .500/450 Black Powder Express cartridge. Damascus barrels and double triggers. Gun is hammerless and features ornate scroll engraving as well as a high-grade hand checkered walnut stock and forend. Furnished with fitted leather case and accessories. Manufactured in 1890s. Values are approximate only. Each gun must be evaluated for configuration, decoration, caliber, and action type. Original casing and accessories may add substantially to value.

Exc.	Fine	V.G.	Good	Fair	Poor
9000	5000	3370	1750	800	560

HENRY REPEATING ARMS COMPANY

Bayonne, New Jersey

Henry Repeating Arms was started in 1996 by Louis Imperato and his son Anthony in Brooklyn, New York, producing the Henry Classic Lever Action .22. Since the first shipments were made in March 1997 more than 1 million have been produced. Henry Repeating Arms takes its name from Benjamin Tyler Henry, the inventor who patented the first repeating rifle in 1860, known as the Henry rifle. There is no affiliation or lineage to Benjamin Tyler Henry or to the New Haven Arms Company. Anthony Imperato secured the trademark to the Henry name in 1996. The company headquarters is now located in Bayonne, New Jersey, and a second manufacturing facility is in Rice Lake, Wisconsin.

RIMFIRE RIFLES

Classic Lever Action

Henry has made more than a million of the original Classic Model. Shoots .22 Short (21 rounds), Long (17) or Long Rifle (15) with a round barrel 18.5" long, overall length of 36.5" and weight of 5.25 lbs. Walnut stock with shotgun buttplate. Fully adjustable rear sight with hooded front. Receiver grooved for 3/8" rings. Note: Add $5 for Youth Model with 16.125" barrel and 13" LOP.

NIB	Exc.	V.G.	Good	Fair	Poor
320	280	230	200	120	80

Classic Carbine

Similar to above with 16.125" barrel, 34" OAL, and large loop lever.

NIB	Exc.	V.G.	Good	Fair	Poor
350	290	250	220	130	80

Youth Model

Similar to carbine above, with overall length of 33".

NIB	Exc.	V.G.	Good	Fair	Poor
300	250	220	180	150	100

Classic Magnum

Chambered in .22 WMR with 19.25" round barrel, 11-round capacity, 37.5" OAL, Checkered walnut stock and forend, weighing 5.5 lbs. Note: Add $50 for .17 HMR with checkered Monte Carlo stock and forend.

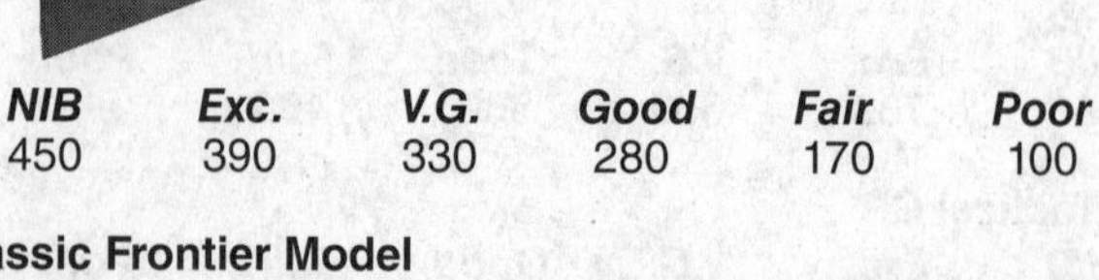

NIB	Exc.	V.G.	Good	Fair	Poor
450	390	330	280	170	100

Classic Frontier Model

Similar to Classic Model but with 20" octagon barrel. Fully adjustable semi-buckhorn rear sight, brass bead front. Receiver grooved for 3/8" rings. Note: Add $85 for 20.5" barrel in .22 WMR or 20" barrel in .17 HMR; Add $25 for 24" barrel in .22 LR; $100 for 24" barrel in .22 WMR; $20 for threaded barrel in all calibers.

NIB	Exc.	V.G.	Good	Fair	Poor
420	350	300	250	150	90

Golden Boy Rimfire

Lever-action rifle in .22 S, L, LR with 20" octagon barrel, "Brasslite" finish receiver, brass buttplate and barrel band, walnut stock and forend and weight of 6.75 lbs. Fully adjustable semi-buckhorn rear sight, brass bead front. Drilled and tapped for scope mounts. Note: Add $50 for .22 WMR with 20.5" octagon barrel; $65 for .17 HMR with 20" octagon barrel.

NIB	Exc.	V.G.	Good	Fair	Poor
490	420	350	300	180	110

Golden Boy Deluxe

Chambered for .22 LR cartridge. Fitted with 20" octagon barrel. Fancy walnut stock. Deeply engraved receiver.

NIB	Exc.	V.G.	Good	Fair	Poor
1400	1200	950	800	500	200

Deluxe Engraved Golden Boy Magnum

Similar to Golden Boy Deluxe, but chambered in .22 WMR. Features deluxe deep-cut German-style engraving on receiver. Introduced 2006.

NIB	Exc.	V.G.	Good	Fair	Poor
1450	1250	1000	820	520	220

Golden Boy Deluxe 3rd Edition

Deluxe models are limited to 1,000 and are currently in the 3rd Edition. As above, but with engraved Brasslite receiver and barrel band, fancy American walnut stock and forend. Note: Add $40 for .22 WMR; Add $70 for .17 HMR.

NIB	Exc.	V.G.	Good	Fair	Poor
1370	1160	990	840	500	300

Silver Boy

Lever-action rimfire rifle similar to Golden Boy, but has a nickel-plated receiver, barrel band and buttplate. The 20" blued barrel is octagon shaped, with Buckhorn adjustable rear sight and bead front. Chambered in .22 LR, .22 WMR or .17 HMR. Also made in youth model with 16.5" barrel, shorter length of pull. Note: Add $50 for .22 Magnum; $75 for .17 HMR.

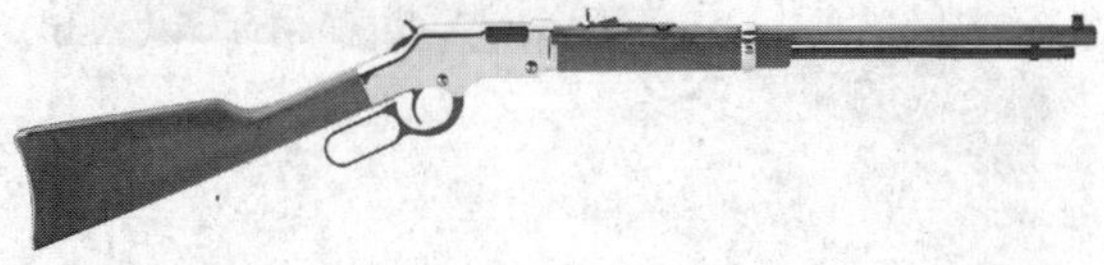

NIB	Exc.	V.G.	Good	Fair	Poor
520	450	400	350	300	280

Varmint Express

Lever-action rifle chambered for .17 HMR cartridge and fitted with 20" round barrel. Checkered American walnut stock. Scope mount included. Magazine capacity 11 rounds. Weight about 5.75 lbs.

NIB	Exc.	V.G.	Good	Fair	Poor
480	400	350	300	200	120

Small Game Rifle and Carbine

Classic model chambered for .22 S, L and LR or .22 WMR. Barrel is 20" or 16.25" for Carbine model. Fully adjustable Skinner peep sight with gold bead front. Large loop lever with walnut stock. Add $85 for .22 WMR.

NIB	Exc.	V.G.	Good	Fair	Poor
450	390	330	280	170	100

Garden Gun

A smoothbore, round 18.5" barrel for .22 LR Shotshells, the Garden Gun has a black ash stock, otherwise as the Classic above.

NIB	Exc.	V.G.	Good	Fair	Poor
370	320	270	230	140	80

Pump-Action Rifle

Introduced in 1999. .22-caliber fitted with 18.25" barrel and chambered for .22 LR cartridge. Walnut stock and adjustable rear sight. Weight about 5.5 lbs. Discontinued.

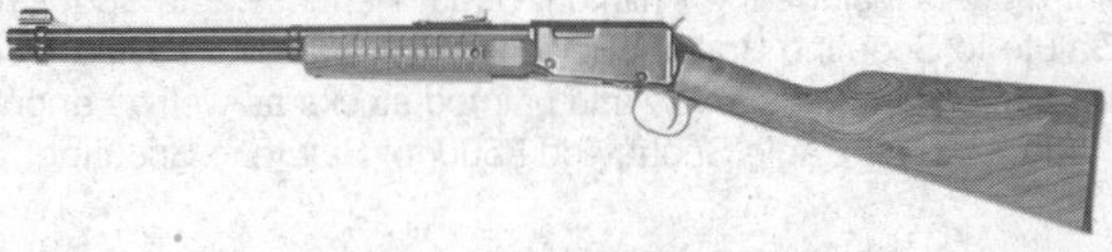

NIB	Exc.	V.G.	Good	Fair	Poor
350	250	180	140	100	80

Mini Bolt

The Mini Bolt-action rifle is chambered in .22 S, L or LR with a 16.25" stainless steel barrel in a 1-piece synthetic stock with 11.5⊠ LOP, weight of 3.25lbs. and OAL of 30.5". Fitted with adjustable Williams Fire Sights using two bright green fiber-optic dots in the rear and a red dot front bead. Stock colors include black, orange and Muddy Girl.

NIB	Exc.	V.G.	Good	Fair	Poor
250	220	180	150	100	60

Pump-Action .22 Octagon Rifle

Pump action rifle with 20" octagon barrel in .22 S, L and LR or .22 WMR. Fitted with semi-buckhorn rear sight and bead front, OAL of 38.5", weight 6 lbs., receiver grooved for 3/8" rings. Note: Add $30 for .22 WMR.

NIB	Exc.	V.G.	Good	Fair	Poor
500	430	360	300	190	110

US Survival AR-7 Rifle

Like the original AR-7 from 1959, the Henry U.S. Survival Rifle is a take-down semi-automatic .22 LR weighing 3.5 lbs. with an OAL of 16.5⊠ with the components stowed in the buttstock. The steel barrel is covered in tough ABS plastic for corrosion resistance. Available in black, True Timber Kanati Camo, and True Timber Viper Western Camo. Equipped with an adjustable rear sight and a blade front sight. Note: Add $50 for camo finishes.

NIB	Exc.	V.G.	Good	Fair	Poor
270	230	190	160	100	60

US AR-7 Rifle w/Survival Pack

The Henry Survival Pack is organized around 3.5-pound black AR-7 and comes in a Grab-and-Go black nylon pack that has Datrex 1000-calorie emergency food packet, Aquamira Frontier Straw, ESEE Fire Steel, Buck Rival 1-hand opening folding knife with 2.75-inch stainless steel blade, H&H Mylar Emergency Hypothermia Blanket, 100' of MIL-C-5040H Type III green camo paracord and a SWAT-T black stretch, wrap, and tuck tourniquet that doubles as a pressure bandage and elastic covering wrap.

NIB	Exc.	V.G.	Good	Fair	Poor
480	400	350	300	180	100

Boy Scouts of America

Henry's has created several rimfire Boy Scouts of America tribute rifles. Current models include the Philmont Scout Ranch, Eagle Scout Tribute and Salute to Scouting Special Editions. All feature increasing levels of ornamentation such as carved and painted stocks as well as engraving. Note: Add $350 for Eagle Scout; Add $500 for Salute to Scouting.

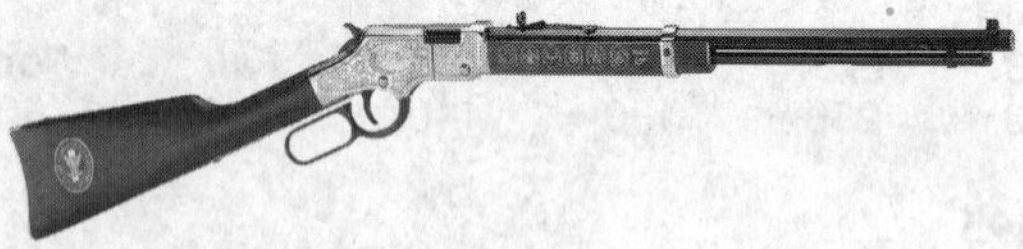

NIB	Exc.	V.G.	Good	Fair	Poor
620	520	450	380	230	140

Mare's Leg .22

Inspired by the gun carried by Steve McQueen in the "Wanted: Dead or Alive" TV series, the Mare's Leg receiver is similar to the Classic but with 12.875" barrel, 10 round capacity (.22 LR; 16 in .22 Short), an abruptly shortened American walnut stock and large loop lever. Note: Add $10 for .22 WMR (9 round capacity).

NIB	Exc.	V.G.	Good	Fair	Poor
400	340	290	250	150	90

SILVER SERIES RIMFIRE

Golden Boy Silver

Lever-action rifle in .22 S, L, LR with 20" octagon barrel, nickel-plated receiver, buttplate and barrel band, walnut stock and forend and weight of 6.75 lbs. Fully adjustable semi-buckhorn rear sight, brass bead front. Drilled and tapped for scope mounts. A Youth Model with 13" LOP and 17" barrel and a Cowboy Action Frontier Carbine "Evil Roy" edition with large loop lever with 17" octagon barrel is priced similarly to the basic model. Note: Add $40 for .22 WMR with 20.5" octagon barrel; $65 for .17 HMR with 20" octagon barrel.

NIB	Exc.	V.G.	Good	Fair	Poor
550	470	400	340	200	120

Silver Eagle

Lever-action rifle in .22 S, L, LR with 20" octagon barrel, engraved in a similar style to the original Henry presented to President Lincoln's Sec. of Navy Gideon Welles in 1860, nickel-plated receiver, buttplate and barrel band, walnut stock and forend and weight of 6.75 lbs. Fully adjustable semi-buckhorn rear sight, brass bead front. Drilled and tapped for scope mounts. Note: Add $30 for .22 WMR with 20.5" octagon barrel; $40 for .17 HMR with 20" octagon barrel.

NIB	Exc.	V.G.	Good	Fair	Poor
770	660	560	480	290	170

American Beauty and American Eagle

Sharing features with the Golden Silver Boy above, the American Beauty's receiver is engraved with an added 14k gold rose, fancy American walnut with 20" octagon barrel in .22 S, L and LR. The American Eagle features a checkered and carved ivory-colored American walnut stock with plain nickel-plated receiver. Note: Add $25 for American Eagle.

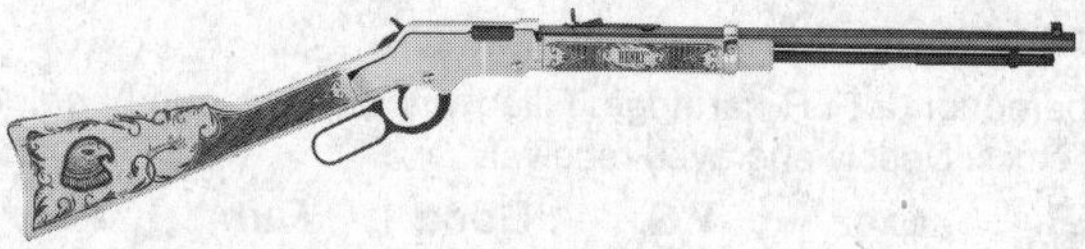

NIB	Exc.	V.G.	Good	Fair	Poor
820	700	590	500	300	180

Golden Eagle and Silver Eagle 2nd Edition

As Silver Eagle above but with a flying eagle as the motif for the engraving. In .22 S, L and LR only. Note: Add $50 for Golden Eagle with 24k gold eagle.

NIB	Exc.	V.G.	Good	Fair	Poor
770	660	560	480	290	170

CENTERFIRE RIFLES

Big Boy Classic Rifle and Carbine

A modern lever action rifle with brass receiver and barrel band, 20" octagon barrel with removable tube magazine, semi-buckhorn rear and white bead front sight. Drilled and tapped for scope mounts. SASS approved, the Big Boy holds 10 rounds chambered for .45 Colt, .44 Magnum/.44 Special, .41 Mag, .357/.38 Spec., .327 Federal Mag/.32 H&R Mag. A carbine version is also available in the calibers and features above, but with 16.5" barrel, holding 7 rounds and with large loop lever. Note: Add $85 for Silver Boy (.45 Colt, .44 Mag and .357 only). Premium for .357 Mag.

NIB	Exc.	V.G.	Good	Fair	Poor
830	700	600	500	300	190

Big Boy Steel Rifles and Carbines

All the calibers and sights as above but with blue-steel receiver and round barrel, checkered walnut stock and forend with solid rubber recoil pad. Weight 7 lbs.

NIB	Exc.	V.G.	Good	Fair	Poor
790	670	570	480	290	180

Big Boy Deluxe Engraved .44 Magnum

Similar to Big Boy, with deluxe deep-cut German-style engraving on receiver. Introduced 2006.

NIB	Exc.	V.G.	Good	Fair	Poor
1350	1100	850	550	280	180

Big Boy .44 Magnum "Wildlife Edition"

Similar to Big Boy .44 Magnum. Forend and buttstock laser-engraved with whitetail deer scenes. Introduced in 2007.

NIB	Exc.	V.G.	Good	Fair	Poor
880	750	620	500	250	120

Big Boy .45 Colt "Cowboy Edition"

Similar to Big Boy .45 Colt. Forend and buttstock laser-engraved with Old West scenes. Introduced in 2007.

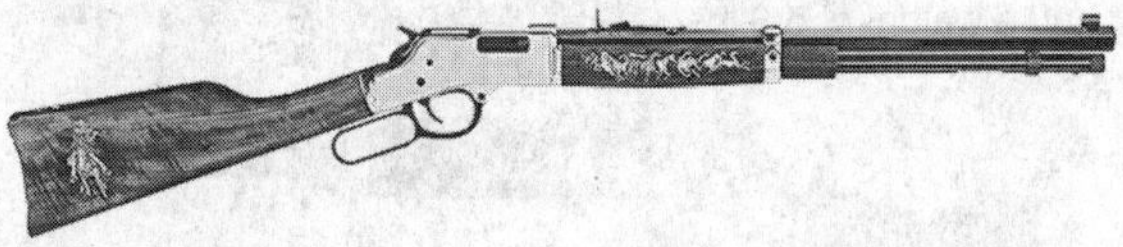

NIB	Exc.	V.G.	Good	Fair	Poor
1350	1100	850	550	280	180

Big Boy X Model

A matte-blue carbine with 17.4" round barrel threaded 5/8-24, chambered in .45 Colt, .44 Mag or .357 Mag, fully adjustable fiber optic sights, drilled and tapped for scope mounts, black synthetic pistol grip stock and forend, solid rubber recoil pad, OAL of 36.3" and a weight of 7.3 lbs. Has 7-round removable tube magazine and the addition of a side loading gate. Large loop lever and M-Lok slots and Picatinny rail under forend.

NIB	Exc.	V.G.	Good	Fair	Poor
830	700	600	500	300	190

Big Boy Case Hardened Rifle and Carbine

The Big Boy action with removable tube magazine system in case-hardened steel with blued 20" barrel (rifle, 10 rounds) or 16.5" (carbine; 7 rounds), semi-buckhorn rear and bead front sight. Drilled and tapped for scope mounts. Calibers include .45 Colt, .44 Mag/.44 Spec., .357 Mag/.38 Spec. Checkered walnut stock and forend, with solid rubber recoil pad. Carbine comes with large loop lever. Introduced in 2018.

NIB	Exc.	V.G.	Good	Fair	Poor
930	790	670	570	340	200

Tribute Series

The Golden Boy Silver lends itself to embellishment and Henry has a growing stable of models with various degrees of engraving and stock carving. Tribute Editions include Texas Tribute, American Rodeo, Shriner Int., Military Service (1st, 2nd) 2nd Amendment, Fraternal Order of Eagles, Coal Miner (1st and 2nd) American Farmer, Law Enforcement, Firefighter, Truckers, American Railroad, Emergency Medical Services, Freemasons and American Oilman (Big Boy .44 Mag). The Patriot Series includes a God Bless America (rimfire and Big Boy) and Stand for the Flag versions. MSRP's range from $990 to $1260, and most will be found in pristine condition. The prices shown below are an average of the high and low prices of all these Tribute rifles rather than a detailed reference. Check Henry's website for the original retail.

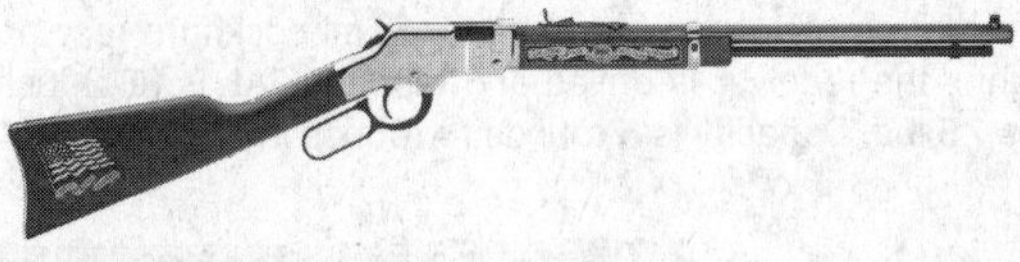

NIB	Exc.	V.G.	Good	Fair	Poor
950	820	690	590	350	210

Big Boy All Weather

In same calibers as above, but with hard-chrome finish on receiver and 20" round barrel, walnut stock with black all-weather coating. Fully adjustable semi-buckhorn sights, drilled and tapped for scope. Rifle length only.

NIB	Exc.	V.G.	Good	Fair	Poor
930	790	670	570	340	200

Big Boy Deluxe 3rd Editions

Current Big Boy Deluxe Editions include the Engraved 3rd Edition and Silver Deluxe Engraved. Same features as the Big Boy Classic, but only in the rifle configuration with 20" octagon barrel in .45 Colt, .44 Mag or .357 Mag. Hand engraved receiver and barrel band, fancy American walnut stock. The Big Boy Silver features a solid aluminum-bronze alloy receiver. Only 1,000 of each caliber are made.

NIB	Exc.	V.G.	Good	Fair	Poor
1750	1490	1260	1080	650	390

Big Boy Special Editions II

A Big Boy Classic in a "Cowboy" edition in .45 Colt or "Wildlife" edition in .44 Mag, both with 20" octagon barrel. The "Cowboy" has a stock depicting a band of cowboys huddled around an open fire. The forearm has the image of a thundering herd of horses, kicking up dust. The Wildlife stock and forearms is engraved with images of elk, white-tailed deer and grouse. The engraving on these editions is then hand painted. Introduced in 2007.

NIB	Exc.	V.G.	Good	Fair	Poor
1280	1080	920	780	470	280

Lever Action

Octagon-barreled brass-frame action has American walnut stock with brass buttplate and barrel band. Round-barreled steel-frame action has checkered walnut stock with solid rubber recoil pad. Both have semi-buckhorn rear and bead front sight and are drilled and tapped for scope mounts. Available in .30-30 or .45-70 with 5-round (.30-30) or 4-round (.45-70) removable tube magazine. Note: Add $90 for brass frame.

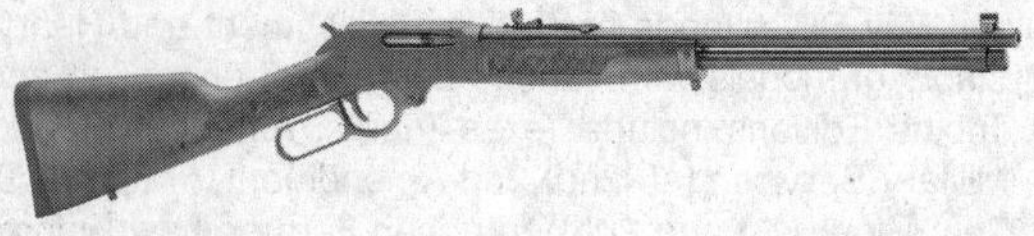

NIB	Exc.	V.G.	Good	Fair	Poor
790	670	570	480	290	180

Side Gate Lever Action

The brass-frame receiver has a removable tube magazine and the addition of a side loading gate with 20" round barrel in .30-30, .35 Rem., .38-55 or .45-70. The checkered walnut stock has a brass buttplate and the checkered forearm a brass barrel band, Semi-buckhorn rear and bead front sights, the receiver is drilled and tapped. OAL is 38.3 inches and weight is 7.5 lbs. Capacity is 5 rounds (4 rounds in .45-70).

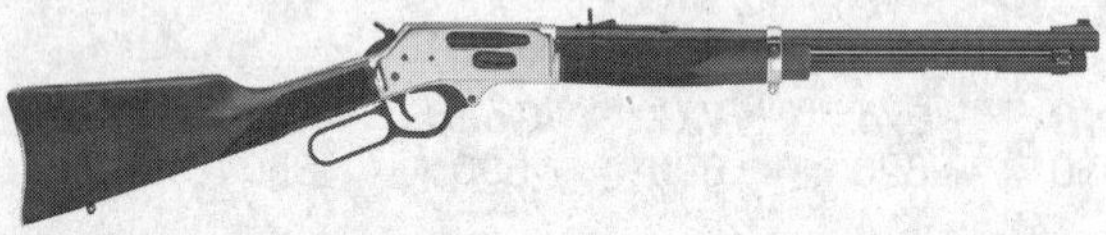

NIB	Exc.	V.G.	Good	Fair	Poor
920	780	660	560	340	200

Lever Action Color Case Hardened

The Lever Action comes with a case-hardened steel receiver with 20" blued barrel, semi-buckhorn rear and bead front sight in .30-30 or .45-70 with removable tube magazine system. Receiver drilled and tapped for scope mounts. Checkered American walnut forend and stock with ventilated rubber recoil pad. The .45-70 comes with pistol grip stock. OAL is 39" (41.1" in .45-70) and weight is 8.54 lbs. (8.1 in .45-70).

NIB	Exc.	V.G.	Good	Fair	Poor
930	790	670	570	340	200

Lever Action All Weather

In same calibers and styles as above, but with hard-chrome finish on receiver and 20" round barrel, and walnut stock with black all-weather coating. Solid recoil pad on .30-30, ventilated pad on .45-70. Fully adjustable semi-buckhorn sights, drilled and tapped for scope.

NIB	Exc.	V.G.	Good	Fair	Poor
930	790	670	570	340	200

Lever Action X

A matte-blue rifle with 19.8" round barrel threaded 5/8-24, chambered in .45-70, fully adjustable fiber optic sights, drilled and tapped for scope mounts, black synthetic pistol grip stock and forend, solid rubber recoil pad, OAL of 38.6" and a weight of 7.4 lbs. Has 4-round removable tube magazine and the addition of a side loading gate. Large loop lever and M-Lok slots and Picatinny rail under forend. New for 2020.

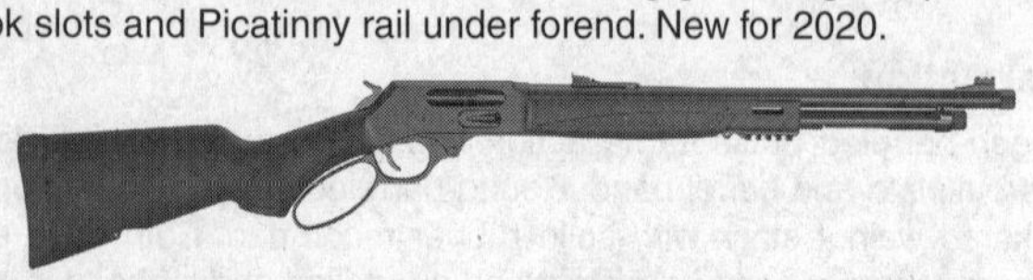

NIB	Exc.	V.G.	Good	Fair	Poor
830	700	600	500	300	190

Lever-Action .30-30

.30-30 caliber Winchester. Features 20" barrel, straight-grip American walnut stock with rubber butt-pad, XS ghost ring sights, blue finish, weight 7 lbs. Also available with brass receiver, octagon barrel and adjustable Marble's buck-horn rear sight, bead front. Note: Add $100 for brass receiver/octagon barrel.

NIB	Exc.	V.G.	Good	Fair	Poor
720	650	500	400	300	200

Lever-Action .45-70

Identical to Lever-Action .30-30 model, except for caliber.

NIB	Exc.	V.G.	Good	Fair	Poor
720	650	500	400	300	200

Lever Action X Model

Caliber: .45-70. Capacity: 4. Barrel: 19.8 in., round blue steel. Stock: Synthetic. Sights: Fiber optic. Weight: 7.4 lbs. Features: Large loop lever, swivel studs, 5/8x24 threaded barrel.

NIB	Exc.	V.G.	Good	Fair	Poor
900	—	—	—	—	—

Mare's Leg

Inspired by the gun carried by Steve McQueen in the "Wanted: Dead or Alive" TV series, the Mare's Leg uses the Classic Big Boy receiver but with 12.9" barrel, 5 round capacity in .45 Colt, .44 Mag or .357 Mag, and large loop lever. Abruptly shortened American walnut stock with a OAL of 25" and a weight of 5.8 lbs.

NIB	Exc.	V.G.	Good	Fair	Poor
890	760	650	550	330	200

.45 Colt

NIB	Exc.	V.G.	Good	Fair	Poor
800	680	500	400	300	200

Original Henry Rifle

A reproduction of the famous "Load on Sunday and shoot all week" Civil War-era Henry rimfire rifle, the new Henry is in centerfire .44-40 or .45 Colt using a replica of the original's toggle-link action, with brass frame and buttplate and 24" or 20" (carbine) blued, octagon barrel with a fancy American walnut stock. Note: Add $500 for case-hardened iron frame; Add $1200 for Engraved 3rd Edition; Add $1500 for Silver Engraved Edition.

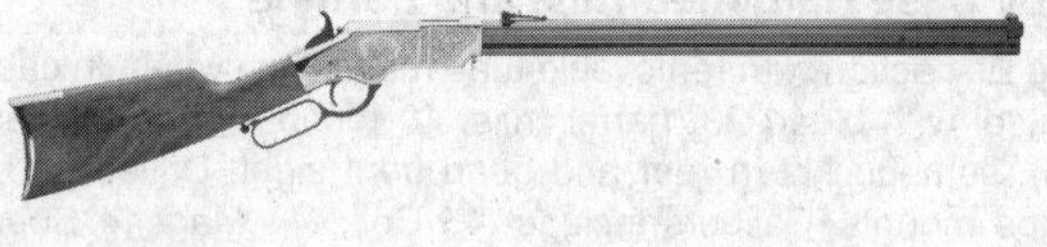

NIB	Exc.	V.G.	Good	Fair	Poor
2050	1750	1480	1260	760	450

Long Ranger

The Long Ranger is a traditional lever action rifle with exposed hammer updated with a geared action in a lightweight alloy receiver and a 6-lug rotary head bolt locking to a rear extension of the barrel. The side-ejecting receiver is drilled and tapped for scope mounts, and has a flush-fit detachable magazine (5-round .223, 4-round in .243, .308, and 6.5 Creedmoor). A 20" (22" in 6.5 C) round, blued barrel, checkered American walnut forend and straight-grip stock with a solid black rubber recoil pad. With or without iron sights. OAL is 40.5" (42.5" in 6.5C), weight is 7 lbs.

NIB	Exc.	V.G.	Good	Fair	Poor
940	800	680	580	350	210

Long Ranger Deluxe

As above but in .223, .243 or .308 with engraved nickel-plated receiver with 24k gold inlays and iron sights.

NIB	Exc.	V.G.	Good	Fair	Poor
1630	1390	1180	1000	600	360

Long Ranger Wildlife Edition

Three deluxe engraved Wildlife Editions have different engraving themes with 24k gold inlay game heads depending on caliber. Themes include a .223 (Coyote), .243 (Antelope) and .308 (Elk). Guns finished as Long Ranger above but with nickel-plated receivers to showcase the engraving.

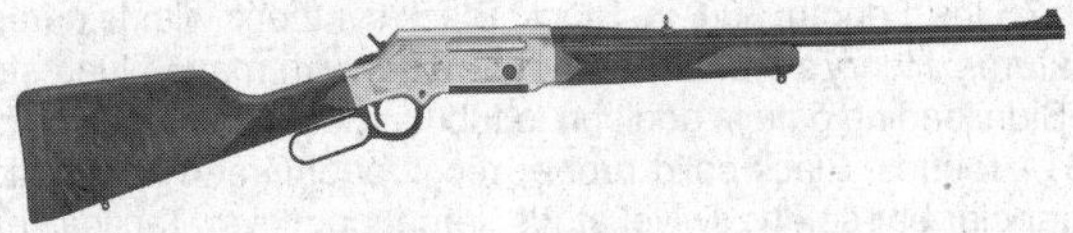

NIB	Exc.	V.G.	Good	Fair	Poor
1630	1390	1180	1000	600	360

Long Ranger Express

Calibers: .223 Rem/5.56 NATO. Capacity: 5-round steel box magazine. Barrel: 16.5-in. threaded round blued steel. Weight: 7 lbs. Length: 37 in. Stock: Birch laminate in black/gray. Sights: Top Picatinny rail. No iron sights. Features: Expansion of the Long Ranger line, this one a more compact platform. Same geared action with side ejection port. Chromed steel bolt with six lugs. Flush fit dropbox magazine with side push-button release. Sling studs, rubber recoil pad. Transfer bar safety. Hammer extension included. Barrel threaded at 5/8x24.

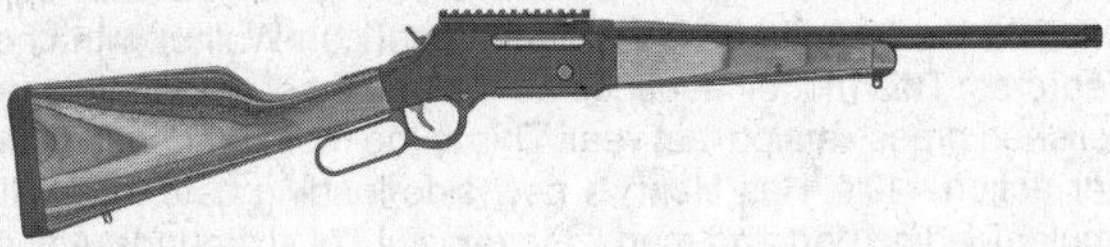

NIB	Exc.	V.G.	Good	Fair	Poor
1190	—	—	—	—	—

Lever Action X Model .410

Gauge: .410 bore, 2.5 in. Capacity: 6-round tubular magazine. Barrel: 19.8 in., round blued steel. Weight: 7.5 lbs. Length: 38.6 in. Stock: Black synthetic with textured panels. Features: Henry's first blacked-out model with matte-blued steel receiver that is drilled and tapped for Weaver 63B mount. Side loading gate in addition to tubular port. Black solid-rubber recoil pad. Fiber-optic front sight, transfer-bar safety, swivel studs, large loop lever, lower Picatinny rail, M-LOK attachment points at forend. Includes Invector choke.

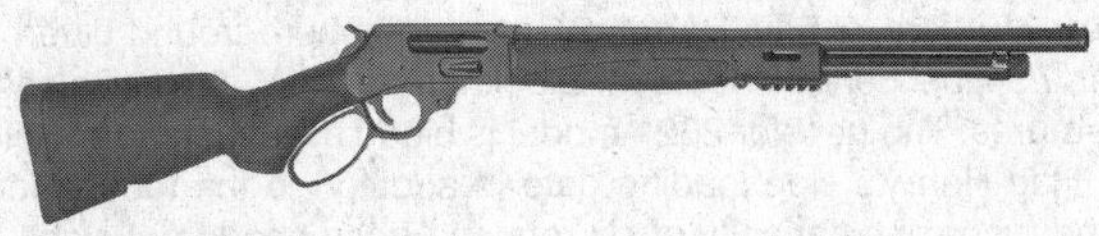

NIB	Exc.	V.G.	Good	Fair	Poor
850	—	—	—	—	—

Acu-Bolt

Chambered for .22 LR, .22 WMR or .17 HMR cartridges. Fitted with 20" barrel. Fiberglass stock. Scope mounts. Weight about 4.25 lbs. Add 10 percent for factory scope. Discontinued.

NIB	Exc.	V.G.	Good	Fair	Poor
320	280	200	150	100	80

Single Shot Rifle

The Single Shot break-open, top-lever rifle comes with steel frame with matte finish or brass frame polished and hardened. Fitted with 22" round barrels, fully adjustable folding leaf rear and brass bead front sights, drilled and tapped for scope mounts. Walnut stocks (pistol grip with solid rubber recoil pad on steel, straight wrist and brass buttplate on brass frames). Extractor only. Weight about 7 lbs with an OAL of 37.5". Calibers include .223, .243, .30-30, .308, .357 Mag, .44 Mag, and .45-70 in steel, and .44 Mag, .357 Mag and .45-70 in brass. A steel-frame Youth Model in .243 with 13" LOP on a pistol grip stock is available. Note: Add $100 for .45-70 with brass frame. Introduced in 2017.

NIB	Exc.	V.G.	Good	Fair	Poor
440	370	320	270	160	100

Brass Wildlife Edition

Highly embellished brass-frame rifles, engraved in .30-30 (20" round barrel) or .45-70 (22" round barrel) with fancy, smooth, straight-grip walnut stock and forend, semi-buckhorn rear and bead sights, drilled and tapped for scope. Brass buttplate and barrel band or forend cap. Large loop lever on .45-70. Note: Add $150 for .45-70.

NIB	Exc.	V.G.	Good	Fair	Poor
1160	990	840	720	430	260

Steel Wildlife Edition

Highly embellished blued steel-frame rifles, engraved with 24k gold inlays in .30-30 (20" round barrel) or .45-70 (18.4" round barrel) with fancy checkered walnut straight-grip stock (.30-30) or pistol grip (.45-70) and forend. Semi-buckhorn rear and bead front sights, drilled and tapped for scope.

NIB	Exc.	V.G.	Good	Fair	Poor
1320	1130	950	810	490	290

Homesteader Carbine

Calibers: 9mm Luger. Barrel: 16.3" round-blued steel. Weight: 6.6 lbs. Stock: American walnut. Features: Henry's first semi-automatic PPC-style rifle. Hard-anodized black receiver finish. Adjustable aperture rear sight and post front. Threaded barrel. Ambidextrous bolt handle. Swivel studs. Tang safety. All models include five- and 10-round Henry proprietary magazines. Additional magazines and adapters are sold separately.

NIB	Exc.	V.G.	Good	Fair	Poor
900	—	—	—	—	—

SHOTGUNS

Single Shot Shotgun

Traditional break-open shotgun in 12, 20 gauge or .410 bore. 3.5" chambers in 12 gauges, 3" in 20 and .410. Features and dimensions similar to Single Shot Rifle including steel or brass frame. The12-gauge barrel is 28", 26" for 20 and .410. Threaded for Rem-Choke tubes. A Modified tube is included. External hammer, no manual safety. A Youth Model is also available in 3" 20 gauge only with 13" LOP. Introduced in 2017.

NIB	Exc.	V.G.	Good	Fair	Poor
440	370	320	270	160	100

Single Shot Slug

Gauge: 12 ga. 3 in. Barrel: 24-in. round blued steel. Weight: 6.88 lbs. Length: 39.5 in. Stock: American Walnut. Features: The company's first slug-hunting shotgun, with a fully-rifled 1:35 twist barrel. This single shot is finished in traditional blued steel and checkered walnut with a black rubber recoil pad. Buttstock has a 14-inch LOP. Sling studs. Rebounding hammer safety. Fiber optic sights. Drilled and tapped for a Weaver 82 base.

NIB	Exc.	V.G.	Good	Fair	Poor
490	—	—	—	—	—

Single Shot Turkey

Gauge: 12 ga. 3.5 in. Barrel: 24-in. round. Weight: 6.78 lbs. Length: 39.5 in. Stock: American Walnut covered in Mossy Oak Obsession camo. Features: The company's first dedicated turkey-hunting shotgun wears full-coverage Mossy Oak Obsession, the official camouflage pattern of the National Wild Turkey Federation. Fiber-optic front and rear sights. Drilled and tapped for a Weaver 82 base. Black solid rubber recoil pad creates a 14-inch LOP. Swivel studs. Rebounding hammer safety. Includes an extended Turkey choke.

NIB	Exc.	V.G.	Good	Fair	Poor
600	—	—	—	—	—

Lever Action .410

Based on the blued, steel-framed .45-70 Lever Action, the .410 has a 20" or 24" barrel with 5-shot removable tube magazines chambered for 2.5" .410 shells only, checkered American walnut forend and pistol grip stock with a ventilated black rubber recoil pad. Weight about 7 lbs. The 24⊠ round barrel, has a removable invector-style full choke, front brass bead, with no rear sight. The compact 20⊠ barreled model has a fixed cylinder bore choke, and standard adjustable semi-buckhorn rear and brass bead front sights. Note: Add $30 for 24" barrel.

NIB	Exc.	V.G.	Good	Fair	Poor
790	670	570	480	290	180

Lever Action Axe .410

Gauge: .410 bore 2.5 in. Barrel: 15.14 in. smoothbore, round blued steel. Weight: 5.75 lbs. Length: 26.4 in. Stock: American Walnut with unique axe-handle-style rear grip. Features: Henry's Axe is most closely related to the handgun-chambered Mare's Leg platform, but this time with a slightly different design and firing .410 shotshells. Both the standard Steel and Brass Axe have a 5-round capacity with the addition of a loading gate. Short barrel takes interchangeable Invector-style chokes and ships with a full tube. Brass front bead, swivel studs, transfer bar safety. Drilled and tapped for optics mounting.

NIB	Exc.	V.G.	Good	Fair	Poor
990	700	600	500	300	190

Side Gate Lever Action .410

Based on the side-loading/removable mag tube .45-70 action, the brass-framed .410 holds 5 rounds in 2.5" shells only, the straight grip stock features deluxe checkering. Semi-buckhorn rear and ramp front with bead sights, receiver drilled and tapped.

NIB	Exc.	V.G.	Good	Fair	Poor
920	780	660	560	340	200

Lever Action X Model .410

Gauge: .410 bore 2.5 in. Barrel: 19.8 in. smoothbore, round blued steel. Weight: 7.5 lbs. Length: 38.6 in. Stock: Black synthetic with textured panels. Features: Henry's first blacked-out model with matte blued steel receiver. Side loading gate in addition to tubular port with magazine capacity of 6+1 rounds. Black solid rubber recoil pad. Green fiber-optic front sight, transfer bar safety, swivel studs, large loop lever. Tactical features include lower Picatinny rail and M-LOK attachment points at forend. Drilled and tapped for a Weaver 63B optics mount. Includes Invector choke.

NIB	Exc.	V.G.	Good	Fair	Poor
880	700	600	500	300	190

Side Gate Lever Action 410 Model H018G-410R

Gauge: .410 bore 2.5in. Barrel: 19.75 in. smoothbore, round blued steel. Weight: 7.09 lbs. Length: 38.1 in. Stock: American Walnut with checkering. Features: This model launches as a blued steel companion to Henry's polished brass version last year. This is the more compact of the pair of lever action 410's. Has Henry's new side-loading gate in addition to the tubular loading port and magazine capacity of six rounds. Adjustable semi-buckhorn rear sight with diamond insert and brass bead front post sight. Black ventilated rubber recoil pad, transfer bar safety, sling swivel studs. Fixed cylinder bore choke.

NIB	Exc.	V.G.	Good	Fair	Poor
850	—	—	—	—	—

Side Gate Lever Action 410 Model H018G-410

Gauge: .410 bore, 2.5 in. Barrel: 24 in. smoothbore, round blued steel. Weight: 7.54 lbs. Length: 42.75 in. Stock: American Walnut with checkering. Features: The new-for-2021 model is blued steel instead of polished brass. Has Henry's side loading gate in addition to the tubular loading port and magazine capacity of six rounds. Brass bead front sight. Black ventilated rubber recoil pad, sling swivel studs. Transfer bar safety. LOP of 14-inches. Drilled and tapped for a Weaver 63B optics base. Threaded for Invector-style chokes with a Full choke supplied.

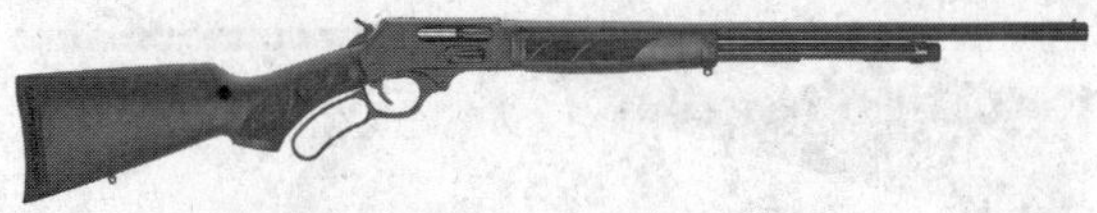

NIB	Exc.	V.G.	Good	Fair	Poor
890	750	650	—	—	—

Side Gate Lever Action 410 Model H024-410

Gauge: .410 bore 2.5 in. Barrel: 19.8 in. smoothbore, round blued steel. Weight: 7.09 lbs. Length: 38.1 in. Stock: American walnut with intricate floral and Henry logo checkering appointments. Features: Polished brass receiver with Henry's new side loading gate in addition to the tubular loading port. Magazine capacity of six rounds. Fully adjustable semi-buckhorn rear sight with diamond insert and ramp front with 0.62-inch ivory bead. Polished brass buttplate, transfer bar safety, sling swivel studs. Fixed cylinder bore choke.

NIB	Exc.	V.G.	Good	Fair	Poor
960	830	700	—	—	—

HERITAGE MANUFACTURING, INC.

Opa Locka, Florida

Stealth

Semi-automatic pistol chambered in 9mm and .40 S&W. Black polymer frame, with stainless steel slide. Barrel length 3.9"; overall 6.3". Magazine capacity 10 rounds. Weight about 20 oz. Offered with black finish, two-tone black chrome, with stainless steel side panels or black chrome.

NIB	Exc.	V.G.	Good	Fair	Poor
280	220	180	150	120	100

Model H25S

Semi-automatic pistol chambered for .25 ACP cartridge. Barrel length 2.25"; overall 4.58"; weight about 13.5 oz. Frame mounted safety. Single-action-only. Available in blue or nickel.

NIB	Exc.	V.G.	Good	Fair	Poor
150	120	100	80	60	50

Sentry

Double-action revolver chambered for .38 Special. Cylinder holds 6 rounds. Barrel length 2". Weight about 23 oz. Blue or nickel finish.

NIB	Exc.	V.G.	Good	Fair	Poor
130	100	80	60	50	30

Rough Rider

Single-action revolver chambered for .22-caliber cartridges. Barrel lengths 4.75", 6.5" and 9". Cylinder holds 6 rounds. Weight about 34 oz. Available in blue or nickel finish.

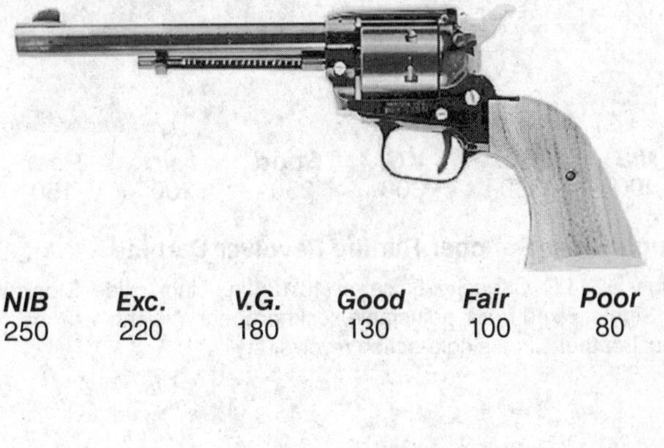

NIB	Exc.	V.G.	Good	Fair	Poor
250	220	180	130	100	80

With Combination Cylinder—.22 Magnum

NIB	Exc.	V.G.	Good	Fair	Poor
280	240	200	150	120	100

With Bird's-Head Grip & Combo Cylinder

NIB	Exc.	V.G.	Good	Fair	Poor
280	250	200	150	120	100

Rough Rider .17 HMR

Introduced in 2004.

NIB	Exc.	V.G.	Good	Fair	Poor
300	260	220	180	120	100

Rough Rider .32

Six-shot revolver chambered for .32 H&R Magnum centerfire (interchangeably .32 S&W, .32 S&W Long). Black satin finish. Offered with 3.5", 4.75" or 6.5" barrels. Weight 35 oz. (6.5" bbl.). 11.785" LOA. Fixed sights. Bird's-head grip available. Discontinued.

NIB	Exc.	V.G.	Good	Fair	Poor
240	190	140	100	80	50

Rough Rider Big-Bore Series

Six-shot steel-frame revolver chambered for .357, .44-40 or .45 Long Colt. Barrel lengths 4.75", 5.5" or 7.5". Weight 36 oz. Fixed sights. Note: Add 10 percent for chrome finish.

NIB	Exc.	V.G.	Good	Fair	Poor
400	350	300	250	200	150

Rough Rider Rancher Rimfire Revolver Carbine

Caliber: .22 LR. Capacity: 6. Barrel: 16.125 in., black oxide. Stock: Walnut. Sights: Fixed front, adjustable buckhorn rear. Weight: 4.12 lbs. Features: Leather sling, single-action revolver-style.

NIB	Exc.	V.G.	Good	Fair	Poor
280	—	—	—	—	—

Rough Rider Tactical Cowboy

Chambered in .22 LR, is also compatible with the .22 WMR cylinder allowing you to shoot either .22 LR or .22 WMR ammo. The barrel is threaded for compensators and suppressors. Caliber: .22 LR, Capacity: 6 rounds, Finish: Black standard. Action Type: Single Action Only. Lands & Grooves: 6. Front Sight: Fiber optic. Rear Sight: Picatinny rail. Safety: Thumb/hammer. Grips: Carbon fiber. Weight: 32.10 oz., Barrel Length: 6.5 in. Overall Length: 11.85 in.

NIB	Exc.	V.G.	Good	Fair	Poor
160	—	—	—	—	—

Barkeep Boot

Caliber: .22 LR. Capacity: 6 rounds. Finish: Black standard. Action Type: Single Action Only. Safety: Thumb/Hammer. Grips: Black, gray pearl, custom wood burnt snake. Weight: 25.5 oz. Barrel Length: 1.68 in. Overall Length: 6.38 in.

NIB	Exc.	V.G.	Good	Fair	Poor
150	—	—	—	—	—

HEROLD

Franz Jaeger
Suhl, Germany

Bolt-Action Rifle

A .22 Hornet bolt-action sporting rifle, with 24" ribbed barrel, adjustable sights, double-set triggers and walnut stock. Imported by Charles Daly and Stoeger Arms prior to WWII.

NIB	Exc.	V.G.	Good	Fair	Poor
—	1500	850	600	400	250

HERTER'S

Waseca, Minnesota

An importer and retailer of European-made firearms. Active until approximately 1980.

REVOLVERS

Guide

A .22-caliber double-action swing-out cylinder revolver, with 6" barrel and 6-shot cylinder. Blued, with walnut grips.

NIB	Exc.	V.G.	Good	Fair	Poor
—	120	100	70	40	30

Power-Mag Revolver

A .357 Magnum, .401 Herter Power Magnum and .44 Magnum caliber single-action revolver, with 4" or 6" barrel and 6-shot cylinder. Blued, with walnut grips. Note: Add 10 percent for .401.

NIB	Exc.	V.G.	Good	Fair	Poor
—	400	320	200	120	80

Western

As above, in .22-caliber.

NIB	Exc.	V.G.	Good	Fair	Poor
—	200	150	120	80	50

RIFLES

J-9 or U-9 Hunter

Mauser-action sporting rifles manufactured in England (J-9) and Yugoslavia (U-9), with 24" barrels and Monte Carlo-style walnut stocks.

NIB	Exc.	V.G.	Good	Fair	Poor
—	480	200	160	100	80

J-9 or U-9 Presentation or Supreme

As above, with checkering and sling swivels.

NIB	Exc.	V.G.	Good	Fair	Poor
—	550	320	200	150	100

HESSE ARMS

Inver Grove Heights, Minnesota

This previous manufacturer of military style firearms was succeeded by Vulcan Armament, which is no longer in business. Values of Hesse Arms products can vary widely.

HEYM, F. W.

Gleichamberg, Germany

Established 1865 in Suhl, Germany, this company was re-established after WWII in Munnerstadt. Company remained there until 1996 when it moved back to a suburb of Suhl. Post-war arms were originally imported by Paul Jaeger of Grand Junction, Tennessee. Double Gun Imports in Dallas, Texas, is the current importer of Heym firearms.

SINGLE-SHOT RIFLES

Model HR-30

Built on Ruger No. 1 falling-block-action. Chambered for most calibers, with 24" round barrel or 26" barrel in Magnum calibers. There is a quarter rib with express sights. Single-set trigger made by Canjar. Rifle engraved with game scene motif. Stock is deluxe hand checkered French walnut, with classic European-style cheekpiece. French case-hardened and blued.

NIB	Exc.	V.G.	Good	Fair	Poor
4000	3500	3000	2500	2000	1000

Model HR-38

As above, with octagonal barrel.

NIB	Exc.	V.G.	Good	Fair	Poor
4600	4200	3600	3000	2300	1200

DOUBLE RIFLES

Model 22 Safety

Over/under combination rifle/shotgun chambered for 16- or 20-gauge over .22 Hornet, .22 WMR, .222 Remington, .222 Remington Magnum, .223, 5.6x50Rmm, 6.5x57Rmm and 7x57Rmm, with 24" barrels. Boxlock action with single trigger, automatic ejectors and automatic decocking mechanism. French case-hardened, blued, with walnut stock.

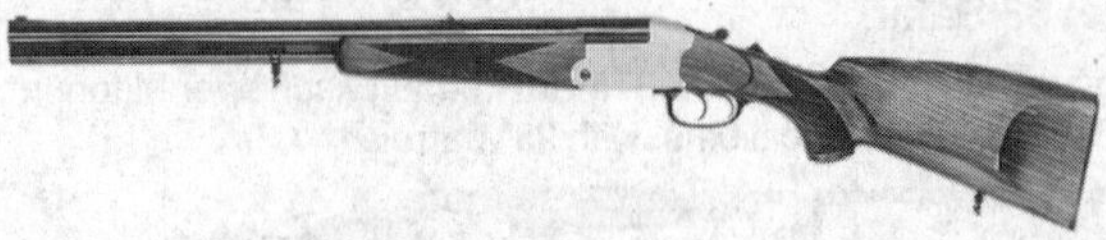

NIB	Exc.	V.G.	Good	Fair	Poor
—	3500	3000	2750	1200	900

Model 77B/55B Over/Under Rifle

Over/under rifle manufactured in a variety of calibers, with 25" barrels. Has open sights and boxlock-action, with Kersten double cross bolts. Action is heavily engraved with game scene motif and silver plated. Has double triggers, cocking indicators, automatic ejectors and select walnut stock. Barrels machined to accept Zeiss scope, with claw mounts.

NIB	Exc.	V.G.	Good	Fair	Poor
—	6000	5500	4000	3250	2500

Model 55BSS

As above with sidelocks.

NIB	Exc.	V.G.	Good	Fair	Poor
—	10500	9500	8500	5000	3500

Model 55BF/77BF

Similar to Model 55B, except one barrel rifled and other smooth in 12-, 16- or 20-gauge.

NIB	Exc.	V.G.	Good	Fair	Poor
—	6000	5500	5000	3250	2500

Model 55BFSS

As above, with sidelocks.

NIB	Exc.	V.G.	Good	Fair	Poor
—	10500	9500	8500	5000	3500

Model 88 B

Large bore double-barrel boxlock rifle, with 24" barrels, automatic ejectors, double triggers and select walnut stock.

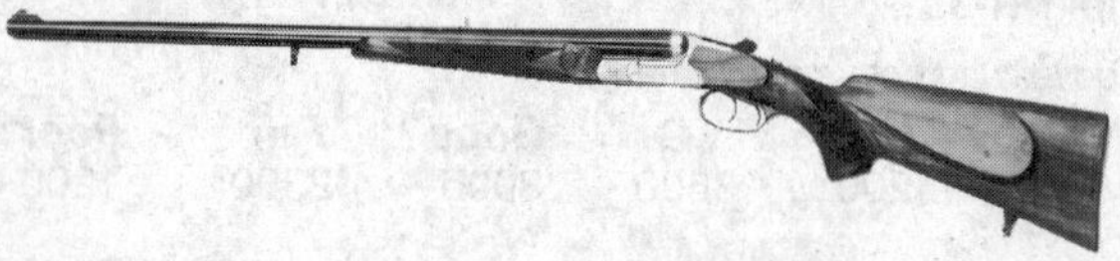

NIB	Exc.	V.G.	Good	Fair	Poor
—	12500	9750	8750	5500	4000

Model 88 BSS

As above with sidelocks.

NIB	Exc.	V.G.	Good	Fair	Poor
20000	18000	15000	10500	6500	5250

Model 88 Safari

As above, but chambered for .375 H&H, .458 Winchester Magnum, .470 or .500 Nitro Express calibers, with 25" barrels.

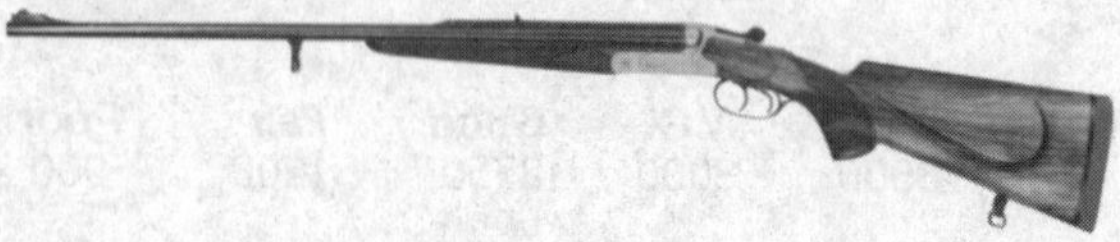

NIB	Exc.	V.G.	Good	Fair	Poor
20000	18000	15000	10000	7000	4750

Model 88B SXS Double Rifle

Calibers/Gauge: .22 Hornet, .300 Win. Mag., .375 H&H Belted Mag., .375 H&H Flanged Mag., .416 Rigby, .416/500 NE, .450/400 NE 3-in., .450 NE 3.25-in., .470 NE, .500 NE, .577 NE, .600 NE, 20 gauge, and more. Barrel: Up to 26 in., Krupp steel, hammer-forged. Stock: Custom select European walnut. Sights: V rear, bead front. Weight: 9 to 13 lbs. Features: Automatic ejectors, articulated front trigger, stocked-to-fit RH or LH, cocking indicators, engraving available. Values are speculative.

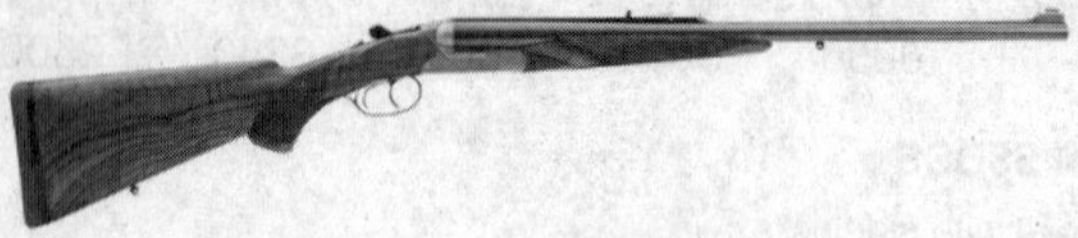

NIB	Exc.	V.G.	Good	Fair	Poor
18000	15000	13000	—	—	—

Model 89B SXS Double Rifle

Calibers/Gauge: .22 Hornet, .300 Win. Mag., 375 H&H Belted Mag., 375 H&H Flanged Mag., .416 Rigby, .416/500 NE, .450/400 NE 3-in., .450 NE 3.25-in., .470 NE, .500 NE, .577 NE, .600 NE, 20 gauge, and more. Barrel: Up to 26 in., Krupp steel, hammer-forged. Stock: Custom select European walnut. Sights: V rear, bead front. Weight: 9-13 lbs. Features: Five frame sizes, automatic ejectors, intercepting sears, stocked-to-fit RH or LH, engraving available. Values are speculative.

NIB	Exc.	V.G.	Good	Fair	Poor
23000	19000	16000	—	—	—

DRILLINGS

Model 33

Boxlock drilling manufactured in a variety of American and European calibers and gauges. 25" barrels, double triggers and extractors. Case-hardened, blued, with walnut stock.

NIB	Exc.	V.G.	Good	Fair	Poor
—	7000	6000	5250	3750	2000

Model 33 Deluxe

Same as above, with game scene engraving.

NIB	Exc.	V.G.	Good	Fair	Poor
—	8500	7000	5750	4500	2500

Model 37

Similar to Model 33 Standard, with full sidelocks.

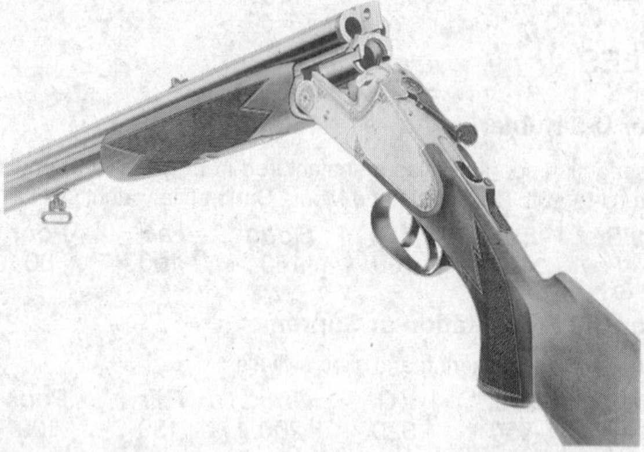

NIB	Exc.	V.G.	Good	Fair	Poor
20000	17500	13000	9500	6000	2500

Model 37 Deluxe

Similar to Model 37, with hand engraved scroll work and fancy walnut stock.

NIB	Exc.	V.G.	Good	Fair	Poor
23500	20000	16500	12000	6000	3000

BOLT-ACTION RIFLES

Model SR-20

Mauser-action sporting rifle manufactured in a variety of calibers, with 21", 24" or 26" barrels, open sights, adjustable or set trigger. Blued, with walnut stock.

NIB	Exc.	V.G.	Good	Fair	Poor
2450	2250	1650	750	600	450

Model SR-20 Alpine

As above, with 20" barrel and Mannlicher stock. Introduced in 1989.

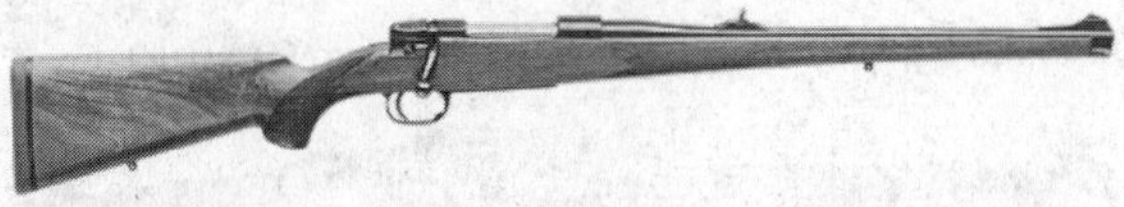

NIB	Exc.	V.G.	Good	Fair	Poor
—	2500	2000	1250	850	600

SR-20 Classic Safari

As above, but chambered for .404 Jeffries, .425 Express and .458 Win. Magnum, with 24" barrel having express sights. Introduced in 1989.

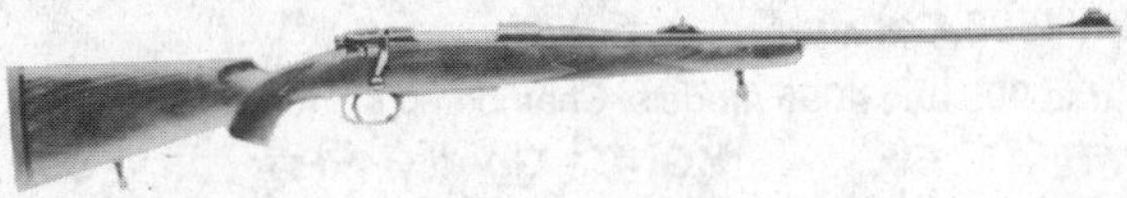

NIB	Exc.	V.G.	Good	Fair	Poor
—	3000	2500	2000	1250	750

SR-20 Classic Sportsman

Features round barrel without sights. Chambered for many calibers from .243 to .375 H&H. Introduced in 1988. Note: Add $100 for Magnum calibers.

NIB	Exc.	V.G.	Good	Fair	Poor
2650	2250	1900	900	500	300

SR-20 Trophy

Similar to above Classic Sportsman, with German bead ramp sight and open quarter rib rear sight. Select walnut stock, with oil-finish. Octagonal barrel and rosewood grip cap.

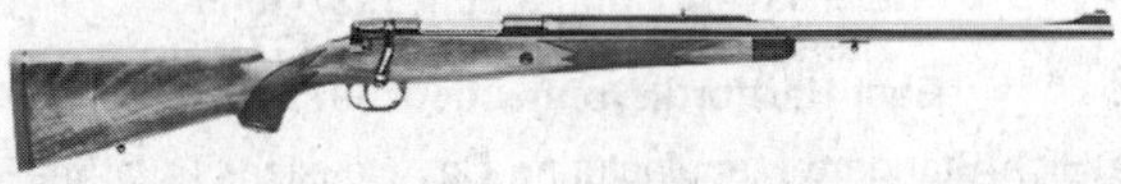

NIB	Exc.	V.G.	Good	Fair	Poor
3000	2500	2250	1800	900	300

Heym Magnum Express

Bolt-action rifle chambered for .338 Lapua, .375 H&H, .416 Rigby, .500 Nitro Express, .500 A-Square and few were built in .600 Nitro Express. Fitted with 24" barrel. Adjustable front sight, three leaf rear express sight. Select hand checkered European walnut stock and many other special features. Introduced in 1989. Note: Add $4,000 for .600 N.E.

NIB	Exc.	V.G.	Good	Fair	Poor
10000	8000	5000	2500	1750	500

Express Bolt-Action Rifle

Calibers: .375 H&H Mag., .416 Rigby, .404 Jeffery, .458 Lott, .450 Rigby. Capacity: 5. Barrel: 24 in., Krupp steel, hammer-forged. Stock: Custom select European walnut. Sights: Iron, barrel-banded front. Weight: 9 to 10.5 lbs. Features: Caliber-specific action and magazine box, classic English sporting rifle, three-position safety. Values are speculative.

NIB	Exc.	V.G.	Good	Fair	Poor
12000	10000	7500	—	—	—

HI-POINT FIREARMS

MKS Supply
Dayton, Ohio

Model C

A 9mm single-action compact semi-automatic pistol, with 3.5" barrel. Magazine capacity 8 rounds. Black or chrome finish. Weight 32 oz.

NIB	Exc.	V.G.	Good	Fair	Poor
120	100	80	80	60	50

Model C Polymer

Same as above, with polymer frame. Weight 28 oz.

NIB	Exc.	V.G.	Good	Fair	Poor
140	110	80	80	60	50

Model C Comp

Introduced in 1998, this 9mm model features 4" barrel with compensator, adjustable sights and 10-round magazine.

NIB	Exc.	V.G.	Good	Fair	Poor
170	130	100	90	80	50

Model JH

All steel construction chambered for .45 ACP, with 4.5" barrel. Magazine capacity 7 rounds. Weight 39 oz.

NIB	Exc.	V.G.	Good	Fair	Poor
180	140	100	80	80	50

Model 40SW

Same as above. Chambered for .40 S&W cartridge, 8-round magazine. Weight 39 oz.

NIB	Exc.	V.G.	Good	Fair	Poor
180	140	100	80	80	50

Model 9mm Polymer (Model 916)

Polymer frame 9mm. Similar to .40- and .45-caliber models.

NIB	Exc.	V.G.	Good	Fair	Poor
160	140	120	100	80	60

Model .45 Polymer

Polymer frame and 4.5" barrel. Chambered for .45 ACP cartridge. Magazine capacity 9 rounds. Weight about 32 oz.

NIB	Exc.	V.G.	Good	Fair	Poor
180	140	100	80	80	50

Model .40 Polymer

As above, but chambered for .40 S&W cartridge, with magazine capacity of 10 rounds. Weight about 32 oz.

NIB	Exc.	V.G.	Good	Fair	Poor
180	140	100	80	80	50

Model CF

Chambered for .380 ACP cartridge. Fitted with polymer frame. Magazine capacity 8 rounds. Barrel length 3.5". Weight 29 oz. Note: Add $25 for compensator model.

NIB	Exc.	V.G.	Good	Fair	Poor
120	100	60	40	30	20

.380 ACP Compensated

Semi-automatic with fully-adjustable 3-dot sights, muzzle compensator, 4" barrel, 31 oz. polymer frame. Two magazines 8 and 10 rounds. Note: Add 50 percent for laser sight.

NIB	Exc.	V.G.	Good	Fair	Poor
150	120	100	80	80	50

Model 4095 Carbine

.40 S&W semi-automatic carbine. Features include all-weather black polymer stock, 10-shot magazine, 17.5" barrel, sling swivels, grip mounted clip release, quick on & off thumb safety, rear peep sight, 32.5" OAL and scope mount. Note: Add $85 for red dot sight.

NIB	Exc.	V.G.	Good	Fair	Poor
280	200	150	100	—	—

Model 995 Carbine

Similar to .40 S&W Carbine. Chambered for 9mm Parabellum.

NIB	Exc.	V.G.	Good	Fair	Poor
250	190	150	100	—	—

Model 4595 Carbine

Similar to 995 and 4095 models. Chambered in .45 ACP.

NIB	Exc.	V.G.	Good	Fair	Poor
300	260	200	150	—	—

Model 3895 Carbine

Like the Model 4595 Carbine but chambered .380 ACP.

NIB	Exc.	V.G.	Good	Fair	Poor
250	190	150	100	—	—

HIGGINS, J. C.
Chicago, Illinois

Sears, Roebuck & Company of Chicago used trade name J.C. Higgins on firearms and other sporting goods it sold between 1946 and 1962. Arms bearing this trade name were manufactured by a variety of American gun makers. See High Standard, Mossberg, etc.

HIGH STANDARD
New Haven, Connecticut 1932-1945
Hamden, Connecticut 1946-1977
East Hartford, Connecticut 1977-1984

See High Standard Manufacturing Co., Houston, TX at the end of this section.

LETTER MODELS

Model B

A .22 LR caliber semi-automatic pistol, with 4.5" or 6.75" round barrel and 10-shot magazine. Blued came with checkered hard rubber grips (later production versions have checkered grips impressed with High Standard monogram). Introduced 1932, with serial numbers beginning at 5000. Early production utilized Hartford parts. Approximately 65,000 made. Note: Add $75 premium for Type-I-B take-down; $75 premium for early models with Hartford Arms front sight, safety and takedown levers; 15 percent premium for box with papers. C&R eligible. Most guns are found in serial number ranges from 5,000 to about 95,894 and 148198 to about 151021.

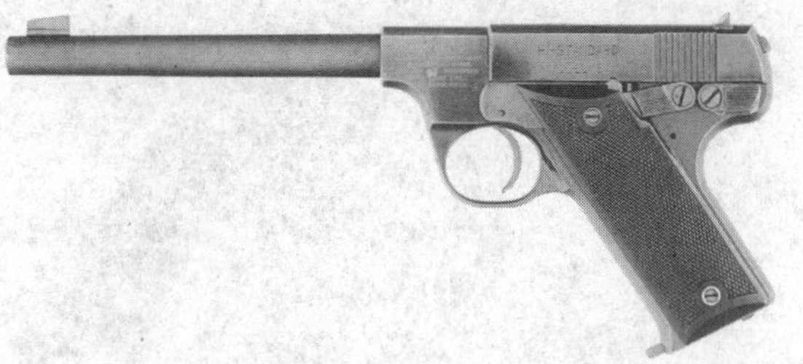

NIB	Exc.	V.G.	Good	Fair	Poor
—	680	550	350	250	150

Model B-US

Version of Model B, with slight contour modifications to back of frame. Approximately 14,000 made for U.S. government in 1942-1943. Most are marked "PROPERTY OF U.S." on top of barrel and on right side of frame. Monogrammed hard rubber grips. Most guns found in serial number range 92344 to about 111631. Note: Add 20 percent premium for box with papers.

NIB	Exc.	V.G.	Good	Fair	Poor
—	880	750	400	300	200

Model C

Like Model B except in .22 Short. Introduced 1936; approximately 4,700 made. Both plain and monogrammed hard rubber grips. Available with 4.5" or 6.75" round barrel. Note: Add $75 premium for I-A take-down; $175 premium for I-B take-down; 15 percent premium for box with papers.

NIB	Exc.	V.G.	Good	Fair	Poor
—	930	800	560	430	250

Model A

Similar to Model B, with checkered walnut grips over an extended grip and adjustable sight. Introduced 1938; approximately 7,300 made. Available with 4.5" or 6.75" round barrel. Same light barrel as Model B. Note: Add $175 premium for I-B take-down; 15 percent premium for box with papers.

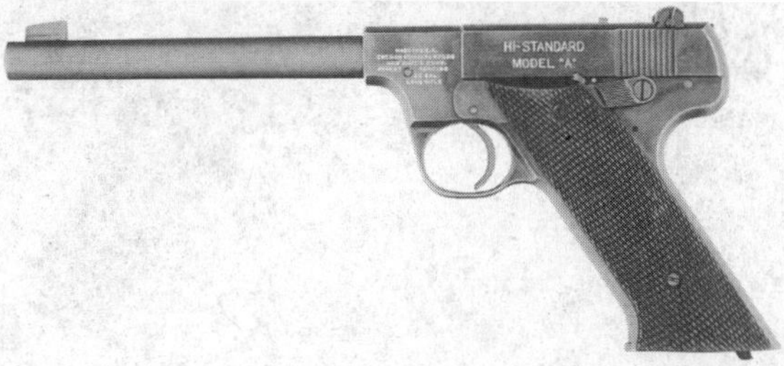

NIB	Exc.	V.G.	Good	Fair	Poor
—	850	700	380	300	200

Model D

Similar to Model A, with heavier weight barrel (middle weight barrel). Available with 4.5" or 6.75" barrel and optional checkered walnut grips. Introduced 1938; approximately 2,500 made. Note: Add $175 premium for I-B take-down; 15 percent premium for box with papers.

NIB	Exc.	V.G.	Good	Fair	Poor
—	1000	850	500	400	300

Model E

Like Model D, with still heavier weight barrel (heavy weight barrel). Available with 4.5" or 6.75" barrel. Checkered walnut grips, with thumbrest. Introduced 1938; approximately 2,600 made. Note: Add $175 for I-B take-down; 18 percent premium for box with papers.

NIB	Exc.	V.G.	Good	Fair	Poor
—	1400	1000	750	500	350

Model S

Not a production model. Like Model B, with a smoothbore. Nine registered as Model S. Additional five with Model C slides are registered, Model C/S. Note ivory bead front sight. Others may exist but only 14 are registered with BATF. Manufactured in 1939 and 1940. Values for both variations are equal. 6.75" barrels. Note: Serial numbers for registered samples. Model S: 48142; 48143; 48144; 48145; 48146; 59458; 59459; 59474 Model C/S: 59279; 59460; 59469; 59473; 59478. This model is too rare to accurately price. Last one sold at auction for $7,500 in 2012.

NIB	Exc.	V.G.	Good	Fair	Poor
—	5250	3950	3000	—	—

HAMMER LETTER MODELS

Second models made. Like letter models, with external hammers.

Model H-B, Type 1 Pre-War

Like Model B, with exposed hammer. Introduced 1940; approximately 2,100 made. Note: Add 15 percent premium for box with papers.

NIB	Exc.	V.G.	Good	Fair	Poor
—	1000	900	750	500	300

Model H-B, Type 2 Post-War

Post-war variation has external safety. Approximately 25,000 made. Note: Add 15 percent premium for box with papers.

NIB	Exc.	V.G.	Good	Fair	Poor
—	650	580	420	350	200

Model H-A

Like Model A, with exposed hammer. Introduced 1940; approximately 1,040 made. Note: Add 15 percent premium for box with papers.

NIB	Exc.	V.G.	Good	Fair	Poor
—	1850	1400	900	750	400

Model H-D

Like Model D, with exposed hammer. Introduced 1940; approximately 6,900 made. Note: Add 15 percent premium for box with papers.

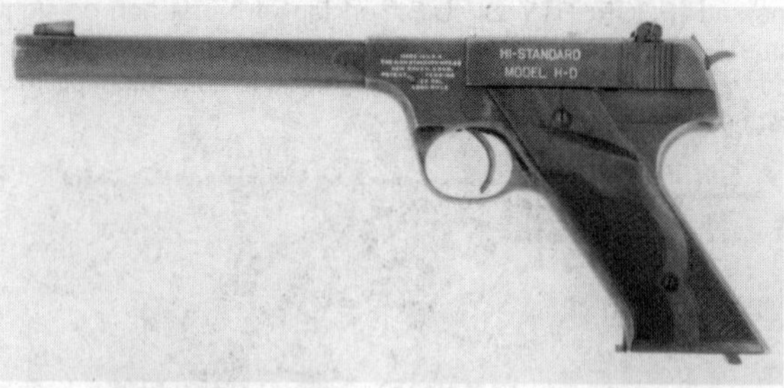

NIB	Exc.	V.G.	Good	Fair	Poor
—	2250	1750	1100	850	400

Model H-E

Like Model E, with exposed hammer. Introduced 1940; approximately 2,100 made. Note: Add 15 percent premium for box with papers.

NIB	Exc.	V.G.	Good	Fair	Poor
—	2200	1700	1050	800	400

Model USA—Model HD

Similar to Model HD, with 4.5" barrel only. Has fixed sights, checkered black hard rubber grips and external safety. Early models blued; later model Parkerized. Introduced 1943; approximately 44,000 produced for U.S. government. Note: Add 20 percent premium for box with papers.

NIB	Exc.	V.G.	Good	Fair	Poor
—	950	850	700	500	300

Model USA—Model HD-MS

Silenced variation of USA Model HD. Approximately 2,000 produced for OSS during 1944 and 1945. 6.75" shrouded barrel. Early models blued; later model Parkerized. Only a few registered with BATFE or civilian ownership. This model is too rare to accurately price.

Model H-D Military

Similar to HD, with external safety. Early production had checkered plastic grips; later production changed to checkered walnut. Introduced 1945; approximately 150,000 produced. Note: Add 15 percent premium for box with papers.

NIB	Exc.	V.G.	Good	Fair	Poor
—	850	750	550	350	200

LEVER LETTER MODELS

Third design models incorporate interchangeable barrels, with lever take-down.

G-.380

A .380-caliber semi-automatic pistol, with 5" barrel and 6-shot magazine. Blued, with checkered plastic grips. Fixed sights. Introduced 1947; discontinued 1950; approximately 7,400 made. High Standard's only production centerfire pistol. Note: Add 10 percent premium for box with papers.

NIB	Exc.	V.G.	Good	Fair	Poor
—	750	550	450	350	200

G-B

Similar characteristics like Model B. with interchangeable 4.5" or 6.75" barrels. Sold with barrel or as combination with both barrels. Fixed sights. Blued, with monogrammed plastic grips. Last short frame model produced. Introduced 1949; discontinued 1950; approximately 4,900 produced. Note: Add $225 premium for factory combination; 15 percent premium for box with papers.

NIB	Exc.	V.G.	Good	Fair	Poor
—	650	550	450	350	200

G-D

Similar characteristics like Model D, with interchangeable 4.5" or 6.75" barrels. Sold with barrel or as combination with both barrels. Adjustable sights. Blued, with checkered walnut grips. Optional checkered thumbrest walnut grips. Introduced 1949; discontinued 1950; approximately 3,300 produced. Note: Add $325 premium for factory combination; $50 premium for factory target grips; 15 percent premium for box with papers.

NIB	Exc.	V.G.	Good	Fair	Poor
—	1050	950	600	400	300

G-E

Similar characteristics like Model E, with interchangeable 4.5" or 6.75" barrels. Sold with barrel or as combination with both barrels. Adjustable sights. Blued, with checkered thumbrest walnut grips. Introduced 1949; discontinued 1950; approximately 2,900 produced. Note: Add $375 premium for factory combination; 15 percent premium for box with papers.

NIB	Exc.	V.G.	Good	Fair	Poor
—	1550	1200	800	450	300

Olympic (commonly called "G-O")

New gun design for competitive shooting in .22 Short caliber. 4.5 or 6.75" barrels. Sold with barrel or as combination with both barrels. Grooved front and backstraps on frame. Adjustable sights. Blued, with checkered thumbrest walnut grips. Introduced 1949; discontinued 1950; approximately 1,200 produced. Model uses a special curved magazine. Few guns will utilize a straight-back magazine. Majority of these Olympics use curved magazine, with a humped back. Note: Add $375 premium for factory combination; $300 for straight magazine variation; 15 percent premium for box with papers.

NIB	Exc.	V.G.	Good	Fair	Poor
—	1800	1450	900	500	300

LEVER NAME MODELS

Fourth design models evolving from lever letter series, with slight changes.

Supermatic

.22 LR caliber pistol, with 10-shot magazine. Heavy round barrel, blued finish, adjustable sights and brown plastic thumbrest grips. Grooved front and backstraps on frame. Available with 4.5" or 6.75" barrels or combination with both barrels. Ribbed barrels and provisions for weights. A 2 and 3 oz. weight were provided with this model, as was a filler strip for when weights were not used. Note: Add $250 for factory combination; 15 percent premium for box with papers.

NIB	Exc.	V.G.	Good	Fair	Poor
—	880	720	620	420	200

Olympic

.22 Short caliber pistol, with 10-shot magazine. Heavy round barrel, blued finish, adjustable sights and brown plastic thumbrest grips. Grooved front and backstraps on frame. Available with 4.5" or 6.75" barrels or combination with both barrels. Ribbed barrels and provisions for weights. Weights of 2 and 3 oz. were provided with this model, as was a filler strip for when weights were not used. Note: Add $250 for factory combination; 15 percent premium for box with papers.

NIB	Exc.	V.G.	Good	Fair	Poor
—	1250	920	780	650	250

Field King

.22 LR caliber pistol, with 10-shot magazine. Heavy round barrel, blued finish, adjustable sights and brown plastic thumbrest grips. Available with 4.5" or 6.75" barrels or combination with both barrels. No rib on barrels or provisions for weights. Note: Add $225 premium for factory combination; 15 percent premium for box with papers.

NIB	Exc.	V.G.	Good	Fair	Poor
—	650	550	450	350	150

Sport King

.22-caliber pistol, with 10-shot magazine. Lightweight round barrel, blued finish, fixed sights and brown plastic thumbrest grips. Available with 4.5" or 6.75" barrels or combination with both barrels. Early models did not have slide holdback when magazine was empty. Early variation without holdback was produced in about twice the quantity as later models incorporating this feature. Note: Add $200 premium for factory combination; $25 premium for guns with holdback feature; 15 percent premium for box with papers.

NIB	Exc.	V.G.	Good	Fair	Poor
—	500	420	350	250	150

100 SERIES MODELS

Fifth design models evolving from lever name series. Series introduced small pushbutton barrel release take-down and deletes shrouded breech.

Supermatic S-100

Like lever take-down Supermatic, with new take-down. Available with 4.5" or 6.75" barrels or combination with both barrel lengths. Grooved front and backstraps on frame. Model produced briefly in 1954. Weights of 2 and 3 oz. were provided with this model, as was filler strip for when weights were not used. Note: Add $250 for factory combination; 15 percent premium for box with papers.

NIB	Exc.	V.G.	Good	Fair	Poor
—	850	750	550	400	200

Olympic O-100

Like lever take-down Olympic, with new take-down. Available with 4.5" or 6.75" barrels or combination with both barrel lengths. Grooved front and backstraps on frame. Model produced briefly in 1954. Weights of 2 and

3 oz. were provided with this model, as was filler strip for when weights were not used. Note: Add $250 for factory combination; 15 percent premium for box with papers.

NIB	Exc.	V.G.	Good	Fair	Poor
—	1200	950	650	500	300

Field King FK-100

Like lever take-down Field King, with new take-down. Available with 4.5" or 6.75" barrels or combination with both barrel lengths. Model produced briefly in 1954. Note: Add $225 premium for factory combination; 15 percent premium for box with papers.

NIB	Exc.	V.G.	Good	Fair	Poor
—	750	650	400	300	200

Sport King SK-100

Like lever take-down Sport King, with new take-down. Available with 4.5" or 6.75" barrels or combination with both barrel lengths. Produced 1954 to 1957. In late 1958, Col. Rex Applegate imported about 300 of these pistols into Mexico. Guns are marked with his company's name "ARMAMEX". Marked "ARMAMEX, MEXICO" on right side of barrel and "SPORT KING/CAL .22 L.R." on left side of barrel. Serial numbers around 870,084-870,383. Note that Applegate guns were made after 102 series was in production. Armamex catalog number 1910. Note: Add $200 premium for factory combination; $250 premium for Armamex version; 10 percent premium for box with papers.

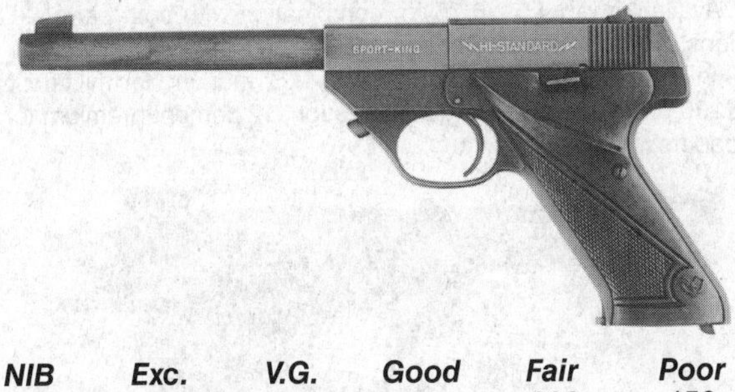

NIB	Exc.	V.G.	Good	Fair	Poor
—	450	400	300	200	150

Sport King Lightweight SK-100

Aluminum frame like Flite King LW-100 in .22 LR caliber. Produced 1956 to 1964. Also available nickel plated 1957 to 1960. Note: Add $150 premium for nickel finish; $200 premium for factory combination; 12 percent premium for box with papers.

NIB	Exc.	V.G.	Good	Fair	Poor
—	520	450	350	280	200

Flite King LW-100

.22 Short caliber semi-automatic pistol, with 10-shot magazine. Blued finish, with black anodized aluminum frame and slide. Brown plastic checkered thumbrest grips. Fixed sights. Available with 4.5" or 6.75" barrels or combination with both barrel lengths. Produced 1954 to 1957. Note: Add $200 for factory combination; 12 percent premium for box with papers.

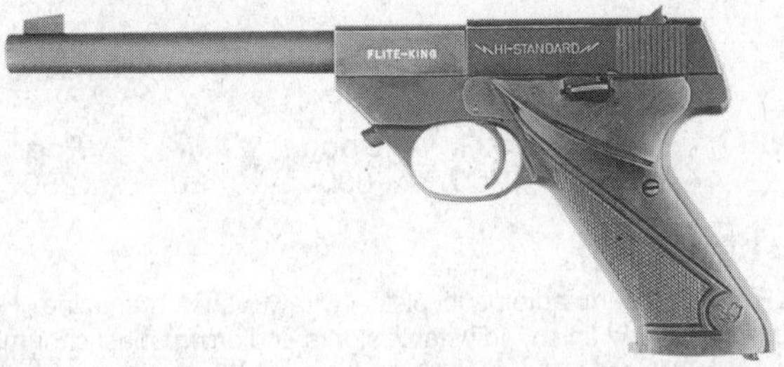

NIB	Exc.	V.G.	Good	Fair	Poor
—	620	520	400	300	200

Dura-Matic M-100

.22 LR caliber semi-automatic pistol, with 10-shot magazine. Striker-fired, fixed sights, blued finish, brown checkered plastic one-piece grip. Take-down by thumb nut. Available with 4.5" or 6.5" barrels or combination with both barrel lengths. Produced briefly in 1954. Note: Add $150 premium for factory combination; 12 percent premium for box with papers.

NIB	Exc.	V.G.	Good	Fair	Poor
—	500	350	300	250	180

101 SERIES MODELS

Sixth design models evolving from 100 series. Series continued small pushbutton barrel release take-down.

Olympic O-101

.22 Short caliber semi-automatic pistol, with 10-shot magazine. Heavy round barrel, blued finish, adjustable sights and brown plastic thumbrest grips. Grooved front and backstraps on frame. Available with 4.5" or 6.75" barrels or combination with both barrel lengths. The 6.75" barrel incorporates a muzzle brake with one slot on either side of front sight. Note: Add $250 premium for factory combination; 13 percent premium for box with papers.

NIB	Exc.	V.G.	Good	Fair	Poor
—	1150	950	800	500	300

Supermatic S-101

.22 LR caliber semi-automatic pistol, with 10-shot magazine. Heavy round barrel, blued finish, adjustable sights and brown plastic thumbrest grips. Grooved front and backstraps on frame. Available with 4.5" or 6.75" barrels or combination with both barrel lengths. The 6.75" barrel incorporates a muzzle brake with one slot on either side of front sight. Produced with U.S. marking for military. Note: Add $250 premium for factory combination; 13 percent premium for box with papers.

NIB	Exc.	V.G.	Good	Fair	Poor
—	780	700	600	420	250

Field King FK-101

.22 LR caliber semi-automatic pistol, with 10-shot magazine. Heavy round barrel, blued finish, adjustable sights and brown plastic thumbrest grips. Available with 4.5" or 6.75" barrels or combination with both barrel lengths. Note: Add $225 premium for factory combination; 15 percent premium for box with papers.

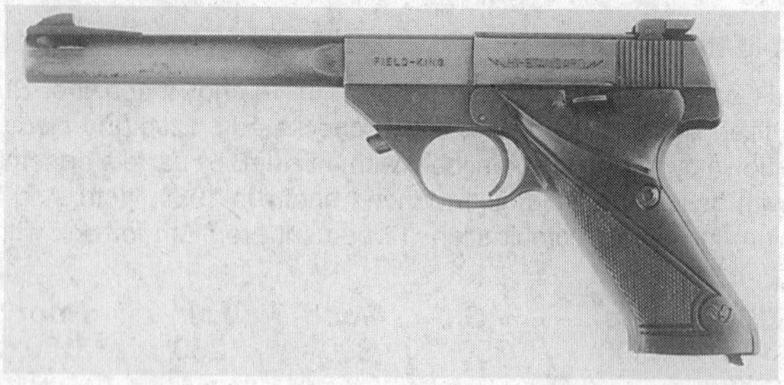

NIB	Exc.	V.G.	Good	Fair	Poor
—	680	550	500	300	200

Dura-Matic M-101

Like Dura-matic M-100, with slightly different locking method for thumb nut take-down. Produced 1954 to 1970. Later appeared renamed "Plinker" M-101 in 1971 to 1973. Plinker not available with both barrel combinations. Slightly modified version was sold by Sears Roebuck & Co. as J. C. Higgins M-80. Note: Add $150 premium for factory combination; 10 percent premium for box with papers.

NIB	Exc.	V.G.	Good	Fair	Poor
—	380	320	250	180	100

Conversion Kits

Kits convert .22 LR to .22 Short and include barrel, aluminum slide and magazine for .22 Short to .22 LR, in which case slide is steel. Prices for kit in original factory boxes. Note: First advertised for 101 Series guns. Later versions were produced for lever take-down guns. Catalog numbers are unknown for conversion kits for lever take-down guns.

NIB	Exc.	V.G.	Good	Fair	Poor
—	600	480	—	—	—

102 & 103 SERIES MODELS

The 102 Series was a major design change. Incorporating a new frame with large pushbutton take-down release. Also new was a superb adjustable sight. Little difference between the two series.

Supermatic Trophy

.22 LR caliber semi-automatic pistol, with 10-shot magazine. Tapered barrel with enlarged register at muzzle end to hold a removable muzzle brake. Super polished blue finish; adjustable sights; 2 and 3 oz. adjustable weights and checkered walnut thumbrest grips. Grooved front and backstraps on frame. Available with 6.75", 8" or 10" barrels. Occasionally sold as combination including two barrels. Premiums for 10" barrels and combinations in original boxes. 5.5" bull barrel available in 103s after April 1962, 7.25" fluted barrels available in 103s after April 1963. Note: Add $125 premium for 8" barrel; $225 premium for 10" barrel; 12 percent premium for box with papers; 14 percent premium for light oak case.

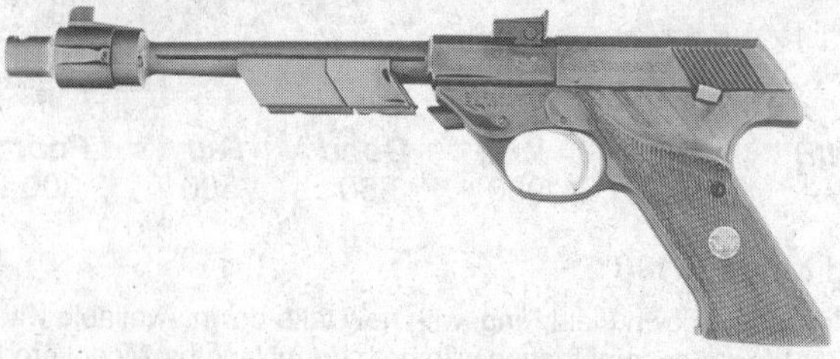

NIB	Exc.	V.G.	Good	Fair	Poor
—	1350	1100	820	500	250

Supermatic Citation

Like Supermatic Trophy, with checkered plastic grips. Blued finish, without trophy's super polished finish. Grooved front and backstraps on frame. 5.5" bull barrel available in 103s after April 1962. Also produced with U.S. marking for military. Note: Add $100 premium for 8" barrel; $200 premium for 10" barrel; 12 percent premiun for box with papers; 18 percent premium for light oak case.

NIB	Exc.	V.G.	Good	Fair	Poor
—	900	820	680	400	200

Supermatic Tournament

.22 LR caliber semi-automatic pistol, with 10-shot magazine. Barrels are round and tapered. Blued finish, adjustable sights and checkered plastic grips. Available with 4.5", 6.75" or combination with both barrels. Combinations available in 102 Series only. 5.5" bull barrel replaced the 4.5" barrel in early 1962. Also produced with U.S. marking for military. Note: Add $200 premium for factory combination; 12 percent premium for box with papers.

NIB	Exc.	V.G.	Good	Fair	Poor
—	720	600	450	300	200

Olympic

.22 Short caliber version of Supermatic Citation. Early models marked "Olympic Citation", changed to "Olympic" only in 1960. Grooved front and backstraps on frame. 6.75", 8" and 10" barrels produced. 5.5" bull barrel available on later 103 production. Note: Add $125 premium for 8" barrel; $225 premium for 10" barrel; $150 premium for "Olympic Citation" marked guns; 12 percent premium for box with papers.

NIB	Exc.	V.G.	Good	Fair	Poor
—	1150	900	750	450	220

Olympic ISU

Like an Olympic only available with 6.75" barrel and integral muzzle brake. Grooved front and backstraps on frame. Note: Add 12 percent premium for box with papers.

NIB	Exc.	V.G.	Good	Fair	Poor
—	1250	950	800	550	250

Olympic Trophy ISU

Olympic ISU with Supermatic Trophy finish. Grooved front and back straps on frame. Produced in 103 Series only. Fewer than 500 produced. Note: Add 10 percent premium for box with papers.

NIB	Exc.	V.G.	Good	Fair	Poor
—	2250	1450	800	550	250

Sport King

.22 LR caliber semi-automatic pistol, with 10-shot magazine. Barrels are light-weight, round and tapered. Blued finish, fixed sights and checkered plastic grips. Available with 4.5", 6.75" or combination with both barrel lengths. Produced 1957 to 1970 and 1974 to 1977. Also available 1974 to 1977 with nickel finish. Note: Add $100 premium for nickel finish; $200 premium for factory combination; 20 percent premium for box with papers.

NIB	Exc.	V.G.	Good	Fair	Poor
—	420	350	300	200	150

Flite King

.22 Short caliber version of Sport King Models 102 and 103. Models have steel frames. Note: Add $200 premium for factory combination; 12 percent premium for box with papers.

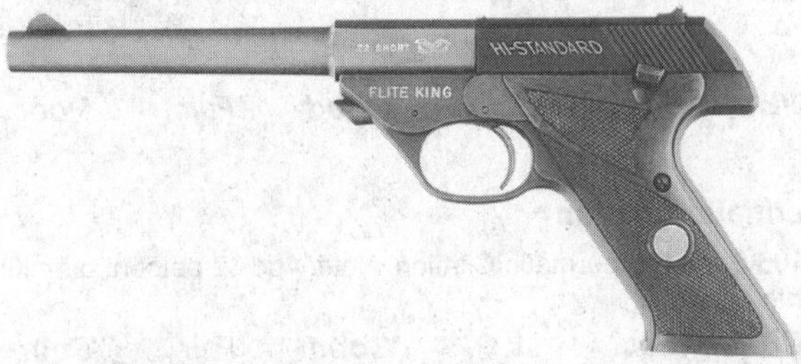

NIB	Exc.	V.G.	Good	Fair	Poor
—	520	450	350	300	200

Sharpshooter

.22 LR caliber semi-automatic pistol, with 10-shot magazine. 5.5" bull barrel, blued finish, adjustable sights, checkered plastic grips. Some produced with Model 103-marked slides. Although the 103-marked guns have 1969 and later serial numbers they were shipped after introduction of Sharpshooter in 1971 and were probably converted from unsold Sport Kings. No premium for 103-marked. Variation without series marked on slide is most plentiful. Produced 1971 to 1977. Note: Add 15 percent premium for box with papers.

NIB	Exc.	V.G.	Good	Fair	Poor
—	600	480	400	300	200

Conversion Kits

Kits convert .22 LR to .22 Short and include barrel, aluminum slide and magazine. Prices for kits in original boxes.

NIB	Exc.	V.G.	Good	Fair	Poor
900	700	580	—	—	—

104 SERIES MODELS

Last of slant grip gun designs. Early production marked "Model 104". Later production unmarked.

Supermatic Trophy

.22 LR caliber semi-automatic pistol, with 10-shot magazine. Super polished blue finish; adjustable sights; 2 and 3 oz. adjustable weights; checkered walnut thumbrest grips. Grooved front and backstraps on frame. Available with 5.5" bull or 7.25" fluted barrels. Both barrels accept removable muzzle brake. Note: Add $150 premium for high polish blue finish; 12 percent premium for box with papers.

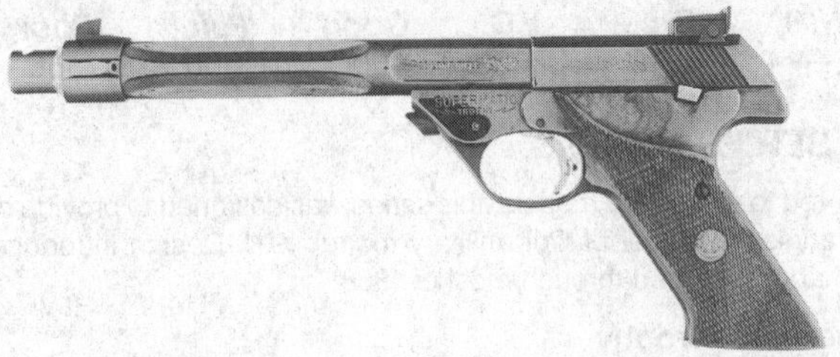

NIB	Exc.	V.G.	Good	Fair	Poor
—	1180	1050	800	450	220

Supermatic Citation

.22 LR caliber semi-automatic pistol, with 10-shot magazine. Blue finish, adjustable sights, 2 and 3 oz. adjustable weights, checkered walnut thumbrest grips. Grooved front and back-straps on frame. Note: Add 12 percent premium for box with papers.

NIB	Exc.	V.G.	Good	Fair	Poor
—	850	750	620	350	180

Olympic

Like 103 Series 8" barrel models. Note: Add 12 percent premium for box with papers.

NIB	Exc.	V.G.	Good	Fair	Poor
—	1300	1150	850	550	300

Olympic ISU

Like 103 model. 6.75" barrel with integral brake. 5.5" version introduced in 1964. Catalogs and price list refer to 9295 as both Olympic and Olympic ISU. Met ISU regulations and included removable muzzle brake and weights. Note: Add 12 percent premium for box with papers.

NIB	Exc.	V.G.	Good	Fair	Poor
—	1200	1000	850	450	250

Victor (Slant Grip)

.22 LR caliber semi-automatic pistol, with 10-shot magazine. 4.5" and 5.5" slab-sided barrels with ventilated or solid ribs. Adjustable sights are integral with rib. Blue finish, barrel tapped for weight, checkered walnut thumbrest grips. Grooved front and backstraps on frame. Probably fewer than 600 of these slant grip Victors in all configurations. Probably fewer than 40 each of 4.5" guns. Trigger adjustable for both pull and over-travel. Most guns in serial number range above 2401xxx with few in ML serial number series. Note: Early ventilated rib barrels were steel and later ones aluminum, without a change in catalog numbers. **BEWARE**—fakes exist. Note: Add $75 premium for steel rib; $200 premium for solid rib; $200 premium for 4.5" barrel; 15 percent premium for box with papers.

Victor with 4.5 solid rib barrel.

NIB	Exc.	V.G.	Good	Fair	Poor
—	3210	2650	1000	650	350

106 SERIES MODELS

Referred to as military models, this series was designed to provide same grip angles and feel of Colt military model 1911. Design introduced in 1965 and continued through most of 1968.

Supermatic Trophy

Like 104 Series Supermatic Trophy, with new military frame. Stippled front and backstraps on frame. Note: Add $100 premium for high polish blue finish; $200 premium for guns with boxes and accessories if factory records verify model numbers; 12 percent premium for box with papers.

NIB	Exc.	V.G.	Good	Fair	Poor
—	1100	850	600	450	200

Supermatic Citation

Like 104 Series Supermatic Citation, with new military frame. Stippled front and backstraps on frame. Note: Add $150 premium for guns with boxes and accessories if factory records verify model numbers; 12 percent premium for box with papers.

NIB	Exc.	V.G.	Good	Fair	Poor
—	850	750	500	300	180

Supermatic Tournament

Like 104 Series Supermatic Tournament, with new military frame. Stippled front and backstraps on frame. Note: Add $125 premium for guns with boxes and accessories if factory records verify model numbers; 12 percent premium for box with papers.

NIB	Exc.	V.G.	Good	Fair	Poor
—	720	650	400	250	180

Olympic

Listed in catalog not in shipping records. Catalog number 9235 for 5.5" barrel. **WARNING:** There is no evidence this model was actually produced.

Olympic ISU

Like 104 Series Olympic ISU, with new military frame. Stippled front and backstraps on frame. Note: Add $200 premium for guns with boxes and accessories if factory records verify model numbers; 12 percent premium for box with papers.

NIB	Exc.	V.G.	Good	Fair	Poor
—	1200	900	700	450	200

107 SERIES MODELS

Evolutionary successor to 106 Series. Series had frame re-designed to eliminate plugging of spring hole produced with old tooling. During time of this series production, MILITARY marking on frame was removed and then later reappeared near the end of traditional serial number series. MILITARY marking is absent from guns with ML prefixed serial numbers. No premium associated with these variations.

Olympic ISU

Like 106 Series Olympic ISU. Note: Add 12 percent premium for box with papers.

NIB	Exc.	V.G.	Good	Fair	Poor
—	1200	900	700	450	200

Olympic ISU 1980 Commemorative

Limited edition of 107 Olympic ISU, with 1,000 produced. "USA" prefix on serial numbers from 0001 to 1000. Engraved right side of slide has five gold ring Olympic logo. Offered with lined presentation case. Note: Prices are for guns with box, papers and presentation case; otherwise deduct $250 for guns in excellent condition.

NIB	Exc.	V.G.	Good	Fair	Poor
—	1750	1250	650	—	—

Supermatic Trophy

Like 106 Series Supermatic Trophy. Note: Add 12 percent premium for box with papers.

NIB	Exc.	V.G.	Good	Fair	Poor
—	980	750	500	250	180

Supermatic Trophy 1972 Commemorative

Limited edition of 107 Supermatic Trophy, with 1000 planned. "T" prefix on serial numbers from 0000 to 999. Engraved right side of slide has five gold ring Olympic logo. Offered with lined presentation case. Only 107 guns listed in shipping records, plus one frame. Couple of proto-types believed to exist in regular serial number series. Prices are for guns in original presentation cases. Note: One fully engraved gun is known.

NIB	Exc.	V.G.	Good	Fair	Poor
7500					

Supermatic Citation

Like 106 Series Supermatic Citation. Note: Add 12 percent premium for box with papers.

NIB	Exc.	V.G.	Good	Fair	Poor
—	850	650	500	250	180

Supermatic Tournament

Like 106 Series Supermatic Tournament. Smooth front and backstraps on frame. Note: Add 12 percent premium for box with papers.

NIB	Exc.	V.G.	Good	Fair	Poor
—	700	550	400	300	180

Sport King

Like 103 Series Sport King, with military frame. Note: Add 12 percent premium for box with papers.

NIB	Exc.	V.G.	Good	Fair	Poor
—	450	400	350	300	180

Sharpshooter

Like 103 Series Sharpshooter, with military frame. Note: Add 12 percent premium for box with papers.

NIB	Exc.	V.G.	Good	Fair	Poor
—	550	450	400	350	180

Survival Kit

An electroless nickel Sharpshooter, with 5.5" barrel in canvas carrying case and extra electroless nickel magazine. Note: Deduct $100 for guns without case; $65 for guns without extra magazine, for guns in excellent condition.

NIB	Exc.	V.G.	Good	Fair	Poor
—	600	480	400	300	180

Victor

.22 LR caliber semi-automatic pistol, with 10-shot magazine. 4.5" and 5.5" slab-sided barrels with ventilated or solid ribs. Adjustable sights are integral with rib. Blue finish, barrel tapped for weight, checkered walnut thumbrest grips. Stippled front and backstraps on frame. Early ventilated ribs were steel; aluminum replaced steel on later ventilated ribs. Still later a clearance groove was added for spent shell ejection behind barrel. Early models marked THE VICTOR on left side of barrel; later guns marked simply VICTOR on left side of frame. Few transition guns marked in both locations. Note: Add $125 premium for steel ribs; $125 premium for solid rib guns, premium for 4.5" barreled guns; $140 premium for Hamden guns (7-digit serial numbers and ML prefix serial numbers below ML 25,000); 12 percent premium for box with papers.

NIB	Exc.	V.G.	Good	Fair	Poor
—	1020	800	700	450	200

10-X

.22 LR caliber semi-automatic pistol, with 10-shot magazine. Matte blue finish, adjustable sights, checkered walnut thumbrest grips painted black. Stippled front and backstraps on frame. Available with 5.5" bull barrel. Assembled by a master gunsmith. Gunsmith's initials stamped in frame under left grip panel. Produced in 1981. Note: Prices are for guns with box and papers including test target, otherwise deduct $175.

NIB	Exc.	V.G.	Good	Fair	Poor
—	2800	2350	1700	800	300

SH SERIES MODELS

Final design produced by High Standard. Change in take-down from large pushbutton introduced with 102 Series and continuing through 107 Series, to hex socket head cap screw take-down.

Supermatic Trophy

Like 107 Supermatic Trophy, with new take-down. Note: Add 10 percent premium for box with papers.

NIB	Exc.	V.G.	Good	Fair	Poor
—	750	700	600	450	200

Supermatic Citation

Like 107 Supermatic Citation, with new take-down. Note: Add 10 percent premium for box with papers.

NIB	Exc.	V.G.	Good	Fair	Poor
—	700	620	550	400	200

Citation II

New gun like Supermatic Citation, with barrel slabbed on sides like Victor and smooth front and backstraps on frame. 5.5" and 7.25" barrels available. Blued finish, adjustable sights. Electroless nickel version utilized in some survival kits. Note: Add 10 percent premium for box with papers.

NIB	Exc.	V.G.	Good	Fair	Poor
—	550	500	400	300	200

Sport King-M

Like 107 Sport King, with new take-down. Electroless nickel finish also available. Note: Add 10 percent premium for box with papers.

NIB	Exc.	V.G.	Good	Fair	Poor
—	350	280	190	150	100

Victor

Like 107 Victor, with new take-down. Only available with 5.5" barrel. Note: Add 10 percent premium for box with papers.

NIB	Exc.	V.G.	Good	Fair	Poor
—	800	700	580	400	200

Sharpshooter-M

Like 107 Sharpshooter, with new take-down. Electroless nickel version utilized in some survival kits. Note: Add 10 percent premium for box with papers.

NIB	Exc.	V.G.	Good	Fair	Poor
—	420	380	300	200	100

10-X

Like 107 10-X, with new take-down. Also available with 7.25" fluted barrel and 5.5" ribbed barrel like Victor. Note: Add $500 premium for 7.25" barrel; $1,000 for ribbed barrel like Victor. Prices are for guns with box and papers including test target, otherwise deduct $150.

NIB	Exc.	V.G.	Good	Fair	Poor
—	2320	1900	1200	750	300

Survival Kit (with carrying case)

Electroless nickel Sharpshooter or electroless nickel Citation II, with 5.5" barrel in canvas carrying case, with an extra electroless nickel magazine. Two different fabrics utilized during production. Note: Deduct $100 for guns without case; $65 for guns without extra magazine, for guns in excellent condition.

NIB	Exc.	V.G.	Good	Fair	Poor
—	620	580	480	300	200

Conversion Kits for Military Frame Guns

Kits convert .22 LR to .22 Short and include barrel, aluminum slide and 2 magazines. Note: Prices are for kits in original boxes.

NIB	Exc.	V.G.	Good	Fair	Poor
—	620	390	—	—	—

DERRINGERS

A .22-caliber or .22 Magnum caliber over/under double-action-only derringer, with 3.50" barrels. Found with three different types of markings.

Type 1 Markings

Type 1 Markings are found on early models which are marked "HI-STANDARD" / "DERRINGER" and have EAGLE logo on left side of barrel. Models marked "D-100" for .22-caliber and "DM-101" for .22 Magnum on left side of barrel. Date range 1962 to about 1967.

Type 2 Markings

Type 2 Markings are found on later models marked "HI-STANDARD" / "DERRINGER" and had TRIGGER logo. Early .22-caliber models marked "D-100" and later .22-caliber models beginning about 1969 were marked "D-101" on left side of barrel. .22 Magnum models marked "DM-101" on left side of barrel. Date range 1967 to about 1970.

Type 3 Markings

Type 3 Markings are found on latest models marked simply "DERRINGER" without HI STANDARD or either logo. These models also marked "D-101" for .22-caliber and "DM-101" for .22 Magnum on left side of barrel.

Blued finish, white or black grips, 1962-1984

NIB	Exc.	V.G.	Good	Fair	Poor
—	450	350	250	120	80

Nickel Finish black grips, introduced 1970

NIB	Exc.	V.G.	Good	Fair	Poor
—	450	350	250	120	80

Electroless Nickel Finish with checkered walnut grips

NIB	Exc.	V.G.	Good	Fair	Poor
—	480	380	250	120	80

Silver-Plated Derringer

A .22 Magnum derringer, with presentation case. Faux black mother of pearl grips. 501 made. Serial numbers SP 0 through SP 500. Produced in 1981.

NIB	Exc.	V.G.	Good	Fair	Poor
—	750	700	500	200	150

Gold-Plated Derringer

Note: Prices for GP serial number guns with presentation case. $100 premium for DM prefix guns in Exc. condition with presentation case; $150 premium for 1960s gold guns in Exc. condition with presentation cases.

NIB	Exc.	V.G.	Good	Fair	Poor
—	800	720	550	200	150

REVOLVERS

POLICE-STYLE REVOLVERS

Revolvers begin with R-100 design series and continue through R-109. Later steel-framed Sentinels carry no design series markings. Changes of design series designations indicate design changes to guns. Only R-105 known to date is a private label gun made for Sears. Design series designations and associated catalog numbers listed are best estimates at time of publication.

Earliest Sentinels in 1955 were in separate serial number series from 1 through approximately 45000. They were included in serial number series common to all handguns. In 1974 they were again put in separate serial number series with S prefix: S101 through S79946. Many later guns had V suffix which indicated gun was visually imperfect, but guaranteed to work properly.

Sentinel Aluminum Frames

A 9-shot single-/double-action revolver, with swing-out cylinder for .22 Short, Long or LR cartridges. Fixed sights. Sentinel snub 2.375" barrel model had bobbed hammer from its introduction until 1960. Beginning in 1961 this changed to standard spur hammer with no change in catalog number. Beginning with R-102 series ejector had a spring return. Available in configurations listed.

High Standard private-labeled aluminum-framed Sentinels for both Sears and Western Auto. From 1957 through 1962 High Standard offered 2.375" snub-barreled Sentinel in three different color anodized frames. These guns had nickel-plated cylinders, triggers and hammers. Grips were round-butt ivory-colored plastic. Note: Add $20 premium for nickel; $20 for R-102 marked guns. Deduct $15 for early models without spring return ejector.

NIB	Exc.	V.G.	Good	Fair	Poor
—	350	280	180	120	100

Gold

NIB	Exc.	V.G.	Good	Fair	Poor
—	1000	850	500	300	200

Turquoise

NIB	Exc.	V.G.	Good	Fair	Poor
—	1200	900	650	300	200

Pink

NIB	Exc.	V.G.	Good	Fair	Poor
—	1200	900	650	300	200

Sentinel Imperial

Has two-piece walnut square-butt grips, ramp front and adjustable rear sights. Note: Add $15 premium for nickel.

NIB	Exc.	V.G.	Good	Fair	Poor
—	380	320	280	150	100

Sentinel Deluxe

Has two-piece walnut square-butt grips and fixed sights. Note: Add $20 premium for nickel.

NIB	Exc.	V.G.	Good	Fair	Poor
—	380	320	280	150	100

Sentinel Snub

Has 2.375" barrel, with round-butt grips. Note: Add $20 premium for nickel.

NIB	Exc.	V.G.	Good	Fair	Poor
—	380	320	280	150	100

Sentinel Steel Frames

Model like Mark I Sentinels without Mark I markings. Offered as a combination with cylinders for .22 LR and .22 Win. Magnum. Prices for guns with both cylinders. Note: Add $25 premium for adjustable sights. Deduct $50 for guns with only one cylinder.

NIB	Exc.	V.G.	Good	Fair	Poor
—	420	380	300	150	100

Kit Gun

A 9-shot single-/double-action revolver, with swing-out cylinder for .22 Short, Long or LR cartridges. Blue finish, aluminum frame, 4.0" barrel and adjustable sights. Wood round-butt grips.

NIB	Exc.	V.G.	Good	Fair	Poor
—	350	300	200	150	100

Camp Gun

A 9-shot single-/double-action revolver, with swing-out cylinder for .22 Short, Long, LR cartridges or .22 Magnum. Available as combination with both cylinders. Blue finished steel frame, adjustable sights. Note: Add $50 premium for combination with both cylinders.

NIB	Exc.	V.G.	Good	Fair	Poor
—	350	300	200	150	100

Sentinel Mark I

A 9-shot single-/double-action revolver, with swing-out cylinder for .22 Short, Long or LR cartridges. Steel frame and fixed sights. Available with blue and nickel finishes in 2", 3" and 4" barrels. Adjustable sights available on 3" and 4" barreled guns only. Wood square-butt grips. Note: Add $25 premium for adjustable sights; $25 for nickel.

NIB	Exc.	V.G.	Good	Fair	Poor
—	350	300	200	150	100

Sentinel Mark IV

Like Mark I above except in .22 Magnum. Note: Add $25 premium for nickel; $25 premium for adjustable sights.

NIB	Exc.	V.G.	Good	Fair	Poor
—	400	350	250	180	120

Sentinel Mark II

A .357 Magnum single-/double-action 6-shot revolver, with swing-out cylinder. Blue finish, steel frame, fixed sights. Produced by Dan Wesson for High Standard. Sold 1974 through 1975.

NIB	Exc.	V.G.	Good	Fair	Poor
—	480	400	320	250	200

Sentinel Mark III

Like Mark II above except with adjustable sights. Sold 1974 through 1975.

NIB	Exc.	V.G.	Good	Fair	Poor
—	500	420	350	280	200

Power Plus

A 5-shot single-/double-action revolver, with swing-out cylinder for .38 Special cartridges. Blue finished steel frame. Only 177 guns produced. Serial numbers between PG 1010 and PG 1273.

NIB	Exc.	V.G.	Good	Fair	Poor
—	650	580	480	300	250

Crusader

A .44 Magnum or .45 Colt caliber double-action swing-out cylinder revolver, with unique geared action. Adjustable sights. 6-shot cylinder. First 51 guns had long barrels, special engraving, gold crusader figure on side plate and anniversary rollmark to commemorate High Standard's 50th Anniversary.

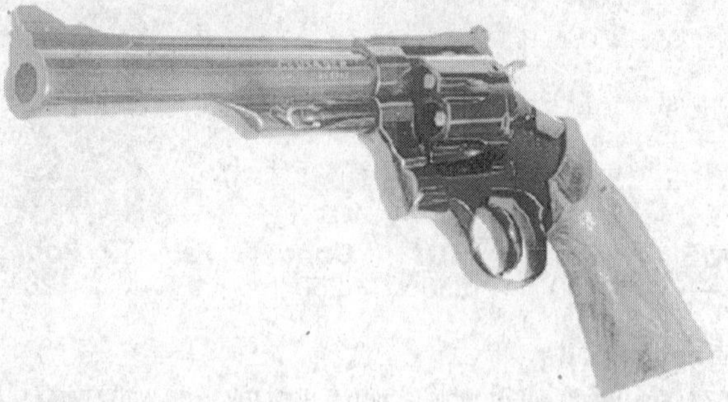

.45 Colt (s/n 000 to 050)

Note: Values are for .45 Colt with serial numbers 000 to 050. Add 10 percent for .44 Magnum; $1,000 for serial numbers 000 and 001 or prototypes C001, C002, C003.

NIB	Exc.	V.G.	Good	Fair	Poor
2500	2000	1500	750	—	—

.45 Colt (s/n over 050)

Note: Prices for serial numbers over 050 in .45 Colt. Add 10 percent for .44 Magnum. Expect to pay a premium for matching set.

NIB	Exc.	V.G.	Good	Fair	Poor
1750	1500	1000	650	—	—

WESTERN-STYLE REVOLVERS

Western-style revolvers begin with W-100 design series and continue through W-106. Later steel-framed Sentinels carry no design series markings. Changes of design series designations indicate design changes to guns. Design series designations and associated catalog numbers listed are best estimates at time of publication.

High Standard private labeled aluminum-framed Western-style revolvers for Sears and Western Auto.

Double Nine with Aluminum Frame

A 9-shot single-/double-action revolver for .22 Short, Long, LR cartridges and all aluminum frame guns. One model has grip straps and triggerguard, with gold plating contrasting with blue frame. Note: Add $50 premium for nickel.

NIB	Exc.	V.G.	Good	Fair	Poor
—	400	320	200	150	100

Double Nine with Steel Frame

Available as .22 Short/Long/LR, .22 Magnum or combination with both cylinders. Note: Add $45 premium for combination models; $50 premium for nickel.

NIB	Exc.	V.G.	Good	Fair	Poor
—	400	320	200	150	100

Longhorn

A 9-shot single-/double-action revolver for .22 Short, Long, LR cartridges and all aluminum frame guns. Blue finish, fixed sights and square-butt grips. One model has grip straps and triggerguard, with gold plating contrasting with blue frame. Sears version exists.

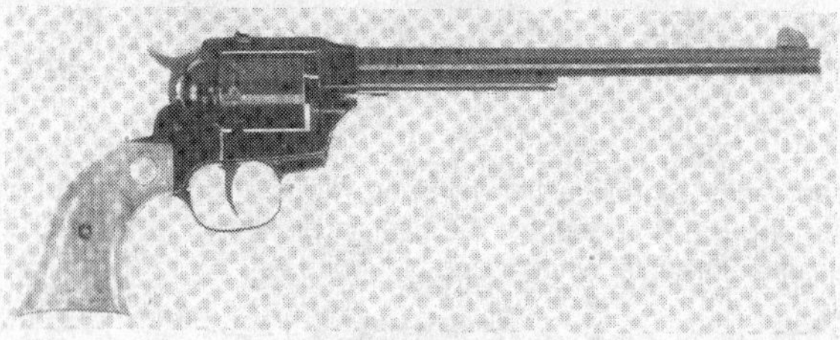

NIB	Exc.	V.G.	Good	Fair	Poor
—	480	450	350	280	200

Longhorns with Steel Frame

Guns available as .22 Short/Long/LR, .22 Magnum or combination with both cylinders. Note: Add $45 premium for combination models; $25 premium for adjustable sights.

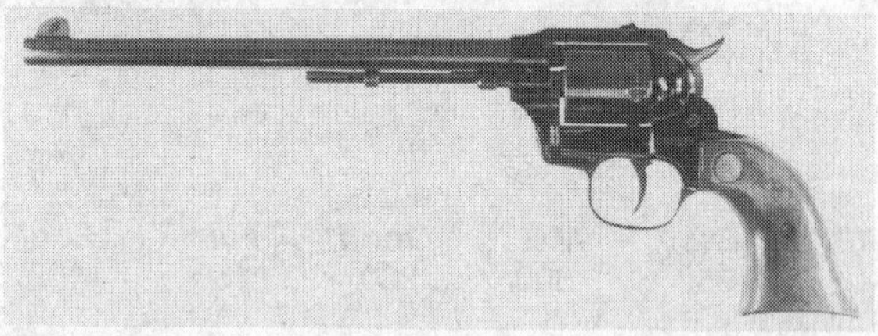

NIB	Exc.	V.G.	Good	Fair	Poor
—	480	450	350	280	200

Marshal

A 9-shot single-/double-action revolver for .22 Short, Long or LR cartridges. Blue finish. Aluminum frame, 5.5" barrel, fixed sights and square-butt stag style plastic grips. Offered in special promotion package, with holster, trigger lock and spray can of G-96 gun scrubber. Price for gun only. Note: Add $40 premium if box, papers and accessories are present and in excellent condition.

NIB	Exc.	V.G.	Good	Fair	Poor
—	350	250	200	150	100

Posse

A 9-shot single-/double-action revolver for .22 Short, Long or LR cartridges. Blue finish, with brass colored grip straps and triggerguard. Aluminum frame, 3.5" barrel, fixed sights and square-butt walnut grips.

NIB	Exc.	V.G.	Good	Fair	Poor
—	450	380	280	150	100

Natchez

A 9-shot single-/double-action revolver for .22 Short, Long or LR cartridges. Aluminum frame, 4.5" barrel, fixed sights and bird's-head style ivory colored plastic grips.

NIB	Exc.	V.G.	Good	Fair	Poor
800	750	650	500	350	200

Hombre

A 9-shot single-/double-action revolver for .22 Short/Long/LR cartridges. Blue or nickel finish. Aluminum frame, 4" barrel, fixed sights and square-butt walnut grips. Note: Add $20 premium for nickel.

NIB	Exc.	V.G.	Good	Fair	Poor
—	420	380	300	250	180

Durango

A 9-shot single-/double-action revolver for .22 Short/Long/LR cartridges. Blue or nickel finish. Aluminum or steel frame, 4.5" or 5.5" barrel, fixed or adjustable sights and square-butt walnut grips. Two models have their grip straps and triggerguard with contrasting plating to blue frame. Note: Add $50 premium for nickel; $25 premium for steel frame; $25 premium for adjustable sights.

NIB	Exc.	V.G.	Good	Fair	Poor
—	420	380	300	250	180

The Gun/High Sierra

A 9-shot single-/double-action revolver for .22 Short, Long or LR cartridges. Available as combination model, with second cylinder in .22 Magnum. Blued finish, with gold plated grip straps and triggerguard. Steel frame, 7" octagonal barrel, fixed or adjustable sights and square-butt walnut grips. Revolver introduced as "The Gun" in February 1973 price list and name changed to "High Sierra" by November 1973 price list. Note that early "The Gun" had neither "High Sierra" markings nor any other name. Note: Add $60 premium for presentation case; $55 premium for combination models; $25 for adjustable sights.

NIB	Exc.	V.G.	Good	Fair	Poor
—	480	420	350	280	200

BLACKPOWDER REVOLVERS

Guns were series of .36-caliber cap-and-ball revolvers that began production in 1974 and ran through 1976. These are reproductions of Confederate copies of Colt Model 1851 Navy. Note: Most Confederate copies of Colt had round barrels not octagonal as found on Colts. Frames were made by High Standard and balance of parts by Uberti. Guns were assembled and finished by High Standard.

Griswold & Gunnison

Blued finish with brass frame. Six-shot single-action. Commemorative gun came with pine presentation case and brass belt plate depicting Georgia state seal. Note: Price is for gun in case with accessories. Deduct $100 for gun only in Exc. condition.

NIB	Exc.	V.G.	Good	Fair	Poor
—	450	380	300	180	100

Leech & Rigdon

Blued finish with steel frame. Six-shot single-action. Commemorative gun came with presentation case and re-production of Civil War belt buckle. Note: Price is for gun in case with accessories. Deduct $100 for gun only in Exc. condition.

NIB	Exc.	V.G.	Good	Fair	Poor
—	450	380	300	180	100

Schneider & Glassick

Blued finish, with steel frame. Six-shot single-action. Commemorative gun came with presentation case and modern version of Confederate "D" guard Bowie knife. Note: Add $450 for Confederate "D" Bowie knife.

NIB	Exc.	V.G.	Good	Fair	Poor
—	450	380	300	180	100

Bicentennial 1776-1976

Blued finish, with steel frame. Six-shot single-action. Guns came with two versions of presentation case. One case is pine marked "High Standard" and trigger logo on lid, with powder flask and silver dollar-sized medallion inside; other a brown leatherette covered case with "American Bicentennial 1776-1976" and contains a pewter Bicentennial belt buckle.

NIB	Exc.	V.G.	Good	Fair	Poor
—	450	380	300	180	100

Special Presentation Bicentennial

100 guns were available in presentation cases, with "US" serial number prefixes. Serial numbers US 11 through US 50 are in walnut presentation cases, with purple fitted lining and pewter Bicentennial belt buckle. Top of case marked "Limited Edition / American Bicentennial / 1776 – 1976". Guns are engraved on frame, cylinder barrel, loading lever, and hammer. Catalog number 9339 has a steel frame, with round barrel; catalog number 9340 has a brass frame, with octagonal barrel.

NIB	Exc.	V.G.	Good	Fair	Poor
—	700	500	350	180	120

SHOTGUNS

High Standard made a series of semi-automatic and slide-action shotguns for Sears, Roebuck & Co. under the J. C. Higgins brand name from late 1940s to late 1950s. Beginning in 1960, similar models were made under the High Standard name. Most of these remained in production until mid 1970s.

SEMI-AUTOMATIC SHOTGUNS

Supermatic Field

Gas-operated semi-automatic shotgun. Blued finish, plain pistol grip walnut stock and forearm, 4-round magazine capacity. Supermatic Field models were superseded by models in Supermatic Deluxe group beginning in 1966. 12-gauge guns have 2.75" chambers; 20-gauge 3" chambers. Note: Slight premium for 20-gauge.

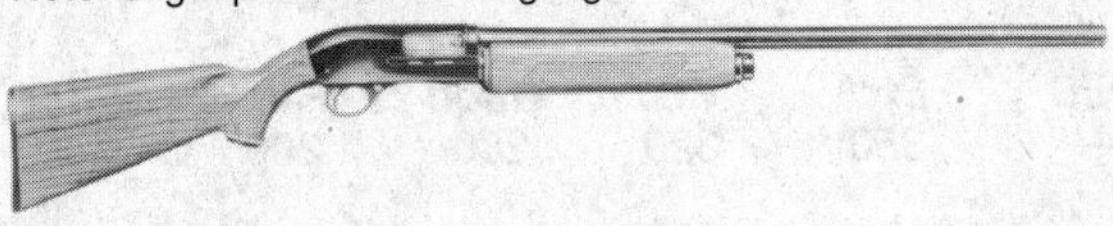

NIB	Exc.	V.G.	Good	Fair	Poor
—	320	300	250	200	100

Supermatic Special

Like Supermatic Field except with 27" barrel and 6-position click-stop adjustable choke. Supermatic Special models were superseded by models in Supermatic Deluxe group beginning in 1966. 12-gauge guns have 2.75" chambers.

NIB	Exc.	V.G.	Good	Fair	Poor
—	320	300	250	200	100

Supermatic Deluxe

Gas-operated semi-automatic shotgun. Blued finish, checkered pistol grip walnut stock and forearm, 4-round magazine. Adjustable choke had 6-click-stop positions. Recoil pad beginning 1966. 12-gauge guns have 2.75" chambers; 20-gauge 3". Note: Add $20 premium for ventilated rib versions.

NIB	Exc.	V.G.	Good	Fair	Poor
—	350	320	280	200	100

Supermatic Citation

Same as Trophy, without ventilated rib. 6-click-stop adjustable choke. Catalog #8220 has compensator integral, with adjustable choke. 12-gauge guns have 2.75" chambers.

NIB	Exc.	V.G.	Good	Fair	Poor
—	320	300	250	200	100

Supermatic Trophy

Gas-operated semi-automatic shotgun. Blued finish, checkered walnut stock and forend, 4-round magazine, 6-click-stop adjustable choke. Catalog #8230 has compensator integral, with adjustable choke. 12-gauge guns have 2.75" chambers; 20-gauge 3".

NIB	Exc.	V.G.	Good	Fair	Poor
—	320	300	250	200	100

Supermatic Duck

Gas-operated semi-automatic shotgun. Chambered for 3" Magnum. Suitable for all 2.75" shells. Blued finish. Checkered pistol grip walnut stock and forearm. Magazine capacity: five 2.75" shells; four 3" shells. Recoil pad. Note: Add $20 premium for ventilated rib versions.

NIB	Exc.	V.G.	Good	Fair	Poor
—	350	320	280	250	130

Supermatic Deer

Like Supermatic Deluxe, with rifle sight. Recoil pad. Receiver tapped for peep sight on catalog #8246. 12-gauge guns have 2.75" chambers.

NIB	Exc.	V.G.	Good	Fair	Poor
—	320	300	250	200	100

Supermatic Skeet

Same features as Supermatic Deluxe except select American walnut stock and forearm. No recoil pad. 12-gauge 2.75" chambers; 20-gauge 3".

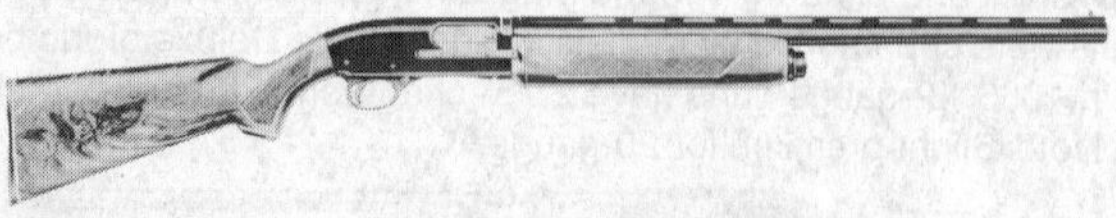

NIB	Exc.	V.G.	Good	Fair	Poor
—	350	320	280	200	100

Supermatic Trap

Same features as Supermatic Deluxe except select American walnut stock and forearm. Recoil pad. Catalog #8266 is Executive Trap model, with Fajen Monte Carlo stock. 12-gauge guns have 2.75" chambers.

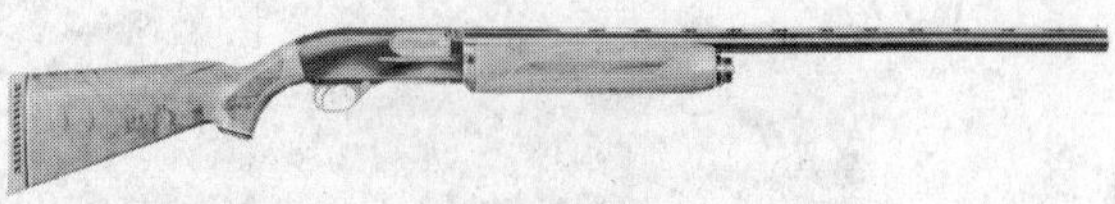

NIB	Exc.	V.G.	Good	Fair	Poor
—	350	320	280	200	100

PUMP SHOTGUNS

Model 200

Economy 12-gauge pump shotgun, sold as part of a promotional package beginning in 1971. Package included Model 200, zippered gun case, plastic trigger lock and G-96 gun lubricant. Prices are for gun alone. Note: Add $30 for gun with complete promotional package.

NIB	Exc.	V.G.	Good	Fair	Poor
—	200	150	120	100	80

Flite King Field

Slide-action shotgun. Blued finish, plain pistol grip walnut stock and forearm. Catalog #8450, magazine capacity: five 2.5" shells; four 3" shells. 12-gauge guns have 2.75" chambers; 20 gauge 3". Note: Add 50 percent for .410 bore.

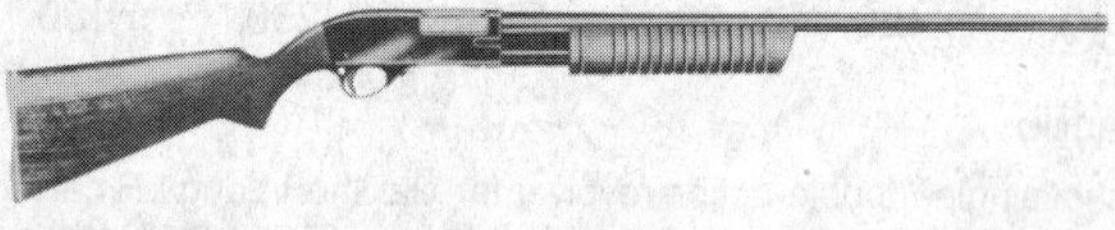

NIB	Exc.	V.G.	Good	Fair	Poor
—	250	220	180	140	100

Flite King Brush

Like Flite King Field, with adjustable rifle sights. Receiver tapped for Williams sight and provision exists for sling swivels. Deluxe models have Williams receiver sight, leather sling with swivels and recoil pad. 12-gauge guns have 2.75" chambers. Note: Add $10 premium for deluxe model.

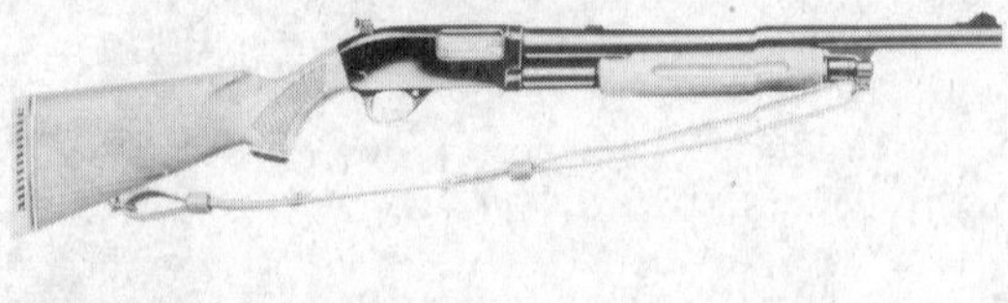

Flite King Brush Deluxe

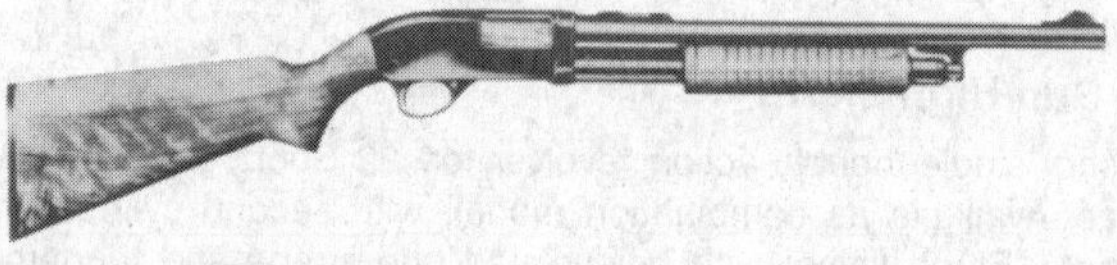

NIB	Exc.	V.G.	Good	Fair	Poor
—	280	240	200	180	140

Flite King Special

Like Flite King Field, with 27" barrel and 6-click-stop adjustable choke. 12-gauge guns have 2.75" chambers; 20-gauge 3".

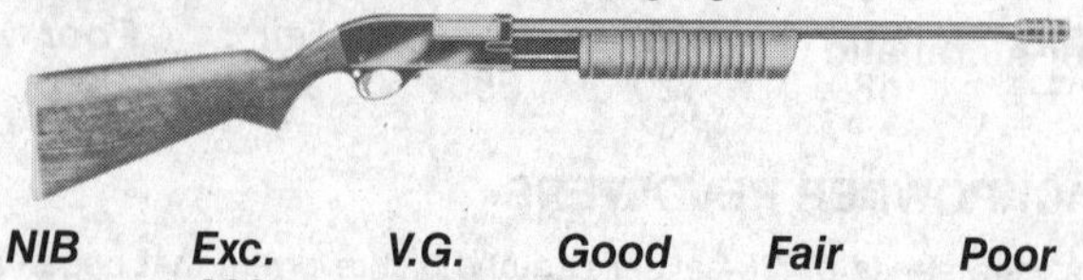

NIB	Exc.	V.G.	Good	Fair	Poor
—	280	220	180	140	100

Flite King Deluxe

Slide-action shotgun. Blued finish, checkered pistol grip walnut stock and forearm, 5-round magazine. Available with-/without ventilated rib. #8411 and #6411 were boys "Converta Pump" sold with two stocks: one youth size, one full. Adjustable choke had 6-click-stop positions. Recoil pad beginning 1966 except .410 models. 12-gauge guns have 2.75" chambers; 16- gauge 2.75"; 20-gauge 3"; 28-gauge 2.75"; .410 bore 3". Note: Add $20 for ventilated rib.

NIB	Exc.	V.G.	Good	Fair	Poor
—	280	250	210	180	140

Flite King Citation

Like Flite King Trophy without ventilated rib. Catalog #8130 has compensator integral, with 6-click-stop position adjustable choke. 12- and 16-gauge guns have 2.75" chambers.

NIB	Exc.	V.G.	Good	Fair	Poor
—	280	220	180	140	100

Flite King Trophy

Slide-action shotgun. Blued finish, checkered pistol grip walnut stock and forearm, 5-round magazine, ventilated rib. Catalog #8140 has compensator integral, with adjustable choke. 12-gauge guns have 2.75" chambers; 20-gauge 3".

NIB	Exc.	V.G.	Good	Fair	Poor
—	280	220	200	180	140

Flite King Skeet

Same features as Flite King Deluxe, except select American walnut stock and forearm. No recoil pad. 12-gauge guns have 2.75" chambers; 20-gauge 3"; 28-gauge 2.75"; .410 bore 3".

NIB	Exc.	V.G.	Good	Fair	Poor
—	320	280	220	180	140

Flite King Trap

Same features as Flite King Deluxe, except select American walnut stock and forearm. Recoil pad. #8166 is Executive Trap model, with Fajen Monte Carlo stock. Catalog #6165 model has provisions for interchangeable barrels. 12-gauge guns have 2.75" chambers. Note: Add $25 for Fajen Monte Carlo stock.

NIB	Exc.	V.G.	Good	Fair	Poor
—	300	250	200	180	140

BOLT-ACTION SHOTGUNS

Model 514

Sears version of this shotgun was recalled for safety considerations in late 1990s.

NIB	Exc.	V.G.	Good	Fair	Poor
—	140	80	60	40	20

POLICE SHOTGUNS

Semi-Automatic

Gas-operated semi-automatic 12-gauge shotgun. Plain oiled pistol grip walnut stock and forearm. Magazine capacity 4 rounds. Recoil pad.

NIB	Exc.	V.G.	Good	Fair	Poor
—	300	250	200	180	120

Model 10-A

Gas-operated semi-automatic 12-gauge shotgun. Bullpup configuration with pistol grip. Integral carrying handle and flashlight on top of gun. Magazine capacity 4 rounds.

NIB	Exc.	V.G.	Good	Fair	Poor
—	1850	1150	800	550	250

Model 10-B

Gas-operated semi-automatic 12-gauge shotgun. Bullpup configuration with pistol grip. Fitted with integral folding carrying handle and mounting provisions for flashlight. Magazine capacity 4 rounds. Carrying case catalog #50284 and attachable flashlight catalog #50285, sold optionally. Note: Values for gun with flashlight.

NIB	Exc.	V.G.	Good	Fair	Poor
—	1700	1000	700	450	200

Pump

Slide-action 12-gauge shotgun. Plain pistol grip oiled walnut stock and forearm—changed from walnut to stained and lacquered birch in mid 1970s. Magazine capacity: #8111/8113 6-rounds; #8104/8129 5-rounds. A 1963 flyer mentions #8105 Flite King Brush 20" and #8107 Flite King Deluxe 20" as riot guns. Data on #8105 and #8107 listed under Flite King Brush.

NIB	Exc.	V.G.	Good	Fair	Poor
—	300	220	150	120	100

IMPORTED SHOTGUNS

Supermatic Shadow Automatic

Gas-operated semi-automatic shotgun in 12- and 20-gauge. Interchangeable barrels. Checkered walnut stock and forearm. Special "airflow" rib. Imported from Nikko in Japan.

NIB	Exc.	V.G.	Good	Fair	Poor
—	450	350	260	200	180

Supermatic Shadow Indy Over/Under

Boxlock over/under 12-gauge shotgun, with selective automatic ejectors and single trigger. Receiver fully engraved. Skipline checkered walnut stock, with pistol grip. Ventilated forearm. Recoil pad. Special "airflow" rib. Imported from Nikko in Japan.

NIB	Exc.	V.G.	Good	Fair	Poor
—	920	850	720	550	350

Supermatic Shadow Seven Over/Under

Like Shadow Indy, with standard size ventilated rib, conventional forearm, no recoil pad, standard checkering and less engraving. Imported from Nikko in Japan.

NIB	Exc.	V.G.	Good	Fair	Poor
—	720	650	520	400	320

RIFLES

Sport King/Flite King

.22-caliber slide-action rifle capable of using Short/Long/LR ammunition interchangeably. 24" barrel, open sights and tubular magazine. Magazine capacity 21 Short, 17 Long or 15 LR.

NIB	Exc.	V.G.	Good	Fair	Poor
—	220	150	80	60	50

Sport King Field

.22-caliber semi-automatic rifle capable of using Short/Long/LR ammunition interchangeably. 22.25" barrel, open sights and tubular magazine. Magazine capacity 21 Short, 17 Long, 15 LR. Walnut stock.

NIB	Exc.	V.G.	Good	Fair	Poor
—	250	200	100	80	50

Sport King Special

Like Sport King Field except Monte Carlo walnut stock, with pistol grip.

NIB	Exc.	V.G.	Good	Fair	Poor
—	220	150	120	100	80

Sport King Deluxe/Sport King Rifle

Sport King Special with a new name. Catalog #6005 is the same gun but called just Sport King. Promotional package offered that included Sport King rifle, zippered gun case, plastic trigger lock and G-96 gun lubricant. This package was catalog #8007. Note: Add a 10 percent premium for complete 8007 package in original box.

NIB	Exc.	V.G.	Good	Fair	Poor
—	280	220	140	100	80

Sport King Carbine

.22 carbine semi-automatic rifle capable of using Short/Long/LR ammunition interchangeably. 18.25" barrel, open sights and tubular magazine. Magazine capacity 17 Short, 14 Long, 12 LR. Straight-grip walnut stock, with barrel band and sling.

NIB	Exc.	V.G.	Good	Fair	Poor
—	220	180	150	100	80

Hi-Power Field Grade

A .270 or .30-06 caliber bolt-action rifle, with 22" barrel, open sights and 4-shot magazine. Blued, with walnut stock.

NIB	Exc.	V.G.	Good	Fair	Poor
—	500	420	300	150	100

Hi-Power Deluxe

Like Field Grade except has Monte Carlo-style stock.

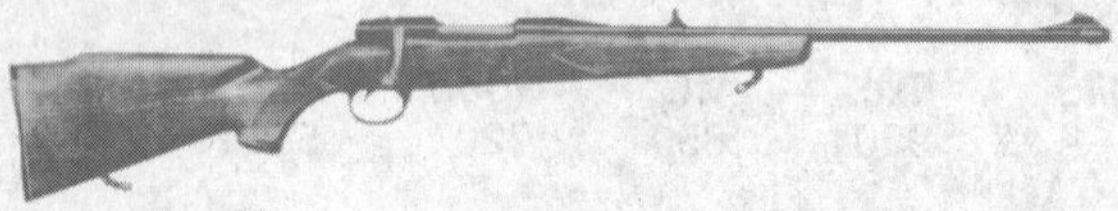

NIB	Exc.	V.G.	Good	Fair	Poor
—	580	500	380	220	150

HIGH STANDARD MANUFACTURING CO.

Houston, Texas

Company established in 1993. Among its employees are several who worked for High Standard Company that closed its doors in Connecticut in 1984. Remaining semi-automatic pistols in this section were made in Houston. This firm expanded in 2004, by purchasing the assets of AMT-Auto Mag and Interarms.

Supermatic Citation

Chambered for .22 LR. Fitted with 5.5" barrel. Matte blue or Parkerized finish. Weight about 44 oz. Discontinued.

NIB	Exc.	V.G.	Good	Fair	Poor
420	320	280	220	180	100

Supermatic Citation MS

Designed for metallic silhouette shooting. Introduced in 1996. Fitted with 10" barrel. Weight about 49 oz. Discontinued.

NIB	Exc.	V.G.	Good	Fair	Poor
800	650	500	400	320	200

Supermatic Tournament

Chambered for .22 LR. Fitted with 5.5" barrel. Matte blue finish. Weight about 44 oz.

NIB	Exc.	V.G.	Good	Fair	Poor
900	750	600	450	320	200

Supermatic Trophy

Offered with 5.5" or 7.25" barrels. Chambered for .22 LR. Adjustable trigger, barrel weights, gold-plated trigger safety, slide stop and magazine catch. Matte blue or Parkerized finish. Weight about 45 oz. Note: Add 10 percent for 7.25 barrel.

NIB	Exc.	V.G.	Good	Fair	Poor
800	650	500	400	320	200

Olympic Model

Chambered for .22 Short. Fitted with 5.5" bull barrel. Blued finish. Weight about 44 oz.

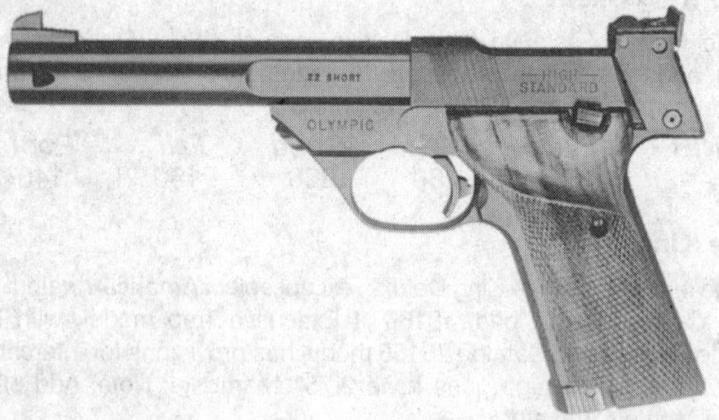

NIB	Exc.	V.G.	Good	Fair	Poor
900	750	600	450	300	150

Olympic ISU

Similar to previous model. Fitted with 6.75" barrel with internal stabilizer. Magazine capacity 5 rounds. Checkered walnut grips. Weight about 45 oz. Discontinued in 1995.

NIB	Exc.	V.G.	Good	Fair	Poor
600	500	350	300	200	150

Olympic Rapid Fire

Introduced in 1996. Chambered for .22 Short cartridge, with 4" barrel, integral muzzle brake and forward mounted compensator. Special grips. Weight about 46 oz. Discontinued.

NIB	Exc.	V.G.	Good	Fair	Poor
1000	850	700	500	420	300

Sport King

Chambered for .22 LR. Fitted with 4.5" or 6.75" barrel. Adjustable rear sight. Weight about 44 oz. Limited edition.

NIB	Exc.	V.G.	Good	Fair	Poor
650	400	220	150	100	80

Victor

With 4.5" barrel and blue or Parkerized finish. Note: Add $75 for adjustable sights.

NIB	Exc.	V.G.	Good	Fair	Poor
800	650	500	400	320	200

10-X

Fitted with 5.5" barrel. Weight about 44 oz. From HS Custom Shop.

NIB	Exc.	V.G.	Good	Fair	Poor
1100	950	800	600	420	300

10-X—Shea Model

Fitted with 4.5" or 5.5" barrel. Limited to 150 pistols per year. Note: Add 10 percent for 5.5 barrel.

NIB	Exc.	V.G.	Good	Fair	Poor
1400	1200	850	750	500	350

Olympic Trophy Space Gun

Semi-automatic pistol chambered in .22 LR. Re-creation of famed competition "Space Gun" from 1960s. Features include 8" or 10" barrel; 10-round magazine; adjustable sights; barrel weight; adjustable muzzle brake; blue-black finish with gold highlights.

NIB	Exc.	V.G.	Good	Fair	Poor
1200	900	800	650	500	200

Model 1911A1

Re-production of standard Colt design imported from the Philippines, where it is made by Armscor. Chambered in .45 ACP or .38 Super. Has 5" barrel with fixed, adjustable or Novak Night Sights. Note: Add $40 for .38 Super; $300 for adjustable or Novak sights.

NIB	Exc.	V.G.	Good	Fair	Poor
450	400	380	350	300	150

HSA-15

An A2 configuration AR-15 style rifle, with 16" or 20" barrel with muzzle brake, 30-shot magazine, fixed or folding stock (carbine). Chambered in .223/5.56 NATO. Previously chambered in 6x45mm.

NIB	Exc.	V.G.	Good	Fair	Poor
800	700	580	420	320	220

HSA-15 Enforcer

M4-style carbine, with 16" barrel. Chambered for 5.56 NATO or .300 Blackout. Features include A2 flash hider, forged aluminum upper and lower receiver, six-position adjustable stock, Picatinny rail.

NIB	Exc.	V.G.	Good	Fair	Poor
1000	850	700	500	—	—

HSA-15 National Match

Chambered in 5.56 NATO, with 20" or 24" heavy fluted barrel. Knight two-stage trigger.

NIB	Exc.	V.G.	Good	Fair	Poor
1100	950	800	650	300	200

HILL, W.J.

Birmingham, England

Hill's Self-Extracting Revolver (Antique)

.32-caliber double-action folding trigger revolver, with 3.75" barrel and 6-shot cylinder. Marked "Hill's Patent Self Extractor". Blued, with walnut grips.

Exc.	Fine	V.G.	Good	Fair	Poor
1020	500	400	300	150	100

HILLIARD, D. H.

Cornish, New Hampshire

Underhammer Pistol (Antique)

.34-caliber under hammer percussion pistol, with varying barrel lengths. Blued, with walnut grips. Active 1842 to 1877. Hillard also made underhamer rifles. Values are similar to those for pistols.

Exc.	Fine	V.G.	Good	Fair	Poor
1500	1200	900	600	400	200

HINO-KUMORO

Tokyo, Japan

7.65mm or 8mm Nambu semi-automatic pistol manufactured in limited quantities between 1905 and 1912. Operation of this pistol involves pulling muzzle forward until slide engages a catch on trigger assembly. Pulling trigger at this point allows barrel to move back and engage cartridge nose into chamber. Squeezing grip safety then allows barrel to slam back into fixed firing pin on breech-block. Very Rare. Prospective purchasers are advised to secure a qualified appraisal prior to acquisition.

NIB	Exc.	V.G.	Good	Fair	Poor
—	18000	14000	9000	7000	3000

HODGKINS, D. C. & SONS

Macon, Georgia

See—BILHARZ, HALL & CO.

HOFER, P.

Feriach, Austria

Gunmaker specializing in double-barrel rifles made strictly to custom order. Value depends on local demand, chamberings and other factors.

HOFFMAN, LOUIS
Vicksburg, Mississippi

Pocket Pistol (Antique)

.41-caliber percussion pocket pistol, with 3" barrel, German silver mounts and walnut stock. Active 1857 to 1886. Hoffman also made plains rifles (q.v.) and other percussion firearms.

Exc.	Fine	V.G.	Good	Fair	Poor
900	520	360	200	100	70

HOLDEN, C. B.
Worcester, Massachusetts

Open Frame Rifle (Antique)

.44 rimfire single-shot rifle, with 28" barrel, open sights, silver plated bronze frame and walnut stock. Barrel marked "C.B. Holden Worcester-Mass.". Produced in limited quantities during mid-1860s.

Exc.	Fine	V.G.	Good	Fair	Poor
3500	2200	1500	750	500	300

HOLECK, EMANUEL
Czechoslovakia

Holeck Rifle

Chambered for .276 cartridge. Semi-automatic rifle submitted for testing for U.S. military trials in 1920s. Barrel length 21.5", with upper portion slotted for operating handle. Rotating dial at barrel band. Rarely encountered. Note: Thanks to Jim Supica for research found in his Old Town Station Dispatch, in which one of these rifles was offered for sale.

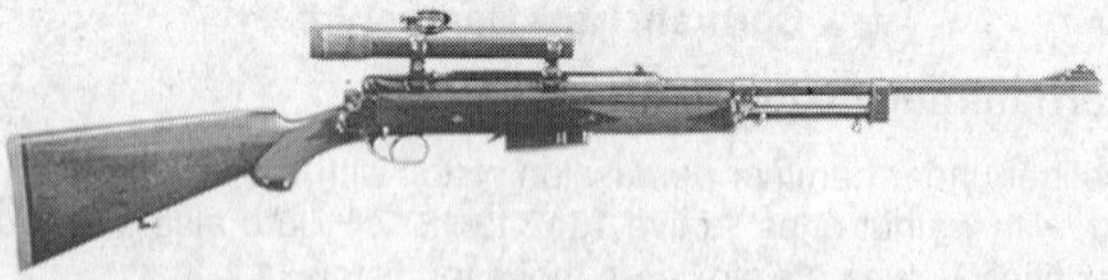

NIB	Exc.	V.G.	Good	Fair	Poor
—	4250	—	—	—	—

HOLLAND & HOLLAND, LTD.
London, England

Established in 1835, Holland & Holland has manufactured a wide variety of shotguns and rifles during its existence. Greater part of these arms are made to custom order.

DOUBLE RIFLES

No. 2 Grade Double Rifle

Sidelock double-barrel rifle produced in a variety of calibers, with 24" barrels, double triggers, automatic ejectors and express sights. Obsolete cartridges could be worth less. Note: Add 50 percent for calibers from .400 to .500; 100 percent for over .500.

NIB	Exc.	V.G.	Good	Fair	Poor
20000	17000	12500	10000	—	—

Royal Side-by-Side Rifle

Higher grade version of No. 2, with more elaborate engraving. Values shown are for .300 H&H. Note: Add 25 percent for larger calibers; 50 to 100 percent for Nitro Express calibers. Add 10000 to 15000 for ejectors.

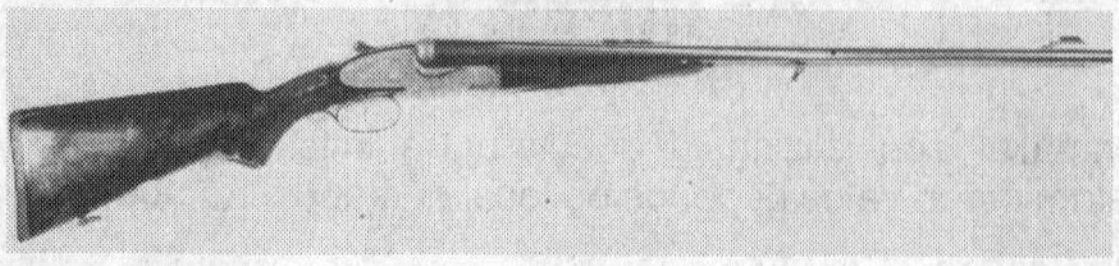

NIB	Exc.	V.G.	Good	Fair	Poor
35000	30000	25000	15000	—	—

H&H .700 Bore Side-by-Side Rifle

.700 H&H double-barrel rifle. Weight about 18 lbs. Currently manufactured. Because of its uniqueness, buyers should seek a qualified appraisal. Current base price approximately $200,000.

BOLT-ACTION RIFLES

Best Quality Rifle

Price depends on caliber and extra cost options. Retail prices for magazine rifles begin around $41,500, depending on value of the dollar. Due to uniqueness of each rifle an independent appraisal is a must prior to sale.

SHOTGUNS

Holland & Holland has been one of Britain's most prestigious makers of custom-made shotguns, all the way back to mid-19th Century. Currently the company makes several side-by-side and over/under models, with prices starting at approximately $75,000. Values of older models range from $8,000 to $10,000 for boxlock designs; $25,000 to $100,000 for sidelocks.

HOLLOWAY ARMS CO.
Ft. Worth, Texas

HAC Model 7

7.62x54mm semi-automatic rifle, with 20" barrel, adjustable sights, integral telescope mount and 20-shot magazine. Black anodized finish, with folding stock. No longer in production.

NIB	Exc.	V.G.	Good	Fair	Poor
2500	2000	1750	1200	600	500

HAC Model 7C

As above, with 16" barrel.

NIB	Exc.	V.G.	Good	Fair	Poor
2750	2500	2000	1400	700	500

HAC Model 7S

As above, with heavy barrel.

NIB	Exc.	V.G.	Good	Fair	Poor
2850	2650	2100	1500	700	500

HOLMES FIREARMS
Wheeler, Arkansas

MP-22

.22-caliber semi-automatic pistol, with 6" barrel and alloy receiver. Anodized black finish, with walnut grip. Manufactured in 1985.

NIB	Exc.	V.G.	Good	Fair	Poor
420	320	250	200	150	100

MP-83

Similar to above in 9mm or .45-caliber. Manufactured in 1985. Note: Several of Holmes pistols have been declared machine guns by BATFE, because of their easy conversion to full automatics. Make sure before purchase that a Class III license is not required.

NIB	Exc.	V.G.	Good	Fair	Poor
550	420	320	250	200	120

HONOR DEFENSE
Gainsville, GA

Manufacturer of polymer frame, striker-fire pistols since 2015.

Honor Guard Sub-Compact

Polymer frame striker fire chambered in 9mm with 3.2-in. barrel. Equipped with 7- or 8-rnd. magazine. Some models have manual thumb safety. Finish available in FDE, OD green, black and a variety of other colors.

NIB	Exc.	V.G.	Good	Fair	Poor
450	390	360	300	280	260

HOOD F. A. CO.
Norwich, Connecticut

Manufacturer of spur trigger .22- or .32-caliber revolvers, with varying length barrels and finishes. Many of these revolvers are found stamped only with trade names. This type of handgun is often referred to as a suicide special to denote its poor quality and lack of reliability.

NIB	Exc.	V.G.	Good	Fair	Poor
—	—	250	140	80	50

HOPKINS & ALLEN
Norwich, Connecticut 1868-1915

Also see XPERT

Hopkins & Allen was best known for inexpensive pocket revolvers. Firms like H&A, H&R and Iver Johnson have been called "Armorers to the Nation's Nightstands" in recognition of the common use of their products. At its peak, H&A was one of the largest American firearms manufacturers with production quantities approaching those of firms like Colt and Winchester. When H&A was formed in 1868, it took over production of Bacon Manufacturing Co. revolvers. Later, it acquired other makers such as Davenport Firearms (1901) and Forehand & Wadsworth (1902). The high-quality Merwin Hulbert & Co. (q.v.) revolvers produced in the 1870s and 1880s are usually found marked with the Hopkins & Allen name on the barrels. Trade names used by H&A on revolvers included Acme, Allen 22, American Eagle, Americus, Aristocrat, Black Prince, Blue Jacket, Blue Whistler, Buckeye, Bulldog, Captain Jack, Creedmoor, Czar, Dictator, Double Action No., Dreadnaught, Duchess, Duke, Encore, Essex, Excelsior, Expert, Forehand Model, Hinsdale, Imperial Arms, Life Guard, Metropolitan Police, Monarch, Morley, Mountain Eagle, Non XL, Old Hickory, Pointer, Range Model, Ranger, Red Jacket, Safety Police, Scott, Swamp Angel, Terror, The Challenge, Toledo Firearms, Towers Police Safety, Tramps Terror, Universal, Wolverine, XL, XLCR, and Xpert. Often these guns would not have the H&A name on them. Other firms also used some of these names for their products. Trade names reported on H&A long guns included Chichester, Cannon Breech, Douglas Arms, Dreadnought, King Nitro, KK, Seminole, and Worlds Fair. This is a recently revised and expanded section. Readers with comments and suggestions are invited to contact the editor.

Dictator .36 perc./.38 Rimfire Model (Antique)

.36-caliber percussion or .38 rimfire single-action revolver, with 4" barrel and 5-shot cylinder. Blued, with walnut grips. Barrel marked "Dictator". Made approximately 6,000 percussion; 5,000 rimfire. Note that this is not the same revolver as the inexpensive H&A Dictator spur-trigger revolver listed below. This model has a traditional triggerguard and an open-top frame, similar to the model listed above.

Exc.	Fine	V.G.	Good	Fair	Poor
2700	1600	1150	700	300	210

Spur-Trigger Revolvers (Antique)

Made in a wide variety of configurations in .22, .30, .32, .38, and .41 rimfire under the H&A name and a wide variety of trade names, the most common of which include XL, Blue Jacket, Ranger, Czar Most of these model names would include a number usually indicating the frame size and caliber, for example In XL's, No.1 or No. 1 ½ - .22 rimfire, No. 2 - .30 or .32 rimfire, No. 3 - .32 rimfire, No. 4 or No. 5- .38 rimfire, and No. 6 - .41 rimfire. Factors that may bring a premium over the prices listed include ornate decoration, unusual configuration, large caliber, or colorful trade name. Substantial premium for long-barrel revolving rifle variation with detachable stock, usually Czar Pocket Rifle, Ranger, and Chichester. Another trade name used was Dictator, which had also been used on the more valuable open-top percussion model listed earlier.

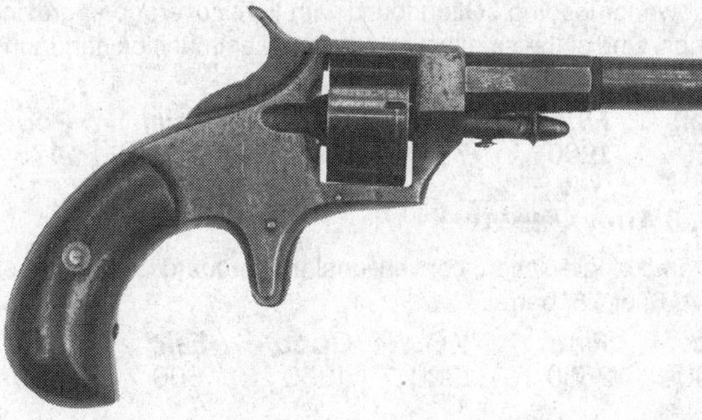

Courtesy Milwaukee Public Museum, Milwaukee, Wisconsin

Exc.	Fine	V.G.	Good	Fair	Poor
250	150	120	100	50	30

Pointer Derringer (Antique)

Unmarked Hopkins & Allen single-shot pistol stamped "Pointer" on barrel. Barrel length 2.75", caliber .22, frame of nickel-plated brass. Barrel swings sideways for loading. Bird's-head walnut grips. Believed about 2,500 made between 1870 and 1890.

Exc.	Fine	V.G.	Good	Fair	Poor
450	380	310	250	100	70

Spur-Trigger Side-Pivot Single-Shot Derringers (Antique)

XL Derringer in .41 rimfire, Pointer in .22 rimfire, and XL Vest Pocket in .22 have barrels that pivot to the side to load.

Exc.	Fine	V.G.	Good	Fair	Poor
350	200	150	100	50	30

Expert Single-Shot Derringer (Antique)

.22 or .30 rimfire with a very unusual design where a breech cover swivels sideways for loading and unloading. The rare Expert Pocket Rifle with 7" barrel and detachable stock is worth a substantial premium.

Exc.	Fine	V.G.	Good	Fair	Poor
700	400	320	250	130	90

Hopkins & Allen derringer (Antique)

.22-caliber single-shot pistol, with hinged 1.75" barrel that pivots downwards for loading. Blued or nickel-plated, with walnut, ivory or pearl grips. Frame marked "Hopkins & Allen Arms Co., Norwich, Conn. U.S.A." Several hundred manufactured in 1880s and 1890s.

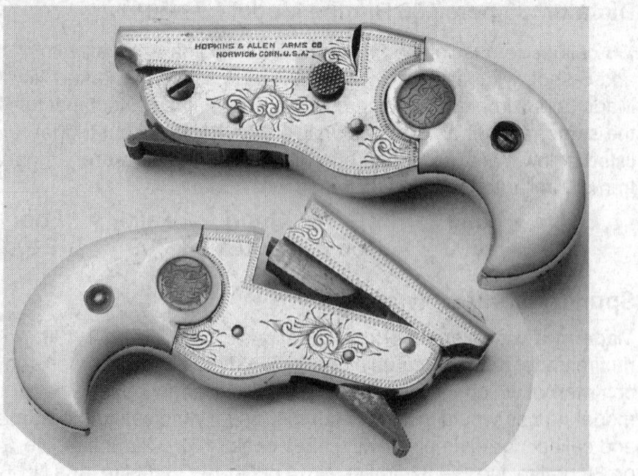

Jim Supica photo

Exc.	Fine	V.G.	Good	Fair	Poor
2750	950	640	330	150	100

Vest Pocket Derringer (Antique)

Hammerless double-action only, extreme birdshead grip, 1.75" barrel pivots down for loading. Often found with light coverage engraving and pearl grips. One of the smallest conventional ammunition handguns ever made.

Exc.	Fine	V.G.	Good	Fair	Poor
2750	1200	750	500	300	175

XL No. 8 Army (Antique)

Large frame single-action, conventional triggerguard, .44 rimfire or centerfire. 4", 6", or 7.5" barrel.

Exc.	Fine	V.G.	Good	Fair	Poor
3200	2500	1920	1350	600	420

XL Navy and XL Police (Antique)

Medium frame single-action, conventional triggerguard, .38 rimfire. XL Navy has square-butt grip frame and 6.5" barrel. XL Police has rounded corners to the grip frame and 4.5" barrel.

Exc.	Fine	V.G.	Good	Fair	Poor
2000	1250	1050	850	350	240

Double-Action Revolvers

These "pocket revolvers" were made in a wide variety of configurations and under a wide variety of names. Most are .22 rimfire, .32 S&W, or .38 S&W. They can be sorted into four major types: Solid-frame exposed hammer revolvers that typically load through a loading gate. Hammerless (concealed-hammer) solid frame. Manual safety worth slight premium. Top-break exposed hammer revolvers. Safety Police variations typically have a pinch-open barrel release instead of the conventional lift-latch found on most. Hammerless (concealed-hammer) top-break revolvers. A novel feature found on some of the conventional hammer revolvers, worth a slight premium, is a patented folding hammer spur. Others were made with bobbed hammer spurs. While most have round butts and relatively short barrels, 4" and 5" barrels are also found. The Range Models have oversize square butt grips with a slight knuckle and 4 ½" or 6" barrels.

NIB	Exc.	V.G.	Good	Fair	Poor
—	350	200	150	90	50

Single Shot Target Pistols

Top-break single shots in .22 rimfire, with 10", 8", or 6" barrels. The New Model Skeleton Stock Target Pistol with 18" barrel and detachable stock is worth a substantial premium.

NIB	Exc.	V.G.	Good	Fair	Poor
—	800	500	300	200	100

Falling Block Rifle (Antique)

.22 to .38-55 caliber single-shot rifle, with 24", 26" or 28" octagonal barrel. Blued, with walnut stock. Manufactured between 1888 and 1892.

Exc.	Fine	V.G.	Good	Fair	Poor
1250	650	490	330	180	120

Schuetzen Rifle

.22 or .25-20 caliber single-shot rifle, with 26" octagonal barrel, double-set trigger and Schuetzen-type buttplate. Blued, with walnut stock.

NIB	Exc.	V.G.	Good	Fair	Poor
—	—	2750	1030	550	200

Double-Barrel Shotguns

Hopkins & Allen also made good quality single-/double-barrel shotguns in large numbers. Many sold under private brand names such as Seminole and King Nitro. Both hammer and hammerless versions were offered. Values vary from $100 to $1000 depending on model and condition.

HOWA MACHINE COMPANY

Japan

Company manufactured bolt-action rifles for Smith & Wesson until 1985 and then for Mossberg in 1986 and 1987. From 1988 to 2000, Howa firearms were imported by Interarms of Alexandria, Virginia. These rifles are now imported by Legacy Sports of Reno, Nevada.

Model 1500 Hunter

.22-250, .223, .243, .270, 7mm Rem. Magnum .308, .30-06, .300 Win. Magnum and .338 Win. Magnum caliber bolt-action sporting rifle, with 22" or 24" barrel and 3- or 5-shot magazine. Blued or stainless steel, with checkered walnut stock. In 2002, offered with black polymer stock. Weight about 7.6 lbs. Note: Add $70 for stainless steel.

NIB	Exc.	V.G.	Good	Fair	Poor
600	500	450	320	220	180

Model 1500 JRS Classic

Offered in blue or stainless steel, with laminated stock. Chambered for .223 through .338 Win. Magnum calibers. Barrel length 22" or 24" depending on caliber. Weight about 8 lbs. Note: Add $70 for stainless steel.

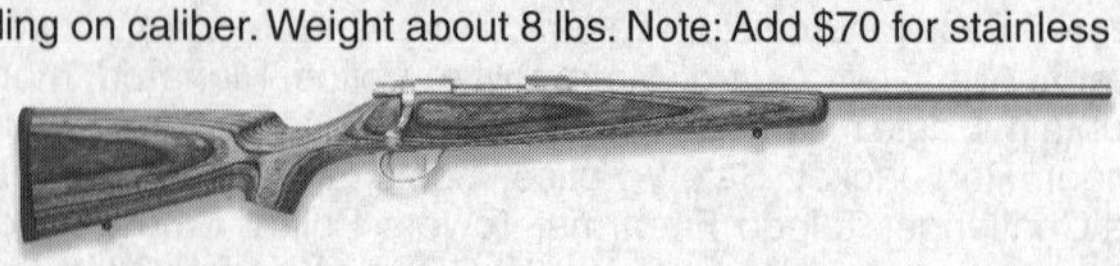

NIB	Exc.	V.G.	Good	Fair	Poor
650	580	500	380	250	200

Model 1500 Mountain

Introduced in 2004. Bolt-action chambered for .243, .308 or 7mm-08 cartridges. Fitted with 20" contoured barrel, no sights, blued finish, black hardwood stock. Stainless steel offered in .308 only. Magazine capacity 5 rounds. Weight about 6.4 lbs. Note: Add $115 for stainless steel.

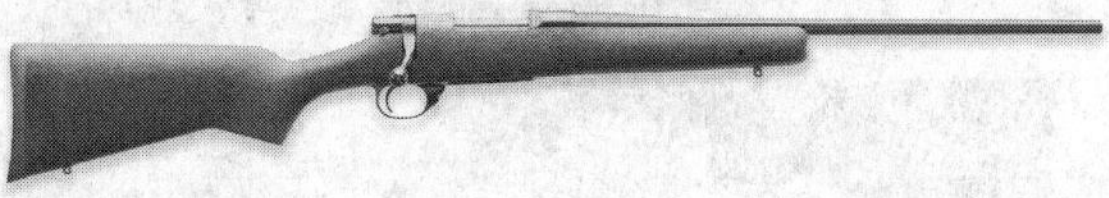

NIB	Exc.	V.G.	Good	Fair	Poor
600	500	450	320	220	180

Model 1500 Trophy

As above, with more finely figured walnut stocks and checkering. Introduced in 1988. No longer imported.

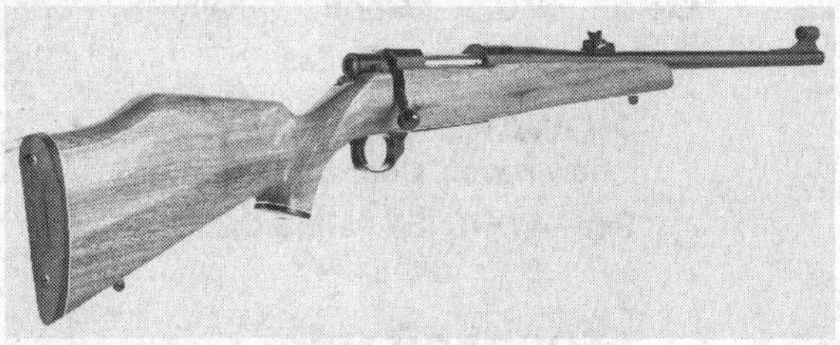

NIB	Exc.	V.G.	Good	Fair	Poor
650	520	450	380	250	200

Model 1500 Varmint

As above in .22-250 or .223 caliber, with 24" heavy barrel. Choice of walnut or synthetic stock in blue or stainless. Weight about 9.3 lbs. Introduced in 1988. Note: Add $70 for stainless steel; $20 for walnut stock.

NIB	Exc.	V.G.	Good	Fair	Poor
650	600	500	380	250	200

Model 1500 Varmint Supreme

Features stainless steel barrel. Chambered for .223, .22-250, .308 and .243. No sights. Choice of black synthetic or laminated stock, with Monte Carlo comb. Note: Add $110 for thumbhole stock.

NIB	Exc.	V.G.	Good	Fair	Poor
650	520	450	380	250	200

Model 1500 Lightning Rifle

Introduced in 1993. Has black composite checkered stock, with schnabel forend. Buttstock is Monte Carlo. Choice of blue or stainless steel. Offered in .223, .22-250, .243, .270, .308, .30-06, 7mm Rem. Magnum, .300 and .338 Win. Magnum. Weight about 7.5 lbs. Note: Add $70 for stainless steel.

NIB	Exc.	V.G.	Good	Fair	Poor
600	520	450	320	220	180

Model 1500 Youth

Chambered for .243, .308 or 7mm-08 cartridge. Barrel length 20". Black hardwood stock, with 1" shorter length of pull than standard. Weight about 6.3 lbs. Introduced in 2004. Note: Add $115 for stainless steel .308 version.

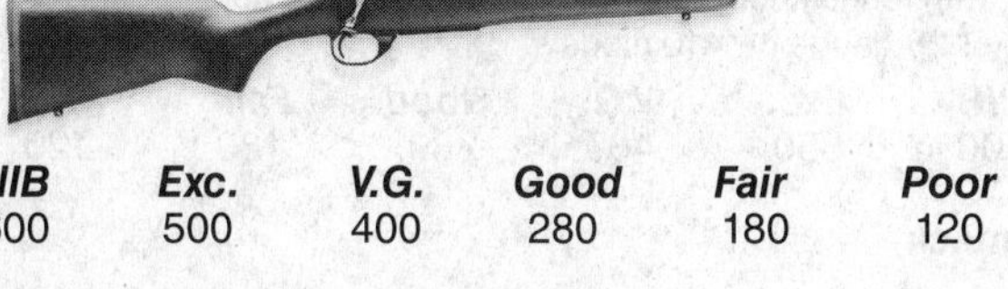

NIB	Exc.	V.G.	Good	Fair	Poor
600	500	400	280	180	120

Model 1500 Thumbhole Sporter

As above, with thumbhole stock. Weight about 8.25 lbs. Note: Add $70 for stainless steel.

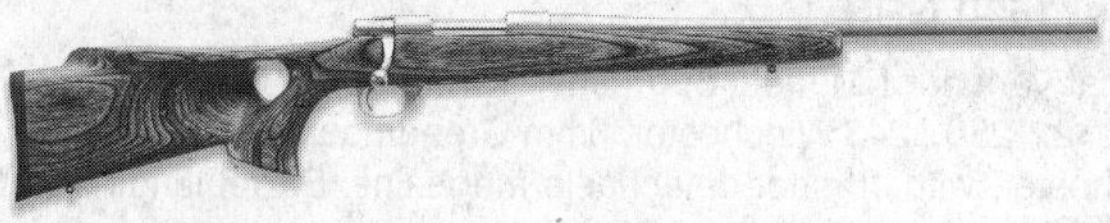

NIB	Exc.	V.G.	Good	Fair	Poor
750	620	500	400	280	150

Model 1500 Custom

Chambered for .300 WSM or .300 Win. Magnum cartridge. Fitted with 22" or 24" barrel, depending on caliber. Polymer or laminated stock. Weight about 8 lbs. Blued or stainless steel. Note: Add $70 for stainless steel.

NIB	Exc.	V.G.	Good	Fair	Poor
950	800	700	500	320	180

Realtree Camo Rifle

Introduced in 1993. Bolt-action features composite stock and 22" barrel. Both metal and stock finish are brown leaf pattern. Receiver is monoblock system, drilled and tapped for scope mounts. Floorplate hinged and magazine holds 5 rounds. Fitted with sling swivel and recoil pad. Offered in .30-06 and .270 calibers. Weight 8 lbs.

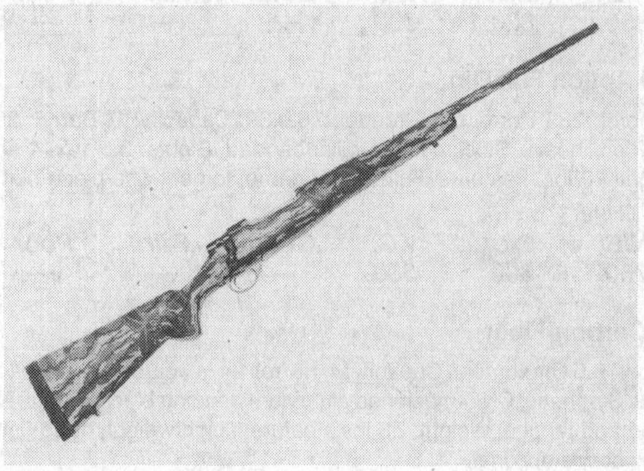

NIB	Exc.	V.G.	Good	Fair	Poor
650	520	400	280	180	120

Texas Safari Rifle

Chambered for .270 Win. or .300 Win. Magnum cartridge. Rifle is modified by gunsmith Bill Wiseman. Blue Teflon finish and 22" or 24" barrel depending on caliber. Laminated stock. Weight about 7.8 lbs.

NIB	Exc.	V.G.	Good	Fair	Poor
1200	800	650	520	400	150

Model 1500 PCS (Police Counter Sniper)

Bolt-action offered in .308 Winchester. Fitted with 24" heavy barrel. Magazine capacity 5 rounds. Available in blue or stainless steel. Walnut or synthetic stock. Weight about 9.3 lbs.

NIB	Exc.	V.G.	Good	Fair	Poor
1200	800	650	520	400	150

Alpine Mountain Rifle

Short-action in .243 Win., 6.5 Creedmoor, 7mm-08 or .308 Win., with 20" barrel and lightweight Hi Tech stock. Cerakote Gray finish on metal parts, OD Green/Black on stock.

NIB	Exc.	V.G.	Good	Fair	Poor
950	820	720	600	400	200

Long Range Rifle

Features 26" heavy threaded barrel. Bell & Carlson Varmint stock, with ventilated forend and raised cheekpiece. Chambered for 6.5 Creedmoor or .308 Winchester. Introduced in 2017.

NIB	Exc.	V.G.	Good	Fair	Poor
850	700	600	—	—	—

Model 1500 GRS

Tactical variant of Model 1500 series. Chambered in .204 Ruger, .223 Rem., .22-250, .243 Winchester, 6mm Creedmoor, 6.5 Creedmoor, .308 Winchester, with 10-shot detachable magazine. Barrel lengths 20", 24" or 26". Heavy barreled action. GRS Berserk stock, with adjustable comb, rubberized grip and forend. Introduced in 2018.

NIB	Exc.	V.G.	Good	Fair	Poor
1050	900	700	—	—	—

Model 1500 H-SA Precision

Available in most popular calibers, with 22" or 24" stock, 26" heavy barrel in some calibers. Main feature is the H-S Precision stock, with Kevlar, fiberglass and carbon fiber material hand-laminated. Aluminum bedding block is machined to dimensions of Howa barreled action. Introduced in 2018.

NIB	Exc.	V.G.	Good	Fair	Poor
950	820	700	—	—	—

Mini Action Full Dip

Calibers: .223 Rem., 6.5 Grendel, 7.62x39. Capacity: 5. Barrel: 20 in., threaded, heavy. Stock: Hogue pillar-bedded. Sights: 3.5-10x44 scope. Weight: 10 lbs. Features: Full-dipped camo, forged, one-piece bolt with locking lugs.

NIB	Exc.	V.G.	Good	Fair	Poor
700	600	530	—	—	—

HS Carbon Fiber

Caliber: 6.5 Creedmoor. Capacity: 4. Barrel: 24 in., carbon-fiber wrapped. Stock: Synthetic, CNC-machined aluminum bedding block. Sights: None, drilled and tapped. Weight: 7.8 lbs. Features: Lightweight, hand-finished stock, scope optional.

NIB	Exc.	V.G.	Good	Fair	Poor
1760	1500	1250	—	—	—

Carbon Elevate

Calibers: .6.5 Grendel, 6.5 Creedmoor, .308 Win., 6.5 PRC. Capacity: Varies by caliber and depending on flush mount or extended magazine. Barrel: 24-in. heavy threaded barrel. Weight: from 4 lbs. 13 oz. Stock: Stocky's Custom carbon-fiber super lightweight design available in natural carbon fiber or Kryptek Altitude. Sights: No sights. Drilled and tapped. Features: Ultra-lightweight bolt-action hunting rifle with AccuBlock lug bed. Three-position safety. Sub-MOA accuracy assurance. HACT two-stage trigger. LimbSaver buttpad. Suppressor-ready. Sub-MOA guarantee. Manufacturer Lifetime Warranty.

NIB	Exc.	V.G.	Good	Fair	Poor
1400	—	—	—	—	—

Gamepro Rimfire

Calibers: .22 LR, .22 WMR, .17 HMR. Capacity: 10. Barrel: 18 in., threaded, blued. Stock: Composite Hogue over-molded. Sights: Picatinny rail. Weight: 9.35 lbs. Features: Guaranteed sub-MOA, two-stage HACT trigger.

NIB	Exc.	V.G.	Good	Fair	Poor
600	500	450	—	—	—

HOWARD-WHITNEY

New Haven, Connecticut.

See—WHITNEY ARMS CO.

HUDSON MFG.

Temple, TX

Manufacturer of polymer frame, striker-fire pistols from 2016 thru 2019.

H9

Polymer-frame striker fire chambered in 9mm with 4.28-in. barrel. Equipped with 15-rnd. magazine, 1911-style trigger, G10 grips, Trijicon sights and Picatinny rail. Finish in black.

NIB	Exc.	V.G.	Good	Fair	Poor
1000	910	810	620	500	400

HUGLU

Turkey

SIDE-BY-SIDES

Bobwhite

Offered in 12-, 20-, 28-gauge and .410 bore, with 26" or 28" barrels with choke tubes. The .410 bore has Fixed chokes. Double triggers with no auto ejectors. Manual safety. Boxlock receiver, with silver finish. Walnut stock, with round knob pistol grip and splinter schnabel forend. Note: Add $200 for 28-gauge or .410 models.

NIB	Exc.	V.G.	Good	Fair	Poor
700	550	400	280	180	120

Ringneck

Similar to Bobwhite, with single trigger, case colored frame and side plates. Choice of round knob pistol-/straight-grip. Forend is beavertail schnabel. Note: Add $200 for 28-gauge or .410 models.

NIB	Exc.	V.G.	Good	Fair	Poor
1000	750	600	500	300	150

OVER/UNDERS

Woodcock

Available in 12-, 20-, 28-gauge and .410 bore. Choice of 26" or 28" ventilated rib barrels, with choke tubes. Fixed chokes on .410. Single trigger. No auto ejectors. Manual safety. Receiver finish is case colored. Checkered walnut stock, with round knob pistol grip and schnabel forend. Note: Add $150 for 28-gauge or .410 models.

NIB	Exc.	V.G.	Good	Fair	Poor
1050	820	600	500	300	150

Woodcock Deluxe

As above in 12-gauge, with auto ejectors and side plates.

NIB	Exc.	V.G.	Good	Fair	Poor
1200	900	750	550	350	180

Redhead

Available in 12-, 20-, 28-gauge and .410 bore. Choice of 26" or 28" ventilated rib barrels, with choke tubes. Fixed chokes on .410. The 20-gauge offered with 24" barrels. Single trigger, no auto ejectors and manual safety. Boxlock receiver with silver finish. Checkered walnut stock, with round knob pistol grip and schnabel forend. Note: Add $150 for 28-gauge or .410 models.

NIB	Exc.	V.G.	Good	Fair	Poor
800	620	500	400	280	150

Redhead Deluxe

As above in 12- and 20-gauge only, with 26" or 28" barrels. Auto ejectors.

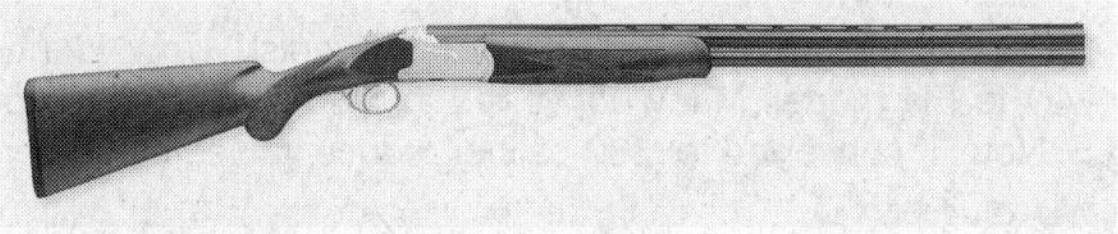

NIB	Exc.	V.G.	Good	Fair	Poor
900	750	680	400	200	100

Mallard

12- or 20-gauge gun fitted with 28" ventilated rib barrels and choke tubes. Double triggers and no auto ejectors. Silver receiver. Checkered walnut stock, with round knob pistol grip and schnabel forend.

NIB	Exc.	V.G.	Good	Fair	Poor
550	420	300	200	150	80

Canvasback

Available in 12-, 20-, 28-gauge and .410 bore. Choice of 26" or 28" ventilated rib barrels, with choke tubes. Fixed chokes on .410. Single trigger, no auto ejectors and manual safety. Black boxlock receiver. Checkered walnut stock, with round knob pistol grip and schnabel forend. Note: Add $150 for 28-gauge or .410 models.

NIB	Exc.	V.G.	Good	Fair	Poor
800	620	500	400	280	150

Canvasback Deluxe

As above in 12- and 20-gauge only, with auto ejectors.

NIB	Exc.	V.G.	Good	Fair	Poor
900	750	680	400	200	100

COWBOY & SINGLE-SHOTS

Cottontail

Single-barrel shotgun in 12- or 20-gauge and .410 bore. Choice of 24" or 28" barrels. Modified choke. No auto ejectors. Silver receiver, with blued barrel. Checkered walnut stock, with pistol grip.

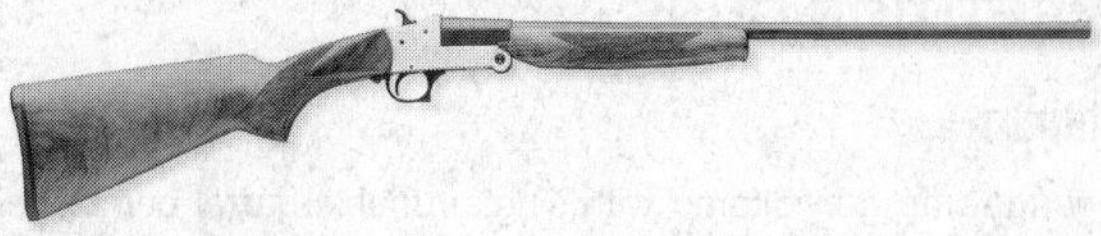

NIB	Exc.	V.G.	Good	Fair	Poor
200	150	100	80	50	20

Durango

Side-by-side shotgun chambered for 12- or 20-gauge, with single trigger and choke tubes. Barrel lengths 20". No auto ejectors. Boxlock receiver is case colored. Checkered walnut grips, with round knob pistol grip and schnabel forend.

NIB	Exc.	V.G.	Good	Fair	Poor
850	650	500	400	280	150

Amarillo

Similar to Durango, with flat-side receiver.

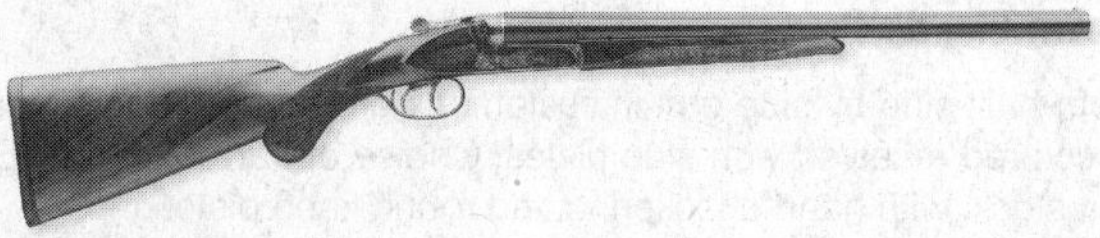

NIB	Exc.	V.G.	Good	Fair	Poor
700	520	400	300	200	120

SEMI-AUTOMATICS

Sharptail

12-gauge 3" gun fitted with choice of 26" or 28" ventilated rib barrels and choke tubes. Black receiver. Checkered walnut stock, with pistol grip. Weight about 7.3 lbs.

NIB	Exc.	V.G.	Good	Fair	Poor
550	420	300	200	150	100

Canadian

As above, with alloy frame and matte black finish. Weight about 7 lbs.

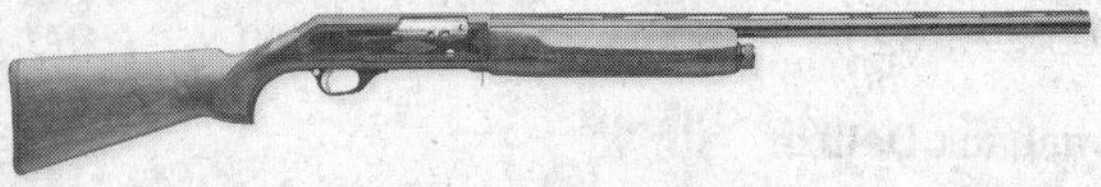

NIB	Exc.	V.G.	Good	Fair	Poor
650	520	400	280	160	120

Teal

A 20-gauge, with 3" chambers. Choice of 26" or 28" ventilated rib barrels, with choke tubes. Black alloy receiver. Checkered walnut stock, with pistol grip.

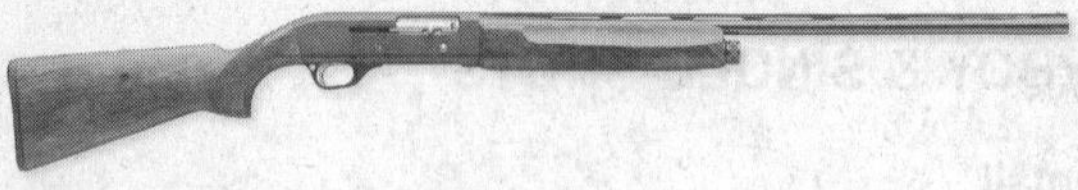

NIB	Exc.	V.G.	Good	Fair	Poor
550	420	300	200	150	100

COMPETITION GUNS

Vandalia Trap

A 12-gauge trap gun offered with single-/double-barrel combo: single-barrel only; double-barrel only. Five choke tubes. Engraved silver receiver. Checkered walnut stock, with pistol grip and adjustable comb. Note: Add $300 for Combo model.

NIB	Exc.	V.G.	Good	Fair	Poor
1900	1400	1000	650	400	200

English Sporter

Sporting clays model chambered for 12-gauge shell. Fitted with 30" barrel. Ten choke tubes. Black receiver. Adjustable comb. Checkered walnut stock, with pistol grip.

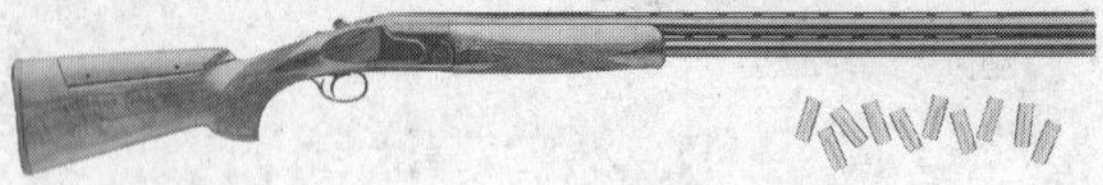

NIB	Exc.	V.G.	Good	Fair	Poor
1900	1400	1000	650	400	200

CUSTOM GRADES

Custom Grade II

Custom-built side-by-side gun in customer's choice of gauge. Engraved case colored receiver, with side plates. Choice of barrel lengths. Select walnut stock, with hand-checkering and round knob pistol grip.

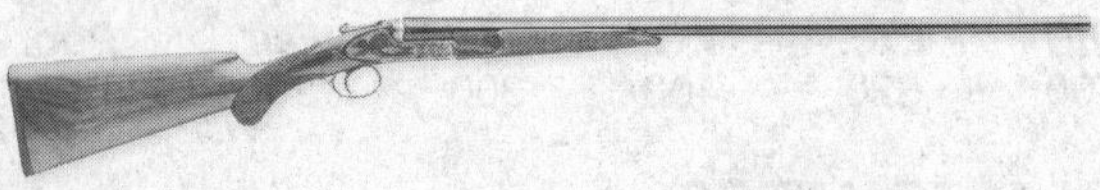

NIB	Exc.	V.G.	Good	Fair	Poor
2200	1600	1200	950	500	300

Custom Grade IV

Custom-built side-by-side features silver scroll engraved receiver, with side plates. Straight-grip stock. Choice of bore and barrel lengths.

NIB	Exc.	V.G.	Good	Fair	Poor
2800	1900	1400	650	600	350

Custom Grade IV with Upgrade

An over/under gun, with extra fancy walnut stock and elaborately engraved silver receiver. Choice of gauge and barrel lengths.

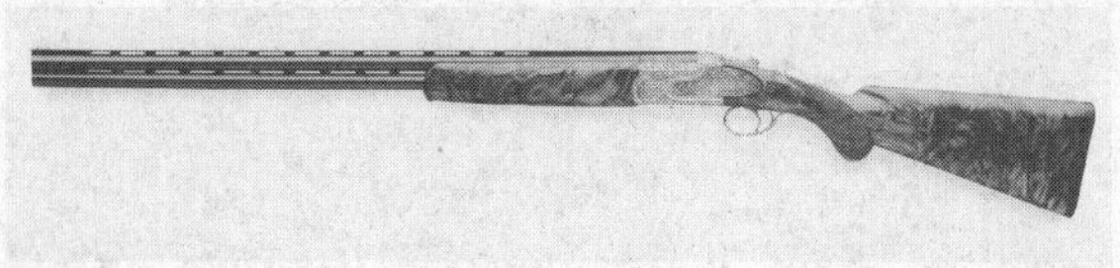

NIB	Exc.	V.G.	Good	Fair	Poor
3150	2200	1600	750	650	350

Custom Grade VI

Highest grade offered, with finest walnut stock and engraving.

NIB	Exc.	V.G.	Good	Fair	Poor
3500	2650	1900	950	780	480

HUNGARY

SA-85M

Pre-ban semi-automatic copy of AKM rifle. Chambered for 7.62x39mm cartridge. Fixed or folding stock.

NIB	Exc.	V.G.	Good	Fair	Poor
1800	1600	1200	850	600	500

HUNT

New Haven, Connecticut

See—WINCHESTER REPEATING ARMS CO.

HUNTER ARMS CO.

Fulton, New York

See—L. C. SMITH

HUSQVARNA

Husqvarna, Sweden

PISTOLS

Model 1907

Copy of FN Browning Model 1903 made for Swedish Army. Identical in every way to FN model. Many converted to .380-caliber and imported into U.S. Note: If converted to .380-caliber reduce values by 50 percent.

Courtesy Orvel Reichert

NIB	Exc.	V.G.	Good	Fair	Poor
—	400	320	220	150	100

Lahti

9mm caliber semi-automatic pistol, with 5.5" barrel and 8-shot magazine. Designed by Aino Lahti and adopted as standard Swedish sidearm in 1940. Note: Add 75 percent for complete military rig, with holsters and magazines.

NIB	Exc.	V.G.	Good	Fair	Poor
—	800	680	480	220	150

BOLT-ACTION RIFLES

Hi-Power

Bolt-action sporting rifle. Manufactured in a variety of calibers, with 24" barrel, open sights and beechwood stock. Manufactured between 1946 and 1951.

NIB	Exc.	V.G.	Good	Fair	Poor
—	500	380	280	200	150

Model 1100 Deluxe

As above, with walnut stock. Manufactured between 1952 and 1956.

NIB	Exc.	V.G.	Good	Fair	Poor
—	550	400	320	250	200

Model 1000 Super Grade

As above, with Monte Carlo-style stock. Manufactured between 1952 and 1956.

NIB	Exc.	V.G.	Good	Fair	Poor
—	580	480	350	250	200

Model 3100 Crown Grade

Bolt-action sporting rifle manufactured in a variety of calibers, with 24" barrel. Walnut stock, with black composition forend tip and pistol grip cap. Manufactured between 1954 and 1972.

NIB	Exc.	V.G.	Good	Fair	Poor
—	580	480	350	300	200

Model 4100 Lightweight

As above, with schnabel forend tip. Manufactured between 1954 and 1972.

NIB	Exc.	V.G.	Good	Fair	Poor
—	580	480	350	300	200

Model 456

As above, with full length Mannlicher-style stock. Manufactured between 1959 and 1970.

NIB	Exc.	V.G.	Good	Fair	Poor
—	600	500	380	320	200

Model 6000

Model 4100, with express folding sights and finely figured walnut stock. Manufactured between 1968 and 1970.

NIB	Exc.	V.G.	Good	Fair	Poor
—	600	500	400	300	200

Model 9000 Crown Grade

Bolt-action sporting rifle. Manufactured in a variety of calibers, with 23.5" barrel, open sights, adjustable trigger and walnut stock. Manufactured in 1971 and 1972.

NIB	Exc.	V.G.	Good	Fair	Poor
—	500	420	350	300	250

Model 8000 Imperial Grade

As above, with engraved magazine floor plate, machine jeweled bolt. Finely figured walnut stock. Manufactured in 1971 and 1972.

NIB	Exc.	V.G.	Good	Fair	Poor
—	680	550	480	400	300

DOUBLE SHOTGUNS

Number of pre-war Husqvarna side-by-side shotguns have been imported over the years. While sturdy excellent shotguns, their collector value is rather limited. Those following values apply only to modern fluid-steel (nitro proofed) guns.

NIB	Exc.	V.G.	Good	Fair	Poor
—	500	420	350	300	250

HY-HUNTER, INC.

Burbank, California

Chicago Cub

.22-caliber folding trigger double-action revolver, with 2" barrel and 6-shot cylinder.

NIB	Exc.	V.G.	Good	Fair	Poor
—	50	40	30	20	20

Detective

.22 or .22 WMR caliber double-action revolver, with 2.5" barrel and 6-shot cylinder. Blued, with plastic grips.

NIB	Exc.	V.G.	Good	Fair	Poor
—	60	50	40	30	20

Frontier Six Shooter (rimfire)

.22 or .22 WMR caliber single-action revolver, with 6-shot cylinder.

NIB	Exc.	V.G.	Good	Fair	Poor
—	120	100	50	40	30

Frontier Six Shooter(centerfire)

As above in .357 Magnum, .44 Magnum or .45 Colt.

NIB	Exc.	V.G.	Good	Fair	Poor
—	220	200	180	100	50

Maxim

.25-caliber semi-automatic pistol, with 2" barrel and 5-shot magazine.

NIB	Exc.	V.G.	Good	Fair	Poor
—	80	60	50	40	30

Military

.22-, .32- or .380-caliber double-action semi-automatic pistol, with 4" barrel and 6-shot magazine.

NIB	Exc.	V.G.	Good	Fair	Poor
—	100	80	60	50	40

Stingray

.25-caliber semi-automatic pistol, with 2.5" barrel and 5-shot magazine.

NIB	Exc.	V.G.	Good	Fair	Poor
—	80	60	50	40	30

Panzer

.22-caliber semi-automatic pistol, with 4" barrel and 7-shot magazine.

NIB	Exc.	V.G.	Good	Fair	Poor
—	80	60	50	40	30

Stuka

Similar to above.

NIB	Exc.	V.G.	Good	Fair	Poor
—	80	60	50	40	30

Automatic Derringer

.22-caliber over/under pocket pistol patterned after Remington Double Derringer.

NIB	Exc.	V.G.	Good	Fair	Poor
—	50	40	30	20	20

Accurate Ace

.22-caliber Flobert-action pistol.

NIB	Exc.	V.G.	Good	Fair	Poor
—	50	40	30	20	20

Favorite

.22 or .22 WMR caliber copy of Steven's single-shot pistol, with 6" barrel and nickel-plated frame.

NIB	Exc.	V.G.	Good	Fair	Poor
—	100	80	70	50	20

Gold Rush Derringer

.22-caliber spur trigger single-shot pistol, with 2.5" barrel.

NIB	Exc.	V.G.	Good	Fair	Poor
—	100	80	70	50	20

Target Model

.22 or .22 WMR bolt-action single-shot pistol, with 10" barrel, adjustable sights and walnut grip.

NIB	Exc.	V.G.	Good	Fair	Poor
—	50	40	30	20	20

HYDE & SHATTUCK
Hatfield, Massachusetts

Derringer (Antique)

.22-caliber spur trigger brass constructed single-shot pistol, with 2.5" barrel and walnut grips. Believed to have been made during 1880s.

Exc.	Fine	V.G.	Good	Fair	Poor
680	200	150	100	50	30

Queen Derringer (Antique)

.22-caliber spur trigger single-shot pistol, with 2.5" half octagonal barrel. Blued or nickel-plated, with walnut grips. Barrel normally marked "Queen" sometimes "Hyde & Shattuck". Manufactured between 1876 and 1879.

Exc.	Fine	V.G.	Good	Fair	Poor
650	400	350	300	150	100

HYPER
Jenks, Oklahoma

Single-Shot Rifle

Custom made falling-block action single-shot rifle. Manufactured in a variety of calibers, barrel lengths, barrel types, and stock styles. Manufactured until 1984.

NIB	Exc.	V.G.	Good	Fair	Poor
—	2750	2000	1750	1450	800

I

I.G.I.
Itaiguns International
Zingone de Tressano, Italy

Domino SP602

.22-caliber semi-automatic target pistol, with 6" barrel and 5-shot magazine (inserted into action from top), adjustable trigger and customized grips.

NIB	Exc.	V.G.	Good	Fair	Poor
—	950	720	620	450	250

Domino OP601

As above in .22 short caliber.

NIB	Exc.	V.G.	Good	Fair	Poor
—	950	720	620	450	250

IAB
Industria Armi Bresciane
Brescia, Italy

S-300

12-gauge boxlock single-barrel trap gun, with 30" or 32" barrels having wide ventilated rib. Walnut trap-style stock.

NIB	Exc.	V.G.	Good	Fair	Poor
—	1600	1320	1050	850	450

C-300 Combo

12-gauge over/under boxlock double-barrel shotgun, with 30" or 32" barrels. Single-selective trigger, automatic ejectors, trap-style walnut stock, accompanied by two extra single barrels.

NIB	Exc.	V.G.	Good	Fair	Poor
—	2850	2300	1880	1500	800

C-300 Super Combo

As above, but more finely finished.

NIB	Exc.	V.G.	Good	Fair	Poor
—	3600	2800	2280	1750	900

IAI-AMERICAN LEGENDS
Houston, Texas

RIFLES

M-888 M1 Carbine

Re-creation of U.S. M1 Carbine in .30-caliber. Barrel length 18". Weight about 5.5 lbs. Uses surplus magazines of 15 to 30 rounds. Comes with 10-round magazine. Options: wooden or metal handguard; walnut or birchwood stock.

NIB	Exc.	V.G.	Good	Fair	Poor
680	580	400	320	200	100

M-333 M1 Garand

Re-manufactured to GI specifications. Fitted with 24" barrel and GI wood stock. Eight-round capacity. Parkerized finish. Weight about 9.5 lbs.

NIB	Exc.	V.G.	Good	Fair	Poor
900	800	620	500	350	150

PISTOLS

M-2000

Government model .45 ACP pistol, fitted with 5" barrel and 7-round magazine. Fixed sights, wood grips and Parkerized finish. Weight about 38 oz.

NIB	Exc.	V.G.	Good	Fair	Poor
480	380	320	250	180	100

M-999

Similar to above model, with rubber-style combat grips, extended slide stop safety and magazine release. Fixed sights. Offered with stainless steel slide and blued frame or all stainless steel. Supplied with 7-round magazine. Weight about 38 oz. Note: Add $25 for stainless steel frame.

NIB	Exc.	V.G.	Good	Fair	Poor
480	350	280	200	120	80

M-777

Same as M-999, fitted with 4.25" barrel. Weight about 36 oz. Note: Add $25 for stainless steel frame.

NIB	Exc.	V.G.	Good	Fair	Poor
480	350	280	200	120	80

M-6000

This .45 ACP pistol, fitted with 5" barrel, plastic grips, extended slide stop safety and magazine release. Safety is ambidextrous. Magazine capacity 8 rounds. Fixed sights. Weight about 38 oz.

NIB	Exc.	V.G.	Good	Fair	Poor
480	380	320	250	180	100

M-5000

Similar to M-6000. Fitted with 4.25" barrel. Weight about 36 oz.

NIB	Exc.	V.G.	Good	Fair	Poor
480	380	320	250	180	100

IGA
Veranopolis, Brazil

Single-Barrel Shotgun

A 12-, 20-gauge or .410 bore single-barrel shotgun, with exposed hammer, 28" barrel and hardwood stock.

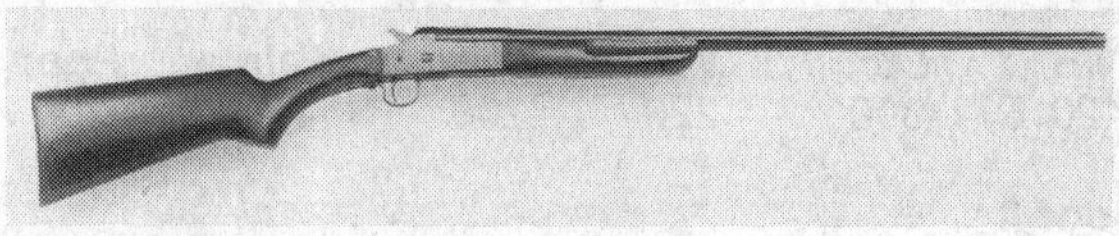

NIB	Exc.	V.G.	Good	Fair	Poor
150	90	80	50	40	30

Single-Barrel Shotgun Youth Model

Offered in 20-gauge and .410 bore. Features 22" barrel and shorter than standard buttstock. Weight 5 lbs.

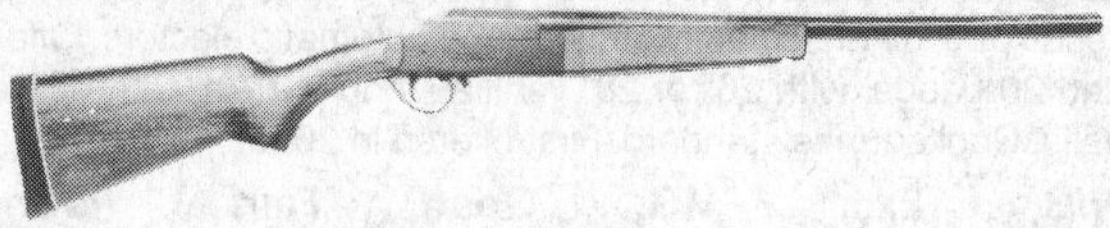

NIB	Exc.	V.G.	Good	Fair	Poor
150	100	80	60	50	40

Coach Gun

A 12- or 20-gauge and .410 bore boxlock double-barrel shotgun, with 20" barrels, double triggers and extractors. Blued, with hardwood stock. Note: Add $50 for nickel finish; $60 for engraved butt stock.

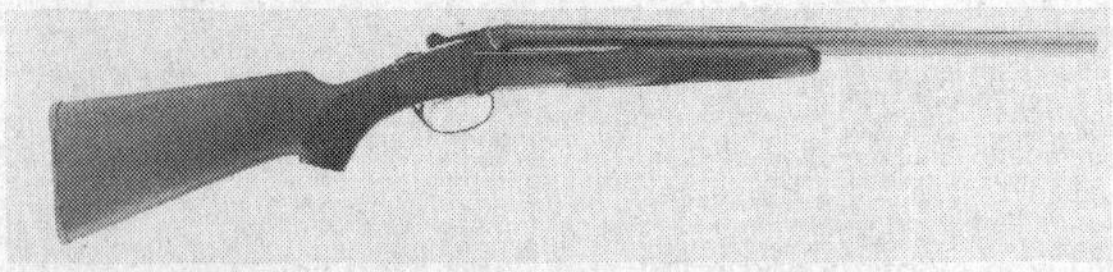

NIB	Exc.	V.G.	Good	Fair	Poor
420	320	250	150	100	80

Standard Side-by-Side Uplander

Offered in 12-, 20-, 28-gauge and .410 bore, with 26" and 28" barrels. Checkered hardwood stock, with pistol-/straight-grip. Weight 6.75 lbs. Note: Add $40 for choke tubes.

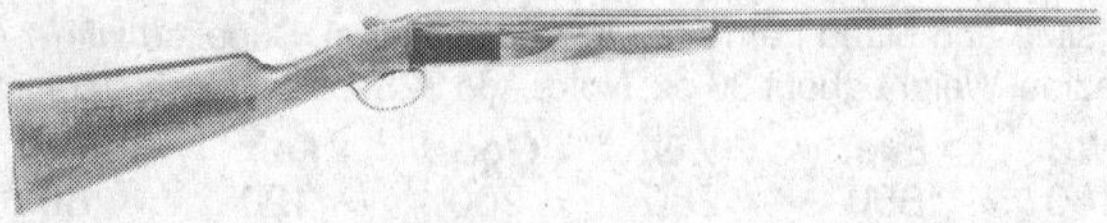

NIB	Exc.	V.G.	Good	Fair	Poor
420	320	250	150	100	80

Uplander Youth

Same as above. Offered in 20-gauge or .410 bore with 24" barrels. Shorter length of pull. Recoil pad standard.

NIB	Exc.	V.G.	Good	Fair	Poor
450	320	250	150	100	80

Uplander Supreme

Introduced in 2000. Features high grade walnut stock with checkering, single-selective trigger, choke tubes and automatic ejectors. Offered in 12- and 20-gauge, with 26" or 28" barrels. Chambered for 3" shells. Soft rubber recoil pad standard.

NIB	Exc.	V.G.	Good	Fair	Poor
600	450	380	300	200	100

Standard Over/Under Condor I

Offered in 12- or 20-gauge, with 26" or 28" barrels. Fitted with extractors and single trigger. Choke tubes are standard. Checkered hardwood stock, with pistol grip and recoil pad. Weight 8 lbs.

NIB	Exc.	V.G.	Good	Fair	Poor
420	300	220	200	150	100

Condor II

Same as above, with double triggers and plastic buttplate.

NIB	Exc.	V.G.	Good	Fair	Poor
400	250	200	150	100	80

Condor Supreme Deluxe

Similar to standard Condor. Has high grade walnut stock, hand-checkering, recoil pad, single-selective trigger and automatic ejectors. Offered in 12- and 20-gauge, with 26" or 28" ventilated rib barrels. Chambered for 3" shells. Choke tubes standard. First offered in 2000.

NIB	Exc.	V.G.	Good	Fair	Poor
550	400	320	200	150	100

Deluxe Over/Under ERA 2000

Offered in 12-gauge only, with 26" or 28" barrels. Fitted with single trigger and extractors. Choke tubes are standard. Barrels are chrome lined and stock is hand-checkered.

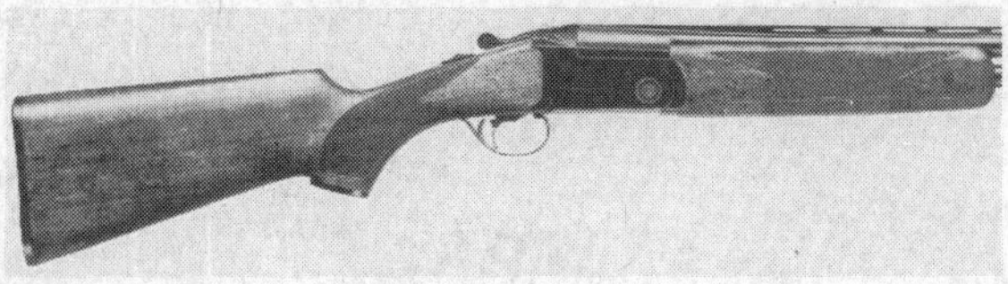

NIB	Exc.	V.G.	Good	Fair	Poor
450	320	250	150	100	80

IMI

See Israel Weapon Industries/Israel Military Industries

INDIAN ARMS CORP.

Detroit, Michigan

Indian Arms .380

.380-caliber semi-automatic pistol, with 3.25" barrel and 6-shot magazine. Made of stainless steel. Finished in white or blued, with walnut grips. Manufactured from 1975 to 1977.

NIB	Exc.	V.G.	Good	Fair	Poor
—	350	250	200	150	100

INDUSTRIA ARMI GALESI

Brescia, Italy

See—GALESI

INDUSTRIA NACIONAL DE ARMAS (INA)

Brazil

Firearms manufacturer 1949 to 1972, making submachine guns for the Brazilian army and inexpensive revolvers for the U.S. market.

INA Tiger

Compact double action revolver in .32 S&W Long or .38 Special caliber.

NIB	Exc.	V.G.	Good	Fair	Poor
280	200	150	110	90	40

INGRAM

Military Armament Corp.
Atlanta, Georgia

MAC 10

9mm or .45-caliber open-bolt semi-automatic pistol, with 5.75" barrel and 32-shot magazine. Anodized, with plastic grips. Discontinued. Note:

Add 20 percent for accessory kit (barrel extension and extra magazine).

NIB	Exc.	V.G.	Good	Fair	Poor
750	500	380	250	180	100

MAC 10AI

As above, but firing from closed-bolt. Note: Add 300 percent for earlier open-bolt model; 20 percent for accessory kit.

NIB	Exc.	V.G.	Good	Fair	Poor
750	600	250	200	150	100

MAC 11

As above in smaller version. Chambered for 9mm cartridge. Note: Add 300 percent for earlier open-bolt model; 20 percent for accessory kit.

NIB	Exc.	V.G.	Good	Fair	Poor
800	650	350	150	100	50

MAC 1911 Classic

Caliber: .45 ACP. Capacity: 8-round magazine. Barrel: 5-in., match-grade bull. Sights: Bomar-type fully adjustable rear, fiber-optic front. Weight: 40.5 oz. Finish: Blue, black chrome or hard chrome. Grips: Hardwood. Features: Checkered frontstrap, skeletonized trigger and hammer, flared and lowered ejection port, wide front and rear slide serrations. Imported from the Philippines by Eagle Imports.

NIB	Exc.	V.G.	Good	Fair	Poor
1000	—	—	—	—	—

MAC 3011 SLD Tactical

Calibers: 9mm, .40 S&W, .45 ACP. Capacity: 14-, 15- or 17-round magazines. Barrel: 5 in.-, match-grade bull. Sights: Bomar-type fully adjustable rear, fiber-optic front. Weight: 46.5 oz. Finish: Blue. Grips: Aluminum. Features: Checkered frontstrap serrations, skeletonized trigger and hammer, flared and lowered ejection port, ambidextrous safety, full dust cover. Imported from the Philippines by Eagle Imports.

NIB	Exc.	V.G.	Good	Fair	Poor
1050	—	—	—	—	—

Rapido

Calibers: 9mm, .38 Super. Capacity: 17-round magazine. Barrels: 5- or 5.5-in., match-grade with compensator. Sights: Optic ready. Weight: 46.5 oz. Finish: Blue. Grips: Aluminum. Features: Checkered frontstrap serrations, combat trigger and hammer, flared and lowered ejection port, ambidextrous safety. Imported from the Philippines by Eagle Imports.

NIB	Exc.	V.G.	Good	Fair	Poor
1650	—	—	—	—	—

INLAND MFG.

Dayton, OH

Manufacturer of M1 Carbine-style rifles, WWII-era 1911A1 pistols and shotguns and modern 1911 pistols. Established 2014.

1911A1 Government Model

Replica of 1911A1 G.I. pistol chambered in .45 ACP with 5-in. barrel. Equipped with 7-rnd. magazine, checkered brown plastic grips, lanyard loop, fixed combat sights. Stainless finish.

NIB	Exc.	V.G.	Good	Fair	Poor
1010	910	800	600	480	380

1911 Custom Carry

1911-style semi-auto handgun chambered in .45 ACP with 5-in. barrel. Equipped with 7-rnd. magazine, Ergo XTR grips, Novak sights, extended beavertail, forward slides serrations. Parkerized finish.

NIB	Exc.	V.G.	Good	Fair	Poor
800	710	610	460	380	280

M1 Advisor

M1 Carbine-style action chambered in .30 Carbine with 12-in. barrel with flash hider. Equipped with 15-rnd. magazine, walnut grip and stock. Parkerized finish.

NIB	Exc.	V.G.	Good	Fair	Poor
1210	1060	910	750	560	430

INTERARMS

Alexandria, Virginia

Importer of arms made by Howa Machine, Star and Walther. This firm no longer in business.

RIFLES

Mark X Viscount

Bolt-action sporting rifle made in a variety of calibers, with 24" barrel, open sights and adjustable trigger. Magazine holds 3 or 5 cartridges. Manufactured in Yugoslavia. Blued, with walnut stock.

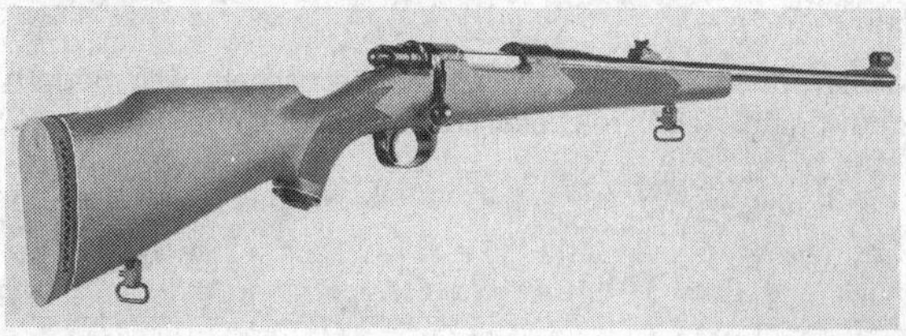

NIB	Exc.	V.G.	Good	Fair	Poor
450	300	250	200	180	120

Mark X Lightweight

As above, with 20" barrel and composition stock. Introduced in 1988.

NIB	Exc.	V.G.	Good	Fair	Poor
450	300	250	200	180	120

Mini Mark X

As above, with short action in .223-caliber only, 20" barrel, open sights and adjustable trigger. Five-shot magazine. Introduced in 1987.

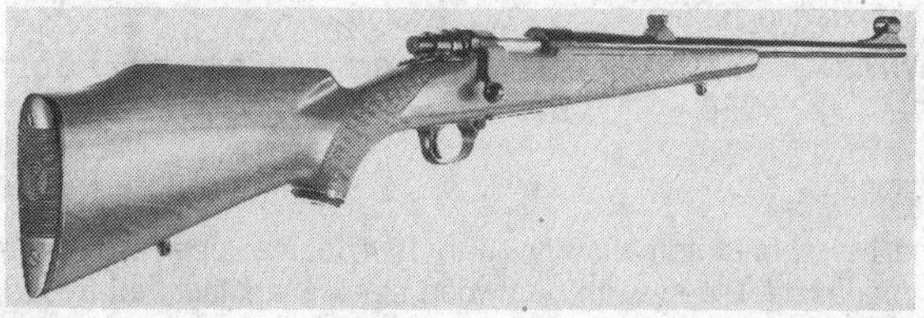

NIB	Exc.	V.G.	Good	Fair	Poor
450	300	250	200	180	120

Mark X American Field

As above, with finely figured walnut stock, ebony forend tip, pistol grip cap, sling swivels and recoil pad. Introduced in 1984.

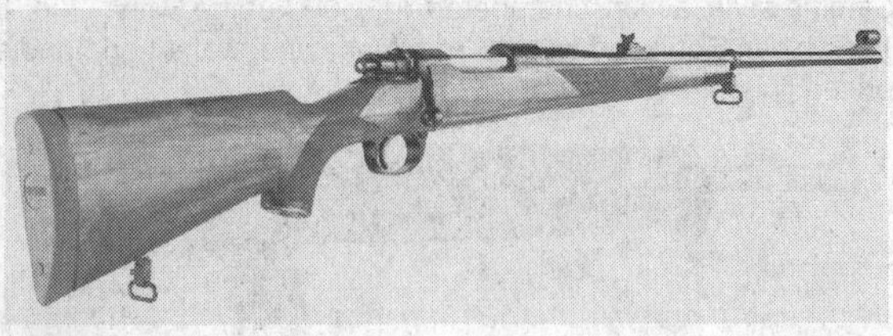

NIB	Exc.	V.G.	Good	Fair	Poor
520	400	350	300	250	180

Whitworth Express Rifle

.375 H&H or .458 Win. Magnum bolt-action sporting rifle, with 24" barrel, express sights and 3-shot magazine. Blued, with walnut stock. Introduced in 1974.

NIB	Exc.	V.G.	Good	Fair	Poor
950	750	550	350	250	200

Whitworth Mannlicher Carbine

.243, .270, 7x57mm, .308 and .30-06 caliber bolt-action rifle, with 20" barrel, open sights, sling swivels and full length stock. Manufactured between 1984 and 1987.

NIB	Exc.	V.G.	Good	Fair	Poor
—	720	550	380	250	200

Cavalier

Bolt-action sporting rifle. Made in a variety of calibers, with modern style stock having rollover cheekpiece. Discontinued.

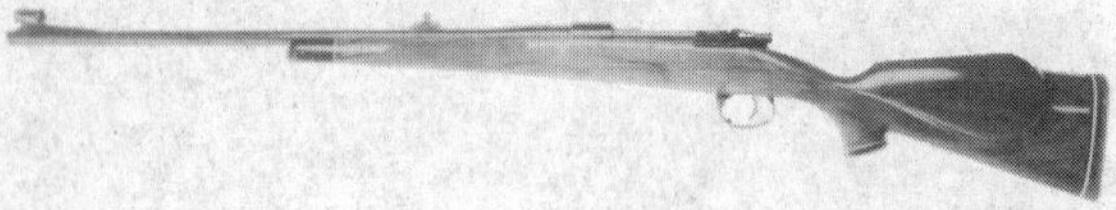

NIB	Exc.	V.G.	Good	Fair	Poor
—	500	400	350	200	150

Mannlicher Carbine

As above, with 20" barrel and full length stock. Discontinued.

NIB	Exc.	V.G.	Good	Fair	Poor
—	600	500	420	280	200

Continental Carbine

As above, with double-set triggers. Discontinued.

NIB	Exc.	V.G.	Good	Fair	Poor
—	620	520	450	300	220

Alaskan Model

Similar to Mark X in .375 H&H or .458 Win. Magnum, with 24" barrel. Discontinued in 1985.

NIB	Exc.	V.G.	Good	Fair	Poor
—	950	750	550	350	200

22-ATD

.22-caliber semi-automatic rifle, with 19.4" barrel, open sights and 11-shot magazine. Blued, with hardwood stock. Manufactured by Norinco. Introduced in 1987.

NIB	Exc.	V.G.	Good	Fair	Poor
200	120	100	60	50	40

HANDGUNS

Helwan Brigadier

9mm semi-automatic pistol, with 4.5" barrel, fixed sights and 8-shot magazine. Blued, with plastic grips. Introduced in 1988.

NIB	Exc.	V.G.	Good	Fair	Poor
380	280	200	180	120	100

FEG R-9

9mm semi-automatic pistol patterned after Browning 35, with 13-shot magazine. Blued, with walnut grips. Manufactured in 1986 and 1987.

NIB	Exc.	V.G.	Good	Fair	Poor
—	350	250	180	140	100

FEG PPH

.380-caliber double-action semi-automatic pistol, with 3.5" barrel and 6-shot magazine. Blued, with plastic grips.

NIB	Exc.	V.G.	Good	Fair	Poor
—	300	180	150	120	100

Mark II AP

Copy of Walther PP. Chambered for .380 ACP or .22 LR cartridge.

NIB	Exc.	V.G.	Good	Fair	Poor
300	180	120	100	80	50

Mark II APK

Copy of Walther PPK. Chambered for .380 ACP cartridge only.

NIB	Exc.	V.G.	Good	Fair	Poor
300	180	120	100	80	50

Mauser Parabellum Karabiner

9mm caliber semi-automatic carbine, with 11.75" barrel and detachable shoulder stock. Fitted in leather case. Note: Only 100 imported into U.S. This arm subject to BATFE registration.

NIB	Exc.	V.G.	Good	Fair	Poor
6500	5750	5000	4000	3000	2250

Mauser Parabellum Cartridge Counter

Re-production of cartridge counter Luger. Fitted in leather case, with only 100 units imported into U.S.

NIB	Exc.	V.G.	Good	Fair	Poor
4000	3000	2500	2000	1500	1000

Virginian Dragoon

Single-action revolver in .357 Magnum, .41 Magnum, .44 Magnum or .45 Colt, with 5", 6", 7.5", 8.75" or 12" barrel, fixed or adjustable sights and 6-shot cylinder. Originally made in Switzerland, then in U.S.A. Discontinued in 1984. Note: Add 20 percent for Swiss manufacture; 15 percent for 12" barrel.

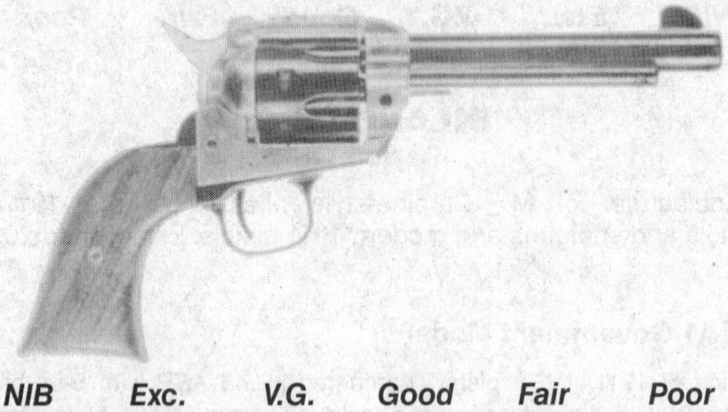

NIB	Exc.	V.G.	Good	Fair	Poor
—	320	280	200	150	100

Stainless Dragoon

As above in stainless steel.

NIB	Exc.	V.G.	Good	Fair	Poor
—	380	300	240	180	100

Virginian Dragoon Silhouette

Similar to stainless Virginia Dragoon, except in .357 or .44 Magnum, with 7.5", 8.375" or 10.5" barrel. Adjustable sights, target grips.

NIB	Exc.	V.G.	Good	Fair	Poor
500	420	350	300	250	150

Dragoon Deputy

Similar to Virginia Dragoon except in .357 or .44 Magnum. Blue finish, with case-hardened frame or stainless and 5" barrel.

NIB	Exc.	V.G.	Good	Fair	Poor
450	380	300	250	200	120

Virginian .22 Convertible

As above in .22-caliber, with 5.5" barrel.

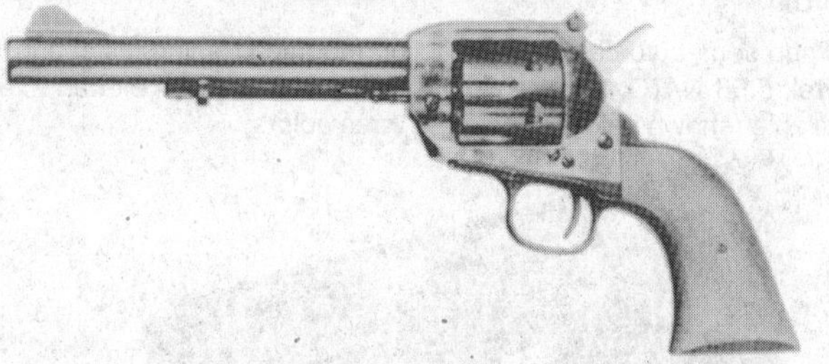

NIB	Exc.	V.G.	Good	Fair	Poor
—	280	200	120	100	80

Virginian Stainless .22 Convertible

As above in stainless steel.

NIB	Exc.	V.G.	Good	Fair	Poor
—	300	220	160	100	80

INTERARMS/HIGH STANDARD

Houston, Texas

In 2000, High Standard Manufacturing Company of Houston, Texas resurrected the Interarms name. They began making several AK-style semi-automatic rifles in U.S.A. Following is a sampling of these models.

AK-47 (7.62x39mm)

NIB	Exc.	V.G.	Good	Fair	Poor
1000	850	700	500	400	250

AKM Series (7.62x39mm)

NIB	Exc.	V.G.	Good	Fair	Poor
550	450	380	300	220	150

AK-74 (5.45x39mm)

NIB	Exc.	V.G.	Good	Fair	Poor
600	500	400	320	280	200

INTERDYNAMICS OF AMERICA

Miami, Florida

KG-9

9mm caliber semi-automatic pistol, with 3" barrel and 36-shot magazine. Manufactured from 1981 to 1983. Note: Earliest models fire from open bolt. Valued at approximately 150 percent of values shown here.

NIB	Exc.	V.G.	Good	Fair	Poor
—	800	650	580	500	300

KG-99

As above, with barrel shroud. Manufactured from 1981 to 1984.

NIB	Exc.	V.G.	Good	Fair	Poor
—	800	650	580	500	300

KG-99 Stainless

As above in stainless steel. Manufactured in 1984.

NIB	Exc.	V.G.	Good	Fair	Poor
—	800	650	580	500	300

KG-99M

More compact version of above. Manufactured in 1984.

NIB	Exc.	V.G.	Good	Fair	Poor
—	800	650	580	500	300

INTRATEC USA, INC.

Miami, Florida

This manufacturer was in business from 1985 to 2000, under the names Intratec and Intratec USA, Inc.

TEC-9

9mm caliber semi-automatic pistol, with 5-in. shrouded barrel and 36-shot magazine. Introduced in 1985.

NIB	Exc.	V.G.	Good	Fair	Poor
700	600	500	430	—	—

TEC-9C

As above, with 16" barrel and folding stock. Manufactured in 1987.

NIB	Exc.	V.G.	Good	Fair	Poor
700	600	500	—	—	—

TEC-9M

As above, with 3-in. barrel and 20-shot magazine. Also made in stainless steel.

NIB	Exc.	V.G.	Good	Fair	Poor
730	630	500	—	—	—

TEC-22 "Scorpion"

Similar to above in .22-caliber, with 4-in. barrel and 30-shot magazine.

NIB	Exc.	V.G.	Good	Fair	Poor
380	330	280	210	180	160

TEC-38

.38-caliber over/under double-action derringer, with 3" barrels. Manufactured between 1986 and 1988.

NIB	Exc.	V.G.	Good	Fair	Poor
—	200	120	90	60	40

IRVING, W.

New York, New York

See REID, JAMES

IRWINDALE ARMS, INC.

Irwindale, California

See—AMT

ISRAEL WEAPON INDUSTRIES (IWI)

Israel

Formerly ISRAEL MILITARY INDUSTRIES (IMI). Israeli manufacturer of military and sporting arms founded as Israel Military Industries (IMI) in the 1930s and renamed Israel Weapon Industries with products most recently imported as IWI, USA. Best known products include Uzi submachine guns and Galil assault rifles, along with semi-auto sporting versions of the same design. IMI/IWI produced guns have been sold in America under other brands, including Action Arms (Uzi Models A&B), Desert Eagle (magnum semi-auto pistols), Magnum Research, and Mossberg (Uzi American arms), and Springfield Armory. Some IWI/IMI made models will be found in those sections.

Galil Rifles

Semi-auto version of Israeli Galil military rifle, design influenced by Kalashnikov AK-47 and Valmet Rk62. Most early models have side-folding stocks.

Model AR (.223)

Note: Add $600 for .308-caliber.

NIB	*Exc.*	*V.G.*	*Good*	*Fair*	*Poor*
3000	2400	2000	1500	900	700

Model ARM

NIB	*Exc.*	*V.G.*	*Good*	*Fair*	*Poor*
3400	2700	2000	1500	900	700

Sniper Rifle

NIB	*Exc.*	*V.G.*	*Good*	*Fair*	*Poor*
8500	7500	6000	4000	3000	2000

Hadar II

NIB	*Exc.*	*V.G.*	*Good*	*Fair*	*Poor*
1300	1100	800	650	500	400

Galil Ace Pistol

8.3" barrel, 30-round mag, 5.56 NATO or 7.62 NATO ($100 premium), with or without side-folding stabilizing brace.

NIB	*Exc.*	*V.G.*	*Good*	*Fair*	*Poor*
1750	1600	1250	—	—	—

Galil Ace Rifle

Current production version of Galil, 5.56 NATO, 7.62x39, or 7.62 NATO ($150 premium), 16" barrel. Changes include last round hold-open, charging handle moved to left side, lighter weight due to polymer components, uses NATO STANAG magazines, telescoping adjustable side-folding stock, Picatinny rails.

NIB	*Exc.*	*V.G.*	*Good*	*Fair*	*Poor*
1800	1650	1300	—	—	—

Zion15

AR/M4-based semi-auto carbine. 16" barrel, 5.56 NATO.

NIB	*Exc.*	*V.G.*	*Good*	*Fair*	*Poor*
840	790	650	—	—	—

Tavor

Bullpup semi-auto carbine with action mounted behind pistol grip. 16.5" barrel. 5.56 NATO, 9mm, .300 Blackout, 7.62 NATO. Left-hand version available (shown below). Choice of three colors.

NIB	*Exc.*	*V.G.*	*Good*	*Fair*	*Poor*
1900	1750	1500	—	—	—

Tavor TS-12

Gauge: 12 ga. 3 in. Barrel: 18.5 in. Length: 28.34 in. Weight: 8.9 lbs. Stock: Synthetic fixed bullpup style, with Black, OD green and FDE color options. Features: Gas-driven semi-automatic bullpup design that feeds from one of three magazine tubes. Each tube holds four 3-in. shells or five 2.75-in. rounds. Max capacity 15 rounds. Includes four sling attachment points, M-LOK rails, and extended Picatinny top rail. Crossbolt safety. Bullhead bolt system. Uses Benelli/Beretta-style Mobil choke tubes.

NIB	*Exc.*	*V.G.*	*Good*	*Fair*	*Poor*
1200	1000	900	—	—	—

Jericho 941

9mm or .41 Action Express double-action semi-automatic pistol, with 4.72" barrel, polygonal rifling, ambidextrous safety and fixed sights. Blued, with plastic grips. Variations include full-size or mid-size, and polymer or steel frames.

NIB	*Exc.*	*V.G.*	*Good*	*Fair*	*Poor*
580	500	400	350	300	200

Jericho Enhanced

Similar to above with Picatinny rail, adjustable backstrap and reconfigured controls.

NIB	*Exc.*	*V.G.*	*Good*	*Fair*	*Poor*
500	430	380	—	—	—

Masada

9mm polymer frame pistol, ambidextrous controls, Picatinny rail, 17-round mag.

NIB	*Exc.*	*V.G.*	*Good*	*Fair*	*Poor*
440	390	330	—	—	—

UZI MODELS

Action Arms Uzi Model A Carbine

Action Arms Uzi Model A Carbine Semi-auto with folding stock, 25-round magazine, 9mm or .45 ACP, Parkerized finished, made by IMI 1981-1983 beginning at serial number SA01001.

Jim Supica photo

NIB	*Exc.*	*V.G.*	*Good*	*Fair*	*Poor*
1900	1600	1250	900	—	—

Action Arms Uzi Model B Carbine

Similar to above with black enamel finish, 9mm, .41 AE, or .45 ACP. Made by IMI 1983-1989 beginning at s/n SA037001.

NIB	*Exc.*	*V.G.*	*Good*	*Fair*	*Poor*
1800	1500	1150	800	—	—

Uzi Pro Pistol

9mm semi-auto micro-Uzi, 4.5” barrel, 25-round mag.

NIB	*Exc.*	*V.G.*	*Good*	*Fair*	*Poor*
1000	880	750	—	—	—

Uzi Mini-Carbine

As above in 9mm or .45-caliber, with 19.75" barrel. No longer imported.

NIB	*Exc.*	*V.G.*	*Good*	*Fair*	*Poor*
2250	1600	1150	800	600	400

Uzi Pistol

As above in 9mm or .45 ACP, with 4.5" barrel, pistol grip, no rear stock and 20-shot magazine. No longer imported.

NIB	*Exc.*	*V.G.*	*Good*	*Fair*	*Poor*
850	700	550	450	350	250

UZI EAGLE PISTOLS

As of 1999, these pistols no longer imported into U.S.

Full Size Model

Introduced in 1997. Double-action pistol chambered for 9mm and .40 S&W cartridge. Barrel length 4.4"; overall length 8.1". Tritium night sights standard.

NIB	*Exc.*	*V.G.*	*Good*	*Fair*	*Poor*
550	430	350	280	200	150

Short Slide Model

Introduced in 1997. Double-action pistol chambered for 9mm, .40 S&W and .45 ACP cartridge. Barrel length 3.7"; overall length 7.5". Tritium night sights standard.

NIB	*Exc.*	*V.G.*	*Good*	*Fair*	*Poor*
600	480	400	330	250	200

Compact Model

Introduced in 1997. Double-action pistol chambered for 9mm, .40 S&W and .45 ACP cartridge. Barrel length 3.5"; overall length 7.2". Tritium night sights standard. Magazine capacity: 8 rounds .45 ACP; 10 rounds other calibers. Double-action-only an option for this model.

NIB	*Exc.*	*V.G.*	*Good*	*Fair*	*Poor*
600	480	400	330	250	200

Polymer Compact Model

Introduced in 1997. Double-action pistol chambered for 9mm and .40 S&W cartridge. Barrel length 3.5"; overall length 7.2". Tritium night sights standard.

NIB	*Exc.*	*V.G.*	*Good*	*Fair*	*Poor*
550	430	350	280	200	150

ITHACA GUN CO.

Upper Sandusky, Ohio

Material was supplied by Walter C. Snyder and is copyrighted in his name. Used with author's permission.

Ithaca Gun Company was founded by William Henry Baker, John VanNatta and Dwight McIntyre. Gun production started during latter half of 1883, at an industrial site located on Fall Creek, Ithaca, New York. Leroy Smith joined the company by 1885 and George Livermore joined the firm in 1887. By 1894, the company was under exclusive control of Leroy Smith and George Livermore. Many of the company's assets were purchased by Ithaca Acquisition Corporation in 1987 and moved to King Ferry, New York, where it operated until May, 1996. Now, dba, Ithaca Gun Company of Upper Sandusky, Ohio.

HAMMER MODELS

Ithaca Baker Model

First model produced by the company was designed by W.H. Baker and manufactured from 1883 through 1887. Offered in six grades; Quality A ($35) through Quality F ($200), in 10- or 12-gauge. All Ithaca-produced Baker models had exposed hammers. Grades above Quality B are seldom encountered and an expert appraisal is recommended.

Quality A Antique

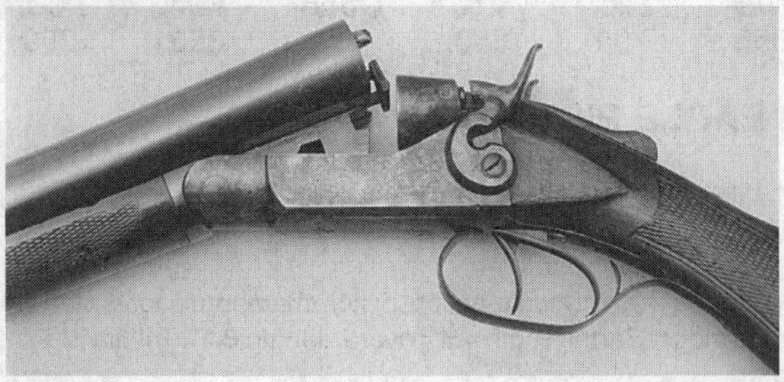

Courtesy Walter C. Snyder

Exc.	Fine	V.G.	Good	Fair	Poor
500	300	250	200	100	70

Quality B

NIB	Exc.	V.G.	Good	Fair	Poor
—	1850	1350	750	300	100

New Ithaca Gun

Introduced in 1888; discontinued during 1915. Like its predecessor, introduced in same seven grades, Quality A through Quality F. Later Quality F was discontinued. By 1900 a "condensed steel" barreled model named Quality X was introduced. New Ithaca Gun was produced in gauges 10-, 12-, 16- and very rarely 20-gauge. Lower grade models carried logo "New Ithaca Gun" usually within a banner on each side of frame. Like its predecessor, grades above Quality B are seldom encountered and an expert appraisal is recommended. 16-gauge guns command a 30 percent price premium. Extremely rare 20-gauge model requires an expert appraisal.

Quality A

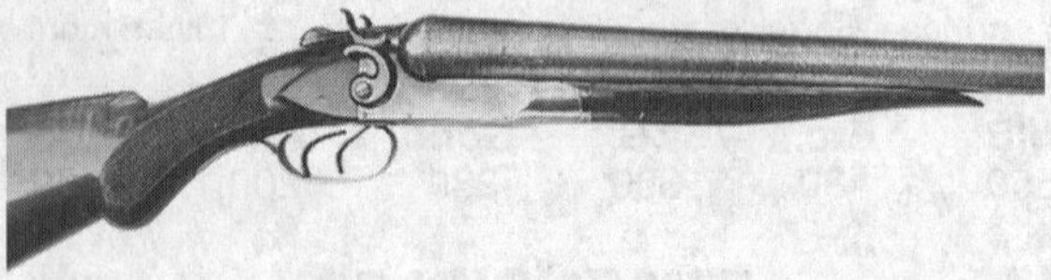

Courtesy Walter C. Snyder

NIB	Exc.	V.G.	Good	Fair	Poor
—	1100	780	300	180	100

Quality AA

NIB	Exc.	V.G.	Good	Fair	Poor
—	1100	780	300	180	100

Quality B Antique

Exc.	Fine	V.G.	Good	Fair	Poor
1350	750	500	300	100	70

Quality X

NIB	Exc.	V.G.	Good	Fair	Poor
—	1300	880	450	220	100

The "New Double Bolted Hammer Gun"

During 1915, Ithaca Gun Company replaced New Ithaca Gun, with model it referred to as our new model two bolt hammer gun". New hammer gun had coil springs powering external hammers. The "two bolt" lock up was accomplished by a bottom bolt and top lever engagement, with rear nub of rib extension. Lower grade models were marked on both sides of frame, with a setter dog and logo "Ithaca Gun Co.". The 1915 catalog is last year hammer guns were advertised, but old records indicate a few were sold as late as 1919.

Grades offered were X, A, AA, B, C, D and E. The 1915 catalog advertised a price of $29 for a Quality A model and $150 for elaborately engraved Quality E. All grades were available in 10-, 12- and 16-gauge. Like the New Ithaca Gun, grades above Quality B are seldom encountered and an expert appraisal is recommended. 16-gauge guns command a 30 percent price premium. Extremely rare 20-gauge model requires an expert appraisal.

Quality A

NIB	Exc.	V.G.	Good	Fair	Poor
—	1300	880	350	220	100

Quality AA

NIB	Exc.	V.G.	Good	Fair	Poor
—	1600	1080	450	250	100

Quality B

NIB	Exc.	V.G.	Good	Fair	Poor
—	1600	1080	450	250	100

Quality X

NIB	Exc.	V.G.	Good	Fair	Poor
—	1600	1080	450	250	100

HAMMERLESS MODELS

First hammerless Ithaca gun was introduced in 1888. All Ithaca double guns were discontinued in 1948. Gauge and grade can usually be found on left front corner of water table of frame. Serial number usually found on right side of same water table on barrel flats and forend iron.

Crass Model

Crass Model, named after Ithaca's Frederick Crass who designed it, was introduced in 1888. Offered in Quality 1 through Quality 7. Quality 1P model with no engraving introduced in 1898. Crass Model underwent three major frame re-designs, before it was discontinued during 1901. Gun was available in 10-, 12- and 16-gauge. Automatic ejectors introduced in 1893. Available in any Quality gun at extra cost. Note: 16-gauge guns will command a 20 percent price premium. Guns above Quality 4 are seldom encountered and an expert appraisal is necessary. Automatic ejectors add $250. Serial number range for Crass Model approximately 7000 to 50000.

Quality 1

NIB	Exc.	V.G.	Good	Fair	Poor
580	400	310	220	100	70

Quality 1-1/2

NIB	Exc.	V.G.	Good	Fair	Poor
580	400	310	220	100	70

Quality 1P

NIB	Exc.	V.G.	Good	Fair	Poor
580	400	310	220	100	70

Quality 2

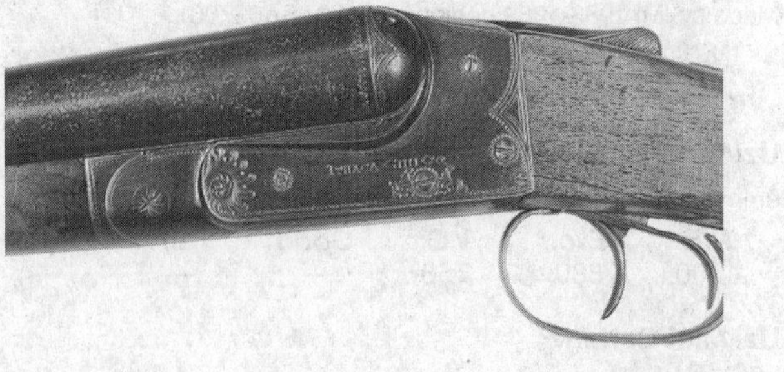

Courtesy Walter C. Snyder

NIB	Exc.	V.G.	Good	Fair	Poor
880	600	420	250	100	70

Quality 3

NIB	Exc.	V.G.	Good	Fair	Poor
1300	780	550	320	100	70

Quality 4

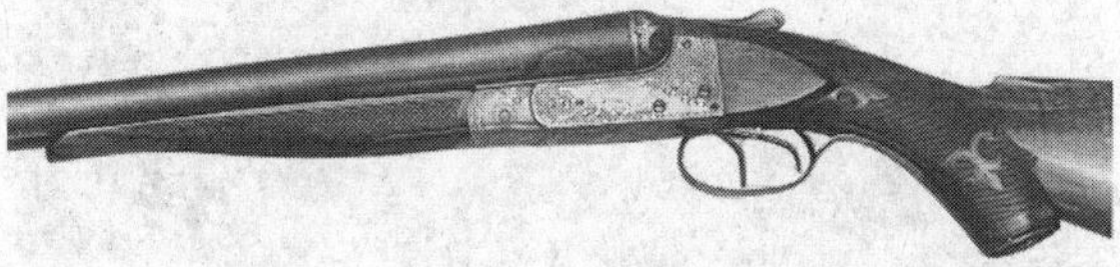

NIB	Exc.	V.G.	Good	Fair	Poor
1850	1080	700	320	100	70

Lewis Model

Chester Lewis, an Ithaca Gun employee, was credited with design of this gun that now bears his name. Gun was bolted through rib extension in addition to traditional under bolt. Available from 1901 through 1906 and offered in Qualities 1 through 7. Made in 10-, 12- and 16-gauge. After 1906, 20-gauge. Automatic ejectors were offered at an added cost. Note: Automatic ejectors add about $250 to grades below Quality 4. Serial number range for Lewis Model approximately 55000 to 123600.

Quality 1

NIB	Exc.	V.G.	Good	Fair	Poor
—	900	580	320	180	100

Quality 1 Special

Courtesy Walter C. Snyder

NIB	Exc.	V.G.	Good	Fair	Poor
—	900	580	320	180	100

Quality 1-1/2

NIB	Exc.	V.G.	Good	Fair	Poor
—	950	600	350	200	100

Quality 2

NIB	Exc.	V.G.	Good	Fair	Poor
—	1150	720	500	220	100

Quality 3

NIB	Exc.	V.G.	Good	Fair	Poor
—	1850	1500	850	420	100

Quality 4

NIB	Exc.	V.G.	Good	Fair	Poor
—	2700	2350	1900	480	100

Quality 5

NIB	Exc.	V.G.	Good	Fair	Poor
—	3700	3150	2100	720	300

Quality 6

NIB	Exc.	V.G.	Good	Fair	Poor
—	6300	4750	3200	780	300

Quality 7

NIB	Exc.	V.G.	Good	Fair	Poor
—	6300	4750	3200	780	300

Minier Model

Minier Model, named after Ithaca's David Minier, was introduced in 1906 and available through 1908. Offered in Qualities Field through 7 and any grade could be ordered with ejectors. Minier Model was first Ithaca gun to use coil springs to power internal hammers. Model was triple bolted, e.g., two fastenings at rib extension and under bolt. Offered in 10-, 12-, 16- and 20-gauge. Note: Automatic ejectors add $250 to guns below Quality 4. Serial number range for Minier Model approximately 130000 to 151000.

Field Grade

NIB	Exc.	V.G.	Good	Fair	Poor
—	1150	720	500	220	100

Quality 1

NIB	Exc.	V.G.	Good	Fair	Poor
—	1150	720	500	220	100

Quality 1 Special

NIB	Exc.	V.G.	Good	Fair	Poor
—	1150	720	500	220	100

Quality 1-1/2

NIB	Exc.	V.G.	Good	Fair	Poor
—	1150	720	500	220	100

Quality 2

NIB	Exc.	V.G.	Good	Fair	Poor
—	1350	700	480	220	100

Quality 3

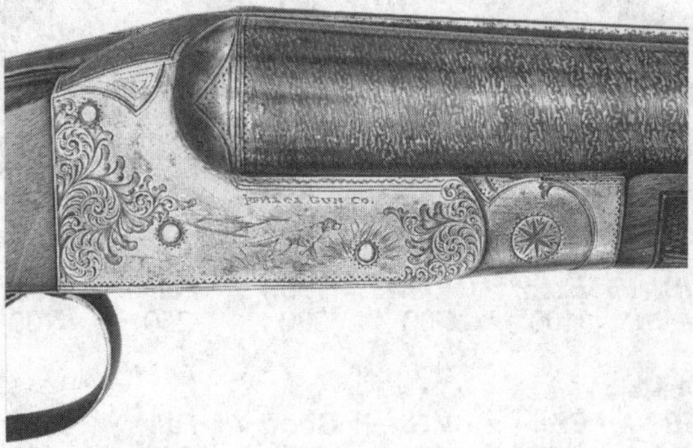

Courtesy Walter C. Snyder

NIB	Exc.	V.G.	Good	Fair	Poor
—	2250	1200	580	450	100

Quality 4

Courtesy Amoskeag Auction Company

NIB	Exc.	V.G.	Good	Fair	Poor
—	2700	1320	880	450	100

Quality 5

NIB	Exc.	V.G.	Good	Fair	Poor
—	3700	3150	2100	720	300

Quality 6

NIB	Exc.	V.G.	Good	Fair	Poor
—	5250	4100	1550	720	300

Quality 7

NIB	Exc.	V.G.	Good	Fair	Poor
—	6800	4300	1700	800	300

Flues Model

Flues Model Ithaca gun, built on three-piece lock mechanism invented and patented by Emil Flues. Introduced in 1908, remained in production through 1926 when it was replaced by Ithaca New Double. Offered in 10-, 12-, 16-, 20- and 28-gauge. Enjoyed longest production life of any Ithaca double gun. Several grades offered beginning with Field Grade and ending with Sousa Special. Flues Model had same bolting system as used on Minier Model. Any grade could have been ordered, with automatic ejectors at an extra cost. Single-selective trigger made by Infallible Trigger Company, offered after 1914 and was first single trigger offered from this company. Note: Add $200 for factory-ordered single trigger; $200 for automatic ejectors on grades lower than Grade 4. Small gauges command a price premium. 20-gauge gun may command up to 50 percent price premium; 28-gauge Field Grade, perhaps as much as 200 percent. Serial number range for Flues approximately 175000 to 399000. Expert appraisals are recommended on higher-grade, small-gauge models, as they are seldom encountered.

Field Grade

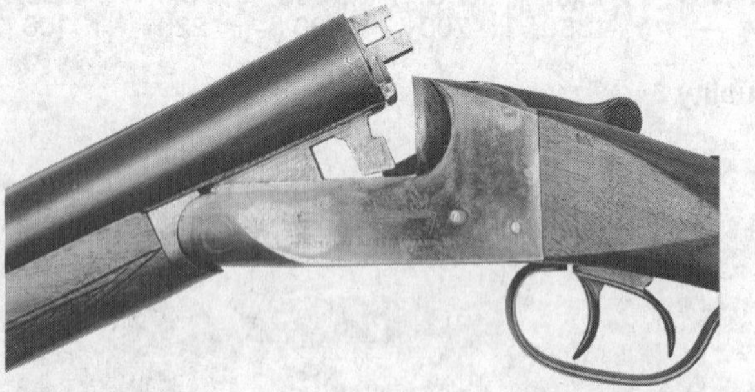

Courtesy Walter C. Snyder

NIB	Exc.	V.G.	Good	Fair	Poor
—	1100	700	380	250	100

Grade 1

NIB	Exc.	V.G.	Good	Fair	Poor
—	1100	700	380	250	100

Grade 1 Special

NIB	Exc.	V.G.	Good	Fair	Poor
—	1100	700	380	250	100

Grade 1-1/2

NIB	Exc.	V.G.	Good	Fair	Poor
—	1250	850	500	350	100

Grade 2

NIB	Exc.	V.G.	Good	Fair	Poor
—	1350	900	580	400	100

Grade 3

NIB	Exc.	V.G.	Good	Fair	Poor
—	2300	1600	800	500	100

Grade 4

NIB	Exc.	V.G.	Good	Fair	Poor
—	2300	1600	800	500	100

Grade 5

NIB	Exc.	V.G.	Good	Fair	Poor
—	2800	2200	1650	600	200

Grade 6

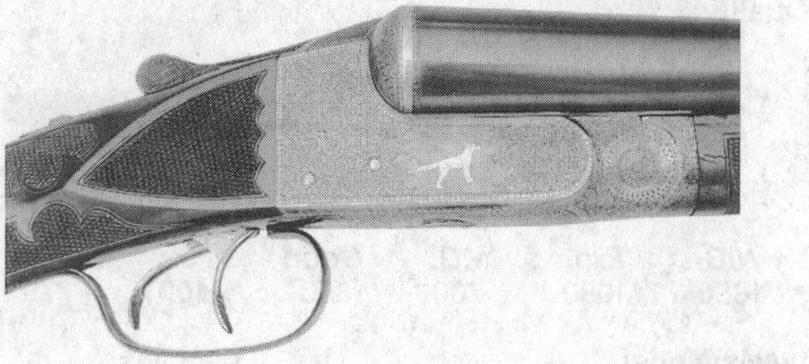

Courtesy Walter C. Snyder

NIB	Exc.	V.G.	Good	Fair	Poor
—	11000	6000	2750	1100	300

Grade 7

NIB	Exc.	V.G.	Good	Fair	Poor
—	11500	7000	3000	1250	300

Sousa

NIB	Exc.	V.G.	Good	Fair	Poor
—	17000	12000	7500	3750	N/A

The New Ithaca Double

New Ithaca Double commonly referred to as NID, manufactured from 1926 to 1948. Has the distinction of being last double gun manufactured by factory. NID was bolted by a single rotary top bolt. External cocking indicators were standard on all NID models until about 1934, when they were eliminated from the design. Selective and non-selective single triggers and automatic ejectors, were optional at additional costs. Special variation of NID was introduced in 1932 to accommodate 10-gauge 3.5" Magnum ammunition and named appropriately, Magnum 10. All NID guns were available in Grades Field, 1, 2, 3, 4, 5, 7 and Sousa (renamed the $1,000 grade after 1936). Magnum 10-gauge and standard 10-, 12-, 16-, 20-, 28-gauge and .410 bore were offered. Note: Like most collectible double guns, smaller gauges command a price premium over 12-gauge model. 16-gauge Field Grade may command a 25 percent price premium; 20-gauge Field Grade may command up to a 50 percent price premium; 28-gauge and .410 caliber Field Grade models, perhaps as much as 250-300 percent. It is recommended that an expert opinion be sought for valuation of high-grade small-gauge models. Of late, Magnum 10-gauge model also commands a price premium. Few of these guns trade and advice of an expert appraiser is suggested. Add $150 for non-selective single trigger; $250 for single-selective trigger; $300 for ventilated rib; $300 for automatic ejectors for grades below Grade 4; $200 for beavertail forearm; $300 for Monte Carlo buttstock.

Field Grade

NIB	Exc.	V.G.	Good	Fair	Poor
—	1100	700	380	250	100

Grade 1

NIB	Exc.	V.G.	Good	Fair	Poor
—	1350	850	480	250	100

Grade 2

Courtesy Walter C. Snyder

NIB	Exc.	V.G.	Good	Fair	Poor
—	1650	900	720	350	100

Grade 3

NIB	Exc.	V.G.	Good	Fair	Poor
—	2600	1600	1080	420	100

Grade 4

NIB	Exc.	V.G.	Good	Fair	Poor
—	3250	2700	1600	480	100

Grade 5

NIB	Exc.	V.G.	Good	Fair	Poor
—	4300	3400	2200	780	200

Grade 7

Values shown are very speculative. Only 22 were manufactured.

NIB	Exc.	V.G.	Good	Fair	Poor
—	50000	42000	35000	—	—

Sousa Grade

NIB	Exc.	V.G.	Good	Fair	Poor
40000	30000	20000	—	—	—

ITHACA CLASSIC DOUBLES (1998-2003)

Special Field Grade

Side-by-side double offered in 16-, 20-, 28-gauge and .410 bore. Choice of matted rib barrel lengths of 26", 28" or 30". Ivory bead front sight. Action is case colored, with light line border engraving. Stock is feather crotch black walnut, with 22 lpi checkering. Choice of pistol-/straight-grip. Double trigger standard. Weight about: 20-gauge 5 lbs. 14 oz.; 28-gauge 5 lbs. 8 oz.; .410 bore 5 lbs. 5 oz.

NIB	Exc.	V.G.	Good	Fair	Poor
6200	4750	4000	1700	800	300

Grade 4E

Available in 16-, 20-, 28-gauge and .410 bore, with 26", 28" and 30" barrels. Has gold plated triggers, jeweled barrel flats and hand tuned locks. Black walnut stock has 28 lpi checkering, with fleur-de-lis pattern. Pistol-/straight-grip stock. Action is hand engraved, with three game scenes and bank note scroll. Case colored frame.

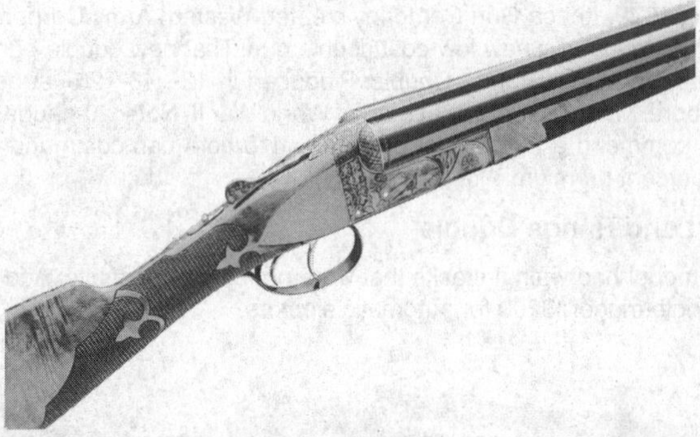

NIB	Exc.	V.G.	Good	Fair	Poor
8000	6000	3000	1750	780	300

Grade 7E

Has all gauges and barrel lengths of above gun. Action is hand engraved, with gold two tone inlays. Exhibition grade black walnut stock, with elaborate patterns. Custom built dimensions.

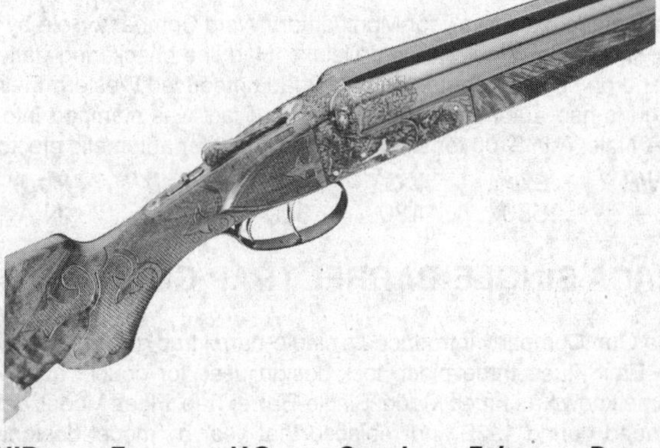

NIB	Exc.	V.G.	Good	Fair	Poor
11000	8750	7500	4250	1100	300

Sousa Grade

Available in same gauges and barrel lengths as above guns. Stocks with presentation grade black walnut and hand carved with 32 lpi checkering. Action hand engraved, with bank note scroll and gold inlays. Entire gun hand-fitted and polished. Extremely limited availability. Special order only. In production from 1998 to 2003.

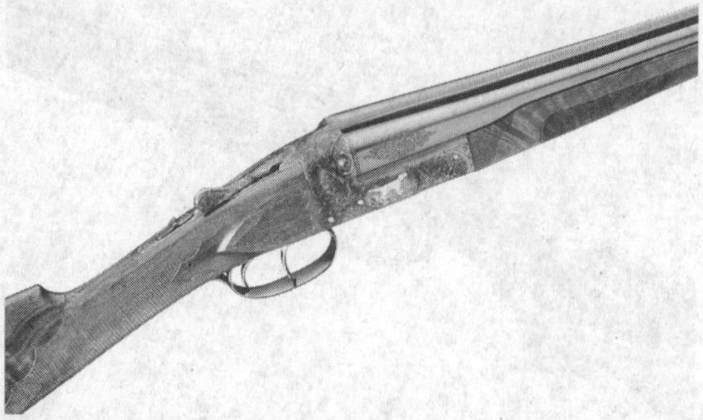

NIB	Exc.	V.G.	Good	Fair	Poor
25000	20000	15000	—	—	—

LEFEVER ARMS COMPANY, INC.

During 1921, Ithaca Gun under the name "The Lefever Arms Company, Inc." introduced a line of lower-cost boxlock guns. See Lefever Arms Company section of this book for prices concerning those guns.

WESTERN ARMS CORPORATION

During 1929, Ithaca Gun Company created Western Arms Corporation, which introduced a new low-cost double gun. That new double gun was named, The Long Range Double. Produced in 12-, 16-, 20-gauge and .410 bore. Model last made at start of World War II. Note: 20-gauge guns often command a 20 percent premium; .410 bore can command up to 250 percent premium.

The Long Range Double

This model had walnut stocks that were not checkered. Note: Add $100 for single trigger; $200 for automatic ejectors.

NIB	Exc.	V.G.	Good	Fair	Poor
—	550	450	200	150	N/A

The Long Range Double Deluxe

Usually made exclusively for Montgomery Ward Company. Sold by them under the name: Western Field Deluxe. Had line checkering pattern at grip and on splinter forend. Many of Ithaca produced Western Field Deluxe guns had automatic ejectors and that fact was stamped into right barrel. Note: Add $100 for single triggers; $200 for automatic ejectors.

NIB	Exc.	V.G.	Good	Fair	Poor
—	580	480	300	150	N/A

ITHACA SINGLE-BARREL TRAP GUNS

Ithaca Gun Company introduced a single-barrel trap gun in 1914. Based upon Emil Flues three piece lock design used for double gun, which become known as Flues Model Single-Barrel Trap. Flues Model was discontinued during 1922 and replaced that year by model designed by Ithaca's, Frank Knickerbocker, commonly referred to as "Knick". Knick Model discontinued in 1988, shortly after Ithaca Acquisition Corp. purchased assets of Ithaca Gun Company. For many years, Ithaca Single-Barrel Trap Gun was the gun of choice for many champion shooters.

Flues Model Single-Barrel Trap Gun (1914 to 1922)

Flues Model trap gun was introduced in 1914. Offered in Grades 4, 5, 6 and 7. Lower cost Victory grade introduced in 1919. Highest cost variety Sousa Special introduced in 1918. All Flues model trap guns were made within same serial number sequence as double guns, but do have letter "T" for Trap following serial number. All Flues Models, with exception of Victory Grade, were produced with an automatic ejector. Rubber anti-recoil pad was an option. Guns having a pre-1916 engraving pattern will command highest prices.

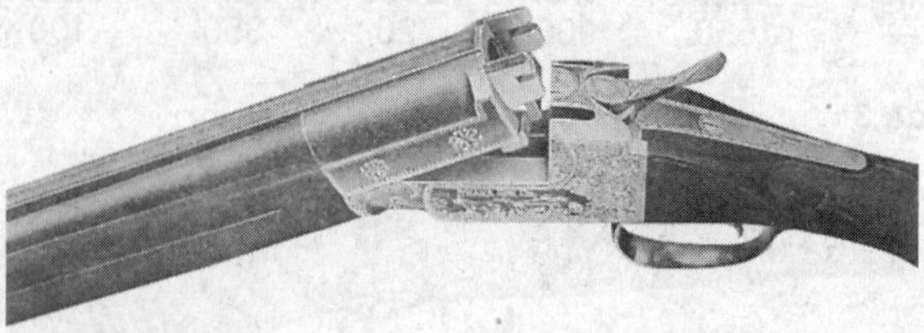

Courtesy Walter C. Snyder

Victory Grade

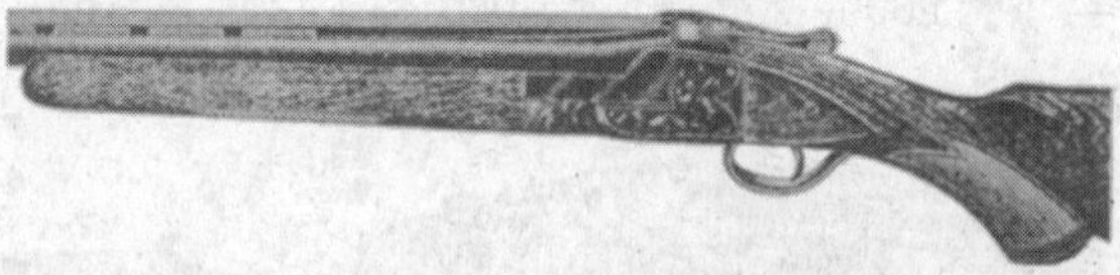

NIB	Exc.	V.G.	Good	Fair	Poor
—	1300	900	700	300	N/A

Grade 4E

NIB	Exc.	V.G.	Good	Fair	Poor
—	2350	1900	1300	400	N/A

Grade 5E

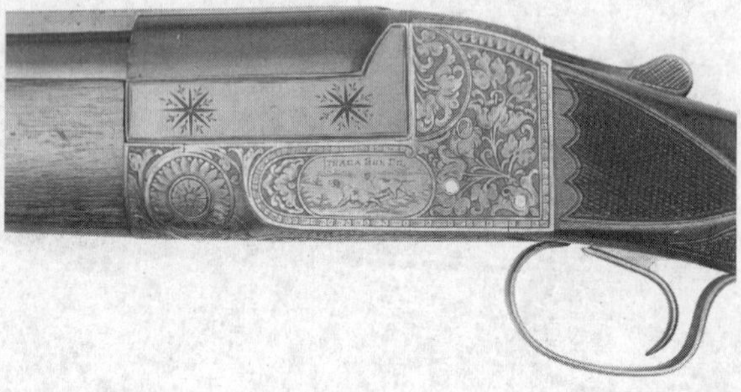

Courtesy Walter C. Snyder

NIB	Exc.	V.G.	Good	Fair	Poor
—	4200	3100	2550	600	N/A

Grade 6E

NIB	Exc.	V.G.	Good	Fair	Poor
—	6300	5250	3200	900	N/A

Grade 7E

NIB	Exc.	V.G.	Good	Fair	Poor
—	8350	6200	4100	1050	N/A

Sousa Grade

NIB	Exc.	V.G.	Good	Fair	Poor
—	16500	11000	9000	2500	N/A

Knick Model Single-Barrel Trap

Knick Model trap gun introduced during 1922. Based on design credited to Frank Knickerbocker. Design was simple and very serviceable. Had been in continuous production until 1988, when it was discontinued. Model available in Victory, 4, 5, 7 and Sousa Special Grades. Sousa was replaced by: $1,000 Grade in about 1936; which was replaced by $2,000 Grade by 1952; $2,500 Grade by 1960; $3,000 Grade by 1965; $5,000 Grade by 1974; finally, Dollar Grade in early 1980s, as cost of production increased. All Knick models were produced with automatic ejector and rubber anti-recoil pad.

Victory Grade

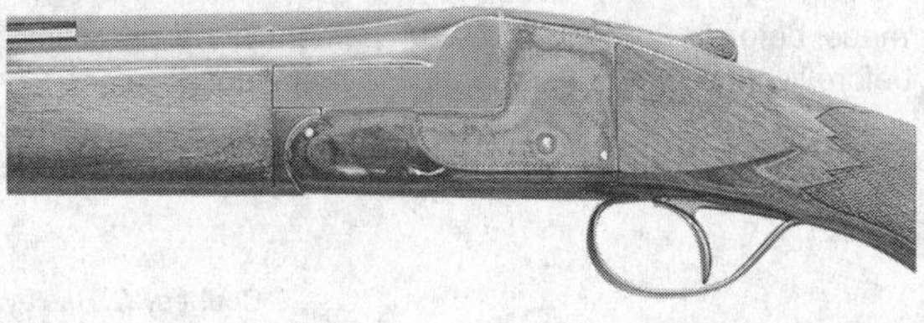

Courtesy William Hammond

NIB	Exc.	V.G.	Good	Fair	Poor
2500	1350	900	700	300	N/A

Grade 4E

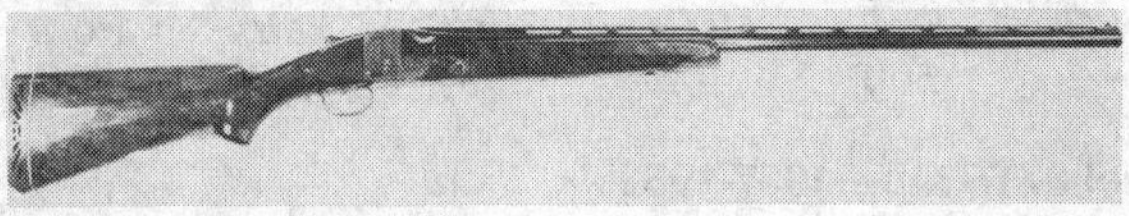

Courtesy C. Hadley Smith

NIB	Exc.	V.G.	Good	Fair	Poor
3300	2450	1950	1100	500	N/A

Grade 5E

NIB	Exc.	V.G.	Good	Fair	Poor
5500	4400	3300	2750	880	N/A

Grade 7E

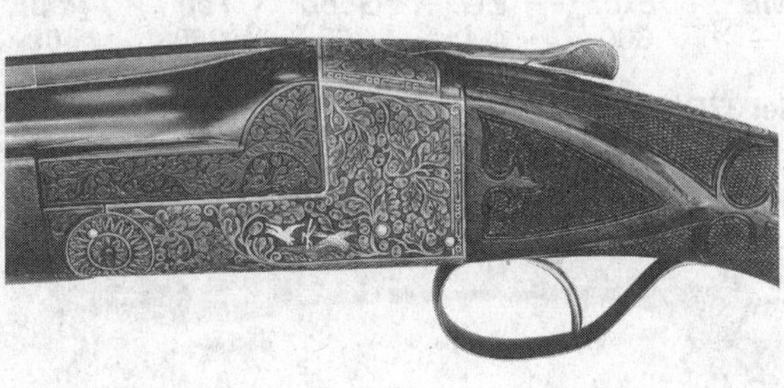

Courtesy Walter C. Snyder

NIB	Exc.	V.G.	Good	Fair	Poor
8800	5500	4450	3300	1100	N/A

Sousa Grade

NIB	Exc.	V.G.	Good	Fair	Poor
19000	11000	6600	4400	N/A	N/A

$1,000 to $2,500 Grades

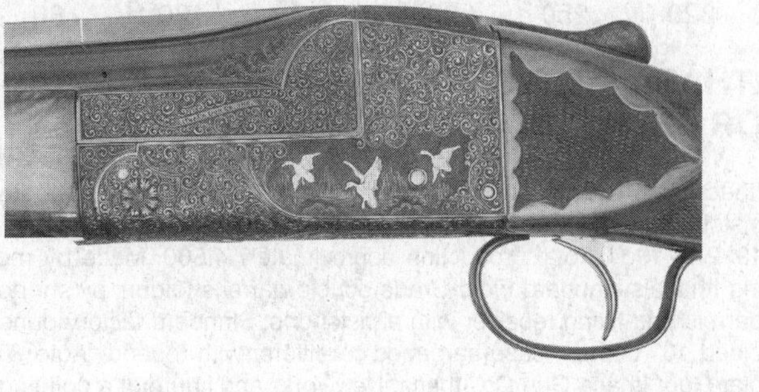

Courtesy Walter C. Snyder

NIB	Exc.	V.G.	Good	Fair	Poor
16500	13500	8800	6500	2200	N/A

$3,000 through the Dollar Grade

NIB	Exc.	V.G.	Good	Fair	Poor
13500	11000	6500	5500	2200	N/A

Century Grade Trap (SKB)

12-gauge boxlock single-barrel shotgun, with 32" or 34" ventilated rib barrel. Automatic ejector. Blued, with walnut stock. Manufactured by SKB during 1970s.

NIB	Exc.	V.G.	Good	Fair	Poor
—	900	700	550	350	300

Century II (SKB)

An improved version of above model.

NIB	Exc.	V.G.	Good	Fair	Poor
—	950	700	600	450	350

ITHACA MODEL 66

Model 66 Supersingle—1963-1978

12-, 20-gauge or .410 bore lever action single-shot shotgun, with 24" barrel. Blued, with walnut stock. Note: Add 50 per premium for 20-gauge and .410 bore.

Courtesy C. Hadley Smith

NIB	Exc.	V.G.	Good	Fair	Poor
300	180	150	120	100	50

Model 66 Youth Grade

Special gun offered for youth market in 20-gauge and .410 bore.

NIB	Exc.	V.G.	Good	Fair	Poor
300	180	150	120	100	50

Model 66 Buck Buster (RS Barrel)

As above in 20-gauge, with Deerslayer 22" barrel fitted with rifle sights.

NIB	Exc.	V.G.	Good	Fair	Poor
320	250	200	150	120	80

Model 66 Vent Rib

NIB	Exc.	V.G.	Good	Fair	Poor
320	250	200	150	120	80

ITHACA AUTO & BURGLAR GUN/NFA, CURIO OR RELIC

Ithaca Auto & Burglar Gun, is a double-barreled 20-gauge smoothbore pistol. Manufactured by Ithaca Gun Company, Ithaca, New York, from 1922 to 1934. Total production approximately 4,500. Made by modifying Ithaca's standard Field Grade double-barrel shotgun, by shortening barrels and fitting receiver with a pistol grip. Standard factory guns had blued 10" barrels, case-hardened receivers, with legend "Auto & Burglar Gun/ Ithaca Gun Co./Ithaca, New York" and figure of a pointing dog stamped on each side. Barrel length on 21 guns inspected varied to 10.25" (typically in increments divisible by .125"), apparently from inexact factory quality control. Ithaca set a $37.50 retail price when gun was in production, but some dealers sold it for $40 or more. Production halted when government ruled Ithaca Auto & Burglar Gun to be a "firearm" in "any other weapon" category under National Firearms Act (NFA) of 1934. This means that it is illegal to possess unless it is currently registered with the BATFE.

There are two variations, termed Model A and Model B. Model A utilizes so-called Flues frame (named after Emil Flues who designed it in 1908). Its distinctive grip has a curving butt and large spur. Model A designed for 2.5" shells and is not considered safe to fire using modern ammunition. Approximately 2,500 Model A Auto & Burglar Guns were manufactured from 1922 to 1925, when Flues model was discontinued.

Model B utilizes so-called NID frame (short for New Ithaca Double). Introduced in 1926 and discontinued in 1948. NID is designed for modern ammunition and 2.75" shells. Has cocking indicators and different pistol grip that is perpendicular to barrel, which lacks distinctive spur. Some Model Bs have been observed with rosettes or "stars" engraved in each side of receiver. Their significance is unknown at this time, but they probably are decorations. Approximately 2,000 Model B Auto & Burglar Guns were manufactured from 1926 to 1934. Values are for legally registered transferable guns.

Model A

Serial numbered from 343336 to 398365

NIB	Exc.	V.G.	Good	Fair	Poor
—	2500	2000	1750	900	500

Model B

Serial numbered from 425000 to 464699

Note: Non-standard or special order guns command premiums of 100 percent or more. Original holsters (marked Auto and Burglar Gun/made by/ITHACA GUN CO./ithaca, n.y.) are extremely rare and worth $300 to $500 or more.

NIB	Exc.	V.G.	Good	Fair	Poor
—	2750	2200	2000	950	550

ITHACA MODEL 37 REPEATER

Ithaca Model 37 Repeater was introduced in 1937 in 12-gauge, 1938 in 16-gauge and 1939 in 20-gauge. It underwent very few design changes throughout its long life, which ended in 1987. Ithaca Acquisition Corp. acquired assets of Ithaca Gun Company during 1987, re-naming the gun Model 87. Name has recently been changed again to M37, after assets of Ithaca Acquisition Corp. were purchased in May of 1996 by Ithaca Gun Company, LLC. All Model 37 guns were chambered only for 2.75 ammunition until 1983, when Magnum with 3" chamber was introduced to some configurations. Most Model 37 guns had blued metal and walnut stocks, with exception of Model 37 Field Grade series, which had matte finished metal and birch stocks. 16-gauge guns were discontinued in 1973. Ithaca Gun closed in April, 2005, but re-opened in 2006 as Ithaca Guns USA of Upper Sandusky, Ohio. Note: 20-gauge guns made before 1968 will generally command a price premium.

Courtesy Keith Kramis

Ithaca Model 37 20 gauge.

Model 37/Standard Grade—1937-1983

Guns made before 1968 will enjoy 15 percent price premium; those made before World War II 30 percent price premium.

Courtesy C. Hadley Smith

NIB	Exc.	V.G.	Good	Fair	Poor
—	350	200	180	120	80

Model 37S/Skeet Grade—1937-1953

Guns made before World War II will enjoy 50 percent price premium.

NIB	Exc.	V.G.	Good	Fair	Poor
—	600	400	350	250	100

Model 37T/Trap—1937-1953

Guns made before World War II will enjoy 50 percent price premium.

NIB	Exc.	V.G.	Good	Fair	Poor
—	600	400	350	250	100

Model 37T/Target—1954-1961

NIB	Exc.	V.G.	Good	Fair	Poor
—	600	400	350	250	100

Model 37R/Solid Rib—1940-1967

Guns made before World War II will enjoy 50 percent price premium.

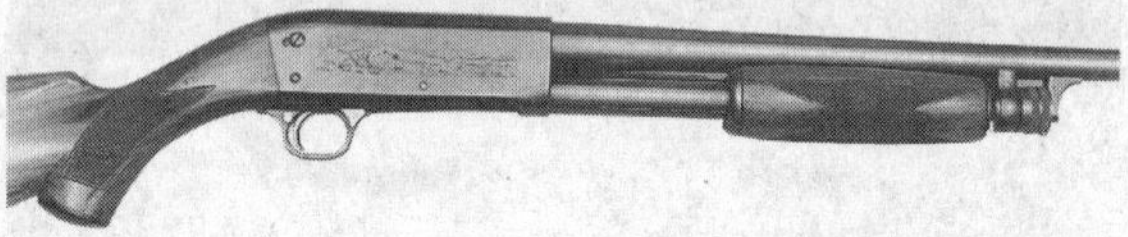

Courtesy Walter C. Snyder

NIB	Exc.	V.G.	Good	Fair	Poor
—	400	280	220	200	80

Model 37 Military Marked (WWII)

One of the scarcest military shotguns. Built in three different configurations; 30" barrel, 20" barrel and 20" barrel with handguard and bayonet lug (Trench Gun). Rare shotgun, proceed with caution. Note: Add $200 for government release papers; 150 percent for Trench Gun configuration.

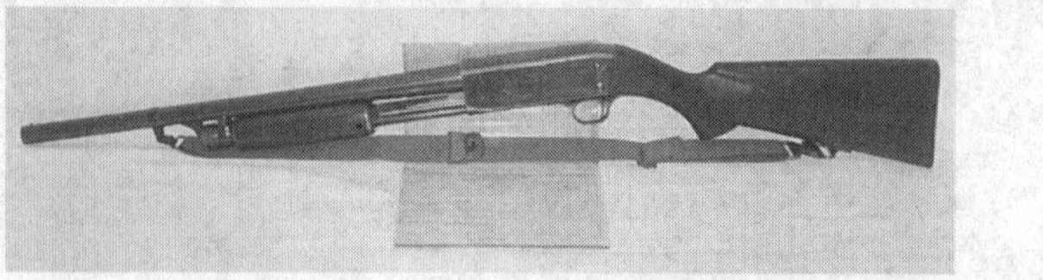

Courtesy Richard M. Kumor, Sr.

NIB	Exc.	V.G.	Good	Fair	Poor
—	2000	1800	1500	—	—

Model 37RD/Deluxe Solid Rib—1954-1962

Courtesy C. Hadley Smith

NIB	Exc.	V.G.	Good	Fair	Poor
—	500	380	300	200	100

Model 37 Deerslayer—1959-1987

All Deerslayer models made before 1968 will enjoy 10 to 20 percent price premium.

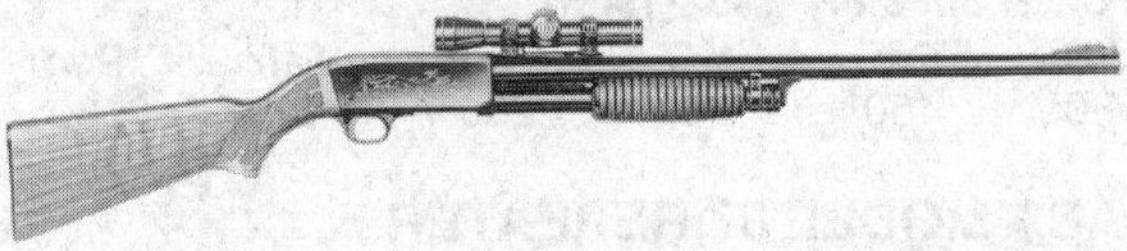

Courtesy C. Hadley Smith

NIB	Exc.	V.G.	Good	Fair	Poor
—	300	250	200	120	80

Model 37 Deluxe Deerslayer—1959-1971

NIB	Exc.	V.G.	Good	Fair	Poor
—	300	250	220	120	80

Model 37 Super Deluxe Deerslayer—1959-1987

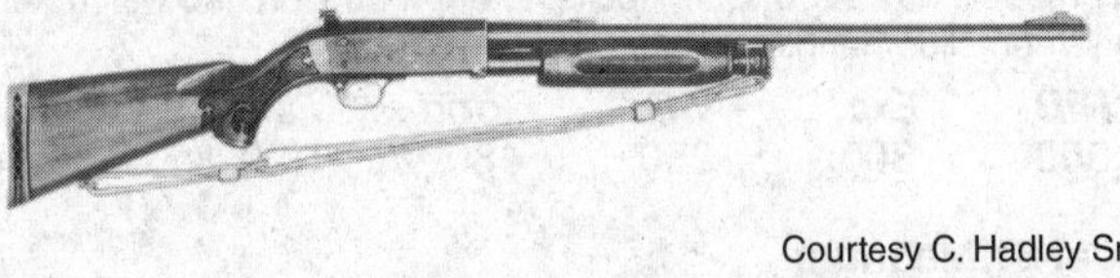

Courtesy C. Hadley Smith

NIB	Exc.	V.G.	Good	Fair	Poor
—	450	320	280	200	100

Model 37 Supreme Grade—1967-1987

NIB	Exc.	V.G.	Good	Fair	Poor
—	700	450	350	200	100

Model 37 Field Grade Standard—1983-1985

NIB	Exc.	V.G.	Good	Fair	Poor
—	350	200	150	120	80

Model 37 Field Grade Vent Rib—1983-1986

NIB	Exc.	V.G.	Good	Fair	Poor
—	350	250	200	120	80

Model 37 Basic Featherlight—1979-1983

Manufactured in 12-gauge only.

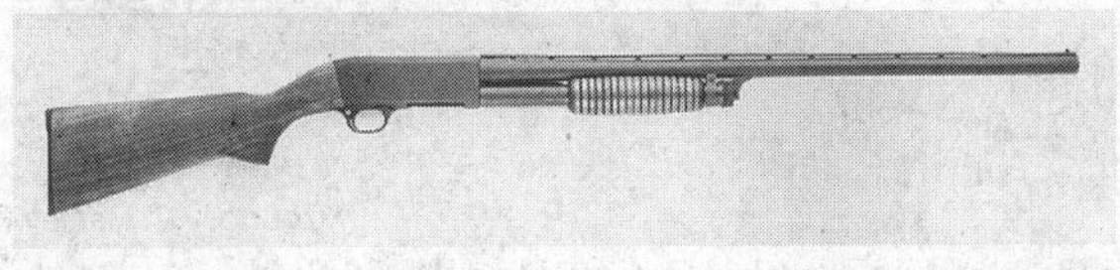

Courtesy Walter C. Snyder

NIB	Exc.	V.G.	Good	Fair	Poor
—	300	250	200	120	80

Model 37V/Vent Rib—1961-1983

Guns made before 1968 will enjoy 10 to 20 percent price premium.

NIB	Exc.	V.G.	Good	Fair	Poor
—	350	300	180	150	80

Model 37RV/Deluxe Vent Rib—1961-1966

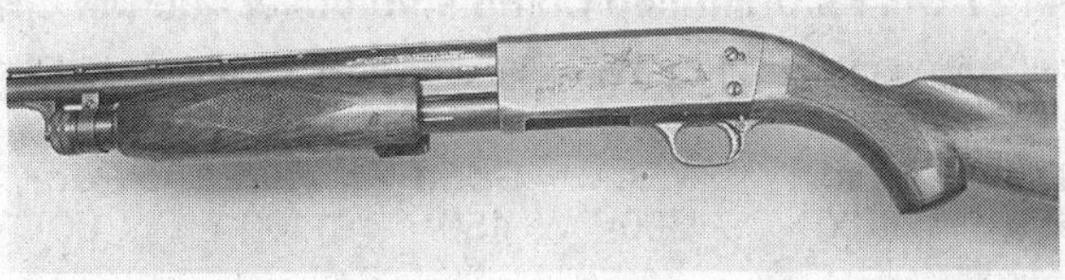

Courtesy Walter C. Snyder

NIB	Exc.	V.G.	Good	Fair	Poor
—	750	500	300	200	80

Model 37D/Deluxe—1955-1977

Guns made before 1968 will enjoy 10 to 20 percent price premium.

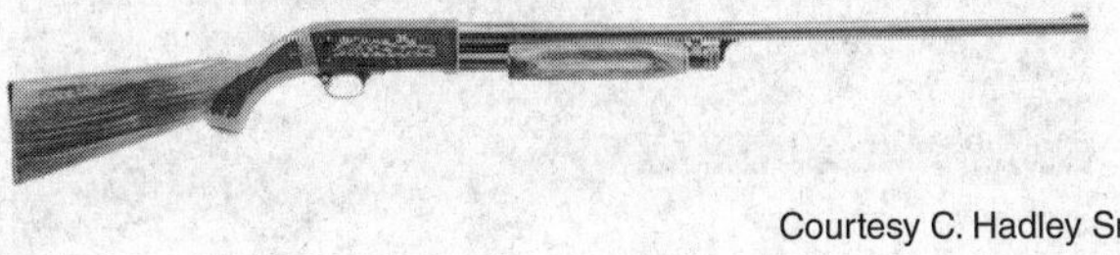

Courtesy C. Hadley Smith

NIB	Exc.	V.G.	Good	Fair	Poor
—	400	250	180	120	80

Model 37DV/Deluxe Vent Rib—1961-1987

Guns made before 1968 will enjoy 10 to 20 percent price premium.

NIB	Exc.	V.G.	Good	Fair	Poor
—	450	300	200	150	100

Model 37 Magnum 3" Chamber—1978-1987

NIB	Exc.	V.G.	Good	Fair	Poor
—	400	300	220	120	80

Model 37 Field Grade Magnum—1984-1987

NIB	Exc.	V.G.	Good	Fair	Poor
—	300	220	180	120	80

Model 37 UltraLight—1978 to 1987

UltraLight had aluminum alloy frame and trigger plate. Barrels marked Ultra Featherlight. Serial number prefaced with the mark "ULT". Both 12- and 20-gauge offered.

NIB	Exc.	V.G.	Good	Fair	Poor
—	480	400	300	150	100

Model 37 English UltraLight—1982-1987

Same as Model 37 UltraLight, with English-style straight-grip stock.

NIB	Exc.	V.G.	Good	Fair	Poor
—	500	450	350	150	100

Model 37 Camo

Introduced in 1985, with green or brown camouflage finish. Offered only in 12-gauge.

NIB	Exc.	V.G.	Good	Fair	Poor
—	350	300	200	150	100

Model 37 Bicentennial

Special model produced during 1976 to commemorate 200th year Anniversary of United States. Gun came with full-length trunk-style hard case and pewter belt buckle numbered to gun. Serial number was prefaced with "U.S.A." Note: Subtract 35 percent if original case and belt buckle are missing.

NIB	Exc.	V.G.	Good	Fair	Poor
650	500	300	200	120	80

Model 37 Ducks Unlimited Commemorative, Auction Grade

Special edition made during 1977. Serial number sequence 40-DU0001 to 40-DU1125.

NIB	Exc.	V.G.	Good	Fair	Poor
650	400	300	150	100	80

Model 37 Ducks Unlimited Commemorative, Trade Grade

Special edition made during 1977. Lower grade version of Auction Grade. Serial number preceded with the mark DU37040.

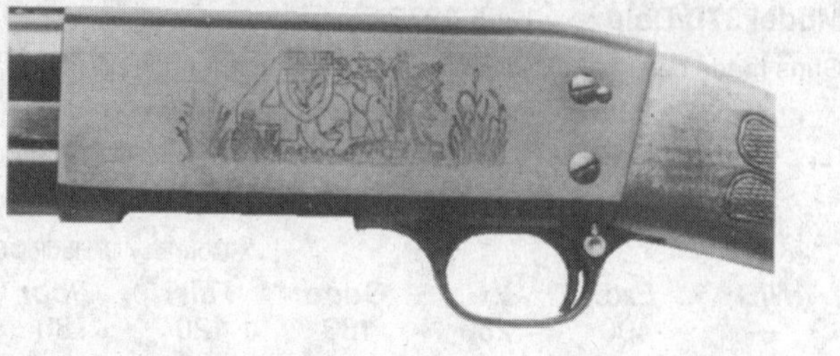

NIB	Exc.	V.G.	Good	Fair	Poor
450	400	350	200	N/A	N/A

Model 37 2500 Series Centennial

Commemorative Model 37 12-gauge shotgun, with silver-plated receiver and press checkered stocks. Manufactured in 1984.

NIB	Exc.	V.G.	Good	Fair	Poor
800	500	300	150	100	80

Model 37 Presentation Series Centennial

Commemorative Model 37 12-gauge shotgun. Gold-plated receiver and high-grade hand-checkered stocks. Manufactured from 1981 to 1986 and later on special order only.

NIB	Exc.	V.G.	Good	Fair	Poor
1500	800	500	150	100	—

Hi-Grade Ithaca Model 37 Guns

Ithaca Gun company offered custom engraving services from its in-house engraver, one of which was retained until about 1972, or through an outside contract engraver, who was usually William Mains. Many customers requested some degree of custom work and guns with various patterns turn up from time to time. Four standard engraving patterns offered to customers: Grade 1; Grade 2; Grade 3 and very elaborate $1,000 Grade pattern. Increasing production costs forced $1,000 Grade to become $2,000 Grade, $2,500 and finally $3,000 Grade over the years. Note: All factory engraved Model 37 guns are rare and require an expert appraiser to determine an accurate value.

$1,000 Grade

Model 37, with engraved receiver, gold inlays and well-figured walnut stock. Manufactured between 1940 and 1942.

NIB	Exc.	V.G.	Good	Fair	Poor
10000	5000	3000	2000	N/A	N/A

$2,000 Grade

Manufactured from 1946 to 1957.

NIB	Exc.	V.G.	Good	Fair	Poor
10000	5000	3000	2000	N/A	N/A

$3,000 Grade

Manufactured from 1958 to 1967.

NIB	Exc.	V.G.	Good	Fair	Poor
8000	4000	2500	1500	N/A	N/A

Model 37 Law Enforcement Weapons

Ithaca Gun Company entered the law enforcement market in 1962. Introduced Model 37 Military and Police (M&P) and Model 37DS Police special (DSPS). M&P Model styled after riot guns, made for various military contracts. DSPS styled after Ithaca Deerslayer. Both models offered with 8-shot capacity after 1968. Chrome finish was an available option after 1976. Both models usually had ring turned slide handles. Only those models available to general public, i.e. barrel lengths of 18" or longer, are listed. Note: Add 25 percent if marked with police department; 20 percent for 8-shot model in NIB or EXC. condition; additional 15 percent for chrome plated models in similar condition.

Military and Police (M&P)—1962-1986

NIB	Exc.	V.G.	Good	Fair	Poor
550	450	250	200	120	80

DS Police Special—1962-1986

NIB	Exc.	V.G.	Good	Fair	Poor
580	450	250	200	120	80

ITHACA MODEL 87 REPEATER

During 1987, many assets of bankrupt Ithaca Gun Company were purchased by Ithaca Acquisition Corporation. Manufacture of Model 37 resumed that summer, after the gun was renamed Model 87. Many models offered by the old company were continued. All Model 87 field guns were produced with ventilated ribs. All Deerslayer models continued rifle sights, used on Model 37 guns.

Model 87 Basic—1989-1994

Early models had birchwood stocks, later production had walnut. All had ring turned slide handles.

NIB	Exc.	V.G.	Good	Fair	Poor
350	300	250	180	120	80

Model 87 Magnum

12- or 20-gauge Magnum slide action shotgun, with 25" barrel. Fitted with screw-in choke tubes and ventilated rib, that is similar to Model 37. Blued, with walnut stock.

NIB	Exc.	V.G.	Good	Fair	Poor
400	350	300	220	150	100

Model 87 Field Grade—1987-1990

Stocks were walnut, with pressed checkering.

NIB	Exc.	V.G.	Good	Fair	Poor
320	250	200	180	120	80

Model 87 Camo—1987-1994

NIB	Exc.	V.G.	Good	Fair	Poor
300	250	200	180	120	80

Model 87 Turkey Gun—1987-1996

Courtesy C. Hadley Smith

NIB	Exc.	V.G.	Good	Fair	Poor
320	250	200	180	120	80

Model 87 Deluxe—1987-1996

Buttstocks and slide handle were walnut, with machine cut checkered pattern.

Courtesy C. Hadley Smith

NIB	Exc.	V.G.	Good	Fair	Poor
380	300	250	200	120	80

Model 87 Ultralite—1987-1990

All IAC manufactured Ultralite guns carry old Model 37 serial number.

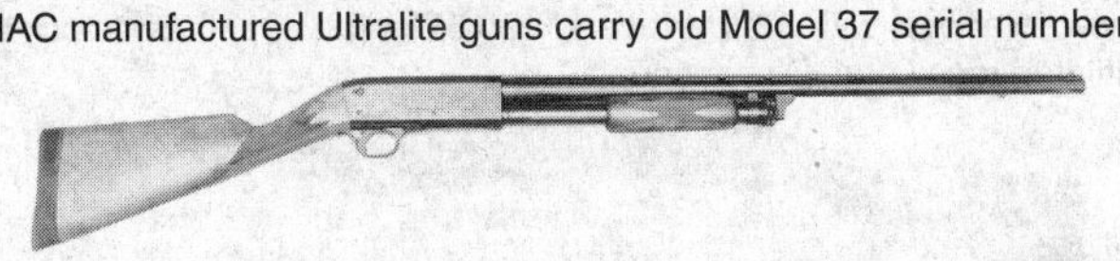

Courtesy C. Hadley Smith

NIB	Exc.	V.G.	Good	Fair	Poor
500	350	250	180	120	80

Model 87 English—1993-1996

Hand-checkered walnut stocks. Slide handle styled after pre-war Model 37 slide handle.

NIB	Exc.	V.G.	Good	Fair	Poor
400	350	250	180	120	80

Model 87 Ultralite Deluxe

NIB	Exc.	V.G.	Good	Fair	Poor
400	350	300	250	120	80

Model 87 Supreme Grade—1987-1996

High grade walnut stocks, with hand-checkering. Metal had extra fine polish and finish.

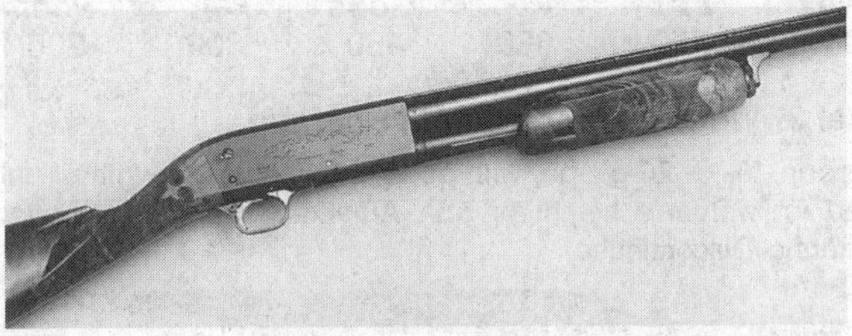

Courtesy C. Hadley Smith

NIB	Exc.	V.G.	Good	Fair	Poor
1000	700	500	300	250	100

Model 87 Deerslayer Basic—1989-1996

Walnut oil-finish butt and slide handle stocks. Slide handle was classic ring turned style.

NIB	Exc.	V.G.	Good	Fair	Poor
300	280	250	200	120	80

Model 87 Deerslayer—1989-1996

Sometimes advertised as Model 87 Deerslayer Field. Buttstock and slide handle were walnut. Usually had pressed checkered pattern. Slide handle was beavertail style.

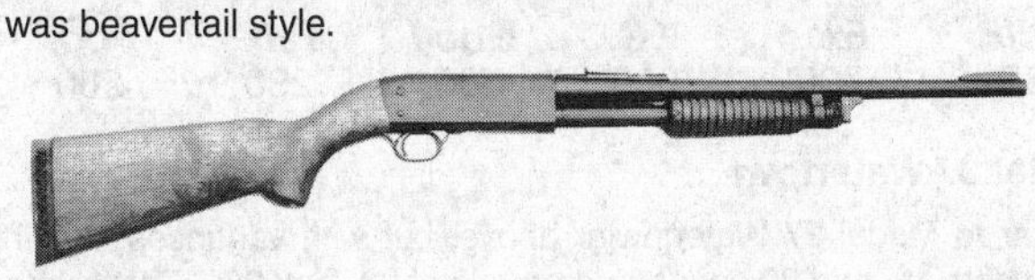

Courtesy C. Hadley Smith

NIB	Exc.	V.G.	Good	Fair	Poor
350	300	250	200	120	80

Model 87 Deluxe Deerslayer—1989-1996

Buttstock and slide handle were walnut, with machine-cut checkering pattern. Slide handle was beavertail.

NIB	Exc.	V.G.	Good	Fair	Poor
400	350	250	200	120	80

Model 87 Deerslayer II—1988-1996

Fixed rifle barrel and Monte Carlo buttstock. Small number of guns specially made with fast twist barrel to handle Brenneke ammunition. Marked "BRENNEKE" on receiver. Note: Brenneke-marked guns will command a 30 percent price premium.

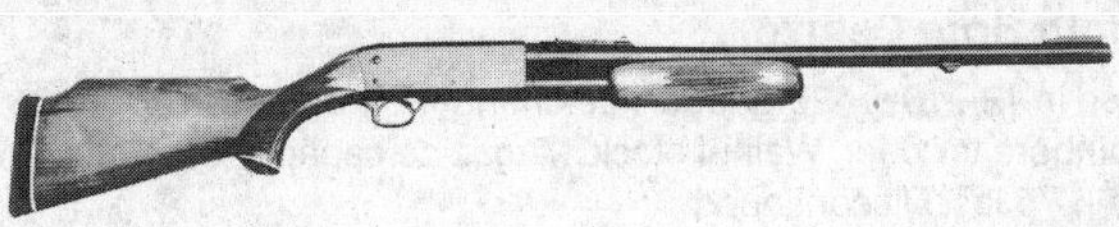

Courtesy C. Hadley Smith

NIB	Exc.	V.G.	Good	Fair	Poor
550	450	350	200	120	80

Model 87 Home Protection and Law Enforcement

Ithaca Acquisition Corporation continued production of many law enforcement firearms produced by Ithaca Gun Company. Only those models available to general public are listed.

Military & Police—1987-1996

Generally produced with non-checkered walnut buttstock and ring turned slide handle, both of which were oil-finished. Note: Add 20 percent for 8-shot model in NIB or excellent condition; additional 15 percent for chrome plated models in similar condition.

NIB	Exc.	V.G.	Good	Fair	Poor
450	400	280	200	120	80

DS Police Special—1987-1996

Produced with pressed checkered or non-checkered walnut buttstock and ring-turned slide handle, both lacquer finished. Metal usually finished with a commercial polished blue, but chrome-plated finish also available. Note: Add 20 percent for 8-shot model in NIB or excellent condition; additional 15 percent for chrome plated models in similar condition.

NIB	Exc.	V.G.	Good	Fair	Poor
450	400	280	200	120	80

NEW MODEL 37 REPEATER

During 1996, assets of bankrupt Ithaca Acquisition Corporation were purchased by a new company named Ithaca Gun Company, LLC. One of the first public actions of the new firm was to re-name Model 87, Model 37. Before resuming production later that year, serial number of new Model 37 is prefaced with letter "M".

Model 37 Featherlight

The current version of the classic pump-gun design patented by John Browning in 1915 and which evolved from the Remington Model 17 and 31 into the Ithaca 37 in 1937. In 12 or 20 gauge with 24", 26", 28", or 30" vent-rib barrel and three choke tubes. TruGlo front sight available on vent-rib models; brass bead on field barrels. Original features include bottom ejection and 4+1 magazine capacity. Stock and forend are grade A walnut; AA and AAA grades are optional. Add $150 for AA wood, $350 for AAA. Seven Combo packages available with vent-rib smoothbore and a choice of 24" Rifled or 24" Cantilevered Rifled barrel. Featherlight with Women's Stock features a unique drop of comb, drop of heel, cast pitch, and toe out. Featherlight with Youth Stock features an adjustable length of pull.

NIB	Exc.	V.G.	Good	Fair	Poor
800	700	500	400	300	200

Model 37 Deerslayer II

Offered in 12- and 20-gauge. Fitted with 20" or 25" barrel, with rifled bores. Barrel fixed to receiver. Magazine capacity 5 rounds. Walnut stock. Weight about 7 lbs. In 2001 a 16-gauge version, with fixed rifled barrel was offered.

NIB	Exc.	V.G.	Good	Fair	Poor
1000	800	650	480	300	200

Smooth Bore Deluxe

Offered in 12-, 16- or 20-gauge. Interchangeable barrels in 20" or 25" and smoothbore for deer. Walnut stock. Magazine capacity 5 rounds. Weight about 6.75 lbs. Discontinued.

NIB	Exc.	V.G.	Good	Fair	Poor
680	400	350	280	200	100

Rifled Deluxe

Same as above in 12- and 20-gauge only, with rifled barrels. Discontinued.

NIB	Exc.	V.G.	Good	Fair	Poor
680	400	350	280	200	100

Model 37 Deerslayer III

Updated slug-only version of classic Model 37 pump-action shotgun, in 12- or 20-gauge. Fully rifled heavy fluted 26" barrel, with 1:28 twist. Bottom ejection. Fancy black walnut stock and forend. Blued barrel and receiver.

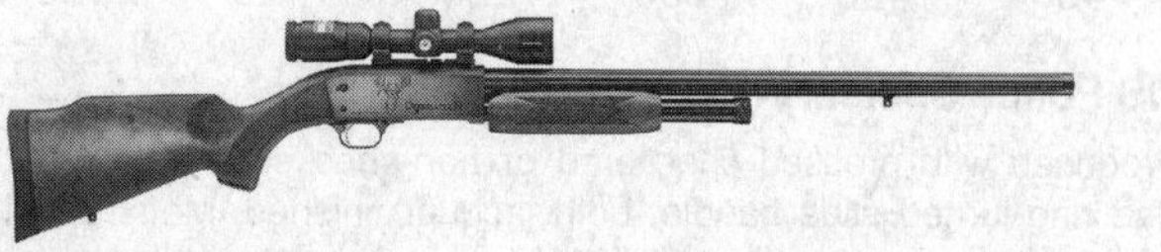

NIB	Exc.	V.G.	Good	Fair	Poor
1300	1100	900	700	500	300

Model 37 28 Gauge

28-gauge pump-action shotgun. Scaled-down receiver, with traditional Model 37 bottom ejection and easy take-down. 24", 26" or 28" barrel, black walnut stock and forend. Available in Fancy "A", Fancy "AA" and Fancy "AAA" grades, with increasingly elaborate receiver engraving and decoration. Blued or chrome receiver finish. Special order only. Values shown are for "Fancy A" grade.

NIB	Exc.	V.G.	Good	Fair	Poor
1100	950	720	600	500	300

Model 37 Deluxe Field

Offered in 12-, 16- and 20-gauge. Interchangeable ventilated rib barrels 26", 28" or 30" (12-gauge only). Walnut stock. Magazine capacity 5 rounds. Weight about 7 lbs. Discontinued.

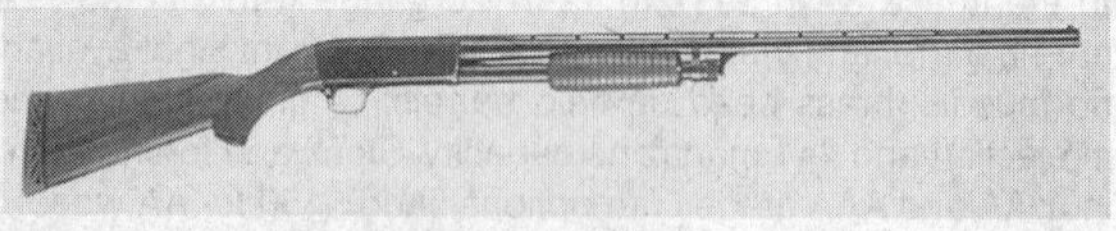

NIB	Exc.	V.G.	Good	Fair	Poor
620	480	380	250	150	100

Model 37 Deluxe Field English Style

Offered in 20-gauge only, with 24", 26" or 28" ventilated rib barrels. Walnut stock. Weight about 7 lbs. Magazine capacity 5 rounds. Discontinued.

NIB	Exc.	V.G.	Good	Fair	Poor
650	480	380	250	150	100

Model 37 Ultra Featherlight Grouse Special

Based on Classic Model 37, with bottom ejection. Features aluminum receiver and 24" ventilated rib barrel, with choke tubes. Straight-grip stock of American black walnut. Discontinued.

NIB	Exc.	V.G.	Good	Fair	Poor
650	520	400	280	150	100

Model 37 Ultra Featherlight Youth

Similar to above, with 22" barrel and 12.75" length of pull. Buttstock with ventilated recoil pad. Discontinued.

NIB	Exc.	V.G.	Good	Fair	Poor
600	480	380	250	150	100

Model 37 Sporting Clays

Features choice of 24", 26" or 28" wide ventilated rib barrels, with Briley choke tubes. Receiver has antiqued finish, with scroll engraving and high grade American black walnut. Discontinued.

NIB	Exc.	V.G.	Good	Fair	Poor
1350	1000	750	580	300	150

Model 37 Trap

Similar features as Sporting Clays, with 30" wide ventilated rib barrel.

NIB	Exc.	V.G.	Good	Fair	Poor
900	750	650	480	300	200

Model 37 Women's Endowment Shotgun

Offered in 16- or 20-gauge, with straight-grip stock. Length of pull designed for woman's height of 5'5". American walnut stock, with cut checkering. Discontinued.

NIB	Exc.	V.G.	Good	Fair	Poor
640	500	380	250	150	100

Model 37 Waterfowler

Available in 12-gauge only, with 28" steel shot barrel. Camo pattern stock. Weight about 7 lbs. Magazine capacity 5 rounds.

NIB	Exc.	V.G.	Good	Fair	Poor
850	700	600	500	280	200

Model 37 Waterfowl

Similar to Model 37 Waterfowler above, but with variances. Waterfowl offers both 12 and 20 gauge and barrels of 28" and 30". Black synthetic stock standard, Perma-Guard finish.

NIB	Exc.	V.G.	Good	Fair	Poor
850	750	620	500	400	300

Model 37 New Classic

Available in 12-, 16- or 20- gauge, with hand-checkered walnut stock. Choice of pistol-/straight-grip. High polish bolt and other component parts. Sunburst recoil pad. Interchangeable ventilated rib barrels are 26" or 28". Weight about 7 lbs. Discontinued.

NIB	Exc.	V.G.	Good	Fair	Poor
810	620	480	380	250	150

Model 37 Turkeyslayer

First version of this model made from 1996 to 2004, with 22" barrel and camo stock. Offered in 12- or 20-gauge. Later model introduced in 2010, in 12-gauge only, with 24" fixed barrel, synthetic stock with matte black or camo finish. Available with laminated thumbhole stock. Other features include Briley extended and ported Extra-Full Turkey choke, lengthened forcing cone, Pachmayr Decelerator recoil pad, Tru-Glo fiber optic front sight. Weight: 7.6 lbs. with standard stock, 8.2 lbs with thumbhole.

NIB	*Exc.*	*V.G.*	*Good*	*Fair*	*Poor*
800	650	550	400	280	200

Model 37 Home Defense

In 12- or 20-gauge, with 18.5" or 20" barrel, rifle sights and matte blue finish. Black synthetic or wood stock, 20" fixed barrel rifle sights. Magazine holds 8 rounds (12-gauge only); 5 rounds (12- or 20-gauge).

NIB	*Exc.*	*V.G.*	*Good*	*Fair*	*Poor*
700	600	500	400	280	200

Model 37 Hogslayer

In 12-gauge, with 20" rifled barrel and sights. Tubular magazine holds 8 rounds. Matte blued barrel, action and finish. Synthetic stock. Discontinued.

NIB	*Exc.*	*V.G.*	*Good*	*Fair*	*Poor*
450	400	360	300	250	200

Ithaca Stakeout II, Pistol Grip Firearm

Introduced 2018. Updated M37-action trench gun in 12 or 20 gauge. 26.75" in total length. 14⊠ chrome-moly barrel, black American walnut grip with ringtail forend. Discontinued. Also available as Inland Manufacturing Stakeout II.

NIB	*Exc.*	*V.G.*	*Good*	*Fair*	*Poor*
800	650	480	300	200	—

MODEL 51

A 12- or 20-gauge semi-automatic shotgun, with 26", 28" or 30" ventilated rib barrels. Blued, with walnut stock. Manufactured from 1970 to 1985 as listed.

Model 51A Standard

Plain barrel. Note: Add $100 for ventilated rib.

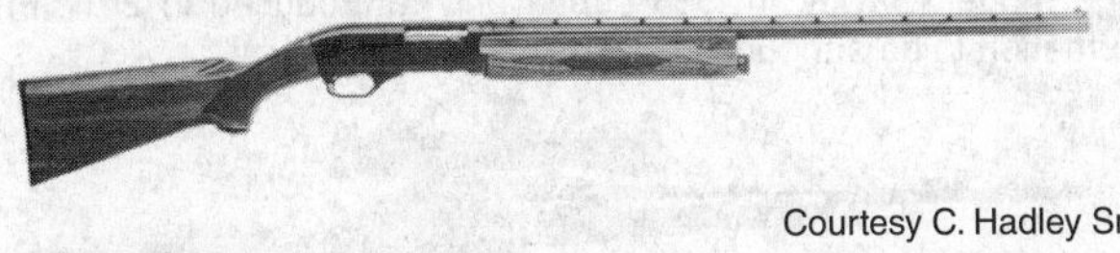

Courtesy C. Hadley Smith

NIB	*Exc.*	*V.G.*	*Good*	*Fair*	*Poor*
—	400	320	250	150	80

Model 51A Magnum

3" chamber. Note: Add $100 for ventilated rib.

NIB	*Exc.*	*V.G.*	*Good*	*Fair*	*Poor*
—	420	350	280	180	80

Model 51A Waterfowler

Matte finished.

NIB	*Exc.*	*V.G.*	*Good*	*Fair*	*Poor*
—	420	350	280	180	80

Model 51A Deerslayer

Courtesy C. Hadley Smith

NIB	*Exc.*	*V.G.*	*Good*	*Fair*	*Poor*
—	320	280	220	150	80

Model 51A Turkey Gun

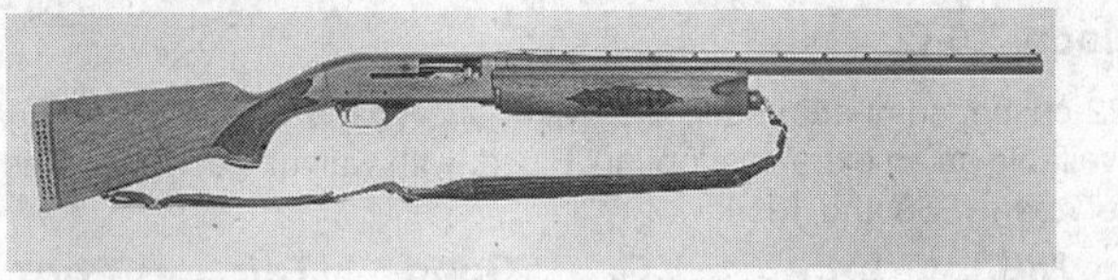

Courtesy C. Hadley Smith

NIB	*Exc.*	*V.G.*	*Good*	*Fair*	*Poor*
—	420	350	280	180	80

Model 51 Supreme Trap

NIB	*Exc.*	*V.G.*	*Good*	*Fair*	*Poor*
—	420	380	320	250	80

Model 51 Supreme Skeet

NIB	*Exc.*	*V.G.*	*Good*	*Fair*	*Poor*
—	450	400	350	280	200

Model 51 Ducks Unlimited Commemorative

NIB	*Exc.*	*V.G.*	*Good*	*Fair*	*Poor*
600	500	380	320	280	200

Model 51 Presentation

Engraved receiver.

NIB	*Exc.*	*V.G.*	*Good*	*Fair*	*Poor*
1500	1250	1000	750	500	300

MAG-10

A 10-gauge Magnum semi-automatic shotgun, manufactured in a variety of barrel lengths, styles and finishes. Manufactured from 1975 to 1986 as listed. Note: Market for Ithaca Mag-10s has declined somewhat, with success of 3.5" 12-gauge load. Apparently because most owners consider their Mag-10s as hunting weapons, not collectors' pieces. Nevertheless, NIB or Excellent+ examples still command fairly high prices, if right buyer can be found.

Standard Grade

NIB	*Exc.*	*V.G.*	*Good*	*Fair*	*Poor*
—	750	650	600	300	250

Standard Vent Rib Grade

NIB	*Exc.*	*V.G.*	*Good*	*Fair*	*Poor*
—	850	700	680	550	250

Deluxe Vent Rib Grade

NIB	*Exc.*	*V.G.*	*Good*	*Fair*	*Poor*
—	1000	780	750	600	250

Supreme Grade

NIB	*Exc.*	*V.G.*	*Good*	*Fair*	*Poor*
—	1100	850	800	700	250

Roadblocker—Military and Police Model

NIB	*Exc.*	*V.G.*	*Good*	*Fair*	*Poor*
—	750	650	600	300	250

Presentation Grade

Engraved, gold-inlaid, 200 made.

NIB	Exc.	V.G.	Good	Fair	Poor
1880	1500	1100	900	750	300

National Wild Turkey Federation

1985 manufacture.

NIB	Exc.	V.G.	Good	Fair	Poor
850	700	600	550	450	350

RIFLES

Model X5-C

.22-caliber semi-automatic rifle, with 7-shot magazine. 10-shot magazine available as an extra cost option. Blued, with walnut stock. Manufactured between 1958 and 1964.

NIB	Exc.	V.G.	Good	Fair	Poor
400	200	150	100	80	50

Model X5T Lightning

.22-caliber tubular feed auto-loading rifle, produced between 1959 and 1963. Some models stocked with curly maple stocks. Note: These guns will command a 25 percent price premium.

NIB	Exc.	V.G.	Good	Fair	Poor
450	180	150	100	80	50

Model X-15 Lightning

Similar to above. Manufactured between 1964 and 1966.

NIB	Exc.	V.G.	Good	Fair	Poor
450	180	150	100	80	50

Model 49 Saddlegun—1961-1979

.22-caliber lever-action single-shot rifle, with 18.5" barrel, fixed sights, alloy receiver and hardwood stock. Offered chambered for .22 Magnum in 1962. Note: Deduct 20 percent for .22 LR.

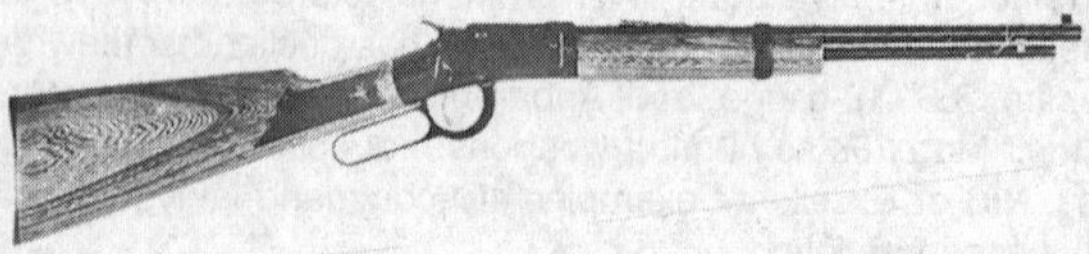

Courtesy C. Hadley Smith

NIB	Exc.	V.G.	Good	Fair	Poor
350	220	180	100	50	20

Deluxe Grade

Fitted with gold plated trigger and hammer. Equipped with sling and sling swivels.

NIB	Exc.	V.G.	Good	Fair	Poor
400	250	200	120	50	20

Presentation Grade

High grade wood and engraved frame.

NIB	Exc.	V.G.	Good	Fair	Poor
420	300	250	200	50	20

Model 49R—1968-1971

Lever-action .22-caliber tubular feed repeater. Magazine capacity 15 LR cartridges.

NIB	Exc.	V.G.	Good	Fair	Poor
350	250	200	150	50	20

Model 72 Saddlegun—1973-1979

.22- or .22 Magnum caliber lever-action rifle, with 18.5" barrel. Tubular magazine, open sights and walnut stock. Made by Erma in Germany.

NIB	Exc.	V.G.	Good	Fair	Poor
300	250	220	200	100	20

LSA-55 or 65

Bolt-action sporting rifle, manufactured in a variety of calibers and barrel lengths, by Tikka of Finland. Imported between 1969 and 1977 in models listed.

LSA-55 Standard

NIB	Exc.	V.G.	Good	Fair	Poor
—	500	350	300	250	180

LSA-55 Deluxe

NIB	Exc.	V.G.	Good	Fair	Poor
—	600	380	320	280	200

LSA-55 Varmint Heavy Barrel

NIB	Exc.	V.G.	Good	Fair	Poor
—	600	400	350	300	220

LSA-55 Turkey Gun

12-gauge by .222 Remington caliber over/under combination rifle/shotgun, with 24.5" barrels, single trigger, exposed hammer and walnut stock. Manufactured in Finland by Tikka between 1970 and 1981.

NIB	Exc.	V.G.	Good	Fair	Poor
—	900	700	450	350	280

LSA-65 Long Action

NIB	Exc.	V.G.	Good	Fair	Poor
—	500	350	300	250	180

LSA-65 Deluxe

NIB	Exc.	V.G.	Good	Fair	Poor
—	600	380	320	280	200

Ithaca Protector

A new bolt-action rifle series designed for precision long-range shooting. Chambered in most popular calibers. Developed in conjunction with a world record holding marksman. Features include a competition-grade barrel and trigger. Advertised to produce 1/2 MOA accuracy or better. Other models include a short-action platform (Guardian) and a long-range model (Savior, in .338 Lapua only). Introduced in 2017. Pricing information to be announced.

NIB	Exc.	V.G.	Good	Fair	Poor
—	—	—	—	—	—

HANDGUNS

Model 1911

First 1911 made by Ithaca since WWII. Chambered in .45 ACP, with hand-lapped carbon steel frame and slide. Checkered front strap, skeletonized hammer and trigger, checkered cocobolo grips and choice of adjustable Novak Combat or Bomar Target sights. Other features include stainless steel Match grade barrel bushing and full-length two-piece guide rod. Optional lockable canvas case. Introduced in 2011. Also available in Carry size, with 4.25" barrel. Note: Add $100 for case.

NIB	Exc.	V.G.	Good	Fair	Poor
1600	1380	1000	750	580	430

X-Caliber

.22- to .44 Magnum caliber single-shot pistol, with 10" or 15" barrels. Featuring dual firing pin system so that interchangeable barrels could be used. Model 20 is blued; Model 30 Teflon coated. Introduced in 1988. Made by Sterling Arms. Note: Add 20 percent premium for .44.

NIB	Exc.	V.G.	Good	Fair	Poor
600	480	300	220	180	120

IVER JOHNSON ARMS & CYCLE WORKS

Middlesex, New Jersey

See—AMAC

Established in 1883 in Fitchburg, Massachusetts. Company has produced a wide variety of firearms during its existence. In 1894, the firm became "Iver Johnson's Arms & Cycle Works." It is perhaps best known as a major manufacturer of inexpensive but serviceable pocket-size revolvers in .22 rimfire, .32 S&W, and .38 S&W calibers, serving the same sizable market niche as Hopkins & Allen and Harrington & Richardson in the late-19th through mid-20th centuries. During that time, beginning in 1890, the Iver Johnson owl's head logo appeared on the grips of most of its revolvers. Its best-known marketing slogan, "Hammer the hammer," referred to a hammer-block safety and frame-mounted firing pin that prevented a revolver from firing accidentally if dropped on the hammer spur, introduced in 1904 on the popular Safety Automatic double-action revolver line. Iver Johnson continued arms production until it was liquidated in 1993. Many 19th century handguns made by Iver Johnson and its predecessor Johnson and Bye are difficult to identify due to the lack of a maker's name on the gun.

HANDGUNS

Antique

Percussion Single-Shot Derringer Antique

Spur-trigger .28, .30, or .32 caliber, 3" barrel, center hammer. Only made in the early 1870s by Johnson & Bye. Trade names include Uncle Sam and Prince with no maker's name.

Exc.	Fine	V.G.	Good	Fair	Poor
350	250	210	180	80	50

Cartridge Derringer Antique

Spur-trigger .22, .32, & .38 rimfire, made 1871 to 1899, first by Johnson & Bye, then Iver Johnson. Side swing barrel for loading. Most are unmarked except for serial (batch) number.

Exc.	Fine	V.G.	Good	Fair	Poor
300	150	120	100	50	30

Spur-Trigger Revolvers Antique

Series of spur trigger single-action revolvers made by Johnson & Bye, in .22, .32, .38, & .41 rimfire. Most bear only trade names such as Defender, Defender 89, Eagle, Encore, Eureka, Favorite, Favorite Navy, Eclipse, Lion, Old Hickory, Smoker, and Tycoon.

Exc.	Fine	V.G.	Good	Fair	Poor
250	150	120	100	50	30

Early Bulldog Type Revolvers

Three different solid-frame double-action models made 1878-1899: American Eagle, small frame .22 rimfire, med. frame .32 rimfire, large frame .38 rimfire; American Bulldog, small frame .22 rimfire, med. frame .32 RF or CF, large frame .38 RF or CF, extra large frame .44 CF (worth premium), with 2" to 6" barrels. Not always marked American Bulldog, trade names included Old Hickory, Lion, British Bulldog, and others. First Models (1882-1886) and Second Models (1887-1899) are recognized by collectors. Boston Bulldog, lightweight version of the American Bulldog in .22 RF, .32 CF, or .38 CF.

NIB	Exc.	V.G.	Good	Fair	Poor
250	150	120	100	50	30

Lovell Safety Double Action Antique

Solid frame double-action revolver in .22, .32, or .38 caliber; swing-out cylinder (unique to this model of Iver Johnson.) Made 1883-1887, this is the only one of the 19th-century solid-frame DA revolvers regularly found marked with the Iver Johnson name.

Exc.	Fine	V.G.	Good	Fair	Poor
190	150	120	100	50	30

U.S. Revolver Co.

United States Revolver Co. was a subsidiary of Iver Johnson. It produced small revolvers similar to the Iver Johnson models in solid frame double-action, hammerless, and top-break double-action configurations. The top-break double-action models lacked the "hammer the hammer" safety feature of the Iver Johnson line. Values are slightly less than those for comparable IJ models.

Safety Automatic Double-Action

.22, .32 CF or .38 CF caliber double-action revolver. Produced in a variety of barrel lengths with-/without exposed hammers. Manufactured between 1893 and 1950.

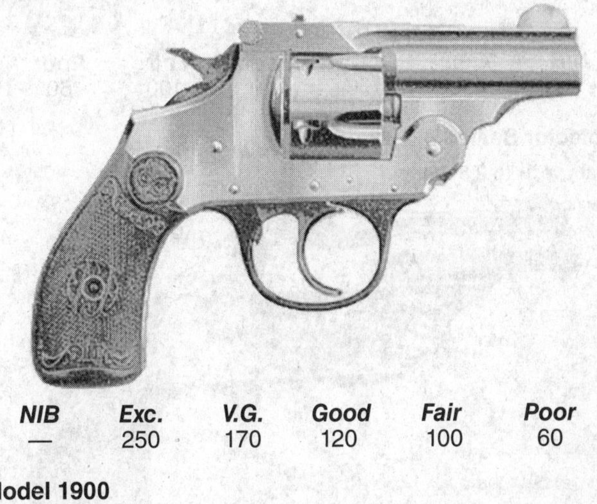

NIB	Exc.	V.G.	Good	Fair	Poor
—	250	170	120	100	60

Model 1900

.22- to .38-caliber double-action revolver, with 2.5", 4.5" or 6" barrel. Blued or nickel-plated. Rubber grips and no cartridge ejecting system. Manufactured between 1900 and 1947.

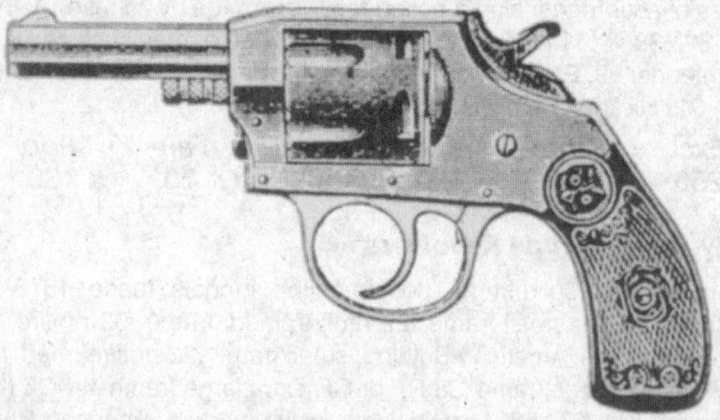

NIB	Exc.	V.G.	Good	Fair	Poor
—	250	170	120	100	60

Safety Cycle Automatic

Similar to Safety Automatic, with 2" barrel.

NIB	Exc.	V.G.	Good	Fair	Poor
—	250	170	120	100	60

Petite

.22 Short caliber hammerless double-action folding trigger revolver, with 1" barrel and 7-shot cylinder. Nickel-plated, with rubber grips. Introduced in 1909.

NIB	Exc.	V.G.	Good	Fair	Poor
—	600	400	300	180	100

Supershot Sealed 8

.22-caliber double-action revolver, with 6" barrel. Counterbored 8-shot cylinder. Blued, with rubber grips. Manufactured from 1919 to 1957.

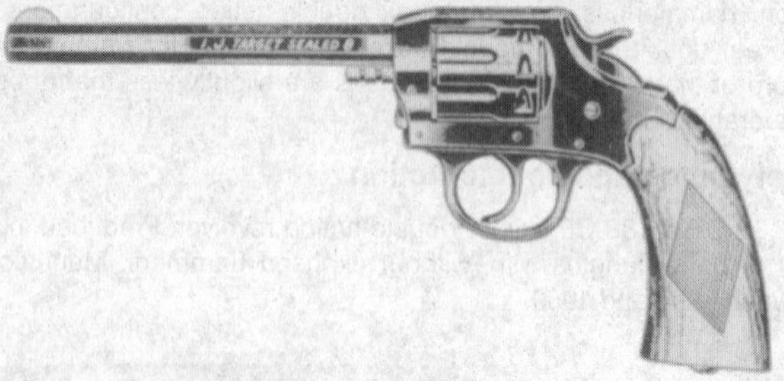

NIB	Exc.	V.G.	Good	Fair	Poor
—	250	170	120	100	60

Protector Sealed 8

As above, with 2.5" barrel.

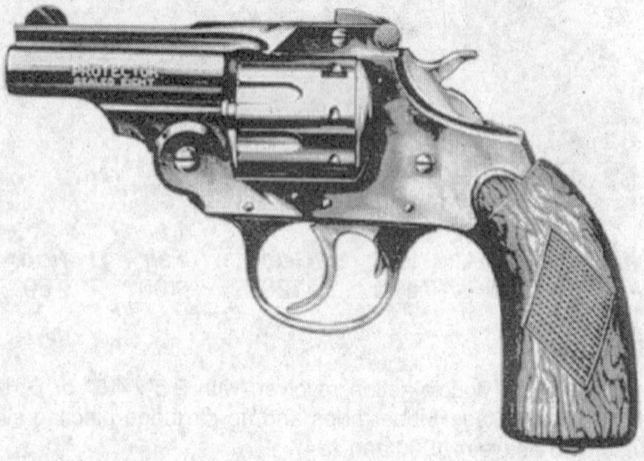

NIB	Exc.	V.G.	Good	Fair	Poor
—	250	170	120	100	60

Supershot 9

Similar to Supershot Sealed 8, with 9-shot un-counterbored cylinder. Manufactured between 1929 and 1949.

NIB	Exc.	V.G.	Good	Fair	Poor
—	250	170	120	100	60

Trigger Cocker Single-Action

.22-caliber single-action revolver, with 6" barrel and 8-shot counterbored cylinder. Blued, with walnut grips. Manufactured between 1940 and 1947.

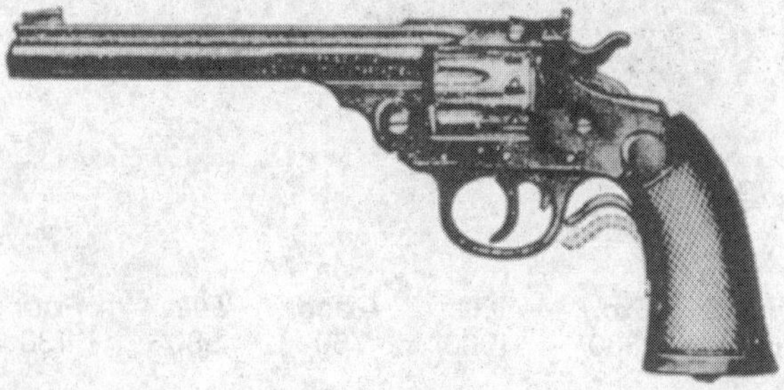

NIB	Exc.	V.G.	Good	Fair	Poor
—	200	120	100	50	20

.22 Target Single-Action

As above, with adjustable sights and grips. Manufactured between 1938 and 1948.

NIB	Exc.	V.G.	Good	Fair	Poor
—	250	190	150	120	60

Model 844

.22-caliber double-action revolver, with 4.5" or 6" barrel. Adjustable sights and 8-shot cylinder. Manufactured in 1950s.

NIB	Exc.	V.G.	Good	Fair	Poor
—	220	140	100	80	40

Model 855

As above, with single-action and 6" barrel. Manufactured in 1950s.

NIB	Exc.	V.G.	Good	Fair	Poor
—	220	140	100	80	40

Model 55A Sportsmen Target

.22-caliber single-action revolver, with 4.75" or 6" barrel. Fixed sights and 8-shot cylinder. Blued, with walnut grips.

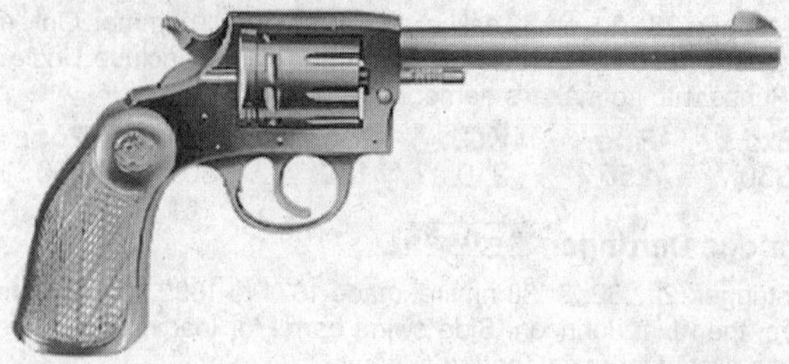

NIB	Exc.	V.G.	Good	Fair	Poor
—	200	120	100	80	40

Model 55S-A Cadet

.22- to .38-caliber single-action revolver, with 2.5" barrel and fixed sights. Blued, with plastic grips. Introduced in 1955.

NIB	Exc.	V.G.	Good	Fair	Poor
—	250	170	120	100	60

Model 57A Target

As above, with 4.5" or 6" barrel and adjustable sights. Manufactured between 1955 and 1975.

NIB	Exc.	V.G.	Good	Fair	Poor
—	180	110	80	60	40

Model 66 Trailsman

.22-caliber double-action revolver, with 6" barrel. Adjustable sights and 8-shot cylinder. Blued, with walnut grips. Manufactured between 1958 and 1975.

NIB	Exc.	V.G.	Good	Fair	Poor
—	120	80	60	50	20

Model 67 Viking

As above, with safety hammer.

NIB	Exc.	V.G.	Good	Fair	Poor
—	120	80	60	50	20

Model 67S Viking Snub

Same as above. Fitted with 2" barrel.

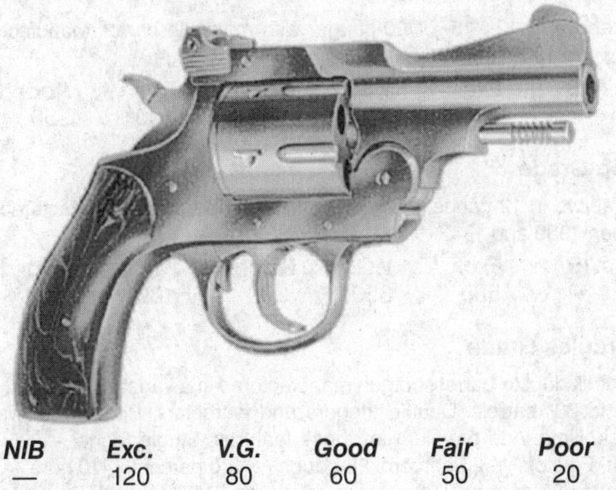

NIB	Exc.	V.G.	Good	Fair	Poor
—	120	80	60	50	20

Model 50

.22- or .22 Magnum single-action revolver, with 4.75" or 6" barrel and 8-shot cylinder. Fixed or adjustable sights. Also known as Sidewinder. Manufactured between 1961 and 1975.

NIB	Exc.	V.G.	Good	Fair	Poor
—	120	80	60	50	20

American Bulldog

.22- to .38-caliber double-action revolver, with 2.5" or 4" barrel. Adjustable sights. Blued or nickel-plated, with plastic grips. Manufactured between 1974 and 1976.

NIB	Exc.	V.G.	Good	Fair	Poor
—	180	100	80	50	20

Rookie

.38-caliber revolver, with 4" barrel and 5-shot cylinder. Blued or nickel-plated, with plastic grips.

NIB	Exc.	V.G.	Good	Fair	Poor
—	180	100	80	50	20

Cattleman Series

Manufactured by Aldo Uberti. Listed under that name in this book.

Model X300 Pony

.380 semi-automatic pistol, with 3" barrel and 6-shot magazine. Blued, with plastic grips. Introduced in 1975.

NIB	Exc.	V.G.	Good	Fair	Poor
—	280	200	160	140	80

Trailsman

.22-caliber semi-automatic pistol, with 4.5" or 6" barrel and 10-shot magazine. Blued, with plastic or walnut grips.

NIB	Exc.	V.G.	Good	Fair	Poor
—	280	200	160	140	80

TP22/TP25 Pistol

.22 or .25 ACP caliber double-action semi-automatic pistol, with 2.8" barrel and 7-shot magazine. Blued or nickel-plated, with plastic grips.

NIB	Exc.	V.G.	Good	Fair	Poor
—	280	200	160	140	80

Enforcer Pistol

M1 Carbine action, .30 cal., in a pistol configuration, 9.5-in. barrel.

NIB	Exc.	V.G.	Good	Fair	Poor
860	750	650	480	390	300

RIFLES

Model X

Bolt action .22-caliber single-shot rifle. Fitted with 22" barrel, open sights and pistol grip. Manufactured between 1927 and 1932.

NIB	Exc.	V.G.	Good	Fair	Poor
—	180	110	90	70	40

Model XA

As above, with Lyman receiver sight swivels, leather strap and ivory bead. Manufactured between 1927 and 1932.

NIB	Exc.	V.G.	Good	Fair	Poor
—	320	220	180	130	80

Model 2X

Fitted with 24" heavy barrel and adjustable sights. Manufactured between 1932 and 1955.

NIB	Exc.	V.G.	Good	Fair	Poor
—	400	300	250	150	100

Li'L Champ

Chambered for .22 LR cartridge. Bolt-action single-shot rifle. Weight about 3 lbs.

NIB	Exc.	V.G.	Good	Fair	Poor
—	120	80	70	50	30

Long Range Rifle

Single-shot bolt-action rifle, chambered for .50-caliber Browning cartridge. Fitted with 29" fluted barrel and adjustable trigger. Bipod. Comes supplied with 20 power Leupold scope. Limited production. Weight about 36 lbs. Manufactured between 1988 and 1993.

NIB	Exc.	V.G.	Good	Fair	Poor
—	4600	4000	3000	2500	1000

JJ 9mm Carbine

Copy of U.S. military M1. Blued finish and hardwood stock. Magazine is 20 rounds. Chambered for 9mm cartridge. Built between 1985 and 1986. Note: Add 10 percent for folding stock. Deduct 5 percent for plastic stock.

NIB	Exc.	V.G.	Good	Fair	Poor
—	500	400	250	180	100

Delta-786 Carbine

Similar to M1 carbine in 9mm only. Matte finish. Manufactured in 1989.

NIB	Exc.	V.G.	Good	Fair	Poor
—	500	400	250	180	100

Carbine .30 Caliber

Similar to M1 carbine and chambered for .30 carbine cartridge. Offered in various stock configurations. Built from 1985 to 1986; again in 1988 to 1993. Note: Add $50 for Paratrooper model. Deduct $75 for Johnson 5.7mm caliber. No premium for stainless steel.

NIB	Exc.	V.G.	Good	Fair	Poor
—	600	480	320	250	150

U.S. Carbine .22 Caliber

Same as above. Chambered for .22 LR or .22 Magnum cartridge. Built in 1985 and 1986; again in 1988. Fitted with 15-round magazine.

NIB	Exc.	V.G.	Good	Fair	Poor
—	350	300	220	150	80

Slide Action Targetmaster

Chambered for .22 LR or .22 Magnum cartridge. Has 15-round tubular magazine. Manufactured between 1985 and 1988; again in 1990.

NIB	Exc.	V.G.	Good	Fair	Poor
—	250	170	120	100	50

Wagonmaster Model EW .22 HBL Lever Action

Chambered for .22 LR or .22 Magnum cartridge. Fitted with hardwood stock. Blued finish. Grooved scope mounts. Built in 1985 and 1986; again between 1988 and 1990.

NIB	Exc.	V.G.	Good	Fair	Poor
—	250	180	130	100	50

Model IJ .22 HB Semi-Automatic (Trail Blazer)

Chambered for .22 LR only, with 10-round magazine. Manufactured only in 1985.

NIB	Exc.	V.G.	Good	Fair	Poor
—	220	130	100	60	40

SHOTGUNS

Champion

Single-barrel shotgun manufactured in a variety of gauges, as well as .44- or .45-caliber, with 26" to 32" barrels. External hammers and automatic ejectors. Blued, with walnut stock. Manufactured between 1909 and 1956.

NIB	Exc.	V.G.	Good	Fair	Poor
—	250	200	150	80	20

Matted Rib Grade

As above in 12-, 16- or 20-gauge, with matte rib barrel. Manufactured between 1909 and 1948.

NIB	Exc.	V.G.	Good	Fair	Poor
—	280	220	180	100	50

Trap Grade

As above in 12-gauge, with 32" ventilated rib barrel. Manufactured between 1909 and 1942.

NIB	Exc.	V.G.	Good	Fair	Poor
—	520	350	280	180	100

Hercules Grade

Boxlock double-barrel shotgun manufactured in a variety of gauges, with 26" to 32" barrels. Double triggers and extractors. Blued, with walnut stock. Note: Add premium for these features: Single trigger — 25 percent, Ejectors — 25 percent, 28-gauge — 100 percent, .410 bore — 100 percent, 20-gauge — 50 percent, 16-gauge — 20 percent, Engraving —

100 percent, and Ventilated rib — 25 percent.

NIB	Exc.	V.G.	Good	Fair	Poor
—	1350	1050	780	550	350

Skeeter Model

As above, but more finely finished. Discontinued in 1946. Note: Add premium for these features: Single trigger — 25 percent, Ejectors — 25 percent, 28-gauge — 100 percent, .410 bore — 100 percent, 20-gauge — 50 percent, 16-gauge — 20 percent, Engraving — 100 percent, Ventilated rib — 25 percent.

NIB	Exc.	V.G.	Good	Fair	Poor
—	2250	1600	1050	750	300

Super Trap

12-gauge boxlock double-barrel shotgun, with 32" Full choked barrels and extractors. Discontinued in 1942. Note: Add 50 percent for Miller single-selective trigger; 35 percent for non-selective single trigger.

NIB	Exc.	V.G.	Good	Fair	Poor
—	2650	2000	1350	850	350

Silver Shadow

12-gauge boxlock over/under shotgun, with 26" or 28" ventilated rib barrels. Double triggers and extractors. Blued, with walnut stock. Manufactured in Italy and imported by Iver Johnson. Note: Available with single trigger, which would increase values listed by approximately 25 percent.

NIB	Exc.	V.G.	Good	Fair	Poor
—	550	400	350	300	200

IVER JOHNSON ARMS, INC.

Rockledge, Florida

This brand was resurrected in 2006, by Iver Johnson Arms, Inc., a new company based in Rockledge, Florida. This company manufactures several 1911-pattern pistols and imports a series of self-defense pump-action shotguns from Turkey. From 2006 to 2009, a four-barreled derringer, Frontier Four and two 1911-type pistols under Raven brand were manufactured.

Frontier Four Derringer

Four-barrel, stainless .22 LR single-action derringer, with unique rotating firing pin. Based on old Sharps derringer. Weight 5.5 oz. Introduced 2006. Discontinued.

NIB	Exc.	V.G.	Good	Fair	Poor
200	150	100	80	50	—

Eagle Target Series 1911 .45

All-steel 7+1 capacity 1911 .45 ACP, with 5" Government or 4.5" Commander barrel. Adjustable white outline rear sight and trigger. Polished blue. Introduced 2006. Note: Add $150 for LR model with accessory rail.

NIB	Exc.	V.G.	Good	Fair	Poor
650	550	420	320	250	150

Eagle Target Series 1911 .22 LR

Aluminum slide and frame, 15+1 capacity 1911 .22 LR, with 5" Government or 4.5" Commander barrel. Weight 19 oz. Adjustable white outline rear sight and trigger. Blued or stainless. Introduced 2006.

NIB	Exc.	V.G.	Good	Fair	Poor
600	500	400	300	200	100

Falcon

All-steel 8+1 capacity 1911 Series 70 .45 ACP, with 4.5" Commander barrel. Fixed sights. Matte blue. Introduced 2010.

NIB	Exc.	V.G.	Good	Fair	Poor
480	420	360	270	220	170

Hawk

All-steel 8+1 capacity Commander size 1911 9mm or 45 ACP, with 4.5" barrel. Fixed sights. Matte blue, polished blue, OD Green, Coyote Tan, Navy Camo, Snow Camo and other Cerakote finishes.

NIB	Exc.	V.G.	Good	Fair	Poor
570	500	430	320	260	200

Raven Series 1911 .45

All-steel 7+1 capacity 1911 .45 ACP, with 5" Government or 4.5" Commander barrel. Fixed sights. Matte blue, Parkerized or two-tone. Introduced 2006. Discontinued.

NIB	Exc.	V.G.	Good	Fair	Poor
550	420	320	250	150	100

Raven Series 1911 .22 LR

Aluminum slide and frame, 15+1 capacity 1911 in .22 LR, with 5" Government or 4.5" Commander barrel. Weight 19 oz. Fixed sights. Matte blued or stainless two-tone finish. Introduced 2006. Discontinued.

NIB	Exc.	V.G.	Good	Fair	Poor
550	420	320	250	150	100

Thrasher Series

All-steel 7+1 capacity Officer size 1911 9mm or 45 ACP, with 3.5" bull barrel Officer size frame. Fixed sights. Matte blue, polished blue, matte stainless, bright chrome.

NIB	Exc.	V.G.	Good	Fair	Poor
560	490	420	300	260	200

1911A1

Several variations of Series 70 type 1911A1 are offered in .45 ACP and 9mm chamberings, in full-size, Commander-size and Officers models. Available in a wide variety of finishes, including matte blue, polished blue, O.D. Green, Coyote Tan, Pink, Zombie and others. Values are for standard blue finish. Note: Add 10 to 15 percent for special finishes.

NIB	Exc.	V.G.	Good	Fair	Poor
500	450	400	300	250	200

PAS Shotgun

Series of pump-action shotguns designed primarily for self-defense use. All are 12-gauge, with light-weight alloy black receivers, black polymer stocks with straight-/pistol grip and choice of sighting systems and accessory rails. Note: Add 10 to 15 percent for pistol grip stock and fiber-optic sights.

NIB	Exc.	V.G.	Good	Fair	Poor
260	220	180	150	120	90

Stryker-12

Gauge: 12 ga., 3 in. Barrel: 20 in., smoothbore with muzzle brake. Length: 43 in. Stock: Black synthetic two-piece, pistol grip stock. Features: This AR-15-style semi-auto shotgun uses a standard AR-15 bolt and mag release. A2-style detachable carry handle with adjustable sight, fiber-optic front sight. Light rails on both sides and bottom of forend. Push button releases the stock and leaves the pistol grip for a modular platform. Cross-bolt safety, thick rubber buttpad. Ships with two MKA 1919 5-round box magazines.

NIB	Exc.	V.G.	Good	Fair	Poor
420	350	280	—	—	—

IXL

New York, New York

Pocket Revolver (Antique)

.31-caliber double-action percussion revolver, with 4" octagonal barrel and 6-shot cylinder. Blued, with walnut grips. Barrel marked "IXL N.York". Approximately 750 made without hammer spurs and 150 with side-mounted hammers during 1850s.

Exc.	*Fine*	*V.G.*	*Good*	*Fair*	*Poor*
2000	1250	920	600	300	210

Navy Revolver (Antique)

As above in .36-caliber. Approximately 100 made, with both center and side-mounted hammers during 1850s.

Exc.	*Fine*	*V.G.*	*Good*	*Fair*	*Poor*
10000	7000	5000	3000	1500	750

J

JACQUESMART, JULES
Liege, Belgium

Le Monobloc

6.35mm semi-automatic pistol, with 2" barrel and 6-shot magazine. Slide marked "Le Monobloc/Pistolet Automatique/Brevefte". Blued, with composition grips. Production ceased in 1914.

Courtesy James Rankin

NIB	Exc.	V.G.	Good	Fair	Poor
—	550	450	350	200	100

JACQUITH, ELIJAH
Brattleboro, Vermont

Revolving Underhammer Rifle (Antique)

Extremely rare .40-caliber percussion revolving rifle, with 34" round/octagonal barrel and 8-shot cylinder. Believed that approximately 25 of these rifles were made in 1838 and 1839. Barrel marked "E. Jaquith Brattleboro. Vt." Prospective purchasers should secure a qualified appraisal prior to acquisition. Values are speculative.

Exc.	Fine	V.G.	Good	Fair	Poor
—	18000	—	—	—	—

JAGER WAFFENFABIK
Suhl, Germany

Jager Semi-Automatic Pistol

7.65mm caliber semi-automatic pistol, with 3" barrel and 7-shot magazine. Largely made from steel stampings. Weight about 23 oz. Blued, with plastic grips. Slide marked "Jager-Pistole DRP Angem". Approximately 5,500 made prior to 1914. Note: Add 50 percent for Imperial proofed examples.

Courtesy Richard M. Kumor, Sr.

NIB	Exc.	V.G.	Good	Fair	Poor
—	500	380	320	180	100

JEFFERY, W. J. & CO. LTD.
London, England

Company produced high quality shotguns and rifles. Their products have been used by wealthy sportsmen for many years. They produced guns under their own banner and also as contractors for other distributors. They made guns sold by Army & Navy Department Store in London. Guns of this type were basically custom-ordered and as such are extremely hard to evaluate on a general basis. We supply estimated values for standard rifle models.

Single-Shot

Built on Farquharson Falling Block action. Chambered for many calibers up to .600 Nitro Express. Also a custom-order gun and barrel length was optional. Usually finish is blued with folding express sights. Select hand-checkered walnut stock. These were high quality firearms and values would be determined, for the most part, by options and embellishments on particular specimens. Individual appraisal is definitely advised. Caliber in which rifle is chambered will also have an effect on value. Obsolete calibers bring less and larger express calibers bring more.

NIB	Exc.	V.G.	Good	Fair	Poor
—	9000	6750	3750	2200	900

Boxlock Double Rifle

Boxlock chambered for many different calibers. Found with top or underlever-action and has folding express sights. Stock and forearm are select hand-checkered walnut and finish is usually blue. This was a custom-order proposition and values can be affected by many variables such as caliber options and embellishment. Damascus barreled hammer guns are worth approximately 50 percent less.

NIB	Exc.	V.G.	Good	Fair	Poor
—	22000	15250	10950	3850	2500

Sidelock Double Rifle

Has detachable sidelocks. Otherwise comparable to boxlock version.

NIB	Exc.	V.G.	Good	Fair	Poor
—	35000	22500	12250	7000	4000

JENISON, J. & CO.
Southbridge, Connecticut

Underhammer Pistol (Antique)

.28-caliber single-shot under hammer percussion pistol, with 4" half-octagonal barrel marked "J.Jenison & Co./Southbridge, Mass.". Blued, with maple or oak grip. Manufactured during 1850s.

Exc.	Fine	V.G.	Good	Fair	Poor
1550	850	620	400	200	140

JENKS CARBINE
Springfield, Massachusetts

Manufacturer—N. P. AMES

Jenks "Mule Ear" Carbine (Antique)

.54-caliber percussion side hammer carbine, with 24.5 round barrel and full-length stock secured by two barrel bands. Lock case-hardened, barrel browned and furniture of brass. Lock marked "N.P.Ames/Springfield/ Mass.". Barrel stamped "Wm.Jenks/USN" followed by inspector's initials. Buttstock carries an inspector's cartouche. Approximately 4,250 made between 1841 and 1846. Some marked "USR" for "U.S. Revenue Cutter Service". These would bring approximately 80 percent premium over values listed. However, prospective purchasers should secure a qualified appraisal prior to acquisition. Premium for first variation with no sling ring behind triggerguard and round (instead of oval) slot for round ball.

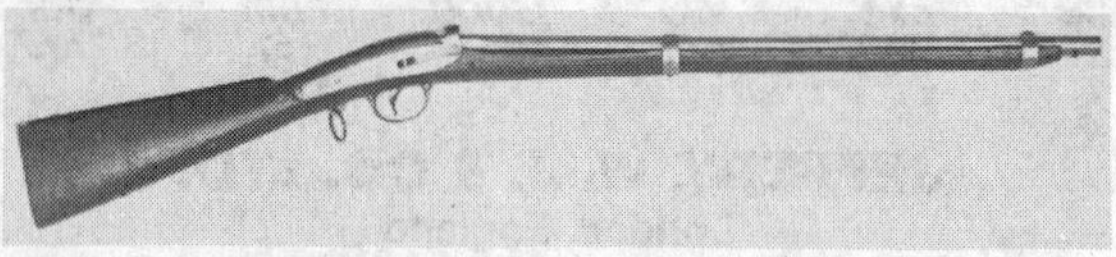

Courtesy Milwaukee Public Museum, Milwaukee, Wisconsin

Exc.	Fine	V.G.	Good	Fair	Poor
4500	3750	2620	1500	600	420

Jenks Navy Rifle (Antique)

As above, with 30" round barrel and full-length stock secured by three barrel bands. Approximately 1,000 made for U.S. Navy in 1841.

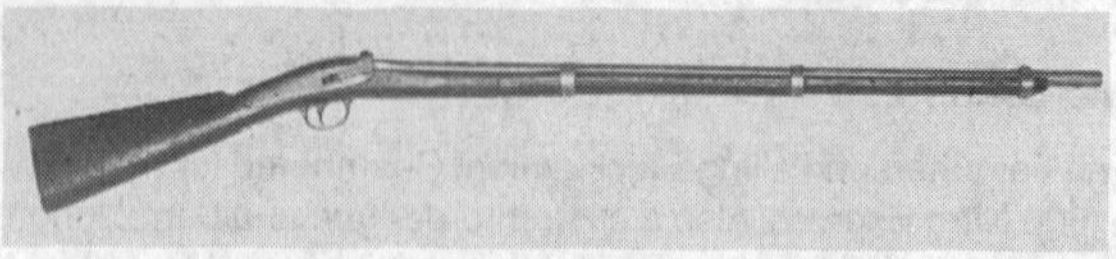

Courtesy Milwaukee Public Museum, Milwaukee, Wisconsin

Exc.	Fine	V.G.	Good	Fair	Poor
5000	4250	3000	1750	750	520

JENKS-HERKIMER
New York

Manufacturer—E. REMINGTON & SON

Mule Ear Carbine (Antique)

Identical to "Mule Ear Carbine" listed in (JENKS CARBINE), except barrel length is 24.25" and lock fitted with Maynard tape primer. Lock marked "Remington's/Herkimer/N.Y." Barrel marked "W. Jenks/USN/ RC/P/Cast Steel". Approximately 1,000 manufactured circa 1846.

Exc.	Fine	V.G.	Good	Fair	Poor
5000	4250	3000	1750	750	520

JENKS-MERRILL
Baltimore, Maryland

An alteration of Jenks Carbine to a breech loading system developed by J.H. Merrill. Conventional sidelock marked "J. H. Merrill Balto./Pat. July 1858". Breech retains mark "Wm.Jenks/ USN". Approximately 300 altered between 1858 and 1860.

Breech Loading Mule Ear Carbine (Antique)

Exc.	Fine	V.G.	Good	Fair	Poor
9750	8500	6000	3500	950	660

JENNINGS
Windsor, Vermont

Manufacturer—ROBBINS & LAWRENCE
See—WINCHESTER REPEATING ARMS

JENNINGS F. A., INC.
Carson City, Nevada

Distributor of arms manufactured by Calwestco in Chino, California and Bryco Firearms in Carson City, Nevada.

J-22

.22-caliber semi-automatic pistol, with 2.5" barrel and 6-shot magazine. Aluminum, finished in bright chrome, Teflon or satin nickel. Plastic or wood grips.

NIB	Exc.	V.G.	Good	Fair	Poor
150	90	80	60	50	40

Bryco Model 25

.25-caliber semi-automatic pistol, with 2.5" barrel and 6-shot magazine. Constructed and finished as above.

NIB	Exc.	V.G.	Good	Fair	Poor
150	90	80	60	50	40

Bryco Model 38

.22, .32 or .380 semi-automatic pistol, with 2.8" barrel and 6-shot magazine. Constructed and finished as above.

NIB	Exc.	V.G.	Good	Fair	Poor
150	90	80	60	50	40

Bryco Model 48

Similar to above, with re-designed triggerguard. Squared forward section. Introduced in 1988.

NIB	Exc.	V.G.	Good	Fair	Poor
150	90	80	60	50	40

JERICHO

See—ISRAEL WEAPON INDUSTRIES/ISRAEL MILITARY INDUSTRIES

JIEFFCO

Liege, Belgium

See—ROBAR ET CIE

JOHNSON, STAN, BYE & CO.

Worcester, Massachusetts

See—IVER JOHNSON ARMS & CYCLE WORKS

Established in 1871 by Martin Bye and Iver Johnson. Company primarily manufactured inexpensive pistols. In 1883 Johnson assumed full control of the company and re-named it Iver Johnson Arms Company.

JOSLYN

Milbury, Massachusetts

Manufacturer—A. H. WATERS

JOSLYN

Springfield, Massachusetts

Manufacturer—SPRINGFIELD ARMORY

Joslyn Breechloading Rifle (Antique)

First mass-produced true breech-loading cartridge firearm. Manufactured in a national armory. Actions were supplied by Joslyn Firearms Company. Chambered for .56-50 rimfire cartridge. Has 35.5" round barrel and full-length stock that is held on by three barrel bands. Lock marked "U.S./Springfield" with "1864" at back. Barrel marked "B. F. Joslyn's Patent/ Oct. 8th, 1861 / June 24th, 1862". Approximately 3,000 manufactured circa 1865. Probably issued to Union forces, but unknown if they saw action before end of Civil War.

Exc.	Fine	V.G.	Good	Fair	Poor
8500	5250	3500	2500	12500	500

Model 1855 "Monkey Tail" Carbine (Antique)

.54-caliber breech-loading single-shot percussion carbine, with 22.5" barrel secured to forend by one barrel band. Blued case-hardened, with brass mounts. Lock marked "A.H.Waters & Co./Milbury, Mass." and patent dates stamped on breech lever. Approximately 1,000 manufactured in 1855 and 1856.

Exc.	Fine	V.G.	Good	Fair	Poor
8000	5000	3500	2500	1250	500

.50-70 Alteration (Antique)

Approximately 1,600 Joslyn rifles re-chambered to fire .50-70 centerfire cartridge. Conversion consisted of re-chambering and drilling a new firing pin hole after rimfire pin was sealed. No specific serial number range in which these conversions were done. Most of these weapons were eventually converted to smoothbores and sold in Africa. Original military specimens are extremely scarce.

Exc.	Fine	V.G.	Good	Fair	Poor
6000	4200	3350	2500	750	520

Model 1855 Rifle (Antique)

Similar to above in .58-caliber, with 38" barrel secured by three barrel bands. Several hundred made in 1856.

Exc.	Fine	V.G.	Good	Fair	Poor
4500	3250	2170	1100	400	280

JOSLYN FIREARMS COMPANY

Stonington, Connecticut

Model 1862 Carbine (Antique)

.52 rimfire breech-loading single-shot carbine, with 22" round barrel secured by one barrel band. Blued case-hardened, with brass mounts. Lock marked "Joslyn Firearms Co./Stonington/Conn.", and patent date marked on barrel. Trigger plate 8" long and upper tang measures 4.5". Approximately 4,000 manufactured in 1862.

Courtesy Milwaukee Public Museum, Milwaukee, Wisconsin

Exc.	Fine	V.G.	Good	Fair	Poor
4750	3700	2600	1500	700	350

Model 1864 Carbine (Antique)

As above, with case-hardened iron mounts, 7" trigger plate and 2" upper tang. Approximately 12,000 made in 1864 and 1865.

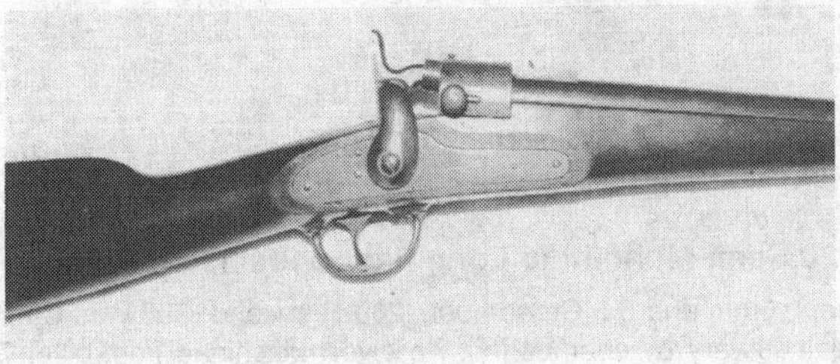

Courtesy Milwaukee Public Museum, Milwaukee, Wisconsin

Exc.	Fine	V.G.	Good	Fair	Poor
4500	3000	2000	1250	700	350

Army Model Revolver

.44-caliber side hammer percussion revolver, with 8" octagonal barrel and 5-shot cylinder. Blued case-hardened, with walnut grips. Barrel marked "B. F. Joslyn/Patd. May 4, 1858". Martially marked examples are worth a premium of approximately 25 percent over values listed.

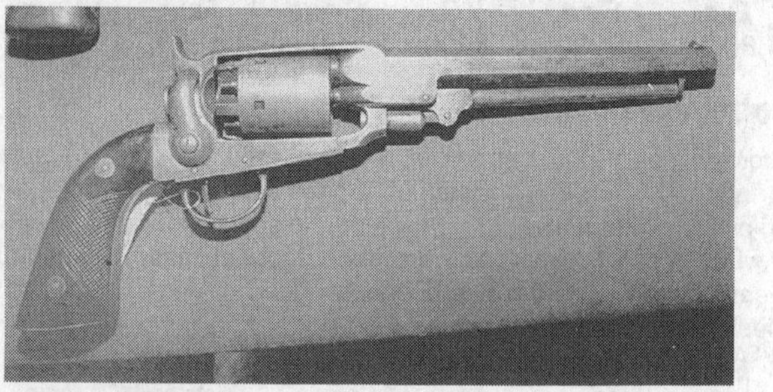

First Model (Antique)

With brass triggerguard and iron butt cap. Approximately 500 made in 1861.

Exc.	Fine	V.G.	Good	Fair	Poor
8750	5250	3250	2000	850	450

Second Model (Antique)

Fitted with iron triggerguard, without butt cap. Approximately 2,500 made in 1861 and 1862.

Exc.	Fine	V.G.	Good	Fair	Poor
8500	5000	3000	2000	850	450

J.P. ENTERPRISES
Hugo, Minnesota

Founded by John Paul, J.P. Enterprises produces high-end competition-grade AR-15s and AR-10s, and a variety of AR parts for the tactical firearms market.

SCR-11 Rifle

Calibers: .223, 6.5 Grendel, .224 Valkyrie, .22 LR. Capacity: Magazines vary by chambering. Receiver: Machined from billet 7075-T6 upper/lower receiver set with left-side charging system on the upper receiver. Matte black hardcoat anodizing on aluminum components. Barrel: JP Supermatch 416R air-gauged, button-rifled, cryogenically treated barrel Thermo-Fit to the receiver, polished stainless, JP Compensator. Stock: Hogue OverMolded, Magpul MOE, Magpul CTR, LUTH-AR "Skullaton," or Mission First Tactical BATTLELINK. Handguard: JP MK III system. Grip: Hogue pistol grip. Sights: Optics ready top rail. Trigger: JP Fire Control Package available in weights of 3.0 to 4.5 lbs. Overall Length: NA. Features: Scaled-down version of the LRP-07 available with the same caliber, barrel, handguard, metal finishing and stock options as the CTR-02. Exaggerated bevel on the magazine well. JP adjustable gas system; choice of JP Low Mass Operating System or JP Full Mass Operating System.

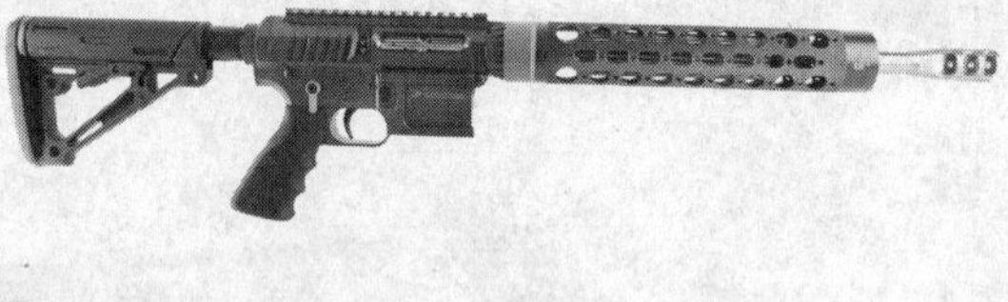

NIB	Exc.	V.G.	Good	Fair	Poor
3500	2100	—	—	—	—

LRI-20 Semi-Monolithic Long Range Precision Rifle

Calibers: 6mm and 6.5 Creedmoor, .260 Rem. and .308 Win. Capacity: Magazines vary by chambering. Receiver: Machined from billet 7075-T6 upper/lower receiver set with left-side charging system on the upper receiver. Matte-black hardcoat anodizing on aluminum components. Barrel: JP Supermatch 416R air-gauged, button-rifled, cryogenically treated barrel Thermo-Fit to the receiver, polished stainless, JP Compensator. Stock: Hogue OverMolded, Magpul MOE, Magpul CTR, LUTH-AR "Skullaton," or Mission First Tactical BATTLELINK. Handguard: JP MK III system (Signature or Rapid configuration). Grip: Hogue pistol grip. Sights: Optics ready top rail. Trigger: JP Fire Control Package available in weights of 3.5 to 4.5 lbs. Features: Scaled-down version of the LRP-07 available with the same caliber, barrel, handguard, metal finishing and stock options as the CTR-02. An exaggerated bevel on the magazine well. A new integral handguard nut stabilizes the barrel mount and front pivot-pin joint. MicroFit Takedown Pins, lightened military-style upper design, dust cover and forward assist paired with dedicated side-charging handle. Thermo-Fit installation. LRI-20 upper assemblies pair with any existing LRP-07 side-charge lower. JP adjustable gas system; JP .308 Low Mass Operating System with JP High-Pressure Enhanced Bolt. Introduced 2019. SEE POLITICAL PANIC PRICING.

NIB	Exc.	V.G.	Good	Fair	Poor
3280	3000	2750	2490	—	—

LRP-07 SERIES

Calibers: .308 Win, .260 Rem., 6.5 Creedmoor, 6mm Creedmoor. Barrels: 16"–22" polished stainless with compensator. Buttstock: A2, ACE ARFX, Tactical Tactical Intent Carbine, Magpul MOE. Grip: Hogue Pistol Grip. Features: Machined upper and lower receivers with a left-side charging system. MKIII handguard. Adjustable gas system. Subtract $200 for LTI-23 Top-Charge Upper.

NIB	Exc.	V.G.	Good	Fair	Poor
3460	3300	3100	2750	—	—

JP-15 Professional Rifle

Calibers: .223, 6.5 Grendel, .300 Blackout, .22 LR. Barrels: 18" or 24". Buttstock: Synthetic modified thumbhole or laminate thumbhole. Grip: Hogue Pistol grip. Basic AR-type general-purpose rifle with numerous options.

NIB	Exc.	V.G.	Good	Fair	Poor
1980	1900	1780	1590	—	—

JP-15 Small-Frame Ready Rifles

Caliber: .223/5.56. Mil-spec forged 7075 receiver set with Magpul MOE trigger guard. Barrel: 16" or 18" JP Supermatch 416R barrel, 1:8" twist, black Teflon finish. JP tactical compensator. Hogue Overmolded buttstock, A2 grip, Rapid Configuration hand guard, rifle length, with JPHG-SM QD sling mount. JP Full Mass Operating System with EnhancedBolt assembly. JP LE Enhanced Reliability Fire Control Package, 4.0 to 4.5 lbs. SEE POLITICAL PANIC PRICING.

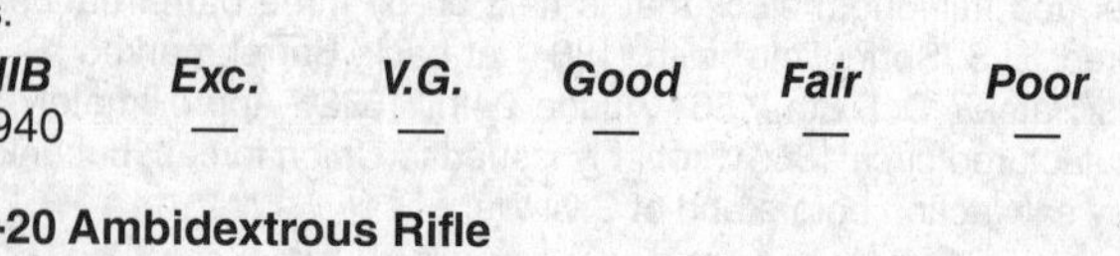

NIB	Exc.	V.G.	Good	Fair	Poor
1580	—	—	—	—	—

JP-15 Large-Frame Ready Rifle

Caliber: 6.5 Creedmoor, .308 Win. Similar to JP-15 Small-Frame Ready Rifles.

NIB	Exc.	V.G.	Good	Fair	Poor
3940	—	—	—	—	—

ASF-20 Ambidextrous Rifle

Caliber: .223/5.56, 6.5 Grendel, .300 AAC Blackout, .22 LR. Combines A-DAC (Ambidextrous Dual Action Catch) system from Radian Weapons with JP Ambi Mag Release. Compatible with any mil-spec pattern upper receiver. Choice of JP Low Mass Operating System, JP Full Mass Operating System, or JP Variable Mass Operating System. Trigger: JP Fire Control Package, 3.0 to 5.0 lbs. Ambi lower receiver. Introduced 2020. SEE POLITICAL PANIC PRICING.

NIB	Exc.	V.G.	Good	Fair	Poor
2360	—	—	—	—	—

JURRAS, LEE

Prescott, Arizona

See—AUTO MAG

While Jurras is best known for manufacturing last model of Auto Mag, he also produced the pistol listed sold by J. & G. Sales in Prescott, Arizona.

Howdah Pistol

.375-, .416-, .460-, .475-, .500-, .577-caliber single-shot pistol, with 12" barrel, adjustable sights and Nitex finish. Built on Thompson/Center Contender frame. Supposedly, approximately 100 produced.

NIB	Exc.	V.G.	Good	Fair	Poor
—	1750	1100	800	650	500

JUSTICE, P. S.

Philadelphia, Pennsylvania

Percussion Rifle (Antique)

.58-caliber percussion rifle, with 35" round barrel secured by two barrel bands, browned barrel, polished lock and brass furniture. Lock marked "P.S. Justice/Philada.". Approximately 2,500 manufactured in 1861.

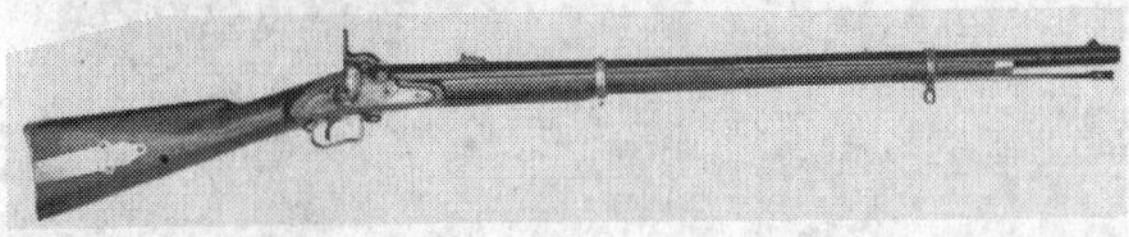

Courtesy Milwaukee Public Museum, Milwaukee, Wisconsin

Exc.	Fine	V.G.	Good	Fair	Poor
2300	1900	1390	880	450	310

K

K.F.C. (KAWAGUCHIYA FIREARMS CO.)

Japan

E-1 Trap or Skeet Over/Under

12-gauge boxlock double-barrel shotgun, with 26" or 30" barrels, competition rib, single-selective trigger and automatic ejectors. Engraved, blued with walnut stock. Manufactured until 1986.

NIB	Exc.	V.G.	Good	Fair	Poor
—	950	800	700	500	300

E-2 Trap or Skeet Over/Under

As above, but more finely finished.

NIB	Exc.	V.G.	Good	Fair	Poor
—	1400	1250	1000	750	350

Field Grade Over/Under

As above, with narrow rib and 26" or 28" barrels. Discontinued in 1986.

NIB	Exc.	V.G.	Good	Fair	Poor
—	650	580	500	400	280

Model 250

12-gauge semi-automatic shotgun, with 26", 28" or 30" barrels fitted for choke tubes. Matte blued, with walnut stock. Manufactured from 1980 to 1986.

NIB	Exc.	V.G.	Good	Fair	Poor
—	350	300	280	200	100

KAHR ARMS

Worcester, Massachusetts

Kahr's parent company, established in 1981, supplies CNC machine tools and applications engineering. In 1986, the company expanded by forming a manufacturing division which provides quality contract machining, manufacturing, and assembly services for diverse industries, including aerospace, automotive, electronics, medical equipment, scientific instrumentation, and telecommunications. Kahr Arms was founded in 1994 on fifteen years of manufacturing service in precision metalworking industries. Kahr incorporates the inherited professional, technical expertise into all its operations. Kahr's corporate headquarters are in Greeley, Pennsylvania. Production and assembly operations are in Worcester, Massachusetts, in the region commonly known as "Gun Valley." In recent years, Kahr has grown, acquiring Auto-Ordnance and Magnum Research. (See AUTO-ORDNANCE and MAGNUM RESEARCH for their specific arms and values.)

K SERIES

Calibers: 9mm, 7-shot; .45 ACP six-shot magazine. Barrel: 3.5". Weight: 25 oz. Length: 6" overall. Grips: Wraparound textured soft polymer. Sights: Blade front, rear drift adjustable for windage; bar-dot combat style. Features: Trigger-cocking double-action mechanism with passive firing pin block. Made of 4140 ordnance steel with a matte black finish. Contact maker for complete price list. Introduced 1994. Made in USA by Kahr Arms.

NIB	Exc.	V.G.	Good	Fair	Poor
900	790	680	500	430	—

K9

The K9 was the first Kahr pistol debuting in 1995. A premium all-steel semi-automatic DAO pistol chambered in 9mm or .40 S&W (Model K40). Ultra-compact size with a Lothar Walther polygonal-rifled barrel of 3.5"; overall length 6"; width at slide .9". Originally available in blue or electroless nickel finish and now in stainless steel. Weight 25 oz. A variety of special models including a K9 Lady's Model with lighter recoil spring have been offered in the past. Note: Add $30 for blackened stainless steel slide; $100 for night sights; $50 for Elite with polished slide; $50 for Gen2, with accessory rail, fiber optic sights, and 3 magazines.

NIB	Exc.	V.G.	Good	Fair	Poor
760	650	550	470	280	170

Lady K9

Same as above, with lightened recoil spring.

NIB	Exc.	V.G.	Good	Fair	Poor
500	380	300	220	120	50

K9 Elite

Introduced in 2003. This 9mm features 3.5" barrel and polished stainless steel slide. Magazine capacity 7 rounds. Weight about 25 oz. Note: Add $110 for night sights.

NIB	Exc.	V.G.	Good	Fair	Poor
580	420	350	280	150	100

K9 Compact Polymer Covert

Same as above, with .5" shorter grip frame. Weight about 17 oz. Magazine capacity 6 rounds. Introduced in 1999.

NIB	Exc.	V.G.	Good	Fair	Poor
620	550	480	320	250	100

25th Anniversary K9

Kahr's "25th Anniversary" limited edition K9 commemorates the 25 years of the K9. Each 25th Anniversary is a proven K9 pistol, chambered in 9mm and made in the United States from stainless steel. The guns are then custom engraved with front and rear slide serrations, slide porting, and a commemorative "25 Years" logo. The barrel and trigger are brightly polished, and the slide and frame finished in Sniper Grey Cerakote. Hogue aluminum grips are custom engraved with aggressive stippling and the new Kahr logo. TruGlo tritium sights, angled to allow 1-handed slide retraction. Comes in a plastic case, with three magazines, and a matching custom 1791 leather holster.

NIB	*Exc.*	*V.G.*	*Good*	*Fair*	*Poor*
1400	1200	1000	—	—	—

K40

Similar to K9, but chambered for .40 S&W cartridge. Magazine capacity 6 rounds. Weight 26 oz. Note: Add 15 percent for night sights.

NIB	*Exc.*	*V.G.*	*Good*	*Fair*	*Poor*
750	650	450	350	250	150

K40 Elite

Introduced in 2003. This .40 S&W features 3.5" barrel and polished stainless steel slide. Magazine capacity 6 rounds, with beveled magazine well. Weight about 26 oz. Note: Add 15 percent for night sights; 10 percent nickel finish; 15 percent black titanium finish; 5 percent K40 stainless steel version.

NIB	*Exc.*	*V.G.*	*Good*	*Fair*	*Poor*
800	700	580	400	300	180

K40 Covert

Similar to K40, with .5 in. shorter grip frame and flush-fitting 5-round magazine. Barrel length 3.5 in. Weight about 25 oz. Finish matte stainless steel.

NIB	*Exc.*	*V.G.*	*Good*	*Fair*	*Poor*
580	420	350	280	150	100

MK9 Elite

Introduced in 2003. This 9mm features 3" barrel and polished stainless steel slide. Magazine capacity 7 rounds. Weight about 24 oz. Note: Add 15 percent for laser grips or night sights.

NIB	*Exc.*	*V.G.*	*Good*	*Fair*	*Poor*
720	600	450	300	180	100

P9 Compact Polymer

Introduced in 1999. This 9mm features 3.5" barrel, with double-action-only trigger. Black polymer frame, with stainless steel slide. Overall length 6"; height 4.5"; weight about 18 oz. Magazine capacity 7 rounds.

NIB	*Exc.*	*V.G.*	*Good*	*Fair*	*Poor*
620	550	480	320	250	100

T SERIES

A premium full-size 9mm or .40 S&W with stainless steel slide and frame, 3.9" or 4" Lothar Walther polygonal-rifled barrel, white bar-dot combat sights, DAO trigger, wood grips, a height of 4.5" to 5", a length of 6" or 6.6" and a weight of about 25 oz. Note: Add $50 for night sights; Add $125 for Elite model with polished slide and night sights.

NIB	*Exc.*	*V.G.*	*Good*	*Fair*	*Poor*
730	620	530	450	270	160

TP SERIES

Calibers: 9mm, .45 ACP. Capacities: TP9 9mm (eight-shot magazine), TP45 .45 ACP (seven or eight shots). Barrels: 4", 5", or 6". Features: Model with a 4" barrel has features similar to KP GEN 2. The 5" model has front and rear slide serrations, white three-dot sights, mount for reflex sights. The 6" model has the same features, plus comes with a Leupold Delta Point Reflex sight.

NIB	*Exc.*	*V.G.*	*Good*	*Fair*	*Poor*
830	700	620	530	480	—

TP9

Introduced in 2004. This 9mm features black polymer frame, with matte stainless steel slide. Fitted with 4" barrel. Weight about 20 oz. Note: Add 15 percent for Novak night sights; $250 for TP9 Gen2, with accessory rail, fiber optic sights, three magazines; $350 for 6" barrel model, with Leupold Delta Point Reflex sight.

NIB	*Exc.*	*V.G.*	*Good*	*Fair*	*Poor*
620	550	480	320	250	100

TP40

Double-action-only semi-automatic pistol chambered in .40 S&W. Black polymer frame, matte stainless slide, 4" barrel, textured polymer grips, 6- or 7-round capacity depending on magazine. Drift-adjustable white bar-dot sights or Novak two-dot tritium sights. Introduced 2006.

NIB	*Exc.*	*V.G.*	*Good*	*Fair*	*Poor*
620	550	480	320	250	100

TP45

Similar design to TP9 and TP40 models, except chambered in .45 ACP. Note: Add $250 for TP45 Gen2, with accessory rail, fiber optic sights, three magazines; $350 for 6" barrel model, with Leupold Delta Point Reflex sight.

NIB	*Exc.*	*V.G.*	*Good*	*Fair*	*Poor*
620	550	480	320	250	100

PM Series

Kahr's PM Series in 9mm, .40 S&W and .45 ACP are premium thin-profile subcompacts for pocket carry. Features include a Lothar Walther 3" polygonal-rifled barrel, smooth DAO trigger, stainless or blackened stainless slide and an option for night sights.

NIB	*Exc.*	*V.G.*	*Good*	*Fair*	*Poor*
650	550	470	400	240	140

PM9

9mm fitted with 3" barrel, blackened stainless steel slide and black polymer frame. Magazine capacity 6 rounds. Weight about 16 oz. Introduced in 2004. Note: Add 15 percent for night sights.

NIB	*Exc.*	*V.G.*	*Good*	*Fair*	*Poor*
700	600	480	320	250	100

PM9 Micro

Fitted with 3" barrel. Chambered for 9mm cartridge. Weight about 16 oz. Polymer frame and stainless steel slide. Introduced in 2002.

NIB	*Exc.*	*V.G.*	*Good*	*Fair*	*Poor*
700	600	400	300	200	100

PM9 Thin Blue Line

As "PM Series" above, with black polymer frame, slide finished with "Armor Black Cerakote" featuring a "Thin Blue Line" down both sides of slide, TruGlo night sights.

NIB	*Exc.*	*V.G.*	*Good*	*Fair*	*Poor*
760	650	550	—	—	—

CM Series

Calibers: 9mm, .45 ACP. Capacities: 9mm (6+1), .45 ACP (5+1). CM45 Model is shown. Barrels: 3", 3.25", (45) Weights: 15.9–17.3 oz. Length: 5.42" overall. Grips: Textured polymer with integral steel rails molded into the frame. Sights: Pinned in polymer sight; drift-adjustable, white bar-dot combat. Features: A conventional rifled barrel instead of the match-grade polygonal barrel on Kahr's PM series; the CM slide stop lever is MIM (metal-injection-molded) instead of machined; the CM series slide has fewer machining operations and uses simple engraved markings instead of roll marking. The CM series are shipped with one magazine instead of two. The slide is machined from solid 416 stainless with a matte finish, each gun is shipped with one six-round stainless steel magazine with a flush baseplate. Magazines are U.S.-made, plasma welded, tumbled to remove burrs and feature Wolff springs. The magazine catch in the polymer frame is all metal and will not wear out on the stainless steel magazine after extended use.

NIB	*Exc.*	*V.G.*	*Good*	*Fair*	*Poor*
450	390	340	300	250	—

MK Series

Kahr's MK Series are thin profile subcompact, pocket carry handguns in 9mm or .40 S&W (also known as the "Covert"). Part of the Premium Series, features include a Lothar Walther 3" polygonal-rifled barrel, DAO trigger, stainless or blackened stainless slide and an option for night sights. Height is 4" with a length of 5.4" and a weight around 23 oz. Note: Add $100 for night sights; Add $175 for Elite model with polished stainless steel slide.

NIB	*Exc.*	*V.G.*	*Good*	*Fair*	*Poor*
780	660	560	480	290	170

MK40

.40 S&W model fitted with 3" barrel. Overall length 5.4"; height 4". Finish matte stainless steel. Magazine capacity 5 rounds. Uses same magazines as K40 Covert. Introduced in 1999.

NIB	Exc.	V.G.	Good	Fair	Poor
700	600	400	300	200	100

MK40 Elite

Introduced in 2003. This .40 S&W features 3" barrel and polished stainless steel slide. Magazine capacity 5 rounds, with beveled magazine well. Weight about 25 oz. Note: Add 10 percent for night sights.

NIB	Exc.	V.G.	Good	Fair	Poor
750	620	520	420	220	150

P Series

The widest array of models including the "TP" and "P" models, these polymer-framed models come in the premium series come chambered in .380 ACP (P380), 9mm (TP9, P9), .40 S&W (TP40, P40) and .45 ACP (TP45, P45). All have a matte stainless steel slide, polygonal-rifled barrel with a length (depending on model) of 2.3" to 3.6" and height of 3.9" to 4.8"; slide width between .75" to 1.00" and weight range between 9.9 oz to 16.8 oz. Note: Deduct $50 for .380 ACP; Add $50 for .45 ACP; Add $100 for P9 with external safety.

NIB	Exc.	V.G.	Good	Fair	Poor
650	550	470	400	240	140

P40

Similar to P9, but chambered for .40 S&W cartridge. Fitted with 3.5" match-grade barrel. Matte stainless steel slide and black polymer frame. Supplied with two 6-round stainless steel magazines. Weight about 19 oz. Introduced in 2001. Note: Add $30 for blackened stainless steel slide; $130 for night sights.

NIB	Exc.	V.G.	Good	Fair	Poor
550	420	320	250	150	80

P45

Introduced in 2005. Chambered for .45 ACP cartridge, with polymer frame and stainless steel slide. Barrel length 3.5". Fixed sights. Magazine capacity 6 rounds. Height 4.8"; overall length 6.3"; slide width 1"; weight about 18.5 oz. Note: Add 15 percent for night sights.

NIB	Exc.	V.G.	Good	Fair	Poor
680	550	380	280	170	120

MK9

9mm model with double-action-only trigger. Barrel length 3"; overall length 5.5"; height 4"; weight about 22 oz. One 6-round and 7-round magazine, with grip extension standard. Fitted with specially designed trigger for shorter trigger stroke. Note: Add 15 percent for night sights or laser grips.

NIB	*Exc.*	*V.G.*	*Good*	*Fair*	*Poor*
700	600	400	300	200	100

CW Series

Caliber: 9mm or .45 ACP. Capacities: 9mm, seven-round magazine; .45 ACP, six-round magazine. Barrels: 3.5" and 3.64". Weight: 17.7–18.7 oz. Length: 5.9"–6.36" overall. Grips: Textured polymer. Similar to the P-Series, but CW Series have conventional rifling, metal-injection-molded slide stop lever, no front dovetail cut, one magazine. Made in USA.

NIB	*Exc.*	*V.G.*	*Good*	*Fair*	*Poor*
430	380	330	300	240	—

CW9

9mm introduced in 2005. Features 3.5" barrel, polymer frame and stainless steel slide. Magazine capacity 7 rounds. Height 4.5"; overall length 6"; slide width .9".

NIB	*Exc.*	*V.G.*	*Good*	*Fair*	*Poor*
480	380	250	200	150	100

CW40

Semi-automatic with textured polymer grip. Chambered for .40 S&W and 6+1 capacity. Double-action, with 3.6" barrel. Adjustable rear sights. Weight 16.8 oz. Introduced 2006.

NIB	*Exc.*	*V.G.*	*Good*	*Fair*	*Poor*
500	380	300	220	120	50

CW 380

Part of the Value Series, the CW 380 compact locked breech in .380 ACP with a conventionally rifled 2.58" barrel, 6+1 capacity, 3.9" height, 4.96" long and 10.2 oz. weight, pinned front sights, metal-injection-molded slide stops. Ships with one magazine. Note: Add $15 for black carbon fiber frame or Kryptek camo frame finish.

NIB	*Exc.*	*V.G.*	*Good*	*Fair*	*Poor*
350	300	260	220	130	80

Wilson Combat Kahr Pistols

Offered in both K9 and K40 models. Customized pistol by Wilson's Gun Shop. Features hard chrome frame, black slide, 30 lpi checkering on front strap, beveled magazine well and several other special features. Initial production was for 50 K40 pistols; 25 K9 pistols. Discontinued.

NIB	*Exc.*	*V.G.*	*Good*	*Fair*	*Poor*
1300	1050	800	550	330	200

Model 1911WGS Deluxe

Model has blued finish, rubber wrap-around grips, with Thompson medallion high profile white dot sights and Thompson bullet logo on slide. Seven-round magazine. Introduced in 2001.

NIB	*Exc.*	*V.G.*	*Good*	*Fair*	*Poor*
580	480	420	300	220	120

P380 .380 ACP Pistol

DAO semi-automatic pocket pistol chambered in .380 ACP. Features include 2.5" Lothar Walther barrel, black polymer frame and grips, stainless steel slide 6+1 capacity. Overall length 4.9"; weight 11.3 oz. Note: Add 15 percent for night sights.

NIB	Exc.	V.G.	Good	Fair	Poor
620	500	400	300	180	80

CT Series

Calibers: 9mm, .45 ACP. Capacities: 9mm (8+1), .45 ACP (7+1). Barrel: 4". Weights: 20–25 oz. Length: 5.42" overall. Grips: Textured polymer with integral steel rails molded into the frame. Sights: Drift adjustable, white bar-dot combat.

NIB	Exc.	V.G.	Good	Fair	Poor
420	370	320	280	230	—

CT45

Chambered for .45 ACP. Listed by manufacturer as part of its Value Series. Features include black polymer frame, matte stainless slide, 4" barrel and textured polymer grips. A double-action-only trigger-cocking system, with locked breech. Browning-type recoil lug, with no magazine disconnect. Overall length 6.6"; weight 24 oz. Similar models with virtually identical features include CT40 in .40 S&W (22 oz.) and CT9 in 9mm (18.5 oz.). Introduced in 2014.

NIB	Exc.	V.G.	Good	Fair	Poor
400	360	320	280	250	200

CT 380

Part of the Value series, The CT380 is a locked-breech pistol with stainless steel slide and polymer frame in .380 ACP with 3" barrel, fixed sights, DAO trigger, 4.4" high, 5.52" long weighing 11.4 oz., and capacity of 7+1. Slide finished in matte stainless or "tungsten." Note: Add $15 for gold finish slide.

NIB	Exc.	V.G.	Good	Fair	Poor
350	300	260	220	130	80

S Series

New in 2019, the new "S" Series 9mm pistols come with an accessory rail on the frame and barrels with conventional rifling. The ST9 Compact has a 3.6" barrel, an overall length of 5.9", and a height of 4.5", front serrations on the slide and white 3-dot sights. Capacity is 7+1 and the pistol ships with two 7-round magazines. The larger S9 has a 4" barrel, has an overall length of 6.5" and a height of 5.08". Capacity is 8+1 and ships with two 8-round magazines. Note: Add $30 for ST9.

NIB	Exc.	V.G.	Good	Fair	Poor
390	330	280	240	150	90

ST9

Double-action only trigger cocking 9mm, with black polymer frame and stainless steel slide. Barrel 4"; overall length 6.5". Weight unloaded 18.5 oz. plus 2.1 oz. for empty magazine, which has 8-round capacity. Other features include drift adjustable two white-dot rear sight, polymer front sight. S9 model is compact version, with 3.6" barrel and 7-round magazine. Introduced in 2017. Note: Add $25 for S9 model.

NIB	Exc.	V.G.	Good	Fair	Poor
400	350	320	—	—	—

ST9 Tig Special Edition

This is a limited edition ST9 model, with part of the proceeds to be donated to the Beyond the Battlefield (BTB) Foundation. Founded by John "Tig" Tiegen and his wife Margaret to support wounded veterans. Engravings on the slide include its number in the series, the TIG logo, Tig's signature and Beyond the Battlefield logo. Chambered in 9mm, features include Black Armor Cerakote stainless steel slide, 4" barrel and textured polymer grip. Introduced in 2018, production limited to 1,000 pistols.

NIB	Exc.	V.G.	Good	Fair	Poor
480	400	340	—	—	—

CM Series

The smallest pistols in Kahr's Value series are the CM models. The CM models' slide is only .90" to .94" wide and machined from solid 416 stainless slide with a matte finish, 3" (9mm), 3.1" .40 S&W), and 3.14" .45ACP) conventionally-rifled barrels. Ships with one stainless steel magazine with a flush baseplate. Note: Add $30 for front night sight; Add $20 Kryptek Camo frame.

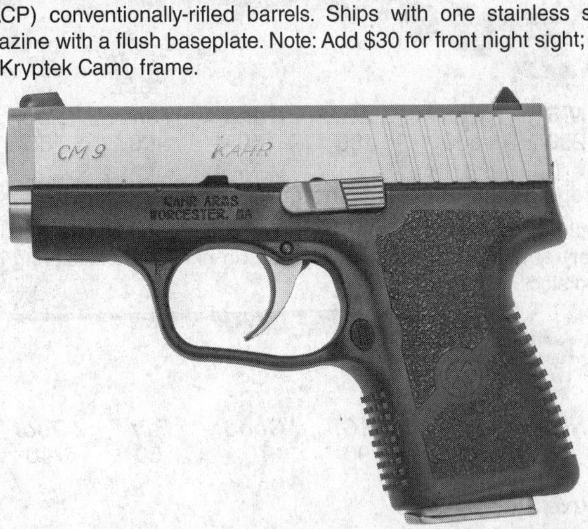

NIB	Exc.	V.G.	Good	Fair	Poor
390	330	280	240	150	90

KASSNAR IMPORTS, INC.

Harrisburg, Pennsylvania

Also see shotgun listings for Churchill and Omega. Both were trade names for modestly priced shotguns imported by Kassnar.

Omega Over/Under Shotgun

12-, 20-, 28-gauge and .410 bore boxlock over/under shotgun, with 26" or 28" ventilated rib barrels, single trigger and extractors. Blued, with walnut stock.

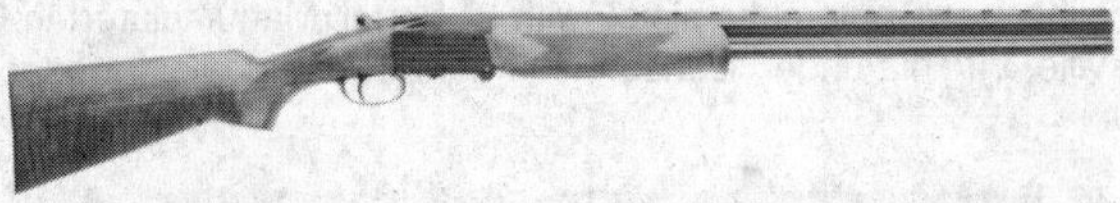

NIB	Exc.	V.G.	Good	Fair	Poor
—	450	300	200	150	130

Standard Over/Under

12-, 20- or 28-gauge and .410 bore boxlock double-barrel shotgun, with 26" or 28" barrels. Ventilated ribs, single trigger and extractors. Blued, with walnut stock.

NIB	Exc.	V.G.	Good	Fair	Poor
350	280	220	200	150	100

Deluxe Over/Under

As above, with more finely figured stock.

NIB	Exc.	V.G.	Good	Fair	Poor
400	320	250	220	180	100

Omega Side-by-Side Shotgun

20-, 28-gauge and .410 bore boxlock double-barrel shotgun, with 26" barrels, double triggers and extractors. Blued, with hardwood stock.

NIB	Exc.	V.G.	Good	Fair	Poor
—	350	250	150	100	80

Standard Side-by-Side

20- or 28-gauge and .410 bore boxlock folding double-barrel shotgun, with 26" barrels. Double triggers and extractors. Blued, with walnut stock.

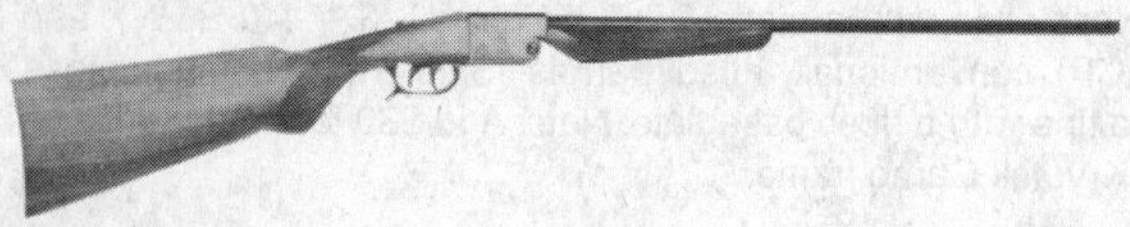

NIB	Exc.	V.G.	Good	Fair	Poor
250	200	180	150	100	80

Omega Single Barreled Shotgun

12-, 20-gauge and .410 bore single-barrel shotgun. Manufactured in a variety of barrel lengths and fitted with an extractor. Blued, with hardwood stock.

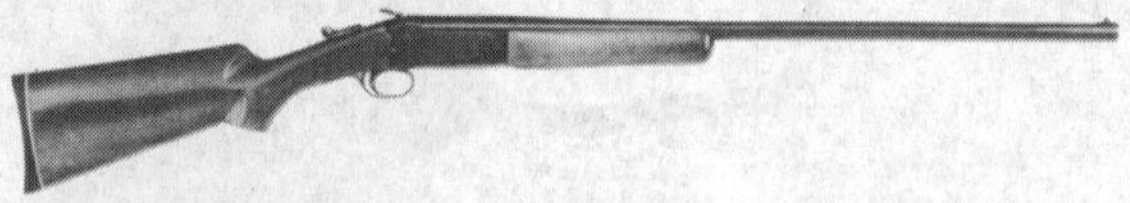

NIB	Exc.	V.G.	Good	Fair	Poor
—	130	90	70	50	40

Deluxe Side-by-Side

As above in .410 bore only, with more finely figured wood.

NIB	Exc.	V.G.	Good	Fair	Poor
300	250	200	180	120	80

KBI, INC.

Harrisburg, Pennsylvania

Company previously imported firearms from several manufacturers. These brands included Charles Daly handguns, shotguns and rifles, which are listed in the "D" section under Daly, Charles.

Kassnar PSP-25

.25-caliber semi-automatic pistol, with 2" barrel. Manufactured in Charlottesville, Virginia under license from Fabrique Nationale. Introduced in 1989.

NIB	Exc.	V.G.	Good	Fair	Poor
280	200	180	150	100	—

KEBERST INTERNATIONAL

Kendall International
Paris, Kentucky

Model 1A

.338 Lapua Magnum, .338-416 Rigby or .338-06 caliber bolt-action rifle, with 24" barrel having integral muzzle brake. Fitted with 3-9 power Leupold telescope. Matte blued, with camouflaged composition stock. Manufactured in 1987 and 1988.

NIB	Exc.	V.G.	Good	Fair	Poor
—	3750	3000	2500	1800	900

KELTEC CNC INDUSTRIES

Cocoa, Florida

PMR30

Caliber .22 WMR, steel barrel and slide, glass reinforced Zytel grip frame. Slide cover, 30-round magazine, single-action trigger, ambidextrous manual safety, fiber optic sights and accessory rail. Fluted 4.3-in. barrel, with matte black finish. Weight 13.6 oz. New 2011.

NIB	Exc.	V.G.	Good	Fair	Poor
510	450	430	340	300	280

CP33

Competition .22 LR pistol with 33-round magazine, 5.5" barrel. Ambidextrous controls, Picatinny rail on top of slide.

NIB	Exc.	V.G.	Good	Fair	Poor
450	380	—	—	—	—

P11

Semi-automatic pistol chambered for 9mm cartridge. Double-action-only. Barrel length 3.1"; overall length 5.6"; weight 14 oz. Magazine capacity 10 rounds. Standard model has blued slide, with black grip. Stainless steel and Parkerized finish are offered as well. Note: Add $100 for stainless steel; $40 for Parkerized finish.

NIB	Exc.	V.G.	Good	Fair	Poor
320	230	180	130	100	80

PF9

9mm concealed carry pistol, similar in configuration to above, 3.1" barrel, 12.7 lbs. weight, 7-round magazine.

NIB	Exc.	V.G.	Good	Fair	Poor
350	290	—	—	—	—

P15

Caliber: 9mm. Capacity: 15-round magazine. Barrel: 4" bull. Grip: Textured polymer. Sights: Adjustable tritium and fiber optic. Length: 5.6" overall. Weight: 14 oz. unloaded. Finish: Matte black. Features: Striker-fire, accessory rail, grip safety.

NIB	Exc.	V.G.	Good	Fair	Poor
370	330	280	260	210	—

P17

Caliber: .22 LR. Capacity: 16-round magazine. Barrel: 3.8 in. Grips: Textured polymer. Sights: Fixed. Length: 6.7 in. overall. Weight: 11.2 oz. unloaded. Finish: Matte black.

NIB	Exc.	V.G.	Good	Fair	Poor
150	—	—	—	—	—

P32

.32-caliber semi-automatic pistol fitted with 2.68" barrel. Double-action-only. Blued slide and frame. Magazine capacity 7 rounds. Overall length 5"; height 3.5"; weight about 6.6 oz. Note: Add $40 for Parkerized finish.

NIB	Exc.	V.G.	Good	Fair	Poor
310	230	180	130	100	80

P3AT

Chambered for .380 cartridge. Fitted with 2.75" barrel. Blued finish. Magazine capacity 6 rounds. Weight about 7.3 oz. Note: Add $40 for Parkerized finish; $60 for hard chrome.

NIB	Exc.	V.G.	Good	Fair	Poor
310	230	180	130	100	50

P40

Similar to P-11, but chambered for .40 S&W cartridge. Barrel length 3.3". Magazine capacity 9 rounds. Blued finish. Weight about 16 oz. Note: Add $40 for Parkerized finish; $60 for hard chrome.

NIB	Exc.	V.G.	Good	Fair	Poor
320	230	180	130	100	80

P50

Caliber: 5.7 x 28mm. Capacity: 20-round magazine. Barrel: 5" bull. Grip: Textured aluminum. Sights: Optics-ready. Length: 15" overall. Weight: 3.2 lbs. unloaded. Finish: Matte black. Features: Uses FN P90 50-round double-stack magazines, QD mount in the butt.

NIB	Exc.	V.G.	Good	Fair	Poor
750	710	700	640	560	—

SUB-2000 Rifle

Introduced in 1996. Semi-automatic rifle chambered for 9mm or .40 S&W cartridge. Barrel length 16.1". Rifle can be folded closed, with overall length of 16". Different grip assembly can be fitted to this rifle allowing for use of different magazines. Weight about 4.6 lbs. Note: Add $100 for Gen 2 model which has threaded barrel, double-stack magazine capability, adjustable stock and other upgraded features.

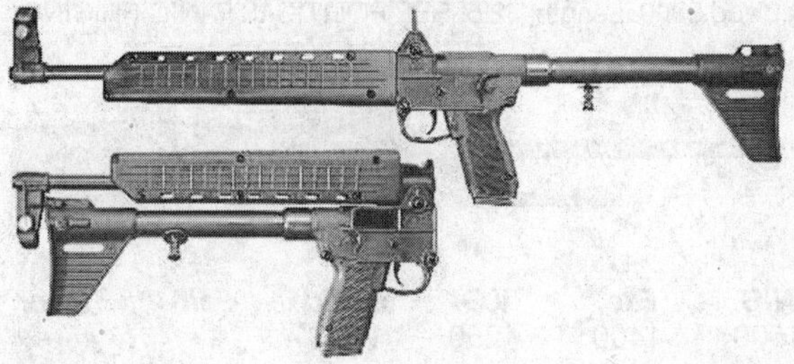

NIB	Exc.	V.G.	Good	Fair	Poor
380	300	180	120	80	50

SU-16 SERIES

Caliber: 5.56 NATO/.223. Capacity: 10-round magazine. Barrels: 16" or 18.5". Minimum length: folded 24.9"; overall, 35.9". Weights: 4.5 to 5 lbs. Magazine storage stock holds two proprietary 10-round magazines. The forend covers an 18.5" barrel and doubles as a bipod. Adjustable sights and an integrated Picatinny-style top rail. Offered in several rifle, carbine, and SBR variations with A, B, C, CA, D9, D12, and E designations. Add $417 for D9 and D12 models. Add $140 for the 'E' gas-piston model, which has a threaded muzzle and six-position stock. SEE POLITICAL PANIC PRICING.

NIB	Exc.	V.G.	Good	Fair	Poor
500	450	400	300	—	—

SU22

.22 LR rifle in configuration similar to above, 16" barrel, 26-round magazine.

NIB	Exc.	V.G.	Good	Fair	Poor
500	430	300	—	—	—

PLR16

5.56mm NATO gas-operated semi-automatic AR-15-style long-range pistol. Windage-adjustable rear sight. Picatinny rail. Muzzle threaded for muzzle brake. 9.2" barrel; weight 51 oz.; 10-round or M-16 magazine. Blued finish polymer construction. Introduced 2006.

NIB	Exc.	V.G.	Good	Fair	Poor
650	550	430	330	200	100

PLR22

.22 LR pistol in similar configuration to above, 9" barrel, 26-round magazine.

NIB	Exc.	V.G.	Good	Fair	Poor
390	300	250	—	—	—

RFB Rifle

Caliber: 7.62 NATO/.308. 20-round FAL-type magazine. Barrel: 18" with threaded muzzle, A2-style flash hider. Weight: 8 lbs. RFB stands for Rifle Forward-ejecting Bullpup. Features: A bullpup short-stroke gas-piston-operated carbine with ambidextrous controls, reversible operating handle, and mil-spec Picatinny rail. Length: 27.5". RFB Hunter has a 24" barrel; add $200. Length: 32.5". SEE POLITICAL PANIC PRICING.

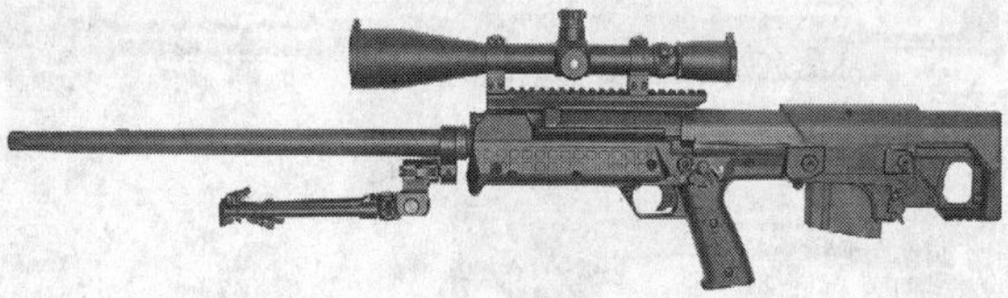

NIB	Exc.	V.G.	Good	Fair	Poor
1500	1400	1250	1000	—	—

RDB17

Bullpup rifle in configuration similar to above, 5.56 NATO, uses AR-15 magazines, 17.3" barrel, downward ejection. Similar models on the same platform include RDB Defender light duty tactical bullpup, $100 premium; RDB Hunter traditional stock & 20" barrel; and RDB Survival, lighter weight at just under 6 lbs.

NIB	Exc.	V.G.	Good	Fair	Poor
1000	880	730	—	—	—

KS7

Single tube 12-ga. bullpup pump shotgun, 18.5" barrel, 6+1 capacity.

NIB	Exc.	V.G.	Good	Fair	Poor
480	430	300	—	—	—

KSG

Dual tube 12-ga. bullpup pump shotgun, 18.5" barrel, 6+6+1 capacity. Also offered in KSG25, 12+12+1 capacity, ($275 premium), and KSG Compact, 5+5+1 capacity ($150 premium).

NIB	Exc.	V.G.	Good	Fair	Poor
700	630	500	—	—	—

KSG410

Gauge: .410 bore. Barrel: 18.5". Stock: Synthetic bullpup style in Black or FDE. Features: Baby bore bullpup touted as "sidekick with no kick." Only 1.7" wide with two magazine tubes. Capacity of 5+5+1 rounds. Fiber-optic sights, top carry handle/sight rail. Overall length of 26.1" keeps it legal as a shotgun. Three-inch chamber.

NIB	Exc.	V.G.	Good	Fair	Poor
420	360	300	—	—	—

KS7 Bullpup

Gauge: 12 ga., 3 in. Capacity: 6+1. Barrel: 18.5 in. Length: 26.1 in. Weight: 5.9 lbs. Stock: Black synthetic bullpup. Features: The pump-action KS7 Bullpup is a compact self-defense shotgun. Carry handle, Picatinny rail, M-LOK mounting points. Rear loading, downward ejection, ambidextrous controls. Cylinder choke.

NIB	Exc.	V.G.	Good	Fair	Poor
380	330	280	—	—	—

KEMPER, SHRIVER & COMPANY

Nashville, Tennessee

Delivered rifles made from sporting arm parts to Ordnance Department at Nashville, from December 1861 to March 1862. In all, 150 arms were assembled. Overall length 48.5"; octagonal barrels shortened 33" and bored to .48-caliber; some fitted with saber bayonet lugs; stocks of military with brass furniture. No sales reported.

KENDALL, INTERNATIONAL

Paris, Kentucky

See—KEBERST INTERNATIONAL

KENDALL, NICANOR

Windsor, Vermont

Underhammer Pistol (Antique)

.31- to .41-caliber under hammer percussion pistol, with 4" to 10" octagonal/round barrels marked "N.Kendall/Windsor,Vt." Browned or blued, with brass mounts and maple grips. Manufactured in 1850s.

Exc.	Fine	V.G.	Good	Fair	Poor
2500	1750	1250	900	500	250

KENO

Derringer (Antique)

.22-caliber single-shot spur trigger pistol, with 2.5" barrel, brass frame and walnut grips. Barrel blued or nickel-plated and marked "Keno".

Exc.	Fine	V.G.	Good	Fair	Poor
1200	650	400	225	150	70

KENTUCKY RIFLE

See AMERICAN LONGRIFLE

KERR

London, England

Kerr Revolver (Antique)

.44-caliber double-action percussion revolver, with 5.5" barrel and 6-shot cylinder. Blued, with walnut grips. Frame marked "Kerr's Patent 648" and "London Armoury Bermondsey".

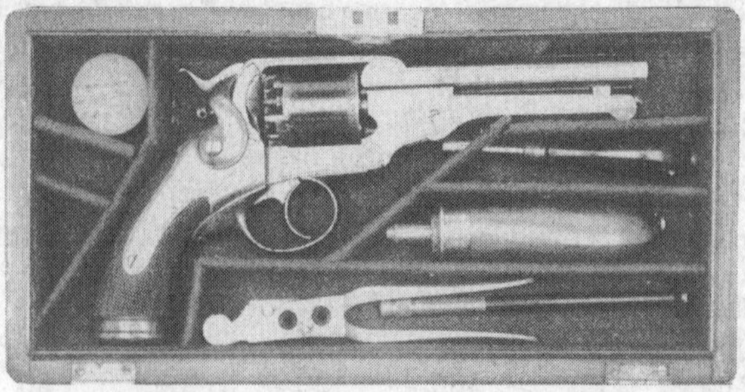

Courtesy Bonhams & Butterfields, San Francisco, California

Exc.	Fine	V.G.	Good	Fair	Poor
4250	2000	1400	800	300	210

KESSLER ARMS CORPORATION

Silver Creek, New York

Bolt-Action Shotgun

12-, 16- or 20-gauge shotgun, with 26" or 28" barrels. Blued, with walnut stock. Manufactured between 1951 and 1953.

NIB	Exc.	V.G.	Good	Fair	Poor
—	120	80	50	30	20

Levermatic Shotgun

12-, 16- or 20-gauge lever-action shotgun, with 26" or 28" barrel. Blued, with walnut stock. Manufactured between 1951 and 1953. A nice low-end collectible.

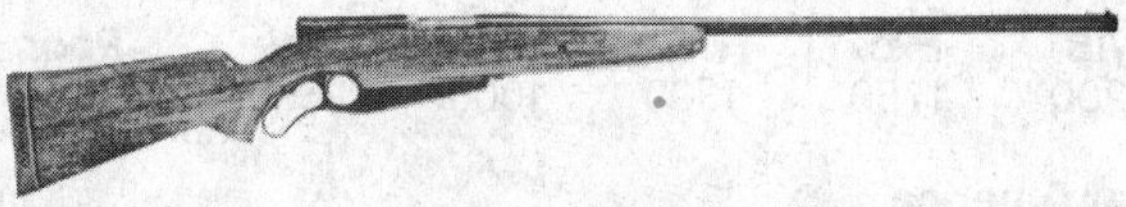

NIB	Exc.	V.G.	Good	Fair	Poor
—	300	280	200	150	80

KETTNER, EDWARD

Suhl, Germany

Drilling

High-quality three-barreled firearm chambered for 12x12- or 16x16-gauge, over various metric rifle cartridges. Barrels 25" in length. Features are ejectors, selective triggers and pop-up rifle sights that appear when rifle barrel is selected. Gun is deep-relief engraved in German style and has a high-grade checkered walnut stock. Manufactured between 1922 and 1939.

NIB	Exc.	V.G.	Good	Fair	Poor
—	—	3200	1700	900	500

KEYSTONE SPORTING ARMS

Milton, Pennsylvania

In 2007 Keystone acquired Chipmunk rifles, makers of small-size .22 rifles.

Crickett Shotgun

.410 ga. 32" OAL small foldable single-shot shotgun for beginning shooters.

NIB	Exc.	V.G.	Good	Fair	Poor
170	—	—	—	—	—

Chipmunk Single-Shot Standard Rifle

A .22 or .22 rimfire Magnum caliber bolt-action rifle, with 16.25" barrel and open sights. Weight about 3.5 lbs. Variations include left handed models, alloy frame models, stock variations, adult rifle, and threaded heavy barrel. Each brings a premium over the standard model.

NIB	Exc.	V.G.	Good	Fair	Poor
190	150	130	100	80	60

4200 My First Shotgun

Gauge: .410 bore. 3 in. Barrel: 18.5 in. Length: 37 in. Stock: Turkish Walnut. Features: Marketed as a Crickett "My First Shotgun," this pump-action baby bore holds 5+1 rounds of 2.75-inch shells or 4+1 rounds of 3 inch. Aluminum receiver with matte blue metalwork. MC-1 choke. Blade-style front sight. Checkered stocks with rubber recoil pad. Length of pull built for small-frame shooters at only 12 in.

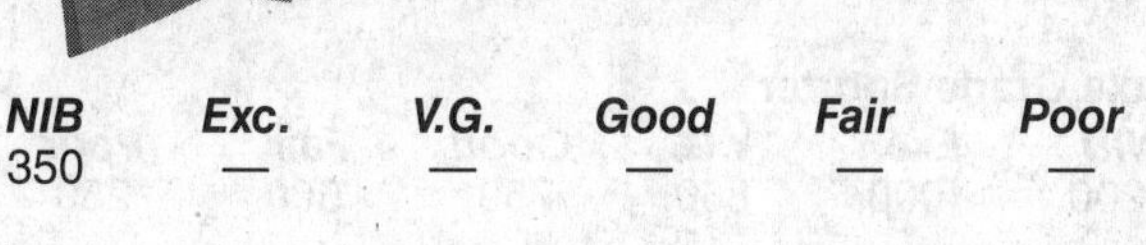

NIB	Exc.	V.G.	Good	Fair	Poor
350	—	—	—	—	—

4100 My First Shotgun

Gauge: .410 bore 3 in. Barrel: 18.5 in. Length: 32 in. Weight: 4.2 lbs. Stock: Turkish Walnut. Features: Marketed as a Crickett "My First Shotgun," this single-shot baby bore uses a folding design. Recoil reducing chamber and soft rubber recoil pad. Aluminum receiver with matte blue metalwork. Blade-style front sight. Checkered stock. Length of pull built for small-frame shooters at 11 inches. Fixed modified choke.

NIB	Exc.	V.G.	Good	Fair	Poor
160	—	—	—	—	—

91/30 Mini-Mosin

Scaled down .22 LR copy of the bolt-action Mosin Nagant.

NIB	Exc.	V.G.	Good	Fair	Poor
390	—	—	—	—	—

Deluxe Chipmunk

As above, with hand-checkered walnut stock.

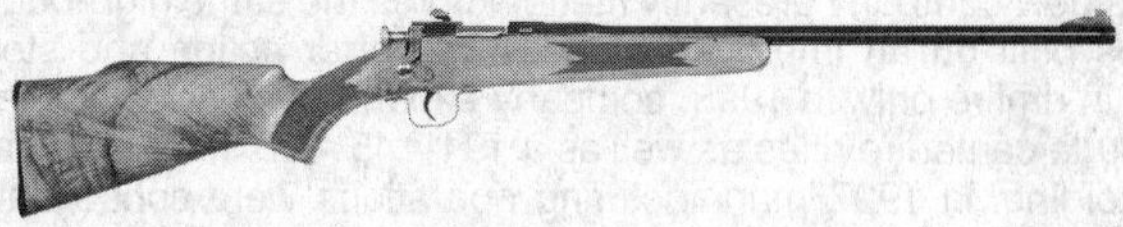

NIB	Exc.	V.G.	Good	Fair	Poor
230	180	140	100	80	60

Chipmunk .17 HMR

Similar to Standard Model. Chambered for .17 HMR cartridge. Introduced in 2002.

NIB	Exc.	V.G.	Good	Fair	Poor
200	160	120	100	80	40

Chipmunk TM

Introduced in 2002. Features a micrometer rear sight. Stock has accessory rail installed and is adjustable for length of pull. Heavy type 18" barrel. Weight about 5 lbs.

NIB	Exc.	V.G.	Good	Fair	Poor
320	250	150	120	100	80

Silhouette Pistol

A .22-caliber bolt-action pistol, with 14.5" barrel, open sights and pistol grip walnut stock. Variations include Crickett Hunter Pistol (worth premium) and Crickett Synthetic Pistol.

NIB	Exc.	V.G.	Good	Fair	Poor
150	130	100	80	60	40

KIMBALL ARMS COMPANY

Detroit, Michigan

Semi-Automatic Pistol

.30-caliber carbine semi-automatic pistol, with 3.5" or 5" barrel. Blued, with plastic grips. Also believed to have been made in .22 Hornet and .357 Magnum, though few legitimate examples have been seen. Manufactured from 1955 to 1958. Approximately 238 made.

Courtesy James Rankin

NIB	Exc.	V.G.	Good	Fair	Poor
—	3000	2000	1500	1000	450

KIMBER MFG., INC.

Elmsford, New York
(previously in Yonkers, New York)

Kimber of Oregon was established in April, 1979 by Greg and Jack Warne. Company produced high quality rimfire and centerfire rifles until going out of business in early 1991. Kimber produced approximately 60,000 rifles during its operation. In April 1993, Greg Warne opened Kimber of America in Clackamas, Oregon. This new company presently manufactures the same high-quality rifles built on an improved Model 82 Sporter action and stock, but in rimfire only. In 1995, company expanded its product line to include centerfire rifles as well as a 1911 .45 ACP semi-automatic pistol line. In 1997, manufacturing operations were consolidated in the New York pistol factory and two factories in Oregon were closed. Guns may be found stamped "Kimber of America", "Kimber, Yonkers, NY" or "Kimber, Clackamas, Oregon".

DISCONTINUED MODELS

Model 82 Classic

.22 LR, .22 Magnum or .22 Hornet bolt-action rifle, with 22" barrel. Furnished without sights; 4- or 5-shot magazine. Blued, with walnut stock. Discontinued in 1988. Note: Add 10 percent for Model 82 Series rifles in .22 Magnum caliber; 15 percent for rifles chambered in.22 Hornet.

NIB	Exc.	V.G.	Good	Fair	Poor
950	800	600	550	450	350

Cascade

As above, with Monte Carlo-style stock.

NIB	Exc.	V.G.	Good	Fair	Poor
950	800	650	600	500	400

Custom Classic

As above in .218 Bee or .25-20.

NIB	Exc.	V.G.	Good	Fair	Poor
1500	1250	720	650	400	300

Mini Classic

Model 82 with 18" barrel. Manufactured in 1988.

NIB	Exc.	V.G.	Good	Fair	Poor
900	750	550	480	400	300

Deluxe Grade

Similar to Custom Classic. Introduced in 1989.

NIB	Exc.	V.G.	Good	Fair	Poor
1500	1250	650	550	450	350

Model 82A Government

.22-caliber bolt-action rifle, with 25" heavy barrel fitted with telescope mounts. Matte blued, with walnut stock. Introduced in 1987.

NIB	Exc.	V.G.	Good	Fair	Poor
680	550	450	380	300	200

Continental

Similar to Custom Classic, with 20" barrel, open sights and full-length Mannlicher-style stock. Introduced in 1987.

NIB	Exc.	V.G.	Good	Fair	Poor
2000	1600	1250	950	400	300

Super Continental

As above, but more finely finished. Discontinued in 1988.

NIB	Exc.	V.G.	Good	Fair	Poor
2200	1750	1300	1000	600	300

Super America

Model 82 more finely finished. Discontinued in 1988.

NIB	Exc.	V.G.	Good	Fair	Poor
2000	1600	950	850	650	500

Super Grade

As above. Introduced in 1989.

NIB	Exc.	V.G.	Good	Fair	Poor
2200	1750	1300	1000	600	480

Centennial

Commemorative rifle moderately engraved. Including special match barrel, skeleton buttplate, hand-selected walnut stock and light engraving. Issued to commemorate 100th Anniversary of .22 LR cartridge. One hundred manufactured in 1987.

NIB	Exc.	V.G.	Good	Fair	Poor
4000	2800	2000	1750	1500	1150

Brownell

In 1986, 500 commemorative rifles were produced in honor of Leonard Brownell. Featuring a high-grade Mannlicher-style full-length walnut stock.

NIB	Exc.	V.G.	Good	Fair	Poor
2800	2250	1500	1200	600	500

MODEL 84 SERIES—DISCONTINUED MODELS

Bolt-action rifle manufactured in a variety of smallbore centerfire calibers, with 22" or 24" barrel and 5-shot magazine. Blued, with walnut stock. Variations are listed.

Classic

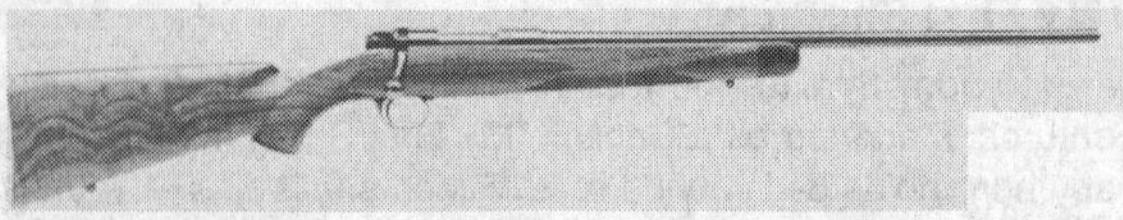

NIB	Exc.	V.G.	Good	Fair	Poor
1200	950	700	400	250	200

Custom Classic

NIB	Exc.	V.G.	Good	Fair	Poor
1500	1100	800	500	350	200

Deluxe Grade Sporter

NIB	Exc.	V.G.	Good	Fair	Poor
1200	1000	850	750	500	250

Continental

NIB	Exc.	V.G.	Good	Fair	Poor
2000	1700	1100	700	500	250

Super Continental

NIB	Exc.	V.G.	Good	Fair	Poor
2000	1700	1100	700	580	250

Super America

NIB	Exc.	V.G.	Good	Fair	Poor
2000	1700	1100	820	600	300

Super Grade

NIB	Exc.	V.G.	Good	Fair	Poor
2100	1800	1200	850	650	300

Ultra Varmint

As above, with 24" stainless steel barrel and laminated birchwood stock. Introduced in 1989.

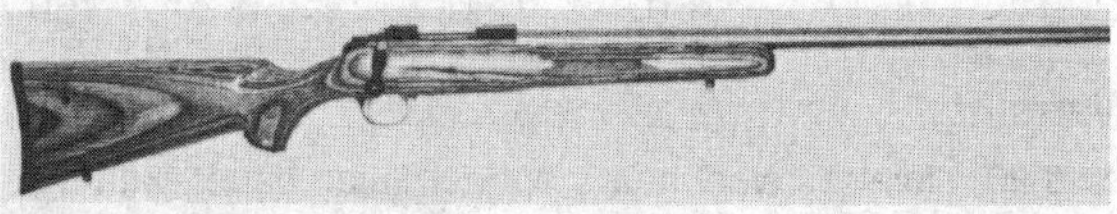

NIB	Exc.	V.G.	Good	Fair	Poor
1500	1100	900	750	550	250

Super Varmint

As above, with walnut stock. Introduced in 1989.

NIB	Exc.	V.G.	Good	Fair	Poor
2000	1600	1200	850	650	300

Predator

.221 Fireball, .223 Rem., 6mm TCU, 7mm TCU or 6x45mm caliber single-shot bolt-action pistol. Based upon Model 84 action, with 14.75" barrel adopted for telescope. Blued, with walnut stock. Available in two grades as listed. Manufactured in 1987 and 1988 only.

Hunter Grade

NIB	Exc.	V.G.	Good	Fair	Poor
1800	1350	950	600	400	300

Super Grade

NIB	Exc.	V.G.	Good	Fair	Poor
2500	2000	1500	1000	500	400

MODEL 89 SERIES/BGR (BIG GAME RIFLES)

Bolt-action sporting rifle, produced in .257 Roberts to .505 Gibbs caliber, with 22" or 24" barrel. Blued, with walnut stock. Variations of this model are listed. Note: Rare calibers (.257 Roberts, 7x57, .375 H&H) will bring a premium of 25 percent or more.

Classic

NIB	Exc.	V.G.	Good	Fair	Poor
800	650	550	400	300	200

Custom Classic

NIB	Exc.	V.G.	Good	Fair	Poor
1000	850	650	450	350	250

Deluxe Grade

NIB	Exc.	V.G.	Good	Fair	Poor
1400	1150	900	650	450	250

Super America

NIB	Exc.	V.G.	Good	Fair	Poor
1800	1250	900	700	500	250

Super Grade

NIB	Exc.	V.G.	Good	Fair	Poor
1800	1250	900	700	500	250

African Grade

Note: Add 10 percent for .375 H&H or .505 Gibbs.

NIB	Exc.	V.G.	Good	Fair	Poor
5500	4250	3200	2400	1200	500

MODEL 82C SERIES—DISCONTINUED MODELS

In 1998 Model 82C series rifles went out of production.

Classic

Bolt-action rifle chambered for .22 LR cartridge. Receiver drilled and tapped for sights. Fitted with 22" barrel. Detachable magazine holds 4 rounds. Stock is plain, with standard grade Claro Walnut. Checkering is 18 lpi, with 4 point side panel pattern. Red rubber butt pad and polished steel pistol grip cap are standard. Weight about 6.5 lbs. Re-introduced in 1989.

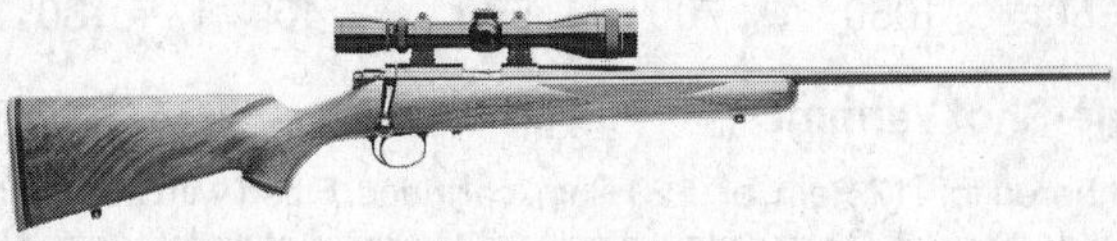

NIB	Exc.	V.G.	Good	Fair	Poor
900	650	500	400	—	—

Super America

Same as above. Fitted with AAA fancy grade Claro Walnut, with ebony tip and beaded cheekpiece. Hand-checkering 22 lpi in a full-coverage pattern. Steel buttplate and pistol grip cap are standard.

NIB	Exc.	V.G.	Good	Fair	Poor
2200	1500	1100	750	300	300

Custom Match

Bolt-action .22-caliber has 22" barrel. Stock AA French walnut, with full coverage checkering. Finish rust blued. Weight about 6.75 lbs.

NIB	Exc.	V.G.	Good	Fair	Poor
2000	1600	950	700	400	200

Custom Shop Super America (Basic)

Same as above. Furnished with a number of special order options that greatly affect value. Seek an independent appraisal before sale.

Stainless Classic Limited Edition

Introduced in 1996. Limited edition Model 82C chambered for .22 LR cartridge. Stainless steel barrel 22" long. A 4-shot magazine included. Production limited to about 600 rifles.

NIB	Exc.	V.G.	Good	Fair	Poor
1900	1750	1100	800	500	300

SVT (Short Varmint/Target)

First introduced in 1996, this .22-caliber rifle is a single-shot. Fitted with 18" stainless steel fluted barrel. Walnut stock is target style, with no checkering. Weight about 7.5 lbs.

NIB	Exc.	V.G.	Good	Fair	Poor
1350	1050	700	500	400	180

HS (Hunter Silhouette)

Introduced in 1997. Features 24" half-fluted barrel. Chambered for .22 LR cartridge. Stock American walnut, with high comb. Trigger fully adjustable. Four-round magazine standard. Weight about 7 lbs.

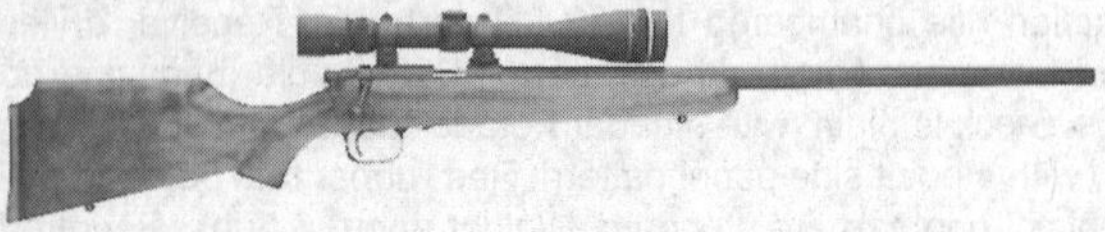

NIB	Exc.	V.G.	Good	Fair	Poor
1350	1050	700	500	400	180

Single-Shot Varmint

Chambered for .17 Rem. or .223 Rem. cartridge. Fitted with 25" stainless steel fluted barrel. Claro walnut stock, with varmint-style forearm. Weight about 7.5 lbs. In 1998, Model 84C series rifle went out of production.

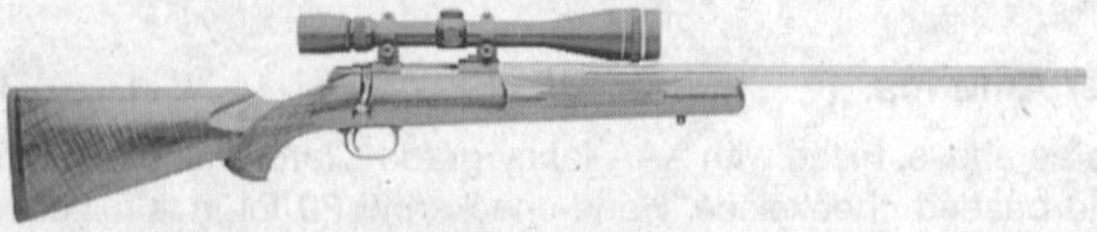

NIB	Exc.	V.G.	Good	Fair	Poor
1500	1180	900	600	400	200

Sporterized Model 98 Swedish Mausers

These are re-conditioned and re-worked Mausers. Fitted with new match grade stainless steel fluted barrels in 24" or 26" depending on caliber. Stock is new synthetic checkered. Chambered in .257 Roberts, .270 Win., .280 Rem., .30-06, 7mm Rem. Magnum, .300 Win. Magnum, .338 Win. Magnum and .220 Swift with 25" barrel. Note: Suggested retail price: $535 for standard calibers; $560 for Magnum.

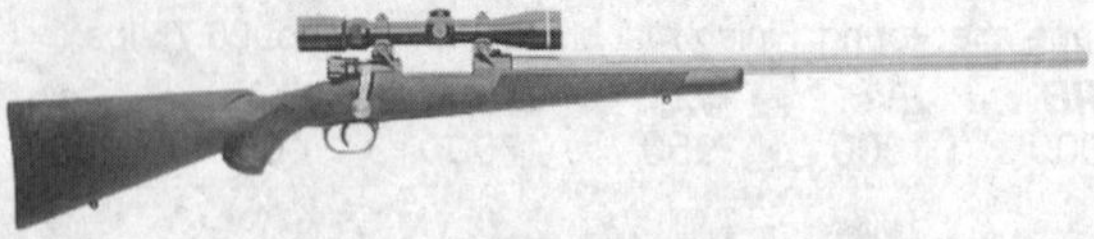

Sporterized Model 96 Swedish Mausers

Similar to above in terms of re-working and re-conditioning. Chambered for these calibers:.22-250 w/stainless steel heavy barrel fluted — Retail $500. .243 Win. — $400 to $465 depending on finish. 6.5x55mm — $340 to $370 depending on finish. 7mm-08 Rem. — $415 to $465 depending on finish. .308 Win. — $415 to $520 depending on finish and barrel configuration.

RECENT PRODUCTION MODELS

17 SERIES

Series of .17 Mach 2 rifles. Introduced in 2005. Features are similar to 22 Series.

Hunter

Fitted with 22" light sporter barrel. No sights. Checkered walnut stock, with black pad and clear stock finish. Magazine capacity 5 rounds. Weight about 6.5 lbs.

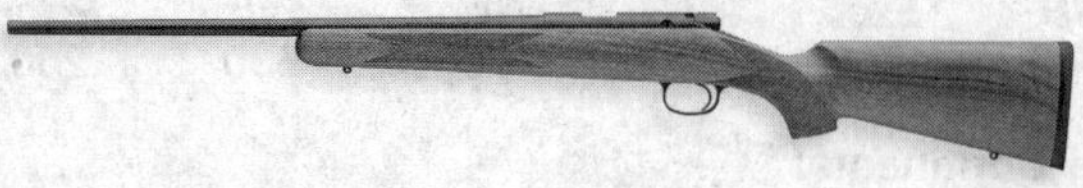

NIB	Exc.	V.G.	Good	Fair	Poor
900	700	500	380	250	120

SVT (Short Varmint/Target) (Centerfire)

Fitted with 18.25" stainless steel bull fluted barrel, with no sights. Checkered walnut stock, with black pad and oil-finish. Magazine capacity 5 rounds. Weight about 7.9 lbs.

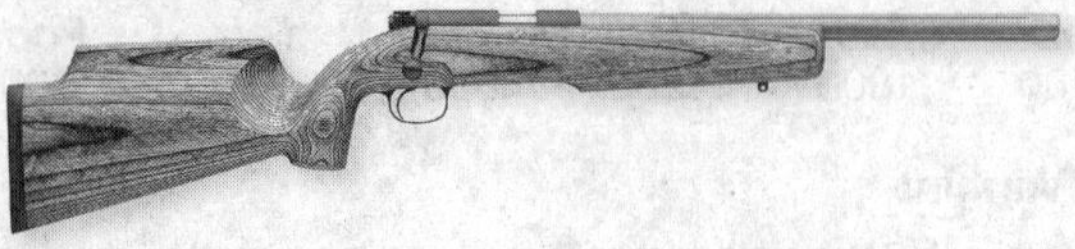

NIB	Exc.	V.G.	Good	Fair	Poor
1200	950	780	580	350	150

Pro Varmint

Features 20" stainless steel heavy sporter fluted barrel, with no sights. Stock gray laminate, with oil-finish and no checkering. Magazine capacity 5 rounds. Weight about 6.75 lbs.

NIB	Exc.	V.G.	Good	Fair	Poor
1150	880	680	500	320	150

Classic Varmint

Fitted with 20" heavy sporter fluted barrel, with no sights. Checkered walnut stock, with oil-finish. Magazine capacity 5 rounds. Weight about 6.5 lbs.

NIB	Exc.	V.G.	Good	Fair	Poor
1200	950	780	580	350	150

22 SERIES

In 1999, Kimber introduced a new line of bolt-action .22-caliber rimfire rifles. First deliveries were made early in 2000. Series built on a totally new design from bolt, to magazine, to barrel. All rifles in this series have 5-round magazine capacity. Line replaces Model 82-C series of rifles.

Classic

.22-caliber rifle fitted with 22" barrel. Fully adjustable trigger. Stock A grade Claro walnut, with 18 lpi checkering. Fitted with Model 70 style safety. Blued finish. Weight about 6.5 lbs.

NIB	Exc.	V.G.	Good	Fair	Poor
1200	950	780	580	350	150

Custom Classic

Fitted with 22" barrel, ebony forend tip, hand-rubbed oil-finish and 24 lpi checkering. Introduced in 2003. Weight about 6.5 lbs.

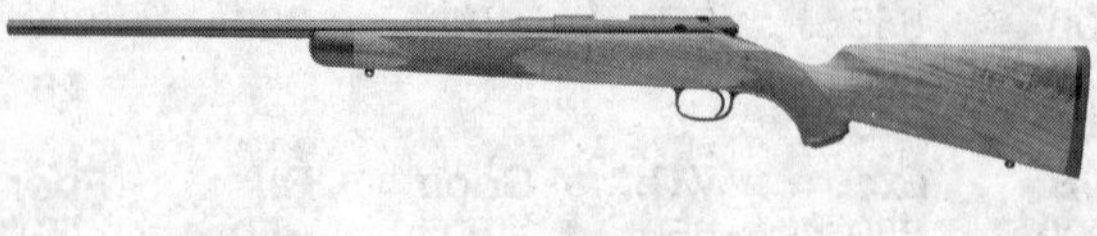

NIB	Exc.	V.G.	Good	Fair	Poor
1420	1100	850	680	450	150

Super America

Features 22" barrel, with fully adjustable trigger. Stock AAA grade Claro walnut, with 22 lpi wrap-around checkering and ebony forend tip. Black recoil pad. Weight about 6.5 lbs.

NIB	Exc.	V.G.	Good	Fair	Poor
1900	1400	1080	780	500	200

SVT (Short Varmint/Target)

Fitted with 18" fluted stainless steel barrel and gray laminated wood stock. High target comb. Weight about 7.5 lbs. In 2004, offered in Mach 2 .17-caliber.

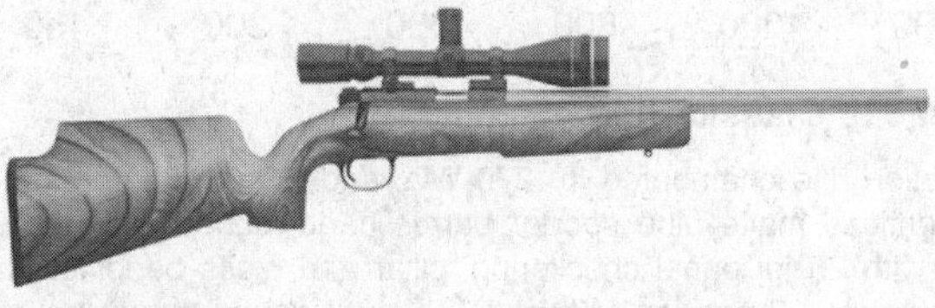

NIB	Exc.	V.G.	Good	Fair	Poor
1150	880	680	500	320	150

Classic Varmint

Introduced in 2003. Features 20" barrel, with hand-rubbed oil-finish and 20 lpi checkering. Weight about 6.5 lbs. In 2004, available in Mach 2 .17-caliber.

NIB	Exc.	V.G.	Good	Fair	Poor
1150	880	680	500	320	150

Pro Varmint

Features heavy fluted 20" stainless steel barrel and gray laminated stock. No sights. Magazine capacity 5 rounds. Weight about 6.75 lbs. Introduced in 2004. Available in Mach 2 .17-caliber.

NIB	Exc.	V.G.	Good	Fair	Poor
1200	950	780	580	350	150

HS (Hunter Silhouette)

Fitted with 24" medium sporter match-grade barrel, with match chambered and half fluting. Walnut stock, with 18 lpi checkering and Monte Carlo comb. Weight about 7 lbs.

NIB	Exc.	V.G.	Good	Fair	Poor
900	700	500	380	250	120

Youth

Introduced in 2002. This .22-caliber rifle fitted with 18.5" barrel. Checkered Claro walnut stock, with 12.25" lop. Weight about 5.25 lbs.

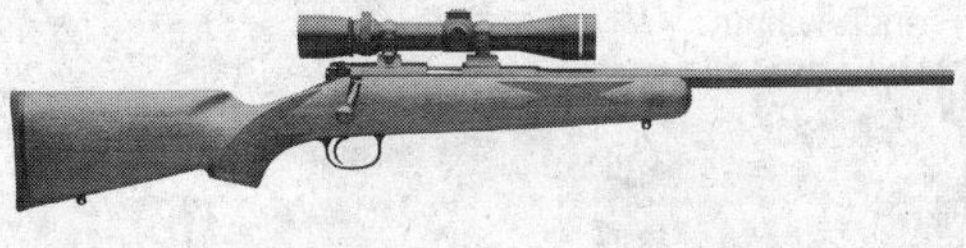

NIB	Exc.	V.G.	Good	Fair	Poor
850	680	500	300	200	100

Hunter

Lower-priced version of Classic.

NIB	Exc.	V.G.	Good	Fair	Poor
800	650	550	400	300	200

Custom Match Limited Edition

Introduced in 2004. Limited edition of 300 rifles. Features checkered French walnut stock of AAA wood and several custom features. Serial numbered from KAN25001-KAN25300.

NIB	Exc.	V.G.	Good	Fair	Poor
2850	2300	—	—	—	—

MODEL 84M SERIES

Classic

Introduced in 2001. Centerfire bolt-action rifle chambered for .243 Win., .260 Rem., 7mm-08 Rem. and .308 Win. In 2005, offered chambered for .22-250 cartridge. Fitted with 22" light sporter match-grade barrel, Claro walnut stock with 20 lpi checkering and satin wood finish. Matted blue finish. Fitted with 1" Pachmayr Decelerator recoil pad. Weight about 5.75 lbs.

NIB	Exc.	V.G.	Good	Fair	Poor
1100	900	700	480	300	150

Montana

Essentially, a stainless steel version of Model 84M Classic with black synthetic stock. Weight about 5.25 lbs. Introduced in 2003.

NIB	Exc.	V.G.	Good	Fair	Poor
1200	950	780	580	350	150

Super America

First offered in 2003. Available in .243, .260 Rem., 7mm-08 Rem. and .308 Win. Fitted with 22" barrel. In 2005, offered chambered for .223 cartridge. Stock select walnut, with 24 lpi checkering. Fitted with ebony forend tip, cheekpiece and hand-rubbed oil-finish. Weight about 5.75 lbs., depending on caliber. Magazine capacity 5 rounds.

NIB	Exc.	V.G.	Good	Fair	Poor
1800	1350	1000	650	320	180

Pro Varmint

Introduced in 2004. Chambered for .22-250 Win. cartridge. Fitted with 24" stainless steel fluted barrel, with no sights. In 2005, offered in .204

Ruger and .223 calibers. Gray laminated stock. Magazine capacity 5 rounds. Weight 7.25 lbs.

NIB	Exc.	V.G.	Good	Fair	Poor
1080	800	580	400	300	150

Varmint

Similar to Classic, fitted with stainless steel 26" match-grade barrel. Chambered for .22-250 Rem. cartridge. In 2005, offered in .204 Ruger caliber. Fitted with .5" solid recoil pad. Weight about 7.4 lbs.

NIB	Exc.	V.G.	Good	Fair	Poor
1000	750	500	380	300	150

SVT

Stock gray laminate, with Monte Carlo comb. Barrel length 18.25" in stainless steel and fluted. Chambered for .223 cartridge. Magazine capacity 5 rounds. Weight about 8.3 lbs.

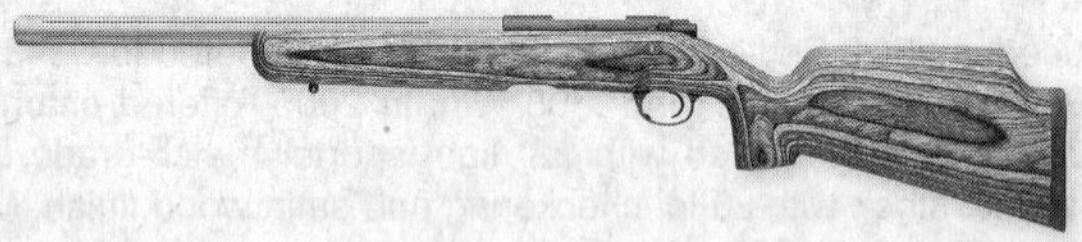

NIB	Exc.	V.G.	Good	Fair	Poor
1200	950	780	580	350	150

LongMaster VT

Bolt-action rifle chambered for .22-250 cartridge. Fitted with 26" fluted stainless steel match-grade barrel. Special laminated target stock. Weight about 10 lbs. No sights. Introduced in 2002.

NIB	Exc.	V.G.	Good	Fair	Poor
1200	950	780	580	350	150

LongMaster Classic

Same features as Model 84M Classic, with 24" fluted stainless steel barrel. Chambered for .308 Win. cartridge. In 2005, offered in .223-caliber. Checkered walnut stock. Weight about 7.25 lbs. Introduced in 2002.

NIB	Exc.	V.G.	Good	Fair	Poor
1200	950	780	580	350	150

LongMaster Pro

Introduced in 2003. Single-shot bolt-action rifle fitted with 24" fluted heavy barrel. Chambered for .308 Win. or .22-250 cartridge. Fitted with synthetic bench-rest stock. Weight about 7.25 lbs.

NIB	Exc.	V.G.	Good	Fair	Poor
1350	1050	700	500	400	180

Open Range Pro Carbon

Calibers: 6.5 Creedmoor, .308 Win. Capacity: 4. Barrel: 24 in., carbon-fiber wrapped, Proof Research. Stock: Carbon fiber. Sights: None, drilled and tapped. Weight: 6 lbs. Features: Sub-MOA accuracy, 84M stainless controlled-round-feed action, three-position safety.

NIB	Exc.	V.G.	Good	Fair	Poor
3000	—	—	—	—	—

Light Police Tactical

Based on Model 84 action, with 24" medium weight fluted match barrel. Black laminated stock and third swivel for bipod. Chambered in .308 Win. or .223 Rem. Introduced in 2007.

NIB	Exc.	V.G.	Good	Fair	Poor
1200	1000	800	600	300	150

Model 84L Classic Rifle

Bolt-action rifle chambered in .270 Win. and .30-06. Features include 24" sightless matte blue sporter barrel; hand-rubbed A-grade walnut stock, with 20 lpi panel checkering; pillar and glass bedding; Mauser claw extractor; 3-position M70-style safety; 5-round magazine; adjustable trigger.

NIB	Exc.	V.G.	Good	Fair	Poor
1000	850	720	400	300	200

Model 84L Montana

Long-action variation of Model 84 action. Chambered in .25-06 Remington, .270 Winchester, .280 Ackley Improved and .30-06 Springfield. Capacity 4-rounds in blind magazine. Kevlar-reinforced carbon fiber stock. Match-grade barrel, chamber and trigger. Free-floating 24" barrel is both pillar and glass bedded. Model 70-type 3-position safety. Weight under 6 lbs. Introduced in 2011.

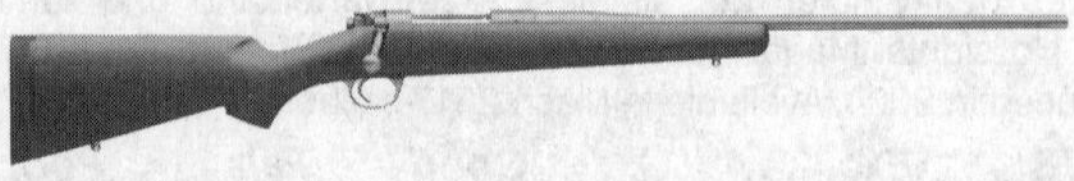

NIB	Exc.	V.G.	Good	Fair	Poor
1150	1000	850	600	300	200

Model 84L Hunter

Similar to 84L Montana, except chambered in .270 Winchester, .280 Ackley Improved and .30-06. Has a detachable magazine and reinforced synthetic stock.

NIB	Exc.	V.G.	Good	Fair	Poor
750	600	500	400	300	200

MODEL 8400 SERIES

Series introduced in 2003. Features smallest action size compatible with WSM family of cartridges.

Classic

Fitted with select walnut stock with 20 lpi checkering. Chambered for WSM calibers: .270, 7mm, .300 and .325. Barrel length 24" with no sights. Magazine capacity 3 rounds. Weight about 6.6 lbs. Note: Add $140 for French walnut.

NIB	Exc.	V.G.	Good	Fair	Poor
1000	800	600	480	300	150

Montana

Features 24" stainless steel barrel, with no sights. Stock black synthetic, with no checkering. Same calibers as Classic. Weight about 6.25 lbs.

NIB	Exc.	V.G.	Good	Fair	Poor
1350	1050	700	500	400	180

Sonora

Features brown laminate stock and 24" barrel. Chambered in .25-06, 7mm Rem., .308 Win., .30-06 or .300 Win. Magnum. Discontinued 2011.

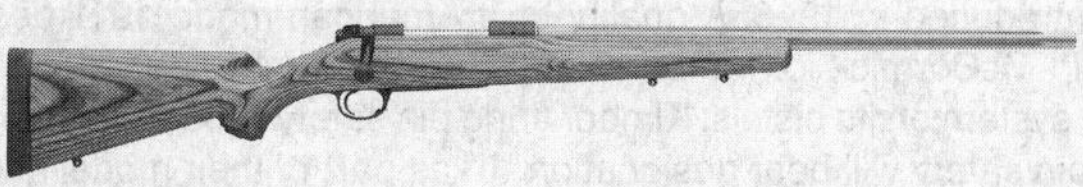

NIB	Exc.	V.G.	Good	Fair	Poor
1100	900	750	600	400	200

Caprivi

Medium-bore variation of Model 8400 with 3-leaf express sight, double cross-bolts, AA-Grade French walnut stock. Chambered in .375 H&H, .416 Rem. or .458 Lott.

NIB	Exc.	V.G.	Good	Fair	Poor
3000	2500	2000	1500	750	400

Talkeetna

Dangerous-game rifle in .375 H&H only. Kevlar stock, single-leaf express sight, 24" barrel.

NIB	Exc.	V.G.	Good	Fair	Poor
1850	1450	1100	900	500	300

Super America

Fitted with AAA walnut stock, with 24 lpi checkering. Cheekpiece and ebony forend tip are standard. Barrel length 24", with no sights. Chambered for same calibers as Classic. Weight about 6.6 lbs.

NIB	Exc.	V.G.	Good	Fair	Poor
1880	1350	1000	650	320	180

Classic Select Grade

Similar to 8400 Classic, with hand-rubbed oil-finished select stock of Claro or French walnut. Introduced 2006.

NIB	Exc.	V.G.	Good	Fair	Poor
1100	900	700	480	300	150

Tactical

24" heavyweight match barrel, stippled black McMillan stock, third swivel for bipod. Chambered in .308 Winchester. Introduced in 2007.

NIB	Exc.	V.G.	Good	Fair	Poor
1650	1200	800	550	300	150

Advanced Tactical

Similar to Model 8400 Tactical, with KimPro II Dark Earth finish, fully-adjustable stock and hard case. Introduced in 2007.

NIB	Exc.	V.G.	Good	Fair	Poor
1800	1350	1000	650	320	180

Advanced Tactical II

Similar to above, with improved and enhanced features. Chambered in 6.5 Creedmoor, .308 Win. or .300 Win. Magnum, with Manners folding stock and adjustable comb, match-grade barrel with muzzle brake, oversized bolt knob, upper and lower Picatinny rails and KimPro II Desert Tan finish.

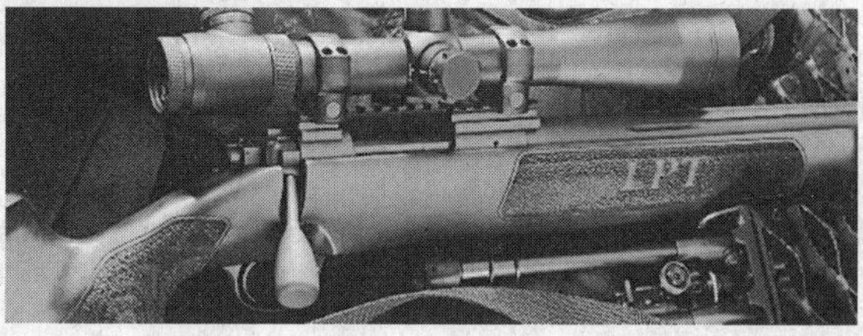

NIB	Exc.	V.G.	Good	Fair	Poor
3600	3000	2400	1750	800	500

Patrol Rifle

Bolt-action tactical rifle chambered in .308 Win. Features include 20" 1:12 fluted sightless matte blue heavy barrel; black epoxy-coated laminated wood stock, with 20 lpi panel checkering; pillar and glass bedding; Mauser claw extractor; 3-position M70-style safety; 5-round magazine; adjustable trigger.

NIB	Exc.	V.G.	Good	Fair	Poor
1300	1100	850	500	350	200

Patrol Tactical

Replacement for Patrol Rifle after 2013. Based on Model 8400 Magnum action. Chambered for .308 Win. or .300 Win. Magnum. Heavy contour and fluted 24" barrel, with match-grade chamber. Reinforced carbon fiber stock, with glass pillar bedding, Pachmayr Decelerator pad. Model 70-type 3-position safety and Mauser claw extractor.

NIB	Exc.	V.G.	Good	Fair	Poor
2000	1700	1300	900	600	300

AUGUSTA SHOTGUNS

Shotguns made in Italy for Kimber. Based on Boss-type action, each model fitted with H-Viz sights and Pachmayr Decelerator recoil pads. Back bored. Single-selective trigger and automatic ejectors. Introduced in 2002.

Sporting

Chambered for 12-gauge shell. Fitted with choice of barrel lengths from 28.5" to 32". Checkered walnut stock, with pistol grip and schnabel forearm. Blued finish, with silver frame. Weight about 7.75 lbs.

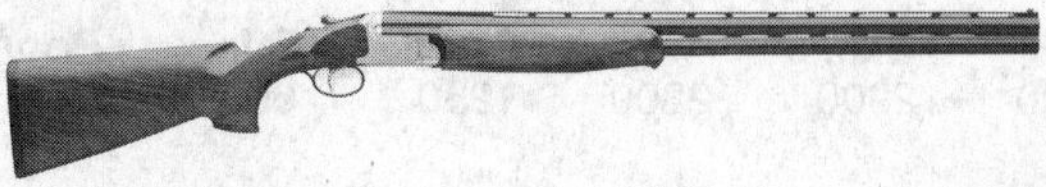

NIB	Exc.	V.G.	Good	Fair	Poor
5000	4500	3000	1750	600	300

Field

Chambered for 12-gauge shell. Choice of barrel lengths from 26" to 27.5". Checkered with pistol grip and beavertail forearm. Weight about 7 lbs.

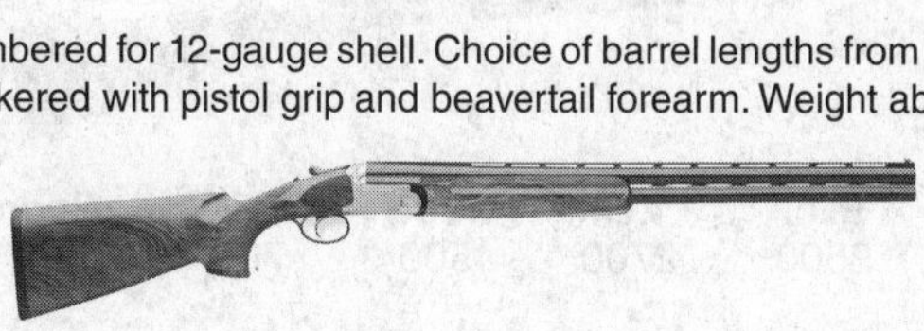

NIB	Exc.	V.G.	Good	Fair	Poor
4750	3900	2650	1500	480	220

Trap

12-gauge offered in barrel lengths from 30" to 34". Beavertail forearm. Wide ramped ventilated rib. Weight about 7.75 lbs.

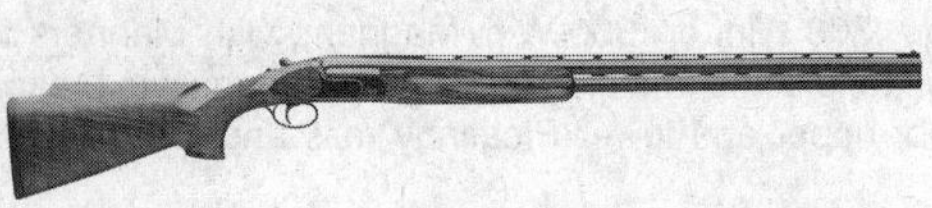

NIB	Exc.	V.G.	Good	Fair	Poor
5200	4700	3000	1750	600	300

Skeet

12-gauge gun. Choice of 26" or 27.5" barrels fitted with 11mm flat rib. Checkered walnut stock, with beavertail forearm. Weight about 7.5 lbs.

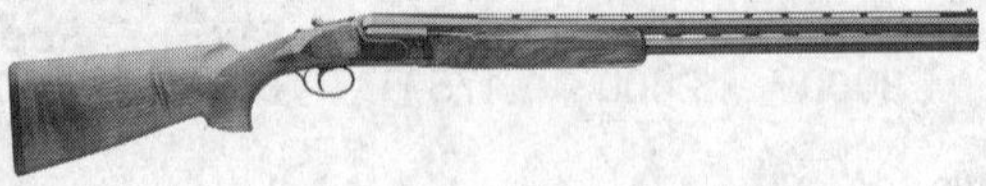

NIB	Exc.	V.G.	Good	Fair	Poor
5200	4700	3000	1750	600	300

VALIER SHOTGUNS

Side-by-side guns introduced into Kimber line in 2005.

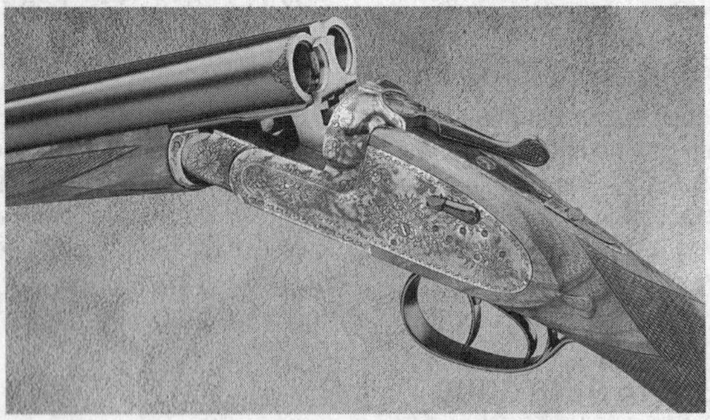

Grade I

Light-weight properly-scaled side-by-side in 16- and 20-gauge. Double triggers and extractors. Choked IC and Mod. Color case-hardened receiver, straight stock and splinter forend. Hand-checkered wood at 24 lpi. Chambered for: 2.75" shells 16-gauge; 3" shells 20-gauge.

NIB	Exc.	V.G.	Good	Fair	Poor
3300	2900	2300	1250	600	300

Grade II

Similar to Valier Grade I, with higher grade wood. Choice of color case blued or bone charcoal receiver in 20-gauge; bone charcoal only in 16-gauge. Automatic ejectors.

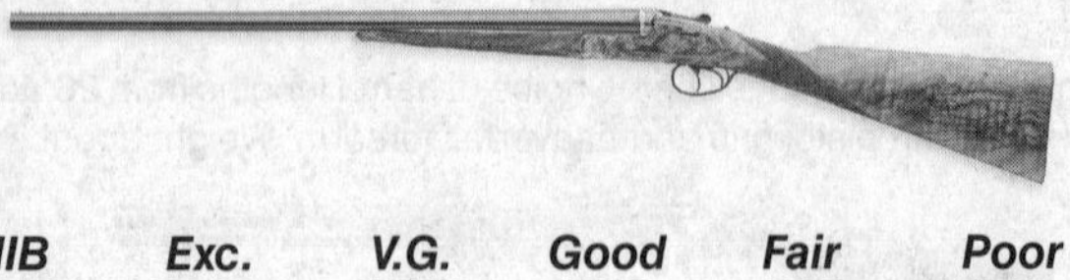

NIB	Exc.	V.G.	Good	Fair	Poor
4900	3500	2700	1500	700	300

MARIAS SHOTGUNS

Grade I

Single trigger sidelock over/under, features scroll hand engraving and bone charcoal case colors, with 24 lpi checkered wood. Grade I available with 28" barrels and Prince of Wales stock in 12- and 20-gauge. Chambered for 3" shells. Automatic ejectors. Comes with 5 choke tubes.

NIB	Exc.	V.G.	Good	Fair	Poor
4600	3300	2300	1200	600	300

Grade II

Similar to Marias Grade I, with higher grade wood. Available in 12-gauge with PW stock or 20-gauge with PW or straight stock in 26", 28" or 30" barrels.

NIB	Exc.	V.G.	Good	Fair	Poor
4900	3500	2700	1500	700	300

CLASSIC .45 PISTOLS

CUSTOM SERIES

First introduced in 1996. A quality built American-made 1911 designed by Chip McCormick for Kimber. Note: In 2001, Kimber phased in a new safety system on its pistols: Kimber firing pin safety. Models with this new firing pin safety will bear designation "II" as part of their model name.

Custom

Barrel length 5", with black oxide finish fixed sights. Black synthetic grips. Magazine capacity 8 rounds. Weight about 38 oz. Note: Add $100 for night sights.

NIB	Exc.	V.G.	Good	Fair	Poor
850	750	650	480	300	150

Custom II

Note: Add $10 for walnut grips; $100 for night sights. For Two-Tone, NIB: 1140.

NIB	Exc.	V.G.	Good	Fair	Poor
820	680	500	380	250	120

Custom Heritage Edition

Chambered for .45 ACP cartridge. Fitted with 5" barrel. Magazine capacity 7 rounds. Checkered front strap, ambidextrous thumb safety, aluminum trigger, hand-checkered rosewood grips, special edition markings on slide. Sights are low-profile fixed. Weight about 38 oz. Introduced in 2000.

NIB	Exc.	V.G.	Good	Fair	Poor
1150	950	700	500	300	150

Custom Stainless II

Similar to Custom in stainless steel. Made in .45 ACP, .38 Super, 9mm and .40 S&W. Note: Add $100 for night sights.

NIB	Exc.	V.G.	Good	Fair	Poor
1000	800	650	480	300	150

Stainless Limited Edition

Similar to Custom Stainless, except for black thumb release, black grip safety, black magazine release button and black barrel bushing. Limited to approximately 1,200 pistols.

NIB	Exc.	V.G.	Good	Fair	Poor
1200	950	780	580	350	150

Custom Target

Custom Target has same features as Custom, with addition of adjustable rear sight.

NIB	Exc.	V.G.	Good	Fair	Poor
820	680	500	380	250	120

Custom TLE II (Tactical Law Enforcement)

Introduced in 2003. Features Meprolight three-dot night sights and 30 lpi checkering on front strap. Magazine capacity 7 rounds. Weight about 38 oz. Note: Add $135 for stainless steel version offered in 2004.

NIB	Exc.	V.G.	Good	Fair	Poor
900	700	500	380	250	120

Custom TLE/RL II

Similar to TLE, with addition of an integral tactical rail. Weight about 39 oz. Introduced in 2004.

NIB	Exc.	V.G.	Good	Fair	Poor
1050	820	680	450	300	150

Stainless II

Chambered for .45 ACP or .40 S&W cartridge. Fitted with 5" barrel and fixed low profile sights. Both frame and slide are satin stainless steel. Magazine capacity: .45 ACP 7 rounds; .40 S&W 8 rounds. Weight about 38 oz.

NIB	Exc.	V.G.	Good	Fair	Poor
860	650	450	280	150	100

Stainless II (polished)

As above, chambered for .38 Super cartridge. Frame and slide are polished stainless steel. Magazine capacity 9 rounds. Weight about 38 oz. Introduced in 2005.

NIB	Exc.	V.G.	Good	Fair	Poor
1150	950	700	500	300	150

Stainless Ultra TLE II

1911-style semi-automatic pistol chambered in .45 ACP. Features include 7-round magazine; full length guide rod; aluminum frame with stainless slide; satin silver finish; checkered frontstrap; 3" barrel; tactical gray double diamond grips; tritium 3-dot night sights.

NIB	Exc.	V.G.	Good	Fair	Poor
1000	900	750	650	500	400

Stainless Target II

Chambered for .45 ACP or .38 Super cartridge, with slide and frame machined from stainless steel. Weight 38 oz.

NIB	Exc.	V.G.	Good	Fair	Poor
980	750	600	400	250	120

Stainless Target II 9mm/10mm

As above, chambered for 9mm or 10mm cartridge. Magazine capacity: 9mm 9-rounds; 10mm 8-rounds. Both pistols produced on a one-run basis only, with production in low hundreds. Introduced in 2003.

NIB	Exc.	V.G.	Good	Fair	Poor
1150	950	700	500	300	150

Stainless Target II (polished)

As above, chambered for .38 Super cartridge. Frame and slide are polished stainless steel. Magazine capacity 9 rounds. Weight about 38 oz.

Introduced in 2005.

NIB	Exc.	V.G.	Good	Fair	Poor
1200	950	780	580	350	150

Stainless Target Limited Edition

Similar to Stainless Target, with black thumb safety, black grip safety, black slide release and black barrel bushing. Limited to approximately 700 pistols. Introduced in 1998.

NIB	Exc.	V.G.	Good	Fair	Poor
900	700	500	380	250	120

Custom Royal

Has all the features of Custom, plus high polish blue finish, hand-checkered walnut grips and long guide rod.

NIB	Exc.	V.G.	Good	Fair	Poor
900	700	500	380	250	120

Custom Royal II

NIB	Exc.	V.G.	Good	Fair	Poor
1500	1100	750	400	250	120

Custom TLE/RL II Special Edition

.45 ACP pistol fitted with 5" barrel and fixed night sights. Steel frame and slide, with tactical accessory rail on frame. Black rubber grips. Black matte finish. Magazine capacity 7 rounds. Weight about 38 oz. Introduced in 2003.

NIB	Exc.	V.G.	Good	Fair	Poor
1150	950	700	500	300	150

Warrior

Introduced in 2005. Chambered for .45 ACP cartridge. Fitted with 5" barrel with night sights. Grips are Kimber G-10 Tactical, with lanyard loop. Accessory rail on frame. KimPro finish. Magazine capacity 7 rounds. Weight about 39 oz.

NIB	Exc.	V.G.	Good	Fair	Poor
1200	950	780	580	350	150

Desert Warrior

Similar to Warrior, with desert tan finish and lighter tan G10 tactical grips.

NIB	Exc.	V.G.	Good	Fair	Poor
1200	950	780	580	350	150

25th ANNIVERSARY LIMITED EDITIONS

Anniversary Custom

Introduced in 2004. Limited edition of 1,911 pistols. Chambered for .45 ACP cartridge. Select walnut grips. Serial numbered: KAPC0001-KAPC1911.

NIB	Exc.	V.G.	Good	Fair	Poor
850	650	450	280	150	100

Anniversary Gold Match

Limited to 500 pistols in .45 ACP. Serial numbered KAPG0001-KAPG0500.

NIB	Exc.	V.G.	Good	Fair	Poor
1200	950	780	580	350	150

Anniversary Match Pair Custom

Matched pair of Custom pistols in .45 ACP. Matching serial numbers and presentation case. Limited to 250 pairs.

NIB	Exc.	V.G.	Good	Fair	Poor
2500	2100	—	—	—	—

GOLD MATCH SERIES

Gold Match

All features of Custom Royal, plus BoMar adjustable sights and fancy checkered diamond grips.

NIB	Exc.	V.G.	Good	Fair	Poor
1200	950	780	580	350	150

Gold Match II

NIB	Exc.	V.G.	Good	Fair	Poor
1200	950	780	580	400	150

Stainless Gold Match

Similar to Gold Match, except slide and frame are stainless steel. Introduced in 1998.

NIB	Exc.	V.G.	Good	Fair	Poor
1200	950	780	580	350	150

Gold Team Match II

Introduced in 2003. This .45 ACP 5" barrel model features stainless steel slide and frame along with Kimber Tactical Extractor with loaded chamber indicator. Front strap checkered 30 lpi and grips are red, white and blue. USA Shooting Team logo. Weight about 38 oz.

NIB	Exc.	V.G.	Good	Fair	Poor
1350	1220	950	580	400	150

Team Match II .38 Super

As above, without external extractor. Limited production run. Introduced in 2003.

NIB	Exc.	V.G.	Good	Fair	Poor
1600	1300	1000	580	400	150

TEN II SERIES

In 2002, Polymer series pistols were upgraded to Ten II series. Added features: firing pin block safety; Kimber-made frame of improved dimensions; external extractor. Original Polymer pistol magazines of 10 and 14 rounds will interchange with newer Ten II Series pistols.

Polymer

Features polymer frame, with matte black oxide slide. Sights are McCormick low profile. Barrel length 5"; overall length 8.75"; weight about 34 oz. One 14-round magazine supplied with gun when new.

NIB	Exc.	V.G.	Good	Fair	Poor
700	600	550	400	200	100

Polymer Stainless

Similar to Polymer model, with stainless steel slide. Weight about 34 oz.

NIB	Exc.	V.G.	Good	Fair	Poor
750	650	550	420	220	120

Polymer Target

Introduced in 1998. Has matte black oxide slide, with adjustable sights and 14-round magazine. Weight about 34 oz.

NIB	Exc.	V.G.	Good	Fair	Poor
950	780	620	450	240	150

Polymer Stainless Target

Same as above, with stainless steel slide. Introduced in 1998.

NIB	Exc.	V.G.	Good	Fair	Poor
950	780	620	450	240	150

Polymer Pro Carry Stainless

Chambered for .45 ACP cartridge, with 4" barrel. McCormick Low Profile sights. Stainless steel slide, with black polymer frame. Weight about 32 oz. Magazine capacity 14 rounds. Introduced in 1999.

NIB	Exc.	V.G.	Good	Fair	Poor
750	680	550	400	200	100

Polymer Stainless Gold Match

Similar to Polymer Gold Match, with addition of stainless steel slide. Chambered for several calibers: .45 ACP; 9mm; .38 Super; .40 S&W. Weight about 34 oz.

NIB	Exc.	V.G.	Good	Fair	Poor
1000	850	780	580	350	150

Pro Carry Ten II

.45 ACP model features 4" bull barrel, with no barrel bushing. Stainless steel slide. Weight about 28 oz.

NIB	Exc.	V.G.	Good	Fair	Poor
850	680	550	400	200	100

Ultra Ten CDP II

Introduced in 2003. Features night sights and rounded edges. Fitted with 3" bull barrel. Chambered for .45 ACP. Weight about 24 oz.

NIB	Exc.	V.G.	Good	Fair	Poor
900	800	700	580	350	150

Gold Match Ten II

.45 ACP 5" barrel model has all standard features of Gold Match. Black polymer frame and blued steel slide. Magazine capacity 14 rounds. Weight about 34 oz.

NIB	Exc.	V.G.	Good	Fair	Poor
1200	950	780	580	350	150

BP Ten II

.45 ACP pistol has 5" barrel and 10-round magazine. Steel slide with polymer frame. Fixed sights. Black matte finish. Weight about 30 oz. Introduced in 2003.

NIB	Exc.	V.G.	Good	Fair	Poor
750	680	550	400	200	100

Pro BP Ten II

As above, with 4" barrel. Weight about 31 oz. Introduced in 2003.

NIB	Exc.	V.G.	Good	Fair	Poor
750	680	550	400	200	100

COMPACT SERIES

Compact

Steel frame and slide. Pistols fitted with 4" bull barrel and shortened grip (.4" shorter than full size). Offered in .45 ACP. Finish is matte black oxide. Grips are black synthetic. Overall length 7.7"; weight about 43 oz. Introduced in 1998.

NIB	Exc.	V.G.	Good	Fair	Poor
680	550	400	300	200	100

Compact Aluminum

Same appearance as Compact, with aluminum frame. Matte black finish. Weight about 28 oz. Introduced in 1998.

NIB	Exc.	V.G.	Good	Fair	Poor
680	550	400	300	200	100

Compact Stainless

Same as Compact model, with stainless steel slide and frame. Offered in both .45 ACP and .40 S&W. Introduced in 1998.

NIB	Exc.	V.G.	Good	Fair	Poor
850	680	550	400	200	100

Compact Stainless II

NIB	Exc.	V.G.	Good	Fair	Poor
900	680	500	380	250	120

Compact Stainless Aluminum

Offered in both .45 ACP and .40 S&W. Features 4" barrel, with stainless steel slide and aluminum frame. Weight about 28 oz. Note: Add $25 for .40 S&W.

NIB	Exc.	V.G.	Good	Fair	Poor
750	600	480	300	200	100

PRO CARRY

Pro Carry II

Introduced in 1998. This .45 ACP or .40 S&W model features full-size aluminum frame and 4" slide and bull barrel. Other features are match-grade trigger, beveled magazine well, full-length guide rod, low-profile combat sights and 7-round magazine. Finish is matte black oxide. Weight about 28 oz. In 2005, was offered in 9mm. For Two-Tone, NIB: 1140.

NIB	Exc.	V.G.	Good	Fair	Poor
850	680	550	400	200	100

Pro Carry II Night Sights

As above fitted with night sights.

NIB	Exc.	V.G.	Good	Fair	Poor
750	680	600	420	250	150

Pro Carry Stainless

Same as Pro Carry, with stainless steel slide. Note: Add $50 for .38 Super

NIB	Exc.	V.G.	Good	Fair	Poor
850	700	550	400	200	100

Pro Carry Stainless Night Sights

As above fitted with night sights.

NIB	Exc.	V.G.	Good	Fair	Poor
950	750	620	450	280	180

Pro TLE/RL II

Introduced in 2005. Features .45 ACP, with 4" barrel and night sights. Slide and frame are steel, with steel finish. Accessory rail on frame. Magazine capacity 7 rounds. Weight about 36 oz.

NIB	Exc.	V.G.	Good	Fair	Poor
1150	950	700	500	300	150

Stainless Pro TLE/RL II

As above, with stainless steel frame and slide. Introduced in 2005.

NIB	Exc.	V.G.	Good	Fair	Poor
1250	920	750	520	350	180

Super Carry Pro

1911-style semi-automatic pistol, chambered in .45 ACP. Features include 8-round magazine; ambidextrous thumb safety; carry melt profiling; full length guide rod; aluminum frame with stainless slide; satin silver finish; super carry serrations; 4" barrel; micarta laminated grips; tritium night sights.

NIB	Exc.	V.G.	Good	Fair	Poor
1300	1120	950	500	300	200

Pro TLE II TFS

This TLE II variation is Threaded For Suppression (TFS). In .45 ACP with 4.5" barrel.

NIB	Exc.	V.G.	Good	Fair	Poor
1050	900	750	600	400	200

Sapphire Pro II

A 9mm limited edition model with 4" barrel, engraving accents on the bright blue polished stainless slide, G-10 grips and 3-dot night sights. Introduced in 2015.

NIB	Exc.	V.G.	Good	Fair	Poor
1500	1300	—	—	—	—

SUPER CARRY SERIES

Super Carry Custom HD

.45 Carry Pro pistols, feature stainless steel slide and frame, match-grade barrel and bushing, ambidextrous thumb safety, beavertail tang, directional serrations on slide, mainspring housing and front strap. Other features include night sights, 8-round magazine, rounded heel and "melt" treatment for easy carrying. Weight 38 oz., 5" barrel and KimPro finish. Super Carry Pro has 4" barrel, Ultra has 3" and 6-round magazine. Introduced in 2011.

NIB	Exc.	V.G.	Good	Fair	Poor
1400	1200	1000	750	300	200

Super Carry Ultra Plus

Combines full-size round-heel frame of Carry Pro, with short slide and 3" barrel of Carry Ultra. Light-weight alloy frame reduces weight to 25 oz., with 8-round magazine. Introduced in 2011.

NIB	Exc.	V.G.	Good	Fair	Poor
1350	1150	960	720	300	200

Solo Carry STS

Micro compact pistol designed for concealed carry. Single-action striker fired 9mm, with stainless steel slide, alloy frame, 6-round magazine, ambidextrous thumb safety and magazine release. Weight 17 oz.; barrel length 2.7"; width 1.2"; overall length 5.5". Finish is KimPro or bright stainless. Mfg. 2011-2017. Note: Add $355 for CDP model, add $80 for DC model, add $400 for Sapphire model.

NIB	Exc.	V.G.	Good	Fair	Poor
700	620	530	390	330	260

ULTRA CARRY II SERIES

Ultra Carry

Chambered for .45 ACP or .40 S&W cartridge. Fitted with 3" barrel and McCormick low profile sights. Grips are black synthetic. Magazine capacity 7 rounds. Weight about 25 oz. Black oxide finish. Introduced in 1999. Note: Add $100 for night sights.

NIB	Exc.	V.G.	Good	Fair	Poor
760	600	480	350	200	100

Ultra Carry II

For Two-Tone, NIB: 1180.

NIB	Exc.	V.G.	Good	Fair	Poor
800	620	500	380	220	120

Ultra Carry Stainless

Same as above, with stainless steel slide. Note: Add $25 for .40 S&W model; $100 for night sights.

NIB	Exc.	V.G.	Good	Fair	Poor
850	650	520	400	240	140

Ultra Carry Stainless II

NIB	Exc.	V.G.	Good	Fair	Poor
880	680	550	420	260	150

Micro Carry

Semi-automatic single-action in .380 ACP. Stainless steel slide with aluminum frame, 1911-style controls with ambidextrous thumb safety. Capacity 6+1. Low-profile 3-dot night sights. Crimson Trace laser grips available (CDP model). Introduced in 2013. Note: Add $200 for CT grips; $300 for Sapphire bright polished blue finish.

NIB	Exc.	V.G.	Good	Fair	Poor
500	420	350	300	220	180

Micro 9

Caliber: 9mm. Capacity: 7-round magazine. Barrel: 3.15 in. Weight: 15.6 oz. Features: The easily concealed Micro 9 features mild recoil, smooth trigger pull and the intuitive operation of a 1911 platform. Micro 9 slides are made to the tightest allowable tolerances, with barrels machined from stainless steel for superior resistance to moisture. All Micro 9 frames are shaped from the finest aluminum for integrity and strength. Lowered and flared ejection ports for flawless ejection and a beveled magazine well for fast, positive loading. In 2020, Kimber offered 15 different Micro 9 models with a total of 26 variations.

NIB	Exc.	V.G.	Good	Fair	Poor
580	500	420	320	250	200

Micro Raptor

Enhanced variation of Micro Carry, with match grade trigger, carry-melt treatment, Zebra wood grips with scale pattern and satin silver or black finish.

NIB	Exc.	V.G.	Good	Fair	Poor
880	750	600	450	350	300

Collector Edition Raptor 1911

Calibers: .45 ACP Capacity: 7- or 8-round magazine. Barrels: 3.15, 3.16 or 5 in. Weight: 15.6–38 oz. Grips: G10 smooth/scaled texture. Sights: Low profile, tritium. Finish: Two-tone bronze. Features: Scale-style slide serrations. Made in the Kimber Custom Shop.

NIB	Exc.	V.G.	Good	Fair	Poor
1500	1250	1000	—	—	—

Collector Edition Raptor Micro 9

Calibers: 9mm Capacity: 7- or 8-round magazine. Barrels: 3.15, 3.16 or 5 in. Weight: 15.6–38 oz. Grips: G10 smooth/scaled texture. Sights: Low profile, tritium. Finish: Two-tone bronze. Features: Scale-style slide serrations. Made in the Kimber Custom Shop.

NIB	Exc.	V.G.	Good	Fair	Poor
950	800	680	—	—	—

Collector Edition Raptor EVO

Calibers: 9mm Capacity: 7- or 8-round magazine. Barrels: 3.15, 3.16 or 5 in. Weight: 15.6–38 oz. Grips: G10 smooth/scaled texture. Sights: Low profile, tritium. Finish: Two-tone bronze. Features: Scale-style slide serrations. Made in the Kimber Custom Shop.

NIB	Exc.	V.G.	Good	Fair	Poor
1000	850	730	—	—	—

Warrior SOC

Full-size 1911-style semi-automatic in .45 ACP. Stainless steel frame, slide, barrel and bushing. Tactical Wedge night sights, Crimson Trace Rail Master laser sights included. Tan/green KimPro finish, textured G-10 grips, lanyard ring.

NIB	Exc.	V.G.	Good	Fair	Poor
1400	1200	1050	850	600	—

Master Carry Series

Semi-automatic 1911-style pistol in .45 ACP. Offered in three sizes: Custom (5" barrel); Pro (4"); Carry (3"). Stainless frame on Custom; aluminum on Pro and Carry. Crimson Trace laser grips included. Other features include 3-dot Tactical Wedge night sights, KimPro II finish, rounded heel grip. Introduced in 2013.

NIB	Exc.	V.G.	Good	Fair	Poor
1420	1220	1100	900	650	—

EVO SP Series

Micro compact pistol designed for concealed carry. Striker fired 9mm, with 3.16-in. barrel, steel slide, alloy frame, 7-round magazine. Weight 19 oz.; overall length 6.1". Finish stainless slide black frame. Introduced 2018. Note: Add $100 for CS model, deduct $20 for TLE model.

NIB	Exc.	V.G.	Good	Fair	Poor
800	700	600	460	360	300

CUSTOM SHOP PISTOLS

Super Jagare

A 10mm model from Kimber Custom Shop designed for hunting. Features include 6" barrel, rounded-heel frame, DeltaPoint Pro optic, Super Carry front strap checkering pattern, Super Carry pattern flattop slide and complete carry melt treatment. Introduced in 2017.

NIB	Exc.	V.G.	Good	Fair	Poor
2400	2100	1850	—	—	—

Centennial Edition 1911

Highly artistic 1911-style semi-automatic pistol, chambered in .45 ACP. Features include color case-hardened steel frame; extended thumb safety; charcoal-blue finished steel slide; 5" match-grade barrel; special serial number; solid smooth ivory grips; nitre blue pins; adjustable sights; presentation case. Edition limited to 250 units. Finished by Doug Turnbull Restoration.

NIB	Exc.	V.G.	Good	Fair	Poor
4000	3600	3200	—	—	—

Royal Carry

Limited edition of 600 pistols. Chambered for .45 ACP. Fitted with 4" barrel with night sights. Hand-checkered rosewood grips. Steel slide and aluminum frame. High polish blue finish. Magazine capacity 7 rounds. Weight about 28 oz. Introduced in 1998.

NIB	Exc.	V.G.	Good	Fair	Poor
1000	800	650	480	300	150

Elite Carry

Introduced in 1998. Limited to 1,200 Custom Shop pistols. Chambered for .45 ACP, with 4" barrel and night sights. Frame aluminum, with black oxide finish. Slide steel, with stainless steel finish. Ambidextrous extended thumb safety, checkered front strap, match trigger and hand-checkered rosewood grips. Magazine capacity 7 rounds. Weight about 28 oz.

NIB	Exc.	V.G.	Good	Fair	Poor
1000	800	650	480	300	150

Gold Guardian

Limited edition custom shop pistols to 300 units. Chambered for .45 ACP. Fitted with 5" barrel, with fixed night sights. Stainless steel slide and frame. Ambidextrous extended thumb safety, match-grade barrel, extended magazine well, match trigger, special markings and serial number. Magazine capacity 8 rounds; weight about 38 oz. Introduced in 1998.

NIB	Exc.	V.G.	Good	Fair	Poor
1500	1200	950	580	400	150

Combat Carry

Chambered for .45 ACP or .40 S&W cartridge, with 4" barrel. Many custom features and special markings. Stainless steel slide and blued frame. Night sights standard. Weight about 28 oz. Introduced in 1999.

NIB	Exc.	V.G.	Good	Fair	Poor
1050	850	680	500	320	160

Gold Combat

Full-size pistol chambered for .45 ACP cartridge. Many custom features. Night sights standard. Special markings. Weight about 38 oz. Blued slide and frame. Introduced in 1999.

NIB	Exc.	V.G.	Good	Fair	Poor
1680	1250	920	700	350	180

Gold Combat II

NIB	Exc.	V.G.	Good	Fair	Poor
1730	1300	920	750	420	200

Gold Combat Stainless

Same as above, with stainless steel slide.

NIB	Exc.	V.G.	Good	Fair	Poor
1720	1300	920	750	420	200

Gold Combat Stainless II

NIB	Exc.	V.G.	Good	Fair	Poor
1680	1250	920	700	350	180

Super Match

Kimber's most accurate .45 ACP pistol. Fitted with 5" barrel and many special features. Adjustable sights. Weight about 38 oz. Stainless steel slide and frame, with two-tone finish. Introduced in 1999.

NIB	Exc.	V.G.	Good	Fair	Poor
1920	1500	900	600	350	180

Super Match II

NIB	Exc.	V.G.	Good	Fair	Poor
1980	1550	900	600	350	180

LTP II

Designed for limited pistol competition. Fitted with external extractor, 5" barrel with tungsten guide rod, flattop serrated slide with adjustable sights, extended and beveled magazine well holding 10 rounds. Front strap has 20 lpi checkering. Weight about 38 oz.

NIB	Exc.	V.G.	Good	Fair	Poor
2100	1580	920	620	380	200

Raptor II

Introduced in 2005. This .45 ACP features 5" barrel with night sights. Blued finished. Scale serrations on front strap and slide, with scaled zebra wood grips. Magazine capacity 8 rounds. Weight about 38 oz.

NIB	Exc.	V.G.	Good	Fair	Poor
1220	920	750	520	350	180

Pro Raptor II

Similar to Raptor II, except a 4" barrel. Weight about 35 oz. Introduced in 2005.

NIB	Exc.	V.G.	Good	Fair	Poor
1100	820	700	500	300	120

Grand Raptor II

.45 ACP pistol, with 5" match-grade stainless steel barrel and adjustable night sights. Black aluminum trigger and rosewood grips. Slide serrations are lizard scale. Stainless steel frame. Slide is matte black and engraved with Custom Shop logo.

NIB	Exc.	V.G.	Good	Fair	Poor
1500	1200	950	580	400	150

Ultra Raptor II

.45 ACP model features 3" ramped match-grade bushing-less bull barrel. Fixed night sights. Ambidextrous thumb safety. Lizard scale slide serrations. Introduced in 2005.

NIB	Exc.	V.G.	Good	Fair	Poor
1250	920	750	520	350	180

Ultra RCP II

Introduced in 2003. Features 3" barrel, aluminum frame and sight rail. Chambered for .45 ACP cartridge. Magazine capacity 7 rounds. Weight 26 oz. No longer in production.

NIB	Exc.	V.G.	Good	Fair	Poor
1300	980	800	550	370	200

Gold Combat RL II

Similar to above model, with premium trigger, KimPro finish and rosewood grips. Magazine capacity 8 rounds. Weight about 38 oz. Introduced in 2003.

NIB	Exc.	V.G.	Good	Fair	Poor
1780	1320	1100	700	420	240

Target Match

Limited edition of 1,000 pistols. Chambered for .45 ACP cartridge. Matte black frame, with adjustable sights. Match-grade barrel and chamber. Solid aluminum trigger. Checkered front strap and underside of trigger-guard. Special serial numbers: KTM0001-KTM1000. Introduced in 2005.

NIB	Exc.	V.G.	Good	Fair	Poor
1400	1050	880	650	400	180

Super America

Billed as Kimber's ultimate top-of-the-line custom 1911. Polished matte blue finish, scroll engraving, mammoth ivory grips, presentation case with matching sheath knife. Introduced 2007.

NIB	Exc.	V.G.	Good	Fair	Poor
3000	2250	1700	1000	600	220

CDP SERIES (Custom Defense Package)

Ultra CDP

Custom shop model features 3" barrel, night sights, hand-checkered rosewood grips and numerous other features. Stainless steel slide and matte black frame. Chambered for .45 ACP cartridge. Magazine capacity 6 rounds. Weight about 25 oz. Introduced in 2000.

NIB	Exc.	V.G.	Good	Fair	Poor
1100	820	700	500	300	120

Ultra CDP II

Compact 1911-style semi-automatic pistol, chambered in .45 ACP. Features include 7-round magazine; ambidextrous thumb safety; carry "melt" profiling; full-length guide rod; aluminum frame with stainless slide; satin silver finish; checkered front strap; 3" barrel; rosewood double diamond Crimson Trace Lasergrips; tritium 3-dot night sights.

NIB	Exc.	V.G.	Good	Fair	Poor
1550	1350	850	520	350	180

Compact CDP

Introduced in 2000. Features 4" bull barrel, night sights, hand-checkered rosewood grips and other custom features. Stainless steel slide and matte black frame. Chambered for .45 ACP cartridge. Magazine capacity 6 rounds. Weight about 28 oz.

NIB	Exc.	V.G.	Good	Fair	Poor
1200	950	780	580	350	150

Compact CDP II

NIB	Exc.	V.G.	Good	Fair	Poor
1250	1000	800	600	350	150

Pro CDP

Similar to Compact CDP, with full length grip. Magazine capacity 7 rounds. Weight about 28 oz. Introduced in 2000.

NIB	Exc.	V.G.	Good	Fair	Poor
1100	820	700	500	300	120

Pro CDP II

NIB	Exc.	V.G.	Good	Fair	Poor
1180	900	780	550	350	150

Custom CDP

.45 ACP full-size pistol fitted with 5" match-grade barrel. Stainless steel slide, with front and rear beveled serrations. Matte black steel frame, with checkered rosewood grips. Night sights standard. Introduced in 2001.

NIB	Exc.	V.G.	Good	Fair	Poor
1200	950	780	580	350	150

Custom CDP II

NIB	Exc.	V.G.	Good	Fair	Poor
1250	1000	800	600	380	160

ECLIPSE II SERIES

Eclipse Custom II

Chambered for .45 ACP cartridge. Fitted with 5" barrel and match-grade bushing. Fixed night sights. Magazine capacity 8 rounds. Weight about 38 oz. Introduced in 2002. In 2005, offered in 10mm. Note: Add $110 for 10mm.

NIB	Exc.	V.G.	Good	Fair	Poor
1180	900	780	550	350	150

Eclipse Target II

Similar to Eclipse Custom II, with addition of adjustable night sights. Introduced in 2002.

NIB	Exc.	V.G.	Good	Fair	Poor
1200	950	780	580	350	150

Eclipse Ultra II

.45 ACP pistol with 3" barrel. Slide machined from stainless steel forging. Front strap checkering. Fixed night sights. Magazine capacity 7 rounds. Weight about 34 oz. Introduced in 2002.

NIB	Exc.	V.G.	Good	Fair	Poor
1100	820	700	500	300	120

Eclipse Pro II

Similar to Eclipse Ultra II. Features full-length grip frame and 4" barrel. Fixed night sights. Introduced in 2002.

NIB	Exc.	V.G.	Good	Fair	Poor
1100	820	700	500	300	120

Eclipse Pro Target II

Similar to Eclipse Pro, with adjustable night sights. Introduced in 2002.

NIB	Exc.	V.G.	Good	Fair	Poor
1190	950	720	520	320	150

TACTICAL SERIES

Series of pistols introduced in 2003. Each pistol has 30 lpi checkering on front strap and under triggerguard, Meprolight three-dot night sights, extended and beveled magazine well, magazines with extended bumper pads, laminated grips and match-grade barrel and chamber.

Tactical Custom II

Chambered for .45 ACP cartridge. Fitted with 5" barrel. Magazine capacity 7 rounds. Weight about 31 oz.

NIB	Exc.	V.G.	Good	Fair	Poor
1250	1000	800	600	380	160

Tactical Pro II

Fitted with 4" barrel. Weight about 28 oz.

NIB	Exc.	V.G.	Good	Fair	Poor
1250	1000	800	600	380	160

Tactical Ultra II

Fitted with 3" barrel. Weight about 25 oz.

NIB	Exc.	V.G.	Good	Fair	Poor
1250	1000	800	600	380	160

COVERT SERIES

Custom Covert II

1911-style semi-automatic carry gun, chambered in .45 ACP. Aluminum frame finished in Desert Tan; steel slide in matte black. 5" barrel with 3-dot sights. Introduced in 2007.

NIB	Exc.	V.G.	Good	Fair	Poor
1500	1200	950	580	400	150

Pro Covert II

Similar to Custom Covert II, with 4" barrel. Introduced in 2007.

NIB	Exc.	V.G.	Good	Fair	Poor
1500	1200	950	580	400	150

Ultra Covert II

Similar to Pro Covert II, with 3" barrel. Introduced 2007.

NIB	Exc.	V.G.	Good	Fair	Poor
1300	980	800	550	370	200

AEGIS SERIES

Pro Aegis II

1911-style semi-automatic carry gun, chambered in 9mm Parabellum. Frame finished in matte aluminum; steel slide in matte black. 4" bull barrel with 3-dot sights. Introduced in 2007.

NIB	Exc.	V.G.	Good	Fair	Poor
1000	800	650	480	300	150

Custom Aegis II

Full-size 1911-style semi-automatic carry gun, chambered in 9mm Parabellum. Aluminum frame finished in matte aluminum; steel slide in matte black. 5" bull barrel with 3-dot sights. Introduced in 2007.

NIB	Exc.	V.G.	Good	Fair	Poor
1100	820	700	500	300	120

Ultra Aegis II

Similar to Pro Aegis II, with 4" barrel. Introduced in 2007.

NIB	Exc.	V.G.	Good	Fair	Poor
1100	820	700	500	300	120

Ultra Onyx II Special Edition

Limited edition model has a deep black Onyx PVD coating and custom engraving. In .45 or 9mm. Features include a rounded heel with ball-milled grooves on front strap, mainspring housing and thin Micarta grips. Barrel length 3", with Tritium night sights. Introduced in 2015.

NIB	Exc.	V.G.	Good	Fair	Poor
1500	1300	—	—	—	—

Aegis Elite Custom OI

This model comes equipped with a Vortex Optics Venom 6MOA red dot sight. Chambered in .45 ACP or 9mm. Barrel is 5" (Elite Pro 4"; Elite Ultra 3"). Green, black and gray G10 grips, rounded heel frame. Other features include 24 lpi front strap checkering, distinctive rear and front slide serrations, KimPro II gray finish and premium aluminum trigger. Introduced in 2018.

NIB	Exc.	V.G.	Good	Fair	Poor
1150	1050	1000	—	—	—

KHX Series

Introduced in 2018. This 9mm or .45 ACP features 5" barrel with night sights. Gray finish. Hexagonal serrations on slide, with Hogue Enhanced MagGrip G10 Grips and mainspring housing. Weight about 38 oz. Note: Deduct $150 for OR (Optic Ready) model.

NIB	Exc.	V.G.	Good	Fair	Poor
1080	960	800	600	500	400

KHX Pro

Introduced in 2018. This 9mm or .45 ACP features 4" barrel with night sights. Gray finish. Hexagonal serrations on slide, with Hogue Enhanced MagGrip G10 Grips and mainspring housing. Weight about 35 oz. Note: Deduct $150 for OR (Optic Ready) model.

NIB	Exc.	V.G.	Good	Fair	Poor
1080	960	800	600	500	400

KHX Ultra

Introduced in 2018. This 9mm or .45 ACP features 3" barrel with night sights. Gray finish. Hexagonal serrations on slide, with Hogue Enhanced MagGrip G10 Grips and mainspring housing. Weight about 25 oz. Note: Deduct $150 for OR (Optic Ready) model.

NIB	Exc.	V.G.	Good	Fair	Poor
1080	960	800	600	500	400

K6 REVOLVER SERIES

Model K6s

Kimber's first revolver, a double-action-only .357 Magnum with 6-shot cylinder, 2" or 3" barrel, fixed sights, stainless steel frame, barrel with smooth satin finish and rubber or walnut grips. Weight about 23 oz. Introduced in 2016. CDP (Custom Defense Package) has superior ergonomics, match-grade trigger, black Diamond-Like Carbon frame, checkered rosewood grips and tritium night sights. DCR (Deluxe Carry Revolver) has same features as CDP, plus fiber optic front sight. LG model has Crimson Trace Lasergrips. Special First Edition model has high-grade mirror-polished finish and Pao Ferro wood grips.

NIB	Exc.	V.G.	Good	Fair	Poor
950	780	680	—	—	—

DCR

NIB	Exc.	V.G.	Good	Fair	Poor
900	820	700	—	—	—

CDP/DC/LG

NIB	Exc.	V.G.	Good	Fair	Poor
1060	950	800	—	—	—

First Edition

NIB	Exc.	V.G.	Good	Fair	Poor
1650	1400	1000	—	—	—

K6s DASA Target

Caliber: .357 Magnum. Capacity: 6 rounds. Barrel: 4 in. Grip: Walnut laminate, oversized. Sights: Fully adjustable rear, fiber-optic front. Features: The DASA is the next evolution of the K6s. The DASA is outfitted with a double- and single-action trigger mechanism. Kimber's K6s revolvers feature the purportedly smallest cylinder capable of housing 6 rounds of .357 Magnum at 1.39-inch diameter, making for a very slim and streamlined package.

NIB	Exc.	V.G.	Good	Fair	Poor
900	750	650	—	—	—

K6s DASA Combat

Caliber: .357 Magnum. Capacity: 6 rounds. Barrel: 4 in. Grip: Walnut laminate, oversized with finger grooves. Sights: Fixed front and rear with white dots. Features: The DASA Combat is outfitted with a double- and single-action trigger mechanism. Kimber's K6s DASA revolvers have a smooth no-stack double-action trigger and a crisp 3.25- to 4.25-lb. single-action pull. The K6s DASA revolvers are equipped with knurled hammer spur.

NIB	Exc.	V.G.	Good	Fair	Poor
850	730	610	—	—	—

K6s DASA Texas Edition

Caliber: .357 Magnum. Capacity: 6 rounds. Barrel: 2 in. Grip: Ivory G10. Sights: Fixed front and rear with white dots. Features: The Texas Edition is adorned with ivory G10 grips with the state motto, name and flag on this special edition. The satin finish has American Western cut scroll engraving on the barrel, frame and cylinder. The K6s DASA Texas Edition revolvers are equipped with knurled hammer spur.

NIB	Exc.	V.G.	Good	Fair	Poor
1230	1050	900	—	—	—

K6s Royal

Caliber: .357 Magnum. Capacity: 6 rounds. Barrel: 2 in. Grip: Walnut. Sights: Fixed brass-bead front and rear with white dots. Features: The K6s Royal features a 2-inch barrel for easy concealment. The dovetailed white-dot rear sight complements the brass-bead front sight. The Royal's stainless steel is hand polished to a high shine and a Dark Oil DLC is applied for a unique look.

NIB	Exc.	V.G.	Good	Fair	Poor
1300	1100	950	—	—	—

RIMFIRE SERIES

Rimfire Custom

Introduced in 2003. This .22-caliber pistol features 5" barrel, with fixed sights and 10-round magazine. Matte black or silver anodized finish. Weight about 23 oz.

NIB	Exc.	V.G.	Good	Fair	Poor
750	520	360	220	150	100

Rimfire Target

As above, with adjustable sights. In 2004, available in .17-caliber Mach 2.

NIB	Exc.	V.G.	Good	Fair	Poor
800	580	400	280	200	120

Rimfire Super

Introduced in 2004. Features serrated flattop slide, with flutes in upper corners, ambidextrous thumb safety, aluminum trigger and two-tone finish. Weight about 23 oz.

NIB	Exc.	V.G.	Good	Fair	Poor
1100	820	700	500	300	120

.22 LR Conversion Kit

Introduced in 1998. Kit features a complete upper assembly: slide, barrel, guide rod, shock buffer and 10-round magazine. Finish satin silver or satin blue. Will fit all Kimber 1911 .45 ACP models. In 2005, offered for .17 Mach 2 cartridge conversion.

NIB	Exc.	V.G.	Good	Fair	Poor
300	250	200	120	80	20

KING PIN

Unknown

See HYDE & SHATTUCK

KIRRIKALE, ENDUSTRISI

Ankara, Turkey

Kirrikale Pistol

7.65 or 9mm short caliber semi-automatic pistol, with 3.5" barrel and 6-shot magazine. Blued, with plastic grips. Slide marked "MKE"; and "Kirrikale Tufek Fb Cal.—". Imported by Firearms Center in Victoria, Texas and Mandall Shooting Supplies. An unauthorized copy of Walther PP, that was imported into U.S. briefly.

NIB	Exc.	V.G.	Good	Fair	Poor
450	350	280	220	150	100

KLEINGUENTHER/KDF, INC.

Kleinguenther Distinctive Firearms
Seguin, Texas

Condor

12-gauge boxlock over/under shotgun, with 28" barrels, ventilated ribs, single-selective trigger and automatic ejectors. Blued, with walnut stock. Manufactured in Italy.

NIB	Exc.	V.G.	Good	Fair	Poor
—	700	600	520	380	280

Brescia

A 12-gauge boxlock double-barrel shotgun, with 28" barrels, double triggers and extractors. Blued, with walnut stock. Manufactured in Italy.

NIB	Exc.	V.G.	Good	Fair	Poor
—	400	320	300	200	120

K-14 Insta Fire Rifle

Bolt-action sporting rifle, manufactured in a variety of calibers, with 24" or 26" barrels furnished without sights. Blued, with Monte Carlo-style walnut stock.

NIB	Exc.	V.G.	Good	Fair	Poor
—	1750	1350	1100	500	250

K-15

Similar to above, with 60-degree bolt angle and accurized barrel. Guaranteed to fire .5" group at 100 yards. Manufactured with a variety of optional features.

NIB	Exc.	V.G.	Good	Fair	Poor
—	1750	1350	1100	500	250

K-15 Pro-Hunter

As above, with matte blued or electroless nickel-plated and fiberglass stock.

NIB	Exc.	V.G.	Good	Fair	Poor
—	1750	1350	1100	500	250

K-15 Swat Rifle

7.62x54mm caliber bolt-action rifle, with 24" or 26" barrel. Furnished without sights. Parkerized finish and 4-shot magazine. Walnut stock.

NIB	Exc.	V.G.	Good	Fair	Poor
—	1800	1400	1150	700	350

K-15 Dangerous Game

As above in .411 KDF caliber.

NIB	Exc.	V.G.	Good	Fair	Poor
—	2500	2000	1300	1000	700

K-16

Bolt-action sporting rifle, manufactured in a variety of calibers, with 24" or 26" barrel. Furnished without sights, single stage adjustable trigger, accurized barrel and Dupont Rynite stock. Produced with a variety of optional features.

NIB	Exc.	V.G.	Good	Fair	Poor
—	1750	1350	1100	500	250

Titan Menor

.222- or .223-caliber bolt-action rifle, with 24" or 26" barrel. Furnished without sights. Monte Carlo-style or standard schnabel tipped walnut stock. Blued.

NIB	Exc.	V.G.	Good	Fair	Poor
—	1200	900	550	400	200

Titan II Standard

As above, with mid-sized action.

NIB	Exc.	V.G.	Good	Fair	Poor
—	1200	900	550	400	200

Titan II Magnum

As above, with long-action. Discontinued in 1988.

NIB	Exc.	V.G.	Good	Fair	Poor
—	1350	1100	680	450	200

Titan .411 KDF Mag.

As above in .411 KDF, with 26" barrel having integral muzzle brake. Blued or electroless nickel-plated, with walnut stock. Discontinued in 1988.

NIB	Exc.	V.G.	Good	Fair	Poor
—	2500	2000	1300	1000	700

K-22

.22-caliber bolt-action rifle, with 21" free floating barrel. Furnished without sights, adjustable trigger and 5-shot magazine. Also known as Mauser 201.

NIB	Exc.	V.G.	Good	Fair	Poor
—	500	400	300	180	100

Deluxe

NIB	Exc.	V.G.	Good	Fair	Poor
—	520	420	320	200	120

Deluxe Custom

NIB	Exc.	V.G.	Good	Fair	Poor
—	650	550	450	380	220

Deluxe Special Select

NIB	Exc.	V.G.	Good	Fair	Poor
—	1150	850	750	650	320

Model 2005

.22-caliber semi-automatic rifle, with 19.5" barrel, open sights and 5-shot magazine. Blued, with walnut stock. Also, available in deluxe model. Imported in 1986.

NIB	Exc.	V.G.	Good	Fair	Poor
250	180	150	100	80	50

Model 2107

.22- or .22-caliber Magnum bolt-action rifle, with 19.5" barrel, open sights and 5-shot magazine. Blued, with walnut stock.

NIB	Exc.	V.G.	Good	Fair	Poor
—	380	320	250	150	100

Model 2112

Deluxe version of Model 2107.

NIB	Exc.	V.G.	Good	Fair	Poor
—	400	320	280	180	120

KLIPZIG & COMPANY

San Francisco, California

Pocket Pistol

.41-caliber single-shot percussion pistol, with 2.5" barrel, German silver mounts and walnut stocks. Manufactured during 1850s early 1860s.

NIB	Exc.	V.G.	Good	Fair	Poor
		1950	980	400	200

KNICKERBOCKER

Made by Crescent Fire Arms Co.

Knickerbocker Pistol NFA

Knickerbocker is a 14" double-barreled 20-gauge smoothbore pistol, manufactured by Crescent Fire Arms Co. of Norwich, Connecticut. On the basis of its hammerless design and dates of production of similarly designed firearms by Crescent, the Knickerbocker was probably manufactured sometime during early 1900s. Receiver is case-hardened and barrels are nickel-plated. Right side of receiver stamped "AMERICAN GUN CO./ NEW YORK U S A"; left side "KNICKERBOCKER". Probably was intended for law enforcement and/or defensive purposes and manufactured using the same techniques used to produce Ithaca Auto & Burglar Gun. Receiver fitted with checkered pistol grip, resembling that of Model 1 and Model 2 smoothbore H&R Handy-Gun. Only known specimen of Knickerbocker bears serial number 200114. Knickerbocker was classified as "any other weapon" under NFA in 1934, because it was originally designed as "a so-called shotgun with a pistol grip"; because it is concealable (see Treasury Department ruling S.T. 772, dated August 6, 1934). Its rarity precludes being able to reliably estimate its value at this time. Possession is illegal unless registered with the BATFE.

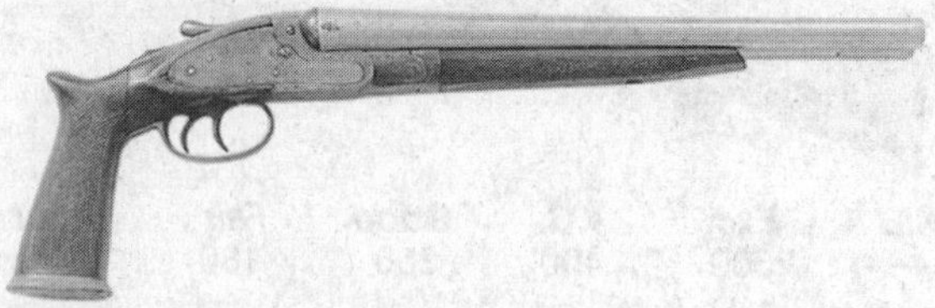

Double-Barrel Shotgun

Knickerbocker was a popular Dutch name for a New Yorker. It was used as a brand on many hammerless sidelock doubles made by Crescent Firearms Co. Valued from $100 to $700 depending on model and condition.

KNIGHT RIFLES

Athens, TN

Company was started in 1985, by Tony Knight. Company produces inline blackpowder muzzleloading rifles and a complete line of accessories.

Disc Magnum

Available in .50-caliber, with choice of blued or stainless steel 24" or 26" barrel. Adjustable rear sight. Checkered stock, with palm swell and rubber recoil pad. Stock offered in black or camo. Adjustable trigger. Weight about 8 lbs. Note: Add $50 for camo finish; $70 for stainless steel.

NIB	Exc.	V.G.	Good	Fair	Poor
350	300	250	220	180	160

Bighorn Magnum

Available in .50-caliber, with choice of 22" or 26" blued or stainless steel barrel. Adjustable rear sight. Checkered stock, with rubber recoil pad. Stock offered in black or camo. Adjustable trigger. Weight about 7.7 lbs. Note: Add $50 for camo finish; $70 for stainless steel.

NIB	Exc.	V.G.	Good	Fair	Poor
250	200	160	130	100	80

T-Bolt Magnum

Available in .50-caliber, with choice of blue or stainless steel 22" or 26" barrel. Adjustable rear sight. Composite stock, with rubber recoil pad. Stock available in camo. Adjustable trigger. Weight about 8 lbs. Note: Add $50 for camo finish; $70 for stainless steel.

NIB	Exc.	V.G.	Good	Fair	Poor
320	260	210	170	130	110

LK-93 Wolverine

Available in .50- or .54-caliber, with choice of 22" blued or stainless steel barrel. Adjustable rear sight. Composite skeleton or thumbhole stock. Stock available in black or camo. Adjustable trigger. Weight about 6.5 lbs. Note: Add $50 for camo finish; $70 for stainless steel; $40 for thumbhole stock.

NIB	Exc.	V.G.	Good	Fair	Poor
250	210	180	150	130	110

LK-93 Wolverine Youth

Same as above, with shorter length of pull. Offered in black stock only.

NIB	Exc.	V.G.	Good	Fair	Poor
250	210	180	150	130	110

American Knight

Available in .50-caliber, with 22" blued barrel. Adjustable rear sight. Black composite stock. Non-adjustable trigger. Weight about 6.3 lbs.

NIB	Exc.	V.G.	Good	Fair	Poor
180	140	110	90	70	60

MK-85 Hunter

Offered in .50- or .54-caliber, with blued finish and walnut stock.

NIB	Exc.	V.G.	Good	Fair	Poor
400	320	260	200	160	130

MK-85 Predator

Stainless steel version of Hunter model. Offered with composite stock or various camo finishes. Note: Add $50 for camo finish.

NIB	Exc.	V.G.	Good	Fair	Poor
450	360	290	230	180	150

MK-85 Stalker

Offered in .50- or .54-caliber, with a variety of stock options. Standard stock is composite. Blued finish. Note: Add $50 for camo finish.

NIB	Exc.	V.G.	Good	Fair	Poor
400	320	260	200	160	130

MK-85 Knight Hawk

Offered in .50- or .54-caliber, with black composite stock and stainless steel.

NIB	Exc.	V.G.	Good	Fair	Poor
500	400	320	260	200	160

MK-86 Shotgun

Available in 12-gauge, with 24" Extra Full choked barrel. Black composite stock, with blued finish.

NIB	Exc.	V.G.	Good	Fair	Poor
500	400	320	260	200	160

HK-94 Hawkeye Pistol

.50-caliber pistol fitted with 12" barrel. Overall length 20"; weight 52 oz. Offered in stainless steel or blued finish. First offered in 1993. Discontinued in 1998. Note: Add $70 for stainless steel.

NIB	Exc.	V.G.	Good	Fair	Poor
300	240	190	150	120	100

Rolling Block Rifle

Rolling Block blackpowder rifle, similar in design to old Remington Rolling Block. 209 primer ignition, .50-caliber barrel rifled for sabots. Finishes include blued/composite, stainless/camo and all-camo. Introduced in 2007. Values shown are for stainless.

NIB	Exc.	V.G.	Good	Fair	Poor
300	240	190	150	120	100

Long Range Hunter

.45-, .50- or .52-caliber bolt-action muzzleloader, with 27" fluted stainless barrel. Said to shoot 4" 3-shot groups at 200 yards. Laminated stock. Introduced in 2007.

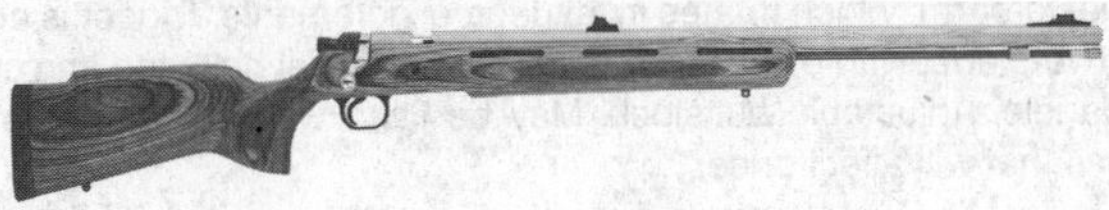

NIB	Exc.	V.G.	Good	Fair	Poor
400	320	260	200	160	130

Knight 500 Muzzleloader

.45 cal. Competition muzzleloader that can be used as a hunting rifle. Full plastic jacket ignition system, 28" handcrafted Green Mountain barrel, Boyd's Custom Stock with aluminum bedding block, free-floated 1:18" twist barrel, adjustable cheekpiece. Timney Fully Adjustable Match Grade Trigger. LOP 13.5", OAL 46", 10 lbs. Other equipment included: Harris Bipod, 50 count of 530-gr. lead bullets., 20-MOA scope rail, 9.5" breech plug removal tool, .45 cal. range rod, custom Knight 500 Carrying Case by SKB. Options include Vortex scopes from $150 to $600. No. MMTE758TAR.

NIB	Exc.	V.G.	Good	Fair	Poor
2000	1600	1280	1020	820	660

Ultra-Lite Muzzleloader

.50 Cal. twist rate 1:28", 24" barrel. 6 lbs. Bell & Carlson Kevlar, aluminum bedding, free floating Green Mountain Barrel, Williams fully adjustable metallic fiber optic sight set. Ignition is 209 Bare Primer, Western No.11 & Musket Cap Nipple. No. MULE704B.

NIB	Exc.	V.G.	Good	Fair	Poor
1120	890	710	570	460	360

Mountaineer Muzzleloader

.45, .50, and .52 caliber. 209 Bare Primer ignition system or Western-legal musket cap & #11 system. Twist rates: .45/1:20 in., 50/1:28 in., .52/1:26 in. 27" fluted stainless steel w/cantilever lug. OAL, 45.5". Straight and thumbhole stocks. Weight: 8.1 to 8.5 lbs. Williams fully adjustable metallic fiber optic sight set, adjustable trigger. Forest Green, Shadow Gray, Nutmeg stock finishes. Pricing for No. MMT707SSG Shadow Gray Straight Stock shown.

NIB	Exc.	V.G.	Good	Fair	Poor
1000	800	640	510	410	330

Bighorn Max 1

.50 Cal, .52 Cal. Current Bighorn line uses ignition system of full plastic jacket, Western No. 11 & Musket Cap Nipple. Twist rates for Green Mountain barrels are 50/1:28", .52/1:26", 26" stainless steel. OAL 44.5", LOP 14.25". Weight (thumbhole) 8.1 lbs., (straight) 8.5 lbs. Williams fully adjustable metallic fiber optic sight set, adjustable trigger. Realtree camo patterns. Ramrod is Easton Carbon Core Ramrod with reverse threaded extendable full brass jag. DynaTek coating on bore and exterior of the barrel.

NIB	Exc.	V.G.	Good	Fair	Poor
560	450	360	290	230	180

KNIGHT'S ARMAMENT COMPANY

Titusville, Florida
(previously in Vero Beach, Florida)

STONER SR-15 RIFLES

SR-15 models are AR pattern rifles chambered for the 5.56 NATO cartridge.

SR-15 E3 Mod 2 Series

Introduced 2018. Mod 2 features a proprietary mid-length gas system, gas block secured with locking ring, E3 round-lug bolt design, URX4 handguard, ambidextrous bolt release, selector and magazine release, drop-in 2-stage trigger, receiver end plate with ambidextrous QD sling swivel sockets, 6-position collapsible stock, fully ambidextrous lower receiver controls, extended charging handle latch, folding front and 200–600 meter rear micro-iron sights are standard features of the SR-15 E3 Mod 2. Specific units in Mod 2 line include M-LOK handguards and 1:7 rifling twist, such as the E3 31900 (16" chrome-lined barrel), E3 Carbine 31946 (14.5" barrel), CQB 31952 (11.5" barrel), and Light Precision Rifle 31973 (18" barrel). Price shown for E3 31900. KeyMod handguard versions also available.

NIB	Exc.	V.G.	Good	Fair	Poor
2700	2300	2000	1700	—	—

SR-15 Match

Chambered for .223 Win. Fitted with target contour 20" free floating barrel. Two-stage match trigger. Flattop receiver. No sights. Weight about 7.9 lbs.

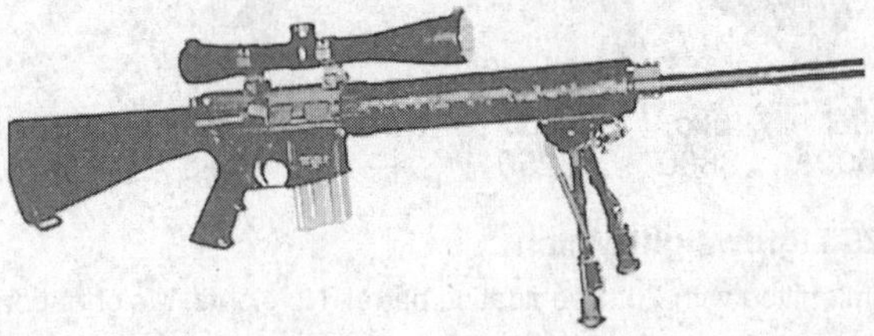

NIB	Exc.	V.G.	Good	Fair	Poor
3000	2500	2150	—	—	—

SR-15 M-5 Rifle

.223 fitted with 20" standard weight barrel, with two-stage target trigger. Handguard employs RAS accessory system. Fitted with flip-up low profile rear sight. Weight about 7.6 lbs.

NIB	Exc.	V.G.	Good	Fair	Poor
1900	1600	1350	—	—	—

SR-15 E3 URX Carbine

Similar to SR-15 M-5, with 16" barrel, telescoping buttstock and vertical forend grip. Introduced 2006.

NIB	Exc.	V.G.	Good	Fair	Poor
2500	2100	1800	—	—	—

SR-15 M4 Carbine

Caliber: 5.56mm NATO. Barrel: 14.5" chrome-lined mil-spec, proprietary mid-length gas system. Free-floated, hammer forged, 1:7" twist. E3 round-lug bolt design; ambidextrous bolt release, selector, and magazine release. M-LOK handguard. Drop-in two-stage trigger. 3-Prong Flash Eliminator. Weight: 6.55 lbs. Length: 33" to 36.5". SEE POLITICAL PANIC PRICING.

NIB	Exc.	V.G.	Good	Fair	Poor
2770	2600	1450	2200	—	—

STONER SR-25 RIFLES

SR-25 models are AR pattern rifles chambered for the 7.62 NATO / .308 Win. cartridge.

SR-25 Match

Chambered for .308-caliber. Fitted with 24" target contour free-floating barrel. Special rifling and twist rate. No sights. Weight about 10.75 lbs.

NIB	Exc.	V.G.	Good	Fair	Poor
4500	3800	3250	—	—	—

SR-25 Lightweight Match

.308 rifle fitted with 20" free-floating barrel. No sights. Weight about 9.5 lbs.

NIB	Exc.	V.G.	Good	Fair	Poor
4000	3400	2900	—	—	—

SR-25 Stoner Carbine

Fitted with 16" free-floating barrel and special short non-slip handguard. Weight about 7.75 lbs.

NIB	Exc.	V.G.	Good	Fair	Poor
4200	3600	3100	—	—	—

SR-25 APC

Latest evolution of 7.62mm NATO carbine. Advanced Precision Carbine (APC) has 16" barrel with flash suppressor, ambidextrous bolt release, safety and magazine release. A drop-in two-stage trigger serves double duty for long or close range shooting. Introduced in 2014.

NIB	Exc.	V.G.	Good	Fair	Poor
5500	4750	4000	—	—	—

SR-25 Tubb Competition Match

Chambered for .308 or .260 cartridge. Has 26" match barrel. Fitted with special forearm, which rotates in 15 degree increments. Trigger is adjustable two-stage, with extended triggerguard. Special bolt stop and charging handle. Adjustable buttstock. May be fitted with several extra cost options that will affect price.

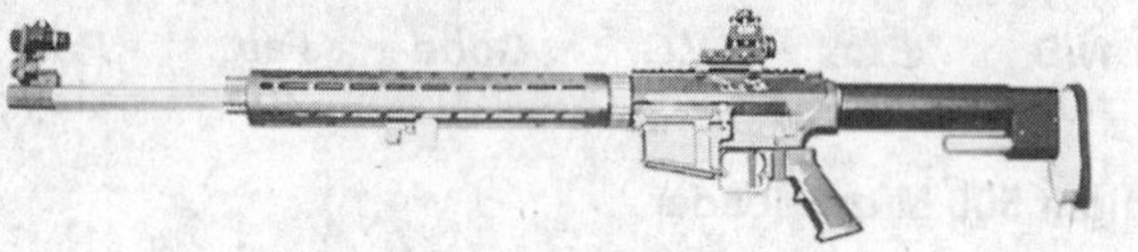

NIB	Exc.	V.G.	Good	Fair	Poor
6250	5250	4500	—	—	—

SR-25 MkII Mod 0 Match Rifle

Introduced in 2004. Features heavy 20" free-floating target grade barrel.

NIB	Exc.	V.G.	Good	Fair	Poor
6500	5500	4750	—	—	—

SR-25 E2 Series

Introduced 2018. 7.62mm NATO chambering. Second evolution of the rifles include ambidextrous bolt release, selector, and magazine release, drop-in 2-stage trigger, 7.62 QDC flash suppressor. Variations with M-LOK handguards include Combat Carbine (CC) 31893 (16" lightweight chrome-lined barrel, 8.4 lbs.), Precision Carbine 31955 (16" medium profile barrel, 5R cut, 1:10 twist, 9 lbs.), E2 SBR DSR 31958 (14.5" 5R barrel 1:10 twist, 9 lbs.), Precision Rifle No. 31961 (20" 5R barrel 1:10 twist, 10.5 lbs.), and others. KeyMod models also available (Nos. 31243, 31184, 31198).

NIB	Exc.	V.G.	Good	Fair	Poor
5000	4250	3500	—	—	—

SR-25 Sporter

NIB	Exc.	V.G.	Good	Fair	Poor
3250	2750	2350	—	—	—

SR-25 Combat Carbine

Caliber: 7.62mm NATO/.308 Win. Ambidextrous bolt release, selector, and magazine release. Drop-in two-stage trigger, 7.62 QDC flash suppressor. Barrel: 16" hammer-forged, chrome-lined, 1:10" twist, 5R cut. M-LOK handguard. Weight: 8.4 lbs. Length: 35.75" to 39.5". Add $875 for the E2 PC variant. SEE POLITICAL PANIC PRICING.

NIB	Exc.	V.G.	Good	Fair	Poor
4780	4500	4250	3870	—	—

SR-30

Chambered in .300 AAC Blackout with QDC flash suppressor, adjustable SOPMOD stock. M-LOK Models include No. 31970 (9.5" 1:7 twist, chrome lined, 6.2 lbs., 27.5" OAL) and DSR (Direct Signature Reduction) No. 32401 (9.5" 1:7 twist, chrome lined, 7.2 lbs., 32" OAL). KeyMod-equipped model is DSR Keymod No. 31222.

NIB	Exc.	V.G.	Good	Fair	Poor
2650	2250	1900	—	—	—

STONER SR-25 RIFLES

SR-50 Rifle

Semi-automatic rifle chambered for .50 BMG cartridge. Magazine feed. Weight about 31 lbs.

NIB	Exc.	V.G.	Good	Fair	Poor
7000	6000	5000	—	—	—

KOHOUT & SPOLECNOST

Kdyne, Czechoslovakia

Mars

6.35 or 7.65mm caliber semi-automatic pistol. Larger caliber having grip safety. Blued, with plastic grips impressed with word "Mars". Slide marked "Mars 7.65 (or 6.35) Kohout & Spol. Kdyne". Manufactured between 1928 and 1945.

NIB	Exc.	V.G.	Good	Fair	Poor
—	350	250	200	150	100

Niva, PZK

Similar to above in 6.35mm caliber.

NIB	Exc.	V.G.	Good	Fair	Poor
—	350	250	200	150	100

KOLB, HENRY M.

Philadelphia, Pennsylvania

Later made by R.F.Sedgley

Over a quarter-million diminutive folding-trigger Baby Hammerless-type revolvers were made in the U.S. from the late 1890s through 1930, first by Henry M. Kolb until 1912, and then by R. F. Sedgley, Inc. This general style of revolver was popular in Europe, where many models by various makers are sometimes lumped together as "velodog" revolvers. However, the only comparable American made gun was the Iver Johnson Petite, with only a small number produced. The Kolb guns typically have a K at the top of their hard rubber grips, and the Sedgley guns an S. Some early guns found with twining vines in that area of the grips may have been made by Columbian Firearms Company. They were offered in two frame sizes. The small-frame models were only 4" overall, with a 1 5/16" barrel and held six .22 Short cartridges. The rarer large-frame models were 5 ¼" overall with a 1 ¾" barrel, and held five .32 S&W short cartridges, with a very rare later variation made for eight .22 Long cartridges. Most guns were nickel plated, with around 15% blued. Most had hard rubber grips, but around 25 percent of them had pearls. Several models and variations are identified in the definitive work on the subject, Baby Hammerless Revolvers by Frank M. Sellers. These may be compiled into six general groups:

- First Model – solid frame, birdshead grips, both small frame and large frame made.
- Model 1910 New Model – solid frame, square grips, both small frame and large frame made.
- Transition Models – similar to solidframe square grip
- Model 1910, with a MODEL (YEAR) marking on the topstrap as minor changes were made. There are 8 different (YEAR) dates ranging from 1910 to 1924.
- Ejector Models – similar to Model 1910 and Transition Models, except with a star ejector to extract cartridge cases. These are also marked MODEL (YEAR) on the topstrap, with the (YEAR) dates ranging from 1924 to 1930.
- New Baby – top-break, small frame.

Trade name Baby Hammerless revolvers are relatively scarce, but include Western Arms Co. and Konqueror in the large-frame models. There are currently few differences in the values of the many small-frame variations.

- First Model – solid frame, birdshead grips, both small frame and large frame made.
- Model 1910 New Model – solid frame, square grips, both small frame and large frame made.
- Transition Models – similar to solidframe square grip
- Model 1910, with a MODEL (YEAR) marking on the topstrap as minor changes were made. There are 8 different (YEAR) dates ranging from 1910 to 1924.
- Ejector Models – similar to Model 1910 and Transition Models, except with a star ejector to extract cartridge cases. These are also marked MODEL (YEAR) on the topstrap, with the (YEAR) dates ranging from 1924 to 1930.
- New Baby – top-break, small frame.

Trade name Baby Hammerless revolvers are relatively scarce, but include Western Arms Co. and Konqueror in the large-frame models. There are currently few differences in the values of the many small-frame variations. Large-frame guns will bring about double what a comparable small frame will bring. Engraved guns, or guns with purse holsters, will bring a premium. Pearl grips and blued guns in nice condition will bring a premium. All variations are somewhat delicate mechanically, and non-working guns will bring less than those that function properly.

Small Frame Baby Hammerless Revolvers

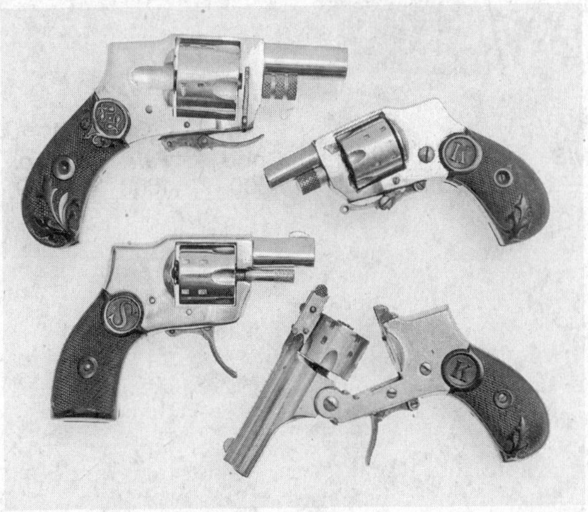

NIB	Exc.	V.G.	Good	Fair	Poor
800	400	300	200	150	80

Large Frame Baby Hammerless Revolvers

NIB	Exc.	V.G.	Good	Fair	Poor
1500	900	550	400	300	150

KOLIBRI/FREDERICH PFANNL
Rehberg, Austria

2.7mm

2.7mm semi-automatic pistol, with 7-round magazine. F.P. trademark on grips, Kolibri name at bottom of grips. Single cartridge may be worth as much as $75!

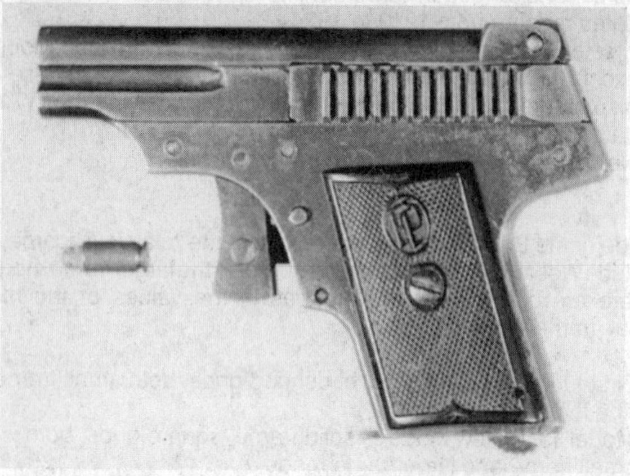

Courtesy James Rankin

NIB	Exc.	V.G.	Good	Fair	Poor
—	2500	1550	850	600	400

3mm

3mm semi-automatic pistol, with 6-round magazine. The 3mm version rarer of the two Kolibri pistols. F.P. trademark on grips.

Courtesy James Rankin

NIB	Exc.	V.G.	Good	Fair	Poor
—	2800	2000	1500	1000	600

KOMMER, THEODOR WAFFENFABRIK
Zella Mehlis, Germany

Model 1

6.35mm semi-automatic pistol, with 8-shot magazine. Blued, with plastic grips. Kommer name on both slide and frame, with T.K. trademark on grips. Manufactured during 1920s.

Courtesy James Rankin

NIB	Exc.	V.G.	Good	Fair	Poor
—	300	250	200	150	90

Model 2

6.35mm semi-automatic pistol, with 6-round magazine. Similar to Model 1906 Browning. Barrel length 2"; weight about 13 oz. Kommer name on slide. Late TH.K. trademark on grips. Manufactured in 1930s.

Courtesy James Rankin

NIB	Exc.	V.G.	Good	Fair	Poor
—	300	250	200	150	90

Model 3

6.35mm semi-automatic pistol, with 9-round magazine. Kommer name on slide. TH.K. trademark on grips. Same as Model 2, with extended grips straps for longer magazine.

Courtesy James Rankin

NIB	Exc.	V.G.	Good	Fair	Poor
—	300	250	200	150	90

Model 4

7.65mm caliber semi-automatic pistol, with 7-shot magazine. Without a grip safety. Similar to FN Model 1901. Barrel length 3"; weight about 20 oz. Slide marked "Waffenfabrik Kommer Zella Mehlis Kal. 7.65". Manufactured between 1936 and 1940.

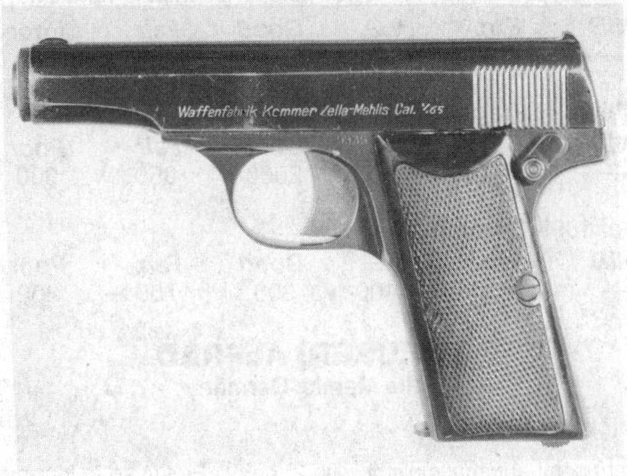

Courtesy James Rankin

NIB	Exc.	V.G.	Good	Fair	Poor
—	380	320	280	180	100

KONGSBERG

Norway

Thumbhole Sporter

Introduced in 1993. This bolt-action rifle chambered for .22-250 and .308 Win. cartridges. Fitted with 23" heavy barrel. Stock is American walnut, with stippled thumbhole grip and wide forend. Cheekpiece is adjustable for height. Weight about 8.5 lbs. Available in both right-/left-hand configurations. Note: Add 10 percent for left-hand model.

NIB	Exc.	V.G.	Good	Fair	Poor
1580	1250	900	550	350	200

Classic Rifle

Also introduced in 1993. Chambered for a wide variety of calibers from .22-250 to .338 Win. Magnum. Fitted with 23" barrel for standard calibers; 26" barrel for Magnum calibers. European walnut stock, with straight comb. Hand-checkered. Open sights. Weight about 7.5 lbs., depending on caliber. Offered in both right-/left-hand configurations. Note: Add 10 percent for left-hand model; 10 percent for Magnum calibers.

NIB	Exc.	V.G.	Good	Fair	Poor
1000	800	650	380	220	120

KOON CUSTOM RIFLES

See—OMEGA FIREARMS

KORRIPHILA

Germany

HSP

7.65mm Luger, .38 Special, 9mm Police, 9mm Luger, 9mm Steyr, 10mm ACP and .45 ACP caliber. Double-action semi-automatic pistol, with 4" barrel made of stainless steel.

NIB	Exc.	V.G.	Good	Fair	Poor
7500	6000	5000	2500	1250	550

HSP—Single-Action Only

NIB	Exc.	V.G.	Good	Fair	Poor
7500	6000	5000	2500	1250	550

Odin's Eye

Essentially same model as above. Same calibers, with choice of 4" or 5" barrel lengths. Frame and slide made of Damascus steel.

NIB	Exc.	V.G.	Good	Fair	Poor
14000	10000	7500	4000	1500	500

KORTH

Germany

See—NIGHTHAWK CUSTOM

Korth started business in Ratzegurg, Germany, in 1954.

Semi-Automatic Pistol

9mm caliber double-action semi-automatic pistol, with 4" barrel, adjustable sights and 13-shot magazine. Other calibers offered: .40 S&W, .357 SIG and 9x21. Optional 5" barrel also offered. Weight about 44 oz. Matte or polished blue, with walnut grips. Introduced in 1985.

NIB	Exc.	V.G.	Good	Fair	Poor
7000	5000	3750	2750	1300	650

Combat Revolver

.22 LR, .22 Magnum, .357 Magnum and 9mm caliber revolver, with 3", 4", 5.25" or 6" barrel and 6-shot cylinder. Barrels and cylinders are interchangeable. Matte or polished blue, with walnut grips.

NIB	Exc.	V.G.	Good	Fair	Poor
5000	3900	3000	1750	1150	700

Match Revolver

Built in same calibers as Combat revolver, with 5.25" or 6" barrel. Adjustable sight notch widths and rear sight. Machined trigger shoe. Adjustable match grips, with oiled walnut and matte finish.

NIB	Exc.	V.G.	Good	Fair	Poor
6250	5000	4000	2250	1500	1000

Korth Sky Hawk Revolver

Imported by Nighthawk Custom. See that listing.

KRAG-JORGENSEN

This was the first bolt-action repeating rifle that used smokeless powder to be adopted by the U.S. government as a service rifle. Adopted as Model 1892, it was similar to the Denmark military rifle, which had been designed by Norwegians Ole Krag and Erik Jorgensen. Most unique part of this design was the side-mounted hinged magazine. With the exception of Model 1898 Practice Rifle, which was chambered for .22 rimfire — all Krag rifles were chambered for .30-40 Government cartridge. From 1892 to 1899, more than a dozen variations were made. Over the years many have been altered or "customized". Values shown here are for unmodified, original rifles. For more on Krag-Jorgensen, see the latest edition of *Standard Catalog of Military Firearms*, available at GunDigestStore.com.

Model of 1892

1st Type, Serial number 1 — 1500 Antique

Exc.	Fine	V.G.	Good	Fair	Poor
12500	6500	4750	3000	900	630

2nd Type, Serial number 1501 — 24562 Antique

Exc.	Fine	V.G.	Good	Fair	Poor
7500	4000	3000	2000	600	420

Model 1892, altered to 1896 Antique

Exc.	Fine	V.G.	Good	Fair	Poor
950	750	600	450	200	140

Model 1896 Antique

Note: Add 10 percent for carbine variation. Rifle values listed. Original 1896 Carbine will bring 50% premium to double rifle values. Beware of rifles modified to carbine configuration. Very rare 1896 Cadet Rifles bring a substantial premium.

Exc.	Fine	V.G.	Good	Fair	Poor
2750	1600	1170	750	300	210

Model 1898

Note: Add a premium of 100 to 120 percent for carbine variation.

NIB	Exc.	V.G.	Good	Fair	Poor
—	1250	900	650	450	200

Model 1898 Practice Rifle (.22 rimfire)

NIB	Exc.	V.G.	Good	Fair	Poor
—	—	4500	2000	850	300

Model 1899 Carbine

NIB	Exc.	V.G.	Good	Fair	Poor
—	1850	1400	900	750	300

KRAUSER, ALFRED

Zella Mehlis, Germany

Helfricht or Helkra

6.35mm semi-automatic pistol, with 2" barrel. Produced in four models: fourth, with enclosed barrel. Blued, with composition grips. Manufactured from 1921 to 1929.

NIB	Exc.	V.G.	Good	Fair	Poor
—	480	400	350	250	150

KRICO

Stuttgart, West Germany

Founded as Junghans & Kriegeskorte in 1878; merged with Kongsberg Small Arms Company in 1991.

Sporting Rifle

.22 Hornet or .222-caliber bolt-action rifle, with 22", 24" or 26" barrels. Single-/double-set trigger, adjustable sights and 4-shot magazine. Blued, with walnut stock. Manufactured between 1956 and 1962.

NIB	Exc.	V.G.	Good	Fair	Poor
—	650	550	480	380	280

Sporting Carbine

As above, with 20" barrel and full-length stock.

NIB	Exc.	V.G.	Good	Fair	Poor
—	680	580	500	400	300

Varmint Special Rifle

Sporting Rifle, with heavier barrel.

NIB	Exc.	V.G.	Good	Fair	Poor
—	650	550	480	380	280

Model 300

.22-caliber bolt-action rifle, with 23.5" barrel, 5-shot magazine and grooved receiver. Blued, with walnut stock. Imported prior to 1989.

NIB	Exc.	V.G.	Good	Fair	Poor
—	700	600	550	400	300

Model 302 and 304

Variations of above. Discontinued in 1986.

NIB	Exc.	V.G.	Good	Fair	Poor
—	700	600	550	400	300

Model 311 Smallbore

.22-caliber bolt-action rifle, with 22" barrel. Double-set triggers, adjustable sights and 5- or 10-shot magazine. Blued, with walnut stock. Not imported after 1988.

NIB	Exc.	V.G.	Good	Fair	Poor
—	320	280	220	150	100

Model 320

As above, with 19.5" barrel and full-length stock. Discontinued in 1988.

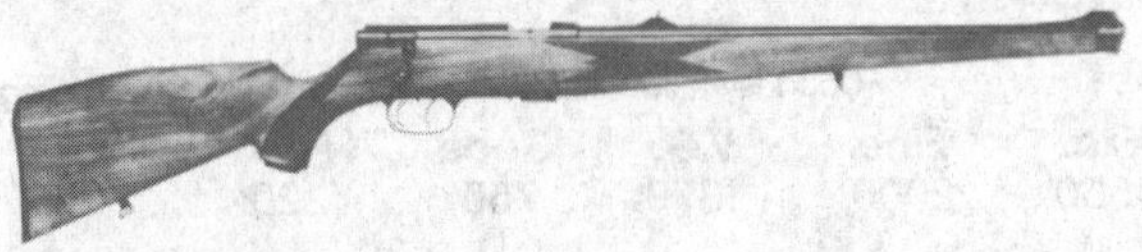

NIB	Exc.	V.G.	Good	Fair	Poor
—	700	600	550	400	300

Model 340

.22-caliber bolt-action rifle, with 21" heavy barrel. Furnished without sights, adjustable trigger and 5-shot magazine. Blued, with walnut stock. Not imported after 1988.

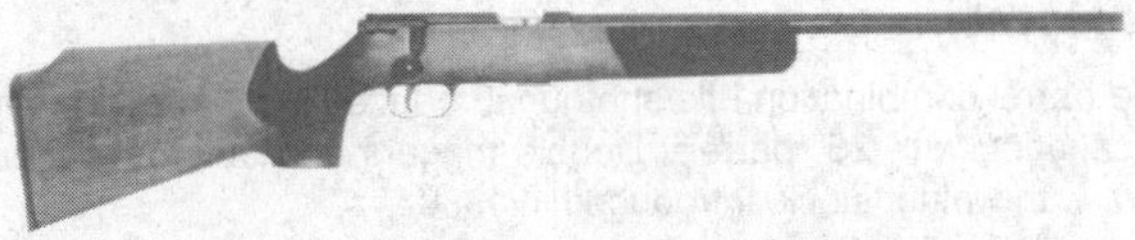

NIB	Exc.	V.G.	Good	Fair	Poor
—	750	620	580	420	320

Model 340 Mini-Sniper

As above, with matte finish. Barrel fitted with muzzle brake. Stock with raised cheekpiece, as well as ventilated handguard.

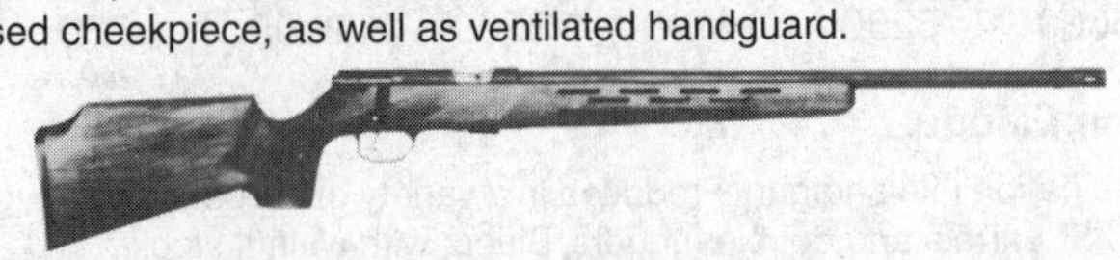

NIB	Exc.	V.G.	Good	Fair	Poor
—	1000	850	750	500	400

Model 340 Kricotronic

Model 340 fitted with electronic trigger. Not imported after 1988.

NIB	Exc.	V.G.	Good	Fair	Poor
—	1450	1000	850	600	500

Model 360S Biathlon Rifle

Introduced in 1991. Features .22 LR straight-pull bolt-action, with 5-round magazine. Fitted with 21.25" barrel and 17 oz. match trigger. Walnut stock, with high comb and adjustable buttplate. Fully adjustable match peep sight. Weight about 9.25 lbs.

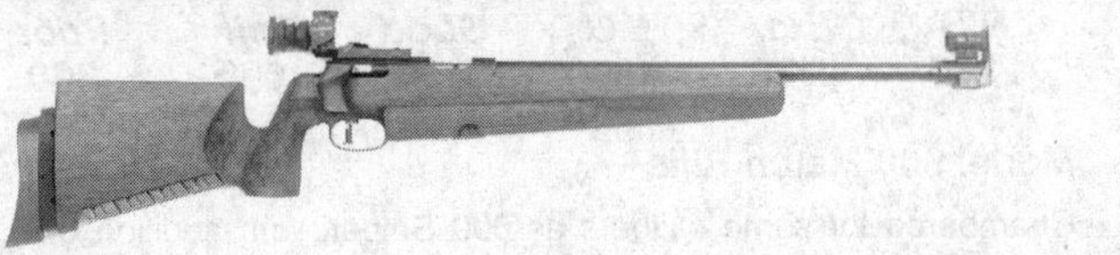

NIB	Exc.	V.G.	Good	Fair	Poor
1950	1350	850	500	300	150

Model 360S2 Biathlon Rifle

Same as above, with black epoxy finished walnut stock, with pistol grip. Weight 9 lbs.

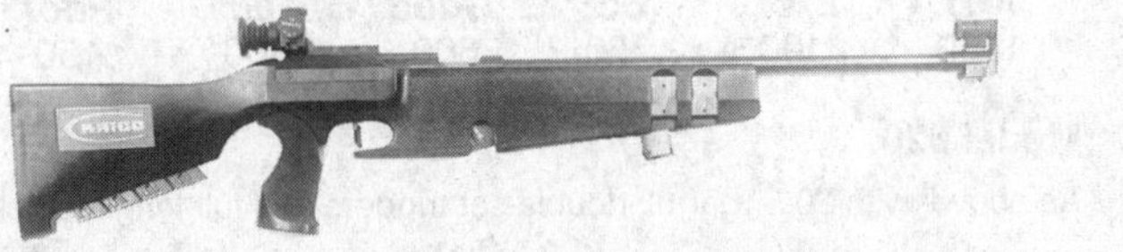

NIB	Exc.	V.G.	Good	Fair	Poor
1500	1250	800	400	200	100

Model 400 Match

Chambered for .22 LR or .22 Hornet. Bolt-action rifle fitted with heavy match 23" barrel, double-set of match triggers and 5-round magazine. Match-style stock of European walnut. Weight about 8.8 lbs.

NIB	Exc.	V.G.	Good	Fair	Poor
900	780	650	500	300	150

Model 400 Sporter

.22 Hornet caliber bolt-action rifle, with 23.5" barrel, open sights and 5-shot magazine. Blued, with walnut stock. Not imported after 1988.

NIB	Exc.	V.G.	Good	Fair	Poor
—	750	620	550	420	320

Model 420

As above, with 19.5" barrel, double-set triggers and full-length stock. Discontinued in 1988.

NIB	Exc.	V.G.	Good	Fair	Poor
—	900	750	680	500	400

Model 440

Similar to Model 340. Not imported after 1988.

NIB	Exc.	V.G.	Good	Fair	Poor
—	950	800	700	500	380

Model 500 Kricotronic Match Rifle

Chambered for .22 LR. Bolt-action rifle fitted with 23.6" barrel and tapered bore. Walnut stock, with match-type adjustable buttplate. Electronic ignition system gives fastest lock time. Weight about 9.4 lbs.

NIB	Exc.	V.G.	Good	Fair	Poor
3900	3000	2400	1650	1000	400

Model 600 Sporter

.17 Rem. to .308 Win. caliber bolt-action rifle, with 23.5" barrel. Open sights and 3-shot magazine. Blued, with walnut stock. Not imported after 1988.

NIB	Exc.	V.G.	Good	Fair	Poor
—	1150	950	880	700	580

Model 600 Sniper Rifle

Bolt-action rifle chambered for .222, .223, .22-250, .243 and 308. Fitted with 25.6" heavy barrel, with flack hider. Stock walnut, with adjustable rubber buttplate. Magazine holds 4 rounds. Weight about 9.2 lbs.

NIB	Exc.	V.G.	Good	Fair	Poor
2900	2100	1500	1100	600	300

Model 600 Match Rifle

Chambered for same calibers as 600 Sniper, with addition of 5.6x50 Magnum. Fitted with 23.6" barrel. Match stock is ventilated in forearm for cooling. Wood is walnut, with cheekpiece. Weight about 8.8 lbs.

NIB	Exc.	V.G.	Good	Fair	Poor
1500	1100	750	600	300	150

Model 620

As above, with 20.5" barrel, double-set triggers and full-length stock.

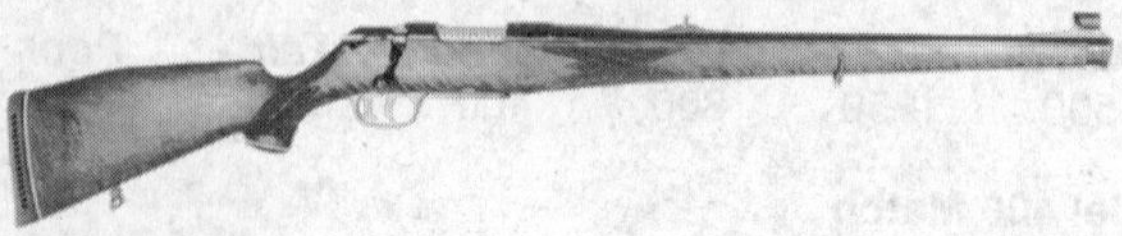

NIB	Exc.	V.G.	Good	Fair	Poor
1500	1100	750	600	300	150

Model 640 Varmint Rifle

Similar to above in .22-250, .222- or .223-caliber, with 23.5" heavy barrel. Not imported after 1988.

NIB	Exc.	V.G.	Good	Fair	Poor
—	1250	1020	920	780	620

Model 640 Sniper Rifle

As above, with matte finish. Discontinued in 1988.

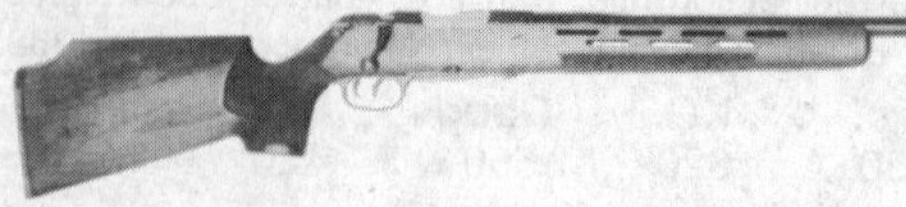

NIB	Exc.	V.G.	Good	Fair	Poor
1500	1100	750	600	300	150

Model 640 Deluxe Sniper Rifle

As above in .223- or .308-caliber, with 23" barrel, stippled stock and adjustable trigger. Not imported after 1988.

NIB	Exc.	V.G.	Good	Fair	Poor
—	1700	1250	1000	750	650

Model 700 Sporter

.270- or .30-06 caliber bolt-action rifle, with 23.5" barrel, open sights, single-set trigger and 3-shot magazine. Blued, with walnut stock. Discontinued in 1988.

NIB	Exc.	V.G.	Good	Fair	Poor
—	1050	850	750	600	500

Model 720

As above, with 20.5" barrel, double-set triggers and full-length stock. Discontinued in 1988.

NIB	Exc.	V.G.	Good	Fair	Poor
—	1200	900	750	600	500

Model 720 Limited Edition

As above in .270-caliber only, with gold-plated furniture and gold highlighted engraving. Not imported after 1988.

NIB	Exc.	V.G.	Good	Fair	Poor
—	2500	2000	1750	1400	900

KRIDER, J. H.

Philadelphia, Pennsylvania

Pocket Pistol (Antique)

.41-caliber percussion pocket pistol, with 3" barrel, German silver furniture and walnut stock. Barrel marked "Krider Phila.". Manufactured during 1850s and 1860s.

Exc.	Fine	V.G.	Good	Fair	Poor
4500	2300	1250	650	350	250

Militia Rifle (Antique)

.58-caliber percussion rifle, with 39" browned barrel. Full-length stock secured by two barrel bands. Lock marked "Krider". Case-hardened and furniture of brass. Several hundred manufactured in 1861.

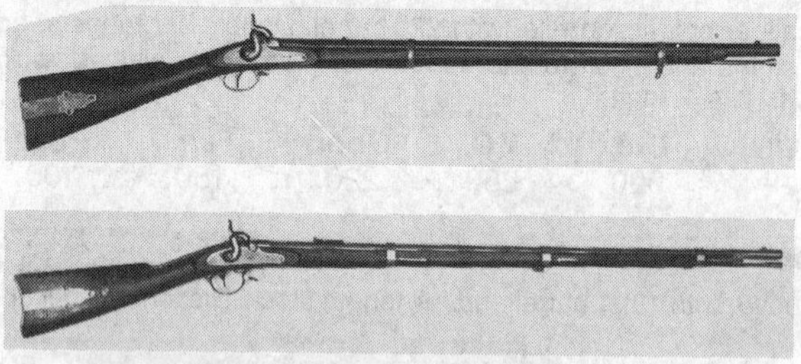

Courtesy Milwaukee Public Museum, Milwaukee, Wisconsin

Exc.	Fine	V.G.	Good	Fair	Poor
4550	2000	1370	750	220	150

KRIEGHOFF, HEINRICH, GUN CO.

Ulm, Germany

Krieghoff-manufactured Lugers are listed in Luger section.

DRILLINGS AND COMBINATION GUNS

Plus Model

Three-barrel combination rifle/shotgun. Produced in a variety of gauges and calibers, with 25" barrels. Double triggers and automatic ejectors. Blued, with walnut stock. Introduced in 1988.

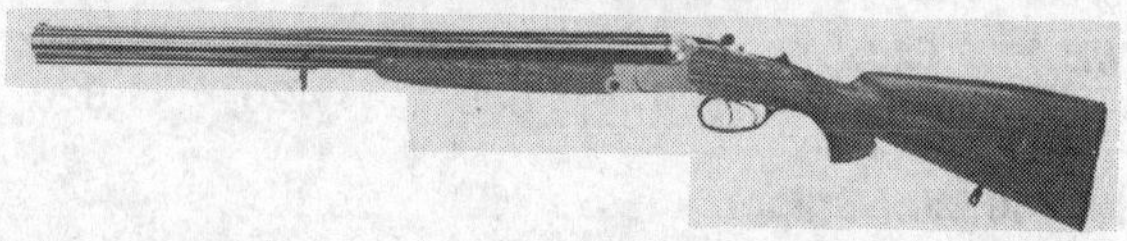

NIB	Exc.	V.G.	Good	Fair	Poor
6600	5250	4100	3500	2000	750

Trumpf Model

Combination rifle/shotgun. Produced in a variety of calibers and gauges, with 25" barrels and double triggers. Blued, with walnut stock.

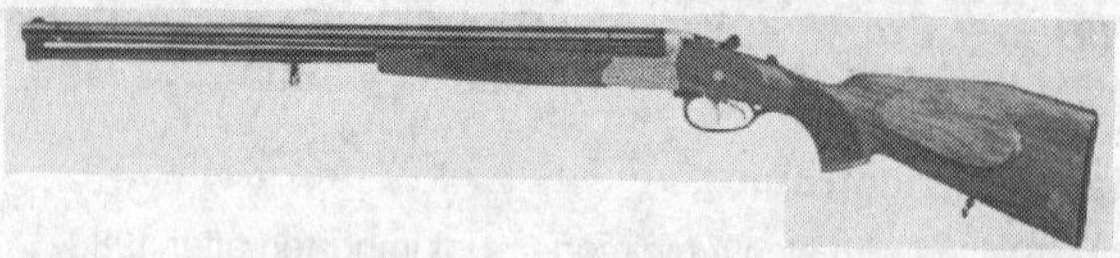

NIB	Exc.	V.G.	Good	Fair	Poor
11000	7700	5100	3500	2000	750

Trumpf Dural

As above lightweight boxlock, with Duraluminum frame. Note: Add $1,850 for single trigger; $450 for free-floating barrel.

NIB	Exc.	V.G.	Good	Fair	Poor
11000	7700	5100	3500	2000	750

Neptun

Combination over/under rifle/shotgun, with sidelocks. Produced in a variety of gauges and calibers. Engraved, blued with walnut stock.

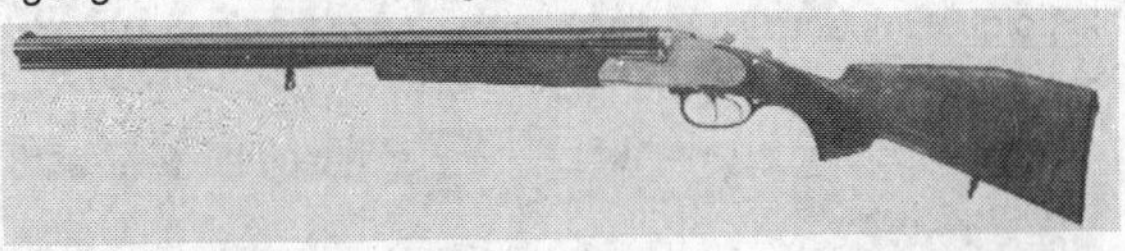

NIB	Exc.	V.G.	Good	Fair	Poor
15000	12000	10500	5000	2500	1500

Neptun Dural

As above lightweight boxlock, with Duraluminum frame.

NIB	Exc.	V.G.	Good	Fair	Poor
15000	12000	10500	5000	2500	1500

Neptun Primus

Neptun, with relief engraving and detachable sidelocks.

NIB	Exc.	V.G.	Good	Fair	Poor
20000	17000	14000	7500	3500	2000

Neptun Primus Dural

As above lightweight sidelock, with Duraluminum frame.

NIB	Exc.	V.G.	Good	Fair	Poor
20000	18000	14000	7500	3500	2000

Optima

Classic drilling combination of side-by-side shotgun barrels over a rifle barrel. Shotgun offered in 12- or 20-gauge; rifle barrel in .308 Win., .30-06 or several popular European cartridges. Features include twin-hammer action, with Universal trigger system, combination cocking device and a set trigger integrated in the front trigger. Values shown are for base model. Many options available.

NIB	Exc.	V.G.	Good	Fair	Poor
10000	8500	6500	5000	3000	900

DOUBLE RIFLES

Many optional engraving patterns available for these double rifles that may affect price. Consult an expert prior to sale.

Teck Over/Under

Boxlock over/under rifle manufactured in a variety of calibers, with 25" barrels. Double triggers, extractors and express sights. Blued, with walnut stock. Note: Add $1,500 for .458 Win. Magnum.

NIB	Exc.	V.G.	Good	Fair	Poor
9000	8250	6600	5000	2250	1500

Ulm Model

As above, with sidelocks.

NIB	Exc.	V.G.	Good	Fair	Poor
15000	12000	10500	7500	3000	2000

Ulm Primus

As above, with detachable sidelocks.

NIB	Exc.	V.G.	Good	Fair	Poor
23500	19500	16500	11500	7000	3000

Ultra

Boxlock over/under rifle offered with several different options. Same caliber or different caliber rifle barrels. Built on 20-gauge frame, with game scene engraving. Weight depends on caliber and combination of calibers, but between 6.5 lbs. and 8 lbs.

NIB	Exc.	V.G.	Good	Fair	Poor
7500	6100	4400	3000	1500	800

Classic

Side-by-side rifle with sideplates. Offered in 7x65R to 9.3x74R calibers, with optional interchangeable 20-gauge shotgun barrel. Single trigger. Choice of standard stock with cheekpiece or classic Bavaria style. Weight about 7.25 to 8 lbs., depending on calibers.

NIB	Exc.	V.G.	Good	Fair	Poor
8800	6900	5000	3500	2000	800

Classic Big Five

Similar to Classic, but chambered for .375 H&H, .375 NE, .458 Win. Magnum, .416 Rigby, .470 NE and .500 NE 3". Double trigger, with hinged front trigger. Weight about 9.25 to 10 lbs., depending on caliber. Interchangeable barrels are optional.

NIB	Exc.	V.G.	Good	Fair	Poor
10900	82500	5100	3500	2000	750

SHOTGUNS

Model 32 Standard

12-, 20-, 28-gauge or .410 bore boxlock over/under shotgun, with 26.5" to 32" barrels. Single-selective trigger and automatic ejectors. Blued, with walnut stock. Discontinued in 1980. Note: Add 50 percent for 28-gauge or .410 two barrel set; 100 percent for four-barrel Skeet set.

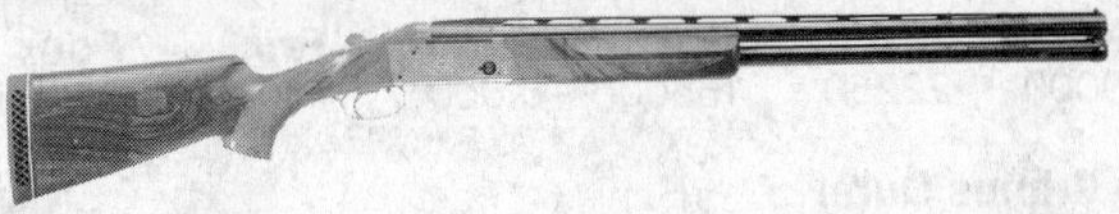

NIB	Exc.	V.G.	Good	Fair	Poor
—	3000	2500	2000	1100	750

San Remo Grade

NIB	Exc.	V.G.	Good	Fair	Poor
—	5000	3750	1900	1400	1000

Monte Carlo Grade

NIB	Exc.	V.G.	Good	Fair	Poor
—	6250	4850	2750	1650	1250

Crown Grade

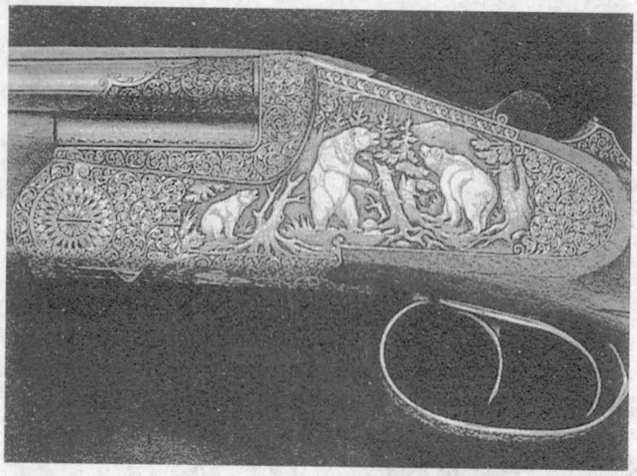

Courtesy Bonhams & Butterfields

NIB	Exc.	V.G.	Good	Fair	Poor
—	8700	6500	4300	2200	1500

Super Crown Grade

NIB	Exc.	V.G.	Good	Fair	Poor
18000	14700	10500	6850	3750	2000

Single Barrel Trap Gun

Model 32, with single 32" to 34" barrel.

NIB	Exc.	V.G.	Good	Fair	Poor
—	3950	3250	1700	1080	600

Teck Over/Under

Similar to Teck double rifle, but offered in 12- and 16-gauge.

NIB	Exc.	V.G.	Good	Fair	Poor
12000	10000	7500	4550	3000	1750

Teck Dural

Same as above, with lightweight aluminum frame.

NIB	Exc.	V.G.	Good	Fair	Poor
12000	10000	7500	4550	3000	1750

Ulm

Sidelock over/under offered in both 12- and 16-gauge.

NIB	Exc.	V.G.	Good	Fair	Poor
20000	16500	13000	8000	4500	3000

Ulm Dural

Lightweight version of above model.

NIB	Exc.	V.G.	Good	Fair	Poor
20000	16500	13000	8000	4500	3000

Ulm Primus

Deluxe version of Ulm series, with sidelocks and extensive engraving.

NIB	Exc.	V.G.	Good	Fair	Poor
30000	22250	16500	12000	7000	3500

Ulm Primus Dural

Lightweight version of above model.

NIB	Exc.	V.G.	Good	Fair	Poor
30000	22250	16500	12000	7000	3500

Ultra

Lightweight over/under gun offered in 12- or 20-gauge.

NIB	Exc.	V.G.	Good	Fair	Poor
—	6250	4850	2750	1650	1250

KS-5 Single Barrel Trap

Boxlock 12-gauge only trap gun, with 32" or 34" ventilated tapered rib barrel. Case-hardened frame, with satin gray finish. Barrel features adjustable point of impact. Offered with screw-in choke tubes. Weight about 8.6 lbs.

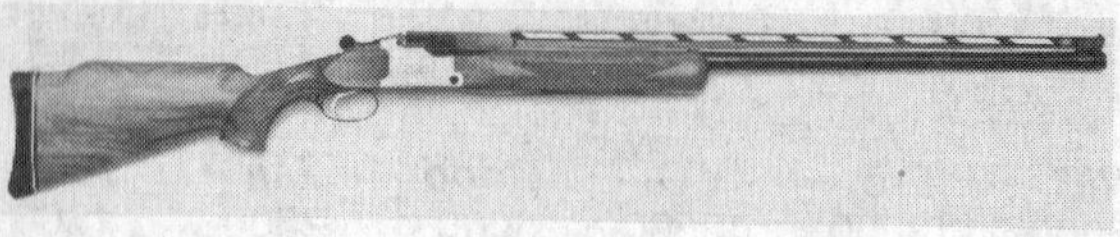

NIB	Exc.	V.G.	Good	Fair	Poor
8000	7500	5900	3650	1250	800

KS-5 Special

Same as above, with adjustable rib and comb.

NIB	Exc.	V.G.	Good	Fair	Poor
8250	7750	6100	3900	1500	1000

K-80 Trap

Boxlock 12-gauge shotgun built to trap dimensions. Offered in many variations. Available in over/under trap, with choice of 30" or 32" ventilated tapered step rib barrels. Single-barrel offered in 32" or 34" tapered step rib lengths. Single-barrels are adjustable for point of impact. Top single-barrel available in 34" length. Trap combos are also offered. All barrels offered with-/without choke tubes. Checkered walnut stock offered in Monte Carlo or straight trap dimensions. Trap gun weight about 8.75 lbs. Prices listed for Standard Grade. Note: Add 70 percent for Bavaria Grade; 100 percent for Danube Grade; 200 percent for Gold Target Grade.

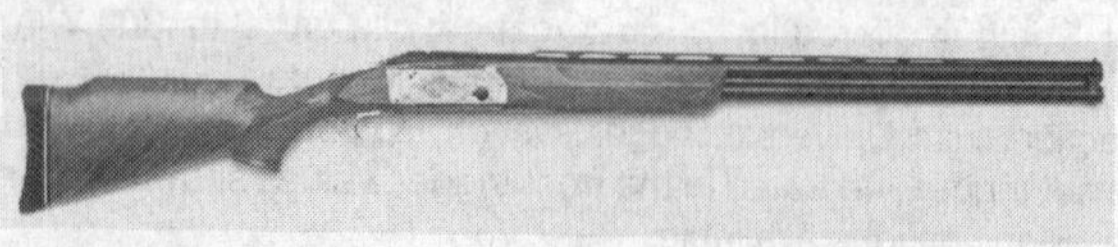

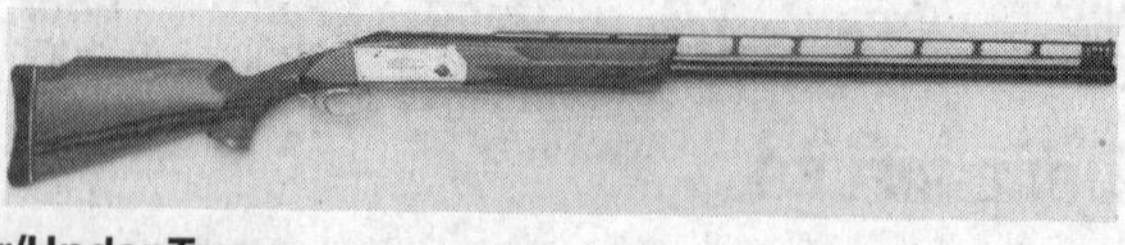

Over/Under Trap

NIB	Exc.	V.G.	Good	Fair	Poor
9800	8000	6000	4200	2500	1000

Unsingle Trap

NIB	Exc.	V.G.	Good	Fair	Poor
11000	9000	7200	5500	3000	1500

Top Single Trap

NIB	Exc.	V.G.	Good	Fair	Poor
11500	10000	8000	6000	3700	1850

Trap Combos

NIB	Exc.	V.G.	Good	Fair	Poor
13000	10700	9600	7400	4300	1900

K-20 Sporting and Field

Compact frame variation of K-80, chambered in 20- or 28-gauge and .410 bore. Barrels are 30" or 32", with five choke tubes and tapered flat rib. Checkered walnut stock, auto ejectors and single-selective trigger. Weight about 7.25 lbs. Available with extra sets of barrels in other two gauges.

NIB	Exc.	V.G.	Good	Fair	Poor
9000	8000	7000	4000	2200	1000

K-20 Sporting

NIB	Exc.	V.G.	Good	Fair	Poor
12000	—	—	—	—	—

K-20 Parcours

NIB	Exc.	V.G.	Good	Fair	Poor
12000	—	—	—	—	—

K-20 Victoria

NIB	Exc.	V.G.	Good	Fair	Poor
12000	—	—	—	—	—

K-80 Sporting Clays

Same frame as trap model, with addition of lightweight alloy model available in 12-gauge only. Barrel lengths: standard weight 28", 30" or 32", with tapered flat rib; lightweight alloy 28" or 30" flat rib barrels. Select European walnut stock, with hand-checkering and supplied with #3 Sporting stock, with schnabel forearm. Weight: standard weight 8.25 lbs.; lightweight alloy 7.75 lbs. Prices listed are for Standard Grade. Note: Add 70 percent for Bavaria Grade; 100 percent for Danube Grade; 200 percent for Gold Target Grade.

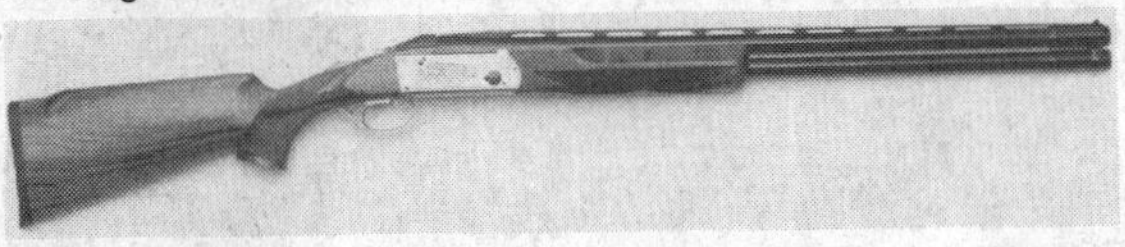

NIB	Exc.	V.G.	Good	Fair	Poor
9500	8000	7000	4000	2200	1000

K-80 Skeet

Offered in a number of variations. Standard and Lightweight skeet, with 28" or 30" tapered or parallel ribs; International skeet, with 28" parallel broadway rib; 4-barrel skeet set in 12-, 20-, 28-gauge and .410 bore, with 8mm rib. Stock hand-checkered select European walnut, with choice of several skeet dimensions. Values listed are for Standard Grade. Note: Add 70 percent for Bavaria Grade; 100 percent for Danube Grade; 200 percent for Gold Target Grade. Optional Engravings available by special order on NIB or Exc. conditions guns: Add $1500 Parcours; $2800 Parcours Special; $1100 Super Scroll; $2900 Gold Super Scroll; $4700 Custom Bavaria over Bavaria Grade price.

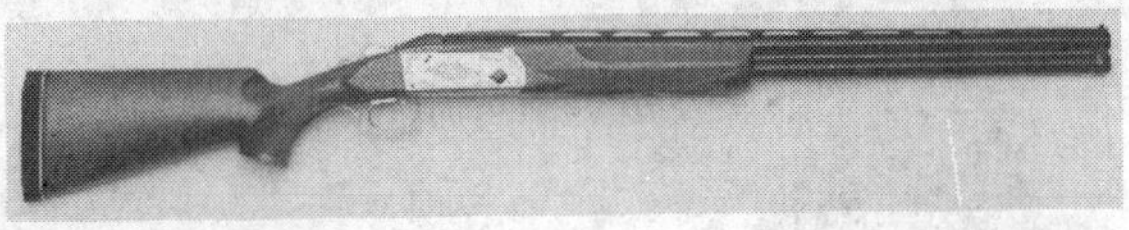

Standard Weight Skeet

NIB	Exc.	V.G.	Good	Fair	Poor
7500	6250	4950	3300	2200	1000

Lightweight Skeet

NIB	Exc.	V.G.	Good	Fair	Poor
7500	6250	4950	3300	2200	1000

International Skeet

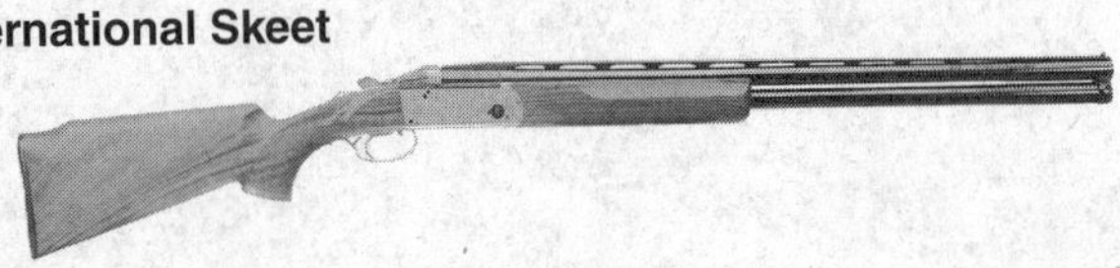

NIB	Exc.	V.G.	Good	Fair	Poor
7500	6250	4950	3300	2200	1000

4 Barrel Set

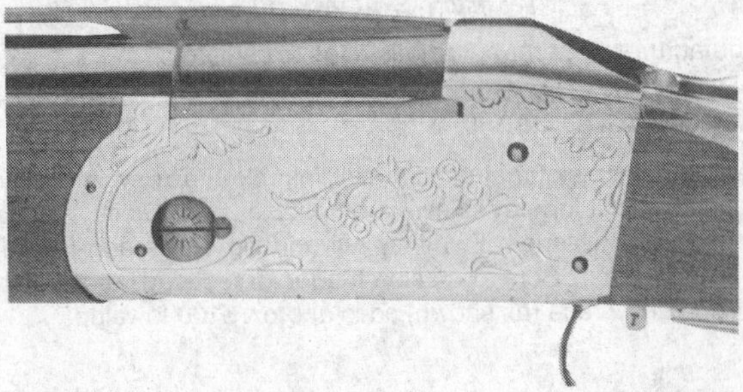

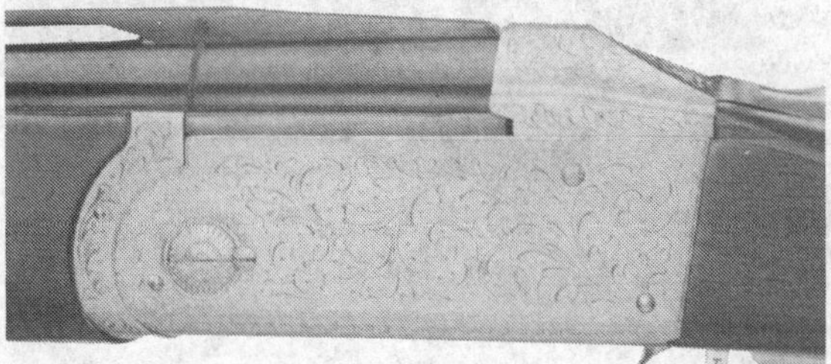

NIB	Exc.	V.G.	Good	Fair	Poor
17000	10000	7600	4400	3300	2200

SIDE-BY-SIDE DOUBLES

Essencia Boxlock

High-grade model introduced in 2003. Has round-body receiver, with English-style scroll engraving and gold highlights. Offered in 12-, 16-, 20- and 28-gauge, with 28" or 30" barrels and Fixed IC/M chokes. Straight-grip Turkish walnut checkered stock, single (non-selective) or double triggers and automatic ejectors. Note: Add $1000 for 28-gauge; $1000 for single trigger.

NIB	Exc.	V.G.	Good	Fair	Poor
22000	17500	15000	10000	3000	800

Essencia Sidelock

Also introduced in 2003. Back-action sidelock on three frame sizes, designed for different gauges. Offered in 12-, 16-, 20- and 28-gauge. Barrel lengths 18", 26.5" or 30", with Fixed chokes or Briley choke tubes. Receiver is color case-hardened, with gold-inlayed engraving. Straight-/pistol grip Turkish walnut checkered stock, single (non-selective) or double triggers and automatic ejectors. Note: Add $1000 for 28-gauge; $1000 for single trigger; $1500 for Briley choke tubes.

NIB	Exc.	V.G.	Good	Fair	Poor
27000	22500	18000	12000	4000	800

KRISS ARMS GROUP (KRISS USA)
Etoy, Switzerland

Manufacturer of semi-automatic rifles and pistols.

Vector SDP/SDP Gen II

Semi-automatic pistol that uses a multilink, blowback system designed to redirect recoil energy down. Compatible with Glock magazines. Equipped with full-length Picatinny rail and flip sights and SB Tactical SBX-K brace. 9mm. Bore axis below trigger for reduced perceived recoil. Stabilizing arm brace (as shown) adds approx. $100 to value.

NIB	*Exc.*	*V.G.*	*Good*	*Fair*	*Poor*
1230	1080	930	680	560	460

Vector CRB

9mm pistol caliber carbine built on same action and general design as the pistol. 16" barrel standard. Variations are offered to meet legal restrictions in MA, NJ, CA, MD, and Canada.

NIB	*Exc.*	*V.G.*	*Good*	*Fair*	*Poor*
1230	1080	930	680	560	460

KRNKA, KAREL
Vienna, Austria

Karel Krnka was a talented firearms inventor, born in 1858. He began his career in firearms design as a member of the Austro-Hungarian army. He made many improvements to their service rifle design. After he left the military, he took the job of head engineer, with ill-fated and short-lived "Gatling Gun Company". This company ceased operations in 1890. Krnka then went to work for the patent office and remained there for a few years. In 1898, he became foreman of Roth Cartridge Company and worked with Roth on firearm designs until the death of Roth in 1909. After this, he became associated with Hertenberger Cartridge Company; and finally in 1922 he moved to Czechoslovakia, where he became a firearms designer for the firm of C.Z. He remained at this post until his death in 1926. He recorded his first firearm patent in 1888 for a mechanical repeater with a ring trigger. His best known innovations are the internal butt magazine, that is loaded by means of a stripper clip and rotating locked bolt, with internal firing pin. These designs were never actually turned into a mass-marketed pistol, but were major contributions in the development of a practical semi-automatic pistol design. Krnka's name is associated with the Model 1867 Russian military conversion of muzzleloading Model 1857 to a breechloading rifle. Various model-name dates have been assigned to early Krnka pistols, including Models 1895, 1897, 1898, 1899 and possibly 1892. The more commonly encountered Roth-Steyr M1907 pistol may be correctly called Roth-Krnka M7. The early Krnka firearms come on the market too seldom to publish a meaningful value estimate by condition. Sales of Krnka Model 1867 conversion rifles have been reported in the $2,000 to $5,000 range. Krnka pistols identified as Model 1895 prototypes have sold in the $13,000 to $16,000 range. Model 1905 Krnka pistols have sold in the $4,000 to $8,000 range.

KSN INDUSTRIES
Israel

Golan

Semi-automatic pistol introduced in 1996. Chambered for 9mm or .40 S&W cartridge. Double-action trigger, with ambidextrous controls. Barrel length 3.9". Magazine capacity: 10 rounds in U.S.; rest of the world 15 rounds 9mm, 11 rounds .40 S&W. Weight 29 oz.

NIB	*Exc.*	*V.G.*	*Good*	*Fair*	*Poor*
650	520	400	320	200	100

Kareen MK II

Single-action semi-automatic pistol, chambered for 9mm cartridge. Barrel length 4.5". Ambidextrous safety and rubber grips. Steel slide and frame. Weight about 34 oz.

NIB	*Exc.*	*V.G.*	*Good*	*Fair*	*Poor*
500	400	250	200	150	100

Kareen MK II—Compact

Same as above, with 3.9" barrel. Weight about 32 oz.

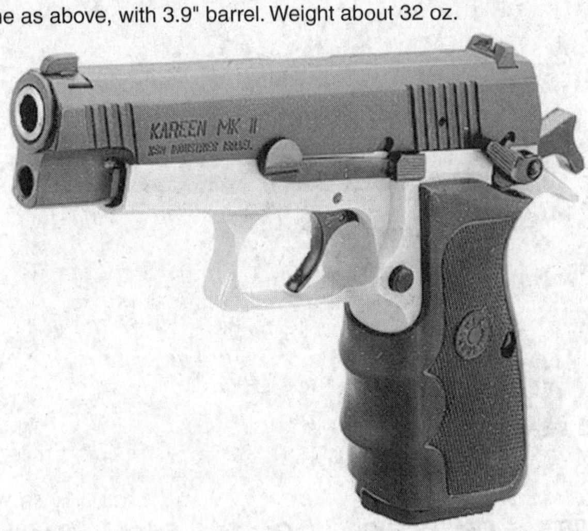

NIB	Exc.	V.G.	Good	Fair	Poor
580	420	320	250	200	150

GAL

Same as full size Kareen. Chambered for .45 ACP cartridge.

NIB	Exc.	V.G.	Good	Fair	Poor
580	420	320	250	200	150

KUFAHL, G. L.
Sommerda, Germany

Kufahl Needle-Fire Revolver

Designed and patented in Britain in 1852 by G.L. Kufahl, who tried unsuccessfully to interest a British company in producing it. He then went to the firm of Rheinmettal Dreyse, where a needle-fire gun was produced in 1838. This company manufactured his design. This revolver was chambered for a unique, totally consumed .30-caliber "cartridge". A lead projectile had the ignition percussion cap affixed to its base, with propellant powder in rear. Firing pin had to be long enough to penetrate the powder charge and hit the percussion cap. This does not sound efficient, but realize that these were the days before cartridges. This revolver has a 3.2" barrel and an unfluted cylinder that holds six shots. It is not bored all the way through, but is loaded from the front. Finish is blued, with a modicum of simple engraving and checkered wood grips that protrude all the way over the trigger. Markings are "Fv.V. Dreyse Sommerda".

NIB	Exc.	V.G.	Good	Fair	Poor
—	—	2950	1600	650	400

KYNOCH GUN FACTORY
Birmingham, England

Established by George Kynoch as a successor firm to Tranter in 1886. The firm ceased operation in 1890. Henry Schlund was the manager, and held patents for their best known product, the Kynoch Schlund revolver.

Kynoch Schlund Revolver

This unusual design was a top-break, auto-eject hammerless (concealed hammer) revolver, with two triggers. The lower trigger that served to rotate the cylinder and cock the hammer while the upper trigger fired the revolver in single-action mode. At least some of the models can be fired by a very heavy pull on the upper trigger. On the early guns, the lower cocking trigger extends below the triggerguard, and on the later models it is inside the large triggerguard, above and in front of the firing trigger. Calibers reported include .476, .450, .43, .380, and .320, with frame sizes appropriate to the chamberings. These guns are rarely encountered and rarely sold, so estimated values are a bit speculative. Large frame/large caliber brings a premium over smaller revolvers. Detachable wire shoulder stock adds 50% to 100% to value.

NIB	Exc.	V.G.	Good	Fair	Poor
6000	4000	2500	1750	1200	600

Kynoch-Dimancea (Antique)

A .38- or .45-caliber double-action hammerless revolver, with 6-shot cylinder. Loading system rather unusual—a spur that resembles a hammer is pulled down allowing barrel and cylinder to pivot and to be pulled forward. During this motion, empty cases are ejected and new ones could be inserted. Marked "The Gatling Arms and Ammunition Co. Birmingham"; also marked "Dimancea Patent".

Exc.	Fine	V.G.	Good	Fair	Poor
2500	1280	1010	750	350	240

L

LAGRESE
Paris, France

Lagrese Revolver

Previous editions listed the Lagrese as a "Large ornate revolver chambered for .43 rimfire cartridge. Has 6.25" barrel, 6-shot fluted cylinder, no topstrap, frame as well as grip straps are cast in one piece, with barrel screwed into frame. It is loaded through a gate and has double-action lock work. Outstanding feature about this well-made revolver is its extremely ornate appearance. There are more sweeps and curves than could be imagined. In general outline somewhat resembles the leMat, though with a single barrel. Engraved and blued, with well-figured curved walnut grips. Marked "Lagrese Bte a Paris". Manufactured in late 1860s." Little information is available on this model. A few references suggest that it is identical to a model in the NRA Museums identified as a Pidault & Cordier revolver chambered for the unique 12mm Perrin cartridge, ca. 1860s. No recent sales known. Additional information would be appreciated, contact editor. Value too rare to estimate.

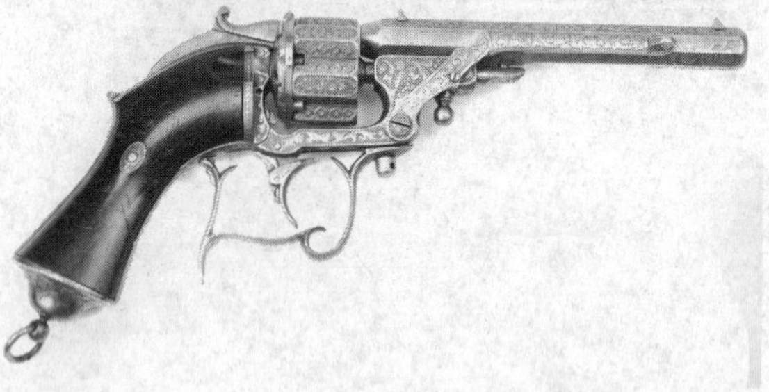

Photo courtesy of NRA Museums

LAHTI
Finland

See—HUSQVARNA

Lahti

Commercial version of Finnish L-35 9mm pistol. Pistols have barrel and triggerguard design of L-35, but barrel extension of Swedish M40. Produced in late 1950s.

Courtesy J.B. Wood

NIB	*Exc.*	*V.G.*	*Good*	*Fair*	*Poor*
—	1250	1000	800	550	300

LAKELANDER
Gulfport, Mississippi

Model 389 Premium

Bolt-action rifle chambered for .270 Win., .308 Win. and .30-06 calibers. Fitted with 22" light-weight barrel. Stock oil-finished walnut, with diamond checkering. Rosewood forend cap, black recoil pad and Monte Carlo buttstock. Weight about 7.6 lbs. Introduced in 1997.

NIB	*Exc.*	*V.G.*	*Good*	*Fair*	*Poor*
1750	1350	950	700	380	200

Model 389 Classic

Similar to 389 Premium above. Offered with traditional checkering and stock (less fancy walnut stock). Weight about 7.3 lbs. Introduced in 1997.

NIB	*Exc.*	*V.G.*	*Good*	*Fair*	*Poor*
1720	1320	920	680	350	150

Model 389 Match-Maker

Bolt-action chambered for .308 cartridge. Fitted with 21.7" barrel. Stock is target style, with adjustable chin support with benchrest-style buttpad. Weight about 8.4 lbs. Introduced in 1997. Note: Add $50 for Magnum calibers.

NIB	*Exc.*	*V.G.*	*Good*	*Fair*	*Poor*
2250	1850	1350	850	580	250

LAMB, H. C. & CO.
Jamestown, North Carolina

Muzzleloading Rifle (Antique)

Chambered for .58-caliber and utilizes percussion ignition system. Has 33" barrel and full-length oak stock held on by two barrel bands. Ramrod mounted under barrel made of iron. All other trim is brass. A bayonet lug at muzzle. Rifle was made for Confederacy and workmanship was crude, as it was on most CSA weapons. Stock marked "H.C.Lamb & Co., N.C." Supposedly 10,000 rifles ordered, but approximately 250 manufactured between 1861 and 1863. Rarity of guns of Confederacy gives them a great deal of collector appeal.

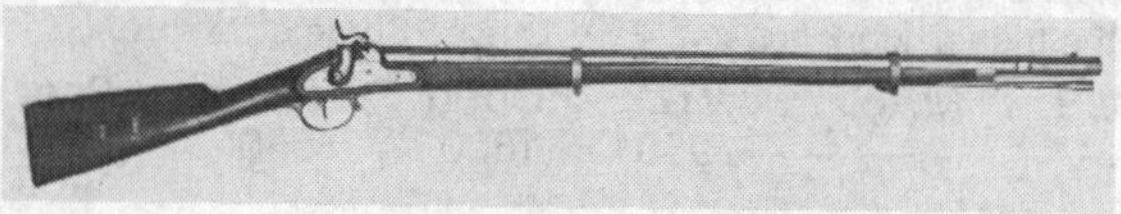

Courtesy Milwaukee Public Museum, Milwaukee, Wisconsin

Exc.	*Fine*	*V.G.*	*Good*	*Fair*	*Poor*
35000	15000	8870	2750	500	350

LAMES
Chiavari, Italy

Skeet or Trap Grade

Over/under shotgun chambered for 12-gauge, with 26" skeet-and-skeet barrels or 30" or 32" Full-choked barrels. Has competition-style wide ventilated rib and automatic ejectors. Trigger single-selective and finish blued. Trap gun has Monte Carlo stock of checkered walnut. Both models feature recoil pads.

NIB	Exc.	V.G.	Good	Fair	Poor
—	700	580	480	380	200

California Trap Grade

Over/under similar to standard trap model, with separated barrels. All other features the same.

NIB	Exc.	V.G.	Good	Fair	Poor
—	780	650	580	480	220

Field Grade

Similar in design to standard trap model, with 3" chambers and barrel lengths of 26", 28" or 30". Field dimensioned stock. Features various choke combinations. Also available with separated barrels of California Trap for an additional 20 percent cost.

NIB	Exc.	V.G.	Good	Fair	Poor
—	480	450	350	250	150

LANBER ARMAS S.A.
Vizcaya, Spain

Model 2072 Slug

Fixed choke double-barrel slug gun, with 3" chambers and 20" barrel. Fiber-optic rifle sights. Weight about 6 lbs. Hard-to-find gun.

NIB	Exc.	V.G.	Good	Fair	Poor
900	800	650	480	300	200

Model 844 ST

12-gauge over/under shotgun, with 26" or 28" ventilated rib barrels. Chokes vary. Features single-selective trigger, extractors and engraved receiver, with blued finish and walnut stock. Manufactured until 1986.

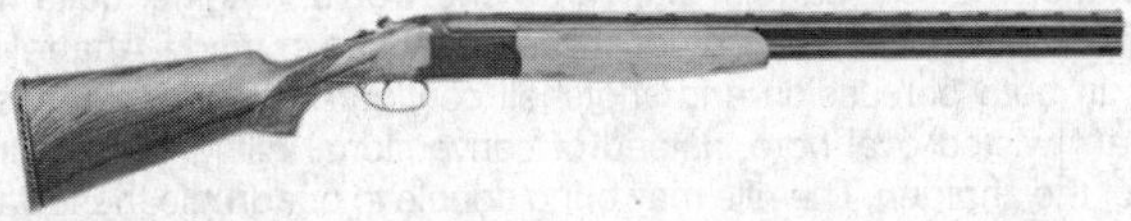

NIB	Exc.	V.G.	Good	Fair	Poor
—	420	350	300	250	180

Model 844 MST

Similar to Model 844 ST except chambered for 3" Magnum. Has 30" Full and Modified choked barrels.

NIB	Exc.	V.G.	Good	Fair	Poor
—	520	450	300	250	180

Model 844 EST

Similar to others, but features automatic ejectors.

NIB	Exc.	V.G.	Good	Fair	Poor
—	580	420	350	300	200

Model 844 EST CHR

Has automatic ejectors and double triggers. All other features same as EST.

NIB	Exc.	V.G.	Good	Fair	Poor
—	550	400	320	280	180

Model 2004 LCH

Over/under chambered for 12-gauge. Features 28" ventilated rib barrels, with screw-in choke tubes. Single-selective trigger, automatic ejectors. Engraved boxlock action that is matte finished, with hand-checkered walnut stock. Discontinued in 1986.

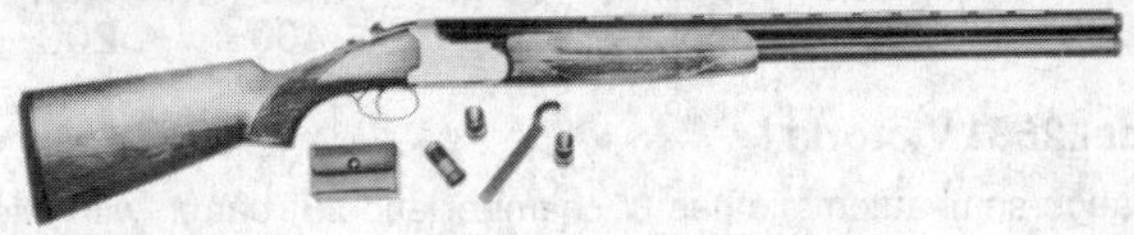

NIB	Exc.	V.G.	Good	Fair	Poor
—	780	650	550	480	380

Model 2008 LCH and Model 2009 LCH

Trap and skeet versions of series. Basic differences in barrel lengths and stock dimensions.

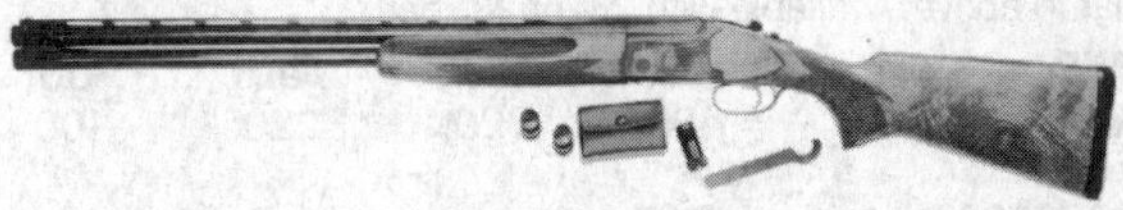

Model 2008 LCH

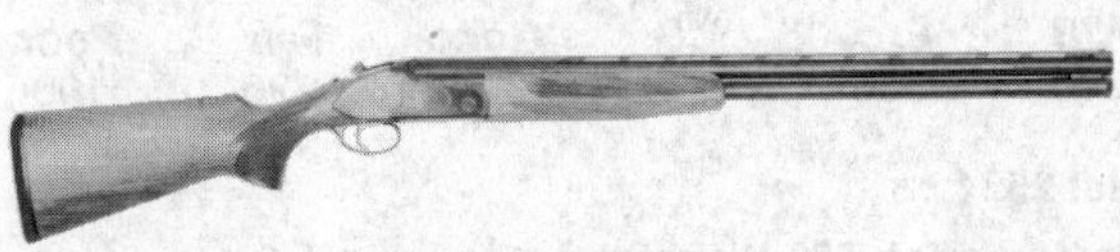

NIB	Exc.	V.G.	Good	Fair	Poor
—	900	750	650	580	480

Model 2067

20-gauge over/under, with 3" chambers. Has 28" barrels, auto ejectors and oil-finished walnut stock. Weight about 6.6 lbs.

NIB	Exc.	V.G.	Good	Fair	Poor
780	650	550	450	380	200

Model 2077 Hunter Light

A 2.75" 12-gauge, with 26" barrels and lightweight alloy receiver. Weight about 6.2 lbs.

NIB	Exc.	V.G.	Good	Fair	Poor
850	720	580	480	400	200

Model 2087 Hunter

12-gauge comes with 3" chambers, auto ejectors, oil-finished walnut stock and 28" or 30" barrel. Weight about 7 lbs.

NIB	Exc.	V.G.	Good	Fair	Poor
780	650	550	450	380	200

Model 2097 Sporting

Sporting clays model in 12-gauge, with 3" chambers and 28" or 30" barrels. Weight about 7.7 lbs. Note: Add $50 for Sporting LUX.

NIB	Exc.	V.G.	Good	Fair	Poor
850	720	580	480	400	200

Model 2088 Rival I

Sporting clays model is 2.75" 12-gauge, with 28" barrels and case-hardened receiver. Weight about 7.6 lbs.

NIB	Exc.	V.G.	Good	Fair	Poor
1600	1300	850	600	400	200

Model 2089 Rival II

This 2.75" 12-gauge sporting clays has 30" barrels, one fixed and other threaded for choke tubes. Blued receiver. Weight about 7.9 lbs.

NIB	Exc.	V.G.	Good	Fair	Poor
1600	1300	850	600	400	200

Model 2070 Becada

This 3" 12-gauge developed for woodcock hunting. Features one Fixed choke barrel; one barrel threaded for chokes. Barrel length 23"; weight about 6 lbs.

NIB	Exc.	V.G.	Good	Fair	Poor
850	720	580	480	400	200

Model 2531 Victoria I

12-gauge semi-automatic has 3" chamber and 28" barrel, with internal choke tube system. Stock oil-finished walnut. Receiver blued. Weight about 6.8 lbs.

NIB	Exc.	V.G.	Good	Fair	Poor
600	500	400	300	200	100

Model 2532 Victoria II

Similar to above. Available with 26" or 28" barrel.

NIB	Exc.	V.G.	Good	Fair	Poor
620	520	420	320	220	100

Model 2532 Victoria II EXT

Similar to above, with 24.5" barrel. External choke tube system.

NIB	Exc.	V.G.	Good	Fair	Poor
620	520	420	320	220	100

Model 2534

Lighter version of 2532. Weight about 6.4 lbs., with 26" barrel.

NIB	Exc.	V.G.	Good	Fair	Poor
620	520	420	320	220	100

Model 2533 Victoria LUX

Semi-automatic 3" 12-gauge. Features brushed silver finish scrollwork and gold mallard on receiver. Barrel 26" or 28". Weight about 6.8 lbs.

NIB	Exc.	V.G.	Good	Fair	Poor
650	550	450	350	250	100

Model 2533 Victoria LUX EXT

As above, with 24.5" barrel. External choke tube system.

NIB	Exc.	V.G.	Good	Fair	Poor
650	550	450	350	250	100

Model 2535 Victoria Slug

Dedicated slug gun has fiber-optic rifle sights atop 24" fixed cylinder barrel.

NIB	Exc.	V.G.	Good	Fair	Poor
650	550	450	350	250	100

LANCASTER, CHARLES

London, England

4-Barreled Pistol Antique

Unique pistol for several reasons. Chambered for .476 rimfire cartridge and four 6.25" barrels. Bore has slightly twisted oval pattern that imparts a spin to bullet. Barrels are hinged at bottom and break downward for loading. Double-action type lockwork, with long difficult trigger pull. Pistol well made and caliber suitably heavy to insure stopping power. Primary goal was military; successful seeing action in Sudan campaigns of 1882 and 1885. This powerful weapon was also popular with big game hunters as a backup sidearm. Finish blued, with checkered walnut grips. Marked "Charles Lancaster (Patent) 151 New Bond St. London". Introduced in 1881. There are smaller-caliber versions of this pistol, with shorter barrels. They are not as well known as large-caliber version and values would be similar as their rarity would be balanced by desirability of large bore models.

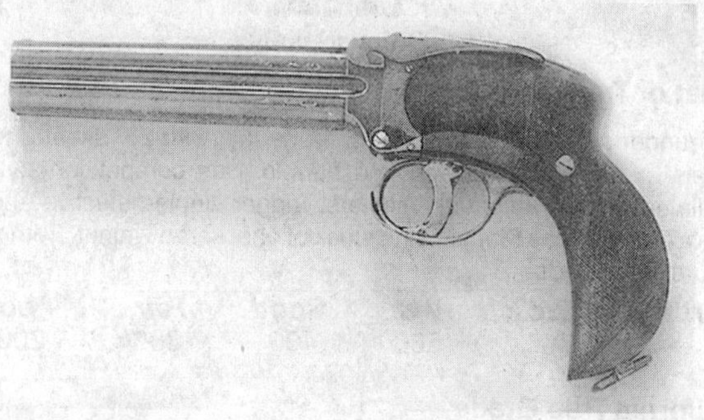

Exc.	Fine	V.G.	Good	Fair	Poor
11000	8000	5000	3000	2000	1250

2-Barreled Pistol Antique

Similar to 4 barreled version, with only two superposed barrels. Chambered for a variety of calibers from .320 to .577. Also chambered for 20-gauge and .410 bore. Advantage to 2 barreled pistol it is lighter and better balanced. The 2 barrel is less common than 4 barrel version.

Courtesy James Rankin

Exc.	Fine	V.G.	Good	Fair	Poor
9000	7000	5000	2000	1500	750

4-Barreled Shotgun or rifle Antique

Also produced a shotgun in 4 barrel configuration. Chambered for 12- or 16-gauge, with 28" barrels. Gun is as one would imagine, quite heavy and poorly balanced; not a great success. Lancaster made 4-barrel shotguns in both percussion and shotshell configuration. The express rifle had an twisted oval bore instead of conventional rifling. Values shown are for the shotgun. The rifle may bring double to quadruple these values.

Exc.	Fine	V.G.	Good	Fair	Poor
10000	7500	5000	2000	1000	700

Bolt-Action Rifle

High-grade sporting rifle chambered for various different calibers. Barrel 24" in length; finish blued with classic-styled hand-checkered walnut stock. Discontinued in 1936.

NIB	Exc.	V.G.	Good	Fair	Poor
—	3500	1900	1250	800	600

LANG, J.

London, England

Maker of high-end British double guns. See ATKIN GRANT & LANG.

Percussion Pistol Antique

Chambered for .60-caliber percussion. Single-barreled muzzleloading pistol, with 3.25" barrel. Essentially a defensive weapon that was well made. Damascus barrels and ornate engraved hammer and frame. In addition to the models listed Lang also made percussion pistols in other configurations, percussion rifles, swivel barrel over/under boxlock pecussion pistols, over/under percussion howdah pistols, pepperboxes, side by side double barrel percussion carriage pistols, and percussion cane guns.

Exc.	Fine	V.G.	Good	Fair	Poor
4510	3000	2050	1100	600	420

Gas Seal Revolver (Antique)

Chambered for .42-caliber percussion and 4.75" barrel. Unfluted cylinder holds 6 shots and spring-loaded to be forced into barrel when cocked, in order to obtain "Gas Seal" feature desired. Revolver was well made and finished. Lightly engraved, with case colored cylinder, blued barrel and frame. Grips are finely checkered walnut. Markings are "J.Lang 22 Cockspur St. London". This type of firearm was forerunner of later designs such as Russian Nagant. Manufactured in 1850s.

Exc.	Fine	V.G.	Good	Fair	Poor
4000	2750	1500	850	500	350

LANGENHAN, FRIEDRICH
Zella Mehlis, Germany

F.L. Selbstlader is not a manufacturer, but the German designation for self-loader used on pistols made by Friedrich Langenhan.

Army Model

Blowback-operated semi-automatic chambered for 7.65mm Auto Pistol cartridge. Has 4" barrel and detachable magazine that holds 8 rounds. Weight about 24 oz. Made with separate breech-block that is held into slide by a screw. This feature doomed pistol to eventual failure, when this screw became worn it could loosen when firing and allow breech-block to pivot upwards—and slide would then be propelled rearward and into the face of shooter. Produced with wood grips.

Courtesy James Rankin

NIB	Exc.	V.G.	Good	Fair	Poor
—	380	300	250	180	100

Open Model

Semi-automatic similar to Army Model, with some minor variations. Open window in frame. Checkered hard rubber grips, with "FL" logo on each side.

Courtesy James Rankin

NIB	Exc.	V.G.	Good	Fair	Poor
—	400	320	280	200	100

Closed Model

Similar to Open Model, with closed frame and other minor variations.

Courtesy James Rankin

NIB	Exc.	V.G.	Good	Fair	Poor
—	400	320	280	200	100

Model 2

Blowback-operated semi-automatic chambered for 6.35mm cartridge. Has 3" barrel and 8-round detachable magazine. Weight about 18 oz. Fires by means of concealed hammer. Breech-block separate from rest of slide and held in place by a heavy crossbolt. Finish blued. Grips are molded checkered black plastic, with monogram "F.L." at top. Slide marked "Langenhan 6.35". Manufactured between 1921 and 1936.

Courtesy James Rankin

NIB	Exc.	V.G.	Good	Fair	Poor
—	380	300	250	200	100

Model 3

Similar to Model 2 except somewhat smaller. Barrel 2.25" in length. Butt only large enough to house a 5-round detachable magazine. Weight about 17 oz. Markings the same with addition of "Model 111" on slide. Manufactured until 1936.

NIB	Exc.	V.G.	Good	Fair	Poor
—	320	280	250	200	150

LANSOM & CO.
See—BALL REPEATING CARBINE

LAR MFG. CO.
West Jordan, Utah

Grizzly Mark I

.357 Magnum, .45 ACP, 10mm or .45 Win. Magnum semi-automatic pistol, with 5.4-, 6.5-, 8- or 10-in. barrel. Millett sights, ambidextrous safety and 7-shot magazine. Parkerized, blued or hard-chrome plated, with rubber grips. Available with cartridge conversion units, telescope mounts or compensator. Weight about 48 oz. Introduced in 1984.

NIB	Exc.	V.G.	Good	Fair	Poor
1400	1200	950	700	400	200

Grizzly Mark II

As above, with fixed sights. Without ambidextrous safety. Manufactured in 1986.

NIB	Exc.	V.G.	Good	Fair	Poor
—	1300	1050	780	480	300

Grizzly Mark IV

Similar to Mark I. Chambered for .44 Magnum cartridge. Barrel lengths 5.4" or 6.5". Choice of blue or Parkerized finish.

NIB	Exc.	V.G.	Good	Fair	Poor
1500	1100	780	500	400	200

Grizzly Mark V

Same as above, but chambered for .50 AE cartridge. Empty weight 56 oz. Note: Add $200 for nickel finish.

NIB	Exc.	V.G.	Good	Fair	Poor
1950	1350	1000	650	420	200

Grizzly State Pistol

Limited edition of 50 Grizzly pistols. Serial numbers match order in which each state was admitted into the union. Each pistol features state outline, state seal and name of state engraved in gold. Supplied with cherrywood fitted case, with glass top. Chambered for .45 Win. Magnum cartridge.

NIB	Exc.	V.G.	Good	Fair	Poor
3000	—	—	—	—	—

Grizzly 50 Big Boar

Single-shot breech-loading rifle chambered for .50-caliber BMG cartridge. Barrel 36" in length. Weight about 30 lbs. Note: Add $100 for Parkerized finish; $250 for nickel frame; $350 for full nickel finish.

NIB	Exc.	V.G.	Good	Fair	Poor
2350	2000	1550	1100	550	300

LARUE TACTICAL
Leander, Texas

Produces a variety of AR pattern rifles and other arms. Some rifle models are also available in Class III short-barrel-rifle configurations. In addition to the production models listed, LaRue has produced limited editions including, Costa Edition 5.56 , UDE (Ultra Dark Earth) Edition 5.56 PredatOBR, FDE 7.62 Heavy Barrel PredatAR rifle (similar to Costa Edition), and 6.5 Grendel FDE Rifle. SEE POLITICAL PANIC PRICING.

OBR (Optimized Battle Rifle)

AR-style series available in 5.56 NATO (.223 Rem.) or 7.62 NATO (.308 Win.). In several variations and barrel lengths. Handguard does not touch barrel at any point, resulting in a weapon that remains cool, even after high rates of fire. There is a continuous upper rail for day/night accessories, plus three 3" Picatinny rail sections to be attached anywhere on the handguard. A two-point adjustable gas selector allows optimum function between suppressed and unsuppressed operation. Barrel lengths available are 16.1", 18" and 20". Adjustable telescoping stock on 16.1" and 18" models.

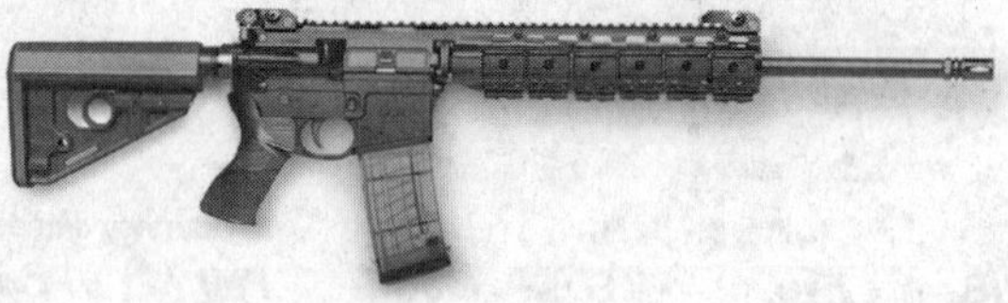

NIB	Exc.	V.G.	Good	Fair	Poor
1900	1600	1350	980	550	250

OBR, 5.56 NATO

Calibers: 5.56 NATO/.223. Barrels: 16.1, 18, or 20 in. Weights: 7.5–9.25 lbs. Features: Manufacturer of several models of AR-style rifles and carbines. Optimized Battle Rifle (OBR) series is made in both NATO calibers. Many AR-type options available. Made in the USA.

NIB	Exc.	V.G.	Good	Fair	Poor
2750	1800	1500	—	—	—

OBR, 7.62 NATO

Same basic features as 5.56 version, with heavier frame for larger calibers. Barrel lengths 16, 18 or 20 in. Has proprietary XTRAXTN chamber for enhanced extraction, with wide range of loads and temperatures.

NIB	Exc.	V.G.	Good	Fair	Poor
4130	2750	2250	—	—	—

PredatAR 5.56

Caliber: 5.56 NATO. Chambered in .223 Wylde. Match-grade barrel, 16" and 18", 1:8" twist, medium-weight contour. Muzzle threaded in 1/2x28, with A2 flash hider. A six-position LaRue RAT Stock and LaRue A-PEG

Grip. Weight: 6.25 lbs. Introduced 2011. SEE POLITICAL PANIC PRICING.

NIB	Exc.	V.G.	Good	Fair	Poor
2180	2000	1890	1680	—	—

PredatAR 7.62

NIB	Exc.	V.G.	Good	Fair	Poor
2700	2500	2100	—	—	—

PredatOBR

Described as a cross between the OBR and the PredatAR models. Can be quickly broken down for storage or transport. Available in 5.56 NATO, 7.62 NATO, .260 caliber, or 6.5 Creedmoor. Barrel lengths are 16.1", 18", or 20" for 5.56 NATO and 7.62 NATO calibers; 20" or 22" for .260 caliber and 6.5 Creedmoor.

PredatOBR 5.56

Caliber: 5.56 NATO. Barrels: 16.1", 18", or 20"; 1:8" twist rate; muzzles threaded 1/2x28. Weights: 7.5 to 9.25 lbs. Manufacturer of several models of AR-style rifles and carbines. Many AR-type options are available. Hybrid between OBR and PredatAR 5.56x45 Rifles. Can be broken down and stored into the optional Rollup Bag and Toolbox. The handguard has a locking stainless-steel QD lever system to slide off the upper assembly in seconds. Barrel can be removed with supplied wrench, no need to remove the gas tube, gas block, or muzzle device. No conventional AR barrel nut; handguard bolts directly to the proprietary upper receiver, free-floating barrel. Zero-MOA upper rail. Adjustable Port Selector Technology gas block for sound suppressor use. LaRue Tactical six-position Retract Action Trigger (R.A.T.) stock, A-PEG grip. Introduced 2012. Made in the USA. SEE POLITICAL PANIC PRICING.

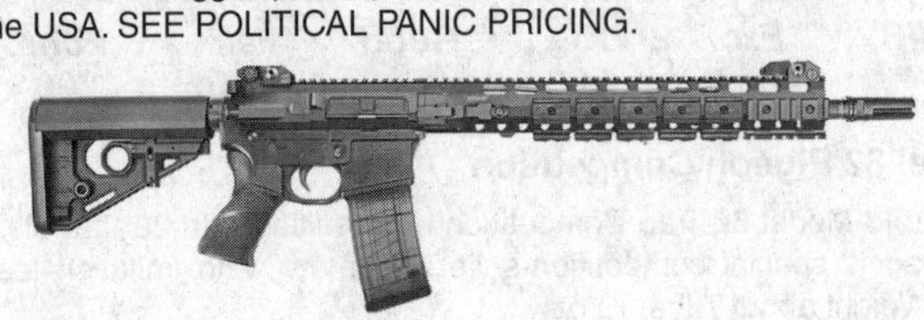

NIB	Exc.	V.G.	Good	Fair	Poor
2700	2500	2200	1890	—	—

PredatOBR 7.62, .260, or 6.5

Calibers: 7.62 NATO, .260 Rem., 6.5 Creedmoor. Barrels: 16.1", 18", or 20"; 1:8" twist rate; muzzles threaded 5/8x24. Weights: 7.5 to 9.25 lbs. Chambering in 6.5 Creedmoor has 20"; 1:7.5" twist. SEE POLITICAL PANIC PRICING.

NIB	Exc.	V.G.	Good	Fair	Poor
4060	3820	3500	3000	—	—

16.1" Black and Tan 5.56

Caliber: 5.56 NATO, 6mm ARC, 6.5 Grendel. Barrels: 16.1", 18", 1:8" twist rate; medium-weight contour, mid-length gas tube, M4 Feed Ramps, and 1/2x28 threaded muzzle. CNC machined LaRue Billet Match Grade Upper mated to LaRue Billet. Full-floating upper handguard with M-LOK attach points, LaRue MBT trigger. LaRue Rat Stock, machined buffer tube, birdcage flash hider installed. Comes in a compact high-impact-polymer case for easy and discreet carry. Add $100 for 6.5 Grendel chambering. SEE POLITICAL PANIC PRICING.

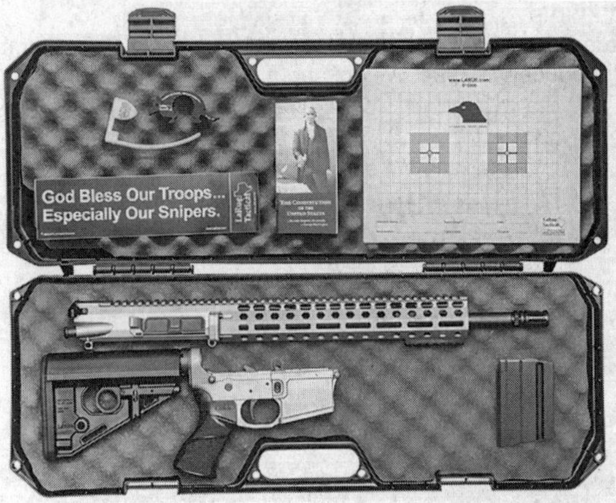

NIB	Exc.	V.G.	Good	Fair	Poor
1940	—	—	—	—	—

LASALLE

France

Slide-Action Shotgun

Chambered for 12- or 20-gauge. Offered with 26", 28" or 30" barrel, with Improved-Cylinder, Modified or Full chokes. Receiver alloy anodized blue and ventilated rib barrel blued. Stock checkered walnut.

NIB	Exc.	V.G.	Good	Fair	Poor
—	280	220	200	150	100

Semi-Automatic Shotgun

Gas-operated semi-automatic shotgun chambered for 12-gauge only. Same barrel length and choke combinations as above. Receiver alloy and stock checkered walnut.

NIB	Exc.	V.G.	Good	Fair	Poor
—	320	250	200	180	100

LASERAIM ARMS

Little Rock, Arkansas

Series I

Offered in 10mm or .45 ACP. Single-action semi-automatic pistol. Fitted with 6" barrel with compensator. Adjustable rear sight. Stainless steel frame and barrel, with matte black Teflon finish. Introduced in 1993. Magazine capacity: 10mm 8-rounds; .45 ACP 7-rounds. Weight about 46 oz.

NIB	Exc.	V.G.	Good	Fair	Poor
650	550	400	300	200	100

Series II

Similar to Series I. Has no compensator. Fitted with 5" barrel. Stainless steel finish. Compact version has 3.375" barrel. Introduced in 1993. Weight: 43 oz. 5" barrel; 37 oz. compact version.

NIB	Exc.	V.G.	Good	Fair	Poor
620	520	380	280	180	100

Series III

Similar to Series II except offered with 5" barrel only. Dual port compensator. Introduced in 1994. Weight about 43 oz.

NIB	Exc.	V.G.	Good	Fair	Poor
650	550	400	300	200	100

LAURONA

Eibar, Spain

Company has manufactured quality shotguns in Spain since 1941, but there has not been a U.S. importer for many years. Last importer was Galaxy Imports of Victoria, Texas, which brought several models of over/under and side-by-side shotguns into the country from about 1967 to early 1990s. One of the unique features of standard Laurona over/under series was a double trigger system, with each trigger acting as a non-selective single trigger. One trigger fired bottom barrel first, then top barrel; other trigger fired top barrel first then bottom barrel. We thank Thomas Barker of Galaxy Imports for information and specifications in these listings.

Model 67

First over/under Laurona chambered for 12-gauge only. Double triggers and 28" ventilated rib barrels, with extractors. Boxlock action. Barrels are blued and stock checkered walnut in 20 lpi skip line checkering.

NIB	Exc.	V.G.	Good	Fair	Poor
—	400	250	150	80	50

Model 71

Similar to Model 67, with minor cosmetic changes and improvements to facilitate ease of manufacturing. Receiver bright chrome, with roll engraving depicting dogs on right side and birds on left. Imported and sold by Sears & Roebuck about 1973-1974. Earlier models had traditional solid center ribbed blued barrels; later models black chrome finished solid ribbed barrels.

NIB	Exc.	V.G.	Good	Fair	Poor
—	450	300	200	100	80

MODEL 82

Similar to Model 71, with auto-ejectors. Chambered for 12-gauge only. All barrels separated without center rib. Black chrome finish and hard chrome bores, with long forcing cones in chambers. Firing pins changed to traditional round type. Many internal parts improved for reliability. Checkering changed from skip diamond to standard 20 lpi. In most respects 82 Models are representative of present-day Laurona over/under shotguns and will share most internal parts. Note: Super Models listed have nickel-finish receivers featuring delicate fine scroll engraving, with black chrome relief. All barrels have very durable rust-resistant black chrome finish.

Model 82 Game

Barrels are 28" with 2.75" or 3" chambers, long forcing cones, hard chrome bores, 5mm rib and chokes. Finish on barrels is black chrome, with nickel receiver with Louis XVI style engraving. Tulip forend, field-style stock, with plastic buttplate. Weight about 7 lbs.

NIB	Exc.	V.G.	Good	Fair	Poor
—	550	400	250	120	100

Model 82 Super Game

Similar to Model 82 Game except more elaborate and very delicate engraving

NIB	Exc.	V.G.	Good	Fair	Poor
—	600	500	300	120	100

Model 82 Trap Combi

Similar to Model 82 Game except for 28" or 29" barrels. Rib is 8mm. Trap stock fitted with rubber recoil pad. Weight about 7.4 lbs.

NIB	Exc.	V.G.	Good	Fair	Poor
—	700	500	350	300	200

Model 82 Trap Competition

Similar to Model 82 Trap Combi except for 13mm aluminum rib, with long white sight. Engraving consists of motifs on sides of receiver. Beavertail fluted forend and Monte Carlo Trap stock, with black rubber special Trap recoil pad. Weight about 8 lbs.

NIB	Exc.	V.G.	Good	Fair	Poor
—	700	500	300	250	200

Model 82 Super Trap (U only)

Similar to Model 82 Trap Competition except for special trap Pachmayr recoil pad, with imitation leather face. Engraving very delicate fine scroll. Weight 7 lbs. 12 oz.

NIB	Exc.	V.G.	Good	Fair	Poor
—	650	500	350	300	250

Model 82 Super Skeet

Similar to Model 82 Super Trap except fitted with 28" barrels, choked Skeet with field-style buttstock and plastic buttplate. Weight about 7 lbs.

NIB	Exc.	V.G.	Good	Fair	Poor
—	650	500	300	250	200

Model 82 Pigeon Competition

Similar to Model 82 Trap Competition except fitted with 28" barrels. Recoil pad is special competition-style Pachmayr, with imitation leather face. Weight about 7 lbs. 13 oz.

NIB	Exc.	V.G.	Good	Fair	Poor
—	650	500	350	300	250

Model 82 Super Pigeon

Similar to Model 82 Super Trap except fitted with 28" barrels. Weight about 7 lbs. 9 oz.

NIB	Exc.	V.G.	Good	Fair	Poor
—	680	580	450	300	250

MODEL 83/84/85

Note: Super Game models listed were available with an extra set of 20-gauge multi-choke barrels in 26" or 28". Add $400 to Exc. value for these barrels. Models with cast-on stocks for left-hand shooters add $50 to Exc. value.

Model 84S Super Game

Similar to Model 82 Super Game except for new single-selective trigger which is designated by "S" in model number. Chambered for 12-gauge 3" Magnum, with 28" barrels and 8mm rib. Weight about 7 lbs.

NIB	Exc.	V.G.	Good	Fair	Poor
—	500	400	350	200	100

Model 83MG Super Game

Similar to Model 82 Super Game except this model was the advent of Laurona's new multi-choke. **CAUTION!** Laurona multi-choke is not compatible with any other brand of screw-in chokes because of black chrome plating on metric threads. Do not attempt to interchange with other guns. Barrel for this model in 12-gauge are 28" in length; 20-gauge 26" or 28". Both are chambered for 3" shell. Rib is 8mm. Weight about 7 lbs.

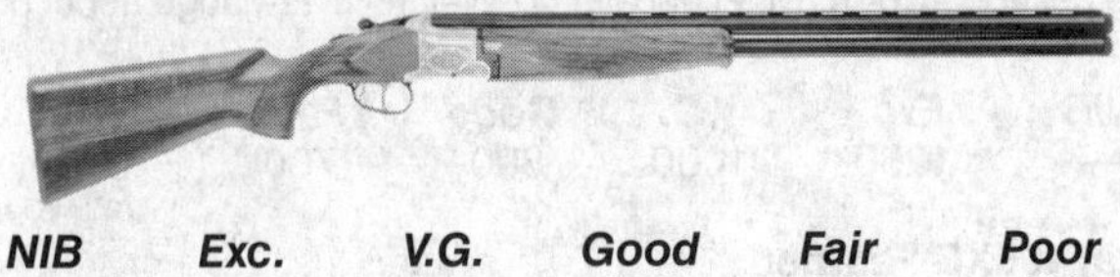

NIB	*Exc.*	*V.G.*	*Good*	*Fair*	*Poor*
—	700	450	350	200	100

Model 85MS Super Game

Similar to Model 83MG Super Game except for single-selective trigger. Chambered for 12- or 20-gauge 3" Magnum. Weight about 7 lbs.

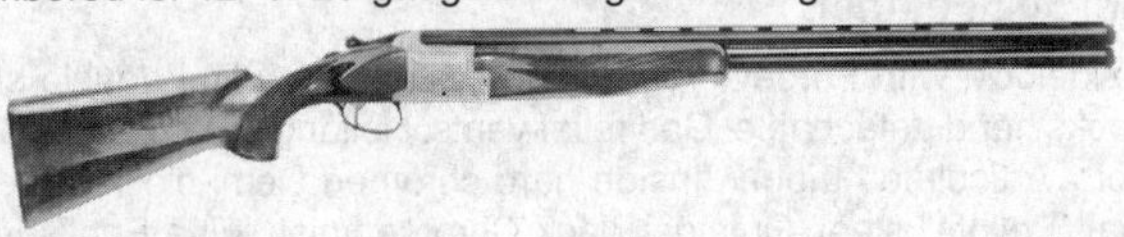

NIB	*Exc.*	*V.G.*	*Good*	*Fair*	*Poor*
—	750	650	450	250	200

Model 84S Super Trap

Single-selective trigger with 29" barrels. Chambered for 2.75" shells, with long forcing cones. Aluminum rib is 13mm wide. Auto ejectors. Receiver nickel plated, with fine scroll engraving and black chrome relief. Beavertail forearm and choice of Monte Carlo or standard Trap stock. Weight about 7 lbs. 12 oz.

NIB	*Exc.*	*V.G.*	*Good*	*Fair*	*Poor*
—	1000	750	550	350	250

Model 85MS Super Trap

Similar to Model 82S Super Trap except multi-choke in bottom barrel with fixed choke on top barrel. Weight about 7 lbs. 12 oz.

NIB	*Exc.*	*V.G.*	*Good*	*Fair*	*Poor*
—	1100	900	700	500	300

Model 85MS Super Pigeon

Similar to Model 85MS Super Trap except with 28" barrels, fixed IM choke on top barrel and multi-choke on bottom barrel. Intended for live bird competition. Weight about 7 lbs. 4 oz.

NIB	*Exc.*	*V.G.*	*Good*	*Fair*	*Poor*
—	1100	900	800	600	300

Model 85MS Special Sporting

Similar to Model 85MS Super Pigeon except for field-style buttstock, with plastic buttplate. Intended for upland game. Weight about 7 lbs. 4 oz.

NIB	*Exc.*	*V.G.*	*Good*	*Fair*	*Poor*
—	1100	900	800	600	300

Model 84S Super Skeet

Similar to Model 85MS Special Sporting except choked Skeet and Skeet. Weight about 7 lbs.

NIB	*Exc.*	*V.G.*	*Good*	*Fair*	*Poor*
—	950	900	800	600	300

OVER/UNDER MODELS SILHOUETTE 300

Guns are basically same as Super series above with these exceptions: Readily identified by white and black chrome stripped receiver, with model engraved on side of receiver. Barrels are multi-choked on both bores and have 11mm steel ribs. Note: Two types of chokes were used. Some guns came with knurl head-type as in Super models and others were made with flush invector style. Later option for ease of changing chokes is knurl long choke, which is a flush-type with a knurl head added. Both later type chokes, flush and knurl long-type, can be used in early multi-choke models, with some extension showing.

Silhouette 300 Trap

Has barrels 29" with 2.75" chambers. Long forcing cones, with hard chrome bores and 11mm rib. Beavertail forearm and straight comb trap stock fitted with ventilated black rubber recoil pad are standard. Weight about 8 lbs.

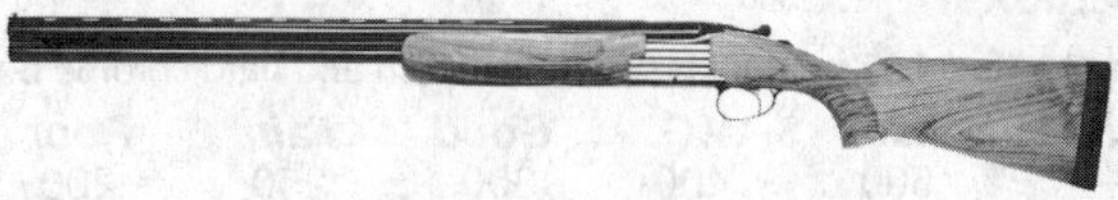

NIB	*Exc.*	*V.G.*	*Good*	*Fair*	*Poor*
—	1100	800	500	200	100

Silhouette 300 Sporting Clays

Similar to Model 300 Trap except with 28" barrels. Some guns came with 3" chambers. Buttstock is field style, with plastic buttplate or hard rubber sporting clay pad. Weight about 8 lbs.

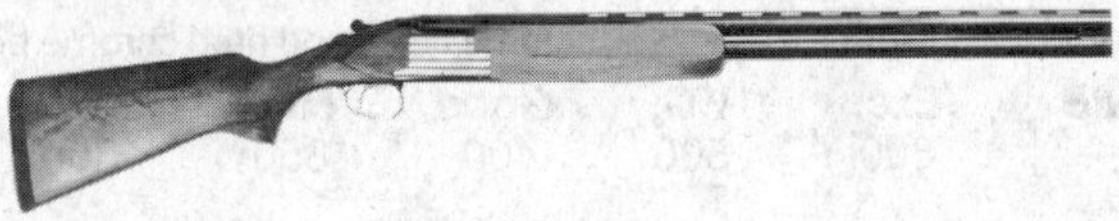

NIB	*Exc.*	*V.G.*	*Good*	*Fair*	*Poor*
—	950	700	600	200	100

Silhouette 300 Ultra Magnum

Similar to Model 300 Sporting Clays except with 3.5" chamber in 12-gauge for waterfowl hunting. Weight about 7 lbs. 8 oz.

NIB	*Exc.*	*V.G.*	*Good*	*Fair*	*Poor*
—	1000	800	500	280	150

SIDE-BY-SIDE SHOTGUNS

Models with "X" after model number were made after 1975 and finished with non-rusting black chrome on barrels and action, with hard chrome bores. Made in 12-, 16- and 20-gauge. Smaller gauges made on special order. Side-by-side shotguns were discontinued by Laurona after 1978 to concentrate on the over/under market.

Model 11

Boxlock action, with triple Greener-type round crossbolt. Independent firing pins bushed into face of the action. Barrels of "Bellota" steel. Made in 12-, 16- and 20-gauge.

NIB	*Exc.*	*V.G.*	*Good*	*Fair*	*Poor*
—	400	350	300	200	150

Model 13

Similar to Model 11, with Purdey-type bolting system. Extractor of double radius.

NIB	*Exc.*	*V.G.*	*Good*	*Fair*	*Poor*
—	400	350	300	200	150

Model 13X

Barrels and action finished in black chrome, with hard chrome bores.

NIB	*Exc.*	*V.G.*	*Good*	*Fair*	*Poor*
—	500	400	300	250	200

Model 13E

Similar to Model 13, with automatic ejectors.

NIB	Exc.	V.G.	Good	Fair	Poor
—	500	400	300	250	200

Model 13XE

Similar to Model 13E except black chrome finish and hard chrome bores.

NIB	Exc.	V.G.	Good	Fair	Poor
—	600	500	400	350	300

Model 15 Economic Pluma

Similar to Model 13 except first model has hard chrome bores.

NIB	Exc.	V.G.	Good	Fair	Poor
—	450	400	300	250	200

Model 15X

Similar to Model 15 except black chrome finish and hard chrome bores.

NIB	Exc.	V.G.	Good	Fair	Poor
—	500	400	300	250	200

Model 15E Economic Pluma

Similar to Model 15, with automatic ejectors.

NIB	Exc.	V.G.	Good	Fair	Poor
—	550	450	350	300	250

Model 15XE

Similar to Model 15E except black chrome finish and hard chrome bores.

NIB	Exc.	V.G.	Good	Fair	Poor
—	600	500	400	350	300

Model 52 Pluma

Boxlock action, with back of action scalloped and artistically engraved in fine English-style scroll. Churchill rib and double radius extractor. Hard chrome bores. Weight about 6 lbs.

NIB	Exc.	V.G.	Good	Fair	Poor
—	750	650	500	400	350

Model 52E Pluma

Similar to Model 52, with automatic ejectors. Weight about 6 lbs. 2 oz.

NIB	Exc.	V.G.	Good	Fair	Poor
—	850	750	600	500	450

SIDE-BY-SIDE SIDELOCKS

Model 103

Blued sidelock, with some light border engraving. Triple Purdey-type bolting system. Extractor of double radius. Barrels of special "Bellota" steel, with hard chrome bores. Made in 12-, 16- and 20-gauge.

NIB	Exc.	V.G.	Good	Fair	Poor
—	900	800	700	500	400

Model 103E

Similar to Model 103, with automatic ejectors.

NIB	Exc.	V.G.	Good	Fair	Poor
—	1000	800	700	600	500

Model 104X

Case colored sidelocks, with Purdey-type bolting system. Extractor with double radius. Fine double safety sidelocks. Gas relief vents. Articulated trigger. Hard chrome bores. Demi-block barrels of special "Bellota" steel. Black chrome barrels. Produced in 12-, 16- and 20-gauge, with smaller bores available on special order.

NIB	Exc.	V.G.	Good	Fair	Poor
—	1200	1000	800	700	600

Model 104XE

Same as Model 104X, with Holland automatic selective ejectors.

NIB	Exc.	V.G.	Good	Fair	Poor
—	1350	1100	900	800	700

Model 105X Feather

Same as Model 104X, with concave rib. Weight in 12-gauge about 6 lbs. 2 oz.

NIB	Exc.	V.G.	Good	Fair	Poor
—	1250	1000	800	700	600

Model 105XE Feather

Same as Model 105X, with Holland automatic selective ejectors.

NIB	Exc.	V.G.	Good	Fair	Poor
—	1400	1250	1000	800	750

Model 502 Feather

Fine sidelock, with Purdey-type bolting system. Very fine double safety sidelocks hand detachable. Gas relief vents. Holland automatic selective ejectors. Articulated trigger. Inside hard chromed Demi-block barrels of special "Bellota" steel. Outside Black Chrome finish. Fine English-style scroll engraving. Marble gray or Laurona Imperial finish. Churchill or concave type rib. Weight 12-gauge about 6.25 lbs. Offered in 12-, 16- and 20-gauge.

NIB	Exc.	V.G.	Good	Fair	Poor
—	2200	1800	1600	1500	1400

Model 801 Deluxe

Same as Model 502 Feather, but engraving is true deluxe Renaissance style. Fully handmade with Imperial finish. First grade walnut stock and forearm.

NIB	Exc.	V.G.	Good	Fair	Poor
—	4400	4000	3750	2750	2250

Model 802 Eagle

Same as Model 801 Deluxe, except highly artistic base relief hand engraving of hunting scenes.

NIB	Exc.	V.G.	Good	Fair	Poor
—	5000	4500	4000	3500	3250

LAW ENFORCEMENT ORDNANCE CORP.

Ridgeway, Pennsylvania

Striker 12

Semi-automatic shotgun designed for self-defense. Chambered for 12-gauge. Has 18.25" cylinder bored barrel. Unique feature about this gun is its 12-round drum magazine. Barrel is shrouded and stock folds. Fixed-stock model also available. Introduced primarily as a law enforcement tool. Original models had 12" barrels and were legal for law enforcement agencies and Class 3 licensed individuals only. Shotgun no longer imported into U.S. Shotgun now classified as a Class III weapon and subject to restrictions of BATFE. Be certain that the particular shotgun is transferable before purchase. If there are any questions contact BATFE before purchase. Striker 12 shotguns in excellent condition may sell for as much as $1500.

LAZZERONI ARMS COMPANY

Tucson, Arizona

All Lazzeroni models are chambered for the company's own proprietary calibers. The 6.17 (.243) Spitfire, 6.53 (.257) Scramjet, 6.71 (.264) Phantom, 7.21 (.284) Tomahawk, 7.82 (.308) Patriot and 8.59 (.338) Galaxy.

Model 2000ST-F

Fitted with 27" match-grade barrel, with fully adjustable trigger and removable muzzle brake. Conventional fiberglass stock.

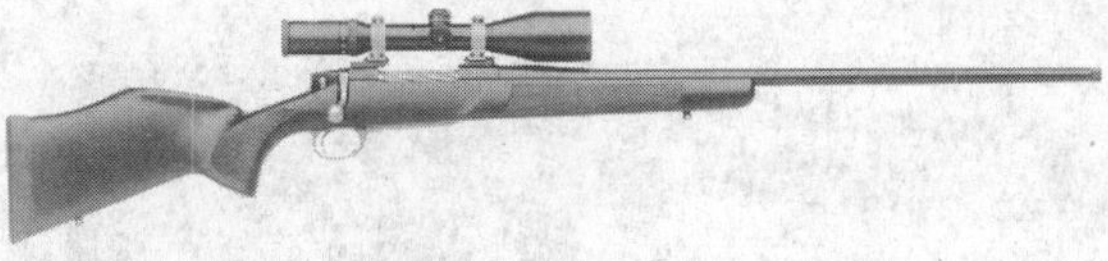

NIB	Exc.	V.G.	Good	Fair	Poor
3700	3000	2200	1500	800	300

Model 2000ST-W

As above, fitted with black wood laminate stock. No longer offered.

NIB	Exc.	V.G.	Good	Fair	Poor
4800	3900	2700	1750	1000	350

Model 2000ST-FW

As above, fitted with conventional fiberglass stock and additional black wood laminate stock. No longer offered.

NIB	Exc.	V.G.	Good	Fair	Poor
5300	4250	3000	2000	1200	500

Model 2000ST-28

Model is 28" barrel variation of Model 2000 ST. Chambered for 7.82 Warbird cartridge. Introduced in 1999.

NIB	Exc.	V.G.	Good	Fair	Poor
5300	4250	3000	2000	1200	500

Model 2000SLR

Model has 28" extra-heavy fluted barrel, with conventional fiberglass stock. Chambered for 6.53 Scramjet, 7.21 Firehawk and 7.82 Warbird.

NIB	Exc.	V.G.	Good	Fair	Poor
3900	3100	2300	1600	900	400

Model 2000SP-F

Fitted with 23" match-grade barrel and Lazzeroni thumbhole fiberglass stock. Chambered for all Lazzeroni calibers.

NIB	Exc.	V.G.	Good	Fair	Poor
3700	3000	2200	1500	800	300

Model 2000SP-W

Same as above, with black wood laminate thumbhole stock. No longer offered.

NIB	Exc.	V.G.	Good	Fair	Poor
4800	3900	2700	1750	1000	350

Model 2000SP-FW

Same as above, but supplied with two stocks: thumbhole fiberglass and black wood laminate. No longer offered.

NIB	Exc.	V.G.	Good	Fair	Poor
5300	4250	3000	2000	1200	500

Model 2000SA

Designed as a lightweight mountain rifle. Chambered for .308, .284 or .338 propriety calibers. Barrel length 24" and fluted except for .338-caliber. Offered in both right-/left-hand models. Stock has Monte Carlo cheekpiece. Weight about 6.8 lbs.

NIB	Exc.	V.G.	Good	Fair	Poor
4000	3100	2300	1600	900	400

Model 2000DG

Offered in Saturn and Meteor calibers only. Fitted with 24" barrel. Fibergrain stock finish, removable muzzle brake and threaded muzzle protector are standard. Weight about 10 lbs.

NIB	Exc.	V.G.	Good	Fair	Poor
4400	3500	2700	1850	1050	450

Model 700ST

Built around a modified Remington 700 action. Fitted with 26" barrel. Chambered for all Lazzeroni long-action calibers except Saturn and Meteor. Weight about 8 lbs. Synthetic stock.

NIB	Exc.	V.G.	Good	Fair	Poor
2400	1850	1550	1200	900	200

Swarovski P.H. 3-12x50 Rifle

NIB	Exc.	V.G.	Good	Fair	Poor
1400	1150	920	600	400	150

Savage 16 LZ

Introduced in 2001. Features 24" stainless steel barrel, synthetic stock. Chambered for 7.82 Patriot and 7.21 Tomahawk cartridges. Weight about 6.8 lbs. Values shown include Cabela's 4.5-14x42mm scope.

NIB	Exc.	V.G.	Good	Fair	Poor
900	780	500	380	200	100

Sako TRG-S

Fitted with 26" stainless steel barrel and synthetic stock. Chambered for 7.82 Warbird and 7.21 Firebird cartridges. Weight about 7.9 lbs. Values shown include Burris 6-14x50mm mil-dot scope.

NIB	Exc.	V.G.	Good	Fair	Poor
1400	1150	920	600	400	150

Model 2005 Global Hunter

Features include precision CNC-machined 17R stainless steel receiver; stainless steel match-grade button-barrel; Jewel competition trigger; titanium firing pin; slim line graphite/composite stock; precision-machined aluminum-alloy floorplate/triggerguard assembly; Vais muzzle brake; and Limbsaver recoil pad. Base price listed.

NIB	Exc.	V.G.	Good	Fair	Poor
6900	5900	4700	3250	1500	500

M2012MTLR Mountain-Lite Long-Range

Bolt action, 26" barrel, 7.3 lbs., available left- or right-hand, stainless steel, composite stock, muzzle brake, 6.53 through 7.82 calibers.

NIB	Exc.	V.G.	Good	Fair	Poor
6000	5500	4500	—	—	—

M2012 Sporter Extra Long-Range

Bolt action, 28" barrel, 8.8 lbs., stainless steel, raised roll over cheekpiece. Composite stock, muzzle brake, 7.82 through 10.57 calibers.

NIB	Exc.	V.G.	Good	Fair	Poor
7500	6850	5500	—	—	—

M2012 Thumbhole Extra Long-Range

Bolt actions, 26" barrel, 7.9 lbs., stainless steel, thumbhole composite stock, muzzle brake, 7.21 through 9.53 calibers.

NIB	Exc.	V.G.	Good	Fair	Poor
7000	6400	5250	—	—	—

M2012 Precision Hunter Extra Long-Range

Bolt action, 26" barrel, 8.9 lbs., stainless steel, adjustable synthetic stock, muzzle brake, 7.21 through 9.53 calibers.

NIB	Exc.	V.G.	Good	Fair	Poor
8400	7200	6000	—	—	—

LE FORGERON

Liege, Belgium

Model 6020 Double Rifle

Boxlock-actioned side-by-side. Chambered for 9.3x74R cartridge. Has 25" barrels, with double triggers and automatic ejectors. Finish blued and pistol grip stock is checkered walnut.

NIB	Exc.	V.G.	Good	Fair	Poor
—	6100	4950	4400	3300	1250

Model 6040

Simply Model 6020, with false sideplates. All other specifications the same.

NIB	Exc.	V.G.	Good	Fair	Poor
—	6900	5750	4950	3850	1500

Model 6030

Double rifle that has true sidelock action and engraved. Deluxe French walnut stock.

NIB	Exc.	V.G.	Good	Fair	Poor
—	11000	8800	8000	6100	2000

Boxlock Shotgun

Side-by-side double-barreled shotgun chambered for 20- or 28-gauge. Barrel lengths optional as are choke combinations. Has single-selective trigger and automatic ejectors. Engraved and blued, with deluxe French walnut stock. Note: Add 20 percent for false sideplates.

NIB	Exc.	V.G.	Good	Fair	Poor
—	5500	4400	3600	2500	1000

Sidelock Shotgun

Similar specifications to boxlock, except it has true sidelock action. Generally more deluxe in materials and workmanship.

NIB	Exc.	V.G.	Good	Fair	Poor
—	13000	12000	9350	7250	2500

LE FRANCAIS

Francais D'Armes et Cycles de St. Etienne
St. Etienne, France

See—MANUFRANCE

Gaulois (Antique)

8mm palm pistol designed by Brun-Latrige. Manufactured by Le Francais. Furnished with 5-round magazine. It was introduced in 1893 as "Mitrailleuse" and renamed Gaulois in 1897, with production continuing through 1910. No. 1, 2, & 3 models were made; values are similar for all three variations.

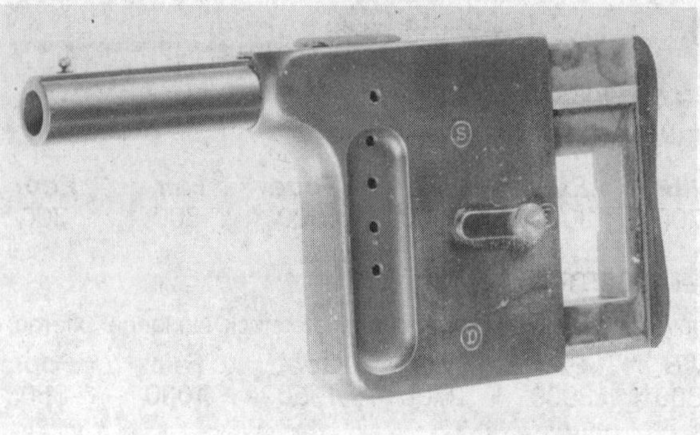

Courtesy James Rankin

Exc.	Fine	V.G.	Good	Fair	Poor
1200	900	700	500	350	200

Le Francais Model 28 (Type Armee)

Unique pistol chambered for 9mm Browning cartridge. A large pistol, with 5" barrel hinged with a tip-up breech. Blowback-operated semi-automatic pistol that has no extractor. Empty cases are blown out of breech by gas pressure. One feature about this pistol that is desirable, it's possible to tip barrel breech forward like a shotgun and load cartridges singly, while holding contents of magazine in reserve. Weapon has fixed sights and blued finish, with checkered walnut grips. Manufactured in 1928.

Courtesy James Rankin

NIB	Exc.	V.G.	Good	Fair	Poor
—	1250	950	750	500	200

Police Model (Type Policeman)

Blowback-operated double-action semi-automatic chambered for .25 ACP cartridge. Has 3.5" barrel and 7-round magazine. Same hinged barrel feature of Model 28. Blued, with fixed sights and Ebonite grips. Manufactured 1913 to 1914.

Courtesy James Rankin

NIB	Exc.	V.G.	Good	Fair	Poor
—	800	650	450	300	150

Officer's Model (Pocket Model)

Also referred to as "Staff Model". Blowback-operated semi-automatic chambered for .25 ACP cartridge. Has 2.5" barrel and concealed hammer. Fixed sights and finish blued. Grips are Ebonite. Manufactured between 1914 and 1938 in two variations: early and second type.

Courtesy James Rankin

Early variation Pocket

NIB	Exc.	V.G.	Good	Fair	Poor
—	300	250	200	150	100

Target Model (Type Champion)

Chambered for 6.35mm cartridge and fitted with 6" barrel. Extended magazine base is for grip purposes, not additional cartridges.

Courtesy James Rankin

NIB	Exc.	V.G.	Good	Fair	Poor
—	900	700	550	400	280

LE MAT
Paris, France

LeMat "Grapeshot Revolver" Antique

Somewhat unique background that makes it a bit controversial among collectors. Foreign-made firearm manufactured in Paris, France, as well as Birmingham, England. Designed and patented by an American, Jean Alexander Le Mat of New Orleans, Louisiana; purchased for use by Confederate States of America and used in Civil War. Curious firearm, as it is a huge weapon that has two barrels. Top 6.5" barrel chambered for .42-caliber percussion and supplied by 9-shot unfluted cylinder that revolves on a 5", .63-caliber smoothbore barrel that doubles as cylinder axis pin. These two barrels are held together by a front and rear ring. Rear sight is a notch in nose of hammer. Attached ramrod on side of top barrel. Weapon marked "Lemat and Girards Patent, London". Finish blued, with checkered walnut grips. Fewer than 3,000 manufactured. Approximately one-half were purchased by Confederate States of America. Made between 1856 and 1865. Both full size and Baby LeMats were also made for pinfire cartridges. Values are similar to those shown for percussion revolvers. Belgian copies of the pinfire LeMat will bring less.

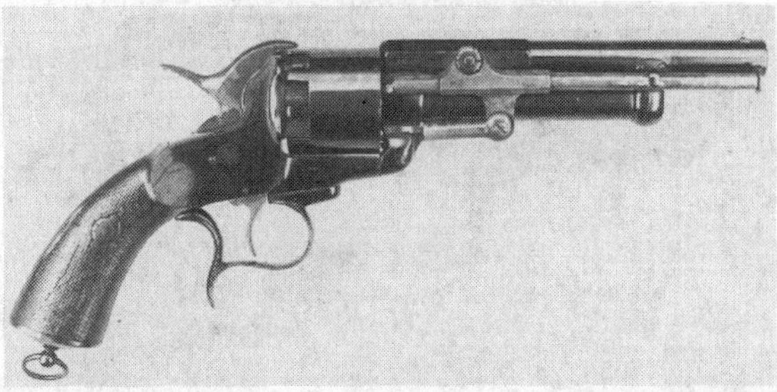

Courtesy Milwaukee Public Museum, Milwaukee, Wisconsin

Exc.	Fine	V.G.	Good	Fair	Poor
30000	25000	16250	7500	1750	1220

Baby LeMat Antique

Similar in appearance (though a good deal smaller in size) to standard model pistol. Chambered for .32-caliber percussion. Has 4.25" top barrel and .41-caliber smoothbore lower barrel. Cylinder is unfluted and holds 9 shots. Barrel marked "Systeme Le Mat Bte s.g.d.g. Paris". Has British proofmarks. Blued, with checkered walnut grips. Scarcest model Le Mat. Only an estimated 100 manufactured. Used by Confederate States of America in Civil War.

Exc.	Fine	V.G.	Good	Fair	Poor
28500	22000	11550	1100	3300	2310

LeMat Revolving Carbine Antique

Chambered for centerfire, rimfire cartridges or percussion. Barrels are half round half octagon and 20" in length. Chambered for a variety of calibers, but usually in percussion .42-caliber, with .62-caliber smoothbore lower barrel. In 2019 Cowans Auction sold the "Finest known" LeMat revolving carbine for $117,500.

Courtesy Little John's Auction Service, Inc., Paul Goodwin photo

Exc.	Fine	V.G.	Good	Fair	Poor
31500	25000	18000	11000	3000	2100

LE PAGE SA.
Liege, Belgium

Pinfire Revolver Antique

Company was in business of revolver manufacture in 1850s. Produced a .40-caliber pinfire revolver, similar to Lefauchaux and other pinfires of the day. Barrel lengths vary and unfluted cylinder holds 6 shots. Pistols are double-action and sometimes found with ornate, but somewhat crude engraving. Finish is blued, with wood grips. Quality of these weapons is fair. They were serviceable, but ammunition created somewhat of a problem. Rather fragile and difficult to handle, with protruding primer pin to contend with. LePage also made other caliber and configuration pinfires. Generally, larger caliber brings more and smaller caliber, especially the small folding trigger models, bring less. Also see LeFaucheux.

Exc.	Fine	V.G.	Good	Fair	Poor
780	320	260	200	120	80

Semi-Automatic Pistol

Semi-automatic pistol, with open top slide and exposed hammer. Chambered for 6.35mm, 7.65mm, 9mm Short and 9mm Long cartridges. Large grip with finger grooves.

Courtesy James Rankin

NIB	Exc.	V.G.	Good	Fair	Poor
—	880	680	520	300	200

Pocket Pistol

Semi-automatic pistol in caliber 6.35mm. Checkered hard rubber grips, with crossed sword and pistol logo of Le Page on each side of grip.

Courtesy James Rankin

NIB	Exc.	V.G.	Good	Fair	Poor
—	320	280	220	180	80

LEBEAU COURALLY

Liege, Belgium

Company has been in business since 1865. Made more guns for royalty than any other gun company in the world. Prices listed are for guns without engraving. Other extra-cost options will affect price. All guns are built to order. Virtually no upper end for values to these infrequently-encountered guns. Values are certainly well in excess of $30,000 for any model in Very Good or better condition.

LEE FIREARMS CO.

Milwaukee, Wisconsin

Lee Single-Shot Carbine Antique

Rare single-shot break-open carbine that pivots to right side for loading. Chambered for .44 rimfire cartridge. Has 21.5" barrel, with hammer mounted in center of frame. Carbine has walnut buttstock, but no forearm and marked "Lee's Firearms Co. Milwaukee, Wisc.". Approximately 450 manufactured between 1863 and 1865. Few surviving examples and one should be wary of fakes.

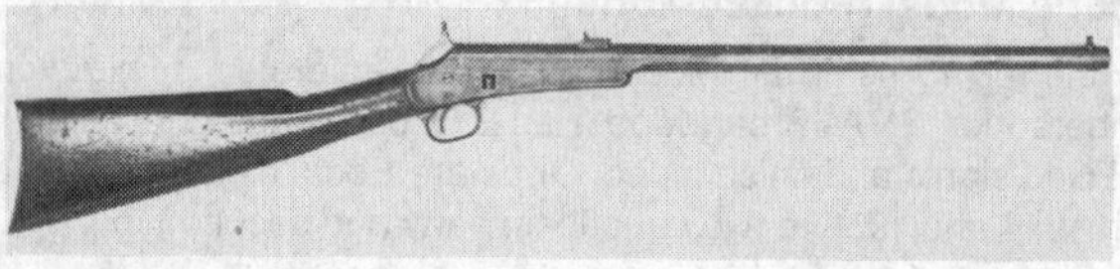

Courtesy Milwaukee Public Museum, Milwaukee, Wisconsin

Exc.	Fine	V.G.	Good	Fair	Poor
10000	8000	5000	2500	1200	600

Lee Sporting Rifle Antique

Similar to military carbine except it has a longer octagonal barrel. Barrel length varied and there were more of these manufactured. Survival rate appears to have been better than for carbine model.

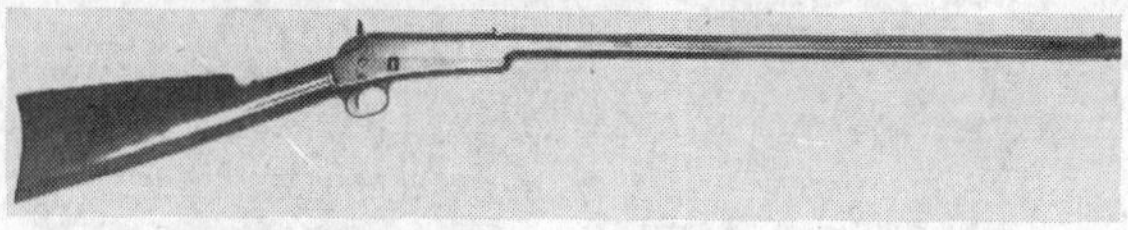

Courtesy Milwaukee Public Museum, Milwaukee, Wisconsin

Exc.	Fine	V.G.	Good	Fair	Poor
3000	1500	800	600	300	150

LEECH & RIGDON

Greensboro, Georgia

Leech & Rigdon Revolver Antique

Confederate revolver patterned after 1851 Colt Navy. Chambered for .36-caliber percussion. Has 6-shot unfluted cylinder. The 7.5" barrel is part-octagonal and has a loading lever beneath it. Frame is open-topped; finish blued, with brass grip straps and walnut one-piece grips. Barrel marked "Leech & Rigdon CSA." Approximately 1,500 revolvers manufactured in 1863 and 1864. All contracted for/by Confederacy and considered to be prime acquisition for collectors. Beware of fakes! Premium for very rare early "Novelty Works" barrel marking.

Courtesy Jim and Caroline Cerny

Exc.	Fine	V.G.	Good	Fair	Poor
42000	27500	19250	11000	6000	3500

LEFAUCHEUX, CASIMER & EUGENE

Paris, France

Pinfire Revolver Antique

LeFaucheux, also spelled LeFauchaux, is a term that has come to be generally applied to a wide range of European made pinfire revolvers from the 2nd half of the nineteenth century. The pinfire ignition system was invented by Casimir Lefaucheux in 1836 and perfected in 1846. In 1852 Casimir's son, Eugene, patented the bored-through cylinder in Europe leading to the introduction of the first effective metallic cartridge revolvers. The LeFaucheux firm was prolific, producing pinfire revolvers for civilian and military markets. Many pinfire revolvers made by other European firms will be found marked "LeFaucheux Sytem" or "LeFaucheux Brevete" or similar wording. This indicates the pinfire system and not necessarily manufacture by the LeFaucheux firm. The pinfire cartridge consists of smooth rimless case that contains powder charge and percussion cap. Pin protrudes from side of this case at rear and when struck by hammer is driven into cap, thereby igniting charge and firing weapon. Pistols for this cartridge are slotted at end of cylinder to allow pins to protrude and be struck by downward blow of hammer. In 1856 the LeFaucheux revolver was adopted by the French Navy - the first metallic cartridge revolver selected as a military sidearm. It was widely used by both sides in the American Civil War. Lefaucheux type revolvers were made in many calibers and configurations. Values shown are generalizations for mid-sized well made revolvers. Premiums are paid for large 11 to 13mm caliber, military issue, purse holsters, ornately decorated specimens, and those with folding blades. Large premiums are paid for high capacity (up to 20 rounds), double barrel pinfire revolvers, or those with fixed blades. Pinfire revolvers will usually bring less if they are poorly made or smaller calibers, including most small folding trigger specimens. Engraving is commonly found on commercial pinfire revolvers, and will not necessarily bring a premium unless expertly rendered. Also see listings for Francotte pinfire revolvers. Reader input in expanding LeFaucheux and pinfire revolver listings is invited.

Exc.	Fine	V.G.	Good	Fair	Poor
700	580	410	250	120	80

LEFEVER ARMS CO.

Syracuse, New York

Founded by Dan Lefever (president), in 1884, who was a pioneer in the field of breech-loading firearms. He was referred to as "Uncle Dan" within the firearms industry. He was responsible for many improvements in double-barrel shotgun design. He developed the automatic hammerless system in late 1880s. He also developed a compensating action that allowed simple adjustments to compensate for action wear. In 1901, he was forced out of the company and organized another company—D.M. Lefever, Sons & Company—also in Syracuse. Dan Lefever died in 1906 and his new company went out of business. The original company was acquired by Ithaca in 1916. They continued to produce Lefever guns until 1948.

Sideplated Shotgun

Double-barrel side-by-side shotgun chambered for 10-, 12-, 16- or 20-gauge. Offered with 26", 28", 30" or 32" barrels, with various choke combinations. Barrels are Damascus or fluid steel. Damascus guns have become collectible and in better condition—very good to excellent—can bring nearly the same price as fluid-steel guns. Features a fractional sidelock, because hammers were mounted in frame and sears and cocking indicators were mounted on sideplates. After serial number 25,000, entire locking mechanism was frame mounted and only cocking indicators remained on sideplates. Double triggers are standard. Finish blued, with checkered walnut stock. A number of variations that differ in amount of ornamentation and quality of materials and workmanship utilized in their construction. Automatic ejectors are represented by the letter "E" after respective grade designation. Shotgun manufactured between 1885 and 1919. We strongly recommend that a qualified appraisal be secured if a transaction is contemplated. Also, an Optimus Grade and Thousand Dollar Grade offered. These are extremely high-grade, heavily ornamented firearms inlaid with precious metals. Extremely rare and evaluating them on a general basis is impossible. Note: All models listed: add 50 percent for 16-gauge; 100 percent for 20-gauge; 10 percent for single-selective trigger.

H Grade

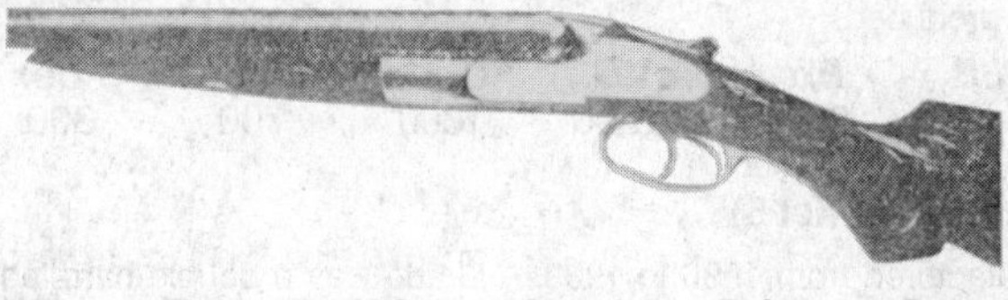

NIB	Exc.	V.G.	Good	Fair	Poor
—	2500	1600	950	550	350

HE Grade

NIB	Exc.	V.G.	Good	Fair	Poor
—	3000	2000	1550	900	650

G Grade

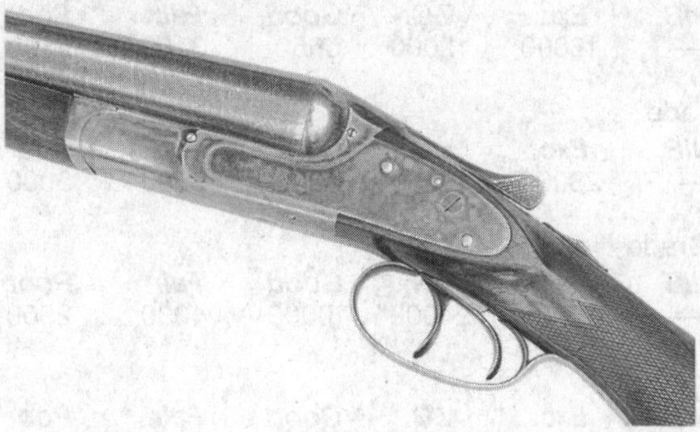

NIB	Exc.	V.G.	Good	Fair	Poor
—	2800	1800	1200	700	420

GE Grade

NIB	Exc.	V.G.	Good	Fair	Poor
—	3500	2300	1800	1000	650

F Grade

NIB	Exc.	V.G.	Good	Fair	Poor
—	3200	2000	1550	900	650

FE Grade

NIB	Exc.	V.G.	Good	Fair	Poor
—	5000	3200	2200	1300	800

E Grade

NIB	Exc.	V.G.	Good	Fair	Poor
—	5500	3700	2400	1400	900

EE Grade

Courtesy Rock Island Auction Company

NIB	Exc.	V.G.	Good	Fair	Poor
—	10000	8000	3100	1850	1150

D Grade

NIB	Exc.	V.G.	Good	Fair	Poor
—	8500	6000	3000	1800	1100

DS Grade

NIB	Exc.	V.G.	Good	Fair	Poor
—	2100	1800	1000	700	500

DE Grade

Courtesy Rock Island Auction Company

NIB	Exc.	V.G.	Good	Fair	Poor
—	10500	8200	4600	2800	1750

DSE Grade

NIB	Exc.	V.G.	Good	Fair	Poor
—	3500	2750	1800	1000	700

C Grade

NIB	Exc.	V.G.	Good	Fair	Poor
—	11000	8500	4200	2400	1500

CE Grade

NIB	Exc.	V.G.	Good	Fair	Poor
—	18000	12000	5650	3400	2100

B Grade

NIB	Exc.	V.G.	Good	Fair	Poor
—	28000	19500	7000	3200	2000

BE Grade

NIB	Exc.	V.G.	Good	Fair	Poor
—	32000	24000	10000	4000	2500

A Grade

NIB	Exc.	V.G.	Good	Fair	Poor
—	40000	34000	16000	6000	3700

AA Grade

NIB	Exc.	V.G.	Good	Fair	Poor
—	50000	40000	25000	8000	5000

LEFEVER, D. M., SONS & COMPANY

Syracuse, New York

In 1901, when Dan Lefever was forced out of Lefever Arms the company he had founded in 1884, he organized another company to produce a line of high-grade boxlock side-by-side doubles. He operated Lefever, D.M. & sons until his death in 1906, at which time the firm closed its doors. During this five-year period, approximately 1,200 shotguns were made in several grades. This makes them quite rare and difficult to evaluate. It is important to get an appraisal from a trusted source before buying or selling. Prices shown are average values.

Lefever Double-Barrel Shotgun

Side-by-side, double-barrel shotgun chambered for 12-, 16- or 20-gauge. Offered with various barrel lengths and choke combinations that were made to order. Features double triggers and automatic ejectors. Single-selective trigger was available as an option. Finish blued, with checkered walnut stock. Individual grades differ in amount of ornamentation and general quality of materials and workmanship utilized in their construction. Discontinued in 1906. There are an "Optimus" and "Uncle Dan" grade, which are top-of-the-line models, that features extremely high quality in materials and workmanship and a great deal of ornamentation. This firearm is extremely rare and seldom found in today's market. It is impossible to evaluate on a general basis. Note: For all models listed: add 50 percent for 20-gauge; 25 percent for single-selective trigger.

O Excelsior Grade—Extractors

NIB	Exc.	V.G.	Good	Fair	Poor
—	2750	2200	1750	950	700

Excelsior Grade—Auto Ejectors

NIB	Exc.	V.G.	Good	Fair	Poor
—	3250	2700	2100	1250	900

F Grade, No. 9

NIB	Exc.	V.G.	Good	Fair	Poor
—	5500	4200	2350	1500	1100

E Grade, No. 8

NIB	Exc.	V.G.	Good	Fair	Poor
—	6500	5200	3200	2400	1700

D Grade, No. 7

NIB	Exc.	V.G.	Good	Fair	Poor
—	9000	7000	4000	2750	2000

C Grade, No. 6

NIB	Exc.	V.G.	Good	Fair	Poor
—	12000	9000	6000	3000	2500

B Grade, No. 5

NIB	Exc.	V.G.	Good	Fair	Poor
—	13000	10500	7000	3500	3000

AA Grade, No. 4

NIB	Exc.	V.G.	Good	Fair	Poor
—	20000	16000	9000	4200	2750

LEFEVER ARMS COMPANY, INC. (ITHACA)

Syracuse, New York

During 1916, Ithaca Gun company purchased the gun making assets of Syracuse, New York based Lefever Arms Company. Between then and World War I, they continued to manufacture the same sideplate gun that had been made in Syracuse until about 1919, when they were discontinued. Prices for those guns are listed in Sideplated Shotgun section. During 1921, Ithaca Gun Company, under the name Lefever Arms Company, Inc., introduced a line of lower cost boxlock guns. Eventually, six different models were produced. Ithaca's Lefever guns were produced in 12-, 16- and 20-gauge and .410 bore. Note: 20-gauge guns often command a price premium of 50 percent; .410 bore gun may command up to 200 percent premium.

Nitro Special

Side-by-side double-barrel shotgun chambered for 12-, 16-, 20-gauge and .410 bore. Barrels were offered in lengths of 26" to 32", with various choke combinations. Features boxlock action, with double triggers and extractors standard. Finish blued, with case colored receiver and checkered walnut stock. Manufactured between 1921 and 1948. Incredible as it may seem, its price at introduction was $29. Note: Add 100+ percent for .410; $100 for single-selective trigger; $200 for automatic ejectors.

NIB	Exc.	V.G.	Good	Fair	Poor
—	600	400	250	200	100

Long Range Single-Barrel Trap and Field (Model 2)

Manufactured from 1927 to 1947. Model 2 was a single-barrel, with no rib. Like Nitro Special it had walnut stocks. Line cut checkered at grip area of buttstock and on forend.

NIB	Exc.	V.G.	Good	Fair	Poor
—	500	300	200	150	100

Single-Barrel Trap Ventilated Rib (Model 3)

Manufactured from 1927 to 1942. Model 3 was a single-barrel, with same ventilated rib used on "Knick" trap gun. Walnut stocks had line cut checkering at grip area of buttstock and on forend.

NIB	Exc.	V.G.	Good	Fair	Poor
—	1200	500	250	150	100

Double-Barrel Ventilated Rib Trap (Model 4)

Manufactured during 1929, but cataloged until 1939. Model 4 was a double-barrel, with ventilated rib barrel. Walnut stocks had line cut checkering at grip area of buttstock and on beavertail forend. Only about 200 units produced.

NIB	Exc.	V.G.	Good	Fair	Poor
—	2000	1200	1000	700	300

A Grade (Model 5)

Manufactured from 1936 to 1939. A Grade was a double-barreled gun. Walnut stocks had pointed checkering cut at grip area of buttstock and on splinter forend. Line engraving outlined its nicely sculptured frame. Note: Add $200 for single trigger; $200 for automatic ejectors; $300 for beavertail forend.

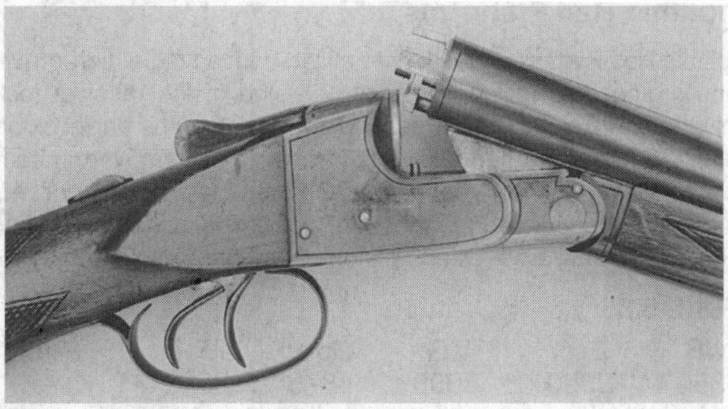

NIB	*Exc.*	*V.G.*	*Good*	*Fair*	*Poor*
—	900	600	400	300	100

Skeet Special (Model 6)

Manufactured from 1936 to 1939. A Grade was a double-barreled gun. Walnut stocks had pointed checkering cut at grip area of buttstock and on beavertail forend. Beavertail forend, single trigger, automatic ejectors, recoil pad and ivory center and front sight were standard. Frame was sculptured and line engraved like Model 5.

NIB	*Exc.*	*V.G.*	*Good*	*Fair*	*Poor*
—	1500	1200	1000	400	100

LEMAN, H. E.
Lancaster, Pennsylvania

Leman Militia Rifle (Antique)

.58-caliber percussion muzzleloader has 33" round barrel. Stock is full-length and held on by two barrel bands. Ramrod mounted under barrel. Trim is brass and barrel browned, with case colored lock. Lock marked "H.E.Leman/Lancaster, Pa." Approximately 500 manufactured between 1860 and 1864. Believed used by Pennsylvania State Militia in Civil War.

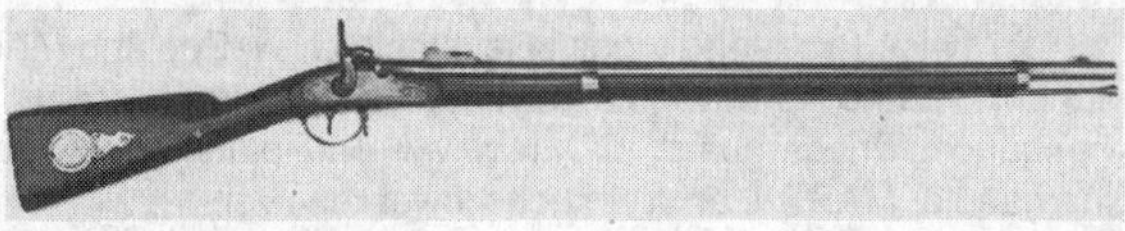

Exc.	*Fine*	*V.G.*	*Good*	*Fair*	*Poor*
4750	2000	1370	750	300	210

LeNovo

– see Oury, D.D.

LENOVO
See—OURY

LEONARD, G.
Charlestown, Massachusetts

Pepperbox (Antique)

.31-caliber four-barreled pepperbox, with concealed hammer. Barrels 3.25" in length. Ring trigger used to cock weapon, while smaller trigger located outside ring is used to fire weapon. Barrels on this pistol do not revolve. Revolving striker inside frame that turns to fire each chamber. Barrels must be removed for loading and capping purposes. Frame is iron and blued, with engraving. Rounded grips are walnut. Barrel stamped "G. Leonard Jr. Charlestown". Fewer than 200 manufactured in 1849 and 1850.

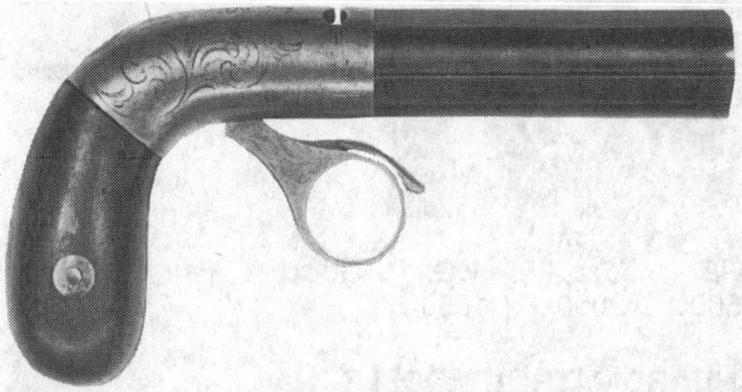

Exc.	*Fine*	*V.G.*	*Good*	*Fair*	*Poor*
1850	720	510	300	150	100

LES, INC.
Skokie, Illinois

Rogak P-18

Based on the Steyr GB service pistol. 9mm caliber double-action semi-automatic pistol, with 5.5" barrel and 18-shot magazine. Stainless steel. Discontinued.

NIB	*Exc.*	*V.G.*	*Good*	*Fair*	*Poor*
—	380	350	300	200	150

LEW HORTON
Westborough, Massachusetts

This company is a full-line distributor of several major firearm manufacturers. They specialize in exclusive special editions of various models.

LEWIS MACHINE & TOOL COMPANY (LMT)
Eldridge, Iowa

LMT Defense (Lewis Machine & Tool Company) manufactures gas-piston and direct-impingement AR-15s, .308s, M203 grenade launchers, suppressors and firearms accessories. The company was founded in 1980 in Milan, Illinois. LMT Defense is known for its Monolithic Rail Platform and is an ISO 9001:2015 certified company and has been a GSA supplier since 2005.

Modular Weapon System

Chambered in 6.5 Creedmoor and 7.62x51 NATO (308 Win.). Direct-impingement operating system, with monolithic rail system on one-piece upper receiver, free-floated cryogenically treated barrel that can quickly be changed to another size, two-stage triggers, 20-shot magazines. Various models follow below.

.308 Modular Weapon System (MWSE)

Gas piston operating system, with monolithic rail system with one-piece upper receiver, free floated cryogenically treated barrel which can quickly be changed to another size, two-stage trigger, 20-shot magazine.

NIB	Exc.	V.G.	Good	Fair	Poor
2500	2000	1550	—	—	—

STANDARD PATROL MODELS

Calibers: 5.56 NATO/.223, 7.62 NATO/.308 Win. Barrels: 16.1", 18", or 20". Weights: 7.5–9.25 lbs. Features: Manufactures a wide range of AR-style carbines with many options. SOPMOD stock, gas piston operating system, monolithic rail platform, tactical sights. SPM=Standard Patrol Model. MARS (Modular Ambidextrous Rifle System), fully ambidextrous. Made in the USA. SEE POLITICAL PANIC PRICING.

Defender-L 5.56

NIB	Exc.	V.G.	Good	Fair	Poor
1930	1830	1600	1490	—	—

Standard 16" 5.56

Calibers: 5.56 NATO/.223. Barrels: 16.1. Weight: 7.5 lbs. Features: SOPMOD stock, gas piston operating system, monolithic rail platform, tactical sights. Modular Ambidextrous Rifle System (MARS) rifles are fully ambidextrous systems. Made in the USA.

NIB	Exc.	V.G.	Good	Fair	Poor
1900	1800	1650	1480	—	—

Defender-H 7.62

Standard flattop upper receiver, with 16" chrome-lined 1:10"-twist barrel, standard semi-automatic bolt carrier group, tactical charging handle, Generation 1 collapsible buttstock. MLKMWS upper receiver, 308MWS lower receiver.

NIB	Exc.	V.G.	Good	Fair	Poor
2500	2400	2200	1980	—	—

6.5 Long Range MLK65-MARS

24" 6.5 Creedmoor stainless steel, 1:8" RH twist barrel. DMR buttstock and the LMT 3-prong flash hider.

NIB	Exc.	V.G.	Good	Fair	Poor
1400	1200	1000	—	—	—

L129A1 Reference Rifle LM308SSR

7.62x51, 16" stainless steel, 1:11.25" rifling. Reference is to the weapon contracted by United Kingdom Ministry of Defence, designated the L129A1. LM308MWS lower receiver features EDM machined two-stage trigger, ambidextrous magazine release and safety selector, endplate with QD swivel point, LMT ergonomic textured grip, and SOPMOD stock.

NIB	Exc.	V.G.	Good	Fair	Poor
3300	2800	2400	—	—	—

MLK MWS Sniper Rifle

20" 7.62x51 (.308) stainless steel 1:11.25" RH twist 5R cut barrel

NIB	Exc.	V.G.	Good	Fair	Poor
2900	2500	2100	—	—	—

Monolithic Rail Platforms

Monolithic Rail Platforms (MRP) are milled from a single high-grade aluminum forging. Two locking bolts on the side of the receiver lock the barrel extension in place. MRP technology engages the barrel extension for a full 360 degrees and allows the barrel to be removed in seconds while minimizing point of impact shift. One receiver can support numerous barrels of varying length, material, and caliber. Chambered in 5.56, 6.8 SPC, .300 BLK. Both DI and piston operation. Barrels length 16 in.

MARS-L 5.56

NIB	Exc.	V.G.	Good	Fair	Poor
2350	2290	2000	1870	—	—

MARS-L 5.56 Piston Rifle

NIB	Exc.	V.G.	Good	Fair	Poor
L	2400	2040	1730	1470	1250

MARS-L PDW 5.56

NIB	Exc.	V.G.	Good	Fair	Poor
2400	2040	1730	1470	1250	1070

MARS-L 5.56 Pistol

NIB	Exc.	V.G.	Good	Fair	Poor
2200	1870	1590	1350	1150	980

MARS-H 7.62

NIB	Exc.	V.G.	Good	Fair	Poor
2700	2600	2410	2200	—	—

MARS-H 6.5 DMR

NIB	Exc.	V.G.	Good	Fair	Poor
2890	2760	2500	2300	—	—

New Zealand Reference Rifle

5.56, 16" 1:7 twist. Two-stage trigger. Resembles New Zealand MARS-L rifle with LMT metric flip-up sights, bayonet lug, Surefire Warcomp flash hider, enhanced triggerguard, QD receiver end plate, ambidextrous charging handle, MARS-L ambidextrous lower receiver.

NIB	Exc.	V.G.	Good	Fair	Poor
2800	2380	2020	1720	1460	1240

Confined Space Weapon

.300 BLK, 12" integrally suppressed barrel; rifling 1:7". The CSW300 upper receiver is mid-length and encloses its combined barrel and suppressor. 16.5" Picatinny top rail, grip stop, MARS-L ambidextrous lower receiver. Introduced 2017.

NIB	Exc.	V.G.	Good	Fair	Poor
4000	3400	2890	2460	2090	1780

MLC Ambidextrous Rifle

NIB	Exc.	V.G.	Good	Fair	Poor
2100	1790	1520	1290	1100	930

Modular Weapon System (MWS)

Chambered in 6.5 Creedmoor and 7.62x51 NATO (308 Win.). Direct-impingement operating system, with monolithic rail system on one-piece upper receiver, free-floated cryogenically-treated barrel that can quickly be changed to another size, two-stage triggers, 20-shot magazines. Various models follow below.

MLOK MARS-H

16", chrome-lined barrel, 1:10 RH twist, two-stage trigger.

NIB	Exc.	V.G.	Good	Fair	Poor
2900	2470	2100	1780	1510	1290

6.5 Long Range

NIB	Exc.	V.G.	Good	Fair	Poor
3200	2720	2310	1970	1670	1420

L129A1 Reference Rifle

NIB	Exc.	V.G.	Good	Fair	Poor
3700	3150	2670	2270	1930	1640

MLK MWS Sniper Rifle

NIB	Exc.	V.G.	Good	Fair	Poor
3200	2720	2310	1970	1670	1420

OTHER LMT MODELS

Sharpshooter 2

S-A bolt carrier group, MARS-H DMR lower receiver. 20" 7.62x51 stainless steel, 1:11.25" RH twist 5R cut barrel.

NIB	Exc.	V.G.	Good	Fair	Poor
3500	2980	2530	2150	1830	1550

CQB Series

Piston operated with CQB/MRP (Close Quarter Battle/Monolithic Rail Platform) upper receiver, 16" chrome lined 5.56" barrel with SOPMOD buttstock and standard trigger group. Also offered in 6.8 SPC. Note: Add $200 for 6.8 SPC.

NIB	Exc.	V.G.	Good	Fair	Poor
1880	1600	1360	1150	980	830

Defender MLCDFDR

5.56, 16" 1:7" rifling. New model is not the Defender 2000, released in 2000.

NIB	Exc.	V.G.	Good	Fair	Poor
1900	1620	1370	1170	990	840

MLC Pistol MLCPISTOL-556

NIB	Exc.	V.G.	Good	Fair	Poor
1900	1620	1370	1170	990	840

Valkyrie MLK Rifle

.224 Val, 20" barrel, 1:7" twist. Two-stage trigger, MLR upper receiver, ambidextrous charging handle, enhanced S-A 6.8 bolt carrier group, MARS-L lower receiver, DMR 5.56 buttstock. Available in three rifle length MRP upper receiver patterns (MRP, SLK, MLR).

NIB	Exc.	V.G.	Good	Fair	Poor
2000	1700	1450	1230	1040	890

Piston

5.56, 16" chrome-lined 1:7" RH twist piston barrel. S-A piston bolt carrier group, MARS-L lower receiver.

NIB	Exc.	V.G.	Good	Fair	Poor
2030	1720	1460	1240	1060	900

LM8

NIB	Exc.	V.G.	Good	Fair	Poor
1950	1660	1410	1200	1020	870

LIDDLE & KAEDING

San Francisco, California

Pocket Revolver (Antique)

Manufactured by Forehand and Wadsworth, but stamped with above name. Company was a dealer in California and had nothing whatsoever to do with production of this revolver. Chambered for .32 rimfire cartridge. Has 3.25" octagonal barrel and 5-shot fluted cylinder. Frame is iron and finish blued, with walnut grips. Few hundred manufactured between 1880 and 1886. Dealer's name marked on top strap.

Exc.	Fine	V.G.	Good	Fair	Poor
580	450	320	200	80	50

LIEGEOISE D ARMES

Liege, Belgium

Side-by-Side Boxlock Shotgun

Double-barreled gun chambered for 12- and 20-gauge. Barrels 28" or 30" in length. Choke combinations are varied. Single trigger and automatic ejectors. Action moderately engraved. Finish blued, with checkered walnut stock.

NIB	Exc.	V.G.	Good	Fair	Poor
—	900	700	500	400	200

Liegeoise Pistol

Semi-automatic pistol in 6.35mm caliber.

Courtesy James Rankin

NIB	Exc.	V.G.	Good	Fair	Poor
—	250	200	180	120	80

LIGNOSE

Suhl, Germany

In 1921, Bergmann Industriewerke was incorporated into Aktiengesellschaft Lignose, Berlin, with a manufacturing division in Suhl.

Liliput Model I

Manufactured in caliber 6.35mm during 1920s.

NIB	Exc.	V.G.	Good	Fair	Poor
—	400	300	200	150	100

Lignose Model 2

Pocket Model in 6.35mm caliber.

Courtesy James Rankin

NIB	Exc.	V.G.	Good	Fair	Poor
—	450	400	350	250	150

Lignose Model 3

Same as Model 2, with 9-round magazine capacity.

NIB	Exc.	V.G.	Good	Fair	Poor
—	750	650	500	400	250

Einhand Model 2A

Unique design resembled Swiss Chylewski. Allows shooter to cock and fire this blowback-operated semi-automatic pistol with one hand (Einhand). Chambered for 6.35mm cartridge. Has 2" barrel. Magazine holds 6 shots. Finish blued, with molded horn grips marked "Lignose". Triggerguard on this pistol has a reverse curve that fits finger and moves backward to cock slide. Short-grip model without Einhard feature was Model 2; long grip model without Einhand was Model 3. First 9,000 to 10,000 examples (all four variations serial numbered in same series) were marketed under Bergmann name; only later Lignose. Manufactured in early 1920s by Bergman Company. Firm merged with Lignose under whose name it was produced.

Courtesy James Rankin

NIB	Exc.	V.G.	Good	Fair	Poor
—	750	650	500	400	250

Einhand Model 3A

Similar to Model 2A, with longer grip that houses 9-shot magazine. All other specifications same as Model 2A.

Courtesy Orvel Reichert

NIB	Exc.	V.G.	Good	Fair	Poor
—	850	700	650	500	300

LILLIPUT

See—MENZ

LINDE A.

Memphis, Tennessee

Pocket Pistol (Antique)

Company manufactured a small concealable firearm, patterned after Henry Deringer Philadelphia-type pistol. Chambered for .41-caliber percussion. Has 2.5" barrel, German silver mountings and walnut stock. Manufactured in 1850s.

Exc.	Fine	V.G.	Good	Fair	Poor
2150	880	590	300	150	100

LINDSAY, JOHN P.

Union Knife Company
Naugatuck, Connecticut

Union Knife Company manufactured Lindsay 2-shot pistols for inventor John P. Lindsay. There are three separate and distinct models listed.

Young America 2 Shot Belt Pistol (Antique)

An oddity. Single-barreled .41-caliber percussion pistol, with double chamber that contains two powder charges and projectiles that are simultaneously fired by two separate hammers. Hammers are released by a single trigger that allows them to fall in proper sequence. 5.5" octagonal barrel contoured into a radical stepped-down shape and spur trigger. Frame is brass, with scroll engraving. Barrel blued and marked "Lindsay's Young America". Estimated to be fewer than 100 manufactured between 1860 and 1862.

Exc.	Fine	V.G.	Good	Fair	Poor
4400	1500	1100	700	300	210

2 Shot Pocket Pistol (Antique)

Smaller version of Belt Pistol. Chambered for same caliber, but has 4" barrel. Approximately 200 manufactured between 1860 and 1862.

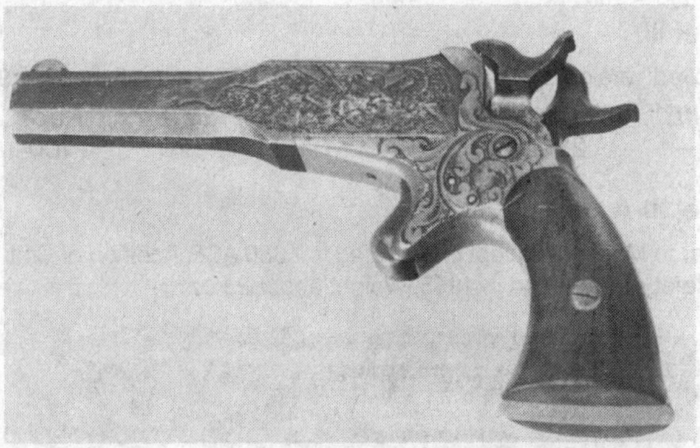

Courtesy W. P. Hallstein III and son Chip

Exc.	Fine	V.G.	Good	Fair	Poor
3500	3000	2050	1100	400	280

2 Shot Martial Pistol (Antique)

Large version of Lindsay design. Chambered for .45-caliber smoothbore. Has 8.5" part-round part-octagonal barrel. Other respects similar to smaller models. Inventor tried to sell this pistol to the government, but was unsuccessful. Estimated 100 manufactured between 1860 and 1862.

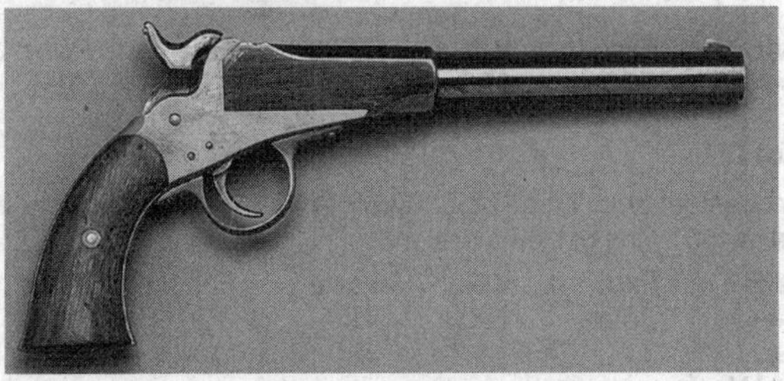

Exc.	Fine	V.G.	Good	Fair	Poor
10000	6500	4000	2200	700	480

LINS, A. F.
Philadelphia, Pennsylvania

Pocket Pistol (Antique)

Chambered for .41-caliber percussion. Copy of Henry Deringer pistol. Has 3" barrel, walnut stock and marked "A. Fred. Lins. Philada." Manufactured between 1855 and 1860.

Exc.	Fine	V.G.	Good	Fair	Poor
2100	1080	710	350	200	140

Rifled Musket (Antique)

Single-shot muzzleloading percussion rifle, chambered for .58-caliber. Has 39" barrel and full-length walnut stock held on by three barrel bands. Iron ramrod mounted under barrel. Mountings are iron. A bayonet lug combined with front sight. Lock marked "A. Fred. Lins/Philada." Rare weapon used by Union forces in Civil War. Approximately 200 manufactured in 1861 and 1862.

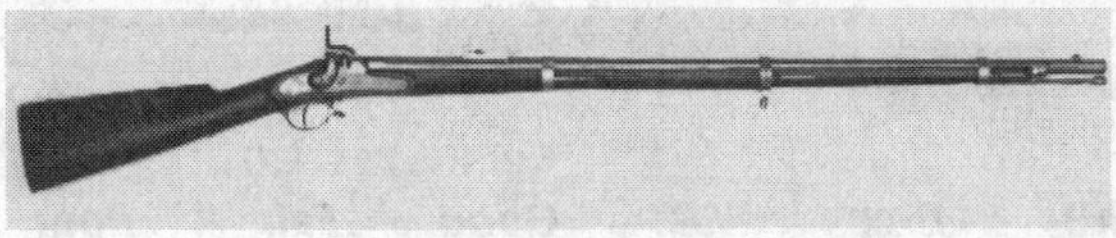

Courtesy Milwaukee Public Museum, Milwaukee, Wisconsin

Exc.	Fine	V.G.	Good	Fair	Poor
5500	2000	1410	820	300	210

LITTLE SHARPS RIFLE MFG. CO.
Big Sandy, Montana

Little Sharps Rifle

Hand-built re-production of single-shot Sharps rifle is 20 percent smaller than original. Chambered for a wide variety of calibers from .22 LR to .375 LSR. A number of extra cost options are available for this rifle. Price listed for basic model.

NIB	Exc.	V.G.	Good	Fair	Poor
3250	2750	2000	1500	900	500

LJUTIC INDUSTRIES
Yakima, Washington

Bi-Matic Semi-Automatic

Custom-built gas-operated semi-automatic shotgun, known for its low level of felt recoil. Chambered for 12-gauge. Has 26" to 32" barrels choked for skeet or trap. Stock specifications are to customer's order. Note: Add 15 percent for interchangeable chokes.

NIB	Exc.	V.G.	Good	Fair	Poor
2750	2100	1300	800	400	200

Dynatrap Single-Barrel

Single-shot trap gun chambered for 12-gauge. Has 33" ventilated rib Full-choke barrel. Features push-button opener and manual extractor. Stock made to trap specifications. Many options affect value.

NIB	Exc.	V.G.	Good	Fair	Poor
2500	1500	1000	800	400	200

Model X-73 Single-Barrel

Similar features to Dynatrap, with high competition rib. Appraisal is recommended. Note: Add 15 percent for interchangeable chokes.

NIB	Exc.	V.G.	Good	Fair	Poor
2750	2100	1300	800	400	200

Mono Gun Single-Barrel

Chambered for 12-gauge. Has 34" ventilated rib barrel. Essentially a custom-order proposition that is available with standard, as well as release trigger. Many value-affecting options available. Note: Add 15 percent for interchangeable chokes.

NIB	Exc.	V.G.	Good	Fair	Poor
6500	5700	4200	3000	1000	—

LTX Model

Deluxe version of Mono Gun, with 33" medium-height ventilated rib. High-grade walnut stock, with fine hand checkering. Options raise values drastically.

NIB	Exc.	V.G.	Good	Fair	Poor
7500	6200	5000	3500	1500	—

Space Gun

Unique single-barrel gun chambered for 12-gauge, with trap choking. Stock and forearm reminds one of a crutch in appearance, but allows shooter to have inline control, with little felt recoil. Barrel, forearm and stock are all on one line. There is a recoil pad and high ventilated rib.

NIB	Exc.	V.G.	Good	Fair	Poor
3750	3000	2250	1500	900	200

Bi-Gun Over/Under

Over/under double chambered for 12-gauge. Has 30" or 32" ventilated rib barrels that are separated. Choking to trap specifications. Stock deluxe hand-checkered walnut.

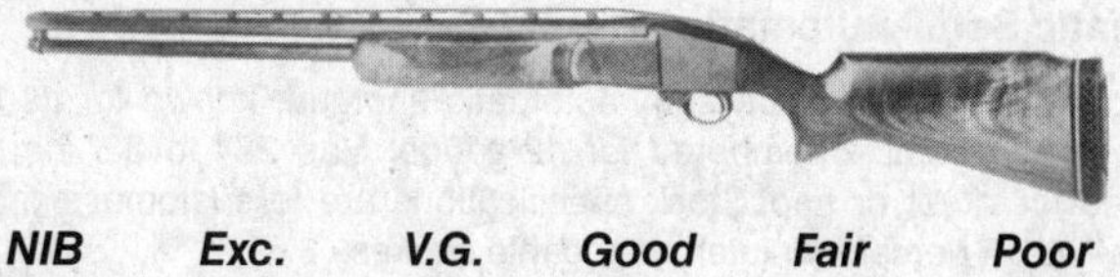

NIB	Exc.	V.G.	Good	Fair	Poor
7250	6000	4000	1000	600	200

Bi-Gun Combo

Over/under Bi-Gun supplied with high ribbed single-barrel, in addition to separated over/under barrels.

NIB	Exc.	V.G.	Good	Fair	Poor
10000	7000	4000	2000	1000	200

LM-6 Super Deluxe

Over/under gun made to customer's specifications. Available in 12-gauge, with barrel lengths from 28" to 34". All other specifications are custom. Note: Add $7,000 for extra single-barrel.

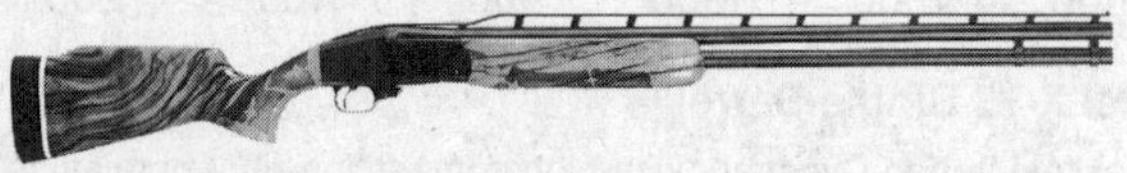

NIB	Exc.	V.G.	Good	Fair	Poor
15000	11500	7500	5000	2500	1000

LLAMA
Philippines

Same firm that was founded in 1904 and produced several inexpensive revolvers and pistols prior to 1931. In 1931, company began to produce a semi-automatic pistol based on Colt Model 1911. They were of high quality and have been sold around the world. After Spanish civil war, company moved its facilities to Vitoria, Spain, where it continued to build handguns under Llama trade name. In 1980s, firm introduced a new line of pistols that were more modern in design and function. Llama pistol is still produced today. For Llama pistols built prior to 1936 slide marking reads: "GABILONDO Y CIA ELOEIBAR (ESPANA) CAL 9MM/.380IN LLAMA". For pistols built after 1936 slide marking reads: "LLAMA GABILONDO Y CIA ELOEIBAR (ESPANA) CAL 9MM .380". Current production Llama pistols will show a slide marking with "LLAMA CAL..." or "GABILONDO Y CIA VITORIA (ESPANA)" and Llama logo. Llama pistols are now made in the Philippines, by Metro Arms and imported into the U.S. by Eagle Imports of Wanamassa, New Jersey.

SEMI-AUTOMATICS

Model I-A

7.65mm blowback design introduced in 1933. Magazine capacity 7 rounds. Barrel 3.62"; overall length 6.3"; weight about 19 oz.

NIB	Exc.	V.G.	Good	Fair	Poor
—	280	220	120	100	80

Model II

Chambered for 9mm Short. Identical to Model I. Introduced in 1933; discontinued in 1936.

NIB	Exc.	V.G.	Good	Fair	Poor
—	260	200	150	120	100

Model III

Improved version of Model II. Introduced in 1936; discontinued in 1954.

NIB	Exc.	V.G.	Good	Fair	Poor
—	280	220	180	120	100

Model III-A

Similar to Model III except chambered for .380 ACP. Addition of Colt-type grip safety. Introduced in 1955. Weight about 23 oz.

NIB	Exc.	V.G.	Good	Fair	Poor
—	300	250	200	120	100

Model IV

Chambered for 9mm Largo or .380 ACP. Not fitted with grip safety. Introduced in 1931. First of Llama designs.

NIB	Exc.	V.G.	Good	Fair	Poor
—	280	220	180	120	100

Model V

Same as Model IV, but intended for export to U.S. Stamped "made in Spain" on slide.

NIB	Exc.	V.G.	Good	Fair	Poor
—	280	220	180	120	100

Model VI

Chambered for 9mm Short, without a grip safety.

NIB	Exc.	V.G.	Good	Fair	Poor
—	280	220	180	120	100

Model VII

Introduced in 1932. Manufactured until 1954. Chambered for .38 Auto cartridge. No grip safety.

NIB	Exc.	V.G.	Good	Fair	Poor
—	400	300	220	150	100

Model VIII

Introduced in 1955. Chambered for .45 ACP, .38 Auto or 9mm Largo. Fitted with a grip safety. Barrel length 5"; overall length 8.5"; weight about 38 oz. Magazine capacity 7 rounds. Note: Many of these pistols marked

".38". Unclear whether these pistols were intended for use with .38 Super cartridge or with milder .38 Automatic. We do not recommend full-house Super loadings in these pistols.

NIB	Exc.	V.G.	Good	Fair	Poor
—	400	300	220	150	100

Model IX

Chambered for 7.65mm Para, 9mm Largo or .45 ACP. Has locked breech, with no grip safety. Built from 1936 to 1954.

NIB	Exc.	V.G.	Good	Fair	Poor
—	400	300	200	150	100

Model IX-A

Version of Model IX. Fitted with a grip safety and 5" barrel. Current production models chambered for .45 ACP only. Weight about 30 oz.

NIB	Exc.	V.G.	Good	Fair	Poor
—	400	300	200	150	100

Model IX-B

Version of Model IX series. Chambered in .45 ACP. Fitted with extended slide release, black plastic grips and target-type hammer. Offered in blue or satin chrome finish.

NIB	Exc.	V.G.	Good	Fair	Poor
400	300	250	180	120	100

Model IX-C

Last large-frame version of Model IX. Chambered for .45 ACP. Fitted with 5.125" barrel. Blade front sight, with adjustable rear. Magazine capacity 10 rounds. Weight about 41 oz.

NIB	Exc.	V.G.	Good	Fair	Poor
400	300	250	200	150	100

Model IX-D

Compact frame version, with 4.25" barrel. Chambered for .45 ACP cartridge. Stocks are black rubber. Fixed front sight, with adjustable rear. Introduced in 1995. Magazine capacity 10 rounds. Weight about 39 oz.

NIB	Exc.	V.G.	Good	Fair	Poor
450	350	250	200	150	100

Model X

First produced in 1935. Chambered for 7.65mm cartridge. No grip safety.

NIB	Exc.	V.G.	Good	Fair	Poor
—	300	220	150	100	80

Model X-A

Version similar to Model X, with a grip safety. Produced from 1954 to present.

NIB	Exc.	V.G.	Good	Fair	Poor
—	300	220	150	100	80

Model XI

Chambered for 9mm Parabellum. Different from previous models with longer curved butt, ring hammer and vertically grooved walnut grips. Magazine capacity 9 rounds. Barrel length 5". Discontinued in 1954.

NIB	Exc.	V.G.	Good	Fair	Poor
—	350	300	250	180	120

Model XI-B

Similar to Model XI, with spur hammer and shorter barrel.

NIB	Exc.	V.G.	Good	Fair	Poor
400	380	280	150	100	80

Model XII-B

Chambered for .40 S&W cartridge. Has compact frame.

NIB	Exc.	V.G.	Good	Fair	Poor
400	380	280	150	100	80

Model XV

Chambered for .22 LR and marked "Especial". Fitted with grip safety. Comes in several finishes and different grip styles. Barrel length 3.6"; overall length 6.5"; weight about 17 oz.

NIB	Exc.	V.G.	Good	Fair	Poor
—	320	280	200	120	100

Model XVI

Deluxe version of Model XV, with engraving, ventilated rib and adjustable sights.

NIB	Exc.	V.G.	Good	Fair	Poor
—	350	280	200	150	100

Model XVII "Especial"

Vest pocket-sized model chambered for .22 Short. Small version of Model XV, with finger-contoured grip.

NIB	Exc.	V.G.	Good	Fair	Poor
—	280	220	180	120	100

Model XVIII

Introduced in 1998. Chambered for .25 ACP cartridge. Offered with gold or chrome finish and stag grips.

NIB	Exc.	V.G.	Good	Fair	Poor
—	300	220	180	150	120

Model Omni

Chambered for .45 ACP or 9mm cartridge. Fitted with 4.25" barrel. Blued finish. Adjustable rear sight. Magazine capacity: 7 rounds .45 ACP; 13 rounds 9mm. Weight about 40 oz. Produced between 1984 and 1986.

NIB	Exc.	V.G.	Good	Fair	Poor
480	350	250	150	120	100

Model Max-I

Introduced in 1995. This 1911 design single-action features 9mm or .45 ACP chambers, with 4.25" or 5.125" barrel. Black rubber grips, with blade front sight and adjustable rear. Weight: 34 oz. compact model; 36 oz. Government model. As of 2016, this model is back in production. Made in the Philippines and imported by Eagle Imports. Note: Add $25 for compact model; $25 for duo-tone model.

NIB	Exc.	V.G.	Good	Fair	Poor
400	350	250	180	150	100

Previous Production Prior to 2006

NIB	Exc.	V.G.	Good	Fair	Poor
420	380	300	220	180	120

New Production

NIB	Exc.	V.G.	Good	Fair	Poor
500	440	380	300	250	200

Model Mini-Max

Chambered for 9mm, .40 S&W or .45 ACP. Furnished with 6-round magazine. Barrel length 3.5". Checkered rubber grips. Introduced in 1996. Weight about 35 oz. Choice of blue, duo-tone, satin chrome or stainless steel finish. As of 2016, this model is back in production. Made in the Philippines and imported by Eagle Imports. Values shown apply to old and new production. Note: Add $40 for satin chrome; $60 for stainless; $20 for duo-tone.

NIB	Exc.	V.G.	Good	Fair	Poor
400	380	280	150	100	80

Mini-Max Sub Compact

Semi-automatic chambered for 9mm, .40 S&W or .45 ACP. Fitted with 3.14" barrel. Overall length 6.5"; height 4.5". Skeletonized combat-style hammer. Grips are black polymer. Weight about 31 oz. Introduced in 1999. Note: Add $40 for satin chrome; $60 for stainless; $20 for duo-tone.

NIB	Exc.	V.G.	Good	Fair	Poor
400	380	280	150	100	80

Model Max-I with Compensator

Similar to Max-I, with addition of compensator. Introduced in 1996. Weight about 42 oz.

NIB	Exc.	V.G.	Good	Fair	Poor
450	400	300	180	120	100

Micro-Max

Chambered for .32 ACP or .380 cartridge. Operates on a straight blowback system, with single-action trigger. Black polymer grips. Barrel length 3.6"; overall 6.5"; height 4.37"; weight about 23 oz. Introduced in 1999. Note: Add $20 for satin chrome finish.

NIB	*Exc.*	*V.G.*	*Good*	*Fair*	*Poor*
400	380	280	150	100	80

Model 82

Large-frame double-action semi-automatic pistol. Features plastic grips, ambidextrous safety, 3-dot sights. Barrel length 4.25"; overall 8"; weight about 39 oz. Choice of blue or satin chrome finish.

NIB	*Exc.*	*V.G.*	*Good*	*Fair*	*Poor*
650	500	350	250	150	100

Model 87 Competition

Chambered for 9mm cartridge. Fitted with integral muzzle compensator. Has a number of competition features such as oversize safety, beveled magazine well, release and 14-round capacity. Offered between 1989 and 1993.

NIB	*Exc.*	*V.G.*	*Good*	*Fair*	*Poor*
1200	920	650	520	300	150

Compact Frame Semi-Automatic

9mm or .45 ACP caliber semi-automatic pistol, with 4.25" barrel and 7- or 9-shot detachable magazine. Blued. Introduced in 1986.

NIB	*Exc.*	*V.G.*	*Good*	*Fair*	*Poor*
350	300	220	150	100	80

Small Frame Semi-Automatic

.22, .32 ACP and .380 ACP caliber semi-automatic pistol, with 3.6875" barrel and 7-shot detachable magazine. Blued or satin chrome finish. Note: Add $75 for satin chrome.

NIB	*Exc.*	*V.G.*	*Good*	*Fair*	*Poor*
350	300	220	150	100	80

Large Frame Semi-Automatic

9mm, .38 Super or .45 ACP caliber semi-automatic pistol, with 5.25" barrel and 7- or 9-shot detachable magazine, depending on caliber. Blued or satin chrome. Note: Add $125 for satin chrome.

NIB	*Exc.*	*V.G.*	*Good*	*Fair*	*Poor*
450	400	300	180	120	100

Mugica

Eibar gun dealer, Jose Mugica, sold Llama pistols under his private trade name. They are marked "mugica-ebir-spain" on slide. These pistols do not seem to have any additional value over and above their respective Llama models. For the sake of clarification, Mugica models are listed with their Llama counterparts:

Mugica Model 101
Mugica Model 101-G
Mugica Model 105
Mugica Model 105-G
Mugica Model 110
Mugica Model 110-G
Mugica Model 120

Llama Model X
Llama Model X-A
Llama Model III
Llama Model III-A
Llama Model VII
Llama Model VIII
Llama Model XI

Tauler

In an arrangement similar to Mugica, a gun dealer in Madrid sold Llama pistols under his own brand name. Most of these pistols were sold in early 1930s to police and other government officials. Most common Llama models were Models I to VIII. Slide inscriptions were in English and had name Tauler in them. No additional value is attached to this private trademark.

REVOLVERS

RUBY EXTRA MODELS

Revolvers produced in the 1950s, were copies of Smith & Wessons. Marked "RUBY EXTRA" on left side of frame. Top of grips had a Ruby medallion. Barrel address stamped: gabilondo y cia elgoeibar espana. Ruby Extra Models represent company's attempts to produce and sell a low-cost revolver.

Model XII

Chambered for .38 Long cartridge. Fitted with 5" barrel and squared butt.

NIB	Exc.	V.G.	Good	Fair	Poor
—	200	150	120	100	80

Model XIII

Chambered for .38 Special. Has a round butt with 4" or 6" ventilated rib barrel. 6" barreled gun fitted with adjustable sights and target grips.

NIB	Exc.	V.G.	Good	Fair	Poor
—	220	180	150	120	100

Model XIV

Offered in .22 LR or .32-caliber. Available in a wide choice of barrel lengths and sights.

NIB	Exc.	V.G.	Good	Fair	Poor
—	200	150	120	100	80

Model XXII Olimpico

Designed as .38 Special target revolver. Features adjustable anatomic grip and rear sight, ventilated rib barrel and a web that joins barrel to ejector shroud.

NIB	Exc.	V.G.	Good	Fair	Poor
—	280	220	150	120	100

Model XXIX Olimpico

Model XXII chambered for .22 LR.

NIB	Exc.	V.G.	Good	Fair	Poor
—	250	200	150	120	100

Model XXVI

Chambered for .22 LR. Features traditional grips and shrouded ejector rod.

NIB	Exc.	V.G.	Good	Fair	Poor
—	180	150	120	100	80

Model XXVII

Similar to above, with 2" barrel. Chambered for .32 Long cartridge.

NIB	Exc.	V.G.	Good	Fair	Poor
—	180	150	120	100	80

Model XXVIII

Chambered for .22 LR. Fitted with 6" barrel. Ramp front sight and adjustable rear.

NIB	Exc.	V.G.	Good	Fair	Poor
—	200	180	150	100	80

Model XXXII Olimpico

A .32 target revolver, with unusual cylinder and frame design.

NIB	Exc.	V.G.	Good	Fair	Poor
—	400	300	250	200	150

Martial

.22 or .38 Special caliber double-action revolver, with 6-round swingout cylinder, 4" or 6" barrel and adjustable sights. Blued, with checkered hardwood grips. Manufactured between 1969 and 1976. Note: Add $500 for engraved chrome; $600 for engraved blue; $1,000 to $3,000 for gold model.

NIB	Exc.	V.G.	Good	Fair	Poor
—	280	220	200	150	120

Comanche I

.22-caliber revolver fitted with 6" barrel and 9-shot cylinder. Rubber grips with adjustable sights. Choice of blue or stainless steel. Weight about 39 oz.

NIB	Exc.	V.G.	Good	Fair	Poor
240	180	120	100	80	50

Comanche II

As above in .38 Special caliber, with 6-shot cylinder. Choice of 3" or 4" barrel. Rubber grips and adjustable sights. Blue or stainless steel. Weight about 30 oz.

NIB	Exc.	V.G.	Good	Fair	Poor
220	180	120	100	80	50

Comanche III

As above in .357 Magnum, with 3", 4" or 6" barrel. Adjustable sights. Rubber grips. Blue or stainless steel. Weight about 30 oz. for 3" or 4" barrel; 39 oz. for 6". Introduced in 1975. Note: Add 20 percent for satin chrome.

NIB	Exc.	V.G.	Good	Fair	Poor
280	220	180	120	100	80

Super Comanche

As above in .357 or .44 Magnum, with 10" ventilated rib barrel and adjustable sights. Blued, with walnut grips. Weight about 47 oz.

NIB	Exc.	V.G.	Good	Fair	Poor
320	250	200	150	100	80

LOEWE, LUDWIG & CO.

Berlin, Germany

See—BORCHARDT

During 1870s and 1880s, this firm manufactured a close copy of Smith & Wesson Russian Model for the Russian government. They are marked "Ludwig Loewe Berlin" on top of barrel. Russian contract guns are marked in Cyrillic.

Loewe Smith & Wesson Russian Revolver Antique

Exc.	Fine	V.G.	Good	Fair	Poor
5000	3500	2300	1500	800	500

LOHNER, C.

Philadelphia, Pennsylvania

Pocket Pistol Antique

.44-caliber single-shot percussion pistol, with 5" barrel, German silver mounts and walnut grip. Barrel marked "C. Lohner". Manufactured during 1850s.

Exc.	Fine	V.G.	Good	Fair	Poor
1600	680	460	250	120	80

LOMBARD, H. C. & CO.

Springfield, Massachusetts

Pocket Pistol Antique

.22-caliber single-shot spur trigger pistol, with 3.5" octagonal barrel. Frame is silver plated, barrel blued and grips are of walnut. Barrel marked "H.C. Lombard & Co. Springfield, Mass.

Exc.	Fine	V.G.	Good	Fair	Poor
650	450	300	200	125	75

LONE STAR RIFLE COMPANY

Conroe, Texas

Company builds custom blackpowder rifles. They are built on a rolling block design and offered in two basic configurations. There are a wide number of options that will affect the price of these rifles.

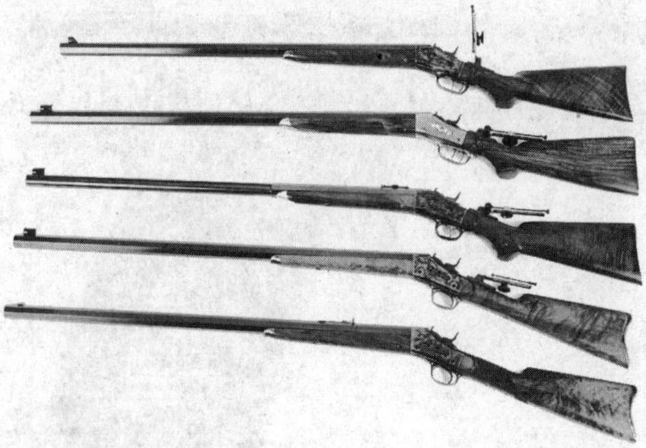

Sporting Rifle

Basic configuration that features straight-grip stock, with semi-crescent butt. Offered in a wide variety of calibers from .32-40 to .50-90. Barrel lengths and configurations, wood, triggers, sights, engraving, finishes, hammers and accessories will greatly affect the final price. Basic retail price: $2195.

Target Rifle

Basic configuration that features straight-grip stock, with semi-crescent butt. Offered in a wide variety of calibers from .32-40 to .50-90. Barrel lengths and configurations, wood, triggers, sights, engraving, finishes, hammers and accessories will greatly affect the final price. Basic retail price: $2195.

LORCIN ENGINEERING CO., INC.

Mira Loma, California

Company in business from 1989 to 1999.

Model L-25

.25-caliber semi-automatic pistol, with 2.5" barrel and 7-shot magazine. Weight 14.5 oz.; overall length 4.8". Introduced in 1989.

NIB	Exc.	V.G.	Good	Fair	Poor
120	100	80	40	30	20

Model LT-25

Same as above, with aluminum alloy frame. Introduced in 1989.

NIB	Exc.	V.G.	Good	Fair	Poor
120	100	80	40	30	20

Model L-22

Chambered for .22 LR cartridge, with 2.5" barrel. Magazine capacity 9 rounds. Introduced in 1989. Weight 16 oz.

NIB	Exc.	V.G.	Good	Fair	Poor
120	100	80	40	30	20

Model L-380

Semi-automatic pistol chambered for .380 ACP cartridge. Barrel length 3.5", with magazine capacity of 7 rounds. Introduced in 1992. Weight about 23 oz.

NIB	Exc.	V.G.	Good	Fair	Poor
120	100	80	40	30	20

Model L-380 10th Anniversary

Same as above, but frame and slide are plated in 24 karat gold. Limited edition model.

NIB	Exc.	V.G.	Good	Fair	Poor
120	100	80	40	30	20

Model L-32

Same as above, but chambered for .32 ACP cartridge. Introduced in 1992

NIB	Exc.	V.G.	Good	Fair	Poor
120	100	80	40	30	20

Model LH-380

Semi-automatic pistol chambered for .380 ACP cartridge. Barrel length 4.5" and magazine capacity 10 rounds. Offered in black, satin or bright chrome finishes.

NIB	Exc.	V.G.	Good	Fair	Poor
150	120	100	80	60	50

Model L-9mm

Same as above, but chambered for 9mm cartridge. Weight 36 oz.

NIB	Exc.	V.G.	Good	Fair	Poor
150	120	100	80	60	50

Derringer

Over/under pistol chambered for .38 Special, .357 Magnum and .45 ACP. Barrel length 3.5"; overall length 6.5".

NIB	Exc.	V.G.	Good	Fair	Poor
140	120	100	60	50	40

LOWELL ARMS CO.

See—ROLLIN WHITE ARMS CO.

LOWER, J. P.

See—SLOTTER & CO.

LUGERS

Various Manufacturers

Just before the turn of the 20th century, Georg Luger re-designed Borchardt semi-automatic pistol so that its mainspring was housed in rear of grip. Resulting pistol was to prove extremely successful and his name has become synonymous with the pistol despite the fact his name never appeared on it.

These companies manufactured Luger pattern pistols at various times.

1. DWM - Deutsch Waffen und Munitions - Berlin, Germany
2. The Royal Arsenal of Erfurt Germany
3. Simson & Company - Suhl, Germany
4. Mauser - Oberndorf, Germany
5. Vickers Ltd. - England
6. Waffenfabrik Bern - Bern, Switzerland
7. Heinrich Krieghoff - Suhl, Germany At least six pre-production

Lugers are known to exist. On later production guns, matching numbered magazines enhance value. Matching magazines are more likely to be found on police Lugers than on military issue models. Unit marked military models will usually bring a premium.

DEUTSCH WAFFEN UND MUNITIONS

1899/1900 Swiss Test Model

4.75" barrel, 7.65mm caliber. Swiss Cross in Sunburst stamped over chamber. Serial range runs to three digits. With fewer than 100 manufactured and only one known to exist, it is one of the rarest Lugers and first true Luger that was produced. Model is far too rare to estimate an accurate value.

1900 Swiss Contract

4.75-in. barrel, 7.65mm caliber. Swiss Cross in Sunburst stamped over chamber. Serial number range 1-5,000, all for military contract.

Courtesy Gale Morgan

Swiss Cross & Sunburst

NIB	Exc.	V.G.	Good	Fair	Poor
—	8000	6750	4000	1500	1000

1900 Commercial

4.75" barrel, 7.65mm caliber. Area above chamber is blank. Serial range 01-19000. Approximately 5,500 manufactured for commercial sale in Germany or other countries. Some have "Germany" stamped on frame. Imported into the U.S. Some were even stamped after bluing.

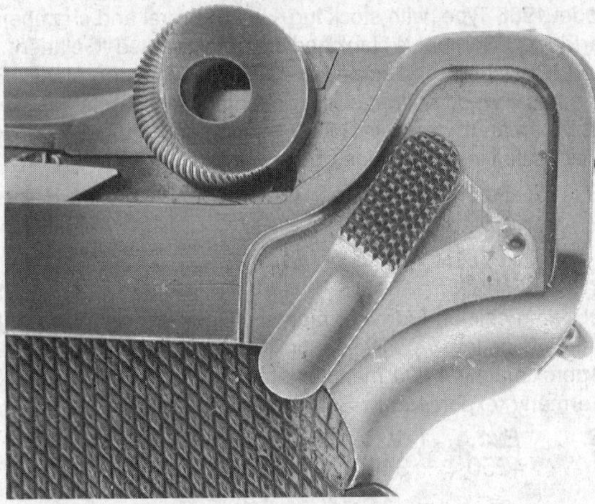

Courtesy Gale Morgan

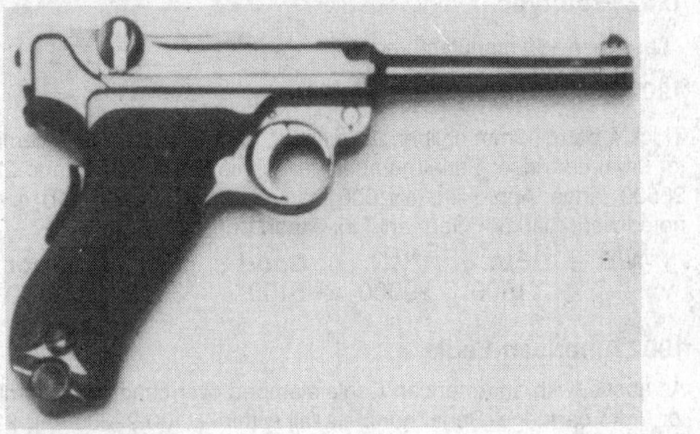

NIB	Exc.	V.G.	Good	Fair	Poor
—	7600	5300	2500	1000	650

1900 American Eagle

4.75" barrel, 7.65mm caliber. American Eagle crest stamped over chamber. Serial range between 2000-200000. Approximately 11,000-12,000 commercial models marked "Germany" and 1,000 military test models, without commercial import stamp. Serial numbers of military lots are between 6100-7100. Note: For these models add a premium of 40 to 50 percent, depending on condition.

NIB	Exc.	V.G.	Good	Fair	Poor
—	5500	4000	2000	850	600

1900 Test Eagle

NIB	Exc.	V.G.	Good	Fair	Poor
—	7500	5000	3000	2000	1500

1900 Bulgarian Contract

Old model 1900 Type, with no stock lug. Has 4.75" barrel and chambered for 7.65mm cartridge. Bulgarian crest stamped over chamber and safety marked in Bulgarian letters. Serial range 20000-21000, with 1,000 manufactured. Military test model and quite rare, as most were re-barreled to 9mm during the time they were used. Even with 9mm versions, approximately 10 are known to exist. Only variation to feature a marked safety before 1904.

Courtesy Gale Morgan

NIB	Exc.	V.G.	Good	Fair	Poor
—	12500	8500	4000	2500	1800

1900 Carbine

11.75" barrel, 7.65mm caliber. Carbines have a gracefully contoured and finely checkered walnut forearm and detachable shoulder stock. Rear sight on this extremely rare variation is a five-position sliding model located on rear link. Area above chamber is blank. Serial range is three digits or under. This may have been a prototype, as less than 100 were produced. Model far too rare to estimate an accurate value.

1902 Prototype

- Less than 150 manufactured.

1902 Commercial—"Fat Barrel"

Thick 4 barrel, 9mm caliber. Area above chamber is blank. Chambered for 9mm cartridge. Serial numbers fall within 22300-22400 and 22900-23500 range. Approximately 600 manufactured. Greater part of those noted were marked "Germany" for export purposes.

NIB	Exc.	V.G.	Good	Fair	Poor
—	11500	9000	5100	3500	1500

1902 American Eagle

As above, with an American Eagle stamped over chamber. Chambered for 9mm cartridge. Serial numbers fall within 22100-22300 and 22450-22900 range. Solely intended for export sales in U.S.A. and all are marked "Germany" on frame. Approximately 700 manufactured.

NIB	Exc.	V.G.	Good	Fair	Poor
—	13000	9500	5500	3000	1300

1902 American Eagle Cartridge Counter

As above, with "Powell Indicating Device" added to left grip. Slotted left grip, with a numbered window that allows visual access to number or rounds remaining in special "indicator magazines". There were 50 Lugers altered in this way at the request of U.S. Board of Ordinance, for U.S. Army evaluation. Serial numbers are 22401-22450. Be especially wary of fakes!

NIB	Exc.	V.G.	Good	Fair	Poor
—	45000	32000	20000	6000	3500

1902 Carbine

11.75" barrel, 7.65mm caliber. Sight has four positions and is silver-soldered to barrel. Stock and forearm were sold with this weapon. Serial range was 21000-22100, 23500-24900 and 50000 to 50100. Approximately 2,500 manufactured for commercial sale in and out of Germany. Many were imported into United States, but none here have been noted with "Germany" export stamp. Note: Prices include matching stock. Add 15 percent premium for 50000 to 50100 serial numbers.

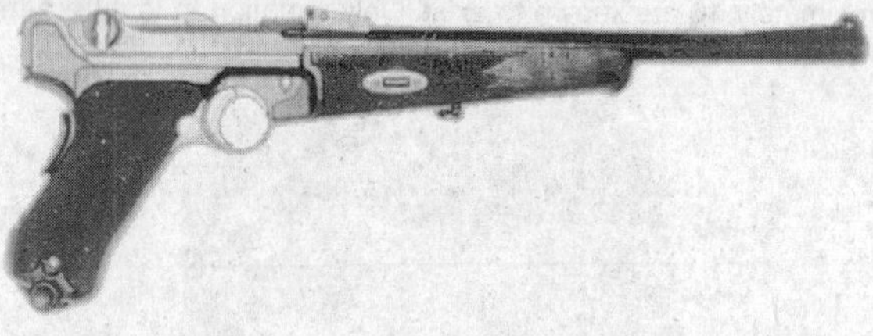

Courtesy Gale Morgan

NIB	Exc.	V.G.	Good	Fair	Poor
—	19000	15000	85000	3000	2000

1902 Presentation Carbine

11.75" barrel, 7.65mm caliber. Carbines have initials of owner gold-inlaid above chamber. Furnished with checkered walnut stock and forearm. Only four have been noted in 9000C serial number range. They have initials "GL" for Georg Luger on back of rear toggle. Too rare to estimate value.

1902/06 Carbine (Transitional)

11.75" barrel, 7.65mm caliber. Assembled from Model 1902 parts with new toggle assembly. Four-position sliding sight silver-soldered to barrel and checkered walnut stock and forearm. Approximately 100 manufactured in 23600 serial number range. Note: Prices include matching stock.

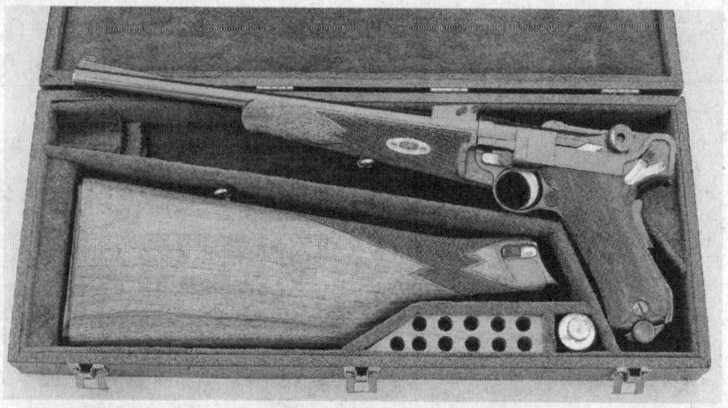

Paul Goodwin photo

NIB	Exc.	V.G.	Good	Fair	Poor
—	17000	14500	8000	5000	3000

1903 Commercial

4" barrel, 7.65mm caliber. Chamber area is blank. Approximately 50 manufactured for export to France. Serial numbered 25000-25050. Extractor on this model marked "CHARGE".

NIB	Exc.	V.G.	Good	Fair	Poor
—	18000	15000	6000	3200	2500

1904 Navy

6" thick barrel, 9mm caliber. Chamber area is blank and extractor marked "Geladen". Safety marked "Gesichert". Approximately 1,500 manufactured in one- to four-digit serial range, for military issue to German Navy. Toggle has a "lock" similar to 1900 types. Note: Advised that a professional appraisal be obtained before purchase.

NIB	Exc.	V.G.	Good	Fair	Poor
—	75000	50000	30000	6000	4500

1906 Navy Commercial

New model 1906 Type, with stock lug. Has 6" barrel and chambered for 9mm cartridge. Chamber is blank and extractor marked "Geladen". Safety marked "Gesichert" and some have "Germany" export stamp. Proper magazine has a wood bottom, with concentric circles on sides. Approximately 2,500 manufactured in 25050-65000 serial range. Produced for commercial sales in and outside of Germany.

NIB	Exc.	V.G.	Good	Fair	Poor
—	6500	4600	2200	1400	900

1906 Commercial

4" barrel, 9mm caliber. Extractor marked "Geladen" and area of frame under safety in its lower position is polished and not blued. Chamber is blank. Approximately 4,000 manufactured for commercial sales. Some have "Germany" export stamp. Serial range is 26500-68000.

NIB	Exc.	V.G.	Good	Fair	Poor
—	4250	3400	1400	750	500

1906 Commercial (Marked Safety)

As above, with area of frame under safety in its lowest position marked "Gesichert". Barrel is 4.75" in length and chambered for 7.65mm cartridge. Approximately 750 manufactured, serial numbered 25050-26800.

NIB	Exc.	V.G.	Good	Fair	Poor
—	5850	4500	1900	800	600

1906 American Eagle

4" barrel, 9mm caliber. Chamber area has the American Eagle stamped on it. Extractor marked "Loaded". Frame under safety at its lowest point is polished and not blued. Has no stock lug. Approximately 3,000 manufactured for commercial sale in U.S.A., in serial range 25800-69000. They were supplied with wooden-based magazines stamped Cal. 9mm.

NIB	Exc.	V.G.	Good	Fair	Poor
—	5500	4000	1200	700	500

1906 American Eagle (Marked Safety)

4.75" barrel, 7.65mm caliber. Frame under safety at its lowest point marked "Gesichert". Approximately 750 manufactured in 25100-26500 serial number range.

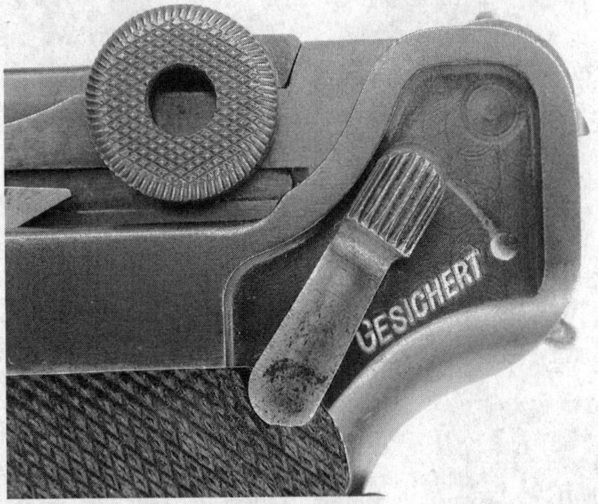

Courtesy Gale Morgan

NIB	Exc.	V.G.	Good	Fair	Poor
—	7000	5000	2000	1200	800

1906 American Eagle 4.75" Barrel

As above, with polished bright safety area. Approximately 8,000 manufactured in 26500-69000 serial range.

NIB	Exc.	V.G.	Good	Fair	Poor
—	3500	2800	1100	700	450

1906 U.S. Army Test Luger .45 Caliber

5" barrel, .45 ACP caliber. Sent to United States for testing in 1907. Chamber is blank, extractor marked "Loaded". Frame is polished under safety lever. Trigger on this model has an odd hook at the bottom. Only five of these pistols were manufactured. Referred to as the "Million Dollar Luger", it is believed that no one has ever paid close to that price. One sold in the late '80s for $430,000. **BUYER CAUTION:** Perfect copies of this model have been made. See John Martz - Custom Lugers at the end of this Luger section.

1906 Swiss Commercial

4.75" barrel, 7.65mm caliber. Swiss Cross in Sunburst appears over chamber. Extractor marked "Geladen". Frame under safety is polished. No stock lug and proofmarks are commercial. Approximately 1,000 manufactured in 35000-55000 serial number range.

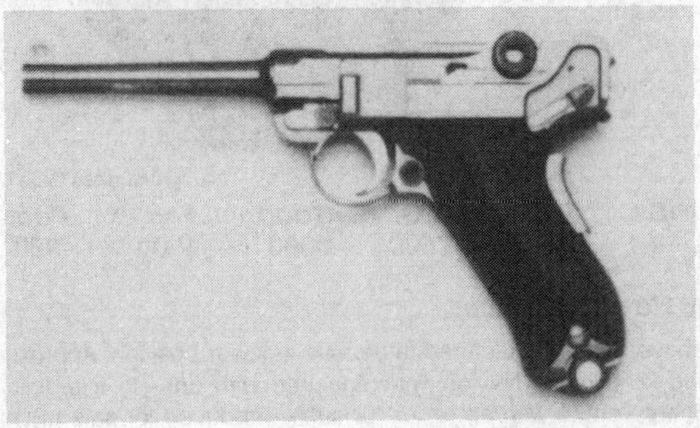

Courtesy Bonhams & Butterfields, San Francisco, California

NIB	Exc.	V.G.	Good	Fair	Poor
—	5800	4700	2500	1400	800

1906 Swiss Military

Swiss Commercial except with military proofmarks.

NIB	Exc.	V.G.	Good	Fair	Poor
—	5500	3800	2200	900	700

1906 Swiss Police Cross in Shield

As above, with shield replacing sunburst on chamber marking. There were 10,215 of both models combined. In 5000-15215 serial number range.

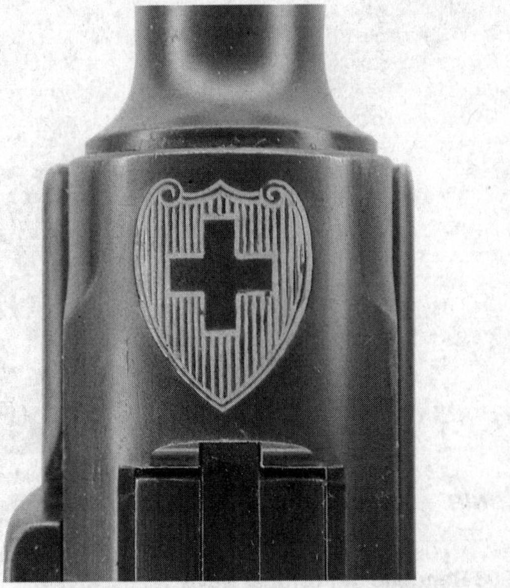

Courtesy Gale Morgan

NIB	Exc.	V.G.	Good	Fair	Poor
—	5500	3800	2200	900	700

1906 Dutch Contract

4" barrel, 9mm caliber. No stock lug and chamber is blank. Extractor marked "Geleden" on both sides and safety marked "RUST", with a curved upward pointing arrow. Manufactured for military sales to Netherlands. Date will be found on barrel of most examples encountered. Dutch re-finished their pistols on a regular basis and marked date on barrels. Approximately 4,000 manufactured, serial numbered between 1 and 4000.

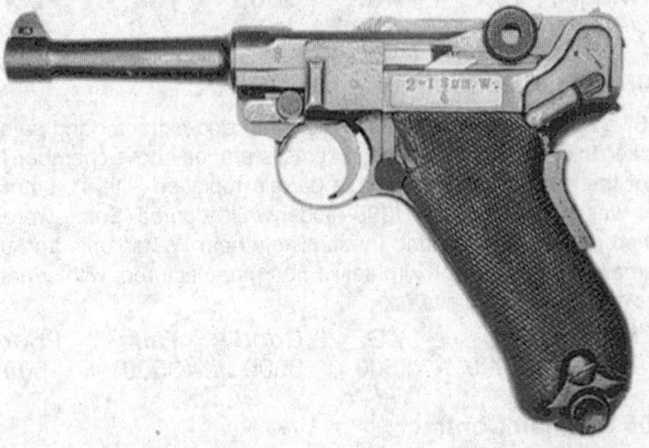

Courtesy Gale Morgan

NIB	Exc.	V.G.	Good	Fair	Poor
—	5000	3500	1500	800	600

1906 Royal Portuguese Navy

4" barrel, 9mm caliber and no stock lug. Royal Portuguese Naval crest, an anchor under a crown, stamped above chamber. Extractor marked "CARREGADA" on left side. Frame under safety is polished. Approximately 1,000 manufactured with one- to four-digit serial numbers.

NIB	Exc.	V.G.	Good	Fair	Poor
—	11000	8000	6500	4000	2500

1906 Royal Portuguese Army (M2)

4.75" barrel, 7.65mm caliber. No stock lug. Chamber area has Royal Portuguese crest of Mannuel II stamped upon it. Extractor marked "CARREGADA". Approximately 5,000 manufactured, with one- to four-digit serial numbers.

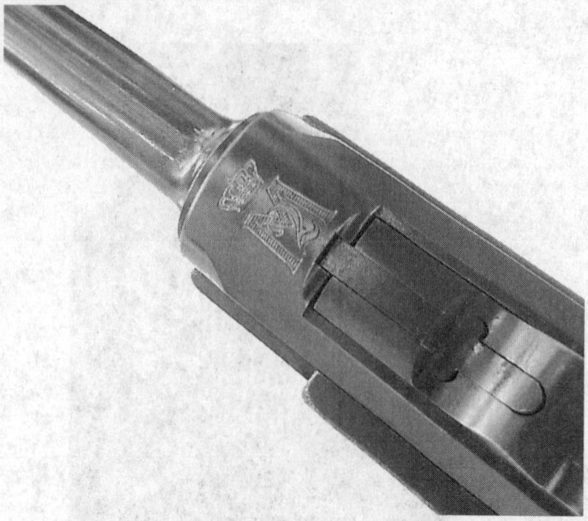

Courtesy Gale Morgan

NIB	Exc.	V.G.	Good	Fair	Poor
—	4000	3200	1200	600	500

1906 Republic of Portugal Navy

4" barrel, 9mm caliber. No stock lug and extractor marked "CARREGADA". Made after 1910, when Portugal had become a republic. Anchor on chamber is under letters "R.P." Approximately 1,000 manufactured, with one- to four-digit serial numbers.

NIB	Exc.	V.G.	Good	Fair	Poor
—	10500	8000	5500	2500	1500

1906 Brazilian Contract

4.75" barrel, 7.65mm caliber. No stock lug and chamber area is blank. Extractor marked "CARREGADA" and frame under safety is polished. Approximately 5,000 manufactured for military sales to Brazil.

NIB	Exc.	V.G.	Good	Fair	Poor
—	3750	2900	1100	750	450

1906 Bulgarian Contract

4.75" barrel, 7.65mm caliber. No stock lug and extractor and safety are marked in cyrillic letters. Bulgarian crest stamped above chamber. Nearly all of the examples located have barrels replaced with 4", 9mm units. This was done after later 1908 model was adopted. Some were refurbished during Nazi era and these pistols bear Waffenamts and usually mismatched parts. Approximately 1,500 manufactured, with serial numbers of one- to four-digits.

NIB	Exc.	V.G.	Good	Fair	Poor
—	10000	7500	5000	3500	1500

1906 Russian Contract

4" barrel, 9mm caliber. No stock lug. Extractor and safety are marked with cyrillic letters. Crossed Nagant rifles are stamped over chamber. Approximately 1,000 manufactured, with one- to four-digit serial numbers; but few survive. An extremely rare variation and caution should be exercised if purchase is contemplated.

Courtesy Gale Morgan

NIB	Exc.	V.G.	Good	Fair	Poor
—	16000	12500	6500	4000	2500

1906 Navy 1st Issue

6" barrel, 9mm caliber. Safety and extractor are both marked in German. Chamber area is blank. There is a stock lug and unique two-position sliding Navy sight is mounted on rear toggle link. Approximately 12,000 manufactured for German Navy, with serial numbers of one- to five-digits. Wooden magazine bottom features concentric rings. Note: Many of these pistols had their safety changed so they were "safe" in lower position. Known as "1st issue altered". Value at approximately 20 percent less.

Courtesy Gale Morgan

NIB	Exc.	V.G.	Good	Fair	Poor
—	12500	7500	3000	1500	950

1906 Navy 2nd Issue

As above, but manufactured to be safe in lower position. Approximately 11,000, 2nd Issue Navies, manufactured with one- to five-digit serial numbers—some with an "a" or "b" suffix. Produced for sale to German Navy.

Courtesy Gale Morgan

NIB	Exc.	V.G.	Good	Fair	Poor
—	7000	4500	2500	1200	700

1908 Commercial

4" barrel, 9mm caliber. No stock lug and chamber area is blank. Extractor and safety are both marked in German and many examples are marked with "Germany" export stamp. Approximately 9,000 manufactured in 39000-71500 serial number range.

NIB	Exc.	V.G.	Good	Fair	Poor
—	5000	3500	750	600	450

1908 Bulgarian

Considered by many to be the most unique Luger manufactured. It has a 4" barrel, "DWM" logo over the chamber, no stock lug, Cyrillic lettered safety and extractor, Bulgarian crest on middle link and no lanyard loop at rear of frame, but rather at lower end of rear grip strap. Nealy 10,000 manufactured, but few survived the heavy wartime use. Extremely rare in V.G. to Exc. condition.

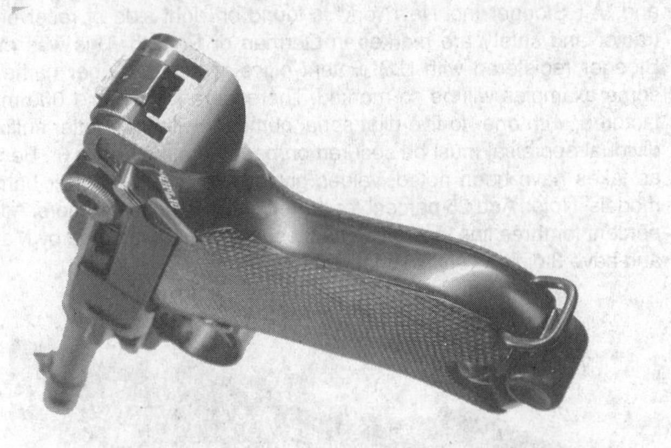

Courtesy Gale Morgan

NIB	Exc.	V.G.	Good	Fair	Poor
—	7500	5500	1500	1000	600

1908 Navy Commercial

6" barrel, 9mm caliber. Has a stock lug, no grip safety and characteristic two-position sliding sight mounted on rear toggle link. Chamber area is blank and safety and extractor are both marked. The "Germany" export stamp appears on some examples. Approximately 1,500 manufactured in 44000-50000 serial number range.

NIB	Exc.	V.G.	Good	Fair	Poor
—	8300	5000	2500	1750	1250

1908 Navy

As above, with "Crown M" military proof. May or may not have concentric rings on magazine bottom. Approximately 40,000 manufactured, with one- to five-digit serial numbers and "a" or "b" suffix. These Lugers are quite scarce, as many were destroyed during and after WWI.

NIB	Exc.	V.G.	Good	Fair	Poor
—	8000	5000	2000	1100	800

1914 Navy

Stamped with dates from 1914-1918 above chamber. Approximately 30,000 manufactured, with one- to five-digit serial numbers with an "a" or "b" suffix. They are scarce, as many were destroyed as a result of WWI. **WARNING:** Many counterfeit pistols reported. Note: Add 10 percent for 1916 date.

NIB	Exc.	V.G.	Good	Fair	Poor
—	6700	4700	2500	950	700

1908 Military 1st Issue

4" barrel, 9mm caliber. No stock lug. Extractor and safety are both marked in German. Chamber is blank. Approximately 20,000 manufactured, with one- to five-digit serial numbers—some with an "a" suffix.

NIB	Exc.	V.G.	Good	Fair	Poor
—	3500	2000	1000	500	350

1908 Military Dated Chamber (1910-1913)

As above, with date of manufacture stamped on chamber.

NIB	Exc.	V.G.	Good	Fair	Poor
—	2500	1700	800	500	350

1913 Commercial

As above, with grip safety. Approximately 1,000 manufactured, with serial numbers 71000-72000; but few have been noted and are considered to be quite rare.

NIB	Exc.	V.G.	Good	Fair	Poor
—	3200	2200	1300	850	600

1914 Military

As above, with stock lug. Chamber dated 1914 - 1918.

NIB	Exc.	V.G.	Good	Fair	Poor
—	2500	1700	600	500	350

1914 Artillery Long Pistol (LP 08)

1914 Artillery Long Pistol (LP 08) Features a nine-position adjustable sight, which has a base that is an integral part of barrel. Has stock lug and furnished with military-style flat board stock and holster rig (see Accessories). Chamber dated from 1914-1918. Safety and extractor are both marked. Developed for artillery and machine gun crews; many thousands were manufactured, with one- to five-digit serial numbers—some have letter suffixes. Quite desirable from a collector's standpoint and is rarer than its production figures would indicate. After the war many were destroyed as the allies deemed them more insidious than other models, for some reason. Note: Add 100 percent to Models stamped with 1914 date. Complete matching rig adds considerably to value.

Courtesy Gale Morgan

NIB	Exc.	V.G.	Good	Fair	Poor
—	5000	3500	1700	1500	900

DWM Double Dated

4" barrel, 9mm cartridge. Date 1920 or 1921 stamped over original chamber date of 1910-1918, creating double-date nomenclature. These are arsenal-reworked WWI military pistols and were then issued to German military and/or police units within provisions of Treaty of Versailles. Many thousands of these Lugers were produced.

NIB	Exc.	V.G.	Good	Fair	Poor
—	2000	1000	550	400	300

1920 Police Rework

As above, except original manufacture date was removed before rework date was stamped. There were many thousands of these produced. Note: It is not unusual to find with one or two "Police Matched" magazines.

NIB	Exc.	V.G.	Good	Fair	Poor
—	1800	1200	500	350	300

1920 Commercial

Similar to above, with 3.5" to 6" barrels in 7.65mm or 9mm calibers. Marked "Germany" or "Made in Germany" for export. Others are unmarked and were produced for commercial sale inside Germany. Some of these pistols are military reworks, with markings and proofmarks removed; others were newly manufactured. Extractors and safety are both marked and chamber is blank. Serial number range one- to five-digits and letter suffixes often appear. Note: Add 15 percent for 9mm.

NIB	Exc.	V.G.	Good	Fair	Poor
4000	2300	1300	950	450	350

1920 Commercial Navy

6" barrel, 9mm caliber. Some have a stock lug; others have been noted without. Chamber area is generally blank, but some have been found with 1914-1918 dates stamped on them. These were reworked by DWM from Military Navy Lugers after WWI for commercial sales. They are marked "Germany" or "Made in Germany" and were sold by Stoeger Arms, among others. Extractor and safety are both marked and unique Navy sight is on rear toggle link. No one knows exactly how many were produced, but they are quite scarce.

NIB	Exc.	V.G.	Good	Fair	Poor
—	9000	5000	2100	1100	850

1920 Commercial Artillery

8" barrel, 9mm caliber. Erfurt-manufactured pistols, as well as DWM-manufactured pistols, were reworked in this manner. Export markings "Germany" or "Made in Germany" are found on most examples. Number produced is not known, but examples are quite scarce.

NIB	Exc.	V.G.	Good	Fair	Poor
—	4500	3000	1100	700	450

1920 Long Barrel Commercial

10" to 24" barrels, 7.65mm or 9mm caliber. Extractor and safety are both marked and an artillery model rear sight is used. Often built to customer's specifications. They are rare and number manufactured is not known.

NIB	Exc.	V.G.	Good	Fair	Poor
—	5000	3450	1500	1000	800

1920 Carbine

11.75" barrel, 7.65mm caliber. Chamber is blank and extractor marked "Geleden" or "Loaded". Safety is not-marked. Carbine has checkered walnut forearm and stock. Most have "Germany" or "Made in Germany" export stamp. There were few of these carbines manufactured for commercial sales in and outside of Germany. Only two-digit serial numbers observed. Note: Prices include stock.

NIB	Exc.	V.G.	Good	Fair	Poor
—	16000	12000	6000	2500	1500

1920 Navy Carbine

Assembled from surplus Navy parts, with distinctive two position sliding navy sight on rear toggle link. Most are marked with export stamp and have naval military proofmarks still in evidence. Safety and extractor are marked and rarely one is found chambered for 9mm cartridge. Few were manufactured.

NIB	Exc.	V.G.	Good	Fair	Poor
—	19500	11000	5250	3000	1700

1920 Swiss Commercial

3.5" or 6" barrels, 7.65mm or 9mm caliber. Swiss Cross in Sunburst stamped over chamber and extractor marked "Geladen". Frame under safety is polished. There were a few thousand produced, with serial numbers in one- to five-digit range, sometimes with a letter suffix.

NIB	Exc.	V.G.	Good	Fair	Poor
—	4000	1800	1200	800	600

1923 Stoeger Commercial

3.5" to 24" barrels, 7.65mm or 9mm caliber. There is a stock lug. Chamber area is blank or has the American Eagle stamped on it. Export stamp and "A.F.Stoeger Inc. New York" is found on right side of receiver. Extractor and safety are marked in German or English. This was model Stoeger registered with U.S. Patent office to secure Luger name and some examples will be so marked. There were less than 1,000 manufactured, with one- to five-digit serial numbers without a letter suffix. Individual appraisal must be secured on barrel lengths above 6". Be wary as fakes have been noted. Values given here are for shorter barreled models. Note: Add 25 percent for barrel length 8 inches or more. Add 50 percent for three line inscription as these were manufactured by Mauser and have 3 digit "v" suffix serial numbers.

Courtesy Gale Morgan

NIB	Exc.	V.G.	Good	Fair	Poor
—	6000	4500	1800	1000	700

Abercrombie & Fitch Commercial 100

Swiss Lugers were made for commercial sale in United States by "Abercrombie & Fitch Co. New York. Made in Switzerland". —in either one or two lines—stamped on top of barrel. Barrel is 4.75" in length and there were 49 chambered for 9mm and 51 chambered for 7.65mm cartridge. Has a grip safety and no stock lug. Swiss Cross in Sunburst stamped over chamber. Extractor is marked, but safety area is polished. Serial range is four digits—some with a letter suffix. This is a rare and desirable Luger. Be careful of fakes on models of this type and rarity.

NIB	Exc.	V.G.	Good	Fair	Poor
—	11000	8000	4500	3000	2000

1923 Commercial

7.5" barrel, 7.65mm caliber. Has a stock lug and chamber area is blank. Extractor and safety are both marked in German. Manufactured for commercial sales in and outside of Germany. Approximately 18,000 produced, with serial numbers in 73500-96000 range.

NIB	Exc.	V.G.	Good	Fair	Poor
—	2500	1800	800	600	450

1923 Commercial Safe & Loaded

As above, except extractor and safety are marked in English "Safe" & "Loaded". Approximately 7,000 manufactured in 73500-96000 serial number range.

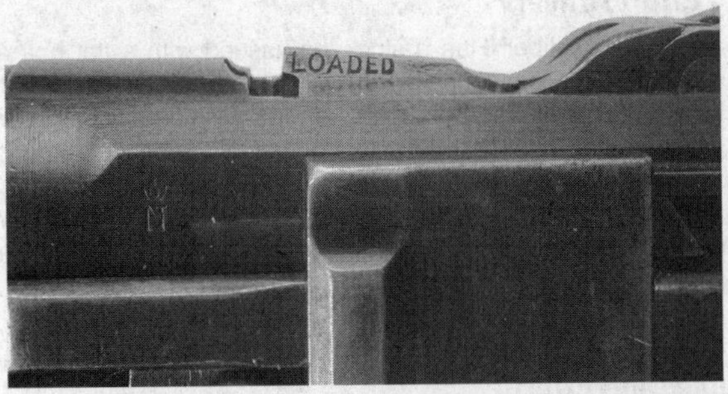

Courtesy Gale Morgan

NIB	Exc.	V.G.	Good	Fair	Poor
—	3500	2200	1000	800	500

1923 Dutch Commercial & Military

4" barrel, 9mm caliber. Has a stock lug and chamber area is blank. Extractor marked in German and safety marked "RUST", with a downward pointing arrow. Sold commercially and to military in Netherlands. Approximately 1,000 manufactured in one- to three-digit serial range, with no letter suffix.

NIB	Exc.	V.G.	Good	Fair	Poor
—	4000	2800	1000	850	550

Royal Dutch Air Force

4" barrel, 9mm caliber. Marked with Mauser Oberndorf proofmark. Serial numbered in 10000 to 14000 range. Safety marked "RUST".

NIB	Exc.	V.G.	Good	Fair	Poor
—	5000	2900	1000	800	550

VICKERS LTD.

1906 Vickers Dutch

4" barrel, 9mm caliber. No stock lug and uses a grip safety. Chamber is blank and extractor marked "Geleden". "Vickers Ltd." stamped on front toggle link. Safety marked "RUST", with an upward pointing arrow. Examples have been found with an additional date as late as 1933 stamped on barrel. Dates indicate arsenal refinishing and in no way detract from value of this variation. Arsenal reworks are matte-finished and originals are a higher-polished rust blue. Approximately 6,100 manufactured in the 4,000-10100 serial-number range.

NIB	Exc.	V.G.	Good	Fair	Poor
—	3800	3000	1800	1200	750

ERFURT ROYAL ARSENAL

1908 Erfurt

4" barrel, 9mm caliber. No stock lug; year of manufacture from 1910-1913 stamped above chamber. Extractor and safety are both marked in German. "ERFURT" under a crown stamped on front toggle link. Many thousands produced as Germany was involved in WWI. Found in one- to five-digit serial range, sometimes with a letter suffix.

NIB	Exc.	V.G.	Good	Fair	Poor
—	2100	1350	600	400	350

1914 Erfurt Military

4" barrel, 9mm caliber. Has a stock lug and date of manufacture over chamber 1914-1918. Extractor and safety are both marked in German and front link marked "ERFURT" under a crown. Finish on this model is rough; as war progressed in 1917 and 1918 finish got worse. Many thousands produced with one- to five-digit serial numbers, some with letter suffixes.

NIB	Exc.	V.G.	Good	Fair	Poor
—	2000	1100	600	400	350

1914 Erfurt Artillery

8" barrel, 9mm caliber. Has a stock lug. Issued with a flat board-type stock and other accessories which will be covered in the section of this book dealing with same. Sight is a nine-position adjustable model. Chamber is dated 1914 and extractor and safety are both marked in German. "ERFURT" under a crown is stamped on front toggle link. A great many manufactured with one- to five-digit serial numbers, some with a letter suffix. Model similar to DWM Artillery, except finish is not as fine.

NIB	Exc.	V.G.	Good	Fair	Poor
—	3750	2200	1100	800	600

Double Date Erfurt

4" barrel, 9mm caliber. Area above chamber has two dates: original 1910-1918 and date of rework, 1920 or 1921. Extractor and safety are both marked in German. Model can be found with or without stock lug. "ERFURT" under a crown is stamped on front toggle link. Police or military unit markings are found on front of grip straps, more often than not. Thousands produced by DWM as well as Erfurt.

NIB	Exc.	V.G.	Good	Fair	Poor
—	1200	700	500	400	350

SIMSON & CO. SUHL, GERMANY

Simson was official re-work firm for German army. Thanks to Edward Tinker for his contributions to this section.

Simson & Co. Rework

4" barrels, 9mm caliber. Chamber is blank, but some examples are dated 1917 or 1918. Forward toggle link stamped "SIMSON & CO. Suhl". Extractor and safety are marked in German. Most examples have stock lugs; some have been noted without them. Only difference between military and commercial models is proofmarks.

NIB	Exc.	V.G.	Good	Fair	Poor
—	2750	1650	900	600	500

Simson Grip Safety Rework

4" barrel, 9mm caliber. Grip safety was added. There is a stock lug. Chamber area is blank; extractor is marked but safety is not. Only a few of these commercial reworks manufactured. Caution should be taken to avoid fakes.

NIB	Exc.	V.G.	Good	Fair	Poor
—	3860	2600	1500	850	550

Simson Dated Military

4" barrel, 9mm caliber. There is a stock lug and year of manufacture from 1925-1926 stamped above chamber (below serial number 700). Extractor and safety both marked in German. Checkered walnut grips of Simson-made Lugers are noticeably thicker than others. This is an extremely rare variation. Few seem to have survived.

NIB	Exc.	V.G.	Good	Fair	Poor
—	5300	2600	1800	900	650

Simson S Code

4" barrel, 9mm caliber. Forward toggle link stamped with Gothic S, possibly for "Simson". It has a stock lug and area above chamber is blank. Extractor and safety are both marked. Grips are also thicker. Fewer than 12,000 manufactured, with one- to five-digit serial numbers—some with letter "a" suffix. Quite rare on today's market. Add $200 to $400 for a matching mag. Up to $1,000 premium for a dated model (1925 or 1926)

NIB	Exc.	V.G.	Good	Fair	Poor
6000	2300	2000	1500	1000	700

EARLY NAZI ERA REWORKS MAUSER

Produced between 1930 and 1933. Normally marked with Waffenamt markings.

Deaths Head Rework

4" barrel, 9mm caliber. Has a stock lug; skull and crossbones are stamped, in addition to date of manufacture, on chamber area. Date was from 1914-1918. Extractor and safety are both marked. Waffenamt proof is present. Thought that this variation was produced for 1930-1933 era "SS" division of Nazi Party. Mixed serial numbers are encountered on this model and do not lower value. A rare Luger on today's market.

NIB	Exc.	V.G.	Good	Fair	Poor
—	3500	1900	950	600	450

Kadetten Institute Rework

4" barrel, 9mm caliber. Has a stock lug and chamber area stamped "K.I." above date 1933. This stood for Cadets Institute, an early "SA" and "SS" officers' training school. Extractor and safety are both marked and Waffenamt is present. Only a few hundred reworked and variation is quite scarce. Be wary of fakes.

NIB	Exc.	V.G.	Good	Fair	Poor
—	4500	2900	1100	800	600

Mauser Unmarked Rework

4" barrel, 9mm caliber. Entire weapon is void of identifying markings. Extensive refurbishing, removal of all markings, re-barreling, etc. Stock lug is present and extractor and safety are marked. Waffenamt proofmark is on right side of receiver. Number manufactured is not known.

NIB	Exc.	V.G.	Good	Fair	Poor
—	2500	1350	850	600	450

MAUSER MANUFACTURED LUGERS 1930-1942 DWM

Mauser Oberndorf

4" barrel, 9mm caliber. Has a stock lug, blank chamber area and marked extractor and safety. Early example of Mauser Luger. Front toggle link is still marked DWM. Leftover parts were intermixed with new Mauser parts in production of this pistol. One of the first Lugers to be finished with "Salt" blue process. Approximately 500 manufactured with one- to four-digit serial numbers, with letter "v" suffix. A rare variation.

NIB	Exc.	V.G.	Good	Fair	Poor
—	8000	6100	2000	1500	900

1934/06 Swiss Commercial Mauser

4.75" barrel, 7.65mm caliber. No stock lug, but has a grip safety. Swiss Cross in Sunburst stamped above chamber. Extractor and safety marked in German. Front toggle link marked with Mauser banner. Approximately 200 manufactured for commercial sale in Switzerland. Variation is very well finished. Serial numbers are all four-digits with a "v" suffix.

NIB	Exc.	V.G.	Good	Fair	Poor
—	8000	6000	4000	1800	1000

1935/06 Portuguese "GNR"

4.75 barrel, 7.65mm caliber. No stock lug, but has a grip safety. Chamber marked "GNR", representing Republic National Guard. Extractor marked "Carregada"; safety "Seguranca". Mauser banner stamped on front toggle link. Exactly 564 manufactured according to original contract records that Portuguese government made public. All have four-digit serial numbers with a "v" suffix.

NIB	Exc.	V.G.	Good	Fair	Poor
—	4500	3300	1800	900	750

1934 Mauser Commercial

4" barrel, 7.65mm or 9mm caliber. Has a stock lug and chamber area is blank. Extractor and safety are marked. Mauser banner stamped on front toggle link. Finish on this pistol was very good. Grips are checkered walnut or black plastic on later models. Few thousand manufactured for commercial sales in and outside of Germany.

NIB	Exc.	V.G.	Good	Fair	Poor
—	5500	3500	1650	1100	700

S/42 K Date

4" barrel, 9mm caliber. Has a stock lug. Extractor and safety are marked. First Luger that utilized codes to represent maker and date of manufacture. Front toggle link marked S/42 in Gothic or script; this was code for Mauser. Chamber area stamped with letter "K" code for 1934 year of manufacture. Approximately 10,500 manufactured, with one- to five-digit serial numbers—some with letter suffixes.

NIB	Exc.	V.G.	Good	Fair	Poor
—	9500	7500	3000	1200	1000

S/42 G Date

As above, with chamber stamped "G" code for year 1935. Gothic lettering was eliminated. Many thousands of this model produced.

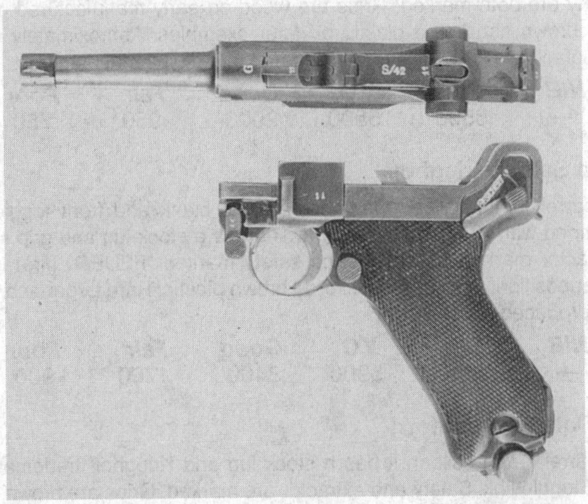

Courtesy Orvel Reichert

NIB	Exc.	V.G.	Good	Fair	Poor
—	4000	2500	1200	650	450

Dated Chamber S/42

4" barrel, 9mm caliber. Chamber area dated 1936-1940. There is a stock lug. Extractor and safety marked. In 1937, rust blue process was eliminated entirely and all subsequent pistols were salt blued. Many thousands manufactured with one- to five-digit serial numbers—some with letter suffix. Note: Rarest variation is early 1937, with rust blued and strawed parts, add 20 percent.

NIB	Exc.	V.G.	Good	Fair	Poor
—	3000	2100	1100	500	400

S/42 Commercial Contract

4" barrel, 9mm caliber. Has a stock lug, chamber area is dated and marked extractor and safety. Unusual feature, although this was a commercial pistol, front toggle link is stamped S/42, which was military code for Mauser. Only a few hundred manufactured, so perhaps toggles were left over from previous military production runs. Serial number range is four-digits, with letter "v".

NIB	Exc.	V.G.	Good	Fair	Poor
—	3750	2500	1200	750	450

Code 42 Dated Chamber

4" barrel, 9mm caliber. New German code for Mauser, number 42, stamped on front toggle link. There is a stock lug. Chamber area dated 1939 or 1940. At least 50,000 manufactured, with one- to five-digit serial numbers; some have letter suffixes.

NIB	Exc.	V.G.	Good	Fair	Poor
—	2500	1400	1000	600	350

41/42 Code

As above, except date of manufacture is represented by final two digits (e.g. 41 for 1941). Approximately 20,000 manufactured, with one- to five-digit serial number range.

NIB	Exc.	V.G.	Good	Fair	Poor
—	4000	2100	1200	800	500

byf Code

As above, with "byf" code stamped on toggle link. Year of manufacture, either 41 or 42, stamped on chamber. Model also made with black plastic and walnut grips. Many thousands produced, with one- to five-digit serial numbers—some with a letter suffix.

NIB	Exc.	V.G.	Good	Fair	Poor
—	3000	1800	950	450	350

Persian Contract 4

4" barrel, 9mm caliber. Has a stock lug and Persian crest stamped over chamber. All identifying markings on this variation—including extractor, safety and toggle—are marked in Farsi, Persian alphabet. There were 1,000 manufactured. Serial numbers are also in Farsi.

NIB	Exc.	V.G.	Good	Fair	Poor
—	7000	5500	3500	2500	2000

Persian Contract Artillery

As above, with 8-in. barrel and nine-position adjustable sight on barrel. All these were issued as complete rigs with holster, matching stock, cleaning rod, and carrying strap. A total of 1,000 were manufactured and sold to Persia. Add 50 percent to value for complete rig.

NIB	Exc.	V.G.	Good	Fair	Poor
—	8500	5500	3500	1750	1000

1934/06 Dated Commercial

4.75" barrel, 7.65mm caliber. Has a grip safety, but no stock lug. Year of manufacture, from 1937-1942, stamped above chamber. Mauser banner stamped on front link. Extractor marked, but safety is not. Approximately 1,000 manufactured, with one- to three-digit serial numbers—some with letter suffix.

NIB	Exc.	V.G.	Good	Fair	Poor
—	4500	3100	1400	900	500

1934 Mauser Dutch Contract

4" barrel, 9mm caliber. Year of manufacture, 1936-1940, stamped above chamber. Extractor marked "Geladen" and safety is marked "RUST", with a downward pointing arrow. Mauser banner stamped on front toggle link. This was a military contract sale. Approximately 1,000 were manufactured, with four-digit serial numbers and letter "v" suffix.

NIB	Exc.	V.G.	Good	Fair	Poor
—	4750	3650	2000	1100	850

1934 Mauser Swedish Contract

4.75" barrel, 9mm or 7.65mm caliber. Chamber dated 1938 or 1939. Extractor and safety are both marked in German. There is a stock lug. Front toggle link stamped with Mauser banner. Only 275 dated 1938; 25 dated 1939 in 9mm; 30 dated 1939 in 7.65mm. Serial number range is four-digits with letter "v" suffix.

NIB	Exc.	V.G.	Good	Fair	Poor
—	6000	3800	2000	1500	700

1934 Mauser Swedish Commercial

4" barrel, 7.65mm caliber. 1940 stamped over chamber; "Kal. 7.65" stamped on left side of barrel. Extractor and safety are both marked and Mauser banner stamped on front toggle link. There is a stock lug. Model is rare. Only a few hundred manufactured, with four-digit serial numbers with letter "w" suffix.

NIB	Exc.	V.G.	Good	Fair	Poor
—	4500	2950	1200	850	600

1934 Mauser German Contract

4" barrel, 9mm caliber. Chamber dated 1939-1942. Front toggle link stamped with Mauser banner. There is a stock lug. Extractor and safety are both marked. Grips are walnut or black plastic. Several thousand manufactured, with one- to five-digit serial numbers—some with letter suffixes. Purchased for issue to police or paramilitary units.

NIB	Exc.	V.G.	Good	Fair	Poor
—	4500	3200	1500	800	550

Austrian Bundes Heer (Federal Army)

4" barrel, 9mm caliber. Chamber is blank and there is a stock lug. Extractor and safety marked in German. Austrian Federal Army Proof stamped on left side of frame above triggerguard. Approximately 200 manufactured, with four-digit serial numbers and no letter suffix.

NIB	Exc.	V.G.	Good	Fair	Poor
—	4000	2350	1200	700	500

Mauser 2 Digit Date

4" barrel, 9mm caliber. Last two digits of year of manufacture—41 or 42—stamped over chamber. There is a stock lug and Mauser banner on front toggle link. Extractor and safety both marked. Proofmarks were commercial. Grips are walnut or black plastic. Approximately 2,000 manufactured for sale to Nazi political groups. They have one- to five-digit serial numbers; some have letter suffix.

NIB	Exc.	V.G.	Good	Fair	Poor
—	3500	2600	1500	900	650

Ku Luger (Prefix or suffix)

4" barrel, 9mm Luger. Probably manufactured by Mauser for German Luftwaffe in early 1940s. Serial number (on left side receiver area) has "Ku" prefix or suffix. Total production estimated at 5000 pieces.

Courtesy Gale Morgan

NIB	Exc.	V.G.	Good	Fair	Poor
—	4750	3000	1200	900	550

KRIEGHOFF MANUFACTURED LUGERS

1923 DWM/Krieghoff Commercial

4" barrel, 7.65mm or 9mm caliber. Chamber dated 1921 or left blank. There is a stock lug. Front toggle marked DWM, as they manufactured this Luger to be sold by Krieghoff. "Krieghoff Suhl" stamped on back above lanyard loop. Second "F" in Krieghoff was defective and all specimens have this distinctive die strike. Safety and extractor are marked in German. Only a few hundred manufactured, with four-digit serial numbers with letter "i" suffix.

NIB	Exc.	V.G.	Good	Fair	Poor
—	5000	3500	1700	900	500

DWM/Krieghoff Commercial

As above, but marked "Heinrich Krieghoff Waffenfabrik Suhl" on right side of frame. Some examples have "Germany" export stamp. Several hundred manufactured, with four-digit serial numbers with a letter suffix.

NIB	Exc.	V.G.	Good	Fair	Poor
—	4800	3650	2000	950	800

Krieghoff Commercial Inscribed Side Frame

4" or 6" barrel, 7.65mm or 9mm caliber. 1,000 were marked "Heinrich Krieghoff Waffenfabrik Suhl" on left side of frame and 500 were devoid of this marking. All have dagger and anchor trademark over "H.K. Krieghoff Suhl" on front toggle link. Extractor and safety are both marked. There is a stock lug and grips are of brown checkered plastic. Approximately 1,500 manufactured, with one- to four-digit serial numbers with "P" prefix.

NIB	Exc.	V.G.	Good	Fair	Poor
—	8500	6400	3000	2000	1000

S Code Krieghoff

4" barrel, 9mm caliber. Krieghoff trademark stamped on front toggle link and letter "S" stamped over chamber. There is a stock lug. Extractor and safety are both marked. Grips are wood on early manufactured pistols and brown checkered plastic on later examples. Approximately 4,500 manufactured for Luftwaffe, with one- to four-digit serial numbers.

NIB	Exc.	V.G.	Good	Fair	Poor
—	8500	5500	2000	950	750

Grip Safety Krieghoff

4" barrel, 9mm caliber. Chamber area is blank and front toggle link stamped with Krieghoff trademark. There is a stock lug and grip safety. Extractor marked "Geleden" and safety marked "FEUER" (fire) in the lower position. Grips are checkered brown plastic. Rare Luger and number produced is not known.

NIB	Exc.	V.G.	Good	Fair	Poor
—	9500	5900	3400	1700	900

36 Date Krieghoff

4" barrel, 9mm caliber. It has a stock lug and Krieghoff trademark on front toggle link. Safety and extractor are marked. Grips are brown plastic. Two-digit year of manufacture, 36, stamped over chamber. Approximately 700 produced in 3800-4500 serial number range.

NIB	Exc.	V.G.	Good	Fair	Poor
—	9000	6000	2600	1200	950

4 Digit Dated Krieghoff

As above, with date of production, 1936-1945, stamped above chamber. Approximately 9,000 manufactured within 4500-14000 serial number range. Note: Add 25 percent for 1942 or 1943 dates; 100 percent for 1944 or 1945.

Courtesy Gale Morgan

NIB	Exc.	V.G.	Good	Fair	Poor
—	7500	6000	3000	1500	750

2nd Series Krieghoff Commercial

4" barrel, 9mm caliber. There is a stock lug and Krieghoff trademark stamped on front link. Chamber area is blank. Extractor and safety are marked. Approximately 500 manufactured for commercial sales inside Germany. Date of manufacture is estimated at 1939-1940. This variation has dark finish that results from bluing without polishing surface, which was done during these years. Grips are coarsely checkered black plastic. Serial number range is one- to three-digits, with a "P" prefix.

NIB	Exc.	V.G.	Good	Fair	Poor
—	6500	4200	2200	1300	800

Post-War Krieghoff

4" barrel, 9mm caliber. There is a stock lug and chamber area is blank. Extractor and safety are marked. Serial numbers in one- to three-digit range are unusually large—about .1875 of an inch. There were 300 post-war Lugers produced for occupation forces. They were assembled from leftover parts and only 150 have Krieghoff trademark on front toggle link—second 150 have blank links.

NIB	Exc.	V.G.	Good	Fair	Poor
—	6000	3500	2000	750	650

Krieghoff Post-War Commercial

As above in 7.65mm caliber. Extractor not marked. Approximately 200 manufactured, with standard-sized two- or three-digit serial numbers. They were supposedly sold to occupation forces in PX stores.

NIB	Exc.	V.G.	Good	Fair	Poor
—	6500	3500	2200	700	550

East German Luger Rework, aka VOPO

Imported between 1996 and 1999, primarily by Miltex of La Plata, Maryland. These Russian re-worked 9mm Luger pistols, were the first surplus Lugers imported to the United States since 1960s military surplus boom. Primarily captured by Soviet troops during WWII, these Lugers may be found with original matching or non-matching numbers. Many were re-marked by the Russians, with examples having re-stamped matching numbers done by steel die or electro penciling. Issued to East German military and Volks Polizei (hence the People's Police, nickname VOPO), most had the walnut grips removed by the Russians, and were stored in barrels of oil to preserve them until they were re-issued to the German Democratic Republic in 1946. It is believed they were removed from East German service by 1958. Black-lined hard rubber or plastic grips made both in Russia and Hungary were fitted to these pistols, as well as the more commonly encountered, East German-made brown checkered plastic grips that has a target-style design at the top. Many VOPO Lugers have Nazi Waffenampt "scrubbed" or a remaining Reich's Eagle with an obliterated swastika. Many are found with no German proofs at all. Snubbed by collectors at first, they now have a following and are a complete area of Luger collecting all to their own. Some re-barreled examples have an East German Crown over N marking on lower barrel, reflecting a replacement.

NIB	Exc.	V.G.	Good	Fair	Poor
—	1280	1100	880	600	300

LUGER ACCESSORIES

Detachable Carbine Stocks

Approximately 13" in length, with sling swivel and horn buttplate.

NIB	Exc.	V.G.	Good	Fair	Poor
—	6500	4500	3000	1000	700

Artillery Stock with Holster

Artillery stock is a flat board style, approximately 13.75" in length. There is a holster and magazine pouches, with straps attached. A desirable addition to Artillery Luger.

NIB	Exc.	V.G.	Good	Fair	Poor
—	3500	2500	1000	800	600

Navy Stock without Holster

As above, but 12.75" in length with metal disc inlaid on left side.

NIB	Exc.	V.G.	Good	Fair	Poor
—	4500	3000	1500	800	400

Ideal Stock/Holster with Grips

Telescoping metal tube stock, with attached leather holster. Used in conjunction with metal-backed set of plain grips that correspond to metal hooks on stock and allow attachment. This Ideal Stock is U.S. patented and is so marked.

NIB	Exc.	V.G.	Good	Fair	Poor
—	3500	2000	1500	700	450

Drum Magazine 1st Issue

A 32-round snail-like affair that is used with Artillery Luger. Also used with adapter in German 9mm sub-machine gun. 1st Issue has a telescoping tube that is used to wind the spring. There is a dust cover that protects interior from dirt.

NIB	Exc.	V.G.	Good	Fair	Poor
—	2500	2000	1500	550	300

Drum Magazine 2nd Issue

As above, with folding spring winding lever.

NIB	Exc.	V.G.	Good	Fair	Poor
—	2000	1700	1000	550	300

Drum Magazine Loading Tool

Tool slipped over magazine and allows spring to be compressed so cartridges could be inserted.

NIB	Exc.	V.G.	Good	Fair	Poor
—	1500	800	500	300	200

Drum Carrying Case

NIB	Exc.	V.G.	Good	Fair	Poor
—	500	350	120	100	50

LATE PRODUCTION MAUSER LUGERS MANUFACTURED DURING THE 1970S

P.08 Interarms

4" or 6" barrel, 7.65mm or 9mm caliber.

NIB	Exc.	V.G.	Good	Fair	Poor
1750	1250	550	400	350	300

Swiss Eagle Interarms

Swiss-style straight front grip strap and American Eagle crest over chamber. Chambered for 7.65mm or 9mm and offered with 4" or 6" barrel.

NIB	Exc.	V.G.	Good	Fair	Poor
1800	950	650	350	320	300

Cartridge Counter

Chambered for 9mm cartridge. Fitted with slotted grip to show cartridge count in magazine.

NIB	Exc.	V.G.	Good	Fair	Poor
2500	1600	1100	750	500	350

Commemorative Bulgarian

Bulgarian crest stamped over chamber. Only 100 produced.

NIB	Exc.	V.G.	Good	Fair	Poor
2200	1600	1100	750	500	350

Commemorative Russian

Crossed Nagant rifles stamped over chamber. Only 100 produced.

NIB	Exc.	V.G.	Good	Fair	Poor
2750	1600	1100	750	500	350

Modern Production Carbine

Splendid re-production produced on limited basis. Workmanship is excellent. Carbine and stock furnished in case.

NIB	Exc.	V.G.	Good	Fair	Poor
6000	4500	4000	3200	2500	2000

JOHN MARTZ CUSTOM LUGERS

Martz Luger Carbine

16" barrel. Fewer than 100 manufactured.

NIB	Exc.	V.G.	Good	Fair	Poor
—	9000	7000	4500	2500	1000

.45 ACP or .357 SIG

6" barrel, .45 ACP caliber. Assembled from two Luger pistols that were split and welded together. Fewer than 100 manufactured.

NIB	Exc.	V.G.	Good	Fair	Poor
—	5500	4000	3000	—	—

Baby Luger 9mm & 7.65mm

Compact Luger pistol. Fewer than 300 produced.

Courtesy Gale Morgan

NIB	Exc.	V.G.	Good	Fair	Poor
—	4000	2500	1500	—	—

Baby Luger .380 ACP

As above in .380-caliber. Seven were manufactured.

Courtesy Gale Morgan

NIB	Exc.	V.G.	Good	Fair	Poor
—	8000	6000	4000	—	—

LUNA
Zella-Mehlis, Germany

Model 200 Free Pistol

.22-caliber Martini action single-shot pistol, with 11" barrel, adjustable sights and walnut grips. Manufactured prior to WWII.

NIB	Exc.	V.G.	Good	Fair	Poor
—	1850	1250	800	500	300

Model 300 Free Pistol

Single-shot target pistol chambered for .22 Short cartridge. Fitted with 11" barrel, set trigger, walnut stocks and forearm, with adjustable palm rest. Built about 1929 to 1939.

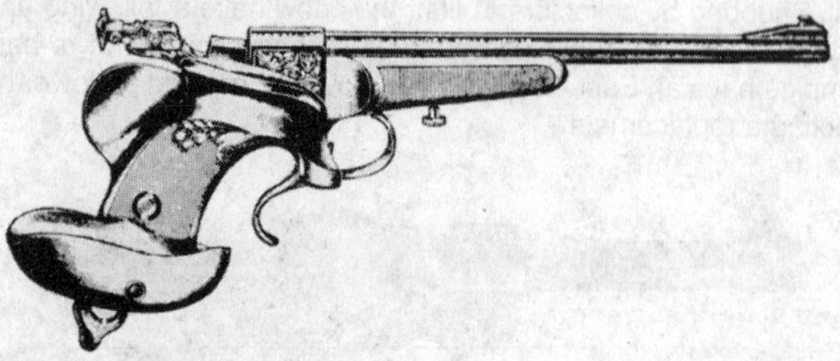

NIB	Exc.	V.G.	Good	Fair	Poor
—	1950	1250	800	500	300

Target Rifle

.22 or .22 Hornet caliber Martini action single-shot rifle, with 20" barrel, adjustable sights and walnut stock. Manufactured prior to WWII.

NIB	Exc.	V.G.	Good	Fair	Poor
—	1800	1350	850	500	250

LWRC INTERNATIONAL
Cambridge, Maryland

A manufacturer of AR-type rifles for military, law enforcement and civilian markets. All models a proprietary short-stroke, self-regulating, gas piston operating system that prevents the gases from contacting the bolt carrier or receiver. LWRC is acronym for Land Warfare Resources Corporation and previously stood for Leitner-Wise Rifle Company, Inc. SEE POLITICAL PANIC PRICING.

M6-A2

Standard carbine available in 5.56 NATO/.223 Rem., with 16.1" barrel (10.5" or 14.7" lengths for LE/Military) and in several AR configurations. Discontinued.

NIB	Exc.	V.G.	Good	Fair	Poor
2000	1700	1350	950	—	—

IC-PSD

Caliber: 5.56 NATO. Barrel: 8.5". Capacity: Magpul PMAG 30-round magazine. Stock: LWRC adjustable compact stock. Sights: Low-profile, flip-up Skirmish Sights. Weight: 5.9 lbs. Trigger: LWRC Enhanced Fire Control Group. Overall Length: 25"-28". Features: Part of the Individual Carbine series of rifles. NFA item. LWRCI Monoforge upper receiver with modular 7" rail system. Nickel-boron coated bolt carrier, LWRCI High-Efficiency 4-Prong Flash Hider. SEE POLITICAL PANIC PRICING.

NIB	Exc.	V.G.	Good	Fair	Poor
2590	2480	2150	1700	—	—

SIX8-A5

Caliber: 6.8 SPC II. Capacity: Magpul 20-round PMAG. Barrel: 14.7", 16.1" in.; 1:10" RH twist, 5/8x24 muzzle threads. Cold hammer-forged, spiral fluted, NiCorr treated. Stock: LWRC adjustable compact stock. Grip: Magpul MOE+. Sights: Low-profile flip-up Skirmish Sights. Weight: 6.5 lbs. Trigger: LWRC Enhanced Fire Control Group. Overall length: 32"-35.25". Features: LWRCI proprietary upper and lower receivers optimized for 6.8 SPC II cartridge; adjustable two-position gas block, Birdcage (A2) Flash Hider; 12-in. user-configurable rail system; ambidextrous charging handle and lower receiver. SEE POLITICAL PANIC PRICING.

NIB	Exc.	V.G.	Good	Fair	Poor
2700	2500	2300	1990	1510	—

REPR

Rapid Engagement Precision Rifle chambered for 7.62 NATO/.308 Win., with 16.1" or 20" barrel. Custom packages including one lower receiver, with two or more barreled uppers are available. Finish colors are black, Flat Dark Earth, Patriot Brown or O.D. Green.

NIB	Exc.	V.G.	Good	Fair	Poor
3500	3000	2700	1900	—	—

IC-SPR

Caliber: 5.56 NATO. Capacity: Magpul PMAG 5.56. Barrel: 14.7", 16.1"; 1:7" RH twist, 1/2x28 muzzle threads. Cold hammer-forged, spiral fluted, NiCorr treated. Stock: LWRC adjustable compact stock. Sights: Low-profile flip-up Skirmish Sights. Weight: 7.0 lbs., 7.3 lbs. SEE POLITICAL PANIC PRICING.

NIB	Exc.	V.G.	Good	Fair	Poor
2430	2300	2130	1980	—	—

IC-A5

Similar to the IC-SPR. Caliber: 5.56 NATO. Barrel: 10.5", 12.7", 14.7", 16.1". Features: Has a low-profile two-position adjustable gas block allowing the shooter to compensate for running a suppressor and a longer modular rail system. SEE POLITICAL PANIC PRICING.

NIB	Exc.	V.G.	Good	Fair	Poor
2700	2570	2390	2000	1650	—

IC-Enhanced

Caliber: 5.56 NATO. Barrel: 12.7", 14.7", 16.1". Features: Includes a Picatinny rail at 12 o'clock, a bayonet lug, and is compatible with accessories like the M320 grenade launcher and the M26 shotgun. Add $170 for FDE and OD Green colors. SEE POLITICAL PANIC PRICING.

NIB	Exc.	V.G.	Good	Fair	Poor
2750	2600	2430	2000	1790	—

REPR MKII

Caliber: 6.5 Creedmoor, 7.62 NATO. Rapid Engagement Precision Rifle. Capacity: Magpul 20-round PMAG. Barrel: 12.7", 16.1", 20", and 22" stainless steel. 1:8" RH twist, 5/8x24 muzzle threads. Stock: Magpul PRS. Grip: Magpul MOE+. Sights: Low-profile flip-up Skirmish Sights. Weight: 10.5 lbs. Trigger: Geissele SSA-E Two-Stage Precision. Overall Length: 43.5". Non-reciprocating side charging handle, 20-position tunable gas block, short-stroke gas piston system, Monoforge upper receiver with integrated rail base, removable top rail design, removable barrel, fully ambidextrous lower receiver controls including bolt catch and release, magazine release, and safety selector. LWRCI Advanced Triggerguard, Skirmish Back-Up Iron Sights, Enhanced 4-Port Ultra Static muzzle brake. Add $560 for a Proof Research carbon-fiber barrel. SEE POLITICAL PANIC PRICING.

NIB	Exc.	V.G.	Good	Fair	Poor
4220	4000	3780	2970	—	—

REPR MKII SC 6.5 Creedmoor Elite

Caliber: 6.5 Creedmoor. Capacity: Magpul 20-round PMAG 6.5 Creedmoor. Barrel: 22 in., Proof Research carbon-fiber or stainless steel barrel, 1:8 in. RH twist, 5/8x24 tpi muzzle threads. Stock: Magpul PRS. Grip: Magpul MOE+. Sights: Low-profile, flip-up Skirmish Sights. Weight: 10.5 lbs. Trigger: Geissele SSA-E 2-Stage Precision. Overall Length: 43.5 in. Features: Rapid Engagement Precision Rifle. Non-reciprocating side charging handle, 20-position tunable gas block, short-stroke gas piston system, Monoforge upper receiver with integrated rail-base, removable top rail design, removable barrel, fully ambidextrous lower receiver controls include bolt catch and release, magazine release and safety selector. LWRCI Advanced Triggerguard, Skirmish Back-Up Iron Sights, Enhanced 4-port Ultra Static muzzle brake.

NIB	*Exc.*	*V.G.*	*Good*	*Fair*	*Poor*
4250	3500	3000	—	—	—

LYMAN
Middletown, Connecticut

Lyman In-Line

Introduced in 1998. Inline muzzleloader offered in .50- or .54-caliber. Fitted with 22" barrel. Hardwood stock. Note: Add $80 for stainless steel version.

NIB	*Exc.*	*V.G.*	*Good*	*Fair*	*Poor*
—	250	210	180	150	130

Deerstalker Rifle

Available in .50- or .54-caliber percussion or flintlock. Fitted with 24" barrel and hardwood stock. Note: Add $40 for flintlock version and $80 for stainless steel version.

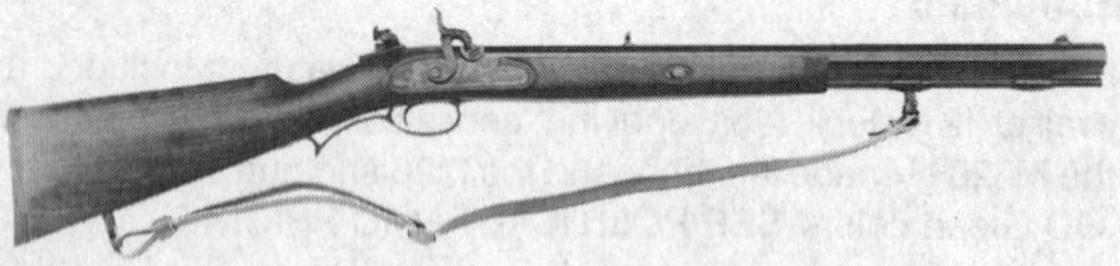

NIB	*Exc.*	*V.G.*	*Good*	*Fair*	*Poor*
420	360	310	260	220	190

Deerstalker Carbine

Same as above, with 21" barrel. Offered in .50-caliber only.

NIB	*Exc.*	*V.G.*	*Good*	*Fair*	*Poor*
420	360	310	260	220	190

Great Plains Rifle

Offered in .50- or .54-caliber flint or percussion. Barrel length 32". Hardwood stock. Note: Add $40 for flintlock version; $25 for left-hand rifles. Early models in Excellent condition are showing significant collector potential. No. 6031102 pricing shown below. Hunter model has 1:32" shallow groove rifled barrel for shooting modern projectiles and is also predrilled and tapped for the optional 57 GPR receiver sight.

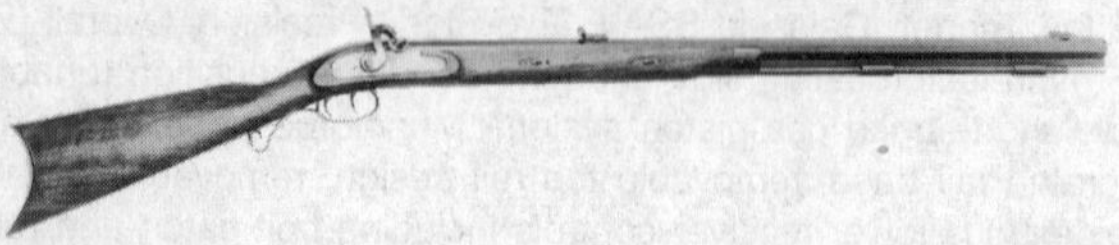

NIB	*Exc.*	*V.G.*	*Good*	*Fair*	*Poor*
580	490	420	350	300	260

Trade Rifle

Offered in .50- or .54-caliber, with 28" octagonal barrel and hardwood stock. Polished brass furniture. Note: Add $25 for flintlock rifle. No. 6032125 pricing shown below.

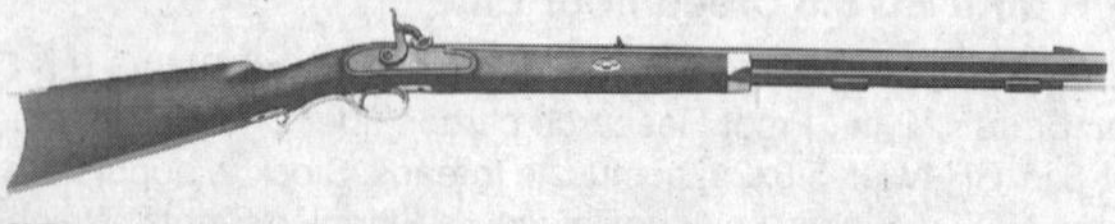

NIB	*Exc.*	*V.G.*	*Good*	*Fair*	*Poor*
420	360	310	260	220	190

Plains Pistol

Available in .50- or .54-caliber percussion.

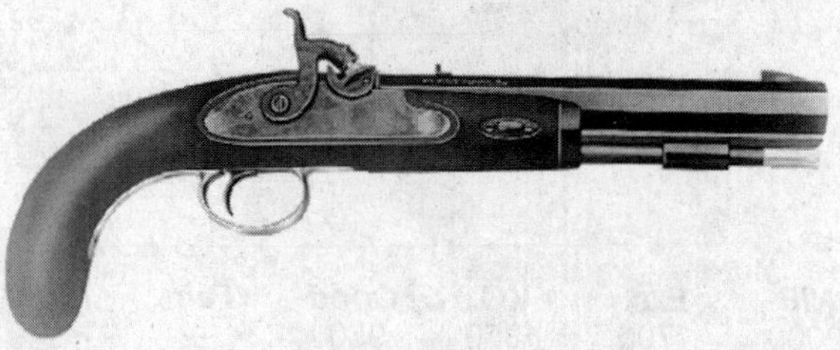

NIB	*Exc.*	*V.G.*	*Good*	*Fair*	*Poor*
350	300	250	220	180	160

Model 1878 Sharps

Replica of famous single-shot in .45-70. Features tang-mounted aperture sight, globe front sight, checkered stock with a comfortable shotgun-style buttplate, laser-engraved sideplate and 30" barrel. Made in Italy by Pedersoli. Imported by Lyman beginning in 2014.

NIB	*Exc.*	*V.G.*	*Good*	*Fair*	*Poor*
1750	1450	1200	900	—	—

Little Sharps

Also known as Ideal Model, this smaller variation of original Sharps was chambered in a wide range of both rimfire and centerfire calibers. Made in Italy by Armi-Sport. Discontinued.

NIB	*Exc.*	*V.G.*	*Good*	*Fair*	*Poor*
1500	1200	850	650	500	350

M

M.O.A. CORP.
Dayton, Ohio

Maximum

Single-shot pistol. Manufactured in a variety of calibers from .22 rimfire to .454 Casull, with 8.5", 10" or 14" barrel, adjustable sights, stainless steel receiver, blued barrel and walnut grip. Introduced in 1986. Note: Add 100 percent for stainless steel barrel.

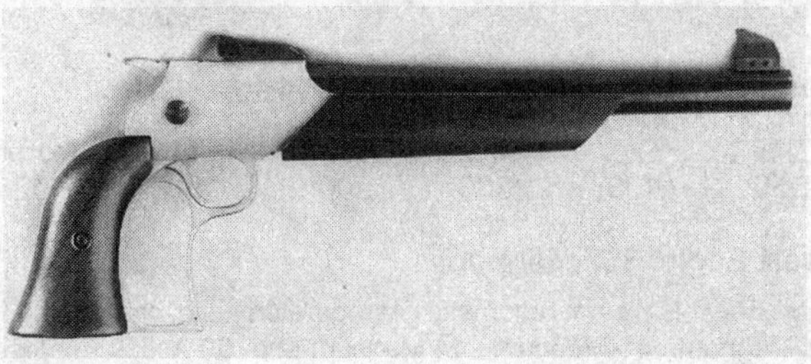

NIB	Exc.	V.G.	Good	Fair	Poor
800	600	480	320	250	120

Carbine

As above, with 18" barrel. Discontinued.

NIB	Exc.	V.G.	Good	Fair	Poor
1000	680	520	350	280	150

MAC

See—INGRAM

MADSEN
Copenhagen, Denmark

Model 47

NIB	Exc.	V.G.	Good	Fair	Poor
—	700	520	400	280	120

MAGNUM RESEARCH, INC.
Pillager, Minnesota

See—DESERT EAGLE

Magnum Research Inc. in Pillager, MN, was founded in 1979 by Jim Skildum and John Risdall and purchased by Kahr Arms in June 2010. Kahr Arms, based in Worcester, Massachusetts, has offices and factories in Massachusetts, Pennsylvania, and Minnesota. The current line includes the BFR (Biggest Finest Revolver), Desert Eagle, Baby Eagle, Desert Eagle 1911, and Magnum Lite Rimfire and Centerfire rifles. Magnum Research Inc., now owned by Kahr Arms, has been responsible for the design and development of the Desert Eagle pistol, and the actual pistols were manufactured by Israel Military Industries (IMI), subsequently shifted to Israeli Weapons Industries (IWI) until 1995, when MRI moved the manufacturing contract to Saco Defense in Saco, Maine. In 1998, MRI moved manufacturing back to IWI. Since 2009 the Desert Eagle Pistol has been produced in the USA at MRI's Pillager, MN facility.

.22 WMR Hogue OverMolded Rifle

NIB	Exc.	V.G.	Good	Fair	Poor
680	580	490	420	250	150

BFR (Long Cylinder)

Single-action revolver, with long cylinder. Past chamberings included .22 Hornet, .475/.480. Currently chambered in .30/30 Win., .444 Marlin, .450 Marlin, .45LC/.410 (Vent-Rib barrel Note: Add about $70), .45/70 Gov't., .460 S&W, .500 S&W (Note: Deduct $100 for the .500 S&W), with 7.5" or 10" barrels. Fitted with adjustable sights and stainless steel finish. Weight about 4 lbs. with 7.5" barrel. Grips include "Bisley" style synthetic or rubber. Introduced in 1998.

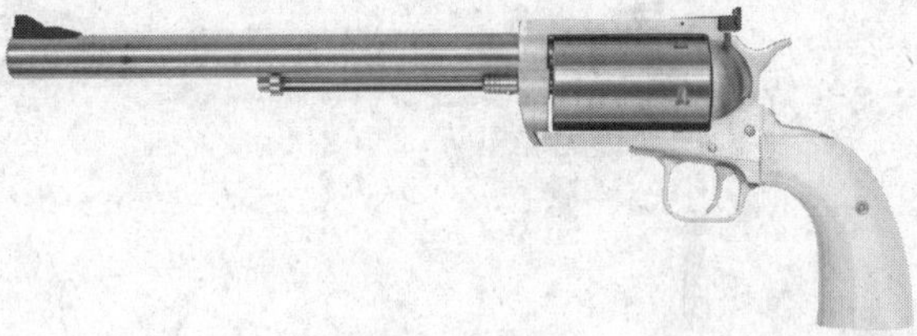

NIB	Exc.	V.G.	Good	Fair	Poor
1100	940	800	680	400	250

BFR Little Max (Short Cylinder)

Single-action revolver has a standard-length cylinder chambered for most magnum cartridges in the past and including the .22 Hornet. Current chamberings (5 or 6 shot depending on caliber) include .357 Magnum, .44 Magnum, .454 Casull, .475 Linebaugh, .50 AE, .500 JRH, and .500 Linebaugh. Fitted with adjustable sights and stainless steel finish. Barrel lengths include 5", 6.5" and 7.5". Weight about 3.5 lbs. with 7.5" barrel. Grips include "Bisley" style synthetic or rubber. Introduced in 1998.

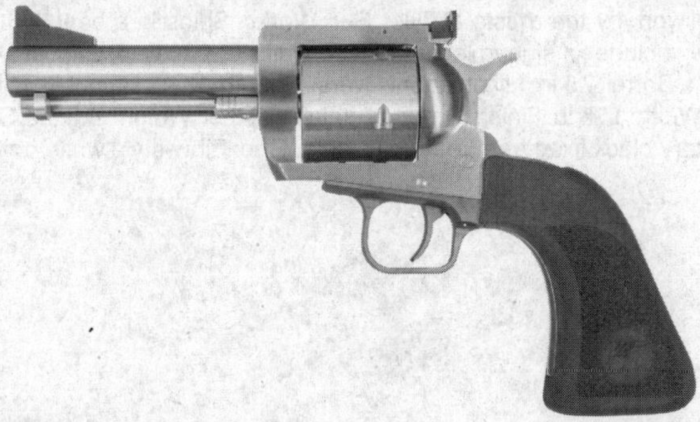

NIB	Exc.	V.G.	Good	Fair	Poor
1100	940	800	680	400	250

BFR Long Frame

Caliber: .350 Legend. Capacity: 6 rounds. Barrel: 7.5, 10 in. Grip: Standard rubber, Bisley, white polymer or black micarta. Sights: Adjustable rear, fixed front. Weight: 4.8, 5 lbs. Features: Built on Magnum Research's long frame and made entirely of 17-4PH stainless steel. The first long frame in six-shot configuration. Two grip frame options available: a standard plow handle with rubber grip, and Magnum Research iteration of a Bisley with white polymer or black micarta grips.

NIB	Exc.	V.G.	Good	Fair	Poor
—	—	—	—	—	—

BFR Short Frame

Caliber: .357 Magnum, .44 Magnum. Capacity: 6 rounds. Barrel: 5, 7.5 in. Grip: Standard rubber, Bisley, white polymer or black micarta. Sights: Adjustable rear, fixed front. Weight: 3.5, 3.65 lbs. Features: Made entirely of super tough 17-4PH stainless steel, BFRs are made in the United States and were designed from the outset to handle powerful revolver cartridges. The pre-eminent single-action hunting revolver. Two grip frame options available: a standard plow handle with rubber grip, and Magnum Research iteration of a Bisley with white polymer or black micarta grips.

NIB	Exc.	V.G.	Good	Fair	Poor
980	—	—	—	—	—

BFR 20th Anniversary

Each hand-crafted 20th Anniversary BFR is part of a limited series, with only 20 pistols to be produced. This custom gun is based on a .45-70 Government long frame model, the first production caliber. A full octagon barrel is added with a custom E-Rod Housing and base pin. Plow-style white polymer grips are hand fit. Exterior surfaces engraved with elegant scrollwork by the artists at Tyler Gun Works. Ships in a beautiful wood case, includes a signed letter of authenticity. Capacity: 5. Caliber: .45/70 Gov't. Barrel: 7.5 in. full octagon. Overall Length: 15-in. Height: 6 in. Cylinder Width: 1.75 in. Finish: Brushed stainless steel. Weight: 4.3 lbs. Sights: Factory black fixed front/rear adjustable. Grip: Plow-style white polymer.

NIB	Exc.	V.G.	Good	Fair	Poor
5250	—	—	—	—	—

IMI SP-21

Semi-automatic double-action pistol. Chambered for 9mm, .40 S&W or .45 ACP cartridge. Barrel length 3.9". Magazine capacity 10 rounds for all calibers. Polymer frame, with steel slide and barrel. Weight about 26 oz. Made in Israel by Israel Military Industries. Discontinued. Flashlight not included

Flashlight not included

NIB	Exc.	V.G.	Good	Fair	Poor
550	400	300	200	150	100

Desert Eagle .357 Magnum

Desert Eagle is a semi-automatic gas-operated pistol chambered for the .357 Magnum, .41 Magnum, .44 Magnum and .50 Action Express. Pistols furnished with a standard 6" barrel, but 10" (currently) and even 14" interchangeable barrels have been offered as options. Mag-Na-Ported interchangeable barrels were once offered, but MRI's muzzle brakes are currently all that is available. Standard material used for frame is steel, with stainless and aluminum also available. Standard finish for these pistols is black oxide, with custom finishes available on special order including gold, stainless steel, satin nickel, bright nickel, polished blue, camo, case hardened, matte chrome, polished chrome, brushed chrome and matte chrome with gold. All of these special order finishes, as well as the optional barrels, will affect the price of these pistols. Prices listed here will reflect standard pistols only.

NIB	Exc.	V.G.	Good	Fair	Poor
1250	900	700	500	400	250

Desert Eagle .41 Magnum/.44 Magnum

Standard barrel length 6", with black oxide finish. Magazine capacity 8 rounds. Weight for standard 63 oz. Note: Add 10 percent for .41.

NIB	Exc.	V.G.	Good	Fair	Poor
1350	900	700	500	400	250

Desert Eagle .50 Action Express

Standard barrel length 10", with black oxide finish. Magazine capacity 7 rounds. Standard weight 72 oz.

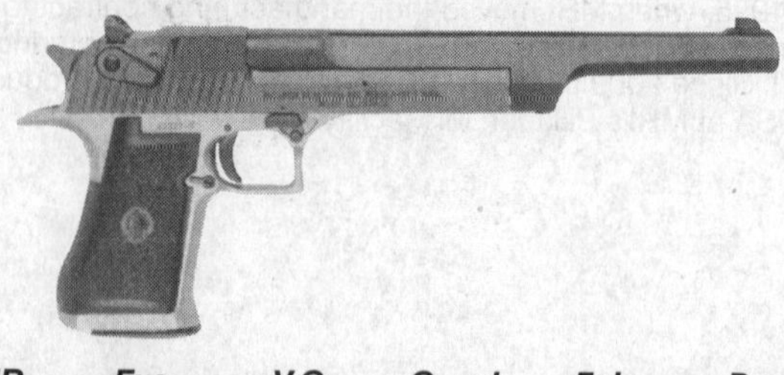

NIB	Exc.	V.G.	Good	Fair	Poor
1450	900	700	500	400	250

Desert Eagle Mark XIX

Introduced in 1996. This new design is manufactured in U.S. and allows interchangeability of barrels to switch calibers between the same receiver. Single receiver can be turned into six different pistols in three Magnum calibers. Available are .50 A.E., .44 Magnum and .357 Magnum in barrel lengths of 6" or 10". Separate magazines are also required. Eight different finishes offered as well. Separate bolt assembly is necessary to convert .44/.50 calibers to .357. There are so many different possibilities with this design that only basic pistol prices are given. Extra barrel assemblies are an additional cost. Some models have under barrel Picatinny rails as well as Weaver scope rail. Note: Custom shop finishes for Desert Eagle pistols are available in satin nickel, bright nickel, polished and deep blued, case hardened, matte hard chrome, polished hard chrome, brushed hard chrome, titanium gold, and gold with tiger stripes. All finishes beyond basic matte black add $100 to $200 to the base price of pistol; add $400 for gold; add $600 for case hardened or gold/tiger stripe finish.

.50A.E. w/6" Barrel

NIB	Exc.	V.G.	Good	Fair	Poor
1450	900	700	500	300	200

.50A.E. w/10" Barrel

NIB	Exc.	V.G.	Good	Fair	Poor
1350	1000	750	500	300	200

.44 Mag. w/6" Barrel

NIB	Exc.	V.G.	Good	Fair	Poor
1250	900	700	450	300	200

.44 Mag. w/10" Barrel

NIB	Exc.	V.G.	Good	Fair	Poor
1350	1000	750	500	300	200

.357 Mag. w/6" Barrel

NIB	Exc.	V.G.	Good	Fair	Poor
1250	900	700	450	300	200

.357 Mag. w/10" Barrel

NIB	Exc.	V.G.	Good	Fair	Poor
1350	1000	750	500	300	200

.440 CorBon w/6" Barrel (1999)

NIB	Exc.	V.G.	Good	Fair	Poor
1200	950	700	600	500	300

.440 CorBon w/10" Barrel (1999)

NIB	Exc.	V.G.	Good	Fair	Poor
1300	1000	750	650	550	320

Bolt Assembly—.44/.50 or .357

NIB	Exc.	V.G.	Good	Fair	Poor
220	180	150	100	80	50

Mark XIX Component System

Introduced in 2000. This system features Mark XIX frame with .44 Magnum 6" and 10" barrels; .50AE with 6" and 10" barrel; .357 Magnum with 6" and 10" barrel. Supplied with ICC aluminum case. Also offered with 6" only barrel components or 10" only barrel components.

6" and 10" Component System

NIB	Exc.	V.G.	Good	Fair	Poor
3990	2990	2500	1880	1150	500

6" Component System

NIB	Exc.	V.G.	Good	Fair	Poor
2580	1900	1500	1200	700	350

10" Component System

NIB	Exc.	V.G.	Good	Fair	Poor
2820	2100	1600	1320	720	400

Mark XIX .429 DE

The Mark XIX Pistol has a new caliber in the .429 DE based on the .50 AE case necked down to .44. Comes with a stainless steel frame and slide; Picatinny bottom rail, Weaver-style top rail; integral muzzle brake, black appointments with 6" barrel and 7-round magazine. A variety of accessory barrels are available in carbon steel in matte black, with Cerakote finish or stainless steel.

NIB	Exc.	V.G.	Good	Fair	Poor
1830	1550	1320	1120	680	400

Baby Eagle

Baby Eagle is a smaller version of Desert Eagle. All-steel construction, extra long slide rail, nylon grips, combat style triggerguard, ambidextrous thumb safety and decocking safety. Double-action design and available in 9mm, .40 S&W, .41 Action Express. Standard finish is black oxide, but matte chrome and brushed are offered as optional finishes. Fixed sights are standard. Fixed night sights and adjustable night sights are options.

.40 S&W (Standard)

Supplied with 4.5" barrel and black oxide finish. Magazine capacity 10 rounds. Empty weight 38 oz.

NIB	Exc.	V.G.	Good	Fair	Poor
500	400	350	300	250	200

9mm (Standard)

Fitted with 4.5" barrel and black oxide finish. Magazine capacity 16 rounds. Empty weight 38 oz.

NIB	Exc.	V.G.	Good	Fair	Poor
500	400	350	300	250	200

.41 Action Express

Has 4.7" barrel and black oxide finish. Magazine capacity 11 rounds. Empty weight 38 oz.

NIB	Exc.	V.G.	Good	Fair	Poor
500	400	350	300	250	200

Short Barrel (Semi-Compact)

This 9mm, .40 S&W or .45 ACP model features 3.6" barrel, with frame-mounted safety. Weight about 36 oz. Magazine holds 10 rounds.

NIB	Exc.	V.G.	Good	Fair	Poor
500	400	350	300	250	200

Short Barrel/Short Grip (Compact)

This 9mm or .40 S&W version has 3.6" barrel and shorter grip (3.25") than standard. Magazine capacity still 10 rounds. Weight about 38 oz. Frame-mounted safety.

NIB	Exc.	V.G.	Good	Fair	Poor
500	400	350	300	250	200

Semi-Compact Polymer

Pistol has a polymer frame and 3.9" barrel chambered for 9mm or .40 S&W cartridge. Weight about 29 oz.

NIB	Exc.	V.G.	Good	Fair	Poor
500	400	320	280	220	180

Compact Polymer

As above, with 3.6" barrel and short grip. Weight about 27 oz.

NIB	Exc.	V.G.	Good	Fair	Poor
500	400	320	280	220	180

Baby Eagle II

Chambered in 9mm, .40 S&W or .45 ACP. Similar features to original model, with improvements. Full size or compact models. Made by IMI in Israel from 2008 to 2014.

NIB	Exc.	V.G.	Good	Fair	Poor
550	450	380	300	250	200

Baby Eagle III

Further evolution of basic Baby Eagle, with slimmer and trimmer frame. Ambidextrous decocker, reversible magazine catch, ergonomic grips and integral accessory rail.

NIB	Exc.	V.G.	Good	Fair	Poor
600	500	420	350	300	200

Baby Eagle III Compact

The same frame, calibers and capacity as the full size, the compact has a shorter slide and 3.85" barrel. Polymer framed models only available in 9mm and .40 S&W. Note: Add about $40 for steel frame.

NIB	Exc.	V.G.	Good	Fair	Poor
550	470	400	340	200	130

Mountain Eagle

Semi-automatic pistol chambered for .22 LR cartridge. Features 6.5" barrel, with adjustable rear sight. Grip is a one-piece molded checkered plastic, with raised side panels. Magazine capacity 15 rounds; 20-round magazine available as an option. Black oxide finish standard. Weight 21 oz.

NIB	Exc.	V.G.	Good	Fair	Poor
280	180	150	120	100	80

Mountain Eagle Target Edition

Similar to standard Mountain Eagle. Fitted with 8" accurized barrel, two-stage target trigger, jeweled bolt, adjustable sights with three interchangeable blades and range case.

NIB	Exc.	V.G.	Good	Fair	Poor
300	220	200	150	120	80

Mountain Eagle Compact Edition

Similar to above, with 4.5" barrel and short grip.

NIB	*Exc.*	*V.G.*	*Good*	*Fair*	*Poor*
300	220	200	150	120	80

Mark XIX L5/L6

Magnum Research introduced two lighter weight models in the Desert Eagle L5 and the L6. Lighter by a pound or two respectively in comparison to other similar Desert Eagle pistols weighing almost 5 pounds. Offered in .50 AE, .44 Magnum and .357 Magnum with 5-inch barrels with integral muzzle brake, hard-coat anodized black aluminum frame, black carbon steel slide and barrel and Hogue rubber grip. Longer barrels are not compatible with the L5. The L6 versions (same calibers as L5 but with 6" barrels) are about 11 oz. lighter than similar Desert Eagles. The L6 is offered with hard-coat anodized black aluminum frame, stainless steel slide and integral muzzle brake, and a Picatinny rail on the frame. The lightweight L5/L6 Desert Eagles take the same magazines as the current steel models. The L5 was introduced in 2006.

NIB	*Exc.*	*V.G.*	*Good*	*Fair*	*Poor*
1580	1350	1150	980	580	350

Lone Eagle

Single-shot rotating breech pistol designed to fire centerfire cartridges. Standard finish black oxide blue luster. Barrel drilled and tapped for scope mounts. Standard barrel length 14". Fixed, adjustable or silhouette sights are offered as options. Stock assembly made from Lexan. Handgun offered in these calibers: .22-250, .223, .22 Hornet, .243, .30-30, .30-06, .308, .357 Magnum, .358 Win., .35 Rem., .44 Magnum, .444 Marlin, 7mm-08, 7mm Bench Rest. Weight between 4 lbs. 3 oz. to 4 lbs. 7 oz. depending on caliber.

NIB	*Exc.*	*V.G.*	*Good*	*Fair*	*Poor*
400	300	280	250	200	120

Lone Eagle (New Model)

Introduced in 1996, this improved Lone Eagle model features 15 interchangeable barreled actions from .22 Hornet to .444 Marlin. Available in both black and chrome actions, with or without muzzle brake. The 7.62x39 action introduced in 1996 also. Sights can be fixed, adjustable or silhouette type. Weight from 4 lbs. 3 oz. to 4 lbs. 7 oz. depending on caliber. Prices listed reflect black action and fixed sights. Note: Add $100 for muzzle brake; $30 for chrome action; $35 for adjustable sights; $130 for silhouette sights.

NIB	*Exc.*	*V.G.*	*Good*	*Fair*	*Poor*
420	320	180	150	120	100

Micro Desert Eagle Pistol

Small-frame DAO pocket pistol chambered in .380 ACP. Features include 2.22" barrel, fixed low-profile sights, steel slide, aluminum alloy frame, nickel-teflon finish, 6-round capacity. Overall length 4.52"; weight 14 oz.

NIB	*Exc.*	*V.G.*	*Good*	*Fair*	*Poor*
450	350	250	200	150	100

Model 1911 Desert Eagle

All Desert Eagle 1911 pistols feature Series 70 slide and frame rails and are offered in either chrome moly or stainless and feature stainless match barrels, G-10 grips, light triggers and stainless beavertail grip safety. The G (5" barrel) and C (4.33" barrel) models are equipped with fixed combat sights. The Undercover "U" (3" barrel) models come with an adjustable rear sight. All feature a solid guide rod, extended manual safety and slide stop, beveled magazine well, extended ejection port, and two magazines. Desert Eagle 1911s chambered in .45 ACP have a traditional feed ramp machined into the frame, while all 9mm pistols have a ramped barrel with fully supported chamber. Only the 1911G models have a traditional barrel bushing in the slide. The 1911C and U models have a bushingless slide and bull barrel allowing the shorter slides of the C and U models to have a longer recoil spring for more reliable function.

NIB	*Exc.*	*V.G.*	*Good*	*Fair*	*Poor*
750	650	500	400	300	200

DE1911 G

Full-size Government model in .45 ACP or 9mm (add about $20) in carbon steel or stainless (add about $60). Some models come with an optional knife (add about $40).

NIB	Exc.	V.G.	Good	Fair	Poor
700	600	510	440	260	150

DE1911 C

Commander-size model with shorter slide and 4.33" barrel in .45 ACP or 9mm (add about $20) in carbon steel or stainless (add about $60). Some models come with an optional knife (add about $40).

NIB	Exc.	V.G.	Good	Fair	Poor
700	600	510	440	260	150

DE1911 U

Undercover model with 3" barrel, shorter frame in .45 ACP with 6-shot magazine or 7-shot 9mm (add about $20) in carbon steel or stainless steel (adds about $60). Some models come with an optional knife (add about $40).

NIB	Exc.	V.G.	Good	Fair	Poor
800	690	580	500	300	180

MR9 / MR40

This family of pistols has a Walther polymer frame, with Magnum Research stainless slide and barrel made in U.S.A. Striker-fired operation, with internal safeties. Offered in 9mm or .40 S&W, with 4", 4.15" or 4.5" barrels. The integral polymer grips have interchangeable palm swells of different sizes.

NIB	Exc.	V.G.	Good	Fair	Poor
500	400	320	250	200	120

Mountain Eagle Rifle

Limited edition rifle (1,000), with Sako action and composite stock. Chambered for .270, .280, .30-06, .300 Win., .338 Win, 7mm Magnum. Introduced in 1994. Additional calibers are .300 Weatherby, .375 H&H, .416 Rem. and 7mm STW. Barrel length 24". Average weight about 7.74 lbs. Note: Add $150 for muzzle brake; $300 for .375 H&H and .416 Rem.; $100 for left-hand actions.

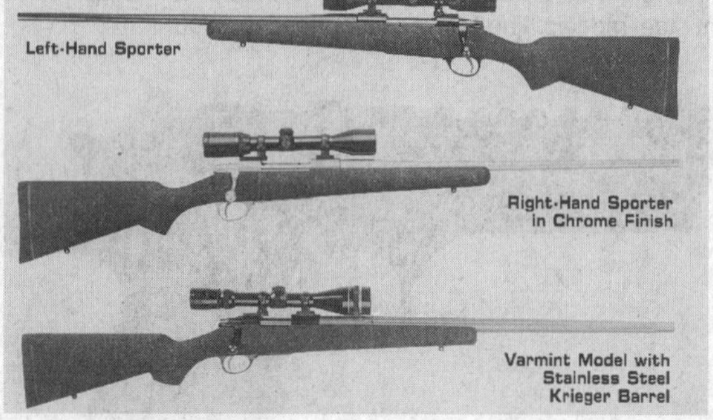

NIB	Exc.	V.G.	Good	Fair	Poor
2300	1700	1150	800	400	180

Mountain Eagle Varmint Edition

Chambered for .222 Rem. and .223 Rem. cartridges. Fitted with 26" stainless Krieger barrel. Kevlar-graphite stock. Weight about 9 lbs. 13 oz.

NIB	Exc.	V.G.	Good	Fair	Poor
2300	1750	1150	800	400	180

Magnum Lite Rimfire Rifles

These older rifles are built with Ruger 10/22 actions with graphite barrels. There are several variations depending on stock configuration. Note: For Clark Custom Upgrades add $130 to price of each Magnum Lite rifle.

Hogue and Fajen Scope-Hi Stock

NIB	Exc.	V.G.	Good	Fair	Poor
650	500	400	300	200	120

Fajen Thumbhole Sporter

NIB	Exc.	V.G.	Good	Fair	Poor
700	550	450	300	200	120

Fajen Thumbhole Silhouette

NIB	Exc.	V.G.	Good	Fair	Poor
800	650	500	300	200	120

Turner Barracuda

NIB	Exc.	V.G.	Good	Fair	Poor
800	650	500	300	200	120

Magnum Lite Centerfire Rifles

Previously built on Sako or Remington 700 actions fitted with graphite barrels. Introduced in 1999 in three models. Discontinued.

Heavy Barrel

Fitted with 26", 1.2" diameter barrel, with 1-in-14 twist. Chambered for .223 cartridge. Weight about 7.8 lbs

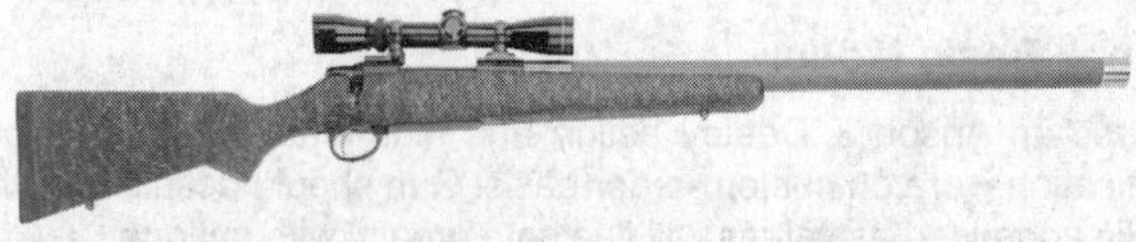

NIB	Exc.	V.G.	Good	Fair	Poor
2300	1700	1150	800	400	300

Sport Taper Barrel

Fitted with 24" tapered barrel. Chambered for .280 Rem., 7mm Magnum, .30-06, .300 Win. Magnum. Weight about 6.4 lbs.

NIB	Exc.	V.G.	Good	Fair	Poor
2300	1700	1150	800	400	300

Tactical Rifle

Introduced in 2000. Features 26" match grade barrel. Chambered for .223, .22-250, .308 or .300 Win. Magnum cartridges. Barrel made from carbon fiber. Action is Remington Model 700. H-S Precision tactical stock, with adjustable comb. Adjustable trigger. Weight about 8.3 lbs.

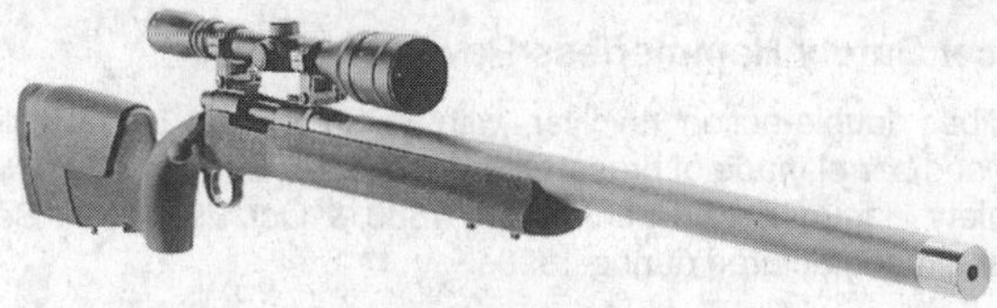

NIB	Exc.	V.G.	Good	Fair	Poor
2400	1800	1250	850	400	300

Current Magnum Lite Rimfire Rifles

Magnum Research MLR rifles are designed and manufactured in the United States. The MLR series in either 22 LR (10 shot) or 22 WMR (9 shot) with a 1-piece, forged 6061-T6 receiver with integral Picatinny rail and black, hard-coat anodizing. Barrel options include: patented carbon, patented Ultra tensioned, stainless steel, or integrally suppressed "TTS-22" barrels of 18" or 19". Stock options are suitable for right and left handed shooters of either polymer or wood. Note: Add $180 for laminate stock.

.22 LR Ultra, Threaded

NIB	Exc.	V.G.	Good	Fair	Poor
500	430	370	300	190	120

.22 WMR Barracuda

NIB	Exc.	V.G.	Good	Fair	Poor
800	690	580	500	300	180

SwitchBolt Magnum Lite Rifle

The SwitchBolt .22 LR rifles are an evolutionary extension tested and perfected on the professional speed shooting circuit. Built in the USA, the SwitchBolt receivers, with integral Picatinny rail, are machined from a 6061-T6 forging, and hard-coat anodized. All barrels are chambered in the 22 Bentz configuration and come with a bolt handle on the left side of a right-handed bolt. The result is an extremely fast and handy configuration for a right-handed shooter, whose trigger hand never has to leave the stock to charge the rifle. The lightweight SwitchBolt rifle is available in many barrel (17" to 20.5") and stock configurations. Note: Add about $180 for laminate stock.

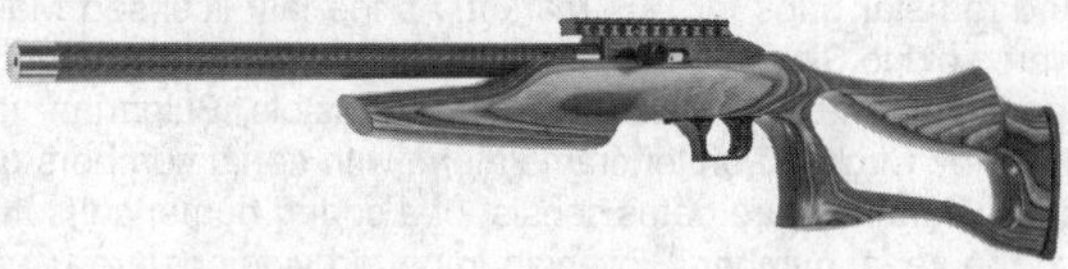

NIB	Exc.	V.G.	Good	Fair	Poor
540	460	390	330	200	120

Current Magnum Lite Centerfire Rifles

Magnum Research now builds the Centerfire line using Defiance Machine actions. The rifle is custom-built to the buyer's specifications and has a base price of $3195. Many options in bottom metal, stocks (including Hogue, XLR, HS Precision and Bell & Carlson), as well as caliber, barrel length and muzzle brakes. Contact Magnum Research for a quote. Prices below reflect the base model.

NIB	Exc.	V.G.	Good	Fair	Poor
2700	2300	1960	1670	1000	600

MAKAROV PISTOL

Makarov

The 9mm Makarov (9x18mm) caliber, 8-shot, semi-automatic, double-action, straight blowback pistol was adopted by the Soviet Union in 1951, to replace older 7.62x25mm Tokarev pistol. Production at Izhevsk factory continued through 1992, following the fall of the USSR. Makarov has a 3.68" barrel and mechanically similar to Walther PP/PPK series of pistols. Makarovs began to arrive in the U.S. in 1993, but due to the 1994 voluntary trade restriction of Russian military arms, importation was halted by 1995. All military versions have red-checkered plastic grips, with the circled star in the center. Makarov was licensed for production in China and Soviet satellites of East Germany and Bulgaria. Manufacture date and Izshevsk factory marking are found on the left frame, with serial number on both left slide flat and frame. Those dated in the 1950s are seldom seen. Note: Add 40 percent for those dated 1959 or earlier. The small quantity of Russian variants sold to East Germany in 1980s—some having German post-unification proof marks—will bring a 30 percent premium. These are also marked "Germany". Some imports marked with "Bulgaria" are known as "sneak" model that mistakenly entered the U.S. and will bring a 20 percent premium. Non-import marked specimens are highly desirable, especially if accompanied by military capture papers, and will raise prices considerably.

NIB	Exc.	V.G.	Good	Fair	Poor
—	700	600	550	400	200

Bulgarian Makarov

Manufactured under license from 1975 to 2007. Production was undertaken at the state factory Number 10 in Kazanlak (under Soviet supervision until 1976). After 1989, factory's name was changed to Arsenal or AD. Some specially made after the fall of communism, with Cerakote finish and red star grips for U.S. market. As the last licensed Makarov, many were sold to Slovenia after the Iron Curtain fell. As the most commonly encountered of all Makarov designed pistols, Bulgarian version is identified by Circle 10 on left frame along with serial numbers on this side as well. Manufacture dates consist of a coded numerical suffix adjacent to the serial number. Slovenian imported versions are usually in new, unfired condition, in cosmoline and if accompanied by holster and maintenance log book, values will increase by 40 percent. Those manufactured in the 1970s appear to fetch a higher price.

NIB	Exc.	V.G.	Good	Fair	Poor
—	580	450	380	280	200

East German Makarov

Similar to Russian made variant, however the blue finish is of a higher quality. Manufactured at Ernst Thaelmann state factory from 1958 (very rare) to 1965. Black plastic checkered grips are without the Soviet star. Identified by a "K100" in a rectangle on left frame adjacent to a small circle in a triangle. Serial number is on both left slide and frame, plus last two digits of manufacture year. Internal parts are serial numbered. A post-unification-made version produced with leftover parts marked SIMON SUHL/THUR is highly desirable and can bring a 50 percent premium, depending on condition. Often considered the "Colt" of Makarov pistols. The Borsig pistol is also reported as a variation of the East German Makarov. If a reader can confirm the existence and values of Borsig pistols in the American collector market, please advise the editor.

NIB	Exc.	V.G.	Good	Fair	Poor
—	780	700	650	500	250

MALIN, F. E.
London, England

Boxlock and sidelock shotguns made by Malin were imported into United States for a number of years. As these arms were all essentially built to specific customer's requirements, values listed are rough estimates only.

Boxlock Basic Model

Features an Anson & Deeley action and high-grade walnut. All other specification were on custom-order basis. Gun should definitely be individually appraised as values will fluctuate greatly with options.

NIB	Exc.	V.G.	Good	Fair	Poor
4800	4000	3500	2500	1850	1000

Sidelock Basic Model

Features Holland & Holland-type detachable sidelock action. All other features (as on boxlock) were on a custom-order basis. This model should also be appraised individually.

NIB	Exc.	V.G.	Good	Fair	Poor
7000	6000	4750	3000	2500	1250

MALTBY, HENLEY AND CO.
New York, New York

See Smith, Otis A.

Maltby Henley & Co. was formed in 1888 as a successor firm to Norwich Falls Pistol Co. and Maltby Curtis & Co. They marketed unique design Otis A. Smith spur-trigger single action top-break and Safety Hammerless solid-frame pocket revolvers."

Spencer Safety Hammerless Revolver (Antique)

.32-caliber double-action revolver, with 3" barrel and 5-shot cylinder. Frame and barrel made of brass. Cylinder of steel. Barrel marked "Spencer Safety Hammerless Pat. Jan. 24, 1888 & Oct. 29, 1889". Several thousand manufactured during 1890s.

Courtesy Mike Stuckslager

Exc.	Fine	V.G.	Good	Fair	Poor
320	220	170	120	80	50

MANHATTAN FIREARMS COMPANY

Norwich, Connecticut
Newark, New Jersey

Founded in 1856, Manhattan was a significant American handgun maker for about two decades, producing over 150,000 handguns, mainly copies of other makers such as percussion pocket single-shot pistols, pepperboxes, Colt-style percussion revolvers (following the expiration of Colt's patent), and S&W-style tip-up .22 rimfire spur-trigger revolvers. The successor company, American Standard Tool, lasted 1868 to 1873.

Bar Hammer Pistol (Antique)

.31-, .34- or .36-caliber single-shot percussion pistol, with 2" or 4" barrel. Hammer marked "Manhattan F.A. Mfg. Co. New York". Blued, with walnut grips. Approximately 1,500 made during 1850s.

Exc.	Fine	V.G.	Good	Fair	Poor
1050	750	520	300	150	100

Shotgun Hammer Pistol (Antique)

.36-caliber bar hammer single-shot percussion pistol, with 5.5" half octagonal barrel marked as above. Blued, with walnut grips. Approximately 500 made.

Exc.	Fine	V.G.	Good	Fair	Poor
1050	750	520	300	150	100

Pepperboxes

.28 caliber (sometimes mistakenly called .31 cal.) bar-hammer double-action percussion pepperbox, with 3", 4" or 5" barrels and 5- or 6-shot barrel groups. Blued & casehardened finishes with walnut grips. Marked "Manhattan F. A. MFG. Co. / New York" with some later specimens dropping the address, and "Cast Steel." Major variations of this pistol are as follows:

Jim Supica photo

PepperboxThree-shot with 3" Barrel (Antique)

Manually rotated barrels.

Exc.	Fine	V.G.	Good	Fair	Poor
1300	900	700	500	300	210

Five-shot with 3", 4", 5" Barrel (Antique)

Automatically rotated barrels.

Exc.	Fine	V.G.	Good	Fair	Poor
1100	650	550	450	250	170

Six-shot with 3" or 4" Barrel (Antique)

Automatic rotation.

Exc.	Fine	V.G.	Good	Fair	Poor
1100	650	550	450	250	170

Six-shot with 5" Barrel (Antique)

Automatic rotation.

Exc.	Fine	V.G.	Good	Fair	Poor
1600	1200	870	550	350	240

Double Action Pepperbox (Antique)

Very rare, different configuration from other Manhattan pepperboxes – 6-shot, .31 cal., oversize triggerguard, nipples protrude straight out from the rear of the barrels, hammer much smaller than other bar-hammers.

Exc.	Fine	V.G.	Good	Fair	Poor
2000	1500	1250	1000	500	350

Pocket Revolver

.31-caliber percussion revolver, with 4", 5" or 6" barrel and 5- or 6-shot cylinder. Blued case-hardened, with walnut grips. Barrel marked "Manhattan Firearms/Manufg. Co. New York" on 5-shot model, serial numbers from 1 to approximately 1,000; "Manhattan Firearms Mfg. Co. New York" on 6-shot model, frame marked "December 27, 1859".

Courtesy Milwaukee Public Museum, Milwaukee, Wisconsin

Series I—Five-Shot (Antique)

Exc.	Fine	V.G.	Good	Fair	Poor
1600	1200	600	400	250	150

Series II—Six-Shot (Antique)

Exc.	Fine	V.G.	Good	Fair	Poor
1600	1200	600	400	250	150

London Pistol Company (Antique)

As above marked "London Pistol Company". Approximately 200 manufactured between 1859 and 1861.

Exc.	Fine	V.G.	Good	Fair	Poor
1400	750	600	450	150	100

.36 Caliber Percussion Revolver

.36-caliber percussion revolver, with 4", 5" or 6.5" octagonal barrel and 5- or 6-shot cylinder. Blued case-hardened, with walnut grips. Approximately 78,000 made between 1859 and 1868. There were five variations.

Courtesy Milwaukee Public Museum, Milwaukee, Wisconsin

Series I Antique

A 5-shot cylinder marked "Manhattan Firearms Mfg. Co. New York". Serial numbers from 1 through 4200. Note: Add 15 percent premium for 6" barreled version.

Exc.	Fine	V.G.	Good	Fair	Poor
2000	1050	800	550	150	100

Series II Antique

As above, with 1859 patent date marked on barrel. Serial range 4200 to 14500.

Exc.	Fine	V.G.	Good	Fair	Poor
2200	1350	950	550	150	100

Series III Antique

A 5-shot cylinder marked "Manhattan Firearms Co. Newark NJ", together with 1859 patent date. Serial numbers from 14500 to 45200.

Exc.	Fine	V.G.	Good	Fair	Poor
2100	1200	850	500	150	100

Series IV Antique

As above, with modified recoil shield. Patent date March 8, 1864 added to barrel inscription. Serial numbers from 45200 to 69200.

Exc.	Fine	V.G.	Good	Fair	Poor
2000	1250	850	450	150	100

Series V Antique

Exc.	Fine	V.G.	Good	Fair	Poor
2100	1350	950	550	200	140

.22 Caliber Pocket Revolver Antique

.22-caliber spur trigger revolver, with 3" barrel and 7-shot cylinder. Blued silver plated, with walnut or rosewood grips. Approximately 17,000 made during 1860s. Fairly close copy of S&W No. 1.

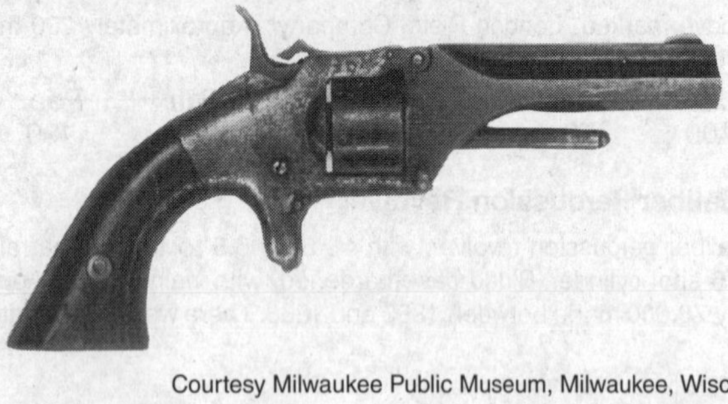

Courtesy Milwaukee Public Museum, Milwaukee, Wisconsin

Exc.	Fine	V.G.	Good	Fair	Poor
550	300	270	250	100	70

Manhattan-American Standard Hero

.34-caliber single-shot percussion pistol, with 2" or 3" round barrel that unscrews for loading. Blued brass frame, with walnut grips. Marked "A.S.T. Co./HERO". Made by American Standard Tool Company, Manhattan's successor. Approximately 30,000 manufactured between 1868 and 1873.

Manhattan Manufactured Antique

Marked "HERO/M.F.A.Co.". Approximately 5,000 produced.

Exc.	Fine	V.G.	Good	Fair	Poor
620	550	400	250	100	70

American Standard Manufactured Antique

Approximately 25,000 produced.

Exc.	Fine	V.G.	Good	Fair	Poor
620	500	360	220	100	70

MANN, FRITZ

Suhl, Germany

6.35mm Pocket Pistol

6.35mm caliber semi-automatic pistol, with 1.65" barrel and 5-shot magazine. Blued, with plastic grips having name "Mann" cast in them. Weight only 9 oz. One of the smallest semi-automatic pistols ever manufactured. Made between 1920 and 1922.

NIB	Exc.	V.G.	Good	Fair	Poor
—	400	300	200	150	100

7.65mm Pocket Pistol

7.65mm or 9mm short semi-automatic pistol, with 2.35" barrel and 5-shot magazine. Blued, with plastic grips that have name "Mann" cast in them. Manufactured between 1924 and 1929.

NIB	Exc.	V.G.	Good	Fair	Poor
—	380	280	200	150	100

MANNLICHER PISTOL

Steyr, Austria

See—STEYR

MANNLICHER SCHOENAUER

Steyr, Austria

Military models and their history, technical data, descriptions and prices see Standard Catalog of Military Firearms under "Austria-Hungary". Currently imported Mannlicher models, see Steyr.

Model 1903 Carbine

6.5x54mm caliber bolt-action rifle, with 17.7" barrel. Rotary magazine capacity 5 rounds. Folding rear leaf sight, double-set triggers and full-length walnut stock. Discontinued prior to WWII.

NIB	Exc.	V.G.	Good	Fair	Poor
—	2200	1650	1300	1000	550

Model 1905 Carbine

As above chambered for 9x56mm cartridge. Discontinued prior to WWII.

NIB	Exc.	V.G.	Good	Fair	Poor
—	1850	1500	1000	750	550

Model 1908 Carbine

As above chambered for 7x57mm or 8x56mm cartridge. Discontinued prior to WWII.

NIB	Exc.	V.G.	Good	Fair	Poor
—	1950	1600	1000	750	550

Model 1910 Carbine

As above chambered for 9.5x57mm cartridge. Discontinued prior to WWII.

NIB	Exc.	V.G.	Good	Fair	Poor
—	1850	1500	1000	750	550

Model 1924 Carbine

As above chambered for .30-06 cartridge. Discontinued prior to WWII.

Serial Number One Guns

The first of any gun model is special for gun collectors and firearm historians alike. Here are some notable examples.

› JIM SUPICA

Photos courtesy of the NRA National Firearms Museum, Rock Island Auction Company and Cody Firearms Museum.

(Above) **U.S. Springfield Armory Sharps Model 1870 2nd Type, s/n 1**
Rock Island Auction photo.

Unique serial numbers on guns were not required before the Gun Control Act of 1968. However, large manufacturers had marked individual guns with identifying numbers well before.

Each gun pictured here can be considered a "serial number one" gun. However, that can mean different things in various contexts. The early common practice was to begin a model with serial number 1 and continue sequentially until the model was eventually discontinued. It might be the beginning of a long and successful production run or a design that proved to be a flop. It might even be an experimental model, with only a handful made and never offered commercially. Before 1968 some gun makers used "batch numbers," beginning with 1 and continuing to 999 or 9999 or some random number and then starting over, resulting in multiple "serial number one" guns of the same model. Some guns may be numbered only with an "assembly number"—usually a one- or two-digit number to keep hand-fitted parts of an individual gun together or identify the worker who assembled it. Others used no numbering, especially on low-cost .22 rifles and single-shot shotguns.

After the 1968 requirement of a unique serial number, some manufacturers began models with an alphanumeric prefix before the number or at a number other than 1. In those cases, the first number of a production run is considered serial number one for that model for our purposes here.

Sometimes manufacturers did limited runs of an existing model decorated as a commemorative or with other special features. Although these will usually have serial numbers that continue from the base model, each may also be marked with a unique number indicating its order in production (such as "1 of 1000," "2 of 1000," etc.). On other rare occasions, a gun might be made for presentation or on a custom order with a particular serial number incorporating the recipient's initials or other significant letters, with the number 1 included.

Occasionally, especially on older and obscure guns, we don't know the significance of the number.

Here's a look at examples of all these.

Colt .40 cal. Navy Model, s/n 1

In the 1850s Colt was looking for a design with more stopping power than its widely successful .36-caliber Model 1851 Navy but handier to carry than the massive .44-caliber Dragoon Model. Colt experimented with a .40-caliber Navy model. This is serial number 1 of a total of only four made. It was kept in the Colt factory collection for over a century. The maker solved the riddle with its .44-caliber Model 1860 Army revolver, based on the 1851 Navy frame, with the front diameter of the cylinder enlarged to accommodate the larger lead ball. Photo: NRA Museums

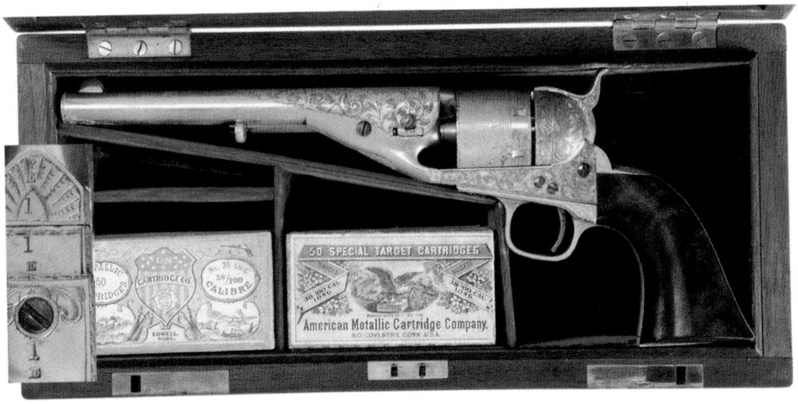

Colt 1861-72 Navy Cartridge Revolver, s/n 1

In 1871 this Colt Naxy was factory engraved and cased, and presented to Colt employee Lewis Sheldon. Rock Island Auction Company sold it for $368,000 in 2012. Photo: Rock Island Auction Company

Smith & Wesson Model 2 "Old Army" Prototype, Assembly Number 1

The Model 2 was a significant advance for handgun design and the fledgling Smith & Wesson firm when it was introduced in 1861. Smith & Wesson's first revolver was the diminutive Model 1 spurtrigger tip-up, first offered in 1857 upon the expiration of Colt's revolver patent. As the first widely successful American handgun chambered for a self-contained metallic cartridge, it represented a significant breakthrough in convenience and ease of loading over the earlier cap and ball percussion revolvers. However, it was chambered for an anemic .22 rimfire blackpowder cartridge dimensionally identical to today's .22 Short.

The Model 2 was upsized and chambered for the larger and more powerful .32 rimfire. This cartridge was hardly an earthshaker, but it represented a definite improvement—enough to gain significant popularity as a private purchase sidearm for Civil War soldiers in a pre-ballistic-gelatin era.

Inspection by several Smith & Wesson experts suggests that this gun is likely an in-house prototype for the Model 2. It is marked on the barrel rib with the standard S&W company marking, and the number "1" is stamped in the usual assembly number locations on the barrel, cylinder and side of the grip frame. There is no marking on the frame butt where the serial number is usually stamped on this model, and some of the dimensions are different from production Model 2s.

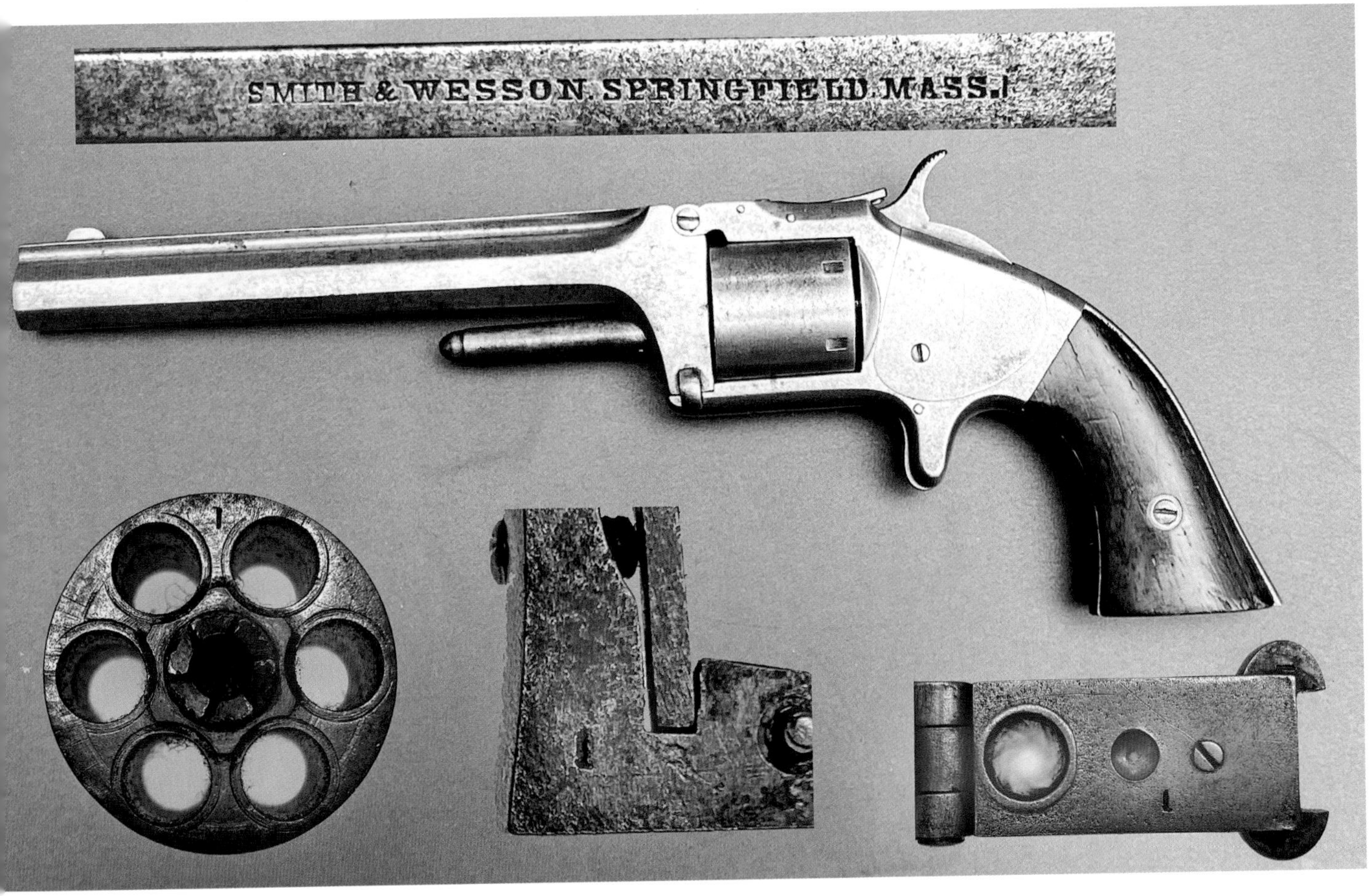

Department-Marked Colts

Just as Wells Fargo marked its messengers' Schofields, some police departments marked its officers' issued sidearms. Each of these Colts appears to be number one of a group of police revolvers.

Colt Official Police marked "L.U.P.D. No. 1"—Shipped to Lehigh University Police Department, .38 Special.

Colt New Service marked "E.C.P.D. No. 1"—Reported to be East Chicago Police Department, .357 Magnum.

(Opposite top) Just Plain Weird

Unknown prototype revolver, s/n Exp No 1—A bizarre combination of features that begs the question, "What were they thinking?" Top-break single-action seven-shot .45 Colt with a unique stirrup-style top latch, a manual safety, and "hand ejector"-style ejection of empty cartridge cases. It is believed to be early post-WWII production, making it one of the earliest stainless steel revolvers. Maker unknown—no other markings.

Novo folding grip revolver, s/n 1—Although folding triggers never gained much traction in America, "Velodog" pocket revolvers enjoyed popularity in Europe as concealable personal defense handguns. The Novo went one better by adding a folding grip, making it possibly the most compact handgun in a conventional caliber, 6.35mm.

Smith & Wesson Schofield, s/n 1

The Schofield was designed for the U.S. military and issued beginning in 1875. Along with the Colt Single Action Army, it saw use in the Indian Wars. Upon decommissioning, many were sold to Wells Fargo for its messengers' use. Wells Fargo had the barrels shortened from 7 to 5 inches and marked the guns as company property "W.F. & CO. EX." on the ejector housing using the S&W serial number as their company accession number. Photo: NRA Museums

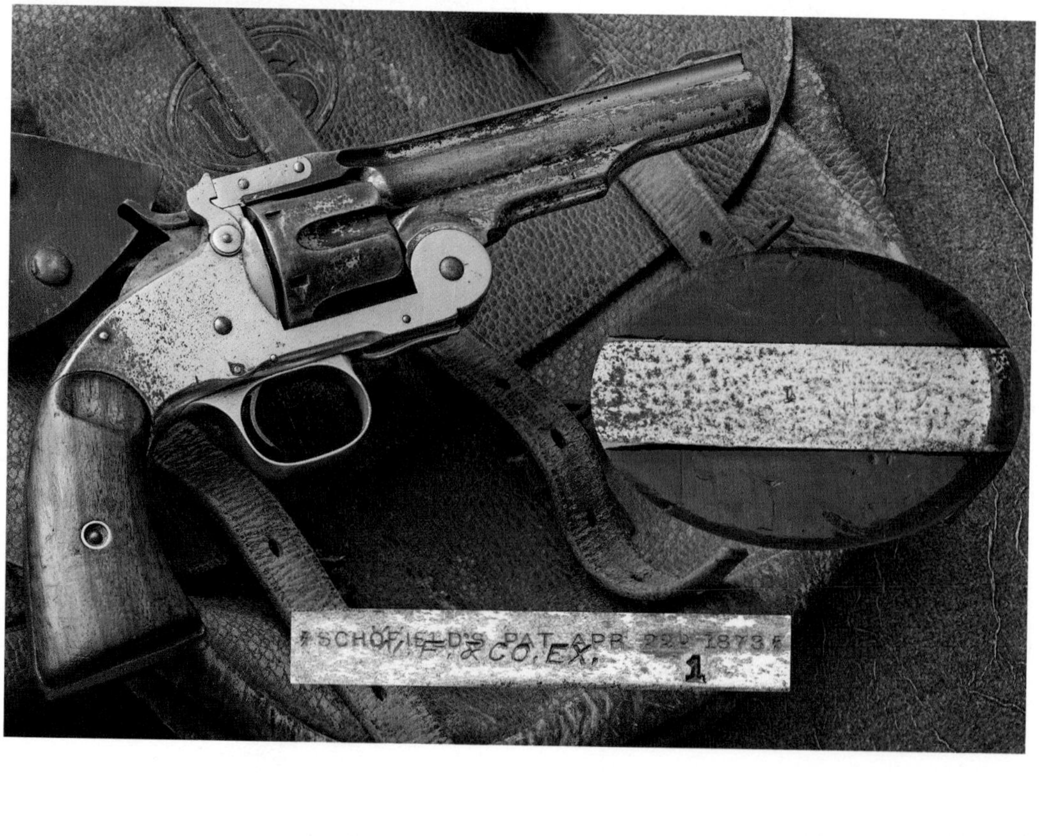

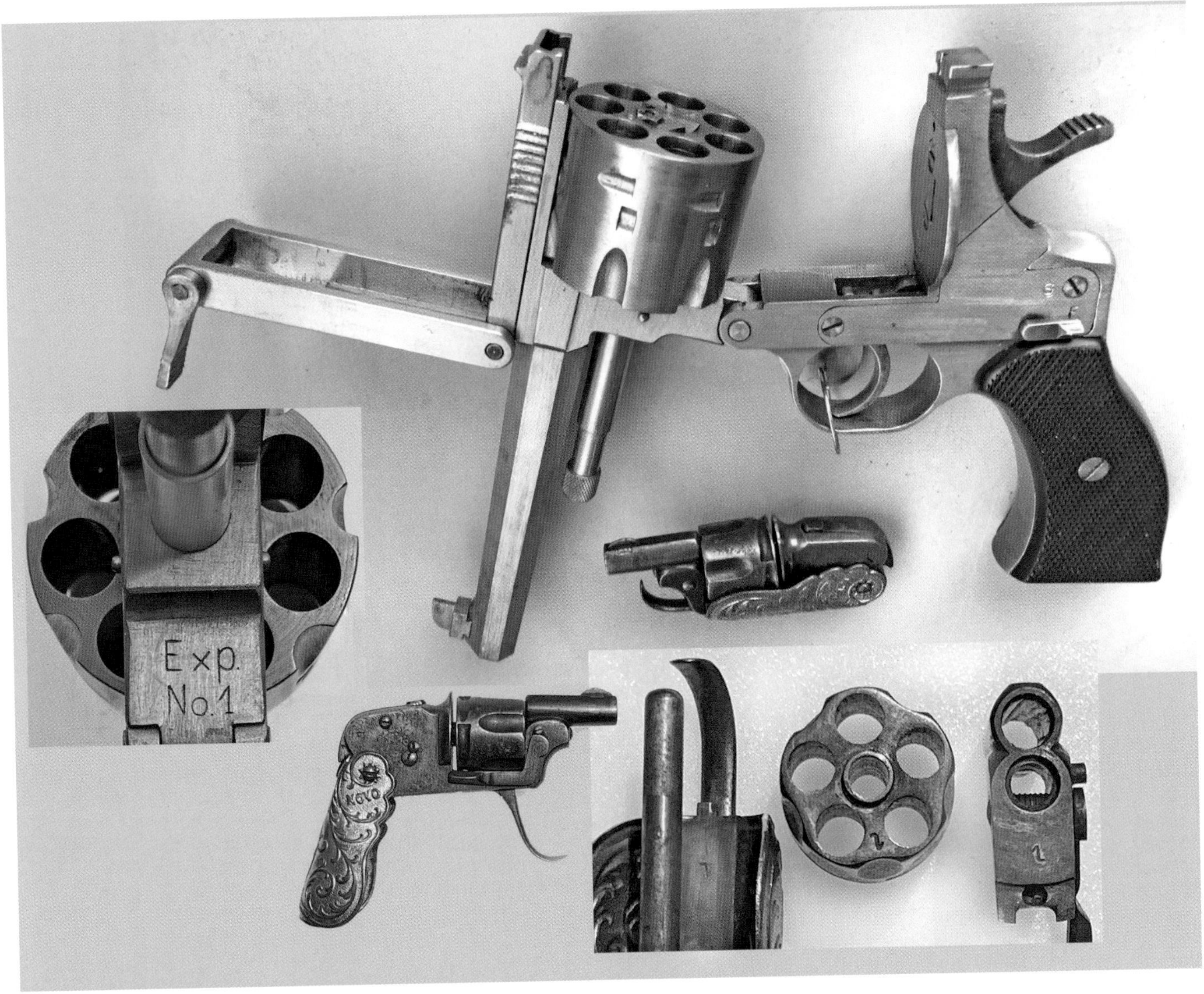

Mystery Single-Action Revolvers

Mikkenger-attributed single-action prototype, s/n 0001—Believed to be a 1970s vintage pre-production .357 Magnum prototype by Mikkenger Arms, a short-lived small maker of high-quality single-action revolvers.

Custom Colt Single Action Army, s/n 1—Custom-built .44 Special revolver, probably by an unknown gunsmith, based on a Colt SAA, probably done mid-20th century. The barrel is shortened, the triggerguard diameter reduced, the trigger curved and a lanyard ring added.

All That Glitters: Commemorative Firearms

In the 1960s both Colt and Winchester offered limited edition variations of their classic models with special decoration commemorating some individual, event, geographical region or concept. Usually, production was limited to a set number of guns. Sometimes the run would be assigned its own serial number range prefixed or suffixed with letters indicating the commemorated subject. Other times the guns would be in the standard serial number of the base model but also be prominently decorated with an individual production number such as "1 of 200," "2 of 200," etc., through "200 of 200." Large distributors have produced similarly numbered limited editions.

Initially these were popular models with a strong association with the old west, most notably the Winchester Model 94 lever actions, Colt Single Action Army revolvers and second-generation Colt reproduction percussion revolvers. Soon other models were added, and other manufacturers jumped on the bandwagon. By the late 1980s the commemorative market cooled significantly. However, firearms companies have continued to offer limited production runs with unique features, sometimes marked with production numbers. Some companies such as Franklin Mint and America Remembers have built businesses on marketing decorated commemorative reproduction blackpowder firearms.

Examples include:

1. Uberti/America Remembers United States Cavalry Commemorative Model 1860 revolver s/n 1—This Calvary Commemorative Model 1860 was copied from the original .44 percussion Colt model.

2. Navy Arms/America Remembers Stonewall Jackson Commemorative LeMat reproduction revolver, s/n 001—This example was presented initially to the Stonewall Jackson House Museum in Lexington, VA. The LeMat was an unusual two-barrel percussion revolver, often associated with some Confederate officers. The upper barrel aligns with the chambers of the nine-shot .42-caliber cylinder. The lower smoothbore barrel serves as the axis around which the cylinder revolves and takes a 20-ga. shotgun load (see inset at the lower right corner of the photo).

Presentation .45 Handguns

These presentation .45s were made for specific individuals with custom number one serial numbers. The first two at far left are 1911 pattern pistols chambered for .45 ACP, and the center photo is a Schofield reproduction in .45 Colt.

New Detonics Series II s/n DVC-JC1—Made for Col. Jeff Cooper, famous firearms trainer and author who played a prominent role in the resurgence of 1911 pattern pistols for defense and police use, this presentation serial number incorporated his initials and slogan "DVC"—Diligentia, Vis, Celeritas—Latin for Accuracy, Power, Speed.

Colt Mk. IV Series 80 Officers Model, s/n RLW-1—Made for Colt historian and author R. L. Wilson.

Smith & Wesson Performance Center Schofield 2000, s/n JWS00001—Made for me incorporating my initials. Thanks, Smith!

3. Lew Horton Limited Edition Smith & Wesson Model 29-6, marked "1 of 100"—The first of a 100-gun run of this .44 Magnum revolver with gold-filled scroll engraving offered by a major S&W distributor.

4. Winchester Model 94 Cherokee Commemorative carbine, s/n CK00001—The first of 9,000 .30-30 lever actions produced in 1978.

5. Winchester Model 94 Canadian Pacific Railway Centennial rifle, s/n—The first of 2,700 made in 1981, caliber .32 Win. Special.

Sixguns by the Dozen

Just in case one commemorative at a time isn't enough, a couple of major manufacturers offered limited edition decorated revolvers in sets of 12.

Colt Kansas Commemorative Series of Frontier Scout .22 revolvers, each s/n 1—In the 1960s at around the time of the Kansas State Centennial, these were offered in three sets of four each—Kansas Cow Towns, Kansas Forts and Kansas Trails. Colt made a total of 500 sets of 12 and assigned serial numbers with letter suffixes indicating the town, trail or fort featured. For example, 1SF would

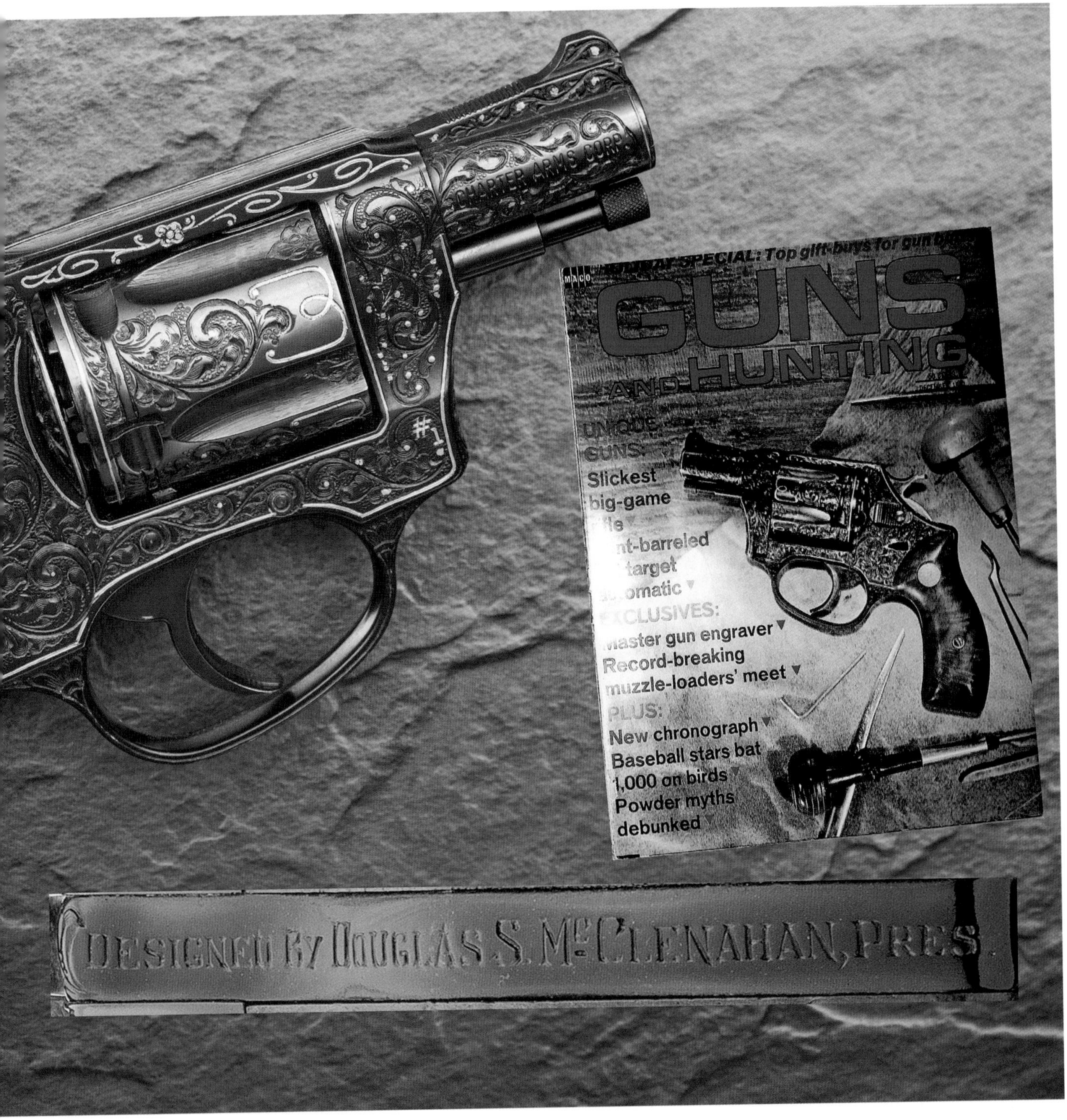

be for the Santa Fe Trail, 1FS would be for Fort Scott, 1KA would represent the Kansas Series Abilene, etc. Most guns were sold individually. The serial number one set was housed in a factory-made three-drawer case, with one themed set in each drawer. Photos: Rock Island Auction Company

Smith & Wesson 12 Revolvers set, each marked "1 of 500"—In the late 1980s S&W introduced new models so rapidly that it was jokingly referred to as the "Gun of the Month Club." In 1990 the firm ran with the concept by offering a set of 12 revolvers with one new variation every month. Five hundred sets were planned with the individual guns in each set marked sequentially "1 of 500" through "500 of 500" on the barrel. Each monthly gun was a classic S&W model in a configuration that had never been offered, and each month featured a laser-etched image from a classic S&W advertising poster from the late 19th through early 20th centuries.

Charter Arms Undercover, s/n 1

Not only the first gun of this model but the first produced by this company. Charter Arms founder Doug McClenahan designed the revolver in 1965 as a lightweight concealed carry five-shot .38 Special that could be priced cheaper than the S&W Chiefs Special. He had the first one decorated by Colt master engraver Alvin White. Guns and Hunting magazine featured it on its cover. Photo: NRA Museums

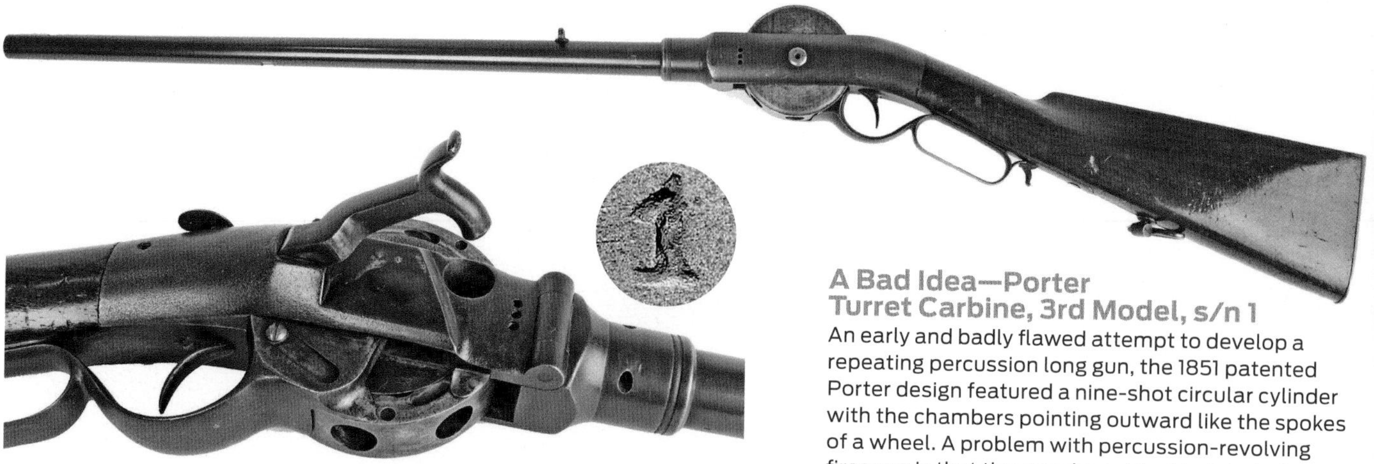

A Bad Idea—Porter Turret Carbine, 3rd Model, s/n 1
An early and badly flawed attempt to develop a repeating percussion long gun, the 1851 patented Porter design featured a nine-shot circular cylinder with the chambers pointing outward like the spokes of a wheel. A problem with percussion-revolving firearms is that they can be subject to "chain fire," where the sparks from a chamber being fired jump to another adjoining chamber, causing that round to fire prematurely while not in line with the rear of the barrel. The problem with the Porter was that one of those chambers always pointed at the shooter's forehead! This example is believed to be one of 10 that the U.S. Ordnance Department purchased.

Magnumitis

TDE AutoMag 180, s/n WJD001—The .44 AutoMag Pistol (.44AMP) cartridge was developed around 1970 to provide .44 Magnum power in an autoloading pistol. A series of since-failed companies, including TDE, AMT, OMC, and AMC, manufactured it in limited numbers. The significance of the serial number is unknown; possibly a custom number for an employee or particular customer.

Wyoming Arms Parker S.S. pistol, s/n SAFARI-1—The 10mm cartridge was designed to provide more power in a semi-auto pistol than the 9mm, with a bullet diameter small enough for double-stack magazines. It enjoyed a period of interest from law enforcement agencies but was largely supplanted by the less powerful but easier-to-shoot .40 S&W cartridge. Wyoming Arms did not last long. The serial number is reportedly a custom one made for a fundraising raffle at a tavern named the Safari Bar.

El Dorado Arms Single-Action .357 Maximum revolver, s/n 001—So, lengthen the .38 Special cartridge to produce the .357 Magnum cartridge, which was a splendid success. Why not lengthen the .357 Mag to make an even more powerful .357 Maximum round? As it turns out, because the .357 Max is a step too far—the power level leads to flame cutting of the topstrap of revolvers. For a brief time El Dorado Arms made these as specialty revolvers for metallic silhouette target competition.

Its Bite Is Worse Than Its Bark

"Bulldog" revolvers were popular compact self-defense handguns from the 1870s through the early 20th century. These were usually small solid-frame double-action pocket-sized revolvers in large calibers.

Westley Richards Royal Irish Constabulary ("RIC") revolver, s/n 1—A six-shot, .450 centerfire, ca. 1870s.

Webley bulldog style revolver, s/n 1—A five-shot .450 centerfire.

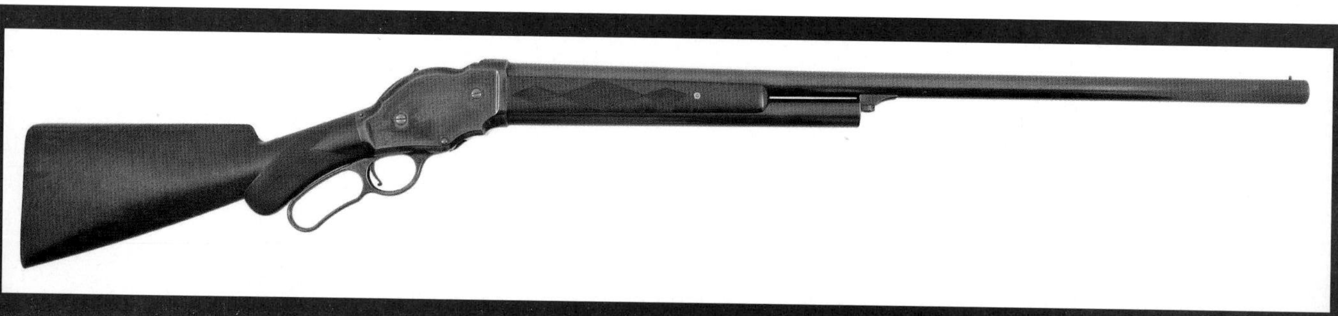

Winchester Milestones

The Cody Firearms Museum at the Buffalo Bill Center of the West is the repository for Winchester's shipping records and factory collection, including these serial number one long guns. Cody Firearms Museum photos.

Winchester Model 1887, s/n 1—This lever action shotgun was one of the first commercially successful repeating single barrel shotguns, although it was replaced on the market within about a decade by handier pump actions.

Winchester Model 1905, s/n 1—One of the earliest semi-auto centerfire rifles to attain significant popularity. The Models 1905 and 1907 featured detachable box magazines long before the AR and AK rifles that are popular today.

Serial Number One "Assault Weapons"

1. IMI/Action Arms Uzi Model A, s/n SA-01001—The first of this 9mm semi-auto Uzi carbine version to be imported into the U.S.

2. Springfield Armory G3, s/n 05000—A semi-auto version of the Heckler & Koch HK91, built by Hellenic Arms in Egypt. This one is the first of this model imported by Springfield and has an aftermarket scope.

3. Maadi Steyr ARM, s/n 00001—The first of this AK based semi-auto, built on Soviet equipment in Egypt.

4. Armco AK47 Sporter, s/n 9000001—The first of this model, designed to comply with the 1994 Assault Weapons Ban. And, it was thoughtfully marked "MAIDE IN CHINA."

The term "assault weapon" is primarily a product of political attempts to restrict semi-automatic firearms with detachable box magazines and other specific features that cosmetically resemble military arms. These anti-gun efforts ignore the fact that the targeted guns function identically to common sporting arms that have been popular for over a century.

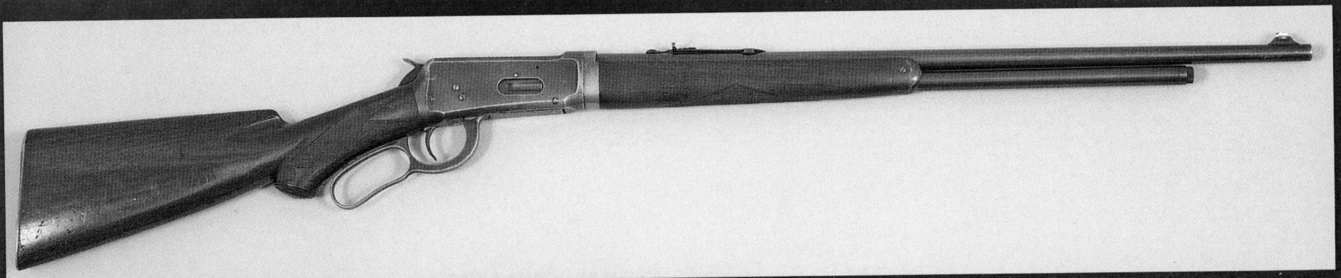

Winchester Model 55, s/n 1—This variant of the Winchester Model 1894 was initially offered in takedown configuration in 1924. Although Model 55 production only lasted eight years with over 20,000 produced, the Model 1894 on which it was based may be considered the quintessential American deer rifle with over seven million sold.

Winchester Model 65, s/n 1—The Model 65 was based on the earlier Model 53 which had been an improvement of the classic Model 1892. With fewer than 5,800 made from 1933 to 1947, the 65 was usually chambered for the .218 Bee cartridge, making it an effective "varmint rifle" in the Winchester lever action rifle line.

Springfield Armory M1A, Serial Numbers X001 and X002

After the U.S. Springfield Armory ceased production of military arms in 1968, Elmer Balance adopted its name for commercial distribution of a semi-auto 7.62 NATO / .308 Win. rifle manufactured by Mel Smith of Valley Ordnance based on the military select-fire M14. Designated the M1A model, these two guns are reported as the first two made, with X001 as the prototype submitted for BATF and patent office approval. Its model marking lacks the circled (T) trademark symbol found on X002 and subsequent production guns. Early manufacture used many surplus military parts. For example, the military wood stock for X002 has a cutout on the right rear of the receiver for a (non-present) selector switch with X001 lacking this cutout. Here, X002 is shown with an added scope and mount.

In further illustration of the absurdities of "assault weapon bans," it's interesting to note that the Springfield Armory M1A and G3 models (previously illustrated) are functionally identical. Both are .308 semi-auto rifles with 20 round detachable box magazines. However, the latter is usually restricted by various bans while the former is generally ignored. This appears to be based on cosmetic differences, with the G3 having the scary pistol grip synthetic stock configuration while the M1A has the more traditional wooden stock.

It's also worth noting that the 5.56 / .223 cartridge fired by most AR pattern rifles, the most commonly cited target of bans, is only about half as powerful as the 7.62 NATO / .308 round of the usually-ignored M1A.

Smith & Wesson Sigma Model 40F, s/n SGM0001

During the 1980s and early 1990s, polymer framed Glock pistols made major headway into the police market previously dominated by S&W. At the same time, demand grew for a cartridge that carried more stopping power than 9mm, but could fit in double stack magazines that wouldn't accommodate the .45 ACP round. In 1994, S&W introduced the polymer frame Sigma, which some alleged stood for "Smith Imitates Glock, Made in America." So much so that Glock sued for patent infringement. The suit was settled. This is the first production Sigma, also one of the earliest pistols chambered for .40 S&W.

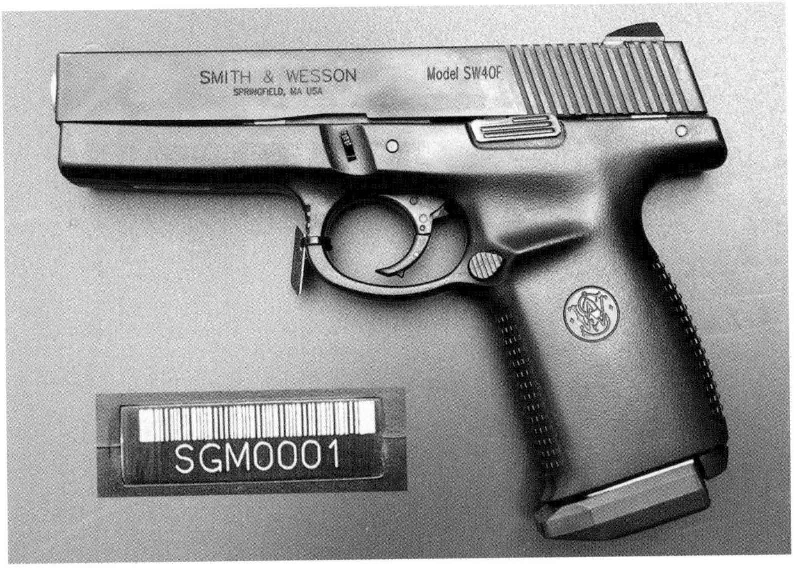

Chinese Military Pattern Arms

Chinese Type 53 carbine, s/n A000001— Patterned on the Russian Mosin Nagant and chambered for the 7.62x54R round. This is believed to be the first serial number of a pre-production run of about 30,000 guns for the Chinese military from their factory 296 in Congquing in 1953.

Chinese SKS Paratrooper, s/n 0001—Short barrel copy of this 7.62x39 semi-auto fixed magazine carbine, made for the American market.

Norinco SKS s/n 001—Standard configuration, made for the American market.

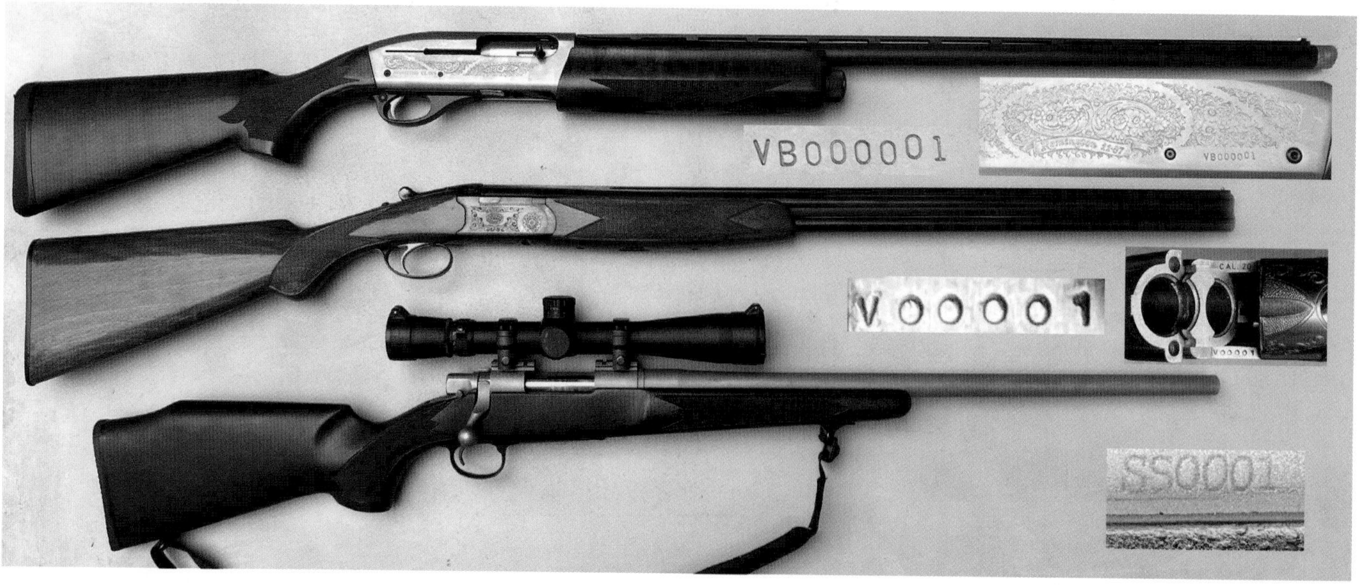

Traditional Action Long Arms

Remington Model 11-87 Sporting Clays, s/n VB000001—12 ga. light contour target barrel semi-auto shotgun.

Beretta BL-3, s/n V00001—20 ga. over-under, manufactured 1968-1976. Believed to be the first one made.

McMillan Super Sniper prototype, s/n SS0001—.308 Win., unmarked except for serial number, represented as the first prototype McMillan Brothers bolt action rifle made by Rock and Kelly McMillan.

Speaking of High Capacity

In the 1980s Calico Light Weapons systems introduced semi-automatic pistols and rifles chambered in 9mm or .22 LR which utilized a cylindrical drum magazine with a standard capacity of 50 rounds, with optional 100 round mags also available. The cartridges set in a helical spiral inside the magazines, which mounted on top of the receiver. The magazines have a folding crank on the rear that is wound to provide spring tension to feed the rounds. These are from the personal collection of former Calico President Michael Miller, and are the first numbered gun of the first production run of each model.

Calico Model M900 carbine, s/n B000001—The first 9mm firearm model made by Calico, introduced in 1989.

Calico M110 pistol, s/n F000001—The second .22 firearm model made by Calico, introduced in 1985.

NIB	Exc.	V.G.	Good	Fair	Poor
—	2750	2250	1750	1000	550

High Velocity Rifle

As above in 7x64mm Brenneke, .30-06, 8x60Smm Magnum, 9.3x62mm and 10.75x68mm caliber, with 23.5" barrel and folding leaf sight. Half-length walnut stock. Discontinued prior to WWII. Note: Add 75 percent for Takedown Model.

NIB	Exc.	V.G.	Good	Fair	Poor
—	2750	2250	1750	1000	550

Model 1950

.257 Roberts, .270 Winchester and .30-06 caliber bolt-action rifle, with 24" barrel and 5-shot rotary magazine. Blued, with half -length walnut stock. Manufactured between 1950 and 1952.

NIB	Exc.	V.G.	Good	Fair	Poor
2000	1600	1250	800	650	450

Model 1950 Carbine

As above, with 20" barrel and full-length stock.

NIB	Exc.	V.G.	Good	Fair	Poor
2200	1750	1250	800	650	450

Model 1950 6.5 Carbine

As above in 6.5x54mm Mannlicher Schoenauer caliber, with 18.5" barrel and full-length stock.

NIB	Exc.	V.G.	Good	Fair	Poor
2300	1900	1400	1000	650	300

Model 1952

Similar to above, with turned back bolt handle. Manufactured between 1952 and 1956.

NIB	Exc.	V.G.	Good	Fair	Poor
2400	2100	1850	1300	650	300

Model 1952 Carbine

Similar to Model 1950 carbine. Additionally in 7x57mm caliber. Manufactured between 1952 and 1956.

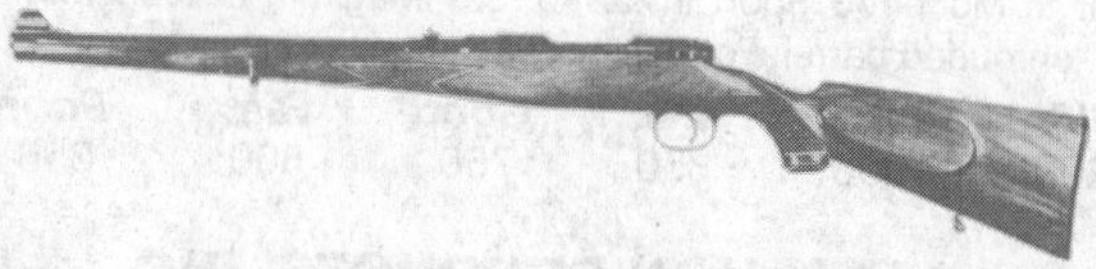

NIB	Exc.	V.G.	Good	Fair	Poor
2450	2100	1850	1300	650	300

Model 1952 6.5mm Carbine

As above in 6.5x54mm Mannlicher Schoenauer caliber, with 18.5" barrel. Manufactured between 1952 and 1956.

NIB	Exc.	V.G.	Good	Fair	Poor
2400	2000	1500	850	650	300

Model 1956 Rifle

.243 or .30-06 caliber bolt-action rifle, with 22" barrel and Monte Carlo-style stock. Manufactured between 1956 and 1960.

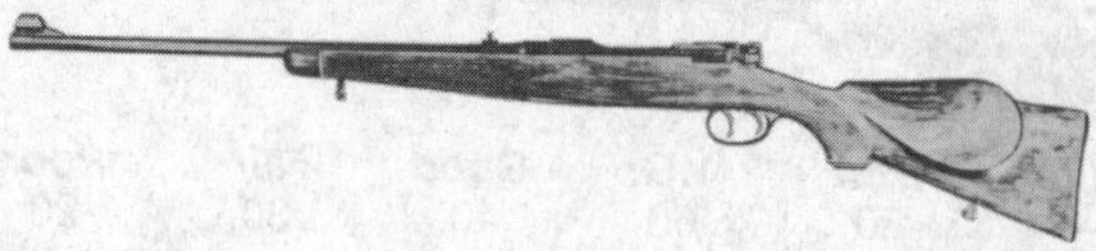

NIB	Exc.	V.G.	Good	Fair	Poor
2100	1900	1700	950	650	300

Model 1956 Carbine

As above, with 20" barrel and full-length stock. Manufactured between 1956 and 1960.

NIB	Exc.	V.G.	Good	Fair	Poor
2100	1900	1700	950	650	300

Model 1961 MCA Rifle

As above modified for easier use with telescopic sight.

NIB	Exc.	V.G.	Good	Fair	Poor
1750	1550	1250	1000	800	650

Model 1961 MCA Carbine

As above, with 20" barrel and half-length stock.

NIB	Exc.	V.G.	Good	Fair	Poor
1950	1650	1250	1100	700	600

Alpine Model

Variant of Model 1961 MCA was chambered in .243 Win. or .30-06. Featured engraving on the bolt handle and oak leaf carving on stock. Manufactured from 1965 to 1967.

NIB	Exc.	V.G.	Good	Fair	Poor
4000	3500	2850	2000	1000	300

Model M72 LM Rifle

Fitted with 23" fluted barrel, double-set or single trigger and full-length stock. Manufactured between 1972 and 1980.

NIB	Exc.	V.G.	Good	Fair	Poor
—	1300	1050	700	550	450

MANUFRANCE

St. Etienne, France

See—LE FRANCAIS

Auto Stand

.22-caliber semi-automatic pistol. Manufactured by Pyrenees and sold by Manufrance under trade name Auto Stand.

NIB	Exc.	V.G.	Good	Fair	Poor
—	250	220	200	150	100

Buffalo Stand

.22-caliber bolt-action pistol, with 12" barrel and adjustable sights. Blued, with walnut stock. Manufactured prior to 1914.

NIB	Exc.	V.G.	Good	Fair	Poor
—	250	220	200	150	100

Le Agent

8mm caliber double-action revolver, with 5" barrel. Blued, with walnut grips.

NIB	Exc.	V.G.	Good	Fair	Poor
—	200	100	180	150	80

Le Colonial

As above, with enclosed hammer.

NIB	Exc.	V.G.	Good	Fair	Poor
—	200	180	150	100	80

LeFrancais

Semi-automatic pistol chambered for 7.65mm cartridge. Built on blowback design. 7.65mm pistols first built in 1950; discontinued 1959. Very few of these pistols are in U.S.

NIB	Exc.	V.G.	Good	Fair	Poor
—	520	420	300	200	100

MANURHIN

Saint-Bonnet-le-Chateau, France

Company manufactured Walther PP and PPK models under license. These are marked "Manufacture de Machines du Haut-Rhin" on left front of slide and "Lic Excl. Walther" on left rear. These arms were imported into U.S.A. in early 1950s by Thalson Import Company of San Francisco, California and later by Interarms. Latter are marked "Mark 11" and "Made in France". Manurhin is now owned by Chapuis Armes. Note: All models add 15 percent for police markings.

Model PP

Similar to Walther Model PP, with revised safety. Discontinued.

NIB	Exc.	V.G.	Good	Fair	Poor
—	400	350	300	220	150

Model PPK/S

Similar to Walther Model PPK/S, with revised safety. Discontinued.

NIB	Exc.	V.G.	Good	Fair	Poor
—	400	350	300	220	150

Model PP Sports

Target version of PP. Chambered for .22-caliber shell. Available in various barrel lengths. Discontinued.

NIB	Exc.	V.G.	Good	Fair	Poor
—	400	350	300	220	150

Model 73 Defense Revolver

.38 Special or .357 Magnum caliber double-action swing-out cylinder revolver, with 2.5", 3" or 4" barrel having fixed sights. Blued, with walnut grips.

NIB	Exc.	V.G.	Good	Fair	Poor
1150	1000	850	750	500	350

Model 73 Gendarmerie

As above, with 5.5", 6" or 8" long barrel and adjustable sights.

NIB	Exc.	V.G.	Good	Fair	Poor
1250	1100	900	800	550	400

Model 73 Sport

Similar to above, with shortened lock time and target-style adjustable sights.

NIB	Exc.	V.G.	Good	Fair	Poor
1250	1100	900	800	550	400

Model 73 Convertible

As above, with interchangeable .22-, .32- or .38-caliber barrels and cylinders.

NIB	Exc.	V.G.	Good	Fair	Poor
2250	1850	1600	1400	950	750

Model 73 Silhouette

Similar to Model 73 Sport in .22 to .357 Magnum caliber, with 10" or 10.75" shrouded barrel. Form fitting walnut grips.

NIB	Exc.	V.G.	Good	Fair	Poor
1200	1050	850	750	500	350

MARATHON PRODUCTS, INC.

Santa Barbara, California

.22 First Shot

.22-caliber single-shot bolt-action rifle, with 16.5" barrel. Overall length 31". Blued, with walnut stock. Manufactured between 1985 and 1987.

NIB	Exc.	V.G.	Good	Fair	Poor
—	80	60	40	30	20

.22 Super Shot

As above, with 24" barrel. Manufactured between 1985 and 1987.

NIB	Exc.	V.G.	Good	Fair	Poor
—	80	60	40	30	20

.22 Hot Shot Pistol

.22-caliber bolt-action pistol, with 14.5" barrel. Blued, with walnut stock. Manufactured in 1986 and 1987.

NIB	Exc.	V.G.	Good	Fair	Poor
—	100	60	40	30	20

Centerfire Rifle

Bolt-action sporting rifle. Manufactured in a variety of calibers, with 24" barrel, open sights, adjustable trigger and 5-shot magazine. Blued, with walnut stock. Manufactured in 1985 and 1986.

NIB	Exc.	V.G.	Good	Fair	Poor
—	320	250	200	150	120

MARBLE'S ARMS & MFG. CO.

Gladstone, Michigan

Marble's Game Getter Gun—NFA, curio or relic

Marble's suspended sales of Game Getter in United States after Treasury Department ruled it was a "firearm" under NFA, but continued sales abroad. Retail price in 1934 was about $24 (12" or 15" barrels) to $26 (18" barrels). Bureau of Internal Revenue removed 18" barrel variation from NFA in a Letter Ruling dated March 1, 1939. Today, 12" and 15" barrel variations are controlled under NFA in "any other weapon" category. If shoulder stock is removed from a 12", 15" or 18" barreled Game Getter, however, ATF has ruled it to be a NFA "firearm" subject to a $200 transfer tax. IMPORTANT! This gun is considered a Class III firearm by the Federal Government. This means that it is illegal to possess unless it has been previously registered with the BATFE. Any transfer must be registered with the BATFE. There is currently no way to legally register an unregistered Class III firearm.

Model 1908

Serial numbered from A to M; then 001 to 10000.

NIB	Exc.	V.G.	Good	Fair	Poor
2750	2200	1600	1150	750	350

Model 1908 was available in two variations. Model 1908A has a flexible rear tang sight and Model 1908B has a filler block. Some confusion about serial numbering exists, because some Marble's factory representatives gave out incorrect information during 1960s and 1970s. According to some letters from this period, on Marble's factory letterhead, serial numbers began with number 700 and ended with 9999. Original factory records, however, disclose that Model 1908 was first shipped from factory in 1909, serial numbered with letters A through M, before beginning numerically with serial number 001 through 10000, when production ended in May, 1914. Serial number 001 was shipped from factory on March 3, 1909 and last Model 1908 was shipped on May 22, 1918.

Markings on Model 1908 are:
Type I (serial 1 to about 4000)
Type II (about serial 4000 to 9999)

LEFT SIDE:
MANUFACTURED BY THE

MARBLE SAFETY AXE CO.
GLADSTONE, MICH. U.S.A.
Marble Arms & Mfg. Co.

MANUFACTURED BY THE

MARBLE SAFETY AXE CO.
GLADSTONE, MICH. U.S.A.
SUCCESSOR

RIGHT SIDE:
Calibers 22 & 44
Patent Allowed

Calibers 22 & 44
Patent Allowed

Each of the markings on right side is enclosed within an elongated circle.

OTHER CHARACTERISTICS: Separate flat buttplate attached with two screws up to approximately serial number 1200; afterwards, a flattened buttplate was integrally formed from same round steel used to form skeleton stock. Early stocks have drop adjustment with a knurled collar .375" diameter by .1875" long; at approximately serial number 2500, collar was changed to .500" by .625" long. Hammer spur is curved down up to approximately serial number 2,000, then curve at hammer is up.

Model 1908 was originally designed for .22 Short, Long or LR and .44 shot and ball ammunition, but the most satisfactory load was long-cased .44-40 that held shot in place with a disk and mouth crimp. The 1915 Marble's catalog stated Model 1908 was available for use with 2" .410 shotgun shell; chambering is slightly different from that of .44-40, but is seldom encountered. Production of Model 1908 was not resumed because of WWI.

Model 1921

NIB	Exc.	V.G.	Good	Fair	Poor
2100	1750	1250	900	500	250

To meet continuing demand for the extremely popular 1908, Marble's produced an entirely new gun in 1921. Grip, folding stock (made from cold-rolled sheet metal and nickel-plated) and other features were redesigned. Serial number range for Model 1921 is 10001 (shipped in October 1921) to 20076. Most production of Model 1921 apparently ended around the time of WWII; however, factory records disclose Marble's was exporting 15" barrel Model 1921s into Canada in 1955, where their registration was not required at that time. Marble's also assembled approximately 200 Model 1921s from parts circa 1960-61 and sold them (without holster) for $200 each.

Model 1921 was originally designed for 2" .410 shotgun shell, but Marble's changed the extractor marking on some guns to 2" or 2.5" to indicate factory rechambering for 2.5" shell, which has been reported to have started in 1924. However, change to a 2.5" chamber may not have been uniform, because both 2" and 2.5" marked guns have been observed in low (14000) and high (19000) serial number ranges. Lowest serial number with 2.5" marking observed so far is 14601. Range from approximately 14500 to 17000 have plastic rather than walnut grips, single-bladed rear sight rather than multiple-blade and blued rather than case-hardened hammer. Outside this range, only 19288 has 2" marking; and number 19692 is marked 2.5". No Model 1921 Game Getters are known to have been factory chambered for 3" .410 shell.

The markings on the Model 1921 are:

LEFT SIDE:
Marble'S
Game Getter Gun
Marble Arms & Mfg.Co.
Gladstone, Mich.U.S.A.
RIGHT SIDE: UPPER BARREL 22 S.L. LR.&N.R.A
LOWER BARREL .44GG & .410 2"

OTHER CHARACTERISTICS: Other barrel markings for Model 1921 in .410 are .410 2" and .410 2.5"; latter appears in serial number range from approximately 15000 to 16600 and in the low 19000 range.

Marble's Game Getter Pistol and other special-order or experimental Game Getters—NFA, curio or relic

Contemporary articles and advertisements in Hunter-Trader-Trapper and some early Marble's catalogs, state that a small number of Model 1908 Game Getters were originally manufactured (with rifled barrels) for .25-20, .32-20 and .38-40 cartridges. An illustrated advertisement in a 1910 issue of Hunter-Trapper-Trader states that 12", 15" and 18" barrel Game Getters were available for delivery in .25-20, .32-20 and .38-40 and that these firearms were designed as over/under rifles with rifled barrels. An article in October 1913 issue of Outdoor Life states that Marble's was manufacturing a Game Getter pistol, with 10" barrels and that any barrel length could be ordered.

Original factory records have confirmed the manufacture of foregoing Game Getters and clarified their designs. All original guns are thus correctly classified as experimental or special-order guns and all are extremely rare. Factory records disclose that about 20 each of Model 1908 were manufactured with .22/25-20 and .22/.32-20 over/under rifled barrels, but barrel lengths are not specified. No .22/.38-40 Model 1908 Game Getters are listed in factory records, but that may not have precluded a later factory alteration to that configuration. It is important to note that any Model 1908 Game Getter with over/under rifled barrels less than 18" in length is currently subject to registration under NFA as a short barreled rifle, with a $200 transfer tax. Under current law, if these firearms are not registered they are contraband and cannot be legally owned unless ATF administratively removes them from NFA as collector's items.

Factory records disclose that eight Model 1908 Game Getter pistols were manufactured and all were shipped to a Minneapolis hardware store. Two specimens have been located: serial number 3810, with a 8" .22/.44 smoothbore barrel, and serial number 3837, with a 10" .22/.44 smoothbore barrel. Inspection of serial numbers 3810 and 3837 (including removal of grips) reveal they were never fitted with shoulder stocks, because the portion of frame which would have accommodated the stock was never machined out to receive one. Under current law, an original Marble's Game Getter pistol is subject to registration under NFA as an "Any Other Weapon" with a $5 transfer tax. According to very incomplete factory records, a relatively small number—about a dozen—Model 1921 Game Getters were manufactured with .22/.38-40 rifled barrels, but barrel lengths are not specified. It is possible that other factory-original configurations exist, such as .22/.25-20 and others.

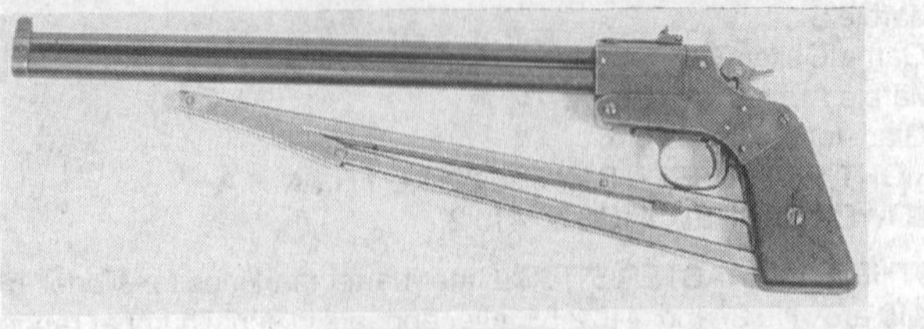

MARGOLIN

Tula, Soviet State Arsenal

Model MT Sports

Semi-automatic .22-caliber pistol, with no barrel weights. Not threaded for a compensator. Barrel length 7.5". Furnished with a black plastic case, with spare magazine and repair parts. Discontinued.

Courtesy Orvel Reichert

NIB	Exc.	V.G.	Good	Fair	Poor
—	600	500	400	300	200

Model MTS-1

.22 short semi-automatic pistol, with 5.9" barrel having an integral muzzle brake (7.4" overall), adjustable walnut grips and 6-shot magazine. Normally accompanied by a wooden case, with cleaning accessories. Discontinued.

Courtesy Orvel Reichert

NIB	Exc.	V.G.	Good	Fair	Poor
—	1300	1020	800	450	350

Model MTS-2

As above in .22 LR, with 5.9" barrel. Discontinued.

NIB	Exc.	V.G.	Good	Fair	Poor
—	1200	900	600	400	350

MARIETTE BREVETTE

Liege, Belgium

A number of European manufacturers produced percussion pepperbox pistols based upon a patent issued to Mariette during 1840s and 1850s. These pistols have detachable barrels that are loaded at breech, double-action ring triggers and internally mounted hammers. Normally blued and foliate engraved.

4" Barrel Pepperbox

NIB	Exc.	V.G.	Good	Fair	Poor
—	—	2250	900	400	—

6" Barrel Pepperbox

NIB	Exc.	V.G.	Good	Fair	Poor
—	—	2250	900	400	—

MARLIN FIREARMS CO.

Madison, North Carolina

Established by John Mahlon Marlin in 1863. Marlin manufactured pistols until 1875, when he began production of Ballard rifles. In 1881, he made his first lever-action repeating rifle for which his company became famous. In recent years, Marlin, along with its subsidiaries Harrington & Richardson/NEF, are now owned by Freedom Group Family of Companies.

BALLARD RIFLES

Antique

Before Marlin production, Ballard rifles were made by Dwight Chapin & Co., Ball & Williams, Merrimack Arms, Brown Manufacturing, and Ballard. Listings for these will be found in the BALLARD section of this book.

MARLIN-BALLARD RIFLES

Antique

Commencing in 1875, Ballard single-shot rifle was made by John Marlin for Schoverling and Daly. In 1881, business was incorporated and became Marlin Firearms Co. All Ballards made from then until 1891, when they were discontinued, were produced under this banner. Only real difference in rifles manufactured during these periods was in markings. Earlier rifles stamped "J.M. Marlin New Haven. Conn. U.S.A./Ballards Patent. Nov. 5, 1861"; post-1881 models stamped "Marlin Firearms Co. New Haven Ct. U.S.A./Patented Feb. 9, 1875/Ballards Patent Nov. 5, 1861".

Ballard Hunters Rifle (Antique)

Resembles earlier Brown Manufacturing Company rifles. Utilizes many leftover parts acquired by Marlin. Chambered for .32, .38 and .44 rimfire and centerfire. Features John Marlin's unique reversible firing pin that allows same gun to use both rimfire and centerfire ammunition simply by rotating firing pin in breech-block. Model still had external ejector and bears J.M. Marlin markings. Approximately 500 manufactured in 1 to 500 serial range. Produced in 1875 and 1876.

Exc.	Fine	V.G.	Good	Fair	Poor
3700	2750	1850	950	400	280

Ballard No. 1 Hunters Rifle (Antique)

Model bears early J.M. Marlin marking only. Manufactured from 1876 until 1880. Discontinued before incorporation. Has 26", 28" and 30" barrel. Chambered for .44 rimfire or centerfire cartridge. Has reversible firing pin and new internal extractor. Production figures are not available. Serial number range between 500 and 4000.

Exc.	Fine	V.G.	Good	Fair	Poor
4500	3000	2000	1000	400	280

Ballard No. 1-1/2 Hunters Rifle (Antique)

Similar to No. 1. Chambered for .45-70, .40-63 and .40-65 cartridges. Does not have reversible firing pin. Barrel length 30" and 32". Manufactured between 1879 and 1883. Found with both early and later markings.

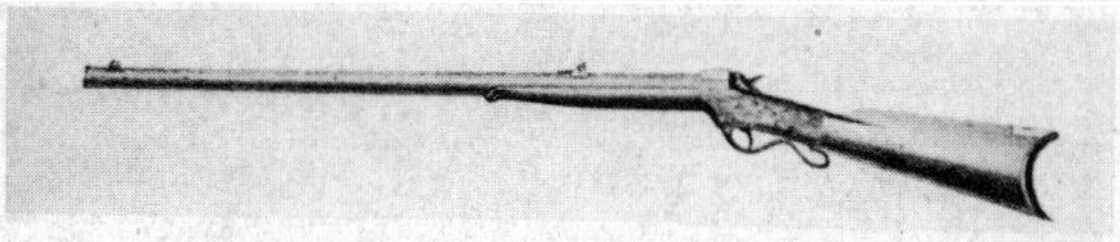

Courtesy Marlin Firearms Co.

Exc.	Fine	V.G.	Good	Fair	Poor
5200	3750	2620	1500	500	350

Ballard No. 1-3/4 "Far West" Hunters Rifle (Antique)

Model made by J. M. Marlin only. Similar to No. 1-1/2. Difference being addition of double-set triggers and a ring on opening lever. Manufactured in 1880 and 1881.

Exc.	Fine	V.G.	Good	Fair	Poor
6300	4750	3370	2000	600	420

Ballard No. 2 Sporting Rifle (Antique)

Chambered for .32, .38 rimfire or centerfire cartridges and .44 centerfire. Has reversible firing pin. Offered in 26", 28" and 30" barrel lengths. Features "Rocky Mountain" sights. Manufactured between 1876 and 1891. Found with both early and late markings.

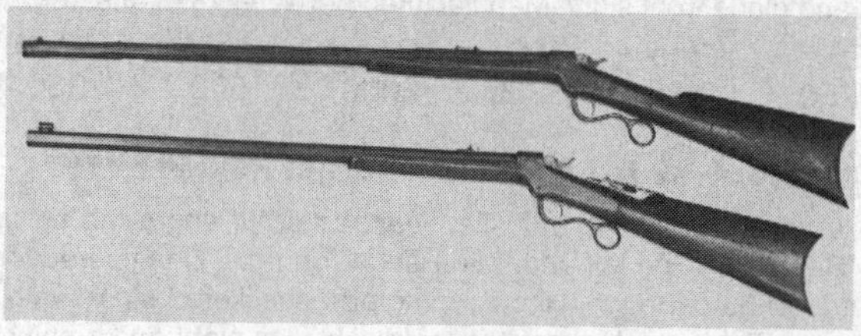

Courtesy Milwaukee Public Museum, Milwaukee, Wisconsin

Exc.	Fine	V.G.	Good	Fair	Poor
3200	2000	1320	650	200	140

Ballard No. 3 Gallery Rifle (Antique)

Similar to No. 2 rifle. Chambered for .22 rimfire cartridge. Has a manually operated external extractor. Sights are same and a 24" barrel was offered in addition to 26", 28" and 30". Manufactured between 1876 and 1891.

Exc.	Fine	V.G.	Good	Fair	Poor
3200	2000	1320	650	200	140

Ballard No. 3F Gallery Rifle (Antique)

Deluxe version of No. 3. Has a pistol grip stock, nickel-plated Schutzen-style buttplate and an opening lever like a repeating rifle. Features a 26" octagonal barrel and oil-finished stock. Manufactured in late 1880s. Quite scarce in today's market.

No. 3 F Fine Gallery Rifle.

Courtesy Marlin Firearms Co.

Exc.	Fine	V.G.	Good	Fair	Poor
6500	4250	3000	1750	500	350

Ballard No. 4 Perfection Rifle (Antique)

Chambered for a number of centerfire calibers from .32-40 to .50-70. Barrel lengths from 26" to 30". Sights are "Rocky Mountain" type. Manufactured between 1876 and 1891.

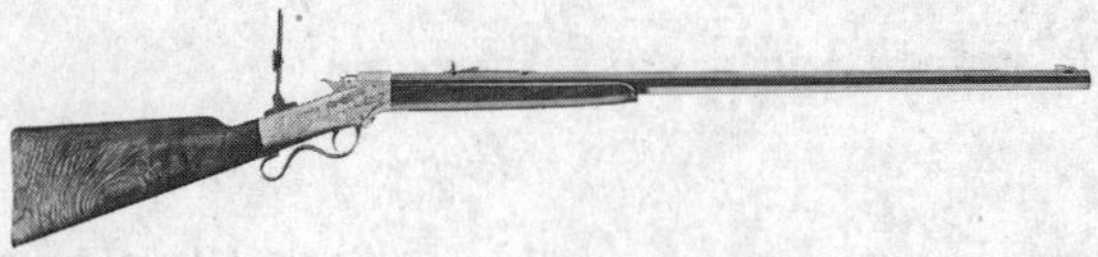

Courtesy Rock Island Auction Company

Exc.	Fine	V.G.	Good	Fair	Poor
6500	4250	3000	1750	500	350

Ballard No. 3-1/2 Target Rifle (Antique)

Similar to No. 4 Perfection Rifle. Has a checkered stock, with shotgun-style buttplate, 30" barrel and tang peep sight with globe front sight. Chambered for .40-65 cartridge. Manufactured from 1880-1882.

Exc.	Fine	V.G.	Good	Fair	Poor
6500	4250	3000	1750	500	350

Ballard No. 4-1/2 Mid Range Rifle (Antique)

Variation of No. 4 Perfection model. Has a higher-grade checkered stock, with shotgun buttplate, 30" part-round part-octagonal barrel. Chambered for .38-40, .40-65 and .45-70 cartridges. Features a Vernier tang peep sight and globe front sight. Manufactured between 1878 and 1882.

Exc.	Fine	V.G.	Good	Fair	Poor
6750	4500	3250	2000	500	350

Ballard No. 4-1/2 A-1 Mid Range Target Rifle (Antique)

Deluxe version of No. 4-1/2" rifle. Features scroll engraving on frame, with "Ballard A-1" on left and "Mid-Range" on right. Chambered for .38-50 and .40-65 cartridge. Has a high-grade checkered stock, with horn forend tip. Sights are highest-grade Vernier tang sight and a spirit lever front sight. Shotgun-/rifle-style butt was optional. Manufactured between 1878 and 1880.

Courtesy Milwaukee Public Museum, Milwaukee, Wisconsin

Exc.	Fine	V.G.	Good	Fair	Poor
9000	7250	5370	3500	750	520

Ballard No. 5 Pacific Rifle (Antique)

Model has a 30" or 32" medium to heavyweight barrel, with a ramrod mounted underneath. Chambered for many different calibers from .38-50 to .50-70. Features "Rocky Mountain" sights, crescent butt, double-set triggers and a ring-style opening lever. Manufactured between 1876 and 1891.

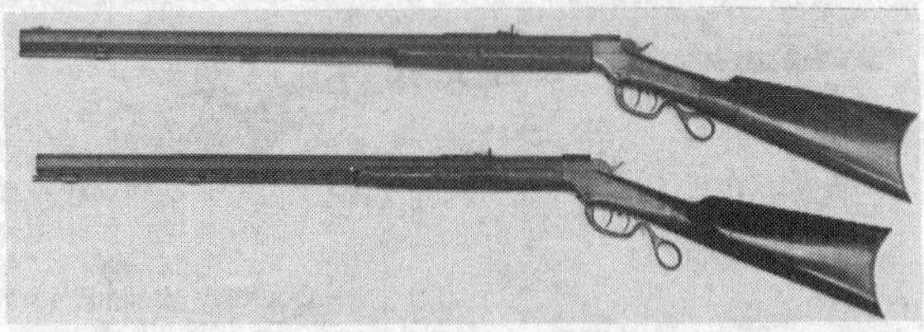

Courtesy Milwaukee Public Museum, Milwaukee, Wisconsin

Exc.	Fine	V.G.	Good	Fair	Poor
5500	4750	3370	2000	500	350

Ballard No. 5-1/2 Montana Rifle (Antique)

Similar to Pacific Rifle, with an extra heavyweight barrel. Chambered for .45 Sharps cartridge only. Features checkered steel shotgun-style buttplate. Manufactured from 1882-1884. Has late markings only.

Courtesy Milwaukee Public Museum, Milwaukee, Wisconsin

Exc.	Fine	V.G.	Good	Fair	Poor
15000	10000	7750	5500	1250	870

Ballard No. 6 Schuetzen Off Hand Rifle (Antique)

Model has a 30" or 32" octagonal barrel. Chambered for .40-65, .44-75 and .38-50 cartridges. Stock is of select walnut in high-combed Schuetzen style. Buttplate is nickel-plated. Receiver is not engraved. Sights are Vernier tang type on rear and a spirit lever front. Triggers are double-set. Opening lever has a ring and spur. Marked J.M. Marlin only. Manufactured between 1876 and 1880.

Exc.	Fine	V.G.	Good	Fair	Poor
—	6500	4500	2500	500	350

Ballard No. 6 Schuetzen Rifle (Antique)

Similar to Off Hand. Produced by later Marlin Firearms Company and was so marked. More deluxe version, with checkered stock, horn forend tip and a fully engraved receiver. Chambered for .32-40 and .38-55 cartridges. Manufactured between 1881 and 1891.

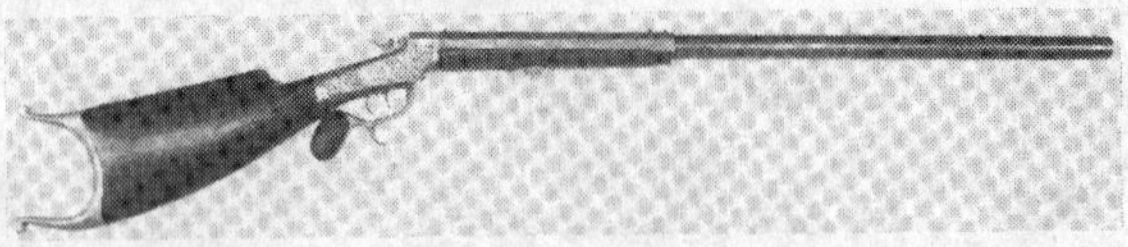

Exc.	Fine	V.G.	Good	Fair	Poor
13000	8500	6500	4500	1250	870

Ballard No. 6-1/2 Off Hand Mid Range Rifle (Antique)

Chambered for .40-54 Everlasting cartridge only. Has 28" or 30" part-round part-octagonal barrel, Schuetzen-style stock, and plain non-engraved receiver. Manufactured between 1880 and 1882.

Exc.	Fine	V.G.	Good	Fair	Poor
9500	5500	4000	2500	500	350

Ballard No. 6-1/2 Rigby Off Hand Mid Range Rifle (Antique)

Chambered for .38-50 and .40-65 cartridges. Features Rigby ribbed-style barrel in 26" and 28" lengths, with Vernier rear and globe front sights. High grade checkered walnut Schuetzen-style stock, with horn forend tip and pistol grip cap. Buttplate nickel-plated. Opening lever of ring type, with single trigger. Extensively engraved receiver. Manufactured from 1880 to 1882.

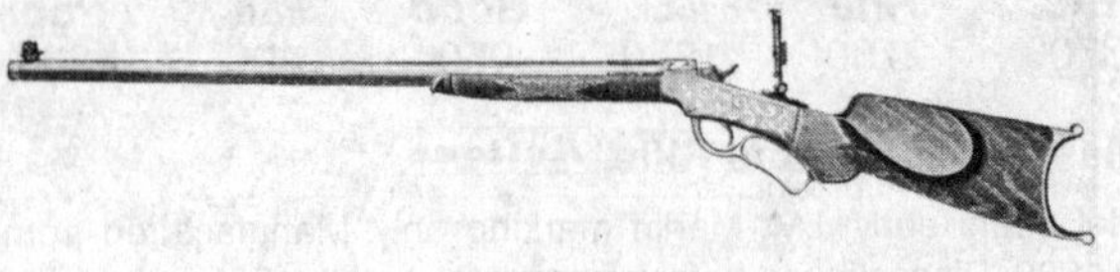

No. 6½ Off-Hand Rifle.

Courtesy Marlin Firearms Co.

Exc.	Fine	V.G.	Good	Fair	Poor
14500	9000	7250	5500	1250	870

Ballard No. 6-1/2 Off Hand Rifle (Antique)

Chambered for .32-40 and .38-55 cartridges. Features barrel lengths 28" and 30". Checkered high-grade walnut Schuetzen-style stock, with nickel-plated buttplate. Forend tip and pistol grip cap are of horn. Receiver engraved. Has single trigger, full-ring opening lever, Vernier tang rear sight and spirit lever front sight. Made by Marlin Firearms Company between 1883 and 1891. Found with later markings only.

Exc.	Fine	V.G.	Good	Fair	Poor
14000	9000	7250	5500	1250	870

Ballard No. 7 "Creedmore A-1" Long Range Rifle (Antique)

Model commonly chambered for .44-100 or .45-100 cartridges. Has 34 part-round part-octagonal barrel. High grade checkered pistol grip stock, with a horn forend tip and shotgun-style butt. Sights are a special 1,300-yard Vernier tang rear and a spirit level front. Another sight base on heel of stock for mounting rear sight for ultra long-range shooting. Opening lever is similar to a repeating rifle. Single trigger featured. Receiver engraved and marked "Ballard A-1" on left and "Long Range" on right. Manufactured between 1876 and 1886. Found with both early and late markings.

Courtesy Milwaukee Public Museum, Milwaukee, Wisconsin

Exc.	Fine	V.G.	Good	Fair	Poor
15000	9700	7600	5500	1250	870

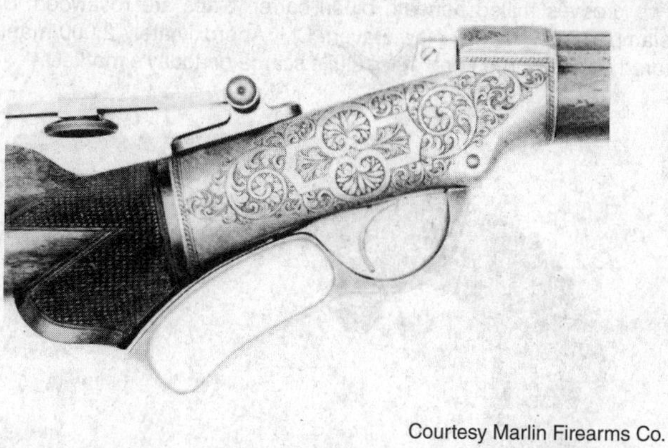

Courtesy Marlin Firearms Co.

Exc.	Fine	V.G.	Good	Fair	Poor
19500	11500	9000	6500	1500	1050

Ballard No. 7 Long Range Rifle (Antique)

Similar to "Creedmore A-1". Slightly less deluxe. Engraving less elaborate. Lettering on receiver is absent. Manufactured between 1883 and 1890. Found with later markings only.

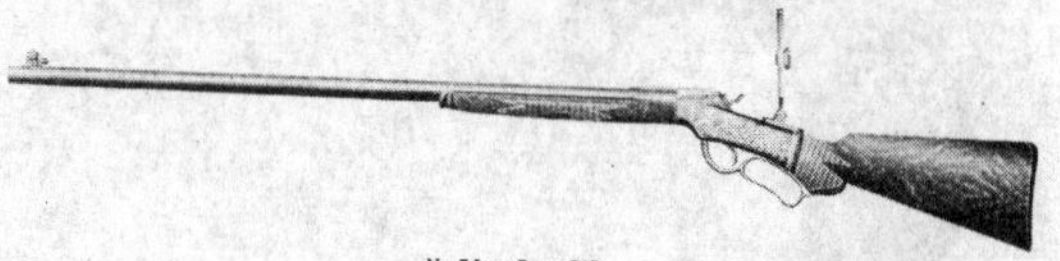

No. 7 Long Range Rifle.

Courtesy Marlin Firearms Co.

Exc.	Fine	V.G.	Good	Fair	Poor
13500	8000	6250	4500	850	590

Ballard No. 7A-1 Long Range Rifle (Antique)

Higher grade version of "Creedmore A-I", with fancier walnut and checkered straight stock. Better sights and deluxe engraving also featured. Manufactured between 1879 and 1883. Found with both markings.

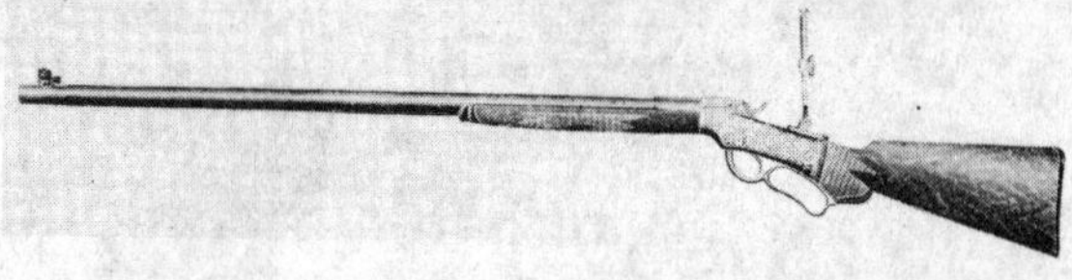

Courtesy Marlin Firearms Co.

Exc.	Fine	V.G.	Good	Fair	Poor
16000	1000	3250	5500	1250	870

Ballard No. 7A-1 Extra Grade Long Range Rifle (Antique)

Highest grade version of No. 7 rifles. Features 34" "Rigby" -type ribbed round barrel. Usually a special-order rifle, with most features to customer specifications. Manufactured in limited numbers between 1879 and 1883. Found with both markings.

Ballard No. 8 Union Hill Rifle (Antique)

Model has 28" and 30" part-round part-octagonal barrel. Chambered for .32-40 and .38-55 cartridges. Checkered pistol grip stock, with nickel-plated buttplate; opening lever is fully enclosed ring as on repeaters. Double-set trigger and a tang peep, with globe front sight. Receiver not engraved. Manufactured between 1884 and 1890. Found only with late markings. This was one of the most popular rifles in Ballard line.

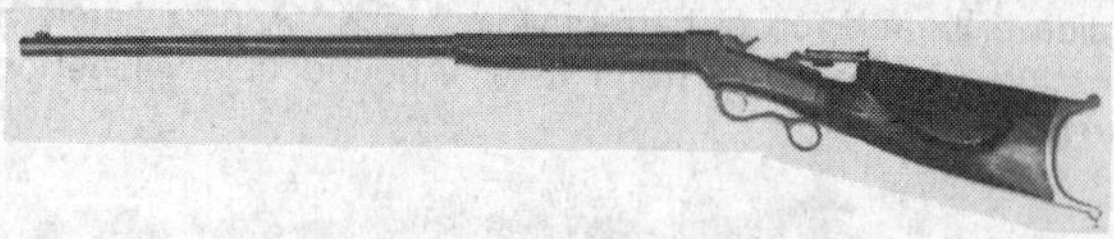

Courtesy Milwaukee Public Museum, Milwaukee, Wisconsin

Exc.	Fine	V.G.	Good	Fair	Poor
7000	4250	3000	1750	500	350

Ballard No. 9 Union Hill Rifle (Antique)

Similar to No. 8. Features a single trigger and better sights. Manufactured between 1884 and 1891. Has later markings only.

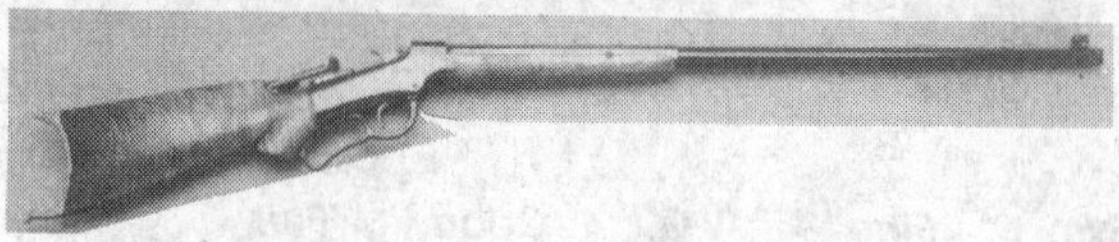

Courtesy Bonhams & Butterfields, San Francisco, California

Exc.	Fine	V.G.	Good	Fair	Poor
7000	4250	3000	1750	500	350

Ballard No. 10 Schuetzen Junior Rifle (Antique)

Simply a heavier barreled version of No. 9. Barrel 32" long. Checkered pistol grip stock is off-hand style. Rear sight Vernier Mid Range. Front sight spirit level type. Popular model. Manufactured between 1885 and 1891. Found with later markings only.

Courtesy Amoskeag Auction Company

Exc.	Fine	V.G.	Good	Fair	Poor
7000	4750	3370	2000	650	450

MARLIN HANDGUNS

1st Model Derringer (Antique)

First handgun produced by Marlin. Barrel 2.0625" long and pivots to side for loading. There is a plunger under the frame that is depressed to free barrel. This device is a Ballard patent. Chambered for .22 rimfire cartridge. No extractor. Frame brass and usually nickel-plated. Has two grooves milled beneath blued barrel. Grips are rosewood. Barrel stamped "J.M. Marlin, New Haven, Ct.". Approximately 2,000 manufactured between 1863 and 1867. Quite scarce on today's market.

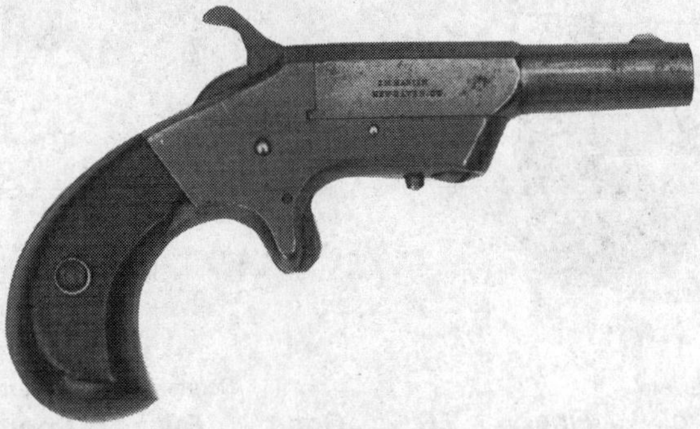

Courtesy Milwaukee Public Museum, Milwaukee, Wisconsin

Exc.	Fine	V.G.	Good	Fair	Poor
1350	750	520	300	100	70

O.K. Model Derringer Antique

O.K. Model chambered for .22, .30 and .32 rimfire cartridges. Barrel 2.125" or 3.125" on .32 rimfire. No extractor. Functions as 1st Model. Frame plated brass, with flat sides. Barrel found blued or nickel-plated. Grips are rosewood. Markings same as on 1st Model, but located on right side of barrel. Top of barrel marked "O.K." Approximately 5,000 manufactured between 1863 and 1870. About double values for rare square butt variation.

Courtesy Marlin Firearms Co.

Exc.	Fine	V.G.	Good	Fair	Poor
1350	750	520	300	100	70

Victor Model Derringer Antique

Similar in appearance to "O.K.". Larger in size and chambered for .38-caliber rimfire cartridge. Barrel 2.6875" long; there was for the first time an extractor. Finish and function unchanged. Right side of barrel stamped "J.M. Marlin/New Haven, Ct./Pat. April 5.1870". "Victor" stamped on top of barrel. Approximately 4,000 manufactured between 1870 and 1881.

Exc.	Fine	V.G.	Good	Fair	Poor
1600	1250	870	500	150	100

Nevermiss Model Derringer

Made in three different sizes. Chambered for .22, .32 and .41 rimfire cartridges. Barrel 2.5" long and swings sideways for loading. Frame plated brass. Barrels blued or nickel-plated. Grips are rosewood. Frame grooved under barrels as on 1st model. There is an extractor. Barrel markings same as on "Victor", with top of barrel marked "Nevermiss". Approximately 5,000 manufactured between 1870 and 1881.

.22 Caliber Model Antique

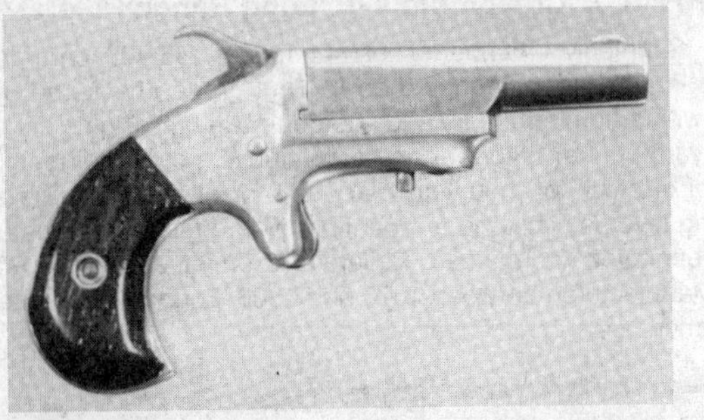

Courtesy Marlin Firearms Co.

Exc.	Fine	V.G.	Good	Fair	Poor
1500	1150	820	500	100	70

.32 Caliber Model Antique

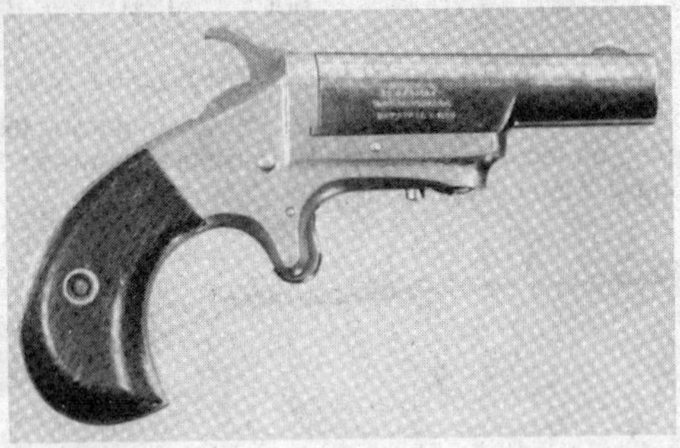

Courtesy Marlin Firearms Co.

Exc.	Fine	V.G.	Good	Fair	Poor
1200	750	550	350	100	70

.41 Caliber Model Antique

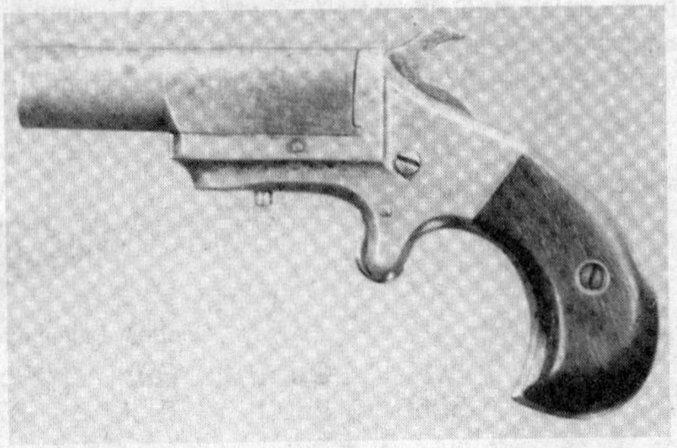

Courtesy Marlin Firearms Co.

Exc.	Fine	V.G.	Good	Fair	Poor
3750	2500	1750	1000	400	280

Stonewall Model Derringer Antique

Identical to .41-caliber "Nevermiss". Top of barrel marked "Stonewall". Rarely encountered.

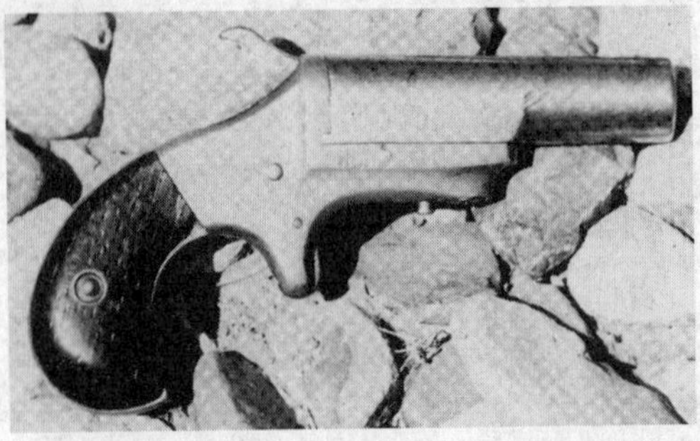

Courtesy Marlin Firearms Co.

Exc.	Fine	V.G.	Good	Fair	Poor
6000	4250	3120	2000	750	520

O.K. Pocket Revolver Antique

Solid-frame spur-trigger single-action revolver. Chambered for .22 rimfire short. Round barrel 2.25" and 7-shot cylinder is unfluted. Frame nickel-plated brass, with blue or nickel-plated barrel. Bird's-head grips are rosewood. Cylinder pin is removable and used to knock empty cases out of cylinder. Top of barrel marked "O.K." and "J.M. Marlin. New Haven, Conn. U.S.A.". Approximately 1,500 manufactured between 1870 and 1875.

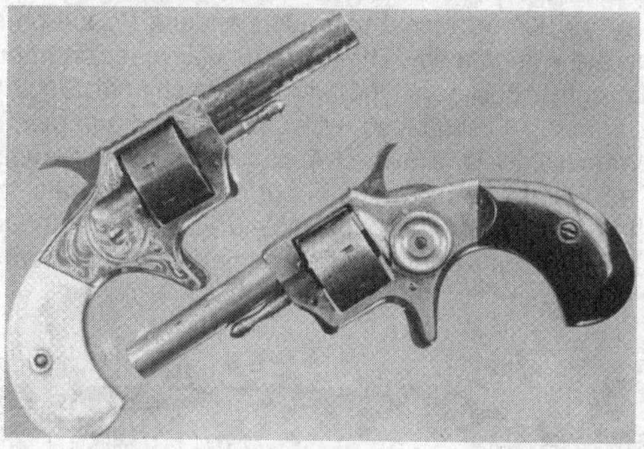

Courtesy Marlin Firearms Co.

Exc.	Fine	V.G.	Good	Fair	Poor
700	500	350	200	80	50

Little Joker Revolver Antique

Similar in appearance to "O.K." revolver. Some are reported to have engraving and ivory or pearl grips. Approximately 500 manufactured between 1871 and 1873.

Exc.	Fine	V.G.	Good	Fair	Poor
800	500	420	350	120	80

J.M. MARLIN STANDARD POCKET REVOLVERS

In 1872, Marlin began production of its Smith & Wesson look-alike. Manhattan Firearms Company had developed a copy of Model 1 S&W .22 cartridge revolver. In 1868, company ceased business and revolvers were produced by American Standard Tool Company until their dissolution in 1873. In 1872, Marlin had entered into an agreement with this company to manufacture these revolvers, which were no longer protected by Rollin White patent after 1869. Marlin revolvers are similar to those made by American Standard. Only real difference being that Marlin grips are of bird's-head round configuration. A contoured grip frame and a patented pawl spring mechanism is utilized on Marlin revolvers.

Marlin XXX Standard 1872 Pocket Revolver

This is the first in a series of four Standard model revolvers. Chambered for .30-caliber rimfire. Earlier model has an octagonal 3.125" barrel; later, a round 3" barrel. There are round and octagonal barrel variations (with unfluted cylinders) and round barrel variations (with short and long fluted cylinders). All barrels are ribbed and tip up for loading. They have plated brass frames and barrels are nickel-plated. Bird's-head grips are of rosewood or hard rubber, bearing the monogram "M.F.A. Co." inside a star. There is a spur trigger. Markings "J.M. Marlin-New Haven Ct." appear on earlier octagonal barreled models. "U.S.A. Pat. July 1. 1873" was added to later round barreled models. All barrels are marked "XXX Standard 1872". Approximately 5,000 of all types manufactured between 1872 and 1887.

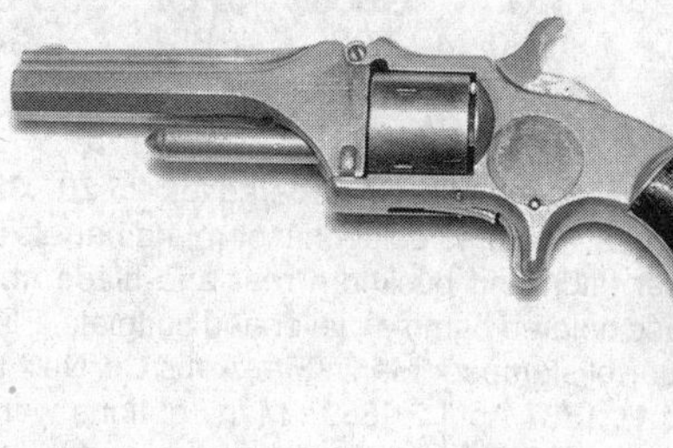

Octagon Barrel—Early Variation Antique

Exc.	Fine	V.G.	Good	Fair	Poor
900	500	400	300	80	50

Round Barrel—Non-Fluted Cylinder Antique

Exc.	Fine	V.G.	Good	Fair	Poor
800	400	340	280	80	50

Round Barrel—Short Fluted Cylinder Antique

Exc.	Fine	V.G.	Good	Fair	Poor
750	350	270	200	80	50

Round Barrel—Long Fluted Cylinder Antique

Exc.	Fine	V.G.	Good	Fair	Poor
750	450	300	150	80	50

Marlin XX Standard 1873 Pocket Revolver

Similar in appearance to XXX Standard 1872. Chambered for .22 Long rimfire and marked "XX Standard 1873". There are three basic variations: early octagonal barrel with non-fluted cylinder; round barrel with non-fluted cylinder; round barrel with fluted cylinder. Function and features same as described for "XXX Standard 1872". Approximately 5,000 manufactured between 1873 and 1887.

Early Octagon Barrel Model Antique

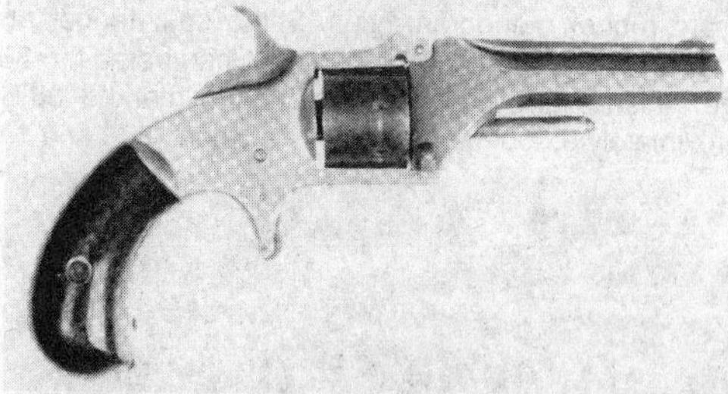

Courtesy Marlin Firearms Co.

Exc.	Fine	V.G.	Good	Fair	Poor
900	600	400	200	100	70

Round Barrel—Fluted Cylinder Antique

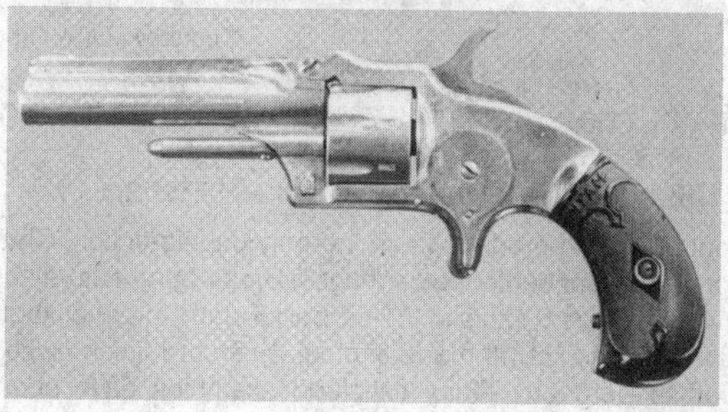

Courtesy Marlin Firearms Co.

Exc.	Fine	V.G.	Good	Fair	Poor
750	500	350	200	80	50

Round Barrel—Non-Fluted Cylinder Antique

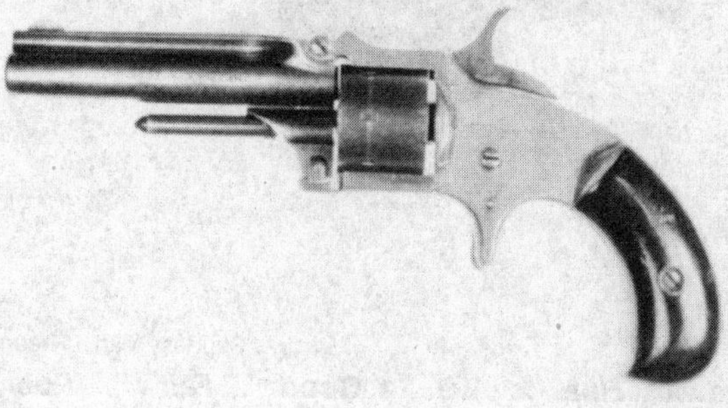

Exc.	Fine	V.G.	Good	Fair	Poor
880	650	520	400	100	70

Marlin No. 32 Standard 1875 Pocket Revolver Antique

Similar in appearance to "XXX Standard 1872". Chambered for .32 rimfire cartridge. 3" round barrel, with a rib. 5-shot cylinder fluted and in two different lengths to accommodate .32 Short or Long cartridge. Finish, function and most markings are same as on previous models, with exception of barrel top marking "No. 32 Standard 1875". Approximately 8,000 manufactured between 1875 and 1887.

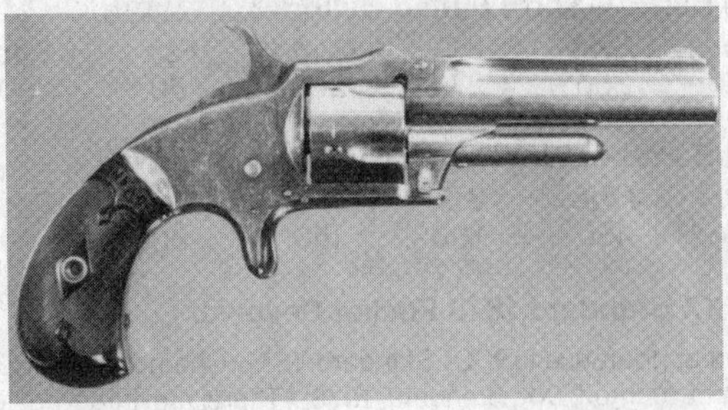

Courtesy Marlin Firearms Co.

Exc.	Fine	V.G.	Good	Fair	Poor
680	450	320	200	80	50

Marlin 38 Standard 1878 Pocket Revolver Antique

Different than its predecessors. Features a steel frame and flat bottom butt, with hard rubber monogram grips. Still a spur trigger and 3.25" ribbed round barrel that tipped up for loading. Chambered for .38 centerfire cartridge. Finish is full nickel plate. Top of barrel marked "38 Standard 1878". Approximately 9,000 manufactured between 1878 and 1887.

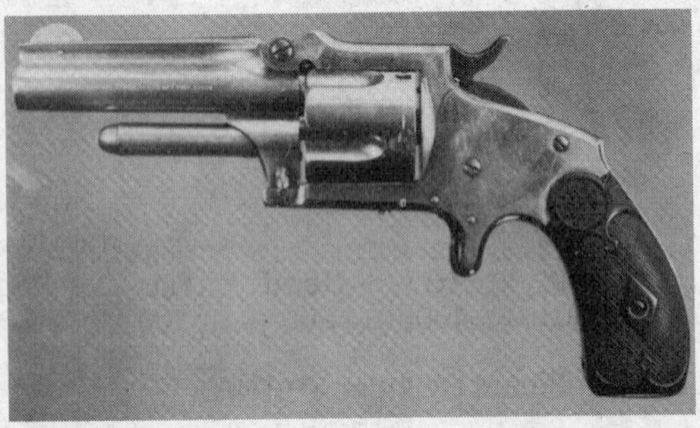

Courtesy Marlin Firearms Co.

Exc.	Fine	V.G.	Good	Fair	Poor
900	600	420	250	80	50

Marlin 1887 Double-Action Revolver Antique

Last handgun Marlin produced and the only double-action. Chambered for .32- or .38-caliber centerfire cartridges. Break-open auto-ejector type. Fluted cylinder holds 6 shots in .32-caliber; 5 shots in .38-caliber. Round ribbed 3.25" barrel. Frame made of steel. Standard finish nickel-plated, with blued triggerguard. Many full-blued examples have been noted. Round butt grips are hard rubber. Top of barrel marked "Marlin Firearms Co. New Haven Conn. U.S.A./Patented Aug. 9 1887". Approximately 15,000 manufactured between 1887 and 1899.

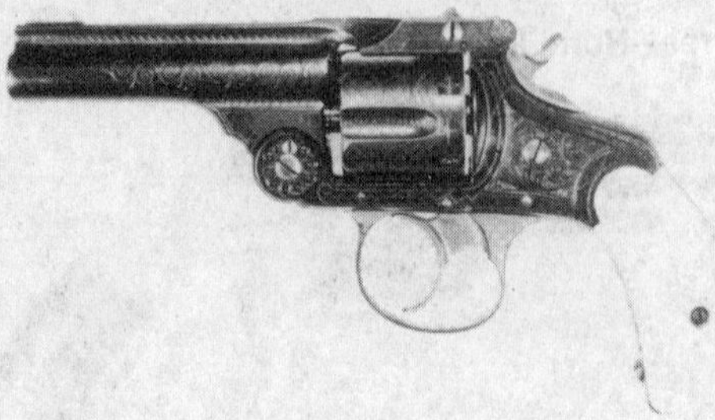

Courtesy Marlin Firearms Co.

Exc.	Fine	V.G.	Good	Fair	Poor
800	500	350	200	80	50

EARLY PRODUCTION MARLIN RIFLES

Antique

Model 1881 Lever-Action Rifle Antique

First Marlin lever-action rifle. Always been regarded as a high quality rifle. Capable of handling large calibers and well received by the shooting public. Chambered for .32-40, .38-55, .40-60, .45-70 and .45-85. The 24", 28" or 30" octagonal barrel is standard. Round barrels were offered and are scarce today. There is a tubular magazine beneath the barrel. Rear sight is buckhorn type, with a blade on front. Ejects its empty cartridges from top. Finish blued, with case colored hammer, lever and buttplate. Walnut stock is varnished. Approximately 20,000 manufactured between 1881 and 1892, but this is not easy to ascertain, as factory records on Marlin rifles are quite incomplete. Note: Add 200-300 percent premium for 1st Models prior to serial number 600; 15 percent premium for .45-70 caliber.

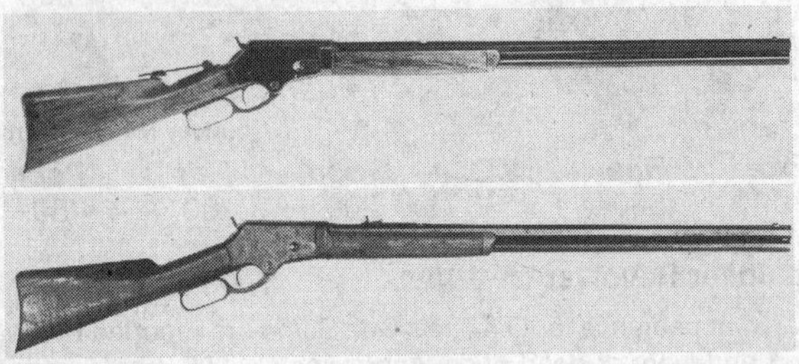

Exc.	Fine	V.G.	Good	Fair	Poor
4000	2250	1000	700	500	250

Lightweight Model Antique

Thinner frame, lever and barrel. Caliber .32-40 and .38-55. Barrels 24" and 28" only.

Exc.	Fine	V.G.	Good	Fair	Poor
2600	1750	1170	600	300	210

Model 1888 Lever-Action Rifle Antique

Chambered for .32-20, .38-40 and .44-40 cartridges. Shorter action was designed (chiefly by Lewis Hepburn) to handle pistol cartridges for which it was chambered. Standard barrel was octagonal, but round barrels were available as special-order items. Top ejecting action. Has buckhorn rear and blade front sight. Finish blued, with case colored hammer, lever and buttplate. Walnut stock varnished. Approximately 4,800 manufactured in 1888 and 1889. As with most of these fine old rifles, many special-order options were available that affect today's market value. Individual appraisal would be necessary for these special models, to ascertain both value and authenticity. Note: Add 40 percent premium for half octagon barrel; 20 percent premium for round barrel.

Exc.	Fine	V.G.	Good	Fair	Poor
3000	2500	1550	600	350	240

Model 1889 Lever-Action Rifle

Marlin's first side-eject solid-top rifle. Chambered for .25-20, .32-20, .38-40 and .44-40 cartridges. Features octagonal or round barrels in lengths from 24" to 32", lever latch and buckhorn rear and blade front sights. Finish blued, with case colored hammer, lever and buttplate. Plain walnut stock is varnished. Barrel stamped "Marlin Fire-Arms Co. New Haven Ct. U.S.A./Patented Oct.11 1887 April 2.1889". Many options were offered. Again one must urge individual appraisal on such variations. Values fluctuate greatly due to some seemingly insignificant variation. Approximately 55,000 manufactured between 1889 and 1899.

Production Model (Antique)

24" barrel.

Exc.	Fine	V.G.	Good	Fair	Poor
1700	1000	720	450	150	100

Short Carbine (Antique)

15" barrel. 327 produced.

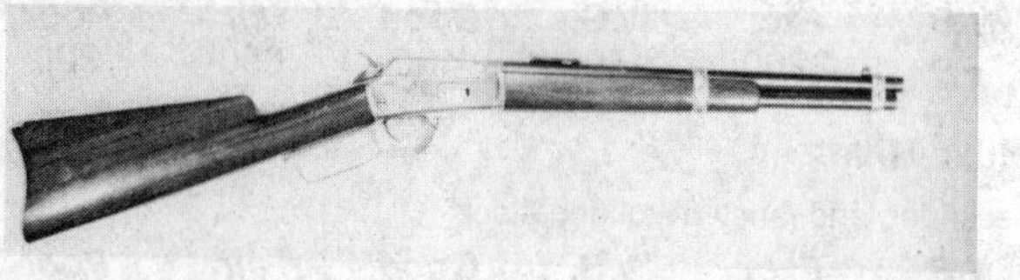

Courtesy Marlin Firearms Co.

Exc.	Fine	V.G.	Good	Fair	Poor
5000	2250	1620	1000	500	350

Carbine 20" Barrel and Saddle Ring on Left Side of Receiver (Antique)

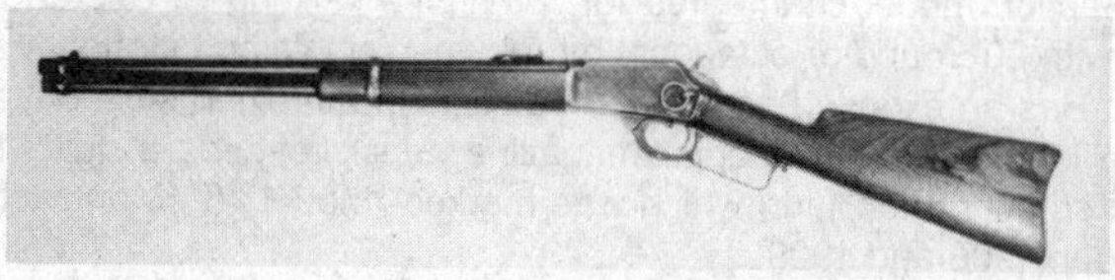

Courtesy Marlin Firearms Co.

Exc.	Fine	V.G.	Good	Fair	Poor
2250	1250	870	500	250	170

Musket (Antique)

30" barrel, with full-length stock. 68 made in .44-40.

Exc.	Fine	V.G.	Good	Fair	Poor
6900	3800	2770	1750	750	520

Model 1891 Lever-Action Rifle

Marlin's first rifle designed to fire .22 rimfire; first repeating rifle to accept .22 Short, Long and LR cartridges interchangeably. Chambered for .32 rimfire and centerfire. The 24" octagonal barrel is standard, with buckhorn rear and blade front sights. Finish blued, with case colored hammer, lever and buttplate. Stock is plain walnut. First variation marked "Marlin Fire-Arms Co. New Haven, Ct. U.S.A./Pat'd Nov.19.1878. April 2.1889. Aug.12 1890" on barrel, with solid-topped frame marked "Marlin Safety". Second variation marked the same with "March 1,1892" added. Approximately 18,650 manufactured between 1891 and 1897.

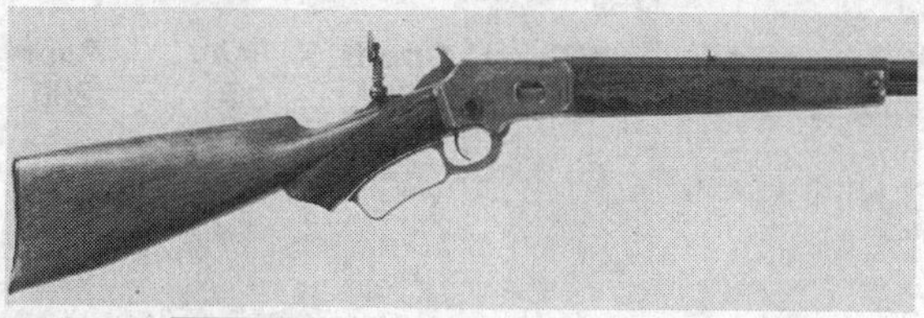

1st Variation (Antique)

.22 rimfire only. Side loading. Approximately 5,000 made.

Exc.	Fine	V.G.	Good	Fair	Poor
2500	1000	770	550	300	210

2nd Variation (Antique)

.22 and .32 rimfire. .32 centerfire. Tube loading Model 1891. Later model tangs (3rd variation). Note: Add 20 percent for .22 rifle with "1891" stamped on tang. Deduct 50 percent for .32-caliber.

Exc.	Fine	V.G.	Good	Fair	Poor
1500	500	400	300	150	100

Model 1892 Lever-Action Rifle

Basically an improved version of Model 1891. Similar to second variation of 1891. Only notable exceptions were tang marking "Model 1892" and "Model 92" on later models. .22 rimfire was scarce in Model 1892. Approximately 45,000 manufactured between 1895 and 1916. There were many options. These special-order guns must be individually appraised to ascertain value and authenticity.

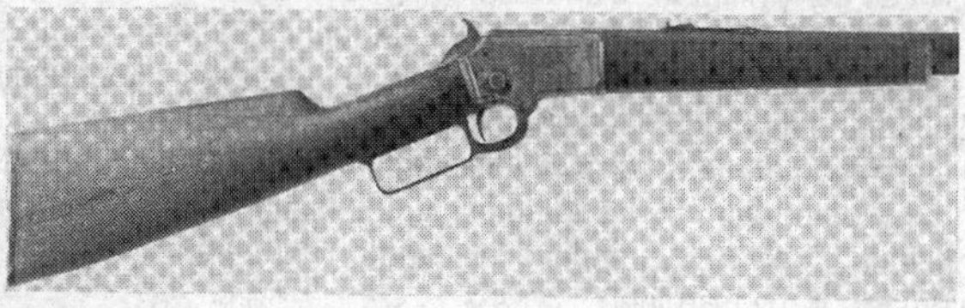

.22 Rimfire

Note: Add 20 percent for antique (pre-1898).

NIB	Exc.	V.G.	Good	Fair	Poor
—	—	1350	400	250	150

.32 Rimfire and Centerfire

NIB	Exc.	V.G.	Good	Fair	Poor
—	—	950	350	150	100

Model 1893 Lever-Action Rifle

First rifle Marlin designed for, then new, smokeless powder cartridges. Chambered for .25-36, .30-30, .32 Special, .32-40 and .38-55. Offered standard: round or octagonal barrel in lengths of 24" to 32"; buckhorn rear and blade front sights. Receiver, lever, hammer and buttplate are case colored. Rest is blued. Stock varnished walnut.

As with all early Marlins, many options were offered and when encountered, will drastically alter value of particular rifle. For this reason, we supply values for basic model and urge securing competent appraisal on non-standard specimens. Barrel on earlier guns marked "Marlin Fire-Arms Co. New Haven, Ct.U.S.A./ Patented Oct.11. 1887.April 2.1889. Aug.1.1893". In 1919, markings were changed to "The Marlin Firearms Corporation/ New Haven, Conn.U.S.A.Patented". Rifles manufactured after 1904 are marked "Special Smokeless Steel" on left side of barrel. Upper tang marked "Model 1893" on early guns; "Model 93" on later specimens. Approximately 900,000 manufactured between 1893 and 1935. Factory records are incomplete on Model 1893.

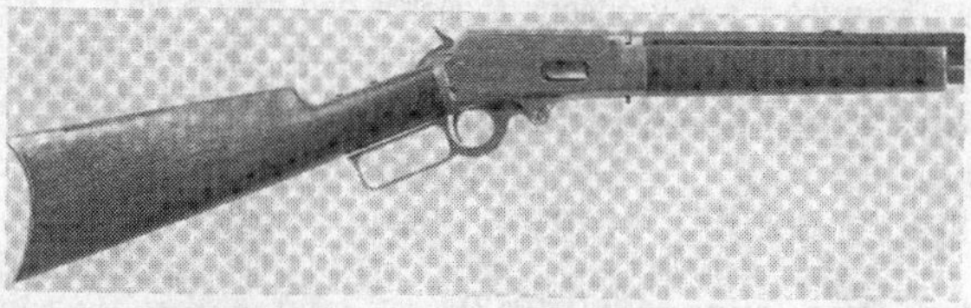

Antique Production (Pre-1898) (Antique)

Pre-1899, usually serial number under 175500

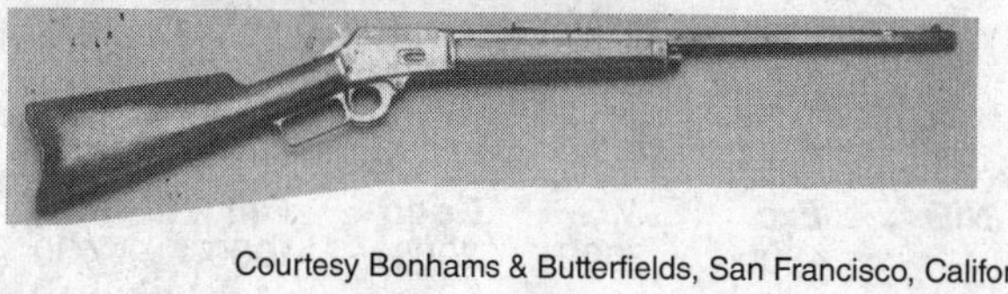

Courtesy Bonhams & Butterfields, San Francisco, California

Exc.	Fine	V.G.	Good	Fair	Poor
4000	2800	1500	1000	600	300

Modern Production 1899-1935

Note: Add 100 percent premium for musket. Deduct 50 percent for B model with blued receiver.

NIB	Exc.	V.G.	Good	Fair	Poor
—	2000	1100	550	350	220

Model 1894 Lever-Action Rifle (Antique)

Similar to Model 1893, with a shorter action. Chambered for .25-20, .32-20, .38-40 and .44-40. Offered standard: 24" to 32" round or octagonal barrels with full-length magazine tubes; buckhorn rear and blade front sights. Finish is case colored receiver, lever, hammer and buttplate. Rest is blued. Walnut stock varnished. First versions marked "Marlin Fire-Arms Co., New Haven, Ct.U.S.A./Patented Oct.11, 1887. April 2,1889". Top of frame marked "Marlin Safety" and model designation is not stamped on tang. These early rifles were chambered for .38-40 and .44-40 only. Later rifles added patent date "Aug. 1, 1893"; "Model 1894" was stamped on tang. On latest versions this was shortened to "Model 94". Approximately 250,000 manufactured between 1894 and 1935. This model was produced with a great many options. Individual appraisal should be secured when confronted with these features. Note: Add 100 percent premium for musket, 25 percent premium for saddle ring carbine, 200 percent premium for "Baby Carbine."

Antique Production (Pre-1898)

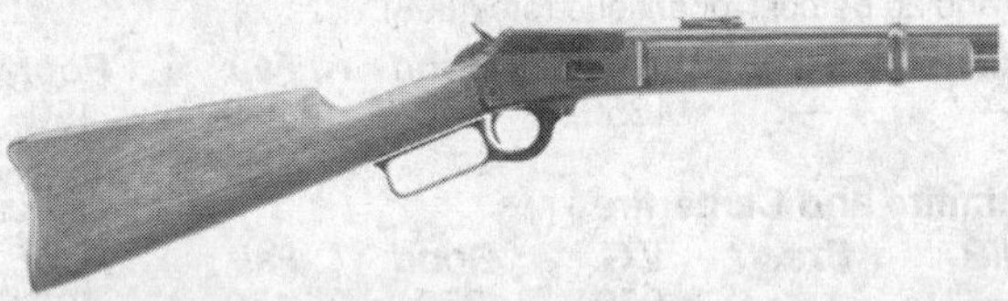

NIB	Exc.	V.G.	Good	Fair	Poor
—	3500	2500	1850	750	350

Moden Production 1899-1937 (Antique)

Note: Add 100 percent premium for musket; 25 percent premium saddle ring carbine; 30 percent premium "Baby" carbine. Usually serial number over 175500, and prior to replacement by the Model 36 in 1937.

Exc.	Fine	V.G.	Good	Fair	Poor
—	2000	1000	650	400	200

Model 1895 Lever-Action Rifle

A large rifle designed to fire larger hunting cartridges. Chambered for .33 W.C.F., .38-56, .40-65, .40-70, .40-83, .45-70 and .45-90. Came standard with: round or octagonal barrels from 26" to 32" in length; bull-length magazine tube; buckhorn rear and blade front sights. Finish is case colored receiver, lever and hammer. Rest is blued. Varnished walnut stock. Barrel markings are same as Model 1894. Top tang marked "Model 1895". After 1896 "Special Smokeless Steel" was stamped on barrel. There were many options available and they have a big effect on value. Approximately 18,000 manufactured between 1895 and 1917.

Antique Production (Pre-1898) (Antique)

Exc.	Fine	V.G.	Good	Fair	Poor
4500	3000	1720	1250	400	280

Modern Production (1899-1917)

Note: Add 75 to 100 percent for rare carbine variations.

NIB	Exc.	V.G.	Good	Fair	Poor
—	4300	3600	2000	1000	400

Model 1897 Lever-Action Rifle

Improved version of Model 1892. Chambered for .22 rimfire only. Came standard with: 24", 26" or 28" round, octagonal or part-round, part-octagonal barrel; buckhorn rear and blade front sights; all were manufactured as take-down rifles. Case colored receiver, lever and hammer. Rest is blued. Walnut stock varnished. Approximately 125,000 manufactured between 1897 and 1917. In 1922, production began with designation changed to "Model 39" which is produced to this day. There were options offered with this rifle that have great effect on value. Take this into consideration and seek qualified appraisal.

Standard Production Rifle

Note: Add 40 percent for first year production antique.

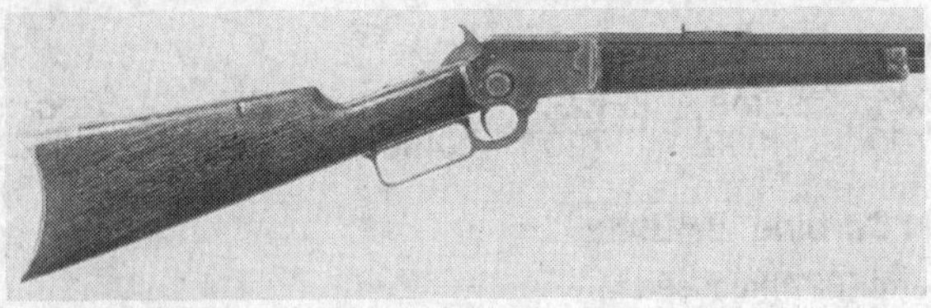

NIB	Exc.	V.G.	Good	Fair	Poor
—	2200	1500	1100	650	200

Deluxe Rifle

Checkering and fancy pistol grip stock.

NIB	Exc.	V.G.	Good	Fair	Poor
—	3000	2000	1500	850	300

POST 1900 PRODUCTION MARLIN RIFLES

Model 18

Slide-action model chambered for .22 rimfire cartridges. Offered standard with 20" round or octagonal barrel, open sights and straight walnut stock. Has an exposed hammer. Blued finish, with blued steel buttplate. There is a half-length tubular magazine. Stock features a quick take-down screw on top tang which was marked "Model 18". Manufactured between 1906 and 1909.

Courtesy Marlin Firearms Co.

NIB	Exc.	V.G.	Good	Fair	Poor
1500	1200	800	650	300	200

Model 20

Slide-action chambered for .22 rimfire cartridges. Offered standard with 24" octagonal barrel and open sight, with an exposed hammer. Only made as a "Takedown" receiver model. Blued, with straight walnut stock. Manufactured between 1907 and 1922.

NIB	Exc.	V.G.	Good	Fair	Poor
1500	1200	800	650	300	200

Model 25

Slide-action chambered for .22 Short only. Not a commercial success. Standard: 23" round or octagonal barrel; open sights. Called a take-down model, but only stock is removable—receiver does not separate. Has an exposed hammer, tubular magazine and straight walnut stock. Finish is blued. Manufactured in 1909 and 1910.

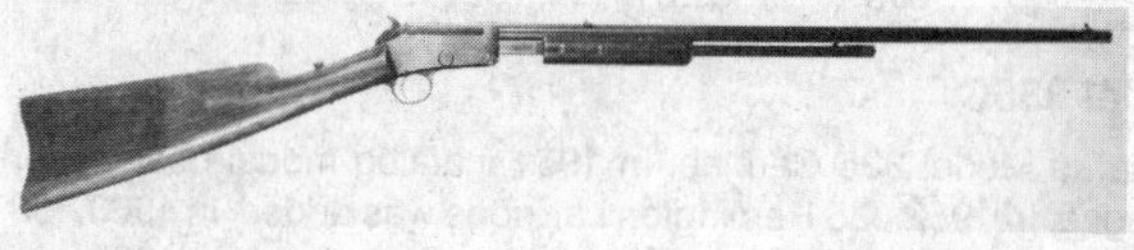

Courtesy Marlin Firearms Co.

NIB	Exc.	V.G.	Good	Fair	Poor
1600	1300	850	700	350	200

Model 27

Centerfire slide-action rifle. Chambered for .25-20 and .32-20 cartridges, also .25-caliber rimfire cartridge. Features 24" octagonal barrel, with two-thirds-length magazine tube that holds 7 shots. Has open sights, blued finish and straight walnut stock with crescent buttplate. Manufactured from 1910 to 1916. Note: Deduct 20 percent chambered for .25 rimfire.

NIB	Exc.	V.G.	Good	Fair	Poor
1500	1200	850	500	350	200

Model 27S

Similar to Model 27, with a sliding button on right side of receiver that permitted gun to be opened while a cartridge was in the chamber. Offered with a round (1913) or octagonal 24" barrel. The .25 rimfire cartridge was added in 1913 to those already available. Introduced in 1910 and manufactured until 1932. Note: Deduct 20 percent chambered for .25 rimfire.

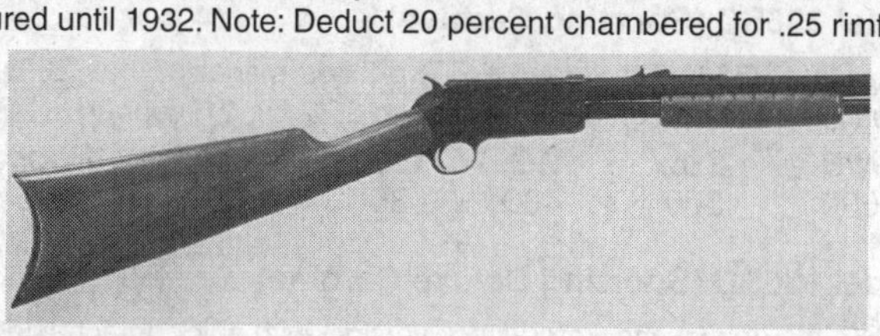

NIB	Exc.	V.G.	Good	Fair	Poor
1500	1200	850	500	350	200

Model 29

Slide action model identical to Model 20, with 23" round barrel and smooth walnut forend instead of a grooved one as found on Model 20. Manufactured between 1913 and 1916. Note: Deduct 20 percent chambered for .25 rimfire.

Courtesy Marlin Firearms Co.

NIB	Exc.	V.G.	Good	Fair	Poor
1500	1200	800	650	300	200

Model 32

First of hammerless slide-action rifles. Chambered for .22 rimfire. Has 24" octagonal barrel and half-length magazine tube. A take-down rifle, with adjustable sights and features "Ballard" rifling. Blued, with a pistol grip walnut stock. Advent of WWI and need for Marlin to produce military arms, cut short production of this model. Manufactured in 1914 and 1915 only.

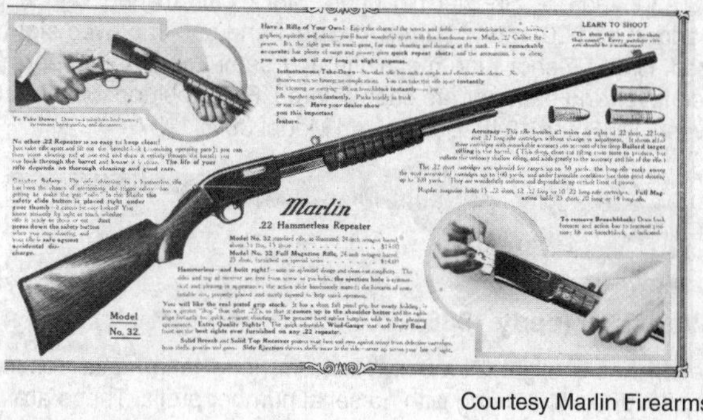

Courtesy Marlin Firearms Co.

NIB	Exc.	V.G.	Good	Fair	Poor
1800	1500	1200	850	400	300

Model 37

Slide-action model same as Model 29, with 24" round barrel and full-length magazine tube. Manufactured between 1913 and 1916.

Courtesy Marlin Firearms Co.

NIB	Exc.	V.G.	Good	Fair	Poor
1200	1000	700	600	300	200

Model 38

Hammerless slide-action introduced after end of WWI to replace Model 32. Similar in appearance. Features Rocky Mountain adjustable rear and ivory bead front sight instead of distinctive round Swebilius sight on Model 32. Manufactured between 1920 and 1930.

NIB	Exc.	V.G.	Good	Fair	Poor
1300	1100	850	650	300	200

Model 40

Slide-action identical to Model 27S centerfire. Barrel marked "Marlin-Rockwell". Top tang stamped "Marlin/Mod. 40". Rare, not many marked in this manner have been noted.

NIB	Exc.	V.G.	Good	Fair	Poor
1600	1300	850	500	350	200

Model 47

Similar to Model 20, with 23" round barrel and improved magazine tube. Has case colored receiver and checkered buttstock. Not offered for sale nor was it listed in Marlin's catalog, but offered free of charge to anyone purchasing four shares of Marlin stock for $100. One other fact about this model: it was the first Marlin to be case colored with new cyanide method, which created a tiger-striped pattern that is peculiar to Model 47.

NIB	Exc.	V.G.	Good	Fair	Poor
—	1000	800	600	300	150

Model 1936, Rifle or Carbine

Lever-action model is a direct descendant of Model 1893. Chambered for .30-30 and .32 Special cartridge. Stock streamlined with a pistol grip added and 20" round barrel. A barrel band and improved sights are utilized. Has a 7-shot tube magazine and semi-beavertail forearm. Receiver, lever and hammer are case colored. Rest is blued. Manufactured between 1936 and 1948. Designated Model 36 in 1937.

1st Variation (early 1936)

Variation has a slight "fish-belly" forearm, long tang, case colored receiver, lever and hammer, with no serial number prefix. These are rare.

NIB	*Exc.*	*V.G.*	*Good*	*Fair*	*Poor*
—	1200	850	400	180	120

2nd Variation (late 1936-1947)

Variation has thicker forearm, short tang and "B" serial number prefix.

NIB	*Exc.*	*V.G.*	*Good*	*Fair*	*Poor*
—	1000	650	300	150	100

Model 36 Rifle or Carbine (1937-1948)

First and Second variations of this lever-action both have case colored receiver and "C" serial number prefix. Second variation tapped for receiver sight.

NIB	*Exc.*	*V.G.*	*Good*	*Fair*	*Poor*
—	800	600	400	200	120

1st & 2nd Variations

NIB	*Exc.*	*V.G.*	*Good*	*Fair*	*Poor*
—	800	600	400	200	120

3rd Variation—Blued Receiver

NIB	*Exc.*	*V.G.*	*Good*	*Fair*	*Poor*
—	600	400	300	180	100

Model 36 Sporting Carbine

Similar to 1936 Carbine, with 20" barrel. Features two-thirds-length magazine tube and holds 6 shots instead of 7. Front sight is a ramp sight with hood.

NIB	*Exc.*	*V.G.*	*Good*	*Fair*	*Poor*
—	800	600	400	200	120

Model 36A-DL Rifle

Lever-action model similar to Model 36A, with deluxe checkered stock. Features sight swivels. Furnished with leather sling.

NIB	*Exc.*	*V.G.*	*Good*	*Fair*	*Poor*
1000	800	650	400	220	150

RECENT PRODUCTION

Recent Production – Variations of Model 336 branded "Model 1894" in calibers such as .44 Magnum, .45 Colt, .32 Magnum, etc. – See listings following Model 336 in the POST 1900 PRODUCTION MARLIN RIFLES section.

MODEL 336

Information on Model 336 provided by the late Doug Murray, author and publisher of *The 336* (1983). Note: Beginning in 1980s, Marlin used "S" suffix on its model numbers (e.g., 336CS, 1895S, etc.) to designate models with new crossbolt safety. This suffix has now been dropped in most cases, even though safety remains.

Model 336 Carbine (R.C. Regular Carbine)

Introduced in 1948. Improved version of Model 36. Features a new-type round bolt chrome-plated, with improved extractor and re-designed cartridge carrier that improved feeding. Chambered for .30-30 and .32 Special cartridges. Has 20" tapered round barrel, with Ballard-type rifling. Finish blued, with receiver top matted to reduce reflections. Pistol grip stock and semi-beavertail forend are of American walnut. Features Rocky Mountain-style rear and bead front sights. Hammer is lowered to facilitate scope mounting.

NIB	*Exc.*	*V.G.*	*Good*	*Fair*	*Poor*
—	480	320	180	120	100

Model 336C

Same as Model 336 Carbine. In 1951, catalog model designation was changed. In 1952, .35 Remington cartridge was added. In 1963, .32 Special was discontinued. This variation was discontinued in 1983.

NIB	*Exc.*	*V.G.*	*Good*	*Fair*	*Poor*
—	480	320	180	120	100

Model 336A

Similar to 336C, with 24" barrel and steel forend tip instead of a barrel band. Magazine tube is two-thirds-length and holds 6 shots. Introduced in 1948 and built until 1962. Re-introduced in 1973; discontinued in 1980. In 1950, .35 Rem. was added. In 1960, .32 Special was discontinued.

NIB	*Exc.*	*V.G.*	*Good*	*Fair*	*Poor*
—	480	320	180	120	100

Model 336ADL

Differs from Model 336A. Has deluxe wood checkered stock and forend, quick detachable swivels, better grade finish and a sling.

NIB	*Exc.*	*V.G.*	*Good*	*Fair*	*Poor*
—	650	500	300	150	120

Model 336SC (Sporting Carbine)

Basically a 336A, with forend tip. Two-thirds magazine has 20" barrel instead of 24" found on 336A. Note: Add 25% for .219 Zipper.

NIB	*Exc.*	*V.G.*	*Good*	*Fair*	*Poor*
600	500	400	350	250	150

Model 336SD (Sporting Deluxe Carbine)

336SC in a deluxe checkered stock version, with quick detachable swivels. Supplied with a sling. Note: Scarce model as only 4,392 were built.

NIB	*Exc.*	*V.G.*	*Good*	*Fair*	*Poor*
—	1000	750	400	200	120

Model 336 MicroGroove Zipper

Advertised as a fast-handling lever-action carbine. Chambered for .219 Zipper cartridges flat trajectory, varmint-type round. Has 20" heavy barrel, which was the feature that doomed it to failure as this was too short to coax maximum performance and accuracy from cartridge. "MicroGroove" rifling that was used did not yield long barrel life; model survived from 1955 through 1959, when it was discontinued. Externally similar to 336SC. Note: First few thousand Zippers were made in standard weight barrels, not heavyweight. These are scarce and found in "M" prefix code number. Add 100 percent.

NIB	*Exc.*	*V.G.*	*Good*	*Fair*	*Poor*
1600	1000	800	600	300	150

Model 336T (Texan)

Straight-stock version of 336C. Chambered for .30-30 cartridge, with 20" barrel. Produced in .35 Rem. from 1953 to 1964; .44 Magnum from 1965 to 1967. Manufactured from 1953-1983.

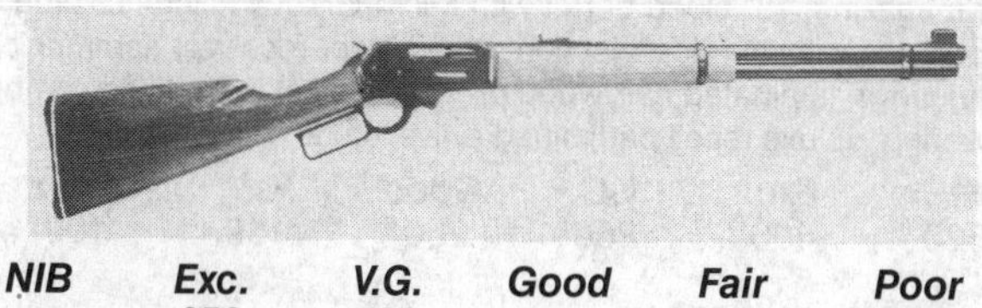

NIB	Exc.	V.G.	Good	Fair	Poor
—	650	480	400	250	180

Model 336DT

Deluxe-stock version of "Texan", with map of Texas and a longhorn carved on butt. Manufactured between 1962 and 1964. Calibers: .30-30 and .35 Rem.

NIB	Exc.	V.G.	Good	Fair	Poor
—	700	550	420	280	180

Model 336 "Marauder"

Simply a 336T, with 16.25 barrel and slimmer forend. Chambered for .30-30 or .35 Rem. cartridges. Has a gold trigger. Drilled and tapped for both scope mounts and receiver sights. Manufactured in 1963 and 1964.

NIB	Exc.	V.G.	Good	Fair	Poor
—	750	680	550	300	150

Model 336 .44 Magnum

This is the 336 "Marauder", with 20" MicroGroove barrel chambered for .44 Magnum cartridge. Holds 10 shots. Introduced in 1963. Not very successful, because of feeding difficulties.

NIB	Exc.	V.G.	Good	Fair	Poor
—	600	450	300	150	100

Model 336 "Centennial"

In 1970, a 100th Year Medallion was embedded into the buttstock of 336 Carbines, 336 Texan and 444 Rifle.

NIB	Exc.	V.G.	Good	Fair	Poor
—	620	500	380	250	150

1970 100th Year Commemorative Matched Pair

Deluxe octagonal barreled .30-30, with engraved receiver and deluxe wood with an inlaid medallion, accompanied by a matching Model 39 .22 rimfire rifle. They are numbered the same and furnished in a deluxe luggage case. There were 1,000 sets manufactured in 1970. These are commemoratives. It should be noted that collectors usually will only show interest if they are new and unfired in original packaging. All accessories and brochures should be included for them to be worth top dollar. Once a commemorative has been used, it has no more value than as a shooter.

NIB	Exc.	V.G.	Good	Fair	Poor
2250	1750	1200	750	500	400

Model 336 "Zane Grey Century"

Introduced in 1972, 100th Year Anniversary birth of Zane Grey, famous Western author. Has 22 octagonal barrel chambered for .30-30. Stock is high grade walnut. Features brass buttplate and pistol grip cap. Zane Grey medallion inlaid into receiver. Manufactured 10,000 in 1972. This is a commemorative rifle and must be new in box to generate top collector appeal.

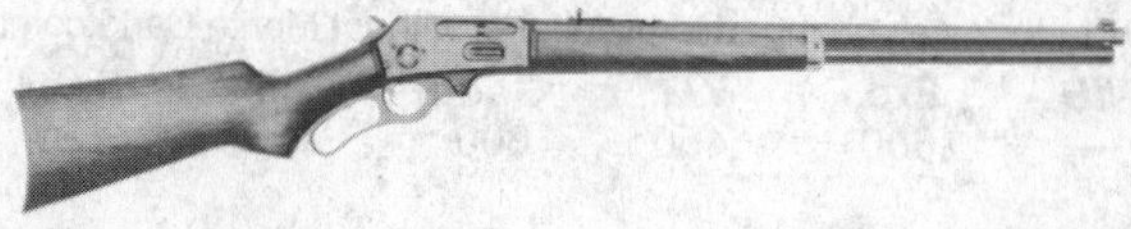

NIB	Exc.	V.G.	Good	Fair	Poor
600	420	280	200	150	100

Model 336 Octagon

Introduced to utilize octagonal barrel making equipment that was on hand from manufacture of commemorative's. Essentially a 336T, with 22" tapered octagonal barrel chambered for .30-30 only. Features full-length magazine tube, slim forend with steel cap and classic-style hard rubber buttplate. Walnut stock is straight and lever square. Finish, including trigger, blued. Made in 1973 only.

NIB	Exc.	V.G.	Good	Fair	Poor
720	600	500	320	180	150

Model 336ER (Extra Range)

Introduced in 1983. Advertised as being chambered for .307 and .356 Winchester cartridges. .307 was never produced. .356 Winchester was supposed to add new capabilities to this classic rifle, but it never caught on with the shooting public. Discontinued in 1986 after only 2,441 Model ERs were manufactured. Has 20" barrel and 5-shot tube magazine.

NIB	Exc.	V.G.	Good	Fair	Poor
—	820	550	300	250	150

Model 336C

Current carbine model of this line. Has a hammer-block safety. Chambered for .30-30, .35 Remington and until 1988, .375 Winchester. Barrel 20" and magazine tube holds 6 shots. Pistol grip stock and semi-beavertail forearm are American walnut. Has been manufactured since 1984. The 1983 model was known as 336C. Had no hammer-block safety. Weight about 7 lbs.

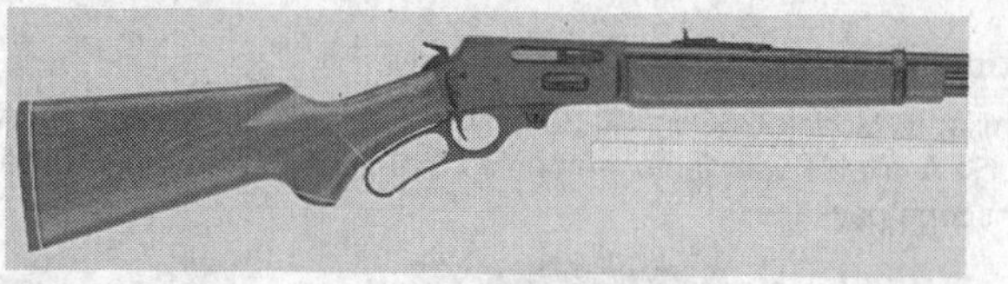

NIB	Exc.	V.G.	Good	Fair	Poor
480	350	220	200	180	150

Model 336SS

Similar to Model 336C in .30-30 only. Stainless steel barrel and receiver.

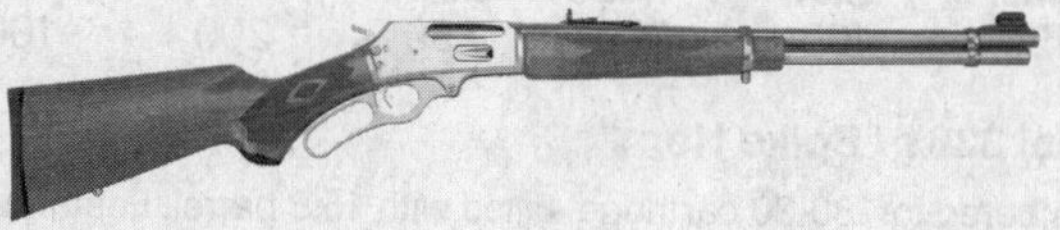

NIB	Exc.	V.G.	Good	Fair	Poor
520	400	250	200	150	100

Model 336LTS

Latest version of old "Marauder" carbine. Dubbed LTS or "Lightweight" instead of Marauder, as it was feared the latter designation would be inappropriate in today's society. Features 16.5" barrel, with full-length tube magazine that holds 5 shots. Walnut stock has straight-grip. Barrel band on forearm. Butt has rubber rifle pad. Introduced in 1988. Discontinued.

NIB	Exc.	V.G.	Good	Fair	Poor
680	450	300	250	200	150

Model 336 Cowboy

Similar to Model 336CS. Available in both .30-30 and .38-55 calibers. Fitted with 24" tapered octagon barrel. Rear sight is Marble buckhorn. Tubular magazine holds 6 rounds. Straight-grip walnut stock has hard rubber buttplate. Weight about 7.5 lbs. First introduced in 1999.

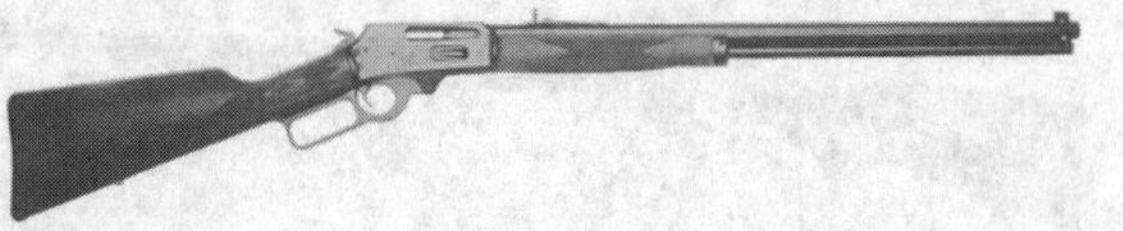

NIB	Exc.	V.G.	Good	Fair	Poor
880	650	520	320	180	150

Model 336M

Introduced in 2000. Chambered for .30-30 cartridge. Features stainless steel receiver and barrel; all other parts are nickel plated. Barrel length 20". Magazine capacity 6 rounds. Checkered walnut stock has Mar-Shield finish. Rubber buttpad. Weight about 7 lbs. Marlin's first stainless steel rifle.

NIB	Exc.	V.G.	Good	Fair	Poor
680	550	420	280	180	120

Model 336CC

Chambered for .30-30 cartridge. Fitted with 20" barrel. Features Mossy Oak Break-Up camo finish. Adjustable rear sight. Weight about 7 lbs. Introduced in 2001.

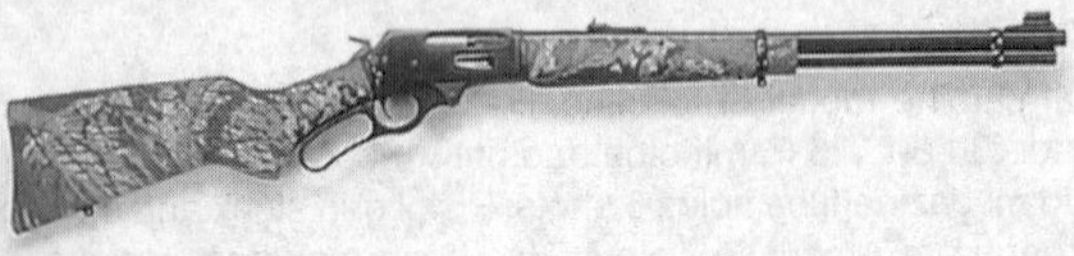

NIB	Exc.	V.G.	Good	Fair	Poor
500	390	320	250	200	100

Model 336W

Similar to Model 336C in .30-30 only. Gold-plated trigger and hardwood stock. Available with factory-mounted 3x9 scope. Note: Add 10 percent for scope package.

NIB	Exc.	V.G.	Good	Fair	Poor
450	400	320	250	200	100

Model 336Y "Spike Horn"

Chambered for .30-30 cartridge. Fitted with 16.5 barrel. Features checkered walnut stock with pistol grip. Magazine capacity 5 rounds. Adjustable rear sight. Weight about 6.5 lbs. Introduced in 2003.

NIB	Exc.	V.G.	Good	Fair	Poor
580	420	300	200	150	100

Model 336XLR

Lever-action chambered in .30-30 or .35 Remington, with 5-shot tubular magazine, 24" stainless steel barrel, along with stainless steel receiver, trigger, triggerguard plate, magazine tube, loading gate and lever. Full pistol grip, swivel studs and Ballard-type rifling precision fluted bolt. Features solid top receiver with side-ejection, adjustable folding semi-buckhorn rear sight, ramp front sight, tapped for scope mount. Designed for Hornady LEVERevolution cartridges. Introduced 2006.

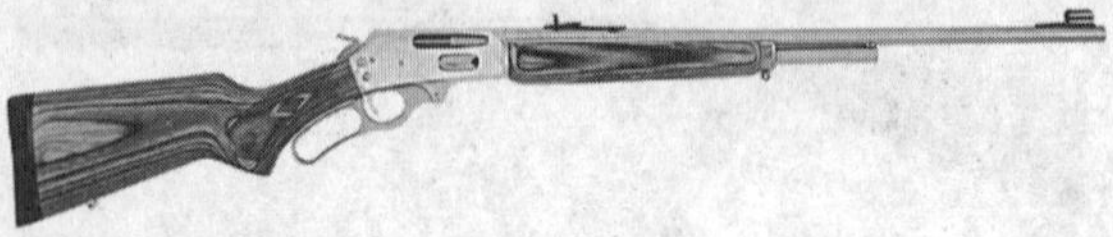

NIB	Exc.	V.G.	Good	Fair	Poor
720	600	480	350	220	180

Model 336BL

Lever-action chambered for .30-30. Features include 6-shot full length tubular magazine; 18" blued barrel with Micro-Groove rifling (12 grooves); big-loop finger lever; side ejection; blued steel receiver; hammer block safety; brown laminated hardwood pistol grip stock with fluted comb; cut checkering; deluxe recoil pad; blued swivel studs.

NIB	Exc.	V.G.	Good	Fair	Poor
520	400	250	200	150	100

Ruger-Made Model 336

Caliber: .30-30 Win., .35 Rem. Barrel: 20.25" round blued. Stock: Walnut pistol-grip style with checkering. Features: New 336 model launch under Ruger ownership. Blued metalwork with forward barrel band. Iron sights with a hooded front. Crossbolt safety. Gold-plated trigger. Low-profile rubber buttpad. Side loading gate. Sling studs. Red and white bullseye stock insert denotes Ruger production Marlins.

NIB	Exc.	V.G.	Good	Fair	Poor
1120	—	—	—	—	—

Model 30AS

Similar to 336CS. Stock made of walnut-finished hardwood instead of genuine American walnut. Chambered for .30-30 only.

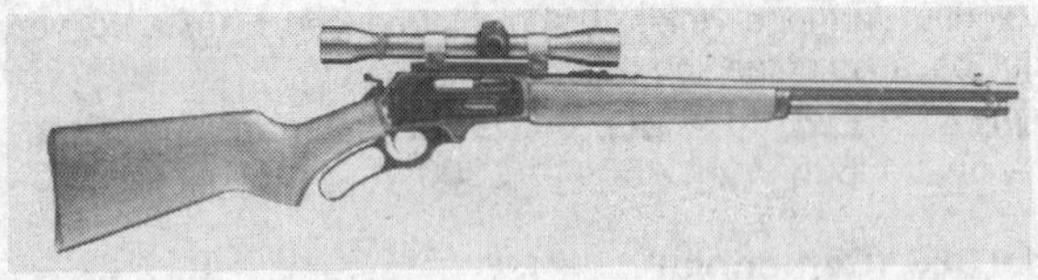

Marlin 30AS with scope

NIB	Exc.	V.G.	Good	Fair	Poor
400	280	200	180	120	100

Model 375

Introduced in 1980. Has 20" MicroGroove barrel. Chambered for .375 Winchester cartridge. Its appearance much the same as Model 336, with walnut pistol stock and steel forend tip. Discontinued in 1983 after 16,315 manufactured.

NIB	Exc.	V.G.	Good	Fair	Poor
620	500	380	250	180	100

MODEL 444

Model 444

Introduced in 1965. Chambered for .444 Marlin. Essentially a Model 336 action modified to accept larger cartridge. Has 24" round barrel that was cut back to 22" in 1971. Holds 5 shots total. When introduced, featured straight-grip Monte Carlo stock and semi-beavertail forend with barrel band. Another band holds the two-thirds-length magazine tube in place. In 1971 stock was changed to pistol grip, without Monte Carlo comb.

NIB	Exc.	V.G.	Good	Fair	Poor
—	600	450	300	180	120

Model 444S

Introduced in 1972. Essentially, later 444 with steel forend tip instead of barrel bands.

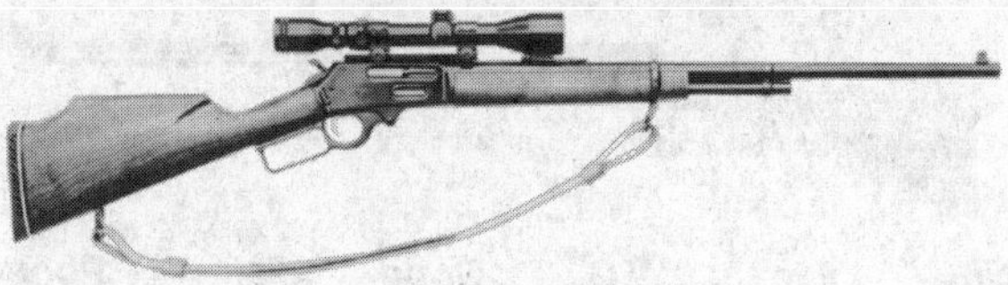

NIB	Exc.	V.G.	Good	Fair	Poor
—	500	350	180	150	120

Model 444SS

In 1984, company added a crossbolt hammer-block safety to 444S and re-designated it 444SS.

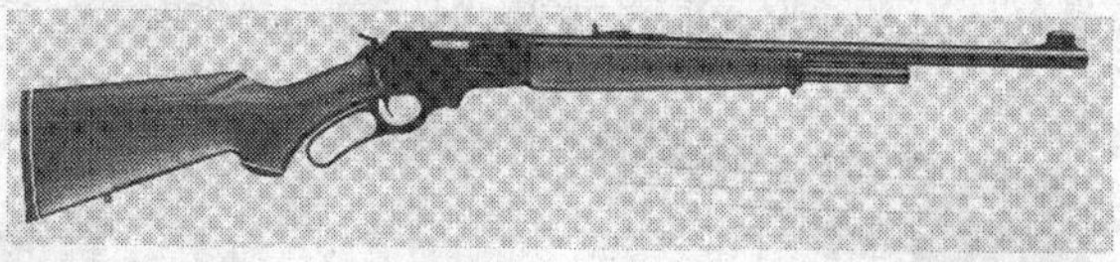

NIB	Exc.	V.G.	Good	Fair	Poor
700	600	500	350	150	120

Model 444P Outfitter

Introduced in 1999. Chambered for .444 Marlin cartridge. Fitted with 18.5" ported barrel. Tubular magazine capacity 5 rounds. Walnut stock, with straight-grip. Ventilated recoil pad standard. Weight about 6.75 lbs. Discontinued 2002.

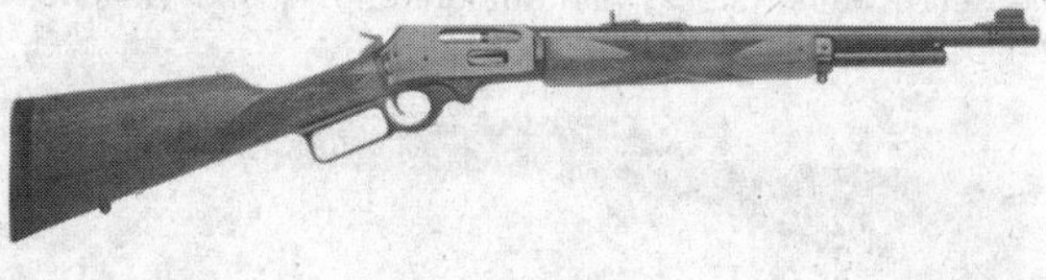

NIB	Exc.	V.G.	Good	Fair	Poor
720	600	420	340	280	200

Model 444XLR

Similar to Model 1895XLR. Chambered in .444 Marlin. Introduced 2006.

NIB	Exc.	V.G.	Good	Fair	Poor
620	500	380	250	180	100

1895 444 150th Anniversary

Caliber: .444 Marlin. Capacity: 6. Barrel: 24 in., half-octagon/half-round, blued. Stock: C-grade American black walnut, pistol grip. Sights: Skinner ladder. Weight: 7 lbs. Features: Engraved receiver with gold inlay, commemorative box, historical checkering.

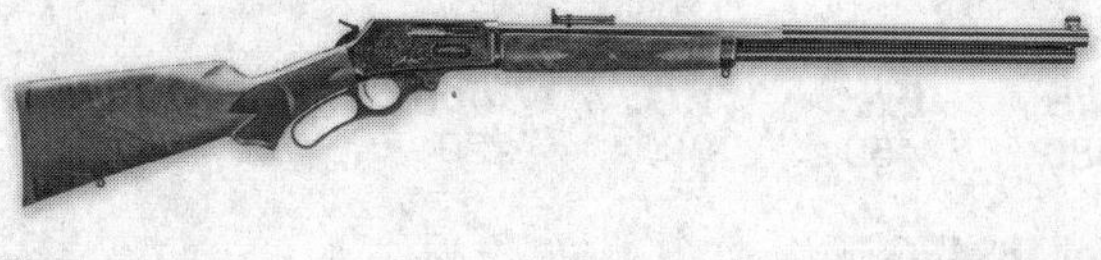

NIB	Exc.	V.G.	Good	Fair	Poor
1800	—	—	—	—	—

MODEL 1894

Model 1894

Production of Model 336 in .44 Magnum was a frustrating experience. Action was simply too long for a short pistol case. In 1969, Marlin reintroduced Model 1894 chambered for .44 Magnum cartridge. Barrel 20". Full-length magazine tube holds 10 rounds. Features adjustable rear and ramp-type front sight. Finish blued, with matted receiver top. Walnut stock has straight-grip; forend a barrel band. From 1969 to 1971 there was a brass saddle ring.

NIB	Exc.	V.G.	Good	Fair	Poor
520	380	300	200	150	100

Model 1894 Octagon Barrel

Basically same as Model 1894, with 20" octagonal barrel. Steel forend tip instead of barrel band. Manufactured 2,957 in 1973 only.

NIB	Exc.	V.G.	Good	Fair	Poor
—	650	520	350	220	100

Model 1894 Sporter

Variation has 20" round barrel, half-length magazine tube that holds 6 shots. Hard rubber classic-style buttplate. Manufactured 1,398 in 1973 only.

NIB	Exc.	V.G.	Good	Fair	Poor
620	480	320	250	180	120

Model 1894P

Introduced in 2000. Chambered for .44 Magnum or .44 Special cartridges. Barrel length 16.25". Magazine capacity 8 rounds. Adjustable rear sight. Blued finish, with bead blasted receiver top. Drilled and tapped for scope mount. Weight about 5.75 lbs.

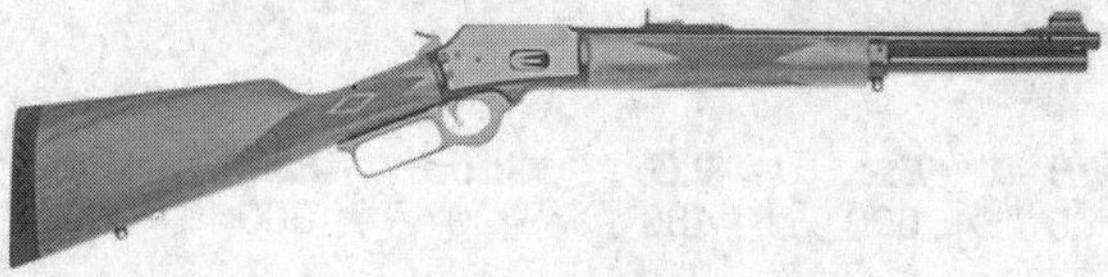

NIB	Exc.	V.G.	Good	Fair	Poor
600	450	380	300	150	100

Model 1894CS

Chambered for .38 Special and .357 Magnum cartridges. Features 18.5" round barrel, with full-length magazine tube and two barrel bands. Holds 9 shots. Walnut straight-grip stock. Manufactured between 1969 and 1984. In 1984, hammer-block crossbolt safety was added and model number was changed to 1894CS. All other specifications remained the same. Model is now known, again, as Model 1894C.

NIB	Exc.	V.G.	Good	Fair	Poor
—	520	380	280	120	100

Model 1894M

Similar to other 1894 rifles. Chambered for .22 Magnum cartridge. Features an outside loading tube magazine that holds 11 shots. Barrel 20". Steel forend tip instead of barrel band. Manufactured between 1983 and 1988. Only produced with crossbolt safety.

NIB	Exc.	V.G.	Good	Fair	Poor
—	550	450	320	280	150

Model 1894S

Introduced in 1984. Chambered for .41 Magnum and .44 Special/.44 Magnum cartridges. In 1988, .45 Colt chambering offered. Barrel 20". Straight-grip stock. Forend has steel cap. Currently produced as Model 1894. Features hammer-block safety.

NIB	Exc.	V.G.	Good	Fair	Poor
550	450	380	280	180	120

Model 1894CL (Classic)

Introduced in 1988. Same basic rifle chambered for old .25-20 and .32-20 cartridges. Also chambered for .218 Bee. Barrel 22". Half-length magazine tube holds 6 shots. Walnut stock has no white spacers. Has black buttplate. Discontinued in 1993. Note: Collector interest has been growing since it was discontinued.

NIB	Exc.	V.G.	Good	Fair	Poor
750	550	450	300	250	150

Model 1894CL (Classic) New

Re-introduced in 2005. Chambered for .32-20 cartridge. Barrel 22", with open sights. Tubular magazine capacity 6 rounds. Checkered straight-grip walnut stock. Weight about 6 lbs. Discontinued.

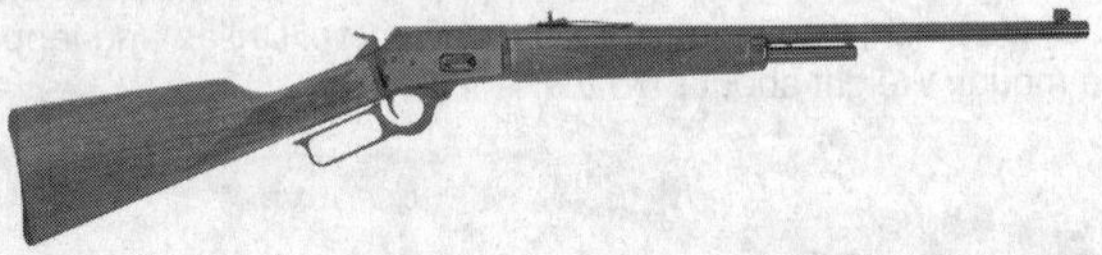

NIB	Exc.	V.G.	Good	Fair	Poor
700	600	480	400	300	120

Model 1894 Century Limited

Anniversary edition of Marlin Model 1894. Limited to 2,500 rifles. Chambered in .44-40 caliber. Frame engraved and case colored. Fitted with 24" octagon barrel with 10-round magazine tube. Stock semi-fancy walnut with straight-grip and cut checkering, with brass crescent buttplate.

NIB	Exc.	V.G.	Good	Fair	Poor
1500	1200	800	600	400	300

Model 1894 Century Limited Employee Edition

Same as above. Limited to 100 rifles. Has finer grade wood. The Marlin man on horse logo inlaid in gold on right side of receiver.

NIB	Exc.	V.G.	Good	Fair	Poor
4000	3500	3000	—	—	—

Model 1894 Cowboy

Introduced in 1996. Lever-action features 24" tapered octagon barrel, with 10-round tubular magazine. Chambered for .45 Long Colt, a popular cartridge for "Cowboy Action Shooting". Straight-grip checkered stock. Flued steel forearm cap. Weight about 7.5 lbs.

NIB	Exc.	V.G.	Good	Fair	Poor
750	600	450	300	220	150

Model 1894 Cowboy 32

As above chambered for .32 H&R Magnum cartridge. Introduced in 2004.

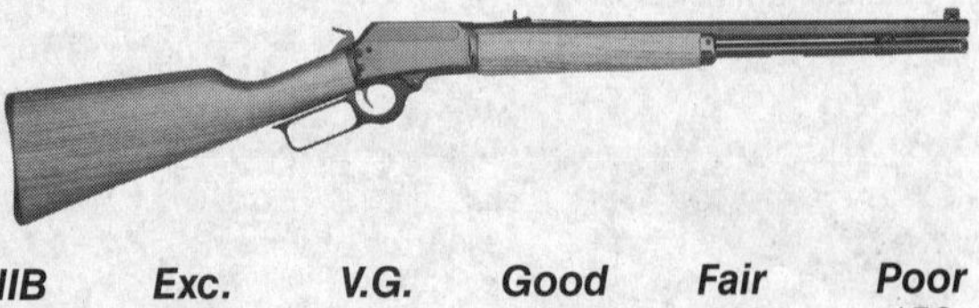

NIB	Exc.	V.G.	Good	Fair	Poor
750	600	450	300	220	150

Model 1894 Cowboy II

Introduced in 1997. Same as Model 1894 Cowboy chambered for several cartridges. Available in .44-40, .357 Magnum .38 Special and .44 Magnum/.44 Special. Made with 20" or 24" barrel. Sources report significant premium currently being charged for .357 Magnum chambering.

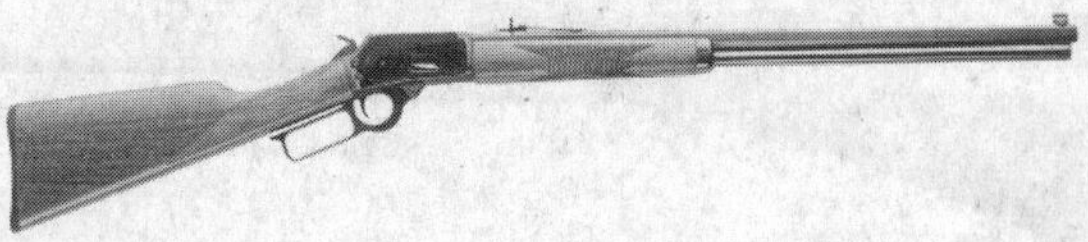

NIB	Exc.	V.G.	Good	Fair	Poor
650	520	300	220	150	100

Model 1894CP

Chambered for .375 Magnum cartridge. Fitted with 16.25" ported barrel. Tubular magazine holds 8 rounds. Checkered American black walnut stock. Adjustable semi-buckhorn rear sight. Receiver drilled and tapped for scope mount. Weight about 5.75 lbs. Introduced in 2001.

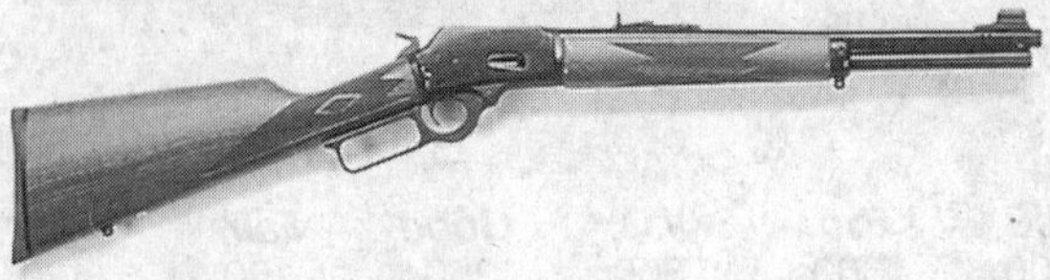

NIB	Exc.	V.G.	Good	Fair	Poor
630	580	450	300	220	100

Model 1894SS

Lever-action chambered for .44 Magnum and .44 Special cartridges. Barrel 20", with 10-round magazine. Stainless steel barrel and receiver. Checkered walnut stock, with straight-grip. Rubber buttpad. Weight about 6 lbs. Introduced in 2002.

NIB	Exc.	V.G.	Good	Fair	Poor
650	500	400	300	200	100

Model 1894PG

Introduced in 2003. Lever-action chambered for .44 Rem. Magnum cartridge. Fitted with 20" barrel. Checkered walnut stock, with pistol grip. Magazine capacity 10 rounds. Adjustable rear sight. Blued finish. Weight about 6.5 lbs.

NIB	Exc.	V.G.	Good	Fair	Poor
580	450	300	220	150	100

Model 1894FG

Lever-action chambered for .41 Rem. Magnum cartridge. Fitted with 20" barrel. Checkered walnut stock, with pistol grip. Magazine capacity 10 rounds. Weight about 6.5 lbs. Introduced in 2003.

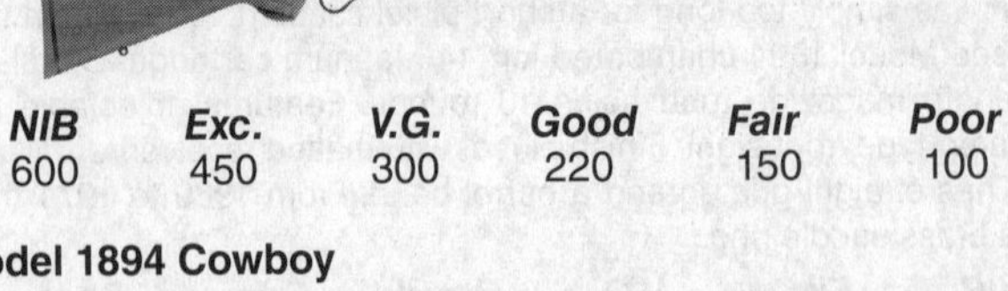

NIB	Exc.	V.G.	Good	Fair	Poor
600	450	300	220	150	100

Model 1894 Cowboy

Fitted with 20" barrel. Chambered for .38 Special cartridge. Designed for Cowboy Action Shooting. Special hand-tuned parts. Magazine capacity 10 rounds. Walnut stock, with straight-grip. Case colored receiver, bolt, trigger plate and lever. Weight about 6 lbs. Introduced in 2002. In 2003, offered chambered for .45 Colt cartridge.

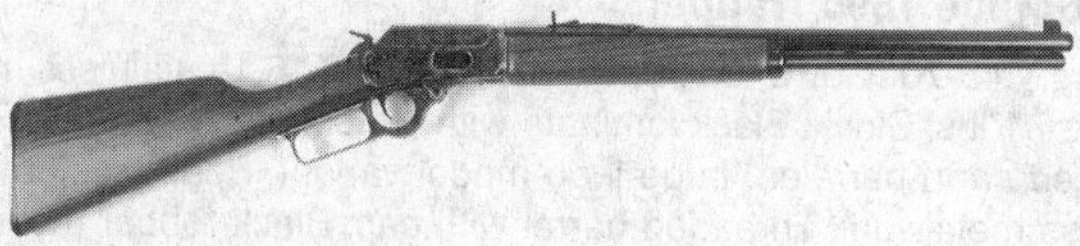

NIB	Exc.	V.G.	Good	Fair	Poor
820	750	600	500	300	150

Marlin 1894 Deluxe

Lever-action chambered in .44 Magnum/.44 Special. Features include 10-shot tubular magazine; squared finger lever; side ejection; richly polished deep blued metal surfaces; solid top receiver; hammer block safety; #1 grade fancy American black walnut straight-grip stock and forend; cut checkering; rubber rifle butt pad; Mar-Shield finish; blued steel forend cap; swivel studs; deep-cut Ballard-type rifling (6 grooves).

NIB	Exc.	V.G.	Good	Fair	Poor
600	500	400	320	250	150

Marlin 1894CSS

Lever-action chambered in .357 Magnum/.38 Special. Features include 9-shot tubular magazine; stainless steel receiver, barrel, lever, trigger and hammer; squared finger lever; side ejection; solid top receiver; hammer block safety; American black walnut straight-grip stock and forend; cut checkering; rubber rifle butt pad; Mar-Shield finish.

NIB	Exc.	V.G.	Good	Fair	Poor
720	600	450	350	300	200

Marlin 1894 CSBL

Chambered in .357/.38 Special, with 7-round capacity. Barrel 16.25", stock gray/black laminated. Other features include Marlin's Big Loop lever; stainless steel barrel, receiver, triggerguard plate and loading gate. Ghost ring sighting system, with mounting rail for optical sights. Introduced in 2011.

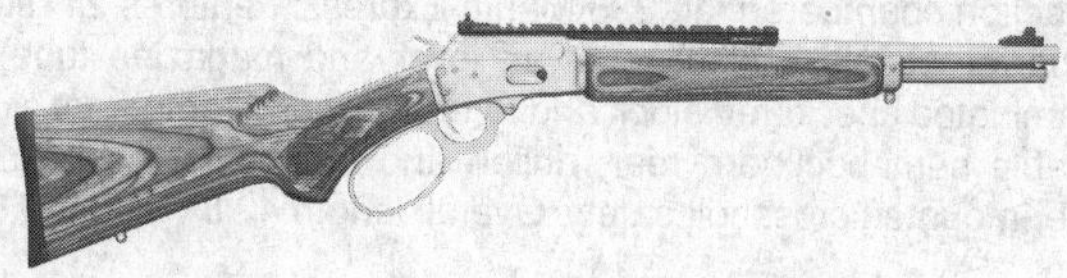

NIB	Exc.	V.G.	Good	Fair	Poor
800	720	600	500	400	300

MODEL 1895

Model 1895 and 1895SS

Model 1895 was re-introduced on Model 336 action, that had been modified to handle .45-70 cartridge. This was done to capitalize on nostalgia wave that descended on the country in early 1970s. Features 22" round barrel, with two-thirds-length magazine tube that holds 4 shots. Walnut stock had straight-grip until Model 1895S was released in 1980, when pistol grip stock was used. In 1983, Model 1895SS with crossbolt hammer-block safety was added; currently produced in this configuration. Note: Add 25 percent for early "B" prefix guns below serial number 12000.

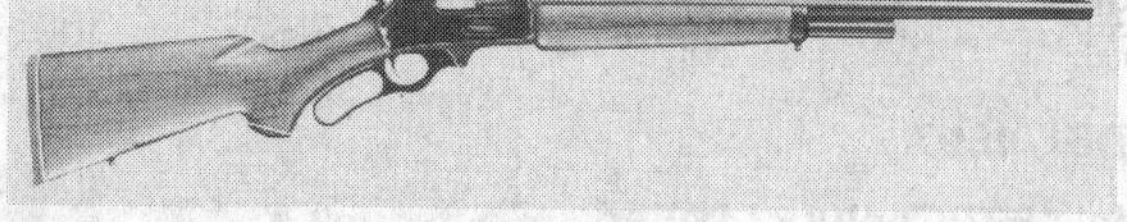

NIB	Exc.	V.G.	Good	Fair	Poor
600	500	320	200	150	100

Model 1895M

Similar to Model 1895. Chambered in .450 Marlin.

NIB	Exc.	V.G.	Good	Fair	Poor
600	500	320	200	150	100

Model 1895 Century Limited

Chambered for .45-70 cartridge. Features: 4-shot tubular magazine; 24" half round/half octagon barrel; semi-fancy walnut stock, with pistol grip. Receiver French grayed and engraved with the Marlin man on one side and two bears on other. Weight about 7.5 lbs. Discontinued. 299 produced.

NIB	Exc.	V.G.	Good	Fair	Poor
1400	1200	900	600	400	200

Model 1895 Century Limited Employee Edition

Similar to above. Limited to 100 rifles. Company logo inlaid in gold on right side; left side has two cow elk and bull elk.

NIB	Exc.	V.G.	Good	Fair	Poor
3200	2700	2250	—	—	—

Model 1895G Guide Gun

Chambered for .45-70 Government cartridge. Has 18.5" ported barrel. Straight-grip walnut stock, with cut checkering and ventilated recoil pad. Adjustable rear sight. Weight about 6.75 lbs. Introduced in 1998.

NIB	Exc.	V.G.	Good	Fair	Poor
650	550	450	350	250	150

Model 1895GS Guide Gun

Introduced in 2001. This .45-70 rifle fitted with 18.5" ported barrel, with 4-round magazine. Stainless steel receiver and barrel. American black walnut stock, with cut checkering and ventilated recoil pad. Adjustable rear semi-buckhorn sight. Weight about 7 lbs. Early models had ported barrel, now discontinued.

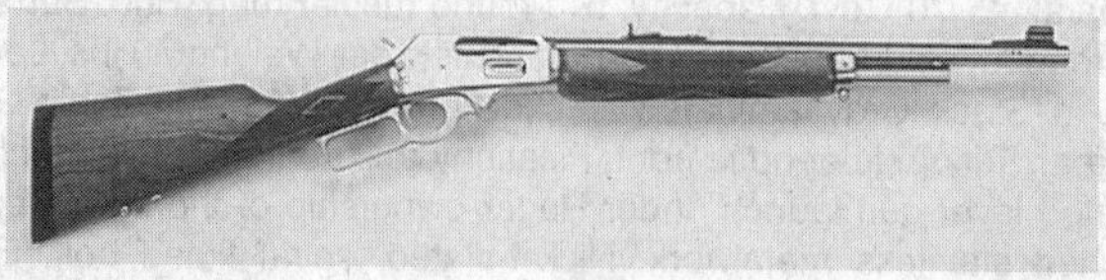

NIB	Exc.	V.G.	Good	Fair	Poor
750	650	550	450	350	100

Model 1895 Cowboy

Chambered for .45-70 cartridge. Fitted with 26" tapered octagon barrel. Tubular magazine has 9-round capacity. Adjustable semi-buckhorn rear sight. American black stock, with cut checkering. Hard rubber butt. Weight about 8 lbs. Introduced in 2001.

NIB	Exc.	V.G.	Good	Fair	Poor
650	550	450	350	200	100

Model 1895XLR

Lever-action chambered in .45-70 Government or .450 Marlin; 4-shot tubular magazine; 24" stainless steel barrel; stainless steel receiver, trigger, triggerguard plate, magazine tube, loading gate and lever. Full pistol grip, swivel studs and Ballard-type rifling precision fluted bolt. Features solid top receiver with side-ejection, adjustable folding semi-buckhorn rear sight, ramp front sight, tapped for scope mount. Designed for Hornady LEVERevolution cartridges. Introduced 2006.

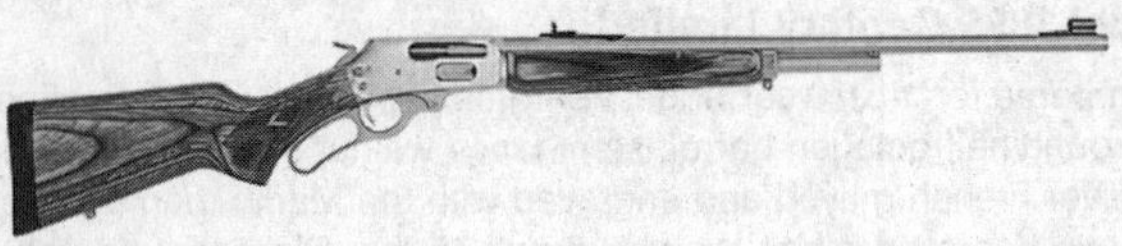

NIB	Exc.	V.G.	Good	Fair	Poor
700	600	520	400	300	150

Model 1895MXLR

Similar to Model 1895XLR. Chambered in .450 Marlin. Introduced 2006.

NIB	Exc.	V.G.	Good	Fair	Poor
700	600	520	400	300	150

Model 1895 SBLR

Similar to Model 1895GS Guide Gun, with stainless steel barrel (18.5"), receiver, large loop lever and magazine tube. Black/gray laminated buttstock and forend, XS ghost ring rear sight, hooded ramp front sight, receiver/barrel-mounted top rail for mounting accessory optics. Chambered in .45-70 Government. Overall length 42.5"; weight 7.5 lbs.

NIB	Exc.	V.G.	Good	Fair	Poor
880	700	600	520	400	150

Model 1895GBL

Lever-action chambered in .45-70 Government. Features include 6-shot full-length tubular magazine; 18.5" barrel, with deep-cut Ballard-type rifling (6 grooves); big-loop finger lever; side ejection; solid-top receiver; deeply blued metal surfaces; hammer block safety; pistol grip two tone brown laminate stock, with cut checkering; ventilated recoil pad; Mar-Shield finish, swivel studs. Introduced 2010.

NIB	Exc.	V.G.	Good	Fair	Poor
550	500	420	350	250	150

Ruger-Made Model 1895 SBL

Calibers: .45-70 Govt. Capacity: 6+1-round tubular magazine. Barrel: 19 in. threaded, cold-hammer-forged stainless steel. Weight: 7.3 lbs. Length: 37.25 in. Stock: Gray laminate with checkering. Sights: Adjustable Ghost ring rear, Tritium fiber-optic front. Picatinny rail. Features: The much-anticipated lever gun launch under Ruger ownership of the Marlin brand. Polished stainless metalwork. Nickel-plated, spiral fluted bolt. Barrel threaded at 11/16x24. Rubber buttpad. Push-button, cross-bolt manual safety and half-cock hammer. Oversized lever loop and slimmed-down forend. Includes swivel studs and offset hammer spur. Marlin horse-and-rider logo laser engraved on the grip. Made in Mayodan, NC. Ruger-made Marlin rifles begin with the serial prefix "RM." Traditional Marlin stock bullseye is now red/white.

NIB	Exc.	V.G.	Good	Fair	Poor
1320	—	—	—	—	—

Ruger-Made 1895 Guide Gun

Caliber: .45-70 Gov't. Barrel: 24" round, cold hammer forged. Weight: 7.4 lbs. Stock: Brown laminate with checkering. Features: Ruger-produced big loop guide gun model variant. Threaded barrel with cap. Semi-buckhorn rear and hooded front sight. Bead blasted satin blued metalwork finish. Nickel-plated bolt. 6+1 capacity. Black rubber recoil pad. Sling studs. Red/White bullseye stock insert denotes Ruger manufacture.

NIB	Exc.	V.G.	Good	Fair	Poor
1120	—	—	—	—	—

Ruger-Made 1895 Trapper

Calibers: .45-70 Gov't. Capacity: 5+1. Barrel: 16.1" stainless round. Weight: 7.1 lbs. Stock: Black laminate with checkering. Features: Ruger-produced short-barreled, large loop model variant. Bead blasted matte stainless metalwork. Threaded barrel with cap. Black rubber recoil pad. Sling studs. Comes standard with Skinner Sights receiver-mounted peep. Red/White bullseye stock insert denotes Ruger manufacture.

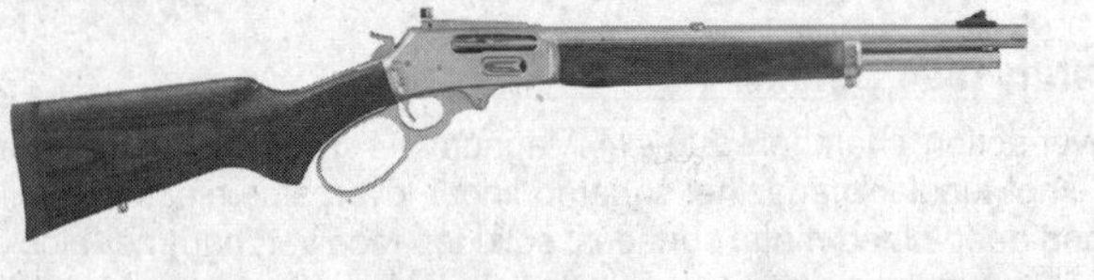

NIB	Exc.	V.G.	Good	Fair	Poor
1300	—	—	—	—	—

Model 308MXLR

Similar to Model 1895MXLR. Chambered in proprietary .308 Marlin Express cartridge.

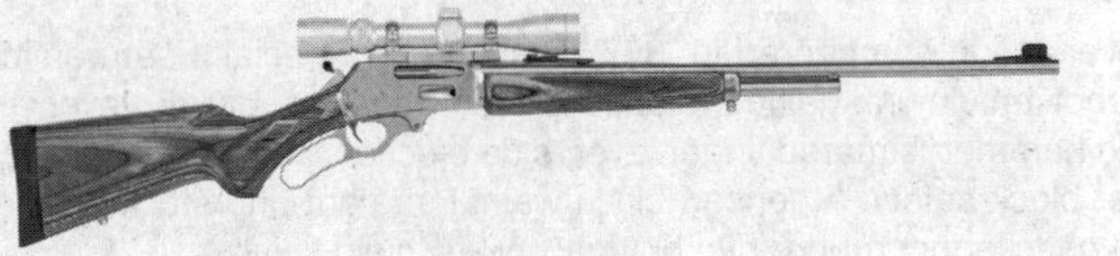

NIB	Exc.	V.G.	Good	Fair	Poor
700	600	520	400	300	150

Model 308MX

Similar to Model 308MXLR, with blued receiver and barrel.

NIB	Exc.	V.G.	Good	Fair	Poor
550	450	350	250	150	100

Model 338MXLR

Lever-action chambered for .338 Marlin Express. Features 24" stainless steel barrel; stainless steel receiver, lever and magazine tube; black/gray laminated checkered stock and forend; hooded ramp front sight and adjustable semi-buckhorn rear; drilled and tapped for scope mounts; receiver-mounted crossbolt safety. Overall length 42.5"; weight 7.5 lbs.

NIB	Exc.	V.G.	Good	Fair	Poor
700	600	520	400	300	150

Model 338MX

Similar to Model 338MXLR, with blued metal. Walnut stock and forend.

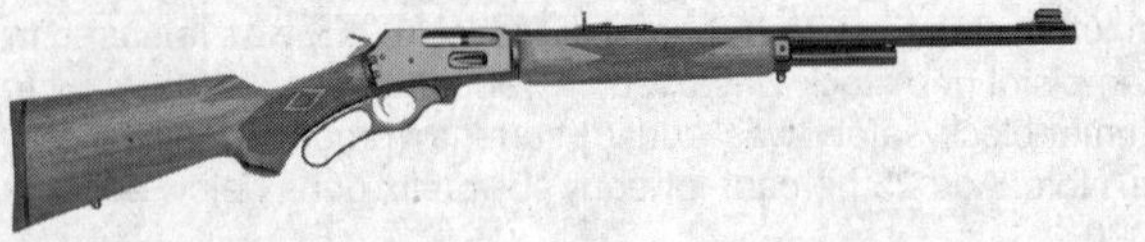

NIB	Exc.	V.G.	Good	Fair	Poor
550	450	350	250	150	100

MODEL 1897

Model 1897 Century Limited

Introduced in 1997. Chambered for .22-caliber cartridge. Commemorates 100th Anniversary of Model 1897. Fitted with 24" half round/half octagon barrel, with adjustable Marble rear sight and Marble front sight, with brass bead. Blued receiver engraved and gold inlaid. Semi-fancy walnut stock. Hard rubber buttplate. Weight about 6.5 lbs.

NIB	Exc.	V.G.	Good	Fair	Poor
1150	950	700	550	300	200

Model 1897 Century Limited Employee Edition

Similar to above, with additional gold engraving on lever. Limited to 100 rifles.

NIB	Exc.	V.G.	Good	Fair	Poor
2000	1650	1250	—	—	—

Model 1897 Cowboy

.22-caliber lever-action rifle. Fitted with 24" tapered octagon barrel, with adjustable Marble buckhorn sight and Marble front sight with brass bead. Full-length tubular magazine holds 26 Shorts, 21 Longs and 19 LR cartridges. Walnut straight-grip stock, with hard rubber buttplate. Weight 7.5 lbs. Introduced in 1999.

NIB	Exc.	V.G.	Good	Fair	Poor
700	550	450	350	200	100

Model 1897 Annie Oakley

Introduced in 1998. This .22-caliber features 18.5" tapered octagon barrel, adjustable Marble rear sight and Marble front sight. Blued receiver roll engraved, with gold signature. Stock straight-grip, with blued end cap. Hard rubber buttplate. Weight about 5.5 lbs.

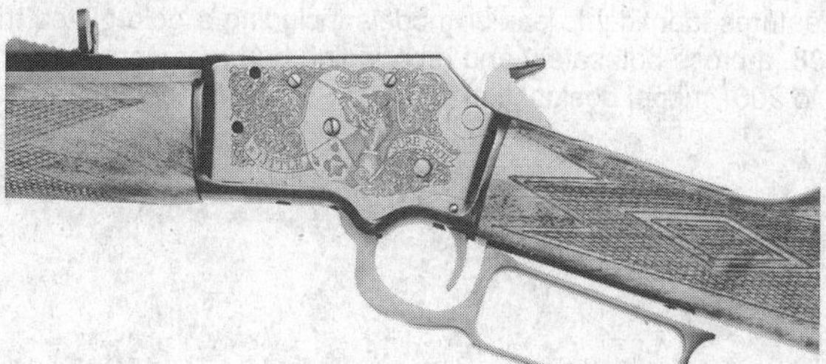

NIB	Exc.	V.G.	Good	Fair	Poor
1200	1000	750	600	400	200

Model 1897 Texan

Chambered for .22-caliber cartridge. Fitted with 20" octagon barrel; walnut stock with straight-grip. Magazine capacity 14 to 21 cartridges depending on type. Weight about 6 lbs. Introduced in 2002.

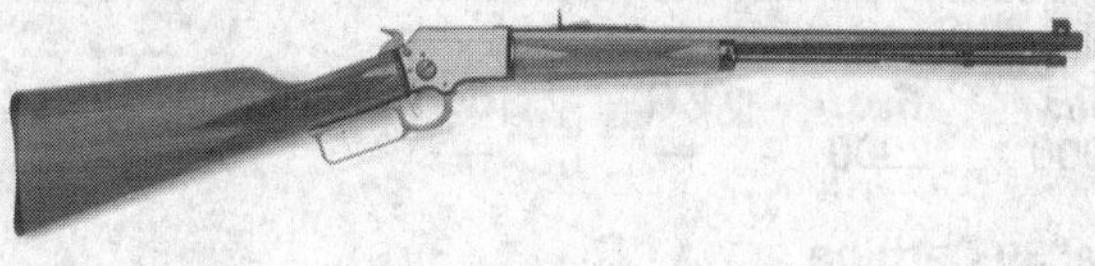

NIB	Exc.	V.G.	Good	Fair	Poor
700	600	400	300	200	120

Glenfield Lever-Action Rifles

Glenfield line of rifles were designed to be sold in large outlet chain stores. Simply cheaper versions that were to be sold for less money. Rifles functioned fine, but birch was used instead of walnut and pressed checkering instead of hand-cut. Manufactured under Glenfield name between 1964 and 1983. There are five models of Lever-Action Glenfields: 30, 30A, 30AS, 30GT and 36G. Chambered for .30-30 cartridge. Basic differences are slight and in most cases, merely cosmetic. They are good serviceable rifles, but have little or no collector interest or investment potential.

NIB	Exc.	V.G.	Good	Fair	Poor
300	250	200	150	120	100

Model 30AW

Lever-action chambered for .30-30 cartridge. Has 20" barrel and 6-round magazine tube. Stock walnut finished birch, with pistol grip cap. Hard rubber buttplate. Introduced in 1998.

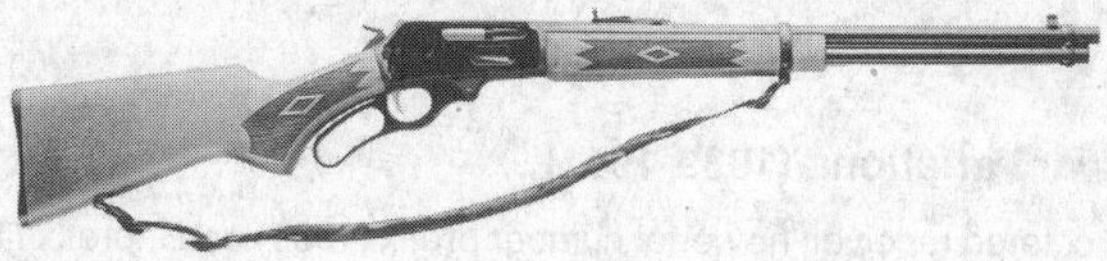

NIB	Exc.	V.G.	Good	Fair	Poor
300	250	200	150	120	100

MODEL 39

Originally evolved from Model 1891, invented by L.L. Hepburn. Model 1891 became Model 1892 and eventually developed into take-down Model 1897. Latter two were produced until 1915, when discontinued in favor of machine gun production for WWI. In 1922, when the company was sold to John Moran and became Marlin Firearms Corp., .22 rimfire lever-action was re-introduced as Model 39. Has been in production in one form or another ever since.

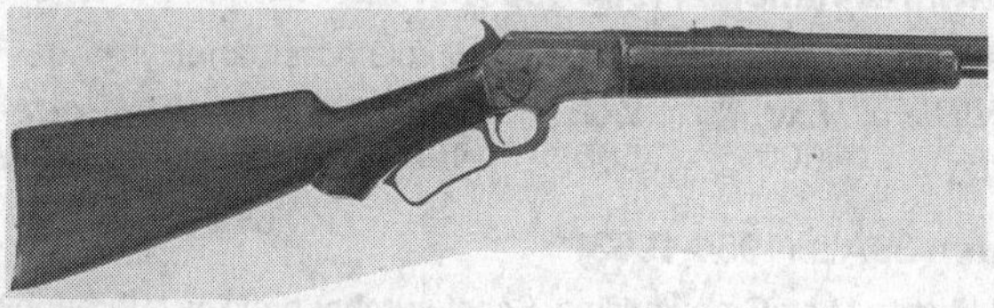

Model 39

Introduced in 1922. Model 39 was chambered for .22 rimfire, had 24" octagonal barrel and take-down receiver. Has full-length magazine tube which holds 25 Shorts, 20 Longs or 18 LR cartridges. Most Model 39s had a spring-loaded button outer magazine tube release. Very early variations had Model '97 type knurled latch release. As Model 39As were being phased in around 1939, many have more modern removable inner magazine tube. Has solid top frame and side ejection, Rocky Mountain rear and ivory bead front sight. Receiver, lever and hammer are case colored; barrel blued. Pistol grip stock and steel-capped forearm are varnished walnut. Manufactured in this form between 1922 and 1938, with a number of options that could affect value and would warrant an individual appraisal. Model 39s with a "star" stamped on tang, were considered high grade guns by factory inspector and will command a premium in better condition examples. Note: Model 39s made prior to 1932 that have no prefix or prefix S on serial number, should not be used with high-speed ammunition. Prefix HS indicates an improved bolt that is safe for this ammunition.

Standard Rifle

NIB	Exc.	V.G.	Good	Fair	Poor
—	4000	3000	2000	1000	750

Deluxe Rifle

Factory checkering, fancy wood and "star" stamp on tang.

NIB	Exc.	V.G.	Good	Fair	Poor
—	4500	3500	2200	1000	750

Model 39A

Improved version of Model 39. Has a heavier tapered round barrel, semi-beavertail forearm and redesigned pistol grip stock. Rubber buttplate was replaced by one of a synthetic fiber; otherwise, specifications were similar to Model 39. Manufactured from 1939 to 1960. Several variations are listed.

Pre-war Variations (1939-1941)

Case colored receiver, no serial number prefix (1939) or "B" prefix (1940-1941).

NIB	Exc.	V.G.	Good	Fair	Poor
—	2200	1400	900	500	400

Post-war Variations (1945-1953)

Serial number prefixes up to letter "K". Ballard-type deep rifling. Note: Add 20 percent premium for C prefix 1st post-war variation, with figured wood.

NIB	Exc.	V.G.	Good	Fair	Poor
—	700	580	420	250	200

Post-war Variations (1954-1956)

Serial number prefixes L, M, N, with MicroGroove barrel.

NIB	Exc.	V.G.	Good	Fair	Poor
—	600	500	400	220	120

Golden 39A's (1954-1963)

Gold trigger, MicroGroove rifling. Serial number prefixes L through W.

NIB	Exc.	V.G.	Good	Fair	Poor
—	550	450	320	200	120

Model 39A Mountie

Basically a carbine version of Model 39A. Features 20" tapered round barrel, straight-grip walnut stock and slimmed-down forearm. Manufactured between 1953 and 1960.

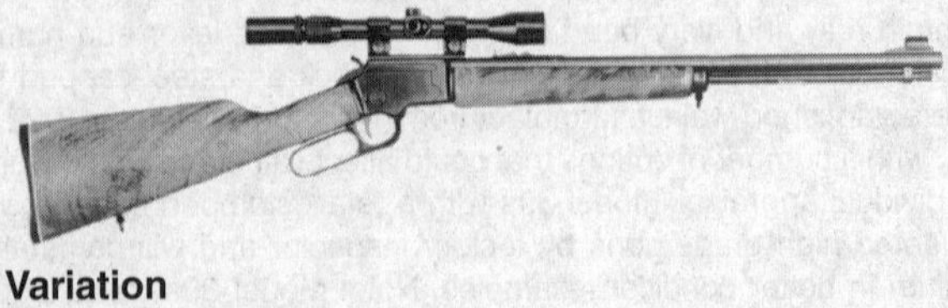

1st Variation

K prefix and 24" barrel, fat forearm. Note: Add 20 percent for slim forearm.

NIB	Exc.	V.G.	Good	Fair	Poor
—	600	450	300	200	100

Standard

NIB	Exc.	V.G.	Good	Fair	Poor
—	450	320	180	120	100

Model 39A 1960 Presentation Model

Released in 1960. Marlin's 90th Anniversary model. Similar to 39A. Has chrome-plated barrel and receiver, with high grade checkered walnut stock and forend. There is a squirrel carved on right side of buttstock. Produced 500 in 1960. This is a commemorative. Desirable to collectors only if NIB with all boxes and papers with which it was originally sold.

NIB	Exc.	V.G.	Good	Fair	Poor
1500	1200	800	650	300	200

Model 39M Mountie 1960 Presentation Model

Carbine version of 90th Anniversary model. Same as 39A, with 20" barrel and straight-grip stock. Manufactured 500 in 1960.

NIB	Exc.	V.G.	Good	Fair	Poor
1500	1200	800	650	300	200

Model 39ADL

Same as 90th Anniversary issue except blued instead of chrome-plated. Manufactured 3,306 between 1960 and 1963.

NIB	Exc.	V.G.	Good	Fair	Poor
1200	900	700	550	300	200

Golden 39A (1960-1983)

Similar to 39A, with gold-plated trigger and sling swivels. Manufactured between 1960 and 1983.

NIB	Exc.	V.G.	Good	Fair	Poor
—	650	550	400	250	120

Golden 39A (1984-2015)

This is the most recent production model of this extremely popular rifle, with features identical to earlier models including a gold-plated trigger. In 1988, a cross-bolt safety and rebounding hammer were added; from 1988 to 2001 model designation was 39AS. Discontinued in 2015.

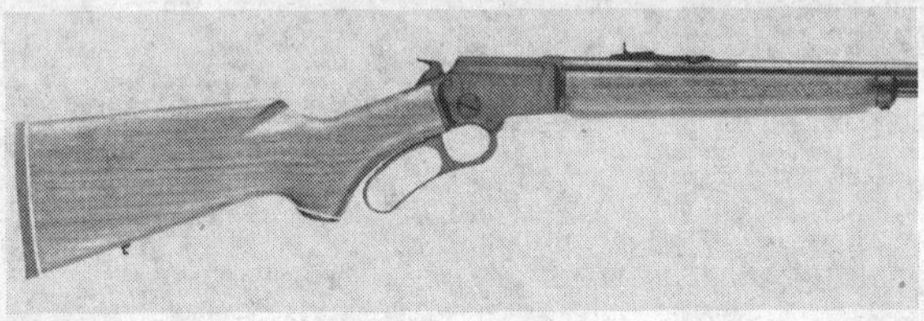

NIB	Exc.	V.G.	Good	Fair	Poor
650	550	420	320	220	200

Model 39A Fancy

Limited Edition Golden 39A. Extra fancy walnut stock, with hand rubbed oil-finish. All metal surfaces deburred with high polish blue finish. Other features include action job, trigger job and clocked screws. A custom rifle made to order by Dakota Arms. Introduced in 2017, with MSRP of $3,195. Very limited production.

NIB	Exc.	V.G.	Good	Fair	Poor
3000	2900	—	—	—	—

Model 39 Carbine

Slimmer lighter version of Model 39A. Features slimmer forend and thinner barrel. Manufactured 12,140 between 1963 and 1967.

NIB	Exc.	V.G.	Good	Fair	Poor
—	550	400	250	180	100

Model 39 Century Limited

Introduction of this model marked 100th Anniversary of the Marlin Company. Features 20" octagonal barrel, with semi-buckhorn rear and brass blade front sight. Stock is fancy walnut, with straight-grip, brass forend tip and buttplate. A medallion inlaid into right side of receiver. Brass plate on stock. Manufactured 34,197 in 1970. As a commemorative, needs to be as it came from the factory to command collector interest.

NIB	Exc.	V.G.	Good	Fair	Poor
950	550	300	150	120	100

Model 39A Article II

Commemorated National Rifle Association's 100th Anniversary in 1971. Has 24" octagonal barrel, high grade walnut pistol grip stock, brass forend tip and buttplate. Right side of receiver has NRA's Second Amendment "Right to Keep and Bear Arms" medallion inlaid. Manufactured in 1971.

NIB	Exc.	V.G.	Good	Fair	Poor
750	450	300	150	120	100

Model 39M Article II

Same as Model 39A Article II, except a carbine version with 20" octagonal barrel and straight-grip stock. Manufactured 3,824 in 1971. As commemorative, NIB condition is essential to collector interest.

NIB	Exc.	V.G.	Good	Fair	Poor
780	480	320	180	150	100

Model 39A Octagon

Produced because the company had machinery and some left-over barrels from two commemorative models produced in 1970 and 1971. A regular production run that was meant to be used and was not a special issue. Has 24" tapered octagonal barrel. Chambered for .22 rimfire cartridges. Pistol grip walnut stock, with steel forend tip. Manufactured 2,551 in 1972 and 1973. This was not a commercially successful model and discontinued for that reason.

NIB	Exc.	V.G.	Good	Fair	Poor
800	600	400	250	200	180

Model 39M Octagon

This is the 20" octagonal barreled carbine version, with straight-grip stock. Manufactured 2,140 in 1973.

NIB	Exc.	V.G.	Good	Fair	Poor
750	600	400	250	200	180

Model 39D

Essentially Model 39M carbine 20" barrel version, with pistol grip stock. Manufactured in 1971; re-introduced in 1973. The 1971 version has white line spacers and pistol grip caps; 1973 version has neither of these features.

NIB	Exc.	V.G.	Good	Fair	Poor
—	620	480	320	200	120

Model 39TDS

Similar to Model 39AS, with 20" carbine barrel and straight-grip stock. Replaced Model 39M. Introduced in 1988. Superseded by current Golden 39A, which is a take-down design.

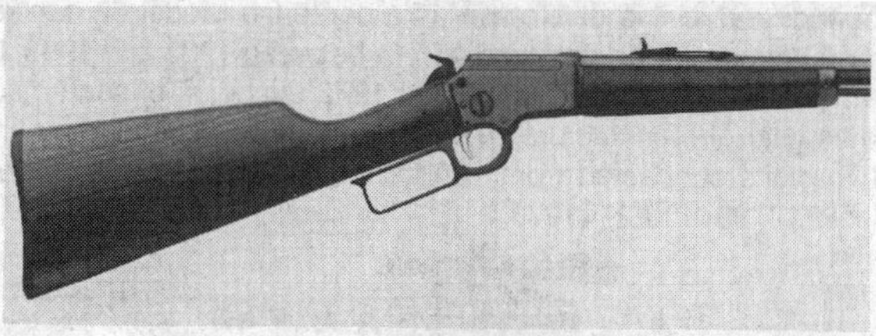

NIB	Exc.	V.G.	Good	Fair	Poor
600	480	300	200	150	100

Model 39AWL

Limited edition of 2,000 rifles distributed solely through Wal-Mart. Fitted with 24.5" octagon barrel, select checkered walnut stock, gold filled engraving and stamped "Wildlife For Tomorrow".

NIB	Exc.	V.G.	Good	Fair	Poor
750	600	400	300	200	120

MODEL 56

Model 56 Levermatic

Streamlined version of lever-action. Features short lever throw and one-piece walnut stock. Round 22" barrel. Chambered for .22 rimfire cartridges, with 7-shot detachable magazine. Open sights. Gold-plated trigger. Receiver made of aluminum after 1956. Manufactured 31,523 between 1955 and 1964.

NIB	Exc.	V.G.	Good	Fair	Poor
—	320	220	150	80	50

Model 56 "Clipper King" Levermatic

Same as Model 56, except specially packaged. Comes with 4X .22 scope. Name Clipper King" stamped on barrel. Buttplate red hard rubber. Manufactured only 152 in 1959.

NIB	Exc.	V.G.	Good	Fair	Poor
—	350	250	180	100	80

MODEL 57

Model 57 Levermatic

Similar to Model 56, with tube magazine and Monte Carlo stock. In 1960, Marlin went back to a steel receiver on this model. Manufactured 34,628 from 1959 to 1965.

NIB	Exc.	V.G.	Good	Fair	Poor
—	320	220	150	80	50

Model 57M Levermatic

Model 57 chambered for .22 Magnum cartridge. Manufactured 66,889 between 1959 and 1969.

NIB	Exc.	V.G.	Good	Fair	Poor
—	450	350	250	180	100

MODEL 62

Model 62 Levermatic

Similar in appearance to Model 57, except chambered for centerfire .256 Magnum cartridge, with 4-shot magazine. In 1966, .30 carbine cartridge was added. This model has a 23" "MicroGroove" barrel, with open sights and walnut one-piece stock. First 4,000 Model 62s were shipped without serial numbers in violation of federal law. Company recalled rifles for numbering; and to this day, owner of a centerfire Model 62 can return rifle for numbering. Manufactured 15,714 between 1963 and 1969. Note: Add 15 percent for .256. From 1969 to 1972, first digit of serial number indicates year of manufacture. In 1973, system was changed by having first two digits subtracted from 100 to find year of production. For example: 2717793=100-27=1973.

NIB	*Exc.*	*V.G.*	*Good*	*Fair*	*Poor*
—	600	480	380	220	100

RIMFIRE RIFLES

Marlin Firearms Company produced a great many bolt-action rifles, both single-shot and repeaters, starting in 1930 and continuing today. These rifles were low-priced and designed primarily as utility rifles. They also manufactured many auto-loaders of the same type during these years. Glenfield name will also be found on these models, as many were produced to be marketed by large chain outlets. These rifles have limited value as collectibles at the present time, but no one can deny that they're durable accurate good-natured little rifles.

Model 70P "Papoose"

Semi-automatic take-down carbine. Chambered for .22 rimfire family of cartridges. Has 16.25 barrel and 7-shot detachable magazine. Supplied with 4X scope. Bright red case that will float if dropped overboard. Stock walnut-finished birch, with pistol grip. Rubber buttplate. Introduced in 1986.

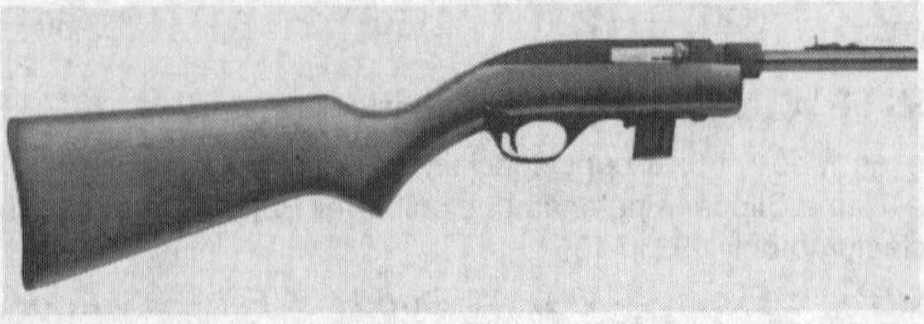

NIB	*Exc.*	*V.G.*	*Good*	*Fair*	*Poor*
280	200	150	100	80	50

Model 70PSS

Same as Model 70P above. Furnished with 10-round magazine. Finished in stainless steel, with synthetic stock. Automatic last shot bolt hold-open.

NIB	*Exc.*	*V.G.*	*Good*	*Fair*	*Poor*
240	180	120	100	80	60

Model 70HC

This is the Model 70 .22 rimfire semi-automatic that has been produced since 1983, with high-capacity 25-round "Banana" magazine.

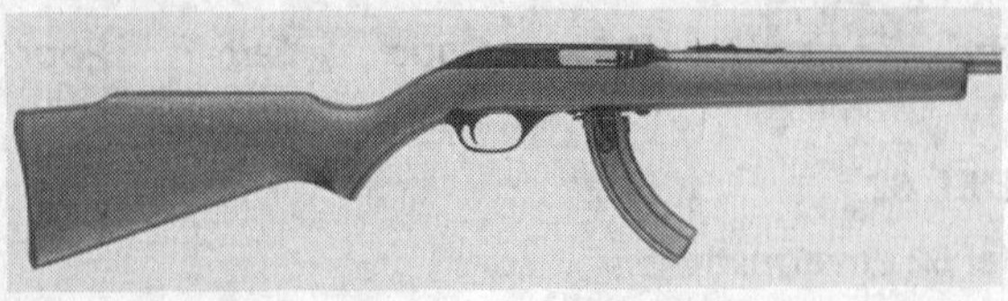

NIB	*Exc.*	*V.G.*	*Good*	*Fair*	*Poor*
200	160	140	110	80	80

Model 9 Camp Carbine

Model has 16.5" barrel. Chambered for 9mm Parabellum pistol cartridge. Has 12- or 20-shot detachable magazine, walnut-finished hardwood pistol grip stock and sandblasted matte-blued finish. Open sights. Receiver drilled and tapped for scope mounting. Introduced in 1985.

NIB	*Exc.*	*V.G.*	*Good*	*Fair*	*Poor*
620	500	400	250	180	120

Model 9N

Similar to Model 9mm Carbine. Furnished with nickel-plated metal parts.

NIB	*Exc.*	*V.G.*	*Good*	*Fair*	*Poor*
650	520	420	280	200	120

Model 45 Camp Carbine

Same as 9mm version. Chambered for .45 ACP cartridge. Has 7-shot detachable magazine. Very hot collectible.

NIB	*Exc.*	*V.G.*	*Good*	*Fair*	*Poor*
680	600	420	300	220	180

Model 922M

First offered in 1993. A semi-automatic .22 Win. Magnum rimfire rifle. Features 7-shot clip; 20.5" MicroGroove barrel; receiver sandblasted, drilled and tapped for scope mounting; Monte Carlo black walnut stock, with rubber rifle buff pad; adjustable rear sight and ramp front sight with hood. Weight 6.5 lbs.

NIB	*Exc.*	*V.G.*	*Good*	*Fair*	*Poor*
550	450	380	220	150	120

Model 995

Semi-automatic .22 LR only rifle. Features 7-shot clip, 18" MicroGroove barrel. Receiver grooved for scope mount and has a serrated non-glare top. Adjustable sights. Monte Carlo American black walnut stock, with checkered pistol grip and forearm. White buttplate spacer standard. Weight 5 lbs. Introduced in 1979.

NIB	*Exc.*	*V.G.*	*Good*	*Fair*	*Poor*
180	110	80	70	60	40

Model 995SS

Same as above, with stainless steel finish. Black fiberglass stock. Introduced in 1995.

NIB	Exc.	V.G.	Good	Fair	Poor
200	120	100	80	60	50

Model 990L

Semi-automatic .22 LR Marlin features tubular 14-round magazine, with 22" MicroGroove barrel. Trigger gold plated. Receiver grooved for scope mount. Stock a two-tone brown birch Monte Carlo. Rubber rifle buttpad standard. Weight 5.75 lbs.

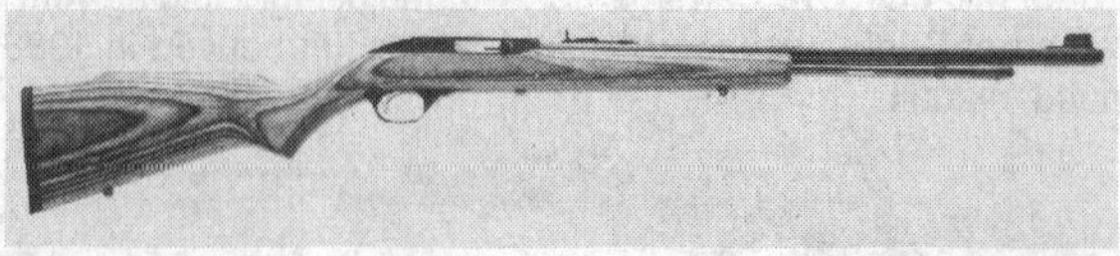

NIB	Exc.	V.G.	Good	Fair	Poor
150	120	100	80	60	50

Model 7000

First offered in 1997. A semi-automatic .22-caliber rifle, with 18" heavy barrel. Magazine holds 10 rounds. Black synthetic stock, with Monte Carlo comb and molded checkering. Receiver grooved for scope mount. No sights included. Weight about 6 lbs.

NIB	Exc.	V.G.	Good	Fair	Poor
200	150	120	100	80	50

Model 7000T

Target rifle fitted with an 18" barrel and recessed muzzle. No sights. Stock laminated red, white and blue with pistol grip. Serrated rubber buttplate adjustable for length of pull, height and angle. Weight about 7.5 lbs. Introduced in 1999.

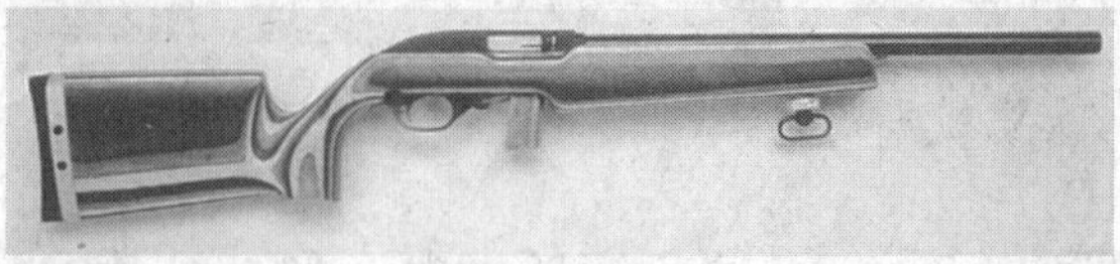

NIB	Exc.	V.G.	Good	Fair	Poor
420	380	320	280	150	100

Model 795

Similar to Model 7000 above, with 18" standard weight barrel. Weight about 5 lbs. Available with 4X scope. Note: Add $5 for scope.

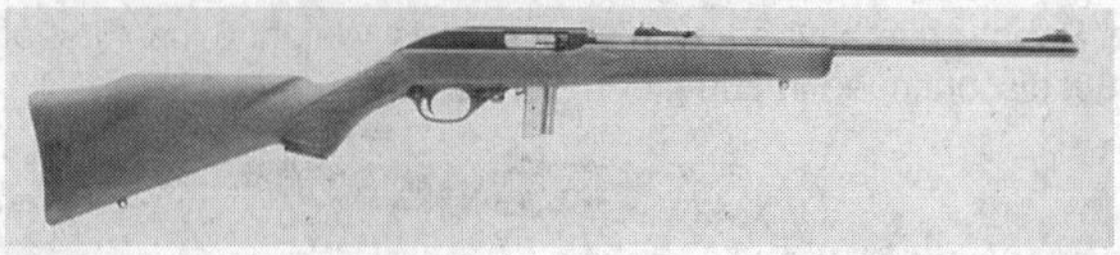

NIB	Exc.	V.G.	Good	Fair	Poor
150	120	—	—	—	—

Model 795SS

As above, with stainless steel action and barrel. Black fiberglass stock. Weight about 4.5 lbs. Introduced in 2002.

NIB	Exc.	V.G.	Good	Fair	Poor
200	150	120	100	80	50

Model 60

Semi-automatic 14-shot .22-caliber LR. Features 22" MicroGroove barrel, with adjustable rear sight. Receiver grooved for scope mount. Stock birch, with Monte Carlo comb. Weight 5.5 lbs. Introduced in 1960.

NIB	Exc.	V.G.	Good	Fair	Poor
180	120	90	60	50	40

Model 60SS

Introduced in 1993. Similar to Model 60. Features stainless barrel, bolt and magazine tube. All other metal parts are nickel plated. Stock is two-tone black/gray laminated birch Monte Carlo.

NIB	Exc.	V.G.	Good	Fair	Poor
280	220	150	120	80	50

Model 60SN

Similar to Model 60SS, with black synthetic stock, molded checkering and swivel studs. Blued metal. Introduced in 2007. Available with factory-mounted 3x9 scope. Note: Add 10 percent for scope package.

NIB	Exc.	V.G.	Good	Fair	Poor
200	150	120	100	80	50

Model 60S-CF

Similar to Model 60SN, with carbon fiber-dipped black synthetic stock.

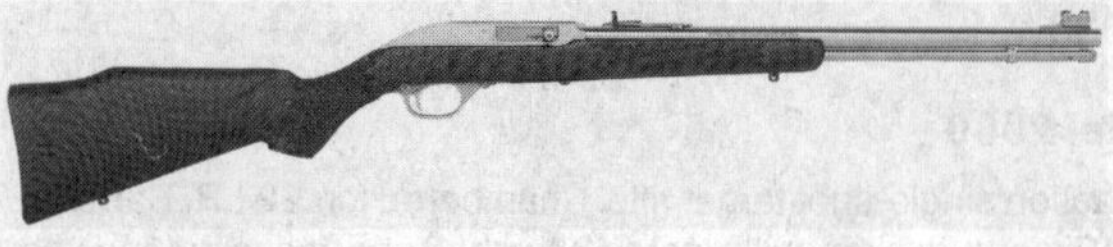

NIB	Exc.	V.G.	Good	Fair	Poor
250	220	180	120	100	80

Model 60SB

Introduced in 1998. Features stainless steel 22" barrel, bolt and magazine tube. Stock birch, with Monte Carlo. Hard rubber buttplate.

NIB	Exc.	V.G.	Good	Fair	Poor
180	120	90	60	50	40

Model 60SSK

Similar to Model 60SB. Addition of black synthetic Monte Carlo stock, with checkering.

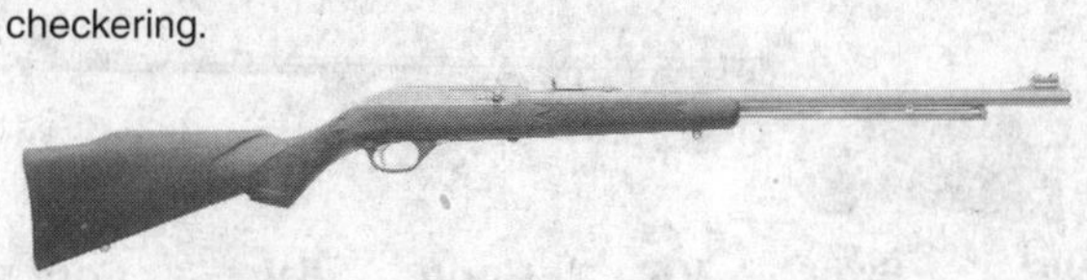

NIB	Exc.	V.G.	Good	Fair	Poor
200	200	150	120	100	80

Model 60C

Similar to Model 60, with Realtree camo finish. Introduced in 2000.

NIB	Exc.	V.G.	Good	Fair	Poor
200	200	150	120	100	80

Model 60DL

Introduced in 2004. Features Monte Carlo hardwood stock, with Walnutone walnut pattern finish. Full pistol grip. Weight about 5.5 lbs.

NIB	Exc.	V.G.	Good	Fair	Poor
180	120	90	60	50	40

Model 60DLX

Semi-automatic rifle chambered for .22 LR. Features include 14-shot tubular magazine; side ejection; manual and automatic last-shot bolt hold-opens; receiver top with serrated non-glare finish; cross-bolt safety; steel charging handle; Monte Carlo American walnut-finished hardwood; full pistol grip; tough Mar-Shield finish; 19" barrel with MicroGroove rifling. Limited availability.

NIB	Exc.	V.G.	Good	Fair	Poor
220	180	120	100	80	50

Model 60 150th Anniversary

Caliber: .22 LR. Capacity: 14. Barrel: 19 in., stainless steel. Stock: Monte Carlo walnut hardwood. Sights: Semi-buckhorn folding rear, ramp front with wide-scan hood. Weight: 5.5 lbs. Features: Cross-bolt safety, commemorative emblem, checkered grip and forearm.

NIB	Exc.	V.G.	Good	Fair	Poor
330	—	—	—	—	—

Model 2000

Bolt-action single-shot target rifle. Chambered for .22 LR. Barrel 22" long MicroGroove design, with match chamber and recessed muzzle. Rear sight fully adjustable target peep sight, with hooded front sight supplied with 10 aperture inserts. Stock Marlin blue fiberglass/Kevlar material, with adjustable buttplate. Aluminum forearm rail, with forearm stop and quick detachable swivel. Weight 8 lbs. Discontinued.

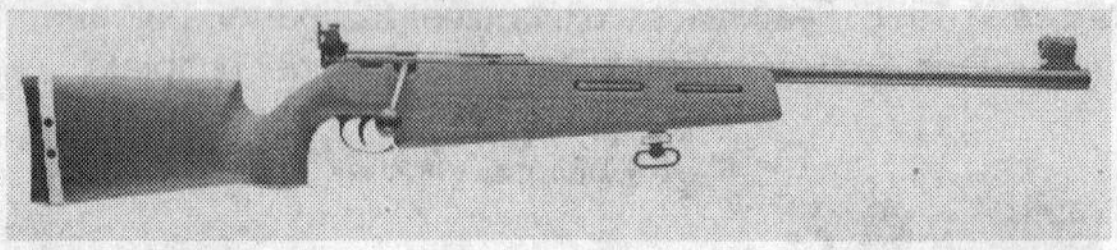

NIB	Exc.	V.G.	Good	Fair	Poor
650	500	400	320	250	200

Model 2000A

A 1996 version of Model 2000. Introduced in 1994. Features adjustable comb and ambidextrous pistol grip. Marlin logo molded into side of buttstock. Weight about 8.5 lbs. Discontinued.

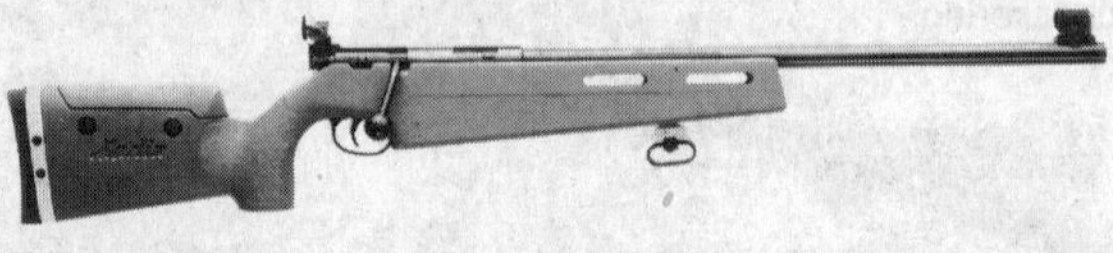

NIB	Exc.	V.G.	Good	Fair	Poor
750	600	500	380	300	250

Model 2000L

Introduced in 1996. Version of Model 2000. Features black/gray laminated stock. Fitted with heavy 22" barrel and match chamber; two-stage target trigger; rubber buttplate adjustable for length of pull, height and angle. Weight about 8 lbs. Discontinued.

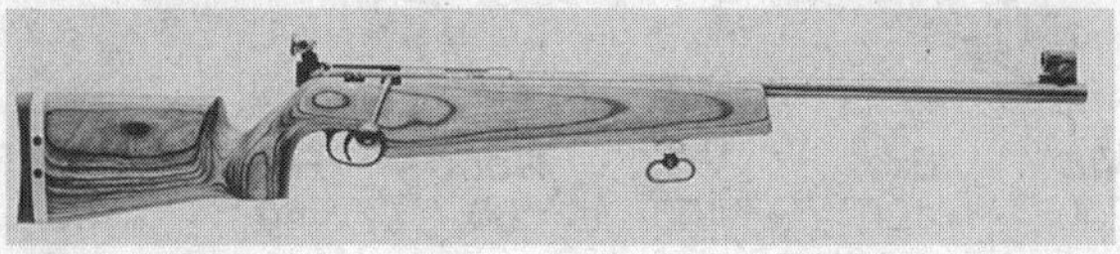

NIB	Exc.	V.G.	Good	Fair	Poor
800	650	550	400	320	250

Model 880

Bolt-action clip-fed rifle. Chambered for .22 LR caliber. Clip is a 7-shot magazine. MicroGroove barrel is 22". Has adjustable folding rear sight and ramp front sight with hood. Weight 5.5 lbs. Introduced in 1988; discontinued in 2004.

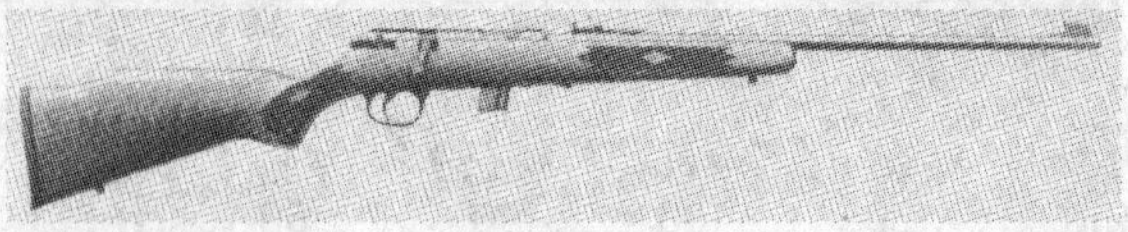

NIB	Exc.	V.G.	Good	Fair	Poor
160	140	110	90	80	50

Model 880SS

Introduced in 1994. This .22-caliber rifle features synthetic stock; stainless steel receiver and 22" barrel; 7-shot magazine standard. Discontinued in 2004.

NIB	Exc.	V.G.	Good	Fair	Poor
250	180	150	120	80	60

Model 880SQ

Similar to Model 880. Fitted with 22" heavy barrel and no sights. Weight about 7 lbs. Introduced in 1996; discontinued in 2004.

NIB	Exc.	V.G.	Good	Fair	Poor
280	220	200	150	100	80

Model 881

Bolt-action .22-caliber rifle has tubular magazine that holds 25 Shorts, 19 Longs and 17 LR. A 22" MicroGroove barrel has adjustable folding rear sight and ramp front sight with hood. Stock black walnut, with Monte Carlo. Rubber rifle buttpad, with sling swivels. Weight 6 lbs. First offered in 1988; discontinued in 2004.

NIB	Exc.	V.G.	Good	Fair	Poor
180	150	120	100	80	60

Model 882SS

Bolt-action magazine rifle chambered for .22 Magnum cartridge. Stainless steel barrel and action, with black synthetic stock. Marlin "Fire Sights" installed. Introduced in 1998; discontinued in 2004.

NIB	Exc.	V.G.	Good	Fair	Poor
220	180	150	100	80	50

Model 25N

Marlin promotional model. Bolt-action rifle chambered for .22 LR only. Seven-shot clip magazine, with 22" MicroGroove barrel. Receiver grooved for scope mount. Walnut finished birch stock. Weight 5.5 lbs.

NIB	Exc.	V.G.	Good	Fair	Poor
120	90	80	70	50	40

Model 25NC

Similar to above, with Mossy Oak Break-Up camo finish. Introduced in 2000.

NIB	Exc.	V.G.	Good	Fair	Poor
120	100	80	70	50	40

Model 25MN

Same as above chambered for .22 Win. Magnum rimfire cartridge. Weight 6 lbs.

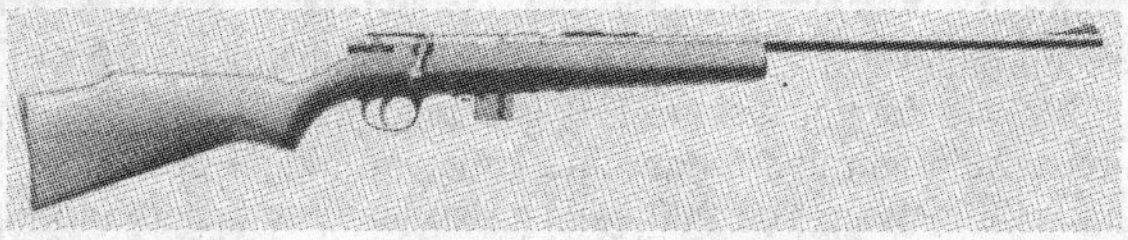

NIB	Exc.	V.G.	Good	Fair	Poor
180	150	120	100	80	60

Model 25MNC

Similar to above, with Mossy Oak Break-Up camo finish. Weight about 6 lbs. Introduced in 2001.

NIB	Exc.	V.G.	Good	Fair	Poor
200	160	120	100	80	60

Model 17V

Introduced in 2002. Bolt-action rifle chambered for .17 Hornady Magnum rimfire cartridge. Fitted with 22" heavy barrel. Hardwood stock. No sights. Magazine capacity 7-round detachable magazine. Weight about 6 lbs.

NIB	Exc.	V.G.	Good	Fair	Poor
220	200	150	120	90	50

Model 17VS

As above, with stainless steel heavy barrel and action. Laminated stock. Weight about 7 lbs. Discontinued.

NIB	Exc.	V.G.	Good	Fair	Poor
280	220	200	150	100	80

Model 15YN "Little Buckaroo"

Marlin promotional model referred to as Little Buckaroo". Bolt-action .22-caliber single-shot rifle for the beginner. Features MicroGroove 16.25" barrel, adjustable rear sight and receiver grooved for scope mount. Birch stock. Weight 4.25 lbs.

NIB	Exc.	V.G.	Good	Fair	Poor
120	100	80	60	50	40

Model 15N

Bolt-action rifle chambered for .22 Short, Long and LR. Fitted with adjustable rear sight. Full size birch stock interchangeable with Model 15YN. Weight about 4.25 lbs. Introduced in 1998.

NIB	Exc.	V.G.	Good	Fair	Poor
180	140	100	80	60	40

Model 15YS (Youth)

Single-shot bolt-action rifle, with shorter-than-standard length of pull. Barrel length 16.25". Hardwood stock. Weight about 4.25 lbs. Introduced in 2002.

NIB	Exc.	V.G.	Good	Fair	Poor
180	140	110	60	50	40

Model 81TS

Bolt-action rifle chambered for .22 Short, Long and LR cartridges. Fitted with 22" barrel and tubular magazine. Comes with black Monte Carlo synthetic stock. Adjustable rear sight. Weight about 6 lbs. Introduced in 1998; discontinued in 2004.

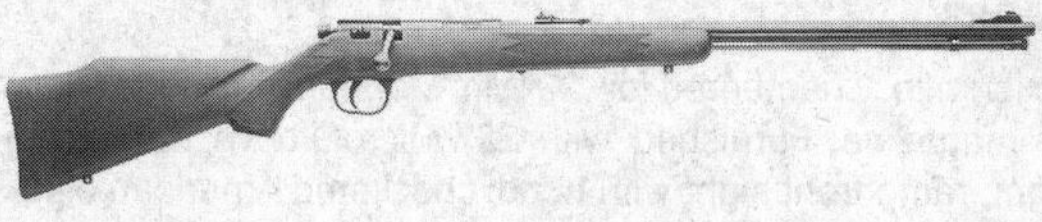

NIB	Exc.	V.G.	Good	Fair	Poor
180	140	110	60	50	40

Model 882

Bolt-action rifle chambered for .22 Win. Magnum rimfire cartridge. A 7-shot clip standard. MicroGroove 22" barrel, with adjustable rear sight and ramp front sight with hood. Receiver grooved for scope mount. Black walnut stock, with Monte Carlo. Rubber rifle butt. Weight 6 lbs. Introduced in 1988; discontinued in 2004.

NIB	Exc.	V.G.	Good	Fair	Poor
280	220	200	150	100	80

Model 882L

Same as above. Furnished with two-tone brown hardwood Monte Carlo stock. Weight 6.25 lbs. Discontinued in 2004.

NIB	Exc.	V.G.	Good	Fair	Poor
280	220	190	140	90	60

Model 882SS

Same as above. Furnished in stainless steel. Black fiberglass stock. Introduced in 1995; discontinued in 2004.

NIB	Exc.	V.G.	Good	Fair	Poor
280	220	200	150	100	80

Model 882SSV

Variation of Model 882. Introduced in 1997. All in stainless steel. Chambered for .22 WMR cartridge. Fitted with nickel plated 7-round magazine and 22" barrel. Stock black synthetic, with molded checkering. Receiver grooved for scope mount. 1" brushed aluminum scope ring mounts included. Weight about 7 lbs. Discontinued in 2004.

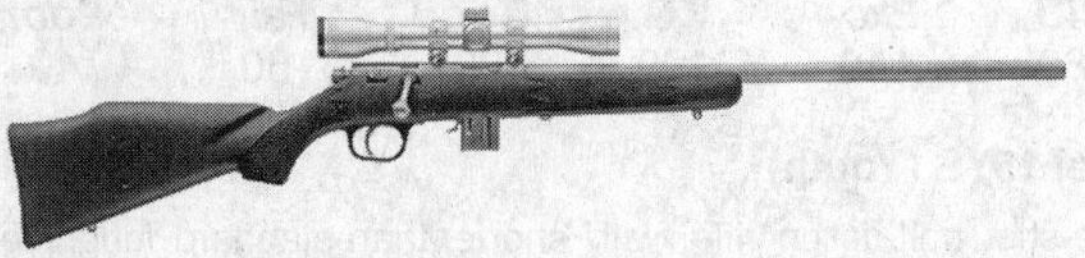

NIB	Exc.	V.G.	Good	Fair	Poor
280	220	200	150	100	80

Model 83TS

Chambered for .22 Win. Magnum cartridge. Fitted with 22" barrel and 12-round tubular magazine. Adjustable rear sight. Bolt-action, with synthetic stock. Weight about 6 lbs. Introduced in 2001; discontinued in 2004.

NIB	Exc.	V.G.	Good	Fair	Poor
250	200	160	140	100	80

Model 883

Bolt-action rifle. Chambered for .22 Win. Magnum cartridge, with 12-shot tubular magazine. Furnished with 22" MicroGroove barrel; adjustable rear sight, ramp front sight with hood; checkered American black walnut stock, with Monte Carlo. Weight 6 lbs. Introduced in 1988; discontinued in 2004.

NIB	Exc.	V.G.	Good	Fair	Poor
280	220	200	150	100	80

Model 883N

Same as above. Furnished with stainless steel barrel, receiver, front breech bolt and striker. All other metal parts, except for sights, are nickel plated. Discontinued in 2004.

NIB	Exc.	V.G.	Good	Fair	Poor
280	220	200	150	100	80

Model 883SS

Introduced in 1993. Similar to Model 883, with all metal parts in stainless steel or nickel. Stock is two-tone brown birch Monte Carlo that is not checkered. Discontinued in 2004.

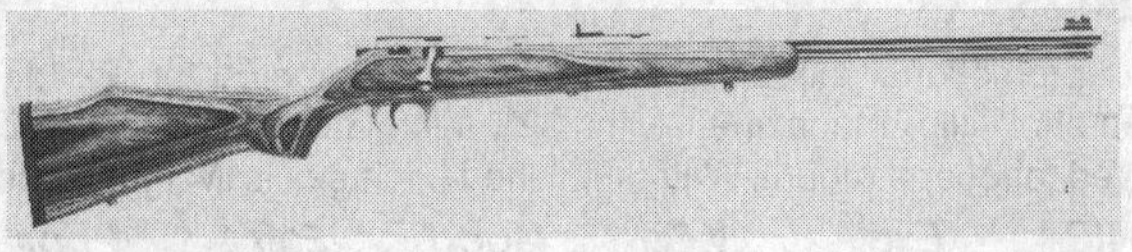

NIB	Exc.	V.G.	Good	Fair	Poor
280	220	190	140	90	60

Model 717M2

Introduced in 2005. Semi-automatic chambered for .17 Mach 2 cartridge. Laminated hardwood stock, with Monte Carlo comb. Fitted with 18" barrel and iron sights. Magazine capacity 7 rounds. Weight about 5 lbs.

NIB	Exc.	V.G.	Good	Fair	Poor
300	250	200	180	150	120

MODEL 900 SERIES

Bolt-action rimfire series was introduced into Marlin line in 2004. Features T-900 fire control system. This is a trigger and safety system that features a wide serrated trigger and improved trigger pull. Safety activation also improved. The 900 series also features drilled and tapped receivers on all models.

Model 915Y Compact

Single-shot .22 rimfire rifle, with 16.25" barrel. Hardwood stock, with impressed checkering. Iron sights.

NIB	Exc.	V.G.	Good	Fair	Poor
200	150	120	100	80	50

Model 915YS Compact

Similar to above, with stainless steel receiver and barrel. No checkering. Fiber optic sights.

NIB	Exc.	V.G.	Good	Fair	Poor
220	180	150	120	100	80

Model 917

Bolt-action rifle chambered in .17 Hornady Magnum rimfire; 7-shot clip magazine; fiberglass-filled synthetic stock with full pistol grip; swivel studs and molded-in checkering. Adjustable open rear sight, ramp front. 22" barrel. Introduced 2006.

NIB	Exc.	V.G.	Good	Fair	Poor
280	220	200	150	100	80

Model 917V

Chambered for .17 HMR cartridge. Fitted with 22" heavy barrel. Hardwood Monte Carlo stock, with full pistol grip. No sights. Detachable magazine with 7-round capacity. Weight about 6 lbs.

NIB	Exc.	V.G.	Good	Fair	Poor
280	220	200	150	100	80

Model 917VR

Similar to Model 917, with fiberglass-filled synthetic stock. Introduced

2006.

NIB	Exc.	V.G.	Good	Fair	Poor
280	220	200	150	100	80

Model 917VS

As above, with gray/black laminated hardwood stock. No sights. Magazine nickel plated. Weight about 7 lbs. Scope bases included.

NIB	Exc.	V.G.	Good	Fair	Poor
280	220	200	150	100	80

Model 917VS-CF

Similar to Model 917VS, with carbon fiber-patterned stock.

NIB	Exc.	V.G.	Good	Fair	Poor
280	220	200	150	100	80

Model 917VSF

Chambered for .17 HMR cartridge. Fitted with 22" heavy stainless steel fluted barrel. No sights. Nickel magazine capacity 7 rounds. Laminated gray stock, with Monte Carlo comb. Weight about 6.75 lbs. Introduced in 2005.

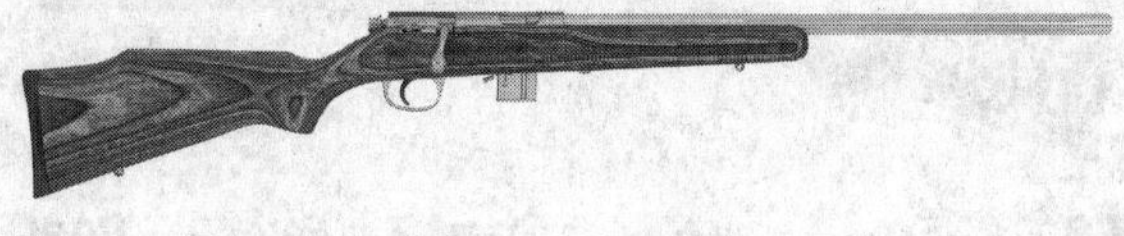

NIB	Exc.	V.G.	Good	Fair	Poor
300	250	200	180	150	120

Model 917VT

Similar to above, with laminated brown thumbhole stock. Introduced 2008.

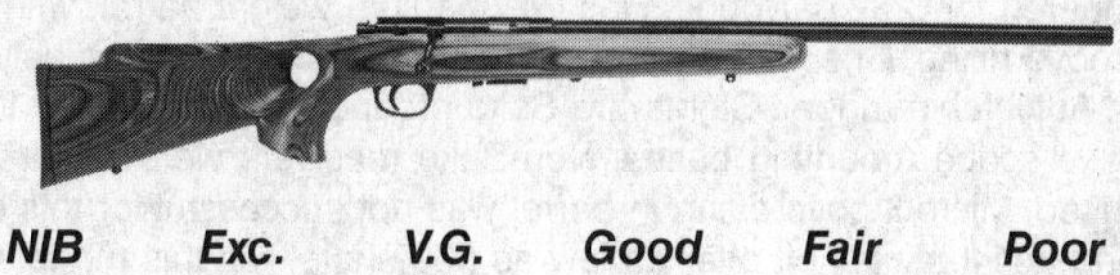

NIB	Exc.	V.G.	Good	Fair	Poor
350	300	250	180	140	110

Model 917VST

Similar to above, with laminated gray/black thumbhole stock. Introduced 2008.

NIB	Exc.	V.G.	Good	Fair	Poor
400	350	300	240	120	100

Model 917M2

Chambered for .17 Mach 2 cartridge. Fitted with 22" heavy barrel. Monte Carlo hardwood stock, with full pistol grip. No sights. Scope bases included. Magazine capacity 7 rounds. Weight about 5.5 lbs.

NIB	Exc.	V.G.	Good	Fair	Poor
300	250	200	180	150	120

Model 917M2S

As above, with Monte Carlo gray/black laminated stock. Full pistol grip. Stainless steel barrel and receiver. Nickel plated magazine.

NIB	Exc.	V.G.	Good	Fair	Poor
320	280	220	200	180	120

Model 925

Chambered for .22 LR cartridge. Fitted with 22" standard weight barrel. Adjustable sights. Monte Carlo hardwood stock. Full pistol grip. Seven-round magazine. Weight about 5.5 lbs.

NIB	Exc.	V.G.	Good	Fair	Poor
220	180	150	120	100	80

Model 925M

As above, with hardwood stock. Full pistol grip. Fitted with 22" standard weight barrel. Adjustable sights. Weight about 6 lbs.

NIB	Exc.	V.G.	Good	Fair	Poor
250	200	160	140	100	80

Model 925RM

Similar to Model 925M, with black fiberglass-filled synthetic stock.

NIB	Exc.	V.G.	Good	Fair	Poor
250	200	160	140	100	80

Model 925MC

As above, with Monte Carlo Mossy Oak Break-up camo stock. Weight about 6 lbs.

NIB	Exc.	V.G.	Good	Fair	Poor
280	220	200	150	100	80

Model 925C

As above, with Monte Carlo hardwood stock in Mossy Oak Break-up camo pattern. Adjustable sights.

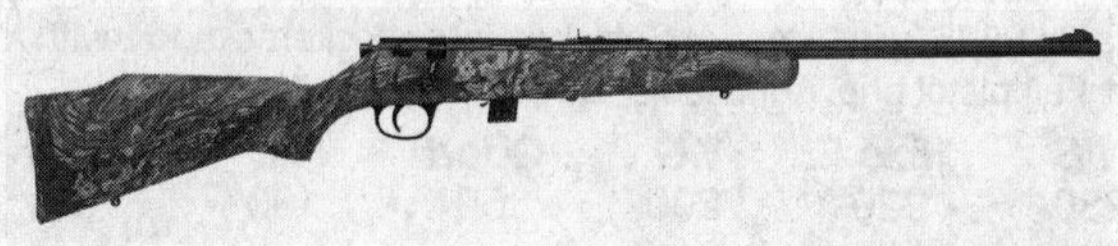

NIB	Exc.	V.G.	Good	Fair	Poor
250	200	160	140	100	80

Model 925R

As above, with factory-mounted 3x9 scope.

NIB	Exc.	V.G.	Good	Fair	Poor
250	200	160	140	100	80

Model 980V

Chambered for .22 LR cartridge. Fitted with 22" heavy barrel. Black fiberglass stock, with Monte Carlo. Full pistol grip. No sights. Magazine capacity 7 rounds. Weight about 7 lbs.

NIB	Exc.	V.G.	Good	Fair	Poor
280	220	200	150	100	80

Model 980S

As above, with standard weight 22" barrel and 7-round nickel plated magazine. Stainless steel barrel and receiver. Adjustable sights. Weight about 6 lbs.

NIB	Exc.	V.G.	Good	Fair	Poor
280	220	200	150	100	80

Model 980S-CF

As above, with carbon fiber stock. Introduced in 2007.

NIB	Exc.	V.G.	Good	Fair	Poor
280	220	200	150	100	80

Model 981T

Chambered to handle interchangeably .22 Short, Long or LR cartridges in a tubular magazine. Black Monte Carlo fiberglass stock, with full pistol grip. Adjustable sights. Fitted with standard weight 22" barrel. Weight about 6 lbs.

NIB	Exc.	V.G.	Good	Fair	Poor
280	220	200	150	100	80

Model 981TS

Bolt-action rifle chambered in .22 S/L/LR. Features include tubular magazine (holds 25 Short, 19 Long or 17 Long Rifle) cartridges; thumb safety; red cocking indicator; black fiberglass-filled synthetic stock, with full pistol grip; molded-in checkering and swivel studs; 22" stainless steel barrel, with MicroGroove rifling (16 grooves). Adjustable semi-buckhorn folding rear sight, ramp front with high visibility orange front sight post; cutaway Wide-Scan hood. Receiver grooved for scope mount; drilled and tapped for scope bases.

NIB	Exc.	V.G.	Good	Fair	Poor
300	250	220	150	100	80

Model 982

Similar to 982S, with American black walnut checkered stock, with Monte Carlo. Full pistol grip. Adjustable sights. Weight about 6 lbs.

NIB	Exc.	V.G.	Good	Fair	Poor
280	220	200	150	100	80

Model 982S

Chambered for .22 WMR cartridge. Fitted with 22" stainless steel barrel. Adjustable sights. Black fiberglass stock, with Monte Carlo. Full pistol grip. Detachable 7-round nickel magazine. Weight about 6 lbs.

NIB	Exc.	V.G.	Good	Fair	Poor
280	220	200	150	100	80

Model 982L

As above, with gray/black laminated stock. Weight about 6.25 lbs.

NIB	Exc.	V.G.	Good	Fair	Poor
300	250	200	180	150	120

Model 982VS

As above, with black fiberglass Monte Carlo stock. Heavy 22" stainless steel barrel. Nickel plated 7-round magazine. No sights. Weight about 7 lbs.

NIB	Exc.	V.G.	Good	Fair	Poor
320	280	220	200	180	120

Model 982VS-CF

As above, with synthetic stock. Dipped carbon-fiber textured finish.

NIB	Exc.	V.G.	Good	Fair	Poor
320	280	220	200	180	120

Model 983

.22 WMR model features Monte Carlo stock of American black walnut, with full pistol grip and checkering.

NIB	Exc.	V.G.	Good	Fair	Poor
280	220	200	150	100	80

Model 983T

Chambered for .22 WMR cartridge. Fitted with 22" barrel. Monte Carlo black fiberglass stock, with checkering. Adjustable sights. Tubular 12-round magazine. Weight about 6 lbs.

NIB	Exc.	V.G.	Good	Fair	Poor
280	220	200	150	100	80

Model 983S

As above, with laminated two-tone stock.

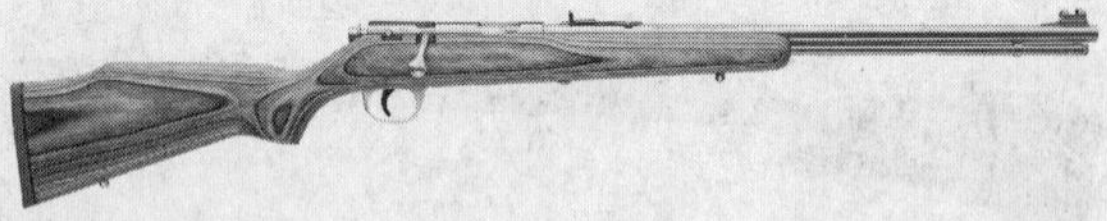

NIB	Exc.	V.G.	Good	Fair	Poor
280	220	200	150	100	80

CENTERFIRE RIFLES

Model 322

Chambered for .222 cartridge. Has 24" medium weight barrel, with MicroGroove rifling. Checkered walnut pistol grip stock. Magazine holds 4 shots. Adjustable trigger. Sights are Sako products. Sako receiver fitted for Sako scope mounting bases. Non-Sako receivers were apparently also used. MicroGroove rifling in barrel was not successful for this caliber and accuracy fell off after as few as 500 shots—so this model was dropped and replaced. Serial numbers were Sako. Manufactured 5,859 between 1954 and 1959.

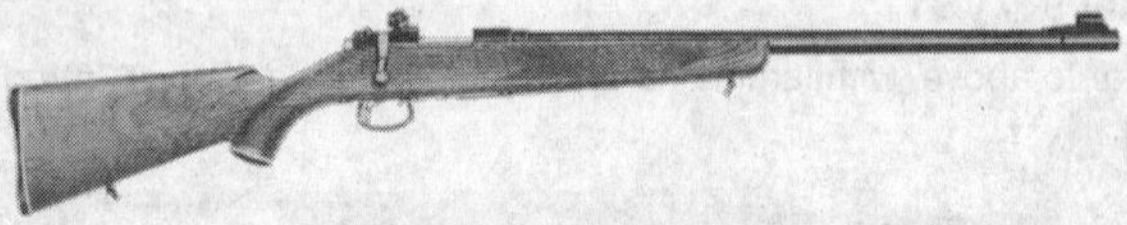

NIB	Exc.	V.G.	Good	Fair	Poor
600	550	450	350	300	200

Model 422

Successor to Model 322. Simply same rifle fitted with 24" featherweight stainless steel barrel. Named "Varmint King". Features Monte Carlo stock, with cheekpiece. Manufactured only 354 between 1956 and 1958.

NIB	Exc.	V.G.	Good	Fair	Poor
950	600	500	400	300	200

Model 455

Built on Fabrique Nationale Belgian Mauser action. Chambered for .308 and .30-06 cartridges. Stainless steel barrel made by Marlin, with 5-shot magazine. Bishop checkered walnut stock, with detachable sling swivels and leather sling. Rear sight Lyman 48; front ramp type, with detachable hood. Receiver drilled and tapped for scope mounts. Trigger adjustable Sako unit. Manufactured 1,079 in .30-06; only 59 in .308 between 1955 and 1959.

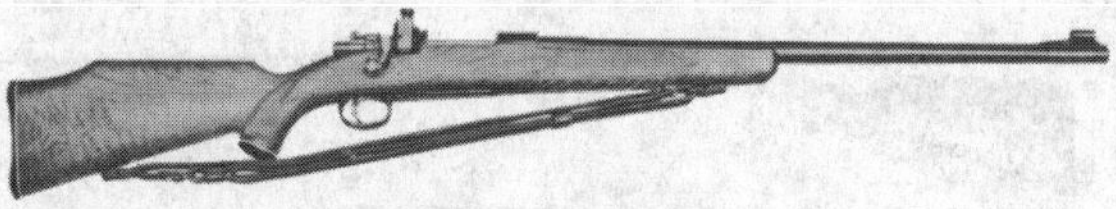

NIB	Exc.	V.G.	Good	Fair	Poor
—	700	600	420	300	200

Model MR-7

Introduced in 1996. American-made bolt-action centerfire rifle of a totally new design. Chambered for .25-06 (first offered in 1997), .243, .270 Win. .280, .308 or .30-06 cartridges. Fitted with 22" barrel. Has American black walnut stock; 4-shot detachable box magazine. Offered with or without sights. Weight about 7.5 lbs. Discontinued 1999.

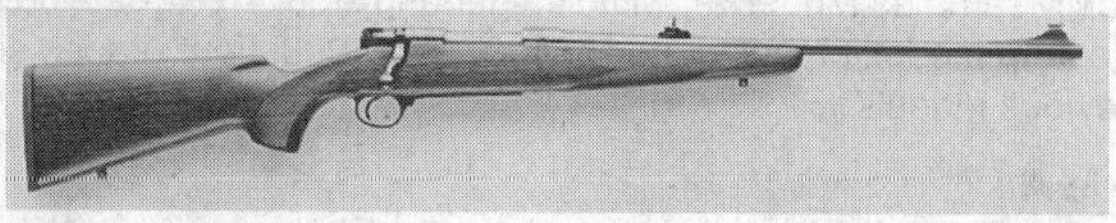

NIB	Exc.	V.G.	Good	Fair	Poor
450	350	300	250	180	150

Model MR-7B

Similar to MR-7. Fitted with 4-round blind magazine; birch stock. Offered in .30-06 or .270; with or without sights. Introduced in 1998; discontinued.

NIB	Exc.	V.G.	Good	Fair	Poor
380	300	250	180	150	100

Model XL7

Introduced in 2008. Centerfire bolt-action rifle, with adjustable Pro-Fire trigger system. 4+1 capacity. Chambered in .25-06, .270 and .30-06. Black synthetic or walnut stock, with raised cheekpiece. Soft-Tech recoil pad. No sights; drilled and tapped for mounts. Short action chambered in 7mm-08, .243 Win, .308 Win and comes in a youth model with shorter stock. Note: Add $50 for factory scope package; Add $25 for camo finish. Discontinued.

NIB	Exc.	V.G.	Good	Fair	Poor
320	280	220	200	180	120

Model XL7C

Similar to above, with Realtree APG HD camo finish.

NIB	Exc.	V.G.	Good	Fair	Poor
350	300	250	180	140	110

Model XS7 Short-Action

Similar to Model XL7. Chambered in 7mm-08, .243 Win. and .308 Win. Note: Add $50 for factory scope package.

NIB	Exc.	V.G.	Good	Fair	Poor
320	280	220	200	180	120

Model XS7Y Youth Rifle

Similar to above, with smaller dimensions.

NIB	Exc.	V.G.	Good	Fair	Poor
320	280	220	200	180	120

Model XS7C Camo

Similar to above, with Realtree APG HD camo stock.

NIB	Exc.	V.G.	Good	Fair	Poor
350	300	250	180	140	110

Model XS7S

Bolt-action rifle similar to Model XS7, with stainless steel barrel, receiver and trigger group. Short action. Discontinued.

NIB	Exc.	V.G.	Good	Fair	Poor
380	320	280	180	150	100

Model XL7

Entry-level bolt-action rifle chambered in .25-06 Rem., .270 Win., .30-06 Spr. Features include 4+1 magazine capacity; pillar bedded 22" barrel; Pro-Fire adjustable trigger system; 2-position safety; red cocking indicator; swivel studs; matte blue/black finish; black synthetic stock, with molded in checkering and Soft-Tech recoil pad. No sights.

NIB	Exc.	V.G.	Good	Fair	Poor
320	280	240	200	150	80

PUMP SHOTGUNS

Model 1898

Made in 12-gauge, with exposed hammer. Has take-down receiver. Walnut pistol grip stock and forend. 5-shot tube magazine. Barrel lengths from 26" to 32". Manufactured between 1898 and 1905.

Grade A

Variation has 30", 32" or 38" barrel. Full choke. Plainest grade.

Courtesy Marlin Firearms Co.

NIB	Exc.	V.G.	Good	Fair	Poor
—	480	420	320	120	80

Grade A Brush or Riot

Same shotgun, with 26" cylinder-bore barrel.

NIB	Exc.	V.G.	Good	Fair	Poor
—	420	380	250	150	100

Grade B

Same as Grade A, with special smokeless steel barrel. Checkered stock.

NIB	Exc.	V.G.	Good	Fair	Poor
—	680	550	350	150	100

Grade C

More deluxe version, with engraving. Fancier wood.

NIB	Exc.	V.G.	Good	Fair	Poor
—	1150	850	550	280	120

Grade D

Variation has Damascus barrel. Greatest amount of engraving.

NIB	Exc.	V.G.	Good	Fair	Poor
—	2100	1400	900	450	250

Model 16

Exactly the same as Model 1898, except chambered for 16-gauge only. Four grades are the same. Manufactured between 1903 and 1910.

Grade A

NIB	Exc.	V.G.	Good	Fair	Poor
—	500	450	400	250	150

Grade B

NIB	Exc.	V.G.	Good	Fair	Poor
—	650	550	400	200	100

Grade C

NIB	Exc.	V.G.	Good	Fair	Poor
—	1100	850	500	300	150

Grade D

NIB	Exc.	V.G.	Good	Fair	Poor
—	2000	1400	950	420	250

Model 17

An exposed-hammer gun, with a solid frame and straight-grip stock. Chambered for 12-gauge, with 30" or 32" barrel. Manufactured between 1906 and 1908.

NIB	Exc.	V.G.	Good	Fair	Poor
—	520	450	280	150	80

Model 17 Brush Gun

Variation similar to standard Model 17, with 26" cylinder-bore barrel.

NIB	Exc.	V.G.	Good	Fair	Poor
—	550	480	320	200	100

Model 17 Riot Gun

Variation has 20" cylinder-bore barrel.

NIB	Exc.	V.G.	Good	Fair	Poor
—	600	520	320	150	120

Model 19

A take-down gun chambered for 12-gauge. Basically an improved and lightened version of Model 1898. Available in same four grades. Manufactured in 1906 and 1907.

Grade A

NIB	Exc.	V.G.	Good	Fair	Poor
—	500	450	250	150	100

Grade B

NIB	Exc.	V.G.	Good	Fair	Poor
—	600	550	500	350	220

Grade C

NIB	Exc.	V.G.	Good	Fair	Poor
—	750	680	5550	420	300

Grade D

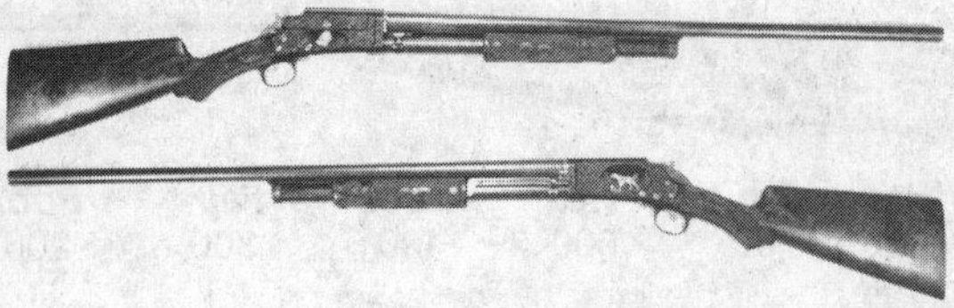

Courtesy Marlin Firearms Co.

NIB	Exc.	V.G.	Good	Fair	Poor
—	1850	1500	1050	400	200

Model 21 "Trap"

Basically same as Model 19, with straight-grip stock. 1907 catalog listed it as a Trap model. Manufactured in 1907 and 1908. Four grades similar to previous models.

Grade A

NIB	Exc.	V.G.	Good	Fair	Poor
—	450	450	300	200	100

Grade B

NIB	Exc.	V.G.	Good	Fair	Poor
—	600	550	350	200	100

Grade C

NIB	Exc.	V.G.	Good	Fair	Poor
—	750	680	500	350	200

Grade D

NIB	Exc.	V.G.	Good	Fair	Poor
—	1600	1300	1050	700	550

Model 24

Actually an improved version of Model 21. Has pistol grip stock and exposed hammer. Features automatic recoil lock on slide; matte rib barrel. Otherwise, quite similar to its predecessor. Manufactured between 1908 and 1917.

Grade A

Courtesy Marlin Firearms Co.

NIB	Exc.	V.G.	Good	Fair	Poor
—	480	400	350	150	100

Grade B

NIB	Exc.	V.G.	Good	Fair	Poor
—	600	550	450	350	220

Grade C

NIB	Exc.	V.G.	Good	Fair	Poor
—	750	680	550	420	300

Grade D

NIB	Exc.	V.G.	Good	Fair	Poor
—	1600	1300	900	600	400

Marlin "Trap Gun"

Unique, in it has no numerical designation and simply known as Trap Gun". A take-down gun, with interchangeable barrels from 16" to 32". Straight-grip buttstock, Quite similar in appearance to Model 24. Manufactured between 1909 and 1912.

NIB	Exc.	V.G.	Good	Fair	Poor
—	1000	700	520	350	200

Model 26

Similar to Model 24 Grade A, with solid frame. 30" or 32" barrels.

NIB	Exc.	V.G.	Good	Fair	Poor
—	520	450	320	120	100

Model 26 Brush Gun

Model has 26" cylinder-bored barrel.

NIB	Exc.	V.G.	Good	Fair	Poor
—	550	480	320	200	100

Model 26 Riot Gun

Variation has 20" cylinder-bored barrel.

NIB	Exc.	V.G.	Good	Fair	Poor
—	600	520	320	150	120

Model 28 Hammerless

First of the Marlin hammerless shotguns. A take-down 12-gauge, with barrels from 26" to 32" in length. Stock has pistol grip. Comes in four grades like its predecessors. Manufactured between 1913 and 1922.

Grade A

NIB	Exc.	V.G.	Good	Fair	Poor
—	400	340	200	100	70

Grade B

NIB	Exc.	V.G.	Good	Fair	Poor
—	600	550	350	350	220

Grade C

NIB	Exc.	V.G.	Good	Fair	Poor
—	750	620	550	420	300

Grade D

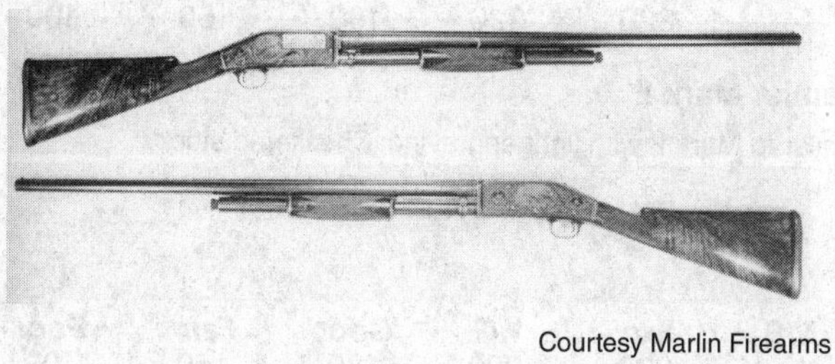

Courtesy Marlin Firearms Co.

NIB	Exc.	V.G.	Good	Fair	Poor
—	1700	1200	800	600	300

Model 28TS Trap Gun

Variation same as Model 28, with 30" Full choke barrel. Matte rib and high-comb straight-grip stock. Manufactured in 1915.

NIB	Exc.	V.G.	Good	Fair	Poor
—	720	600	520	420	300

Model 28T Trap Gun

Variation is deluxe model similar to Model 28TS, with engraving, high-grade walnut and hand checkering. Manufactured in 1915.

NIB	Exc.	V.G.	Good	Fair	Poor
—	750	620	550	420	300

Model 30

Improved version of Model 16, 16-gauge shotgun. Features similar, with addition of improved take-down system and automatic recoil lock on slide. Manufactured between 1910 and 1914.

Grade A

NIB	Exc.	V.G.	Good	Fair	Poor
—	550	480	350	200	100

Grade B

NIB	Exc.	V.G.	Good	Fair	Poor
—	600	550	450	200	100

Grade C

NIB	Exc.	V.G.	Good	Fair	Poor
—	750	680	550	250	150

Grade D

NIB	Exc.	V.G.	Good	Fair	Poor
—	1400	1200	1000	700	550

Model 30 Field Grade

Similar to Model 30 Grade B, with 25" Modified-choke barrel. Straight-grip stock. Manufactured in 1913 and 1914.

NIB	Exc.	V.G.	Good	Fair	Poor
—	450	380	250	150	100

Model 31

Smaller version of Model 28 Hammerless take-down. Chambered for 16- and 20-gauge. Barrel lengths 26" and 28". Available in usual four grades. Various different chokes. Manufactured between 1915 and 1922.

Grade A

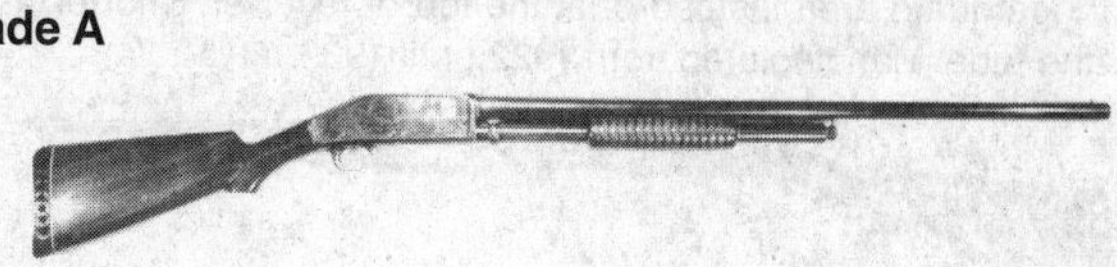

Courtesy Marlin Firearms Co.

NIB	Exc.	V.G.	Good	Fair	Poor
—	500	450	350	150	100

Grade B

NIB	Exc.	V.G.	Good	Fair	Poor
—	600	550	450	250	150

Grade C

NIB	Exc.	V.G.	Good	Fair	Poor
—	750	680	550	300	150

Grade D

NIB	Exc.	V.G.	Good	Fair	Poor
—	1400	1200	1000	600	300

Model 42/42A

Originally listed as Model 42, but in the second year of production, designation was changed to /42A for no apparent reason than standardization of models. Similar to Model 24, except barrel markings are different. Still an exposed hammer take-down gun chambered for 12-gauge. Manufactured between 1922 and 1933.

NIB	Exc.	V.G.	Good	Fair	Poor
—	380	320	200	150	100

Model 43A

Hammerless model quite similar to Model 28, with different markings and less attention to finishing detail. Manufactured between 1923 and

1930.

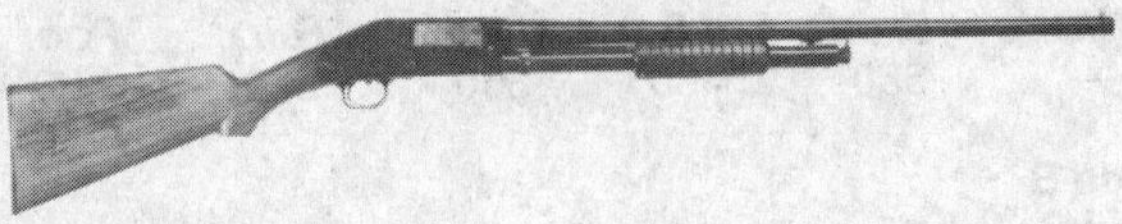

NIB	Exc.	V.G.	Good	Fair	Poor
—	400	350	250	150	80

Model 43T

Same as Model 43A take-down hammerless, with 30" or 32" matte rib barrel. Straight-grip stock of high grade walnut, with non-gloss oil-finish. Fitted recoil pad. Manufactured between 1922 and 1930.

NIB	Exc.	V.G.	Good	Fair	Poor
—	500	450	350	200	100

Model 43TS

Custom-order version of Model 43T. Same in all respects, except stock could be ordered to any specifications shooter desired. Manufactured between 1922 and 1930.

NIB	Exc.	V.G.	Good	Fair	Poor
—	700	620	550	250	150

Model 44A

Similar to Model 31. Advertised as its successor. Hammerless take-down chambered for 20-gauge. Features improved bolt opening device located in triggerguard area instead of at the top of receiver. Shorter 4-shot magazine tube. Manufactured from 1922 until 1933.

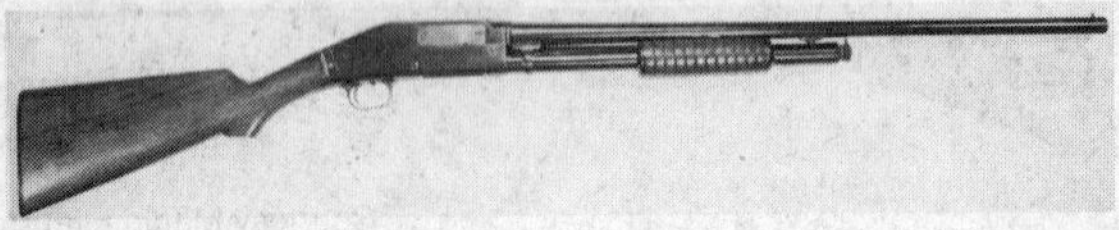

Courtesy Marlin Firearms Co.

NIB	Exc.	V.G.	Good	Fair	Poor
—	480	400	280	150	100

Model 44S

Similar to Model 44A, with higher grade walnut stock. Featured hand-cut checkering.

NIB	Exc.	V.G.	Good	Fair	Poor
—	500	420	300	200	100

Model 49

12-gauge exposed-hammer take-down. Combines features of Model 42 and Model 24. Basically a lower-priced model that was never listed in Marlin catalog. Part of Frank Kenna's money-raising program—anyone who purchased four shares of stock for $25 per share was given one, free of charge. Manufactured between 1925 and 1928.

NIB	Exc.	V.G.	Good	Fair	Poor
—	700	620	550	250	150

Model 53

Hammerless take-down 12-gauge that was not in production for long. Theorized that Model 53 was produced to use up old parts on hand when Model 43 was introduced. Manufactured in 1929 and 1980.

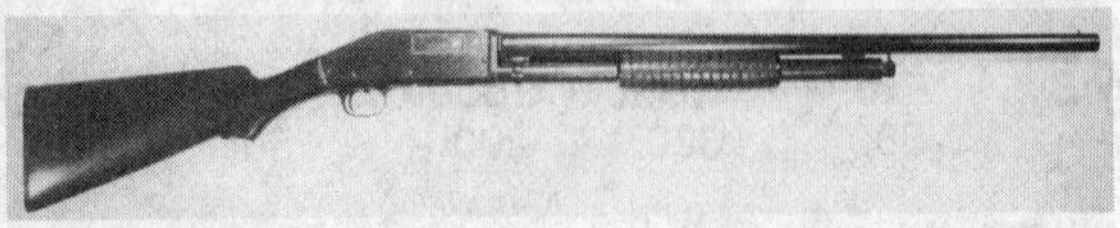

Courtesy Marlin Firearms Co.

NIB	Exc.	V.G.	Good	Fair	Poor
—	450	400	280	180	120

Model 63

Last of the slide-action shotguns produced by Marlin until Model 120 in 1971. Hammerless take-down 12-gauge. Replaced Model 43A in Marlin catalog. Had improvements over earlier guns, but its introduction during Depression did little to bolster sales. Offered free of charge to anyone purchasing four shares of Marlin stock at $25 per share. Manufactured between 1931 and 1933.

NIB	Exc.	V.G.	Good	Fair	Poor
—	500	450	350	200	100

Model 63T

Trap-grade version of Model 63. Has better grade hand-checkered stock. Fitted recoil pad and oil-finish. Manufactured between 1931 and 1933.

NIB	Exc.	V.G.	Good	Fair	Poor
—	600	520	450	200	120

Model 63TS

Variation same as Model 63T, except stock dimensions were custom-made to customer's specifications. Manufactured between 1931 and 1933.

NIB	Exc.	V.G.	Good	Fair	Poor
—	700	620	550	250	150

Premier Mark I

Made by Manufrance and called LaSalle. Marlin was able to purchase them, without barrels at a good enough price, for Marlin to barrel and market them under their own name. This model is 12-gauge only. Alloy receiver and seven interchangeable barrels in 26" to 30" lengths. Various chokes. Plain stock is French walnut. Biggest problem with this gun is that the lightweight (6 lbs.) produced severe recoil and less than enjoyable to shoot. In production from 1959 through 1963, with approximately 13,700 sold.

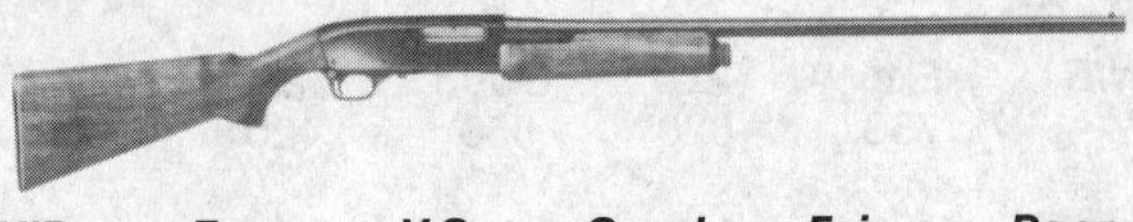

NIB	Exc.	V.G.	Good	Fair	Poor
—	320	220	180	150	100

Premier Mark II

Similar to Mark I, with light engraving. Checkered stock.

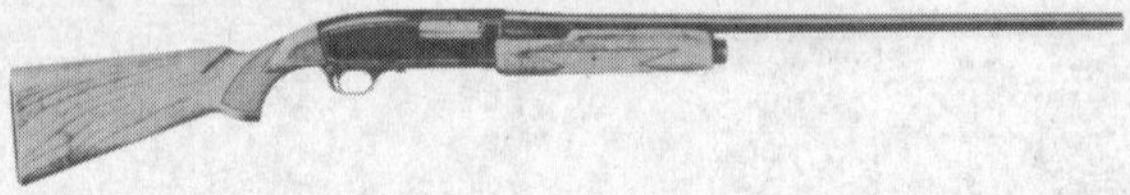

NIB	Exc.	V.G.	Good	Fair	Poor
—	320	220	180	150	100

Premier Mark IV

Similar to Mark II, with more engraving on receiver. Note: Add 10 percent for ventilated rib.

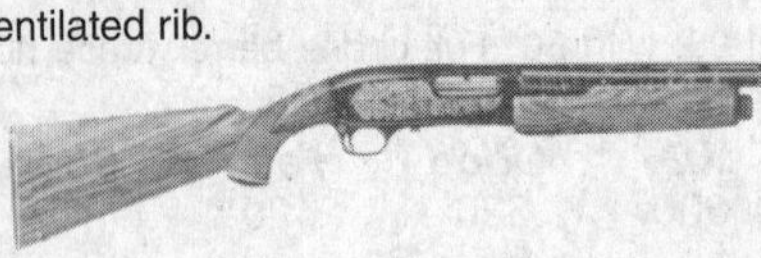

NIB	Exc.	V.G.	Good	Fair	Poor
—	320	220	180	150	100

Model 120

Styled to resemble Winchester Model 12. Advertised as an all steel and walnut shotgun. Offered with interchangeable barrels from 26" to 40". Various chokes were available. Checkered walnut stock, with fitted recoil pad. Tube magazine holds 5 shots, 4 in 3". Trap Model available (1973-1975); slug gun (1974-1984). Manufactured between 1971 and 1985. A really nice gun, if a bit heavy. Note: Add 10 percent for 36" "Long Tom" barrel.

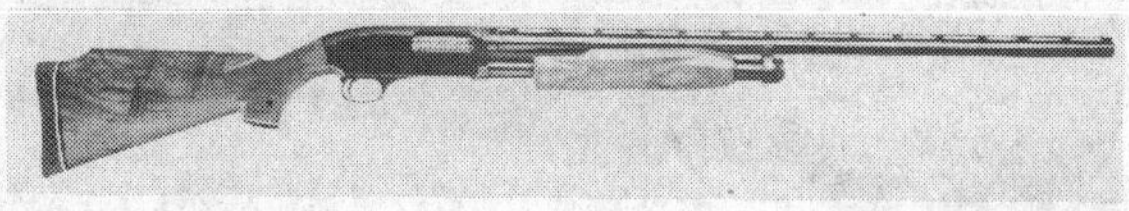

NIB	Exc.	V.G.	Good	Fair	Poor
—	350	300	250	150	120

Model 778 (Glenfield)

Similar to Model 120, with walnut finished hardwood stock instead of walnut. Glenfield name stamped on it. Manufactured between 1979 and 1984.

NIB	Exc.	V.G.	Good	Fair	Poor
—	280	220	180	120	100

OVER/UNDER & TOP-BREAK SHOTGUNS

Model 60 Single-Barrel Shotgun

Break-open exposed-hammer top lever-opening 12-gauge, with 30" or 32" Full-choke barrel. Pistol grip stock. Approximately 60 manufactured in 1923.

NIB	Exc.	V.G.	Good	Fair	Poor
—	400	350	250	150	80

Model 90 Over/Under Shotgun

Produced in response to a request from Sears Roebuck, that Marlin should manufacture an over/under shotgun for Sears to market in their stores. Guns produced for Sears have prefix 103 in their serial numbers and marked "Ranger" before WWII and "J.C. Higgins" after the war. Prior to 1945, they were not marked Marlin; after that date Sears requested that the company stamp their name on the guns. They were also produced as Marlin Model 90 during the same period. Chambered for 12-, 16- and 20-gauge, as well as .410 bore. The 16- and 20-gauge guns first offered in 1937, with 26" or 28" barrels. In 1939, .410 bore was first offered with 26" barrel and 3" chambers. Barrels are 26", 28" or 30", with various chokes. Action is boxlock with extractors. Guns made prior to 1950 were solid between the barrels; after that date there was a space between barrels. Can be found with double-/single triggers and checkered walnut stock. Ventilated rib offered as an option beginning in 1949. Be aware that this model was also available as a combination gun in .22 LR/.410, .22 Hornet/.410 and .218 Bee/.410. Approximately 34,000 Model 90s manufactured between 1937 and 1963. Note: Add 33 percent single trigger; 25 percent 20-gauge; 300 percent .410 bores; 300 percent premium combination guns. There are other rare gauge and barrel combinations that may affect value.

Marlin Model 90 Combination Gun

NIB	Exc.	V.G.	Good	Fair	Poor
—	550	420	350	280	200

LEVER-ACTION SHOTGUNS

Model .410 Lever-Action Shotgun (Original)

Unique venture for Marlin Company—a lever-action shotgun based on Model 1893 action. Longer loading port, modified tube magazine that held 5 shots and smoothbore barrel chambered for .410 shot shell. Finish blued, with walnut pistol grip stock and grooved beavertail forend. Hard rubber rifle-type buttplate. Available with 22" or 26" Full-choke barrel. This gun was also part of the stock purchase plan and was given free of charge to anyone purchasing four shares at $25 per share. Also cataloged for sale. Manufactured between 1929 and 1932.

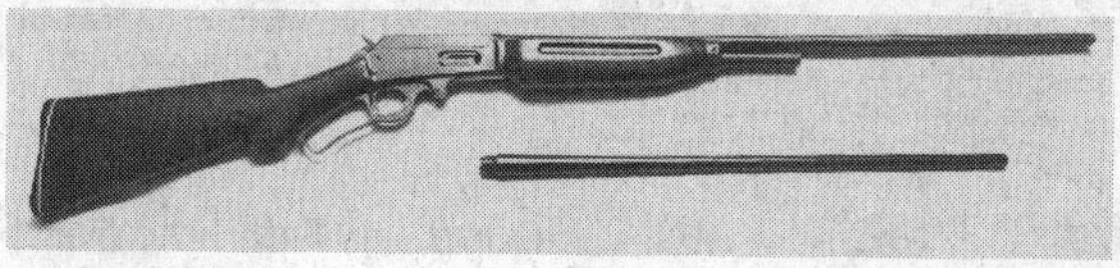

Courtesy Mike Stuckslager

NIB	Exc.	V.G.	Good	Fair	Poor
—	1600	1000	650	500	200

Model .410 Deluxe (Original)

Variation was never cataloged. Essentially same as standard version, with hand-checkered stock. Forend does not have grooves as found on standard model. Be wary of fakes!

NIB	Exc.	V.G.	Good	Fair	Poor
—	2200	1200	800	400	200

Model .410 (New)

Lever-action shotgun chambered for 2.5" .410 shot shell. Checkered walnut stock, fluorescent front sight. Based on Model 336 action. Discontinued.

NIB	Exc.	V.G.	Good	Fair	Poor
700	620	550	450	300	—

Model 410XLR 410 XLR

New in 2009. Latest Marlin .410 shotgun. Built on M1895 chassis. Chambered for 2.5" .410 shot shells. Receiver and barrel stainless. Stock laminated wood.

NIB	Exc.	V.G.	Good	Fair	Poor
750	680	580	450	300	—

Model 1895 410 Bore

Gauge: .410 bore, 2.5 in. Capacity: 4+1. Barrel: 22 in. round barrel. Length: 40.5 in. Weight: 7.25 lbs. Stock: American black walnut, straight stock. Features: Marlin re-enters the lever-action shotgun market with a .410 bore. Standard loop, polished blue, adjustable semi-buckhorn rear sight. Choice of two models, one with a fixed cylinder bore and the other with three flush-mount interchangeable chokes (IM, LM, F).

NIB	Exc.	V.G.	Good	Fair	Poor
840	—	—	—	—	—

BOLT-ACTION SHOTGUNS

Model 50DL

Bolt-action 12-gauge shotgun. Available with 28" modified barrel, black synthetic stock. Ventilated recoil pad standard. Brass bead front sight. Weight about 7.5 lbs.

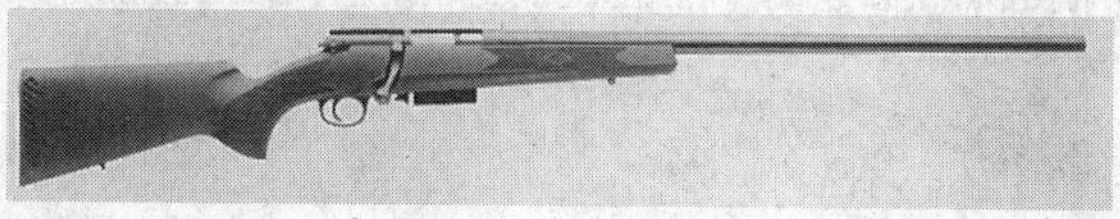

NIB	Exc.	V.G.	Good	Fair	Poor
300	280	220	150	120	100

Model 55

Chambered for 12-, 16- and 20-gauge, with Full or adjustable choke. Barrels 26" or 28". Bolt-action, with 2-shot box magazine. Pistol grip stock is plain. Manufactured between 1950 and 1965.

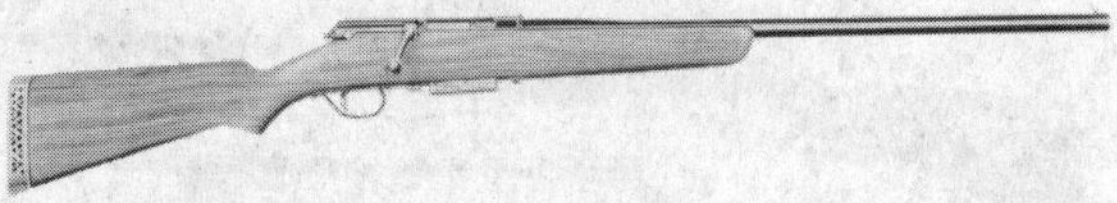

NIB	Exc.	V.G.	Good	Fair	Poor
—	220	180	100	50	20

Model 55 Swamp Gun

Simply Model 55, with 3" Magnum 20" barrel. Adjustable choke. Manufactured between 1963 and 1965.

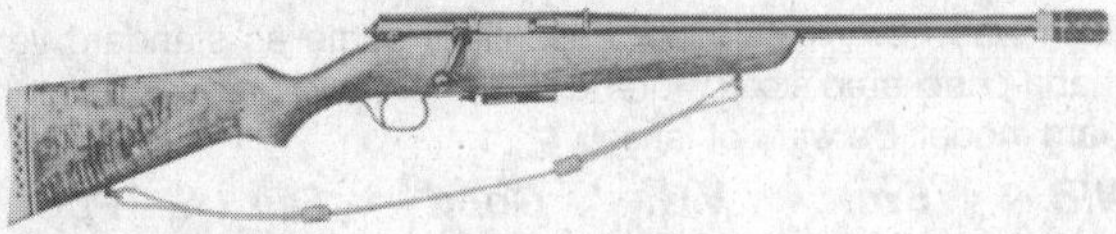

NIB	Exc.	V.G.	Good	Fair	Poor
—	300	250	180	80	50

Model 55 Goose Gun

Model 55, with 3" chamber, 36" Full choke 12-gauge barrel. Recoil pad and sling. Introduced in 1962.

NIB	Exc.	V.G.	Good	Fair	Poor
380	250	180	150	80	50

Model 55S Slug Gun

Model 55, with 24" Cylinder Bore barrel. Rifle sights. Manufactured between 1974 and 1983.

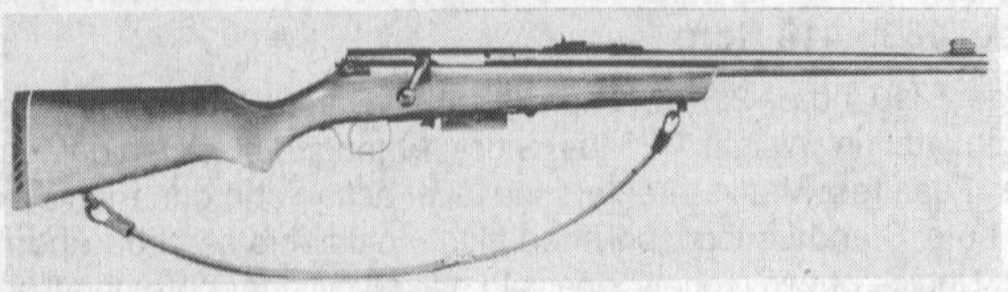

NIB	Exc.	V.G.	Good	Fair	Poor
—	250	200	150	100	50

Model 5510 Goose Gun

Chambered for 3.5" 10-gauge. Has 34" Full choke barrel. Recoil pad and sling. Manufactured between 1976 and 1985.

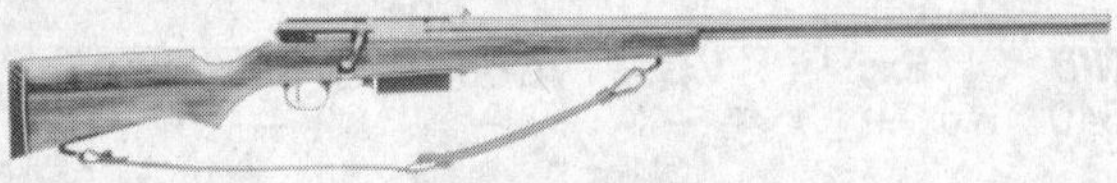

NIB	Exc.	V.G.	Good	Fair	Poor
—	400	300	250	180	100

Model 55GDL

Bolt-action shotgun fitted with 36" Full choke barrel. Reinforced black synthetic stock. Magazine holds two rounds. Ventilated recoil pad standard. Weight about 8 lbs. First introduced in 1997; discontinued.

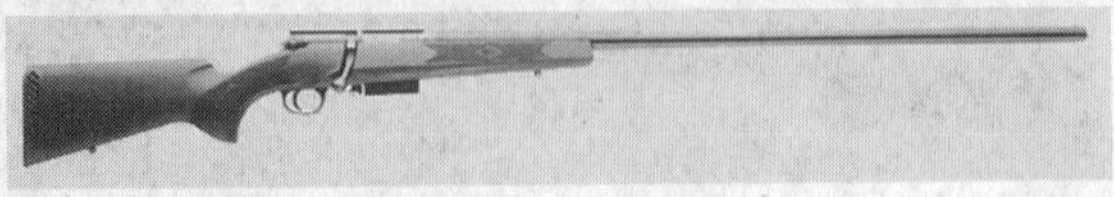

NIB	Exc.	V.G.	Good	Fair	Poor
350	320	280	200	150	100

Model 512 Slugmaster

Introduced in 1994. Bolt-action shotgun features rifled 21" barrel. Equipped with two-shot detachable magazine. Ventilated recoil pad. Special scope also provided. Weight about 8 lbs. Discontinued.

NIB	Exc.	V.G.	Good	Fair	Poor
350	320	280	200	150	100

Model 512DL Slugmaster

Introduced in 1997. Bolt-action features black synthetic stock, with fully rifled 21" barrel. Chambered for 12-gauge shell. A two-round magazine is standard. Adjustable rear sight, with ramp front sight. In 1998, furnished with "Fire Sights". Receiver drilled and tapped for scope mount. Weight about 8 lbs. Discontinued.

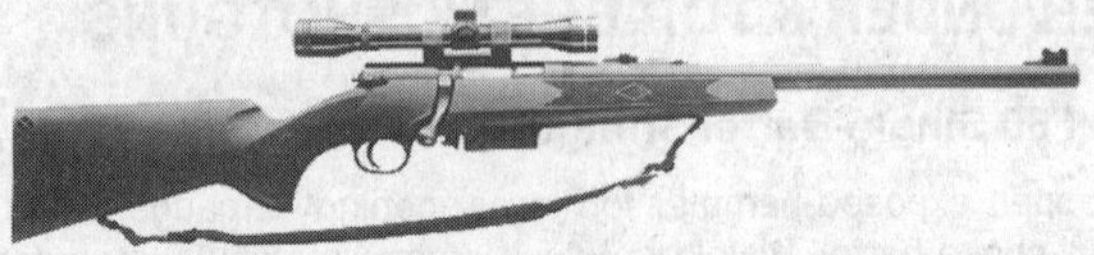

NIB	Exc.	V.G.	Good	Fair	Poor
400	250	200	150	120	100

Model 512P

Introduced in 1999. Similar to Model 512 DL, with addition of 21" fully rifled and ported barrel. Fire sights standard. Weight about 8 lbs. Discontinued.

NIB	Exc.	V.G.	Good	Fair	Poor
400	250	200	150	120	100

Model 25MG

Bolt-action .22 Win. Magnum shot shell only. Fitted with 22" smoothbore barrel. Has 7-round magazine. Hardwood stock. Weight about 6 lbs. First introduced in 1999.

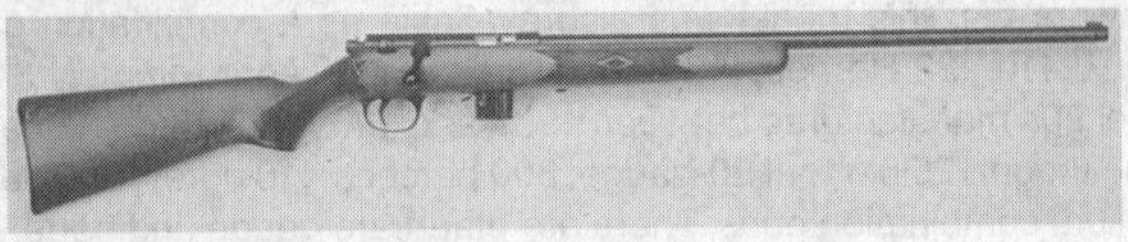

NIB	Exc.	V.G.	Good	Fair	Poor
220	180	140	120	100	80

MODERN L.C. SMITH SHOTGUNS

Modern line of L.C. Smith shotguns made in Europe. Imported into USA under Marlin name from 2005 to 2009.

Model LC410-DB

Side-by-side .410 bore, with fleur-de-lis checkered walnut stock, single selective trigger, selective automatic ejectors, three choke tubes (IC, M, F) and 26" chrome-lined barrels, with solid rib and bead front sight. Case colored receiver has gold game bird embossed on side and bottom.

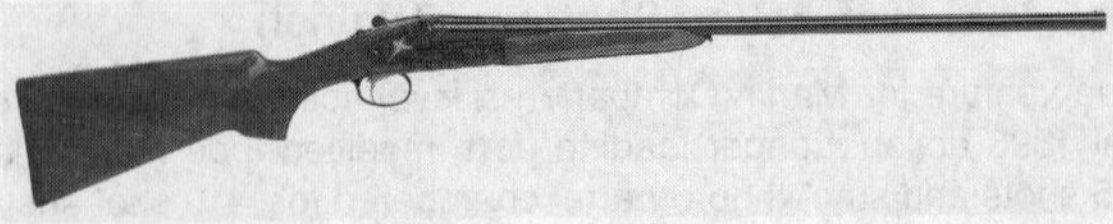

NIB	Exc.	V.G.	Good	Fair	Poor
1800	1750	1400	900	600	300

Model LC28-DB

Similar to above in 28-gauge.

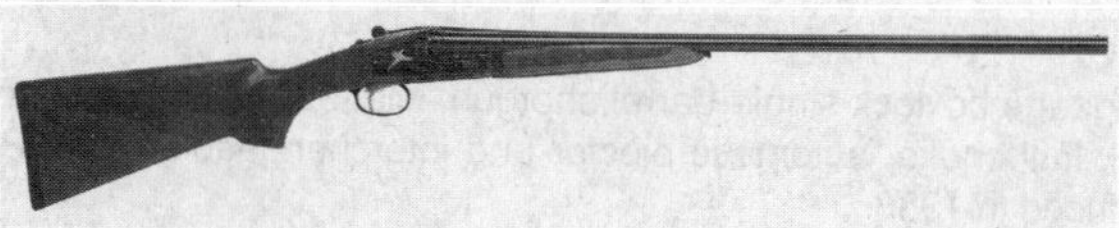

NIB	Exc.	V.G.	Good	Fair	Poor
1900	1850	1500	1000	750	300

Model LC12-DB

12-gauge double barrel features 3" chambers, single trigger, selective automatic ejectors, three choke tubes (IC, M, F), 28" barrels, with solid rib and bead front sight. Walnut stock checkered. Has fluted comb, beavertail forearm and recoil pad. Case coloring on receiver and side plates.

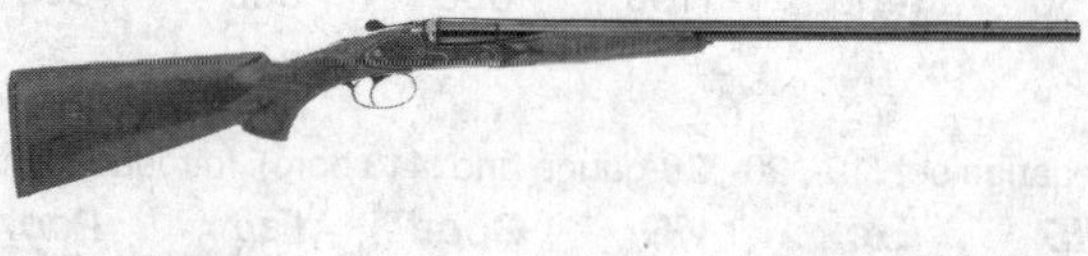

NIB	Exc.	V.G.	Good	Fair	Poor
1400	1280	880	700	350	200

Model LC20-DB

Similar to above in 20-gauge.

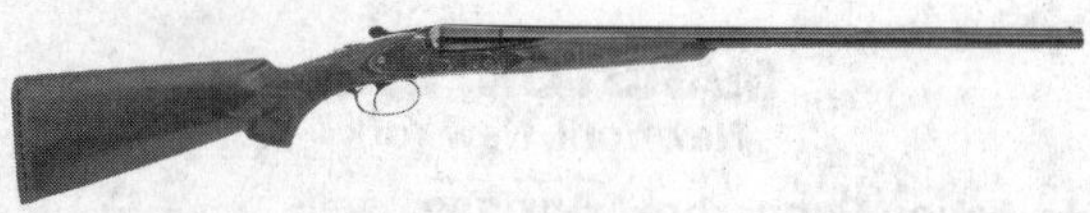

NIB	Exc.	V.G.	Good	Fair	Poor
1600	1500	1100	800	400	200

Model LC12-OU

Over/under features 3" chambers, single selective trigger, selective automatic ejectors, automatic safety, three choke tubes (IC, M, F), 28" barrels, with ventilated rib and bead front sight. Checkered walnut stock, with fluted comb. Recoil pad. Case coloring on receiver and sideplates.

NIB	Exc.	V.G.	Good	Fair	Poor
950	820	600	450	300	200

Model LC20-OU

Similar to above in 20-gauge.

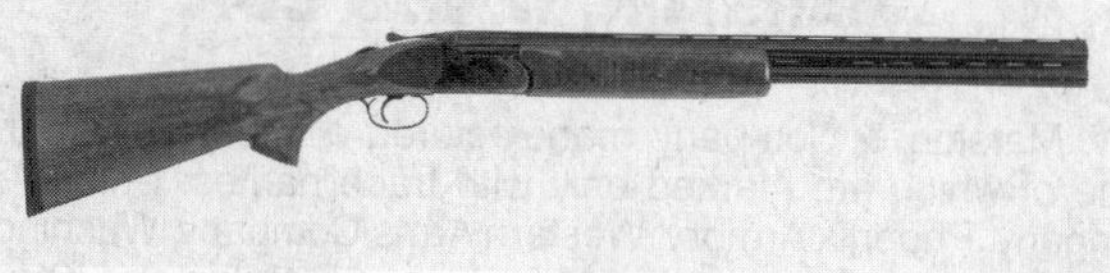

NIB	Exc.	V.G.	Good	Fair	Poor
950	820	600	450	300	200

MODERN MUZZLELOADERS

Model MLS-50/54

Marlin inline muzzleloaders were introduced in 1997. They are stainless steel. Available in .50- or .54-caliber. Barrel 22" long. Adjustable Marble rear sight, ramp front sight with brass bead. Drilled and tapped for scope mount. Black synthetic stock, with molded checkering. Weight about 7 lbs. Discontinued. Not particularly easy to take down for cleaning.

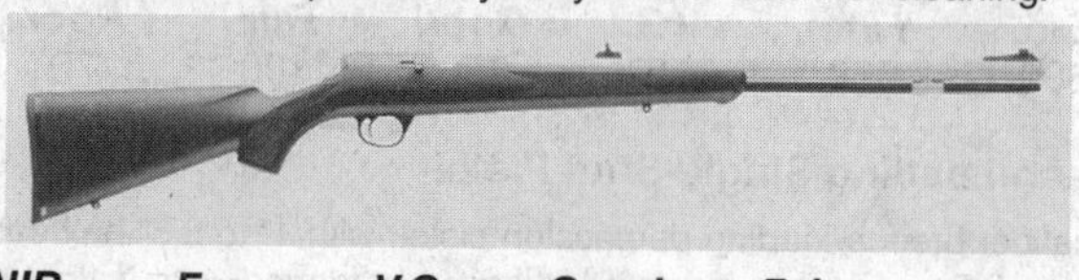

NIB	Exc.	V.G.	Good	Fair	Poor
300	220	200	150	80	50

MAROCCHI ARMI

Brescia, Italy

Model 2000

12-gauge Magnum single-shot, with 28" barrel, exposed hammer and automatic ejector. Blued, with walnut stock.

NIB	Exc.	V.G.	Good	Fair	Poor
—	100	80	60	50	40

Field Master I

12-gauge over/under, with 26" or 28" ventilated rib barrels fitted for choke tubes, single trigger and automatic ejectors. Blued French case-hardened, with walnut stock.

NIB	Exc.	V.G.	Good	Fair	Poor
—	500	400	300	200	150

Field Master II

As above, with single-selective trigger.

NIB	Exc.	V.G.	Good	Fair	Poor
—	520	450	350	220	180

CONQUISTA SERIES

Grade I is standard grade, with special polished steel finish and machine engraved. Stock and forearm are select walnut, with hand-checkered 20 lpi. Grade II has roll engraved game scenes. Stock is select figured walnut. Grade III is hand engraved by a master engraver featuring game scenes. Finely figured walnut stock.

Sporting Clays Model

Offered in 12-gauge, with 28", 30" or 32" ventilated rib barrels. Screw in chokes are standard. Adjustable trigger. Weight about 8 lbs.

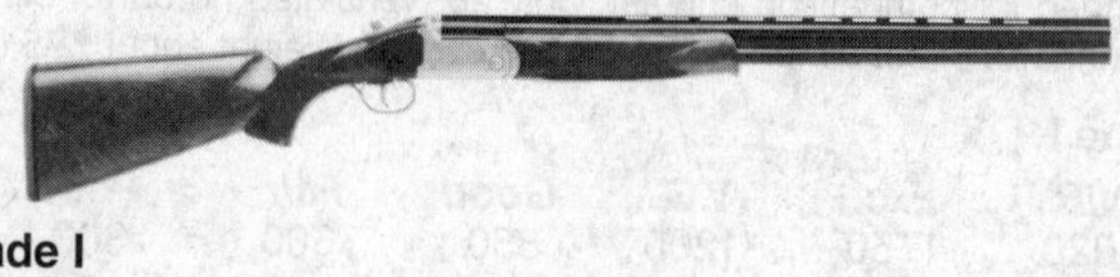

Grade I

NIB	Exc.	V.G.	Good	Fair	Poor
1950	1700	1180	850	600	300

Grade II

NIB	Exc.	V.G.	Good	Fair	Poor
2350	1900	1480	950	700	350

Grade III

NIB	Exc.	V.G.	Good	Fair	Poor
3350	2850	1820	1150	800	400

Sporting Light—Grade I

Same as above, but slightly smaller dimensions. Available in 28" or 30" barrel length. Weight about 7.5 lbs.

NIB	Exc.	V.G.	Good	Fair	Poor
2050	1700	1180	850	600	300

Sporting Clays Left-Hand Model—Grade I

Same as Sporting Clays Model. Designed for left-handed shooter.

NIB	Exc.	V.G.	Good	Fair	Poor
2150	1700	1180	850	600	300

Lady Sport Model

Offered in 12-gauge only, with 28" or 30" ventilated rib barrels. Slightly smaller dimensions for women. Weight 7.75 lbs.

Grade I

NIB	Exc.	V.G.	Good	Fair	Poor
2150	1700	1180	850	600	300

Spectrum Grade—Colored Frame

NIB	Exc.	V.G.	Good	Fair	Poor
2100	1750	1200	850	600	300

Lady Sport Left-Handed

Same as above for left-handed shooters.

Grade I

NIB	Exc.	V.G.	Good	Fair	Poor
2100	1750	1200	850	600	300

Spectrum Grade

NIB	Exc.	V.G.	Good	Fair	Poor
2180	1800	1220	850	600	300

Trap Model

Built for competition shooter. Features 30" or 32" ventilated rib barrels. Trap dimension stock. Weight about 8.25 lbs.

Grade I

NIB	Exc.	V.G.	Good	Fair	Poor
2020	1750	1200	850	600	300

Grade II

NIB	Exc.	V.G.	Good	Fair	Poor
2400	1950	1500	1000	750	350

Grade III

NIB	Exc.	V.G.	Good	Fair	Poor
3400	2700	18900	1500	800	400

Skeet Model

Designed for competition shooter. Only 28" ventilated rib barrel offered as standard. Skeet dimension stock and chokes. Weight about 7.75 lbs.

Grade I

NIB	Exc.	V.G.	Good	Fair	Poor
2020	1750	1200	850	600	300

Grade II

NIB	Exc.	V.G.	Good	Fair	Poor
2420	1950	1520	1000	750	350

Grade III

NIB	Exc.	V.G.	Good	Fair	Poor
3400	2700	1900	1500	800	400

Classic Doubles Model 92

Offered in 12-gauge only, with 30" ventilated rib barrels. Adjustable trigger. Walnut stock, with 18 lpi checkering. Weight about 8.12 lbs.

NIB	Exc.	V.G.	Good	Fair	Poor
1650	1350	880	600	500	250

Model 99—Grade I

Over/under gun. Features silver-grayed receiver; boxlock action, with single-selective trigger; pistol grip stock; schnabel forearm. Sporting models offered with 28", 30" or 32" barrels; trap with 30" or 32" barrels; skeet with 28" or 30" barrels. All barrels supplied with five extended choke tubes.

NIB	Exc.	V.G.	Good	Fair	Poor
3120	2350	1800	750	700	300

Model 99—Grade III

Has all the above features in addition to five flush-mounted choke tubes. Silver game scene engraved receiver.

NIB	Exc.	V.G.	Good	Fair	Poor
5200	3400	2200	950	800	300

FT I

A 12-gauge boxlock single-barrel shotgun, with 32" or 34" ventilated rib barrel. Full choke, automatic ejector and interchangeable stock. Blued. Introduced in 1986.

NIB	Exc.	V.G.	Good	Fair	Poor
950	750	650	550	450	300

FTC

As above, with two sets of barrels (a single ventilated rib trap barrel and a set of over/under ventilated rib barrels). In a fitted case. Introduced in 1986.

NIB	Exc.	V.G.	Good	Fair	Poor
1750	1400	1150	800	650	500

FS-4

A four gauge set (12-, 20-, 28-gauge and .410 bore). Introduced in 1986.

NIB	Exc.	V.G.	Good	Fair	Poor
2500	2100	1750	1500	1100	750

MARS

See—GABBET-FAIRFAX or BERGMANN

MARSTON, S.W.

New York, New York

Double-Action Pepperbox Antique

.31-caliber double-action percussion pepperbox, with 5" barrel group and ring trigger. Blued, with walnut grips. Manufactured between 1850 and 1855.

Exc.	Fine	V.G.	Good	Fair	Poor
2000	1120	860	600	250	170

2-Barrel Pistol Antique

.31- or .36-caliber revolving barrel 2-shot pistol, with ring trigger. Barrel marked "J.Cohn & S.W.Marston-New York". Blued brass frame, with walnut grips. Manufactured during 1850s.

Exc.	Fine	V.G.	Good	Fair	Poor
2700	1250	850	450	200	140

MARSTON, W. W. & CO.

New York, New York

W.W. Marston & Company manufactured a variety of firearms, some of which are marked only with trade names: Union Arms Company, Phoenix Armory, Western Arms Company, Washington Arms Company, Sprague and Marston and Marston and Knox.

Double-Action Single-Shot Pistol Antique

.31- or .36-caliber bar hammer percussion pistol, with 2.5" or 5" half octagonal barrel. Blued, with walnut grips. Manufactured during 1850s.

Exc.	Fine	V.G.	Good	Fair	Poor
650	320	230	150	100	70

Single-Shot Double-Action Pistol Antique

.31- or .36-caliber percussion pistol, with 4" or 6" barrel. Blued, with walnut grips. Manufactured during 1860s.

Exc.	Fine	V.G.	Good	Fair	Poor
680	580	410	250	100	70

Breech-Loading Single-Shot Pistol

.36-caliber breech-loading percussion pistol, with 4" to 8.5" half octagonal barrel. Brass or iron frame. Blued case-hardened, with walnut grips. Approximately 1,000 manufactured in 1850s.

Courtesy Milwaukee Public Museum, Milwaukee, Wisconsin

Breech-Loading PistolBrass Frame Antique

Exc.	Fine	V.G.	Good	Fair	Poor
4400	3600	2620	1650	500	350

Iron Frame Antique

Exc.	Fine	V.G.	Good	Fair	Poor
3900	3000	2050	1100	300	210

Three-Shot Percussion Pocket Pistol Antique

Very rare .31-cal. superposed-barrels 3-shot percussion pistol; unusual rising hammer design. Too rare to value.

Double-Action Pepperbox Antique

.31-caliber double-action 6-shot percussion pepperbox, with 4" or 5" barrel groups. Bar hammer. Blued case-hardened, with walnut grips. Manufactured during 1850s.

Courtesy Milwaukee Public Museum, Milwaukee, Wisconsin

Exc.	Fine	V.G.	Good	Fair	Poor
3200	2500	1820	1150	300	210

Pocket Revolver Antique

.31-caliber percussion revolver, with 3.25" to 7.5" barrel and 6-shot cylinder. Blued, with walnut grips. Approximately 13,000 manufactured between 1857 and 1862. Seven different Types are recognized. Values are similar for all.

Exc.	Fine	V.G.	Good	Fair	Poor
2000	1100	600	400	200	100

Navy Revolver Antique

.36-caliber percussion revolver, with 7.5" or 8.5" octagonal barrel and 6-shot cylinder. Blued, with walnut grips. Manufactured between 1857 and 1862. Some examples marked "The Union Arms Co." or "Western Arms Co."

Exc.	Fine	V.G.	Good	Fair	Poor
3100	1400	1000	600	200	140

3-Barrel Derringer Antique

.22-caliber 3-barreled spur-trigger pocket pistol, with sliding knife blade mounted on left side of 3" barrel group. Blued silver-plated, with walnut grips. Barrel marked "Wm. W. Marston/New York City". Approximately 1,500 manufactured between 1858 and 1864.

Knife Blade Model Antique

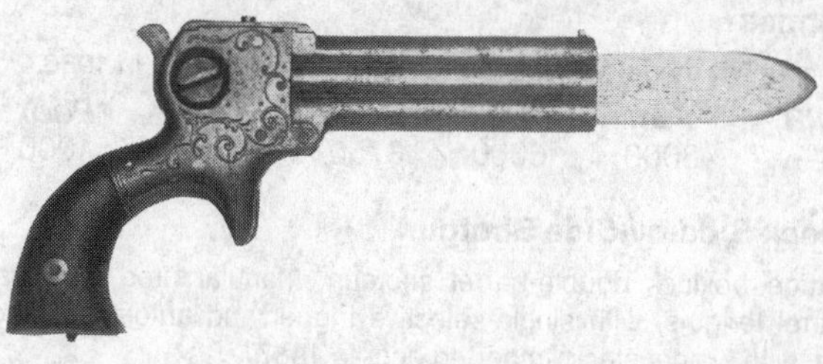

Courtesy Milwaukee Public Museum, Milwaukee, Wisconsin

Exc.	Fine	V.G.	Good	Fair	Poor
6000	4100	2870	1650	400	280

Without Knife Antique

Courtesy Milwaukee Public Museum, Milwaukee, Wisconsin

Exc.	Fine	V.G.	Good	Fair	Poor
2550	2000	1390	780	200	140

3-Barrel Derringer .32 Caliber Antique

Similar to above in .32-caliber, with 3" or 4" barrels. Not fitted with knife blade. Approximately 3,000 manufactured between 1864 and 1872.

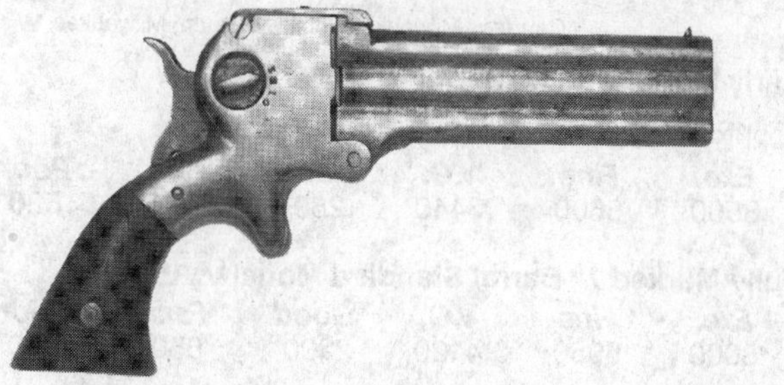

Courtesy Milwaukee Public Museum, Milwaukee, Wisconsin

Exc.	Fine	V.G.	Good	Fair	Poor
3750	3000	1910	820	200	140

MASQUELIER, S. A.

Liege, Belgium

Carpathe

.243, .270, .7x57mm, 7x65Rmm or .30-06 caliber single-shot rifle, with 24" barrel, adjustable trigger and sights. Blued, with engraved receiver. Walnut stock. Imported until 1986.

NIB	Exc.	V.G.	Good	Fair	Poor
—	3750	2950	1950	1250	750

Express

.270, .30-06, 8x57JRSmm or 9.3x74Rmm caliber over/under double-barrel rifle, with 24" barrels, single-selective trigger and automatic ejectors. Blued engraved, with walnut stock. Not imported after 1986.

NIB	Exc.	V.G.	Good	Fair	Poor
—	3800	2950	1950	1250	750

Ardennes

As above, but made on custom order only. Discontinued in 1986.

NIB	Exc.	V.G.	Good	Fair	Poor
—	8000	6000	3750	2500	1000

Boxlock Side-by-Side Shotgun

12-gauge boxlock double-barrel shotgun. Manufactured in a variety of barrel lengths, with single-selective trigger and automatic ejectors. Blued, with walnut stock. Imported prior to 1987.

NIB	Exc.	V.G.	Good	Fair	Poor
—	4750	3500	2500	1500	850

Sidelock Side-by-Side Shotgun

Similar to above, with detachable sidelocks. Finely engraved. Imported prior to 1987.

NIB	Exc.	V.G.	Good	Fair	Poor
—	14500	11750	7000	5000	1750

MASSACHUSETTS ARMS CO.
Chicopee Falls, Massachusetts

Wesson & Leavitt Dragoon

.40-caliber percussion revolver, with 7-in. round barrel, 6-shot cylinder and side-mounted hammer. Blued case-hardened, with walnut grips. Approximately 800 manufactured in 1850 and 1851.

Courtesy Milwaukee Public Museum, Milwaukee, Wisconsin

Early Model with 6" Barrel (Antique)

Approximately 30 made.

Exc.	Fine	V.G.	Good	Fair	Poor
8500	6600	3440	280	750	520

Fully Marked 7" Barrel Standard Model (Antique)

Exc.	Fine	V.G.	Good	Fair	Poor
8000	6050	4120	2200	650	450

Wesson & Leavitt Belt Revolver (Antique)

.31-caliber percussion revolver, with 3" to 7" round barrel and 6-shot cylinder. Similar in appearance to above. Approximately 1,000 manufactured in 1850 and 1851.

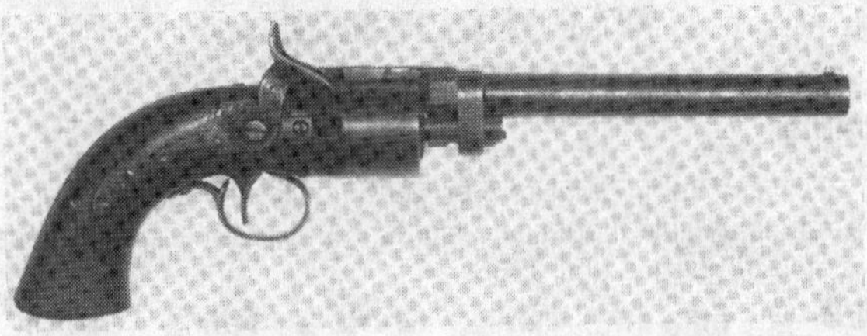

Courtesy Milwaukee Public Museum, Milwaukee, Wisconsin

Exc.	Fine	V.G.	Good	Fair	Poor
3000	1900	1350	900	600	300

Revolving Rifle (Antique)

A .40-caliber percussion revolving rifle, with 16- to 24-in. round barrel and 6-shot cylinder. Blued, with walnut stock. Approximately 25 made in 1849.

Exc.	Fine	V.G.	Good	Fair	Poor
19000	10000	5500	3500	2000	1000

Maynard Primed Belt Revolver (Antique)

Similar to above, with Maynard tape primer. Approximately 1,000 manufactured between 1851 and 1857.

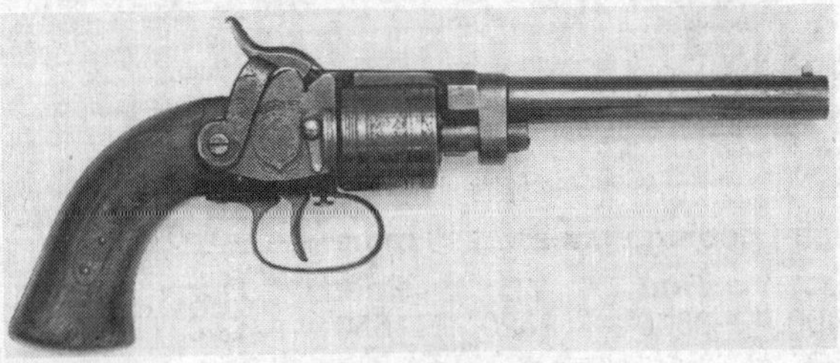

Courtesy Milwaukee Public Museum, Milwaukee, Wisconsin

Exc.	Fine	V.G.	Good	Fair	Poor
3700	2750	1810	880	400	200

Maynard Primed Pocket Revolver (Antique)

Similar to above in .28- or .30-caliber, with 2.5" to 3.5" octagonal or round barrels. Approximately 3,000 made between 1851 and 1860.

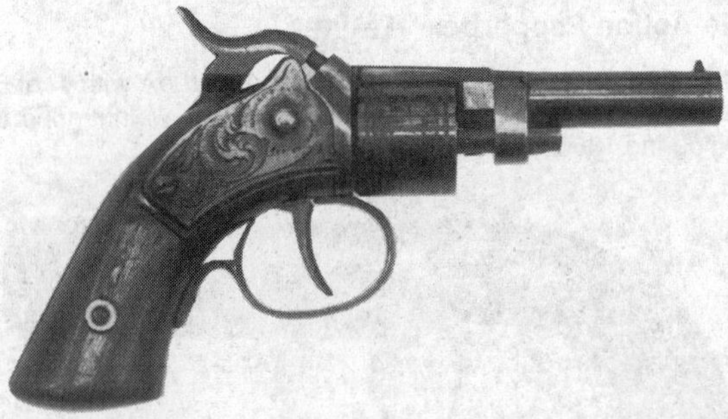

Courtesy Milwaukee Public Museum, Milwaukee, Wisconsin

Exc.	Fine	V.G.	Good	Fair	Poor
3000	2250	1500	700	300	150

Adams Patent Navy Revolver (Antique)

As above in .36-caliber, with 6" octagonal barrel. Approximately 600 of the 1,000 made were purchased by U.S. government. Note: Those bearing inspection marks will bring approximately a 20 percent premium over values listed.

Courtesy Milwaukee Public Museum, Milwaukee, Wisconsin

Exc.	Fine	V.G.	Good	Fair	Poor
5000	3500	2500	1900	1200	700

Single-Shot Pocket Pistol (Antique)

.31-caliber single-shot percussion pistol, with 2.5" to 3.5" half octagonal barrel. Maynard tape primer. Barrel marked "Mass. Arms Co/Chicopee Falls" and primer door "Maynard's Patent Sept. 22, 1845". Blued case-hardened, with walnut grips. Manufactured in 1850s.

Exc.	Fine	V.G.	Good	Fair	Poor
4000	2750	1830	920	600	300

MAYNARD CARBINE

Single-shot breech-loader chambered for .35- or .50-caliber percussion. Round 20" barrel. Triggerguard is a lever that pivots barrel in break-open fashion when lowered. Finish blued, with case colored frame. Buttstock walnut and there is no forend. This carbine was designed by same Maynard who invented the tape primer system. There are two models—a 1st and 2nd. They were made for both sporting use and as a U.S. Martial carbine; 2nd Model was used considerably during Civil War.

1st Model (Antique)

Marked "Maynard Patentee/May 27, 1851/June 17, 1856". Has iron patchbox; curved buttplate; Maynard tape primer system; tang sight. Later production fitted with a sling swivel. Approximately 400 of these carbines are U.S. marked. Total manufactured in late 1850s is unknown.

Courtesy Milwaukee Public Museum, Milwaukee, Wisconsin

U.S. Martially Marked (Antique)

Values are speculative.

Exc.	Fine	V.G.	Good	Fair	Poor
6500	4050	3020	2000	700	480

Commercial Model (Antique)

Premium for examples in possible confederate state purchase serial number ranges 1900 to 4100; expert evaluation recommended.

Exc.	Fine	V.G.	Good	Fair	Poor
6000	3500	2120	1250	400	280

2nd Model (Antique)

Chambered for .50-caliber only. Does not have tape primer system or tang sight. There is no patchbox. Buttplate is not as curved as on 1st Model. Marked "Manufactured By/Mass. Arms Co./Chicopee Falls". Approximately 20,000 manufactured between 1860 and 1865. Used by Union forces during Civil War.

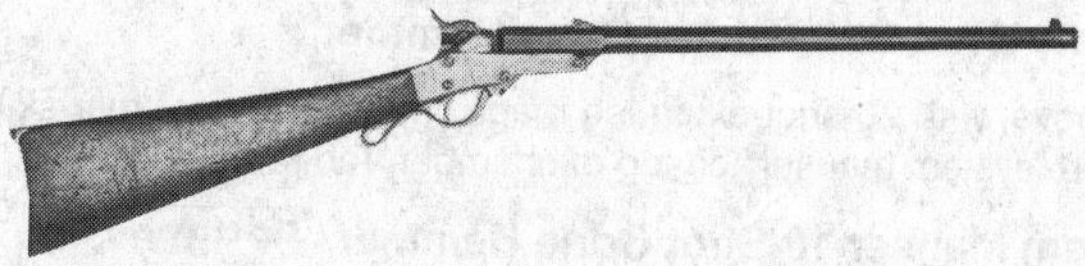

Courtesy Milwaukee Public Museum, Milwaukee, Wisconsin

Exc.	Fine	V.G.	Good	Fair	Poor
2500	2050	1370	700	500	350

Maynard Patent Sporting Rifle (Antique)

Sporting rifles bearing designations Model 1865, 1873 and 1882 were manufactured in a wide variety of calibers, gauges, stock styles, finishes and options.

Courtesy Milwaukee Public Museum, Milwaukee, Wisconsin

Exc.	Fine	V.G.	Good	Fair	Poor
2500	1650	1150	660	200	140

MASTERPIECE ARMS

Comer, Georgia

Manufacturer of tactical chassis-style bolt-action rifles for the target and tactical markets.

BA PMR Competition Rifle

Calibers: .308 Win., 6mm Creedmoor, 6.5 Creedmoor. Capacity: 10. Barrel: 26 in., M24 stainless steel, polished. Stock: Aluminum chassis. Sights: None, optional package with MPA 30mm mount and Bushnell scope. Weight: 11.5 lbs. Features: Built-in inclinometer, MPA/Curtis action, match-grade chamber.

NIB	Exc.	V.G.	Good	Fair	Poor
2500	—	—	—	—	—

MATEBA ARMS

Italy

AutoRevolver

Introduced in 2000. Chambered for .357 Magnum or .44 Magnum, with 4", 6" or 8" barrel. Features single-action trigger that has a reciprocating cylinder that fires from bottom chamber rather than top. Firing of the gun cocks hammer and cycles action for next round. Available with or without compensator. Offered in blue or nickel finish. Extra barrels available. Distributed in USA by American Western Arms (AWA). Note: Add $50 for nickel finish; $140 for extra barrel. Deduct $80 for guns without compensator.

Courtesy Supica's GunHeritage.com photo by Stoney Roberts

AutoRevolver

NIB	Exc.	V.G.	Good	Fair	Poor
2700	2000	1500	1000	—	—

AutoRevolver Carbine

Similar in principle to a handgun, with 16" or 18" barrel. Walnut buttstock, pistol grip and forend.

NIB	Exc.	V.G.	Good	Fair	Poor
1800	1300	1000	700	500	300

MATRA MANURHIN DEFENSE

Mulhouse, France

See—MANURHIN

MAUNZ MFG., INC.

Maumee, Ohio

Manufacturer (1970s-1980s) of high-end law enforcement and competition rifles based primarily on M14 military rifle.

Model 77 Service Match Rifle

Semi-automatic rifle chambered in .308 Winchester. Other chamberings on custom order. 22" barrel standard; medium and heavy barrels available. Charcoal gray parkerized finish. Custom rifles had heavyweight Kevlar or graphite/fiberglass stocks covered in black gelcoat. Red/white/blue stocks were also produced. 300 produced.

NIB	Exc.	V.G.	Good	Fair	Poor
—	2500	2250	2000	1850	1500

Model 87 Maunz Match Rifle

Semi-automatic rifle chambered in .308 Winchester and 6.30 Maunz. Limited .338 and .45 Maunz chamberings on custom order. Sold only to Master competitors and American Shooters Union members.

NIB	Exc.	V.G.	Good	Fair	Poor
—	2500	2200	2000	1500	1200

Model 57 M1A

Semi-automatic rifle chambered in .30-06, .276 and .308 Winchester. Also .45 Maunz (rare). M1 Garand receiver, with M14 parts and National Match barrels. Custom-built glass-bedded stock. Approximately 200 made.

NIB	Exc.	V.G.	Good	Fair	Poor
—	1500	1250	1000	800	600

Model 67 Match Grade for Practice

Semi-automatic rifle chambered in .308 Winchester, 6.30 Maunz and .45 Maunz. Camp Perry stamped. Not allowed for Service Rifle competition. Combination of M1 Garand and M14 parts. Approximately 250 made.

NIB	Exc.	V.G.	Good	Fair	Poor
—	2000	1800	1500	1200	1500

MAUSER WERKE

Established in 1869 by Peter and Wilhelm Mauser, this company came under effective control of Ludwig Loewe and Company of Berlin in 1887. In 1896, latter company was reorganized under name Deutsches Waffen und Munition as it is better known, DWM. Note: Historical information, technical details, photos and prices on military Mausers see Standard Catalog of Military Firearms, 8th Edition, Gun Digest Books 2016.

Early Model 98 Sporting Rifles

Wide variety of commercial Model 98 Sporting Rifles were made. Most of which had 23.5" ribbed barrels, open sights, 5-shot magazines, single-/double-set triggers and full or semi-pistol grip stocks.

Type A—Short Action

NIB	Exc.	V.G.	Good	Fair	Poor
—	10000	9000	7200	3500	1000

Type A—Medium Action

NIB	Exc.	V.G.	Good	Fair	Poor
—	7000	5000	4000	2000	1000

Type A—Long Action

NIB	Exc.	V.G.	Good	Fair	Poor
—	8000	6000	5000	2500	1000

Type B

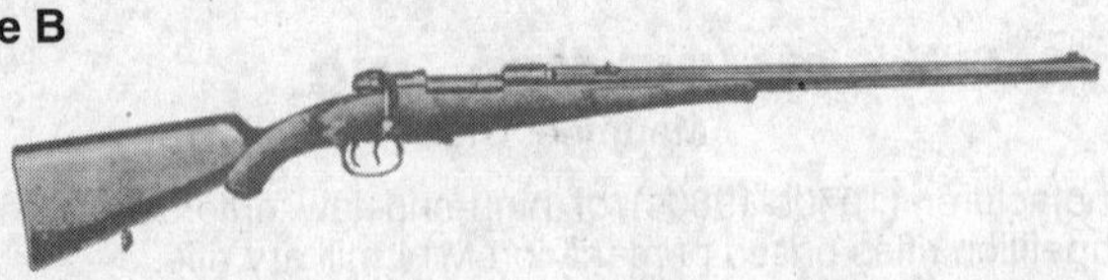

NIB	Exc.	V.G.	Good	Fair	Poor
—	4800	3500	2300	1400	500

Type K

NIB	Exc.	V.G.	Good	Fair	Poor
—	7500	6500	4000	2000	700

Type M

NIB	Exc.	V.G.	Good	Fair	Poor
—	5500	5000	4000	2800	900

Type S

NIB	Exc.	V.G.	Good	Fair	Poor
—	5500	5000	4000	2800	900

MODEL 1896 BROOMHANDLE MAUSER PISTOL

Manufactured from 1896 to 1939. Model 1896 Pistol was produced in a wide variety of styles as listed. It is recommended that those considering purchase of any models listed should consult Breathed & Schroeders's System Mauser (Chicago 1967) as it provides detailed descriptions and photographs of various models. Note: Prices listed are for pistol only. A correct matching stock/holster will add approximately 40 percent to value of each category. Non-matching stock/holster will add $350 and $600 to prices.

"BUYER BEWARE" ALERT by Gale Morgan: I have personally seen English Crest, U.S. Great Seal, unheard-of European dealers, aristocratic Coats-of-Arms and Middle East Medallions beautifully photo-etched into magazine wells and rear panels of some really common wartime commercials, with price tags that have been elevated to $2,500 plus. They are quite eye-catching and if they are sold as customized/modified Mausers, seller can price the piece at whatever the market will bear. However, if sold as a factory original—BUYER BEWARE.

Six-Shot Step-Barrel Cone Hammer

7.63mm semi-automatic pistol, with 5.5" barrel, fixed rear sight and checkered walnut grips. Marked "Ruecklauf Pistole System Mauser, Oberndorf am/Neckar 1896". Very few were manufactured. Too rare to price.

Twenty-Shot Step-Barrel Cone Hammer

As above, with 20-shot extended magazine and tangent rear sight. Engraved "system mauser" on top of chamber. Too rare to price.

System Mauser 10-Shot Cone Hammer (Antique)

As above, with fixed or tangent rear sight. Step barrel (pictured) is very rare as is tapered barrel. Magazine capacity 10 rounds.

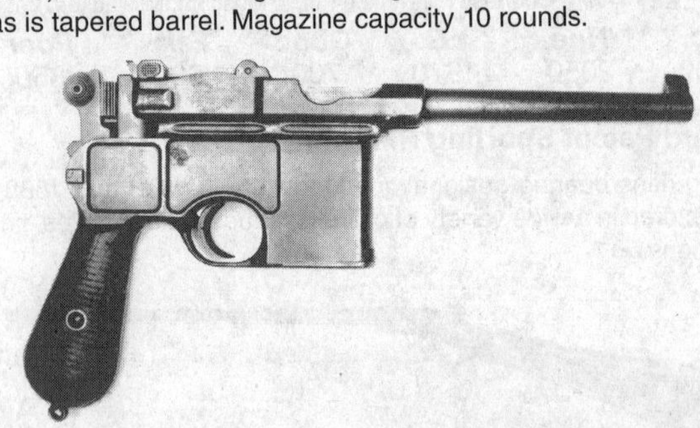

Courtesy Joe Schroeder

Exc.	Fine	V.G.	Good	Fair	Poor
17000	12000	10000	8000	7000	4900

Six-Shot Standard Cone Hammer (Antique)

Similar to above, with no step in barrel, 6-shot magazine and marked "Waffenfabrik Mauser, Oberndorf A/N" over the chamber. May have fixed, or rarely, tangent rear sight.

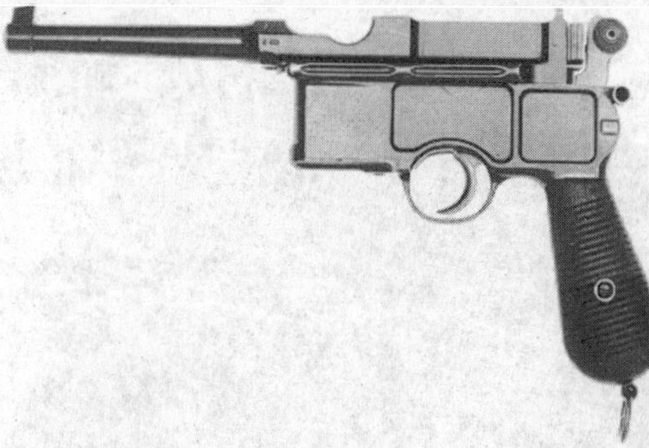

Courtesy Joe Schroeder

Exc.	Fine	V.G.	Good	Fair	Poor
12000	6750	5620	4500	3000	2100

Twenty-Shot Cone Hammer (Antique)

As above, with extended magazine holding 20 cartridges. May have panels or flat sides.

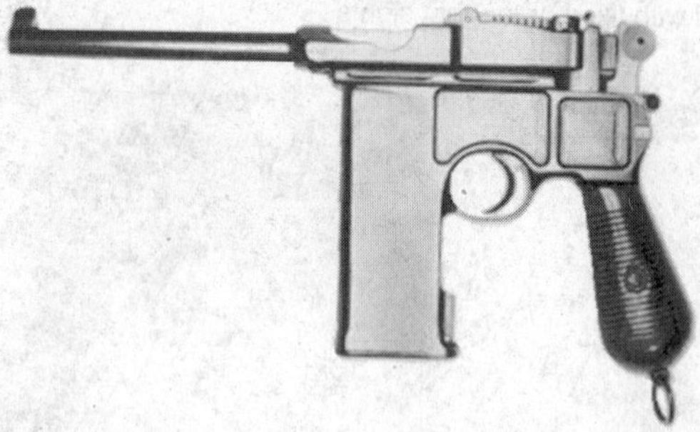

Courtesy Joe Schroeder

Exc.	Fine	V.G.	Good	Fair	Poor
35000	20000	15000	10000	7000	4900

Standard Cone Hammer (Antique)

As above, with 10-shot magazine and 23-groove grips. Price includes matching stocks.

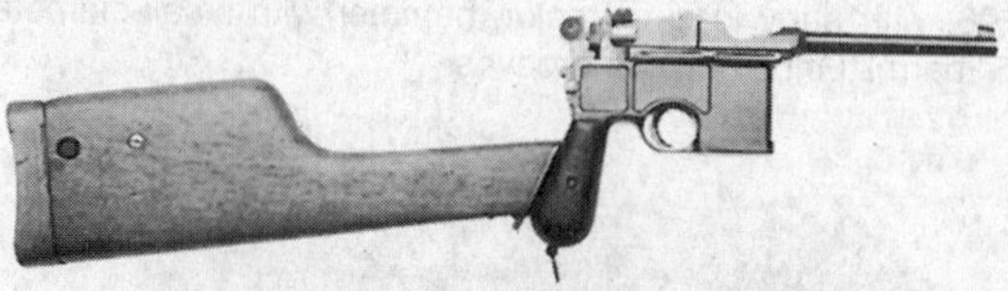

Courtesy Rock Island Auction Company

Exc.	Fine	V.G.	Good	Fair	Poor
6500	4000	2750	1750	1000	700

Fixed Sight Cone Hammer (Antique)

Similar to standard Cone Hammer, except fixed integral sight is machined into barrel extension.

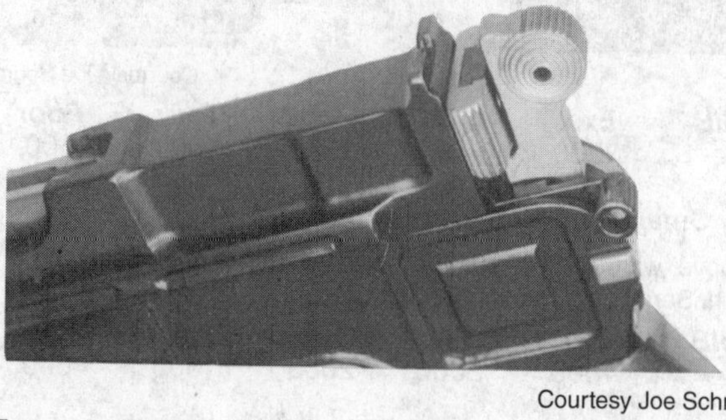

Courtesy Joe Schroeder

Exc.	Fine	V.G.	Good	Fair	Poor
7000	4500	3000	2000	1000	700

Turkish Contract Cone Hammer (Antique)

As above, but sight marked in Farsi and bearing crest of Sultan Abdul-Hamid II on frame. Approximately 1,000 were made.

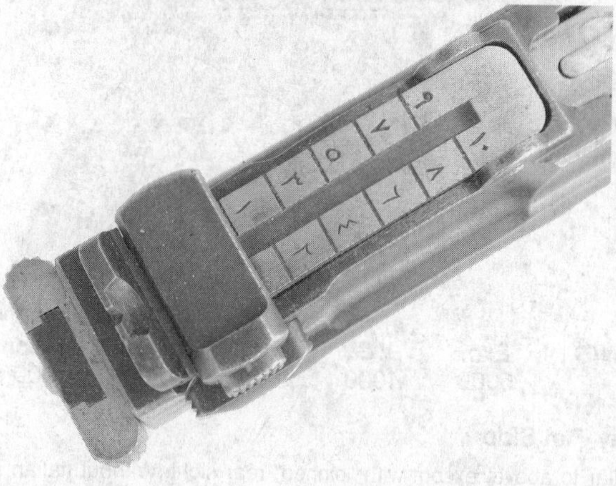

Courtesy Gale Morgan

Courtesy Joe Schroeder

Exc.	Fine	V.G.	Good	Fair	Poor
15000	8500	6750	5000	2000	1400

Early Transitional Large Ring Hammer

Variation has same characteristics of "Standard Cone Hammer", except hammer has larger open ring.

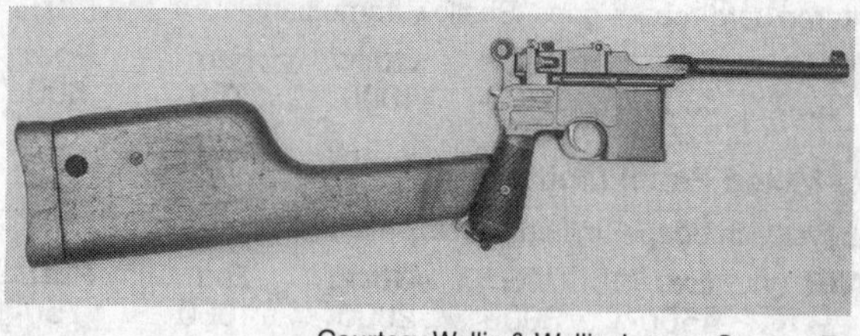

Courtesy Wallis & Wallis, Lewes, Sussex, England

NIB	Exc.	V.G.	Good	Fair	Poor
—	5500	4000	2500	1150	800

Model 1899 Flat Side—Italian Contract

Similar to above, with 5.5" barrel, adjustable rear sight and frame sides milled flat. Left flat of chamber marked with "DV" proof. Approximately 5,000 manufactured in 1899.

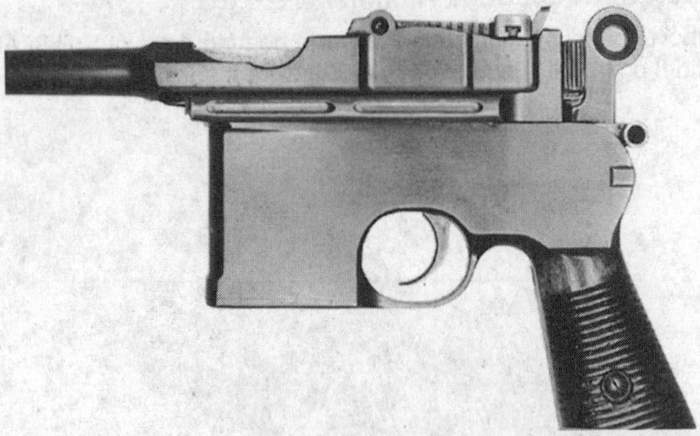

Courtesy Joe Schroeder

NIB	Exc.	V.G.	Good	Fair	Poor
—	6000	4000	2000	1200	900

Early Flat Side

Similar to above, except with "pinned" rear sight. Without Italian markings.

NIB	Exc.	V.G.	Good	Fair	Poor
—	5000	3500	2800	1000	750

Late Flat Side

Similar to above, with an integral pin mounted adjustable rear sight. Often marked with dealer's names such as "Von Lengerke & Detmold, New York".

NIB	Exc.	V.G.	Good	Fair	Poor
—	4000	3200	2000	1000	750

Flat Side Bolo

Similar to above, with 3.9" barrel, fixed sights. Checkered walnut grips. Very rare.

NIB	Exc.	V.G.	Good	Fair	Poor
—	7500	6000	4000	3000	2000

Early Large Ring Hammer Bolo

As above, with milled frame, adjustable rear sight. Grooved wood or hard rubber grips cast with a floral pattern. 10-shot magazine.

NIB	Exc.	V.G.	Good	Fair	Poor
—	4700	3700	2000	1500	1000

Shallow-Milled Panel Model

Full size. Similar to above, with 5.5" barrel. Either 23-groove walnut or checkered hard rubber grips. Shallow frame panels.

NIB	Exc.	V.G.	Good	Fair	Poor
—	3800	2700	1000	750	500

Deep-Milled Panel Model

As above, with deeper milled panels on sides of receiver.

NIB	Exc.	V.G.	Good	Fair	Poor
—	4500	3000	2000	1000	750

Late Large Ring Hammer Bolo

Similar to Early Large Ring Hammer Bolo, with late style adjustable rear sight.

Courtesy Joe Schroeder

NIB	Exc.	V.G.	Good	Fair	Poor
—	4000	3000	2000	1000	750

Six-Shot Large Ring Bolo

Similar to above Large Ring Bolo, with 6-shot magazine. May be equipped with fixed or tangent sights.

Courtesy James Rankin

NIB	Exc.	V.G.	Good	Fair	Poor
—	8900	6500	5000	3000	1800

Early Small Ring Hammer Model, Transitional

Model 96, with early long extractor, hammer with small-diameter hole and 5.5" barrel. Grips have 34 grooves.

Courtesy Joe Schroeder

NIB	Exc.	V.G.	Good	Fair	Poor
—	3200	2000	1500	1000	500

Early Small Ring Hammer Bolo Model

As above, with 3.9" barrel. Wood or hard rubber grips cast with a floral pattern. Serial numbers in 40,000 range.

NIB	Exc.	V.G.	Good	Fair	Poor
—	4500	3000	2000	1500	600

Six-Shot Small Ring Hammer Model

As above, with 27-groove walnut grips.

NIB	Exc.	V.G.	Good	Fair	Poor
—	8500	6500	3000	1800	1000

Standard Pre-war Commercial

Model 96, with 5.5" barrel, late-style adjustable rear sight and 34-groove walnut grips or checkered hard rubber grips. Often found with dealers markings such as "Von Lengerke & Detmold".

Courtesy Joe Schroeder

NIB	Exc.	V.G.	Good	Fair	Poor
—	3500	2500	1200	650	300

9mm Export Model

As above in 9mm Mauser, with 34-groove walnut grips.

NIB	Exc.	V.G.	Good	Fair	Poor
—	3750	2250	1500	1000	700

Mauser Banner Model

Standard pre-war features, except chamber stamped with Mauser Banner trademark and 32-groove walnut grips. Approximately 10,000 were manufactured.

Courtesy Joe Schroeder

NIB	Exc.	V.G.	Good	Fair	Poor
—	4500	3200	2300	1100	600

Persian Contract

Persian rampant lion on left rear panel. Prospective purchasers should secure a qualified appraisal prior to acquisition. Serial numbers in 154000 range.

NIB	Exc.	V.G.	Good	Fair	Poor
—	5500	4200	3000	1400	1000

Standard Wartime Commercial

Identical to pre-war Commercial Model 96, except it has 30-groove walnut grips. Rear of hammer stamped "NS" for new safety. Many also bear German or Austrian military acceptance proofs.

Courtesy Gale Morgan

NIB	Exc.	V.G.	Good	Fair	Poor
—	2500	1750	1000	500	350

9mm Parabellum Military Contract

As above in 9mm Parabellum caliber, with 24-groove grips. Stamped with large "9" filled with red paint. Note: Add 20 percent to full rig.

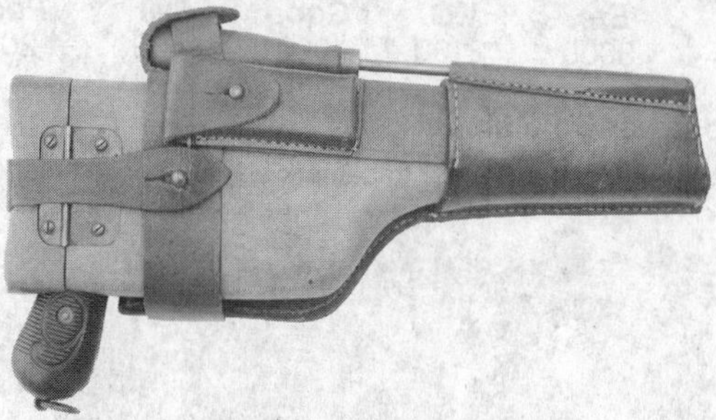

NIB	Exc.	V.G.	Good	Fair	Poor
—	3500	2500	1000	700	450

1920 Rework

Model 96 modified to barrel length of 3.9" and in 7.63mm Mauser or 9mm Parabellum caliber. Often encountered with police markings.

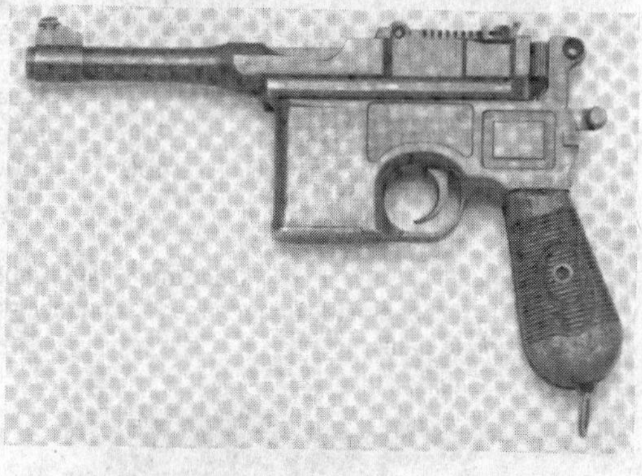

Courtesy Joe Schroeder

NIB	Exc.	V.G.	Good	Fair	Poor
—	1750	1000	500	400	350

Luger Barreled 1920 Rework

Similar to above. Fitted with Luger 4" barrel or a sighted Luger barrel-band, 12- or 23-groove walnut grips and 9mm caliber.

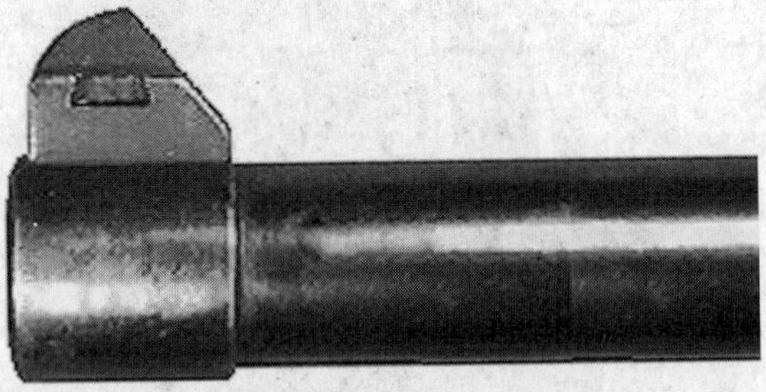

Courtesy Gale Morgan

NIB	Exc.	V.G.	Good	Fair	Poor
—	2500	1200	700	500	450

Early Post-war Bolo Model

Model 96 in 7.63mm caliber, with 3.9" barrel, adjustable rear sight and 22-groove walnut grips.

NIB	Exc.	V.G.	Good	Fair	Poor
—	3000	2100	1000	400	200

Late Post-war Bolo Model

As above, with Mauser Banner trademark stamped on left rear panel.

Courtesy Gale Morgan

NIB	Exc.	V.G.	Good	Fair	Poor
—	3000	2000	1000	400	200

French Gendarme Model

Standard Model 96 fitted with 3.9" barrel. Checkered hard rubber grips. Although reputed to have been made under a French contract, no record of that has been found to date.

Courtesy James Rankin

NIB	Exc.	V.G.	Good	Fair	Poor
—	4500	3000	1000	600	350

Early Model 1930

7.63mm caliber Model 96, with 5.2" barrel, grooved side rails, 12-groove walnut grips and late-style safety. Note: Add 25 percent with correct stocks.

Courtesy Gale Morgan

NIB	Exc.	V.G.	Good	Fair	Poor
—	3000	2000	1700	800	500

Late Model 1930

Similar to above, except for solid receiver rails.

NIB	Exc.	V.G.	Good	Fair	Poor
—	3500	2200	1700	800	400

Model 1930 Removable Magazine

Similar to above, with detachable magazine. Prospective purchasers should secure a qualified appraisal prior to acquisition. Too rare to price.

CARBINE MODELS

Cone Hammer Flat Side Carbine

7.63mm caliber carbine, with 11.75" full length "rib" barrel, early adjustable sight, flat frame and detachable buttstock. Prospective purchasers should secure a qualified appraisal prior to acquisition. Too rare to price. Note: Watch for fakes.

Large Ring Hammer Transitional Carbine

Similar to above, with milled frame panels. Prospective purchasers should secure a qualified appraisal prior to acquisition.

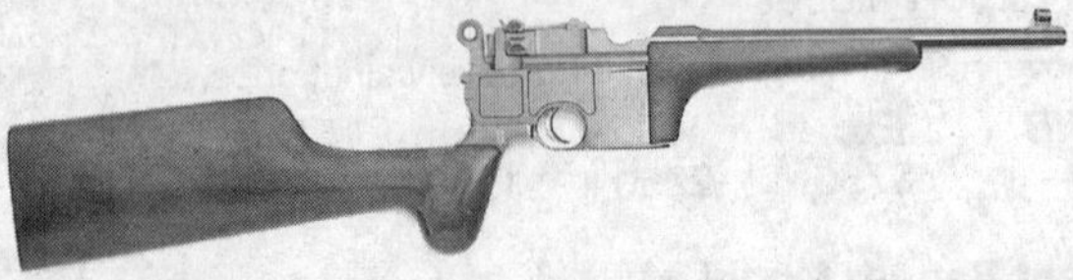

NIB	Exc.	V.G.	Good	Fair	Poor
—	25000	18000	11000	5000	3000

Large Ring Hammer Flatside Carbine

Similar to above, with 14.5" barrel. Prospective purchasers should secure a qualified appraisal prior to acquisition.

NIB	Exc.	V.G.	Good	Fair	Poor
—	23000	17000	10000	5000	3000

Small Ring Hammer Carbine

Similar to above, with hammer having a smaller diameter hole at its tip. Prospective purchasers should secure a qualified appraisal prior to acquisition. Some late carbines were chambered for 9mm export.

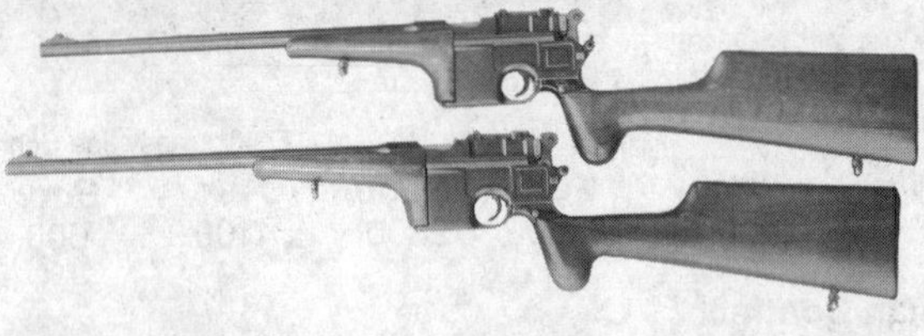

NIB	Exc.	V.G.	Good	Fair	Poor
—	21000	18000	15000	6000	4000

CHINESE COPIES

Chinese Marked, Handmade Copies

Crude copies of Model 96 and unsafe to fire.

NIB	Exc.	V.G.	Good	Fair	Poor
—	500	400	350	250	180

Taku-Naval Dockyard Model

Approximately 6,000 very good quality copies of Model 96 were made at Taku-Naval Dockyard. In several variations, both flat and paneled sides.

NIB	Exc.	V.G.	Good	Fair	Poor
—	3500	2000	1000	600	400

Shansei Arsenal Model

Approximately 8,000 Model 96 pistols were manufactured in .45 ACP caliber. Copies of Model 96 were made by Unceta (Astra) and Zulaica y Cia (Royal) and marketed by the firm of Beistegui Hermanos. These copies are covered in their own sections of this text. Note: Within past several years, a large quantity of Model 96 pistols exported to or made in China have been imported into United States. It has been reported that some newly made copies of Shansei .45 were recently exported from China. Proceed with caution.

Shansei Panel Marking

Courtesy Gale Morgan

NIB	Exc.	V.G.	Good	Fair	Poor
—	5000	3500	2250	1500	1300

MAUSER POCKET PISTOLS

Model 1910

6.35mm (.25 ACP) caliber pistol, with 3" barrel, 9-shot magazine. Checkered walnut or (scarce) hard rubber wrap-around grip. Early examples (below serial 60,000 or so) have a pivoting take-down latch above triggerguard and are identified as "Sidelatch" models by collectors. Later production Models 1910s are often identified as Model 1910/14. Manufactured from 1910 to 1934.

Sidelatch Model

NIB	Exc.	V.G.	Good	Fair	Poor
—	1200	900	600	300	300

Later Production (Model 1910/14)

NIB	Exc.	V.G.	Good	Fair	Poor
—	550	300	200	150	100

Model 1914

Larger version of Model 1910. Chambered for 7.65mm Browning (.32 ACP), with 3.5" or (rarely) 4.5" barrel. Very early examples up to serial 2500 or so had a contoured hump on slide and are called "Humpbacks" by collectors; these bring a considerable premium. Model 1914s with police or military markings bring a small premium. Manufactured between 1914 and 1934.

Model 1914 "Humpback"

NIB	Exc.	V.G.	Good	Fair	Poor
—	4000	3000	1750	800	400

Model 1914 (later)

NIB	Exc.	V.G.	Good	Fair	Poor
—	480	300	200	150	100

Model 1912/14

While Mauser's pocket pistols were very successful on the commercial market, Mauser was also trying to develop a larger caliber pistol for military use. Most successful of these was Model 1912/14, though only about 200 were ever made. A few of these did reach commercial market and it's likely the pistol would have continued in production had WWI not broken out. Higher serial numbered guns were slotted for Model 1896-style holster stock. Few of these also had tangent sights. Note: Add 50 percent for shoulder stock.

NIB	Exc.	V.G.	Good	Fair	Poor
—	38000	30000	22000	10000	5000

Model WTP I

Mauser's first post-WWI new design. First vest pocket pistol, with 2.5" barrel and 6-shot magazine. Grips were plastic wrap-around, with one, two or three grip screws depending on production period. Production ended in late 1930s, when WTP II was introduced.

NIB	Exc.	V.G.	Good	Fair	Poor
—	750	500	400	250	150

Model WTP II

WTP II was a much more compact design than its predecessor, with 2" barrel and separate grip panels instead of Mauser's usual wrap-around grip. Production was limited by the outbreak of WWII, so WTP II is much scarcer than WTP I. Under French occupation, at least several hundred WTP II's were assembled and sold; these can be identified by their very low electric penciled serial numbers and lack of German proofing. Brings a slight premium over pre-war German manufactured pistols.

Courtesy Gale Morgan

NIB	Exc.	V.G.	Good	Fair	Poor
—	1250	900	700	350	200

Model 1934

In response to competition from Walther and others, in 1934 Mauser spruced up its aging 1910/14 and 1914 pistols with a new high-polish finish and form-fitting swept back grips. Nickel finish was offered, but is very rare (50 percent premium, but beware of re-nickeled blued guns). The 7.65mm pistols became popular with both military and police, but those so marked can bring a considerable premium.

Courtesy Orvel Reichert

6.35mm

NIB	Exc.	V.G.	Good	Fair	Poor
—	520	320	250	200	120

7.65mm Commercial

NIB	Exc.	V.G.	Good	Fair	Poor
—	450	320	250	200	120

7.65mm Eagle L proofed

NIB	Exc.	V.G.	Good	Fair	Poor
—	680	450	300	250	150

7.56mm Large Eagle over M (Navy)

NIB	Exc.	V.G.	Good	Fair	Poor
—	1200	750	450	300	200

MODEL HSc

HSc was a totally new design. Chambered for 7.65mm Browning. Featuring double-action lockwork and partially concealed external hammer. Introduced just as WWII broke out. HSc was produced through the war for both commercial sale and military use. Serials started at 700,000 and first 1500 or so had grip screws located near bottom of grip and bring a large premium. Finish deteriorated as war progressed. Some HSc pistols were even produced under French occupation after the war ended. Note: Add 20 percent for Waffenamt markings; 50 percent for Navy marked front straps.

Courtesy Orvel Reichert

Low Grip Screw Model

As above, with screws that attach grip located near bottom of grip. Highly-polished blue checkered walnut grips. Early address without lines and has Eagle N proof. Some have been observed with Nazi Kreigsmarine markings. Approximately 2,000 were manufactured.

NIB	Exc.	V.G.	Good	Fair	Poor
—	8000	5000	1800	750	650

Early Commercial Model

Highly polished blued finish, checkered walnut grips, standard Mauser address on slide and Eagle N proofmark. Floorplate of magazine stamped with Mauser Banner.

NIB	Exc.	V.G.	Good	Fair	Poor
—	750	500	350	180	120

Transition Model

As above, but not as highly finished.

NIB	Exc.	V.G.	Good	Fair	Poor
—	520	400	300	150	100

Early Nazi Army Model

Courtesy Orvel Reichert

NIB	Exc.	V.G.	Good	Fair	Poor
—	650	550	400	200	120

Late Nazi Army Model

NIB	Exc.	V.G.	Good	Fair	Poor
—	450	380	250	150	100

Early Nazi Navy Model

NIB	Exc.	V.G.	Good	Fair	Poor
—	1350	1000	750	400	300

Wartime Nazi Navy Model

NIB	Exc.	V.G.	Good	Fair	Poor
—	1100	800	650	400	200

Early Nazi Police Model

NIB	Exc.	V.G.	Good	Fair	Poor
—	600	500	420	250	180

Wartime Nazi Police Model

NIB	Exc.	V.G.	Good	Fair	Poor
—	500	400	350	250	180

Wartime Commercial Model

As above, without acceptance markings on triggerguard.

NIB	Exc.	V.G.	Good	Fair	Poor
—	420	350	300	200	120

French Manufactured Model

Blued or Parkerized, with walnut or plastic grips. Triggerguard marked on left side with monogram "MR".

NIB	Exc.	V.G.	Good	Fair	Poor
—	380	280	220	150	100

Model HSc Post-war Production

In late 1960s, Mauser resumed production of HSc in both 7.65mm and 9mm Browning short (.380). Five thousand post-war HSc pistols were specially marked with an American eagle and bring a slight premium over standard marked pistols. In 1980s, Mauser licensed HSc production to Gamba in Italy, which produced an enlarged frame version of HSc, with a double-column magazine. In both German and Italian production, .380s bring about a 20 percent premium over .32s.

Mauser Production (.32)

NIB	Exc.	V.G.	Good	Fair	Poor
—	520	450	300	180	120

Gamba Production

In recent years Mauser has licensed several firms other than Gamba to produce pistols bearing Mauser trademark, such as Browning Hi Power knockoff made in Hungary. In 1999, Mauser was bought by SIG-Sauer and a new large caliber Mauser pistol was announced.

NIB	Exc.	V.G.	Good	Fair	Poor
—	600	480	320	200	100

MAUSER RIFLES—RECENT PRODUCTION

In February 1999, SIGARMS announced acquisition of Mauser line of small arms. Current production is in Isny, Germany. Some Mauser rifles were imported and distributed by SIGARMS and later Briley Manufacturing, located in Houston, Texas. Beginning in 2009, Mauser rifles are imported by Mauser USA, San Antonio, Texas.

Model 2000

.270, .308 or .30-06 caliber bolt-action rifle, with 24" barrel, open sights and 5-shot magazine. Blued, with checkered walnut stock. Manufactured between 1969 and 1971 by Heym.

NIB	Exc.	V.G.	Good	Fair	Poor
—	600	450	300	200	150

Model 3000

As above, with 22" barrel, no sights and Monte Carlo-style stock. Manufactured from 1971 to 1974 by Heym.

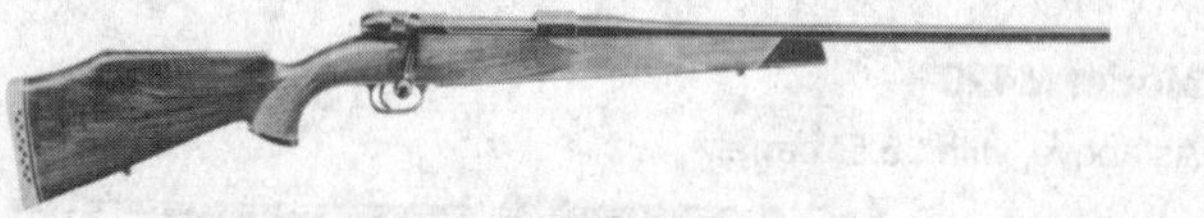

NIB	Exc.	V.G.	Good	Fair	Poor
—	600	450	300	200	150

Model 3000 Magnum

As above in 7mm Rem. Magnum, .300 Win. Magnum and .375 H&H Magnum caliber, with 26" barrel and 3-shot integral magazine. Blued, with checkered walnut stock. Produced by Heym.

NIB	Exc.	V.G.	Good	Fair	Poor
—	680	520	380	250	200

Model 4000

Similar to Model 3000 in .222- or .223-caliber, with folding open sights. Produced by Heym.

NIB	Exc.	V.G.	Good	Fair	Poor
—	550	400	250	200	150

Model 225

.243 to .300 Weatherby Magnum caliber bolt-action rifle, with 24" or 26" barrel, no sights, adjustable trigger and 3- or 5-shot magazine. Blued, with walnut stock.

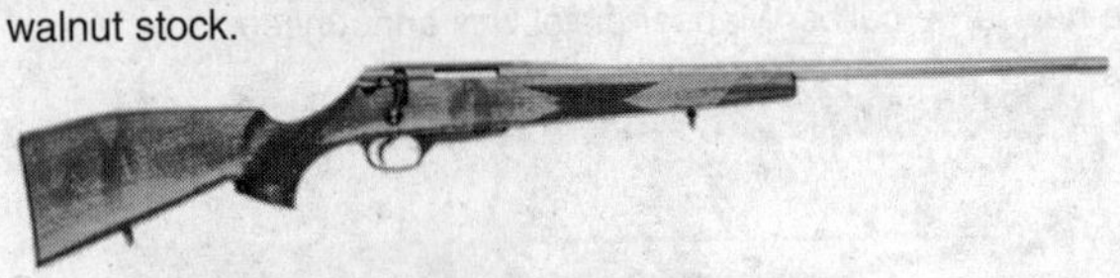

NIB	Exc.	V.G.	Good	Fair	Poor
1400	1250	1000	750	600	500

Model ES340

.22-caliber single-shot bolt-action rifle, with 25.5" barrel, open sights and walnut stock. Manufactured before WWII.

NIB	Exc.	V.G.	Good	Fair	Poor
—	300	250	220	180	120

Model DSM34

Similar to above, with 25" barrel and full-length walnut stock. Manufactured prior to WWII.

NIB	Exc.	V.G.	Good	Fair	Poor
—	320	280	250	200	150

Model MS420B

Similar to above, with 25" barrel and 5-shot magazine. Manufactured before WWII.

NIB	Exc.	V.G.	Good	Fair	Poor
—	380	320	300	280	200

Model ES350

.22-caliber single-shot bolt-action rifle, with 27.5" barrel. Checkered pistol grip walnut stock. Manufactured before WWII.

NIB	Exc.	V.G.	Good	Fair	Poor
—	450	400	380	350	280

Model M410

Similar to above, with 23.5" barrel and 5-shot magazine. Manufactured before WWII.

NIB	Exc.	V.G.	Good	Fair	Poor
—	380	320	300	280	200

Model M420

As above, with 25.5" barrel.

NIB	Exc.	V.G.	Good	Fair	Poor
380	320	300	280	200	—

Model EN310

.22-caliber single-shot bolt-action rifle, with 19.75" barrel, open sights and plain walnut stock. Manufactured before WWII.

NIB	Exc.	V.G.	Good	Fair	Poor
—	250	220	200	150	100

Model EL320

As above, with 23.5" barrel. Checkered walnut stock.

NIB	Exc.	V.G.	Good	Fair	Poor
—	280	250	220	180	120

Model KKW

.22-caliber single-shot bolt-action rifle, with 26" barrel, ladder rear sight and full-length walnut stock. Manufactured prior to WWII.

NIB	Exc.	V.G.	Good	Fair	Poor
—	400	350	300	220	150

Model MS350B

.22-caliber bolt-action rifle, with 26.75" barrel, adjustable rear sight and 5-shot magazine. Blued, with walnut stock.

NIB	Exc.	V.G.	Good	Fair	Poor
—	480	400	350	280	200

Model ES340B

Similar to above in single-shot form.

NIB	Exc.	V.G.	Good	Fair	Poor
—	380	300	250	180	100

Model MM41OBN

.22-caliber bolt-action rifle, with 23.5" barrel, adjustable sights and 5-shot magazine. Blued, with walnut stock.

NIB	Exc.	V.G.	Good	Fair	Poor
—	400	350	300	200	120

Model MS420B

As above, with 26.75" barrel and target-style stock.

NIB	Exc.	V.G.	Good	Fair	Poor
—	400	350	300	200	120

Model 107

Bolt-action rifle chambered for .22 LR. Barrel length 21.6". Box magazine has 5-shot capacity. Beechwood checkered Monte Carlo stock is full size, with pistol grip plastic buttplate. Rear sight adjustable. Metal finish blue. Weight about 5 lbs.

NIB	Exc.	V.G.	Good	Fair	Poor
260	220	180	150	120	100

Model 201 Standard

Features 21" medium heavy free-floating barrel. Receiver accepts all rail mounts. Drilled and tapped for scope mount. Magazine capacity 5-shot. Chambered for.22 LR or .22 WMR cartridge. Beechwood stock is hand checkered, with plastic buttplate. Monte Carlo stock fitted with cheekpiece. Weight about 6.5 lbs.

NIB	Exc.	V.G.	Good	Fair	Poor
600	500	350	200	150	100

Model 66 Standard

Centerfire bolt-action rifle. Fitted with European walnut hand-checkered oil-finished half stock design. Rosewood forends and pistol grip caps are standard. Fitted with rubber recoil pad and 1" quick disconnect sling swivels. Interchangeable 24" barrels in standard calibers: .243 Win., .270, .308, .30-06, 5.6x57, 6.5x57, 7.64 and 9.3x62. Weight about 7.5 lbs.

NIB	Exc.	V.G.	Good	Fair	Poor
1700	1450	1100	700	550	350

Model 66 Magnum

Same as above. Chambered for 7mm Rem. Magnum, .300 and .338 Win. Magnum, 6.5x68, 8x86S, 9.3x64. Fitted with 26" barrel. Weight about 7.9 lbs.

NIB	Exc.	V.G.	Good	Fair	Poor
1800	1550	1200	800	600	400

Model 66 Safari

Same as above. Chambered for .375 H&H and .458 Win. Magnum. Fitted with 26" barrel. Weight about 9.3 lbs.

NIB	Exc.	V.G.	Good	Fair	Poor
2600	2000	1250	850	650	400

Model 66 Stuzen

Same as Standard Model 66. Fitted with a full stock. Barrel length 21". Calibers same as Standard. Weight about 7.5 lbs.

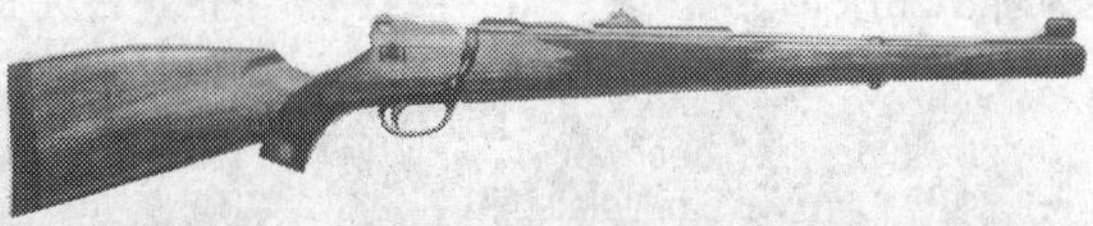

NIB	Exc.	V.G.	Good	Fair	Poor
2500	2100	1500	800	600	400

IDF Mauser Rifle Model 66SP

Bolt-action rifle chambered for .308 Win. cartridge. Adjustable trigger for pull and travel. Barrel length 27". Specially designed stock has broad forend and thumbhole pistol grip. Cheekpiece adjustable as is recoil pad. Supplied with case. This rifle is military issue. Fewer than 100 imported into U.S. by Springfield Armory.

NIB	Exc.	V.G.	Good	Fair	Poor
2250	1580	1100	850	650	400

Model 77

Fitted with a 24" barrel. Bolt-action rifle chambered for .243, .270, 6.5x57, 7x64, .308 and .30-06 calibers. Detachable box magazine. Set trigger. Walnut stock, with cheekpiece. Hand-checkering. Weight about 7.25 lbs.

NIB	Exc.	V.G.	Good	Fair	Poor
1250	950	800	650	450	200

Model 77 Ultra

Fitted with a 20" barrel. Chambered for 6.5x57, 7x64 and .30-06 calibers. Weight about 7.5 lbs.

NIB	Exc.	V.G.	Good	Fair	Poor
1250	950	800	650	450	200

Model 77 Mannlicher

Similar to Ultra Model, with full-length Mannlicher stock. Set trigger. Weight about 7.5 lbs.

NIB	Exc.	V.G.	Good	Fair	Poor
1250	950	800	650	450	200

Model 77 Big Game

Chambered for .375 H&H Magnum cartridge. Fitted with a 26" barrel. Weight about 8.5 lbs.

NIB	Exc.	V.G.	Good	Fair	Poor
1100	900	750	600	500	200

Model 86-SR

Introduced in 1993. Bolt-action .308 is sometimes referred to as "Specialty Rifle". Fitted with a laminated wood and special match thumbhole or fiberglass stock, with adjustable cheekpiece. Stock has rail in forearm and adjustable recoil pad. Magazine capacity 9 rounds. Finish a non-glare blue. Barrel length with muzzle brake 28.8". Many special features are found on this rifle from adjustable trigger weight to silent safety. Mauser offers many options on this rifle that will affect price. Weight about 11 lbs.

NIB	Exc.	V.G.	Good	Fair	Poor
9500	7500	5000	3500	1800	1000

Model 93 SR

Introduced in 1996. A tactical semi-automatic rifle chambered for .300 Win. Magnum or .338 Lapua cartridge. Barrel length 25.5"; overall length 48.4". Barrel fitted with a muzzle brake. Magazine capacity: 6 rounds .300; 5 rounds .338-caliber. Weight about 13 lbs.

NIB	Exc.	V.G.	Good	Fair	Poor
10000	9000	7500	5000	3500	1500

Model 96

Bolt-action rifle chambered for .25-06, .270 Win., 7x64, .308 or .30-06 cartridge. Fitted with a 22" barrel (24" Magnum calibers) and has a 5-round top loading magazine. Receiver drilled and tapped. Checkered walnut stock. No sights. Weight about 6.25 lbs.

NIB	Exc.	V.G.	Good	Fair	Poor
700	600	500	300	120	100

Model 99 Standard

Bolt-action centerfire sporting rifle. Offered with two stock designs: classic with straight oil-finish stock or high luster with cheekpiece and schnabel forend and Monte Carlo with rosewood forend tip and pistol grip cap. Chambered for standard calibers: .243, .25-06, .270, .308, .30-06, 5.6x57, 6.5x57, 7x57, 7x64. Barrel length 24"; weight about 8 lbs.

NIB	Exc.	V.G.	Good	Fair	Poor
900	700	600	500	400	300

Model 99 Magnum

Same as above. Chambered for Magnum calibers: 7mm Rem. Magnum, .257 Wby., .270 Wby., .300 Wby., .300 and .338 Win. Magnum, 8x68S and 9.3x64. Fitted with 26" barrel. Weight about 8 lbs.

NIB	Exc.	V.G.	Good	Fair	Poor
950	750	650	550	400	300

CURRENT MAUSER RIFLE PRODUCTION

M98

In four models, the classic Model 1898 double-square-bridge, controlled-round-feed bolt action, the M98 is barreled and stocked in deluxe high-grade walnut. Standard calibers: 7x57, 8x57IS, 9.3x62, .308, .30-06 with 22" barrels; Magnum calibers: .375 H&H, .416 Rigby, .450 Rigby with 24.4" barrels. Price shown for Standard, Add $3000 for Magnums.

NIB	Exc.	V.G.	Good	Fair	Poor
8300	7000	6000	5000	3000	1800

M03

Offered in several variants and grades. Chambered in a wide range of popular calibers from .222 Remington to .375 H&H Magnum. Built on traditional Mauser square-bridge action. Features include barrel interchangeability and manual cocking system, with safety/cocking lever at rear of bolt. Made by Blaser. Values shown are for basic model, with synthetic stock. Higher grade wood and various levels of engraving are available at extra cost. Note: Currently Special Order only.

NIB	Exc.	V.G.	Good	Fair	Poor
—	3400	2800	2000	1000	400

M12

Modern Mauser design, with solid steel construction, checkered walnut or synthetic stock with Prince of Wales pistol grip, three-position safety, detachable magazine and short 60-degree bolt lift. Offered in .22-250 Rem., .243 Win., .270 Win., .308 Win., .30-06, 7mm Rem. Mag., .300 Win. Mag., .338 Win. Mag., 6.5x55SE, 7x64, 8x57IS, 9.3x62. Several variations are available, with barrel lengths of 19", 22" or 24.5" with or without sights. Introduced in 2013. Note: Add $500 for walnut stock.

NIB	Exc.	V.G.	Good	Fair	Poor

M18

The latest Mauser rifle is a modern bolt action chambered in .243 Win., 6.5 C, 6.5 PRC, .270 Win., 7mm Rem. Mag., .308 Win., .30-06 and .300 Win. Mag. Barrel length is 21 3/4" for standard calibers, 24" for magnums. The polymer stock has swivel studs, grip inlays and recoil pad. Other features include an adjustable trigger and detachable 5-shot magazine. Introduced in 2018.

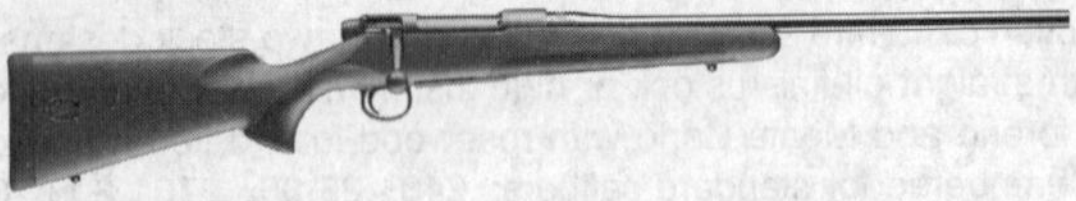

NIB	Exc.	V.G.	Good	Fair	Poor
600	520	480	300	150	100

M18 Savanna

Calibers: .223 Rem., .243 Win., 6.5 PRC, 6.5 Creedmoor, .270 Win., .308 Win., .30-06 Spfld., 7mm Rem. Mag., .300 Win. Mag. Capacity: 5-round magazine standard; 10-rounders available. Barrel: 21.75 or 24.5-in. cold-hammer forged, German-steel, threaded. Weight: 6.5–6.8 lbs. Length: 41.7–44.0 in. Stock: Savanna Tan Polymer with grip inserts. Sights: No iron sights. Drilled and tapped. Features: Adjustable trigger. Sixty-degree oversized bolt. Three-position safety. Removeable recoil pad section with interior buttstock storage. Sub-MOA guarantee and 10-year warranty.

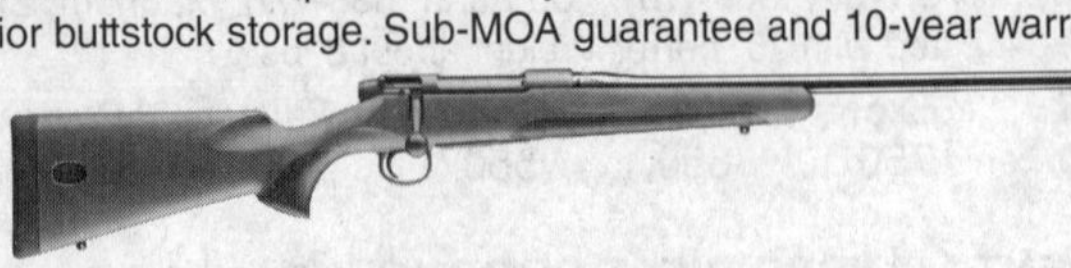

NIB	Exc.	V.G.	Good	Fair	Poor
740	—	—	—	—	—

CURRENT MAUSER PRODUCTION PISTOLS

Model 80 SA

Single-action semi-automatic pistol. Based on Browning Hi-Power design. Chambered for 9mm Parabellum cartridge. Barrel length 4.66"; magazine capacity 14 rounds; weight about 35 oz.

NIB	Exc.	V.G.	Good	Fair	Poor
550	480	300	180	120	100

Model Compact DA

Same as above, with double-action trigger. Shorter barrel 4.13". Weight about 33 oz.

NIB	Exc.	V.G.	Good	Fair	Poor
340	320	250	180	120	100

Model 90 DA

Similar to Model 80, with double-action trigger.

NIB	Exc.	V.G.	Good	Fair	Poor
550	480	300	180	120	100

Model M2 (Imported by SIG ARMS)

Introduced in 2000. Chambered for .45 ACP, .40 S&W or .357 SIG cartridges. Has an aluminum alloy frame and steel slide. Action is an enclosed hammerless striker-fired design. Barrel length 3.5". Fixed sights. Weight about 29 oz. Magazine capacity: 8 rounds .45 ACP; 10 rounds .40 S&W and .357 SIG.

NIB	Exc.	V.G.	Good	Fair	Poor
480	400	300	200	150	100

MAVERICK ARMS, INC.

Subsidiary of O. F. Mossberg & Sons, Inc.
Eagle Pass, Texas

Model 88

12-gauge Magnum slide-action shotgun, with 28" or 30" barrels, anodized receiver, composition stock. Introduced in 1989.

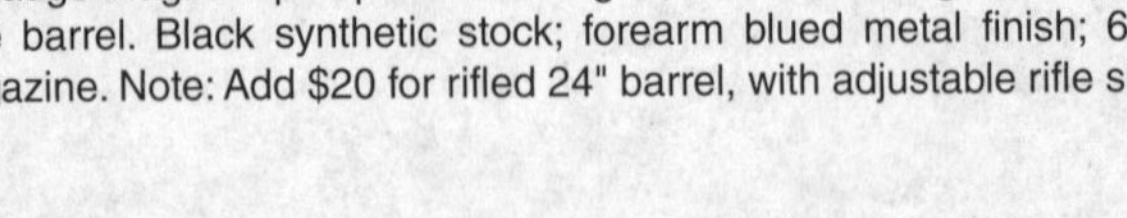

NIB	Exc.	V.G.	Good	Fair	Poor
250	150	120	100	80	50

Model 88 Slug Pump Shotgun

12-gauge Magnum pump-action shotgun, with interchangeable cylinder-bore barrel. Black synthetic stock; forearm blued metal finish; 6-shot magazine. Note: Add $20 for rifled 24" barrel, with adjustable rifle sights.

NIB	Exc.	V.G.	Good	Fair	Poor
300	200	100	80	60	50

Model 88 Six-Shot Security Model

12-gauge Magnum pump-action shotgun, with 6-shot magazine. Interchangeable 18.5" Cylinder-Bore Fixed choke barrel; rugged black synthetic stock and forearm; blued metal finish; brass front sight bead, are also included. Note: Add 5 percent for 8-shot Security Model, with 20" cylinder-bore Fixed choke barrel; 10 percent for heat shield.

NIB	Exc.	V.G.	Good	Fair	Poor
300	200	100	80	60	50

Model HS-12

A 12-gauge over/under shotgun offered in several variations. Field model has 28" barrels, with Improved-Cylinder and Modified choke tubes, selective single trigger, extractors and synthetic stock; Tactical model has an 18.5" barrel and Picatinny rails. Note: Add $50 for this model.

NIB	Exc.	V.G.	Good	Fair	Poor
400	380	320	250	200	100

Shockwave CTC Laser Saddle Model

NIB	Exc.	V.G.	Good	Fair	Poor
550	—	—	—	—	—

930 Special Purpose Chainsaw

NIB	Exc.	V.G.	Good	Fair	Poor
500	—	—	—	—	—

MAYNARD CARBINE

See Massachusetts Arms Co.

MAYNARD/PERRY

Keen, Walker & Co.
Danville, Virginia

Brass Framed Carbine (Antique)

Overall length 40"; barrel length 22.5"; caliber .54. Browned blued barrel, brass frame and walnut stock. Manufactured in 1861 and 1862. Values are speculative.

Exc.	Fine	V.G.	Good	Fair	Poor
33000	14000	11000	8000	1500	1050

McMILLAN FIREARMS

Phoenix, Arizona

A manufacturer of custom rifles including hunting, tactical and hybrid models.

Legacy

Built on McMillan G31 short action in .223, .243, .260 Rem., .308 Win. or .300 WSM, with 22" or 24" match-grade barrel. Walnut, graphite or laminate stock. Machined one-piece aluminum hinged floorplate. Various options available.

NIB	Exc.	V.G.	Good	Fair	Poor
5500	4700	3700	2500	800	300

Heritage

Built on G31 long action in 6.5-284, .284 Win., 7mm Rem. Magnum, .30-06, .300 Win. Magnum, with 24" or 26" match-grade barrel. Other features similar to Legacy model.

NIB	Exc.	V.G.	Good	Fair	Poor
5600	4800	3800	2600	900	300

TAC-Series

Available in .308 Win., .300 Win. Magnum, .338 Lapua or .416 Barret with medium heavy free-floating contour or fluted barrel. Muzzle brake is optional. A-3 or A-5 fiberglass tactical stock available in various colors with adjustable cheekpiece and length of pull. Detachable 5-shot magazine or hinged floorplate.

NIB	Exc.	V.G.	Good	Fair	Poor
5000	4200	3200	2000	900	300

TAC-50 A1

Chambered in .50 BMG with 29" match-grade free-floating fluted Navy contour barrel with Picatinny rail, threaded muzzle and muzzle brake. McMillan TAC-50 stock has an adjustable cheekpiece and A1 bipod. Detachable magazine holds 5 rounds.

NIB	Exc.	V.G.	Good	Fair	Poor
9000	8000	7000	—	—	—

M. B. ASSOCIATES-GYROJET

San Ramon, California

Established in 1960 by R. Maynard and Art Biehl. M. B. Associates produced Gyrojet pistols and carbines from 1962 to 1970. Basically a hand held rocket launcher, shooting a 12mm or 13mm spin stablized rocket cartridge, composed of four-part solid rocket fuel. Nose of the round was forced rearward onto a stationary firing pin, igniting fuel, expelling round and recocking for next shot. These were not very accurate and led to MBA's demise. Ammunition typically sells for $35 per round or more. By Dave Rachwal.

Mark I Model A Commemorative

13mm pistol cased with Goddard Commemorative Medal and 10 dummy rounds. Black anodized finish, with walnut grips.

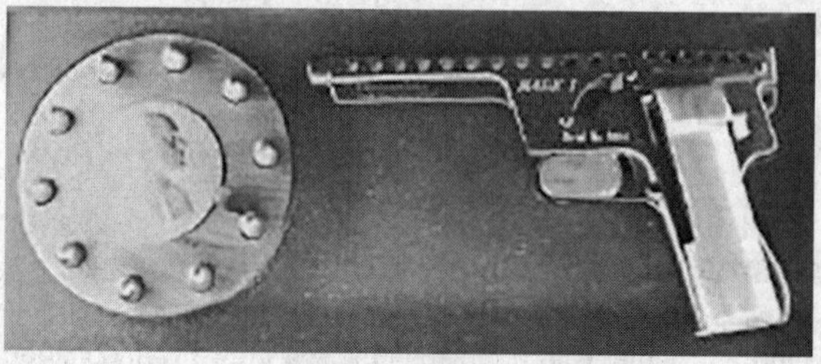

NIB	Exc.	V.G.	Good	Fair	Poor
—	2200	1500	1200	900	500

Mark I Model B Commemorative

13mm pistol cased with Goddard Commemorative Medal and 10 dummy rounds. Black with walnut grips; or antique nickel with pearlite grips.

NIB	Exc.	V.G.	Good	Fair	Poor
—	1900	1700	1000	600	300

Mark I Model B

13mm pistol cardboard box. Black anodized, with walnut grips usually. Produced in many variations and finishes.

NIB	Exc.	V.G.	Good	Fair	Poor
—	1000	800	650	400	200

Mark II Model C

12mm pistol. Black anodized, with walnut grips. Manufactured for 12mm round to conform with 1968 gun control act, because 13mm is .51-caliber and 12mm is .49-caliber.

NIB	Exc.	V.G.	Good	Fair	Poor
—	1000	800	650	400	200

Mark I Model A Carbine

13mm black anodized finish, with walnut stock and carrying handle.

NIB	Exc.	V.G.	Good	Fair	Poor
—	2500	2200	1700	1000	600

Mark I Model B Carbine

13mm antique nickel finish, with walnut stock. Sporter carbine had flared muzzle and sleek lines.

NIB	Exc.	V.G.	Good	Fair	Poor
—	1500	800	900	400	200

McMILLAN & CO. INC., G.
(Later: Harris/McMillan Gunworks, Harris Gunworks)
Phoenix, Arizona

Competition Model

Custom order bolt-action rifle in .308, 7mm-08 and .300 Win. Magnum caliber. Barrel length, stock type and dimensions to customer's specifications. Introduced in 1988.

NIB	Exc.	V.G.	Good	Fair	Poor
1700	1500	1150	800	600	300

Model 86 Sniper's Rifle

Custom order rifle in .308 Win. or .300 Win. Magnum calibers, with synthetic stock. Choice of scope systems. Introduced in 1988.

NIB	Exc.	V.G.	Good	Fair	Poor
3250	2700	1900	1100	600	300

Model 86 System

As above, with Ultra scope mounting system, bipod and fitted case. Introduced in 1988.

NIB	Exc.	V.G.	Good	Fair	Poor
3700	3250	2300	1800	850	550

Model 87 Long Range Sniper's Rifle

Large stainless steel, single-shot bolt-action rifle in .50 BMG caliber. Featuring 29" barrel, with an integral muzzle brake. Camouflaged synthetic stock. Weight 21 lbs. Accurate to 1,500 meters. Introduced in 1988.

NIB	Exc.	V.G.	Good	Fair	Poor
6000	5200	4000	2750	1000	500

Model 87 System

As above, with bipod and 20X Ultra scope mounting system. Fitted case. Introduced in 1988.

NIB	Exc.	V.G.	Good	Fair	Poor
6500	5700	4400	3150	1200	600

Signature Model

Bolt-action sporting rifle. Manufactured in a variety of calibers up to .375 H&H, with 22" or 24" stainless barrel. Composition stock and 3- or 4-shot magazine. Introduced in 1988.

NIB	Exc.	V.G.	Good	Fair	Poor
2200	1750	1250	800	600	300

Signature Stainless

Same as above, with barrel and action made of stainless steel. Fiberglass stock. Left-/right-hand model. .416 Rigby also offered in this configuration. Introduced in 1990.

NIB	Exc.	V.G.	Good	Fair	Poor
2500	2050	1650	1000	750	400

Signature Alaskan

Introduced in 1989. Offered in .270, .280 Rem., .30-06, 7mm Rem. Magnum, .300 Win. Magnum, .300 Wby. Magnum, .358 Win. Magnum, .340 Wby. Magnum, .375 H&H. Match-grade barrel from 22" to 26" in length. Single leaf rear sight, barrel band front sight.

NIB	Exc.	V.G.	Good	Fair	Poor
3000	2700	2000	1500	950	500

Signature Titanium Mountain

Offered in calibers from .270 Win. to 7mm Rem. Magnum. Match-grade barrel produced from titanium. Stock is graphite. Weight about 6.5 lbs.

NIB	Exc.	V.G.	Good	Fair	Poor
3500	3000	2500	1800	950	500

Signature Varminter

Available in calibers .223, .22-250, .220 Swift, .243, 6mm Rem., .25-06, 7mm-08, .308. Barrel lengths from 22" to 26". Heavy barrel configuration, with hand-bedded fiberglass stock. Field bipod is standard. Introduced in 1989.

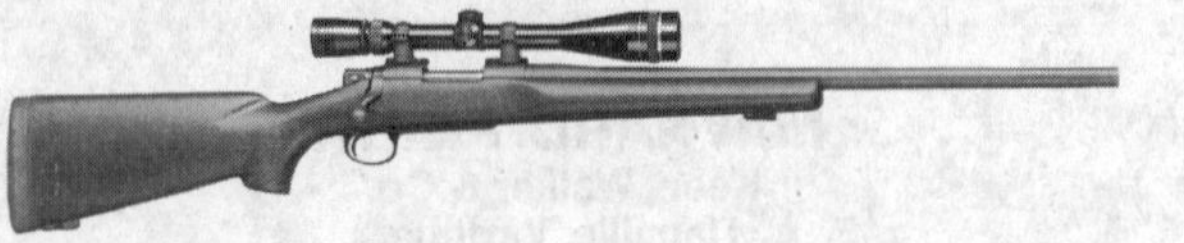

NIB	Exc.	V.G.	Good	Fair	Poor
2500	2000	1500	900	600	400

Talon Safari

Bolt-action rifle offered in various calibers from .300 Win. Magnum to .458 Win. Magnum. Stainless steel 24" barrel, 4-round magazine, fiberglass stock. Introduced in 1989. Weight about 10 lbs.

NIB	Exc.	V.G.	Good	Fair	Poor
3750	3250	2200	6500	950	500

Talon Sporter

Offered in calibers from .25-06 to .416 Rem. Magnum. 24" barrel with no sights. Built on pre-1964 Winchester Model 70 action. Choice of walnut or fiberglass stock. Weight about 7.5 lbs.

NIB	Exc.	V.G.	Good	Fair	Poor
2500	2000	1750	1250	600	250

Model 300 Phoenix Long Range Rifle

Introduced in 1992. Chambered for .300 Phoenix cartridge. Fitted with 28" barrel. No sights. Fiberglass stock. Weight about 12.5 lbs.

NIB	Exc.	V.G.	Good	Fair	Poor
3000	2500	2050	1450	600	350

Model 40 Sniper

Bolt-action rifle chambered for .308 cartridge. Introduced in 1990. Fitted with 24" match-grade heavy weight barrel. No sights. Weight about 9 lbs.

NIB	Exc.	V.G.	Good	Fair	Poor
2500	2000	1500	1150	500	300

Model 92 Bullpup

Single-shot rifle chambered for .50-caliber BMG. Fitted with 26" barrel. No sights. Fiberglass bullpup stock. First introduced in 1995.

NIB	Exc.	V.G.	Good	Fair	Poor
4500	3750	2800	2200	1000	500

Model 93 SN

Bolt-action rifle chambered for .50 BMG. Fitted with 29" barrel with muzzle brake. Magazine holds 10 rounds. No sights. Weight about 21.5 lbs. Folding fiberglass stock. Introduced in 1995.

NIB	Exc.	V.G.	Good	Fair	Poor
4750	4250	3500	2450	1450	750

McMillan LRHR

Long Range Hunting Rifle, designed for precision shooting. Custom made bench-rest tolerances in a long or short action. Chambered in .243 Win., .308 Win., 7mm Rem., .300 Win. and .338 Lapua Magnum. Action is pillar-bedded. Barrel lengths: 24", 26" or 27", depending on caliber. McMillan A-3 fiberglass stock is standard.

NIB	Exc.	V.G.	Good	Fair	Poor
4750	4000	3000	2500	—	—

MEAD & ADRIANCE

St. Louis, Missouri

See ALLEN, ETHAN

Retailer marking found on a variety of percussion handguns, most notably Ethan Allen.

MENDENHALL, JONES & GARDNER

Greensboro, North Carolina

Confederate Percussion Rifle (Antique)

.58-caliber percussion rifle, with 33" barrel. Full-length walnut stock secured by two barrel bands. Finished in white, with lock marked "M.J.&G.,N.C.". As with all confederate arms, beware of fakes.

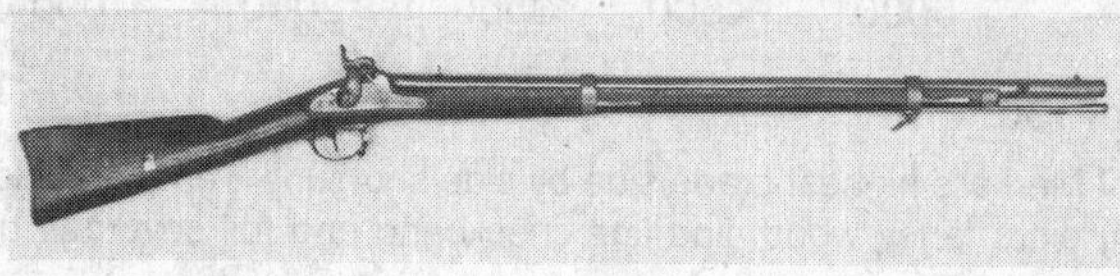

Exc.	Fine	V.G.	Good	Fair	Poor
—	33000	23500	14000	5000	3500

MENZ, AUGUST

Suhl, Germany

Established prior to WWI to manufacture Beholla pistols. Company was purchased by Lignose in 1937.

Menta

Identical to Beholla, which is listed separately.

NIB	Exc.	V.G.	Good	Fair	Poor
—	350	250	200	150	100

Liliput

4.25mm caliber semi-automatic pistol, with 2" barrel and 6-shot magazine. Overall length 3.5"; weight 10 oz. Slide marked "Liliput Kal. 4.25". Also manufactured in 6.35mm caliber; overall length 4". Blued, with composition grips.

NIB	Exc.	V.G.	Good	Fair	Poor
—	800	600	450	300	200

Menz Model II

As above in 7.65mm caliber.

NIB	Exc.	V.G.	Good	Fair	Poor
—	400	300	250	200	120

Menz VP Model

Similar to Model II in 6.35mm caliber, with 2.35" barrel, 6-shot magazine. Fitted with a cocking indicator.

NIB	Exc.	V.G.	Good	Fair	Poor
—	400	300	250	200	120

Model III

Total re-design. Quality is much better than previous Menz pistols. Has a closed-top slide, fixed barrel, exposed hammer. Similar to Model 1910 Browning. Produced until 1937.

NIB	Exc.	V.G.	Good	Fair	Poor
—	450	350	300	250	150

MERCURY

Liege, Belgium

Model 622 VP

.22-caliber semi-automatic rifle, with 20" barrel, open sights and 7-shot magazine. Blued, with walnut stock. Manufactured by Robar & Son.

NIB	Exc.	V.G.	Good	Fair	Poor
—	320	280	250	200	120

MERCURY(2)

Eibar, Spain

Double-Barreled Shotgun

10-, 12- or 20-gauge Magnum boxlock double-barrel shotgun, with 28" or 32" barrels, double triggers and extractors. Blued, with walnut stock. Note: Add 75 percent for 10-gauge.

NIB	Exc.	V.G.	Good	Fair	Poor
—	320	250	220	180	120

MERIDEN FIREARMS CO.

Meriden, Connecticut

Also see TRIPLETT & SCOTT

Pocket Pistol

A successor to Andrew Fryberg & Sons, Meriden made guns for Sears and other mail-order catalogs approx.1905-1918. In addition to shotguns, they made .32 and .38 double-action top-break revolvers in both exposed hammer and concealed hammer models. Some sources list these revolvers produced as early as 1895, possibly by Fryberg. They were sold under a wide variety of trade names including Secret Service Special, Eastern Arms, New England Firearms, Federal Fire Arms, and Howard Arms Co. Other manufacturers also made revolvers for Sears using some of these same trade names, even if the gun had a different configuration. Some of the design features that help identify some but not all of the Meriden-made revolvers include sharp angle on grip backstrap knuckle (hammerless models), "Napoleon hat" front sight on some, hard rubber grips with blank logo circle at top, and large serif font s/n on butt."

NIB	Exc.	V.G.	Good	Fair	Poor
—	—	380	200	80	50

Double-Barrel Shotguns

From 1905-1918 Meriden Fire Arms Co., successor to A.J. Aubrey, made 12-, 16- and 20-gauge sidelock double-barrel shotguns. These were better quality hammer and hammerless side-by-sides fitted with twist laminated Damascus and steel barrels in grades A to G. Some of these guns were beautifully engraved by same artisans who worked for Parker Bros. and other Connecticut gunmakers. Prices in 1910 ranged from $40 to $250, but they represented great value for the money, as they were superior to the popular Crescent guns which they closely resembled. Current values depend on model, grade, gauge and condition. Difficult to find examples in excellent condition as these were sold by Sears to customers who put them to hard use. In good condition their current values range from $250 for plain Janes to $3,500 or more for top grades, of which few specimens are known.

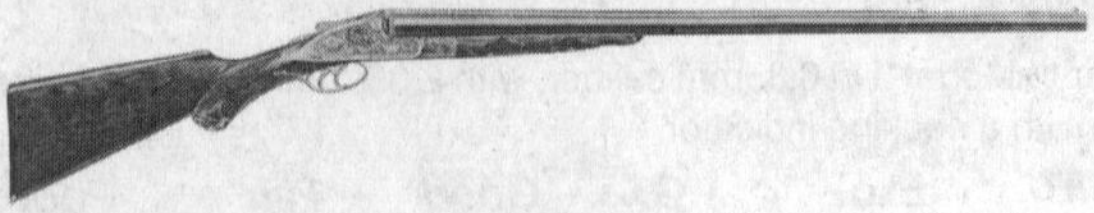

Single-Barrel Shotguns and Rifles

Meriden Fire Arms Co. also made many single-barrel shotguns and rifles. Current values are determined by growing collector interest and condition.

MERKEL, GEBRUDER

Suhl, Germany

Merkel brothers began manufacturing rifles and shotguns in Suhl, Germany in 1898. Company is best known for its over/under and side-by-side shotguns, but has also produced double-barreled express rifles, drillings with various rifle/shotgun combinations, falling block single-shot rifles and bolt-action rifles. Many experts consider Merkels to be equal in quality to some of the better Italian and English guns. Because of the company's long and complex history, including years during which it operated behind the Iron Curtain, there are many un-catalogued models that may be encountered. Merkel firearms are imported by Merkel USA, a subsidiary of Steyr Arms in Trussville, Alabama.

SIDE-BY-SIDE SHOTGUNS

Model 8

Self-cocking Deeley boxlock action, with cocking indicators. Locking mechanism is a Greener cross-bolt, with double-barrel locking lug. Triggers are single-selective or double. Safety is automatic and tang mounted. Has an extractor. Offered in 12- and 16-gauge with 28" solid rib barrels; 20-gauge with 26.75" barrels. Available with straight-/pistol grip oil-finished walnut stock. Receiver case colored, with light scroll engraving. Weight about: 12- and 16-gauge 6.8 lbs.; 20-gauge 6 lbs.

NIB	Exc.	V.G.	Good	Fair	Poor
1500	1150	900	600	500	400

Model 117/117E

Offered in 12- and 16-gauge, with various barrel lengths. Featured a boxlock action, with double triggers and extractors. Ejectors were available under "E" designation. Boxlock action body was scrupled at rear with fine line scroll engraving.

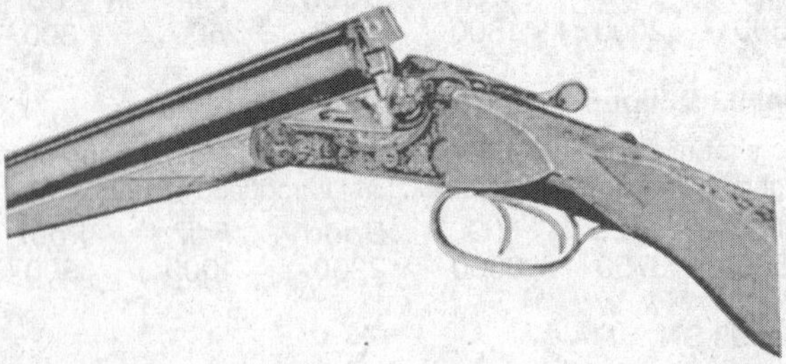

NIB	Exc.	V.G.	Good	Fair	Poor
—	6000	4350	1950	1000	500

Model 118/118E

Offered in 12- and 16-gauge. Similar to above model, with slightly more engraving and better wood. Some engraving coverage on breech end of barrels.

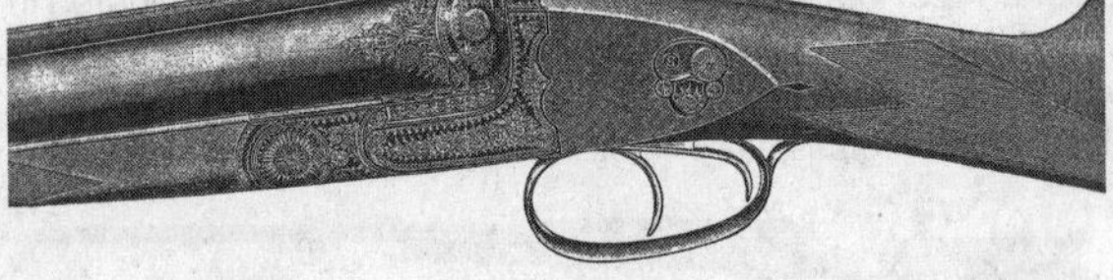

NIB	Exc.	V.G.	Good	Fair	Poor
—	7100	4900	2800	1200	650

Model 124/125

Similar to above models, but supplied with extractors for Model 124 and ejectors for Model 125. Both models have more engraving coverage with game scenes. Finer checkering and fancy wood is seen on this model.

Model 124

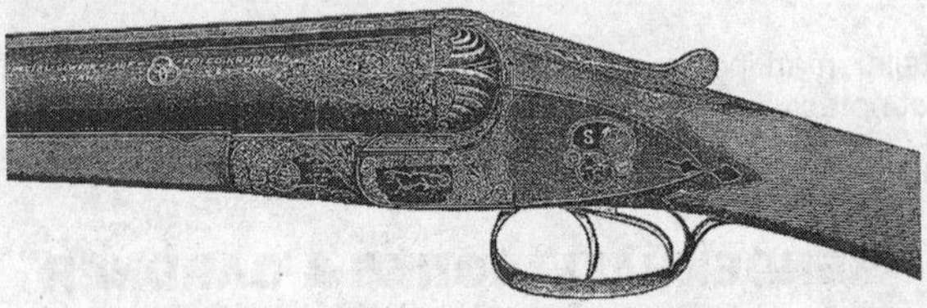

NIB	Exc.	V.G.	Good	Fair	Poor
—	5400	4350	2500	1500	700

Model 125

NIB	Exc.	V.G.	Good	Fair	Poor
—	6000	4600	3500	2000	1000

Model 130

One of Merkel's highest grade side-by-side shotguns. Featured sidelock action, extra fancy wood, fine line checkering and full coverage game scene engraving.

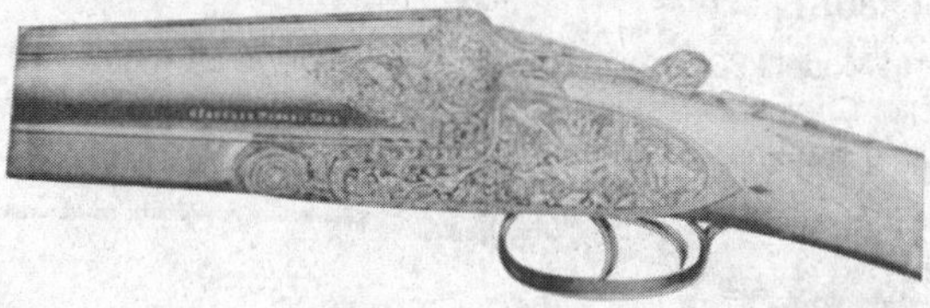

NIB	Exc.	V.G.	Good	Fair	Poor
—	25500	17500	10000	3200	300

Model 126

Similar to Model 130. Fitted with removable sidelocks. H&H-style ejectors.

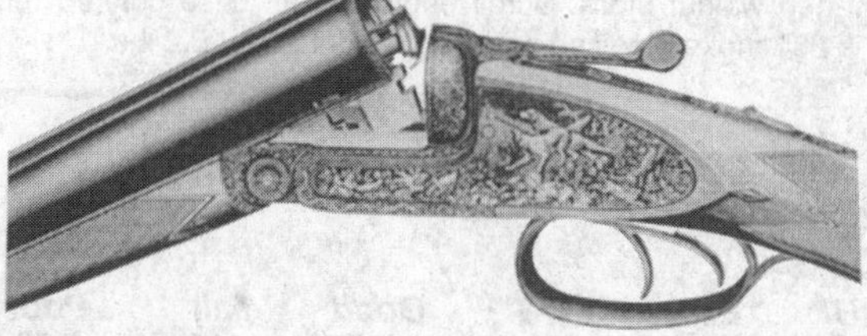

NIB	Exc.	V.G.	Good	Fair	Poor
—	22000	17000	9000	5000	700

Model 170

Offered in 12-gauge only, with automatic ejectors. Boxlock action engraved, with fine full coverage scroll.

NIB	Exc.	V.G.	Good	Fair	Poor
—	6000	4900	3900	2500	300

Model 127

Merkel's finest side-by-side shotgun. Sidelock action featured full coverage fine line scroll engraving of the best quality.

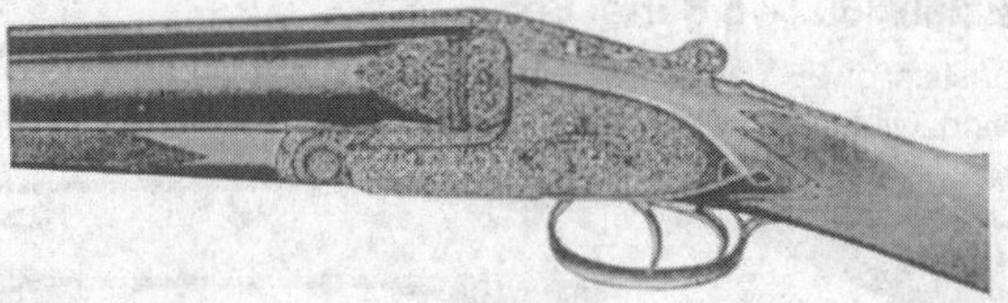

NIB	Exc.	V.G.	Good	Fair	Poor
—	25000	19500	14500	6000	300

Model 47E

Same as above. Fitted with ejectors. Offered in 12-, 16- or 20-gauge. Supplied with fitted luggage case.

NIB	Exc.	V.G.	Good	Fair	Poor
4000	3400	2300	1200	600	200

Model 147

Same as Model 8. Silver/grayed receiver, with fine engraved hunting scenes, engraved border and screws. Discontinued.

NIB	Exc.	V.G.	Good	Fair	Poor
3700	3250	2300	1100	600	200

Model 147E

Same as above. Fitted with ejectors. Offered in 12-, 16-, 20- or 28-gauge. Supplied with fitted luggage case.

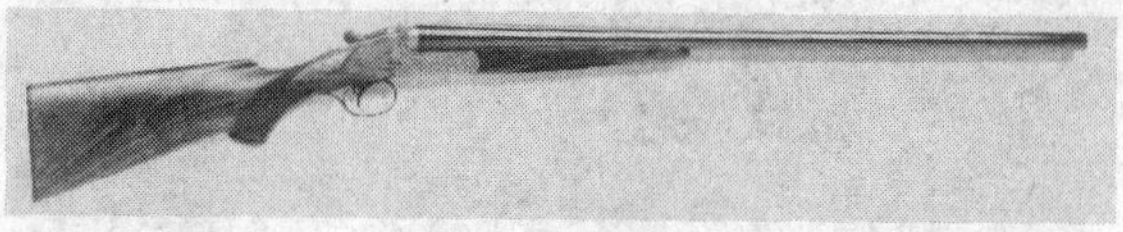

NIB	Exc.	V.G.	Good	Fair	Poor
7200	6500	5000	3250	1200	400

Model 147EL

Similar to Model 147E, with fancy walnut stock. Supplied with fitted luggage case.

NIB	Exc.	V.G.	Good	Fair	Poor
6500	5500	4650	3600	1300	400

Model 122

Features same specifications as above models, but has false sideplates. Fitted with ejectors. Receiver is silver/gray, with fine engraved hunting scenes on false sideplates, engraved border and screws.

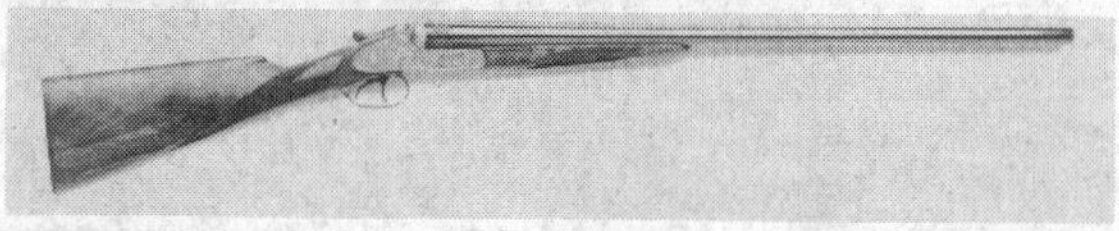

NIB	Exc.	V.G.	Good	Fair	Poor
4000	3500	3000	1900	950	300

Model 47SL

Same as above, with scroll engraving in place of hunting scenes.

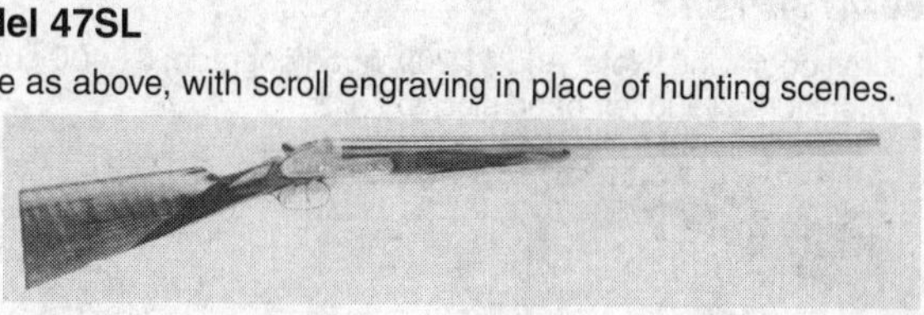

NIB	Exc.	V.G.	Good	Fair	Poor
8200	6100	4400	3000	1750	300

Model 147SL

Features true H&H style sidelocks, with cocking indicators. Gauge and barrel lengths as above. Stock fancy walnut. Weight: 20-gauge 6.4 lbs.; 28-gauge about 6.1 lbs.

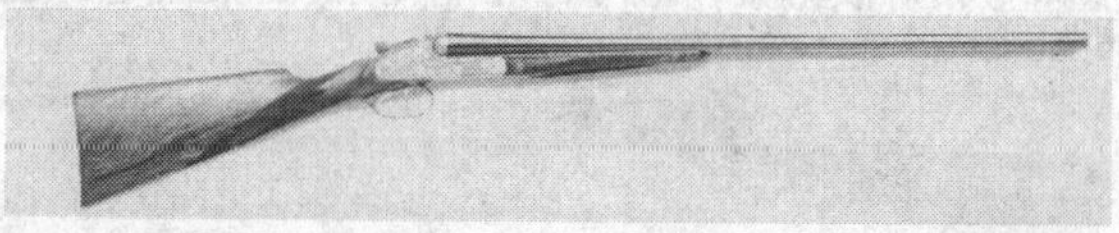

NIB	Exc.	V.G.	Good	Fair	Poor
10000	7000	5500	3850	2250	300

Model 147SSL

Similar to Model 147SL. Fitted with removable sideplates. Fancy walnut stock. Supplied with fitted luggage case.

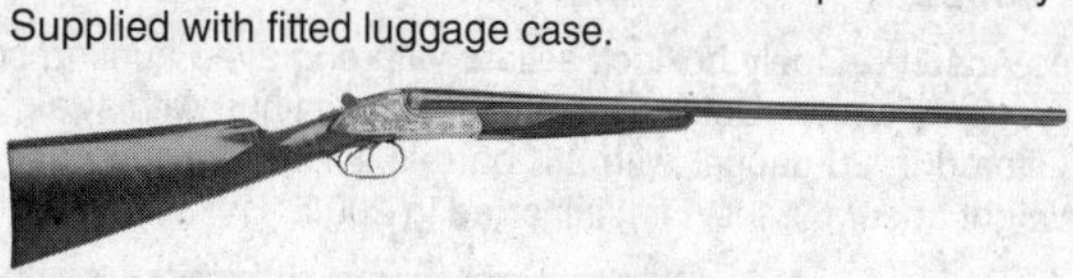

NIB	Exc.	V.G.	Good	Fair	Poor
8800	6500	5200	3000	2500	300

Models 247S/347S

Same as Model 147S, with different types of engraving.

Model 247S

Large scroll engraving.

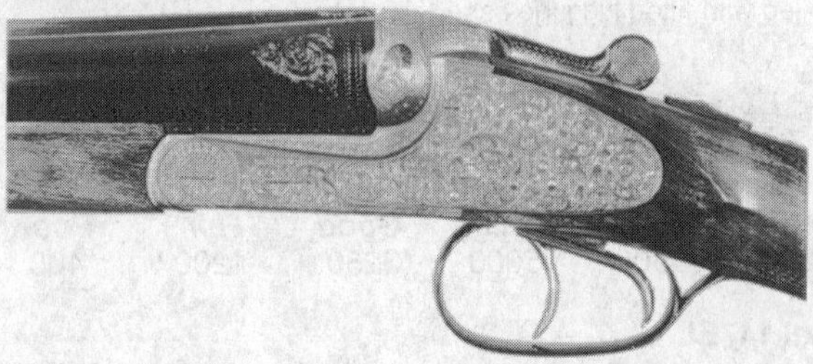

NIB	Exc.	V.G.	Good	Fair	Poor
7700	5800	4400	2500	2000	300

Model 347S

Medium scroll engraving.

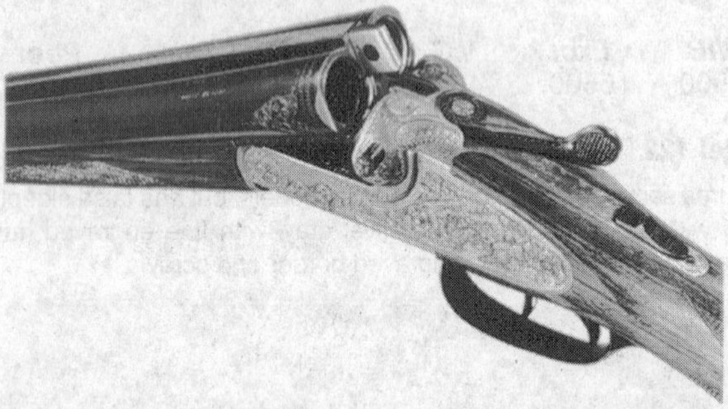

NIB	Exc.	V.G.	Good	Fair	Poor
7100	6100	4950	3850	2250	300

Model 447SL

Small scroll engraving. Note: Add $1,200 wood upgrade; $1,400 custom stock dimensions; $900 left-hand stocks.

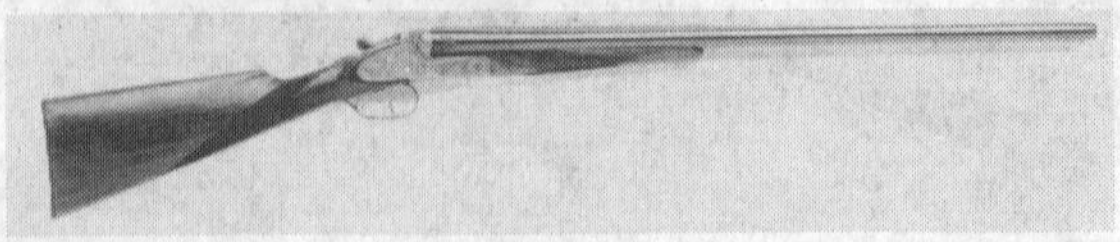

NIB	Exc.	V.G.	Good	Fair	Poor
9900	7300	6000	4400	2700	300

Model 280

Boxlock gun chambered for 28-gauge shell. Fitted with 28" barrels choked Improved Cylinder and Modified. Double triggers with ejectors. Straight-grip walnut stock. Scroll engraving, with case colored receiver. Weight about 5.2 lbs.

NIB	Exc.	V.G.	Good	Fair	Poor
4000	3600	2650	1900	950	300

Model 280EL

Features Anson & Deely boxlock action, with engraved hunting scenes on a silver/gray action. Double triggers. Fancy walnut, with straight-grip stock. Offered in 28-gauge, with 28" barrels. Fitted luggage case standard. Weight about 5.2 lbs. First imported in 2000.

NIB	Exc.	V.G.	Good	Fair	Poor
6500	5500	3850	2500	1500	300

Model 280SL

Similar to Model 280EL, with English-style scroll engraving on H&H style sidelocks. Choice of pistol-/straight-grip fancy walnut stock. Fitted luggage case standard. First imported in 2000.

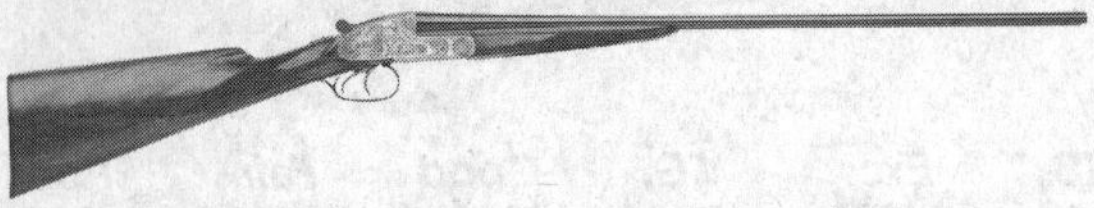

NIB	Exc.	V.G.	Good	Fair	Poor
10500	9000	7500	5000	2000	500

Model 360

Boxlock model same as Model 280, but chambered for .410 bore. Straight-grip walnut stock. Scroll engraving on case colored receiver. Barrel is 28" choke Modified and Full. Weight about 5.2 lbs.

NIB	Exc.	V.G.	Good	Fair	Poor
4200	3600	2650	1400	800	300

Model 360EL

Same as Model 280EL, but chambered for .410 shell. Fitted with 28" barrels. Fancy walnut. Fitted case. Weight about 5.5 lbs. First imported in 2000.

NIB	Exc.	V.G.	Good	Fair	Poor
7000	5700	4100	2750	1300	300

Model 360SL

Same as Model 360EL, with English-style scroll engraving on H&H style sidelocks. Choice of pistol-/straight-grip stock. First imported in 2000.

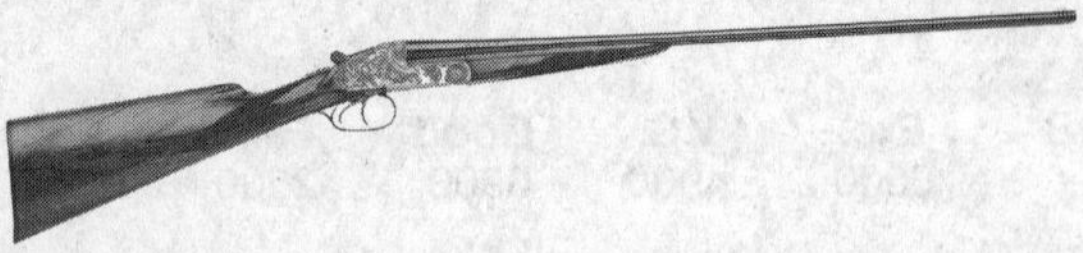

NIB	Exc.	V.G.	Good	Fair	Poor
10500	8100	5900	3750	1600	300

Model 280/360 Two Barrel Set

Set consists of 28 gauge 28" barrel; .410 bore 28" barrel, with scroll engraving. Oil-finish walnut stock. Double triggers. Straight-grip stock.

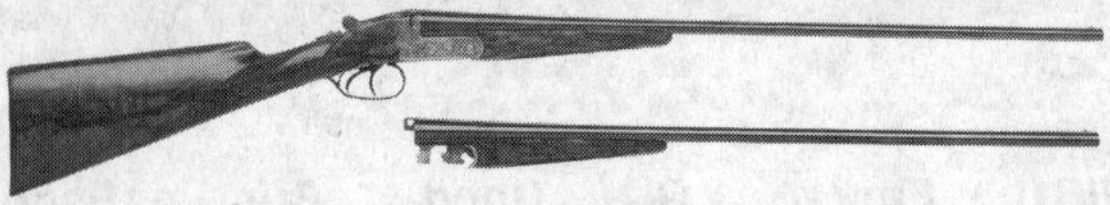

NIB	Exc.	V.G.	Good	Fair	Poor
6500	6000	5000	3750	1600	500

Model 280/360EL Two Barrel Set

Set consists of 28-gauge 28" barrel; .410 bore 28" barrel, with engraved hunting scenes. Fancy walnut stock. Double triggers. Straight-grip stock. First imported in 2000.

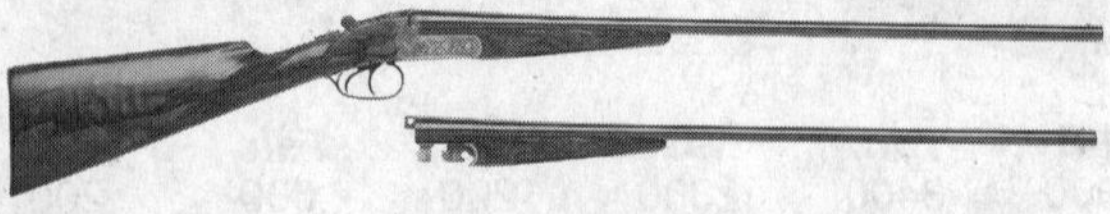

NIB	Exc.	V.G.	Good	Fair	Poor
9500	8000	6000	3750	1600	500

Model 280/360SL Two Barrel Set

Same as above, with English-style scroll engraving. Choice of pistol-/straight-grip stock. First imported in 2000.

NIB	Exc.	V.G.	Good	Fair	Poor
15500	11500	8000	5500	3500	500

Model 1620

Boxlock side-by-side gun chambered for 16-gauge shell. Fitted with 28" barrels; double triggers; barrel chokes Improved Cylinder and Modified; ejectors; straight-grip walnut stock, with oil-finish; case colored receiver; light scroll engraving; fitted luggage case. Weight about 6.1 lbs. Note: Add $2,300 two-barrel set. Second set 20-gauge 28" barrels.

NIB	Exc.	V.G.	Good	Fair	Poor
4200	3600	2500	1800	1000	300

Model 1620E

Similar to Model 1620, with fine engraved hunting scenes on silver/gray receiver.

NIB	Exc.	V.G.	Good	Fair	Poor
5000	4000	3000	2000	1000	300

Model 1620EL

As above, with high-grade walnut straight-grip stock and deeply engraved hunting scenes. Note: Add $2,900 two-barrel set. Second set 20-gauge 28" barrels.

NIB	Exc.	V.G.	Good	Fair	Poor
6000	5000	3850	2200	1100	300

Model 1620SL

Similar to 1620 models above, with grayed sidelocks with deeply engraved hunting scenes. High-grade walnut stock, with oil-finish. Weight 6.6 lbs. Note: Add $3,800 two-barrel set. Second set 20-gauge 28" barrels.

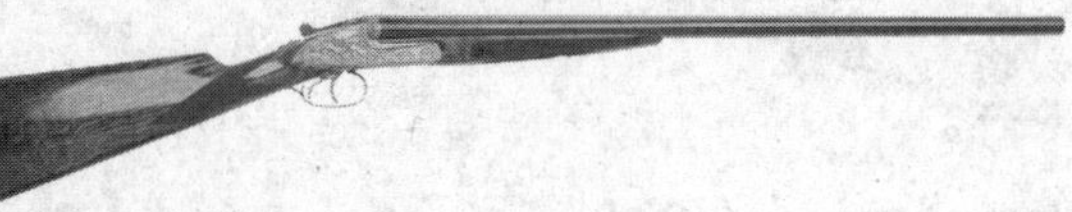

NIB	Exc.	V.G.	Good	Fair	Poor
11000	8400	6100	3750	1800	500

Model 1622

Introduced in 2006. This 16-gauge boxlock side-by-side features full sideplates; case-hardened receiver with cocking indicators; ejectors; single-selective or double triggers; pistol grip or English style stock. Fixed IC and Mod. chokes. Note: Add 50 percent for 2-barrel set. Second set 20-gauge 28" barrels.

NIB	Exc.	V.G.	Good	Fair	Poor
4000	3200	2550	1700	1400	300

Model 1622E

Similar to 1622, with fine engraved hunting scenes on silver/gray receiver.

NIB	Exc.	V.G.	Good	Fair	Poor
7500	5700	4100	2750	1300	300

Model 1622EL

Similar to Model 1622E, with luxury grade wood. Note: Add 30 percent for 2-barrel set. Second set 20-gauge 28" barrel.

NIB	Exc.	V.G.	Good	Fair	Poor
8800	6500	5200	3000	2500	300

OVER/UNDER SHOTGUNS

Model 102E

Was Merkel's standard over/under boxlock model. Offered in 12-gauge 28" barrels; 16-gauge 26" barrels. Both fitted with double triggers, semi-pistol grip and ejectors.

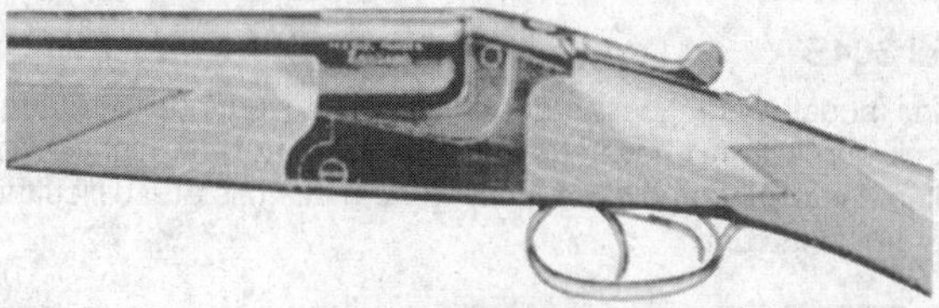

NIB	Exc.	V.G.	Good	Fair	Poor
—	1800	1450	1100	650	400

Model 103E

Similar to standard, with more English scroll engraving coverage and better wood. Was offered in 12-, 16- and 20-gauge.

NIB	Exc.	V.G.	Good	Fair	Poor
—	2450	1650	1350	950	600

Model 204E

Essentially a Model 203E, with finer engraving. Discontinued prior to 1939.

NIB	Exc.	V.G.	Good	Fair	Poor
—	8000	6800	5000	2750	1900

Model 301E

Boxlock model with scalloped action. Chambered for 12-, 16-, 20-, 24-, 28- and 32-gauge. Engraving is an English scroll. Triggerguard is horn. Double triggers. Pistol grip is standard. Produced prior to 1939.

NIB	Exc.	V.G.	Good	Fair	Poor
—	5800	5000	4000	2000	1850

Model 302E

Similar to Model 301E. Fitted with sideplates. Full-coverage engraving features game scenes. Produced prior to WWII.

NIB	Exc.	V.G.	Good	Fair	Poor
—	13250	11000	8250	4400	2000

Model 303 Luxus

Over/under Merkel is custom built to customer's specifications. Each gun is unique. Should be appraised by a knowledgeable individual who is familiar with quality European shotguns.

NIB	Exc.	V.G.	Good	Fair	Poor
27500	20000	16500	—	—	—

Model 304E

Pre-war model was highest grade in Merkel's over/under shotgun line. Sidelock gun with full coverage scroll engraving of the highest quality. Fine line checkering and extra fancy wood make this gun difficult to appraise due to its rarity.

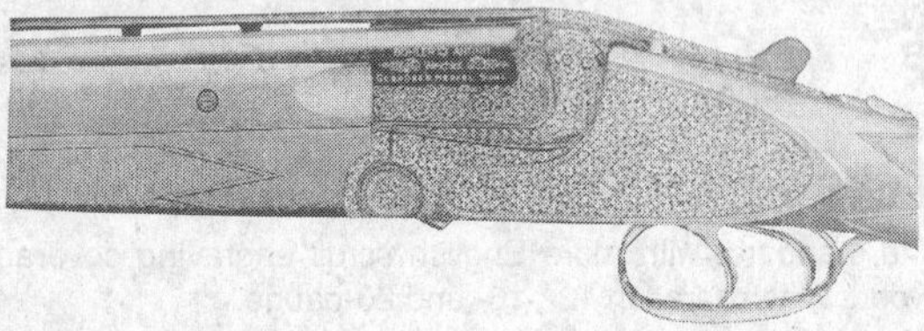

Model 400E

Higher grade over/under fitted with Kersten crossbolt, finer engraving and fancy wood. Merkel offered this grade in 12-, 16-, 20-, 24-, 28- and 32-gauge, with choice of barrel lengths. Produced prior to 1939.

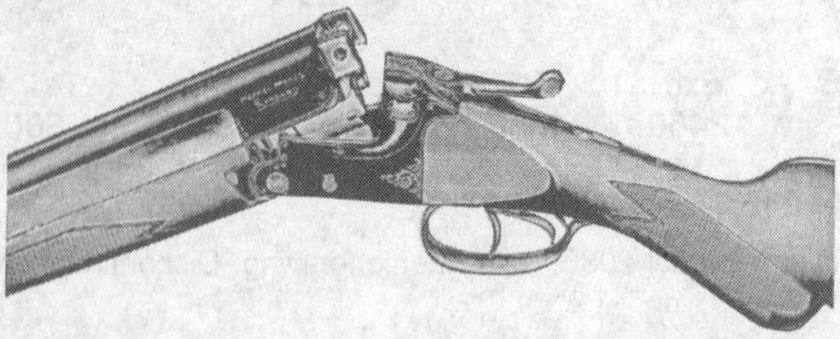

NIB	Exc.	V.G.	Good	Fair	Poor
—	1950	1450	1000	600	400

Model 401E

Similar to model above, with full coverage game scene engraving.

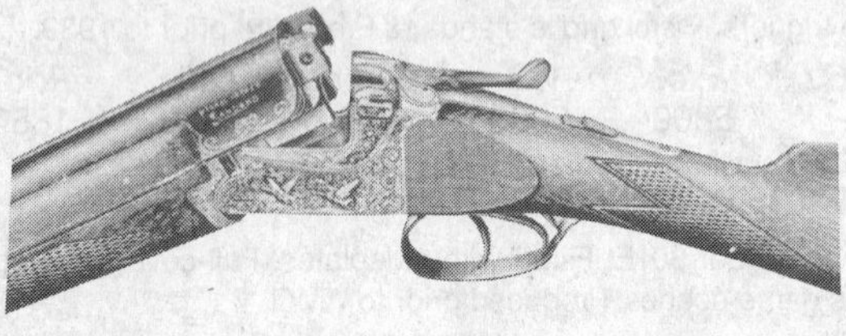

NIB	Exc.	V.G.	Good	Fair	Poor
—	2750	2000	1350	800	600

Model 200E

Action on this model is a self-cocking Blitz, where hammers are attached to trigger plates. Locking mechanism is a Kersten double crossbolt lock, with release. Trigger may be single-selective or double. Manual safety is mounted on tang. Fitted with coil spring ejectors. Offered in 12- and 16-gauge with 28" solid rib barrels; 20-gauge with 26.75" barrels. Oil-finished stock offered with straight-/pistol grip. Receiver case colored, with engraved border and screws. Weight: 12-gauge 7 lbs.; 16-gauge 6.8 lbs.; 20-gauge 6.4 lbs.

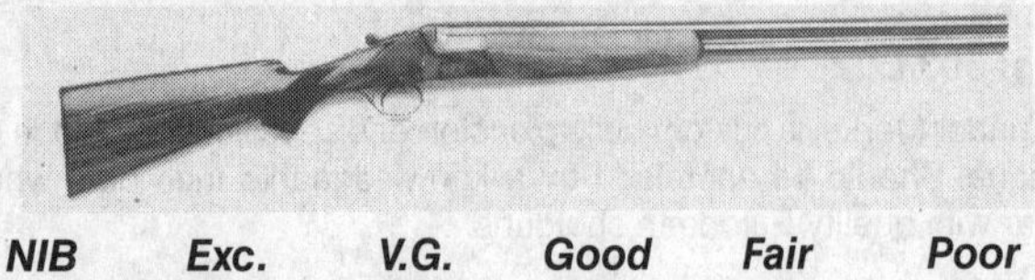

NIB	Exc.	V.G.	Good	Fair	Poor
2900	2200	1650	1000	800	500

Model 200ES

Features a Blitz action, with cocking indicators and Kersten double cross bolt lock, with release. Trigger is single-selective, with tang-mounted manual safety. Coil spring ejectors are standard. Offered in 12-gauge only, with 26.75" or 28" ventilated rib barrel. Walnut stock has skeet dimensions, with pistol grip. Receiver silver/gray, with 112 coverage scroll engraving, engraved borders and screws. Weight about 7.3 lbs.

NIB	Exc.	V.G.	Good	Fair	Poor
4400	3600	2750	2200	1500	1000

Model 200ET

Same as Model 200ES in trap configuration. Ventilated rib barrel length offered is 30".

NIB	Exc.	V.G.	Good	Fair	Poor
4700	3850	3000	2250	1750	1000

Model 200SC (Sporting Clays)

Introduced in 1995. Offered in 12-gauge only, with 3" chambers and 30" barrels with ventilated rib. Fitted with a single-selective trigger adjustable for length of pull. Special walnut oil-finished stock, with 26 lpi checkering. Pistol grip and Pachmayr Sporting Clays recoil pad standard. Weight about 7.6 lbs. Note: Add $500 with Briley choke tubes.

NIB	Exc.	V.G.	Good	Fair	Poor
7200	6000	3300	1500	900	450

Model 201E

Same as Model 200E, with silver/gray receiver with fine engraved hunting scenes, engraved border and screws.

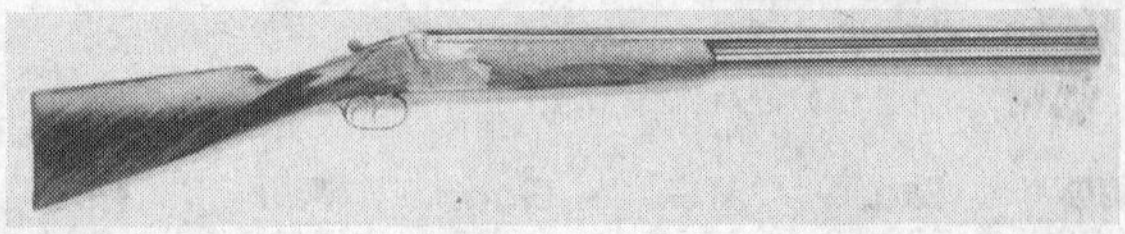

NIB	Exc.	V.G.	Good	Fair	Poor
3700	3100	2500	1650	1000	750

Model 201ES

Same as Model 200SC, with full coverage scroll engraving.

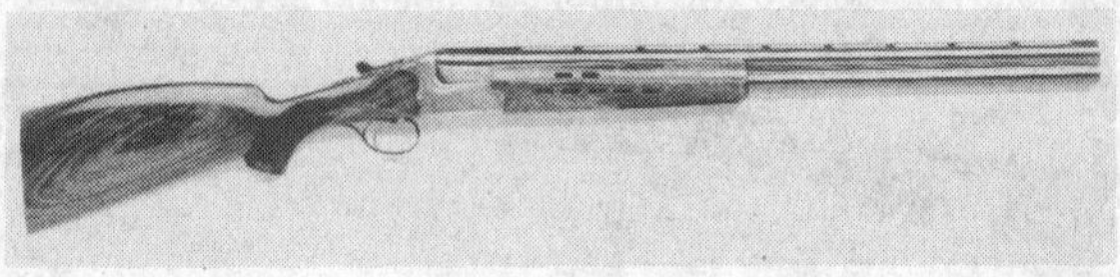

NIB	Exc.	V.G.	Good	Fair	Poor
4950	4050	3300	2500	2000	1000

Model 201ET

Same as Model 210ES. Fitted with 30" barrel and trap stock dimensions.

NIB	Exc.	V.G.	Good	Fair	Poor
4950	4100	3300	2750	2000	1000

Model 202E

Same basic specifications as Model 201E. Fitted with false sideplates with cocking indicators.

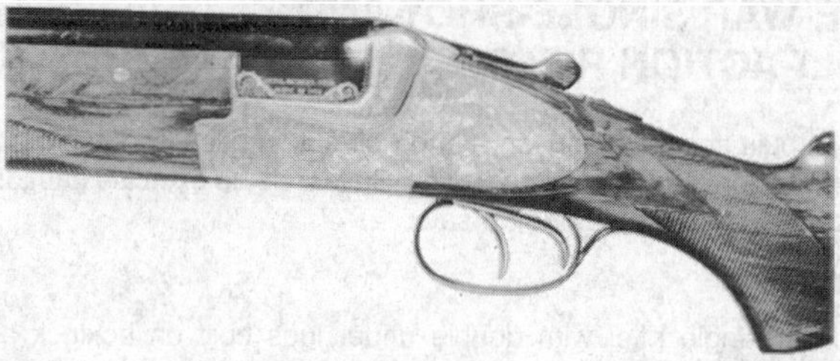

NIB	Exc.	V.G.	Good	Fair	Poor
8200	5500	3850	2500	1500	1000

Model 203E

Has true H&H style sidelocks, with cocking indicators. Sideplates are removable with cranked screw. Gauge selection and barrel are same as those listed above. Silver/gray receiver has English-style large scroll engraving. Discontinued.

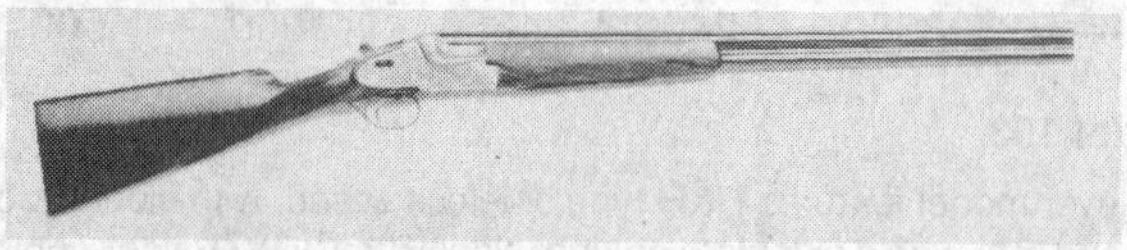

NIB	Exc.	V.G.	Good	Fair	Poor
13500	10400	8250	5000	2500	1000

Model 303E

Same as Model 203E, with detachable sidelock plates with integral retracting hook. Model 303E has medium scroll work engraving and H&H type ejectors.

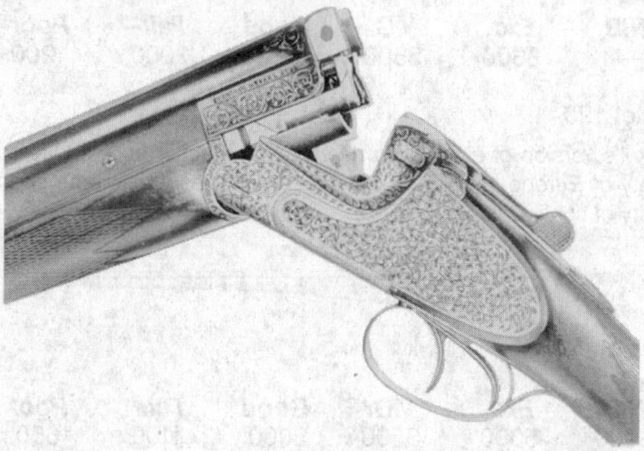

NIB	Exc.	V.G.	Good	Fair	Poor
18700	16500	13400	7500	5000	2500

Model 303EL

Features H&H style sidelocks that are quick detachable without tools. Receiver engraved with hunting scenes. Offered in 12-, 20- and 28-gauge. Double triggers. Fancy walnut stock, with pistol-/straight-grip. Weight about: 12-gauge 7 lbs.; 20-, 28-gauge 6.4 lbs. Fitted luggage case standard.

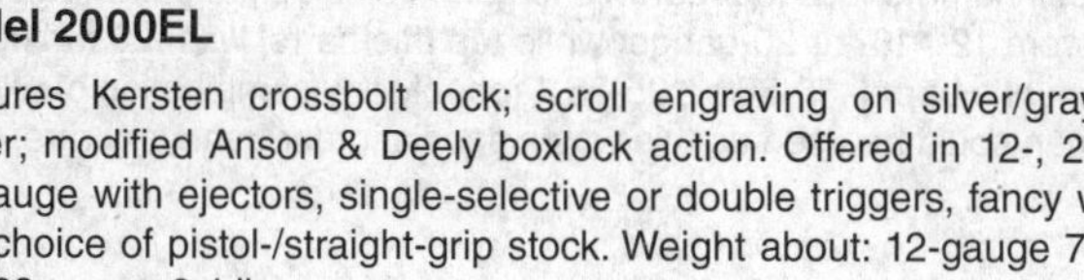

NIB	Exc.	V.G.	Good	Fair	Poor
26000	18700	13000	7500	5000	2500

Model 2000EL

Features Kersten crossbolt lock; scroll engraving on silver/gray receiver; modified Anson & Deely boxlock action. Offered in 12-, 20- or 28-gauge with ejectors, single-selective or double triggers, fancy wood and choice of pistol-/straight-grip stock. Weight about: 12-gauge 7 lbs.; 20-, 28-gauge 6.4 lbs.

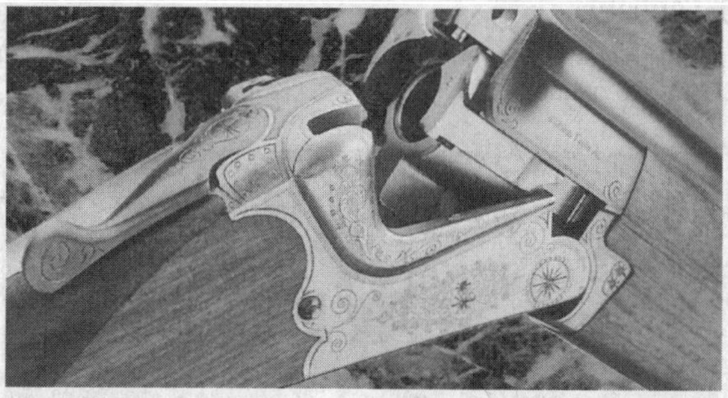

NIB	Exc.	V.G.	Good	Fair	Poor
6000	5100	3600	2200	1500	750

Model 2000EL Sporter

Similar to above model. Fitted with 30" barrels 12-gauge; 28" barrels 20- and 28-gauge.

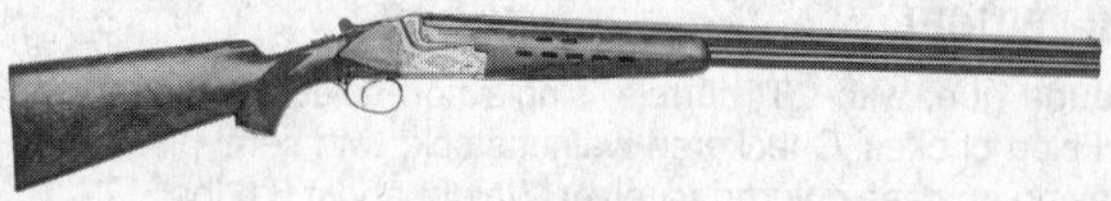

NIB	Exc.	V.G.	Good	Fair	Poor
6000	5200	3600	2200	1500	750

Model 2000CL

Introduced in 2005. Chambered for 12-, 20- or 28-gauge, with 28" barrels choked Improved Cylinder and Modified. Scroll engraved receiver, with case colors. Single-selective trigger, with auto ejectors. High grade wood, with semi-pistol grip and straight-grip.

NIB	Exc.	V.G.	Good	Fair	Poor
7700	5800	3750	2200	1500	750

Model 2000CL Sporter

As above in 12-gauge, 30" barrels with ventilated rib; 20- and 28-gauge, 28" barrels with solid rib. Pistol grip stock. Introduced in 2005.

NIB	Exc.	V.G.	Good	Fair	Poor
8100	6100	3750	2200	1500	750

Model 2001EL

Similar to Model 2000, with finely engraved hunting scenes. Offered in 12-, 20-, 28-gauge.

NIB	Exc.	V.G.	Good	Fair	Poor
11000	9350	7500	5000	2000	900

Model 2001EL Sporter

Same as above, with 30" barrels 12-gauge; 28" barrels 20- and 28-gauge.

NIB	Exc.	V.G.	Good	Fair	Poor
13000	11000	9000	6500	3000	1100

Model 2002EL

Features finely engraved hunting scenes, with arabesque style. Offered in 12-, 20-, 28-gauge.

NIB	Exc.	V.G.	Good	Fair	Poor
11000	8800	6000	4400	2200	1200

Model 2016EL

16-gauge gun, with 28" barrels, single non-selective trigger and ejectors. Fixed chokes. Checkered walnut stock, with semi-pistol grip. Scroll engraving on case colored receiver. Weight about 6.6 lbs.

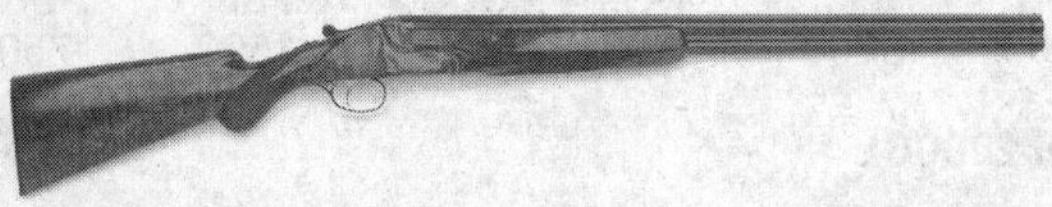

NIB	Exc.	V.G.	Good	Fair	Poor
8750	7000	5000	3000	1500	750

Model 2016EL Two Barrel Set

As above, with extra set of 20-gauge 28" barrels with Fixed chokes.

NIB	Exc.	V.G.	Good	Fair	Poor
12000	10500	8000	5000	3000	1000

Model 2116EL

16-gauge model similar to above, with game scene engraving on case colored receiver.

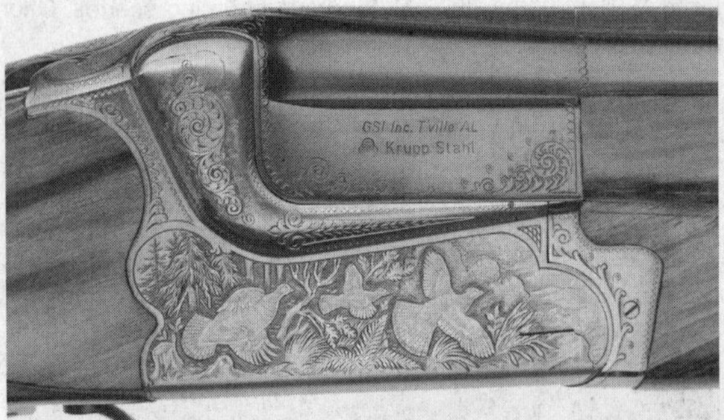

NIB	Exc.	V.G.	Good	Fair	Poor
10500	8500	6750	5000	2000	1000

Model 2116EL Two Barrel Set

As above, with extra set of 20-gauge 28" barrels with Fixed chokes.

NIB	Exc.	V.G.	Good	Fair	Poor
14500	12000	9000	7000	2900	2000

PRE-WAR SINGLE-SHOT AND BOLT-ACTION RIFLES

Merkel built special single-shot and bolt-action rifles. Produced prior to WWII. Seldom seen in United States. Buyer should exercise caution and seek expert assistance prior to sale.

Model 180

Top-lever single rifle, with double under lugs built on boxlock action. Stock is .750 with pistol grip. Commonly referred to as a stalking rifle. Offered in a variety of European calibers. Rare Merkel.

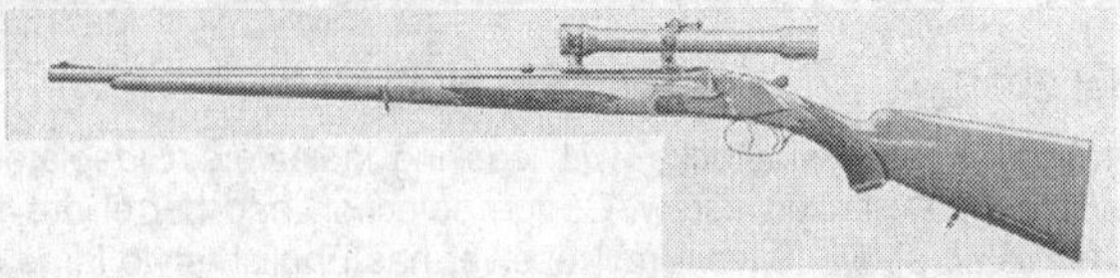

NIB	Exc.	V.G.	Good	Fair	Poor
—	3300	2400	1650	1000	500

Model 183

Top-lever model features H&H type sidelock action, with sidelock on left side and removable sideplate on right side. Fitted with straight-grip stock, full-length forearm with sling swivels, fine line checkering and fancy wood. Rare rifle.

NIB	Exc.	V.G.	Good	Fair	Poor
—	8300	5500	3850	2000	1200

Model 190

Merkel's version of a Sporting rifle built on Mauser action. Offered in a variety of European calibers. Special order rifles that will be seen in a variety of configurations.

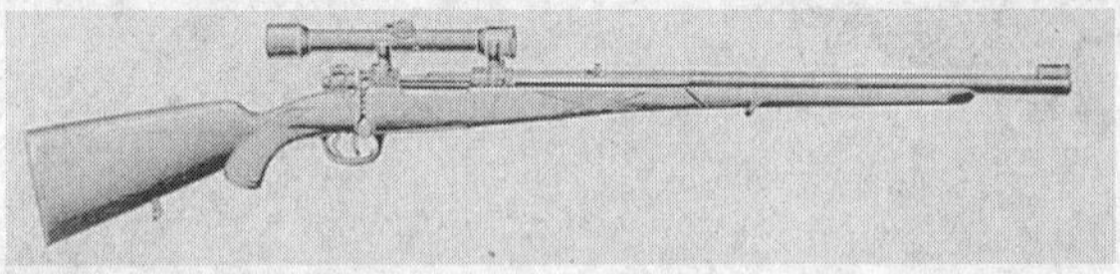

NIB	Exc.	V.G.	Good	Fair	Poor
6000	5000	3500	2000	1100	650

DOUBLE RIFLES, COMBINATION GUNS, DRILLINGS

Model 410E

Merkel's base boxlock model with ejectors. Produced prior to WWII.

NIB	Exc.	V.G.	Good	Fair	Poor
—	2500	1950	1350	750	500

Model 411E

Similar to above, with addition of a small coverage of scroll engraving.

NIB	Exc.	V.G.	Good	Fair	Poor
—	2750	2200	1650	1100	600

Model 300

Boxlock hammerless four barrel shotgun/rifle combination. Shotgun barrels were 12-, 16- or 20-gauge; while top rifle barrel was .22 rimfire with bottom rifle barrel .30-30 or .25-35. Probably any combination of rifle and shotgun could be used as this was a special order gun. Very rare.

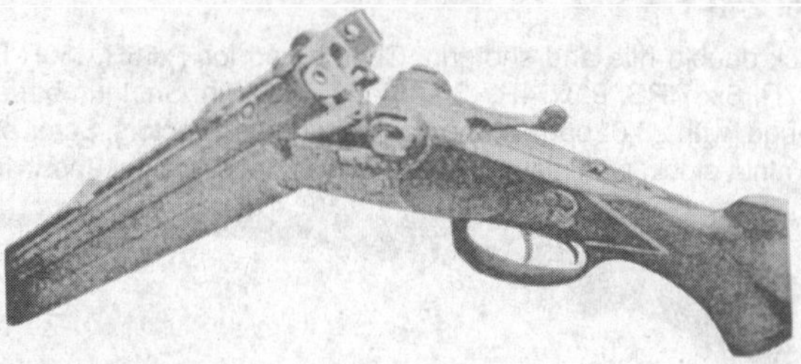

Model 311E

Combination gun has additional English scroll engraving.

NIB	Exc.	V.G.	Good	Fair	Poor
—	8600	7200	5500	2250	1250

Model 312E

Fitted with sideplates and game scene engraving.

NIB	Exc.	V.G.	Good	Fair	Poor
—	10400	9000	7500	4000	2000

Model 313E

Model has sidelocks, with fine full coverage scroll engraving. Expert appraisal is recommended due to this model's rarity and unique features.

NIB	Exc.	V.G.	Good	Fair	Poor
18000	13000	11750	8800	4400	2000

Model 314E

Sidelock model is also rare and unique. Expert appraisal is recommended prior to sale. Extra barrels will frequently be seen with this model.

Model 128E

Side-by-side double rifle is a droplock design, with scroll and game scene engraving. Wood is Circassian walnut, with fine line checkering. Offered in a variety of European calibers.

Model 132E

Similar to Model 128E, with full coverage scroll engraving and fancy wood.

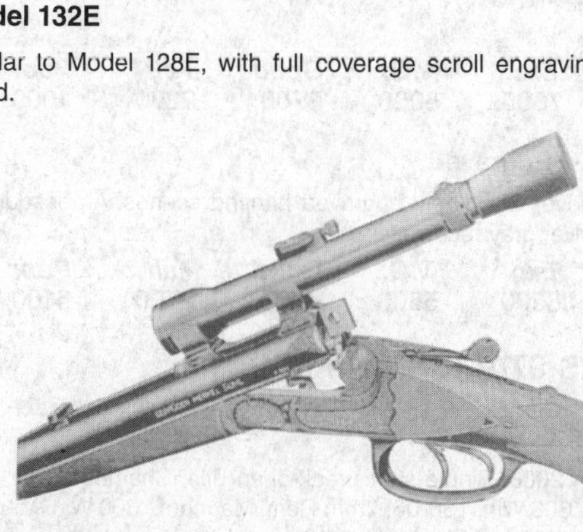

Model 140-1

Features Greener crossbolt scroll engraving, with case-hardened receiver. Extractors and double triggers, with pistol grip stock are standard. Offered in a wide variety of European and American calibers.

NIB	Exc.	V.G.	Good	Fair	Poor
6500	5200	4100	2900	2000	1000

Model 140-1.1

Same as above, with finely engraved hunting scenes.

NIB	Exc.	V.G.	Good	Fair	Poor
7400	6100	4400	2900	2000	1000

Model 140-2

Double rifle has an Anson & Deely boxlock action. Double triggers. Barrel length 23.6". Chambered for .375 H&H, .416 Rigby and .470 NE. Pistol grip stock, with cheekpiece on oil-finish walnut. Weight about 10.7 lbs. depending on caliber.

NIB	Exc.	V.G.	Good	Fair	Poor
11500	8250	6000	3750	2200	1500

Model 140-2.1

Similar to one above. Engraved with African game scenes.

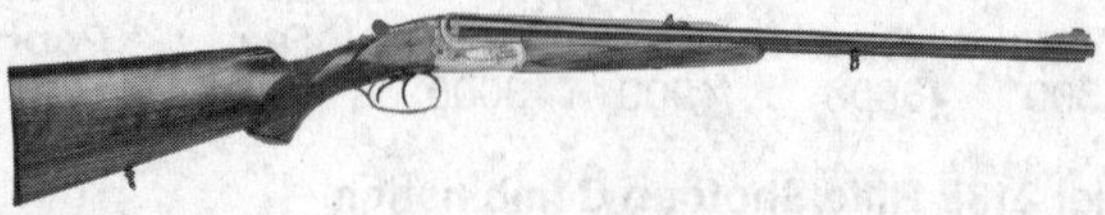

NIB	Exc.	V.G.	Good	Fair	Poor
13400	9300	6600	3750	2200	1500

Model 150-1

Features an arabesque engraving on silver/gray receiver. Extractors, double triggers and pistol grip are standard.

NIB	Exc.	V.G.	Good	Fair	Poor
8250	6600	5100	3000	2000	900

Model 150-1.1

Same as above, with finely engraved hunting scenes.

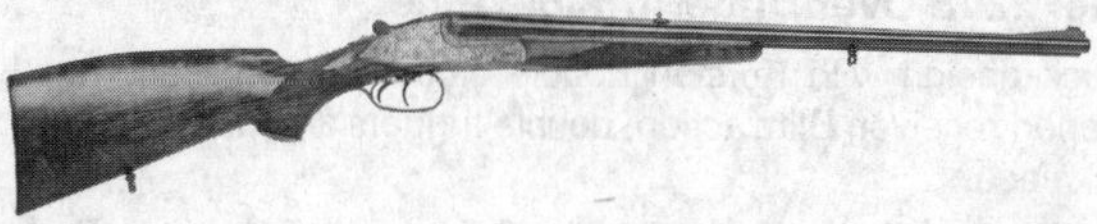

NIB	Exc.	V.G.	Good	Fair	Poor
9500	7700	6000	3500	2500	1000

Model 160S Luxus Double Rifle

Double rifle is part of Luxus series. Features highest quality sidelock action, wood and fittings. Offered in .222 Rem., 5.6x5OR Magnum, .243, 6.5x57R, 7x57, 7x65, .3006, .30R Blaser, 8x57IRS, 8x57RS, .308 Win. and 9.3x74R. Weight about 8 lbs. An expert appraisal should be sought prior to sale, due to unique nature of this model.

NIB	Exc.	V.G.	Good	Fair	Poor
15000	12500	8500	5750	4300	1200

Model 160S-2.1

Same as above, with finely engraved hunting scenes. Chambered for

.470 Nitro Express. Weight about 11 lbs.

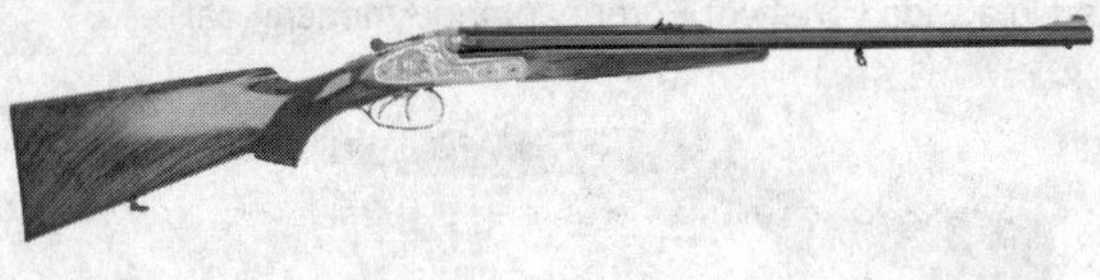

NIB	Exc.	V.G.	Good	Fair	Poor
28500	20750	16500	12000	7500	1500

Model 211E Rifle/Shotgun Combination

Over/under model features gray metal boxlock action, with hunting scenes. Top barrel available in 12-, 16- or 20-gauge; bottom barrel offered in .22 Hornet, 5.6R Magnum, 5.6R, .222 Rem., .243 Win., 6.5x55, 6.5x57R, 7x57R, 7x65R, .30-06, 8x57IRS, 9.3x74R and .375 H&H Magnum. Barrel has a solid rib. Trigger is single-selective. Select walnut stock is hand-checkered. Weight about 7 lbs.

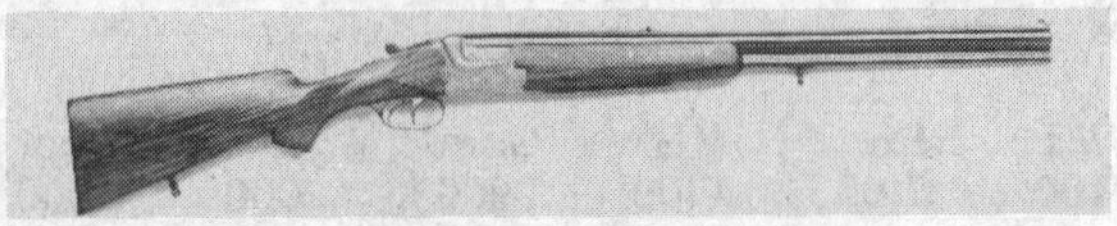

NIB	Exc.	V.G.	Good	Fair	Poor
6600	4950	3850	2250	1500	700

Model 210E Rifle/Shotgun Combination

Same as above. Features scroll engraved case-hardened receiver. Discontinued.

NIB	Exc.	V.G.	Good	Fair	Poor
6900	5500	4400	2750	1200	700

Model 211E Rifle/Shotgun Combination

Similar to above, with finely engraved hunting scenes.

NIB	Exc.	V.G.	Good	Fair	Poor
8300	6600	4900	3000	1500	750

Model 213E Rifle/Shotgun Combination

Combination gun features sidelocks, with English-style large scroll engraving on silver/gray receiver. Fitted with double triggers and pistol grip with cheekpiece.

NIB	Exc.	V.G.	Good	Fair	Poor
13000	10000	8200	5500	1900	900

Model 313E Rifle/Shotgun Combination

Same as above, with finer scroll engraving and fancy wood.

NIB	Exc.	V.G.	Good	Fair	Poor
19000	15000	8250	6500	2000	1000

Model 220E Over/Under Double Rifle

Boxlock design with Kersten double crossbolt, scroll engraved case-hardened receiver, Blitz action, double triggers and pistol grip stock with cheekpiece.

NIB	Exc.	V.G.	Good	Fair	Poor
10000	6600	4950	3800	1700	820

Model 221E Over/Under Double Rifle

Similar to above, with game scene engraving on silver/gray receiver.

NIB	Exc.	V.G.	Good	Fair	Poor
12500	9350	6300	4500	2300	900

Model 223E Over/Under Double Rifle

Fitted with sidelocks. Features English-style arabesque engraving in large scrolls on silver/gray receiver.

NIB	Exc.	V.G.	Good	Fair	Poor
16000	14000	11000	8000	4200	1000

Model 240-1

Boxlock double rifle and shotgun. Chambered for 7x65R, .30R Blaser, 6.5x57R, 8x57IRS, 9.3x74R, .30-06 and .308 Win. Shotgun barrels are 20-gauge, with 23.6" barrels and double triggers. Ejectors. Scroll engraving. Walnut stock, with pistol grip and cheekpiece. Weight about 10 lbs.

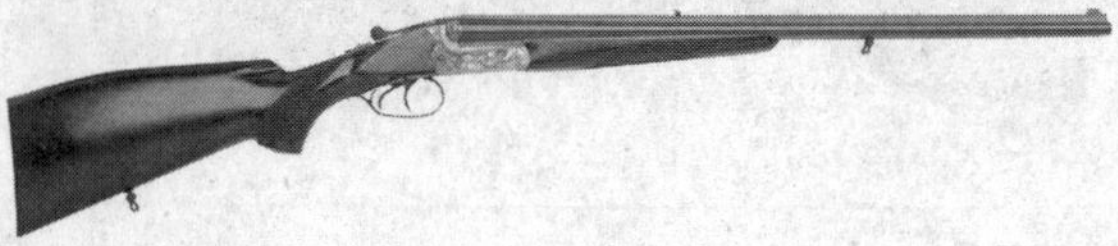

NIB	Exc.	V.G.	Good	Fair	Poor
8000	6300	5000	4000	3000	1300

Model 240-1.1

As above, with hunting scene engraving on grayed receiver.

NIB	Exc.	V.G.	Good	Fair	Poor
9100	7100	6000	5000	4000	1500

Model 323E Over/Under Double Rifle

Similar to above, with finer engraving.

NIB	Exc.	V.G.	Good	Fair	Poor
25000	19000	13500	9500	3200	1500

Model 95K Drilling

Three-barrel shotgun/rifle combination. Top two barrels are chambered for 12-, 16- or 20-gauge; bottom barrel available in rifle calibers from .22 Hornet to .375 H&H Magnum. Action is a boxlock design, with scroll engraving on borders and screws. Stock is select grade walnut, with raised comb, pistol grip with cap, cheekpiece and plastic butt-plate. Weight about 7.7 lbs. Discontinued

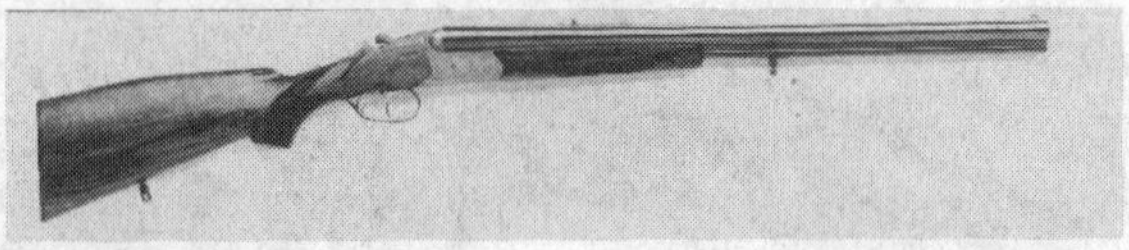

NIB	Exc.	V.G.	Good	Fair	Poor
9400	7400	4700	3000	2000	1000

Model 96K

Similar to above, with scroll engraving on case-hardened frame.

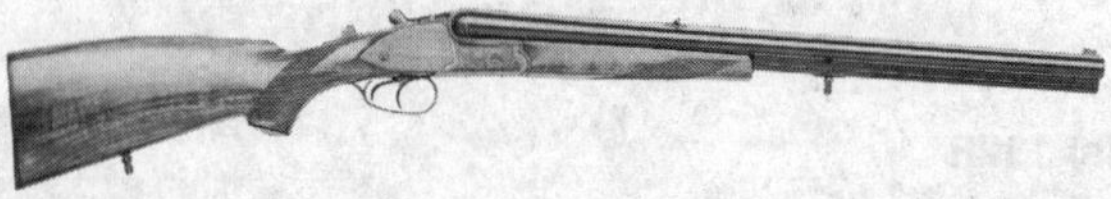

NIB	Exc.	V.G.	Good	Fair	Poor
9800	7800	5000	3700	2200	1000

Model 96K—Engraved

Same as above, with finely engraved hunting scenes. Arabesque engraving on silver/gray receiver.

NIB	Exc.	V.G.	Good	Fair	Poor
11000	8500	5500	4000	2700	1100

K-SERIES STALKING RIFLES

K1 (K3) Jagd

Introduced in 2003. Single-shot break-open rifle. Chambered for .243, 270, 7x57R, .308 Win., .30-06, 7mm Rem. Magnum, .300 Win. Magnum and 9.3x74R cartridge. Fitted with 23.6" barrel. Hunting scene engraving. Weight about 5.4 lbs. This model's name was changed in 2012 to K3 Jagd. Note: Add $400 premium for full-length Mannlicher stock.

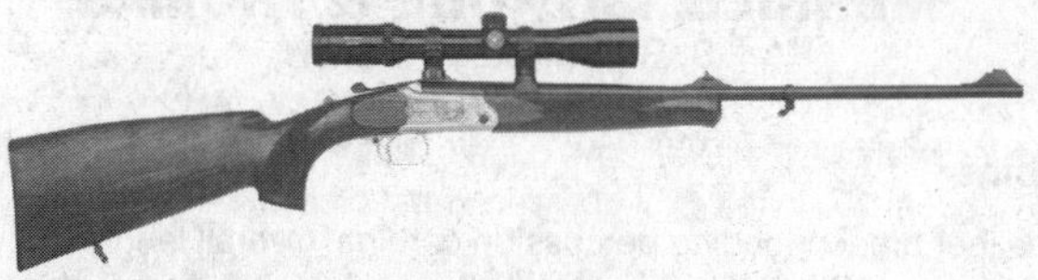

NIB	Exc.	V.G.	Good	Fair	Poor
3200	2750	1900	1600	1100	600

K2 (K4)

High-grade variation of K1/K3 series with octagon barrel, deep-relief hand-engraved hunting scenes, hand-carved high-grade walnut stock. Higher grade versions were made in 2005 and 2006 with values of up to 100 percent of those shown here.

NIB	Exc.	V.G.	Good	Fair	Poor
12500	11000	9000	6500	—	—

POST-WAR BOLT-ACTION RIFLES

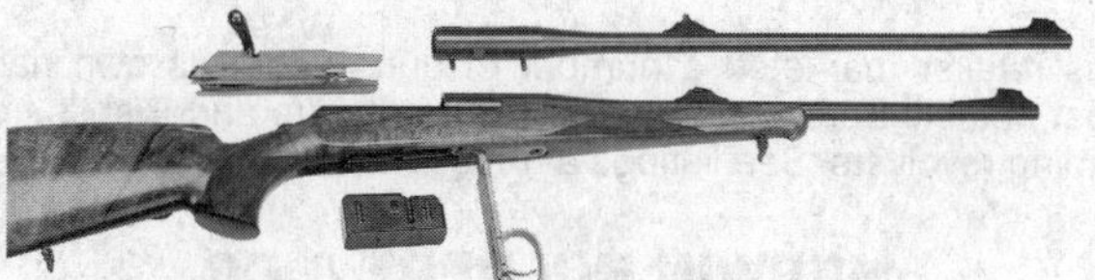

KR-1 Premium

Short-stroke bolt-action rifle. Chambered for .243, .308 or .30-06 and 7mm Rem. Magnum and .300 Win. Magnum calibers. Barrel length for standard calibers 20" or 22"; Magnum calibers 22" or 24". Checkered walnut stock, with hog-back comb. Magazine capacity 3 rounds. Single-set trigger. Interchangeable barrels. Arabesque engraving on bolt housing and trigger plate. Select walnut stock, with Bavarian cheekpiece. Weight about 6.4 lbs. depending on caliber and barrel length. Introduced in 2005. Note: Add $200 for Magnum calibers.

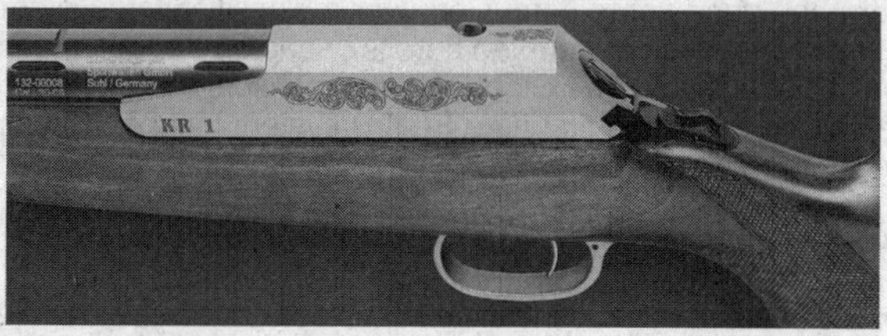

NIB	Exc.	V.G.	Good	Fair	Poor
3000	2200	1600	1000	500	200

KR-1 Weimar

As above, with rounded bolt housing. Hand-chiseled-engraving, with game scenes. Trigger and lockbolt head are gold titanium nitride plated. Select walnut stock, with rosewood forearm tip and Bavarian double fold cheekpiece. Introduced in 2005. Note: Add $200 for Magnum calibers.

NIB	Exc.	V.G.	Good	Fair	Poor
10000	8800	7100	5500	3000	600

RX Helix

Straight-pull bolt-action take-down rifle, with a universal-length action that accommodates calibers from .222 Rem. to .300 Win. Magnum. Two-piece stock is No. 2-grade checkered walnut. Interchangeable barrels are available in many calibers. Introduced in 2013. Values shown are for standard model. Several higher-grade versions are available at prices up to $10,000.

NIB	Exc.	V.G.	Good	Fair	Poor
3350	2800	2100	1600	800	300

Helix Explorer

Explorer model has synthetic stock and most features of RX Helix.

NIB	Exc.	V.G.	Good	Fair	Poor
2550	2000	1500	1250	500	200

MHR 16

A modern bolt-action rifle at an affordable price. Available in both wood-/synthetic-stocked versions. The MHR 16 rifle features a cold-forged and precision-machined receiver. Bolt has three lugs for maximum strength and safety, and a 60-degree throw. Receiver is mated to a cold-hammer-forged barrel in a standard contour. Features include a detachable box magazine which is removable by way of a release built to surround the triggerguard. Safety is located behind the bolt handle and acts directly upon the sear. It also features a separate chamber lock, which allows safe unloading while keeping the safety "on". Available in standard and Magnum calibers: .243 Win., 6.5x55, .270 Win., .308 Win., .30-06, 9.3x62, .300 Win. Magnum and 7 Rem. Magnum. Introduced in 2017, with a MSRP starting at $799.

NIB	Exc.	V.G.	Good	Fair	Poor
700	600	480	400	320	220

SEMI-AUTOMATIC RIFLES

SR1 Semi-Auto

Gas-operated semi-automatic rifle chambered in .223 Rem., .308 Win., .30-06 and .300 Win. Magnum, plus several European calibers. Features include a free-floating 20" barrel, checkered walnut stock and forend, Battue rib rear sight with adjustable front. Stock has adjustable drop and cast off.

NIB	Exc.	V.G.	Good	Fair	Poor
1750	1500	1100	800	400	200

MERRILL
Fullerton, California

Sportsman

Single-shot pistol manufactured in a variety of calibers. Either 9" or 12" octagonal barrel having a wide ventilated rib, adjustable sights and integral telescope mounts. Blued, with walnut grips. Note: Add $100 Interchangeable barrels; $25 wrist support.

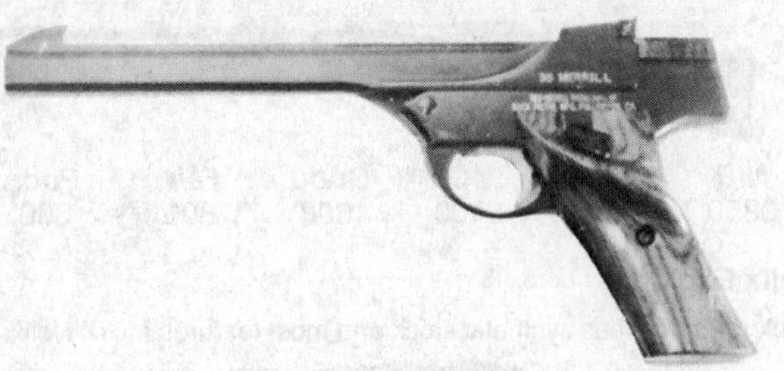

NIB	Exc.	V.G.	Good	Fair	Poor
—	700	580	320	180	120

MERRILL, JAMES H.
Baltimore, Maryland

Merrill Rifle (Antique)

Single-shot breech-loading rifle. Chambered for .54-caliber. Utilizes percussion ignition system. Breech opens for loading by lifting and pulling back on a lever. Barrel 33" in length. Full-length walnut stock held on by two barrel bands. Mountings and patchbox are brass; lock is case colored, with browned barrel. Lock marked "J.H. Merrill Balto./Pat. July 1858". There are military acceptance marks on stock. Approximately 775 of these rifles manufactured and purchased by government for use during Civil War. Made in 1864 and 1865. Values are for Civil War rifle. Hunting percussion rifles with Merrill markings bring less.

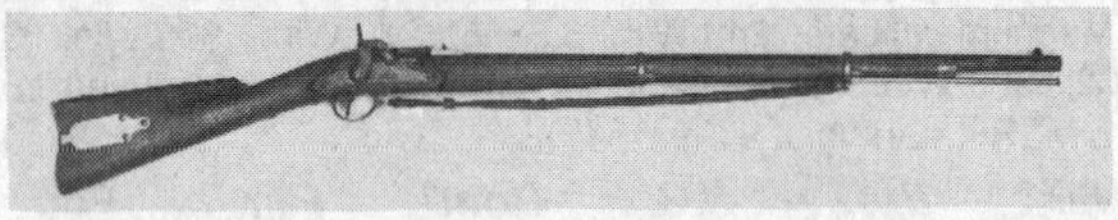

Courtesy Milwaukee Public Museum, Milwaukee, Wisconsin

Exc.	Fine	V.G.	Good	Fair	Poor
10000	8000	6000	4000	2000	1000

Merrill Carbine

Similar in appearance to rifle, except barrel length is 22"; stock only half-length with one barrel band. There are some variations that are quite subtle in appearance, but which have a considerable effect on values. We recommend that an independent appraisal be secured. Values given are for standard 1st and 2nd Types. Approximately 15,000 total manufactured. Most were used in Civil War.

1st Type (Antique)

No eagle stamped on lock. Breech lever is flat.

Courtesy Milwaukee Public Museum, Milwaukee, Wisconsin

Exc.	Fine	V.G.	Good	Fair	Poor
3750	2750	2120	1500	500	350

2nd Type (Antique)

Eagle stamped on lock. Stock has no patchbox. Breech lever has a round tip.

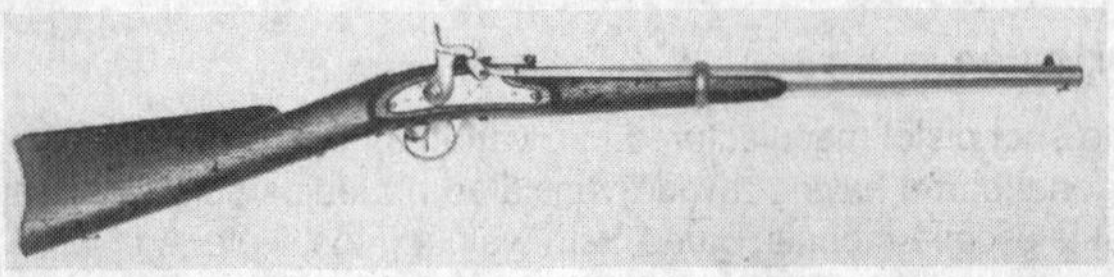

Courtesy Milwaukee Public Museum, Milwaukee, Wisconsin

Exc.	Fine	V.G.	Good	Fair	Poor
4250	3000	2370	1750	600	420

MERRILL, LATROBE & THOMAS
S. Remington—Maker
Ilion, New York

Carbine

.58-caliber breech-loading percussion carbine. Overall length 38"; barrel 21". Lock marked "S. Remington/ Ilion, N.Y."; barrel "Merrill, Latrobe & Thomas/Baltimore, Md./Patent Applied For". Approximately 170 made in 1855.

NIB	Exc.	V.G.	Good	Fair	Poor
—	—	45000	35000	12500	700

MERRIMACK ARMS
See—BROWN MANUFACTURING CO.

MERWIN & BRAY
Worcester, Massachusetts

See BACON. Also see PLANT'S MANUFACTURING CO.

This retailer marketed a number of guns under its own name, most notably Bacon single shot .22 derringers and Plant's front-loading revolvers. See listings at those makers.

MERWIN HULBERT & CO.
New York, New York

Merwin Hulbert & Co., New York City, founder Joseph Merwin, had previously been involved in Merwin & Bray. Merwin Hulbert & Co. or its principals were also involved in Phoenix Rifle, Evans Rifle Company, American Cartridge Company and Hopkins & Allen of Norwich, CT. Most Merwin Hulbert revolvers will be marked with Hopkins & Allen name, in addition to Merwin Hulbert. They were made for a fairly brief period, with most production apparently taking place during 1870s & early 1880s.

There has been some confusion over a classification system for MH revolvers. System adopted here is based on distinctions listed in Art Phelps' book, The Story of Merwin Hulbert & Co. Firearms. We believe this is the first time Phelps system has been adapted to a list format.

LARGE-FRAME MERWIN HULBERT SIXGUNS

There has been a marked increase in interest in Merwin Hulbert & Co. over the past decade, with many coming to recognize them as one of the pre-eminent makers of large-frame revolvers used in the American West. Total production of large-frame revolvers has been estimated at a few thousand by some sources. However, frequency with which they are encountered suggests possibly greater production.

MH used a unique system of opening, loading & unloading their revolvers which was supposed to allow selective ejection of spent shells, leaving remaining cartridges in place. A latch on bottom of frame is pushed toward rear of gun and barrel and cylinder are rotated to right (clockwise, as viewed from rear of revolver) 90 degrees. Barrel and cylinder are then pulled forward, far enough to allow empty brass to fall free. This system required exceptional quality machining and some modern authorities are on record as considering Merwin Hulbert to have the finest workmanship of all revolvers of that era. All are .44-caliber 6-shot large-frame revolvers. Beyond that, to fully identify a large-frame Merwin Hulbert, you must specify the following:

1. MODEL DESIGNATION — First Model has an open top and scoop flutes, round barrel and two small screws above triggerguard. Second Model similar to first, except with only one screw above triggerguard. Third Model has a top-strap with standard flutes and a round barrel. Fourth Model is similar to third, except it has a ribbed barrel. Open-top 1st and 2nd Models seem to be more sought after. 4th Model is rare and will bring a premium from a serious Merwin collector.

2. FRONTIER ARMY or POCKET ARMY — Frontier Army models have a square butt and were made in 1st through 4th models. Pocket Army models have a bird's-head butt, with a pointed extension with lanyard hole and are found in 2nd or 3rd Model configuration. Generally, Frontier Army will bring more than Pocket Army.

3. SINGLE-ACTION or DOUBLE-ACTION — Topstrap models 3rd and 4th were manufactured in both single- and double-action. Single-action models tend to bring more.

4. BARREL LENGTH — Standard barrel length on Frontier Army 1st, 2nd & 3rd Models is 7", with 5.5" barrel common on 4th Model. Standard barrel length on Pocket Army was a more "pocket-sized" 3.5". However somewhat ironically, bird's-head butt models marked "Pocket Army" were also produced with full length 7" barrels. Generally, these longer barrels will bring a bit more than shorter ones.

5. CALIBER — Most common is .44-40 (designated "Winchester Calibre 1873"). Merwins were also chambered for .44 Merwin Hulbert (somewhat similar to S&W .44 American cartridge) and .44 Russian. Less common calibers may bring a small premium from serious Merwin collectors.

6. FOREIGN COPIES — Merwin Hulbert design was relatively widely copied during the period of use, particularly in Spain. It seems that much of this production may have gone to Mexico and some found their way to U.S. Although these Spanish copies may bear markings such as "System Merwin Hulbert" or other usage of words "Merwin Hulbert", they generally will not be found with Hopkins & Allen marking. Spanish firms making Merwin copies included Orbea Hermanos and Anitua y Charola. These Spanish copies may bring half or less of what an original Merwin will bring and it can sometimes take a fairly experienced eye to tell the difference.

7. ENGRAVING — Special order engraving was available and it was usually executed in a distinctive and colorful "punch dot" style, which has come to be associated with Merwins (although it is occasionally encountered on other makes of firearms). For a long time, this style was somewhat dismissed as a bit crude and lacking in artistry. However, a new appreciation of Merwin engraving has emerged and factory engraved pieces will bring a significant premium. Often, a panel scene depicts an animal, object or landmark. These panel scenes have an almost "folk art" quality to them and will enhance value further. Engraved Merwins are sometimes encountered with engraving filled with colored enamel, quite rare, and if original, this will bring a further premium.

8. FINISH — Vast majority were nickel plated. Original blued guns will bring a premium.

Courtesy Supica's Old Town Station

Top: Open Top Pocket Army. Bottom: Topstrap Double-Action Pocket Army

First Model Frontier Army, .44 Open Top (Antique)

Two screws, square butt, 7" barrel.

Exc.	Fine	V.G.	Good	Fair	Poor
5500	3000	2250	1500	500	350

Second Model Frontier Army, .44 Open Top (Antique)

One screw, square butt, 7" barrel.

Exc.	Fine	V.G.	Good	Fair	Poor
4500	2750	1870	1000	500	350

Second Model Pocket Army, .44 Open Top (Antique)

Bird's-head butt. 3.5" barrel standard, 7" will bring a premium.

Exc.	Fine	V.G.	Good	Fair	Poor
3500	2000	1350	700	400	280

Third Model Frontier Army, Single-Action, .44 Topstrap (Antique)

Square butt, 7" barrel.

Exc.	Fine	V.G.	Good	Fair	Poor
3750	2250	1520	800	450	310

Third Model Frontier Army, Double-Action, .44 Topstrap (Antique)

Square butt, 7" barrel.

Exc.	Fine	V.G.	Good	Fair	Poor
3250	1750	1220	700	400	280

Third Model Pocket Army, Single-Action, .44 Topstrap (Antique)

Bird's-head butt. 3.5" barrel standard, 7" will bring a premium.

Exc.	Fine	V.G.	Good	Fair	Poor
3250	1750	1220	700	400	280

Third Model Pocket Army, Double-Action, .44 Topstrap (Antique)

Bird's-head butt. 3.5" barrel standard, 7" will bring a premium.

Exc.	Fine	V.G.	Good	Fair	Poor
3000	1600	1120	650	400	280

Fourth Model Frontier Army, Single-Action, .44 Topstrap (Antique)

Ribbed barrel, scarce. 5.5" barrel seems to be most common, also offered in 7" and 3.5".

Exc.	Fine	V.G.	Good	Fair	Poor
5000	2750	1770	800	550	380

Fourth Model Frontier Army, Double-Action, .44 Topstrap (Antique)

Ribbed barrel. Barrel lengths as above.

Exc.	Fine	V.G.	Good	Fair	Poor
4750	2500	1620	750	550	380

SMALL-FRAME MERWIN HULBERT POCKET REVOLVERS

.32 & .38 centerfire revolvers were manufactured with unique Merwin Hulbert twist-open system, like large frame revolvers. They were often advertised as chambered for .32 MH & Co. or .38 MH & Co. cartridges, but it appears as if these cartridges may have been essentially the same as .32 S&W and .38 S&W rounds. Of course, Merwin Hulbert revolvers were manufactured for original lower pressure blackpowder loadings of these cartridges. Saw-handled grip frames were standard, although some were manufactured with distinctive Pocket Army type pointed "skullcrusher" bird's-head grip frames. These will generally bring a premium. Most common barrel length for most models is 3.5", with 5.5" barrels somewhat scarcer in most models and 2.75" barrels quite scarce and worth a premium. A number of police departments purchased small frame Merwin Hulbert revolvers in late 19th century. Department marked guns will bring a premium.Note that .44-caliber "Pocket Army" model is a large-frame and listed in section above. .22 Merwin Hulbert revolver is the only one not to use MH twist-open system. It is, instead, a tip-up revolver closely resembling S&W Model One.

First Pocket Model Single-Action (Antique)

Spur-trigger, cylinder pin exposed at front of frame, round loading aperture in recoil shield (no loading gate), five-shot .38, scarce.

Exc.	Fine	V.G.	Good	Fair	Poor
1250	800	550	300	180	120

Second Pocket Model Single-Action (Antique)

Spur-trigger, cylinder pin exposed, sliding loading gate, five-shot .38.

Exc.	Fine	V.G.	Good	Fair	Poor
1000	650	460	280	150	100

Third Pocket Model Single-Action Spur-Trigger (Antique)

Enclosed cylinder pin, sliding loading gate, five-shot .38.

Exc.	Fine	V.G.	Good	Fair	Poor
950	600	410	220	120	80

Third Pocket Model Single-Action w/Triggerguard (Antique)

Five-shot .38.

Exc.	Fine	V.G.	Good	Fair	Poor
1000	680	480	280	150	100

Double-Action Pocket Model, Small Frame (Antique)

.32-caliber five-shot. Patent marked folding hammer spur will bring a small premium.

Exc.	Fine	V.G.	Good	Fair	Poor
1000	750	400	250	150	80

Double-Action Pocket Model, Medium Frame (Antique)

Usually .38 five-shot. Scarce, .32 seven-shot will bring 25- to 50 percent premium. Patent marked folding hammer spur will bring a small premium.

Exc.	Fine	V.G.	Good	Fair	Poor
1500	1000	600	350	200	100

Tip-Up .22 Spur-Trigger (Antique)

.22 rimfire, S&W patent infringement, looks similar to S&W Model. One Third Issue. Scarce. "Made by Merwin Hulbert & Co. for Smith & Wesson" marking will bring a small premium.

Exc.	Fine	V.G.	Good	Fair	Poor
1000	650	460	280	180	120

MERWIN HULBERT RIFLES

Very similar in design to Hopkins & Allen single-shot breech-loaders. Advertised in .22 and .32 rimfire, as well as .32 WCF, .38 WCF and .44 WCF. May have been offered in .32-40 and .38-55 chamberings. A 20-gauge shotgun barrel was offered separately for these rifles. Features included set trigger, rebounding hammer, pistol grip stock and take-down. Seldom encountered, Merwin Hulbert name on these should bring a premium over standard Hopkins & Allen single-shot rifles. A small frame "Merwin Hulbert & Co's. Junior" rifle was also offered, chambered for .22 rimfire.

METRO ARMS CORPORATION

Imported from the Philippines by Eagle Imports
Wanamassa, New Jersey

MAC 3011

This is a competition model in .40 S&W or .45 ACP. Has a wide-body high-capacity magazine, fiber-optic front sight and fully adjustable rear. Features include ramped match-grade bull barrel, ambidextrous safety.

NIB	Exc.	V.G.	Good	Fair	Poor
900	800	650	500	300	200

MAC 1911

A series of 1911-style pistols in .45 ACP, with 4.25" or 5" barrel. Standard 1911 configurations, with enhancements including Novak or Bomar sights, custom hardwood grips, 8-shot magazines. Bobcut grip-frame on 4.25" model (shown). Bullseye model has 6" barrel, combat hammer and trigger, flared and lowered ejection port, large magazine well, front and rear slide serrations.

Standard Model 5 bbl.

NIB	Exc.	V.G.	Good	Fair	Poor
850	750	650	500	300	200

Bobcut Model 4.25 bbl.

NIB	Exc.	V.G.	Good	Fair	Poor
750	650	550	400	300	200

Bullseye Model 6 bbl.

NIB	Exc.	V.G.	Good	Fair	Poor
1000	900	750	650	400	200

METROPOLITAN ARMS CO.

New York, New York

Established in February 1864, company manufactured copies of Colt Model 1851 and 1861 Navy Revolvers, as well as copies of Colt Model 1862 Police Revolver. Two of the firm's principle officers were Samuel and William Syms (formerly of Blunt & Syms) and it is believed that they were responsible for production. Curiously although, most Metropolitan pistols were produced during 1864 to 1866 period. Company itself was not dissolved until 1920.

1851 Navy Revolver

.36-caliber percussion revolver, with 7.5" octagonal barrel and 6-shot cylinder. Blued case-hardened, with walnut grips. Barrel marked "Metropolitan Arms Co. New York". Approximately 6,000 made during 1860s. Those bearing H.E. Dimick markings are worth considerably more than standard marked examples.

Standard Navy Model (Antique)

Exc.	Fine	V.G.	Good	Fair	Poor
—	4100	2750	1400	500	350

H.E. Dimick Navy Model (Antique)

Exc.	Fine	V.G.	Good	Fair	Poor
—	8000	5500	3000	850	590

1861 Navy Revolver (Antique)

.36-caliber percussion revolver, with 7.5" round barrel and 6-shot cylinder. Loading lever of rack-and-pinion type. Blued case-hardened, with walnut grips. Barrel marked "Metropolitan Arms Co. New York". Approximately 50 made in 1864 and 1865.

Exc.	Fine	V.G.	Good	Fair	Poor
—	8000	5650	3300	950	660

Police Revolver (Antique)

.36-caliber percussion revolver, with 4.5", 5.5" or 6.5" round barrels and fluted 5-shot cylinder. Blued case-hardened, with walnut grips. Barrel normally marked "Metropolitan Arms Co. New York", although examples have been noted without any markings. Approximately 2,750 made between 1864 and 1866.

Exc.	Fine	V.G.	Good	Fair	Poor
2400	1650	1150	650	250	170

MIDWEST INDUSTRIES

Waukesha, Wisconsin

Wisconsin-based Midwest Industries produces a dizzying array of AR-15 rifles, carbines and parts in calibers .223, .308, and .300 Blackout. Typical examples include:

COMBAT RIFLE SERIES

Caliber: 5.56 NATO/.223 Rem., .223 Wylde. Barrels: 16", 18", 20". Upper receiver: Forged 7075 T6 aluminum, M16/M4 specs, M4 feed ramps, hardcoat anodized Mil 8625 Type-3 Class-2 Finish, .250" takedown pins. MI M16 bolt carrier group, MI-CRM12.625 Combat series handguard, M-LOK compatible. Criterion barrels, mid-Length hybrid profile, 1:8" twist, .223 Wylde chamber, chrome-lined, .625 diameter. A2 flash hider. Lower receiver: Receiver rear takedown pin detent hole threaded for a 4-40 set screw, mil-spec-diameter buffer tube. Magpul CTR buttstock, MOE grip, MOE triggerguard. Heavy-duty quick-detach end plate. SEE POLITICAL PANIC PRICING.

Combat Rifle 16"

NIB	Exc.	V.G.	Good	Fair	Poor
1260	1100	900	700	—	—

Combat Rifle 18"

NIB	Exc.	V.G.	Good	Fair	Poor
1280	1120	920	920	720	—

Combat Rifle 20"

NIB	Exc.	V.G.	Good	Fair	Poor
1380	1220	1010	830	—	—

Combat Rail Series

Caliber: .300 AAC Blackout. Capacity: AR-15-pattern magazines. Barrel: 16 in., Criterion 1:8 twist, stainless-nitride finish, A2 flash hider, .625 in. diameter. Upper/Lower Receivers: Forged 7075 aluminum, M16/M4 specs. Stock: Magpul CTR buttstock. Grip: Magpul MOE. Sights: Optics-ready top rail, laser engraved T-marks. Weight: 6.2 lbs. for MI-FC-300CRM12. Trigger: NA. Overall Length: NA. Features: MI-CRM Combat series handguards, M-LOK compatible. Hard-coat anodized Mil 8625 Type 3, Class 2 finish, M4 feed ramps, .250-in. takedown pins, M16 bolt carrier group. Works with standard AR-15 components and magazines, receiver rear takedown pin detent hole threaded for a 4-40 set screw. Models denote handguard lengths.

NIB	Exc.	V.G.	Good	Fair	Poor
1200	1000	850	—	—	—

SLH Firearms

Caliber: .300 AAC Blackout. Capacity: AR-15-pattern magazines. Barrel: 16 in., Criterion 1:7 twist, stainless-nitride finish, A2 flash hider, .750 in. diameter. Upper/Lower Receivers: Forged 7075 aluminum, M16/M4 specs. Stock: Magpul CTR buttstock. Grip: Magpul MOE. Sights: Optics-ready top rail, laser engraved T-marks. Weight: 6.2 lbs. for MI-FN300SLH12. Trigger: NA. Overall Length: NA. Features: MI-SLH 12-in. Slim Line Handguards, M-LOK compatible. Hard-coat anodized Mil 8625 Type 3, Class 2 finish, M4 feed ramps, .250 in. takedown pins, M16 bolt carrier group. Works with standard AR-15 components and magazines, receiver rear takedown pin detent hole threaded for a 4-40 set screw. Models denote handguard lengths. Discontinued

NIB	Exc.	V.G.	Good	Fair	Poor
1100	930	800	—	—	—

MI .308 Rifles

Caliber: .308 Win. Capacity: (1) Magpul 10 round; accepts SR-25 pattern magazines. Barrel: 16", 18"; Criterion 1:10" twist, stainless-nitride finish. Upper/Lower Receivers: Forged 7075 aluminum. Stock: Magpul Gen 3 PRS buttstock. Grip: Magpul MOE. Sights: Optics-ready top rail. Weight: 8.2 lbs. for MI-10F-16M. Features: Midwest Industries .308 Bolt carrier group, 12" M-LOK handguard, two-chamber enhanced muzzle brake, mid-length gas system .750" gas block, MI-HDEP heavy-duty quick-detach end plate. Add $50 for 18" Criterion barrel. Introduced 2015. SEE POLITICAL PANIC PRICING.

NIB	Exc.	V.G.	Good	Fair	Poor
1600	1400	1190	930	—	—

MI Tactical Response Rifle

Caliber: 5.56 NATO/.223 Rem. Weight: 6.25 lbs. Outfitted with Magpul CTR Stock, MOE grip, MOE triggerguard, heavy duty quick detach end plate MI-HDEP, and has Custom Tactical Response logo laser engraved on the receiver. Barrel: 16", 1:8" twist. Weight: 6.5 lbs. SEE POLITICAL PANIC PRICING.

NIB	Exc.	V.G.	Good	Fair	Poor
1400	1290	1000	780	—	—

MIIDA
Marubeni America Corp.
Japan

Model 612
12-gauge boxlock over/under shotgun, with 26" or 28" ventilated rib barrels, single-selective trigger, automatic ejectors. Blued, with walnut stock. Imported between 1972 and 1974.

NIB	Exc.	V.G.	Good	Fair	Poor
—	900	750	600	400	250

Model 612 Skeet
As above, with 27" Skeet choked barrels. Some engraving. Imported between 1972 and 1974.

NIB	Exc.	V.G.	Good	Fair	Poor
—	900	750	600	400	250

Model 2100 Skeet
Similar to Model 612, with more engraving coverage.

NIB	Exc.	V.G.	Good	Fair	Poor
—	950	800	650	450	300

Model 2200 Trap or Skeet
As above, with 30" trap or 27" skeet bored barrels. More finely engraved. Imported between 1972 and 1974.

NIB	Exc.	V.G.	Good	Fair	Poor
—	1100	850	700	450	300

Model 2300 Trap or Skeet
More finely finished Model 2200. Imported from 1972 until 1974.

NIB	Exc.	V.G.	Good	Fair	Poor
—	1200	900	750	500	300

Model GRT Trap or GRS Skeet
12-gauge boxlock shotgun. Fitted with false sideplates, 27" skeet or 29" Full choked barrels, single-selective trigger, automatic ejector. Imported between 1972 and 1974.

NIB	Exc.	V.G.	Good	Fair	Poor
—	2250	1850	1250	800	500

MILLER ARMS
Sturgis, South Dakota

Miller rifle models are made by Dakota Arms, which is now part of the Remington group. Note: There are a large number of extra costs options available for these rifles.

Standard Rifle
Single-shot falling block rifle. Fitted with 26" round barrel. Chambered for centerfire cartridges up to .375-caliber. Stock is checkered XXX walnut, with pistol grip. Quarter rib scope base. Weight depends on caliber.

NIB	Exc.	V.G.	Good	Fair	Poor
5000	4000	3000	2000	700	350

Low Boy
Features 24" half round/half octagon barrel. All other features as above.

NIB	Exc.	V.G.	Good	Fair	Poor
5000	4000	2250	1300	700	350

Model F
Similar to standard rifle, with addition of 26" octagon barrel, tang sight. Globe front sight. All calibers to .45-110.

NIB	Exc.	V.G.	Good	Fair	Poor
5500	4750	3000	2200	1300	500

MILTECH
Los Altos, California

Company rebuilds and refinishes selected military firearms. All firearms are thoroughly inspected for safety and are considered safe to shoot. All firearms have their original receivers and markings. These rifles are not stamped with Miltech name, but do have a unique Miltech pine crate serial numbered to gun as standard. Company will verify it did the rebuild if asked. All guns come with manual, sling and other selected accessories depending on model.

German Mauser Model 98k

NIB	Exc.	V.G.	Good	Fair	Poor
1500	1150	900	750	550	300

M1 Garand
Note: Add $225 for International Harvester and Winchester.

NIB	Exc.	V.G.	Good	Fair	Poor
1600	1200	850	700	500	300

M1D Garand

NIB	Exc.	V.G.	Good	Fair	Poor
2950	2500	1900	1350	700	400

M1 Carbine
Note: Add $200-300 for Rockola and Winchester.

NIB	Exc.	V.G.	Good	Fair	Poor
1300	1050	800	580	380	200

Model 1941 Johnson

NIB	Exc.	V.G.	Good	Fair	Poor
5000	4000	3000	2000	1000	500

Model 1903 Springfield

NIB	Exc.	V.G.	Good	Fair	Poor
1500	1150	900	750	550	300

Model 1903A3 Springfield

NIB	Exc.	V.G.	Good	Fair	Poor
1500	1150	900	750	550	300

Model 1903 Mark I Springfield

NIB	Exc.	V.G.	Good	Fair	Poor
1550	1220	980	800	580	320

Model 1917 U.S. Enfield

NIB	Exc.	V.G.	Good	Fair	Poor
1500	1150	900	750	550	300

MINNEAPOLIS F. A. CO.

Minneapolis, Minnesota

Palm Pistol (Antique)

.32-caliber radial cylinder pistol, with 1.75" barrel. Manufactured by Ames Manufacturing Company (see Ames entry). Nickel-plated, with hard rubber grips. Sideplates marked "Minneapolis Firearms Co." and "The Protector". Several thousand sold during 1890s.

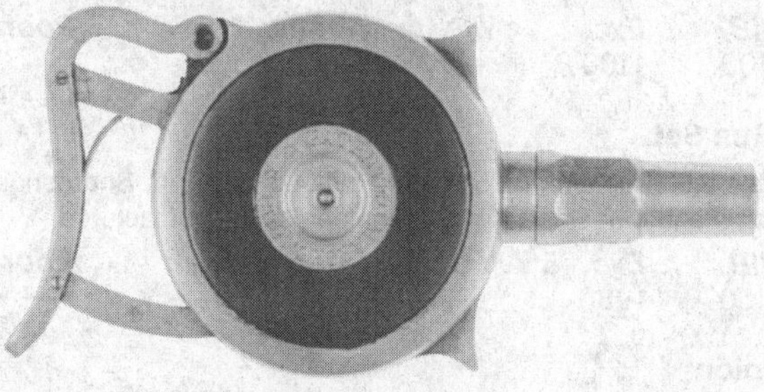

Exc.	*Fine*	*V.G.*	*Good*	*Fair*	*Poor*
2250	1850	1400	950	500	300

MIROKU B. C.

Miroku, Japan

Firearms produced by this manufacturer have been imported and marketed by a variety of companies such as Charles Daly, Browning, Winchester and SKB.

MITCHELL ARMS, INC.

Santa Ana, California

Importer and distributor of foreign-made firearms. Company no longer in business. However, some Mitchell models were available under Brolin Arms through 1998. Brolin Arms was no longer in business as of 1999. Company also imported Yugoslavian-manufactured semi-automatic AK-47 rifles in 7.62x39mm, as well as 7.62x54mm. SEE POLITICAL PANIC PRICING.

RIFLES

Galil

.22 or .22 Magnum caliber copy of Galil rifle. Introduced in 1987.

NIB	*Exc.*	*V.G.*	*Good*	*Fair*	*Poor*
500	400	300	150	120	100

MAS

.22 or .22 Magnum caliber copy of French MAS Bullpup Service Rifle. Introduced in 1987.

NIB	*Exc.*	*V.G.*	*Good*	*Fair*	*Poor*
400	320	200	150	120	100

AK-22

.22 or .22 Magnum caliber copy of AK-47 rifle. Introduced in 1985.

NIB	*Exc.*	*V.G.*	*Good*	*Fair*	*Poor*
400	300	250	120	100	80

M-16

.22 rimfire copy of Colt AR-15. Introduced in 1987.

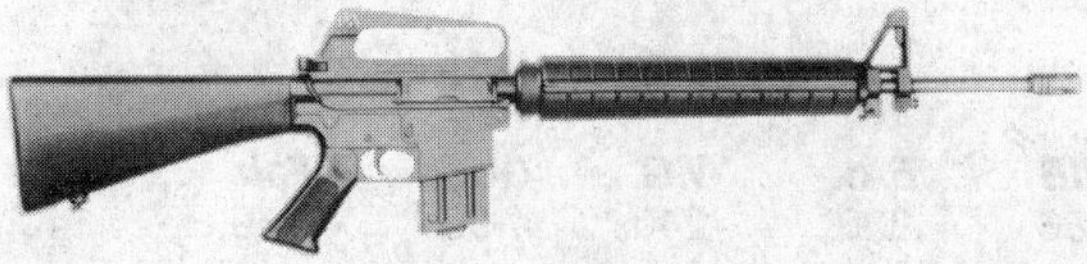

NIB	*Exc.*	*V.G.*	*Good*	*Fair*	*Poor*
320	250	150	120	100	80

PPSH-30/50

.22 or .22 Magnum caliber copy of PPSH Submachine gun.

NIB	*Exc.*	*V.G.*	*Good*	*Fair*	*Poor*
380	320	220	150	80	60

HANDGUNS

Trophy II

Semi-automatic pistol chambered for .22 LR cartridge. Offered in 7.25" fluted or 5.5" bull barrel. Barrels are interchangeable. Trigger adjustable for weight and pull. Walnut grips, with thumbrest standard.

NIB	*Exc.*	*V.G.*	*Good*	*Fair*	*Poor*
560	430	380	330	260	200

Citation II

Similar to Trophy II, with matte satin finish.

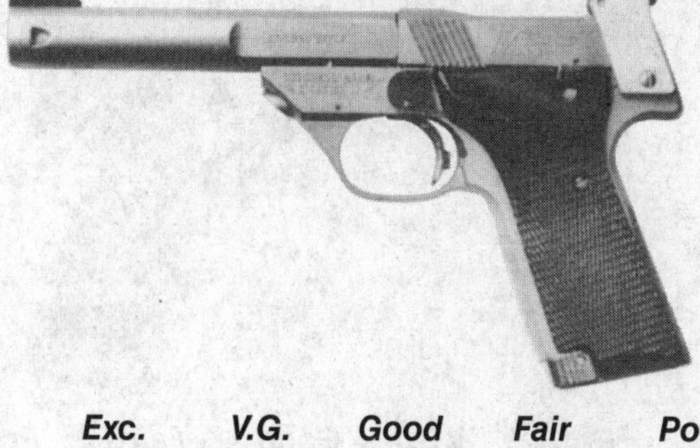

NIB	*Exc.*	*V.G.*	*Good*	*Fair*	*Poor*
400	300	220	200	180	160

Sharpshooter II

Stainless steel target pistol, with 5.5-in. bull barrel to which barrel weights can be added. Fully adjustable rear sight. Checkered walnut grips standard.

NIB	Exc.	V.G.	Good	Fair	Poor
380	330	240	190	170	140

Olympic I.S.U.

Competition pistol features 6.75-in. barrel, with integral stabilizer. Rear sight adjustable as is trigger. Barrel weights adjustable and removable.

NIB	Exc.	V.G.	Good	Fair	Poor
660	580	480	420	280	230

Victor II

.22-caliber pistol built from stainless steel. Has interchangeable barrels in 4.5- or 5.5-in. lengths. Barrels have full length ventilated ribs, checkered walnut grips with thumbrest. Gold plated trigger is adjustable.

NIB	Exc.	V.G.	Good	Fair	Poor
510	430	380	280	230	200

Victor II with Weaver Rib

NIB	Exc.	V.G.	Good	Fair	Poor
520	450	380	280	180	120

High Standard Collectors' Association Special Editions

Limited run of Mitchell's version of High Standard pistol, with special roll marking on slide "High Standard / Collectors Association / Special Edition" and a special serial number series with HSCA prefix. Manufactured by Pastucek Industries, Fort Worth, Texas.

Three Gun Set

Includes Trophy II, Olympic ISU and Victor II. Eleven sets manufactured.

NIB	Exc.	V.G.	Good	Fair	Poor
1400	1100	—	—	—	—

Six Gun Set

Includes 5.5" Trophy II, 6.75" Olympic II, 4.5" Victor II, Sharpshooter II, Citation II and 4.5" Sport King II. Nineteen sets manufactured.

NIB	Exc.	V.G.	Good	Fair	Poor
2450	1980	—	—	—	—

Skorpion

.32-caliber semi-automatic pistol, with 4.75" barrel. Either 20- or 30-shot magazine. Blued, with plastic grips. Imported from Yugoslavia in 1987 and 1988 only.

NIB	Exc.	V.G.	Good	Fair	Poor
—	600	500	420	350	180

Spectre

9mm caliber semi-automatic pistol, with 8" shrouded barrel. Either 30- or 50-shot magazine. Blued, with plastic grips. Also produced with 18" barrel and folding buttstock. Imported from Yugoslavia in 1987 and 1988.

NIB	Exc.	V.G.	Good	Fair	Poor
—	600	500	420	350	180

MITCHELL'S MAUSERS
Fountain Valley, California

Black Arrow

.50-caliber bolt-action rifle, with 5-round box magazine. Fitted with recoil compensator, iron sights, bipod.

NIB	Exc.	V.G.	Good	Fair	Poor
6000	5000	4000	2700	1600	500

Centurion

Double-action revolver, with 4" or 6" barrel. Chambered for .357 Magnum cartridge. Blued or stainless steel.

NIB	Exc.	V.G.	Good	Fair	Poor
700	550	400	300	200	100

Valkyrie

Chambered for .44 Magnum cartridge. Choice of 4" or 6" barrel. Blued or stainless steel.

NIB	Exc.	V.G.	Good	Fair	Poor
900	700	500	400	300	200

Gold Series '03

Chambered for 9mm, .40 S&W or .45 ACP cartridge. Built on Model 1911 Government Model. Blued or stainless steel.

NIB	Exc.	V.G.	Good	Fair	Poor
800	600	450	320	250	150

Escalade

Slide-action shotgun chambered for 12-gauge shell. Fitted with 18.5" barrel; 28" ventilated rib barrel; 22" barrel with Turkey choke. Turkish walnut stock. Blued.

NIB	Exc.	V.G.	Good	Fair	Poor
400	300	250	200	150	100

Sabre

Semi-automatic 12-gauge shotgun. Choice of 22" or 28" ventilated rib barrel. Blued.

NIB	Exc.	V.G.	Good	Fair	Poor
500	400	350	300	250	150

Mauser M98 North American

Bolt-action rifle fitted with Mauser 98 action. Offered in most standard hunting calibers. Note: Add $2,000 for Magnum calibers.

NIB	Exc.	V.G.	Good	Fair	Poor
7000	6000	4500	2280	1500	400

Mauser M98 Varmint

As above chambered for .22-250 or .220 Swift.

NIB	Exc.	V.G.	Good	Fair	Poor
6000	5000	3500	1780	1000	300

Mauser M98 African/Alaskan

Chambered for heavy calibers up to .500 Jeffery.

NIB	Exc.	V.G.	Good	Fair	Poor
8000	7500	6500	2500	1500	500

MK ARMS, INC.

Irvine, California

Model 760

9mm caliber semi-automatic carbine, with 16" shrouded barrel, fixed sights and 14-, 24- or 36-shot magazine. Parkerized with folding stock. Introduced in 1983.

NIB	Exc.	V.G.	Good	Fair	Poor
950	700	580	400	250	120

MKE

Ankara, Turkey

Kirrikale

7.65mm or 9mm short semi-automatic pistol, with 4" barrel and 7-shot magazine. Unauthorized copy of Walther PP. Blued, with plastic grips.

NIB	Exc.	V.G.	Good	Fair	Poor
450	380	280	220	150	100

MODESTO SANTOS CIA.

Eibar, Spain

Action, Corrientes, and M.S.

6.35mm or 7.65mm caliber semi-automatic pistol of low quality. Marked on slide "Pistolet Automatique Model 1920". Blued, with composition grips having monogram "M.S." cast in them. Manufactured between 1920 and 1935.

NIB	Exc.	V.G.	Good	Fair	Poor
—	280	180	120	80	50

Action

6.35mm or 7.65mm semi-automatic pistol. Marked on slide "Pistolet Automatique Modele 1920". Often found bearing trade name "Corrientes" as well as maker's trademark "MS".

NIB	Exc.	V.G.	Good	Fair	Poor
—	280	180	120	80	60

MONTENEGRIN-GASSER

See—GASSER, LEOPOLD

MONTENEGRIN REVOLVERS (Antique)

"Montenegrin" refers to a wide variety of large revolvers chambered for the massive 11.36x36mmR cartridge. They were made by various makers in Austria, Belgium, and Spain. They are found in five- or six-shot configurations. The best known manufacturer is Gasser (see GASSER, LEOPOLD). The type was introduced around 1870. The name comes from the King of Montenegro declaring that all male citizens had the duty to own a Gasser-pattern revolver. Most are double action. The three major types include open-top frame, top-break auto-eject, and solid-frame. Most have a rounded grip frame somewhat like the Mauser Broomhandle pistol. Most do not have a maker or model name. Decorations such as engraving and ivory or bone grips are relatively common, but if nice may add to the value.

Jim Supica photo

Exc.	Fine	V.G.	Good	Fair	Poor
700	500	450	400	200	140

MOORE'S PATENT FIREARMS CO.

Brooklyn, New York

In 1866, this company became known as National Arms Company.

No. 1 Derringer (Antique)

.41-caliber spur trigger all metal pistol, with 2.5" barrel. Blued or silver-plated. Approximately 10,000 manufactured between 1860 and 1865. Also marketed as No. 1 Derringer by Colt Company after they purchased National Arms Company in 1870.

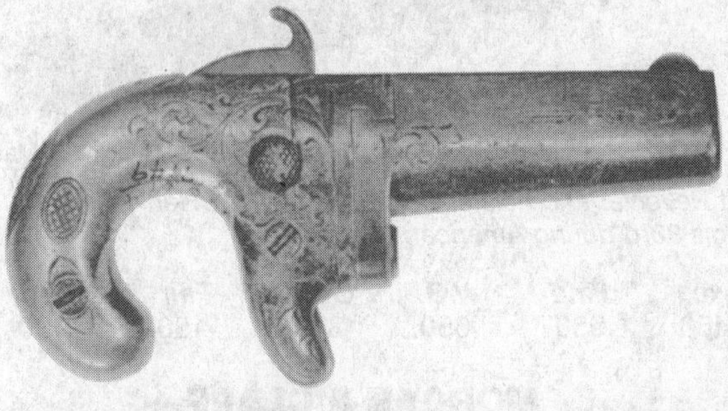

Courtesy Milwaukee Public Museum, Milwaukee, Wisconsin

1st Variation Marked "Patent Applied For" (Antique)

Exc.	Fine	V.G.	Good	Fair	Poor
3200	2500	1800	1100	600	350

2nd Variation Marked "D. Moore Patented Feb. 19 1861" Antique

Exc.	Fine	V.G.	Good	Fair	Poor
2200	1500	1100	700	400	200

Standard Model Marked "Moore's Pat F.A. Co." Antique

Exc.	Fine	V.G.	Good	Fair	Poor
1800	1200	800	500	350	200

National Arms Co. Production. Antique

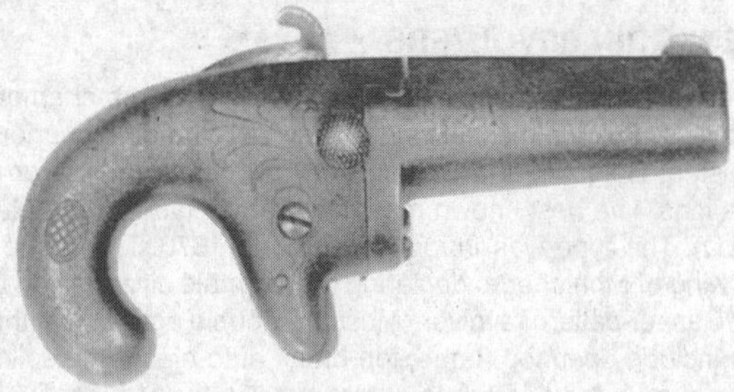

Courtesy Milwaukee Public Museum, Milwaukee, Wisconsin

Exc.	Fine	V.G.	Good	Fair	Poor
1800	1200	800	500	350	200

Iron Model Antique

Exc.	Fine	V.G.	Good	Fair	Poor
2000	1300	850	500	350	200

Pocket Revolver Antique

.32 teat fire caliber spur trigger revolver, with round 3.25" barrel and 6-shot cylinder. Blued or silver plated, with walnut grips. Approximately 30,000 manufactured between 1864 and 1870.

Exc.	Fine	V.G.	Good	Fair	Poor
800	550	410	280	100	70

Belt Revolver Antique

.32 rimfire caliber revolver, with 4", 5" or 6" octagonal barrel and 7-shot cylinder. Barrel and cylinder blued. Brass frame sometimes silver-plated, with walnut grips. Barrel marked "D. Moore Patent Sept. 18, 1860". Several thousand manufactured between 1861 and 1863.

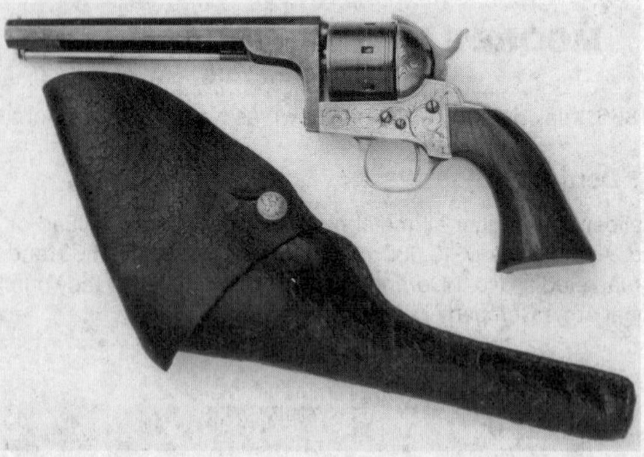

Courtesy Rudolph R. Massenzi

Belt Revolver and holster belonging to Capt. Henry Kellogg, Illinois 33rd during American Civil War.

Exc.	Fine	V.G.	Good	Fair	Poor
1450	950	650	350	150	100

MORGAN & CLAPP
New Haven, Connecticut

Single-Shot Pocket Pistol Antique

.22- or .23-caliber spur trigger single-shot pistol, with 3.5" octagonal barrel. Blued silver-plated frame, with walnut grips. Barrel marked "Morgan & Clapp New Haven". Active 1864 to 1867.

Exc.	Fine	V.G.	Good	Fair	Poor
1150	650	450	250	100	70

MORINI
Italy

C-80 Standard

.22-caliber single-shot pistol, with free floating 10" barrel, match sights. Adjustable frame and grips. Discontinued in 1989.

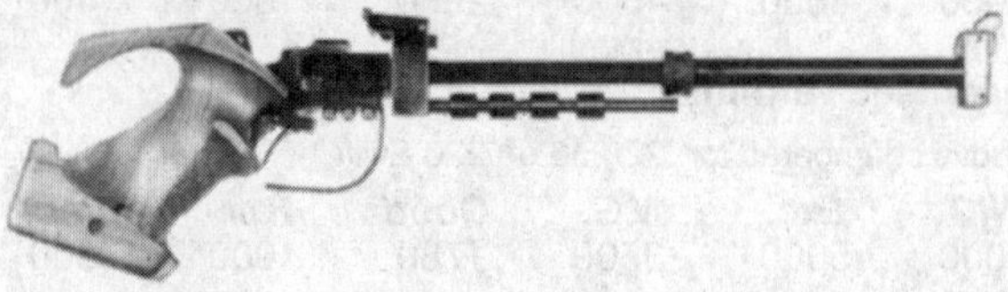

NIB	Exc.	V.G.	Good	Fair	Poor
—	1100	800	680	550	250

CM-80 Super Competition

As above, with trigger adjustable from 5 to 120 grams pressure, Plexiglass front sight, polished finish. Discontinued in 1989.

NIB	Exc.	V.G.	Good	Fair	Poor
—	1200	900	750	650	300

Model 84E Free Pistol

Introduced in 1995. Competition single-shot pistol features 11.4" barrel chambered for .22 LR. Adjustable electronic trigger and sights. Weight about 44 oz.

NIB	Exc.	V.G.	Good	Fair	Poor
1650	1150	900	700	500	200

MORRONE
Hope Valley, Rhode Island

See—RHODE ISLAND ARMS COMPANY

MORSE
Greenville, South Carolina
State Armory

Morse Carbine

Overall length 40"; barrel length 20"; caliber .50 (other calibers are known to have been made on an experimental basis). Round barrel blued; frame brass; stock walnut or beechwood. Approximately 1,000 manufactured during Civil War.

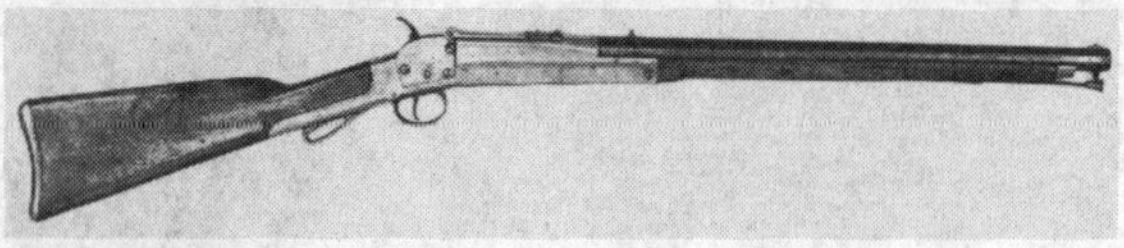

Courtesy Milwaukee Public Museum, Milwaukee, Wisconsin

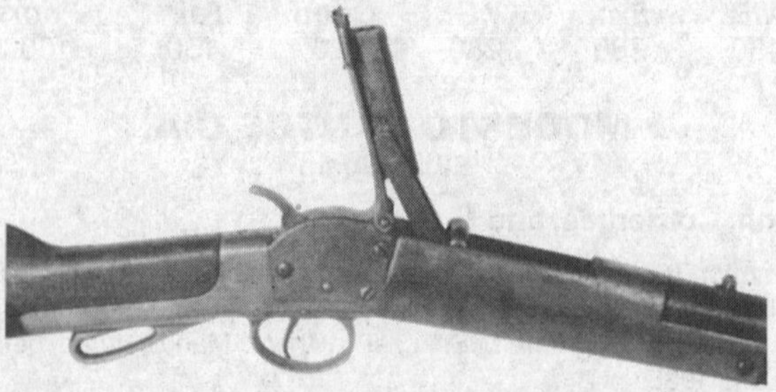

NIB	Exc.	V.G.	Good	Fair	Poor
—	—	27000	23000	7500	1500

MOSSBERG, O. F. & SONS, INC.

North Haven, Connecticut

Founded by Oscar F. Mossberg in 1892 at Fitchburg, Massachusetts. Company for a time was located at Chicopee Falls, Massachusetts and since 1962 has been in North Haven, Connecticut. Oldest family-owned firearms manufacturer in America.

HANDGUNS

Brownie

.22-caliber four-barreled pocket pistol, with revolving firing pin. Resembles a semi-automatic. Manufactured from 1906 to approximately 1940. Premium for in box with papers.

NIB	Exc.	V.G.	Good	Fair	Poor
750	450	320	300	220	150

Model 715P

AR-style semi-automatic .22 LR pistol. Has 25-round magazine, 6" barrel with A2-style muzzle brake, full-length Picatinny top rail and short ventilated quad-rail forend and pistol grip synthetic stock. Adjustable front and rear sights or 1x30mm red dot sight. Note: Add $40 for Red Dot Combo model; $100 for Duck Commander, with Realtree Max-5 camo finish.

NIB	Exc.	V.G.	Good	Fair	Poor
280	240	210	180	150	120

MC1sc

Sub-compact 9mm semi-auto pistol; polymer frame, stainless slide, 3.4" barrel, 19 oz., integrated safety on trigger face, Mossberg safe takedown system. Clear-count transparent 6 and 7 round magazines. Optional features include crossbolt safety, stainless two-tone, tritium night sights.

NIB	Exc.	V.G.	Good	Fair	Poor
400	350	300	—	—	—

MC2C

Caliber: 9mm. Capacity: 11- or 14-round magazine. Barrel: 3.4". Grips: Textured polymer. Sights: Fixed, three-dot, optics-ready. Length: 6.2" overall. Weight: 19.5 oz. unloaded. Finish: Matte black. Features: Accessory rail, forward slide serrations.

NIB	Exc.	V.G.	Good	Fair	Poor
480	420	360	330	270	—

MC2SC

Caliber: 9mm. Capacity: 11- or 14-round magazine. Barrel: 3.4 in. Grips: Textured polymer. Sights: Fixed, 3-dot, optics-ready. Length: 6.2 in. overall. Weight: 19.5 oz. unloaded. Finish: Matte black. Features: Accessory rail, forward-slide serrations.

NIB	Exc.	V.G.	Good	Fair	Poor
550	—	—	—	—	—

RIFLES

Model K

.22-caliber slide-action rifle, with 22" barrel, tubular magazine, internal hammer and take-down system. Blued, with walnut stock. Discontinued in 1931.

NIB	Exc.	V.G.	Good	Fair	Poor
—	350	250	150	80	50

Model M

As above, with 24" octagonal barrel. Manufactured from 1928 and 1931.

NIB	Exc.	V.G.	Good	Fair	Poor
—	350	250	150	80	50

Model L

.22-caliber Martini-style single-shot take-down rifle, with 24" barrel. Manufactured from 1927 to 1932.

NIB	Exc.	V.G.	Good	Fair	Poor
—	600	480	350	180	100

Misc. Bolt-Action Rifles

Beginning in 1930, Mossberg company manufactured a variety of utilitarian single-shot and repeating bolt-action rifles. Later they introduced a similar line of semi-automatic rifles. As these arms were intended for extensive use and were low-priced, values for them may be categorized as listed.

Bolt-Action Rifles (Various Models)

Various Bolt-Action Rifles

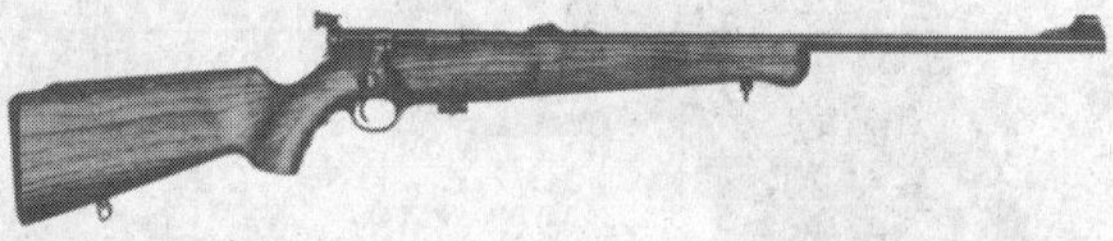

Model 140B

NIB	Exc.	V.G.	Good	Fair	Poor
400	300	200	100	80	50

Semi-Automatic Rifles

Model 50
Model 51
Model 51M
Model 151K
Model 151M
Model 152
Model 152K
Model 350K
Model 351C
Model 351K
Model 352K
Model 432

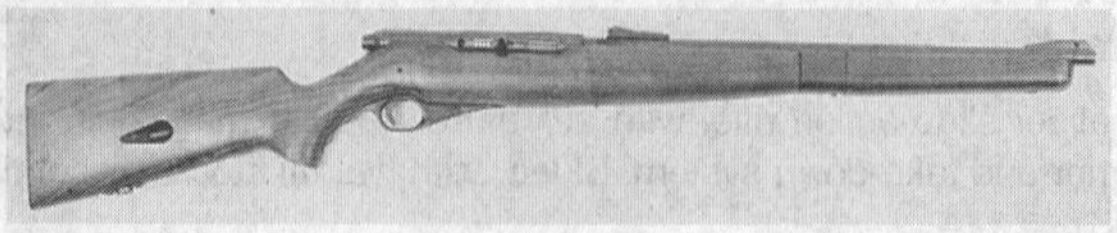

Model 51M

NIB	Exc.	V.G.	Good	Fair	Poor
350	300	200	150	100	50

Targo Smoothbore Series

Early 1940s, Mossberg produced a series of bolt-action .22 rimfire rifles, with smoothbore barrels. Rifles were mainly designed for clay target game called Targo, in which shooters used .22 LR shot ammunition. Game never achieved much popularity. Rifled barrel section several inches long could be attached to muzzle, which allowed use of standard ammunition. Some models came with a smoothbore attachment that extended length of barrel. Other accessories included clay target launcher that attached to barrel, case designed for rifle and supply of small clay targets. There were several model variations: single shot (Model 26T), two repeater models with 7-round magazines (42T and 42TR) and fourth version with an extended 15-round clip (B42T). Most of these rifles were produced from 1940-1942 and again in late '40s, after WWII. Two models were introduced briefly in early 1960s, Model 320TR single shot and 340TR repeater. Note: Add 50 percent for original case and all original accessories; 20 percent for Model 26T or B42T0 rarest models of this series.

NIB	Exc.	V.G.	Good	Fair	Poor
500	420	350	250	200	100

Model 400 Palomino

.22-caliber lever-action rifle, with 22" barrel, open sights and tubular magazine. Also made with 18.5" barrel. Blued, with walnut stock. Manufactured from 1959 to 1964.

NIB	Exc.	V.G.	Good	Fair	Poor
350	300	200	150	100	50

Model 702 Plinkster

Introduced in 2004. This .22-caliber semi-automatic rifle fitted with 18" barrel and adjustable sights. Detachable 10-round magazine. Blued finish. Choice of black synthetic, hardwood, synthetic thumb-hole, solid pink, pink camo or Mossy Oak New Break-up camo finish stock. Weight about 4 lbs. Also available as scope package (add 10 percent). Tiger maple or carbon fiber stock and chromed barrel and receiver. By 2008, a variety of color and stock options, including a modern synthetic version of Mossberg's old flip-down forend and thumb-hole stocks had been added to line. These will bring more or less than values listed, according to local demand.

NIB	Exc.	V.G.	Good	Fair	Poor
180	140	110	80	50	20

Model 702 International Plinkster

Features 21" chrome barrel, with iron sights. Black synthetic stock. Weight about 4.5 lbs. Note: Add $75 for muzzle brake.

NIB	Exc.	V.G.	Good	Fair	Poor
200	160	120	90	60	40

Flex 22 Tactical

Based on action of Model 702, with tactical features including pistol grip, adjustable stock, muzzle brake, top mounted rail and 25-round magazine.

NIB	Exc.	V.G.	Good	Fair	Poor
320	280	220	180	150	120

Model 817 Varmint

Introduced in 2008. Offered by Mossberg International features 21" free-floating blued or brushed chrome barrel, hardwood or black synthetic stock, factory Weaver mounts, detachable box magazine and .17 HMR chambering.

NIB	Exc.	V.G.	Good	Fair	Poor
180	150	120	100	80	50

Tactical .22

AR-styled rimfire auto-loading rifle, with 18" free-floating barrel. Matte blue finish. Matte black synthetic stock, with fixed or adjustable length of pull. Magazine capacity 10 or 25 rounds. Quad forend for unlimited mounting opportunities of optical or light systems. Peep rear and front post sight are standard.

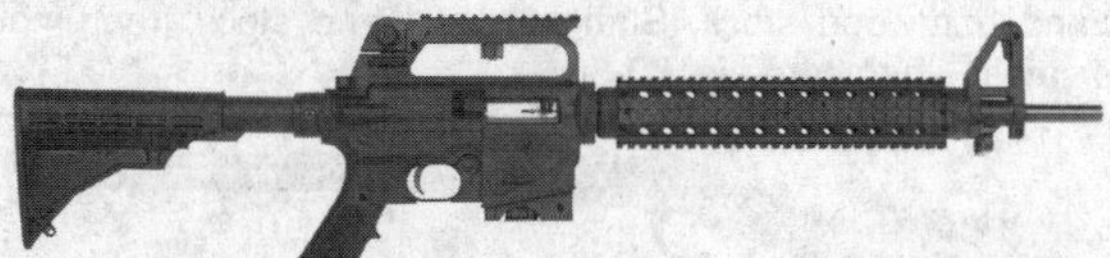

NIB	*Exc.*	*V.G.*	*Good*	*Fair*	*Poor*
240	200	160	120	100	80

Blaze

Semi-automatic rifle chambered for .22 LR, with polymer stock, 16.5" barrel. Choice of adjustable iron sights or Dead Ringer Holographic Green Dot sight with four reticle configurations. Capacity: 10- or 25-round magazine. Finish: black or camo (Kryptec Highlander, Muddy Girl or Wild Fire). Introduced in 2015. Note: Add $65 for Green Dot sight model; $60 for camo finish.

NIB	*Exc.*	*V.G.*	*Good*	*Fair*	*Poor*
180	150	120	90	60	50

Blaze-47

Semi-automatic rifle chambered for .22 LR, with 10- or 25-round magazine. Design is patterned after AK-47 profile, with 16.5" barrel, fiber-optic adjustable rear and raised front sight, synthetic or wood stock. Synthetic stock adjustable for length of pull. Introduced in 2015. Note: Add $50 for wood stock.

NIB	*Exc.*	*V.G.*	*Good*	*Fair*	*Poor*
300	250	200	150	120	100

Model 715T Flat-Top

AR-style semi-automatic chambered for .22 LR, with 10- or 25-round magazine, 6-position stock with adjustable length of pull, black or Moonshine Muddy Girl finish. Barrel length 16.25"; weight 5.5 lbs. Choice of mounted front and adjustable rear sights or 30mm Red Dot sight. Note: Add $50 for Moonshine Muddy Girl finish (shown).

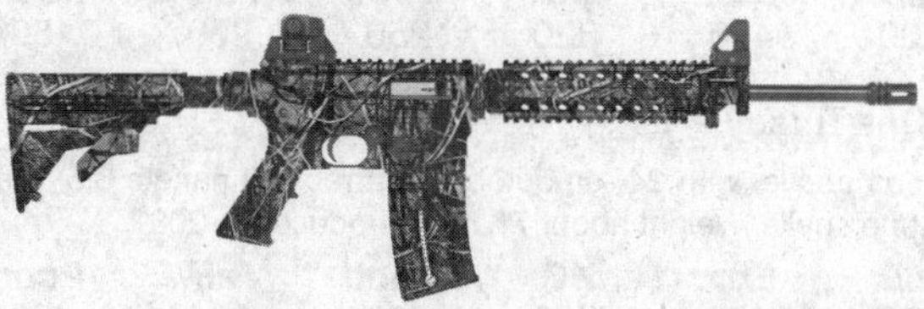

NIB	*Exc.*	*V.G.*	*Good*	*Fair*	*Poor*
340	300	250	200	160	120

Model 100 ATR (All-Terrain Rifle)

Introduced in 2005. Bolt-action rifle chambered for .270 or .30-06 calibers. Fitted with 22" barrel. No sights. Choice of black synthetic, synthetic walnut or camo stock. Matte blue or all-weather finish. Weight about 7 lbs.; .243, 308. Also available as 3X9 scope package. Note: Add 10 percent for scope; $40 for all-weather finish.

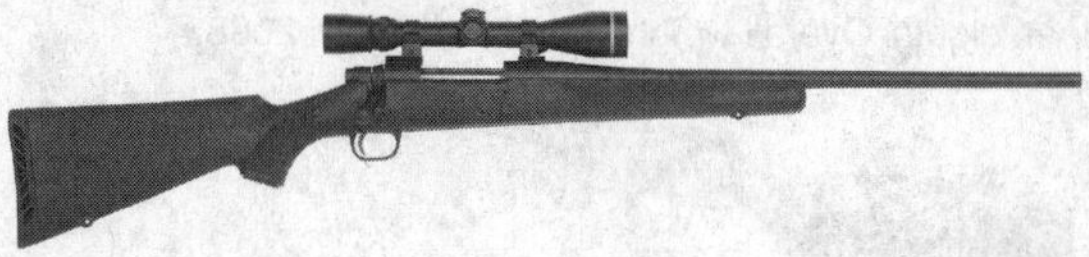

NIB	*Exc.*	*V.G.*	*Good*	*Fair*	*Poor*
360	300	250	200	150	100

Model 100 ATR Night Train

Similar to above, with black synthetic stock, factory-mounted 4x16 scope, bipod and .308 Winchester chambering. Introduced 2008.

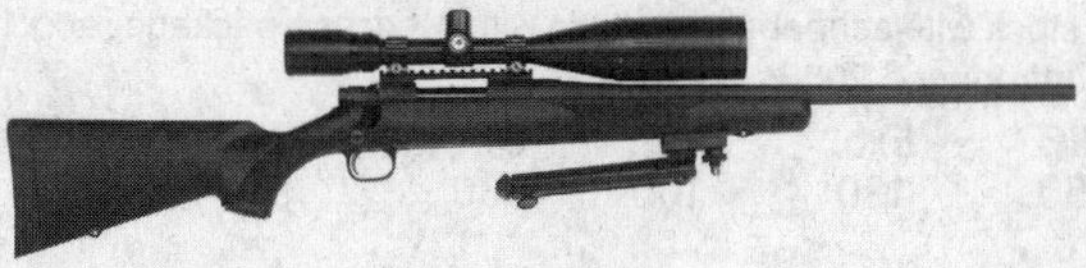

NIB	*Exc.*	*V.G.*	*Good*	*Fair*	*Poor*
380	320	280	220	160	120

Model 100 ATR Super Bantam

Similar to Model 100 ATR. Chambered only in .243 and .308. No sights. Synthetic black stock adjustable for length of pull. Introduced in 2007.

NIB	*Exc.*	*V.G.*	*Good*	*Fair*	*Poor*
360	300	250	200	150	100

Model 800

Bolt-action rifle manufactured in a variety of calibers, with 22" barrel and folding leaf rear sight. Blued, with walnut stock. Introduced in 1967.

NIB	*Exc.*	*V.G.*	*Good*	*Fair*	*Poor*
400	320	200	150	100	80

Model 800D

As above, with comb stock, rosewood forend tip and pistol grip cap. Manufactured from 1970 to 1973.

NIB	*Exc.*	*V.G.*	*Good*	*Fair*	*Poor*
400	300	250	200	150	100

Model 800V

As above, with 24" heavy barrel not fitted with sights. Introduced in 1968.

NIB	*Exc.*	*V.G.*	*Good*	*Fair*	*Poor*
400	300	220	150	100	80

Model 800M

As above, with Mannlicher-style stock.

NIB	*Exc.*	*V.G.*	*Good*	*Fair*	*Poor*
500	380	250	200	150	100

Model 800SM

As above, with 4X scope.

NIB	*Exc.*	*V.G.*	*Good*	*Fair*	*Poor*
550	420	280	220	150	100

Model 801 Half-Pint Plinkster

Entry-level .22 LR single-shot rifle, with removable magazine plug to allow insertion of 10-round magazine. 16" barrel, hardwood stock, adjustable open sights. Overall weight 4 lbs. Introduced 2008.

NIB	Exc.	V.G.	Good	Fair	Poor
150	120	100	80	50	20

Model 802 Plinkster

Bolt-action rifle chambered in .22 LR, with 18" steel barrel. Black synthetic stock with schnabel. Available with 4X scope package (add 10 percent). Introduced 2006.

NIB	Exc.	V.G.	Good	Fair	Poor
150	120	100	80	50	20

Model 817 Plinkster

Similar to Model 802 Plinkster. Chambered in .17 HMR. Introduced in 2007.

NIB	Exc.	V.G.	Good	Fair	Poor
180	150	120	100	80	50

Model 810

.270 to .338 Win. Magnum caliber bolt-action rifle, with 22" or 24" barrel. Fitted with folding rear sight. Blued, with Monte Carlo-style stock. Introduced in 1970.

NIB	Exc.	V.G.	Good	Fair	Poor
—	280	250	200	150	100

Model 472C

.30-30 or .35 Rem. caliber lever-action rifle, with 20" barrel, open sights and tubular magazine. Blued, with walnut stock. Introduced in 1972.

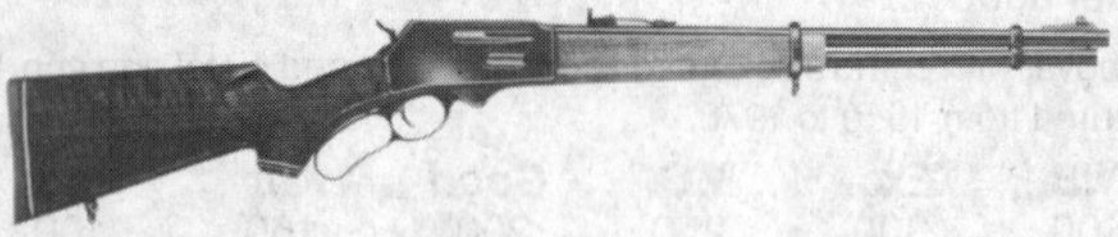

NIB	Exc.	V.G.	Good	Fair	Poor
—	250	200	150	100	80

Model 472P

As above, with pistol grip stock. Not fitted with saddle ring.

NIB	Exc.	V.G.	Good	Fair	Poor
—	250	200	150	100	80

Model 472 One in Five Thousand

As above, with etched receiver, brass buttplate, saddle ring and barrel band. Total 5,000 made in 1974.

NIB	Exc.	V.G.	Good	Fair	Poor
—	400	350	300	200	150

Model 479 PCA

Similar to Model 472C in .30-30 caliber, with 20" barrel. Blued, with walnut stock.

NIB	Exc.	V.G.	Good	Fair	Poor
—	250	200	150	100	80

Model 479 RR (Roy Rogers)

As above, with gold-plated trigger, barrel band and "Roy Rogers" signature. Total 5,000 made in 1983.

NIB	Exc.	V.G.	Good	Fair	Poor
—	320	250	200	150	100

Model 464 Lever-Action Centerfire

Side-loading top-ejecting lever rifle, with button-rifled 20" barrel, blued finish and hardwood stock. Straight-/pistol grip stock. Tang-mounted thumb safety. Chambered in .30-30.

NIB	Exc.	V.G.	Good	Fair	Poor
—	400	350	300	200	150

Model 464 Lever-Action Rimfire

Rimfire version of above, with 18" barrel.

NIB	Exc.	V.G.	Good	Fair	Poor
—	380	300	250	200	150

SSi-One Sporter

Introduced in 2000. Single-shot rifle chambered for .223, .243, 270 Win., .308 and .30-06 cartridges. Fitted with 24" barrel, without sights. Matte blue finish. Checkered walnut stock. Weight about 8 lbs. Interchangeable barrels including 12-gauge.

NIB	Exc.	V.G.	Good	Fair	Poor
480	370	300	220	180	120

SSi-One Varmint

Similar to single-shot model above. Fitted with 24" bull barrel chambered for .22-250 cartridge. Walnut stock. Weight about 10 lbs. Introduced in 2000. Interchangeable barrels.

NIB	Exc.	V.G.	Good	Fair	Poor
480	370	300	220	180	120

SSi-One Slug

Single-shot model similar to other SSi-One guns. Fitted with 24" fully rifled 12-gauge barrel. Walnut stock. Weight about 8 lbs. Interchangeable barrels. Introduced in 2000.

NIB	Exc.	V.G.	Good	Fair	Poor
500	400	320	250	200	150

SSi-One Turkey

Same as above, with 24" smoothbore barrel. Will handle 3.5" Magnum 12-gauge shells. Weight about 7.5 lbs. Introduced in 2001.

NIB	Exc.	V.G.	Good	Fair	Poor
500	400	320	250	200	150

Model 1500

.223 to .338 Win. Magnum bolt-action rifle, with 22" or 24" barrel, 5- or 6-shot magazine and various sights. Blued, with hardwood or walnut stock. Manufactured by Howa in Japan. Also known as Smith & Wesson

Model 1500. Offered in 1986 and 1987.

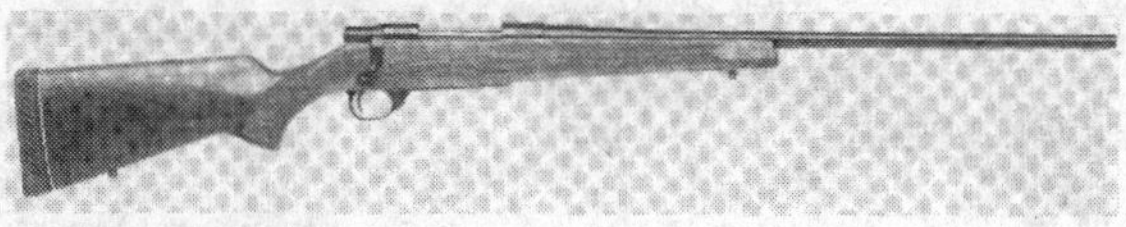

Mountaineer Grade I

NIB	Exc.	V.G.	Good	Fair	Poor
—	350	250	220	150	120

Mountaineer Grade II

NIB	Exc.	V.G.	Good	Fair	Poor
—	320	280	250	180	120

Varmint

24" heavy barrel.

NIB	Exc.	V.G.	Good	Fair	Poor
—	350	300	280	200	150

Model 1550

As above in .243, .270 or .30-06 caliber. Offered in 1986 and 1987.

NIB	Exc.	V.G.	Good	Fair	Poor
—	320	280	250	180	120

Model 1700 LS

Similar to above in same calibers, with 22" barrel not fitted for sights. Machine jeweled bolt and knurled bolt handle. Blued, with walnut stock. Schnabel forend. Offered in 1986 and 1987.

NIB	Exc.	V.G.	Good	Fair	Poor
—	400	350	280	200	150

Mossberg 4x4

Bolt-action centerfire rifle. Chambered in .25-06, .270, .30-06, 7mm Rem. Magnum, .300 Win. Magnum, .338 Win. Magnum. Barrel length 22" (iron sight) or 24" (sightless). Detachable box magazine, two-position safety. Walnut, laminated or black synthetic stock, with lightening cutouts in butt and forend. Scope package also available. Introduced in 2007.

NIB	Exc.	V.G.	Good	Fair	Poor
480	380	300	220	180	120

Mossberg 4X4 Classic Stock Synthetic

Similar to above, with black synthetic stock. Marinecote metal surfaces.

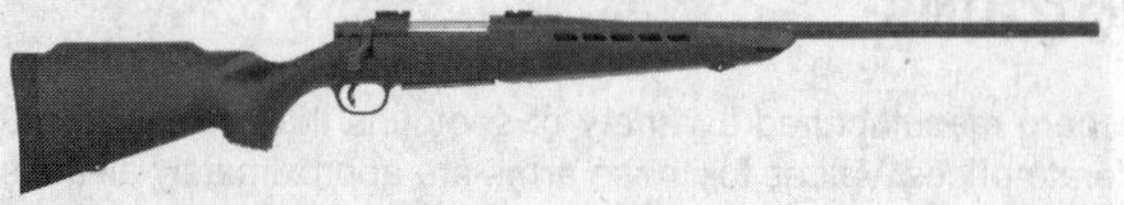

NIB	Exc.	V.G.	Good	Fair	Poor
—	450	350	280	200	120

Mossberg 4X4 Scoped Combo

Similar to above, with matte blue finish and 3x9 scope. Various stock compositions, including laminate.

NIB	Exc.	V.G.	Good	Fair	Poor
—	450	350	280	200	120

Mossberg 4X4 Classic Walnut Stock

Similar to above, with checkered walnut stock.

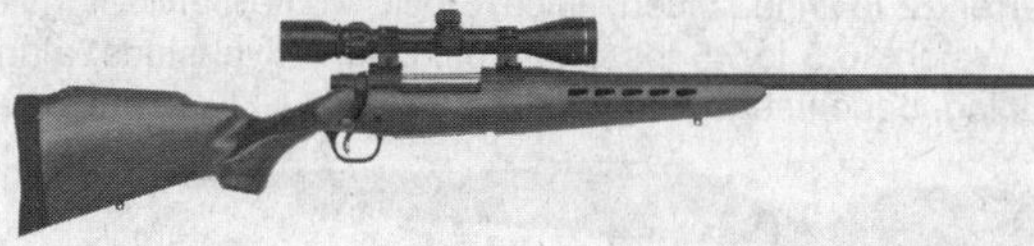

NIB	Exc.	V.G.	Good	Fair	Poor
—	500	450	350	220	150

Patriot

Bolt action chambered in .22-250 Rem., .243 Win., .25-06, .270 Win., 7mm-08 Rem., 7mm Rem. Magnum, .308 Win., .30-06, .300 Win. Magnum, .338 Win. Magnum and .375 Ruger. Features include 22" fluted barrel, adjustable trigger, choice of fiber-optic iron sights or scope base. Finish is matte black or Marinecote. Available with black synthetic, laminate or walnut stock, as shown in photo. Also available with Mossy Oak camo finish. Introduced in 2015. Note: Add $50 for walnut stock; $75 for camo.

NIB	Exc.	V.G.	Good	Fair	Poor
340	300	280	200	180	120

Patriot Predator

Offered in .243 Win., 6.5 Creedmoor, .308 Win. Gray synthetic stock, LBA adjustable trigger, fluted and threaded 22" barrel, oversized bolt handle, spiral fluted bolt, top-mount Picatinny rail/scope bases and 4-round box magazine. MSRP $441. Introduced in 2017.

NIB	Exc.	V.G.	Good	Fair	Poor
380	—	—	—	—	—

Patriot Revere

A high-grade variant with 2.0 grade walnut stock, with oil-finish, fine line checkering, rosewood forend tip and grip cap with contrasting maple spacer. Streamlined and checkered bolt handle. Chambered for .243 Win., 6.5 Creedmoor, .270 Win., .308 Win., .30-06, .300 Win. Magnum. MSRP $823. Introduced in 2017.

NIB	Exc.	V.G.	Good	Fair	Poor
750	620	500	420	350	200

Patriot Vortex Scoped Combo

As above, but includes Vortex Crossfire II 3-9x40mm scope featuring Dead-Hold BDC reticle

NIB	Exc.	V.G.	Good	Fair	Poor
470	400	320	250	200	150

Patriot Night Train I

Tactical variation chambered in .308 Win. with 4-16x50mm scope, Picatinny rails, adjustable bipod and black synthetic or OD green stock. Night Train II and III models in .308 Win. or .300 Win. Magnum have suppressor-ready threaded barrels with SilencerCo muzzle brake and neoprene cheek-raising kit with interchangeable insert pads. Note: Add $150 for Night Train 2 or 3.

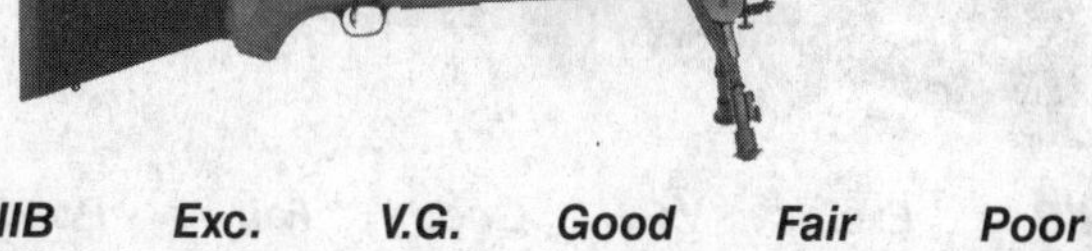

NIB	Exc.	V.G.	Good	Fair	Poor
550	500	450	350	300	250

Patriot Long Range Hunter

Calibers: .308 Win., 6.5 Creedmoor, 6.5 PRC, .300 Win. Mag. Capacity:

3 to 5. Barrel: 22 to 24 in., blued, fluted. Stock: Monte Carlo. Sights: Picatinny rail. Weight: 6.5 to 7.5 lbs. Features: Dual swivel studs, aluminum pillar bedding, benchrest-type forend.

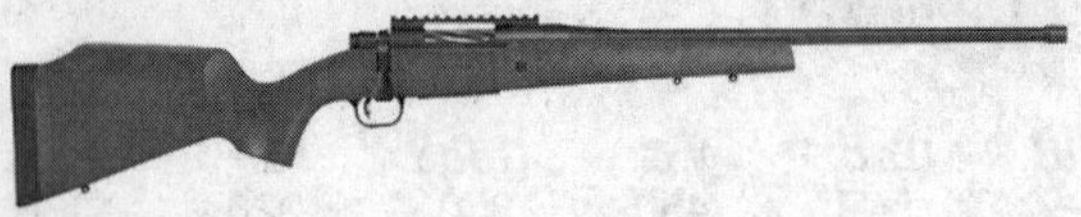

NIB	Exc.	V.G.	Good	Fair	Poor
660	—	—	—	—	—

Patriot LR Tactical

Caliber: 6.5 Creedmoor, 6.5 PRC, .308 Win. Barrel: 22", 24" medium bull threaded. Stock: MDT adjustable for LOP and cheek rest. Features: Latest hunting-meets-long-range competition bolt action with the most popular Patriot features plus additional upgrades. M-LOK forend slots. 20 MOA Picatinny rail. Aluminum V-Block bedding. AICS magazine with either seven- or 10-round capacity.

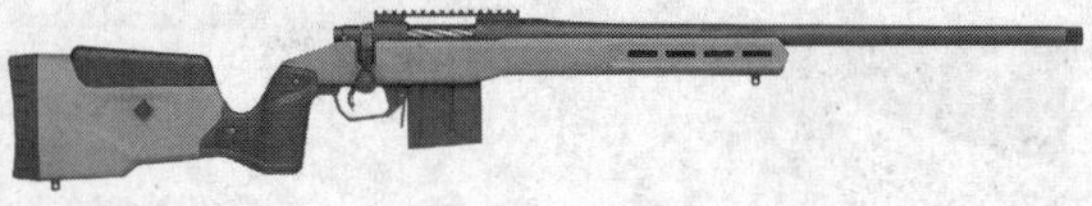

NIB	Exc.	V.G.	Good	Fair	Poor
970	—	—	—	—	—

Model MVP Flex

Bolt-action centerfire in .223/5.56 or .308/7.62 NATO. Feeds from any AR-15 or AR-10 magazine. Synthetic FLEX system stock. Barrel 18.5" or 20" with or without threaded muzzle and flash hider (on 18.5" model). Also available in Predator/Varmint variation with target-style laminated stock; Patrol Model with 16.25" barrel in .223, .308 or .300 Blackout. Note: Deduct 10 percent for Predator/Varmint; 25 percent for Patrol model.

NIB	Exc.	V.G.	Good	Fair	Poor
850	700	620	500	400	300

MVP Precision

Similar to MVP Flex. Chambered in 6.5 Creedmoor or .308 Win. Barrel 20". Matte hard anodized chassis, Luth MBA 3 adjustable stock, with M-Lok forend. New in 2018.

NIB	Exc.	V.G.	Good	Fair	Poor
1150	1000	900	—	—	—

MVP Long Range

Like other MVP bolt designs, accepts and feeds from standard AR-style magazines. The 7.62mm NATO models accept both M1A/M14 and AR10-style magazines (LR308/SR25). Available in 5.56 NATO/.223, 6.5 Creedmoor, 7.62 NATO/.308. Long range OD green pillar-bedded stock, with push-button adjustable comb with a rubberized Mosscote cheek-rest, patented LBA Adjustable Trigger (3-7 lbs.), oversized bolt handle and Picatinny rail. All barrels are threaded for suppressors or muzzle brakes and come with a protective thread cap. MSRP $975. Introduced in 2017.

NIB	Exc.	V.G.	Good	Fair	Poor
850	—	—	—	—	—

MVP Patrol

.300 AAC Blackout. 16.25-in. barrel. 6.5-lb. weight. 36.5-in. length. 10+1-round capacity.

NIB	Exc.	V.G.	Good	Fair	Poor
580	—	—	—	—	—

MMR Carbine

AR-style semi-auto rifle; 5.56 NATO, 16.25" barrel, telescoping stock, 7 lbs. Discontinued.

NIB	Exc.	V.G.	Good	Fair	Poor
950	880	800	—	—	—

MMR Pro

AR-style semi-auto rifle; 5.56 NATO, 18" fluted stainless barrel, telescoping stock, 7 lbs. Discontinued.

NIB	Exc.	V.G.	Good	Fair	Poor
1400	1300	1200	—	—	—

Model MMR Hunter

AR-15 style semi-automatic carbine in .223/5.56 NATO, with 20" free-floated barrel, start SE-1 pistol grip, fixed A-2 stock, round aluminum handguard, flattop receiver. Available in black, Mossy Oak Brush or Mossy Oak Treestand camo. Available in several other variations including Tactical model. Discontinued.

NIB	Exc.	V.G.	Good	Fair	Poor
880	790	700	600	450	300

SHOTGUNS

Mossberg manufactured a variety of shotguns that were sold at low to moderate prices. Values for these arms are approximately all the same.

Miscellaneous Bolt-Action Shotguns

Model 73
Model 173
Model 173Y
Model 183D
Model 183K
Model 183T
Model 185D
Model 185K
Model 190D
Model 190K
Model 195D
Model 195K
Model 385K
Model 385T
Model 390K
Model 390T
Model 395K
Model 395S
Model 395T

NIB	Exc.	V.G.	Good	Fair	Poor
—	150	120	90	60	40

Model 695

Introduced in 1969. Bolt-action shotgun chambered for 12-gauge shell. Barrel length 22" with rifled or plain bore. Finish matte blue. In 1997, offered with 22" plain ported barrel with rifled bore. Magazine capacity 3 rounds. Weight about 7.5 lbs.

NIB	Exc.	V.G.	Good	Fair	Poor
280	220	180	150	120	100

Model 695 Camo

Introduced in 2000. Same as standard Model 695, with addition of woodland camo finish.

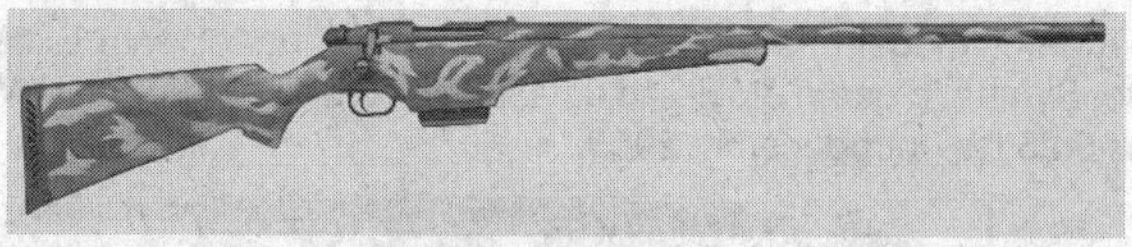

NIB	Exc.	V.G.	Good	Fair	Poor
380	320	280	250	200	150

Model 200K

12-gauge slide-action shotgun, with 28" barrel and Mossberg select choke. Blued, with composition slide handle. Walnut stock. Manufactured from 1955 to 1959.

NIB	Exc.	V.G.	Good	Fair	Poor
—	150	120	100	80	50

MAVERICK 88 SERIES

Maverick 88 Cruiser

Gauges: 12 ga., 3 in., 20 ga., 3in. Capacity: 5+1 or 7+1 capacity. Barrels: 18.5 in., 20 in. Length: 28.125-30.375 in. Weight: 5.5-6.0 lbs. Stock: Black synthetic pistol grip. Features: Fixed cylinder bore choke, blued metalwork, bead front sight, cross-bolt safety.

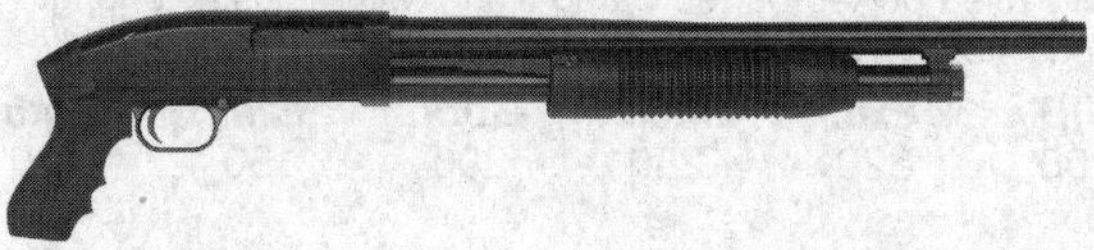

NIB	Exc.	V.G.	Good	Fair	Poor
190	—	—	—	—	—

Maverick 88 Field

Gauges: 12 ga., 20 ga. Barrels: 22", 26", 28". ventilated rib. Stock: Synthetic Mossy Oak Bottomland camo. Features: Three new All-Purpose Field camo variants. A 3-inch chamber, 5+1-round capacity. Dual extractors, twin action bars, steel-to-steel lockup, and anti-jam elevator for reliable operation. The 22" Bantam model shortens LOP to 12". Modified choke tube included, but Maverick 88 accessories are interchangeable with the Mossberg 500.

NIB	Exc.	V.G.	Good	Fair	Poor
250	210	—	—	—	—

MODEL 500 SERIES

12-, 20-gauge or .410 bore slide-action shotgun. Manufactured in a variety of barrel lengths and styles as listed.

Model 500 Centennial (2019)

This Limited Edition run of 750 units celebrated the company's 100th anniversary. Nickel-plated 12 gauge 3" receiver engraved with the Mossberg 100th Anniversary logo on the right side, and a pair of flushing ruffed grouse on the left, highlighted in 24-karat gold. Special serial numbers MCE0000 to MCE0750. Traditional high-gloss walnut stock and forend with fine checkering on the pistol grip and wrapping around the underside of the forend. Red rubber recoil pad. Jeweled bolt, gold-plated trigger, high-polish blue-metal finish. 28" vent-rib barrel comes with Mossberg's interchangeable Accu-Choke choke tubes (F, M, IC). Overall Length: 47.5⊠, about 7.5 lbs.

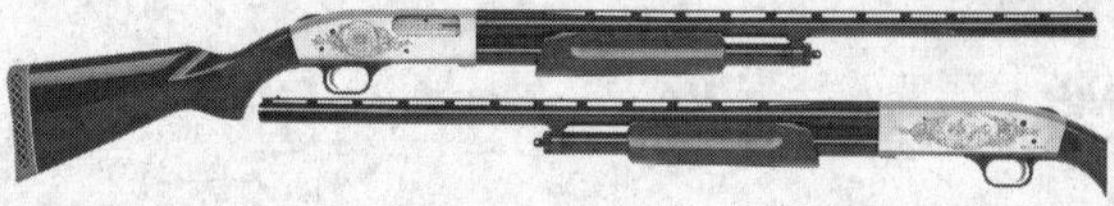

NIB	Exc.	V.G.	Good	Fair	Poor
1000	—	—	—	—	—

Model 500 Regal

NIB	Exc.	V.G.	Good	Fair	Poor
—	250	200	150	100	80

Model 500 Field Grade

NIB	Exc.	V.G.	Good	Fair	Poor
280	250	200	150	100	80

Model 500 Steel Shot

Chrome bore.

NIB	Exc.	V.G.	Good	Fair	Poor
—	300	250	200	120	100

Model 500 Slugster

Crown grade, iron sights.

NIB	Exc.	V.G.	Good	Fair	Poor
—	280	250	200	150	100

Model 500 Camper

18.5" barrel, camo case.

NIB	Exc.	V.G.	Good	Fair	Poor
—	300	280	220	180	100

Model 500 Hi-Rib Trap

NIB	Exc.	V.G.	Good	Fair	Poor
—	280	250	200	150	100

Model 500 Super Grade

NIB	Exc.	V.G.	Good	Fair	Poor
—	300	280	220	180	100

Model 500 Pigeon Grade

NIB	Exc.	V.G.	Good	Fair	Poor
—	380	300	250	200	120

Model 500 Pigeon Grade Trap

NIB	Exc.	V.G.	Good	Fair	Poor
—	450	380	300	250	180

Model 500 Persuader

Riot gun, 18.5" barrel 12-gauge; 20" barrel 20-gauge (added 2008).

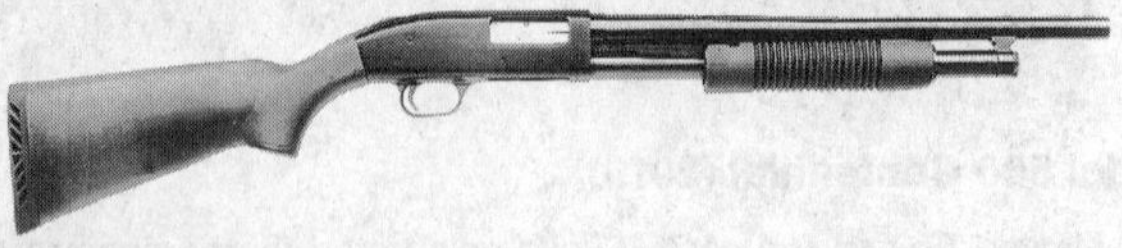

NIB	Exc.	V.G.	Good	Fair	Poor
300	280	220	180	100	80

Model 500 Persuader Retrograde (2019)

18.5" (6-shot) cylinder-bore barrel, single front brass bead sight, blued metal finish, and full-length walnut stock and corncob forend.

NIB	Exc.	V.G.	Good	Fair	Poor
500	400	300	—	—	—

Model 500 Mariner

Marinecote finish.

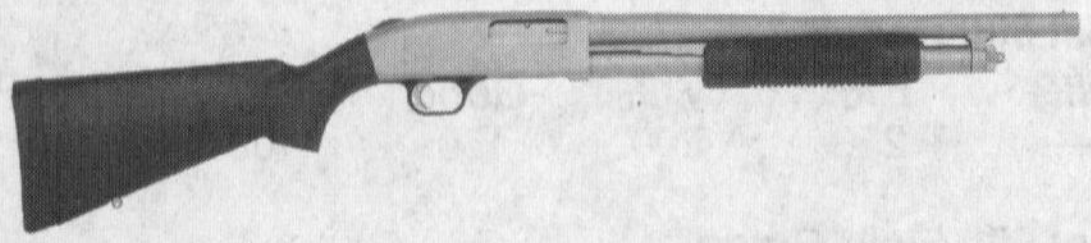

NIB	Exc.	V.G.	Good	Fair	Poor
400	320	220	200	150	120

Model 500 Cruiser

Pistol grip only.

NIB	Exc.	V.G.	Good	Fair	Poor
380	300	250	200	120	100

Model 500 Muzzleloader Combo

NIB	Exc.	V.G.	Good	Fair	Poor
350	320	280	220	200	150

Model 500 Turkey Bottomland 410 Bore (2019)

.410 bore comes with a 26" vent rib, fixed full-choke barrel, fiber-optic front sight, and is fully-camouflaged with Mossy Oak Bottomland.

NIB	Exc.	V.G.	Good	Fair	Poor
380	290	200	—	—	—

Model 500 Turkey (2023)

Gauges: 20 ga., .410 bore. Barrels: 22" to 24". Stock: Synthetic Mossy Oak Greenleaf camo. Features: Two new optics-ready turkey hunting variants. Receiver machined for direct mounting of RMSc-pattern optics. 5+1-round capacity. Fiber-optic front sight. Has a 3" chamber. X-Factor ported choke tube.

NIB	Exc.	V.G.	Good	Fair	Poor
590	500	—	—	—	—

Model 500 Bantam

Introduced in 1996. Slightly smaller overall than full-size guns. Chambered for 20-gauge shell. Fitted with 22" shotgun barrel; 24" rifled ventilated rib barrel. Walnut stock. Weight about 6.9 lbs.

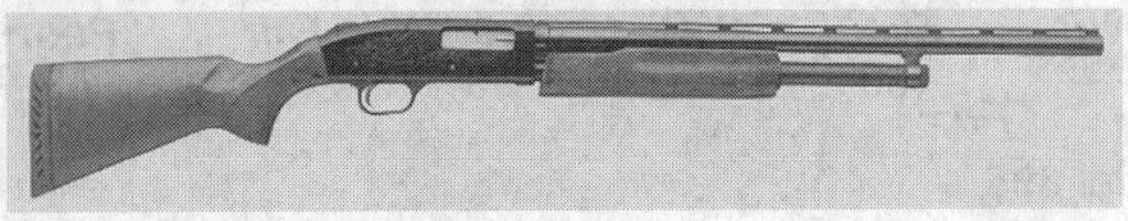

NIB	Exc.	V.G.	Good	Fair	Poor
280	220	200	150	120	100

Model 500 Super Bantam Field

Introduced in 2005. Features 20-gauge 3" chamber, with 22" ventilated rib barrel with choke tubes. Blued finish. Synthetic stock, with adjustable length of pull. Weight about 5.25 lbs.

NIB	Exc.	V.G.	Good	Fair	Poor
320	280	180	120	100	80

Model 500 Super Bantam Turkey

20-gauge 3" model has 22" ventilated rib ported barrel, with Extra Full choke. Synthetic camo stock. Adjustable stock for length of pull. Weight about 5.25 lbs. Introduced in 2005.

NIB	Exc.	V.G.	Good	Fair	Poor
380	320	250	180	150	100

Model 500 Super Bantam Slug

20-gauge model features full rifled 24" ported barrel, with adjustable sights. Synthetic stock, with blue or camo finish. Weight about 5.25 lbs. Introduced in 2005. In 2008, a version with an integrated scope base was added to this series.

NIB	Exc.	V.G.	Good	Fair	Poor
380	320	250	180	150	100

Model 500 Super Bantam Combo

Introduced in 2005. Features 22" ventilated rib barrel, with choke tubes; 24" fully rifled ported barrel. Camo finish, with adjustable length of pull synthetic stock. Weight about 5.25 lbs.

NIB	Exc.	V.G.	Good	Fair	Poor
400	320	280	200	150	120

Model 500 Bullpup

12-gauge slide-action Bullpup shotgun, with 18.5" or 20" shrouded barrel. Matte black finish, with composition stock. Introduced in 1986; discontinued. Values shown are for 6-shot version. Note: Add 25 percent for 8-shot.

NIB	Exc.	V.G.	Good	Fair	Poor
600	500	380	250	150	100

Model 500 Slug Gun Viking Grade

Introduced in 1996. A 12-gauge with 24" rifled barrel; iron sights; green synthetic stock. Note: In 1997, Mossberg introduced ported barrels on some of its slug models. These ported barrels will be seen on rifled barrels only.

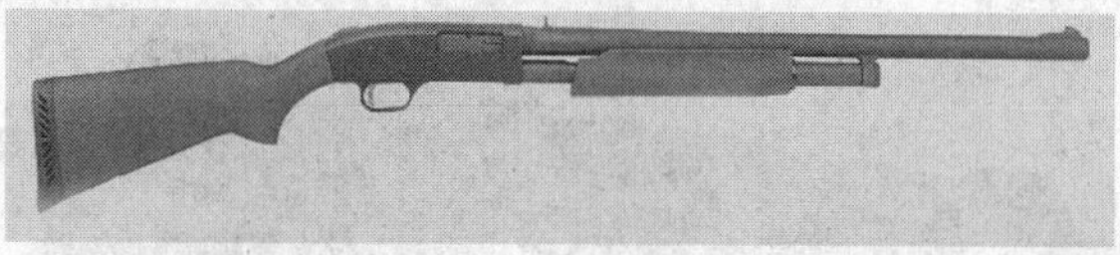

NIB	Exc.	V.G.	Good	Fair	Poor
300	280	220	180	100	80

Model 500 Grand Slam Turkey

12- or 20-gauge 3" gun. Introduced in 2004. Offered with 20" ventilated rib barrel; adjustable fiber optic sights; ported Extra Full choke tube. Available in Realtree Hardwood or Mossy Oak Break-Up camo pattern. Weight about: 7 lbs. 12-gauge; 6.75 lbs. 20-gauge.

NIB	Exc.	V.G.	Good	Fair	Poor
380	320	250	180	150	100

Model 500 Flyway Series

Introduced in 2005. A 12-gauge 3.5", with 28" ventilated rib barrel with fiber optic front sight. Choke tubes. Advantage camo synthetic stock. Weight about 7.5 lbs.

NIB	Exc.	V.G.	Good	Fair	Poor
400	320	220	200	150	120

Model 500 FLEX

Introduced in 2012, this variant of Model 500 series features FLEX TLS (Tool-less Locking System), which allows user a simple method of changing stocks, forends and recoil pad. Chambered for 12- or 20-gauge and offered in Hunting and Tactical variations. Also available in Combo models with two barrels, one for hunting and one for home security: Deer/Security; Turkey/Security; Waterfowl/Security. Duck Commander has fiber optic sight, Realtree Max-5 camo finish on stock and forend, OD Green finish on metal parts, special engraving of Duck Commander logo on synthetic stock.

Flex Hunting

NIB	Exc.	V.G.	Good	Fair	Poor
500	420	350	280	220	200

Flex Tactical

NIB	Exc.	V.G.	Good	Fair	Poor
550	480	400	320	280	220

Flex Deer/Security Combo

NIB	Exc.	V.G.	Good	Fair	Poor
700	600	480	350	300	220

Flex Turkey/Security; Waterfowl/Security

NIB	Exc.	V.G.	Good	Fair	Poor
600	500	400	320	280	220

Flex Duck Commander

NIB	Exc.	V.G.	Good	Fair	Poor
650	550	450	400	300	200

Flex 500 Super Bantam — All-Purpose (2019)

NIB	Exc.	V.G.	Good	Fair	Poor
330	250	200	—	—	—

Flex 500 Youth Combo Field/Deer (2019)

NIB	Exc.	V.G.	Good	Fair	Poor
480	400	300	—	—	—

Model 500 Combo

500 series has a total of nine combination sets available to choose from. They are combination of shotgun barrels and rifled barrels for different hunting applications. Offered in both 12- and 20-gauge sets of same gauge only.

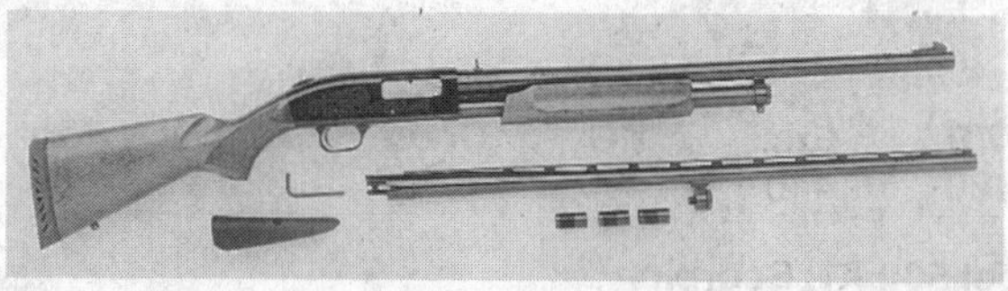

NIB	Exc.	V.G.	Good	Fair	Poor
400	320	280	220	180	120

Model 500 Field/Deer Scoped Combo (2019)

12 and 20 gauge, 3" chambers. Matte-blue metal finishes combined with a black-synthetic forend and dual comb stock. Two barrels are included: a 26" vent rib, Accu-Set choked barrel with dual bead sights and a 24" ISB (cantilever), fully-rifled barrel topped with a Dead Ringer 2.5x20 scope. 7.25 lbs., length 46.5"/44.5".

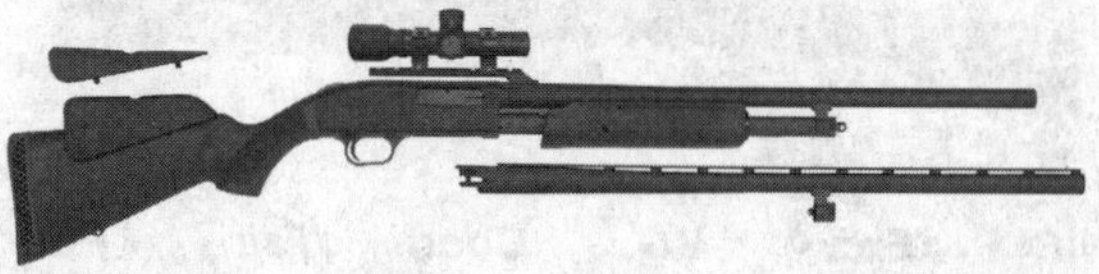

NIB	Exc.	V.G.	Good	Fair	Poor
350	250	150	—	—	—

Model 500 USA

Introduced in 1997. Similar to military model. Has Parkerized finish, with heavy-duty sling swivels. Fitted with plain 20" barrel choked Cylinder. Stock black synthetic. Magazine capacity 6 rounds. Weight about 7.2 lbs.

NIB	Exc.	V.G.	Good	Fair	Poor
250	200	180	150	120	100

Model 500 HS (Home Security)

Chambered for .410 shell. Fitted with 18.5" barrel. Magazine capacity 5 rounds. Synthetic stock and blue finish. Note: In 1999, Mossberg offered a .50 muzzleloader 24" fully rifled barrel that will fit directly onto any six-shot Model 500.

NIB	Exc.	V.G.	Good	Fair	Poor
350	320	280	220	200	150

Model 500 Rolling Thunder

Home Defense/Tactical is a 3" 12-gauge. Featuring pistol grip, 23" barrel with heat shield and recoil-reducing stabilizer and 6-round capacity.

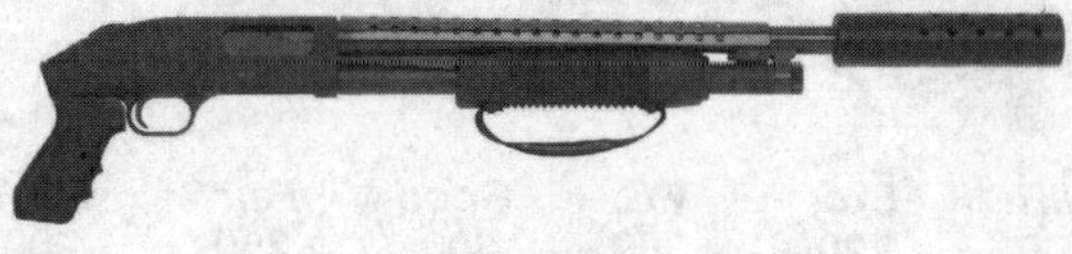

NIB	Exc.	V.G.	Good	Fair	Poor
400	320	280	220	180	120

Model 500 Tactical Cruiser "Door Buster"

Similar to above, with serrated muzzle. A TALO exclusive.

NIB	Exc.	V.G.	Good	Fair	Poor
520	420	320	220	180	120

Model 500 Tactical

An 8-shot pump has 20" barrel and ghost ring sights. Black synthetic pistol grip stock can be adjusted to provide 10.75" to 14.625" length of pull. Weight 6.25 lbs. Capacity 7+1. Matte blue finish.

NIB	Exc.	V.G.	Good	Fair	Poor
480	440	400	370	320	280

Model 500 ATI Scorpion

Top-of-the-line tactical Model 500 outfitted with various features from Advanced Technology International Co. (ATI). Including 6-position stock with adjustable cheek, Scorpion rear pad and grip, ATI Halo Heatshield, two 2" accessory rails and removable top rail, and three add-a-shell units that mount in nine different positions on the gun. Model 500 features include an ambidextrous safety, dual extractors, twin action bars and anti-jam elevator. Introduced in 2016, with limited availability only through a Talo Group distributor.

NIB	Exc.	V.G.	Good	Fair	Poor
600	500	—	—	—	—

Model 500 ATI Tactical (2019)

18.5" Cylinder-bore barrel with ATI heat shield and two, 2.75-inch sections of Picatinny rail. Magazine tube holds five 12-gauge 3" magnum or six 2.75" shells. A machined, anodized aluminum, ATI Halo Side Saddle attaches to the 500's receiver, holding up to 9 ATI shell holders (6 left and 3 right.) The Side Saddle is also drilled and tapped for a top Picatinny rail, and one is included. The rail is grooved along its centerline to serve as the rear sight. A winged-post front sight attaches to the end of the heat shield. Stocks are ATI's polymer Akita forend and the company's Scorpion TacLite pistol grip stock, the latter having 3.3 inches of length-of-pull adjustment in six different positions and has adjustable comb.

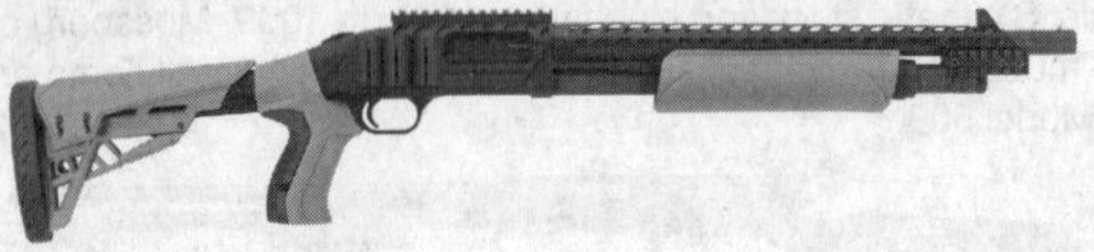

NIB	Exc.	V.G.	Good	Fair	Poor
430	330	—	—	—	—

Model 500 Magpul

This variation of Model 500 Tactical shotgun features Magpul SGA stock, with adjustable length of pull and interchangeable cheek riser. Barrel 18.5" with 6-shot capacity; 20" with 8-shots. Introduced in 2014.

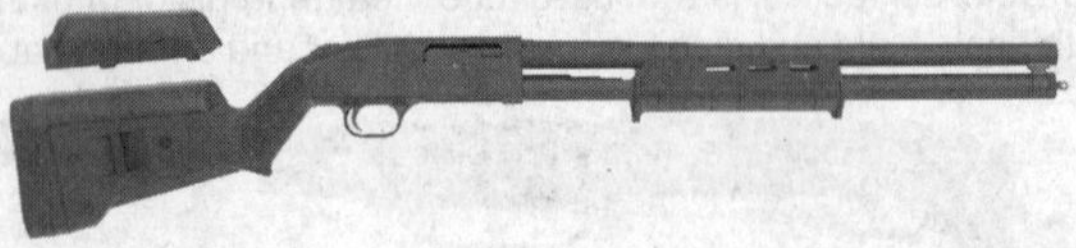

NIB	Exc.	V.G.	Good	Fair	Poor
500	420	380	300	250	200

Model 500 JIC (Just In Case)

Survival model is a 3" 12-gauge. Featuring pistol grip, 18.5" barrel and weatherproof pack tube. Three different models available with different finishes and accessory packages. Note: Add 15 percent for nickel finish; 10 percent for JIC II with black finish in black nylon case.

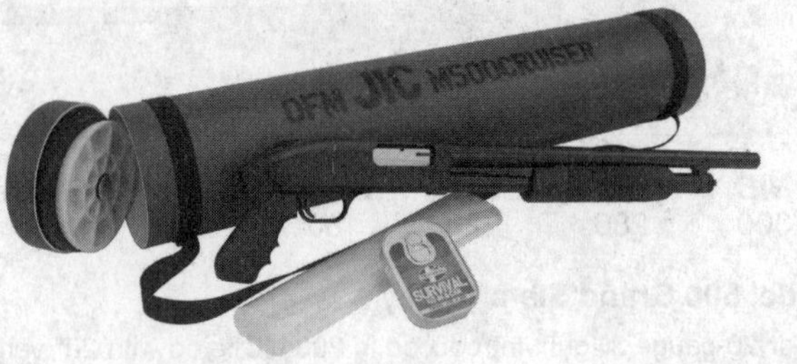

NIB	Exc.	V.G.	Good	Fair	Poor
380	320	250	180	150	100

Model 505 Youth

Offered in 20-gauge or .410 bore. Fitted with 20" ventilated rib barrel with choke tubes 20-gauge; Fixed Modified choke .410 bore. Wood stock, with recoil pad. Blued finish. Weight about 5.25 lbs.

NIB	Exc.	V.G.	Good	Fair	Poor
320	280	180	120	100	80

Model 510 Mini Shotgun

Compact pump-action shotgun. Based on Model 500 action. Chambered in 3" 20-gauge and .410 bore. Features include 18.5" ventilated rib barrel with Interchangeable (20-gauge) or Fixed (.410 bore) choke, black synthetic stock, inserts to adjust length of pull from 10.5" to 11.5" and 4-shot capacity. Weight 5 lbs.

NIB	Exc.	V.G.	Good	Fair	Poor
320	280	180	120	100	80

MODEL 535 SERIES

Model 535 ATS (All Terrain Shotgun) Field

Introduced in 2005. This 12-gauge 3.5" model features 28" ventilated rib barrel with choke tubes. Blued finish, with checkered wood stock and pistol grip. Weight about 6.75 lbs.

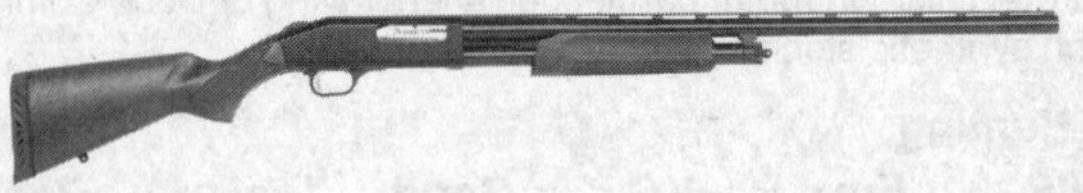

NIB	Exc.	V.G.	Good	Fair	Poor
380	320	250	180	150	100

Model 535 ATS Turkey

As above, with 22" ventilated rib barrel with Extra Full choke. Fiber optic front sight. Synthetic stock, with matte blue or camo finish. Weight about 6.5 lbs. Introduced in 2005. Note: Add $55 for camo finish.

NIB	Exc.	V.G.	Good	Fair	Poor
380	320	250	180	150	100

Model 535 ATS Waterfowl

Fitted with 28" ventilated rib barrel with choke tubes. Fiber optic front sight. Synthetic stock, with matte blue or camo finish. Weight about 6.75

lbs. Introduced in 2005. Note: Add $55 for camo finish.

NIB	Exc.	V.G.	Good	Fair	Poor
380	320	250	180	150	100

Model 535 ATS Slugster

Fitted with fully rifled 24" ventilated rib barrel with adjustable sights. Choice of matte blue or camo finish. Synthetic stock. Weight about 7 lbs.

NIB	Exc.	V.G.	Good	Fair	Poor
380	320	250	180	150	100

Model 535 ATS Combos

Set offered in several different configurations: Field/Deer 28" and 24"; Turkey/Deer 22" and 24"; Turkey/Slug/Waterfowl 22" and 28". Weight from 6.5 to 7 lbs. depending on barrel length. Introduced in 2005. Note: Add $55 for camo finish.

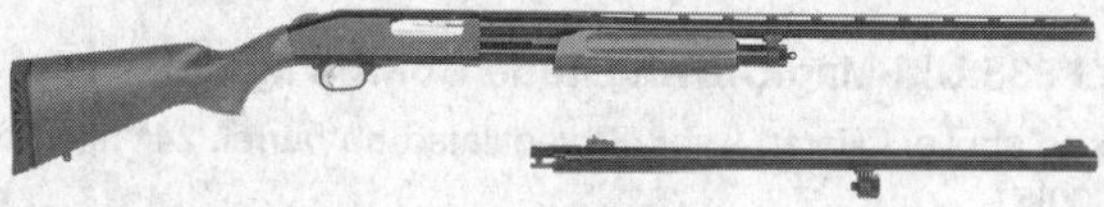

NIB	Exc.	V.G.	Good	Fair	Poor
480	400	350	220	150	180

MODEL 590 SERIES

Model 590 Special Purpose

Fitted with 20" shrouded barrel, bayonet lug, Parkerized or blued finish. Speed feed stock. Ghost ring sights. Introduced in 1987. Weight about 7.25 lbs.

NIB	Exc.	V.G.	Good	Fair	Poor
320	280	200	180	120	100

Model 590 Mariner

Marinecote finish.

NIB	Exc.	V.G.	Good	Fair	Poor
420	350	280	220	150	100

Model 590DA

12-gauge introduced in 2000. Features 6-round tubular magazine and 18.5" barrel. Choice of plain bead sight or ghost ring. Choke is Fixed Modified. Weight about 7 lbs. A 14" barreled model also offered, but NFA rules apply. Note: Add $50 for ghost ring sights.

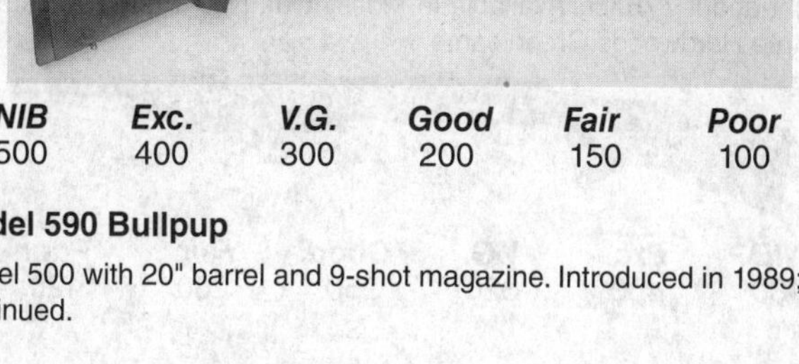

NIB	Exc.	V.G.	Good	Fair	Poor
500	400	300	200	150	100

Model 590 Bullpup

Model 500 with 20" barrel and 9-shot magazine. Introduced in 1989; discontinued.

NIB	Exc.	V.G.	Good	Fair	Poor
600	500	400	250	200	120

Model 590A1 Blackwater

A 12-gauge pump with 3" chamber, 20" long heavy-walled barrel, measures 41" overall. Ghost ring/AR-style sights. Length of pull 13.875". Features synthetic Speedfeed stock and Parkerized finish. Thumb safety atop receiver. Capacity 8+1 rounds; weight 7.25 lbs. Blackwater logo etched on receiver.

NIB	Exc.	V.G.	Good	Fair	Poor
580	500	420	350	300	150

Model 590 Tri Rail

Pump chambered for 3" 12-gauge loads. Features protective heat shield on 20" barrel. Overall length 40.875". Has synthetic Speedfeed stock. Bead front sight. Tri-Rail forend, with removable side rails and integral bottom rail. Extended magazine gives an 8+1 capacity. Matte blue finish. Length of pull 13.8". Weight 7.25 lbs.

NIB	Exc.	V.G.	Good	Fair	Poor
540	490	440	390	300	150

Model 590 A1

Features adjustable aluminum stock and ghost ring sights. Heavy-walled barrel 20" long. Length of pull can be adjusted between 10.5" and 14.25". Weight 7.5 lbs. Capacity 8+1. Parkerized finish.

NIB	Exc.	V.G.	Good	Fair	Poor
480	420	320	250	200	120

Model 590 A1 Retrograde (2019)

9-shot 12 gauge has a 20-inch heavy-walled, Cylinder bore barrel with a heat shield, bayonet lug and Ghost Ring sights. Parkerized finish; metal trigger assembly; metal safety button; full-length walnut stock and corncob forend.

NIB	Exc.	V.G.	Good	Fair	Poor
680	600	500	—	—	—

Mossberg 590 Thunder Ranch 12 Gauge (2019)

18.5-inch (6-shot) cylinder bore, standoff barrel with matte-blue finish. Front red-fiber-optic bead sight. Synthetic stock and tri-rail corncob forend, both in KUIU Vias camouflage. Thunder Ranch logo is engraved on the right side of the receiver.

NIB	Exc.	V.G.	Good	Fair	Poor
450	350	—	—	—	—

Model 590 Shockwave

Compact variant of 590 series, with bird's-head pistol grip and Cylinder choked 14" barrel. Available in 12-, 20-gauge or .410 bore. Includes features found on other 590 models: ambidextrous thumb safety, dual extractors, positive steel-to-steel lockup, twin action bars and an anti-jam elevator. Bureau of Alcohol, Tobacco, Firearms & Explosives has confirmed the 590 Shockwave as a "firearm" per the Gun Control Act

(GCA), but not a Class 3/NFA firearm. This only speaks to its federal status. There could be local state laws that prohibit the sale of this gun in your state. Consult your State Police for clarification. As with any other pistol grip firearm, the buyer must be 21 years of age and a resident of the state where it is purchased. MSRP $455. Introduced in 2017.

NIB	Exc.	V.G.	Good	Fair	Poor
400	350	300	280	200	180

Model 590 Shockwave Mag-Fed

Magazine-fed variant, with 11-round capacity. Introduced in 2018.

NIB	Exc.	V.G.	Good	Fair	Poor
600	500	450	—	—	—

Model 590S Shockwave

Gauge: 12 ga. 1.7–3 in. Barrel: 14.375 and 18.5 in. Length: 26.37–30.75 in. Weight: 5.3–5.5 lbs. Stock: Black synthetic with Raptor grip and corncob forend with strap. Features: The upgraded 590S version of the pistol grip Shockwave is built to cycle any length shells without adapter or adjustment, from 1.75 to 3-in. Bead front sight, matte blued metalwork, shorter-barreled model uses heavy-walled barrel. Both feature fixed cylinder bore choke.

NIB	Exc.	V.G.	Good	Fair	Poor
570	—	—	—	—	—

Model 590S

Gauge: 12 ga. 3 in. with 1.75-in. short shell and 2.75 in. capability. Barrel: 18.5 or 20 in., matte blued. Length: 39.5–41 in. Weight: 6.75–7.25 lbs. Stock: Black Synthetic with fixed LOP; Model with Ghost ring sights uses tactical stock with M-LOK attachment points. Features: Standard model with 18.5-in. barrel allows capacities of 9+1, 6+1, or 5+1. Model with 20-in. barrel and ghost ring sights has capacities of 13+1, 8+1, or 7+1. The former uses a fixed cylinder bore. The latter features the Accu-Choke system with cylinder bore choke included. Both models cycle all length of shells without adapters or adjustment.

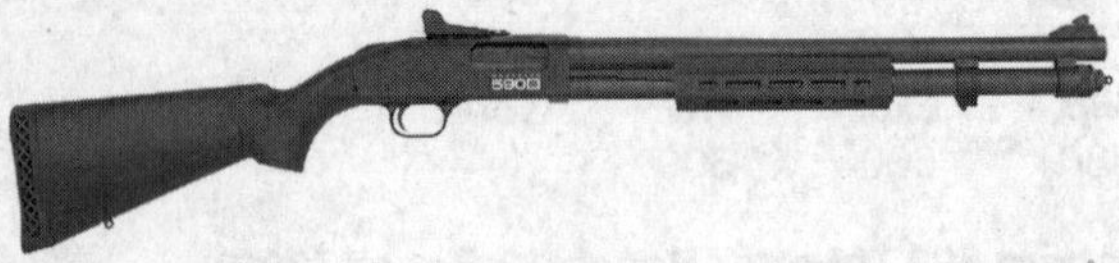

NIB	Exc.	V.G.	Good	Fair	Poor
560	—	—	—	—	—

MODEL 835 SERIES

Model 835 Ulti-Mag

12-gauge Magnum slide-action shotgun. Features 24" or 28" ventilated rib barrel fitted for choke tubes; 6-shot magazine; composition camo or walnut stock; barrel is ported. Introduced in 1988. In 1998, offered with Shadow Grass camo pattern on both stock and barrel. In 1999, offered with Woodland camo. Weight 7.3 to 7.7 lbs. In 2000, offered with Realtree Hardwoods camo finish.

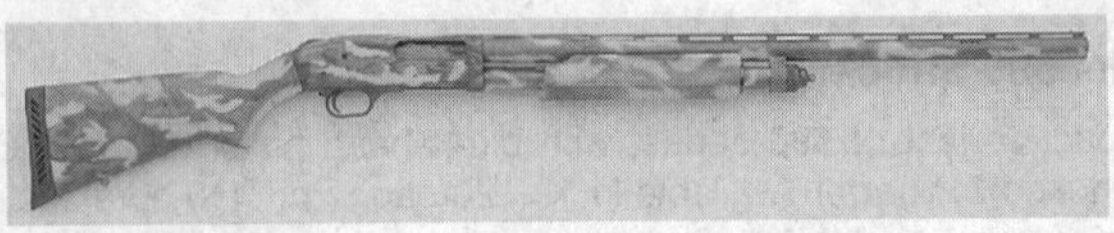

Woodland Camo

NIB	Exc.	V.G.	Good	Fair	Poor
420	350	280	220	150	100

Model 835 Ulti-Mag Viking Grade

Introduced in 1996. Features 12-gauge 3.5" Magnum chamber. Green synthetic stock. Modified choke tube. Furnished with 28" ventilated rib barrel.

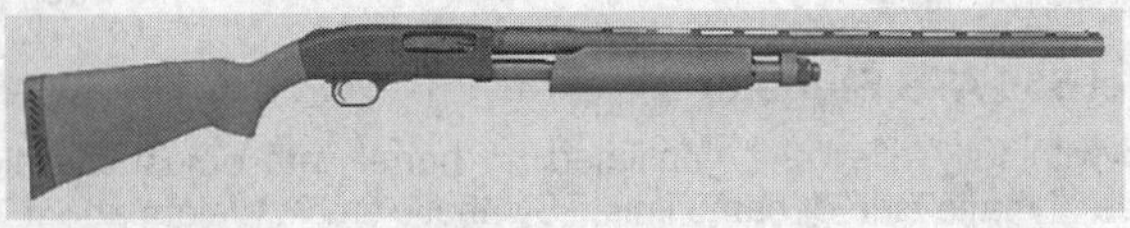

NIB	Exc.	V.G.	Good	Fair	Poor
300	250	200	180	120	100

Model 835 Ulti-Mag Crown Grade

Features checkered walnut stock, with fluted comb. Chambered for 12-gauge with 3.5" chamber. Offered in 24" or 28" ventilated rib barrels, with blued or camo finish. Weight about 7.3 to 7.7 lbs.

NIB	Exc.	V.G.	Good	Fair	Poor
380	300	220	200	150	100

Model 835 Ulti-Mag Crown Grade Combo Model

Same as above. Offered with 28" ventilated rib barrel; 24" rifled barrel. Iron sights.

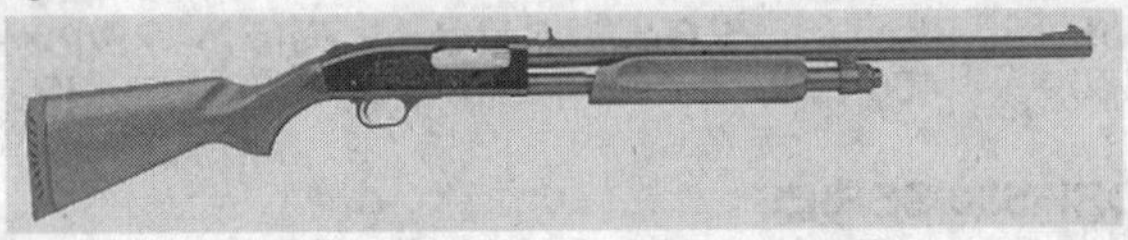

NIB	Exc.	V.G.	Good	Fair	Poor
420	320	250	220	180	150

Model 835 Ulti-Mag Combo Field/Deer (2019)

NIB	Exc.	V.G.	Good	Fair	Poor
350	300	250	200	—	—

Model 835 Ulti-Mag Grand Slam Turkey

Introduced in 2004. This 12-gauge 3.5" features 20" ventilated rib overbored barrel, with Extra Full ported choke tube. Magazine capacity 6 rounds 2.75" shells; 5 rounds 3"; 4 rounds 3.5". Adjustable fiber optic sights. Available in Realtree Hardwoods camo or Mossy Oak Break-Up. Weight about 7.25 lbs.

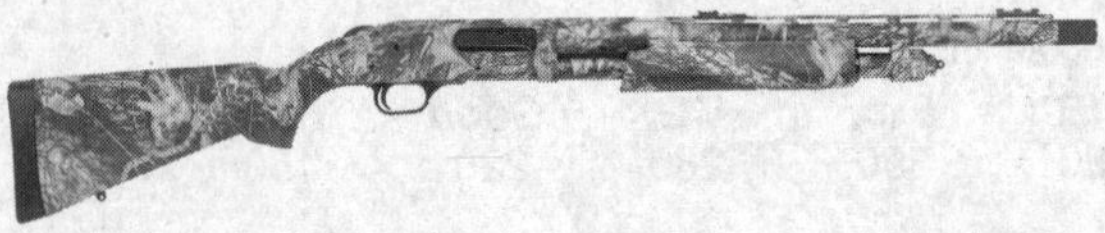

NIB	Exc.	V.G.	Good	Fair	Poor
400	320	280	220	180	120

Model 835 Ulti-Mag Thumbhole Turkey

New in 2006. Dedicated pump-action 12-gauge turkey. Features thumbhole stock and overbored barrel. Chambered for 3.5" shells. X-Factor ported choke tube. Barrel 20". Adjustable fiber-optic front and rear sights. Weight about 7.75 lbs. Available in Mossy Oak New Break-Up camo or Realtree Hardwoods Green camo.

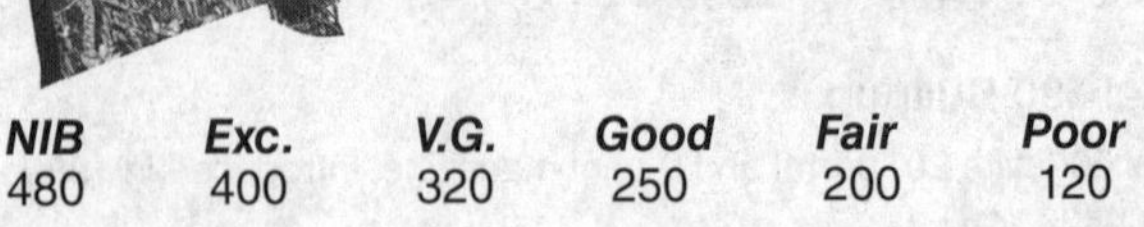

NIB	Exc.	V.G.	Good	Fair	Poor
480	400	320	250	200	120

Model 835 Ulti-Mag Tactical Turkey

Same as above, with extended pistol grip stock that is adjustable for length of pull from 10.75" to 14.5".

NIB	Exc.	V.G.	Good	Fair	Poor
480	400	320	250	200	120

835 Ulti-Mag Tactical Turkey (2019)

NIB	Exc.	V.G.	Good	Fair	Poor
380	300	250	200	—	—

Model 835 Ulti-Mag Turkey (2023)

Gauges: 12 ga. Barrels: 24". Stock: Synthetic in Mossy Oak Greenleaf camo. Features: Turkey-specific, optics-ready. Receiver machined for direct mounting of RMSc-pattern optics. A 5+1-round capacity. Magnum 3.5" chamber. Full Mossy Oak Greenleaf coverage.

NIB	Exc.	V.G.	Good	Fair	Poor
630	570	—	—	—	—

Model 835 Wild Turkey Federation

As above, with Wild Turkey Federation medallion inlaid in stock. Introduced in 1989.

NIB	Exc.	V.G.	Good	Fair	Poor
480	400	320	250	200	120

Model 835 American Field

12-gauge has checkered walnut stock, 28" ventilated rib barrel with Modified choke tube. Weight about 7.7 lbs.

NIB	Exc.	V.G.	Good	Fair	Poor
300	280	220	200	150	100

Model 835 Ulti-Mag Duck Commander

Same features as 835 Ulti-Mag slide-action series, with addition of Max-5 Realtree camo, premium Tru-Glo/Tru-Bead dual color front fiber optic sight, logo of Duck Commander TV show engraved on stock and American flag bandana. Introduced in 2014.

NIB	Exc.	V.G.	Good	Fair	Poor
620	550	400	320	250	150

MODEL 930 SERIES

12-gauge 3" chamber semi-automatic shotgun series. Introduced in 2005.

Model 930 Field

12-gauge 3" gun fitted with 26" or 28" ventilated rib barrels with choke tubes. Barrel is ported. Checkered walnut stock, with recoil pad. Magazine capacity 5 rounds. Blued finish. Weight about 7.75 lbs.

NIB	Exc.	V.G.	Good	Fair	Poor
500	400	300	200	—	—

Model 930 All Purpose Field

Current (2019) Field version, 28" barrels only, walnut 85110 has front bead sight. Synthetic 85127 has fiber-optic front.

NIB	Exc.	V.G.	Good	Fair	Poor
500	400	300	200	—	—

Model 930 Turkey

Fitted with synthetic stock and 24" ventilated-rib ported barrel. Chokes are Extra Full extended tubes. Offered with camo finish. Weight about 7.5 lbs.

NIB	Exc.	V.G.	Good	Fair	Poor
550	450	350	250	—	—

Model 930 Turkey Pistol Grip

Similar to above, with full pistol grip stock, matte black or Mossy Oak Obsession camo finish overall.

NIB	Exc.	V.G.	Good	Fair	Poor
550	450	350	250	—	—

Model 930 Waterfowl

Fitted with 28" ventilated rib ported barrel with choke tubes. Choice of matte blue or camo finish. Weight about 7.75 lbs. Note: Add $100 for camo finish.

NIB	Exc.	V.G.	Good	Fair	Poor
600	500	400	300	200	100

Model 930 Snow Goose

Finished stock-to-muzzle in Kryptec's Yeti camouflage.

NIB	Exc.	V.G.	Good	Fair	Poor
600	500	400	300	200	100

Model 930 Combo Deer/Waterfowl

Comes with 24" fully-rifled bore and adjustable rifle sights and 28" vent rib barrel with fiber-optic front.

NIB	Exc.	V.G.	Good	Fair	Poor
500	400	300	200	100	—

Model 930 Pro Waterfowl

Similar to 930 Waterfowl. Upgraded features including ported barrel, fiber-optic front sight, Mossy Oak Shadow Grass Blades camo and Stock Drop System that provides drop-at-comb adjustment. Current designation (2019) is Pro-Series Waterfowl 85141, pricing for which is reflected below.

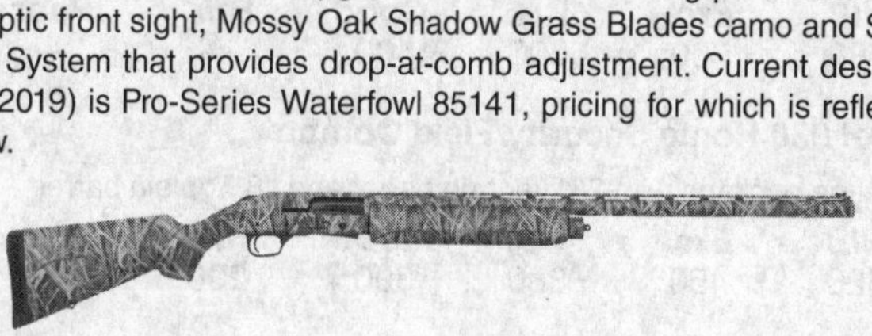

NIB	Exc.	V.G.	Good	Fair	Poor
600	500	400	300	200	100

Model 930 Pro Sporting

Designed for clay target shooting in 12 gauge, with 28" ported barrel, ventilated rib, HiViz sights and Briley extended choke tubes. Special sporting clays walnut stock, with adjustable drop. Designed in collaboration with professional shooting instructors Gil and Vicki Ash. Introduced in 2016. Current designation (2019) is Pro-Series Sporting 85139, pricing for which is reflected below. Weight 7.75 lbs., length 48.5".

NIB	Exc.	V.G.	Good	Fair	Poor
780	700	600	—	—	—

Model 930 Slugster

Older model features 24" ventilated rib ported barrel, with plain or Monte Carlo synthetic stock. Matte-blue or camo finish. Weight about 7.5 lbs. Note: Add $100 for camo finish. Current model (2019) Slugster 85232 only available in matte-blued with integral cantilever scope base, pricing for which is reflected below.

NIB	Exc.	V.G.	Good	Fair	Poor
500	400	300	—	—	—

Model 930 Tactical

Older issue was a 3" 12 gauge with 18.5" barrel and Cylinder bore. Synthetic stock, with matte-black finish. Note: Add $75 for ventilated heat shield. Current model (2019) is called 930 Tactical 8 Shot 85322, which lacks the heat shield. Pricing for current model is reflected below.

NIB	Exc.	V.G.	Good	Fair	Poor
500	400	300	200	100	—

Model 930 Road Blocker

Similar to above with muzzle brake.

NIB	Exc.	V.G.	Good	Fair	Poor
530	430	330	230	180	130

Model 930 SPX

Billed as "home security" model, 3" 12-gauge SPX has 7-round magazine tube, 18.5" barrel, Picatinny rail, ghost ring rear sight and fiber-optic front. Note: Deduct 10 percent for white dot sights. Nomenclature for this model has changed to Tactical SPX, and comes in three 2019 models: 930 Tactical 8-Shot SPX 85360, and 930 Tactical 8-Shot SPX Pistol Grip 85223 and 85370. The 85223 has a tan metal finish, while the 85370 is all black. Pricing for current model is reflected below.

NIB	Exc.	V.G.	Good	Fair	Poor
780	700	600	500	—	—

Model 930 Home Security/Field Combo

12-gauge package with 28" vent rib barrel and 18.5" plain barrel.

NIB	Exc.	V.G.	Good	Fair	Poor
520	450	380	300	200	100

Model 930 Hunting Turkey/Field

NIB	Exc.	V.G.	Good	Fair	Poor
500	400	300	200	100	—

Model 930 Thunder Ranch 12 Gauge (2019)

Autoloading shotgun features an 18.5" (5-shot) Cylinder bore, standoff barrel with matte-blue finish. Front red-fiber-optic bead sight. Thunder Ranch logo is engraved on the right side of the receiver.

NIB	Exc.	V.G.	Good	Fair	Poor
540	440	350	—	—	—

930 JM Pro-Series Autoloaders

Introduced 2016. Developed with Jerry Miculek to meet the needs of Team Miculek in 3-gun competition. Upgraded features include boron nitride-coated gas pistons, piston rings, magazine tubes, hammers, sears, return spring plungers, and return spring tubes. Shell stops, bolt slides, and elevators receive additional finishing, which reduces overall friction on internal parts. 22" and 24" barrels, 9- and 10-shot magazine tube capacity. Vent ribs, fiber-optic front sight, Accu-Set chokes, matte-blued metal finish, black synthetic stocks on 85118 and 85119; 85133 is Kryptek Typhon finish. Weight, 7.75 lbs., length, 44.5".

NIB	Exc.	V.G.	Good	Fair	Poor
630	550	480	400	300	—

MODEL 935 MAGNUM SERIES

Introduced in 2004.

Model 935 Magnum Waterfowl Synthetic

12-gauge 3.5" gun features 26" or 28" ventilated rib overbored barrel with choke tubes. Fiber optic bead. Matte black finish, with black synthetic stock. Weight about 7.75 lbs.

NIB	Exc.	V.G.	Good	Fair	Poor
550	450	350	250	150	120

Model 935 Magnum Waterfowl Camo

12-gauge 3.5" semi-automatic. Available with 26" or 28" ventilated rib overbored barrel, with fiber optic bead and choke tubes. Offered with Mossy Oak Break-Up or Advantage Max-4 camo pattern. Magazine capacity 5 rounds 3"; 4 rounds 3.5". Weight about 7.75 lbs.

NIB	Exc.	V.G.	Good	Fair	Poor
600	500	400	250	200	130

Model 935 Magnum Slugster

Similar to above, with 24" fully rifled barrel and sights, Realtree AP camo overall.

NIB	Exc.	V.G.	Good	Fair	Poor
600	500	400	250	200	130

Model 935 Magnum Turkey/Deer Comb

Similar to above, with interchangeable 24" Turkey barrel. Mossy Oak New Break-up camo overall.

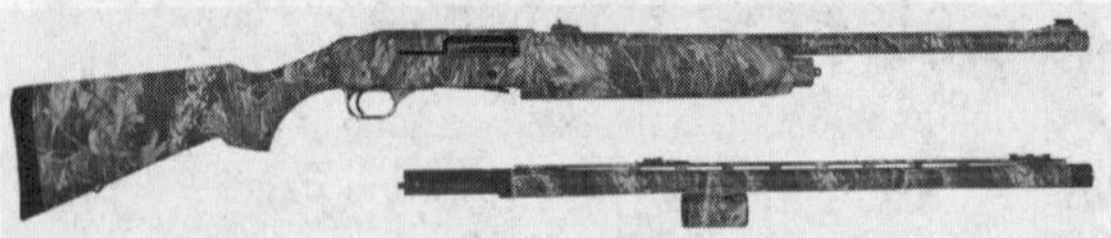

NIB	Exc.	V.G.	Good	Fair	Poor
700	600	500	350	280	150

Model 935 Magnum Turkey Camo

Older 12-gauge 3.5" model features 24" ventilated rib overbored barrel with adjustable fiber-optic sights. Ultra Full choke tube. Offered in Mossy Oak Break-Up or Hardwoods HD-Green. Weight about 7.75 lbs. The 2019 model 81046 has 22" vent-rib overbored barrel, all in MO Bottomland.

NIB	Exc.	V.G.	Good	Fair	Poor
550	450	350	250	—	—

Model 935 Magnum Turkey Pistol Grip

Similar to above, with full pistol grip stock.

NIB	Exc.	V.G.	Good	Fair	Poor
630	530	430	280	230	150

Model 935 Magnum Turkey Synthetic

As above, with 24" ventilated rib overbored barrel with Ultra Full choke tube. Weight about 7.75 lbs.

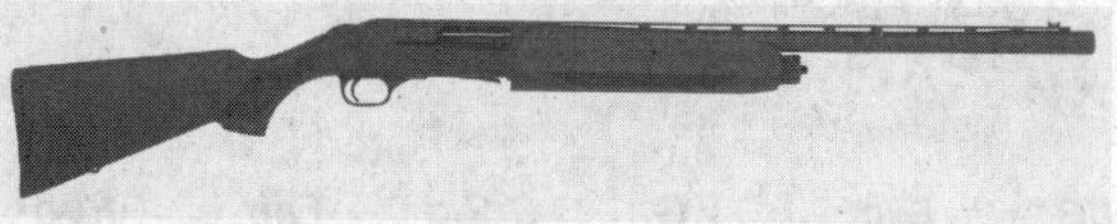

NIB	Exc.	V.G.	Good	Fair	Poor
550	450	350	250	150	130

Model 935 Magnum Waterfowl/Turkey Combo

Similar to above, with 24" Turkey; 28" Waterfowl barrels. Mossy Oak New Break-up finish overall.

NIB	Exc.	V.G.	Good	Fair	Poor
800	650	500	400	250	150

Model 935 Grand Slam Turkey

12-gauge 3.5" model features 22" ventilated rib overbored barrel with Extra Full ported choke tube. Adjustable fiber optic sights. Offered in Realtree Hardwoods Green or Mossy Oak Break-Up camo pattern. Camo sling included. Weight about 7.5 lbs.

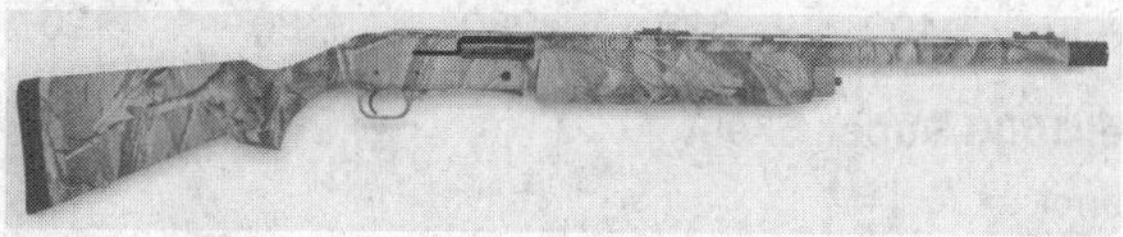

NIB	Exc.	V.G.	Good	Fair	Poor
650	550	450	280	230	150

Model 935 Magnum

Chambered for 12-gauge 3.5" Magnum. Semi-automatic model offered in waterfowl or turkey versions, with several camo options and barrel lengths. Note: Add $100 for full camo coverage; $150 for Grand Slam model with ported barrel; $200 for pistol grip stock.

NIB	Exc.	V.G.	Good	Fair	Poor
600	520	430	350	250	150

Model 935 Duck Commander

Same features as 935 Magnum semi-automatic series, with addition of Max-5 Realtree camo, premium Tru-Glo/Tru-Bead dual color front fiber optic sight, logo of Duck Commander TV show engraved on stock and American flag bandana. Introduced in 2014.

NIB	Exc.	V.G.	Good	Fair	Poor
830	750	600	450	300	200

Model 935 Pro Waterfowl

Introduced 2016. 3.5" chamber 12 gauge with boron nitride internal finishes; stainless-steel recoil spring PRO-SERIES WATERFOWL engraved receiver; Mossy Oak Shadowgrass Blades camo; fiber-optic front sight; three choke tube set; and Stock Drop System. Current designation (2019) is Pro-Series Waterfowl 82042, pricing for which is reflected below.

NIB	Exc.	V.G.	Good	Fair	Poor
650	550	450	350	250	—

MODEL 940 SERIES

Model 940 JM Pro

Auto-loading competition 12 ga. shotgun designed in conjunction with champion shooter Jerry Miculek; 24" barrel, 9+1 shell capacity.

NIB	Exc.	V.G.	Good	Fair	Poor
1000	900	800	—	—	—

940 Pro Snow Goose

Gauge: 12 ga. 3 in. Barrel: 28-in. vent rib. Length: 50.75 in. Weight: 8.25 lbs. Stock: True Timber Viper Snow camo synthetic, adjustable for LOP, cast and drop. Features: High-capacity 12+1 in the extended magazine tube, unique to the Snow Goose model. LOP adjustable from 13–14.25 in. TriComp fiber-optic front sight. X-Factor extended choke tube. Metalwork finished in Battleship Gray Cerakote.

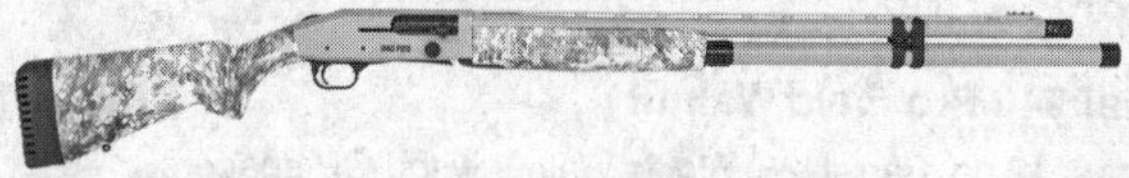

NIB	Exc.	V.G.	Good	Fair	Poor
1040	—	—	—	—	—

940 Pro Turkey

Gauge: 12 ga. 3 in. Barrel: 18 or 24-in. vent rib. Length: 39.25–44.75 in. Weight: 7.25–7.5 lbs. Stock: Synthetic in Mossy Oak Greenleaf camo, adjustable for LOP, cast and drop. Features: Turkey-specific variants of the 940 Pro lineup, these with shorter barrels, Greenleaf camo, and fitted with X-Factor XX-Full Turkey choke tubes. Optics-ready cutout. Compsight fiber optics. LOP adjustable from 13–14.25 in. Both models carry 4+1-round capacity.

NIB	Exc.	V.G.	Good	Fair	Poor
1020	—	—	—	—	—

940 Pro Waterfowl

Gauge: 12 ga. 3 in. Barrel: 18 or 24-in. vent rib. Length: 39.25–44.75 in. Weight: 7.25–7.5 lbs. Stock: Synthetic in Mossy Oak Greenleaf camo, adjustable for LOP, cast and drop. Features: Turkey-specific variants of the 940 Pro lineup, these with shorter barrels, GreenlGauge: 12 ga. 3 in. Barrel: 28-in. vent rib. Length: 48.75 in. Weight: 7.75 lbs. Stock: Synthetic in True Timber Prairie camo, adjustable for LOP, cast and drop. Features: Waterfowl-specific variant of the 940 Pro lineup. Includes a set of X-Factor extended choke tubes, TriComp fiber-optic front sight. Oversized controls. LOP adjustable from 13–14.25 inches. 4+1-round capacity. eaf camo, and fitted with X-Factor XX-Full Turkey choke tubes. Optics-ready cutout. Compsight fiber optics. LOP adjustable from 13–14.25 in. Both models carry 4+1-round capacity.

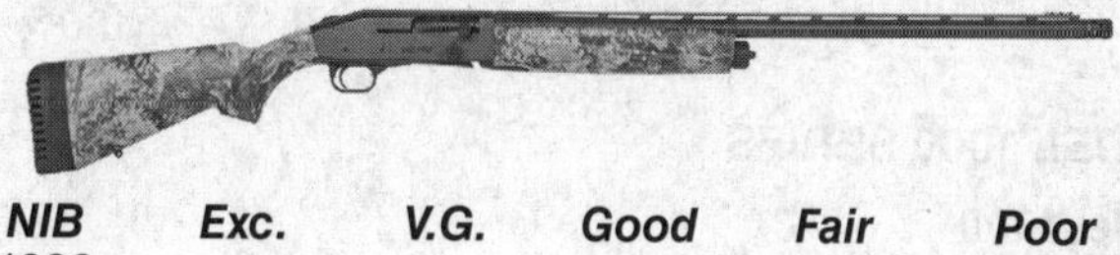

NIB	Exc.	V.G.	Good	Fair	Poor
1000	—	—	—	—	—

940 Pro Field

Gauge: 12 ga. 3 in. Barrel: 28-in. vent rib. Length: 47.5 in. Weight: 7.75 lbs. Stock: Black synthetic, adjustable for LOP, cast and drop. Features: Field hunting variant of the 940 Pro lineup. Includes an Accu-Set of choke tubes. Fiber-optic front sight, matte blue metalwork finish. Oversized controls. Sling studs. LOP adjustable from 13–14.25 inches. 4+1-round capacity.

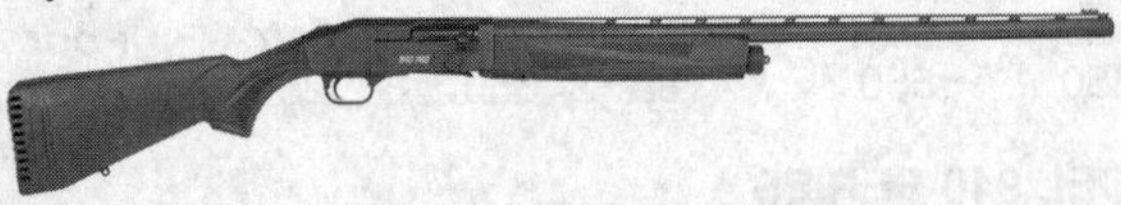

NIB	Exc.	V.G.	Good	Fair	Poor
870	—	—	—	—	—

Model 940 Pro Tactical-Holosun Combo

Gauges: 12 ga. Barrels: 18.5". Stock: Black synthetic. Features: Same system as 940 Pro family with the receiver machined for direct micro-dot optics mounting and a Holosun HS407K along with a fiber-optic front.

NIB	Exc.	V.G.	Good	Fair	Poor
1210	1100	—	—	—	—

Model 940 Pro Field Walnut

Gauges: 12 ga. Barrel: 28". Stock: Walnut with LOP spacers.

NIB	Exc.	V.G.	Good	Fair	Poor
960	870	—	—	—	—

MODEL 3000 SERIES

Model 3000

12- or 20-gauge slide-action shotgun. Manufactured in a variety of barrel lengths and styles. Blued, with walnut stock. Also known as Smith & Wesson Model 3000.

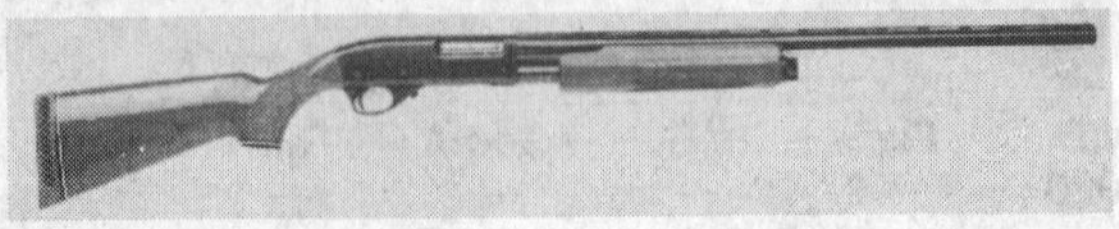

NIB	Exc.	V.G.	Good	Fair	Poor
—	320	250	180	120	80

Model 3000 Waterfowl

As above, with matte finish. Fitted with sling swivels and accompanied by a camouflage sling. Produced in 1986.

NIB	Exc.	V.G.	Good	Fair	Poor
—	350	280	200	150	100

Model 3000 Law Enforcement

As above, with 18.5" or 20" Cylinder Bore barrel. Manufactured in 1986 and 1987.

NIB	Exc.	V.G.	Good	Fair	Poor
—	380	280	200	150	100

MODEL 1000 SERIES

Model 1000

12- or 20-gauge semi-automatic shotgun. Manufactured in a variety of barrel lengths and styles. Receiver of an aluminum alloy and blued. Also known as Smith & Wesson Model 1000. Offered in 1986 and 1987.

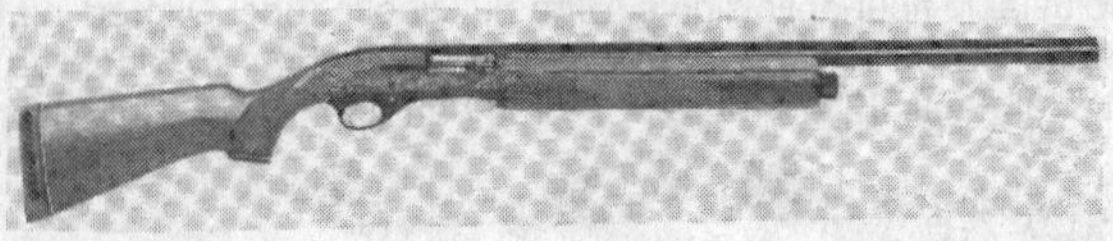

NIB	Exc.	V.G.	Good	Fair	Poor
—	300	250	200	150	100

Model 1000 Slug

As above, with 22" barrel fitted with rifle sights. Offered in 1986 and 1987.

NIB	Exc.	V.G.	Good	Fair	Poor
—	320	250	200	120	100

Model 1000 Super Series

As above, with steel receiver. Self-regulating gas system that allows use of standard or Magnum shells.

NIB	Exc.	V.G.	Good	Fair	Poor
—	380	300	250	150	100

Model 1000 Super Waterfowl

Matte finish.

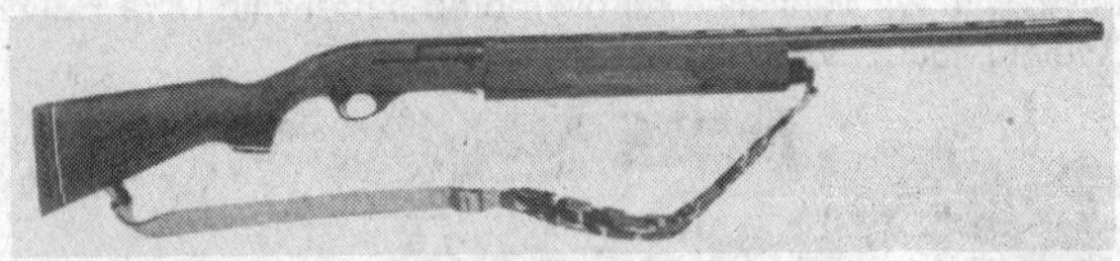

NIB	Exc.	V.G.	Good	Fair	Poor
—	380	300	250	150	100

Model 1000 Super Slug

Rifle sights.

NIB	Exc.	V.G.	Good	Fair	Poor
—	380	300	250	150	100

Model 1000 Super Trap

30" high rib barrel.

NIB	Exc.	V.G.	Good	Fair	Poor
—	400	320	280	180	120

Model 1000 Super Skeet

25" barrel.

NIB	Exc.	V.G.	Good	Fair	Poor
—	400	320	280	180	120

MODEL 9200 SERIES

Has a variety of configurations. A 12-gauge semi-automatic, with walnut or camo synthetic stock. Barrel lengths 22" to 28". Weight 7 to 7.7 lbs.

Model 9200 Viking Grade

NIB	Exc.	V.G.	Good	Fair	Poor
350	300	280	200	100	80

Model 9200 USST Crown Grade

NIB	Exc.	V.G.	Good	Fair	Poor
400	350	300	200	100	80

Model 9200 Combos

NIB	Exc.	V.G.	Good	Fair	Poor
480	420	350	250	150	100

Model 9200 Special Hunter

28" ventilated rib barrel, with synthetic stock.

NIB	Exc.	V.G.	Good	Fair	Poor
480	420	350	250	150	100

Model 9200 Deer Combo

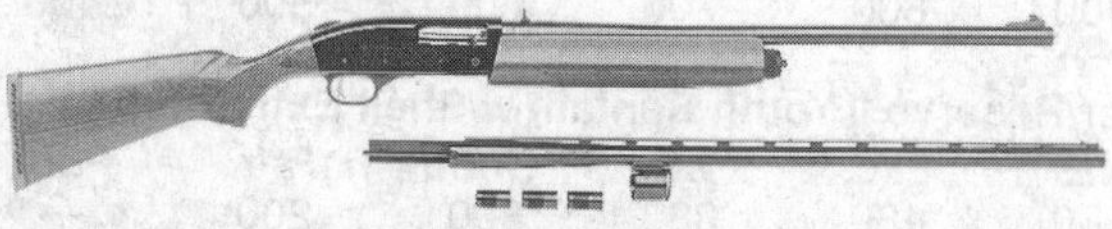

NIB	Exc.	V.G.	Good	Fair	Poor
480	420	350	250	150	100

Model 9200 Turkey Camo

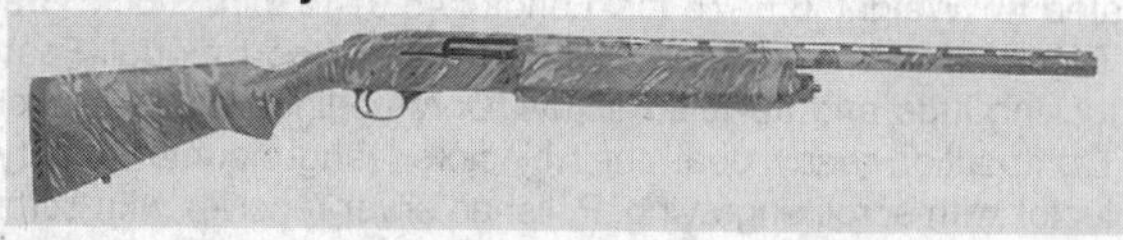

NIB	Exc.	V.G.	Good	Fair	Poor
480	420	350	250	150	100

Model 9200 Crown Grade Bantam

NIB	Exc.	V.G.	Good	Fair	Poor
400	350	300	250	120	80

Model 9200 Jungle Gun

12-gauge auto-loader fitted with plain 18.5" barrel with bead sight. Barrel choked Cylinder. Chambers are 2.75". Magazine capacity 5 rounds. Parkerized finish. Synthetic stock.

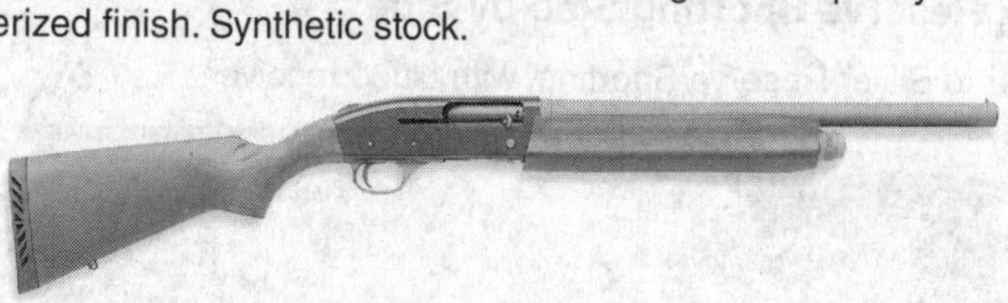

NIB	Exc.	V.G.	Good	Fair	Poor
520	450	320	200	150	120

MODEL SA SERIES

Model SA-20

Introduced in 2008. 20-gauge autoloader chambered for 3" shells. Field models have 26" or 28" ventilated rib barrel and come with five choke tubes (Sport Set). Weight about 6 to 6.5 lbs. Black synthetic stocks on 75771/75772; walnut on 75789. Youth Bantam model has 1" shorter length of pull and 24" barrel. Weight about 5.6 lbs. Turkey model 75790 has 22" barrel with fiber-optic 3-dot sights. Stock finish is MO Obsession. Weight, 5.5lbs., length 40.5". The Railed Pistol Grip 75780 has a ghost ring rear and fiber-optic front sight. LOP, 12.75". Synthetic black pistol grip stock.

NIB	Exc.	V.G.	Good	Fair	Poor
450	350	250	—	—	—

Model SA-20 Tactical

Mossberg's SA-20 Tactical Autoloader in 20-gauge only. Easy-Load elevator facilitates fast one-handed reloading. Top-mounted Picatinny-style rail accommodates optical sights, while magazine tube rail allows mounting lights, lasers and other accessories. Ghost ring rear and fiber optic front sights. Gas-operated action. Capacity 4+1. Cylinder-bore barrel 20" long. Available with conventional black synthetic or synthetic pistol grip stock. Weight about 6 lbs.

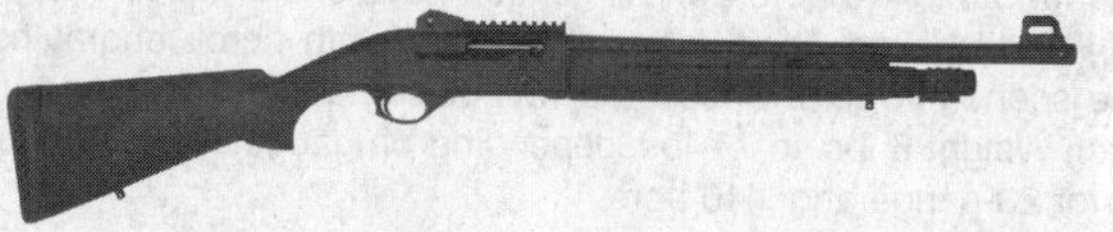

NIB	Exc.	V.G.	Good	Fair	Poor
480	440	400	370	320	280

Model SA-28

Identical to SA-20 except in 28-gauge, with 26" barrel. Introduced in 2017. SA-28 Youth Bantam All Purpose Field 75769 introduced 2018.

NIB	Exc.	V.G.	Good	Fair	Poor
550	450	350	—	—	—

Model SA-410 Field

Gauge: .410 bore, 3 in. Capacity: 4+1. Barrel: 26 in., ventilated rib. Weight: 6.5 lbs. Length: 46 in. Stock: Black synthetic. Features: Mossberg offers the baby bore for small-game and field hunters as well as light recoiling plinking with this lightweight gas-driven autoloader. Metalwork is finished in matte blue. Brass front bead, fixed 13.75 in. length of pull, ventilated rubber buttpad. Cross-bolt safety, easy-load elevator. Includes Sport Set flush fit chokes (F, IM, M, IC, C).

NIB	Exc.	V.G.	Good	Fair	Poor
530	—	—	—	—	—

Model SA-410 Turkey

Gauge: .410 bore, 3 in. Capacity: 4+1. Barrel: 26 in., ventilated rib. Weight: 6.5 lbs. Length: 46 in. Stock: Synthetic stock with Mossy Oak Bottomland camouflage. Features: Mossberg expands its baby-bore turkey lineup with this gas-driven semi-automatic. Both the stocks and metalwork wear full camouflage coverage. Rear fiber-optic ghost-ring sight and front green fiber-optic. Top Picatinny rail for easy optics mounting. Cross-bolt safety, easy-load elevator. Ships with an XX-Full Extended Turkey choke.

NIB	Exc.	V.G.	Good	Fair	Poor
650	—	—	—	—	—

Model 5500 MKI I

12-gauge semi-automatic shotgun. Supplied with 26" barrel 2.75" shells; 28" barrel 3" shells. Blued, with walnut stock. Introduced in 1989.

NIB	Exc.	V.G.	Good	Fair	Poor
300	240	200	180	150	120

RESERVE SERIES

Introduced in 2005 and 2008. Over/under and side-by-side guns in 12-, 20-, 28-gauge and .410 bore. Made in Turkey.

SILVER RESERVE SERIES

Gauge: Options depend on model, but include 12 ga. 3 in., 20 ga. 3 in., 28 ga. 2.75 in., and .410 bore 3 in., as well as a 20-ga. Youth. Barrels: 26-

or 28-in. ventilated rib. Weight: 6.5–7.5 lbs. Length: 42.25–45 in. Stock: Choice of black synthetic or satin Black Walnut, depending upon model, as well as a Youth-sized model with shorter LOP. Features: Matte blue barrel finish. Satin silver receiver on all except the synthetic model with a matte blue receiver. Dual shell extractors. Tang-mounted safety/barrel selector. Includes flush-mount Field set of five chokes (Cyl, IC, M, IM, F).

NIB	*Exc.*	*V.G.*	*Good*	*Fair*	*Poor*
580	—	—	—	—	—

Silver Reserve Field Over/Under

Ventilated rib barrels offered in: 12-gauge 28"; 20-gauge 26" or 28"; 28-gauge 26"; .410 bore 26". All gauges have choke tubes except .410 with Fixed chokes. Steel silvered receiver, with scroll engraving and game scenes in gold. Checkered walnut stock, with recoil pad. Single trigger. Weight 6 lbs. to 7.7 lbs. depending on gauge. Note: Add 20 percent for 28-gauge and .410 bore.

NIB	*Exc.*	*V.G.*	*Good*	*Fair*	*Poor*
600	500	300	200	150	100

Silver Reserve Sporting Over/Under

As above in 12-gauge only, with 28" ventilated 10mm rib barrels with choke tubes and ported barrels. Weight about 7.7 lbs.

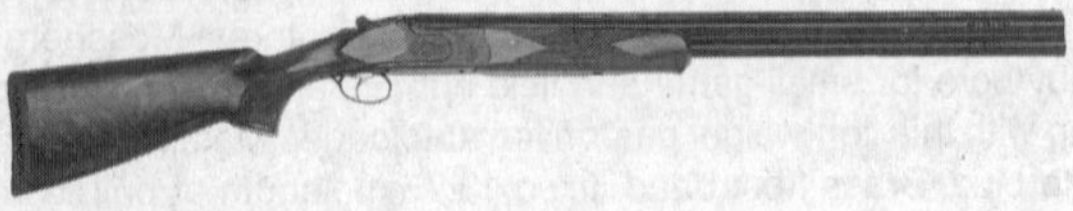

NIB	*Exc.*	*V.G.*	*Good*	*Fair*	*Poor*
700	600	420	300	220	120

Silver Reserve II Sport

Competition model in 12-gauge only with 28" ported barrels, extended choke tubes and fiber optic front sight. Super Sport has wider rib, dual bead sights and stock with ajustable comb. Note: Add $200 for Super Sport.

NIB	*Exc.*	*V.G.*	*Good*	*Fair*	*Poor*
800	700	550	400	300	250

Silver Reserve Side-by-Side

New in 2008. Blued barrels lengths: 12-gauge 26" or 28"; 20- and 28-gauge 26". Stock and forend select black walnut, with satin finish. Receiver satin-finished silver, with scroll engraving. Bores chrome-plated. All models come with five choke tubes. Weight: 7.2 lbs. 12-gauge; 6.4 to 6.5 lbs. 20- and 28-gauge.

NIB	*Exc.*	*V.G.*	*Good*	*Fair*	*Poor*
850	750	600	450	250	150

Silver Reserve II Field

This model replaced the Silver Reserve Field in 2012. Upgraded walnut stock has satin finish, silver receiver has more elaborate engraving than earlier model. In 12-, 20- or 28-gauge.

NIB	*Exc.*	*V.G.*	*Good*	*Fair*	*Poor*
900	800	680	500	350	250

Silver Reserve II Field w/Shell Extractors

In 2014, this model replaced the Silver Reserve Field II (2011). Upgraded walnut stock has satin finish, silver receiver has more elaborate engraving than earlier model. In 12, 20 or 28 gauge and .410 bore.

NIB	*Exc.*	*V.G.*	*Good*	*Fair*	*Poor*
600	500	400	300	200	—

Silver Reserve II Field Combo 12/20 gauge w/Shell Extractors

NIB	*Exc.*	*V.G.*	*Good*	*Fair*	*Poor*
850	750	650	550	450	—

Silver Reserve II Sport w/Shell Ejectors

NIB	*Exc.*	*V.G.*	*Good*	*Fair*	*Poor*
780	680	580	500	400	—

Silver Reserve II Super Sport w/Shell Ejectors

NIB	*Exc.*	*V.G.*	*Good*	*Fair*	*Poor*
900	800	700	600	500	400

Silver Reserve II Youth Bantam w/Shell Extractors

NIB	*Exc.*	*V.G.*	*Good*	*Fair*	*Poor*
580	480	380	300	200	—

GOLD RESERVE SPORTING SERIES

Gauge: 12 ga. 3 in., 20 ga. 3 in., and .410 bore 3 in. Barrels: 28 or 30 in. ventilated rib. Weight: 6.5–7.5 lbs. Length: 45.0–48.0 in. Stock: Grade-A Satin Black Walnut. Adjustable stock on Super Sport model. Features: Dual locking lugs and Jeweled action. Chrome-lined bores and chambers. Competition-ready dual shell ejectors. Tang-mounted safety/barrel selector with scroll engraving. Polished silver receiver with scroll-engraved receiver with 24-Karat gold inlay on the underside receiver. Black Label variants wear polished black receiver with same embellishments. Includes set of five Extended Sport chokes (SK, IC, M, IM, F).

NIB	*Exc.*	*V.G.*	*Good*	*Fair*	*Poor*
930	—	—	—	—	—

Onyx Reserve Sporting Side-by-Side

Similar to Silver Reserve Sporting, with blued receiver.

NIB	*Exc.*	*V.G.*	*Good*	*Fair*	*Poor*
800	700	580	400	220	150

MOUNTAIN ARMS
Ozark, Missouri

Wildcat

Similar to Rau Arms Wildcat (q.v.) and Garcia Bronco, with plastic stock inserts. Take-down model offered as well. Estimated 6,243 produced 1971-1978. First several thousand bore Rau Arms label.

NIB	*Exc.*	*V.G.*	*Good*	*Fair*	*Poor*
220	180	120	100	60	40

MOUNTAIN RIFLES, INC.
Palmer, Alaska

Mountaineer

Bolt-action rifle introduced in 1997. Built on Remington action with Model 70 style bolt release. Factory muzzle brake installed with open sights. Timney trigger standard. Stock fiberglass. Finish Parkerized. Chambered for many different calibers from .223 Rem. to .416 Rem., including Dakota and Weatherby cartridges. Weight starts about 6 lbs. depending on caliber. Several options that will affect price. Left-hand offered as an option.

NIB	Exc.	V.G.	Good	Fair	Poor
2200	1750	1400	1100	750	300

Super Mountaineer

Similar to Mountaineer, but bolt is fluted and hollow. Barrel is match-grade stainless steel, with muzzle brake. Kevlar/Graphite stock. Wide variety of calibers. Weight starts about 4.25 lbs. depending on caliber.

NIB	Exc.	V.G.	Good	Fair	Poor
2900	2350	1900	1500	1000	400

Pro Mountaineer

Built on Winchester Model 70 action. Premium match-grade barrel, with muzzle brake. Model 70 trigger. Stainless steel matte finish. Kevlar/Graphite stock. Wide variety of calibers. Weight starts about 6 lbs.

NIB	Exc.	V.G.	Good	Fair	Poor
2900	2350	2350	1900	1500	400

Pro Safari

Built on MRI action with controlled feed. Premium match-grade barrel. Timney trigger. Matte blue finish. Exhibition grade walnut stock, with custom bottom metal. Weight starts about 7 lbs. depending on caliber. Caliber from .223 to .458 Lott.

NIB	Exc.	V.G.	Good	Fair	Poor
4500	3500	2300	1750	1200	500

Ultra Mountaineer

Built on MRI action, with premium match-grade barrel and muzzle brake. Timney trigger. Parkerized finish. Kevlar/Graphite stock. Calibers from .223 to .505 Gibbs. Weight begins at 5 lbs. depending on caliber. Note: Add $500 for Rigby-length calibers.

NIB	Exc.	V.G.	Good	Fair	Poor
3000	2500	2200	1900	1500	400

MUGICA, JOSE
Eibar, Spain

See—LLAMA

Trade name found on Llama pistols that were manufactured by Gabilondo.

MURFREESBORO ARMORY
Murfreesboro, Tennessee

Established in 1861 by William Ledbetter. Made copies of U.S. Model 1841 Rifle complete with patchbox and double strapped nose cap. Barrel bands pinned to stock. Between 270 and 390 made from October 1861 through March 1862. Overall length 48.75"; barrel length 33"; .54-caliber. Unmarked except for serial number on various parts including barrel.

Antique

Previous editions reported this as maker follows: "Established in 1861 by William Ledbetter. Made copies of U.S. Model 1841 Rifle complete with patchbox and double strapped nose cap. Barrel bands pinned to stock. Between 270 and 390 made from October 1861 through March 1862. Overall length 48.75"; barrel length 33"; .54-caliber. Unmarked except for serial number on various parts including barrel." However, we have been unable to confirm this from other sources, and have found no recorded sales. Reader input is invited."

Exc.	Fine	V.G.	Good	Fair	Poor
—	—	—	—	—	—

MURPHY & O'CONNELL
New York, New York

Pocket Pistol **Antique**

Murphy & O'Connell are listed in Sellers' book "American Gunsmiths" as a maker of derringers in New York, New York from 1857-1858. No other references or sales have been found. Reader input is invited."

Exc.	Fine	V.G.	Good	Fair	Poor
—	—	—	—	—	—

MURRAY, J. P.
Columbus, Georgia

Percussion Rifle **Antique**

.58-caliber percussion rifle, with 33" barrel, full stock and brass mounts. Also made with 23.5" to 24" barrel as a carbine. Lock marked "J.P. Murray/Columbus Ga.". Several hundred manufactured between 1862 and 1864. As with most confederate arms, sales are rare and values are speculative.

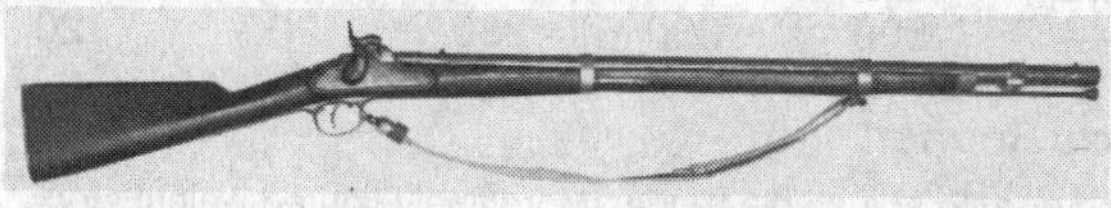

Courtesy Milwaukee Public Museum, Milwaukee, Wisconsin

Exc.	Fine	V.G.	Good	Fair	Poor
50000	33000	23500	14000	7000	3000

MUSGRAVE
Republic of South Africa

RSA NR I Single-Shot Target Rifle

.308-caliber single-shot bolt-action rifle, with 26" barrel, match sights, adjustable trigger. Target-style stock made of walnut. Manufactured between 1971 and 1976.

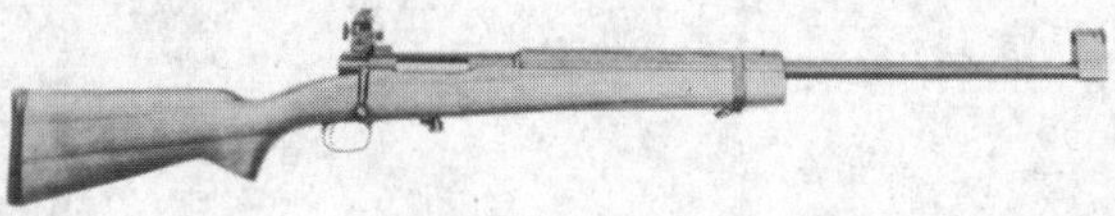

NIB	Exc.	V.G.	Good	Fair	Poor
—	550	420	300	220	120

Valiant NR6

.243, .270, .308, .30-06 and 7mm Rem. Magnum caliber bolt-action sporting rifle, with 24" barrel, open sights. English-style stock. Imported from 1971 to 1976.

NIB	Exc.	V.G.	Good	Fair	Poor
—	450	350	280	180	120

Premier NR5

As above, with 26" barrel. Pistol grip Monte Carlo-style stock. Discontinued in 1976.

NIB	Exc.	V.G.	Good	Fair	Poor
—	550	450	320	220	150

MUSKETEER RIFLES

Firearms International/Garcia
Washington, D.C.

Sporter

.243 to .300 Win. Magnum caliber bolt-action rifle, with 24" barrel without sights. Monte Carlo-style stock. Imported between 1963 and 1972. Note: Add 20 percent for Magnum chamberings.

NIB	Exc.	V.G.	Good	Fair	Poor
—	500	380	280	200	120

Deluxe Sporter

As above, with adjustable trigger. More finely figured walnut stock.

NIB	Exc.	V.G.	Good	Fair	Poor
—	550	400	300	200	120

Carbine

Sporter, with 20" barrel.

NIB	Exc.	V.G.	Good	Fair	Poor
—	500	380	280	200	120

N

NATIONAL ARMS CO.

Brooklyn, New York

See—MOORE'S PATENT FIREARMS CO.

Successor to Moore's Patent Firearms Company in 1865. Purchased by Colt Company in 1870.

Large Frame Teat-Fire Revolver (Antique)

.45 teat fire caliber revolver with 7.5" barrel and 6-shot cylinder. Blued or silver-plated with walnut grips. Barrel marked "National Arms Co. Brooklyn". Exact number made is unknown. Estimated fewer than 30. Too rare to value. Recent auction sales include a no-finish example sold for $3,250 in 2020, and a 40% blue example sold for $16,100 in 2018.

No. 2 Derringer (Antique)

.41-caliber spur trigger pocket pistol with 2.5" barrel. Blued or silver-plated with walnut grips. Later manufactured by Colt Company as their No. 2 Derringer.

Courtesy Rock Island Auction Company

Exc.	*Fine*	*V.G.*	*Good*	*Fair*	*Poor*
1750	1300	920	550	150	100

NAVY ARMS COMPANY

Martinsburg, West Virginia

Founded in 1957 by the late Val Forgett, Jr. Over the years, this company has imported many blackpowder and modern surplus firearms and replicas. Many of the models imported are classified as curios and relics. In 2012, Navy Arms now operated by Val Forgett III, temporarily suspended the importation side of the business. Presently the company is working with Winchester and Turnbull Manufacturing Co. on marketing a series of Winchester Model 1873 rifles. Shown on these following pages are examples of the many firearms that have been imported by Navy Arms.

SHOTGUNS

Model 83

12- or 20-gauge Magnum over/under shotgun. Manufactured in a variety of barrel lengths and styles, with double triggers and extractors. Blued, engraved, with walnut stock. Introduced in 1985.

NIB	*Exc.*	*V.G.*	*Good*	*Fair*	*Poor*
500	400	280	200	180	100

Model 93

As above, with automatic ejectors.

NIB	*Exc.*	*V.G.*	*Good*	*Fair*	*Poor*
580	480	300	250	200	100

Model 95

As above, with single trigger and screw-in choke tubes.

NIB	*Exc.*	*V.G.*	*Good*	*Fair*	*Poor*
600	500	350	250	200	100

Model 96 Sportsman

As above in 12-gauge only, with gold-plated receiver.

NIB	*Exc.*	*V.G.*	*Good*	*Fair*	*Poor*
600	500	350	250	200	100

Model 100

12-, 20-, 28-gauge or .410 bore over/under boxlock shotgun, with 26" ventilated rib barrels, single trigger and extractors. Blued, chrome-plated, with walnut stock. Introduced in 1989. Note: Add 20 percent for .410.

NIB	*Exc.*	*V.G.*	*Good*	*Fair*	*Poor*
450	350	200	150	100	80

Model 100 Side-by-Side

12- or 20-gauge Magnum boxlock double-barrel shotgun, with 27.5" barrels, double triggers and extractors. Blued, with walnut stock. Imported between 1985 and 1987.

NIB	*Exc.*	*V.G.*	*Good*	*Fair*	*Poor*
—	480	350	250	200	100

Model 150

As above, with automatic ejectors.

NIB	*Exc.*	*V.G.*	*Good*	*Fair*	*Poor*
—	500	380	300	220	120

Model 105

12- or 20-gauge and .410 bore folding single-barrel shotgun, with 26" or 28" blued barrel, chrome-plated engraved receiver and hardwood stock. Introduced in 1985.

NIB	*Exc.*	*V.G.*	*Good*	*Fair*	*Poor*
120	80	80	60	50	40

Model 105 Deluxe

As above, with ventilated rib barrel. Checkered walnut stock.

NIB	*Exc.*	*V.G.*	*Good*	*Fair*	*Poor*
150	100	80	80	60	40

REPLICA LONG GUNS

Harpers Ferry Flint Rifle

Copy of 1803 rifle in original .54-caliber. Features rust blued 35" barrel. Weight 8.5 lbs.

NIB	*Exc.*	*V.G.*	*Good*	*Fair*	*Poor*
500	350	240	170	120	80

Harpers Ferry "Journey of Discovery Rifle"

Similar to Harpers Ferry Flint Rifle above, with oil-finished walnut stock and brass fittings. Brass patchbox engraved Lewis and Clark's 'Journey of Discovery'; 1803 to 1806". Introduced in 2003.

NIB	*Exc.*	*V.G.*	*Good*	*Fair*	*Poor*
600	420	290	210	140	100

Brown Bess Musket

Replica copy of second model used between 1760 and 1776. Bright finish on metal and one-piece walnut stock, with polished brass locks. Barrel length 42"; weight 9.5 lbs.

NIB	Exc.	V.G.	Good	Fair	Poor
600	420	290	210	140	100

Brown Bess Carbine

Same as above. Fitted with 30" barrel. Weight 7.75 lbs.

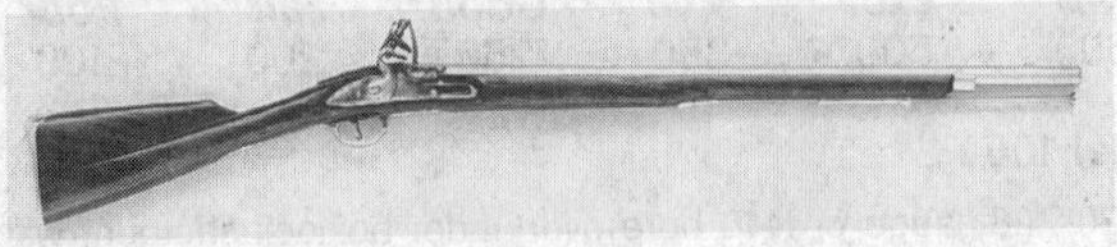

NIB	Exc.	V.G.	Good	Fair	Poor
600	420	290	210	140	100

1777 Charleville Musket

Copy of French flintlock in .69-caliber. Fittings are steel, with brass front sight and flashpan. Barrel length 44.625"; weight about 8.75 lbs

NIB	Exc.	V.G.	Good	Fair	Poor
650	460	320	220	160	110

1777 Standard Charleville Musket

Same as above, with polished steel barrel and select walnut stock.

NIB	Exc.	V.G.	Good	Fair	Poor
650	460	320	220	160	110

1816 M.T. Wickham Musket

Furnished in .69-caliber, with steel ramrod and button head. Brass flashpan and walnut stock standard.

NIB	Exc.	V.G.	Good	Fair	Poor
550	380	270	190	130	90

1808 Springfield Musket

A U.S. copy of 1763 Charleville musket, with 1808 Springfield markings. Barrel length 44"; weight 8.75 lbs.

NIB	Exc.	V.G.	Good	Fair	Poor
700	490	340	240	170	120

Pennsylvania Long Rifle

Offered in percussion or flintlock ignition. Choice of .32- or .45-caliber. Has octagonal 40.5" rust blued barrel, polished lock, double-set triggers and brass furniture on walnut stock. Weight 7.5 lbs.

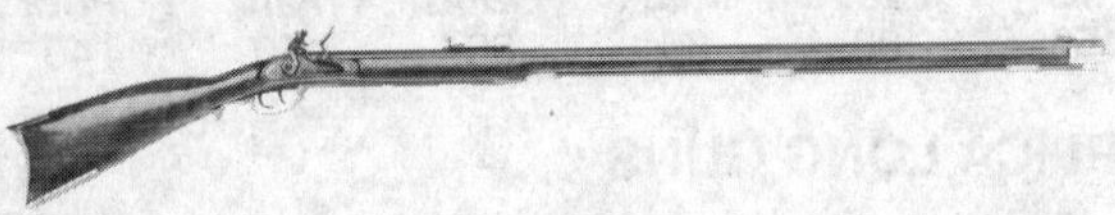

Percussion

NIB	Exc.	V.G.	Good	Fair	Poor
400	280	200	140	100	70

Flintlock

NIB	Exc.	V.G.	Good	Fair	Poor
420	280	200	140	100	70

Kentucky Rifle

Offered in percussion or flintlock ignition. Has blue steel barrel, case colored lockplate and polished brass patchbox inletted into walnut stock. Available in .45- or 50-caliber. Barrel length 35"; weight 6 lbs. 14 oz.

Percussion

NIB	Exc.	V.G.	Good	Fair	Poor
400	280	200	140	100	70

Flintlock

NIB	Exc.	V.G.	Good	Fair	Poor
380	260	180	130	90	60

Mortimer Flintlock Rifle

Offered in .54-caliber, with rust blued barrel, walnut stock with cheekpiece and checkered straight-grip. Has external safety and sling swivels. Barrel length 36"; weight 9 lbs. Optional shotgun barrel. Made by Pedersoli. Note: Add $240 for optional shotgun barrel.

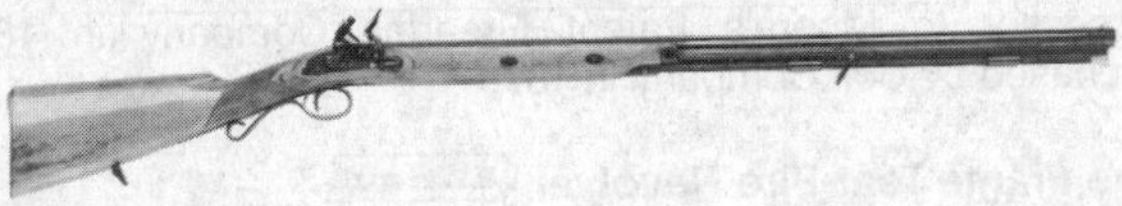

NIB	Exc.	V.G.	Good	Fair	Poor
700	490	340	240	170	120

Tryon Creedmoor Rifle

.45-caliber features heavy blued 33" octagonal barrel, hooded front sight, adjustable tang sight, double-set triggers, sling swivels and walnut stock. Weight about 9.5 lbs.

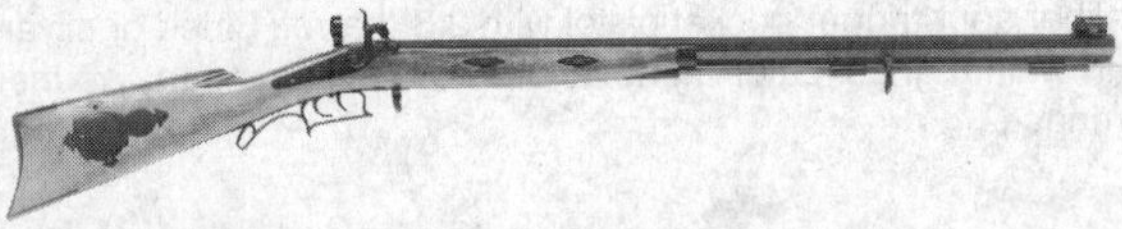

NIB	Exc.	V.G.	Good	Fair	Poor
600	420	290	210	140	100

Standard Tryon Rifle

Same as above, without target sights.

NIB	Exc.	V.G.	Good	Fair	Poor
650	460	320	220	160	110

Deluxe Tryon Rifle

Same as above, with polished and engraved lock and patchbox.

NIB	Exc.	V.G.	Good	Fair	Poor
620	440	310	210	150	100

Parker-Hale Whitworth Rifle

Replica of British sniper rifle in .451-caliber. Used by Confederates during Civil War. Round 36" barrel. Features globe front sight and ladder rear. Walnut stock hand-checkered. Weight 9 lbs. 10 oz. Note: Add $150 for limited edition telescope.

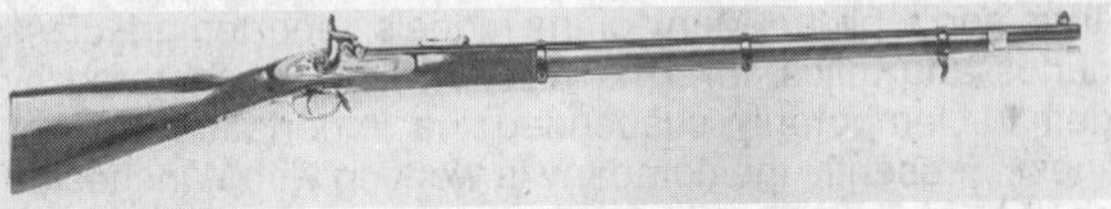

NIB	Exc.	V.G.	Good	Fair	Poor
680	470	330	230	160	110

Parker-Hale Volunteer Rifle

.451-caliber rifle, with hand-checkered walnut stock. Fitted with 32" barrel, with globe front sight and ladder rear. Weight 9.5 lbs.

NIB	Exc.	V.G.	Good	Fair	Poor
600	420	290	210	140	100

Parker-Hale 3 Band Volunteer Rifle

Same basic specifications as Whitworth rifle. Furnished with Alexander Henry rifling.

NIB	Exc.	V.G.	Good	Fair	Poor
500	350	240	170	120	80

Rigby Target Rifle

1880s replica chambered for .451-caliber. Fitted with adjustable front sight and vernier tang sight. Lock, breech plug, triggerguard, buttplate and escutcheons are case colored. Barrel length 32"; weight 7 lbs. 12 oz.

NIB	Exc.	V.G.	Good	Fair	Poor
450	320	220	150	110	80

1861 Springfield Rifle

.58-caliber replica. Fitted with 1855-style hammer. Barrel length 40"; weight 10 lbs. 4 oz.

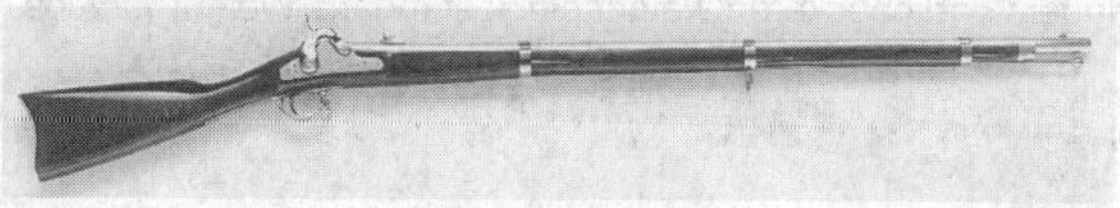

NIB	Exc.	V.G.	Good	Fair	Poor
350	240	170	120	80	60

Model 1873 Springfield Officer's Trapdoor

Features single-set trigger, case colored breech-block, deluxe walnut stock, adjustable rear peep sight with Beech front sight. Chambered for .45-70 cartridge. Fitted with 26" round barrel. Weight about 8 lbs. Introduced in 2003.

NIB	Exc.	V.G.	Good	Fair	Poor
900	750	500	350	300	200

1862 C.S. Richmond Rifle

Confederate rifle is .58-caliber. Faithful reproduction of those produced at Richmond Armory. Barrel length 40"; weight 10 lbs. 4 oz.

NIB	Exc.	V.G.	Good	Fair	Poor
420	300	210	150	100	70

J.P. Murray Carbine

Confederate cavalry .58-caliber carbine. Has case colored lock and brass furniture on walnut stock. Barrel length 23.5"; weight 8 lbs. 5 oz.

NIB	Exc.	V.G.	Good	Fair	Poor
320	230	160	110	80	60

1863 Springfield Rifle

Exact replica of famous Springfield Musket. Barrel length 40", with 3 barrel bands. All metal parts are finished bright. Weight 9.5 lbs.

NIB	Exc.	V.G.	Good	Fair	Poor
420	300	210	150	100	70

1841 Mississippi Rifle

Also known as "Yager" rifle. Offered in .54- or .58-caliber. Barrel length 33"; weight 9.5 lbs.

NIB	Exc.	V.G.	Good	Fair	Poor
320	230	160	110	80	60

Zouave Rifle

Civil War replica is .58-caliber. Polished brass hardware and blued 33" barrel. Weight 9 lbs.

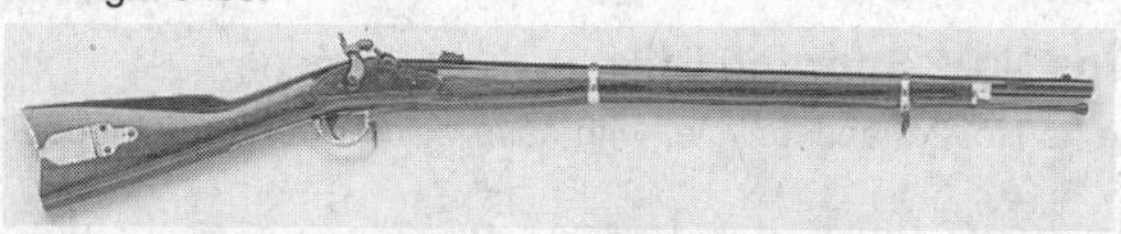

NIB	Exc.	V.G.	Good	Fair	Poor
320	230	160	110	80	60

Parker-Hale 1861 Musketoon

Made by Gibbs Rifle Company using 130-year-old gauges for reference. This .577-caliber replica features 24" barrel, with folding ladder military sight. Stock is walnut and lock case colored. All furniture polished brass. Weight 7.5 lbs.

NIB	Exc.	V.G.	Good	Fair	Poor
320	230	160	110	80	60

Navy Arms Musketoon

Same as above. Manufactured in Italy.

NIB	Exc.	V.G.	Good	Fair	Poor
320	230	160	110	80	60

Parker-Hale 1858 Two Band Musket

.577-caliber model based on 1858 Enfield naval pattern. Fitted with military sight graduated to 1,100 yards. Case colored lock. Walnut stock with brass fittings. Barrel length 33"; weight 8.5 lbs.

NIB	Exc.	V.G.	Good	Fair	Poor
420	300	210	150	100	70

Navy Arms 1858 Two Band Musket

Same as above. Built in Italy.

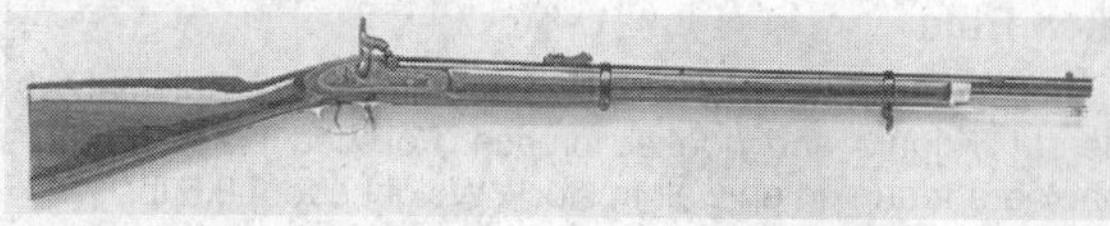

NIB	Exc.	V.G.	Good	Fair	Poor
320	230	160	110	80	60

Parker-Hale Three Band Musket

Replica based on design produced between 1853 and 1863. Rear sight based on an 1853 model graduated to 900 yards. Fitted with case colored lock. Walnut stock with brass furniture. Barrel length 39"; weight 9 lbs.

NIB	Exc.	V.G.	Good	Fair	Poor
480	330	230	160	110	80

Navy Arms Three Band Musket

Same as above. Produced in Italy.

NIB	Exc.	V.G.	Good	Fair	Poor
350	240	170	120	80	60

Navy Arms Revolving Carbine

Fitted with 20" barrel. Chambered for .357 Magnum, .44-40 or .45 Colt cartridge. Has revolving 6-shot cylinder. Straight-grip stock with brass buttplate and triggerguard. Action based on Remington Model 1874 revolver. Introduced in 1968; discontinued 1984.

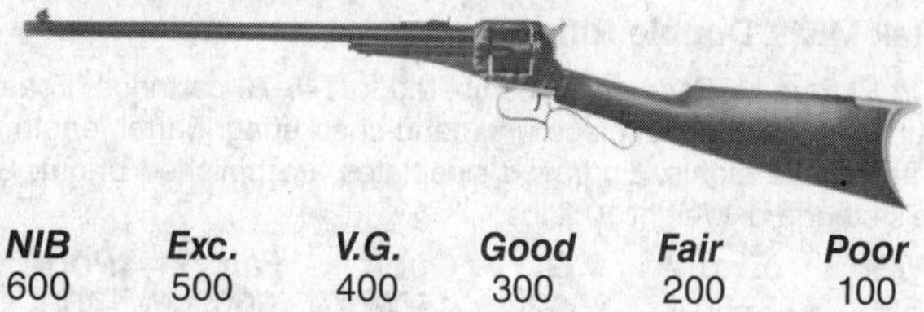

NIB	Exc.	V.G.	Good	Fair	Poor
600	500	400	300	200	100

1859 Sharps Infantry Rifle

.54-caliber copy of three band Sharps. Barrel length 30". Case-hardened receiver and patchbox. Blued barrel and walnut stock. Weight about 8.5 lbs.

NIB	Exc.	V.G.	Good	Fair	Poor
800	560	390	270	190	130

1859 Berdan Sharps Rifle

Similar to 1859 Sharps, with double-set triggers.

NIB	Exc.	V.G.	Good	Fair	Poor
900	630	440	310	220	150

Ithaca/Navy Hawken Rifle

Offered in .50- or. 54-caliber percussion. Features 31.5" rust blued octagon barrel. Percussion lockplate case colored. Rest of hardware blued, with exception of nose cap and escutcheons. Weight about 9 lbs. 13 oz.

NIB	Exc.	V.G.	Good	Fair	Poor
300	210	150	100	70	50

Hawken Rifle

Features case colored lock, 28" blued octagon barrel, adjustable sights, double-set triggers and hooked breech. Polished brass furniture and patchbox are mounted on walnut stock. Weight about 8.5 lbs.

NIB	Exc.	V.G.	Good	Fair	Poor
200	140	100	70	50	30

Hawken Hunter Rifle

Offered in .50-, .54- or .58-caliber. Features blued hardware, adjustable sights, case colored lock and hooked breech. Walnut stock hand-checkered, with cheekpiece. Rubber recoil pad standard. Barrel length 28".

NIB	Exc.	V.G.	Good	Fair	Poor
200	140	100	70	50	30

Hawken Hunter Carbine

Same as above. Fitted with 22.5" barrel. Weight about 6 lbs. 12 oz.

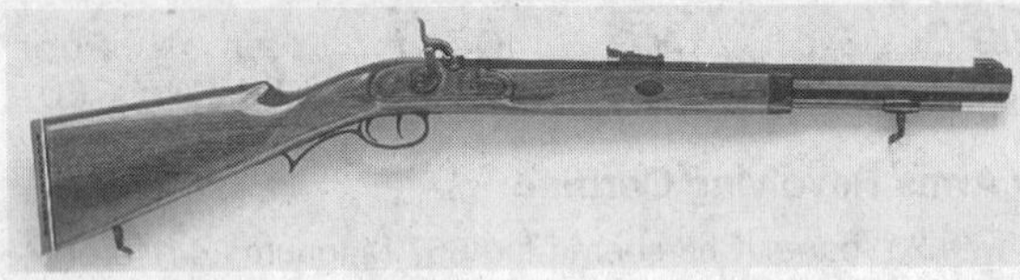

NIB	Exc.	V.G.	Good	Fair	Poor
200	140	100	70	50	30

Kodiak MKIV Double Rifle

Built in Europe by Pedersoli. Chambered for .45-70 cartridge. Features walnut stock, with cheekpiece and hand-checkering. Barrel length 24", with adjustable sights. Engraved sideplates are polished bright. Sling swivels standard. Weight 10.2 lbs.

NIB	Exc.	V.G.	Good	Fair	Poor
4500	3350	2500	1500	600	400

Mortimer Flintlock or Percussion Shotgun

Replica of 12-gauge English Mortimer. Features waterproof pan, roller frizzen (flintlock only), external safety. All parts case colored. Barrel length 36"; weight 7 lbs.

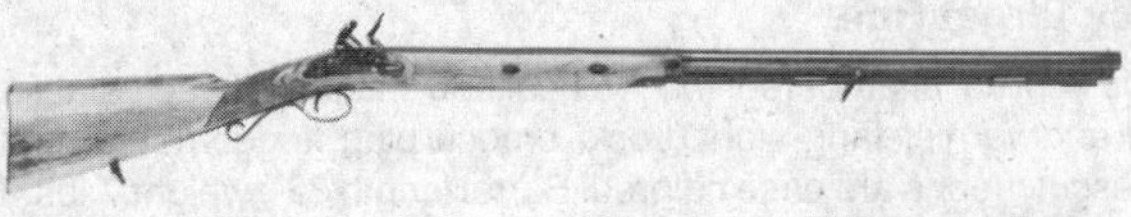

NIB	Exc.	V.G.	Good	Fair	Poor
980	800	600	500	400	200

Fowler Shotgun

12-gauge side-by-side, with straight-grip stock. Features hooked breech and 28" blued barrels. Sideplates are engraved and case colored. Double triggers and checkered walnut stock standard. Weight 7.25 lbs.

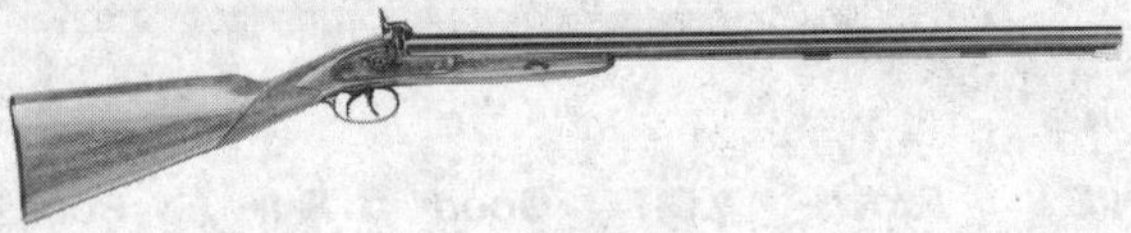

NIB	Exc.	V.G.	Good	Fair	Poor
550	400	300	250	200	100

Navy Arms Steel Shot Magnum

Same as above in 10-gauge. Weight 7 lbs. 9 oz.

NIB	Exc.	V.G.	Good	Fair	Poor
580	400	300	120	100	80

T&T Shotgun

Turkey and trap have straight-grip stock and 28" barrel choked Full and Full. Locks are case colored and engraved. Checkered walnut stock. Weight 7.5 lbs.

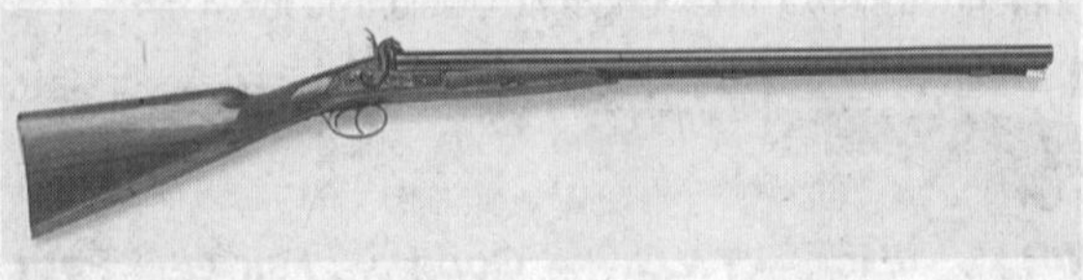

NIB	Exc.	V.G.	Good	Fair	Poor
400	280	200	140	100	70

Japanese Tanegashima Matchlock

A .50-caliber, with 41" barrels. Weight 8.5 lbs.

NIB	Exc.	V.G.	Good	Fair	Poor
800	560	390	270	190	130

SINGLE-SHOT CARTRIDGE RIFLES

1873 Sharps No. 2 Creedmoor

Chambered for .45-70 cartridge. Fitted with 30" round barrel. Polished nickel receiver. Target-grade rear tang sight and globe front, with inserts. Checkered walnut stock, with pistol grip. Weight about 10 lbs. Introduced in 2002.

NIB	Exc.	V.G.	Good	Fair	Poor
1430	1000	750	550	380	200

Sharps No. 2 Silhouette Rifle

Identical to standard No. 2, with full octagon barrel. Weight about 10.5 lbs. Introduced in 2003.

NIB	Exc.	V.G.	Good	Fair	Poor
1320	1000	750	550	380	200

Sharps No. 2 Sporting Rifle

Same as No. 2 standard rifle, with case colored receiver. Introduced in 2003.

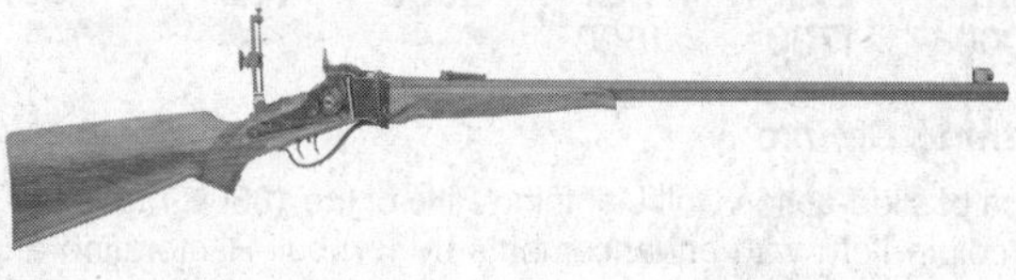

NIB	Exc.	V.G.	Good	Fair	Poor
1420	1000	750	550	380	200

1873 Sharps Quigley

Chambered for .45-70 cartridge. Fitted with heavy 34" octagon barrel. Case-hardened receiver with military patchbox. Open sights. Weight about 13 lbs. Introduced in 2002.

NIB	Exc.	V.G.	Good	Fair	Poor
1600	1250	900	620	400	220

1874 Sharps Infantry Rifle

Fitted with 30" round barrel. Chambered for .45-70 cartridge. Blued barrel, with case-hardened receiver. Walnut stock, with 3 barrel bands. Weight about 8.5 lbs.

NIB	Exc.	V.G.	Good	Fair	Poor
1150	800	600	400	300	150

1874 Sharps Sniper Rifle

Same as 1874 Infantry rifle, with double-set triggers.

NIB	Exc.	V.G.	Good	Fair	Poor
1200	850	650	450	320	150

Sharps Cavalry Carbine

Breech-loading .54-caliber carbine, with 22" blued barrel. Military-style sights, walnut stock and saddle bar with ring are standard. Weight 7 lbs. 12 oz.

NIB	Exc.	V.G.	Good	Fair	Poor
1050	800	600	400	300	150

Sharps Cavalry Carbine Cartridge Model

Same as above. Chambered for .45-70 Government cartridge.

NIB	Exc.	V.G.	Good	Fair	Poor
1150	800	600	400	300	150

1874 Sharps Plains Rifle

Features case colored receiver, blued barrel and checkered walnut stock. Offered in .44-70 or .54-caliber percussion. Barrel length 28.5"; weight 8 lbs. 10 oz.

NIB	Exc.	V.G.	Good	Fair	Poor
800	560	390	270	190	130

1874 Sharps Sporting Rifle

Similar to above. Features full pistol grip, 32" medium weight octagonal barrel, double-set triggers and case colored frame. Weight about 10.75 lbs.

NIB	Exc.	V.G.	Good	Fair	Poor
1000	700	490	340	240	170

1874 Sharps Buffalo Rifle

Chambered for .45-70 or .45-90 cartridge. Fitted with 28" heavy octagon barrel. Buttstock checkered. Weight about 12 lbs.

NIB	Exc.	V.G.	Good	Fair	Poor
1320	1000	750	550	380	200

1874 Sharps No. 3 Long Range Rifle

Built by Pedersoli. Fitted with 34" medium weight octagon barrel, globe target front sight and match-grade rear tang sight. Double-set trigger. Case-hardened frame. Walnut stock. Weight about 11 lbs.

NIB	Exc.	V.G.	Good	Fair	Poor
2000	1600	1200	900	750	400

Rolling Block Buffalo Rifle

Replica of Remington Buffalo rifle. Fitted with 26" or 30" octagonal or half octagonal barrel, case colored receiver, blade front sight and notch rear, brass triggerguard and walnut stocks. Tang drilled and tapped for tang sight.

NIB	Exc.	V.G.	Good	Fair	Poor
750	600	480	300	200	100

Half Octagon Barrel Model

NIB	Exc.	V.G.	Good	Fair	Poor
750	600	480	300	200	100

"John Bodine" Rolling Block Rifle

Chambered for .45-70 cartridge. Fitted with 30 octagon barrel. Double-set triggers. Match-grade rear tang sight. Weight about 12 lbs. Introduced in 2002.

NIB	Exc.	V.G.	Good	Fair	Poor
1550	1150	800	580	350	200

1885 High Wall

Chambered for .45-70 cartridge. Fitted with 30" medium heavy octagon barrel. Case colored receiver, target sights and walnut stocks. Also available with 28" round barrel. Note: Deduct $100 for Buckhorn sights; $60 for 28" barrel.

NIB	Exc.	V.G.	Good	Fair	Poor
900	720	600	500	400	200

1873 Springfield Infantry Rifle

Copy of Trapdoor Springfield. Chambered for .45-70. Fitted with 32.5" barrel. Walnut stock. Case-hardened breechlock. Weight about 8.25 lbs.

NIB	Exc.	V.G.	Good	Fair	Poor
980	800	600	500	400	200

1873 Springfield Cavalry Carbine

Same as above, with 22" barrel. Weight about 7 lbs.

NIB	Exc.	V.G.	Good	Fair	Poor
880	700	600	500	400	200

REPLICA LEVER-ACTION RIFLES

1873 Winchester Rifle

Replica features case colored receiver, blued octagon 24" barrel and walnut stocks. Offered in .44-40 or .45 Long Colt. Weight about 8 lbs. 4 oz.

NIB	Exc.	V.G.	Good	Fair	Poor
900	720	600	500	400	200

1873 Winchester Carbine

Same specifications as rifle. Fitted with 19" round barrel, blued receiver and saddle ring. Weight 7 lbs. 4 oz.

NIB	Exc.	V.G.	Good	Fair	Poor
900	720	600	500	400	200

1873 Winchester Sporting Rifle

Features 24.25" octagonal barrel, case colored receiver and checkered pistol grip. Offered in .44-40 or. 45 Long Colt. Weight about 8 lbs. 14 oz.

NIB	Exc.	V.G.	Good	Fair	Poor
950	750	650	520	400	200

1873 Sporting Long Range Rifle

Similar to Winchester Sporting Rifle. Chambered for .44-40 cartridge. Fitted with 30" octagon barrel. Long-range rear tang sight. Weight about 7.5 lbs. Introduced in 2002.

NIB	Exc.	V.G.	Good	Fair	Poor
1080	850	750	620	500	250

1873 Border Model

Introduced in 2000. Features 20" blued octagon barrel, with buckhorn rear sight. Magazine capacity 10 rounds. Walnut checkered pistol grip stock, with oil-finish. Chambered for .357 Magnum, .44-40 or .45 Colt cartridge.

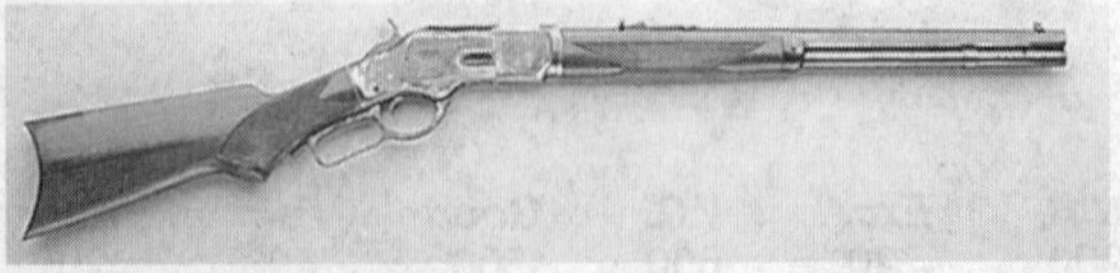

NIB	Exc.	V.G.	Good	Fair	Poor
980	800	700	550	450	220

Winchester/Turnbull Model 1873 Rifle

Available exclusively from Navy Arms, this is a faithful reproduction of the "Gun That Won The West". Chambered in .45 Colt or .357 Magnum, with a Turnbull color case-hardened frame, deluxe checkered American walnut stock and forend, 20" or 24.250" octagonal barrel, semi-buckhorn rear and gold bead front sight. Introduced in 2014.

NIB	Exc.	V.G.	Good	Fair	Poor
2250	1800	1600	1200	900	450

Winchester Model 1873 Centennial Rifle

Two variations of High-Grade Model 1873 rifles made to celebrate the centennial of the Cody Firearms Museum. Detailed description in previous editions. 1,000 Presentation Models originally sold at $3,500. 200 Exhibition Models originally sold at $8,000.

Winchester Model 1892 Coyote Killer

Like Model 1873 rifle created by Winchester and Turnbull, this Model 1892 has a Grade 1 American walnut checkered stock and forend, bone-charcoal color case-hardened frame, Marble's semi-buckhorn rear and gold bead front sight mounted on a full octagonal barrel. Chambered in .44 Magnum or .45 Colt. Barrel length 20"; weight 6 lbs. Introduced in 2016.

NIB	Exc.	V.G.	Good	Fair	Poor
2000	1700	1500	—	—	—

Lightning Deluxe

Replica of slide-action Colt Lightning Rifle of the 1880s, made by Davide Pedersoli in Italy, with enhancements by Turnbull Restoration and Mfg. Co. Chambered in .357 Magnum or .45 Colt. Features include hand-selected and expertly checkered Grade 1 American walnut stock and forend, bone-charcoal color case-hardened receiver, high-polish full octagonal barrel in 20" or 24". Sights are semi-buckhorn rear and gold bead dovetail front. Introduced in 2016.

NIB	Exc.	V.G.	Good	Fair	Poor
1950	1750	1450	—	—	—

Lightning Slide Action

Standard model of Deluxe model, made by Pedersoli. Imported from 2010 to 2012. Same features with standard walnut stock and case colored finish.

NIB	Exc.	V.G.	Good	Fair	Poor
1000	850	700	550	450	300

1866 "Yellowboy" Rifle

Features brass receiver, 24 octagon barrel and walnut stocks. Weight 8.5 lbs.

NIB	Exc.	V.G.	Good	Fair	Poor
850	680	520	450	300	150

1866 "Yellowboy" Carbine

Same as above. Fitted with 19 round barrel and saddle ring. Weight 7 lbs. 4 oz.

NIB	Exc.	V.G.	Good	Fair	Poor
850	680	520	450	300	150

1866 "Yellowboy" Short Rifle

Introduced in 2000. Features 20 barrel with buckhorn rear sight. Walnut stock with oil-finish. Receiver is yellow brass. Chambered for .38 Special, .44-40 or .45 Colt cartridge. Magazine capacity 10 rounds.

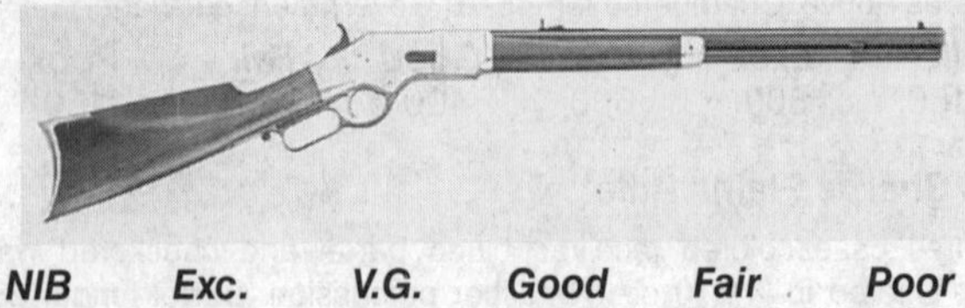

NIB	Exc.	V.G.	Good	Fair	Poor
850	680	520	450	300	150

Iron Frame Henry

Replica of famous and rare .44-40 Iron Frame Henry. Features case colored frame. Barrel length 24"; weight 9 lbs.

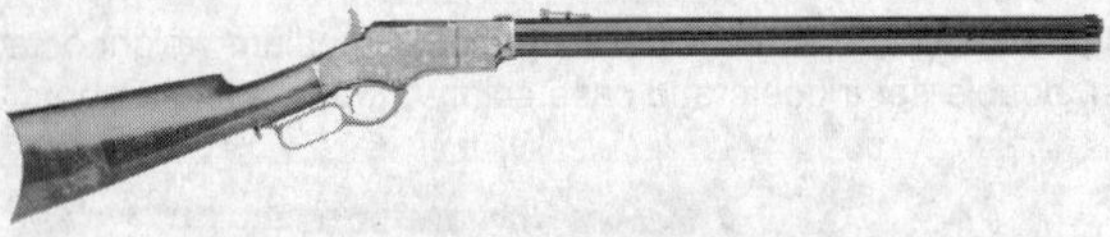

NIB	Exc.	V.G.	Good	Fair	Poor
920	750	650	500	400	200

Blued Iron Frame Henry

Same as above. Furnished with highly polished blued receiver.

NIB	Exc.	V.G.	Good	Fair	Poor
920	750	650	500	400	200

Military Henry

Based on brass frame military version of Henry rifle. Furnished with sling swivels mounted on left side. Buttplate fitted with trap door. Caliber .44-40; barrel length 24"; weight 9 lbs. 4 oz.

NIB	Exc.	V.G.	Good	Fair	Poor
900	720	620	500	400	200

Henry Carbine

Brass frame carbine version. Features 22" barrel. Chambered for .44-40 cartridge. Weight 8 lbs. 12 oz.

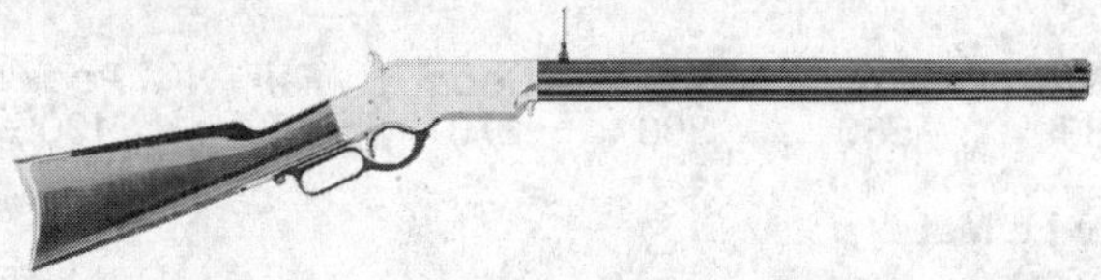

NIB	Exc.	V.G.	Good	Fair	Poor
880	700	600	500	400	200

Henry Trapper

Replica not based on actual Henry. Fitted with unique 16.5" barrel. Brass frame model. Weight 7 lbs. 7 oz. Chambered for .44-40 cartridge.

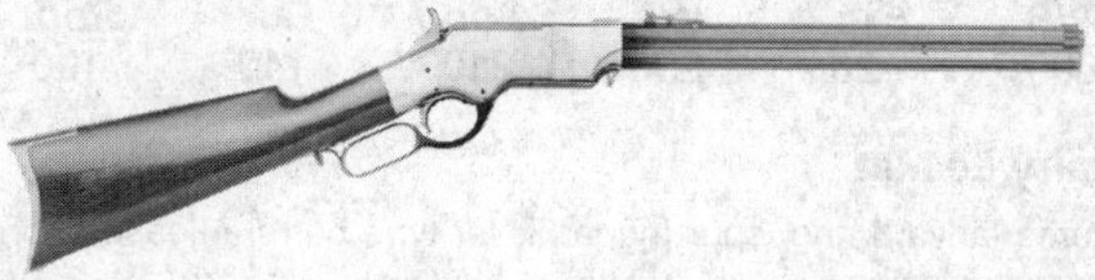

NIB	Exc.	V.G.	Good	Fair	Poor
880	700	600	500	400	200

1892 Rifle

Lever-action rifle chambered for .357 Magnum, .44-40, .45 Colt or .32-20 cartridge. Octagon 24.25" barrel. Walnut stock, crescent butt and blued or case colored receiver. Weight about 6.25 lbs.

NIB	Exc.	V.G.	Good	Fair	Poor
520	420	350	300	250	200

1892 Short Rifle

Same as above, with 20" octagon barrel. Weight about 6.25 lbs.

NIB	Exc.	V.G.	Good	Fair	Poor
520	420	350	300	250	200

1892 Carbine

Similar to short rifle. Fitted with 20" round barrel. Saddle ring on left side of receiver. Weight about 5.75 lbs.

NIB	Exc.	V.G.	Good	Fair	Poor
450	350	300	250	200	150

1892 Brass Frame Carbine

Same as above, with polished brass receiver.

NIB	Exc.	V.G.	Good	Fair	Poor
450	350	300	250	200	150

1892 Brass Frame Rifle

Same as carbine, with polished brass receiver.

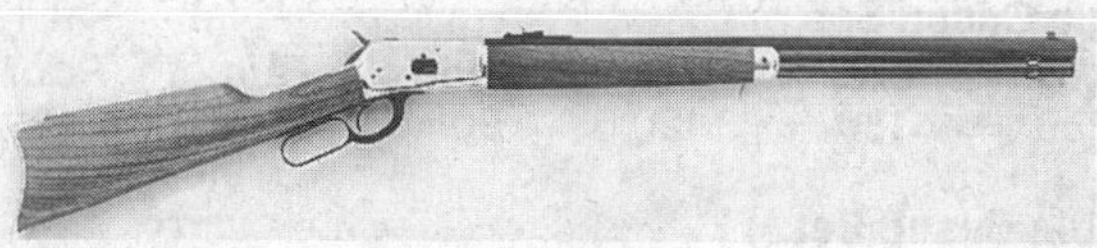

NIB	Exc.	V.G.	Good	Fair	Poor
520	420	350	300	250	200

No. 2 Creedmoor Target Rifle

Reproduction of Remington No. 2 Creedmoor. Features case colored receiver, tapered 30" octagonal barrel, hooded front sight, Creedmoor tang sight and walnut stock, with checkered pistol grip. Furnished in .45-70 Government. Weight 9 lbs.

NIB	Exc.	V.G.	Good	Fair	Poor
900	720	620	500	400	200

HANDGUNS

Le Page Pistol

.44-caliber percussion pistol. Has 10.25" tapered octagon barrel, adjustable single-set trigger. Lock, triggerguard and buttcap engraved. Hand-checkered walnut stocks. Weight 36 oz.

NIB	Exc.	V.G.	Good	Fair	Poor
380	260	180	130	90	60

Single Cased Set

NIB	Exc.	V.G.	Good	Fair	Poor
500	350	240	170	120	80

Double Cased Set

NIB	Exc.	V.G.	Good	Fair	Poor
900	630	440	310	220	150

Flintlock

Same as above, with flintlock ignition. Weight 41 oz.

NIB	Exc.	V.G.	Good	Fair	Poor
420	300	210	150	100	70

Smoothbore Flintlock Pistol

Same as above, with smoothbore.

NIB	Exc.	V.G.	Good	Fair	Poor
420	300	210	150	100	70

Smoothbore Flintlock Pistol Single Cased Set

NIB	Exc.	V.G.	Good	Fair	Poor
280	190	140	90	70	50

Smoothbore Flintlock Pistol Double Cased Set

NIB	Exc.	V.G.	Good	Fair	Poor
450	320	220	150	110	80

Kentucky Pistol

Percussion replica of a pistol developed in 1840s. Has 10.125" blued barrel, case colored lock, brass furniture and triggerguard, with walnut stock. Weight 32 oz.

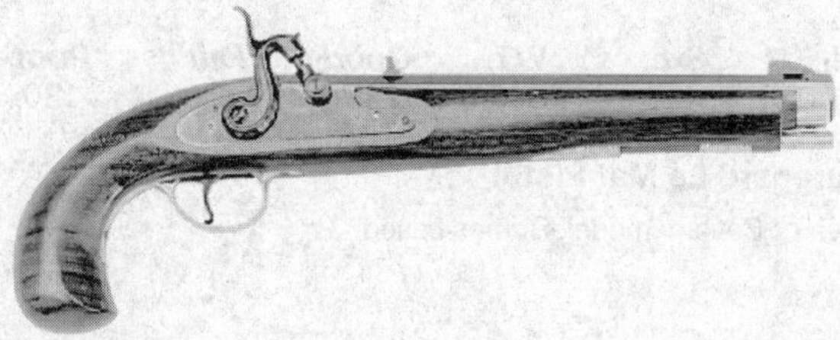

NIB	Exc.	V.G.	Good	Fair	Poor
200	140	100	70	50	30

Single Cased Set

NIB	Exc.	V.G.	Good	Fair	Poor
250	180	120	90	60	40

Double Cased Set

NIB	Exc.	V.G.	Good	Fair	Poor
450	320	220	150	110	80

Flintlock Pistol

Same as above, with flintlock ignition.

NIB	Exc.	V.G.	Good	Fair	Poor
180	120	90	60	40	30

Flintlock Pistol Single Cased Set

NIB	Exc.	V.G.	Good	Fair	Poor
350	280	220	180	120	80

Flintlock Pistol Double Cased Set

NIB	Exc.	V.G.	Good	Fair	Poor
550	450	350	280	180	100

Harpers Ferry Pistol

Has .58-caliber rifled 10" barrel. Case-hardened lock and walnut stock. Weight about 39 oz.

NIB	Exc.	V.G.	Good	Fair	Poor
250	180	120	90	60	40

Pistol Single Cased Set

NIB	Exc.	V.G.	Good	Fair	Poor
280	190	140	90	70	50

LE MAT PISTOLS

18th Georgia Le Mat Pistol

9-shot .44-caliber percussion revolver has 7.625" blued barrel and engraved cylinder. Engraved banner on left side of frame reads "DEO VINDICE". Hammer and trigger case colored. Stock checkered walnut. Comes with Le Mat mould and velvet draped French fitted case. Weight 55 oz.

NIB	Exc.	V.G.	Good	Fair	Poor
700	490	340	240	170	120

Beauregard Le Mat Pistol

Replica of Cavalry model. Comes cased.

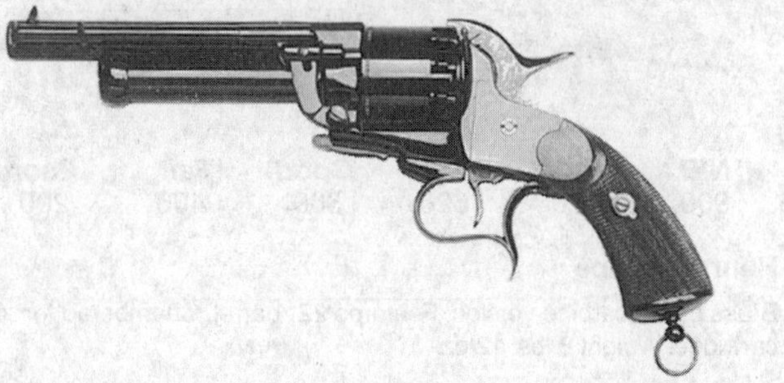

NIB	Exc.	V.G.	Good	Fair	Poor
800	560	390	270	190	130

Navy Le Mat

Features knurled pin barrel release and spur barrel selector.

NIB	Exc.	V.G.	Good	Fair	Poor
600	420	290	210	140	100

Army Le Mat

Features knurled pin barrel release and cross pin barrel selector.

NIB	Exc.	V.G.	Good	Fair	Poor
600	420	290	210	140	100

Cavalry Le Mat

Features lanyard ring, spur trigger, lever type barrel release and cross pin barrel selector.

NIB	Exc.	V.G.	Good	Fair	Poor
600	420	290	210	140	100

Starr Double-Action Model 1858 Army

Double-action revolver chambered for .44-caliber. Fitted with 6" barrel. Blued finish. Weight about 48 oz.

NIB	Exc.	V.G.	Good	Fair	Poor
250	180	120	90	60	40

Starr Single-Action Model 1863 Army

Fitted with 8" barrel. Chambered for .44-caliber. Blued finish and walnut stock. Weight about 48 oz.

NIB	Exc.	V.G.	Good	Fair	Poor
250	180	120	90	60	40

1862 New Model Police

Replica based on Colt .36-caliber pocket pistol of the same name. Features half fluted and re-dated cylinder. Case colored frame and loading gate. Polished brass triggerguard and backstrap. Barrel length 5.5"; weight 26 oz.

NIB	Exc.	V.G.	Good	Fair	Poor
250	180	120	90	60	40

1862 New Model Book-Style Cased Set

NIB	Exc.	V.G.	Good	Fair	Poor
250	180	120	90	60	40

Paterson Revolver

Replica is 5-shot .36-caliber. Cylinder scroll engraved with stagecoach scene. Hidden trigger drops down when hammer is cocked. Barrel length 9"; weight 43 oz.

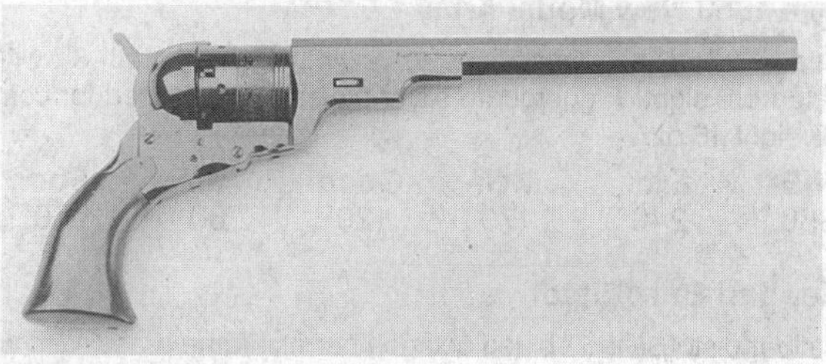

NIB	Exc.	V.G.	Good	Fair	Poor
420	300	210	150	100	70

Engraved Paterson Revolver

Features hand engraving with silver inlays.

NIB	Exc.	V.G.	Good	Fair	Poor
480	330	230	160	110	80

1851 Navy

Colt replica offered in .36- or .44-caliber. Naval battle scene engraved in cylinder. Octagon 7.5" barrel. Triggerguard and backstrap polished brass. Walnut grips are hand-rubbed. Weight 32 oz. Note: Add $100 for optional shoulder stock.

NIB	Exc.	V.G.	Good	Fair	Poor
250	180	120	90	60	40

Single Cased Set

NIB	Exc.	V.G.	Good	Fair	Poor
280	190	140	90	70	50

Double Cased Set

NIB	Exc.	V.G.	Good	Fair	Poor
450	320	220	150	110	80

1851 Navy Conversion

Replica of Colt 1851 Navy cartridge conversion. Offered in .38 Special or .38 Long Colt. Choice of 5.5" or 7.5" barrels. Weight about 40 oz.

NIB	Exc.	V.G.	Good	Fair	Poor
480	420	350	250	150	100

Augusta 1851 Navy Pistol

Available with 5" or 7.5" barrel. Engraved with "A" coverage.

NIB	Exc.	V.G.	Good	Fair	Poor
250	180	120	90	60	40

Model 1851 Navy Frontiersman

Introduced in 2003. Features 5" .36-caliber barrel. Receiver, loading lever and hammer case colored. Barrel and cylinder charcoal blued. Fitted with German silver backstrap and walnut grips.

NIB	Exc.	V.G.	Good	Fair	Poor
250	180	120	90	60	40

Reb Model 1860 Pistol

Replica of Confederate Griswold and Gunnison revolver. Features blued round 7.5" barrel. Brass frame, triggerguard and backstrap. Offered in .36- or .44-caliber. Weight 44 oz.

NIB	Exc.	V.G.	Good	Fair	Poor
150	100	70	50	40	20

Reb 1860 Sheriff's Model

Same as above. Fitted with 5" barrel. Weight 40 oz.

NIB	Exc.	V.G.	Good	Fair	Poor
150	100	70	50	40	20

1847 Walker Dragoon

Replica of rare Colt .44-caliber revolver. Barrel and cylinder blued. Frame and loading lever case colored. Barrel length 9"; weight 75 oz.

NIB	Exc.	V.G.	Good	Fair	Poor
320	230	160	110	80	60

Single Cased Set

NIB	Exc.	V.G.	Good	Fair	Poor
380	260	180	130	90	60

Single Deluxe Cased Set

NIB	Exc.	V.G.	Good	Fair	Poor
450	320	220	150	110	80

1860 Army Pistol

.44-caliber features case colored frame and loading lever. Blued barrel, cylinder and backstrap. Triggerguard brass. Cylinder engraved with battle scene. Barrel length 8"; weight 41 oz.

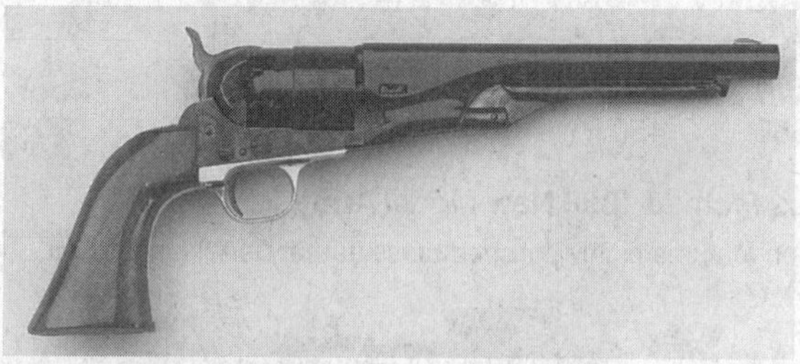

NIB	Exc.	V.G.	Good	Fair	Poor
250	180	120	90	60	40

Single Cased Set

NIB	Exc.	V.G.	Good	Fair	Poor
280	190	140	90	70	50

Double Cased Set

NIB	Exc.	V.G.	Good	Fair	Poor
450	320	220	150	110	80

1860 Army Conversion

Chambered for .38 Special or .38 Long Colt. Fitted with 5.5" or 7.5" barrel. Blued finish. Walnut grips. Weight about 40 oz.

NIB	Exc.	V.G.	Good	Fair	Poor
420	300	210	150	100	70

1858 New Model Remington-Style Pistol

Replica has solid frame as did original. Frame and 8" barrel blued. Triggerguard brass. Walnut grips standard. Weight 40 oz.

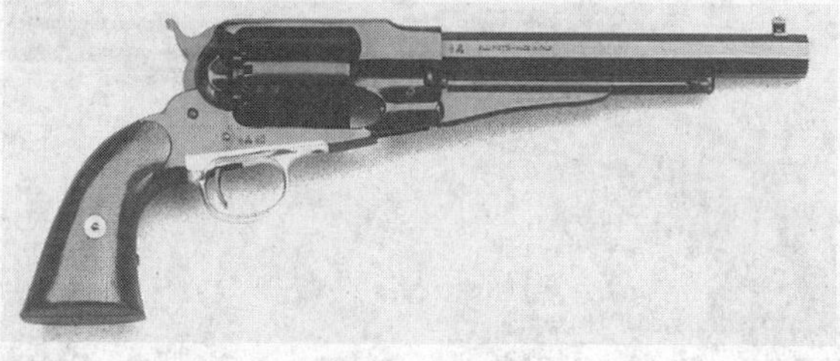

NIB	Exc.	V.G.	Good	Fair	Poor
250	180	120	90	60	40

Single Cased Set

NIB	Exc.	V.G.	Good	Fair	Poor
320	230	160	110	80	60

Double Cased Set

NIB	Exc.	V.G.	Good	Fair	Poor
450	320	220	150	110	80

Stainless Steel 1858 New Model Army

Same as above in stainless steel. Weight 40 oz.

NIB	Exc.	V.G.	Good	Fair	Poor
380	280	220	150	100	80

Single Cased Set

NIB	Exc.	V.G.	Good	Fair	Poor
380	280	220	150	100	80

Double Cased Set

NIB	Exc.	V.G.	Good	Fair	Poor
550	450	380	280	200	10

Brass Framed 1858 New Model Army

Version features highly polished brass frame. Barrel length 7.75".

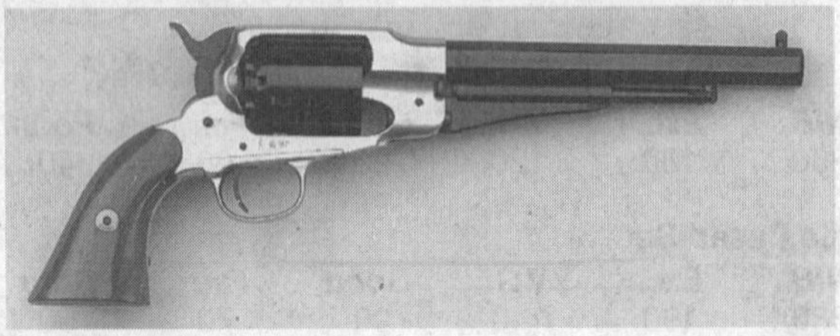

NIB	Exc.	V.G.	Good	Fair	Poor
150	100	70	50	40	20

Single Cased Set

NIB	Exc.	V.G.	Good	Fair	Poor
200	140	100	70	50	30

Double Cased Set

NIB	Exc.	V.G.	Good	Fair	Poor
320	230	160	110	80	60

1858 Target Model

Same as above. Features patridge front sight and adjustable rear. Barrel length 8".

NIB	Exc.	V.G.	Good	Fair	Poor
250	180	120	90	60	40

Deluxe 1858 New Model Army

Replica built to exact dimensions as original. Barrel length 8", with adjustable front sight. Triggerguard silver plated. Action tuned for competition. Weight 46 oz.

NIB	Exc.	V.G.	Good	Fair	Poor
350	240	170	120	80	60

Spiller and Burr Pistol

.36-caliber pistol, with 7" blued octagon barrel. Frame brass, with walnut grips. Weight 40 oz.

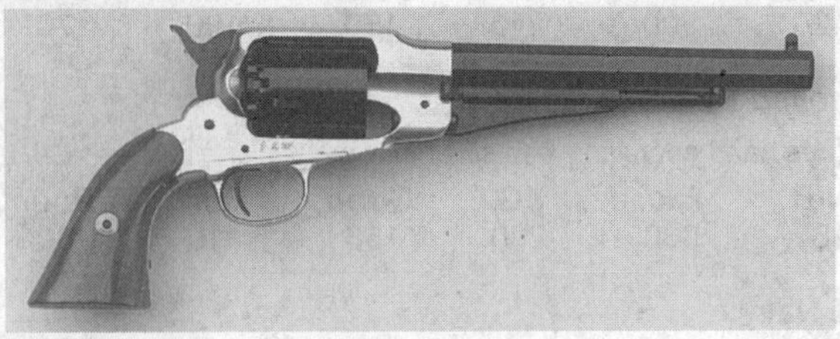

NIB	Exc.	V.G.	Good	Fair	Poor
300	210	150	100	70	50

Single Cased Set

NIB	Exc.	V.G.	Good	Fair	Poor
320	230	160	110	80	60

Double Cased Set

NIB	Exc.	V.G.	Good	Fair	Poor
400	280	200	140	100	70

Rogers and Spencer

Features 7.5" blued barrel and frame. Offered in .44-caliber. Walnut grips. Weight 48 oz.

NIB	Exc.	V.G.	Good	Fair	Poor
300	210	150	100	70	50

"London Gray" Rogers and Spencer Pistol

Same as above, with burnished satin chrome finish.

NIB	Exc.	V.G.	Good	Fair	Poor
300	210	150	100	70	50

Rogers and Spencer Target Model

Same as standard. Fitted with adjustable target sights.

NIB	Exc.	V.G.	Good	Fair	Poor
320	230	160	110	80	60

1861 Navy Conversion

Replica of cartridge conversion 1861 Navy. Chambered for .38 Special or .38 Long Colt. Fitted with 5.5" or 7.5" barrel. Weight about 40 oz.

NIB	Exc.	V.G.	Good	Fair	Poor
480	420	350	250	150	100

1872 Colt Open Top

Features 5.5" or 7.5" barrel. Case-hardened frame. Blued barrel and cylinder. Silver-plated brass triggerguard and backstrap. Walnut grips. Chambered for .38-caliber cartridge. Weight about 40 oz.

NIB	Exc.	V.G.	Good	Fair	Poor
500	380	220	180	150	120

1873 Colt-Style Single-Action Army

Replica features case colored frame and hammer. Blued round barrel in 3", 4.75", 5.5" or 7.5" lengths. Triggerguard and cylinder blued. Offered in .44-40, .45 Long Colt, .357 Magnum and .32-20.

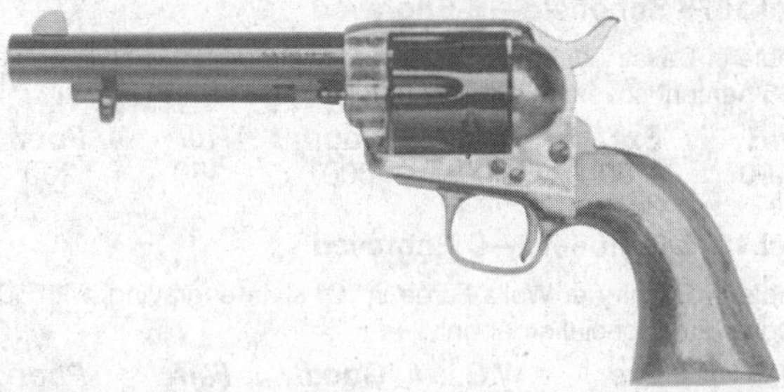

NIB	Exc.	V.G.	Good	Fair	Poor
500	380	220	180	150	120

Model 1873 SAA Stainless Gunfighter

Introduced in 2003. Same as standard 1873. Features all stainless steel construction. Offered in .45 Colt and .357 Magnum caliber. Choice of 4.75", 5.5" or 7.5" barrel. Weight about 45 oz. depending on barrel length.

NIB	Exc.	V.G.	Good	Fair	Poor
520	400	250	200	150	120

Economy Model 1873 S.A.A.

Same as above, with brass triggerguard and backstrap.

NIB	Exc.	V.G.	Good	Fair	Poor
320	250	200	150	120	100

Nickel 1873 S.A.A.

NIB	Exc.	V.G.	Good	Fair	Poor
520	400	250	200	150	120

1873 U.S. Cavalry Model

.45 Long Colt features U.S. arsenal stampings, case colored frame and walnut grips. Barrel length 7.5"; weight 45 oz.

NIB	Exc.	V.G.	Good	Fair	Poor
500	380	220	180	150	120

1873 Pinched Frame Model

Replica of "pinched" frame 1873. "U" shape rear sight notch. Chambered for .45 Colt, with 7.5" barrel.

NIB	Exc.	V.G.	Good	Fair	Poor
500	380	220	180	150	120

1873 Flat Top Target

Features windage adjustable rear sight on flattop frame. Spring loaded front sight. Barrel length 7.5". Offered in .45 Colt. Weight about 40 oz. Introduced in 1998.

NIB	Exc.	V.G.	Good	Fair	Poor
500	380	220	180	150	120

Deputy Single-Action Army

Similar to Model 1873, with bird's-head grip. Barrel lengths 3", 3.5", 4" and 4.75". Chambered for .44-40 and .45 Colt.

NIB	Exc.	V.G.	Good	Fair	Poor
400	320	250	200	150	100

Shootist Model S.A.A.

Reproduction of Colt 1873. Parts are interchangeable with originals. Blued barrel, cylinder, triggerguard and backstrap. Case-hardened frame and hammer. Walnut grips. Offered in 4.75", 5.5" and 7.5" barrel lengths. Chambered for .357 Magnum, .44-40 or .45 Colt.

NIB	Exc.	V.G.	Good	Fair	Poor
500	380	220	180	150	120

Scout Small Frame Revolver

Identical to Colt 1873 SAA, with smaller dimensions. Offered in .38 Special. Choice of 4.75" or 5.5" barrel. Weight about 30 oz. Introduced in 2003.

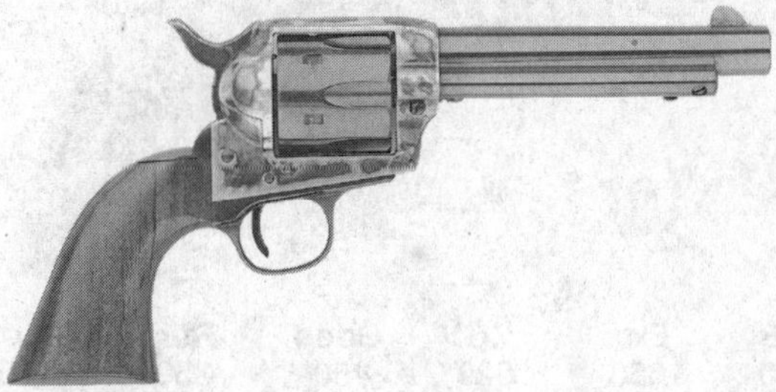

NIB	Exc.	V.G.	Good	Fair	Poor
400	320	250	200	150	100

Deluxe 1873 Colt Revolver

Chambered for .32-20 cartridge. Features bright charcoal blue barrel, with case colored frame and hammer. Walnut grips. Fitted with 5.5" barrel. Limited production. Weight about 41 oz.

NIB	Exc.	V.G.	Good	Fair	Poor
500	380	220	180	150	120

Bisley Model

Features famous Bisley grip. Barrel lengths 4.75", 5.5" and 7.5". Chambered for .44-40 or .45 Colt.

NIB	Exc.	V.G.	Good	Fair	Poor
500	380	220	180	150	120

Bisley Flat Top Target

Similar to Bisley, with 7.5" barrel. Flattop frame, with adjustable front sight and windage adjustable rear. Chambered for .44-40 or .45 Colt. Weight about 40 oz.

NIB	Exc.	V.G.	Good	Fair	Poor
520	400	250	200	150	120

1875 Remington-Style Revolver

Frame case colored. All other parts blued except brass triggerguard. Available in .44-40 or .45 Long Colt. Furnished with walnut grips. Barrel length 7.5"; weight 41 oz.

NIB	Exc.	V.G.	Good	Fair	Poor
500	380	220	180	150	120

1890 Remington-Style Revolver

Modified version of 1875 model. Offered in .44-40 or .45 Long Colt. Web under barrel has been eliminated. Blued 5.5" steel barrel and frame. Lanyard loop on bottom of walnut grips. Weight 39 oz.

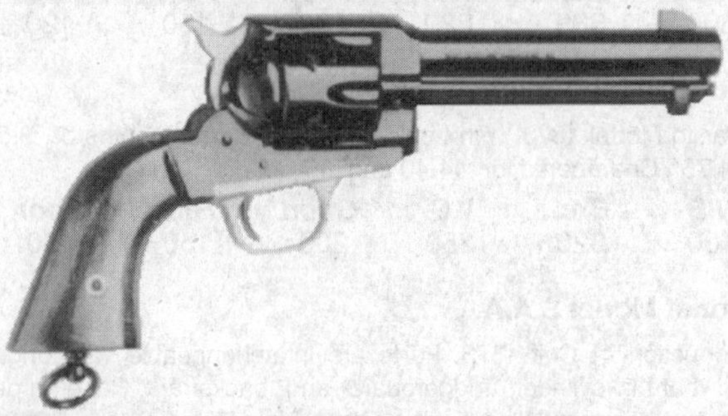

NIB	Exc.	V.G.	Good	Fair	Poor
500	380	220	180	150	120

TOP BREAK REVOLVERS

Model 1875 Schofield—Wells Fargo 5" barrel

NIB	Exc.	V.G.	Good	Fair	Poor
750	650	520	450	350	120

Model 1875 Schofield—Cavalry 7" barrel

Reproduction of S&W Model 3 top-break revolver in .44-40 or .45 Long Colt. Cavalry model has 7 barrel; Wells Fargo model 5". Weight about 39 oz.

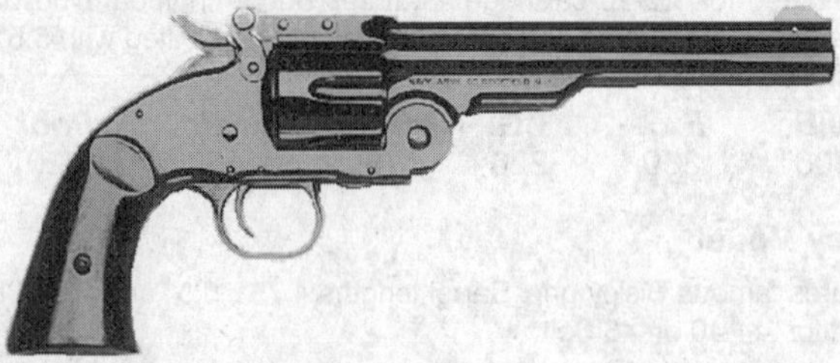

NIB	Exc.	V.G.	Good	Fair	Poor
750	650	520	450	350	120

Model 1875 Schofield—Deluxe

Charcoal blue finish with gold inlays and "A" style hand-engraving. Available in Cavalry or Wells Fargo model. Special order only.

NIB	Exc.	V.G.	Good	Fair	Poor
1700	1400	1000	800	500	300

Model 1875 Schofield—B Engraved

Available in Cavalry or Wells Fargo model. Grade "B" is style engraved, with 35 percent coverage. Special order only.

NIB	Exc.	V.G.	Good	Fair	Poor
1400	1100	800	600	350	200

Model 1875 Schofield—C Engraved

Available in Cavalry or Wells Fargo in "C" style engraving, with 50 percent coverage. Special order only.

NIB	Exc.	V.G.	Good	Fair	Poor
1150	950	800	680	60	280

Model 1875 Schofield Founder's Model

Introduced in 2003 to honor Val Forgett, Sr. and Aldo Uberti. Features charcoal blued barrel and cylinder. Color case-hardened receiver, backstrap, triggerguard and trigger. Grip white ivory polymer. Limited production. Special serial number prefix of "VF".

NIB	Exc.	V.G.	Good	Fair	Poor
750	650	520	450	350	120

Model 1875 Schofield—Hideout

Short-barrel variation of Schofield. Fitted with 3.5" barrel. Chambered for .44-40 or .45 Colt cartridge. Weight about 38 oz.

NIB	Exc.	V.G.	Good	Fair	Poor
750	650	520	450	350	120

New Model Russian

Built around single-action Smith & Wesson Model 3. Chambered for .44 Russian cartridge. Fitted with 6.5" barrel. Case colored spur triggerguard, latch and hammer. Blued frame, barrel and cylinder. Walnut grips. Weight about 40 oz. Introduced in 1999.

NIB	Exc.	V.G.	Good	Fair	Poor
750	650	520	450	350	120

MILITARY SURPLUS ARMS

SKS Type 56 w/Scope Rail

Semi-automatic gas-operated rifle. Chambered for 7.62x39 cartridge. Has 10-round clip. Fitted with scope-rail on left side of receiver. Barrel length 20.5"; weight 8 lbs.

NIB	Exc.	V.G.	Good	Fair	Poor
400	320	250	200	150	100

Standard SKS Type 56

Same as above, without scope-rail.

NIB	Exc.	V.G.	Good	Fair	Poor
400	320	250	200	150	100

Standard SKS Type 56 With Scope and Bipod

NIB	Exc.	V.G.	Good	Fair	Poor
400	320	250	200	150	100

SKS "Cowboy's Companion" Carbine

Barrel length version 16.5. Weight 7 lbs. 8 oz.

NIB	Exc.	V.G.	Good	Fair	Poor
400	320	250	200	150	100

Military Version

NIB	Exc.	V.G.	Good	Fair	Poor
400	320	250	200	150	100

SKS "Hunter" Carbine

Checkered composite Monte Carlo stock, with full-length pull. Comes with 5-round magazine.

NIB	Exc.	V.G.	Good	Fair	Poor
400	320	250	200	150	100

TT-Olympia Pistol

Reproduction of Walther target pistol. Chambered for .22 LR. Barrel length 4.625"; weight 27 oz.

NIB	Exc.	V.G.	Good	Fair	Poor
280	200	150	120	100	50

TU-90 Pistol

Based on Tokagypt pistol. Features wrap-around grip, with thumbrest. Barrel length 4.5"; weight 30 oz.

NIB	Exc.	V.G.	Good	Fair	Poor
250	190	120	80	50	40

TU-111 Mauser

Replica of Mauser 111 9mm pistol, with 5.250" barrel and 10- or 20-shot magazine. Made in China, with limited importation into U.S. in early '90s.

NIB	Exc.	V.G.	Good	Fair	Poor
1000	800	650	500	350	150

TU-KKW Training Rifle

Based on 98 Mauser. Chambered for .22 LR cartridge. Fitted with military sights, bayonet lug, cleaning rod and take-down disc. Comes with detachable 5-round box magazine. Barrel length 26"; weight 8 lbs.

NIB	Exc.	V.G.	Good	Fair	Poor
320	280	200	150	100	60

TU-KKW Sniper Trainer

Same as above, with 2.75 power Type 89 scope. Quick detachable mounting system.

NIB	Exc.	V.G.	Good	Fair	Poor
380	320	280	200	150	100

TU-33/40 Carbine

Based on WWII Mauser G 33/40 mountain carbine. Chambered for .22 LR or 7.62x39 cartridge. Barrel length 20.75"; weight 7.5 lbs.

NIB	Exc.	V.G.	Good	Fair	Poor
320	280	200	150	100	—

JW-15 Rifle

Bolt-action design based on BRNO Model 5 action. Chambered for .22 LR. Features adjustable sights, sling swivels, detachable 5-round magazine. Top of receiver dovetailed for easy scope mounting. Barrel 24" long; weight 5 lbs. 12 oz.

NIB	Exc.	V.G.	Good	Fair	Poor
100	80	70	60	50	40

Martini Target Rifle

.444 or .45-70 caliber single-shot Martini-action rifle, with 26" or 30" octagonal barrel, tang sight and walnut stock. Offered between 1972 and 1984.

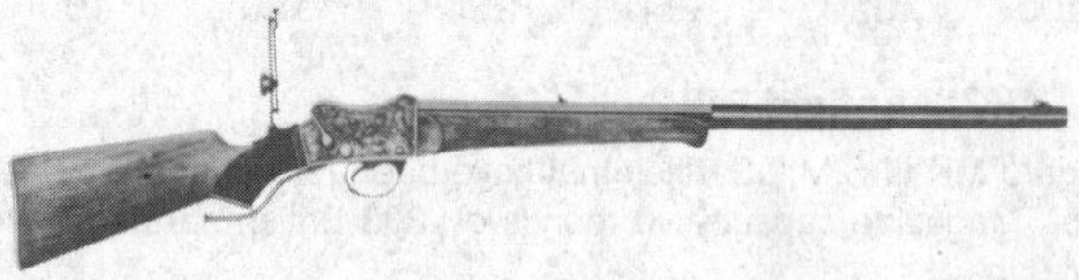

NIB	Exc.	V.G.	Good	Fair	Poor
—	620	500	400	300	150

Parker-Hale Sniper Rifle

See—Parker-Hale.

RPKS-74

5.56mm or 7.62x39mm caliber semi-automatic rifle, with 19" barrel. Patterned after Russian AK series rifles.

NIB	Exc.	V.G.	Good	Fair	Poor
550	450	380	280	200	10

No. 5 Enfield Jungle Carbine

Replica chambered for .303 British cartridge. Fitted with cupped buttplate and flashider. Barrel length 20.5". Magazine capacity 10 rounds. Weight about 7 lbs.

NIB	Exc.	V.G.	Good	Fair	Poor
380	320	280	200	150	100

No. 6 Enfield Jungle Carbine

Reproduction chambered for .303 British cartridge, with 20.5" barrel and flashider. Weight about 7 lbs. 10 round magazine.

NIB	Exc.	V.G.	Good	Fair	Poor
380	320	280	200	150	100

Ishapore 2A No. 1 MK III Rifle

Refinished rifle with 25" barrel. Chambered for .308 Win. cartridge. Magazine capacity 12 rounds. Weight about 9.3 lbs.

NIB	Exc.	V.G.	Good	Fair	Poor
350	250	200	150	100	80

2A Tanker Carbine

Replica with short 20" barrel. Chambered for .308 Win. Magazine capacity 12 rounds. Weight about 8.7 lbs.

NIB	Exc.	V.G.	Good	Fair	Poor
380	320	280	200	150	100

MK III Tanker Carbine

Similar to above. Chambered for .303 British cartridge. Magazine capacity 10 rounds.

NIB	Exc.	V.G.	Good	Fair	Poor
380	320	280	200	150	100

Lithgow No. 1 MK III Rifle

Rifles in unissued condition. Barrel length 25". Chambered for .303 British cartridge. Magazine capacity 10 rounds. Weight about 9 lbs.

NIB	Exc.	V.G.	Good	Fair	Poor
400	320	250	200	150	100

No. 1 MK III Enfield Rifle

Standard MK III S.M.L.E. rifles that have been refinished. Barrel length 25.25". Magazine capacity 10 rounds of .303 British cartridge. Weight about 9 lbs.

NIB	Exc.	V.G.	Good	Fair	Poor
380	320	280	200	150	100

No. 4 Tanker Carbine

Cut-down version of No. 4 MK I Enfield. Barrel length 20.5". Chambered for .303 British cartridge. Magazine capacity 10 rounds. Weight about 8.2 lbs.

NIB	Exc.	V.G.	Good	Fair	Poor
350	250	200	150	100	80

No. 4 MK I Enfield Rifle

Reconditioned rifle. Barrel length 25". Magazine capacity 10 rounds of .303 British cartridge. Weight about 8.6 lbs.

NIB	Exc.	V.G.	Good	Fair	Poor
350	250	200	150	100	80

Savage No. 4 MK I Rifle

Chambered for .303 British cartridge, with 25" barrel. Stocks are unissued. Magazine capacity 10 rounds. Weight about 8.7 lbs.

NIB	Exc.	V.G.	Good	Fair	Poor
380	320	280	200	150	100

Luger

.22-caliber semi-automatic pistol, with 4", 6" or 8" barrel, fixed sights and 10-shot magazine. Blued, with walnut grips. Manufactured in U.S.A. - 1986 and 1987.

NIB	Exc.	V.G.	Good	Fair	Poor
—	320	280	220	180	120

Grand Prix Silhouette Pistol

.30-30, .44 Magnum, 7mm Special and .45-70 caliber single-shot pistol, with 13.75" barrel. Adjustable sights and aluminum heat-disbursing rib. Matte-blued, walnut grips and forearm. Manufactured in 1985.

NIB	Exc.	V.G.	Good	Fair	Poor
—	450	380	300	220	150

NEAL, W.

Bangor, Maine

Underhammer Pistol Antique

.31-caliber under hammer percussion pistol, with 5" to 8" barrels. Iron frame and walnut grip. Barrel marked "Wm. Neal/Bangor, Me.". William Neal was also a maker of underhammer rifles. SEE NOTE ON UNDERHAMMERS & DERRINGERS at Line 510 & 511.

Exc.	Fine	V.G.	Good	Fair	Poor
1350	1000	720	450	150	100

NEPPERHAN FIREARMS CO.

Yonkers, New York

Pocket Revolver Antique

.31-caliber percussion revolver, with 3.5" to 6" barrels and 5-shot cylinder. Blued case-hardened, with walnut grips. Barrel marked "Nepperhan/Fire Arms Co" and on some additionally "Yonkers New York". Latter worth a slight premium over values listed. Approximately 5,000 made during 1860s.

Exc.	Fine	V.G.	Good	Fair	Poor
1400	1000	690	380	200	140

NESIKA BAY PRECISION, INC.

Sturgis, South Dakota

Sporter Rifle

As of 2020, the Nesika website only lists a Sporter Model bolt-action rifle; stainless steel action and barrel, Timney set trigger, Leupold bases, composite stock, guaranteed MOA accuracy. Calibers .260 Rem., 7mm-08 Rem., .308 Rem., .30-06 Springfield, .280 Rem., 7mm Rem. Mag, .300 Win Mag, & 6.5x284. The last three calibers have 26" barrels, the others 24".

NIB	Exc.	V.G.	Good	Fair	Poor
3500	3000	—	—	—	—

Hunting Rifles

Offered in a number of different calibers. Several stock options to choose from. All rifles fitted with adjustable trigger.

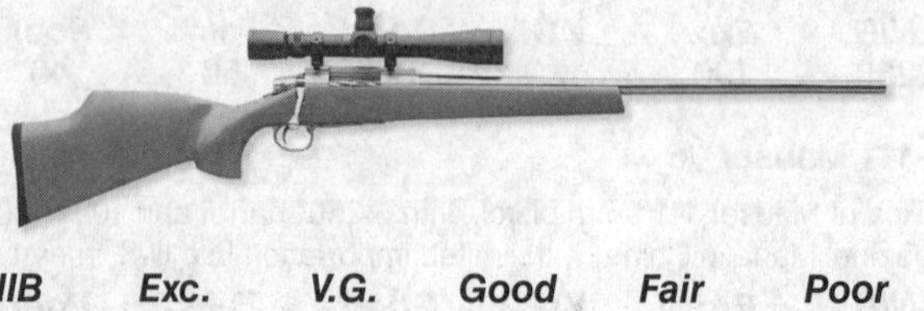

NIB	Exc.	V.G.	Good	Fair	Poor
4000	2900	2300	1500	750	400

Varmint Rifles

Offered in a variety of calibers, barrel lengths and weights. Single-shot or repeater.

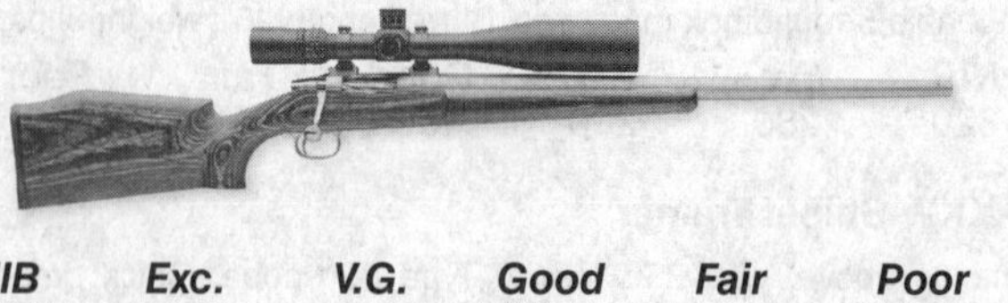

NIB	Exc.	V.G.	Good	Fair	Poor
3500	2900	2300	1500	750	400

Urban Tactical Rifle

Chambered for .308 cartridge. Fitted with 20" fluted barrel. Detachable box magazine. Weight about 10 lbs. Note: Add $100 for .300 Win. Magnum; 5-10 percent for Heavy Tactical version.

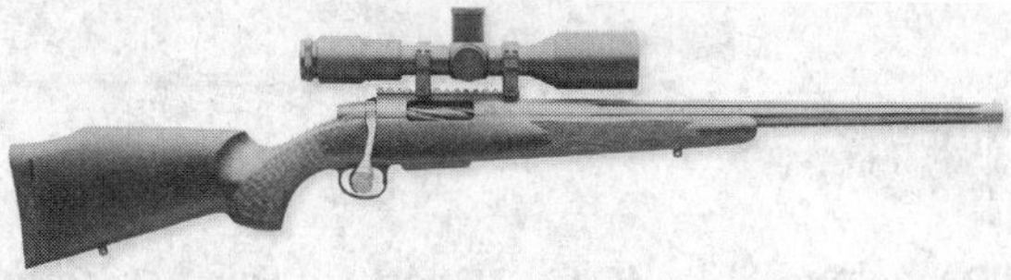

NIB	Exc.	V.G.	Good	Fair	Poor
5800	4800	3500	2700	800	500

NEW ENGLAND FIREARMS CO.

Madison, North Carolina

Formerly located in Gardner, Massachusetts, New England Firearms (NEF) is part of the Freedom Group of gun companies headquartered in Madison, NC. Some models have been marketed under both the NEF brand and H&R 1871. After 2007, the NEF brand has been seen only on imported models.

Model R22

.22 Magnum or .32 H&R Magnum double-action revolver, with 2.5", 4" or 6" barrel. Cylinder 6- or 9-shot. Blued or nickel-plated, with walnut grips. Introduced in 1988.

NIB	Exc.	V.G.	Good	Fair	Poor
150	100	80	70	60	40

Excell

Introduced in 2005. Chambered for 12-gauge 3" shell. Fitted with 28" ventilated rib barrel, with choke tubes. Checkered black synthetic stock. Magazine capacity 5 rounds. Weight about 7 lbs.

NIB	Exc.	V.G.	Good	Fair	Poor
450	380	300	220	150	100

Excell Waterfowl

As above, with Realtree Advantage Wetlands camo finish. Introduced in 2005.

NIB	Exc.	V.G.	Good	Fair	Poor
480	400	320	250	180	120

Excell Turkey

Fitted with 22" barrel with choke tubes and fiber optic front sight. Realtree Advantage Hardwoods camo finish. Weight 7 lbs. Introduced in 2005.

NIB	Exc.	V.G.	Good	Fair	Poor
480	400	320	250	180	120

Excell Combo

Has black synthetic stock and two barrels: 28" ventilated rib with choke tubes; 24" rifled barrel. Weight about 7 lbs. depending on barrel length. Introduced in 2005.

NIB	Exc.	V.G.	Good	Fair	Poor
500	420	340	260	180	140

Pardner

12-, 16-, 20-gauge or .410 bore single-shot shotgun, with 24", 26" or 28" barrel. Blued, with walnut stock. Introduced in 1987.

NIB	Exc.	V.G.	Good	Fair	Poor
150	100	80	70	60	40

Pardner Youth

Similar to above. Offered only in 20-, 28-gauge and .410 bore. Fitted with 26" barrel. Weight between 5 and 6 lbs.

NIB	Exc.	V.G.	Good	Fair	Poor
150	100	80	70	60	40

Special Purpose

Similar model offered only in 10-gauge. Available in several different configurations: 10-gauge with hardwood stock 28" barrel; camo model with 28" barrel or 32" barrel choked Modified; black matte finish model with 24" barrel with screw-in turkey Full choke. Weight about 9.5 lbs.

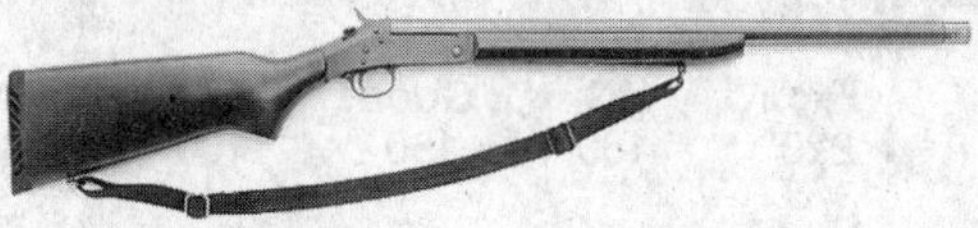

Special Purpose Turkey Gun

NIB	Exc.	V.G.	Good	Fair	Poor
250	180	120	100	80	50

Pardner Pump Turkey

Chambered for 12-gauge 3" shell. Fitted with 22" barrel with Turkey choke tube. Magazine capacity 5 rounds. Weight about 7.5 lbs. Introduced in 2005.

NIB	Exc.	V.G.	Good	Fair	Poor
280	220	180	120	100	80

Pardner Pump Walnut Shotgun

12- or 20-gauge pump-action shotgun, with American walnut furniture, 26" or 28" ventilated rib barrel, 3" chamber and screw-in choke tube. Weight 7.5 lbs.

NIB	Exc.	V.G.	Good	Fair	Poor
—	280	220	180	120	100

Pardner Pump Synthetic Shotgun

Similar to above, with black synthetic buttstock and forend.

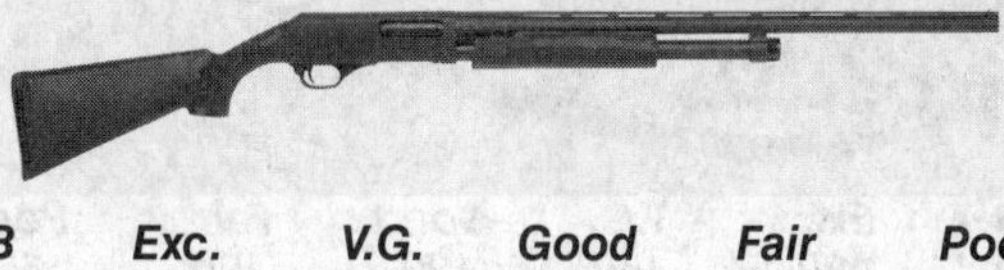

NIB	Exc.	V.G.	Good	Fair	Poor
—	220	180	150	100	80

Pardner Pump Field Shotgun

Similar to above, with Realtree APG HD camo finish.

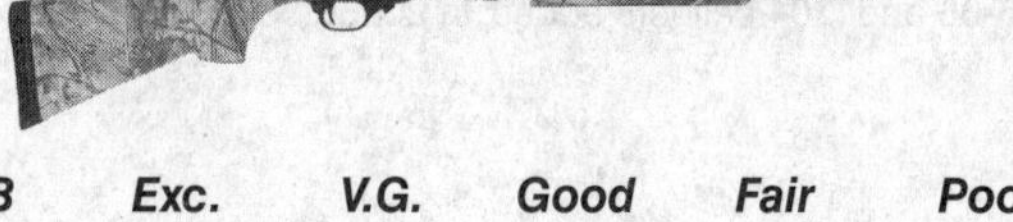

NIB	Exc.	V.G.	Good	Fair	Poor
—	280	220	180	120	100

Pardner Pump Compact Field Shotgun

Similar to above, with 1.25" shorter length of pull and 21" barrel.

NIB	Exc.	V.G.	Good	Fair	Poor
—	220	180	150	100	80

Pardner Pump Compact Walnut Shotgun

Similar to Pardner Pump Walnut, with 1.25" shorter length of pull and 21" barrel. Weight 6.25 lbs.

NIB	Exc.	V.G.	Good	Fair	Poor
—	220	180	150	100	80

Pardner Pump Compact Synthetic Shotgun

Similar to above, with black synthetic buttstock and forend.

NIB	Exc.	V.G.	Good	Fair	Poor
—	220	180	150	100	80

Pardner Pump Combo

Introduced in 2005. Features two 12-gauge 3" barrels. One 28" with ventilated rib and choke tubes other 22" rifled slug barrel. Walnut stock. Weight about 7.5 lbs. depending on barrel length.

NIB	Exc.	V.G.	Good	Fair	Poor
280	220	180	120	100	80

Pardner Pump Protector

Similar to Pardner Pump, with matte black finish throughout. Synthetic buttstock and forend. Also available with carbon fiber dipped stock.

NIB	Exc.	V.G.	Good	Fair	Poor
—	220	180	150	100	80

Survivor

Based on single-shot break-action design. Rifle or shotgun fitted with synthetic stock, with integral storage compartments. Offered in .410/.45 Colt, 12- and 20-gauge, .223 Rem. and .357 Magnum. Barrel length 22". Weight about 6 lbs.

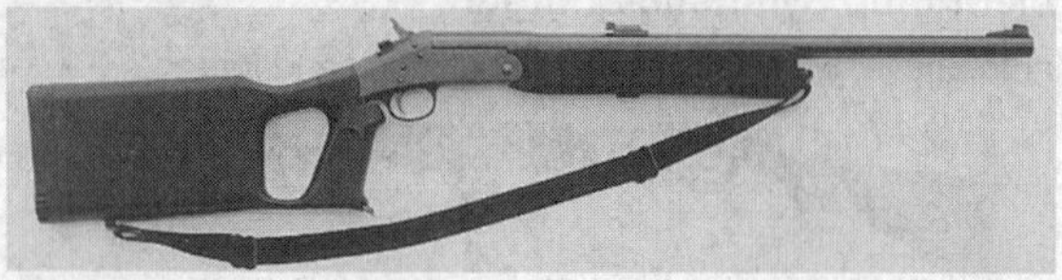

NIB	Exc.	V.G.	Good	Fair	Poor
200	180	150	120	100	80

Handi-Rifle (aka Handi-Gun)

.22 Hornet, .223, .243, .270, .280, .30-30, .44 Magnum or .45-70 caliber version of above. A 22" barrel fitted with open sights. Blued, with walnut stock. Introduced in 1989. In 2003, offered in stainless steel. In 2004, .22-250, .25-06 and .204 calibers added. In 2005, .500 S&W added.

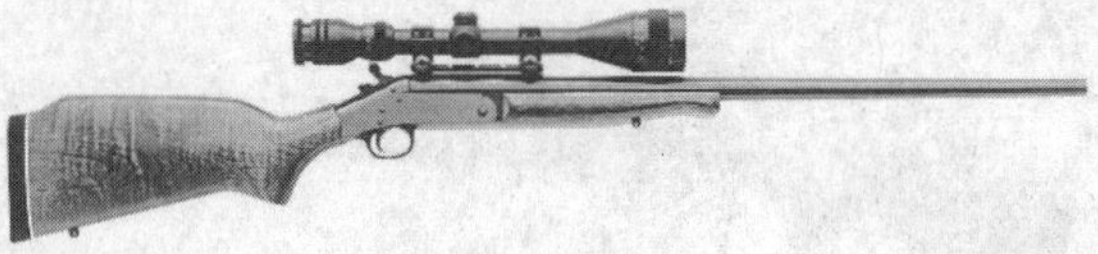

NIB	Exc.	V.G.	Good	Fair	Poor
280	200	150	120	100	80

Tracker

Single-shot break-open shotgun. Offered in 12- and 20-gauge, with rifled or cylinder bore barrel both 24" long. Equipped with adjustable rifle sights. Weight about 6 lbs.

NIB	Exc.	V.G.	Good	Fair	Poor
150	120	100	80	60	50

Super Light Rifle

Single-shot rifle chambered for .22 Hornet or .223 Rem. Fitted with 20" lightweight barrel. Choice of scope mount, no sights or adjustable rear sight and ramp front sight. Black polymer stock, with semi-beavertail forend. Weight about 5.5 lbs.

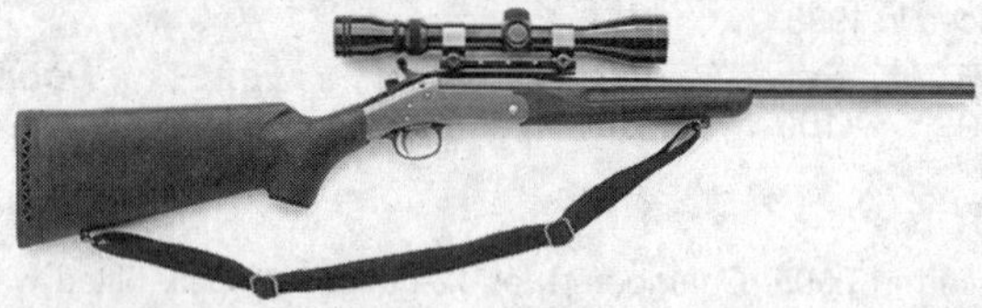

NIB	Exc.	V.G.	Good	Fair	Poor
180	120	100	80	60	50

Huntsman

Blackpowder gun, with break-open action. Hardwood pistol grip stock. Fitted with 24" barrel. Chambered for .45- or .50-caliber slug. Recoil pad. Weight about 6.5 lbs. Introduced in 2002. In 2003, offered in stainless steel.

NIB	Exc.	V.G.	Good	Fair	Poor
180	120	100	80	60	50

Tracker II

Combination two-barrel set. Blackpowder and 12-gauge slug barrel. Case colored frame. Hardwood stock.

NIB	Exc.	V.G.	Good	Fair	Poor
280	220	180	120	100	—

Handi-Rifle Combo

Combination two-barrel set. .50 blackpowder and .243 Win. barrel. Hardwood stock. No iron sights.

NIB	Exc.	V.G.	Good	Fair	Poor
280	220	180	120	100	—

Sportster

Single-shot .22-caliber Short/LR or .22 WMR rifle, with 20" barrel. No iron sights. Black polymer Monte Carlo stock, with matte black metal finish. Scope mount rail. Weight about 5.5 lbs.

NIB	Exc.	V.G.	Good	Fair	Poor
180	120	100	80	60	50

Sportster Youth

As above, with standard stock. Weight about 5.25 lbs.

NIB	Exc.	V.G.	Good	Fair	Poor
180	120	100	80	60	50

Sportster .17 HMR

Single-shot chambered for .17 HMR cartridge. Fitted with 22" heavy varmint barrel. No iron sights. Black polymer Monte Carlo stock, with matte black metal finish. Weight about 7 lbs.

NIB	Exc.	V.G.	Good	Fair	Poor
180	120	100	80	60	50

Sportster .17 M2

As above chambered for .17 Mach 2 cartridge. Introduced in 2005.

NIB	Exc.	V.G.	Good	Fair	Poor
180	120	100	80	60	50

Sportster SL

Semi-automatic rifle chambered for .22 LR cartridge. Fitted with 19" barrel. Walnut finished hardwood stock, with Monte Carlo and pistol grip. Adjustable sights. 10-round magazine. Weight about 5.5 lbs. Introduced in 2004.

NIB	Exc.	V.G.	Good	Fair	Poor
150	120	100	80	60	50

Sportster Versa-Pack

Two-barrel set: 22" .410 barrel; other 20" .22-caliber barrel. Hardwood stock, with straight-grip. Iron sights. Weight about 5.5 lbs.

NIB	Exc.	V.G.	Good	Fair	Poor
250	180	120	100	80	50

Sidekick Muzzleloader

Introduced in 2004. Features break-open-action, side lever release chambered for .50-caliber ball. Barrel length 24" or 26". American hardwood stock, with pistol grip and recoil pad. Black matte finish or stainless steel. Adjustable fiber optic sights. Weight about 6.5 lbs. Note: Add $70 for stainless steel.

NIB	Exc.	V.G.	Good	Fair	Poor
200	160	120	100	80	50

NEWBURY ARMS CO.

Catskill, New York
Albany, New York

Derringer (Antique)

Newbury made .22 and .32 rimfire single shot derringer; too rare to value. Rock Island Auction sold a good refurbished .22 for $3450 in 2015. Two-shot models are also reported in side-by-side or horizontal swivel configuration - possibly one-of prototypes.

Pocket Revolver (Antique)

.26-caliber double-action percussion revolver, with 5" barrel and C-shaped exposed trigger. Blued, with iron or brass frame and walnut grips. Barrel marked "Newbury Arms Co. Albany". Produced in limited numbers between 1855 and 1860.

Exc.	Fine	V.G.	Good	Fair	Poor
7800	6900	4950	3000	750	520

NEWBURY, FREDERICK

Pocket Model Revolver

Percussion revolver, .26 cal., nipples covered by shield, very few known, too rare to value. A number of unusual variations have been reported, possibly prototypes.

NEWCOMB, H. G.

Natchez, Mississippi

Maker of muzzleloading percussion derringers and long guns. Seldom encountered. Also See note on UNDERHAMMER PISTOLS & DERRINGERS at lines 510 & 511

Pocket Pistol (Antique)

NEWTON ARMS CO.

Buffalo, New York

Also known as Buffalo Newton Rifle Company and Charles Newton Rifle Company. In operation from 1913 to 1932. Note: Any rifles listed chambered for a Newton caliber, will bring a premium over standard calibers of about 25 percent.

Newton-Mauser Rifle

.256 Newton caliber bolt-action rifle, with 24" barrel and double-set triggers. Blued, with walnut stock. Manufactured circa 1914.

NIB	Exc.	V.G.	Good	Fair	Poor
—	—	1300	850	500	300

Standard Rifle First Type

.22, .256, .280, .30, .33 and .35 Newton as well as .30-06 caliber bolt-action rifle, with 24" barrel. Open or aperture sights and double-set triggers. Blued, with walnut stock. Manufactured between 1916 and 1918.

Courtesy Amoskeag Auction Company, Inc.

NIB	Exc.	V.G.	Good	Fair	Poor
—	2500	2150	1500	900	400

Standard Rifle Second Model

.256, .30, or .35 Newton as well as .30-06 caliber bolt-action rifle as above, with Enfield-style bolt handle. Manufactured after 1918.

NIB	Exc.	V.G.	Good	Fair	Poor
—	2500	2150	1500	900	400

Buffalo Newton Rifle

As above marked "Buffalo Newton Rifle Company".

NIB	Exc.	V.G.	Good	Fair	Poor
—	2000	1650	1000	600	300

NEW ULTRA LIGHT ARMS

Granville, West Virginia

Previously known as Ultra Light Arms, this manufacturer makes a variety of bolt-action rifles fitted with Douglas barrels of varying lengths, custom triggers and reinforced graphite stocks. Values listed are for base models. Note: Forbes Rifles, LLC makes a production-grade version of Model 24B rifle. See that listing.

Model 20 Ultimate Mountain Rifle

Weight 4.5 lbs., with 22" barrel. Composte stock, with choice of colors or camo finish. Adjustable trigger. No sights. Offered in left-/right-hand. The Model 20 is offered in three variations — Model 20 Short, a short action for calibers .17 Rem. through .30 Rem. AR; (4.75 lbs. total weight); Model 20 long action for .308 length cartridges, (5 lbs.); and Model 20 Varmint, varminter stock and 2.5" wide forend, 7.5 lbs.

NIB	Exc.	V.G.	Good	Fair	Poor
3250	2750	2500	1850	900	500

Model 20 RF Rimfire

Weight about 4.5 lbs., with 22" barrel. Stock synthetic, with choice of colors or camo finish. No sights. Adjustable trigger. Available as single-shot or repeater.

NIB	Exc.	V.G.	Good	Fair	Poor
1450	1300	1100	600	450	250

Model 20 Hunter's Pistol

Bolt-action repeating pistol designed with serious hunter in mind. Offered in various popular calibers, with 14" high-quality Douglas heavy barrel. Has 5-shot magazine. Matte blued, with reinforced graphite Kevlar stock. Introduced in 1987.

NIB	Exc.	V.G.	Good	Fair	Poor
1250	1000	800	620	500	300

Model 24 (Long Action) Ultimate Plains Rifle

Weight about 5.25 lbs., with 22" barrel.

NIB	Exc.	V.G.	Good	Fair	Poor
3100	2750	2500	1850	900	500

Model 28 Magnum

Weight about 5.75 lbs., with 24" barrel.

NIB	Exc.	V.G.	Good	Fair	Poor
3500	3050	2750	1950	900	500

Model 28 Short Ultimate Alaskan Model

This was originally designed to handle the 6.5mm and .350 Remington Magnums but works just as well with the .300 Winchester Short Magnums. Weight is 5.75 pounds.

NIB	Exc.	V.G.	Good	Fair	Poor
3500	3050	2750	1950	900	500

Model 32 Professional Hunter

This is designed to handle the .375 H&H Magnum and other cartridges based on the .404 Jeffery. A dangerous game rifle for the African or Alaskan professional hunter. Weight is 7.25 pounds.

NIB	Exc.	V.G.	Good	Fair	Poor
3500	3050	2750	1950	900	500

Model 40 Magnum Ultimate African Rifle

Weight about 7.5 lbs., with 26" barrel.

NIB	Exc.	V.G.	Good	Fair	Poor
3300	3050	2750	1950	900	500

Model 90

Muzzleloading rifle built with .45- or .50-caliber barrel. Graphite stock. Williams sights. Barrel length 28". Adjustable trigger. Weight about 6 lbs.

NIB	Exc.	V.G.	Good	Fair	Poor
950	750	600	480	350	200

Model 290

Blackpowder model with 209 Primer ignition, .45- or .50-caliber, 24" button-rifled barrel, Timney trigger, Kevlar stock with recoil pad, sling swivels, scope mount.

NIB	Exc.	V.G.	Good	Fair	Poor
1200	1100	900	750	650	300

NICHOLS & CHILDS

Conway, Massachusetts

Percussion Belt Revolver (Antique)

.34-caliber percussion revolver, with 6" round barrel and 6-shot cylinder. Blued or browned, with walnut grips. Estimated fewer than 25 made in 1838. Too rare to value.

Revolving Percussion Rifle (Antique)

.36- or .40-caliber percussion rifle, with 22", 26" or 30" barrel and 5-, 6-, 7- or 9-shot cylinder. Blued or browned, with walnut stock and patchbox. Believed approximately 150 made between 1838 and 1840. Too rare to value. In 2018 Amoskeag Auction sold one in about good condition for $5,750

NIGHTHAWK CUSTOM

Berryville, Arkansas

Nighthawk custom manufactures high-end custom 1911 pistols with a wide variety of features. Variations from one model to another may be subtle. Some models are offered in California compliant versions.

PISTOLS

Custom Talon/Talon II

1911-style semi-automatic with 5" (Talon) or 4.25" (Talon II) barrel. Fixed or adjustable sights. Several other barrel lengths/finishes available.

NIB	Exc.	V.G.	Good	Fair	Poor
3000	2500	1800	1200	700	300

Custom Predator

1911-style semi-automatic with 4.25"or 5" barrel. Fixed or adjustable sights. Several other barrel lengths/finishes available.

NIB	Exc.	V.G.	Good	Fair	Poor
3000	2400	1850	1400	750	300

GRP

Global Response Pistol. 1911-style semi-automatic, with 4.25" or 5" barrel. Fixed or adjustable sights. Several other barrel lengths/finishes available.

NIB	Exc.	V.G.	Good	Fair	Poor
2750	2200	1550	1200	700	300

HEINIE SIGNATURE SERIES

Competition, Government Recon or Officer Compact configurations, all chambered in 9mm. 5" barrel except for Compact which is 4.25". Heinie Slant Pro sights. Recon has accessory rail. Many custom features.

NIB	Exc.	V.G.	Good	Fair	Poor
3100	2700	2100	1600	1000	350

Heinie Long Slide

Same features as Signature Series, except with 6" match-grade barrel, checkered front strap, black Perma Kote ceramic-based finish. Chambered in .45 ACP or 10mm.

NIB	Exc.	V.G.	Good	Fair	Poor
3500	3000	2200	1150	800	500

Heinie Lady Hawk

Medium-frame 1911-style pistol in 9mm or .45 ACP. Match-grade 4.25" barrel, titanium blue Perma Kote finish, with hard-chrome controls. Sights are Heinie Straight-Eight Slant Pro. Ultra-thin chain link front and backstrap for reduced grip circumference.

NIB	Exc.	V.G.	Good	Fair	Poor
3100	2700	2100	1600	1000	350

Heinie Lady Hawk 2.0

Similar features and dimensions as standard version, plus DLC (Diamond-like Coating) finish or optional stainless steel, Rose Gold finish on controls and barrel, and custom Obsidian/Abalone/Zinc grips. Introduced in 2018.

NIB	Exc.	V.G.	Good	Fair	Poor
4200	3600	3000	—	—	—

The Bull

Full-size model, with 5" bull barrel.

NIB	Exc.	V.G.	Good	Fair	Poor
3400	2950	2100	—	—	—

Bull Officer

Caliber: 9mm. Capacity: 8-round magazine. Barrel: 3.8 in. Grips: Textured carbon fiber. Sights: Fixed, Heinie Ledge Black rear/fiber-optic front. Length: 7.85 in. overall. Weight: 38.2 oz. unloaded. Finish: Black nitride. Features: Bull nose and French border on slide, ultra-high-cut front grip strap, dehorned.

NIB	Exc.	V.G.	Good	Fair	Poor
3600	3000	2200	—	—	—

Falcon

Full-size 1911 design with Coyote Tan, black or OD Green finish. Dimpled grip, front and rear cocking serrations, Heinie Ledge rear sight. Chambered in 9mm, 10mm or .45 ACP.

NIB	Exc.	V.G.	Good	Fair	Poor
3000	2500	2000	1500	800	350

Bob Marvel Custom 1911

Features Nighthawk/Marvel Everlast Recoil System, which allows a shooter to go at least 10,000 rounds before a spring change is necessary. Felt recoil and muzzle flip are also reduced. Other features include fully adjustable sights that have been recessed into the slide and dehorned, hand stippling on top of slide and a one-piece mainspring housing/magwell.

NIB	Exc.	V.G.	Good	Fair	Poor
3800	3000	2300	1650	800	340

T3

Compact 1911-style pistol, with Officers-size frame and Commander-size slide and barrel. All steel frame and slide, horizontally slanted serrations on mainspring housing and rear of slide, blue or stainless finish. Other features include Heinie Slant-Pro Straight Eight night sights, custom lightweight aluminum trigger and extended mag well. Designed by renowned custom pistolsmith Bob Marvel. Chambered in 9mm, .40 S&W or .45 ACP. Compact T4 model has similar features to T3, with 3.8" barrel and ultra-thin grips. Available in 9mm only.

NIB	Exc.	V.G.	Good	Fair	Poor
3100	2600	2000	1450	800	300

Hi-Power

Nighthawk's customized Browning Hi-Power 9mm. Upgrades include stippled frame and triggerguard, select Cocobolo checkered grips, extended beavertail, Heinie Slant-Pro rear sight gold bead front and contoured magazine well. Introduced in 2016. With the discontinuance of the Browning Hi-Power in 2018, production of the Nighthawk Custom model also came to an end. A series of 50 limited editions and another 10 high-grade engraved models were announced in mid 2018 but no prices were available. The values shown here are for models produced in 2016 and 2017.

NIB	Exc.	V.G.	Good	Fair	Poor
3000	2500	2000	1200	800	500

Agent 2

Full-size model in .45 or 9mm with 10-round magazine. Forged Government Model frame has lightened recon rail, faceted slide with side windows, Agency front and rear slide serrations, Railscales G10 grips, match-grade bushing barrel, one-piece mainspring housing/mag well, high-cut front strap, Heinie Ledge rear, fiber optic front sight. Introduced in 2018.

NIB	Exc.	V.G.	Good	Fair	Poor
4100	3500	2900	—	—	—

Agent 2 Commander

Calibers: 9mm, .45 ACP. Capacity: 10-round magazine. Barrel: 4.25 in. Grips: G10 Railscale texture. Sights: Fixed, Heinie Ledge Black rear/gold-bead front. Length: 7.85 in. overall. Weight: 38.6 oz. unloaded. Finish: Smoke Cerakote. Features: Accessory rail, faceted slide with side windows, one-piece mainspring housing/mag well, ultra-high-cut front grip strap.

NIB	Exc.	V.G.	Good	Fair	Poor
4500	3750	2500	—	—	—

War Hawk Series

Available in full-size or compact models. Barrel 5" on Government model frame; 4.25" on Officer's size. Among the custom-style features are front and rear multi-faceted slide serrations, one-piece machined and checkered mainspring housing/mag well, high-cut front strap, lightweight aluminum match trigger, G10 Hyena Brown grips, red fiber-optic front sight, Jardine Hook rear sight and War Hawk engraved logo on slide. Numerous upgrades available. Introduced in 2015.

NIB	Exc.	V.G.	Good	Fair	Poor
3500	3000	2650	1800	900	400

Kestrel

Chambered in .45 ACP. Designed for concealed carry. Based on a full-size frame, with a compact "Commander" size 4.25" barrel. Custom features including Heinie Straight Eight night sights, match-grade crowned and recessed barrel, reduced frame circumference and ultra-thin Nighthawk Alumagrips. Introduced in 2016.

NIB	Exc.	V.G.	Good	Fair	Poor
3300	2900	2000	1100	700	400

VIP

Very Impressive Pistol (VIP) is the top-of-the-line from Nighthawk. Features the company's finest customizations including a classic antique nickel finish, hand-engraving throughout, ivory grips, 14k gold bead front sight, custom vertical front strap, mainspring serrations and a handsome Cocobolo presentation case. Introduced in 2016.

NIB	Exc.	V.G.	Good	Fair	Poor
7200	6200	5000	3800	2000	700

Vice President

Caliber: 9mm. Capacity: 10-round magazine. Barrel: 4.25 in. Grips: G10 Railscale Ascend texture. Sights: Fixed, Heinie Straight Eight Ledge rear/tritium front. Length: 7.4 in. overall. Weight: 32 oz. unloaded. Finish: Black DLC. Features: Gold titanium nitride barrel, heavy angle slide-lightening cuts, one-piece mainspring housing/mag well, ultra-high-cut front grip strap, dehorned.

NIB	*Exc.*	*V.G.*	*Good*	*Fair*	*Poor*
4100	3500	2900	—	—	—

Thunder Ranch

Caliber: 9mm, .45 ACP. Capacity: 8-round (.45 ACP), 10-round (9mm) magazine. Barrel: 5 in. Grips: Textured linen micarta. Sights: Fixed, Heinie Black Ledge rear/gold-bead front. Length: 8.6 in. overall. Weight: 41.3 oz. unloaded. Finish: Smoked nitride. Features: Custom front- and rear-cocking serrations, lanyard-loop mainspring housing, GI-Style nub thumb safety and custom engraving.

NIB	*Exc.*	*V.G.*	*Good*	*Fair*	*Poor*
3300	2200	2300	—	—	—

Colt Series 70

Caliber: .45 ACP. Capacity: 7-round magazine. Barrel: 5 in. Grips: Textured linen micarta. Sights: Fixed, retro rear/gold-bead front. Length: 8.75 in. overall. Weight: 39 oz. unloaded. Finish: Smoked nitride. Features: Match-grade solid short trigger, fully machined disconnector, retro hammer, Nighthawk Custom beavertail grip safety, mainspring housing and match barrel bushing.

NIB	*Exc.*	*V.G.*	*Good*	*Fair*	*Poor*
2000	1800	—	—	—	—

Silent Hawk

Commander-size 9mm model. Threaded 4.25" barrel with protector, tri-cut slide top, Heinie Tritium suppressor night sights and Nitride Black Out finish. Introduced in 2016.

NIB	*Exc.*	*V.G.*	*Good*	*Fair*	*Poor*
3800	3000	2200	1150	800	500

REVOLVERS

KORTH REVOLVER SERIES

Nighthawk Custom is now importing three high-grade revolvers made by Korth in Germany. Sky Hawk is a 9mm revolver, with a 2" barrel. Due to its proprietary ejection system no moon clips are required. Frame and parts are fully machined from billet steel and aluminum. Features include gold bead front sight, Hogue grips, DLC coated frame and lanyard. Mongoose model is chambered for .357 Magnum, with 3", 4", 5.25" or 6" barrel with a solid raised rib, adjustable rear sight and skeletonized hammer. Super Sport model is .357 Magnum, with 6" Walther polygonal barrel, Picatinny rails on each side of barrel and Hogue grips with finger grooves. These models were all introduced in 2017.

Sky Hawk

NIB	*Exc.*	*V.G.*	*Good*	*Fair*	*Poor*
1600	1500	1400	—	—	—

Mongoose

NIB	*Exc.*	*V.G.*	*Good*	*Fair*	*Poor*
3200	3000	2800	—	—	—

Korth-Nighthawk Custom Mongoose

Caliber: .357 Mag. Optional 9mm cyl. Barrel lengths: 2.75", 3", 4", 5.25", and 6" Full-lug with black DLC finish A silver DLC-finished .357 Magnum Mongoose is available with 4", 5.25", or 6" barrel configurations.

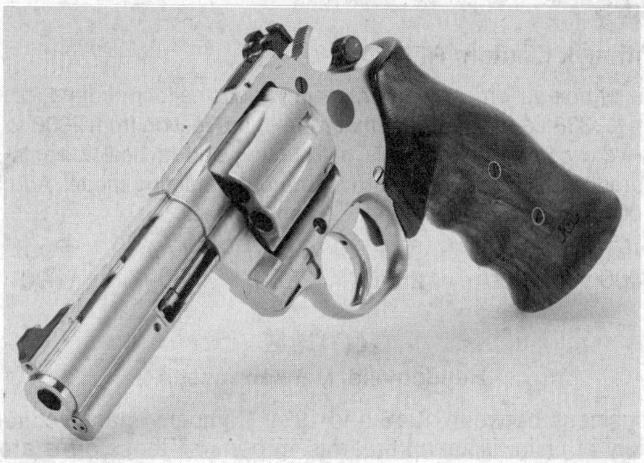

NIB	*Exc.*	*V.G.*	*Good*	*Fair*	*Poor*
2770	—	—	—	—	—

Super Sport

NIB	*Exc.*	*V.G.*	*Good*	*Fair*	*Poor*
4300	4000	3600	—	—	—

Nighthawk/Korth-Waffen NXR Revolver

Caliber: .44 Magnum. Capacity: 6 rounds. Barrel: 6 in. Grip: Ivory G10. Sights: Adjustable rear, fast-changeable front. Weight: 3.05 lbs. Features: The NXR is a futuristic-looking stainless steel double-action revolver that is black DLC-finished. Comes equipped with a removable under-barrel balancing lug/weight. Picatinny rail on top of barrel and underneath for easy accessory mounting.

NIB	*Exc.*	*V.G.*	*Good*	*Fair*	*Poor*
5300	4500	3500	—	—	—

Korth-Nighthawk Custom Vintage

Caliber: .357 Magnum. Barrel: 4" or 6" half-lug. Color-casehardened frame and barrel and charcoal blue cylinder.

NIB	*Exc.*	*V.G.*	*Good*	*Fair*	*Poor*
6750	—	—	—	—	—

SHOTGUNS

Overseer Shotgun

Slide-action 12-gauge with 6 + 1 capacity, hand-honed action and rails, tactical ghost-ring rear and fiber optic front sights, Hogue overmolded stock and forend, black Cerakote finish. Other optional features include Magpul stock and forend, ported barrel, Surefire Z2X Combat Light and Shadow Urban Tan finish. Add $150 for Magpul stock, $250 for ported barrel, $350 for Surefire Combat Light.

NIB	*Exc.*	*V.G.*	*Good*	*Fair*	*Poor*
1300	1000	800	650	400	300

RIFLES

Nighthawk Custom Rifle

Series of bolt-action centerfire rifles in various calibers from .222 Remington to .338 Lapua Magnum that were in production from 2008 to 2011. Most were competition models but hunting and tactical variants were also produced. Prices shown are for the basic hunting model. Add $250 to $600 for tactical model, depending on options.

NIB	Exc.	V.G.	Good	Fair	Poor
3400	3000	2500	2000	1200	600

NOBLE

Haydenville, Massachusetts

In business between 1946 and 1971. Company manufactured a variety of plain utilitarian firearms. In general, these arms are all worth approximately the same, that is, less than $200 in excellent condition. Noble firearms represent an attractive opportunity for beginning collectors, as most can be had very inexpensively.

RIFLES

Model 10

.22-caliber bolt-action single-shot rifle, with 24" barrel. Pistol grip stock with no checkering. Open sights. Produced in late 1950s.

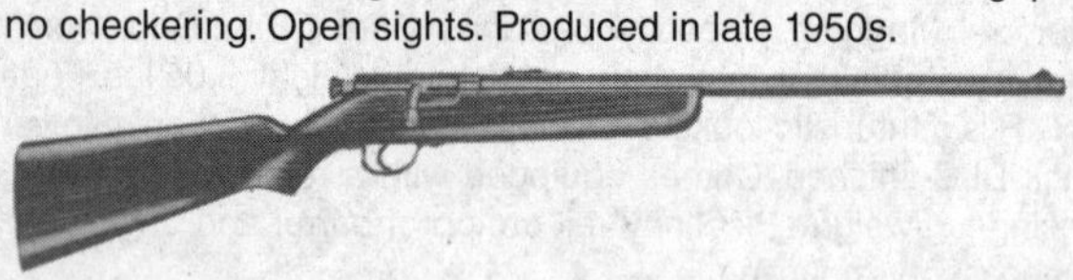

NIB	Exc.	V.G.	Good	Fair	Poor
—	80	60	50	40	30

Model 20

.22-caliber bolt-action rifle. Fitted with 22" barrel. Open sights. Produced from late 1950s to early 1960s.

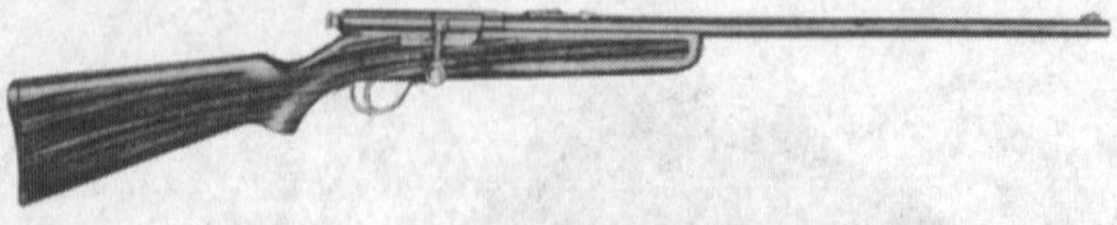

NIB	Exc.	V.G.	Good	Fair	Poor
—	80	60	50	40	30

Model 33

.22-caliber slide-action rifle. Fitted with 24" barrel and tubular magazine. Tenite stock. Produced from late 1940s to early 1950s.

NIB	Exc.	V.G.	Good	Fair	Poor
—	80	70	60	50	40

Model 33A

Same as above, with wood stock.

NIB	Exc.	V.G.	Good	Fair	Poor
—	80	60	50	40	30

Model 222

Single-shot bolt-action rifle chambered for .22-caliber cartridge. Plain pistol grip stock.

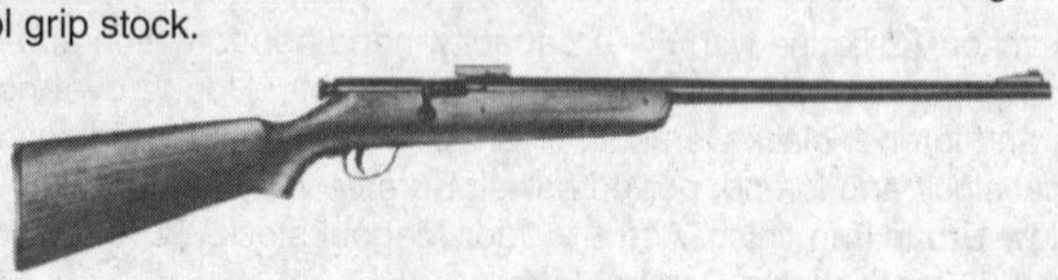

NIB	Exc.	V.G.	Good	Fair	Poor
—	80	80	60	50	40

Model 235

Rather dopey but kinda cute .22-caliber slide-action rifle, with 24" barrel. Tubular magazine. Plain pistol grip stock and grooved slide handle.

NIB	Exc.	V.G.	Good	Fair	Poor
—	200	120	80	60	50

Model 275

.22-caliber lever-action rifle, with tubular magazine. Fitted with 24" barrel. Plain stock has semi-pistol grip.

NIB	Exc.	V.G.	Good	Fair	Poor
—	180	100	80	60	50

SHOTGUNS

Model 40

Hammerless slide-action shotgun chambered for 12-gauge shell. Fitted with tubular magazine, 28" barrel with multi choke. Plain pistol stock, with grooved slide handle.

NIB	Exc.	V.G.	Good	Fair	Poor
—	120	100	80	70	50

Model 50

Same as above, without multi choke.

NIB	Exc.	V.G.	Good	Fair	Poor
—	120	90	80	60	50

Model 60

Hammerless slide-action shotgun in 12- or 16-gauge. Tubular magazine. Fitted with 28" barrel with adjustable choke. Plain pistol grip stock, with grooved slide handle.

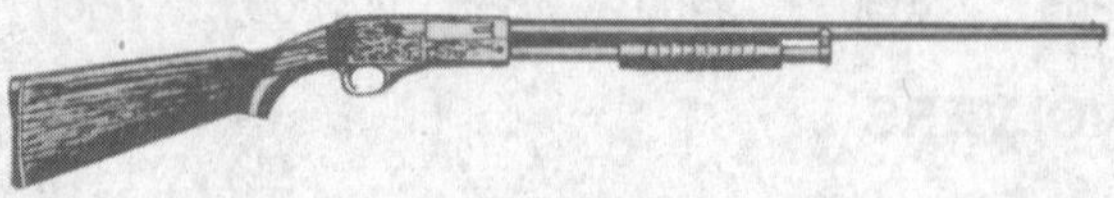

NIB	Exc.	V.G.	Good	Fair	Poor
—	180	150	120	100	80

Model 65

Same as above, without adjustable choke.

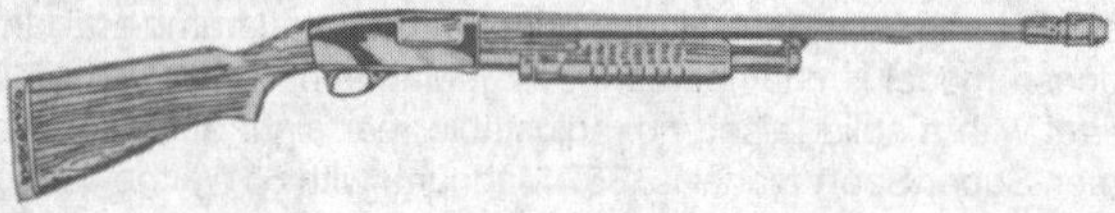

NIB	Exc.	V.G.	Good	Fair	Poor
—	150	120	100	80	60

Model 66CLP

Offered in 12- or 16-gauge. Slide-action shotgun fitted with 28" plain barrel and keyed lock fire control system.

NIB	Exc.	V.G.	Good	Fair	Poor
—	160	140	110	80	70

Model 66RCLP

Similar to above, with 28" ventilated rib barrel. Checkered pistol grip stock. Adjustable choke standard.

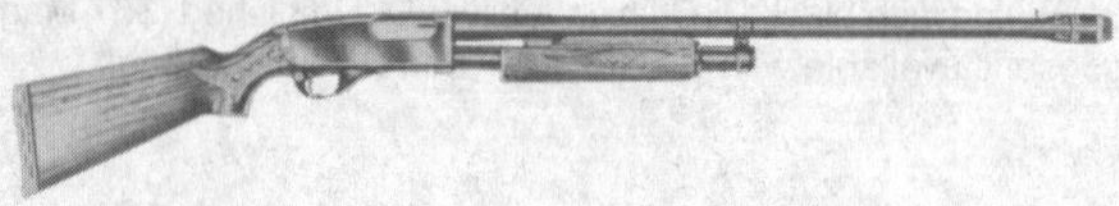

NIB	Exc.	V.G.	Good	Fair	Poor
—	200	180	150	120	100

Model 66RLP

Same as above, without adjustable choke.

NIB	Exc.	V.G.	Good	Fair	Poor
—	180	150	120	100	80

Model 66XL

Similar to above, with plain barrel. Checkering only on slide handle.

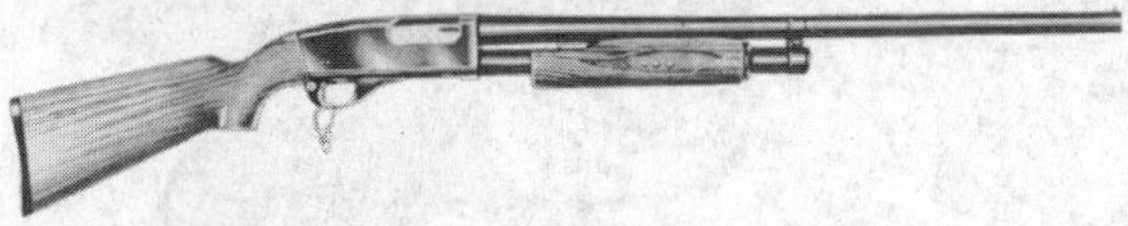

NIB	Exc.	V.G.	Good	Fair	Poor
—	150	120	100	80	60

Model 70CLP

Similar to Model 66 series. Offered in .410 bore, with 26" barrel and adjustable choke. Both buttstock and slide handle checkered.

NIB	Exc.	V.G.	Good	Fair	Poor
—	180	150	120	100	80

Model 70RCLP

Variation fitted with 26" ventilated rib barrel.

NIB	Exc.	V.G.	Good	Fair	Poor
—	200	180	150	120	100

Model 70RLP

Has ventilated rib barrel. No adjustable choke.

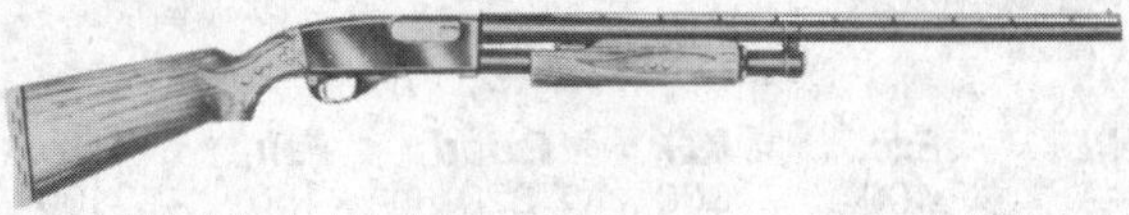

NIB	Exc.	V.G.	Good	Fair	Poor
—	180	150	120	100	80

Model 70XL

This version has no adjustable choke. Fitted with 26" ventilated rib barrel. Stock checked.

NIB	Exc.	V.G.	Good	Fair	Poor
—	120	100	80	70	60

Model 602RCLP

Hammerless slide-action shotgun chambered for 20-gauge shell. Fitted with 28" ventilated barrel and adjustable choke. Checkered pistol grip stock, with slide handle.

NIB	Exc.	V.G.	Good	Fair	Poor
—	220	200	180	120	100

Model 602CLP

Same as above, with plain barrel.

NIB	Exc.	V.G.	Good	Fair	Poor
—	180	150	120	100	80

Model 602RLP

Same as Model RCLP, without addition of adjustable choke device.

NIB	Exc.	V.G.	Good	Fair	Poor
—	200	180	150	120	100

Model 602XL

Same as above, with only slide handle checkered.

NIB	Exc.	V.G.	Good	Fair	Poor
—	150	120	100	80	60

Model 662

20-gauge slide-action shotgun. Has plain aluminum barrel, with checkered pistol grip and slide handle. Receiver is made from aluminum. Produced in late 1960s.

NIB	Exc.	V.G.	Good	Fair	Poor
—	200	180	150	120	100

Model 80

Semi-automatic inertia-operated shotgun. Chambered for .410 shell. Fitted with 26" barrel, plain pistol stock with slotted forearm. Produced in early to mid 1960s.

NIB	Exc.	V.G.	Good	Fair	Poor
—	250	200	150	120	100

Model 166L

12-gauge slide-action shotgun, with key lock system. Fitted with 24" barrel bored for rifled slug. Lyman peep rear sight with post front. Checkered pistol and slide handle.

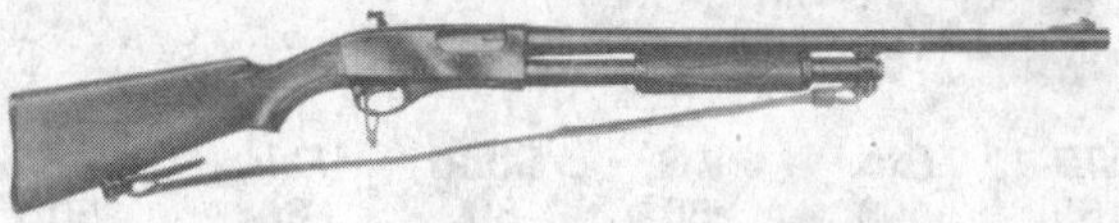

NIB	Exc.	V.G.	Good	Fair	Poor
—	250	200	150	120	100

Model 420

Box lock design side-by-side shotgun, with double triggers. Offered in 12-, 16-, 20-gauge and .410 bore. Barrel length 28" for all gauges; except .410 is 26". Lightly engraved frame. Checkered walnut stock and splinter forearm.

NIB	Exc.	V.G.	Good	Fair	Poor
—	300	250	200	150	100

Model 450E

Similar to Model 420, with addition of automatic ejectors. Not offered in .410 bore. Checkered pistol grip stock, with beavertail forearm. Produced in late 1960s.

NIB	Exc.	V.G.	Good	Fair	Poor
—	350	280	220	180	120

NORINCO

Peoples Republic of China
China North Industries Corp.

Norinco is a state-owned conglomerate in China. Exported firearms to United States from 1988 to 1995. Importation of Norinco firearms was banned in conjunction with 1994 Crime Bill and various trade sanctions against China, with the exception of several shotguns that were marketed between 1999 and 2002.

ATD .22

.22-caliber semi-automatic rifle, with 19.4" barrel and 11-shot magazine located in butt. Blued, with hardwood stock. Importation began in 1987.

NIB	Exc.	V.G.	Good	Fair	Poor
200	150	120	100	80	50

EM-321

.22-caliber slide-action rifle, with 19.5" barrel and 10-shot tubular magazine. Blued, with hardwood stock. Introduced in 1989.

NIB	Exc.	V.G.	Good	Fair	Poor
150	100	80	80	60	50

Model HL-12-203 Shotgun

12-gauge boxlock over/under shotgun, with 30" ventilated rib barrels fitted for choke tubes. Single trigger and automatic ejectors. Blued, with hardwood stock. Introduced in 1989.

NIB	Exc.	V.G.	Good	Fair	Poor
400	320	280	220	180	120

Model HL-12-102 Shotgun

12-gauge slide-action shotgun, with 28" barrel and 3-shot magazine. Blued, with hardwood stock. Introduced in 1989.

NIB	Exc.	V.G.	Good	Fair	Poor
280	220	200	180	120	100

Model 97 Hammer Pump

Similar in appearance to Winchester Model 1897 shotgun. Fitted with 20" barrel with cylinder choke. Hardwood stock.

NIB	Exc.	V.G.	Good	Fair	Poor
380	280	200	150	100	80

Type 54-1 Tokarev

7.62x25mm caliber semi-automatic pistol, with 4.6" barrel, fixed sights and 8-shot magazine. Blued, with plastic grips. Imported in 1989.

NIB	Exc.	V.G.	Good	Fair	Poor
—	300	250	200	100	80

1911 A1

Steel-framed clone of 1911 .45 A1 semi-automatic. Very popular with competition shooters as a platform for custom guns. No longer imported.

NIB	Exc.	V.G.	Good	Fair	Poor
—	400	350	200	100	80

Model 213 Pistol

Copy of Browning P-35 semi-automatic pistol. Sold in 1988 only.

NIB	Exc.	V.G.	Good	Fair	Poor
—	250	200	150	100	80

Type 59 Makarov

.380 or 9mm Makarov caliber double-action semi-automatic pistol, with 3.5" barrel and 8-shot magazine. Blued, with plastic grips.

NIB	Exc.	V.G.	Good	Fair	Poor
—	280	250	220	180	120

SKS Rifle

7.62x39mm caliber semi-automatic rifle, with 20.5" barrel. Folding bayonet and 10-shot fixed or 30-shot detachable magazine. Blued, with hardwood stock. Importation began in 1988.

NIB	Exc.	V.G.	Good	Fair	Poor
—	400	300	220	150	100

Type 84S AK

Similar to AKS service rifle in 5.56mm caliber, with 16" barrel and 30-shot magazine.

NIB	Exc.	V.G.	Good	Fair	Poor
900	800	700	550	350	200

Type 84S-1

As above, with under-folding metal stock.

NIB	Exc.	V.G.	Good	Fair	Poor
1050	900	750	580	380	220

Type 84S-3

As above, with composition stock.

NIB	Exc.	V.G.	Good	Fair	Poor
1000	850	700	600	400	220

NORTH AMERICAN ARMS

Provo, Utah

Originally launched as Rocky Mountain Arms in 1971 producing firearms designed by Dick Casull, the firm was known for the creation of single-action revolvers named "The world's largest and smallest." Renamed "North American Arms," NAA then became a subsidiary of aerospace firm Talley Manufacturing. Purchased by Teleflex in the 1980s, the new owner in turn sold NAA to Sandy Chisholm (current president) in 1991. NAA's current focus is on stainless steel Mini-Revolvers in .22 Short, .22 Long Rifle or .22 Winchester Magnum Rimfire with spur triggers, short barrels, and (since 1998) small centerfire automatics. The business has remained in Provo, Utah, for the last 25 years.

Mini-Revolver

.22 or .22 Magnum caliber spur trigger revolver, with 1" or 2.5" barrel and 5-shot cylinder. Stainless steel, with plastic or laminated rosewood grips.

Introduced in 1975. Made in styles listed.

Mini-Revolver Standard Rimfire Version

Single-action Mini revolver in .22 Short, .22 LR or .22 WMR with barrels from 1 1/8" to 1 5/8", and Rosewood bird's head grips. The 5-shot .22 LR with 1 1/8" barrels has a weight of 4.6 oz (6.2 oz in .22 WMR), width of .88" (1.06" in WMR), height of 2.38" (2.81" in .22 WMR) and an overall length of about 4" (4.63" in WMR). Sights are a fixed notch in the frame and a 1/2-moon front. Note: Add $10 for .22 WMR; Add $30 for ported magnum.

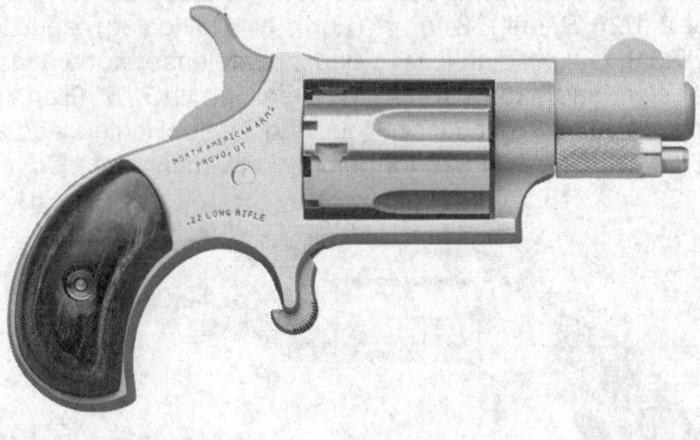

NIB	Exc.	V.G.	Good	Fair	Poor
200	170	140	120	70	50

Mini-Revolver Magnum 2-Cylinder Convertible

Similar to the Standard Rimfire above, the 5-shot .22 WMR version of the Mini revolver can be ordered with an extra .22 LR cylinder.

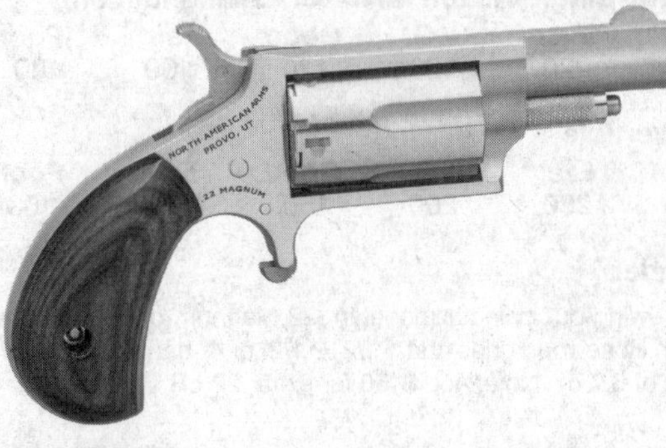

NIB	Exc.	V.G.	Good	Fair	Poor
230	200	170	140	70	50

Belt Buckle Versions

A belt buckle enclosing a Mini .22 LR with 1 1/8" barrel on a belt of 1" to 1 1/2" wide. Also available with a skeleton belt buckle. Note: Deduct $50 for skeleton buckle set. Deduct $30 for skeleton buckle with .22 WMR.

NIB	Exc.	V.G.	Good	Fair	Poor
250	120	180	150	90	60

Holster Grip

The Mini revolver can be had with a folding grip extension in .22 LR with 1 1/8" or 1 5/8" barrel. Note: Add $15 for .22 WMR. Add $30 for .22 WMR/.22LR.

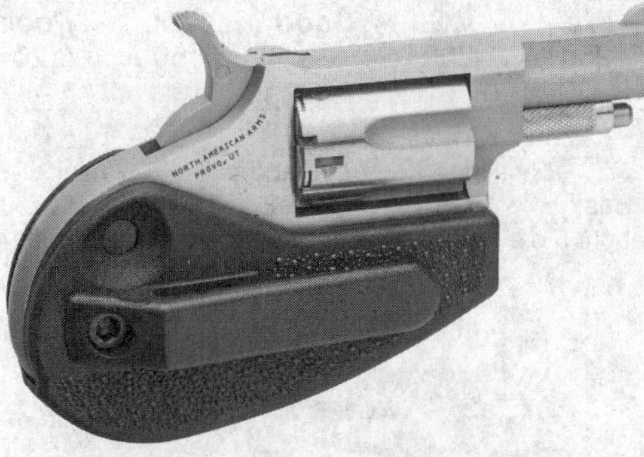

NIB	Exc.	V.G.	Good	Fair	Poor
220	190	160	140	80	50

Mini-RevolverViper Belt Buckle Version

NIB	Exc.	V.G.	Good	Fair	Poor
220	180	150	—	120	100

Magnum Version

NIB	Exc.	V.G.	Good	Fair	Poor
210	170	150	130	110	100

Mini-Revolver .17 Caliber Model

Available in .17 HMR, .17 Mach 2 or convertible, with both cylinders. Note: Add $35 for convertible model. Deduct $20 for .17 Mach 2. Deduct $20 for .17 Mach 2. Discontinued.

NIB	Exc.	V.G.	Good	Fair	Poor
180	160	140	120	100	80

Mini-RevolverStandard 3 Gun Set

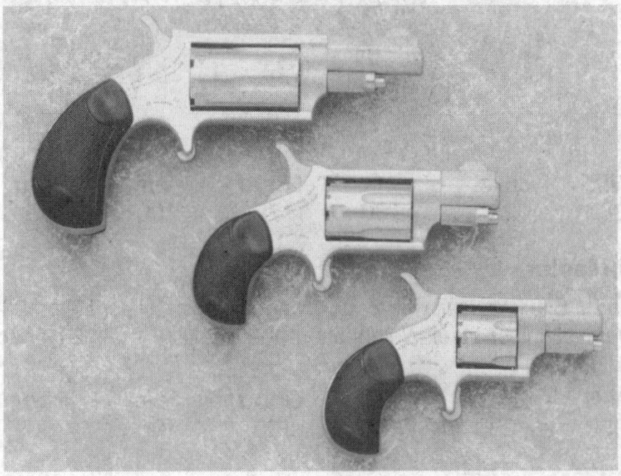

NIB	Exc.	V.G.	Good	Fair	Poor
720	580	400	350	300	220

Deluxe 3 Gun Set

NIB	Exc.	V.G.	Good	Fair	Poor
800	650	480	420	380	280

Cased .22 Magnum

NIB	Exc.	V.G.	Good	Fair	Poor
350	250	200	—	150	120

Companion

Percussion .22-caliber cap-and-ball mini revolver. Has 1.125" barrel. Overall length 4.6"; weight about 5 oz. Note: Add about $50 for Earl model with 4" barrel.

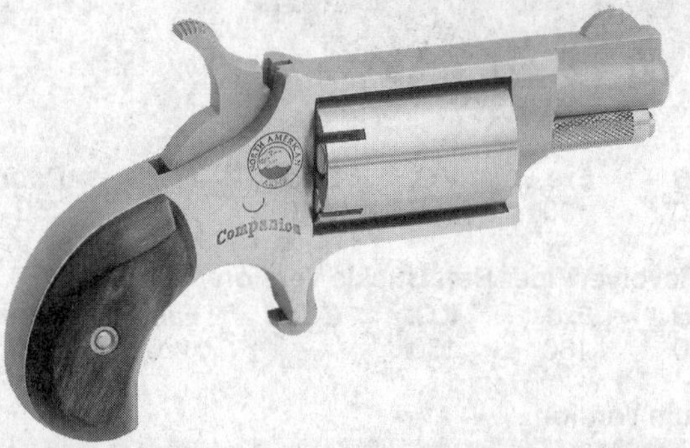

NIB	Exc.	V.G.	Good	Fair	Poor
220	190	160	140	80	50

Super Companion

Same as above, with longer cylinder. Has 1.62" barrel. Weight about 7 oz.

NIB	Exc.	V.G.	Good	Fair	Poor
200	160	150	120	100	80

Black Widow

Five-shot fixed-sight revolver, with 2" or 4" barrel and oversize black rubber grips. Chambered for .22 LR or .22 Win. Magnum stainless steel. Weight about 8.8 oz. Note: Add $20 for adjustable sights.

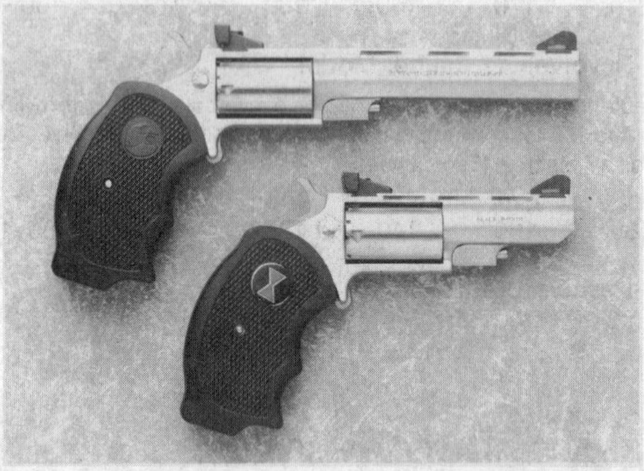

NIB	Exc.	V.G.	Good	Fair	Poor
280	220	180	120	100	80

Mini-Master

Similar to Black Widow, with 2" or 4" barrel. Choice of .22 LR or .22 Win. Magnum stainless steel. Weight about 10.7 oz. Note: Add $20 for adjustable sights.

NIB	Exc.	V.G.	Good	Fair	Poor
280	220	180	120	100	80

Pug

A .22 LR or .22 WMR with 1" heavy barrel, over-sized pebble-textured rubber grips, fixed, dovetailed, XS White Dot Sights. Note: Add $40 for XS tritium front sight; Add $20 for 2-cylinder set.

NIB	Exc.	V.G.	Good	Fair	Poor
280	240	200	170	100	60

Sheriff, Earl and Hogleg

Single-action mini-revolver patterned after the 1858-style Remington percussion revolver. Chambered in .22 WMR. Features include octagonal barrel 2 1/2" (Sheriff), 3" or 4" (Earl), or 6" (Hogleg), spur trigger, 5-shot cylinder, faux loading-lever cylinder pin release, wood grips, fixed notch rear sight and barleycorn front. Overall length 7.75" (Earl), height 3.13", width .94" and weight 6.8 oz. Note: Add $10 for Hogleg; Add $25 for extra .22 LR cylinder; Add $20 for percussion version (see Companion model).

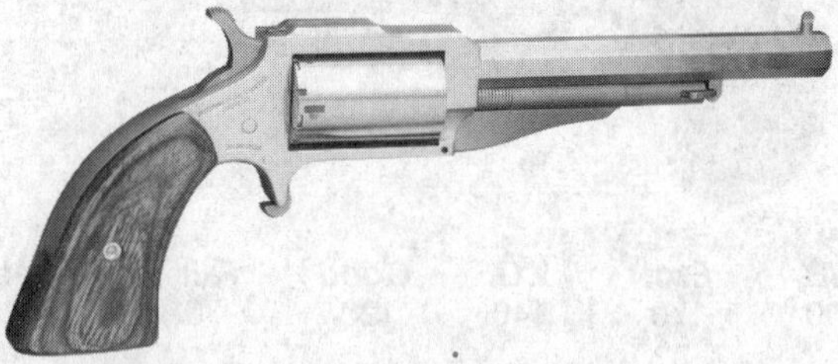

NIB	Exc.	V.G.	Good	Fair	Poor
250	120	180	150	90	60

"The Earl" Single-Action Revolver.22 Magnum only

NIB	Exc.	V.G.	Good	Fair	Poor
250	220	180	120	100	80

.22 convertible

NIB	Exc.	V.G.	Good	Fair	Poor
300	280	200	150	120	100

Sidewinder

A 5-shot swing-out cylinder model in .22 Magnum or .22 LR. Stainless steel, with Rosewood grips and 1 1/2", 2 1/2" or 4" barrel. Length of about 5", weight of 6.7 oz. Note: Add $150 for extra .22 LR cylinder.

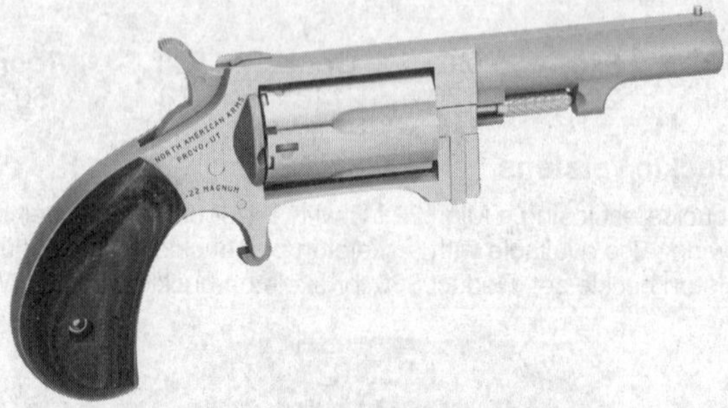

NIB	Exc.	V.G.	Good	Fair	Poor
260	130	190	150	100	60

Single-Action Revolver

Polished stainless steel single-action revolver. Chambered for .45 Win. Magnum and .450 Magnum Express cartridge. Has 7.5" barrel and 5-shot cylinder. Transfer bar safety and walnut grips. Discontinued.

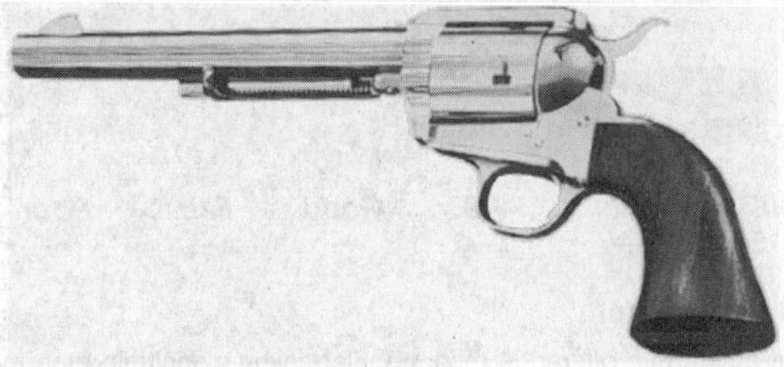

NIB	Exc.	V.G.	Good	Fair	Poor
1300	1200	950	700	400	250

Guardian .32 ACP

Semi-automatic double-action-only pocket pistol. Chambered in proprietary bottlenecked .25 NAA or .32 ACP. Magazine capacity 6+1 rounds. Barrel length 2.2"; overall length 4.4"; weight empty 13.5 oz. Introduced in 1998. Note: Add 25 percent for Crimson Trace laser grips; Add $20 for Integrated Locking System.

NIB	Exc.	V.G.	Good	Fair	Poor
350	300	250	220	130	80

Guardian .380 ACP

Similar to above. Chambered in proprietary bottlenecked .32 NAA or .380 ACP cartridge. Barrel length 2.5". Magazine capacity 6+1 rounds. Weight about 19 oz. Note: Add 25 percent for Crimson Trace laser grips. Add $20 for Integrated Locking System.

NIB	Exc.	V.G.	Good	Fair	Poor
390	330	280	240	140	90

The Ranger II

Top-break revolver in .22 LR or .22 WMR, star ejector, full ribbed barrel of 1 5/8", 2 1/2", 4" long, bead blast finish, weight of about 8 oz. Note: Add $100 for extra cylinder/extractor assembly.

NIB	Exc.	V.G.	Good	Fair	Poor
470	400	340	290	170	100

Custom, Curious & Collectibles

NAA offers limited production of the revolvers and pistols for consumers as well as "dealer exclusives" with a wide array of special finishes. Currently, revolvers may be found fully case hardened in colors with a variety of grip options; 24K gold plated with synthetic pearl grips; carbon steel with blued finish and a variety of grips; and an engraved Guardian pistol with synthetic pearl grips in all calibers. Values for NIB will be from $340 to $500 depending on original retails and options. Most will be found in NIB to V.G. conditions.

NORTH AMERICAN ARMS CORP.

Toronto, Canada

Brigadier

.45 ACP caliber semi-automatic pistol, with 5" barrel, 8-shot magazine and alloy frame. Weight 4.5 lbs. Produced in limited quantity between 1948 and 1951. Rarely if ever seen. Note: Value should be in excess of $5000 in Excellent or better condition.

NORTH AMERICAN SAFARI EXPRESS

Liege, Belgium

See—FRANCOTTE

Trade name used by Francotte on their double rifles imported and distributed by Armes De Chasse of Chads Ford, Pennsylvania.

NORTH & COUCH

New York, New York

Animal Trap Gun

.28- or .30-caliber percussion pepperbox, with 1.75" or 2.12" barrel group. Hammer made with-/without spur. Marked "North & Couch, Middletown, Conn." or "North & Couch New York". Manufactured during 1860s. All barrels fire simultaneously. Intended to be set as an untended trap gun, firing when the bait is pulled (a truly horrid idea). Unlike most animal trap guns, these models could also be fired as a pistol by pulling the trigger.

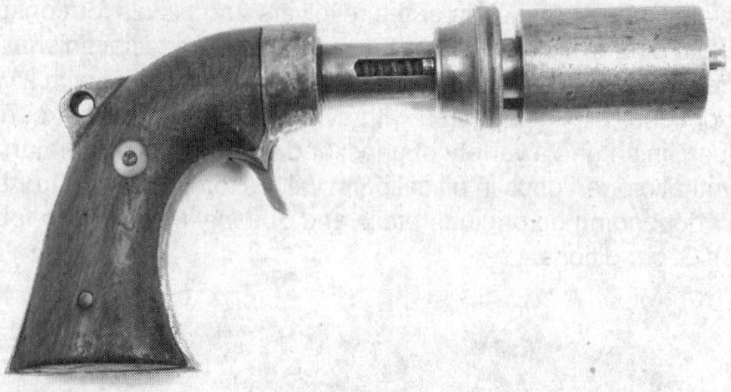

Photo courtesy NRA Museums

Disk Hammer Model (Antique)

Exc.	Fine	V.G.	Good	Fair	Poor
2500	1850	1270	700	300	210

Spur Hammer Model (Antique)

Exc.	Fine	V.G.	Good	Fair	Poor
3000	2750	1820	900	350	240

NORTON ARMAMENT CORPORATION

Mt. Clemens, Michigan

See—BUDISCHOWSKY

Firm manufactured Budischowsky Model TP-70 semi-automatic pistols prior to 1979. After that date, these arms were made by American Arms and Ammunition Company. Values below are for early Michigan production. Note: Deduct 15 percent for later Florida and Utah production.

NIB	Exc.	V.G.	Good	Fair	Poor
—	500	380	250	120	100

NOSLER CUSTOM

Bend, Oregon

Model 21

Calibers: 22 Nosler, 6.5 Creedmoor, 6.5 PRC, 26 Nosler, 27 Nosler, .280 Ackley Improved, 28 Nosler, .308 Win., .300 Win. Mag., 30 Nosler, 33 Nosler, .375 H&H Magnum. Capacity: 3 or 4 rounds depending on caliber. Barrel: 22- or 24-in. Shilen match-grade stainless Weight: 6.8–7.1 lbs. Length: 41.625–44.5 in. Stock: McMillian Hunters Edge Sporter 100% carbon fiber painted in all-weather epoxy-style finish. Sights: No iron sights; contoured to accept any standard two-piece scope base that would otherwise fit a Remington 700. Features: Nosler's new rifle design for 2022 with a blueprinted action, wire EDM machined receiver, spriral-fluted, one-piece, nitride coated bolt. TriggerTech Frictionless Release trigger. M16-style extractor and fire control group feature tool-less takedown. LOP of 13.5-in. with one-inch recoil pad. Threaded barrel with knurled cover.

NIB	Exc.	V.G.	Good	Fair	Poor
2600	—	—	—	—	—

Model 21 Carbon Chassis Hunter

Calibers: 6.5 Creedmoor, 6.5 PRC, 28 Nosler, .300 Win. Mag. Barrel: 24", 26" Proof Sendero contour carbon-fiber threaded. Weight: 6.9 lbs. (short actions) 7.1 lbs. (long action) Stock: MDT HNT26 collapsible. Features: Nosler's first chassis rifle on the Model 21 bolt-action family. Blueprinted action with magnesium alloy frame. Fluted bolt with nitride coating. TriggerTech Primary trigger. ARCA rail.

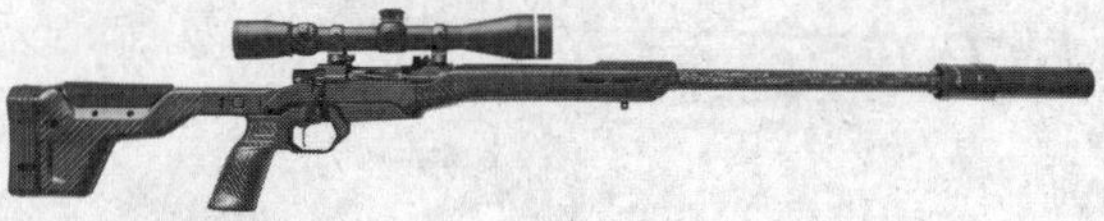

NIB	Exc.	V.G.	Good	Fair	Poor
5150	—	—	—	—	—

Model 48 Custom

A bolt-action rifle offered in most popular calibers, including the manufacturer's proprietary cartridges: 22 Nosler (.223), 26 Nosler (6.5), 28 Nosler (7mm), 30 Nosler (.308) and 33 Nosler (.338). Other calibers from .243 Win. to .458 Win. Magnum. Every Model 48 Custom Rifle includes these features: upgraded Match-grade, stainless steel, hand-lapped barrel, custom 3-pound trigger pull, glass and stainless steel pillar bedding, Kevlar carbon fiber stock, Cerakote and Micro Slick metal finish, accuracy test with prescribed Nosler ammunition guaranteed .75" or better 3-shot groups at 100 yards, or 1" for belted Magnums and calibers .35 and up. Options include a choice of several stock colors, two or three-position safety, barrel lengths from 20" to 26", muzzle brake, iron sights, left-hand action. All optional items at additional cost. Several package variants have been produced including Leupold or Swarvoski optics. In addition to the variations of the Model 48 listed below, Nosler has recently offered the following, with MSRP:
Model 48 Mountain Carbon Rifle - $3,140
Model 48 Liberty - $1,935
Model 48 Long Range Rifle - $2,675
Model 48 LR Carbon Long Range Rifle - $3,190
Model 48 Independence Handgun – single shot bolt action.

NIB	Exc.	V.G.	Good	Fair	Poor
2200	1800	1500	1100	700	300

Model 48 Professional

Custom made on Nosler action, with glass-bedded Aramid Fiber reinforced composite stock. Match-grade hand-lapped stainless steel barrel. Custom 3-pound trigger, 2-position safety, choice of fixed or detachable magazine. Available in most popular calibers from .22-250 to 9.3x62mm.

NIB	Exc.	V.G.	Good	Fair	Poor
2500	2100	1850	1200	600	350

Model 48 Heritage

Features a fancy grade walnut checkered stock, 2-position safety, match-grade free-floated barrel and hinged floorplate. Offered in most popular calibers.

NIB	Exc.	V.G.	Good	Fair	Poor
1750	1500	1100	700	500	250

Model 48 Independence Handgun

Bolt-action single-shot pistol; 15" barrel. .22 Nosler, 6mm Creedmoor, .34 Nosler, 6.5 Creedmoor, 7mm-08, or .308 Win. The similar Model 48 NCH (Nosler Custom Handgun) includes a muzzle brake.

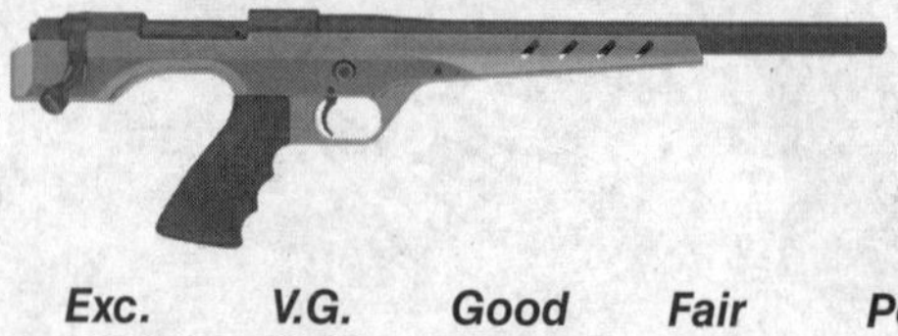

NIB	Exc.	V.G.	Good	Fair	Poor
1500	1250	950	—	—	—

Model 48 NCH (Nosler Custom Handgun)

Calibers: 22 Nosler, 7mm-08, 6mm Creedmoor, 6.5 Creedmoor, .308 Winchester. Standard barrel length 15" with 12" to 18" barrels available upon request. Stock: CNC machined 6061-T6 aircraft-grade aluminum. Bedded action. Free-floated barrel. Finish: Variety of Cerakote colors and combinations. Action: single-shot, solid bottom receiver. Brake: Harrell's Precision Tactical 4-Port is available. Grip: Accepts standard AR-15 grips. Ships with Hogue OverMolded rubber grip with finger grooves. Barrel: Shilen 416R stainless heavy contour. Threaded at the muzzle, supplied with thread protector. Barrel fluting is available for an additional charge.

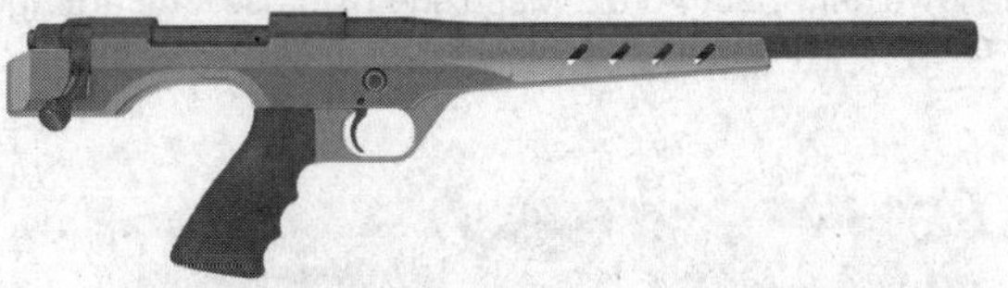

NIB	Exc.	V.G.	Good	Fair	Poor
1870	1650	1400	—	—	—

Custom Rifle (Limited Edition)

Built on Nosler action, with integral scope bases, hand-lapped stainless steel barrel, glass bedded American walnut stock with 20 lpi checkering. Comes with choice of three VX3 Leupold scopes with matching serial number and custom reticle designed for different chamberings. Limited to 500 rifles per series. Offered in .300 WSM, .280 Ackley Improved, .338 Win. Magnum.

NIB	Exc.	V.G.	Good	Fair	Poor
4000	3750	3200	2600	—	—

Varmageddon

AR-15 style semi-automatic in .223 Rem. Features include 18" Noveske stainless barrel, with 1/2 x 28 muzzle threads, low profile gas block, Noveske backup iron sights, forged Vltor upper receiver. Comes with Leupold CDS VX3 4.5-14x50 scope and mounts, Harris bi-pod, soft case and two boxes of Nosler Varmageddon ammo. Made for Nosler by Noveske Rifleworks. New in 2013

NIB	Exc.	V.G.	Good	Fair	Poor
2100	1850	1600	1400	—	—

NOVESKE RIFLEWORKS

Grants Pass, Oregon

Maker of AR-style firearms, parts and accessories.

Gen 4 N4 PDW

Calibers: 5.56 NATO, 6.5 Grendel, .300 BLK. Barrel: 16", stainless steel hammer-forged, muzzle thread pitch 1/2×28. Twist: 1:7". Low-profile adjustable gas block, direct impingement. PDW-style collapsible stock. M-LOK free-float handguard, Magpul MBUS PRO folding sights, and a Geissele Super Badass charging handle. Full-length Picatinny rail, ambidextrous safety selector. SEE POLITICAL PANIC PRICING.

NIB	Exc.	V.G.	Good	Fair	Poor
2790	2600	2430	2100	—	—

Chainsaw Rifle

Caliber: 5.56 NATO/.223 Rem. Noveske's forged product offering based on a hybrid of Gen 1 and Gen 4 designs. Barrel: 16" 416R stainless, 1:7" twist. Hand-polished Noveske Match Chamber, mid-length gas tube system. Noveske marked gas block: Low-profile .750" journal pinned to the barrel. M4 barrel extension w/extended hand-polished feed ramps, 1/2x28 muzzle threads with an A2 birdcage flash hider. Noveske Chainsaw forged upper receiver with extended feed ramps. Radian Raptor LT charging handle. Phosphate-coated bolt carrier, full auto compatible, chrome-lined carrier bore, and key. Properly staked Grade 8 American-made gas key bolts. Phosphate bolt made from Carpenter 158 heat-treated steel, MPI tested. GEN 4 NSR-15 (M-LOK) free-floating handguard. A flared magazine well. Magpul-enhanced aluminum triggerguard. ALG Defense Advanced Combat Trigger. Stock: Magpul MOE SL. Grip: Magpul MOE K2. Length collapsed: 35 1/4" 6.8 lbs. One 30-rd. Gen 3 PMAG. Introduced 2022. SEE POLITICAL PANIC PRICING.

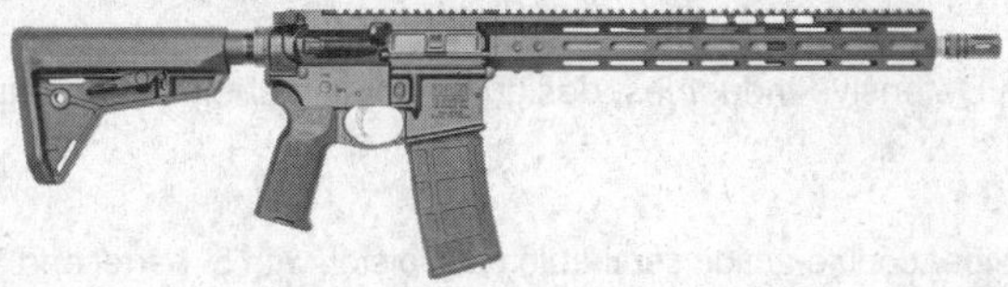

NIB	Exc.	V.G.	Good	Fair	Poor
1980	—	—	—	—	—

NORWICH PISTOL CO.

Norwich, Connecticut

Established in 1875 by New York retailer Maltby, Curtis & Company. This firm manufactured a wide variety of inexpensive spur trigger revolvers that were sold under these trade names: America, Bulldozer, Challenge, Chieftain, Crescent, Defiance, Hartford Arms, Maltby Henley, Metropolitan Police, Nonpariel, Norwich Arms, Parole, Patriot, Pinafore, Prairie King, Protector, Spy, True Blue, U.M.C. Winfield Arms. Company ceased operations in 1881. Value for any of its arms listed is approximate.

NIB	Exc.	V.G.	Good	Fair	Poor
—	—	300	200	80	50

NOVO

See—OURY

NOWLIN MANUFACTURING COMPANY

Claremore, Oklahoma

Match Classic

This 1911 pistol has a wide range of features. Can be chambered in 9mm, .38 Super, 9x23, .40 S&W and .45 ACP. Has 5" barrel, adjustable trigger, checkered main spring housing, hardwood grips, front and rear cocking serrations. Price listed for basic pistols. Options will greatly affect price.

NIB	Exc.	V.G.	Good	Fair	Poor
1600	1250	800	600	400	250

Compact Carry

Similar to Match Classic, with exception of 4" barrel on full-size frame. Again, options will greatly affect price.

NIB	Exc.	V.G.	Good	Fair	Poor
1500	1100	700	500	300	200

Match Master

These hand-built pistols offered choice of S.T.I., Caspian Hi-Cap or Nowlin STD Government frames. Available in 9mm, 9x23, .38 Super, .40 S&W and .45 ACP. Many special features included in standard pistol. Many extra cost options are available. Note: Add $140 for hard chrome finish.

NIB	Exc.	V.G.	Good	Fair	Poor
2400	1750	1200	800	600	300

O

O.D.I.
Midland Park, New Jersey

Odin Defensive Industries, design by Louis Wilhelm Seecamp.

Viking

.45-caliber double-action semi-automatic pistol, with 5" barrel and 7-shot magazine. Stainless steel, with teak grips. Manufactured in 1981 and 1982.

NIB	Exc.	V.G.	Good	Fair	Poor
700	620	380	300	200	100

Viking Combat

As above, with 4.25" barrel.

NIB	Exc.	V.G.	Good	Fair	Poor
700	620	380	300	200	100

O.K.
See—MARLIN

O'CONNELL, DAVID
New York, New York

Pocket Pistol (Antique)

.41-caliber percussion pocket pistol, with 2.5" barrel, German silver mounts and walnut stock. Manufactured during 1850s. Also See note on UNDERHAMMER PISTOLS & DERRINGERS at lines 510 & 511

Exc.	Fine	V.G.	Good	Fair	Poor
3650	3000	2010	1020	300	210

O'DELL, STEPHEN
Natchez, Mississippi

Pocket Pistol (Antique)

.34- to .44-caliber percussion pocket pistol, with 2" to 4" barrel, German silver mounts and walnut stock. Manufactured during 1850s. Also See note on UNDERHAMMER PISTOLS & DERRINGERS at lines 510 & 511

Exc.	Fine	V.G.	Good	Fair	Poor
6750	6000	4250	2500	950	660

OBREGON
Mexico City, Mexico

This is a .45-caliber semi-automatic pistol, with 5" barrel. Similar to Colt M1911A1, with combination side and safety latch on left side of frame. Breech is locked by rotating barrel, instead of Browning swinging link. This unusual locking system results in a tubular front end appearance to pistol. Originally designed for Mexican military, it was not adopted as such and only about 1,000 pistols were produced and sold commercially. Pistol is 8.5" overall; weight about 40 oz. Magazine holds seven cartridges. A rare pistol; independent appraisal suggested prior to sale.

NIB	Exc.	V.G.	Good	Fair	Poor
—	5000	3750	2500	1750	900

OHIO ORDNANCE INC.
Chardon, Ohio

Model 1918A3 Self-Loading Rifle

Semi-automatic version of famed Browning Automatic Rifle. Chambered for .30-06 cartridge. Has a 20-round magazine. Introduced in this configuration in 1996. Note: Add $200 for .308 or 8mm caliber guns. Deduct 10 percent for bakelite stock.

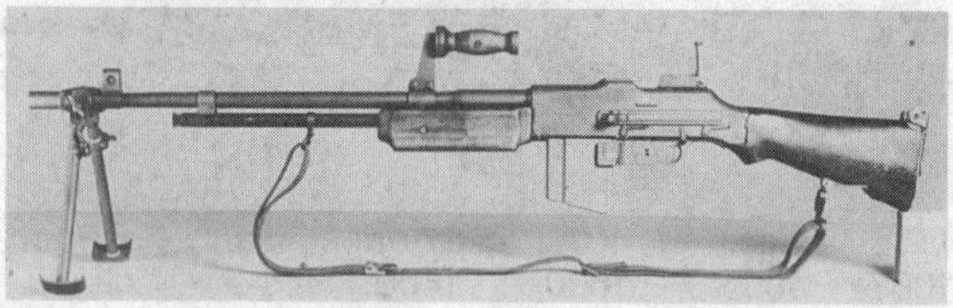

NIB	Exc.	V.G.	Good	Fair	Poor
6250	5000	3750	—	—	—

Colt Browning Water Cooled Gun

Introduced in 2001. Semi-automatic version of famous Browning Model 1928 belt-fed machine gun. Features .30-06 or 7.65 Argentine caliber belt-fed gun, with tripod, wooden ammo box, water hose, water can and one 250 cloth belt. Note: Add $200 for .308 or 8mm caliber guns.

NIB	Exc.	V.G.	Good	Fair	Poor
4750	3750	2750	—	—	—

1919A4

Semi-automatic version of air-cooled belt-fed .30-caliber 1919 machine gun. Chambered for .308/7.62 NATO.

NIB	Exc.	V.G.	Good	Fair	Poor
3500	2800	2000	1250	1100	500

OJANGUREN Y VIDOSA
Eibar, Spain

This typical Eibar company produced mediocre firearms from early 1920s. Forced out of business during Spanish Civil War.

Apache (Model 1920)

Typical Eibar Browning copy chambered for 6.35mm cartridge. Low quality associated with most Spanish arms of this era. Slide marked "Pistole Browning Automatica Cal. 6.35 Apache". Finish is blued. Plastic grips have a head with a beret and word "Apache" molded into them.

NIB	Exc.	V.G.	Good	Fair	Poor
—	250	180	120	80	50

7.65mm

As above chambered for 7.65mm cartridge.

Courtesy James Rankin

NIB	Exc.	V.G.	Good	Fair	Poor
—	280	220	190	100	80

Ojanguren

Trade name this company used to cover line of revolvers they produced in 1930s. Produced two in .32-caliber and two chambered for .38 Special cartridge. Similar in appearance and barrel lengths of 3" or 6". Finishes are blued, with plastic grips. One of the .38-caliber models "Legitimo Tanque" is a reasonably well-made gun that was popular with Spanish target shooters. These guns have little collector or practical value and are all priced alike.

NIB	Exc.	V.G.	Good	Fair	Poor
—	180	120	100	80	50

Tanque

Blowback-operated semi-automatic chambered for 6.35mm cartridge. Has a 1.5" barrel and is actually an original design, which was rarely found on Eibar guns of this period. Has an oddly shaped slide and barrel is retained by means of a screw in front of frame. It has a 6-shot magazine and slide marked "6.35 Tanque Patent". Plastic grips have a tank molded into them and word "Tanque", as well as letters "O&V".

NIB	Exc.	V.G.	Good	Fair	Poor
—	180	120	100	80	50

OLD WEST GUN CO.

Houston, Texas

See—CIMARRON ARMS

An importer of reproduction firearms primarily manufactured by Aldo Uberti of Italy. In 1987, this company purchased the inventory of Allen Firearms and subsequently changed their name to Cimarron Arms.

OLYMPIC ARMS, INC.

Olympia, Washington

This company was in business for more than 60 years, first as a barrel maker and later as a manufacturer of bolt-action and AR-style rifles. In the 1980s, company bought Safari Arms, a manufacturer of 1911-style pistols. Many of these models remained in production under the Safari name until 2004, when they were changed to the Olympic brand. In 2014, the company announced that all handgun production was being discontinued. In 2017 the company announced it was closing. The notice turned out to be premature, and as of Summer 2020, Olympic Arms remains in business. Brian Schuetz, son of founder Bob Schuetz, is now President. Current production is focused on AR-type rifles.

PISTOLS

Black Widow

.45-caliber semi-automatic pistol, with 3.9" barrel and 6-shot magazine. Nickel-plated, with ivory Micarta grips with a spider engraved on them.

NIB	Exc.	V.G.	Good	Fair	Poor
700	580	450	350	300	200

Enforcer

.45-caliber semi-automatic pistol, with 3.8" barrel and 6-shot magazine. Parkerized, anodized or nickel-plated, with rubber grips. Weight about 36 oz.

NIB	Exc.	V.G.	Good	Fair	Poor
900	750	600	450	300	200

Match Master

As above, with 5" barrel and 7-shot magazine. Weight about 40 oz.

NIB	Exc.	V.G.	Good	Fair	Poor
650	500	400	350	300	200

Match Master 6"

Same as above, with 6" barrel and slide. Weight about 44 oz.

NIB	Exc.	V.G.	Good	Fair	Poor
680	550	400	350	300	200

Cohort

Fitted with 4" bull barrel. Full size frame. Magazine capacity 7 rounds. Weight about 38 oz.

NIB	Exc.	V.G.	Good	Fair	Poor
800	650	500	400	300	200

Safari G.I.

Built on Match Master frame, with 5" barrel and fixed sights. Finish is flat black Parkerized. Checkered walnut grips.

NIB	Exc.	V.G.	Good	Fair	Poor
600	450	400	350	300	200

Schuetzen Pistol Works Big Deuce

Made in Olympic Arms specialty shop called, Schuetzen Pistol Works. Marked "Schuetzen Pistol Works" on slide and "Safari Arms" on frame. Introduced in 1995. Semi-automatic pistol chambered for .45 ACP cartridge. Fitted with 6" barrel, smooth walnut grips and a number of other custom features. Magazine capacity 7 rounds. Weight about 40 oz. Black slide, with stainless steel frame.

NIB	Exc.	V.G.	Good	Fair	Poor
950	800	700	500	280	150

Schuetzen Pistol Works Crest

Similar to above model with same markings. This version features .45 ACP pistol, with 4.5", 5" or 5.5" barrel. Checkered walnut grips. Offered in both right-/left-hand configurations. Stainless steel finish. Introduced in 1993. Weight about 39 oz. depending on barrel length. Note: Left-hand model will bring a small premium.

NIB	Exc.	V.G.	Good	Fair	Poor
800	650	500	400	280	150

Schuetzen Pistol Works Griffon

Similar to above specialty models. This version fitted with 5" barrel and smooth walnut grips. Magazine capacity 10 rounds. Stainless steel finish. Numerous custom features. Introduced in 1995.

NIB	Exc.	V.G.	Good	Fair	Poor
1300	1150	980	650	400	200

Schuetzen Pistol Works Carrier

Special built model along the lines of Detonics Score Master, with adjustable sights.

NIB	Exc.	V.G.	Good	Fair	Poor
700	600	500	400	250	150

Black-Tac

Semi-automatic .45 ACP pistol treated with "black-tac" process – advantages of hard chrome without its drawbacks such as embrittlement.

NIB	Exc.	V.G.	Good	Fair	Poor
800	650	500	400	280	150

Constable

Semi-automatic pistol chambered for .45 ACP, with 4" barrel, 5.75" sight radius, 7+1 capacity, weight 35 oz. Introduced 2006.

NIB	Exc.	V.G.	Good	Fair	Poor
950	800	700	500	280	150

Custom Street Deuce

Semi-automatic chambered for .45 ACP, with 5.2" bull barrel, 7" sight radius, 7+1 capacity, weight 38 oz. Many options. Introduced 2006.

NIB	Exc.	V.G.	Good	Fair	Poor
1300	1150	980	650	400	200

Custom Journeyman

Semi-automatic chambered for .45 ACP, with 4" bull barrel, 6" sight radius, 6+1 capacity, weight 35 oz. Many options. Introduced 2006.

NIB	Exc.	V.G.	Good	Fair	Poor
1100	800	680	500	300	150

Trail Boss

Semi-automatic pistol in Westerner line chambered for .45 ACP, with 6" barrel, 8" sight radius, 7+1 capacity, weight 43 oz. Introduced 2006.

NIB	Exc.	V.G.	Good	Fair	Poor
950	800	700	500	280	150

Westerner

Semi-automatic pistol chambered for .45 ACP, with 5" barrel, 7" sight radius, 7+1 capacity, weight 39 oz. Introduced 2006.

NIB	Exc.	V.G.	Good	Fair	Poor
950	800	700	500	280	150

Wolverine

Polymer-frame ventilated rib replica of old "ray gun" .22 Whitney Wolverine semi-automatic pistol.

NIB	Exc.	V.G.	Good	Fair	Poor
300	260	250	200	150	100

RIFLES

SGW Ultra Match (PCR-1)

Match grade copy of AR-15, with 20" or 24" barrel. Not fitted with carrying handle. Weight about 10 lbs.

NIB	Exc.	V.G.	Good	Fair	Poor
—	900	770	—	—	—

Model PCR-2

Similar to above, with 16" match-grade barrel, post front and E2 rear sight. Weight about 8.2 lbs.

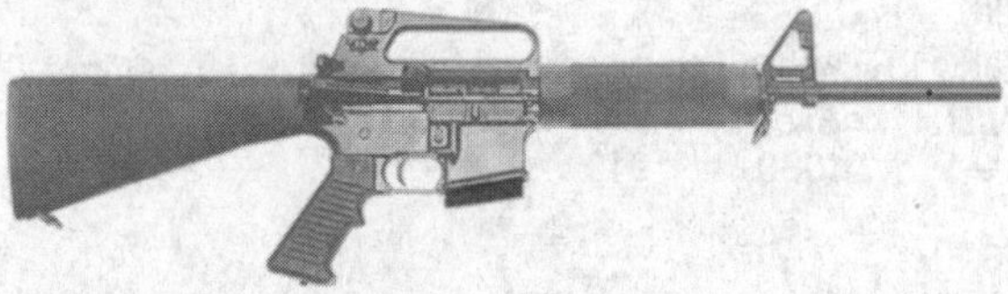

NIB	*Exc.*	*V.G.*	*Good*	*Fair*	*Poor*
—	830	700	—	—	—

Model PCR-3

Same as above, with forged T-12 upper receiver.

NIB	*Exc.*	*V.G.*	*Good*	*Fair*	*Poor*
—	830	700	—	—	—

Model PCR-4

Fitted with 20" steel barrel. Post front sight and A-1 style rear sight. Weight about 8.5 lbs.

NIB	*Exc.*	*V.G.*	*Good*	*Fair*	*Poor*
—	700	600	—	—	—

Model PCR-5

Similar to above, with 16" barrel. Weight about 7 lbs.

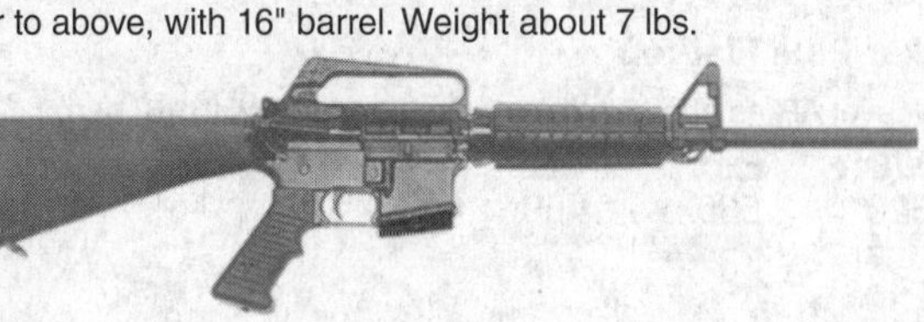

NIB	*Exc.*	*V.G.*	*Good*	*Fair*	*Poor*
—	700	600	—	—	—

Model PCR-6

AR-15 style rifle chambered for 7.62x39 Russian caliber. Fitted with 16" barrel. Post front sight and A-1 style rear sight. Weight about 7 lbs.

NIB	*Exc.*	*V.G.*	*Good*	*Fair*	*Poor*
—	750	640	—	—	—

Model PCR-7 "Eliminator"

Shortened version of PCR-4. Fitted with 16 barrel, A2: handguard, stock and pistol grip. Weight about 7.6 lbs.

NIB	*Exc.*	*V.G.*	*Good*	*Fair*	*Poor*
—	750	640	—	—	—

Model PCR-Service Match

.223-caliber rifle has 20" stainless steel match barrel. Fitted with post front sight and E-2 style rear sight. Weight about 8.7 lbs.

NIB	*Exc.*	*V.G.*	*Good*	*Fair*	*Poor*
1080	910	780	—	—	—

Ultra CSR Tactical Rifle

Bolt-action rifle chambered for .308 Win. cartridge. Barrel length 26". Magazine capacity 5 rounds. Tactical-style stock is black synthetic, with aluminum bedding block. Comes complete with scope rings and Harris bipod in a hardcase. Weight about 9.4 lbs.

NIB	*Exc.*	*V.G.*	*Good*	*Fair*	*Poor*
1100	940	800	—	—	—

Model CAR-97

Chambered for .223 cartridge or optional 9mm, .40 S&W or .45 ACP pistol cartridges. Fitted with 16" barrel and non-collapsible CAR-style stock. Overall length 34"; weight about 7 lbs. Note: Add $50 for pistol cartridge conversion.

NIB	*Exc.*	*V.G.*	*Good*	*Fair*	*Poor*
—	700	600	—	—	—

Model OA-93-CAR

Features include OA-93 FT recoil-reducing upper, 16" chrome-moly barrel, with Phantom flash hider and side-folding buttstock.

NIB	*Exc.*	*V.G.*	*Good*	*Fair*	*Poor*
—	1050	900	—	—	—

UM-1P

Gas-operated .223 semi-automatic target rifle based on AR-15 chassis. Features include 24" stainless steel bull barrel, anodized finish, pistol grip with bottom swell, Picatinny rail, Harris bipod and competition trigger.

NIB	*Exc.*	*V.G.*	*Good*	*Fair*	*Poor*
—	1200	1030	—	—	—

UM-1

Similar to UM-1P, with 20" stainless steel bull barrel, standard pistol grip, no bipod.

NIB	*Exc.*	*V.G.*	*Good*	*Fair*	*Poor*
—	1100	930	—	—	—

SM-1P

Tricked-out AR-15 in .223 with 20" stainless steel barrel, free-floating sleeve handguard, carry handle upper or Picatinny rail flattop, pneumatic recoil buffer, Bob Jones interchangeable sight system, competition trigger and Maxhard receivers.

NIB	*Exc.*	*V.G.*	*Good*	*Fair*	*Poor*
1400	1190	1010	—	—	—

SM-1

Similar to SM-1P, with standard receivers, trigger and sights. No pneumatic recoil buffer.

NIB	*Exc.*	*V.G.*	*Good*	*Fair*	*Poor*
1080	920	780	—	—	—

ML-1

Similar to SM-1, with 16" barrel, flash hider, 6-position collapsible buttstock and free-floating aluminum tube handguard.

NIB	*Exc.*	*V.G.*	*Good*	*Fair*	*Poor*
980	830	700	—	—	—

ML-2

Similar to ML-1, with flattop upper receiver. Picatinny rails, standard buttstock and bull barrel.

NIB	*Exc.*	*V.G.*	*Good*	*Fair*	*Poor*
1050	900	760	—	—	—

K3B

Features include 16" chrome-moly barrel with flash-hidefully adjustable rear sight, 6-position collapsible buttstock and carbine-length handguard.

NIB	*Exc.*	*V.G.*	*Good*	*Fair*	*Poor*
—	700	600	—	—	—

K3B-M4

Similar to K3B, with M4S fiberite handguard with heatshield. Overall length 32.25".

NIB	Exc.	V.G.	Good	Fair	Poor
—	750	640	—	—	—

K3B-CAR

Similar to K3B, with 30.5" overall length.

NIB	Exc.	V.G.	Good	Fair	Poor
—	700	600	—	—	—

K3B-FAR

Similar to K3B, with featherweight barrel. Weight 5.84 lbs.

NIB	Exc.	V.G.	Good	Fair	Poor
—	700	600	—	—	—

K4B

Similar to K3B, with 20" barrel and rifle-length fiberite handguard.

NIB	Exc.	V.G.	Good	Fair	Poor
—	750	640	—	—	—

K4B-A4

Similar to K4B, with ventilated FIRSH rifle-length handguard.

NIB	Exc.	V.G.	Good	Fair	Poor
—	810	690	—	—	—

K7 Eliminator

Similar to K4B, with 16" barrel, extended handguard and sight radius of 20" barreled models.

NIB	Exc.	V.G.	Good	Fair	Poor
780	660	560	—	—	—

K8

Similar to ML-2, with 20" barrel and extended aluminum tube handguard.

NIB	Exc.	V.G.	Good	Fair	Poor
—	800	680	—	—	—

K8-MAG

Similar to K8, with 24" bull barrel and chambered in .223 WSM, .243 WSM or .25 WSM.

NIB	Exc.	V.G.	Good	Fair	Poor
1130	960	810	—	—	—

K9/K10/K40/K45

Similar to K30. Chambered respectively for 9mm Parabellum, 10mm, .40 S&W and .45ACP. Models use converted surplus military magazines.

NIB	Exc.	V.G.	Good	Fair	Poor
850	720	610	—	—	—

K9-GL/K40-GL

Similar to K9 and K40. Accepts standard Glock pistol magazines.

NIB	Exc.	V.G.	Good	Fair	Poor
960	820	690	—	—	—

K16

Similar to K8, with 16" bull chrome-moly barrel.

NIB	Exc.	V.G.	Good	Fair	Poor
750	640	540	—	—	—

LTF

Features include 16" chrome-moly barrel, free-floating FIRSH handguard with Picatinny rails, ACE FX skeleton stock, ERGO pistol grip and multiple-aperture flip-up sight system.

NIB	Exc.	V.G.	Good	Fair	Poor
—	1080	910	—	—	—

LT-M4

Similar to LTF, with 16" stainless steel barrel.

NIB	Exc.	V.G.	Good	Fair	Poor
—	1080	910	—	—	—

GI-16

Basic AR-15-inspired semi-automatic rifle chambered in .223. 16" chrome-moly barrel, with flash-hider, 6-position collapsible buttstock, carbine-length handguard and rear sight adjustable for windage only.

NIB	Exc.	V.G.	Good	Fair	Poor
750	640	540	—	—	—

Plinker Plus

Similar to GI-16, with standard buttstock.

NIB	Exc.	V.G.	Good	Fair	Poor
630	530	450	—	—	—

Plinker Plus 20

Similar to Plinker Plus, with 20" barrel and rifle-length handguard.

NIB	Exc.	V.G.	Good	Fair	Poor
650	550	470	—	—	—

Plinker Plus Flat-top

Entry-level AR as above in flat-top configuration with 16” barrel; .223.

NIB	Exc.	V.G.	Good	Fair	Poor
620	530	450	—	—	—

K30

Similar to GI-16 chambered in .30 Carbine. Includes Magnum well insert to accept military-spec magazines.

NIB	Exc.	V.G.	Good	Fair	Poor
780	660	560	—	—	—

OA-93-PT

Similar to OA-93-CAR, with F8R handguard, vertical grip, post-ban muzzle brake, and detachable stock.

NIB	Exc.	V.G.	Good	Fair	Poor
900	770	650	—	—	—

Gamestalker

Sporting AR-style rifle chambered in .223, .243, .25 WSSM and .300 OSSM. Features include forged aluminum upper and lower; flattop receiver with Picatinny rail; gas block front sight; 22" stainless steel fluted barrel; free-floating slotted tube handguard; camo finish overall; ACE FX skeleton stock.

NIB	Exc.	V.G.	Good	Fair	Poor
1150	980	830	—	—	—

UMAR

AR-type rifle in .22-250 caliber.

NIB	Exc.	V.G.	Good	Fair	Poor
1080	910	780	—	—	—

AR-TYPE PISTOLS

Model OA-93-PT

Similar to OA-93-CAR, with F8R handguard, vertical grip, post-ban muzzle brake and detachable stock.

NIB	Exc.	V.G.	Good	Fair	Poor
1300	1050	900	—	—	—

OA-96

Model has 6" barrel with pistol grip only, no buttstock. The 30-round magazine is pinned and cannot be detached. Break-open-action allows loading with stripper clips. Overall length 15.75"; weight about 4.2 lbs.

NIB	Exc.	V.G.	Good	Fair	Poor
1000	750	640	—	—	—

OA-98

Similar to OA-93, with lightening holes on grip mount and magazine. Fitted with 6" barrel. No vertical grip. Weight about 3 lbs. No buttstock.

NIB	Exc.	V.G.	Good	Fair	Poor
1300	900	770	—	—	—

K23P Pistol

AR-type pistol, 6.5" barrel. Chambered for .223, 9mm, 10mm, .40 S&W, or .45ACP.

NIB	Exc.	V.G.	Good	Fair	Poor
800	680	580	—	—	—

K24P Pistol

As above, except with 11.5" barrel.

NIB	Exc.	V.G.	Good	Fair	Poor
750	640	540	—	—	—

OMEGA FIREARMS CO.

Flower Mound, Texas

Custom rifles by Harold Koon. Features will vary and will impact value. Approximately 1,000 Omega rifles produced before the rights were sold to Hi-Shear, which produced a few more as the Omega III rifle. Hood previously produced as Alpha Arms of Dallas TX and Ranger Arms of Gainesville TX.

Omega Bolt-Action Rifle

A .25-06 to .358 Norma Magnum bolt-action rifle, with 22" or 24" barrel, octagonal bolt, adjustable trigger and rotary magazine. Blued, with two-piece walnut or laminated stock. Discontinued circa 1975.

NIB	Exc.	V.G.	Good	Fair	Poor
—	2500	1850	—	—	—

OMEGA SHOTGUNS BY KASSNAR

See—KASSNAR IMPORTS, INC.

Omega Over/Under Shotgun

12-, 20-, 28-gauge and .410 bore boxlock over/under shotgun, with 26" or 28" ventilated rib barrels, single trigger and extractors. Blued, with walnut stock.

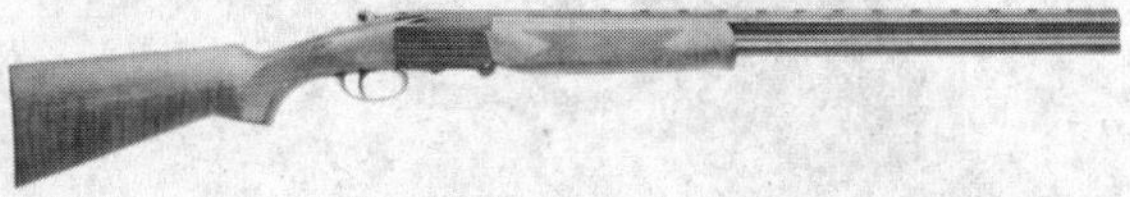

NIB	Exc.	V.G.	Good	Fair	Poor
—	450	300	200	150	130

Omega Side-by-Side Shotgun

20-, 28-gauge and .410 bore boxlock double-barrel shotgun, with 26" barrels, double triggers and extractors. Blued, with hardwood stock.

NIB	Exc.	V.G.	Good	Fair	Poor
—	350	250	150	100	80

Omega Single Barreled Shotgun

12-, 20-gauge and .410 bore single-barrel shotgun. Manufactured in a variety of barrel lengths and fitted with an extractor. Blued, with hardwood stock.

NIB	Exc.	V.G.	Good	Fair	Poor
—	130	90	70	50	40

OMEGA GUNS

Russelville, Arkansas

Founded 2001. Maker of roller-lock semi-auto firearms.

Gideon Shadow

Recoil-operated pistol based on H&K UMP. 9mm, .40 S&W, 10mm, and .45ACP calibers are interchangeable by swapping barrel, bolt and magazine.

NIB	Exc.	V.G.	Good	Fair	Poor
1700	1450	—	—	—	—

OM9 Series Pistols

Semi-auto roller lock pistol; 9mm, uses 30 round MP5 magazines. Variations include OM9-FS with 8.85" barrel, OM9-RS with 5.5" barrel, and OM9-K with 3" barrel.

NIB	Exc.	V.G.	Good	Fair	Poor
1650	1400	—	—	—	—

AK-47

Semi-auto AK pattern rifle, 7.62x39. MSRP $1,600.

OMEGA ARMS USA, LLC

Heath, Ohio

Turkish-made arms, primarily Regent pistols and AR-platform shotguns and rifles. Distributed by LKCI, LLC, Newark, Ohio.

AR 12T

Semi-auto tactical shotgun, adjustable stock, adjustable gas system, 12 ga.

NIB	*Exc.*	*V.G.*	*Good*	*Fair*	*Poor*
730	650	—	—	—	—

AR 12

Semi-auto tactical shotgun, fixed synthetic stock 12 ga. similar to above.

NIB	*Exc.*	*V.G.*	*Good*	*Fair*	*Poor*
500	430	—	—	—	—

S12

Semi-auto sporting shotgun, 12 ga., wood stock. Variations include S12S synthetic stock, S12ST black or white chrome with pistol grip synthetic stock.

NIB	*Exc.*	*V.G.*	*Good*	*Fair*	*Poor*
300	250	—	—	—	—

S12 STM

Semi-auto tactical shotgun, 12 ga. No sales information available. Not currently imported by LKCI.

P12

Pump-action shotgun, 12 ga. Variations include white chrome finish, P12D pistol grip stock, P12M wood stock.

NIB	*Exc.*	*V.G.*	*Good*	*Fair*	*Poor*
240	190	—	—	—	—

Quantum Arms Mag 1618

Bolt-action shotgun, 20 ga. with several stock options available, rifle sights. No sales information available. Not currently imported by LKCI.

Regent 45

1911-type semi-auto pistol, .45 ACP. Variations found in different models include 5" barrel or compact 4" barrel and original 1911 configuration or updated with high visibility sights, beavertail girp safety and oversized safety. Stainless steel models add $100. Also offered in 9mm as the Regent M9 Model.

NIB	*Exc.*	*V.G.*	*Good*	*Fair*	*Poor*
430	380	—	—	—	—

1911-type semi-auto pistol, .45 ACP. Variations found in different models include 5" barrel or compact 4" barrel and original 1911 configuration or updated with high visibility sights, beavertail girp safety and oversized safety. Stainless steel models add $100. Also offered in 9mm as the Regent M9 Model.

NIB	*Exc.*	*V.G.*	*Good*	*Fair*	*Poor*
430	380	—	—	—	—

Regent BR9

Browning High Power pattern semi-auto pistols, 9mm. Add $40 for stainless steel model.

NIB	*Exc.*	*V.G.*	*Good*	*Fair*	*Poor*
530	450	—	—	—	—

Browning High Power pattern semi-auto pistols, 9mm. Add $40 for stainless steel model.

NIB	*Exc.*	*V.G.*	*Good*	*Fair*	*Poor*
530	450	—	—	—	—

Regent P9

Compact SA/DA polymer frame semi-auto pistol, 9mm, 4" barrel. No sales information available. Not currently imported by LKCI.

Regent SP

9mm semi-auto SA/DA pistol, 9mm, 5.1" barrel, available in black Cerakote as Regent SP1 or white chrome as Regent SP2.

NIB	Exc.	V.G.	Good	Fair	Poor
400	350	—	—	—	—

Regent T

9mm semi-auto SA/DA pistol, 9mm, 5.4" barrel, available in black Cerakote as Regent T1 or white cerakote as Regent T2.

NIB	Exc.	V.G.	Good	Fair	Poor
380	330	—	—	—	—

OPUS SPORTING ARMS, INC.

Long Beach, California

Opus One

A .243, .270 or .30-06 caliber bolt-action rifle, with 24" barrel, well figured walnut stock and ebony pistol grip cap as well as forend tip. Built on Model 70 Winchester action. Manufactured in 1987 and 1988.

NIB	Exc.	V.G.	Good	Fair	Poor
—	2250	1600	1150	700	350

Opus Two

As above in 7mm Rem. Magnum and .300 Win. Magnum.

NIB	Exc.	V.G.	Good	Fair	Poor
—	2500	1750	1250	750	350

Opus Three

As above in .375 H&H and .458 Win. Magnum.

NIB	Exc.	V.G.	Good	Fair	Poor
—	3000	2000	1500	900	500

ORBEA HERMANOS

Eibar, Spain

The Orbea family began making firearms around 1538. Orbea Hermanos was founded in 1859, and in 1897 the name was changed to Orbea y Cia. In 1936 it discontinued firearms manufacture and focused on bicycles, which it continues making today. It was possibly the largest and best of several Spanish handgun manufacturers of the era. Other Spanish makers of the time producing similar products included Garate Anitua, Euskaro, and Trocala Aranzaral. Eibar was the center of Spanish arms manufacture, much as Liege was for Belgium. Guns made by these firms, and others that were possibly unmarked other than "Fabricada en Eibar" (or similar), will have values much the same as or a bit less than the Orbea products. Orbea primarily made copies of firearms by other firms, including Lefaucheux pinfire revolvers, Kerr revolvers, Berdan carbines, Remington carbines, S&W Russian Model revolvers, Merwin Hulbert revolvers, S&W .44 Double-Action top-break revolvers, and S&W Hand Ejector revolvers. Orbea made military sales to Italy, the Philippines, Romania, Spain, United Kingdom (WWI England, Royal Ulster Constabulary, and New South Wales Police Force), and France. Spanish handguns by Orbea and others will sometimes be found with exquisite gold damascene decoration, and these pieces will bring substantial premiums for their artistry and rarity. This maker's listing is recently expanded, and reader input on Orbea and other Spanish revolvers is invited.

Pocket Pistol

6.35mm semi-automatic pistol, with 2.5" barrel. Blued, with plastic grips. Slide marked "Orbea y Cia Eibar Espana Pistola Automatica Cal. 6.35". Manufactured about 1918 to 1936.

NIB	Exc.	V.G.	Good	Fair	Poor
—	250	180	120	80	50

Kerr Type Antique

Kerr pattern percussion revolver. Few sales observed.

Exc.	Fine	V.G.	Good	Fair	Poor
—	—	—	1000	—	0

Lefaucheux Pinfire Type Antique

12mm pinfire revolver. Smaller caliber Orbea pinfires bring less.

Exc.	Fine	V.G.	Good	Fair	Poor
900	500	400	300	200	140

Mod. 1884

Also known as the Ona, a top-break .44 Russian double-action revolver based on the S&W .44 Double Action model. About 10,000 were purchased by England for use in WWI in .455 caliber, grips marked 1914, and these will bring a premium with British military markings.

NIB	Exc.	V.G.	Good	Fair	Poor
—	950	650	400	350	200

Hand Ejector Revolver

Some variations are known as Model 1905 or Model 1922. Generally patterned on the S&W .38 HE, calibers .22, .32, & .38.

NIB	Exc.	V.G.	Good	Fair	Poor
—	300	230	150	80	50

ORTGIES, HEINRICH & CO.

Erfurt, Germany

Ortgies Pistol

6.35mm or 7.65mm semi-automatic pistol, with 2.75" or 3.25" barrel. Blued, with walnut grips. Slide marked "Ortgies & Co. Erfurt". After 1921, these pistols were manufactured by Deutsche Werke. Note: Deduct $100 for 6.35 mm.

NIB	Exc.	V.G.	Good	Fair	Poor
—	550	300	180	120	80

ORVIS

Sunderland, Vermont

Importer and retailer of sporting goods including foreign manufactured firearms. Orvis sells some of these side-by-side and over/under guns under its own name. Most are made by Beretta, Arrieta or other Italian manufacturers. Values approximate those of similar models made by gunmakers.

OSBORN, S.
Canton, Connecticut

Underhammer Pistol (Antique)

.34-caliber under hammer percussion pistol, with 7" half octagonal barrel, brass mounts and walnut grip. Barrel marked "S. Osborn/Canton, Conn." Also see "Andrus & Osborn." See note on UNDERHAMMER PISTOLS & DERRINGERS at lines 510 & 511"

Exc.	Fine	V.G.	Good	Fair	Poor
800	550	400	250	120	80

OSGOOD GUN WORKS
Norwich, Connecticut

Duplex Revolver (Antique)

.22-caliber spur trigger revolver, with two super-imposed barrels: upper most .22-caliber; lower .32-caliber. Cylinder with eight .22 chambers. Hammer fitted with movable firing pin so pistol can be used as a revolver or single-shot, with .32-caliber barrel. Blued or nickel-plated, with hard rubber grips. Barrel marked "Osgood Gun Works-Norwich Conn." and "Duplex". An unknown quantity manufactured during 1880s.

Courtesy Milwaukee Public Museum, Milwaukee, Wisconsin

Exc.	Fine	V.G.	Good	Fair	Poor
1600	900	600	350	200	150

OURY, D.D.
Liege, Belgium

LeNovo Folding Revolver

Also found marked "Novo." Unique small hammerless (concealed hammer) double-action revolver with folding trigger and folding grip patented by D.D. Oury in 1909. Lever on right side releases barrel so cylinder and barrel may be removed for loading and unloading. Made by various Belgian makers, reportedly including Ancion Marx, Bertrand Jules, Francotte, Galand, G. Riga, Henrion, H. Mahillon, Dassy et Heuschen, Scholberg, and possibly others. Manufacturer name may not appear on revolver but Oury patent is usually stamped in the metal. Five-shot 6.35mm (.25ACP) or six-shot 5mm Novo (rare.) Metal grip has ornate decoration usually including LENOVO or NOVO marking. Engraving, if present, may add to value.

Jim Supica photo

NIB	Exc.	V.G.	Good	Fair	Poor
—	4000	3000	2000	1000	500

OVERTON, JOHN
Nashville, Tennessee

Formerly armorer at Harpers Ferry Armory. He delivered 81 rifles copying U.S. Model 1841, with saber bayonet lug on right side of barrel. Unmarked externally but are serial numbered internally. Overall length ca. 48.75"; barrel length 33"; .54-caliber.

NIB	Exc.	V.G.	Good	Fair	Poor
—	—	18500	14000	5500	2000

OWA
Osterreiche Werke Anstalt
Vienna, Austria

OWA Pocket Pistol

6.35mm semi-automatic pistol, with 2" barrel. "OWA" logo cast in grips. Blued, with plastic grips. Manufactured between 1920 and 1925.

Courtesy Orvel Reichert

NIB	Exc.	V.G.	Good	Fair	Poor
—	400	320	200	150	1000

P

P.38
GERMAN WWII SERVICE PISTOL

Note: For history, technical data, descriptions, photos and prices see: Standard Catalog of Military Firearms.

WALTHER COMMERCIAL

Commercial version of P.38 is identified by commercial proofmarks of a crown over N or an eagle over N. Production started around serial number 1000 and went through 26659. First of commercial pistols and a high-quality well made gun, with complete inscription on left slide. Few of these early pistols were equipped with checkered wooden grips. Quality decreased as war progressed. Many variations of these commercial models and values can range up to more than $30,000. Suggested these pistols be appraised and evaluated by an expert. For post-war Walther P.38 pistols, see Walther section.

Few of Walther Commercial Model variations are listed.

MOD HP

H Prefix w/rectangular firing pin

NIB	Exc.	V.G.	Good	Fair	Poor
—	3200	2000	950	750	450

MOD HP Early w/High Gloss Blue

NIB	Exc.	V.G.	Good	Fair	Poor
—	3000	1750	750	600	400

MOD HP .30 caliber, extremely rare

NIB	Exc.	V.G.	Good	Fair	Poor
—	28000	—	—	—	—

MOD HP Early w/High Gloss Blue & Alloy Frame

NIB	Exc.	V.G.	Good	Fair	Poor
—	10000	6500	3500	2000	1000

MOD HP Croatian Contract

100 built, 6 known

NIB	Exc.	V.G.	Good	Fair	Poor
—	10000	—	—	—	—

MOD HP Late w/Military Blue Finish

Note: Add $500 for "Eagle/359" on right side.

NIB	Exc.	V.G.	Good	Fair	Poor
—	2000	1400	750	550	350

MOD P38—Late with Military Blue

1800 produced.

NIB	Exc.	V.G.	Good	Fair	Poor
—	2700	1750	750	600	400

ac45 Zero Series

1,200 made.

NIB	Exc.	V.G.	Good	Fair	Poor
—	2800	1750	750	600	400

WALTHER MILITARY

ZERO SERIES

First Issue

NIB	Exc.	V.G.	Good	Fair	Poor
—	11000	9000	6000	3500	1500

Second Issue

NIB	Exc.	V.G.	Good	Fair	Poor
—	9000	7200	5250	2000	1000

Third Issue

NIB	Exc.	V.G.	Good	Fair	Poor
—	3500	2200	1250	800	500

480 CODE

NIB	Exc.	V.G.	Good	Fair	Poor
—	8000	6000	4000	1750	1000

AC CODES

This variation follows 480 code.

AC (no date)

NIB	Exc.	V.G.	Good	Fair	Poor
—	9000	7500	5000	3000	2000

AC40

NIB	Exc.	V.G.	Good	Fair	Poor
—	3800	2500	1750	1000	600

Standard

NIB	Exc.	V.G.	Good	Fair	Poor
—	3000	2000	1200	700	500

AC41

1st Variation

NIB	Exc.	V.G.	Good	Fair	Poor
—	2200	1100	700	500	350

2nd Variation

NIB	Exc.	V.G.	Good	Fair	Poor
—	2000	1000	700	450	300

3rd Variation

NIB	Exc.	V.G.	Good	Fair	Poor
—	1500	800	600	400	300

AC42

1st Variation

Note: Add $800 for "byf" Mauser code.

NIB	Exc.	V.G.	Good	Fair	Poor
—	1300	550	400	350	280

2nd Variation

NIB	Exc.	V.G.	Good	Fair	Poor
—	1100	500	400	300	250

AC43

1st Variation

NIB	Exc.	V.G.	Good	Fair	Poor
—	900	450	300	250	200

2nd Variation

NIB	Exc.	V.G.	Good	Fair	Poor
—	900	450	300	250	200

Single Line Slide

NIB	Exc.	V.G.	Good	Fair	Poor
—	1200	550	450	350	250

AC44

Note: Add $300 for FN frame (Eagle/140).

NIB	Exc.	V.G.	Good	Fair	Poor
—	800	450	300	250	200

AC45

Note: Add $200 for pistols with Czech barrels; barrel code "fnh."

1st Variation

NIB	Exc.	V.G.	Good	Fair	Poor
—	800	450	300	250	200

2nd Variation

NIB	Exc.	V.G.	Good	Fair	Poor
—	950	500	320	300	250

3rd Variation

NIB	Exc.	V.G.	Good	Fair	Poor
—	750	400	300	250	200

MAUSER MILITARY

byf42

NIB	Exc.	V.G.	Good	Fair	Poor
—	2200	1200	700	500	300

byf43

NIB	Exc.	V.G.	Good	Fair	Poor
—	950	550	300	250	200

byf44

Note: Add $100 for dual-tone finish (combination of blue/gray components).

NIB	Exc.	V.G.	Good	Fair	Poor
—	950	550	300	250	200

AC43/44—FN slide

NIB	Exc.	V.G.	Good	Fair	Poor
—	2200	1200	720	550	400

SVW45

German Proofed

NIB	Exc.	V.G.	Good	Fair	Poor
—	2900	2000	1300	550	400

French Proofed

NIB	Exc.	V.G.	Good	Fair	Poor
—	650	400	300	250	200

SVW46— French Proofed

NIB	Exc.	V.G.	Good	Fair	Poor
—	800	500	400	350	300

MAUSER "POLICE" P.38

byf/43

NIB	Exc.	V.G.	Good	Fair	Poor
—	2500	1700	1200	800	500

byf/44

NIB	Exc.	V.G.	Good	Fair	Poor
—	2500	1700	1200	800	500

ac/43

NIB	Exc.	V.G.	Good	Fair	Poor
—	5000	3500	2000	1250	800

ac/44

NIB	Exc.	V.G.	Good	Fair	Poor
—	5000	3500	2000	1250	800

svw/45

NIB	Exc.	V.G.	Good	Fair	Poor
—	6000	4500	2500	1600	1000

SPREEWERKE MILITARY

cyq

Eagle /211 on frame

2 known.

NIB	Exc.	V.G.	Good	Fair	Poor
—	5000	—	—	—	—

1st Variation

NIB	Exc.	V.G.	Good	Fair	Poor
—	1400	1000	750	600	500

Standard Variation

Note: Add $250 if A" or "B" prefix.

NIB	Exc.	V.G.	Good	Fair	Poor
—	800	400	280	250	200

Zero Series

Note: Add $250 for AC43- or AC44-marked "FN" slide.

NIB	Exc.	V.G.	Good	Fair	Poor
—	1250	550	400	350	280

POST-WAR PISTOLS

Standard Slides

NIB	Exc.	V.G.	Good	Fair	Poor
—	400	250	200	180	150

Single Line Code (Rare)

NIB	Exc.	V.G.	Good	Fair	Poor
—	1000	550	350	250	200

Manurhin

NIB	Exc.	V.G.	Good	Fair	Poor
—	400	300	200	180	150

P.A.F.

Pretoria Small Arms Factory
Pretoria, South Africa

P.A.F. Junior

.22- or .25-caliber semi-automatic pistol, with 2" barrel and 6-shot magazine. Blued, with plastic grips. Slide marked "Junior Verwaardig in Suid Afrika Made in South Africa". Manufactured during 1950s.

NIB	Exc.	V.G.	Good	Fair	Poor
—	350	250	120	100	70

PAGE-LEWIS ARMS CO.

Chicopee Falls, Massachusetts

Model A Target

.22-caliber single-shot lever-action rifle, with 20" barrel and open sights. Blued, with walnut stock. Manufactured from 1920 to 1926.

NIB	Exc.	V.G.	Good	Fair	Poor
—	300	220	180	120	100

Model B Sharpshooter

As above, with 24" barrel and longer forend.

NIB	Exc.	V.G.	Good	Fair	Poor
—	300	220	180	120	100

Model C Olympic

As above, with 24" barrel and improved sights.

NIB	Exc.	V.G.	Good	Fair	Poor
—	380	280	200	150	100

Challenge Model 49

Single-shot .22 LR boy's rifle. Manufactured cira 1925-1930. Stamped on top of barrel "Page Lewis Arms Co., Chicopee Falls, Mass USA/22 LR" Model 49. 22" long barrel, fixed front and rear sights.

NIB	Exc.	V.G.	Good	Fair	Poor
—	150	100	80	50	40

PALMETTO ARMORY

From 1849-1852, Palmetto Armory attempted to provide southern arms manufacturing during the secession crisis leading to the Civil War. Considered a secondary Confederate weapon; beware of fakes and reproductions.

Model 1841 Percussion Rifle Antique

Copy of U.S. Model 1841 "Mississippi Rifle" with brass patchbox, very few known to exist.

Exc.	Fine	V.G.	Good	Fair	Poor
—	—	7000	4500	3000	1500

Model 1842 Percussion Pistol Antique

.54-caliber U.S. 1842-pattern muzzleloading pistol, palmetto tree lockplate marking. Numerous fakes were produced in the 1950s and since. Buyer beware.

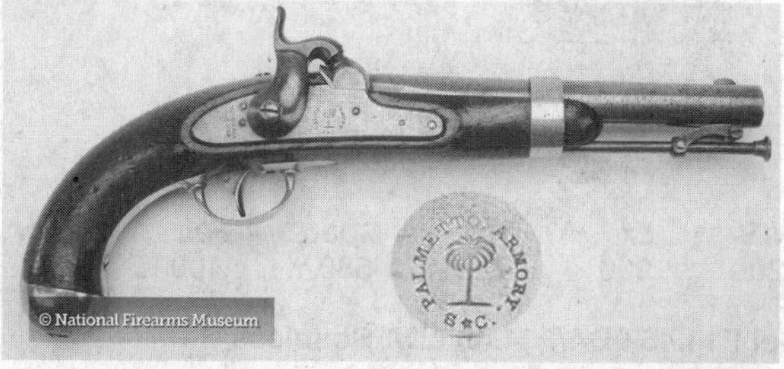

Photo courtesy of NRA Museums

Exc.	Fine	V.G.	Good	Fair	Poor
15000	7500	5000	3000	2000	1000

Model 1842 Percussion Musket Antique

Muzzleloading U.S. 1842-pattern .69-caliber musket; brass barrel bands and bayonet lug, palmetto tree lockplate marking. Mostly smoothbore — rifled model worth premium.

Exc.	Fine	V.G.	Good	Fair	Poor
—	15000	10000	5000	3000	1500

Percussion Conversion of U.S. M1816 Flintlock Musket Antique

Various original makers, .69 caliber, conversions are usually marked "SO CAROLINA."

Exc.	Fine	V.G.	Good	Fair	Poor
—	7000	5000	3000	1500	1050

PALMER

Windsor, Vermont
E. G. Lamson & Co.

Palmer Bolt-Action Carbine Antique

.50-caliber single-shot bolt-action carbine, with 20" round barrel, walnut half-stock and full sidelock. Blued and case-hardened. Receiver marked "Wm. Palmer / Patent / Dec.22, 1863" and lock "G.Lamson & Co./ Windsor, Vt." Approximately 1,000 made in 1865.

Exc.	Fine	V.G.	Good	Fair	Poor
4250	2500	1750	1250	650	350

PALMETTO STATE ARMORY

Columbia, South Carolina

Maker of AR-style rifles and parts, as well as AK-pattern guns and handguns.

PA-15

Chamber: 5.56 NATO. Barrel: 16" 4150V Chrome Moly Vanadium Steel, Nitride finish. Barrel Profile: A2 style. Twist Rate: 1:7." M4 extension. Mid-length gas system, Low-profile .750" gas block. Upper receiver: M4 flat top with feed ramps. Handguard: PSA 13.5." Lightweight M-Lok free-float rail. Bolt Steel: Carpenter 158. Bolt Carrier Steel: 8620. Staked gas key. PSA AR-15 Enhanced Polished Trigger (EPT). Mil-spec buffer tube. Magpul MOE Carbine six-position collapsible stock. (1) 30-round magazine (where available by law). Backup Sights: Magpul MBUS. Length: 32." SEE POLITICAL PANIC PRICING.

NIB	Exc.	V.G.	Good	Fair	Poor
600	500	400	290	—	—

GEN 3 PA-10

Caliber: 6.5 Creedmoor, .308 Win. Barrels: 18" or 20," stainless-steel heavy barrel, adjustable gas block. Buttstock: PSA classic M4 stock, Black six-position adjustable. Handguards: PSA classic polymer mid-length handguard, Keymod- or M-LOK-compatible free-floated. SEE POLITICAL PANIC PRICING.

NIB	Exc.	V.G.	Good	Fair	Poor
840	—	—	—	—	—

H&R M16A1

Caliber: 5.56 NATO. Copy of the gas-operated semi-automatic M16A1 with a 20" barrel. Harrington & Richardson was one of only four manufacturers to have made an official M16 variant for the U.S. military. Fixed synthetic stock, A2 carry handle receiver, smooth rifle-length handguard, A2 front sight. Includes sling swivels, 20-round magazine. SEE POLITICAL PANIC PRICING.

NIB	Exc.	V.G.	Good	Fair	Poor
1200	—	—	—	—	—

PANTHER

See—DPMS

PARA USA (PARA-ORDNANCE)

Previously known as Para-Ordnance of Scarborough, Ontario, Canada. In 2009, company relocated to Pineville, North Carolina. In January, 2012, assets of Para USA were purchased by Freedom Group, parent company of Remington, Marlin, Bushmaster and several other companies. On Feb. 9, 2015, Remington Outdoor Company (formerly Freedom Group) announced that the Para USA trademark was being discontinued and its handgun models would be integrated into the Remington brand and manufactured in a new facility in Huntsville, Alabama. See Remington R1 Limited Double Stack in Remington section.

Custom Series

Manufactured from 2013 to 2015. 1911-style pistols in a wide range of models. Caliber: .45 ACP, 9mm, or .40 S&W. Capacity: 8-, 10-, 14-, 16- or 18-round magazine. Barrel: 3" (Executive Agent and Executive Carry), or 5" (Pro Custom 10.45, Pro Custom 14.45, Pro Custom 16.40, and Pro Comp). Fiber optic front sight, adjustable rear sight. Note: Deduct $40 for Executive Agent and Executive Carry.

NIB	*Exc.*	*V.G.*	*Good*	*Fair*	*Poor*
1470	1230	930	680	560	440

Tomasie Custom

Similar to Custom series. Manufactured from 2013 to 2015. 1911-style pistols in a wide range of models. Caliber: .40 S&W. Capacity: 16-round magazine. Barrel: 5". Fiber-optic front sight, adjustable rear sight.

NIB	*Exc.*	*V.G.*	*Good*	*Fair*	*Poor*
2030	1700	1280	940	770	600

Para Elite Series

In 2013, Para USA introduced a new family of 1911-style pistols in a wide range of models. Caliber: .45 ACP, 9mm (Elite LS Hunter only). Capacity: 6, 7 or 8 rounds; 9 rounds (9mm LS Hunter). Barrel: 3", 4" or 5" (.45 models), 6" (9mm LS Hunter). Pro Model has Ed Brown mag well, HD extractor, checkered front strap and mainspring housing, Trijicon sights. Note: Add $250 for Pro Model; $200 LS Hunter.

NIB	*Exc.*	*V.G.*	*Good*	*Fair*	*Poor*
850	780	650	500	—	—

Para 1911 100th Anniversary

Classic 1911 styling to commemorate centennial of design. Caliber .45 ACP, military-style thumb and grip safeties, solid muzzle bushing and hammer. Three-dot sights. Weight 39 oz., 5" barrel, Covert Black finish. Smooth Cocobolo grips. Comes with one 7- and 8-round magazine.

NIB	*Exc.*	*V.G.*	*Good*	*Fair*	*Poor*
920	780	660	500	350	200

Model P14.45

Similar in appearance to Colt Government model. This .45 ACP semi-automatic pistol features 5" barrel, flared ejection port, combat style hammer, beveled magazine well and 13-round magazine. Overall length 8.5"; weight 40 oz. for steel and stainless steel version; 31 oz. for alloy frame model. Finish black except for stainless steel model. Note: Add $50 for steel frame; $45 for stainless steel; $30 for duo-tone.

NIB	*Exc.*	*V.G.*	*Good*	*Fair*	*Poor*
700	550	500	400	300	200

Model P14.45 Limited

Similar to above. Extra features such as full-length recoil guide, beavertail grip safety, adjustable rear sight, competition hammer, lowered ejection port, front and rear slide serrations and trigger overtravel stop. Match-grade barrel. Choice of black carbon steel or stainless steel finish. Weight about 40 oz.

NIB	*Exc.*	*V.G.*	*Good*	*Fair*	*Poor*
1200	900	720	580	400	200

Model P14.45 LDA/P14.45 LDA Stainless

Essentially same as P14.45, with double-action trigger. Offered in black carbon steel only. Weight about 40 oz. First introduced in 1999. Note: Add $50 for stainless steel.

NIB	*Exc.*	*V.G.*	*Good*	*Fair*	*Poor*
800	600	400	350	220	150

Model P16.40

Essentially same as Model 14.45, except chambered for .40 S&W cartridge. Magazine capacity 15 rounds. Note: Add $50 for steel frame; $45 for stainless steel; $30 for duo-tone.

NIB	*Exc.*	*V.G.*	*Good*	*Fair*	*Poor*
800	600	400	350	220	150

Model P16.40 Limited

Similar to above. Extra features such as full-length recoil guide, beavertail grip safety, adjustable rear sight, competition hammer, lowered ejection port, front and rear slide serrations and trigger over-travel stop. Match-grade barrel. Black carbon steel finish.

NIB	*Exc.*	*V.G.*	*Good*	*Fair*	*Poor*
1200	900	720	580	400	200

Model P16.40 LDA

Double-action version of P16.40 in black carbon steel only. First offered in 1999.

NIB	*Exc.*	*V.G.*	*Good*	*Fair*	*Poor*
800	600	400	350	220	150

Model P13.45

Introduced in 1994. This .45 ACP model features 4.25" barrel, with 13-round magazine. Grip .25" longer than 12.45 model. Offered in light alloy, carbon or stainless steel. Overall length 7.75"; height 5.25"; weight about 36 oz. in steel version, 28 oz. in alloy version. Note: Add $50 for steel frame; $45 for stainless steel; $30 for duo-tone.

NIB	*Exc.*	*V.G.*	*Good*	*Fair*	*Poor*
600	450	350	300	200	100

Model P13.45/P12.45 Limited

Similar to above, with extra features such as full-length recoil guide, beavertail grip safety, adjustable rear sight, competition hammer, lowered ejection port, front and rear slide serrations and trigger over-travel stop. Match-grade barrel. Black carbon steel finish.

P13.45

NIB	*Exc.*	*V.G.*	*Good*	*Fair*	*Poor*
800	600	400	350	220	150

Model P12.45 LDA/P12.45 LDA

Fitted with 3.5" barrel and 12-round magazine. Features double-action trigger. Finish black. Weight about 34 oz. Introduced in 2000. Note: Add $50 for stainless steel.

NIB	*Exc.*	*V.G.*	*Good*	*Fair*	*Poor*
750	600	450	300	200	100

Model P12.45/P12.40

Similar to Model P14 but in a smaller package. Introduced in 1993. Has all the same features as Model P14. Magazine capacity 11 rounds. Available in alloy, steel or stainless steel. Weight 24 oz. in alloy; 33 oz. in steel. P12.40 is same model chambered for .40 S&W cartridge. Note: Add $50 for steel frame; $45 for stainless steel; $30 for duo-tone.

NIB	*Exc.*	*V.G.*	*Good*	*Fair*	*Poor*
800	600	400	350	220	150

Model P10.45/P10.40/P10.9

Introduced in 1996. At the time, was smallest semi-automatic .45 ACP in production. Overall length 6.5"; height 4.5". Magazine capacity 10 rounds. Barrel length 3.5". Offered in stainless steel, duo-tone or black alloy finish. Chambered for .40 S&W and 9mm cartridge. Weight about 31 oz. for stainless; 24 oz. for alloy. Note: Add $50 for steel frame; $45 for stainless steel; $30 for duo-tone.

NIB	*Exc.*	*V.G.*	*Good*	*Fair*	*Poor*
600	450	350	300	0	100

Model P10.45 Limited

Similar to above. Extra features such as full-length recoil guide, beavertail grip safety, adjustable rear sight, competition hammer, lowered ejection port, front and rear slide serrations and trigger over-travel stop. Match-grade barrel. Black carbon steel finish.

NIB	Exc.	V.G.	Good	Fair	Poor
650	500	400	300	200	100

Model P18.9

Chambered for 9mm cartridge. Fitted with 5" barrel. Finish stainless steel. Rear sight adjustable; dovetail front sight. Magazine capacity 18 rounds (10 rounds for US and Canada). Weight about 40 oz.

NIB	Exc.	V.G.	Good	Fair	Poor
780	620	500	350	200	120

Model P18.9 LDA

Double-action version of P18-9. Offered in black carbon steel only. Introduced in 1999.

NIB	Exc.	V.G.	Good	Fair	Poor
780	620	500	350	200	120

Model C7.45 LDA (Para Companion)

.45 ACP pistol fitted with 3.5" barrel. Stainless steel slide and frame. Low profile fixed sights. Magazine capacity 7 rounds. Weight about 32 oz.

NIB	Exc.	V.G.	Good	Fair	Poor
700	550	400	300	200	100

Model C6.45 LDA (Para Carry)

Similar to above, with 3" barrel and 6-round magazine. Weight about 30 oz.

NIB	Exc.	V.G.	Good	Fair	Poor
750	580	550	380	200	100

Model Stealth Carry

Introduced in 2005. Chambered for .45 ACP cartridge. Fitted with 3" barrel with Novak adjustable sights. LDA trigger. Black slide, frame and polymer grips. Magazine capacity 6 rounds. Weight about 30 oz.

NIB	Exc.	V.G.	Good	Fair	Poor
850	680	550	420	300	150

Model Para CCW

Introduced in 2003. This .45 ACP model features 4.25" barrel, with stainless steel receiver and frame. Magazine capacity 7 rounds. Fitted with LDA trigger system. Weight about 34 oz.

NIB	Exc.	V.G.	Good	Fair	Poor
900	800	650	500	350	120

Model Para Companion Carry Option

Similar to CCW above. Fitted with 3.5" barrel. Weight about 32 oz. Introduced in 2003.

NIB	Exc.	V.G.	Good	Fair	Poor
780	580	400	300	200	100

Model Tac-Four

.45 ACP model features LDA trigger system. Fitted with 4.25" barrel and stainless steel slide and frame. Early models shipped with two pre-ban 13-round magazines. Later models will ship with two 10-round magazines. Weight about 36 oz. Introduced in 2003.

NIB	Exc.	V.G.	Good	Fair	Poor
900	800	650	500	350	120

Model Tac-Four LE

Same as above. Shipped with two 13-round magazines to certified law enforcement only, back in the ban days.

NIB	Exc.	V.G.	Good	Fair	Poor
900	800	650	500	350	120

SINGLE-ACTION, SINGLE-STACK MODELS

PARA PXT SERIES

In 2004, company introduced new extractor called Power Extractor (PXT). Company also added a number of new finishes and features for its PXT line. All Para pistols have integral ramp barrels that are of match-grade quality. All pistols have full-length guide rod, match trigger, flared ejection port, extended slide lock safety, beavertail grip safety, Cocobolo stocks with gold medallion and high-visibility low-mount dovetail three-dot sights. Para introduced five finishes: 1. Sterling—All stainless steel, black slide with polished sides. 2. Stealth—Black slide, black frame with black fire controls. 3. Black Watch—Black slide, green frame with green fire controls on hi-cap models and black controls on single-stack models. 4. Regal—Black slide, black frame with stainless steel fire controls. 5. Spec Ops—Green slide, green frame with black fire controls.

Model LTC

This .45 ACP pistol has 4.25" ramped match barrel, with steel receiver and Regal finish. Fixed 3-dot sights. Cocobolo wood grips, with gold medallion. Magazine capacity 7 rounds. Weight about 37 oz.

NIB	Exc.	V.G.	Good	Fair	Poor
900	800	580	400	350	320

Model LTC Alloy

As above, with alloy frame. Weight about 28 oz.

NIB	Exc.	V.G.	Good	Fair	Poor
900	780	560	380	330	300

Model LTC Stainless

Same as Model LTC, with stainless steel frame and slide. Weight about 35 oz. Introduced in 2005.

NIB	Exc.	V.G.	Good	Fair	Poor
1050	920	620	520	480	430

Hawg 9

Chambered for 9mm cartridge. Fitted with 3" ramped barrel. Alloy receiver and steel slide. Fixed 3-dot sights. Black slide, frame and polymer stocks. Stainless steel fire controls. Weight about 24 oz.; 12-shot magazine. Introduced in 2005.

NIB	Exc.	V.G.	Good	Fair	Poor
960	880	660	550	450	350

Hawg 7

Caliber .45 ACP, single-action trigger, stainless steel slide, alloy frame with Griptor grooves, extended thumb and grip safeties, fiber optic front and 2-dot rear sights, 7-round magazine. Weight 32 oz., 3.5" barrel with Covert Black finish. Introduced in 2011.

NIB	Exc.	V.G.	Good	Fair	Poor
900	780	580	530	360	290

Model OPS

.45 ACP pistol fitted with 3.5" barrel. Has stainless steel frame and slide. Low mount fixed sights. Cocobolo grips. Magazine capacity 7 rounds. Weight about 32 oz. Introduced in 2005.

NIB	Exc.	V.G.	Good	Fair	Poor
1100	980	740	540	440	340

Model 1911

.45 ACP model has 5" barrel, with steel receiver and Regal finish. Magazine capacity 7 rounds. Weight about 39 oz.

NIB	Exc.	V.G.	Good	Fair	Poor
780	580	400	300	200	100

1911 SSP

7+1 capacity .45 ACP 1911-style semi-automatic, with 5" barrel. Competition triggers and hammers. Fixed sights. Cocobolo grip panels. Weight 39 oz.

NIB	Exc.	V.G.	Good	Fair	Poor
920	800	680	500	400	180

GI Expert LTC

Caliber .45 ACP, single-action trigger, Commander-length stainless slide on alloy frame, extended grip safety, competition trigger, fiber-optic front, and 2-dot rear sights. Weight 28 oz., 4.25" barrel with Covert Black finish. Magazine capacity 8 rounds.

NIB	Exc.	V.G.	Good	Fair	Poor
800	700	530	380	330	290

1911 Wild Bunch

Designed for SASS Traditional and Modern "Wild Bunch" shooting matches. Class 1911 features. Caliber .45 ACP, traditional thumb and grip safeties, hammer, solid trigger, recoil system, 7-round magazine, plain sights and barrel without integral ramp. Weight 39 oz., 5" barrel with Covert Black finish. Introduced in 2011.

NIB	Exc.	V.G.	Good	Fair	Poor
950	780	530	380	330	280

HIGH-CAPACITY, SINGLE-ACTION MODELS

PARA PXT SERIES

Warthog

Introduced in 2004. This .45 ACP pistol fitted with 3" barrel. Receiver is alloy. Black slide and frame, with stainless steel fire controls. Overall length 6.5"; height 4.5". Magazine capacity 10 rounds. Weight about 24 oz. In 2005, chambered for 9mm cartridge.

NIB	Exc.	V.G.	Good	Fair	Poor
920	800	680	500	400	180

Stainless Warthog

Stainless .45 ACP with 10+1 capacity. Barrel 3", weight 31 oz. Fixed 3-dot sights and plastic grips. Introduced 2006.

NIB	Exc.	V.G.	Good	Fair	Poor
890	830	700	530	430	200

Stealth Warthog

Chambered for .45 ACP cartridge. Fitted with 3" ramped barrel. Black alloy slide, frame and fire controls. Tritium night sights. Extended slide lock, beavertail grip and firing pin. Weight about 24 oz. Introduced in 2004.

NIB	Exc.	V.G.	Good	Fair	Poor
850	680	550	420	300	150

Slim Hawg

.45 ACP pistol with 6+1 capacity. Single-stack single-action 1911. Barrel 3", weight 30 oz. Stainless construction, checkered wood grips. Fixed 3-dot sights. Introduced 2006.

NIB	Exc.	V.G.	Good	Fair	Poor
850	680	550	420	300	150

Lite Hawg 9

Double-stack 12+1 capacity single-action 9mm in non-reflective black finish. Barrel 3", weight 31.5 oz. Fixed 3-dot sights. Introduced 2006.

NIB	Exc.	V.G.	Good	Fair	Poor
850	680	550	420	300	150

P12.45

.45 ACP model fitted with 3.5" barrel. Has stainless steel receiver and finish. Magazine capacity 10 or 12 rounds. Weight about 34 oz.

NIB	Exc.	V.G.	Good	Fair	Poor
800	620	500	400	150	120

P13.45

.45 ACP pistol has 4.25" barrel, with stainless steel receiver and Spec Ops finish. Magazine capacity 10 or 13 rounds. Weight about 36 oz.

NIB	Exc.	V.G.	Good	Fair	Poor
750	580	550	380	200	100

Midnight Blue P14-45

Double-stack 14+1 single-action .45 ACP in non-reflective black. 5" barrel, fixed 3-dot sights and black plastic grips. Introduced 2006.

NIB	Exc.	V.G.	Good	Fair	Poor
750	580	550	380	200	100

Hi-Cap LTC

Introduced in 2005. Chambered for .45 ACP cartridge. Fitted with 4.25" barrel with low mount fixed sights. Slide and frame are green, with black fire controls. Black polymer grips. Magazine capacity 14 rounds. Weight about 37 oz.

NIB	Exc.	V.G.	Good	Fair	Poor
850	680	550	420	300	150

Stealth P14.45

.45 ACP model fitted with 5" barrel. Has steel receiver with Stealth finish. Magazine capacity 10 or 14 rounds. Weight about 40 oz.

NIB	Exc.	V.G.	Good	Fair	Poor
850	680	550	420	300	150

P14.45

As above, with stainless steel receiver and finish.

NIB	Exc.	V.G.	Good	Fair	Poor
920	800	680	500	400	180

14.45 Tactical

Based upon classic Para-Ordnance 14.45 high-capacity 1911 design in .45 ACP. Stainless steel slide and frame, with 14-round double-stack magazine. Custom features include Ed Brown National Match barrel, bushing, slide stop and checkered mainspring housing; Dawson Precision mag well; ambidextrous thumb safeties; extended grip tang and accessory rail. Sights are adjustable rear and fiber optic front. Covert Black finish. Weight 42 oz., barrel length 5". PXT Tactical model same except for single-stack frame, 8-round magazine, 4.25" barrel and weight of 36 oz.

NIB	Exc.	V.G.	Good	Fair	Poor
1350	1150	880	650	350	200

P18.45

Chambered for 9mm Parabellum cartridge. Fitted with 5" barrel. Receiver and finish stainless steel. Magazine 10 or 18 rounds. Weight about 40 oz.

NIB	Exc.	V.G.	Good	Fair	Poor
850	680	520	380	200	120

HIGH-CAPACITY SINGLE-ACTION LIMITED MODELS

S12.45 Limited

.45 ACP pistol has 3.5" barrel, with stainless steel receiver and Sterling finish. Magazine capacity 10 or 12 rounds. Weight about 34 oz. Introduced in 2005.

NIB	Exc.	V.G.	Good	Fair	Poor
920	800	680	500	400	180

S13.45 Limited

.45 ACP pistol with 4.25" barrel. Stainless steel receiver and Sterling finish. Spurless hammer. Magazine capacity 10 or 13 rounds. Weight about 36 oz.

NIB	Exc.	V.G.	Good	Fair	Poor
920	800	680	500	400	180

Stealth S14.45 Limited

.45 ACP pistol fitted with 5" barrel. Has steel receiver with Stealth finish. Magazine capacity 10 or 14 rounds. Weight about 40 oz.

NIB	Exc.	V.G.	Good	Fair	Poor
920	800	680	500	400	180

S14.45 Limited

As above, with stainless steel receiver and Sterling finish.

NIB	Exc.	V.G.	Good	Fair	Poor
1000	800	600	450	280	220

Long Slide Limited

Lengthened barrel and slide for competition or hunting. Caliber .435 ACP. Weight 41 oz., barrel length 6". Front and rear slide serrations, ambidextrous thumb safeties, extended grip safety, adjustable rear and fiber optic front sight, 14-round magazine and stainless finish. Introduced in 2011.

NIB	Exc.	V.G.	Good	Fair	Poor
1200	1020	820	650	450	300

Stealth S16.40 Limited

Chambered for .40 S&W cartridge. Fitted with 5" barrel. Receiver steel with Stealth finish. Magazine capacity 10 or 16 rounds. Weight about 40 oz.

NIB	Exc.	V.G.	Good	Fair	Poor
1100	950	750	500	400	180

S16.40 Limited

As above, with stainless steel receiver and Sterling finish.

NIB	Exc.	V.G.	Good	Fair	Poor
920	800	680	500	400	180

18.9 Limited

Chambered for 9mm Parabellum. Features include stainless steel slide and frame with dual grasping grooves, 18-round magazine, adjustable rear and fiber optic front sight, ambidextrous thumb safeties, extended grip tang and competition trigger. Weight 40 oz., barrel length 5". Finish bright stainless.

NIB	Exc.	V.G.	Good	Fair	Poor
1100	880	750	580	350	200

Todd Jarrett .40 USPSA P-16

Limited edition 16+1 (or 10+1) .40 S&W custom competition pistol, with adjustable rear and fiber optic front sight. 5" barrel, weight 40 oz. Covert non-reflective black or Sterling finish.

NIB	Exc.	V.G.	Good	Fair	Poor
1500	1250	900	680	450	200

Todd Jarrett .45 USPSA

Limited edition 8+1 .45 ACP caliber custom competition pistol, with adjustable rear and fiber optic front sight. 5" barrel, weight 39 oz. Covert non-reflective black or stainless finish.

NIB	Exc.	V.G.	Good	Fair	Poor
1500	1250	900	680	450	200

1911 BLACK OPS SERIES

Manufactured from 2012 to 2015. 1911-style pistols. Caliber: .45 ACP. Capacity: 8-, 10-, or 14-round magazine. Barrel: 5". Tritium night sights. G10 grips. IonBond black finish. Blacks Ops skull engraving on slide.

NIB	Exc.	V.G.	Good	Fair	Poor
1270	1080	830	630	530	400

1911 Black Ops Ltd.

Similar to above. Checkered wood grips. Manufactured from 2012 to 2013. Capacity: 8-round magazine.

NIB	Exc.	V.G.	Good	Fair	Poor
1270	1080	830	630	530	400

1911 Black Ops 10.45

Similar to above. Capacity: 10-round magazine. Weight 41 oz.

NIB	Exc.	V.G.	Good	Fair	Poor
1320	1100	830	630	530	400

1911 Black Ops 14.45

Similar to above. Capacity: 14-round magazine. Weight 41 oz.

NIB	Exc.	V.G.	Good	Fair	Poor
1320	1100	830	630	530	400

1911 Black Ops Combat

Similar to above. Capacity: 14-round magazine. 5.5" threaded barrel. Weight 41 oz.

NIB	Exc.	V.G.	Good	Fair	Poor
1340	1130	830	630	530	400

1911 Black Ops Recon

Similar to above. Caliber .45 ACP or 9mm. Capacity: 14 (.45 ACP) or 18 (9mm) round magazine. 4.25" barrel. Weight 41 oz.

NIB	Exc.	V.G.	Good	Fair	Poor
1320	1100	830	630	530	400

LDA, DOUBLE ACTION, SINGLE STACK CARRY OPTION

Companion II

Caliber .45 ACP, Light Double-Action (LDA) trigger, Commander-length stainless slide on full-size stainless frame, extended grip safety, fiber optic front sight and 8-round magazine. Weight 35 oz., 4.25" barrel, with Covert Black finish. Introduced in 2011.

NIB	Exc.	V.G.	Good	Fair	Poor
780	650	550	400	300	200

Carry Model

.45 ACP model has 3" barrel and stainless steel receiver and finish. Magazine capacity 6 rounds. Weight about 30 oz.

NIB	Exc.	V.G.	Good	Fair	Poor
920	800	680	500	400	180

Stealth Carry

Similar to above, with Stealth finish and Novak adjustable sights.

NIB	Exc.	V.G.	Good	Fair	Poor
920	800	680	500	400	180

CCO (Companion Carry Option)

.45 ACP model fitted with 3.5" barrel. Receiver and finish stainless steel. Magazine capacity 7 rounds. Weight about 32 oz.

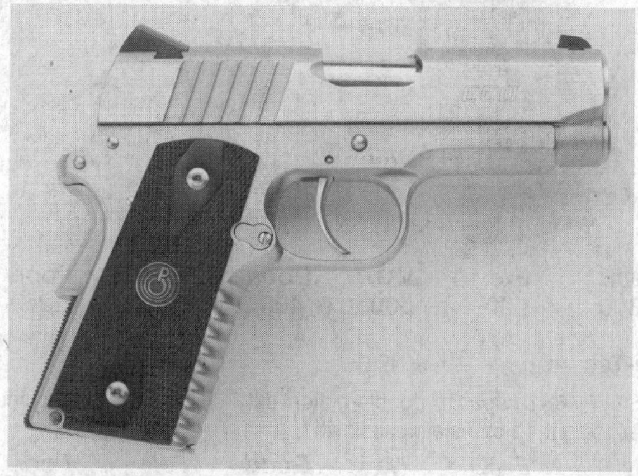

NIB	Exc.	V.G.	Good	Fair	Poor
850	700	580	400	300	120

CCW

Similar to above, with 4.45" barrel. Weight about 34 oz.

NIB	Exc.	V.G.	Good	Fair	Poor
850	700	580	400	300	120

DOUBLE-ACTION ONLY, SINGLE-STACK MODELS

Black Watch Companion

.45 ACP pistol fitted with 3.5" barrel. Receiver stainless steel with Black Watch finish. Magazine capacity 7 rounds. Weight about 32 oz.

NIB	Exc.	V.G.	Good	Fair	Poor
850	680	520	380	200	120

TAC-S

Chambered for .45 ACP cartridge, with 4.45" barrel. Steel receiver and Spec Ops finish. Magazine capacity 7 rounds. Weight about 35 oz.

NIB	Exc.	V.G.	Good	Fair	Poor
750	580	550	380	200	100

Black Watch SSP

.45 ACP pistol has 5" barrel, with steel receiver and Black Watch finish. Fixed 3-dot sights. Match trigger. Cocobolo wood grip, with gold medallion. Magazine capacity 7 rounds. Weight about 39 oz.

NIB	Exc.	V.G.	Good	Fair	Poor
750	580	550	380	200	100

SSP

Similar to above, with stainless steel receiver and finish.

NIB	Exc.	V.G.	Good	Fair	Poor
800	620	500	400	150	120

LDA, DOUBLE ACTION, SINGLE STACK LIMITED MODELS

Stealth Limited

.45 ACP pistol has 5" barrel, with adjustable sights. Receiver steel with Stealth finish. Magazine capacity 7 rounds. Weight about 40 oz.

NIB	Exc.	V.G.	Good	Fair	Poor
850	700	580	400	300	120

Limited

.45 ACP model has 5" barrel. Stainless steel receiver with Sterling finish. Magazine capacity 7 rounds. Weight about 40 oz. Adjustable sights.

NIB	Exc.	V.G.	Good	Fair	Poor
920	800	680	500	400	180

LDA, DOUBLE ACTION, HIGH-CAPACITY CARRY OPTION SERIES

Carry 12

.45 ACP pistol with 3.5" barrel. Fitted with night sights. Receiver and finish stainless steel. Magazine capacity 10 or 12 rounds. Weight about 34 oz.

NIB	Exc.	V.G.	Good	Fair	Poor
850	700	580	400	300	120

Tac-Four

.45 ACP model fitted with 4.35" barrel. Stainless steel receiver with Spec Ops finish. Magazine capacity 10 or 13 rounds. Sights are 3-dot. Weight about 36 oz.

NIB	Exc.	V.G.	Good	Fair	Poor
850	700	580	400	300	120

Tac-Five

Light double-action 9mm with 18+1 capacity. 5" barrel, weight 37.5 oz., stainless finish, adjustable rear sight, plastic grips.

NIB	Exc.	V.G.	Good	Fair	Poor
850	700	580	400	300	120

LDA, DOUBLE-ACTION, HIGH-CAPACITY MODELS

Stealth Hi-Cap .45

.45 ACP pistol has 5" barrel, with steel receiver and Stealth finish. Spurless hammer. Sights are 3-dot. Magazine capacity 10 or 14 rounds. Weight about 40 oz.

NIB	Exc.	V.G.	Good	Fair	Poor
800	620	500	400	150	120

Hi-Cap .45

Similar to above, with stainless steel receiver and finish.

NIB	Exc.	V.G.	Good	Fair	Poor
800	620	500	400	150	120

Colonel

.45 ACP pistol fitted with 4.25" barrel, with low mount fixed sights. Slide and frame are green, with black fire controls. Black polymer grips. Magazine capacity 14 rounds. Weight about 37 oz. Introduced in 2005.

NIB	Exc.	V.G.	Good	Fair	Poor
800	620	500	400	150	120

Hi-Cap .40

Chambered for .40 S&W cartridge. Fitted with 5" barrel and 3-dot sights. Stainless steel receiver and finish. Magazine capacity 10 or 16 rounds. Weight about 40 oz.

NIB	Exc.	V.G.	Good	Fair	Poor
800	620	500	400	150	120

Stealth Hi-Cap 9

9mm pistol fitted with 5" barrel with 3-dot sights. Steel receiver with Stealth finish. Magazine capacity 10 or 18 rounds. Weight about 40 oz.

NIB	Exc.	V.G.	Good	Fair	Poor
800	620	500	400	150	120

Hi-Cap 9

Similar to above, with stainless steel receiver and finish.

NIB	Exc.	V.G.	Good	Fair	Poor
850	700	580	400	300	120

Covert Black Nite-Tac

Introduced in 2005. This .45 ACP pistol fitted with 5" barrel and covert black finish. Low mount fixed sights. Magazine capacity 14 rounds. Weight about 40 oz.

NIB	Exc.	V.G.	Good	Fair	Poor
850	700	580	400	300	120

Nite-Tac

As above, with stainless steel frame and slide. Introduced in 2005.

NIB	Exc.	V.G.	Good	Fair	Poor
800	620	500	400	150	120

Nite-Tac .40

.40 S&W 16+1 capacity double-action duty pistol, with fixed sights. 5" barrel, weight 40 oz., stainless finish.

NIB	Exc.	V.G.	Good	Fair	Poor
800	620	500	400	150	120

Nite-Tac 9

9mm 18+1 double-action duty pistol, with fixed sights. 5" barrel, weight 40 oz., stainless finish.

NIB	Exc.	V.G.	Good	Fair	Poor
800	620	500	400	150	120

LDA, DOUBLE ACTION, HIGH CAPACITY, LIMITED

Hi-Cap Limited .40

.40 S&W pistol has 5" barrel with 3-dot sights. Stainless steel receiver with Sterling finish. Magazine capacity 16 rounds. Weight about 40 oz.

NIB	Exc.	V.G.	Good	Fair	Poor
1000	880	720	580	400	200

Stealth Hi-Cap Limited 9

Chambered for 9mm cartridge. Fitted with 5" barrel with 3-dot sights. Receiver steel with Stealth finish. Magazine capacity 18 rounds. Weight about 40 oz.

NIB	Exc.	V.G.	Good	Fair	Poor
1000	880	720	580	400	200

Hi-Cap Limited 9

As above, with stainless steel receiver and Sterling finish.

NIB	Exc.	V.G.	Good	Fair	Poor
1200	980	820	650	450	220

Stealth Hi-Cap Ltd .45

.45 ACP pistol has 5" barrel with 3-dot sights and spurless hammer. Receiver steel with Stealth finish. Magazine capacity 10 or 14 rounds. Weight about 40 oz.

NIB	Exc.	V.G.	Good	Fair	Poor
1000	880	720	580	400	200

Hi-Cap Limited .45

Similar to above, with stainless steel receiver and Sterling finish.

NIB	Exc.	V.G.	Good	Fair	Poor
1100	980	820	650	450	220

SEMI-AUTO RIFLES

TTR RIFLE SERIES

Para's Tactical Target Rifle based on AR platform, with 16.5" barrel, 30-round magazine. Chambered in .223 Rem./5.56x45 NATO. Flattop upper receiver, full-length Picatinny rail, short or long-rail forearm, adjustable buttstock. Delayed impingement gas system, front and rear flip-up sights. Accepts all M16 and AR-15 magazines. Manufactured 2009 - 2011.

NIB	Exc.	V.G.	Good	Fair	Poor
1950	1700	1450	1100	900	400

Para Ordnance Model TTR (Tactical Target Rifle)

AR-15 type rifle using a delayed gas impingement system that permits the use of a folding stock. Produced only for a few years.

NIB	Exc.	V.G.	Good	Fair	Poor
1950	1950	1500	—	—	—

Para-Ordnance Model LR-300 (Light Rifle 300)

Description and values similar to above. Originally produced by Z-M Weapons (see listing).

PARDINI

Italy

Italian maker of competition pistols and air pistols. Several variations designed for specific shooting disciplines such as Bullseye, Olympic Free Pistol, or Rapid Fire. Current specific model names with MSRP include: PDM Free Pistol Mechanical, .22 LR - $2,600; HPACP5, .32 ACP, 5" barrel for NRA Bullseye - $2,750; HPACP6, .32 ACP, 6" barrel for NRA Bullseye – $2,850; HPNew, .32 S&W for NRA Centerfire - $2,650; SPBE5, Bullseye, 5" barrel, .22 LR - $2,550; SPBE6, Bullseye 6" barrel, .22 LR - $2,650; SPBE6C, Bullseye Champion Set, .22 LR - $2,800; SPNew, for International Sport Pistol, .22 LR - $2,450; SPRF, Rapid Fire, .22 LR - $2,800. As reflected above, values for most models and variations are within about a 10% to 20% range of other models. Listings below are general model descriptions, including previously produced models.

Standard Target Pistol

.22-caliber semi-automatic pistol, with 4.7" barrel, adjustable rear sight and trigger. Blued, with two sizes of walnut grips. One suitable for use by ladies. Introduced in 1986.

NIB	Exc.	V.G.	Good	Fair	Poor
2000	1500	1000	—	—	—

Rapidfire Pistol

Similar to above in .22 Short, with alloy bolt, 4.6" barrel and enclosed grip. Weight about 43 oz. Introduced in 1995.

NIB	Exc.	V.G.	Good	Fair	Poor
2000	1500	1000	—	—	—

Centerfire Pistol

Similar to standard model in .32 S&W caliber. Introduced in 1986.

NIB	Exc.	V.G.	Good	Fair	Poor
2000	1500	1000	—	—	—

Free Pistol

.22-caliber single-shot pistol, with 9.8" barrel, adjustable sights and grip. Furnished with barrel weights. Weight about 35 oz. Introduced in 1995.

NIB	Exc.	V.G.	Good	Fair	Poor
2300	1750	1200	—	—	—

GT Pistol

NRA IPSC pistol in .45 ACP or 9mm. Model variations include GT455B & GT455S — 5" barrel .45 ACP in black or silver; GT456B & GT456S — same except 6" barrel; GT95B & GT95S — 5" barrel 9mm in black or silver; GT96B & GT96S — same except 6" barrel. Also advertised as available in .40 S&W.

NIB	Exc.	V.G.	Good	Fair	Poor
2500	2000	1700	—	—	—

PARKER
Springfield, Massachusetts

4-Shot Pistol

.33-caliber percussion pistol, with 4" half-octagonal barrel and 4-shot sliding chamber. Marked "Albert Parker/Patent Secured/Springfield, Mass." Original finish unknown, with walnut grips. Prospective purchasers are advised to secure a qualified appraisal prior to acquisition.

NIB	*Exc.*	*V.G.*	*Good*	*Fair*	*Poor*
—	—	15000	13500	6000	2000

PARKER BROS.
Meriden, Connecticut

Perhaps best known of all American shotgun manufacturers. Established by Charles Parker shortly after the Civil War. This company has produced a wide variety of shotguns in a number of different styles over the years. In early 1930s, company was purchased by Remington Arms Company.

VH

12-, 16-, 20-, 28-gauge or .410 bore boxlock double-barrel shotgun. Manufactured in a variety of barrel lengths with double triggers and extractors. Blued case-hardened receiver, with walnut stock. Only 2,297 guns had single triggers; only 3,983 had straight-grip stocks. Approximately 78,659 were made: 10-gauge—20, 12-gauge—51,901, 16-gauge—14,446, 20-gauge—10,406, 28-gauge—1,417, .410 bore—469. Also made with automatic ejectors and known as Model VHE. The E suffix was used on all models to denote automatic ejectors. Note: Add 40 percent VHE; 60 percent 20-gauge; 500 percent 28-gauge and .410 bore.

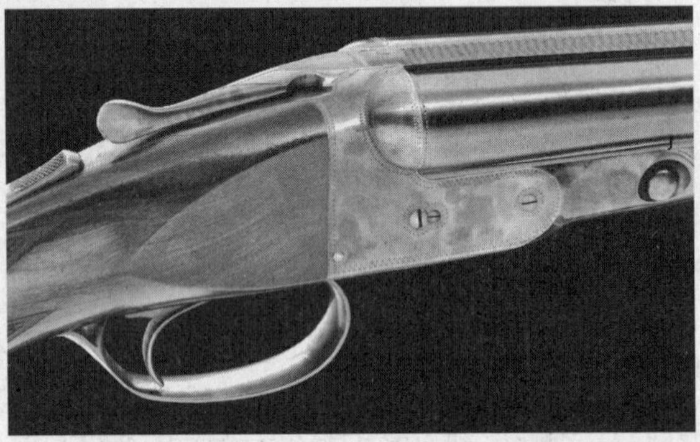

Courtesy Bonhams & Butterfields

NIB	*Exc.*	*V.G.*	*Good*	*Fair*	*Poor*
—	5500	4500	3500	2750	1850

PH

Similar to above, with a small amount of scroll engraving. Slightly better grade of walnut. Approximately 1,339 were made: 10-gauge—798, 12-gauge—839, 16-gauge—208, 20-gauge—204, 28-gauge—5, .410 bore—4. Note: Add 40 percent PHE (ejectors); 60 percent 20-gauge; extremely rare 28-gauge and .410 bore models, prices can command a 1000 percent premium.

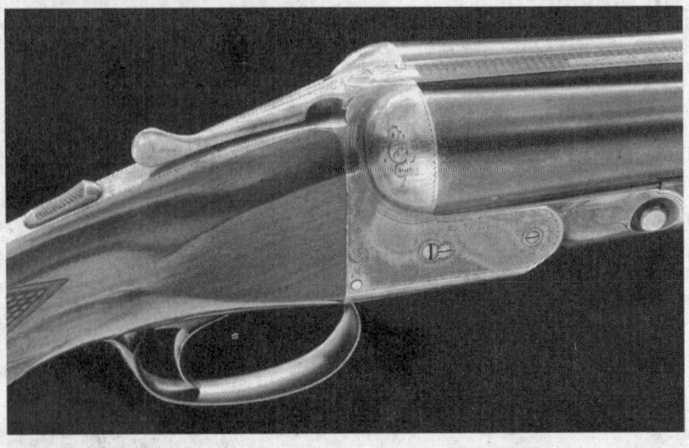

Courtesy Bonhams & Butterfields

NIB	*Exc.*	*V.G.*	*Good*	*Fair*	*Poor*
—	6000	5200	4200	3200	2000

GH

Similar to above, with a modest amount of scroll and game scene engraving. Barrels marked "Parker Special Steel". Only about 430 G grades were built with straight-grip stocks. Approximately 4,291 were made: 8-gauge—11, 10-gauge—63, 12-gauge—2,501, 16-gauge—607, 20-gauge—990, 28-gauge—91, .410 bore—28. Note: Add 35 percent GHE (ejectors); 15 percent 16-gauge; 50 percent 20-gauge; 300 percent 28-gauge; 500 percent .410 bore.

NIB	*Exc.*	*V.G.*	*Good*	*Fair*	*Poor*
—	7500	6800	4500	4000	2500

DH

As above, but more finely finished. Engraving coverage more profuse. Most modern D grade guns were fitted with Titanic barrels. Only about 280 were built with Parker single triggers; about 280 built with ventilated ribs. Approximately 9,346 were made: 8-gauge—10, 10-gauge—45, 12-gauge—6,330, 16-gauge—1,178, 20-gauge—1,536, 28-gauge—187, .410 bore—60. Note: Add 35 percent DHE (ejectors); 15 percent 16-gauge; 50 percent 20-gauge; 300 percent 28-gauge; 500 percent .410 bore.

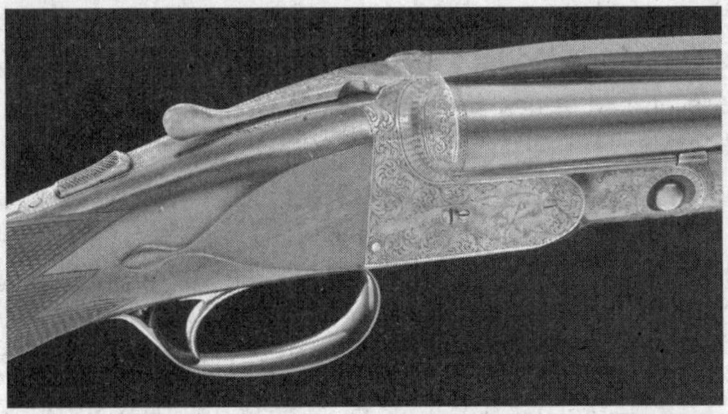

Courtesy Bonhams & Butterfields

NIB	*Exc.*	*V.G.*	*Good*	*Fair*	*Poor*
—	8000	7500	6000	4500	3000

CH

As above, with more scroll and game scene engraving coverage. Marked with Acme steel barrels. Only about 93 C grades had straight-grip stocks. Approximately 697 were made: 8-gauge—2, 10-gauge—9, 12-gauge—410, 16-gauge—105, 20-gauge—149, 28-gauge—16, .410 bore—6. Note: Add 35 percent CHE (ejectors); 10 percent 16-gauge; 40 percent 20-gauge; 400 percent 28-gauge; 700 percent .410 bore.

NIB	Exc.	V.G.	Good	Fair	Poor
—	14000	11000	10000	8000	4000

BH

As above, but offered in a variety of different styles of engraved decoration. Only about 66 guns had straight-grip stocks, 29 had beavertail forends, 20 were built with ventilated ribs and 57 had single triggers. Approximately 512 were made: 10-gauge—2, 12-gauge—317, 16-gauge—71, 20-gauge—109, 28-gauge—13. Note: Prospective purchasers are advised to secure qualified appraisal prior to acquisition. Add 35 percent BHE (ejectors); 15 percent 16-gauge; 50 percent 20-gauge; 300 percent 28-gauge. .410 bore very rare. Only 4 are known to have been made.

NIB	Exc.	V.G.	Good	Fair	Poor
—	22000	18500	14000	12000	5000

AH

As above, but highly engraved with finely figured walnut stocks. Most had Acme steel barrels. About 42 A grade guns were built with straight-grip stocks. Approximately 167 were made: 10-gauge—1, 12-gauge—92, 16-gauge—23, 20-gauge—44, 28-gauge—6, .410 bore—1. Note: Add 30 percent AHE (ejectors); 25 percent 16-gauge; 75 percent 20-gauge; 300 percent 28-gauge; .410 bore "priceless" as only one is believed to have been made.

NIB	Exc.	V.G.	Good	Fair	Poor
—	45000	40000	28000	15000	5000

AAH

As above, with Whitworth or Peerless barrels. Not made in .410 bore. Engraving is more extensive and of first quality. Only 1 AA grade has ventilated rib, 10 were built with single trigger and 95 had straight-grip stocks. Approximately 238 were made: 10-gauge—2, 12-gauge—185, 16-gauge—19, 20-gauge—27, 28-gauge—5. Note: Due to rarity of this grade, prospective purchasers are advised to secure qualified appraisal prior to acquisition. Add 30 percent AAHE (ejectors); 35 percent 16-gauge; 75 percent 20-gauge; 250 percent 28-gauge.

NIB	Exc.	V.G.	Good	Fair	Poor
—	80000	65000	45000	20000	3000

A-1 Special

As above, but made strictly on special order. Not manufactured in .410 bore. Two A-1 Specials were built with ventilated rib, 7 had single triggers, 3 had beavertail forends and 24 were built with straight-grip stocks. Approximately 79 were made: 12-gauge—55, 16-gauge—6, 20-gauge—11, 28-gauge—7. Note: Add 35 percent 16-gauge; 75 percent 20-gauge; 400 percent 28-gauge.

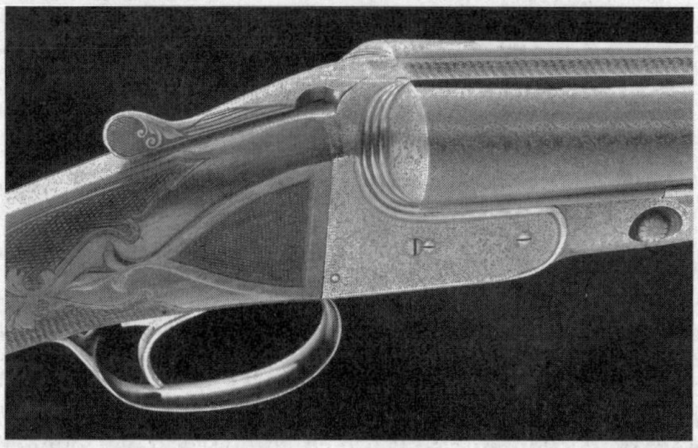

NIB	Exc.	V.G.	Good	Fair	Poor
—	120000	100000	80000	50000	20000

Single-Barrel Trap

12-gauge single-shot, with 30", 32" or 34" barrel. Automatic ejector and walnut stock. Produced in a variety of grades as listed. Prospective purchasers are advised to secure a qualified appraisal prior to acquisition.

S.C. Grade

NIB	Exc.	V.G.	Good	Fair	Poor
—	9000	8500	6500	3500	1500

S.B. Grade

NIB	Exc.	V.G.	Good	Fair	Poor
—	11000	10000	8000	5000	2000

S.A. Grade

NIB	Exc.	V.G.	Good	Fair	Poor
—	15000	14000	12000	8000	5000

S.A.A. Grade

NIB	Exc.	V.G.	Good	Fair	Poor
—	35000	30000	25000	15000	5000

S.A-1 Special Grade

NIB	Exc.	V.G.	Good	Fair	Poor
—	40000	35000	30000	15000	5000

Under Lifter Hammer Gun

Side hammer double-barrel shotgun. Manufactured in a variety of gauges, with barrel release located in front of triggerguards. Damascus barrels, case-hardened locks, blued furniture with walnut stocks. Manufactured during 1870s and later.

NIB	Exc.	V.G.	Good	Fair	Poor
—	6000	3200	1500	800	600

Trojan

12-, 16- or 20-gauge boxlock double-barrel shotgun. Manufactured in a variety of barrel lengths, with double triggers and extractors. Only 27 Trojans were built with single triggers. Blued case-hardened receiver, with walnut stock. Approximately 33,000 were made: 12-gauge—21,977, 16-gauge—6,573, 20-gauge—5450. Note: Add 20 percent 16-gauge; 40 percent 20-gauge;

NIB	Exc.	V.G.	Good	Fair	Poor
—	3800	3000	2000	1000	600

PARKER GUN

Parker Gun, a division of Remington Arms Company, offers a current production of this classic shotgun. Made by Connecticut Shotgun Manufacturing Co., the AAHE Grade is offered only in 28-gauge. This made-to-order gun is priced from $49,000 and must be ordered directly from Remington, P.O. Box 700, Madison, NC 27025.

PARKER FIELD & SONS

London, England

Gas Seal Revolver (Antique)

.42-caliber percussion revolver, with 6" barrel and 6-shot cylinder. Blued case-hardened, with walnut grips. Manufactured during 1860s. Very rare. Values are speculative.

Exc.	Fine	V.G.	Good	Fair	Poor
2500	1950	1420	900	450	310

PARKER-HALE LTD.

Birmingham, England 1890-1992

S&W Revolver Conversion

Conversion of S&W 38-100 Hand Ejector British WWII military-era revolver from .38 S&W to .38 Special or .22 LR done by Parker Hale. Replaced sights.

NIB	Exc.	V.G.	Good	Fair	Poor
—	350	250	200	150	100

Model 1200

.22-250 to .300 Win. Magnum bolt-action rifle, with 24" barrel and open sights. Blued, with walnut stock. The Model 82 is a military version of the 1200TX target rifle, worth substantial premium.

NIB	Exc.	V.G.	Good	Fair	Poor
700	550	450	400	350	250

Model 1100 Lightweight

As above, with 22" barrel and 4-shot magazine. Introduced in 1985.

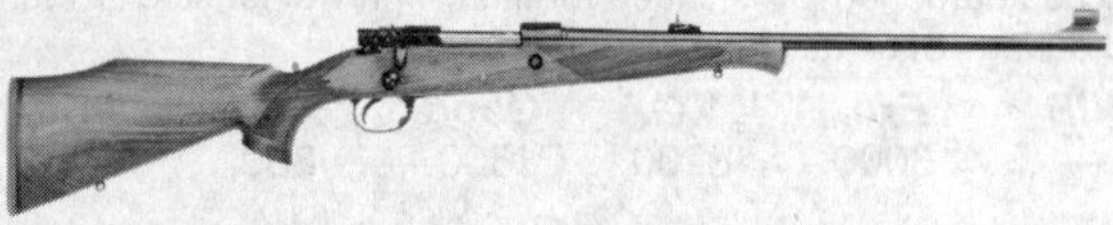

NIB	Exc.	V.G.	Good	Fair	Poor
600	480	400	300	250	200

Model 81 Classic

.22-250 to 7mm Rem. Magnum bolt-action rifle, with 24" barrel and open sights. Blued, with walnut stock. Introduced in 1985.

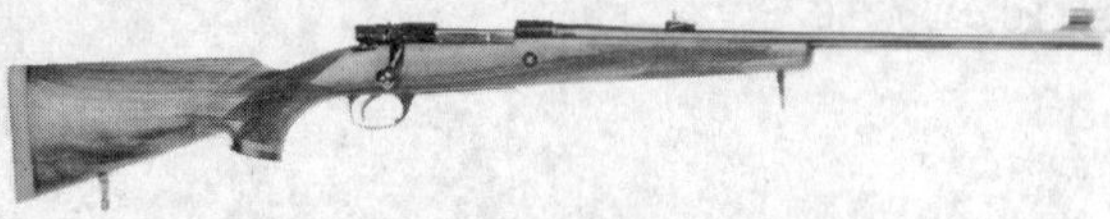

NIB	Exc.	V.G.	Good	Fair	Poor
880	750	600	500	400	350

Model 81 African

As above in .375 H&H caliber. Introduced in 1986.

NIB	Exc.	V.G.	Good	Fair	Poor
1750	1200	1100	700	500	350

Model 84 Target

Similar to Model 81 in .308-caliber. Has adjustable rear sights and cheekpiece.

NIB	Exc.	V.G.	Good	Fair	Poor
1300	1000	800	600	450	250

Model 85 Sniper

As above, with scope and bipod.

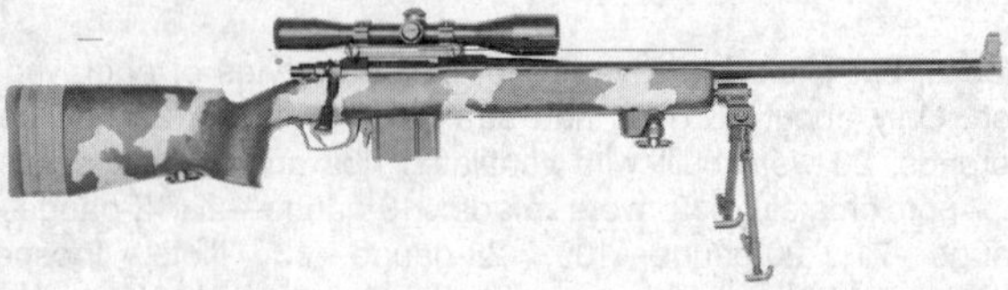

NIB	Exc.	V.G.	Good	Fair	Poor
3250	2500	980	—	—	—

Model 640E Shotgun

12-, 16- or 20-gauge boxlock double-barrel shotgun. Manufactured in a variety of barrel lengths with double triggers and extractors. Blued French case-hardened, with walnut stock. Introduced in 1986.

NIB	Exc.	V.G.	Good	Fair	Poor
580	450	400	300	250	200

Model 640A

As above, with pistol grip, beavertail forend and single trigger. Introduced in 1986.

NIB	Exc.	V.G.	Good	Fair	Poor
680	550	500	400	300	200

Model 645E

As above, but more finely finished and engraved.

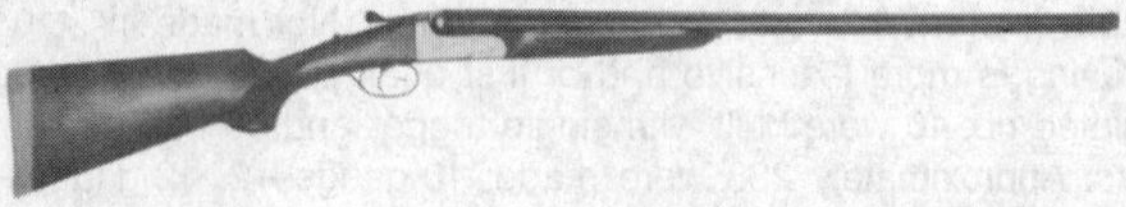

NIB	Exc.	V.G.	Good	Fair	Poor
700	550	500	400	300	200

Model 670E

Sidelock double-barrel shotgun made on special order. Introduced in 1986.

NIB	Exc.	V.G.	Good	Fair	Poor
3000	2500	1850	1200	750	400

Model 680E—XXV

As above, with case-hardened lockplates and 25" barrels.

NIB	Exc.	V.G.	Good	Fair	Poor
3000	2500	1850	1200	750	400

BLACKPOWDER REPRODUCTIONS

1853 Enfield Rifle Musket

Three-band version in .577-caliber. Barrel length 39". Rear sight graduated to 900 yards. Weight about 9 lbs.

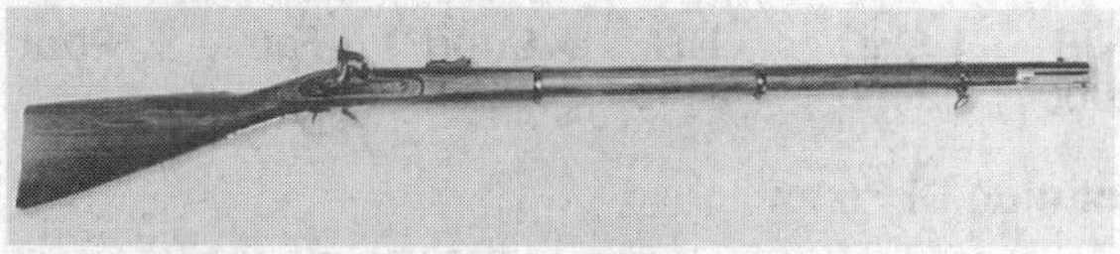

NIB	Exc.	V.G.	Good	Fair	Poor
600	480	380	250	180	80

1858 Enfield Naval Pattern Rifle

Naval version with 2-bands in .577-caliber. Barrel length 33". Walnut stock, with brass furniture. Rear sight adjustable to 1100 yards. Weight about 8.5 lbs.

NIB	Exc.	V.G.	Good	Fair	Poor
550	420	320	200	120	50

1861 Enfield Artillery Carbine Musketoon

Artillery version in .577-caliber, with 24" barrel. Walnut stock, with brass furniture. Rear sight adjustable to 600 yards. Weight about 7.5 lbs.

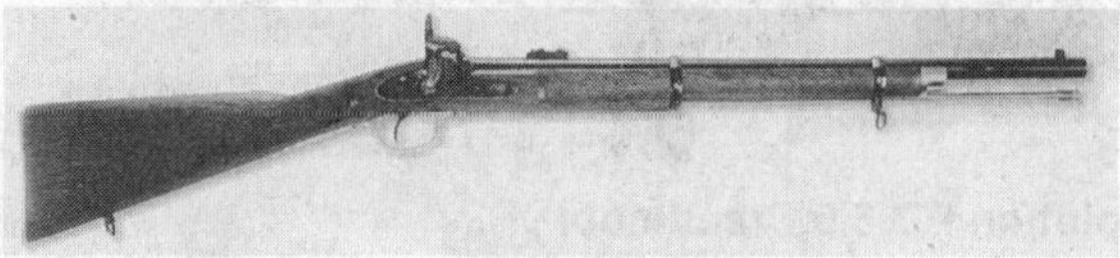

NIB	Exc.	V.G.	Good	Fair	Poor
550	420	320	200	120	50

Whitworth Military Target Rifle

Model in .451-caliber. Barrel length 36". Weight about 9.9 lbs.

NIB	Exc.	V.G.	Good	Fair	Poor
880	700	550	400	200	100

Whitworth Sniping Rifle

Same as above, with brass scope and mounts.

NIB	Exc.	V.G.	Good	Fair	Poor
1400	1050	800	550	300	150

Volunteer Percussion Target Rifle

Rifle in .451-caliber. Fitted with 33" barrel. Two-banded design, with walnut stock and brass furniture. Adjustable rear sight. Weight about 9.5 lbs.

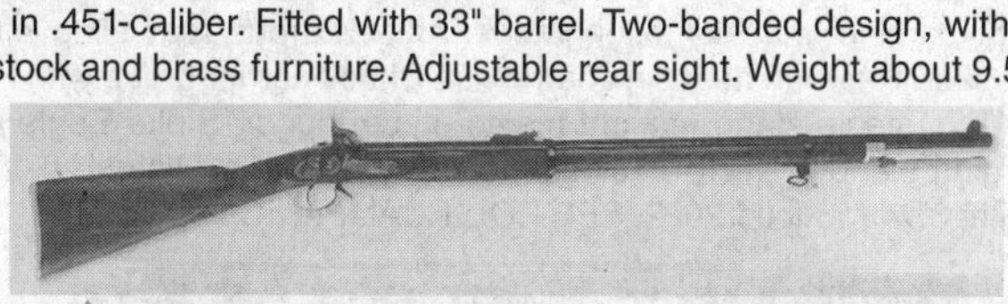

NIB	Exc.	V.G.	Good	Fair	Poor
850	650	550	400	200	100

PARKER REPRODUCTIONS
Japan

Company had exact reproductions of Parker D, DHE, B and A-1 Special shotguns made in Japan. They are of the finest quality and workmanship. Styles of engraving and features of these shotguns correspond exactly to original Parker Arms. Following values are a starting point.

DHE Grade

Side-by-side shotgun offered in 12-, 20- and 28-gauge. Barrel lengths 26" or 28" with solid matte rib. Stocks are select walnut, with choice of pistol-/straight-grip. Choice splinter or beavertail forearms offered. Single-/double triggers available. Receiver case colored and scroll engraved with game scenes to match original Parker DHE grade. Weight: 12-gauge 6.75 lbs.; 20-gauge 6.5 lbs.; 28-gauge 5.3 lbs.

12 Gauge

Note: Add 30 percent 20-gauge.

NIB	Exc.	V.G.	Good	Fair	Poor
4300	3500	2800	1800	1200	400

16/20 Combination

Introduced in 1993. Limited to 500 sets. Offered with 28" barrels only. This set features 16-gauge barrel on 20-gauge frame. Weight 6.25 lbs.

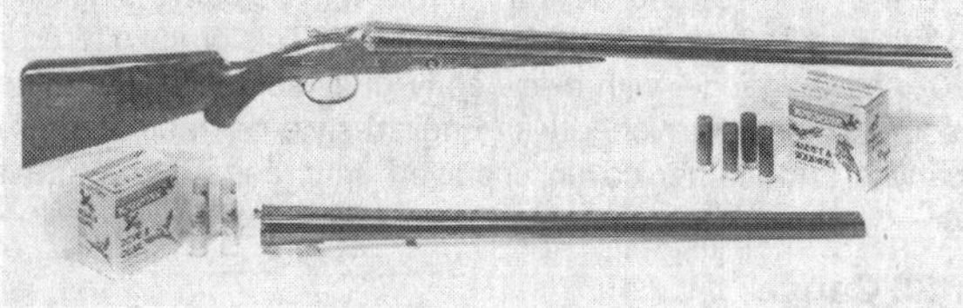

NIB	Exc.	V.G.	Good	Fair	Poor
11000	8900	7500	3500	2000	650

28 Gauge

NIB	Exc.	V.G.	Good	Fair	Poor
6000	4250	3000	2000	1400	400

28 Gauge/.410 Bore Combination

Note: Add $990 for additional barrel; $170 for beavertail forearm. D Grade three-barrel sets are offered in 16/20/20 combinations for additional $2300.

NIB	Exc.	V.G.	Good	Fair	Poor
15000	12000	9000	7500	3000	1000

DHE Grade Steel-Shot Special

Offered in 12-gauge only, with 28" barrels. Fitted with 3" chambers and special chrome lined barrels. Weight 7 lbs.

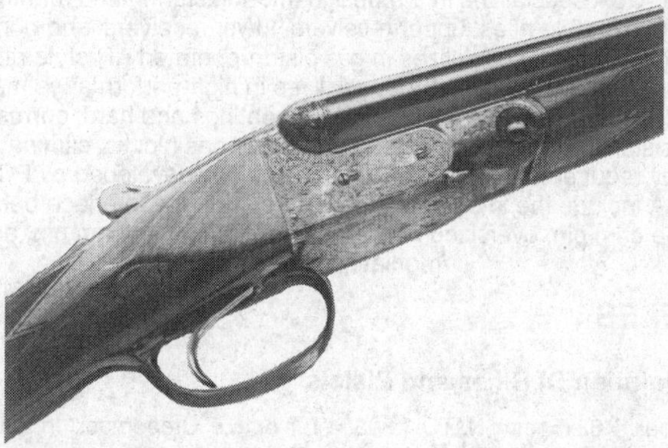

NIB	Exc.	V.G.	Good	Fair	Poor
6000	5000	3950	2200	1200	400

BHE Grade Limited Edition

Features engraving similar to original Parker BHE Grade. Fancy walnut stocks with fine line checkering was standard. Offered in 12-, 20- and 28-gauge. A 28-gauge/.410 bore combination was also offered. Only 100 shotguns in this grade produced in 1989. Note: Add 20 percent for 20-gauge; 150 percent for 28-gauge or .410 bore.

NIB	Exc.	V.G.	Good	Fair	Poor
8500	6500	5000	2250	900	450

2-Barrel Set

NIB	Exc.	V.G.	Good	Fair	Poor
25000	22000	15000	10000	6000	3000

A-1 Special

Introduced in 1988. Grade featured fine scroll engraving and presentation French walnut, with custom checked pattern. Stock was hand-carved with fleur-de-lis and features 32 lpi checkering. Grip cap was rosewood and gold or gold initial plate on straight-grip guns. Gold wire was used on breech end on barrels. Serial numbers were in gold relief as were the word "SAFE" and "L" and "R" on models with selective single trigger. Barrel flats and frame water table were jeweled. This grade offered in 12-, 16-, 20- and 28-gauge, with a few early guns sold with 28-gauge/.410 bore combinations. Furnished with English-style oak-and-leather case, with canvas and leather cover, engraved snap caps and engraved oil bottle.

12 or 20 Gauge

NIB	Exc.	V.G.	Good	Fair	Poor
16000	11500	9000	6500	5000	700

28 Gauge

NIB	Exc.	V.G.	Good	Fair	Poor
20000	15000	10000	7000	3500	600

28 Gauge & .410 Combination

NIB	Exc.	V.G.	Good	Fair	Poor
35000	30000	23000	12000	7000	4000

16 Gauge and 20 Gauge Combination

NIB	Exc.	V.G.	Good	Fair	Poor
35000	32000	24000	15000	7500	4000

A-1 Special Custom Engraved

A custom A-1 Special hand-engraved to each individual customer's specifications. Only limited number of these shotguns were built. Initial price in 1989 was $10,500. Sky's the limit on a gun of this sort.

PATRIOT ORDNANCE FACTORY, INC.

Phoenix, Arizona

POF-USA specializes in the design, manufacturing and marketing of AR-style rifles, upper receivers, lower receivers, and gun accessories. It specializes in gas piston-operated AR-style rifles. Began in 2002. POF-USA specializes in high-performance metal finishes and coatings, including NP3 coatings and hard, corrosion-resistant, nitride heat-treated barrels and gas blocks, eliminating any requirement for lubrication. Innovations developed by POF-USA include the integral bolt-carrier key with the interface behind the cam pin, oversized heat-sink barrel nut, roller cam pin, and regulating gas plug.

RIFLES

Revolution DI Rifles and Pistols

Caliber: 7.62x51mm NATO (.308 Win.) or 6.5 Creedmoor. Introduced 2019. Similar to PD Revolution, but with direct-impingement operation, nine-position adjustable Dictator gas block and Renegade rail. Weight: 6.8 lbs. Barrel: 16.5", 18.5" for .308 Win.; 20" and 22" for 6mm CM and 6.5 CM. Gen 4 ambi lower receiver. Add $134 for Burnt Bronze or Tungsten finishes. Introduced 2019. SEE POLITICAL PANIC PRICING.

NIB	Exc.	V.G.	Good	Fair	Poor
2600	2400	2150	1890	—	—

Revolution DI Pistol

Introduced 2019. Direct Impingement .308 Win., 12.5" barrel, 11.5" Renegade Rail. 6.31 lbs. Black Anodized 01599 or Burnt Bronze 01600.

NIB	Exc.	V.G.	Good	Fair	Poor
2350	2000	1700	1440	1230	1040

Revolution PD Rifles and Pistols

6.5 Creedmoor introduced 2019. Also, .308 Win. Piston-driven guns use 5.56 bolt carrier and other 5.56 parts to reduce size and weight, 7.3 lbs. Edge handguard with four built-in QD mounts, 5-position adjustable gas piston.

Revolution PD 6.5 Creedmoor

20" barrel, 14.5" M-LOK MRR handguard. 9.38 lbs. Burnt Bronze model number 01565.

NIB	Exc.	V.G.	Good	Fair	Poor
2400	2040	1730	1470	1250	1070

Revolution PD .308 Win.

16.5" barrel, same handguard as above. 7.3 lbs. Burnt Bronze model number is 01467.

NIB	Exc.	V.G.	Good	Fair	Poor
2400	2040	1730	1470	1250	1070

Revolution PD Pistol .308 Win.

12.5" barrel, 11.5" M-LOK MRR handguard. 7.0 lbs.

NIB	Exc.	V.G.	Good	Fair	Poor
2280	1930	1640	1400	1190	1010

Wonder Rifle DI

Caliber: 5.56 NATO. Direct impingement. Barrel: 16.5" match-grade Nitride heat-treated Puritan barrel, 1:8" twist, 1/2x28 barrel threads. Lightweight carbine with some upgrades. Ambidextrous rear sling mount, Renegade Rail with heat sink barrel nut, DI bolt carrier group with Roller Cam Pin, single-stage straight match-grade trigger, Strike Eagle Ambi Charging Handle, Micro B single-port muzzle brake. Weight: 6.18 lbs. Length: 3". Introduced 2022. SEE POLITICAL PANIC PRICING.

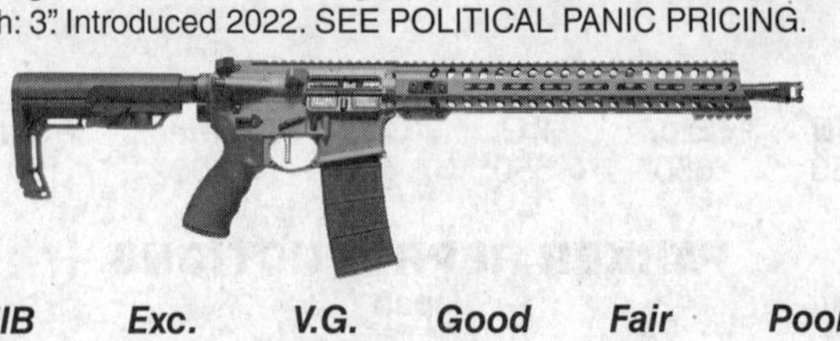

NIB	Exc.	V.G.	Good	Fair	Poor
1680	1500	1300	1050	—	—

Constable Rifle 5.56

16" barrel, direct impingement. 14.5" rail, 6.14 lbs. Black anodized.

NIB	*Exc.*	*V.G.*	*Good*	*Fair*	*Poor*
900	770	650	550	470	400

Constable Rifle .300 BLK (2019)

16" barrel, direct impingement. 14.5" rail, 6.14 lbs. Black anodized.

NIB	*Exc.*	*V.G.*	*Good*	*Fair*	*Poor*
900	770	650	550	470	400

Constable Rifle 7.62x39 (2019)

16" barrel, direct impingement. 14.5" rail, 6.14 lbs. Black anodized.

NIB	*Exc.*	*V.G.*	*Good*	*Fair*	*Poor*
900	770	650	550	470	400

Constable Pistol 5.56 (2019)

10.5" barrel, direct impingement. 9" Renegade Rail. 5.53 lbs. Black anodized.

NIB	*Exc.*	*V.G.*	*Good*	*Fair*	*Poor*
1000	850	720	610	520	440

Renegade+ DI Rifles and Pistols

5.56, .224 Valkyrie, .223 Wylde, and .300 BLK chamberings introduced in 2016. Utilizes DIctator adjustable gas system (yes, the capital DI shows it's a direct-impingement design) with nine settings to fine-tune the rifle to a given ammunition and/or suppressor. Straight gas tube and comes with a special tool for adjusting.

Renegade+ Rifle 5.56

Includes Renegade+ Rifle .300 BLK. Both with 16.5" barrel, direct impingement. 14.5" rail, 6.3 lbs. 1:8 twist for 5.56, 1:7 twist for .300 BLK. 34" collapsed length. Black anodized model numbers shown. Burnt Bronze finishes also available.

NIB	*Exc.*	*V.G.*	*Good*	*Fair*	*Poor*
1700	1450	1230	1040	890	750

Renegade+ SPR 5.56

Includes Renegade+ SPR 01180 .223 Wylde and Renegade+ SPR 01480. Chambered .224 Valkyrie, 5.56 and .223 Wylde have 18.5" barrels, .224 Val. has 20" barrel. All have 14.5" rails, 7.7 to 7.9 lbs. Black anodized model numbers shown. Burnt Bronze finishes also available.

NIB	*Exc.*	*V.G.*	*Good*	*Fair*	*Poor*
1750	1490	1260	1080	910	780

Revolution Gas Piston & Direct Impingement Rifles and Pistols

E2 dual-extraction technology helps dislodge cartridge cases. Modular Railed Receiver (M.R.R) is a two-piece upper assembly with a free-floating monolithic handguard. One-piece high-phosphorus nickel coated gas piston and direct impingement bolt carriers with mechanical key built into the body and positioned behind the cam pin. Chrome-plated bolt, extractor, and firing pin. Oversized heat-sink barrel nut, nitride heat-treated triple port muzzle brake. Button pulled chrome-moly 5R barrels with polygonal rifling, nitride heat-treated. Single-stage non-adjustable drop-in triggers with 3.5-, 4-, and 4.5-pound pull weights in aluminum housings. Trigger, disconnect, and hammer are wire EDM cut from American A2 tool steel, nitride heat-treated. KNS Precision stainless steel non-rotating anti-walk pins. Mil-Spec aluminum anti-tilt buffer tube. Patented roller cam pin with NP3-coated roller head. Several chamberings and barrel lengths.

Renegade+ Pistol 5.56

Includes Renegade+ Pistol 01462 .300 BLK. 10.5" barrel, direct impingement. 9" Renegade Rail. 5.94 lbs. Black anodized model number shown. Burnt Bronze finish also available.

NIB	*Exc.*	*V.G.*	*Good*	*Fair*	*Poor*
1760	1490	1270	1080	920	780

Edge Series Gas-Piston Rifles and Pistols

5.56, .300 BLK, .308 Win., and 6.5 Creedmoor chamberings in gas-piston designs. Gas system consists of a FAL-type gas cylinder plug, a chrome-lined gas cylinder with a chrome-plated stainless steel piston, and operating rod that impinges against a reinforced bolt carrier key. Introduced 2017 as improved line.

P415 Edge Rifle 5.56

Caliber: 5.56 NATO. Gas-piston operation. Barrel: 16.5". Rail length: 14.5". Weight: 7 lbs. Collapsed length: 34". E2 Extraction Technology, complete ambidextrous fire controls, modular free-floating rail platform, redesigned handguard. Add $134 for Burnt Bronze, Olive Drab, and Tungsten finishes. SEE POLITICAL PANIC PRICING.

NIB	*Exc.*	*V.G.*	*Good*	*Fair*	*Poor*
2100	1980	1700	1550	1230	—

P415 Edge Pistol 5.56

Same as P415 Edge Pistol 01513 .300 BLK. Pistols have 10.5" barrels, 9" MRR rails, 6.4 lbs. Black anodized model numbers shown. Burnt Bronze finishes also available.

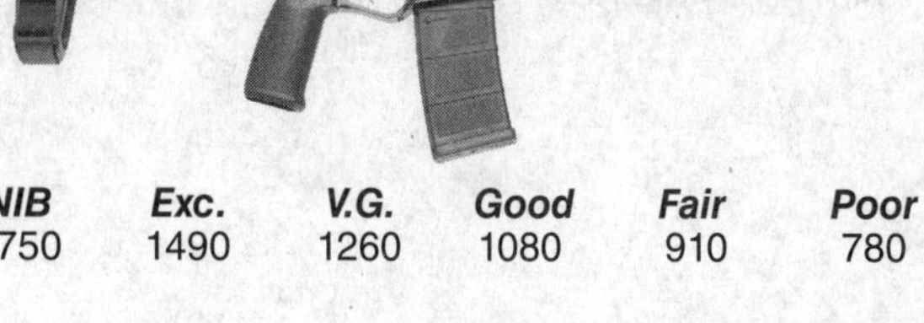

NIB	*Exc.*	*V.G.*	*Good*	*Fair*	*Poor*
1750	1490	1260	1080	910	780

P308 Edge Rifle 01568

Similar to P308 Edge Rifle/SPR 01572. .308 Win. chambering, 1:10 twist barrels, 14.5" M-Rails. Rifle has 16.5" barrel. SPR has 18.5" barrel. 8.4 and 9.46 lbs., respectively. 35" OAL collapsed. Black anodized model numbers shown. Burnt Bronze finishes also available.

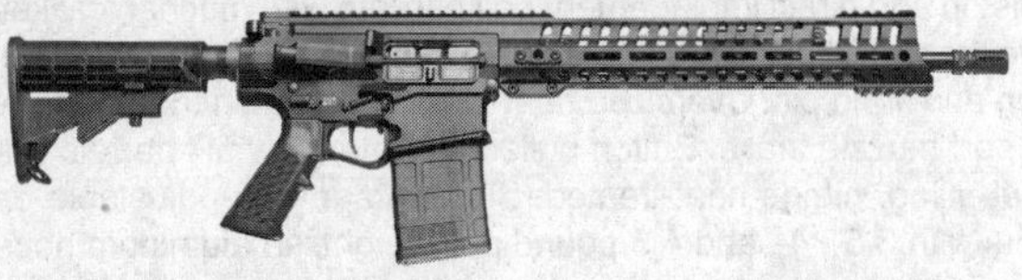

NIB	Exc.	V.G.	Good	Fair	Poor
1750	1490	1260	1080	910	780

P6.5 Edge Rifle

6.5 Creedmoor chambering, 1:8 twist barrels, 14.5" MMR handguard. 16.5" (01570) or 20" (01574) barrel. 8.4 and 9.7 lbs., respectively. 35" OAL collapsed. Black anodized model numbers shown. Burnt Bronze finishes also available.

NIB	Exc.	V.G.	Good	Fair	Poor
2150	1830	1550	1320	1120	950

Rogue Rifle

Caliber: 7.62x51mm NATO (.308 Win.) Capacity: One Magpul 20-round magazine. Barrel: 16.5", 1:8" twist, 5/8x24 tpi muzzle threads, match-grade stainless steel, Micro-B muzzle brake. Stock: Mission First Tactical. Sights: None, optics-ready with top Picatinny rail. Weight: 5.9 lbs. Trigger: 4.5-lb. POFUSA drop-in trigger system with KNS anti-walk pins. Length: 34". Roller cam pin with NP3-coated roller head. Introduced 2020. Add $134 for Patriot Brown or Olive Drab finishes. SEE POLITICAL PANIC PRICING.

NIB	Exc.	V.G.	Good	Fair	Poor
1980	1800	1600	1250	—	—

Rogue Pistol

.308 Win., 12.5" barrel, 11" Renegade Rail. 5.6 lbs., 29.5" OAL.

NIB	Exc.	V.G.	Good	Fair	Poor
1700	1450	1230	1040	890	750

Prescott Rifle

Caliber: 6mm Creedmoor, 6.5 Creedmoor. Built on Rogue platform. Weight: 7 lbs. Barrel: 20". Collapsed length: 41". Introduced 2021. Add $134 for Patriot Brown finish. Add $215 for 6mm Creedmoor chambering. SEE POLITICAL PANIC PRICING.

NIB	Exc.	V.G.	Good	Fair	Poor
2150	2000	1800	1530	1100	—

Minuteman Rifle

Caliber: 5.56 NATO, .350 Legend. Direct Impingement. Nitride heat-treated barrel, 16.5". Features: Rear QD ambidextrous sling swivel plate, anti-tilt buffer tube, ambidextrous Strike Eagle charging handle. 3.5-lbs. straight match-grade trigger. Mid-length gas system. 6.2 lbs. 34" length. Introduced 2022. Add $134 for Patriot Brown or Tungsten finishes. SEE POLITICAL PANIC PRICING

NIB	Exc.	V.G.	Good	Fair	Poor
1520	1400	1220	980	—	—

Tombstone

Caliber: 9mm Luger. Barrel: 16.5" free-floating, fluted steel. Weight: 5.75 lbs. Stock: Black synthetic Magpul SGA. Features: Accepts the same 10- and 20-round magazines as the company's Phoenix pistols. 10.5" Modular Receiver Rail (MRR) with M-LOK slots and Pic rails. Ghost ring iron sights. Crossbolt safety. Threaded muzzle with removable dual port brake. Single-stage 3.5-lb. nonadjustable trigger.

NIB	Exc.	V.G.	Good	Fair	Poor
1830	—	—	—	—	—

PEABODY

Providence, Rhode Island
Providence Tool Company

For historical information, photos and data on Peabody military rifles see Standard Catalog of Military Firearms.

Peabody Rifle and Carbine (Antique)

.43 Spanish, .443, .45 Peabody, .45-70, .50 or .50-70 caliber single-shot rifle, with 33" or 20" (carbine) barrel. Full-length or half-stock. Receiver marked "Peabody's Patent July 22, 1862 / Manf'd by Providence Tool Co. Prov. R.I." Blued, with walnut stock. Produced in large quantities during 1860s and 1870s.

Courtesy Milwaukee Public Museum, Milwaukee, Wisconsin

Exc.	Fine	V.G.	Good	Fair	Poor
1950	1400	1000	600	350	200

Sporting Rifle (Antique)

As above in sporting configuration. Barrels 26" or 28". Frame marked, "Peabody's Patent, July 22, 1862 / Manf'd by Providence Tool Co., Prov. R.I.". Blued case-hardened, with walnut stock. Manufactured approximately 1866 to 1875.

Exc.	Fine	V.G.	Good	Fair	Poor
5500	3000	2050	1100	400	280

PEABODY-MARTINI SPORTING RIFLES

Creedmoor (Antique)

.40-90 or .44-100 caliber Martini-action single-shot rifle, with 32" round/octagonal barrel, butt-mounted vernier rear sight, combination wind gauge and spirit level front sight. Receiver marked, "Peabody & Martini Patents" and barrel "Manufactured by the Providence Tool Co. Providence R.I. U.S.A.". Blued case-hardened, with walnut stock.

Courtesy Milwaukee Public Museum, Milwaukee, Wisconsin

Exc.	Fine	V.G.	Good	Fair	Poor
8250	3850	2750	1650	550	380

Creedmoor Mid-Range Antique

Similar to above in .40-70 or .40-90 caliber, with 28" round/octagonal barrel, vernier tang sight and wind gauge front. Blued case-hardened, with walnut stock.

Exc.	Fine	V.G.	Good	Fair	Poor
6600	3700	2550	1400	400	280

What Cheer Antique

Creedmoor, without pistol grip.

Exc.	Fine	V.G.	Good	Fair	Poor
6600	3600	2470	1350	400	280

What Cheer Mid-Range Antique

Mid-Range Creedmoor, without pistol grip.

Exc.	Fine	V.G.	Good	Fair	Poor
5500	3100	2100	1100	300	210

Kill Deer Antique

.45-70 caliber single-shot Martini-action rifle, with 28" or 30" round/octagonal barrels, adjustable tang rear sight and globe front. Blued case-hardened, with walnut stock.

Exc.	Fine	V.G.	Good	Fair	Poor
8250	4700	3170	1650	500	350

PEAVEY, A. J.

South Montville, Maine

Knife-Pistol

.22-caliber single-shot knife pistol. Constructed of steel and brass, with folding trigger. Sideplates marked "A.J. Peavy Pat. Sept. 5, '65 & Mar. 27, '66". Produced between 1866 and 1870.

NIB	Exc.	V.G.	Good	Fair	Poor
—	—	6000	4000	2750	700

PECARE & SMITH

New York, New York

Four-Shot Pepperbox Antique

.28 or .31 cal., four shot barrel cluster just under 4 inches long, folding trigger, double-action with bar hammer. Premium for single-action variant with hammer spur for cocking.

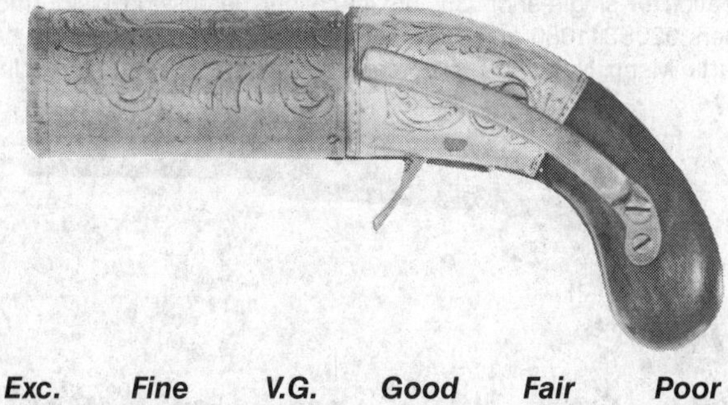

Exc.	Fine	V.G.	Good	Fair	Poor
4800	3000	2150	1300	350	240

PepperboxTen-Shot Pepperbox (rare) Antique

.28-caliber 10-shot percussion pepperbox, with folding trigger and 4" barrel group enclosed within an iron casing. Premium for rare variation with ribbed barrels cluster and nipple shield.

Exc.	Fine	V.G.	Good	Fair	Poor
9500	6600	4670	2750	600	420

PEDERSEN, JOHN D.

Denver, Colorado & Jackson, Wyoming

See—Standard Catalog of Military Firearms (GunDigestStore.com)

PEDERSEN CUSTOM GUNS

North Haven, Connecticut

Division of O.F. Mossberg Company. Operated between 1973 and 1975.

Model 4000 Shotgun

Mossberg Model 500 slide-action shotgun. In 12-, 20-gauge or .410 bore, with 26", 28" or 30" ventilated rib barrels. Blued engraved, with walnut stock. Manufactured in 1975.

NIB	Exc.	V.G.	Good	Fair	Poor
—	400	350	250	200	100

Model 4000 Trap

Chambered for 12-gauge only, with 30" Full choke barrel. Monte Carlo stock, with factory recoil pad.

NIB	Exc.	V.G.	Good	Fair	Poor
—	500	400	300	200	100

Model 4500

As above, with reduced amount of engraving.

NIB	Exc.	V.G.	Good	Fair	Poor
—	420	320	220	180	100

Model 4500 Trap

Same as Model 4000 Trap, with less engraving.

NIB	Exc.	V.G.	Good	Fair	Poor
—	400	350	250	200	100

Model 1500

12-gauge Magnum over/under shotgun, with 26", 28" or 30" ventilated rib barrels, single-selective trigger and automatic ejectors. Blued, with walnut stock. Weight about 7.5 lbs. depending on barrel length. Manufactured between 1973 and 1975.

NIB	Exc.	V.G.	Good	Fair	Poor
—	900	780	550	300	200

Model 1500 Skeet

Similar to above. Fitted with 27" barrels, skeet-style stock and chokes.

NIB	Exc.	V.G.	Good	Fair	Poor
—	950	820	600	350	200

Model 1500 Trap

Fitted with Monte Carlo-style stock. Choice of 30" or 32" barrels.

NIB	Exc.	V.G.	Good	Fair	Poor
—	950	820	600	350	200

Model 1000

As above in two grades of decoration. Manufactured between 1973 and 1975.

Grade I

NIB	Exc.	V.G.	Good	Fair	Poor
—	1750	1250	800	500	200

Grade II

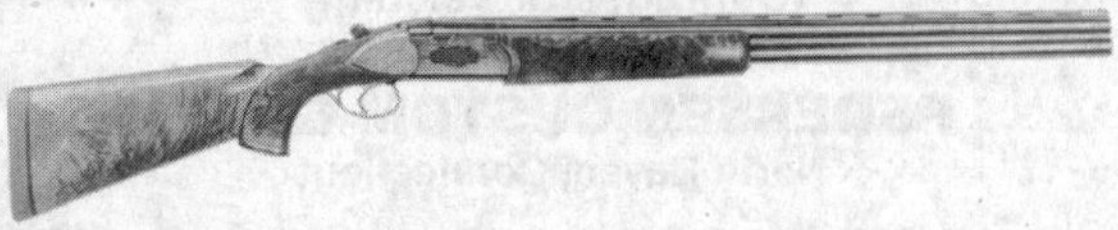

NIB	Exc.	V.G.	Good	Fair	Poor
—	1500	1000	750	400	200

Model 1000 Magnum

Chambered for 12-gauge 3" shell. Fitted with 30" barrels.

Grade I

NIB	Exc.	V.G.	Good	Fair	Poor
—	1600	1200	800	500	200

Grade II

NIB	Exc.	V.G.	Good	Fair	Poor
—	1400	1100	750	400	200

Model 1000 Skeet

Offered in 12-gauge only, with 26" or 28" barrels. Skeet-style stock and chokes.

Grade I

NIB	Exc.	V.G.	Good	Fair	Poor
—	1750	1250	800	400	200

Grade II

NIB	Exc.	V.G.	Good	Fair	Poor
—	1500	1000	750	400	200

Model 1000 Trap

Chambered for 12-gauge. Fitted with 30" or 32" barrels. Trap-style Monte Carlo stock.

Grade I

NIB	Exc.	V.G.	Good	Fair	Poor
—	1600	1200	800	500	200

Grade II

NIB	Exc.	V.G.	Good	Fair	Poor
—	1400	1100	750	400	200

Model 2000

12- or 20-gauge boxlock double-barrel shotgun, with 26", 28" or 30" barrels. Single-selective trigger and automatic ejectors. Produced in two grades of decoration. Manufactured in 1973 and 1974.

Grade I

NIB	Exc.	V.G.	Good	Fair	Poor
—	2000	1500	1000	600	200

Grade II

NIB	Exc.	V.G.	Good	Fair	Poor
—	1750	1250	800	400	200

Model 2500

12- or 20-gauge boxlock double-barrel shotgun, with 26" or 28" barrels. Double triggers and automatic ejectors. Blued, with walnut stock.

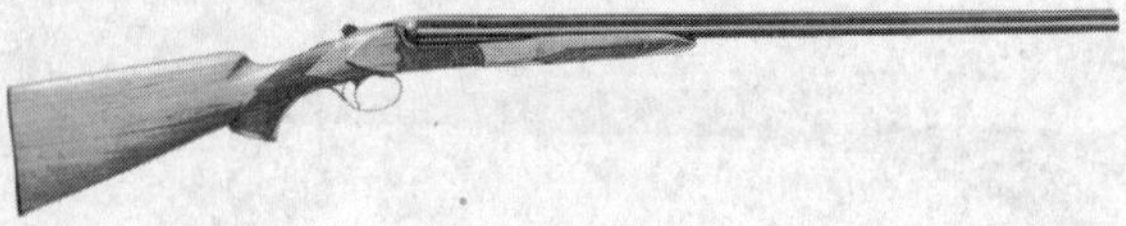

NIB	Exc.	V.G.	Good	Fair	Poor
—	400	300	250	150	200

Model 3000

Mossberg Model 810 bolt-action rifle. Manufactured in .270 to .338 Win. Magnum caliber, with 22" or 24" barrel with open sights. Produced in three grades.

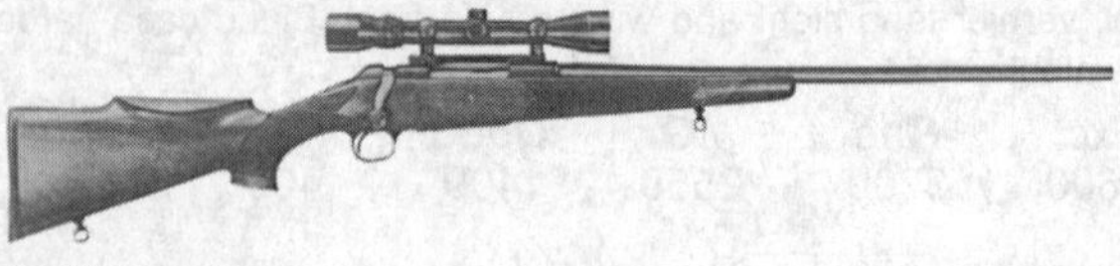

Grade III—Plain

NIB	Exc.	V.G.	Good	Fair	Poor
—	450	400	350	150	200

Grade II

NIB	Exc.	V.G.	Good	Fair	Poor
—	520	420	350	150	200

Grade I

NIB	Exc.	V.G.	Good	Fair	Poor
—	800	650	500	200	200

Model 4700

Mossberg Model 472 lever-action in .30-30 or .35 Rem. caliber, with 24" barrel and 5-shot tubular magazine. Blued, with walnut stock.

NIB	Exc.	V.G.	Good	Fair	Poor
—	450	380	280	180	100

PEDERSOLI, DAVIDE

Brescia, Italy

Davide Pedersoli & Co. was founded in 1957 by the late Davide Pedersoli. In nearly half-century since, Pedersoli has established itself as a manufacturer of extremely high-quality replica and modern firearms. Pedersoli products are frequently marked with importer's or retailer's name (e.g., Dixie Gun Works or Cabela's) rather than Pedersoli brand, usually at widely varying discounts. Many muzzleloading rifles and pistols are available in kit form at reduced prices. Note: Rapidly-fluctuating currency markets can result in values for newly-imported Pedersoli guns being 10-15 percent higher than values listed below.

HANDGUNS

Mang In Graz Pistol

Recreation of single-shot .38- or .44-caliber percussion pistol, model numbers 020S341380 and 020S341440, respectively. Made circa 1850 by Martin Mang. Note: Add 10 percent for Match; 20 percent for Deluxe.

NIB	Exc.	V.G.	Good	Fair	Poor
1600	1360	1160	980	840	710

Kuchenreuter Pistol

Recreation of single-shot .38- or .44-caliber percussion pistol, model numbers 020S300380 and 020S300440, respectively. Made circa 1854 by Bartholomaus Kuchenreuter of Steinweg, Germany. Note: Add 20 percent for deluxe.

NIB	Exc.	V.G.	Good	Fair	Poor
—	1850	1570	1340	1140	970

Mortimer Pistol

Recreation of single-shot .44-caliber pistol. First made circa 1810 by H. W Mortimer & Son of London. Smooth or rifled barrel. Percussion (020C981440) and flint versions available. Note: Add 10 percent for match model; 20 percent for deluxe.

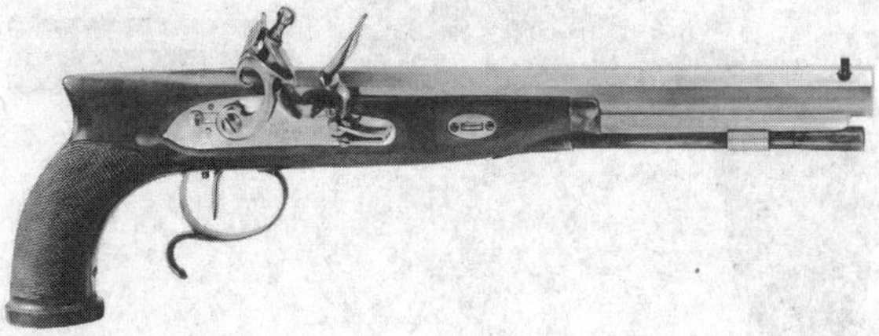

NIB	Exc.	V.G.	Good	Fair	Poor
1000	850	720	610	520	440

LePage Dueller

Recreation of single-shot .31-, .36- or .44-caliber dueling pistol. Made by Henry LePage circa 1840. Percussion and flint versions available. .Note: Add 20 percent for deluxe.

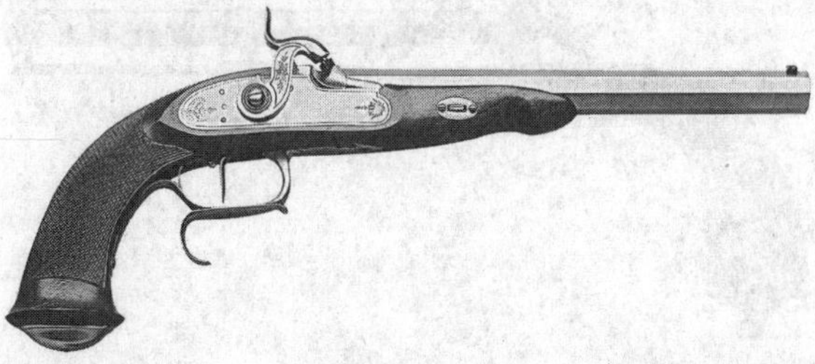

NIB	Exc.	V.G.	Good	Fair	Poor
1000	850	720	610	520	440

Charles Moore Dueling Pistol

Recreation of single-shot .36- or .44-caliber dueling pistol. Made by Charles Moore of London circa 1800. Percussion and flint versions available. Note: Add 10 percent for target model.

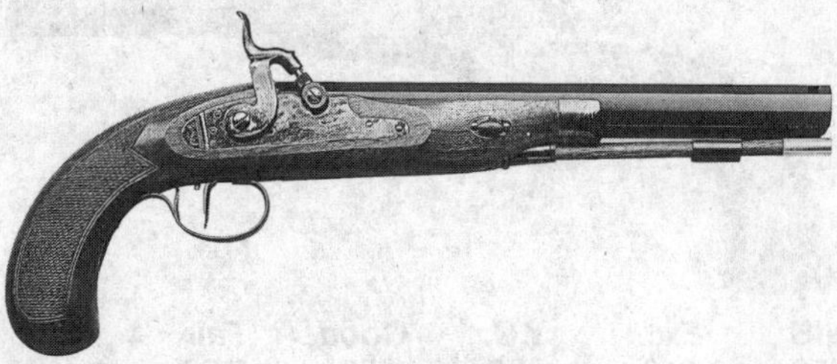

NIB	Exc.	V.G.	Good	Fair	Poor
700	600	510	430	360	310

Carleton Underhammer Pistol

Recreation of saw-handled .36-caliber underhammer percussion pistol. circa 1850.

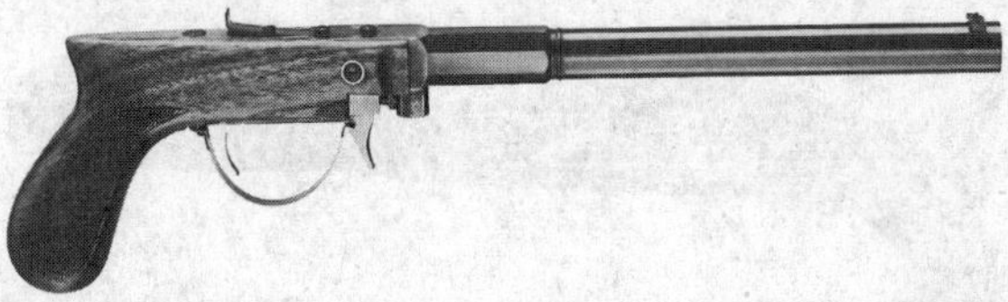

NIB	Exc.	V.G.	Good	Fair	Poor
900	760	650	550	470	400

Remington Pattern Target Revolver

Replica of Remington "1858-style" .44-caliber percussion revolver.

NIB	Exc.	V.G.	Good	Fair	Poor
900	760	650	550	470	400

Rogers & Spencer Target Percussion Target Revolver

Replica of .44-caliber Rogers and Spencer revolver, that didn't quite make it in time for Civil War.

NIB	Exc.	V.G.	Good	Fair	Poor
500	420	360	310	260	220

Kentucky Pistol

Recreation of single-shot .45-, .50- and .54-caliber pistol of American colonial era, percussion model numbers 020S310450, 020S310500, and 020S310540, respectively. Flint versions available. Note: Add 50 percent for "Silver Star" models.

NIB	Exc.	V.G.	Good	Fair	Poor
450	380	320	280	240	200

Bounty Pistol

Similar to Kentucky Pistol standard version, with 16" barrel. .45- or .50-caliber only.

NIB	Exc.	V.G.	Good	Fair	Poor
570	480	410	350	300	250

Navy Moll Pistol

Similar to Kentucky pistol, with brass trim. Flint and percussion versions available. .45-caliber.

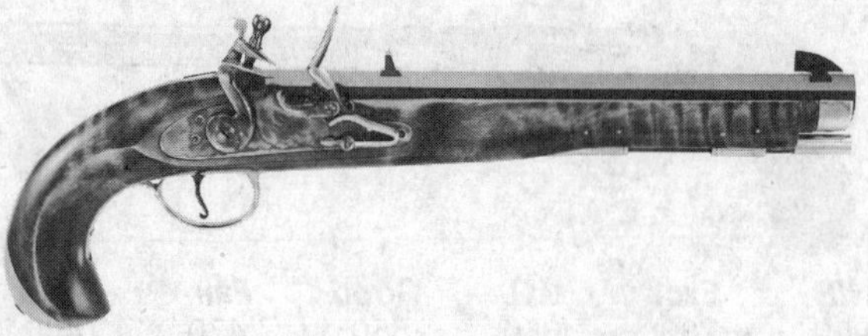

NIB	Exc.	V.G.	Good	Fair	Poor
620	530	450	380	320	280

Harper's Ferry Pistol

Recreation of .58-caliber flintlock pistol procured for U. S. Navy in 1806.

NIB	Exc.	V.G.	Good	Fair	Poor
600	510	430	370	310	270

Queen Anne Pistol

Recreation of English 17th-century cannon-barrel flintlock pistol. .50-caliber smoothbore barrel. Steel or brass construction.

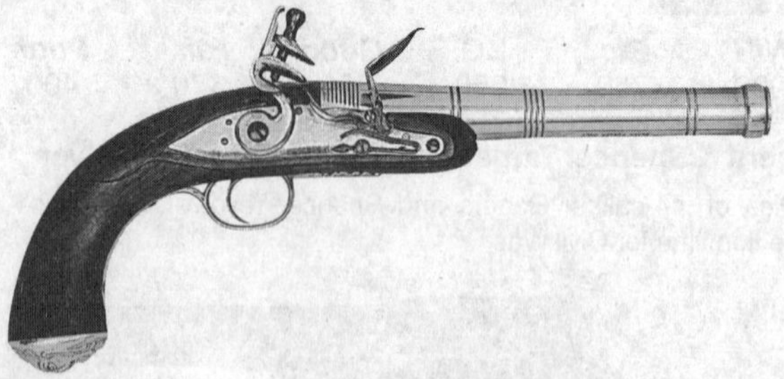

NIB	Exc.	V.G.	Good	Fair	Poor
500	420	360	310	260	220

An IX Pistol

Recreation of .69-caliber Napoleonic flintlock cavalry pistol of 1803. Brass trim.

NIB	Exc.	V.G.	Good	Fair	Poor
740	630	540	450	390	330

An XIII Pistol

Simplified 1806 version of An IX pistol.

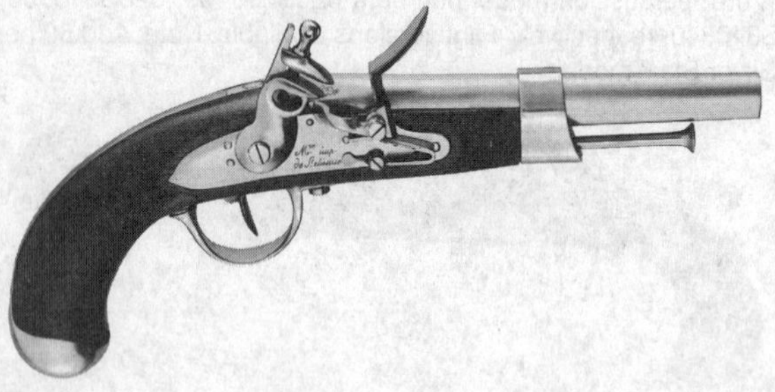

NIB	Exc.	V.G.	Good	Fair	Poor
750	640	540	460	390	330

Remington Rider Derringer

Recreation of Remington Rider single-shot .177 percussion parlor pistol. Available in white or with case-hardened gold-toned or engraved/silvered finish. Pricing for basic model.

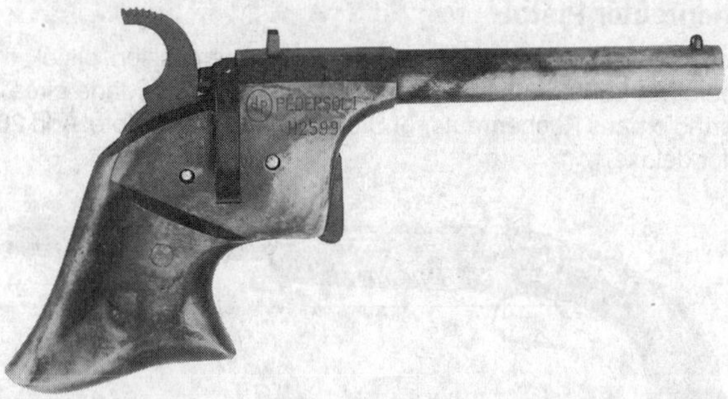

NIB	Exc.	V.G.	Good	Fair	Poor
200	170	140	120	100	90

Derringer Liegi

Recreation of circa 1850 screw-barrel percussion pocket pistol, with folding trigger and bag grip. .44-caliber. Note: Add 10 percent for engraved model.

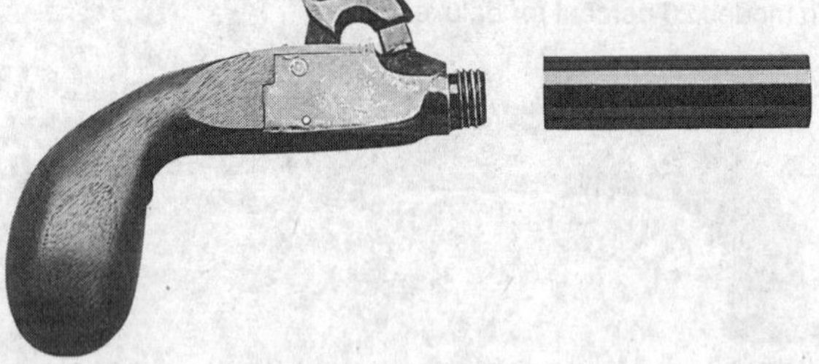

NIB	Exc.	V.G.	Good	Fair	Poor
240	200	170	150	120	110

Zimmer Pistol

Recreation of circa 1850 single-shot percussion parlor pistol. .177-caliber; fluted-grip with butt cap. Discontinued.

NIB	Exc.	V.G.	Good	Fair	Poor
210	180	150	130	110	90

Saloon Pistol

Recreation of circa 1850 single-shot percussion parlor pistol. .36- or .177-caliber. Discontinued.

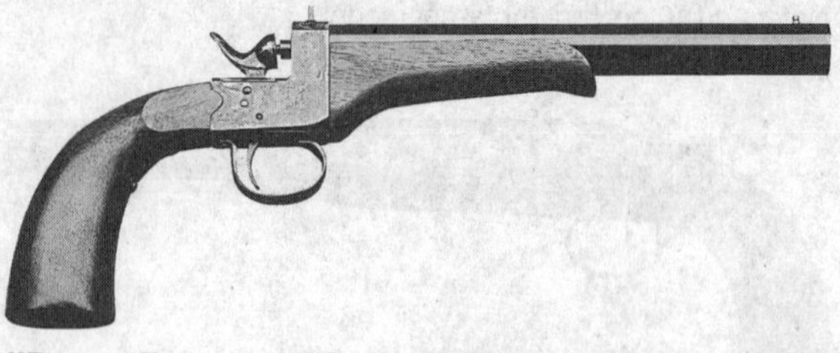

NIB	Exc.	V.G.	Good	Fair	Poor
250	210	180	150	130	110

RIFLES

Swivel-Breech Rifle

Muzzleloading over/under rotating percussion rifle in .45-, .50- or .54-caliber. Browned barrel, walnut stock. Discontinued.

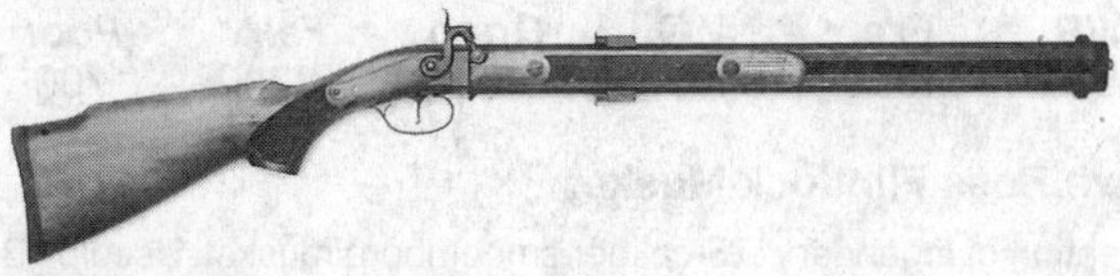

NIB	Exc.	V.G.	Good	Fair	Poor
600	510	430	370	310	270

Bristlen a Morges Standard Rifle

.35-cal. (010S235350) or .44-cal. (010S235440). Recreation of 1850-vintage percussion target rifle made by Marc Bristlen of Morges, Switzerland. Schuetzen-style buttplate, double triggers, false muzzle. Shoots elongated conica bullet. Note: Add 20% for deluxe model.

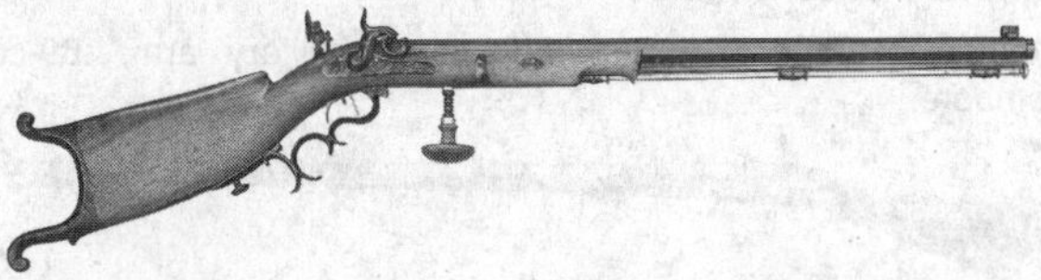

NIB	Exc.	V.G.	Good	Fair	Poor
2400	2040	1730	1470	1250	1060

Waadtlander Target Rifle

Similar to Bristlen a Morges target rifle. Rifled for .45-caliber round ball (010S2344500). Note: Add 20% for deluxe version.

NIB	Exc.	V.G.	Good	Fair	Poor
2500	2120	1810	1540	1300	1110

Swiss Match Rifle

Similar to Waadtlander Target Rifle in flintlock, with 29.5" barrel. No. 010S250450.

NIB	Exc.	V.G.	Good	Fair	Poor
1500	1280	1080	920	780	660

Wurttemberg Mauser (1857 Württembergischen)

Replica of 1857 Mauser military percussion rifle. Shoots .54 Minie ball. No. 010S290547. Designed for 100m target shooting.

NIB	Exc.	V.G.	Good	Fair	Poor
1700	1440	1230	1040	890	750

Gibbs Rifle

Recreation of 1865-vintage long-range percussion rifle made by George Gibbs of London. Shoots elongated .40- or .45-caliber conicals, model numbers 010S225400 and 010S225450, respectively.

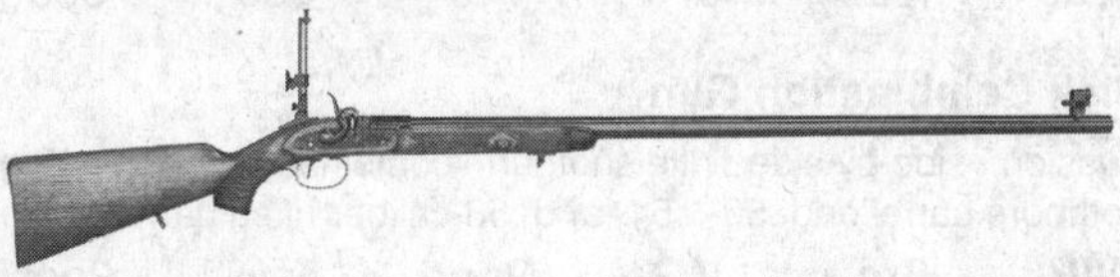

NIB	Exc.	V.G.	Good	Fair	Poor
1950	1660	1410	1200	1020	860

Tryon Rifle

Recreation of noteworthy American percussion plains rifle circa 1850. .45-, .50- or .54-caliber. Model numbers 010S219450, 010S219500, and 010S219540, respectively. Note: Add 50% for maple stock, 35% for Creedmoor model, 25% for Deluxe Target.

NIB	Exc.	V.G.	Good	Fair	Poor
1100	940	800	680	570	490

Mortimer Standard Rifle

Recreation of arms made circa 1850 by H. W Mortimer & Son of London. Percussion and flint versions available. Various configurations including Target, Target Deluxe, Deluxe, Whitworth Standard, and Whitworth Deluxe, and 12-gauge fowler. Price shown for Mortimer Standard 010S240540, caliber .54.

NIB	Exc.	V.G.	Good	Fair	Poor
1580	1340	1140	970	820	700

Indian Trade Musket

Recreation of 18th-century flintlock smoothbore as typified by colonial and early 19th-century trading companies. .20-gauge 010S282020.

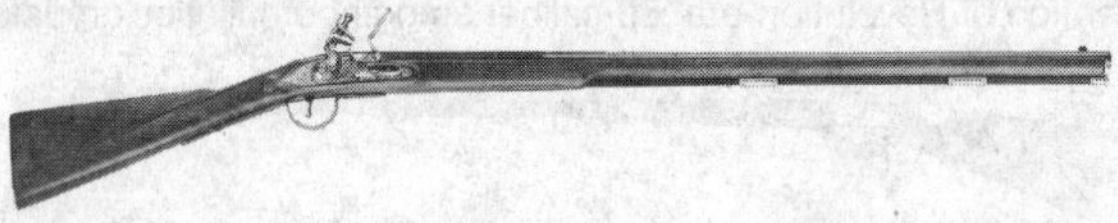

NIB	Exc.	V.G.	Good	Fair	Poor
1100	940	800	680	570	490

Frontier Rifle

Recreation of typical American hunting rifle circa 1800-1840. .32-, .36-, .45-, .50- and .54-caliber versions available in flintlock and percussion. Various barrel lengths.

NIB	Exc.	V.G.	Good	Fair	Poor
820	700	600	510	430	370

Kentucky Rifle

Recreation of Pennsylvania-style rifle circa 1800. .32-, .45- and .50-caliber percussion or flintlock. Note: Add 35% for "Silver Star" model.

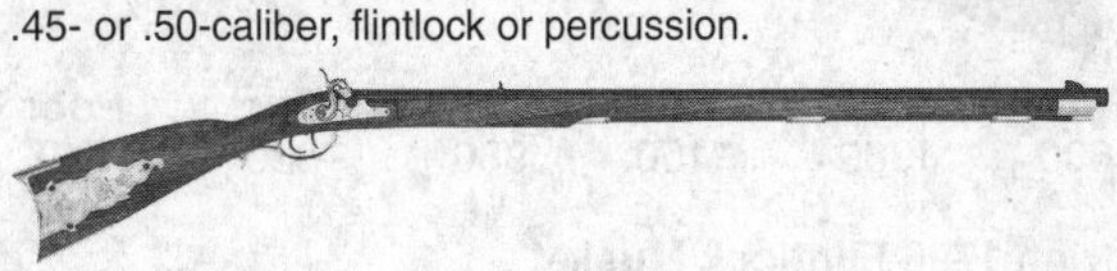

NIB	Exc.	V.G.	Good	Fair	Poor
620	520	440	380	320	270

Alamo Rifle

Re-creation of long rifle used in Mexican War of 1840s. Double triggers; .32-, .45- or .50-caliber, flintlock or percussion.

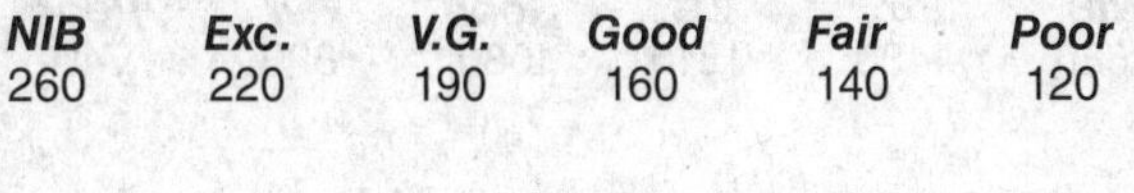

NIB	Exc.	V.G.	Good	Fair	Poor
900	760	650	550	470	400

Cub

Scaled-down Pennsylvania-type rifle in .36-, .45- or .50-caliber. Percussion or flint. Note: Add 25% for flint.

NIB	Exc.	V.G.	Good	Fair	Poor
260	220	190	160	140	120

Country Hunter

Exceedingly simple half-stock .50-caliber percussion (010S237500, price for below) or flintlock rifle (010S236500).

NIB	Exc.	V.G.	Good	Fair	Poor
680	570	490	420	350	300

Jäger Hunter Rifle

Massive, decidedly Germanic .54-caliber percussion (010S233540, price for below) or flintlock rifle (010S232540) based on Teutonic hunting arms, circa 1750–1850.

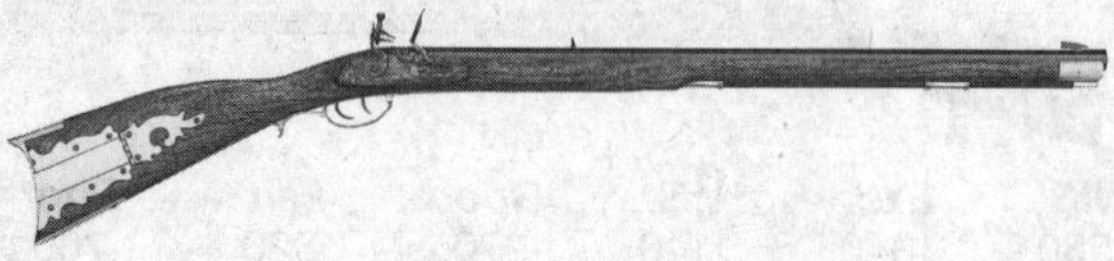

NIB	Exc.	V.G.	Good	Fair	Poor
1350	1150	980	830	700	600

Leger 1763 Charleville Musket

Recreation of Revolution-era .69-caliber smoothbore flintlock musket.

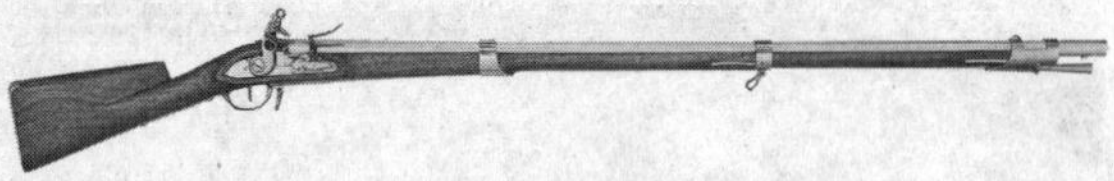

NIB	Exc.	V.G.	Good	Fair	Poor
1400	1190	1010	860	730	620

Revolutionnaire 1777 Musket

Similar to Charleville musket in detail. Patterned after muskets used in French Revolution.

NIB	Exc.	V.G.	Good	Fair	Poor
1350	1150	980	830	700	600

Corrige An IX

Similar to Revolutionnaire 1777 musket. Differing in details of frizzen, etc.

NIB	Exc.	V.G.	Good	Fair	Poor
1490	1270	1080	920	780	660

An IX Dragoon Musket

Similar to Corrige An IX musket, with 40.5" cavalry-length barrel.

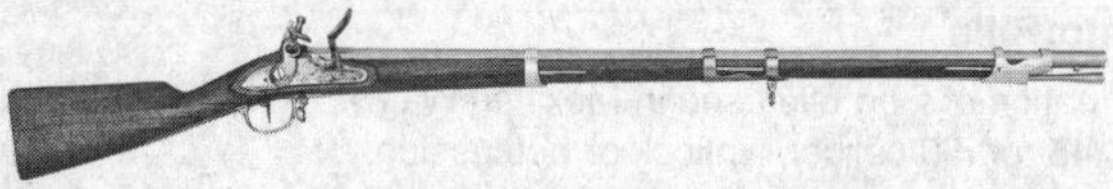

NIB	Exc.	V.G.	Good	Fair	Poor
1600	1360	1150	980	830	710

Austrian 1798 Flintlock Musket

Similar to 1777 musket, with Austrian modifications in barrel bands, bayonet mount, etc.

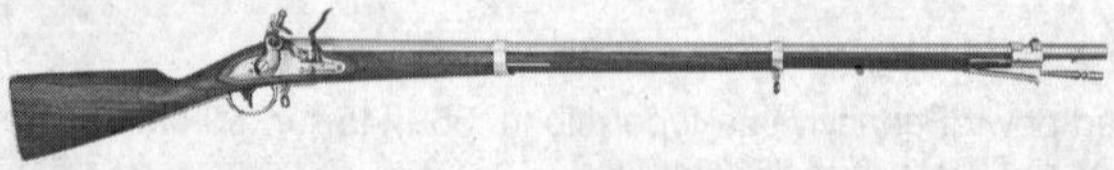

NIB	Exc.	V.G.	Good	Fair	Poor
1680	1430	1210	1030	880	740

Prussian 1809 Flintlock Musket

Similar to French 1777 musket in .75-caliber with "Potsdam" markings.

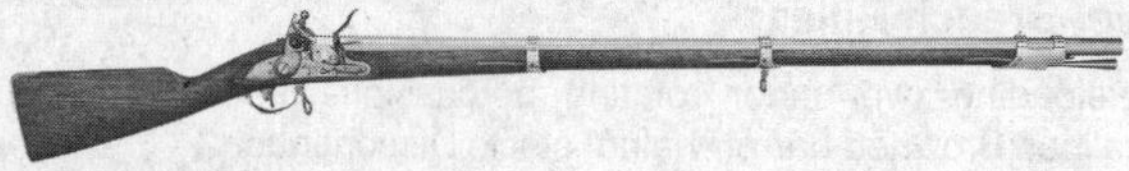

NIB	Exc.	V.G.	Good	Fair	Poor
1590	1350	1150	980	830	700

Brown Bess Flintlock Musket

Recreation of legendary .75-caliber smoothbore musket. Used by British troops before, during and after American Revolutionary War.

NIB	Exc.	V.G.	Good	Fair	Poor
1200	1020	870	740	630	530

Springfield 1795 Musket

Recreation of America's first indigenous military arm, .69-caliber smoothbore.

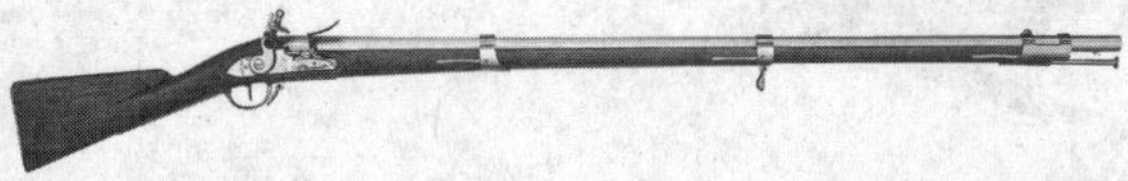

NIB	Exc.	V.G.	Good	Fair	Poor
1590	1350	1150	980	830	700

Harper's Ferry 1816 Musket

Recreation of U.S. martial .69-caliber smoothbore flintlock musket.

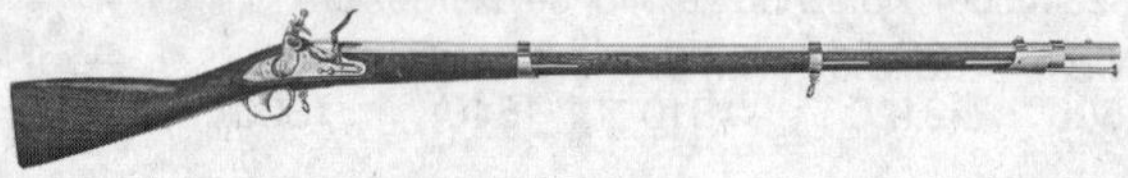

NIB	Exc.	V.G.	Good	Fair	Poor
1530	1300	1100	940	800	680

Rocky Mountain Hawken

Faithful recreation of legendary plains rifle, .54-caliber.

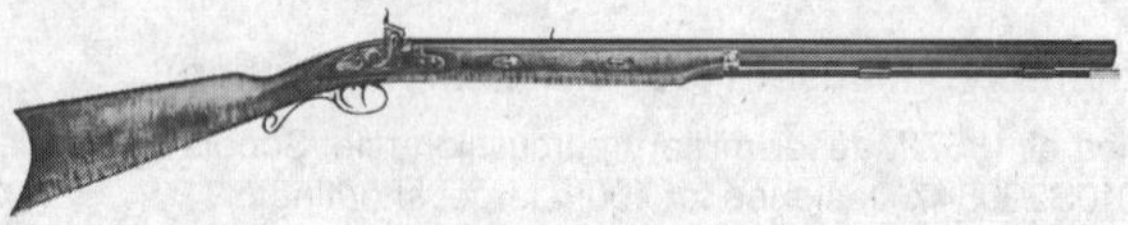

NIB	Exc.	V.G.	Good	Fair	Poor
1260	1070	910	770	660	560

Springfield 1861 Rifle

Recreation of .58-caliber percussion rifle. Used in American Civil War.

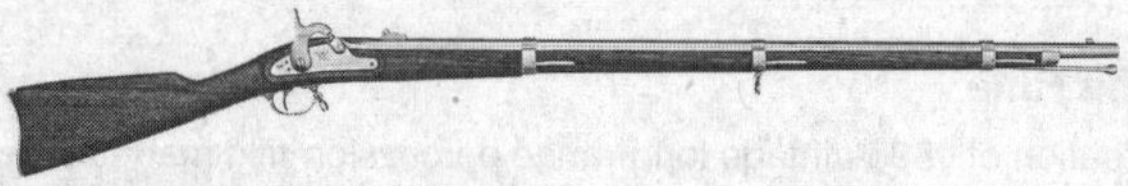

NIB	Exc.	V.G.	Good	Fair	Poor
1200	1020	870	740	630	530

Kodiak Combination Gun

Percussion side-by-side rifle/shotgun combination, with 12-gauge smoothbore barrel and .50-, .54- and .58-caliber rifled barrel.

NIB	Exc.	V.G.	Good	Fair	Poor
1200	1020	870	740	630	530

Kodiak Express MK VI

Side-by-side double percussion rifle in .50-, .54-, and .58-caliber, respectively model numbers 010S661500, 010S661540, and 010S661580. Sights regulated to 75 yards.

NIB	Exc.	V.G.	Good	Fair	Poor
1300	1100	940	800	680	580

Model 86/71 Boarbuster

Calibers: .45-70 Govt. Capacity: 5-round tubular magazine. Barrel: 19-in. round. Weight: 7.93–8.25 lbs. Length: 37-7/16 in. Stock: Varied by model. Sights: Scout-style Picatinny rail and fiber-optic iron sights. Receiver drilled and tapped for side scope mounts. Features: Big-bore lever action based on the 1886. Several models use two-piece, interchangeable loop loading lever on several models. Pedersoli's Boarbuster line is comprised of five model variants. Mark II wears coated black Walnut with Silicon grip film adjustable cheek piece and Bronze Cerakote metal finish. HV-1 wears orange and black HV-1 camo stocks with Silicon grip film and black Cerakote. Evolution is a classic model with selected Walnut stocks, Silver Cerakote receiver, and blued barrel. Shadow uses gray techno-polymer stock with adjustable cheek riser and ghost ring sights in place of Picatinny rail. Guidemaster wears camo stocks and fully chromed metalwork.

NIB	Exc.	V.G.	Good	Fair	Poor
1630	—	—	—	—	—

Rolling Block Rifle

Replica of famous Remington rolling block single-shot rifle, circa 1867-1890. Various centerfire chamberings and configurations including Baby carbine. Prices shown are for standard version in .45-70.

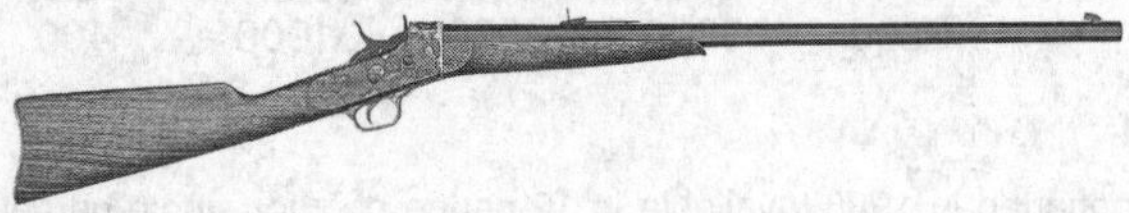

NIB	Exc.	V.G.	Good	Fair	Poor
950	880	700	550	380	200

1859 Sharps Cavalry Carbine

Replica of Sharps percussion carbine with 22" barrel, patchbox and elevator sight; .54-caliber. Available as Infantry Rifle with 30" barrel.

NIB	Exc.	V.G.	Good	Fair	Poor
1200	1020	870	740	630	530

1862 Robinson Confederate Sharps

Similar to 1859 Sharps carbine, with different barrel band, receiver details and rear sight.

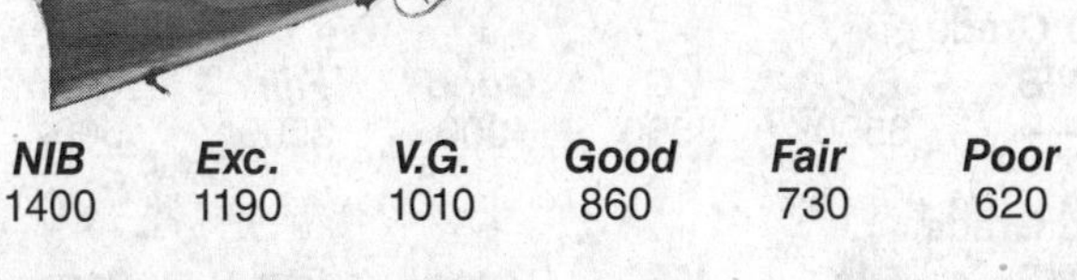

NIB	Exc.	V.G.	Good	Fair	Poor
1400	1190	1010	860	730	620

Sharps 1863 Sporting Rifle

Replica of Sharps sporting rifle, with 32" barrel, set trigger and sculpted forend; .45- or .54-caliber. .45-caliber version rifled for elongated conicals.

NIB	Exc.	V.G.	Good	Fair	Poor
1500	1280	1080	920	780	660

1874 Sharps

High-quality replica of first Sharps chambered for metallic cartridges. Chamberings include .45-70, .45-90, .45-110, .45-120, .50-70 and .50-90. Several variations available including Sporting Standard Sporting, Cavalry Rifle, Cavalry Carbine, Sporting Deluxe, Sporting Extra Deluxe, Silhouette Standard, Silhouette Deluxe, Boss, Business Rifle, Buffalo, Billy Dixon, Long Range, Quigley, Creedmore #2 and Competition Standard. Prices given are for Standard Sporting model.

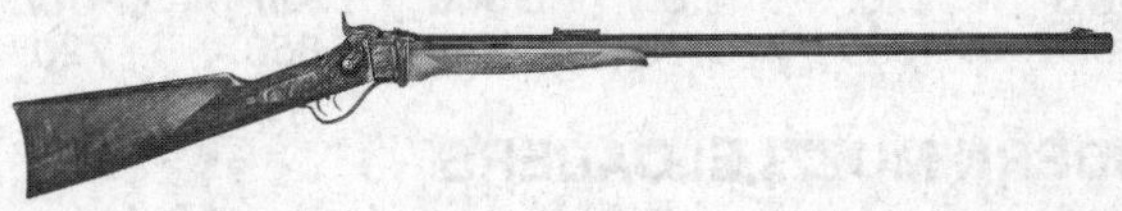

NIB	Exc.	V.G.	Good	Fair	Poor
1100	850	600	420	300	200

1873 Trapdoor Springfield

Replica of famous single-shot cartridge rifle chambered in .45-70. Several variations available including Standard Rifle, Standard Carbine, Officer's Model and Long Range Model. Prices given are for Standard Rifle. Note: Add 30% for deluxe models.

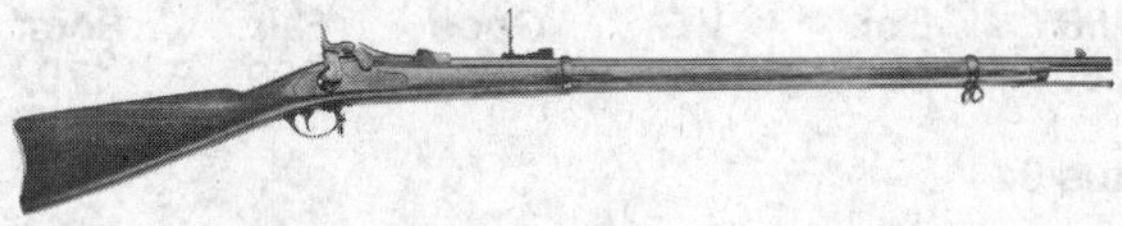

NIB	Exc.	V.G.	Good	Fair	Poor
1100	850	600	420	300	200

Kodiak Mark IV Express Rifle

Side-by-side double rifle chambered for .45-70 cartridge.

NIB	Exc.	V.G.	Good	Fair	Poor
4500	3750	3000	2000	900	300

Pedersoli Lightning Rifle

Updated replica of Model 1883 Colt Lightning Magazine Rifle. Pump action with magazine disconnector. Chambered for .44-40 and .45 Colt.

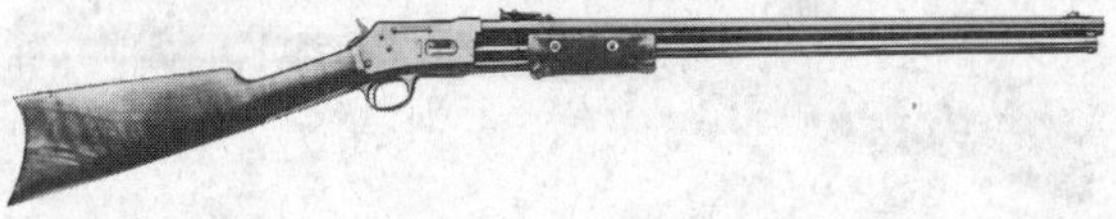

NIB	Exc.	V.G.	Good	Fair	Poor
1100	850	600	420	300	200

SHOTGUNS

Side By Side Shotgun Standard

Muzzleloading shotguns in 10-, 12- and 20-gauge. Prices given are for basic version in 12-gauge.

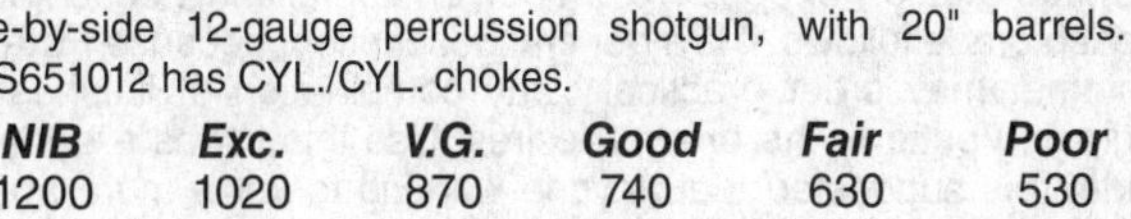

NIB	Exc.	V.G.	Good	Fair	Poor
1060	900	770	650	560	470

Coach Shotgun

Side-by-side 12-gauge percussion shotgun, with 20" barrels. No. 010S651012 has CYL./CYL. chokes.

NIB	Exc.	V.G.	Good	Fair	Poor
1200	1020	870	740	630	530

Mortimer Shotgun Standard

Recreation of 12-gauge Fowlers. Made circa 1830-1850 by H. W Mortimer & Son of London. Percussion and flint versions available.

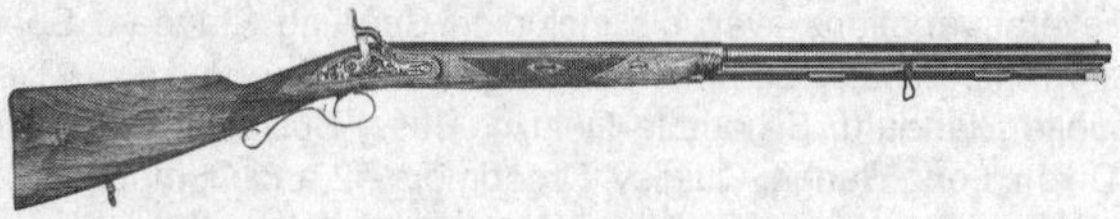

NIB	Exc.	V.G.	Good	Fair	Poor
1620	1380	1170	1000	850	720

MODERN MUZZLELOADERS

Denali

Inline .50-caliber muzzleloader, with lever-operated break-open action. Walnut/blue or camo/blue finish. Note: Add 15 percent for camo.

NIB	Exc.	V.G.	Good	Fair	Poor
380	320	280	230	200	170

Brutus 94

Inline .50-caliber muzzleloader. Blued/composite, blued/synthetic or stainless/blued/walnut finish. Note: Add 15 percent for camo.

NIB	Exc.	V.G.	Good	Fair	Poor
310	260	220	190	160	140

Brutus Ovation

Inline .50-caliber muzzleloader, with interchangeable barrels. Developed in cooperation with Mid-Western Outdoor Specialties and so marked. One-piece stock. Blued/hardwood or blued/camo finish. Note: Add 15 percent for camo.

NIB	Exc.	V.G.	Good	Fair	Poor
300	260	220	180	160	130

Rolling Block Percussion Rifle

.50-caliber muzzleloading version of Remington rolling block rifle. Blued/hardwoods or blued/camo finish.

NIB	Exc.	V.G.	Good	Fair	Poor
300	260	220	180	160	130

PERAZZI

Brescia, Italy

Company founded in 1957. During 1970s, Ithaca and Winchester imported and sold Perazzi shotguns. Perazzi has now taken over its own importation and distribution in United States, with creation of Perazzi USA, Inc. In addition, each model may be available in different grades. These grades are based on type of finish, engraving and wood quality. Vast majority of Perazzi shotguns that are sold in this country are Standard Grade guns. According to Perazzi USA, these Standard Grade guns account for approximately 98 percent of North American sales. Therefore, it is unlikely that shooter or collector will encounter high-grade Perazzi guns. It should be pointed out that in some models no Extra Grade or Extra Gold Grade shotguns have ever been sold in United States. For benefit of reader, an approximate description of each grade follows. It is a general description, because Perazzi customer may order practically any combination of finishes or engraving patterns he or she desires. Use this list as a general guide. It is suggested that anyone wanting to know more about Perazzi guns buy a copy of Karl Lippard's book, Perazzi Shotguns. He can be reached at P.O. Box 60719, Colorado Springs, CO.

OUT-OF-PRODUCTION SHOTGUNS

Note: Very high premiums on early SCO and higher grades.

COMP 1-SB TRAP (Standard Grade)

Single-barrel trap gun in 12-gauge only, with 32" or 34" ventilated rib barrel.

NIB	Exc.	V.G.	Good	Fair	Poor
—	2500	1750	1000	750	500

COMP 1-TRAP (Standard Grade)

Over/under version of above model.

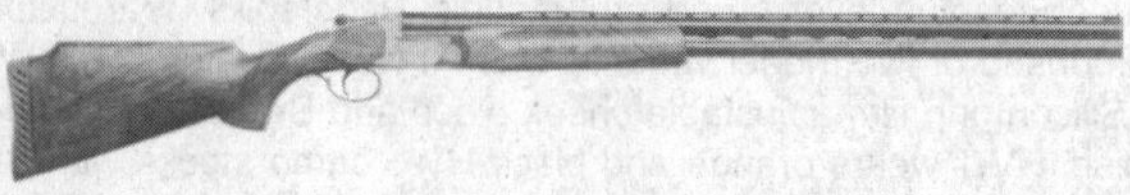

NIB	Exc.	V.G.	Good	Fair	Poor
—	4800	4000	3000	2250	500

Light Game Model (Standard Grade)

Offered in 12-gauge, with 27.5" ventilated rib barrel. Trigger group not detachable. Produced between 1972 and 1974.

NIB	Exc.	V.G.	Good	Fair	Poor
—	6250	4750	3000	1400	500

MT-6 Model (Standard Grade)

Offered in 12-gauge, with tapered ventilated rib. Trigger group not removable. Discontinued in 1983.

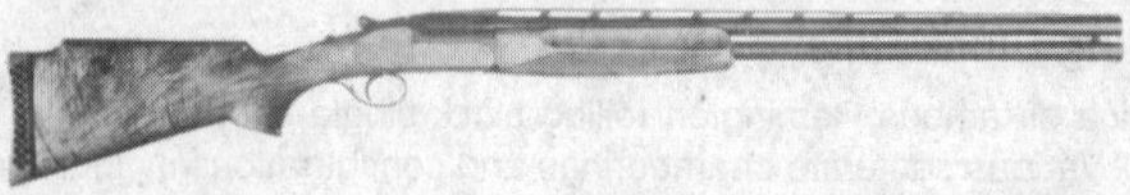

NIB	Exc.	V.G.	Good	Fair	Poor
—	3800	3000	2000	1000	400

MX3

Discontinued in 1988. Available in 12-gauge only for single-barrel trap, over/under trap, combination trap, skeet and sporting configurations. Note: Add 50 percent for Combination Trap Guns.

Standard Grade

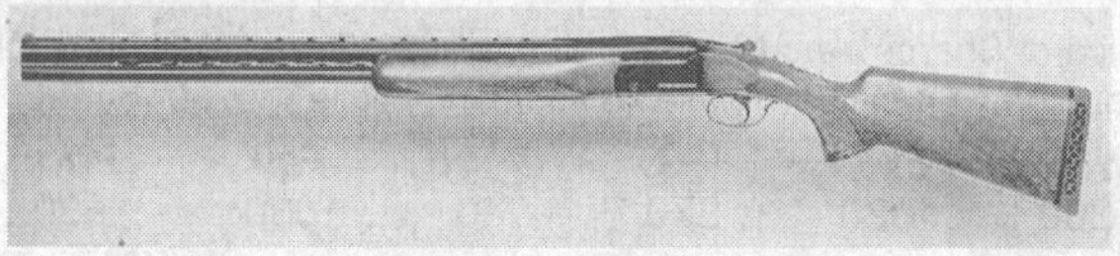

NIB	Exc.	V.G.	Good	Fair	Poor
—	3500	3000	2250	1750	400

SC3 Grade

NIB	Exc.	V.G.	Good	Fair	Poor
—	5000	4000	3000	2200	500

SCO Grade

NIB	Exc.	V.G.	Good	Fair	Poor
—	6500	5500	4000	2500	500

Gold Grade

NIB	Exc.	V.G.	Good	Fair	Poor
10000	8500	5900	2700	—	700

Grand American Special

Introduced in 1988. Features high ramped rib similar to MX3 model. Forend was grooved. Discontinued in 1991. Offered in these trap configurations: single-barrel, combination and over/under.

Standard Grade

NIB	Exc.	V.G.	Good	Fair	Poor
—	5250	4250	3500	2000	700

SC3 Grade

NIB	Exc.	V.G.	Good	Fair	Poor
—	6500	5250	4500	3000	700

SCO Grade

NIB	Exc.	V.G.	Good	Fair	Poor
—	8000	6500	5500	3750	700

Gold Grade

NIB	Exc.	V.G.	Good	Fair	Poor
—	10000	7500	6000	4000	700

SCO Grade w/Sideplates

NIB	Exc.	V.G.	Good	Fair	Poor
—	13500	10000	7500	6000	700

Gold Grade w/Sideplates

NIB	Exc.	V.G.	Good	Fair	Poor
—	15000	12000	8500	6500	700

SHO Model

Over/under sidelock model available in 12-gauge only, in both Type 1 and Type 2 configurations. Type 1 does not have rebounding firing pins and worth approximately 50 percent less than; Type 2 models that are fitted with rebounding firing pins. No parts available in this country or at the factory for Type 1 guns. An expert appraisal recommended for this model due to its unique features.

SHO model features silver finish with fine scroll engraving, with game scenes to customer's specifications. Select walnut stock built to customer's dimensions, with fine line checkering. Custom built shotgun. Special order only. Sky's the limit.

DHO Model

Side-by-side shotgun offered in 12-gauge only. Has full sidelocks and silver receiver finish. Scroll and game scene engraving of same quality as SHO Model. Fancy walnut stock, with fine line checkering. An expert appraisal recommended for this model due to its unique features. Special order only. Sky's the limit.

DHO Extra Gold

Available in any gauge and barrel length combination. Only finest presentation walnut and checkering. Totally custom built shotgun. Special order only. Sky's the limit.

RECENT PRODUCTION SHOTGUNS

MX7 Standard Grade

Introduced in 1993. Over/under trap offered in 12-gauge, with 29.5" or 31.5" over/under barrels with 32" or 34" single-barrel. Has a non-renewable trigger group feathering fixed coil spring trigger mechanism. Trigger is selective and works in conjunction with safety catch. Ventilated rib is ramped on Combo Trap model. Walnut stock custom made to customer's dimensions.

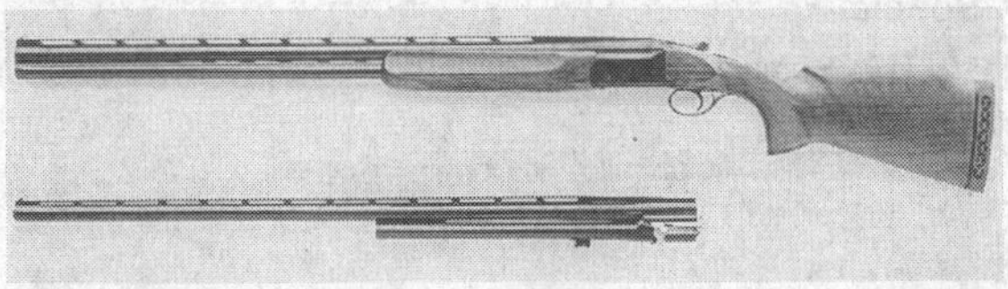

NIB	Exc.	V.G.	Good	Fair	Poor
—	4500	3200	2500	1750	700

MX7C Standard Grade

Introduced in 1993. Offered in 12-gauge, with non-renewable trigger group. Has coil spring mechanism, fully selective in conjunction with safety. Offered in 27.5", 29.5" or 31.5" flat ventilated rib barrels. Screw-in chokes are standard. Walnut stock custom made to customer's dimensions. Forend is beavertail.

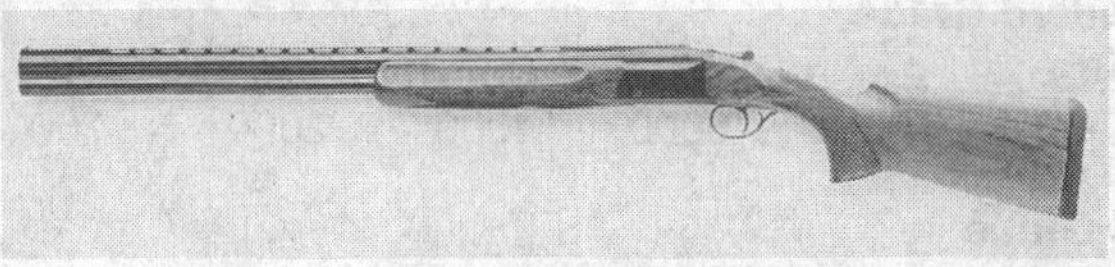

NIB	Exc.	V.G.	Good	Fair	Poor
—	5500	4000	3000	2000	700

MX8 SERIES

MX8/20-8/20C

Introduced in 1993. Offered in 20-gauge, with 26" or 27.625" ventilated rib barrels. Trigger group removable. Stock is high-grade walnut custom made to customers' specifications. Forend is round. MX8/20 supplied with Fixed chokes; MX8/20C has 5 screw-in choke tubes. Note: Add $400 for MX8/20C values.

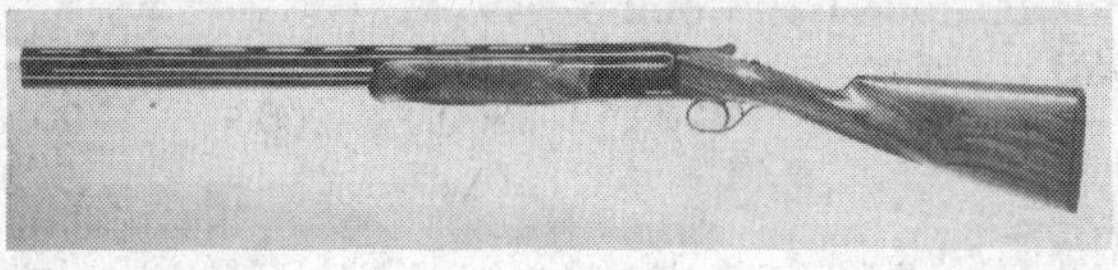

Standard Grade

NIB	Exc.	V.G.	Good	Fair	Poor
10500	9000	7000	5000	2250	—

SC3 Grade

NIB	Exc.	V.G.	Good	Fair	Poor
16500	13500	10000	8000	4000	—

SCO Grade

NIB	Exc.	V.G.	Good	Fair	Poor
32000	25000	20000	14000	7000	—

MX8/20

First introduced in 1993. Features removable trigger group. Available in 20-gauge only. Choice of 27.5", 28.375", 29.5" flat ventilated rib barrels. Choice of Fixed or screw-in chokes on sporting model. Stock custom made to customer's dimensions, with beavertail forend.

Standard Grade

NIB	Exc.	V.G.	Good	Fair	Poor
10000	8500	6500	4800	2000	—

SC3 Grade

NIB	Exc.	V.G.	Good	Fair	Poor
16000	14500	12000	7500	3000	—

SCO Grade

NIB	Exc.	V.G.	Good	Fair	Poor
30000	24000	17500	12000	5000	—

MX8 Special

Features low contour ventilated rib, adjustable trigger and grooved forend. Note: Some SCO engraving patterns on early models have sold in $30,000 to $45,000 price range, depending on engraver. Get an expert appraisal. Beware of counterfeits.

Standard Grade

NIB	Exc.	V.G.	Good	Fair	Poor
8500	7200	6000	4000	2000	700

SC3 Grade

NIB	Exc.	V.G.	Good	Fair	Poor
17500	14500	11000	7000	3000	1000

SCO Grade

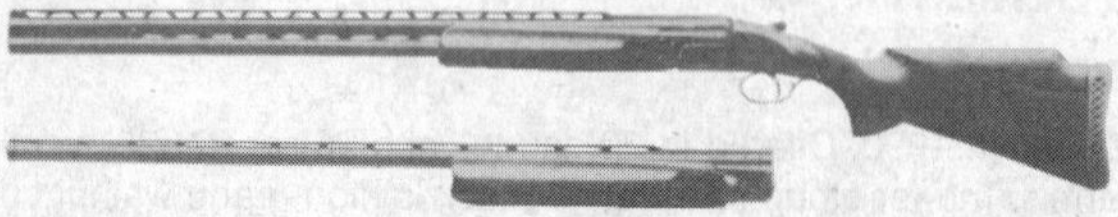

NIB	Exc.	V.G.	Good	Fair	Poor
29000	23000	14000	8000	5000	700

Standard Grade Trap Combo

NIB	Exc.	V.G.	Good	Fair	Poor
—	7500	5000	3500	2000	700

MX9

Introduced in 1993. Features removable inserts on rib to adjust point of impact; walnut stock with adjustable comb. Offered in 12-gauge with 32" or 34" barrel. Screw-in chokes in trap configuration and single-barrels in Trap/Combo models. Competition version also offered with unique ventilated rib inserts to correct for point of impact. Trigger group removable. Available in several different grades of ornamentation.

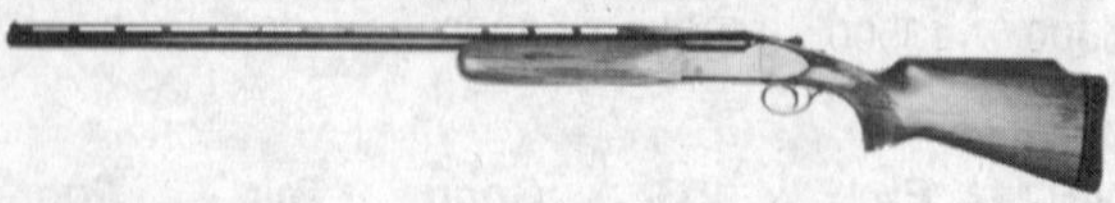

Standard Grade

NIB	Exc.	V.G.	Good	Fair	Poor
—	6500	5000	3500	1800	700

SC3 Grade

NIB	Exc.	V.G.	Good	Fair	Poor
—	11500	6000	5000	3000	700

SCO Grade

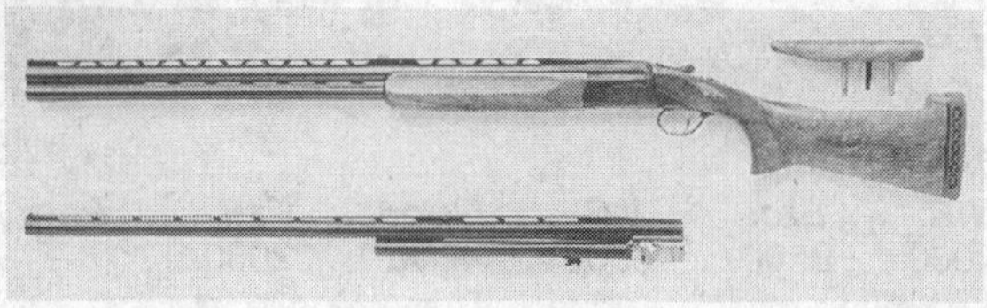

NIB	Exc.	V.G.	Good	Fair	Poor
—	18000	8000	7000	3500	7000

Standard Grade Trap Combo

NIB	Exc.	V.G.	Good	Fair	Poor
—	9500	6500	5000	3500	900

MX10

Introduced in 1993. Single-Barrel Trap models feature different method of rib height and pattern adjustment. Has adjustable stock. Available in 12-gauge with 32" or 34" barrels. Trap/Combo models offered in 12-gauge with 29.5" or 31.5" over/under barrels with 32" or 34" single-barrel. Chokes are Fixed. Competition models offered in 12- and 20-gauge with choice of 29.5" or 31.5" barrel for 12-gauge and 29.5" barrel for 20-gauge. Ventilated rib height adjustable as is comb position on stock. Trigger removable.

DB81 Special

Offered in 12-gauge only. Features high ramped ventilated rib. Trigger adjustable, with internal selector. Barrel lengths 29.5" or 31.5". Note: Add $1,000 for two forends and two triggers for Trap/Combo models.

Standard Grade

NIB	Exc.	V.G.	Good	Fair	Poor
—	8700	6500	5200	2500	700

SC3 Grade

NIB	Exc.	V.G.	Good	Fair	Poor
—	11000	8000	7000	3500	700

SCO Grade

NIB	Exc.	V.G.	Good	Fair	Poor
—	17500	12500	10000	6500	700

MX10Standard Grade

NIB	Exc.	V.G.	Good	Fair	Poor
—	8250	7000	6000	4300	700

SC3 Grade

NIB	Exc.	V.G.	Good	Fair	Poor
—	10000	8500	7000	5200	700

SCO Grade

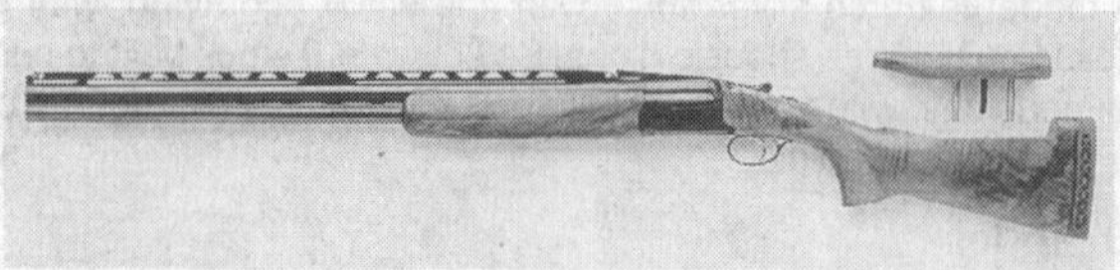

MX 10 Competition model

NIB	Exc.	V.G.	Good	Fair	Poor
—	13500	11000	8500	6750	700

Standard Grade Combo Model

NIB	Exc.	V.G.	Good	Fair	Poor
—	15000	13000	10500	5000	700

TM1 Special Standard Grade

Basic single-barrel Perazzi. Trap model offered in 12-gauge, with 32" or 34" barrel. Trigger adjustable.

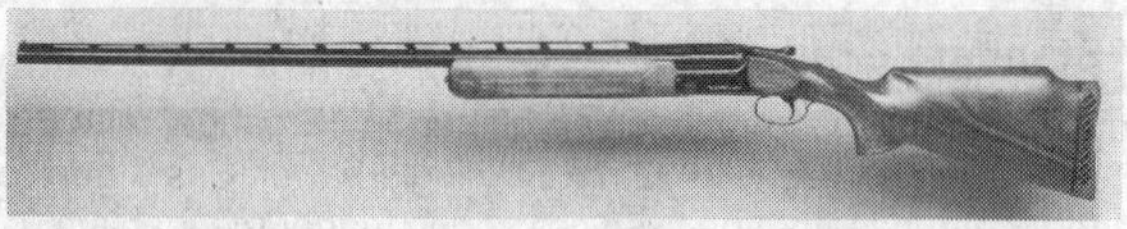

NIB	Exc.	V.G.	Good	Fair	Poor
4000	3000	2000	1250	850	700

TMX Special

Similar to TM1 Special, with select walnut.

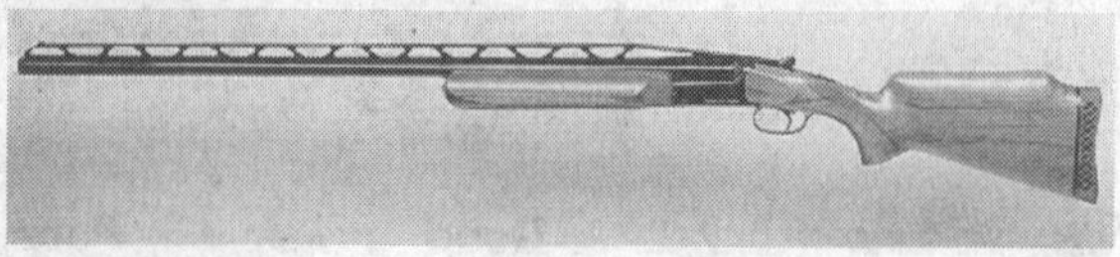

Standard Grade

NIB	Exc.	V.G.	Good	Fair	Poor
—	5000	4200	2700	1900	700

SCO Grade

NIB	Exc.	V.G.	Good	Fair	Poor
—	8000	6000	5000	2100	700

TM9

Top-single model with sculpted nickel or blue frame. Note: Add $1200 for TM9X model with adjustable rib and comb, in V.G. or better condition.

NIB	Exc.	V.G.	Good	Fair	Poor
6800	5500	3700	2500	2000	800

COMPETITION MODELS

Competition versions are over/under shotguns in trap, skeet, pigeon and sporting models. Stock dimensions based on particular model chosen. Trap models feature trap stock dimensions and forearm designed for that purpose. Other models have their own particular specifications. However, prices are based on a common style referred to by Perazzi as Competition. Thus, all models within this group are priced the same regardless of specific type. The Mirage name for competition guns was discontinued in 1998.

Mirage Special Standard Grade

Features adjustable trigger. Available in 12-gauge, with choice of 27.5", 28.375", 29.5" or 31.5" ventilated rib barrels.

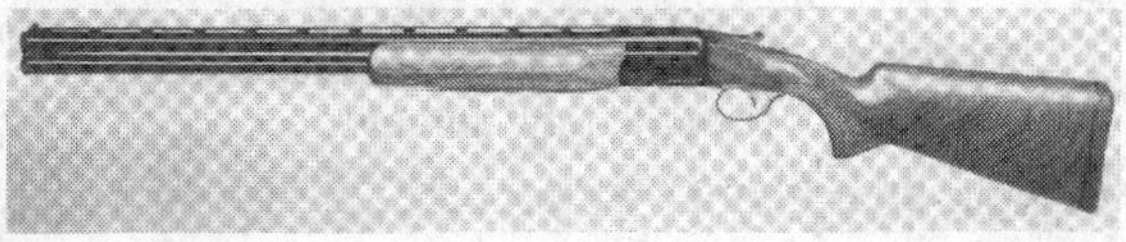

NIB	Exc.	V.G.	Good	Fair	Poor
—	5500	3750	2500	1100	700

Mirage Special Sporting Standard Grade

Similar to Mirage Special, with external trigger selection and screw-in chokes. Offered in 12-gauge only. Choice of 27.5", 28.375" or 29.5" ventilated rib barrels.

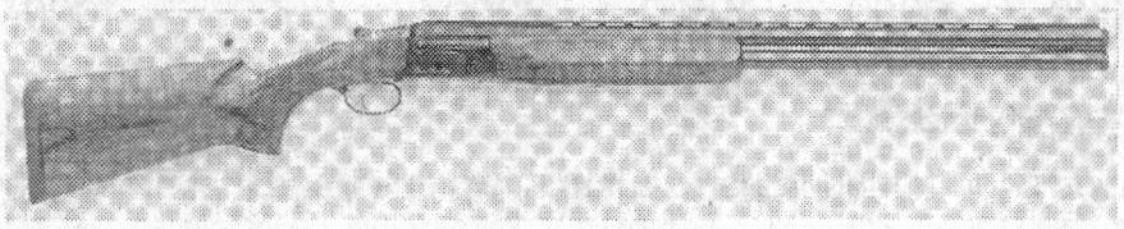

NIB	Exc.	V.G.	Good	Fair	Poor
—	4500	3250	2500	1100	700

Mirage Special Sporting Classic Standard Grade

Features same basic specifications as Mirage Special Sporting. Addition of scroll border on receiver and triggerguard. Wood is slightly higher quality. Offered in 12-gauge only, with 27.5", 28.375" or 29.5" ventilated rib barrels.

NIB	Exc.	V.G.	Good	Fair	Poor
—	4500	3250	2500	1100	700

Mirage MX8 Sporting Standard Grade

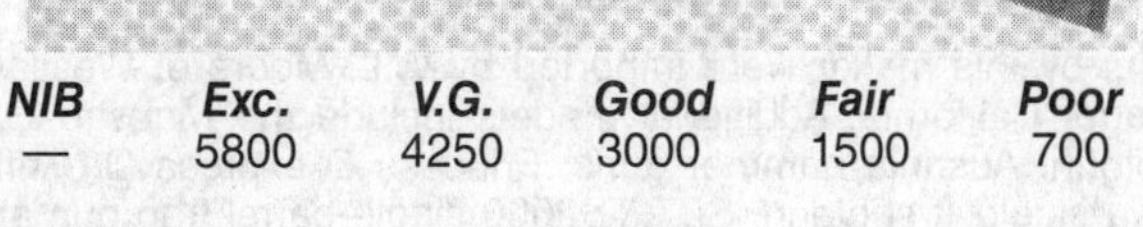

NIB	Exc.	V.G.	Good	Fair	Poor
—	5800	4250	3000	1500	700

SCO Model

Similar to MX8. Offered only in 12-gauge. Barrel lengths from 27.5" to 31.5". Trigger adjustable instead of removable.

NIB	Exc.	V.G.	Good	Fair	Poor
—	10500	6000	4500	3000	700

Mirage Special 4-Gauge Set

Similar to Mirage Special in appearance and specifications. Fitted with four barrel sets with 27.62" barrels in 12-, 20-, 28-gauge and .410 bore. Note: Add $2,000 for 28.37" barrels; $3,000 for 29.5" barrels.

Standard Grade

NIB	Exc.	V.G.	Good	Fair	Poor
—	—	10000	7000	4500	700

SC3 Grade

NIB	Exc.	V.G.	Good	Fair	Poor
—	21000	15000	10000	7500	700

SCO Grade

NIB	Exc.	V.G.	Good	Fair	Poor
—	28000	19000	12500	8500	700

MX12/12C

Offered in 12-gauge only, with 26.75" or 27.5" ventilated rib barrels. Single-selective trigger nonrefillable. Walnut stock fitted with schnabel forend. Receiver has light-scroll engraved border. MX12 supplied with Fixed chokes; MX12C fitted with 5 screw-in choke tubes. Note: Add $400 to MX12 prices to get MX12C values.

Standard Grade

NIB	Exc.	V.G.	Good	Fair	Poor
11000	9000	6800	4500	2000	1000

SC3 Grade

NIB	Exc.	V.G.	Good	Fair	Poor
18000	15000	12000	9000	5000	1200

SCO Grade

NIB	Exc.	V.G.	Good	Fair	Poor
30000	26000	20000	15000	10000	3000

MX20/20C

Offered in 20-gauge. Features non-removable trigger group. Frame smaller than 12-gauge. Offered with 26" or 27.5" ventilated rib barrels. MX20 has Fixed chokes; MX20C supplied with 5 screw-in choke tubes. Note: Add $400 to MX20 prices to get MX20C values.

Standard Grade

NIB	Exc.	V.G.	Good	Fair	Poor
11500	9000	6800	4500	2000	1000

SC3 Grade

NIB	Exc.	V.G.	Good	Fair	Poor
18500	15000	12000	9000	5000	1200

SCO Grade

NIB	Exc.	V.G.	Good	Fair	Poor
32000	25000	20000	13500	7000	3000

MX28 and MX410

Introduced in 1993, these two models feature a non-removable trigger group and special small frame for each. MX28: .28-gauge weight about 5.5 lbs.; MX410: .410 bore weight slightly less. Both supplied with Fixed chokes, flat ribs, custom made stocks and round forends. Each model offered with choice of 26" or 27.5" barrels. Both MX28 and MX410 are priced the same.

Standard Grade

NIB	Exc.	V.G.	Good	Fair	Poor
21000	16000	12000	9000	6000	1000

SCO Grade

NIB	Exc.	V.G.	Good	Fair	Poor
42000	36000	29000	20000	10000	3000

MX-2000

In 12-, 20-, 28-gauge or .410 bore in several grades and styles. Standard features include fixed or removable trigger group, choke tubes or Fixed chokes, fixed or adjustable ventilated rib and comb. Prices shown are for Game, Sporting, Pigeon, Skeet and Trap models. Note: Add 50 percent for Gold grades, which have higher levels of engraving, gold inlays and wood.

NIB	Exc.	V.G.	Good	Fair	Poor
8750	7750	6000	4200	3000	1000

MX-2005

This un-single model has a 34" barrel with extra-high 5-notch adjustable rib, removable trigger group and adjustable comb.

NIB	Exc.	V.G.	Good	Fair	Poor
8500	7500	5500	4000	2800	1000

High Tech 2020

Gauge: 12 ga., 3 in. Barrels: 27-9/16 in., 28-3/8 in., 29-1/2 in., 30-3/4 in., 31-1/2 in., flat ramped stepped 9/32 x 3/8 in. rib. Weight: 8 lbs.-8 lbs., 8 oz. Stock: Oil-finish, high-grade walnut, HT design standard or custom adjustable. Features: The competition grade High Tech 2020 is made in Italy. Logo engraving across silver-finish receiver. Hand-cut checkering, blued-steel barrels. Removeable trigger group with coil or flat springs and selector. Ventilated mid-rib. Interchangeable chokes available on demand.

NIB	Exc.	V.G.	Good	Fair	Poor
20500	—	—	—	—	—

DC12

Side-by-side 12 ga.; barrel lengths from 26.75" to 31.5". Removable trigger group with flat springs. English-style or pistol grip stock; game or beavertail forend. Values not available at press time.

PERRIN, L.
Paris, France

Manufacturers of revolvers chambered for the unique Perrin cartridges. Low production. Engraved specimens worth premium.

Model 1859 (Antique)

Double-action-only revolver with no hammer spur chambered for the 12mm Perrin thick rim cartridge. Various types are recognized, all rare in the U.S. Some reportedly used in Civil War.

Exc.	Fine	V.G.	Good	Fair	Poor
2900	1500	1170	850	400	280

Model 1865 (Antique)

Double-action revolver with hammer spur and anchor-shaped loading gate spring; 12mm Perrin. Related Model 1865-69 has a reinforced frame. Later centerfire models are known; values are similar.

Exc.	Fine	V.G.	Good	Fair	Poor
2900	1500	1170	850	400	280

Knife Revolver (Antique)

Double-action revolver with no hammer spur and knife blade integral with barrel; 9mm Perrin. Rare; values are speculative.

Exc.	Fine	V.G.	Good	Fair	Poor
6000	4000	2500	1750	900	600

PERRY & GODDARD
Renwick Arms Co.
New York, New York

Derringer

.44-caliber single-shot spur trigger pistol, with 2" octagonal barrel. Blued or silver-plated, with walnut or gutta-percha grips. Barrel may be swiveled so either end can serve as chamber and marked "Double Header/ E.S. Renwick". Extremely rare, estimated that only 25 were ever made. Too rare to estimate.

PERRY PATENT FIREARMS CO.
Newark, New Jersey

Perry Single-Shot Pistol

.52-caliber breech-loading percussion pistol, with 6" round barrel. Blued, with walnut grips. Barrel marked "Perry Patent Firearms Co./Newark, N.J." Approximately 200 made between 1854 and 1856 in two styles.

1st Type (Antique)

Long contoured triggerguard opening lever.

Exc.	Fine	V.G.	Good	Fair	Poor
8000	6000	4500	3000	2000	1000

2nd Type (Antique)

S curved shorter triggerguard. Automatic primer feed that protrudes from butt.

Exc.	Fine	V.G.	Good	Fair	Poor
8000	6000	4500	3000	2000	1000

Perry Carbine (Antique)

.54-caliber breech-loading percussion carbine, with 20.75" barrel and half-length walnut stock secured by one barrel band. Blued, with case-hardened lock. Approximately 200 were made.

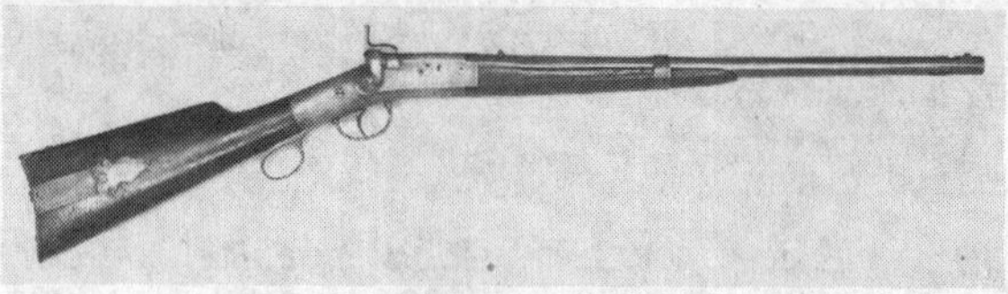

Courtesy Milwaukee Public Museum, Milwaukee, Wisconsin

Exc.	Fine	V.G.	Good	Fair	Poor
20000	12000	7500	5000	3500	1500

PERUGINI & VISINI
Brescia, Italy

Arms by this maker were imported by W.L. Moore of Westlake Village, California. Additional models include the Maestro O/U shotgun, Ausonia hammer guns, Princess D express O/U rifle, Nova sidelock shotgun, SBT TS2000 single-barrel trap gun and Ausonia hammer guns. As with most high-end sporting arms makers, values will vary greatly depending on engraving and special features. Exact model designation may not always be readily apparent from examining the arm. These listings should be considered as examples of the values that the general type of gun may bring, and each gun should be evaluated individually.

Liberty Model

Side-by-side 12-, 20-, 28-gauge and .410 bore shotgun, with 28" barrels. Anson & Deeley action with double Purdy lock. Blued overall, with checkered walnut stock.

NIB	Exc.	V.G.	Good	Fair	Poor
7500	6000	4500	2500	1250	750

Classic Model

12- or 20-gauge double-barrel shotgun, with H&H-style sidelock and double Purdy lock. Barrels are 28". Single trigger and automatic ejectors. Sidelocks and mounts engraved and blued. Well figured checkered walnut stock.

NIB	Exc.	V.G.	Good	Fair	Poor
15000	11500	9500	4000	2000	1000

Bolt-Action Rifle

Mauser-type bolt-action rifle. Available in a variety of chamberings, with 24" or 26" barrels. Sights not furnished. Well figured checkered walnut stock.

NIB	Exc.	V.G.	Good	Fair	Poor
6500	4250	3000	1500	900	500

Deluxe Bolt-Action Rifle

As above, with first quality walnut stocks and case.

NIB	Exc.	V.G.	Good	Fair	Poor
7500	5000	3500	1500	1000	600

Eagle Single-Shot

Anson & Deeley single-shot rifle. Fitted with 24" or 26" barrels, open sights, automatic ejector and adjustable trigger. Stock of checkered walnut.

NIB	Exc.	V.G.	Good	Fair	Poor
7500	4250	4000	1500	1000	600

Boxlock Express Rifle

Anson & Deeley action double-barrel rifle. Chambered for .444 Marlin or 9.3x74R cartridges. Barrel length 24". Fitted with express sights. Double triggers and automatic ejectors. Receiver case-hardened. Barrels and mounts blued. Checkered walnut stock.

NIB	Exc.	V.G.	Good	Fair	Poor
7000	5500	3750	2000	1500	500

Magnum Over/Under

Anson & Deeley action over/under rifle. Available in .375 H&H and .458 Win. Magnum. Barrels are 24" and fitted with express sights. Double triggers and automatic ejectors. Receiver and barrels blued. Stock checkered walnut.

NIB	Exc.	V.G.	Good	Fair	Poor
7000	5500	3750	2000	1500	500

Super Express Rifle

H&H-style sidelock double-barrel rifle, with 24" barrel. Fitted with express sights. Available in a variety of chamberings. Receiver and sidelocks case-hardened or bright finish. Fully engraved. Checkered walnut stock.

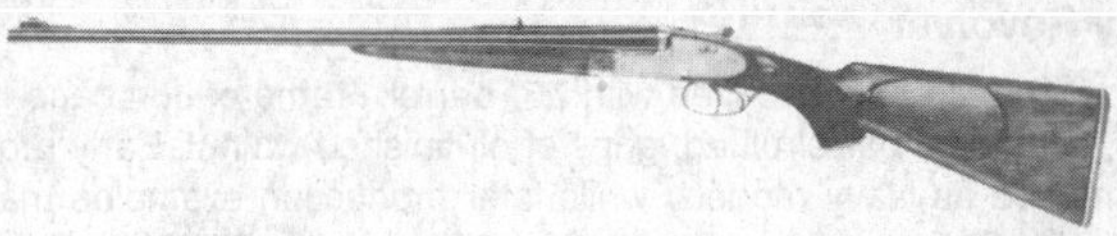

NIB	Exc.	V.G.	Good	Fair	Poor
20000	17500	13000	10000	6500	1000

Victoria Side-by-Side Rifle

Similar to Boxlock Express Rifle. Chambered for .30-06, 7x65R or 9.3x74R cartridges. Barrels were 24" or 26". Double triggers and automatic ejectors. Blued, with minimal engraving. Stock checkered walnut.

NIB	Exc.	V.G.	Good	Fair	Poor
6500	5250	4000	3000	1500	750

Selous Side-by-Side Rifle

First quality double-barrel express rifle, with 24" or 26" barrels. Fully detachable H&H-style sidelocks, double triggers and automatic ejectors. Fully engraved, with well figured checkered walnut stocks.

NIB	Exc.	V.G.	Good	Fair	Poor
22500	17500	12500	6000	3000	1500

PETTENGILL C. S.

New Haven, Connecticut
Rogers, Spencer & Co.
Willowvale, New York

Pocket Revolver

Hammerless double-action .31-caliber percussion revolver, with 4" octagonal barrel. Frame of brass or iron. Blued barrel. Grips of oil-finished walnut. First and Second Models marked "Pettengill's Patent 1856" as well as "T.K. Austin". Third Model marked "Pettengill Patent 1856" and "Raymond and Robitaille Patented 1858". Approximately 400 manufactured in late 1850s early 1860s.

1st Model Antique

Brass frame.

Exc.	Fine	V.G.	Good	Fair	Poor
4000	3000	2000	1100	500	300

2nd Model Antique

Iron frame.

Exc.	Fine	V.G.	Good	Fair	Poor
2850	2100	1500	1000	500	300

3rd Model Antique

Iron frame and improved action.

Exc.	Fine	V.G.	Good	Fair	Poor
2750	2000	1500	1000	500	300

Navy Revolver Antique

As above in .34-caliber, with 4.5" barrel and 6-shot cylinder. Frame of iron, blued overall and grips of walnut. Marked "Pettengill's Patent 1856" and "Raymond & Robitaille Patented 1858". Approximately 900 manufactured in late 1850s early 1860s.

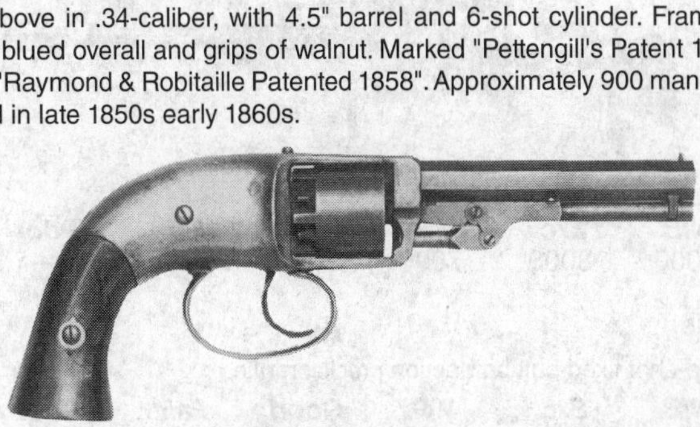

Courtesy Milwaukee Public Museum, Milwaukee, Wisconsin

Exc.	Fine	V.G.	Good	Fair	Poor
4000	2000	1500	1000	500	350

Army Revolver (Antique)

As above in .44-caliber. Fitted with 7.5" barrel. Frame of iron case-hardened, octagonal barrel blued, grips of oil-finished walnut. Early production marked as Navy models, while later production examples marked "Petengill's Patent 1856, pat'd July 22, 1856 and July 27, 1858". Believed 3,400 made in 1860s. Note: Some examples will be found with government inspector's marks and worth approximately 25 percent more.

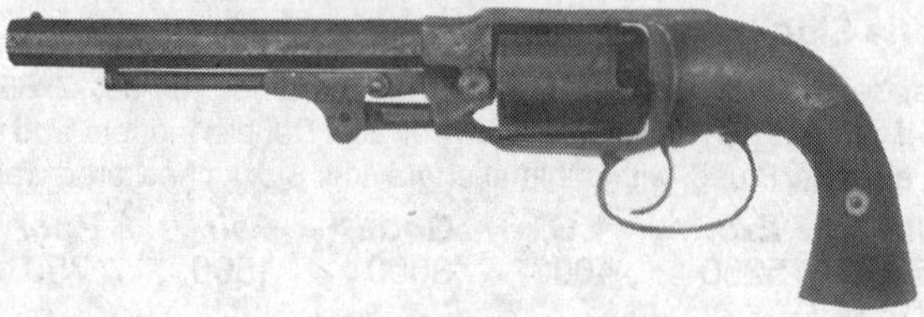

Courtesy Milwaukee Public Museum, Milwaukee, Wisconsin

Exc.	Fine	V.G.	Good	Fair	Poor
10000	6000	3500	2250	1500	900

PFANNL, FRANCOIS

Krems, Austria

Erika

4.25mm semi-automatic pistol, with hinged barrel assembly. Barrel length 1.5" or 2.25". Grips marked "Erika". Approximately 3,500 made between 1912 and 1926.

NIB	Exc.	V.G.	Good	Fair	Poor
—	3000	2500	1750	900	500

PGM PRECISION

France

Model PGM

Highly sophisticated semi-automatic rifle. Designed and built on modular component system. Barrel change is fast. Available calibers .308 Win., .300 Savage, 7mm-08, .243 and .22-250. Match-grade barrel length 23.4". Fully adjustable trigger and buttstock. Adjustable bipod. Five-round magazine standard. Weight about 13 lbs.

NIB	Exc.	V.G.	Good	Fair	Poor
13500	9000	7000	3500	1750	1000

Hecate 2

Bolt-action sniper rifle in .50 BMG. Standard anti-materiel rifle of French Army. 7-round detachable box magazine. New U.S. sales currently restricted to law enforcement and military.

NIB	Exc.	V.G.	Good	Fair	Poor
9000	7000	6000	—	—	—

Mini Hecate 2

Bolt-action rifle, .338 Lapua Magnum.

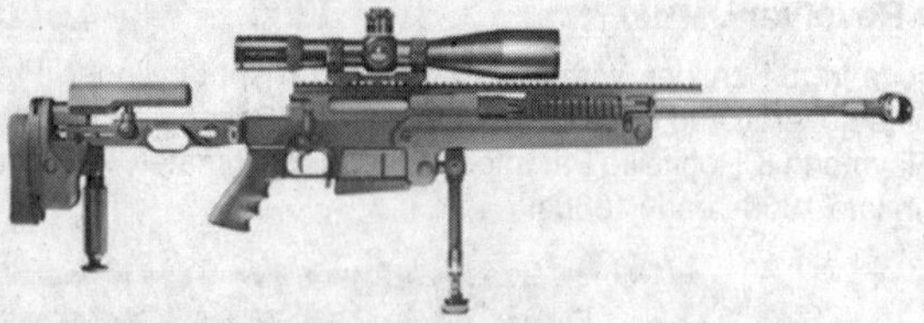

NIB	Exc.	V.G.	Good	Fair	Poor
9000	8000	7000	—	—	—

Ludis

Single-shot fixed-butt bolt-action precision rifle.

NIB	Exc.	V.G.	Good	Fair	Poor
4750	4000	3000	—	—	—

Ultima Ratio

Bolt-action rifle; .308 Win or 6.5 Creedmoor.

NIB	Exc.	V.G.	Good	Fair	Poor
6500	5750	5000	—	—	—

PHILLIPS & RODGERS INC.

Huntsville, Texas

Medusa Model 47

Introduced in 1996. Unique multi-caliber revolver. Designed to chamber, fire and extract almost any cartridge. Using 9mm, .357 or .38 cartridges—total of about 25 different calibers. Barrel length 2.5", 3", 4", 5" or 6". Rubber grips and interchangeable front sights. Finish is matte blue. Rarely if ever encountered. Discontinued.

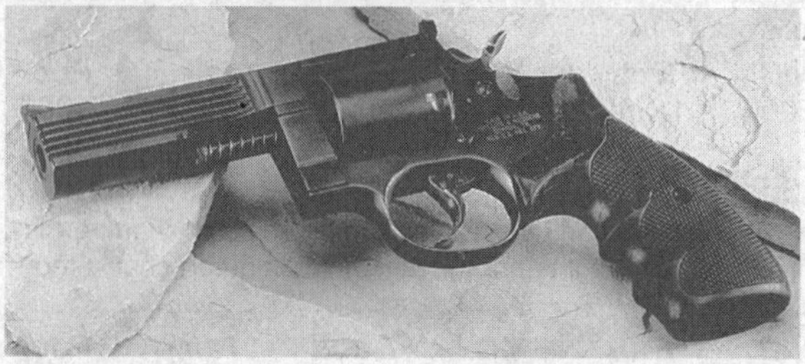

NIB	Exc.	V.G.	Good	Fair	Poor
2000	1500	1000	—	—	—

Ruger 50 Conversion

Conversion executed on a new revolver converts .44 Magnum Ruger into .50 Action Express. Stainless steel or blue, with 5-shot cylinder. Barrel length 6.5".

NIB	Exc.	V.G.	Good	Fair	Poor
1000	800	550	450	280	150

PHOENIX

Lowell, Massachusetts

Pocket Pistol

Rare .25 ACP semi-automatic pistol, with 2.25" barrel and 6-round magazine. Receiver and slide blued. Grips are hard rubber. Manufactured during 1920s.

NIB	Exc.	V.G.	Good	Fair	Poor
—	950	700	350	200	100

PHOENIX ARMS

Ontario, California

HP22

Pocket-size semi-automatic pistol chambered for .22 LR cartridge. Barrel length 3"; magazine capacity 11 rounds. Offered in bright chrome or polished blue finish. Black checkered grips. Top of gun fitted with ventilated rib. Overall length 4.1"; weight about 20 oz.

NIB	Exc.	V.G.	Good	Fair	Poor
180	120	90	60	40	20

HP25

Same as above. Chambered for .25 ACP cartridge. Magazine capacity 10 rounds.

NIB	*Exc.*	*V.G.*	*Good*	*Fair*	*Poor*
180	120	90	60	40	20

HP22/HP25 Target

Conversion kit to convert HP22/HP25 into target pistol. Kit includes extended ventilated rib barrel and convertible 10-round magazine. Finish blue or nickel.

NIB	*Exc.*	*V.G.*	*Good*	*Fair*	*Poor*
100	80	60	40	30	20

Raven

Small pocket-size semi-automatic pistol chambered for .25 ACP cartridge. Magazine capacity 6 rounds. Barrel length 2.4", with fixed sights. Offered in 3 finishes: bright chrome, satin nickel or polished blue. Grips ivory, pink pearl or black. Overall length 4.8"; weight about 15 oz.

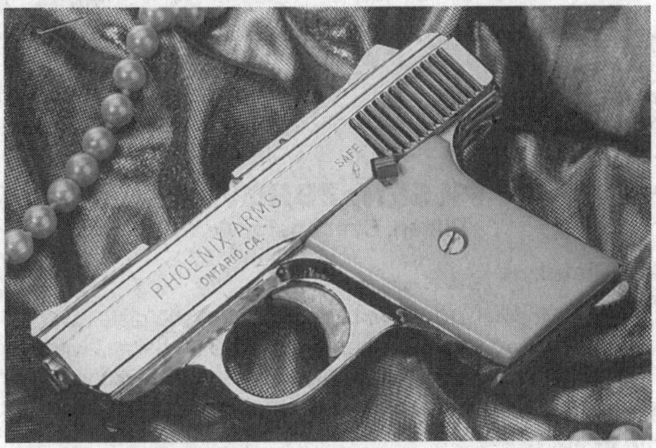

NIB	*Exc.*	*V.G.*	*Good*	*Fair*	*Poor*
180	120	90	60	40	20

PHOENIX ARMS CO.

Liege, Belgium

See—ROBAR and DE KIRKHAVE

PICKERT, FRIEDRICH

Arminius Waffenfabrik
Zella-Mehlis, Germany

Firm produced revolvers bearing trade name "Arminius". Revolvers manufactured by Pickert are of double-action type, with or without exposed hammers. Some models fitted with ejectors, while others have removable cylinders. Calibers and barrel lengths vary. After WWII, trade name was acquired by Hermann Wiehauch.

Arminius 7.65mm

Five-shot concealed hammer revolver in 7.65mm caliber. Arminius head on grips.

Courtesy James Rankin

NIB	*Exc.*	*V.G.*	*Good*	*Fair*	*Poor*
—	350	220	180	120	90

Arminius Single-Shot Target Pistol

Single-shot target pistol chambered for .22-caliber cartridge. Some built under name PICKERT. Arminius name seen on frame.

Courtesy James Rankin

NIB	*Exc.*	*V.G.*	*Good*	*Fair*	*Poor*
—	900	700	600	400	300

Pickert Revolver

Similar to Arminius revolver, with half-round half-octagon barrel. Chambered for 7.54mm cartridge.

Courtesy James Rankin

NIB	*Exc.*	*V.G.*	*Good*	*Fair*	*Poor*
—	280	220	180	150	100

PIDAULT & CORDIER

See - LA GRESE

PIEPER, HENRI & NICOLAS

Liege, Belgium

Originally founded by Henri Pieper in 1859. Company was reorganized in 1898, when his son Nicolas assumed control. Firm perhaps best known for a series of semi-automatic pistols that are listed below. Pieper also manufactured a bewildering variety of drillings, combination guns, cape guns, rook rifles, salon rifles and even volley guns. These guns must be evaluated on their own merits and their value strictly a function of what the market will bear.

Pieper Model 1907

6.35 or 7.65mm semi-automatic pistol. Featuring hinged barrel assembly 2.5" in length. Receiver and barrel blued. Grips hard rubber with firm's trademark cast in them. Model 1907 variation does not have hinged barrel assembly. Model 1908 also known as "Basculant"; Model 1918 as "Demontant".

Courtesy Orvel Reichert

NIB	Exc.	V.G.	Good	Fair	Poor
—	250	150	120	100	80

Model 1908/Basculant

Tipping barrel pistol chambered for 6.35mm Auto cartridge. Similar in appearance to Model 1907, with several improvements. Front end of barrel retained by a pivot bolt. Recoil spring rod had a hook that engaged lug on slide.

Courtesy Orvel Reichert

NIB	Exc.	V.G.	Good	Fair	Poor
—	280	180	150	120	100

Pieper Bayard Revolver

In competition with Nagant gas seal revolver, Henri Pieper developed a superior design. Revolvers of this type have 5" barrels and chambered for 8mm cartridges. First model had automatic ejection system; second utilized swing-out cylinder. Standard finish blued. Checkered hard rubber grips.

NIB	Exc.	V.G.	Good	Fair	Poor
—	1000	750	500	250	100

Legia

Patterned after that of Browning. Chambered for 6.35mm cartridge. Standard magazine holds 6 rounds; 10-round available.

NIB	Exc.	V.G.	Good	Fair	Poor
—	250	150	120	100	80

Bayard

6.35, 7.65 or 9mm short semi-automatic pistol, with 2.5" barrel. Standard magazine capacity 6 rounds. Slide stamped "Anciens Etablissement Pieper Liege, Belgium".

NIB	Exc.	V.G.	Good	Fair	Poor
—	250	150	120	100	80

PIETTA, F.LLI
Gussago, Italy

This is a manufacturer of current and replica firearms, best known for its single-action revolvers. These models are imported by Cimarron, Taylor's and Co., Heritage, Cabela's, Dixie Gun Works and Navy Arms. Refer to these importers under their individual listings.

1858 General Custer

Caliber: .44, 6-shot. Barrel: 8 in., blued. Grips: Two-piece wood. Sights: Open. Weight: 2.7 lbs. Features: Nickel-plated triggerguard, color case-hardened hammer, laser engraving.

NIB	Exc.	V.G.	Good	Fair	Poor
360	—	—	—	—	—

PILSEN, ZBROVKA
Pilsen, Czechoslovakia

Pocket Pistol

Essentially a Model 1910 Browning semi-automatic pistol, without grip safety. Pistol was 7.65mm caliber and had 3.5" barrel, with 6-round magazine. Slide marked "Akciova Spolecnost drive Skodovny zavody Zbrovka Plzen". Standard finish blued. Grips hard rubber. Manufactured during 1920s.

NIB	Exc.	V.G.	Good	Fair	Poor
—	300	200	150	120	100

PIOTTI
Brescia, Italy

Italian gun making firm located in Gardone Val Trompia in province of Brescia. Shotguns are hand crafted and limited to a few each year. Each gun made to individual specifications. Many consider them one of the best double shotguns made in the world today. Actions are Anson & Deeley boxlock or Holland & Holland sidelock. Several features offered on these shotguns at no additional cost: type of stock and forearm, barrel length and chokes, rib, action shape and finish.

Other features are considered extra cost options and will affect value of gun. These are: single triggers, detachable sidelocks, automatic safety, recoil pads, upgraded wood, engraving and multi-gauge sets. With exception of a few grades, Piotti guns are available in 10-, 12-, 16-, 20-, 28-gauge and .410 bore. Depending on gauge, barrel lengths are from 25" to 32".

Model Piuma (BSEE)

Firm's standard boxlock offering. Available in 12-gauge to .410 bore. Features ejectors and scalloped frame. Fine scroll and rosette engraving standard. Note: Around serial number 9000 or 1989, Piotti began building Model BSEE to same standards as King Model. Therefore, guns below serial number 9000 deduct about 40 percent from prices listed.

NIB	Exc.	V.G.	Good	Fair	Poor
20000	15000	7500	6000	4000	700

Westlake Model

Piotti's second quality model. Features case colored receiver, with gold line work. Offered in 12-, 16- and 20-gauge. Discontinued in 1989.

NIB	Exc.	V.G.	Good	Fair	Poor
13000	10500	8000	6000	3500	700

Over/Under Gun

Features King 2 engraving, which has light border scroll with 10 percent coverage. Custom engraving patterns available at extra charge.

NIB	Exc.	V.G.	Good	Fair	Poor
44750	33500	25000	17500	10000	1000

Model King No. I

Features sidelock with fine line scroll engraving, with full coverage. Gold crown inlaid on top lever prior to 1989. H&H or Purdey-style engraving. Select walnut, with hand-checkering standard. Chambered from 10-gauge to .410 bore.

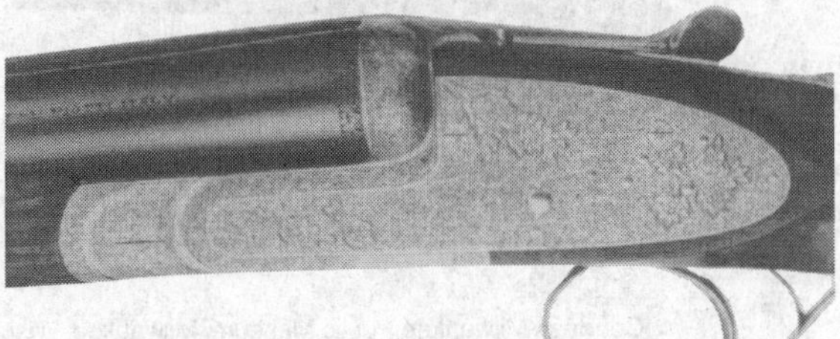

NIB	Exc.	V.G.	Good	Fair	Poor
33000	25000	18000	12500	8000	2700

Monte Carlo Model

Less expensive version of King Model. Had H&H or Purdey-style engraving. Discontinued in 1989. Upgraded and became part of King Model. This occurred around serial number 9000.

NIB	Exc.	V.G.	Good	Fair	Poor
14000	10000	7000	6000	3500	700

Model King Extra

Similar to King No. 1, with addition of a number of engraving styles from English to game scenes with gold inlays. Because of the wide variety of engraving patterns offered, it is advisable to secure a qualified appraisal before purchase.

Model Lunik

Fitted with H&H sidelocks. Engraving is Renaissance-style relief cut scroll. Gold crown inlaid on top lever. Offered in gauges from 10- to .410 bore.

NIB	Exc.	V.G.	Good	Fair	Poor
33000	25000	18000	12000	7000	1700

Model Monaco

Sidelock model features all the best Piotti has to offer. Extra attention paid to hand-work and fitting. Only finest European hardwoods used. Available in 10-gauge to 410 bore. Offered with three different types of engraving designated No. 1, No. 2 and No. 4.

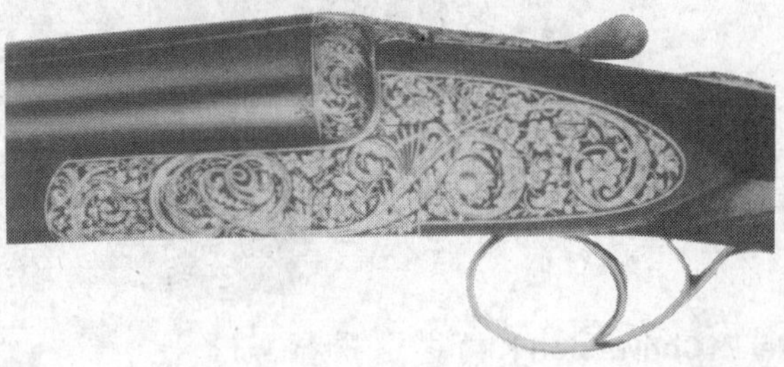

No. 1 or No. 2

NIB	Exc.	V.G.	Good	Fair	Poor
47500	40000	28000	19500	12000	2000

No. 3

NIB	Exc.	V.G.	Good	Fair	Poor
50000	43000	32000	22000	13000	2000

No. 4

NIB	Exc.	V.G.	Good	Fair	Poor
55000	47000	36000	28000	—	—

PLAINFIELD MACHINE CO.

Dunelien, New Jersey

Super Enforcer

Cut-down version of U.S. M1 Carbine, with 12" barrel and pistol grip. Finish blued. Stocks walnut.

NIB	Exc.	V.G.	Good	Fair	Poor
—	600	480	380	220	100

M1 Carbine

Commercial reproduction of U.S. M1 Carbine. Finish blued. Walnut stock.

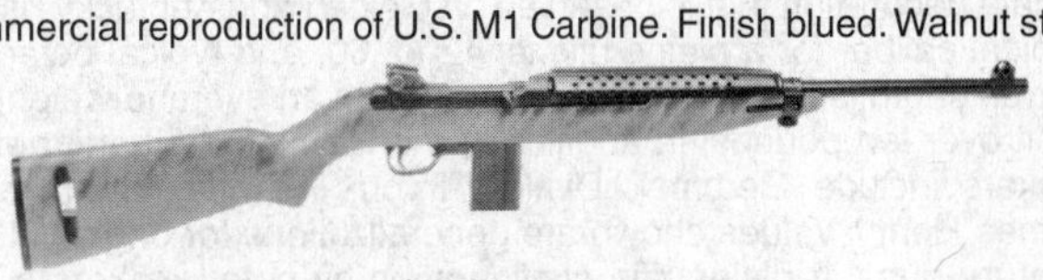

NIB	Exc.	V.G.	Good	Fair	Poor
—	400	350	220	150	100

M1 Paratrooper Carbine

As above, with telescoping wire buttstock and walnut forend.

NIB	Exc.	V.G.	Good	Fair	Poor
—	480	380	280	200	120

PLAINFIELD ORDNANCE CO.

Middlesex, New Jersey

Stainless steel .22-caliber semi-automatic pistol, with 10-shot magazine and 1" barrel. Also available in .25 ACP. Conversion kits were available.

Model 71Conversion Kit

NIB	Exc.	V.G.	Good	Fair	Poor
—	50	40	30	20	20

.22 or .25 Caliber Pistol

NIB	Exc.	V.G.	Good	Fair	Poor
—	180	120	100	80	50

Model 72

As above, with alloy frame.

NIB	Exc.	V.G.	Good	Fair	Poor
—	180	120	100	80	50

PLAINS RIFLE

"Plains rifle" is a generic description for a type of muzzleloading percussion rifle originally developed by the Hawken brothers in St. Louis for the needs of hunters and trappers in the Great Plains and Rocky Mountain west, beginning in the 1820s. Although they were made into the 20th century, plains rifles were mostly replaced after the Civil War by mass-produced breech loaders. They differed from the earlier American long rifle (or "Kentucky rifle") in having shorter barrels and larger caliber in half-stock rather than full-stock configuration. They generally do not have the ornate decoration that is observed on Golden Age Kentucky rifles. Typical caliber for a plains rifle is .42 to .60, and typical octagon barrel length is in the 32" to 38" range, with an average weight of a bit over ten pounds. In addition to the Hawken brothers, noted makers include Gemmer, Dimick, Tryon, Henry Lehman, and James Henry. Values shown are generalizations for original 19th century guns in plains rifle configuration by noted makers such as these. Original Hawken made plains rifles may bring double or more, and unmarked plains rifles or those by lesser-known makers may bring half or less.

General Type (Antique)

Exc.	Fine	V.G.	Good	Fair	Poor
10000	7000	5000	2500	1200	600

PLANT'S MANUFACTURING CO.

New Haven, Connecticut

Maker of front-loading early cartridge revolvers. Also found marked "Eagle Arms"

Army Model Revolver

Large single-action revolver. Chambered for .42-caliber cup-primed cartridge that loads from front of cylinder. Barrel length 6" and octagonal form with rib. Frame made of brass or iron. Finish blued, with walnut or rosewood grips. Interchangeable percussion cylinders also made for these revolvers. If present, values would be increased approximately 30 percent. Revolver was marketed by Merwin & Bray. Approximately 1,500 of 1st and 2nd Models manufactured; 10,000 of 3rd Model in 1860s.

1st Model Brass Frame (Antique)

Exc.	Fine	V.G.	Good	Fair	Poor
2500	1100	700	500	300	200

1st Model Iron Frame (Antique)

Exc.	Fine	V.G.	Good	Fair	Poor
2500	1100	700	500	300	200

2nd Model Rounded Brass Frame (Antique)

Exc.	Fine	V.G.	Good	Fair	Poor
3500	1600	1000	700	500	250

2nd Model Iron Frame (Antique)

As above, with iron frame.

Exc.	Fine	V.G.	Good	Fair	Poor
2300	900	650	500	300	200

3rd Model (Antique)

As above, with flat brass frame.

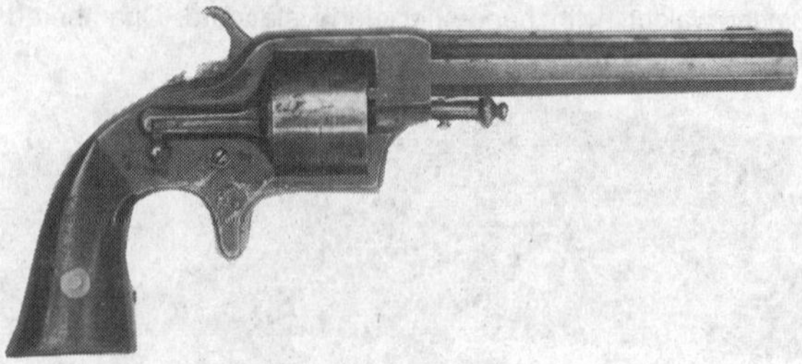

Courtesy Milwaukee Public Museum, Milwaukee, Wisconsin

Exc.	Fine	V.G.	Good	Fair	Poor
2000	1000	850	500	350	200

Pocket Revolver (Antique)

Similar to Army model described above except chambered for .30-caliber cartridges. Barrel length 3.5", 5-shot cylinder. Frame normally silver plated, barrel and cylinder blued and grips of rosewood or walnut. Model encountered with a variety of retailer's markings: Eagle Arms Co., New York, "Reynolds, Plant & Hotchkiss, New Haven, Ct.", and "Merwin & Bray Firearms Co., N.Y." Approximately 20,000 were made.

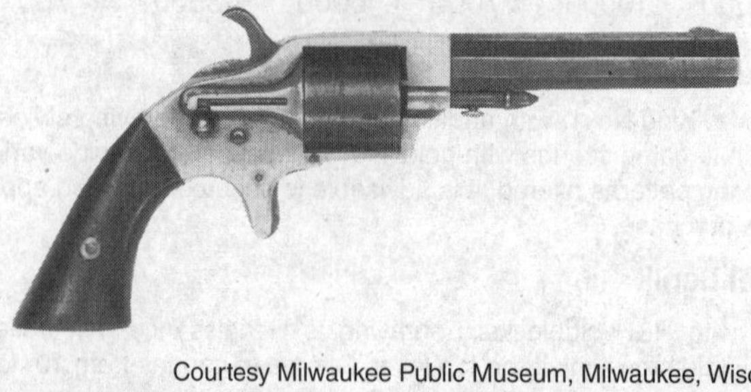

Courtesy Milwaukee Public Museum, Milwaukee, Wisconsin

Exc.	Fine	V.G.	Good	Fair	Poor
1250	800	550	350	250	150

POINTER
Hopkins & Allen
Norwich, Connecticut

Pointer Derringer (Antique)

See Hopkins & Allen

POINTER - LEGACY SPORTS INTERNATIONAL
Reno, Nevada

Pointer is a Turkish-made shotgun brand distributed in the U.S. by Legacy Sports International. Legacy, a subsidiary of Fuller Global based in Alexandria, Virginia, purchased the inventory of Interarmco on Jan. 1, 2000. In December 2005, Legacy moved from Virginia to Reno, Nevada. On January 1, 2006, it officially opens its doors in Reno and, on January 2016, moved into its new and current location, doubling the size of its previous facility. LSI currently imports Howa rifles and accessories (Howa Machinery, LTD in Japan), Lithgow Arms rifles (Australia), Nikko Stirling optics and accessories (Japan), Citadel rifles, shotguns, handguns and accessories (Armscor, Phillippines), and Pointer semi-auto shotguns (Armsan, Turkey) and Pointer over/under shotguns (Kahn, Turkey).

SEMI-AUTO SHOTGUNS

Phenoma

Introduced 2019. Available in 12, 20, 28 gauge and .410 in 3" or 3.5" (12 gauge) chambers. 28" chrome-moly lined barrel, proofed for steel shot. 3/8" dovetail accessory rail on top of receiver. Fiber-optic sight, raised ventilated rib, gas-operated cycling system, single-round magazine cut-off, hard case included. Five chokes included (C, IC, M, IM, F). Black synthetic standard stock, but several camo patterns and walnut are available.

NIB	Exc.	V.G.	Good	Fair	Poor
400	300	250	—	—	—

Phenoma Cerakote & Wood

Introduced 2019. Similar to Phenoma but with oil-rubbed Turkish Walnut stocks and bronze or gray Cerakote barrels and receivers. Laser-Etched models have camo patterns cut onto Cerakote finishes.

NIB	Exc.	V.G.	Good	Fair	Poor
480	400	320	—	—	—

Pointer SCT

Introduced 2019. 12 gauge, 3" chamber, black synthetic stock. SCT Clay features a 30" clays barrel, soft-touch synthetic stock, sporting raised rib, 5+1 capacity, fiber-optic rear and front sight, matte-black finish, stock drop and LOP spacers. MC-3 Extended Beretta/Benelli Mobil Chokes. Similar to SCT Clay, SCT Competition has 24" barrel and oversize charging handle.

NIB	Exc.	V.G.	Good	Fair	Poor
500	400	—	—	—	—

OVER/UNDER SHOTGUNS

Pointer Arista

Introduced 2019. Available in 12, 20, 28 gauge and .410 bore, 28" chrome-lined barrel. Youth has 26" barrel in 20 gauge and .410. Turkish walnut stocks and floral coin finish receiver, 5 chokes (C, IC, M, IM, F), fiber-optic front sight, raised and ventilated rib.

NIB	Exc.	V.G.	Good	Fair	Poor
500	400	—	—	—	—

Pointer Clays Over/Under

Available in 12 gauge 3", 28" or 30" chrome-moly lined and ported carbon-steel barrels. Wide ventilated raised rib, five chokes (SK, IC, M, IM, F), shell ejectors. Turkish walnut stock with adjustable comb.

NIB	Exc.	V.G.	Good	Fair	Poor
820	650	520	—	—	—

Pointer 1000 Field 12-Gauge Over/Under Shotgun

NIB	Exc.	V.G.	Good	Fair	Poor
430	350	220	—	—	—

Pointer MXL Deluxe

NIB	Exc.	V.G.	Good	Fair	Poor
550	450	350	—	—	—

Pointer SCT

Introduced 2019. Basic and Deluxe lines. Available in 12 gauge 3" chambers. 30" ported carbon-steel barrels. Ventilated raised rib, five chokes (SK, IC, M, IM, F), shell ejectors. Oil-rubbed Turkish walnut stock; adjustable comb on Deluxe version. Similar single-barrel Trap model.

Pointer SCT Basic

NIB	Exc.	V.G.	Good	Fair	Poor
700	650	500	—	—	—

Pointer SCT Deluxe

NIB	Exc.	V.G.	Good	Fair	Poor
920	800	750	—	—	—

Pointer SCT Basic Trap

NIB	Exc.	V.G.	Good	Fair	Poor
800	750	—	—	—	—

Pointer SCT Deluxe Trap

NIB	Exc.	V.G.	Good	Fair	Poor
920	800	750	—	—	—

POLY-TECHNOLOGIES, INC./POLY-TECH
China

SKS

Semi-automatic rifle. Chambered for 7.62x39mm cartridge, with 20.5" barrel and 10-shot fixed magazine. Based on Soviet Siminov carbine. Finish blued. Stock and handguard made of Chinese hardwood.

NIB	Exc.	V.G.	Good	Fair	Poor
500	430	300	200	130	80

AKS-762

Semi-automatic version of Chinese-type 56 Assault rifle. Chambered for 7.62x39mm cartridge, with 16.5" barrel. Furnished with 20-round magazine and Chinese bayonet. Finish blued. Stock is hardwood. Note: Add $250 folding stock model; 15 percent for milled receiver.

NIB	Exc.	V.G.	Good	Fair	Poor
950	800	680	500	350	200

AK-47/S

Chambered for 7.62x39 cartridge. Note: Add $350 folding stock model; $15 with Soviet-style bayonet.

NIB	Exc.	V.G.	Good	Fair	Poor
1350	1150	850	750	600	400

M-14/S

Reproduction of U.S. M14 rifle. Chambered for 7.62mm cartridge, with 22" barrel and 20-round magazine. Finish blued. Stock is hardwood.

NIB	Exc.	V.G.	Good	Fair	Poor
1000	880	680	500	350	200

POND, LUCIUS, W.
Worchester, Massachusetts

Pocket Revolver (Antique)

Single-action spur trigger .32-caliber revolver, with octagonal barrels of 4", 5" or 6" length. Barrel top strap and cylinder pivot upwards for loading. Made with brass or iron frames. A screwdriver fitted in butt. Revolvers were an infringement of Rollin White's patent, they were discontinued. Some revolvers found with inscription "Manuf'd. for Smith & Wesson Pat'd. April 5, 1855". These examples worth approximately 20 percent more than values listed.

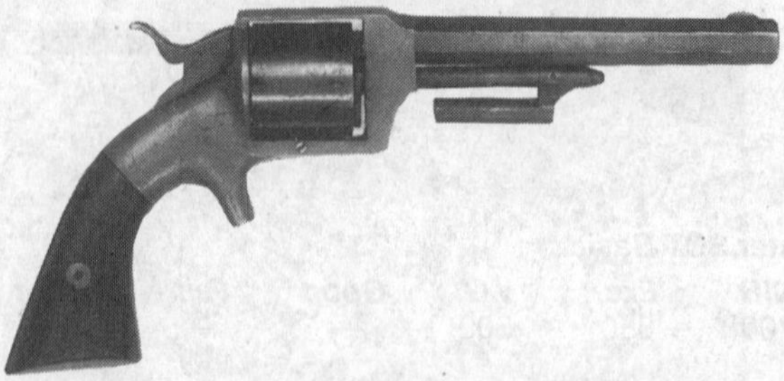

Courtesy Milwaukee Public Museum, Milwaukee, Wisconsin

Brass Framed Revolver (Antique)

Exc.	Fine	V.G.	Good	Fair	Poor
1100	880	610	350	100	70

Iron Framed Revolver (Antique)

Exc.	Fine	V.G.	Good	Fair	Poor
1000	780	540	300	80	50

Separate Chamber Revolver (Antique)

To avoid Rollin White patent, this revolver chambered for .22- or .32-caliber rimfire cartridges that fit into separate steel chamber inserts that can be removed from front of cylinder for loading. The .22-caliber version has 3.5" octagonal barrel with 7-round unfluted cylinder; .32-caliber version has 4", 5" or 6" octagonal barrel and 6-shot unfluted cylinder. Frames are silver-plated brass. Barrels and cylinders blued. Grips of walnut. Standard markings include "L.W. Pond, Worcester, Mass." and patent dates. Approximately 2,000 manufactured in .22-caliber; 5,000 in .32-caliber between 1863 and 1870.

.22 Caliber Version (Antique)

Exc.	Fine	V.G.	Good	Fair	Poor
1750	1400	970	550	150	100

.32 Caliber Version (Antique)

Exc.	Fine	V.G.	Good	Fair	Poor
1750	1400	970	550	150	100

PORTER, P. W.
New York, New York

Turret Revolver (Antique)

Extremely rare 9-shot vertical cylinder .41-caliber percussion revolver, with 5.25" round barrel. Triggerguard is also a lever that turns cylinder and cocks hammer. Automatic primer system also fitted to this revolver. Manufactured during 1850s in an unknown quantity. Rare. Values are speculative.

Exc.	Fine	V.G.	Good	Fair	Poor
20000	12500	8000	5000	3000	1500

Turret RifleMemphis Model with Canister Magazine (Antique)

Fitted with a 30-shot round canister magazine over turret. Made in Tennessee and extremely rare. Most often canisters are not encountered and values reflect this. Approximately 25 made..40 caliber. Very rare. Values are extremely speculative. Add premium for intact cylindrical canister magazine mounted above the turret magazine (total capacity 38 rounds).

Exc.	Fine	V.G.	Good	Fair	Poor
40000	30000	20000	12500	5000	2500

9-shot vertical cylinder .44-caliber rifle, with 26" or 28" octagonal barrel. Only markings are "Address P.W. Porter/New York". Four variations of this rifle known. The 22" barreled carbine would command 25 percent premium. Approximately 1,250 manufactured during 1850s.

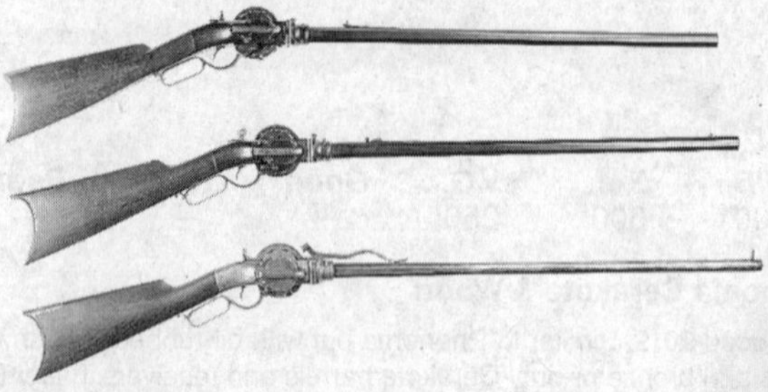

1st Model (New York) (Antique)

Exc.	Fine	V.G.	Good	Fair	Poor
15000	12000	8000	5000	3500	1500

2nd Model (New York) (Antique)

Model has screw-off cover over magazine.

Exc.	Fine	V.G.	Good	Fair	Poor
12500	9000	6000	3750	2500	1000

3rd Model (New York) (Antique)

As above, without automatic primer magazine. Nipples are exposed.

Exc.	Fine	V.G.	Good	Fair	Poor
10000	8000	5000	3500	2000	1000

PRAHA ZBROJOVKA
Prague, Czechoslovakia

Established in 1918 by A. Novotny. Company ceased operations in 1926.

VZ2L

7.65mm semi-automatic pistol. Patterned after Model 1910 Browning, without grip safety. Barrel length 3.5", magazine capacity 6 rounds, grips of wood. Slide marked "Zbrojowka Praga Praha".

NIB	Exc.	V.G.	Good	Fair	Poor
—	400	250	200	150	100

Praga 1921

6.35mm semi-automatic pistol, with slide of stamped steel cut with a finger groove at front. Folding trigger. Barrel 2" in length. Slide marked "Zbrojowka Praga Praha Patent Cal 6.35". Grips of molded plastic, with name "Praga" cast in them. A dangerous feature of this pistol is that it is striker-fired with no hammer. Intended to be carried fully loaded and cocked in the pocket with absolutely no safety of any kind. I do not recommend this. Folding trigger does not spring out until slide is drawn back slightly by using finger groove in front of it.

NIB	Exc.	V.G.	Good	Fair	Poor
—	380	220	200	150	100

PRAIRIE GUN WORKS
Winnipeg, Manitoba, Canada

M-15

Lightweight mountain rifle chambered for .22-250, 6mm-284, .25-284, 6.5-284, 7mm-08, .308 Win. and most short calibers. Built on Remington 700 action, with 20" lightweight barrel. Stock is Kevlar and comes in green, black or gray. Barrel length usually 20". Weight about 4.75 lbs.

NIB	Exc.	V.G.	Good	Fair	Poor
2600	2200	1750	1200	800	500

M-18

Similar to above. Chambered for long-action calibers. Fitted with barrel lengths from 22" to 24". Weight about 5.25 lbs.

NIB	Exc.	V.G.	Good	Fair	Poor
2600	2200	1750	1200	800	500

PRANDELLI & GASPARINI
Brescia, Italy

Boxlock Side-by-Side Shotgun

Good quality double-barrel 12- or 20-gauge shotgun, with 26" or 28" barrels. Single-selective trigger, automatic ejectors and Anson & Deeley action. Blued, stock of select walnut.

NIB	Exc.	V.G.	Good	Fair	Poor
—	2500	1750	1100	700	450

Sidelock Side-by-Side Shotgun

Similar to above, with full sidelocks.

NIB	Exc.	V.G.	Good	Fair	Poor
—	3500	2650	1500	900	500

Boxlock Over/Under Shotgun

Over/under double-barrel 12- or 20-gauge shotgun, with 26" or 28" barrels, single triggers and automatic ejectors. Blued, with select walnut stock.

NIB	Exc.	V.G.	Good	Fair	Poor
—	2750	1850	1200	900	350

Sidelock Over/Under Shotgun

As above, with full sidelocks.

NIB	Exc.	V.G.	Good	Fair	Poor
—	3000	2500	1800	950	450

PRATT, GEORGE
Middletown, Connecticut

Trap Gun

Doubled-barreled stationary burglar alarm or animal trap gun. Chambered for .38-caliber centerfire. Barrel 4" in length. All components are made of cast iron, with galvanized finish. Barrels and action mounted on round base, which can turn 360 degrees. Patent date "Dec. 18, 1883" marked on gun. Many manufactured between 1880 and early 1890s.

NIB	Exc.	V.G.	Good	Fair	Poor
—	—	1800	1200	500	150

PRATT, H.
Roxbury, Massachusetts

Underhammer Pistol (Antique)

.31-caliber percussion single-shot pistol, with 8.5" octagonal barrel. Frame marked "H. Pratt's/ Patent". Manufactured during 1850s.

Exc.	Fine	V.G.	Good	Fair	Poor
1700	1350	1000	650	200	140

PRECISION SMALL ARMS
Aspen, Colorado

PSA-25

Semi-automatic pistol chambered for .25 ACP. Barrel length 2.13-in.; magazine capacity 6 rounds. Frame and slide steel alloy. Weight 9.5 oz.; overall length 4.11 in.. Grips black polymer. Standard finish black oxide. Modeled after Browning Baby. Note: Add $50 brushed chrome finish; $75 stainless steel.

NIB	Exc.	V.G.	Good	Fair	Poor
660	560	510	400	350	250

PSA-25 Stainless Steel

NIB	Exc.	V.G.	Good	Fair	Poor
710	610	510	460	360	260

Featherweight Model

Same as above, with aluminum frame. Chrome slide with gold-plated trigger.

NIB	Exc.	V.G.	Good	Fair	Poor
1000	850	700	480	250	100

Diplomat Model

Black oxide, with gold highlights and ivory grips.

NIB	Exc.	V.G.	Good	Fair	Poor
1000	850	700	500	400	200

Montreaux Model

Gold plated with ivory grips.

NIB	Exc.	V.G.	Good	Fair	Poor
820	750	600	450	300	200

Renaissance Model

Same as above, with hand-engraved steel frame and slide. Antique stain chrome finish.

NIB	Exc.	V.G.	Good	Fair	Poor
2600	2100	1600	1200	700	300

Imperiale

Inlaid gold filigree over blue, with scrimshawed ivory grips.

NIB	Exc.	V.G.	Good	Fair	Poor
3300	2750	2100	1500	850	350

PREMIER
Italy and Spain

Trade name used by various retailers on shotguns manufactured in Italy and Spain that were imported during late 1950s and early 1960s.

Regent Side-by-Side Shotgun

Double-barrel shotgun, with 26" to 30" barrels. Available in all standard gauges. Receiver blued, stock of walnut. Normally found with pistol grip and beavertail forend.

NIB	Exc.	V.G.	Good	Fair	Poor
—	450	250	200	150	100

Regent Magnum

As above chambered for 3.5" 10-gauge Magnum cartridge. Barrels 32" in length and choked Full and Full.

NIB	Exc.	V.G.	Good	Fair	Poor
—	500	300	250	200	150

Brush King

Identical to Regent Model, except fitted with 22" Modified and Improved Cylinder barrels. Straight-grip English-style stock.

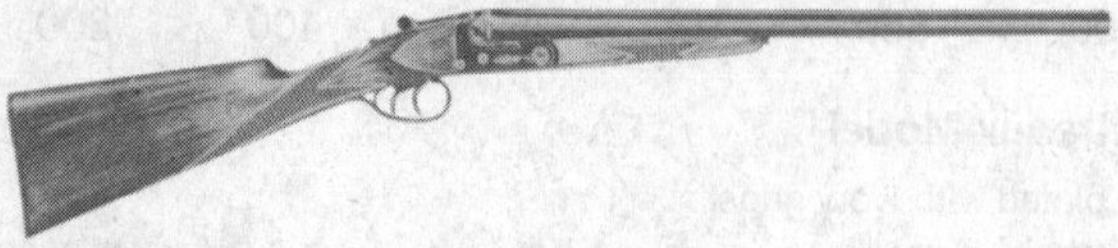

NIB	Exc.	V.G.	Good	Fair	Poor
—	500	380	250	200	150

Ambassador Model

More ornate version of Regent Model.

NIB	Exc.	V.G.	Good	Fair	Poor
—	600	450	300	250	180

Presentation Custom Grade

Custom-order shotgun, with game scenes and gold and silver inlays.

NIB	Exc.	V.G.	Good	Fair	Poor
—	2500	1750	1250	850	400

PRESCOTT, E. A.
Worcester, Massachusetts

Percussion Pocket Revolver (Antique)

.31-caliber percussion spur trigger revolver, with 4" or 4.25" octagonal barrel and 6-shot cylinder. Frame brass. Grips walnut. Believed approximately 100 manufactured during 1860 and 1861. Variations include birdshead butt or square-butt, short frame or long frame, and humped frame. These can have an impact on value. May be found unmarked or with trade names.

Exc.	Fine	V.G.	Good	Fair	Poor
6000	4000	3000	2000	1000	600

Pocket Revolver (Antique)

.22- or .32-caliber spur trigger revolver, with 3" or 4" barrel. .22-caliber version has 7-shot cylinder; .32 caliber 6-shot cylinder. Standard markings "E.A. Prescott Worchester Mass. Pat. Oct. 2, 1860". Approximately 1,000 manufactured between 1862 and 1867.

Exc.	Fine	V.G.	Good	Fair	Poor
1050	820	580	350	100	70

Navy Revolver (Antique)

Single-action revolver fitted with conventional trigger. Chambered for .38 rimfire cartridges, with 7.25" octagonal barrel. Unfluted cylinder holds 6 shots. Frame silver-plated brass or blued iron; barrel and cylinder blued, with walnut grips. Barrel marked "E.A. Prescott, Worcester, Mass. Pat. Oct. 2, 1860". Believed several hundred manufactured between 1861 and 1863. Iron frame model will bring a small premium.

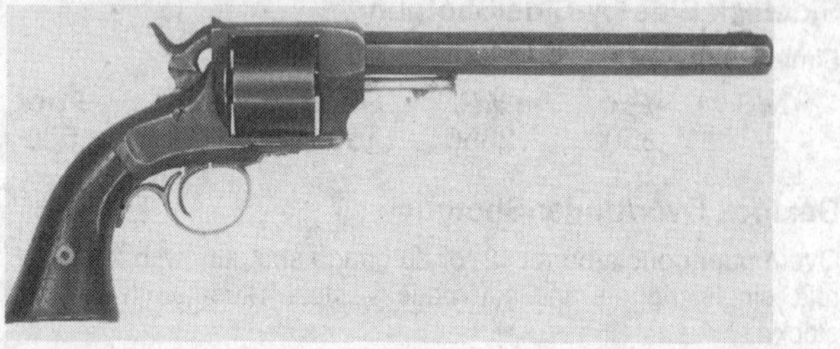

Courtesy Milwaukee Public Museum, Milwaukee, Wisconsin

Exc.	Fine	V.G.	Good	Fair	Poor
5000	3500	2000	1200	950	500

Army Revolver (Antique)

Similar in appearance to Navy model, with larger frame. Chambered for .44-caliber rimfire cartridge. Fitted with 9" octagon barrel, with extractor rod and loading gate on right side of frame. Very rare. Values listed are speculative.

Exc.	Fine	V.G.	Good	Fair	Poor
—	20000	15000	9000	3000	2000

Prescott S&W Style Pocket & Belt Revolver (Antique)

Although similar in appearance to early Smith & Wesson revolvers, Prescott has a solid frame. Available in .22- or .32-caliber: .22-caliber has 3" barrel; .32-caliber 5.75" barrel. Markings are identical found on Pocket Revolver. Approximately 300 manufactured between 1861 and 1863.

Exc.	Fine	V.G.	Good	Fair	Poor
1150	820	570	320	100	70

PRESCOTT PISTOL CO.
Hatfield Massachusetts

Manufacturer of good quality cartridge handguns in the mid-1870s.

Pocket Revolvers (Antique)

Limited production in several configurations and variations in .22, .32, .38, and .41 rimfire calibers. Most are single-action solid-frame spur-trigger revolvers, although open-top and double-action bulldog style models were also made. Most are not marked with the Prescott name. Specific Model designations include Paragon, Star (marked with five-pointed star), and the smaller .22 Comet. The open-top model, DA bulldog model, and revolvers in .41 rimfire will bring a premium over the values listed. Additional information from readers is invited.

Exc.	Fine	V.G.	Good	Fair	Poor
800	600	400	300	200	125

Single Action .44 (Antique)

Large brass frame single action; appearance is similar to Forehand & Wadsworth Old Model Army. Extremely rare, values are speculative.

Exc.	Fine	V.G.	Good	Fair	Poor
—	15000	8000	5000	3000	1000

Magazine Derringer (Antique)

.32 rimfire repeating derringer with mag tube mounted under barrel; very rare, values are speculative.

Exc.	Fine	V.G.	Good	Fair	Poor
—	3500	2000	1500	750	400

PRETORIA
Pretoria, South Africa

See—P.A.F.

PRINZ
Germany

Grade 1 Bolt-Action Rifle

High quality bolt-action rifle. Chambered for .243, .30-06, .308, 7mm Rem. Magnum or .300 Win. Magnum cartridges. Barrel length 24", double-set triggers available. Finish blued. Stock oil-finished select walnut. Introduced in 1989.

NIB	Exc.	V.G.	Good	Fair	Poor
1200	950	700	450	320	150

Grade 2 Bolt-Action Rifle

As above, with rosewood forend tip. Pistol grip cap.

NIB	Exc.	V.G.	Good	Fair	Poor
1300	1080	750	480	350	180

Tip Up Rifle

High quality single-shot rifle. Available in a variety of American cartridges. Barrel length 24". Not furnished with sights. Finish blued, stock of select walnut.

NIB	Exc.	V.G.	Good	Fair	Poor
3000	2250	1700	1140	850	300

Model 85 "Princess"

Combination 12-gauge shotgun and rifle, with 24 or 26" barrels, double triggers and automatic ejectors. Finish blued, stock of select walnut.

NIB	Exc.	V.G.	Good	Fair	Poor
3500	2850	2100	1650	1000	300

PROFESSIONAL ORDNANCE, INC.
Ontario, California

Company was purchased by Bushmaster.

Carbon-15 Pistol--Type 97

Introduced in 1996. Semi-automatic pistol built on carbon fiber upper and lower receiver. Chambered for 5.56 cartridge. Has 7.25" fluted stainless steel barrel. Ghost ring sights are standard. Magazine is AR-15 compatible. Quick detach compensator. Furnished with 10-round magazine. Weight about 46 oz. Note: Pistol has several options that will affect value.

NIB	Exc.	V.G.	Good	Fair	Poor
920	700	550	420	300	150

Carbon-15 Rifle—Type 97

Similar to above. Fitted with 16" barrel, quick detachable buttstock and compensator, Weaver type mounting base. Overall length 35"; weight about 3.9 lbs.

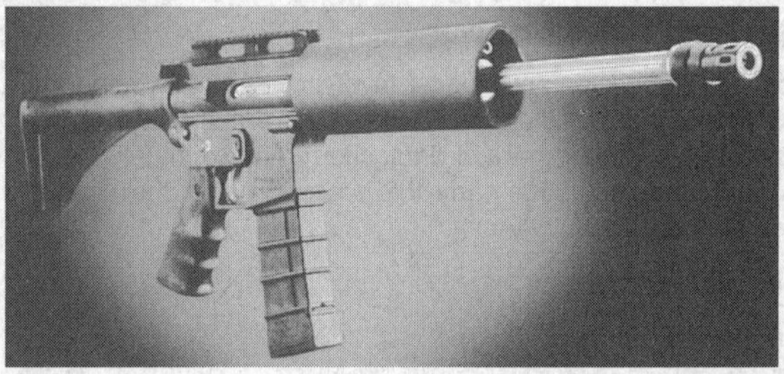

NIB	Exc.	V.G.	Good	Fair	Poor
950	720	600	500	350	150

Carbon-15 Rifle—Type 97S

Introduced in 2000. Rifle incorporated several new features. Fore-grip is double walled and insulated with a sheet of ultra-lightweight alumina silica ceramic fiber. Recoil buffer has been increased in size by 30 percent for less recoil. New ambidextrous safety has been added. New multi carry silent sling with Hogue grip standard. Weight about 4.3 lbs.

NIB	Exc.	V.G.	Good	Fair	Poor
1280	950	700	550	380	150

Carbon-15 Pistol--Type 21

Introduced in 1999. Features light profile stainless steel 7.25" barrel. Ghost ring sights are standard. Optional recoil compensator. A 30-round magazine standard until supplies are exhausted. Weight about 40 oz.

NIB	Exc.	V.G.	Good	Fair	Poor
920	700	550	420	300	150

Carbon-15 Rifle—Type 21

Fitted with 16" light profile stainless steel barrel. Quick detachable stock, weaver mounting base. Introduced in 1999. Weight about 3.9 lbs.

NIB	Exc.	V.G.	Good	Fair	Poor
1150	900	650	500	320	120

PROOF RESEARCH

Columbia Falls, Montana

Since 2012, PROOF Research has conducted R&D into advanced composites for weapons and industrial systems, and is best known for its carbon-fiber barrel wraps on a custom basis and proprietary for manufacturers.

Ascension

Caliber: 6.5 Creed, 6.5 PRC, 7mm Rem. Mag., 7mm PRC, 28 Nosler, .308 Win., .300 Win. Mag., .300 WSM, 300 PRC. Barrel: 20" to 26" Proof carbon-fiber wrapped, match-grade Sendero weight. Weight: 5 lbs., 5 oz. to 6 lbs., 4 oz. Stock: PROOF carbon-fiber Monte Carlo-style in multiple colors/patterns. Features: High Country Hunter bolt-action rifle built on a titanium Zermatt Arms receiver. TriggerTech trigger. Threaded barrel with protector; brakes available for an upcharge. Multiple Cerakote action colors. Split rail base. BDL-style magazine. 1/2 MOA accuracy guarantee.

NIB	Exc.	V.G.	Good	Fair	Poor
7500	—	—	—	—	—

PROTECTION

Protection Pocket Revolver

.28-caliber percussion spur-trigger revolver, with 3.25" octagonal barrel and 6-shot cylinder. Roll engraved with police arrest scene. Frame brass. Grips walnut. Cylinder marked "Protection". Approximately 1,000 manufactured during late 1850s early 1860s. Very rare and few sales knows. Values are very speculative.

1st Model (Antique)

Roll engraved cylinder.

Exc.	Fine	V.G.	Good	Fair	Poor
1500	1150	800	450	100	70

2nd Model (Antique)

Plain cylinder above serial no. 650.

Exc.	Fine	V.G.	Good	Fair	Poor
1300	950	650	350	100	70

PTR

Aynor, SC

Manufacturer of H&K/CEMTE type roller delayed blowback rifles and pistols.

PTR 51

Semi-automatic pistol chambered in .308 Win./7.62 NATO with either a 7.5- or 8.5-in. barrel. Polymer pistol grip, stamped steel receiver. Compatible with M4 buffer tubes. Weight is 7.9 pounds.

NIB	Exc.	V.G.	Good	Fair	Poor
1130	1010	870	710	590	410

9KT PTR 603

Semi-automatic. Similar to H&K SP5K but with 5.16-in. barrel, top rail, open sights, polymer pistol grip, and 30-round polymer magazine.

NIB	Exc.	V.G.	Good	Fair	Poor
1760	1540	1380	1000	800	660

PTK INTERNATIONAL, INC.

Atlanta, Georgia

See—POLY-TECHNOLOGIES, INC.

PULASKI ARMORY

Pulaski, Tennessee

Founded in 1861, this firm produced rifles for State of Tennessee. Overall length 48.5" to 49.5"; round barrels 32.5" to 33.25"; caliber .54. Resembles U.S. Model 1841 Rifles without patchbox. Had single screw sporting locks, with diamond-shaped ferrules. Usually marked on barrel "PULASKI T. C.S.A. 61". Production estimated about 300.

Confederate Military Rifle (Antique)

Very rare. Values are speculative.

Exc.	Fine	V.G.	Good	Fair	Poor
—	—	—	10000	5000	—

PUMA

Model 92 Rifle

Copy of Winchester lever-action rifle. Fitted with 24" octagon barrel. Chambered for .44 Magnum, .357 Magnum, .454 Casull or .45 Colt cartridge. Offered in a variety of finishes: stainless steel; blued; blued and brass; blued and case colored. Fitted with crescent butt and hardwood stock. Note: Add $50 for stainless steel.

NIB	Exc.	V.G.	Good	Fair	Poor
550	420	350	280	200	100

Model 92 Carbine

Also available with 20" round barrel. Chambered as above, plus .454 Casull and .480 Ruger. Fitted with a shotgun butt. Note: Add $50 for stainless steel.

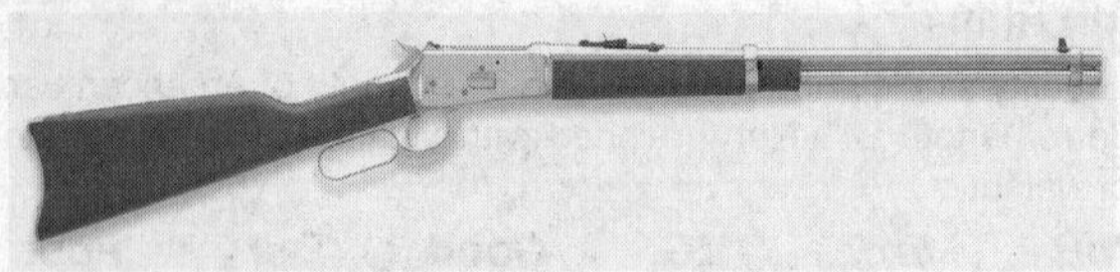

NIB	Exc.	V.G.	Good	Fair	Poor
550	420	350	280	200	100

Model 92 Trapper

Introduced in 2004. Features 16" barrel, with large-loop lever and saddle ring. Available in all calibers noted above.

NIB	Exc.	V.G.	Good	Fair	Poor
550	420	350	280	200	100

PPS22

New in 2009. A .22 LR version of Soviet PPSh sub-machine gun. Comes with one 50-round drum magazine.

NIB	Exc.	V.G.	Good	Fair	Poor
580	480	350	280	200	100

PURDEY, J. & SONS LTD.

London, England

Purdey is one of the finest manufacturer of shotguns, double-barrel and bolt-action rifles in the world. Virtually all their products are made on special order and impossible to establish general values. Prospective purchasers are advised to seek qualified guidance prior to acquisition of any arms made by this maker. Prices listed are for standard guns with no extras. Below, are approximate base prices for new custom shotguns and rifles based on the exchange rate between English pound and U.S. dollar as of September, 2014. Prices do not include VAT, which is approximately 20 percent. These guns are made to order to buyer's specifications and can be made in any gauge or caliber.

CURRENT PRODUCTION

Purdey's website currently catalogs the following types of custom-made long guns, each made to the buyer's specifications.

- Bolt action rifles in .30-06, .375 bore, .416 bore, .300 Win Mag, .308 Win or .375 H&H.
- Hammerless side-by-side shotguns in 20 ga., various configurations.
- Hammerless over-under shotguns in 12 ga. or 20 ga. various configurations.
- Hammerless double rifles in 9.3x74R

Each gun must be evaluated individually. Recently made Purdeys in relatively simple configuration showing wear or refinished have sold at auction for under $10,000 while their best guns in excellent condition may bring well into the six figures.

OLDER MANUFACTURED SHOTGUNS AND RIFLES

Best Quality Game Gun

Note: Add 50 percent for 20-gauge; 80 to 100 percent for 28-gauge or .410 bore.

NIB	Exc.	V.G.	Good	Fair	Poor
40000	35000	27500	20000	8000	—

Best Quality Heavy Duck Gun

NIB	Exc.	V.G.	Good	Fair	Poor
24000	20000	12500	7500	5000	—

Best Quality Over/Under

Note: Add 50 percent for 20-gauge; 100 percent for 28-gauge.

NIB	Exc.	V.G.	Good	Fair	Poor
50000	42000	32000	25000	9000	—

Double Rifle

.300 H&H

NIB	Exc.	V.G.	Good	Fair	Poor
—	55000	47500	40000	25000	—

.375 H&H

NIB	Exc.	V.G.	Good	Fair	Poor
—	70000	60000	50000	35000	—

.470 N.E.

NIB	Exc.	V.G.	Good	Fair	Poor
—	90000	75000	65000	45000	—

.600 N.E.

NIB	Exc.	V.G.	Good	Fair	Poor
—	100000	85000	70000	55000	—

PYRENEES

Hendaye, France

Founded in 1923, this company has produced a variety of models. Most popular of which was "Unique" series. Prior to 1939, a variety of trade names were marked on their products such as these: Superior, Capitan, Cesar, Chantecler, Chimere Renoir, Colonial, Prima, Rapid Maxima, Reina, Demon, Demonmarine, Ebac, Elite, Gallia, Ixor, Le Majestic, St. Hubert, Selecta, Sympathique, Touriste, Le Sanspariel, Le Tout Acier, Mars, Perfect, Triomphe Francais, Unis & Vindex. Following 1939, this company's products are simply stamped "Unique". Note: During World War II, production at this company was taken over by the Nazis. Consequently, the various models listed will be found with German inspection marks. These arms are worth approximately 25 percent more than values listed.

Model 10 Unique

6.35mm semi-automatic pistol similar to Model 1906 Browning. Slide marked "Le Veritable Pistolet Francais Unique". Introduced in 1923.

NIB	Exc.	V.G.	Good	Fair	Poor
—	300	200	160	100	80

Model 11

As above, with grip safety and loaded chamber indicator.

NIB	Exc.	V.G.	Good	Fair	Poor
—	320	220	200	150	100

Model 12

As above, without loaded chamber indicator.

NIB	Exc.	V.G.	Good	Fair	Poor
—	300	200	160	100	80

Model 13

As above, with 7-shot magazine.

NIB	Exc.	V.G.	Good	Fair	Poor
—	300	200	160	100	80

Model 14

As above, with 9-shot magazine.

NIB	Exc.	V.G.	Good	Fair	Poor
—	300	200	160	100	80

Model 15

As above in 7.65mm caliber. Introduced in 1923.

NIB	Exc.	V.G.	Good	Fair	Poor
—	300	200	160	100	80

Model 16

As above, with 7-shot magazine.

Courtesy Orvel Reichert

NIB	Exc.	V.G.	Good	Fair	Poor
—	300	200	160	100	80

Model 17

As above, with 9-shot magazine.

NIB	Exc.	V.G.	Good	Fair	Poor
—	320	220	200	150	100

Model 18

7.65mm caliber semi-automatic pistol. Patterned after Model 1920 Browning, without grip safety.

NIB	Exc.	V.G.	Good	Fair	Poor
—	300	200	160	100	80

Model 19

As above, with 7-shot magazine.

NIB	Exc.	V.G.	Good	Fair	Poor
—	300	200	160	100	80

Model 20

As above, with 9-shot magazine.

NIB	Exc.	V.G.	Good	Fair	Poor
—	320	220	200	150	100

Model 21

As above chambered for 9mm short cartridge.

NIB	Exc.	V.G.	Good	Fair	Poor
—	320	220	200	150	100

POST-WAR UNIQUE

Model BCF66

9mm short semi-automatic pistol, with 3.5" barrel, open top slide and external hammer. Slide marked "Armes Unique Hendaye BP France". Blued finish. Plastic grips.

NIB	Exc.	V.G.	Good	Fair	Poor
—	300	200	160	100	80

Model C

Virtually identical to Model 17 listed above. Slide marked "7.65 Court 9 coups Unique". Blued finish. Plastic grips with trademark "PF" in a circle cast into them.

NIB	Exc.	V.G.	Good	Fair	Poor
—	250	180	150	120	80

Model F

Identical to Model C, except chambered for 9mm Short cartridges. Magazine capacity 8 rounds.

NIB	Exc.	V.G.	Good	Fair	Poor
—	300	200	160	100	80

Model D

.22-caliber semi-automatic pistol, with barrels ranging from 4" to 7.5" in length. The 7.5" barreled version fitted with muzzle brake. Magazine capacity 10 rounds. Finish blued, plastic grips.

NIB	Exc.	V.G.	Good	Fair	Poor
—	280	220	200	150	120

Model DES/VO

Identical to Model D, but chambered for .22 Short cartridges.

NIB	Exc.	V.G.	Good	Fair	Poor
—	280	220	200	150	120

Model L

Similar to Model D, except chambered for .22, .32 ACP and 9mm Short cartridges. Available with steel or alloy frame.

NIB	Exc.	V.G.	Good	Fair	Poor
—	300	200	160	100	80

Model DES 69

As above, with better quality sights, special trigger and improved grips.

NIB	Exc.	V.G.	Good	Fair	Poor
—	320	220	200	150	100

Model 2000

Courtesy John J. Stimson, Jr.

NIB	Exc.	V.G.	Good	Fair	Poor
1250	950	780	500	350	150

Q

QUACKENBUSH
Herkimer, New York

Quackenbush Safety Cartridge Rifle

Single-shot take-down boy's rifle. Chambered for .22 rimfire cartridges in .22 Short or .22 Long. Barrel length 18". Weight about 4.5 lbs. All metal parts nickel-plated. Breech swings to side for loading. Stock of walnut. Manufactured between 1886 and about 1920. Approximately 50,000 produced. Quackenbush also made nickel-plated nutcrackers. Who'd'a thought?

NIB	Exc.	V.G.	Good	Fair	Poor
—	—	800	650	300	150

Junior Safety Rifle

Same as above, with skeleton stock. Built between 1893 and 1920. About 7,000 guns manufactured. Weight about 4 lbs.

NIB	Exc.	V.G.	Good	Fair	Poor
—	—	950	600	200	100

Bicycle Rifle

Chambered for .22 cartridge. Fitted with 12" barrel. Skeleton wire pistol grip.

NIB	Exc.	V.G.	Good	Fair	Poor
—	—	1300	750	350	150

QUINABAUG MFG. CO.
Southridge, Massachusetts

Underhammer Pistol (Antique)

.31-caliber percussion under hammer pistol, with barrels from 3" to 8" in length. Frame of blued iron, grips of walnut or maple. Top of frame marked "Quinabaug Rifle M'g Co. Southbridge, Mass." Barrels are normally marked "E. Hutchings & Co. Agents". Manufactured during 1850s.

Exc.	Fine	V.G.	Good	Fair	Poor
1900	1400	1000	600	200	140

R

R. G. INDUSTRIES
Miami, Florida
Rohm Gmbh
Sontheim/Brenz, Germany

An importer of inexpensive handguns of dubious quality that ceased operations in 1986.

RG-25

A .25-caliber semi-automatic pistol. Available blued or chrome-plated finish.

NIB	Exc.	V.G.	Good	Fair	Poor
—	80	60	50	20	0

RG-16

A double-barrel .22-caliber chrome-plated derringer.

NIB	Exc.	V.G.	Good	Fair	Poor
—	80	60	50	20	0

RG-17

As above, except chambered for. 38 Special cartridge.

NIB	Exc.	V.G.	Good	Fair	Poor
—	80	70	60	20	0

RG-14

A .22-caliber double-action revolver, with 4" barrel and 6-shot cylinder. Blued finish, plastic grips.

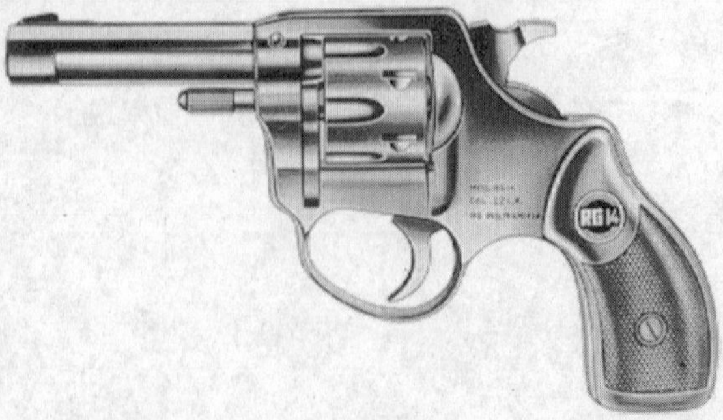

NIB	Exc.	V.G.	Good	Fair	Poor
—	80	70	60	20	0

RG-30

A .22 LR or Magnum double-action revolver. Blued finish, plastic grips.

NIB	Exc.	V.G.	Good	Fair	Poor
—	80	60	50	20	0

RG-40

A .38 Special double-action revolver, with swing-out cylinder. Blued finish, plastic grips.

NIB	Exc.	V.G.	Good	Fair	Poor
—	80	70	60	20	0

RG-57

A .357 or .44 Magnum double-action revolver, with 6-shot cylinder. Blued finish, checkered wood grips.

NIB	Exc.	V.G.	Good	Fair	Poor
—	80	70	60	20	0

RG-63

A .22-caliber double-action revolver resembling Colt Model 1873.

NIB	Exc.	V.G.	Good	Fair	Poor
—	80	70	60	20	0

RG-66

A .22 or .22 Magnum single-action revolver patterned after Colt Model 1873.

NIB	Exc.	V.G.	Good	Fair	Poor
—	90	70	50	20	0

RG-66T

As above, with adjustable sights.

NIB	Exc.	V.G.	Good	Fair	Poor
—	90	70	50	20	0

RG-74

A .22-caliber double-action revolver, with swing-out cylinder.

NIB	Exc.	V.G.	Good	Fair	Poor
—	80	60	60	20	0

RG-88

A .357 Magnum double-action revolver, with swing-out cylinder.

NIB	Exc.	V.G.	Good	Fair	Poor
—	80	60	60	20	0

R.E.
Valencia, Spain

Initials R.E. stand for "Republica Espana." This copy of Spanish Army Model 1921, also known as Astra 400, was produced between 1936 and 1939 during Spanish Civil War by the Republican forces. This variation can be identified by

RE monogram on butt and the absence of any manufacturer's stampings.

NIB	Exc.	V.G.	Good	Fair	Poor
—	480	320	250	180	100

RADICAL FIREARMS

Stafford, Texas

Texas-based Radical Firearms is a Title II NFA gun manufacturer with a full line of AR-style rifles and carbines, as well as full-auto machine guns and parts.

AR PATTERN RIFLES

Various configurations in 5.56 NATO or 7.62x39. Special features may add to these values. Slight premium for .300 Blackout. Add 25% for .458 SOCOM or 6.5 Grendel chambering.

NIB	Exc.	V.G.	Good	Fair	Poor
575	500	425	—	—	—

.350 Legend

Caliber: .350 Legend. Capacity: .350 Legend magazine. Barrel: 16 in., 1:14 twist, 4140 chrome-moly vanadium steel, Melonite finish, Big Bore Contour, A2 flash hider, 5/8x32 tpi muzzle thread. Upper/Lower Receivers: Forged 7075 T6, M4 Mil-Std upper with oversized ejection port, forward assist and dust cover. Type III anodizing. Stock: B5 Bravo, 6-position. Handguard: Free-float M-LOK hybrid rail, 15 in. Sights: None, full length top rail. Weight: NA. Trigger: Mil-Std. Length: 33-37.5 in. Features: Carbine-length gas system, low-profile gas block, Mil-Std charging handle, carbine Mil-Std buffer tube. Discontinued.

NIB	Exc.	V.G.	Good	Fair	Poor
900	700	500	—	—	—

.308 Winchester

Caliber: .308 Win. Capacity: 20-round, .308 magazines. Barrel: 18 in., 1:10 twist, 5/8x24 tpi muzzle threads, RF-MS Compensator. Upper/Lower Receivers: 7075 T6 billet aluminum, DPMS Pattern High, Type III anodizing with forward assist and dust cover. Stock: Mission First Tactical Minimalist. Sights: None, full length top rail. Weight: NA. Trigger: Mil-Std. Length: 33-37.5 in. Features: Mid-length gas system, M-LOK Thin Rail Handguard, 15 in. Discontinued.

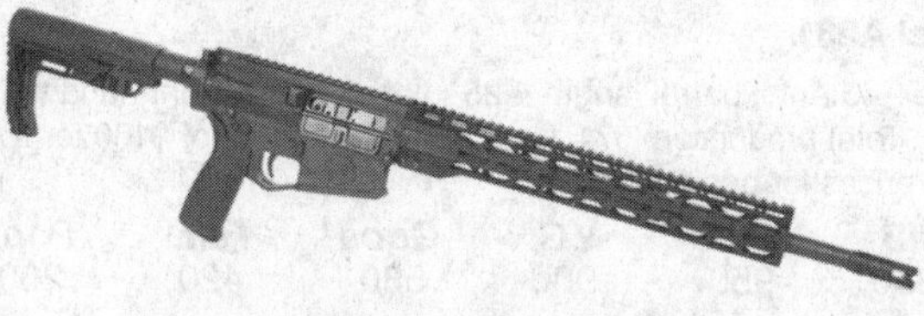

NIB	Exc.	V.G.	Good	Fair	Poor
1100	750	600	—	—	—

RADIAN WEAPONS

Redmond, Oregon

Formerly AXTS Weapons Systems, makers of custom-order upgraded AR-pattern rifles, also available in kit form. Example pricing is for base model.

Model One

AR pattern semi-auto rifle, available on custom-order basis; 5.56 NATO or .300 Blackout, 16" barrel.

NIB	Exc.	V.G.	Good	Fair	Poor
2200	1900	—	—	—	—

RADOM

Radom, Poland

For history, technical data, descriptions, photos and prices see the Standard Catalog of Military Firearms.

VIS-35 Reissue

An exact copy of original VIS-35 pistol. Limited to 100 pistols, with fewer than that number imported into U.S. Importer, "Dalvar of USA" is stamped on barrel. Note: Deduct 50 percent for "non-eagle" version.

NIB	Exc.	V.G.	Good	Fair	Poor
2300	2000	1500	—	—	—

FB P-64

Polish semi-automatic, straight blowback pistol in 9mm Makarov caliber. Produced from 1964 to 1983. P-64 replaced older Polish-made PW wz.33, a licensed Tokarev copy, and was manufactured by Fabrika Broni in Radom, Poland. This 6-shot pistol has a 3.3" barrel and is very similar in size to the Walther PPK. Also similar mechanically, but no external slide latch is present, as empty magazine locks the slide in the open position. Major drawback is its heavy felt recoil, replaced in 1984. Huge quantities have been imported to the United States from the late 2000s until recently. Features a blue finish, plastic wrap-around grips, marked "P-64" and "9mm" on left slide flat. Serial number and date of manufacture on right side.

NIB	Exc.	V.G.	Good	Fair	Poor
—	280	240	220	200	150

FB P-83

Superbly made replacement for older P-64, the P-83 is an 8-shot 9mm Makarov caliber, straight blowback semi-automatic pistol, with large comfortable lined wrap-around rubber grips. Also known as Vanad pistol, it is dimensionally similar to the Russian Makarov. (Vanad is a reference to vanadium, an alloy used to strengthen steel). Produced at the Polish Fabrika Broni factory. Has a 3.5" barrel, with a unique take-down system by which the triggerguard slides forward, as opposed to being pulled down as required on most Makarov-size pistols. P-83 was used by Polish forces in the Yugoslav and Iraq Wars, and is still a reserve issue item in Polish military and police forces. Imported to the United States beginning in late 2000s.

NIB	Exc.	V.G.	Good	Fair	Poor
—	400	350	300	280	220

RAM-LINE COMPANY
Grand Junction, Colorado

Ram-Tech

This series of budget-priced .22 semi-automatic pistols was made in the early 1990s by the Ram-Line Company, a manufacturer of gunstocks, magazines and gun parts. Alloy receiver, single-action operation, 4.5", 5.5" or 7.5" barrel (Target Model). Discontinued in 1995. >b>Note: Add $50 for Target Model.

NIB	Exc.	V.G.	Good	Fair	Poor
200	160	120	90	80	60

RANDALL FIREARMS CO.
Sun Valley, California

This company was in operation from 1983 to 1985. It was the first manufacturer to mass-produce 1911-type pistols in stainless steel. Also, the first to make a mirror-image left-hand variation. Many models were offered, most in .45 ACP or 9mm. Records show only two samples were chambered in .38 Super. Total production of Randall Firearms Co. was almost 10,000 pistols.

Model A111

Caliber .45 Auto; barrel length 5"; round-slide top, right-hand with fixed sights. Total production: 3,431. Note: Add a premium of $100 for Exc. thru Good prices for original box.

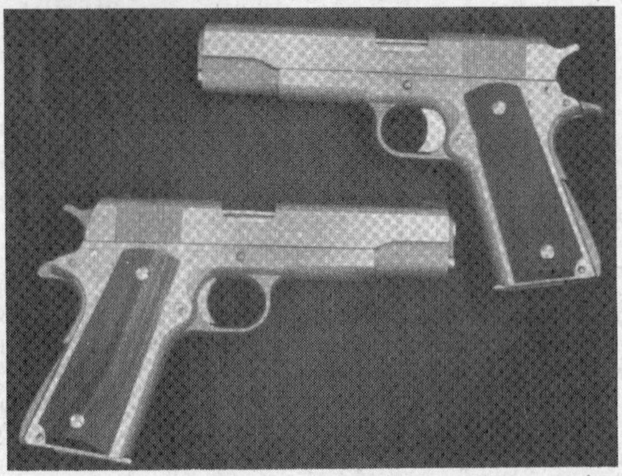

Photo by Steve Comus

"Randall matched set, serial-number RFOO010C. Made for the TV series Magnum PI". ""

NIB	Exc.	V.G.	Good	Fair	Poor
1050	950	650	400	350	200

Model A121

Caliber .45 Auto; barrel length 5"; flat-slide top, right-hand with fixed sights. Total production: 1,067. Note: Add a premium of $100 for Exc. thru Good prices for original box.

NIB	Exc.	V.G.	Good	Fair	Poor
1150	1000	800	420	380	200

Model A131

Caliber .45 Auto; barrel length 5"; flat-slide top, right-hand with Millet sights. Total production: 2,083. Note: Add a premium of $100 for Exc. thru Good prices for original box.

Photo by Larry Gray

Randall A131/SO in .451 Detonics Magnum with Randall memorabilia.

NIB	Exc.	V.G.	Good	Fair	Poor
1300	1050	880	550	400	200

Model A112

Caliber 9mm; barrel length 5"; round-slide top, right-hand with fixed sights. Total production: 301. Note: Add a premium of $100 for Exc. thru Good prices for original box.

NIB	Exc.	V.G.	Good	Fair	Poor
1350	950	900	580	420	200

Model A211

Caliber .45 Auto; barrel length 4.25"; round-slide top, right-hand with fixed sights. Total production: 922. Note: Add a premium of $100 for Exc. thru Good prices for original box.

NIB	Exc.	V.G.	Good	Fair	Poor
1150	1000	800	420	380	200

Model A231

Caliber .45 Auto; barrel length 4.25"; flat-slide top, right-hand with Millet sights. Total production: 574. Note: Add a premium of $100 for Exc. thru Good prices for original box.

NIB	Exc.	V.G.	Good	Fair	Poor
1350	950	900	580	420	200

Model A311

Caliber .45 Auto; barrel length 4.25"; round-slide top, right-hand with fixed sights. Total production: 361. Note: Add a premium of $100 for Exc. thru Good prices for original box.

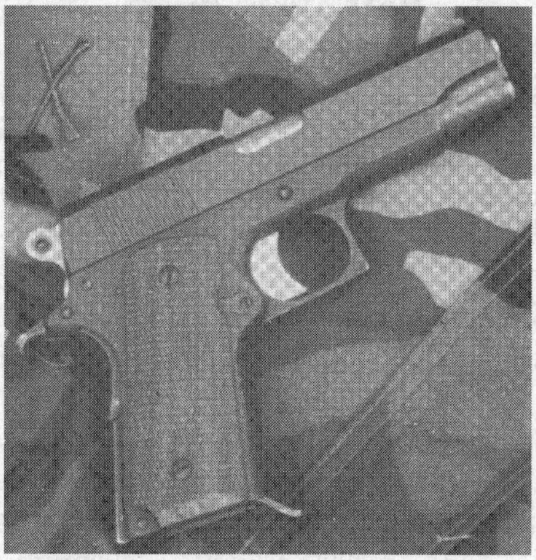

Photo by Steve Comus

A311B black oxide LeMay special order by Soldier of Fortune magazine for field testing in El Salvador.

NIB	Exc.	V.G.	Good	Fair	Poor
1700	1380	1150	900	700	300

Model A331 Curtis LeMay

Caliber .45 Auto; barrel length 4.25"; flat-slide top, right-hand with Millet sights. Total production: 293.

NIB	Exc.	V.G.	Good	Fair	Poor
1800	1480	1250	950	740	300

Model B111

Caliber .45 Auto; barrel length 5"; round-slide top, left-hand with fixed sights. Total production: 297. Note: Add a premium of $100 for Exc. thru Good prices for original box.

NIB	Exc.	V.G.	Good	Fair	Poor
1900	1550	1200	980	700	300

Model B121

Caliber .45 Auto; barrel length 5"; flat-slide top, left-hand with fixed sights. Total production: 110. Note: Add a premium of $100 for Exc. thru Good prices for original box.

NIB	Exc.	V.G.	Good	Fair	Poor
2250	1780	1450	1000	750	300

Model B131

Caliber .45 Auto; barrel length 5"; flat-slide top, left-hand with Millet sights. Total production: 225. Note: Add a premium of $100 for Exc. thru Good prices for original box.

Photo by Steve Comus

B131/SO left-hand service model with custom Chuck Stapel knife.

NIB	Exc.	V.G.	Good	Fair	Poor
2080	1700	1400	880	700	300

RANDALL MAGAZINES

.45 LeMay—Right-Hand

NIB	Exc.	V.G.	Good	Fair	Poor
100	90	80	80	—	—

.45 LeMay—Dogleg Right-Hand

NIB	Exc.	V.G.	Good	Fair	Poor
80	70	70	70	—	—

.45 LeMay—Left-Hand

NIB	Exc.	V.G.	Good	Fair	Poor
150	130	120	120	—	—

.45 LeMay—Dogleg Left-Hand

NIB	Exc.	V.G.	Good	Fair	Poor
140	130	120	120	—	—

.45 Service—Right-Hand

NIB	Exc.	V.G.	Good	Fair	Poor
60	40	40	40	—	—

.45 Service—Left-Hand

NIB	Exc.	V.G.	Good	Fair	Poor
120	120	100	100	—	—

9mm Service—Right-Hand

NIB	Exc.	V.G.	Good	Fair	Poor
120	120	100	100	—	—

9mm Service—Left-Hand

NIB	Exc.	V.G.	Good	Fair	Poor
200	180	150	150	—	—

Randall made a number of models with extremely low production. These rarely come onto the market and values are speculative. These include:

- Model A122 - Caliber 9mm; barrel length 5 in.; flat-slide top, right-hand with fixed sights. Total production: 18. NIB 1900.
- Model A212 Caliber 9mm; barrel length 4.25 in.; round-slide top, right-hand with fixed sights. Total production: 76. NIB 1450.
- Model A232 Caliber 9mm; barrel length 4.25 in.; flat-slide top, right-hand with Millet sights. Total production: 5. NIB 2400.
- Model A312 Caliber 9mm; barrel length 4.25 in.; round-slide top, right-hand with fixed sights. Total production: 2. NIB 3750.
- Model A332 Caliber 9mm; barrel length 4.25 in.; flat-slide top, right-hand with Millet sights. Total production: 9. NIB 2250.
- Model B122 Caliber 9mm; barrel length 5 in.; flat-slide top, left-hand with fixed sights. Total production: 2. NIB 4000.
- Model B123 Caliber .38 Super; barrel length 5 in.; flat-slide top, left-hand with fixed sights. Total production: 2. NIB 4000.
- Model B311 Caliber .45 Auto; barrel length 4.25 in.; round-slide top, left-hand with fixed sights. Total production: 52. NIB 2250.
- Model B312 Caliber 9mm; barrel length 4.25 in.; round-slide top, left-hand with fixed sights. Total production: 9. NIB 3750.
- Model B331 Caliber .45 Auto; barrel length 4.25 in.; flat-slide top, left-hand with Millet sights. Total production: 45. NIB 2500.
- Model C311 Caliber .45 Auto; barrel length 4.25 in.; round-slide top, right-hand with fixed sights. Total production: 1. NIB 4250.
- Model C332 Caliber 9mm; barrel length 4.25 in.; flat-slide top, right-hand with Millet sights. Total production: 4. NIB 1900.
- Model B321 SET. NIB 24500.
- Model A111/111 Matched Set. NIB 9200.
- Austrian Randall Total production: 5. Due to the rarity, values for this model are very speculative. An expert appraisal is advised.

RANGER ARMS, INC.
Gainesville, Texas

.22 Rifle

Bolt-action rifle produced in .22 LR. Checkered walnut Monte Carlo stock. Manufactured early 1970s.

NIB	Exc.	V.G.	Good	Fair	Poor
—	200	150	100	80	50

Statesman

Bolt-action rifle produced in various centerfire calibers, with 22" barrel, no sights and checkered walnut stock. Standard finish blued. Manufactured early 1970s.

NIB	Exc.	V.G.	Good	Fair	Poor
—	900	750	600	350	200

Statesman Magnum

As above, chambered for Magnum calibers, with 24" barrel.

NIB	Exc.	V.G.	Good	Fair	Poor
—	950	800	650	380	200

Senator

As above, with a better finish.

NIB	Exc.	V.G.	Good	Fair	Poor
—	1000	850	700	520	250

Senator Magnum

As above, chambered for Magnum cartridges.

NIB	Exc.	V.G.	Good	Fair	Poor
—	1150	900	750	580	250

Governor

As above, with better walnut and finer lined checkering.

NIB	Exc.	V.G.	Good	Fair	Poor
—	1300	1050	800	600	300

Governor Magnum

As above, chambered for Magnum cartridges.

NIB	Exc.	V.G.	Good	Fair	Poor
—	1540	1200	950	750	300

RAPTOR ARMS CO.
Shelton, Connecticut

Raptor Bolt-Action Rifle

Economy-class rifle introduced in 1997. Chambered for .270-, .30-06, .243-, .25-06 and .308-calibers. Fitted with 22" barrel and black synthetic checkered stock. An upgrade model was available with wooden stock. Adjustable trigger. Weight about 7.5 lbs.

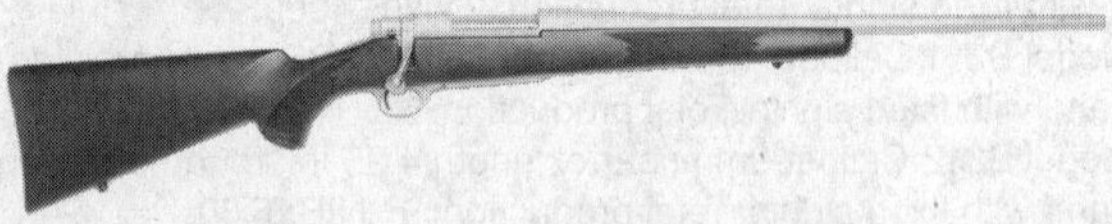

NIB	Exc.	V.G.	Good	Fair	Poor
280	220	180	120	100	80

Peregrine Bolt-Action Rifle

Similar to above, with checkered hardwood stock. Special order.

NIB	Exc.	V.G.	Good	Fair	Poor
280	220	180	120	100	80

RAST & GASSER
See—GASSER

RAU ARMS CORP.
El Dorado, Kansas

Wildcat

Single-shot pivoting-barrel .22 rimfire rifle. Skeletonized stock, with walnut or mahogany inset. Forend acts as extractor. Similar in overall look to FIE/Garcia Bronco in .22 only. Mfg. 1969-1970, with 2500-3000 produced. Later produced by Mountain Arms. See that listing.

Model 500

Blued, with walnut stock insert.

NIB	Exc.	V.G.	Good	Fair	Poor
300	200	150	100	80	40

Model 600 Deluxe

Chrome finish, with mahogany stock insert.

NIB	Exc.	V.G.	Good	Fair	Poor
320	220	180	120	100	50

RAVELL
Barcelona, Spain

Maxim Double Rifle

H&H-styled sidelock double-barrel rifle. Available in .375 H&H or 9.3x74R, with 23" barrels having express sights. Double triggers and automatic ejectors. Sidelocks and mounts engraved. Stock of well figured walnut. Normally fitted with a recoil pad.

NIB	Exc.	V.G.	Good	Fair	Poor
4500	3500	2750	1850	1250	850

RAVEN ARMS
Industry, California

P-25

A .25-caliber semi-automatic pistol, with 2.75" barrel and 6-round magazine. Available with blued, chrome or nickel-plated finish and walnut grips. Manufacture ceased in 1984.

NIB	Exc.	V.G.	Good	Fair	Poor
—	100	80	50	40	20

MP-25

As above, with die-cast frame and imitation ivory grips.

NIB	Exc.	V.G.	Good	Fair	Poor
110	80	60	40	40	20

READ & WATSON
Danville, Virginia

During 1862 and 1863, Read & Watson produced approximately 900 altered Hall rifles for State of Virginia. These arms were made from Hall rifles issued to the state prior to the Civil War. Original breech-loading mechanisms were removed and a brass breech piece or receiver was secured in their place. New buttstocks were fitted and original Hall furniture was reused. Carbines have an overall length of 42.125"; barrel length 26"; in .52-caliber. Position and style of serial numbers varies.

Antique

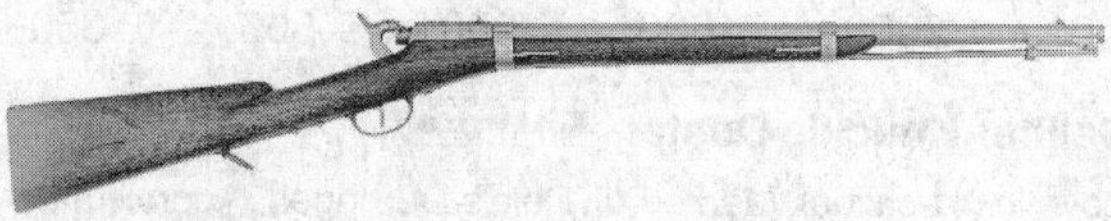

Exc.	Fine	V.G.	Good	Fair	Poor
18500	15500	12000	7000	4000	2000

RED ARROW WEAPONS
Fork Union, Virginia

Founded by Kip Campbell of the Red Arrow television show, a manufacturer of AR-style rifles and carbines.

RAW15 .300 Blackout

Caliber: .300 BLK. Barrel: 16" free-floated Melonite-coated 4150 chrome-moly barrel, 1:8" twist, DB15 556 muzzle brake, threaded 5/8×24. Red accents on black-anodized hardcoat finish. CMC 2.5-lb. single-stage trigger, pistol-length gas system, Magpul CTR stock, Magpul K2+ grip, M-Lok forend. Length: 32.5" to 36.25". Weight: 6.9 lbs. Handguard: 15". RAW M-LOK Battle Rail. Ambidextrous safety selector, MagPul K2+ Grip, MagPul CTR Stock, Magpul P-Mag 30 rd. Introduced: 2022. 5.56 NATO, 6.5 CM, and .308 Win. chamberings also available. Based in Fork Union, Virginia. SEE POLITICAL PANIC PRICING.

NIB	Exc.	V.G.	Good	Fair	Poor
1350	—	—	—	—	—

REEDER, GARY CUSTOM GUNS
Flagstaff, Arizona

Company offers complete guns as listed below. It also offers custom options built on customer guns as well. An extensive number of custom options is available on any of these models. Prices listed below reflect the standard for that particular model. Retail prices only are listed below due to lack of active secondary market for these limited edition guns. Reeder is a custom manufacturer, or re-stylist, working primarily with Ruger frames. Previous editions included listings of about 43 examples of various Reeder custom guns, some with pictures. These can still be found on the Standard Catalog of Firearms website Since many of Reeder's guns are made to custom specs, their value is largely a matter of finding the right buyer. In general, previous listings suggested that Reeder guns built in standard calibers on Ruger frames may sell for in the 1200 to 1500 range when NIB, and 1000 to 1300 when Exc. A few models in extra-large caliber models such as .500 S&W or .500 Maximum listed at double to triple those values.

REFORM
August Schuler
Suhl, Germany

Reform Pistol

A 6.35 or .25 ACP four barreled double-action pistol. Constructed so that barrel unit rises upward when trigger is pulled. Superficially resembles a semi-automatic pistol. Blued, with hard rubber grips. Manufactured between 1906 and about 1913.

NIB	Exc.	V.G.	Good	Fair	Poor
—	1750	1200	950	600	380

REGENT
See—OMEGA ARMS

REID, JAMES
New York, New York

James Reid manufactured guns in New York City 1861-1865 and Catskill New York 1868-1883. His serial numbers ran consecutively through all models. His early Model 1 revolver will also be found marked James P. Fitch, Phoenix Revolver, Wm. Irving, and Holey Mfg. Co.

Single-Shot Derringer Antique

.22-caliber spur trigger single-shot pistol, with 2.75" half octagonal barrel. Silver plated brass frame, blued barrel and rosewood grips. Barrel marked "W. Irving". Manufactured in 1860s. Note: .32-caliber variation has 3" barrel and worth approximately 40 percent more than values listed.

Exc.	Fine	V.G.	Good	Fair	Poor
1050	480	340	200	120	80

Model 1 Revolver Antique

Spur trigger .22-caliber revolver, with 3.5" octagonal barrel and 7-shot unfluted cylinder. Blued, with walnut grips. Barrel marked "J. Reid, New York". Approximately 500 manufactured between 1862 and 1865. Sometimes marked with different maker names. Guns marked "Wm Irving, New York" or "Holey Mfg. Co. Lakeview Conn" will bring a premium.

Exc.	Fine	V.G.	Good	Fair	Poor
1200	950	650	400	100	70

Model 2 Revolver Antique

As above in .32-caliber. Barrel marked "Address W.P. Irving, 20 Cliff Street. N.Y." or "James P. Fitch. N.Y." Approximately 1,300 manufactured between 1862 and 1865.

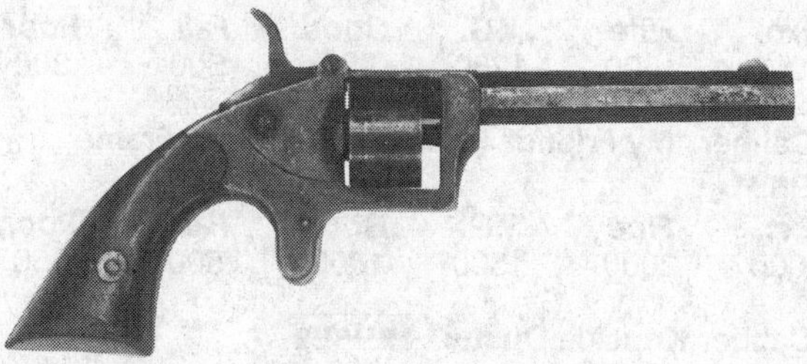

Exc.	Fine	V.G.	Good	Fair	Poor
1200	950	650	400	100	70

Model 3 Revolver (Antique)

Similar to above, with grip angle sharpened. Chambered for .32 rimfire cartridge, with 4.75" barrel. Cylinder chambers are threaded so that percussion nipples can be inserted. Barrel marked "J. Reid N.Y. City". Approximately 300 made between 1862 and 1865.

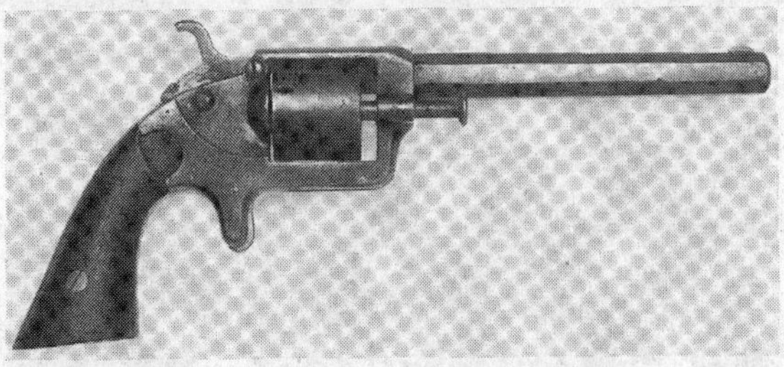

Exc.	Fine	V.G.	Good	Fair	Poor
1550	1380	960	550	200	140

Model 4 Revolver (Antique)

As above, with barrel lengths varying from 3.75" to 8". Approximately 1,600 manufactured between 1862 and 1865.

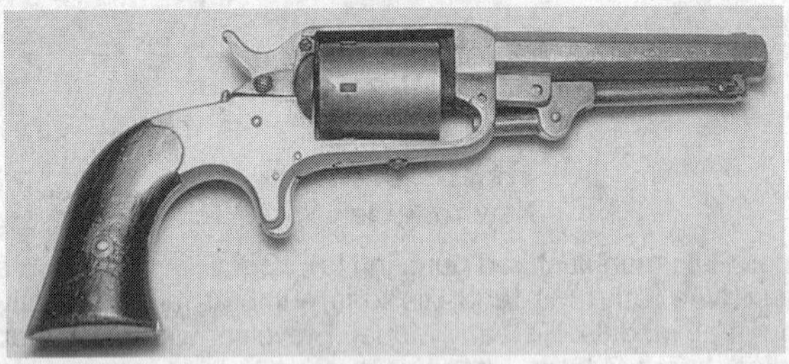

Exc.	Fine	V.G.	Good	Fair	Poor
1550	1380	960	550	200	140

"My Friend" Knuckle Duster

A 7-shot .22 .32, or .41 rimfire revolver. Constructed entirely of metal, without a barrel. Frame of silver-plated brass or blued iron. Marked My Friend Patd. Dec. 26, 1865". Grip is formed with a finger hole so that the pistol can be used as a set of brass knuckles.

Courtesy W.P. Hallstein III and son Chip

.22 Caliber "My Friend" Knuckle Duster - (Brass Frame)Brass Frame (Antique)

Exc.	Fine	V.G.	Good	Fair	Poor
2000	1600	1250	900	500	300

.22 Caliber "My Friend" Knuckle DusterIron Frame (Antique)

Exc.	Fine	V.G.	Good	Fair	Poor
3000	2000	1500	1000	500	350

.32 Caliber Knuckle Duster (Antique)

As above in .32-caliber. Approximately 3,400 manufactured between 1869 and 1884.

Brass Frame (Antique)

Exc.	Fine	V.G.	Good	Fair	Poor
2200	1750	1420	1100	500	350

Iron Frame (Antique)

Exc.	Fine	V.G.	Good	Fair	Poor
3000	2000	1600	1200	500	350

.41 Caliber Knuckle Duster (Antique)

As above in .41-caliber. Marked "J. Reid's Derringer". Approximately 300 manufactured between 1875 and 1878.

Exc.	Fine	V.G.	Good	Fair	Poor
15000	9000	7750	6500	2000	1400

Model No. 1 Knuckle Duster (Antique)

As above with 3" barrel. Approximately 350 made between 1875 and 1880.

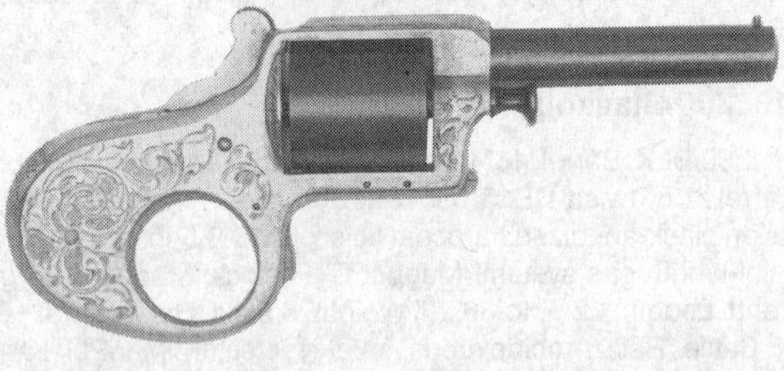

Courtesy W.P. Hallstein III and son Chip

Exc.	Fine	V.G.	Good	Fair	Poor
2750	1300	1070	850	250	170

Model No. 2 Knuckle Duster (Antique)

As above with 1.75" barrel. Approximately 150 made between 1875 and 1880.

Exc.	Fine	V.G.	Good	Fair	Poor
3000	1700	1470	1250	600	420

Model No. 3 Derringer (Antique)

A .41-caliber revolver, with 3" octagonal barrel and 5-shot fluted cylinder. Frame silver-plated. Blued barrel and cylinder. Approximately 75 made between 1880 and 1884.

Exc.	Fine	V.G.	Good	Fair	Poor
2500	1200	1100	1000	500	350

Model No. 4 Derringer (Antique)

As above, with brass frame and walnut grips. Marked "Reid's Extra". Approximately 200 made during 1883 and 1884.

Exc.	Fine	V.G.	Good	Fair	Poor
1500	1000	850	700	400	280

New Model Knuckle Duster (Antique)

Similar to Model 2, with 2" barrel and 5-shot cylinder. Barrel marked "Reid's New Model .32 My Friend". Approximately 150 made in 1884.

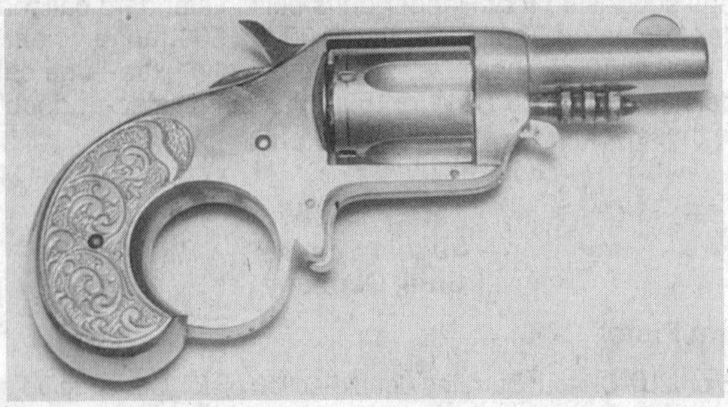

Exc.	Fine	V.G.	Good	Fair	Poor
1500	1050	850	650	400	280

REISING ARMS CO.
Hartford, Connecticut

Standard Model

A .22-caliber semi-automatic pistol, with hinged 6.5" barrel and 10-round magazine. Standard finish blued, however, nickel-plated versions are known. Slide marked with company's name and patent dates. Bakelite grips impressed with a bear's head and motto "Reising, It's A Bear". Manufactured in both New York City and Hartford during 1920s. CAUTION: High-velocity ammunition should not be used in these pistols.

Courtesy John J. Stimson, Jr.

New York Manufacture

NIB	Exc.	V.G.	Good	Fair	Poor
—	900	750	500	300	100

Hartford Manufacture

NIB	Exc.	V.G.	Good	Fair	Poor
—	450	350	280	180	100

REMINGTON ARMS COMPANY, INC.
Ilion, New York

Founded in 1816 by Eliphalet Remington. Company has distinction of being oldest firearms manufacturing firm in United States. Since 1856, it has been known by four different names: between 1856 and 1888, E. Remington & Sons; 1888-1910, Remington Arms Company; 1910-1925, Remington Arms U.M.C. Company (Union Metallic Cartridge Company); and 1925 to present, Remington Arms Company. In 2020, RemArms acquired the Remington Firearms legacy manufacturing facility in Ilion, NY, and now builds Remington firearms.

1st Model Remington-Beals Revolver (Antique)

A .31-caliber 5-shot percussion revolver, with 3" octagonal barrel. Cylinder turning mechanism mounted on left outside frame. Blued case-hardened, silver-plated, brass triggerguard and gutta-percha grips. Barrel marked, "F. Beal's Patent, June 24, '56 & May 26, '57"; frame "Remington's Ilion, N.Y.". Approximately 5,000 manufactured in 1857 and 1858.

Courtesy Milwaukee Public Museum, Milwaukee, Wisconsin

Exc.	Fine	V.G.	Good	Fair	Poor
2750	2000	1400	900	650	400

2nd Model Remington-Beals Revolver (Antique)

Spur trigger .31-caliber 5-shot percussion revolver, with 3" octagonal barrel. Blued case-hardened, with squared gutta-percha grip. Barrel marked "Beals Patent 1856 & 57, Manufactured by Remingtons Ilion, N.Y.". Approximately 1,000 manufactured between 1858 and 1860.

Exc.	Fine	V.G.	Good	Fair	Poor
5000	4000	3500	2500	1200	600

3rd Model Remington-Beals Revolver (Antique)

A .31-caliber 5-shot percussion revolver, with 4" octagonal barrel. Loading lever mounted beneath barrel. Blued case-hardened, with gutta-percha grips. Barrel marked "Beals Pat. 1856, 57, 58" and also "Manufactured by Remingtons, Ilion, N.Y.". Approximately 1,500 manufactured in 1859 and 1860.

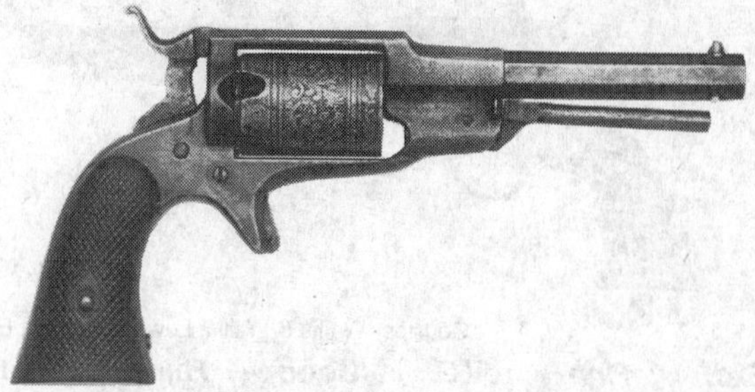

Courtesy Milwaukee Public Museum, Milwaukee, Wisconsin

Exc.	Fine	V.G.	Good	Fair	Poor
3500	2500	1750	1250	800	500

Remington-Rider Pocket Revolver (Antique)

Double-action .31-caliber percussion revolver, with 3" barrel and 5-shot cylinder. Most of these revolvers were blued but a few were nickel-plated case-hardened, with gutta-percha grips. This model also encountered altered to .32 rimfire. Barrel marked "Manufactured by Remingtons, Ilion, N.Y., Riders Pt. Aug. 17, 1858, May 3, 1859". Approximately 20,000 manufactured between 1860 and 1873. Note: Cartridge variation worth approximately 20 percent less than original percussion version.

Exc.	Fine	V.G.	Good	Fair	Poor
2000	1250	800	400	275	150

Remington-Beals Army Revolver (Antique)

A .44-caliber percussion revolver, with 8" barrel and 6-shot cylinder. Blued case-hardened, with walnut grips. Barrel marked "Beals Patent Sept. 14, 1858 Manufactured by Remington's Ilion, New York". Approximately 2,500 manufactured between 1860 and 1862. Note: Martially marked example extremely rare and would be worth approximately 35 percent additional. Add approx. 25% for U.S. military issue.

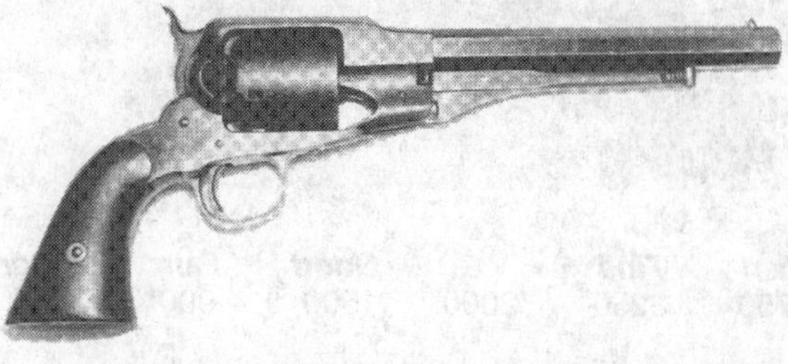

Exc.	Fine	V.G.	Good	Fair	Poor
6380	5420	5010	4610	3920	2740

Remington-Beals Navy Revolver (Antique)

Similar in appearance to Remington-Beals Army Revolver in .36-caliber, with 7.5" octagonal barrel. First examples of this model were fitted with a loading lever that would not allow cylinder pin to be completely removed. These examples are worth approximately 80 percent more than standard model. Approximately 1,000 of these revolvers were purchased by the United States government and martially marked examples are worth approximately 40 percent more than values listed below. Manufactured from 1860 to 1862. Total production of approximately 15,000. Add substantial premium for U.S. military issue.

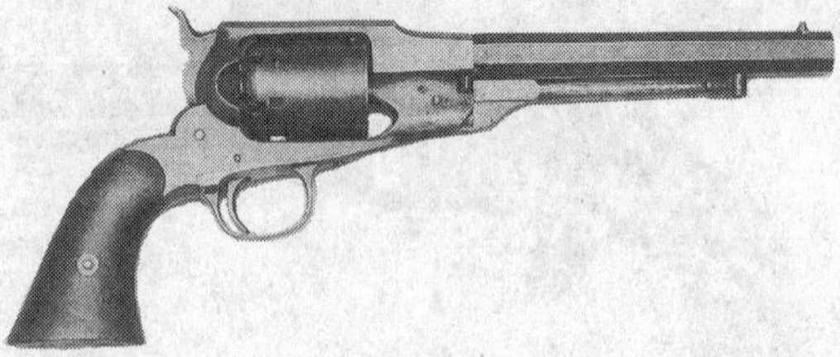

Courtesy Wallis & Wallis, Lewes, Sussex, England

Exc.	Fine	V.G.	Good	Fair	Poor
6000	4000	2250	1400	800	500

1861 Army Revolver (Antique)

A .44-caliber percussion revolver, with 8" octagonal barrel and 6-shot cylinder. Loading lever cut with a slot so that cylinder pin can be drawn forward without lever being lowered. Blued case-hardened, with walnut grips. Barrel marked "Patented Dec. 17, 1861 Manufactured by Remington's, Ilion, N.Y.". Some examples were converted to .46-caliber rimfire cartridge and would be worth approximately 25 percent more than original martially marked standard percussion model. Approximately 12,000 manufactured in 1862. This model also known as "Old Army Model".

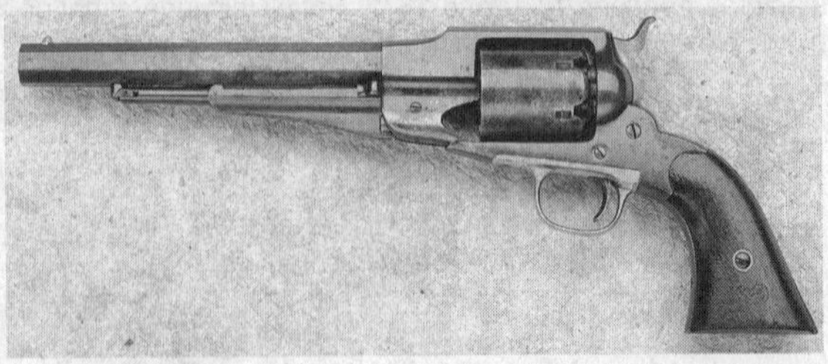

Paul Goodwin photo

Exc.	Fine	V.G.	Good	Fair	Poor
5000	3500	2500	1800	1000	600

1861 Navy Revolver (Antique)

As above in .36-caliber, with 7.25" octagonal barrel. Blued case-hardened, with walnut grips. Also found altered to .38 metallic cartridge. Cartridge examples are worth approximately 35 percent less than percussion versions. Approximately 8,000 manufactured in 1862. Note: Add 25 percent for martial.

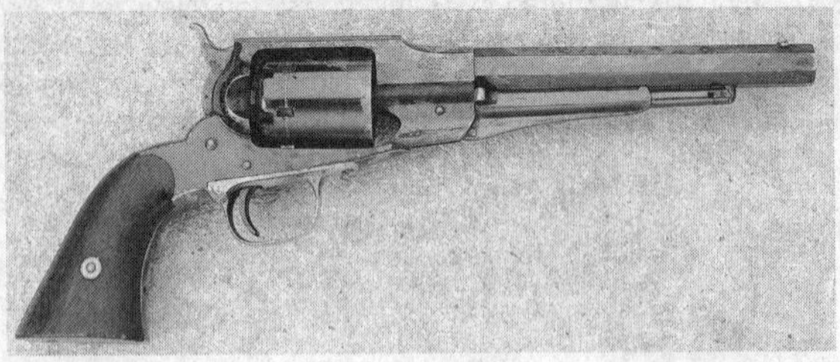

Paul Goodwin photo

Exc.	Fine	V.G.	Good	Fair	Poor
4750	3250	2000	1500	900	500

New Model Army Revolver (Antique)

"A .44-caliber 6-shot percussion revolver, with 8" octagonal barrel. Blued case-hardened, with walnut grips. Barrel marked "Patented Sept. 14, 1858 E. Remington & Sons, Ilion, New York, U.S.A. New Model". Approximately 132,000 made between 1863 and 1873."

Standard Model—Military Version (Antique)

Exc.	Fine	V.G.	Good	Fair	Poor
6500	3750	2000	1200	900	600

Civilian Model—No Government Inspector's Markings (Antique)

Exc.	Fine	V.G.	Good	Fair	Poor
4500	3250	2000	1100	800	500

.44 or .46 Cartridge Conversion (Antique)

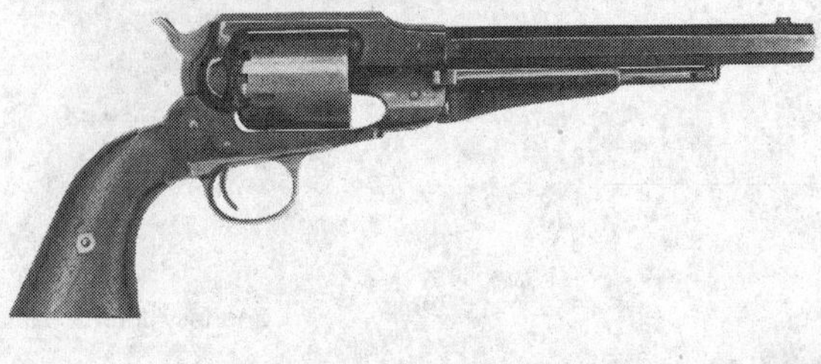

Courtesy Milwaukee Public Museum, Milwaukee, Wisconsin

Exc.	Fine	V.G.	Good	Fair	Poor
3500	2700	1500	1100	750	500

New Model Navy Revolver

As above in .36-caliber, with 7.23" octagonal barrel. Approximately 22,000 made between 1863 and 1875.

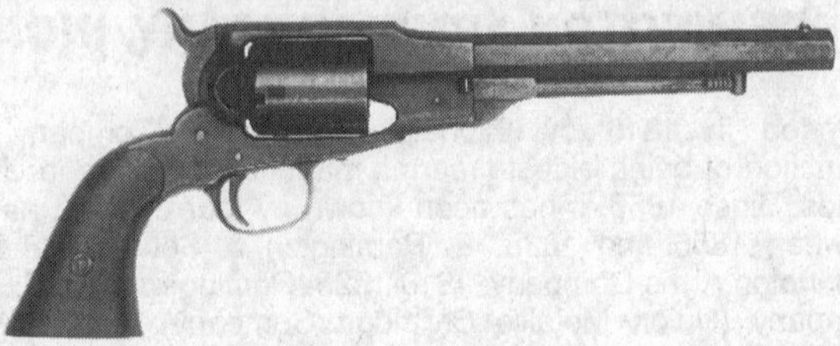

Courtesy Milwaukee Public Museum, Milwaukee, Wisconsin

Military Version (Antique)

Exc.	Fine	V.G.	Good	Fair	Poor
6000	4000	2500	1500	1000	650

Civilian Version (Antique)

Exc.	Fine	V.G.	Good	Fair	Poor
5500	3250	2100	1200	900	550

.38 Cartridge Conversion—1873 to 1888 (Antique)

Exc.	Fine	V.G.	Good	Fair	Poor
5000	3000	2000	1100	750	500

New Model Single-Action Belt Revolver (Antique)

As above with 6.5" barrel. Blued or nickel-plated case-hardened, with walnut grips. Sometimes encountered altered to .38 cartridge. Cartridge examples are worth approximately 25 percent less than values listed below. Approximately 3,000 made between 1863 and 1873. Note: Blued models will command a premium.

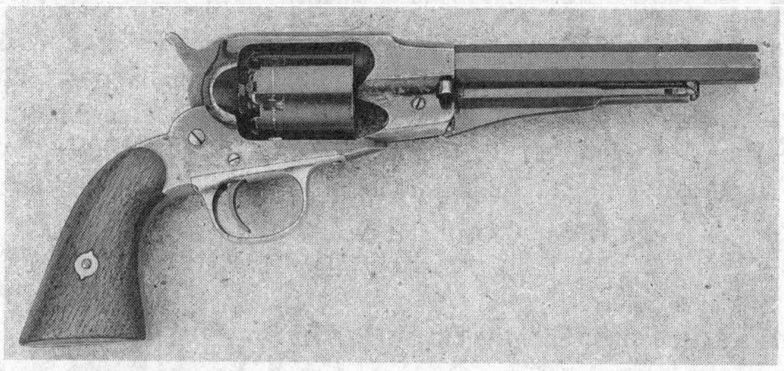

Paul Goodwin photo

Exc.	Fine	V.G.	Good	Fair	Poor
4200	2800	1900	1000	500	350

Remington-Rider Double-Action Belt Revolver (Antique)

Double-action .36-caliber percussion revolver, with 6.5" octagonal barrel marked "Manufactured by Remington's, Ilion, N.Y. Rider's Pt. Aug. 17, 1858, May 3, 1859". Blued or nickel-plated case-hardened, with walnut grips. Also found converted to cartridge and such examples would be worth approximately 20 percent less than values listed below. Several hundred of this model were made with fluted cylinders and are worth a premium of about 25 percent. Approximately 5,000 made between 1863 and 1873. Cased gun w/ accessories described as "finest known" reported sold by Rock Island Auction for T40,250 in 2018.

Courtesy Milwaukee Public Museum, Milwaukee, Wisconsin

Exc.	Fine	V.G.	Good	Fair	Poor
4000	3000	2000	1500	1000	500

New Model Police Revolver (Antique)

A .36-caliber percussion revolver, with octagonal barrels ranging from 3.5" to 6.5" and 5-shot cylinder. Blued or nickel-plated case-hardened, with walnut grips. Also found converted to cartridge and such examples would be worth approximately 20 percent less than values listed below. Approximately 18,000 manufactured between 1863 and 1873. Note: Blued models will command a premium.

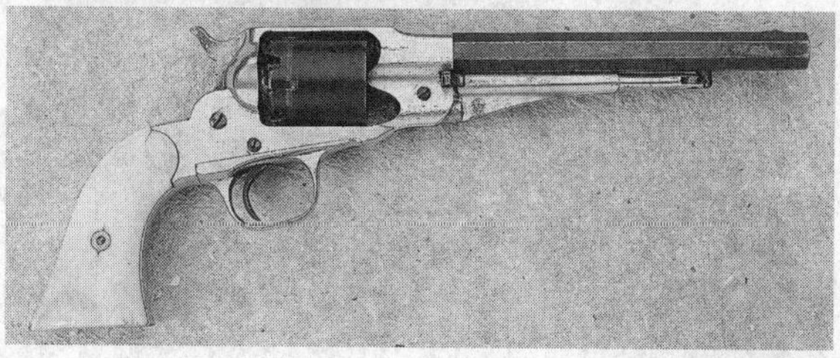

Paul Goodwin photo

Exc.	Fine	V.G.	Good	Fair	Poor
4000	2000	1200	1000	600	350

New Model Pocket Revolver

A .31-caliber spur trigger percussion revolver, with octagonal barrels ranging from 3" to 4.5" in length and 5-shot cylinder. Blued or nickel-plated case-hardened, with walnut grips. Barrel marked "Patented Sept. 14, 1858, March 17, 1863 E. Remington & Sons, Ilion, New York U.S.A. New Model.". Approximately 25,000 manufactured between 1863 and 1873. Note: Add 15 percent for blued models.

1st Version (Antique)

Brass frame and trigger.

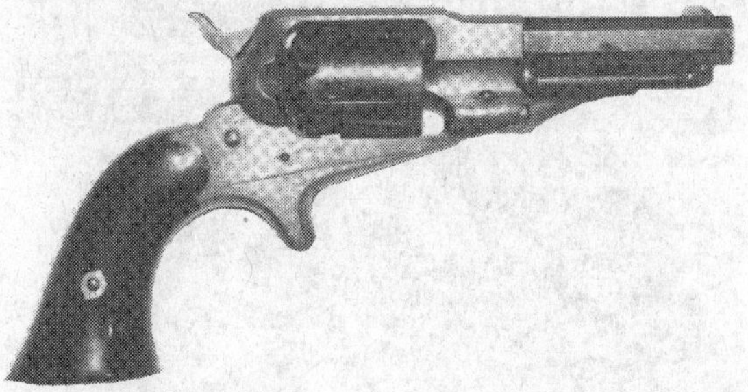

Exc.	Fine	V.G.	Good	Fair	Poor
3200	1800	1550	1300	300	210

2nd Version (Antique)

Iron frame, brass trigger.

Exc.	Fine	V.G.	Good	Fair	Poor
2500	1500	1200	1000	600	350

3rd Version (Antique)

Iron frame, iron trigger.

Exc.	Fine	V.G.	Good	Fair	Poor
2500	1500	1200	1000	600	350

.32 Cartridge Conversion (Antique)

Exc.	Fine	V.G.	Good	Fair	Poor
1500	850	500	350	250	150

Remington-Rider Derringer (Antique)

Small silver-plated brass single-shot .17-caliber percussion pistol, with 3" round barrel. Barrel marked "Rider's Pt. Sept. 13, 1859". Approximately 1,000 manufactured between 1860 and 1863. Beware of fakes. Rare. Values are speculative.

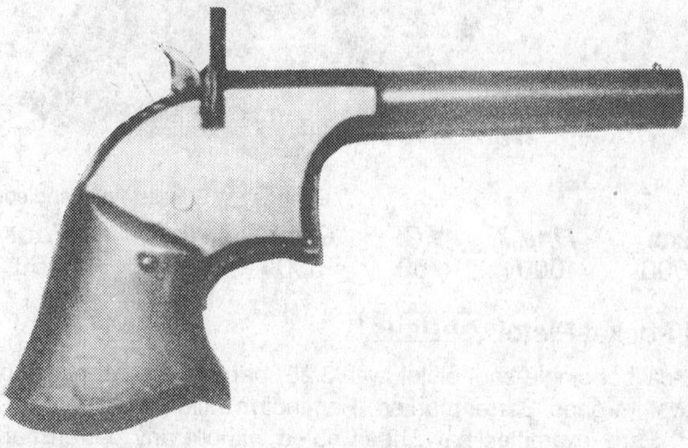

Exc.	Fine	V.G.	Good	Fair	Poor
12000	7500	5000	3000	1500	800

Zig-Zag Derringer (Antique)

A 6-shot .22-caliber revolving barrel pocket pistol, with barrels 3.25" in length. Barrels are cut with zigzag grooves, which are part of the revolving mechanism. Trigger formed as a ring that when moved forward and rearward turns the barrels and cocks the internal hammer. Barrel group marked "Elliot's Patent Aug. 17, 1858 May 29, 1860" as well as "Manufactured by Remington's Ilion, N.Y.". Approximately 1,000 manufactured in 1861 and 1862.

Paul Goodwin photo

Exc.	Fine	V.G.	Good	Fair	Poor
10000	7500	4500	2500	1100	600

Remington-Elliot Derringer Antique

A 5-shot .22-caliber or 4-shot .32-caliber pepperbox pistol, with a revolving firing pin. Blued or nickel-plated, with hard rubber grips. Barrel group marked "Manufactured by E. Remington & Sons, Ilion, N.Y. Elliot's Patents May 19, 1860 - Oct.1, 1861". Approximately 25,000 manufactured between 1863 and 1888.

5-shot .22 caliber Antique

Exc.	Fine	V.G.	Good	Fair	Poor
3600	1500	1000	750	350	150

4-shot .32 caliber Antique

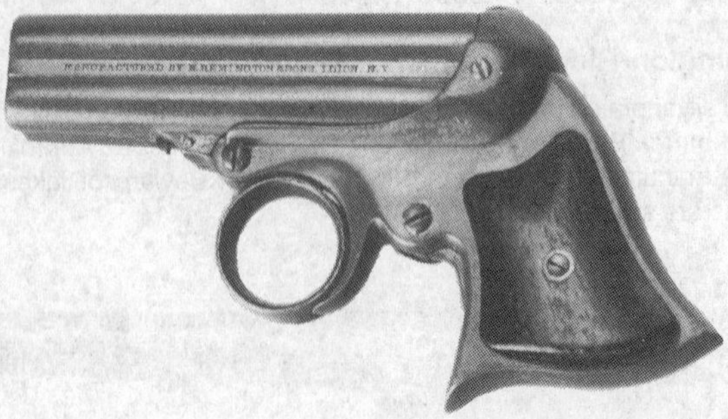

Courtesy W.P. Hallstein III and son Chip

Exc.	Fine	V.G.	Good	Fair	Poor
2000	1000	750	500	300	150

Vest Pocket Pistol Antique

A .22-caliber single-shot pistol, with 3.25" barrel. Blued or nickel-plated, with walnut grips. Barrel marked "Remington's Ilion, N.Y. Patent Oct. 1, 1861". Early examples have been noted without any barrel markings. Approximately 25,000 manufactured from 1865 to 1888. Note: Add 35 percent premium for blued models.

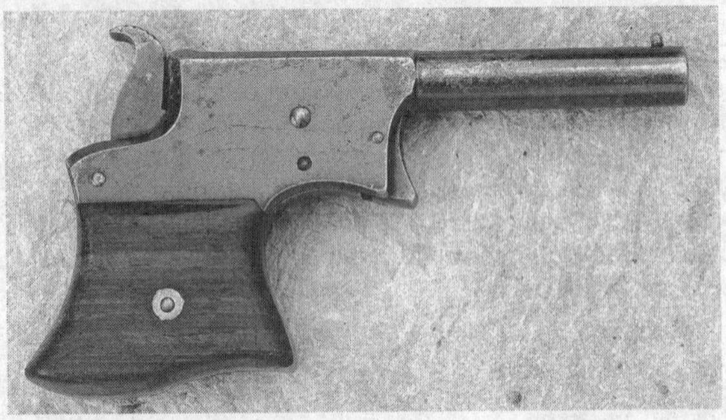

Paul Goodwin photo

Exc.	Fine	V.G.	Good	Fair	Poor
2000	1200	800	500	300	200

Large-Bore Vest Pocket Pistol Antique

As above in .30-, .32- or .41-caliber, with barrel lengths of 3.5" or 4". Blued or nickel-plated, with walnut or rosewood grips. Barrel markings as above, except for the addition of patent date, November 15, 1864. Smaller caliber versions are worth approximately 20 percent more than .41-caliber. Approximately 10,000 manufactured from 1865 to 1888. Note: Add 35 percent premium for blued models.

Exc.	Fine	V.G.	Good	Fair	Poor
3500	1250	700	450	300	175

Remington-Elliot Single-Shot Derringer Antique

A .41-caliber single-shot pistol, with 2.5" round barrel. Blued or nickel-plated, with walnut, ivory or pearl grips. Barrel marked "Remingtons, Ilion, N.Y. Elliot Pat. Aug. 27, 1867". Approximately 10,000 manufactured between 1867 and 1888. Note: Add 35 percent premium for blued models. For all variations of Remington Over/Under Derringer below, examine closely for broken or cracked barrel hinge and subtract from value accordingly.

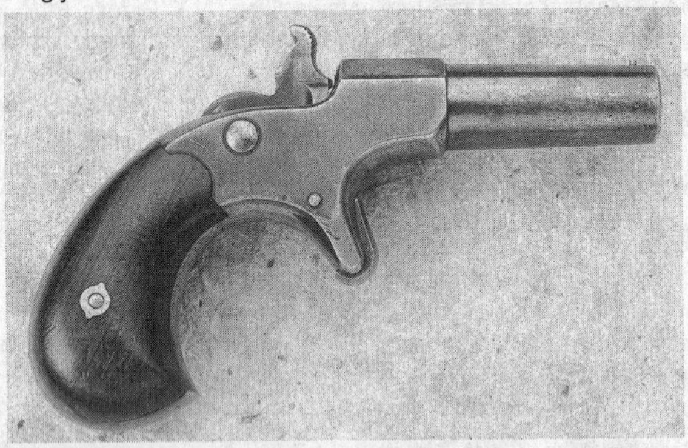

Exc.	Fine	V.G.	Good	Fair	Poor
2500	1200	800	400	120	80

REMINGTON OVER/UNDER DERRINGERS

Double-barrel .41-caliber pocket pistol, with 3" round barrels that pivot upward for loading. There is a lock bar to release barrels on the right side of frame. Firing pin raises and lowers automatically to fire each respective barrel. It has a spur trigger and bird's-head grip. Finish blued or nickel-plated and featured with walnut, rosewood or checkered hard rubber grips. Examples with factory pearl or ivory grips would be worth a small premium. Approximately 150,000 manufactured between 1866 and 1935.

Derringer Early Type I Antique

Manufactured without an extractor, this type marked "E.Remington & Sons, Ilion, N.Y." on one side and "Elliot's Patent Dec. 12, 1865" on other side of barrel rib. Only a few hundred manufactured in 1866. Note: Add 25 percent premium for blued models.

Exc.	Fine	V.G.	Good	Fair	Poor
8000	5000	4500	4000	3000	2100

Type I Mid-Production Antique

As above fitted with an extractor. Manufactured in late 1860s. Note: Add 25 percent premium for blued models.

Exc.	Fine	V.G.	Good	Fair	Poor
5000	4000	3250	2500	1200	840

Type I Late Production Antique

Fitted with an automatic extractor and marked on top of barrel rib. Manufactured from late 1860s to 1888. Note: Add 25 percent premium for blued models.

Exc.	Fine	V.G.	Good	Fair	Poor
3400	2200	1600	1000	200	140

Type II Antique

Marked "Remington Arms Co., Ilion, N.Y." on barrel rib. Manufactured between 1888 and 1911. Note: Add 25 percent premium for blued models.

Exc.	Fine	V.G.	Good	Fair	Poor
2750	1250	700	500	300	200

Type III

Marked "Remington Arms - U.M.C. Co., Ilion, N.Y." on barrel rib. Manufactured between 1912 and 1935. Note: Add 40 percent if there is no "L" in the serial number. For Type III models, blue or nickel prices are the same.

NIB	Exc.	V.G.	Good	Fair	Poor
2500	1500	1150	800	500	350

Remington-Rider Magazine Pistol Antique

A 5-shot .32-caliber magazine pistol, with spur trigger and 3" octagonal barrel. Magazine located beneath barrel and can be loaded from front. Blued nickel-plated or case-hardened, with walnut, pearl or ivory grips. Barrel marked "E.Remington & Sons, Ilion, N.Y. Riders Pat. Aug. 15, 1871". Approximately 10,000 manufactured between 1871 and 1888. Note: Add 50 percent premium for blued finish.

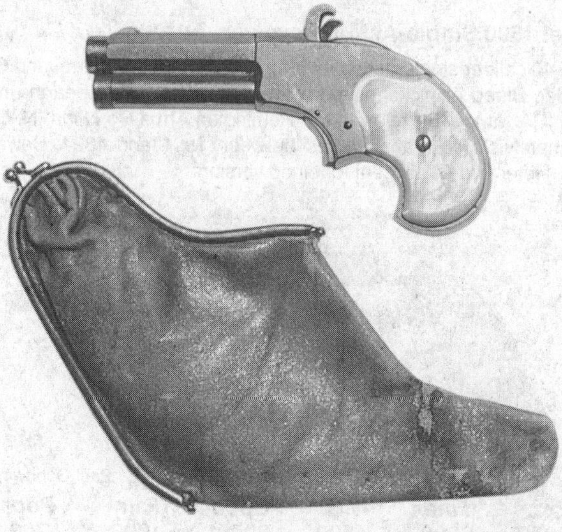

Courtesy William F. Krause

Exc.	Fine	V.G.	Good	Fair	Poor
1950	820	580	350	150	100

Cane Gun Antique

Single-shot firearm built into a walking stick/cane. Made in both .31 cal. percussion and .32 rimfire versions; .22RF rare and worth premium. In addition to plain handle, also offered with large or small dog's head handle, worth premium.

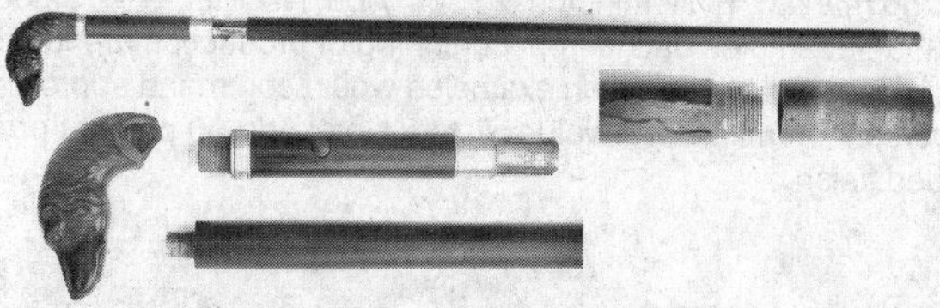

Jim Supica photo

Exc.	Fine	V.G.	Good	Fair	Poor
6000	4000	3250	2500	1000	700

Model 1865 Navy Rolling Block Pistol Antique

Spur trigger single-shot rolling block .50-caliber rimfire cartridge pistol, with 8.5" round barrel. Blued case-hardened, with walnut grips and forend. Barrel marked "Remingtons, Ilion N.Y. U.S.A. Pat. May 3d Nov. 15th, 1864 April 17th, 1866". Examples bearing military inspection marks are worth approximately 25 percent more than values listed below. Examples are also found altered to centerfire cartridge and these are worth approximately 10 percent less than values listed below. Approximately 6,500 manufactured between 1866 and 1870.

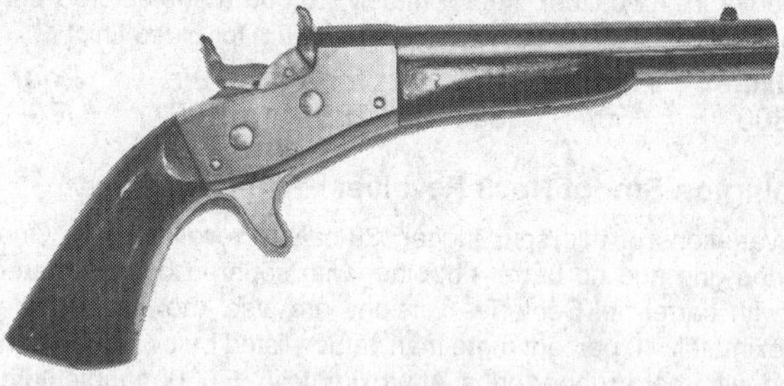

Exc.	Fine	V.G.	Good	Fair	Poor
6000	3500	2000	1000	650	400

Model 1867 Navy Rolling Block Pistol Antique

A .50-caliber single-shot rolling block pistol, with 7" round barrel. Blued case-hardened, with walnut grips and forend. Majority of these pistols were purchased by the United States government. Civilian examples without inspection marks are worth approximately 30 percent more than values listed.

Exc.	Fine	V.G.	Good	Fair	Poor
4500	3000	2000	1000	500	300

Model 1871 Army Rolling Block Pistol Antique

A .50-caliber rolling block single-shot pistol, with 8" round barrel. Blued case-hardened, with walnut grips and forend. Distinguishing feature is a rearward extension at top of the grip and a squared butt. Approximately 6,000 manufactured between 1872 and 1888. Engraved ivory-stocked versions, as pictured below, will bring considerable premiums.

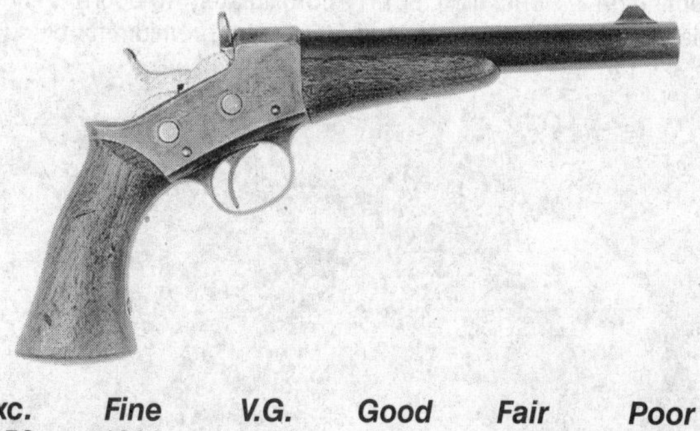

Exc.	Fine	V.G.	Good	Fair	Poor
2350	1800	1340	880	400	280

Remington-Smoot No. 1 Revolver Antique

A .30-caliber spur trigger revolver, with 2.75" octagonal barrel and 5-shot fluted cylinder. Blued or nickel-plated, with walnut or hard rubber grips.

Barrel rib marked "E. Remington & Sons, Ilion, N.Y. Pat. W. S. Smoot Oct. 21, 1873". Examples dating from beginning of production are found with a revolving recoil shield. Such examples would command approximately 300 percent premium over values listed. Note: Add 50 percent premium for blued finish.

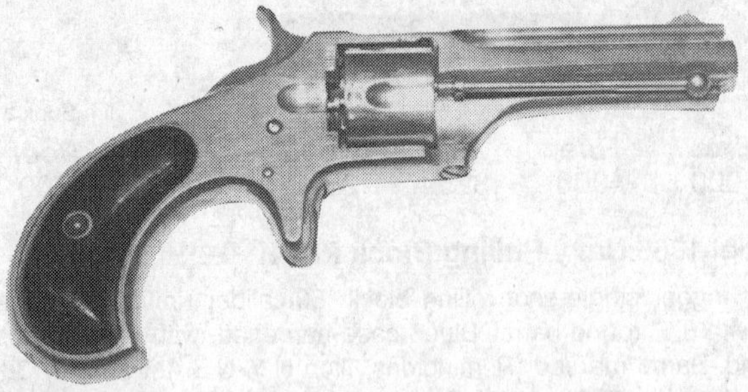

Exc.	Fine	V.G.	Good	Fair	Poor
1650	1100	890	680	250	170

Remington-Smoot No. 2 Revolver Antique

As above in .32-caliber. Approximately 20,000 manufactured between 1878 and 1888. Note: Add 50 percent premium for blued finish.

Exc.	Fine	V.G.	Good	Fair	Poor
800	450	350	280	100	70

Remington-Smoot No. 3 Revolver Antique

Two variations of this spur trigger .38-caliber revolver exist. One with rounded grip and no barrel rib; other with squared back, squared butt grip with barrel rib. Centerfire versions are also known and are worth approximately 10 percent more than values listed below. Blued or nickel-plated, with hard rubber grips. Approximately 25,000 manufactured between 1878 and 1888. Note: Add 50 percent premium for blued finish.

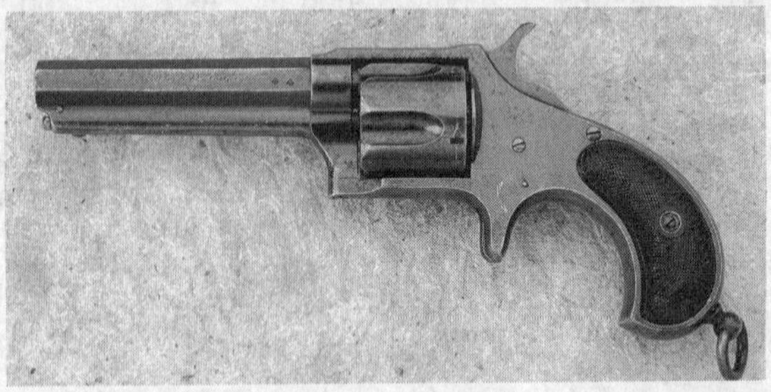

Paul Goodwin photo

Exc.	Fine	V.G.	Good	Fair	Poor
800	450	350	320	100	70

New No. 4 Revolver Antique

A .38- or .41-caliber spur trigger revolver, with 2.5" barrel and no ejector rod. Blued or nickel-plated, with hard rubber grips. Barrel marked "E. Remington & Sons, Ilion, N.Y.". Approximately 10,000 manufactured between 1877 and 1888. Note: Add 50 percent premium for blued finish.

Paul Goodwin photo

Exc.	Fine	V.G.	Good	Fair	Poor
780	480	350	220	100	70

Remington Iroquois Revolver Antique

A .22-caliber spur trigger revolver, with 2.25" barrel and 7-shot cylinder. Blued or nickel-plated, with hard rubber grips. Barrel marked "Remington, Ilion, N.Y." and "Iroquois". Some examples will be found without Remington markings. Approximately 10,000 manufactured between 1878 and 1888. Note: Add 50 percent premium for blued finish.

Exc.	Fine	V.G.	Good	Fair	Poor
1100	820	600	380	150	100

Model 1875 Single-Action Revolver Antique

A .44 Rem., .44-40 or .45-caliber single-action revolver, with 7.5" barrel. Blued or nickel-plated case-hardened, with walnut grips. Some examples found fitted with a lanyard ring at butt. Barrel marked "E. Remington & Sons Ilion, N.Y. U.S.A.". Approximately 25,000 manufactured between 1875 and 1889. Note: Add 40 percent for blued version.

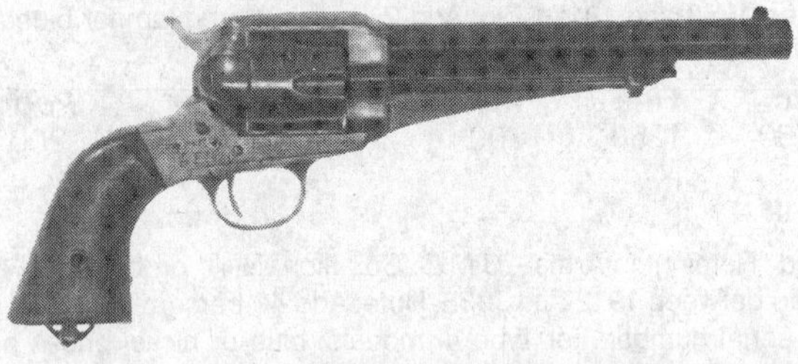

Courtesy Milwaukee Public Museum, Milwaukee, Wisconsin

Exc.	Fine	V.G.	Good	Fair	Poor
10000	6000	4500	3000	1000	700

Model 1888 Single-Action Revolver Antique

Transitional Model between 1875 and 1890 Models, .44-40 cal., 5.5" to 5.75" barrel, ejector housing similar to Model 1890 (no web). Model 1890s with cut barrels are sometimes passed off as Model 1888s, buyer beware. Premium for original blue finish.

Exc.	Fine	V.G.	Good	Fair	Poor
9000	5000	4000	2750	1000	650

Model 1890 Single-Action Revolver Antique

A .44-40 caliber single-action revolver, with 5.5" or 7.5" barrel and 6-shot cylinder. Blued or nickel-plated, with hard rubber grips bearing monogram "RA" at top. Barrel marked "Remington Arms Co., Ilion, N.Y.". Approximately 2,000 manufactured between 1891 and 1894. Beware of fakes. Note: Add 40 percent for blued version.

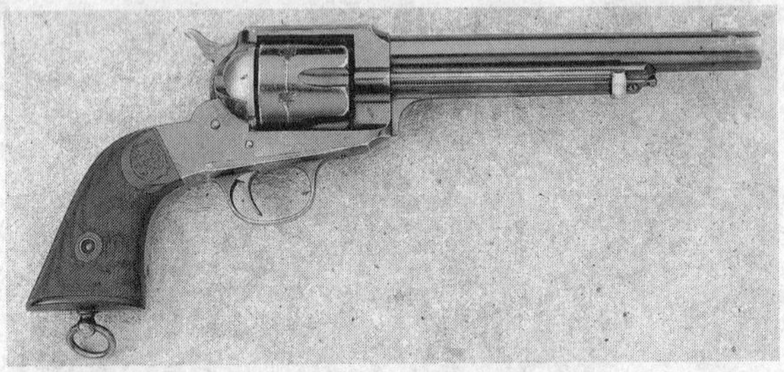

Paul Goodwin photo

Exc.	Fine	V.G.	Good	Fair	Poor
10000	6000	4500	3000	1000	700

Model 1891 Target Rolling Block Pistol Antique

A .22, .25 Stevens or .32 S&W caliber single-shot rolling block pistol, with 10" half octagonal barrel fitted with target sights. Blued case-hardened, with walnut grips and forend. Barrel marked "Remington Arms Co. Ilion, N.Y."; frame "Remingtons Ilion N.Y. U.S.A. Pat. May 3 Nov. 15, 1864 April 17, 1866 P S". An extremely rare pistol, with slightly more than 100 manufactured between 1892 and 1898. Prospective purchasers are advised to secure a qualified appraisal prior to acquisition.

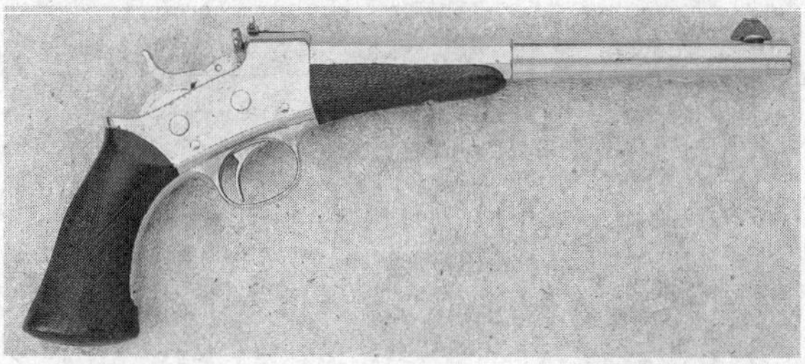

Paul Goodwin photo

Exc.	Fine	V.G.	Good	Fair	Poor
3700	2750	1000	650	500	350

Model 1901 Target Rolling Block

As above, except bridge block thumb piece has been moved out of the line of sight and rear sight mounted on frame instead of barrel. Approximately 735 manufactured between 1901 and 1909.

Paul Goodwin photo

NIB	Exc.	V.G.	Good	Fair	Poor
—	4000	3650	2750	1200	500

Mark III Signal Pistol

A 10-gauge spur trigger flare pistol, with 9" round barrel. Frame of brass and barrel of iron finished matte black, with walnut grips. Barrel marked "The Remington Arms - Union Metallic Cartridge Co., Inc. Mark III, Remington Bridgeport Works Bridgeport, Connecticut U.S.A.". Approximately 25,000 manufactured between 1915 and 1918.

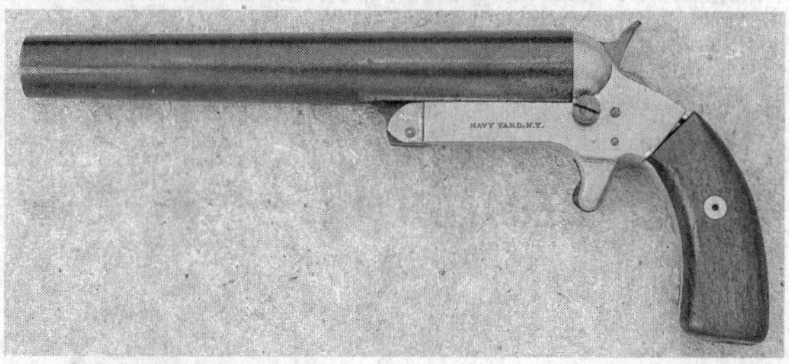

Paul Goodwin photo

NIB	Exc.	V.G.	Good	Fair	Poor
—	—	720	380	110	60

Model 51

A .32- or .380-caliber semi-automatic pistol, with 3.5" barrel. Magazines capable of holding 7 or 8 cartridges depending on caliber. Blued, with hard rubber grips having legend "Remington UMC" in a circle at top. Slide marked "The Remington Arms - Union Metallic Cartridge Co., Inc. Remington Ilion Wks. Ilion, N.Y. U.S.A. Pedersen's Patents Pending". Later versions carried a 1920 and 1921 patent date. Early examples have 9 grooves on slide; later models 15 grooves, with frame marked "Remington Trademark". Early variations are worth approximately 10 percent more than values listed below; .32-caliber examples are worth approximately 25 percent additional. Approximately 65,000 manufactured between 1918 and 1934.

Courtesy Orvel Reichert

NIB	Exc.	V.G.	Good	Fair	Poor
—	750	580	350	120	80

Model 53

Built in 1917 for U.S. government test in .45 ACP. Similar to Model 51, except for size and an external hammer. Tested by US Army and Navy. Overall length 8.25"; weight about 35 oz.; magazine capacity 7 rounds. Too rare to price.

Courtesy James Rankin

1911R1 SERIES

Model 1911R1

Combines traditional 1911 features with modern touches. Caliber .45 ACP. Carbon steel slide and frame, traditionally styled trigger, hammer, recoil system, walnut grips, 7-round magazine, thumb and grip safeties. Dovetailed front and rear sights, with white dots, lowered and flared ejection port. Weight 38.5 oz., 5" barrel and Satin Black Oxide or stainless finish. Model 1911 Enhanced has match-grade barrel and bushing, front cocking serrations, extended thumb safety and beavertail tang, textured grips, adjustable rear and fiber-optic front sights and lightweight trigger and hammer. Introduced 2010. Note: Add $50 for stainless finish. A Commander version available with 4.25" barrel.

NIB	Exc.	V.G.	Good	Fair	Poor
600	520	440	350	200	150

Model 1911R1 Centennial

Same features as 1911R1, with special Centennial engravings on slide, Centennial serial number range, dovetailed brass-bead front and black serrated rear sight. Custom grips with Remington medallions.

NIB	Exc.	V.G.	Good	Fair	Poor
1100	920	800	600	—	—

Model 1911R1 Centennial Limited Edition

Same features as above, plus uniquely engraved slide with gold banner, custom charcoal blued finish, 24-karat gold front sight, smooth exhibition grade walnut grips. Each Limited Edition model is hand assembled and comes in a custom wood presentation case. Introduced in 2011. Production scheduled for only 300 units.

NIB	Exc.	V.G.	Good	Fair	Poor
2000	1900	1800	—	—	—

Model 1911R1 200th Year Anniversary Commemorative

Full size 1911 in .45 ACP, with black oxide finish and Commemorative engraved walnut grips. Note: Add 100% for the Limited Edition model, with engraving and gold inlay, high polished slide and frame, and C-Grade walnut grips. Limited to 2,016 units in the year 2016.

NIB	Exc.	V.G.	Good	Fair	Poor
700	600	500	420	350	300

Model 1911R1 Double Stack

Standard 1911R1 features plus a double-stack high-capacity magazine. Offered in 9mm, .40 S&W, .45 ACP. Has adjustable match-grade trigger, adjustable rear and fiber optic front sights, ambidextrous safety, checkered front strap and mainspring housing. Introduced in 2017. MSRP $1,399.

NIB	Exc.	V.G.	Good	Fair	Poor
1250	1100	900	—	—	—

Model 1911R1 Recon

A Commander-size variant of Double Stack model with 4.5-inch barrel. Available in .45 ACP (15-round magazine) or 9mm (18). Features include accessory rail, PVD finish, front and rear tritium night sights, wide front and rear cocking serrations, and G10 grips. New in 2018.

NIB	Exc.	V.G.	Good	Fair	Poor
1080	950	850	650	—	—

Model 1911R1 Enhanced

Same features and dimensions as other 1911R1 models, with custom enhancements. In .45 ACP, with 8-round magazine. Adjustable rear sight and fiber optic front. Hardwood checkered grips. Front and rear slide serrations, with checkered mainspring housing. Aluminum anodized trigger. Match-grade barrel and bushing. Carbon steel frame and slide, with satin black oxide finish. Custom carrying case. Introduced 2012; stainless version 2013. Available in Commander version, with 4.25" barrel. Note: Add $150 for optional threaded barrel; $50 for stainless finish.

NIB	Exc.	V.G.	Good	Fair	Poor
880	780	680	550	400	350

Model 1911R1 Carry

Same general specifications as other 1911R1 models. Added features include: all sharp edges have been dehorned; Novak combat sights, with tritium front sight; Cocobolo checkered grips; Beavertail grip safety, with checkered memory bump; rear slide serrations, with checkered mainspring housing and front strap; aluminum anodized trigger; match-grade barrel and bushing; carbon steel frame and slide, with satin black oxide finish. Custom carrying case. 8+1 capacity. Introduced 2013. Available in Commander version, with 4.25" barrel.

NIB	Exc.	V.G.	Good	Fair	Poor
1000	900	800	500	450	350

Remington-UMC Commemorative 1911

Limited edition replica of Remington manufactured military 1911 made in 1918 and 1919. This edition limited to 4,000 units made in 2014.

NIB	Exc.	V.G.	Good	Fair	Poor
2400	2000	1600	—	—	—

Model 1911R1 Hunter

Chambered for 10mm. Features a 6" barrel, adjustable and skeletonizd trigger, extended beavertail grip safety and adjustable sights. Introduced in 2016.

NIB	Exc.	V.G.	Good	Fair	Poor
1180	1000	850	—	—	—

R1 Ultralight Executive

Compact model with 3.5-inch match-grade barrel, aluminum frame, rounded frame and mainspring housing, extended beavertail grip safety, front and rear titanium night sights, adjustable trigger, PVD slide finish. New in 2018.

NIB	Exc.	V.G.	Good	Fair	Poor
1050	900	800	600	—	—

Model R51

Sub-compact 9mm with double-action-only operation, 3.4" barrel, low-profile fixed sights, grip safety, ambidextrous magazine release and 7+1 capacity. Introduced in 2014. In July of 2014, Remington stopped production of R51 and announced a recall of the pistol due to reports of functioning problems. Anyone who purchased an early production R51 may return it to Remington and receive a new one, along with two additional magazines and a custom Pelican case. To find out if your R51 is subject to the recall, contact Remington at (800) 243-9700. You will be asked to provide your name, address, telephone number and serial number of your pistol. Production of R51 resumed in August of 2016, with what Remington describes as a perfected design. Among updated features are a fast re-set polymer trigger, a more aggressive extractor and an enhanced recoil spring. Note: Add $200 for Crimson Trace Laser.

NIB	Exc.	V.G.	Good	Fair	Poor
320	300	260	220	200	150

Model RP9/RP45

These striker-fired polymer frame pistols are similar to other popular models, except RP9 and RP45 have high-capacity magazines, 15 rounds .45 ACP, 18 for 9mm. Features include safety-in-trigger, 3-dot sights and interchangeable backstraps. Introduced in 2016.

NIB	Exc.	V.G.	Good	Fair	Poor
420	380	320	—	—	—

Model RM380

Mini-compact double-action only pistol chambered in .380 ACP with 6+1 capacity and 2.9" stainless steel barrel. Slide is all steel and frame aluminum. Overall length 5.27"; weight empty 12.2 oz.; height 3.86"; width .94". Other features include a fully functional slide stop and ambidextrous magazine release. Magazine release is located at the rear of the triggerguard. Introduced in 2015.

NIB	Exc.	V.G.	Good	Fair	Poor
380	340	300	280	—	—

RIFLES

Model 1841 "Mississippi Rifle" Antique

A .54-caliber percussion rifle, with 33 barrel. Full stock secured by two barrel bands. Lock case-hardened marked (Remington's Herkimer N.Y.). Barrel browned and furniture of brass. Stock fitted with brass patchbox on right side. Approximately 20,000 manufactured between 1846 and 1855.

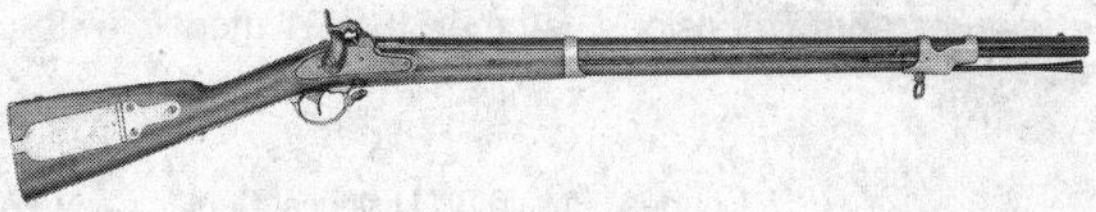

Paul Goodwin photo

Exc.	Fine	V.G.	Good	Fair	Poor
2200	1870	1730	1590	1350	940

Model 1861 U.S. Rifle Musket Antique

A .58-caliber percussion rifle, with 40" barrel. Full length stock secured by three barrel bands. Lock marked "Remington's Ilion, N.Y.". Finished in white, with walnut stock. Approximately 40,000 manufactured between 1864 and 1866.

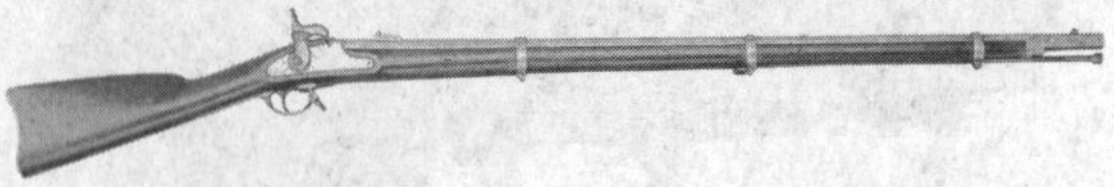

Paul Goodwin photo

Exc.	Fine	V.G.	Good	Fair	Poor
4250	3610	3340	3070	2610	1820

Model 1863 Zouave Rifle Antique

A .58-caliber percussion rifle, with 33" barrel. Full length stock secured by two barrel bands. Lock case-hardened marked "Remington's Ilion N.Y.". Barrel blued and furniture of brass. Approximately 12,500 manufactured between 1862 and 1865.

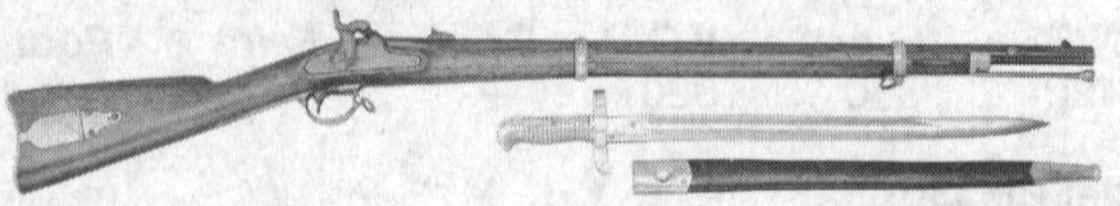

Paul Goodwin photo

Exc.	Fine	V.G.	Good	Fair	Poor
5000	3000	2000	1200	700	500

Breech-Loading Carbine Antique

A .46 or .50 rimfire single-shot rolling block carbine, with 20" barrel. Blued case-hardened, with walnut stock. Tang marked "Remington's Ilion, N.Y. Pat. Dec. 23, 1863 May 3 & Nov. 16, 1864". The .50-caliber version worth approximately 15 percent more than .46-caliber. Approximately 15,000 .50-caliber variations were made, most of which were sold to France. Approximately 5,000 carbines were made in .46-caliber. Manufactured from 1864 to 1866.

Paul Goodwin photo

Exc.	Fine	V.G.	Good	Fair	Poor
3750	3000	2500	1500	750	350

Revolving Rifle Antique

A .36- or. 44-caliber revolving rifle, with 24" or 28" octagonal barrels and 6-shot cylinder. Triggerguard formed with scrolled finger extension at rear. Blued case-hardened, with walnut stock. These rifles are also encountered converted to cartridge and would be worth approximately 20% less than percussion values listed below. Barrel marked "Patented Sept. 14, 1858 E. Remington & Sons, Ilion, New York, U.S.A. New Model". The .44-caliber model will bring a premium of about 15 percent and is rare. Approximately 1,000 manufactured between 1866 and 1879.

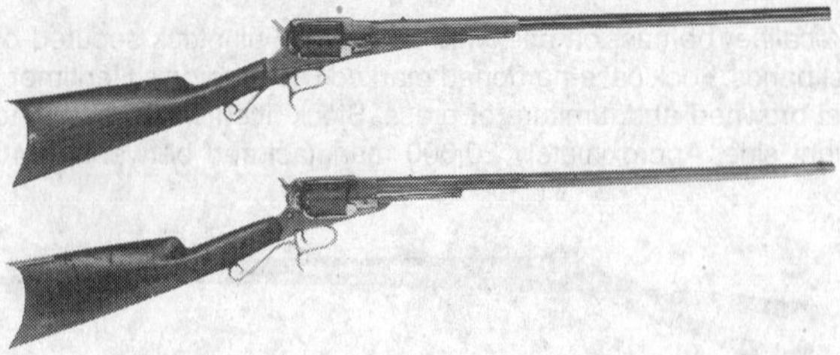

Courtesy Buffalo Bill Historical Center, Cody, Wyoming

Exc.	Fine	V.G.	Good	Fair	Poor
11500	8000	6750	5500	900	630

Remington-Beals Rifle Antique

A .32- or .38-caliber sliding barrel single-shot rifle, with octagonal barrels of 24", 26" or 28" length. Barrel can be moved forward by lowering triggerguard/lever. This model found with frames made of brass or iron, the latter being worth approximately 20 percent more than values listed below. Walnut stock. Barrel marked "Beals Patent June 28, 1864 Jan. 30, 1866 E. Remington & Sons, Ilion, New York.". Approximately 800 manufactured between 1866 and 1888. Few examples are known to have been factory engraved. Prospective purchasers are advised to secure a qualified appraisal prior to acquisition.

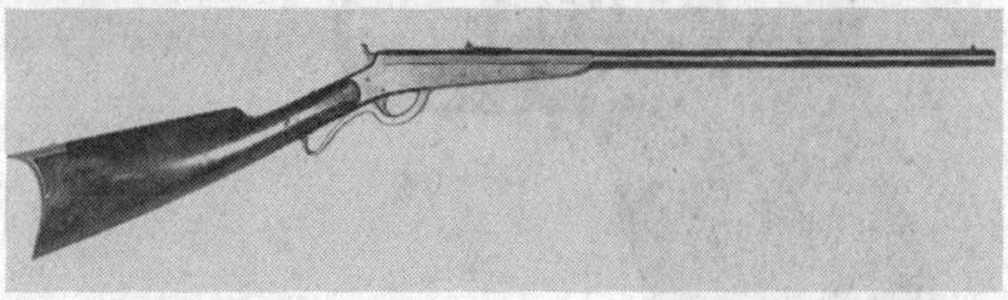

Courtesy Milwaukee Public Museum, Milwaukee, Wisconsin

Exc.	Fine	V.G.	Good	Fair	Poor
3000	1500	850	500	300	175

U.S. Navy Rolling Block Carbine Antique

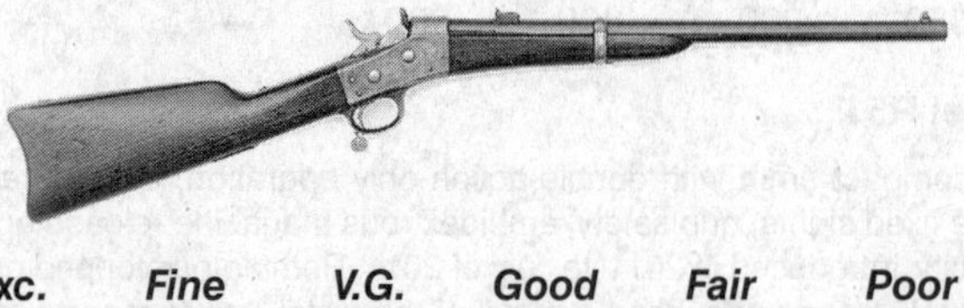

Exc.	Fine	V.G.	Good	Fair	Poor
4000	2750	1870	1000	350	240

Model 1867 Navy Cadet Rifle Antique

Paul Goodwin photo

Exc.	Fine	V.G.	Good	Fair	Poor
3500	1400	1050	700	350	240

Rolling Block Military Rifles Antique

Exc.	Fine	V.G.	Good	Fair	Poor
900	750	570	400	100	70

FOREIGN CONTRACT ROLLING BLOCK MILITARY RIFLES

Antique

Consolidated and contributed by George Layman.

Remington Danish Model 1867

This was the first quantity contract sold overseas by Remington in 1867. Denmark ordered 42,000 rifles and 1,800 carbines in 11mm Danish Remington rimfire cartridge. Two-line address on tang started with REMINGTON'S and April 17, 1866 patent. Barrel 36", with long saber bayonet lug and three barrel bands spring retained. Produced under license in Denmark, original Remington-made version is not commonly encountered. Tang markings of Kjobenhavn Tojhuis and year indicate a Danish copy which is very common in the United States. Prices below reflect the original Remington product.

Rifle Antique

Exc.	Fine	V.G.	Good	Fair	Poor
880	650	570	500	350	240

Carbine Antique

Exc.	Fine	V.G.	Good	Fair	Poor
1150	880	760	650	400	280

Remington Swedish Contract Model Antique

In 1868, Sweden procured 10,000 complete Remington rifles and 20,000 actions. They immediately began production under license from Remington. It is often difficult to determine an original Remington made variant due to many examples having half-Swedish half-Remington components. Most of the original 10,000 Remington rifles had serialized barrels. Actions on this contract had serial numbers as well and date of 1868. Sweden manufactured dozens of domestic variants based on Remington action produced by Husqvarna, Carl Gustaf and other makers. Original Remington product had a 35" barrel, short saber bayonet lug and two-line tang address similar to Danish version. Caliber is 12.11mm Swedish Remington rimfire. Prices below indicate Remington-made rifle.

Exc.	*Fine*	*V.G.*	*Good*	*Fair*	*Poor*
1000	780	640	500	400	280

Remington Egyptian Model

One of the largest contracts received by Remington was from Egypt. Only hard copy evidence is first contract of 30,000 rifles signed in London on 30 June, 1869, as the others were likely destroyed by a fire at Remington factory in 1939. It is estimated almost a quarter of a million were sold up to 1878-82. 149,000 were purchased by France in the war of 1870-71. Thousands have been imported to U.S. since the 1960s. Most are well worn from desert exposure and show extreme wear and replaced parts. A whole host of different Arabic markings may be encountered. Egypt also purchased carbines and musketoons in mid to late 1870s as well, but their numbers are unknown, however, condition of most are similar to the aforementioned. Those Egyptian rifles sold to France are the only specimens that occasionally surface in any appreciable condition. Leftover Egyptian models were catalogued by Remington up to 1882 and were sometimes advertised as French Model.

Rifle Antique

Exc.	*Fine*	*V.G.*	*Good*	*Fair*	*Poor*
800	450	370	300	280	190

Carbine Antique

Exc.	*Fine*	*V.G.*	*Good*	*Fair*	*Poor*
980	650	550	450	380	260

Musketoon Antique

Exc.	*Fine*	*V.G.*	*Good*	*Fair*	*Poor*
1000	850	710	580	400	280

Remington Spanish Model Antique

Advertised commercially from 1875 through 1902, this .43 Spanish caliber Remington Rolling Block accounts for largest number of production, with something over 1.5 million sold from 1869 to 1910. A tremendous amount of variation exists here, with differences as indicated below. Original Spanish Contract Model. Spain purchased over 90,000 rifles in three contracts from 1869 to 1873. Early slot extractor, three-band rifle with no provision for saber bayonet lug, leaf adjustable rear sight, spring held barrel bands. All have REMINGTON ILION, NY address and are found with various locally applied Spanish government and Cuban garrison markings. Those having 75 percent case colors or more will reap the higher price accordingly. First-year contract version with its concave breech-block is scarce and will reap a 50 percent premium depending on condition. Those Remington Spanish Model rifles of the Third and final contract were overproduced by several thousand more than Spain had originally ordered for the 1873 contract. In reality, Spain cancelled the receipt of close to 5,500 .43 Spanish-caliber rifles remaining in the contract, as the in-country licensed production had caught up with demand. Among the known purchasers of the surplus Spanish Model rifles was Meiji Era Japan, which since 1868 had made at least three sizeable orders of the surplus Remington rolling block rifles of the 1868 Swedish contract. In 1873, Japan ordered close to 2,400 of the Spanish Model rifles but demanded they be reamed and re-chambered to its in-country Remington caliber of 12.11mm Swedish Remington centerfire. In 1881, about 978 rifles were sold to the Kingdom of Korea with the remainder sold as surplus to Hong Kong in 1885. These are very scarce variations and practically all are stamped with the Japanese Kanji characters of "Surplus/Disposed Rifle" with a Japanese/Chinese character numeration on the right side of the chamber. They are otherwise identical to the original second and third Spanish contract rifles, aside from the 12.11mm chambering. Few of these have survived and no more than three have been viewed by the author, but it is certain there are more in circulation. Many may well have been re-chambered during the 1960s re-barreling craze of surplus rolling block rifles and carbines. Prices for these three-band rifles are basically high in any condition.

Exc.	*Fine*	*V.G.*	*Good*	*Fair*	*Poor*
700	580	480	380	200	140

Japanese Contract Model Rolling Block Antique

Values are speculative.

Exc.	*Fine*	*V.G.*	*Good*	*Fair*	*Poor*
1800	1400	1250	1100	950	660

Post 1874 Catalogued Generic Spanish Model Antique

Equipped with the improved rotary extractor, this configuration accounts for a majority of sales for the next 36 years. Screw retained barrel bands, tang markings prior to 1887 have E. REMINGTON & SONS with 1874 as the final patent year. All have 35.5" barrels, except where indicated. From 1888 until the end of production, REMINGTON ARMS COMPANY marked on tang which reflects the reorganization of the company. Realistically speaking, any Remington Rolling Block rifle whether re-chambered or modified from other versions that were sold by the company or its agents Schuyler, Hartley & Graham, (which would by 1900 become M. Hartley and Company) in .43 Spanish caliber was listed as "Spanish Model". Listed are the four sub-categories in addition to cataloged generic variants manufactured after 1874 and priced accordingly. Note: Standard Generic Spanish Model (add 20% if Long or Short combination bayonet lug is present).

Exc.	*Fine*	*V.G.*	*Good*	*Fair*	*Poor*
700	400	370	350	200	140

Argentine Model of 1879 Antique

One of the most unusual and very well built special order export versions of Spanish Model was this .43 Spanish caliber Rolling Block of which Remington produced an estimated 50,000 rifles and carbines. Its Knox-form chamber is stamped Model Argentino 1879 E.N. on top flat, and equipped with an Austrian Werndl type rear sight, three screw retained barrel bands and long saber bayonet lug. It is, however, the most commonly encountered of all Remington Rolling Block rifles in .43 Spanish caliber, as the Argentine government sold well over 25,000 to US surplus importers between 1959 and 1962. Ninety percent or more of both rifles and carbines were re-blued and refinished by the host country to a practically like new condition, complete with cosmoline. Inexperienced buyers should be cautious as some dealers in the past have offered these as in "arsenal fresh new condition". Those in original condition with both un-refinished metal and wood bring significantly higher prices as they are not common. Any Argentine Model without the stamping over the chamber, and having a short saber bayonet lug is one of 2,500 ultra-rare Honduran contract rifles, which were nothing more than modified surplus Argentine variants. These are difficult to price, but normally reap a far higher tag than the standard 1879 Argentine model. The prices below reflect the common refinished variation. Note: Add 100% for those Model 1879 Argentine rifles and carbines showing 80 to 100 percent case colors and all original raised grain wood and deep blue finish.

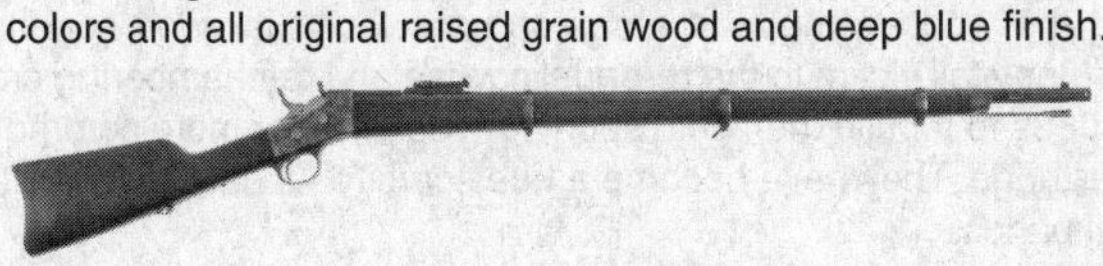

Exc.	*Fine*	*V.G.*	*Good*	*Fair*	*Poor*
580	450	410	380	250	170

Greek Contract Transformed Spanish Model (Antique)

This variation is part of 9,000 to 13,000 surplus Greek 1869 Contract Models that were diverted from Greece and sold to France during Franco-Prussian War of 1870-71. Remington pressured Greece into canceling their contract to reap a higher price from the French. The original caliber of Greek Model was .42 Russian Berdan, which is practically identical to .43 Spanish, aside from the larger diameter neck and bullet of the latter. Sold later as surplus by the French to American military arms dealers such as Schuyler, Hartley and Graham. Practically all had their chambers throated out to accept larger .43 Spanish bullet diameter and sold as "Spanish Model" rifles or "Greek Rifles Bushed for Spanish Cartridge" to Central and South American countries. All have spring retained three-band long saber bayonet lug. Furthermore, aside from REMINGTON'S marking on the tang, all have a crown on the left frame, chamber flat, and on each barrel band. Some may be identified by a Circle G on left butt stock. Those that were not modified to .43 Spanish and remain in original .42 Russian Berdan caliber, will bring a premium of 75%. This may be determined by attempting to chamber a .43 Spanish cartridge of which .125" will protrude if in the original caliber. This variant of the Spanish Model is not common.

Exc.	*Fine*	*V.G.*	*Good*	*Fair*	*Poor*
700	480	410	350	300	210

Egyptian Transformed Spanish Model (Antique)

This version of Spanish Model was modified from existing stocks of surplus over-runs of Remington .43 Egyptian caliber rifle. Between 1878 and 1882, Remington had no customers for left-over Egyptian contract rifles. They had their agents convert these to .43 Spanish by shortening barrels to 33.875" and reaming chambers to accept smaller dimensions of Spanish cartridge. Most are encountered in well used condition, however, they are easily identified. Aside from shorter barrel length, rear sight is 1" from forward edge of receiver and most have a short combination saber bayonet lug. Also, a small "H" cartouche is found on left receiver, as well as on the flat of the bayonet lug, which indicates Hartley the primary contractor who had the conversions completed. Practically all of these rifles have three-screw retained barrel bands. Those which have two barrel bands and an even shorter 29.125" barrel are rare and 40% should be added to below listed prices.

Exc.	*Fine*	*V.G.*	*Good*	*Fair*	*Poor*
600	420	360	300	250	170

Guatemalan Marked Spanish Model (Antique)

Guatemala was a prolific customer of Remington's Rolling Block since 1870. However, late REMINGTON ARMS CO. tang-dated versions are the only known Spanish Models having EJERCITO DE GUATEMALA (Army of Guatemala) stamped over the chamber between the receiver and rear sight. Nearly all these rifles display heavy usage and pitting along the wood-to-metal fit areas and are found in good condition at best. Many fell victim to the re-barreling vise and re-chambering craze in the 1960s to rebuild them into sporting-type rifles for more common .45-70 cartridge. They have become a true scarcity. All have screw-retained barrel bands.

Exc.	*Fine*	*V.G.*	*Good*	*Fair*	*Poor*
980	700	600	500	380	260

Remington Civil Guard Model (Antique)

Named after the Spanish Civil Guard, but never been proven to be issued to them. Essentially a Spanish Model rifle, with two bands and 30.5" barrel, all chambered for .43 Spanish cartridge. Many were sold to Cuban volunteer regiments serving Spain, with most found thus far with a number stamped on the wood at the front tang of the buttplate. Numbers appear limited and were advertised in factory catalogs dated as late as 1882. Ironically, records show Argentina procured a small number of them. Rare.

Exc.	*Fine*	*V.G.*	*Good*	*Fair*	*Poor*
1200	850	720	600	380	260

Spanish Model Carbine (Antique)

These saddle ring carbines remained part of the lineup until 1902, with most having a 20.5" barrel. Argentine variants are marked identically, having Knoxform chamber as well. Some factory carbines have both saddle ring and sling swivels. An especially rare factory carbine is those with a full-length, two-band forearm (150% should be added to their prices). Single carbine barrel band with two-position 100-, 300- and 500-yard sight. Locally applied markings such as a Crown over RV (Regiment of Volunteers) on Spanish/Cuban versions will add 10% to 20%, depending on the condition. Noteworthy is that RV-marked Cuban carbines are usually re-chambered to the improved .43 Reformado cartridge, which is interchangeable with the Spanish Remington cartridge.

Exc.	*Fine*	*V.G.*	*Good*	*Fair*	*Poor*
750	500	460	420	380	260

Remington Springfield Transformed Model (Antique)

Offered as late as 1882, this .58-caliber Berdan centerfire was one of the early ventures of Rolling Block. Remington action was fitted to surplus .58-caliber muzzleloading Springfield parts that were transformed into a breechloader. Though an obsolete, low-powered, short-range number, it still remained popular. However, it is believed Remington had large numbers on hand and kept them in the catalog hoping certain customers would eventually buy them out. There were two models: Short Transformed, with 36" barrel and two spring-held barrel bands; Long Transformed, with three barrel bands and 39" barrel. The former is the scarcer of the two and 30% should be added to the below-listed prices for the Long Transformed variant. The Dominican Republic was one of the last recorded customers purchasing a quantity as late as 1888. Both versions are scarce.

Exc.	*Fine*	*V.G.*	*Good*	*Fair*	*Poor*
1200	750	650	550	380	260

New York State Militia (Antique)

Rolling block in .50-70 caliber. High hammer spur, and breechblock lever sticks out to the right side instead of vertically. Rifle has 36-in. barrel with three barrel bands. Saddle ring carbine has a 22-in. barrel. In 1872 about 15,000 were made for the New York National Guard. May be found with inspector H.B.H. and US N.Y. markings. Carbines will bring about a 20% premium.

Model 1897/1902

First advertised in late 1896. First April, 1897 catalog listed Remington's new Smokeless Powder Small Bore Military Rifle as Model 1896 until end of the year when it became Model 1897. Major difference being M 1896 had a 1x.25" sight base which used a pinned sight blade. Model 1897 was modified to use a more practical .25x.25" barleycorn type front sight. Model 1896 was offered in 7mm Spanish Mauser, 7.65mm

Mauser, .30/40 Krag, 6mm (.236 Remington) and 7.62/.30 Remington. Model 1896 is not commonly encountered, however, an example in either latter two calibers will increase prices with a 90% premium as both are very rare calibers. Later Model 1897 was not catalogued in these two scarce chamberings. When in excellent to very good condition, add 25 percent premium for M1896 in any caliber. Following October 22, 1901 improved rotary automatic extractor patent, Model 1897 dispensed with earlier side slot extractor. Introduced in early 1902, improved Model 1897 unofficially became known as Model 1902 given its first year of production, with updated automatic extractor. At the end of 1900s, so-called M1902 was equipped with a banded front sight and a more cost effective ramp type rear sight and leaf. In modern times, such an addition became known as Model 1910 for collector convenience, but again was not an official Remington Arms Company term. By this time calibers were limited to 7mm Mauser and .30/40 Krag chambering. Over 98,000 7mm Remington Model 1897/02/10 rifles were produced until 1918. These later versions may often be found in practically new, unissued condition with bright case colors. Several thousand were unsold until 1921, when most were transferred to warehouses of Remington agents and wholesalers to be sold at almost fire sale prices. Note: Add 20% premium for .30/40 Krag caliber example.

NIB	Exc.	V.G.	Good	Fair	Poor
—	2000	900	650	450	380

French Contract Model of 1914

France practically put Rolling Block tooling into full production following 1914-15 World War One French Contract. These rifles were essentially so called M1910, however, all are chambered in 8mm Lebel French service cartridge. Ironically with 100,291 produced, they have highest production record of Remington Military Rolling Block of smokeless powder era. Not a common item due to their post war distribution to numerous French colonial areas as Indo-China etc. They may be found in every condition from near excellent to poor, however, they are one of the most sought after given their First World War connection. Stocks usually have unit markings and individual serial numbers

NIB	Exc.	V.G.	Good	Fair	Poor
—	2400	1300	800	650	400

NO. 1 ROLLING BLOCK SPORTING RIFLE

Standard No. 1 Sporting Rifle (Antique)

Single-shot rolling block rifle. Produced in a variety of calibers from .40-50 to .50-70 centerfire, as well as .32, .44 and .46 rimfire. Standard octagonal barrel lengths were 28" or 30".

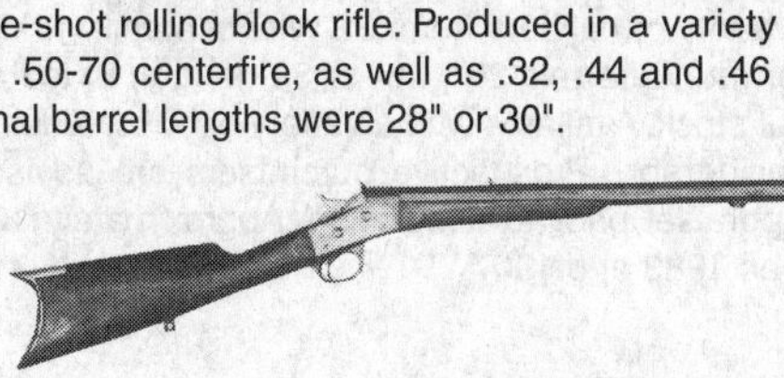

Courtesy Milwaukee Public Museum, Milwaukee, Wisconsin

Exc.	Fine	V.G.	Good	Fair	Poor
5000	2500	2000	1500	500	350

Long-Range Creedmoor Rifle (Antique)

A .44-90, .44-100 or .44-105 caliber rolling block rifle, with 34" half-octagonal barrel, long-range vernier tang sights and globe front. Blued case-hardened, with walnut stock and checkered pistol grip. Rifle was available with a number of optional features. A qualified appraisal should be secured if those features are in doubt. Produced from 1873 to 1890.

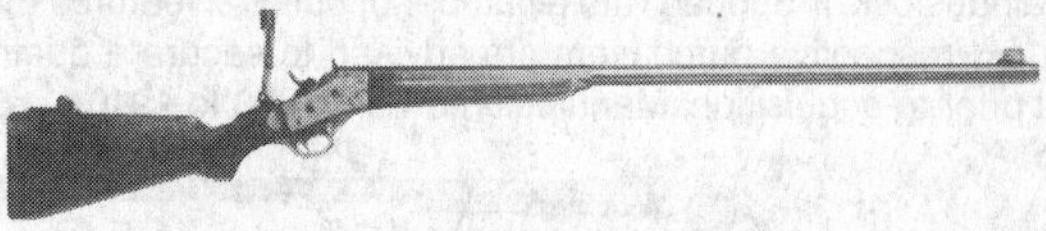

Courtesy Bonhams & Butterfields, San Francisco, California

Exc.	Fine	V.G.	Good	Fair	Poor
10000	7000	3000	2000	1500	800

Mid-Range Target Rifle (Antique)

As above, except chambered for .40-70, .44-77, .45-70 or .50-70 caliber, with 28" or 30" half-octagonal barrels. Produced from 1875 to 1890.

Exc.	Fine	V.G.	Good	Fair	Poor
6000	2750	2250	1750	950	500

Short-Range Rifle (Antique)

As above, chambered for cartridges between .38- and .44-caliber, with 26" or 30" round or octagonal barrels. Open rear sight, with Beach front sight. Walnut stock is checkered. Produced from 1875 to 1890.

Exc.	Fine	V.G.	Good	Fair	Poor
5000	2750	2210	1680	250	170

Black Hills Rifle (Antique)

As above in .45-60 caliber, with 28" round barrel. Fitted with open sights and plain straight-grip stock. Produced from 1877 to 1882.

Exc.	Fine	V.G.	Good	Fair	Poor
5000	2750	2210	1680	250	170

No.1 Rolling Block Shotgun (Antique)

As above in 16-gauge, with 30" or 32" Damascus or fluid steel barrels. Produced from 1870 to 1892.

Exc.	Fine	V.G.	Good	Fair	Poor
1650	1200	970	750	150	100

Baby Carbine (Antique)

As above, with 20" thin round barrel. Chambered for .44-40 cartridge. Fitted with a saddle ring on left side of frame. Blued case-hardened, with walnut stock and carbine buttplate. Manufactured from 1892 to 1902.

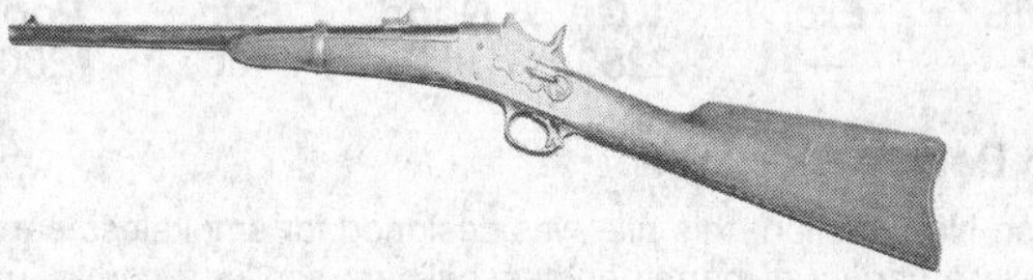

Exc.	Fine	V.G.	Good	Fair	Poor
4250	2250	1570	900	500	250

Model 1-1/2 Sporting Rifle (Antique)

Lightweight variation of above, using 1.25" wide No. 1 rolling block action. Chambered for rimfire cartridges from .22 to .38 Extra Long, as well as centerfire cartridges from .32-20 to .44-40. Medium weight octagonal barrels from 24" to 28" in length, with open rear and blade-type front sight. Blued case-hardened, with walnut stock. Several thousand manufactured between 1888 and 1897.

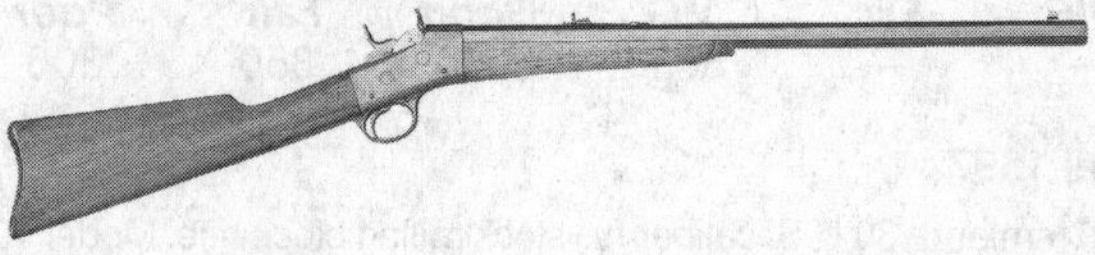

Paul Goodwin photo

Exc.	Fine	V.G.	Good	Fair	Poor
3000	1200	800	500	300	200

Model 2 Sporting Rifle

As above using No. 2 action. Chambered for various cartridges from .22- to .38-caliber, with 24" or 26" octagonal barrels. Blued case-hardened, with walnut stock. Produced with a number of optional features that affect its value. Prospective purchasers are advised to secure a qualified appraisal prior to acquisition. Manufactured from 1873 to 1910.

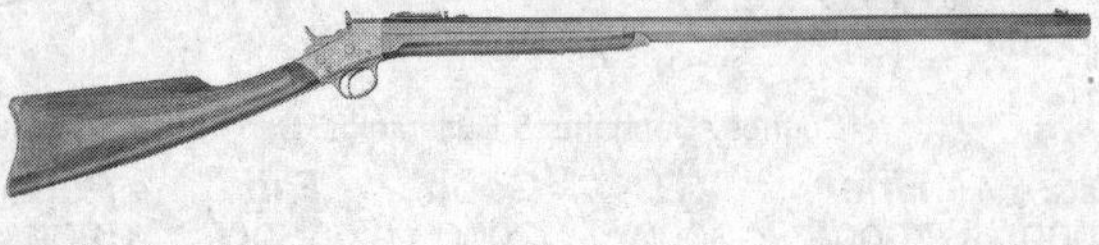

Paul Goodwin photo

NIB	Exc.	V.G.	Good	Fair	Poor
—	3200	2200	700	250	100

No. 4 Rolling Block Rifle

Built on lightweight No. 4 action. Available in .22, .25 Stevens or .32-caliber, with 22.5" or 24" octagonal barrel. Blued case-hardened, with walnut stock. Take-down version was also made and these are worth approximately 10 percent more than values listed. Approximately 50,000 manufactured between 1890 and 1933.

NIB	Exc.	V.G.	Good	Fair	Poor
—	1300	1000	400	200	80

No. 4 S Military Rifle

At the request of United States Boy Scouts in 1913, Remington Company designed a military style rifle having a 28" barrel and full-length forend secured by one barrel band. A short upper handguard was also fitted and a bayonet stud is found at the muzzle. In 1915, designation of this model was changed from "Boy Scout" to "Military Model". Approximately 15,000 manufactured between 1913 and 1923.

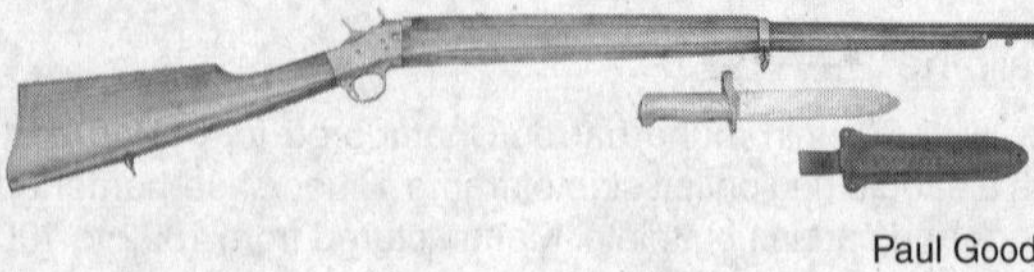

Paul Goodwin photo

NIB	Exc.	V.G.	Good	Fair	Poor
—	—	2250	950	400	280

No. 5 Rolling Block Rifle

Built on No. 5 action, this rifle was designed for smokeless cartridges. Made in a variety of barrel lengths, calibers and in a carbine version. Blued case-hardened, with walnut stock.

NIB	Exc.	V.G.	Good	Fair	Poor
—	—	2250	800	350	100

No. 5 Sporting or Target Rifle

Chambered for .30-30, .303 British, 7mm, .30 U.S., .32-40, .32 U.S. and .38-55 cartridges. Offered with 28" or 30" round barrels. Features a plain straight-grip stock, with half-length forend. Has open rear sights and was available with double-set triggers that would add approximately 10 percent to value. Manufactured between 1898 and 1905.

NIB	Exc.	V.G.	Good	Fair	Poor
—	—	5750	2250	850	300

Model 1897

A 7x57mm and .30 U.S. caliber full stock rolling block rifle. Model 1902 is of identical form, except it was fitted with an automatic ejector. Manufactured from 1897 to 1902.

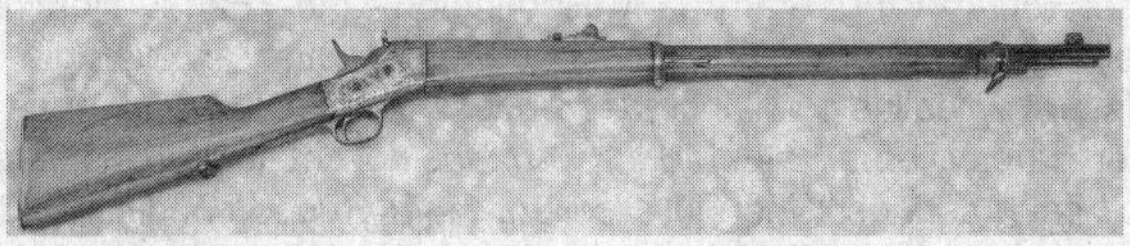

Paul Goodwin photo

NIB	Exc.	V.G.	Good	Fair	Poor
—	2800	1250	550	250	100

Carbine

As above fitted with 20" round barrel and half-length forend secured by one barrel band.

NIB	Exc.	V.G.	Good	Fair	Poor
—	—	1750	750	350	100

No. 6 Falling Block Rifle

Lightweight small rifle designed expressly to be used by young boys. Chambered for .22 rimfire cartridge, as well as .32 Short or Long. Also produced with smoothbore barrel to be used with shot cartridges. Round barrel 20" in length. Has a take-down action, with barrel held on by a knurled knob underneath the frame. It is a lightweight rolling block, with a thin operating knob on the breech. Finish is blued overall. Early models featured case colored frame and these versions would be worth approximately 10 percent additional. Has a straight-grip walnut stock, with a small forearm. Over 250,000 manufactured between 1902 and 1903.

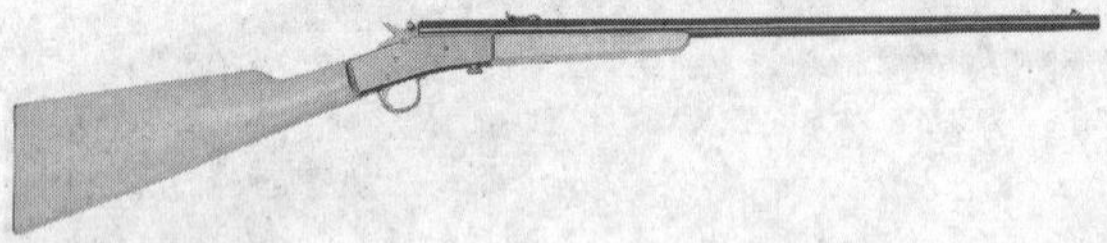

Paul Goodwin photo

NIB	Exc.	V.G.	Good	Fair	Poor
—	750	480	300	100	80

No. 7 Rolling Block Rifle

Readily identifiable by its accentuated checked pistol grip. Available in .22 or .25-10 Stevens caliber, with 24", 26" or 28" half octagonal barrels. Fitted with a tang mounted aperture rear sight. Blued case-hardened, with walnut stock. Approximately 1,000 manufactured between 1903 and 1911.

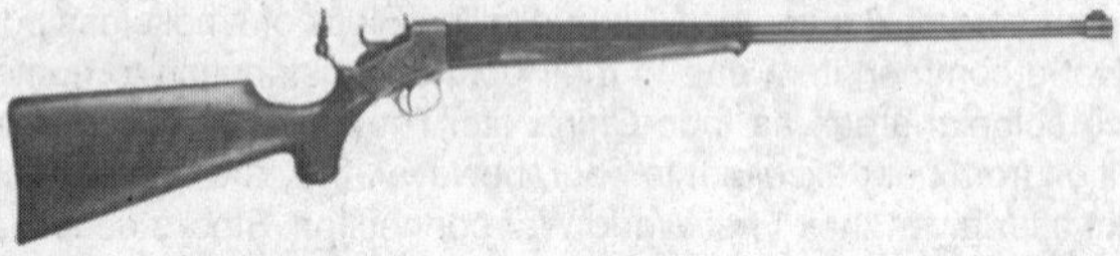

NIB	Exc.	V.G.	Good	Fair	Poor
—	7500	6000	4000	2000	500

REMINGTON-HEPBURN RIFLES

Remington-Hepburn No. 3 Rifle (Antique)

Lever activated falling block single-shot rifle designed by Lewis Hepburn. Available in a variety of calibers from .22 Win. centerfire to .50-90 Sharps. Octagonal or round barrels 26", 28" or 30" length. Blued case-hardened, with walnut stock. Available with a variety of optional features that affect value considerably. Prospective purchasers are advised to secure a qualified appraisal prior to acquisition. Approximately 10,000 manufactured between 1883 and 1907.

Exc.	Fine	V.G.	Good	Fair	Poor
7500	5000	3500	2000	400	280

Remington-Hepburn No. 3 Match Rifle

As above fitted with a high comb buttstock and nickel-plated Schuetzen buttplate. Manufactured in various calibers from .25-20 Stevens to .40-65, with 30" half octagonal barrels. Model was made in two versions: "A Quality" with plain stock, tang mounted rear sight and a Beach front sight; "B Quality" with checkered walnut stock having a cheek-rest, checkered forend, vernier rear sight and combination wind gauge and spirit level front sight. Double-set triggers were also available and these would add approximately 10 percent to values listed below. Approximately 1,000 manufactured between 1883 and 1907.

A Quality (Antique)

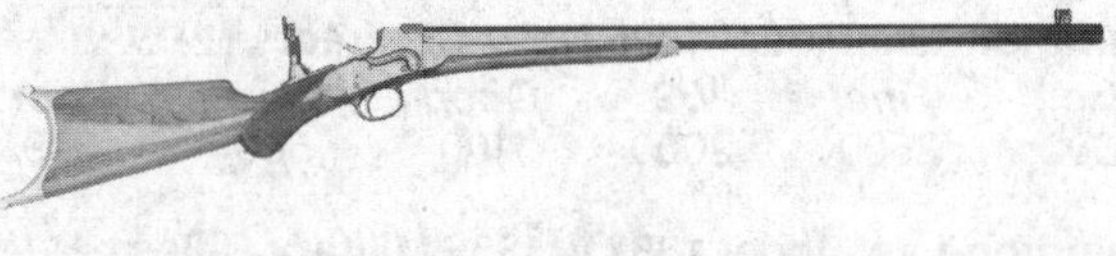

Paul Goodwin photo

Exc.	Fine	V.G.	Good	Fair	Poor
8800	6000	4250	2500	500	350

B Quality (Antique)

Paul Goodwin photo

Exc.	Fine	V.G.	Good	Fair	Poor
90000	6500	4650	2800	600	420

Remington-Hepburn No. 3 Long-Range Creedmoor Rifle (Antique)

As above in .44-caliber, with 32" or 34" half-octagonal barrel. Long-range vernier rear sight, combination wind gauge and spirit level front sight. Deluxe checkered walnut stock and rubber shotgun buttplate. Produced with a number of optional features that affect value. Prospective purchasers are advised to secure a qualified appraisal prior to acquisition. Manufactured from 1880 to 1907.

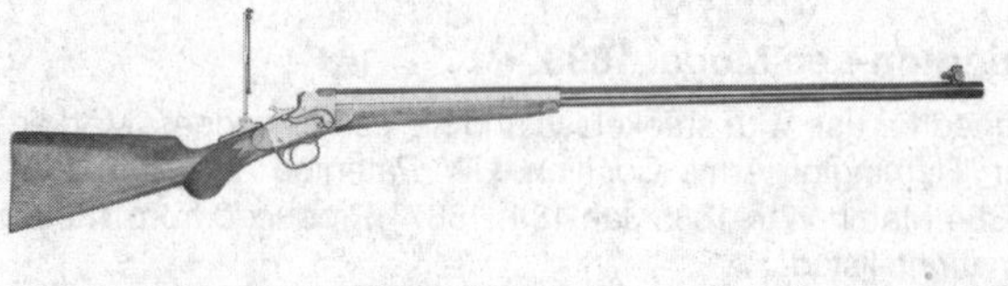

Paul Goodwin photo

Exc.	Fine	V.G.	Good	Fair	Poor
8500	4750	3270	1800	350	240

Remington-Hepburn No. 3 Mid-Range Creedmoor Rifle (Antique)

As above chambered for .40-65 cartridge. Fitted with 28" barrel.

Exc.	Fine	V.G.	Good	Fair	Poor
8500	4750	3270	1800	350	240

Remington-Hepburn No. 3 Long-Range Military Rifle

Rare variation chambered for .44-20 Rem. cartridge. Has round 34" barrel and full-length forearm held on by two barrel bands. Blued case colored finish. Stock is walnut. There are two basic versions: plain grade has un-checkered straight-grip stock, with military-type sights; fancy grade features high-grade checkered pistol grip stock, with full-length checkered forend, vernier tang sight, wind gauge and spirit lever front sight. A few manufactured in the 1880s.

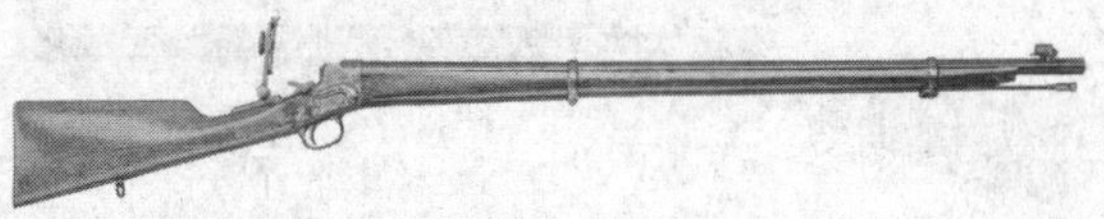

Paul Goodwin photo

Plain Grade (Antique)

Exc.	Fine	V.G.	Good	Fair	Poor
6000	3000	2100	1200	400	280

Fancy Grade (Antique)

Exc.	Fine	V.G.	Good	Fair	Poor
8000	4000	2750	1500	600	420

Remington-Hepburn No. 3 Schuetzen Match Rifle

As above instead of side lever the action is raised or lowered by means of lever on the triggerguard. Chambered for various popular cartridges. Offered with 30" or 32" part-octagonal heavy barrel. Features vernier tang sight, with hooded front sight. Standard with double-set triggers and palm rest. Finish blued and case colored, with high-grade checkered walnut stock and forend. Has ornate Swiss-type Schuetzen buttplate. Also known as "Walker-Hepburn Rifle". There were two versions available. One, standard breech-loader with Remington Walker-marked barrel; the other, a muzzleloading variation fitted with a removable false muzzle. This version was supplied with brass bullet starter and other accessories. Prospective purchasers are advised to secure a qualified appraisal prior to acquisition.

Breechloading Version (Antique)

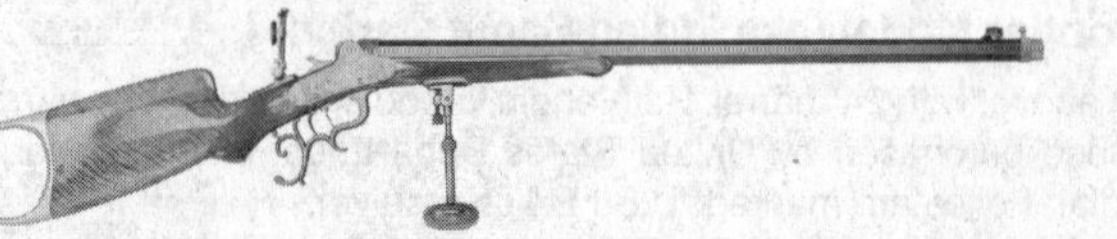

Exc.	Fine	V.G.	Good	Fair	Poor
27500	12500	8000	3500	900	630

Muzzleloading Version (Antique)

Exc.	Fine	V.G.	Good	Fair	Poor
42500	17500	11250	5000	1500	1050

Remington-Hepburn No. 3 High-Power Rifle

Model No. 3 also available in a variety of smokeless cartridges: .30-30, .30-40, .32 Special, .32-40 and .38-55. Standard barrel lengths were 26", 28" or 30". Produced from 1900 to 1907.

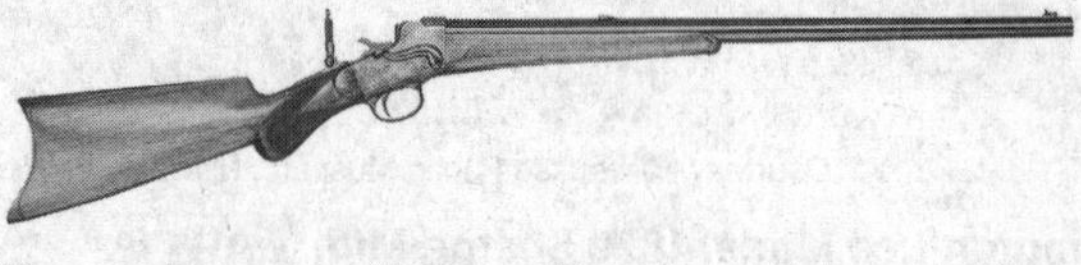

NIB	Exc.	V.G.	Good	Fair	Poor
—	4000	2500	1750	650	250

REMINGTON-KEENE MAGAZINE RIFLE

Bolt-action rifle chambered for .40, .43 and .45-70 centerfire cartridges, with 22", 24.5", 29.25" or 32.5" barrels. Readily identifiable by exposed hammer at end of the bolt. Blued case-hardened hammer and furniture, with walnut stock. Receiver marked "E. Remington & Sons, Ilion, N.Y." together with patent dates 1874, 1876 and 1877. Magazine on this rifle was located beneath the barrel. Receiver fitted with a cut-off so that rifle could be used as a single-shot. Approximately 5,000 manufactured between 1880 and 1888 in variations listed.

Sporting Rifle (Antique)

24.5" barrel.

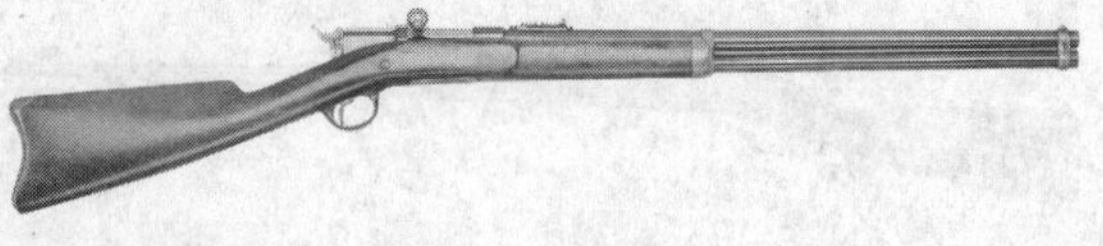

Exc.	Fine	V.G.	Good	Fair	Poor
5000	2500	1200	800	400	250

Army Rifle Antique

Barrel length 32.5". Full-length stock secured by two barrel bands.

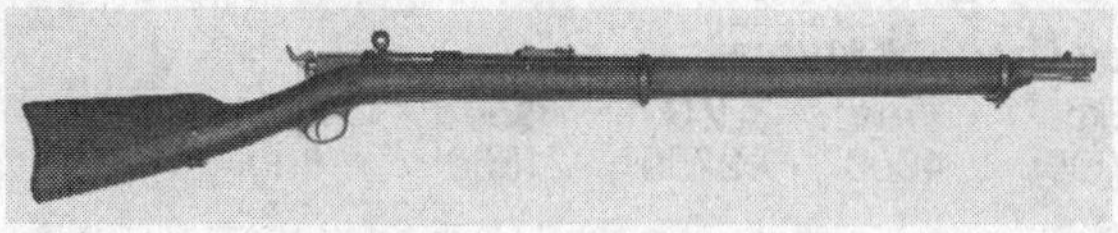

Courtesy Milwaukee Public Museum, Milwaukee, Wisconsin

Exc.	Fine	V.G.	Good	Fair	Poor
—	3500	2220	950	450	310

Navy Rifle Antique

As above, with 29.25" barrel.

Exc.	Fine	V.G.	Good	Fair	Poor
—	4500	3120	1750	450	310

Carbine Antique

As above, with 22" barrel. Half-length forend secured by one barrel band.

Exc.	Fine	V.G.	Good	Fair	Poor
5750	3250	2250	1250	350	240

Frontier Model (aka Indian Scout Carbine) Antique

As above, with 24" barrel. Half-length forend secured by one barrel band. Those purchased by United States Department of Interior for arming Indian Police are marked "U.S.I.D." on receiver.

Exc.	Fine	V.G.	Good	Fair	Poor
12000	9000	8500	5000	2500	1200

REMINGTON-LEE RIFLES

Remington-Lee Magazine Rifle Antique

Designed by James Paris Lee. Rifles of this type were originally manufactured by Sharps Rifle Company in 1880. Remington Company began production of this model in 1881, after Sharps Company ceased operations. Approximately 100,000 Lee magazine rifles manufactured between 1880 and 1907. Their variations are listed.

Courtesy Milwaukee Public Museum, Milwaukee, Wisconsin

Remington-Lee Model 1879 Sharps Mfg. Antique

Barrel length 28", with full-length stock secured by two barrel bands. Barrel marked "Sharps Rifle Co. Bridgeport, Conn." and "Old Reliable" in rectangular cartouche. Approximately 300 made prior to 1881.

Exc.	Fine	V.G.	Good	Fair	Poor
4750	3000	2500	2000	600	420

Remington-Lee Model 1879 U.S. Navy Model Antique

Exc.	Fine	V.G.	Good	Fair	Poor
2800	1600	1170	750	250	170

Remington-Lee Model 1879 Sporting Rifle Antique

Barrel length 28" or 30"; .45-70 or .45-90 caliber. Checkered pistol grip stock, with sporting-style forend. Markings on receiver as above. Approximately 450 made.

Exc.	Fine	V.G.	Good	Fair	Poor
2500	1750	1220	700	250	170

Remington-Lee Model 1879 Military Rifle Antique

Identical to Navy model, except chambered for .43 Spanish cartridge. Limited number were produced in .45-70 caliber. Spanish versions are worth approximately 25 percent less than values listed below. Approximately 1,000 made. Majority of these rifles were for export.

Exc.	Fine	V.G.	Good	Fair	Poor
2200	1250	870	500	150	100

Remington-Lee Model 1882 Army Contract Antique

Exc.	Fine	V.G.	Good	Fair	Poor
4000	2500	2000	1100	500	300

Remington-Lee Model 1885 Navy Contract Antique

Exc.	Fine	V.G.	Good	Fair	Poor
4000	2500	2000	1100	500	300

Remington-Lee Model 1882 & 1885 Military Rifles Antique

Barrel length 32". Full-length stock secured by two barrel bands. Chambered for .42 Russian, .43 Spanish, .45 Gardner or .45-70 cartridges. Values for those rifles not in .45-70 caliber would be approximately 25 percent less than those listed. Approximately 10,000 Model 1882 rifles made; 60,000 Model 1885 rifles. Two models can be differentiated by the cocking piece on the bolt of Model 1885 is larger. Majority of these rifles made for foreign contracts and commercial sales.

Exc.	Fine	V.G.	Good	Fair	Poor
3000	2500	1850	1200	300	210

Remington-Lee Model 1882 & 1885 Sporting Rifle Antique

As above chambered for .45-70 and .45-90 caliber, with 26" or 30" octagonal barrels and walnut sporting stocks. Approximately 200 made.

Exc.	Fine	V.G.	Good	Fair	Poor
2700	2000	1450	900	250	170

Remington-Lee Model 1882 & 1885 Carbine Antique

As above, with 24" barrel and half-length forend secured by one barrel band. Prospective purchasers are advised to secure a qualified appraisal prior to acquisition.

Exc.	Fine	V.G.	Good	Fair	Poor
2700	2000	1450	900	250	170

Remington-Lee Model 1899

Designed for use with smokeless and rimless cartridges. Marked on receiver "Remington Arms Co. Ilion, N.Y. Patented Aug. 26th 1884 Sept. 9th 1884 March 17th 1885 Jan 18th 1887". Produced from 1889 to 1907 in variations listed.

Military Rifle

NIB	Exc.	V.G.	Good	Fair	Poor
—	3000	2000	1000	400	200

Military Carbine

NIB	Exc.	V.G.	Good	Fair	Poor
—	3200	2200	1250	500	250

Remington-Lee Sporting Rifle

As above, with 24", 26" or 28" round or octagonal barrel. Half-length sporting stock, with checkered pistol grip. Approximately 7,000 manufactured.

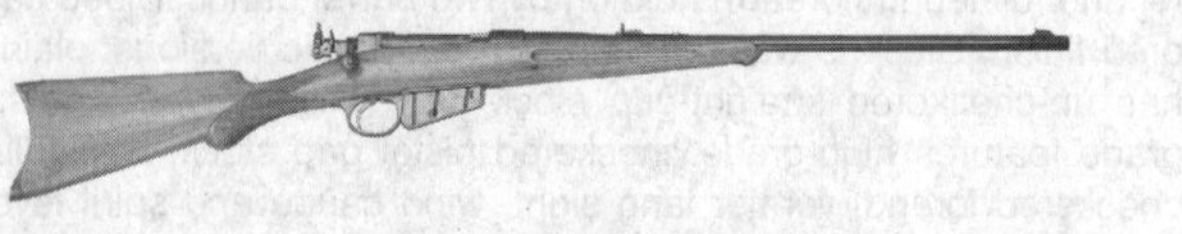

NIB	Exc.	V.G.	Good	Fair	Poor
—	3000	2400	2000	900	250

Remington Lebel Bolt-Action Rifle

NIB	Exc.	V.G.	Good	Fair	Poor
—	—	750	450	150	100

Remington Mosin-Nagant Bolt-Action Rifle

NIB	Exc.	V.G.	Good	Fair	Poor
—	—	600	300	100	80

U.S. Model 1917 Magazine Rifle

NIB	Exc.	V.G.	Good	Fair	Poor
—	—	1250	600	150	100

Remington-Whitmore Model 1874

Sidelock double-barrel shotgun, combination shotgun/rifle or double-barrel rifle, with 28" or 30" fluid steel barrels. Also available with Damascus barrels. Barrels released by pushing forward the top lever. Blued case-hardened, with straight-/semi-pistol grip walnut stock. Barrels marked "A. E. Whitmore's Patent Aug. 8, 1871, April 16, 1872". Rib between barrels marked "E. Remington & Sons, Ilion, N.Y.". Several thousand manufactured between 1874 and 1882.

Shotgun (Antique)

Exc.	Fine	V.G.	Good	Fair	Poor
1750	850	650	450	100	70

Combination Gun (Rare) (Antique)

Exc.	Fine	V.G.	Good	Fair	Poor
4250	3200	2350	1500	300	210

Double Rifle (Antique)

Very rare.

Exc.	Fine	V.G.	Good	Fair	Poor
9000	4250	2870	1500	500	350

Model 1882 Shotgun (Antique)

Sidelock double-barrel 10- or 12-gauge shotgun, with 28" or 30" fluid steel or Damascus barrels. Blued case-hardened, with checkered pistol grip stock and hard rubber buttplate. Barrels are marked "E. Remington & Sons, Ilion, N.Y." and lock marked "Remington Arms Co.". Has a conventional top lever that moves to the side. Offered with optional engraving. Such models should be individually appraised. Approximately 7,500 manufactured between 1882 and 1889.

Exc.	Fine	V.G.	Good	Fair	Poor
1250	750	520	300	150	100

Model 1883 through 1889 Shotgun (Antique)

Sidelock 10-, 12- or 16-gauge double-barrel shotgun, with fluid steel or Damascus barrels 28" to 32" in length. Models 1883, 1885, 1887 and 1889 are all somewhat alike, varying only in form of their hammers and internal mechanisms. Blued case-hardened checkered pistol grip stock, with a grip cap. Available in a variety of styles including highly engraved models that should be individually appraised. Approximately 30,000 manufactured between 1883 and 1909.

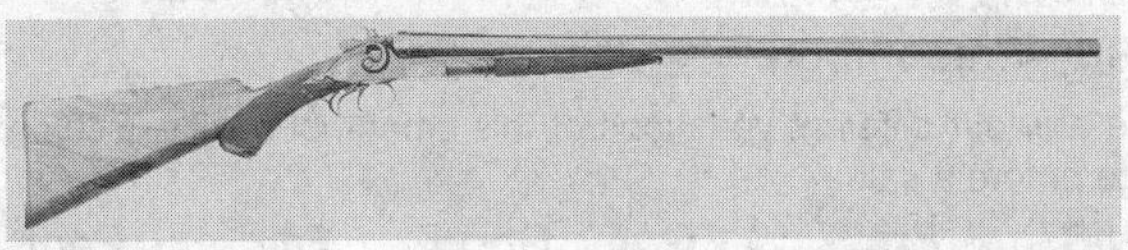

Exc.	Fine	V.G.	Good	Fair	Poor
1800	1100	950	800	200	140

Model 1893 (No. 9)

Single-barrel hammer gun in 10-, 12-, 16-, 20-, 24- and 28-gauge. Barrel lengths from 28" to 34". Case colored frame, with hard rubber buttplate.

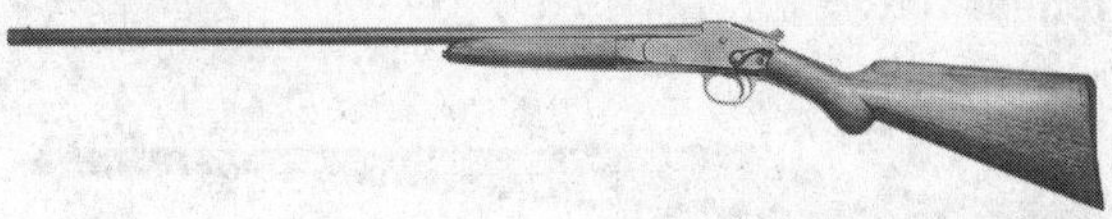

Courtesy William F. Krause

NIB	Exc.	V.G.	Good	Fair	Poor
—	—	—	600	250	100

Hammerless Shotgun Model 1894

Boxlock 10-, 12- or 16-gauge double shotgun, with fluid steel or Damascus barrels 26" to 32" in length. Blued case-hardened, with pistol grip stock. Available in a variety of styles. It is advised that highly engraved examples should be individually appraised. Note: Add 25 percent premium for fluid steel barrels.

NIB	Exc.	V.G.	Good	Fair	Poor
—	1750	1250	750	300	100

Model 1900 Shotgun

As above in 12- and 16-gauge only. Same cautions apply to highly engraved examples.

NIB	Exc.	V.G.	Good	Fair	Poor
—	1500	1000	600	250	100

Model 8 Rifle

A .25, .30, .32 or .35 Rem. semi-automatic rifle. Featuring 22" barrel, with open sights. Barrel covered by a full- length tube that encloses the recoil spring. Blued, with walnut stock. Approximately 60,000 made between 1906 and 1936 in styles listed. Note: Add 35 percent for .25 Rem. Some collectors will pay and demand, prices substantially in excess of those listed below for Grades C, D and E

Standard Grade

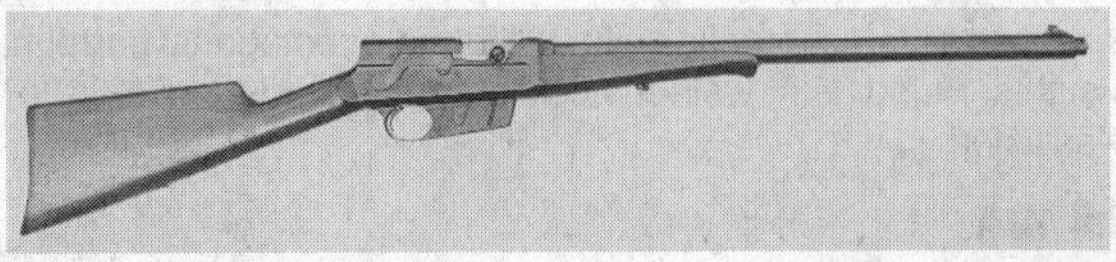

Courtesy Remington Arms

NIB	Exc.	V.G.	Good	Fair	Poor
1400	1200	800	550	250	120

Model 8A

Checkered stock.

NIB	Exc.	V.G.	Good	Fair	Poor
1600	1300	900	600	300	150

Model 8C

NIB	Exc.	V.G.	Good	Fair	Poor
3000	2500	1500	900	500	300

8D Peerless

Light engraving.

NIB	Exc.	V.G.	Good	Fair	Poor
6000	5000	3500	1750	800	400

8E Expert

NIB	Exc.	V.G.	Good	Fair	Poor
7500	6000	4000	2250	1100	450

8F Premier

Heavily engraved.

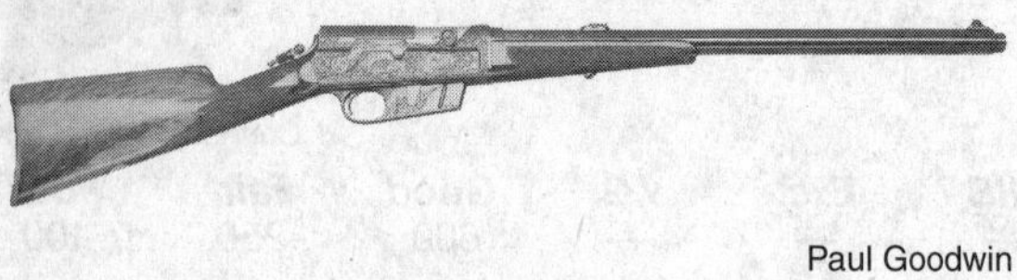

Paul Goodwin photo

NIB	Exc.	V.G.	Good	Fair	Poor
10000	8500	7500	3750	1600	700

Model 81 Woodsmaster

Improved variation of Model 8. Chambered for same calibers (but not .25 apparently) as well as .300 Savage cartridge. Produced from 1936 to 1950 in styles listed. Note: Add 300 percent for police model, with detachable 15-round magazine.

Standard Grade

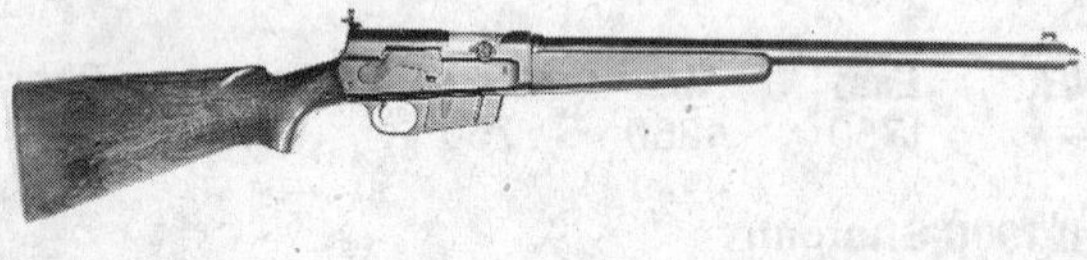

NIB	Exc.	V.G.	Good	Fair	Poor
1100	900	750	500	250	120

Model 81A

NIB	Exc.	V.G.	Good	Fair	Poor
1200	1000	850	500	250	120

81D Peerless

Engraved.

NIB	Exc.	V.G.	Good	Fair	Poor
7500	6000	4000	2250	1100	450

81F Premier

Heavily engraved.

NIB	Exc.	V.G.	Good	Fair	Poor
10000	8500	7500	3750	1600	700

Model 12 or 12A

A .22-caliber slide-action rifle, with 22" round or octagonal barrel having open sights. Blued, with walnut stock. Manufactured from 1909 to 1936 in styles listed.

Model 12A

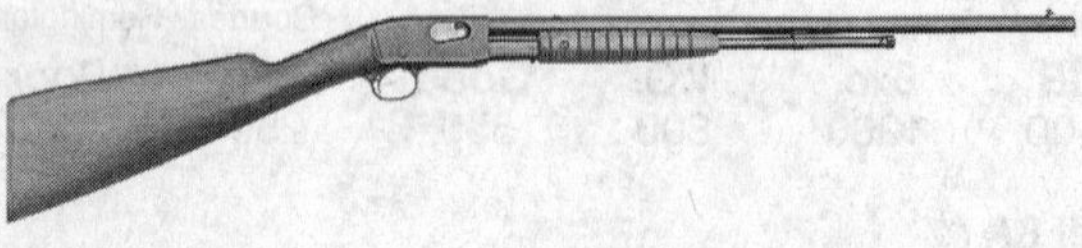

NIB	Exc.	V.G.	Good	Fair	Poor
1200	1050	900	600	220	150

Model 12B

.22 Short Gallery Model.

NIB	Exc.	V.G.	Good	Fair	Poor
2000	1800	1200	900	400	150

Model 12C

24" octagon barrel.

NIB	Exc.	V.G.	Good	Fair	Poor
1400	1150	950	650	300	180

12C N.R.A. Target

Limited production.

NIB	Exc.	V.G.	Good	Fair	Poor
2400	2100	1400	1000	500	300

Model 12CS

.22 Remington Special.

NIB	Exc.	V.G.	Good	Fair	Poor
1500	1250	1000	800	400	180

12D Peerless

Light engraving.

NIB	Exc.	V.G.	Good	Fair	Poor
7000	6000	5000	3000	1500	750

12E Expert

NIB	Exc.	V.G.	Good	Fair	Poor
8500	7200	6000	3500	2000	1000

12F Premier

Heavily engraved.

Paul Goodwin photo

NIB	Exc.	V.G.	Good	Fair	Poor
10000	9000	5250	3150	1500	800

Model 121 and/or 121A

A .22-caliber slide-action rifle, with 24" round barrel. Blued, with walnut stock. Manufactured from 1936 to 1954 in styles listed.

Standard Grade

NIB	Exc.	V.G.	Good	Fair	Poor
1000	850	650	500	180	100

121D Peerless

Engraved.

NIB	Exc.	V.G.	Good	Fair	Poor
6500	5000	3750	1800	1000	500

121F Premier

Heavily engraved.

NIB	Exc.	V.G.	Good	Fair	Poor
9000	7500	5250	3150	1500	800

Model 121S

.22 WRF.

NIB	Exc.	V.G.	Good	Fair	Poor
1200	1050	900	600	350	250

121SB—Smoothbore

There are four different variations of this smoothbore rifle. Seek expert advice before a sale.

NIB	Exc.	V.G.	Good	Fair	Poor
1500	1350	1100	650	400	300

Model 14 or 14A

A .25, .30, .32 or .35 Rem. caliber slide-action rifle, with 22" round barrel and open sights. Blued, plain walnut stock. Manufactured from 1912 to 1936. Note: Add 85 percent for .25 Remington.

NIB	Exc.	V.G.	Good	Fair	Poor
—	900	750	500	300	200

Model 14R

As above, with 18.5" barrel.

NIB	Exc.	V.G.	Good	Fair	Poor
—	1500	800	500	300	200

Model 14-1/2

As above, except chambered for .38-40 or .44-40 cartridge, with 22.5" barrel. Carbine with 18.5" barrel, known as Model 14-1/2R, would be worth approximately 10 percent more than values listed. Manufactured from 1912 to 1922.

NIB	Exc.	V.G.	Good	Fair	Poor
—	2000	1250	700	350	250

Model 16

A .22-caliber (Rem. Automatic, not interchangeable with anything else) semi-automatic rifle, with 22" barrel and open sights. Blued, with walnut stock. Later production examples were known as Model 16A. Manufactured from 1914 to 1928. Note: Peerless and Premier Grades have engraving and higher grades of walnut. Add 400 percent premium for Peerless grade; 700 percent for Premier grade.

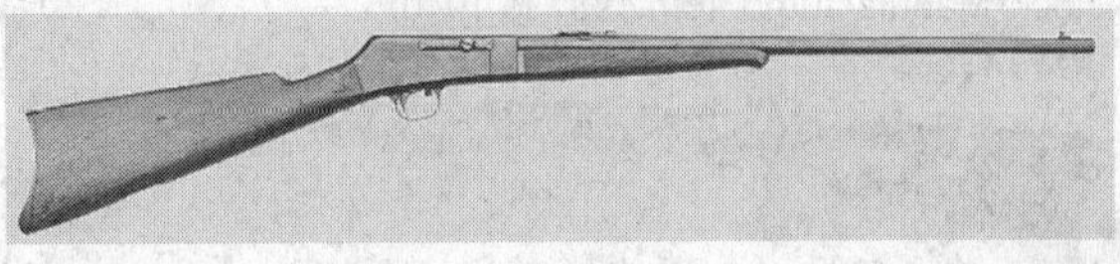

Courtesy Remington Arms

NIB	Exc.	V.G.	Good	Fair	Poor
1500	1100	900	600	400	200

Model 141

A .30, .32 or .35 Rem. caliber slide-action rifle, with 24" barrel having open sights. Blued, with plain walnut stock. Later production versions were known as Model 141A. Manufactured from 1936 to 1950.

Courtesy Remington Arms

NIB	Exc.	V.G.	Good	Fair	Poor
1000	800	650	500	250	180

Model 141 Special Grade

This model has a higher-grade checkered walnut stock and forend. Note: Add 200 percent premium for engraved Peerless Grade; 300 percent for Premier Grade with more elaborate engraving.

NIB	Exc.	V.G.	Good	Fair	Poor
1800	1600	1200	900	600	300

Model 25

A .25-20 or .32-20 caliber slide-action rifle, with 24" barrel having open sights. Blued, with walnut stock. Later production examples were known as Model 25A. Carbine version with an 18" barrel as Model 25R. Manufactured from 1923 to 1936. Note: Add 100 percent for rifles with 18" barrels.

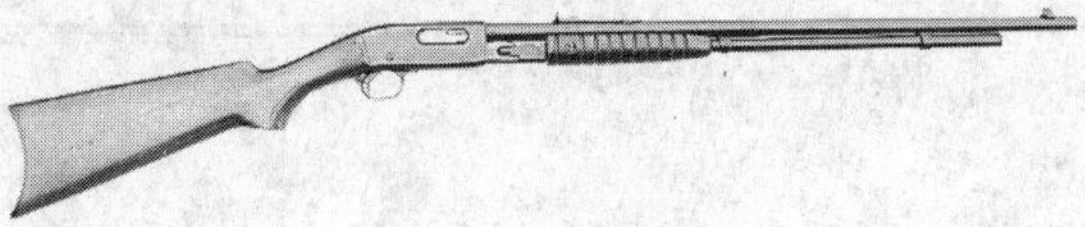

NIB	Exc.	V.G.	Good	Fair	Poor
—	1000	750	400	250	200

Model 24

Designed by John M. Browning. Semi-automatic rifle in .22-caliber, with 19" barrel and open sights. Blued, with walnut pistol grip stock. Later production versions known as Model 24A. Produced from 1922 to 1935.

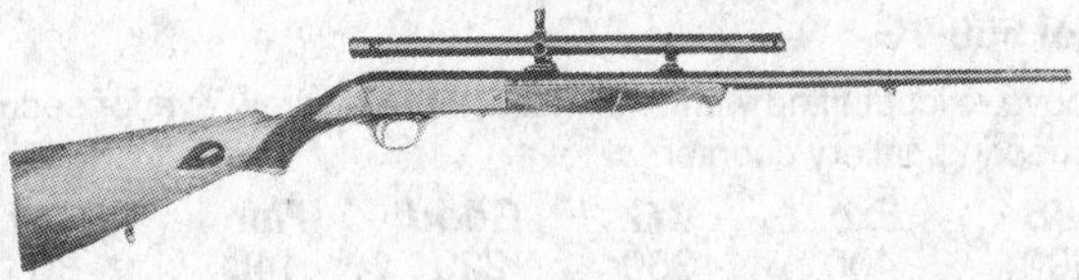

Courtesy Wallis & Wallis, Lewes, Sussex, England

NIB	Exc.	V.G.	Good	Fair	Poor
1200	1000	600	400	200	100

Model 241 Speedmaster

A .22-caliber take-down semi-automatic rifle, with 24" barrel and open sights. Blued, with walnut stock. Later production versions known as Model 241A. Approximately 56,000 made between 1935 and 1949 in styles listed.

NIB	Exc.	V.G.	Good	Fair	Poor
1200	800	650	550	350	200

Model 241

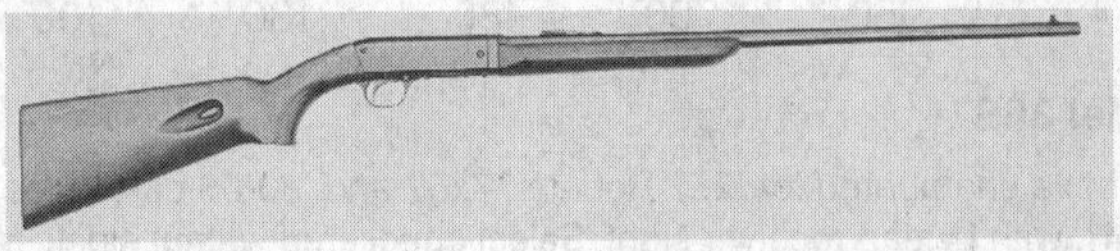

Courtesy Remington Arms

NIB	Exc.	V.G.	Good	Fair	Poor
750	550	400	250	200	150

241D Peerless

Engraved.

NIB	Exc.	V.G.	Good	Fair	Poor
6500	5000	3750	1800	1000	500

241E Expert

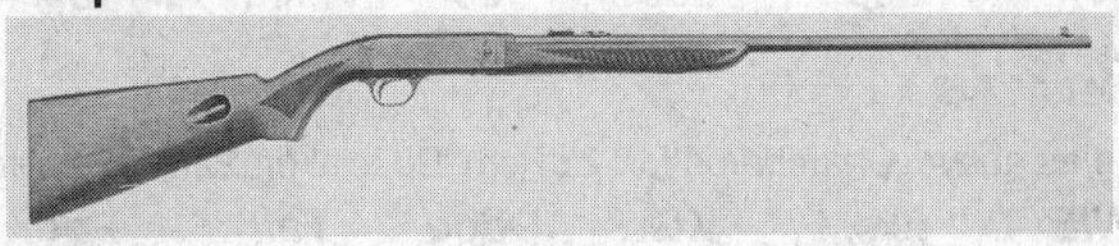

NIB	Exc.	V.G.	Good	Fair	Poor
8000	7500	4000	2250	1200	800

241F Premier

Heavily engraved.

NIB	Exc.	V.G.	Good	Fair	Poor
10000	9000	5250	3150	1500	800

Model 550A

A .22 Short, Long or LR caliber semi-automatic rifle, with 24" barrel and open sights. Blued, with walnut pistol grip stock. Approximately 220,000 made between 1941 and 1971.

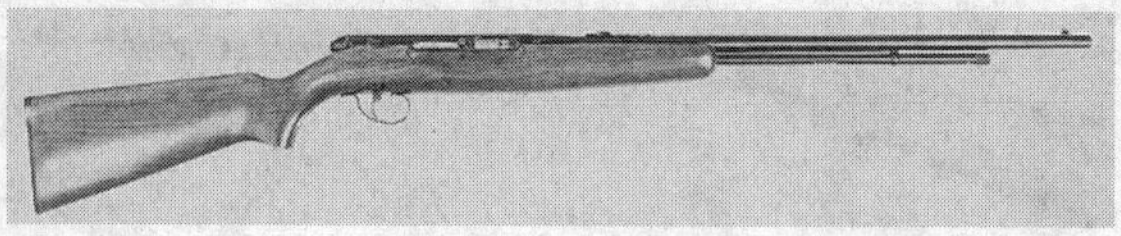

NIB	Exc.	V.G.	Good	Fair	Poor
—	350	280	150	100	80

Model 550P

As above, with aperture rear sight.

NIB	Exc.	V.G.	Good	Fair	Poor
—	380	300	180	120	100

Model 550-2G

As above, except fitted with shell deflector and screw eye for securing it to a shooting gallery counter.

NIB	Exc.	V.G.	Good	Fair	Poor
500	400	380	220	140	80

Model 30A "Express"

Sporting rifle using U.S. Model 1917 Enfield bolt-action. Chambered for various Rem. cartridges as well as 7x57mm and .30-06 cartridges. Barrel length 22. Checkered walnut stock. Carbine model fitted with 20" barrel was known as Model 30R. Manufactured from 1921 to 1940.

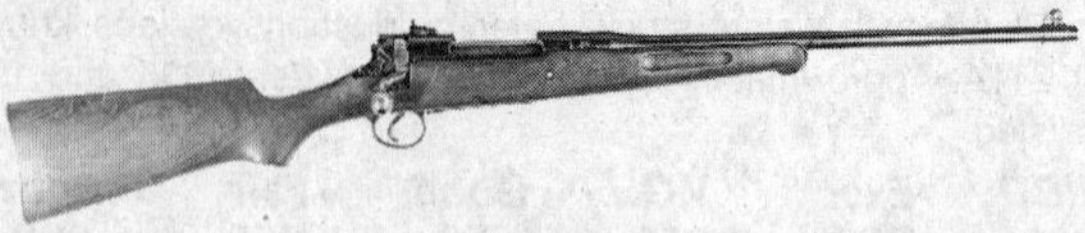

Courtesy Remington Arms

NIB	Exc.	V.G.	Good	Fair	Poor
—	950	700	480	180	100

Model 30S

As above chambered for .257 Roberts, 7x57 and .30-06 cartridges. Barrel 24", with Lyman receiver sight. Select checkered walnut stock. Manufactured from 1930 to 1940.

NIB	Exc.	V.G.	Good	Fair	Poor
—	1300	980	500	250	150

Model 41A "Targetmaster"

A bolt-action rimfire rifle chambered for .22-caliber Short, Long and LR. Barrel 27, with open rear sight and bead front. Pistol grip stock is plain. Produced from 1936 to 1940.

NIB	Exc.	V.G.	Good	Fair	Poor
—	300	200	150	100	50

Model 41AS

Same as above. Chambered for .22 Rem. Special or .22 WRF cartridge.

NIB	Exc.	V.G.	Good	Fair	Poor
—	280	180	120	100	80

Model 41P

Same as Model 41A, with addition of rear peep sight and hooded front.

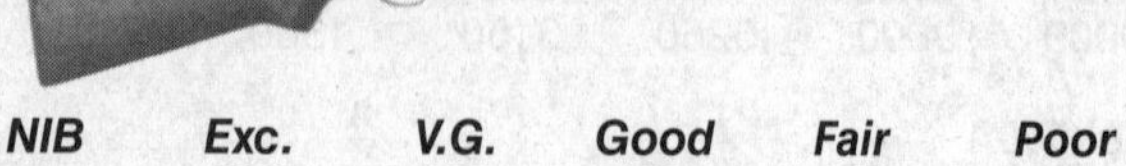

NIB	Exc.	V.G.	Good	Fair	Poor
—	320	220	180	120	50

Model 41SB

Same as Model 41A, except used with .22 shot cartridge. Barrel is smoothbore.

NIB	Exc.	V.G.	Good	Fair	Poor
—	350	280	200	150	80

Miscellaneous Remington Bolt Action Rimfires, 1930-1970

From 1930 to 1970, Remington Company produced a variety of single-shot and repeating .22-caliber rifles. Values for these are much the same, consequently, they are listed for reference only.

Model 33
Model 33 NRA
Model 34
Model 34 NRA
Model 341 A
Model 341 P
Model 341 SB
Model 510
Model 510 P
Model 510 SB

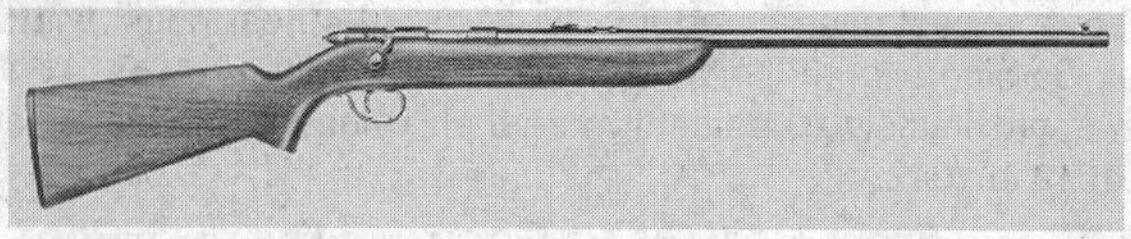

Courtesy Remington Arms

Model 510

NIB	Exc.	V.G.	Good	Fair	Poor
300	250	200	120	80	50

Model 37

A .22-caliber bolt-action magazine target rifle, with heavy 28" barrel. Featuring target-sights and telescope bases. Blued, with walnut target style stock. Manufactured from 1937 to 1940.

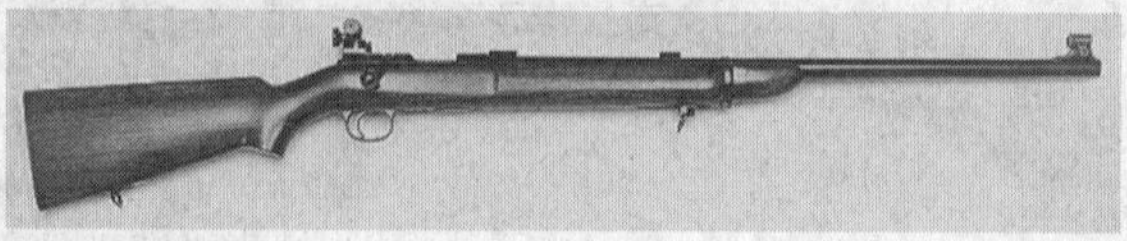

Courtesy Remington Arms

NIB	Exc.	V.G.	Good	Fair	Poor
1200	1000	600	400	300	250

Model 37-1940

As above, with improved lock, trigger pull and redesigned stock. Manufactured from 1940 to 1954.

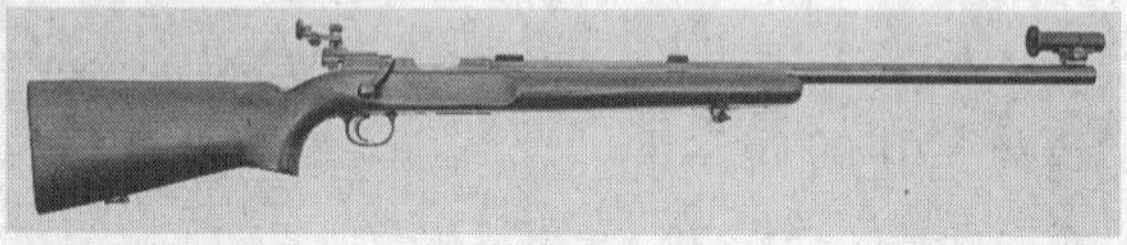

Courtesy Remington Arms

NIB	Exc.	V.G.	Good	Fair	Poor
1300	1100	750	500	300	200

Model 504

This .22-caliber bolt-action rifle was introduced in 2004. Barrel 20", with no sights. American walnut stock, with checkering and pistol grip. Satin blue metal finish. 6-round flush mounted detachable magazine. Receiver drilled and tapped for scope mounts. Weight about 6 lbs. Discontinued 2006. Also was chambered in .17 Mach 2 and .17 HMR.

NIB	Exc.	V.G.	Good	Fair	Poor
650	550	400	300	200	100

Model 504 Custom

Introduced in 2005. Features fancy walnut stock.

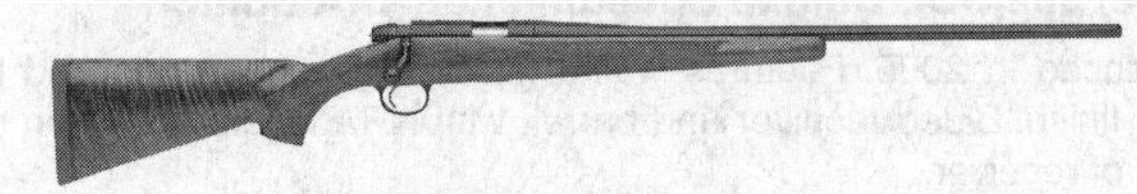

NIB	Exc.	V.G.	Good	Fair	Poor
1500	1300	1000	650	300	200

Model 504-T LS HB

Introduced in 2005. Features 20" heavy barrel, with blued finish. Chambered for .22 LR or .17 HMR cartridge. Brown laminate stock, with Monte Carlo comb. Weight about 8.5 lbs.

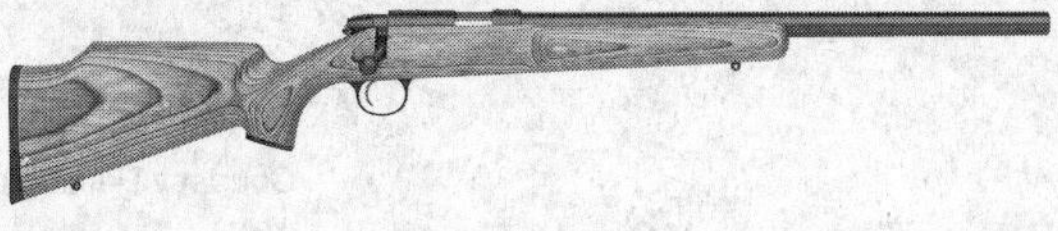

NIB	Exc.	V.G.	Good	Fair	Poor
800	680	480	280	250	150

Model 541 S Custom

A .22-caliber bolt-action magazine rifle, with 24" barrel. Blued, with scroll engraved receiver. Checkered walnut stock having a rosewood pistol grip cap and forend tip. Manufactured from 1972 to 1984.

NIB	Exc.	V.G.	Good	Fair	Poor
700	600	500	380	200	120

Model 541T

As above, drilled and tapped for telescopic sights. Introduced in 1986.

NIB	Exc.	V.G.	Good	Fair	Poor
380	280	200	180	120	80

Model 541T Heavy Barrel

Same as standard 541-T, with exception of 24" heavy barrel. First introduced in 1993.

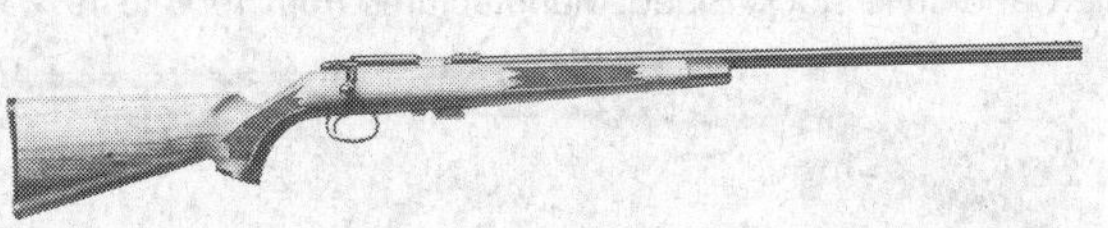

NIB	Exc.	V.G.	Good	Fair	Poor
450	350	300	250	200	120

Model 547

High-quality magazine-fed .17 or .22 rimfire sporter, with walnut stock, crowned muzzle, tuned trigger and other goodies. Suspiciously similar to defunct Model 504. Dealer exclusive for 2007.

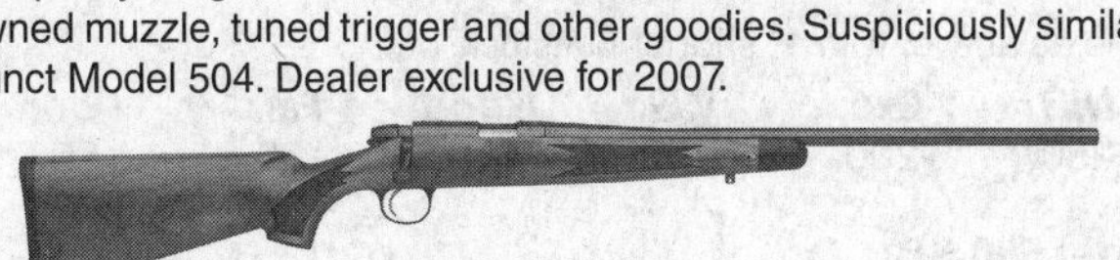

NIB	Exc.	V.G.	Good	Fair	Poor
1000	780	600	400	280	200

Model 511 Scoremaster

A .22-caliber bolt-action magazine sporting rifle, with 22" barrel. Blued, with walnut stock. Six-round magazine.

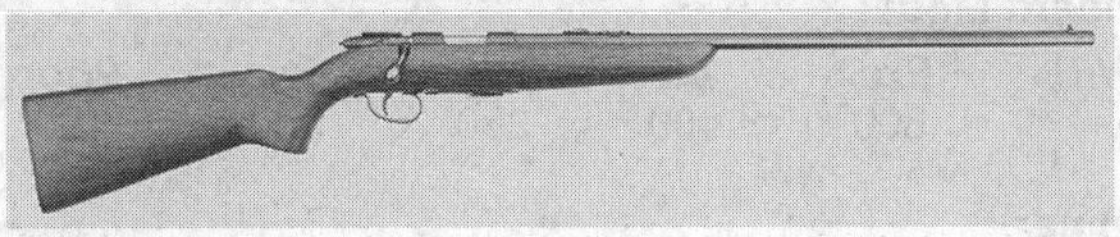

NIB	Exc.	V.G.	Good	Fair	Poor
380	320	250	180	120	80

Model 512

Bolt-action .22 rimfire repeater identical to 511, except with tubular magazine located beneath the barrel. Capacity is 15 LR, 17 Long and 22 Short cartridges. Manufactured from 1940 to 1962. All 500 series models (510, 511, 512, 513 and 521) feature a red cocking indicator at rear of bolt.

NIB	Exc.	V.G.	Good	Fair	Poor
400	350	280	200	150	100

Model 513 TR Matchmaster

A .22-caliber bolt-action magazine target rifle, with heavy 27" barrel and Redfield aperture rear sight. Blued, with target-style walnut stock. Manufactured from 1940 to 1969.

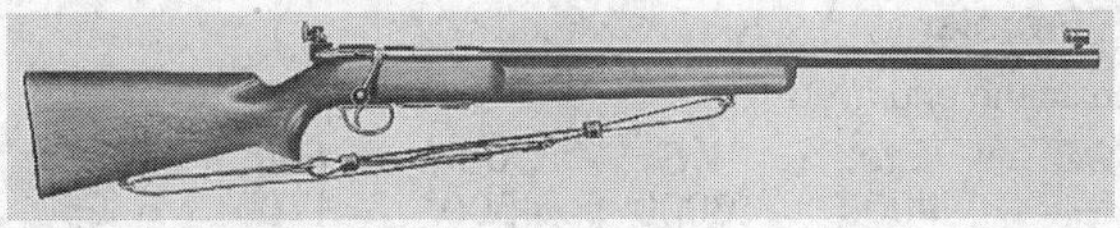

NIB	Exc.	V.G.	Good	Fair	Poor
500	400	300	200	150	100

Model 513 S

As above, with Marble sights and checkered walnut sporting-style stock. Manufactured from 1941 to 1956.

NIB	Exc.	V.G.	Good	Fair	Poor
950	800	700	480	380	220

Model 514

Bolt-action single-shot .22 rimfire rifle manufactured from 1948 to 1971. Total of 770,932 were made, with standard barrels and sights. Another 5,617 were made with Routledge Bore barrels, which were meant for use only with .22 LR Shot loads and came with a shotgun-style bead front sight. These rifles have 24" smoothbore barrel, with bore diameter of .22" that opens up to .40 for the last 12". Routledge Bore Model 514 was never in Remington catalog and available only on special order. Design originated with Michigan trap shooter and gunsmith Fred Routledge in 1938. Note: Add $100 for Routledge barrel.

NIB	Exc.	V.G.	Good	Fair	Poor
300	250	200	120	80	50

Model 521 TL Jr.

A .22-caliber bolt-action magazine target rifle, with heavy 25" barrel and Lyman sights. Blued, with target-style walnut stock. Manufactured from 1947 to 1969.

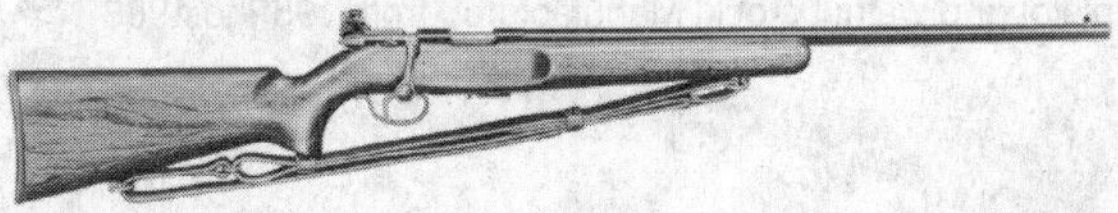

NIB	Exc.	V.G.	Good	Fair	Poor
400	350	250	180	120	80

Model 760

Slide-action sporting rifle chambered for various popular centerfire cartridges from .222 up to .35 Rem. cartridge, with 22" round barrel and open sights. Features detachable box magazine. Blued, with checkered walnut pistol grip stock. Manufactured between 1952 and 1982. Examples of this rifle chambered for .222, .223, .244 and .257 Roberts are worth a premium of 100 to 200 percent over other calibers. Produced in styles listed.

Standard Model

NIB	Exc.	V.G.	Good	Fair	Poor
—	500	400	280	200	150

Carbine

18.5" barrel.

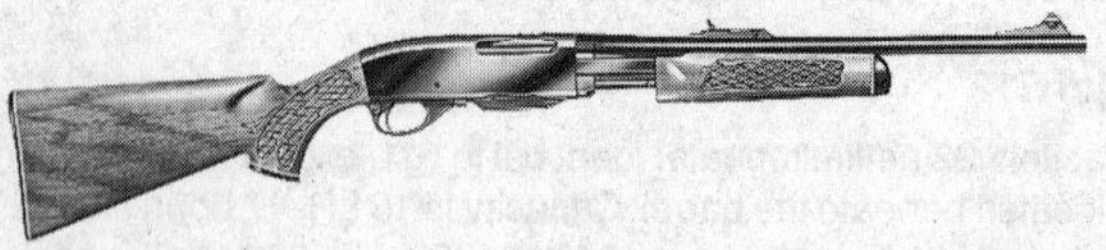

NIB	Exc.	V.G.	Good	Fair	Poor
—	520	400	280	200	150

760D Peerless

Engraved.

NIB	Exc.	V.G.	Good	Fair	Poor
—	5000	3500	2250	1100	450

760F Premier

Game scene engraved.

NIB	Exc.	V.G.	Good	Fair	Poor
—	9000	6000	4500	1700	550

760F Gold Inlaid

NIB	Exc.	V.G.	Good	Fair	Poor
—	10000	7000	5250	2200	750

Bicentennial

1976 only.

NIB	Exc.	V.G.	Good	Fair	Poor
—	550	500	300	200	150

ADL

NIB	Exc.	V.G.	Good	Fair	Poor
—	520	400	280	200	150

BDL

Basketweave checkering.

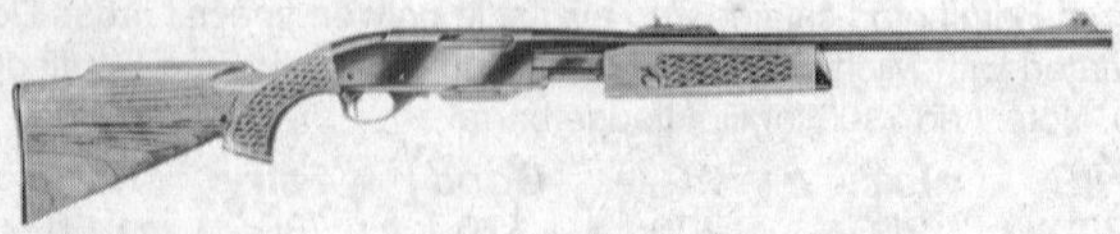

NIB	Exc.	V.G.	Good	Fair	Poor
—	520	400	280	200	150

Model 552A Speedmaster

A .22-caliber semi-automatic rifle, with 23" barrel and open sights. Blued, with pistol grip walnut stock. Manufactured from 1959 to 1988.

NIB	Exc.	V.G.	Good	Fair	Poor
300	250	220	150	80	50

Model 552 BDL

As above, with more fully figured stock and impressed checkering. Introduced in 1966. This is the only U.S.-made .22 semi-automatic that functions with Short, Long and LR ammunition.

NIB	Exc.	V.G.	Good	Fair	Poor
550	480	400	300	200	100

Model 552 BDL Deluxe Speedmaster NRA Edition

Introduced in 2005. Features walnut stock, with checkering and high gloss finish. Blued receiver and barrel, with NRA logos etched on both sides of receiver.

NIB	Exc.	V.G.	Good	Fair	Poor
520	400	300	200	120	100

Model 572 Fieldmaster

A .22-caliber slide-action rifle, with 21" barrel and open sights. Blued, with walnut stock. Manufactured from 1955 to 1988.

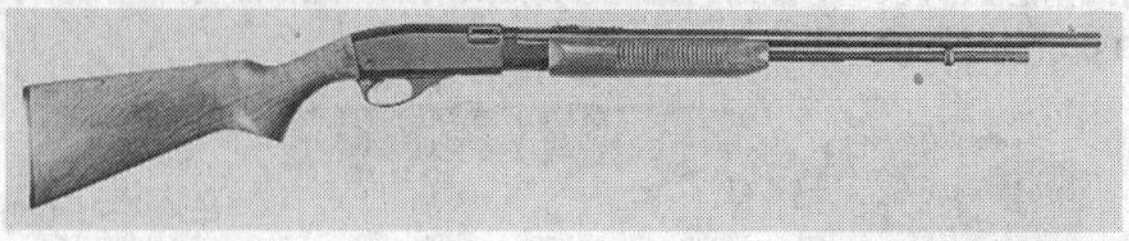

Courtesy Remington Arms

NIB	Exc.	V.G.	Good	Fair	Poor
350	300	220	150	80	50

Model 572 BDL

As above, with more fully figured walnut stock and impressed checkering. Introduced in 1966.

NIB	Exc.	V.G.	Good	Fair	Poor
550	480	400	300	200	100

Model 572SB

Same as Model 572, with a smoothbore barrel. Chambered for .22 LR shot cartridge.

NIB	Exc.	V.G.	Good	Fair	Poor
320	280	200	120	80	60

Model 572 BDL Smoothbore

Similar to Model 572, with unrifled barrel for use with shot cartridges. Introduced as a special production item in 2007.

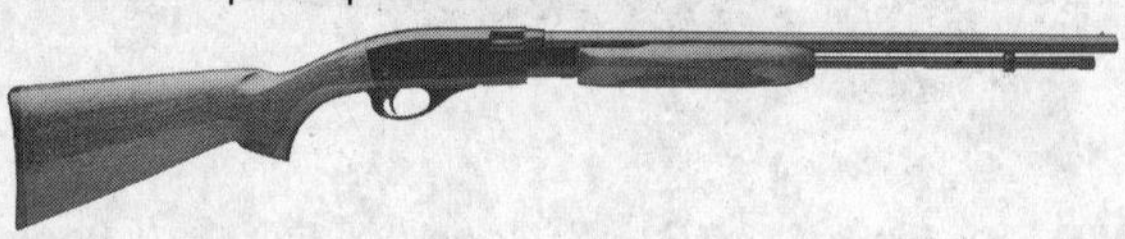

NIB	Exc.	V.G.	Good	Fair	Poor
650	580	400	350	110	80

Model 580

A .22-caliber single-shot bolt-action rifle, with 24" barrel, open sights and Monte Carlo-style stock. Blued. Manufactured from 1968 to 1978.

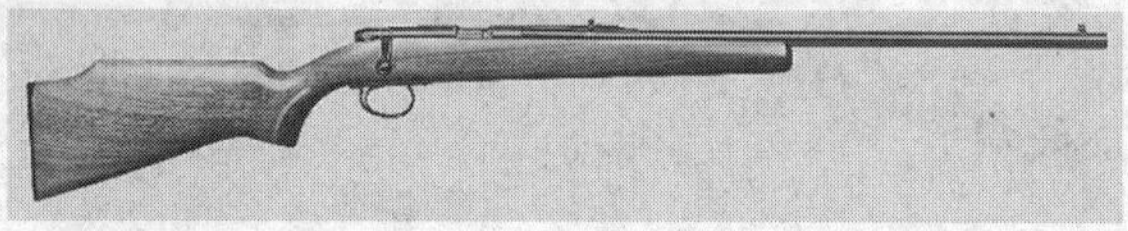

Courtesy Remington Arms

NIB	Exc.	V.G.	Good	Fair	Poor
—	250	200	150	80	50

Model 580 BR

Same as above, with 1" shorter buttstock.

NIB	Exc.	V.G.	Good	Fair	Poor
250	200	150	180	80	50

Model 580 SB

Same as Model 580, with smoothbore barrel for .22 LR shot cartridges.

NIB	Exc.	V.G.	Good	Fair	Poor
300	250	180	120	80	50

Model 581

A .22-caliber bolt-action magazine rifle. Blued, with 24" barrel and walnut stock. Manufactured from 1967 to 1983.

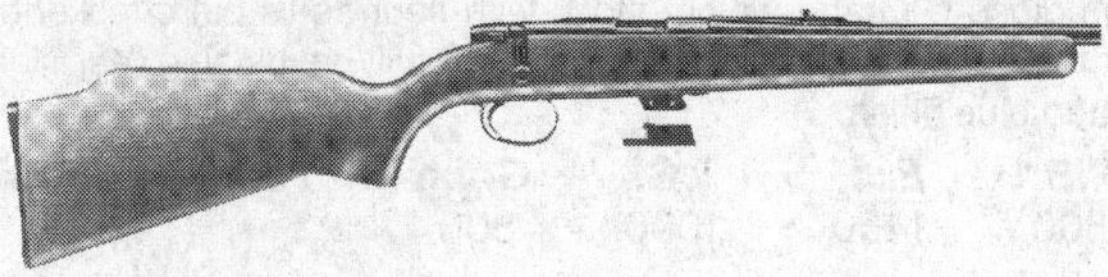

NIB	Exc.	V.G.	Good	Fair	Poor
300	250	180	120	80	50

Model 581 Left-Hand

Same as above. Built for left-handed shooter.

NIB	Exc.	V.G.	Good	Fair	Poor
300	250	180	120	80	50

Model 581-S

As above, fitted with 5-round detachable magazine. Introduced in 1986.

NIB	Exc.	V.G.	Good	Fair	Poor
300	250	180	120	80	50

Model 582

As above, fitted with tubular magazine in place of detachable box magazine. Manufactured from 1967 to 1983.

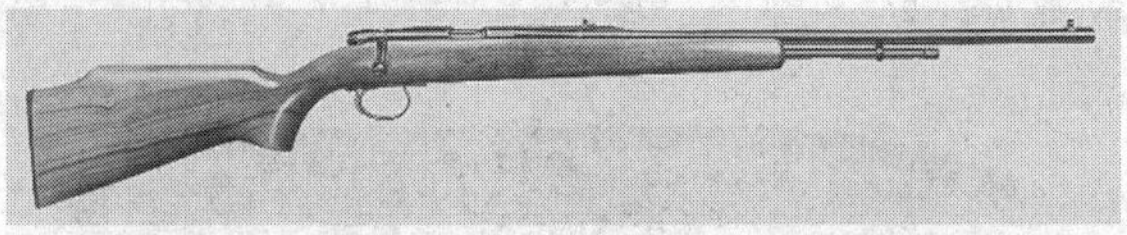

Courtesy Remington Arms

NIB	Exc.	V.G.	Good	Fair	Poor
300	250	180	120	80	50

Model 591

A 5mm rimfire Magnum bolt-action rifle, with 24" barrel and Monte Carlo-style stock. Approximately 20,000 made between 1970 and 1973.

NIB	Exc.	V.G.	Good	Fair	Poor
450	300	220	180	120	80

Model 592

As above, with tubular magazine. Approximately 7,000 made.

NIB	Exc.	V.G.	Good	Fair	Poor
450	300	220	180	120	80

Model 740

Semi-automatic rifle, with 22" barrel and detachable box magazine. Chambered in .244 Rem., .280 Rem., .308 or .30-06. Blued, with plain walnut stock. Also available with 18.5" barrel that would be worth approximately 10 percent more than values listed below. Manufactured from 1955 to 1960. Note: Add 30 percent premium for .244 Rem.

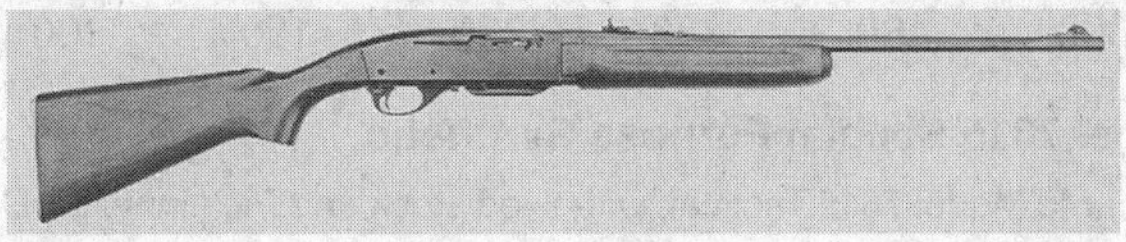

NIB	Exc.	V.G.	Good	Fair	Poor
—	300	220	200	150	100

ADL

As above, with a checkered walnut pistol grip stock.

NIB	Exc.	V.G.	Good	Fair	Poor
—	350	250	220	150	100

BDL

As above, with a more finely figured walnut stock.

NIB	Exc.	V.G.	Good	Fair	Poor
—	400	280	250	150	100

Peerless Grade

Higher grade wood, scroll engraving.

NIB	Exc.	V.G.	Good	Fair	Poor
3600	2800	2000	—	—	—

Premier Grade

Best grade walnut, extensive engraving throughout. Note: Add $2000 for gold inlays.

NIB	Exc.	V.G.	Good	Fair	Poor
7000	6000	3000	—	—	—

Model 742

A 6mm Rem., .243, .280, .30-06 or .308-caliber semi-automatic rifle, with 22" barrel and 4-shot magazine. Also available with 18" barrel in calibers .308 and .30-06 that are worth approximately 10 percent more than values listed below. Blued, with checkered walnut stock. Manufactured from 1960 to 1980.

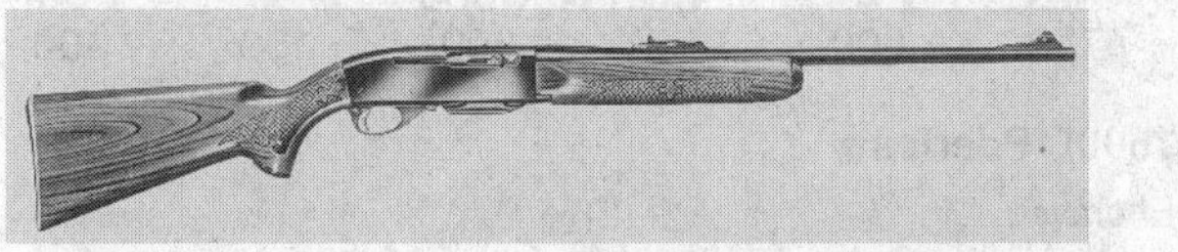

Courtesy Remington Arms

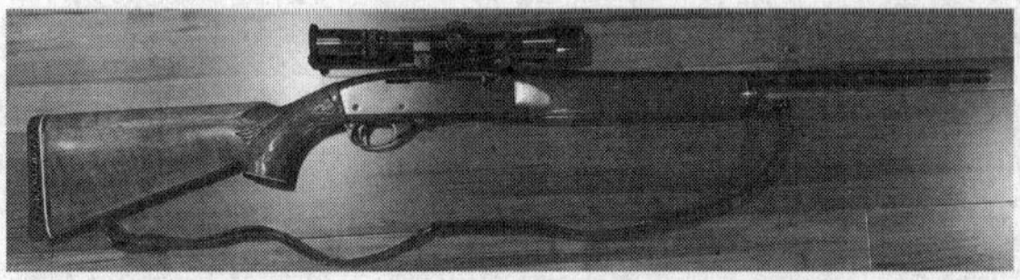

Courtesy Keith Kramis

Remington Woodsmaster Model 742 in 30-06.

NIB	Exc.	V.G.	Good	Fair	Poor
—	350	280	250	150	100

BDL Standard Grade

As above, with Monte Carlo-style stock and basketweave checkering.

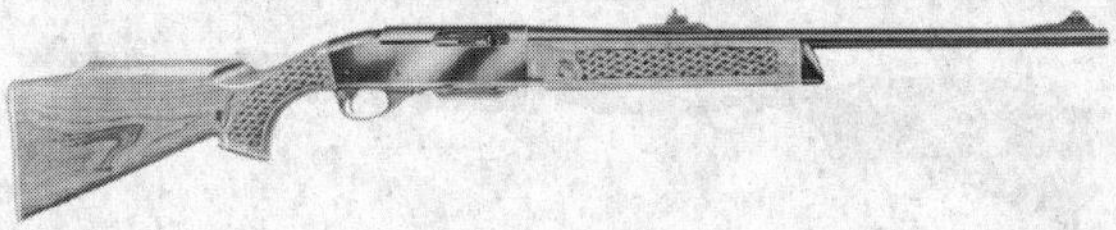

NIB	Exc.	V.G.	Good	Fair	Poor
—	380	280	220	180	120

742D Peerless

Engraved.

NIB	Exc.	V.G.	Good	Fair	Poor
—	5000	3500	2250	1100	450

742F Premier (Game Scene)

NIB	Exc.	V.G.	Good	Fair	Poor
—	9000	6000	4500	1700	550

742F Premier (Gold Inlaid)

NIB	Exc.	V.G.	Good	Fair	Poor
—	10000	7000	5250	2200	750

Bicentennial

Mfg. 1976 only.

NIB	Exc.	V.G.	Good	Fair	Poor
—	550	500	300	200	150

Model 76 Sportsman

A .30-06 slide-action rifle, with 22" barrel and 4-shot magazine. Blued, with walnut stock. Manufactured from 1985 to 1987.

NIB	Exc.	V.G.	Good	Fair	Poor
—	320	220	180	120	80

Model 7600

Variation of the above. Chambered for a variety of cartridges from 6mm Rem. to .35 Whelen, with 22" barrel and detachable magazine. Also available with 18.5" barrel. Blued, with checkered walnut stock. In 1996, fine line engraving on receiver was offered as standard.

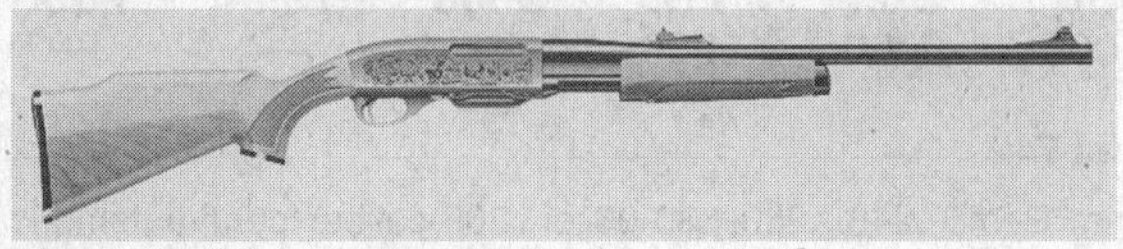

Model 7600 with engraving

Standard Grade

NIB	Exc.	V.G.	Good	Fair	Poor
750	600	500	300	150	100

7600D Peerless

Engraved.

NIB	Exc.	V.G.	Good	Fair	Poor
—	5000	3500	2250	1100	450

7600F Premier

Game scene engraved.

NIB	Exc.	V.G.	Good	Fair	Poor
—	9000	6000	4500	1700	550

Premier

Gold inlaid.

NIB	Exc.	V.G.	Good	Fair	Poor
—	10000	7000	5250	2200	750

Synthetic

Same as standard grade Model 7600, with black synthetic stock. A .30-06 carbine version is also available. Introduced in 1998.

NIB	Exc.	V.G.	Good	Fair	Poor
510	380	280	200	150	100

Special Purpose

Same configuration as standard Model 7600. Equipped with a special finish on both the wood and metal that is non-reflective. First offered in 1993.

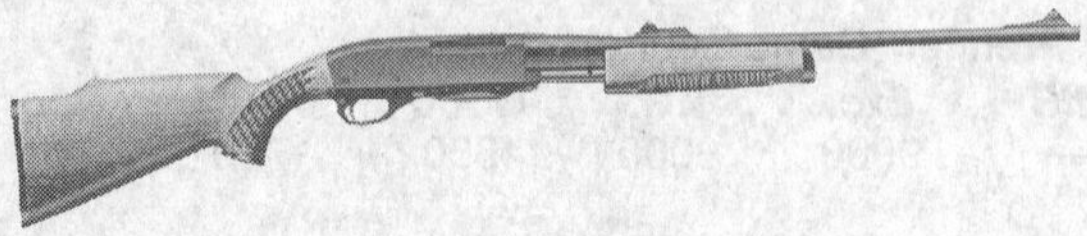

NIB	Exc.	V.G.	Good	Fair	Poor
600	480	350	220	150	100

Model 7600 200th Year Anniversary Edition

A limited edition made only in 2016 to commemorate the 200th anniversary of the Remington company. A total of 2,016 rifles were produced in .30-06 featuring a 24-carat gold inlay of founder Eliphalet Remington, a high gloss C Grade walnut stock with fleur-de-lis cut checkering and black forend tip, a hooded ramp front and fully adjustable rear sight and polished blue finish.

NIB	Exc.	V.G.	Good	Fair	Poor
1600	1450	1000	800	—	—

7600P Patrol

Introduced in 2002. Chambered for .308 cartridge. Fitted with 16.5" barrel. Synthetic stock, with matte black finish. Parkerized finish on metal. Wilson Combat rear ghost ring sights, with AO front sight. Weight about 7 lbs.

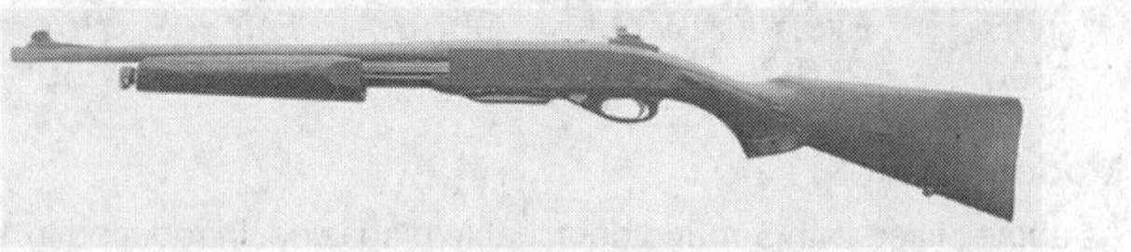

NIB	Exc.	V.G.	Good	Fair	Poor
600	480	350	220	150	100

Model 7600 Buckmasters ADF (American Deer Foundation)

Introduced in 1997. Built only for that year. Chambered for .30-06 cartridge. Limited edition item. Fitted with 22" barrel and special fine line engraved receiver.

NIB	Exc.	V.G.	Good	Fair	Poor
600	480	350	220	150	100

Model Six

Centerfire slide-action rifle, with 22" barrel and 4-shot detachable magazine. Blued, with walnut stock. Manufactured from 1981 to 1987. Chambered in 6mm Rem., .243 Win., .270 Win., .308 Win., .30-06. Discontinued in 1987. Note: Add 50 percent for 6mm Rem.

NIB	Exc.	V.G.	Good	Fair	Poor
750	600	450	350	200	120

Model 7615 Tactical Pump Carbine

Pump-action rifle based on Model 7600 action. Chambered in .223 Rem., with 16.5" barrel. Folding synthetic stock. Introduced in 2007.

NIB	Exc.	V.G.	Good	Fair	Poor
600	480	350	220	150	100

Model 7615 Special Purpose Synthetic

Similar to Model 7615 Tactical, with fixed stock and Picatinny rail. Dealer exclusive for 2007.

NIB	Exc.	V.G.	Good	Fair	Poor
620	500	380	250	180	120

Model 7615 Camo Hunter

Similar to Model 7615 Tactical, with fixed buttstock and entirely camo-finished except for action parts and triggerguard assembly. Introduced in 2007.

NIB	Exc.	V.G.	Good	Fair	Poor
650	520	400	260	200	150

Model 7615 Ranch Carbine

Similar to Model 7615 Tactical, with fixed walnut buttstock and forend. 18.5" barrel. No iron sights. Drilled and tapped for scope mounts. Introduced in 2007.

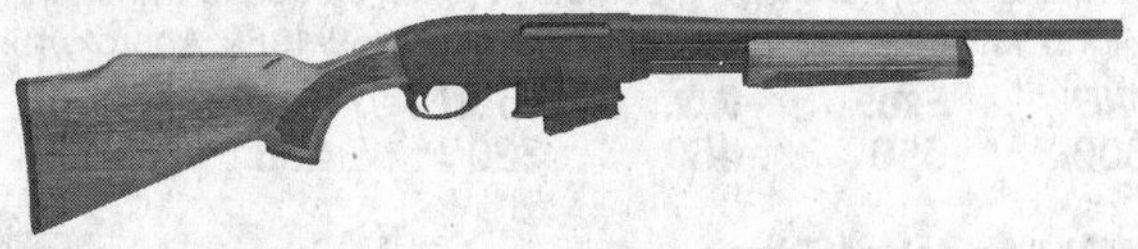

NIB	Exc.	V.G.	Good	Fair	Poor
620	500	380	250	180	120

Model 74 Sportsman

A .30-06 caliber semi-automatic rifle, with 22" barrel and 4-shot detachable magazine. Blued, with walnut stock. Manufactured from 1985 to 1987.

NIB	Exc.	V.G.	Good	Fair	Poor
—	350	250	180	120	80

Model Four

As above, with select Monte Carlo-style stock. Manufactured from 1982 to 1987.

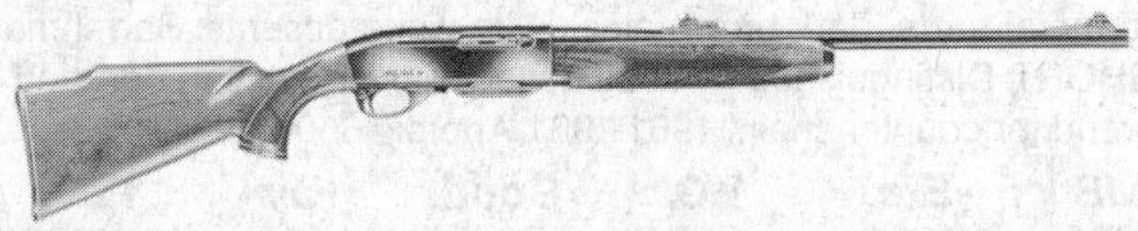

NIB	Exc.	V.G.	Good	Fair	Poor
650	500	400	350	280	180

Model 7400

A semi-automatic rifle with 22" barrel. Chambered for .243, .270, .280, .30-06, .308 and .35 Whelen. Blued with checkered walnut stock. Average weight about 7.5 lbs. Introduced in 1982. In 1996, offered with fine line engraving on receiver as standard.

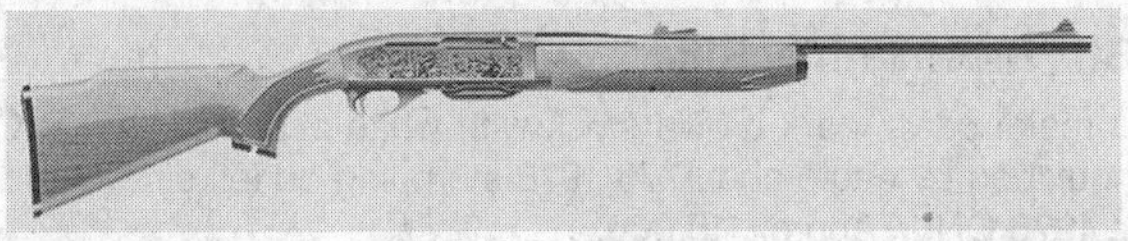

NIB	Exc.	V.G.	Good	Fair	Poor
600	480	350	250	200	100

Synthetic

Similar to Model 7400, with black non-reflective synthetic stock. A .30-06 carbine also offered. Introduced in 1998.

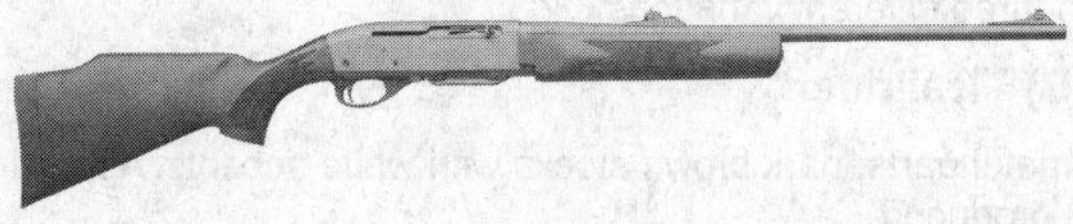

NIB	Exc.	V.G.	Good	Fair	Poor
550	400	300	200	150	100

Weathermaster

Introduced in 2003. Semi-automatic features weather-resistant black synthetic stock and matte nickel-plated receiver, barrel and magazine. Barrel length 22", with iron sights. Chambered for .30-06 or .270 Win. cartridges. Weight about 7.5 lbs.

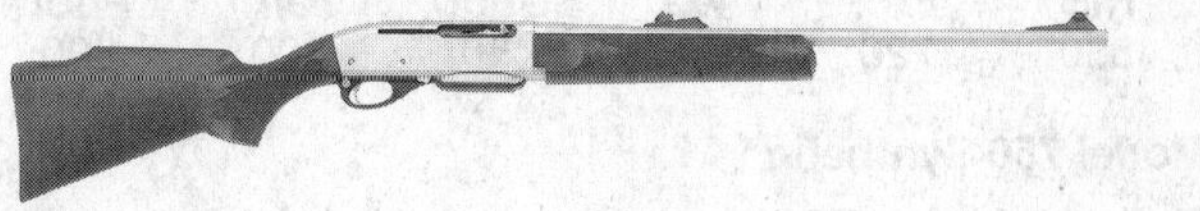

NIB	Exc.	V.G.	Good	Fair	Poor
650	520	400	300	200	100

Carbine

Same as above, with 18.5" barrel. Chambered for .30-06 cartridge.

NIB	Exc.	V.G.	Good	Fair	Poor
550	400	300	200	150	100

Special Purpose

Same configuration as standard Model 7400. Equipped with special finish on both the wood and metal that is non-eflective. First offered in 1993.

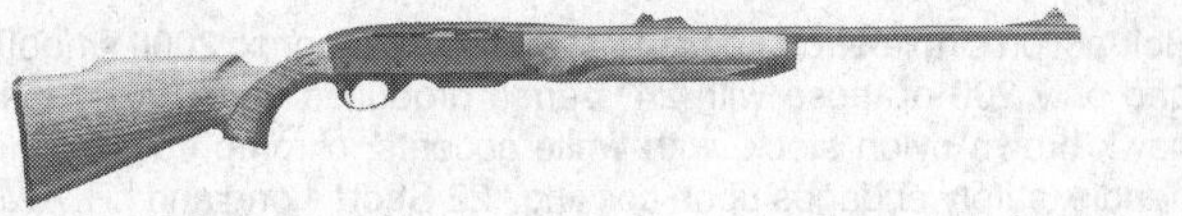

NIB	Exc.	V.G.	Good	Fair	Poor
450	350	300	250	200	100

Buckmasters ADF (American Deer Foundation)

Introduced in 1997. Built only in that year as a limited model. Chambered for .30-06 cartridge. Fitted with 22" barrel. Special fine line engraving and polished blue finish. American walnut stock, with Monte Carlo and cut checkering. Weight is 7.5 lbs.

Close-up detail on engraving for Model 7400 Buckmasters ADF

NIB	Exc.	V.G.	Good	Fair	Poor
600	500	400	300	200	100

Model 7400 Custom Grade

Custom Shop model available in three levels of engraving, gold inlay, wood grade and finish, metal work finish, recoil pad/buttplate and dimensions. Each gun should be individually appraised prior to sale.

F Grade

NIB	Exc.	V.G.	Good	Fair	Poor
—	9000	6000	4500	1700	550

F Grade with Gold Inlay

NIB	Exc.	V.G.	Good	Fair	Poor
—	10000	7000	5250	2200	750

Model 750 Woodsmaster

This model replaced the 7400 family of semi-automatic rifles in 2006. Features include an improved gas-operating system and lower profile. Standard model has walnut stock; rifle version has 22" barrel; carbine has 18.5" barrel. Discontinued in 2017.

NIB	Exc.	V.G.	Good	Fair	Poor
880	720	600	450	300	200

Model 750 Synthetic

Similar to Model 750 Woodsmaster, with black synthetic stock and forend. Introduced in 2007.

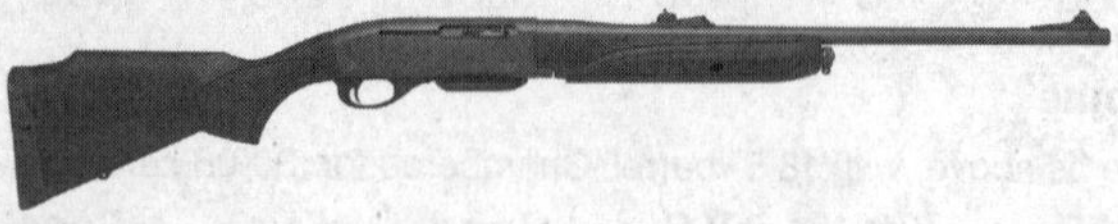

NIB	Exc.	V.G.	Good	Fair	Poor
620	550	400	300	220	120

NYLON SERIES .22 RIFLES

Model 10 Nylon

Bolt-action single-shot. Approximately 10,700 (approx. 2000 smoothbore and only 200 of those with 24" barrel) produced from 1962-1964. Mohawk brown nylon stock, with white accents, chrome spoon style bolt handle, safety engages upon cocking, .22 Short, Long and LR. Available in both rifled and smoothbore versions (smoothbore barrels are marked "smoothbore") and barrel lengths of 19.5" and 24". Note: Add 100%+ for 24" versions; 100%+ for NIB.

Courtesy Remington Arms

10 (model)

NIB	Exc.	V.G.	Good	Fair	Poor
—	700	600	500	300	200

10 (SB)

NIB	Exc.	V.G.	Good	Fair	Poor
—	1000	800	700	500	450

Model 11 Nylon

Bolt-action repeater, 6- or 10-round metal box magazine. Approximately 22,500 produced from 1962-1964. Mohawk brown nylon stock, with white accents, chrome spoon style bolt handle, manual right side safety. .22 Short, Long or LR. Barrel lengths 19.5" and 24". Note: Add 100% for 24" version.

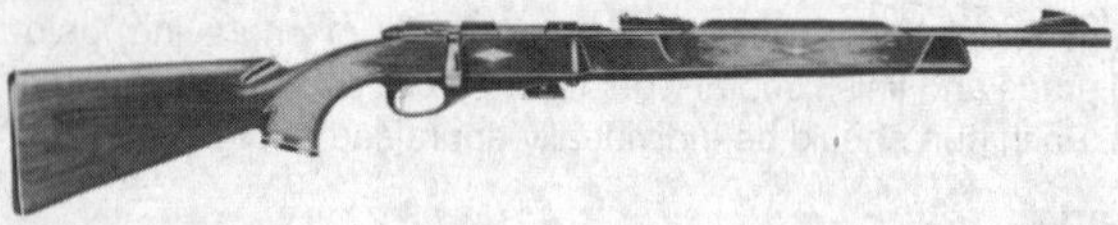

NIB	Exc.	V.G.	Good	Fair	Poor
—	480	380	300	280	180

Model 12 Nylon

Bolt-action repeater, 14-round external tubular magazine under the barrel. Approximately 27,600 produced from 1962-1964. Mohawk brown nylon stock, with white accents, chrome spoon-style bolt handle, manual right side safety. .22 Short, Long or LR. Barrel lengths 19.5" and 24". Note: Add 100% for 24" version.

NIB	Exc.	V.G.	Good	Fair	Poor
—	480	380	300	280	180

Model 66 Nylon

Semi-automatic, 19.5" barrel, 14-round tubular magazine fed through buttplate. In excess of 1,000,000 produced from 1959-1987. Seven different variations of style and color were sold. Non-serialized prior to 1968 gun control act of 1968. An "A" prefix was added to serialization in 1977.

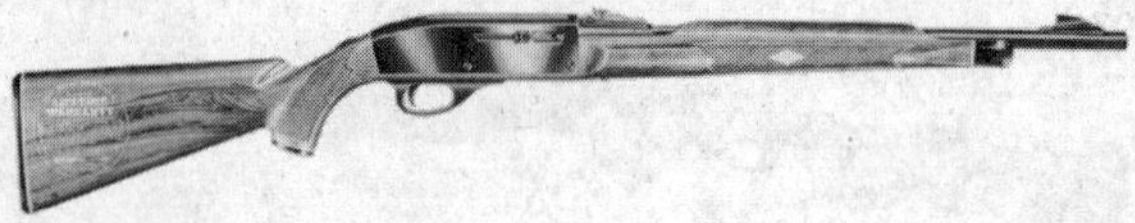

66 (MB) "Mohawk" Brown

Blued metal parts, dark chocolate brown stock with white accents, .22 LR ONLY. 1959-1987. Approx. 678,000.

NIB	Exc.	V.G.	Good	Fair	Poor
400	350	300	150	120	100

66 (SG) "Seneca" Green

Blued metal parts, dark olive green stock (often confused with MB in artificial light) with white accents, .22 LR ONLY, 1959-1962. Approx. 45,000.

NIB	Exc.	V.G.	Good	Fair	Poor
600	550	450	320	280	180

66 (AB) "Apache" Black

Bright chrome plated metal parts, black stock with white accents, .22 LR ONLY. 1962-1983. Approx. 220,000.

NIB	Exc.	V.G.	Good	Fair	Poor
600	500	420	350	250	120

66 (BD) "Black Diamond"

Blued metal parts, black stock with black diamonds in forend. Remainder of accents are white, .22 LR ONLY, 1978-1987. Approx. 56,000.

NIB	Exc.	V.G.	Good	Fair	Poor
450	420	380	300	250	150

66 (GS) "Gallery Special"

Blued metal parts, dark brown stock with white accents. Barrel marked .22 SHORT. Distinguished by shell deflector over ejection port and loop on forend for counter chain. 1961-1981. Approx. 6500.

NIB	Exc.	V.G.	Good	Fair	Poor
1300	1200	950	700	450	300

66 (AN) "150th Anniversary Rifle"

Blued metal parts, dark brown stock with white accents, .22 LR ONLY. Distinguished by 150th Anniversary stamping on left side of receiver cover. 1966 ONLY. Approx. 4,000.

NIB	Exc.	V.G.	Good	Fair	Poor
750	700	600	450	300	250

66 (BI) "Bicentennial Rifle"

Blued metal parts, dark brown stock with white accents, .22 LR ONLY. Distinguished by eagle and 1776/1976 stamping on left side of receiver cover. 1976 ONLY. Approx. 10,000.

NIB	Exc.	V.G.	Good	Fair	Poor
700	600	500	320	280	200

Model 76 Nylon

Only lever-action repeater Remington ever produced. 19.5" barrel, 14-round tubular magazine, fed through buttplate. Produced from 1962-1964 in three different variations.

76 (MB) "Trailrider"

Blued metal parts, dark brown stocks with white accents. Approximately 25,300 produced.

NIB	Exc.	V.G.	Good	Fair	Poor
—	1700	600	500	380	250

76 (AB) "Trailrider"

Bright chrome metal parts, black stock with white accents. Approximately

1,600 produced.

NIB	Exc.	V.G.	Good	Fair	Poor
—	2000	800	700	500	400

76 (not cataloged)

Blued metal parts, black stock with white accents. Production numbers do not exist.

NIB	Exc.	V.G.	Good	Fair	Poor
—	1800	680	600	400	300

Model 77 Nylon

Known as 77 (MB): Semi-automatic, 19.5" barrel, 5-round plastic box magazine. Blued metal parts, dark brown stock with white accents. .22 LR ONLY. 1970-1971, approx. 15,300 produced. This model was replaced by Model 10C in 1972. Note: Add 100% for NIB.

NIB	Exc.	V.G.	Good	Fair	Poor
—	500	380	300	200	150

Model 10C Nylon

Known as 10C. Identical copy of 77 (MB), except box magazine capacity was increased to 10 rounds. 1972-1978. Approx. 128,000 produced. Note: Add 50% for NIB.

NIB	Exc.	V.G.	Good	Fair	Poor
—	320	280	220	180	100

Model 77 Apache Nylon

Known as "APACHE 77". Semi-automatic, 19.5" barrel, 10-round plastic box magazine. Metal parts coated with black "teflon-like" finish, bright green stock with swirls of orange, brown and black (highly variable), not to be confused with the 66 (SG). Rifle was contracted as an "exclusive" run, marketed by K-Mart. Number manufactured is hazy, but estimates run from 54,000 to over 100,000. Produced from 1987-1989. Note: Add 100% for NIB.

NIB	Exc.	V.G.	Good	Fair	Poor
—	350	250	200	140	120

Model 522 Viper

Introduced in 1993. A new Remington .22 rimfire caliber semi-automatic design. Black stock made from synthetic resin, while receiver is made from a synthetic as well. Features 20" barrel and 10-shot detachable clip. Weight 4.6 lbs.

NIB	Exc.	V.G.	Good	Fair	Poor
160	120	100	80	60	40

MODEL 597 SERIES

Model 597

Introduced in 1997. Automatic .22 LR rimfire. Features carbon steel barrel, with alloy receiver. All metal has a non-reflective matte black finish. Stock is dark gray synthetic. Barrel length 20". Weight about 5.5 lbs.

NIB	Exc.	V.G.	Good	Fair	Poor
220	150	100	70	50	20

40X Sporter

Introduced in 1998. This version of Model 597 has a blued finish, with hardwood stock and beavertail-style forearm. Magazine capacity 10 rounds.

NIB	Exc.	V.G.	Good	Fair	Poor
220	150	100	70	50	20

Stainless Sporter

Same as Model 597SS. Fitted with hardwood stock. Introduced in 2000.

NIB	Exc.	V.G.	Good	Fair	Poor
280	200	150	100	80	20

LSS

This version of Model 597 is similar to above, with addition of a laminated stock and stainless steel finish.

NIB	Exc.	V.G.	Good	Fair	Poor
300	220	180	120	100	50

SS

This version is also chambered for .22 LR. Has a stainless steel barrel on an alloy receiver. Stock is gray synthetic, with beavertail style forearm. Magazine capacity 10 rounds. Weight about 5.5 lbs. Introduced in 1998.

NIB	Exc.	V.G.	Good	Fair	Poor
240	180	120	100	80	20

HB

Introduced in 2001. Features 20" carbon steel heavy barrel. Chambered for .22 LR cartridge. Fitted with brown laminated stock. No sights. Weight about 6 lbs.

NIB	Exc.	V.G.	Good	Fair	Poor
280	220	160	120	80	20

HB Magnum

Same as model above. Chambered for .22 Win. Magnum cartridge. Introduced in 2001.

NIB	Exc.	V.G.	Good	Fair	Poor
420	320	200	160	120	50

Magnum

Features 20" carbon steel barrel, alloy receiver and black synthetic stock. Chambered for .22 Win. Magnum cartridge. Weight about 6 lbs.

NIB	Exc.	V.G.	Good	Fair	Poor
350	250	200	150	100	50

Magnum LS

Chambered for .22 Magnum. Receiver and barrel blued, with gray laminated hardwood stock and beavertail-style forearm. Magazine capacity 10 rounds. Introduced in 1998. In 2003, also offered chambered for .17 HMR cartridge.

NIB	Exc.	V.G.	Good	Fair	Poor
380	280	200	140	100	50

Custom Target

Available on special order from Custom Shop. Chambered for .22 LR cartridge. Has 20" stainless steel heavy target barrel, without sights. Stock green laminated-wood target-style, with pistol grip. Trigger custom tuned. Weight about 7.5 lbs. Introduced in 1998.

NIB	Exc.	V.G.	Good	Fair	Poor
600	480	400	280	200	150

Custom Target Magnum

Similar to model above. Chambered for .22 Win. Magnum. Weight about 8 lbs. Introduced in 1998. Special order item only.

NIB	Exc.	V.G.	Good	Fair	Poor
750	600	500	380	250	180

LSS

Similar to Model 597, with laminated stock, stainless barrel and 3-9X scope. Dealer exclusive for 2007.

NIB	Exc.	V.G.	Good	Fair	Poor
280	200	150	100	80	20

Synthetic Scope Combo

"Package rifle" similar to Model 597, with 3-9X scope included. Introduced in 2007.

NIB	Exc.	V.G.	Good	Fair	Poor
300	220	180	120	100	50

TVP (Target/Varmint/Plinker)

Ultra-funky .22 LR autoloader built on Model 597 chassis. Features include bolt-guidance system, with twin tool-steel guide rails; laminated skeletonized wood stock; non-glare matte finish; 10-shot metal detachable magazine; last-shot hold-open bolt for added safety. Scope rail. Introduced in 2008.

NIB	Exc.	V.G.	Good	Fair	Poor
530	460	400	280	180	120

Yellow Jacket

Similar to above, with yellow and black laminated stock.

NIB	Exc.	V.G.	Good	Fair	Poor
500	400	220	150	100	80

Blaze Camo

Model 597, with synthetic stock molded in screamin' blaze orange and black.

NIB	Exc.	V.G.	Good	Fair	Poor
280	220	160	120	80	20

Pink Camo

Similar to above, with pink – yes pink – and black camo-pattern stock.

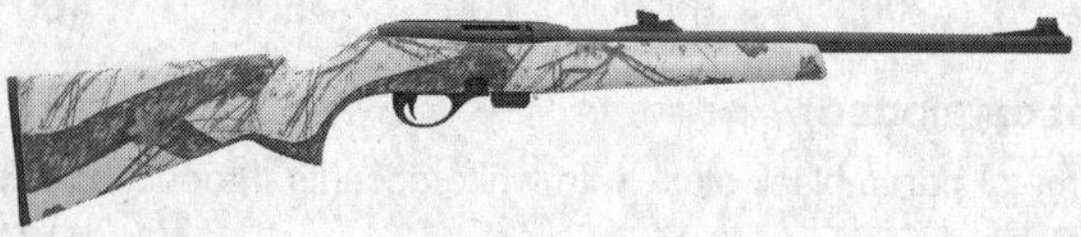

NIB	Exc.	V.G.	Good	Fair	Poor
280	220	160	120	80	20

FLX

Similar to Model 597 Blaze/Pink camo, with FLX Digital Camo stock.

NIB	Exc.	V.G.	Good	Fair	Poor
280	220	160	120	80	20

AAC

Same features as other 597 models, except it has 16.5" barrel that will accept AAC flash hider, muzzle-break or suppressor. Staggered-stack magazine holds 10 rounds. Weight 5.5 lbs.

NIB	Exc.	V.G.	Good	Fair	Poor
200	160	140	120	100	80

VTR - Quad Rail

Semi-automatic rifle chambered in .22 LR. Styled to resemble AR. Features include matte blued finish; black synthetic stock; 16" barrel; Pardus A2-style collapsible pistol grip stock; quad-rail free-floated tube; 10-round magazine.

NIB	Exc.	V.G.	Good	Fair	Poor
400	360	320	280	210	150

VTR A-2 Fixed Stock

Similar to VTR - Quad Rail, with fixed A2-style stock. Standard handguard, with quad rail.

NIB	Exc.	V.G.	Good	Fair	Poor
400	360	320	280	210	150

VTR Collapsible Stock

Similar to VTR A-2 Fixed Stock, with Pardus A2-style collapsible pistol grip stock.

NIB	Exc.	V.G.	Good	Fair	Poor
400	360	320	280	210	150

VTR A-TACS Camo

Semi-automatic rifle chambered in .22 LR. Styled to resemble AR. Features include ATACS camo finish overall; 16" barrel; Pardus A2-style collapsible pistol grip stock; round handguard without rails; receiver-mounted optics rail; 10-round magazine.

NIB	Exc.	V.G.	Good	Fair	Poor
520	460	420	350	280	180

Model Five

.22 rimfire bolt-action sporter. Calibers .22 LR, .22 WMR, .17 HMR; five-shot detachable magazine; barrel 22" blued, with iron sights; receiver blued for scope mounts; stock laminated walnut, with QD swivels. Introduced 2006. Note: Add 10 percent for .22 WMR.

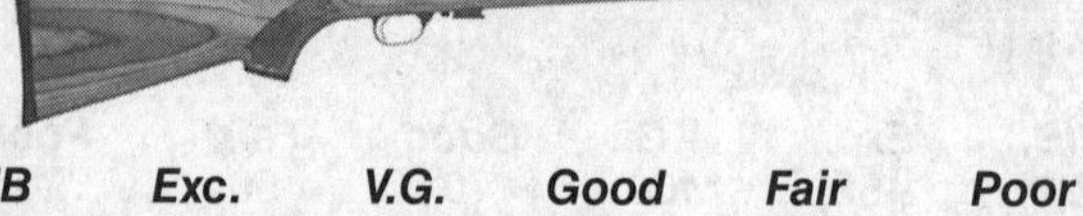

NIB	Exc.	V.G.	Good	Fair	Poor
300	250	180	120	80	20

MODEL 40X SERIES

40X Target Rifle

A .22-caliber rimfire single-shot bolt-action rifle, with heavy 28" barrel. Fitted with Redfield Olympic sights or telescopic sight bases. Blued, with walnut target-style stock having a hard rubber buttplate. Manufactured from 1955 to 1964. Note: Add $125 with sights.

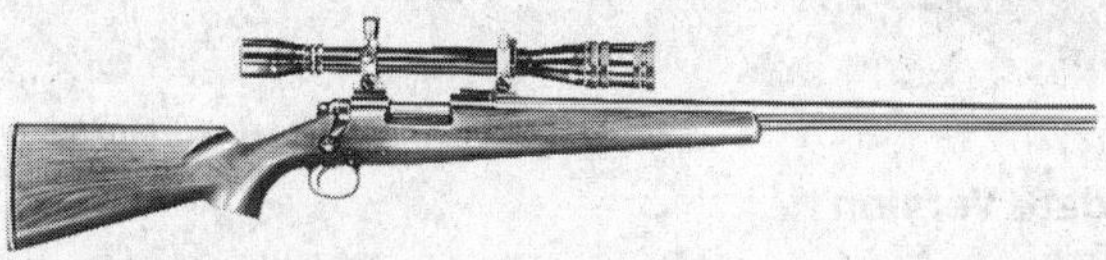

Courtesy Remington Arms

NIB	Exc.	V.G.	Good	Fair	Poor
1380	1170	1000	850	500	300

Sporter

As above, with 24" barrel, 5-shot magazine. Walnut sporting-style stock. Fewer than 700 made between 1969 and 1980.

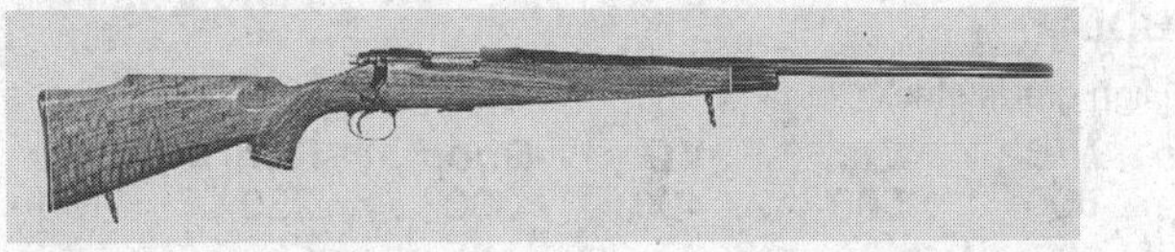

Courtesy Remington Arms

NIB	Exc.	V.G.	Good	Fair	Poor
4500	3750	3000	2250	1000	500

40X Centerfire Target

Chambered for .222, .222 Magnum, .308 or .30-06 centerfire cartridges. Manufactured from 1961 to 1964.

NIB	Exc.	V.G.	Good	Fair	Poor
1100	950	700	500	300	200

40XB Rangemaster Centerfire

Features blue or stainless steel barrel, receiver and bolt. Receiver drilled, tapped and fitted with 27.25" heavy target barrel. Trigger fully adjustable. Choice of walnut or synthetic stock. Starting in 1998, offered with a special laminated thumbhole stock. Offered in calibers from .222 to .300 Win Mag. Rifle built to order in Custom Shop. Made since 1964. Note: Add $300 for thumbhole stock.

NIB	Exc.	V.G.	Good	Fair	Poor
2100	1800	1320	1000	600	250

40XB BR

A benchrest Custom Shop version of above model. Has 22" stainless heavy barrel. Chambered for .22 BR Rem. Adjustable trigger. Built to order.

NIB	Exc.	V.G.	Good	Fair	Poor
1200	1000	850	600	450	200

40XBBR Benchrest

An advanced version of the above model with 27 ¼-inch stainless steel barrel, satin-finished walnut stock with front swivel block and forend guide rail, straight-comb with cheekpiece. Hand-fitted barreled action epoxy bedded to stock, single-shot or repeater, externally adjustable trigger, left-hand version available. Made to order in Custom Shop.

NIB	Exc.	V.G.	Good	Fair	Poor
3300	2500	1900	1400	800	350

40XB Tactical Rifle

First offered in 2003. Bolt-action rifle features Teflon-coated stainless steel 27.25" barrel. Chambered for .308 Win cartridge. Fitted with H.S. Precision tactical stock, with vertical pistol grip. Remington 40-X trigger.

NIB	Exc.	V.G.	Good	Fair	Poor
2500	2100	1600	1200	700	350

40XS Tactical

Bolt-action rifle chambered in .308 Win. or .338 Lapua Magnum. Features include 416 stainless steel Model 40-X 24" 1:12 barreled action; black polymer coating; McMillan A3 series stock, with adjustable length of pull and comb; adjustable trigger and all-steel triggerguard; Harris bipod, with quick-adjust swivel lock; Leupold Mark IV 3.5-10x40mm long-range M1 scope with Mil Dot reticle; Badger Ordnance all-steel Picatinny scope rail and rings. Note: Deduct 50% if without Leupold scope, Harris Bipod, Badger Ordnance Picatinny rail.

NIB	Exc.	V.G.	Good	Fair	Poor
4000	3600	3000	2000	—	—

40XR KS Sporter

Rimfire model in .22 LR or .22 WMR. Sporter contoured 24" barrel, Kevlar stock, no sights. Magazine capacity 5+1. Made from 1994 to 2000.

NIB	Exc.	V.G.	Good	Fair	Poor
1500	1200	850	600	450	350

40XR Custom Sporter

From Remington Custom Shop, high-grade version of 40X rimfire, with specifications made to order. In .22 LR or .22 WMR. Limited production.

NIB	Exc.	V.G.	Good	Fair	Poor
4200	3750	3200	2400	1500	500

40XS Tactical System

Current Custom Shop bolt-action rifle built on blueprinted short action. Features include 416 stainless steel Model 40-X 24" barreled action; black polymer coating; McMillan A5 series stock, with adjustable length of pull and comb; adjustable trigger and all-steel triggerguard; Harris bipod, with quick-adjust swivel lock; Leupold Mark IV 3.5-10x40mm long range M1 scope with Mil Dot reticle; Badger Ordnance all-steel Picatinny scope rail and rings. Turner AWS tactical sling with swivels. Note: Deduct 40% if without Leupold scope, Harris Bipod, Badger Ordnance Picatinny rail.

NIB	Exc.	V.G.	Good	Fair	Poor
7200	6100	5200	4400	—	—

40XS Tactical HB System

Current Custom Shop 40-X blueprinted receiver custom bedded in a McMillan A5 series stock with adjustable length-of-pull and comb height, chambered in 308 Win (1:12" twist), .300 Win (1:12" twist), .338 Lapua Magnum (detachable 5-round magazine); Harris bipod, Leupold Mark IV 3.5-10x40mm long range M1 scope with Mil Dot reticle, Badger Ordnance all-steel Picatinny scope rail and rings, all-steel triggerguard, Turner AWS tactical sling with swivels. Note: Deduct 35% if without Leupold scope, Harris Bipod, Badger Ordnance Picatinny rail.

NIB	Exc.	V.G.	Good	Fair	Poor
7000	6000	5000	4000	—	—

40X TDR (Tactical Deployment Rifle)

Current Custom Shop 40-X chrome moly short-action blueprinted receiver, stainless steel button rifle and hand-lapped barrel, Bell & Carlson Premium stock, 40-X Trigger, 1-piece steel triggerguard, 20 MOA S.A. clip-slotted Picatinny rail, enhanced bolt knob, double pinned bolt handle, ACC 51T muzzle brake, 1/2 MOA accuracy guarantee.

NIB	Exc.	V.G.	Good	Fair	Poor
2800	2300	1750	1200	—	—

40X TIR (Target Interdiction Rifle)

Current Custom Shop 40-X chrome moly short-action blueprinted receiver, 24" stainless steel button rifle and hand-lapped barrel, black HS PST25 Tactical, vertical stock with adjustable LOP/cheekrest, 40-X Trigger, 1-piece steel triggerguard, 20 MOA S.A. clip-slotted Picatinny rail, enhanced bolt knob, double pinned bolt handle, ACC 51T muzzle brake, 1/2 MOA accuracy guarantee.

NIB	Exc.	V.G.	Good	Fair	Poor
3500	2950	2500	2000	—	—

Model XR-100 Rangemaster

Introduced in 2005. Features 26" barrel. Chambered for .204 Ruger, .223 or .22-250 calibers. Black laminate stock, with thumbhole and ventilated forearm. Adjustable trigger. Blued finish. Weight about 9.12 lbs.

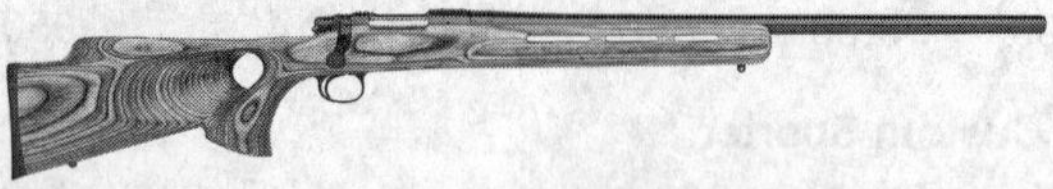

NIB	Exc.	V.G.	Good	Fair	Poor
880	680	500	400	280	150

Model XC KS

Custom Shop position rifle, with 24" stainless steel heavy barrel. Chambered for .223 Rem. and .308 Win. cartridges. Kevlar stock, with palm rail. Weight about 11 lbs.

NIB	Exc.	V.G.	Good	Fair	Poor
2650	2220	1850	1400	800	400

Model 673 Guide Rifle

Introduced in 2003. Bolt-action rifle features 22" ventilated rib barrel. Chambered for 6.5mm Rem. Magnum, .308, .300 RUM or .350 Rem. Magnum cartridge. Adjustable rear sight. Stock is dark and light tan laminate, with checkering. Magazine capacity three rounds. Weight about 7.5 lbs. Discontinued 2006. Slight premium for .300 RUM.

NIB	Exc.	V.G.	Good	Fair	Poor
650	520	400	300	200	150

Model 720A

A .257 Roberts, .270 or .30-06 bolt-action sporting rifle, with 22" barrel and 5-shot integral magazine. Blued, with checkered walnut stock. Approximately 2,500 manufactured from 1941 to 1944. Another 1,000 or so were made in 1942 for the U.S. Navy, mostly in .30-06 with a few in .270 and .257 Roberts. Note: Add 100 percent for .270; 150 percent for .257 Roberts.

Courtesy Remington Arms

NIB	Exc.	V.G.	Good	Fair	Poor
1400	1200	1000	700	300	200

Model 721

A .264 Magnum, .270, .280 or .30-06 bolt-action rifle, with 24" barrel and 4-shot magazine. Blued, with plain walnut stock. Manufactured from 1948 to 1962.

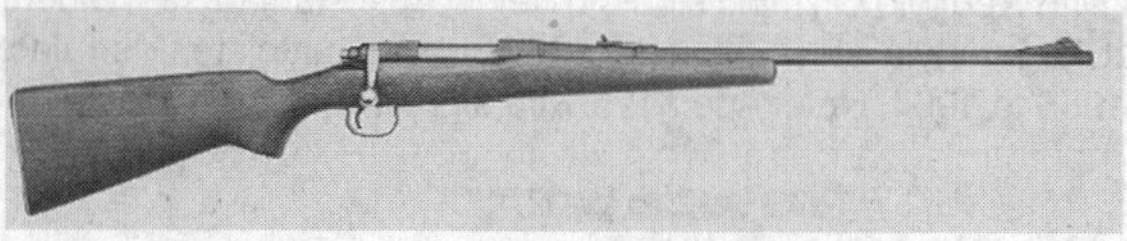

Courtesy Remington Arms

Standard Version

NIB	Exc.	V.G.	Good	Fair	Poor
500	450	350	200	150	100

ADL

Checkered stock.

NIB	Exc.	V.G.	Good	Fair	Poor
550	480	380	250	200	120

BDL

High grade stock.

NIB	Exc.	V.G.	Good	Fair	Poor
600	500	400	300	250	150

Model 721A Magnum

.300 H&H or .264 Win.

NIB	Exc.	V.G.	Good	Fair	Poor
650	550	400	350	280	150

Model 722

Short-action variation of Model 721. Chambered for .222 Rem., .222 Rem. Magnum, .243 Win., .244 Rem., .257 Roberts, .300 Savage, .308 Win. BDL models featured high-grade select walnut stocks; ADL had checkered stocks. Made from 1948 to 1962. Note: Add 25 percent for BDL; 10 percent for ADL; 25 percent for .222 Rem. Magnum, .243, .257 or .308 chamberings.

NIB	Exc.	V.G.	Good	Fair	Poor
550	450	350	200	150	100

Model 725 ADL

Short-lived but well-made model. Offered in .222 Rem., .243 Win., .244 Rem., .270 Win., .280 Rem., and .30-06 Springfield. 4-round magazine capacity (5 in .222). Adjustable open rear sight, hooded ramp front. Checkered walnut stock, with Monte Carlo comb, sling swivels. Barrel length: 22" (24" .222). Weight about 7 lbs. Made from 1958 to 1961. Note: Add $150 for .280 Rem. if NIB or Exc.

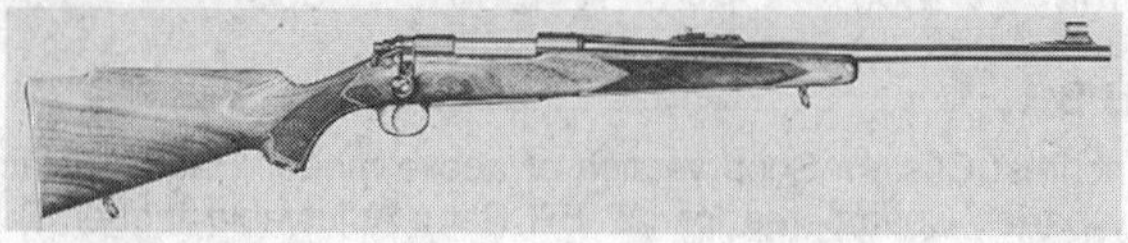

Courtesy Remington Arms

NIB	Exc.	V.G.	Good	Fair	Poor
900	800	520	280	220	150

Model 725 Kodiak

A .375 H&H Magnum or .458 Win. Magnum bolt-action sporting rifle, with 26" barrel, muzzle brake, open sights and 3-shot magazine. Blued, with checkered walnut stock. Manufactured in 1961. Very limited production.

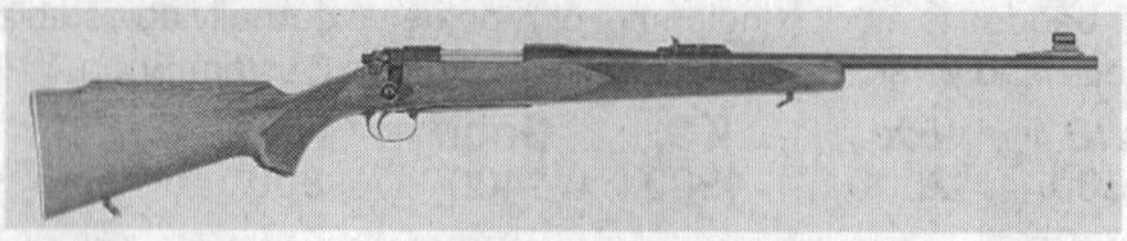

NIB	Exc.	V.G.	Good	Fair	Poor
6000	5000	4000	3000	1500	500

Model 78 Sportsman

Centerfire bolt-action sporting rifle, with 22" barrel and 4-shot magazine. Blued, with walnut stock. Introduced in 1985. Calibers: .223, .243, .270, .308, .30-06.

NIB	Exc.	V.G.	Good	Fair	Poor
340	280	220	200	150	100

Model 600

Centerfire bolt-action sporting rifle, with 18.5" ventilated rib barrel and checkered walnut stock. Manufactured from 1964 to 1967. Calibers: .222 Rem., .223 Rem., 6mm Rem., .243, .308, .35 Rem. Note: Add 100 percent for .223 Rem.

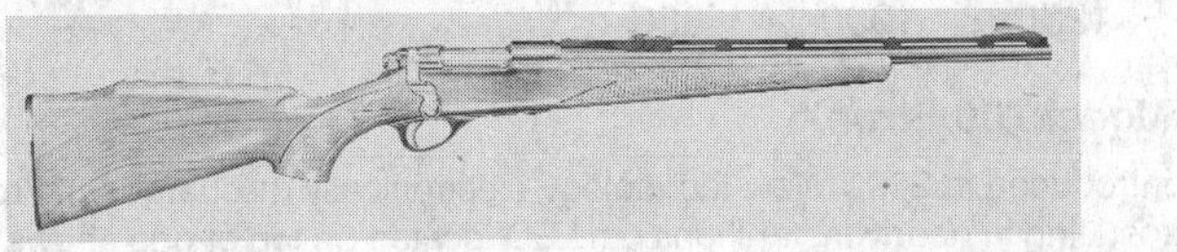

Courtesy Remington Arms

NIB	Exc.	V.G.	Good	Fair	Poor
650	550	450	350	220	150

Model 600 Mohawk

As above, with plain barrel. Chambered only for .222 Rem., .243 Win. or .308 Win. cartridges. Manufactured from 1971 to 1979.

NIB	Exc.	V.G.	Good	Fair	Poor
—	450	380	220	180	120

Model 600 Magnum

As above, chambered for 6.5mm Rem. Magnum and .350 Rem. Magnum cartridges. Stock of laminated walnut and beechwood. Manufactured from 1965 to 1967.

NIB	Exc.	V.G.	Good	Fair	Poor
—	1000	750	600	450	200

Model 660

Improved version of Model 600. Manufactured from 1968 to 1971. Note: Add 100 percent for .223 Rem.

NIB	Exc.	V.G.	Good	Fair	Poor
700	600	420	350	250	200

Model 660 Magnum

As above, chambered for 6.5mm Rem. Magnum or .350 Rem. Magnum cartridges. Fitted with laminated stock.

NIB	Exc.	V.G.	Good	Fair	Poor
—	1000	750	600	450	200

RIFLES

MODEL 700 SERIES

Model 700 Alpha 1

Caliber: .223 Rem., .22-250 Rem., .243 Win., 6.5 Creed, 7mm-08 Rem., .270 Win,. .308 Win., .30-06 Spfld., 7mm Rem. Mag., .300 Win. Mag. Barrel: 22", 24" fluted 5R w/ Black Cerakote. Stock: AG Composite Gray Speckled Synthetic. Features: First rifle launch from new RemArms. Precision ground recoil lug. Enlarged ejection port. Timney Elite Hunter trigger. Tool-less firing pin disassembly. Aluminum Obendorf-style triggerguard. Included Picatinny rail mount. Longer internal magazine for greater case lengths.

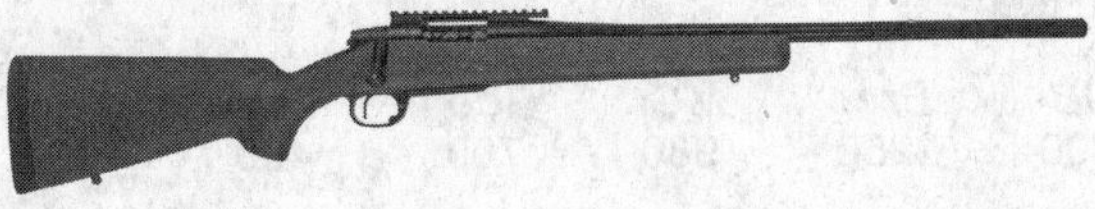

NIB	Exc.	V.G.	Good	Fair	Poor
1900	—	—	—	—	—

Model 700 ADL

Introduced in 1962 along with the 700 BDL upgraded variation. From 1962–1963 barrels were 20 inches for standard calibers, 23 ½ for magnums. This changed to 22 and 24 inches in 1964. Current production is with 24" or 26" barrel on Magnums. Offered in many variations. Original walnut stock had pressed checkering. Current synthetic stock is black with checkering, recoil pad and sling swivel studs, includes factory mounted and boresighted 3-9X scope. Note: Add about $100 for stainless steel. Now offered in .223 Rem, .22-250, .243, 6.5C, .270, .308, .30-06 and 7mm Rem Mag, .300 Win Mag. Add $100 to $200 for 20-inch barrel (1962–1963) depending on condition, add another $100 for .222 Rem. Mag. or .280 Rem. w/20-inch bbl.

Courtesy Remington Arms

NIB	Exc.	V.G.	Good	Fair	Poor
460	400	300	250	150	100

Model 700 ADL Synthetic Youth

Introduced in 1998. Has a shortened synthetic stock, with 13" lop. Offered in .243 and .308 Win. Discontinued 2005.

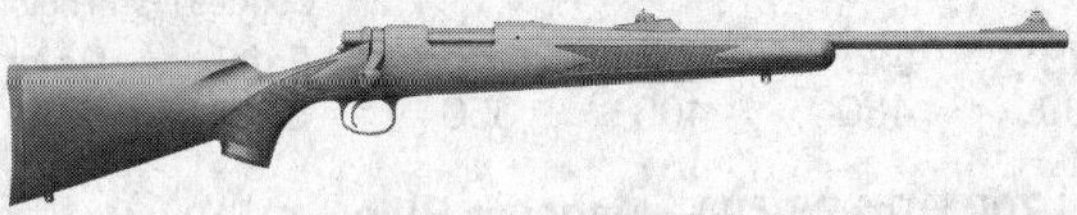

NIB	Exc.	V.G.	Good	Fair	Poor
450	380	320	280	160	100

Model 700 BDL

Introduced in 1962 as an upgraded variation of 700 ADL, the traditional BDL has a hinged floorplate, wood stock, cut checkering, black forend tip and pistol grip cap, finished in polished blue with iron sights. Offered in short and long actions, a wide variety of calibers from .17 Rem. to .375 RUM have been offered over the years. Current calibers include, .243, .270 Win, 7mm Rem Mag, .30-06, in barrel lengths of 22", 24" (7mm Rem Mag). Note: Add $100-$200 for .222 Rem. Mag, 6.5 Rem. Mag, .350 Rem. Mag. Add $30 for 7 Mag.

Courtesy Remington Arms

NIB	Exc.	V.G.	Good	Fair	Poor
800	700	600	400	280	200

Model 700 BDL Stainless Fluted

Matte wood stock, 24" (short and standard length actions), 26" (magnums). Calibers include .257 Wby. Mag, .270 Win, .270 WSM, 7-08, 7mm Rem Mag, .30-06, .300 WSM. Add $30 for magnums; add $90 for WSMs.

NIB	Exc.	V.G.	Good	Fair	Poor
1100	1000	850	720	440	370

Model 700 SPS LH (Left Hand)

Currently offered in long- or short-action hunting models and a heavy-barrel varmint with matte blue metal and synthetic stock. Calibers include .223, .22-250, .243, .270 Win, 7-08, .308, .30-06, .300 Win Mag. (Add $30 for Varmint)

NIB	Exc.	V.G.	Good	Fair	Poor
730	620	520	450	270	160

Model 700 BDL (DM)

Same as BDL above, with detachable magazine. Introduced in 1995, discontinued 2004.

NIB	Exc.	V.G.	Good	Fair	Poor
720	520	400	300	220	150

Model 700 BDL LH (Left-Hand)

Offered in selected calibers for left-hand shooters. They are: .270 Win., 7mm Rem. Magnum, .30-06 and .300 Rem. Ultra Magnum.

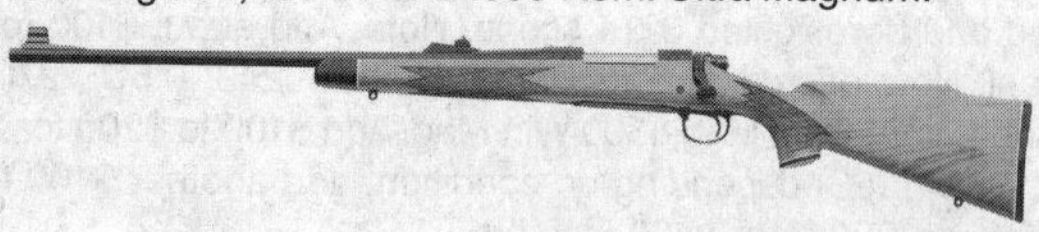

NIB	Exc.	V.G.	Good	Fair	Poor
600	500	450	320	250	150

Model 700 BDL LSS

Introduced in 1996. Has laminated stock and stainless steel action, barrel, and bolt in most popular chamberings in long and short actions. Note: Add about $40 for Left Hand versions in magnums. Discontinued 2004.

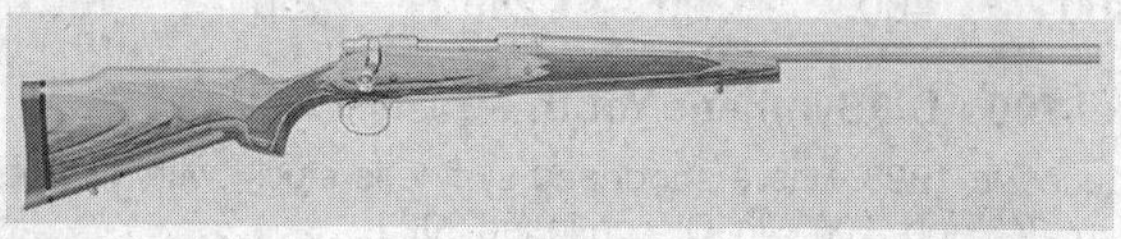

Courtesy Remington Arms

NIB	Exc.	V.G.	Good	Fair	Poor
600	480	400	350	300	200

Model 700 BDL SS DM—Magnum Rifle

Introduced in 1996. Fitted with factory installed muzzle brake on Magnum calibers: 7mm Rem Mag, 7mm STW, .300 Win. Mag, .300 Wby. Mag, .338 Win. Mag. and .338 Rem. Ultra Mag. Weight about 7.5 lbs. Discontinued 2004.

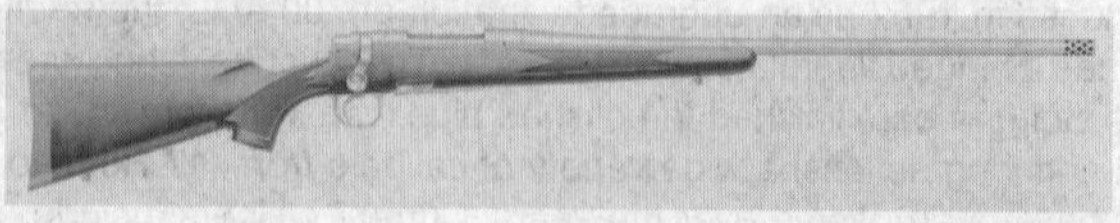

Courtesy Remington Arms

NIB	Exc.	V.G.	Good	Fair	Poor
780	650	500	300	200	150

Model 700 BDL SS

Fitted with a stainless steel barrel and black synthetic stock. No sights, barrel lengths of 24" to 26" (magnums). Weight about 7.325 lbs., in most popular calibers. Made from 1992–2004.

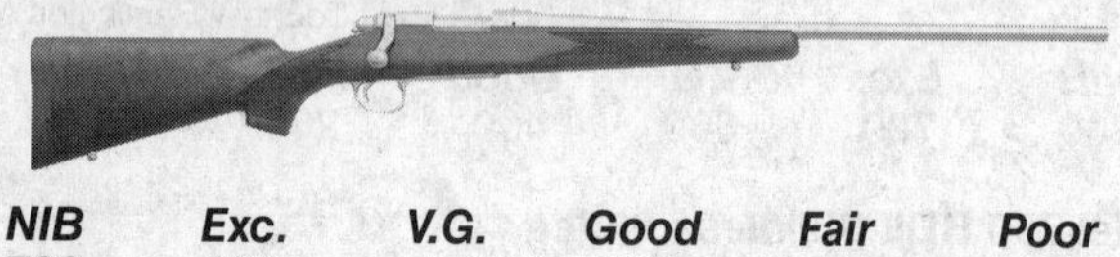

NIB	Exc.	V.G.	Good	Fair	Poor
780	620	500	400	300	180

Model 700 BDL SS Camo Special Edition (RMEF)

Special edition rifle for Rocky Mountain Elk Foundation. Fitted with 24" barrel. Chambered for .300 Rem. Ultra Mag cartridge. Camo stock, with stainless steel receiver and barrel. Weight about 7.5 lbs. Introduced in 2001. In 2002, 7mm Rem. Ultra Magnum chambering was added for one year only. In 2003, .300 Rem. Ultra Magnum was offered. Made 2001–2004.

NIB	Exc.	V.G.	Good	Fair	Poor
840	650	500	400	300	180

Model 700 50th Anniversary Edition

Manufactured in 2012 only. A recreation of original M700 BDL of 1962. Satin finished walnut stock with cheekpiece, cut fleur-de-lis checkering, whiteline spacers, black forend grip caps and recoil pad. Laser engraving on floorplate commemorates the 50th Anniversary. Barrel length 24". Chambered for 7mm Rem. Magnum, the cartridge that was introduced with Model 700 BDL.

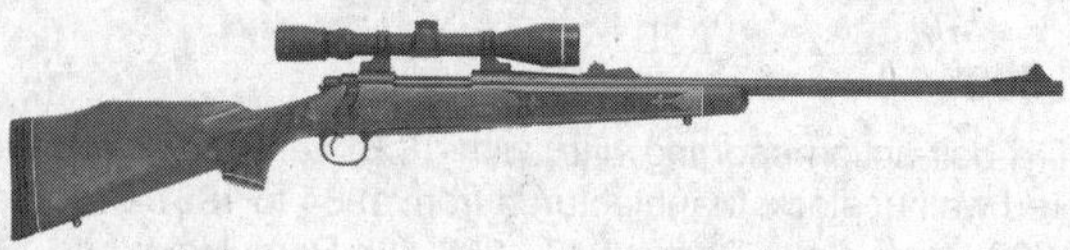

NIB	Exc.	V.G.	Good	Fair	Poor
1250	1000	850	—	—	—

Model 700 EtronX

Introduced in 2000. New technology electronically discharges the round resulting in nearly instant ignition. LED located on top of grip shows safe or fire and chamber status. Also, a low battery indicator and malfunction indicators as well. Fitted with 26" stainless steel fluted barrel. Stock is fiberglass and graphite reinforced with Kevlar. Chambers are .220 Swift, .22-250 Rem and .243 Win cartridges. Average weight about 8.88 lbs. Gun was unsuccessful in the marketplace but is now considered an almost-prime collectible. Discontinued 2004.

NIB	Exc.	V.G.	Good	Fair	Poor
1500	1320	1180	720	500	300

Model 700 Sendero

Model 700 configuration chambered for .25-06, .270, 7mm Rem Mag, .300 Win Mag. Fitted with synthetic stock and 24" or 26" heavy barrel. Made from 1994 to 2002.

NIB	Exc.	V.G.	Good	Fair	Poor
600	480	400	300	200	150

Model 700 Sendero SF

Introduced in 1996. Features stainless steel fluted barrel. Synthetic stock, with full-length bedding. Weight about 8.5 lbs. Chambered for most calibers as standard Sendero above, including 7mm STW, 7mm SAUM, 7mm Rem Ultra Mag, .300 RSAUM, .300 Rem Ultra Mag, .300 Win Mag and .300 Wby Mag. Made between 1996 and 2004.

NIB	Exc.	V.G.	Good	Fair	Poor
900	800	600	450	350	200

Model 700 Sendero SF-II

Similar to Sendero SF, with HS Precision synthetic stock, 26" heavy, stainless fluted barrel. Currently chambered in .25-06, .264 Win Mag, 7mm Rem Mag, .300 Win Mag and .300 RUM. Introduced 2006.

NIB	Exc.	V.G.	Good	Fair	Poor
1280	1080	850	550	350	280

Model 700 Sendero Composite

Features a composite barrel of graphite fiber, with stainless steel liner. Stock is synthetic. Calibers include .25-06, 7mm STW and .300 Win. Magnum. Barrel length 26". Made 1999 only.

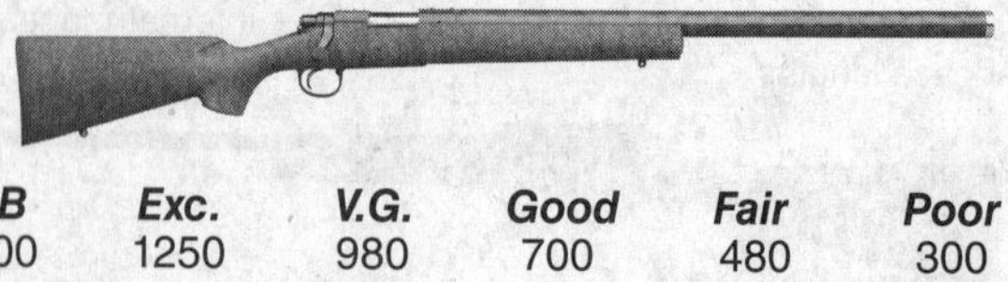

NIB	Exc.	V.G.	Good	Fair	Poor
1400	1250	980	700	480	300

Model 700 Mountain Rifle

Lightweight rifle with tapered 22" blued barrel in checkered walnut stock. Made from 1986 to 1994. Add $100–$150 for .257 Roberts or 7x57

Mauser.

NIB	Exc.	V.G.	Good	Fair	Poor
420	320	250	200	150	100

Model 700 KS Mountain Rifle

As Mountain Rifle above, with lightweight Kevlar stock, blue or stainless. Made 1986–2004; 2006–2008.

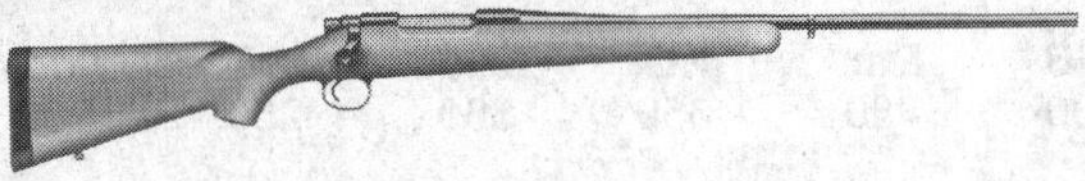

NIB	Exc.	V.G.	Good	Fair	Poor
750	700	600	500	400	300

Model 700 Mountain Rifle (DM)

Same as standard Mountain Rifle, with detachable magazine and satin walnut stock. In 1998, available in .260 Rem caliber. Made from 1995 to 2006.

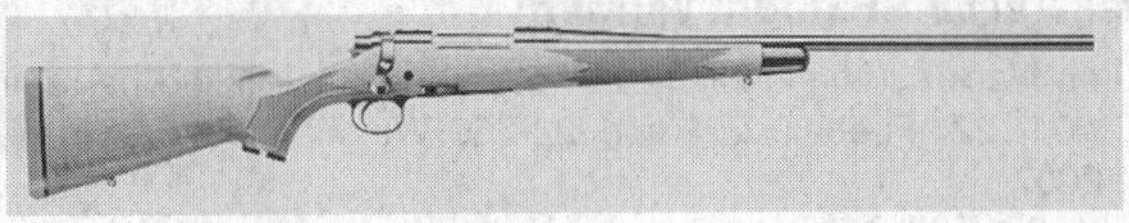

Courtesy Remington Arms

NIB	Exc.	V.G.	Good	Fair	Poor
780	580	420	300	250	180

Model 700 Mountain Rifle Stainless Synthetic

Current offering same as Mountain Rifle, with stainless steel receiver, bolt and barrel in Bell & Carlson synthetic stock. Offered in .25-06, .270, 7-08, .280, .308 and .30-06. All calibers supplied with 22" barrel.

NIB	Exc.	V.G.	Good	Fair	Poor
980	820	700	420	250	200

Model 700 LSS Mountain Rifle

Introduced in 1999. Fitted with two-tone laminated stock, with black forend tip and cheekpiece. Stainless steel barrel and action. Offered in .260 Rem, 7-08, .270 Win and .30-06. Barrel length 22". Weight about 6.5 lbs. Made 1999–2010.

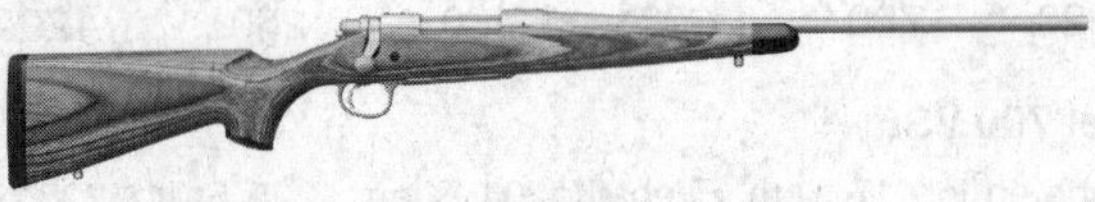

NIB	Exc.	V.G.	Good	Fair	Poor
830	620	450	300	200	100

Model 700 Safari Grade

As Model 700 BDL. Chambered for 8mm Rem. Magnum, .375 H&H, 8mm Rem Mag, .416 Rem Mag or .458 Win Mag cartridges with 24" barrel and 3-shot magazine. Blued, with finely figured walnut checkered stock. Model KS Safari Grade was fitted with Kevlar stock and would be worth approximately 20% more than values listed. Made from 1962–2000.

NIB	Exc.	V.G.	Good	Fair	Poor
1500	1300	1000	700	400	300

Model 700 RS

Chambered for .270 Win., .280 Rem. or .30-06 cartridges. 22" barrel and 4-shot magazine. Blued, with DuPont Rynite stock. Manufactured 1987–1988.

NIB	Exc.	V.G.	Good	Fair	Poor
—	550	420	350	250	150

Model 700 FS

As above, with Kevlar stock. Made 1987–1988.

NIB	Exc.	V.G.	Good	Fair	Poor
—	550	480	400	300	200

Model 700 BDL European

Features oil finish stock, with Monte Carlo comb, raised cheekpiece, fine-line checkering, hinged floorplate, sling swivel studs, hooded ramp front sight and adjustable rear sight. Offered in .243, .270, .280, 7mm-08, 7mm Rem. Mag., .30-06 and .308. Discontinued 1994.

NIB	Exc.	V.G.	Good	Fair	Poor
680	400	350	300	250	200

Model 700 BDL Stainless Synthetic

Features stainless steel receiver, barrel and bolt. Synthetic stock has straight comb, raised cheekpiece and hinged floorplate. Metal finished in a black matte non-reflective finish. Available in 14 calibers from .223 to .338 Win. Mag. All barrel lengths regardless of caliber are 24". Made 1992–2004

NIB	Exc.	V.G.	Good	Fair	Poor
750	600	500	300	200	150

Model 700 BDL Stainless Synthetic (DM)

Same as above, with detachable magazine. Made 1995–2004.

NIB	Exc.	V.G.	Good	Fair	Poor
800	650	520	350	200	150

Model 700 CDL Classic Deluxe

Introduced in 2004. Features classic-style checkered walnut stock, with black forend tip and grip cap. Polish blue metal. Hinged floorplate, and most popular cartridges chambered over the years. Currently chambered for .243, .25-06, .270, 7mm-08, 7mm Rem. Mag, .30-06, .300 Win. Mag. Standard calibers are fitted with 24" barrel; Magnum calibers have 26" barrel. Weight about 7.5 lbs. depending on caliber (add $20 for magnums). Limited edition 100th Anniversary edition offered in 2012 only in .375 H&H. Note: Add $300 to $400, depending on condition.

NIB	Exc.	V.G.	Good	Fair	Poor
880	750	630	380	230	200

Model 700 CDL SF

As above, but with satin stainless steel action and fluted barrel, chambered in .257 Wby. Mag, .270 Win, .270 WSM, 7-08, 7mm Rem. Mag, .30-06 and .300 Win. Mag. Add $30 for magnums; add $90 for WSMs.

NIB	Exc.	V.G.	Good	Fair	Poor
1000	850	720	440	260	200

Model 700 CDL Boone and Crockett

Similar to Model 700 CDL, with B&C laser-engraved barrel. Dealer exclusive for 2007.

NIB	Exc.	V.G.	Good	Fair	Poor
750	560	400	300	200	120

Model 700 CDL SF Ltd.

Model 700 CDL SF Ltd. Similar to Model 700 CDL SF, satin walnut stock, stainless steel action and fluted barrel, with engraved floorplate. Beginning in 2006, Remington produced this model only in one caliber each year, as follows: .30-06 (2006); .17 Fireball (2007); .260 Rem (2008); .257 Roberts (2009); .280 Rem (2010); 6mm Rem (2011); 7mm Rem Mag (2012); .300 Win Mag (2013); .223 Rem (2014); .22-250 (2015); .35 Whelen (2016); .260 (2017); 6.5 C (2018); .25-06 (2019).

NIB	Exc.	V.G.	Good	Fair	Poor
1050	900	750	450	270	200

Model 700 Titanium

Introduced in 2001. Features titanium receiver drilled and tapped for scope mounts. Fitted with 22" stainless steel barrel. Chambered for both Long and Short calibers. Synthetic stock. Weight about 5.25 lbs. In 2002, .308 Win. chambering added. Made 2001–2006.

NIB	Exc.	V.G.	Good	Fair	Poor
1270	950	700	500	300	180

Model 700 Varmint Special

Model 700 BDL with 24" heavy barrel in walnut stock in calibers .222, .223, .22-250, .243, 6mm Rem, .25-06, 7-08 and .308, made from 1967–1994.

NIB	Exc.	V.G.	Good	Fair	Poor
830	620	450	300	200	100

Model 700 Varmint Synthetic

Heavy-barreled Model 700 in synthetic Kevlar fiberglass and graphite stock matte black finish. Action in aluminum bedding block. Offered in .22-250, .223 and .308 calibers. In 1993, .220 Swift was briefly added. Made 1992-2004.

NIB	Exc.	V.G.	Good	Fair	Poor
600	480	400	350	300	200

Model 700 VS SF (Varmint Synthetic Stainless Fluted)

Model 700 stainless steel barrel, receiver and action fitted with 26" heavy, fluted barrel in synthetic stock. Offered in .223, .220 Swift, .22-250, 243 and .308. Barrel Fluted, Ported model offered as 700VS SF-P.

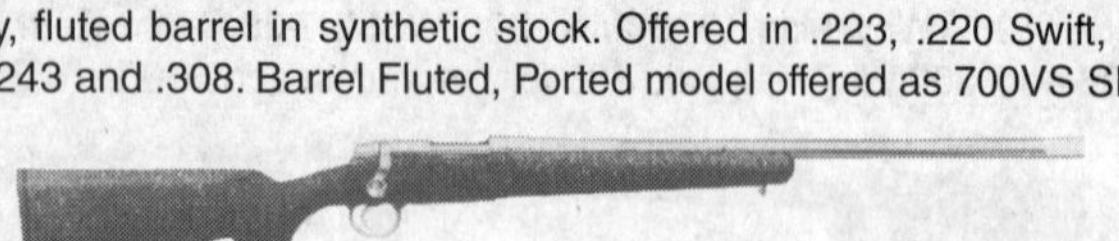

NIB	Exc.	V.G.	Good	Fair	Poor
800	650	500	400	300	150

Model 700 Varmint Special Wood

Same as above, but furnished with walnut stock. Offered in these calibers: .222, .22-250, .223, 6mm, .243, 7mm-08 and .308.

NIB	Exc.	V.G.	Good	Fair	Poor
820	680	520	400	300	150

Model 700 Varmint Laminated Stock (VLS)

Laminated stock with palm swell and beavertail forend, 26" heavy barrel, current calibers include .204, .223, .22-250, .243, and .308. Also available in brown laminate thumbhole stock. Introduced in 1995.

Courtesy Remington Arms

Model 700 VLS with beavertail forearm.

NIB	Exc.	V.G.	Good	Fair	Poor
900	780	650	390	250	200

Model 700 VS Composite (Varmint Synthetic Composite)

Fitted with a graphite fiber composite barrel. Chambered in .223, .22-250 or .308. Synthetic stock. Barrel length 26". Weight 7.9 lbs. Custom shop offering from 1999–2000.

NIB	Exc.	V.G.	Good	Fair	Poor
1550	1250	950	600	420	300

Model 700 LV SF (Light Varmint)

Features black synthetic stock, 22" stainless steel, fluted barrel in .17 Rem, .204, .221 Fireball, .223 and .22-250. Weight about 6.75 lbs. Made 2004–2007.

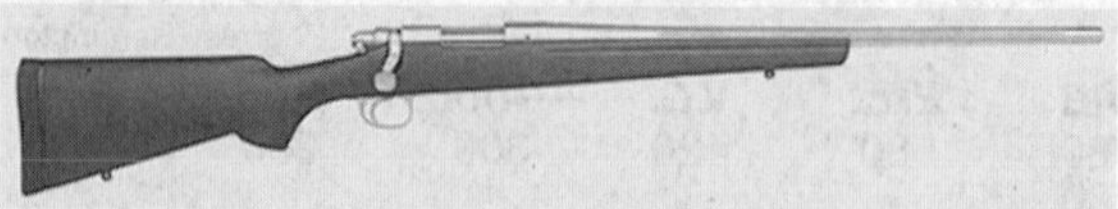

NIB	Exc.	V.G.	Good	Fair	Poor
950	700	480	300	220	120

Model 700 VS SF II

Features varmint synthetic stock, with stainless steel action and stainless fluted 26" barrel. Chambered for .204 Ruger, .220 Swift, .223 and .22-250. Weight about 8.5 lbs. Made 2005–2011.

NIB	Exc.	V.G.	Good	Fair	Poor
1020	780	600	480	250	120

Model 700 VSF

Chambered for .17 Rem. Fireball, .204 Ruger, .220 Swift, .223 or .22-250. Fitted with 26" blued, fluted, heavy barrel. Tan synthetic stock. Weight about 8.5 lbs. Made 2005–2007.

NIB	Exc.	V.G.	Good	Fair	Poor
930	700	480	300	220	120

Model 700 LSS LH (Laminated Stock SS Left-Hand)

Introduced in 1998. Features stainless steel barreled action, with satin finish. Stock similar to BDL style, with Monte Carlo comb and cheekpiece, with hinged floorplate. Barrel 24", with no sights. Offered in .270, .30-06, 7mm Rem. Magnum and .300 Win. Magnum.

NIB	Exc.	V.G.	Good	Fair	Poor
700	550	400	300	250	150

Model 700 VTR (Varmint Tactical Rifle)

Carbon steel action, matte finished with heavy 22" barrel with integral muzzle brake in flat dark earth or black (.223 and .308 only) stock with overmolded grips, tactical bolt knob, Picatinny rail and bipod in .223, .22-250, .260 and .308.

NIB	*Exc.*	*V.G.*	*Good*	*Fair*	*Poor*
980	830	700	600	360	220

Model 700 SPS (Special Purpose Synthetic)

Introduced in 2005. Features an improved synthetic stock, RS recoil pad and hinged floorplate, matte blue finish. Calibers include .223, .243, 6.5 Creedmoor, .260, 7-08, 7mm Rem Mag, .308, .270, .270 WSM, .308, .30-06, .300 WSM, .300 Win. Mag., .300 RUM. Weight about 7.5 lbs. depending on caliber and barrel length. Compact models with shorter lop have 20" barrel in .243 and .308 only; 24" barrels standard, 26" on magnums. Note: Add about $80 for Mossy Oak camo. Add $40 for 20" barrel and threaded muzzle.

NIB	*Exc.*	*V.G.*	*Good*	*Fair*	*Poor*
730	620	520	450	270	160

Model 700 SPS LH (Left Hand)

Similar to Model 700 SPS, but for left-handed shooters. Calibers limited to .270, .30-06, (24" barrel) 7mm Rem Mag, .300 Win Mag (26" barrel). Compact model shorter lop, and 20" barrel in .243 and. .308.

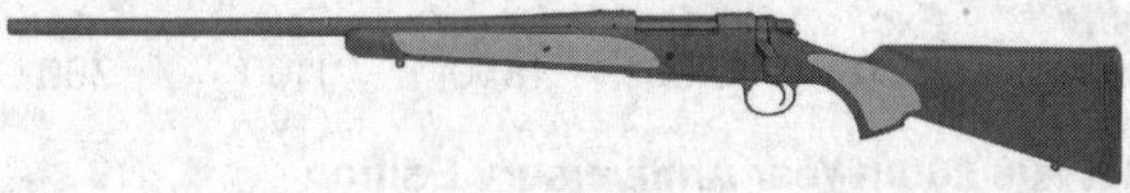

NIB	*Exc.*	*V.G.*	*Good*	*Fair*	*Poor*
730	620	520	450	270	160

Model 700 SPS Varmint

Varmint version of Model 700 SPS, with 26" heavy-contour barrel. Synthetic stock, with weight-reducing cuts in forend and twin swivels. Current chamberings include .203, .223, .22-250, .243 and .308 Win. Left-hand version in all but .204. Introduced in 2007.

NIB	*Exc.*	*V.G.*	*Good*	*Fair*	*Poor*
760	650	550	470	280	170

Model 700 SPS Long Range

Chambered for .25-06, 7mm Rem Mag, .30-06, .300 Win Mag, and .300 RUM with 26-inch barrel, no sights. Black synthetic Bell & Carlson M40 stock. Add $60 for stainless steel (magnums only).

NIB	*Exc.*	*V.G.*	*Good*	*Fair*	*Poor*
760	650	550	470	280	170

Model 700 SPS Dangerous Game

Similar to 700 SPS but chambered in .375 H&H Magnum. A TALO exclusive. Discontinued.

NIB	*Exc.*	*V.G.*	*Good*	*Fair*	*Poor*
680	550	400	280	200	150

Model 700 SPS DM

Same as Model SPS above, with detachable magazine. Matte blue finish. Made 2005–2010.

NIB	*Exc.*	*V.G.*	*Good*	*Fair*	*Poor*
580	450	300	200	150	100

Model 700 SPS Stainless

As above, with matte stainless steel barrel and action. Same calibers and barrel lengths as above, but no compact models. Introduced in 2005.

NIB	*Exc.*	*V.G.*	*Good*	*Fair*	*Poor*
840	720	600	520	300	180

Model 700 SPS Youth

Offered in both Long and Short action calibers. Features barrel lengths of 20" and 22" depending on caliber. Weight about 7 lbs. Introduced in 2005. Current SPS Compact models (see SPS above) feature a 1" shorter stock with spacers to adjust lop.

NIB	*Exc.*	*V.G.*	*Good*	*Fair*	*Poor*
520	420	280	180	120	100

Model 700 SPS Tactical

Similar to Model 700 Police, with 20" barrel and calibers .223 and .308. Laser-engraved tactical barrel. Dealer exclusive for 2007.

NIB	*Exc.*	*V.G.*	*Good*	*Fair*	*Poor*
800	680	500	380	250	180

Model 700 SPS Tactical AAC

Short, heavy, threaded barrel 700 short action with 16 1/2" barrel in .223, .300 AAC, and .308; 20" barrel in .308 and 22" in 6.5 Creedmoor. Hogue green overmolded stock with matte finish metal. Note: Subtract $55 for unthreaded 20" barrel (.223 and .308); add $33 for 6.5 in Coyote Tan stock, threaded. Introduced 2013.

NIB	*Exc.*	*V.G.*	*Good*	*Fair*	*Poor*
720	600	520	300	220	180

Model 700 VTR A-TACS Camo with Scope

Bolt-action rifle chambered in .223 and .308 Win. Features include ATACS camo finish overall; triangular contour 22" barrel with integral muzzle brake; black over-mold grips; 1:9 (.223) or 1:12 (.308) twist; factory-mounted scope. Discontinued.

NIB	*Exc.*	*V.G.*	*Good*	*Fair*	*Poor*
880	750	620	550	380	220

Model 700 XCR

Features stainless steel action and barrel, synthetic stock, rubber grip and forearm panels, hinged floorplate and RS recoil pad. Chambered for .270 Win, .280 Rem, 7mm Ultra Mag, .30-06, .300 WSM and .300 Win.

Mag. cartridges. Barrel lengths 24" and 26" depending on caliber. Weight around 7.5 lbs. depending on caliber. Note: Add $25 for Magnum calibers. Made 2005–2009.

NIB	Exc.	V.G.	Good	Fair	Poor
860	650	500	380	300	120

Model 700 XCR Tactical

Current model features 26" stainless steel barrel finished in black TriNyte, synthetic OD green tactical stock with full-length bedding block and hinged floorplate. Chambered in .308, .300 Win. Mag. and .338 Lapua. Barrel lengths 26". Compact model in .308 with 20" barrel. Note: Add $975 for .338 Lapua.

NIB	Exc.	V.G.	Good	Fair	Poor
1300	1100	950	700	570	350

Model 700 XCR Compact Tactical

Similar to above, with Black TriNyte PVD coating OD green stock; hinged floorplate magazine; dual front swivel studs and rear stud; free-floating 20" barrel with LTR-style fluting; 40-X externally adjustable trigger; tactical-style 1 in 9" (.223-caliber) or 1 in 12" twist (.308-caliber). Chambered in .223 and .308.

NIB	Exc.	V.G.	Good	Fair	Poor
1400	1150	880	650	480	200

Model 700 XCR RMEF Limited Edition

RMEF XCR in 7mm Rem Mag (2005), .300 WSM (2006), .300 RUM (2007 and 2010), 7mm RUM (2008), .30-06 (2009), 700 XCR II RMEF rifle in .25-06 (2012) .257 Wby Mag (2013). Features include 26" barrel, with Black TriNyte finish and nickel floorplate in a variety of camo finished stocks.

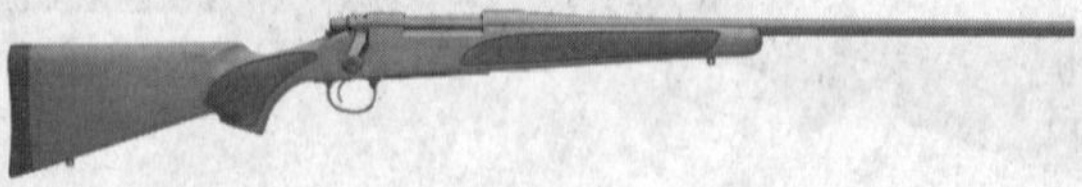

NIB	Exc.	V.G.	Good	Fair	Poor
950	850	750	—	—	—

Model 700 SPS Tactical II

Available in .223 Rem., .300 Black Out or .308 Win. Threaded muzzle, with 16.5" heavy barrel: 1/2 x 28 on .223 Rem., 5/8 x 24 on .300 Black Out and .308 Win. Hogue Chillie Green Overmolded stock and X-Mark Pro trigger. Introduced 2013.

NIB	Exc.	V.G.	Good	Fair	Poor
700	600	500	450	—	—

Remington 700 XCR II

Bolt-action rifle chambered in .25-06, .270, .280, 7mm Rem Mag, 7mm RUM, .30-06, .300 WSM, .300 Win Mag, .300 RUM, .338 Win Mag, .338 RUM, .375 H&H, .375 RUM. Features include black TriNyte corrosion control system coating; coated stainless steel barrel and receiver; olive drab green Hogue overmolded synthetic stock; SuperCell recoil pad; X-Mark Pro Trigger System; 24" or 26" barrel depending on chambering. Note: Add $30 for standard magnums; $80 for .300 WSM. Discontinued.

NIB	Exc.	V.G.	Good	Fair	Poor
820	740	600	500	350	200

Remington 700 XCR II - Bone Collector Edition

Similar to Remington 700 XCR II, with Realtree AP HD camo stock. Made 2010–2011.

NIB	Exc.	V.G.	Good	Fair	Poor
900	780	680	550	380	220

Model 700 Classic

Limited edition model. Furnished with a straight comb, satin finished walnut stock, sling swivel studs and hinged magazine floorplate. Series began in 1981. Each year Remington offered Model 700 Classic in a special chambering, concluding the series in 2005. Note: Add 25% for .250 Savage, .257 Roberts, 6.5x55, or 7x57.

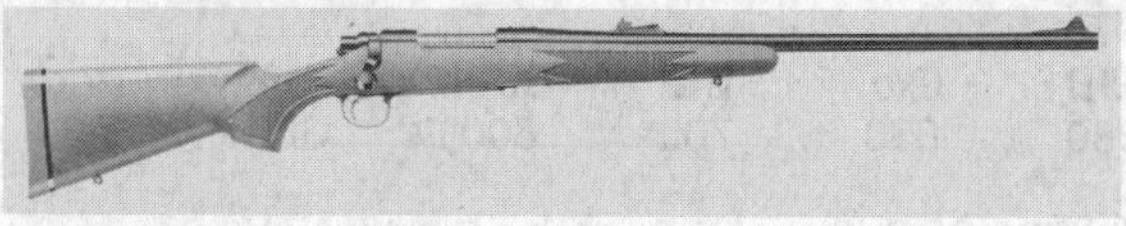

Courtesy Remington Arms

NIB	Exc.	V.G.	Good	Fair	Poor
900	700	600	500	350	250

Model 700 Custom

Special order rifle available in American, English or California walnut. Stock can be fitted to customer's own dimensions. Engraving available as is a large selection of calibers. Custom Grade Model 700 Custom rifles should be priced individually with an appraisal obtained.

Model 700 Custom "C" Grade

Made from 1964–1983, 2003–2004 and reintroduced in 2006. Custom Shop bolt-action rifle in high-polish blue. Fitted with fancy walnut BDL-style Monte Carlo stock and rosewood forend tip and grip cap. Offered in all standard calibers. Barrel length 24" for all calibers, except magnums which are 26".

NIB	Exc.	V.G.	Good	Fair	Poor
3000	2550	2200	1850	1100	700

Model 700 200th Year Anniversary Edition

A limited edition made only in 2016 to commemorate the 200th anniversary of the Remington company. A total of 2,016 rifles were produced in 7mm Remington Magnum featuring a 24-carat gold inlay of founder Eliphalet Remington, a high gloss C Grade walnut stock with fleur-de-lis cut checkering and black forend tip, a hooded ramp front and fully adjustable rear sight and polished blue finish.

NIB	Exc.	V.G.	Good	Fair	Poor
2200	1900	1700	1200	—	—

Model 700 AWR (Alaskan Wilderness Rifle)

Formerly built in Custom Shop to order, now cataloged. BDL stainless steel barreled action on Grayboe synthetic stock. Fitted with 24" or 26" barrel. All metal parts finished in black Cerakote. Currently offered in .270, 7mm Rem Mag, .30-06, .300 RUM, .300 Win Mag, .338 RUM and .338 Win Mag.

NIB	Exc.	V.G.	Good	Fair	Poor
1150	980	830	700	420	250

Model 700 APR (African Plains Rifle)

Custom Shop model features hinged floorplate, 26" barrel and blue metal finish. Stock laminated Monte Carlo style, with cheekpiece. Fitted with black rubber recoil pad, calibers include 7mm Rem Mag, 7mm STW, 7mm RUM, .300 Win, .300 RUM, .300 Wby. Mag., .338 Win. Mag., 338 RUM, .375 H&H and .375 RUM. Weight about 7.75 lbs. Made 1994-2004, 2006-2011.

NIB	Exc.	V.G.	Good	Fair	Poor
2400	2000	1500	1000	500	250

Model 700 ABG (African Big Game)

Custom Shop rifle fitted with laminated stock, matte finished receiver, barrel and 3-round detachable magazine. Chambered for .375 Rem Ultra Mag, .375 H&H, .416 Rem Mag and .458 Win Mag. Introduced in 2001. Many extra cost options are offered for Custom Shop firearms. Discontinued in this basic configuration.

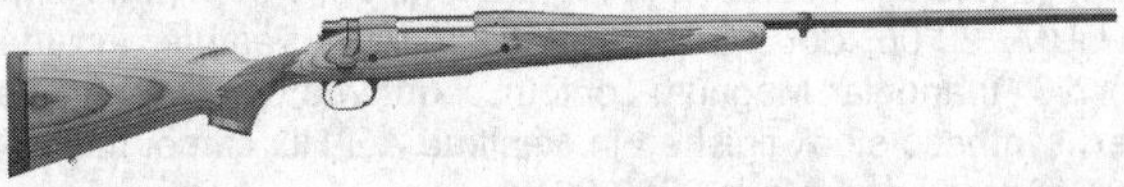

NIB	Exc.	V.G.	Good	Fair	Poor
2750	2350	1800	1250	750	350

Model 700 Safari Custom KS

Model 700 Safari KS in blue or stainless steel has a special reinforced Kevlar stock in a non-reflective gray finish in 8mm Rem. Mag. (blued only), .375 H&H, .416 Rem. Mag. and .458 Win. Mag. Made (most configurations) 1989-2004; 2006-2011. Add $175 for stainless.

NIB	Exc.	V.G.	Good	Fair	Poor
2200	1800	1500	900	600	300

Model 700 North American Custom

Matte blue or stainless steel "Blueprinted" Custom Shop Model 700 action, bedded to a Bell & Carlson Stock in Remington Green, Desert Tan, or Black, most calibers available with 24" (standard) or 26" (magnum) fluted or unfluted barrel, 40X trigger, accuracy guarantee. Add $200 for stainless.

NIB	Exc.	V.G.	Good	Fair	Poor
2000	1700	1450	1220	740	450

Model 700 Ultimate Sheep Rifle

Collaboration with Jason Hairston of KUIU mountain gear, the 5.6-lb. Custom Shop rifle has a titanium 700 short action in 6.5 Creedmoor (any other short-action caliber chambered; SAUM and WSM calibers require stainless steel action), 20" Proof Research carbon fiber barrel with muzzle brake, Manners EH-8 stock, spiral-flute bolt, aluminum floorplate, firing pin and bolt shroud.

NIB	Exc.	V.G.	Good	Fair	Poor
5000	4250	3500	—	—	—

Model 700 Custom Sendero SS

"Blueprinted" Custom Shop Model 700 short or long, right or left handed actions, 24" (standard) or 26" (magnum) Sendero profile fluted or unfluted barrel with .930" muzzle, Bell & Carlson synthetic stock in green, tan or black, 40X trigger, accuracy guarantee.

NIB	Exc.	V.G.	Good	Fair	Poor
2120	1800	1550	920	550	300

Model 700 Safari KS Stainless

New addition to Remington line in 1993. Safari KS Stainless has a special reinforced Kevlar stock in a non-reflective gray finish. Checkering is 18 lpi. Offered in these calibers: .375 H&H Magnum, .416 Rem. Magnum and .458 Win. Magnum.

NIB	Exc.	V.G.	Good	Fair	Poor
2200	1800	1500	900	600	300

Model 700 Police

Many calibers and configurations in short or long actions, usually with heavy barrels matte or Parkerized metal in synthetic stocks. Although not available for civilian sales, Remington occasionally sells overruns on the commercial market. Usually found chambered in .223 cartridge or .308 with 26" heavy barrel.

NIB	Exc.	V.G.	Good	Fair	Poor
850	680	500	400	200	120

Model 700 Police DM

Same as above. Chambered for .308 Win (1-12" twist) or .300 Win Mag (1-10" twist). Detachable magazine standard. Note: Add $20 for .300 Win. Magnum.

NIB	Exc.	V.G.	Good	Fair	Poor
850	680	500	400	200	120

Model 700 Police Lightweight Tactical

Chambered for .308 Win. cartridge. Fitted with 20" fluted barrel (1-12" twist). Stock is slim composite Kevlar, with dual front swivel studs. Parkerized finish. Detachable magazine. Weight about 7.5 lbs. Introduced in 1998.

NIB	Exc.	V.G.	Good	Fair	Poor
700	550	400	300	200	120

Model 700 Target Tactical Rifle

Bolt-action rifle chambered in .308 Win. Features include: 26" triangular counterbored barrel, textured green Bell & Carlson varmint/tactical stock, with adjustable comb and length of pull; adjustable trigger; satin black oxide finish metal; hinged floorplate; SuperCell recoil pad. Overall length 45.75". Weight 11.75 lbs. Introduced in 2009.

NIB	Exc.	V.G.	Good	Fair	Poor
1800	1550	1180	850	680	300

Model 700 Tactical Chassis

Variation of M700 Tactical rifle built on a MDT TAC21 Chassis. Magpul fully adjustable stock and pistol grip. 24" or 26" free-floating barrel. Chambered in .308 Win., .300 Win. Magnum or .338 Lapua. Features include a full-length MIL-STN-1914 accessory rail, stainless steel barreled action with black Cerakote finish, target tactical bolt handle, AAC 51-T muzzle brake and X-Mark Pro adjustable trigger. Introduced in 2014.

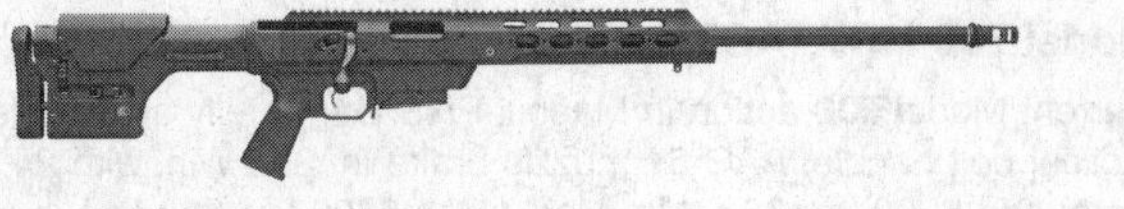

NIB	Exc.	V.G.	Good	Fair	Poor
2500	2100	1700	—	—	—

Model 700 VTR Varmint-Tactical Rifle

Bolt-action rifle chambered in .17 Rem. Fireball, .204 Ruger, .22-250, .223 Rem., .243 Win. and .308 Win. VTR Desert Recon with digital desert camo stock in .223 and .308 only. Features include: 22" triangular counterbored barrel; olive drab overmolded or Digital Tiger TSP Desert Camo stock with ventilated semi-beavertail forend; tactical-style dual swivel mounts for bipod; matte blue. Overall length 41.625". Weight 7.5 lbs. Made 2008-2013.

NIB	Exc.	V.G.	Good	Fair	Poor
750	620	500	380	200	120

Model 700 VTR Desert Recon

Similar to above, with Digital Desert Camo stock. Chambered for .223 and .308 Win. only.

NIB	Exc.	V.G.	Good	Fair	Poor
750	620	500	380	200	120

Model 700 PCR

The 700 Precision Chassis Rifle mates a short action 700 with an aluminum chassis, 24" heavy barrel with 5R rifling, free-floated aluminum handguard and Magpul PRS Gen-3 stock, and 5-round Magpul detachable magazine. Chambered in 6.5 Creedmoor, .260 Rem., and .308 Win.

NIB	Exc.	V.G.	Good	Fair	Poor
1000	860	740	440	260	200

Model 700 PCR Enhanced

Calibers: .308 Win., .260 Rem., 6.5 Creedmoor. Capacity: 5. Barrel: 24 in., cold hammer-forged, 5R rifling, threaded. Stock: Anodized aluminum chassis, Magpul Gen 3 PRS. Sights: Picatinny rail. Weight: 11 lbs. Features: Aluminum handguard with square drop, X-Mark Pro adjustable trigger, tactical bolt knob.

NIB	Exc.	V.G.	Good	Fair	Poor
1000	—	—	—	—	—

Model 700 Magpul

The Model 700 with tactical bolt knob in a 1-piece adjustable Magpul Hunter stock with threaded barrel, 5-round detachable magazine, 20" to 24" barrel depending on caliber, Cerakote finish. Comes in 6mm Creedmoor, 6.5 Creedmoor, .260 Rem., .308 Win., and .300 Win. Mag. Note: Add $75 for a 10-round magazine and bipod in the Enhanced Model.

NIB	Exc.	V.G.	Good	Fair	Poor
1000	850	720	430	260	200

Model 700 MDT TAC21

Current Model 700 action in Magpul PRS Gen 3 fully adjustable stock, tactical bolt handle, AAC 51 muzzle brake in .308 Win. with 24" barrel. Note: Add $200 for .300 Win. Mag. (24"); $600 for .338 Lapua with 26" barrel.

NIB	Exc.	V.G.	Good	Fair	Poor
2500	2100	1750	1000	650	300

Model 700 Stainless 5R

Three models featuring the stainless 700 BDL action, H-S Precision 1-piece stock, heavy barrel, 20"-26" barrel. Calibers include .223 Rem., 6.5 Creedmoor, .260 Rem., .308 Win., .300 Win. Mag. Note: Add $50 for barrel threaded for suppressor; add $150 for Gen 2 threaded and black Cerakote.

NIB	Exc.	V.G.	Good	Fair	Poor
950	800	680	400	300	250

Model 700 XHR Extreme Hunting Rifle

Bolt-action rifle chambered in .243, .25-06, .270, 7-08, 7mm Rem Mag, 7mm RUM, .30-06, .300 Win. Mag. and .300 RUM. Features include: 24", 25" or 26" triangular Magnum-contour counterbored barrel; adjustable trigger; synthetic stock finished in Realtree AG HD camo; matte finish, SuperCell recoil pad. Made 2009-2010.

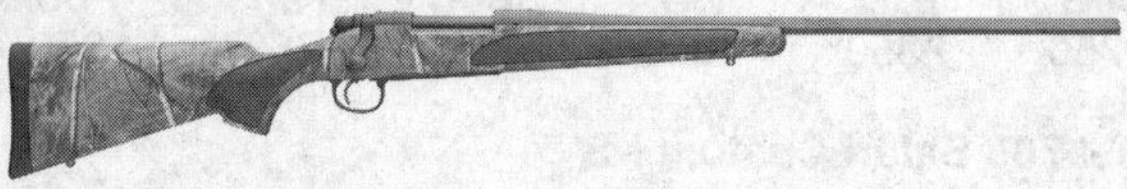

NIB	Exc.	V.G.	Good	Fair	Poor
850	680	500	400	250	150

Model 700 SPS Buckmasters Edition

Similar to Model 700 SPS with 20" to 26" barrel, logo engraved floorplate and Realtree Hardwoods camo stock. Also available in Youth model (20" barrel). Chambered in .243, .270, 7mm-08, 7mm Rem. Mag., .30-06 and .300 Win. Mag. Made 2007-2010.

NIB	Exc.	V.G.	Good	Fair	Poor
600	500	400	320	250	150

Model 700 Alaskan Ti

Lightweight (6.25 lbs.) version of Model 700, with titanium receiver, 24" fluted stainless barrel and Bell & Carlson synthetic stock. Chambered in a variety of long, short and super-short cartridges. Introduced in 2007-2009.

NIB	Exc.	V.G.	Good	Fair	Poor
1750	1350	1050	780	500	200

Model 700 LSS 50th Anniversary of .280 Remington

Similar to Model 700 LSS, in .280 Rem. Dealer exclusive for 2007.

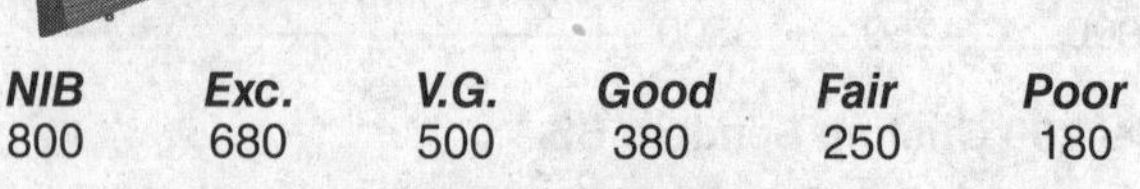

NIB	Exc.	V.G.	Good	Fair	Poor
800	680	500	380	250	180

Model 700 VL SS Thumbhole

Similar to Model 700 VS Composite, with brown laminated thumbhole stock and stainless steel barrel. Introduced in 2007.

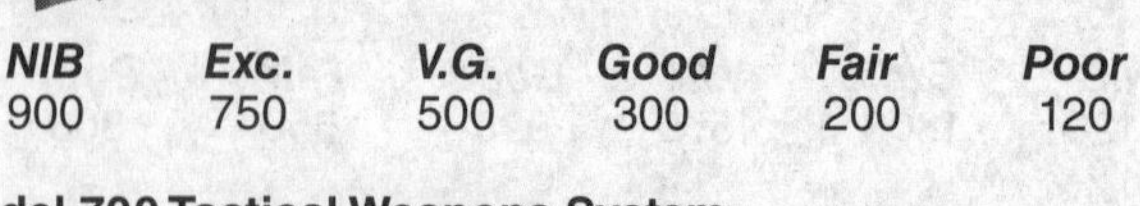

NIB	Exc.	V.G.	Good	Fair	Poor
900	750	500	300	200	120

Model 700 Tactical Weapons System

This set designed for law enforcement use. Features Model 700 Police chambered for .308 Win. cartridge, 24" barrel (1-12" twist) and detachable magazine. Furnished with Leupold VARI X III scope, with rings and base; Harris 1A2 bipod, sling, lens covers and case.

NIB	Exc.	V.G.	Good	Fair	Poor
2500	2000	1650	1150	800	500

Model 700 CP

Calibers: .223 Rem., .300 BLK, .308 Win., 6.5 Creedmoor. Capacity: 10-round magazine. Barrels: 10.5, 12.5 in. Grips: Magpul MIAD. Sights: Optic-ready, Picatinny-style rail. Length: 21.75 in. overall without brace. Weight: 5.9 to 7.05 lbs. unloaded. Finish: Hard-coat anodized, black Cerakote. Features: Rear QD mount or SBA3 arm brace, uses Model 700 short action, X-Mark Pro trigger, M-LOK handguard, oversized bolt knob and magazine release.

NIB	Exc.	V.G.	Good	Fair	Poor
800	—	—	—	—	—

Model 710

Sleeved polymer action with 3-lug bolt locking to barrel extension (until 2004; steel receiver thereafter). Chambered for .243, .270 Win. or .30-06. Fitted with 22" barrel and dark gray synthetic stock. Detachable box magazine. Supplied with pre-mounted Bushnell Sharpshooter 3-9X scope. Later, .243, 7mm Rem. Mag. and .300 Win. Mag. chamberings added. Youth Model added in 2006 in .243 only. Made 2001-2006.

NIB	Exc.	V.G.	Good	Fair	Poor
420	360	300	260	150	100

Model 710 Youth

Similar to Model 710, with 20" barrel and 39.5" overall length. Chambered in .243 Win. Introduced 2006.

NIB	Exc.	V.G.	Good	Fair	Poor
380	280	220	200	150	100

Model 783 Synthetic

Bolt-action repeater in .223, .22-250, .243, .270, 7-08, 7mm Rem. Mag., .308, .30-06, .300 Win. Mag. Short and long cylindrical action, with 22" (standard) or 24" (magnum) barrel attached via external nut, matte finish, injection-molded synthetic stock, pillar bedded, detachable box magazine, recoil pad and Crossfire trigger. Compact model available. New in 2013. Note: Add $45 with 3-9X scope mounted and boresighted. Add $100 for Mossy Oak Break-up stock with 3-9X scope mounted and boresighted.

NIB	Exc.	V.G.	Good	Fair	Poor
360	330	300	250	200	120

Model 783 VL (Varmint Laminate)

As 783 above with 26" heavy barrel, black oxide finish, in .223, .22-250, .243, 6.5 Creedmoor and .308 Win. Oversized bolt handle with Picatinny rail added.

NIB	Exc.	V.G.	Good	Fair	Poor
620	530	450	380	230	140

Model 783 HBT (Heavy Barrel Threaded)

As 783 above with threaded, 16.5" barrel, flat dark earth stock, tactical bolt handle, Picatinny rail, in .223, 6.5 Creedmoor, .300 AAC and .308 Win. All but the .300 AAC available with 24" heavy, threaded barrel. Note: Add $10 for 6.5 Creedmoor in 24" barrel.

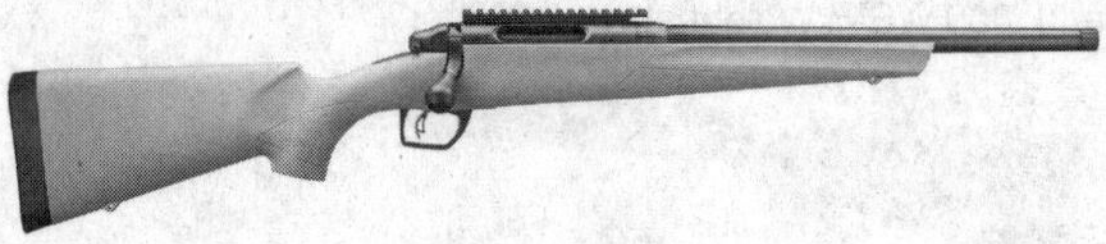

NIB	Exc.	V.G.	Good	Fair	Poor
460	390	330	280	170	100

Model 783 Walnut

As 783 above but in American black walnut stock, 22" (standard) or 24" (magnum) barrel, in .223, 6.5 Creedmoor, .270, 7mm Rem. Mag, .308, .30-06 and .300 Win. Mag. Note: Add $185 for Vortex Crossfire II scope mounted and boresighted.

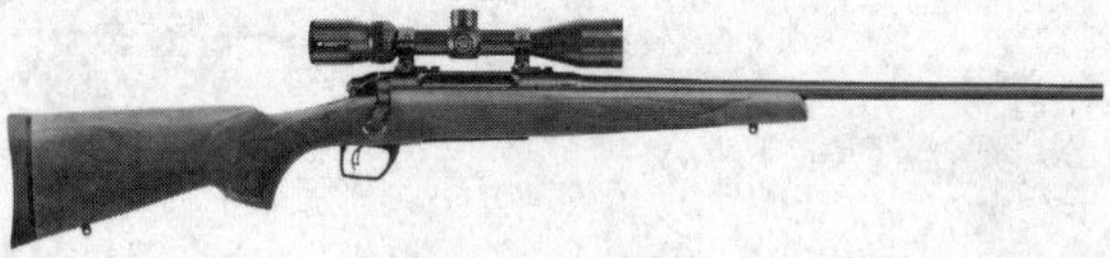

NIB	Exc.	V.G.	Good	Fair	Poor
420	380	300	250	150	100

Model 788

Centerfire bolt-action sporting rifle, with 22" or 24" barrel and plain walnut stock. An 18" barrel carbine was also manufactured and worth approximately 10 percent more than values listed below. Manufactured from 1967 to 1983. Note: Add 30% premium for .44 Magnum; 25% for .30-30; 20% for 7mm-08 caliber; and 40% for left-hand models in 6mm and .308.

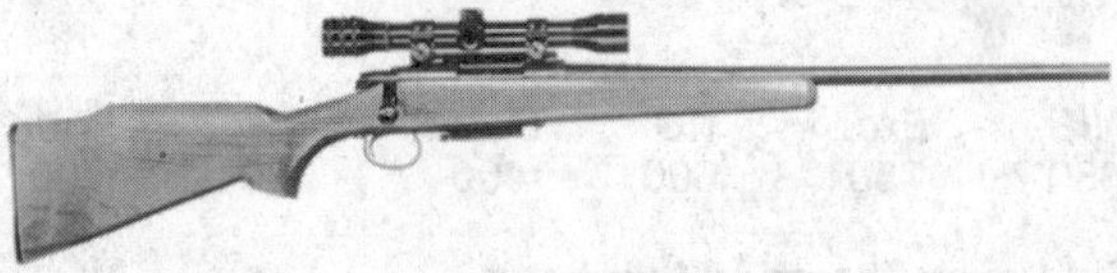

NIB	Exc.	V.G.	Good	Fair	Poor
600	500	420	380	300	250

Model Seven

Centerfire bolt-action sporting rifle, with 18.5" barrel and 4- or 5-shot magazine. Blued, with checkered walnut stock. Chambered for .17 Rem., .222 Rem., .223 Rem., .243 Rem., 6mm Rem., .260 Rem., 7mm-08 Rem. and .308 Win. Introduced into Remington product line in 1982.

NIB	Exc.	V.G.	Good	Fair	Poor
600	480	320	280	200	100

Model Seven FS

As above, with Kevlar stock, Parkerized metal, iron sights. Made from 1987–1989.

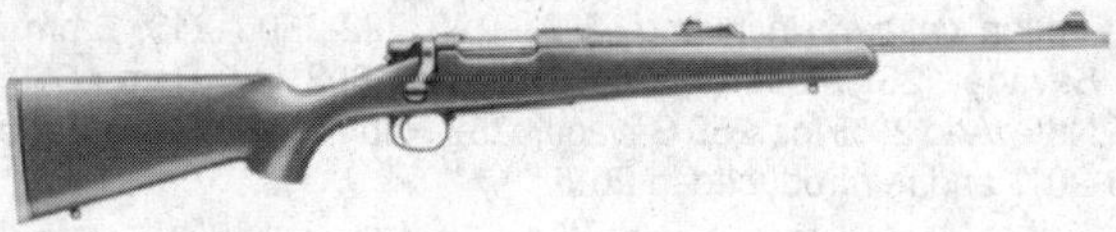

NIB	Exc.	V.G.	Good	Fair	Poor
600	520	450	380	280	150

Model Seven Synthetic

Updated Synthetic short-action series in .223, .243, .260, 7mm-08 Rem and .308 Win 20" matte blue barrel and matte black stock. Externally adjustable X-Mark Pro trigger is standard. No sights. Weight about 6 lbs. Compact version has 18" barrel, chambered in .243 or 7-08 only.

NIB	Exc.	V.G.	Good	Fair	Poor
620	520	450	350	200	120

Model Seven SS (Stainless Synthetic)

Introduced in 1994. Features stainless steel barrel, receiver and bolt with matte finish. Fitted with 20" barrel and hinged floorplate. Synthetic stock is textured black. Currently available in .223, .243, 6mm Rem, .260, 7-08, .308 and .300 WSM. Weight about 6.25 lbs.

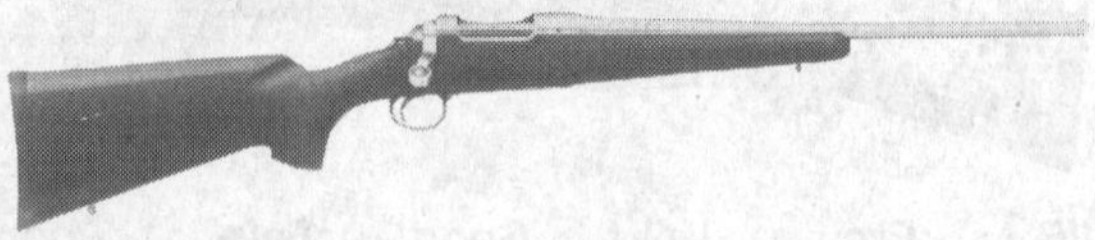

NIB	Exc.	V.G.	Good	Fair	Poor
700	600	520	400	280	200

Model Seven LSS

Has stainless steel barrel and action. Fitted with satin finished laminated stock. Chambered for .22-250, .243, and 7mm-08 Rem. Weight about 6.5 lbs. Made from 2000-2003.

NIB	Exc.	V.G.	Good	Fair	Poor
620	500	380	300	200	100

Model Seven LS

Has blued barrel and action (a stainless version was offered previously). Fitted with satin finished laminated stock, 18.5" barrel and iron sights. Chambered in .223, .243, 7mm-08 and .308.

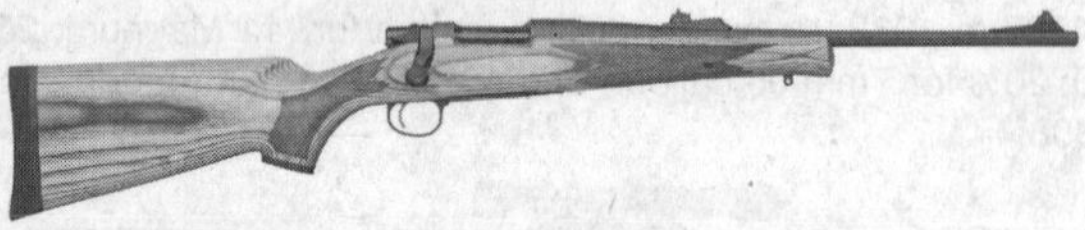

NIB	Exc.	V.G.	Good	Fair	Poor
880	750	600	400	300	200

Model Seven Threaded Synthetic

Threaded matte blue 16 1/2" barrel camo synthetic stock in .308 and .300 AAC.

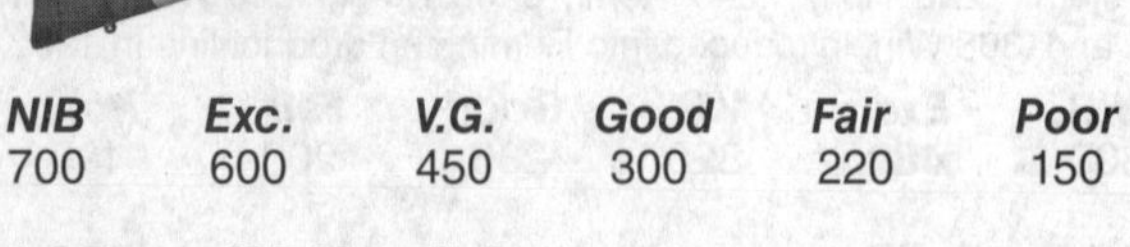

NIB	Exc.	V.G.	Good	Fair	Poor
700	600	450	300	220	150

Model Seven MS Mannlicher

Available through Remington Custom Shop. Features 20" barrel, with Mannlicher stock made from brown laminated wood. Available in most short-action calibers including .222, .223, .22-250, .243, 6mm Rem, .250 Savage, .257 Roberts, .260, 7mm-08, .308, .35 Rem, .350 Rem Mag. Note: Add 20% for .250 Savage, .257 Roberts, .35 Rem. Made from 1993-2011 and reintroduced in 2015.

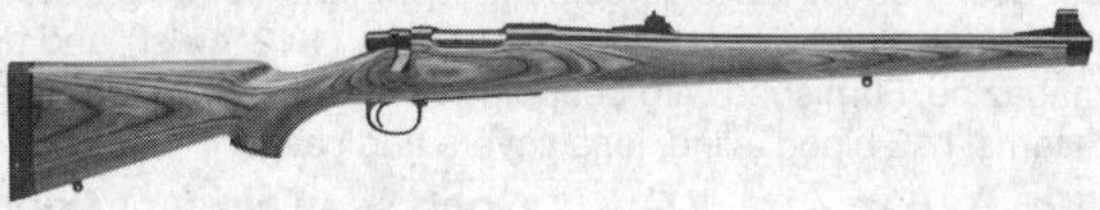

NIB	Exc.	V.G.	Good	Fair	Poor
2500	2200	1850	1300	700	300

Model Seven Custom

Custom Shop blueprinted Model Seven action with 20" barrel, iron sights currently available in most short-action calibers. In McMillan stock with black Cerakote metal finish.

NIB	Exc.	V.G.	Good	Fair	Poor
2600	2200	1850	1300	700	300

Model Seven AWR

Alaskan Wilderness Model has black synthetic stock, stainless steel action and 22" barrel with black matte Teflon finish. Weight 6.125 lbs. Detachable 3-shot magazine. A Remington Custom Shop offering chambered in 6.8 SPC, 7mm RSAUM or .300 RSAUM. Replaced by Model Seven AWR II in 2008. Came with 20" or 22" stainless steel barrel, Bell & Carlson olive green fiberglass stock and hinged floorplate. Chamberings include .260, .270 WSM, 7mm-08, 7mm RSAUM, .308 Win, .300 WSM, .300 RSAUM and .350 Rem Mag. Made 2002-2011. Note: Add 10% for AWR II, made from 2008-2011.

NIB	Exc.	V.G.	Good	Fair	Poor
2400	1800	1500	500	350	250

Model Seven Youth

First offered in 1993. A youth version of standard Model Seven. Buttstock is 1" shorter than standard. Available in 6mm, .243 and 7mm-08. In 1998, available in .260 Rem. caliber.

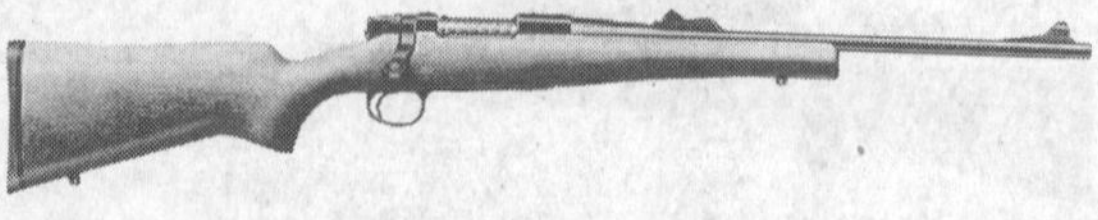

NIB	Exc.	V.G.	Good	Fair	Poor
600	500	350	220	180	100

Model Seven CDL

Current compact centerfire bolt-action sporting rifle currently with 20" barrel. Blued, with checkered walnut stock. Chambered in many short-action calibers over the years, currently in .243, .260, 7mm-08 and .308.

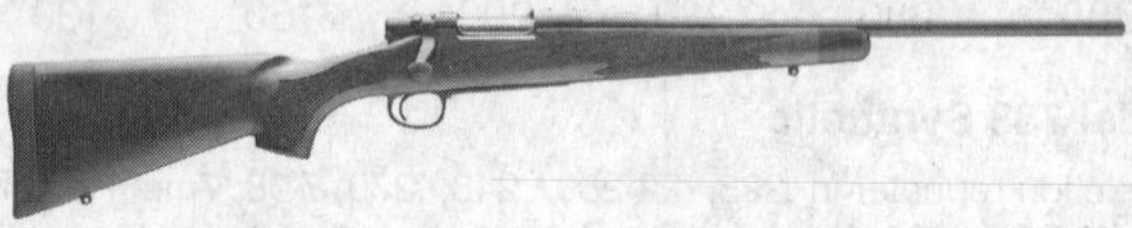

NIB	Exc.	V.G.	Good	Fair	Poor
880	750	600	400	280	200

Model Seven XCR Camo

Similar to Model Seven LSS, with camo stock, fluted barrel and weather resistant coating. Chambered in .243, 7mm-08, .308, .270 WSM and .300 WSM. Made 2007 only.

NIB	Exc.	V.G.	Good	Fair	Poor
780	650	500	400	280	180

Model Seven 25th Anniversary Version

Classic deluxe-style walnut stock offered in 7mm-08 only, with 25th Anniversary medallion inset at pistol grip cap area. High-sheen blued finish on receiver bolt and 22" standard-contour barrel. X-Mark Pro Trigger and

SuperCell recoil pad. Made 2008 only.

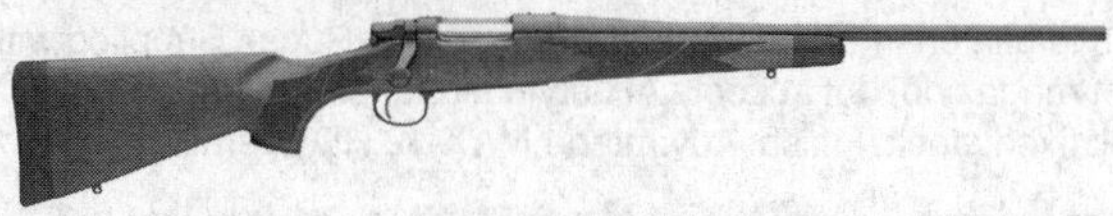

NIB	Exc.	V.G.	Good	Fair	Poor
950	700	550	350	250	150

Model Seven Predator

Similar to Model Seven, uses Model 700 BDL action, with full coverage in Mossy Oak Brush camo; fluted Magnum contour 22" barrel; synthetic stock as on Model Seven XCR; X-Mark Pro Trigger. Chambered in .17 Rem. Fireball, .204, .223, .22-250 and .243. Introduced in 2008, now discontinued.

NIB	Exc.	V.G.	Good	Fair	Poor
800	650	500	400	280	180

Model 770

Package rifle similar to Model 710, with redesigned bolt assembly and magazine catch. Chambered in .243, .270, 7mm-08, .308, .30-06 and .300 WM with 22" or 24" barrel. Available in Youth model chambered in .243 only with shortened stock and 20" barrel. Introduced in 2007. In 2008, a version with stainless steel barrel and receiver and full camo finish was introduced. A 3-9X Bushnell scope is included. Note: Add $60 for camo finish or stainless steel. Discontinued in 2014.

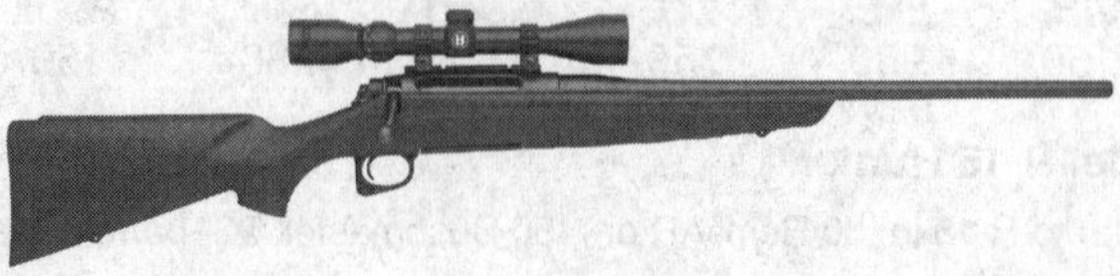

NIB	Exc.	V.G.	Good	Fair	Poor
330	280	240	200	120	80

Model 770 Youth

Similar to Model 770, with shorter stock and barrel.

NIB	Exc.	V.G.	Good	Fair	Poor
380	280	200	160	90	50

Model 715 Sportsman

Similar to Model 770. Dealer exclusive for 2007.

NIB	Exc.	V.G.	Good	Fair	Poor
380	280	200	160	90	50

Model 798

Long-action sporting rifle built on Zastava 98 Mauser action. Calibers: .243, .308, .30-06, .270, .300 Win. Mag., .375 H&H, .458 Win. Mag. Barrel 22" or 24" blued, sightless. Stock brown laminated, with recoil pad. Claw extractor, 2-position safety, hinged floorplate. Note: Add 10% for magnum chamberings; 30% for .375 H&H and .458 Win. Made 2006-2008.

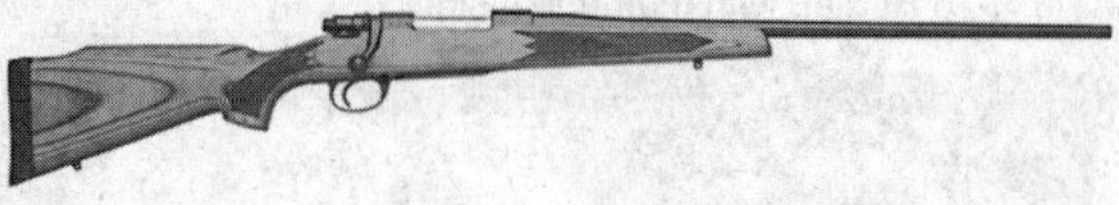

NIB	Exc.	V.G.	Good	Fair	Poor
580	400	300	200	120	100

Model 798 Stainless Laminate

Similar to Model 798, with laminated stock and stainless barrel. Chambered in .243, .25-06, .270, .30-06, 7mm Magnum, .300 Win. Mag. and .375 H&H Magnum. Introduced in 2007. Discontinued. Note: Add 25% for .375.

NIB	Exc.	V.G.	Good	Fair	Poor
650	480	350	250	180	120

Model 798 SPS

Similar to Model 798, with blued barrel and black synthetic stock. Introduced 2008. Discontinued.

NIB	Exc.	V.G.	Good	Fair	Poor
580	400	300	200	120	100

Model 798 Safari

Similar to Model 798. Chambered in .375 H&H or .458 Win. Mag. Introduced 2008. Discontinued.

NIB	Exc.	V.G.	Good	Fair	Poor
900	760	620	500	400	250

Model 799

Similar to Model 798, but short-action without recoil pad. Calibers .22 Hornet, .222 Rem., .22-250, .223, 762X39. Introduced 2006. Discontinued.

NIB	Exc.	V.G.	Good	Fair	Poor
520	400	300	200	120	100

Model 1816 Commemorative Flint Lock Rifle

Introduced in 1995. Features .50-caliber 39" octagonal barrel. Stock is hand-finished extra fancy curly maple. Built for one year only. Special order only.

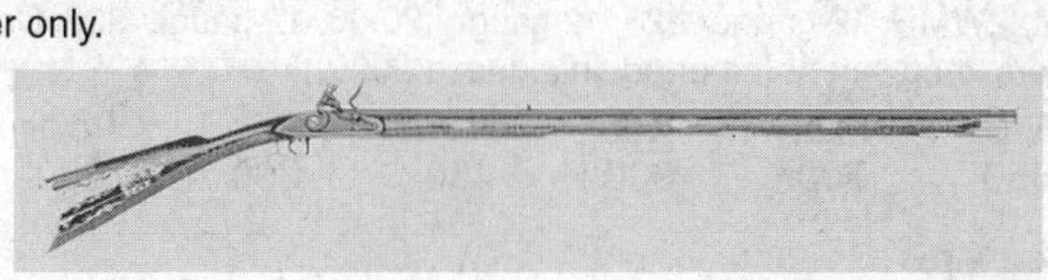

Courtesy Remington Arms

NIB	Exc.	V.G.	Good	Fair	Poor
4900	4160	3540	3010	2560	2170

Remington No. 1 Rolling Block Mid-Range

Classic rifle reintroduced in 1997 to Remington line. Features 30" half-octagon, half-round barrel. Chambered for .45-70 Government cartridge. Designed for use with black powder and lead cast bullets. Receiver is case colored. All barrel, receiver and metalwork markings match original rifle. Rear tang-mounted vernier sight and front globe sight, with interchangeable inserts. Single-set trigger is standard. Steel buttplate. Weight about 9.75 lbs.

NIB	Exc.	V.G.	Good	Fair	Poor
2750	2400	1750	1200	700	400

Remington Mid-Range Sporter Rolling Block

Introduced in 1998. Features 30" round barrel, with pistol grip sporter stock. Adjustable rear sight. Chambered for .30-30, .444 Marlin and .45-70 Government. A number of extra cost options are available, including barrels, sights, fancy wood, etc. Prices listed below are for standard model.

NIB	Exc.	V.G.	Good	Fair	Poor
2500	2100	1500	900	600	350

Model SPR18 Single Shot Rifle

Break-action rifle, with silvertone receiver and fluted barrel. Calibers .223, .243, .270, .30-06, .308. Weight 6.75 lbs. Imported. Introduced 2005.

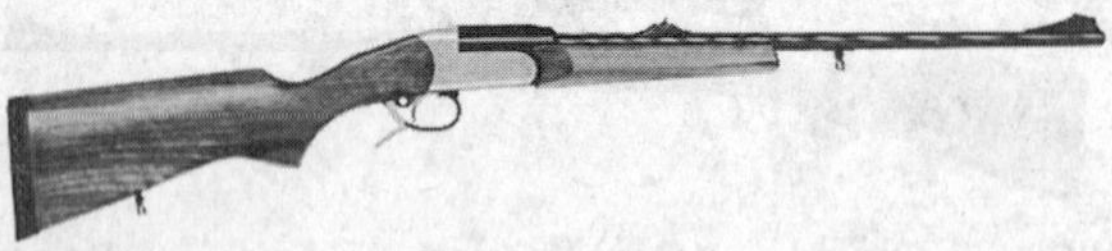

NIB	Exc.	V.G.	Good	Fair	Poor
260	220	180	150	100	80

Model SPR22 Double Rifle

Top-lever operated break-action SXS double rifle in .30-06 and .45-70. Double triggers, tang safety. Barrels can be regulated via jackscrew. Imported. Introduced 2005.

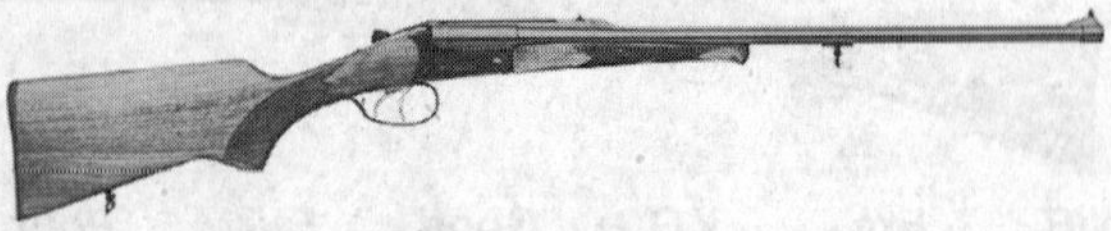

NIB	Exc.	V.G.	Good	Fair	Poor
1000	850	700	600	450	300

Model SPR94 Combo Gun

Over/under rifle/shotgun. Combinations .410/.22 rimfire, .410/.17HMR, .410/.22WMR, 12-gauge/.223, 12-gauge/.30-06, 12-gauge/.308. Double triggers, tang safety. Imported. Introduced 2005.

NIB	Exc.	V.G.	Good	Fair	Poor
850	700	600	450	300	200

Model 412

Compact single-shot chambered for .22 LR. 19.5" blued barrel, hardwood stock. Introduced 2006.

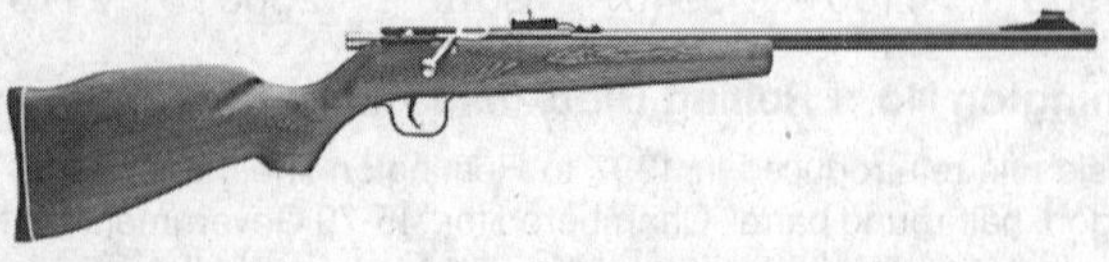

NIB	Exc.	V.G.	Good	Fair	Poor
160	120	100	80	50	20

Model R-15 VTR Predator Rifle

AR-style rifle chambered for .223 Rem. or .204 Ruger. Supplied with one 5-shot magazine, but accepts AR-style higher-cap magazines. 22" fluted barrel; fixed stock. Finish: Advantage MAX-12 HD overall.

NIB	Exc.	V.G.	Good	Fair	Poor
1100	900	700	500	250	130

Model R-15 VTR Predator Carbine

Similar to above, with 18" barrel.

NIB	Exc.	V.G.	Good	Fair	Poor
1100	900	700	500	250	130

Model R-15CS VTR Predator Carbine

Similar to above, with collapsible buttstock.

NIB	Exc.	V.G.	Good	Fair	Poor
1150	950	750	550	280	150

Model R-15 Hunter

Similar to R-15 in .30 Rem. AR or .450 Bushmaster, 22" barrel, Realtree AP HD camo.

NIB	Exc.	V.G.	Good	Fair	Poor
1200	980	750	550	280	150

Model R-15 VTR Byron South Edition

.223, 18" barrel, Advantage MAX-1 HD camo.

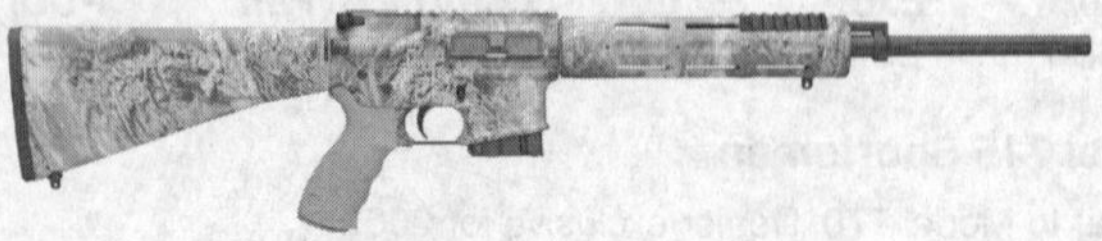

NIB	Exc.	V.G.	Good	Fair	Poor
1200	980	750	550	280	150

Model R-15 VTR SS Varmint

As above, with 24" stainless steel barrel.

NIB	Exc.	V.G.	Good	Fair	Poor
1200	980	750	550	280	150

Model R-15 VTR Thumbhole

Similar to R-15 Hunter, with thumbhole stock.

NIB	Exc.	V.G.	Good	Fair	Poor
1300	1080	850	600	300	150

Model R-15 MOE

Semi-automatic .223 (AR-15 type), with AAC 51 Tooth Brakeout flash hider, Magpul Grip and triggerguard, competition two-stage trigger finished in Mossy Oak Brush camo. Available with: 16" barrel with collapsible stock and mid-length forend; 18" carbine with fixed stock and Dissipator forend; 18" barrel carbine with collapsible stock and Dissipator forend; 22" barrel rifle with fixed stock and Dissipator forend. Introduced 2013.

NIB	Exc.	V.G.	Good	Fair	Poor
1200	1050	800	700	—	—

Model R-25 Modular Repeating Rifle

Enhanced AR-style semi-automatic rifle. Chambered in .243, 7mm-08 and .308 Win. Features include 20" chrome-moly barrel, single-stage trigger, four-round magazine, aluminum alloy upper and lower Mossy Oak Treestand camo finish overall. Overall length 38.25"; weight 7.75 lbs.

NIB	Exc.	V.G.	Good	Fair	Poor
1500	1250	900	700	300	200

Model R-25 GII

The next generation R-25. Features include a downsized but stronger rifle with a matched pair of forged anodized Teflon-coated upper and lower receivers. Also, a lighter bolt carrier and improved extractor/ejector system, free-floated barrel and Hogue rubber pistol grip. Introduced in 2015.

NIB	Exc.	V.G.	Good	Fair	Poor
1550	1300	950	—	—	—

MODERN MUZZLELOADERS

Model 700 ML

Introduced in 1996. An inline design and first built on a modern action. Chambered for .50- or .54-caliber bullet. Fitted with synthetic stock and rubber recoil pad. Barrel length 24". Weight about 7.75 lbs. Camo stock option added in 1997. Discontinued 2006.

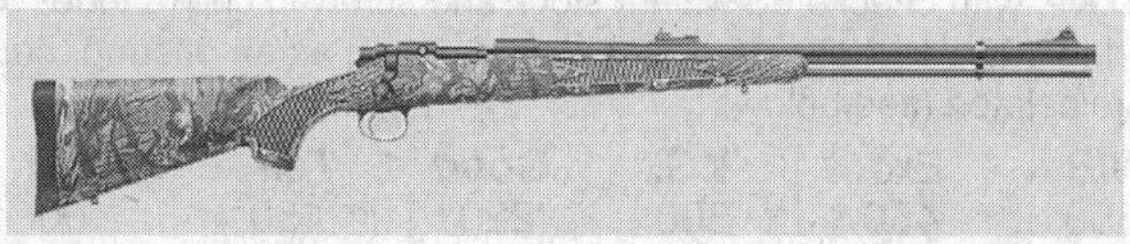

Courtesy Remington Arms

NIB	Exc.	V.G.	Good	Fair	Poor
—	300	260	220	180	160

Model 700 ML Custom

Introduced in 1997. Similar to above featuring satin metal finish and gray laminated thumbhole stock, with roll-over cheekpiece. Discontinued.

NIB	Exc.	V.G.	Good	Fair	Poor
—	420	360	310	260	220

Model 700 MLS

Same as above, with stainless steel barrel and action. Discontinued.

Courtesy Remington Arms

NIB	Exc.	V.G.	Good	Fair	Poor
—	300	260	220	180	160

Model 700 MLS Custom

Similar to above model, with satin stainless steel finish and two-toned gray laminated thumbhole stock, with roll-over cheekpiece. Introduced in 1997. Discontinued.

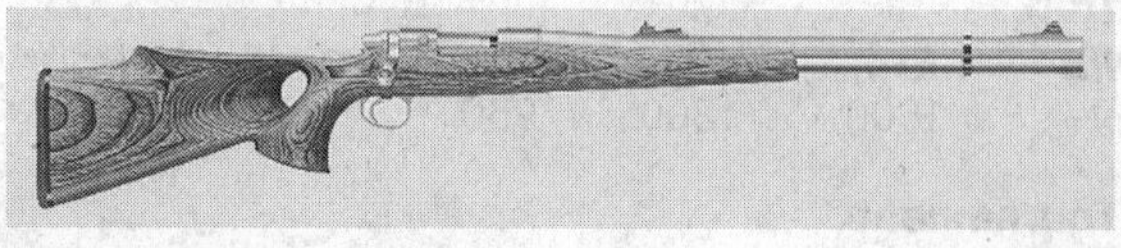

NIB	Exc.	V.G.	Good	Fair	Poor
—	480	400	340	290	250

Model 700 ML Youth

Similar to Model ML. Shortened stock, with 13" lop and rubber recoil pad. Discontinued.

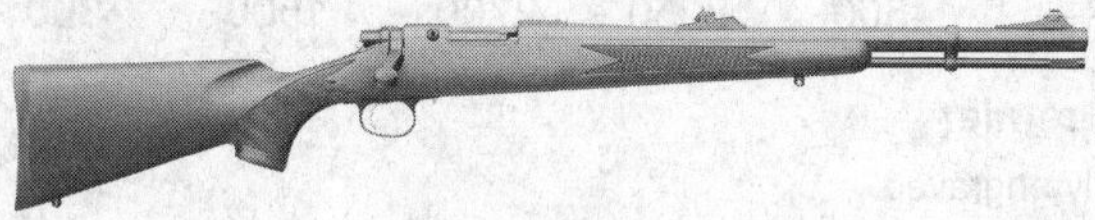

NIB	Exc.	V.G.	Good	Fair	Poor
—	300	260	220	180	160

Model 700 Ultimate Muzzle Loader

Model introduces Ultimate Muzzle Loader (UML) ignition system. Uses a unique brass case containing a Remington 9.5 large-Magnum rifle primer that is push fed into breech plug, creating a gas seal in the flash hole of the primer. Can handle up to a 200-grain Magnum powder charge for velocities over 2,400 fps. Features include .50-caliber fluted stainless barrel and laminate or Bell & Carlson synthetic stock. Introduced in 2014.

NIB	Exc.	V.G.	Good	Fair	Poor
900	760	650	550	470	400

Genesis Muzzleloaders

Fixed-breech hammer-fired muzzleloaders manufactured in a variety of configurations. Imported. Manufactured from 2006 to 2008.

NIB	Exc.	V.G.	Good	Fair	Poor
180	150	130	110	90	80

SHOTGUNS

Model 11

12-, 16- or 20-gauge semi-automatic shotgun, with barrels ranging in length from 26" to 32". Designed by John M. Browning. Produced under license from Fabrique Nationale. Blued, with checkered walnut stock. Approximately 300,000 made from 1911 to 1948. Note: Add 30% for solid or ventilated rib to listed values.

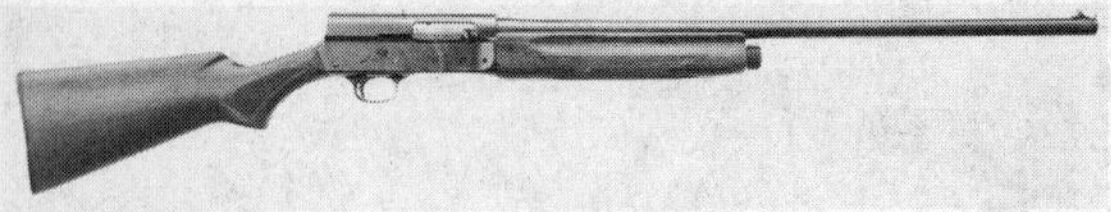

NIB	Exc.	V.G.	Good	Fair	Poor
—	800	650	500	400	300

11B Special

Engraved.

NIB	Exc.	V.G.	Good	Fair	Poor
—	1400	1100	600	500	400

11C Trap

NIB	Exc.	V.G.	Good	Fair	Poor
—	1600	1300	950	450	220

11D Tournament

NIB	Exc.	V.G.	Good	Fair	Poor
—	2200	1600	1000	600	450

11E Expert

Engraved.

NIB	Exc.	V.G.	Good	Fair	Poor
—	4500	3250	2700	1500	300

11F Premier

Heavily engraved.

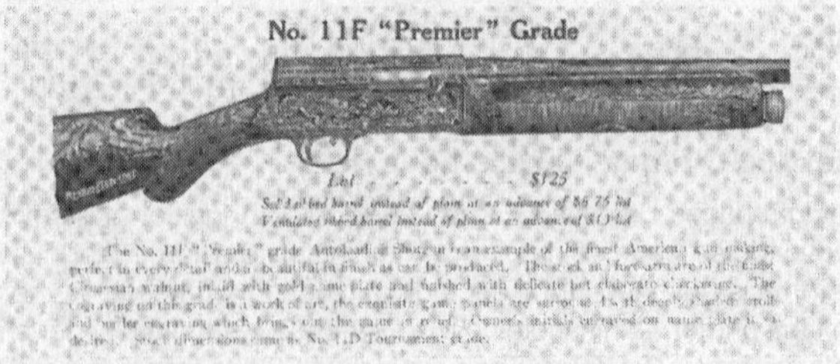

NIB	Exc.	V.G.	Good	Fair	Poor
—	9000	7000	5000	3500	500

11R

20" barrel riot gun.

NIB	Exc.	V.G.	Good	Fair	Poor
—	1000	850	700	500	400

Model 10A

A 12-, 16- or 20-gauge slide-action shotgun. Barrels ranging from 26" to 32". Take-down blued, with plain walnut stock. Manufactured from 1907 to 1929.

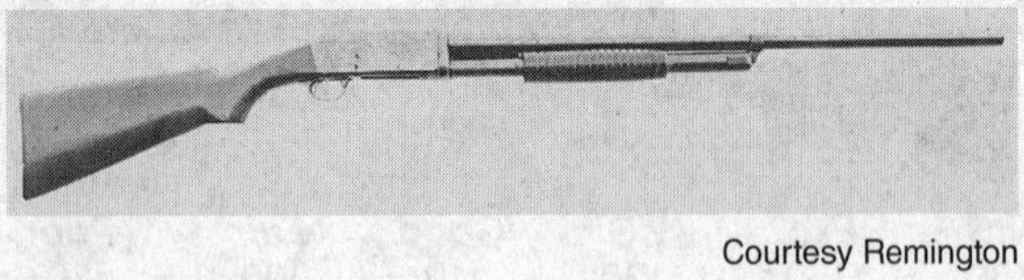

Courtesy Remington Arms

NIB	Exc.	V.G.	Good	Fair	Poor
—	380	300	250	200	100

Model 17

A 20-gauge slide-action shotgun. Barrels from 26" to 32". Take-down blued, with plain walnut stock. Approximately 48,000 made from 1917 to 1933. Note: Add 25% for ventilated rib.

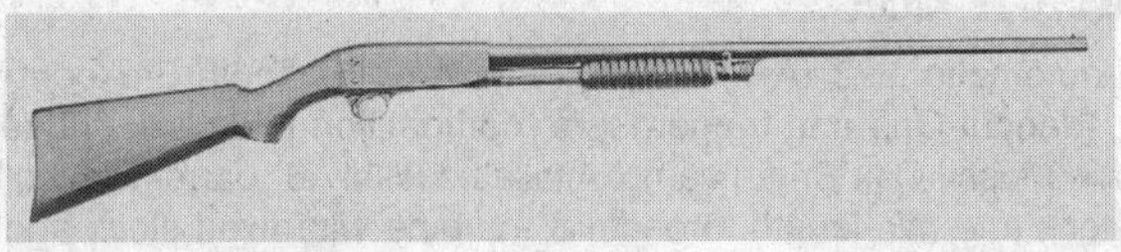

Courtesy Remington Arms

NIB	Exc.	V.G.	Good	Fair	Poor
—	400	300	250	180	100

Model 29

As above, chambered for 12-gauge cartridge. Approximately 24,000 manufactured from 1929 to 1933. Note: Add 40% for 32" barrels; 25% for ventilated rib.

NIB	Exc.	V.G.	Good	Fair	Poor
—	450	350	300	200	180

Model 31

A 12-, 16- or 20-gauge slide-action shotgun. Barrels from 26" to 32". Magazine capacity 2 or 4 rounds. Take-down blued, with walnut stock. Approximately 160,000 made from 1931 to 1949. Note: Add 50% for 32" barrel; 40% for early models with checkered stocks; 25% for solid or ventilated rib; 25% for early banded barrels.

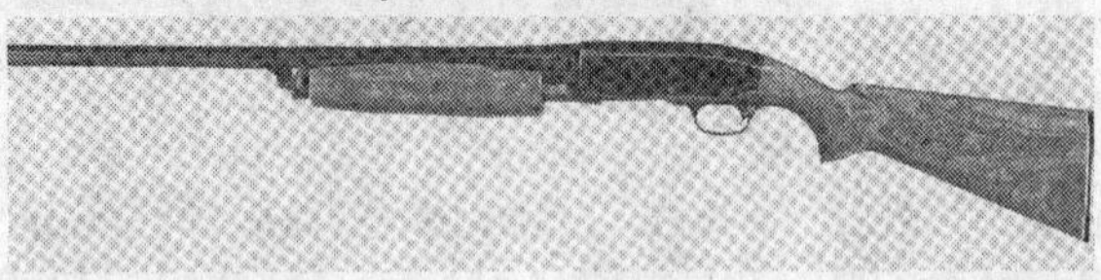

NIB	Exc.	V.G.	Good	Fair	Poor
—	450	320	280	200	120

MODEL 870 SERIES

Model 870 Wingmaster

A 12-, 16- or 20-gauge slide-action shotgun, with 26", 28" or 30" barrels and 5-shot tubular magazine. Blued, with plain walnut stock. Manufactured from 1950 to 1963. Note: Add 10% for ventilated rib.

NIB	Exc.	V.G.	Good	Fair	Poor
—	450	300	220	150	100

Model 870 Field Wingmaster

As above, with checkered walnut stock and screw-in choke tubes. Introduced in 1964. In 1980, 16-gauge was dropped as an offering, but was later reinstated (see below).

NIB	Exc.	V.G.	Good	Fair	Poor
550	450	300	220	150	100

Model 870 Field Wingmaster 16 Gauge

In 2002, 16-gauge was reintroduced into the Wingmaster line. Offered with 26" or 28" ventilated rib barrel and choke tubes. Walnut stock, with blued finish. Weight about 7 lbs. Offered in 16-gauge in other configurations listed.

NIB	Exc.	V.G.	Good	Fair	Poor
—	480	380	250	200	100

Model 870 Wingmaster NRA Edition

A 12-gauge 3" gun, with 28" ventilated rib barrel and choke tubes. Walnut stock, with checkering. Blued receiver, with NRA logos on both sides. Introduced in 2005.

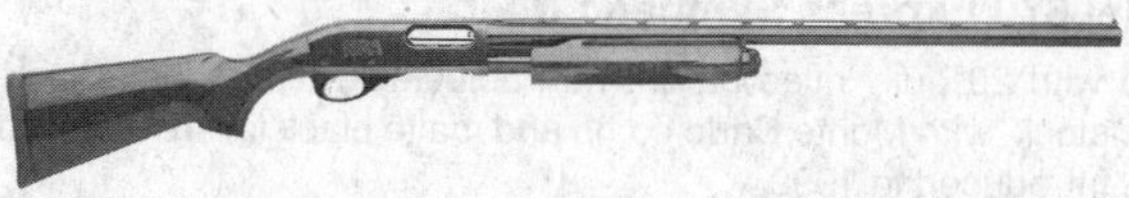

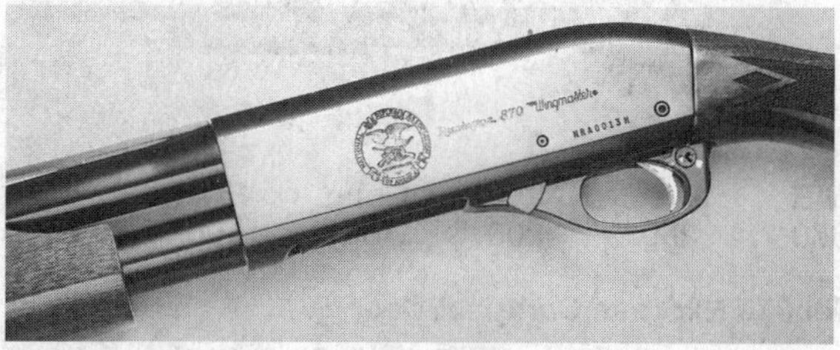

NIB	Exc.	V.G.	Good	Fair	Poor
—	450	300	220	150	100

Model 870 Wingmaster Jr.

Introduced in 2005. Features a 20-gauge gun, with 18.75" ventilated rib barrel and choke tubes. Checkered walnut stock, with recoil pad. Blued finish. Weight about 6 lbs.

NIB	Exc.	V.G.	Good	Fair	Poor
400	320	240	180	100	—

Model 870 Field Wingmaster Small Bores

Introduced in 1999. Now offered in both 28-gauge and .410 bore. Checkered walnut stock. High-polish blue finish. Both guns are fitted with 25" barrels. 28-gauge has RemChokes while .410 comes with Fixed Modified chokes. Weight about 6 lbs. Price listed is for .410 bore. Note: Add $50 for 28 gauge.

Wingmaster 28 gauge

NIB	Exc.	V.G.	Good	Fair	Poor
700	600	510	430	370	310

Model 870 Magnum

As above chambered for 12- or 20-gauge. 3" Magnum shells. Introduced in 1964. Choke tubes introduced in 1987.

NIB	Exc.	V.G.	Good	Fair	Poor
—	420	300	220	150	100

Model 870 Express

As above for 3", 12-gauge shells, with 28" ventilated rib and one choke tube. Parkerized, with matte finished stock. Introduced in 1987.

NIB	Exc.	V.G.	Good	Fair	Poor
340	290	240	210	180	150

Model 870 Express Synthetic

NIB	Exc.	V.G.	Good	Fair	Poor
340	290	240	210	180	150

Model 870 Express Synthetic Youth

NIB	Exc.	V.G.	Good	Fair	Poor
300	250	200	150	100	80

Model 870 Express Jr. NWTF Edition

20-gauge model fitted with 18.75" ventilated rib barrel, with choke tubes. Synthetic stock has camo finish. Metal matte black. Weight about 6 lbs. Introduced in 2005.

NIB	Exc.	V.G.	Good	Fair	Poor
320	250	200	150	100	80

Model 870 Express Super Magnum

Similar to 870 Express, but chambered for 3.5" 12 gauge. Offered in walnut stock, with blued 28" barrel. Matte black synthetic, with 26" or 28" barrel or various camo finishes. Also available as a combo, with extra 20" rifled deer barrel. Introduced in 1998. Note: Add $100 for camo; 20% for combo with deer barrel.

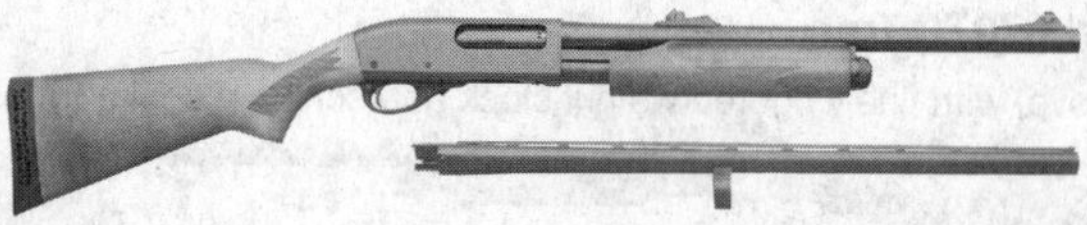

NIB	Exc.	V.G.	Good	Fair	Poor
420	330	220	180	120	100

Model 870 Express Super Magnum Fall Flight

Chambered for 12-gauge, with 2.75", 3" or 3.5" shells. Fitted with 30" ventilated rib barrel and choke tubes. Skyline Fall Flight camo finish. Weight about 7.75 lbs. Introduced in 2005.

NIB	Exc.	V.G.	Good	Fair	Poor
480	380	280	220	180	150

Model 870 Express Synthetic Super Mag Turkey-Waterfowl Camo

Pump action shotgun. Chambered in 12-gauge, 2.75" to 3.5" shells. Features include full Mossy Oak Bottomland camo coverage; 26" barrel with HiViz fiber-optics sights; Wingmaster HD Waterfowl and Turkey Extra Full RemChokes; SuperCell recoil pad; drilled and tapped receiver.

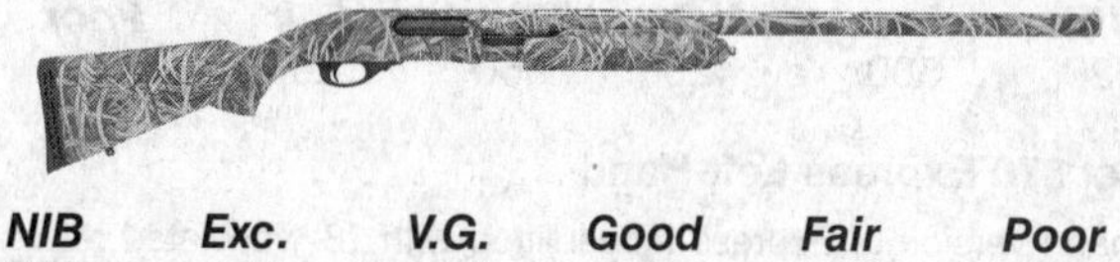

NIB	Exc.	V.G.	Good	Fair	Poor
520	440	380	320	200	150

Model 870 Super Mag Turkey-Predator Camo with Scope

Pump action shotgun chambered in 12-gauge, 2.75" to 3.5" shells. Features include 20" barrel; TruGlo red/green selectable illuminated sight mounted on pre-installed Weaver-style rail; black padded sling; Wingmaster HD Turkey/Predator RemChoke; full Mossy Oak Obsession camo coverage; ShurShot pistol grip stock, with black overmolded grip panels; TruGlo 30mm Red/Green Dot Scope pre-mounted.

NIB	Exc.	V.G.	Good	Fair	Poor
580	500	420	350	200	150

Model 870 Express Trap

New (in 2020) 870 Express Trap, 12 ga., 3 in., 30-in. barrel. Hardwood Monte Carlo stock with raised comb, mid-bead, ivory front target sight, gold trigger. Ships with three choke tubes.

NIB	Exc.	V.G.	Good	Fair	Poor
550	—	—	—	—	—

Model 870TA Trap

As above, with competition ventilated rib and checkered stock. Produced in 12-gauge only. Discontinued in 1986.

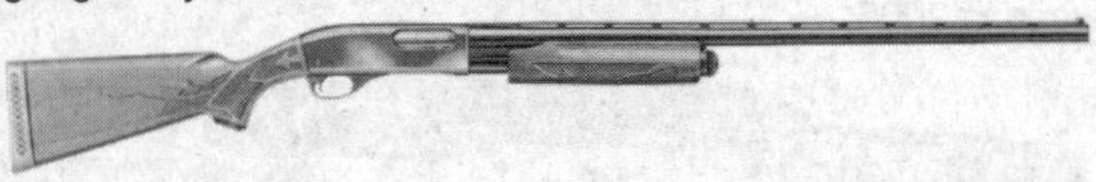

NIB	Exc.	V.G.	Good	Fair	Poor
500	400	300	200	150	100

Model 870TB Trap

As above, with 28" or 30" Full choke, ventilated rib barrel and trap-style walnut stock. Manufactured from 1950 to 1981.

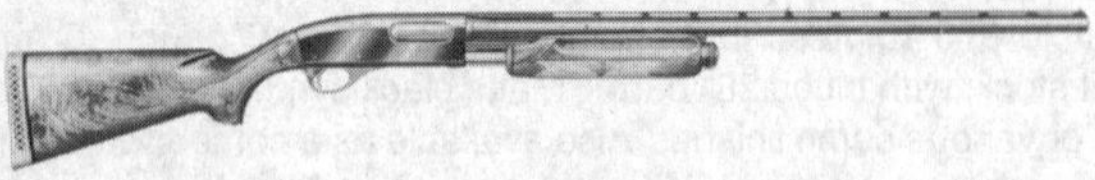

NIB	Exc.	V.G.	Good	Fair	Poor
—	450	320	280	200	120

Model 870TC Trap

As above, with finely figured walnut stock and screw-in choke tubes.

NIB	Exc.	V.G.	Good	Fair	Poor
580	480	400	350	250	150

Model 870 Express Deer Gun

Fitted with 20" fully rifled barrel, iron sights and Monte Carlo stock. Also offered with 20" IC rifle sighted barrel. Available in 12-gauge only.

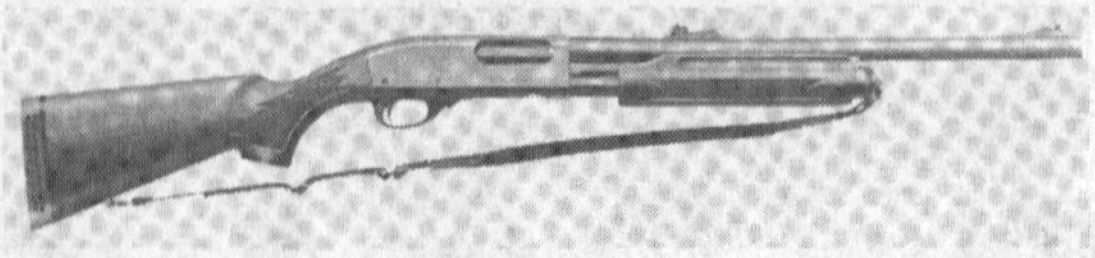

NIB	Exc.	V.G.	Good	Fair	Poor
370	310	270	230	190	160

Model 870 Express Deer/Turkey Combo

This 3" 12-gauge has a 21" barrel threaded for RemChokes for turkey hunting and 23" rifled slug barrel, with cantilever scope mount for deer hunting. Receiver and barrel are matte black; synthetic stock is Mossy Oak Break-Up camo.

NIB	Exc.	V.G.	Good	Fair	Poor
620	500	420	350	250	150

Model 870 Express Left-Hand

Left-hand version of Express model fitted with 28" ventilated rib barrel. Checkered hardwood stock. Black matte finish.

NIB	Exc.	V.G.	Good	Fair	Poor
360	280	200	150	100	80

Model 870 Express Synthetic Turkey Camo

12-gauge pump-action shotgun chambered for 2.75" and 3" shells. Features include 21" ventilated rib bead-sighted barrel; standard Express finish on barrel and receiver; Turkey Extra Full RemChoke; synthetic stock with integrated sling swivel attachment.

NIB	Exc.	V.G.	Good	Fair	Poor
440	380	320	280	200	150

Model 870 Express Super Magnum Turkey

This 12-gauge gun will handle 2.75", 3" or 3.5" shells. Fitted with 23" ventilated rib barrel, black synthetic stock and matte black metal finish. Weight about 7.25 lbs. Introduced in 1999.

NIB	Exc.	V.G.	Good	Fair	Poor
390	290	200	150	100	80

Model 870 Express Synthetic Deer

Fitted with 20" fully rifled barrel, with adjustable rifle sights. Black synthetic stock, with Monte Carlo comb and matte black finish. Weight about 7 lbs. Introduced in 1999.

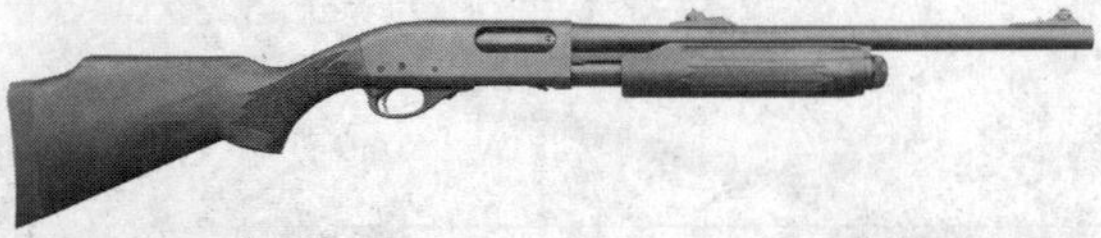

NIB	Exc.	V.G.	Good	Fair	Poor
370	280	200	150	100	80

Model 870 Express Compact Deer

20-gauge; similar to Model 870 Express Synthetic Deer, with smaller dimensions.

NIB	Exc.	V.G.	Good	Fair	Poor
420	300	200	150	100	80

Model 870 Express Compact Pink Camo

20-gauge; similar to Model 870 Express, with pink camo synthetic stock.

NIB	Exc.	V.G.	Good	Fair	Poor
370	280	200	150	100	80

Model 870 Express Compact Synthetic

Similar to above, with matte black synthetic stock.

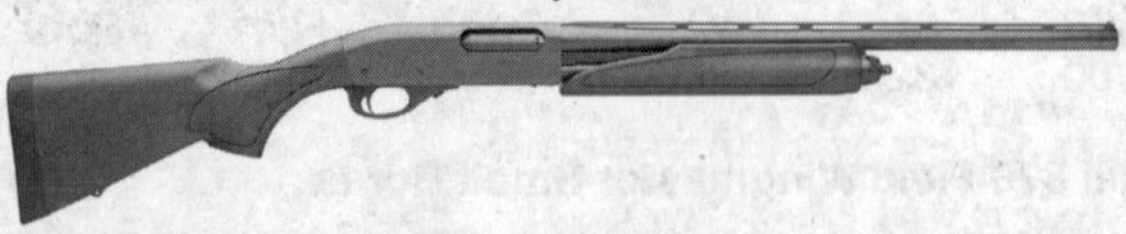

NIB	Exc.	V.G.	Good	Fair	Poor
370	280	200	150	100	80

Model 870 Express Compact Camo

Similar to above, with camo buttstock and forend.

NIB	Exc.	V.G.	Good	Fair	Poor
400	300	220	150	100	80

Model 870 Express Compact Jr.

Similar to above, with shorter barrel and lop.

NIB	Exc.	V.G.	Good	Fair	Poor
370	280	200	150	100	80

Model 870 Express Combos

Offered in both 12- and 20-gauge, with 26" ventilated rib modified barrel and 20" fully rifled deer barrel.

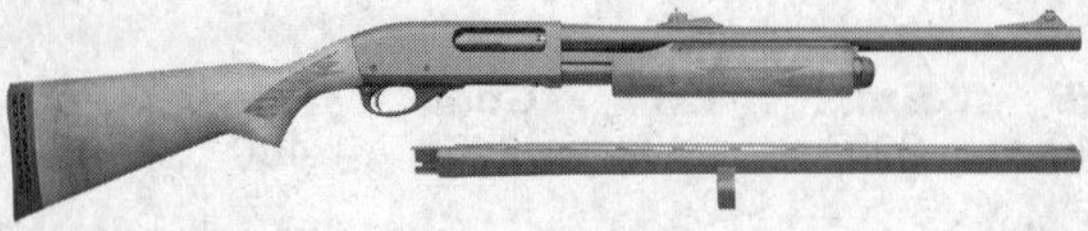

NIB	Exc.	V.G.	Good	Fair	Poor
500	400	250	200	150	100

Model 870 Express Youth Gun

Available in 20-gauge only. Built for children. Has 13" length of pull and 21" ventilated rib barrel. Sold with Modified RemChoke tube.

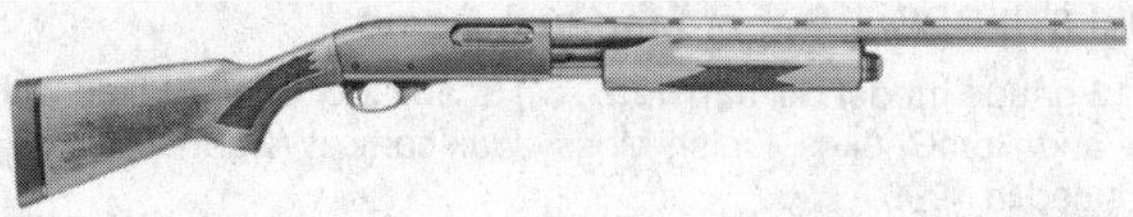

NIB	Exc.	V.G.	Good	Fair	Poor
330	250	200	150	120	100

Model 870 Express Turkey

Furnished in 12-gauge, with 21" ventilated rib barrel. Extra-full RemChoke Turkey tube.

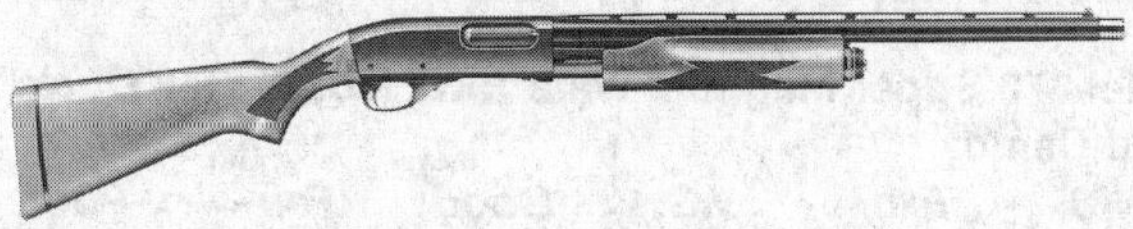

NIB	Exc.	V.G.	Good	Fair	Poor
340	250	180	150	120	100

Model 870 Express Camo Turkey

Similar to Express Turkey, with complete coverage of camo stock. Metal is matte black.

NIB	Exc.	V.G.	Good	Fair	Poor
400	300	220	150	100	80

Model 870 20 Gauge Express Youth Camo Turkey

Similar to Model 870 Express Camo. In 20-gauge, with shortened stock (13" lop).

NIB	Exc.	V.G.	Good	Fair	Poor
400	300	220	150	100	80

Model 870 Express Small Game

Offered in 20-gauge or .410 bore. Has a non-reflective metal and wood finish. The .410 bore furnished with 25" ventilated rib Full choke barrel; 20-gauge available with 26" or 28" ventilated rib barrel, with Modified RemChoke tube.

NIB	Exc.	V.G.	Good	Fair	Poor
220	200	180	150	120	100

Model 870 Express HD (Home Defense)

Introduced in 1995. Features 18" 12-gauge barrel, with cylinder barrel and front bead sight. Weight about 7.25 lb.

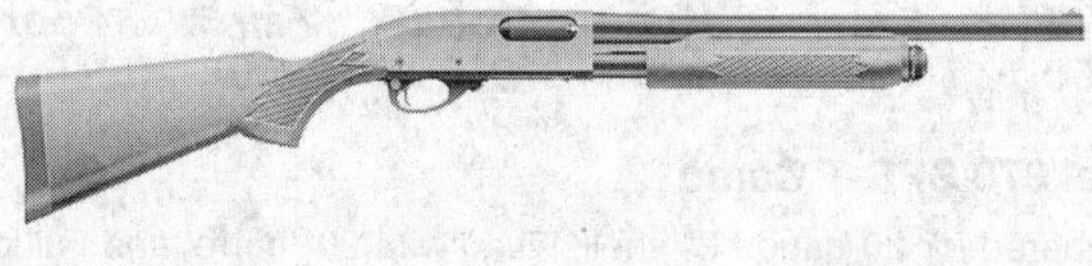

Courtesy Remington Arms

NIB	Exc.	V.G.	Good	Fair	Poor
340	250	180	150	120	100

Model 870 Classic Trap

Introduced in 2000. Features special fine line engraving, with gold inlays. Stock is select walnut, with Monte Carlo comb, 30" barrel, with contoured ventilated rib. Ventilated recoil pad, with white-line spacers. Choke tubes. Weight about 8 lbs.

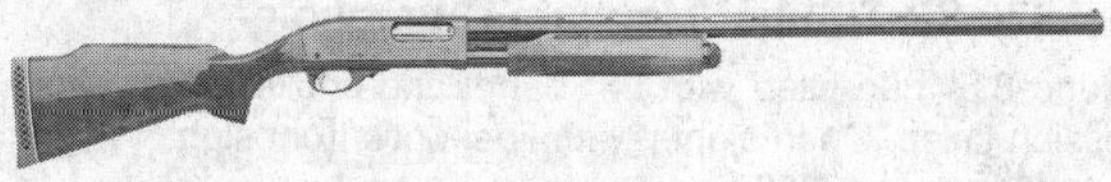

NIB	Exc.	V.G.	Good	Fair	Poor
680	550	450	300	200	—

Model 870 Special Field

Pump-action shotgun available in 12- or 20-gauge. Features English-style straight-grip stock, 21" ventilated rib barrel and slim shortened slide handle. Weight: 12-gauge 7 lbs.; 20-gauge 6.25 lbs. Comes with a set of RemChoke tubes.

NIB	Exc.	V.G.	Good	Fair	Poor
650	550	380	250	150	100

Model 870 Rifled Deer Gun

New 20-gauge model introduced in 1994. Features fully rifled 20" barrel. Has a new scope rail design that is more rigid. Finish blue and Monte Carlo stock walnut. Equipped with recoil pad and checkering.

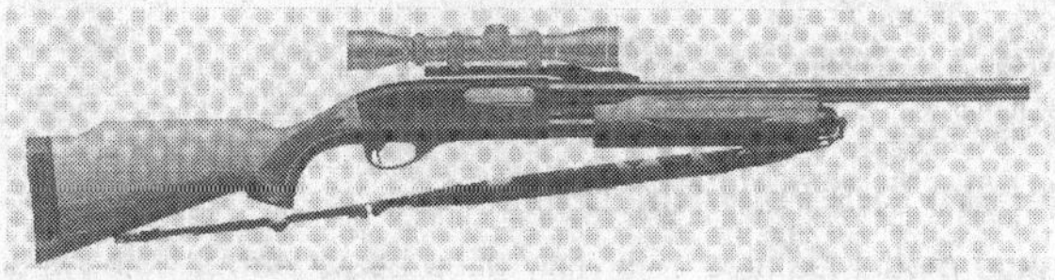

NIB	Exc.	V.G.	Good	Fair	Poor
450	400	350	300	200	100

Model 870 Brushmaster Deer Gun

12-gauge slide-action shotgun. Fitted with 20" RemChoke plain barrel and Monte Carlo stock. Available for left-/right-hand shooters.

NIB	Exc.	V.G.	Good	Fair	Poor
350	300	250	200	150	100

Model 870 Express Youth Turkey Camo

Similar to model above. Chambered for 20-gauge shell. Finished with Realtree Camo. Weight about 6 lbs.

NIB	Exc.	V.G.	Good	Fair	Poor
400	300	220	150	120	100

Model 870 Youth Deer Gun

Chambered for 20-gauge shell. Fitted with 21" Full choked barrel. Realtree Camo finish. Magazine capacity 4 rounds. Weight about 6 lbs.

NIB	Exc.	V.G.	Good	Fair	Poor
350	300	250	200	150	100

Model 870 Security

Offered in 12-gauge only. This personal protection shotgun has 18.5" Cylinder-choked plain barrel, with front bead sight.

NIB	Exc.	V.G.	Good	Fair	Poor
350	300	250	200	150	100

Model 870 SPS-Camo

Offered in 12-gauge only. Choice of 26" or 28" ventilated rib barrel, with RemChoke tubes. Wood and metal are finished in brown camo color. Introduced in 2001.

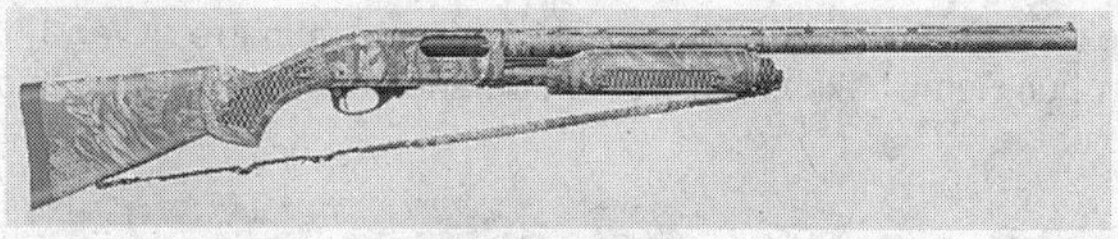

NIB	Exc.	V.G.	Good	Fair	Poor
600	420	320	220	180	120

Model 870 SPS Super Magnum Camo

Chambered for 12-gauge shells, with chambers that will handle both 3" and 3.5" Magnum, as well as all 2.75" shells. Barrel 23", with ventilated rib and RemChokes. Finish Mossy Oak camo. Weight about 7.25 lbs. Introduced in 1999.

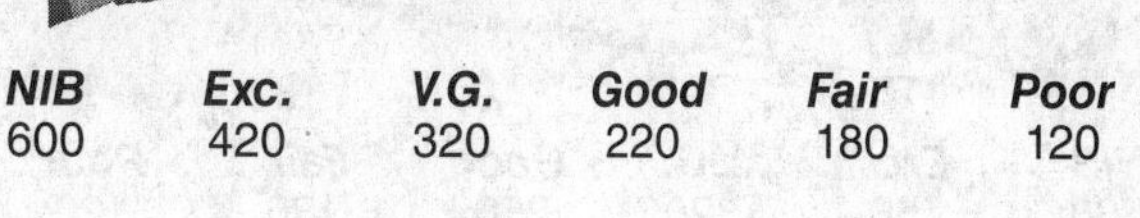

NIB	Exc.	V.G.	Good	Fair	Poor
600	420	320	220	180	120

Model 870 SPS-BG Camo

First time available in 1993. Features 12-gauge 20" plain barrel, with IC and Turkey Super Full RemChoke tubes. Wood and metal are finished in brown camo color.

NIB	Exc.	V.G.	Good	Fair	Poor
400	300	220	180	120	100

Model 870 SPS Fully Rifled Deer Gun

20-gauge model features 18.5" fully rifled heavy barrel, with no sights. Receiver has cantilever scope mount. Black synthetic stock. Black matte finish. Weight about 8 lbs. Magazine capacity 4 rounds. Introduced in 2004.

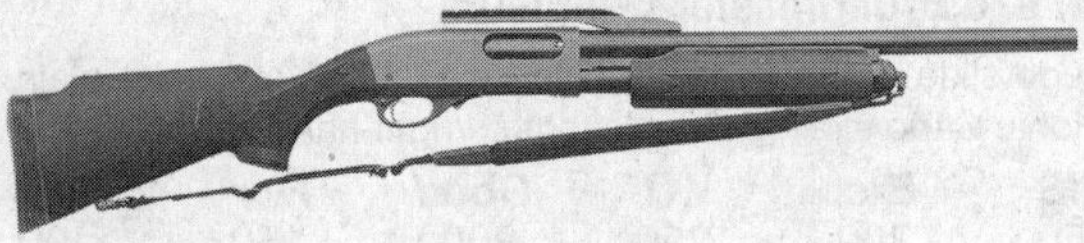

NIB	Exc.	V.G.	Good	Fair	Poor
500	380	250	180	120	100

Model 870 SPS Super Slug Deer Gun

Features 23" fully rifled modified contour barrel which is equipped with a barrel mounted cantilever scope mount. Stock is black synthetic. Weight about 8 lbs. Introduced in 1999.

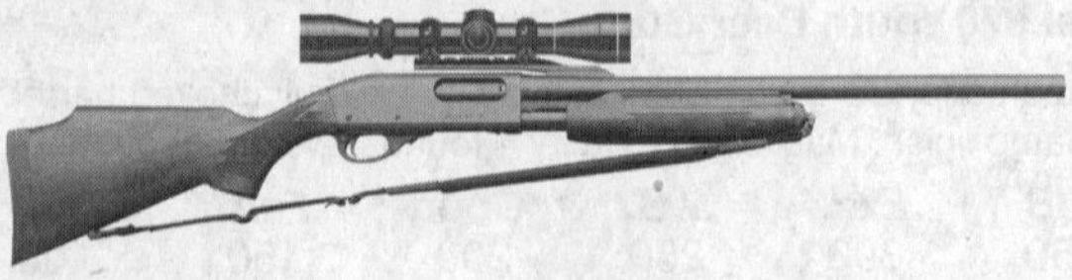

NIB	Exc.	V.G.	Good	Fair	Poor
600	420	320	250	180	100

Model 870 SPS-T

12-gauge model comes standard with 21" ventilated rib barrel, RemChoke tubes in IC and Turkey Super Full, black synthetic stock and black matte finish.

NIB	Exc.	V.G.	Good	Fair	Poor
580	480	400	350	250	150

Model 870 SPS-T Camo

Same as above, with exception of 21" ventilated rib barrel. IC and Turkey Super Full RemChoke tubes. Both wood and metal are finished in green camo color.

NIB	Exc.	V.G.	Good	Fair	Poor
600	420	320	250	180	100

Model 870 SPS-T Youth Turkey Camo

Finished in Mossy Oak Break-Up. Chambered for 12-gauge shell. Fitted with 20" Super Full choke. Weight about 7.125 lbs. Introduced in 2001.

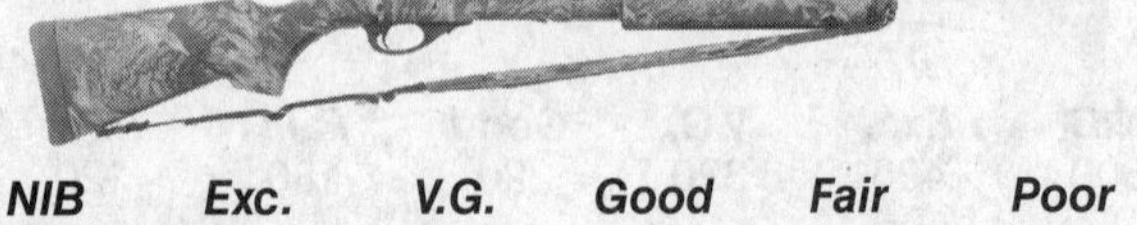

NIB	Exc.	V.G.	Good	Fair	Poor
560	450	320	250	180	120

Model 870 SPS-T Super Magnum Camo

This 12-gauge model will handle 2.75", 3" and 3.5" shells. Fitted with 23" barrel and RemChokes. Finish Mossy Oak camo. Weight about 7.25 lbs. Introduced in 1999.

NIB	Exc.	V.G.	Good	Fair	Poor
620	420	320	250	180	120

Model 870 Super Magnum Waterfowl, Mossy Oak Duck Blind Camo

NIB	Exc.	V.G.	Good	Fair	Poor
590	—	—	—	—	—

Model 870 SPS-T Camo NWTF 25th Anniversary

Fitted with 21" barrel that has special fibe- optic sighting system. NWTF logo on left side of receiver. Introduced in 1998.

NIB	Exc.	V.G.	Good	Fair	Poor
600	450	320	250	180	120

Model 870 SPS-T Super Mag

Similar to Model 870 SP-T Thumbhole, with pistol grip stock and ventilated rib barrel.

NIB	Exc.	V.G.	Good	Fair	Poor
630	450	350	280	200	150

Model 870 SPS-T/20

20-gauge turkey gun features 3" chamber, 23" ventilated rib barrel, R3 recoil pad and full coverage in Mossy Oak New Break-Up camo. Drilled and tapped for scope mount.

NIB	Exc.	V.G.	Good	Fair	Poor
550	450	320	250	200	150

Model 870 SPS-T Camo

Chambered for 20-gauge 3" shell. Fitted with 20" barrel and Full choke. Stock is Mossy Oak camo. Fiber optic front sight. Weight about 6 lbs. Introduced in 2003.

NIB	Exc.	V.G.	Good	Fair	Poor
600	450	320	250	180	120

Model 870 SP-T Super Magnum Thumbhole

12-gauge 3.5" gun fitted with 23" barrel and choke tubes. Mossy Oak Obsession finish. Open sights, with fiber-optic front sight. Weight about 8 lbs. Introduced in 2005.

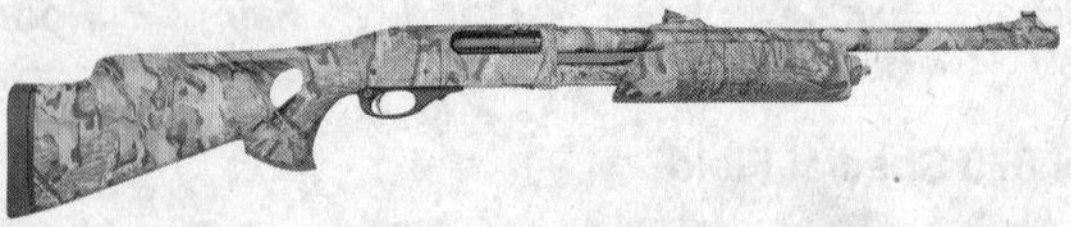

NIB	Exc.	V.G.	Good	Fair	Poor
650	500	350	250	180	120

Model 870 Dale Earnhardt Limited Edition

12-gauge with 28" ventilated rib barrel and choke tubes. Checkered walnut stock. Receiver engraved with Earnhardt's likeness and gold signature. High polish blue finish. Weight about 8 lbs. Introduced in 2005.

NIB	Exc.	V.G.	Good	Fair	Poor
650	500	350	250	180	120

Model 870 Marine Magnum

This 12-gauge shotgun has a nickel finish on the inside and outside of receiver and barrel. Synthetic stock checkered. The 18" barrel is bored cylinder. Fitted with 7-round magazine. Sling swivel studs are standard.

NIB	Exc.	V.G.	Good	Fair	Poor
560	320	280	220	180	120

Model 870 SPS

Offered in 12-gauge only. Synthetic stock and black matte finish. Barrel 26" or 28", with ventilated rib and RemChoke tubes.

NIB	Exc.	V.G.	Good	Fair	Poor
320	280	220	180	120	100

Model 870 SPS-Deer

Available with 20" rifle and plain barrel. This 12-gauge shotgun has black synthetic stock and black matte finish. First introduced in 1993.

NIB	Exc.	V.G.	Good	Fair	Poor
550	450	320	250	200	150

Model 870 Police

This model comes in a wide variety (21) of 12-gauge configurations. Fitted with barrel from 14" (Class III), 18" or 20". Most with Parkerized finish, although some variations have blued finish. Wood, folding, Speed-feed or synthetic stock. Rifle or bead sights. Some configurations with ghost ring and tritium night sights. Some variations have 7- or 8-round magazine extensions, depending on barrel length.

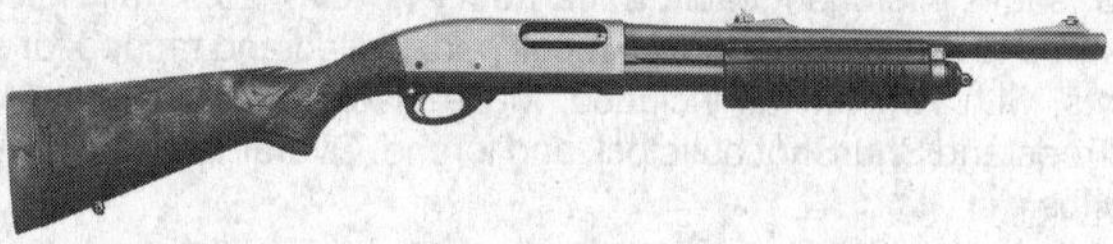

NIB	Exc.	V.G.	Good	Fair	Poor
650	520	400	300	220	120

Model 870 Tac-2 SpecOps Stock

Tactical 3" 12-gauge. Available with Knoxx pistol grip or folding stock. Barrel 18", with fixed Cylinder choke. Magazine capacity 6 shells. Weight 7 lbs.

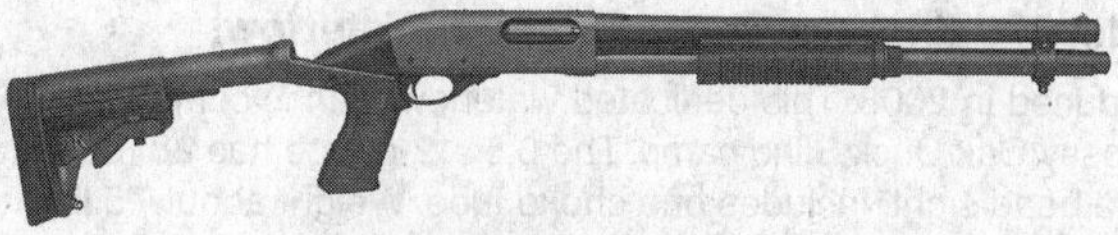

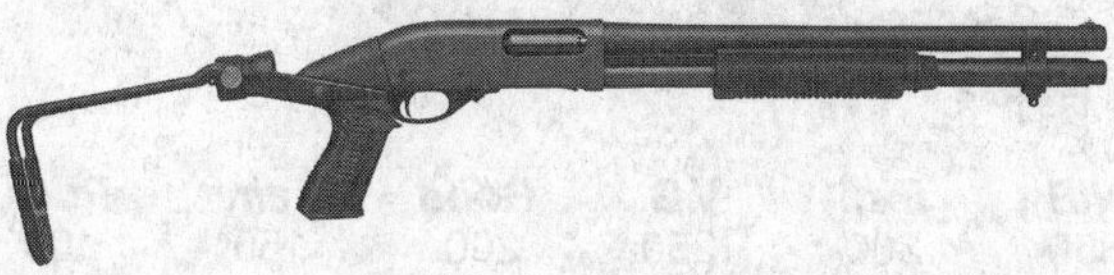

NIB	Exc.	V.G.	Good	Fair	Poor
620	420	320	250	180	120

Model 870 Tac-3 Speedfeed IV

Tactical 3" 12-gauge, with pistol grip stock and 20" barrel. Extended 7-round magazine. Weight 7.5 lbs.

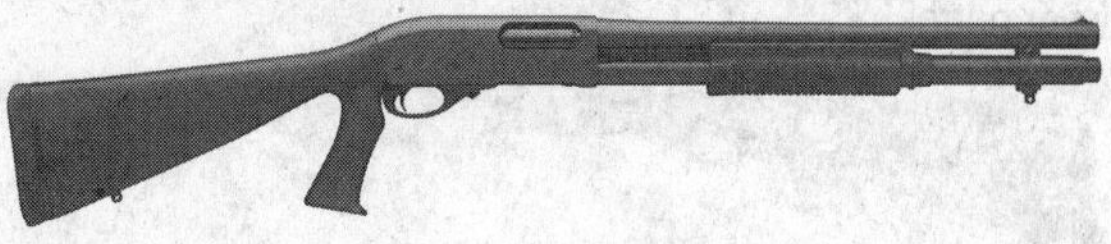

NIB	Exc.	V.G.	Good	Fair	Poor
600	450	320	250	180	120

Model 870 Tac-3 Folder

As above, with Knoxx Spec-Ops folding stock. Weight 7 lbs.

NIB	Exc.	V.G.	Good	Fair	Poor
600	450	320	250	180	120

Model 870 Express Tactical Side Folder

Introduced 2019. 12 gauge 81210 and 20 gauge 81223 include side-folding stock that reduces OAL 11" when folded. Tapco AK Pattern SAW grip, with positive hand stops on the forend and a hand strap. 6+1 capacity, 18.5" Remchoke barrel. Soft touch cheekpiece, M-Lok compatible forend, drilled and tapped teceiver, QD cup attachment points, Supercell recoil pad that works with adjustable LOP kit. Remchoke threaded muzzle.

NIB	Exc.	V.G.	Good	Fair	Poor
430	350	280	—	—	—

Model 870 Express Tactical A-TACS Camo

Pump-action shotgun chambered for 2.75" and 3" 12-gauge. Features include full A-TACS digitized camo; 18.5" barrel; extended ported Tactical RemChoke; SpeedFeed IV pistol grip stock with SuperCell recoil pad; fully adjustable XS ghost ring sight rail with removable white bead front sight; 7-round capacity with factory-installed 2-shot extension; drilled and tapped receiver; sling swivel stud.

NIB	Exc.	V.G.	Good	Fair	Poor
600	520	450	380	280	180

Model 870 Custom Grade

Custom Shop model available in three levels of engraving, gold inlay, wood grade and finish, metal work finish, recoil pad/buttplate and dimensions.

D Grade

NIB	Exc.	V.G.	Good	Fair	Poor
3000	200	1100	—	—	—

F Grade

NIB	Exc.	V.G.	Good	Fair	Poor
6000	4000	2250	—	—	—

F Grade with Gold Inlay

NIB	Exc.	V.G.	Good	Fair	Poor
10000	7500	5000	—	—	—

Model 870 SP-T Thumbhole

Introduced in 2005. This 3.5" 12-gauge is designed specifically for turkey hunting. Full coverage in Mossy Oak Obsession camo and thumbhole stock. The 23" barrel features fiber-optic adjustable rifle sights and is drilled and tapped for scope mounting. Includes R3 recoil pad, sling, swivels and Turkey Super Full choke tube.

NIB	Exc.	V.G.	Good	Fair	Poor
620	420	320	250	180	120

Model 870 Special Purpose Thumbhole

Laminated stock 12-gauge slug gun, with 3" chamber and 23" fully rifled cantilever barrel.

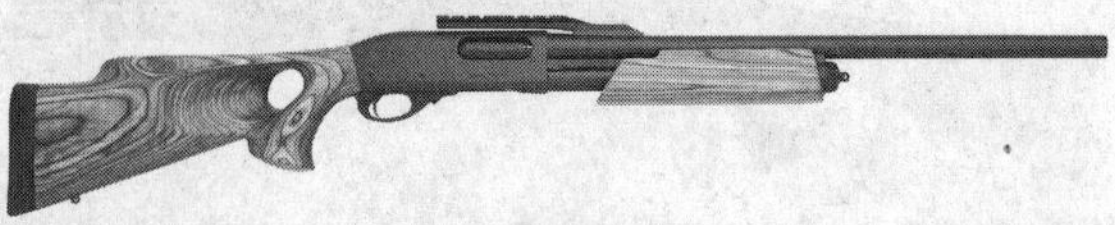

NIB	Exc.	V.G.	Good	Fair	Poor
520	480	350	280	200	150

Model 870 XCS Marine Magnum

New in 2007, this weather-resistant 870 is a 3" 12-gauge, with full black TriNyte coverage, 18" fixed Cylinder barrel and 7-round capacity. Weight 7.5 lbs.

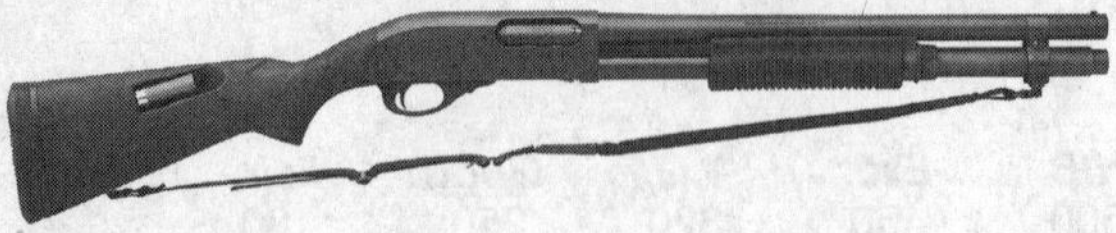

NIB	Exc.	V.G.	Good	Fair	Poor
680	500	400	300	200	120

Model 870 SPS MAX Gobbler

Dedicated turkey gun is a 3.5" 12-gauge. Featuring length-adjustable Knoxx SpecOps stock, 23" barrel, fiber-optic rifle sights, Turkey Super Full choke tube and full coverage in Realtree APG camo. Drilled and tapped for Weaver style mount. Weight 8 lbs.

NIB	Exc.	V.G.	Good	Fair	Poor
650	550	420	350	220	150

Model 870 20 Gauge Lightweight Magnum

Fixed-choke, high-gloss 3" version of Model 870 Wingmaster, with impressed checkering. Introduced mid-1980s. Also chambers 2.75" shells. Discontinued.

NIB	Exc.	V.G.	Good	Fair	Poor
550	450	320	250	200	150

Model 870 Wingmaster 100th Anniversary

Commemorative Edition 12-gauge celebrating 100 years of Remington pump shotguns (dating from introduction of Model 10 in 1908). Introduced in 2008. Offered only for one year. Gold-inlaid logos on both sides of receiver and "B" Grade American walnut stock, with high-gloss finish. Includes three choke tubes.

NIB	Exc.	V.G.	Good	Fair	Poor
880	600	480	350	200	120

Model 870 200th Year Anniversary Commemorative Edition

A limited edition made only in 2016 to commemorate the 200th anniversary of the Remington company. A total of 2,016 Model 870 12-gauge shotguns were produced featuring a 24-carat gold inlay of founder Eliphalet Remington, a high gloss C Grade walnut stock with fleur-de-lis cut checkering, 26-inch barrel with a ventilated rib, and polished blue finish.

NIB	Exc.	V.G.	Good	Fair	Poor
1400	1100	900	700	—	—

Model 870 American Classic

Part of Remington American Classic series honoring some of the great models of the 20th century. Inaugurating this line in 2014, is this special edition Model 870 pump action and a comparable Model 1100 semi-automatic. Features include a higher B-grade walnut stock, gold filled engraving and ventilated recoil pad, with white outline as was found on the originals.

NIB	Exc.	V.G.	Good	Fair	Poor
1000	850	700	600	400	300

Model 870 with Claro Walnut

This 2008 upgrade to 870 Wingmaster. Features semi-fancy claro walnut stock and forend. Available in 3" 12- and 20-gauge, with 28" and 26" barrels, respectively. Three choke tubes included.

NIB	Exc.	V.G.	Good	Fair	Poor
880	600	480	350	200	120

Model 870 Express Magnum ShurShot Cantilever

This 3" 12-gauge has a 23" fully rifled barrel, with cantilever scope mount. Matte black finish. Weight about 7.75 lbs.

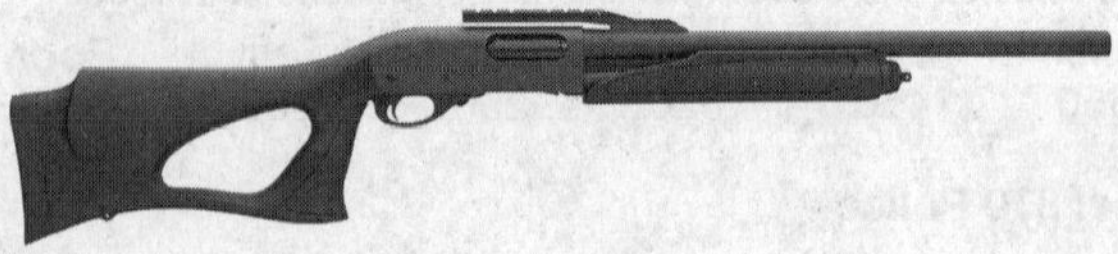

NIB	Exc.	V.G.	Good	Fair	Poor
550	450	320	250	200	150

Model 870 SPS ShurShot Synthetic Super Slug

Pump-action shotgun based on 870 platform. Chambers 12-gauge 2.75" and 3" shells interchangeably. Extra-heavy (1" dia.) 25.5" fully rifled barrel pinned to receiver. SuperCell recoil pad. Drilled and tapped for scope mounts, with Weaver rail included. Matte black metal surfaces, Mossy Oak Treestand ShurShot buttstock and forend. Overall length 47". Weight 7.875 lbs.

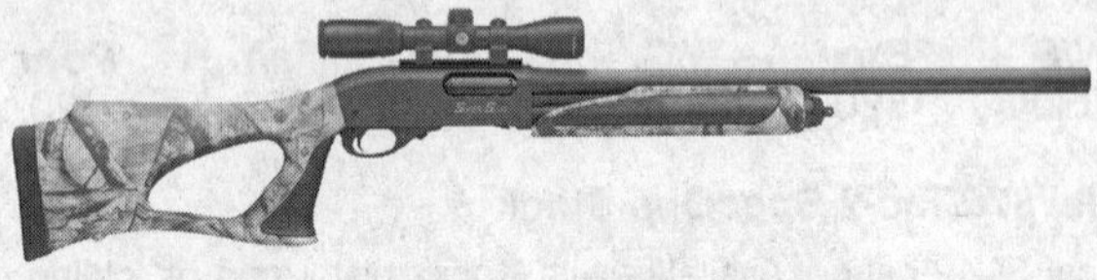

NIB	Exc.	V.G.	Good	Fair	Poor
640	540	460	390	330	280

Model 870 Express Super Magnum Waterfowl

Introduced in 2008. This dedicated waterfowl gun is completely finished in Mossy Oak Duck Blind camo. The 3.5" 12-gauge has 28" barrel, HiViz single bead sight. Includes one choke tube. Weight about 7.5 lbs.

NIB	Exc.	V.G.	Good	Fair	Poor
350	300	250	200	150	100

Model 870 Express Magnum ShurShot Turkey

Turkey-dedicated model has matte black finish, with ShurShot pistol grip/thumbhole stock. Forend finished in Mossy Oak Obsession camo. The 3" 12-gauge has 21" barrel. Includes a Turkey Extra Full choke tube. Weight about 7.5 lbs.

NIB	Exc.	V.G.	Good	Fair	Poor
580	490	420	350	300	260

Model 870 SPS ShurShot Turkey

New in 2008. This 12-gauge chambered for shells up to 3.5". Features Remington's ShurShot pistol grip/thumbhole stock. Fully covered in Realtree's APG HD camo. Has 23" non-ventilated rib barrel outfitted with fiber-optic rifle-type sights and includes an extended Turkey RemChoke. Weight about 7.5 lbs.

NIB	Exc.	V.G.	Good	Fair	Poor
620	500	400	300	200	120

Model 870 Express Tactical

Similar to Model 870, in 12-gauge only (2.75" and 3" interchangeably) with 18.5" barrel, Tactical RemChoke extended/ported choke tube, black synthetic buttstock and forend, extended magazine tube, gray powder-coat finish overall. 38.5" overall length. Weight 7.5 lbs.

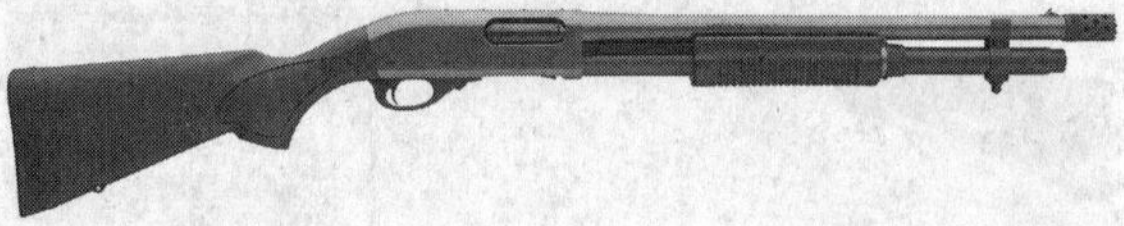

NIB	Exc.	V.G.	Good	Fair	Poor
580	460	320	250	200	150

Model 870 Express Tactical with Ghost Ring Sights

Similar to Model 870 Express Tactical, with top-mounted accessories rail and XS ghost ring rear sight.

NIB	Exc.	V.G.	Good	Fair	Poor
470	400	340	290	240	210

Model 870 Tactical Desert Recon

Tactical version 870 features Digital Tiger desert camo on synthetic stock and forend. Olive-drab powder-coated barrel and receiver. Available with 18" (6-round mag. capacity) or 20" (7-round mag. capacity) barrel. Speedfeed I (shell holding) or Speedfeed IV (pistol grip) stock. Note: Add 10% for Speedfeed IV stock.

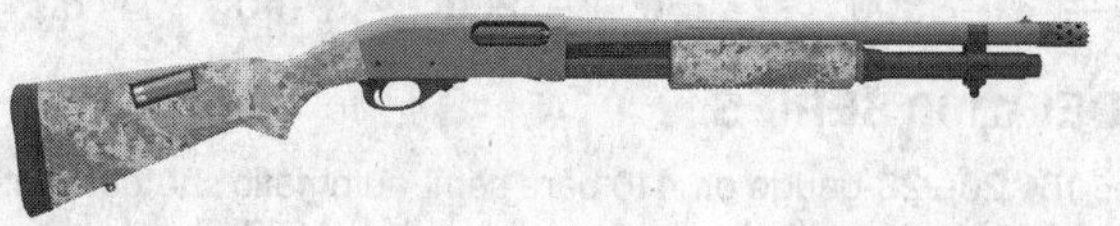

NIB	Exc.	V.G.	Good	Fair	Poor
620	500	400	300	200	120

Model 870 DM

New 2018. In 12 gauge only with 18.5" cylinder-bore barrel and 3" chamber. Detachable 6-round magazine. Stocks are hardwood (81351) or black synthetic (81350) with textured gripping surfaces, corn-cob style forend, Super Cell Recoil pad. Magpul version 81352 has Magpul SGA stock and forend, XS Ghost Ring sights and tactical rail. The Model 870 DM Tactical 81360 adds Rem choke barrel with ported tactical choke and pistol grip tactical stock. DM Predator 81354 comes in Kryptek Highlander full camo ShurShot stock and tactical forend with TruLock extended XFull predator/turkey and XFull hog chokes.

NIB	Exc.	V.G.	Good	Fair	Poor
340	290	250	210	180	150

Model 870 DM Hardwood

NIB	Exc.	V.G.	Good	Fair	Poor
390	330	280	240	200	170

Model 870 DM Magpul

NIB	Exc.	V.G.	Good	Fair	Poor
570	490	410	350	300	250

Model 870 DM Tactical

NIB	Exc.	V.G.	Good	Fair	Poor
570	490	410	350	300	250

Model 870 DM Predator

NIB	Exc.	V.G.	Good	Fair	Poor
570	480	410	350	300	250

Model 870 Tac-14

Introduced 2017 in 12 gauge (81230) and 20 gauge (81145). This is a non-NFA 14" barrel configuration attached to a pump-action receiver. Has a Shockwave Raptor pistol grip, Magpul M-Lok forend. Cylinder-bore barrel with bead sight, steel receiver, black oxide finish, and 26.2" overall length. 5.6 lbs. Synthetic black stock. The 870 Tac-14 was designed and manufactured by Remington as a "firearm" and is not governed by the National Firearms Act (NFA). No ATF NFA registration or tax stamp is required, but state and local laws may apply.

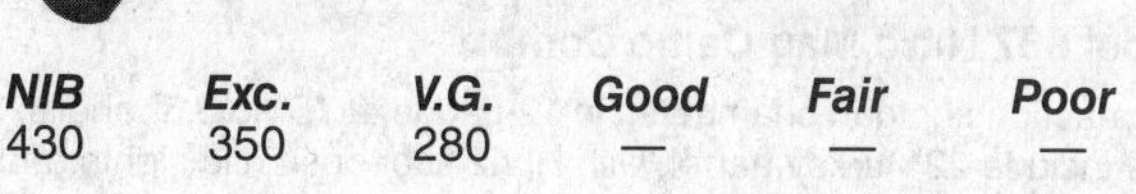

NIB	Exc.	V.G.	Good	Fair	Poor
430	350	280	—	—	—

REMARMS 870 SERIES

Model 870 Fieldmaster (2023)

Gauges: 12 ga., 20 ga. Barrels: 26", 28" (21" Compact 20-ga. model available). Stock: Standard-grade American Walnut. Features: New RemArms pump action in the old Express style, now called Fieldmaster. Milled steel receiver. Twin action bars. Matte black metalwork. Ventilated rib barrel with single front bead. Drilled and tapped receiver. A left-hand 12-gauge model is available. Includes three flush Rem chokes.

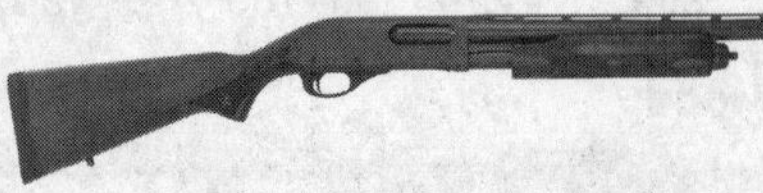

NIB	Exc.	V.G.	Good	Fair	Poor
550	490	400	300	—	—

Model 870 Fieldmaster Synthetic (2023)

Gauges: 12 ga. (20 ga. Compact only). Barrels: 26", 28" (12 ga.), 21" (20 ga.) Stock: Black synthetic. Features: New RemArms pump action in the old Express style, now called Fieldmaster Synthetic. Milled steel receiver. Twin action bars. Matte black metalwork. Adjustable comb insert available. Drilled and tapped receiver. Includes three flush Rem chokes.

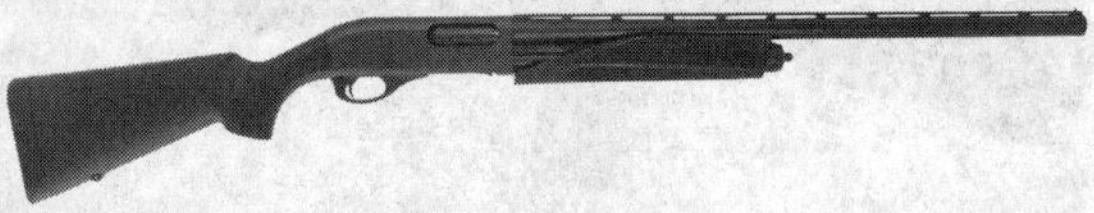

NIB	Exc.	V.G.	Good	Fair	Poor
500	440	380	300	—	—

MODEL 887 SERIES

Model 887 Nitro Mag Pump Shotgun

Pump-action shotgun based on Model 870. Chambers 2.75", 3" and 3.5" 12-gauge shells interchangeably. Black matte ArmorLokt rustproof coating throughout. SuperCell recoil pad. 28" barrel, with solid rib. Hi-Viz front sight, with interchangeable light tubes. Black synthetic stock, with contoured grip panels.

NIB	Exc.	V.G.	Good	Fair	Poor
—	380	320	270	230	200

Model 887 Nitro Mag Waterfowl

Similar to above, with Advantage Max-4 camo overall.

NIB	Exc.	V.G.	Good	Fair	Poor
—	400	340	290	250	210

Model 887 Bone Collector Edition

Pump-action shotgun chambered in 12-gauge, 2.75" to 3.5" shells. Features include ArmorLokt rustproof coating; synthetic stock and forend; 26" barrel; full camo finish; integral swivel studs; SuperCell recoil pad; solid rib and HiViz front sight. Bone Collector logo.

NIB	Exc.	V.G.	Good	Fair	Poor
560	480	400	340	250	150

Model 887 Nitro Mag Camo Combo

Pump-action shotgun chambered in 12-gauge, 2.75" to 3.5" shells. Features include 22" turkey barrel, with HiViz fiber-optic rifle sights and 28" waterfowl, with HiViz sight; extended Waterfowl and Super Full Turkey RemChokes are included; SuperCell recoil pad; synthetic stock and forend, with specially contoured grip panels; full camo coverage.

NIB	Exc.	V.G.	Good	Fair	Poor
620	540	460	380	320	200

Model 887 Nitro Mag Tactical

Pump-action shotgun chambered in 12-gauge, 2.75" to 3.5" shells. Features include 18.5" barrel, with ported extended tactical RemChoke; 2-shot magazine extension; barrel clamp, with integral Picatinny rails; ArmorLokt coating; synthetic stock and forend, with specially contour grip panels.

NIB	Exc.	V.G.	Good	Fair	Poor
450	400	350	280	200	150

Model 878 Automaster

As above in 12-gauge only. Approximately 60,000 made from 1959 to 1962.

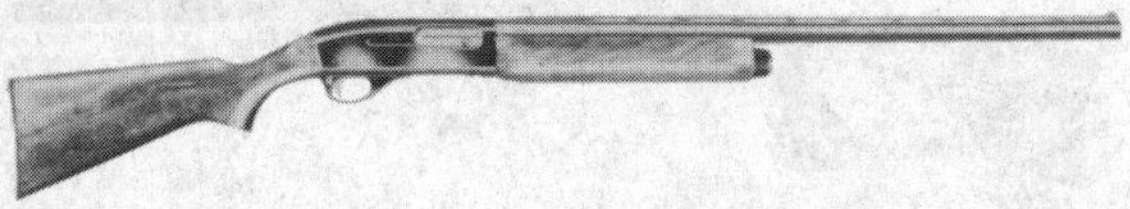

NIB	Exc.	V.G.	Good	Fair	Poor
—	350	250	180	120	80

Model 48 Sportsman

A 12-, 16- or 20-gauge semi-automatic shotgun, with 26", 28" or 32" barrels and 3-shot tubular magazine. Blued. with checkered walnut stock. Approximately 275,000 made from 1949 to 1959. Note: Add 20% for ventilated rib.

NIB	Exc.	V.G.	Good	Fair	Poor
—	320	300	250	180	100

Model 11-48

As above, with addition of 28-gauge and .410 bore. Approximately 425,000 made from 1949 to 1968. Note: Add 20% for 20-gauge; 100% for 28-gauge or .410 bore.

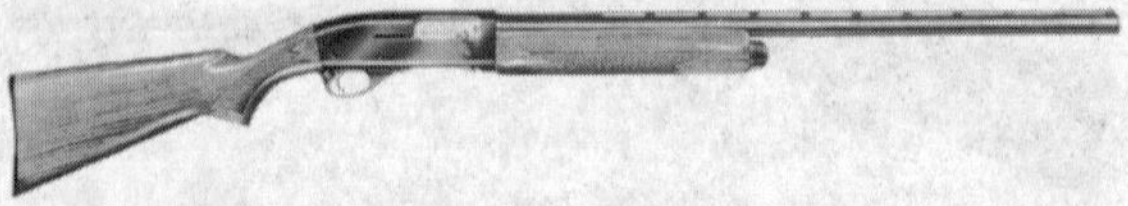

NIB	Exc.	V.G.	Good	Fair	Poor
—	300	250	200	150	80

Model 58 Sportsman

A 12-, 16- or 20-gauge semi-automatic shotgun, with 26", 28" or 30" barrels and 3-shot tubular magazine. Receiver is scroll engraved and blued. Checkered walnut stock. Approximately 270,000 made from 1956 to 1963. Note: Add 50% for skeet model.

NIB	Exc.	V.G.	Good	Fair	Poor
—	300	250	200	150	80

MODEL 1100 SERIES

A 12-, 16-, 20-, 28-gauge or .410 bore semi-automatic shotgun, with barrels from 26" to 30". Fitted with choke tubes after 1987. Blued, with checkered walnut stock. Manufactured beginning in 1963. Note: Smaller bore versions are worth approximately 20 percent more than values listed.

NIB	Exc.	V.G.	Good	Fair	Poor
550	450	350	200	150	100

Model 1100 Classic Field

Introduced in 2003. Chambered for 16-gauge shell. Fitted with choice of 26" or 28" ventilated rib barrel, with RemChoke tubes. Checkered walnut stock, with pistol grip. High polish blue finish. Magazine capacity 4 rounds. Weight about 7 to 7.25 lbs. depending on barrel length.

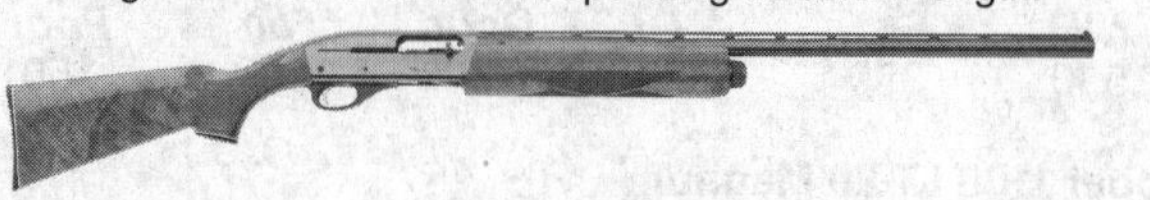

NIB	Exc.	V.G.	Good	Fair	Poor
800	600	450	300	200	100

Model 1100 Small Gauge

Available in 20-, 28-gauge or .410 bore. Fitted with 25" ventilated rib barrels. 28-gauge and .410 have Fixed chokes, while 20-gauge has RemChoke tubes.

NIB	Exc.	V.G.	Good	Fair	Poor
500	450	400	350	250	150

Model 1100 Youth Gun

Offered in 20-gauge only, with 21" ventilated rib 2.75" barrel. Stock has special 13" length of pull. Gun supplied with a set of RemChoke tubes.

NIB	Exc.	V.G.	Good	Fair	Poor
600	400	350	300	200	150

Model 1100 Youth Synthetic

Fitted with 21" ventilated rib barrel, this 20-gauge gun has a 1" shorter length of pull than standard. Matte black finish. Black synthetic stock. Weight about 6.5 lbs. Introduced in 1999.

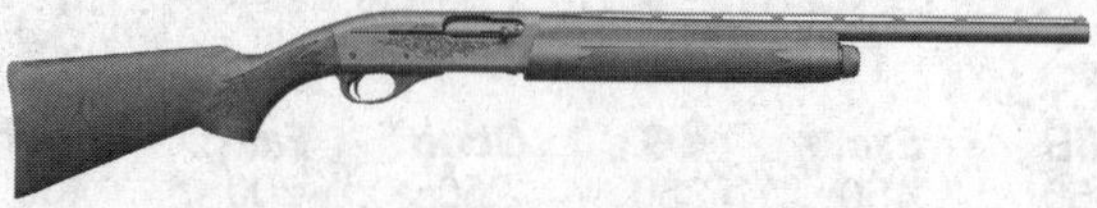

NIB	Exc.	V.G.	Good	Fair	Poor
580	400	300	220	150	100

Model 1100 Youth Synthetic Camo

Same as model above, with Realtree camo finish and chambered for 20-gauge 3" Magnum shells. Weight about 6.75 lbs. Introduced in 1999.

NIB	Exc.	V.G.	Good	Fair	Poor
700	480	320	220	180	100

Model 1100 Tournament Skeet

Offered in 20-, 28-gauge and .410 bore. The 28-gauge and .410 come with 25" Skeet choked ventilated rib barrels; 20-gauge supplied with 26" Skeet choked ventilated rib barrel.

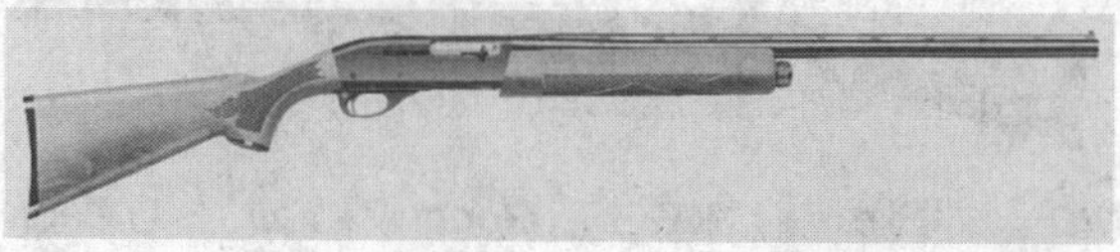

Courtesy Remington Arms

NIB	Exc.	V.G.	Good	Fair	Poor
800	650	500	400	250	150

Model 1100 Tournament Skeet, 12 Gauge

Introduced in 2003. Fitted with 26" light contour ventilated rib barrel. Stock semi-fancy walnut. Receiver rolled-marked "tournament skeet". Supplied with extended choke tubes and gold-plated trigger. Weight about 7.75 lbs.

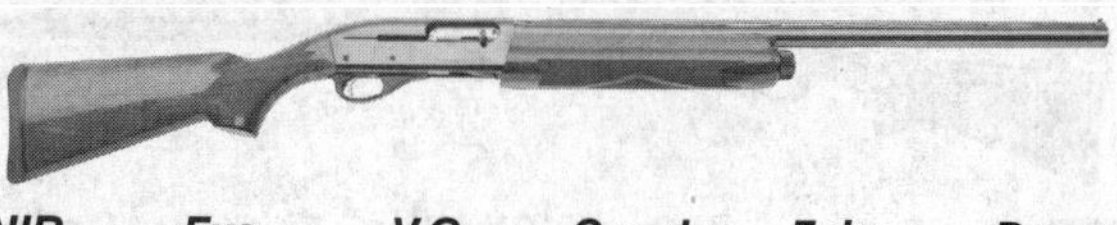

NIB	Exc.	V.G.	Good	Fair	Poor
650	500	400	300	200	100

Model 1100 Classic Trap

Features 30" low-profile ventilated rib barrel. Stock semi-fancy walnut, with Monte Carlo comb and ventilated recoil pad. Receiver has fine line engraving, with gold inlays. Trigger is gold. Weight about 8.25 lbs.

NIB	Exc.	V.G.	Good	Fair	Poor
1050	890	760	640	550	470

Model 1100 Sporting 12

Introduced in 2000. This 12-gauge features 28" low profile ventilated rib barrel. Stock walnut, with cut checkering and Sporting Clays-style recoil pad. Gold trigger and fine line engraving on receiver. Weight about 8 lbs.

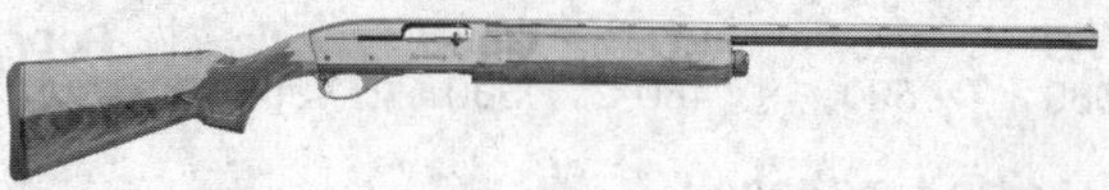

NIB	Exc.	V.G.	Good	Fair	Poor
940	800	680	580	490	420

Model 1100 Sporting 20

High grade walnut stock, with glass finish and recoil pad. Fitted with 28" barrel, with target sights. Interchangeable chokes. Introduced in 1998.

NIB	Exc.	V.G.	Good	Fair	Poor
950	800	680	580	490	420

Model 1100 Sporting 28

Introduced in 1996. Chambered for 28-gauge shell. Fitted with interchangeable chokes and 25" ventilated rib barrel. Stock is walnut, with Tournament grade checkering and recoil pad.

NIB	Exc.	V.G.	Good	Fair	Poor
1000	850	720	620	520	440

Model 1100 Sporting 410

NIB	Exc.	V.G.	Good	Fair	Poor
1020	860	730	620	530	450

Model 1100 Competition Master

Introduced in 2003. Features 12-gauge gun chambered for 2.75" shell. Fitted with 22" ventilated rib barrel, with RemChokes and fiber optic front sight. Has gray synthetic stock, with matte black finish on receiver and barrel. Magazine extension has 8-round capacity. Receiver mounted ammo carrier for seven extra shells. Weight about 8 lbs. Designed for practical shooting competition.

NIB	Exc.	V.G.	Good	Fair	Poor
720	600	420	400	300	150

Model 1100 Competition

Introduced in 2005. Chambered for 12-gauge shells, with 2.75" chamber. Fitted with 30" target style barrel, with 10mm ventilated rib. Extended choke tubes. Receiver nickel plated. Stock semi-fancy American walnut, with checkering and a high-gloss finish. Adjustable comb offered as an option. Weight about 8 lbs. Note: Add $175 for the adjustable comb model.

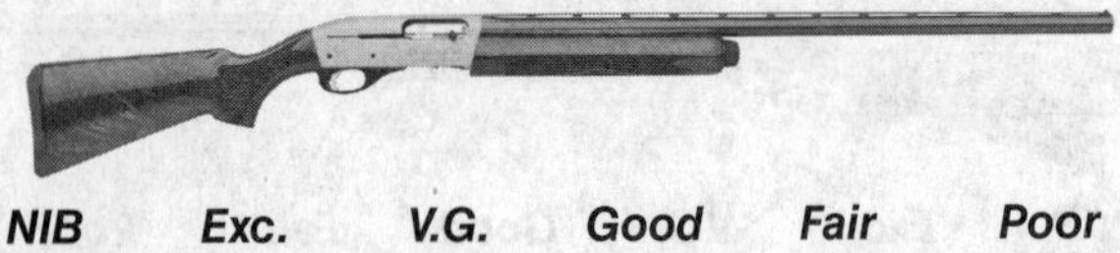

NIB	Exc.	V.G.	Good	Fair	Poor
950	780	650	520	350	180

Model 1100 LT-20

20-gauge model features choice of 26" or 28" ventilated rib barrels, with RemChoke tubes. Blue finish and walnut Monte Carlo stock. Recoil pad and cut checkering are standard. Weight 6.75 to 7 lbs. depending on barrel length.

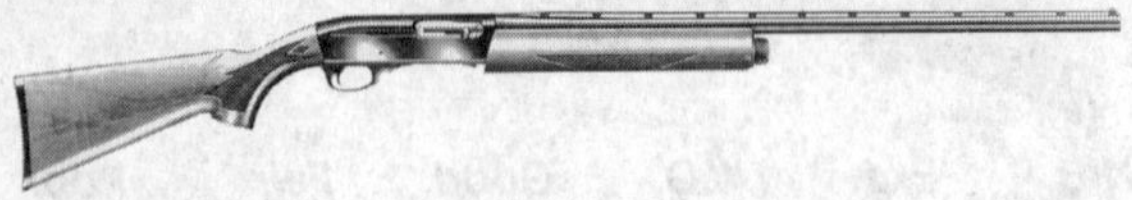

NIB	Exc.	V.G.	Good	Fair	Poor
600	450	400	300	200	150

Model 1100 LT-20 "Limited"

20-gauge lightweight Model 1100 Field gun. Stock 1 shorter than standard and 23" barrel for youthful beginner shooters of smaller stature.

NIB	Exc.	V.G.	Good	Fair	Poor
680	520	480	380	280	200

Model 1100 1 OF 3000

Remington announced Model 1100 Limited Edition "One of Three Thousand", in September, 1980. High grade gun, with positive cut checkered fancy American walnut wood, fitted rosewood grip cap, thin brown butt pad, 14K gold trimmed and etched with hunting scenes on receiver. All metal parts including receiver, barrel, bolt and magazine cap have a high-luster finish. Available only in 1980.

NIB	Exc.	V.G.	Good	Fair	Poor
2000	1600	1000	800	400	250

Model 1100 Special Field

In 12-, 20-gauge or .410 bore. Shorter variation of standard 1100. Barrel length was originally 21" (1983-1993); changed to 23" from (1994 to 1999) when model was discontinued. Checkered walnut stock, with straight-grip. Ventilated rib on all models. Note: Add 20% for .410 bore.

NIB	Exc.	V.G.	Good	Fair	Poor
600	500	400	350	300	150

Model 1100 TBMC Trap Gun

12-gauge, with 30" ventilated rib barrel in Full or Modified trap chokes. Featured a figured and checkered stock and forend. Had a rubber recoil pad. Monte Carlo-style stock was optional. A left-hand version was also available. Due to a shortage of American walnut, in mid-year, Remington began fitting some Model 1100 and Model 870 Field Grade shotguns with lightweight mahogany stocks and forends.

NIB	Exc.	V.G.	Good	Fair	Poor
720	650	480	400	300	150

Model 1100 LT-20 Deer Gun

Same as above, with 21" barrel, adjustable sights and Improved Cylinder choke. Satin finish with American walnut stock. Weight about 6.5 lbs.

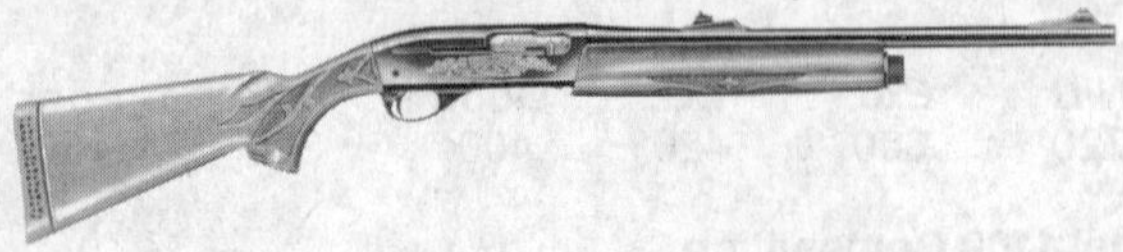

NIB	Exc.	V.G.	Good	Fair	Poor
520	450	400	300	200	150

Model 1100 LT-20 Synthetic

Same as above, with synthetic stock and recoil pad.

NIB	Exc.	V.G.	Good	Fair	Poor
550	380	320	280	200	150

Model 1100 LT-20 Magnum

20-gauge Model 1100 chambered for 3" 20-gauge shell. Fitted with 28" ventilated rib barrel, with interchangeable chokes. Checkered walnut stock. Weight about 7 lbs.

NIB	Exc.	V.G.	Good	Fair	Poor
580	400	400	300	200	150

Model 1100 LT-20 Synthetic Camo NWTF 25th Anniversary

Fitted with 21" barrel and special fiber optic sighting system. NWTF logo on left side of receiver. Introduced in 1998.

NIB	Exc.	V.G.	Good	Fair	Poor
650	520	450	300	250	120

Model 1100 Synthetic

Introduced in 1995. Furnished with black synthetic stock, with black matte metal finish. Available in both 12- and 20-gauge. Weight about 6.75 to 7 lbs. depending on barrel length. In 2003, offered chambered for 16-gauge shell.

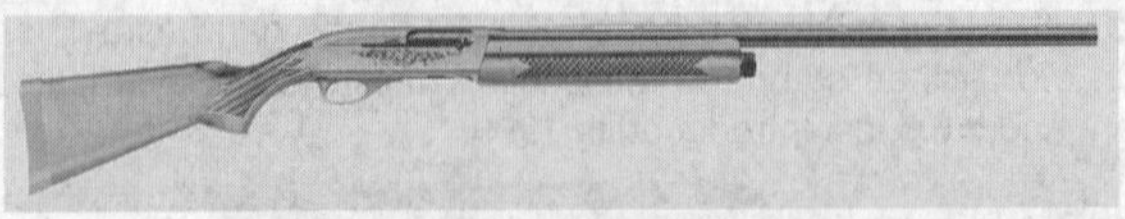

Courtesy Remington Arms

NIB	Exc.	V.G.	Good	Fair	Poor
550	450	350	250	200	100

Model 1100 Synthetic Deer Gun

Same as above, with 21" fully rifled barrel with cantilever rail for scope mounting. Furnished with 2.75" chamber. Stock black synthetic, with checkering and Monte Carlo-style cheekpiece. Recoil pad standard.

NIB	Exc.	V.G.	Good	Fair	Poor
520	450	400	300	200	150

Model 1100 Competition Synthetic

Super-tuned for competitive shooters. Overbored 30" barrel, with lengthened forcing cones. Optimized for 2.75" target loads and light field loads. Receiver and all internal parts have nickel-Teflon finish. Synthetic stock has SuperCell recoil pad. 12-gauge only. Weight 8.25 lbs.

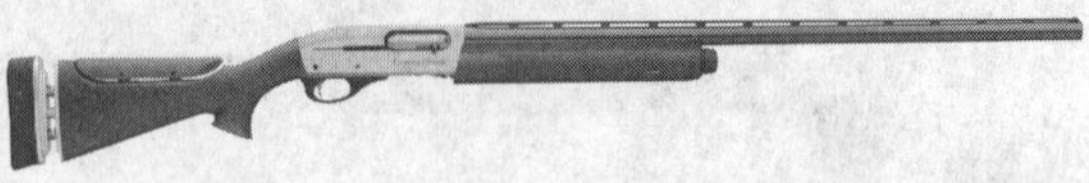

NIB	Exc.	V.G.	Good	Fair	Poor
980	840	710	600	510	440

Model 1100 Custom Grade

Custom Shop model available in three levels of engraving, gold inlay, wood grade and finish, metal work finish, recoil pad/buttplate and dimensions. Each gun should be individually appraised prior to sale.

D Grade

NIB	Exc.	V.G.	Good	Fair	Poor
3000	200	1100	—	—	—

F Grade

NIB	Exc.	V.G.	Good	Fair	Poor
6000	4000	2250	—	—	—

F Grade with Gold Inlay

NIB	Exc.	V.G.	Good	Fair	Poor
10000	7500	5000	—	—	—

Model 1100 G3

Introduced in 2006. Updated 1100 features Realwood high gloss semi-fancy stock and forend. Available in 12- and 20-gauge, with 26" or 28" barrel. Chambered for 3" shells. Includes 5 ProBore chokes for 12-gauge; 5 Remchokes for 20-gauge. R3 recoil pad and high-grade travel case. Left-handed version added in 2008.

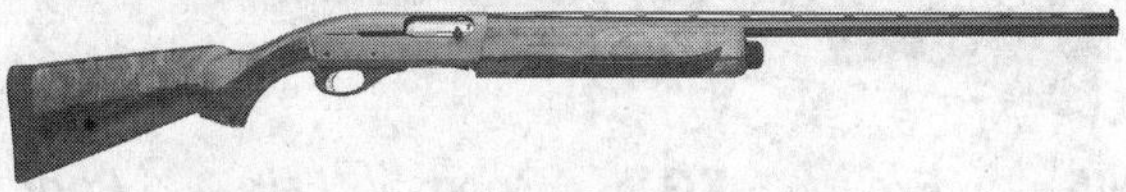

NIB	Exc.	V.G.	Good	Fair	Poor
820	600	450	300	220	150

Model 1100 Tactical Speedfeed IV

All-black 2.75" 12-gauge has 18" barrel, with Fixed Improved Cylinder choke and Speedfeed IV stock. Extended 6-round magazine. Weight 7.5 lbs.

NIB	Exc.	V.G.	Good	Fair	Poor
820	600	450	300	220	150

Model 1100 Tactical Standard Stock

Tactical 2.75" 12-gauge has 22" barrel threaded for RemChokes. Extended 8-round magazine.

NIB	Exc.	V.G.	Good	Fair	Poor
820	600	450	300	220	150

Model 1100 Premier Sporting

Introduced in 2008. A dedicated sporting clays gun. Comes in 12-, 20-, 28-gauge and .410 bore, with 2.75" chamber (3" in .410). Polished nickel receiver, with fine-line embellishments and gold accents. Stock and forend are semi-fancy American walnut, with high-gloss finish. Full line of Briley choke tubes and Premier Sporting hard case are included. Weight about: 8 lbs. 12-gauge; 7 lbs. 20-gauge; 6.5 lbs. 28-gauge and .410 bore. Note: Add 5% for 28-gauge and .410 bore.

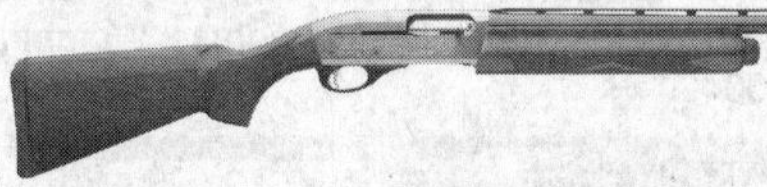

NIB	Exc.	V.G.	Good	Fair	Poor
1150	1000	850	680	480	300

Model 1100 50th Anniversary Limited Edition

Model 1100s most popular semi-automatic shotgun in the world. To commemorate 50 years of service to shooters, this Limited Edition model has machine-cut engraved receiver, with gold fill and high-grade walnut stock. White diamond grip cap and white line spacer recall the style of stock in 1963. In 12-gauge only, with 28" ventilated rib barrel. Introduced 2013, with limited production.

NIB	Exc.	V.G.	Good	Fair	Poor
1800	1600	1400	—	—	—

Model 1100 200th Anniversary Limited Edition

A limited edition made only in 2016 to commemorate the 200th anniversary of the Remington company. A total of 2,016 Model 1100 12-gauge shotguns were produced featuring a 24-carat gold inlay of founder Eliphalet Remington, a high gloss C Grade walnut stock with fleur-de-lis cut checkering, 28-inch barrel with a ventilated rib, and polished blue finish.

NIB	Exc.	V.G.	Good	Fair	Poor
1400	1100	900	700	—	—

Model 1100 American Classic

Introduced 2014. Special edition Model 1100 semi-automatic and comparable Model 870 pump action. Features include higher B-grade walnut stock, gold filled engraving and ventilated recoil pad with white outline, as was found on the originals. Chambered in 12 gauge (83016) and 20 gauge (83018).

NIB	Exc.	V.G.	Good	Fair	Poor
1100	940	800	680	570	490

Model 1100 American Classic 20 Gauge

NIB	Exc.	V.G.	Good	Fair	Poor
1350	1150	980	830	700	600

MODEL 11-87 SERIES

Model 11-87 Premier

A 3" 12-gauge semi-automatic shotgun, with 26" to 32" ventilated rib barrels having screw-in choke tubes. Blued, with checkered walnut stock. Weight about 7.75 lbs. Introduced in 1987. In 1999, offered in a left-hand version.

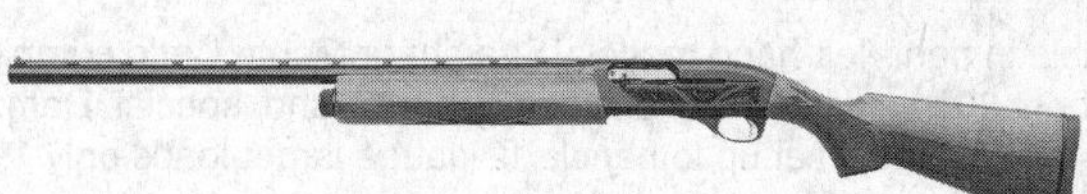

Model 11-87 Premier left-hand model

NIB	Exc.	V.G.	Good	Fair	Poor
700	600	450	300	200	150

Model 11-87 Premier 20 Gauge

Introduced in 1999. Built on a small frame receiver. Will chamber both 2.75" and 3" shells. Available in both 26" and 28" ventilated rib barrels, with twin beads. Barrels are built for RemChokes. Stock walnut, with gloss finish. Weight about 7 lbs.

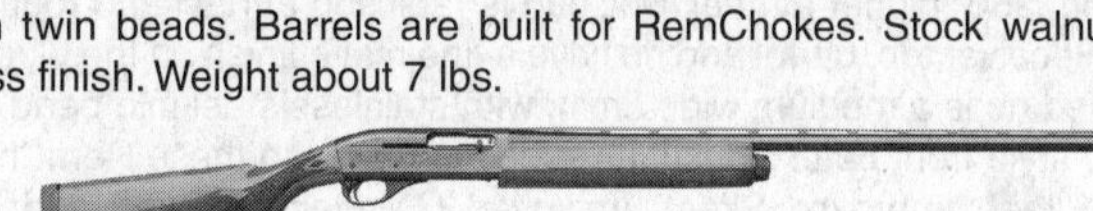

NIB	Exc.	V.G.	Good	Fair	Poor
680	580	420	300	220	120

Model 11-87 Dale Earnhardt Tribute

Introduced in 2003 to honor Dale Earnhardt. This 12-gauge fitted with 28" ventilated rib barrel and walnut stock with checkering. Engraved on receiver is a likeness of Earnhardt, his signature and scroll work inlayed in gold. Serial numbers start with "DE3." Weight about 7.75 lbs.

NIB	Exc.	V.G.	Good	Fair	Poor
680	580	420	300	220	120

Model 11-87 Upland Special

Offered in 12- or 20-gauge, with 23" barrel and twin bead sights. Chambered for 3" shells. Stock walnut, with straight-grip. Choke tubes standard. Weight about: 7.25 lbs. 12-gauge; 6.5 lbs. 20-gauge. Introduced in 2000.

NIB	Exc.	V.G.	Good	Fair	Poor
720	600	450	300	220	120

Model 11-87 Premier Cantilever Scope Mount Deer Gun

Semi-automatic has a Monte Carlo stock. Option of barrel-mounted scope (not included). Optional with fully rifled barrel 21" long, with 1-in-35" twist. Also available in 21" non-rifled barrel, with Rifled and IC RemChoke tubes. Available in 12-gauge only. Sling swivel studs and camo are standard.

NIB	Exc.	V.G.	Good	Fair	Poor
800	680	400	300	200	150

Model 11-87 Premier Trap

Available in right-/left-hand models. Straight or Monte Carlo comb. 2.75" chamber, 30" ventilated rib overbored barrel and special Rem. Trap choke tubes. Model set up to handle 12-gauge target loads only.

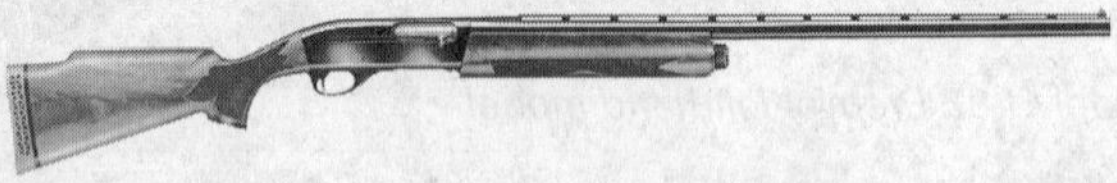

NIB	Exc.	V.G.	Good	Fair	Poor
520	480	420	300	200	150

Model 11-87 Premier SC (Sporting Clays)

Features special target stock, with 3.16" length of pull longer than standard and .250" higher at heel. Butt pad is radiused at heel and rounded at toe. Receiver top, barrel and rib have a fine matte finish on the blueing. Ventilated rib is a medium wide 8mm, with stainless steel mid bead and Bradley-style front bead sight. Gun supplied new with these RemChoke tubes: Skeet, Improved Skeet, Improved Cylinder, Modified and Full. Supplied from factory with a two-barrel custom fitted hard case.

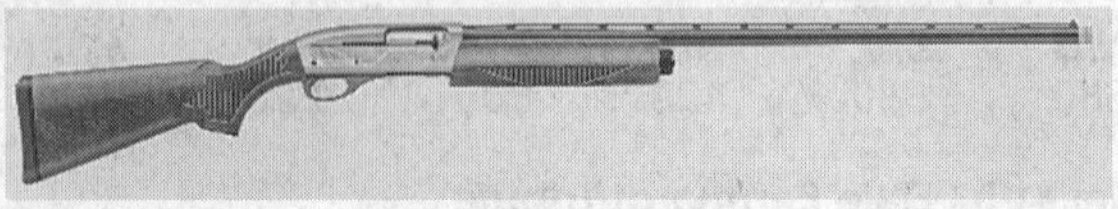

Courtesy Remington Arms

*Remington Model 11-87 Sporting Clays with nickel-plated receiver
and ported barrel*

NIB	Exc.	V.G.	Good	Fair	Poor
750	600	450	350	200	150

Model 11-87 SC NP (Sporting Clays Nickel-Plated)

Same as above, with nickel-plated receiver.

NIB	Exc.	V.G.	Good	Fair	Poor
800	650	500	400	300	200

Model 11-87 SPS-BG Camo

12-gauge fitted with rifle sighted 21" barrel, with brown camo finish on stock and metal parts. Introduced in 1993.

NIB	Exc.	V.G.	Good	Fair	Poor
520	480	420	300	200	150

Model 11-87 SPS-T Camo

Same as above, but supplied with 21" ventilated rib barrel with IC and Turkey Super Full RemChoke tubes. Camo finish is green. Introduced in 1993.

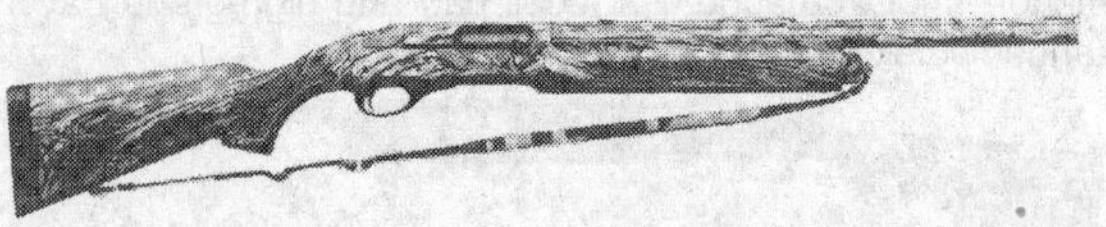

NIB	Exc.	V.G.	Good	Fair	Poor
550	450	350	250	200	150

Model 11-87 SPS

12-gauge furnished with 26" or 28" ventilated rib barrel, with IC Mod. and Full RemChoke tubes. Stock black synthetic material and metal finished in black matte. In 1997, a camo version was introduced.

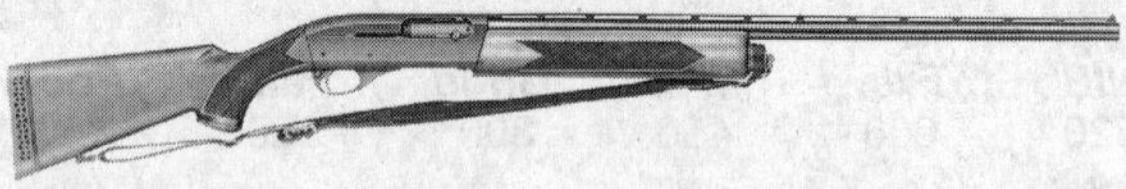

NIB	Exc.	V.G.	Good	Fair	Poor
500	400	300	250	200	150

Model 11-87 SPS-Deer

Same as above, with 21" rifled sighted barrel. First introduced in 1993.

NIB	Exc.	V.G.	Good	Fair	Poor
520	480	420	300	200	150

Model 11-87 Waterfowl

12-gauge gun fitted with 28" ventilated rib barrel with choke tubes and Hi-Viz sights. Camo pattern is Mossy Oak Shadow-grass. Weight about 8.25 lbs. Introduced in 2004.

NIB	Exc.	V.G.	Good	Fair	Poor
920	700	600	500	350	180

Model 11-87 SPS-T

Same as above, with 21" ventilated rib barrel with IC and Turkey Super Full RemChoke tubes. In 1997, a camo version was introduced.

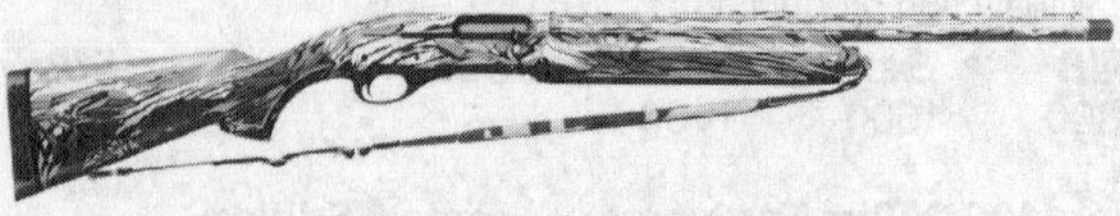

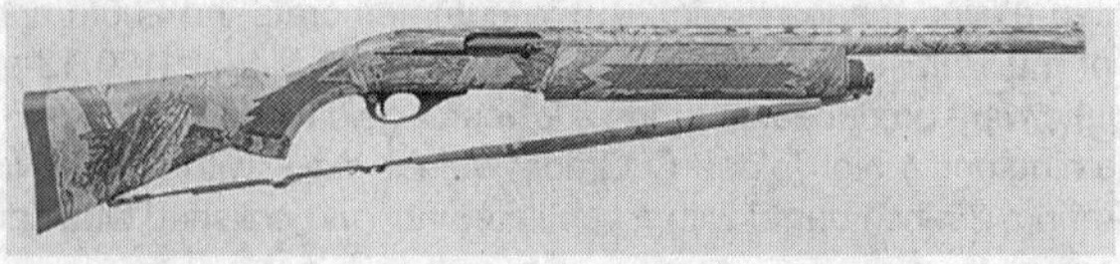

NIB	Exc.	V.G.	Good	Fair	Poor
520	480	420	300	200	150

Model 11-87 SPS-T Camo NWTF 25th Anniversary

Model has 21" barrel, with special fiber optic sighting system. NWTF logo on left side of receiver. Introduced in 1998.

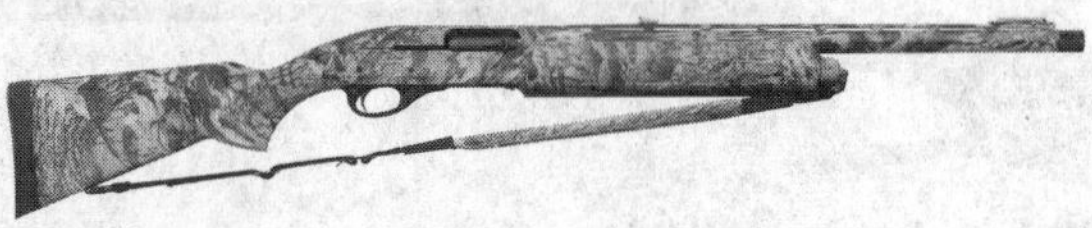

NIB	Exc.	V.G.	Good	Fair	Poor
700	600	420	300	200	150

Model 11-87 SP Super Magnum

Introduced in 2000. Chambered for 12-gauge 3.5" Magnum shell. Fitted with 26" or 28" ventilated rib barrel. Walnut stock, with flat finish. Recoil pad. Matte black finish. Weight about 8.25 lbs.

NIB	Exc.	V.G.	Good	Fair	Poor
680	500	350	300	120	100

Model 11-87 SPS Super Magnum

Same as above, with black synthetic stock. Introduced in 2000. Weight about 8.25 lbs.

NIB	Exc.	V.G.	Good	Fair	Poor
680	500	350	300	120	100

Model 11-87 SPS-T Super Magnum (NWTF Edition)

Introduced in 2005. Features 12-gauge 3.5" chamber, 23" barrel with choke tubes and iron sights. Mossy Oak Obsession camo stock, with Monte Carlo comb. Weight about 8 lbs.

NIB	Exc.	V.G.	Good	Fair	Poor
950	780	650	520	350	180

Model 11-87 Police

Offered chambered for 12-gauge shells. Features synthetic stock, 18" barrel with bead rifle or ghost ring sights and 7-shot magazine extension. Note: Add $20 for rifle sights; $60 for ghost ring sights.

NIB	Exc.	V.G.	Good	Fair	Poor
680	500	350	300	120	100

Model 11-87 Custom Grade

Custom Shop model available in three levels of engraving, gold inlay, wood grade and finish, metal work finish, recoil pad/buttplate and dimensions.

D Grade

NIB	Exc.	V.G.	Good	Fair	Poor
3000	200	1100	—	—	—

F Grade

NIB	Exc.	V.G.	Good	Fair	Poor
6000	4000	2250	—	—	—

F Grade with Gold Inlay

NIB	Exc.	V.G.	Good	Fair	Poor
10000	7500	5000	—	—	—

Model 11-87 Sportsman Synthetic

Introduced in 2005. Features black synthetic stock, with choice of 12- or 20-gauge 3" chambers; 26" or 28" barrels with Mod. choke tube. Weight about 7.75 to 8.25 lbs. depending on gauge and barrel length. Compact model 83626 has 21" barrel and adjustable LOP.

NIB	Exc.	V.G.	Good	Fair	Poor
680	500	350	300	120	100

Model 11-87 Sportsman Super Magnum

In 2008, Remington added this 3.5" version of 11-87 Sportsman. Has 28" barrel. Weight 8.25 lbs.

NIB	Exc.	V.G.	Good	Fair	Poor
750	620	550	400	300	200

Model 11-87 Sportsman Rifled

A 12-gauge 3" gun, with 21" rifled barrel with cantilever scope mount. Black synthetic stock, with black metal finish. Weight about 8.5 lbs. Introduced in 2005.

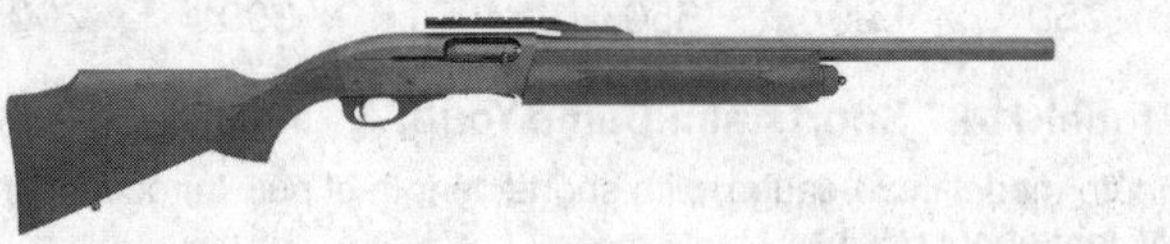

NIB	Exc.	V.G.	Good	Fair	Poor
680	500	350	300	120	100

Model 11-87 Sportsman Youth

A 20-gauge 3" gun, with 21" ventilated rib barrel and choke tubes. Black synthetic stock. Length of pull 13". Weight about 6.5 lbs. Introduced in 2005.

NIB	Exc.	V.G.	Good	Fair	Poor
600	450	400	300	200	150

Model 11-87 Sportsman Compact Synthetic

Similar to Model 11-87 black synthetic, with reduced overall dimensions.

NIB	Exc.	V.G.	Good	Fair	Poor
700	600	500	350	220	150

Model 11-87 Sportsman Youth Camo

Same as above, with full coverage in Mossy Oak Break-Up camo.

NIB	Exc.	V.G.	Good	Fair	Poor
750	620	550	400	300	180

Model 11-87 Sportsman NRA Edition

This 12-gauge 3" model fitted with 28" ventilated rib barrel, with choke tubes. Synthetic stock, with Mossy Oak New Break-Up camo. NRA logo on left side of matte black receiver. Introduced in 2005.

NIB	Exc.	V.G.	Good	Fair	Poor
680	500	350	300	120	100

Model 11-87 SP Thumbhole

Laminated thumbhole stock 12-gauge slug gun, with 3" chamber and 21" fully rifled cantilever barrel.

NIB	Exc.	V.G.	Good	Fair	Poor
700	600	500	350	220	150

Model 11-87 SPS-T Super Magnum

Similar to above, with pistol grip stock and ventilated rib barrel.

NIB	Exc.	V.G.	Good	Fair	Poor
750	620	550	400	300	200

Model 11-87 SP-T Thumbhole

This 12-gauge with 3.5" chamber is made specifically for turkey hunting. Camouflaged in Mossy Oak Obsession, with R3 recoil pad and thumbhole stock. The 23" barrel has fiber-optic adjustable rifle sights and drilled and tapped for scope mounting. Includes a Turkey Super Full choke tube and sling/swivels. Introduced 2006.

NIB	Exc.	V.G.	Good	Fair	Poor
750	620	550	400	300	200

Model 11-87 Sportsman Camo

New in 2007. Camo version of Sportsman comes in 12- and 20-gauge, with 26" or 28" barrel. Finished in Mossy Oak Break-Up camo.

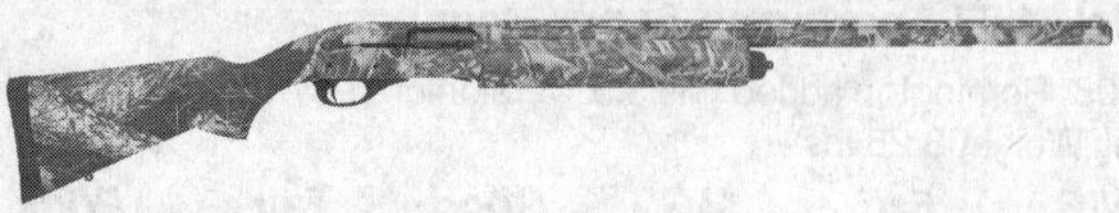

NIB	Exc.	V.G.	Good	Fair	Poor
750	620	550	400	300	200

Model 11-87 Sportsman Camo Rifled

Camo 12-gauge slug gun, with 21" barrel and cantilever scope mount.

NIB	Exc.	V.G.	Good	Fair	Poor
750	620	550	400	300	200

Model 11-87 Sportsman Camo Youth

Youth model in 20-gauge, with shorter length of pull. Introduced in 2007. Weight about 6.5 lbs.

NIB	Exc.	V.G.	Good	Fair	Poor
700	600	500	350	220	150

Model 11-87 Sportsman Field

Semi-automatic shotgun chambered in 12- and 20-gauge, 2.75" and 3" shells. Features include 26" (20-gauge) or 28" (12-gauge) barrel; ventilated rib; RemChokes (one supplied); satin-finished walnut stock and forend with fleur-de-lis pattern; dual sights; nickel-plated bolt and trigger.

NIB	Exc.	V.G.	Good	Fair	Poor
680	580	440	350	220	150

Model 11-87 Sportsman Super Mag Synthetic

Semi-automatic shotgun chambered in 12-gauge, 3.5" shells. Features include black matte synthetic stock and forend; rubber overmolded grip panels on stock and forend; black padded sling; HiViz sights featuring interchangeable light pipe; 28" ventilated rib barrel; SuperCell recoil pad; RemChoke.

NIB	Exc.	V.G.	Good	Fair	Poor
730	650	550	420	250	180

Model 11-87 Sportsman Super Mag Shurshot Turkey

Similar to above, with ambidextrous ShurShot pistol grip stock; full Realtree APG HD coverage; 23" barrel with fully adjustable TruGlo rifle sights. Wingmaster HD Turkey Choke included.

NIB	Exc.	V.G.	Good	Fair	Poor
880	750	620	500	300	180

Model 11-87 SPS Super Magnum Waterfowl

This 3.5" 12-gauge finished in Mossy Oak Duck Blind camo. Has 30" barrel and includes three chokes. Weight 8.25 lbs.

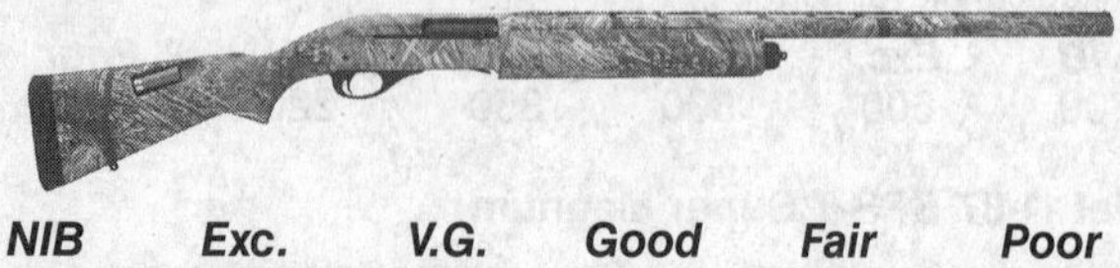

NIB	Exc.	V.G.	Good	Fair	Poor
950	780	650	520	350	180

Model 11-87 Sportsman Super Mag ShurShot Turkey

New in 2008. Specialized turkey shotgun, with ShurShot stock is a 3.5" chamber 12-gauge with 23" non-ventilated rib barrel. Comes with fiber-optic rifle-type sights and synthetic stock and forend. Gun fully covered in Realtree APG HD camo. Weight about 7.6 lbs.

NIB	Exc.	V.G.	Good	Fair	Poor
800	700	550	450	300	180

Model 11-87 Sportsman Super Magnum Waterfowl

Full coverage in Mossy Oak Duck Blind camo. Shell-holding Speedfeed stock and three choke tubes.

NIB	Exc.	V.G.	Good	Fair	Poor
850	720	600	480	320	200

Model 11-87 Sportsman ShurShot Cantilever

Dedicated slug gun in 3" 12-gauge features 23" fully rifled barrel, with cantilever scope mount. Is matte black, with synthetic stock and forend finished in Realtree Hardwoods HD camo. Weight about 8 lbs.

NIB	Exc.	V.G.	Good	Fair	Poor
850	720	600	480	320	200

Model 11-96 Euro Lightweight

Introduced in 1996. Based on Model 11-87 action. Two ventilated rib barrel lengths are offered: 26" and 28" supplied with three RemChokes. Fine line engraving on receiver and checkered Claro walnut stocks are standard. Blued finish. Weight about 7 lbs. Made for one year only.

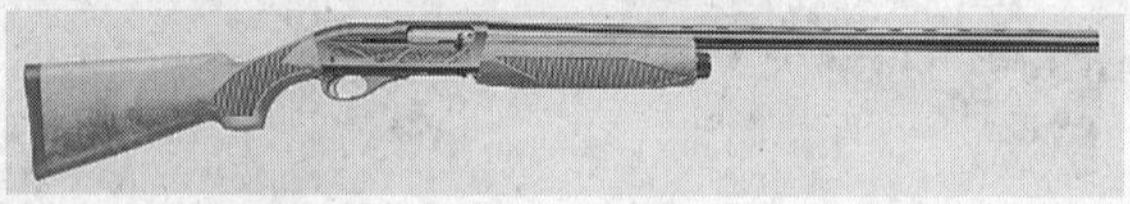

NIB	Exc.	V.G.	Good	Fair	Poor
1000	880	620	500	320	200

Model SP-10

A 3.5" 10-gauge semi-automatic shotgun, with 26" or 30" ventilated rib barrels having screw-in choke tubes. Matte blued, with checkered walnut stock.

NIB	Exc.	V.G.	Good	Fair	Poor
1500	1280	950	780	600	300

Model SP-10 Magnum Camo

Introduced in 1993. This 10-gauge semi-automatic designed for turkey or deer hunter. Available with 26" or 30" ventilated rib barrel or 22" deer barrel. Additional barrel option is 23" ventilated rib barrel, with camo finish. All barrels are fitted with RemChoke tubes.

NIB	Exc.	V.G.	Good	Fair	Poor
1550	1320	1000	820	620	320

Model SP-10 Magnum Camo NWTF 25th Anniversary

A special fiber optic sighting system. "NWTF" logo on left side of receiver. Barrel length 23". Introduced in 1998.

NIB	Exc.	V.G.	Good	Fair	Poor
1550	1320	1000	820	620	320

Model SP-10 Synthetic

Features black synthetic stock, with 26" barrel. Chambered for 10-gauge shells. Matte black metal finish. Choke tubes standard. Introduced in 2000. Weight about 10 lbs.

NIB	Exc.	V.G.	Good	Fair	Poor
1300	1150	900	780	580	300

Model SP-10 RC/VT

This 10-gauge introduced in 2005. Fitted with 26" ventilated rib barrel, with choke tubes. Mossy Oak Obsession finish. Weight about 10.75 lbs.

NIB	Exc.	V.G.	Good	Fair	Poor
1300	1150	900	780	580	300

Model SP-10 Custom Grade

Custom Shop model available in three levels of engraving, gold inlay, wood grade and finish, metal work finish, recoil pad/buttplate and dimensions. Limited production or activity on used gun market. Price estimates for NIB models start at $2000 to $3000 and vary depending on quality of custom features.

Model SP-10 Magnum Waterfowl

New in 2007. A synthetic stock 3.5" 10-gauge waterfowl specific model, with Mossy Oak Duck Blind camo finish and 26" barrel. Includes three Briley ported choke tubes. Weight about 10.9 lbs.

NIB	Exc.	V.G.	Good	Fair	Poor
1550	1320	1000	820	620	320

Model SP-10 Magnum Thumbhole Camo

Special turkey model features synthetic thumbhole stock and complete Mossy Oak Obsession camo finish. Barrel is 23". Briley ported Turkey choke included. Weight 10.9 lbs.

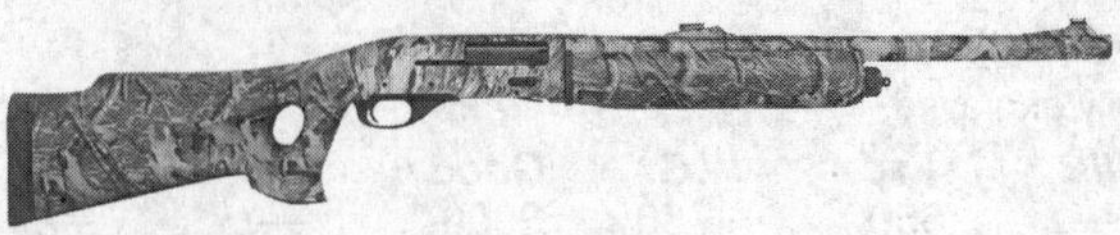

NIB	Exc.	V.G.	Good	Fair	Poor
1650	1500	1200	900	680	350

Model 105CTi

New in 2006. Ultralight gas-operated 12-gauge autoloader. Features advanced recoil reduction and bottom feed and ejection. Available with 26" or 28" barrel. Satin finish walnut stock. Chambered for 3" shells. Includes three ProBore chokes. Weight about 7 lbs. Discontinued in 2009.

NIB	Exc.	V.G.	Good	Fair	Poor
1180	950	800	600	480	280

Versa Max

Versa Max gas-operated semi-automatic shoots everything from 2.75" target loads to 3.5" Magnums. Synthetic stock in black and camo finishes is adjustable for length-of-pull, drop-of-comb and cast. 12-gauge only; 26" and 28" barrels; 7.7 lbs. Introduced in 2010. Also available with Wood-Tech stock finish, Realtree and Mossy Oak camo, Tactical model and special-finish "Zombie" models. Values shown are for standard Synthetic stock 81042. Note: Add $250 for camo finishes or Tactical model; $175 for Wood-Tech or Zombie finishes.

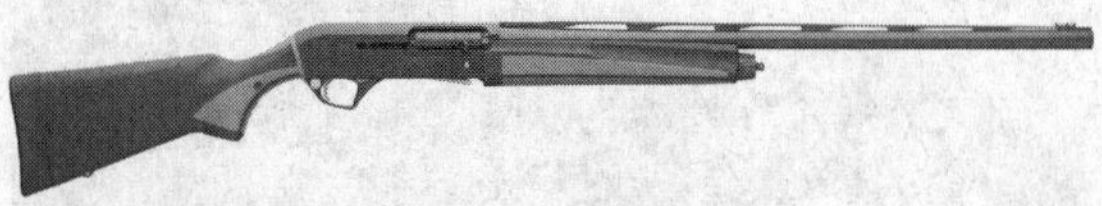

NIB	Exc.	V.G.	Good	Fair	Poor
1000	850	720	610	520	440

Versa Max Sportsman

MO Bottomland or Realtree Edge, 26 in. R

NIB	Exc.	V.G.	Good	Fair	Poor
1170	—	—	—	—	—

Model V3 Field Sport

Latest generation of Remington semi-automatic shotgun operates on Versaport gas system. Handles all ammo from 2.75" target loads to 3" Magnums. Barrel length 26" or 28". Stock choice: black synthetic (83400), camo synthetic or American walnut satin-finished, all with adjustable length of pull. Introduced in 2015. Note: Add $100 for camo or walnut stock. V3 Field Sport Compact 83402 added in 2019 without vent rib and with 13" LOP.

NIB	Exc.	V.G.	Good	Fair	Poor
620	500	400	300	200	—

V3 Field Sport Compact

NIB	Exc.	V.G.	Good	Fair	Poor
650	520	400	300	200	—

Model V3 Field Sport NWTF

Mossy Oak Obsession, 26 in.

NIB	Exc.	V.G.	Good	Fair	Poor
940	—	—	—	—	—

V3 Waterfowl Pro

Introduced 2019, V3 Waterfowl Pro 83435 has a Cerakoted receiver and barrel. Other upgrades include fiber-optic front sight and steel mid bead, included sling, three extended black chokes (IC, M, F), drop and cast adjustment shims included, modernized oversized bolt handle, bolt release, and ergonomic oversized safety; redesigned loading port.

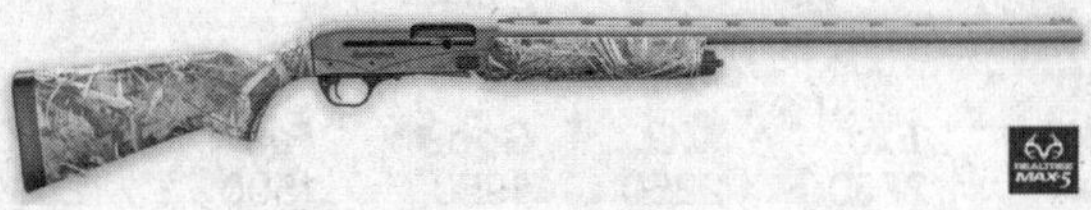

NIB	Exc.	V.G.	Good	Fair	Poor
900	720	580	450	—	—

V3 Turkey Pro

Introduced 2019. Realtree Timber camo finish; comes with a 40-yard factory-bore-sighted Truglo optic and Truglo Headbanger choke tube, 83445.

NIB	Exc.	V.G.	Good	Fair	Poor
900	720	580	450	—	—

V3 Tac-13

Introduced 2019 in 12 (83392) gauge. Brings the Versaport semi-auto gas system to this platform.

NIB	Exc.	V.G.	Good	Fair	Poor
800	680	580	—	—	—

V3 Tactical

Addition of two tactical models to the V3 lineup with the same VersaPort self-regulating gas system that works with any shotshell from 2.75 in. to 3 in. Capacity: 6+1. Both wear an 18.5 in. barrel and oversized controls. One model with rifle sights, the other with a vent rib and bead sights.

NIB	Exc.	V.G.	Good	Fair	Poor
910	—	—	—	—	—

V3 Competition Tactical

Addition of competition tactical model to the exiting V3 lineup. This 12 ga. uses the same Versa-Port technology to self-regulate for any shotshell from 2.75 in. to 3in. Capacity: 8+1. Features: 22-inch barrel with Hi-Viz front sight and low-profile, dovetail-rib mounting rear sight and oversized controls.

NIB	Exc.	V.G.	Good	Fair	Poor
1000	—	—	—	—	—

Model 32

A 12-gauge over/under shotgun, with 26", 28" or 30" separated barrels and single-selective trigger. Approximately 15,000 made from 1932 to 1942. Add 10% for solid or ventilated rib.

Standard Grade

NIB	Exc.	V.G.	Good	Fair	Poor
—	2500	2250	1600	1250	1000

Skeet

NIB	Exc.	V.G.	Good	Fair	Poor
—	2750	2250	1950	1500	1250

TC

NIB	Exc.	V.G.	Good	Fair	Poor
—	2750	2500	2250	1750	1450

TC 32D Grade

NIB	Exc.	V.G.	Good	Fair	Poor
3000	2000	1100	—	—	—

TC 32F Grade

NIB	Exc.	V.G.	Good	Fair	Poor
6000	4000	2250	—	—	—

TC 32E Expert

NIB	Exc.	V.G.	Good	Fair	Poor
10000	7500	5000	—	—	—

Model 3200

A 12-gauge over/under shotgun, with 26", 28" or 30" separated ventilated rib barrels, single-selective trigger and automatic ejector. Blued, with checkered walnut stock. Manufactured from 1972 to 1984.

Field Grade

NIB	Exc.	V.G.	Good	Fair	Poor
—	800	720	600	450	300

Magnum

3" chambers.

NIB	Exc.	V.G.	Good	Fair	Poor
—	1000	850	750	550	300

Skeet

NIB	Exc.	V.G.	Good	Fair	Poor
—	1200	1000	800	600	300

4-Gauge Set

NIB	Exc.	V.G.	Good	Fair	Poor
—	5500	4750	3500	2450	1500

Trap

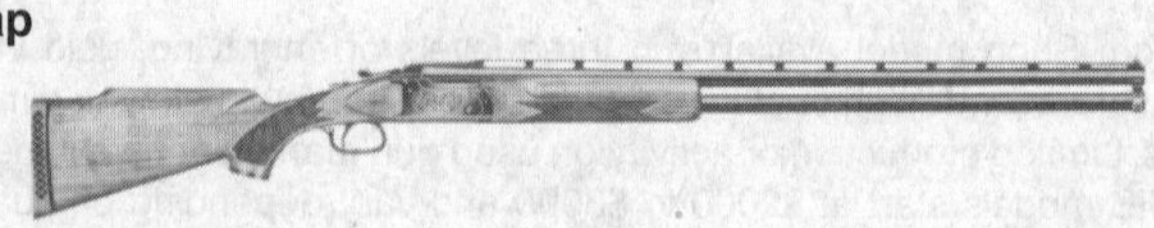

NIB	Exc.	V.G.	Good	Fair	Poor
—	1200	1000	800	600	300

Special Trap

Deluxe wood.

NIB	Exc.	V.G.	Good	Fair	Poor
—	1350	1150	750	700	300

Competition Trap

Engraved.

NIB	Exc.	V.G.	Good	Fair	Poor
—	2750	2000	1350	950	300

Premier

Heavily engraved.

NIB	Exc.	V.G.	Good	Fair	Poor
—	5500	4750	3900	—	—

"One of One Thousand"

1,000 produced.

NIB	Exc.	V.G.	Good	Fair	Poor
—	3500	3000	2500	—	—

Model 300 Ideal

This 12-gauge over/under shotgun was introduced in 2000. Offered with choice of 26", 28" or 30" barrels. Single-selective trigger and automatic ejectors. Metal finish blue. Stock walnut, with semi-gloss finish. Solid black recoil pad. Weight about 7.62 lbs. for 28" barrels. Dropped from production in 2001.

NIB	Exc.	V.G.	Good	Fair	Poor
1650	1400	1150	700	580	300

Model 90-T Single-Barrel Trap

Offered in 12-gauge only. Single-barrel trap fitted with 32" or 34" over-bored Full choke barrel.

NIB	Exc.	V.G.	Good	Fair	Poor
3600	2500	1450	1100	600	300

Model 90-T Single-Barrel Trap (High Rib)

Same as described above, with exception of an adjustable high rib for shooters who prefer a more open target picture and higher head position.

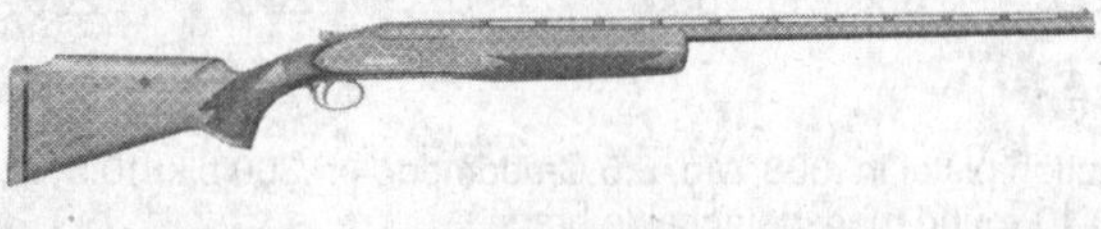

NIB	Exc.	V.G.	Good	Fair	Poor
3600	2500	1450	1100	600	300

Model 332

Reintroduction in 2002 of famous Remington Model 32. Features mechanical set trigger, automatic ejectors, with choice of ventilated rib barrel lengths in 26", 28" and 30". Checkered walnut stock. Black oxide metal finish. Chambered for 12-gauge, with 3" chambers. Weight about 7.75 lbs. depending on barrel length.

NIB	Exc.	V.G.	Good	Fair	Poor
1250	900	750	600	400	250

Remington Peerless

Introduced in 1993. New Remington over/under shotgun offered in 12-gauge only. Available in 26", 28" and 30" ventilated rib barrel lengths. Fitted with RemChoke tubes (IC, M, F). Sideplates are removable. Stock American walnut. Production stopped in 1998.

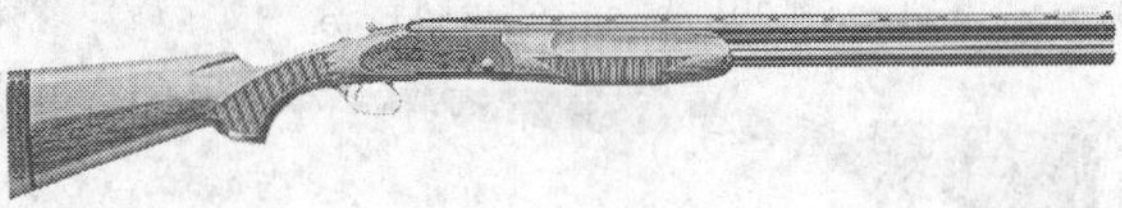

NIB	Exc.	V.G.	Good	Fair	Poor
1250	900	750	600	400	250

Model 396 Sporting

Introduced in 1996. Over/under shotgun designed for sporting clay shooting. Offered in 12-gauge only, with 30" barrels. Chokes are interchangeable RemChoke system. Fancy American stock, with satin finish. Scroll engraving on receiver and blue finish. Weight about 8 lbs.

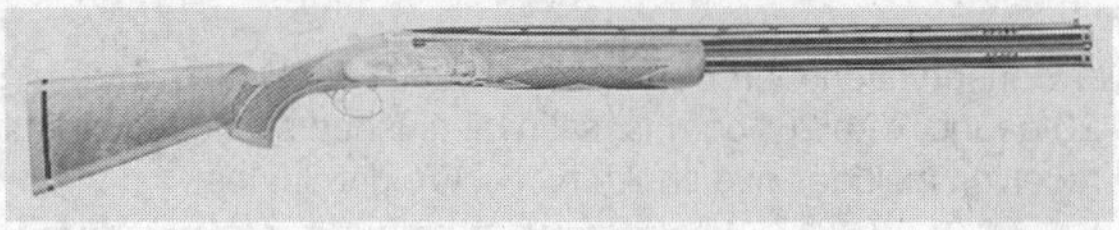

Courtesy Remington Arms

NIB	Exc.	V.G.	Good	Fair	Poor
2150	1700	1150	880	500	300

Model 396 Skeet

Same as above, with choice of 28" or 30" barrels.

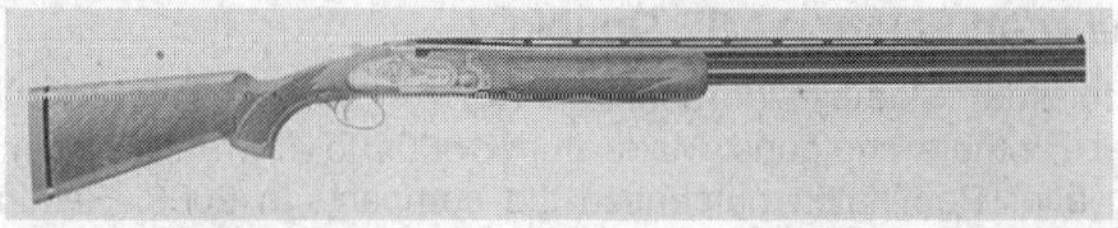

Courtesy Remington Arms

NIB	Exc.	V.G.	Good	Fair	Poor
2150	1700	1150	880	500	300

Model 396 Custom Grade

Custom Shop model available in three levels of engraving, gold inlay, wood grade and finish, metal work finish, recoil pad/buttplate, and dimensions. Each gun should be individually appraised prior to sale. Limited production or activity on used gun market. Price estimates for NIB models start at $2000 to $3000 and vary depending on quality of custom features.

PREMIER SERIES OVER/UNDERS

Introduced in 2006. Italian-made over/unders in Premier Series. Feature premium figured walnut stocks, schnabel forends, ProBore chokes, 3" chambers (2.75" in 28-gauge). Includes a hardside case.

STS Competition

This 12-gauge with 28", 30" or 32" over-bored barrels has an engraved nickel-plated receiver and high-gloss finished stock. Weight about 7.8 lbs. Note: Add 15% for adjustable-stock model.

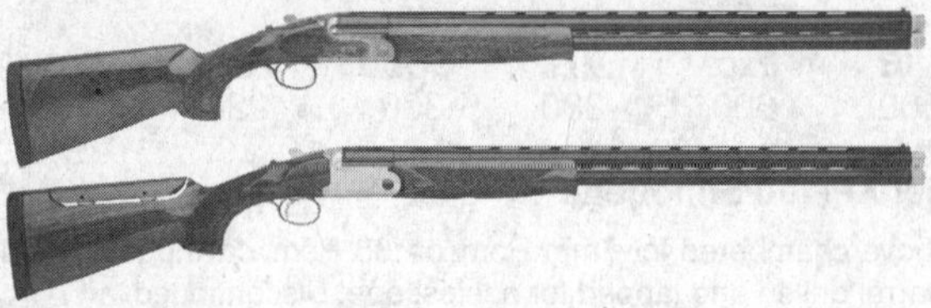

NIB	Exc.	V.G.	Good	Fair	Poor
1500	1300	950	700	550	300

Field Grade

Available in 12-, 20- and 28-gauge, with satin finish and nickel receiver. Barrel length 26" or 28". Includes three Flush chokes. Weight about: 6.5 lbs. 20- and 28-gauge; 7.5 lbs. 12-gauge.

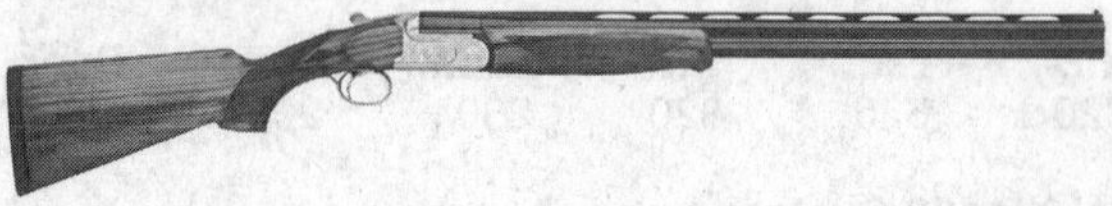

NIB	Exc.	V.G.	Good	Fair	Poor
1400	1200	900	650	500	300

Upland Grade

As above, with oil-finish stock. Case colored receiver, with gold game bird scene.

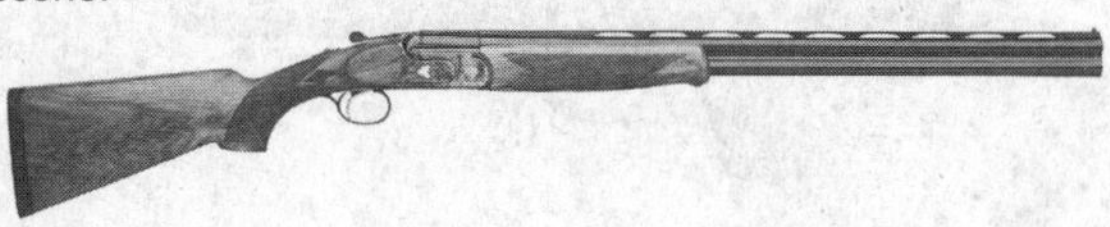

NIB	Exc.	V.G.	Good	Fair	Poor
1450	1250	900	680	520	300

RGS

Special Conservation Gun of the Year, in 2007, for Ruffed Grouse Society. A 20-gauge, with 26" barrels, satin oil-finished stock and satin black oxide receiver. Includes five choke tubes. Weight 6.5 lbs.

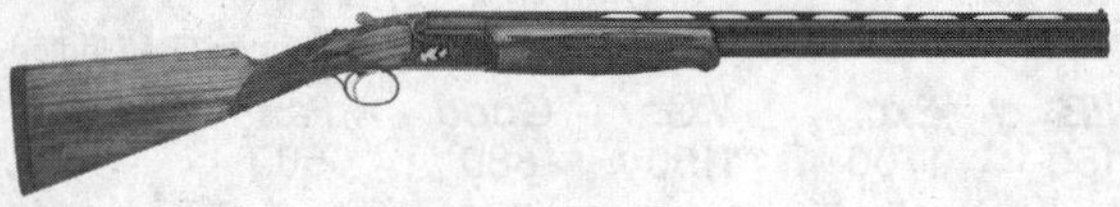

NIB	Exc.	V.G.	Good	Fair	Poor
1650	1400	1150	700	580	300

Remington Parker AAHE Double

Built to order. Side-by-side double is exact in every respect to original Parker Brothers shotguns. Made from 1860s to 1937 and again until 1942, after Remington purchased the company. In 2006, Remington partnered with Connecticut Shotgun Mfg. Co., to build high-grade AAHE model. Offered in 28-gauge only, with many options including stock dimensions and engraving patterns. Prices start at $49,000.

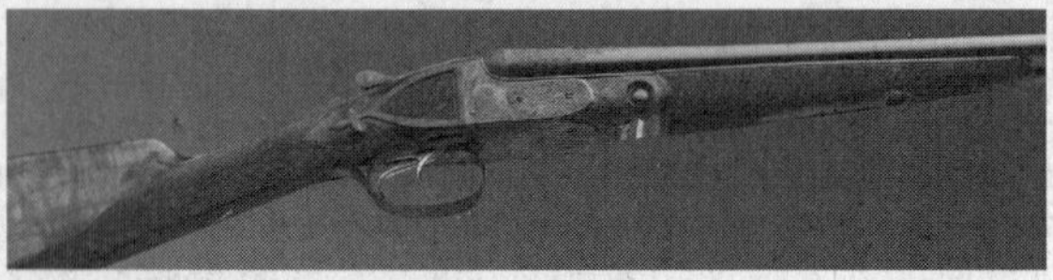

BOLT-ACTION HANDGUNS

Model XP-100

A .221 Rem. Fireball or .223 Rem. caliber bolt-action single-shot pistol. Available with or without 14.5" ventilated rib barrel and adjustable sights. Blued, with nylon stock. Introduced in 1963. Discontinued.

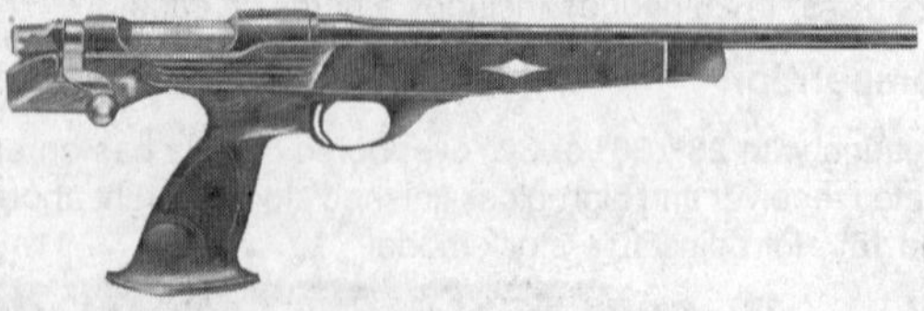

NIB	Exc.	V.G.	Good	Fair	Poor
800	600	380	300	220	180

Model XP-100 Silhouette

As above chambered for 7mm Rem. or .35 Rem. cartridges. Fitted with 15" barrel drilled and tapped for a telescope. Discontinued.

NIB	Exc.	V.G.	Good	Fair	Poor
720	520	320	250	200	120

Model XP-100 Custom

Custom-made version of above, with 15" barrel. Nylon or walnut stock. Available in .223 Rem., .250 Savage, 6mm Benchrest, 7mm Benchrest, 7mm-08 or .35 Rem. calibers. Introduced in 1986. Discontinued.

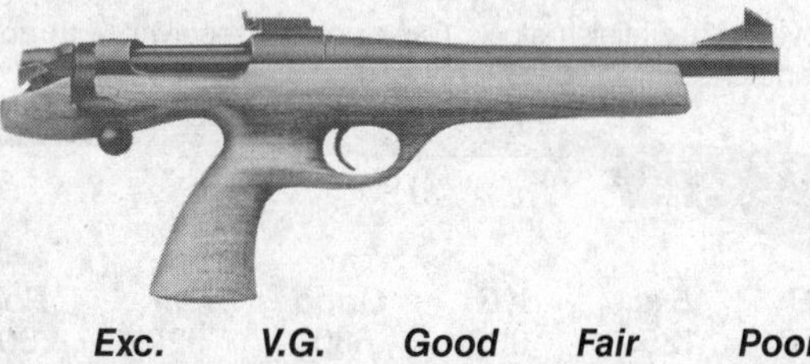

NIB	Exc.	V.G.	Good	Fair	Poor
950	800	650	550	420	300

Model XP-100 Hunter

Features laminated wood stock, 14.5" drilled and tapped barrel and no sights. Offered in these calibers: .223 Rem., 7mm BR Rem., 7mm-08 Rem., and .35 Rem. Discontinued.

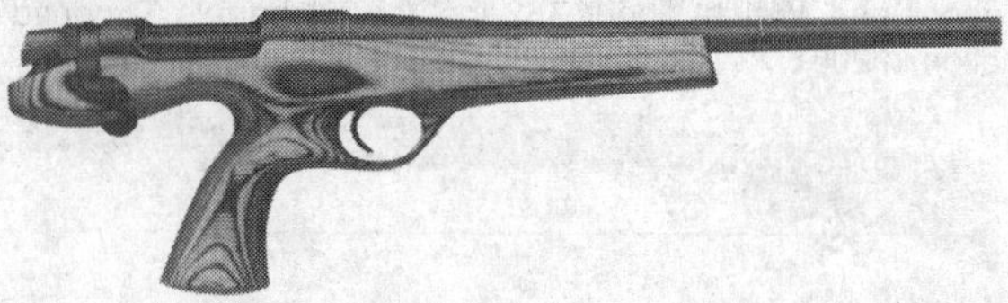

NIB	Exc.	V.G.	Good	Fair	Poor
800	680	380	300	250	180

Model XP-100R Repeater

Introduced in 1998. Chambered for .22-250, .223, .260 and .35 Rem. cartridges. Fitted with 14.5" barrel that is drilled and tapped for sights. Receiver drilled and tapped for scope mounts. Fiberglass stock. Weight about 4.5 lbs. Manufactured 1998. Discontinued.

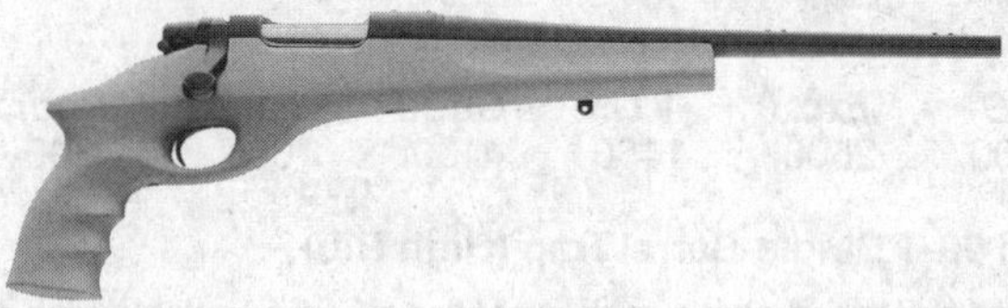

NIB	Exc.	V.G.	Good	Fair	Poor
950	800	500	450	220	200

700CP

Bolt-action pistol in .308 Win, 6.5 Creedmoor, or .300 blk; 10.5" or 12.5" barrel; 10-round mag; detachable brace.

NIB	Exc.	V.G.	Good	Fair	Poor
900	750	—	—	—	—

SPARTAN GUNWORKS BY REMINGTON

Imported firearms introduced into Remington line in 2004; discontinued 2009.

Model SPR 210

Side-by-side with single-selective trigger and auto ejectors. Boxlock receiver is nickel. Fitted with 26" or 28" barrels, with choke tubes in 12- and 20-gauge. Fixed chokes in 28-gauge and .410 bore. Also offered with 20" barrel, with choke tubes and blued receiver. Checkered walnut stock, with recoil pad. Weight about 6.75 lbs. depending on gauge and barrel length. Note: Add $30 for 28 gauge and .410 bore.

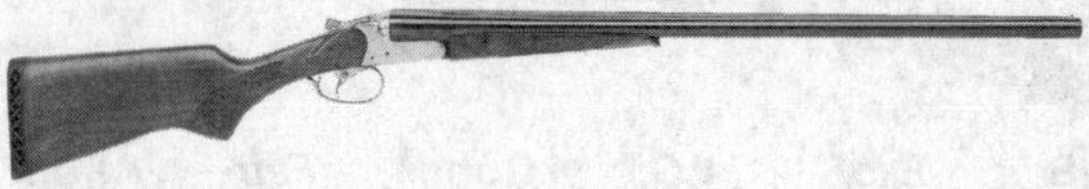

NIB	Exc.	V.G.	Good	Fair	Poor
480	400	350	220	180	100

Model SPR 220

Double trigger model, with 20" barrels and choke tubes. Extractors. Nickel or blued receiver. Walnut stock, with recoil pad. Weight about 6.25 lbs.

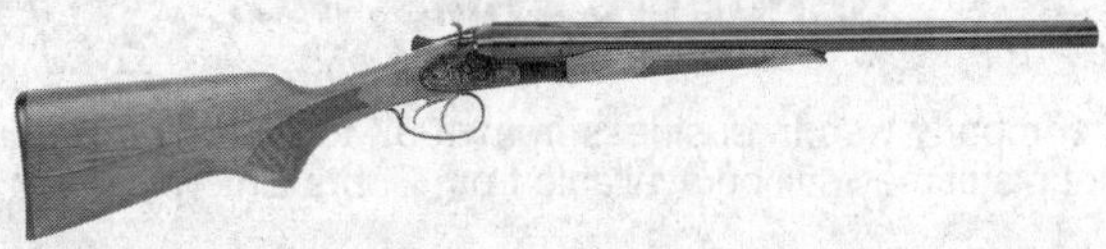

NIB	Exc.	V.G.	Good	Fair	Poor
420	380	300	200	150	100

Model SPR 310

An over/under gun chambered for 12-, 20-, 28-gauge and .410 bore. Choice of 26" or 28" ventilated rib barrels, with choke tubes; or 26" barrels for 28-gauge and .410 bore. Single-selective trigger and auto ejectors. Checkered walnut stock, with recoil pad. Weight about 7.5 lbs.

NIB	Exc.	V.G.	Good	Fair	Poor
480	400	350	220	180	120

Model SPR 310S

Chambered for 12- and 20-gauge 3" shell. Fitted with 29.5" (12-gauge) or 28.5" (20-gauge) ported barrels with choke tubes. Checked walnut stock, with recoil pad. Weight about 7.5 lbs.

NIB	Exc.	V.G.	Good	Fair	Poor
700	600	480	350	280	200

Model SPR 100/Sporting

Single-shot chambered for 12-, 20-gauge or .410 bore. Fitted with 29.5" (12-gauge), 28.5" (20-gauge) or 26" (.410) barrel. Single trigger, with ejectors or extractors. Youth model offered with 24" barrel chambered for .410 bore. Checkered walnut stock, with recoil pad. Weight about 6.25 lbs. Note: Add $40 for Sporting models.

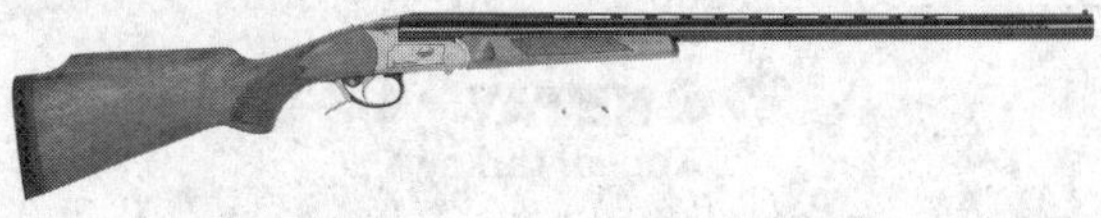

NIB	Exc.	V.G.	Good	Fair	Poor
250	180	120	100	80	50

Model SPR 18

Single-shot rifle chambered for .223, .243, .270 or .30-06 calibers. Nickel receiver. Fitted with 23.5" barrel, with iron sights. Checkered walnut stock, with recoil pad. Weight about 6.75 lbs.

NIB	Exc.	V.G.	Good	Fair	Poor
280	200	150	120	100	80

Model SPR 22

Side-by-side double rifle chambered for .30-06 or .45-70 calibers. Fitted with 23.5" barrels. Blued receiver and checkered walnut stock, with recoil pad. Weight about 7.5 lbs.

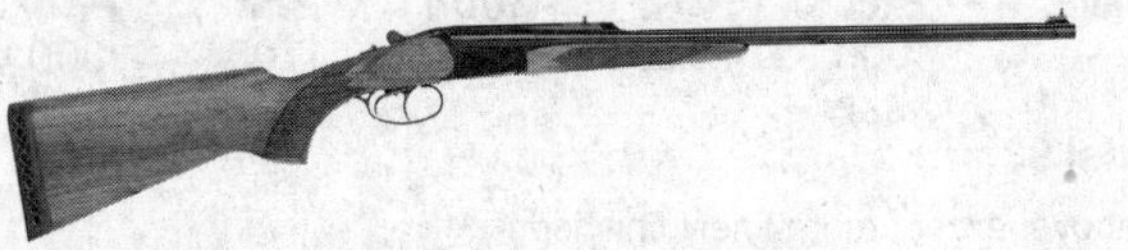

NIB	Exc.	V.G.	Good	Fair	Poor
1000	820	700	580	400	250

Model SPR 94

Features an over/under rifle/shotgun combination. Chambered for .410/17HMR, .410/.22WMR, 12-/.223, 12-/.30-06 or 12-/.308. Fitted with 24" barrel, with iron sights. Checkered walnut stock, with recoil pad. Blued receiver. Weight about 8 lbs. depending on combination. Note: Add 30% for centerfire models.

NIB	Exc.	V.G.	Good	Fair	Poor
380	300	220	150	100	80

REMINGTON CUSTOM SHOP

Remington Custom Shop builds a number of specialty rifles and shotguns as well as specific custom guns for its customers. Remington will build a wide number of special features from special wood type, finish and styling options to engraving. These special order features add considerably to the cost of a gun and will affect its price. Custom Shop can be reached at 605-347-4686 for current prices and availability.

REMINGTON 180TH ANNIVERSARY LIMITED EDITION RIFLES AND SHOTGUNS

Remington manufactured 180 each of these firearms to commemorate the founding of the company in 1816: Model 700, Model 7600, Model 7400, Model 870, and Model 11-87. These firearms featured fine line hand-engraving, with gold embellishments. Rifles were chambered for .30-06 cartridge, with 22" barrels; shotguns were chambered for 12-gauge shell, with 26" ventilated rib barrels with RemChokes. All guns had blue finishes, with high gloss semi-fancy walnut stocks. Any estimate about current values would be quite speculative. If sold in a five-gun set, each should have matching serial numbers. Suggested retail price for the five-gun set was $6,925 in 1996. Individual guns carried these suggested retail prices:

Model 700 180th Anniversary Commemorative—$1,372
Model 7400 180th Anniversary Commemorative—$1,372
Model 7600 180th Anniversary Commemorative—$1,332
Model 870 180th Anniversary Commemorative—$1,305
Model 11-87 180th Anniversary Commemorative—$1,465

RENETTE, GASTINNE
Paris, France

Gastinne Renette, established 1840, made and sold high-end decorated firearms. He was gunmaker to the emperor of France and the King of Spain. Their 19th-century pistols included both percussion arms and breechloaders using the distinctive Rennette dropping block system. In the 20th century, they were best known for high-end sporting arms, often with custom features and engraving. As with all such arms, an expert hands-on evaluation is indicated to establish a likely market value. Prices listed here should be considered examples.

SHOTGUNS

Model 105

Anson & Deeley action 12- or 20-gauge double-barrel shotgun. Available in a variety of barrel lengths, with double triggers and automatic ejectors. Blued case-hardened, with checkered walnut stock.

NIB	Exc.	V.G.	Good	Fair	Poor
—	4000	3200	2500	1700	300

Model 98

As above, except more finely finished.

NIB	Exc.	V.G.	Good	Fair	Poor
—	5200	4500	3500	2800	300

Model 202

A 12- or 20-gauge sidelock double-barrel shotgun. Made only on custom order. French case-hardened. Blued, with checkered walnut stock.

NIB	Exc.	V.G.	Good	Fair	Poor
—	9000	7000	5000	3450	300

Model 353

Custom manufactured double-barrel shotgun, with detachable sidelocks. Highly finished.

NIB	Exc.	V.G.	Good	Fair	Poor
—	35000	30000	1700	8000	500

RIFLES

Type G Rifle

A .30-06, 9.3x74R or .375 H&H double-barrel rifle, with 24" barrels, express sights, double triggers and automatic ejectors. Engraved. Blued, with checkered walnut stock.

NIB	Exc.	V.G.	Good	Fair	Poor
—	5500	3700	3000	2000	650

Type R Deluxe

As above, engraved with hunting scenes and more finely figured walnut stock.

NIB	Exc.	V.G.	Good	Fair	Poor
—	7000	5000	3400	2900	750

Type PT President

As above, inlaid in gold with extremely well figured walnut stock.

NIB	Exc.	V.G.	Good	Fair	Poor
—	8000	6400	4000	3500	950

Mauser Bolt-Action

Custom-made bolt-action rifle built on a Mauser action. Choice of calibers and stock styles. Base price listed.

NIB	Exc.	V.G.	Good	Fair	Poor
—	11000	9000	6500	3000	750

Deluxe Mauser Bolt-Action

Same as above, with fancy wood and other options.

NIB	Exc.	V.G.	Good	Fair	Poor
—	20000	14000	9000	6500	1250

PISTOLS

Pistols (Antique)

Wide range of configurations of target, travelers', and dueling pistols from the 1840s through 1880s. Values of both muzzleloading and breechloading are similar for similar quality and condition. Casings with accessories and cased pairs (usually referred to as "dueling pistols") will bring a premium.

Exc.	Fine	V.G.	Good	Fair	Poor
4000	2000	1620	1250	600	420

RENWICK ARMS CO.

See—PERRY & GODDARD

REPUBLIC ARMS, INC.

Chino, California

This company was in business from 1997 to 2001. The Republic Patriot pistol may still be available from Cobra Enterpises.

RAP 440

Pistol chambered for .40 S&W or 9mm cartridges. A double-/single-action operation. Fitted with 3.75" barrel. Magazine capacity 7 rounds. Grips are two-piece black plastic. Weight about 32 oz. Sights are three dot, with fixed ramp front and windage adjustable rear. Introduced in 1998. Imported by TSF of Fairfax, Virginia.

NIB	Exc.	V.G.	Good	Fair	Poor
550	450	300	200	150	100

Republic Patriot

Double-action-only .45 ACP caliber pistol, with 3" barrel and fixed sights. Black polymer frame, with checkered grips and stainless steel slide. Magazine capacity 6 rounds. Weight about 20 oz. Introduced in 1997.

NIB	Exc.	V.G.	Good	Fair	Poor
320	250	200	150	100	80

RETAY

Konya, Turkey

Founded in 2006, a Turkish firearm manufacturer primarily in the market of affordable semi-automatic shotguns.

RETAY GPS XL

Gauge: 12 ga. 3.5 in. Barrel: 28 in. Weight: oz. Stock: Black or camo ABS synthetic. Features: Retay's pump-action GPS expands to the XL, chambering magnum rounds. GPS, short for Geometric Pump System, uses a short-travel pump action with a frictionless forend design. Anodized aluminum receiver, chrome-lined barrel with elongated, back-bored forcing cones. Crossbolt safety. Milled aluminum trigger housing and guard. Integral sling swivel mounts. Red fiber-optic front sight. Rubber recoil pad. Ships with MaraPro chokes.

NIB	Exc.	V.G.	Good	Fair	Poor
360	—	—	—	—	—

Gordion

Gauge: 12 ga., 3 in. Barrels: 26 in., 28 in., ventilated rib. Weight: 6.5-6.75 lbs. Stock: Choice of black synthetic, several Realtree camo patterns, or Turkish walnut. Features: The Turkish-made Gordion line of semi-automatics uses an inertia-plus action and bolt system. Oversized SP controls, quick unload system, TruGlo red front sight. Choice of matte or polished black receiver and barrel, or full camouflage coverage. Easy-Load port as well as Easy Unload system that allows the magazine tube to be emptied without racking the action. Includes a stock adjustment ship kit, TSA airline-approved hard case, and five flush choke tubes (F, IM, M, IC, S).

NIB	Exc.	V.G.	Good	Fair	Poor
900	750	650	—	—	—

Gordion Turkey

Similar to Gordion. Turkey variant with 24-in. barrel, Realtree or Mossy Oak camo.

NIB	Exc.	V.G.	Good	Fair	Poor
930	780	650	—	—	—

Masai Mara

Gauges: 12 ga., 3.5 in., 20 ga., 3 in. Barrels: 26 in., 28 in., ventilated rib. Weight: 6.5-6.75 lbs. Stock: Choice of synthetic in black or numerous camouflage patterns or two grades of Turkish walnut. Features: The Turkish-made Masai Mara line of semi-automatics uses an inertia-plus action and bolt system. Oversized controls, Easy Unload system, TruGlo red fiber-optic front sight. Options in Cerakote metalwork or anodized finishes. Push-button removeable trigger group for both safety and easy field cleaning. Microcell rubber recoil pad. Includes a TSA airline-approved hard case and ships with five flush choke tubes (F, IM, M, IC, S).

NIB	Exc.	V.G.	Good	Fair	Poor
1100	850	700	—	—	—

Upland Grade 2

NIB	Exc.	V.G.	Good	Fair	Poor
1150	—	—	—	—	—

Upland Grade 3

NIB	Exc.	V.G.	Good	Fair	Poor
1700	—	—	—	—	—

Comfort Grade 2

NIB	Exc.	V.G.	Good	Fair	Poor
1340	—	—	—	—	—

Comfort Grade 4

NIB	Exc.	V.G.	Good	Fair	Poor
1890	—	—	—	—	—

SP Air King Waterfowl Camo/Cerakote

NIB	Exc.	V.G.	Good	Fair	Poor
1440	—	—	—	—	—

SP Air King Waterfowl Cerakote

NIB	Exc.	V.G.	Good	Fair	Poor
1440	—	—	—	—	—

Masai Mara Warden

Gauge: 12 ga., 3 in. Barrel: 18.5 in. Weight: 6.6 lbs. Stock: Black Synthetic. Features: The Turkish-made Masai Mara line of semi-automatics uses an inertia-plus action and bolt system. Oversized controls, quick unload system, Picatinny rail, extended charging handle, ghost-ring sights. Push-button removeable trigger group. Microcell rubber recoil pad. Includes a hard case and ships with five MaraPro choke tubes.

NIB	Exc.	V.G.	Good	Fair	Poor
1000	800	700	—	—	—

GPS

Gauge: 12 ga. 3 in. Barrel: 18.5 in. Weight: 6 lbs. 9 oz. Stock: Black ABS synthetic. Features: Retay's first pump-action shotgun is the GPS, short for Geometric Pump System. Extra-short travel pump action. Anodized aluminum receiver. 5+1-round capacity. Chrome-lined barrel with elongated, back-bored forcing cones. Crossbolt safety. Milled aluminum trigger housing and guard. Integral sling swivel mounts. Beavertail adapter for optics mounting. High visibility front blade sight. Comfort rubber recoil pad. Ships with removeable MaraPro chokes (S, M, F).

NIB	Exc.	V.G.	Good	Fair	Poor
300	250	200	—	—	—

RETOLAZA HERMANOS

Eibar, Spain

Brompetier

Folding trigger 6.35mm or 7.65mm caliber double-action revolver, with 2.5" barrel. Safety mounted on left side of frame. Manufactured until 1915.

NIB	Exc.	V.G.	Good	Fair	Poor
—	250	120	80	70	40

Gallus or Titan

A 6.35mm semi-automatic pistol. Normally marked "Gallus" or "Titan". Blued, with plastic grips.

NIB	Exc.	V.G.	Good	Fair	Poor
—	280	150	100	80	50

Liberty, Military, Retolaza, or Paramount

A 6.35mm or 7.65mm semi-automatic pistol, with 3" barrel and 8-shot magazine. Slide marked with any of the trade names listed above.

NIB	Exc.	V.G.	Good	Fair	Poor
—	280	150	100	80	50

Puppy

Folding trigger .22-caliber double-action revolver, with 5-shot cylinder. Trade name "Puppy" stamped on barrel.

NIB	Exc.	V.G.	Good	Fair	Poor
—	180	120	80	50	20

Stosel

A 6.35mm semi-automatic pistol. Marked on slide "Automatic Pistol Stosel No. 1 Patent". Blued, with plastic grips.

NIB	Exc.	V.G.	Good	Fair	Poor
—	280	150	100	80	50

Titanic

A 6.35mm semi-automatic pistol, with 2.5" barrel. Slide marked "1913 Model Automatic Pistol Titanic Eibar". Blued, with plastic grips.

NIB	Exc.	V.G.	Good	Fair	Poor
—	280	150	100	80	50

REUNIES

Liege, Belgium

Dictator

A 6.35mm semi-automatic pistol, with 1.5" barrel and 5-shot magazine. Name "Dictator" together with company's details stamped on slide. Features bolt of tubular form, front end of which is hollow and encloses the barrel breech. Manufactured from 1909 to about 1925.

NIB	Exc.	V.G.	Good	Fair	Poor
—	280	150	100	80	50

Texas Ranger or Cowboy Ranger

Patterned after Colt Model 1873 revolver. A .38 Special caliber, barrel 5.5" and marked with company's details. Legends: "Cowboy Ranger" or "Texas Ranger". Manufactured from 1922 to 1931.

NIB	Exc.	V.G.	Good	Fair	Poor
—	350	200	100	80	50

REUTH, F.
Hartford, Connecticut

Animal Trap Gun (Antique)

Cast iron .28- to .50-caliber percussion trap gun. Single-/double-barrel 3.5" or 5" in length. Firearm fires a barbed arrow and is triggered by a cord attached to an animal trap or bait. Barrels marked "F. Reuth's Patent, May 12, 1857". Several hundred made between 1858 and 1862. Note: Single-barrel model more common than double-barrel and worth approximately 20 percent less.

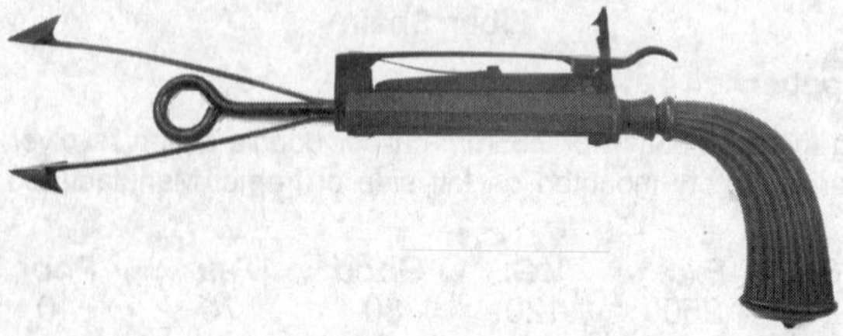

Photo courtesy of NRA Museums

Exc.	Fine	V.G.	Good	Fair	Poor
2000	1650	1100	550	150	100

REXIO DE ARMAS (COMANCHE)
Argentina

RS 22

A 9-shot revolver chambered for .22 LR cartridge. Choice of blued or stainless steel frame. Fixed or adjustable sights. Barrel lengths 4" or 6". Fitted with rubber grips. Note: Add $30 for stainless steel.

NIB	Exc.	V.G.	Good	Fair	Poor
240	180	150	120	80	50

RS 22M

Same as above, chambered for .22 Win. Magnum cartridge. Note: Add $30 for stainless steel.

NIB	Exc.	V.G.	Good	Fair	Poor
240	180	150	120	80	50

RJ 22

Chambered for .22 LR cartridge. Fitted with 3", 4" or 6" barrel. Checkered walnut or synthetic grips. Adjustable rear sight. Blued finish.

NIB	Exc.	V.G.	Good	Fair	Poor
180	120	100	80	50	20

RJ 38

Same as above, chambered for .38 Special cartridge.

NIB	Exc.	V.G.	Good	Fair	Poor
180	120	100	80	50	20

RS 357

Same as above, chambered for .357 Magnum cartridge. Offered with 3", 4" or 6" barrels. Note: Add $30 for stainless steel.

NIB	Exc.	V.G.	Good	Fair	Poor
240	180	120	100	80	50

Outfitter Single-Shot

Break-down single pistol. Chambered for .45 Colt/.410 .22 LR or .22 Win. Magnum. Blued 10" barrel, with synthetic grip. Weight about 43 oz.

NIB	Exc.	V.G.	Good	Fair	Poor
200	150	—	—	—	—

Outfitter Single-Shot Compact

Same as above, with 6" barrel in .22 Win. Magnum or .45 Colt/.410.

NIB	Exc.	V.G.	Good	Fair	Poor
200	150	120	100	80	50

RHEINMETALL
Sommerda, Germany

Dreyse 6.35mm Model 1907

A 6.35mm semi-automatic pistol, with 2" barrel. Manual safety and 6-shot magazine. Weight about 14 oz. Slide marked "Dreyse". Blued, with hard rubber grips having trademark "RFM" molded in them. Patent for this design issued in 1909 to Louis Schmeisser.

Courtesy James Rankin

NIB	Exc.	V.G.	Good	Fair	Poor
—	400	250	200	150	100

Dreyse 7.65mm Model 1907

As above, chambered for 7.65mm cartridge. Barrel 3.6", with 7-shot magazine. Weight about 25 oz. Blued, with horn grips.

Courtesy Orvel Reichert

NIB	Exc.	V.G.	Good	Fair	Poor
—	300	200	150	120	80

Dreyse 9mm

As above, chambered for 9mm cartridge. Barrel 5", with 8-shot magazine. Weight about 37 oz. Slide marked "Rheinische Mettallwaaren Und Maschinenfabrik, Sommerda". Blued, with hard rubber grips. Manufactured prior to 1916 and in small numbers.

Courtesy James Rankin

NIB	Exc.	V.G.	Good	Fair	Poor
—	4500	3750	2500	1500	750

Rheinmetall 32

A 7.65mm semi-automatic pistol, with 3.65" barrel and 8-shot magazine. Slide marked "Rheinmetall ABT. Sommerda". Blued, with walnut grips. Overall length 6.5"; weight about 23.5 oz. Production began in 1920.

Courtesy James Rankin

NIB	Exc.	V.G.	Good	Fair	Poor
—	350	220	180	120	90

Rheinmetall 9mm

A 9mm version of Rheinmetall. Built in 1935 to compete with 9mm Parabellum German military pistols of that time. It was unsuccessful.

Courtesy James Rankin

NIB	Exc.	V.G.	Good	Fair	Poor
—Too Rare To Price—			—	—	—

Dreyse Light Rifle or Carbine

Model 1907 in caliber 7.65 Browning. Fitted with a fixed stock and 6-round magazine.

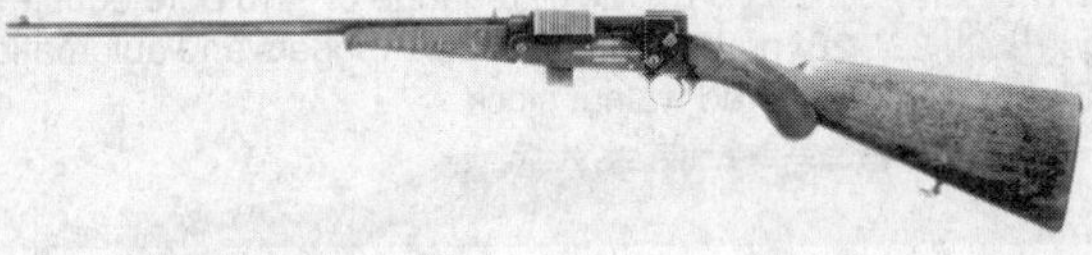

NIB	Exc.	V.G.	Good	Fair	Poor
—	1850	1400	1150	700	300

RHODE ISLAND ARMS CO.
Hope Valley, Rhode Island

Morrone

A 12- or 20-gauge over/under boxlock shotgun, with 26" or 28" barrels, single trigger and automatic ejectors. Blued, with straight-/pistol grip walnut checkered stock. 450 made in 12-gauge; 50 in 20-gauge. Manufactured from 1949 to 1953.

NIB	Exc.	V.G.	Good	Fair	Poor
—	1700	1200	850	600	350

RICHLAND ARMS CO.
Blissfield, Michigan

This company, which ceased operation in 1986, imported a variety of Spanish-made shotguns.

Model 41 Ultra Over/Under

A 20-, 28-gauge or .410 bore double-barrel shotgun, with 26" or 28" ventilated rib barrels, single non-selective trigger and automatic ejectors. French case-hardened receiver and checkered walnut stock.

NIB	Exc.	V.G.	Good	Fair	Poor
—	300	250	200	150	100

Model 747 Over/Under

As above in 20-gauge only, with single-selective trigger.

NIB	Exc.	V.G.	Good	Fair	Poor
—	420	350	300	250	180

Model 757 Over/Under

Greener-style boxlock 12-gauge double-barrel shotgun, with 26" or 28" ventilated rib barrels, double triggers and automatic ejectors. Finished as Model 747.

NIB	Exc.	V.G.	Good	Fair	Poor
—	300	250	200	180	120

Model 787 Over/Under

As above, fitted with screw-in choke tubes.

NIB	Exc.	V.G.	Good	Fair	Poor
—	450	380	320	280	200

Model 808 Over/Under

A 12-gauge double-barrel shotgun, with 26", 28" or 30" ventilated rib barrels, single trigger and automatic ejectors. Blued, with checkered walnut stock. Manufactured in Italy from 1963 to 1968.

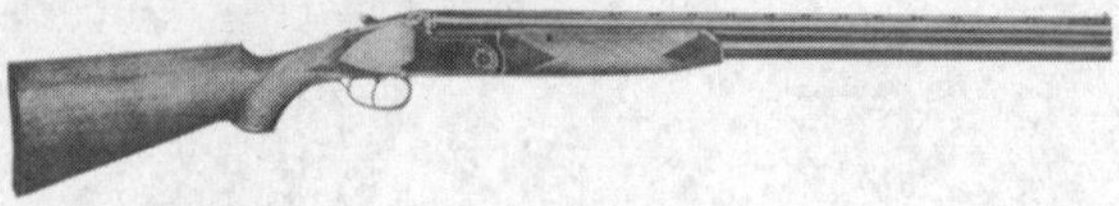

NIB	Exc.	V.G.	Good	Fair	Poor
—	420	350	300	250	180

Model 80 LS

A 12-, 20-gauge or .410 bore single-barrel shotgun, with 26" or 28" barrels. Blued, with checkered walnut stock.

NIB	Exc.	V.G.	Good	Fair	Poor
—	180	120	100	80	60

Model 200

Anson & Deeley-style 12-, 16-, 20-, 28-gauge or .410 bore double-barrel shotgun, with 22", 26" or 28" barrels, double triggers and automatic ejectors. Blued, with checkered walnut stock.

NIB	Exc.	V.G.	Good	Fair	Poor
—	350	300	250	200	120

Model 202

As above, with an extra set of interchangeable barrels. Imported from 1963 to 1985.

NIB	Exc.	V.G.	Good	Fair	Poor
—	320	280	220	180	100

Model 711 Magnum

As above, chambered for 3" shells and fitted with 30" or 32" barrels.

NIB	Exc.	V.G.	Good	Fair	Poor
—	350	300	250	200	150

Model 707 Deluxe

As above, more finely finished and fitted with well figured walnut stocks.

NIB	Exc.	V.G.	Good	Fair	Poor
—	350	300	250	200	150

RICHMOND ARMORY

Richmond, Virginia

Carbine (Antique)

This weapon was manufactured for use by Confederate States of America and is extremely collectible. This muzzleloading carbine chambered for .58-caliber percussion. Has a 25" round barrel and full-length stock that is held on by two barrel bands. Manufactured from parts that were captured at Harper's Ferry Armory in 1861. Locks are marked "Richmond, VA" and dated from 1861 to 1865. There are sling swivels in front of triggerguard and on the front barrel band; a third swivel is on the underside of buttstock. Quantity manufactured is not known. Made between 1861 and 1865. Rare. Values are speculative.

Courtesy Milwaukee Public Museum, Milwaukee, Wisconsin

Exc.	Fine	V.G.	Good	Fair	Poor
—	—	12000	6000	3000	700

Musketoon (Antique)

Weapon similar to the carbine, except barrel is 30" in length and front sight is also the bayonet lug. There is no sling swivel on buttstock. Manufactured between 1861 and 1865.

Exc.	Fine	V.G.	Good	Fair	Poor
—	—	7000	4000	2000	700

Rifled Musket (Antique)

Also similar to the Carbine, with 40" barrel and full-length stock held on by three barrel bands. Front sling swivel is on the middle barrel band instead of front band. Manufactured between 1861 and 1865. As with most confederate arms, extremely rare in better than VG condition. Also, "Assembled" specimens of confederate arms always bring less.

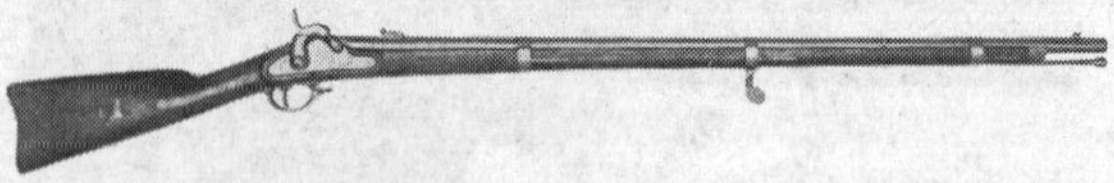

Courtesy Milwaukee Public Museum, Milwaukee, Wisconsin

Exc.	Fine	V.G.	Good	Fair	Poor
—	—	7500	4500	2000	700

RIEDL RIFLE CO.

Westminster, California

Single-Shot Rifle

Company produced custom order dropping block single-shot rifles in a variety of calibers and barrel lengths. Rifles were normally fitted only with telescopic or target sight bases. Blued, with checkered walnut stock. Premium for African or Magnum chamberings.

NIB	Exc.	V.G.	Good	Fair	Poor
—	1750	1500	1250	750	400

RIFLESMITH INC.

Sheridan, Montana

See—AXTELL RIFLE CO.

RIGBY, JOHN & CO., LTD.

London, England

This company was established in the 18th century in U.K. and has produced a wide variety of firearms over the years. It traces its roots back to 1735 in Dublin, where the company was known for its percussion dueling pistols. A branch was opened in London in 1865, where some of the world's finest double rifles were made for more than 130 years, many of them made to order. In 1997, a group of investors acquired the company and moved it to Paso Robles, California, where a limited number of Rigby models were manufactured for several years. In 2010, an investor group from Texas bought the company and returned it to London, where Paul Roberts of J. Roberts and Sons was contracted to make rifles. The L&O Group, which owns Mauser, Blaser and Sauer, purchased the company in 2013. It was relocated to a new facility in Pensbury Place, London in 2014. The classic Rigby double guns made from the mid-1800s through the late-1990s must be evaluated on an individual basis, like other British high-end sporting arms. Depending on configuration, condition, engraving, casing, etc., values may run through five figures into six figures. The values listed below are for recent production arms.

RIFLES

MAGAZINE RIFLES, CURRENT PRODUCTION

Magazine Rifle

Utilizing a Mauser action, this rifle is available in a number of calibers, barrel lengths and 3- or 5-shot magazine. Checkered walnut stock.

Courtesy Faintich Auction Service, Paul Goodwin photo

NIB	Exc.	V.G.	Good	Fair	Poor
—	12500	10000	7000	4000	1000

Big Game Rifle

Available on a single-/double-square bridge Mauser action in .375 H&H, .416 Rigby or .450 Rigby calibers. Classic features of original Rigby rifles include 3-position wing safety, express sights, quarter rib, extractor and Turkish walnut stock, with traditional checkering pattern. Barreled actions are built in Germany by Mauser, as was done with original Rigby rifles a century ago. Higher-grade wood, engraving and color case-hardening are available. Deluxe model has premium finish and features; Vintage model traditional stock and specifications. Note: Prices shown are based on BP=USD exchange rate in July, 2016 and do not include British VAT. Add 20 percent for Deluxe or Vintage model.

NIB	Exc.	V.G.	Good	Fair	Poor
8000	7000	6000	—	—	—

London Best Rifle

Bespoke magazine rifle custom made to buyer's specifications in any caliber, with highest grade walnut and engraving. Price starts about $125,000 based on exchange rate as of July, 2016.

African Express

Utilizing a square bridge Mauser action. Chambered for .375 H&H, .404 Gibbs, .416 Rigby, .458 Win. Magnum, .505 Gibbs cartridges. Barrel lengths vary from 20" to 24"; 4-shot magazine standard.

NIB	Exc.	V.G.	Good	Fair	Poor
—	25000	20000	15000	10000	2000

Single-Shot Rifle

Utilizing a Farquharson falling block action, this rifle is chambered for a variety of cartridges. Has a 24" barrel. Receiver finely engraved and blued. Stock of well figured walnut.

NIB	Exc.	V.G.	Good	Fair	Poor
—	8000	7000	5500	2500	600

Second Quality Boxlock Double Rifle

Double-barrel rifle chambered for cartridges from .275 Magnum to .577 Nitro Express, with 24" to 28" barrel. Fitted with express sights, double triggers and automatic ejectors. Blued, with light engraving. Checkered walnut stock.

NIB	Exc.	V.G.	Good	Fair	Poor
—	20000	17000	11000	5500	900

Best Quality Boxlock Double Rifle

As above, but more finely engraved. Better quality walnut stocks.

NIB	Exc.	V.G.	Good	Fair	Poor
—	30000	22500	15000	7500	1000

Best Quality Sidelock Double Rifle

As above, but fitted with full sidelocks. Best bouquet engraving. Finely figured walnut stocks.

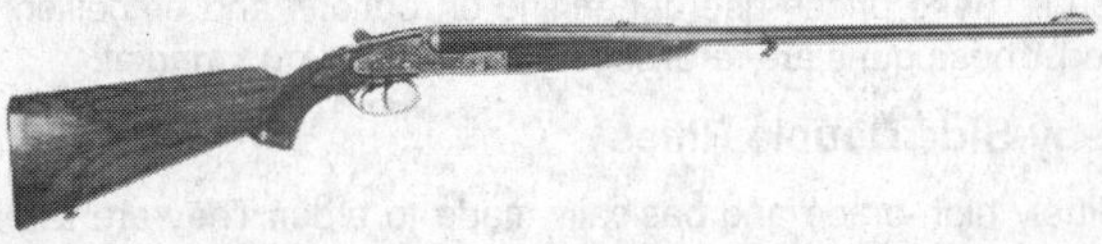

NIB	Exc.	V.G.	Good	Fair	Poor
—	50000	42500	33000	15000	1500

SHOTGUNS

Sidelock Double

Offered in all gauges, with choice of barrel lengths, chokes, stock dimensions, grip and forend styles. Double triggers and automatic ejectors. Prices shown are for Sandringham Grade. Regal Grade has higher grade wood and engraving. Made in London prior to 1998. Note: Add 20 percent for Regal Grade; 30 percent for 20-gauge; 40 percent for 28-gauge or .410 bore.

NIB	Exc.	V.G.	Good	Fair	Poor
9000	7500	6000	4500	3000	1000

Boxlock Double

Same features and options as above, except boxlock action. Prices shown are for Chatsworth Grade. Sackville Grade has higher grade wood and engraving. Made in London prior to 1998. Note: Add 30 percent for Sackville Grade; 20 percent for 20-gauge; 30 percent for 28-gauge or .410 bore.

NIB	Exc.	V.G.	Good	Fair	Poor
4500	3700	2800	2000	1500	500

RIGDON, ANSLEY & CO.

Augusta, Georgia

This is a successor to the firm of Leech & Rigdon, and the revolvers are very similar. As with all Confederate arms, beware of fakes and reproductions. Expert evaluation is recommended. Sales are rare, so the values listed are speculative.

1851 Colt Navy Type (Antique)

A .36-caliber percussion revolver, with 7.5" barrel and 6-shot cylinder. Blued, with walnut grips. Initial production examples marked "Augusta, GA. C.S.A."; later models "C.S.A." Approximately 1,000 manufactured in 1864 and 1865.

Courtesy Milwaukee Public Museum, Milwaukee, Wisconsin

Early Production Model (Antique)

Exc.	Fine	V.G.	Good	Fair	Poor
—	45000	36250	27500	12000	8400

Standard Production Model (Antique)

Exc.	Fine	V.G.	Good	Fair	Poor
—	40000	30000	20000	9000	6300

RIPOMANTI, GUY
St. Etienne, France

Side-by-Side Shotgun

High-grade shotgun offered on a strictly made-to-order basis. There is a boxlock model that begins at $8,500; a sidelock that is priced from $22,500. These prices rise depending on options and embellishments desired. These guns are rarely seen on the used-gun market.

Side-by-Side Double Rifles

Extremely high-grade and basically made to order. They are rarely encountered on today's market. They have been imported since 1988. They range in price from $11,000 up.

Over/Under Double Rifle

Boxlock action over/under chambered for 9.3x74R cartridge. Barrels are 23.5" and have express sights. There are double triggers and automatic ejectors. Highly engraved and features high-grade hand-checkered walnut stock.

NIB	*Exc.*	*V.G.*	*Good*	*Fair*	*Poor*
12500	9750	7750	5000	4000	900

RIVERSIDE ARMS CO.
Chicopee Falls, Massachusetts

See—STEVENS, J. ARMS CO.

Double-Barrel Shotguns

Brand name used by J. Stevens Arms Co. on many good quality double-barrel shotguns. Value depends on model, gauge and condition. From $100 to $1,600. See also Stevens.

Courtesy William Hammond

RIZZINI, BATTISTA
Bresica, Italy

Note: There are a number of extra cost options for Rizzini guns that can greatly affect price. Extra barrels and upgraded wood are such options.

SHOTGUNS

BR 460

Gauge: 12 ga., 3 in. Barrels: 30 in., 32 in., with 10mm x 6mm ventilated rib. Length: 43-45 in. Weight: 8.3 lbs. Stock: Walnut with hand-rubbed oil finish and adjustable comb. Features: These Rizzini O/U Competition guns are produced in Skeet, Sporting, Trap, and Double Trap, each with different characteristics. Choice of fixed or interchangeable chokes and fixed, adjustable or ramped rib. Stock checkered at 28 LPI. White rounded style front sight with silver mid-bead. Rubber buttpad. Either standard or long forcing cones depending on model. Ships with hard case and velvet stock sleeve.

NIB	*Exc.*	*V.G.*	*Good*	*Fair*	*Poor*
6750	—	—	—	—	—

Aurum Light

Over/under model features 24.5" to 27.5" ventilated rib barrel. Figured oil-finish walnut stock, with hand-checkering and pistol grip. Game scene engraved receiver. Auto ejectors and single-selective trigger. Weight about 6 lbs. Made in 12-, 16-, 20-, 28-gauge and .410 bore. Note: Add $500 for 28 gauge or .410 bore.

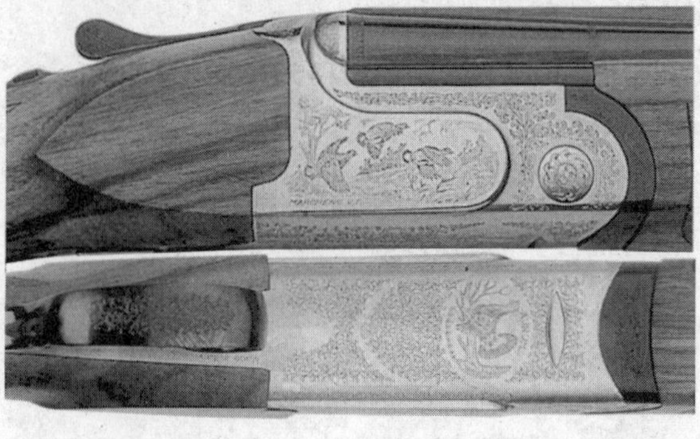

Courtesy William Larkin Moore & Co.

NIB	*Exc.*	*V.G.*	*Good*	*Fair*	*Poor*
3000	2600	2000	1500	900	500

Artemis Classic

Features engraved sideplates with game scenes. Offered in 12-, 16-, 20-, 28-gauge and.410 bore. Barrel lengths from 24" to 27.5". Auto ejectors and single-selective trigger. Figured walnut stock, with hand-checkering and pistol grip. Weight about 6 lbs.

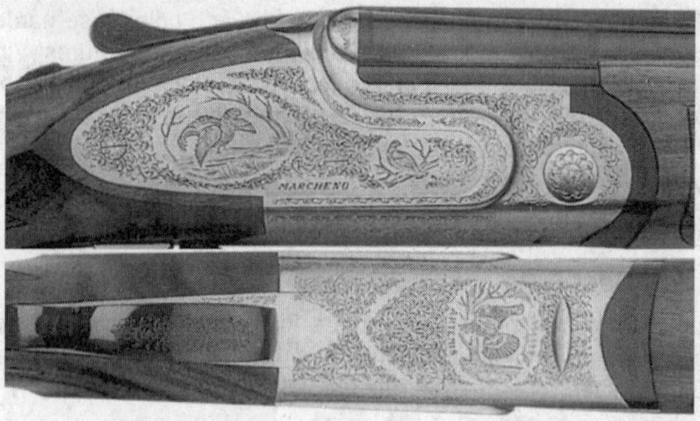

Courtesy William Larkin Moore & Co.

NIB	*Exc.*	*V.G.*	*Good*	*Fair*	*Poor*
3200	2700	2300	1900	1000	500

Artemis Deluxe

Similar to standard Artemis, with addition of gold inlaid game scenes and fancy walnut stock. Cased.

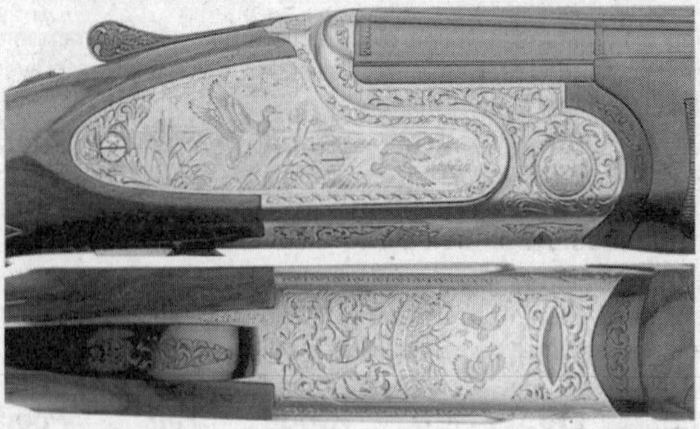

NIB	*Exc.*	*V.G.*	*Good*	*Fair*	*Poor*
6000	4200	3500	2500	1250	600

Artemis EL

Features sideplates, with hand-engraved English scroll and game scenes. Extra fancy walnut stock. Cased.

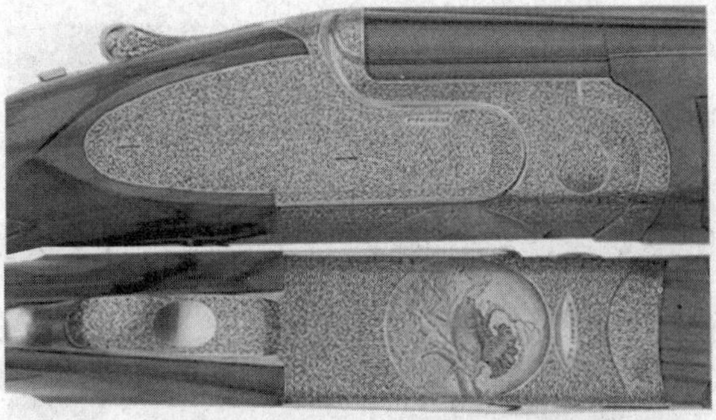

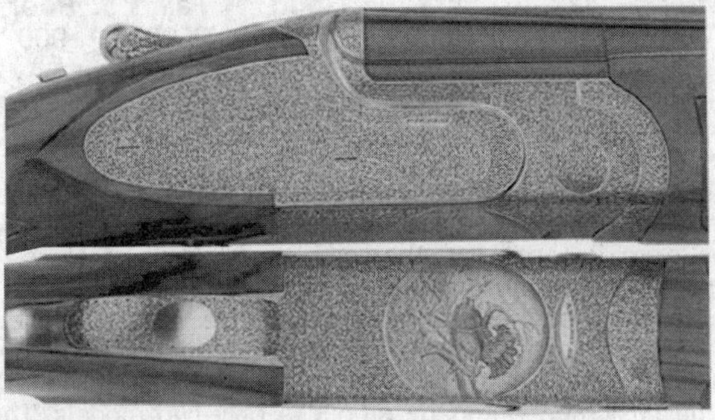

NIB	Exc.	V.G.	Good	Fair	Poor
18000	13500	10000	8000	6000	900

Upland EL

NIB	Exc.	V.G.	Good	Fair	Poor
4000	3500	3000	2500	1250	600

S780 Emel

Boxlock model offered in 12-, 16-, 20-, 28-gauge or .410 bore. Barrel lengths from 24" to 27.5". Hand-engraved receiver, with game scenes. Auto ejectors and single-selective trigger. Fancy walnut stock, with hand-checkering. Leather case. Weight about: 12-gauge 6.8 lbs.; smaller gauges 6 lbs.

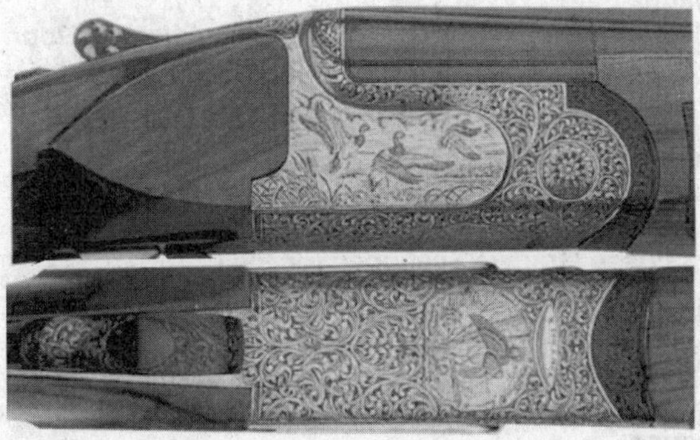

NIB	Exc.	V.G.	Good	Fair	Poor
13500	11000	8750	7000	4250	900

S782 Emel Field Classic

Similar to S792, with addition of hand-engraved gold inlaid game scenes.

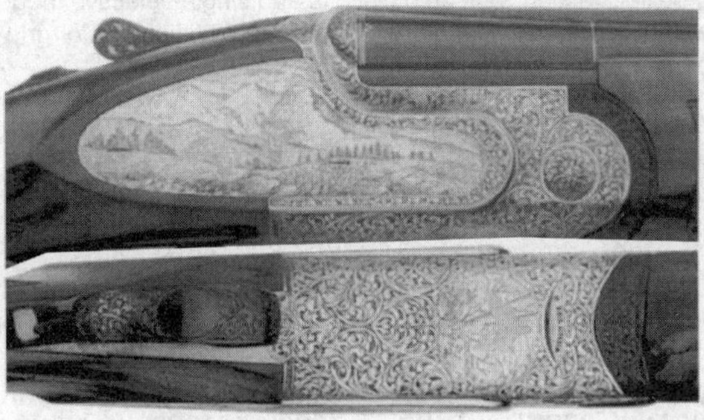

NIB	Exc.	V.G.	Good	Fair	Poor
15000	13000	10000	8750	5700	900

S790 Emel Field

Similar to S780, with exception of thistle-leaf style engraving pattern.

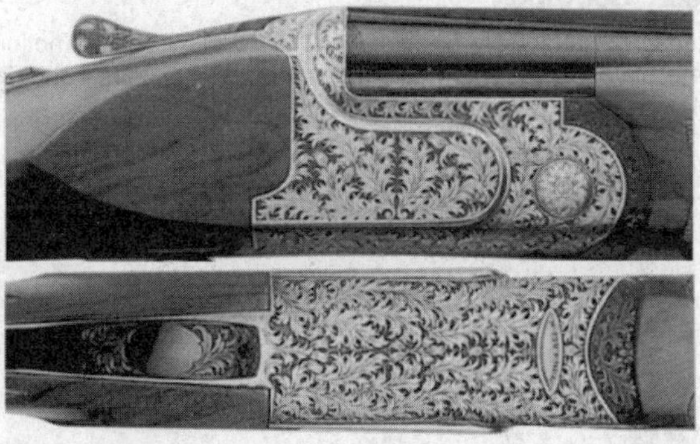

NIB	Exc.	V.G.	Good	Fair	Poor
10500	8000	6500	5000	4250	900

S792 Emel Field

Features sideplates engraved with English scroll and game scenes. Extra select walnut stock. Available in 12-, 16-, 20-, 28-gauge and .410 bore. Barrel lengths from 24" to 27.5".

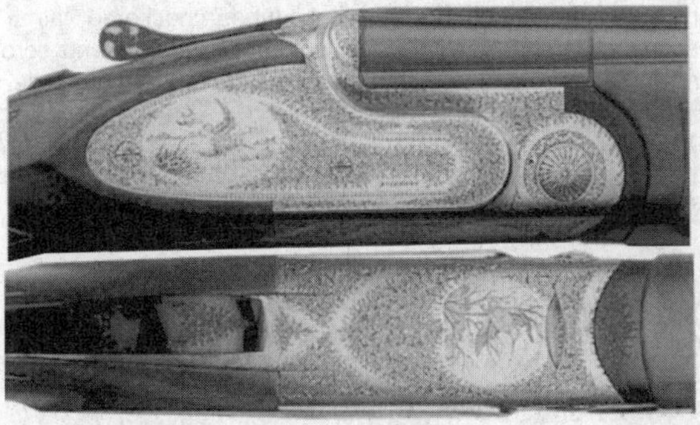

NIB	Exc.	V.G.	Good	Fair	Poor
11000	9750	8000	6750	5000	900

Premier Sporting

Offered in 12- or 20-gauge. Choice of barrel lengths from 27.5" to 31.5". Blued boxlock action, with auto ejectors and single-selective trigger. Select walnut stock, with hand-checkering and oil-finish. Pistol grip stock and beavertail forend. Weight about 7.5 lbs.

NIB	Exc.	V.G.	Good	Fair	Poor
3000	2750	2100	1600	900	500

Sporting EL

NIB	Exc.	V.G.	Good	Fair	Poor
3750	2800	2200	1750	980	600

S790 EL Sporting

Offered in 12-gauge only. Barrels from 27.5" to 31.5". Boxlock action, with chrome plate. Auto ejectors and single-selective trigger. Fancy walnut pistol grip stock. Weight about 7.5 lbs.

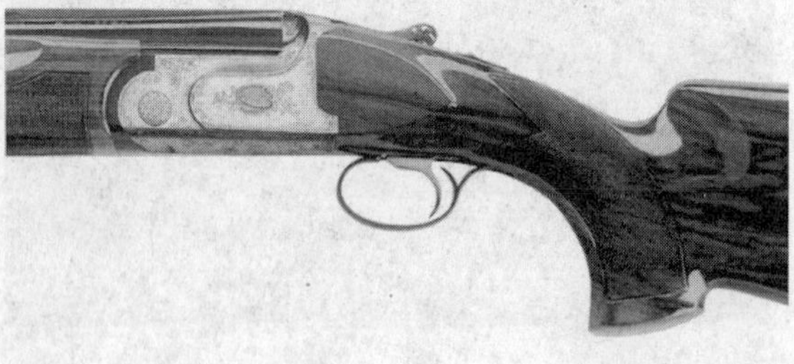

NIB	Exc.	V.G.	Good	Fair	Poor
7500	6250	5000	3750	2900	800

Rizzini Omnium

Model represents entry level of Rizzini over/unders, but it has features not found on comparably priced guns. These include jeweled monoblocs, braised ribs, precisely regulated trigger and blued or coin finish. Other features are interchangeable choke tubes, checkered walnut stock with schnabel forend, ventilated rib, automatic ejectors and scroll engraving. In 12- or 20-gauge, with frame sizes appropriate to gauge. Note: Add $200 for Omnium Light, with coin finish.

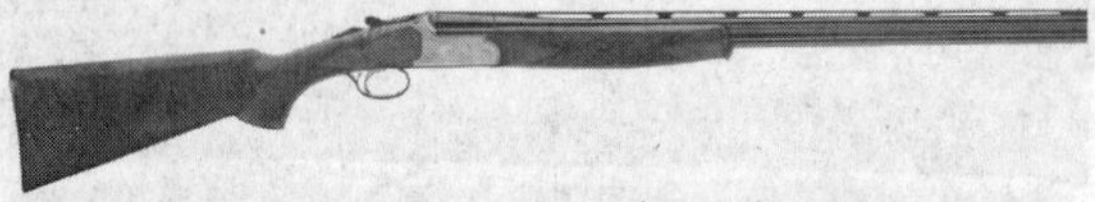

NIB	Exc.	V.G.	Good	Fair	Poor
2250	1880	1550	1000	750	300

EXPRESS RIFLES

Express 90 L

Over/under chambered for 7x65R, 8x57JRS, 9.3x74R, .30-06, .308 Win., .444 Marlin. Barrel length 16". Boxlock action, with case colored receiver. Auto ejectors and single trigger. Pistol grip walnut stock, with Bavarian cheekpiece. Hand-checkered oil-finish stock. Weight about 8 lbs.

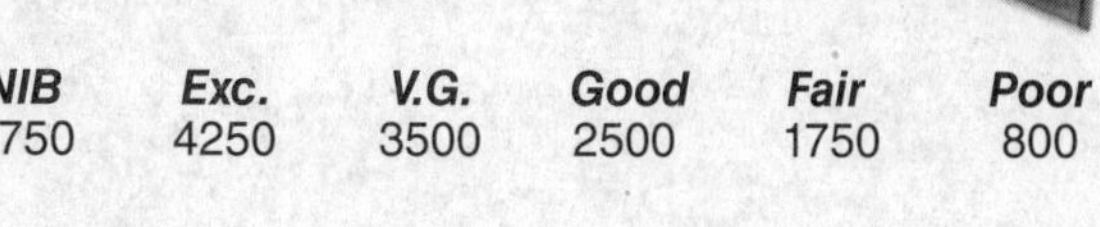

NIB	Exc.	V.G.	Good	Fair	Poor
4750	4250	3500	2500	1750	800

Express 92 EL

Same calibers as above. Sideplates engraved with English scroll and game scenes. Extra select walnut stock, with pistol grip and round cheekpiece.

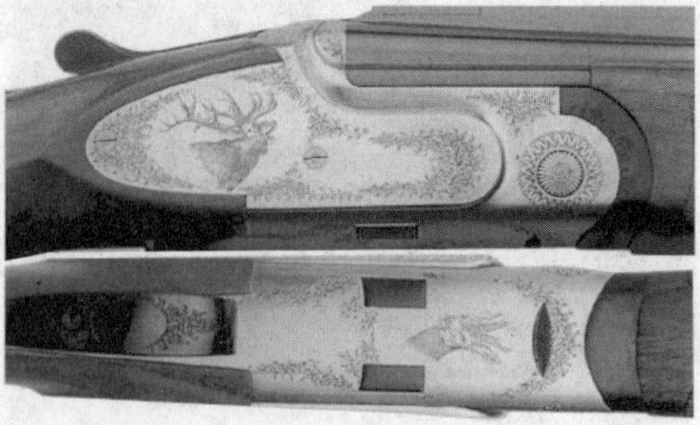

NIB	Exc.	V.G.	Good	Fair	Poor
11000	9500	8000	5500	2500	900

RIZZINI, FRATELLI

Brescia, Italy

Early guns were manufactured with Antonio Zoli. As a result, these were off-the-shelf guns of lower prices. These early guns were imported by Abercombie and Fitch of New York. Some of these guns will be stamped with A&F address on the barrel. These side-by-side guns have a boxlock action. Note: At the present time, this Italian gun company builds about 24 shotguns a year. Each gun is highly individualized for the customer. Company produces only two models. These are listed to give the reader some idea of the value of one of these models. None of these models includes the cost of engraving. Multi barrel set and multi gauge sets are extra. Rizzini models with serial numbers above #1709 have their own patented action, and prices listed reflect that action. Guns listed have a H&H style action and should deduct approximately 30 percent from prices listed.

Lusso Grade

12 gauge

NIB	Exc.	V.G.	Good	Fair	Poor
3200	2850	2200	1600	900	400

20 gauge

NIB	Exc.	V.G.	Good	Fair	Poor
3700	3250	2800	2200	1500	550

28 gauge and .410 bore

NIB	Exc.	V.G.	Good	Fair	Poor
4000	3600	3000	2500	1700	600

Extra Lusso Grade—Scalloped receiver

12 gauge

NIB	Exc.	V.G.	Good	Fair	Poor
4800	4150	3250	2700	1500	700

20 gauge

NIB	Exc.	V.G.	Good	Fair	Poor
5450	4600	3500	2900	1650	700

28 gauge

NIB	Exc.	V.G.	Good	Fair	Poor
5850	4900	3750	3250	1900	700

.410 bore

NIB	Exc.	V.G.	Good	Fair	Poor
6250	5250	3900	3500	2350	750

Model R-1

Available in 12-gauge to .410 bore. Barrels from 25" to 30", single-/double trigger, pistol-/straight-grip, rib, barrel length and chokes are standard items. Features H&H sidelock action.

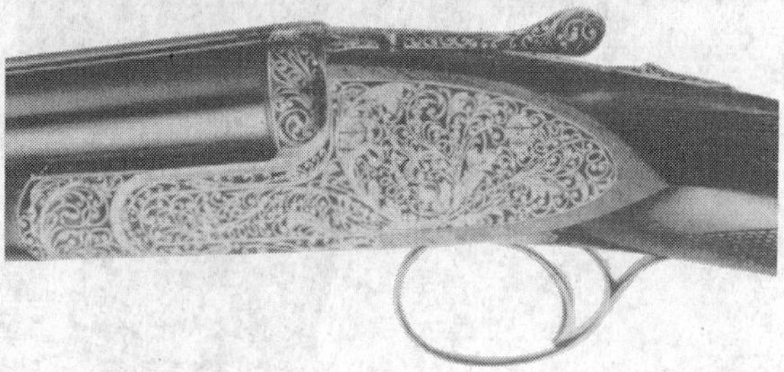

12, 16, or 20 gauge

NIB	Exc.	V.G.	Good	Fair	Poor
85000	72000	57500	40000	—	—

28 gauge or .410 bore

NIB	Exc.	V.G.	Good	Fair	Poor
90000	76000	62000	45000	—	—

Model R-2

Has a boxlock action and removable inspection plate on the bottom of frame. Stock and forearm fitted with Turkish Circassian walnut. Offered in 12-gauge to .410 bore.

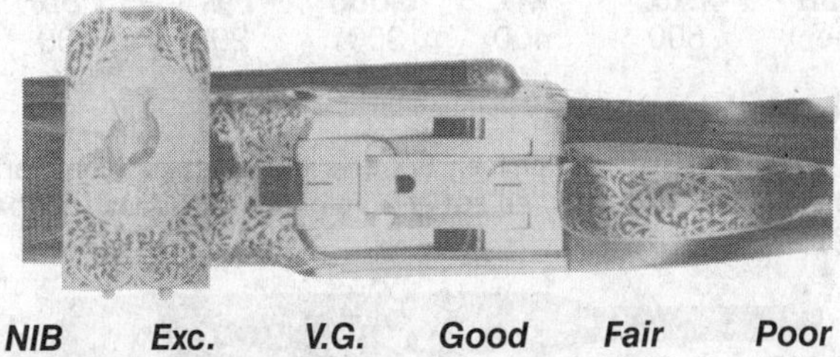

NIB	Exc.	V.G.	Good	Fair	Poor
17000	14000	1000	7500	5000	700

ROBAR AND de KIRKHAVE

Liege, Belgium

Model 1909-1910

A 6.35mm or 7.65mm caliber semi-automatic pistol, with 3" barrel. Barrel located under the recoil spring housing. Slide marked "Pistolet Automatique Jieffeco Depose Brevete SGDG". Blued, with plastic grips. Manufactured from 1910 to 1914. Copy of Browning Model 1900.

Courtesy James Rankin

NIB	Exc.	V.G.	Good	Fair	Poor
—	500	400	300	200	100

Model 1911

Semi-automatic pistol in caliber 6.35mm. Same as Model 1909-1910. Slide serrations have been added at the muzzle.

Courtesy James Rankin

NIB	Exc.	V.G.	Good	Fair	Poor
—	500	400	300	200	100

Model 1912

Semi-automatic pistol in caliber 7.65mm. Similar to Model 1909-1910. Slide serrations have been added at the muzzle.

Courtesy James Rankin

NIB	Exc.	V.G.	Good	Fair	Poor
—	500	400	300	200	100

Melior Model 1907

Semi-automatic pistol in calibers 6.35mm and 7.65mm. Barrel located under the recoil spring housing.

Courtesy James Rankin

NIB	Exc.	V.G.	Good	Fair	Poor
—	500	400	300	200	100

Melior Model 1913-1914

Semi-automatic pistol in caliber 6.35mm and 7.65mm. Same as Model 1907, with slide serrations at the muzzle.

NIB	Exc.	V.G.	Good	Fair	Poor
—	500	400	300	200	100

Melior Pocket Model

Semi-automatic pistol in 6.35mm caliber. Nearly identical to Jieffeco's made by the same company, Robar. Manufactured in 1920s and imported into U.S. by Phoenix Arms Company, Mass. Phoenix name appears on the pistol. Model resembles the FN Browning Model 1910.

Courtesy James Rankin

NIB	Exc.	V.G.	Good	Fair	Poor
—	350	250	180	120	80

Melior Vest Pocket Model

Semi-automatic pistol in caliber 6.35mm, with open-top slide. Blue finish, with black checkered rubber grips. Robar logo "ROC" on each grip.

Courtesy James Rankin

NIB	Exc.	V.G.	Good	Fair	Poor
—	300	250	200	150	100

Melior Model .22 Long Rifle

Semi-automatic pistol chambered for .22 LR cartridge. Very similar in appearance to Pocket Model, with no squeeze grip safety.

Courtesy James Rankin

NIB	Exc.	V.G.	Good	Fair	Poor
—	500	400	300	200	100

Melior Model .22 Target

Semi-automatic in .22 LR caliber. Barrel is detachable so that various lengths may be used. Knurled nut at front of the slide allows for barrel changes.

Courtesy James Rankin

NIB	Exc.	V.G.	Good	Fair	Poor
—	500	400	300	200	100

New Model Jieffeco (7.65mm)

In the 1920s, Robar and de Kirkhave introduced a New Model, Jieffeco. Similar to FN Browning Model 1910. At this time, the right to import Jieffeco into the U.S. was arranged with Davis Warner Arms Corp., New York, whose company name was used on the pistol. Model is a semi-automatic pistol in caliber 7.65mm. On the slide is "Pistolet Automatique Jieffeco Repose".

Courtesy James Rankin

NIB	Exc.	V.G.	Good	Fair	Poor
—	350	250	180	120	80

New Model Jieffeco (6.35mm)

Similar to 7.65mm model, this compact variation is chambered in 6.35mm or .25 ACP. On the slide is "Pistolet Automatique Jieffeco Made in Liege, Belgium. Davis Warmer Arms Corporation, New York".

Courtesy James Rankin

NIB	Exc.	V.G.	Good	Fair	Poor
—	350	250	180	120	80

Mercury

As above in .22-caliber. Imported by Tradewinds of Tacoma, Washington. Slide marked "Mercury Made in Belgium". Blue or nickel-plated. Manufactured from 1946 to 1958.

NIB	Exc.	V.G.	Good	Fair	Poor
—	200	150	120	100	80

ROBAR COMPANIES

Phoenix, Arizona

This company has been building precision rifles, shotguns and pistols since 1983.

Current Production Bolt Action Rifles

SR-21E

The SR21E bolt-action precision rifle uses the Modular Driven Technology ESS chassis system mated with an accurized Remington 700 action and match-grade barrel. Barrel lengths from 18 to 26" chambered in 6mm C, 6.5 Creedmoor, .308 Win, .300 Win. Mag., .338 Lapua. Only base price shown. Many custom extras available.

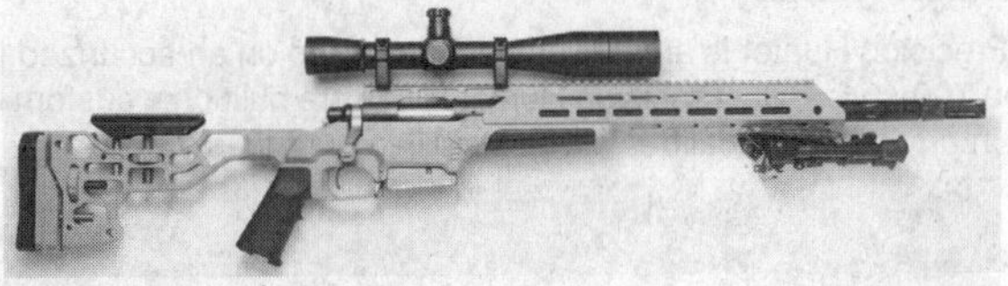

NIB	Exc.	V.G.	Good	Fair	Poor
4000	3400	2900	2450	1480	900

QR2

The Robar QR2 Quick Response Multi-Purpose Rifle System is a precision tactical rifle built on a Remington 700-style BDL to serve multiple functions from close quarters to long range. The QR2 features a Monte-Carlo style ambidextrous stock with a built-in ergonomic palm swell, rear sling swivel stud and a short accessory rail in the forend. Any standard centerfire caliber available.

NIB	Exc.	V.G.	Good	Fair	Poor
3700	3100	2650	2280	1350	800

SR60

The SR60 is a rugged, dependable, easy-to-use rifle with a proven track record with military, law enforcement and civilian marksmen. Based on an accurized Remington 700 action, the SR60 features an ambidextrous Monte Carlo style stock that is the same design as used on the U.S. Marine Corps M40A1 rifle. Any standard centerfire caliber available.

NIB	Exc.	V.G.	Good	Fair	Poor
4000	3400	2900	2450	1480	900

SR90

The SR90 is designed for the advanced marksman, and is the result of collaboration with military and law enforcement marksmen on a Remington 700-style BDL. Using Robar's exclusive ambidextrous stock with built-in ergonomic palm swells, thumb rests and a more vertically orientated pistol grip, the stock has an adjustable cheekpiece and 3-way adjustable buttplate. The accurized action is mated with a fluted stainless steel match-grade barrel and aluminum pillar bedded to the stock with a free-floating barrel channel. Any standard centerfire caliber available.

NIB	Exc.	V.G.	Good	Fair	Poor
4400	3750	3180	2700	1600	980

Precision Hunter

The Precision Hunter is an all-weather rifle based on an accurized Remington 700-style BDL. Precision Hunter Rifles are built on a custom basis only, in any standard caliber with a McMillan hunting-style stock.

NIB	Exc.	V.G.	Good	Fair	Poor
4000	3400	2900	2450	1480	900

Robar Patriot Tactical Shotgun

Built on a Remington Model 870. Features 18" barrel, express sights, seamless extended magazine tube, side-saddle shell carrier, Wolff springs, etc.. Roguard/NP3 finish.

NIB	Exc.	V.G.	Good	Fair	Poor
760	600	500	400	300	100

Robar Spec Ops Tactical Shotgun

Similar to model above. Fitted with tactical ghost ring night sights, safety and sling.

NIB	Exc.	V.G.	Good	Fair	Poor
990	800	700	600	400	100

Robar Elite Tactical Shotgun

Features a number of special options: Robar choke with forcing cone; modified bolt; Pachmayr pad; etc.

NIB	Exc.	V.G.	Good	Fair	Poor
1700	1350	1000	880	600	300

Robar MK I Tactical Rifle

Built on Remington Model 700 action, with 24" heavy factory barrel. Chambered for .308 or .223 cartridge. Fitted with gray Choate Ultimate sniper stock, Robar bipod and adjustable trigger. Roguard/MP3 finish.

NIB	Exc.	V.G.	Good	Fair	Poor
3400	2900	2250	1600	900	300

Robar MK II Tactical Rifle

As above, chambered for .308 cartridge only. Special trigger job and special hand finish of internal parts and chamber.

NIB	Exc.	V.G.	Good	Fair	Poor
3400	2900	2250	1600	900	300

ROBBINS & LAWRENCE

Windsor, Vermont

Pepperbox (Antique)

A .28- or .31-caliber percussion 5 barrel pistol, with barrel groups measuring 3.5" or 4.5" in length. Ring trigger, blued iron frame with simple scroll engraving. Browned barrels are marked "Robbins & Lawrence Co. Windsor, VT. Patent. 1849". Barrel groups for this pistol were made in two types: fluted in both calibers; ribbed in .31-caliber only. Approximately 7,000 made between 1851 and 1854.

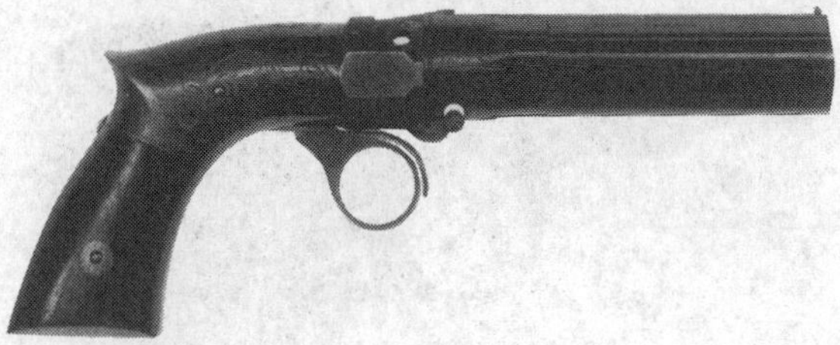

Exc.	Fine	V.G.	Good	Fair	Poor
2700	2200	1500	800	400	280

ROBERTS DEFENSE

Oshkosh, Wisconsin

This manufacturer of 1911-type semi-automatic pistols started production in 2013. All models are chambered in .45 ACP or 9mm and are hand fitted throughout the entire assembly process.

Operator Series

Offered in full- or Commander-size, with forged steel frame and true Picatinny rail. Dark Ops model has black nitride frame and slide. Desert Ops model has Flat Dark Earth Ceracote frame and black nitride slide. Note: Add $200 for 9mm if VG or better condition.

NIB	Exc.	V.G.	Good	Fair	Poor
2000	1650	1250	1000	400	200

Recon Series

In full-size Commander or Officer frame sizes, with 3.5", 4.25" or 5" barrel lengths. Models have a lightweight alloy frame, black finish and fiber optic front sights. Note: Add $200 for 9mm if VG or better condition.

NIB	Exc.	V.G.	Good	Fair	Poor
2000	1650	1250	1000	400	200

Super Grade Custom Series

These models come in all three frame sizes. Choice of all stainless or stainless frame, with black nitride slide. Grips are checkered wood. All components are of match-grade quality. Note: Add $200 for 9mm if VG or better condition.

NIB	Exc.	V.G.	Good	Fair	Poor
2200	1800	1500	1200	300	250

ROBERTSON
Philadelphia, Pennsylvania

Pocket Pistol (Antique)

A .41-caliber single-shot percussion derringer. Barrels ranging in length from 3" to 4.5". Barrel marked "Robertson, Phila.".

Exc.	Fine	V.G.	Good	Fair	Poor
2000	1650	1070	500	200	140

ROBINSON ARMAMENT CO.
Salt Lake City, Utah

Super VEPR

Semi-automatic rifle made in Russia. Chambered for .308, .223 or 7.62x39mm cartridge. Uses an RPK-type receiver. Chrome lined 21.65" barrel. Walnut thumbhole stock. Black oxide finish. Weight about 8.5 lbs.

NIB	Exc.	V.G.	Good	Fair	Poor
1200	800	680	500	400	200

M-96 Expeditonary Rifle

Chambered for .223 or 7.62x39mm cartridge. Can use AK or AR magazines. Quick-change barrel. Adjustable gas-operating system. Can interchange calibers without tools. Built in U.S.A.

NIB	Exc.	V.G.	Good	Fair	Poor
1750	1400	1100	800	580	300

M-96 Carbine

As above, with shorter barrel.

NIB	Exc.	V.G.	Good	Fair	Poor
1750	1400	1100	800	580	300

M-96 Top Fed

Same specifications as rifle, but magazine is fitted to top of receiver.

NIB	Exc.	V.G.	Good	Fair	Poor
1900	1550	1180	900	620	350

XRC-L

AR-type semi-auto rifle which can be ordered with multiple options. The light frame XRC-L is available in calibers such as 5.56, .300 Blk, 7.62x39, 6.8 SPC, .224 Valk, and 6.5 Gren. Available in the following variations: Competition ($300 premium); Standard exposed gas block; Standard buried gas block; Mini buried gas block; Micro. Values are for base models.

NIB	Exc.	V.G.	Good	Fair	Poor
1500	1200	1000	—	—	—

XCR-M

Like above with medium frame for calibers such as .308 Win, .243 Win, .260 Rem, and 6.5 CM. Same variations available as for XCR-L. Values are for base models.

NIB	Exc.	V.G.	Good	Fair	Poor
2400	2200	1800	—	—	—

ROBINSON, ORVIL
See—ADIRONDACK ARMS COMPANY

ROBINSON, S.C.
Richmond, Virginia

From December, 1862 through March 1, 1863, S.C. Robinson produced copies of the Sharps carbine. These arms had an overall length of 38.5", with .52-caliber barrels 21.5" long. Lockplates were marked "S.C. ROBINSON/ARMS MANUFACTORY/ RICHMOND VA/1862" along with the serial number. Barrels were marked forward of the rear sight "S.C. ROBINSON/ARMS MANUFACTORY," as well as "RICHMOND VA/1862" to rear of the sight. Total number made estimated to be slightly more than 1,900.

In March, 1863, Robinson factory was taken over by Confederate States Government. Carbines produced after that date are only stamped with the serial number on their lockplates and "RICHMOND VA" on their barrels. Total number made in excess of 3,400.

Robinson Sharps (Antique)

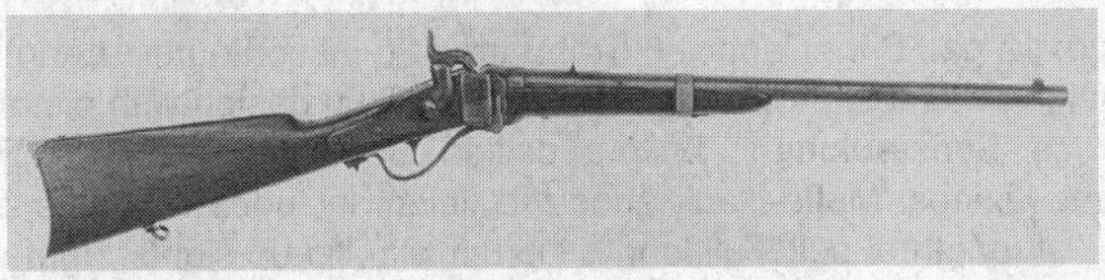

Exc.	Fine	V.G.	Good	Fair	Poor
37000	30000	19650	9300	5000	2000

Confederate Sharps (Antique)

Exc.	Fine	V.G.	Good	Fair	Poor
32000	27500	17870	8250	5000	2000

ROCK ISLAND ARMORY (TRADE NAME OF ARMSCOR)
Pahrump, Nevada

Arms Corp. of the Philippines manufactures firearms under both Armscor and Rock Island brand names. For Armscor models, see that listing.

M1911-A1 FSP

Full-size 1911-pattern pistol in 9mm, .38 Super or .45 ACP. Blue, Duracoat, stainless or two-tone finish, front and rear slide serrations, rubber grips, standard or night sights. In standard or high-capacity variations. FS Match Model has fiber optic front sight, bobbed hammer, checkered walnut grips. Also available in compact version (CSP), with 3.5" barrel. Note: Add $200 for FS Match; $100 for Meprolight night sights.

NIB	*Exc.*	*V.G.*	*Good*	*Fair*	*Poor*
420	380	320	300	250	220

TCM

1911-style series chambered for .22 TCM cartridge. Centerfire round based on necked-down 9mm case, with .223 bullet. In standard, mid-size or target variations. Introduced 2013. Also available chambered for similar .22 TCM9R cartridge.

NIB	*Exc.*	*V.G.*	*Good*	*Fair*	*Poor*
750	680	600	500	—	—

M2011-A1

High capacity or single-stack configurations in .45 ACP or high-capacity 9mm. Features include fiber optic front and adjustable white-dot rear sights, combat hammer, extended grip and thumb safeties and tactical accessory rail.

NIB	*Exc.*	*V.G.*	*Good*	*Fair*	*Poor*
600	520	450	400	300	220

MAPP

Single-/double-action design based on CZ-75 series. In 9mm with 16-shot magazine, 3.5" or 4" barrel, Picatinny rail, adjustable rear sight, ambidextrous safety. Also available chambered for .22 TCM9R cartridge.

NIB	*Exc.*	*V.G.*	*Good*	*Fair*	*Poor*
450	400	350	300	250	220

TCM Rifle

Bolt-action model made in 9mm or .22 TCM, with removable 17-shot box magazine, synthetic stock, skeletonized trigger, Parkerized finish and fixed or adjustable sights.

NIB	*Exc.*	*V.G.*	*Good*	*Fair*	*Poor*
750	680	500	400	300	200

Pro Match Ultra Big Rock

A 10mm model with 6" barrel, choice of single-stack or high-capacity magazine. Note: Add $150 for high-capacity model. Introduced in 2015.

NIB	*Exc.*	*V.G.*	*Good*	*Fair*	*Poor*
1000	850	720	500	300	200

VRBP-100

Gauge: 12 ga., 3 in. Capacity: 5+1. Barrel: 20 in. contoured. Length: 32 in. Weight: 7.94 lbs. Stock: Black polymer bullpup design with pistol grip. Features: Semi-automatic bullpup design. Compatible with all VR Series magazines. Matte-black anodized finish. Includes rubber spacers to adjust length of pull. Full length top rail with flip-up sights, right-sided Picatinny accessory rail. Ships with three interchangeable chokes.

NIB	*Exc.*	*V.G.*	*Good*	*Fair*	*Poor*
660	—	—	—	—	—

VRPA-40

Gauge: 12 ga., 3 in. Capacity: 5+1. Barrel: 20 in., contoured. Length: 55.11 in. Weight: 6.9 lbs. Stock: Black synthetic. Features: The VRPA40 marks the more affordable pump action addition to the VR family of shotguns. Magazine fed, aluminum heat shield, fiber-optic front sight, adjustable rear sight, Picatinny rail. Marine black anodized, compatible with VR series 9-round magazines. Mobil chokes.

NIB	*Exc.*	*V.G.*	*Good*	*Fair*	*Poor*
340	—	—	—	—	—

VR-82

Gauge: 20 ga. 3 in. Barrel: 18 in. contoured. Length: 38 in. Weight: 7.5 lbs. Stock: Black polymer thumbhole style. Features: The semi-automatic VR82 is the little brother of the VR80. Built of 7075 T6 aluminum for lighter weight. Magazine fed with 5+1 capacity but also accepts VR-series 10- and 20-round mags. Ambidextrous controls, flip-up sights, barrel shroud. Forend accepts most aftermarket accessories. Compatible with most buffer tube stocks and pistol grips. Black anodized finish. Mobil choke.

NIB	*Exc.*	*V.G.*	*Good*	*Fair*	*Poor*
640	—	—	—	—	—

VRF-14

Gauge: 12 ga. Barrel: 14 in. Length: 26 in. Weight: 6.6 lbs. Stock: Black polymer with full-top forend and sling adapter rear. Features: Semi-automatic short-barreled firearm in 12-ga. Pistol grip style designed to be fired from the hip. Built with a 7075 aluminum receiver, Bufferbolt system, and full-length top Picatinny rail. Flip-up front and rear sights. Five-round magazine included, but also compatible with VR-Series 9 and 19-round mags.

NIB	*Exc.*	*V.G.*	*Good*	*Fair*	*Poor*
520	—	—	—	—	—

VRPF-14

Gauges: 12 ga. Barrel: 14.1". Stock: Black synthetic with F-Grip. Features: Handheld pump-action defense shotgun. Like other VR series, is magazine-fed, and mags are interchangeable. Bead front sight. Overall length of 26.1". Includes sling adapter and forend strap. Chambered for 2.75" or 3" loads.

NIB	*Exc.*	*V.G.*	*Good*	*Fair*	*Poor*
400	340	290	—	—	—

PF14

Gauges: 12 ga. Barrel: 14.1". Stock: Black synthetic with F-Grip. Features: Handheld pump-action defense shotgun with five-round capacity. Bead front sight. Overall length of 26.1". Includes sling adapter and forend strap. Chambered for 2.75" or 3" loads.

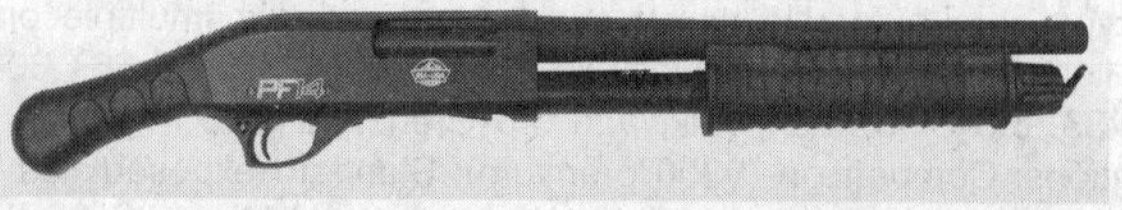

NIB	*Exc.*	*V.G.*	*Good*	*Fair*	*Poor*
320	280	200	—	—	—

ALL GENERATION SHOTGUN SERIES

Gauge: 12 ga. 3 in., 20 ga. 3 in., .410 bore 3 in. Barrel: 18.5, 26, 28 in. smoothbore contoured. Length: 41.0–48.2 in. Weight: 7.10–8.82 lbs. Stock: Black polymer with LOP spacers and adjustable cheek rest for customized fit. Features: Pump-action shotgun designed to accommodate a wide range of ages and physical sizes of shooters. The All Generation Series includes multiple models designed to customize the fit. Comes packaged with multiple stock spacers and an adjustable comb and ergonomic forend. Lightweight aluminum receiver with anodized finish. Magazine tube capacity 5+1 rounds in all chamberings. Bead front sight. Black rubber recoil pad. Interchangeable chokes (F, M, IM) except 18.5-inch barreled option, which has a Slug Choke.

NIB	Exc.	V.G.	Good	Fair	Poor
220	—	—	—	—	—

ROCK RIVER ARMS, INC.
Colona, Illinois

Manufacturer of AR-style rifles and carbines, and a series of 1911-style pistols. SEE POLITICAL PANIC PRICING.

PISTOLS

Elite Commando

Built on a National Match frame, with 4" National Match slide with double serrations and lowered ejection port (5" barrel optional). Front strap is 30 lpi. Night sights standard. Aluminum trigger and many more custom features. Checkered Cocobolo grips. Guaranteed 2.5" groups at 50 yards. Chambered for .45 ACP cartridge.

NIB	Exc.	V.G.	Good	Fair	Poor
1720	1300	950	780	500	300

Standard Match

Many of the same features as above model, without night sights. Also chambered for .45 ACP cartridge.

NIB	Exc.	V.G.	Good	Fair	Poor
1020	750	600	450	300	200

National Match Hardball

Similar features as above models, with adjustable rear Bomar sight and dovetail front. Chambered for .45 ACP cartridge.

NIB	Exc.	V.G.	Good	Fair	Poor
2200	1900	1500	1000	500	300

Bullseye Wadcutter

Features Rock River slide scope mount. Guaranteed to shoot 1.5" groups at 50 yards. Chambered for .45 ACP.

NIB	Exc.	V.G.	Good	Fair	Poor
2200	1900	1500	1000	520	320

Basic Limited Match

Similar to Bullseye Wadcutter, with Bomar adjustable rear sight and dovetail front. Chambered for .45 ACP. Previously offered in .38 Super, 9mm, .40 S&W

NIB	Exc.	V.G.	Good	Fair	Poor
1700	1300	950	750	520	320

Limited Match

Match pistol comes standard with many custom features. Guaranteed to shoot 1.5" groups at 50 yards. Chambered for .45 ACP. Previously offered in .38 Super, 9mm, .40 S&W.

NIB	Exc.	V.G.	Good	Fair	Poor
3200	2800	2000	1500	850	400

Hi-Cap Basic Limited

Model gives customer a choice of STI, SVI, Para-Ordnance or Entreprise frames. Many special features. Chambered for .45 ACP. Note: Add $200 for Para-Ordnance or Entreprise frames.

NIB	Exc.	V.G.	Good	Fair	Poor
1900	1500	1200	800	580	300

Ultimate Match Achiever

An IPSC-style pistol, with scope and three port muzzle compensator. Many special features. Chambered for .38 Super cartridge.

NIB	Exc.	V.G.	Good	Fair	Poor
2250	1750	1150	800	580	350

Match Master Steel

Bianchi-style pistol, with scope and three port muzzle brake. Chambered for .38 Super Cartridge.

NIB	Exc.	V.G.	Good	Fair	Poor
2350	1850	1200	850	600	380

Basic Carry

Introduced in 2005. This .45 ACP model features 5" match barrel, checkered front strap, lowered and flared ejection port, Novak rear sight, dehorned for carry and rosewood grips. Many other special features.

NIB	Exc.	V.G.	Good	Fair	Poor
1520	1150	820	680	500	300

Pro Carry

Similar to Basic Carry, with 4.25", 5" or 6" barrel. Choice of Heinie or Novak tritium sights and polished finish; guaranteed to shoot 2.5" group at 50 yards with select ammunition. Other options available.

NIB	Exc.	V.G.	Good	Fair	Poor
1800	1400	1100	680	500	250

Tactical Pistol

This .45 ACP pistol fitted with a 5" slide, with front serrations and match-grade barrel. Heine or Novak rear sight, checkered front strap, tactical mag catch and safety. Dehorned for carry. Rosewood grips. Introduced in 2005. Note: Add $200 for Black "T" finish.

NIB	Exc.	V.G.	Good	Fair	Poor
1920	1450	1200	800	580	300

Limited Police Competition 9mm

9mm model features 5" slide, with double serrations. Three position rear sight and dovetail front. Checkered front strap. Deluxe blued finish and grips. Many other special features. Introduced in 2005. Note: Add $200 for Black "T" finish.

NIB	Exc.	V.G.	Good	Fair	Poor
2310	1750	1150	800	580	350

Unlimited Police Competition 9mm

Similar to above, with additional special features such as 6" slide. Introduced in 2005. Note: Add $200 for Black "T" finish.

NIB	Exc.	V.G.	Good	Fair	Poor
2310	1750	1150	800	580	350

1911 Poly

Polymer-frame version of full-size 1911 pistol, with steel slide, Parkerized finish, Commander-style hammer, skeletonized trigger, fixed sights. Includes two magazines and polymer holster.

NIB	Exc.	V.G.	Good	Fair	Poor
820	720	500	400	300	200

RIFLES

CAR A2

These are AR-15-style rifles. Chambered for .223 cartridge. Fitted with 16" barrel, with CAR handguards. Two stage trigger. Choice of A2 or non-collapsible buttstock and black or green furniture. Weight about 7 lbs. Note: Add $25 for non-collapsible buttstock.

NIB	Exc.	V.G.	Good	Fair	Poor
930	790	670	570	480	410

CAR A2M

Same as above, with mid-length handguard. Note: Add $25 for non-collapsible buttstock.

NIB	Exc.	V.G.	Good	Fair	Poor
930	790	670	570	480	410

CAR A4

Similar to models above, with flattop receiver and CAR handguard. Note: Add $25 for non-collapsible buttstock.

NIB	Exc.	V.G.	Good	Fair	Poor
930	790	670	570	480	410

CAR A4M

Flattop receiver with mid-length handguard. Note: Add $25 for non-collapsible buttstock.

NIB	Exc.	V.G.	Good	Fair	Poor
850	720	610	520	440	380

Standard A2

AR-15-style rifle fitted with 20" barrel. Chambered for .223 cartridge. Two-stage trigger. Fixed stock and full-length handguard. Weight about 8.2 lbs.

NIB	Exc.	V.G.	Good	Fair	Poor
850	720	610	520	440	380

National Match A2

Features .22 Wylde chamber, with 20" Wilson air-gauged match stainless steel barrel. A2 receiver. Two-stage trigger. Free-float high temp thermo mold handguard. Match sights. Weight about 9.7 lbs.

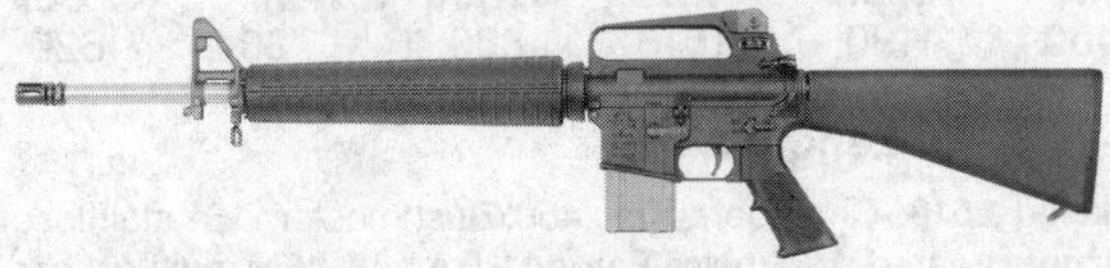

NIB	Exc.	V.G.	Good	Fair	Poor
1150	980	830	710	600	510

Standard A4 Flattop

Same as Standard A2, with flattop receiver.

NIB	Exc.	V.G.	Good	Fair	Poor
950	810	690	580	500	420

Varmint Rifle

Flattop model fitted with 24" stainless steel barrel, without sights. Chambered for .223 cartridge. Fixed stock. Two-stage trigger. Weight about 9.5 lbs.

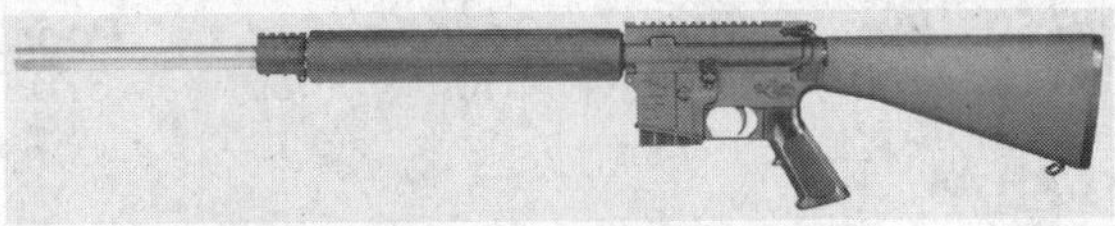

NIB	Exc.	V.G.	Good	Fair	Poor
1280	1080	920	780	670	570

Varmint EOP (Elevated Optical Platform)

Chambered for .223 Wylde. Fitted with Wilson air-gauged bull stainless steel barrel. Choice of 16", 18", 20" and 24" barrel lengths. Free-float aluminum handguard. National Match two-stage trigger. Weight about: 8.2 lbs with 16" barrel; 10 lbs with 24" barrel. Note: Add $10 for each barrel length over 16".

NIB	Exc.	V.G.	Good	Fair	Poor
1150	980	830	710	600	510

Advanced Tactical Hunter

Chambered for 5.56/.223 Rem. Carbine-style adjustable stock, 18" cryogenically treated stainless steel barrel with tactical muzzle brake. Half-quad free-floating mid-length handguard, winter-designed triggerguard, two-stage trigger. Numerous options. Introduced in 2011.

NIB	Exc.	V.G.	Good	Fair	Poor
1050	890	760	650	550	470

NM A2-DCM Legal

Fitted with 20" stainless steel barrel. National Match sleeve and specially selected upper and lower to ensure tight fit. Special high temp handguards. Two-stage trigger. National Match sights. Weight about 9 lbs.

NIB	Exc.	V.G.	Good	Fair	Poor
1150	980	830	710	600	510

Government Model

Chambered for .223 cartridge. Fitted with 16" Wilson chrome barrel with A2 flash hider. National Match two-stage trigger. A4 upper receiver. Flip-up rear sight. EOTech M951 light system. Surefire M73 Quad Rail handguard, and 6 position tactical CAR stock. Weight about 8.2 lbs.

NIB	Exc.	V.G.	Good	Fair	Poor
2100	1790	1520	1290	1100	930

Tactical CAR A4

.223-caliber rifle has 16" Wilson chrome barrel, with A2 flash hider. A4 upper receiver, with detachable carry handle. Two-stage National Match trigger. R-4 handguard. Six-position tactical CAR stock. Weight about 7.5 lbs.

NIB	Exc.	V.G.	Good	Fair	Poor
830	700	600	510	430	370

Elite CAR A4

As above, with mid-length handguard. Weight about 7.7 lbs.

NIB	Exc.	V.G.	Good	Fair	Poor
830	700	600	510	430	370

Tactical CAR UTE (Universal Tactical Entry) 2

.223-caliber rifle has 16" Wilson chrome barrel, with A2 flash hider. R-2 handguard. Upper receiver UTE2, with standard A4 rail height. Two-stage trigger and 6 position CAR tactical stock. Weight about 7.5 lbs.

NIB	Exc.	V.G.	Good	Fair	Poor
900	770	650	550	470	400

Elite CAR UTE 2

As above, with mid-length handguard. Weight about 7.7 lbs.

NIB	Exc.	V.G.	Good	Fair	Poor
930	790	670	570	480	410

Entry Tactical

.223 model features 16" Wilson chrome barrel, with R-4 profile. A4 upper receiver, with detachable carry handle. National Match two-stage trigger. Six-position tactical CAR stock. R-4 handguard. Weight about 7.5 lbs

NIB	Exc.	V.G.	Good	Fair	Poor
830	700	600	510	430	370

TASC Rifle

Features 16" Wilson chrome barrel, with A2 flash hider. A2 upper receiver, with windage and elevation rear sight. R-4 handguard. A2 buttstock. Weight about 7.5 lbs.

NIB	Exc.	V.G.	Good	Fair	Poor
850	720	610	520	440	380

Texas Rifle

In 5.56 NATO or .223 Rem. Wylde chamber. Rock River Texas XL free-float handguard in Magpul FDE, Barret Bronze or Burnt Bronze finish. Two-stage trigger, winter triggerguard, directionally tuned and ported muzzle brake. Has a mid-length gas system and low-profile gas block. Handguard has a full-length rail with 2.5" rail at 3, 6 and 9 o'clock. A2 or CAR stock, Hogue pistol grip. Introduced in 2015.

NIB	Exc.	V.G.	Good	Fair	Poor
1500	1280	1080	920	780	670

LAR SERIES

Calibers: .223/5.56, .223 Wylde chamber. Rifles and carbines available with a wide range of options, including left-hand versions. Individual nameplates include All Terrain Hunter (ATH), Coyote Carbine, Fred Eichler Series, NM A4, Operator ETR, Predator Pursuit, RRage, X-Series, and others. SEE POLITICAL PANIC PRICING.

NIB	Exc.	V.G.	Good	Fair	Poor
850	710	590	450	—	—

LAR-15 Lightweight

Features a chrome moly 16" lightweight barrel, with carbon fiber handguard in several variants, 6-position tactical stock, low-profile gas block. In 5.56 NATO/.223. Weight 5.6 to 6 lbs. Introduced in 2015.

NIB	Exc.	V.G.	Good	Fair	Poor
1200	1020	870	740	630	530

LAR-15 X-1 Rifle

Featuring .223 Wylde chamber, a hybrid chamber designed to better accept both 5.56 NATO and .223 Rem. ammo. Forged upper and lower receivers, 18" fluted stainless barrel with Rock River Beast or Hunter muzzle brake and low-profile gas block are other features. Buttstock is RRA A2 or CAR, with Hogue Rubber pistol grip and RRA's TRO-XL extended-length free-float rail handguard. The X-1 Rifle is available in other variations and chamberings, including 6.5 SPCII, .458 Socom and 7.62 NATO.

LAR-15 X-1 Rifle .223 Wylde

NIB	Exc.	V.G.	Good	Fair	Poor
1200	1020	870	740	630	530

LAR-15 X-1 6.8 SPCII, .300 AAC, .458 Socom

NIB	Exc.	V.G.	Good	Fair	Poor
1200	1020	870	740	630	530

LAR-15 X-1 7.62 NATO

NIB	Exc.	V.G.	Good	Fair	Poor
1400	1190	1010	860	730	620

LAR 47 X-1

Chambered for 7.62x39mm cartridge. This model has an 18" fluted barrel, muzzle brake, extended free-floating rail, Operator A2 or CAR stock, with Hogue pistol grip. Introduced in 2015.

NIB	Exc.	V.G.	Good	Fair	Poor
1400	1190	1010	860	730	620

LAR-15M Mid-Length A4

Introduced 2019. Chambered in .450 Bushmaster, 16" stainless steel barrel, cryo treated, 1:24 twist. Forged RRA LAR-15M multi-caliber lower receiver and A4 upper receiver. 13" lightweight M-LOK free float rail.

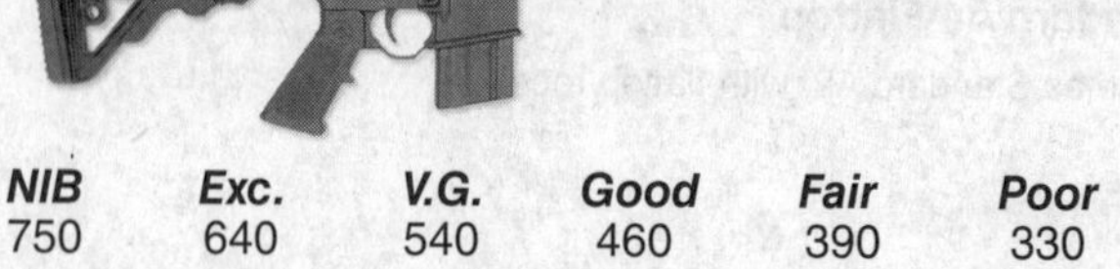

NIB	Exc.	V.G.	Good	Fair	Poor
750	640	540	460	390	330

LAR-BT6 .338 Lapua Magnum

Chambering added in 2022. Barrel: 24" black nitride stainless steel, 1:10" twist, four-port brake. RRA Ultra Match two-stage trigger. Quick takedown design. Weight: 13.5 lbs. Length: 48". Introduced 2020. SEE POLITICAL PANIC PRICING.

NIB	*Exc.*	*V.G.*	*Good*	*Fair*	*Poor*
5300	5000	4680	4050	3590	—

Precision Rifle LAR-BT3

Similar to Enhanced Mid-Length A4. Barrel: 18 in. Weight: 8.5 lbs. Length: 36.5 to 39 in. Introduced 2020.

NIB	*Exc.*	*V.G.*	*Good*	*Fair*	*Poor*
1450	1350	1150	—	—	—

Varmint Rifle LAR-BT3

Caliber: .308 Win. Barrel: 20", 1:10" twist, fluted-stainless steel heavy, cryogenically treated. Stock: RRA six-position NSP-2 CAR. Grip: Hogue Rubber. Sights: None, optics-ready full-length top rail. Weight: 9.8 lbs. Trigger: RRA Two Stage. Length: 37" to 39.75". Features: RRA lightweight free-float rail, 17" extended, M-LOK compatible. Introduced 2020. SEE POLITICAL PANIC PRICING.

NIB	*Exc.*	*V.G.*	*Good*	*Fair*	*Poor*
1700	1600	1400	1150	980	—

LAR-BT3 X-Series X-1 Rifle

Caliber: .308 Win. Barrel: 18" or 20". Weight: 8.5-9.7 lbs. Length: 36.5" to 41". Introduced 2022. SEE POLITICAL PANIC PRICING.

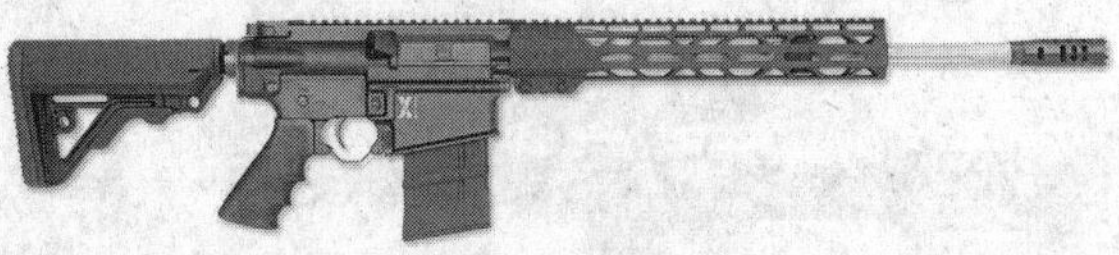

NIB	*Exc.*	*V.G.*	*Good*	*Fair*	*Poor*
1940	—	—	—	—	—

Operator ETR LAR-BT3 .308 Carbine

Caliber: .308 Win. Barrel: 16" chrome-lined, 1:10" twist. Weight: 8.2 lbs. Length: 34.5" retracted. Stock: RRA six-Position NSP-2 CAR Stock. Hogue Beavertail Grip. Trigger: RRA Two-Stage Ultra Match Trigger. Introduced 2022. SEE POLITICAL PANIC PRICING.

NIB	*Exc.*	*V.G.*	*Good*	*Fair*	*Poor*
1250	—	—	—	—	—

LAR-15 RRAGE CARBINE

Introduced 2018. 5.56mm semi-auto with monolithic-style upper receiver/handguard design. Extruded 6061T aluminum flattop upper receiver and free-float handguard. Full-length MS1913 top rail, M-LOK rail configuration. Chrome moly barrel, A2 flash suppressor, carbine-length gas system with a low-profile gas block, single-stage trigger, A2 grip, and the RRA six-position tactical carbine buttstock. Specialized colors +$250. Introduced 2019: 3G Model with 15" RRAGE 3G Handguard.

RRAGE 16" Barrel

1:9 twist, 6.25 lbs., 36" OAL, RRA single-stage trigger. Other models include Tac-Black Carbine DS1850T, Patriotic Carbine DS1850P, and Alpine Carbine DS1850A.

NIB	*Exc.*	*V.G.*	*Good*	*Fair*	*Poor*
700	600	510	430	370	310

RRAGE 3G, 16" Barrel

1:9 twist, 6.5 lbs., 36" OAL, RRA single-stage trigger.

NIB	*Exc.*	*V.G.*	*Good*	*Fair*	*Poor*
700	600	510	430	370	310

R9 COMPETITION BT-9 SERIES

Introduced 2019. Chambered in 9x19mm. New series of semi-autos designed to work with Glock-style magazines. RRA billet aluminum lower receiver with a Glock-compatible flared magazine well. Winter-style triggerguard, latest extruded aluminum upper receiver. Pistols are standard with RRA lightweight free-float M-LOK-compatible handguards.

BT91700 9mm Carbine

Two-stage trigger, 16" chrome moly barrel, RRAGE 3G handguard. RRA 6-position Operator CAR buttstock and Hogue overmolded pistol grip.

NIB	*Exc.*	*V.G.*	*Good*	*Fair*	*Poor*
1400	1190	1010	860	730	620

BT92133 9mm Pistol

7-inch moly barrel with 1/2-36 threads, SB Tactical SBA3 pistol brace, RRA overmolded A2 pistol grip, two-stage trigger.

NIB	*Exc.*	*V.G.*	*Good*	*Fair*	*Poor*
1300	1110	940	800	680	580

BT92142 9mm Pistol

Same configuration as the BT92133, but with a chrome-lined 10.5" barrel plus a 7.25" Lightweight Free-Float handguard.

NIB	Exc.	V.G.	Good	Fair	Poor
1300	1110	940	800	680	580

LAR-22 Rifles

Introduced 2019. .22 LR chamberings in Tactical Carbine, Mid A4, NM A4 CMP Trainer, and Pistol lines.

LAR-22 Tactical Carbine

Tactical Carbine comes with forged-aluminum upper and lower receivers or polymer receiver set. Free-floated, chrome-moly barrel, lightweight, M-Lok-compatible handguard. 16" barrel with 1:16-inch twist, 1/2-28 TPI threaded muzzle, A2 flash hider.

Model 22L1264A

NIB	Exc.	V.G.	Good	Fair	Poor
670	570	480	410	350	300

Model 22L1264P

NIB	Exc.	V.G.	Good	Fair	Poor
580	490	420	360	300	260

LAR-22 Mid AR

More traditional AR-style rifle.

Model 22L1855A Aluminum Receiver

NIB	Exc.	V.G.	Good	Fair	Poor
560	480	410	340	290	250

Model 22L1855P Polymer Receiver

NIB	Exc.	V.G.	Good	Fair	Poor
470	400	340	290	240	210

LAR-22 NM A4 CMP Trainer

Serves as a practice gun for CMP National Match-type competition.

Model 22L1289

NIB	Exc.	V.G.	Good	Fair	Poor
930	790	670	570	490	410

Model 22L2132A Aluminum Receiver

NIB	Exc.	V.G.	Good	Fair	Poor
700	590	500	430	360	310

Model 22L2132P Polymer Receiver

NIB	Exc.	V.G.	Good	Fair	Poor
610	510	440	370	320	270

Enhanced Mid-Length A4 BT-3

Caliber: .308/7.62x51mm. Capacity: 20. Barrel: 16 in., 1:10 twist, 5/8-24 tpi muzzle threads, fluted stainless steel heavy, cryogenically treated, A2 flash hider. Upper/Lower Receivers: RRA BT-3 Billet A4 Upper; RRA BT-3 Billet lower. Stock: RRA 6-position Operator CAR. Sights: None, optics-ready full-length top rail. Weight: 8.2 lbs. Trigger: RRA Two-Stage. Length: 35 to 37.5 in. Features: Low-profile gas block, mid-length gas system, RRA lightweight free-float rail, 13-in. extended, M-LOK compatible. Introduced 2020.

NIB	Exc.	V.G.	Good	Fair	Poor
1300	1110	940	800	680	580

RBG

Calibers: .308 Win., 7.62mm, 6.5 Creedmoor. Capacity: 6. Barrel: 20, 22, 24 in., stainless steel, fluted. Stock: KRG chassis. Sights: 20 MOA rail. Weight: 10 to 10.5 lbs. Features: Sub-MOA accuracy, oversized bolt handle, Trigger Tech trigger.

NIB	Exc.	V.G.	Good	Fair	Poor
4250	3600	3000	—	—	—

20-Inch Select Target Rifle BT-3

Similar to Enhanced Mid-Length A4. Barrel: 20 in. Weight: 8.6 lbs. Length: 42 in. Stock: Magpul Gen3 Precision Rifle. Hogue Grip. Introduced 2020.

NIB	Exc.	V.G.	Good	Fair	Poor
1800	1500	1300	—	—	—

ASCENDANT SERIES

Caliber: .223 Wylde, .350 Legend, .450 Bushmaster. Length: 38.125" (collapsed). Weight: 9.4 lbs. Barrel: 18" 416R fluted stainless steel, media-blasted, cryo-treated. Handguard: RRA 13" lightweight, M-LOK, full 12-o'clock Picatinny rail. Trigger: TriggerTech Diamond Single-Stage AR-15 trigger, adjustable from 1.5 to 4 lbs. of pull weight. Magpul PRS Lite stock, Hogue overmolded rubber grip, ambidextrous Radian Raptor charging handle. Also includes Vortex Viper HS 4-16X44mm riflescope or Vortex Strike Eagle 1-6X24mm optic. Introduced 2023. SEE POLITICAL PANIC PRICING.

AR1562.A .223 Wylde

NIB	Exc.	V.G.	Good	Fair	Poor
3000	—	—	—	—	—

350L1562.A .350 Legend

NIB	Exc.	V.G.	Good	Fair	Poor
2800	—	—	—	—	—

450B1562.A .450 Bushmaster

NIB	Exc.	V.G.	Good	Fair	Poor
2800	—	—	—	—	—

ROGERS & SPENCER
Utica, New York

Army Revolver (Antique)

.44-caliber 6-shot percussion revolver, with 7.5" octagonal barrel. Barrel marked "Rogers & Spencer/Utica, N.Y." Blued case-hardened hammer, with walnut grips bearing inspector's mark "RPB". Approximately 5,800 made between 1863 and 1865.

Courtesy Milwaukee Public Museum, Milwaukee, Wisconsin

Exc.	Fine	V.G.	Good	Fair	Poor
4500	2500	1750	1000	550	380

ROGUE RIFLE COMPANY
Prospect, Oregon

See—KEYSTONE

ROGUE RIVER RIFLEWORKS
Paso Robles, California

Boxlock Double Rifle

These rifles are custom fitted and available in any barrel length or caliber from .22 Hornet to .577 NE. Anson & Deeley boxlocks. Choice of finish, forend, engraving, wood and various other options. Each rifle should be appraised individually before a sale. Prices listed are for basic rifle, with no extras.

NIB	Exc.	V.G.	Good	Fair	Poor
17500	15000	12000	9500	5000	900

Sidelock Double Rifle

These rifles are custom fitted and available in any barrel length or caliber from .22 Hornet to .577 NE. Holland & Holland pattern sidelocks. Choice of finish, forend, engraving, wood and various other options. Each rifle should be appraised individually before a sale. Prices listed are for basic rifle, with no extras.

NIB	Exc.	V.G.	Good	Fair	Poor
50000	42500	30000	17000	7500	900

ROHM GMBH
Sonthein/Brenz, Germany

This company produced a variety of small handguns that were imported into the United States prior to the Gun Control Act of 1968. These included several types of double-action and single-action revolvers, .25 semi-automatics and derringers. Most of these were marketed under the RG name. In early 1970s, the company established a manufacturing facility in Miami. Most of these same models were made there, until the company went out of business in 1986. These firearms were low-priced, utility models and there is little collector's interest. Values would be in the $100 to $125 range, or less. Also see R.G. Industries.

ROHRBAUGH
Bayport, New York

The Rohrbaugh company closed its doors in 2014. Remington purchased the company later that year and in 2015 introduced the Remington RM380, a pistol based on the Rohrbaugh 380/380S design.

Rohrbaugh

Introduced in 2004. A very small pistol made in 9mm or .380 ACP. Offered with-/without sights. Magazine capacity 6 rounds. Barrel length 2.9"; height 3.7"; length 5.2"; slide width .812"; weight about 12.8 oz. Values shown are for basic model.

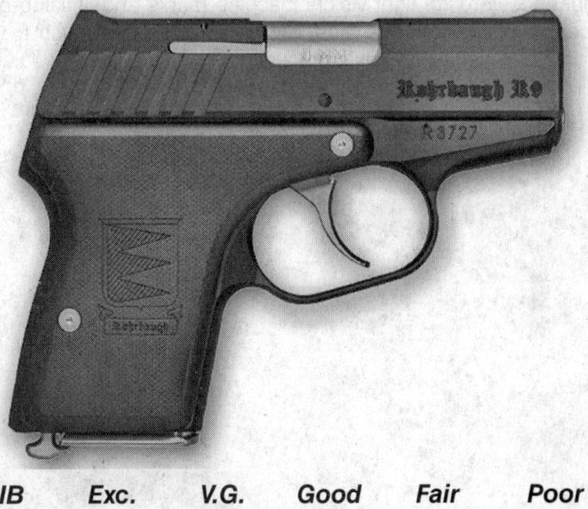

NIB	Exc.	V.G.	Good	Fair	Poor
1000	850	780	600	400	200

ROMARM
Bucharest, Romania

Carpati 74

This seven-shot blowback pistol in 7.65mm Browning (.32 ACP) caliber was official Romanian military and police sidearm from 1974 to 1992. Much like Hungarian FEG series of military pistols, Carpati M74 has a two-tone, dura aluminum frame and blue steel slide and other components. Model unique given its curved forward lower frame. Currently retained in inventory by Romanian army and still used by police on a limited scale. A large number were sold to German Democratic Republic in early 1980s for use by that country's various government sub-agencies. Majority of those entering the United States in mid 1990s were East German surplus. These are identified by the drilled lower left grip which retains East German style, inserted lanyard cord. Imported in limited numbers, all appear to have been mistakenly stamped by importer with "FEG Hungary" due to their similar appearance to Hungarian RK 59, R 61 and PA 63. Few to none have been imported with the country of origin being Romania. They are among the scarcest of post-communist era imported semi-automatic pistols.

NIB	Exc.	V.G.	Good	Fair	Poor
—	500	450	300	280	150

Carpati 95

In 1995, ROMARM state factory introduced a commercial copy of older Carpati 74. It was Romania's intention to enter the post Eastern Bloc surplus boom with a new pistol. Carpati 95 is a 7-shot semi-automatic pistol in Walther PPK class. Chambered for .380 ACP. An updated version of Mdl 74 which included an ambidextrous safety on the slide, black plastic thumbrest grips and a finger grip magazine floorplate. Primarily imported by Century International, it is believed to have entered the U.S. in limited quantities between 1996 to 1999. They came in a pasteboard box, with cleaning brush and spare magazine. Marked ROMARM Carpati 95 and Cugir factory diamond on left slide, its quality is somewhat less than its original ancestor with light visible machine marks and ill-fitting grips. A serviceable pistol none the less, its final finish leaves much to be desired. It is believed to be still in production, however, present sales have been limited to Europe. Not commonly encountered.

NIB	Exc.	V.G.	Good	Fair	Poor
300	280	250	200	180	150

ROMERWERKE
Suhl, Germany

Romer

A .22-caliber semi-automatic pistol, with 2.5" or 6.5" barrel and 7-shot magazine. Barrels are interchangeable and marked "Kal. .22 Long Rifle"; slide marked "Romerwerke Suhl". Blued, with plastic grips. Manufactured between 1924 and 1926.

NIB	Exc.	V.G.	Good	Fair	Poor
—	620	500	450	320	220

RONGE, J. B.
Liege, Belgium

Bulldog

A .32-, .380- or .45-caliber double-action revolver, with 3" barrel. Unmarked except for monogram "RF" on grips. Various trade names have been noted on these revolvers and are believed to have been applied by retailers. Manufactured from 1880 to 1910.

NIB	Exc.	V.G.	Good	Fair	Poor
—	250	150	100	80	50

ROSS RIFLE CO.
Quebec, Canada

Designed by Sir Charles Ross, this controversial straight-pull action rifle was made in a wide range of commercial and military variations from 1903 to 1917. In recent years, some models have become quite collectible. Models listed are a sampling of the many different variations. Note: Some models should not be fired before they are checked by a gunsmith familiar with the Ross design.

Mark I

Barrel length 28"; .303-caliber. "Harris Controlled Platform Magazine" can be depressed by external lever to facilitate loading.

Courtesy Buffalo Bill Historical Center, Cody, Wyoming

NIB	Exc.	V.G.	Good	Fair	Poor
—	1800	1500	1000	600	400

Mark I Carbine

As above, with 22" barrel.

NIB	Exc.	V.G.	Good	Fair	Poor
—	1600	1200	800	500	300

Mark II

As above, with modified rear sight.

NIB	Exc.	V.G.	Good	Fair	Poor
—	2000	1600	1100	650	400

Mark III (Military)

Introduced in 1910, with improved lockwork and stripper clip guides. Note: Mark III and Model 1910 (M10) rifles can be very dangerous to fire if bolt has been taken apart and incorrectly reassembled. DO NOT FIRE one of these rifles without having it examined by a gunsmith who is totally familiar with the Ross design.

Courtesy Buffalo Bill Historical Center, Cody, Wyoming

NIB	Exc.	V.G.	Good	Fair	Poor
—	1900	1550	1050	600	400

Mark III/M-10 Sporter Rifle

.280 Ross or .303-caliber straight-pull sporting rifle, with 24" barrel and open sights. Blued, with checkered walnut stock. Note: Mark III and Model 1910 (M10) rifles can be very dangerous to fire if bolt has been taken apart and incorrectly reassembled. DO NOT FIRE one of these rifles without having it examined by a gunsmith who is totally familiar with the Ross design.

Courtesy Buffalo Bill Historical Center, Cody, Wyoming

.280 Ross Caliber

NIB	Exc.	V.G.	Good	Fair	Poor
—	2000	1600	1100	600	400

.303 British Caliber

NIB	Exc.	V.G.	Good	Fair	Poor
—	1600	1250	850	400	300

ROSSI, AMADEO

See—LEOPOLDO, BRAZIL

Rossi handguns are manufactured under license by Taurus.

SHOTGUNS

Overland Shotgun

An exposed hammer sidelock 12-, 20-gauge or .410 bore double-barrel shotgun, with 26" or 28" barrels and double triggers. Manual extractors. Blued, with walnut stock. Discontinued in 1988.

NIB	Exc.	V.G.	Good	Fair	Poor
250	220	200	150	100	80

Squire Shotgun

A 12-, 20-gauge or .410 bore double-barrel shotgun, with 20", 26" or 28" barrels, double triggers and manual ejectors. Blued, with walnut stock.

NIB	Exc.	V.G.	Good	Fair	Poor
350	300	250	200	150	100

Field Grade Shotgun

Single-shot tip-open gun, with oil-finish hardwood stock, low profile hammer and pistol grip. No checkering. Offered in 12-, 20-gauge or .410 bore. Barrel length 28"; weight about; 5.25 lbs. 12- and 20-gauge; 4 lbs. .410 bore.

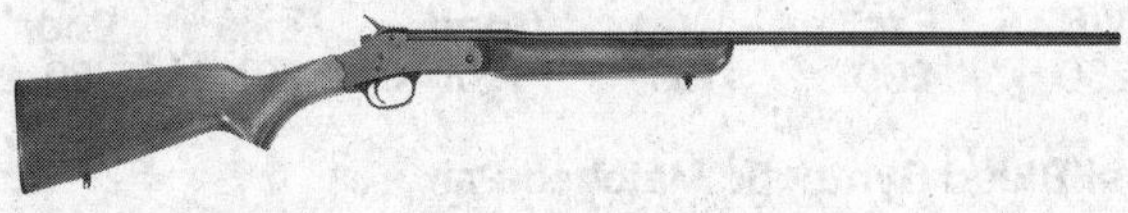

NIB	Exc.	V.G.	Good	Fair	Poor
120	80	50	20	—	10

Youth Model Shotgun

Same as above, with shorter length of pull and 22" barrel. Offered in 20-gauge and .410 bore only. Weight about: 5 lbs. 20-gauge; 3.75 lbs. .410 bore.

NIB	Exc.	V.G.	Good	Fair	Poor
120	80	50	20	—	10

Matched Pair Combo Guns

Model matches single-barrel shotgun, with .22 LR barrel. Offered in 12-/.22, 20-/.22 and .410/.22. Adjustable sights on rifle barrel. Blued finish.

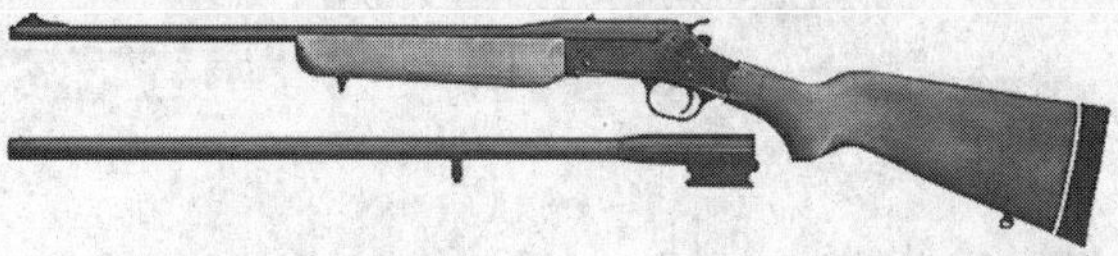

NIB	Exc.	V.G.	Good	Fair	Poor
160	120	100	60	50	20

Stainless Matched Pair Combo Guns

Similar to above, with stainless barrel/receiver. Introduced 2008.

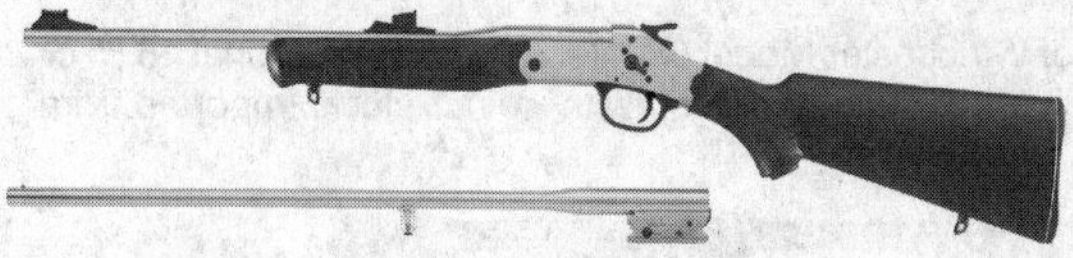

NIB	Exc.	V.G.	Good	Fair	Poor
200	160	120	100	80	50

Trifecta

Similar to Matched Pair, with black synthetic stock and blued barrel; includes easily interchangeable .243 Win. or .44 Magnum, .22 Long Rifle and 20-gauge barrels.

NIB	Exc.	V.G.	Good	Fair	Poor
300	250	200	150	100	80

Turkey Gun

Introduced in 2008. A specialized version of Roosi's 12-gauge single-shot shotgun. Features 3.5" chamber, fiber optic sights, drilled and tapped barrel, included scope mount base and removable Briley Extended Turkey Choke.

NIB	Exc.	V.G.	Good	Fair	Poor
200	160	120	100	80	50

Rossi Circuit Judge

Revolving shotgun chambered in .410 bore (2.5" or 3") .45 Colt. Based on Taurus Judge handgun. Features include 18.5" barrel; fiber optic front sight; 5-round cylinder; hardwood Monte Carlo stock.

NIB	Exc.	V.G.	Good	Fair	Poor
600	480	400	320	250	180

Tuffy Single Shot 410 Turkey

Gauge: .410 bore 3 in. Barrel: 26 in. Length: 41 in. Weight: 58.80 oz. Stock: Olive drab green polymer thumbhole-style with integral buttstock shell holders. Features: Part of Rossi's single-shot, break-action Tuffy family, the new 410 Turkey has an extended barrel length and gobbler-specific choke. Polymer receiver with steel frame structure. Matte black finish metalwork. Bead front sight. Picatinny top rail for easy optics mounting. Sling swivels. Black rubber buttpad. Transfer bar safety. Extended Extra Full Turkey choke.

NIB	Exc.	V.G.	Good	Fair	Poor
190	150	130	—	—	—

RIFLES

Model 62

Copy of Winchester Model 62 rifle. Round or octagonal 16.5" or 23" barrels. Blued or stainless steel; with walnut stock. Imported from 1988 to 1998.

NIB	Exc.	V.G.	Good	Fair	Poor
200	160	120	100	80	50

Model 59

As above, in .22 Magnum caliber.

NIB	Exc.	V.G.	Good	Fair	Poor
250	200	150	110	80	60

Model 92

Copy of Winchester Model 1892. Chambered for .357 Magnum, .44 Magnum, .45 Colt or .44-40. Barrels 16" or 20". Blued, with walnut stock. Engraved version of this model worth approximately 20 percent more than the values listed. Note: Add $75 for stainless steel version introduced in 1997.

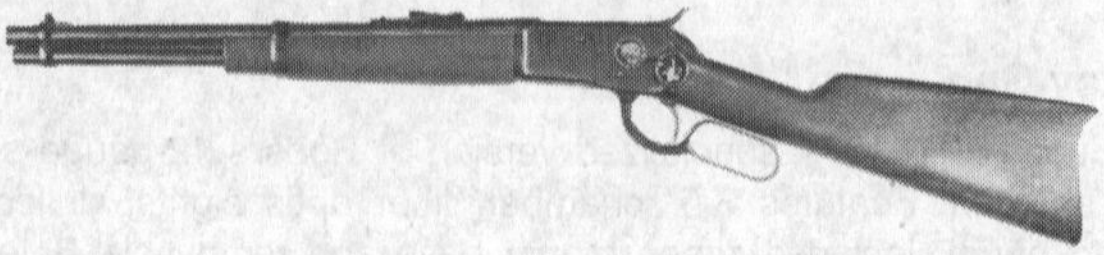

NIB	Exc.	V.G.	Good	Fair	Poor
480	350	300	220	180	100

Model 92 Rifle

Introduced in 1997. Fitted with 24" half-octagon barrel and brass blade front sight. Magazine capacity 13 rounds of .45 Colt. Weight about 6.8 lbs.

NIB	Exc.	V.G.	Good	Fair	Poor
500	380	320	250	200	120

Rossi Rio Grande

Variation of Model 92. Chambered for .45-70 plus .410-bore shotshell. Side ejection and hammer extension allow a scope to be mounted easily. Scope-mounting rail is atop the receiver. Barrel is 20", with adjustable rear open sight, bead front. Hardwood stock with recoil pad. Cross bolt safety.

NIB	Exc.	V.G.	Good	Fair	Poor
500	400	350	280	200	100

Model 92 Large Loop

Has 16" barrel. Chambered for .44 Magnum or .45 Colt cartridge. Weight about 5.5 lbs. Finish is blue. Introduced in 1997.

NIB	Exc.	V.G.	Good	Fair	Poor
480	350	300	220	180	100

Model 65

Similar to Model 92. Chambered for .44 Special or .44 Magnum cartridge. Barrel length 20". Blued, with walnut stock. Introduced in 1989.

NIB	Exc.	V.G.	Good	Fair	Poor
500	380	320	250	200	120

Single-Shot Rifle

Offered in a variety of configurations. Chambered for .22 LR, .22 Magnum, .357 Magnum, .44 Magnum, .45 Colt, .223 Rem., .243-calibers. Fitted with 23" barrel, wood stock and choice of matte blue or stainless steel finish. Weight varies from 4.75 lbs. to 6.25 lbs. depending on caliber. Note: Add $30 for stainless steel; $10 for .357 and .44; $30 for .223 or .243.

NIB	Exc.	V.G.	Good	Fair	Poor
220	180	120	100	80	50

Single Shot Rifle—Heavy Barrel

Chambered for .223, .243, .22-250. Fitted with 23" heavy barrel and plain wood stock. Matte blue finish. Weight about 7 lbs. Introduced in 2005.

NIB	Exc.	V.G.	Good	Fair	Poor
230	180	120	100	80	50

Muzzleloading Rifle

Rifle has .50-caliber bore. Fitted with 23" barrel. Hardwood stock, with recoil pad. Weight about 6.3 lbs. Introduced in 2003. Blue or stainless steel. Note: Add $35 for matte stainless steel finish.

NIB	Exc.	V.G.	Good	Fair	Poor
160	130	100	80	50	20

Muzzleloader Matched Pair

A .50-caliber muzzleloader, with an extra 20-gauge, .243 or .270 barrel. All matched pairs come with blued finish. Price listed for 20-gauge barrel. Note: Add $40 for .243; $150 for .270.

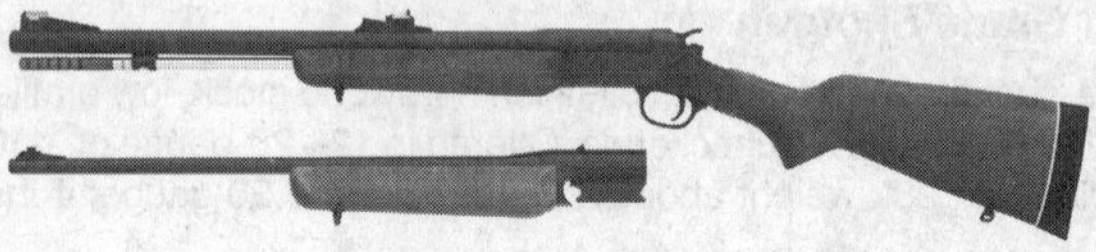

NIB	Exc.	V.G.	Good	Fair	Poor
250	200	150	100	80	50

Rossi Blued Synthetic Matched Pair

Single-shot combo outfit consisting of interchangeable rifle and shotgun barrels. Synthetic stock, blued barrel and receiver. Combinations include 12- or 20-gauge/.22LR, .22 WMR, .17 HMR, .223, .243, .270, .308, .30-06 and .410 bore/.22 LR or .410 bore/.17 HMR. Youth and full-size versions available.

NIB	Exc.	V.G.	Good	Fair	Poor
250	200	150	100	80	50

Rossi Stainless Synthetic Matched Pair

Single-shot combo outfit consisting of interchangeable rifle and shotgun barrels. Synthetic stock, stainless barrel and receiver. Combinations include 12- or 20-gauge/.22LR, .22 WMR, .17 HMR, .223, .243, .270, .308, .30-06 and .410 bore/.22 LR or .410 bore/.17 HMR. Youth and full-size versions available.

NIB	*Exc.*	*V.G.*	*Good*	*Fair*	*Poor*
280	220	160	120	90	50

Rossi Wizard

Single-shot rifle chambered in 23 different rimfire/centerfire/shotshell/muzzleloading configurations. Features include drop-barrel action; quick toolless barrel interchangeability; fiber optic front sight; adjustable rear sight, with barrel-mounted optics rail; hardwood or camo Monte Carlo stock.

NIB	*Exc.*	*V.G.*	*Good*	*Fair*	*Poor*
220	200	180	150	110	80

Rossi Ranch Hand

Based upon Rossi's R92 lever-action rifle. Calibers: .38/.357, .44 Magnum or .45 Colt. Barrel length 12"; overall length 24"; weight 4.9 lbs. (empty). Large loop lever 6-round tubular magazine, shortened hardwood buttstock. Open buckhorn rear sight, bead front. Blue or case-hardened carbon steel receiver, with saddle ring.

NIB	*Exc.*	*V.G.*	*Good*	*Fair*	*Poor*
450	400	320	250	200	100

Rio Bravo Gold

Caliber: .22 LR. Capacity: 15-round tubular magazine. Barrel: 18-in. round. Weight: 5.5 lbs. Length: 36 in. Stock: German Beechwood. Sights: Traditional Buckhorn iron sights. Features: New "Gold" version of Rossi's lever-action rimfire based on the R92 centerfire. PVD gold receiver and lever finish with polished black on remaining metalwork. Hammer fired with cross-bolt safety. Sling studs.

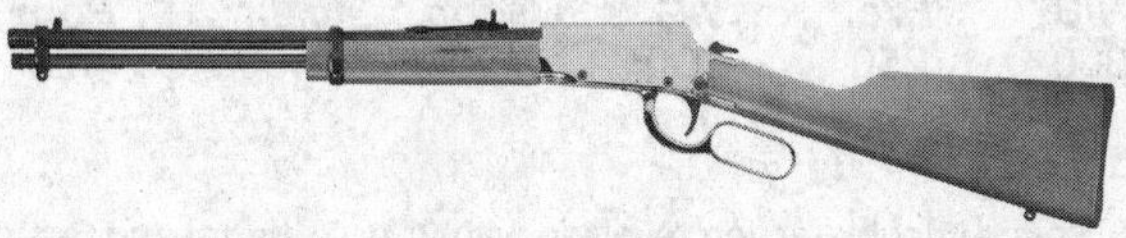

NIB	*Exc.*	*V.G.*	*Good*	*Fair*	*Poor*
420	—	—	—	—	—

HANDGUNS

Model 51

A .22-caliber double-action revolver, with 6" barrel, adjustable sights and 6-shot cylinder. Blued, with walnut grips. Imported prior to 1986.

NIB	*Exc.*	*V.G.*	*Good*	*Fair*	*Poor*
—	150	100	80	50	40

Model 511 Sportsman

As above, with 4" barrel. Made of stainless steel, with walnut grips. Introduced in 1986.

NIB	*Exc.*	*V.G.*	*Good*	*Fair*	*Poor*
220	200	150	120	100	80

Model 461

A 6-round revolver chambered for .357 Magnum cartridge. Fitted with 2" barrel. Rubber grips and blued finish. Weight about 26 oz.

NIB	*Exc.*	*V.G.*	*Good*	*Fair*	*Poor*
300	220	200	150	120	80

Model 462

Same as above, with stainless steel finish.

NIB	*Exc.*	*V.G.*	*Good*	*Fair*	*Poor*
350	280	220	160	140	90

Rossi RP63

Caliber: .357 Magnum. Capacity: 6 rounds. Barrel Length: 3" Rear Sight: Fixed. Front Sight: Removable serrated blade. Finish: Stainless steel. Grips: Rubber. Small-sized frame. Overall Length: 7.95" Overall Height: 5.20" Overall Width 1.46" Overall Weight: 27.30 oz. (unloaded). Safety: Hammer block.

NIB	*Exc.*	*V.G.*	*Good*	*Fair*	*Poor*
350	—	—	—	—	—

Rossi RM66

Caliber: 357 Magnum. Capacity: 6 rounds. Rear Sight: Adjustable. Front Sight: Removable serrated blade. Finish: Stainless steel. Barrel Length: 6". Grips: wrap-around rubber. Medium-sized frame. Overall Length: 11.14" Overall Height: 5.47" Overall Width 1.46" Overall Weight: 34.40 oz. (unloaded). Safety: Hammer block.

NIB	Exc.	V.G.	Good	Fair	Poor
470	—	—	—	—	—

Model 68S

This new version introduced in 1993. Features a shrouded ejector rod and fixed sights. Chambered for .38 Special cartridge. Offered with 2" or 3" barrel. Grips wood or rubber. Finish blue or nickel. Weight about 23 oz.

NIB	Exc.	V.G.	Good	Fair	Poor
180	150	120	100	80	60

Model 69

As above in .32 S&W caliber, with 3" barrel and 6-shot cylinder. Imported prior to 1986.

NIB	Exc.	V.G.	Good	Fair	Poor
—	120	100	80	50	40

Model 70

As above in .22-caliber, with 3" barrel and 6-shot cylinder. Imported prior to 1986.

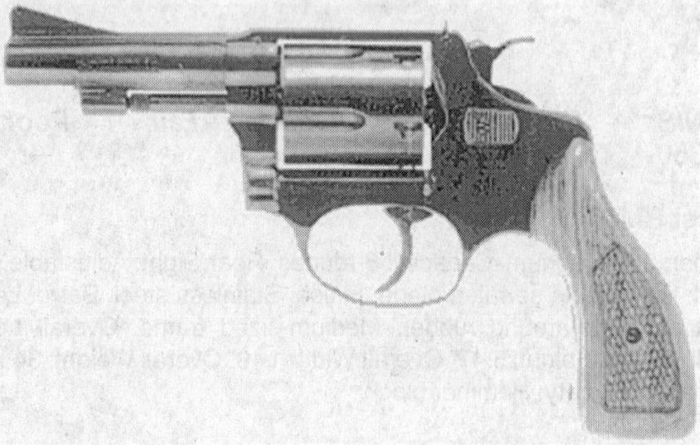

NIB	Exc.	V.G.	Good	Fair	Poor
—	120	100	80	50	40

Model 84

Stainless steel .38 Special caliber double-action revolver, with ribbed 3" or 4" barrel. Blued, with walnut grips. Imported in 1985 and 1986.

NIB	Exc.	V.G.	Good	Fair	Poor
—	180	150	120	100	80

Model 851

As above, with 3" or 4" ventilated rib barrel and adjustable sights.

NIB	Exc.	V.G.	Good	Fair	Poor
200	180	150	120	100	80

Model 981 Plinker

A double-action .22 LR revolver with an 8-shot swing-out cylinder. Barrel in 2, 4 or 6-inch lengths with ventilated rib, fiber optic front and adjustable rear sight. Also made in .22 WMR caliber as Model R99.

NIB	Exc.	V.G.	Good	Fair	Poor
300	250	200	180	150	120

Model 68

A .38 Special double-action revolver, with 2" or 3" barrel and 5-shot cylinder. Blued or nickel-plated, with walnut grips.

NIB	Exc.	V.G.	Good	Fair	Poor
220	180	150	120	100	80

Model 31

A .38 Special caliber double-action revolver, with 4" barrel and 5-shot cylinder. Blued or nickel-plated, with walnut grips. Imported prior to 1986.

NIB	*Exc.*	*V.G.*	*Good*	*Fair*	*Poor*
220	180	150	120	100	80

Model 677

First introduced in 1997. Chambered for .357 Magnum cartridge. Matte blue finish, with 2" barrel and black rubber grips. Weight about 26 oz.

NIB	*Exc.*	*V.G.*	*Good*	*Fair*	*Poor*
300	250	200	150	120	100

Model 88S

Introduced in 1993. This improved model has the same features of Model 68, with addition of a stainless finish. Chambered for .38 Special cartridge. Fitted with 2" or 3" barrel. Available with wood or rubber grips. Cylinder holds 5 cartridges. Weight about 22 oz.

NIB	*Exc.*	*V.G.*	*Good*	*Fair*	*Poor*
320	280	220	160	140	100

Model 351

Chambered for .38 Special +P cartridge. Fitted with 2" barrel and rubber grips. 5-round cylinder. Blued finish. Weight about 24 oz.

NIB	*Exc.*	*V.G.*	*Good*	*Fair*	*Poor*
300	250	200	150	120	100

Model 352

Same as above, with stainless steel finish.

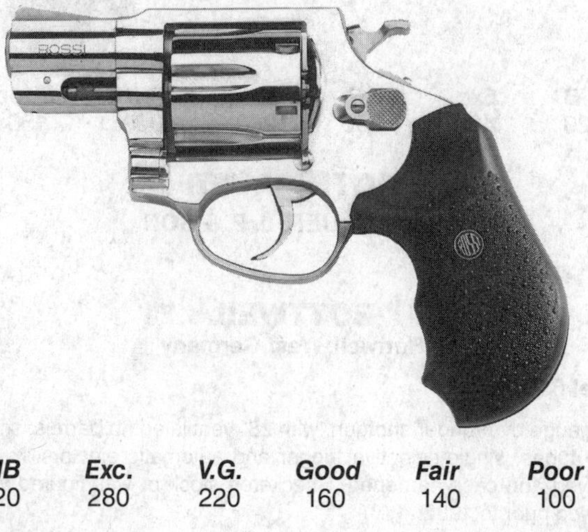

NIB	*Exc.*	*V.G.*	*Good*	*Fair*	*Poor*
320	280	220	160	140	100

Model 951

A .38 Special caliber double-action revolver, with 3" or 4" ventilated rib barrel and 6-shot cylinder. Blued, with walnut grips. Introduced in 1985.

NIB	*Exc.*	*V.G.*	*Good*	*Fair*	*Poor*
300	250	200	150	120	100

Model 971

As above in .357 Magnum caliber, with solid ribbed 4" barrel and enclosed ejector rod. Adjustable sights. Blued, with walnut grips. Introduced in 1988.

NIB	*Exc.*	*V.G.*	*Good*	*Fair*	*Poor*
300	250	200	150	120	100

Model 971 Comp

Introduced in 1993. Similar to Model 971, with the addition of a compensator on 3.25" barrel. Overall length 9"; weight 32 oz. Chambered for .357 Magnum cartridge.

NIB	*Exc.*	*V.G.*	*Good*	*Fair*	*Poor*
340	260	200	150	120	100

Model 971 Comp Stainless

As above, but constructed of stainless steel with checkered black rubber grips. Introduced in 1989.

NIB	*Exc.*	*V.G.*	*Good*	*Fair*	*Poor*
350	280	220	150	120	100

Model 972

Revolver; 6-shot polished stainless double-action .357 Magnum. Adjustable rear sight and red insert on front sight. 6" barrel, rubber grip, 35 oz. Uses Taurus security system. Introduced 2006.

NIB	Exc.	V.G.	Good	Fair	Poor
380	300	250	150	120	100

Model 877

Introduced in 1996. This 6-shot revolver chambered for .357 Magnum cartridge. Fitted with 2" heavy barrel. Stainless steel, with black rubber grips. Weight about 26 oz.

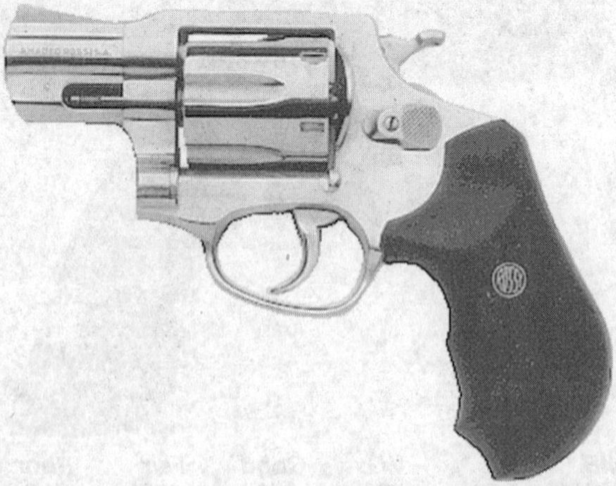

NIB	Exc.	V.G.	Good	Fair	Poor
350	280	220	150	120	100

Model 89

As above in .32 S&W caliber, with 3" barrel.

NIB	Exc.	V.G.	Good	Fair	Poor
320	280	220	160	140	100

Model 971 VRC (vented rib compensator)

Introduced in 1996. Features choice of 2.5", 4" or 6" ventilated rib barrel, with integral compensator. Stainless steel, with black rubber grips. Weight from 30- to 39 oz. depending on barrel length.

NIB	Exc.	V.G.	Good	Fair	Poor
380	300	250	150	120	100

Model 988 Cyclops

Introduced in 1997. Chambered for .357 Magnum cartridge. Fitted with four recessed compensator ports on each side of muzzle. Offered in 6" or 8" barrel lengths. 6-shot double-action revolver. Weight about: 44 oz. 6" model; 51 oz. 8" model. Stainless steel finish.

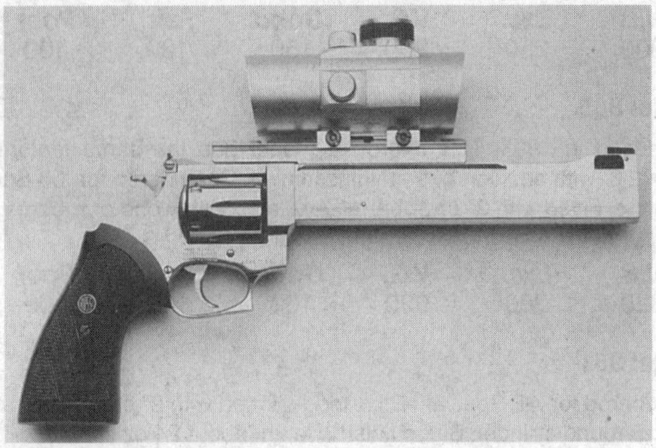

Cyclops with scope mounted

NIB	Exc.	V.G.	Good	Fair	Poor
520	480	350	280	200	150

Model 720

Double-action revolver chambered for .44 Special. Features 5-round cylinder and 3" barrel. Overall length 8"; weight about 27.5 oz. Finish stainless steel.

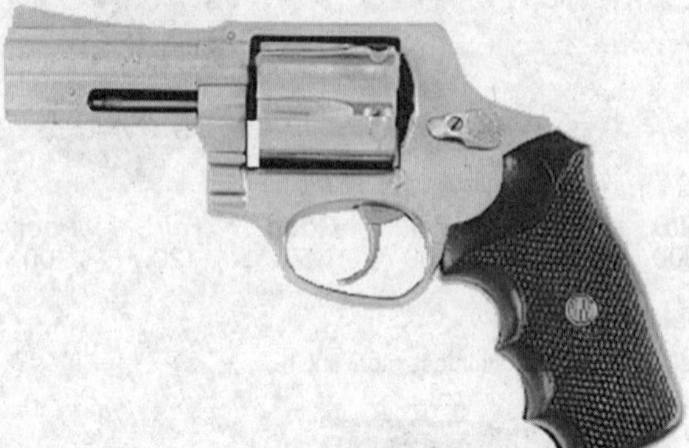

NIB	Exc.	V.G.	Good	Fair	Poor
420	400	350	280	200	150

ROTH-SAUER

See—SAUER, J. P. & SON

ROTTWEIL

Rottweil, West Germany

Model 650

A 12-gauge over/under shotgun, with 28" ventilated rib barrels, screw-in choke tubes, single-selective trigger and automatic ejectors. Receiver engraved and case-hardened. Checkered stock of well figured walnut. Imported prior to 1987.

NIB	Exc.	V.G.	Good	Fair	Poor
—	900	700	550	420	150

Model 72

A 12-gauge over/under shotgun, with 28" ventilated rib barrels, screw-in choke tubes, single-selective trigger and automatic ejectors. Blued, with well figured checkered walnut stock. Imported prior to 1988.

NIB	Exc.	V.G.	Good	Fair	Poor
—	2200	1550	980	650	350

Model 72 American Skeet

As above, with 26.75" ventilated rib barrel, single-selective trigger and automatic ejectors. Receiver also engraved. Imported prior to 1988.

NIB	Exc.	V.G.	Good	Fair	Poor
—	2200	1550	980	650	350

Model 72 Adjustable American Trap

As above, with 34" ventilated rib barrel adjustable to point of impact. Imported prior to 1987.

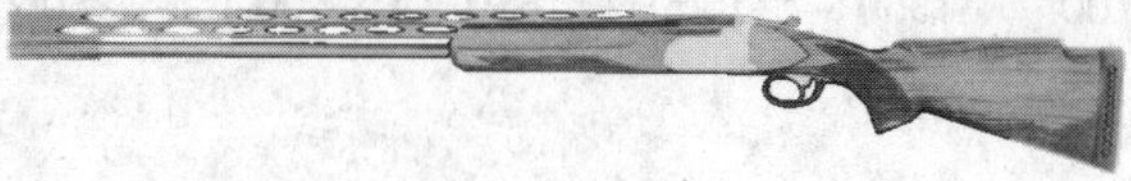

NIB	Exc.	V.G.	Good	Fair	Poor
—	2200	1550	980	650	350

Model 72 American Trap

As above, without the barrel being adjustable to point of impact.

NIB	Exc.	V.G.	Good	Fair	Poor
—	2100	1450	880	550	300

Model 72 International Skeet

As above, with 26.75" ventilated rib barrels choked Skeet. Imported prior to 1988.

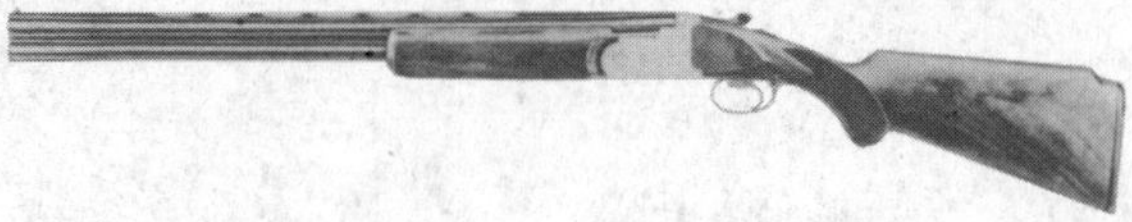

NIB	Exc.	V.G.	Good	Fair	Poor
—	2100	1450	880	550	300

Model 72 International Trap

As above, with 30" high ventilated rib barrels that are choked Improved, Modified and Full. Imported prior to 1988.

NIB	Exc.	V.G.	Good	Fair	Poor
—	2100	1450	880	550	300

ROYAL AMERICAN SHOTGUNS
Woodland Hills, California

Model 100

A 12- or 20-gauge over/under shotgun, with 26", 28" or 30" ventilated rib barrels, double triggers and extractors. Blued, with walnut stock. Imported from 1985 to 1987.

NIB	Exc.	V.G.	Good	Fair	Poor
—	550	380	250	180	150

Model 100AE

As above, with single trigger and automatic ejectors.

NIB	Exc.	V.G.	Good	Fair	Poor
—	650	480	280	200	180

Model 600

A 12-, 20-, 28-gauge or. 410 bore double-barrel shotgun, with 25", 26", 28" or 30" ventilated rib barrels, double triggers and extractors. Blued, with walnut stock. Imported from 1985 to 1987.

NIB	Exc.	V.G.	Good	Fair	Poor
—	600	420	300	200	180

Model 800

A 28-gauge or .410 bore detachable sidelock double-barrel shotgun, with 24", 26" or 28" barrels, double triggers and automatic ejectors. Blued French case-hardened, with English-style walnut stock. Imported from 1985 to 1987.

NIB	Exc.	V.G.	Good	Fair	Poor
—	1550	1200	900	680	400

RUBY ARMS COMPANY
Guernica, Spain

Ruby

A 6.35mm or 7.35mm caliber semi-automatic pistol, with 3.5" barrel and 6-shot magazine. Slide marked "Ruby". Blued, with plastic grips.

NIB	Exc.	V.G.	Good	Fair	Poor
—	280	180	120	80	50

RUGER
See—STURM, RUGER CO.

RUPERTUS, JACOB
Philadelphia, Pennsylvania

Pocket Model Revolver (Antique)

Smaller version of Army and Navy model. Chambered for .25-caliber percussion. It has no loading lever but has a 3.125" octagonal barrel. Approximately 12 manufactured in 1859. Extremely rare; values are speculative.

Exc.	Fine	V.G.	Good	Fair	Poor
11000	8250	5920	3600	950	660

Double-Barrel Pocket Pistol (Antique)

A .22-caliber double-barrel pistol, with 3" round barrels and a spur trigger. Hammer fitted with a sliding firing pin. Blued, with walnut grips.

Exc.	Fine	V.G.	Good	Fair	Poor
4000	3000	1700	900	500	350

Army Revolver (Antique)

An extremely rare revolver. Chambered for .44-caliber percussion. Has a 7.25" octagon barrel, with an integral loading lever that pivots to the side instead of downward. Hammer is mounted on the side and there is a pellet priming device located on the backstrap. There is only one nipple on the breech that lines up with top of the cylinder. Cylinder is unfluted and holds 6-shots. Finish is blued, with walnut grips; frame marked "Patented April 19, 1859". There were less than 12 manufactured in 1859. It would behoove one to secure a qualified independent appraisal if a transaction were contemplated. Due to rarity, listed values are speculative.

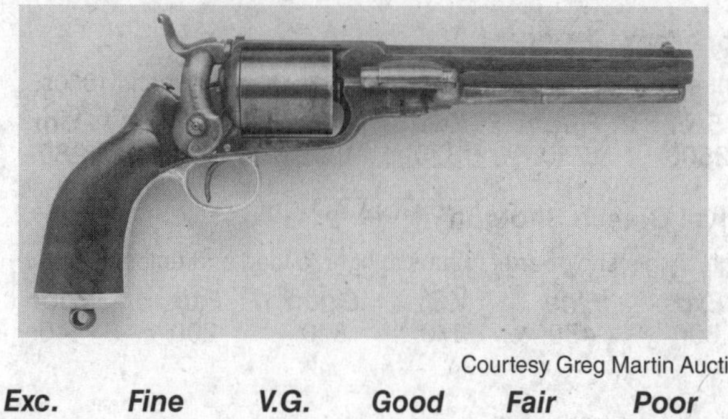

Courtesy Greg Martin Auctions

Exc.	Fine	V.G.	Good	Fair	Poor
20000	11000	8500	6000	3000	2100

Navy Revolver (Antique)

This model equally as rare as Army model. Chambered for .36-caliber percussion. Otherwise, quite similar in appearance to Army model. Approximately 12 manufactured in 1859. Both of these revolvers were manufactured for test purposes and were not well-received by the military, so further production was not accomplished. Due to rarity, listed values are speculative.

Exc.	Fine	V.G.	Good	Fair	Poor
17000	12000	9500	7000	3000	2100

Single-Shot Pocket Pistol (Antique)

A .22, .32, .38 or .41 rimfire single-shot pistol, with half-octagonal barrels ranging in length from 3" to 5". Barrel marked "Rupertus Pat'd. Pistol Mfg. Co. Philadelphia". Blued, with walnut grips. Approximately 3,000 made from 1870 to 1885. Note: The .41-caliber variety is worth approximately 200 percent more than the values listed.

Exc.	Fine	V.G.	Good	Fair	Poor
900	650	430	220	80	50

Spur Trigger Revolver (Antique)

A .22-caliber revolver, with 2.75" barrel and unfluted 7-shot cylinder. Top strap marked "Empire Pat., Nov. 21, 71". Blued or nickel-plated, with walnut grips. Also made in .32 and .32 rimfire, with 5-shot semi-fluted cylinder. A larger model in .41 rimfire with 5-shot semi-fluted cylinder was made with top strap marked "Empire 41". Made during 1870s and 1880s. Note: Add 20 percent for .41-caliber.

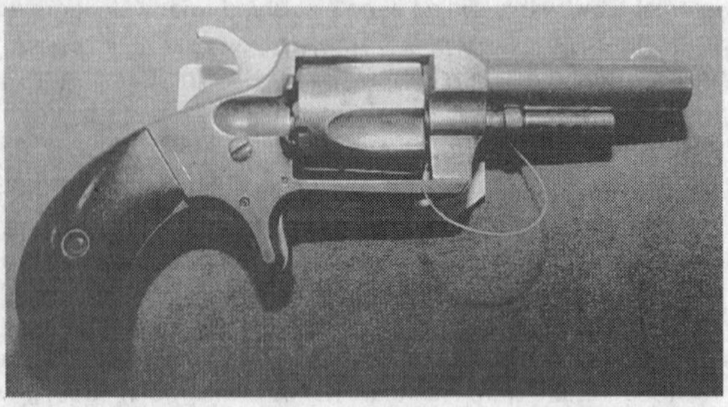

Exc.	Fine	V.G.	Good	Fair	Poor
450	250	210	180	100	70

Pepperbox (Antique)

Eight-shot .22 rimfire pepperbox. About 3,000 made in the 1860s.

Exc.	Fine	V.G.	Good	Fair	Poor
2500	1750	1370	1000	400	280

Swivel-Breech Shotgun (Antique)

12 ga. single shot; barrel rotates to right to load and unload.

Exc.	Fine	V.G.	Good	Fair	Poor
800	450	370	300	200	140

RWS
Dynamit Nobel
Nurenberg, Germany

Model 820 S

A .22-caliber target rifle, with 24" heavy barrel and adjustable aperture sights. Trigger is fully adjustable. Three-position adjustable match stock, with stippled pistol grip and forend. Discontinued in 1986.

NIB	Exc.	V.G.	Good	Fair	Poor
1650	1280	980	620	450	250

Model 820 SF

As above, with a heavier barrel. Discontinued in 1986.

NIB	Exc.	V.G.	Good	Fair	Poor
1700	1350	1000	550	400	250

Model 820 K

Offhand "Running Boar" model of above, with lighter barrel. Furnished without sights. Discontinued in 1986.

NIB	Exc.	V.G.	Good	Fair	Poor
1700	1350	1000	550	400	250

S

S.A.E.
Miami, Florida

S.A.E. was an importer of Spanish shotguns, some of very fine quality. Most notable of these is the S.A.E. line of Sarasqueta shotguns from Eibar, Spain. Not all S.A.E. shotguns are marked with the maker's name.

Model 210S

A 12-, 20-gauge or .410 bore double-barrel shotgun, with 26" or 28" barrels. Double triggers and manual extractors. Blued French case-hardened, with checkered walnut stock. Imported in 1988.

NIB	Exc.	V.G.	Good	Fair	Poor
—	480	400	300	220	150

Model 340X

Holland & Holland-style sidelock 10- or 20-gauge double-barrel shotgun, with 26" barrels. Double triggers and automatic ejectors. Blued case-hardened, with checkered English-style walnut stock. Imported in 1988.

NIB	Exc.	V.G.	Good	Fair	Poor
—	850	680	500	400	200

Model 209E

As above, except also chambered for .410 bore cartridges and more finely engraved. Imported in 1988.

NIB	Exc.	V.G.	Good	Fair	Poor
—	1100	850	700	550	250

Model 70

A 12- or 20-gauge over/under shotgun, with 26" ventilated rib barrels, screw-in choke tubes, single trigger and automatic ejectors. Modestly engraved receiver is blued or French case-hardened. Stock of finely figured walnut. Imported in 1988.

NIB	Exc.	V.G.	Good	Fair	Poor
—	500	380	250	200	100

Model 66C

12-gauge over/under shotgun, with 26" or 30" ventilated rib barrels choked for skeet or trap, single trigger and automatic ejectors. Boxlock action fitted with false sideplates, which are engraved and gold inlaid. Blued, with checkered Monte Carlo-style stock and beavertail forearm. Imported in 1988.

NIB	Exc.	V.G.	Good	Fair	Poor
—	1100	850	700	580	300

S.E.A.M.
Eibar, Spain

This retailer sold a number of pistols produced by the firm of Urizar, prior to 1935.

Praga

A 7.65-caliber semi-automatic pistol marked "Praga Cal 7.65" on the slide. Blued, with plastic grips impressed with trademark "S.E.A.M.".

NIB	Exc.	V.G.	Good	Fair	Poor
—	280	180	120	90	60

S.E.A.M.

A 6.35mm semi-automatic pistol, with 2" barrel. Slide marked "Fabrica de Armas SEAM". Blued, with black plastic grips having trademark "SEAM" cast into them.

NIB	Exc.	V.G.	Good	Fair	Poor
—	250	180	120	90	60

Silesia

As above in 7.65mm caliber, with 3" barrel. Slide stamped with "Silesia".

NIB	Exc.	V.G.	Good	Fair	Poor
—	250	180	120	90	60

S.W.D., INC.
Atlanta, Georgia

See—COBRAY

SABATTI

See—EUROPEAN AMERICAN ARMORY CORP.

SACKET, D. D.
Westfield, Massachusetts

Underhammer Pistol (Antique)

A .34- or .36-caliber single-shot percussion pistol, with half octagonal 3" or 4" barrel marked "D. D. Sacket/Westfield/Cast Steel". Manufactured during 1850s.

Exc.	Fine	V.G.	Good	Fair	Poor
1550	1200	870	550	160	110

SACO DEFENSE, INC.

See—CROSSFIRE

SAFARI ARMS
Phoenix, Arizona

In operation from 1978 to 1987. Company was purchased by Olympic Arms of Olympia, Washington, in 1987. The models listed were produced by that company under the Safari name until 2004, when most were rebranded under Olympic Arms.

Enforcer

A .45-caliber semi-automatic pistol, with 3.9" barrel and 5-shot magazine. Patterned after Colt Model 1911. Blued, Armaloy, electroless nickel-plate or Parkerized finish, with checkered walnut or neoprene grips.

NIB	Exc.	V.G.	Good	Fair	Poor
700	600	500	400	350	150

Match Master

As above, with 5" barrel.

NIB	Exc.	V.G.	Good	Fair	Poor
700	600	500	400	350	150

Black Widow

As above, with ivory Micarta grips etched with a black widow.

NIB	Exc.	V.G.	Good	Fair	Poor
700	600	500	400	350	150

Model 81

As above, without grip etching. Also offered in .38-caliber.

NIB	Exc.	V.G.	Good	Fair	Poor
800	700	600	500	400	200

Model 81L

As above, with 6" barrel.

NIB	Exc.	V.G.	Good	Fair	Poor
850	750	650	550	450	200

Ultimate Unlimited

Bolt-action single-shot pistol, with 15" barrel. Chambered for a variety of cartridges. Blued, with laminated stock.

NIB	Exc.	V.G.	Good	Fair	Poor
850	750	650	550	450	200

Survivor I Conversion Unit

Conversion unit lifted to Model 1911 frame that alters that pistol to a bolt-action carbine. Barrel length 16.25", caliber .223, folding stock.

NIB	Exc.	V.G.	Good	Fair	Poor
300	280	250	200	150	100

Counter Sniper Rifle

A .308-caliber bolt-action target rifle, with heavy 26" barrel and 20-round detachable magazine. Matte blued, with colored composite stock.

NIB	Exc.	V.G.	Good	Fair	Poor
1200	1050	850	650	450	200

SAIGA

Izhevsk, Russia

A series of AK type rifles and shotguns manufactured in Russia by Izhmash. Also see E.A.A.

RIFLES

Model IZ-114, AZ-132

Kalashnikov-type semi-automatic rifle chambered in .223 Rem. (IZ-114) or 7.62x39mm (IZ-132). Black synthetic or wood stock and forearm, 16" or 20.5" barrel. Imported by several companies including EAA, U.S. Sporting Goods and others.

NIB	Exc.	V.G.	Good	Fair	Poor
900	750	600	—	—	—

Model AZ-139

Same as above, except in .308 Win. and 22" barrel.

NIB	Exc.	V.G.	Good	Fair	Poor
1100	950	750	—	—	—

Model 100

Hunting style semi-automatic rifle, with synthetic stock in .223, 7.62x39, .308 or .30-06. Magazine capacity 3 or 10 rounds.

NIB	Exc.	V.G.	Good	Fair	Poor
700	600	500	—	—	—

SGL 21/31

Russian-made series with stamped receivers, Warsaw or NATO stock in Desert Sand, OD Green or Plum finish. Black polymer folding stock available. Features include bayonet lug, double-stage trigger, scope rail. Chambered for 7.62x39mm (21) or 5.45x39mm (31). Note: Add $400 for SGL 31.

NIB	Exc.	V.G.	Good	Fair	Poor
1100	900	750	—	—	—

SHOTGUNS

Model 109

Semi-automatic shotgun based on AK-47 design. In 12-, 20-gauge or .410 bore. Black synthetic stock and forearm, 5- or 10-shot magazine. Note: Add $75 for .410 bore.

NIB	Exc.	V.G.	Good	Fair	Poor
900	750	630	—	—	—

SAKO

Riihimaki, Finland

Note: Arms produced by this company prior to 1972 are worth approximately 25 percent more than arms of the same type produced thereafter. Prices for fair and poor condition reflect worth of the action. In 2000, Beretta Holding Co. purchased Sako and distributes product line through Beretta U.S.A.

Standard Sporter

Bolt-action magazine rifle produced in a wide variety of calibers, with varying barrel lengths, etc. Blued, with checkered walnut stocks.

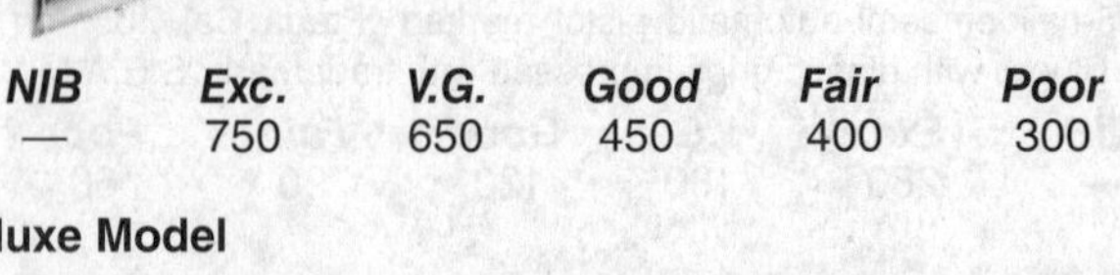

NIB	Exc.	V.G.	Good	Fair	Poor
—	750	650	450	400	300

Deluxe Model

As above, with engraved floorplate and checkered Monte Carlo-style stock. Featuring rosewood pistol grip cap and forend tip.

NIB	Exc.	V.G.	Good	Fair	Poor
—	900	750	600	450	400

Finnbear

As above, with a long action available in a variety of large bore calibers. Fitted with 20" or 23.5" barrel. Blued, with checkered stock. For .458 Win. Magnum (only 20 produced), values double. Note: Add 15 percent for other Magnum chamberings or Deluxe version; 20 percent for Mannlicher Carbine version.

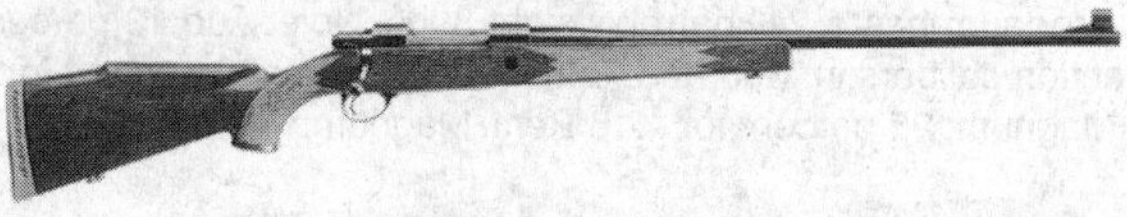

NIB	Exc.	V.G.	Good	Fair	Poor
—	1000	850	650	400	300

Forester

As above, with a shorter action suitable for use with intermediate cartridges. Note: Add 20 percent for Mannlicher Carbine version.

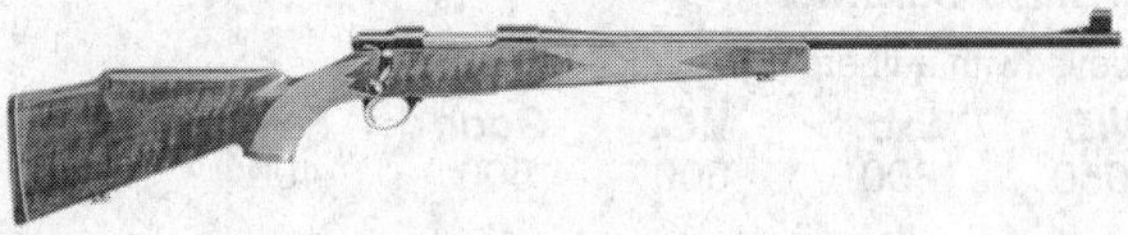

NIB	Exc.	V.G.	Good	Fair	Poor
—	1000	850	650	400	300

Vixen

As above, with a short action. Note: Add 20 percent for Mannlicher Carbine version.

NIB	Exc.	V.G.	Good	Fair	Poor
—	1000	850	650	400	300

FN Action

Manufactured from 1950 to 1957. This model utilized a Fabrique Nationale manufactured receiver. Chambered for .270 Win. and .30-06 cartridges. Otherwise, as above.

NIB	Exc.	V.G.	Good	Fair	Poor
—	800	600	480	400	300

FN Magnum Action

As above, with a long action for .300 and .375 H&H.

NIB	Exc.	V.G.	Good	Fair	Poor
—	900	700	550	400	300

Anniversary Model

A 7mm Rem. Magnum bolt-action rifle, with 24" barrel. Blued, checkered walnut stock. A total of 1,000 manufactured. As with any commemorative firearm, this model should be NIB to realize its full resale potential.

NIB	Exc.	V.G.	Good	Fair	Poor
2500	850	750	450	400	300

Finnwolf

A 4-shot lever-action rifle produced in .243- and .308-calibers. Blued, checkered walnut stock. Manufactured from 1962 to 1974.

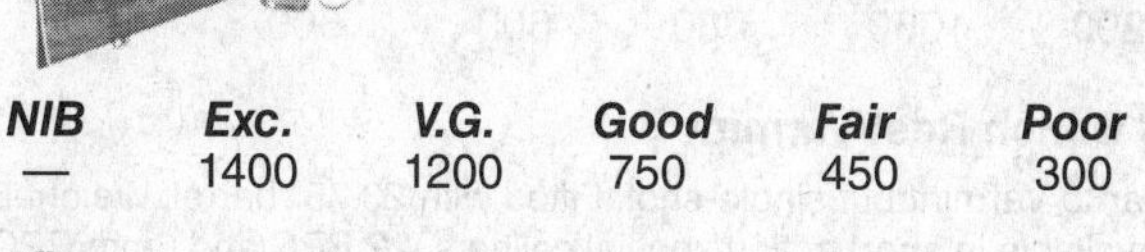

NIB	Exc.	V.G.	Good	Fair	Poor
—	1400	1200	750	450	300

Finnfire

Bolt-action rifle chambered for .22 LR cartridge. Fitted with 22" barrel and choice of iron or no sights. European walnut stock. A 5-shot detachable magazine is standard. Weight about 5.25 lbs.

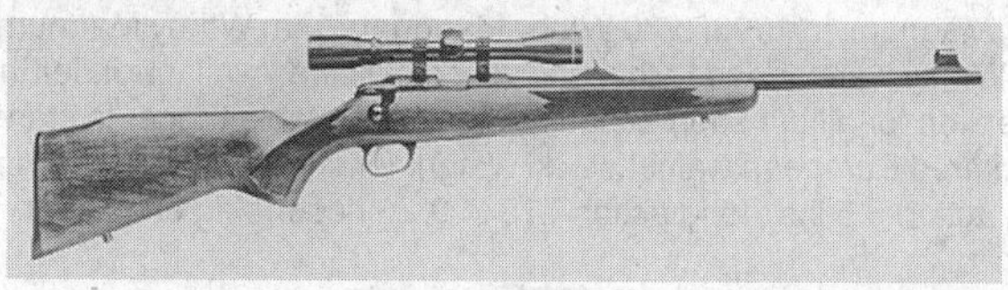

Courtesy Stoeger

NIB	Exc.	V.G.	Good	Fair	Poor
1150	950	700	580	400	300

Finnfire Heavy Barrel

Same as above, with a heavy barrel.

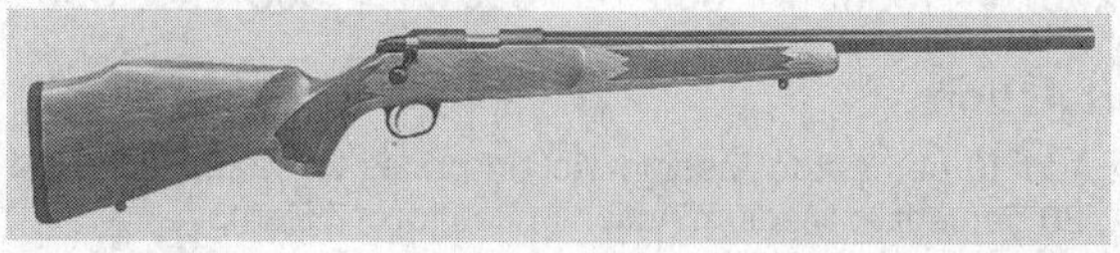

Courtesy Stoeger

NIB	Exc.	V.G.	Good	Fair	Poor
1150	950	700	580	400	300

Finnfire Hunter

Introduced in 2000. Bolt-action model chambered for .22 LR cartridge. Fitted with 22" barrel and Sako 75 style select walnut stock. Weight about 5.75 lbs.

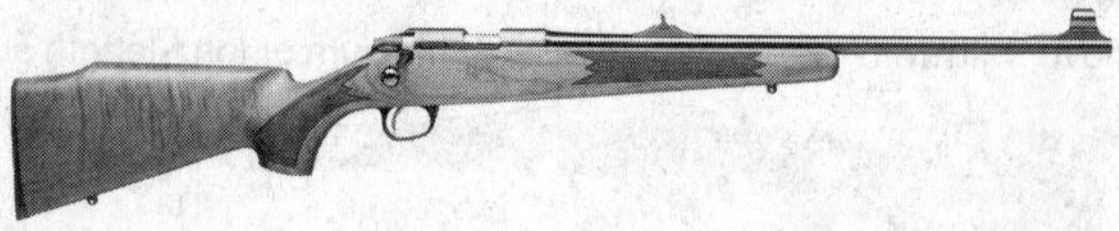

NIB	Exc.	V.G.	Good	Fair	Poor
1150	950	700	580	400	300

Finnfire Sporter

Chambered for .22 LR cartridge and built on P94S action. Has a walnut stock, with adjustable cheekpiece and buttplate spacer system that allows for length of pull and buttplate angle adjustment. Trigger is adjustable. Introduced in 1999.

NIB	Exc.	V.G.	Good	Fair	Poor
1150	950	700	580	400	300

Sako Quad Combo

Introduced in 2005. Bolt-action rifle features four interchangeable barrels in four different rimfire calibers. Black synthetic stock. Detachable 5-round magazine. Included barrels are: .22 Long Rifle; .22 WMR; .17 HMR; .17 Mach 2. All 22" in length. Blued finish. Weight about 5.75 lbs. Note: NIB price for rifles with only one barrel is $948. Extra barrels are $260 each.

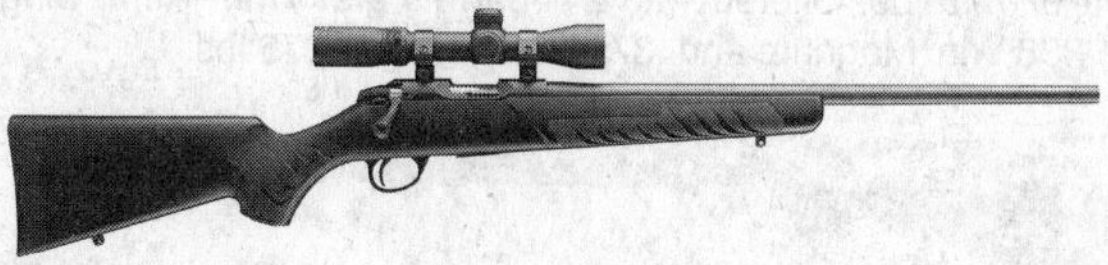

NIB	Exc.	V.G.	Good	Fair	Poor
1450	1300	1080	800	500	300

Hunter

Offered in three action lengths: short; medium; long. Short action calibers available are: .17 Rem., .222, .223 in 21.25" barrel. Medium action calibers are: .22-250, .243, .308 and 7mm-08 in 21.75" barrel. Long action calibers are: .25-06, .270 Win., .280 Rem., .30-06 for 22" barrel length. In 24" barrel the long action calibers are: 7mm Rem. Magnum,

.300 Win. and .300 Wby. Magnum, .338 and .375 Win. Magnum and .416 Rem. Magnum. In 1996, .270 Wthby Magnum, 7mm Wthby Magnum and .340 Wthby were added to the long action calibers. Available in left-handed version for all but short action calibers. Adjustable trigger is standard. Checkered European walnut stock. Weight for short action 6.25 lbs.; medium action 6.5 lbs.; long action 7.75 to 8.25 depending on caliber.

Medium Action

NIB	Exc.	V.G.	Good	Fair	Poor
1200	1050	880	600	500	300

Short Action

Note: Add 10 percent to Medium Action prices for .222 Rem. and .223 Rem.; 20 percent to Medium Action prices for .17 Rem.

Long Action

Note: Add 10 percent for long action calibers in .300 and .338 Win. Magnum; 20 percent for .375 H&H Magnum; 25 percent for .416 Rem. Magnum.

NIB	Exc.	V.G.	Good	Fair	Poor
1400	1180	1000	750	600	300

Carbine

As above, with 18.5" barrel. Produced with medium or long-length action.

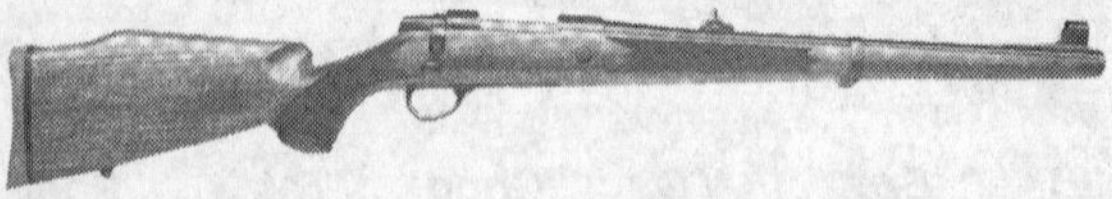

NIB	Exc.	V.G.	Good	Fair	Poor
1200	1050	880	600	500	300

Long Range Hunting Rifle

Similar to long action Hunter. Fitted with 26" fluted barrel. Chambered for .25-06, .270 Win., 7mm Rem. Magnum and .300 Win. Magnum. Introduced in 1996. Note: Add 10 percent to medium action prices for .222 Rem. and .223 Rem.; 20 percent to medium action prices for .17 Rem.

NIB	Exc.	V.G.	Good	Fair	Poor
1500	1300	1050	880	650	300

Laminated Model

Features laminated checkered hardwood stock made up of 36 layers. Solid recoil pad is standard as are quick detachable sling swivels. Available in both medium and long action calibers. Medium action calibers are: .22-250, .243, .308 and 7mm-08 with 21.75" barrel; weight of 6.5 lbs. Long action calibers are: .25-06, .270, .280, .30-06 with 22" barrel; weight of 7.75 lbs. Offered with 24" barrels are: 7mm Rem. Magnum, .300, .338 Win. Magnum and .375 H&H ; weight 7.75 lbs.

Medium Action

Note: Add 10 percent to prices for .222 Rem. and .223 Rem.; 20 percent for .17 Rem.

NIB	Exc.	V.G.	Good	Fair	Poor
1200	1050	880	600	500	300

Long Action

Note: Add 10 percent for long action calibers in .300 and .338 Win. Magnum; 20 percent for .375 H&H Magnum; 25 percent for .416 Rem. Magnum.

NIB	Exc.	V.G.	Good	Fair	Poor
1400	1180	1000	750	600	300

FiberClass

Features a black plain fiberglass stock. Offered in long action calibers only. The .25-06, .270, .280 and .30-06 are fitted with 22" barrels; weight 7.25 lbs. The 7mm Rem. Magnum, .300 Win. Magnum, .338 Win. Magnum and .375 H&H are fitted with 24" barrel; weight 7.25 lbs. The .416 Rem. Magnum has a 24" barrel; weight 8 lbs. Note: Add 10 percent for long action calibers in .300 and .338 Win. Magnum; 20 percent for .375 H&H Magnum; 25 percent for .416 Rem. Magnum.

NIB	Exc.	V.G.	Good	Fair	Poor
1050	800	600	500	400	400

FiberClass Carbine

As above, with a fiberglass stock.

NIB	Exc.	V.G.	Good	Fair	Poor
1050	800	600	500	400	400

Carbine

Features a Mannlicher-style stock, with two-piece forearm. Has a checkered walnut stock, with oil-finish. Offered in both medium and short actions, all with 18.5" barrels. Medium action .243 and .308; weight 6 lbs.; long action calibers .270 and .30-06; weight 7.25 lbs.; .338 Win. Magnum and .375 H&H; weight 7.75 lbs. Note: Add 10 percent for long action calibers in .338 Win. Magnum; 20 percent for .375 H&H Magnum.

Medium Action

NIB	Exc.	V.G.	Good	Fair	Poor
1200	1050	880	600	500	300

Long Action

Note: Add 10 percent for long action calibers in .338 Win. Magnum; 20 percent for .375 H&H Magnum.

NIB	Exc.	V.G.	Good	Fair	Poor
1200	1050	880	600	500	300

Varmint-Heavy Barrel

Checkered walnut stock features an extra wide beavertail forearm, with oil-finish. Offered in both short and medium action. All are fitted with 23" heavy barrel weighing 8.5 lbs. Short action calibers are: .17 Rem., .222 and .223; medium action calibers are: .22-250, .243, .308 and 7mm-08.

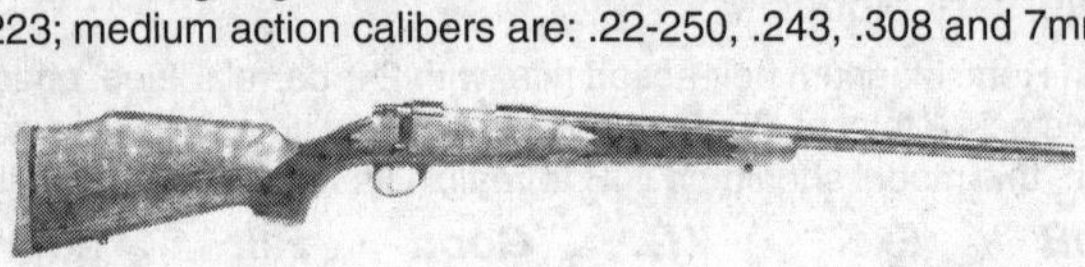

Short Action

Note: Add 10 percent for .222 and .223 Rem.; 20 percent for .17 Rem.

NIB	Exc.	V.G.	Good	Fair	Poor
1200	1050	880	600	500	300

Medium Action

NIB	Exc.	V.G.	Good	Fair	Poor
1200	1050	880	600	500	300

PPC Bench Rest/Varmint

Similar to Varmint but single-shot. Fitted with 23.75" barrel. Weight 8.75 lbs. Available in short action special calibers .22 PPC and 6mm PPC.

NIB	Exc.	V.G.	Good	Fair	Poor
1350	1150	980	650	500	300

Classic Grade

Hand-checkered select walnut stock, with matte lacquer finish is featured on this grade. Offered in medium and long action. Long action rifles are offered in left-hand model. Medium action caliber is .243 Win., with 21.75" barrel; weight 6 lbs. Long action calibers: .270, .30-06 and 7mm Rem. Magnum. with 24" barrels; weight about 7.5 lbs.

NIB	Exc.	V.G.	Good	Fair	Poor
1200	1050	880	600	500	300

Deluxe Grade

Features a high grade European walnut stock, with hand-cut basket weave checkering. Forend tip and grip are fitted with rosewood. English-style recoil pad is standard. Long action models are offered in left-hand configuration. Like the Hunter model short, medium and long actions are available in the same calibers, barrel lengths and weights..

Medium Action

NIB	Exc.	V.G.	Good	Fair	Poor
1400	1180	1000	750	600	300

Short Action

Note: Add 10 percent for .222 and .223 Rem.; 20 percent for .17 Rem.

Long Action

Note: Add 10 percent for long action calibers in .300 and .338 Win. Magnum; 20 percent for .375 H&H Magnum; 25 percent for .416 Rem. Magnum; $100 for left-hand models.

NIB	Exc.	V.G.	Good	Fair	Poor
1400	1180	1000	750	600	300

Super Grade/Super Deluxe

Similar to Deluxe Grade. Offered with fancy walnut stock and oak-leaf carving. Floorplate and triggerguard are engraved. Pistol grip cap has inlaid silver plate. Offered in same actions and calibers as Hunter and Deluxe Grades.

Medium Action

NIB	Exc.	V.G.	Good	Fair	Poor
2500	1750	1200	750	620	300

Short Action

Note: Add 10 percent for .222 and .223 Rem.

Long Action

Note: Add 10 percent for long action calibers in .300 and .338 Win. Magnum; 20 percent for .375 H&H Magnum; 25 percent for .416 Rem. Magnum.

NIB	Exc.	V.G.	Good	Fair	Poor
2500	1750	1200	750	620	300

Safari Grade

As above, chambered for .300 Win. Magnum, .338 Win. Magnum or .375 H&H cartridges.

NIB	Exc.	V.G.	Good	Fair	Poor
2700	2500	1900	1100	800	400

MODEL 75 SERIES

Introduced in March 1997. Based on a new design by Sako. Each of the five different action sizes is manufactured for a specific range of calibers. Its action, barrel and stocks are all redesigned components. Offered in a variety of configurations and calibers. Sako actions are offered separately in carbon steel, white and stainless steel.

Model 75 Hunter

Available in five different action sizes for calibers from .17 Rem. to .416 Rem. Magnum. Weight varies from 6.37 lbs. to 9 lbs. Barrel lengths from 22" to 24.37". Choice of checkered walnut stock or black synthetic stock. All Hunter models are sold without sights as standard, but open sights are an option. Magazine is detachable except for .300 Rem. Ultra Magnum and .416 Rem. Magnum. Single-set trigger is an option. In 2003, a left-hand model was offered in .270 Win and .30-06. In 2004, .270 WSM and .300 WSM calibers were added. Note: Add $30 for long action calibers from .270 to .416.

NIB	Exc.	V.G.	Good	Fair	Poor
1420	1050	700	500	400	300

Model 75 Stainless Synthetic

Same as above, but available with synthetic stock and stainless steel barrel and action. Offered in calibers from .22-250 to .375 H&H. Note: Add $30 for long action calibers.

NIB	Exc.	V.G.	Good	Fair	Poor
1500	1100	750	600	400	300

Model 75 Deluxe

Features all the elements of Hunter model. Plus, special checkering on select walnut stock with special black finish. All models have a hinged floorplate. In 2004, .270 WSM and .300 WSM calibers were added. Weight about 7.75 lbs. Note: Add $100 for long action calibers.

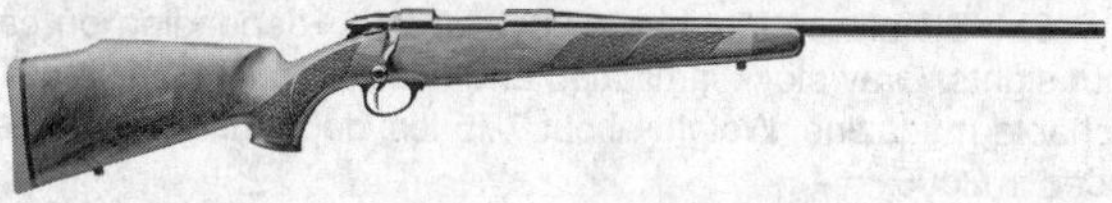

NIB	Exc.	V.G.	Good	Fair	Poor
1600	1050	800	700	500	400

Model 75 Big Game Deluxe

Similar to M75 Deluxe, except chambered for .416 Rem. Magnum cartridge. Fitted with iron sights.

NIB	Exc.	V.G.	Good	Fair	Poor
1600	1050	800	700	500	400

Model 75 Varmint

Chambered for .17 Rem., .222 Rem., .223 and .22-250, all with 24" heavy barrels. In 1999, Sako added .22 PPC and 6mm PPC calibers. Other calibers are .260 Rem., .308 and .204 Ruger. Weight about 8.4 lbs. Walnut stock.

NIB	Exc.	V.G.	Good	Fair	Poor
1250	950	750	600	450	400

Model 75 Varmint Set Trigger

As above, with single-set trigger. Introduced in 2005.

NIB	Exc.	V.G.	Good	Fair	Poor
1550	1100	880	700	500	400

Model 75 Varmint Stainless

Introduced in 1999. Similar to Varmint 75, with stainless steel barrel. Magazine is detachable, but can be loaded through the ejection port. Trigger is adjustable. Offered in all calibers as the standard Model 75 Varmint. Weights vary from about 8 lbs. to 8.6 lbs. Stock is laminated.

NIB	Exc.	V.G.	Good	Fair	Poor
1200	1050	880	600	500	300

Model 75 Varmint Stainless Set Trigger

As above, with stainless steel barrel and receiver. Laminated stock. Weight about 9 lbs. Introduced in 2005.

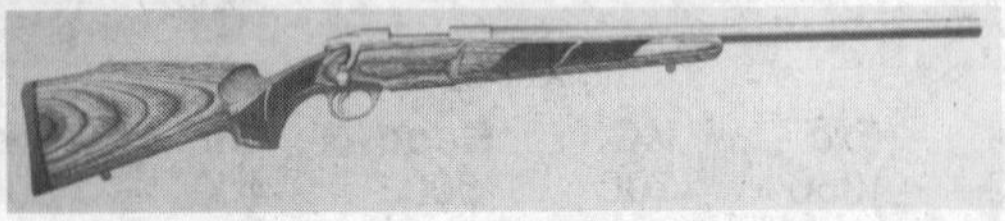

NIB	Exc.	V.G.	Good	Fair	Poor
1400	1180	1000	750	600	300

Model 75 Finnlight

Introduced in 2001. Bolt-action rifle features short, medium and long action calibers. Stainless steel barrel lengths from 20.25" to 22.5" depending on caliber. Barrels are fluted. Synthetic stock. Weight about 6.5 lbs. depending on caliber. In 2003, offered in .300 WSM caliber.

NIB	Exc.	V.G.	Good	Fair	Poor
1300	1080	900	650	500	300

Model 75 Grey Wolf

Bolt-action rifle chambered for a wide variety of calibers from .223 to 7mm WSM. Stainless steel barrel 22.5" or 24.3" depending on caliber, without sights. Gray stock laminated and checkered. Rubber recoil pad. Detachable magazine. Weight about 7.75 lbs. depending on caliber. Introduced in 2005.

NIB	Exc.	V.G.	Good	Fair	Poor
1400	1180	1000	750	600	300

Model 75 Custom Deluxe

Introduced in 2003. Features an oil-finished premium-grade walnut stock, with a special fine-line checkering pattern. Factory recoil pad. Chambered for .270 Win or .30-06 cartridges.

NIB	Exc.	V.G.	Good	Fair	Poor
3250	2500	1900	1100	800	400

Model 75 Custom Single Shot

Introduced in 2004. Single-shot model chambered for .308 cartridge. Fitted with 23.625" heavy fluted stainless steel barrel, without sights. Checkered laminated stock, with beavertail forearm. Weight about 9 lbs.

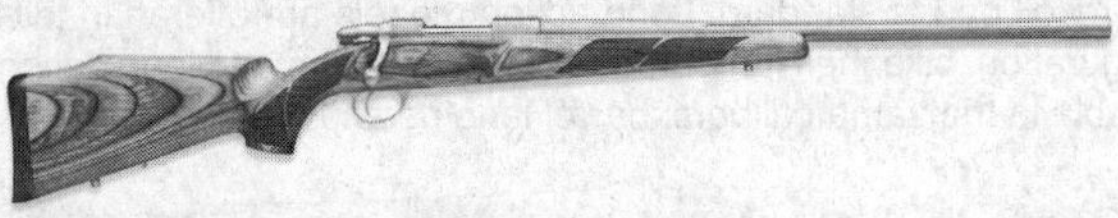

NIB	Exc.	V.G.	Good	Fair	Poor
3250	2500	1900	1100	550	400

Model 75 Super Deluxe

A special order rifle. Advise obtaining an expert opinion before a sale. Prices listed are for the base rifle.

NIB	Exc.	V.G.	Good	Fair	Poor
2500	2100	1600	1280	600	400

Model 78

A .22 or .22 Hornet bolt-action rifle, with 22" barrel. Blued, with checkered walnut stock. Discontinued in 1986.

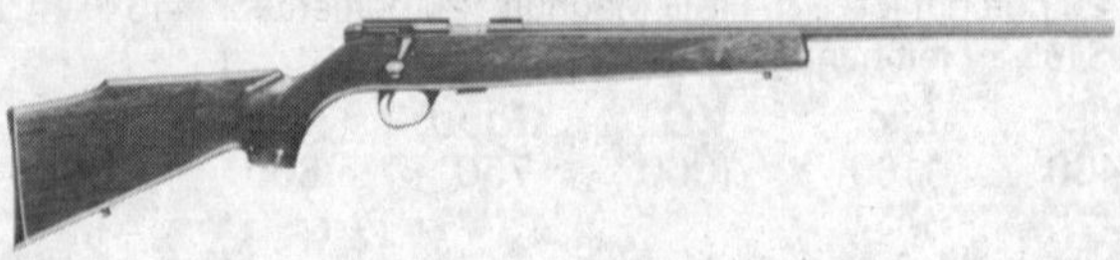

NIB	Exc.	V.G.	Good	Fair	Poor
—	850	680	500	380	250

Model 2700 Finnsport

A .270 to .300 Win. Magnum bolt-action rifle, with 22" barrel. Blued, checkered walnut stock. Discontinued in 1985.

NIB	Exc.	V.G.	Good	Fair	Poor
—	900	750	600	480	200

Safari 80th Anniversary Model

Limited edition rifle. Built on Sako 75 Magnum long action. Chambered for .375 H&H cartridge. Match-grade heavy barrel. Select grade walnut stock, with straight comb and ebony forend tip. Quarter rib. Equipped with Swarovski PV-1 1.25x24 scope. Engraved floorplate. Supplied with hand-made leather case, with cleaning accessories. Limited to 80 rifles worldwide. Serial numbers 200101 to 200180.

NIB	Exc.	V.G.	Good	Fair	Poor
15950	12500	8500	—	—	—

Sako 85 Hunter

Bolt-action centerfire rifle. Chambered in short and long calibers ranging from .223 Rem. to .375 H&H Magnum. Controlled round feeding. Checkered walnut stock. Satin blued sightless 22.4375", 22.875" or 24.375" barrel. Introduced in 2007. Note: Add 30 percent premium for .375.

NIB	Exc.	V.G.	Good	Fair	Poor
1100	900	780	600	480	300

Sako 85 Stainless Synthetic

Similar to Sako 85 Hunter, with stainless steel receiver and barrel. Introduced 2007; discontinued 2008.

NIB	Exc.	V.G.	Good	Fair	Poor
1200	1000	880	650	520	350

Sako 85 Synthetic

Similar to 85 Hunter, with coated black synthetic stock and black matte metal finish. Chambered in 6.5x55, .270 Win., .308 Win., .30-06. Introduced in 2014.

NIB	Exc.	V.G.	Good	Fair	Poor
1500	1250	950	650	400	250

Sako 85 Finnlight

Similar to Sako 85 Stainless Synthetic, with recoil pad and ultra-lightweight synthetic stock. Chambered in long and short cartridges ranging from .243 to .300 Win. Magnum. Introduced 2007.

NIB	Exc.	V.G.	Good	Fair	Poor
1550	1100	880	700	500	400

Sako 85 Finnlight II

Introduced 2019 as update to the Finnlight line. Improved lightweight RTM fiberglass stock with carbon fiber bedding and adjustable cheek riser, rubberized grip zones. Overall weight from 6.17-6.83 pounds. Barrels from 20-24". Calibers from .22-250 to .300 Win. Mag.

NIB	Exc.	V.G.	Good	Fair	Poor
2200	2000	1600	—	—	—

Sako 85 Varmint

Similar to Sako 85 Hunter, with recoil pad and 7.5 oz. set trigger. Chambered in .204 Ruger, .243, .22-250 or .308. Introduced 2007.

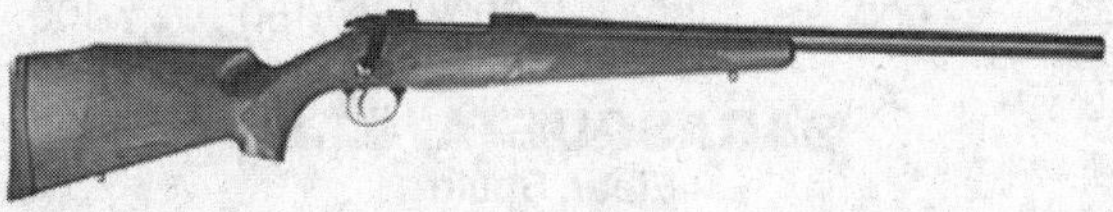

NIB	Exc.	V.G.	Good	Fair	Poor
1300	1080	900	650	500	300

Sako 85 Laminated SS Varmint

Similar to Sako 85 Varmint, with laminated stock and stainless steel barrel. Introduced 2007.

NIB	Exc.	V.G.	Good	Fair	Poor
1400	1180	1000	750	600	300

A-7 American Bolt-Action Rifle

Bolt-action rifle chambered in .22-250, .243 Win., .25-06, .260 Rem., .270 Win., .270 WSM, .300 WSM, .30-06, .300 WM, .308 Win., .338 Federal, .7mm Rem. Magnum, 7mm-08. Features include blued or stainless barrel (22.4375" standard, 24.375" Magnum) and receiver, black composite stock with sling swivels and recoil pad, two-position safety, adjustable trigger, detachable 3+1 box magazine. Weight 6.3 lbs. to 6.13 lbs.

NIB	Exc.	V.G.	Good	Fair	Poor
850	720	580	400	300	200

A-7 Big Game Roughtech

Same features as A-7 American, with Roughtech synthetic pistol grip stock and fluted or heavy barrel. Chambered in .270 Win., 7mm Rem. Magnum, .308 Win., 30-06, .300 Win. Magnum.

NIB	Exc.	V.G.	Good	Fair	Poor
1000	880	700	550	400	250

A-7 Long Range Roughtech

Similar to Big Game Roughtech, with 26" barrel and wide forend. Chambered in .25-06, 7mm Rem. Magnum, .308 Win., .300 Win. Magnum. Introduced in 2016.

NIB	Exc.	V.G.	Good	Fair	Poor
1250	1000	900	—	—	—

A-7 Tecomate

Chambered in .270 WSM (23" barrel) or .300 WSM (24.25") barrel. Magazine capacity 4 rounds. Features a new Bell & Carlson Medalist composite stock. Integral aluminum bedding system CNC produced from aircraft quality 6061-T6 aluminum. Flat bottom receiver. Stainless action. Introduced in 2011.

NIB	Exc.	V.G.	Good	Fair	Poor
1200	1020	850	600	300	100

Sako Classic Deluxe

High grade version of Model 85. Oil-finished walnut stock, with palm swell and cheekpiece, pronounced pistol grip, rosewood pistol and forend tip. Barrel band for sling swivel. Free-floating barrel. All metal parts are highly polished and blued. Medium or long action depending upon caliber. Adjustable trigger. Open sights are available. Five cartridges available to include .270 Win., 7x64, .30-06, .370 Sako Magnum and .375 H&H. Introduced in 2011.

NIB	Exc.	V.G.	Good	Fair	Poor
3450	3100	2600	2000	1600	500

Sako 85 Bavarian

Available in full-length (shown) or carbine style. Offered in most standard calibers, plus 6.5x55 Swedish. Comes with set trigger and adjustable express sights. Stock is oil-finished high-grade checkered walnut, with rosewood grip and forend caps. Carbine has full-length Mannlicher-style stock, with Bavarian-style comb and cheekpiece. Note: Add 15 percent for Carbine model.

NIB	Exc.	V.G.	Good	Fair	Poor
1950	1750	1400	1000	750	250

Sako 85 Kodiak

Weatherproof design has stainless steel barrel and action. Gray laminated stock reinforced with two crossbolts. Free-floating bull barrel in 21", 22.5" or 24.3" lengths. Offered in calibers from .22-250 to .375 H&H.

NIB	Exc.	V.G.	Good	Fair	Poor
1750	1520	1200	800	450	200

Sako Black Bear Series

Model 85 variation available in short and medium actions only. Short action chambered in .308 Win. or .338 Federal; medium action in .30-06, 8x57 JS, 9.3x62 and 9.3x66 (.370) Sako. Controlled feeding, detachable magazine, single-stage adjustable trigger. Black injection molded stock, with Soft Touch areas around pistol grip and forend. Open sights are available. Scope can be mounted to integral Sako mounting system on receiver. Bull barrel, free-floating and hammer forged. Brown Bear model has similar features, but with brown laminated hardwood stock. Chambered in .338 Win. Magnum or .375 H&H. Introduced in 2011.

NIB	Exc.	V.G.	Good	Fair	Poor
1600	1350	1100	950	600	300

TRG-S

Features a unique cold-forged receiver. Stock is special reinforced polyurethane Monte Carlo, without checkering. Recoil pad has spacer for adjustable length of pull. Trigger is adjustable. Detachable magazine holds 5 rounds. Offered in a variety of calibers from .243 to .375 H&H. Non-Magnum calibers fitted with 22" barrel; weight 7.75 lbs.; Magnum calibers fitted with 24" barrel; weight 7.75 lbs. In 1996, .270 Wby. Magnum, 7mm Wby. Magnum, .340 Wby. Magnum and 6.5x55S were added.

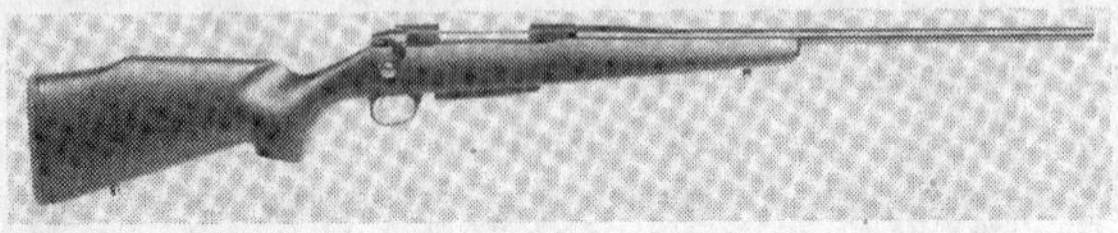

NIB	Exc.	V.G.	Good	Fair	Poor
1000	850	680	500	350	250

TRG-21

Receiver similar to TRG-S, with polyurethane stock featuring a unique design. Chambered for .308 cartridge. Trigger is adjustable for length and two-stage pull; also for horizontal or vertical pitch. Has several options that would affect price; muzzle brake, one-piece scope mount, bipod, quick detachable sling swivels and military nylon sling. Offered in .308 Win. only. Fitted with 25.75" barrel; weight 10.5 lbs.

NIB	Exc.	V.G.	Good	Fair	Poor
2500	2000	1500	1000	600	400

TRG-22

Similar to TRG-21. Meets exact specifications to comply with Finish military requirements. Chambered for .308 cartridge. Introduced in 2000. Offered in both green and black finish. Weight about 10.25 lbs. Note: Add $2,250 for folding stock version.

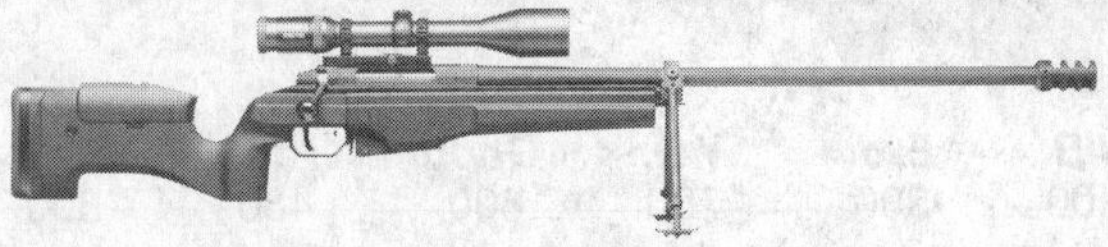

NIB	Exc.	V.G.	Good	Fair	Poor
3000	2400	1850	1250	800	500

TRG-41

Exactly the same as TRG-21, except chambered for .338 Lapua Magnum cartridge.

NIB	Exc.	V.G.	Good	Fair	Poor
3000	2500	2000	—	—	—

TRG-42

Similar to TRG-41. Meets exact specifications to comply with Finish military requirements. Chambered for .338 Lapua or .300 Win. Magnum cartridge. Introduced in 2000. Weight about 11.25 lbs.

NIB	Exc.	V.G.	Good	Fair	Poor
4000	3000	2000	—	—	—

SAM, INC.

Special Service Arms Mfg., Inc.
Reston, Virginia

Model 88 Crossfire

Semi-automatic combination 12-gauge/.308-caliber shotgun/rifle, with 7-shot shotgun magazine and 20-shot rifle magazine. Barrel length 20". Matte black finish, with composition stock. This weapon can be fired in either mode by means of a selector switch mounted on receiver.

NIB	Exc.	V.G.	Good	Fair	Poor
1900	1500	1180	800	550	300

SAMCO GLOBAL ARMS, INC.

Miami, Florida

This firm imports a variety of military surplus firearms, that under current law, are marked with the importer's name.

SARASQUETA, FELIX

Eibar, Spain

Merke

A 12-gauge over/under double-barrel shotgun, with 22" or 27" ribbed and separated barrels, non-selective trigger and manual extractors. Blued, checkered walnut stock. Imported in 1986 only.

NIB	Exc.	V.G.	Good	Fair	Poor
—	500	380	200	150	100

SARASQUETA, J. J.

Eibar, Spain

Model 107E

A 12-, 16- or 20-gauge boxlock double-barrel shotgun, with a variety of barrel lengths, double triggers and automatic ejectors. Blued, with checkered walnut stock. Discontinued in 1984.

NIB	Exc.	V.G.	Good	Fair	Poor
—	420	300	280	220	100

Model 119E

As above, with a more finely figured walnut stock.

NIB	Exc.	V.G.	Good	Fair	Poor
—	520	400	380	320	150

Model 130E

As above, but engraved.

NIB	Exc.	V.G.	Good	Fair	Poor
—	950	700	600	450	250

Model 131E

As above, with considerably more engraving.

NIB	Exc.	V.G.	Good	Fair	Poor
—	1350	900	800	650	350

Model 1882 E LUXE

As above, with a single-selective trigger and gold inlays. Silver inlaid version is sold for approximately 10 percent less.

NIB	Exc.	V.G.	Good	Fair	Poor
—	1750	1250	900	650	350

SARASQUETA, VICTOR

Eibar, Spain

Model 3

A 12-, 16- or 20-gauge boxlock or sidelock double-barrel shotgun. Available in a variety of barrel lengths, with double triggers and automatic ejectors. Blued, with checkered straight stock. Sidelock version is worth approximately 20 percent more than values listed. Basic Model 3 was offered in a variety of grades featuring different amounts of engraving and better quality wood. These shotguns are listed under the model designations of 4 to 12E.

NIB	Exc.	V.G.	Good	Fair	Poor
—	650	500	450	350	300

Model 4

NIB	Exc.	V.G.	Good	Fair	Poor
—	1200	1000	880	600	300

Model 4E (Auto-ejectors)

NIB	Exc.	V.G.	Good	Fair	Poor
—	1600	1400	1100	800	400

Model 203

NIB	Exc.	V.G.	Good	Fair	Poor
—	700	600	520	420	320

Model 203E

NIB	Exc.	V.G.	Good	Fair	Poor
—	900	750	620	480	380

Model 6E

NIB	Exc.	V.G.	Good	Fair	Poor
—	1400	1250	880	520	420

Model 7E

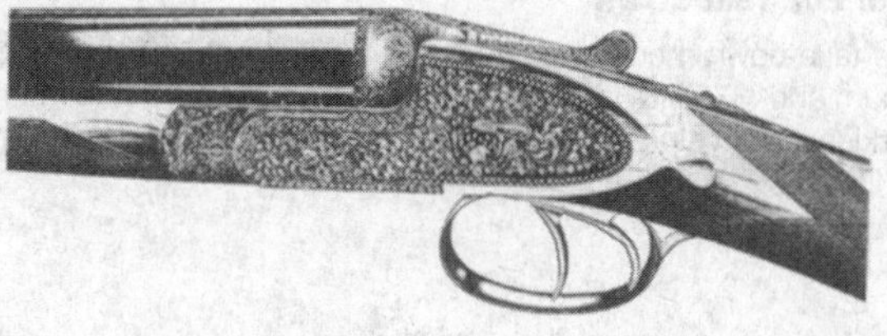

NIB	Exc.	V.G.	Good	Fair	Poor
—	1500	1350	1000	750	480

Model 10E

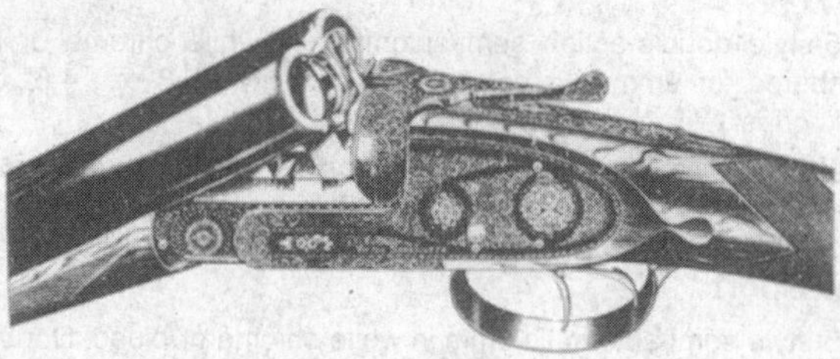

NIB	Exc.	V.G.	Good	Fair	Poor
—	2600	2100	1650	950	750

Model 11E

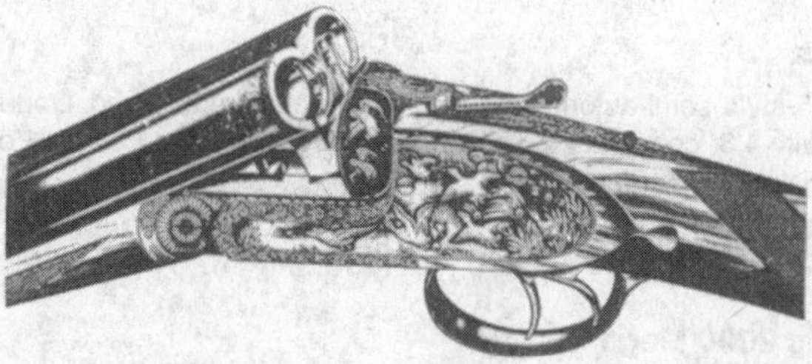

NIB	Exc.	V.G.	Good	Fair	Poor
—	3000	2600	2000	1150	850

Model 12E

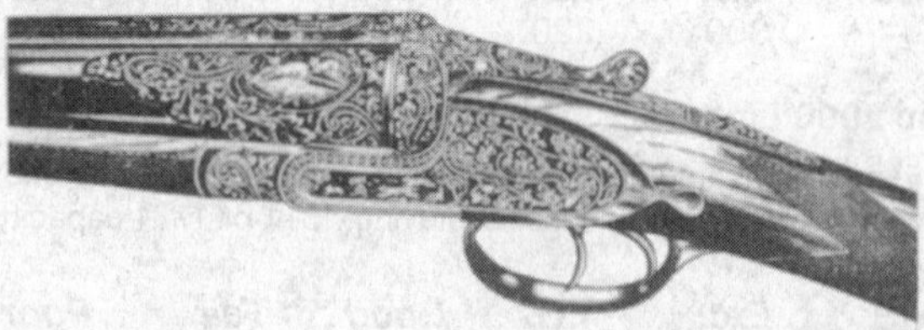

NIB	Exc.	V.G.	Good	Fair	Poor
—	3200	2850	2200	1300	1000

SARDIUS

Israel

SD-9

A 9mm double-action semi-automatic pistol, with 3" barrel and 6-shot magazine. Matte black finish, with composition grips. Imported since 1988.

NIB	Exc.	V.G.	Good	Fair	Poor
420	300	250	200	150	100

SARSILMAZ

Mercan/Istanbul, Turkey

Professional

CZ-75-style compensated semi-automatic in white chrome finish chambered for 9mm. Single-action with adjustable trigger, laser engraving. 16- or 18-round capacity. 42.3 oz.; 5.1" barrel. MSRP: $437.

K2

CZ-75-style double-action semi-automatic in white chrome or blued. Chambered for 9mm. 16- or 18-round capacity. 35.3 oz.; 4.6" barrel. Plastic grips.

NIB	*Exc.*	*V.G.*	*Good*	*Fair*	*Poor*
—	300	220	180	120	50

Kama Sport

CZ-75-style semi-automatic 9mm in white chrome or blued. Double-action with 3.9" compensated barrel, laser engraving. 15+1 or 17+1 capacity. 35.4 oz. Plastic grips.

NIB	*Exc.*	*V.G.*	*Good*	*Fair*	*Poor*
—	320	250	200	140	50

Kama

CZ-75-style semi-automatic 9mm in white chrome or blued. Double-action with 4.3" compensated barrel, laser engraving. 15+1 or 17+1 capacity. 35.4 oz.; 7.7". Plastic grips.

NIB	*Exc.*	*V.G.*	*Good*	*Fair*	*Poor*
—	300	220	180	120	50

Kilinc 2000 Mega

CZ-75-style semi-automatic 9mm in white chrome or blued. Double-action with 4.7" barrel. 16- or 18-round capacity. 35 oz. Plastic grips. Fixed sights.

NIB	*Exc.*	*V.G.*	*Good*	*Fair*	*Poor*
—	300	220	180	120	50

Kilinc 2000 Light

CZ-75-style semi-automatic 9mm in white chrome, blued or camo. Double-action with 4.7" barrel, laser engraving. 15+1 or 17+1 capacity. 35.4 oz. Plastic grips.

NIB	*Exc.*	*V.G.*	*Good*	*Fair*	*Poor*
—	300	220	180	120	50

Hancer 2000/2000 Light

CZ-75-style semi-automatic 9mm in white chrome or blued. Double-action with 3.9" barrel, laser engraving. 13+1 capacity. 33.5 oz. (25.4 oz. Light model). Plastic grips.

NIB	*Exc.*	*V.G.*	*Good*	*Fair*	*Poor*
—	300	220	180	120	50

Bernardelli

CZ-75-style double-action semi-automatic in 9mm. Black/white or blued finish. The 15+1 model has a 4.7" barrel, 27 oz., Plastic grips. The 13+1 model has a 3.9" barrel; 26.7 oz. Plastic grips, fixed sights.

NIB	*Exc.*	*V.G.*	*Good*	*Fair*	*Poor*
—	300	220	180	120	50

SAUER & SOHN, J. P.

Suhl and Eckernfoerde, Germany

Oldest firearms manufacturing firm in Germany. Founded in 1751 in Suhl. During this period the company produced high quality handguns and long guns. In 1938, it introduced a new double-action semi-automatic pistol, Sauer 38H. Pistol had the first decocking lever ever used on a mass produced pistol. In 1951, company relocated to Eckernfoerde where it continued to produce high quality firearms. Note: Model 90 Supreme and Model 202 have been imported by SIGARMS Inc. Sauer USA in San Antonio, Texas is current importer. Sauer firearms have also been sold by Colt (rifles), Charles Daly (shotguns), and Weatherby (rifles). Pricing updates by Jim Cate.

Bolt-Action Rifle

Mauser action sporting rifle. Chambered for a variety of cartridges, with 22" or 24" barrel featuring a raised rib. Double-set triggers, express sights. Blued, with checkered walnut stock. Manufactured prior to WWII.

NIB	*Exc.*	*V.G.*	*Good*	*Fair*	*Poor*
—	1250	900	6500	400	300

Model 200

Bolt-action rifle chambered for a variety of cartridges. Short or medium length actions, 24" barrels, set trigger, 4-round magazine. Blued, checkered walnut stock. Discontinued 1987. Note: Add $235 for extra barrels.

NIB	*Exc.*	*V.G.*	*Good*	*Fair*	*Poor*
1350	1050	700	500	420	350

Model 200 Lightweight

As above, with an alloy receiver. Discontinued in 1987.

NIB	*Exc.*	*V.G.*	*Good*	*Fair*	*Poor*
—	1100	900	550	320	250

Model 200 Lux

As above, with finely figured walnut stock, rosewood pistol grip cap and forend tip. Gold-plated trigger and machine jewelled bolt. Imported prior to 1988.

NIB	*Exc.*	*V.G.*	*Good*	*Fair*	*Poor*
—	1200	950	700	480	400

Model 200 Carbon Fiber

Fitted with a carbon composition stock. Imported in 1987 and 1988.

NIB	*Exc.*	*V.G.*	*Good*	*Fair*	*Poor*
—	1300	1100	800	500	400

Model 202 Supreme

Bolt-action rifle with a barrel change feature. Fitted with adjustable two-stage trigger, quick-change fluted barrel, black rubber recoil pad and removable box magazine. Stock is select American claro walnut, with high gloss finish and rosewood forend and grip cap. Buttstock has a Monte Carlo comb and cheekpiece. Offered in .243, .270, .308, .30-06 calibers; barrel length 23.6"; weight about 7.7 lbs. Supreme Magnum series available in 7mm Magnum, .300 Win. Magnum, .375 H&H Magnum calibers; barrel length 26"; weight about 8.4 lbs.

NIB	*Exc.*	*V.G.*	*Good*	*Fair*	*Poor*
2700	2000	1350	1000	750	400

Model 202 Takedown

A true take-down model. Introduced in 2003. Chambered for .300 Win. Magnum and .375 H&H. Other calibers will be offered in the future. Fancy Turkish walnut stock, with Monte Carlo and rosewood forend tip. Base price listed.

NIB	Exc.	V.G.	Good	Fair	Poor
5700	4400	2900	2000	1200	400

Model S202 Wolverine

Similar to Model 202 Supreme above, with 25.6" barrel, beavertail forend and adjustable cheekpiece. Chambered in various varmint calibers.

NIB	Exc.	V.G.	Good	Fair	Poor
—	2300	1950	1500	1050	400

Model S202 Highland

Similar to Model 202 Supreme above, with 20" barrel, schnabel forend and easily-detachable buttstock. Chambered in .308 Win. and various European cartridges.

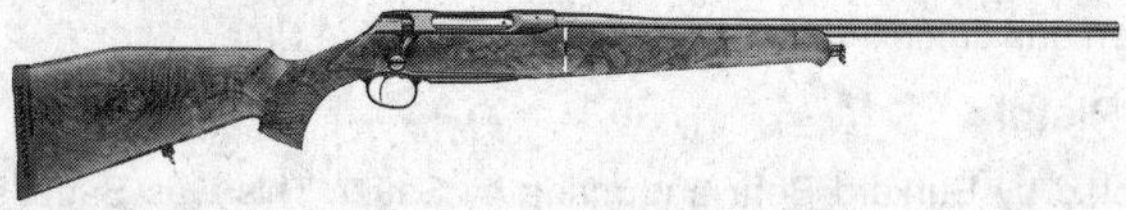

NIB	Exc.	V.G.	Good	Fair	Poor
3500	2800	2250	1500	1050	400

Model S202 Forest

Carbine-style version of Model 202 Highland above. Intended specifically for drive hunts. Has standard forend and 25.6" barrel. Chambered in various varmint calibers.

NIB	Exc.	V.G.	Good	Fair	Poor
—	2500	1950	1500	1050	400

Model S202 Hardwood

Similar to Model 202 Highland above. Oddly enough, with a synthetic stock with orange inserts. Chambered in .308 Win. and various European cartridges.

NIB	Exc.	V.G.	Good	Fair	Poor
3300	2600	2100	1500	1050	400

Model S202 Match

Target version of Model 202, with 26.8" match barrel, wide forend. Chambered in .300 Win. Magnum and 6.5x55 Swedish.

NIB	Exc.	V.G.	Good	Fair	Poor
—	2500	1950	1500	1050	400

Model S202 Outback

Similar to Model 202 Hardwood above, with lightweight construction and plain black synthetic stock

NIB	Exc.	V.G.	Good	Fair	Poor
3000	2500	1950	1500	1050	400

Model S202 Team Sauer

Classically-styled sporter version of Model 202, with heavy medium or Magnum-weight barrel. Walnut Monte Carlo stock. Chambered in various European and American long-action cartridges from 6.5x55 Swedish up to .300 Win. Magnum.

NIB	Exc.	V.G.	Good	Fair	Poor
—	1950	1600	1250	800	400

Model 90

Bolt-action rifle produced in a number of calibers and in all action lengths, with 23" or 26" barrels. Detachable magazine. Blued, with checkered walnut stock.

NIB	Exc.	V.G.	Good	Fair	Poor
—	1300	1100	680	500	300

Model 90 Stutzen

As above, with a full-length Mannlicher-style stock. Imported prior to 1990.

NIB	Exc.	V.G.	Good	Fair	Poor
—	1350	1150	720	550	350

Model 90 Safari

Model 90 made for use with .458 Win. Magnum cartridge. Fitted with a 24" barrel. Imported from 1986 to 1988. Note: Model 90 Series of bolt-action rifles was available in a deluxe version that differed with grade of workmanship and materials utilized. This deluxe series would be worth approximately 60 percent additional.

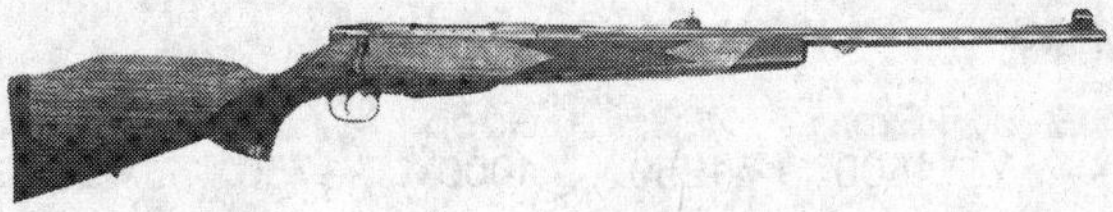

NIB	Exc.	V.G.	Good	Fair	Poor
—	2300	2000	1250	900	400

Model 90 Supreme

Similar to above, with gold-plated trigger, machine jewelled bolt and finely figured checkered walnut stock. Introduced in 1987.

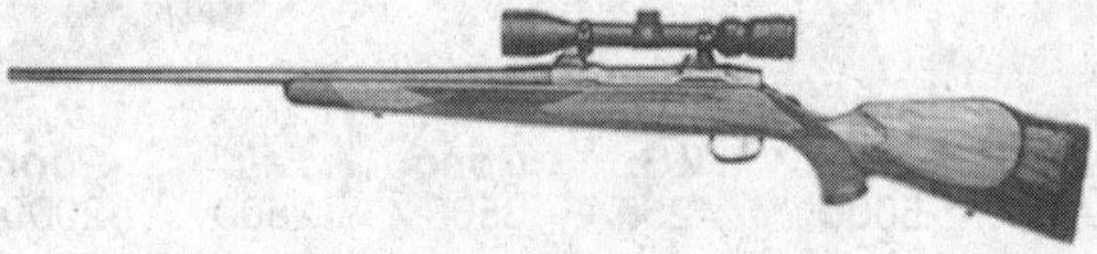

NIB	Exc.	V.G.	Good	Fair	Poor
—	2500	2200	1420	1000	400

SSG-3000

See entry in SIG-Sauer section.

SG 550 Sniper

Note: For other current Sauer rifles see SIGARMS.

NIB	Exc.	V.G.	Good	Fair	Poor
5500	4750	3880	2700	2000	500

SHOTGUN/RIFLE COMBINATIONS

Luftwaffe M30 Survival Drilling

Double-barrel 12-gauge by 9.3x74R combination shotgun/rifle, with 28" barrels. Blued, with checkered walnut stock and marked with Nazi inspection. Stampings on stock and barrel breech. Normally furnished with an aluminum case. Note: Add 50 percent to prices for case.

NIB	Exc.	V.G.	Good	Fair	Poor
20000	15000	9500	6000	3250	1500

Model 3000 Drilling

Chambered for a variety of gauges and calibers. Built upon a boxlock action, with a Greener crossbolt. Action is lightly engraved. Blued, checkered walnut stock.

NIB	Exc.	V.G.	Good	Fair	Poor
5500	3700	2750	2000	1500	1250

Model 54 Combo

Combination rifle/shotgun. Chambered for a variety of gauges and calibers, with an action as above. Discontinued in 1986.

NIB	Exc.	V.G.	Good	Fair	Poor
—	3000	2250	1750	1400	1200

SHOTGUNS

Model 60

A 12-, 16- or 20-gauge double-barrel boxlock shotgun. Produced in a variety of barrel lengths, with double triggers and manual extractors. Blued, with checkered walnut stock. Produced prior to WWII.

NIB	Exc.	V.G.	Good	Fair	Poor
—	1300	950	720	550	400

Royal Model

A 12- or 20-gauge boxlock double-barrel shotgun, with 26", 28" or 30" barrels. Single-selective triggers, with automatic ejectors. Frame is scalloped. Blued, with checkered walnut stock. Manufactured from 1955 to 1977.

NIB	Exc.	V.G.	Good	Fair	Poor
—	1500	1250	1000	750	500

Grade I Artemis

A 12-gauge sidelock double-barrel shotgun, with 28" barrels, single-selective trigger and automatic ejector. Engraved, blued with checkered walnut stock. Manufactured from 1966 to 1977.

NIB	Exc.	V.G.	Good	Fair	Poor
—	5000	4250	3500	2500	2000

Grade II Artemis

As above, but more finely finished.

NIB	Exc.	V.G.	Good	Fair	Poor
—	6500	5750	4750	3500	3000

Model 66

A 12-gauge sidelock double-barrel shotgun, with 26", 28" or 30" barrel. Single-selective trigger and automatic ejectors. Blued, checkered walnut stock. Produced in three different grades that have different degrees of engraving. Produced from 1966 to 1975.

Grade I

NIB	Exc.	V.G.	Good	Fair	Poor
—	2000	1800	1500	1150	800

Grade II

NIB	Exc.	V.G.	Good	Fair	Poor
—	3000	2800	2500	2150	1800

Grade III

NIB	Exc.	V.G.	Good	Fair	Poor
—	3750	3500	2850	2500	2000

SL5 Turkey

Gauge: 12 ga. 3 in. Barrel: 18.5-in. deep-drilled, chrome-lined, with stepped rib. Weight: 7 lbs. Stock: Fixed synthetic pistol grip style in choice of three Mossy Oak camo patterns: Obsession, Bottomland, or New Bottomland. Features: Durable inertia-driven semi-automatic with black anodized receiver. Oversized bolt handle and release button. Removeable Picatinny rail. Cervellati recoil pad and sling attachments. Red single-bead LPA front fiber-optic sight. Made in Italy and backed by 10-year warranty. Ships with three chokes: flush cylinder, extender CRIO Plus Modified, and Carlson extended turkey choke.

NIB	Exc.	V.G.	Good	Fair	Poor
1080	—	—	—	—	—

SL-5 Waterfowl

Gauges: 12 ga. Barrels: 26", 28", 30" chrome-lined with stepped rib Stock: Synthetic with the choice of black or Fred Bear Old School camouflage. Features: Latest addition to the inertia-driven semi-automatic line. Steel upper receiver and aluminum lower. Magnum 3.5" chamber. Extended bolt handle and release button. Cervellati recoil pad. Rubberized comb. Ships with five Crio Plus extended chokes.

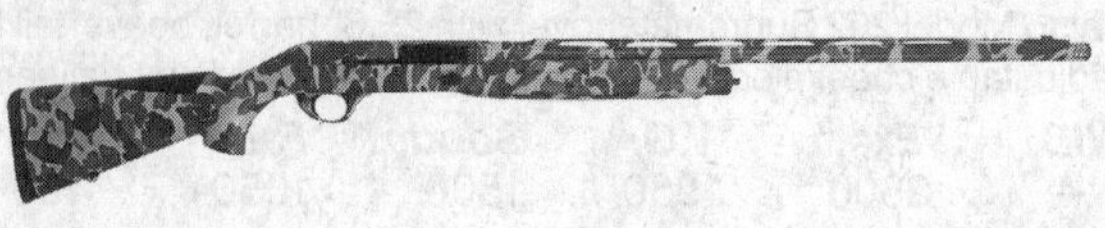

NIB	Exc.	V.G.	Good	Fair	Poor
1440	1370	—	—	—	—

PISTOLS

Written and compiled by our very good friend Jim Cate.

Bär Pistol

Invented by Burkard Behr and made by Sauer. This was Sauer's first modern small pistol. It has stacked barrels (over/under configuration) that allow the shooter to fire two shots, rotate the barrel and then fire two more shots before loading. It was first patented in Germany in 1897 and in the USA in 1899. It shoots the 7mm Bär cartridge only. (DO NOT ATTEMPT TO FIRE THE .25 ACP/6.35mm CARTRIDGE IN THIS PISTOL.) It was made from 1897 to 1911 or 1912. Some pistols have Bakelite grips; some have diamond-pattern checkered wood grips. A case extractor rod screws into the bottom of the frame. No triggerguard. Note: Add $150 for original box and instructions.

NIB	Exc.	V.G.	Good	Fair	Poor
—	1500	1100	450	280	–

Roth-Sauer Model

Very first automatic pistol produced by J.P. Sauer & Son. Designed by Karl Krinka for George Roth. Available only in 7.65 Roth-Sauer caliber. A locked breech design, beautifully finished and extremely well made. Later this design was modified and became the Roth-Steyr military pistol, which was adopted by Austria in 1907. A difficult-to-find pistol.

NIB	Exc.	V.G.	Good	Fair	Poor
—	2800	2000	1000	500	300

SAUER MODEL 1913 FIRST SERIES

First Series, which incorporates an extra safety button on the left side of frame near trigger. Rear sight is simply a milled recess in the cocking knob itself. Serial number range runs from 1 to approximately 4750. First series is found only in 7.65mm caliber. All were for commercial sales as far as can be determined. Some were tested by various militaries, no doubt.

A. European variation—all slide legends are in the German language.
B. English Export variation—slide legends are marked, J.P. Sauer & Son, Suhl - Prussia, "Sauer's Patent" Pat'd May 20 1912.

Both were sold in thick paper cartons or boxes, with the color being a reddish purple with gold colored letters, etc. Examples of the very early European variation are found with the English language brochure or manual as well as an extra magazine, cleaning brush and grease container. These were shipped to England or the U.S. prior to Sauer producing the English Export variation. Note: Original box with accessories and manual: Add $500 if complete and in very good to excellent condition.

A. European variation:

NIB	Exc.	V.G.	Good	Fair	Poor
—	1500	900	650	400	250

B. English Export variation

NIB	Exc.	V.G.	Good	Fair	Poor
2300	1900	1300	800	500	300

SAUER MODEL 1913 SECOND SERIES

Extra safety button eliminated. Rear sight acts as cocking knob retainer.

Commercial variation

Normal European/German slide markings are normally found; however it has been called to my attention that there are English Export pistols in this SECOND SERIES. They have the English markings on the slide which are similar to those found on FIRST SERIES Model 1913. This is applicable to both the 7.65mm and 6.35mm Model 1913/19 pistols. These are exceptionally scarce pistols and should command at least a 50 percent premium, perhaps more due to their rarity. This commercial variation had factory manuals printed in English, Spanish and German which came with the cardboard boxed pistols. Note: With the original Sauer box, accessories and manual: Add $300 if in very good to excellent condition.

Caliber 7.65mm variation

NIB	Exc.	V.G.	Good	Fair	Poor
—	600	450	300	250	100

Caliber 7.65 variation with all words in English (i.e Son, Prussia, etc.)

NIB	Exc.	V.G.	Good	Fair	Poor
—	900	600	450	300	200

Police Variations

These will be standard German Commercial configuration, but always having Zusatzsicherung (additional safety) added to pistol. Safety is found between regular safety lever and top of left grip. Police used both calibers 7.65mm and 6.35mm, but 7.65mm was predominant. After early part of 1930s, 6.35mm was not available to police departments. Thus, 6.35mm police marked Sauer is rather scarce in relation to 7.65mm caliber. Few in 7.65mm are dated 1920 on left side of frame and were used by auxiliary policemen in Bavaria. Normal police property markings are on front or rear grip straps. Most were originally issued with at least two magazines and police accepted holster. Mags were usually numbered and holsters are found with and without pistol numbers. Note: Add 10 percent for one correctly numbered magazine; 20 percent if found with both correctly numbered magazines; 30 percent if found with correct holster and magazines.

Caliber 6.35mm police marked with Zusatzsicherung—RARE!

NIB	Exc.	V.G.	Good	Fair	Poor
—	625	400	300	200	80

Caliber 7.65mm police marked without Zusatzsicherung

NIB	Exc.	V.G.	Good	Fair	Poor
—	650	400	280	180	120

Caliber 7.65mm police marked with Zusatzsicherung

NIB	Exc.	V.G.	Good	Fair	Poor
—	650	400	280	180	120

R.F.V. (Reich Finanz Verwaltung)

This Sauer variation is rarely found in any condition. R.F.V. markings and property number could be 1 to 4 digits. This variation is found in both calibers. Used by the Reich's Customs and Finance department personnel.

Caliber 6.35mm R.F.V. marked pistols

NIB	Exc.	V.G.	Good	Fair	Poor
—	1300	950	600	350	250

Caliber 7.65mm R.F.V. marked pistols

NIB	Exc.	V.G.	Good	Fair	Poor
—	1000	750	500	300	200

Imperial Military Variations

Normal German commercial variations of the time period. Either Imperial Eagle acceptance marking applied on front of triggerguard and having small Imperial Army inspector's acceptance marking (crown over a scriptic letter) on right side of frame close to Nitro proof; or just Imperial Army inspector's marking alone. Usually pistols are found in 40000 to 85000 range. However, quantity actually of Imperial Military accepted is quite low even though thousands were privately purchased by officer corps. There are examples in 6.35mm which are Imperial Military accepted, but these are very scarce. Note: Add 30 percent for 6.35mm.

Caliber 7.65mm Imperial Military accepted pistols

NIB	Exc.	V.G.	Good	Fair	Poor
—	2000	1000	550	300	150

SAUER MODEL 1913 THIRD SERIES

This series has an extra safety (Zusatzsicherung) noted on left side of frame to left of the grip. This device blocked the trigger-bar internally. These were sold commercially. A few were exported with GERMANY noted on them and to a very few police departments. Police examples will have grip-strap markings including property number of the pistol.

Caliber 7.65mm Commercial with Zusatzsicherung

NIB	Exc.	V.G.	Good	Fair	Poor
1750	850	650	400	280	150

Police with Zusatzsicherung and police grip-strap markings

NIB	Exc.	V.G.	Good	Fair	Poor
2850	2000	1300	600	300	150

POST WWI AND WWII VARIATIONS

Paramilitary marked Sauer pistols of the 1925-35 period

Very few Model 1913 pistols would have been marked by paramilitary groups or organizations of this period. Usually this marking is no more than a series of numbers above another series of numbers, such as 23 over 12. These are found usually on the left side of frame next to left grip. Most of these numbers are indicative of property numbers assigned to a particular pistol belonging to a particular SA Group, Stahlhelm or right-wing organization such as Red Front (early communist). Any pistol of this type should be examined by an expert to determine if it is an original example.

NIB	Exc.	V.G.	Good	Fair	Poor
—	1500	800	500	200	100

Norwegian police usage, post WWII

After the war was over, many surplus German weapons were put back into use by the government of Norway. Germans had occupied this country and large numbers of weapons remained when the fighting ended. This included a large number of surplus Sauer pistols being utilized by the police (POLITI) forces. Most of the Sauers that were used by the Politi, which have been imported into the U.S. have been Model 1913; however, there were a number of Model 1930 pistols which reached our country as well. All examples, regardless of model, have the word POLITI stamped on the slide as well as a rampant lion on a shield under a crown marking. Following this is the property number. This number is also stamped into the left side of the frame. Most saw much usage during the post-war period. All are in 7.65mm caliber.

NIB	Exc.	V.G.	Good	Fair	Poor
—	650	480	300	150	100

Model 19 in 6.35mm

This particular pistol must be divided into three (3) sub-variations. This variation appears to be in a serial number range of its own. First sub-variation appears to run from 1 to 40000. It is highly doubtful if this quantity was manufactured. Second sub-variation incorporates a Zusatzsicherung or Additional Safety which can be seen between the normal safety lever and top of the left grip. It locked the trigger bar when in use. This second range appears to run from approximately serial number 40000 to 51000 which probably was continuous in the number produced. Lastly, third sub-variation examples were manufactured during or after 1926. Triggerguard has a different shape; slide has a greater area of vertical milled finger grooves; added Additional safety (Zusatzsicherung) now acts as the hold open device as well. These are found up to approximately 57000. Then a few examples of the first sub-variation are found from 57000 up to about 62500. This was, no doubt, usage of remaining parts. Note: Any commercial pistol could be special ordered with a factory nickel finish, special grip material (pearl, wood, etc.) as well as different types of engraving. It would be in your best interest to have these pistols examined by an expert.

Caliber 6.35mm first sub-variation

NIB	Exc.	V.G.	Good	Fair	Poor
—	580	480	300	150	80

Caliber 6.35mm second sub-variation

NIB	Exc.	V.G.	Good	Fair	Poor
—	600	480	300	150	80

Caliber 6.35mm third sub-variation

NIB	Exc.	V.G.	Good	Fair	Poor
—	700	550	500	200	100

Caliber 6.35mm English export variation—RARE!

NIB	Exc.	V.G.	Good	Fair	Poor
—	1300	1000	580	400	200

1926 Export Model

This variation's name comes from actual Sauer factory records found in the Suhl Archive. An interim pistol produced during 1926 to early 1929 period. Found only in 7.65mm caliber. This was an advancement of the normal 1913 design, which included changes in: (1) safety lever's design that became a slide hold open device as well; (2) shape of the frame was altered in that the triggerguard became more streamlined and the rear of frame was shortened and serrations were added to the slide as well as cocking knob. These are found in 162000 to 169000 range in relatively small clusters. Two to four thousand are presumed to have been manufactured. A scarce Sauer pistol! To date, none have been seen in nickel.

NIB	Exc.	V.G.	Good	Fair	Poor
2800	1400	900	550	300	150

W.T.M.-Westentaschen Model—Vest Pocket Model

Several variations of vest pocket pistols were manufactured. First was called Model 1920 by the Sauer firm. We usually refer to it as Model 1924. Pistol, as well as all other W.T.M. examples, were designed to carry in your pocket. Quite small in size and found only in 6.35mm or .25 ACP caliber. Later in 1928, an updated version became available and was referred to as Model 1928. These differed in internal parts design and slide configuration. Bottom of grip marked "Cal.6.35.28.". Last version appeared in 1933 and still utilized same grips, but trigger and other small parts differed. All three were available in blue or nickel finish, engraving and fancy grip material. Very few Model 1933 had stainless steel (NIROSTA marked) barrels.

Model 1920

Serrations on front and rear of slide.

NIB	Exc.	V.G.	Good	Fair	Poor
1800	1200	850	300	200	80

Model 1928

"Cal. 6.35.28" on black Bakelite grips.

NIB	Exc.	V.G.	Good	Fair	Poor
2000	1500	900	400	200	80

Model 1933—RARE!

Different type of trigger. Found in 253000 to early 254000 serial number range. Note: Add $200 factory nickel; $250 factory engraving; $250 exotic grip material; $500 factory paper box with cleaning brush, extra magazine and brochure; $750 in original factory imitation leather covered metal presentation case with accessories; $500 NIROSTA marked stainless barrel.

NIB	Exc.	V.G.	Good	Fair	Poor
3000	2000	1250	650	300	150

MODEL 1930 VARIATIONS

Dutch Models

These different types of Dutch pistols will have JOH MUNTS - AMSTERDAM on left side of slide. Grips are usually mottled gray color. Sauer manufactured different pistols for Dutch police, Navy, Army, Department of Finance, S.M.N. (Steam Ships Netherlands) and possibly other agencies. Note: Accessories: cleaning rod, brush, aluminum oil bottle and manuals, add accordingly.

Dutch Police

First variation manufactured w/o adjustable front sight and lanyard loop.

NIB	Exc.	V.G.	Good	Fair	Poor
—	1030	900	450	250	120

Amsterdam Police

Manufactured w/o adjustable sight, but having lanyard loop.

NIB	Exc.	V.G.	Good	Fair	Poor
1750	1400	1100	800	450	200

Navy

Made w/o adjustable sight. Anchor & Crown marked on rear grip strap.

NIB	Exc.	V.G.	Good	Fair	Poor
2500	2000	1500	900	450	200

S.M.N.

Found with and w/o adjustable front sights, no lanyard loop. S.M.N. marked horizontally near bottom of rear grip strap.

NIB	Exc.	V.G.	Good	Fair	Poor
2750	2000	1300	900	450	200

Department of Finance

Found with and w/o adjustable front sight, no lanyard loop. DF over date-1933 on rear grip strap.

NIB	Exc.	V.G.	Good	Fair	Poor
2750	2100	1500	600	300	150

1930 Commercial Model

These pistols were for sale in Germany and other countries through normal commercial outlets. Very few are factory nickeled, engraved or both; some are with NIROSTA marked barrels and a very few were made in Duralumin or Dural. Standard caliber was 7.65mm, but a very limited number were made in .22 LR (.22 Long). Standard grip material is black Bakelite. Most of the regular pistols were purchased by military officers, some went to paramilitary groups such as the SA. Note: Add $100 for any variation listed with nickel finish; $500 for engraving; $600 for both nickel and engraving; $750 for nickel, engraving and with a fancy grip material (pearl or ebony, etc.).

Standard Commercial

NIB	Exc.	V.G.	Good	Fair	Poor
1750	1450	1100	800	450	200

Standard Commercial with NIROSTA marked barrel, 7.65mm

NIB	Exc.	V.G.	Good	Fair	Poor
2500	1850	1200	800	450	200

Standard Commercial in .22 LR (.22 Long)—RARE!

NIB	Exc.	V.G.	Good	Fair	Poor
—	3700	2200	1750	600	300

Duralumin (Dural) Variation, 7.65mm

NIB	Exc.	V.G.	Good	Fair	Poor
—	3700	3000	2250	1300	450

BEHORDEN MODEL

Behorden (Authority) Model is different from Model 1930. It has a trigger safety and a loaded indicator provided.

Behorden Commercial

These are normally found with a high polished blued finish. Were available with a nickel finish, engraving, or both, as well as fancy grip material and NIROSTA marked barrel. Regular caliber is 7.65mm, but a very few are known in .22 LR that are probably proto-type pistols. Note: Add $100 for nickel finish; $250 for engraving; $350 for both; $500 with nickel, engraving and a fancy grip material; $500 for NIROSTA marked stainless barrel; 300 percent for .22-caliber.

NIB	Exc.	V.G.	Good	Fair	Poor
2250	1300	750	450	350	200

Late Behorden Commercial

These are actually Model 1930 pistols found in 220000 to 223000 serial number range. They do not have trigger safety and/or indicator pin.

NIB	Exc.	V.G.	Good	Fair	Poor
—	800	500	350	200	120

Duralumin Model (Dural)

Frame and slide are made of Duralumin material. These are rare pistols! Note: Add $250 for stainless barrel.

Blue Anodized Variation

Found with and w/o NIROSTA marked barrels.

NIB	Exc.	V.G.	Good	Fair	Poor
8000	6000	4000	2500	1500	850

Nonanodized Variation

Found with and w/o NIROSTA marked barrels.

NIB	Exc.	V.G.	Good	Fair	Poor
7000	4000	3500	2500	1500	850

Presentation Examples of Anodized and Nonanodized Variations

Please consult an expert for pricing.

Police Models

Examples will be found with police acceptance on the left side of triggerguard. In a few cases on the front or rear grip straps. Black Bakelite grips are standard.

Sunburst K Police Acceptance

Non-adjustable front sight (a round blade).

NIB	Exc.	V.G.	Good	Fair	Poor
—	1400	950	550	300	200

Sunburst K Police Acceptance

Adjustable front sight.

NIB	Exc.	V.G.	Good	Fair	Poor
—	1500	1000	750	400	220

Diamond in Sunburst Police Acceptance

All known are with the adjustable front sight.

NIB	Exc.	V.G.	Good	Fair	Poor
—	2200	1700	1000	400	220

Grip Strap Marked Variations

(Having abbreviations of a city and property number of the pistol on grip strap.) Very few of these are known. Examples are S.Mg. 52, Sch. 78, etc.

NIB	Exc.	V.G.	Good	Fair	Poor
—	1700	1000	680	350	150

MODEL 36/37

These very few pistols are all prototype Sauer pistols which preceded Model 38. They are in 210,000 range. Please consult an expert to determine value! EXTREMELY RARE.

MODEL 38 AND 38-H (H MODEL) VARIATIONS

Model 38

This pistol started at 260000. Crown N Nitro proofed, has cocking/decocking lever, loaded indicator pin and is double-action. High polish blue in 7.65mm (standard production pistol); found without thumb safety on slide; with pinned mag release. VERY RARE.

One Line Slide Legend Variation (pinned magazine release button - no screw)

Crown N proofs. Approximately 250 produced. Extremely rare!

NIB	Exc.	V.G.	Good	Fair	Poor
—	3800	3000	2000	600	300

Two Line Slide Legend Variation (pinned magazine release button - no screw)

C/N proofs, blued, with pinned magazine release (about 850 produced) VERY RARE. Note: Add $250 factory nickel; $1000 engraving; $500 NIROSTA marked barrel.

NIB	Exc.	V.G.	Good	Fair	Poor
—	2600	2000	1500	500	280

Two Line Slide Legend Variation (magazine release button - with screw)

C/N proofs, blued, magazine release button retained by a screw. RARE. Note: Add $250 factory nickel; $350 factory chrome; $1000 engraving; $500 NIROSTA marked barrel.

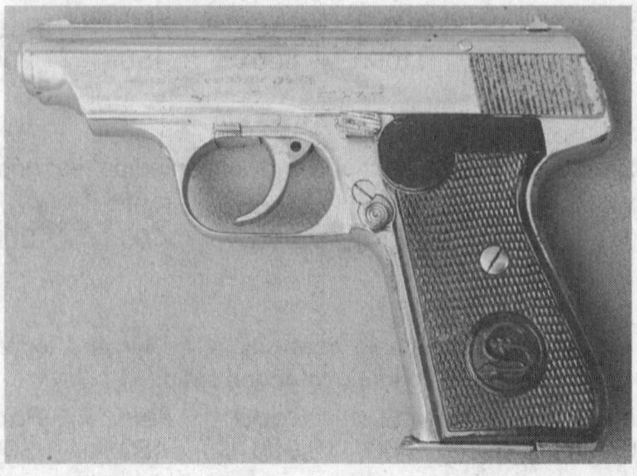

NIB	Exc.	V.G.	Good	Fair	Poor
—	2500	1500	900	500	280

SA der NSDAP Gruppe Thuringen Marked Variation

Blued, C/N proofs, with magazine release button held by a screw. VERY RARE.

NIB	Exc.	V.G.	Good	Fair	Poor
—	7500	5000	3000	750	280

Model 38 pistols converted to H Models by Sauer factory

Currently fewer than 30 known examples in collections. Thumb safety levers were added. Unique milling on left side of slide determines these pistols in 262xxx, 263xxx and 264xxx ranges. Includes SA der NSDAP Gruppe Thringen marked pistols.

NIB	Exc.	V.G.	Good	Fair	Poor
—	3500	2000	1000	450	—

Model 38-H or H Model

This model has a thumb safety on the slide, CROWN N NITRO proof, high polish blued finish, a cocking/decocking lever, double-action. Found in 7.65mm caliber as the standard production pistol. This model is found only with two line slide legend or logo. Type 1, variation 2.

Standard Commercial Variation

Note: Add $100 for factory nickel (factory chromed has not been identified); $1000 for factory engraving; $250 for exotic grip material; $500 for NIROSTA marked stainless barrel.

NIB	Exc.	V.G.	Good	Fair	Poor
—	1650	1050	700	400	180

SA der NSDAP Gruppe Thuringia Variation

Same as Standard above. Having SA markings on slide, with blued finish. VERY RARE. Note: Add $1200 for SA marked Akah holster in excellent condition.

NIB	Exc.	V.G.	Good	Fair	Poor
—	6000	4000	2500	900	400

L.M. Model

(Leicht Model-lightweight model); frame and slide made of DURAL (Duralumin), in the 264800 range, with thumb safety and regular black Bakelite grips. EXTREMELY RARE.

NIB	Exc.	V.G.	Good	Fair	Poor
—	8500	6000	4000	2000	1000

Flash Light Model

Only four known examples of this variation. Battery flash light attached by four screws to pistol. Carried by SS night patrol at the Reich's chancellory in Berlin. No specific markings, but known serial numbers are 266814, 266842, 266845.

NIB	Exc.	V.G.	Good	Fair	Poor
—Too Rare To Price—			—	—	—

Police Accepted Variation

Found with Police Eagle C acceptance on left triggerguard and having Crown N proofs. RARE.

NIB	Exc.	V.G.	Good	Fair	Poor
—	3500	3000	2000	600	180

TYPE TWO MODEL 38-H (H MODEL)

There are no Model 38 pistols in Type Two description, only H Model with thumb safety. These begin at serial number 269100 and have Eagle N Nitro proofs, with blued high polish finish and black Bakelite grips. Normal caliber is 7.65mm.

H Model - Type Two

Standard Commercial

Note: Add $1500 boxed examples complete with factory manual, clean ring rod, all accessories, extra magazine, etc.; $250 factory nickel; $350 factory chrome; $1000 factory engraving.

NIB	Exc.	V.G.	Good	Fair	Poor
4000	3000	2000	800	350	200

.22 Caliber Variation

Slide and magazines marked CAL. .22 LANG. (Some with steel frame and slides; some with Dural frames and slides.) Found in 269900 range. Very Rare.

NIB	Exc.	V.G.	Good	Fair	Poor
—Too Rare To Price—			1000	600	

Jager Model

Special order pistol in .22-caliber. Similar in appearance to Walther's 1936 Jagerschafts pistol. Very rare.

NIB	Exc.	V.G.	Good	Fair	Poor
—	18000	11000	5000	2000	600

Police Eagle C and Eagle F Acceptance Variations

First Eagle N (post January 1940) police accepted pistols. Found in 270000 to 276000 ranges. Note: Add 50 percent for E/F.

NIB	Exc.	V.G.	Good	Fair	Poor
—	2000	1200	750	400	200

German Military Variation Double Eagle 37

First official military accepted range of 2,000 pistols. In a range found between 271000 to 273000. Two Eagle 37 military acceptance marks found on triggerguard.

NIB	Exc.	V.G.	Good	Fair	Poor
—	4500	3000	1500	800	300

Second Military Variation

Pistols found with high polish finish. Have only one Eagle 37 acceptance mark. Letter H found on all small parts.

NIB	Exc.	V.G.	Good	Fair	Poor
—	2200	1600	950	450	200

Police Eagle C Acceptance

This variation includes remainder of high polish blued police accepted pistols. Note: Add $50 matching magazine; $200 both matching mags and correct police holster; $300 both matching mags and correct matching numbered police accepted and dated holster.

NIB	Exc.	V.G.	Good	Fair	Poor
—	1750	1200	900	400	180

TYPE THREE 38-H MODEL (H MODEL)

Terminology used because the change of exterior finish of Sauer pistols. Due to urgency of the war, order was received not to polish exterior surfaces of pistols, as had been done previously. Also a change in formulation of grip's material. Later in this range there will be found stamped parts, zinc triggers and magazine bottoms, etc. used to increase pistol's production. Type Three has a full slide legend.

H Model - Type Three

Military Accepted

One Eagle 37 Waffenamt mark.

NIB	Exc.	V.G.	Good	Fair	Poor
—	1000	750	500	300	150

Commercial

Only Eagle N Nitro proof marks. Note: See Type Two Commercial. Prices apply here also.

NIB	Exc.	V.G.	Good	Fair	Poor
1000	800	500	400	250	150

Police Accepted with the Police Eagle C Acceptance

Note: See Type Two Police. Prices apply here also.

NIB	Exc.	V.G.	Good	Fair	Poor
—	1000	750	400	250	150

TYPE FOUR 38-H MODEL (H MODEL)

Continuation of pistol as described in Type Three, except J.P. Sauer & Sohn, Suhl legend is dropped from slide and only CAL. 7.65 is found on left side. Word PATENT may or may not appear on right side. Many are found with a zinc trigger.

H Model - Type Four

Military Accepted

NIB	Exc.	V.G.	Good	Fair	Poor
—	850	650	400	280	150

Commercial Boxed

Having only Eagle N Nitro proofs. Note: See Type Two Commercial info. Prices apply here also.

NIB	Exc.	V.G.	Good	Fair	Poor
3500	1200	850	600	300	200

Police Accepted with the Police Eagle C Acceptance

Note: See Type Two Price info. Prices apply here also.

NIB	Exc.	V.G.	Good	Fair	Poor
—	850	650	450	300	150

Eigentum NSDAP SA Gruppe Alpenland Slide Marked Pistols

Unique pistols found in 456000 and 457000 serial number ranges. Has thumb safety levers on slides.

NIB	Exc.	V.G.	Good	Fair	Poor
8500	4500	3500	2000	750	400

NSDAP SA Gruppe Alpenland Slide Marked Pistols

Unique pistols found in 465000 serial number range. Has thumb safety levers on slide.

NIB	Exc.	V.G.	Good	Fair	Poor
8500	4500	3500	2500	600	400

Himmler Presentation Pistols

These desirable pistols have high polish finish with DEM SCHARF-SCHUTZEN - H. HIMMLER on left side of slide (with no other markings) and J.P. SAUER & SON over CAL. 7.65 on right side (opposite of normal). Pistols came in imitation leather cover metal cases, with cloth interiors having a cleaning brush, extra magazine and cartridges. Very rare pistols! Extremely rare if cased! Only 12 are known presently.

NIB	Exc.	V.G.	Good	Fair	Poor
40000	38500	25000	18000	5000	1500

Model 38

To speed up production even more thumb safety (Handsicherung-Hammer safety) was eliminated. Side continues to be marked only with CAL. 7.65. Frame's serial number changes from right side to left at 472000, with overlaps up to 489000.

Military Accepted

One Eagle 37 Waffenamt mark.

NIB	Exc.	V.G.	Good	Fair	Poor
—	700	500	400	250	180

Commercial Boxed

Only the Eagle N Nitro proofs. Note: See Type Two Commercial info. Prices apply here also.

NIB	Exc.	V.G.	Good	Fair	Poor
2000	900	500	350	250	180

Police Accepted with Police Eagle C Acceptance

NIB	Exc.	V.G.	Good	Fair	Poor
—	700	500	400	300	200

Police Accepted with Police Eagle F Acceptance

NIB	Exc.	V.G.	Good	Fair	Poor
—	1250	800	600	320	200

TYPE FIVE MODEL 38 & H MODEL PISTOLS

Two different basic variations of Type Five Sauer pistols. May or may not have thumb safety lever on slide. Main criteria is whether frame is factory numbered as per normal and follows chronological sequence of those pistols in preceding model. After frames were used which were already numbered and finished upon arrival of U.S. Army, last variation came about. Neither variation has any Nitro proof marks. Note: There are some pistols which have post-war Russian Crown N Nitro proofs. Russians assembled or refurbished a very few pistols after U.S. Army left Suhl after the war. Several have been found with newly made barrels in 7.65mm, with C/N proof. Hard to find Sauer!

First Variation

Factory numbered sequential frames starting on or near serial number 506800. Slides and breech-blocks may or may not match.

NIB	Exc.	V.G.	Good	Fair	Poor
—	600	500	300	220	100

Second Variation

Started with serial number 1; made from mostly rejected parts, generally have notched triggerguards, may or may not be blued, no Nitro proofs, slides may or may not have factory legends, etc. Approximately 300 assembled. Definitely rare Sauer pistols.

NIB	Exc.	V.G.	Good	Fair	Poor
—	1000	800	500	300	150

REVOLVERS

Medallion

Post-war production double-action revolver with swing-out cylinder, adjustable sights, 4 or 6-inch barrel. Made in .38 Special or .22 LR.

NIB	Exc.	V.G.	Good	Fair	Poor
–	400	300	250	120	90

Trophy

As above with fixed sights, 3, 4 or 6-inch barrel.

NIB	Exc.	V.G.	Good	Fair	Poor
–	400	300	250	120	90

MARSHAL SINGLE-ACTION ARMY REVOLVERS (HAWES)

J.P. Sauer made a western-styled series of revolvers for the Hawes company. These were based in part on the appearance of the Colt SAA.

Silver City

A .22 LR or WMR 6-shot single action with 5.5-inch barrel and fixed sights.

NIB	Exc.	V.G.	Good	Fair	Poor
—	150	120	100	50	20

Western

A .357, .44 Mag., .45 ACP, .45 Colt, .44-40, 9mm, .22 LR, .22WMR single-action revolver with fixed sights, blue or nickel finish.

NIB	Exc.	V.G.	Good	Fair	Poor
—	350	280	200	100	80

SAVAGE ARMS CORPORATION

Utica, New York
Westfield, Massachusetts

RIFLES

Model 1895 (Antique)

A Savage .303-caliber lever-action rifle with 26" or 30" barrel and 5-shot rotary magazine. Identifiable by hole in breech-bolt. Barrel marked "Savage Repeating Arms Co. Utica, N.Y. U.S.A. Pat. Feb. 7, 1893, July 25, 1893. CAL. .303". Blued, with walnut stock. Approximately 8,000 manufactured between 1895 and 1899. Note: Add 100% for carbine version.

Courtesy Rock Island Auction Company

Exc.	Fine	V.G.	Good	Fair	Poor
5000	3750	2870	2000	900	630

Model 1895 Anniversary Edition

A .308-caliber reproduction of Model 1895, with 24" octagonal barrel. Engraved receiver, walnut stock with schnabel forend. Brass crescent buttplate, brass medallion inlaid in stock. Manufactured 9,999 in 1970.

NIB	Exc.	V.G.	Good	Fair	Poor
950	780	600	450	300	200

MODEL 99 SERIES

Model 1899-A 22" Barrel Short Rifle

Chambered for .303, .30-30, .25-35, .32-40, .38-55. Serial number range from 10000 to 220000. Produced from 1899 to 1922. Same cocking indicator as 1899-A rifle. Note: Add 50% for .25-35, .32-40, and .38-55 calibers.

NIB	Exc.	V.G.	Good	Fair	Poor
—	1600	100	600	300	100

Model 1899-A 26" Round Barrel Rifle

A .25-35, .30-30, .303 Savage, .32-40 or .38-55, .300 Savage caliber lever-action rifle with 26 barrel marked "Savage Arms Company, Utica, N.Y. Pat. Feb. 7, 1893, July 25.'93, Oct.3.'99 .CAL.30". Manufactured between 1899 and 1926/27. Blued, with walnut stock. Serial number range 10000 to 300000. Block cocking indicator on bolt to s/n 90000 then changed to pin indicator on tang. Note: Add 50% for .25-35, .32-40, and .38-55 calibers.

Courtesy Rock Island Auction Company

NIB	Exc.	V.G.	Good	Fair	Poor
—	1500	1000	600	250	100

Model 1899-B 26" Octagon Barrel Rifle

In calibers .303, .30-30, .25-35, .32-40, .38-55. Manufactured between 1899 and 1915. Serial number range 10000 to 175000. Same cocking indicator as 1899-A rifle. Note: Add 50% for .25-35, .32-40, and .38-55 calibers.

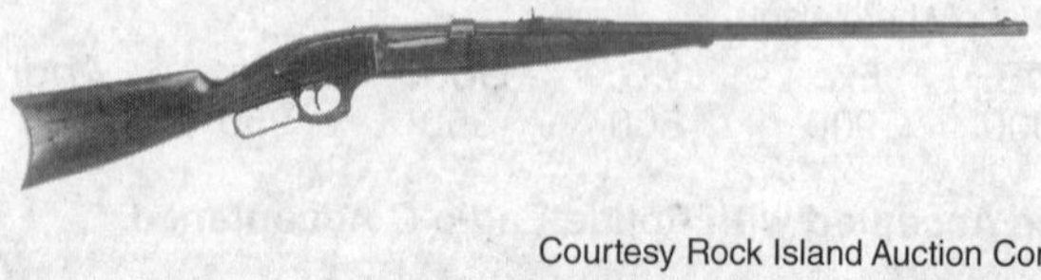

Courtesy Rock Island Auction Company

NIB	Exc.	V.G.	Good	Fair	Poor
—	1900	1300	800	350	150

Model 1899-C 26" Half Octagon Barrel Rifle

In calibers .303, .30-30, .25-35, .32-40, .38-55. Manufactured between 1899 and 1915. Serial number range 10000 to 175000. Same cocking indicator as 1899-A rifle. Note: Add 50% for .25-35, .32-40, and .38-55 calibers.

Courtesy Rock Island Auction Company

NIB	Exc.	V.G.	Good	Fair	Poor
—	2300	1700	1100	400	150

Model 1899-D Military Musket

Chambered for .303 Savage only, with 28" barrel. Fitted with full military stocks. Produced from 1899 to 1915. Several hundred produced for Canadian Home Guard during WWI. These will have rack number on buttplate.

NIB	Exc.	V.G.	Good	Fair	Poor
7500	6500	5000	3700	1000	400

Model 1899-F Saddle Ring Carbine

Fitted with 20" barrel only in calibers .303, .30-30, .25-35, .32-40, .38-55. Built from 1899 to 1919 in serial number range 19000 to 200000. Same cocking indicator as 1899-A rifle. Earliest style with barrel band is rarest variation. Note: Add 100% for .25-35, .32-40 and .38-55 calibers; add 200% for barrel band carbine.

Courtesy Rock Island Auction Company

NIB	Exc.	V.G.	Good	Fair	Poor
—	2400	1600	1000	700	350

Model 1899-CD Deluxe Rifle

In calibers .303, .30-30, .25-35, .32-40, .38-55. Serial number range 50000 to 175000. Built from 1905 to 1917. Same cocking indicator as 1899-A rifle. Standard Deluxe 1899 rifle with 26" round, octagon or half octagon barrel with pistol grip stock and checkering. Take-down barrel or short 22" barrel. Note: Add 30% for .25-35, .32-40, and .38-55 calibers.

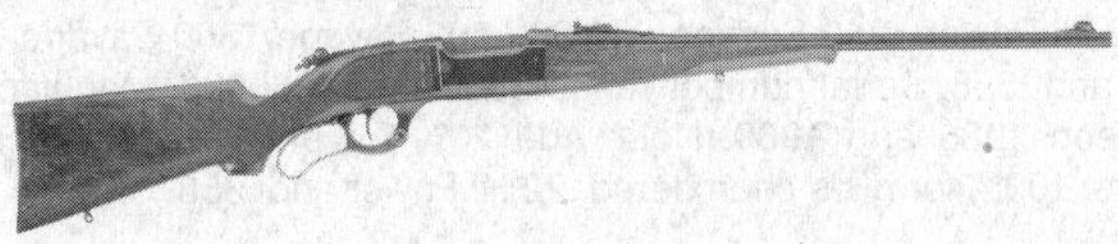

Courtesy Rock Island Auction Company

NIB	Exc.	V.G.	Good	Fair	Poor
—	3000	2200	1600	600	250

Model 1899-H Featherweight Rifle

Chambered for .303, .30-30, .25-35, and .22 HP Savage in 20" barrel. Serial number range 50000 to 220000. Built from 1905 to 1919. Revolutionary .22 HP cartridge introduced in this model in 1912. Most 1899-Hs are found with take-down barrels. Note: Add 50% for .25-35; add 25% for .22 HP.

Paul Goodwin photo

NIB	Exc.	V.G.	Good	Fair	Poor
—	1900	1400	700	300	100

Model 1899 .250-3000 Savage Rifle

Deluxe Model 1899 was developed to introduce Charles Newton designed .250-3000 Savage cartridge. Fitted with 22" featherweight take-down barrel, pistol grip, checkered perch belly stock, unique checkered trigger. Built from 1914 to 1921. Serial number range 146500 to 237500.

NIB	Exc.	V.G.	Good	Fair	Poor
—	1800	1500	800	350	100

Model 99-B 26"/24" Standard Weight Takedown

Chambered for .303, .30-30, and .300 Savage. Serial number range 200000 to 344000. Produced from 1920 to 1934. In 1926 a new 24 barrel with ramp front sight was introduced.

NIB	Exc.	V.G.	Good	Fair	Poor
—	1200	900	500	300	100

Model 99-C 22" Standard Weight Short Rifle

Chambered for .303, .30-30, and .300 Savage. Serial number range 238000 to 290000. Built from 1922 to 1926. This model looks like a shortened 26 rifle but with a heavily crowned muzzle.

NIB	Exc.	V.G.	Good	Fair	Poor
—	1100	800	500	200	100

Model 99-D 22" Standard Weight Takedown Rifle

Chambered for .303, .30-30, and .300 Savage. Serial number range 238000 to 290000. Built from 1922 to 1926. Same heavily crowned muzzle as 99-C.

NIB	Exc.	V.G.	Good	Fair	Poor
—	1200	900	500	200	100

Model 99-E Lightweight Rifle

Chambered for .22 HP, .30-30, .303, .250-3000, and .300 Savage. Manufactured between 1922 and 1934. Serial number range 238000 to 344000. In 1926 new ramp front sight introduced. Note: Add 25% for .22 Hi Power and .250-3000 calibers.

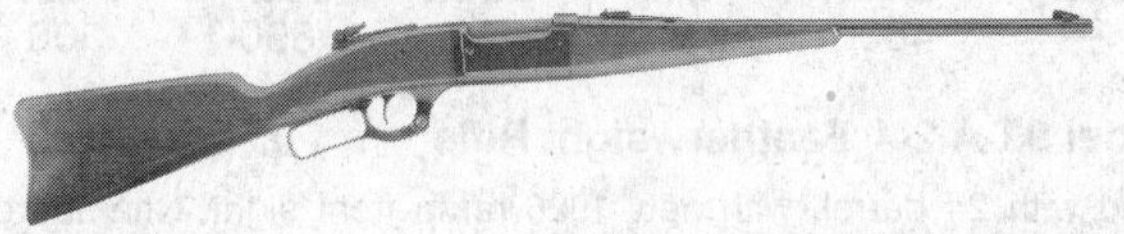

Courtesy Rock Island Auction Company

NIB	Exc.	V.G.	Good	Fair	Poor
—	1450	950	600	300	100

Model 99-F Lightweight Takedown Rifle

As above, but in lightweight take-down barrels in 20", 22" and 24". Chambered for .22 HP, .30-30, .303, .250-3000 and .300 Savage. These were tapered lightweight barrels. Manufactured between 1920 and 1940. Serial number range 200000 to 398000. In 1926, new ramp front sight introduced. Early versions look similar to Model 1899-H featherweight. In 1938, checkered stocks offered. Rare option. Note: Add 50% for .22 HP and .250-3000; add 75% for 1938 checkered stocks.

NIB	Exc.	V.G.	Good	Fair	Poor
—	1700	1200	700	300	100

Model 99-G Deluxe Takedown Pistol Grip Rifle

Calibers and barrel lengths as above, with pistol grip checkered stock. Manufactured between 1922 and 1941. Serial number range 238000 to 407000. No take-down Model 99s made after 1941. Note: Add 50% for .22 Hi Power; add 25% for .250-3000.

Courtesy Rock Island Auction Company

NIB	Exc.	V.G.	Good	Fair	Poor
—	1950	1400	800	300	100

Model 99-H Carbine/Barrel Band Carbine

Fitted with 20" or 22" barrels. Chambered for .30-30, .303, .250-3000 and .300 Savage. Serial number range 220000 to 400000. Built between 1923 and 1940. Distinctive plain stocks with no flat pads on side of buttstock. Curved carbine-style butt-plate. In 1931, barrel band added to forend, then commonly called "barrel band carbine". In 1935, flat pads added to buttstock sides, plus front ramp sight. Note: Add 50% for 1935 barrel band carbine; add 25% for .250-3000 and .300 Savage.

Courtesy Rock Island Auction Company

NIB	Exc.	V.G.	Good	Fair	Poor
—	1200	800	500	200	100

Combination Cased Set .300 Savage/.410 Barrel

Fitted with 22" or 24" barrels, with .410 barrels and .300 Savage in Model 99-F, 99-G or 99-K configuration. In black fitted case. Serial number range 240000 to 350000. Built from 1922 to 1934. BE AWARE: barrel address on .410 barrel matches that on the rifle barrel; and .410 barrel takes up correctly on the receiver; and case fits the .410 barrel and receiver.

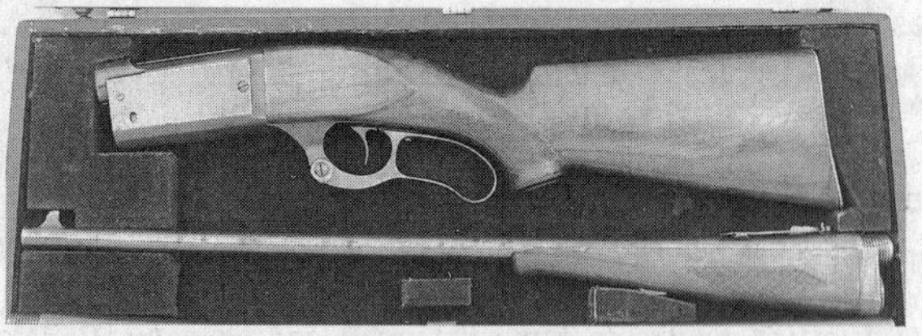

Courtesy Amoskeag Auction Company

NIB	Exc.	V.G.	Good	Fair	Poor
—	4000	2500	1500	800	300

Model 99-A 24" Featherweight Rifle

Fitted with 24 barrel, with new 1926 ramp front sight. Chambered for .303, .30-30 or .300 Savage. Serial number range 290000 to 370000. Built from 1926 to 1937. Buttplate older 1899 crescent style.

NIB	Exc.	V.G.	Good	Fair	Poor
—	900	700	5500	250	80

Model 99-K Deluxe Engraved Rifle

Premier Savage Model 99, with engraved receiver. Fitted with checkered pistol grip stock of select American walnut and take-down frame. Hand honed and fitted. Chambered for .22 HP, .30-30, .303, .250-3000 and .300 Savage. Barrels 22" or 24". Serial number range 285000 to 398000. Manufactured between 1926 and 1940. Note: Add 30% for .22-caliber Hi Power. Some of these models found with cased set with .410 barrel, add $700 for V.G. case and barrels.

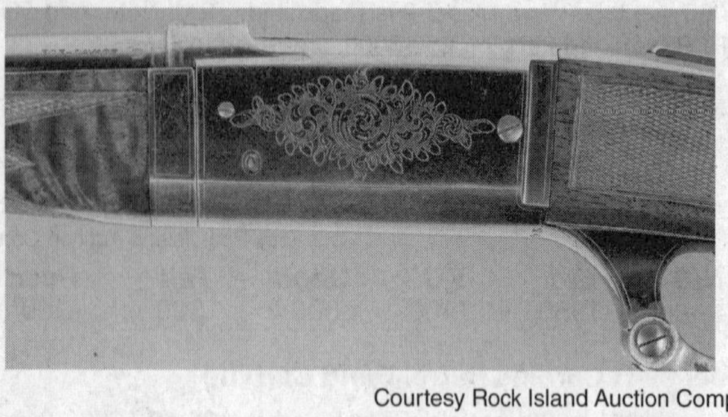

Courtesy Rock Island Auction Company

NIB	Exc.	V.G.	Good	Fair	Poor
3800	3200	2500	2000	1000	500

Model 99-R Heavy Stocked Rifle

Features heavy pistol grip checkered stock, with rounded forend tip. Barrels 22" or 24". Chambered for .250-3000, .303, .300 Savage, .308, .243 and .358-calibers. Serial number range 340000 to 1060000. Manufactured between 1932 and 1960. Note: Add 50% for .358; add 100% for rare uncataloged .30-30. Approximately 10 made for A.F. Stoeger of N.Y.C. for N.Y. State Police in 1935 in serial number range 348600. Most of these are found with Redfield No. 102 side peep sight and .250" rack number stamped in stock below pistol grip.

Courtesy Rock Island Auction Company

NIB	Exc.	V.G.	Good	Fair	Poor
—	1300	800	550	200	100

Model 99-RS Special Sights

As above, with Lyman aperture rear tang sight. In 1940, changed to Redfield micrometer tang sight. First model fitted with Savage quick-release sling swivels. No .30-30 calibers made in this model. Manufactured between 1932 and 1942. Note: Add 50% for .358.

Courtesy Rock Island Auction Company

NIB	Exc.	V.G.	Good	Fair	Poor
—	1500	1000	600	350	200

Model 99-EG Standard Weight Rifle

Produced with plain uncheckered pistol grip stock until 1940. Available in .22 Hi Power, .250 Savage, .30-30, .303 Savage, .300 Savage, .308, .243 and .358. Serial number range 350000 to 1060000. Manufactured between 1935 and 1960. Note: Add 20% for pre-1940 uncheckered stocks; 100% for rifles chambered .22 Hi Power and .358.

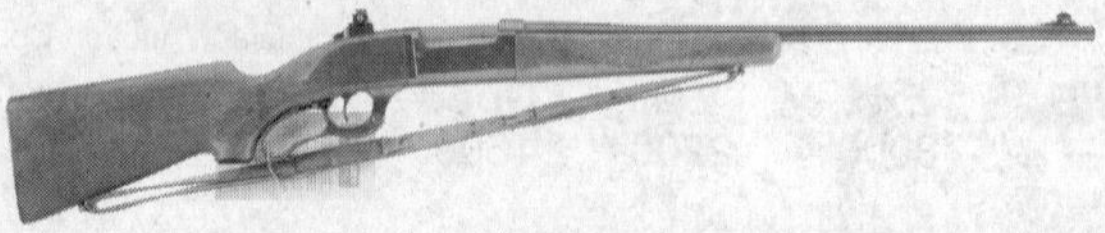

Courtesy Rock Island Auction Company

NIB	Exc.	V.G.	Good	Fair	Poor
—	900	650	400	200	80

Model 99-T Deluxe Featherweight Rifle

Classic short barrel deluxe Model 99, with semi-beavertail forend and distinct long checkering pattern. Fitted with 20" or 22" barrels. Chambered for .250-3000, .30-30, .303, .22 HP or .300 Savage. Serial number range 350000 to 400000. Manufactured between 1935 and 1940. Note: Add 100% for .22 Hi Power caliber; add 20% for .250-3000.

Courtesy Rock Island Auction Company

NIB	Exc.	V.G.	Good	Fair	Poor
2000	1750	1200	800	450	200

Model 99-F Featherweight Rifle

First Savage made with model designation visible on outside. Located at rear on right side of barrel. True featherweight with slender 22" barrel, lightweight stocks with butt end hollowed out. Chambered for .250-3000, .300 Savage, .308, .243, .284 and .358-calibers. Built from 1955 to 1973. Note: Add 75% for .284 and .358-calibers; add 50% for .250 Savage.

NIB	Exc.	V.G.	Good	Fair	Poor
1200	1000	800	500	250	80

Model 99-DL Deluxe Monte Carlo Rifle

Deluxe version of Model 99EG. Available in .243, .250 Savage, .300 Savage, .284, .358 and .308 calibers. Monte Carlo-style stock. Manufactured between 1960 and 1973. Note: Add 75% for .358 and .284 calibers.

NIB	Exc.	V.G.	Good	Fair	Poor
900	800	550	350	200	100

Model 99-E Economy Rifle

Ugly duckling of Savage line. Model 99-E lacked many standard features such as left side cartridge counter, tang sight holes, walnut stocks and capped pistol grip. Fitted with 20", 22" or 24" barrels. Chambered for .250-3000, .300 Savage, .243 and .308-calibers. Built from 1960 to 1984. Note: Model 99-E was the last original rotary magazine. Production was discontinued in 1984 for Model 99.

NIB	Exc.	V.G.	Good	Fair	Poor
850	750	580	380	150	50

Model 99-C Clip Magazine Rifle

Recent production model in .22-250, .243, .284 Win., 7mm-08 or .308-caliber. Barrel 22" and open sights. Blued, with walnut stock. Features clip magazine, first modification to Model 99 in 66 years. Introduced in 1965. Dropped from production and reintroduced in 1995 in .243 and .308-calibers. Weight about 7.75 lbs. Note: Add 50% for .22-250, .284 and 7mm-08.

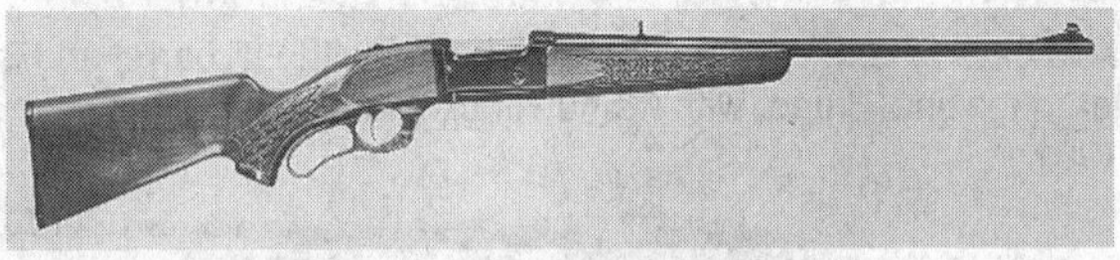

NIB	Exc.	V.G.	Good	Fair	Poor
850	550	400	250	150	50

Model 99-DE Citation Grade Rifle

Premier Savage with engraved receiver. Nickel-like finish and impressed checkering on select walnut stocks. Marked 99-M. Offered in .243, .284 and .308 calibers, with 22" barrel only. Manufactured between 1965 and 1970. Note: Add 30% for .284 caliber.

NIB	Exc.	V.G.	Good	Fair	Poor
1750	1600	1200	700	400	200

Model 99-PE Presentation Grade Rifle

Presentation grade Model 99, with engraved receiver. Hand-checkered finely figured walnut stock. Mountain lion on right side of receiver and elk on left side. Chambered for .243, .284 and .308 caliber, with 22" barrel. Manufactured between 1965 and 1970. Note: Add 30% for .284 caliber.

NIB	Exc.	V.G.	Good	Fair	Poor
2500	2000	1500	800	500	300

Model 99-A Saddle Gun

Variation of original Model 99A, with 20" or 22" barrel. Chambered for .243, .250 Savage, .300 Savage, .308 and .375 caliber. Serial number range in new "A" series on left side. Manufactured between 1971 and 1982. Note: Add 25% for .375 caliber.

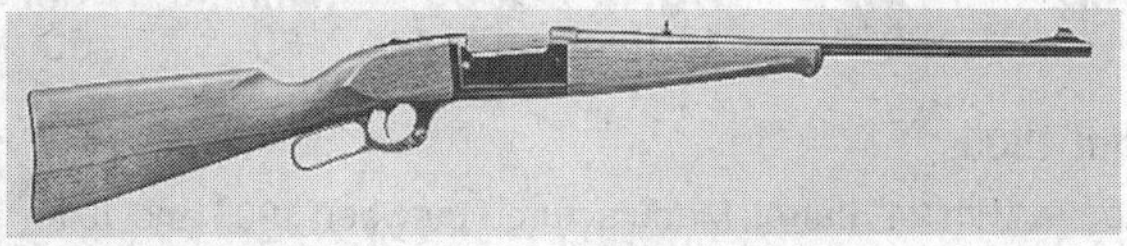

NIB	Exc.	V.G.	Good	Fair	Poor
1200	800	500	400	300	200

Model 99-.358 and 99-.375 Brush Guns

Similar to Model 99-A straight-grip saddle gun, but in .358 and .375 Win. (1980) calibers. Has plain grooved forend, rubber recoil pad. Serial number range in new "A" series on left side. Built from 1977 to 1980. Note: Add 25% for .358 Win. caliber.

NIB	Exc.	V.G.	Good	Fair	Poor
1200	800	500	400	300	200

Model 99-CD Deluxe Clip Model

North American classic rifle, with distinct stocks of checkered walnut. Long grooved forend, deep shaped pistol grip, Monte Carlo stock with cheekpiece. Fitted with 22" barrel. Chambered for .250-3000, .308 or .243. Serial number range in new "A" series on left side. Built from 1975 to 1980.

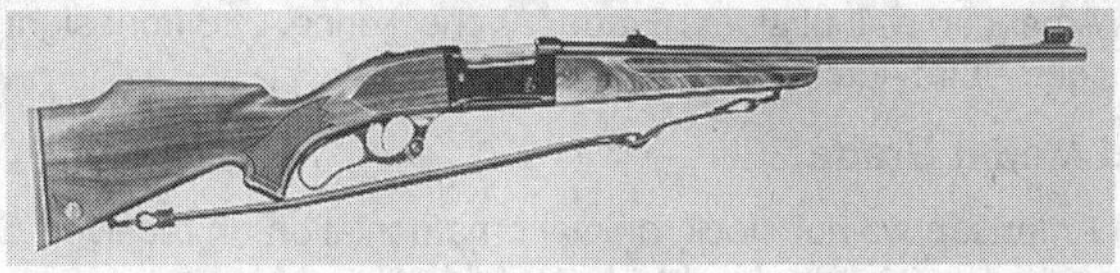

NIB	Exc.	V.G.	Good	Fair	Poor
1100	850	600	400	300	200

Model 99-CE (Centennial Edition)

Introduced in 1995. Limited edition to 1,000 rifles. Serial numbers from AS0001 to AS1000. Chambered for .300 Savage cartridge. Engraved receiver with gold inlays. Select American walnut stock, with Monte Carlo comb.

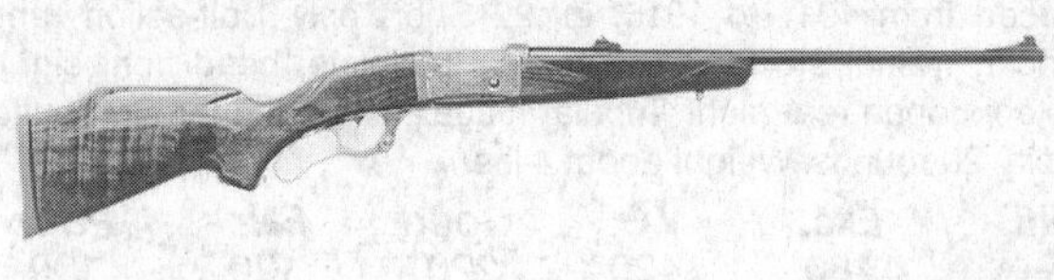

Courtesy Savage Arms

NIB	Exc.	V.G.	Good	Fair	Poor
1600	1300	900	750	500	250

Model 1903

A .22-caliber slide-action rifle, with 24" octagon barrel having open sights. Blued, with walnut stock. Manufactured between 1903 and 1922. Note: Late model rifles have updated slide handle. Pistol grip stock in same style as Model 1914.

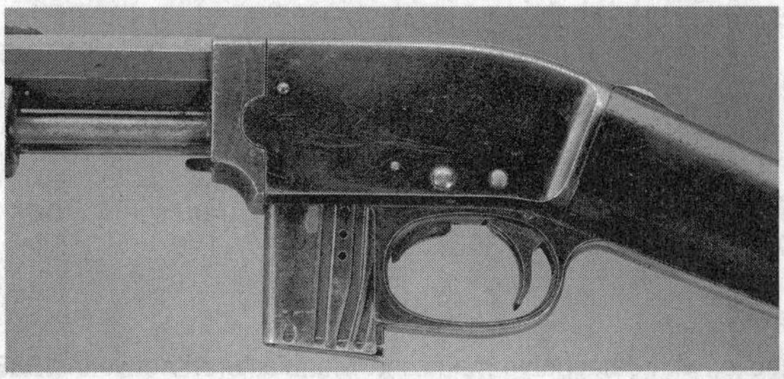

Courtesy Rock Island Auction Company

NIB	Exc.	V.G.	Good	Fair	Poor
600	500	400	250	150	100

Model 1903 Gallery Model

Same general specifications as Model 1903, except for a mechanical counter attached to record shots fired.

NIB	Exc.	V.G.	Good	Fair	Poor
700	600	500	350	150	100

Model 1903 Factory Engraved Models

These models are seldom seen. Secure a qualified appraisal prior to sale. Note: Add premiums as shown.

Grade EF

Grade "B" checkering, fancy English walnut stock, Savage 22B front sights, 21B rear sight. Note: Add 50%.

Expert Grade

Fancy American walnut stock, Grade "A" engraving, Grade "B" checkering, standard sights. Note: Add 150%.

Grade GH

Plain American walnut stock, Grade "A" checkering, 22B front sight, 21B rear sight. Note: Add 50%.

Gold Medal Grade

Plain American walnut stock, animal ornamentation on receiver, Grade "A" checkering, standard sights. Note: Add 60%.

Model 1909

As above, with 20" barrel. Manufactured between 1909 and 1915.

NIB	Exc.	V.G.	Good	Fair	Poor
700	600	500	350	150	100

Model 1911

Produced from 1911 to 1915, in .22 Short only. Bolt-action repeater. American walnut stock. Shotgun steel buttplate, bead front sight with adjustable open rear sight. Tubular magazine loaded through buttstock, capacity 20 rounds. Weight about 4 lbs.

NIB	Exc.	V.G.	Good	Fair	Poor
—	480	420	220	120	100

Model 1912

A .22-caliber semi-automatic rifle, with 20" barrel, open sights and in take-down form. Magazine capacity 7 rounds. Blued, with walnut stock. Manufactured between 1912 and 1916. Weight about 4.5 lbs.

NIB	Exc.	V.G.	Good	Fair	Poor
900	750	500	300	120	90

Model 6

Similar to above, with 24" barrel and tubular magazine. Walnut stock checkered prior to 1938; plain after 1965.

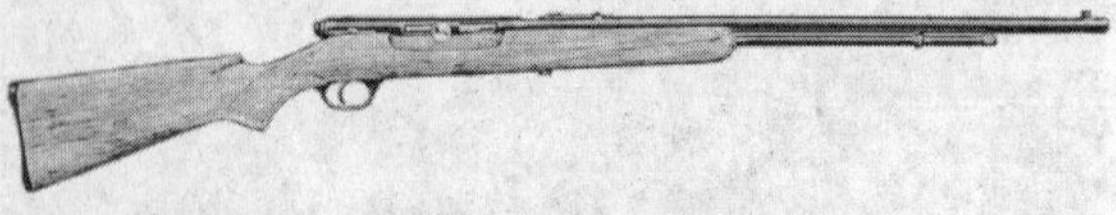

NIB	Exc.	V.G.	Good	Fair	Poor
—	350	300	200	120	50

Model 7

As above, with detachable magazine. Manufactured between 1938 and 1954.

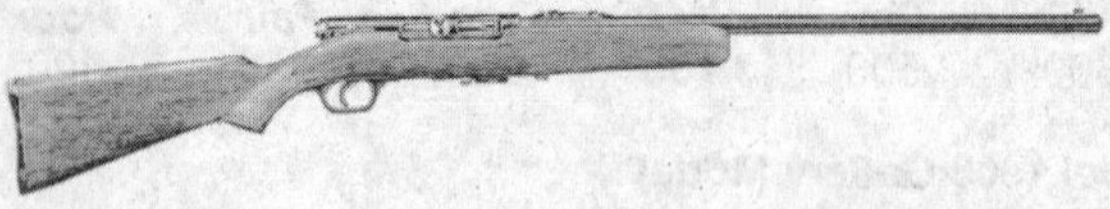

NIB	Exc.	V.G.	Good	Fair	Poor
—	350	300	200	120	50

Model 1914

As above, with 24" octagonal barrel. Manufactured between 1914 and 1926.

NIB	Exc.	V.G.	Good	Fair	Poor
—	350	300	200	120	50

Model 25

A .22-caliber slide-action rifle, with 24" octagonal barrel, open sights and tubular magazine. Blued, with plain walnut stock. Manufactured between 1925 and 1929.

Courtesy Rock Island Auction Company

NIB	Exc.	V.G.	Good	Fair	Poor
—	450	350	250	200	120

Model 29

Similar to above, with 22" octagonal barrel, later changed to round on post-war rifles. Checkered walnut stock, later changed to plain on post-war rifles. Manufactured between 1929 and 1967.

NIB	Exc.	V.G.	Good	Fair	Poor
—	450	320	200	150	100

Model 170

A .30-30 or .35 Rem. caliber slide-action rifle, with 22" barrel and 3-shot tubular magazine. Blued, with walnut stock. Manufactured between 1970 and 1981.

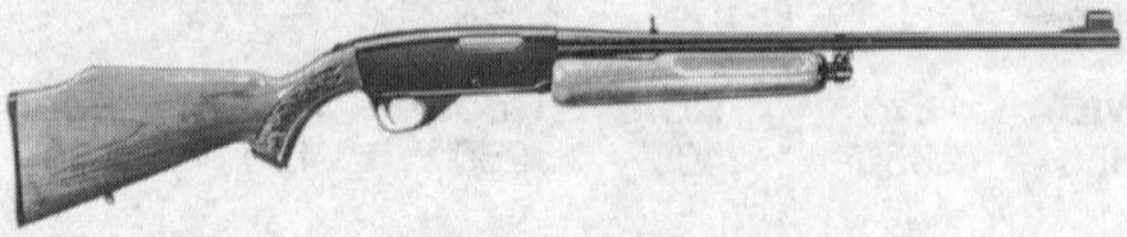

NIB	Exc.	V.G.	Good	Fair	Poor
—	550	400	250	180	100

Model 1904

A .22-caliber single-shot bolt-action rifle, with 18" barrel and walnut stock. Manufactured between 1904 and 1931. Note: After 1915 this model became known as Model 04.

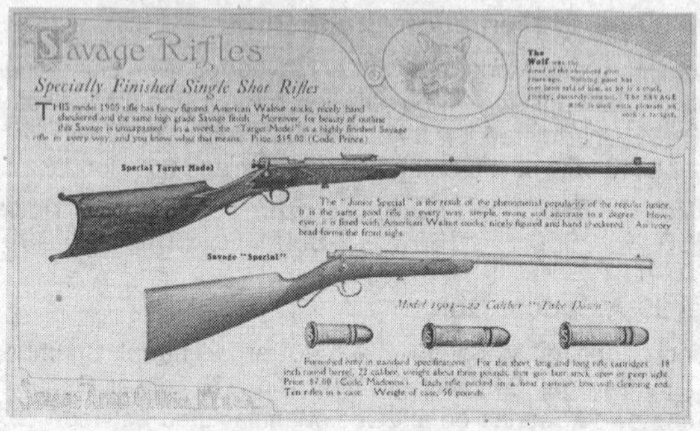

NIB	Exc.	V.G.	Good	Fair	Poor
—	200	150	100	80	50

Model 1905

As above, with 24" barrel. Manufactured between 1905 and 1919.

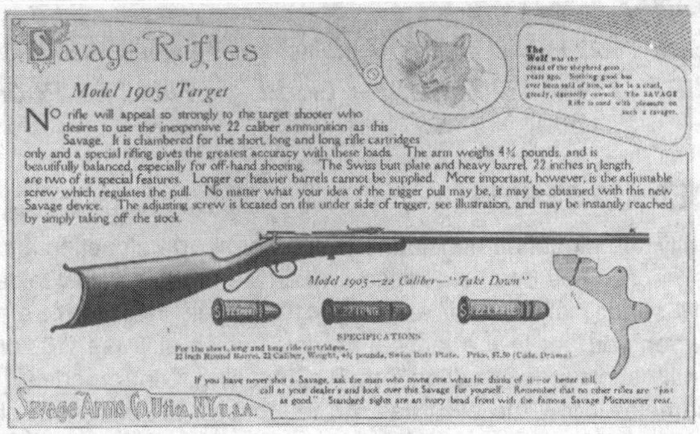

NIB	Exc.	V.G.	Good	Fair	Poor
—	200	150	100	80	50

Model 1905 Style "B"

Same as Model 1905 Target, with shotgun buttplate.

NIB	Exc.	V.G.	Good	Fair	Poor
—	380	300	200	150	50

Model 1905 Special Target Rifle

Same as Model 1905 Target Rifle, except for hand-checkered fancy American walnut stock.

NIB	Exc.	V.G.	Good	Fair	Poor
—	450	320	250	150	100

Model 19 NRA

A .22-caliber bolt-action rifle, with 25" barrel, detachable magazine and full-length military-style stock. Approximately 50,000 manufactured between 1919 and 1937.

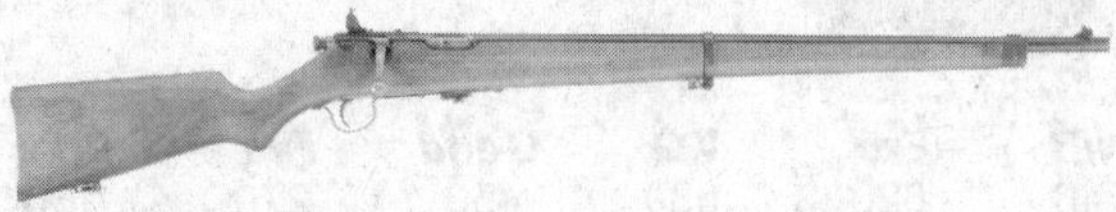

NIB	Exc.	V.G.	Good	Fair	Poor
—	400	250	180	100	80

Model 19L

As above, with Lyman receiver sight. Manufactured between 1933 and 1942.

NIB	Exc.	V.G.	Good	Fair	Poor
—	420	280	220	200	150

Model 19M

As above, with 28" barrel. Fitted with telescope sight bases. Manufactured between 1933 and 1942.

NIB	Exc.	V.G.	Good	Fair	Poor
—	400	250	180	100	80

Model 19H

Model 19 chambered for .22 Hornet. Manufactured between 1933 and 1942.

NIB	Exc.	V.G.	Good	Fair	Poor
—	600	480	350	300	200

Model 3

A .22-caliber single-shot bolt-action rifle, with 24" barrel, open sights and walnut stock. Manufactured between 1933 and 1952.

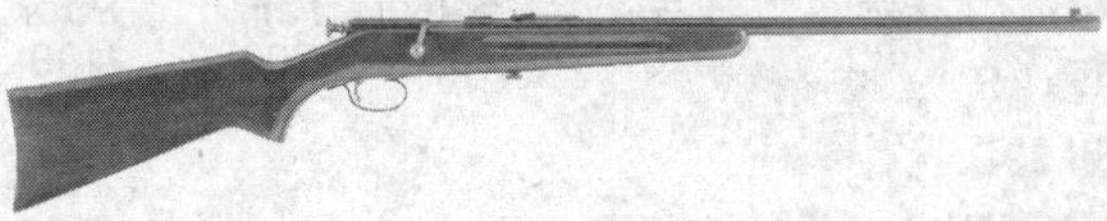

NIB	Exc.	V.G.	Good	Fair	Poor
—	200	150	100	80	50

Model 4

Similar to above, with 24" barrel and 5-shot magazine. Produced from 1932 to 1964.

NIB	Exc.	V.G.	Good	Fair	Poor
—	200	150	100	80	50

Model 4M

As above, in .22 Magnum. Produced from 1960 to 1964.

NIB	Exc.	V.G.	Good	Fair	Poor
—	220	180	110	80	50

Model 5

Model 4, with a tubular magazine. Manufactured between 1933 and 1964.

NIB	Exc.	V.G.	Good	Fair	Poor
—	200	150	100	80	50

Model 1922

A variation of Model 19 NRA, with sporting-style stock and schnabel forend. Fitted with 23" round barrel. Chambered for .22-caliber cartridge. Superceded Model 23; looks like Model 23 Sporter. Introduced in 1922; discontinued 1923. Very rare.

NIB	Exc.	V.G.	Good	Fair	Poor
—	750	600	480	300	200

Model 23A

Bolt-action .22 LR rifle introduced in 1923. Features 5-round detachable box magazine and 23" barrel with open sights. Large loading port on left side of receiver permitted easy single-shot loading. Plain stock, with pistol grip and schnabel forend. A varnish wood finish was applied to this model. Production stopped in 1933.

NIB	Exc.	V.G.	Good	Fair	Poor
—	350	280	150	120	100

Model 23AA

An improved version of Model 23A. Introduced in 1933. Features better speed lock, redesigned stock with oil-finish. Receiver tapped for No. 15 Savage extension peep sight. Weight about 6 lbs. Production ceased in 1942.

NIB	Exc.	V.G.	Good	Fair	Poor
—	400	300	200	150	120

Model 23B

Similar to Model 23A, except chambered for .25-20 cartridge. Barrel length 25", forearm a full 1.5" wide beavertail. Receiver tapped for peep sight, magazine capacity 4 rounds. Production from 1923 to 1940.

NIB	Exc.	V.G.	Good	Fair	Poor
—	380	320	250	200	100

Model 23C

Same configuration as Model 23B, with exception of caliber .32-20. Manufactured from 1923 to 1946.

NIB	Exc.	V.G.	Good	Fair	Poor
—	380	320	250	200	100

Model 23D

Same configuration as Model 23B, only chambered for .22 Hornet cartridge. Manufactured from 1932 to 1948.

NIB	Exc.	V.G.	Good	Fair	Poor
—	380	320	250	200	100

Model 1920

A .250-3000 or .300 Savage bolt-action rifle, with 22" or 24" barrel, open sights and 5-shot magazine. Blued, with walnut stock and schnabel forend. Manufactured between 1920 and 1929. An improved version introduced in 1926, that was heavier and had a Lyman #54 peep sight.

NIB	Exc.	V.G.	Good	Fair	Poor
—	1000	600	460	300	200

Model 40 (Old Model)

Similar to above, in .250-3000, .300 Savage, .30-30 and .30-06 caliber. Manufactured between 1928 and 1940.

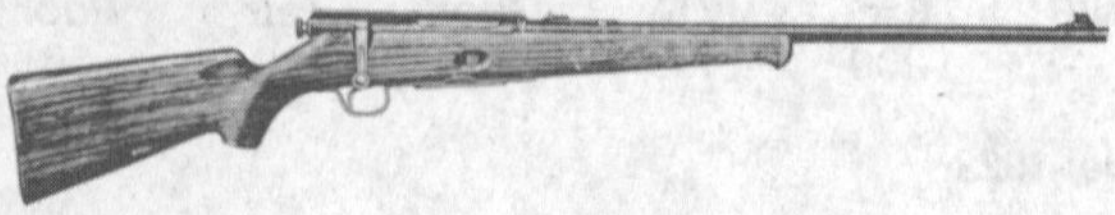

NIB	Exc.	V.G.	Good	Fair	Poor
—	420	350	300	250	180

Model 45 Super

Similar to Old Model 40, with Lyman receiver sight and checkered walnut stock. Manufactured between 1928 and 1940.

NIB	Exc.	V.G.	Good	Fair	Poor
—	400	350	300	200	150

Model 35

A .22-caliber bolt-action rifle, with 22" barrel, open sights and 5-shot magazine. Blued, with Monte Carlo-style hardwood stock.

NIB	Exc.	V.G.	Good	Fair	Poor
—	180	150	120	80	50

Model 46

As above, with a tubular magazine. Manufactured between 1969 and 1973.

NIB	Exc.	V.G.	Good	Fair	Poor
—	180	150	120	80	50

Model 340

A .22 Hornet, .222 Rem., .223 or .30-30 caliber bolt-action rifle, with 22" or 24" barrel. Open sights and 4- or 5-shot magazine. Blued, with plain walnut stock. Manufactured between 1950 and 1985.

NIB	Exc.	V.G.	Good	Fair	Poor
—	380	320	250	200	100

Model 342

As above, in .22 Hornet caliber. Manufactured between 1950 and 1955.

NIB	Exc.	V.G.	Good	Fair	Poor
—	380	320	250	200	100

MODEL 110 SERIES

Currently, the model nomenclature of "10" for short bolt action and "110" for long action has been simplified and all the models below folded into the 110 series, followed by a name (110 Hunter, 110 Storm, etc.), except when you get to the tactical models, which still use "10" or "110" to identify short or long action length. Confusing. Other models (12/112 for example) follow the old rules. An impressive list of caliber choices for the most popular models includes .204, .223, .22-250, .243, 6mm Creedmoor, .25-06, 6.5 Creedmoor, 6.5x284, .260 Rem., .270 Win., .270 WSM, 7mm-08, 7mm Rem. Mag., .308, .30-06, .300 WSM, .300 Win. Mag., .338 Win. Mag. Many calibers can be special ordered if not listed for a specific model, and the custom shop offers even more choices. The AccuTrigger is standard. In 2020 Accu-Fit adjustable stock became available.

Model 110 Storm and Hunter

A blue or stainless steel action and 22" or 24" barrel, depending on chambering. The "Storm" has the most chamberings, which include 17 choices between .223 and .300 Win. Mag., and 10 calibers for left-hand versions. Comes with detachable magazine, black synthetic AccuStock with AccuFit inserts for comb height and buttstock spacers for LOP. Weight about 7.5 lbs. Note: Add $135 for Classic with matte blue metal, wood stock adjustable for comb height and LOP; Deduct about $100 for 110 Hunter in blued carbon steel, or 110 Varmint with blued heavy barrel in three chamberings.

NIB	Exc.	V.G.	Good	Fair	Poor
740	620	530	450	270	160

Model 110 High Country

Long or short action with detachable box magazine and 22" or 24" medium contour threaded and fluted barrel, PVD finish and fluted bolt. True Timber Strata Camo AccuStock with AccuFit. Muzzle brake on magnum calibers only. Note: Deduct $210 for "Predator" in short-action calibers, blued, heavy 22" or 24" barrel, Mossy Oak Mountain Terra Camo Stock; deduct $120 for "Bear Hunter" in magnum calibers with stainless steel, threaded 23" barrel in Mossy Oak Break-up Country stock.

NIB	Exc.	V.G.	Good	Fair	Poor
960	820	700	590	350	220

Model 110 Long Range Hunter

Blued long or short carbon-steel action, medium-contour 26" barrel with adjustable muzzlebrake, hinged floorplate, AccuStock with AccuFit, in nine chamberings from 6.5 Creedmoor to .300 Win. Mag. Add about $200 for .338 Lapua and fixed muzzle brake.

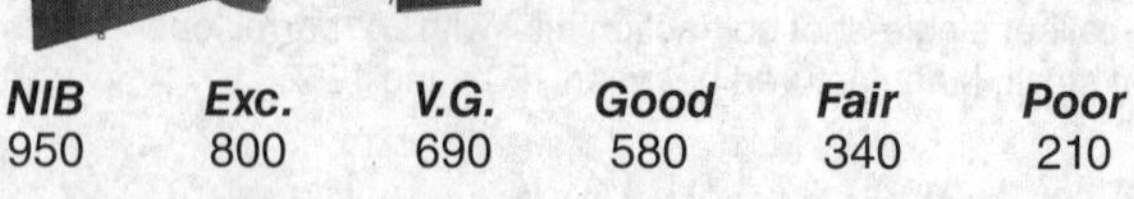

NIB	Exc.	V.G.	Good	Fair	Poor
950	800	690	580	340	210

Models 110 Scout and Tactical

The "Scout" model comes in short action with iron peep sights and forward-mounted base for Intermediate Eye Relief scope, short 16.5" barrel in .223, .308, .338 Federal and .450 Bushmaster, Magpul AI magazine with Flat Dark Earth AccuStock with AccuFit, and fixed muzzle brake. Note: Deduct $30 for "Tactical" and "Tactical Desert" with 20" or 24" threaded barrel in 6mm C, 6.5 C or .308; add $80 for "Wolverine" with 18" barrel in .450 Bushmaster with fixed muzzle brake.

NIB	Exc.	V.G.	Good	Fair	Poor
700	500	430	360	220	130

Model 110 Carbon Tactical

Calibers: 6.5 Creedmoor, .308 Win., 6.5 PRC. Capacity: 10-round AICS magazine. Barrel: 22-in. Proof Research stainless steel, carbon-fiber wrapped, threaded. Length: 42 in. Weight: 7.65 lbs. Stock: Synthetic AccuFit with included interchangeable LOP spacers and comb risers. Features: Factory blueprinted Model 110 bolt action. User-adjustable AccuTrigger. Tactical knurled bolt handle. One-piece 20-MOA rail. Beavertail forend with three sling studs.

NIB	Exc.	V.G.	Good	Fair	Poor
1650	—	—	—	—	—

Model 110 Carbon Predator

Caliber: .223 Rem., .22-250 Rem., 6mm ARC, 6.5 Creedmoor, .308 Win., .300 Blackout. Barrel: 16", 18", 22" Proof Research carbon-fiber-wrapped stainless steel. Weight: 6.5 to 7.2 lbs. Stock: Synthetic gray with AccuFit system. Features: Latest addition to the 110 bolt-action family, now with lighter weight carbon-fiber barrel. AICS detachable box magazine. Spiral-fluted bolt. Threaded barrel. Swivel studs. Two-piece Weaver bases included.

NIB	Exc.	V.G.	Good	Fair	Poor
1530	—	—	—	—	—

Model 110 APEX XP

Short or long action in 17 caliber choices from .223 to .338 Win. Mag., with 20", 22" or 24" blue, carbon steel barrel (depending on caliber), black synthetic stock adjustable for LOP, detachable box magazine, and Vortex Crossfire II 3-9x40 mounted and boresighted on 1-piece rail. Eleven chamberings in left hand. Note: Add $50 for "Apex Storm" stainless steel as above; "Muddy Girl" camo stock in some short action calibers; "Predator" with Mossy Oak Mountain Terra camo, threaded carbon steel heavy barrel, Vortex Crossfire II 4-12 x 44 scope; Deduct $60 for "Engage Hunter" in 16 calibers, with Bushnell 3-9X.

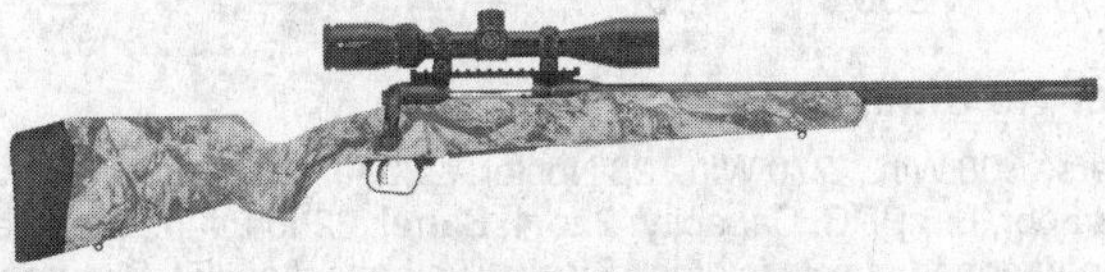

NIB	Exc.	V.G.	Good	Fair	Poor
500	430	360	310	180	110

Models 110 Hog, Brush and Lightweight

Hog Hunter XP in synthetic stock adjustable for LOP, detachable box magazine, with 20" .223, .308, .338 Fed. blue barrel. Note: Add $150 for Lightweight (5.6 lbs.) stainless steel 20" barrel on skeletonized receiver, in six calibers from .223 to .270 Win; Add $200 for Brush Hunter in stainless steel with 20" 5/8-24 threaded barrel in .338 Win. Mag. or .375 Ruger; Add $300 for "Wolverine" in .450 Bushmaster with AccuFit stock and 18" barrel with ported muzzle brake.

NIB	Exc.	V.G.	Good	Fair	Poor
510	440	340	300	180	110

Model 10/110 Stealth

Factory blueprinted action, 16.5", 20" or 24" threaded heavy fluted 5R-rifled barrel in .223, 6.5 Creedmoor or .308, detachable box magazine, matte black chassis and collapsible stock. Note: Add $80 for 110 in .300 Win. Mag.; add $120 for .338 Lapua. Add $590 for 10/110 BA Stealth in Monolithic Aluminum Chassis; add $870 for .300 Win. Mag.; add $970 for .338 Lapua. Left-hand models available.

NIB	Exc.	V.G.	Good	Fair	Poor
1050	890	750	640	380	230

Model 10/110 FCP HS Precision

Short or long action in HS Precision stock with 24" barrel in .308 or .300 Win. Mag. Note: Add $420 for .338 Lapua; add $110 for GRS adjustable buttstock in .308, 6mm Creedmoor, 6.5 Creedmoor or 6.5 PRC.

NIB	Exc.	V.G.	Good	Fair	Poor
1140	970	820	700	420	250

Model 110 Sporter

Bolt-action rifle manufactured in a variety of calibers. Barrel 22", open sights and 4-shot magazine. Blued, with walnut stock. Manufactured between 1958 and 1963.

NIB	Exc.	V.G.	Good	Fair	Poor
400	320	250	180	120	100

Model 110-M

Similar to above, in 7mm Magnum to .338 Win. Magnum. Manufactured between 1963 and 1969.

NIB	Exc.	V.G.	Good	Fair	Poor
400	320	280	200	150	120

Model 110-D

Similar to Model 110, in .22-250 to .338 Win. Magnum, with detachable magazine. Manufactured between 1966 and 1988.

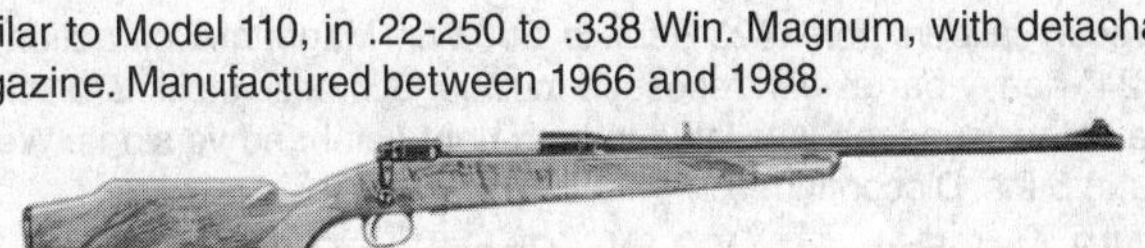

NIB	Exc.	V.G.	Good	Fair	Poor
400	300	250	200	150	100

Model 110-P Premier Grade

As above, with finely figured walnut stock, rosewood forend tip and pistol grip cap. Manufactured between 1964 and 1970.

NIB	Exc.	V.G.	Good	Fair	Poor
650	580	450	320	250	200

Model 110-PE

As above, with an engraved receiver, magazine floorplate and triggerguard. Manufactured between 1968 and 1970.

NIB	Exc.	V.G.	Good	Fair	Poor
900	800	700	500	400	300

Model 110-F

DuPont Rynite stock and sights. Discontinued.

NIB	Exc.	V.G.	Good	Fair	Poor
450	400	350	300	250	200

Model 110-FX

As above without sights. Discontinued.

NIB	Exc.	V.G.	Good	Fair	Poor
400	350	300	250	200	150

Model 110-FP

Composite stock and 24" heavy barrel. In 2003, Savage AccuTrigger was added. Discontinued.

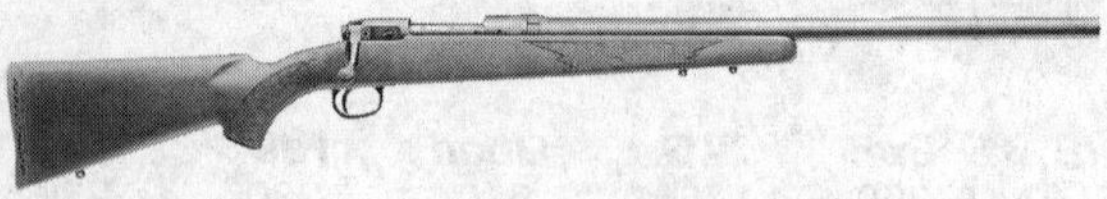

NIB	Exc.	V.G.	Good	Fair	Poor
600	450	320	220	150	150

Model 110-G

Checkered hardwood stock and sights. Discontinued.

NIB	Exc.	V.G.	Good	Fair	Poor
420	320	280	220	180	120

Model 110-GX

As above without sights. Discontinued.

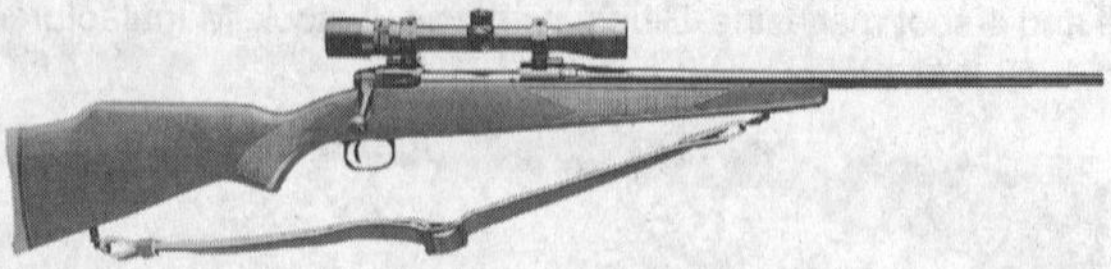

NIB	Exc.	V.G.	Good	Fair	Poor
400	300	250	200	150	100

Model 110-CY

Compact version of Model 110 series. Shorter length of pull on a walnut stock and 22" barrel. Overall length 42.5"; weight about 6.5 lbs. Chambered in .223, .243, .270, .300 Savage and .308-calibers. Discontinued.

NIB	Exc.	V.G.	Good	Fair	Poor
400	300	250	200	150	100

Model 110-FP Tactical

Offered in calibers from .223 Rem. to .300 Win. Magnum. Bolt-action rifle has 24" heavy barrel with recessed muzzle. Synthetic stock is black, as are all other surfaces. Available in both right-/left-hand versions. Weight about 8.5 lbs. Discontinued.

NIB	Exc.	V.G.	Good	Fair	Poor
600	450	320	220	150	150

Model 110-FP Duty

Introduced in 2002. Chambered for .308 cartridge. Features 24" free-floating barrel, with open sights. Black synthetic stock. Third swivel stud for bipod. Matte blue finish. Magazine capacity 4 rounds. Weight about 8.5 lbs. Discontinued.

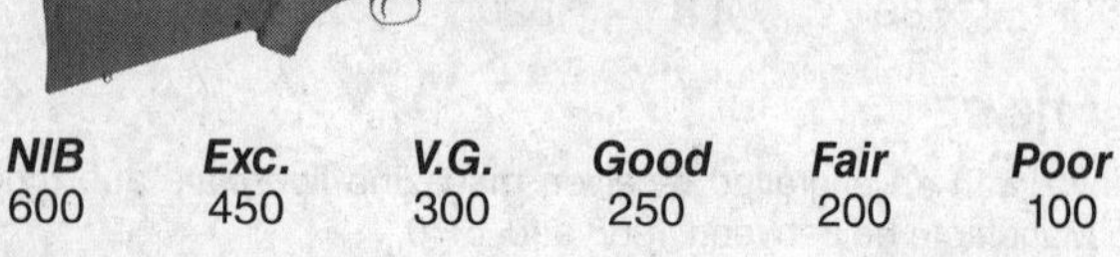

NIB	Exc.	V.G.	Good	Fair	Poor
600	450	300	250	200	100

Model 110-FP-LE1

Similar to Model 110FP-Duty (.308), with 20" barrel. No sights. Weight about 8.25 lbs. Introduced in 2002, discontinued.

NIB	Exc.	V.G.	Good	Fair	Poor
500	380	280	220	180	100

Model 110-FP-LE2

Same as above, but fitted with 26" barrel. Weight about 8.75 lbs. Introduced in 2002, discontinued.

NIB	Exc.	V.G.	Good	Fair	Poor
500	380	280	220	180	100

Model 110-50th Anniversary

Short-action rifle commemorating 50th Anniversary of Model 10. Chambered in .300 Savage, with 22" barrel. 1000 numbered rifles, high-luster blued barrel and action, unique checkering pattern on select walnut stock, high-grade hinged floorplate, scroll pattern on receiver, 24-karat gold plated double-barrel bands, 24-karat gold plated AccuTrigger, embossed recoil pad.

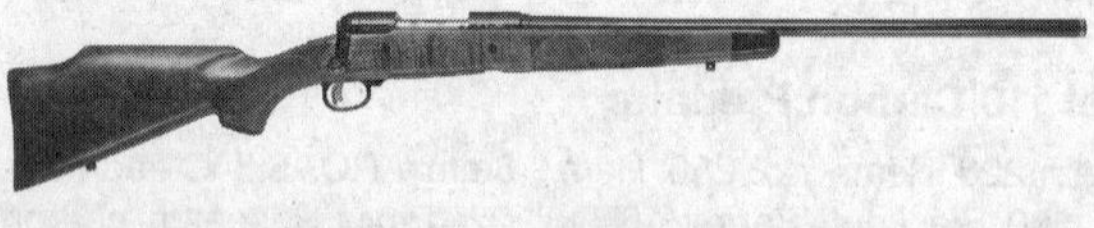

NIB	Exc.	V.G.	Good	Fair	Poor
1000	750	600	480	300	200

Model 110 BA Law Enforcement Rifle

Bolt-action rifle chambered for .300 Win. Magnum and .338 Lapua Magnum. Features include: aluminum stock; Savage's innovative three-dimensional bedding system; interchangeable buttstocks; pistol grips; three-sided accessory rail; 5-round detachable magazine; high-efficiency muzzle brake; Magpul PRS adjustable stock; 26" carbon steel barrel.

NIB	Exc.	V.G.	Good	Fair	Poor
1900	1650	1400	1100	700	300

Model 110 Hunter Series

Offered in several variations and most popular calibers including .204 Ruger .223, .22-250, .243 .25-06, .260 Rem., 6.5 Creedmoor, .270 Win., 7mm-08, .280 Ackley Improved, .308, .30-06, .300 Win Mag, 338 Fed., .338 Win., .375 Ruger. Barrel length from 20 to 26 inches depending on model and caliber. Detachable magazine with 3 or 4-shot capacity. AccuStock has gray finish, soft grip surfaces, adjustable length of pull. Prices shown are for standard Hunter model. Add $250 for Bear Hunter, add $350 for Long Range Hunter, deduct $150 for Hog Hunter. Introduced in 2018.

NIB	Exc.	V.G.	Good	Fair	Poor
650	550	480	—	—	—

Model 110 Ultralite

Calibers: .308 Win., .270 Win., 28 Nosler, .280 AI, .30-06, .300 WSM, 6.5 Creedmoor, 6.5 PRC. Capacity: 2 to 4. Barrel: 22 to 24 in., matte-black, carbon-wrapped stainless steel. Stock: Synthetic, AccuFit. Sights: None, drilled and tapped, no scope included. Weight: 6 lbs. Features: Spiral-fluted bolt, detachable box magazine, Proof Research rifled barrel.

NIB	Exc.	V.G.	Good	Fair	Poor
1280	—	—	—	—	—

Model 110 Precision

Calibers: .308 Win., .300 Win. Mag, .338 Lapua, 6.5 Creedmoor. Capacity: 5, 8/10. Barrel: 20 to 24 in., carbon steel, heavy, threaded. Stock: Aluminum chassis. Sights: Picatinny rail. Weight: 8.9 lbs. Features: BA muzzle brake, skeletonized stock with adjustable comb height and LOP.

NIB	Exc.	V.G.	Good	Fair	Poor
1280	—	—	—	—	—

Model 110 Elite Precision

Calibers: .223 Rem., 6mm Creedmoor, 6.5 Creedmoor, .308 Win., .300 Win. Mag., .300 PRC, .338 Lapua. Capacity: 5- or 10-round AICS-pattern detachable box magazine. Barrel: 26 or 30 in stainless steel. Weight: 12.6–14.95 lbs. Stock: Modular Driven Technologies (MDT) Adjustable Core Competition aluminum chassis with Grey Cerakote finish. Sights: 20 MOA rail. Features: Factory blueprinted action. ARCA Rail along entire length of chassis. Titanium Nitride bolt body. User-adjustable AccuTrigger. MDT vertical grip. Self-timing taper aligned muzzle brake on short action calibers only.

NIB	Exc.	V.G.	Good	Fair	Poor
1840	—	—	—	—	—

Model 110 Tactical

Offered in .308 Win. or 6.5 Creedmoor with 10-shot detachable magazine. Barrel is 20 or 24 inches, threaded and fluted with heavy contour. AccuStock has gray finish, soft grip surfaces, AccuFit adjustable system, top Picatinny rail. Weight is 8.65 pounds. Available with right or left-hand operation. Introduced in 2018.

NIB	Exc.	V.G.	Good	Fair	Poor
680	580	500	—	—	—

Model 110 Ultralight

Lightweight 5.8-lb. bolt action in .308 Win, detachable box magazine, carbon fiber-wrapped stainless steel barrel, skeletonized frame, adjustable trigger and stock. Introduced 2020.

NIB	Exc.	V.G.	Good	Fair	Poor
1400	1250	1000	—	—	—

Model 110 PCS (PISTOL CHASSIS SYSTEM)

Calibers: 6.5 Creedmoor, .308 Win., .350 Legend, .300 AAC BLK., .223 Rem. Features: Carbon steel, matte black, barrel and receiver. Medium-contour 10.5-in. barrel, with threaded muzzle (5/8x24). Machined aluminum, 1-piece chassis with 7-in. free-floating modular forend with M-LOK slots and Cerakote finish. 1-Piece 0-MOA rail. Left-hand bolt, right-side eject. Spiral fluted bolt body. 2.5 to 6-lb. user-adjustable AccuTrigger, Picatinny rail at rear of chassis. Accepts most AR-15 pistol grips. Barricade grooves milled into the front of the magazine well, ambidextrous magazine release and AICS magazine.

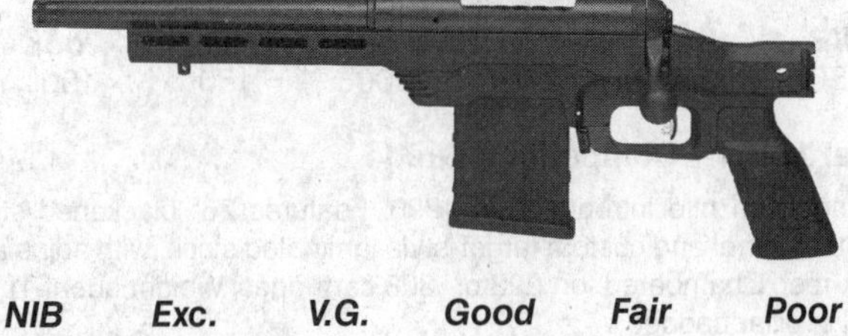

NIB	Exc.	V.G.	Good	Fair	Poor
750	—	—	—	—	—

MODEL 111 SERIES

Model 11/111 Lady Hunter

High-comb walnut stock designed for a woman's physique with a 12.5" LOP, lightweight receiver, 20" barrel in .243, 7mm-08, 6.5 Creedmoor, .308, .270 or .30-06. Detachable box magazine; weight 6–6.5 lbs. The "Lightweight Hunter" weighs a 1/2 lb. less, is in a straight-comb walnut stock, 20" barrel on skeletonized receiver with fluted bolt. (Add $100.)

NIB	Exc.	V.G.	Good	Fair	Poor
780	660	560	480	280	170

Model 11/11 Trophy XP

Matte blue action and 22" or 24" barrel, 17 caliber choices from .204 to .338 Win. Mag., in black synthetic stock with detachable box magazine, 3-9x40 Nikon scope mounted and boresighted. A compact model with 12.5 LOP and 20" barrel is available. Both models in right or left hand. Note: Add $70 for Muddy Girl camo Compact; add $90 for hardwood stock; add $130 for stainless steel. Add $40 more for WSMs in all models.

NIB	Exc.	V.G.	Good	Fair	Poor
550	440	370	320	190	120

Model 111 Classic Hunter Series

All models under this series are fitted with a classic American designed straight comb stock with pistol grip. Chambered in 13 different calibers from .223 Rem. to .338 Win. Magnum. Weights vary with caliber and stock type, but range from 6.365 to 7 lbs. Models are fitted with a detachable or internal magazine. All Hunter series rifles are drilled and tapped for scope mounts.

Model 111G

Top loading, with walnut stock and recoil pad. Chambered for .25-06, .270, .30-06, 7mm Rem. Magnum and .300 Win. Magnum. Fitted with 22" or 24" barrel, depending on caliber with iron sights. Weight about 7 lbs.

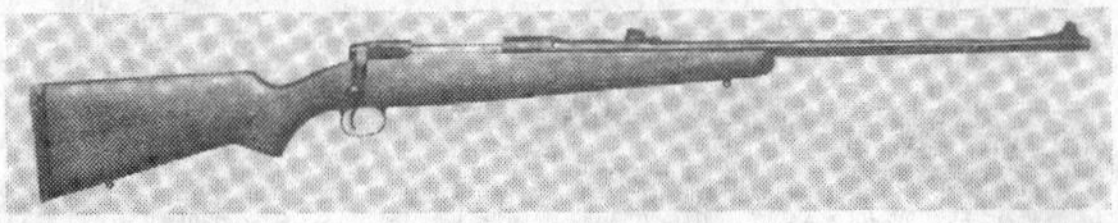

NIB	Exc.	V.G.	Good	Fair	Poor
500	380	280	200	150	100

Model 111GCNS

A long-action model as above, with 22" or 24" barrel depending on caliber with no sights. Introduced in 2005.

NIB	Exc.	V.G.	Good	Fair	Poor
520	400	320	250	180	100

Model 111GC

Detachable magazine with walnut stock and recoil pad. Discontinued.

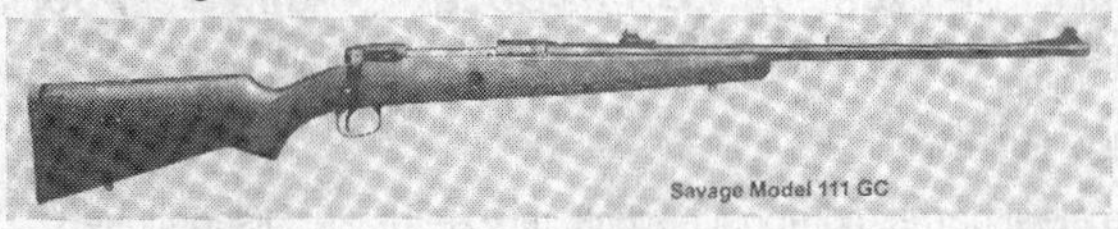

NIB	Exc.	V.G.	Good	Fair	Poor
450	350	300	250	200	150

Model 111GL

Same as Model 111G, with left-hand action.

NIB	Exc.	V.G.	Good	Fair	Poor
480	350	250	200	150	100

Model 111F

Top loading, with graphite stock. Chambered for .25-06, .270, .30-06, 7mm Rem. Magnum, .300 Win. Magmum and .338 Win. Magnum. Fitted with 22" or 24" barrel, with iron sights. Weight about 6.75 lbs.

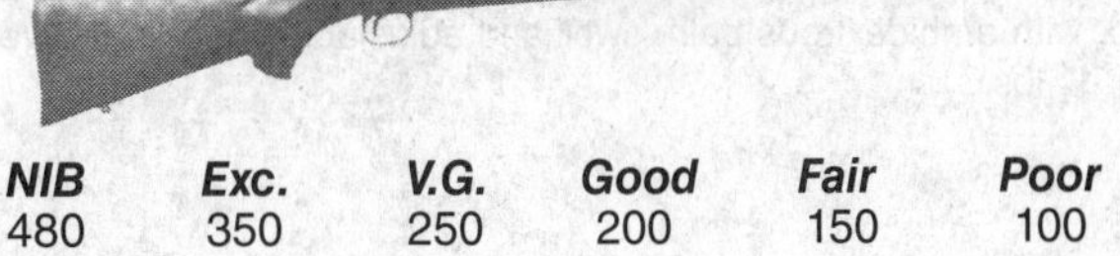

NIB	Exc.	V.G.	Good	Fair	Poor
480	350	250	200	150	100

Model 111FL

As above, with left-hand action.

NIB	Exc.	V.G.	Good	Fair	Poor
480	350	250	200	150	100

Model 111FC

Detachable magazine with graphite stock. Discontinued.

NIB	Exc.	V.G.	Good	Fair	Poor
450	350	300	250	200	150

Model 111FCNS

Introduced in 2005. Chambered for .25-06, .270, .30-06, 7mm Rem. Magnum, .300 Win. Magnum and .338 Win. Magnum. Fitted with 22" or 24" barrel, no sights. Black synthetic stock. Weight about 6.75 lbs., depending on caliber.

NIB	Exc.	V.G.	Good	Fair	Poor
500	380	280	—	—	—

Model 111FXP3

Top loading, with graphite stock and 3x9 scope. Rings, bases and sling.

NIB	Exc.	V.G.	Good	Fair	Poor
520	400	350	300	200	150

Model 111FCXP3

Same as above, with detachable magazine.

NIB	Exc.	V.G.	Good	Fair	Poor
520	400	350	300	200	150

Model 111FAK

Blued steel barrel, composite stock, muzzle brake. Discontinued.

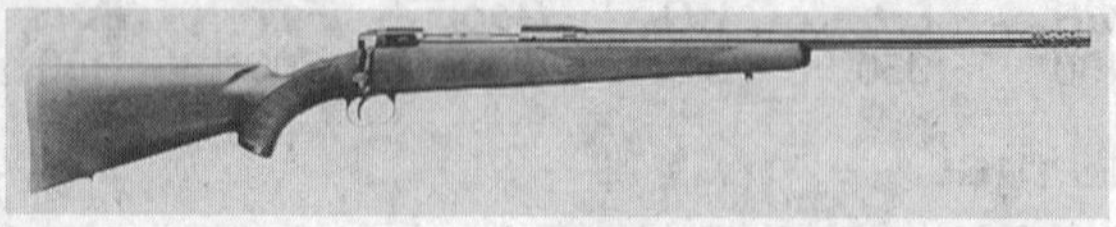

NIB	Exc.	V.G.	Good	Fair	Poor
450	350	300	250	200	150

MODEL 112 SERIES

Model 112BT / 112BT-S (Long Action)

Introduced for the first time in 1994. A competition grade rifle. Chambered for .223 Rem. and .308 Win. Features 26" heavy stainless steel barrel, fitted to an alloy steel receiver. In 1995, .300 Win. Magnum was added and referred to as Model 112BT-S. Barrel finish black. Stock laminated, with ambidextrous palm swell and adjustable cheek-rest. Weight about 11 lbs.

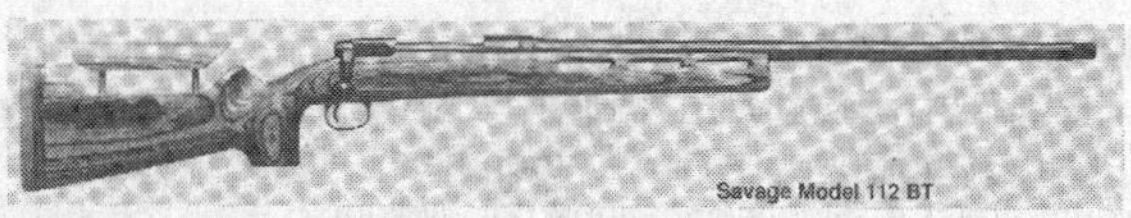

Savage Model 112 BT

NIB	Exc.	V.G.	Good	Fair	Poor
1020	850	700	500	300	250

Model 112 Series Varmint Rifles

Series of varmint rifles feature 26" barrels. Offered with composite or laminated wood stocks. All Model 112s are top loading. Drilled and tapped for scope mounting. Available in .223, .22-250 and .220 Swift. Configuration weight about: 10.5 lbs. BV; 9 lbs. FV.

Model 112BVSS (Long Action)

Laminated wood stock, with high comb and ambidextrous palm swell. Fitted with stainless steel barrel, bolt and triggerguard. In 1996, .300 Win. Magnum, 7mm Rem. Magnum, .308 Win., .30-06 and .25-06 were added.

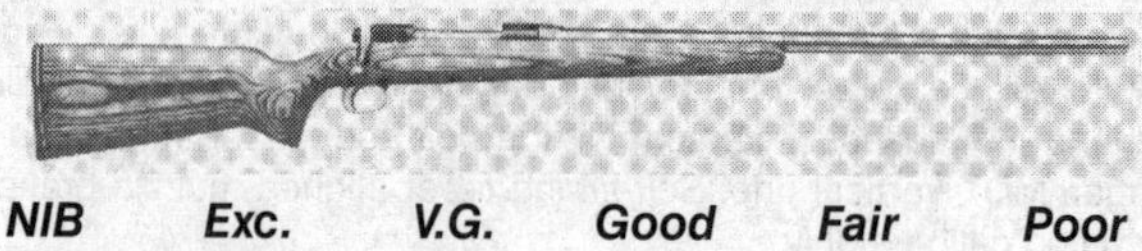

NIB	Exc.	V.G.	Good	Fair	Poor
720	550	400	280	200	150

Model 112BVSS-S

Same as above, but single shot.

NIB	Exc.	V.G.	Good	Fair	Poor
600	450	320	220	150	150

Model 112FVSS

Fitted with stainless steel barrel and composite stock. In 1995, a stainless steel "fluted" barrel and several new calibers were added: 300 Win. Magnum, 7mm Rem. Magnum, .25-06 Rem. In 2003, Savage AccuTrigger was added.

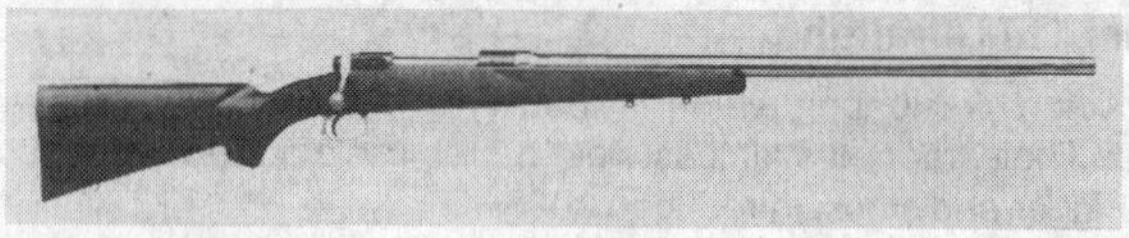

NIB	Exc.	V.G.	Good	Fair	Poor
480	400	350	300	200	150

Model 112FVSS-S

Single-shot version of above model.

NIB	Exc.	V.G.	Good	Fair	Poor
480	400	350	300	200	150

Model 112FV

Similar to above, with a blued barrel.

NIB	Exc.	V.G.	Good	Fair	Poor
380	300	250	200	150	100

Model 112BT—Competition Grade

A competition rifle introduced in 1996. Features 26" blackened stainless steel barrel and custom target-style laminated stock, with adjustable cheek-rest. Chambered for .223 or .308 cartridges. Weight about 11 lbs. Barrel is pillar bedded.

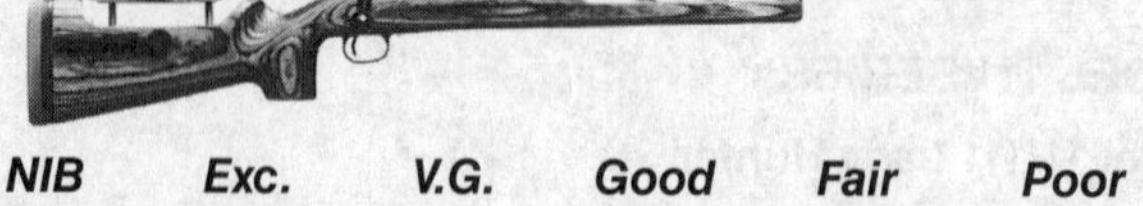

NIB	Exc.	V.G.	Good	Fair	Poor
950	850	700	500	300	250

Model 112 Magnum Target

Long range target/tactical rifle in .338 Lapua Magnum. Single-shot with long-action, target AccuTrigger, 26" heavy barrel and gray laminate stock.

NIB	Exc.	V.G.	Good	Fair	Poor
1000	800	650	500	300	200

MODEL 114 SERIES

Model 114C—Classic

Introduced in 2000. Features select grade oil-finished walnut stock, with cut checkering. No sights. Chambered for .270 and .30-06, with 22" barrel; 7mm Magnum and .300 Win. Magnum, with 24" barrel.

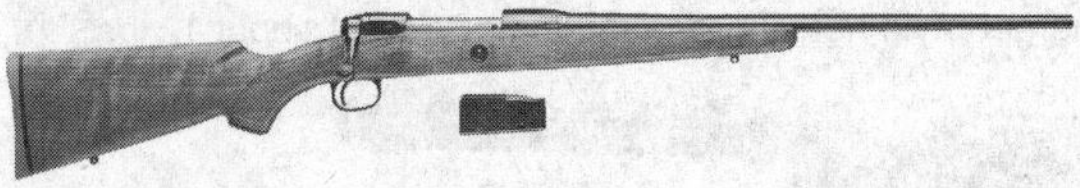

NIB	Exc.	V.G.	Good	Fair	Poor
620	450	320	220	—	—

Model 114CE—Classic European

Introduced in 1996. Chambered for .270 Win., .30-06, 7mm Rem. Magnum and .300 Win. Magnum. Barrel lengths 22" or 24", depending on caliber. Oil-finished stock, with skip line checkering and cheekpiece. Schnabel type forend tip. Rubber recoil pad and pistol grip cap are standard. High-luster blue finish. Weight about 7.12 lbs. Discontinued.

Courtesy Savage Arms

NIB	Exc.	V.G.	Good	Fair	Poor
550	480	400	350	300	150

Model 114CU

Has select grade walnut oil-finished stock. Finish, high polish blue and bolt has laser-etched Savage logo. Detachable magazine standard. Receiver drilled and tapped for scope mount. Offered in .270, .30-06, 7mm Rem. Magnum and .300 Win. Magnum. Weight about 7.125 lbs. Discontinued.

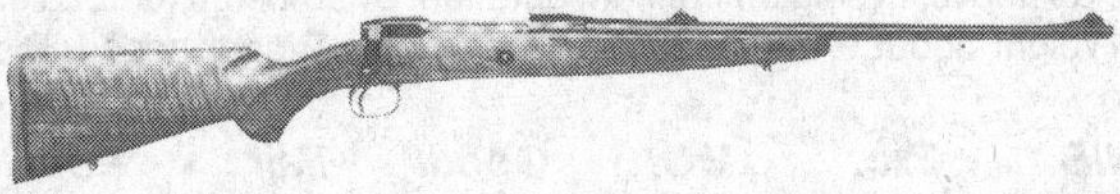

NIB	Exc.	V.G.	Good	Fair	Poor
500	420	320	250	200	150

Model 114U—Ultra

Introduced in 1999. Features high gloss walnut stock, with custom checkering. Blued finish is high luster, with laser-etched Savage logo on bolt body. Chambered for .270 Win., .30-06, 7mm-08 Rem. and .300 Win. Magnum. Barrel length 22" or 24". Weight about 7 lbs.

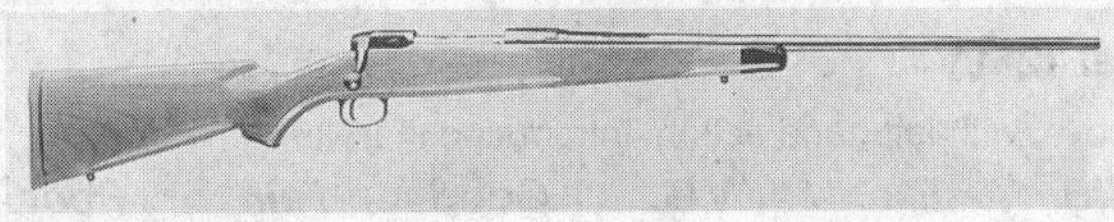

NIB	Exc.	V.G.	Good	Fair	Poor
500	420	320	250	200	150

MODEL 116 SERIES

This series of rifles feature graphite stocks and stainless steel barreled actions. An adjustable muzzle brake is also included. All rifles in the 116 series are drilled and tapped for scope mounts.

Model 116FCSAK (Long Action)

Features a detachable box magazine. Fluted 22" barrel. Offered in .270, .30-06, 7mm Rem. Magnum, .300 Win. Magnum and .338 Win. Magnum. Weight about 6.5 lbs.

NIB	Exc.	V.G.	Good	Fair	Poor
660	500	380	250	180	180

Model 116FSAK (Long Action)

Same as above, with on-off choice for muzzle brake given to shooter. AccuTrigger added in 2004.

NIB	Exc.	V.G.	Good	Fair	Poor
600	450	320	220	180	180

Model 116BSS

Introduced in 2001. Features laminated stock. Chambered for .270 Win., .30-06, 7mm Rem. Magnum, .300 Win. Magnum and .300 Rem. Ultra Magnum. Fitted with 24" or 26" stainless steel barrel. No sights. Weight about 7.5 lbs. Discontinued.

NIB	Exc.	V.G.	Good	Fair	Poor
620	500	360	220	180	180

Model 116FSS (Long Action)

Standard configuration for 116 series. Features top-loading action, with 22" or 24" barrel. No muzzle brake. Weight about 6.75 lbs. Offered in 7 calibers from .223 to .338 Win. Magnum. AccuTrigger added in 2004.

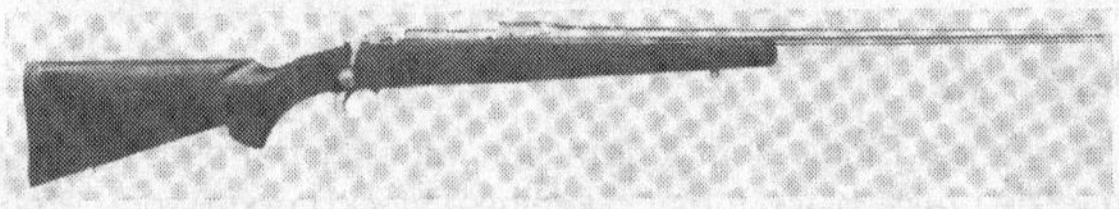

NIB	Exc.	V.G.	Good	Fair	Poor
550	480	380	300	200	150

Model 116FCS

Same as above, with stainless steel removable box magazine.

NIB	Exc.	V.G.	Good	Fair	Poor
550	480	380	300	200	150

Model 116FSK—Kodiak (Long Action)

Features top-loading action, with 22" barrel and muzzle brake. Weight about 7.25 lbs.

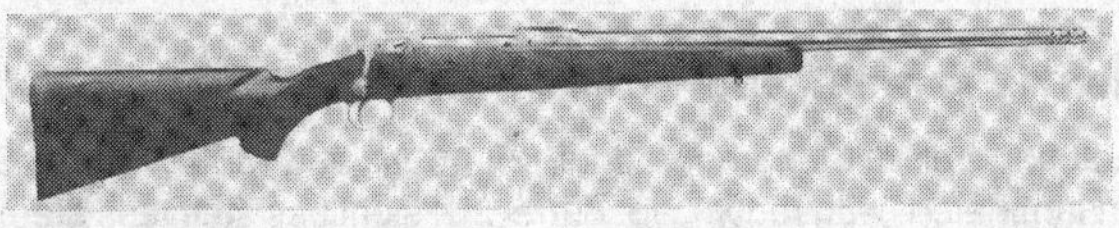

NIB	Exc.	V.G.	Good	Fair	Poor
580	500	380	300	200	150

Model 116SE—Safari Express

Introduced in 1994. Features select-grade walnut stock, with ebony tip and deluxe checkering. Offered in .300 Win. Magnum, .338 Win. Magnum and .458-calibers. In 1995, .425 Express cartridge added. In 2000, stainless steel action and barrel, with adjustable muzzle brake. Weight about 8.5 lbs. Discontinued.

NIB	Exc.	V.G.	Good	Fair	Poor
1100	950	780	600	480	300

Model 116US

Introduced in 1995. Features stainless steel action and barrel, high-gloss

American walnut stock, with ebony tip and custom checkering. Offered in .270 Win., .30-06, 7mm Rem. Magnum and .300 Win. Magnum. Barrel 22" or 24". Discontinued.

NIB	Exc.	V.G.	Good	Fair	Poor
600	500	400	300	250	200

MODEL 12 SERIES VARMINT

Introduced in 1998, this series features short action heavy barrel line of rifles designed for long-range shooting.

Model 12 Varmint

Stainless steel action and 26" fluted heavy barrel in .204, .223 .22-250, .243, .308 and .300 WSM (add $50). Laminated stock with detachable magazine. Note: Deduct $30 for 12 BVSS (fewer calibers, simpler stock); add $115 for 12 BTCSS with laminated thumbhole stock. Add $460 for single-shot Long Range Precision Varmint in HS Precision stock in .204, .223, .22-250 and 6mm Norma BR.

NIB	Exc.	V.G.	Good	Fair	Poor
1020	870	740	620	380	220

Model 12 Palma, F/TR, F Class, Benchrest

Palma is a stainless steel single-shot with 30" heavy barrel in .308, in adjustable laminate stock, Target AccuTrigger. F/TR as above with 30" heavy barrel in .223 or .308 with laminate stock (Deduct $640). F Class comes in flat-bottom laminate stock, 30" heavy barrel in 6mm Norma BR or 6.5-284 Norma (Deduct $500.) Weight 11.5–13.3 lbs. Benchrest comes dual port left-load/right ejection with 29" heavy barrel in 6mm Norma, 6.5x284 or .308 (Deduct ($500).

NIB	Exc.	V.G.	Good	Fair	Poor
1870	1590	1350	1080	650	390

Model 12/112

Magnum Target Single-shot long action with 26" barrel in .338 Lapua with muzzle brake, blued metal in laminate stock. Long Range Precision is a repeater with 26" barrel in .243, 6.5 Creedmoor or .260 Rem, blued metal in HS Precision stock. (Add $115.)

NIB	Exc.	V.G.	Good	Fair	Poor
1020	870	740	620	380	220

Long Range Precision Varminter

Single-shot bolt-action chambered in .204 Ruger, .223 or .22-250. Features include AccuTrigger and oversized bolt handle. Composite stock, sightless stainless steel fluted barrel. Weight 11.25 lbs. Introduced 2006.

NIB	Exc.	V.G.	Good	Fair	Poor
900	750	600	450	300	200

Model 112 Varmint, Low Profile

Long-action bolt rifle chambered for .25-06 (4) and .300 WM (3). Stock brown laminated, with recoil pad. Barrel 26" sightless stainless steel bull. Weight 11.25 lbs.

NIB	Exc.	V.G.	Good	Fair	Poor
600	480	350	200	150	100

Target Actions Only

Stainless steel single-shot, right-hand bolt actions with a choice of left port, right port or dual port, right-side eject (Add $45). Bolt head options include .223 or standard, comes with barrel locknut, recoil lug, trigger-guard and Target AccuTrigger.

NIB	Exc.	V.G.	Good	Fair	Poor
590	500	420	360	220	130

Model 12BVSS

Features 26" fluted stainless steel barrel, recessed crown and brown laminated stock, with beavertail forend. Chambered for .223, .22-250 and .308. Magazine capacity 4 rounds. Weight about 9.5 lbs. Introduced in 1998. In 2003, Savage AccuTrigger added.

NIB	Exc.	V.G.	Good	Fair	Poor
720	550	400	280	200	100

Model 12BVSS-S

Same as above, in single-shot version. Chambered for .223 and .22-250. Weight 9 lbs. In 2003, Savage AccuTrigger added.

NIB	Exc.	V.G.	Good	Fair	Poor
720	550	400	280	200	150

Model 12BVSS-SXP

Introduced in 2003. Single-shot chambered for .223 Rem. or .22-250 Rem. Fitted with 26" stainless steel fluted barrel. Savage AccuTrigger. Stock target-style heavy prone laminate. Weight about 12 lbs.

NIB	Exc.	V.G.	Good	Fair	Poor
680	520	400	280	200	150

Model 12BTCSS

Similar to Model 12BVSS, with laminated thumbhole Monte Carlo stock. Short-action and detachable box magazine.

NIB	Exc.	V.G.	Good	Fair	Poor
720	550	400	280	200	100

Model 12FVSS

Stainless steel 26" fluted barrel and synthetic stock. Offered in .223, .22-250 and .308 calibers. Weight about 9 lbs. Introduced in 1998. A left-hand version also offered. In 2003, Savage AccuTrigger added.

NIB	Exc.	V.G.	Good	Fair	Poor
600	500	380	250	200	100

Model 12FVSS-S

Same as above, in single-shot configuration. Chambered for .223 or .22-250. Weight about 9 lbs. In 2003, Savage AccuTrigger added. Discontinued.

NIB	Exc.	V.G.	Good	Fair	Poor
550	450	320	220	180	100

Model 12FV (Short Action)

Similar to other 12 Series rifles, with blued action and 26" non-fluted barrel. Synthetic stock. Chambered for .223 or .22-250. Weight about 9 lbs. Introduced in 1998. In 2003, Savage AccuTrigger added.

NIB	Exc.	V.G.	Good	Fair	Poor
580	500	380	300	200	150

Model 12FLV

As above, with left-hand action. Introduced in 2005.

NIB	Exc.	V.G.	Good	Fair	Poor
580	500	380	300	200	150

Model 12VSS—Varminter (Short Action)

Introduced in 2000. Features Choate adjustable black synthetic stock. Heavy fluted stainless steel barrel. Box magazine holds 4 rounds. Chambered for .223 or .22-250. Weight about 15 lbs. In 2003, Savage AccuTrigger added.

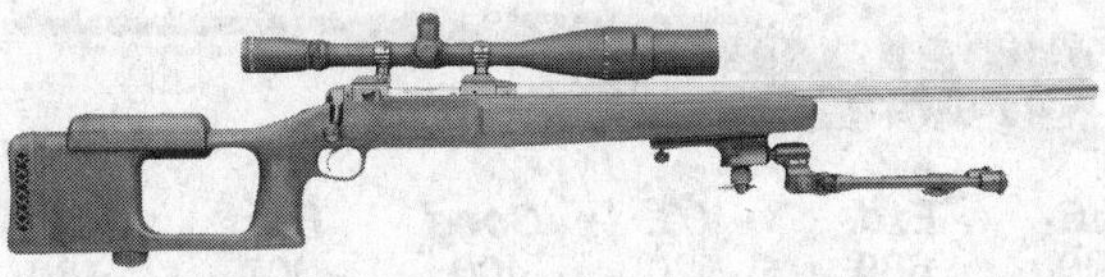

NIB	Exc.	V.G.	Good	Fair	Poor
700	520	380	280	200	100

Model 12 Varminter Low Profile

Introduced in 2004. Chambered for .223 Rem. or .22-250. Fitted with 26" heavy fluted stainless steel barrel, with no sights. Low-profile laminated stock, with extra wide beavertail forearm. Adjustable trigger. Available as a repeater or single-shot. Weight about 10 lbs.

NIB	Exc.	V.G.	Good	Fair	Poor
600	500	380	250	200	100

Model 12 LRPV Long Range Precision Varminter

Similar to Model 12 FVSS, with 30" stainless bull barrel and various accurizing refinements. Chambered in .204 Ruger, .223 Rem. and .22-250. Introduced in 2007. Available in single-shot and 4+1 repeating versions.

NIB	Exc.	V.G.	Good	Fair	Poor
850	700	580	420	300	150

Model 12 FCV Varmint Rifle

New model includes AccuStock, with beavertail forend, AccuTrigger, detachable box magazine and heavy fluted barrel.

NIB	Exc.	V.G.	Good	Fair	Poor
680	600	520	450	300	150

Model 12 F-Class Target Rifle

International-class target rifle chambered in 6.5x284 Norma. Ventilated forend, laminated "under-hold" target stock, oversize bolt knob, AccuTrigger, 30" stainless barrel. Also available in Model 12F/TR version, with conventional buttstock and elevated cheekpiece. Introduced in 2007.

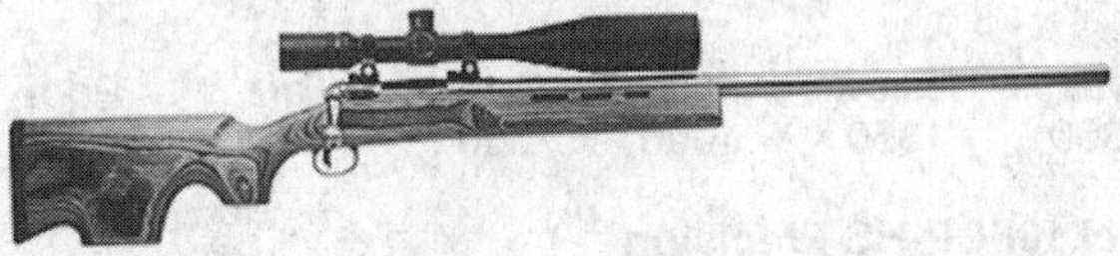

NIB	Exc.	V.G.	Good	Fair	Poor
1200	1000	750	600	480	200

Model 12 Long Range Precision

Target series rifle with target-style AccuTrigger, HS Precision fiberglass matte black stock. Fluted 26" barrel. Detachable magazine with 4-round capacity. Weight 11 lbs.; overall length 46.25". Chambered for .243 Win., .260 Rem. or 6.5 Creedmoor.

NIB	Exc.	V.G.	Good	Fair	Poor
920	820	700	550	400	250

Model 12 Palma

Target rifle designed for Palma Trophy Match competition in .308 Win. Single-shot, with 30" stainless steel heavy barrel, laminated adjustable stock and Savage AccuTrigger.

NIB	Exc.	V.G.	Good	Fair	Poor
1800	1520	1250	900	500	250

MODEL 40 VARMINT HUNTER

Model 40 Varmint Hunter

Introduced in 2004. Chambered for .22 Hornet or .223 Rem. Fitted with 24" heavy barrel, with no sights. Laminated stock, with wide beavertail forearm. Blued. Single shot. Weight about 7.75 lbs. Note: Add $30 for .223 Rem.

NIB	Exc.	V.G.	Good	Fair	Poor
400	300	250	200	150	100

MODEL 10 SERIES

Model 10FP—Tactical (Short Action)

Short-action chambered for .223 or .308 calibers. Fitted with 24" barrel. Black synthetic stock. Drilled and tapped for scope mount. Weight about 8 lbs. Introduced in 1998. In 2003, Savage AccuTrigger added. Premium for Choate or McMillan stock.

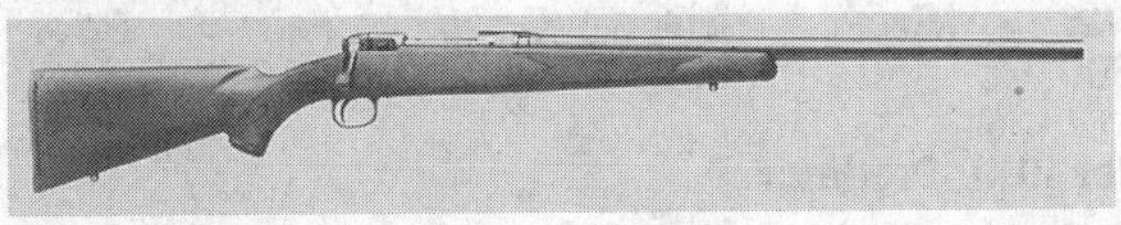

NIB	Exc.	V.G.	Good	Fair	Poor
540	450	320	220	150	100

Model 10FLP

Same as above, in left-hand. In 2003, Savage AccuTrigger added.

NIB	Exc.	V.G.	Good	Fair	Poor
550	450	320	220	150	100

Model 10FM—Sierra

Introduced in 1998. Features 20" barrel chambered for .223, .243 or .308. In 2002, .300 WSM caliber added. Black synthetic stock. Magazine capacity 4 rounds. Weight about 6 lbs. Discontinued.

NIB	Exc.	V.G.	Good	Fair	Poor
500	400	300	150	120	100

Model 10FCM—Sierra

Introduced in 2005. Features 20" light barrel, with detachable magazine. Chambered for .243, 7mm-08 Rem., .308, .270 and .300 WSM. Black synthetic stock. Weight about 6.25 lbs.

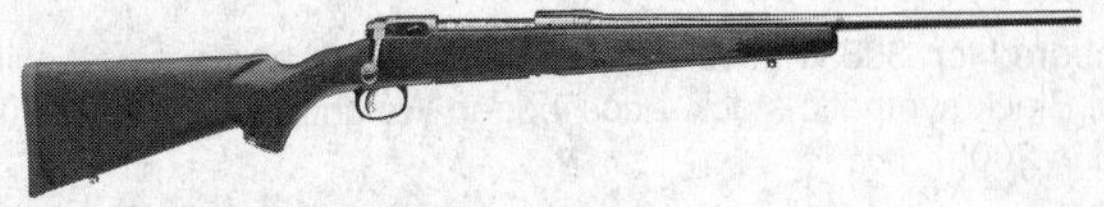

NIB	Exc.	V.G.	Good	Fair	Poor
550	450	320	220	150	100

Model 10FCM—Scout Rifle

Chambered for 7mm-08 Rem. or .308 Win. Fitted with 20" barrel, removable ghost ring rear sight, one-piece scope mount and other special features. Weight about 6.2 lbs. Introduced in 1999; discontinued 2005; reintroduced 2007.

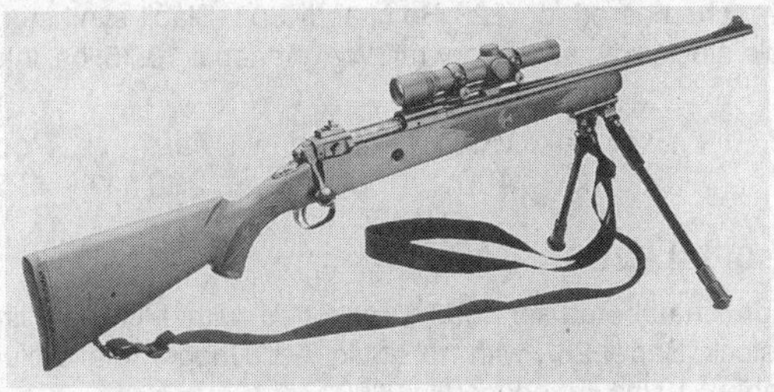

NIB	Exc.	V.G.	Good	Fair	Poor
540	450	320	220	150	100

Model 10GY Youth

Similar to Model 10FM. Features shortened hardwood stock. Fitted with 22" barrel and open sights. Chambered for .223, .243 or .308. Weight about 6.25 lbs. Introduced in 1998.

NIB	*Exc.*	*V.G.*	*Good*	*Fair*	*Poor*
450	320	220	160	120	100

Model 10 Predator Hunter

Similar to Model 10FCM. Overall camo finish, 22" medium-contour barrel and AccuTrigger. Chambered in .204 Ruger, .22-250 and .223. Introduced in 2007. Note: Savage Predator line of rifles now includes a version with new AccuStock, Savage launched in 2009. This version has AccuStock, AccuTrigger, detachable box magazine and medium-contour fluted barrel. Stock finished in Realtree Advantage Max 1 and metal is matte black. MSRP is $945.

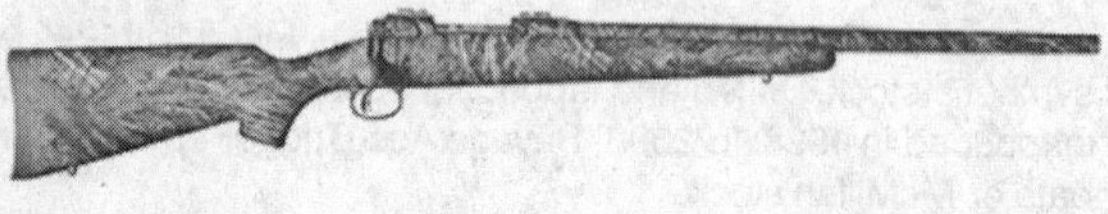

NIB	*Exc.*	*V.G.*	*Good*	*Fair*	*Poor*
600	480	350	280	200	100

Model 10XP Predator

Package rifle with factory-mounted scope. Entirely covered in camo finish. Barrel 22". Chambered in .204, .223 and .22-250. Introduced in 2008.

NIB	*Exc.*	*V.G.*	*Good*	*Fair*	*Poor*
650	500	400	300	220	120

Model 10XP Predator Hunter Bolt-Action Rifle Package

Bolt-action rifle similar to Model 10. Chambered in .223, .204, .22-250 or .243 Win. Includes 4-12x40 scope, 22" barrel, AccuTrigger, choice of Realtree Snow or Mossy Oak Brush camo overall.

NIB	*Exc.*	*V.G.*	*Good*	*Fair*	*Poor*
720	580	420	320	250	150

LAW ENFORCEMENT SERIES

Model 10FP-LE1

Chambered for .308 Win. cartridge. Fitted with 20" heavy barrel, with no sights. Black synthetic stock. AccuTrigger. Weight about 8.25 lbs. Introduced in 2003.

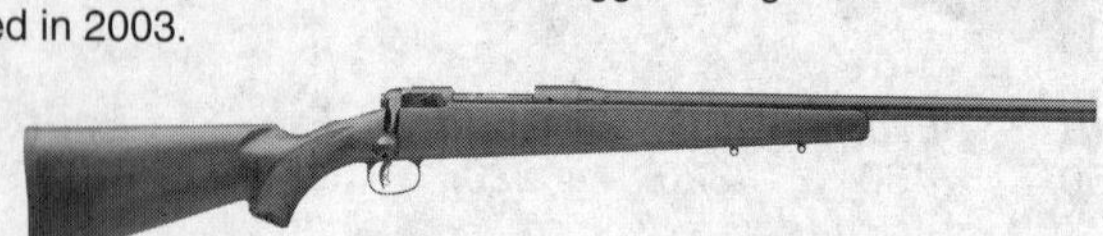

NIB	*Exc.*	*V.G.*	*Good*	*Fair*	*Poor*
550	450	320	220	150	100

Model 10FP-LE1A

As above, chambered for .223 Rem. and .308. Black synthetic Choate adjustable stock, with accessory rail. Weight about 10.75 lbs. Introduced in 2003.

NIB	*Exc.*	*V.G.*	*Good*	*Fair*	*Poor*
650	500	400	300	220	120

Model 10FP-LE2B

Bolt-action chambered for .308 Win. Fitted with McMillan fiberglass tactical stock. Barrel 26", with no sights. AccuTrigger. Matte blue finish. Weight about 10 lbs. Introduced in 2003.

NIB	*Exc.*	*V.G.*	*Good*	*Fair*	*Poor*
800	680	520	400	300	180

Model 10FP-LE2

Introduced in 2003. Features 26" barrel. Chambered for .308 Win. Fitted with black synthetic stock. AccuTrigger. Weight about 8.75 lbs.

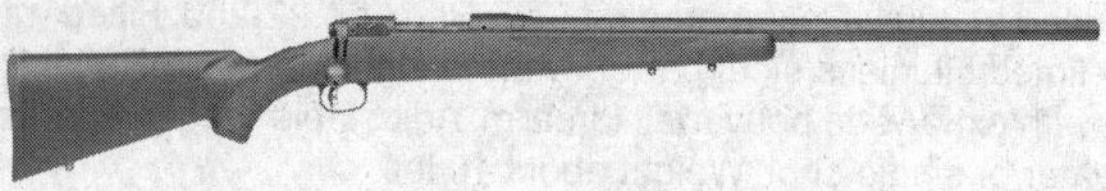

NIB	*Exc.*	*V.G.*	*Good*	*Fair*	*Poor*
650	500	400	300	220	120

Model 10FP-LE2A

Chambered for .223 or .308. Fitted with 26" heavy barrel, with no sights. Black synthetic Choate adjustable stock, with accessory rail. Weight about 11.25 lbs. Introduced in 2003.

NIB	*Exc.*	*V.G.*	*Good*	*Fair*	*Poor*
720	580	420	320	250	150

Model 10FPXP-LEA

This item is a package of both rifle and scope with accessories. Features Model 10FP, with 26" barrel and black synthetic stock. Leupold 3.5-10x40 black matte scope, with Mil Dot scope covers and one-piece base. Harris bipod and heavy duty aluminum case. Weight about 10.5 lbs. Introduced in 2003.

NIB	*Exc.*	*V.G.*	*Good*	*Fair*	*Poor*
1950	1450	1100	700	450	300

Model 10FPXP-LE

As above, with Choate adjustable stock and accessory rail. Weight about 11.25 lbs. Introduced in 2003.

NIB	*Exc.*	*V.G.*	*Good*	*Fair*	*Poor*
1800	1350	1000	600	350	200

Model 10FCP-HS Precision

Similar to Model 110FP-LE1, with one-piece HS Precision synthetic target stock and detachable box magazine. Introduced in 2007.

NIB	*Exc.*	*V.G.*	*Good*	*Fair*	*Poor*
650	500	400	300	220	120

Model 10FCP Choate

Similar to Model 10FP-LE1, with Choate synthetic stock. Introduced in 2007.

NIB	*Exc.*	*V.G.*	*Good*	*Fair*	*Poor*
680	540	400	300	220	120

Model 10FCP McMillan

Similar to Model 10FP-LE1, with synthetic McMillan precision stock. Introduced in 2007.

NIB	*Exc.*	*V.G.*	*Good*	*Fair*	*Poor*
1100	900	720	580	400	200

Model 10FPXP-HS Precision

Similar to Model 10FPXP-LEA, with HS Precision Tactical Stock. Introduced 2006.

NIB	Exc.	V.G.	Good	Fair	Poor
1720	1500	1250	800	600	300

Model 10FP-HS

Similar to Model 10FP-LE1, with HS Precision Tactical stock. Introduced 2006.

NIB	Exc.	V.G.	Good	Fair	Poor
950	800	620	480	300	200

Model 10 Precision Carbine

Similar to Model 10, with 20" medium-contour barrel, synthetic camo AccuStock. Chambered in .223 or .308.

NIB	Exc.	V.G.	Good	Fair	Poor
800	680	520	400	300	180

Model 10FLCP

Similar to Model 10 FCP, in left-hand configuration, with standard or AccuStock.

NIB	Exc.	V.G.	Good	Fair	Poor
800	680	520	400	300	180

Model 10 BAS Law Enforcement Bolt-Action Rifle

Bolt-action repeater based on Model 10 action. Has 24" fluted heavy barrel with muzzle brake, M4-style collapsible buttstock, pistol grip with palm swell, all-aluminum AccuStock, Picatinny rail for mounting optics. Chambered in .308 Win.

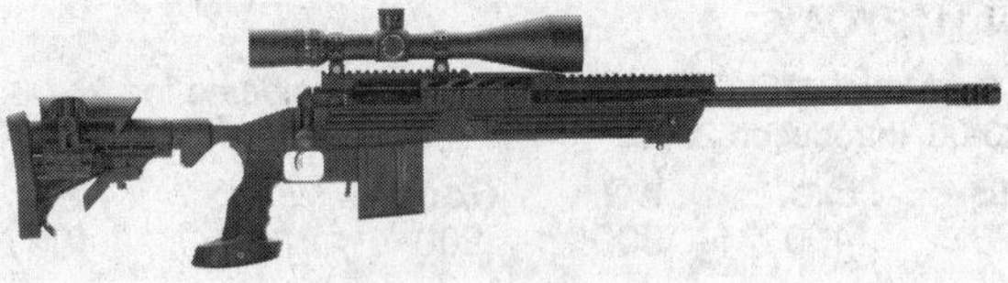

NIB	Exc.	V.G.	Good	Fair	Poor
1600	1350	1000	750	500	300

Model 10 BAT-S

Similar to above, with multi-adjustable buttstock.

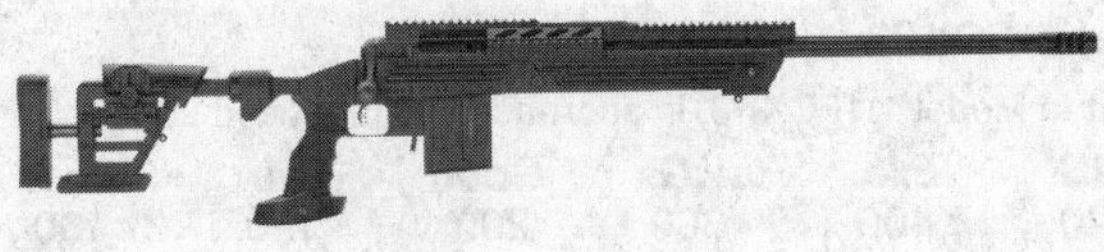

NIB	Exc.	V.G.	Good	Fair	Poor
1700	1400	1080	800	550	320

MSR-15 SERIES

MSR-15 Recon 2.0

Calibers: 5.56 NATO/.223 Rem. Barrel: 16.125" 1:8" 5R rifling; Melonite QPQ finish. Direct-impingement operation. Nickel-boron coated trigger, free-float handguard, Magpul adjustable buttstock and pistol grip. Recon 1.0 introduced 2017. Recon 2.0 introduced 2021. 7.3 lbs. Length: 33.5" to 36.75". SEE POLITICAL PANIC PRICING.

NIB	Exc.	V.G.	Good	Fair	Poor
830	710	600	500	—	—

MSR-15 Recon LRP

Similar to 2.0 except chambered in 22 Nosler, .224 Valkyrie, 6.8 SPC. 18" barrel with 1:7 5R rifling and adjustable gas block. Magpul CTR buttstock and tunable muzzle brake. SEE POLITICAL PANIC PRICING.

NIB	Exc.	V.G.	Good	Fair	Poor
1000	900	700	570	—	—

MSR-15 Long Range

Similar to the Recon LRP, except chambered only in .224 Valkyrie. 22" stainless Savage barrel, custom-length low-profile, gas block, custom free-float handguard. SEE POLITICAL PANIC PRICING.

NIB	Exc.	V.G.	Good	Fair	Poor
2050	1910	1750	1590	—	—

MSR-10 Hunter

Calibers: 6.5 Creedmoor, 308 Win. Barrels: 16" 1:10" 5R. 7.8 lbs. 35" to 39" length. Free-float forend, custom-forged lower receiver, and Magpul adjustable buttstock and pistol grip. SEE POLITICAL PANIC PRICING.

NIB	Exc.	V.G.	Good	Fair	Poor
1450	1320	1190	920	—	—

MSR-10 Long Range

Similar to the MSR-10 Hunter, but with a 20" carbon-steel barrel. Built on a compact frame with a non-reciprocating side-charging handle. SEE POLITICAL PANIC PRICING.

NIB	Exc.	V.G.	Good	Fair	Poor
2140	2000	1800	1520	1100	—

MSR-10 Precision

Similar to the MSR-10 Hunter, but with 22.5" stainless-steel heavy barrel. 18" Arca handguard, Magpul PRS stock, TangoDown Battlegrip Flip Grip, +2 gas system. 44" long, 11.4 lbs. SEE POLITICAL PANIC PRICING.

NIB	Exc.	V.G.	Good	Fair	Poor
2000	1900	1720	1590	1260	—

BLACKPOWDER RIFLES

MODEL 10ML SERIES MUZZLELOADER

Model 10ML-II

Fitted with .50-caliber 24" barrel, with adjustable sights. Synthetic stock. Blued finish. Weight about 7.75 lbs.

NIB	Exc.	V.G.	Good	Fair	Poor
530	380	300	200	150	100

Model 10MLSS-II

As above in stainless steel.

NIB	Exc.	V.G.	Good	Fair	Poor
590	380	320	200	150	100

Model 10ML-II Camo

Introduced in 2002. Has camo stock finish, with blued barrel and action.

NIB	Exc.	V.G.	Good	Fair	Poor
570	420	300	200	150	100

Model 10MLSS-II Camo

Has camo stock finish, with stainless steel barrel and action. Introduced in 2002.

NIB	Exc.	V.G.	Good	Fair	Poor
620	480	350	200	150	100

Model 10MLBSS-II

Features brown laminate stock, with stainless steel action and barrel. Weight 8.75 lbs. Introduced in 2002.

NIB	Exc.	V.G.	Good	Fair	Poor
660	500	380	200	150	100

Model 10ML-IIXP

Introduced in 2002. Has blued action and barrel, with synthetic stock. Fitted with 3-9x40mm scope. Weight 9.25 lbs.

NIB	Exc.	V.G.	Good	Fair	Poor
570	420	300	200	150	100

Model 10MLSS-IIXP

Same as above, with stainless steel barrel and action.

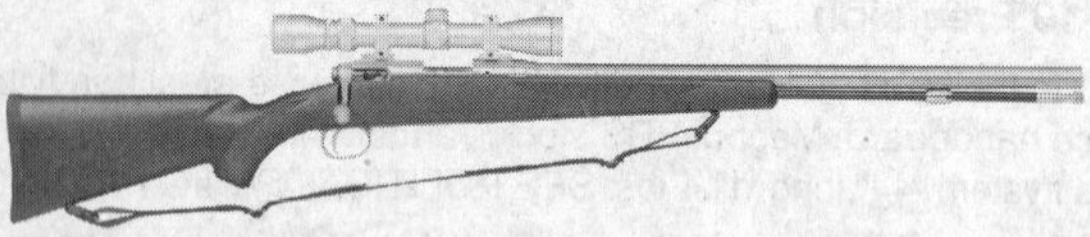

NIB	Exc.	V.G.	Good	Fair	Poor
620	480	350	200	150	100

RIFLES

MODEL 11 SERIES

Model 11F

Features short-action chambered for .223, .22-250, .243 or .308. Barrel 22", with open sights. Black synthetic stock. Weight about 6.75 lbs. Introduced in 1998.

NIB	Exc.	V.G.	Good	Fair	Poor
480	350	250	180	120	100

Model 11FCNS

Introduced in 2005. Chambered for .22-250, .243, 7mm-08, .308, .270 WSM, .7mm WSN and .300 WSM. Barrel 22" or 24", without sights. Detachable box magazine. Black synthetic stock. Weight about 6.5 lbs.

NIB	Exc.	V.G.	Good	Fair	Poor
500	380	250	180	120	100

Model 11 Lightweight Hunter

Chambered for five standard cartridges, plus 6.5 Creedmoor. Lightweight at 5.5 lbs. Satin-finished American walnut wood stock. AccuTrigger, detachable box magazine, matte blue barrel and action with spiral fluted bolt. Barrel 20".

NIB	Exc.	V.G.	Good	Fair	Poor
750	650	500	400	250	150

Model 11G

Chambered for .223, .243, .22-250 or .308. Fitted with 22" barrel. Wood stock has fancy checkered pattern, black recoil pad and gold medallion. Fitted with open sights. Weight about 6.75 lbs. Introduced in 1998.

NIB	Exc.	V.G.	Good	Fair	Poor
500	380	250	180	120	100

Model 11BTH

Laminated thumbhole stock version of Model 11. Chambered in .204, .223, .22-250 and .22 Hornet. Blued 22" barrel.

NIB	Exc.	V.G.	Good	Fair	Poor
620	480	350	200	150	100

Model 11GCNS

Introduced in 2005. Chambered for .22-250, .243, 7mm-08, .308, .270 WSM, 7mm WSM and .300 WSM. Fitted with 22" or 24" barrel, without sights. Checkered walnut stock. Detachable box magazine. Weight about 6.75 lbs.

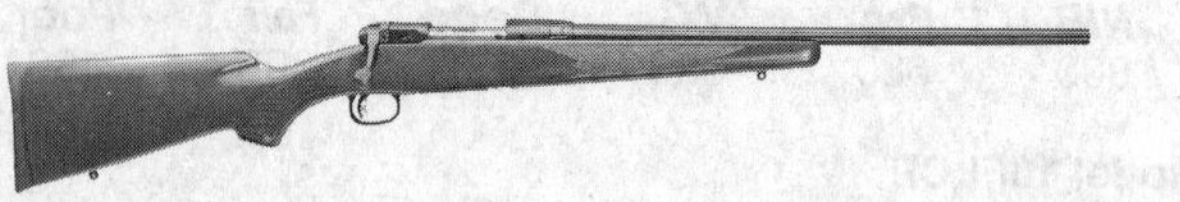

NIB	Exc.	V.G.	Good	Fair	Poor
520	400	300	200	150	100

Model 11FYCAK

Short-action youth model chambered in .243, 7mm-08 and .308. Blue 22" barrel, with muzzle brake. No sights. Stock black composite. Weight 6.5 lbs.; overall length 41.5". Introduced 2006.

NIB	Exc.	V.G.	Good	Fair	Poor
520	400	300	200	120	100

Model 111FYCAK

Similar to Model 11FYCAK, but long-action chambered for .25-06, .270 and .30-06. Introduced 2006.

NIB	Exc.	V.G.	Good	Fair	Poor
520	400	300	200	120	100

Model 111FHNS

Similar to Model 111FCNS, with hinged floorplate. Introduced 2006.

NIB	Exc.	V.G.	Good	Fair	Poor
520	400	300	200	120	100

Model 11FCXP3

Similar to Model 111FCXP3, in short-action. Introduced 2006.

NIB	Exc.	V.G.	Good	Fair	Poor
520	400	300	200	120	100

Model 11FYCXP3

Similar to Model 11FCXP3, in youth version chambered in .243 Win.

NIB	Exc.	V.G.	Good	Fair	Poor
450	320	250	180	150	100

MODEL 14 SERIES

Model 14 Classic

Short-action chambered for .22-250, .243, .270 WSM, 7mm-08, .300 WSM and .308. Barrel polished blue 22" or 24", without sights. Stock select lacquered walnut, with contrasting forend. Introduced 2006. Also available in American Classic version with optional left-hand action.

NIB	Exc.	V.G.	Good	Fair	Poor
600	500	400	300	200	100

Model 14 Left Hand

Similar to above in left-hand. Chambered in .250 and .300 Savage only. Suggested retail price: $779.

Model 114 Classic

Similar to Model 14 Classic, in long-action. Chambered for .270, 7mm RM and .300 WM. Introduced 2006. Also available in American Classic version with optional left-hand action.

NIB	Exc.	V.G.	Good	Fair	Poor
620	480	350	200	150	100

Model 14 Euro Classic

Similar to Model 14 Classic, with iron sights. Introduced 2006.

NIB	Exc.	V.G.	Good	Fair	Poor
620	480	350	200	150	100

Model 114 Euro Classic

Similar to Model 114 Classic, with iron sights. Introduced 2006.

NIB	Exc.	V.G.	Good	Fair	Poor
620	480	350	200	150	100

Model 14/114 American Classic Stainless

Traditional design has an oil-finished American walnut stock. Features wrap-around checkering, black forend tip and no Monte Carlo. Available in short-/long-action versions. Short-action chambered for .243 or .308 Win.; long-action .270 Win., .30-06 and 7mm Rem. Magnum. All with 22" barrel. Introduced in 2011.

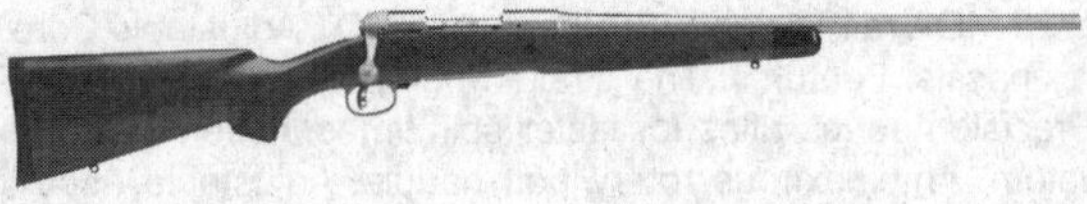

NIB	Exc.	V.G.	Good	Fair	Poor
820	750	650	500	350	150

MODEL 16 SERIES

Model 16FSS

Short-action with top-loading design. Magazine capacity 4 rounds. Chambered for .223, .243 or .308. Fitted with 22" stainless steel barrel. Black synthetic stock. Introduced in 1998.

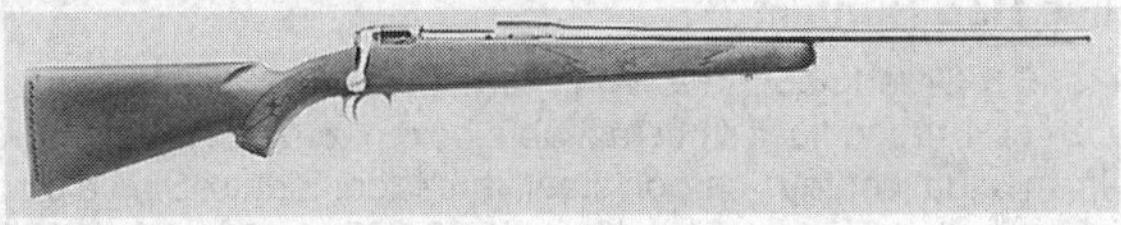

NIB	Exc.	V.G.	Good	Fair	Poor
550	420	320	250	200	100

Model 16FLSS

Same as above, with left-hand action.

NIB	Exc.	V.G.	Good	Fair	Poor
550	420	320	250	200	100

Model 16FCSAK

Introduced in 2005. Chambered for .243, 7mm-08 Rem., .308, .270 WSM, 7mm WSM and .300 WSM. Fitted with 22" or 24" barrel. Detachable box magazine. Black synthetic stock. Weight about 7.5 lbs.

NIB	Exc.	V.G.	Good	Fair	Poor
660	500	400	300	200	100

Model 16FCSS

Chambered for .22-250, .243, 7mm-08 Rem., .308, .270 WSM, 7mm WSM and .300 WSM. Fitted with 22" or 24" barrel. Detachable box magazine. Black synthetic stock. Weight about 6.5 lbs. Introduced in 2005.

NIB	Exc.	V.G.	Good	Fair	Poor
570	420	380	250	180	120

Model 16BSS

Introduced in 2002. Features short-action chambered for 7mm RSUM, .300 RSUM and .300 WSM cartridges. Fitted with 24" stainless steel barrel, drilled and tapped for scope mounts. Laminated stock with cut checkering. Weight about 7.75 lbs. Discontinued.

NIB	Exc.	V.G.	Good	Fair	Poor
640	480	400	300	200	100

Model 16FHSAK

Similar to Model 116FHSAK, but short-action only. Introduced 2006.

NIB	Exc.	V.G.	Good	Fair	Poor
600	480	350	200	150	100

Model 16FHSS

Similar to Model 16FSS, with hinged floorplate. Introduced 2006.

NIB	Exc.	V.G.	Good	Fair	Poor
600	480	350	200	150	100

MODEL 25 SERIES

Model 25 Lightweight Varminter

Short-action rifle chambered in .204 and .223. Medium-contour fluted barrel, with recessed target crown, free-floating sleeved barrel, dual pillar bedding, three locking lugs, 60-degree bolt lift, AccuTrigger adjustable from 2.5 to 3.25 lbs., detachable box magazine. Weight 8.25 lbs.

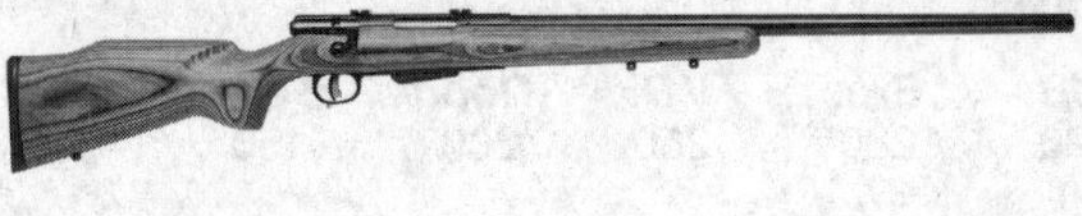

NIB	Exc.	V.G.	Good	Fair	Poor
580	450	320	250	150	100

Model 25 Varminter

Short, bolt-action repeating varmint rifle weighing 6.9–8.25 lbs., with light or heavy barrel in .17 Hornet, .204, .22 Hornet .222 and .223 in black synthetic stock. Note: Add $50 for Real Tree Max 1 camo; add $155 for heavy barrel in laminate stock; add $210 for heavy barrel in thumbhole laminate stock.

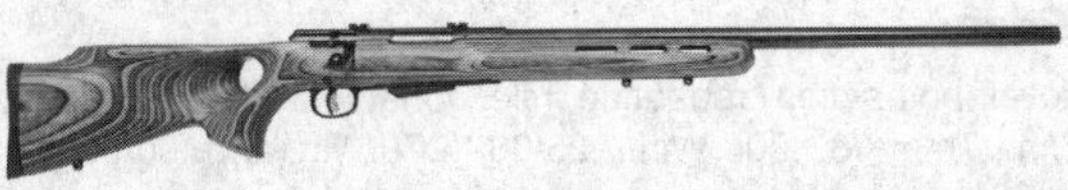

NIB	Exc.	V.G.	Good	Fair	Poor
540	450	390	320	200	120

Model 25 Classic Sporter

Short-action rifle chambered in .204 and .223. Free-floating sleeved barrel, dual pillar bedding, three locking lugs, 60-degree bolt lift, AccuTrigger adjustable from 2.5 to 3.25 lbs. Detachable box magazine. Satin lacquer American walnut stock, with contrasting forend tip and wrap-around checkering. Discontinued.

NIB	Exc.	V.G.	Good	Fair	Poor
600	480	350	200	150	100

Model 25 Walking Varminter

Chambered for .204 Ruger, .22 Hornet, .222 Rem., .223 Rem. and 5.7x28mm. Features 22" barrel sleeved for rigidity. Triple pillar bedding and Weaver scope bases. Has three-lug bolt, with 60-degree throw to allow mounting of a large diameter. AccuTrigger standard. Center feed detachable magazine and synthetic stock.

NIB	Exc.	V.G.	Good	Fair	Poor
480	420	350	250	200	150

AXIS SERIES

Axis

Currently available as Axis, Axis XP and Axis II XP in long- or short-actions in 8 caliber choices from .223 Rem. to .30-06 Springfield in 10 different models. Detachable box magazine. Standard, Compact and left-hand models available. Synthetic stock, with camo or black matte finish. Drilled and tapped for scope mounts. Also available with 3-9x40 Weaver scope mounted. Only Axis II models come with the AccuTrigger. Previously called "The Edge". Note: Add 15% for camo stock; 20% for scope; 30% for pillar bedded hardwood stock; 50% for stainless.

NIB	Exc.	V.G.	Good	Fair	Poor
320	280	250	200	150	120

Axis II Precision

Calibers: .243 Win., .223 Rem, .270 Win., .30-06, .308 Win., 6.5 Creedmoor. Capacity: 5 to 10. Barrel: 22 in., carbon steel, button-rifled heavy, threaded w/cap. Stock: Aluminum MDT chassis. Sights: Picatinny rail. Weight: 9.9 lbs. Features: AccuTrigger, adjustable comb height and LOP spacers, AICS magazine.

NIB	Exc.	V.G.	Good	Fair	Poor
850	—	—	—	—	—

Axis Edge

Entry-level bolt-action repeating rifle. Chambered in .223, .22-250, .243 Win., 7mm-08, .308 Win., .25-06, .270 Win. and .30-06. Features include 22" matte black barrel, synthetic black stock, 4-round capacity detachable box magazine, drilled and tapped for scope mounts. Also available in camo finish (Edge Camo); XP variation (with 3x9 scope); Camo XP (with camo finish and scope). In 2011, the name of this model was changed to Axis. Note: Add 15% for camo stock; 20% for scope. Discontinued.

NIB	Exc.	V.G.	Good	Fair	Poor
320	280	250	200	150	120

Savage Edge Bolt Action Rifle

Entry-level bolt-action repeating rifle. Chambered in .223, .22-250, .243 Win., 7mm-08, .308 Win., .25-06, .270 Win. and .30-06. Features include 22" matte black barrel, synthetic black stock, 4-round capacity detachable box magazine, drilled and tapped for scope mounts. Also available in camo finish (Edge Camo); XP variation (with 3x9 scope); Camo XP (with camo finish and scope). In 2011, the name of this model was changed to Axis. Note: Add 15% for camo stock; 20% for scope.

NIB	Exc.	V.G.	Good	Fair	Poor
300	260	220	200	150	100

IMPULSE SERIES

Impulse Predator

Calibers: .22-250 Rem., .243 Win., 6.5 Creedmoor, .308 Win. Capacity: 10-round AICS-style magazine with ambidextrous release. Barrel: 20-in. medium contour, threaded. Sights: Single piece 20 MOA rail machined into receiver. Length: 41.25 in. Weight: 8.75 lbs. Stock: Mossy Oak Terra Gila camouflage AccuStock with AccuFit user-adjustable system. Features: New straight-pull bolt action uses HexLock bolt system. Ambidextrous rotary bolt handle. Tang safety. Free-floating, tool-free, interchangeable bolt head. Four-bolt barrel clamp system. Adjustable AccuTrigger. Matte black aluminum receiver. Removeable and user adjustable round bolt knob handle.

NIB	Exc.	V.G.	Good	Fair	Poor
1250	—	—	—	—	—

Impulse Elite Precision

Calibers: 6mm Creedmoor, 6.5 Creedmoor, .308 Win., 6.5 PRC, .300 Win. Mag., .300 PRC, .338 Lapua. Capacity: 5- or 10-round AICS magazine with ambidextrous release. Barrel: 26 or 30 in. precision button-rifled, stainless steel, modified Palma contour, with muzzle brake. Sights: Integral 20 MOA rail. Weight: 13.7 lbs. Stock: MDT Adjustable Core Competition chassis. Features: The straight-pull bolt action moves to Savage's Precision series rifles for faster split times. Action uses HexLock bolt system. Ambidextrous rotary bolt handle. Adjustable AccuTrigger. Matte black aluminum receiver. Removeable and user-adjustable round bolt knob handle. ARCA rail forend with M-LOK slots.

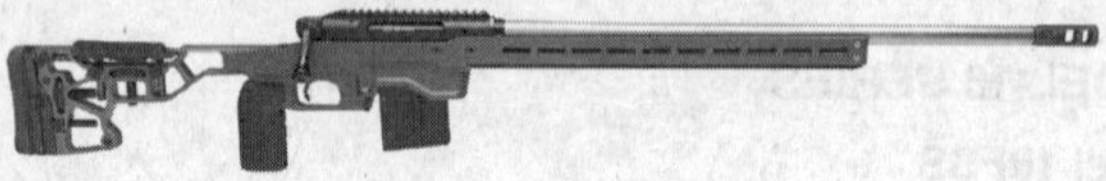

NIB	Exc.	V.G.	Good	Fair	Poor
2380	—	—	—	—	—

Impulse Hog Hunter

Calibers: 6.5 Creedmoor, .308 Win., .30-06 Spfld., .300 Win. Mag. Capacity: 3- or 4-round flush-fit detachable box magazine. Barrel: 18-, 20-, or 24-in. medium contour, carbon steel, threaded. Sights: Single piece 20 MOA rail machined into receiver. Length: 39.25–44.25 in. Weight: 8.41–9.1 lbs. Stock: OD Green Sporter-style AccuStock with AccuFit user-adjustable system. Features: New straight pull bolt action uses HexLock bolt system. Ambidextrous rotary bolt handle. Tang safety. Free-floating, tool-free, interchangeable bolt head. Four-bolt barrel clamp system. Adjustable AccuTrigger. Matte black aluminum receiver. Removeable and user adjustable round bolt knob handle.

NIB	Exc.	V.G.	Good	Fair	Poor
—	—	—	—	—	—

Impulse Mountain Hunter

Caliber: 6.5 Creedmoor, 6.5 PRC, .308 Win., 28 Nosler, 7mm PRC, .300 WSM, .300 Win. mag. Barrel: 22", 24" Proof Research carbon-fiber-wrapped stainless steel. Weight: 7.16 to 7.44 lbs. Stock: Synthetic gray with AccuFit system. Features: Latest addition to the straight-pull family. Aluminum receiver with integral 20-MOA rail. Carbon-fiber barrel. Threaded muzzle with included brake. Detachable box magazine. Ambidextrous, removable, multi-position bolt handle.

NIB	Exc.	V.G.	Good	Fair	Poor
2230	—	—	—	—	—

RIMFIRE RIFLES

Note: As of 2006, virtually all Savage rimfire rifles (with exception of 30G and semi-automatics) were equipped with AccuTrigger as a standard feature.

Model 60

A .22-caliber semi-automatic rifle, with 20" barrel, open sights and tubular magazine. Blued, with Monte Carlo-style walnut stock. Manufactured between 1969 and 1972.

NIB	Exc.	V.G.	Good	Fair	Poor
—	100	80	70	50	40

Model 64G

Introduced in 1996. Semi-automatic .22 Long rifle has 20.25" barrel and 10-shot detachable magazine. Finish is blue. Monte Carlo stock, with checkered pistol grip. Bead front sight, with adjustable open rear sight standard. Weight about 5.5 lbs.

NIB	Exc.	V.G.	Good	Fair	Poor
160	120	90	60	50	40

Model 64GXP

As above, with unmounted 4x15mm scope.

NIB	Exc.	V.G.	Good	Fair	Poor
170	120	100	80	60	50

Model 64BTV

Similar to Model 64, with laminated thumbhole stock.

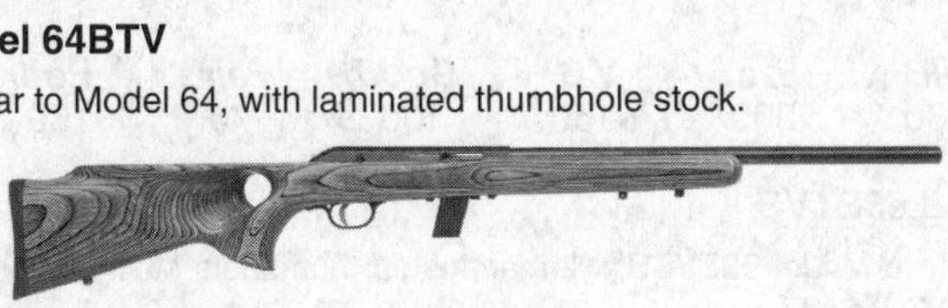

NIB	Exc.	V.G.	Good	Fair	Poor
170	120	100	80	60	50

Model 64F

Introduced in 1997. Features black synthetic stock, with blue finish. Chambered for .22 LR. Fitted with 20.25" barrel. Weight about 5.5 lbs.

NIB	Exc.	V.G.	Good	Fair	Poor
140	120	90	60	50	20

Model 64FSS

Similar to above, with stainless steel action and barrel. Introduced in 2002.

NIB	Exc.	V.G.	Good	Fair	Poor
200	150	110	80	50	20

Model 64FV

Introduced in 1998. Features heavy 21" target barrel, with no sights. Black synthetic stock standard. Chambered for .22 LR cartridge. Weight about 6 lbs. Discontinued.

NIB	Exc.	V.G.	Good	Fair	Poor
150	120	90	60	50	20

Model 64FVXP

Similar to Model 64FV, with scope package. Introduced 2006.

NIB	Exc.	V.G.	Good	Fair	Poor
190	150	110	80	50	20

Model 64FVSS

Similar to Model FV, with stainless steel action and barrel. Introduced in 2002. Discontinued.

NIB	Exc.	V.G.	Good	Fair	Poor
220	180	120	100	80	50

Model 64FXP

A package model that offers a .22 LR gun, with 20.25" barrel. Detachable 10-round magazine. Open sights and 4x15mm scope. Introduced in 1998. Weight about 5.25 lbs.

NIB	Exc.	V.G.	Good	Fair	Poor
150	120	90	60	50	20

Model 88

As above, with hardwood stock. Manufactured between 1969 and 1972.

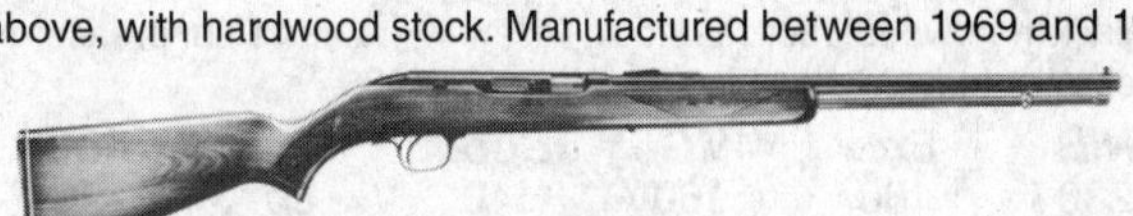

NIB	Exc.	V.G.	Good	Fair	Poor
—	100	80	70	50	40

Model 90 Carbine

As above, with 16.5" barrel and carbine-style stock. Forend secured by one barrel band. Discontinued.

NIB	Exc.	V.G.	Good	Fair	Poor
—	100	80	70	50	40

Model A-17

Current Savage bolt-action rimfires come in a wide array of models from youth single-shot to magnum repeaters all with button rifled barrels and AccuTrigger. Repeaters have 5- or 10-round detachable box magazines.

NIB	Exc.	V.G.	Good	Fair	Poor
400	350	—	—	—	—

Rascal

Single-shot blued .22 LR youth model with 16.125" barrel, synthetic stock with 11.25" LOP in 8 colors and Gator camo (add $42). A left hand model is available with black or pink stock. Weight: 2.71 lbs. Note: Add $29 for 1/2-28-threaded heavy barrel with scope blocks; Add $124 for 1/2-28-threaded heavy barrel Target model (4.42 lbs.) in black hardwood tactical-style stock, oversize bolt handle and scope rail; Add $90 for bi-pod. First introduced in 2012.

NIB	Exc.	V.G.	Good	Fair	Poor
160	140	120	100	60	40

Rascal Minimalist

Caliber: .22 LR. Capacity: single shot. Barrel: 16.125-in. carbon steel, threaded with protector. Length: 30.625 in. Weight: 3.5 lbs. Stock: Minimalist hybrid laminate design in two color options. Features: Addition to the micro-sized Rascal single shot, bolt-action family. Blued carbon steel receiver. Manual safety. Cocks by lifting the bolt. Unloads without pulling the trigger. 11-degree target crown. Adjustable peep sight. Sling studs. User-adjustable AccuTrigger. Feed ramp. ChevCore Laminate technology with Boyd's stock in two color options: Pink/Purple or Teal/Gray. Short 11.5-in length of pull. Package includes ear plugs and firearms lock.

NIB	Exc.	V.G.	Good	Fair	Poor
240	—	—	—	—	—

Model 93 Magnum Series

Bolt-action repeater with 21" or 22" blue or stainless steel barrel in .17 HMR or .22 WMR in black synthetic, hardwood or camo stock. F Model Notes: Add $60–$90 for camo stock; Add $70 for 3-9 scope mounted; Add $100 for threaded barrel; Add $80 for stainless steel barrel. G Model Notes: Add $10 for hardwood stock and $40 for heavy barrel; Add $400 for black hardwood Tactical stock, Picatinny rail and suppressor-ready barrel. Weight 5–6.5 lbs. First introduced in 1996.

NIB	Exc.	V.G.	Good	Fair	Poor
230	180	160	140	80	50

Model 93 Varmint Laminate

Varmint model with laminate stock and blued or stainless steel heavy barrel in .17 HMR or .22 WMR. Note: Add $35 for stainless steel; Add $40 for Thumbhole stock; Add $130 for spiral-fluted heavy barrel; Add $240 for Evolution laminate stock. Weight 6.5–7.25 lbs.

NIB	Exc.	V.G.	Good	Fair	Poor
350	280	220	190	120	70

Model 93G

Introduced in 1996. Bolt-action repeating rifle chambered for .22 WMR cartridge. Fitted with 20.75" barrel, with 5-shot magazine. Walnut-stained hardwood stock, with cut checkering. Open sights standard. Weight about 5.75 lbs. In 2001, offered in left-hand version (Model 93GL).

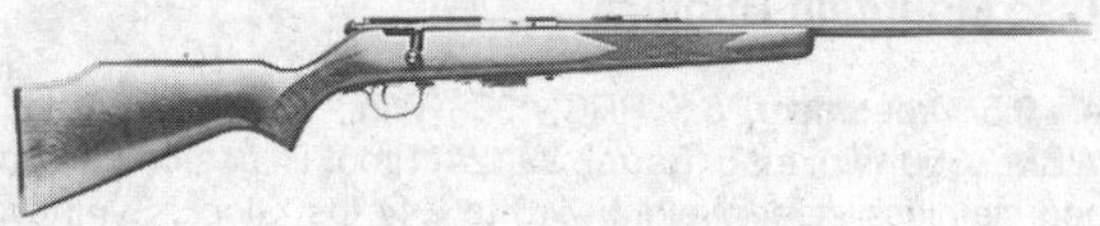

NIB	Exc.	V.G.	Good	Fair	Poor
200	150	100	80	60	50

Model 93FS

This .22 WMR model features stainless steel finish, with 20.75" barrel and black synthetic stock. Five-round magazine. Front bead sight and sporting rear. Introduced in 1997. Weight about 5.5 lbs. Discontinued.

NIB	Exc.	V.G.	Good	Fair	Poor
200	150	100	80	60	50

Model 93 Classic

Similar to Model 93G, with sporter-weight barrel. Oil-finished premium walnut stock. AccuTrigger. Introduced in 2007.

NIB	Exc.	V.G.	Good	Fair	Poor
480	380	320	200	150	100

Model 93 Classic Thumbhole

Similar to above, with thumbhole stock.

NIB	Exc.	V.G.	Good	Fair	Poor
520	400	300	200	120	100

Model 93XP

.22 WMR package gun, with 22" barrel and factory-mounted 3x9 scope. Overall finish in Mossy Oak Brush camo.

NIB	Exc.	V.G.	Good	Fair	Poor
400	320	250	150	100	80

Model 93FVSS

Features 21" heavy barrel chambered for .22 WMR cartridge. Recessed target muzzle and stainless steel barreled action. Equipped with black synthetic stock. Magazine capacity 5 rounds. Weight about 6 lbs. Introduced in 1998.

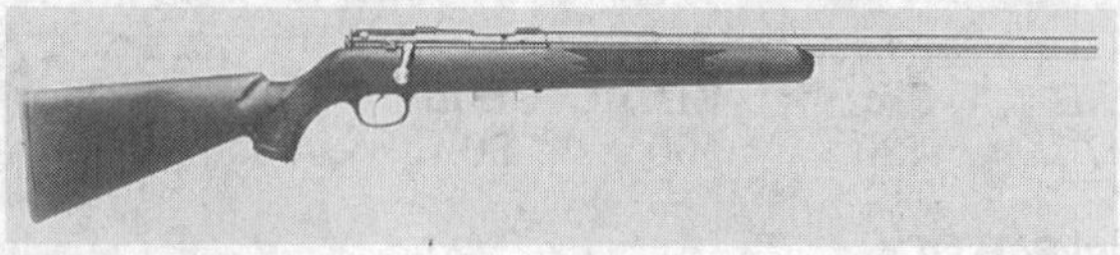

NIB	Exc.	V.G.	Good	Fair	Poor
280	200	150	100	70	50

Model 93BTVS

Similar to Model 93FVSS, with laminated thumbhole stock. Introduced in 2007.

NIB	Exc.	V.G.	Good	Fair	Poor
400	320	250	150	100	80

Model 93F

Similar to above, with blued finish. Synthetic stock, with open sights. Weight about 5 lbs. Introduced in 1998.

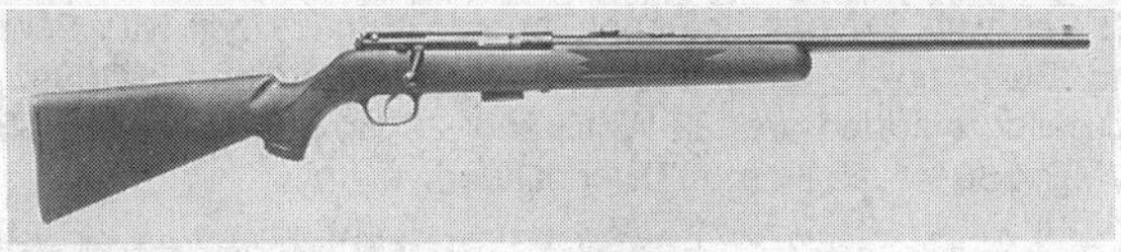

NIB	Exc.	V.G.	Good	Fair	Poor
180	120	100	60	50	20

Model 93R17-F

Bolt-action rifle chambered for .17 HMR cartridge. Fitted with 20.75" barrel, no sights. Black synthetic stock. Magazine capacity 5 rounds. Blued finish. Weight about 5 lbs. Introduced in 2003.

NIB	Exc.	V.G.	Good	Fair	Poor
220	180	120	100	80	50

Model 93R17-BVSS

Similar to above, with 21" stainless steel barrel, no sights and laminated hardwood stock. Weight about 6 lbs. Introduced in 2003.

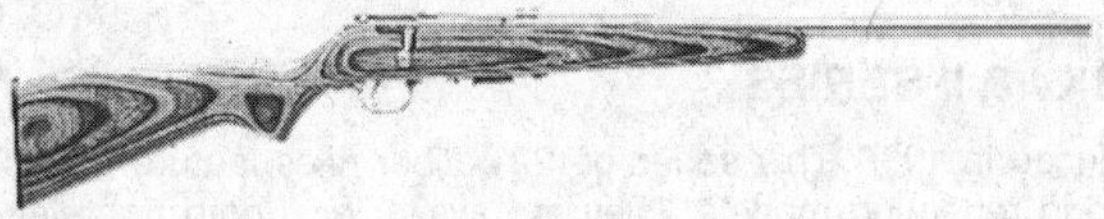

NIB	Exc.	V.G.	Good	Fair	Poor
320	250	190	120	80	50

Model 93R17-FSS

This .17 HMR caliber rifle has 20.75" stainless steel barrel, no sights and black synthetic stock. Weight about 5 lbs. Introduced in 2003.

NIB	Exc.	V.G.	Good	Fair	Poor
250	180	130	100	80	50

Model 93R17-Camo

As above, with Realtree Hardwoods camo stock. Weight about 5 lbs. Introduced in 2003.

NIB	Exc.	V.G.	Good	Fair	Poor
250	180	130	100	80	50

Model 93R17-FVSS

As above, with 21" stainless steel heavy barrel. Weight about 6 lbs. Introduced in 2003.

NIB	Exc.	V.G.	Good	Fair	Poor
280	210	150	120	80	50

Model 93R17-GV

This .17 HMR model has walnut finished hardwood checkered stock. Heavy 21" barrel, no sights. Blued finish. Weight about 6 lbs. Introduced in 2003. Left-hand model available.

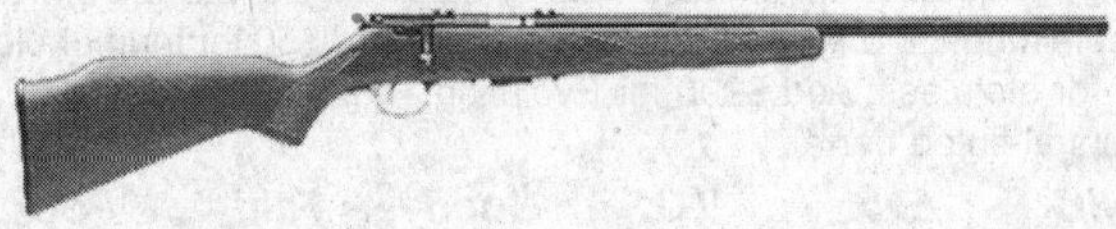

NIB	Exc.	V.G.	Good	Fair	Poor
230	180	120	100	80	50

Model 93R17-GVXP

Similar to Model 93R17-GV, with scope package. Introduced 2006.

NIB	Exc.	V.G.	Good	Fair	Poor
250	180	130	100	80	50

Model 93R17-FXP

Similar to Model 93R17-F, with scope package. Introduced 2006.

NIB	Exc.	V.G.	Good	Fair	Poor
250	180	130	100	80	50

Model 93FVSS-XP

Similar to Model 93FVSS, with scope package. Introduced 2006.

NIB	Exc.	V.G.	Good	Fair	Poor
300	220	150	120	80	50

Model 93FSS

Similar to discontinued Model 93FS, with no sights and AccuTrigger. Introduced 2006.

NIB	Exc.	V.G.	Good	Fair	Poor
280	210	150	120	80	50

Model 93FV

Similar to Model 93F, with AccuTrigger. Introduced 2006.

NIB	Exc.	V.G.	Good	Fair	Poor
250	180	130	100	80	50

Model 93R17-BTVS

Similar to Model 93R17-BVSS, with laminated thumbhole stock. Introduced 2006.

NIB	Exc.	V.G.	Good	Fair	Poor
350	300	240	200	150	100

Model 93R17-BLTVS

Similar to above, in left-hand. Suggested retail price: $441.

Model 93R17-BV

Similar to Model 93R17-GV, with brown laminated stock. Wide beavertail forend. Introduced 2006.

NIB	Exc.	V.G.	Good	Fair	Poor
350	300	240	200	150	100

Model 93R17 Classic

Similar to Model 93R17, with sporter-weight barrel and oil-finished premium walnut stock. AccuTrigger. Introduced in 2007.

NIB	Exc.	V.G.	Good	Fair	Poor
450	340	300	200	140	100

Model Mark II BRJ

Similar to Mark II Model 93. Features spiral fluting pattern on heavy barrel, blued finish and Royal Jacaranda wood laminate stock. In .22 LR, .22 WMR or .17 HMR.

NIB	Exc.	V.G.	Good	Fair	Poor
400	350	300	250	200	100

Model Mark II TRR-SR

Similar to Mark II Model 93. Features heavy barrel, matte finish and tactical-style wood stock.

NIB	Exc.	V.G.	Good	Fair	Poor
480	420	350	300	250	150

Model CUB-G (Mini-Youth)

Introduced in 2003. Single-shot bolt-action rifle chambered for .22-caliber cartridge. Barrel length 16". Walnut-stained hardwood stock is proportionally scaled down. Weight about 3.3 lbs. In 2005, offered in .17 HM2. Discontinued.

NIB	Exc.	V.G.	Good	Fair	Poor
160	120	100	80	50	20

Model CUB-T

Similar to Model CUB-G, with laminated thumbhole stock. Introduced in 2007. Discontinued.

NIB	Exc.	V.G.	Good	Fair	Poor
240	200	140	100	80	50

B-SERIES

A bolt-action rimfire with 21" barrel in .17 HMR, .22 LR and .22 WMR with a higher comb synthetic stock, vertical pistol grip, top-tang safety and 10-round detachable rotary magazine, drilled and tapped for scope mounts, iron sights on some models. Weight 5.25–6.4 lbs. Notes: Add $20 for HMR and WMR; Add $30 for heavy barrel; $115 for stainless steel; Add $65 for 16.25" threaded heavy barrel and 1-piece scope rail; Add $160 for hardwood stock and iron sights. Introduced in 2017.

NIB	Exc.	V.G.	Good	Fair	Poor
220	190	160	140	80	50

Model B - Mag

Designed expressly for the hot .17 WSM with 22" barrel in black synthetic stock, 8-round rotary magazine. Note: Add $20 for heavy barrel; Add $100 for stainless steel barrel in thumbhole laminate stock; Add $130 for matte blue sporter in laminate stock; Add $175 for matte blue heavy barrel in target stock with beavertail forend. First introduced in 2013.

NIB	Exc.	V.G.	Good	Fair	Poor
330	280	240	200	120	70

B-Series Precision

Calibers: .22 LR, .22 WMR, .17 HMR. Capacity: 10-round detachable magazine. Barrel: 18 in heavy carbon steel, threaded. Weight: from 5 lbs. 5 oz. Stock: MDT one-piece billet aluminum chassis with adjustable LOP and comb height. Sights: None. One-piece Picatinny rail. Features: B-Series Precision rifles are built for target performance. They include the B22 in .22 LR, B22 Magnum in .22 WMR, and B17 in .17 HMR. Adjustable AccuTrigger with red trigger detail. For Precision Lite 18-in. carbon-fiber barrel wrap NIB is $880.

NIB	Exc.	V.G.	Good	Fair	Poor
590	—	—	—	—	—

Model 30G "Stevens Favorite"

Based on Stevens Favorite model. Lever-action single-shot .22-caliber rifle. Fitted with 21" half octagonal barrel. Walnut stock with Schnabel forend. Blued finish. Weight about 4.25 lbs. Introduced in 1999. Additional calibers added are .22 WMR and .22 Hornet. Note: Add $35 for .22WMR; $60 for .22 Hornet. Discontinued.

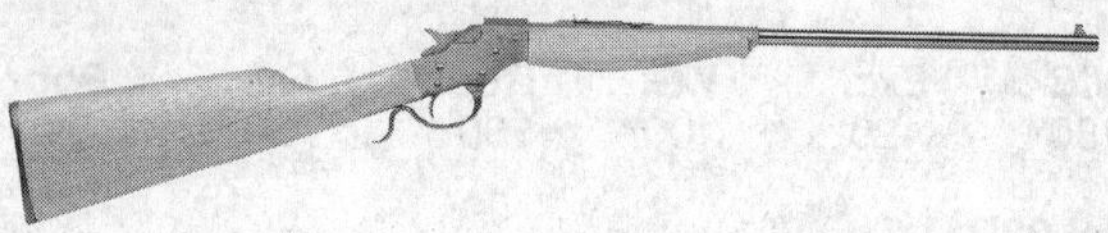

NIB	Exc.	V.G.	Good	Fair	Poor
320	280	220	150	100	50

Model 30G "Favorite" Takedown

Introduced in 2004. Has a take-down feature. Offered in: .17 HMR with 21" full octagon barrel, sights and scope base included; .22 LR with 21" half octagon barrel and sights. Note: Add $65 for .17 HMR model. Discontinued.

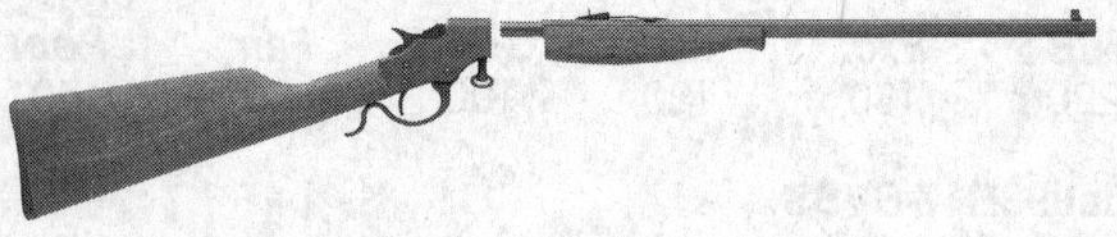

NIB	Exc.	V.G.	Good	Fair	Poor
320	280	220	150	100	50

MARK I & II SERIES

Introduced in 1996. This series of .22-caliber rifles feature both single-shot and repeating models. They are available in both right-/left-hand models.

Models Mk I FVT and G

A full-size single-shot bolt action .22 LR with heavy 21" barrel, target peep and globe front sights in black synthetic stock. A left-hand model is available. The G model is a sporter model in full size or youth, hardwood stock with iron sights (Deduct $200). "G" first introduced in 1996; "F" in 1998.

NIB	Exc.	V.G.	Good	Fair	Poor
400	340	280	240	150	90

Mark I-GY (Youth Model)

Same as above, with 19" barrel and shorter buttstock. Weight about 5 lbs.

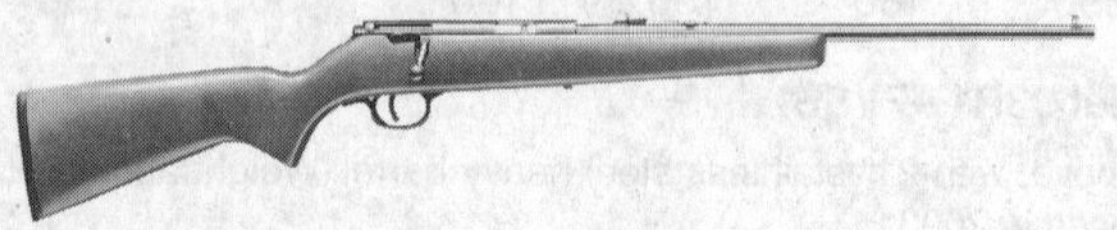

NIB	Exc.	V.G.	Good	Fair	Poor
150	100	80	70	60	50

Mark I-GSB Smoothbore

This version of Mark I is a smoothbore model made for .22-caliber shot cartridges. Barrel length 20.75". Weight about 5.5 lbs. Discontinued.

NIB	Exc.	V.G.	Good	Fair	Poor
150	100	80	70	60	50

Model MK II Laminates

Mk II bolt-action in laminate stock includes conventional and thumbhole. Blued, stainless or spiral-fluted blue or stainless 21" .22 LR barrel. Detachable magazine. Weight 6.5-7.5 lbs. Note: Add $50 for thumbhole; $50 more for stainless; Add $200 for Evolution Thumbhole stock with stainless spiral-fluted barrel.

NIB	Exc.	V.G.	Good	Fair	Poor
350	280	220	190	120	70

Model Mk II F and G Series

A full-size blued, carbon steel bolt-action rifle with 21" sporter or heavy barrel in .17 M2 (limited models) or .22 LR (all models) in 10 different stock configurations (not counting sub-models in left-hand or youth) including black synthetic, tactical, target and camo. Detachable magazine; weight from 5-7.5 lbs. Note: Add $15 for G model in hardwood stock (also comes in a Compact with 16" barrel and 12.9" LOP, and left hand in both Standard and Compact); Add $90 for .17 M2 or .22 LR with 3-9X scope mounted; Add $250 for heavy barrel and peep rear and globe front sights; Add $400 for Tactical stock, heavy barrel threaded for suppressor. First introduced in 1998.

NIB	*Exc.*	*V.G.*	*Good*	*Fair*	*Poor*
200	160	140	120	80	40

Mark II-GY (Youth Model)

Same as above, with 19" barrel and shorter stock.

NIB	*Exc.*	*V.G.*	*Good*	*Fair*	*Poor*
170	120	90	70	60	50

Mark II-GXP

Same as Mark II-G, but includes an unmounted 4x15mm scope. Discontinued.

NIB	*Exc.*	*V.G.*	*Good*	*Fair*	*Poor*
130	100	80	70	60	50

Mark II-FSS

Stainless steel .22-caliber rifle, with 20.75" barrel and 10-round magazine. Receiver dovetailed for scope mounting. Stock black synthetic. Weight about 5 lbs.

NIB	*Exc.*	*V.G.*	*Good*	*Fair*	*Poor*
210	150	110	80	60	40

Mark II-LV

Fitted with 21" heavy barrel, in .22-caliber. Laminated hardwood stock, with cut checkering. Blue finish and 10-round magazine. Weight about 6.5 lbs. Introduced in 1997. Discontinued.

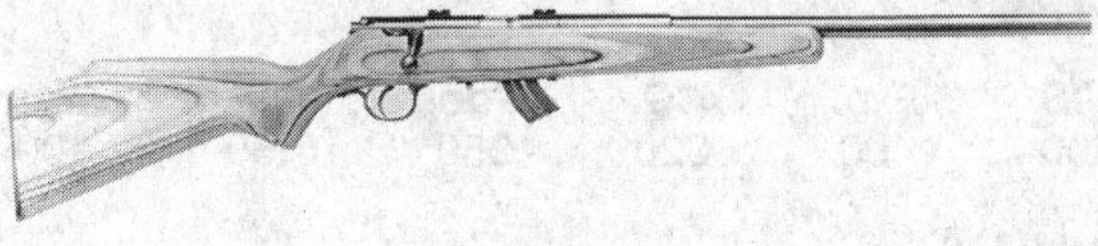

NIB	*Exc.*	*V.G.*	*Good*	*Fair*	*Poor*
200	150	110	80	60	40

Mark II-FXP

Similar to Mark II-F, with 4x15mm scope. Weight about 5.25 lbs. Introduced in 1998.

NIB	*Exc.*	*V.G.*	*Good*	*Fair*	*Poor*
160	110	80	70	60	40

Mark II Camo

Similar to Mark II-F, with forest camo synthetic stock. Introduced 2006.

NIB	*Exc.*	*V.G.*	*Good*	*Fair*	*Poor*
200	160	140	100	80	50

Mark II-FV

Introduced in 1998. Features 21" heavy barrel, with blue alloy steel receiver. Stock black synthetic. Detachable magazine capacity 5 round. Weight about 6 lbs. In 2006, .17 Hornady Mach 2 added.

NIB	*Exc.*	*V.G.*	*Good*	*Fair*	*Poor*
220	150	110	80	60	40

Mark II-FVXP

Similar to Mark II-FV, with scope package. Introduced 2006.

NIB	*Exc.*	*V.G.*	*Good*	*Fair*	*Poor*
250	200	150	120	80	50

Mark II-FVT

Similar to Mark II-FV, with rear peep sight and hooded front. Introduced 2006.

NIB	*Exc.*	*V.G.*	*Good*	*Fair*	*Poor*
320	250	200	140	100	80

Mark II-BV

Features 21" stainless steel bull barrel, without sights. Brown laminate stock. Chambered in .22 LR. Introduced 2006.

NIB	*Exc.*	*V.G.*	*Good*	*Fair*	*Poor*
300	220	180	150	100	80

Mark II BTV

Similar to above, with laminated thumbhole ventilated stock. AccuTrigger. Blued receiver and bull barrel.

NIB	*Exc.*	*V.G.*	*Good*	*Fair*	*Poor*
380	320	250	150	120	100

Mark II BVTS

Similar to above, with stainless barrel and receiver. Available in right-/left-hand (BTVLS) configuration. Suggested retail price: $393 (standard); $441 (left-hand).

NIB	*Exc.*	*V.G.*	*Good*	*Fair*	*Poor*
400	350	260	160	140	120

Mark II Classic

Similar to Mark II-FV, with sporter-weight barrel. Oil-finished premium walnut stock. AccuTrigger. Introduced in 2007. Note: Add $50 for thumbhole stock.

NIB	*Exc.*	*V.G.*	*Good*	*Fair*	*Poor*
400	350	300	220	150	100

Mark II Minimalist

Choice of green or brown Boyd's Minimalist laminate stock design.

NIB	*Exc.*	*V.G.*	*Good*	*Fair*	*Poor*
330	—	—	—	—	—

A22 SERIES

A22 BNS-SR

Caliber: .22 LR. Capacity: 10. Barrel: 18 in., carbon steel. Stock: Laminated wood. Sights: Two-piece Weaver bases, no scope included. Weight: 6.6 lbs. Features: Ergonomic stock, AccuTrigger, straight blowback semi-auto.

NIB	Exc.	V.G.	Good	Fair	Poor
400	350	280	—	—	—

A22 Takedown

Calibers: .22 LR. Barrel: 18". Weight: 6.3 lbs. Stock: Black synthetic adjustable. Features: Latest addition to the semi-auto A22 family, now in a takedown version, which breaks in half with a twist. Threaded barrel with low-profile sights. Crossbolt safety, adjustable AccuTrigger. Storage compartment in pistol grip and magazine compartment in cheek riser. Has 0 MOA rail with a see-through iron sight channel. Includes 10-round rotary magazine.

NIB	Exc.	V.G.	Good	Fair	Poor
420	—	—	—	—	—

MODEL 900 SERIES

First offered in 1996. Series consists of .22-caliber rimfire target rifles in various configurations. All available in both right-/left-hand versions. Discontinued.

Model 900B—Biathlon

Features hardwood stock, with 5-round magazine, carrying and shooting rails, butt hook and hand stop. Barrel 21" and comes with snow cover. Receiver sight are peep variety. Front sight has 7 aperture inserts as standard. Weight about 8.25 lbs.

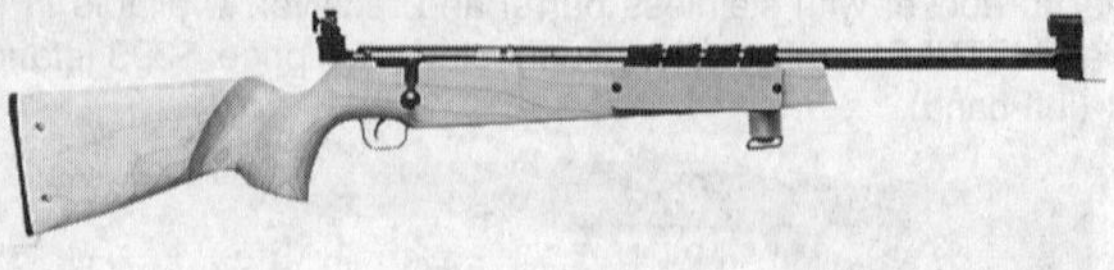

NIB	Exc.	V.G.	Good	Fair	Poor
480	400	350	300	200	120

Model 900 TR—Target

Has one-piece hardwood stock, with shooting rail and hand stop. Rear sight adjustable peep and front sight has 7 aperture inserts. Barrel length 25". Five-shot magazine standard. Weight about 8 lbs.

NIB	Exc.	V.G.	Good	Fair	Poor
400	320	280	220	150	100

Model 900S—Silhouette

Version features 21" heavy barrel, with recessed target style crown. Fitted with one-piece silhouette-style stock, with high comb and satin walnut finish. Receiver drilled and tapped for scope mount. Weight about 8 lbs.

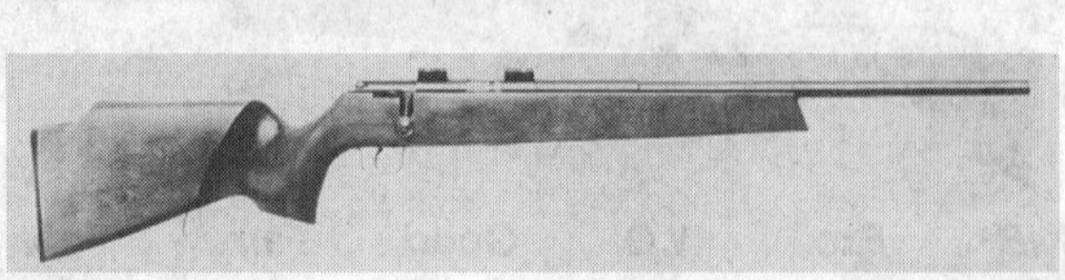

NIB	Exc.	V.G.	Good	Fair	Poor
400	320	280	220	150	100

Model 24

External hammer combination rifle/shotgun, with 24" barrels. Blued, with walnut stock. Manufactured from 1950 to 1965 in a variety of styles. Standard chambering .22 by .410.

NIB	Exc.	V.G.	Good	Fair	Poor
550	500	400	320	250	150

Model 24S

Similar to above, except has side-mounted operating lever. Available with 20-gauge lower barrel.

NIB	Exc.	V.G.	Good	Fair	Poor
450	380	320	250	200	150

Model 24MS

Similar to above, except rifle barrel chambered for .22 WMR.

NIB	Exc.	V.G.	Good	Fair	Poor
600	520	420	350	280	180

Model 24DL

Satin chrome, with checkered stock.

NIB	Exc.	V.G.	Good	Fair	Poor
—	450	380	320	180	120

Model 24 Field—Lightweight Version

NIB	Exc.	V.G.	Good	Fair	Poor
—	450	380	280	150	100

Model 24C

Nickel finish.

NIB	Exc.	V.G.	Good	Fair	Poor
—	450	380	280	150	100

Model 24VS

.357 Magnum or .357 Maximum/20 gauge, nickel finish.

NIB	Exc.	V.G.	Good	Fair	Poor
680	580	450	400	300	200

Model 24F

DuPont Rynite stock.

NIB	Exc.	V.G.	Good	Fair	Poor
500	400	320	250	150	100

Model 2400

Combination 12-gauge by .222- or .308-caliber over/under rifle/shotgun, with 23.5" barrels and Monte Carlo-style stock. Made by Valmet. Imported between 1975 and 1980.

NIB	Exc.	V.G.	Good	Fair	Poor
—	700	580	450	350	280

Model 389

Over/under design with 12-gauge 3" Magnum shotgun barrel over rifle barrel. Chambered for .222 Rem. or .308 Win. Double triggers, hammerless action, checkered walnut stock. Made in 1988 and 1989.

NIB	Exc.	V.G.	Good	Fair	Poor
800	700	600	450	350	200

Model 42

Over/under design with .22 Long rifle or WMR rifle barrel over .410 shotgun barrel. Separated barrels, with black synthetic stock and sling swivels. Opens with lever in front of triggerguard. New in 2013

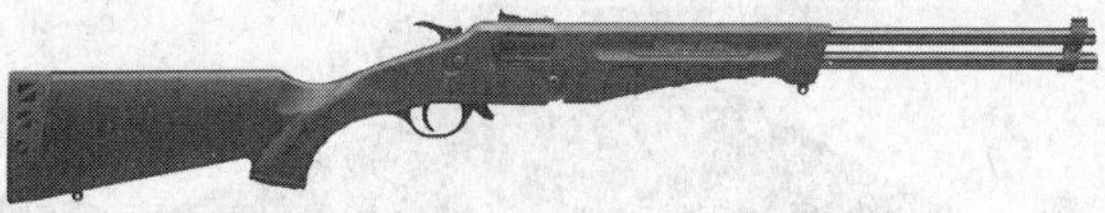

NIB	Exc.	V.G.	Good	Fair	Poor
400	350	300	—	—	—

SAVAGE SHOTGUNS

Model 21

Slide-action shotgun built between 1920 and 1928. Chambered for 12-gauge, with 26", 28", 30" or 32" barrel. Walnut pistol grip stock and slide handle. Take-down. Almost identical to famous Winchester Model 12. Offered in a number of different configurations including standard grade, Trap grade, Tournament grade and Riot Model. About 13,000 built.

NIB	Exc.	V.G.	Good	Fair	Poor
—	300	260	220	180	160

Model 28

Slide-action shotgun is an improved version of Model 21. Manufactured from 1928 to 1934. There are several variations including: Model 28-A standard grade; Model 28-B standard grade with raised matted rib; Model 28-C; Riot; Model 28-D Trap grade; in 1931, Model 28-3 an improved version with checkering and roll marked game scenes on receiver.

NIB	Exc.	V.G.	Good	Fair	Poor
—	300	260	220	180	160

Model 30

A 12-, 16-, 20-gauge and .410 bore slide-action shotgun, with 26" to 30" ventilated rib barrels. Blued, with walnut stock. Manufactured between 1958 and 1978.

NIB	Exc.	V.G.	Good	Fair	Poor
—	220	190	160	140	120

Model 210FT

Introduced in 1997. A 12-gauge bolt-action shotgun, with camouflage finish. Chambered for 3" shells. Fitted with 24" barrel. 2-round magazine. Weight about 7.5 lbs. Drilled and tapped for scope mounting.

NIB	Exc.	V.G.	Good	Fair	Poor
580	500	420	350	200	120

Model 210F

Introduced in 1996. Bolt-action shotgun has 24" rifled barrel for slugs. Chambered for 3" 12-gauge shell. No sights. Magazine holds 2 rounds. Weight about 7.5 lbs.

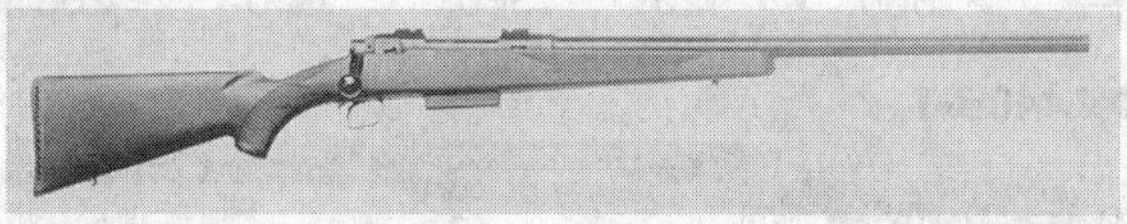

NIB	Exc.	V.G.	Good	Fair	Poor
500	420	360	310	260	220

Model 210F Slug Warrior Camo

As above, with camo stock.

NIB	Exc.	V.G.	Good	Fair	Poor
600	520	450	380	220	150

Model 220

A 12-, 16-, 20-gauge or .410 bore boxlock single-barrel shotgun, with 26" to 32" barrels. Blued, with walnut stock. Manufactured between 1938 and 1965.

NIB	Exc.	V.G.	Good	Fair	Poor
—	100	80	70	50	40

Model 220 Turkey w/Extended X-Full Choke

NIB	Exc.	V.G.	Good	Fair	Poor
640	—	—	—	—	—

Model 212 Slug Gun

NIB	Exc.	V.G.	Good	Fair	Poor
—	600	510	430	370	310

Model 212 Turkey w/Extended X-Full Choke

Gauges: 12 ga., 3 in., 20 ga., 3 in. Barrel: 22 in., carbon steel. Weight: 7.34-7.75 lbs. Length: 43 in. Stock: Synthetic AccuFit stock with included LOP and comb inserts. Thumbhole model uses gray wood laminate. Features: The bolt-action Savage models 212 and 220, so named for their chamberings, are available in Slug, Slug Camo, Thumbhole, Left-Handed and Turkey models. Choice of button-rifled slug barrels or smoothbore. Detachable box magazine, thread-in barrel headspacing. User adjustable AccuTrigger and AccuStock internal chassis. Oversized bolt handle, Picatinny optics rail, sling studs, rubber buttpad.

NIB	Exc.	V.G.	Good	Fair	Poor
700	—	—	—	—	—

Model 242

A .410 bore boxlock double-barrel over/under shotgun, with 26" barrels, single trigger, extractors and exposed hammer. Manufactured between 1977 and 1981.

Courtesy Nick Niles, Paul Goodwin photo

NIB	Exc.	V.G.	Good	Fair	Poor
—	650	550	470	400	340

Model 312 Field Over/Under

NIB	Exc.	V.G.	Good	Fair	Poor
—	580	500	420	360	300

Model 312 Trap

NIB	Exc.	V.G.	Good	Fair	Poor
—	620	520	440	380	320

Model 312 Sporting Clay

NIB	Exc.	V.G.	Good	Fair	Poor
—	600	510	430	360	310

Model 320

This is a side-by-side model.

NIB	*Exc.*	*V.G.*	*Good*	*Fair*	*Poor*
—	800	650	500	400	300

Model 320 Field

NIB	*Exc.*	*V.G.*	*Good*	*Fair*	*Poor*
—	800	600	450	300	200

Model 330

A Valmet manufactured 12- or 20-gauge over/under shotgun, with 26", 28" or 30" barrels. Single-selective trigger and extractors. Blued, with walnut stock. Imported between 1970 and 1978.

Courtesy Nick Niles, Paul Goodwin photo

NIB	*Exc.*	*V.G.*	*Good*	*Fair*	*Poor*
—	500	420	360	300	260

Model 333

As above, with ventilated rib and automatic ejectors. Imported between 1973 and 1980.

NIB	*Exc.*	*V.G.*	*Good*	*Fair*	*Poor*
—	650	550	470	400	340

Model 333T

As above, with 30" barrel and trap-style stock. Imported between 1972 and 1980.

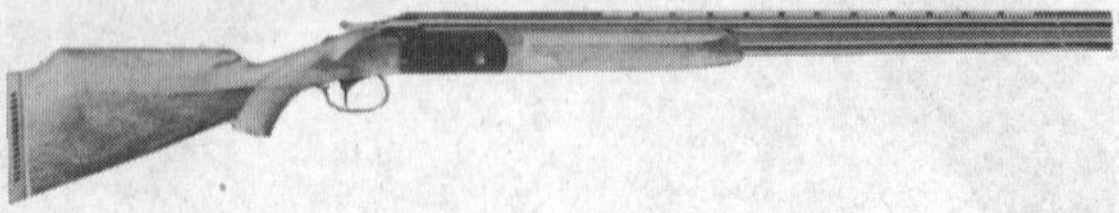

NIB	*Exc.*	*V.G.*	*Good*	*Fair*	*Poor*
—	550	470	400	340	290

Model 411 Upland Sporter

See—STEVENS.

Model 412

.410 bore adapter.

NIB	*Exc.*	*V.G.*	*Good*	*Fair*	*Poor*
—	80	60	50	40	30

Model 412F

.410 bore adapter.

NIB	*Exc.*	*V.G.*	*Good*	*Fair*	*Poor*
—	50	40	40	40	20

Model 420

A 12-, 16- or 20-gauge boxlock over/under shotgun with 26", 28" or 30" barrels. Double triggers and extractors. Manufactured between 1937 and 1943.

Courtesy Nick Niles, Paul Goodwin photo

NIB	*Exc.*	*V.G.*	*Good*	*Fair*	*Poor*
—	380	330	280	240	200

Model 420 with Single Trigger

NIB	*Exc.*	*V.G.*	*Good*	*Fair*	*Poor*
—	440	370	320	270	230

Model 430

As above, with checkered walnut stock and solid barrel rib. Produced from 1937 to 1943.

NIB	*Exc.*	*V.G.*	*Good*	*Fair*	*Poor*
—	440	370	320	270	230

Model 430 with Single Trigger

NIB	*Exc.*	*V.G.*	*Good*	*Fair*	*Poor*
—	480	400	340	290	250

Model 440

An Italian made 12- or 20-gauge boxlock over/under shotgun, with 26", 28" or 30" ventilated rib barrels. Single-selective trigger and extractors. Blued, with walnut stock. Manufactured between 1968 and 1972.

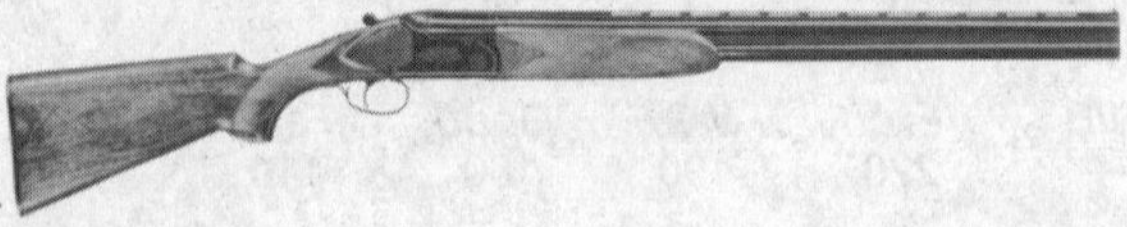

NIB	*Exc.*	*V.G.*	*Good*	*Fair*	*Poor*
—	500	420	360	300	260

Model 440A

Courtesy Nick Niles, Paul Goodwin photo

NIB	*Exc.*	*V.G.*	*Good*	*Fair*	*Poor*
—	500	420	360	300	260

Model 440B-T

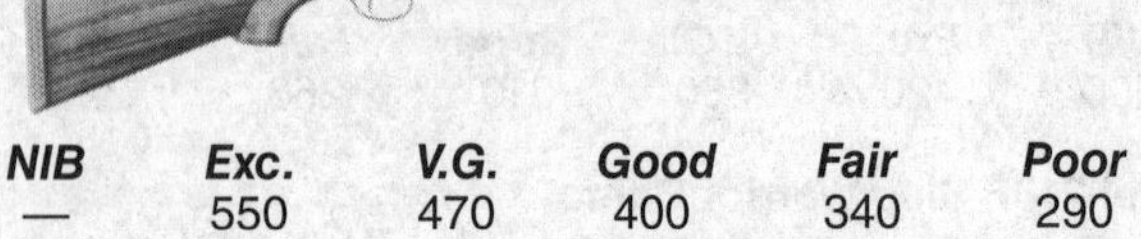

NIB	*Exc.*	*V.G.*	*Good*	*Fair*	*Poor*
—	550	470	400	340	290

Model 444

NIB	*Exc.*	*V.G.*	*Good*	*Fair*	*Poor*
—	600	500	400	300	200

Model 440T

A 12-gauge Model 440, with 30" barrels and trap-style stock. Imported between 1969 and 1972.

NIB	*Exc.*	*V.G.*	*Good*	*Fair*	*Poor*
—	600	500	400	300	200

Model 444B

NIB	*Exc.*	*V.G.*	*Good*	*Fair*	*Poor*
—	700	550	400	300	250

Model 444 Deluxe

As above, with more finely figured stock and automatic ejectors. Imported between 1969 and 1972.

NIB	*Exc.*	*V.G.*	*Good*	*Fair*	*Poor*
—	550	470	400	340	290

Model 550

A 12- or 20-gauge boxlock side-by-side double-barrel shotgun, with 26", 28" or 30" barrels. Single triggers and automatic ejectors. Blued, with hardwood stock. Manufactured between 1971 and 1973. Barrels built by Valmet.

Courtesy Nick Niles, Paul Goodwin photo

NIB	*Exc.*	*V.G.*	*Good*	*Fair*	*Poor*
—	280	230	200	170	140

Model 720

A 12- or 16-gauge semi-automatic shotgun, with 26" to 32" barrels. Blued, with walnut stock. Manufactured between 1930 and 1949.

NIB	*Exc.*	*V.G.*	*Good*	*Fair*	*Poor*
—	220	190	160	140	120

Model 726 Upland Sporter

As above, with 2-shot magazine. Manufactured between 1931 and 1949.

NIB	*Exc.*	*V.G.*	*Good*	*Fair*	*Poor*
—	280	230	200	170	140

Model 740C Skeet

Model 726, with 24.5" barrel. Features a Cutts compensator and skeet-style stock. Manufactured between 1936 and 1949.

NIB	*Exc.*	*V.G.*	*Good*	*Fair*	*Poor*
—	300	260	220	190	160

Model 745

Model 720, in 12-gauge with alloy receiver and 28" barrel. Manufactured between 1940 and 1949.

NIB	*Exc.*	*V.G.*	*Good*	*Fair*	*Poor*
—	280	230	200	170	140

Model 755

A 12- or 16-gauge semi-automatic shotgun, with 26" to 30" barrels. Blued, with walnut stock. Also available with Savage Super Choke. Manufactured between 1949 and 1958.

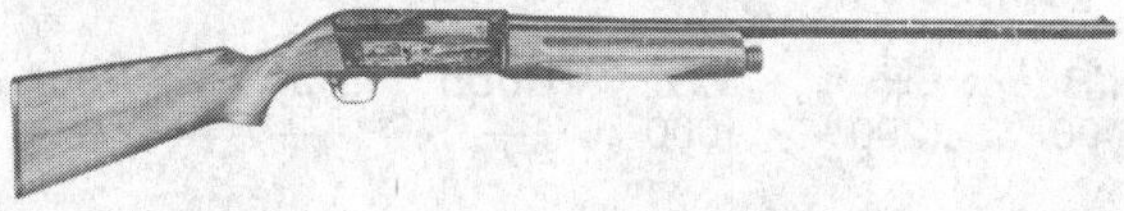

NIB	*Exc.*	*V.G.*	*Good*	*Fair*	*Poor*
—	260	220	190	160	140

Model 750

A 12-gauge semi-automatic shotgun, with 26" or 28" barrel. Model 750SC fitted with Savage Super Choke; Model 750AC with Poly Choke. Blued, with walnut stock. Manufactured between 1960 and 1967.

NIB	*Exc.*	*V.G.*	*Good*	*Fair*	*Poor*
—	280	230	200	170	140

Model 750SC

NIB	*Exc.*	*V.G.*	*Good*	*Fair*	*Poor*
—	280	240	210	180	150

Model 750AC

NIB	*Exc.*	*V.G.*	*Good*	*Fair*	*Poor*
—	280	240	210	180	150

Model 775

As above, with alloy receiver. Manufactured between 1950 and 1966.

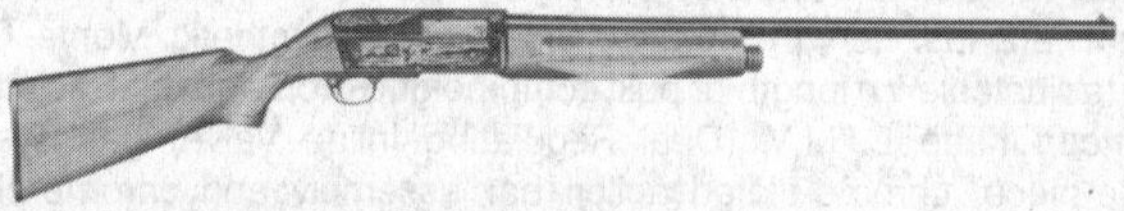

NIB	*Exc.*	*V.G.*	*Good*	*Fair*	*Poor*
—	280	230	200	170	140

RENEGAUGE SERIES

Renegauge

Gauge: 12 ga., 3 in. Capacity: 4+1.Barrels: 26 in., 28 in., fluted with steel ventilated rib. Weight: 7.9-8 lbs. Length: 47.5-49.5 in. Stock: Black synthetic stock with Monte Carlo style cheekpiece, adjustable for length of pull, comb height, drop and cast. Features: American-made D.R.I.V. (Dual Regulating Inline Valve) gas system. Single-piece, chrome-plated action-bar assembly and chrome-plated reciprocating components. Melonite-finished external metalwork. Stock rod buffer to reduce felt recoil. Red fiber-optic sight, competition-ready easy-loading port, oversized controls. Includes three Beretta/Benelli-style chokes (IC, M, F) and hard case.

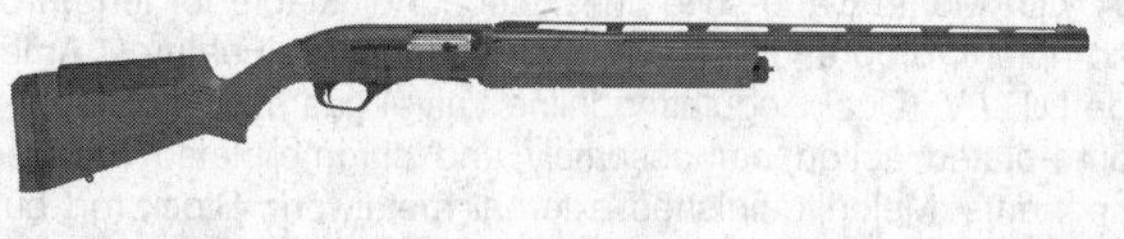

NIB	*Exc.*	*V.G.*	*Good*	*Fair*	*Poor*
1400	1200	1000	—	—	—

Renegauge Turkey

Gauge: 12 ga. 3 in. Barrel: 24-in. fluted carbon steel with ventilated rib. Weight: 7.8 lbs. Length: 49.5 in. Stock: Camo synthetic stock with Monte Carlo-style cheekpiece, adjustable for length of pull, comb height, drop and cast with included inserts. Choice of Mossy Oak Bottomland or Mossy Oak Obsession camouflage finishes. Features: American-made D.R.I.V. (Dual Regulating Inline Valve) gas system. Single-piece, chrome-plated action bar assembly and chrome-plated reciprocating components. Stock rod buffer to reduce felt recoil. Red fiber-optic front sight, competition-ready loading port, oversized controls. 4+1 round capacity. Includes four Beretta/Benelli style chokes (EF, F, IC, M) and hard case.

NIB	Exc.	V.G.	Good	Fair	Poor
1400	1200	1000	—	—	—

Renegauge Waterfowl

Gauge: 12 ga. 3 in. Barrel: 26- or 28-in. fluted carbon steel with ventilated rib. Weight: 7.8 lbs. Lengths: 47.5–49.5 in. Stock: Camouflage synthetic stock with Monte Carlo-style cheekpiece, adjustable for length of pull, comb height, drop and cast with included inserts. Mossy Oak Shadow Grass Blades camouflage. Features: American-made D.R.I.V. (Dual Regulating Inline Valve) gas system. Single-piece, chrome-plated action bar assembly and chrome-plated reciprocating components. Stock rod buffer to reduce felt recoil. Red fiber-optic sight, competition-ready easy loading port, oversized controls. 4+1 round capacity. Includes three Beretta/Benelli style chokes (IC, M, F) and hard case.

NIB	Exc.	V.G.	Good	Fair	Poor
1400	1200	1000	—	—	—

Renegauge Competition

Gauge: 12 ga. 3in. Barrel: 24-in. fluted carbon steel with ventilated rib. Weight: 8.2 lbs. Length: 46.2 in. Stock: Black synthetic Monte Carlo style, adjustable for length of pull, comb height, drop and cast. Features: American-made D.R.I.V. (Dual Regulating Inline Valve) gas system. Single-piece, chrome-plated action bar assembly and chrome-plated reciprocating components. Stock rod buffer to reduce felt recoil. Extended magazine tube with 9+1 capacity. Melonite finished barrel and Red Cerakote receiver. Hi-Viz Tri-Comp front sight. Competition-ready loading port, oversized controls. Extended Skeet2 Light Mod (.015-in.) choke tube of Beretta/Benelli-style.

NIB	Exc.	V.G.	Good	Fair	Poor
1700	1500	1200	—	—	—

Renegauge Field

Gauge: 12 ga. 3 in. Barrel: 26 or 28 in. fluted carbon steel with ventilated rib. Weight: 7.9–8.0 lbs. Length: 47.5–49.5 in. Stock: Grey synthetic stock with Monte Carlo-style cheekpiece. Adjustable for length of pull, comb height, drop and cast with included inserts. Features: American-made D.R.I.V. (Dual Regulating Inline Valve) gas system. Single-piece, chrome-plated action bar assembly and chrome-plated reciprocating components. Melonite-finished external metalwork. Stock rod buffer to reduce felt recoil. Red fiber-optic sight, competition-ready easy-loading port, oversized controls. 4+1 round capacity. Includes three Beretta/Benelli style chokes (IC, M, F) and hard case.

NIB	Exc.	V.G.	Good	Fair	Poor
1300	1000	850	—	—	—

Renegauge Prairie

Gauge: 12 ga. 3 in. Barrel: 28 in. fluted carbon steel with ventilated rib. Weight: 7.9 lbs. Length: 49.5 in. Stock: Camo synthetic sporter style, adjustable for length of pull, comb height, drop and cast with included inserts. Features: American-made D.R.I.V. (Dual Regulating Inline Valve) gas system. Single-piece, chrome plated action bar assembly and chrome-plated reciprocating components. True Timber Prairie camouflage stock finish with Brown Sand Cerakote metalwork. Stock rod buffer to reduce felt recoil. Red fiber-optic sight, competition-ready easy-loading port, oversized controls. 4+1 round capacity. Includes three Beretta/Benelli style chokes (IC, M, F) and hard case.

NIB	Exc.	V.G.	Good	Fair	Poor
1400	1200	1000	—	—	—

Renegauge Security

Gauge: 12 ga. 3 in. Barrel: 18.5 in. Melonite-treated, fluted, with ventilated rib. Length: 40 in. Weight: 7.3 lbs. Stock: Matte gray synthetic with adjustable LOP, comb height, and drop/cast. Features: Savage's self-regulating DRIV gas system. One-piece chrome-plated action bar and reciprocating components. Stock rod buffer to reduce recoil. Adjustable ghost ring sights and one-piece rail. Oversized controls. Includes three flush choke tubes (IC, M, F) and hard case.

NIB	Exc.	V.G.	Good	Fair	Poor
1340	—	—	—	—	—

Model FA-1

Savage Fox semi-automatic shotgun, imported from Japan in 1981 and 1982. Marked KTG. Offered in 12-gauge only, with 28" or 30" ventilated rib barrels. Walnut stock, with cut checkering. Magazine capacity 4 rounds. Weight about 7.5 lbs.

NIB	Exc.	V.G.	Good	Fair	Poor
—	250	210	180	150	130

Model FP-1

Similar to above, with 3" chambers and 5-round magazine.

NIB	Exc.	V.G.	Good	Fair	Poor
—	350	300	250	200	150

Savage Fox A Grade

A new version of a Fox side-by-side in 12 or 20 gauge with double triggers, H&H-type automatic ejectors, Anson & Deeley boxlock action, and an American walnut stock with cut checkering, an English-style straight grip, splinter forend and oil finish. Offered with 26 or 28-inch barrels with interchangeable choke tubes (full, modified, improved cylinder.) Made for Savage by Connecticut Shotgun Co. Introduced in 2018.

NIB	Exc.	V.G.	Good	Fair	Poor
4750	4040	3430	2920	2480	2110

SAVAGE FOX B MODELS

Fox Model B was introduced about 1939, by Savage, for the hunter who wanted better fit and finish than offered by Stevens brand Model 530. Made in many variations until 1988. Note: Values shown are for 12 gauge. Add 15% for 16 gauge; 50% for 20 gauge; 100% for .410 bore.

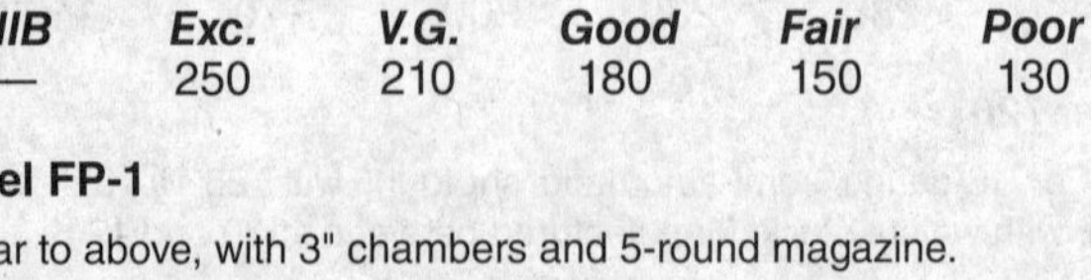

Fox Model B—Utica, NY

NIB	Exc.	V.G.	Good	Fair	Poor
700	600	500	380	250	200

Fox Model B—Chicopee Falls, Mass. (later Westfield, Mass.)

Courtesy Nick Niles, Paul Goodwin photo

NIB	Exc.	V.G.	Good	Fair	Poor
600	500	380	250	200	120

Fox Model B—Single Trigger

NIB	Exc.	V.G.	Good	Fair	Poor
750	620	500	380	250	200

Fox Model BDL

NIB	Exc.	V.G.	Good	Fair	Poor
750	620	500	380	250	200

Fox Model BDE

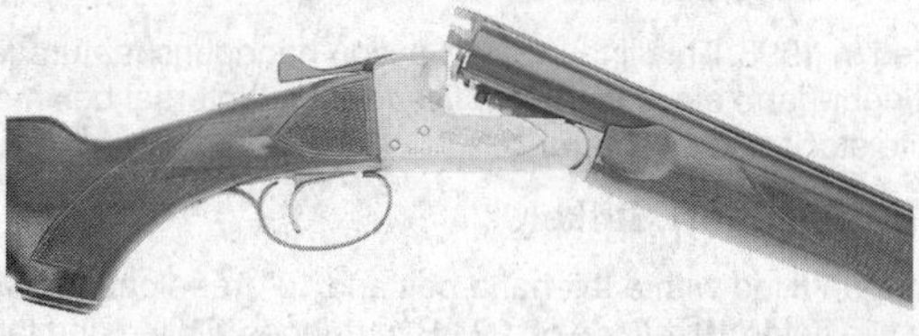

Courtesy Nick Niles, Paul Goodwin photo

NIB	Exc.	V.G.	Good	Fair	Poor
650	550	400	300	200	150

Fox Model BSE

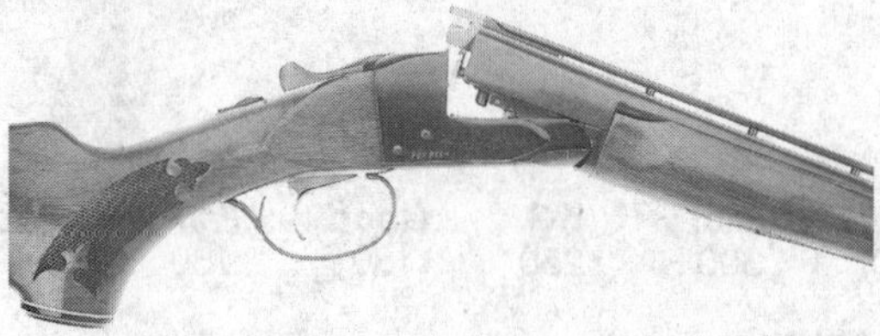

Courtesy Nick Niles, Paul Goodwin photo

NIB	Exc.	V.G.	Good	Fair	Poor
750	620	500	380	250	200

Fox Model BE

NIB	Exc.	V.G.	Good	Fair	Poor
800	700	600	480	300	200

Milano

Italian-made over/under available in 12-, 20-, 28-gauge and .410-bore. On frames scaled to match. All with 28" barrels and 3" chambers. Single-selective trigger. Three choke tubes (fixed IC and Mod. on .410-bore). Automatic ejectors.

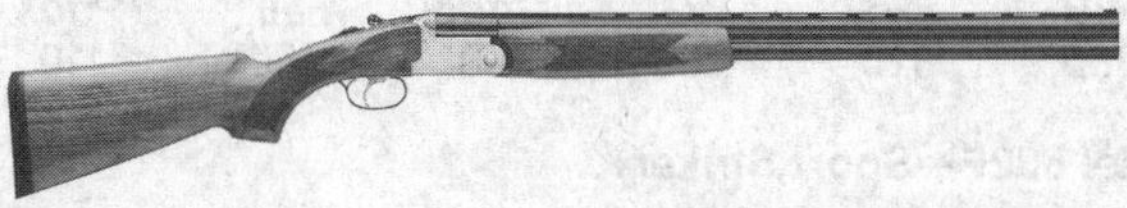

NIB	Exc.	V.G.	Good	Fair	Poor
1380	1170	990	840	720	610

PISTOLS

Elbert Searle was granted a patent on an automatic pistol, which utilized the bullet's torque to twist barrel into a locking position with slide. Patent also featured a double-row staggered magazine which increased capacity over ordinary pistols. Patent was sold to Savage and first Savage automatic pistol Model 1907 was produced. Note: Savage automatic pistols with original cardboard box will bring between $200 and $500 premium. Instruction pamphlet, cleaning brush or other advertising material is present, price will escalate. Savage had four pistol finishes. The majority were blued, 800 were nickeled, about equally distributed in both calibers, four were plated with silver, and just 12 were Gold plated. Eight grip styles were available: a) Steel. b) Black rubber. c) Plain pearl. d) Pearl with "SAC" logo insert in pearl. e) Pearl grips with Indian Head logo. f) Plain trapezoidal pearl grips (no logo). Early Model 1907 pearl grips both plain and with SAC logos are held in place using a kind of clip design inside the magazine well. They are not affixed with screws. f) A very few plain (unchecked) highly figured walnut wood grips and, lastly, g) Rectangular grips where two pearl plates are affixed by rivets to black rubber grips. The "trapezoidal" grips and the Indian Heads logo grips are affixed with one screw as are the plain rectangular mother of pearl grips. Most fancy pistols were engraved except for several "plain" nickel-finished guns. Most engraved pistols were 1907 Models in both .32 and .380 cal., a few Model 1915s in both calibers, and a very few Model 1917 pistols. Records indicate that only approximately 100 pistols were factory engraved. Engraving fell into 3 categories: "A"— Protector Grade the lowest form, "B"— Monitor grade, the middle grade (very few were produced), and "C" — "Special grade, having the most coverage. Records indicate buyers opted for grade "A" or "C', with very few choosing the middle 'B' grade which means it is a real "find". Prices usually must be negotiated due to the rarity of finishes, engraving and grips. Engraved and plated pistols command premium prices depending on finish and grade of engraving. Pistols with special pearl grips can add a premium of $1,000-$1,250. Factory cased pistols are extremely rare. Factory provenance is strongly recommended before purchasing a pistol with special features. Thanks to Dr. Steve Rettke for 2023 edits to this section.

Model 1907

A .32 or .380 semi-automatic pistol, with 3.75" or 4.25" barrel and 9- or 10-shot magazine. Blued, with hard rubber rectangular grips. This model is often incorrectly termed Model 1905 or Model 1910. Note: The .380-caliber worth approximately 30% more than values listed.

NIB	Exc.	V.G.	Good	Fair	Poor
—	800	600	400	250	150

Model 1907 Portugese Contract

Similar to commercial guns, with a lanyard ring same as French contract model. Original Portugese pistols will have Portugese Crest on grips. Only about 1,150 of these pistols were produced and those with crest grips are very rare. Proceed with caution. With original Portugese box add $500.

NIB	Exc.	V.G.	Good	Fair	Poor
—	2000	1750	1250	800	500

Model 1915 Hammerless

Similar to Model 1907, except fitted with grip safety and internal hammer. Approximately 6,500 pistols produced in .32-caliber and 3,900 in .380-caliber. Manufactured between 1915 and 1917. Rarest of regular-production Savage automatic pistols.

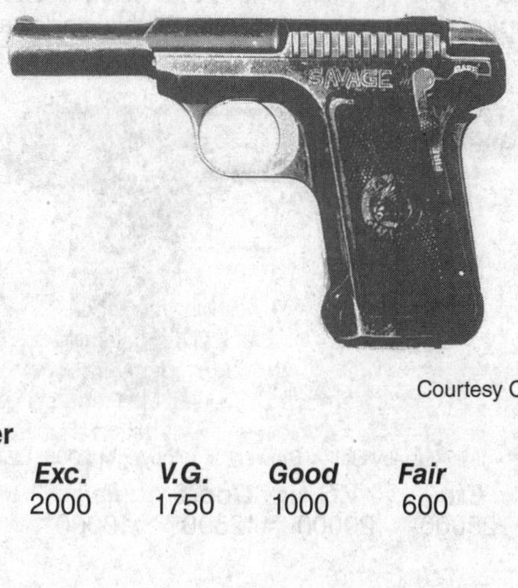

Courtesy Orvel Reichert

.32 Caliber

NIB	Exc.	V.G.	Good	Fair	Poor
—	2000	1750	1000	600	300

.380 Caliber

NIB	Exc.	V.G.	Good	Fair	Poor
—	3000	2500	1200	800	400

Model 1917

As above, with external hammer and without grip safety. Form of grip frame widened in kind of trapezoidal shape. Manufactured between 1917 and 1928. Note: Add $3090 for .380.

NIB	Exc.	V.G.	Good	Fair	Poor
—	900	700	600	300	200

Model 6.35mm

A small number of .25-caliber Savage pistols manufactured between 1915 and 1919. Perhaps less than 25 were built. There are two major variations of this pistol. First, wide or 10-serrations grip; second 27-serrations grip variation. This change occured around 1917. Magazine capacity was 6 to 7 rounds. Very rare. Seldom sold, so values are speculative. Add premium for low serial numbers.

Courtesy Bailey Brower, Jr., Copyright 2005, Bailey Brower, Jr.

NIB	Exc.	V.G.	Good	Fair	Poor
—	17500	15000	13500	12000	—

Model 1907 Test Pistol

Manufactured in 1907 in .45 ACP. Pistol was tested in U.S. Army trials. About 290 pistols produced for these trials. Double-stack magazine held 8 rounds.

Courtesy Bailey Brower, Jr., Copyright 2005, Bailey Brower, Jr

NIB	Exc.	V.G.	Good	Fair	Poor
—	25000	20000	12500	10000	7000

Model 1910 Test Pistol

A modified Model 1907, with heavier slide that was not concave like Model 1907. A total of nine Model 1910s built. Too rare to price.

Model 1911 Test Pistol

This example was completely modified with a longer and thinner grip. Checkered wood grips were attached by friction instead of screws. Slide release was modified. A full grip safety was added. Heavier serrated hammer (cocking lever) was added. Four of these pistols were built. Serial #1 has never been located. Too rare to price.

Model 101

.22-caliber single-shot pistol, resembling a revolver with 5.5" barrel. Blued, with hardwood grips. Made in Chicopee Falls or Westfield, Mass. Manufactured between 1960 and 1968. Ten to twelve guns were non-firing and used for children's play and salesmen's samples. Instead of serial numbers these were stamped "Dummy." Very rare. Valued at $600.

NIB	Exc.	V.G.	Good	Fair	Poor
—	300	250	150	130	100

500 HANDGUN SERIES

Introduced in 1998. This line of short-action handguns feature left-hand bolt and right-hand ejection. All are fitted with an internal box magazine, composite stock and 14" barrel.

Model 501F—Sport Striker

This handgun fitted with a left-hand bolt and 10" free-floating barrel. Detachable clip holds 10 rounds of .22 LR cartridges. Drilled and tapped for scope mount. Weight about 4 lbs. Introduced in 2000.

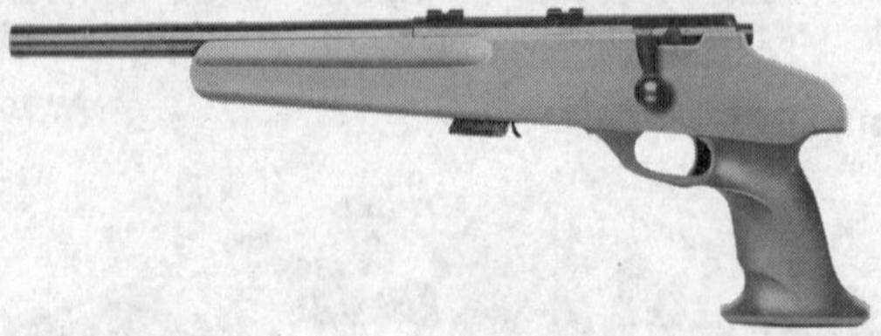

NIB	Exc.	V.G.	Good	Fair	Poor
350	300	250	180	150	100

Model 501FXP

Introduced in 2002. Similar to above. Fitted with 1.25-4x28mm scope with soft case.

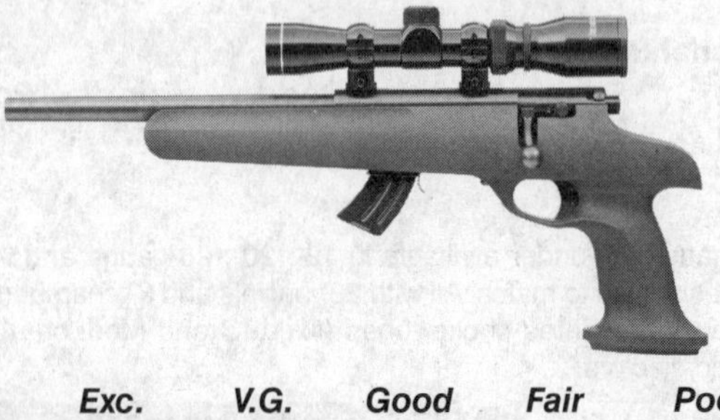

NIB	Exc.	V.G.	Good	Fair	Poor
380	320	260	200	160	110

Model 502F—Sport Striker

Same as 501F, but chambered for .22 WMR cartridge. Magazine capacity 5 rounds. Introduced in 2000.

NIB	Exc.	V.G.	Good	Fair	Poor
380	320	260	200	160	110

Model 503F—Sport Striker

Same as Model 502F-Sport Striker, but chambered for .17 HMR cartridge. Blued finish. Weight about 4 lbs. Introduced in 2003.

NIB	Exc.	V.G.	Good	Fair	Poor
380	320	260	200	160	110

Model 503FSS—Sport Striker

As above, with stainless steel action and barrel.

NIB	Exc.	V.G.	Good	Fair	Poor
400	350	290	210	180	120

Model 510F Striker

Blued barrel action. Chambered for .22-250, .243 or .308-calibers. Weight about 5 lbs.

NIB	Exc.	V.G.	Good	Fair	Poor
480	400	350	300	180	150

Model 516FSS

Similar to model above, with stainless steel barreled action.

NIB	Exc.	V.G.	Good	Fair	Poor
500	420	360	310	200	150

Model 516FSAK

Features stainless steel barreled action, with adjustable muzzle brake.

NIB	Exc.	V.G.	Good	Fair	Poor
520	450	400	340	220	160

Model 516FSAK Camo

As above, with Realtree Hardwood camo stock. Chambered for .300 WSM cartridge. Weight about 5.5 lbs. Introduced in 2002.

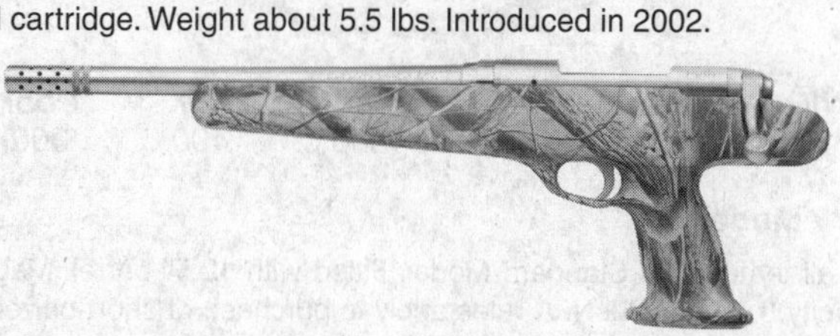

NIB	Exc.	V.G.	Good	Fair	Poor
600	520	450	300	240	80

Model 516BSS

Fitted with laminated thumbhole stock, left-hand bolt for right-hand ejection, 14" barrel. Chambered for .223, .243, 7mm-08 Rem., .260 Rem. and .308 Win. calibers. Magazine capacity 2 rounds. Weight about 5 lbs. Introduced in 1999.

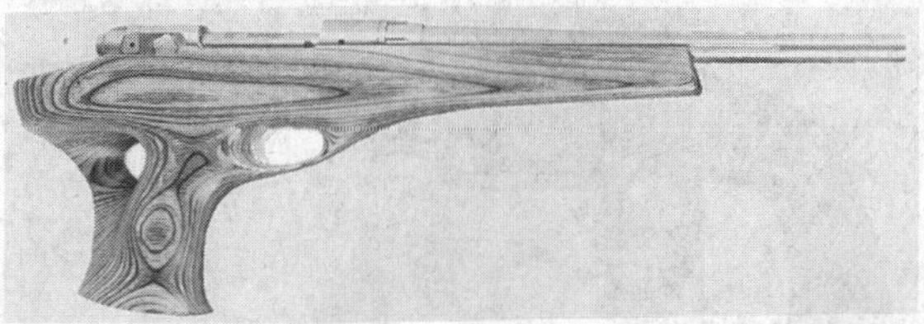

NIB	Exc.	V.G.	Good	Fair	Poor
600	520	450	300	240	80

Model 516BSAK

Similar to model above. Chambered for .223 or .22-250 cartridges. The 14" barrel fitted with an adjustable muzzle brake. Introduced in 1999.

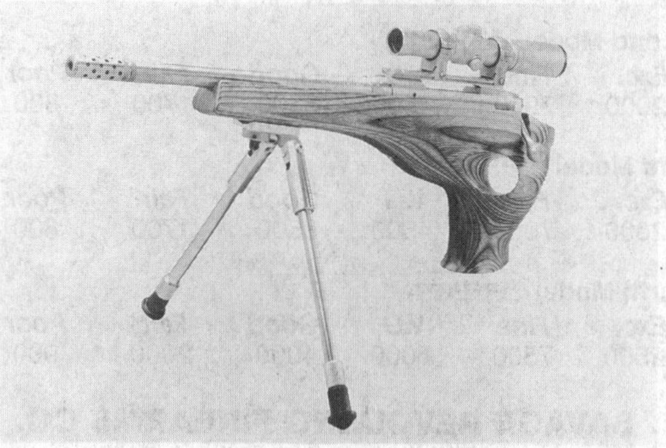

NIB	Exc.	V.G.	Good	Fair	Poor
600	520	450	300	240	80

Stance

Calibers: 9mm. Capacity: seven, eight, or 10 rounds. Barrel: 3". Grip: Textured polymer. Sights: Three white-dot system. Finishes: Cerakote black, gray, or FDE. Features: Polymer frame with chassis system.

NIB	Exc.	V.G.	Good	Fair	Poor
400	380	310	300	260	—

SAVAGE & NORTH
Middletown, Connecticut

Figure 8 Revolver

A .36-caliber percussion revolver with 7" octagonal barrel and 6-shot cylinder. Barrel marked "E. Savage, Middletown. CT./H.S. North. Patented June 17, 1856". Four models of this revolver are: (1) with a rounded brass frame and mouths of the chamber fitting into the end of barrel breech; (2) with a rounded iron frame and modified loading lever that is marked "H.S. North, Patented April 6, 1858"; (3) with a flat-sided brass frame having a round recoil shield; (4) with an iron frame. Approximately 400 manufactured between 1856 and 1859. A very rare .28 caliber "Pocket Model" will bring a substantial premium.

First Model (Antique)

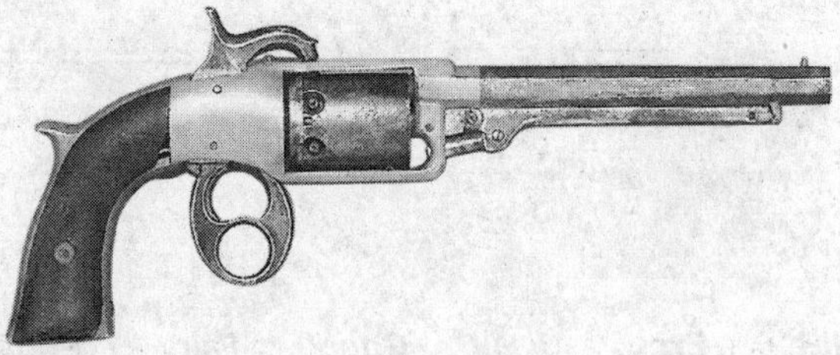

Courtesy Bonhams & Butterfields

First Model Figure 8 Revolver

Exc.	*Fine*	*V.G.*	*Good*	*Fair*	*Poor*
16500	8000	6000	4500	2300	950

Second Model (Antique)

Exc.	*Fine*	*V.G.*	*Good*	*Fair*	*Poor*
12000	7000	4500	3500	1700	800

Third Model (Antique)

Exc.	*Fine*	*V.G.*	*Good*	*Fair*	*Poor*
12000	7000	4500	3500	1700	800

Fourth Model (Antique)

Exc.	*Fine*	*V.G.*	*Good*	*Fair*	*Poor*
12500	7500	5000	4000	2000	900

SAVAGE REVOLVING FIREARMS CO.

Middletown, Connecticut

Navy Revolver (Antique)

A .36-caliber double-action percussion revolver, with 7" octagonal barrel and 6-shot cylinder. Frame marked "Savage R.F.A. Co./H.S. North Patented June 17, 1856/Jan. 18, 1859, May 15, 1860". Approximately 20,000 manufactured between 1861 and 1865. About 12,000 purchased by U.S. Government.

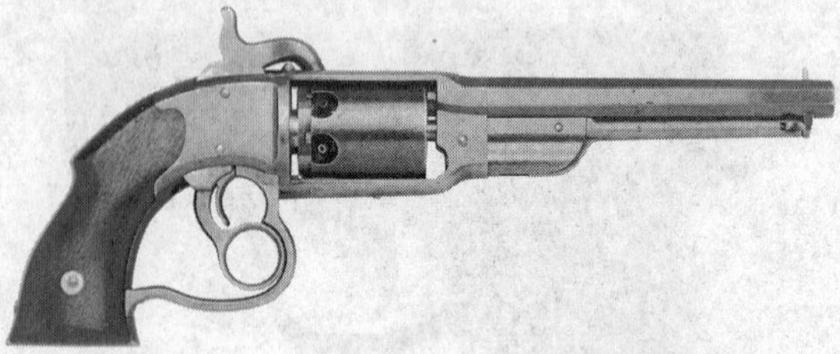

Courtesy Greg Martin Auctions

Exc.	*Fine*	*V.G.*	*Good*	*Fair*	*Poor*
5000	2000	1450	900	600	420

SCATTERGUN TECHNOLOGIES

Formerly—Nashville, Tennessee
Berryville, Arkansas

Note: In 1999, Scattergun Technologies was purchased by Wilson Combat and became a division of Wilson Combat.

TR-870

Model based on Remington Model 870 slide-action shotgun. Offered in a wide variety of configurations with different features. Standard model fitted with 18" barrel and chambered for 12-gauge shell. Stock is composite, with recoil pad. Tactical forend has flashlight built in. Ghost ring rear sight. Front sight has tritium insert. Six-round shell carrier on left side of receiver. Introduced in 1991. Weight for standard model about 9 lbs. Prices listed are for standard model.

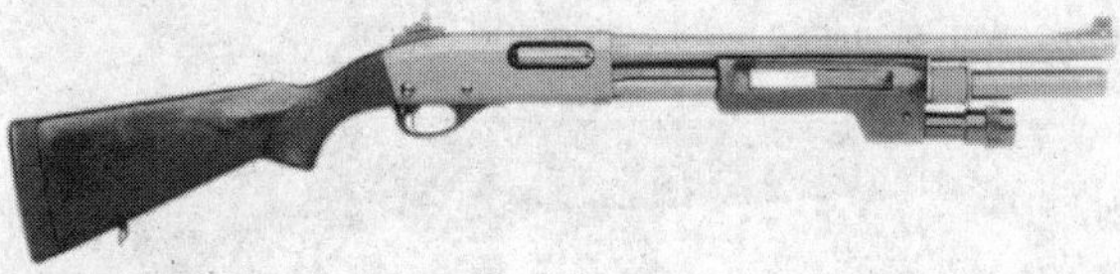

NIB	*Exc.*	*V.G.*	*Good*	*Fair*	*Poor*
1000	800	650	550	300	200

WILSON COMBAT CURRENT PRODUCTION MODELS

Note: Add $100 to all models with Armor-Tuff finish

Standard Model

Based on Remington 12-gauge 3" 870 Magnum. This model fitted with 18" cylinder bore barrel. Adjustable ghost ring rear sight, with tritium front. Seven-round extended magazine. Side saddle shell carrier. Synthetic stock. Tactical sling standard. Parkerized finish. Fitted with SUREFIRE tactical light.

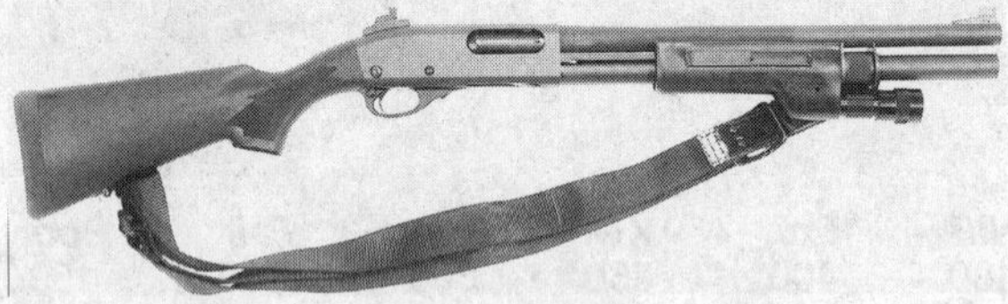

NIB	*Exc.*	*V.G.*	*Good*	*Fair*	*Poor*
1150	850	620	500	400	300

Border Patrol Model

Similar to Standard Model, without tactical light. A 14" barrel is offered. All NFA rules apply to purchase of short barrel shotgun.

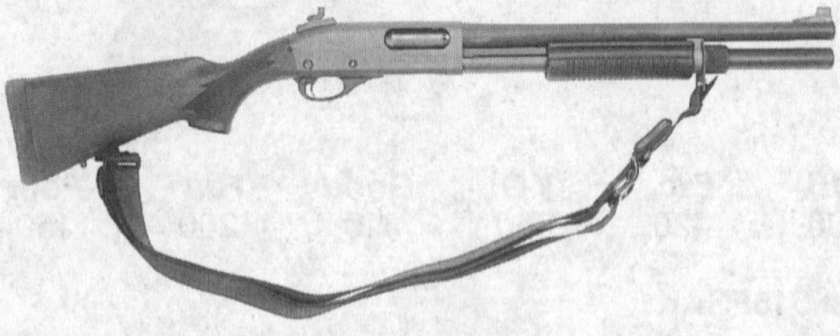

NIB	*Exc.*	*V.G.*	*Good*	*Fair*	*Poor*
880	650	480	300	200	150

Professional Model

Features all Standard Model components. Fitted with a 14" barrel. Magazine capacity 6 rounds. All NFA rules apply to purchase of short barrel shotgun.

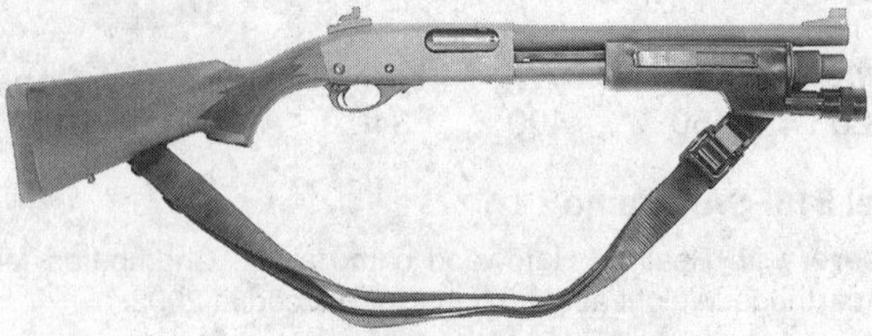

NIB	*Exc.*	*V.G.*	*Good*	*Fair*	*Poor*
1180	880	650	500	400	300

Entry Model

Has all features of Standard Model. Fitted with 12.5" barrel. Magazine capacity 5 rounds. All NFA rules apply to purchase of short barrel shotgun.

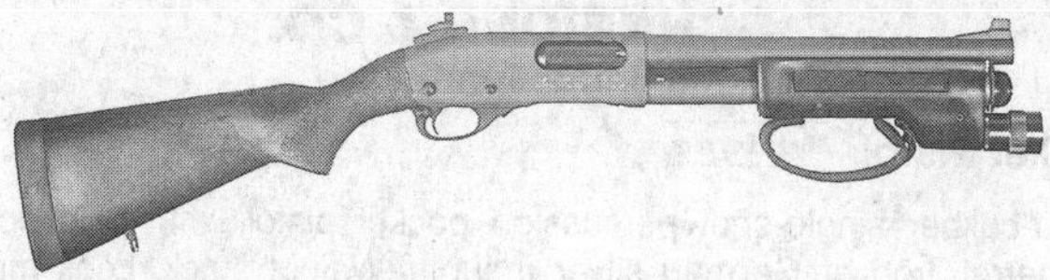

NIB	*Exc.*	*V.G.*	*Good*	*Fair*	*Poor*
950	700	600	500	400	300

K-9 Model

Built on Remington 12-gauge 3" 11-87 Magnum semi-automatic. Fitted with ghost ring rear sights and tritium front. Extended magazine holds 7 rounds. Barrel 18". Synthetic stock, with side saddle shell carrier. Parkerized finish.

NIB	*Exc.*	*V.G.*	*Good*	*Fair*	*Poor*
1080	800	700	600	500	350

SWAT Model

Similar to K-9 model. Fitted with tactical light and 14" barrel. All NFA rules apply to purchase of short barrel shotgun.

NIB	*Exc.*	*V.G.*	*Good*	*Fair*	*Poor*
1350	1000	800	650	550	400

Rob Haught Special

Based on the Remington 870 pump gun with options chosen by veteran law enforcement officer Rob Haught. Features include 18.4-inch cylinder bore barrel with 3-inch chamber, fiber optic front and adjustable rear sights, Magpul SGA stock and MOE M-lok forend, extended magazine tube with 5 + 1 capacity, plus Mesa Tactical 4-round shell carrier.

NIB	*Exc.*	*V.G.*	*Good*	*Fair*	*Poor*
1080	920	780	600	–	–

SCCY INDUSTRIES

South Daytona, Florida

CPX

Hammer-fired double-action-only compact 9mm pistol, with black polymer frame. Stainless steel slide and barrel. Black or matte stainless finish. Available with/without thumb safety. Introduced 2012.

NIB	*Exc.*	*V.G.*	*Good*	*Fair*	*Poor*
280	250	230	180	150	100

CPX-3

Ultra compact model chambered for .380 ACP. Magazine capacity 10 rounds, plus one in the chamber. CPX-3 utilizes a unique and exclusive Quad-Lock system that provides improved barrel stability and accuracy. Introduced in 2016.

NIB	*Exc.*	*V.G.*	*Good*	*Fair*	*Poor*
300	260	220	200	150	100

DVG SERIES

Caliber: 9mm. Capacity: 10-round magazine. Barrel: 3.1." Weight: 15.5 oz. Length: 6" overall. Grips: Integral with a polymer frame. Sights: white dot front and optics-ready. Features: Zytel polymer frame, steel slide, aluminum alloy receiver machined from bar stock. Striker-fire with 5.5-lb. trigger pull. Made in USA.

NIB	*Exc.*	*V.G.*	*Good*	*Fair*	*Poor*
310	250	200	190	150	—

SCHALK, G. S.

Pottsville, Pennsylvania

Rifle Musket Antique

A .58-caliber percussion rifle, with 40" round barrel. Full-length stock secured by three barrel bands. Barrel marked "G. Schalk Poftsville 1861". Finished in white, with walnut stock. Approximately 100 manufactured. Rarely encountered, values are very speculative. Schalk also made percussion target rifles and other arms.

Courtesy Milwaukee Public Museum, Milwaukee, Wisconsin

Exc.	Fine	V.G.	Good	Fair	Poor
6900	3300	2020	750	500	350

SCHALL & CO.
New Haven, Connecticut

Manufactured the Fiala repeating pistol for Fiala. Later, after Fiala's bankruptcy, Schall provided parts, repair service and produced repeating pistols with the Schall name. Marketed by Schall between 1930 and 1935.

Repeating Pistol

A .22-caliber pistol, with 10-shot magazine. Tapered 6.5" barrel, with fixed sights and blued finish. Rear sight much simpler than those on Fiala. Grips are wood, with ribs running lengthwise. Typically marked "schall & co./new haven, conn usa" but guns exist with no markings. Note: Original Fiala pistols had 7.5" barrels, but not so the Schalls (a fact revealed to us by our friend Jack in Florida).

Courtesy Dr. Jon Miller

NIB	Exc.	V.G.	Good	Fair	Poor
—	500	420	320	190	170

SCHMIDT, HERBERT
Ostheim, West Germany

Model 11, Liberty 11, and Eig Model E-8

A .22-caliber double-action revolver, with 2.5" barrel and 6-shot cylinder. Blued, with plastic grips.

NIB	Exc.	V.G.	Good	Fair	Poor
—	120	80	60	40	20

Model 11 Target

As above, with 5.5" barrel and adjustable sights.

NIB	Exc.	V.G.	Good	Fair	Poor
—	150	120	80	40	30

Frontier Model or Texas Scout

.22-caliber revolver, with 5" barrel and 6-shot cylinder. Blued, with plastic grips.

NIB	Exc.	V.G.	Good	Fair	Poor
—	120	80	60	40	20

SCHMIDT & COMPANY, E.
Houston, Texas

Pocket Pistol (Antique)

A .45-caliber percussion single-shot pistol, with 2.5" barrel. German silver mounts and walnut stock. Barrel marked "E. Schmidt & Co. Houston". Manufactured between 1866 and 1870.

Exc.	Fine	V.G.	Good	Fair	Poor
9000	4400	2700	1000	350	240

SCHNEIDER & CO.
Memphis, Tennessee

Pocket Pistol (Antique)

A .41-caliber single-shot percussion pocket pistol, with 3.5" octagonal barrel. Iron or German silver mounts. Walnut stock. Lock marked "Schneider & Co./Memphis, Tenn." Manufactured 1859 and 1860.

Exc.	Fine	V.G.	Good	Fair	Poor
4500	1850	1250	650	300	210

SCHNEIDER & GLASSICK
Memphis, Tennessee

Pocket Pistols (Antique)

A .41-caliber percussion pocket pistol, with 2.5" barrel. German silver mounts and walnut stock. Barrel marked "Schneider & Glassick, Memphis, Tenn." Manufactured 1860 to 1862.

Exc.	Fine	V.G.	Good	Fair	Poor
7000	5250	3870	2500	800	560

Percussion Revolver (Antique)

Rare Confederate revolver based on the Colt 1851 Navy, only about 50 made in 1861–1862. As with all CSA arms, beware of fakes and reproductions — expert evaluation is essential. Values listed are speculative since this gun rarely comes on the market.

Exc.	Fine	V.G.	Good	Fair	Poor
—	80000	60000	40000	20000	14000

SCHOUBOE
See—DANSK REKYLRIFFEL SYNDIKAT

SCHUERMAN ARMS, LTD.
Scottsdale, Arizona

Model SA40

Introduced in 2004. Bolt-action rifle chambered for a wide variety of calibers from Short-action to Long Magnum. Offered in both right-/left-hand models. Barrel lengths from 20" to 26" in stainless steel. No sights. Stock laminated fiberglass sporter-style. Retail prices start at $5440. Note: There are a number of extra costs options that may be ordered with this model. These options will affect price.

SCHULER, AUGUST
Suhl, Germany

Reform

A 6.35mm caliber four-barreled pocket pistol, with 2.5" barrels. Barrel unit rises as trigger is pulled. Blued, with walnut or hard rubber grips. Manufactured between 1907 and 1914.

NIB	Exc.	V.G.	Good	Fair	Poor
—	850	750	650	450	300

SCHULTZ & LARSEN
Ofterup, Denmark

Model 47 Match Rifle

A .22-caliber single-shot bolt-action rifle, with 28" barrel. Adjustable sights and trigger. Blued, with ISU-style stock.

NIB	Exc.	V.G.	Good	Fair	Poor
—	800	650	550	400	250

Model 61 Match Rifle

As above, fitted with a palm rest.

NIB	Exc.	V.G.	Good	Fair	Poor
—	1000	850	750	600	300

Model 62 Match Rifle

Similar to above. Manufactured for centerfire cartridges.

NIB	Exc.	V.G.	Good	Fair	Poor
—	1250	900	750	650	350

Model 54 Free Rifle

Similar to above, with 27" barrel and ISU stock.

NIB	Exc.	V.G.	Good	Fair	Poor
—	950	800	700	550	300

Model 68 DL

A .22-250 to .458 Win. Magnum bolt-action rifle, with 24" barrel. Adjustable trigger. Well figured walnut stock.

NIB	Exc.	V.G.	Good	Fair	Poor
—	850	700	600	450	200

SCHWARZLOSE, ANDREAS
Berlin, Germany

Military Model 1898 (Standart)

Semi-automatic pistol, with 6.5" barrel. Rotary locked bolt, 7-shot magazine and adjustable rear sight. Chambered for 7.63x25mm Borchardt cartridge. Weight about 28 oz. Blued, with walnut grips. Pistol was neither a commercial or military success, and fewer than 500 were made. (CAUTION: Although the 7.63x25mm Mauser cartridge will chamber, it's too powerful for this firearm).

NIB	Exc.	V.G.	Good	Fair	Poor
—	24000	20000	12000	5500	3000

SEARS, ROEBUCK & CO. BRAND
Chicago, Illinois

Double-Barrel Shotguns

Between 1892 and 1988, the world's largest mail order house carried a huge inventory of sporting doubleguns, including any foreign and domestic brands whose makers did not object to Sears' famous price discounts. To increase sales volume, however, Sears also created its own brands which they supported with innovative design, extravagant advertising claims, unbeatable pricing and excellent quality control. These doubles, like many other firearm products handled by Sears, were listed in its very detailed semi-annual catalog from about 1892, when the company first offered doubleguns, until about 1988 when social and political pressures made the company stop handling firearms.

Sears marketing people gave birth to and successfully exploited many house and private brands which we no longer associate with Sears at all. In fact, many of these brands clearly rollmarked on guns are now unfamiliar to many collectors. Frequently seen and important in the market segment which many might describe as affordable doubles are some of the most often seen Sears trade names or brands. Listed in chronological order: T. Barker, S.R. & Co., Triumph, Thomas Barker, Sam Holt, Chicago Long Range Wonder, American Bar Lock, Meriden Fire Arms Co., Norwich, A. J. Arbrey Gun Co., New England, Gladiator, Berkshire, Ranger, Eastern Arms Co., J.C. Higgins, Sears, and Ted Williams. These guns were of good quality but sold at bargain prices which gave them tremendous appeal. They were made for Sears to Sears' specifications by a number of American firms and a few foreign ones as well, all of which produced excellent shotguns under their own names. Among the best-known American companies were J. Stevens, Savage Arms, A.H. Fox, High Standard, N.R. Davis, Crescent Firearms, Ithaca, A. Fyrberg, Colton Mfg. Co., Marlin, Hunter Gun Co., Baker Gun Co., and probably a few others. Among the foreign makers were AYA, H. Pieper, Janssen, SKB, Rossi, CBC, and A. Zoli.

Sears customers were not aware of this, but they did trust Sears name and bought many millions of these shotguns over nearly 100 years that Sears was in the business. Today these guns are becoming recognized as interesting and valuable collectibles in their own special niche. Their values range from $100 to $3,500 or more depending on make, model, decoration, if any, and relative rarity.

SEAVER, E.R.
New York, New York

Pocket Pistol (Antique)

A .41-caliber percussion pocket pistol, with 2.5" barrel. German silver mounts. Walnut stock.

Exc.	Fine	V.G.	Good	Fair	Poor
2300	1820	1400	980	400	280

SECURITY INDUSTRIES
Little Ferry, New Jersey

Model PSS - Police Security Special

A .38 Special double-action revolver, with 2" barrel. Fixed sights and 5-shot cylinder. Stainless steel, with walnut grips. Manufactured between 1973 and 1978.

NIB	Exc.	V.G.	Good	Fair	Poor
—	250	150	120	100	80

Model PM357

As above, with 2.5" barrel. In .357 Magnum caliber. Manufactured between 1975 and 1978.

NIB	Exc.	V.G.	Good	Fair	Poor
—	300	200	180	150	100

Model PPM357

As above, with 2" barrel. Hammer without a finger spur. Manufactured between 1975 and 1978.

NIB	Exc.	V.G.	Good	Fair	Poor
—	300	200	180	150	100

SEDCO INDUSTRIES, INC.
Lake Elsinore, California

Company in business from 1988 to 1990.

Model SP22

A .22-caliber semi-automatic pistol, with 2.5" barrel. Blackened or nickel-plated, with plastic grips. Introduced in 1989.

NIB	Exc.	V.G.	Good	Fair	Poor
120	90	60	50	40	20

SEDGELY, R. F., INC.
Philadelphia, Pennsylvania

R.F. Sedgely produced specialized bolt-action rifles using Model 1903 Springfield action. As these arms were for the most part custom order pieces, it is impossible to provide standardized values. It should be noted that his prime engraver was Rudolph J. Kornbrath. Sedgely also made a .22-caliber Baby Hammerless model revolver. See KOLB.

SEECAMP, L. W. CO., INC.
Milford, Connecticut

LWS .25 ACP Model

A .25-caliber semi-automatic pistol, with 2" barrel. Fixed sights and 7-shot magazine. Stainless steel, with plastic grips. Approximately 5,000 manufactured between 1982 and 1985.

NIB	Exc.	V.G.	Good	Fair	Poor
500	400	300	200	150	100

LWS .32 ACP Model

A .32-caliber double-action semi-automatic pistol, with 2" barrel and 6-shot magazine. Matte or polished stainless steel, with plastic grips.

NIB	Exc.	V.G.	Good	Fair	Poor
520	450	400	350	200	150

Matched Pair

Matched set of the above, with identical serial numbers. Total of 200 sets made, prior to 1968.

NIB	Exc.	V.G.	Good	Fair	Poor
—	900	800	700	500	—

LWS .380 Model

Same as .32-caliber, but chambered for .380 cartridge. Essentially same weight and dimensions as .32-caliber pistol. Introduced in 1999.

NIB	Exc.	V.G.	Good	Fair	Poor
600	550	480	350	—	—

SEEKINS PRECISION
Lewiston, Idaho

NOTE: Founded in 2004, this Idaho-based maker originally started producing extremely tough scope rings and later expanded into AR-style and precision bolt-action chassis rifles.

Havak Element

Calibers: .308 Win., 6mm Creedmoor, 6.5 PRC, 6.5 Creedmoor. Capacity: 3 to 5. Barrel: 21 in., Mountain Hunter contour, spiral fluted, threaded. Stock: Carbon composite. Sights: 20 MOA picatinny rail. Weight: 5.5 lbs. Features: Timney Elite Hunter trigger, M16-style extractor, 7075 aerospace aluminum/stainless steel body.

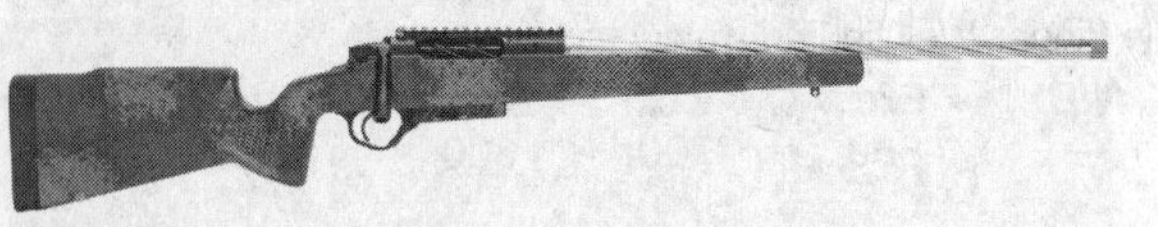

NIB	Exc.	V.G.	Good	Fair	Poor
2000	1700	1500	—	—	—

Havak HIT

Calibers: 6mm GT, 6mm Creedmoor, 6.5 Creedmoor, .308 Win., 6.5 PRC. Capacity: Varies by chambering, compatible with single- or double-stack AICS magazines. Barrel: 24 in. 416 SS LT Tactical contour, threaded, with 5R rifling. Sights: 20 MOA rail. Length: 43.5 in; 34.5 in. folded. Weight: 11.5 lbs. Stock: Chassis-style, folding, available in black and FDE. Features: Bolt-action chassis rifle. A Pro version for competition is planned to follow. Changeable bolt head, M16-style extractor, integrated recoil lug. Quick-change barrel system. R700 trigger compatibility. Integral 20 MOA Picatinny rail. Carbon-fiber cheek piece, fully adjustable recoil pad, and toolless LOP adjustment.

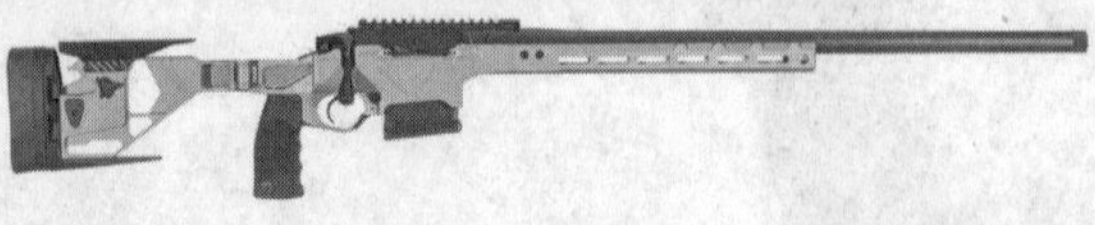

NIB	Exc.	V.G.	Good	Fair	Poor
2000	—	—	—	—	—

SP15

Chamber: .223 Wylde/5.56 NATO. The company's entry-level platform. Barrel: 16", 1:7" twist 5R chromoly. Muzzle device: Seekins NEST Flash Hider 1/2x28. Receivers: SP15 7075-T6 billet upper/lower receiver set. Handguard: 15" SP15 M-LOK. Gas Block: Seekins Low-Profile Adjustable Gas Block. Trigger: Mil-spec. Stock: Six-position adjustable carbine stock. Weight: 7 lbs. Based in Lewiston, Idaho. SEE POLITICAL PANIC PRICING.

NIB	Exc.	V.G.	Good	Fair	Poor
890	800	670	500	—	—

SP15 DMR

Chambers: .223 Wylde/5.56 NATO, 6mm ARC. Similar to the SP15, but with a Seekins 10X stock. SEE POLITICAL PANIC PRICING.

NIB	Exc.	V.G.	Good	Fair	Poor
1750	1630	1500	1250	1000	—

NX15

Chamber: .223 Wylde/5.56 NATO. Similar to SP15, but with higher-level components, including an upgraded Timney trigger, NX15 skeletonized upper/lower receiver set and NOX handguard, and ambidextrous controls. Barrel: 16" 1:8" twist 5R 416 stainless steel. Weight: 7 lbs. SEE POLITICAL PANIC PRICING.

NIB	Exc.	V.G.	Good	Fair	Poor
1750	1620	1500	1250	1000	—

SEMMERLING

Waco, Texas

See—AMERICAN DERRINGER CORPORATION

SERBU FIREARMS

Tampa, Florida

BFG-50 Rifle

A .50-caliber single-shot bolt-action rifle. Fitted with 29.5" barrel. Also offered with 36" barrel. Parkerized finish. Weight about 22 lbs.

NIB	Exc.	V.G.	Good	Fair	Poor
2200	1600	1280	1000	—	—

BFG-50 Carbine

As above, fitted with 22" barrel. Weight about 17 lbs.

NIB	Exc.	V.G.	Good	Fair	Poor
2000	1600	1280	1000	—	—

BFG-50A

A gas-operated semi-automatic take-down rifle, with 25" barrel. Parkerized finish. Magazine capacity 10 rounds. Weight about 25 lbs.

NIB	Exc.	V.G.	Good	Fair	Poor
7000	6000	4500	3000	—	—

RN-50

Single-shot break-open .50 BMG rifle.

NIB	Exc.	V.G.	Good	Fair	Poor
1200	1000	900	—	—	—

SHARPS ARMS CO., C.

Big Timber, Montana

Company was founded in 1975 in Richland, Washington and moved to Big Timber, Montana, in 1980. It also produced custom-built rifles, including Model 1877 Sharps and others, to individual customer specifications. Models listed are standard production, without extras.

Model 1874 Sharps Hartford Sporting Rifle

Chambered for a number of popular blackpowder calibers. Fitted with 26", 28" or 30" tapered octagon barrel and double-set triggers. American walnut stock, with Hartford semi-cresent steel butt. Silver nose cap. Case colored receiver, with blued barrel. Optional sights. Weight about 10 lbs.

NIB	Exc.	V.G.	Good	Fair	Poor
1900	1650	1350	1200	800	500

Model 1874 Bridgeport Sporting Rifle

As above, with Bridgeport checkered steel butt. Schnabel-style forend.

NIB	Exc.	V.G.	Good	Fair	Poor
1750	1500	1350	1200	1000	500

Model 1875 Carbine—Hunters Rifle

Offered in a variety of calibers from .38-55 to .50-70. Fitted with choice of tapered round military-style barrels. Lengths 22", 24" or 26". Full buckhorn and silver blade sights. Semi-cresent military-style butt, with slender forend. Case colored receiver and blued barrel. Double-set triggers.

NIB	Exc.	V.G.	Good	Fair	Poor
1650	1400	1300	1200	1000	500

Model 1874 Boss Gun

Features engraved receiver, XXX fancy walnut, 34" #1 heavy tapered octagon barrel, long range tang sight, buckhorn rear sight globe with post front sight, and Hartford nose cap. Calibers offered from .38-55 to .50-100. Weight about 13.5 lbs. with 34" #1 barrel. Note: Add $750 for Grade II; $1,500 for Grade III.

NIB	Exc.	V.G.	Good	Fair	Poor
4400	3250	2250	1500	1000	500

Model 1875 Target & Sporting Rifle

Offered in a variety of calibers. Fitted with 30" heavy tapered round barrel. American walnut stock, with pistol grip. Case colored receiver, with blued barrel. Single trigger. Price listed without sights.

NIB	Exc.	V.G.	Good	Fair	Poor
1500	1300	1080	900	780	400

Model 1875 Classic Rifle

Features a receiver with octagon top. Tapered octagon barrel lengths from 26" to 30". American walnut stock, with straight-grip and crescent butt. Single trigger. German steel nose cap. Case colored receiver, with blued barrel. Weight about 9.5 lbs. with 30" barrel. Priced without sights.

NIB	Exc.	V.G.	Good	Fair	Poor
1500	1300	1080	900	780	400

Model 1885 High Wall Sporting Rifle

Offered with 26", 28" or 30" tapered octagon barrel. Calibers from .22 to .45-120. Single trigger. American walnut stock, with straight-grip and oil-finish. Checkered steel butt plate. Schnabel forend. Priced without sights. Weight about 9.25 lbs. with 30" barrel.

NIB	Exc.	V.G.	Good	Fair	Poor
1600	1350	1200	1000	750	400

Model 1885 High Wall Classic Rifle

As above, with crescent butt. Stock with cheek-rest. Silver inlay in forend.

NIB	Exc.	V.G.	Good	Fair	Poor
1700	1450	1250	1000	750	400

Model 1879 Hepburn Rifle

Based on the No. 3 Remington Hepburn single-shot rifle. 30" tapered octagon barrel standard.

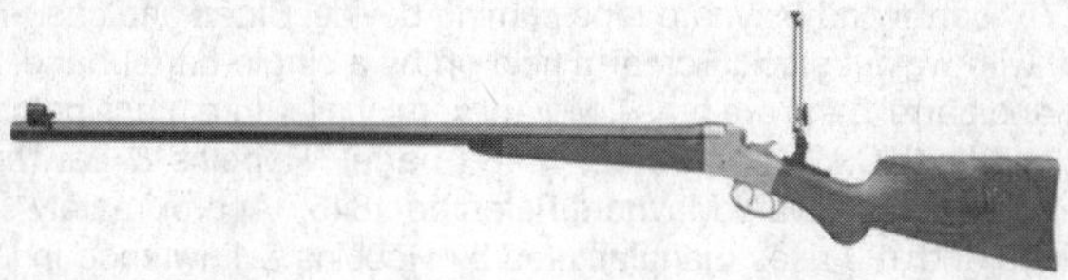

NIB	Exc.	V.G.	Good	Fair	Poor
3000	2700	2500	—	—	—

Hopkins & Allen Rifle

Single-shot rimfire rifle, 16-22" barrel, .22LR, .22 Win. Mag. or .17 HMR. Introduced 2019.

NIB	Exc.	V.G.	Good	Fair	Poor
830	780	650	—	—	—

SHARPS RIFLE COMPANY
Glenrock, Wyoming

SRC 25-45 Rifle

This AR-pattern rifle is chambered for .25-45 Sharps cartridge, a proprietary round based on a .223 case necked up to .257. The "45" refers to length of the .223 case in millimeters. (Factory ammo with a Speer 87-grain bullet and Federal cases with the correct head stamp is available from Sharps Rifle Co.). Rifle uses AR-15 magazines and available in several configurations. Price shown is for base model. Introduced in 2015.

NIB	Exc.	V.G.	Good	Fair	Poor
1100	1000	800	—	—	—

SHARPS RIFLE MANUFACTURING COMPANY
Hartford, Connecticut

First Sharps rifles to be manufactured were made by A.S. Nippes of Mill Creek, Pennsylvania. Later they were made by Robbins & Lawrence of Windsor, Vermont. It wasn't until 1855, that Sharps established his own factory in Hartford, Connecticut. After his death in 1874, the company was reorganized as Sharps Rifle Company and remained in Hartford until 1876 when it moved to Bridgeport, Connecticut. It effectively ceased operations in 1880. The following descriptions are just a brief guide and are by no means exhaustive.

Model 1849 Antique

Breech-loading .44-caliber percussion rifle, with 30" barrel having a wooden cleaning rod mounted beneath it. Breech activated by the triggerguard lever. There is an automatic disk-type capping device on right side of receiver. Finish blued and case colored. Stock is walnut, with a brass patchbox, buttplate and forend cap. Marked "Sharps Patent 1848". Approximately 200 manufactured in 1849 and 1850 by A.S. Nippes Company.

Exc.	Fine	V.G.	Good	Fair	Poor
23000	18000	12750	7500	1500	1050

Model 1850 Antique

As above, with Maynard priming mechanism mounted on breech. Marked "Sharps Patent 1848" on breech; barrel "Manufactured by A.S. Nippes Mill Creek, Pa." Priming device marked "Maynard Patent 1845". Approximately 200 manufactured in 1850. Also known as 2nd Model Sharps.

Exc.	Fine	V.G.	Good	Fair	Poor
21000	15000	10500	6000	1200	840

Model 1851 Carbine Antique

Single-shot breech-loading percussion rifle, in .36-, .44- or .52-caliber. A 21.75" barrel and Maynard tape priming device. Blued and case-hardened, with walnut stock. Forearm held on by a single-barrel band. Buttplate and barrel band are brass. Military versions feature brass patchbox. Tang marked "C. Sharps Patent 1848"; barrel "Robbins & Lawrence"; priming device "Edward Maynard Patentee 1845". Approximately 1,800 carbines and 180 rifles manufactured by Robbins & Lawrence in Windsor, Vermont, in 1851. Note: Those bearing U.S. inspection marks are worth approximately 75 percent more than values listed.

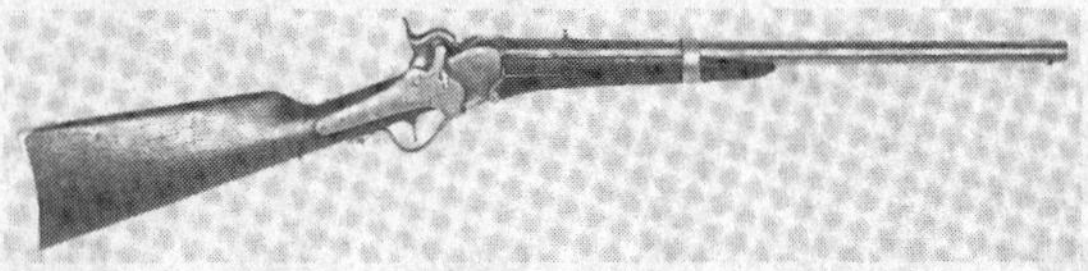

Courtesy Milwaukee Public Museum, Milwaukee, Wisconsin

Exc.	Fine	V.G.	Good	Fair	Poor
12000	9500	6870	4250	1000	700

Model 1852 Antique

Similar to above, with Sharps' Patent Pellet Primer. Barrel marked "Sharps Rifle Manufg. Co. Hartford, Conn.". Blued, case-hardened brass furniture and walnut stock. Manufactured in carbine, rifle, sporting rifle and shotgun form. Approximately 4,600 carbines and 600 rifles made between 1853 and 1855.

Military Carbine Antique

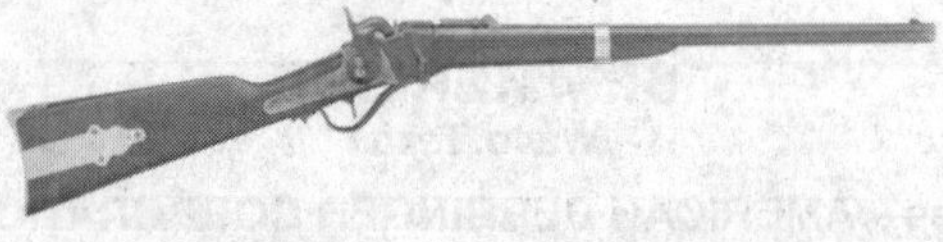

Courtesy Bonhams & Butterfields

Exc.	Fine	V.G.	Good	Fair	Poor
9000	6750	4870	3000	750	520

Military Rifle Antique

Exc.	Fine	V.G.	Good	Fair	Poor
12500	9750	6870	4000	1000	700

Sporting Rifle Antique

Exc.	Fine	V.G.	Good	Fair	Poor
6500	4250	3000	1750	500	350

Shotgun Antique

Values are speculative due to rarity. Beware of rifled arms bored-out to smoothbore configuration.

Exc.	Fine	V.G.	Good	Fair	Poor
—	10000	8000	6000	2500	800

Model 1853 Antique

As above, without spring retainer for lever hinge being mounted in the fore-stock. Approximately 10,500 carbines and 3,000 rifles made between 1854 and 1858.

Military Carbine Antique

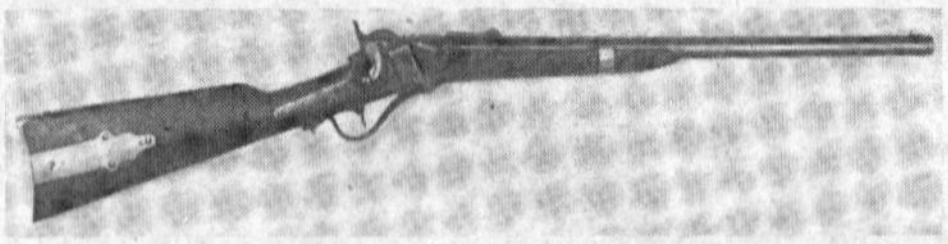

Courtesy Milwaukee Public Museum, Milwaukee, Wisconsin

Exc.	Fine	V.G.	Good	Fair	Poor
8500	6250	4500	2750	750	520

Military Rifle Antique

Exc.	Fine	V.G.	Good	Fair	Poor
12000	9500	6750	4000	1000	700

Sporting Rifle Antique

Courtesy Bonhams & Butterfields

Exc.	Fine	V.G.	Good	Fair	Poor
4500	2750	2000	1250	450	310

Shotgun Antique

Courtesy Bonhams & Butterfields

Exc.	Fine	V.G.	Good	Fair	Poor
4300	2500	1750	1000	450	310

Model 1855 (Antique)

As above, in .52-caliber. Fitted with Maynard tape primer marked "Edward Maynard Patentee 1845". Approximately 700 made between 1855 and 1856. About 12 were made in a Sporting Rifle configuration, extremely rare and worth premium.

Exc.	Fine	V.G.	Good	Fair	Poor
9000	7000	5000	4250	1000	700

Model 1855 U.S. Navy Rifle (Antique)

As above, with 28" barrel, full-length stock and bearing U.S. Navy inspection marks. Approximately 260 made in 1855. Values listed are for the 27" barrel Navy rifle. US Navy carbines with 18" barrels may bring a premium of around 50% (rare - 100 made). US Army carbines marked "U.S./JH" (650 made) may bring a 30% premium.

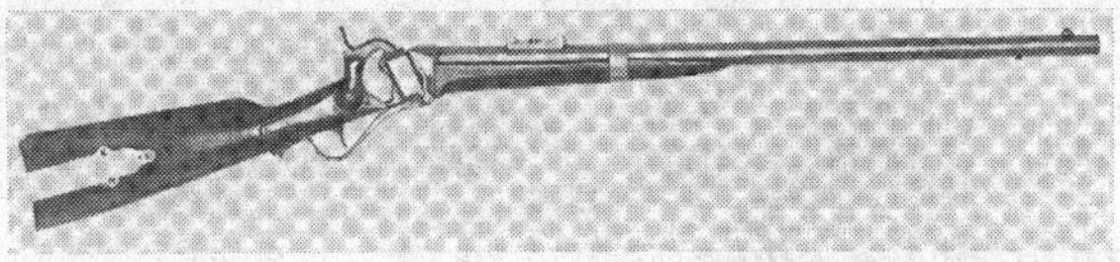

Courtesy Milwaukee Public Museum, Milwaukee, Wisconsin

Exc.	Fine	V.G.	Good	Fair	Poor
13000	10500	7250	4000	1000	700

Model 1855 British Carbine (Antique)

Model 1855 with British inspection marks. Approximately 6,800 made between 1855 and 1857.

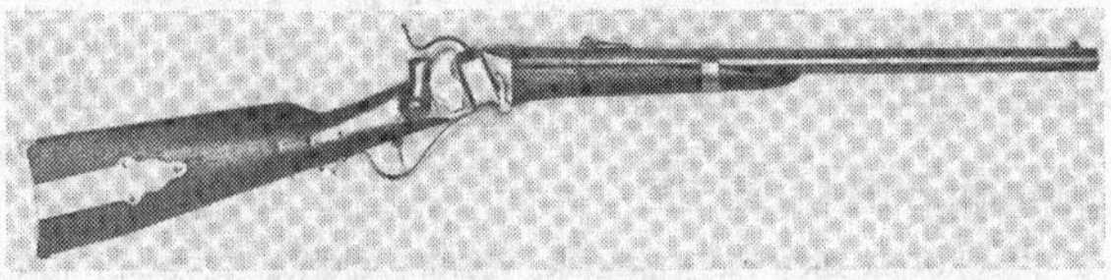

Courtesy Milwaukee Public Museum, Milwaukee, Wisconsin

Exc.	Fine	V.G.	Good	Fair	Poor
8750	6250	4620	3000	850	590

SHARPS STRAIGHT BREECH MODELS

New Model 1859 Carbine (Antique)

Similar to above models, with breech opening cut on an almost vertical angle. .52 caliber, 22" barrel. Standard production had iron furniture and patchbox. Early production with brass furniture and patchbox will bring a 30% to 50% premium.

22" Barrel, Brass Mountings (Antique)

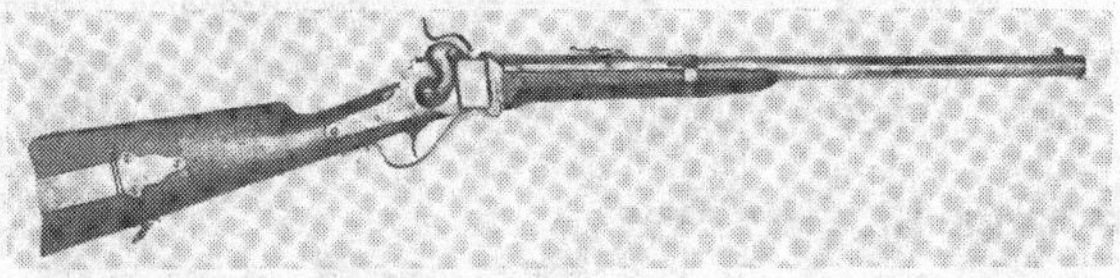

Courtesy Milwaukee Public Museum, Milwaukee, Wisconsin

Exc.	Fine	V.G.	Good	Fair	Poor
8200	6250	4370	2500	500	350

Iron Mountings (Antique)

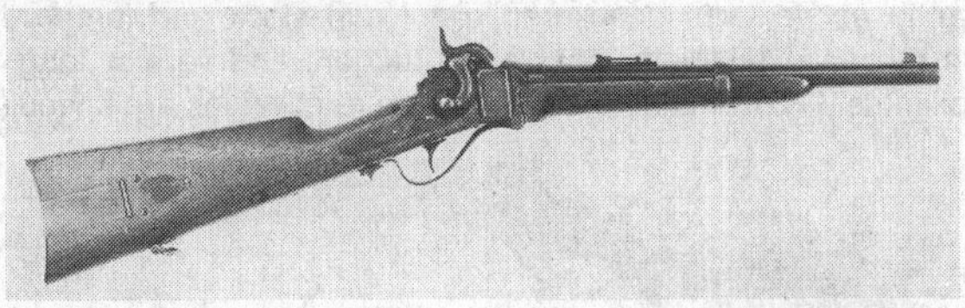

Courtesy Milwaukee Public Museum, Milwaukee, Wisconsin

Exc.	Fine	V.G.	Good	Fair	Poor
—	3250	2370	1500	500	350

New Model 1863 Carbine (Antique)

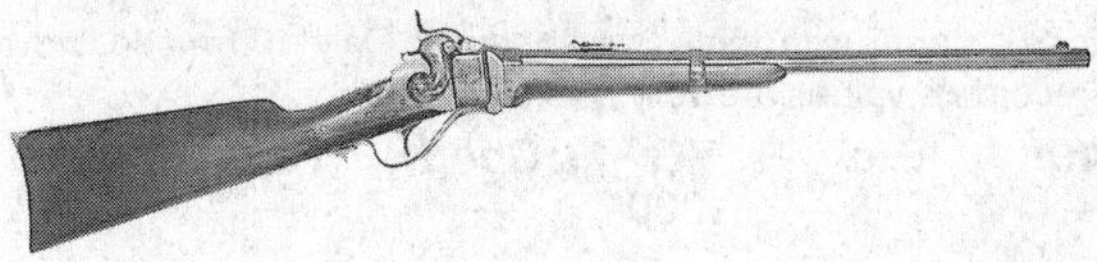

Courtesy Mike Stuckslager

Exc.	Fine	V.G.	Good	Fair	Poor
5000	3250	2370	1500	500	350

New Model 1863 Rifle (Antique)

Without bayonet lug.

Exc.	Fine	V.G.	Good	Fair	Poor
4500	3750	2620	1500	500	350

New Model 1865 Rifle (Antique)

Without bayonet lug.

Exc.	Fine	V.G.	Good	Fair	Poor
4200	3250	2120	1000	500	350

New Model 1865 Carbine (Antique)

Exc.	Fine	V.G.	Good	Fair	Poor
4500	3750	2750	1750	500	350

New Model 1859 Military Rifle (Antique)

Standard configuration has 30" barrel. Some had double set triggers. They are found with either a lug for a sabre bayonet or adapted for a socket bayonet. Around 600 were made with a extra long 36" barrel, and will bring a premium. Rifles which can be documented as issued to Col. Berdan's U.S. Sharpshooters Regiments will bring a significant premium.

Coffee-Mill Model (Antique)

Some Sharps' carbines were fitted with coffee-mill style grinding devices set into their buttstocks. **CAUTION:** These arms are exceptionally rare and extreme caution should be exercised prior to purchase. FAKES EXIST.

Courtesy Milwaukee Public Museum, Milwaukee, Wisconsin

Exc.	Fine	V.G.	Good	Fair	Poor
65000	42500	28750	15000	5000	3500

Straight Breech Metallic Cartridge Conversions (Antique)

In 1867, approximately 32,000 Model 1859, 1863 and 1865 Sharps were altered to .52-70 rimfire and centerfire caliber.

Courtesy Mike Stuckslager

Exc.	Fine	V.G.	Good	Fair	Poor
5500	4250	3120	2000	600	420

New Model 1869

A .40-50 to .50-70 caliber model produced in a military form, with 26", 28" or 30" barrels; as a carbine with 21" or 24" barrels and in a sporting version with various barrel lengths. Forend stock fitted with a pewter tip. Approximately 650 made.

Carbine (Antique)

.50-70, saddle ring on frame.

Exc.	Fine	V.G.	Good	Fair	Poor
5500	4250	3000	1750	500	350

Military Rifle

.50-70, 30" barrel with three barrel bands. Only 100 made, no recent sales recorded, values are very speculative.

NIB	Exc.	V.G.	Good	Fair	Poor
—	—	1000	—	—	—

Sporting Rifle Antique

26" barrel, .44-77 and .50-70.

Exc.	Fine	V.G.	Good	Fair	Poor
15000	10000	6000	3500	1000	500

Model 1870 Springfield Altered

Chambered for .50-70 caliber. Fitted with 35.5" barrel, with two barrel bands. Walnut stock. Case-hardened lock and breechlock. Buttplate stamped "US". Made for government trials, with a total of around 1,000 rifles and 300 carbines produced.

First Type Antique

Most common, straight breech.

Courtesy Bonhams & Butterfields

Exc.	Fine	V.G.	Good	Fair	Poor
8000	6000	4000	2000	900	400

Second Type Antique

Model 1874 action, serial #1 to 300.

Exc.	Fine	V.G.	Good	Fair	Poor
10000	8000	6000	3000	1200	500

Carbine Antique

22" barrel converted to centerfire. Values are speculative.

Exc.	Fine	V.G.	Good	Fair	Poor
10500	8250	6620	5000	1250	870

Model 1874

Manufactured in a variety of calibers, barrel lengths and stock styles. Barrel markings are of three forms: initially, "Sharps Rifle Manufg. Co. Hartford, Conn." ; then, "Sharps Rifle Co. Hartford, Conn." ; finally "Sharps Rifle Co. Bridgeport, Conn." As of 1876 "Old Reliable" was stamped on barrels. This marking usually found on Bridgeport-marked rifles only. Major styles of this model are listed. Sharps rifles documented as shipped to Montana, Wyoming, and other "buffalo hunting" destinations will generally bring a premium.

Military Carbine Antique

.50-70, 21" barrel (460 made). Values are speculative

Exc.	Fine	V.G.	Good	Fair	Poor
7950	5500	4120	2750	750	520

Military Rifle Antique

In .45-70 and .50-70 centerfire caliber, with 30" barrel. Full-length forend secured by three barrel bands. Approximately 1,800 made.

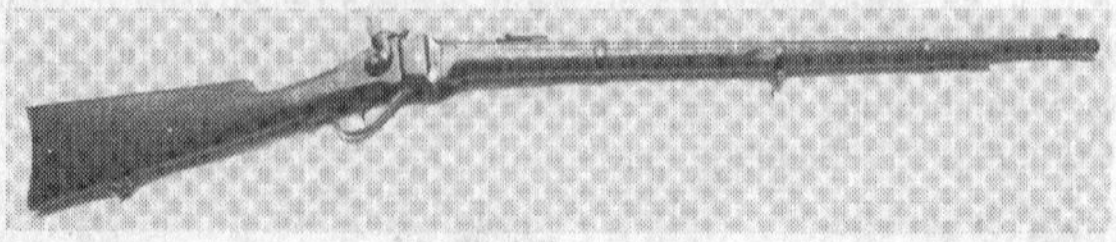

Courtesy Dennis Callender

Exc.	Fine	V.G.	Good	Fair	Poor
7500	5000	3620	2250	750	520

Hunter's Rifle Antique

In .40, .44, .45-70 and .50-70 caliber, with 26", 28" or 30" round barrels. Open sights. Approximately 600 manufactured.

Exc.	Fine	V.G.	Good	Fair	Poor
8000	6250	4500	2750	800	560

Business Rifle Antique

In .40-70 and .45-75 Sharps caliber, with 26", 28" or 30" round barrel. Adjustable sights and double-set triggers. Approximately 1,600 manufactured.

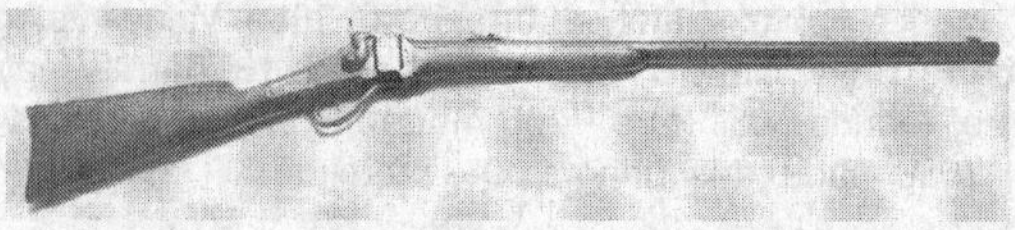

Courtesy Mike Stuckslager

Exc.	Fine	V.G.	Good	Fair	Poor
7750	6000	4620	3250	1000	700

Sporting Rifle Antique

Offered in a variety of calibers, barrel lengths weights and styles, stock styles. Approximately 6,000 manufactured.

Courtesy Milwaukee Public Museum, Milwaukee, Wisconsin

Exc.	Fine	V.G.	Good	Fair	Poor
15000	8500	6250	4000	1500	1050

Creedmoor Rifle Antique

With a checkered pistol grip stock, vernier sights, combination wind gauge and spirit level front sight, set trigger and shotgun style butt. Approximately 150 made.

Exc.	Fine	V.G.	Good	Fair	Poor
40000	20000	13000	8500	3500	1500

Mid-Range Rifle Antique

Similar to above, with crescent buttplate. Approximately 180 made.

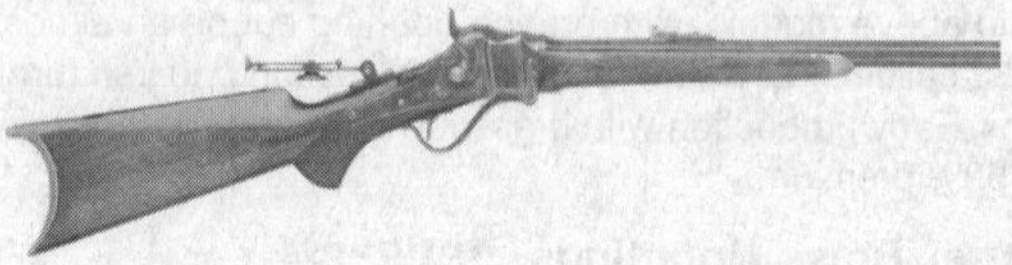

Courtesy Bonhams & Butterfields

Exc.	Fine	V.G.	Good	Fair	Poor
22500	15000	10750	6500	1500	1050

Long-Range Rifle Antique

As above, with 34" octagonal barrel. Approximately 425 manufactured.

Exc.	Fine	V.G.	Good	Fair	Poor
23000	16500	11250	6000	1500	1050

Schuetzen Rifle Antique

Similar to above, with checkered pistol grip stock and forend. Large Schuetzen style buttplate, double-set triggers and vernier tang sight. Approximately 70 manufactured. Sales are rare; values are speculative.

Courtesy Bonhams & Butterfields

Exc.	Fine	V.G.	Good	Fair	Poor
22500	15000	10000	5000	2500	1000

Model 1877 Antique

Similar to Model 1874. In .45-70 caliber, with 34" or 36" barrel. Barrel marked "Sharps Rifle Co. Bridgeport, Conn. Old Reliable". Approximately 100 manufactured in 1877 and 1878.

Exc.	Fine	V.G.	Good	Fair	Poor
30000	10000	7500	5000	2000	1400

MODEL 1878 SHARPS-BORCHARDT

An internal hammer breech-loading rifle. Manufactured from 1878 to about 1880. Frame marked "Borchardt Patent Sharps Rifle Co. Bridgeport Conn. U.S.A.". Note: Be advised that actions on Borchardt Sporting Rifles are worth a minimum of $750. Military actions are not as difficult to locate as Sporting actions. For the sake of continuity, rifles in poor condition but with usable actions are priced at the minimum of $750. For variations with fewer than 300 specimens made, values are very speculative due to few sales.

Model 1878 Sharps Borchardt Carbine Antique

Approximately 385 made in .45-70 caliber, with 24-in. barrel. Forend secured by one barrel band.

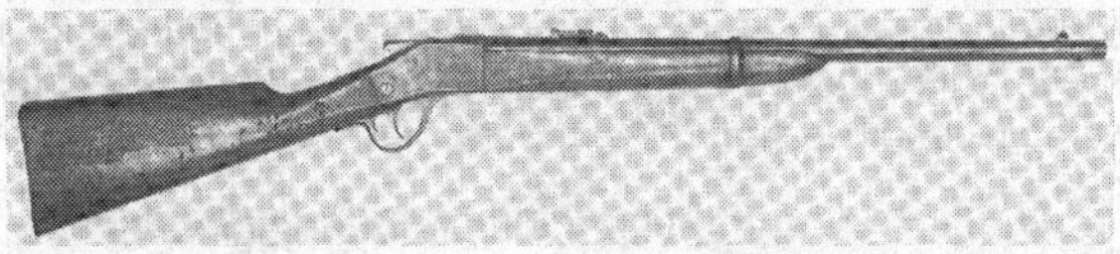

Courtesy Milwaukee Public Museum, Milwaukee, Wisconsin

Exc.	Fine	V.G.	Good	Fair	Poor
5000	4000	2750	1500	750	520

Model 1878 Sharps Borchardt Military Rifle Antique

Approximately 12,000 made in .45-70 caliber, with 32.25" barrels. Full stocks secured by two barrel bands.

Courtesy Bonhams & Butterfields

Exc.	Fine	V.G.	Good	Fair	Poor
3000	2000	1500	900	750	520

Model 1878 Sharps Borchardt Sporting Rifle Antique

Approximately 1,600 made in .45-70 caliber, with 30 round or octagonal barrels.

Exc.	Fine	V.G.	Good	Fair	Poor
6000	4000	3000	1200	750	520

Model 1878 Sharps Borchardt Hunter's Rifle Antique

Approximately 60 made in .40-caliber, with 26" barrels. Plain walnut stocks.

Exc.	Fine	V.G.	Good	Fair	Poor
4500	1750	1370	1000	750	520

Model 1878 Sharps Borchardt Business Rifle Antique

Approximately 90 made, with 28" barrels in .40-caliber. Only 89 made - very rare. Values are extremely speculative.

Exc.	Fine	V.G.	Good	Fair	Poor
10000	6000	3500	2500	1500	750

Model 1878 Sharps Borchardt Officer's Rifle Antique

Approximately 50 made in .45-70 caliber, with 32" barrels. Checkered walnut stocks. Due to rarity, values are speculative.

Exc.	Fine	V.G.	Good	Fair	Poor
7500	3750	2620	1500	750	520

Model 1878 Sharps Borchardt Express Rifle Antique

Approximately 30 made in .45-70 caliber, with 26" barrels. Set triggers and checkered walnut stocks.

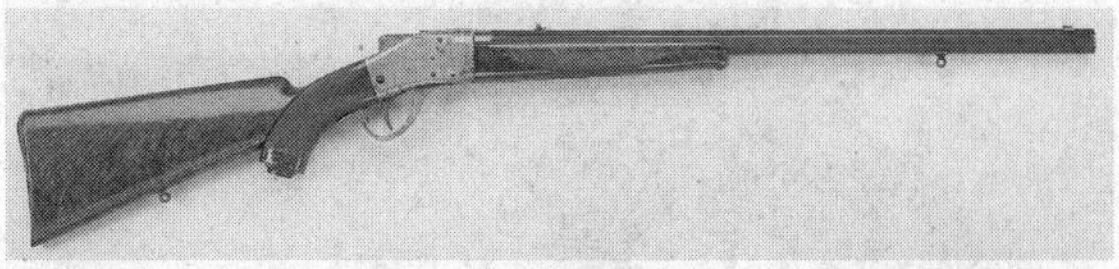

Courtesy Little John's Auction Service, Inc., Paul Goodwin photo

Exc.	Fine	V.G.	Good	Fair	Poor
12500	6000	4000	2000	800	560

Model 1878 Sharps Borchardt Short-Range Rifle Antique

Approximately 155 made in .40-caliber, with 26" barrels. Venier rear sights, wind gauge front sight. Checkered walnut stock.

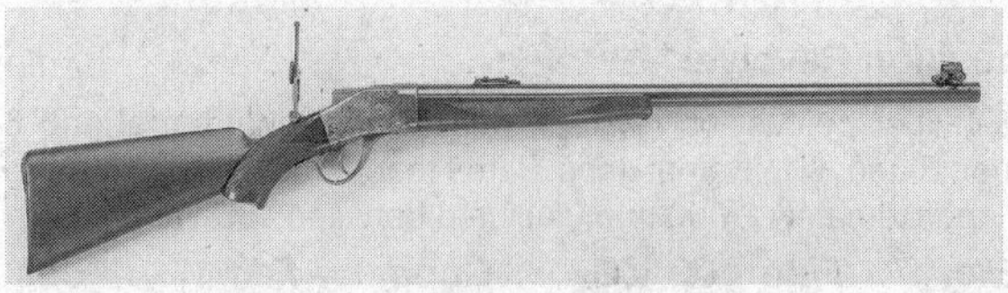

Courtesy Little John's Auction Service, Inc., Paul Goodwin photo

Exc.	Fine	V.G.	Good	Fair	Poor
10000	5000	3000	1000	800	560

Model 1878 Sharps Borchardt Mid-Range Rifle Antique

Similar to above, with 30" barrel. Approximately 250 manufactured.

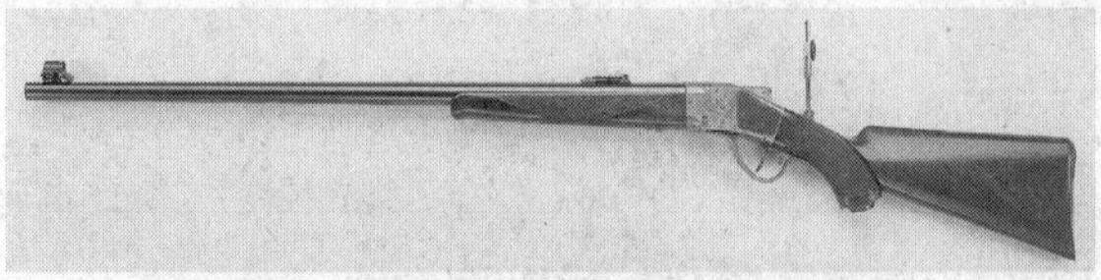

Courtesy Little John's Auction Service, Inc., Paul Goodwin photo

Exc.	Fine	V.G.	Good	Fair	Poor
10000	6500	5000	3000	1500	630

Model 1878 Sharps Borchardt Long-Range Rifle Antique

Similar to above, with different sights. Approximately 230 manufactured.

Courtesy Amoskeag Auction Company

Exc.	Fine	V.G.	Good	Fair	Poor
16000	6500	4500	2500	900	630

C.Sharps Pistol Rifle Antique

A .31- or .38-caliber breech-loading percussion rifle resembling above. Manufactured in a variety of barrel lengths. Blued case-hardened, with walnut stock having German silver mounts.

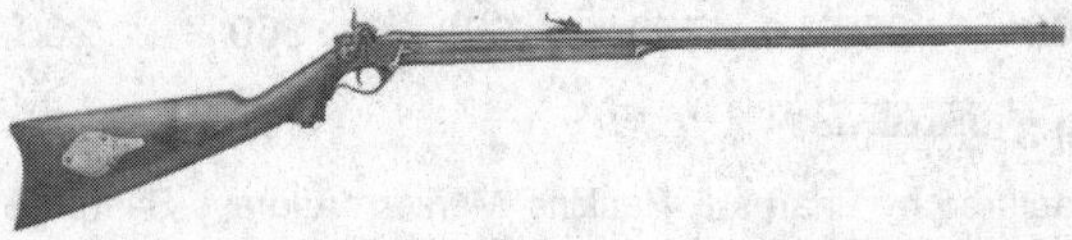

Courtesy Bonhams & Butterfields

Exc.	Fine	V.G.	Good	Fair	Poor
6800	4750	3620	2500	750	520

SHARPS & HANKINS

Sharps & Hankins Breechloading Single-Shot Pistol Antique

A .31-, .34- or .36-caliber breech-loading percussion pistol, with 5- or 6.5-in. round barrels. Blued case-hardened, with walnut stock.

Courtesy Buffalo Bill Historical Center, Cody, Wyoming

Exc.	Fine	V.G.	Good	Fair	Poor
9500	7000	5500	4000	1500	600

Percussion Revolver Antique

A .25-caliber percussion revolver, with 3" octagonal barrel and 6-shot cylinder. Blued, with walnut grips. Barrel marked "C. Sharps & Co., Phila. Pa.". Approximately 2,000 manufactured between 1857 and 1858.

Exc.	Fine	V.G.	Good	Fair	Poor
4250	3000	2120	1250	500	350

4-Shot Pepperbox Pistols Antique

Between 1859 and 1874, these companies manufactured 4 barrel cartridge pocket pistols in a variety of calibers, barrel lengths and finishes. Barrels slide forward for loading. Major models are listed.

Courtesy Buffalo Bill Historical Center, Cody, Wyoming

Model 1 Antique

Manufactured by C. Sharps & Co., in .22 rimfire caliber.

Exc.	Fine	V.G.	Good	Fair	Poor
800	600	420	250	100	70

Model 2 Antique

As above, in .30 rimfire caliber.

Exc.	Fine	V.G.	Good	Fair	Poor
1200	900	750	600	350	200

Model 3 Antique

Manufactured by Sharps & Hankins. Marked "Address Sharps & Hankins Philadelphia Penn." on frame. Caliber .32 Short rimfire.

Exc.	Fine	V.G.	Good	Fair	Poor
1000	850	650	500	300	150

Model 4 Antique

Similar to above in .32 Long rimfire, with rounded bird's-head grip.

Courtesy John J. Stimson, Jr.

Exc.	Fine	V.G.	Good	Fair	Poor
1000	850	650	500	300	150

Sharps & Hankins Model 1861 Navy Rifle Antique

A .52 Sharps & Hankins caliber breech-loading single-shot rifle, with 32.75" barrel. Full stock secured by three barrel bands. Blued case-hardened, with walnut stock. Approximately 700 made in 1861 and 1862. A few were made with leather barrel covers; worth premium.

Courtesy Milwaukee Public Museum, Milwaukee, Wisconsin

Exc.	Fine	V.G.	Good	Fair	Poor
6000	4000	3000	2000	700	480

Sharps & Hankins Model 1862 Navy Carbine Antique

A .24-caliber breech-loading carbine, with 24" leather covered barrel. Case-hardened, with walnut stock. Frame marked "Sharps & Hankins Philada.". Approximately 8,000 manufactured between 1861 and 1862.—To bring full value for Exc, Fine, & VG specimens the leather barrel cover must be intact.

Courtesy Milwaukee Public Museum, Milwaukee, Wisconsin

Exc.	Fine	V.G.	Good	Fair	Poor
5000	3500	2500	1500	700	480

Model 1862 Short Cavalry Carbine Antique

Similar to above, with 19" blued barrel. Approximately 500 manufactured.

Exc.	Fine	V.G.	Good	Fair	Poor
5000	3500	2750	2000	700	480

Model 1862 Army Model Antique

Similar to above, with 24" barrel that does not have a leather covering. Approximately 500 purchased by the Army.

Exc.	Fine	V.G.	Good	Fair	Poor
4750	3000	2370	1750	700	480

SHATTUCK, C. S.

Hatfield, Massachusetts

Double-Barrel Shotguns Antique

In addition to single-barrel shotguns, Shattuck made about 1,000 hammerless doubles.

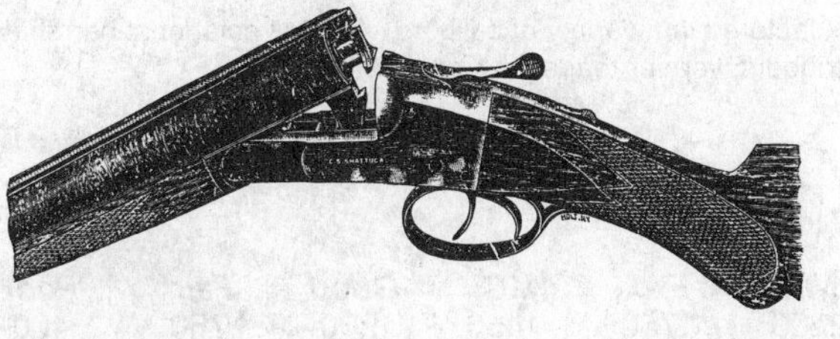

Courtesy Nick Niles

Exc.	Fine	V.G.	Good	Fair	Poor
500	400	350	300	200	140

Boom (Antique)

A .22-caliber spur trigger revolver, with 2" octagonal barrel and 6-shot cylinder. Nickel-plated, with rosewood or walnut grips. Barrel marked "Boom" and "Pat. Nov. 4. 1879". Manufactured during 1880s. Rarely encountered, values are speculative.

Exc.	Fine	V.G.	Good	Fair	Poor
400	150	120	100	80	50

Pocket Revolver (Antique)

A .32-caliber spur trigger revolver, with 3.5" octagonal barrel and 5-shot cylinder. Nickel-plated, with hard rubber grips. Barrel marked "C. S. Shattuck Hatfield, Mass. Pat. Nov. 4, 1879". Manufactured during 1880s. One of the first production revolvers with a side-swing cylinder, albeit one that rotates on a horizontal axis. Bizarre tribute grips feature profiles of assassinated presidents Lincoln and Garfield.

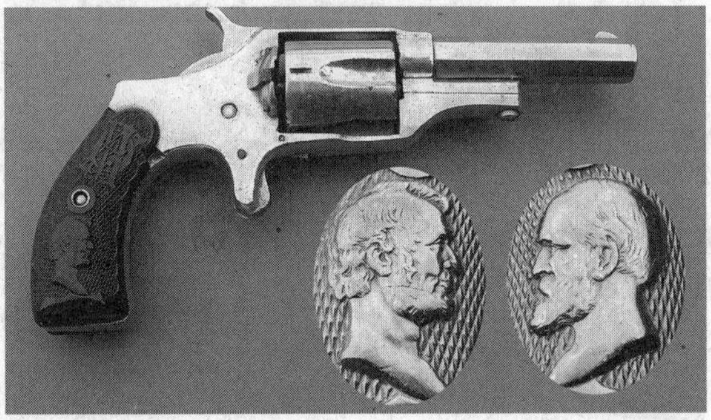

Jim Supica photo

Exc.	Fine	V.G.	Good	Fair	Poor
700	450	250	150	100	70

SHAW & LEDOYT
Stafford, Connecticut

Underhammer Pistol (Antique)

A .31-caliber under hammer percussion pistol, with 2.5" to 3.5" half-octagonal barrel. Blued, with brass mounted walnut grip. Frame marked "Shaw & LeDoyt/Stafford. Conn.". Manufactured during 1850s.

Exc.	Fine	V.G.	Good	Fair	Poor
1750	1300	900	550	150	100

SHAWK & McLANAHAN
St. Louis, Missouri

Navy Revolver (Antique)

A .36-caliber percussion revolver, with 8" round barrel and 6-shot cylinder. Blued, with brass frame and walnut grips. Marked "Shawk & McLanahan, St. Louis, Carondelet, Mo.". Produced in limited quantities prior to 1860. Values are speculative due to rarity.

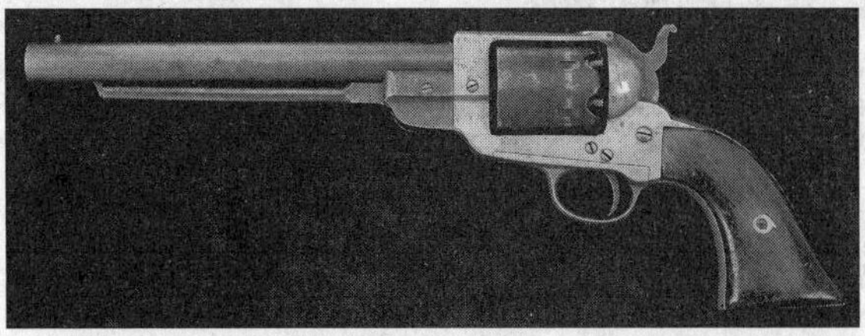

Courtesy Little John's Auction Service, Inc., Paul Goodwin photo

Exc.	Fine	V.G.	Good	Fair	Poor
30000	20000	10000	7500	4000	2000

SHERIDAN PRODUCTS, INC.
Racine, Wisconsin

Knockabout/Model D

A .22-caliber single-shot pistol, with 5" barrel. Fixed sights. Blued, with plastic grips. Manufactured between 1953 and 1960.

NIB	Exc.	V.G.	Good	Fair	Poor
—	350	220	180	100	50

SHILEN RIFLES, INC.
Ennis, Texas

Model DGA Bench Rest Rifle

Centerfire single-shot bolt-action rifle, with 26" barrel. Fiberglass or walnut stock.

NIB	Exc.	V.G.	Good	Fair	Poor
—	1750	1400	1100	850	500

Model DGA Sporter

A .17 Rem. to .308 Win. caliber bolt-action sporting rifle, with 24" barrel without sights. Blued, with walnut stock.

NIB	Exc.	V.G.	Good	Fair	Poor
—	1750	1400	1100	850	500

Model DGA Varminter

As above, in varmint calibers with 25" barrel.

NIB	Exc.	V.G.	Good	Fair	Poor
—	1750	1400	1100	850	500

Model DGA Silhouette Rifle

As above, in .308 Win. only.

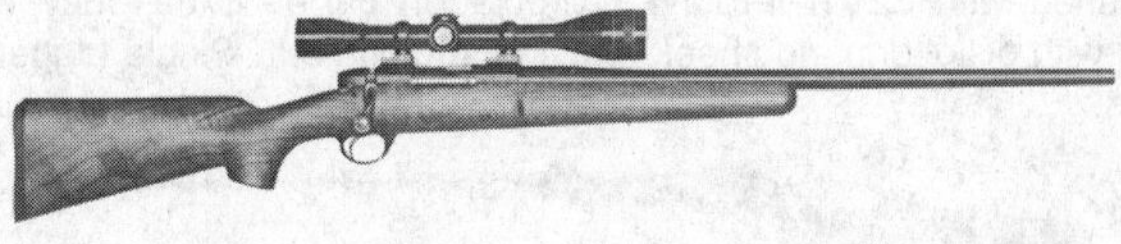

NIB	Exc.	V.G.	Good	Fair	Poor
—	1750	1400	1100	850	500

SHILOH RIFLE MFG. CO., INC.
Big Timber, Montana

Established in Farmingdale, New York, in 1976, this company moved to Big Timber, Montana, in 1983 with the name Shiloh Products. Changed its name to Shiloh Rifle Manufacturing Co. in that same year. In 1985, the company began marketing its products factory direct. In 1991, Robert, Phyllis and Kirk Bryan purchased the company. Those interested in Sharps reproduction rifles manufactured by this company are advised to contact them in Big Timber. NOTE: Company will build a rifle to customers' specifications. It is, therefore, possible that many of these rifles have special-order features that are not reflected in the base model price. Since Shiloh is in effect a custom (or at least semi-custom) manufacturer, rifles listed here are representative but not inclusive.

Model 1863 Military Rifle

A .54-caliber percussion rifle, with 30" barrel, single-/double-set triggers. Full-length walnut stock secured by three barrel bands.

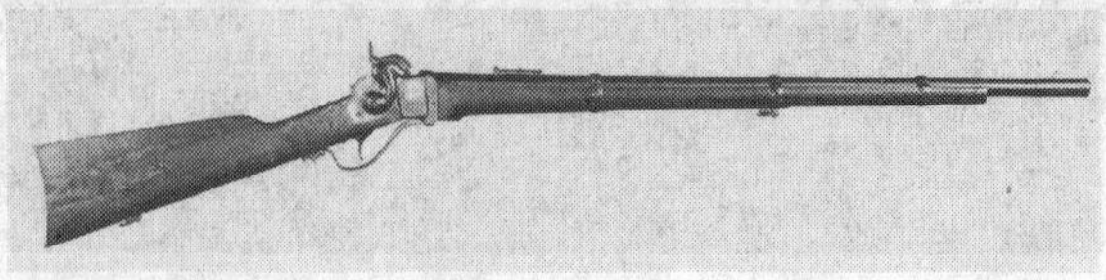

NIB	Exc.	V.G.	Good	Fair	Poor
1900	1650	1100	900	700	500

Model 1863 Sporting Rifle

As above, with 30" octagonal barrel, sporting sights and half-length stock.

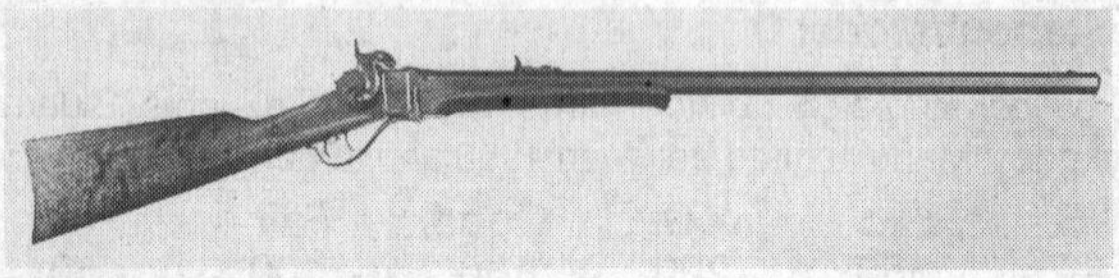

NIB	Exc.	V.G.	Good	Fair	Poor
1800	1550	1050	850	600	450

Model 1863 Military Carbine

Model 1863, with 22" round barrel. Carbine stock secured by one barrel band.

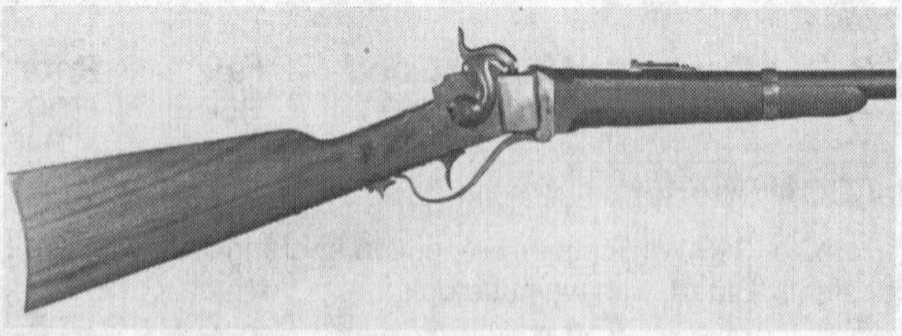

NIB	Exc.	V.G.	Good	Fair	Poor
1900	1650	1100	900	700	500

Model 1862 Confederate Robinson

As above, with 21.5" barrel, brass buttplate and barrel band.

NIB	Exc.	V.G.	Good	Fair	Poor
1900	1650	1100	900	700	500

Model 1874 Creedmoor Target Rifle

Furnished with 32" half-round half-octagon barrel. Extra-fancy wood stock with pistol grip, no cheek-rest and shotgun butt. Single trigger. No sights.

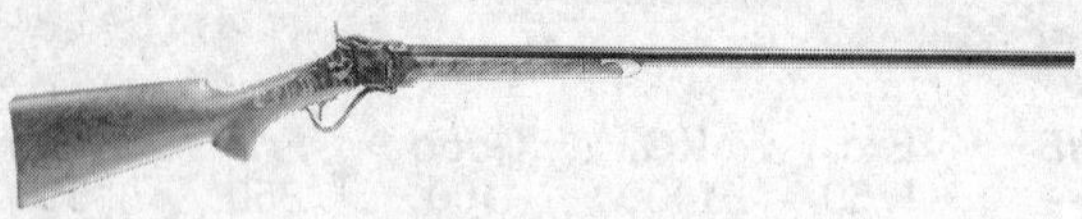

NIB	Exc.	V.G.	Good	Fair	Poor
2700	2250	1700	1300	800	500

Model 1874 Buffalo Rifle (Quigley)

Offered in .45-70 or .45-110, with 34" heavy octagon barrel. Mid-range tang sight, with globe front sight. Semi-buckhorn rear sight. Double-set triggers. Military buttstock, with patchbox. No cheek-rest. Straight-grip stock.

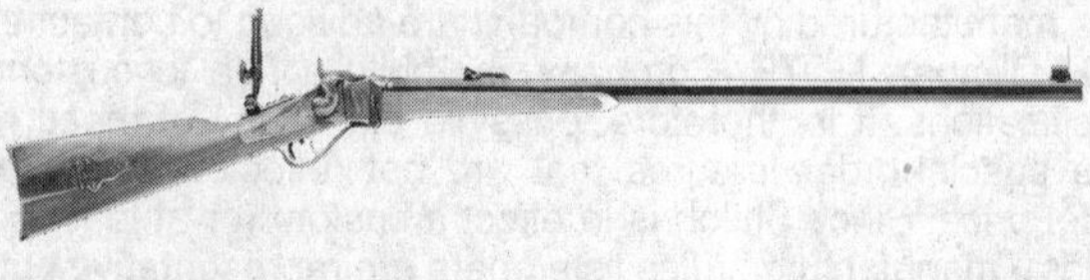

NIB	Exc.	V.G.	Good	Fair	Poor
3300	2750	2100	1700	1200	500

Model 1874 Long Range Express Rifle

Manufactured in a variety of calibers, with 34" octagonal barrel, double-set triggers, vernier rear sight and globe front.

NIB	Exc.	V.G.	Good	Fair	Poor
2200	1750	1450	1200	750	400

Model 1874 Montana Roughrider Rifle

As above, with octagonal or half-octagonal barrels from 24" to 34".

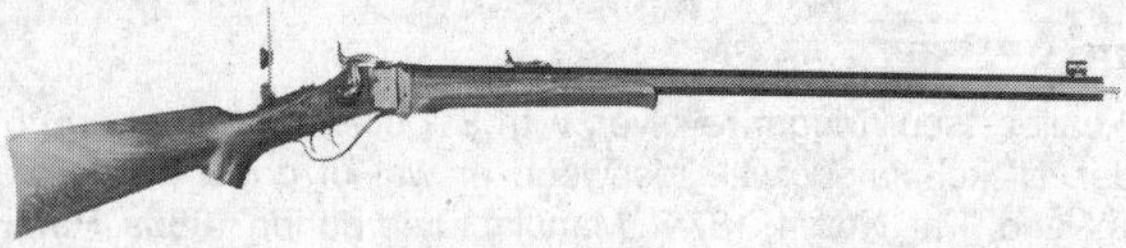

NIB	Exc.	V.G.	Good	Fair	Poor
2200	1750	1450	1200	750	400

Saddle Rifle

As above, with 26" barrel. Shotgun butt.

NIB	Exc.	V.G.	Good	Fair	Poor
2200	1750	1450	1200	750	400

No. 1 Sporter Deluxe Rifle

Similar to above, with 30" octagonal barrel.

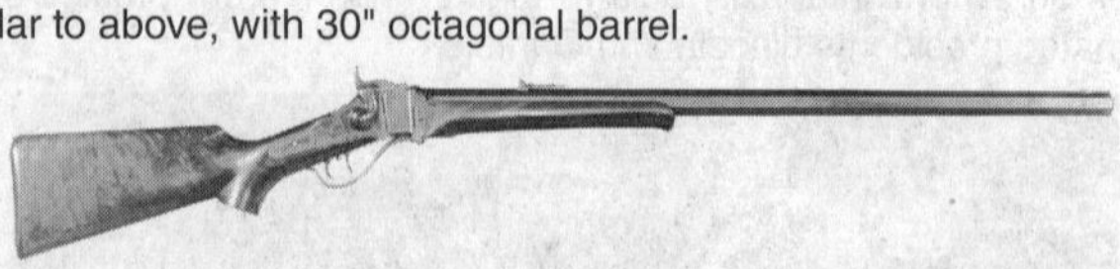

NIB	Exc.	V.G.	Good	Fair	Poor
2200	1750	1450	1200	750	400

No. 3 Standard Sporter

As above, with military-style stock.

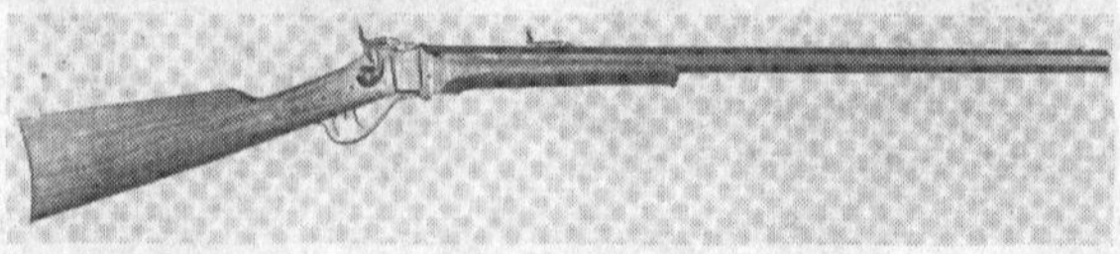

NIB	Exc.	V.G.	Good	Fair	Poor
2200	1750	1450	1200	750	400

Business Rifle

As above, with heavy 28" barrel.

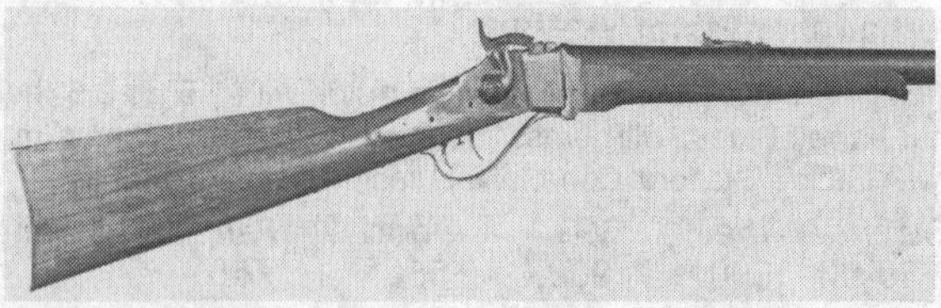

NIB	Exc.	V.G.	Good	Fair	Poor
2200	1750	1450	1200	750	400

Model 1874 Military Rifle

Model 1874, with 30" round barrel, military sights. Full-length stocks secured by three barrel bands.

NIB	Exc.	V.G.	Good	Fair	Poor
2200	1750	1450	1200	750	400

Model 1874 Carbine

Similar to above, with 24" round barrel.

NIB	Exc.	V.G.	Good	Fair	Poor
2000	1550	1150	750	500	300

Jaeger

Model 1874, with 26" half-octagonal barrel, open sights and pistol grip stock with shotgun butt.

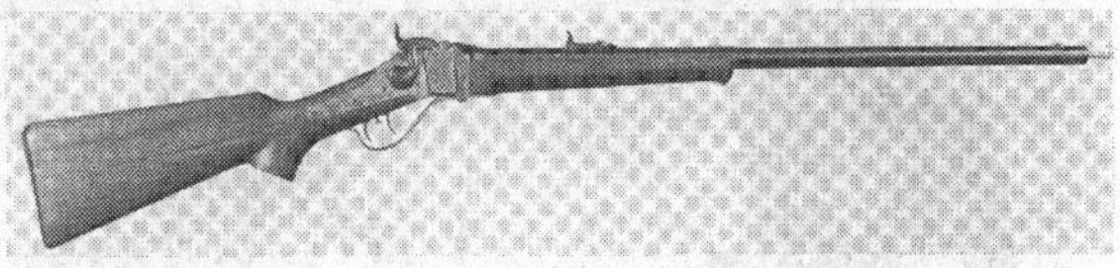

NIB	Exc.	V.G.	Good	Fair	Poor
2200	1750	1450	1200	750	400

Hartford Model

Reproduction of Sharps Hartford Model.

NIB	Exc.	V.G.	Good	Fair	Poor
2200	1750	1450	1200	750	400

Model 1874 Military Carbine

Similar to Military Rifle, with 22" round barrel.

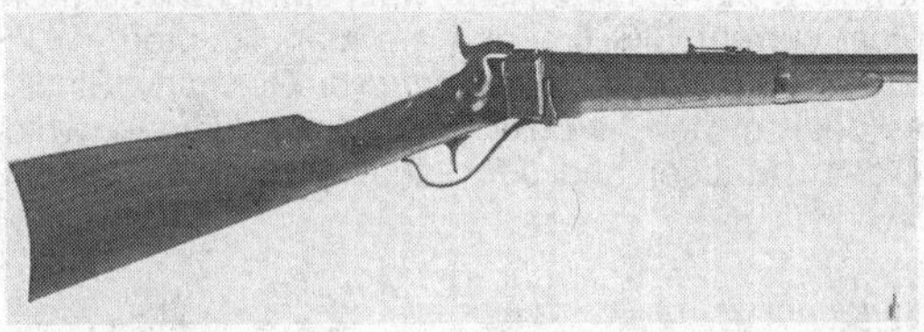

NIB	Exc.	V.G.	Good	Fair	Poor
2200	1750	1450	1200	750	400

SIACE SHOTGUNS

See—DAKOTA ARMS

SIG

Neuhausen, Switzerland

P 210

Pistol introduced in 1947. Standard issue sidearm of Swiss military from 1949 to 1975. Also issued to Danish Army as Model M49. Chambered in 9mm Parabellum, 7.65 (.30 Luger) and .22 Long rifle, with 8-round magazine. A .22 conversion kit also available for centerfire models. Short-recoil operated single-action pistol, with frame-mounted manual safety and 4.75" barrel. Several variations of original P210 were imported into U.S. from 1950s until about 1987, with limited importation of a few more models until 2007. Upgraded and improved version introduced in 2011 as P210 Legend. See listing under SIG Sauer. Note: Add premium of 40 to 50 percent for .22 LR conversion kit.

P210 Danish Army Model M49

NIB	Exc.	V.G.	Good	Fair	Poor
3000	2500	2000	1500	800	400

P 210-1

Fixed sights, walnut grips, polished finish. Imported until 1986.

NIB	Exc.	V.G.	Good	Fair	Poor
2600	2200	1700	1100	500	350

P 210-2

Fixed sights, plastic or wood grips, matte finish. Imported 1987 to 2002. Note: Add 50 percent premium for West German Police model, with loaded chamber indicator.

NIB	Exc.	V.G.	Good	Fair	Poor
2000	1600	1000	750	400	300

P 210-5

Adjustable sights, extended frame and barrel (5"), wood or rubber grips, matte finish, adjustable trigger. Push-button magazine release. Limited importation from 1997 to 2007.

NIB	Exc.	V.G.	Good	Fair	Poor
3000	2250	1650	1000	600	400

P 210-6

As above, with 4.75" barrel.

NIB	Exc.	V.G.	Good	Fair	Poor
3000	2250	1650	1000	600	400

P210-7

In .22 LR caliber. Fewer than 500 made.

NIB	Exc.	V.G.	Good	Fair	Poor
4500	3500	2800	2000	1000	400

P210-8

Special order target model, with adjustable sights, wood grips, heavy frame. Available from 2001 to 2003 only. Limited importation.

NIB	Exc.	V.G.	Good	Fair	Poor
3800	3200	2650	1800	1000	400

SIG-HAMMERLI

Lenzburg, Switzerland

Model P240 Target Pistol

A .32 S&W Long Wadcutter or .38 Midrange caliber semi-automatic pistol, with 5.9" barrel. Adjustable rear sight and trigger. 5-shot magazine. Blued, with adjustable walnut grips. Imported prior 1987.

Courtesy John J. Stimson, Jr.

NIB	Exc.	V.G.	Good	Fair	Poor
—	1300	1150	950	750	600

.22 Conversion Unit

Barrel, slide and magazine used to convert the above to .22-caliber.

NIB	Exc.	V.G.	Good	Fair	Poor
—	500	450	400	300	200

Model P208S

Semi-automatic target pistol chambered for .22 LR cartridge. Barrel length 5.9", with adjustable sights. Sight radius 8.2". Trigger has adjustable pull weight, travel, slack weight and creep. Grips are stippled walnut, with adjustable palm shelf. Weight about 37 oz. empty.

NIB	Exc.	V.G.	Good	Fair	Poor
1900	1600	1300	1100	750	500

Model P280

Semi-automatic pistol chambered for .22 LR cartridge or .32 S&W Long Wadcutter. Single-action-only. Barrel length 4.6", with sight radius of 8.7". Adjustable sights. Trigger adjustable for pull weight, take-up, let-off and creep. Stippled walnut grip, with adjustable palm shelf. Weight: 35 oz. .22-caliber; 42 oz. .32-caliber. Magazine capacity: .22-caliber 6 rounds; .32-caliber 5 rounds.

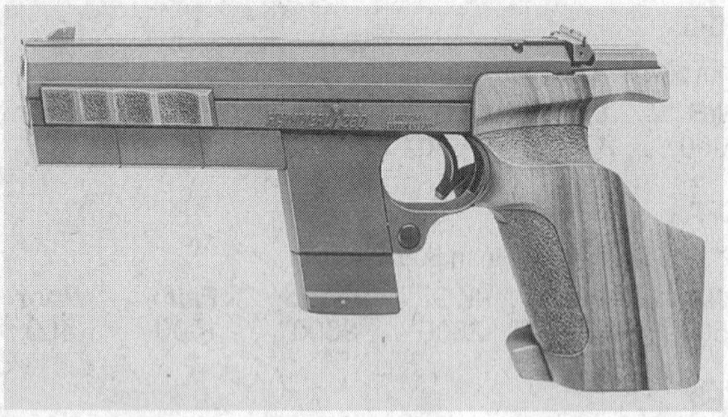

NIB	Exc.	V.G.	Good	Fair	Poor
1200	10000	800	650	500	300

Model P160/162

.22 LR single-shot pistol designed for international free pistol competition. Barrel length 11.3", with sight radius of 14.6". Trigger fully adjustable as are sights. Stippled walnut grips, with adjustable palm shelf and rake angle. Model 160 has a mechanical trigger; Model 162 fitted with an electric trigger.

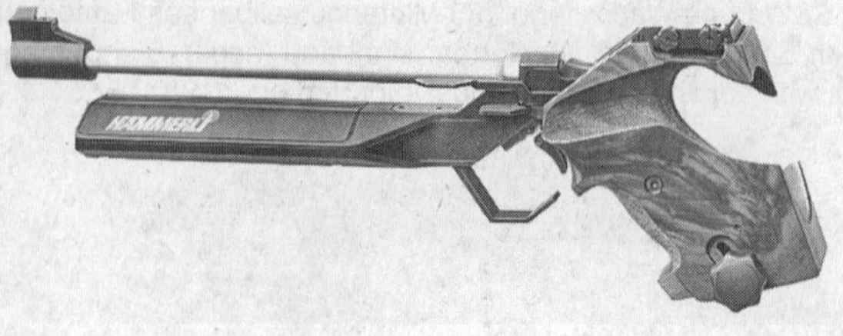

NIB	Exc.	V.G.	Good	Fair	Poor
2300	2000	1700	1250	800	400

Trailside PL 22

Introduced in 1999. Semi-automatic pistol chambered for .22 LR cartridge. Barrel length 4.5" or 6", with fixed sights. Synthetic grips. Two-tone finish. Magazine capacity 10 rounds. Weight about: 28 oz. with 4.5" barrel; 30 oz. with 6" barrel. Note: Add $90 for 6" barrel.

NIB	Exc.	V.G.	Good	Fair	Poor
580	500	380	300	200	100

Trailside PL 22 Target

Similar to PL 22, with addition of adjustable sights and walnut grips. Introduced in 1999. Note: Add $25 for 6" barrel.

NIB	Exc.	V.G.	Good	Fair	Poor
600	520	400	320	220	120

Trailside Competition

Introduced in 2004. This .22-caliber model features 6" barrel, with adjustable competition grip and sights. Counterweights and two-tone finish. Magazine capacity 10 rounds. Weight about 36 oz.

NIB	Exc.	V.G.	Good	Fair	Poor
800	680	500	420	300	150

SIGARMS/SIG-SAUER

Eckernforde, Germany
Neuhausen, Switzerland
Exeter, New Hampshire

In 1985, SIG established a U.S. presence by opening SIG Arms in Exeter, New Hampshire. Name was changed to Sig-Sauer in 2007. Most current SIG firearms are manufactured in U.S., but some are imported from Switzerland or Germany. Since 2000, SIG has been owned by Luke and Ortmeier Group, which also owns Blaser, Mauser and J.P. Sauer. SEE POLITICAL PANIC PRICING.

PISTOLS

P210

Model reintroduced into U.S. in 2001. Based on Swiss military version first built in 1949. Designed primarily as a target pistol. Furnished in four different variations. All variations chambered for 9mm cartridge. Note: Older P210 models imported before 1968 without importer stamps and pistols built during late 1940s and early 1950s, may bring a premium to collectors. Be aware that extra barrels, conversion kits and other special order features will add additional value.

P210 Legend

Updated variation of P210. Features include side-mounted magazine release, improved and extended beavertail, black Nitron finish and choice of fixed or adjustable sights. Available only in 9mm. Introduced in 2011. Made in Germany. Note: Add $200 for adjustable sights.

NIB	Exc.	V.G.	Good	Fair	Poor
2000	1850	1500	1100	700	400

P210 Target

Similar to above. 5" barrel. Target trigger. Adjustable sights. Checkered walnut grip. Weight 36.9 oz. Nitron finish.

NIB	Exc.	V.G.	Good	Fair	Poor
1700	1480	1230	930	680	560

P220

High-quality double-action semi-automatic pistol chambered for .38 Super, .45 ACP and 9mm Parabellum. Has 4.41" barrel and fixed sights. Features decocking lever that was found originally on Sauer Model 38H. Two versions of this Pistol--one with bottom magazine release (commonly referred to as European model); other with release on side (commonly referred to as American model), as on Model 1911 Colt. Frame is lightweight alloy, matte-finished and available in blue, nickel or K-Kote finish. Black plastic grips. .45 ACP magazine capacity 7 rounds, weight 25.7 oz.; .38 Super magazine capacity 9 rounds, weight 26.5 oz.; 9mm magazine holds 9 rounds, overall weight 26.5 oz. Manufactured from 1976 and still in production. The 9mm and .38 Super versions are no longer in production. Prices listed are for guns with standard blue finish. Note: Add $40 K-Kote finish; $40 nickel slide; $100 stainless steel. In 2004, a blued version with tactical rail was offered.

P220 with tactical rail.

NIB	Exc.	V.G.	Good	Fair	Poor
820	600	400	300	200	150

P220 .22

As above chambered for .22 LR cartridge.

NIB	Exc.	V.G.	Good	Fair	Poor
500	400	300	200	150	100

P220 ST

As above chambered for .45 ACP cartridge. Features stainless steel frame and slide, with tactical rail. Also includes a SIGARMS tactical knife and aluminum carrying case. Weight about 39 oz.

NIB	Exc.	V.G.	Good	Fair	Poor
880	700	550	420	300	150

P220 Sport

Introduced in 1999. This .45 ACP pistol similar to P220. Addition of 5.5" barrel, with stainless steel compensator. Frame and slide are stainless steel. Magazine capacity 7 rounds. Weight about 44 oz.

NIB	Exc.	V.G.	Good	Fair	Poor
1400	1250	1000	780	500	300

P220R SAO

An 8+1 or 10+1 capacity single-action semi-automatic. Chambered for .45 ACP. Polymer grip and Nitron finish, 4.4" barrel, weight 30.4 oz., 5-lb. trigger. Picatinny rail. Introduced 2006.

NIB	Exc.	V.G.	Good	Fair	Poor
750	600	480	350	200	150

P220R DAK

Semi-automatic with 8+1 or 10+1 capacity. Chambered for .45 ACP. Polymer grip and Nitron finish, 4.4" barrel, weight 30.4 oz., 7.5-lb. trigger. Picatinny rail. Introduced 2006.

NIB	Exc.	V.G.	Good	Fair	Poor
880	700	600	480	350	200

P220 SAS

An 8+1 capacity double-action semi-automatic. Chambered for .45 ACP. Fixed sights, wood grips, 4.4" barrel, weight 30.4 oz., 6.5-lb. trigger. Introduced 2006.

NIB	Exc.	V.G.	Good	Fair	Poor
1000	880	720	600	400	200

P220 Carry SAS

An 8+1 capacity double-action semi-automatic. Chambered for .45 ACP. Fixed sights, wood grips, 3.9" barrel, weight 30.4 oz., 6.5-lb. trigger. Introduced 2006.

NIB	Exc.	V.G.	Good	Fair	Poor
900	800	700	550	400	200

P220 Carry

An 8+1 or 10+1 capacity single-/double-action semi-automatic. Chambered for .45 ACP. Fixed sights, polymer grips, 3.9" barrel, weight 30.4 oz. Introduced 2006.

NIB	Exc.	V.G.	Good	Fair	Poor
880	720	600	450	350	200

P220R Equinox

An 8+1 or 10+1 capacity single-/double-action semi-automatic. Chambered for .45 ACP. Fixed sights, wood grips, 4.4" barrel, weight 30.4 oz. Introduced 2006.

NIB	Exc.	V.G.	Good	Fair	Poor
1200	1050	750	600	450	300

P220R Carry Equinox

An 8+1 or 10+1 capacity single-/double-action semi-automatic. Chambered for .45 ACP. Fixed sights, wood grips, 3.9" barrel, weight 30.4 oz. Introduced 2006.

NIB	Exc.	V.G.	Good	Fair	Poor
880	700	580	450	350	200

P220 Langdon Edition

.45 ACP pistol introduced in 2004. Features 4.4" barrel, Nill wood grips, fiber optic sight, competition rear sight, front serrations, short trigger and other special features. Two-tone finish. Magazine capacity 8 rounds. Weight about 41 oz. Manufactured 500.

NIB	Exc.	V.G.	Good	Fair	Poor
1300	1050	800	600	450	250

P220 Combat

Similar to P220, with sand-colored alloy slide and steel frame. Threaded barrel for suppressor. Capacity 8+1 or 10+1. Designed for SOCOM side-arm trials. Introduced in 2007.

NIB	Exc.	V.G.	Good	Fair	Poor
1100	950	750	600	400	200

P220 Match

Similar to P220, with 5"barrel. Adjustable sights. Introduced 2007.

NIB	Exc.	V.G.	Good	Fair	Poor
950	800	680	500	300	150

P220 Super Match

Super-accurized version of P220 Match, with single-action only trigger, beavertail safety and custom wood grips. Limited edition.

NIB	Exc.	V.G.	Good	Fair	Poor
1200	980	850	600	400	200

P220 Compact

Similar to P220, with 3.9" barrel and 6+1 capacity. Single-action only or single-/double-action. Various finishes, grip and sight options.

NIB	Exc.	V.G.	Good	Fair	Poor
950	800	680	500	380	200

P220 Elite

Similar to P220, with SIG's new Short Reset Trigger (SRT). Beavertail safety, front cocking serrations, front strap checkering, SIGLITE\xa8 night sights and custom wood grips. Introduced in 2008. Also available in single-action only model.

NIB	Exc.	V.G.	Good	Fair	Poor
950	800	680	500	380	200

P220 Elite Stainless

Similar to above in stainless. Introduced 2008.

NIB	Exc.	V.G.	Good	Fair	Poor
1250	1100	880	650	450	200

P220 Carry Elite Stainless

Compact version of above, with 3.9" barrel; chambered in .45 ACP; 8-round capacity. Introduced 2008.

NIB	Exc.	V.G.	Good	Fair	Poor
1250	1100	880	650	450	200

P220 Platinum Elite

Fine-tuned enhanced version of P220 Elite, with front cocking serrations, front strap checkering, SIGLITE adjustable combat night sights and custom aluminum grips.

NIB	Exc.	V.G.	Good	Fair	Poor
1000	820	700	550	400	200

P220 Extreme

Two-tone black Nitron/stainless finish, with front slide serrations, SIGLITE night sights, Hogue G10 grips

NIB	Exc.	V.G.	Good	Fair	Poor
1000	850	750	600	450	350

P220 Hunter

Similar to above. 10mm, 8-round magazine. 5" match barrel. Adjustable rear sight, fiber-optic front. Textured G10 grip. Weight 39.4 oz. Kryptek camo finish.

NIB	Exc.	V.G.	Good	Fair	Poor
1630	1400	1230	960	630	530

P220 Legion

Similar to above. 10mm or .45 ACP, 8-round magazine. 4.4" or 5" match barrel. DA/SA or SAO trigger. Adjustable rear sight, fiber-optic front. Textured G10 grip with Legion medallion. Weight 30.4 oz. Legion gray finish. Note: Add $480 for 10mm.

NIB	Exc.	V.G.	Good	Fair	Poor
1420	1300	1070	800	700	500

P220 Legion Compact

Similar to above. 9mm, .357 SIG or .40 S&W, 12- or 15-round magazine. 3.9" barrel. DA/SA or SAO trigger. Night sights. Textured G10 grip with Legion medallion. Weight 34.4 oz. Legion gray finish. Note: Add $480 for RX optic model.

NIB	Exc.	V.G.	Good	Fair	Poor
1410	1300	1070	800	600	500

P224

Sub-compact variation of P220/229 series, with double-stack magazine, steel slide, alloy frame, black wood grips and SIGLITE night sights. In 9mm, .357 Sig or .40 S&W. Available with DA/SA or DAK trigger. Introduced in 2012

NIB	Exc.	V.G.	Good	Fair	Poor
1000	880	680	500	400	250

P225

Similar to Model P220, except chambered for 9mm cartridge. More compact pistol, with 3.86" barrel. Has 8-shot detachable magazine and adjustable sights. Finish is matte blue, K-Kote or electroless nickel plate, with black plastic grips. Overall length 7.1"; height 5.2"; weight 26.1 oz. No longer in production. Note: Add $70 K-Kote finish; $70 nickel slide.

NIB	Exc.	V.G.	Good	Fair	Poor
620	580	500	400	200	150

P225 Limited

This 9mm 3.9" model features Novak low-carry rear sight, three magazines, SIG-Sauer range bag. Introduced in 2004. Weight about 26 oz.

NIB	Exc.	V.G.	Good	Fair	Poor
800	620	500	400	280	150

P225-A

Reintroduction of P225 model. Several changes include an enhanced Short Reset Trigger and single-stack frame size. Chambered in 9mm, with 8-round magazine. Introduced in 2016. Note: Add $100 for night sights.

NIB	Exc.	V.G.	Good	Fair	Poor
1030	880	780	540	430	350

P226

Full-size high-capacity pistol, with 4.41" barrel. Chambered for 9mm or .40 S&W cartridge. In 1996, available chambered for .357 SIG cartridge, with 15- or 20-round detachable magazine and high-contrast sights. Blued, electroless nickel-plated or polymer finish (known as K-Kote). Overall length 7.7"; height 5.5"; weight 26.5 oz. Introduced in 1983. In 2003, available with integral rail system on frame. In 2004, offered with optional Crimson Trace laser grips. Note: Add $50 for K-Kote finish; $50 for nickel slide; $125 for Crimson Trace laser grips.

NIB	Exc.	V.G.	Good	Fair	Poor
820	600	550	450	300	200

P226BR .22

Similar to above in .22 LR. Note: Add $125 for Crimson Trace laser grips.

NIB	Exc.	V.G.	Good	Fair	Poor
550	480	350	250	180	100

P226 Navy Seal

Special limited edition 9mm pistol fitted with 4.4" barrel. Special serial numbers from "nsw0001" and above. Black finish.

NIB	Exc.	V.G.	Good	Fair	Poor
1400	900	750	550	400	300

P226 ST

Similar to P226, with stainless steel frame and slide. Offered in 9mm, .40 S&W and .357 SIG. Barrel length 4.4". Magazine capacity 10 rounds. Weight about 39 oz. Features include reverse two-tone finish, 3-dot sights and Hogue rubber grips. Very limited production in 2004 and 2005.

NIB	Exc.	V.G.	Good	Fair	Poor
1000	850	700	580	400	200

P226 Sport Stock

Introduced in 2002, this 9mm pistol features heavy match barrel and adjustable rear sight. Hand tuned. Specifications same as P226 ST. Available by special order only.

NIB	Exc.	V.G.	Good	Fair	Poor
1600	1450	1200	950	700	300

P226 Sport

Introduced in 2001. Similar to other SIG Sport models. Chambered for 9mm Luger cartridge. Stainless steel slide and frame. Adjustable target sights and competition barrel weight.

NIB	Exc.	V.G.	Good	Fair	Poor
1350	1180	1000	850	700	300

JP226 Jubilee Pistol

Variation is a special limited edition of P226. Each gun carries a special serial number prefixed JP. Grips are hand carved select European walnut. Slide and frame covered with solid gold wire inlays. Trigger, hammer, decocking lever, slide catch lever and magazine catch are all gold plated. Each pistol comes in custom fitted hard case of full leather. No longer imported into U.S. Fewer than 250 imported between 1991 and 1992.

NIB	Exc.	V.G.	Good	Fair	Poor
1800	1500	1200	900	700	400

P226R DAK

Introduced in 2005. Features double-action-only DAK trigger system, with double strike capability. Chambered for 9mm, .357 SIG or .40 S&W cartridge. Barrel 4.4". Fixed sights. Magazine capacity 10, 12 or 15 rounds. Weight about: 32 oz. 9mm; 34 oz. .357 SIG or .40 S&W.

NIB	Exc.	V.G.	Good	Fair	Poor
900	780	600	450	300	200

P226 X-Five

Single-action model chambered for 9mm or .40 S&W cartridge. Fitted with 5" barrel. Adjustable rear sight and trigger pull. Slide has front cocking serrations. Checkered Nill wood grips. Magazine capacity: 19 rounds 9mm; 14 rounds .40 S&W. Stainless steel finish. Weight about 47 oz.

NIB	Exc.	V.G.	Good	Fair	Poor
1700	1520	1280	900	550	300

P226 Tactical

9mm pistol has 4.98" extended threaded barrel. Fixed sights. Alloy frame. Magazine capacity 15 rounds. Weight about 32 oz. Black finish. Ellett Brothers exclusive. Introduced in 2005.

NIB	Exc.	V.G.	Good	Fair	Poor
900	800	600	450	300	150

P226 SAS

Double-action semi-automatic, with 12+1 capacity. Chambered for .40 S&W. Fixed sights, wood grips, 4.4" barrel, weight 34 oz., 6.5-lb. trigger. Introduced 2006.

NIB	Exc.	V.G.	Good	Fair	Poor
880	750	600	480	300	150

P226R Equinox

An 10+1 or 12+1 capacity single-/double-action semi-automatic. Chambered for .40 S&W. Fixed sights, wood grips, 4.4" barrel, weight 34 oz. Introduced 2006.

NIB	Exc.	V.G.	Good	Fair	Poor
1180	1020	880	700	550	350

P226 SCT

All black Nitron finished P226. Featuring front cocking serrations, SI-

GLITE rear night sight, TruGlo tritium fiber optic front sight. Comes with four newly designed 20-round magazines for 9mm; or four 15-round magazines for .40 S&W.

NIB	Exc.	V.G.	Good	Fair	Poor
950	820	700	580	400	200

P226 Elite

Introduced in 2008. Similar to P226, with redesigned short-reset trigger and improved ergonomics. Chambered in 9mm, .40 S&W and .357 SIG. Model P226 Enhanced Elite has same features as P226 Elite, with addition of ergonomic one-piece reduced-reach polymer grips.

NIB	Exc.	V.G.	Good	Fair	Poor
1050	900	820	680	450	250

P226 Elite Stainless

Similar to above in stainless steel.

NIB	Exc.	V.G.	Good	Fair	Poor
1100	1000	900	750	480	280

P226 Platinum Elite

Fine-tuned enhanced version of P226 Elite, with front cocking serrations, front strap checkering, SIGLITE adjustable combat night sights and custom aluminum grips.

NIB	Exc.	V.G.	Good	Fair	Poor
1250	1180	950	780	500	300

Mosquito

Model essentially a P226 reduced to 90 percent of its original size. Double-/single-action trigger fitted with 3.98" barrel. Chambered for .22 Long rifle cartridge. Polymer frame with Picatinny rail. Fixed sights. Magazine capacity 10 rounds. Weight about 24.5 oz. Black finish. Introduced in 2005.

NIB	Exc.	V.G.	Good	Fair	Poor
320	300	250	200	150	100

P226 SAO

Single-action only variation of Model P226. Made in Germany. Introduced 2013.

NIB	Exc.	V.G.	Good	Fair	Poor
1100	1000	850	600	450	350

P226 Legion

Similar to P226 SAO. Has custom G-10 grips, SIGLITE X-ray high visibility night sights, enhanced checkering on front strap and triggerguard, reduced and contoured beavertail and Legion gray finish. Introduced in 2016.

NIB	Exc.	V.G.	Good	Fair	Poor
1410	1300	1070	800	600	500

P226 MK25 Navy Model

A 9mm semi-automatic model, with black Nitron or Flat Dark Earth finish, Picatinny rail and night sights. Added touch of an anchor engraved on the slide.

NIB	Exc.	V.G.	Good	Fair	Poor
1000	900	750	500	400	250

P227

A .45 ACP chambered semi-automatic, with a slender double-stack 10-round magazine. Comes in several variations, with 3.9 or 4.4-in. barrel. Edges are dehorned and models available with/without a Picatinny rail. SIGLITE night sights are standard. Note: Add $100 for Equinox model, with wood grips. No longer in production.

NIB	Exc.	V.G.	Good	Fair	Poor
950	850	720	450	380	200

P228

Compact version of P226 fitted with 3.86" barrel. Chambered for 9mm cartridge. Available in blue, K-Kote or nickel finish, with black grips. Overall length 7.1"; height 5.4"; weight 26.1 oz. Made from 1990 to 1997; reintroduced 2004 to 2006. Note: Add $50 K-Kote finish; $50 nickel slide.

NIB	Exc.	V.G.	Good	Fair	Poor
720	600	480	350	200	150

P228 (New Model)

Reintroduced in 2013. Black Nitron or stainless two-tone finish. Standard single-/double-action operation, SIGLITE night sights, two 15-round magazines.

NIB	Exc.	V.G.	Good	Fair	Poor
1000	850	700	500	400	350

P229

Similar to P228 except chambered for .40 S&W cartridge. Has blackened stainless steel slide and lightweight aluminum alloy frame. Slide slightly larger to accommodate more powerful cartridge. In 1996, 9mm chamber also offered. Overall length 7.1"; height 5.4"; weight 27.54 oz. Magazine capacity 12 rounds. Introduced in 1992. In 1994, a new caliber for this model was introduced: .357 SIG developed by Federal. Magazine capacity 12 rounds.

NIB	Exc.	V.G.	Good	Fair	Poor
800	680	550	400	250	150

P229 Nickel

Same as standard P229. with full nickel finish over stainless steel slide and alloy frame. Weight about 27.5 oz. Introduced in 1998.

NIB	Exc.	V.G.	Good	Fair	Poor
850	520	600	450	280	180

P229 Stainless

Introduced in 2005. Same features as standard P229 except for stainless steel slide and frame. Weight about 41 oz. Magazine capacity 12 rounds.

NIB	Exc.	V.G.	Good	Fair	Poor
900	780	600	480	300	150

P229 Sport

Chambered for .357 SIG cartridge. Fitted with 4.8" barrel, with muzzle compensator. Adjustable target sights. Both frame and slide are stainless steel. Magazine capacity 10 rounds. Weight about 41 oz. Introduced in 1998.

NIB	Exc.	V.G.	Good	Fair	Poor
1500	1350	1180	950	600	400

P229 Limited

.40 S&W pistol features 3.9" barrel with fixed sights. Stainless steel slide with Nitron finish. Scroll engraving on top of slide, high polished 24 kt gold accents on trigger, hammer, magazine catch and grip screws. Hardwood grips.

NIB	Exc.	V.G.	Good	Fair	Poor
950	820	680	500	350	200

P229 Combo

Chambered for .40 S&W cartridge and fitted with 3.9" barrel. Fixed sights. Black Nitron finish. Spare barrel chambered for .357 SIG included. Magazine capacity 10 rounds. Weight about 30 oz. Introduced in 2004.

NIB	Exc.	V.G.	Good	Fair	Poor
900	780	620	450	300	180

P229 Elite

Features ergonomic beavertail grip, front cocking serrations, front strap checkering, SIGLITE night sights, custom wood grips and new Short Reset Trigger (SRT). Available in 9mm and .40 S&W. P229 Enhanced Elite has same features as P229 Elite, with addition of ergonomic one-piece reduced-reach polymer grips.

NIB	Exc.	V.G.	Good	Fair	Poor
1100	900	820	680	450	250

P229 Platinum Elite

Fine-tuned enhanced version of P229 Elite, with front cocking serrations, front strap checkering, SIGLITE adjustable combat night sights and custom aluminum grips.

NIB	Exc.	V.G.	Good	Fair	Poor
1100	900	800	700	480	300

P229R DAK

Introduced in 2005. Features double-action only DAK trigger system, with double strike capability. Chambered for 9mm, .357 SIG or .40 S&W cartridge, with 4.4" barrel. Fixed sights. Magazine capacity 10, 12 or 15 rounds. Weight about: 32 oz. 9mm; 34 oz. .357 SIG or .40 S&W.

NIB	Exc.	V.G.	Good	Fair	Poor
850	520	600	450	280	180

P229 SCT

All black Nitron finished P229 featuring front cocking serrations, SIGLITE rear night sight, TruGlo tritium fiber optic front sight. Comes with four newly designed 17-round magazines for 9mm; or four 14-round magazines for .40 S&W.

NIB	Exc.	V.G.	Good	Fair	Poor
1100	950	800	680	500	300

1911 C3

Compact 1911-style autoloader features 7+1 capacity, two-tone finish, custom rosewood grips and 4.2" barrel. Alloy frame gives an unloaded weight of just under 30 oz.

NIB	Exc.	V.G.	Good	Fair	Poor
900	780	600	480	300	150

1911 Platinum Elite

1911-style 8+1 autoloader in .45 ACP, 5"barrel, Nitron frame, aluminum grips. Introduced in 2008.

NIB	Exc.	V.G.	Good	Fair	Poor
1100	950	800	680	500	300

1911 Platinum Elite Carry

Compact version of above, with 4.5" barrel. Introduced in 2008.

NIB	Exc.	V.G.	Good	Fair	Poor
1250	1020	880	750	580	350

1911-22

Same dimensions as standard 1911 pistol. Caliber .22 LR, alloy frame and slide, 10-round magazine, blowback operated, extended thumb safety, extended beavertail grip safety, magazine disconnect safety, skeletonized hammer and trigger. Weight 18 oz. Nitron finish.

NIB	Exc.	V.G.	Good	Fair	Poor
340	280	240	200	160	100

1911 Scorpion

Caliber .45 ACP, stainless steel slide and frame, 8-round magazine, extended thumb safety, extended beavertail grip safety, skeletonized hammer and flat trigger, checkered front strap and mainspring housing, Low-Mount night sights and accessory rail. Frame and slide has Cerkote desert tan finish, grips are Hogue G10 Magwell with Piranha texture.

NIB	Exc.	V.G.	Good	Fair	Poor
980	850	700	500	300	150

Emperor Scorpion Full-Size

NIB	Exc.	V.G.	Good	Fair	Poor
1200	1000	980	930	790	—

Fastback Emperor Scorpion Carry

NIB	Exc.	V.G.	Good	Fair	Poor
1380	1200	1080	980	900	—

Model GSR

.45 ACP pistol introduced in 2004. Fitted with 5" barrel. Single-action only. Offered with white stainless steel frame and slide or blued frame and slide. Also offered with black Nitron finish. Tac rail standard. Hand-fitted. Magazine capacity 8 rounds. Weight about 39 oz.

NIB	Exc.	V.G.	Good	Fair	Poor
1000	850	680	500	300	150

1911 STX

From SIG SAUER Custom Shop. This is a two-tone non-railed 1911, with Nitron slide over a natural stainless frame. Frame and slide are carefully machined and hand-fitted and dehorned for comfortable carry. Other features include match-grade barrel, extended ambidextrous thumb safety, beavertail safety with speed bump, checkered front strap and mainspring housing. Custom wood grips.

NIB	Exc.	V.G.	Good	Fair	Poor
1000	970	950	800	750	—

Fastback Nightmare Carry

NIB	Exc.	V.G.	Good	Fair	Poor
1300	1100	1000	940	800	—

1911 TACOPS TB

Tactical Operations model has an integral accessory rail, ambidextrous safety, Ergo XT grips, low profile night sights and threaded barrel.

NIB	Exc.	V.G.	Good	Fair	Poor
1000	850	680	500	300	150

REVOLUTION SERIES

Revolution

All-stainless frames and slides in four configurations. Novak night sights, rose/diamondwood custom grips. Stainless or Nitron finish. 8+1 capacity, 45 ACP, single-action, 5" barrel, 40.3 oz. Introduced 2006.

NIB	Exc.	V.G.	Good	Fair	Poor
900	780	600	480	300	150

Revolution Custom STX

Single-action .45 ACP stainless semi-automatic with 8+1 capacity. Adjustable combat night sights and custom wood grip panels, 5" barrel, 40.6 oz. Introduced 2006.

NIB	Exc.	V.G.	Good	Fair	Poor
1100	950	800	680	500	300

Revolution TTT

Stainless semi-automatic with 8+1 capacity. Single-action .45 ACP. Adjustable combat night sights and custom wood grip panels, 5" barrel, 40.3 oz. Introduced 2006.

NIB	Exc.	V.G.	Good	Fair	Poor
1000	850	680	580	420	300

Revolution XO

Single-action .45 ACP stainless semi-automatic with 8+1 capacity. Polymer grip panels. 8.65" LOA, 5" barrel, 40.3 oz. Introduced 2006.

NIB	Exc.	V.G.	Good	Fair	Poor
900	780	600	480	300	150

Revolution Target

Single-action .45 ACP stainless semi-automatic with 8+1 capacity. Adjustable target night sights. Custom wood grip panels, 5" barrel, 40.3 oz. Stainless or Nitron finish. Introduced 2006.

NIB	Exc.	V.G.	Good	Fair	Poor
950	820	650	500	320	150

Revolution Carry

Single-action .45 ACP stainless semi-automatic with 8+1 capacity. Fixed sights. Custom wood grip panels, 4" barrel, 35.4 oz. Stainless or Nitron finish. Introduced 2006.

NIB	Exc.	V.G.	Good	Fair	Poor
900	780	600	480	300	150

Revolution Compact

Stainless semi-automatic single-action .45 ACP with 6+1 capacity. Fixed sights. Custom wood grip panels, 4" barrel, 30.3 oz. Stainless or Nitron finish. Introduced 2006.

NIB	Exc.	V.G.	Good	Fair	Poor
950	820	650	500	320	150

Revolution Compact SAS

Dehorned version of Revolution Compact.

NIB	Exc.	V.G.	Good	Fair	Poor
950	820	650	500	320	150

Revolution Compact C3

Similar to Revolution Compact, with black anodized alloy frame and stainless or Nitron finish slide.

NIB	Exc.	V.G.	Good	Fair	Poor
950	820	650	500	320	150

Revolution Custom Compact RCS

Stainless semi-automatic single-action .45 ACP with 6+1 capacity. Fixed sights. Custom wood grip panels, 4" barrel, 30.3 oz. Stainless or Nitron finish. Introduced 2006.

NIB	Exc.	V.G.	Good	Fair	Poor
950	820	650	500	320	150

P238

Compact .380 single-action with 1911-style controls, but no grip safety. Offered in many grip and finish variations. Ambidextrous safety available. Note: Add $100 for rosewood grips or Hogue rubber grips; $50 for ambidextrous safety.

NIB	*Exc.*	*V.G.*	*Good*	*Fair*	*Poor*
640	550	450	400	300	200

P938

Slightly larger version of P238. Chambered in 9mm. Other features similar to P238. Available with many grip and finish options.

NIB	*Exc.*	*V.G.*	*Good*	*Fair*	*Poor*
700	620	520	450	350	220

P239

Introduced in 1996. Chambered for 9mm, .40 S&W or .357 SIG cartridge. Double-/single-action or double-action only. Barrel 3.6" long. Overall length 6.6"; weight 25 oz. Fitted with a single-column magazine: 7 rounds .357 SIG; 8 rounds 9mm. Discontinued. Note: All of the above SIG pistols from P220 to P239 are available with "SIGLITE" night sights. Add $80 for these optional sights. Also was offered with Crimson Trace Lasergrips. Add $250 for this option.

NIB	*Exc.*	*V.G.*	*Good*	*Fair*	*Poor*
900	750	600	400	200	150

P239 Limited

This .40 S&W features rainbow titanium slide, trigger, hammer, grip screws and control levers. Magazine capacity 7 rounds. Weight about 27 oz. Introduced in 2004.

NIB	*Exc.*	*V.G.*	*Good*	*Fair*	*Poor*
900	750	600	400	200	150

P230

Semi-automatic compact pocket-type pistol. Chambered for .22 LR, .32 ACP, .380 ACP and 9mm Ultra. Has 3.62-in. barrel. 10-, 8- or 7-round magazine. Weight between 16.2 oz. and 20.8 oz. Finish blued or stainless, with black plastic grips. Manufactured from 1976. In 1996, a two-tone finish was offered. No longer in production. Note: Add $85 for stainless steel finish; $35 for stainless steel slide.

NIB	*Exc.*	*V.G.*	*Good*	*Fair*	*Poor*
480	460	350	260	220	200

P232

Improved model of P230. Incorporates numerous changes to improve function and reliability. Basic features, operation and dimensions remain the same as P230.

NIB	*Exc.*	*V.G.*	*Good*	*Fair*	*Poor*
450	380	300	250	200	150

P232 (1998 Model)

In 1998, this model has as standard features night sights and Hogue grips, with an all stainless steel finish. Chambered for .380 ACP. Has 7-round magazine. Weight about 21 oz.

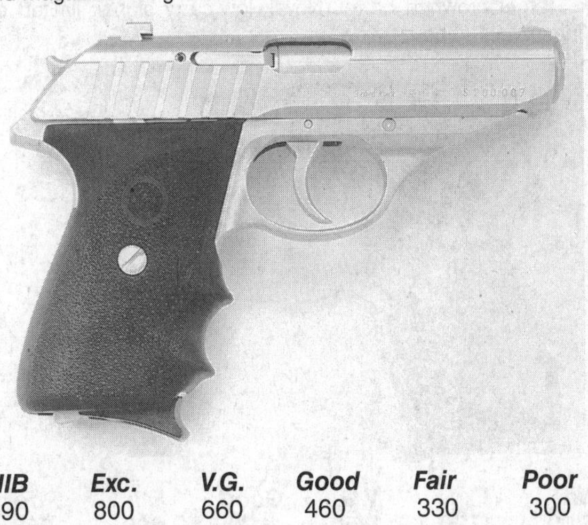

NIB	*Exc.*	*V.G.*	*Good*	*Fair*	*Poor*
890	800	660	460	330	300

P232 Limited

This .380 pistol features a black finish, night sights and satin nickel accents. Hogue rubber grips with finger grooves. Magazine capacity 7 rounds. Weight about 28 oz. Introduced in 2004.

NIB	Exc.	V.G.	Good	Fair	Poor
580	450	380	250	200	100

P245 Compact

Introduced in 1999. Chambered for .45 ACP cartridge. Fitted with 3.9" barrel. Magazine capacity 6 rounds. Overall length 7.3"; weight about 28 oz. Available finishes are blue and K-Kote. SIGLITE night sights also available.

NIB	Exc.	V.G.	Good	Fair	Poor
780	650	500	380	250	150

P245 Custom Shop

Introduced in 2004. This .45 ACP pistol limited to 75 guns. Features Teflon-impregnated nickel slide, frame, trigger, hammer, etc. Hand-tuned action. Target crowned barrel. Novak low-carry sights, limited edition markings. Weight about 27 oz.

NIB	Exc.	V.G.	Good	Fair	Poor
2100	1700	1450	1000	600	350

P250

Modular pistol comes in full, compact (shown) and sub-compact size. Offered in 9mm, .357 SIG, .380 ACP (sub-compact only), .40 S&W and .45 ACP. Double-stack magazine capacity 17 rounds (9mm & .380), 14 rounds (.357 & .40), 10 rounds (.45). Design allows shooter to change calibers, grip size and model size. Double-action-only operation. Features include an accessory rail, Nitron slide finish, contrast or SIGLITE night sights. A compact .22 rimfire version is available, with similar features. Note: Add $80 for night sights. Deduct $50 for .22 rimfire version.

NIB	Exc.	V.G.	Good	Fair	Poor
420	380	350	300	250	180

P290

New micro-compact pistol for concealed carry. Caliber 9mm Parabellum is double-action only, with stainless steel slide, polymer frame, 6-round magazine, three-dot sights and removable grip panels. Weight 20.5 oz., barrel length 2.9". Finish is Nitron or two-tone stainless. Available with detachable laser sight. Note: Add $70 for laser sight.

NIB	Exc.	V.G.	Good	Fair	Poor
450	400	380	320	280	200

P320

Double-action only available in 9mm, .40 S&W, .357 SIG or .45 ACP. Barrel length 4.7". Double-stack magazine capacity (rounds): 10 (.45), 14 (.357 and .40), 17 (9mm). Other features include SIGLITE night sights, interchangeable grip panels and black Nitron finish. Also available in compact (3.9" barrel) and sub-compact (3.6") models. Disassembly process uses a take-down lever and does not require pulling the trigger. M17 variant of P320 has been selected by U.S. Army to replace Beretta M9 service pistol. Note: On August 8, 2017, SIG SAUER issued a press release with the following information: P320 meets U.S. standards for safety, including American National Standards Institute (ANSI), Sporting Arms Ammunition Manufacturer's Institute, Inc. (SAAMI), National Institute of Justice (NIJ), as well as rigorous testing protocols for global military and law enforcement agencies. Recent events indicate that dropping the P320 beyond U.S. standards for safety may cause an unintentional discharge. As a result of input from law enforcement, government and military customers, SIG has developed a number of enhancements in function, reliability and overall safety, including drop performance. SIG

SAUER is offering these enhancements to its customers. Details of this program are available at sigsauer.com. The M17 variant of P320, selected by the U.S. government as U.S. Army's Modular Handgun System (MHS), is not affected by the Voluntary Upgrade.

NIB	Exc.	V.G.	Good	Fair	Poor
600	520	450	350	300	200

P320 RX

Same specifications as full-size P320, plus slide-mounted reflex optical sight.

NIB	Exc.	V.G.	Good	Fair	Poor
800	700	600	400	300	250

P320 RXP Full-Size

Caliber: 9mm. Capacity: 17-round magazine. Barrel: 4.7 in. Grips: Textured polymer. Sights: Romeo1Pro red dot, suppressor contrast 3-dot. Length: 8 in. overall. Weight: 30 oz. unloaded. Finish: Nitron.

NIB	Exc.	V.G.	Good	Fair	Poor
780	—	—	—	—	—

P320 RXP Compact

Caliber: 9mm. Capacity: 15-round magazine. Barrel: 3.9 in. Grips: Textured polymer. Sights: Romeo1Pro red dot, suppressor contrast 3-dot. Length: 7.2 in. overall. Weight: 26 oz. unloaded. Finish: Nitron.

NIB	Exc.	V.G.	Good	Fair	Poor
780	—	—	—	—	—

P320 RXP XFull-Size

Caliber: 9mm. Capacity: 17-round magazine. Barrel: 4.7 in. Grips: Textured polymer. Sights: Romeo1Pro red dot, suppressor contrast 3-dot. Length: 8 in. overall. Weight: 30 oz. unloaded. Finish: Nitron.

NIB	Exc.	V.G.	Good	Fair	Poor
780	—	—	—	—	—

P320 XFive Legion

Caliber: 9mm. Capacity: 17-round magazine. Barrel: 5 in. Grips: Textured polymer. Sights: Dawson Precision adjustable rear, fiber-optic front, optic ready. Length: 8.5 in. overall. Weight: 43.5 oz. unloaded. Finish: Legion gray. Features: TXG tungsten infused heavy XGrip module, slide has lightening cuts, Henning Group aluminum magazine basepads.

NIB	Exc.	V.G.	Good	Fair	Poor
920	—	—	—	—	—

P320P320 TACOPS

Variant of P320 in 9mm only. Large grip and magazine, with 21-round capacity. Comes with four magazines. Fiber optic front, SIGLITE rear sights. Note: Add $50 for compact model, with 3.9" threaded barrel.

NIB	Exc.	V.G.	Good	Fair	Poor
680	600	500	400	300	250

P320 X-Five

The X-Series grip module is exclusive to this line. Features a deeper triggerguard undercut, higher backstrap and an extended beavertail. Also has a removable grip weight for improved balance, removable magazine funnel and extended slide catch lever. X-Five has the straight trigger that breaks at 90 degree. The 5" bull barrel is equipped with Dawson Precision fiber optic front and fully adjustable rear sights. Each P320 X-Five includes four 21-round steel magazines.

NIB	Exc.	V.G.	Good	Fair	Poor
850	750	600	500	350	200

P320 M17

Similar to above. Civilian version of U.S. military M17. 9mm, 17-round magazine. 4.7" barrel. Striker-fire trigger. Night sights. Weight 29.6 oz. Coyote tan finish.

NIB	Exc.	V.G.	Good	Fair	Poor
770	660	580	440	340	300

P320-M18

Caliber: 9mm. Capacity: 17-round magazine. Barrel: 3.9 in. Grips: Textured polymer. Sights: Siglite front/night rear, optic ready. Length: 7.2 in. overall. Weight: 28.1 oz. unloaded. Finish: Coyote tan. Features: Commercial version of U.S. Military M18, manual thumb safety.

NIB	Exc.	V.G.	Good	Fair	Poor
600	—	—	—	—	—

P365

A micro-compact striker-fired 9mm model with 10-round magazine, 3.1-inch barrel, stainless steel frame and slide, XRAY-3 day/night sights, fully textured polymer grip, accessory rail, front and rear slide serrations. Introduced in 2018.

NIB	Exc.	V.G.	Good	Fair	Poor
600	500	430	340	280	260

P365 XL

Caliber: 9mm. Capacity: 12-round magazine. Barrel: 3.7 in. Grips: Textured polymer. Sights: Optic-ready, Day/Night sights. Length: 6.6 in. overall. Weight: 20.7 oz. unloaded. Finish: Nitron. Features: Grip with integrated carry mag well and extended beavertail, flat trigger and optic-ready slide.

NIB	Exc.	V.G.	Good	Fair	Poor
590	—	—	—	—	—

P365 XL RomeoZero

Caliber: 9mm. Capacity: 12-round magazine. Barrel: 3.7 in. Grips: Textured polymer. Sights: RomeoZero red dot, Xray3 front sight. Length: 6.6 in. overall. Weight: 20.7 oz. unloaded. Finish: Nitron. Features: Grip with integrated carry mag well and extended beavertail, and flat trigger.

NIB	Exc.	V.G.	Good	Fair	Poor
680	—	—	—	—	—

P365SAS

Caliber: 9mm. Capacity: 10-round magazine. Barrel: 3.1 in. Grips: Textured polymer. Sights: Flush-mounted FT Bullseye fiber-tritium night sight. Length: 5.8 in. overall. Weight: 17.8 oz. unloaded. Finish: Nitron. Features: Ported slide and barrel, Sig Anti Snag (SAS) treatment.

NIB	Exc.	V.G.	Good	Fair	Poor
550	—	—	—	—	—

SIG PRO SERIES

SP2340

Introduced in 1998. Chambered for .357 SIG or .40 S&W cartridge. Built on a polymer frame with accessory rails on the dust cover. Barrel length 3.9". Standard finish blue. Weight about 28 oz. Comes with two sets of interchangeable grips and two 10-round magazines. Available in single-/double-action or double-action only.

SP2340 with laser sights.

NIB	Exc.	V.G.	Good	Fair	Poor
650	520	450	380	300	150

SP2009

Similar to SP2340. Chambered for 9mm cartridge. Weight about 25 oz. Magazine capacity 10 rounds.

NIB	Exc.	V.G.	Good	Fair	Poor
500	420	350	220	180	100

SP2022

Chambered for 9mm, .357 SIG or .40 S&W cartridges. Fitted with 3.85" barrel, with fixed sights. Polymer frame. Black finish. Weight about 27 to 30 oz. Magazine capacity 10 or 12 rounds, depending on caliber.

NIB	Exc.	V.G.	Good	Fair	Poor
580	450	320	250	200	150

SHOTGUNS

Model SA3 Hunter

Introduced in 1997. Over/under shotgun chambered for 20-gauge shell. Fitted with 26" or 28" barrels. Single-selective trigger and automatic ejectors. Stock figured walnut, with pistol grip. Receiver polished steel, with engraved game scenes. Weight about 6.8 lbs.

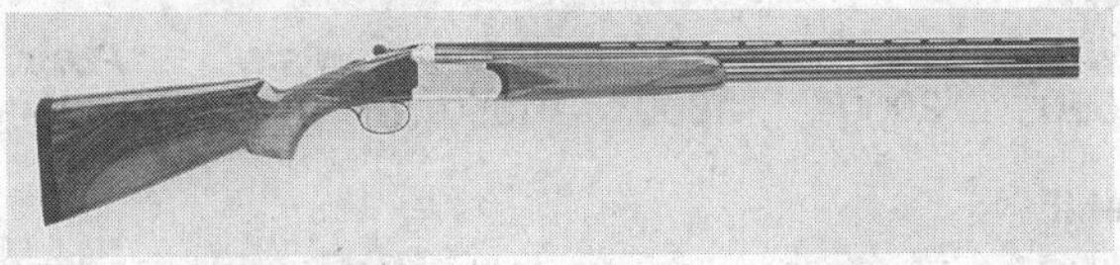

NIB	Exc.	V.G.	Good	Fair	Poor
1200	1050	750	600	400	300

Model SA3 Sporting

12-gauge over/under introduced in 1998. Features 28" or 29.5" barrel, with wide 11mm rib. Front and mid-target sights. Both barrels and action blued. Walnut stock, with pistol grip and recoil pad. Weight about 7.3 lbs.

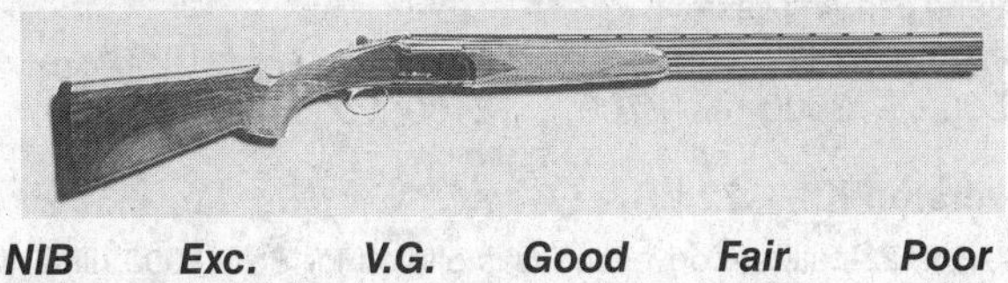

NIB	Exc.	V.G.	Good	Fair	Poor
1680	1250	1000	700	500	400

Model SA5 Sporting

Introduced in 1998. This 12-gauge fitted with choice of 28" or 29.5" barrels. Single-selective trigger and automatic ejectors are standard. Barrels fitted with 10mm rib. Receiver polished steel, with engraved clay target on each side. Weight about 7.6 lbs.

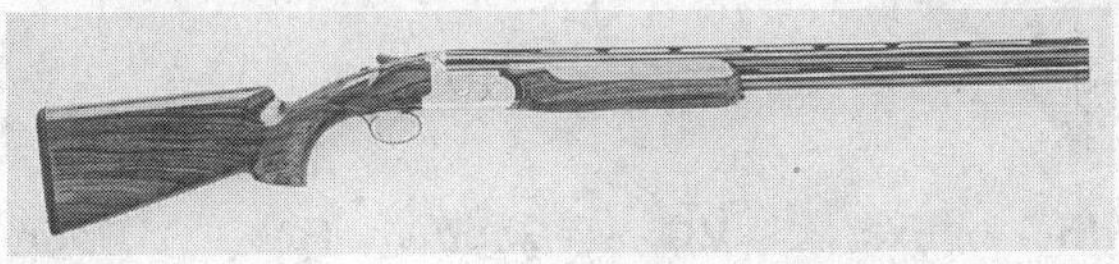

NIB	Exc.	V.G.	Good	Fair	Poor
2500	2000	1500	1100	750	500

AURORA SERIES

These shotguns were first imported and introduced into SIG product line in 2000. They are made in Italy by B. Rizzini. All guns in this series are over/under guns.

Aurora TR Field Shotguns

All the TR field guns offered in 12-, 20-, 28-gauge and .410 bore. All have single triggers and ejectors. Barrel lengths 26" or 28". Weights vary:7 lbs. 12-gauge; to 6 lbs. .410. Select walnut stock, with oil-finish. Cut checkering of 20 lpi. Choke tubes on 12- and 20-gauge; Fixed chokes on 28-gauge and .410 bore.

TR 20U

Features a boxlock action, with case-hardened frame. No engraving. Straight-grip stock.

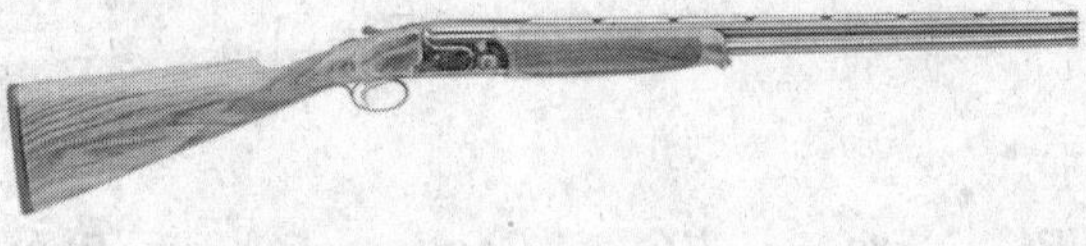

Aurora TR 20U 28 gauge

NIB	Exc.	V.G.	Good	Fair	Poor
2000	1750	1480	1200	900	400

TR 20

Features a boxlock action, with nickel finish and no engraving. Pistol grip.

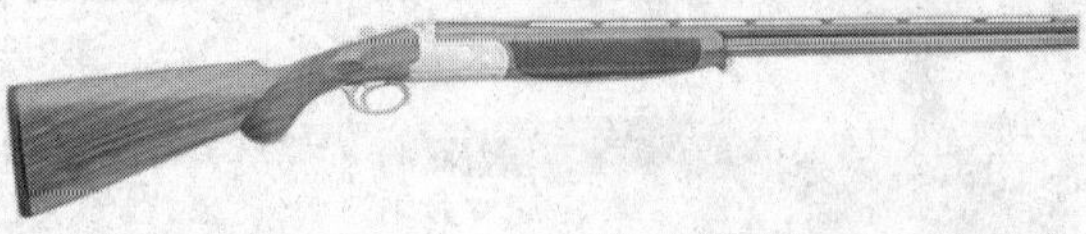

Aurora TR 20 .410 bore

NIB	Exc.	V.G.	Good	Fair	Poor
1850	1500	1320	1000	750	300

TR 30

Features case-hardened action, with side plates. No engraving. Pistol grip.

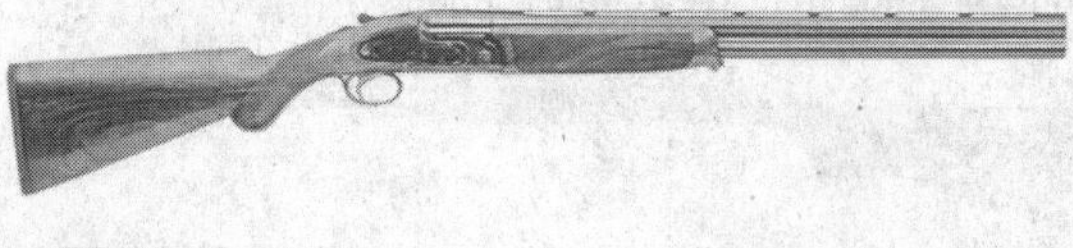

Aurora TR 30 12 gauge

NIB	Exc.	V.G.	Good	Fair	Poor
2220	1850	1550	1380	1000	400

TR 40 Silver

Features silver action and side plates with gold inlaid game scenes. Pistol grip.

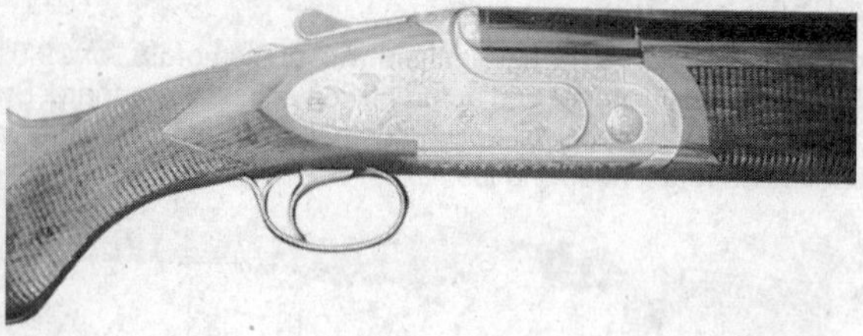

NIB	Exc.	V.G.	Good	Fair	Poor
2580	2100	1550	1200	950	450

TR 40 Gold

Features case-hardened action and side plates with gold inlaid game scenes. Pistol grip.

NIB	Exc.	V.G.	Good	Fair	Poor
2680	2000	1450	1100	800	500

New Englander

Introduced in 2000 jointly by SIG and L.L. Bean. This over/under chambered in 12- and 20-gauge. Choice of 26" or 28" barrels. Single-selective trigger, auto ejectors, choke tubes all standard. L.L. Bean logo inlaid in gold on receiver. Select turkish walnut stock, with oil-finish. Prince of Wales-style pistol grip and rubber recoil pad.

NIB	Exc.	V.G.	Good	Fair	Poor
2000	1500	1200	900	700	350

TT 25 Competition

Offered in 12- and 20-gauge, with 28" to 32" barrels for 12-gauge; 28" or 30" barrels for 20-gauge. Choke tubes. Single-selective auto ejectors are standard. Wide competition ventilated rib. Pistol grip on select walnut stock, with 20 lpi checkering. Weight about: 12-gauge 7.25 lbs.; 20-gauge 6.75 lbs.

Aurora TT 25 12 gauge

NIB	Exc.	V.G.	Good	Fair	Poor
2000	1500	1200	900	700	350

TT45

Similar to TT25, with addition of case-hardened receiver and side plates with engraving and gold inlay game scenes.

NIB	Exc.	V.G.	Good	Fair	Poor
3280	2800	2200	1780	1300	450

RIFLES

SIG AMT

Semi-automatic rifle chambered for .308 cartridge. Fitted with 19" barrel and wooden buttstock and forearm. Folding bipod standard. Box magazine capacity 5, 10 or 20 rounds. Weight about 10 lbs. Built from 1960 to 1974.

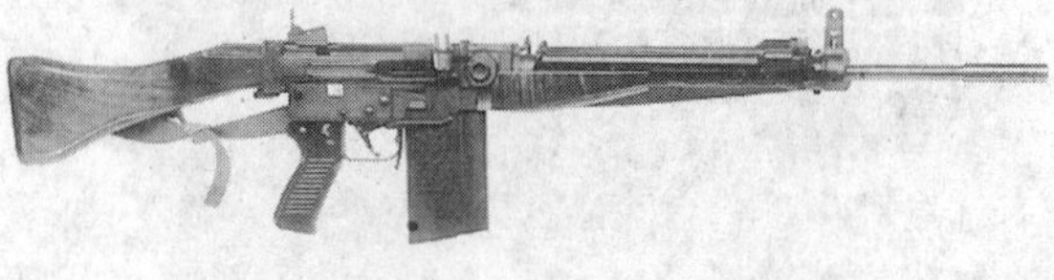

Courtesy Rock Island Auction Company

NIB	Exc.	V.G.	Good	Fair	Poor
8000	6800	5800	4000	3000	2000

SIG PE-57

Similar to above. Chambered for 7.5x55 Swiss cartridge.

NIB	Exc.	V.G.	Good	Fair	Poor
15000	12000	10000	8500	7000	4000

SIG 550

Semi-automatic rifle chambered for .223 cartridge. Fitted with 18" barrel.

NIB	Exc.	V.G.	Good	Fair	Poor
18000	12000	10000	8500	7000	4000

SIG 551

Same as above. Fitted with 16" barrel.

NIB	Exc.	V.G.	Good	Fair	Poor
10500	9500	7500	4000	2000	1000

SSG 2000

High-grade bolt-action sniping-type rifle. Chambered for .223, 7.5mm Swiss, .300 Wby. Magnum and .308 Win. Has a 24" barrel and 4-round box magazine. Furnished without sights. Finish matte blue, with thumbhole-style stippled walnut stock with adjustable cheekpiece. Discontinued in 1986.

NIB	Exc.	V.G.	Good	Fair	Poor
8000	6000	3500	2700	1500	—

SSG 3000

Chambered for .308 Win. cartridge. Fitted with 23.4" barrel and ambidextrous McMillian Tactical stock. Magazine capacity 5 rounds. Overall length 46.5"; weight about 12 lbs. Model comes in three different packages.

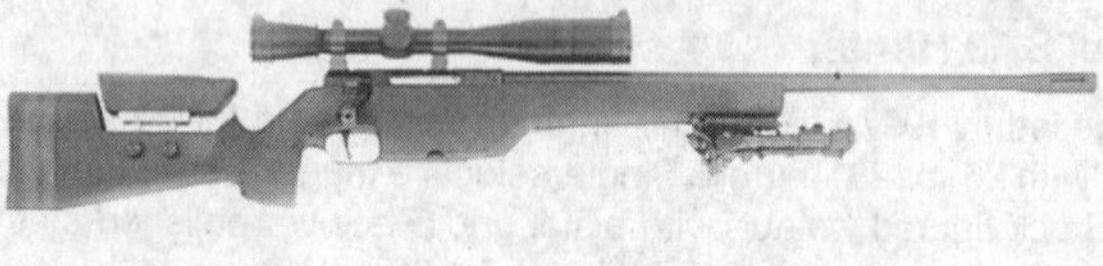

Level I

NIB	Exc.	V.G.	Good	Fair	Poor
2550	2000	1600	1350	950	600

Level II

At this level a Leupold Vari-X III 3.5-10x40mm Duplex scope and Harris bipod, with carrying case.

NIB	Exc.	V.G.	Good	Fair	Poor
3500	2750	2300	1700	1200	600

Level III

Supplied with Leupold Mark 4 M1-10x40mm Mil-Dot Scope, with Harris bipod and carrying case.

NIB	Exc.	V.G.	Good	Fair	Poor
4500	3500	2700	2400	1500	700

Conversion Kit—.22 LR

In 2001, a .22-caliber conversion was offered for SSG 3000 rifle. Kit includes a heavy contured barrel bolt and 5-round magazine.

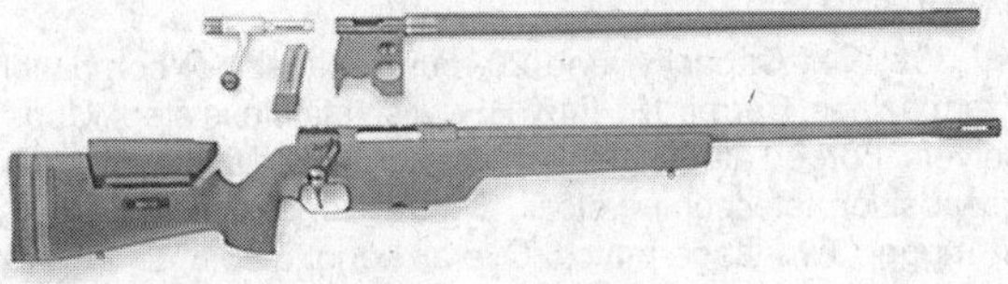

NIB	Exc.	V.G.	Good	Fair	Poor
750	—	—	—	—	—

Model SHR 970

Introduced in 1998. Bolt-action rifle chambered for .25-06 Rem., .270, .280 Rem., .30-06 or .308 cartridges. Has a 22" barrel. Receiver drilled and tapped for scope mounts. Detachable box magazine. Stock black synthetic or walnut. Barrels are interchangeable. Weight about 7.2 lbs. Note: Add $30 for walnut stock.

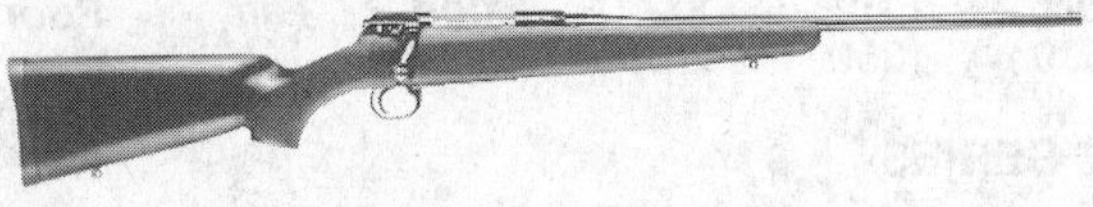

NIB	Exc.	V.G.	Good	Fair	Poor
720	650	580	400	300	200

Model SHR 970 Magnum

Same as above, but chambered for 7mm Rem. Magnum or .300 Win. Magnum. Barrel length 24". Weight about 7.4 lbs. Note: Add $30 for walnut stock.

NIB	Exc.	V.G.	Good	Fair	Poor
780	720	620	450	350	250

Model SHR 970 Tactical

Introduced in 2000. Features a McMillan stock, non-reflective metal coating, heavy fluted contoured barrel, integral muzzle brake. Chambered for .308 Win. or .300 Win. Magnum cartridges. Receiver drilled and tapped for scope mount. Stock has a fitted rubber recoil pad.

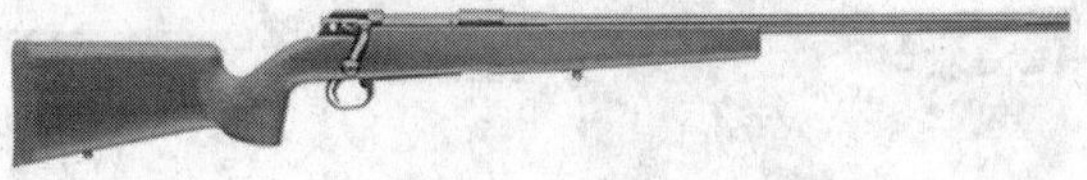

NIB	Exc.	V.G.	Good	Fair	Poor
1400	1200	1000	780	600	400

Model 202 Standard

Bolt-action rifle features synthetic or Turkish walnut stock. Bolt is jeweled. Detachable 3-round box magazine. Offered in standard calibers from .22-250 to .30-06 and Magnum calibers from 7mm Rem. Magnum to .375 H&H Magnum. Barrel length 24" for standard calibers; 26" for Magnum calibers. Weight about 7.5 lbs.

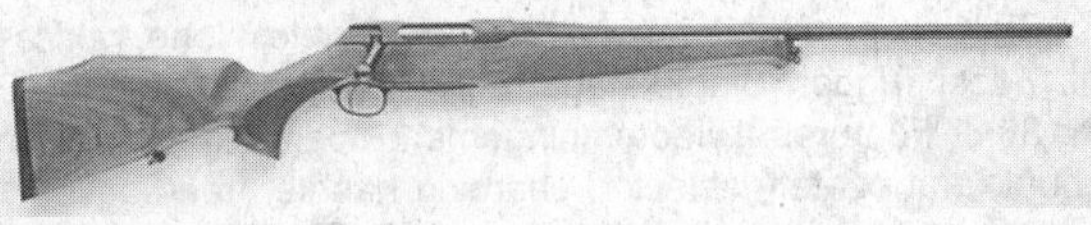

NIB	Exc.	V.G.	Good	Fair	Poor
1650	1200	980	750	600	400

Model 202 Lightweight

Features a black synthetic stock, fluted barrel. Chambered for .22-250, .243, .25-06, .270 or .30-05 calibers. Barrel length 24". Magazine capacity 3 rounds. Alloy receiver and quick change barrel system are standard. Weight about 6.5 lbs. Introduced in 2001.

NIB	Exc.	V.G.	Good	Fair	Poor
1600	1150	920	700	550	350

Model 202 Varmint

Chambered for .22-250, .243 or .25-06 cartridge. Fitted with 26" fluted bull barrel. Stock Turkish walnut, with adjustable cheekpiece. Three-round detachable box magazine. Quick change barrel system. Weight about 9.5 lbs.

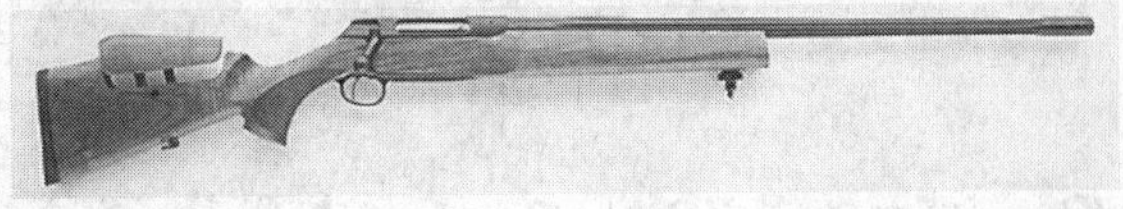

NIB	Exc.	V.G.	Good	Fair	Poor
1600	1150	920	700	550	350

Model 202 Supreme

Bolt-action model chambered for .243, .25-06, 6.5x55 Swedish, .270 Win., .308 Win. or .30-06. Fitted with 24" barrel. Synthetic or walnut stock. Magazine capacity 3 rounds. Weight about 7.7 lbs. No sights. Note: Add $50 for walnut stock.

NIB	Exc.	V.G.	Good	Fair	Poor
1800	1650	1400	1100	800	400

Model 202 Supreme Magnum

As above, but chambered for 7mm Rem. Magnum, .300 Win. Magnum, .300 Wby. Magnum or .375 H&H Magnum. Magazine capacity 3 rounds. Synthetic or walnut stock. Weight about 8.4 lbs. Note: Add $50 for walnut stock.

NIB	Exc.	V.G.	Good	Fair	Poor
1880	1720	1480	1150	850	450

SIG 556

Generally similar to SIG 556, but made in USA. Chambered in 5.56 NATO. Collapsible stock, 16" mil-spec barrel, Picatinny rail and all the trendy tactical goodies. Introduced 2006.

NIB	Exc.	V.G.	Good	Fair	Poor
1700	1400	1200	900	700	500

SIG 556 Classic SWAT

Features a 16" military grade cold hammer forged barrel. Chambered in 5.56mm NATO, with a twist rate of 1 in 7". High performance flash suppressor, vented tactical quad rail forearm machined from aircraft grade aluminum alloy and hard coat anodized for durability, quad rail with four Picatinny rails, Picatinny equipped receiver. Rifle comes standard with flip-up combat front and rear sight system. Trigger housing machined from an aircraft grade aluminum alloy forging, with a hard-coat anodized finish designed to survive extreme conditions. Rifle comes equipped with a smooth two-stage trigger, ambidextrous safety and designed to accept standard AR magazines.

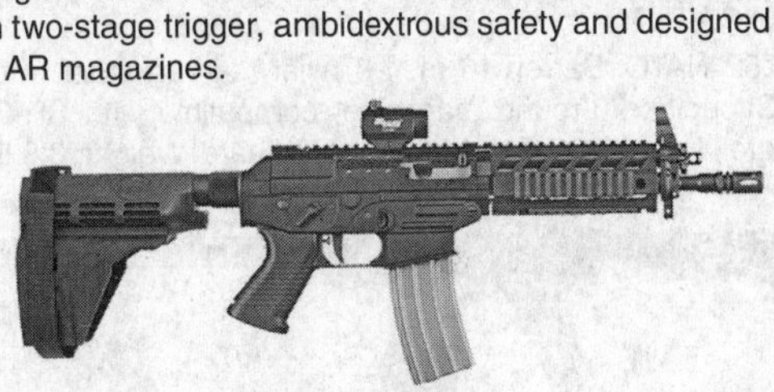

NIB	Exc.	V.G.	Good	Fair	Poor
1800	1500	1250	900	700	500

SIG 556 HOLO

Similar to above, with holographic sight. Without quad rail and other features.

NIB	Exc.	V.G.	Good	Fair	Poor
2200	1870	1590	1350	1150	980

SIG 556 DMR

Sniper version of SIG 556 SWAT, with bipod and other accurizing features.

NIB	Exc.	V.G.	Good	Fair	Poor
2100	1790	1520	1290	1100	930

SIG 516 Gas Piston Rifle

AR-style rifle chambered in 5.56 NATO. Original versions include 14.5", 16", 18" or 20" chrome-lined barrel; free-floating aluminum quad rail forend with four M1913 Picatinny rails; threaded muzzle with standard (0.5x28TPI) pattern; aluminum upper and lower receiver is machined; black anodized finish; 30-round magazine; flattop upper; various configurations available. New G2 versions only available as 5.56/16", introduced 2016.

NIB	Exc.	V.G.	Good	Fair	Poor
1530	1300	1100	940	800	680

SIG 516 G2 Patrol

Caliber: 5.56 NATO. Features: AR-style rifle with included 30-round magazine, 16" chrome-lined barrel with muzzle brake; free-floating, aluminum quad Picatinny rail, Magpul MOE adjustable stock, black-anodized or Flat Dark Earth finish, various configurations available. SEE POLITICAL PANIC PRICING.

NIB	Exc.	V.G.	Good	Fair	Poor
1080	940	800	620	—	—

SIG 716 Tactical Patrol Rifle

Caliber: 7.62 NATO/.308 Win., 6.5 Creedmoor. Features: AR-10-type rifle. Gas-piston operation with three-round position (four-position optional) gas valve; 16", 18", or 20" chrome-lined barrel with threaded muzzle and nitride finish; free-floating aluminum quad rail forend with four M1913 Picatinny rails; telescoping buttstock; the lower receiver is machined from a 7075-T6 Aircraft grade aluminum forging; upper receiver, machined from 7075-T6 aircraft grade aluminum with integral M1913 Picatinny rail. SEE POLITICAL PANIC PRICING.

NIB	Exc.	V.G.	Good	Fair	Poor
1950	1810	1630	1470	—	—

SIG 716G2 DMR

Caliber: 7.62 NATO. Barrel: 16 in. 1:8 twist, carbon steel, with 5/8x24 threads. Capacity: 20-round magazine, compatible with SR-25 magazines. Overall Length: 35.8 in. M-LOK handguard. Weight: 8.8 lbs.

NIB	Exc.	V.G.	Good	Fair	Poor
2800	2210	1880	1600	1360	1150

SIG 716G2 DMR 6.5 Creedmoor

NIB	Exc.	V.G.	Good	Fair	Poor
2730	2320	1970	1670	1420	1210

SIG 716i Tread

Caliber: .308 Win. Capacity: one 20-round magazine, compatible with SR-25 magazines. Barrel: 16", 1:10" RH twist, stainless steel. Upper/Lower Receivers: Forged aluminum, hardcoat anodized finish. Stock: Magpul SL-K six-position telescoping stock. Sights: None, optics ready. Weight: 8.5 lbs. Trigger: Two-stage match. Overall Length: 33.8" to 37". Features: Direct-impingement operating system, integral QD mount, ambi safety selector, charging handle, free-floating 15" M-LOK handguard. SEE POLITICAL PANIC PRICING.

NIB	Exc.	V.G.	Good	Fair	Poor
1500	1350	1200	1000	—	—

M400 SERIES

M400

Caliber: 5.56 NATO. AR-style rifle with Direct Impingement system, 20-in. chrome-lined barrel with muzzle brake; free-floating M-LOK handguard with lightening cuts, 3-chamber compensator, Magpul SLK 6-position adjustable stock, various configurations available.

NIB	Exc.	V.G.	Good	Fair	Poor
700	—	—	—	—	—

SIG M400 Elite

A true AR platform tactical rifle with 16" Nitride treated barrel, 7075-T6 aircraft grade aluminum forged lower receiver and direct-impingement operating system with rotating locking bolt. Offered in a wide range of variations, with many options. Values shown are for standard (Classic) model.

NIB	Exc.	V.G.	Good	Fair	Poor
1100	940	800	680	570	490

M400 Tread

Caliber: 5.56 NATO/.223 Rem. Capacity: one 30-round magazine, comparable with AR-15 types. Barrel: 16", 1:8" RH twist, stainless steel. Upper/Lower Receivers: Forged aluminum, hardcoat anodized finish. Stock: Magpul SL-K six-position telescoping stock. Sights: None, optics-ready. Weight: 7 lbs. Trigger: Single-stage, polished hardcoat trigger. Overall Length: 30.8". Features: Direct-impingement operating system, integral QD mount, ambi safety selector, charging handle, free-floating 15" M-LOK handguard, mid-length gas system. SEE POLITICAL PANIC PRICING.

NIB	Exc.	V.G.	Good	Fair	Poor
880	780	620	500	—	—

M400 Classic

Caliber: 5.56 NATO. AR-style rifle with Direct Impingement system, 20" chrome-lined barrel with muzzle brake; free-floating M-LOK handguard with lightening cuts, three-chamber compensator, Magpul SLK six-position adjustable stock, various configurations available. SEE POLITICAL PANIC PRICING.

NIB	Exc.	V.G.	Good	Fair	Poor
700	—	—	—	—	—

M400 Tread Predator

Chambering: 5.56 NATO. MSR platform designed for predator hunting. Aluminum frame, Cerakote Elite Jungle finish, lightweight adjustable, 16". 1:8" twist stainless threaded barrel with thread protector, lightened free-float M-LOK 15" Predator handguard, hardened polished trigger, ambidextrous controls. Ships with five-round magazines. Length: 35.5". Height: 7.5". Width: 2.5". Weight (with magazine): 7.5 lbs. Compatible with a full line of Tread accessories. Introduced March 2021. SEE POLITICAL PANIC PRICING.

NIB	Exc.	V.G.	Good	Fair	Poor
1000	—	—	—	—	—

SIG M400 Tread Pistol

Caliber: 5.56 NATO. Capacity: 30-round magazine. Barrel: 11.5 in. Grips: Textured polymer. Sights: Optic-ready, Picatinny rail. Length: 27 in. overall. Weight: 6 lbs. unloaded. Finish: Black hard cast anodized. Features: Free-floating M-LOK handguard, Blade 2.0 brace, single-stage trigger.

NIB	Exc.	V.G.	Good	Fair	Poor
740	630	540	450	390	330

M400 Tread Coil

Similar to M400 Tread, but with popular features: Matchlite Duo Trigger, 13" lightweight M-LOK handguard, Tread Romeo5 red-dot sight, vertical foregrip. SEE POLITICAL PANIC PRICING.

NIB	Exc.	V.G.	Good	Fair	Poor
1000	900	790	600	—	—

SIG M400 Elite Vanish

Introduced 2018. .223 Rem. Lightweight 2-Stage Matchlite Duo Trigger, 20" heavy-contour barrel with precision crown. Also, free-floating M-LOK 15" handguard, Kuiu Vias camo finish, fixed Magpul MOE stock, and MOE grip. One 10-round mag with 5-round limiter.

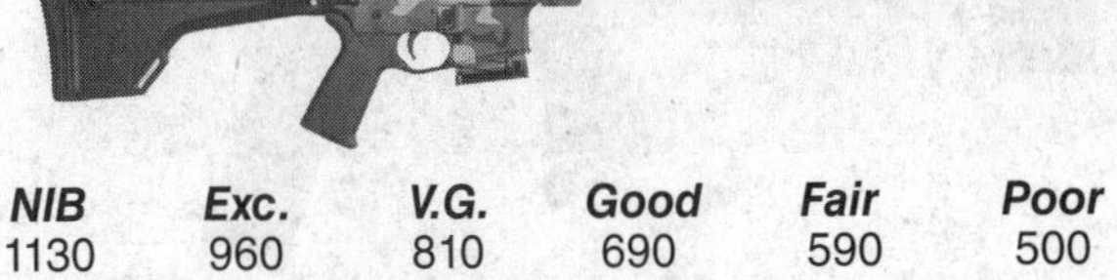

NIB	Exc.	V.G.	Good	Fair	Poor
1130	960	810	690	590	500

SIG M400 Elite TI California Compliant

5.56 NATO. Titanium Cerakote receiver finish, free-floating M-LOK handguard, 6 position telescoping stock, Enhanced SIG Trigger, lightweight, 16" 1:7 nitride barrel, SIG Micro-light Gas Block. 36.5" OAL, 6.5 lbs.

NIB	Exc.	V.G.	Good	Fair	Poor
1330	1130	960	810	690	590

SIG M400 Enhanced Carbine

NIB	Exc.	V.G.	Good	Fair	Poor
1130	960	810	690	590	500

M400-DH3 Rifle

Caliber: .223 Rem. or 5.56 NATO (.223 Wylde chamber). Specialized version released under world champion 3-Gun competitor and Team SIG Shooter Daniel Horner's DH3 brand. The M400-DH3 Rifle is a SIG Direct Impingement (SDI) aluminum frame rifle with a Cerakote Elite Titanium finish. DH3 fully adjustable competition stock, two-stage adjustable Timney trigger, 16". 1:8" twist fluted stainless barrel, three-chamber compensator, low-profile 3-Gun handguard with M-LOK mounts, ambidextrous controls including bolt catch/release. Ships with one 30-round magazine. Length: 34.5". Height: 7.5". Width: 2.5". Weight (with magazine): 7 lbs. Introduced June 2022. SEE POLITICAL PANIC PRICING.

NIB	Exc.	V.G.	Good	Fair	Poor
1600	—	—	—	—	—

MCX SERIES

SIG MCX

AR-15 variant in 5.56 NATO or .300 AAC Blackout, gas-piston operating system. Has a SIG SAS folding stock, SIG grip, mil-spec AR trigger, aluminum KeyMod handguard and 16" barrel. Modular design allows easy caliber interchangeability. Also offered in pistol version. Introduced in 2015.

NIB	Exc.	V.G.	Good	Fair	Poor
1780	1510	1280	1090	930	790

SIG MCX Patrol

NIB	Exc.	V.G.	Good	Fair	Poor
1400	1190	1010	860	730	620

SIG MCX Virtus Patrol Rifle

Calibers: 5.56 NATO, 7.62x39mm or .300 Blackout. Features: AR-style rifle. Modular system allows switching between calibers with conversion kit. Features include a 16-in. barrel, aluminum KeyMod handguards, ambi controls and charging handle, choice of side-folding or telescoping stock, auto-regulating gas system to all transition between subsonic and supersonic loads. SEE POLITICAL PANIC PRICING.

NIB	Exc.	V.G.	Good	Fair	Poor
2750	2600	2300	1950	1600	—

SIG MCX Virtus Patrol .300 Blackout

NIB	Exc.	V.G.	Good	Fair	Poor
1950	1660	1410	1200	1020	870

SIG MCX Virtus SBR .300 Blackout

5.56 (11.5" barrel) or .300 Blackout (5.5" barrel), black or FDE colors.

NIB	Exc.	V.G.	Good	Fair	Poor
2050	1740	1480	1260	1070	910

SIG MCX Virtus Tacops

.300 BLK. Pistol variant in the MCX series with side-folding Pivoting Contour Brace. 6.75" 1:5-twist suppressor designed barrel. Two-stage Matchlite Trigger. Talo Distributors Exclusive. 27.5" OAL, 8" tall, 8 lbs.

NIB	Exc.	V.G.	Good	Fair	Poor
2200	1870	1590	1350	1150	980

SIG MCX Virtus Pistol

5.56 or .300 Blackout, black or FDE colors.

NIB	Exc.	V.G.	Good	Fair	Poor
2200	1870	1590	1350	1150	980

SIG MCX Rattler Canebrake

.300 BLK. Suppressor-ready platform with an SD handguard and inert training device. To have a suppressed MCX system, unthread the inert training device, install your suppressor, and select the appropriate gas setting for your ammunition. Two-stage flat-blade match trigger, Cerakote E190 finished upper and lower, a folding coyote-tan PCB, and one 30-round polymer 300 Blackout Magpul magazine.

NIB	Exc.	V.G.	Good	Fair	Poor
2700	2300	1950	1660	1410	1200

SIG MCX Rattler PCB

.300 BLK. Free-floating M-LOK handguards matched with a PDW upper and 5.5" barrel, 1:5 twist. Gas piston operation, 23" long, 2.8" wide, 8.0" tall. 5.1 lbs.

NIB	Exc.	V.G.	Good	Fair	Poor
2530	2150	1820	1550	1320	1120

SIG MCX Rattler SBR

Similar to Rattler PCB, has thin, durable folding stock.

NIB	Exc.	V.G.	Good	Fair	Poor
2750	2340	1990	1700	1440	1220

MCX-Spear LT

Caliber: 5.56 NATO, 7.62x39mm, .300 Blk. 16" carbon-steel barrel on rifle; 11.5" and 9" for SBRs and pistols. Lightened handguard with attachment screws for additional rigidity and a lightened profile barrel. Ambidextrous bolt catch and release, minimalist, AR-15-style trigger compatibility. Interchangeable barrels, Rocksett SIG QD suppressor-ready flash hider. Barrel twist for 7.62x39 is 1:9.5"; for 5.56 NATO, 1:7". Length: 34.5". Height: 7.5" w/o magazine. 5/8x24 muzzle threads on 7.62x39mm barrel, 1/2x28 tpi on 5.56. Weight: 7.6 lbs. Introduced: Sept. 2022. SEE POLITICAL PANIC PRICING.

NIB	Exc.	V.G.	Good	Fair	Poor
2500	2350	—	—	—	—

MCX-Spear 277

Caliber: 6.5 Creedmoor, 7.62 NATO, .277 SIG Fury/6.8x51. Special edition commercial variant of the MCX-SPEAR is a gas-piston semi-automatic, some of which are chambered in .277 SIG Fury, a civilian variant of the U.S. Army's 6.8x51 hybrid ammunition. Features a six-position adjustable folding stock, ambidextrous controls, two-stage match-grade trigger and an adjustable gas system. The MCX-Spear will also include a free-float, M-LOK handguard with a full-length Picatinny top rail for mounting optics. Barrel: 16", 1:7" barrel twist, interchangeable. Both non-reciprocating side and rear charging handles, fully ambidextrous controls including bolt release, and two-position adjustable gas piston. Comes with two boxes of .277 SIG Fury ammunition. Length: 34.1". Height: 7.97". Width: 2.98". Weight (w/magazine): 8.38 lbs. Rifle, SBR, and Pistol variants. Introduced: Feb. 2023. MSRP is for first-run special edition rifle. SEE POLITICAL PANIC PRICING.

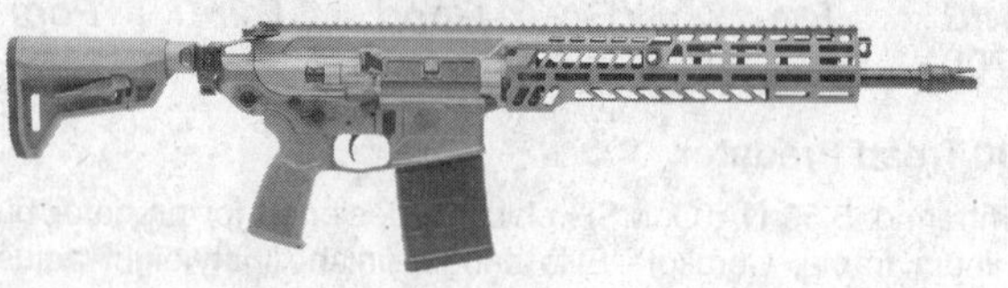

NIB	Exc.	V.G.	Good	Fair	Poor
4580	4200	—	—	—	—

SIG MPX SERIES

9x19mm. Submachine gun introduced in 2013. Select-fire gun uses a short-stroke gas piston system and a rotating bolt, ambidextrous controls. In 2015, several semi-auto variations were made available to the civilian market.

SIG MPX PCC

Caliber: 9mm Luger. Gas-piston operation. Barrel: 16", 1:10" twist, carbon steel. M13.5x1mm muzzle threads. Magazine: MPX 30-rd polymer mag. Trigger: Timney Single Stage. Overall Length: 35.25". Accessory Rail: M-LOK. Weight: 6.63 lbs. SEE POLITICAL PANIC PRICING.

NIB	Exc.	V.G.	Good	Fair	Poor
2000	1850	1600	1350	1000	—

SIG MPX Copperhead

9x19. Elite Series Cerakoted upper receiver, with an integrated stock knuckle lower, 3.5" 1:10-twist barrel with integrated muzzle brake. Pivoting Contour Brace (PCB), dual-sided selector switch, magazine release, charging handle and bolt release. Operates from a fully-closed and locked rotating bolt, short-stroke gas piston. 14.5" long, 2.4" wide, 8" tall, 4.5 lbs.

NIB	Exc.	V.G.	Good	Fair	Poor
1750	1490	1260	1080	910	780

SIG MPX K Pistol

Redesigned 2019. 9x19. Closed bolt gas piston system, modular design allows for multiple handguard and barrel lengths and is ready to go for suppressor use. For 2019, the K featured the SIG PCB folding brace and an updated M-Lok handguard and a Timney MPX Single Stage Trigger co-designed by Timney and SIG. OAL, 22.25"; overall width, 2.4"; height 8"; 4.5" barrel, 1:10 twist; 5 lbs. MPX magazine type.

NIB	Exc.	V.G.	Good	Fair	Poor
1900	1620	1370	1170	990	840

BOLT-ACTION RIFLES

Sauer SSG 3000

Imported by SIG-Sauer from 2000 to 2012. A 5-round bolt-action sniper rifle chambered in .308 Win. Heavy-contoured hammer forged barrel fitted with flash suppressor/muzzle brake to provide greater accuracy, with reduced muzzle signature. Both barrel and receiver feature black oxide finish to eliminate glare. Short, smooth 60-degree bolt throw allows for rapid operation. Like safety release bolt action is quiet. Massive six-lug lockup system used to give greater strength and accuracy. Pistol grip and fully adjustable stock give shooter a custom fit. Trigger adjustable for trigger position, trigger take up, let-off point and trigger pull weight. Receiver features dovetail that will accept a wide range of sighting systems, including factory available M1913 rail. Price include Leupold Vari-X III 3.5-10x40 scope.

NIB	Exc.	V.G.	Good	Fair	Poor
4000	3550	2700	2000	1200	600

SIG 50

Bolt-action tactical rifle chambered for .50 BMG cartridge. Designed for ultra long-range tactical applications. Match-grade trigger set for 3.5 lbs. Stock has adjustable cheekpiece, pistol grip and length of pull. Barrel 29" heavy fluted with muzzle brake. Full length machined rails allow mounting of accessories. Fluted bolt, heavy duty steel bipod, Duracoat coating. Weight 23.5 lbs. Introduced in 2011.

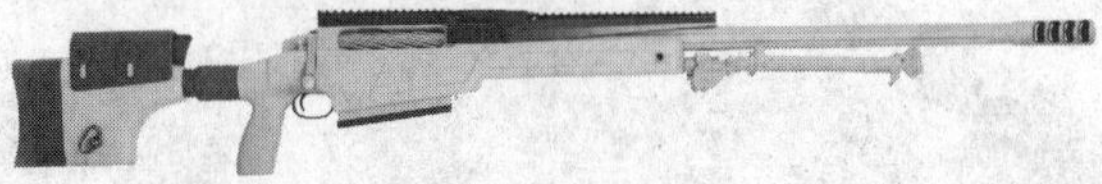

NIB	Exc.	V.G.	Good	Fair	Poor
8300	7400	6350	—	—	—

Cross Rifle

Calibers: .277 Sig Fury, .308 Win., 6.5 Creedmoor. Capacity: 5. Barrel: 16 to 18 in., stainless steel. Stock: Sig precision, polymer/alloy, folding. Sights: Picatinny rail. Weight: 6.5 to 6.8 lbs. Features: M-LOK rail, two-stage match trigger.

NIB	Exc.	V.G.	Good	Fair	Poor
1700	1500	1250	—	—	—

SILMA
Italy

See—DAN ARMS

STANDARD MODELS

Model 70 EJ

Over/under chambered for 12- or 20-gauge shell, with 28 ventilated rib barrels and choke tubes. Single-selective trigger and auto ejectors. Checkered walnut stock. Weight about: 12-gauge 7.6 lbs.; 20-gauge 6.9 lbs. Silver engraved receiver.

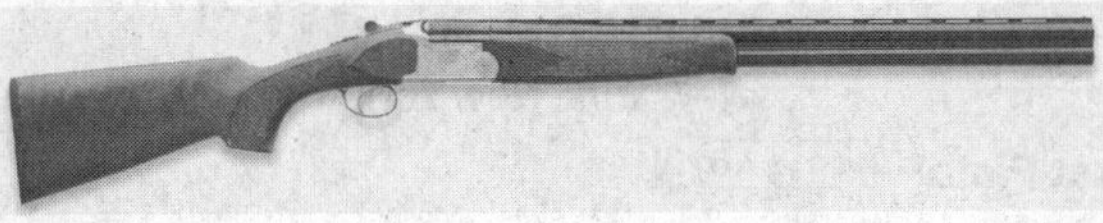

12 Gauge

NIB	Exc.	V.G.	Good	Fair	Poor
950	800	680	500	300	200

20 Gauge

NIB	Exc.	V.G.	Good	Fair	Poor
880	720	600	400	260	150

DELUXE MODELS

Model 70 EJ

Over/under chambered for 12- or 20-gauge shell, with 28" ventilated rib barrels and choke tubes. Single-selective trigger and auto ejectors. Checkered walnut stock. Weight about: 12-gauge 7.6 lbs.; 20-gauge 6.9 lbs. Silver engraved receiver.

12 Gauge

NIB	Exc.	V.G.	Good	Fair	Poor
1050	750	600	480	350	200

20 Gauge

NIB	Exc.	V.G.	Good	Fair	Poor
950	700	550	420	300	180

28 and .410 Gauge

NIB	Exc.	V.G.	Good	Fair	Poor
1080	800	650	520	400	250

Superlight

Offered in 12- or 20-gauge, with 28" barrels and choke tubes. Checkered select walnut stock. Receiver made from alloy steel. Weight about: 12-gauge 6.7 lbs.; 6.3 lbs. 20-gauge.

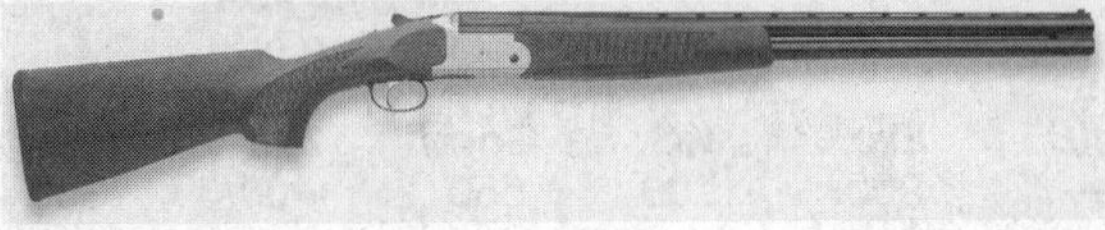

NIB	Exc.	V.G.	Good	Fair	Poor
1100	820	680	550	420	280

Clays Model

Designed for sporting clays. Chambered for 12-gauge 3" shell. Fitted with 28" barrel, choke tubes and wide ventilated rib. Checkered select walnut stock.

NIB	Exc.	V.G.	Good	Fair	Poor
1300	980	780	620	500	400

SIMPLEX
Unknown

Simplex

German design based on Bergmann-Mars pistol. An 8mm caliber semi-automatic pistol, with 2.6" barrel. Front mounted 5-round magazine. Blued, with hard rubber grips having trade name "Simplex" cast in them. Manufactured from 1901 to around 1906. Early samples may have come from Germany; later pistols are thought to have been produced in Belgium.

NIB	Exc.	V.G.	Good	Fair	Poor
—	1650	1050	550	400	200

SIMPSON, R. J.
New York, New York

Pocket Pistol (Antique)

A .41-caliber single-shot percussion pocket pistol, with 2.5" barrel. German silver mounts and walnut stock. Manufactured during 1850s and 1860s.

Exc.	Fine	V.G.	Good	Fair	Poor
2400	1750	1220	700	300	210

SIMSON & COMPANY
Suhl, Germany

See—LUGER

NOTE: Models listed and pictured are taken from a mid-1930s Simson catalog. Because the company was Jewish-owned, Nazis took control in mid-1930s changing the name to "Berlin Suhler Waffen". Prices are estimates.

SHOTGUNS

Model 235

Side-by-side shotgun chambered for 12- or 16-gauge, with Anson & Deely action. Scalloped frame, with scroll engraving. Walnut stock, with pistol grip. Double triggers.

Courtesy Jim Cate

NIB	Exc.	V.G.	Good	Fair	Poor
—	900	700	550	400	350

Model 73

Similar to above, with more scroll engraving coverage.

Courtesy Jim Cate

NIB	Exc.	V.G.	Good	Fair	Poor
—	950	750	600	400	350

Model 74

Features deep cut game scene engraving. Select walnut stock, with fine-line checkering.

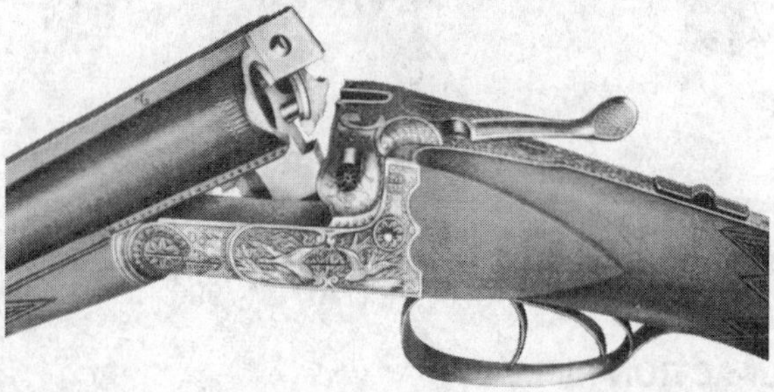

Courtesy Jim Cate

NIB	Exc.	V.G.	Good	Fair	Poor
—	1100	800	600	450	350

Model 74E

Same as above, with automatic ejectors.

Courtesy Jim Cate

NIB	Exc.	V.G.	Good	Fair	Poor
—	1200	850	650	450	350

Model 76

Side-by-side fitted with game scene engraved side plates. Offered in 12- or 16-gauge.

Courtesy Jim Cate

NIB	Exc.	V.G.	Good	Fair	Poor
—	1400	1100	800	550	400

Model 76E

As above, with automatic ejectors.

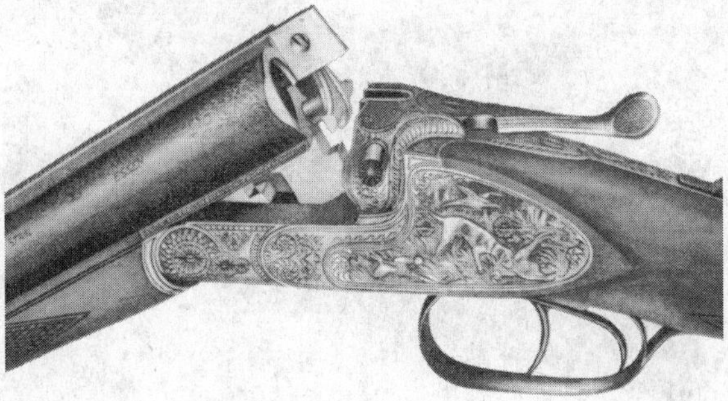

Courtesy Jim Cate

NIB	Exc.	V.G.	Good	Fair	Poor
—	1500	1200	850	550	400

PISTOLS

Model 1922

A 6.35mm semi-automatic pistol, with 2" barrel and 6-shot magazine. Slide marked "Selbstlade Pistole Simson DRP" and "Waffenfabrik Simson & Co Suhl". Blued, with black plastic grips.

NIB	Exc.	V.G.	Good	Fair	Poor
—	600	480	400	300	100

Model 1927

Similar to above, with slimmer frame. Stamped with trademark of three overlapping triangles having letter "S" enclosed.

NIB	Exc.	V.G.	Good	Fair	Poor
—	600	480	400	300	100

SIRKIS INDUSTRIES, LTD.

Ramat-Gan, Israel

SD9

A 9mm double-action semi-automatic pistol, with 3" barrel, fixed sights and 7-shot magazine. Blued, with plastic grips. Also known as Sardius.

NIB	Exc.	V.G.	Good	Fair	Poor
—	320	280	220	180	100

Model 35 Match Rifle

A .22-caliber single-shot bolt-action rifle, with 26" free-floating barrel, adjustable rear sight and trigger. Blued, with walnut stock.

NIB	Exc.	V.G.	Good	Fair	Poor
—	600	550	500	400	200

Model 36 Sniper's Rifle

A 7.62x54mm caliber semi-automatic rifle, with 22" barrel. Matte blued, with composition stock.

NIB	Exc.	V.G.	Good	Fair	Poor
—	680	600	550	450	200

SKB ARMS COMPANY

Omaha, Nebraska

This respected Japanese manufacturer began making shotguns for U.S. market in 1960s. Made various models for Browning, Weatherby and other American brands. In 1970s, SKB began marketing many models under its own name. End of 2009, SKB factory closed its doors. Final inventory was purchased by G. U. Inc. of Omaha, Nebraska. As of mid 2013, G.U. Inc. began importing several shotgun models from Turkey under the SKB brand. Approximately 1967 to 1977, Ithaca imported a series of over/under and side-by-side shotguns from SKB. These models were virtually identical to other SKB-made guns and had the same model numbers. Values shown in this section also apply to Ithaca guns.

SIDE-BY-SIDE GUNS

Model 100

Boxlock 12- or 20-gauge double-barrel shotgun, with 25" to 30" barrels. Single-selective trigger and automatic ejectors. Blued, with walnut stock. Imported prior to 1981. Discontinued.

NIB	Exc.	V.G.	Good	Fair	Poor
1020	870	740	630	540	460

Model 150

As above, with some engraving. A beavertail forearm and figured walnut stock. Imported from 1972 to 1974.

NIB	Exc.	V.G.	Good	Fair	Poor
1020	870	740	630	540	460

Model 200

As above, with French casehardened and scalloped receiver. Discontinued.

NIB	Exc.	V.G.	Good	Fair	Poor
1350	1150	980	830	700	600

Model 200E

As above, with English-style stock. Imported prior to 1989.

NIB	Exc.	V.G.	Good	Fair	Poor
1700	1440	1230	1040	890	750

Model 280

Same as Model 200, but fitted with straight-grip stock. Discontinued.

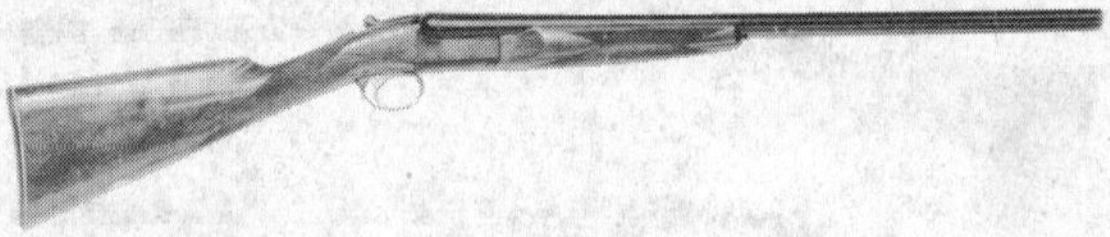

NIB	Exc.	V.G.	Good	Fair	Poor
1420	1210	1030	880	740	630

Model 300

As above, with more engraving. Figured walnut stock. Discontinued.

NIB	Exc.	V.G.	Good	Fair	Poor
1420	1210	1030	880	740	630

Model 385

Similar to Model 300, but chambered for 12-, 20- or 28-gauge shell. Scroll engraved frame, with semi-fancy walnut pistol-/straight-grip stock. Limited quantities imported. Weight about 7 lbs. Discontinued.

NIB	Exc.	V.G.	Good	Fair	Poor
2300	1960	1660	1410	1200	1020

Model 385 2 Barrel Set

Same as above, with 20- and 28-gauge set of 26" or 28" barrels. Discontinued.

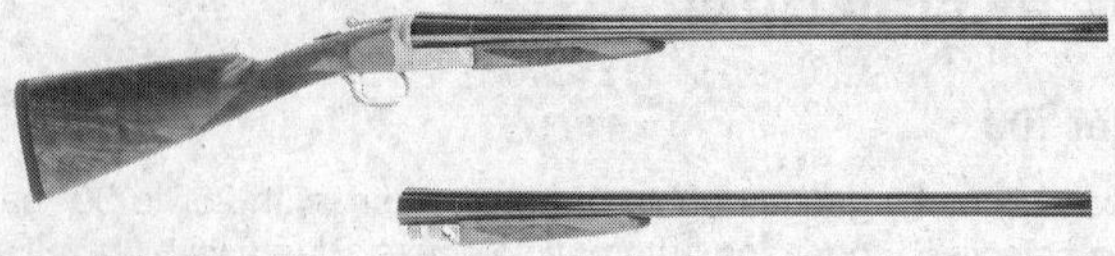

NIB	Exc.	V.G.	Good	Fair	Poor
3100	2640	2240	1900	1620	1380

Model 385 Sporting Clays

Chambered for 12-, 20- or 28-gauge. Fitted with 28" barrel. Pistol grip stock. Weight about 7 lbs. Discontinued. Note: Add $900 for extra set of 20- or 28-gauge barrels.

NIB	Exc.	V.G.	Good	Fair	Poor
2200	1870	1590	1350	1150	980

Model 400E

As above, with engraved false sideplates and English-style stock. Imported prior to 1990.

NIB	Exc.	V.G.	Good	Fair	Poor
2100	1780	1520	1290	1100	930

Model 480E

As above, with French casehardened receiver and more finely figured walnut stocks. Discontinued.

NIB	Exc.	V.G.	Good	Fair	Poor
1700	1440	1230	1040	890	750

Model 485

Features engraved sideplate boxlock action. Chambered for 12-, 20- or 28-gauge, with 26" or 28" barrels. Choke tubes. Weight about 7.7 lbs. Discontinued.

NIB	Exc.	V.G.	Good	Fair	Poor
2850	2420	2060	1750	1490	1260

Model 485 2 Barrel Set

Same as above, with extra set of barrels in 20/28-gauge combinations with 26" barrels. Choice of pistol-/straight-grip stock. Discontinued.

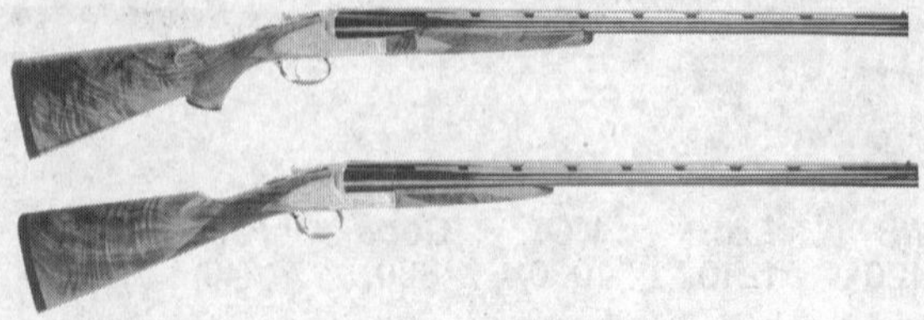

NIB	Exc.	V.G.	Good	Fair	Poor
3800	3230	2750	2330	1980	1690

OVER/UNDER GUNS

MODEL 85TSS SERIES

This series, introduced in 2004, features a low-profile boxlock action. Fitted with an inertia trigger (12- and 20-gauge), mechanical on 28-gauge and .410 bore. Single-selective trigger, with manual safety. Silver nitride finish. Barrels have automatic ejectors, ventilated rib and choke tubes. Pigeon porting is optional. Stocks are American walnut, with matte finish. Fitted with Pachmayr recoil pad. Adjustable comb stock is optional.

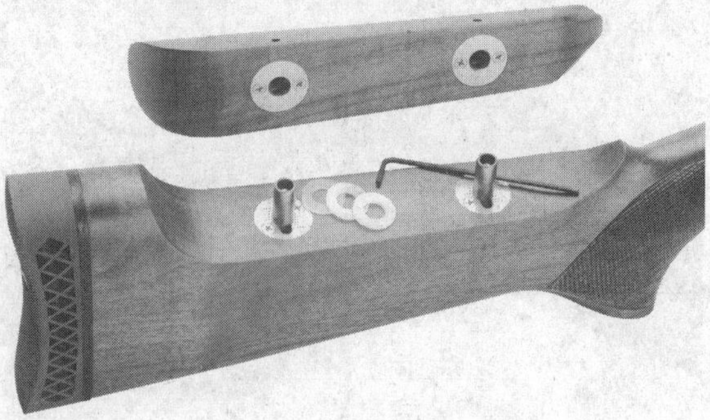

Close-up of adjustable comb

Model 85TSS Sporting Clays

Chambered for 12-, 20-, 28-gauge and .410 bore. Features 28", 30" or 32" barrels on 12-gauge; 28" or 30" barrels on small bore guns. Choke tubes. Fixed or adjustable comb. Choice of multiple barrel sets. Weight about: 12 gauge 8.5 lbs.; 7.5 lbs. smaller bore guns. Note: Add $175 for adjustable comb; $1,200 for two- barrel sets; $2,800 for three-barrel 20-, 28-gauge and .410 sets.

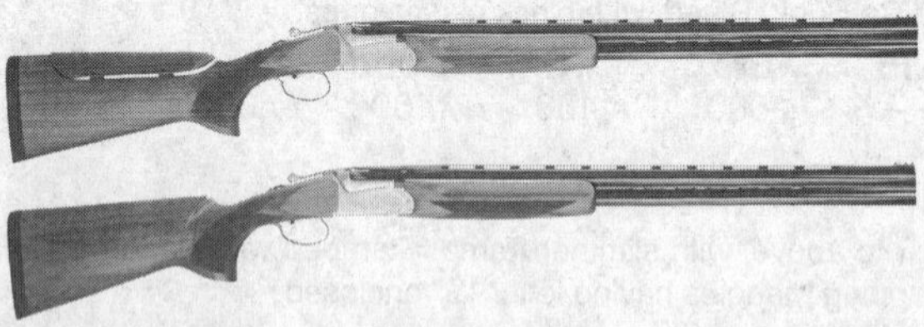

NIB	Exc.	V.G.	Good	Fair	Poor
1880	1600	1420	1080	800	450

Model 85TSS Trap

This 12-gauge 3" trap model fitted with 30" or 32" back-bored barrels, with adjustable 12mm rib. Fixed or adjustable comb, with-/without Monte Carlo. Weight about 8.75 lbs. Note: Add $175 for adjustable comb.

NIB	Exc.	V.G.	Good	Fair	Poor
1900	1620	1370	1170	990	840

Model 85TSS Trap Unsingle

A single-barrel trap gun, with 32" or 34" adjustable rib barrel. Standard comb or Monte Carlo, with-/without adjustable comb. Weight about 9 lbs. Note: Add $175 for adjustable comb.

NIB	Exc.	V.G.	Good	Fair	Poor
2050	1740	1480	1260	1070	910

Model 85TSS Trap Unsingle Combo

Features 32" or 34" single-barrel and 30" or 32" over/under barrels. Barrel rib adjustable. Monte Carlo or standard stock, with-/without adjustable comb. Note: Add $175 for adjustable comb.

NIB	Exc.	V.G.	Good	Fair	Poor
3000	2550	2170	1840	1570	1330

Model 85TSS Skeet

Offered in 12-, 20-, 28-gauge and .410 bore. 12-gauge offered with 28", 30" or 32" back-bored barrels, with 9.5mm rib; small gauges offered with 28" or 30" back-bored barrels, with 8.5mm rib. Weight about: 12-gauge 8.35 lbs.; 7.5 lbs. smaller gauges. Fixed or adjustable comb. Note: Add $175 for adjustable comb; $2,800 for three-barrel set.

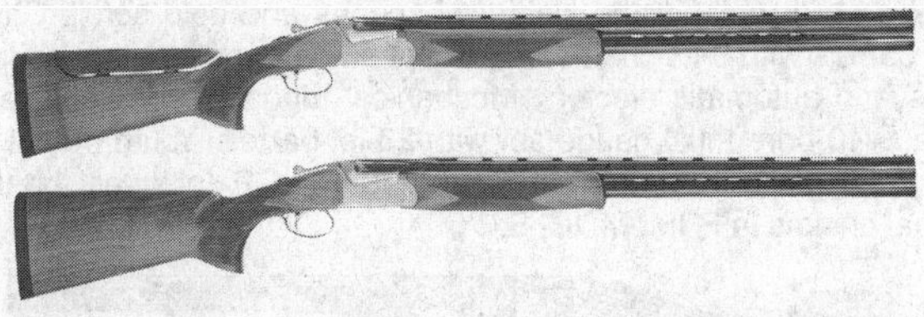

NIB	Exc.	V.G.	Good	Fair	Poor
1900	1620	1370	1170	990	840

Model 500

A 12-, 20-, 28-gauge or .410 bore over/under shotgun, with 26", 28" or 30" ventilated rib barrels. Blued, with walnut stock. Imported from 1966 to 1979.

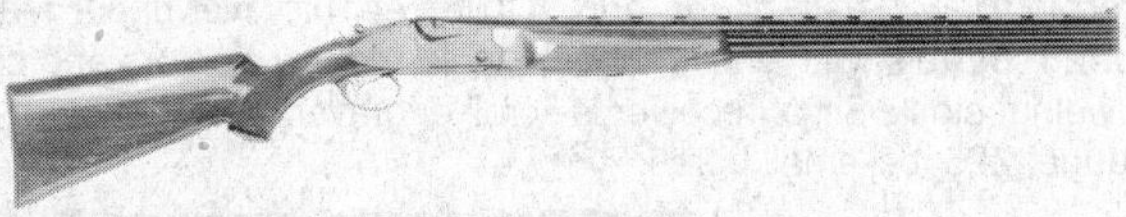

NIB	Exc.	V.G.	Good	Fair	Poor
900	760	650	550	470	400

Model 505 Field

The 505 Series also produced in sporting clays, trap and skeet configurations. Valued at approximately 10% additional.

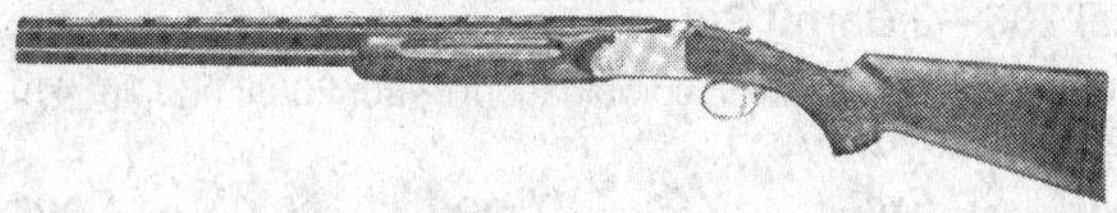

NIB	Exc.	V.G.	Good	Fair	Poor
1200	1020	870	740	630	530

Model 505 3-Gauge Skeet Set

As above, with 3 sets of barrels.

NIB	Exc.	V.G.	Good	Fair	Poor
2780	2360	2000	1700	1450	1230

Model 585

Similar to Model 505, but offered in 12-, 20-, 28-gauge and .410 bore. Barrel lengths 26" or 28". Weight: 7.25 lbs. small bores; 8 lbs. 12-gauge.

NIB	Exc.	V.G.	Good	Fair	Poor
1400	1190	1010	860	730	620

Model 585 Gold Package

Has all the features of 585 series, with addition of a gold-plated trigger, gold-plated game scenes and schnabel forend. Blued or silver receiver.

NIB	Exc.	V.G.	Good	Fair	Poor
1600	1360	1160	980	840	710

Model 585 Skeet

Offered in 12-, 20- or 28-gauge and .410 bore, with 28" barrels. Skeet stock and beavertail forearm. Black recoil pad. Weight about 8 lbs. 12-gauge.

NIB	Exc.	V.G.	Good	Fair	Poor
1420	1210	1030	880	740	630

Model 585—3 Barrel Skeet Set

Fitted with 20-, 28-gauge and .410 bore barrels. Skeet choked.

NIB	Exc.	V.G.	Good	Fair	Poor
3200	2720	2310	1960	1670	1420

Model 585—3 Barrel Skeet Set Gold Package

Same as above, with engraving. Silver or blued receiver.

NIB	Exc.	V.G.	Good	Fair	Poor
3400	2890	2460	2090	1780	1510

Model 585 Youth/Ladies

Similar to 585, with shortened length of pull to 13.5". Weight about: 6.6 lbs. 20-gauge; 7.5 lbs. 12-gauge.

NIB	Exc.	V.G.	Good	Fair	Poor
1400	1190	1010	860	730	620

Model 585 Youth Gold Package

Same as above, with gold trigger, gold-plated game scenes and schnabel forend. Silver or blued receiver.

NIB	Exc.	V.G.	Good	Fair	Poor
1600	1360	1160	980	840	710

Model 585 Upland

Similar to 585 series, except for straight-grip stock. Offered in 12-, 20-, 28-gauge, all with 26" barrels. Weight about: 7.75 lbs. 12-gauge; 6.75 lbs. 20-, 28-gauge.

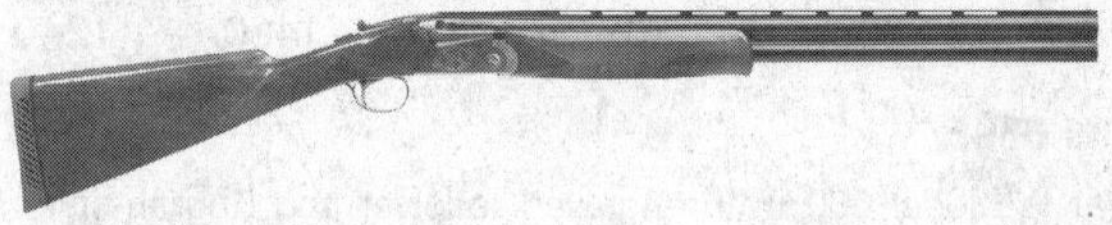

NIB	Exc.	V.G.	Good	Fair	Poor
1400	1190	1010	860	730	620

Model 585 Upland Gold Package

This model has additional gold package features of gold trigger, gold game scenes and schnabel forend. Silver or blued receiver.

NIB	Exc.	V.G.	Good	Fair	Poor
1600	1360	1160	980	840	710

Model 600

Similar to Model 585, with silver-plated receiver.

NIB	Exc.	V.G.	Good	Fair	Poor
1180	1000	850	720	610	520

Model 600 Magnum

As above, chambered for 3", 12-gauge cartridges. Imported from 1969 to 1972.

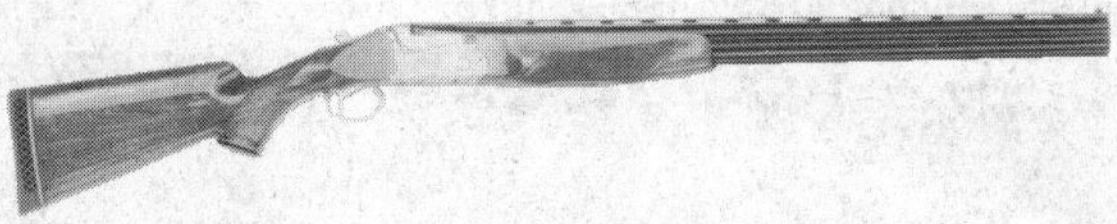

NIB	Exc.	V.G.	Good	Fair	Poor
—	900	680	520	380	200

Model 600 Trap Gun

As above, with 30" or 32" barrels trap choked, with high comb walnut stock.

NIB	Exc.	V.G.	Good	Fair	Poor
1180	1000	850	720	610	520

Model 600 Skeet Gun

As above, chambered for 12-, 20-, 28-gauge or .410 bore cartridges, with 26" or 28" barrels that are skeet choked.

NIB	Exc.	V.G.	Good	Fair	Poor
1180	1000	850	720	610	520

Model 600 Skeet Combo Set

As above, with an extra set of three interchangeable barrels. Furnished with a carrying case.

NIB	Exc.	V.G.	Good	Fair	Poor
2550	2170	1840	1570	1330	1130

Model 605

Similar to Model 600, with engraved and French case-hardened receiver. Note: 605 Series also available in trap or skeet configurations. Values are similar.

NIB	Exc.	V.G.	Good	Fair	Poor
1300	1100	940	800	680	580

Model 605 3-Gauge Skeet Set

As above, with three extra sets of barrels.

NIB	Exc.	V.G.	Good	Fair	Poor
2800	2380	2020	1720	1460	1240

Model 680E

Similar to Model 600, with engraved receiver and English-style stock. Imported from 1973 to 1976.

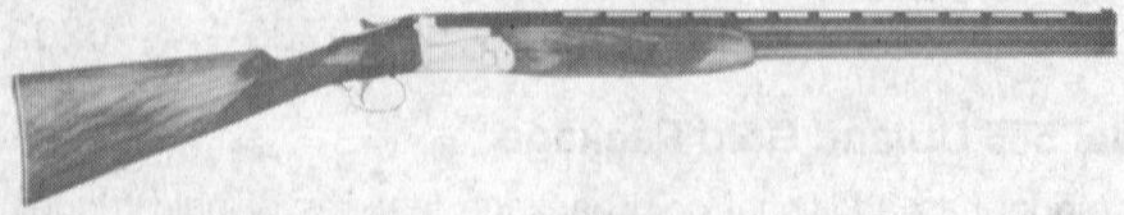

NIB	Exc.	V.G.	Good	Fair	Poor
1350	1150	980	830	700	600

Model 685

Over/under shotgun offered in 12-, 20-, 28-gauge and .410 bore. Barrel lengths 26" or 28", with choke tubes. Engraved receiver has a silver finish, with gold inlays. Walnut stock is semi-fancy.

NIB	Exc.	V.G.	Good	Fair	Poor
1500	1280	1080	920	780	670

Model 700 Trap Gun

Similar to Model 600 Trap, with a wider rib. Additional engraving. Figured walnut stock. Imported from 1969 to 1975.

NIB	Exc.	V.G.	Good	Fair	Poor
1280	1080	920	780	670	570

Model 700 Skeet Gun

As above, with skeet chokes.

NIB	Exc.	V.G.	Good	Fair	Poor
1700	1350	1050	780	500	350

Model 720 Field

Gauge: 12, 20, 28 ga., .410 bore. Barrel: 26, 28, 30 in. Weight: 6 lbs. 10 oz. –7 lbs. 14 oz. Stock: Select Grade II Turkish Walnut. Features: The 720 Field is built on a boxlock receiver, cut with CNC machines from a solid billet of chrome-moly steel. Brushed white chrome receiver is laser engraved with upland and waterfowl scenes and gold scroll. Chrome-lined barrels with 3-in. chambers (except 28 ga.) and lengthened forcing cones and automatic ejectors. Mechanical trigger. Also available as a 28-ga./.410-bore multi-gauge set with 28-in. barrels. Youth model available in 20 ga. with 26-in. barrels and 13-in. LOP. Includes top-thread internal chokes in F, IM, M, IC, S.

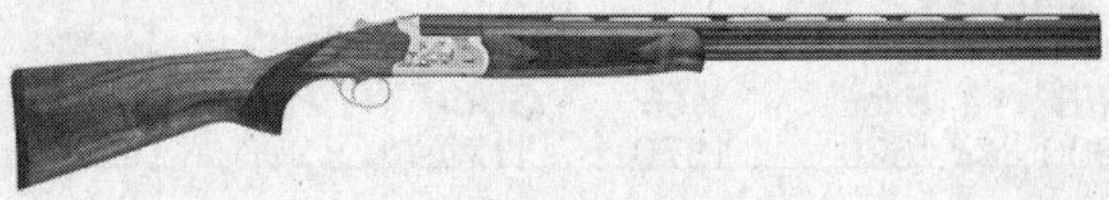

NIB	Exc.	V.G.	Good	Fair	Poor
1430	—	—	—	—	—

Model 785

Offered in 12-, 20-, 28-gauge and .410 bore. This over/under features 26" or 28" barrels, with choke tubes. Single trigger, ejectors and checkered walnut stock. Silver receiver is scroll engraved. Weight about: 8 lbs. 12-gauge; 7.25 lbs. small bores.

NIB	Exc.	V.G.	Good	Fair	Poor
1880	1590	1360	1150	980	830

Model 785—2 Barrel Set

These two barrel sets are in combination 12/20, 20/28 and 28/.410 bore, with 26" and 28" barrels.

NIB	Exc.	V.G.	Good	Fair	Poor
2700	2300	1950	1660	1410	1200

Model 785 Sporting Clays

Chambered for 12-, 20-, 28-gauge. Barrels lengths from 28" to 32" in 12 gauge; 28" in 20 and 28 gauge. Recoil pad standard. Note: Add $900 for Sporting Clays set.

NIB	Exc.	V.G.	Good	Fair	Poor
2000	1700	1440	1220	1040	880

Model 785 Skeet

Offered in 12, 20, 28 gauge and .410 bore, with 28" barrels. Recoil pad standard.

NIB	Exc.	V.G.	Good	Fair	Poor
2250	1750	1150	1400	900	500

Model 785 3-Gauge Skeet Set

Furnished with 12, 20, 28 gauge barrel, all 28" in length. Weight about 7.3 lbs.

NIB	Exc.	V.G.	Good	Fair	Poor
4400	3250	2500	1700	1200	600

Model 785 Trap

Offered in 12-gauge, with-/without Monte Carlo stock. Barrel lengths 30" or 32". Ventilated recoil pad standard.

NIB	Exc.	V.G.	Good	Fair	Poor
1950	1660	1410	1200	1020	860

Model 785 Trap Combo

Features 30" or 32" over/under barrels, with a single 32" or 34" barrel. Standard stock or Monte Carlo.

NIB	Exc.	V.G.	Good	Fair	Poor
2950	2510	2130	1810	1540	1310

Model 800 Trap Gun

As above, with trap chokes and more engraving. Imported from 1969 to 1975.

NIB	Exc.	V.G.	Good	Fair	Poor
1500	1270	1080	920	780	660

Model 800 Skeet Gun

As above in 12 or 20 gauge, with 26" or 28" skeet-choked barrels. Imported from 1969 to 1975.

NIB	Exc.	V.G.	Good	Fair	Poor
1500	1270	1080	920	780	660

Model 880 Crown Grade

A false sidelock 12-, 20-, 28-gauge or .410 bore boxlock double-barrel shotgun, with single-selective trigger and automatic ejectors. Engraved sideplates and receiver are French case-hardened. Figured walnut stock is checkered. Imported prior to 1981.

NIB	Exc.	V.G.	Good	Fair	Poor
2050	1740	1480	1260	1070	910

Model 885

A false sidelock 12, 20, 28 gauge or .410 bore boxlock shotgun. Similar to Model 800.

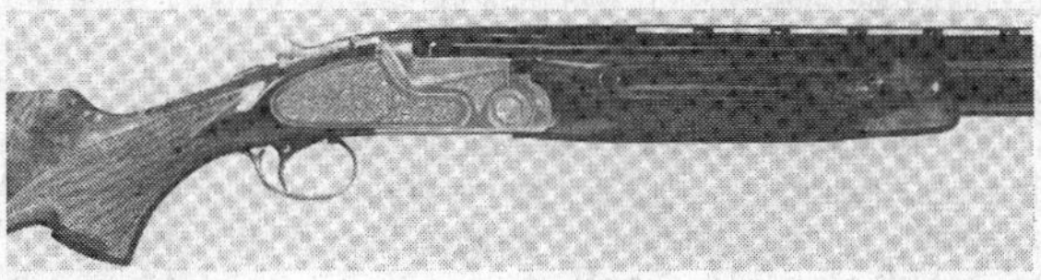

NIB	Exc.	V.G.	Good	Fair	Poor
2000	1700	1440	1230	1040	890

Model 5600

Over/under gun offered in 12-gauge only, in trap or skeet configurations.

NIB	Exc.	V.G.	Good	Fair	Poor
1100	940	800	680	570	490

Model 5700

Similar to above, with light scroll engraving on receiver. Figured walnut stock.

NIB	Exc.	V.G.	Good	Fair	Poor
1520	1300	1100	940	800	680

Model 5800

Similar to Model 5600, with more engraving coverage on receiver. Fancy walnut stock. Note: Add 100% premium for Custom Deluxe model.

NIB	Exc.	V.G.	Good	Fair	Poor
2500	2120	1800	1530	1300	1110

GC 7

This over/under series was last produced by SKB. Three versions offered: Game Bird, Clays and Trap. Game Bird and Clays made in 12, 20, 28 gauge and .410 bore, with Trap only in 12 gauge. All models made on a low-profile boxlock action, with Greener-type crossbolt, automatic ejectors and single-selective trigger. Barrels are 26" to 34", with lengthened forcing cones and Briley choke tubes. Each series made in three grades, with escalating levels of engraving and wood quality. Prices shown for Grade I. Note: Add 20% to 30% for Grade II; 40% to 50% for Grade III. Multi-barrel sets can bring up to 100% premium.

OVER/UNDER GUNS

Game Bird

NIB	Exc.	V.G.	Good	Fair	Poor
1500	1200	900	750	500	400

Clays and Trap

NIB	Exc.	V.G.	Good	Fair	Poor
1600	1300	1000	800	600	400

SLIDE ACTION

Model 7300

12- or 20-gauge slide-action shotgun. Blued, with walnut stock. Imported prior to 1981.

NIB	Exc.	V.G.	Good	Fair	Poor
—	300	260	220	180	160

Model 7900

As above, but skeet choked.

NIB	Exc.	V.G.	Good	Fair	Poor
—	300	260	220	180	160

POST 2013 PRODUCTION

Model 300

A 12- or 20-gauge semi-automatic shotgun, with 26", 28" or 30" barrels. Blued, with walnut stock. Imported from 1968 to 1972. Note: Add 20% for ventilated rib barrel.

NIB	Exc.	V.G.	Good	Fair	Poor
—	450	400	350	300	200

Model 1300

Redesigned version of Model 300, with ventilated rib barrel and screw-in choke tubes. Imported since 1988.

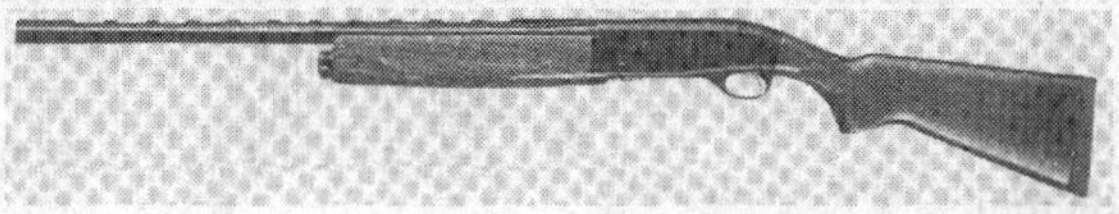

NIB	Exc.	V.G.	Good	Fair	Poor
450	400	350	300	200	150

Model XL 900 MR

A 12-gauge semi-automatic shotgun, with 26" to 30" ventilated rib barrels. Etched alloy receiver. Checkered walnut stock. Imported prior to 1981.

NIB	Exc.	V.G.	Good	Fair	Poor
—	480	420	380	320	200

Model 1900

As above, but also chambered for 20-gauge shells. Available with 22", 26" or 28" ventilated rib barrels. Screw-in choke tubes. Blued, with walnut stock.

NIB	Exc.	V.G.	Good	Fair	Poor
500	420	380	300	250	180

Model 3000

Similar to above, with modified receiver design. Imported prior to 1990.

NIB	Exc.	V.G.	Good	Fair	Poor
—	480	400	350	250	150

Model 90 TSS

Over/under in 12 or 20 gauge, with features designed for trap, skeet or sporting clays. Features include a stock with adjustable comb and length of pull. High ventilated rib. Skeet has fixed stock. Imported from Turkey. Note: Deduct $250 for skeet model.

NIB	Exc.	V.G.	Good	Fair	Poor
1500	1300	1050	800	450	200

Model 7000 SL

A true side-lock model featuring H&H 7-pin removable sidelocks, with safety sears. Premium grade Turkish walnut stock, with extensive fine-line hand-checkering on grip, butt and forend. Special order only. Made in Turkey.

NIB	Exc.	V.G.	Good	Fair	Poor
5800	5200	4500	—	—	—

Model 200 Field

Side-by-side made in 20-, 28-gauge and .410 bore, with oil-finished hand-checkered Turkish walnut stock. Prince of Wales pistol grip and beavertail forend. Sculpted and hand-engraved boxlock receiver has bison bone charcoal case hardening. Other features include single selective trigger, automatic ejectors, bright blue finish and five interchangeable choke tubes. Imported from Turkey. Note: Add $150 for 28-gauge or .410 bore.

NIB	Exc.	V.G.	Good	Fair	Poor
1750	1500	1220	900	450	200

Model 200 Sporting

Same general features as 200 Field grade. Also available in 12-gauge. Barrel lengths 28" or 30" in all gauges and have a raised ventilated rib. Note: Add $100 for 28-gauge or .410 bore.

NIB	Exc.	V.G.	Good	Fair	Poor
2100	1820	1500	1100	500	250

Model 250 Field

Same features as 200 Field, except has engraved decorative sideplates.

NIB	Exc.	V.G.	Good	Fair	Poor
2200	1850	1700	1300	550	300

Model 590

Over/under in 12- or 20-gauge, with features similar to Model 200 side-by-side series. Imported from Turkey.

NIB	Exc.	V.G.	Good	Fair	Poor
1100	900	750	600	300	200

F.A.I.R. Carrera One HR

Gauge: 12 ga. 3 in. Barrels: 30 in. chrome-lined with 15mm wide high vent rib. Optional 28, 30 in. Weight: 7.5 lbs. with mounted chokes. Stock: Selected European Walnut with ergonomic sporting design and XR-Stock adjustment system (comb/heel) Monte Carlo style, in bright oil finish. Features: FAIR's latest sporting O/U with oversize cross-locking bolt on double lugs, this HR variant with a high rib. Black bright action with golden clay pigeon and model names. Triple-depth laser engraving, black selective single trigger, top tang manual safety, long-stroke automatic ejectors. Oil-resistant ventilated rubber recoil pad. Fine-pitch laser checkering. Fiber-optic front sight. Technichoke XP70 system with 5 tubes (F, IM, M, IC, C). Packed in V500SP case.

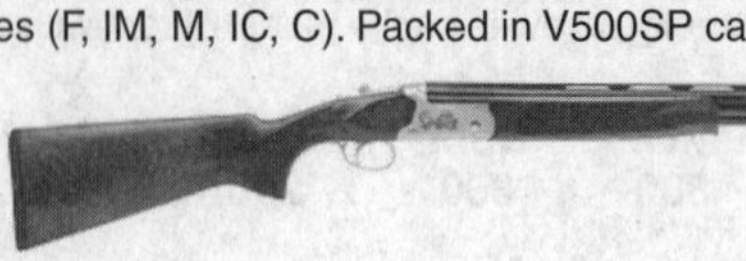

NIB	Exc.	V.G.	Good	Fair	Poor
2030	—	—	—	—	—

Model IS300

Semi-automatic in 12-gauge only. Operates on an inertia-recoil action. Available with synthetic, camo or oil-finished walnut stock. Back-bored barrels and competition choke tube system. Made in Turkey. Note: Deduct $75 for synthetic stock.

NIB	Exc.	V.G.	Good	Fair	Poor
600	500	400	300	200	100

SINGLE BARREL

Century III

Single-barrel trap gun in 12-gauge, with 30" or 32" ventilated rib barrel, fixed or adjustable Grade II walnut stock, lengthened forcing cone, competition choke tube system, laser engraving. Made in Turkey. Note: Add $150 for adjustable stock.

NIB	Exc.	V.G.	Good	Fair	Poor
1000	850	700	500	350	200

SLOTTER & CO.
Philadelphia, Pennsylvania

Pocket Pistol (Antique)

A .41-caliber percussion pocket pistol, with 2.5" to 3.5" barrel. German silver mounts and walnut stock. Marked "Slotter & Co. Phila.". Manufactured during 1860s.

Exc.	Fine	V.G.	Good	Fair	Poor
5000	2500	1570	950	250	170

SMITH AMERICAN ARMS COMPANY
Springfield, Massachusetts

Smith Carbine (Antique)

A .50-caliber breech-loading percussion carbine, with 21.75" round barrel having an octagonal breech. Blued case-hardened, with walnut stock. Barrel marked "Address/Poultney & Trimble/Baltimore, USA" and frame "Smith's Patent/June 23, 1857" as well as "American Arms Co./Chicopee Falls". Approximately 30,000 manufactured, most of which were purchased by the United States government. Sales agents were Poultney & Trimble of Baltimore, Maryland.

Exc.	Fine	V.G.	Good	Fair	Poor
2750	1200	850	500	200	140

SMITH, L. C.
Syracuse, New York
Hunter Arms Company
Fulton, New York

One of the finest American-made double-barrel shotguns and very collectible in today's market. It was manufactured between 1880 and 1888 in Syracuse, New York; and between 1890 and 1945 in Fulton, New York, by Hunter Arms Company. In 1945, Marlin Firearms Company acquired Hunter Arms, and the L.C. Smith was made until 1951. In 1968, L.C. Smith was resurrected for five years, and production ceased in 1973. Marlin brought the L.C. Smith brand to market with models imported from Italy from 2004 to 2010. Values given are approximate for standard production models; and we strongly feel that competent, individual appraisals should be secured, especially on the rarer and higher grade models, if a transaction is contemplated.

Values given are for fluid steel, hammerless guns only. Damascus-barreled guns have become collectible if they are in very good or better condition, and values are approximately the same as for the fluid steel models. Damascus guns in less than good condition are worth considerably less.

Early Hammerless Shotguns

Models listed were manufactured between 1890 and 1913. They are chambered for 10-, 12-, 16- and 20-gauge. Produced with various barrel lengths and choke combinations. Feature full sidelock actions. Difference in models and their values is based on degree of ornamentation and quality of materials and workmanship utilized in their construction. General values furnished are for 10-, 12- or 16-gauge only.

Note: Add 50 percent for 20-gauge; 25 percent premiun for 10- and 16-gauge; $250 for single-selective trigger; 30 percent for automatic ejectors.

00 Grade

60,000 manufactured.

NIB	Exc.	V.G.	Good	Fair	Poor
—	2050	1800	1300	650	400

0 Grade

30,000 manufactured.

NIB	Exc.	V.G.	Good	Fair	Poor
—	2150	1900	1400	700	450

No. 1 Grade

10,000 manufactured.

NIB	Exc.	V.G.	Good	Fair	Poor
—	3150	2600	1950	800	550

No. 2 Grade

13,000 manufactured.

NIB	Exc.	V.G.	Good	Fair	Poor
—	3500	2900	1620	900	700

No. 3 Grade

4,000 manufactured.

NIB	Exc.	V.G.	Good	Fair	Poor
—	4250	3400	2280	1000	750

Pigeon Grade

1,200 manufactured.

NIB	Exc.	V.G.	Good	Fair	Poor
—	8500	7500	5000	3000	1500

No. 4 Grade

500 manufactured.

NIB	Exc.	V.G.	Good	Fair	Poor
—	10000	9000	7000	4500	2400

A-1 Grade

700 manufactured, all damascus, no 20-gauge.

NIB	Exc.	V.G.	Good	Fair	Poor
—	8000	7000	5000	3000	1500

No. 5 Grade

500 manufactured.

NIB	Exc.	V.G.	Good	Fair	Poor
—	12000	11000	8000	6500	3000

Monogram Grade

100 manufactured.

NIB	Exc.	V.G.	Good	Fair	Poor
—	18000	15000	11000	7500	4500

A-2 Grade

200 manufactured.

NIB	Exc.	V.G.	Good	Fair	Poor
—	25000	21000	16000	10000	6000

A-3 Grade

20 manufactured. Too rare to generalize a value.

Later Production Hammerless Shotguns

These were manufactured at Fulton, New York, between 1914 and 1951. They are side-by-side double-barrel shotguns. Chambered for 12-, 16-, 20-gauge and .410 bore. Offered with various barrel lengths and choke combinations. Feature a full sidelock action. Available with double-/single triggers, extractors and automatic ejectors. Finishes are blued and case colored, with checkered walnut stocks that are straight, semi-pistol grip or pistol grip configurations. Various models differ as to degree of ornamentation and quality of materials and workmanship utilized in their construction. These are highly collectible American shotguns. Because these guns were manufactured as late as 1951, mint original specimens and even unfired new in box guns will be offered for sale occasionally. These guns are worth considerably more than excellent condition guns and more than ever an individual, expert authentication and appraisal is recommended if a transaction is anticipated.

Note: Values supplied are for 12-gauge only. Add 25 percent premium for 16-gauge; 50 percent premium for 20-gauge; 200 percent premium for .410 bore (field grade); 300 to 400 percent for higher grades; $250 for single-selective triggers; 30 percent premium for automatic ejectors.

Courtesy Milwaukee Public Museum, Milwaukee, Wisconsin

Field Grade

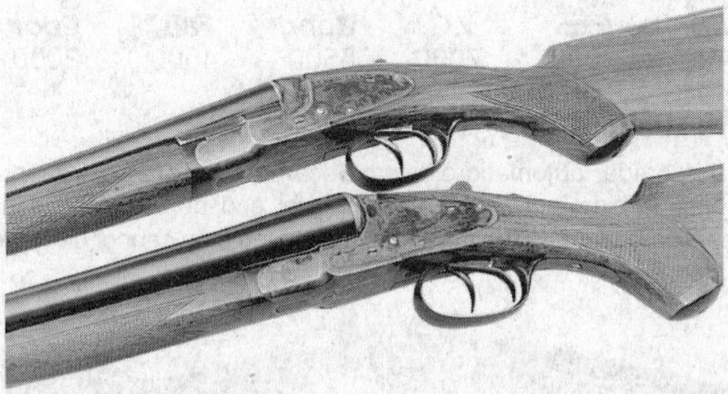

Courtesy William Hammond

L.C. Smith 12 gauge and .410 bore Field Grade

NIB	Exc.	V.G.	Good	Fair	Poor
—	2500	1600	1120	700	350

Specialty Grade

Courtesy William Hammond

NIB	Exc.	V.G.	Good	Fair	Poor
—	5000	4000	3000	2000	1000

Skeet Special Grade

Courtesy William Hammond

NIB	Exc.	V.G.	Good	Fair	Poor
—	4500	3500	2700	1800	900

Premier Skeet Grade

NIB	Exc.	V.G.	Good	Fair	Poor
—	5200	4200	3000	2000	1000

Eagle Grade

NIB	Exc.	V.G.	Good	Fair	Poor
—	8000	7000	5500	4000	2000

Crown Grade

With this grade, automatic ejectors became standard equipment. The .410 bore is extremely rare in this model and non-existent in higher grades. There were only six manufactured, and they cannot be generally evaluated.

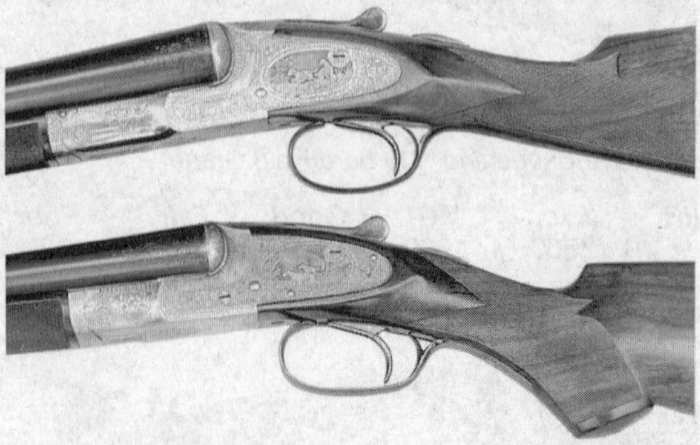

Courtesy William Hammond

12 and 20 gauge Crown Grades

NIB	Exc.	V.G.	Good	Fair	Poor
—	12000	10000	7500	5000	3000

Ideal Grade

With this grade, automatic ejectors became standard equipment. The .410 is extremely rare in this model and non-existent in higher grades. There were only six manufactured, and they cannot be generally evaluated.

NIB	Exc.	V.G.	Good	Fair	Poor
—	3200	2500	1700	900	500

Trap Grade

With this grade, automatic ejectors became standard equipment. The .410 is extremely rare in this model and non-existent in higher grades. There were only six manufactured, and they cannot be generally evaluated.

NIB	Exc.	V.G.	Good	Fair	Poor
—	4000	3000	2500	1500	1000

Monogram Grade

There were two higher grades offered: Premier Grade and Deluxe Grade. They are extremely rare, and there have not been enough transactions to generally evaluate them. This version is offered standard, with automatic ejectors and single-selective trigger.

NIB	Exc.	V.G.	Good	Fair	Poor
—	18000	15000	10000	6000	3500

HUNTER ARMS BOXLOCKS

These shotguns are inexpensive high quality boxlocks. Built with quality equal to Field Grade L.C. Smith. Receiver, forend iron, triggerguard and triggers are all machined from forgings. Durability of these guns has proven to be excellent.

Fulton Model

Utility side-by-side boxlock shotgun, chambered for 12-, 16-, 20-gauge and .410 bore. Offered with various barrel lengths and choke combinations. Has double triggers and extractors, with non-selective single trigger option. Values given are for 12-gauge only. Note: Add 50 percent premium for 20-gauge; 250 percent premium for .410 bore; 25 percent for 16-gauge; $150 for single trigger.

NIB	Exc.	V.G.	Good	Fair	Poor
—	1150	920	600	420	150

Fulton Special

Slightly higher grade version of Fulton Model. Featuring modest engraving and pointed checkering. Note: Add 50 percent premium for 20-gauge; 25 percent for 16-gauge; $200 for single trigger.

Courtesy William Hammond

NIB	Exc.	V.G.	Good	Fair	Poor
—	1400	1050	750	500	200

Hunter Special

Similar to Fulton Model, but features L.C. Smith rotary locking bolt. Note: Add 75 percent premium for 20-gauge; 300 percent premium for .410 bore; 25 percent for 16-gauge.

Courtesy William Hammond

NIB	Exc.	V.G.	Good	Fair	Poor
—	1100	950	750	500	200

Single Barrel Trap Guns

High quality break-open single-shot trap guns, chambered for 12-gauge only. Feature 32" or 34" ventilated rib barrels that are Full-choked. Have boxlock actions and are standard with automatic ejectors. Finish blued and case colored. Checkered walnut stock, with recoil pad. Various models differ in amount of ornamentation and quality of materials and workmanship utilized in their construction. A total of approximately 2,650 manufactured between 1917 and 1951. Although these firearms are actually rarer and just as high in quality as their side-by-side counterparts, they are simply not as collectible as the side-by-side variations.

Note: Only two Premier Grade and three Deluxe Grade trap guns manufactured. This rarity makes it unrealistic to give an estimate of values. Beware of fakes.

Olympic Grade

NIB	Exc.	V.G.	Good	Fair	Poor
—	3000	2200	1500	900	500

Specialty Grade

NIB	Exc.	V.G.	Good	Fair	Poor
—	4500	3500	2000	1000	800

Crown Grade

NIB	Exc.	V.G.	Good	Fair	Poor
—	9000	6700	4500	2500	1500

Monogram Grade

NIB	Exc.	V.G.	Good	Fair	Poor
—	16000	10000	7500	5000	2500

1968 Model

Side-by-side double-barrel shotgun. Chambered for 12-gauge, with 28" ventilated rib barrel, choked Full and Modified. Features sidelock action, with double triggers and extractors. Finish blued and case colored, with checkered walnut stock. Offered by Marlin between 1968 and 1973. These are less desirable than earlier models because of manufacturing expedients used. Investment cast receiver rather than machined forgings were used. Cyanide case-hardening replaced bone charcoal hardening and aluminum ventilated ribs were used. A thin brown polymer layer was used to create the fit between lock plates and buttstock, which is a departure from traditional fitting.

NIB	Exc.	V.G.	Good	Fair	Poor
1750	1480	1100	850	450	300

1968 Deluxe Model

Similar to 1968 Model, but features a Simmons floating rib and beavertail-type forearm. Manufactured by Marlin between 1971 and 1973.

NIB	Exc.	V.G.	Good	Fair	Poor
2200	1800	1350	1100	700	400

L.C. SMITH 2005-2009 (MARLIN)

These L.C. Smith models were made in Italy or Spain and imported into the U.S. under the Marlin name. See listings under Marlin section.

SMITH, OTIS A.

Rockfall, Connecticut

Otis A. Smith produced unique design pocket revolvers including top-break single-action spur-trigger pocket pistols and Safety Hammerless revolvers. Smith revolvers tended to be higher quality than many other pocket revolvers of the era. They usually had a brass barrel and frame. Although iron versions were also made in smaller numbers, they generally do not bring a premium. Maltby Henley & Co. was a major marketing agent for Otis Smith revolvers.

United States Arms Co. .44 CF/RF Revolver (Antique)

.44 rimfire and centerfire single-action revolver, with 7" barrel and integral ejector. Hammer nose fitted with two firing pins so rimfire or centerfire cartridges can be used interchangeably. Barrel marked "United States Arms Company - New York"; topstrap "No. 44". Blued, with hard rubber or rosewood grips. Manufactured in limited quantities. Circa 1870 to 1875.

Exc.	Fine	V.G.	Good	Fair	Poor
4750	3250	2250	1250	500	350

Model 1883 Shell-Ejector (Antique)

Spur-trigger top-break single-action revolver; .32 centerfire, 3.25" barrel, five-shot. Unique features include brass barrel & frame, push-rod ejector mounted under barrel, and firing pin mounted in T-shaped latch. Also found marked "New Model" or "Newest Model."

Exc.	Fine	V.G.	Good	Fair	Poor
500	280	190	100	80	50

Safety Hammerless (Antique)

Also known as Model 1892, manufactured in the 1890s. Most common configuraton is .32 centerfire, five-shot, 3" barrel. Also made in larger frame .38 and smaller frame .22 models, either of which will bring a premium. Unusual solid-frame double-action-only concealed hammer revolver. Barrel and frame are one-piece and usually made of brass. The rarer iron construction does not bring a premium. Other unusual features include a serrated wheel-type safety mounted on the frame knuckle and a latch on the frame top-strap that allows the cylinder to rotate freely for loading. Often marked Maltby Henley & Co., other trade names include Spencer, J.N. Scott, Parker, Columbia Armory, or New York Arms Co.

Exc.	Fine	V.G.	Good	Fair	Poor
500	280	190	100	80	50

SMITH & WESSON

Springfield, Massachusetts

Since 1857 Smith & Wesson has staked its headquarters in Springfield, Massachusetts with manufacturing operations in Holton, Maine and other operations in Columbia, Missouri. Partnership with Horace Smith & Daniel B. Wesson was from 1856–1874. Family owned by the Wesson Family from 1874–1965. Smith & Wesson became a subsidiary of Bangor-Punta from 1965–1983. Between 1983–1987, Smith & Wesson was owned by the Lear Siegler Co. On May 22, 1987, it was sold to R.L.Tomkins, a British holding company. In 2001, Tomkins sold the concern to Saf-T-Hammer, an Arizona-based safety and security company. SEE POLITICAL PANIC PRICING. Edited by Rex Halfpenny for 2023 value updates.

SMITH & WESSON ANTIQUE HANDGUNS

Listed in the following order:
- Volcanic type S&W lever action pistols, see Winchester section.
- Tip-up revolvers, from .22 to .32, 1857-1875
- Top-break revolvers, from .32 to .45, 1870-1913
- Single shot pistols, 1893-1936

A surprising number of early S&Ws are still found in their original boxes, even for older models. This can add up to 100% to the value of the pistol.

TIP-UP REVOLVERS

Single-action spur-trigger rimfire revolvers. Releasing latch on bottom front of frame allows the barrel to be tipped up and the cylinder removed for loading and unloading. Empties are punched out using the ejector stud mounted under the barrel. Model 1 – small frame .22 seven-shot; Model 1 ½ medium-small frame .32 five-shot; Model 2 medium frame .32 six-shot.

Model 1, 1st Issue Revolver

This was the first metallic-cartridge arm produced by Smith & Wesson. It is a small revolver that weighs about 10 oz. Chambered for .22 Short rimfire cartridge. Octagonal barrel 3.25" long. Holds 7 cartridges. Barrel and non-fluted cylinder pivot upward upon release of the latch under the frame. Has a square butt with rosewood grips. Oval brass frame is silver-plated. Barrel and cylinder are blued. Barrel is stamped with company name and address; patent dates also appear. Sides of frame are rounded on the 1st issue. Other characteristics which distinguish the more valuable 1st issue from later issues include a perfectly round side plate and a hinged hammer spur. Smith & Wesson manufactured approximately 11,000 of these revolvers between 1857 and 1860. Since this was the first of its kind, it is not difficult to understand the need for the number of variations within this model designation. Many small improvements were made on the way to the next model. These variations are as follows:

1st Type Antique

Serial range 1 to low 200s. Revolving recoil shield, bayonet type catch on frame. They are too rare to make a meaningful estimate. Depending on condition, might sell in the low- to mid-five figures. Rare; values are speculative.

Exc.	Fine	V.G.	Good	Fair	Poor
60000	40000	20000	12000	8000	5000

2nd Type Antique

Serial range low 200s to 1130. Improved recoil plate.

Exc.	Fine	V.G.	Good	Fair	Poor
10000	6000	4250	2500	1200	700

3rd Type Antique

Serial range 1130 to low 3000s. Bayonet catch dropped for spring-loaded side catch.

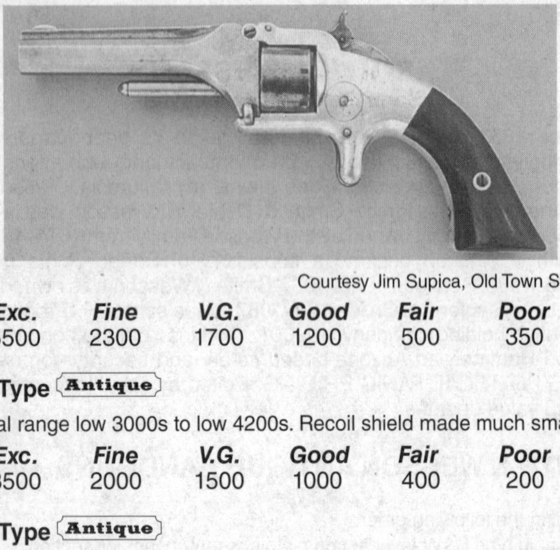

Courtesy Jim Supica, Old Town Station

Exc.	Fine	V.G.	Good	Fair	Poor
5500	2300	1700	1200	500	350

4th Type Antique

Serial range low 3000s to low 4200s. Recoil shield made much smaller.

Exc.	Fine	V.G.	Good	Fair	Poor
3500	2000	1500	1000	400	200

5th Type Antique

Serial range low 4200s to low 5500s. Has 5-groove rifling instead of 3.

Exc.	Fine	V.G.	Good	Fair	Poor
3000	2000	1500	1000	400	200

6th Type Antique

Serial range low 5500s to end of production at about 11670. A cylinder ratchet replaced revolving recoil shield.

Exc.	Fine	V.G.	Good	Fair	Poor
2800	2700	1200	1000	250	170

Model 1, 2nd Issue Antique

Similar in appearance to 1st Issue, this 2nd Issue variation has several notable differences that make identification rather simple. Sides of frame on 2nd Issue are flat not rounded as on 1st Issue. Sideplate is irregular in shape—not round like on 1st Issue. Barrel is 3.1875" in length and stamped "Smith & Wesson" while cylinder is marked with three patent dates: April 3, 1858, July 5, 1859 and December 18, 1860. There have been 2nd Issue noted with full silver or nickel-plating. Smith & Wesson manufactured approximately 115,000 of these revolvers between 1860 and 1868. Serial numbers started around 11000 where 1st Issue left off and continued to 126400. Approximately 4,400 revolvers marked "2D Quality" on barrels. These revolvers were slightly defective and were sold at a lesser price. They will bring approximately 100% premium on today's market. Early production with a straight-edged sideplate, usually found in the 11000 to 12000 s/n range, will bring double values.

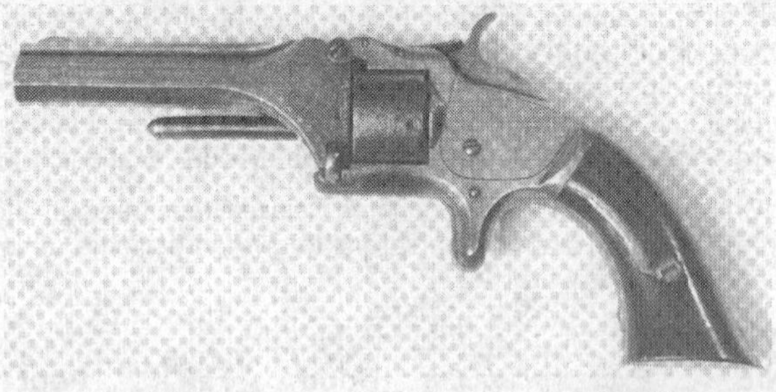

Courtesy Mike Stuckslager

Exc.	Fine	V.G.	Good	Fair	Poor
1250	900	600	350	200	100

Model 1, 3rd Issue

This is a redesigned version of its fore-runners. Another .22 Short rimfire 7-shot revolver, this model has a fluted cylinder and round barrel with a raised rib. This variation was manufactured totally from wrought iron. Three patent dates are stamped on top of ribbed barrel as is "Smith & Wesson". Features bird's-head type grips of rosewood and fully blued nickel-plated or two-toned. Frame nickel, barrel and cylinder blued. There are two barrel lengths offered: 3.25" and 2.6875". Shorter barrel introduced in 1872. Serial numbering began with #1 and continued to 131163. They were manufactured between 1868 and 1882. Model 1, 3rd Issue was last of tip-up style produced by Smith & Wesson. Short Barrel Version. Rare variation will bring double these values or more.

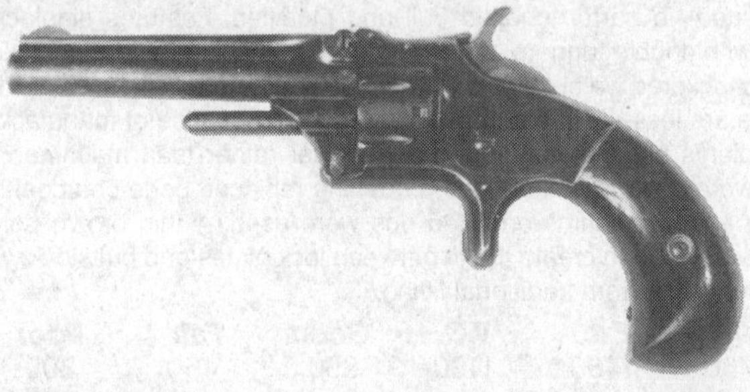

Courtesy Mike Stuckslager

NIB	Exc.	V.G.	Good	Fair	Poor
1500	800	600	400	200	100

Standard Barreled Version Antique

Exc.	Fine	V.G.	Good	Fair	Poor
500	300	250	200	100	70

Model 1-1/2 1st Issue (1-1/2 Old Model) Antique

This model was the first of .32-caliber rimfire Short revolvers that S&W produced. It is a larger version of Model 1, but is physically similar in appearance. Model 1-1/2 was offered with 3.5" octagonal barrel. Has a 5-shot non-fluted cylinder and square butt with rosewood grips. In 1866, a 4" barrel version was produced for a short time. Estimated about 200 were sold. Finish blued or nickel-plated. Serial numbering, on this model, ran from 1 to 26300; interestingly to note, S&W had most of the parts for this revolver manufactured on contract by King & Smith of Middletown, Connecticut. Smith & Wesson merely assembled and finished them. They were produced between 1865 and 1868. Note: Add 50% premium for 4" barrel variation.

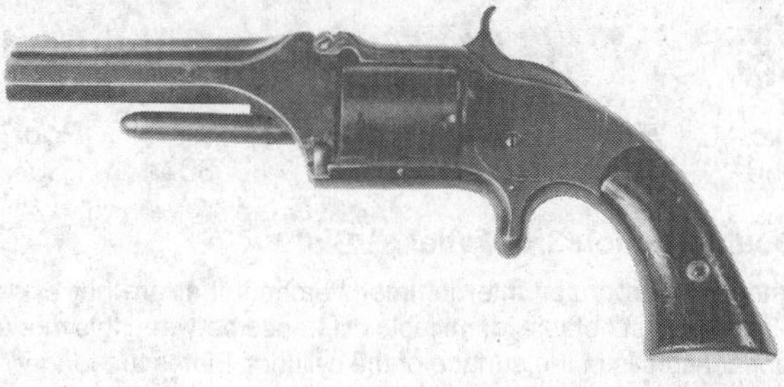

Courtesy Mike Stuckslager

Exc.	Fine	V.G.	Good	Fair	Poor
750	500	450	350	200	100

Model 1-1/2 Transitional Model (Antique)

Approximately 650 of these were produced by fitting 1st Issue cylinders and barrels to 2nd Issue frames. They also have 1st Model octagon barrels, with 2nd Model bird's-head grips. These revolvers fall into serial number range 27200-28800.

Exc.	Fine	V.G.	Good	Fair	Poor
4000	3000	2000	1500	750	400

Model 1-1/2 2nd Issue (1-1/2 New Model)

Factory referred to this model as New Model 1-1/2 and it is an improved version of 1st Issue. Somewhat similar in appearance with a few notable exceptions. Barrel is 2.5" or 3.5" in length, round with a raised rib. Grip is of bird's-head configuration and 5-shot cylinder is fluted. Chambered for .32 Long rimfire cartridge. Cylinder stop located in the top frame instead of bottom. Finish and grip material are the same as 1st Issue. Approximately 100,700 manufactured between 1868 and 1875.

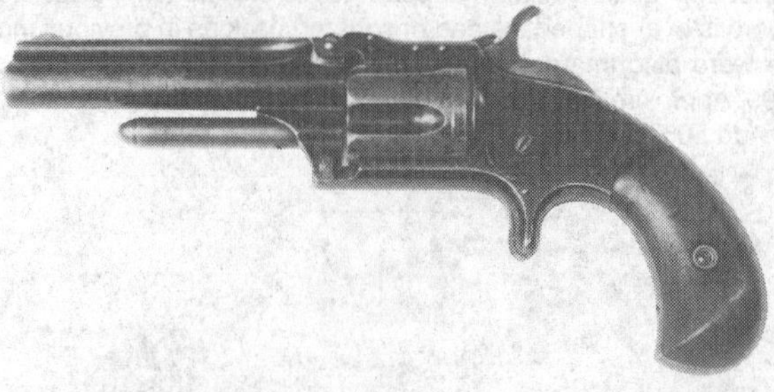

Courtesy Mike Stuckslager

3.5" Barrel (Antique)

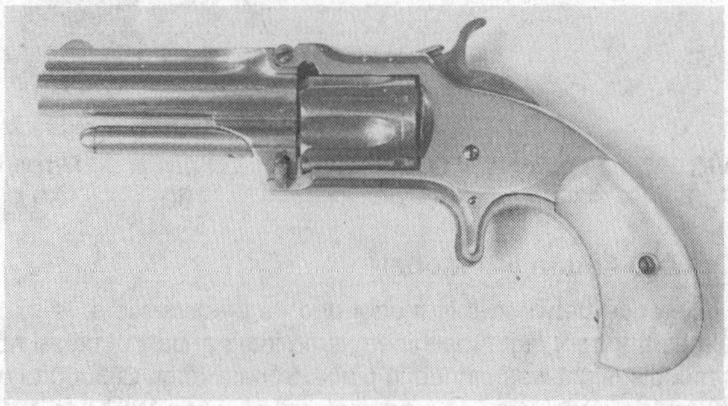

Courtesy Mike Stuckslager

Exc.	Fine	V.G.	Good	Fair	Poor
650	380	280	180	100	70

2.5" Barrel (Antique)

Rare. Watch for fakes.

Exc.	Fine	V.G.	Good	Fair	Poor
1100	600	470	350	100	70

Model Number 2 or Old Army Model

Similar in appearance to Model 1, 2nd Issue, this revolver was extremely successful from a commercial standpoint. Released just in time for commencement of hostilities in the Civil War. Smith & Wesson had, in this revolver, the only weapon able to fire self-contained cartridges and be easily carried as a backup by soldiers going off to war. This resulted in a backlog of more than three years, before the company finally stopped taking orders. Chambered for .32 Long rimfire cartridge, has a 6-shot non-fluted cylinder and 4", 5" or 6" barrel lengths. Has a square butt with rosewood grips and blued or nickel-plated. Approximately 77,155 manufactured between 1861 and 1874. Rare. "Scarce."

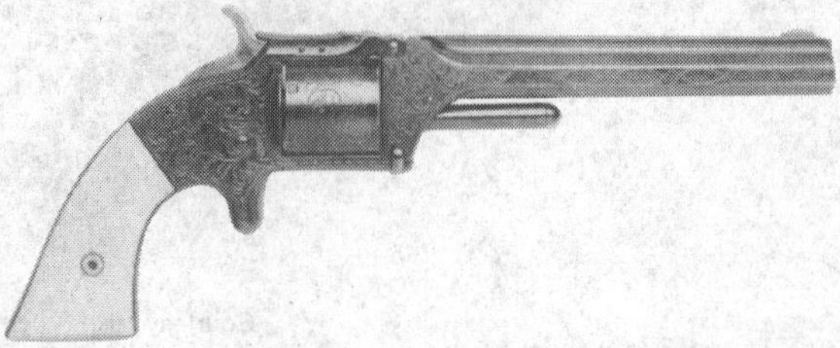

Model 2 Army or Old Model5" or 6" Barrel (Antique)

Standard barrel.

Exc.	Fine	V.G.	Good	Fair	Poor
2000	1200	700	450	300	210

4" Barrel (Antique)

Note: A slight premium for early two-pin model. For rare 8" model add 800%. Rare; use caution, values are speculative.

Exc.	Fine	V.G.	Good	Fair	Poor
6000	3650	2570	1500	500	350

TOP-BREAK REVOLVERS

To load and unload, a latch is released at the rear of the barrel allowing the barrel & cylinder to tip-forward. Cartridges are automatically ejected upon opening. Listed in order of frame size:

- Small frame: Model 1 ½ - .32 caliber five-shot. Single Action, Double Action, Safety Hammerless
- Medium frame: Model 2 - .38 caliber five-shot. Single Action, Double Action, Safety Hammerless
- Large frame: Model 3 - .44 or .45 caliber six-shot. American, Russia, Schofield, New Model No. 3, Double Action.

.32 Single-Action (so-called "1-1/2 Frame" Centerfire)

This model represented the first .32 S&W centerfire caliber top-break revolver that automatically ejected spent cartridges upon opening. Similar in appearance to Model 1-1/2 2nd Issue. This model has a 5-shot fluted cylinder and bird's-head grip of wood or checkered hard rubber. Offered with barrel lengths of 3, 3.5", 6", 8" and 10". The 8" and 10" barrel are rare and were not offered until 1887. Rare long barrels worth premium, Very rare short original 2.5" barrel worth significant premium, perhaps as much as 10X in highest condition grades. This model pivots downward on opening. Features a rebounding hammer that made the weapon much safer to fully load. Approximately 97,599 manufactured between 1878 and 1892.

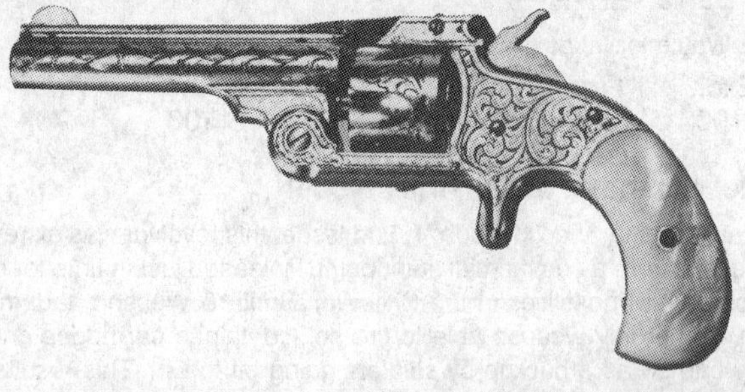

Courtesy W.P. Hallstein III and son Chip

Early Model w/o Strain Screw—Under #6500 Antique

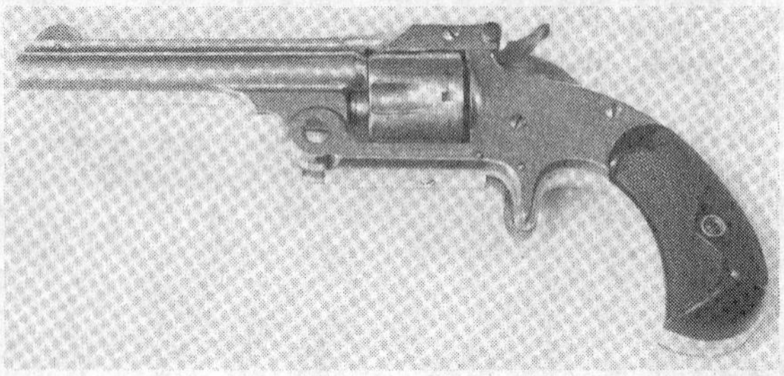

Courtesy Mike Stuckslager

Exc.	Fine	V.G.	Good	Fair	Poor
600	300	240	180	80	50

Later Model with Strain Screw Antique

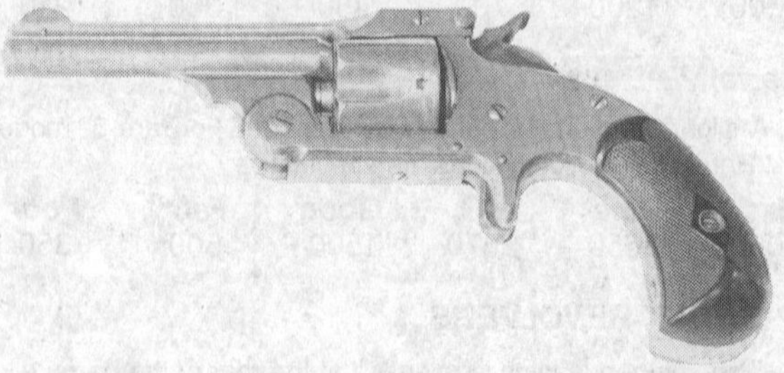

Courtesy Mike Stuckslager

Exc.	Fine	V.G.	Good	Fair	Poor
450	300	220	150	80	50

8" or 10" Barrel Antique

Very rare; use caution. Values are speculative.

Exc.	Fine	V.G.	Good	Fair	Poor
4500	2500	1650	800	400	280

.32 Double-Action 1st Model Antique

This is one of the rarest of all S&W revolvers. There were only 30 manufactured. It also has a straight-sided sideplate which weakened the revolver frame. Perhaps this was the reason that so few were made. This model was the first break-open double-action automatic-ejecting .32 that S&W produced. Features a 3" round barrel with raised rib, 5-shot fluted cylinder and round butt with plain smooth black hard rubber grips. Finish blued or nickel-plated. All 30 of these revolvers were manufactured in 1880. Serial range 1-30. Note: Rarity makes valuation speculative.

Exc.	Fine	V.G.	Good	Fair	Poor
12000	7500	5750	4000	1000	700

.32 Double-Action 2nd Model Antique

This revolver is chambered for .32 S&W cartridge. Has 3" round barrel with a raised rib. The 5-shot cylinder is fluted. Finish blued or nickel plated. It is a top-break design with a round butt. Grips are checkered or floral-embossed hard rubber, with S&W monogram. This model has an oval sideplate, eliminating the weakness of 1st Model. Serial Range 31-22172. Approximately 22,142 manufactured between 1880 and 1882.

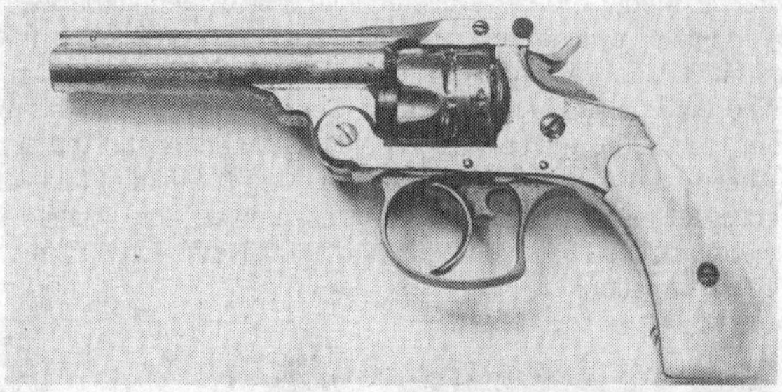

Courtesy Mike Stuckslager

Exc.	Fine	V.G.	Good	Fair	Poor
350	220	200	180	80	50

.32 Double-Action 3rd Model Antique

This model incorporates internal improvements that are not evident in appearance. Most notable identifiable difference between this model and its predecessors is in the surface of the cylinder. Flutes are longer; there is only one set of stops instead of two; free groove is no longer present. Serial Range 22173-43405. Approximately 21,232 manufactured in 1882 and 1883.

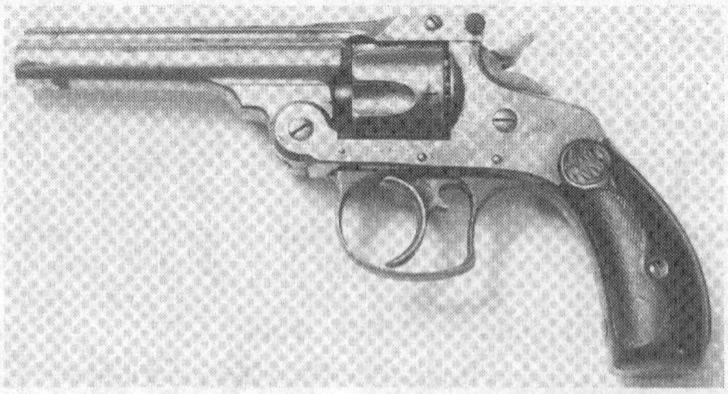

Courtesy Mike Stuckslager

Exc.	Fine	V.G.	Good	Fair	Poor
350	220	200	180	80	50

.32 Double-Action 4th Model

This model is quite similar in appearance to 3rd Model, except the trigguard is oval-shaped instead of squared back as in previous models. There were also internal improvements. Serial Range 43406-to about 282999. Approximately 239,600 manufactured between 1883 and 1909. Note: Add 50% premium for revolvers built before 1898.

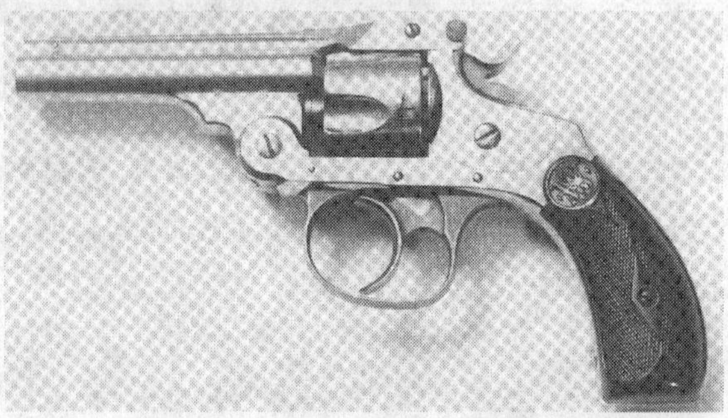

Courtesy Mike Stuckslager

NIB	Exc.	V.G.	Good	Fair	Poor
500	430	280	200	130	80

.32 Double-Action 5th Model

Only difference between this model and its predecessors, is that this model has the front sight machined as an integral part of barrel rib. On other models, sight was pinned in place. Serial Range 283000 to about 32764. Approximately 44,641 manufactured between 1909 and 1919.

Courtesy Mike Stuckslager

NIB	Exc.	V.G.	Good	Fair	Poor
—	500	380	250	120	100

SAFETY HAMMERLESS

This model was a departure from what was commonly being produced at this time. Some attribute the Safety Hammerless design to D.B. Wesson's hearing that a child had been injured by cocking and firing one of the company's pistols. This story has never been proven. Nevertheless, concealed hammer and grip safety make this an ideal pocket pistol for those needing concealability in a handgun. This is a small revolver chambered for .32 S&W and .38 S&W cartridges. It has a 5-shot fluted cylinder. Offered with 2", 3" and 3.5" round barrel, with raised rib. Butt is rounded and has checkered hard rubber grips, with S&W logo. Finish blue or nickel plated. Revolver is a top-break automatic-ejecting design; 1st Model has latch for opening located in the rear center of top strap instead of at the sides. Latch is checkered for a positive grip. This model is commonly referred to as "Lemon Squeezer," because the grip safety must be squeezed as it is fired.

Courtesy Mike Stuckslager

Bicycle Gun

Smith & Wesson manufactured some of their .32 and .32 Safety Hammerless models with shorter than usual barrels - usually 2", but sometimes 1.5". These are called "Bicycle Guns" and will bring a substantial premium, sometimes two to four times what a standard barrel will bring. Beware of cut barrels - S&W would not cut through their barrel address to make a short barrel gun. Original shorter than standard barrels on .32 & .38 Double Action models will also bring a premium.

Courtesy Supica's GunHeritage.com

.32 Safety Hammerless (aka .32 New Departure or .32 Lemon Squeezer) 1st Model Antique

Push button latch serial number 1- 91417. Built 1888-1902. Note: Add 50% premium for revolvers built before 1898.

Exc.	Fine	V.G.	Good	Fair	Poor
600	350	280	200	100	50

.32 Safety Hammerless 2nd Model

T-bar latch pinned front sight. Serial number 91418-169999. Built 1902 to 1909.

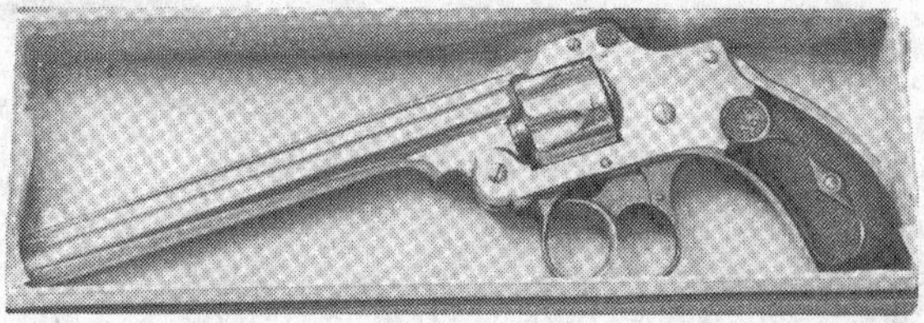

Courtesy Mike Stuckslager

NIB	Exc.	V.G.	Good	Fair	Poor
—	550	350	200	100	50

.32 Safety Hammerless 3rd Model

T-bar latch integral forged front sight. Serial number 170000-242981. Built 1909 to 1937. Note: Add 200% for 2" barrel Bicycle Model.

NIB	Exc.	V.G.	Good	Fair	Poor
—	550	350	200	100	50

.38 Single-Action 1st Model (Baby Russian) Antique

This model is sometimes called "Baby Russian." A top-break automatic-ejecting revolver chambered for .38 S&W centerfire cartridge. Offered with 3.25" or 4" round barrel. Raised rib has a 5-shot fluted cylinder and finished in blue or nickel plating. A 5" barrel was added as an option a short time later. Butt is rounded, with wood or checkered hard rubber grips inlaid with S&W medallion. It has a spur trigger. Approximately 25,548 manufactured in 1876 and 1877, of which 16,046 were nickel; 6,502 blued.

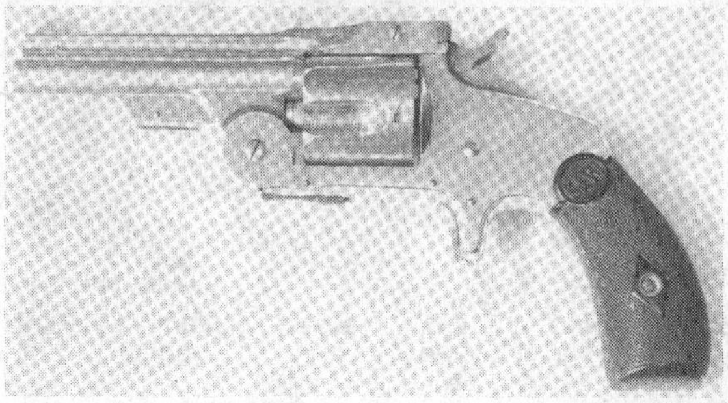

Courtesy Mike Stuckslager

Exc.	Fine	V.G.	Good	Fair	Poor
1200	900	620	350	150	100

.38 Single-Action 2nd Model

With the exception of an improved and shortened extractor assembly and availability of additional barrel lengths of 3.25", 4", 5", 6", 8" and 10", with 8" and 10" barrel lengths being the most rare, this model is quite similar in appearance to 1st Model. Approximately 108,225 manufactured between 1877 and 1891.

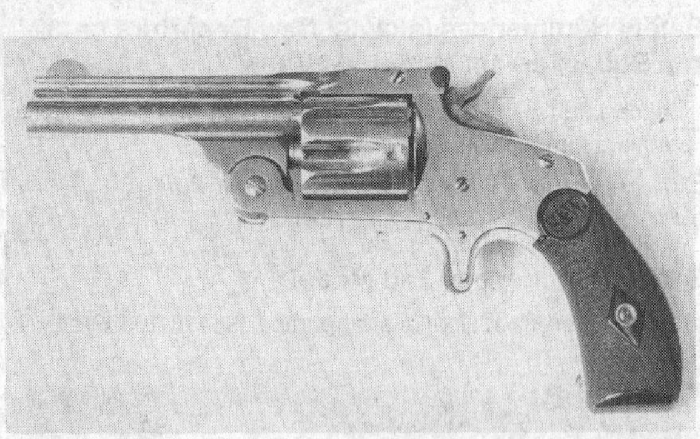

Courtesy Mike Stuckslager

3.25", 4", 5", and 6" Barrel Lengths Antique

Small premium for 5" or 6" lengths.

Exc.	Fine	V.G.	Good	Fair	Poor
450	350	250	200	100	50

8" and 10" Barrel Antique

Very rare, use caution. Values are speculative.

Exc.	Fine	V.G.	Good	Fair	Poor
4000	2250	1600	950	500	350

.38 Single-Action 3rd Model (Model of 1891) Antique

This model differs from first two models because it is fitted with a triggerguard. Chambered for .38 S&W centerfire cartridge. Has a 5-shot fluted cylinder and is a top-break design with automatic ejection upon opening. Barrel lengths are 3.25", 4" and 6". Finish blued or nickel-plated. Butt is rounded, with checkered hard rubber grips featuring S&W medallions. Approximately 26,850 manufactured between 1891 and 1911. Also sold with matching single shot barrel or multiple barrels. Cased sets will bring multiples of the listed value. See also "1st Model Single Shot" listing.

Courtesy Mike Stuckslager

Exc.	Fine	V.G.	Good	Fair	Poor
2500	1200	800	600	200	140

.38 Single-Action Mexican Model Antique

This extremely rare model is quite similar in appearance to 3rd Model Single-Action. Notable differences are flat hammer sides, with no outward flaring of spur. Spur trigger assembly was not made integrally with the frame, but a separate part added to it. One must exercise extreme caution as S&W offered a kit that would convert the triggerguard assembly of Third Model to spur trigger of Mexican Model. This, coupled with the fact that both models fall within the same serial range, can present a real identification problem. Another feature of Mexican Model is absence of a half cock. The exact number of Mexican Models manufactured between 1891 and 1911 is unknown but estimated that the number is about 2,000.

Exc.	Fine	V.G.	Good	Fair	Poor
3650	1500	1220	950	400	280

.38 Double-Action 1st Model Antique

Similar in appearance to .32 1st Model. Having a straight cut side-plate but chambered for .38 S&W cartridge. Grips are checkered. Serial Range 1-about 4000. Manufactured circa 1880.

Exc.	Fine	V.G.	Good	Fair	Poor
650	400	320	250	80	50

.38 Double-Action 2nd Model Antique

Similar in appearance to .32 2nd Model but chambered for .38 S&W cartridge. Approximately 115,000 manufactured between 1880 and 1884. Serial range about 4001-119000.

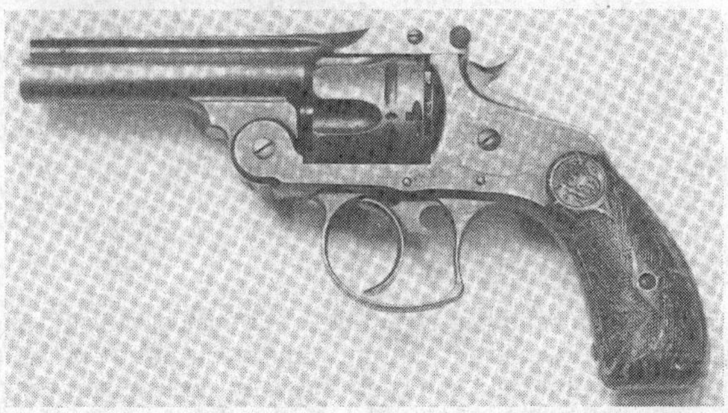

Courtesy Mike Stuckslager

Exc.	Fine	V.G.	Good	Fair	Poor
380	220	210	200	100	70

.38 Double-Action 3rd Model

Essentially the same in appearance as .32 Model but chambered for .38 S&W cartridge. Also offered with 3.25", 4", 5", 6", 8" and 10" barrel. There were numerous internal changes in this model, similar to .32 Double-Action 3rd Model. Serial Range 119001 to 3227000. Approximately 203,700 manufactured between 1884 and 1895.

8- and 10-In. Barrel Antique

Rare, use caution. Values are speculative.

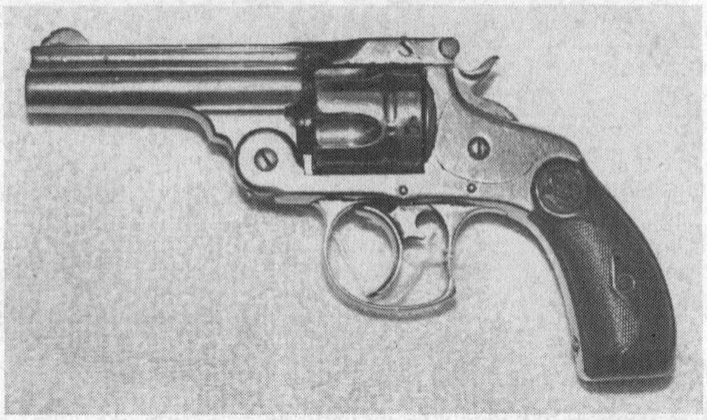

Courtesy Mike Stuckslager

Exc.	Fine	V.G.	Good	Fair	Poor
2500	1500	1150	800	200	140

Standard Barrel Antique

Exc.	Fine	V.G.	Good	Fair	Poor
450	320	260	200	80	50

.38 Double-Action 4th Model

This is .38 S&W version of 4th Model. Identical in outward appearance to 3rd Model. Relocation of sear was the main design change in this model. Serial Range 322701 to 539000. Approximately 216,300 manufactured between 1895 and 1909. Note: Add 20% premium for revolvers built before 1898.

NIB	Exc.	V.G.	Good	Fair	Poor
—	500	230	220	150	80

.38 Double-Action 5th Model

This model same as .32, except chambered for .38 S&W cartridge. Serial Range 529001 to 554077. Approximately 15,000 manufactured between 1909 and 1911.

Courtesy Mike Stuckslager

NIB	Exc.	V.G.	Good	Fair	Poor
—	520	380	220	150	80

.38 Double-Action Perfected

A unique top-break, with both a barrel latch similar to other top-breaks and thumb-piece similar to hand ejectors. Also the only top-break where triggerguard is integral to the frame, rather than a separate piece. Produced from 1909 to 1920 in their own serial number range 1-59400.

NIB	Exc.	V.G.	Good	Fair	Poor
900	600	520	300	160	80

.38 Safety Hammerless 1st Model (Antique)

Z-bar latch. Serial number range 1 to 5250. Made 1887 only. Note: Add 50% for 6" barrel. Rare!

Exc.	Fine	V.G.	Good	Fair	Poor
1200	600	350	250	100	70

.38 Safety Hammerless 2nd Model (Antique)

Push button latch protrudes above frame. Serial number 5251-42483. Built 1887-1890.

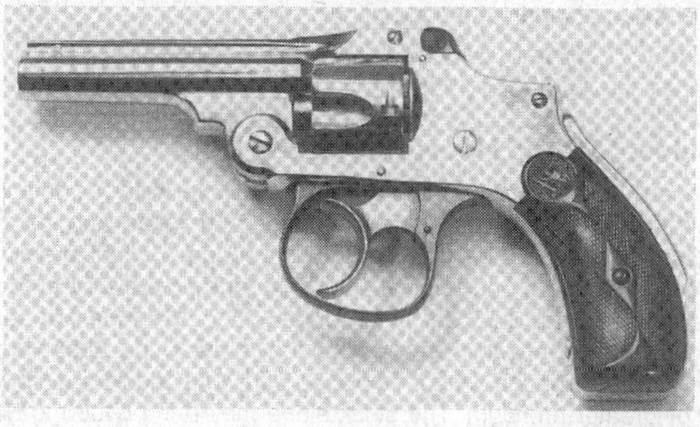

Courtesy Mike Stuckslager

Exc.	Fine	V.G.	Good	Fair	Poor
400	300	210	180	100	70

.38 Safety Hammerless 3rd Model (Antique)

Push button latch flush with frame. Serial number 42484-116002. Built 1890-1898.

Exc.	Fine	V.G.	Good	Fair	Poor
400	300	200	160	100	70

.38 Safety Hammerless Army Test Revolver (Antique)

Approximately 100 sold to U.S. government in 1890. They have 3rd Model features, but in 2nd Model serial number range 41333-41470. Fitted with 6" barrels and marked "US". Caution: Be wary of fakes. Note: Rarity makes valuation speculative.

Exc.	Fine	V.G.	Good	Fair	Poor
10000	7500	5750	4000	—	—

.38 Safety Hammerless 4th Model

Produced in .38 S&W only. The only difference in 4th Model and 3rd Model is adoption of standard T-bar type of barrel latch as found on most of the top-break revolvers. ".38 S&W Cartridge" was also added to the left side of barrel. Approximately 104,000 manufactured between 1898 and 1907. Serial number range 116003 to 220000.

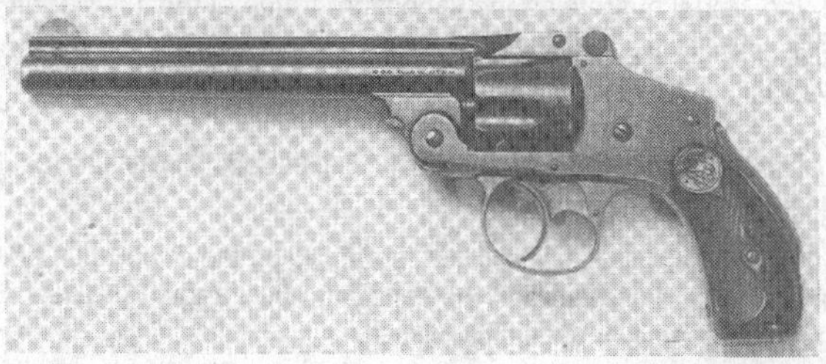

Courtesy Mike Stuckslager

NIB	Exc.	V.G.	Good	Fair	Poor
—	450	340	280	110	50

.38 Safety Hammerless 5th Model

Last of the "Lemon Squeezers". Only appreciable difference between this model and 4th Model is the front sight blade on 5th Model is an integral part of the barrel, not a separate blade pinned onto the barrel. Approximately 41,500 manufactured between 1907 and 1940. Serial number range 220001 to 261493. Note: Add 50% for 2" barrel version.

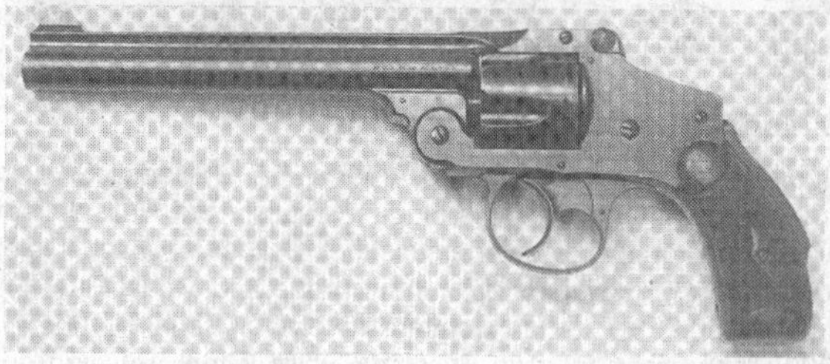

Courtesy Mike Stuckslager

NIB	Exc.	V.G.	Good	Fair	Poor
—	500	400	280	110	50

.44 Frame Model Number Three

The Model Three designation refers to the large-frame top-break revolvers. These fall into five major groups, chronologically by date of introduction: American Model, Russian Model, Schofield, New Model Number Three, and Double Action. Refer to The Standard Catalog of Smith & Wesson, available at GunDigestStore.com, for detailed background.

First Model American

This model represented a number of firsts for Smith & Wesson Company. It was first of the top-break automatic ejection revolvers. Also first Smith & Wesson in a large caliber (chambered for .44 S&W American cartridge as well as .44 Henry rimfire on rare occasions). Also known as 1st Model American. This large revolver offered with an 8" round barrel with a raised rib as standard. Barrel lengths of 6" and 7" were also available. It has a 6-shot fluted cylinder and square butt with walnut grips. Blued or nickel-plated. Interesting to note, this model appeared three years before Colt's Single-Action Army and perhaps, more than any other model, was associated with the historic American West. Only 8,000 manufactured between 1870 and 1872. Note: Add 25% for "oil hole" variation found on approximately first 1,500 guns; 50% for unusual barrel lengths other than standard 8". Original "Nashville Police" marked guns worth a substantial premium. About 200 made in .44 Henry rimfire will bring 25% to 50% premium.

Model 3 American 1st ModelFirst Model American Standard Production (Antique)

Note: Add 25 percent for "oil hole" variation found on approximately first 1,500 guns; 50 percent for unusual barrel lengths other than standard 8". Original "Nashville Police" marked guns worth a substantial premium.

Exc.	Fine	V.G.	Good	Fair	Poor
7000	3500	2500	1500	700	350

Transitional American ModelTransition Model (Antique)

Serial number range 6466-6744. Shorter cylinder (1.423"). Improved barrel of 2nd Model but retains the flat bottom frame of the 1st Model.

Exc.	Fine	V.G.	Good	Fair	Poor
6000	3000	2250	1500	800	560

First Model American U.S. Army OrderU.S. Army Order (Antique)

One thousand produced with "U.S." stamped on top of barrel. "OWA" on left grip. They are scattered in the serial number range 125-2199. Slight premium for scarce original nickel finish.

Exc.	Fine	V.G.	Good	Fair	Poor
17500	7500	5250	3000	1200	700

Model 3 American 2nd ModelSecond Model American (Antique)

Standard configuration 8" barrel, .44 American caliber. Other barrel lengths will bring a premium if factory original. .44 Rimfire chambering will bring a slight premium. Substantial premium for rare specimens with original detachable shoulder stock. Serial number range approx. 8000 to 32800, manufactured 1872-1874.

Exc.	Fine	V.G.	Good	Fair	Poor
5000	3000	2120	1250	700	350

First Model Russian (Old Old Model)

Configuration is about identical to American 2nd Model. S&W made several internal changes to this model to satisfy the Russian government. Markings on this revolver are distinct. Caliber for which it is chambered, .44 S&W Russian, is different from the 2nd Model Russian. Approximately 20,000 Russian-Contract revolvers. Serial number range 1-20000. They are marked in Russian Cyrillic letters. Russian double-headed eagle stamped on rear portion of barrel, with inspector's marks underneath it. All contract guns have 8" barrels and lanyard swivels on the butt. These are rarely encountered, as most were shipped to Russia. Commercial run of this model numbered approximately 4,655. Barrels are stamped in English and include the words "Russian Model". Some are found with 6" and 7" barrels, as well as standard 8". There were also 500 revolvers that were rejected from the Russian contract series and sold on the commercial market. Some of these are marked in English; some, Cyrillic. Some have the Cyrillic markings ground off and English restamped. Manufactured from 1871 to 1874. Guns with Cyrillic barrel markings may bring up to 25% premium.

Model 3 Russian 1st Model First Model RussianCommercial Model (Antique)

Exc.	Fine	V.G.	Good	Fair	Poor
5250	3200	2000	1250	700	400

Second Model Russian (Old Model) (Antique)

This revolver was known as "Old Model Russian". This is a complicated model to understand as there are many variations within the model designation. Serial numbering is quite complex as well and values vary due to relatively minor model differences. Before purchasing this model, it would be advisable to read reference materials solely devoted to this firearm. Chambered for .44 S&W Russian, with some scarce variations in .44 Henry rimfire cartridge. It has a 7" barrel and a round butt featuring a projection on the frame that fits into the thumb web. Grips are walnut and finish blue or nickel-plated. Triggerguard has a reverse curved spur on the bottom. Approximately 85,200 manufactured between 1873 and 1878. Variations include: Russian Contract Cyrillic marked – 10% premium, Japanese Navy, anchor with 2 wavy lines marked – 10% premium, .44 Henry Rimfire variations. Flat tipped triangular firing pin, Commercial - 500 made – 25% premium, 1st Turkish Contract, s/n range 1-1000 – 25-50% premium, 2nd Turkish Contract in standard s/n range – 25% premium

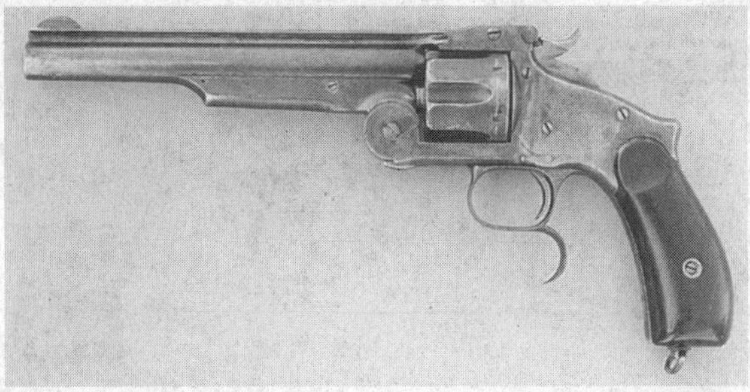

Courtesy Jim Supica, Old Town Station

Exc.	Fine	V.G.	Good	Fair	Poor
4000	2000	1250	850	600	400

Third Model Russian (New Model) (Antique)

Model 3 Russian 3rd ModelThis revolver is also known as "New Model Russian". Factory referred to this model as Model of 1874 or Cavalry Model. Chambered for .44 S&W Russian and .44 Henry rimfire cartridge. Barrel is 6.5" and round butt is the same humped-back affair as 2nd Model. Grips are walnut and finish blue or nickel plated. Most notable differences in appearance between this model and 2nd Model are shorter extractor housing under the barrel and integral front sight blade instead of pinned-on one found on previous models. In addition to S&W production for the commercial market and Russian military, the German firm of Ludwig and Lowe and the Russian Tula arsenal made copies of this gun for the Russian military. These and other variations impact values. Refer to Standard Catalog of Smith & Wesson available at GunDigestStore.com for details. Approximately 60,638 manufactured between 1874 and 1878. Variations include: Japanese Navy, anchor with 2 wavy lines marked – 10% premium; .44 Henry Rimfire. Turkish contract or commercial – 25% premium; Russian Contract Cyrillic marked - Made by S&W – 10% premium; Made by Ludwig & Loewe – 10% premium; Made by Tula Russian arsenal – 20% premium

Exc.	Fine	V.G.	Good	Fair	Poor
4000	2000	1250	850	600	400

Shoulder Stocked Model Threes

American and Russian Models were available with a detachable shoulder stock. The stocks are very rare and fakes and reproductions are known. A gun cut for stock may bring a slight premium. A gun accompanied by an original stock may bring double what the gun alone would bring. Shoulder stocked New Model Number Threes, although still rare, are a bit more common, notably the Australian Colonial Police variation listed below. A gun with stock may bring a 50% or greater premium. The stock alone may bring $1000 to $2000. Schofields and Double Actions with what appear to be period shoulder stocks are known to exist but these were not offered by the factory.

First Model Schofield US Contract (Antique)

Designed for the U.S. Army in caliber .45 S&W, 7" barrel, blued, top-break single-action with automatic ejection. Unlike other Model 3's the Schofield's latch is mounted on the frame instead of on the barrel. Schofield patent markings on ejector housing, 3,000 issued, U.S. Marked on the butt. It is also reported that 35 civilian models were made. These civilian 1st Models are extremely rare and can bring a substantial premium over US issued 1st Models, so expert evaluation is essential. Serial range 1-3035, circa 1875. Premium for "San Francisco Police" variation with large numeral on backstrap.

Exc.	Fine	V.G.	Good	Fair	Poor
9500	5250	3870	2500	1200	850

Second Model Schofield (Civilian 2nd Model Schofield) (Antique)

Similar to the 1st Model Schofield with most noticeable differences being circles on each side of the frame-mounted latch, and serial number range. The vast majority were military issue, and are "US" marked on butt. See comments on modified surplus guns and Wells Fargo Schofields at the listing for First Model Schofields above. In total, 646 Civilian Models were made, but despite their relative rarity they bring about the same value as the more common U.S.-issue Schofields. Serial range 3036-8969. Circa 1876-1877.

Exc.	Fine	V.G.	Good	Fair	Poor
9000	5000	3750	2500	1200	850

Model 3 Schofield 2nd ModelSecond Model Schofield "US" Contract Antique

4,000 issued.

Exc.	Fine	V.G.	Good	Fair	Poor
8000	4500	3500	2250	1200	800

Schofield Surplus Models and Variations Antique

Distributor modifications — After military use, many Schofields were sold as surplus and modified by distributers, who sometimes refinished the guns and shortened the barrel to 5". These modified guns will bring less than guns in original configuration, perhaps 50% of what an original unaltered Schofield will bring. Wells Fargo — The famous Wells Fargo Express Company purchased a number of these shortened 5" barrel surplus Schofields and marked them on the ejector housing "W F & CO (or CO'S) EXP" along with the gun's serial number. These "Wells Fargo Schofields" will bring close to the value of an original unaltered US Schofield. Beware of fake markings. San Francisco Police — Some Schofields are found with large 2- or 3-digit numbers stamped near the top of the backstrap. These have traditionally been "San Francisco Police" models, sent to California at the time of the Sandlot Riots. They will bring a slight premium. Civilian Models — See comments at 1st and 2nd Model Schofield listings above.

Model 3 Schofield—Surplus ModelsWells Fargo & Co. Model Antique

Exc.	Fine	V.G.	Good	Fair	Poor
8000	4000	3000	2000	850	500

Surplus Cut Barrel—Not Wells Fargo Antique

Exc.	Fine	V.G.	Good	Fair	Poor
4000	2500	1600	1200	700	500

New Model Number Three Antique

Always interested in perfecting Model 3 revolver D.B. Wesson redesigned and improved old Model 3 in hopes of attracting more sales. Russian contracts were almost filled, so the company decided to devote the effort necessary to improve on this design. In 1877, this project was undertaken. Extractor housing was shortened; cylinder retention system was improved; shape of grip was changed to a more streamlined and attractive configuration. This New Model was available with a 3.5", 4", 5", 6", 6.5", 7", 7.5" or 8" barrel length, with 6-shot fluted cylinder. The 6.5" barrel and .44 S&W Russian chambering is the most often encountered variation of this model, but the factory considered the 3.5" and 8" barrels as standard and these were kept in stock as well. New Model No. 3 was also chambered for .32 S&W, .32-44 S&W, .320 S&W Rev. Rifle, .38 S&W, .38-40, .38-44 S&W, .38 US (.38 Colt), .41 S&W, .44 Henry rimfire, .44 S&W American, .44-40, .45 S&W Schofield, .450 Rev., .45 Webley, .455 MkI and .455 MkII. They are blued or nickel-plated and have checkered hard rubber grips, with S&W logo molded into them, or walnut grips. There are many sub-variations within this model designation and the potential collector should secure detailed reference material that deals with this model. Approximately 35,796 of these revolvers manufactured between 1878 and 1912. Nearly 40 percent were exported to fill contracts with Japan, Australia, Argentina, England, Spain and Cuba. There were some sent to Asia, as well. Proof marks or military marks of these countries or factory shipping records will establish their provenance. Variations of the New Mod. No. 3 include: Maryland Militia – US, HN, and DAL markings – 200 made – maybe double standard value; Revenue Cutter Service – US purchase, no special markings, i.d. by serial number – 50% premium; Turkish Model – .44 Henry Rimfire; P, U, & AFC markings, own s/n range 1-5461 – 50% to 100% premium; Japanese Navy – usually with Anchor marking – possible slight premium; Japanese Artillery – Japanese kanji on ejector housing – 25% to 50% premium; Argentine Model – marked EJERCITO ARGENTNO, 2,000 made – 50% to 100% premium; Australian Colonial Police with detachable shoulder stock – double value if stock included; Unusual configurations – rare barrel lengths, rare calibers, and special order sights all add to the value of a gun, depending on the rarity of the variation. Related models – several models shared the same configuration but were offered as distinct models in their own serial number ranges. Their listings follow this one and include: New Model No. 3 Target Model; New Model No. 3 Frontier Model; New Mod. No. 3 38 Winchester Model; Revolving Rifle – based on New Mod. No. 3 frame

Exc.	Fine	V.G.	Good	Fair	Poor
4000	3000	2000	1250	800	500

New Model No. 3 Target Model Antique

Similar in appearance to standard New Model No. 3 but was the company's first production target model. It has a 6.5" round barrel, with a raised rib and 6-shot fluted cylinder. Finished in blue or nickel-plated. Grips are walnut or checkered hard rubber, with S&W logo molded into them. Chambered in.32-44 Target or .38-44 Target. Designation of .44 referred to the frame size, i.e. a .32 caliber built on a .44 caliber frame. Approximately 4,333 manufactured between 1887 and 1910.

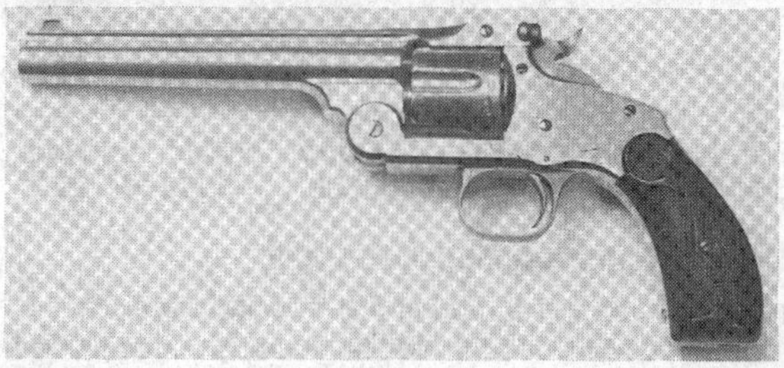

Courtesy Mike Stuckslager

Exc.	Fine	V.G.	Good	Fair	Poor
3500	2000	1250	850	600	400

New Model No. 3 Frontier Model Antique

Another model similar in appearance to standard New Model No. 3. It has a 4", 5" or 6.5" barrel. Chambered for .44-40 Win. centerfire cartridge. Because the original New Model No. 3 cylinder was 1.4375" in length, this would not accommodate the longer .44-40 cartridge. Cylinder on No. 3 Frontier was changed to 1.5625" in length. Later the company converted 786 revolvers to .44 S&W Russian and sold them to Japan. Around 800 of these were converted to .44 Russian for sale to Japan; worth about 10% less. This model is blued or nickel-plated and has checkered grips of walnut or hard rubber. They are serial numbered in their own range from 1 through 2072. Manufactured from 1885 until 1908. This model was designed to compete with Colt Single-Action Army, but was not successful.

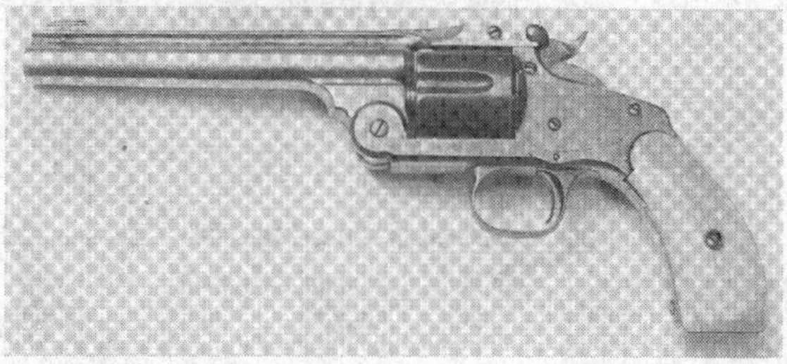

Courtesy Mike Stuckslager

Exc.	Fine	V.G.	Good	Fair	Poor
4500	3000	2000	1400	850	500

New Model No. 3 Frontier Single-Action.44-40—Commercial Model Antique

Exc.	Fine	V.G.	Good	Fair	Poor
5000	2500	1870	1250	500	350

Japanese Purchase Converted to .44 S&W Russian Antique

Exc.	Fine	V.G.	Good	Fair	Poor
4000	3000	2000	1000	500	350

New Model No. 3—.38 Winchester Antique

This variation was the last of New Model No. 3s to be introduced. Chambered for .38-40 Win. it was cataloged from 1900 until 1907, but reliable sources report that all frames were made prior to 1899. If true, that would make this model an antique. Finish blue or nickel-plate. Grips are checkered hard rubber or walnut. Barrel lengths of 4" or 6.5" were offered. This model was not at all popular, as only 74 were manufactured in their own serial range 1 through 74. Today's collectors are extremely interested in this extremely rare model. Note: Rarity makes valuation speculative.

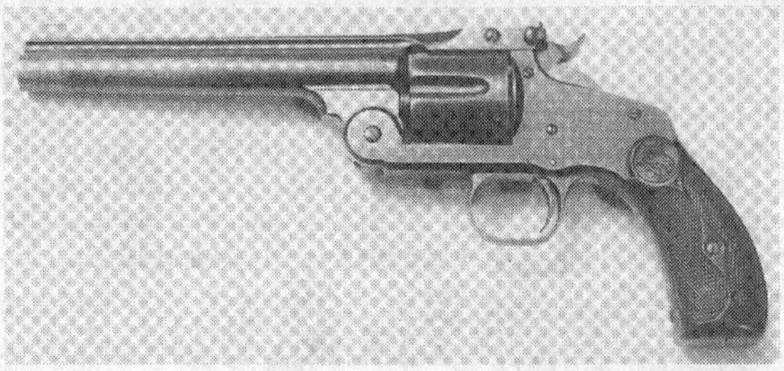

Courtesy Mike Stuckslager

Exc.	Fine	V.G.	Good	Fair	Poor
10000	6000	4000	2500	1000	500

.44 Double-Action 1st Model Antique

A top-break double-action revolver that automatically ejects the spent cartridge cases upon opening. Also known as "The New Model Navy". Standard chambering is .44 S&W Russian; other calibers very rare and worth premium. Target sights available by special order, and worth a premium if factory original. Standard barrel lengths are 4", 5", 6" and 6.5" round, with a raised rib. A 3.5" barrel was produced on this model by special request. Collectors should be aware that the barrel for this model and New Model No. 3 were interchangeable and the factory did in fact use barrels from either model. Serial number on rear of the barrel should match number on the butt, cylinder and barrel latch. Cylinder holds 6-shots and is fluted. It has double sets of stop notches and long free grooves between the stops. It is serial numbered in its own range, beginning at 1. Approximately 54,000 manufactured between 1881 and 1913.Approximately 54,000 manufactured between 1881 and 1913.

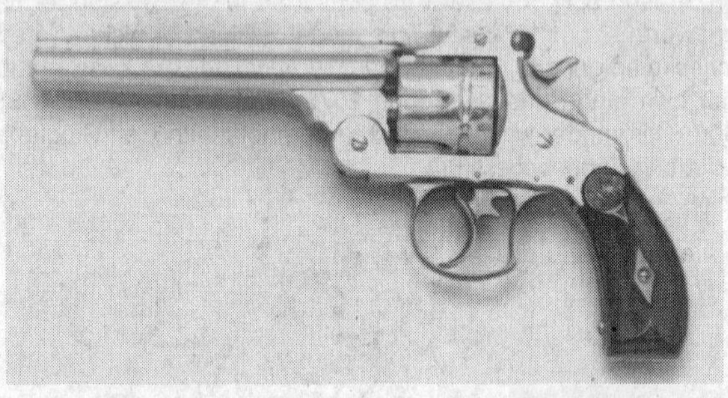

Courtesy Bonhams & Butterfields, San Francisco, California

Exc.	Fine	V.G.	Good	Fair	Poor
3000	1500	950	650	400	280

Model .44 Double-Action Wesson Favorite Antique

Favorite is basically a lightened version of 1st Model D.A. .44. Barrel is thinner and offered in 5" length only. There are lightening cuts in the frame between triggerguard and cylinder; cylinder diameter was smaller and there is a groove milled along the barrel rib. Favorite chambered for .44 S&W Russian cartridge. Has a 6-shot fluted cylinder, with same double-cylinder stop notches and free grooves as 1st Model Double-Action .44. Company name and address, as well as patent dates, are stamped into edge of the cylinder instead of on barrel rib. Serial-numbered in the same range, between 9000 and 10100. Revolver was most often nickel-plated, but also offered blued. Grips are walnut or checkered hard rubber, with S&W logo molded in. Approximately 1,000 manufactured in 1882 and 1883. Use caution when purchasing a blued model. Note: Rarity makes valuation speculative. Add 25% for blued finish.

Exc.	Fine	V.G.	Good	Fair	Poor
9000	5000	3750	2500	1000	500

Model .44 Double-Action Frontier Antique

Chambered for .44-40 cartridge. This is a separate model from .44 Double-Action 1st Model. It has a longer 19/16" cylinder like the later .44 double-action 1st Model's. Produced from 1886 to 1916 with their own serial number range. Approximately 15,340 built.

Exc.	Fine	V.G.	Good	Fair	Poor
3000	1500	1000	700	400	280

.38 Winchester Double-Action

Similar to .44 Double-Action 1st Model, except for chamber. Fitted with long cylinder. Approximately 276 produced, in their own serial number range, from 1900 to 1910.

NIB	Exc.	V.G.	Good	Fair	Poor
—	—	5500	3000	1250	800

1st Model Single-Shot

This unusual pistol combines the frame of a .38 Single-Action 3rd Model, with a single-shot barrel. This model is a top-break and functions exactly as revolver models do. Barrel length 6", 8" or 10". Chambered for .22 LR, .32 S&W and .38 S&W. Finish blue or nickel plated, with square butt. Grips are checkered hard rubber extension types for a proper target Hold. This pistol is considered quite rare on today's market, as only 1,251 manufactured between 1893 and 1905. Serial number range is quite wide as it is shared with the 38 Single action 3rd model revolver 1-28107.

.22 L.R. Antique

Premium for .32 & .38 caliber specimens. Substantial premium for multi-caliber set, and higher premium for a set with .38 Single Action Revolver Model 1891 cylinder & barrel.

Exc.	Fine	V.G.	Good	Fair	Poor
1500	1000	800	600	400	280

2nd Model Single-Shot

2nd Model Single-Shot has a frame with the recoil shield removed. Chambered for .22 LR only. Offered with 10" barrel. Finish blue or nickel plated. Grips are checkered hard rubber extension types. Approximately 4,617 manufactured between 1905 and 1909. Original serial number range 1-4617.

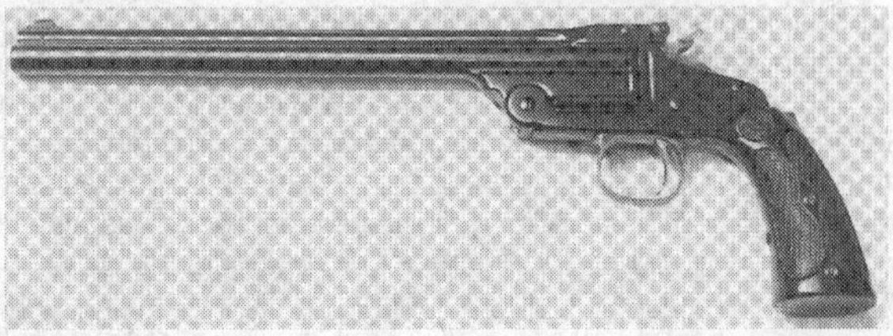

Courtesy Mike Stuckslager

NIB	Exc.	V.G.	Good	Fair	Poor
—	1500	1100	650	350	180

3rd Model Single-Shot

Basic difference between this model and 2nd Model is that this pistol could be fired double-action as well as single-action. Frame came from double-action perfected model. Manufactured 6,949 between 1909 and 1923. Serial number range is considered as 4617-11641. Easy to confirm as the trigger is in the middle of the triggerguard.

Courtesy Mike Stuckslager

NIB	Exc.	V.G.	Good	Fair	Poor
—	2000	1400	1200	600	300

Straight Line Single-Shot

Unique pistol that very much resembles a semi-automatic. Barrel is 10" in length and pivots to left for loading. Chambered for .22 LR cartridge. Finished in blue, with walnut grips inlaid with S&W medallions. Hammer is straight-line in function and does not pivot. Manufactured 1,870 between 1925 and 1936. Serial range 1-1870.

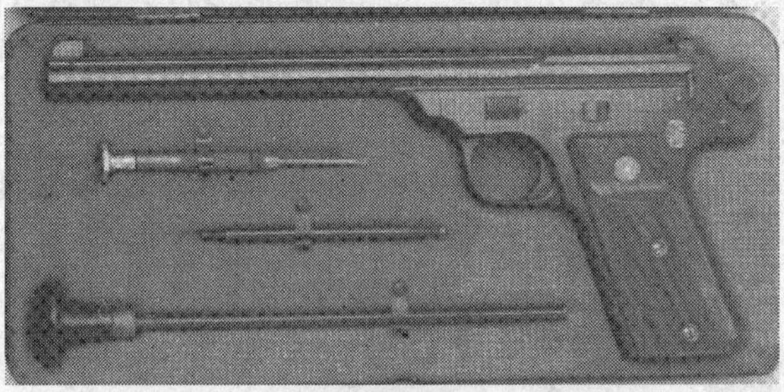

Courtesy Bonhams & Butterfields, San Francisco, California

NIB	Exc.	V.G.	Good	Fair	Poor
—	2500	1750	1200	750	400

HAND EJECTORS

With the development of the Hand Ejector Models and swing-out cylinders, Smith & Wesson opened the door to several new advancements in the revolver field. The new system allowed for a solid frame, making the handguns much stronger than the old top-break designs. The company also developed different basic frame sizes and gave them letter designations. I frame, which later developed into slightly larger J frame, (and later still the J Magnum frame for .357 Magnum) was used for .22-32 and small concealable .38 revolvers. The medium K frame was used for .38 duty-/target-type weapons. N frame was a heavy-duty frame used for larger .357-, .44- and .45-caliber revolvers. Hand ejectors went through many evolutionary changes over the years, and many of these changes will affect the value for collectors. In 1957, S&W began changing its named model Hand Ejectors to numbered models. For example, the .38 Military & Police model became the Model 10. The early pre-1957 Hand Ejectors covered in this section are sometimes called Pre-Models by collectors — i.e. a .38 Hand Ejector made in the early 1950s might be called a "Pre-Model 10." The post-1956 numbered models are covered in the section that follows this one.

SMITH & WESSON MODERN HANDGUNS

.22 CALIBER

.22 Ladysmith 1st Model

Designed primarily as a defensive weapon for women. Small size and caliber made it ideal for that purpose. Chambered for .22 Long cartridge. Has 7-shot fluted cylinder. Barrel lengths 3" and 3.5". Weight 9.625 oz. Blued or nickel-plated. Round butt, with checkered hard rubber grips. Checkered cylinder-latch button on left side of frame. Approximately 4,575 manufactured between 1902 and 1906.

NIB	Exc.	V.G.	Good	Fair	Poor
—	2500	1500	900	650	450

.22 Ladysmith 2nd Model

Essentially, quite similar in appearance to 1st Model. Difference being in pull-forward cylinder-latch located under the barrel, replacing button on left side of frame. New method allowed lockup front and back for greater action strength. Barrel length 2.25" was dropped; caliber and finishes the same. Approximately 9,374 manufactured between 1906 and 1910; serial number range 4576 to 13950.

Courtesy Mike Stuckslager

NIB	Exc.	V.G.	Good	Fair	Poor
—	2300	1500	900	500	300

.22 Ladysmith 3rd Model

Quite different in appearance to 2nd Model. Features square butt and smooth walnut grips, with inlaid S&W medallions. Barrel lengths remained the same, with addition of 2.25" and 6" variation. Under barrel cylinder lockup was not changed, nor caliber and finishes. Approximately 12,200 manufactured between 1910 and 1921; serial number range 13951 to 26154. Note: Add 50% premium for 2.25" and 6" barrel lengths.

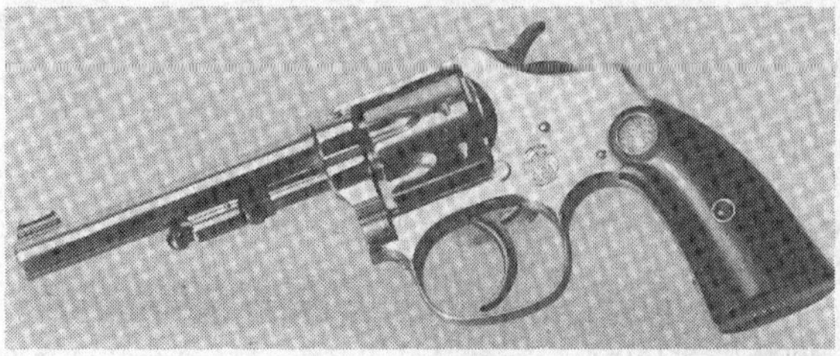

Courtesy W.P. Hallstein III and son Chip

NIB	Exc.	V.G.	Good	Fair	Poor
—	2300	1500	900	500	300

.22-32 Hand Ejector

This is a very interesting model from a collector's point of view. Phillip B. Bekeart, a San Francisco firearms dealer, requested that S&W manufacture a .22-caliber target-grade revolver on the heavier .32 frame. He believed in his idea so passionately, that he immediately ordered 1,000 guns for himself. This initial order is found within serial number range 1 to 3000 and are known to collectors as the authentic Bekearts. Remainder of the extensive production run are simply .22-32 Hand Ejectors. Chambered for .22 LR cartridge and a 6-shot fluted cylinder, with 6" barrel. Finish blue, with square butt and checkered extension-type walnut grips. There were only 292 revolvers of his initial order delivered to Mr. Bekeart, but the first 1,000 pistols are considered to be True Bekearts. Production number of each respective pistol is stamped into the base of the extended wooden grips. S&W went on to manufacture several hundred thousand of these revolvers between 1911 and 1953.

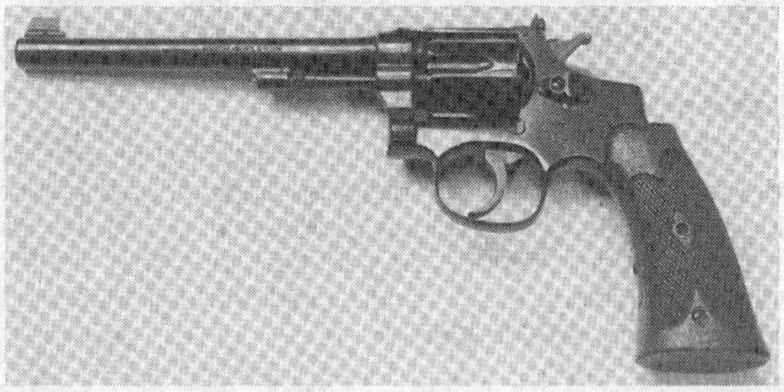

Courtesy Mike Stuckslager

.22-32 HE Standard Model

NIB	Exc.	V.G.	Good	Fair	Poor
3500	2800	1200	600	500	250

.22-32 HE Bekeart Model

Serial number range 138226 to 139275, in .32 Hand Ejector series. Production number stamped on butt. Professional appraisal should be secured.

NIB	Exc.	V.G.	Good	Fair	Poor
—	3000	1500	1000	800	300

.22-32 Target Model of 1953 (Pre-Model 35)

Made on improved I-frame, .22 LR, 6-in. barrel, target sights. Shares s/n range with 1953 Kit Gun, produced 1953-1969.

NIB	Exc.	V.G.	Good	Fair	Poor
2250	1700	850	600	350	200

.22-32 Hand Ejector.22-32 Kit Gun (Pre WWII)

Same features as Standard Model .22 hand Ejector, built on the round butt I frame with a smaller grip frame and 4-in. barrel. Serial range 525670-536684 in the 32 Hand Ejector series. Built from 1935-1941.

NIB	Exc.	V.G.	Good	Fair	Poor
2500	2000	2400	1600	600	250

.22-32 Kit Gun Airweight (Pre-Model 43)

Similar to the steel .22/32 Kit gun but made with aluminum alloy frame and cylinder. Serial range from 5000-135465. 3½-inch steel barrel. 2 in. rare. Made 1954-1974.

NIB	Exc.	V.G.	Good	Fair	Poor
2000	1500	800	500	350	250

K-22 Outdoorsman/ K-22 1st Model

Pre-war version of K-22 K-frame, 6-in. barreled revolver. Chambered for .22 Short, Long and Long Rifle. Walnut grips, adjustable rear sight, no ribbed barrel. Manufactured from 1931 to 1940. In 1940, name was changed to K-22 Masterpiece and an improved adjustable rear sight was added. S&W short action was another improvement., serial number range 632,124-682,419.

NIB	Exc.	V.G.	Good	Fair	Poor
3000	1750	850	700	500	300

K-22 3rd Model / K22 Masterpiece (postwar)

First use of a ribbed barrel to reduce glare. Target sights. Serial range starting with a "K" from K101 to the end of the K series. Continued as the Model 17 in 1957.

NIB	Exc.	V.G.	Good	Fair	Poor
2500	2000	1600	1000	500	300

K-22 2nd Model / K22 Masterpiece

First use of the micrometer click rear sight. Add 100% premium. Only about 1,000 K-22 Masterpieces manufactured in 1940 in serial number range 682,420-696,952.

NIB	Exc.	V.G.	Good	Fair	Poor
3000	1750	1500	850	500	300

K-22 Combat Masterpiece (Pre-Model 18)

Similar to K-22 masterpiece with a 4-inch barrel, target sights. K serial prefix Made from 1949-1985.

NIB	Exc.	V.G.	Good	Fair	Poor
2500	2000	1600	1000	500	300

.22 Military and Police (Pre Model 45)

Square butt K-frame with fixed sights, 4-inch barrel with small production of 6 inch. Wide serial range in the M&P "S" series and "C" series. 1948-1978. Never cataloged.

NIB	Exc.	V.G.	Good	Fair	Poor
3000	2250	1600	1000	500	300

.32 CALIBER

.32 Hand Ejector Model of 1896 or .32 Hand Ejector 1st Model (Antique)

This model was the first time S&W made a revolver with a swing-out cylinder. Interestingly, there is no cylinder latch; but the action opens by pulling forward on the exposed portion of the cylinder pin. This frees the spring tension and allows the cylinder to swing free. Another novel feature of this model is the cylinder stop location, which is located in the top of the frame over the cylinder. Chambered for .32 S&W Long cartridge, has a 6-shot fluted cylinder and offered with 3.25", 4.25" and 6" long barrels. Available with a round or square butt, has checkered hard rubber grips and is blued or nickel-plated. Factory installed target sights were available by special order. Company name, address and patent dates are stamped on the cylinder instead of barrel. Approximately 19,712 manufactured between 1896 and 1903.

Courtesy Mike Stuckslager

Exc.	Fine	V.G.	Good	Fair	Poor
650	400	270	200	150	100

.32 Hand Ejector Model of 1903

Quite different from its predecessor. Cylinder locks front and back; cylinder stop located in bottom of frame and familiar sliding cylinder latch found on left side of frame. Barrel lengths 3.25, 4.25 and 6 in. The 6-shot cylinder is fluted. Chambered for .32 S&W Long. Offered blued or nickel-plated. Round butt grips are checkered hard rubber. Approximately 19,425 manufactured in 1903 and 1904; serial number range 1 to 19425.

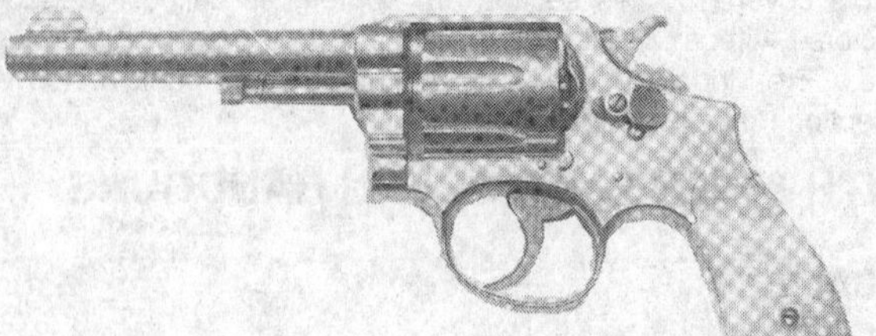

Courtesy Mike Stuckslager

NIB	Exc.	V.G.	Good	Fair	Poor
2000	1500	1100	800	400	250

.32 Hand Ejector Model of 1903, 1st through 5th Change

Collectors recognize five changes of the .32 HE Model of 1903. Values are similar for all five, impacted a bit by scarcity of production. The identifying characteristics of the five changes are listed below, following values.

NIB	Exc.	V.G.	Good	Fair	Poor
1800	1000	600	400	200	150

.32 Hand Ejector Model of 1903 1st Change

Serial number range 19426 to 51126. Approximately 31,700 manufactured between 1904 and 1906.

.32 Hand Ejector Model of 1903 2nd Change

Produced from 1906 to 1909. Serial number range 51127 to 95500. Total of 44,373 manufactured.

.32 Hand Ejector Model of 1903 3rd Change

Produced from 1909 to 1910. Serial number range 95501 to 96125. Total of 624 manufactured.

.32 Hand Ejector Model of 1903 4th Change

Produced in 1910. Serial number range 96126 to 102500. Total of 6,374 manufactured.

.32 Hand Ejector Model of 1903 5th Change

Produced from 1910-1917. Serial number range 102500-263000. Total of 160,500 manufactured.

NIB	Exc.	V.G.	Good	Fair	Poor
1500	1200	600	400	250	150

.32 Hand Ejector Third Model

Produced from 1911 to 1942. Serial number range 263001 to 536684. Total of 273,683 manufactured.

NIB	Exc.	V.G.	Good	Fair	Poor
—	650	500	380	250	150

.32 Hand Ejector postwar (Pre-Model 30)

Similar to 3rd Model, Produced from 1911-1942. Serial number range 536685-712953.

NIB	Exc.	V.G.	Good	Fair	Poor
1100	800	600	400	300	150

.32 Regulation Police (Prewar)

Wide serial range from 260000-536000. Made from 1917-1942. Serial number on the front tang. Not Regulation Police marked. Target Models available at 3X standard model.

NIB	Exc.	V.G.	Good	Fair	Poor
1350	1200	600	300	150	—

.32 Regulation Police (Postwar) Pre-Model 31

Wide serial range from about 536000-712953. Made from 1946-1960. Not "Regulation Police" marked. 196 Target Models made available at 3X standard model.

NIB	Exc.	V.G.	Good	Fair	Poor
2000	1200	900	600	250	150

K-32 Hand Ejector First Model

One of the rarest pre-war K-frame revolvers. Chambered for .32 S&W Long cartridge. Fewer than 100 were made between 1936 and 1941. After WWII, this model was part of the K-22/K-32/K-38 Masterpiece series of 6-in. barreled target-sighted revolvers. Due to its rarity, an expert appraisal is essential. Serial range 653388-682207. Values are speculative due to rarity.

NIB	Exc.	V.G.	Good	Fair	Poor
—	18000	13500	9000	3500	800

K-32 Masterpiece (Pre Model 16)

.32 Long. Postwar continued from the First Model with click adjustable sights. Wide serial range. Made 1946-1974.

NIB	Exc.	V.G.	Good	Fair	Poor
—	18000	13500	9000	3500	800

K-32 Combat Masterpiece

S&W produced a limited number (estimated at 10) of 4-in. barreled K-32 revolvers. Never given a number designation, as they were discontinued before 1957 when the numbering system began.

NIB	Exc.	V.G.	Good	Fair	Poor
6500	4000	3500	1900	1350	300

.32-20 CALIBER

.32-20 Hand Ejector

.32-20 (.32 WCF). All 32-20 HE revolvers are similar to the corresponding 38 Special Hand Ejector models in appearance. Variations include 1st Model, Model 1902 (2nd Model), Model of 1905 (3rd Model), with various changes. Values are similar for all Models and Changes with fluctuations depending on scarcity – the fewer produced, the greater the premium.

NIB	Exc.	V.G.	Good	Fair	Poor
1800	1300	700	450	275	150

.32-20 Hand Ejector 1st Model

.32-20 available in 4", 5" or 6.5" barrel lengths. Serial range 1-5311. Made 1899-1902.

.32-20 Hand Ejector 2nd Model (Model of 1902)

4,499 were produced; serial number range 5312-9811. Made 1902-1905

.32-20 Hand Ejector Model of 1902 1st Change

Serial range 9812-18125. Made 1903-1905. 8,313 .32-20s were produced.

.32-20 Hand Ejector Model of 1905

Serial number range spans 18126-22426, or 4,300 produced. Made 1905-1906.

.32-20 Hand Ejector Model of 1905 1st Change

Serial number range was 22427-33500, with 11,073 sold. Made 1906-1909.

.32-20 Hand Ejector Model of 1905 2nd Change

Serial number range between 33501 to 45200, with 11,699 produced. Made 1906-1909 with overlap with 1st change.

.32-20 Hand Ejector Model of 1905 3rd Change

Serial range 45201-65700. Made 1909-1915.

.32-20 Hand Ejector Model of 1905 4th Change

Offered in 4, 5 or 6 in., produced from 1915-1940, serial number range from 65701-144684.

NIB	Exc.	V.G.	Good	Fair	Poor
2200	1600	900	400	250	150

.38 CALIBER

.38 Hand Ejector Military & Police 1st Model or Model of 1899 Army-Navy Revolver

Early swing-out cylinder revolver. No front lockup for action. Release on left side of frame. Chambered for the new cartridge .38 S&W Special. Has 6-shot fluted cylinder. Offered with 4, 5, 6, 6 1/2-in. barrels. Finish is blued or nickel-plated; grips are checkered walnut or hard rubber. Manufactured between 1899-1902: serial number range 1-20975.

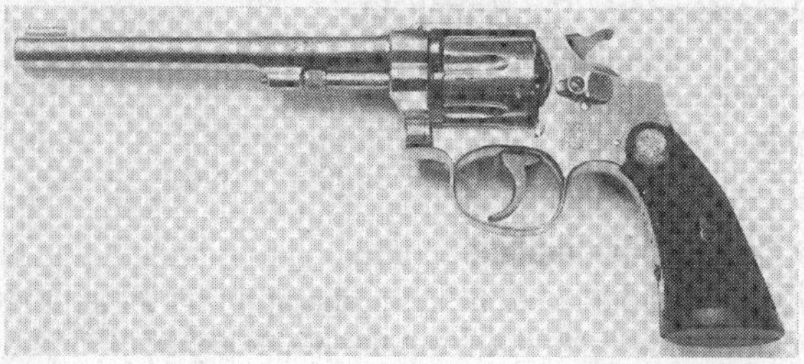

Courtesy Mike Stuckslager

NIB	Exc.	V.G.	Good	Fair	Poor
—	1750	1300	800	500	300

.38 Hand Ejector Military & Police 1st Model or Model of 1899U.S. Navy Model

Produced 1,000 in 1900. .38 S&W Special, 6-in. barrel, blued with checkered walnut grips. "U.S.N." stamped on butt. Serial number range 5000 to 6000.

NIB	Exc.	V.G.	Good	Fair	Poor
—	3500	2600	1500	750	400

U.S. Army Model

Produced 1,000 in 1901. Same as Navy Model except marked "U.S.Army/ Model 1899" on butt. "K.S.M." and "J.T.T." on grips. Serial number range 13001 to 14000.

NIB	Exc.	V.G.	Good	Fair	Poor
—	3500	2600	1500	750	400

Commercial Model

NIB	Exc.	V.G.	Good	Fair	Poor
—	1500	1200	800	450	350

.38/200 British Service Revolver (Model K200)

Similar to the Victory model made for the British Commonwealth countries. .38 S&W with 200-grain bullet, 4.5- or 6-in. barrels. Typically will have British military marks. A significant number of these were converted to .38 Special for sale back to the American market, and these will bring less than original caliber guns.

NIB	Exc.	V.G.	Good	Fair	Poor
—	850	550	400	250	150

.38 Hand Ejector M&P Model of 1902

The 2nd Model is similar in appearance to the 1st Model. Major difference is the addition of the front lockup under the barrel and ejector rod was increased in diameter. Barrel lengths were 4, 5, 6 or 6.5 in.; Offered in round butt only configuration. Approximately 12,827 manufactured 1902-1903; serial number range 20976-33803.

NIB	Exc.	V.G.	Good	Fair	Poor
—	1200	900	500	250	100

.38 Hand Ejector M&P Model of 1902, 1st Change

Built from 1903-1905. This variation represents change to the square butt, which made for better shooting control and standardized frame shape. Available in 4-, 5- or 6.5-in. barrel lengths. Manufactured 28,645. Serial number range 33804-62449.

NIB	Exc.	V.G.	Good	Fair	Poor
—	1100	800	400	250	100

.38 Hand Ejector Model of 1905

A continuation of .38 M&P Hand Ejector series. Built from 1905 to 1906. Available in 4-, 5-, 6- and 6.5-in. barrels. Finished in blue or nickel, with round or square butt. The .38-caliber serial number range 62450-73250, with about 10,800 produced. Note: Prices for the following four variations will be the same as those noted above.

NIB	Exc.	V.G.	Good	Fair	Poor
—	950	550	400	350	150

1st Change

Produced from 1906-1908. Barrel lengths, finish and butt styles like original model of 1905. The 1st change was produced in serial number range 73251-120000, with 46,749 made.

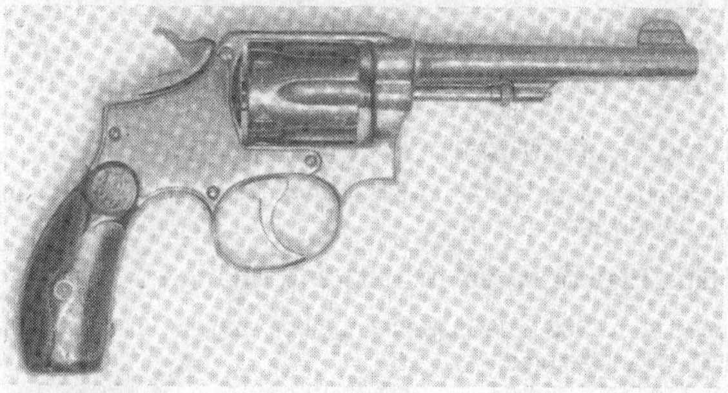

2nd Change

Produced from 1908-1909. Only internal changes were made to this model. Best approach to differentiate this model is by serial number. The serial number range is from 120001-146899, with 26,898 produced.

3rd Change

Produced from 1909 to 1915. The 3rd Change variation available only in 4- or 6-in. barrel lengths. The .38-caliber serial number range between 146900-241703, with 94,803 made.

Courtesy Mike Stuckslager

4th Change

Last variation was also the longest production run. Produced from 1915-1942. Barrel lengths: 2, 4, 5 or 6 in.; The .38-caliber serial number range is from 241704-1000000.

Courtesy Mike Stuckslager

Victory Model

Manufactured during WWII, with sandblasted and Parkerized finish, lanyard swivel and smooth walnut grips. Serial number has a V prefix. Available only in 2- and 4-in. barrel lengths. Victory Model discontinued April 27, 1945, with serial number VS811119. Note: Add 75% premium for topstrap marked Navy; 100% premium for Navy variation with both topstrap and side plate marked; 125% premium for Navy variation marked "N.Y.M.I."; unknown premium amount for revolvers marked "U.S.G.C." or "U.S.M.C.". Exercise caution.

NIB	Exc.	V.G.	Good	Fair	Poor
1800	900	600	500	400	180

Victory Model K-200 British Service Revolver

Very similar to the Victory model made from the British Commonwealth countries. .38 S&W with 200-grain bullet, 4-, 5- or 6-in. barrels. Value will be less for revolvers converted to .38 Special.

NIB	Exc.	V.G.	Good	Fair	Poor
—	850	550	350	250	150

USAF M-13 (Aircrewman)

Manufactured from 1951 to 1957 for the U.S. Air Force on the thinner Model 12 aluminum K-frame. Chambered in .38 Special and have an alloy frame and cylinder. Pilots and other flight-crew members carried them for emergency use. The Air Force ultimately rejected the model because of problems encountered with the alloy cylinder, and most were destroyed. Because of this, the Aircrewman is one of the rarest modern-day Smith & Wesson revolvers. Serial numbers in C247000 to C406000 range. It is not known how many still exist, but estimated at 250. Genuine model is seldom seen for sale. Numerous fakes have been documented, so it is strongly suggested that a knowledgeable S&W expert be consulted for an appraisal.

NIB	Exc.	V.G.	Good	Fair	Poor
—	17000	12000	3500	1500	750

Baby Aircrewman

A few (605) "Baby" Aircrewman 5-shot revolvers with an A.F.No. xxxx serial number were made on the S&W J-frame, and it is believed that fewer than 15 of these guns still exist. Because of the rarity of these two models and few actual transactions that have occurred in recent years, it is not possible to list meaningful values. Another 605 were made on the "K" frame with the same serial number prefix; fewer than 10 of these are known to exist intact. Reported Rock Island Auction sales of Baby Aircrewmen: 2016 - $25,875; 2020 - $36,000; 2021 - $40,250 (Excellent condition).

.38 Regulation Police (prewar)

I-frame (slightly shorter than J-frame) in .38 S&W, five-shot, 4" barrel. Round butt grip frame with square butt wood grips. S/n 1 to 54474, 1917-1940.

NIB	Exc.	V.G.	Good	Fair	Poor
1300	950	700	500	300	200

.38 Regulation Police (postwar) Pre-Model 33

Similar to above. S/n 54475 to 122678, 1949-1957.

NIB	Exc.	V.G.	Good	Fair	Poor
900	600	400	330	200	100

.38/32 Terrier (prewar)

Similar to above. S/n 54475 to 122678, 1949-1957.

NIB	Exc.	V.G.	Good	Fair	Poor
1300	950	700	500	300	200

.38/32 Terrier (postwar) Pre-Model 32

Similar to above. S/n 54475 to 122678, 1949-1957.

NIB	Exc.	V.G.	Good	Fair	Poor
900	600	400	330	200	100

.38 M&P (Pre-Model 10)

.38 Special, postwar production with a new safety hammer block with "S" serial prefix and later became a "C" serial prefix. Many variations.

NIB	Exc.	V.G.	Good	Fair	Poor
1700	900	600	450	250	150

.38/200 M&P Postwar (Pre-Model 11)

Chambered in .38 S&W. Made postwar for the British Commonwealth countries. "S" and "C" serial number prefix. Never cataloged.

.38 M&P Airweight (Pre-Model 12)

.38 Special. Thinner K Frame size with an aluminum alloy frame and cylinder, later changed to a steel cylinder in 1954. Produced from 1952-1957 with the introduction of model numbers to be known as the Model 12. "C" serial prefix. Commonly with 2- and 4-in. barrels with 1 known factory 5-in.

NIB	Exc.	V.G.	Good	Fair	Poor
2500	1700	1200	600	250	150

K-38 Masterpiece (Pre-Model 14)

.38 Special, 6-shot w/6-in. barrel, "K" serial prefix, with Patridge front sight.

NIB	Exc.	V.G.	Good	Fair	Poor
1500	800	500	300	250	150

K-38 Combat Masterpiece (Pre-Model 15)

.38 Special, 6-shot w/4-in. barrel with combat front sight "K" serial prefix.

NIB	Exc.	V.G.	Good	Fair	Poor
1500	1000	700	600	250	150

.38 Chiefs Special (Pre-Model 36)

.38 Special. Introduction of the J-Frame with 5-shot cylinder. In its own serial range. Sports either a 2-in. barrel or with low production of 3-in. and target models later known as the Model 50. Premium for 3" barrel or target sights. See listings for Model 36 and Model 50.

NIB	Exc.	V.G.	Good	Fair	Poor
1600	1200	900	650	300	150

.38 Chiefs Special Airweight (Pre-Model 37)

.38 Special, J-Frame size 5-shot aluminum frame and early alloy cylinders, later changes to steel. Models with 2- and some production of 3-in. barrels.

NIB	Exc.	V.G.	Good	Fair	Poor
1500	900	500	300	200	150

.38 Bodyguard Airweight (Pre-Model 38)

.38 Special J-frame size with a shrouded hammer. 5-shot, steel cylinders only, 2- and rare 3-in. barrels.

NIB	Exc.	V.G.	Good	Fair	Poor
1500	730	400	300	250	180

.38 Centennial (Pre-Model 40)

.38 Special, J-frame size, Fully concealed hammer, 5-shot steel frame and cylinder. 2-in. only.

NIB	Exc.	V.G.	Good	Fair	Poor
2000	1500	800	300	200	150

.38 Centennial Airweight (Pre-Model 42)

.38 Special, J-frame size, fully concealed hammer, 5-shot aluminum frame, and early aluminum cylinder (37 made with aluminum cylinder) changed to steel. 2" only.

NIB	Exc.	V.G.	Good	Fair	Poor
1750	1200	650	300	250	180

.38-44 N-frame .38 Special Revolvers

The .38-44 cartridge was a souped-up version of the .38 Special, loaded in the same case, and S&W introduced these N-frame revolvers to handle these heavy loads. There is significant collector interest in these post-WWII transitional models, and this section will be expanded in future editions. For now, we'll list values ranges for the more common models, along with price adjustment to be made for the more rare pieces. Heavy Duty models have fixed sights and Outdoorsman models have adjustable sights. Also see listings for Model 20 and Model 23.

38-44 Heavy Duty (Pre-Model 20)

25% premium for 6.5-in. barrel or post-war transition model.

NIB	Exc.	V.G.	Good	Fair	Poor
2750	1750	900	750	400	300

.38-44 Outdoorsman (Pre-Model 23)

25% premium for post-war transition models.

NIB	Exc.	V.G.	Good	Fair	Poor
2850	1850	1200	1000	700	300

.357 MAGNUM

.357 Registered Magnum

In the early 1930s, a gun writer named Phillip B. Sharpe, became interested in the development of high performance loads to be used in then-popular .38-44 Heavy Duty S&W revolvers. He repeatedly urged S&W to produce a revolver especially made to handle these high-pressure loads. In 1934, S&W asked Winchester to produce a new cartridge that would create the ballistics that Sharpe was seeking. This new cartridge was made longer than standard .38 Special case, so that it could not inadvertently be fired in an older gun. S&W never felt that this would be a commercially popular venture and from the onset visualized ".357 Magnum" as a strictly deluxe hand-built item. They were to be individually numbered, in addition to serial number, and registered to the new owner. New Magnum was to be the most expensive revolver in the line. This gun went on the market in 1935, and one was presented to FBI Director, J. Edgar Hoover. The gun was to become a tremendous success. S&W could only produce 120 per month, and this did not come close to filling orders. The ".357 Magnum", as it was designated, continued as one of the company's most popular items. Factory Registered Model was built on the N-frame. It could be custom ordered with any barrel length from 3.5" up to 8.75". Finish is blue and grips are checkered walnut. This model was virtually handbuilt and test targeted. A certificate of registration was available from the factory upon request of the buyer with each revolver. The registration number was stamped on the yoke of revolver, with the prefix "Reg.". This practice of numbering and registering each revolver ceased in 1938, after 5,500 were produced. Note: For top NIB dollar, all accessories and registration letter must be present.

Supica photo

NIB	Exc.	V.G.	Good	Fair	Poor
15000	8000	6000	4000	3000	1500

Pre-war .357 Magnum

Same as Factory Registered Model, without the individual. "REG" registration numbering in the frame yoke cutout. Approximately 1,150 manufactured between 1938 and 1941. Production ceased for WWII weapons production.

NIB	Exc.	V.G.	Good	Fair	Poor
8000	6500	5000	3500	1500	500

.357 Magnum Transitional Post-War

Similar to Pre-war .357 Magnums, but with micrometer click rear sight and S serial number prefix. Only about 142 made 1946-1949. Very rare, values are speculative.

NIB	Exc.	V.G.	Good	Fair	Poor
—	18000	12000	8000	4000	1500

Post-War .357 Magnum (Pre-Model 27)

Around 1950 the .357 Magnum was introduced with improvements, including the short throw hammer, with standard barrel lengths of 3.5, 5, 6, 6.5, and 8-3/8 in. Premium for 3.5-in. barrel.

NIB	Exc.	V.G.	Good	Fair	Poor
4000	3000	1300	1000	600	300

The Highway Patrolman (Pre-Model 28)

Chambered in .357 Magnum. The postwar .357 Magnum revolver was extremely popular among law enforcement officers. Many police agencies were interested in purchasing such a weapon — except for cost. In 1954, S&W produced a new model called at the time, "Highway Patrolman". Had all desirable performance features of the deluxe Model 27 but lacked cosmetic features that drove up price. Finish is a matte blue; rib sandblasted instead of checkered or serrated; grips standard checkered walnut. Barrel lengths 4 in. and 6.5 in. On late models, 6.5-in. barrel reduced to 6 in., as on all S&Ws. Designation changed to Model 28 in 1957. S&W discontinued Model 28 in 1986. Note: Add 25% premium for pre-Model 28. Beware, most nickel variations seen are refinished, though a very few factory nickel examples exist and are worth multiples of prices listed below. Three engineering changes.

NIB	Exc.	V.G.	Good	Fair	Poor
1800	1200	900	700	400	250

.357 Combat Magnum (Pre-Model 19)

Introduced in 1954 at the urging of Bill Jordan, a competition shooter with U.S. Border Patrol, who went on to become a respected gun writer.

Built on "K-Frame" and was first medium-frame revolver chambered for the powerful .357 Magnum cartridge. Since its inception, this model has been one of S&W's most popular revolvers. First revolver to be introduced as a four-screw model. Originally offered with 4-in. heavy barrel with extractor shroud; 6 in. became available in 1963. Finish blued or nickel plated. Grips are checkered walnut. Goncalo Alves target stocks first appeared in 1959. In 1968, a 2.5-in. round butt version was introduced. Became the Model 19.

NIB	Exc.	V.G.	Good	Fair	Poor
2800	2000	1200	800	500	300

.44 CALIBER

.44 Hand Ejector 1st Model (Triple Lock)

Also known by collectors as ".44 Triple Lock" or "The New Century." The Triple Lock nickname came from a separate locking device located on extractor rod shroud that is used in addition to usual two locks. Chambered for .44 S&W Special cartridge or .44 S&W Russian. On a limited basis, also chambered in .44-40, .45 Colt, .455 Mark II and .38-40. Fluted cylinder holds 6-shots. Barrel offered in standard lengths of 5 or 6.5 in. Limited quantity of 4" barrels produced. Finish blued or nickel-plated; grips checkered walnut with gold S&W medallion on later models. Approximately 15,375 manufactured between 1908 and 1915. Note: Add 100% premium for factory target sights.

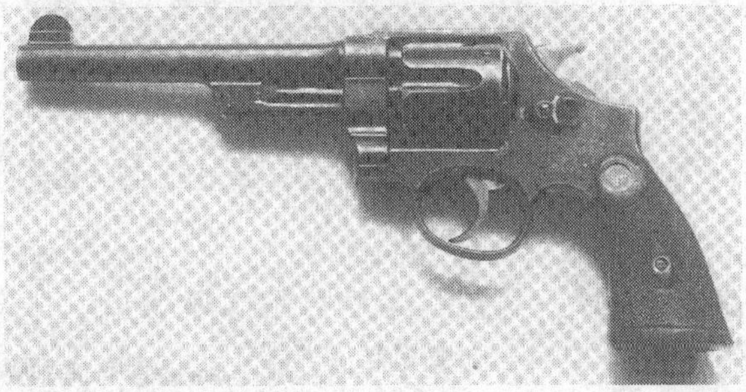

.44 HE 1st - .44 S&W Special

NIB	Exc.	V.G.	Good	Fair	Poor
6000	3500	2500	1500	750	400

.44 HE 1st - Other Calibers (Rare)

NIB	Exc.	V.G.	Good	Fair	Poor
10000	7000	4000	2000	1000	500

.44 Hand Ejector 2nd Model

Quite similar in appearance to 1st Model. Major difference, elimination of third or triple lock device and heavy ejector rod shroud. Other changes are internal and not readily apparent. Standard in .44 S&W Special chambering, but offered rarely in .38-40, .44-40 and .45 Colt. Specimens have been noted with adjustable sights in 6.5" barrel lengths. Standard barrel lengths 4", 5" and 6.5". Approximately 17,510 manufactured between 1915 and 1937, serial number range 15376-60000. Note: Add 50% premium for factory target sights. Standard chambering is .44 Special, add 75% to 100% for rare original .38-40, .44-40 or .45 Colt caliber.

.44 HE 2nd - (.44 S&W Special)

NIB	Exc.	V.G.	Good	Fair	Poor
5000	2000	1200	800	400	200

.44 HE 2nd - .38-40, .44-40 or .45 Colt

Very few factory models were made in these calibers. Values shown are speculative. Use caution and consult an expert appraiser.

NIB	Exc.	V.G.	Good	Fair	Poor
—	5000	4000	2800	1000	500

.44 Hand Ejector 3rd Model or Model of 1926

Similar in appearance to 2nd Model but brought back the heavy ejector rod shroud of 1st Model, without triple lock device. Barrel lengths 4, 5 and 6.5 in. Manufactured between 1926-1949. Add 50 percent premium for factory target sights. Standard chambering is .44 Special, add 50% to 100% for rare original .44-40 or .45 Colt caliber.

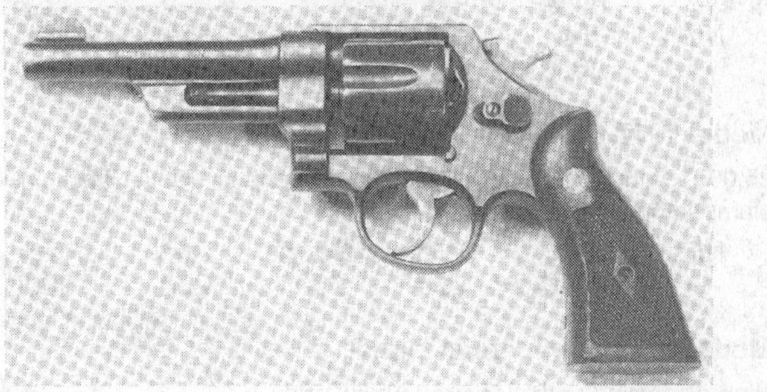

Courtesy Mike Stuckslager

.44 HE 3rd - .44 S&W Special

NIB	Exc.	V.G.	Good	Fair	Poor
6000	3000	2000	1500	1000	500

.44 HE 3rd - .44-40 or .45 Colt

Very few factory models made in these calibers. Values shown are speculative. Use caution and consult an expert appraiser.

NIB	Exc.	V.G.	Good	Fair	Poor
—	5500	4500	3000	1000	500

.44 Hand Ejector 4th Model Military (Model of 1950) Pre-Model 21

Similar to above, fixed sights, .44 Special, 4" or 5" barrel (6.5" rare, worth premium). S/n S75000 to S263000 with 1,200 made 1950-1957.

NIB	Exc.	V.G.	Good	Fair	Poor
6500	3000	1500	900	500	250

.44 Hand Ejector 4th Model Target (Model of 1950 Target) Pre-Model 24

As above but with adjustable target rear sight, .44 Special, 5" or 6.5" barrel (4" scarce, 5" rare, 5.5" very rare – all worth premiums). S/n S75000 to S263000 with 5,050 made 1950-1957.

NIB	Exc.	V.G.	Good	Fair	Poor
4000	2000	1000	700	400	250

The .44 Magnum (Pre-Model 29)

For more background, see Model 29 listing. This listing will be expanded in future editions. The first production .44 Magnum revolver was, at the time, as Detective Callahan said in the movie Dirty Harry, "The world's most powerful handgun." Values shown are for four-screw Pre-Model 29s, add 50% premium for earlier five-screw models. Add premium for 4-in. barrel.

NIB	Exc.	V.G.	Good	Fair	Poor
5000	3000	2000	1200	600	500

.45 CALIBER

.45 Hand Ejector U.S. Service Model of 1917

WWI was on the horizon and it seemed certain that the United States would become involved. S&W people began to work with Springfield Armory to develop a hand ejector model that would fire .45-caliber Government cartridge. This was accomplished in 1916 by the use of half-moon clips. New revolver is quite similar to .44 Hand Ejector in appearance. It has a 5.5" barrel, blued finish with smooth walnut grips and a lanyard ring on the butt. Designation "U.S.Army Model 1917" is stamped on the butt. After the war broke out, the government was not satisfied with S&W's production and actually took control of the company for the duration of the war. This was the first time that the company was not controlled by a Wesson. Factory records indicate that there were 163,476 Model 1917s manufactured between 1917 and 1919, the WWI years. After the war, sale of these revolvers continued on a commercial and contract basis until 1949, when this model was finally dropped from the

S&W product line.

Model 1917 Military Model

NIB	Exc.	V.G.	Good	Fair	Poor
—	2000	1000	750	500	250

Model 1917 Brazilian Contract

25,000 produced for Brazilian government in 1938. Brazilian crest stamped on sideplate.

NIB	Exc.	V.G.	Good	Fair	Poor
—	1100	750	600	250	200

Model 1917 Commercial Model

High-gloss blue and checkered walnut grips.

Courtesy Mike Stuckslager

NIB	Exc.	V.G.	Good	Fair	Poor
—	2500	1500	1100	500	300

.455 Mark II Hand Ejector 1st Model

Designed the same as .44 Hand Ejector 1st Model, with no caliber stamping on the barrel. Barrel length 6.4 in. Of the 5,000 revolvers produced, only 100 sold were commercial guns, rest were military. Produced between 1914 and 1915. Commercial model worth a premium.

NIB	Exc.	V.G.	Good	Fair	Poor
—	1200	1000	700	400	200

.455 Mark II Hand Ejector 2nd Model

Similar to first model, without an extractor shroud. Barrel length also 6.5 in. Serial number range 5000 to 74755. Manufactured from 1915 to 1917.

NIB	Exc.	V.G.	Good	Fair	Poor
—	1300	1050	600	350	180

Model 1917 Heritage

Recent limited edition reintroduction. Chambered for .45 ACP cartridge. Fitted with a 5.5-in. heavy tapered barrel. High-profile front blade sight, with fixed rear. Checkered service grips, with lanyard ring. Offered in blue, case colored or military finish. Shipped in a S&W collectible box. Note: Add $60 for case color finish.

NIB	Exc.	V.G.	Good	Fair	Poor
1200	900	600	450	300	150

NUMBERED MODEL REVOLVERS

With the development of the Hand Ejector models and swing-out cylinders, Smith & Wesson opened the door to several new advancements in the revolver field. The new system allowed for a solid frame, making the weapon stronger than the old top-break design. The company also developed different basic frame sizes and gave them letter designations. The I frame, which later developed into a slightly larger J frame (and later still the J Magnum frame for 357 Magnum), was used for .22-32 and small concealable .38 revolvers. The Medium K frame is used for .38 duty-/target type weapons. The N frame was a heavy-duty frame used for larger .357-, .44- and .45-caliber revolvers. The Hand ejector went through many evolutionary changes over the years. In 1957, all S&W models were given numerical designations (the number stamped in the yoke cut) — Model 10, Model 14, etc. Models are cataloged here by their numerical designations, a brief description given, and current values offered. It is important to note that the S&W revolvers we see marketed by the company today have undergone many changes in reaching their present configuration. Early models featured five screws in their construction, not counting grip screws. Four screws fastening side plate and another through the front of triggerguard that retained cylinder stop plunger. The first change involved elimination of the top side plate screw and five-screw Smith &Wessons became four-screw. Later, the frame was changed to eliminate the cylinder stop plunger screw, and a three-screw was created. Some models offered with flat cylinder latch that was serrated instead of familiar checkering. In 1982, attaching the barrel to the frame was changed, and the familiar pinned barrel was eliminated. At the same time, the recessed cylinder commonly found on Magnum models was also eliminated. All these factors have a definite effect on the value and collectability of a particular S&W handgun. Note: Pre-model number designations are listed in parentheses after the model number. Premiums up to 100 percent can apply to some of these handguns if accompanied by the original box and if both gun and box are in excellent or better condition. See Performance Center pages at the end of the Smith & Wesson section for these handguns' special and limited editions.

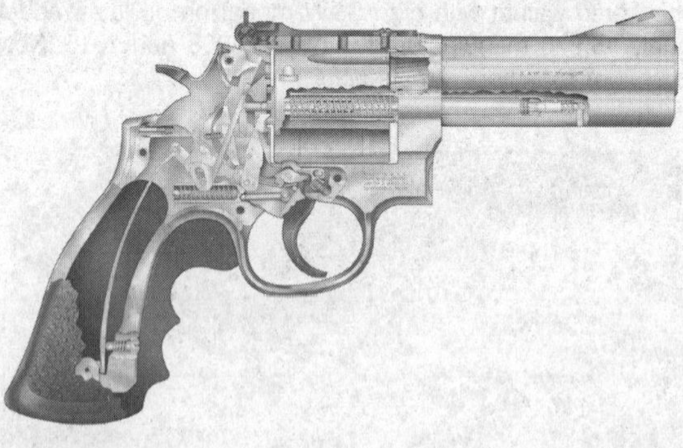

Courtesy Smith & Wesson.

Model 10 (.38 Military & Police)

.38 Special. This model has been in production in one configuration or another since 1899. It was always the mainstay of S&W line. Originally known as .38 Military and Police Model. The Model 10 is built on the K, or medium frame, and was always meant as a duty gun. Offered with 2-, 3-, 4-, 5- or 6-in. barrel. Currently only 4 and 6 in. are available. Round or square butt, chambered for .38 S&W Special. Offered in blue or nickel-plate, with checkered walnut grips. Model designation stamped on yoke on all S&W revolvers. The model 10, with many other modern S&W pistols, underwent 14 engineering changes. These changes may affect value of the revolver, and an expert should be consulted.

NIB	Exc.	V.G.	Good	Fair	Poor
1000	700	450	400	250	150

Model 10-14 Classic

Single-/double-action K-frame revolver chambered in .38 Special. Features include bright blue steel frame and cylinder, checkered wood grips, 4" barrel, adjustable Patridge-style sights.

NIB	Exc.	V.G.	Good	Fair	Poor
600	500	450	380	280	150

Model 11 (.38/200 British)

.38 S&W. First produced in 1947, S&W received many contracts for this service pistol. Nicknamed .38/200 British Service Revolver. S&W sold many of these models throughout 1950s and 1960s. Several rare variations of this model will greatly affect its value. Consult an expert if special markings and barrel lengths are encountered. Four known engineering changes. Never cataloged.

NIB	Exc.	V.G.	Good	Fair	Poor
1200	900	600	500	400	300

Model 15-8 Heritage Lew Horton

Chambered for .38 S&W Special. Fitted with 4-in. barrel. Grips are S&W checkered target. Adjustable rear sight. Offered in nickel or color case-hardened.

NIB	Exc.	V.G.	Good	Fair	Poor
1000	800	—	—	—	—

Model 12 (.38 Military & Police Airweight)

.38 Special. Model 12 was introduced in 1952. Starting serial number C223999. Merely a Model 10, with lightweight alloy frame and cylinder. In 1954, alloy cylinder was replaced with one of steel that added an additional 4 oz. in weight. Discontinued in 1986. Note: Add 40% for aluminum cylinder. Four known engineering changes.

NIB	Exc.	V.G.	Good	Fair	Poor
—	700	500	250	120	100

Model 13 (.357 Military & Police)

Simply a Model 10 M&P fitted with a heavy barrel and chambered for .357 Magnum. Introduced in 1974. Discontinued in 1999. Blued finish. Five Engineering changes. Large Premium for very rare U.S. Air Force model.

NIB	Exc.	V.G.	Good	Fair	Poor
1000	800	600	450	200	150

Model 13 .357 Performance Center

A Lew Horton exclusive. Features a 3-in. barrel with 4 Mag-Na-Ports, a bobbed hammer for double-action-only, chambered charge holes, beveled cylinder, contoured grip and thumb latch for speed loader clearance, overtravel trigger stop and FBI grips. Limited to 300 guns. Suggested Retail Introductory Price: $730

NIB	Exc.	V.G.	Good	Fair	Poor
1500	1200	—	—	—	—

Model 14 (K-38 Masterpiece)

.38 Special. Also known as "K-38." In 1957, "Model 14" stamped on yoke. Offered in 6-in. barrel, with adjustable sights. In 1961, single-action version with faster lock time offered. Discontinued in 1981. Note: Add 25% for single action. Eight engineering changes.

NIB	Exc.	V.G.	Good	Fair	Poor
1100	750	600	400	300	200

Model 14 Classic

Recreation of vintage Model 14 revolver, chambered in .38 Special +P. Six-shot cylinder, 6-in. barrel with pinned Patridge front sight and micro-click rear. Carbon steel frame. Cylinder with blued or nickel finish. Weight 34.5 oz.

NIB	Exc.	V.G.	Good	Fair	Poor
800	680	520	400	280	150

Model 14 Classic (nickel)

Same as above, with nickel finish. Discontinued.

NIB	Exc.	V.G.	Good	Fair	Poor
900	780	600	500	380	200

Model 15 (K-38 Combat Masterpiece)

.38 Special. Also known as "Combat Masterpiece." Produced at request of law enforcement officers who wanted "K-38" fitted with a 4-in. barrel. Produced from 1950-1987. Nine engineering changes.

NIB	Exc.	V.G.	Good	Fair	Poor
1200	900	550	400	300	200

Model 15-9 McGivern Heritage Performance Center

Similar to above model, but fitted with 5-in. barrel and checkered diamond grips. Engraved side plate of McGivern's speed record. Blue finish.

NIB	Exc.	V.G.	Good	Fair	Poor
1000	800	—	—	—	—

Model 15 Classic

Identical to Model 14 Classic, except with 4" barrel.

NIB	Exc.	V.G.	Good	Fair	Poor
800	680	520	400	280	150

Model 16 (K-32 Masterpiece)

Also known as "K-32" until 1957. Identical in appearance to the Model 14, except chambered for .32 S&W. Model 16 did not enjoy the commercial popularity like the Model 14 and was dropped from the line in 1973. Only 3,630 K-32s/Model 16s were sold between 1947-1973. Reintroduced in 1990 in .32 Magnum; discontinued 1993. Note: Add 25% for 1946-1957 production (no Model 16 marking). Four engineering changes.

Courtesy Mike Stuckslager

NIB	Exc.	V.G.	Good	Fair	Poor
3500	3000	2500	1500	500	200

Model 16-4 (.32 H&R Magnum)

Reintroduced in 1990, in .32 H&R Magnum with a full-lug barrel, available in 4, 6 and 8-3/8 in. and discontinued 1993. Very desirable. 50% premium for 4-in. barrel.

NIB	Exc.	V.G.	Good	Fair	Poor
2000	1500	800	500	300	200

Model 17

Chambered for .22-caliber cartridge. Fitted with 6-in. barrel, Patridge front sight and adjustable rear. Four-screw side plate. Diamond checkered S&W walnut grips. Blue or case-colored finish. Note: Add $30 for case colored finish.

NIB	Exc.	V.G.	Good	Fair	Poor
1400	1000	750	600	250	200

Model 17-8 10-Shot

Introduced in 1996. New version of old Model 17. Has a 10-round aluminum cylinder for its .22 LR cartridges. Features 6-in. full-lug barrel, with Patridge front sight and adjustable rear. Hammer is semi-target-style and trigger a smooth combat style. Finish matte black and grips are Hogue black rubber. Drilled and tapped for scope mounts. Weight about 42 oz. Discontinued 1999.

NIB	Exc.	V.G.	Good	Fair	Poor
1400	1000	700	500	300	200

Model 17-8 Heritage

Numerical designation S&W placed on the "K-22" in 1957. Target model .22 rimfire revolver popular since its introduction in 1946. Offered in 4-, 6- and 8.375-in. barrel lengths, with all target options. The 8.375" barrel dropped from the product line in 1993. Finish blued, with checkered walnut grips. Nine engineering changes. 6-shot CNC frame in modern Heritage Series.

Courtesy Mike Stuckslager

NIB	Exc.	V.G.	Good	Fair	Poor
1200	800	—	—	—	—

Model 17 Masterpiece Classic

Recreation of K-22 Masterpiece in .22 LR. Blue finish, 6" barrel, adjustable rear sight and wood grips.

NIB	Exc.	V.G.	Good	Fair	Poor
850	730	550	400	280	150

Model 18 (K-22 Combat Masterpiece)

Model designation for 4-in. barrel "Combat Masterpiece" with combat sights. Chambered for.22 rimfire. Discontinued 1985 and reintroduced in 2009 as part of the Classic Series. Seven engineering changes.

NIB	Exc.	V.G.	Good	Fair	Poor
—	1000	750	550	250	200

Model 18-7 Classic

Recreation of K-22 Combat Masterpiece in .22 LR., adjustable rear sight and wood grips. Note: Common type no lower values needed.

NIB	Exc.	V.G.	Good	Fair	Poor
850	730	550	400	280	150

Model 19 (.357 Combat Magnum)

Introduced in 1954 at the urging of Bill Jordan, a competition shooter with U.S. Border Patrol. He went on to become a respected gun writer. Built on "K-Frame" and was first medium frame revolver chambered for powerful .357 Magnum cartridge. Since its inception, Model 19 has been one of S&W's most popular revolvers. First revolver to be introduced as a four-screw model. Originally offered with 4-in. heavy barrel with extractor shroud; the 6 in. became available in 1963. Finish blued or nickel plated. Grips are checkered walnut. Goncalo Alves target stocks first appeared in 1959. In 1968, a 2.5-in. round butt version was introduced. Model 19 has been basis for many commemoratives, including Texas Ranger/with Bowie Knife and Oregon State Police/with Belt Buckle. Discontinued 1999. Eight engineering changes.

Model 19, 19-1

Note: Add 40% for nickel finish.

NIB	Exc.	V.G.	Good	Fair	Poor
2500	1800	1000	600	300	200

Model 19-2, 19-3, 19-4

NIB	Exc.	V.G.	Good	Fair	Poor
1600	1100	900	600	300	200

Model 19-5 through 19-8

NIB	Exc.	V.G.	Good	Fair	Poor
1200	900	700	500	300	200

Model 19-P Peruvian Contract

No sights, scarce.

NIB	Exc.	V.G.	Good	Fair	Poor
1500	1200	900	700	500	300

Model 19 (.357 Combat Magnum)Oregon State Police Cased with Buckle

NIB	Exc.	V.G.	Good	Fair	Poor
900	—	—	—	—	—

Combat Magnum (Pre-Model 19, 1954-1958)

Note: Add 50% for nickel finish.

NIB	Exc.	V.G.	Good	Fair	Poor
2250	1500	1100	850	500	300

Model 19-7 .357 Magnum K-Comp Performance Center (1994 Pre-lock)

Same gun as F-Comp, but furnished with black matte finish. Sold through stocking dealers on an unlimited basis. Suggested Retail Introductory Price: $800

NIB	Exc.	V.G.	Good	Fair	Poor
1800	1500	1200	—	—	—

Model 19-9 .357 Magnum Carry Comp Performance Center (With Lock)

NIB	Exc.	V.G.	Good	Fair	Poor
1100	900	700	—	—	—

Model 19-9 Classic

NIB	Exc.	V.G.	Good	Fair	Poor
650	550	500	—	—	—

Model 19-4 Various Commemoratives & Specials

Most commemoratives values realized are about the same or even less than regular issue examples in like condition with exceptions for local, departmental or historical interest. Some include:

Model 19 Texas Ranger Commemorative

Introduced in 1973. Supplied with 4-in. barrel and cased. Edition limited to 10,000. 8,000 of these had knives. Serial numbers TR 1-TR 10000. Original Retail Introductory Price: $1,250. w/ knife MSRP $1,500.

Model 20 (.38/.44 Heavy Duty)

Known as ".38/.44 Heavy Duty" before the change to numerical designations. This model was brought out in 1930, in response to requests from law enforcement personnel for a more powerful sidearm. This model, along with the .38-44 S&W Special cartridge, was an attempt to solve this problem. It was manufactured with a standard 5-in. long barrel but has been noted rarely as short as 3.5 in. and as long as 8.375 in. Built on the large N-frame. Blued or nickel-plated, with checkered walnut grips. Eventually the popularity of the .357 Magnum made the Model 20 superfluous and it was discontinued in 1966. Numbered model specimens are scarcer than pre-Model Heavy Duties. Total post-war production was about 20,000 revolvers. Two engineering changes.

Courtesy Mike Stuckslager

NIB	Exc.	V.G.	Good	Fair	Poor
2000	1500	1100	700	500	300

Model 21 (1950 Military)

Known as the "1950 Military" and "4th Model .44 Hand Ejector", before the Model 21 designation was given in 1957. Chambered for the .44 Special cartridge and equipped with fixed sights. Built on N frame and is quite rare. Manufactured only 1,200 in 16 years of production. Discontinued 1966. Two engineering changes.

NIB	Exc.	V.G.	Good	Fair	Poor
3500	3000	2000	1000	750	500

Model 21-4 Thunder Ranch .44 Special

Limited edition variation is a 4-in. barreled .44 Special, with gold-plated logo of legendary Arizona shooting school on the frame.

NIB	Exc.	V.G.	Good	Fair	Poor
1100	800	700	—	—	—

Model 21-4 Classic

Replica of vintage Model 21 N-frame revolver in .44 Special. Six-shot cylinder. Carbon steel frame, 4-in. barrel, fixed sights. Blued, case colored or nickel finish. Altamont wood grips. Introduced 2007. Less common than Thunder Ranch issue but values are similar.

NIB	Exc.	V.G.	Good	Fair	Poor
900	750	520	400	280	150

Model 22 (1950 .45 Military)

.45 ACP. Known as the "1950 .45 Military" before 1957. Introduced in 1951. Similar in appearance to the Model 21, except chambered for .45 Auto Rim or .45 ACP cartridge. Half-moon clips are used with the latter. Estimated that around 178 Model-marked guns were made between 1957-1966 in the serial range of S185000-S263000. Two Engineering changes. Values listed are speculative due to rarity.

NIB	Exc.	V.G.	Good	Fair	Poor
9000	6000	4000	2500	1200	600

Model 22 Thunder Ranch .45 ACP

Limited edition six-shot single-/double-action chambered for .45 ACP. Blued, with 4-in. tapered barrel. Weight 37.5 oz. Cocobolo grips engraved with Thunder Ranch insignia. Fixed sights. Serial numbers begin with TRR0000. 2005.

NIB	Exc.	V.G.	Good	Fair	Poor
1300	1000	800	—	—	—

Model 22-4 Classic

Replica of vintage Model 22 N-frame revolver in .45 ACP. Six-shot cylinder. Carbon steel frame, 4-in. barrel, fixed sights. Blued, case colored or nickel finish. Altamont wood grips. Introduced 2007. (Blue, 10% Nickel, + 20% Case Color)

NIB	Exc.	V.G.	Good	Fair	Poor
1000	900	800	—	—	—

Model 22 of 1917 Classic

Similar to Model 22 Classic, without ejector rod shroud and with lanyard ring on butt. Replica of U.S. Army WWI-era revolver. Introduced 2007.

NIB	Exc.	V.G.	Good	Fair	Poor
1100	900	700	—	—	—

Model 23 (.38-44 Outdoorsman)

.38 Special. The ".38-44 Outdoorsman" was the model name of this N-frame revolver before the 1957 designation change. Simply Model 20, with adjustable sights. Introduced in 1931, as a heavy-duty sporting handgun with hunters in mind. S&W produced 4,761 of these pre-war revolvers. Features 6.5-in. barrel. Blued finish. First S&W to have the new checkered walnut "Magna" grips. After 1949, this revolver was thoroughly modernized and had the later ribbed barrel. A total of 8,365 manufactured before it was discontinued in 1966; 6,039 were of the modernized configuration. Numbered model specimens are scarcer than pre-Model Outdoorsmen. Two engineering changes.

Courtesy Mike Stuckslager

NIB	Exc.	V.G.	Good	Fair	Poor
3000	2300	1800	1200	600	300

Model 24, 24-1, 24-2 (.44 Target Model of 1950, S serial range)

.44 Special. Introduced as the .44 Target Model of 1950. Simply the N-frame Model 21, with adjustable target sights. Quite popular with long-range hand gunning devotees and their leader, Elmer Keith. Introduction of .44 Magnum in 1956, began the death knell of Model 24. Finally discontinued in 1966. S&W produced a total of 5,050 Model 24s. Reintroduced in 1983 and 1984 — and then was dropped again. Note: Add 25% for 4-in. barrel; 40% for 5 in. Six engineering changes.

NIB	Exc.	V.G.	Good	Fair	Poor
5000	4000	3000	2000	1500	1000

Model 24-3, 24-4

NIB	Exc.	V.G.	Good	Fair	Poor
2000	1500	1100	800	500	250

Model 24-5 Heritage

Chambered for .44 Special cartridge. Fitted with a 6.5-in. tapered barrel. McGivern gold-bead front sight, with adjustable rear. Four-screw side-plate, chamfered charge holes, checkered diamond grips. Note: Add $60 for case-colored finish.

NIB	Exc.	V.G.	Good	Fair	Poor
1400	1100	900	—	—	—

Model 24-6 Classic

In .44 Special, with 6.5-in. barrel. Wood grips, with square butt and adjustable rear sight.

NIB	Exc.	V.G.	Good	Fair	Poor
1400	1100	750	—	—	—

Model 25 (.45 Target Model of 1950)

Prior to model designation change in 1957. this model was known as .45 Target Model of 1955. An improved version of 1950 Target .45. Features a heavier barrel 4-, 6.5- or 8-in. in length, with blued or nickel-plated finish. All target options were offered. Chambered for .45 ACP or .45 Auto-rim cartridges. Note: Add 100% premium for .45 Colt. 14 Engineering changes to date, values here apply to Model 25 and 25-1.

NIB	Exc.	V.G.	Good	Fair	Poor
2200	1600	1200	950	650	500

Model 25-2

Discontinued modern version of Model 25. Chambered in .45 ACP. The 6.5-in. barrel is shortened to 6 in. Available in a presentation case.

NIB	Exc.	V.G.	Good	Fair	Poor
1800	1300	800	700	400	200

Model 25-3 125th Anniversary with Case

Introduced in 1977. Limited edition of 10,000. Serial numbers SW0000-SW10000. Deluxe models marked 25-4. Original Retail Introductory Price: $350.

NIB	Exc.	V.G.	Good	Fair	Poor
1400	1100	—	—	—	—

Model 25-4 through 25-9

NIB	Exc.	V.G.	Good	Fair	Poor
1500	1200	800	500	300	150

Model 25-7 - 5" Matte Black Unfluted

NIB	Exc.	V.G.	Good	Fair	Poor
2500	2000	1500	1200	—	—

Model 25-13 Mountain Gun

Introduced in 2004. This .45 Colt N-frame round butt model features 4-in. tapered barrel, with black blade front sight and adjustable rear. Cocobolo wood grips. Blued finish. Weight about 40 oz.

NIB	Exc.	V.G.	Good	Fair	Poor
1400	1100	700	500	—	—

Model 25 Performance Center

Similar to Model 24, but chambered for .45 Colt cartridge. Blue or case colored finish. Note: Add $30 for case-colored finish.

NIB	Exc.	V.G.	Good	Fair	Poor
1200	780	600	450	300	150

Model 25-10 to 25-12 6.5" Heritage/Performance Center

Similar to Model 24 but chambered for .45 Colt cartridge. Blue or case-colored finish. Note: Add $30 for case-colored finish.

NIB	Exc.	V.G.	Good	Fair	Poor
1400	1100	700	500	—	—

Model 25-14 Classic

Identical to Model 24 Classic, except chambered for .45 Colt.

NIB	Exc.	V.G.	Good	Fair	Poor
900	700	—	—	—	—

Model 26 (1950 .45 Target)

Numerical designation of 1950 .45 Target Model. This large N-frame revolver is basically the same as Model 25, but has a lighter, thinner barrel. This caused its unpopularity among competitive shooters who wanted a heavier revolver. This brought about Model 25 and the demise of Model 26, in 1961. Manufactured only 2,768.

NIB	Exc.	V.G.	Good	Fair	Poor
4000	3300	2500	1700	1000	500

Model 26-1 Georgia State Police Commemorative

Introduced in 1988/1989. 45 Colt Supplied with 5-in. barrel. Total production of 802 guns. Known Serial numbers BBY00354-BBY0434.Original Retail Introductory Price: $405.

NIB	Exc.	V.G.	Good	Fair	Poor
1400	1100	900	—	—	—

Model 27 (.357 Magnum)

.357 Magnum. In 1948, after the end of WWII, production of this revolver again commenced with a new rebound slide-operated hammer block and short throw hammer were utilized. Barrel lengths offered were 3.5, 5, 6, 6.5 and 8.375 in. In 1957, model designation was changed to Model 27. In 1975, target trigger, hammer and Goncalo Alves target grips were made standard. Some additional variations may be of interest to the collector. Around serial number SI71584, the three-screw sideplate model was first produced. In 1960, designation -1 was added to model indicating change to a left hand thread to extractor rod. In 1962, cylinder stop was changed which disposed the need for a plunger spring hole in front of triggerguard. Change was indicated by a -2 behind model number. Note: Add 25% for 3.5- or 5-in. barrel. 300%+ premium for scarce postwar pre-1950 Transition Model. Eight engineering changes.

Model 27 (no dash)

Premiums for short barrels 5 in. or less.

NIB	Exc.	V.G.	Good	Fair	Poor
3000	2000	1500	1200	800	400

Model 27-1

NIB	Exc.	V.G.	Good	Fair	Poor
5000	3000	2000	1500	800	450

Model 27-2

NIB	Exc.	V.G.	Good	Fair	Poor
2000	1400	1100	900	600	400

Model 27-3 through 27-6

NIB	Exc.	V.G.	Good	Fair	Poor
1500	1100	800	600	400	300

Model 27-3 50th Anniversary Commemorative

Introduced in 1985. Supplied with 5-in. barrel and cased. Limited edition to 2,500 guns. Serial numbers REG0001-REG2500. Original Retail Introductory Price: N/A.

NIB	Exc.	V.G.	Good	Fair	Poor
1500	1200	900	700	500	300

Model 27-7 (8-Shot Prelock)

NIB	Exc.	V.G.	Good	Fair	Poor
3000	2500	2000	1500	800	500

Model 27-8 (8-Shot with Lock)

NIB	Exc.	V.G.	Good	Fair	Poor
2000	1500	1100	800	500	350

Model 27-9 Classic

Reintroduction of vintage Model 27. Available in blue or bright nickel finish. 6.5-in. barrel, walnut grips. Introduced 2008. Note: Add 25% for 75th Anniversary Model.

NIB	Exc.	V.G.	Good	Fair	Poor
1100	900	700	—	—	—

Model 28 (Highway Patrolman)

.357 Magnum, N-Frame. The Model 27 revolver was extremely popular among law enforcement officers. Many police agencies were interested in purchasing such a weapon — except for cost. In 1954, S&W produced a new model called at the time, "Highway Patrolman". It had all desirable performance features of deluxe Model 27, but lacked cosmetic features that drove up price. Finish matte blue; rib sandblasted instead of checkered or serrated; grips standard checkered walnut. Barrel lengths 4 and 6.5 in. On late models, 6.5-in. barrel reduced to 6 in., as on all S&Ws. Designation changed to Model 28 in 1957. S&W discontinued the Model 28 in 1986. Note: 3 engineering changes.

Model 28

Note: 28-1 rare, 100% premium.

NIB	Exc.	V.G.	Good	Fair	Poor
1800	1400	900	600	400	200

Model 28-2, 28-3

NIB	Exc.	V.G.	Good	Fair	Poor
1400	900	750	600	400	200

Model 29 (.44 Magnum)

Early 1950s, handgun writers under leadership of Elmer Keith, were in the habit of loading .44 Special cartridge to high performance levels and firing them in existing .44 Hand Ejectors. They urged S&W to produce a revolver strong enough to consistently fire these heavy loads. In 1954, Remington at the request of S&W, produced .44 Magnum cartridge which were longer so that they would not fit in chambers of older .44 Special guns. First .44 Magnum became available for sale in early 1955. First 500 were made with 6.5-in. barrel; 4 in. became available later that year. In 1957, model designation was changed to 29 and 8.375-in. barrel was introduced. Available in blue or nickel-plate. Came standard with all target options. Offered in a fitted wood case. Model 29 is considered by many knowledgeable people to be the finest revolver S&W has ever produced. Older Model 29 revolvers are in a different collector category than most modern S&W revolvers. Early four-screw models can be worth 100% premium in excellent condition. These early models were produced from 1956 to 1958. Approximately 6,500 were sold. One must regard these revolvers on a separate basis and have them individually appraised for proper valuation. In 1993, the 4-in. barrel dropped from production. 10 Engineering changes with multiple variations. Rare 5-in. barrel will bring 3X to 5X standard values for Model 29, 29-1, and 29-2. Nickel worth premium, especially on early guns. Note that many model variations exist, values posted below are for standard configurations. Premiums for short barrels (5 in. or less), unfluted cylinders, and limited editions.

Model 29 (no dash)

NIB	Exc.	V.G.	Good	Fair	Poor
4000	2600	2000	1000	700	350

Model 29-1 (Rare)

NIB	Exc.	V.G.	Good	Fair	Poor
11000	4000	3000	2000	1000	500

Model 29-2

NIB	Exc.	V.G.	Good	Fair	Poor
2500	1800	900	750	600	300

Model 29-3 through 29-7 (Prelock)

Premium for 29-7.

NIB	Exc.	V.G.	Good	Fair	Poor
1500	1200	900	700	500	250

Model 29-5 Classic DX

25% premium for 5 in.

NIB	Exc.	V.G.	Good	Fair	Poor
2500	2000	1500	900	600	300

Model 29-8 through 29-10 Internal Lock

Small premium for various special limited editions.

NIB	Exc.	V.G.	Good	Fair	Poor
1400	1100	900	700	—	—

Model 29-9 Performance Center Heritage and "American Pride" Issues

NIB	Exc.	V.G.	Good	Fair	Poor
1500	1100	900	—	—	—

Model 29-3 Elmer Keith Commemorative

Introduced in 1986. Supplied with 4" barrel. Gun etched in gold. Limited edition of 2,500 guns. Serial numbers EMK0000-EMK0100 for Deluxe models and EMK 010-EMK2500 for standard model. Original Retail Introductory Price: $850. Deluxe NIB $1,400.

NIB	Exc.	V.G.	Good	Fair	Poor
1100	—	—	—	—	—

Model 29 Mountain Gun

Lightweight version of the Model 29. .44 Magnum, 4" tapered barrel, round butt grip frame. Embellished Model 29-6 made for the S&W Collectors Association worth 50% or more premium.

NIB	Exc.	V.G.	Good	Fair	Poor
1500	900	700	500	380	250

Fiftieth Anniversary Model 29

Commemorative edition of classic .44 Magnum. Carbon steel, with polished blue finish. Double-action 6-shot. 6.5" barrel, weight 48.5 oz. Cocobolo wood grips, with 24kt Gold Anniversary logo. Fifty were hand engraved, and these will bring double the values below.

NIB	Exc.	V.G.	Good	Fair	Poor
1500	1000	550	350	200	150

Other Variations of Model 29

Among the numerous variations and limited editions are the Silhouette, Classic, Classic DX, and Magna Classic. These will bring varying premiums similar to the premiums for comparable variations of the Model 629 stainless steel .44 Magnum.

Model 29 Heritage

Similar to Model 24 and Model 25, but chambered for .44 Magnum cartridge. Oversized wood grips. Blue or nickel finish. Was to be produced in 2002 only. Serial numbers begin with "DBW2005".

NIB	Exc.	V.G.	Good	Fair	Poor
1100	900	600	450	300	150

Model 29 Classic

Replica of original (1956) Model 29 N-frame revolver in .44 Magnum. Six-shot cylinder. Carbon steel frame, 6.5" barrel, fixed sights. Blued or nickel finish, with/without engraving. Altamont wood grips. Introduced 2007.

NIB	Exc.	V.G.	Good	Fair	Poor
1200	1000	750	500	380	200

Model 30 (The .32 Hand Ejector)

.32 S&W. Built on the small I-frame. Based on .32 Hand Ejector Model of 1903. This older model was dropped from production in 1942. Reintroduced in 1949, in a more modern version but still referred to as .32 Hand Ejector. In 1957, model designation was changed to Model 30. In 1960, this frame size was dropped and J-frame, which had been in use since 1950, became standard for Model 30. S&W stamped -1 behind the model number to designate this important change in frame size. Chambered for .32 S&W Long cartridge. Has a 6-shot cylinder and 2-, 3-, 4- and 6-in. barrel lengths. Fixed sights and blued or nickel-plated. Butt is round, with checkered walnut grips. Discontinued in 1976. One engineering change.

Courtesy W.P. Hallstein III and son Chip

NIB	Exc.	V.G.	Good	Fair	Poor
1000	800	600	400	250	150

Model 31 (.32 Regulation Police)

.32 S&W. Same as Model 30, with a square butt. It was known as .32 Regulation Police before 1957. Discontinued 1991. Three engineering changes.

NIB	Exc.	V.G.	Good	Fair	Poor
1000	750	600	400	250	150

Model 32 (.38/.32 Terrier)

.38 S&W. Known as Terrier prior to 1957, was introduced in 1936. Essentially a .38 Regulation Police chambered for .38 S&W, with 2" barrel and round butt. Like Model 30 and 31, this revolver was originally built on I-frame, which was changed to J-frame in 1960. The -1 behind model number signifies this change. Offered in blue or nickel-plate. Has a 5-shot cylinder, fixed sights and checkered walnut grips. Discontinued in 1974. One engineering change.

NIB	*Exc.*	*V.G.*	*Good*	*Fair*	*Poor*
900	700	600	400	200	100

Model 032 (Rare)

A limited production version with alloy frame and steel cylinder was produced as Model 032 chambered in .32 H&R Magnum. Thought to be cosmetically flawed model 632. 6-shot cylinder, add 30%.

NIB	*Exc.*	*V.G.*	*Good*	*Fair*	*Poor*
2000	1600	1100	800	400	200

Model 33 (.38 Regulation Police)

.38 S&W. Simply the .38 Regulation Police, with a square butt and 4-in. barrel. Chambered for .38 S&W. Factory referred to this model as .38/32 revolver. Also built on small I-frame and later changed to J-frame in 1960. Discontinued in 1974. One engineering change.

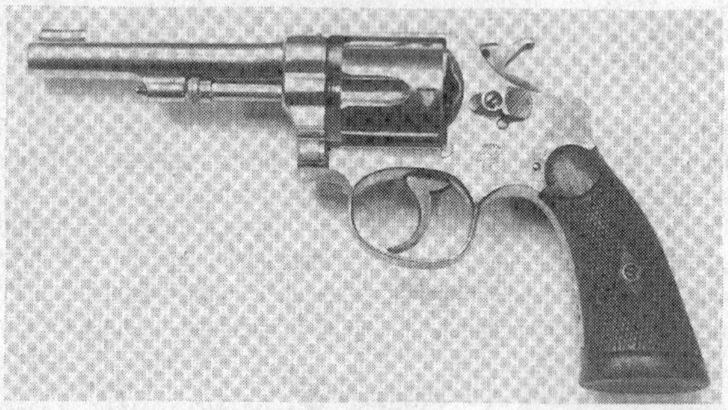

Courtesy Mike Stuckslager

NIB	*Exc.*	*V.G.*	*Good*	*Fair*	*Poor*
900	700	550	400	200	100

Model 34 (.22/.32 Kit Gun)

.22 Long Rifle. Introduced in 1936 as .22-32 Kit Gun. Has a 2- or 4-in. barrel, round or square butt and adjustable sights. Underwent several modifications before it reached its present form. S&W modernized this revolver in 1953, with addition of a coil mainspring and micro-click sights. Model 34 is built on this improved version. Revolver is a .32 Hand Ejector chambered for .22 rimfire. Built on I-frame until 1960, when changeover to improved J-frame occurred. The -1 behind model number indicates this variation. Offered blued or nickel-plate. Add premiums for early variations: Model 34 (no dash) add 50%; Model 34-1 add 40%. Two engineering changes.

Courtesy Mike Stuckslager

NIB	*Exc.*	*V.G.*	*Good*	*Fair*	*Poor*
1200	900	700	500	200	100

Model 35 (.22/.32 Target)

A square-butt, 6-in. barreled version of .22/32 Hand Ejector. Known prior to 1957 as .22/32 Target. Underwent same changes as Model 34. Discontinued in 1973.

Courtesy Mike Stuckslager

NIB	*Exc.*	*V.G.*	*Good*	*Fair*	*Poor*
1500	1200	900	500	300	200

Model 36 (.38 Chief's Special)

Chiefs Special five-shot J-frame as listed above with factory target sights, with round butt or square butt. The same configuration (Chiefs Special with target sights) was also produced as the Model 50. See Model 50 listing for more information on all Chiefs Special Target model designations.

NIB	*Exc.*	*V.G.*	*Good*	*Fair*	*Poor*
800	550	400	300	150	100

Model 36 (Chief's Special Target)

Known as Chief's Special. Introduced in 1950. Built on J-frame. Chambered for .38 Special cartridge. Holds 5 shots. Has a 2- or 3-in. barrel. Initially offered in a round butt. In 1952, a square-butt version was released. Finished in blue or nickel-plate, with checkered walnut grips. A 3-in. heavy barrel was first produced in 1967, and became standard in 1975. The 2-in. barrel dropped from production in 1993. Ten engineering changes.

Courtesy W.P. Hallstein III and son Chip

NIB	*Exc.*	*V.G.*	*Good*	*Fair*	*Poor*
1500	1200	800	400	200	150

Model 36-10 Classic

Replica of vintage Model 36 Chief's Special in .38 Special. Five-shot cylinder. Carbon steel frame, 1.875- or 3-in. barrel, fixed sights. Blued, case-colored or nickel finish. Altamont wood grips. Introduced 2007.

NIB	Exc.	V.G.	Good	Fair	Poor
700	600	500	—	—	—

Model 36LS (.38 Ladysmith)

Similar to Model 36, with exception only offered with 2-in. barrel. Rosewood grips and soft carrying case, standard. Weight 20 oz.

NIB	Exc.	V.G.	Good	Fair	Poor
850	550	400	300	150	100

Model 37

Introduced in 1952 as Chief's Special Airweight. Initially had an alloy frame and cylinder. In 1954, following many complaints regarding damaged revolvers, cylinders were made of steel. Barrel lengths, finishes and grip options on Airweight are the same as on standard Chief Special. In 1957, Model 37 designation was adopted. These early alloy frame and cylinder revolvers were designed to shoot only standard velocity .38 Special cartridges. Use of high-velocity ammunition was not recommended by the factory. Note: All 1998 and later production models were rated for +P ammunition. Three engineering changes.

NIB	Exc.	V.G.	Good	Fair	Poor
800	700	500	300	200	150

Model 38 (Airweight Bodyguard)

Introduced in 1955 as Airweight Bodyguard. This was a departure from S&W's usual procedure in that the alloy-framed version came first. Chambered for .38 Special and available with 2-in. barrel standard. Although a 3-in. barrel was offered, it is rarely encountered. Frame of Bodyguard is extended to conceal and shroud the hammer, but at the same time allows hammer to be cocked by the thumb. This makes this model an ideal pocket revolver, as it can be drawn without catching on clothing. Available blue or nickel-plated, with checkered walnut grips. Note: All 1998 and later production models were rated for +P ammunition. Three engineering changes.

NIB	Exc.	V.G.	Good	Fair	Poor
700	500	350	300	200	150

Model 40 Centennial

Introduced in 1952 as Smith & Wesson's 100th Anniversary and appropriately called "Centennial Model." A Safety Hammerless design. Built on J-frame. Features a fully concealed hammer and grip safety. Chambered for .38 Special cartridge. Offered with 2-in. barrel blued or nickelplate. Grips are checkered walnut. Centennial discontinued in 1974.

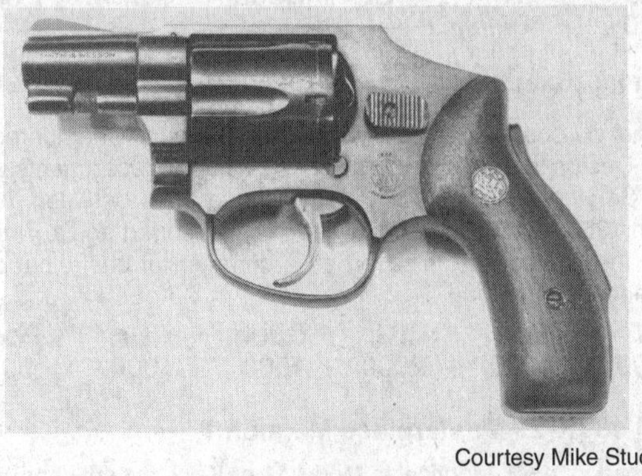

Courtesy Mike Stuckslager

NIB	Exc.	V.G.	Good	Fair	Poor
900	800	550	350	200	150

Model 40/42 Centennial Classic

Recreation of 5-shot J-frame model. Designed for double-action-only operation, with fully concealed hammer and grip safety. Model 40 has a steel frame; weight 19 oz. Model 42 has an alloy frame; weight 13 oz.

NIB	Exc.	V.G.	Good	Fair	Poor
700	600	500	400	300	200

Model 42—Airweight Centennial

Identical in configuration to Model 40, except furnished with an aluminum alloy frame. Discontinued in 1974. Editors Note: First 37 pre-Model 42s were manufactured with aluminum alloy cylinders. Weight 11.1/4 oz., compared to 13 oz. for standard model. Balance of Model 42 production was with steel cylinders. Add 300% for extremely rare aluminum alloy cylinder variation. Circa 1952-1974. Model 42-1 reintroduced in 2009.

NIB	Exc.	V.G.	Good	Fair	Poor
1200	900	600	400	200	100

Model 042 Centennial Airweight

Produced in 1992, but not catalogued. Chambered for .38 Special. Fitted with 2-in. barrel. Frame is alloy. Marked "MOD 042." No grip safety. Blued finish. Weight about 16 oz. Supposedly a reworked Model 642 "blemish gun" distributed through a national wholesaler.

NIB	Exc.	V.G.	Good	Fair	Poor
1200	780	590	380	200	100

Model 43 (.22/.32 Kit Gun Airweight)

Built on J-frame. Chambered for .22 rimfire. Offered in round or square butt, with checkered walnut grips. Has 3.5-in. barrel, adjustable sights and blued or nickel-plated. Frame made of aluminum alloy. Except for this, identical to Model 34 or .22/.32 Kit Gun. This model has a rare 2" barrel configuration as well as very limited production in .22 WRM. Introduced in 1954; discontinued in 1974.

Courtesy Mike Stuckslager

NIB	Exc.	V.G.	Good	Fair	Poor
800	650	500	300	200	100

Model 43C

8-round .22 LR.

NIB	Exc.	V.G.	Good	Fair	Poor
700	600	—	—	—	—

Model 45 (Post Office - Rare)

A special purpose K-frame Military & Police Model. Chambered for .22 rimfire. Designed as a training revolver for police departments and U.S. Postal Service. Manufactured in limited quantities between 1948 and 1957. In 1963, production abruptly began and ended again. There were 500 of these revolvers released on a commercial basis, but they are rarely encountered.

NIB	Exc.	V.G.	Good	Fair	Poor
6000	4000	2000	1500	1000	500

Model 48 (K-22 Masterpiece Magnum)

Introduced in 1959. Identical to Model 17 or K-22, except chambered for .22 WRM cartridge. Offered in 4-, 6- and 8.375-in. barrel lengths. Blued finish. Discontinued in 1986. Reintroduced in 2010. Seven engineering changes.

NIB	Exc.	V.G.	Good	Fair	Poor
1800	1500	1300	900	500	200

Model 48-7 Classic

Single-/double-action K-frame revolver chambered in .22 Magnum rimfire (.22 MRF). Features include bright blue steel frame and cylinder, checkered wood grips, 4- or 6-in. barrel, adjustable Patridge-style sights.

NIB	Exc.	V.G.	Good	Fair	Poor
700	650	600	—	—	—

Model 49 (Bodyguard)

Introduced in 1959. Identical in configuration to Model 38, except frame is made of steel. Three engineering changes, discontinued 1997.

NIB	Exc.	V.G.	Good	Fair	Poor
1000	800	650	400	250	200

Model 50 Chief's Special Target

Five-shot J-frame revolver in .38 Special with adjustable sights. Chiefs Special Target models were introduced in 1955 before S&W began numbering its revolver models in approximately 1957 (see listing for Model 36 Chiefs Special Target). In 1962, the factory began calling this configuration the Model 50, but production guns were still stamped Model 36 until about 1973 when the model marking was changed to Model 50. However, some production runs of Chiefs Special Target Models continued to be marked Model 36, including batches in 1973, 1975 (213 3" heavy barrel Model 36-1s), 1976 (three 2" nickel models), and 1989 (2,000 satin blue 3" full-lug Model 36-6s).

NIB	Exc.	V.G.	Good	Fair	Poor
1900	1400	900	500	300	200

Model 51 (.22/.32 Kit Gun Magnum)

Simply Model 34, chambered for .22 Win. Magnum rimfire. First introduced in 1960, beginning with serial number 52637. Available in both round and square butt, with round butt variation having a total production of only 600. Model 51 discontinued in 1974.

NIB	Exc.	V.G.	Good	Fair	Poor
1500	1000	800	500	300	200

Model 53 (.22 Magnum Jet)

Introduced in 1961. Chambered for .22 Jet, a Remington cartridge. Barrel lengths 4", 6", and 8.375". Finish blued. Sights were adjustable. Furnished with cylinder inserts that would allow .22 rimfire cartridges to be fired. Frame had two firing pins. Approximately 15,000 produced before it was discontinued in 1974. Price includes guns with individual chambered inserts. Note: Add $150 for the auxiliary .22 LR cylinder. One engineering change.

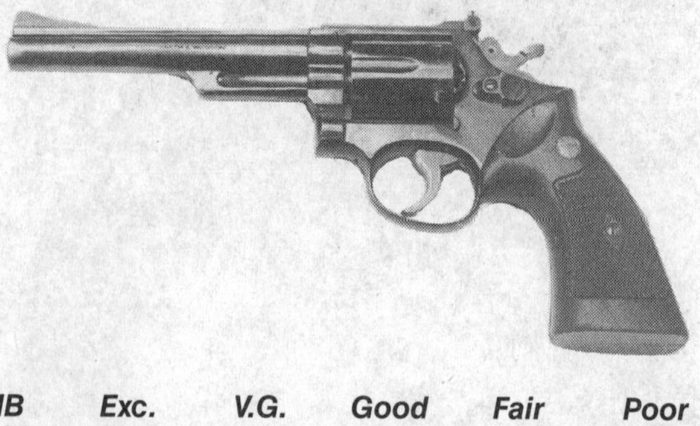

NIB	Exc.	V.G.	Good	Fair	Poor
2500	1800	1200	900	600	300

Model 56 (KXT-38 USAF - Rare)

Introduced in 1962. A 2-in. heavy barrel built on the K-frame. Chambered for .38 Special. Marked "U.S." on backstrap. Total of 15,205 produced. Discontinued in 1964. Most were reportedly destroyed by the Air Force. About 35 have been found to date. Values are speculative due to rarity.

NIB	Exc.	V.G.	Good	Fair	Poor
10000	8000	6000	4000	2000	1000

Model 57

Introduced in 1964. Chambered for .41 Magnum cartridge. Built on N frame. Offered in 4", 6", and 8.375" barrel lengths. Blued frame and adjustable sights. Model designations are: 57-1 1982; 57-2 1988; 57-3 1990; 57-4 1993. Add 25% for nickel finish; 100 percent premium for pre-1969 model with "S" serial number prefix. Six engineering changes.

NIB	Exc.	V.G.	Good	Fair	Poor
2200	1800	1200	500	300	200

Model 57-6 Classic

NIB	Exc.	V.G.	Good	Fair	Poor
900	800	—	—	—	—

Model 58

Chambered for .41 Magnum and fitted with fixed sights. Offered in blued or nickel finish, with 4" barrel. Checkered walnut grips are standard. Introduced in 1964. One engineering change.

NIB	Exc.	V.G.	Good	Fair	Poor
1800	1100	900	500	300	200

Model 60

Introduced in 1965. Similar to Model 36, but in stainless steel. Offered with a 2" barrel, with fixed sights, walnut grips and smooth trigger. The 3" barrel version comes with a full underlug, adjustable sights, serrated trigger and rubber grips. Weight about: 2" version 20 oz.; 3" version 25 oz. In 1996, this model offered chambered for .357 Magnum cartridge, with a 2.125" barrel. Weight about 23 oz. This model also offered in .38 Special-only. Add 50% for 2-in. Model 60s with adjustable sights. 18 engineering changes.

Model 60 Pre-Lock 2"

10% premium for 3" barrel.

NIB	Exc.	V.G.	Good	Fair	Poor
1600	800	600	450	300	200

Model 60LS (LadySmith)

Chambered for .38 Special, with 2" barrel and stainless steel frame and cylinder. "LadySmith" marked. New version offered in 1996, chambered for .357 Magnum cartridge.

NIB	Exc.	V.G.	Good	Fair	Poor
700	500	400	350	200	150

Model 60 Pro Series

Similar to Model 60, in .38/.357 with night front sights, "high-hold" enforcing walnut grips, 3" barrel and matte stainless finish. Introduced 2008.

NIB	Exc.	V.G.	Good	Fair	Poor
800	700	600	—	—	—

Model 60 5"

Has a 5" barrel. Introduced in 2005.

NIB	Exc.	V.G.	Good	Fair	Poor
750	650	550	400	250	200

Model 60-14 Internal Lock

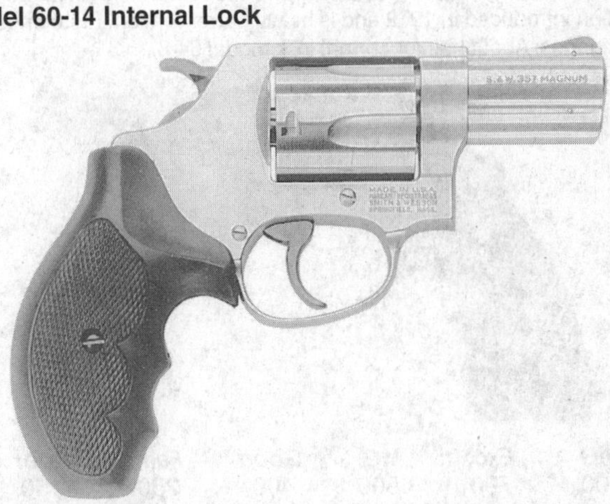

NIB	Exc.	V.G.	Good	Fair	Poor
700	650	500	—	—	—

Model 60 Carry Comp Performance Center

Introduced in the summer of 1993. This J-frame revolver fitted with a 3" full underlug barrel, with integral compensator. Charge holes are radiused for quick loading. Action tuned by Performance Center. Pistol rated for +P ammunition. Grips are fancy wood contoured for speed loaders. This Lew Horton revolver limited to 300 guns. Special serial numbers. Suggested Retail Introductory Price: $795

NIB	Exc.	V.G.	Good	Fair	Poor
1800	1600	1400	—	—	—

Model 63

.22 Long Rifle. Introduced in 1977. Simply Model 34 made of stainless steel. Four engineering changes.

NIB	Exc.	V.G.	Good	Fair	Poor
1200	700	500	450	300	200

Model 64 (Military & Police Stainless)

Stainless steel version of Model 10 M&P. Introduced in 1970. Model 64-1 variation introduced in 1972 and is heavy barrel version. Eight engineering changes. About half for current lock model 64-8.

NIB	Exc.	V.G.	Good	Fair	Poor
900	700	500	400	250	150

Model 65 (.357 Military & Police Heavy Barrel Stainless)

Stainless steel version of Model 13 M&P .357 Magnum. Manufactured 1972-2004. Add 20% premium for 3" barrel or for LadySmith model. Eight engineering changes.

NIB	Exc.	V.G.	Good	Fair	Poor
1000	800	600	500	250	150

Model 66 (.357 Combat Magnum Pre-Lock)

Released in 1970. Stainless steel version of Model 19 or Combat Magnum. Chambered for .357 Magnum. Has adjustable sights, square butt with checkered walnut grips and initially offered with a 4" barrel. In 1974, a 2.5" barrel, round butt version was made available. Also available in a 6" barrel, with all target options until discontinued in 1993. Reintroduced in 2014. Seven engineering changes.

NIB	Exc.	V.G.	Good	Fair	Poor
1300	1000	800	700	500	200

Model 66 Performance Center

A RSR exclusive. Chambered for .357 Magnum cartridge. Fitted with 3" barrel. Red ramp front sight. Stainless steel finish. Limited edition. Suggested Retail Introductory Price: $490

NIB	Exc.	V.G.	Good	Fair	Poor
1200	—	—	—	—	—

Model 66 .357 Magnum F-Comp Performance Center Pre-Lock

Performance Center revolver designed as a carry gun. Furnished with 3" ported barrel and full underlug. Thumb-piece has been cut down to accommodate all speed loaders. Charge holes are countersunk. K-frame action has been custom tuned. Rear sight is a fully adjustable black blade, while front sight features a Tritium dot night sight. Furnished with a round butt combat-style rubber grip. Stainless steel finish. Weight about 35 oz. A Lew Horton special limited edition of 300 units. Note: In 2003, this revolver was produced for all S&W stocking dealers. Suggested Retail Introductory Price: $800

NIB	Exc.	V.G.	Good	Fair	Poor
3000	2000	1400	1000	—	—

Model 66-4 Super K Performance Center 3" Ported

NIB	Exc.	V.G.	Good	Fair	Poor
5000	3000	2000	—	—	—

Model 66-6 Internal Lock

NIB	Exc.	V.G.	Good	Fair	Poor
700	600	—	—	—	—

Model 66-6 .357 Magnum Performance Center F-Comp Internal Lock

NIB	Exc.	V.G.	Good	Fair	Poor
2000	1400	1000	—	—	—

Model 67 (.38 Combat Masterpiece)

Introduced in 1972. Stainless steel version of Model 15, with 4" barrel. Chambered for .38 Special cartridge. Model designation changes are as follows: None: 1972-1977; -1: 1977-1988; -2: 1988-1993; -3: 1993-present. Six engineering changes.

NIB	Exc.	V.G.	Good	Fair	Poor
800	650	500	400	200	150

Model 68

Identical to a Model 66 except chambered in .38 Special only for the CA Highway Patrol. Approx. 6,000 manufactured from 1977-1988. Usually marked CHP with an OHB over stamp.

NIB	Exc.	V.G.	Good	Fair	Poor
2000	1500	1200	900	—	—

Model 69

Built on the L-frame. A five-shot .44 Magnum, with 4.25" barrel and stainless finish. Sights are Smith & Wesson's classic white-outline adjustable rear and red-ramp front. Grips are synthetic, with finger grooves. Introduced in 2014.

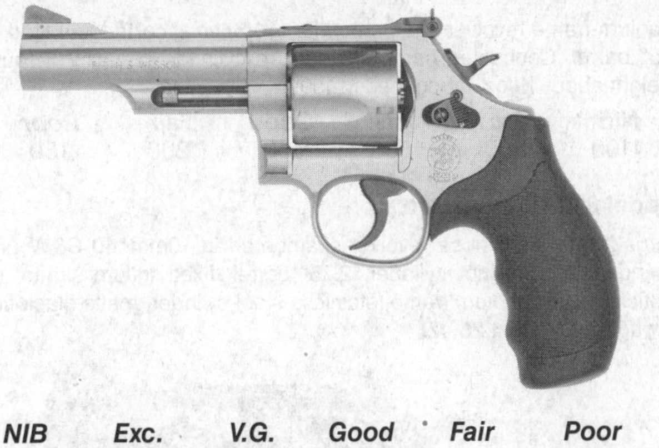

NIB	Exc.	V.G.	Good	Fair	Poor
900	800	—	—	—	—

Model 73

Produced in 1973. Built on a special "C" size frame. Cylinder holds 6 rounds. Chambered for .38 Special cartridge. Fitted with 2" barrel. Total of 5,000 built. All but 20 were destroyed. Marked "MOD 73" on yoke. Rare. Values are speculative.

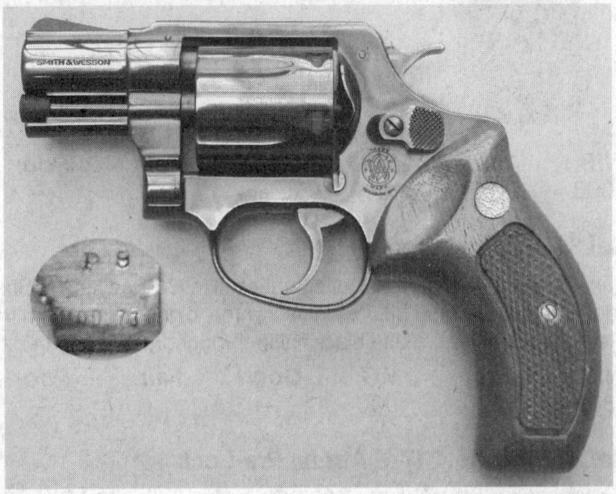

Courtesy Jim Supica, Old Town Station

NIB	Exc.	V.G.	Good	Fair	Poor
10000	8000	6500	5000	4000	2000

Model 242

Medium-frame aluminum revolver chambered for .38 Special +P cartridge. Semi-concealed hammer and 2.5" barrel. Pinned black ramp front sight. Black rubber boot grips. Seven-round titanium cylinder. Matte alloy and titanium finish. Weight about 19 oz. Introduced in 1999; discontinued.

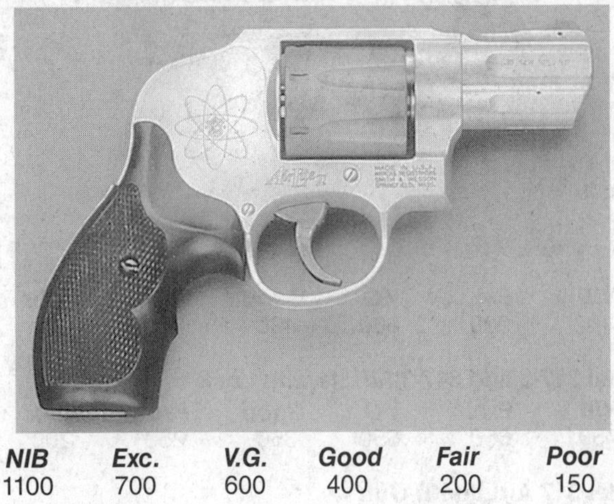

NIB	Exc.	V.G.	Good	Fair	Poor
1100	700	600	400	200	150

Model 296

Medium-frame revolver chambered for .44 Special cartridge. Fitted with 2.5" barrel. Concealed hammer. Titanium cylinder, capacity 5 rounds. Weight about 19 oz. Introduced in 1999.

NIB	Exc.	V.G.	Good	Fair	Poor
1100	800	600	400	200	150

Model 310 Night Guard

Large-frame snub nose revolver chambered in 10mm/.40 S&W (interchangeable). Six-shot cylinder, 2.75" barrel, fixed tritium sights, synthetic grips. Scandium frame, stainless steel cylinder, matte black finish throughout. Weight 28 oz.

NIB	Exc.	V.G.	Good	Fair	Poor
3000	2000	1000	—	—	—

Model 315 Night Guard

Medium-frame snubnose revolver chambered in .38 Special +P. Six-shot cylinder, 2.5" barrel, fixed tritium sights, synthetic grips. Scandium frame, stainless steel cylinder, matte black finish throughout. Weight 24 oz.

NIB	Exc.	V.G.	Good	Fair	Poor
1800	1200	900	—	—	—

Model 317 AirLite, 317-1, AirLite Pre-Lock

8-round revolver introduced in 1997. Chambered for .22 LR cartridge. Fitted with 2" barrel, serrated ramp front sight and fixed rear. Dymondwood boot grips. Produced from stainless steel and aluminum alloy on a J-frame. Weight about 9.9 oz. Three engineering changes.

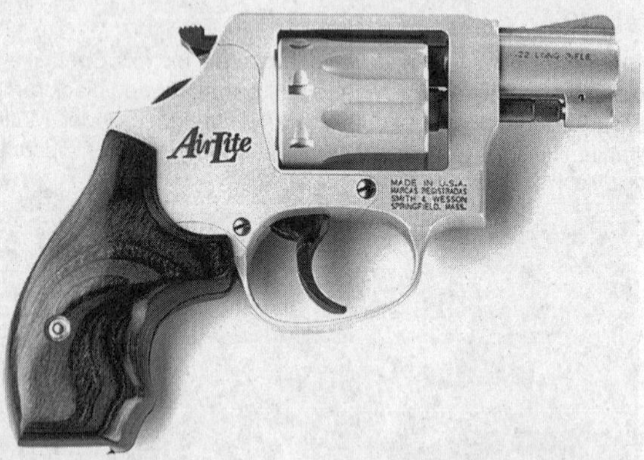

NIB	Exc.	V.G.	Good	Fair	Poor
1100	900	600	400	300	200

Model 317-2 and 317-3 AirLite with Lock

NIB	Exc.	V.G.	Good	Fair	Poor
750	650	550	350	250	200

Model 317 AirLite Kit Gun

Version of the Model 317 introduced in 1998. Fitted with a 3" barrel, with adjustable rear sight. Choice of Dymondwood grips or Uncle Mike's Combat grips. Weight about 12 oz. In 2001, offered with Hi-Viz green dot front sight.

NIB	Exc.	V.G.	Good	Fair	Poor
700	550	420	300	200	150

Model 317 AirLite Ladysmith

Features a 2" barrel and Dymondwood grips. Display case standard. Soft carry case standard. Weight about 10 oz.

NIB	Exc.	V.G.	Good	Fair	Poor
700	550	430	300	200	150

Model 325PD Airlite SC

Double-action-only revolver built on large N-frame. .45 ACP; 6-shot cylinder; 2-3/4" barrel, with adjustable Patridge sights. Matte black finish on Scandium/alloy frame. Introduced 2004-2012. Weight about 21.5 oz.

NIB	Exc.	V.G.	Good	Fair	Poor
1500	1000	700	—	—	—

Model 325Sc 2"

NIB	Exc.	V.G.	Good	Fair	Poor
1800	1500	1100	—	—	—

Model 325 2.5" Night Guard

A 2.5" snubbie chambered for .45 ACP. Tritium sights, Scandium alloy frame, matte black finish overall. Neoprene grips. Introduced 2008.

NIB	Exc.	V.G.	Good	Fair	Poor
1800	1400	900	—	—	—

Model 325PD 4" Thunder Ranch Performance Center

NIB	Exc.	V.G.	Good	Fair	Poor
1500	1300	900	—	—	—

Model 327/M&P R8

Double-action-only revolver built on large N-frame. .357 Magnum/.38 Special; 8-shot cylinder; 5" barrel, with adjustable Patridge sights with interchangeable inserts. Matte black finish on Scandium/alloy frame. Introduced 2007-2012.

NIB	Exc.	V.G.	Good	Fair	Poor
1750	1500	1000	—	—	—

Model 327 Night Guard

Large-frame snubnose revolver chambered in .357 Magnum/.38 Special +P (interchangeable). Six-shot cylinder, 2.5" barrel, fixed tritium sights, synthetic grips. Scandium frame, stainless steel cylinder, matte black finish throughout. Weight 27.6 oz.

NIB	Exc.	V.G.	Good	Fair	Poor
2200	1500	1000	—	—	—

Model 327Sc 2" Carry Performance Center

Introduced in 2004. This 8-shot model chambered for .357 Magnum cartridge. Barrel length 2" with dovetail .260 orange ramp. Scandium alloy frame, with stainless steel barrel, titanium cylinder and shroud. Black oxide finish except for gray cylinder. Cocobolo wood grips. Weight about 21 oz. Suggested Retail Price: $1,226.

NIB	Exc.	V.G.	Good	Fair	Poor
2000	1600	1100	—	—	—

Model 329PD Airlite SC

Double-action-only revolver built on large N-frame. .44 Magnum; 6-shot titanium cylinder; 4" barrel, with adjustable Patridge sights. Matte black finish on Scandium/alloy frame. Orange dot front sight and adjustable rear. Introduced 2003-date. Weight 26.5 oz.

NIB	Exc.	V.G.	Good	Fair	Poor
1200	1000	900	—	—	—

Model 329 Night Guard

Large-frame snubnose revolver chambered in .44 Magnum/.44 Special (interchangeable). Six-shot cylinder, 2.5" barrel, fixed tritium sights, synthetic grips. Scandium frame, stainless steel cylinder, matte black finish throughout. Weight 29.3 oz.

NIB	Exc.	V.G.	Good	Fair	Poor
3000	2000	1500	—	—	—

Model 331 AirLite

Chambered for .32 H&R Magnum cartridge on a J-frame. Barrel length 1.875". Exposed hammer offers single-/double-action. Frame aluminum, as is barrel shroud and yoke. Cylinder is titanium. Barrel has a stainless steel liner. Matte finish. Because the revolver is made from aluminum and titanium, it has a two-tone appearance because of the two different materials. Choice of wood or rubber boot grips. Capacity 6 rounds. Weight about: 12 oz. with rubber grip; 11.2 oz. with wood grip. Introduced in 1999.

NIB	Exc.	V.G.	Good	Fair	Poor
2000	1500	900	—	—	—

Model 332 AirLite

Similar to Model 331 above, with a concealed hammer and double-action configuration. Weight: 12 oz. with rubber grips; 11.3 oz. with wood grips.

NIB	Exc.	V.G.	Good	Fair	Poor
2000	1500	900	—	—	—

Model 337 AirLite

Model has an aluminum frame, exposed hammer and titanium cylinder. Front sight is black and pinned. Smooth trigger. Cylinder capacity 5 rounds. Chambered for .38 Special +P ammo. Barrel length 1.875". Wood or rubber grips. Weight about: 11.2 oz. with wood grips; 12 oz. with rubber grips. Manufactured 1999-2004.

NIB	Exc.	V.G.	Good	Fair	Poor
1300	950	700	500	350	250

Model 337 Kit Gun

Similar to Model 337. Fitted with 3" barrel. Adjustable rear sight. Weight about 13.5 oz. In 2001, offered with HiViz green dot front sight.

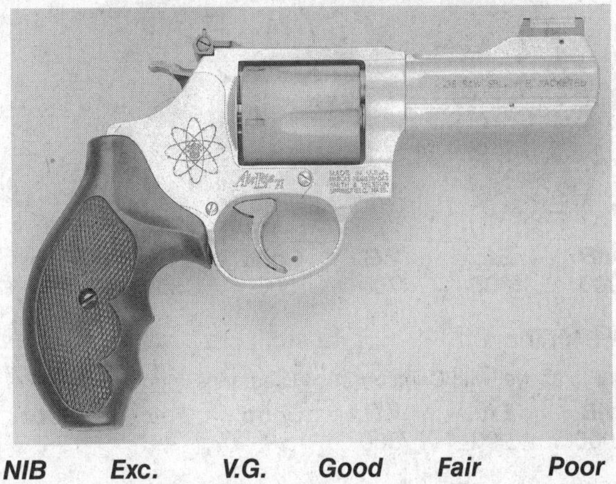

NIB	Exc.	V.G.	Good	Fair	Poor
1100	900	600	400	300	250

Model 337PD

Similar to Model 337, with matte black finish over aluminum frame. Hogue Bantam grips. Weight 10.7 oz. Introduced in 2000.

NIB	Exc.	V.G.	Good	Fair	Poor
1000	700	500	400	300	250

Model 340

Introduced in 2001. Hammerless model features Scandium alloy frame. Fitted with 1.875" barrel. Chambered for .357 Magnum cartridge, with 5-round cylinder. Matte stainless gray finish. Pinned black front sight. Hogue Bantam grips standard. Weight about 12 oz. Similar configuration with different finish and markings also offered as the M&P 340, introduced 2007. Also offered as the M&P 340 CT with Crimson Trace laser grips, add $100 to value.

NIB	Exc.	V.G.	Good	Fair	Poor
800	600	500	300	200	150

Model 340 M&P

Double-action-only revolver built on Centennial (hammerless) J-frame. .357 Magnum/.38 Special; 5-shot cylinder; 1.87" barrel with fixed night sights. Matte black finish on Scandium/alloy frame. Introduced 2007.

NIB	Exc.	V.G.	Good	Fair	Poor
900	700	500	400	300	250

Model 340PD

Same as Model 340, with gray/black finish. Introduced in 2001.

NIB	Exc.	V.G.	Good	Fair	Poor
900	800	700	500	300	250

M&P 340CT

Similar to above, with Crimson Trace Lasergrips. Introduced 2007.

NIB	Exc.	V.G.	Good	Fair	Poor
1000	900	800	—	—	—

Model 342 AirLite Centennial

Similar to the Model 340 in .38 Special +P, with double-action-only concealed hammer. Weight: 11.3 oz. with wood grips; 12 oz. with rubber grips. Introduced in 1998-2004.

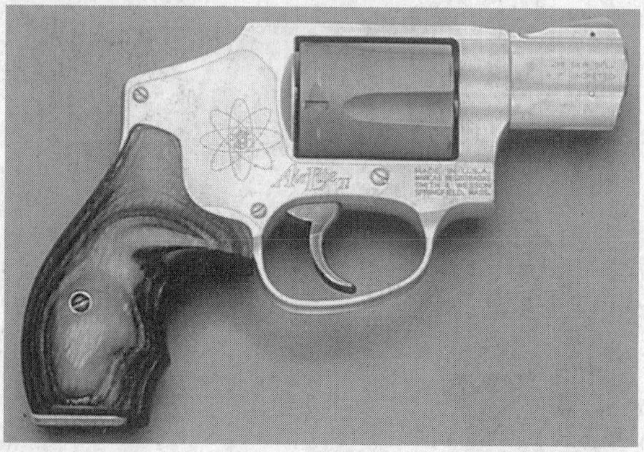

NIB	Exc.	V.G.	Good	Fair	Poor
700	550	430	300	200	150

Model 342 Airlite Ti

NIB	Exc.	V.G.	Good	Fair	Poor
900	700	550	400	300	250

Model 342PD

Similar to Model 337, with matte black finish over aluminum frame. Hogue Bantam grips. Weight about 10.8 oz. Introduced in 2000.

NIB	Exc.	V.G.	Good	Fair	Poor
1100	900	700	500	300	250

Model 351c

NIB	Exc.	V.G.	Good	Fair	Poor
600	550	500	400	300	250

Model 351PD

7-shot revolver chambered for .22 Magnum cartridge. Fitted with 1.875" barrel. Black oxide finish. Rubber grips. HiViz sights. Weight about 10.6 oz. 2004-date.

NIB	Exc.	V.G.	Good	Fair	Poor
700	600	500	400	300	250

Model 357PD .41 Magnum

Double-action-only revolver built on large N-frame. .41 Magnum; 6-shot titanium cylinder; 4" barrel, with adjustable Patridge sights. Matte black finish on Scandium/alloy frame. Wood grip Orange dot front sight and adjustable rear. Introduced 2005-2010. Weight 26.5 oz.

NIB	Exc.	V.G.	Good	Fair	Poor
2000	1500	1250	—	—	—

Model 357NG Night Guard .41 Magnum

Large-frame snubnose revolver chambered in .41 Magnum. Six-shot cylinder, 2.75" barrel, fixed tritium sights, synthetic grips. Scandium frame, stainless steel cylinder, matte black finish throughout. Weight 29.7 oz.

NIB	Exc.	V.G.	Good	Fair	Poor
3000	2500	1800	—	—	—

Model 360Sc Airlite

.357 Magnum. J-frame model with a Scandium alloy frame, exposed hammer and 5-shot titanium cylinder. Fixed sights on a 1.875" barrel. Matte stainless gray finish. Weight about 12 oz. Introduced in 2001-date. Similar configuration with different finish and markings also offered as the M&P 360, which was introduced 2007.

NIB	Exc.	V.G.	Good	Fair	Poor
700	600	500	—	—	—

Model 360 M&P 3" Slabside

Double-action-only revolver built on Chief's Special (hammered) J-frame. .357 Magnum/.38 Special; 5-shot cylinder; 1.87" barrel with fixed night sights. Matte black finish on Scandium/alloy frame. Introduced 2007.

NIB	Exc.	V.G.	Good	Fair	Poor
700	550	400	—	—	—

Model 360 Kit Gun

Version of M360 is fitted with 3.125" barrel, HiViz green dot front sight and adjustable rear. Weight about 14.5 oz. Introduced in 2001.

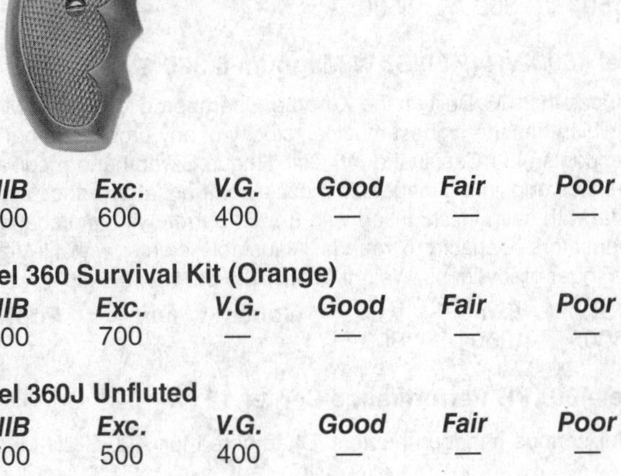

NIB	Exc.	V.G.	Good	Fair	Poor
700	600	400	—	—	—

Model 360 Survival Kit (Orange)

NIB	Exc.	V.G.	Good	Fair	Poor
900	700	—	—	—	—

Model 360J Unfluted

NIB	Exc.	V.G.	Good	Fair	Poor
700	500	400	—	—	—

Model 386Sc/S

Single-/double-action L-frame revolver in .38/.357 Magnum. 7-shot cylinder, 2.5" barrel, Patridge front sight, adjustable rear, Scandium/alloy frame, matte black finish, rubber grips. Introduced 2007.

NIB	Exc.	V.G.	Good	Fair	Poor
1500	1300	900	—	—	—

Model 386Sc Mountain Lite 3"

Manufacutured 2001-2012. L-frame model with 6-shot cylinder chambered for .357 Magnum cartridge. Fitted with 3.125" barrel, HiViz green dot front sight and adjustable rear. Scandium alloy frame, with matte stainless gray finish. Weight about 18.5 oz. Hogue Batam grips.

NIB	Exc.	V.G.	Good	Fair	Poor
1500	1200	600	—	—	—

Model 386PD Pre-Lock

Same as Model 386Sc, with gray/black finish and 2.5" barrel, red ramp front sight and adjustable rear. Weight about 17.5 oz.

NIB	Exc.	V.G.	Good	Fair	Poor
1500	1250	800	—	—	—

Model 386 XL Hunter 6"

Single-/double-action L-frame revolver chambered in .357 Magnum. Features 6" full-lug barrel, 7-round cylinder, Hi-Viz fiber-optic front sight, adjustable rear, Scandium frame, stainless steel cylinder, black matte finish, synthetic grips. Very scarce gun.

NIB	Exc.	V.G.	Good	Fair	Poor
1500	1100	900	—	—	—

Model 386PD Lock

NIB	Exc.	V.G.	Good	Fair	Poor
1300	1100	700	—	—	—

Model 386 Night Guard

Medium-frame snubnose revolver chambered in .357 Magnum/.38 Special +P (interchangeable). Seven-shot cylinder, 2.5" barrel, fixed tritium sights, synthetic grips. Scandium frame, stainless steel cylinder, matte black finish throughout. Weight 24.5 oz.

NIB	Exc.	V.G.	Good	Fair	Poor
2500	2000	1500	—	—	—

Model 396 Mountain Lite 3"

L-frame revolver chambered for .44 Special cartridge. Fitted with 5-round titanium cylinder and aluminum alloy frame. Barrel length 3" with green HiViz front sight and adjustable rear. Introduced in 2000. Weight 19 oz.

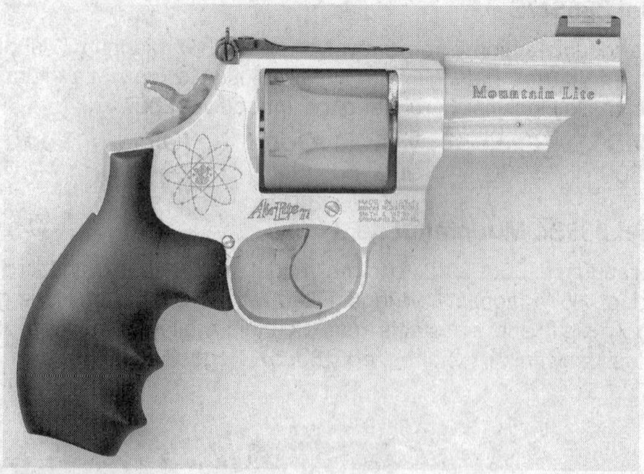

NIB	Exc.	V.G.	Good	Fair	Poor
1500	1200	800	—	—	—

Model 396 Night Guard

Medium-frame snubnose revolver chambered in .44 Special. Five-shot cylinder, 2.5" barrel, fixed tritium sights, synthetic grips. Scandium frame, stainless steel cylinder, matte black finish throughout. Weight 24.2 oz.

NIB	Exc.	V.G.	Good	Fair	Poor
2000	1600	1200	—	—	—

Model 430

J-frame double-action-only revolver chambered in .32 S&W. 6-shot cylinder, 1.87" barrel, fixed front and rear sights, synthetic grips. Aluminum alloy frame, stainless steel cylinder. Marked "Airweight" Matte black finish throughout. Export to Portugal. Rare in U.S. Introduced 2009.

NIB	Exc.	V.G.	Good	Fair	Poor
2900	2500	2000	—	—	—

Model 431PD

J-frame double-action- revolver chambered in .32 H&R Magnum. 6-shot cylinder, 1.87" barrel, fixed front and rear sights, synthetic grips. Aluminum-alloy frame, stainless steel cylinder. Chiefs Special design, Matte black finish throughout. 2004-2006.

NIB	Exc.	V.G.	Good	Fair	Poor
1200	800	400	—	—	—

Model 432PD

J-frame double-action- only revolver chambered in .32 H&R Magnum. 6-shot cylinder, 1.87" barrel, fixed front and rear sights, synthetic grips. Aluminum alloy frame, stainless steel cylinder. Centennial design, Matte black finish throughout. 2004-2005.

NIB	Exc.	V.G.	Good	Fair	Poor
900	750	550	—	—	—

Model 437

J-frame double-action revolver chambered in .38 Special +P. 5-shot cylinder, 1.87" barrel, fixed front and rear sights, synthetic grips. Aluminum-alloy frame, stainless steel cylinder. Chiefs Special design, Matte black finish throughout. 2009-2011. Scarce. Available in two tone and "Molon Labe" inscribed.

NIB	Exc.	V.G.	Good	Fair	Poor
450	400	350	—	—	—

Model 437 Ellett Bros. Black/S 2-Tone 1 of 100

NIB	Exc.	V.G.	Good	Fair	Poor
500	400	350	—	—	—

Model 438

J-frame double-action-only revolver chambered in .38 Special +P. 5-shot cylinder, 1.87" barrel, fixed front and rear sights, synthetic grips. Aluminum alloy frame, stainless steel cylinder. Matte black finish throughout. Scarce. Also available in two tone and "Molon Labe" inscribed.

NIB	Exc.	V.G.	Good	Fair	Poor
700	500	400	—	—	—

Model 442 Centennial Airweight

5-shot revolver chambered .38 Special. Equipped with 2" barrel, aluminum alloy frame and carbon steel cylinder. Has a fully concealed hammer. Weight 15.8 oz. Front ramp sight serrated and rear sight a fixed square notch. Rubber combat grips from Michael's of Oregon are standard. Finish blue/black or satin nickel. Introduced in 1993. Note: Current production models now rated for +P ammunition. Two engineering changes.

NIB	Exc.	V.G.	Good	Fair	Poor
500	450	300	200	150	100

Model 460 Airweight Performance Center (.38 Special) Scarce

Chambered for .38 Special cartridge. Fitted with 2" Mag-Na-Ported barrel and 5-shot cylinder. Fixed sights. Eagle Secret Service grips. Weight about 16 oz. Limited to 450 revolvers. Introduced in 1994.

NIB	Exc.	V.G.	Good	Fair	Poor
1150	800	500	—	—	—

Model 460 XVR (.460 S&W Magnum 8.375")

Introduced in 2005. Built on the X-frame. Chambered for .460 S&W Magnum, which has the highest muzzle velocity of any production handgun. Also accepts .454 Casull and .45 Colt. Hogue Sorbothane recoil-reducing K-L size grip, interchangeable muzzle compensator. 5-shot, stainless material with satin finish. Fitted with 8.375" barrel, with interchangeable compensators. Capacity 5 rounds. Adjustable sights, with Hi-Viz front sight. Finger groovegrips. Weight about 72.5 oz.

NIB	Exc.	V.G.	Good	Fair	Poor
1600	1250	900	—	—	—

Model 460XVR Performance Center 12"

Built for serious handgun hunters. Chambered for .460 S&W Magnum.

Stainless steel cylinder, frame and barrel. 5-round capacity. Adjustable rear and removable Partridge front sight. Other features include sling swivels, dual accessory rails and synthetic grips. Weight a hefty 79.2 oz. Fluted 12" barrel, with compensator. Reintroduced in 2011, by Performance Center. Suggested Retail Introductory Price: $1,619.

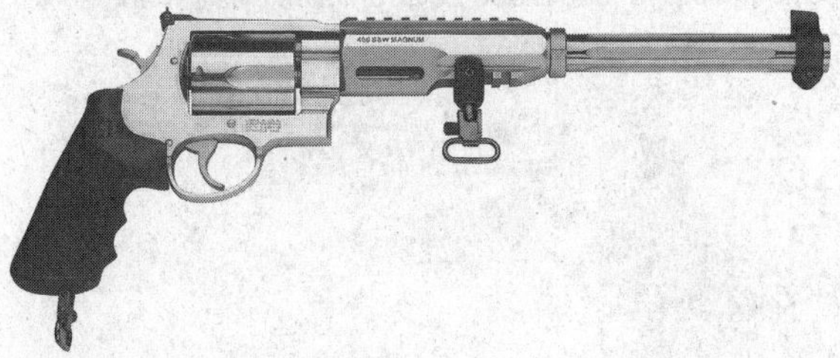

NIB	Exc.	V.G.	Good	Fair	Poor
1500	1200	900	—	—	—

Model 460 XVR Performance Center 14"

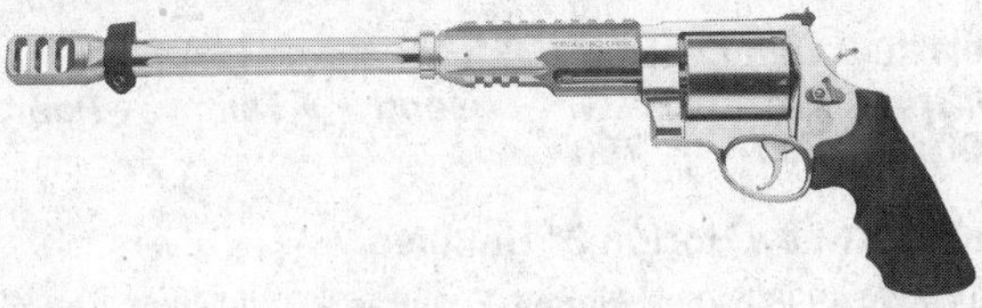

NIB	Exc.	V.G.	Good	Fair	Poor
1700	1400	1100	—	—	—

Model 460XVR Performance Center 2-Tone Ellett Bros. and Bone Collector

NIB	Exc.	V.G.	Good	Fair	Poor
2200	1700	1200	—	—	—

Model 460XVR 3", XVR 3.5", 460V4 4", and 460V5 5"

NIB	Exc.	V.G.	Good	Fair	Poor
1600	1300	1000	—	—	—

Model 460ES 2 3/4" (Emergency Survival)

NIB	Exc.	V.G.	Good	Fair	Poor
4000	3000	1500	—	—	—

Model 460V

X-frame double-action trigger and 4" barrel model. 5" barrel in .460 S&W Magnum caliber. Weight 62.5 oz. Introduced 2006.

NIB	Exc.	V.G.	Good	Fair	Poor
1200	1000	750	600	400	300

Model 500 Various Barrels from 4" to 8.375"

Introduced in 2003. Chambered for .500 S&W Magnum cartridge. Fitted with 8.375" barrel, with compensator. Built on the X-frame. Cylinder holds 5 rounds. Stainless steel frame and barrel. Interchangeable front blade sight and adjustable rear. K-L frame size Hogue Sorbothane grips. Weight about 72.5 oz. In 2004, offered with a 4" barrel, with compensator. Weight about 56 oz. Introduced in 2008, 6.5" model. Note: Add $135 for 4" barrel model. Add 50% for complete as new Bear Protection Kit.

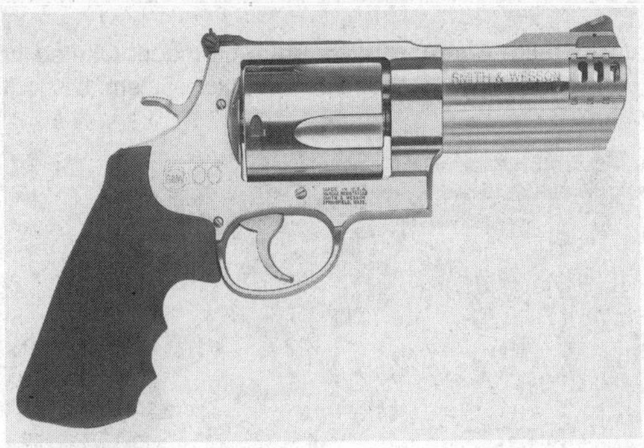

S&W Model 500 with a 4" barrel.

NIB	Exc.	V.G.	Good	Fair	Poor
1200	1100	900	—	—	—

Model 500 Magnum Hunter Performance Center 10.5"

Introduced in 2003. Chambered for .500 S&W cartridge. Fitted with a 10.5" barrel, with compensator. Sling swivel studs and sling are standard. Orange dovetail ramp front sight and adjustable rear. Stainless steel, with glass bead finish. Hogue rubber grips. Weight about 82 oz.

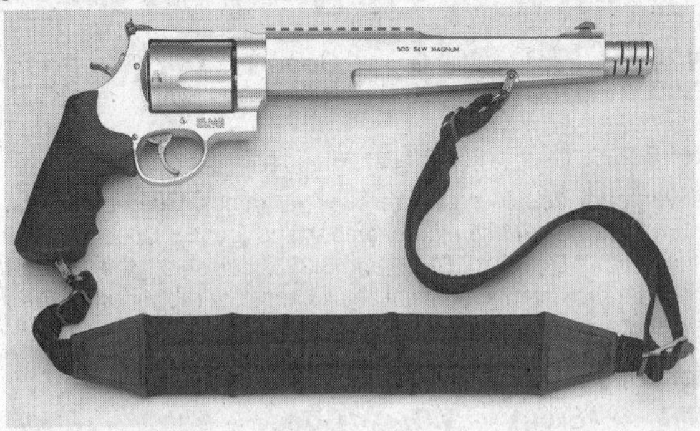

NIB	Exc.	V.G.	Good	Fair	Poor
1800	1500	1100	—	—	—

Model 500 Performance Center 3.5"

NIB	Exc.	V.G.	Good	Fair	Poor
1700	1400	1100	—	—	—

Model 500ES Emergency Survival

NIB	Exc.	V.G.	Good	Fair	Poor
3000	2500	2000	—	—	—

Model 520 (New York State Police)

Chambered for .357 Magnum and fitted with fixed sights. Offered in blued finish, with 4" barrel on an N-Frame for the New York State Police but not delivered. Checkered walnut grips are standard. Produced in 1980 only.

NIB	Exc.	V.G.	Good	Fair	Poor
2000	1500	1000	—	—	—

Model 520 Model of 2005

Chambered for .357 Magnum and fitted with adjustable sights. Offered in blued finish, with 4" barrel on an N Frame with 7-shot scandium cylinder. Checkered walnut grips are standard. Produced in 2005 only. Limited production.

NIB	Exc.	V.G.	Good	Fair	Poor
1000	780	550	400	—	—

Model 544 Texas Wagon Train

Chambered in 44/40 introduced 1986. 6-shot. N-frame commemorative for the Texas Wagon Train. 5" barrel, a total of 4,782 manufactured.

NIB	Exc.	V.G.	Good	Fair	Poor
1500	1200	900	750	—	—

Model 547

Introduced in 1980. Chambered for 9mm cartridge. Offered with 3" or 4" barrel. Finish is blued. Finger-type extractor system. Discontinued in 1985. Scarce.

NIB	Exc.	V.G.	Good	Fair	Poor
1800	1600	1200	1000	500	250

Model 581

Six-shot double-action revolver (L-frame). Chambered for .357 Magnum cartridge. It will also chamber and fire .38 Special cartridges. Available 4" barrel. Blued frame and cylinder, w/ fixed sights, walnut Magna or rubber grips. 1980-1988.

NIB	Exc.	V.G.	Good	Fair	Poor
1500	1100	800	500	300	250

Model 586

Six-/seven-shot double-action revolver (L-frame). Chambered for .357 Magnum cartridge. It will also chamber and fire .38 Special cartridges. Available with 2.5", 3", 4", 5", 6" and 8.375" barrel lengths. Blued frame and cylinder, adjustable sights, walnut Magna or rubber grips. 7-shot offered in limited production.

Model 586 Pre-Lock

NIB	Exc.	V.G.	Good	Fair	Poor
1500	1100	600	500	500	250

Model 586-8 Classic with Lock

NIB	Exc.	V.G.	Good	Fair	Poor
850	700	600	—	—	—

Model 586 L Comp Performance Center with Lock

NIB	Exc.	V.G.	Good	Fair	Poor
1100	800	700	—	—	—

Model 610 Pre-Lock

This N-frame model chambered for 10mm cartridge. Fitted with a variety of barrel lengths. Adjustable rear sight. Six-round non-fluted cylinder. Hogue rubber combat grips. Stainless steel finish. Weight about 50 oz. for 4" model. Reintroduced in 2007. Add 25% for non-fluted cylinder.

NIB	Exc.	V.G.	Good	Fair	Poor
1900	1200	1000	700	500	250

Model 610-2 Performance Center 6.5" Pre-Lock

Introduced in 1998. Chambered for 10mm cartridge. Fitted with a 6.5" full-lug barrel and unfluted cylinder. Hogue grips are standard. Adjustable rear sight. Interchangeable front sight. Weight about 52 oz. Premiums: pre-lock add 30%, 5" barrel add 20%, unfluted cylinder add 20%.

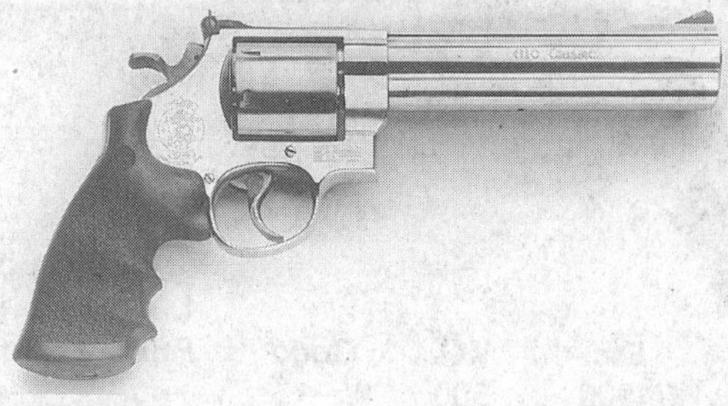

NIB	Exc.	V.G.	Good	Fair	Poor
2200	1700	—	—	—	—

Model 610-3 with Lock

NIB	Exc.	V.G.	Good	Fair	Poor
900	800	700	—	—	—

Model 610-1 Lew Horton 3" Unfluted

Introduced in 1998 by Lew Horton. Features a 3" full-lug barrel. Chambered for 10mm cartridge. Nonfluted cylinder, red ramp front sight and white outline rear. Rosewood grips. Limited to 300 revolvers.

NIB	Exc.	V.G.	Good	Fair	Poor
3000	2500	1800	—	—	—

Model 617 to 617-4 Early Pre-Lock

Identical to Model 17 but furnished with stainless steel frame and cylinder. 4", 6", and 8-3/8" barrels, 6-shot cylinder with 10-shot available in 1996. 1989-date. Six engineering changes.

NIB	Exc.	V.G.	Good	Fair	Poor
1600	1200	800	700	500	250

Model 617-5, 617-6 with Lock

NIB	Exc.	V.G.	Good	Fair	Poor
1250	1000	600	400	300	200

Model 619

Chambered for .357 Magnum cartridge. Fitted with 4" two-piece semi-lug two-piece barrel with fixed sights. Stainless steel frame and barrel. Capacity 7 rounds. Medium-frame. Weight about 37.5 oz. Rubber grips. Introduced 2005-2006. Discontinued.

NIB	Exc.	V.G.	Good	Fair	Poor
1000	750	500	400	300	200

Model 620

Like Model 619, with a 4" barrel, adjustable rear sight and red ramp front. Weight about 37.9 oz. Introduced in 2005-2009. Discontinued.

NIB	Exc.	V.G.	Good	Fair	Poor
1100	800	600	500	300	200

Model 624 Model of 1985 .44 Target

Stainless steel version of Model 24. Fitted with a 4" or 6.5" barrel. Pachmayr SK/GR gripper stocks as standard. Designed for pin shooting. Weight about 45 oz. 1985-1988. 30% Premium for 3" model.

NIB	Exc.	V.G.	Good	Fair	Poor
1400	1100	900	600	400	250

Model 625 IDPA

Like Model 625-2 but fitted with 4" barrel, Patridge front sight and adjustable rear. Hogue grips. Introduced in 2002. Weight about 43 oz.

NIB	Exc.	V.G.	Good	Fair	Poor
900	800	700	580	400	200

Model 625-2 Model of 1988 5"

Stainless steel version of Model 25-2. Fitted with a 5" barrel. Pachmayr SK/GR gripper stocks as standard. Designed for pin shooting. Weight about 45 oz. 11 engineering changes over all Model 625 variations.

NIB	Exc.	V.G.	Good	Fair	Poor
1600	1200	850	700	450	300

Model 625-3 3"

NIB	Exc.	V.G.	Good	Fair	Poor
1600	1300	1000	800	500	300

Model 625-3 Model of 1989 3", 4", 5"

NIB	Exc.	V.G.	Good	Fair	Poor
1500	1200	1000	800	500	300

Model 625-4 Model of 1989

NIB	Exc.	V.G.	Good	Fair	Poor
1400	1200	850	700	450	300

Model 625-4 Springfield Armory

NIB	Exc.	V.G.	Good	Fair	Poor
1200	1000	800	650	400	300

Model 625-5 .45 Colt 4", 5"

NIB	Exc.	V.G.	Good	Fair	Poor
1500	1200	900	700	500	300

Model 625-6 Model of 1989 5"

NIB	Exc.	V.G.	Good	Fair	Poor
1200	1000	800	650	500	300

Model 625-6/625-7 Mountain Gun .45 Colt/45 ACP 4"

NIB	Exc.	V.G.	Good	Fair	Poor
1500	1200	1000	700	500	300

Model 625-6, 626-7 .45 Colt Light Hunter Performance Center 6"

NIB	Exc.	V.G.	Good	Fair	Poor
2800	1900	1400	1200	—	—

Model 625-6 Hunter 6" (Heavy Slab-Sided)

NIB	Exc.	V.G.	Good	Fair	Poor
3000	2300	1800	1300	—	—

Model 625 JM (Jerry Miculek)

Introduced in 2005. Chambered for .45 ACP cartridge. Fitted with a 4" full-lug barrel, with Patridge front sight and adjustable rear. Capacity 6 rounds. Wood grips. Weight 43 oz.

NIB	Exc.	V.G.	Good	Fair	Poor
850	700	600	430	300	150

Model 625—5.25" Performance Center

Introduced in 2001. Features special Jerry Miculek Hogue laminated combat grip. Chambered for .45 ACP cartridge. Fitted with 5.25" barrel. Stainless steel finish. Interchangeable gold bead front sight and adjustable rear. Weight 42 oz. Camfour exclusive.

NIB	Exc.	V.G.	Good	Fair	Poor
1200	1000	800	—	—	—

Model 625 Mountain Gun

First time offered in 1996. Chambered for .45 Colt cartridge. Fitted with 4" tapered barrel, with ramp front sight and adjustable rear. Frame drilled and tapped for scope mount.

NIB	Exc.	V.G.	Good	Fair	Poor
1000	800	600	300	200	130

Model 625 Performance Center

Introduced in 1998. Chambered for .45 ACP or .45 Colt cartridge. Fitted with a 3" full-lug barrel, fluted cylinder and rosewood grips. Limited to 150 revolvers in each chambering.

NIB	Exc.	V.G.	Good	Fair	Poor
1100	—	—	—	—	—

Model 625-6 Light Hunter Performance Center

Large-frame revolver chambered for .45 Colt. Fitted with 6" Mag-Na-Ported barrel, with integral Weaver-style base. Stainless steel finish and black Hogue rubber grips. Drift adjustable Millet front and fully adjustable rear sight. Offered in limited quantities. Introduced in 1997 by RSR.

NIB	Exc.	V.G.	Good	Fair	Poor
2200	1800	1500	—	—	—

Model 625-7 Light Hunter Performance Center

Like Model 625-6 Light Hunter with fluted cylinder.

NIB	Exc.	V.G.	Good	Fair	Poor
1800	1500	1250	—	—	—

Model 625 4" V-Comp Performance Center

Chambered for .44 Magnum cartridge. Fitted with a 4" barrel and removable three-port compensator. Front sight is a red ramp, with black adjustable rear. Hogue wood combat grips. Furnished with aluminum case. Weight 43 oz. Finish stainless steel. Distributed by RSR. Introduced in 1999.

NIB	Exc.	V.G.	Good	Fair	Poor
3000	2000	1400	1000	—	—

Model 625-7 Performance Center 5"

NIB	Exc.	V.G.	Good	Fair	Poor
2300	2000	1600	1000	—	—

Model 625-8 (Jerry Miculek) 3" or 4" with Lock

NIB	Exc.	V.G.	Good	Fair	Poor
1100	850	700	—	—	—

Model 625-8 4" Performance Center with Lock

NIB	Exc.	V.G.	Good	Fair	Poor
1100	1000	800	—	—	—

Model 625-8 Classic Hunter 5"

NIB	Exc.	V.G.	Good	Fair	Poor
1200	900	650	500	—	—

Model 625-9 .45 Colt 4" Mountain Gun

NIB	Exc.	V.G.	Good	Fair	Poor
900	800	700	—	—	—

Model 625-10 2"

NIB	Exc.	V.G.	Good	Fair	Poor
2000	1600	1200	—	—	—

Model 627-0, 627-1, 627-2 (Pre-Lock 6-Shot, 5.5")

Special edition stainless steel version of Model 27. First offered with a 5.5" barrel and 6-shot unfluted cylinder. Originally Manufactured in 1989 as the 627 and 627-0, followed by the 627-1 and 627-2. After that, the 627 continued as an 8-shot Performance Center product. Approximately 4,500 produced at introduction. Values listed are for the Model 627, 627-0 "Model of 1989," 627-1, and 627-2. The 627-PC, 627-3, and higher are Performance Center models. Seven engineering changes.

NIB	Exc.	V.G.	Good	Fair	Poor
2200	1800	1400	900	700	300

Model 627-3 V-Comp 5"

NIB	Exc.	V.G.	Good	Fair	Poor
2500	2000	1500	—	—	—

Model 627-3 V-Comp 3"

NIB	Exc.	V.G.	Good	Fair	Poor
S	3580	2750	2400	—	—

Model 627-5 Pro Series

Introduced in 2008. An eight-shot .357 revolver, with stainless steel frame, adjustable sights, 4" barrel and various accurizing refinements.

NIB	Exc.	V.G.	Good	Fair	Poor
900	800	680	500	300	150

Model 627-PC, 627-3 (Performance Center Pre-Lock 8-Shot 5")

Chambered for .357 Magnum cartridge. Has an 8-round capacity. Drilled and tapped, with adjustable sights on a 5" tapered and contoured barrel. Tuned action. Hogue wood grips. Satin stainless steel finish. Weight about 44 oz. A Lew Horton exclusive. Introduced in 1997. Pre-lock. 25% premium for special editions in high grades: 2 5/8" UDR, 3" V-Comp, 4" V-Comp, 6.5".

NIB	Exc.	V.G.	Good	Fair	Poor
2500	2000	1600	1200	800	350

Model 627 Ultimate Defense Revolver (UDR)—8-Shot Performance Center

Chambered for .357 Magnum. Fitted with an 8-round unfluted cylinder recessed for full moon clips. Barrel length 2.625". Adjustable rear sight and drift adjustable front. Wooden eagle boot grips. Weight about 38 oz. Introduced in 1999. Furnished with aluminum case. Pre-lock.

NIB	Exc.	V.G.	Good	Fair	Poor
2500	2000	1750	—	—	—

Model 627-4 (.38 Super with Lock)

Chambered in .38 Super for competition shooters, 5.5" barrel with removable compensator and 8-shot unfluted titanium cylinder. This important model introduced the internal hammer lock in 2002.

NIB	Exc.	V.G.	Good	Fair	Poor
2100	1700	1300	900	700	350

Model 627-5 (Scarce Non-PC 8-Shot 4")

NIB	Exc.	V.G.	Good	Fair	Poor
2000	1500	1200	—	—	—

Model 627-5 (Current Production Variations)

NIB	Exc.	V.G.	Good	Fair	Poor
1200	1100	900	—	—	—

Model 627-5 V-Comp Two-Tone

NIB	Exc.	V.G.	Good	Fair	Poor
1600	1200	900	—	—	—

Model 629

Simply a stainless steel version of Model 29. Chambered for .44 Magnum. In 2002, offered with HiViz sights. 1979-date. Many variations spanning eight engineering changes. Premium for 3".

NIB	Exc.	V.G.	Good	Fair	Poor
2000	1500	1200	900	500	300

Model 629 Classic

This model has additional features that standard Model 629 does not have such as chamfered cylinder, full-lug barrel, interchangeable front sights, Hogue combat grips, and drilled and tapped frame to accept scope mounts.

NIB	Exc.	V.G.	Good	Fair	Poor
1200	900	600	400	300	200

Model 629-2, 629-3, 629-4 Mountain Gun

Limited edition 6-shot revolver. Introduced in 1993. Features 4" barrel chambered for .44 Magnum. Built on large N-frame. Made from stainless steel and drilled and tapped for scope mounts. Equipped with Hogue round butt rubber mono-grip. Standard sights are a pinned black ramp front sight and adjustable black rear blade. Weight about 40 oz. Reintroduced in 1999.

NIB	Exc.	V.G.	Good	Fair	Poor
1900	1650	800	500	400	300

Model 629-4 Backpacker

A 1994 variation of Model 629. Built on N-frame, with round butt. Cylinders are fluted and chamfered. Barrel length 3", with adjustable rear sight. Finish is stainless steel and Hogue rubber grips are standard. Weight about 40 oz. 100% premium for unfluted cylinder.

NIB	Exc.	V.G.	Good	Fair	Poor
1600	1200	700	550	400	300

Model 629-4 Classic Powerport

Introduced in 1996. Offers an integral port, with 6.5" full-lug barrel. Patridge front sight is pinned and rear sight fully adjustable. Frame drilled and tapped for scope mounts. Synthetic Hogue combat-style grips are standard. Weight about 52 oz.

NIB	Exc.	V.G.	Good	Fair	Poor
1600	1200	700	550	400	300

Model 629 Extreme Performance Center

Chambered for .44 Magnum cartridge. Fitted with a 12" barrel, with sling swivel. Bomar sights. Rubber grips.

Model 629-1 Alaska 1988 Iditarod Commemorative

Introduced in 1987. Limited to 545 guns. Serial numbers from AKI0001-AKI0545.

NIB	Exc.	V.G.	Good	Fair	Poor
1100	—	—	—	—	—

Model 629-2 Classic Hunter Full-Lug Unfluted 6"

NIB	Exc.	V.G.	Good	Fair	Poor
2000	1500	1000	900	500	—

Model 629-3 Hunter I Performance Center

Known by collectors as the "Heavy Hunter." Introduced in 1992 by Lew Horton and Performance Center. Limited edition revolver features a new heavy barrel design that utilizes a 6" under barrel weight system, ported with fluted cylinder. Action has been custom tuned. Barrel has an integral scope mount. Chambered for .44 Magnum. Special finger groove grips are standard. Special serial numbers.

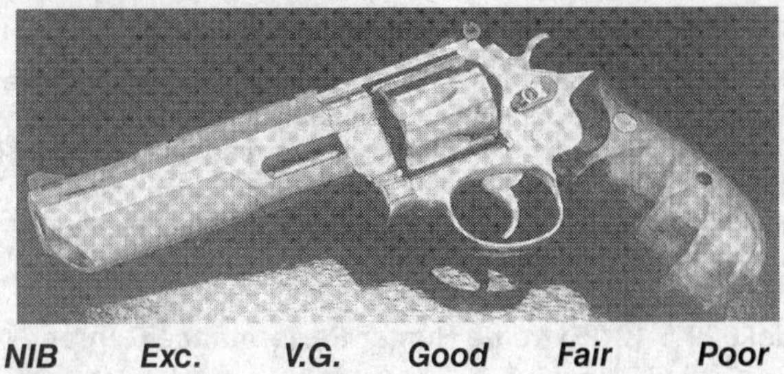

NIB	Exc.	V.G.	Good	Fair	Poor
2750	2000	1600	—	—	—

Model 629-3 Carry Comp Performance Center

Introduced in 1992 by Lew Horton and Performance Center. Limited edition revolver chambered for .44 Magnum cartridge. Features an integral ported 3" barrel, fluted cylinder, radiused charge holes, dovetail front and fixed groove rear sight. Fitted with a rubber combat grip. Action is custom by Performance Center. Special serial numbers.

NIB	Exc.	V.G.	Good	Fair	Poor
1600	1300	1000	—	—	—

Model 629-3, 629-4, 629-5 Classic

Pre-lock full-lug, barrel marked "Classic" or "Classic DX" 25% premium.

NIB	Exc.	V.G.	Good	Fair	Poor
1600	1000	800	600	400	300

Model 629-4 Hunter II Performance Center

Another Lew Horton/Performance Center limited edition revolver. Features 2x Nikon scope, with steel see-through rings. Barrel is Mag-Na-Ported and incorporates Performance Center's under-barrel weight arrangement. Action is custom tuned. Supplied with a ballistic nylon range carry bag. Special serial numbers.

NIB	Exc.	V.G.	Good	Fair	Poor
2200	1700	1400	—	—	—

Model 629-4 Light Hunter Performance Center

Features 6" slabside barrel, ported, full-length rail, 6-shot unfluted cylinder. Introduced 1994.

NIB	Exc.	V.G.	Good	Fair	Poor
2200	1500	1200	—	—	—

Model 629-4 Light Hunter Plus Performance Center

Features 7.5" slabside barrel, ported, full-length rail, 6-shot unfluted cylinder. Introduced 1995.

NIB	Exc.	V.G.	Good	Fair	Poor
2300	1700	1200	—	—	—

Model 629-4 Master Hunter Performance Center

Features 7.5" slabside barrel, ported, no rail, no sights scope only, 6-shot unfluted cylinder. Introduced 1997.

NIB	Exc.	V.G.	Good	Fair	Poor
2000	1500	1200	—	—	—

Model 629-4 Comped Hunter Performance Center

Offered through RSR. Features 6" barrel, with 4-port detachable compensator. Cylinder unfluted. Sights are adjustable. Fitted with Altamount wood grips. Tuned action. Stainless steel. Weight about 59 oz.

NIB	Exc.	V.G.	Good	Fair	Poor
1600	1250	1100	—	—	—

Model 629-4 Magnum Hunter Trail Boss Performance Center

Exclusive to RSR. Limited edition chambered for .44 Magnum cartridge. Fitted with 3" barrel. Stainless steel finish.

NIB	Exc.	V.G.	Good	Fair	Poor
2000	1500	1200	—	—	—

Model 629-4 Carry Comp II Performance Center

Limited edition 1993 offering by Lew Horton and Performance Center. Similar to 1992 Model 629 Carry Comp, except this 1993 model has a special unfluted cylinder and fully adjustable rear sight. Special serial numbers. Suggested Retail Introductory Price: $1,000

NIB	Exc.	V.G.	Good	Fair	Poor
2000	—	—	—	—	—

Model 629-5 12" Extreme Hunter Performance Center

Introduced in 2000. This Lew Horton revolver fitted with a 12" barrel, with Patridge front sight and Wilson silhouette adjustable rear. Hogue Combat grips. Finish glassbead stainless steel. Comes with a Waller 21" gun rug. Weight about 65 oz. A 7.5" version introduced in 2008.

NIB	Exc.	V.G.	Good	Fair	Poor
1400	1100	900	—	—	—

Model 629-5 Compensated Hunter Performance Center

Chambered for .44 Magnum cartridge. Fitted with 7.5" barrel, with compensator. Barrel also has a removable stainless steel scope mount. Open sights fitted with adjustable orange ramp front and adjustable rear. Rosewood grips. 6-round cylinder. Weight 52 oz. Talo exclusive. Introduced in 2001.

NIB	Exc.	V.G.	Good	Fair	Poor
1400	1100	900	—	—	—

Model 629-5 Stealth Hunter Performance Center

Fitted with 7.5" ported barrel. Chambered for .44 Magnum cartridge. 6-round cylinder. Finish is black-T and NATO green. Red ramp Millett front sight and adjustable rear. Hogue rubber combat grips standard. Furnished with lockable aluminum case. Weight about 56 oz. Introduced in 2001. Camfour Distributor exclusive.

NIB	Exc.	V.G.	Good	Fair	Poor
1500	1200	950	—	—	—

Model 629-5 Comped Hunter Performance Center

Chambered for .44 Magnum cartridge. Built with a 7.5" barrel, with a tapered full-length lug and compensator. Front sight is drift adjustable orange ramp and adjustable rear. Stainless steel, with glass bead finish. Removable scope mount. Rosewood grips. Weight about 52 oz. Introduced in 2003.

NIB	Exc.	V.G.	Good	Fair	Poor
1800	1500	1100	—	—	—

Model 629-5 Magna Classic Performance Center

NIB	Exc.	V.G.	Good	Fair	Poor
2000	1500	1100	—	—	—

Model 629 2 5/8" UDR

Prelock premium 100%.

NIB	Exc.	V.G.	Good	Fair	Poor
1300	1000	—	—	—	—

Model 629-5, 629-6 V-Comp Performance Center

30% premium for 2.6".

NIB	Exc.	V.G.	Good	Fair	Poor
1600	1400	1100	—	—	—

Model 629-7 Competitor 6" PC

Ventilated slab side with lock.

NIB	Exc.	V.G.	Good	Fair	Poor
1400	1200	900	—	—	—

Model 629-6 Compensated Hunter 7.5" (With Lock)

NIB	Exc.	V.G.	Good	Fair	Poor
1200	950	—	—	—	—

Model 629-7 Magnum Hunter 7.5" Two-Tone with Removable Compensator

NIB	Exc.	V.G.	Good	Fair	Poor
1700	1200	900	—	—	—

Model 629-8 Hunter 8.375" Fluted Barrel

NIB	Exc.	V.G.	Good	Fair	Poor
1400	1100	900	—	—	—

Model 629-6 through 629-10 w/Lock Classic Series

NIB	Exc.	V.G.	Good	Fair	Poor
1000	800	600	—	—	—

Model 631

Chambered for .32 Magnum cartridge. Fitted with 2" (fixed sights); 4" (adjustable sights) barrel. Stainless steel finish. Weight 22 oz. Produced in 1990.

NIB	Exc.	V.G.	Good	Fair	Poor
1800	1400	1000	750	500	200

Model 631 Lady Smith

Like Model 631, with rosewood grips and laser-etched. Fitted with 2" barrel.

NIB	Exc.	V.G.	Good	Fair	Poor
1800	1400	1000	750	500	200

Model 632 Centennial 2" or 3"

Like other Centennial models but chambered for .32 H&R Magnum cartridge. Standard with 2" barrel, stainless steel cylinder and aluminum alloy frame. 1991-1992.

NIB	Exc.	V.G.	Good	Fair	Poor
2200	1700	1100	—	—	—

Model 632 PowerPort Pro 3" Black or Stainless

J-frame revolver chambered in .327 Federal Magnum. Six-shot cylinder, 3" full-lug ported barrel with full-length extractor. Pinned, serrated front sight, adjustable rear. Synthetic grips. Stainless steel frame and cylinder.

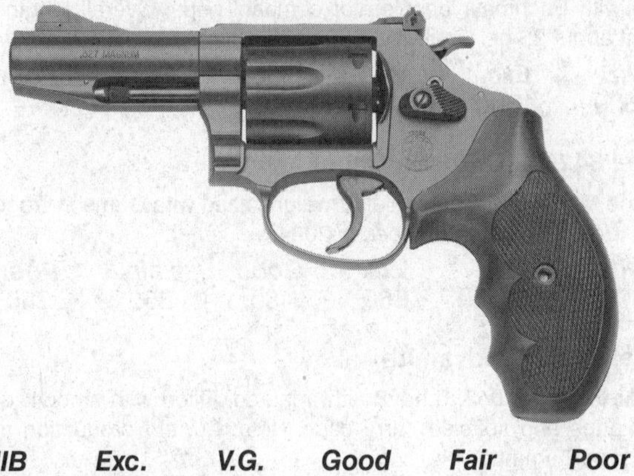

NIB	Exc.	V.G.	Good	Fair	Poor
2000	1500	1000	—	—	—

Model 637 Chiefs Special Airweight

Similar to Model 37, 5-shot .38 Special with aluminum frame and stainless steel cylinder with satin finish. Note: Current production models are now rated for +P ammunition. Special for 1989 and 1996-date. Premium for early examples.

NIB	Exc.	V.G.	Good	Fair	Poor
480	430	390	370	300	200

Model 637 Carry Combo

Like the Model 637 Chiefs Special Airweight Stainless but supplied with Kydex carry holster. Introduced in 2004.

NIB	Exc.	V.G.	Good	Fair	Poor
480	430	390	370	300	200

Model 637 Power Port Pro Series

Aluminum J-frame revolver, with stainless steel cylinder. Chambered for .38 Special (5 shots). 2 1/8" ported black stainless barrel. Introduced 2008. Dealer sets pricing.

NIB	Exc.	V.G.	Good	Fair	Poor
500	430	400	380	300	240

Model 637CT

Same as Model 637, with Crimson Trace Lasergrips.

NIB	Exc.	V.G.	Good	Fair	Poor
500	430	400	380	320	240

Model 638

Similar to Model 38 with stainless steel cylinder and aluminum frame, shrouded hammer, and stainless steel finish. Special for 1989 and 1996-date. Note: Current production models now rated for +P ammunition.

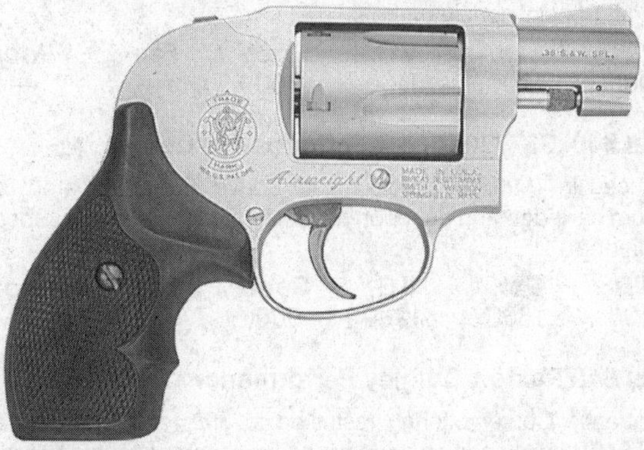

NIB	Exc.	V.G.	Good	Fair	Poor
530	480	450	400	350	200

Model 640 Centennial .38 Special

Stainless steel version of Model 40. Furnished with 2" or 3" barrel. Both frame and cylinder are stainless steel. The 3" barrel no longer offered as of 1993. As of 1998, also offered in .38 Special-only version.

NIB	Exc.	V.G.	Good	Fair	Poor
700	650	600	450	350	240

Model 640 Centennial .357 Magnum

Introduced in 1995. This version of Model 640 chambered for .357 cartridge. Fitted with 2-1/8" barrel. Stainless steel, with a fixed notch rear sight and pinned black ramp front sight. Length 6.75". Weight 25 oz.

NIB	Exc.	V.G.	Good	Fair	Poor
780	700	650	600	400	250

Model 640 Carry Comp Performance Center

Introduced in 1991 by Lew Horton and Performance Center. Chambered for .38 S&W Special, with a strengthened action to handle +P loads. Fitted with heavy 2.625" barrel, with unique integral barrel compensator. Front sight replaceable and adjustable for windage. Rear sight a fixed groove. Custom trigger job and custom tuned action are also part of the package. Special serial numbers.

NIB	Exc.	V.G.	Good	Fair	Poor
1900	1500	1100	800	—	—

Model 640 .357 Quadport Performance Center

Introduced in 1996. Similar to model above, but chambered for .357 Magnum cartridge and quadported. Limited to 190 revolvers. Special serial numbers.

NIB	Exc.	V.G.	Good	Fair	Poor
2100	1600	1200	900	—	—

Model 640 Paxton Quigley Performance Center

Performance Center offering restricted to 300 revolvers. Built around Model 640. Limited edition handgun has a 2" compensated barrel, windage adjustable front sight, specially tuned action and tapestry soft gun case. Each gun has a distinct serial number range.

NIB	Exc.	V.G.	Good	Fair	Poor
1800	1500	1100	900	—	—

Model 642 Centennial Airweight

Similar to Model 640, with exception of a stainless steel cylinder and aluminum alloy frame. Furnished with 2" or 3" barrel. Discontinued in 1992 and reintroduced in 1996-date. Note: Current production models now rated for +P ammunition. Two engineering changes with many variations.

NIB	Exc.	V.G.	Good	Fair	Poor
530	450	350	—	—	—

Model 640 Centennial Powerport Performance Center

Introduced in 1996. A Lew Horton exclusive. Fitted with a 2-1/8" barrel, with integral compensator. Front sight is a black blade, with Tritium insert and rear is a fixed notch. Cylinder holds five .357 or .38 rounds. Stainless steel, with Pachmayr decelerator compact grips. Overall length 6.75"; weight about 25 oz. Limited to 300 units.

NIB	Exc.	V.G.	Good	Fair	Poor
1600	1300	1000	900	—	—

Model 642CT (Crimson Trace)

Like the Model 642 Centennial Airweight, fitted with Crimson Trace laser grips. Weight 15 oz. Introduced in 2004.

NIB	Exc.	V.G.	Good	Fair	Poor
600	580	550	450	350	250

Model 642LS Ladysmith

Similar to Model 642, "LadySmith" marked. Fitted with smooth combat wood grips and softside carry case. Note: Current production models rated for +P ammunition.

NIB	Exc.	V.G.	Good	Fair	Poor
550	500	450	400	300	200

Model 642 PowerPort Pro Series

Similar to Model 642, with gray aluminum frame and black stainless ported barrel. Dealer sets pricing. Introduced 2008.

NIB	Exc.	V.G.	Good	Fair	Poor
550	500	450	400	300	200

Model 646

Introduced in 2000. Chambered for .40 S&W cartridge. Built on the L frame. Fitted with 4" barrel, with full lug. Six-round titanium cylinder.

Stainless steel finish. Adjustable rear sight. Hogue rubber grips. Fitted with a target trigger and hammer. Drilled and tapped for scope. Weight 52.5 oz. Discontinued.

NIB	Exc.	V.G.	Good	Fair	Poor
2500	2200	1500	1000	700	350

Model 647

Introduced in 2003. Chambered for .17 HMR cartridge. Fitted with 8-3/8" barrel, with full lug. Six-round cylinder capacity. Stainless steel finish. Adjustable rear sight. Hogue rubber grips. Fitted with a target trigger and hammer. Drilled and tapped for scope. Weight 52.5 oz. Discontinued.

NIB	Exc.	V.G.	Good	Fair	Poor
1800	1300	1100	900	600	400

Model 647 Varminter Performance Center

Introduced in 2003. Chambered for .17 HMR cartridge. Fitted with a 12" fluted barrel, with removable black Patridge front sight and adjustable rear. Integral scope mount on barrel. 6-round cylinder. Stainless steel finish. Weight 54 oz.

NIB	Exc.	V.G.	Good	Fair	Poor
3000	2300	900	—	—	—

Model 648 Pre-Lock

Identical to Model 617 but chambered for .22 Magnum rimfire cartridge. Pre-lock 1989. Two engineering changes.

NIB	Exc.	V.G.	Good	Fair	Poor
1700	1250	800	700	—	—

Model 648-2 with Lock

Introduced in 2003. Medium frame revolver chambered for .22 WMR cartridge. Fitted with 6" full-lug barrel. Pinned Patridge front sight and adjustable rear. New extractor system. Drilled and tapped for scope mount. Stainless steel finish. Weight 45 oz.

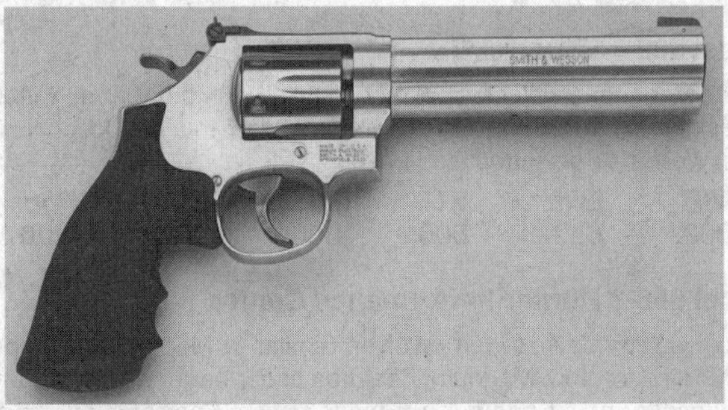

NIB	Exc.	V.G.	Good	Fair	Poor
850	750	650	550	—	—

Model 649 (Bodyguard Stainless)

Stainless steel version of Model 49. Introduced in 1985-1998. Also available in .357 Magnum. As of 1996, offered in .357 Magnum-only version.

NIB	Exc.	V.G.	Good	Fair	Poor
750	700	600	500	400	200

Model 650

Introduced in 1983. Stainless steel model built on a J-frame, with 3" heavy barrel. Chambered for .22 WRM. Has a round butt and fixed sights. Discontinued in 1988.

NIB	Exc.	V.G.	Good	Fair	Poor
1800	1300	900	700	500	300

Model 651

[[J-frame model introduced in 1983. Stainless steel version of Model 51. .22 Magnum Kit Gun manufactured between 1983 and 1987. Chambered for .22 WRM. Fitted with a 4" barrel. Stainless steel finish and adjustable sights. Designation changes are: [None] 1983-1988; [-1] 1988-1990; [-2] 1988-1990.

]] NIB	Exc.	V.G.	Good	Fair	Poor
1900	1500	1000	700	400	300

Model 651-1 2" RSR

A limited edition revolver by RSR. Chambered for .22 WMR cartridge. Fitted with a 2" barrel and boot grips. Stainless steel finish.

NIB	Exc.	V.G.	Good	Fair	Poor
2000	1600	1300	900	500	300

Model 657

A stainless steel version of Model 57. Introduced in 1986-2005. In 2001, this model reintroduced again with 7.5" barrel, with pinned front sight and adjustable rear sight. Hogue rubber combat grips. Weight 52 oz. Premium for 3".

NIB	Exc.	V.G.	Good	Fair	Poor
1800	1500	1200	800	600	250

Model 657 Classic Performance Center

Offered in limited quantities of 350 units. This Lew Horton/Performance Center revolver features an unfluted cylinder and 6.5" barrel on a drilled and tapped N-frame. Chambered for .41 Magnum cartridge. Fitted with adjustable rear sight. Special serial numbers.

NIB	Exc.	V.G.	Good	Fair	Poor
1900	1500	1000	800	—	—

Model 657 Defensive Performance Center

Introduced in 1999 by Lew Horton. This .41 Magnum revolver fitted with 2-5/8" barrel, with drift adjustable Millet front sight and fully adjustable rear sight. Stainless steel finish, with 6-shot unfluted cylinder. Hogue combat grips. Weight about 40 oz. Furnished with aluminum case.

NIB	Exc.	V.G.	Good	Fair	Poor
1800	1400	1200	900	—	—

Model 657-3 Hunter Performance Center

Introduced in 1995. A RSR Wholesale Guns exclusive. Fitted with an integral weaver base, Mag-Na-Ported 6" barrel with Millet red ramp front sight and adjustable rear. Stainless steel finish, special serial numbers, chamfered charge holes and adjustable trigger stop. Limited to 500 guns.

NIB	Exc.	V.G.	Good	Fair	Poor
3000	2500	2000	1500	—	—

Model 657-3 Light Hunter Performance Center

Features 6" slab sided ported barrel with unfluted cylinder. Introduced 1995.

NIB	Exc.	V.G.	Good	Fair	Poor
2500	2000	1500	1000	—	—

Model 681 4"

Six-shot double-action revolver (L-frame). Chambered for the .357 Magnum cartridge. It will also chamber and fire .38 Special +P cartridges. Available with 4" barrel length. Stainless steel frame and cylinder, fixed sights, walnut Magna or rubber grips. Introduced in 1980. See Performance Center section for limited editions. 1980-1992. Reintroduced as 681-4 in 1996 with 7-shot cylinder. Discontinued 2001. Add 50%.

NIB	Exc.	V.G.	Good	Fair	Poor
1400	1000	900	600	400	250

Model 681-4 Quadport 3" Performance Center

A Lew Horton revolver limited to 300 guns, with special serial numbers. This 7-shot revolver has a 3" underlug quadport barrel. Action is tuned, cylinders are chamfered, and trigger has an overtravel stop. Sights are fixed combat type. Pre-lock version.

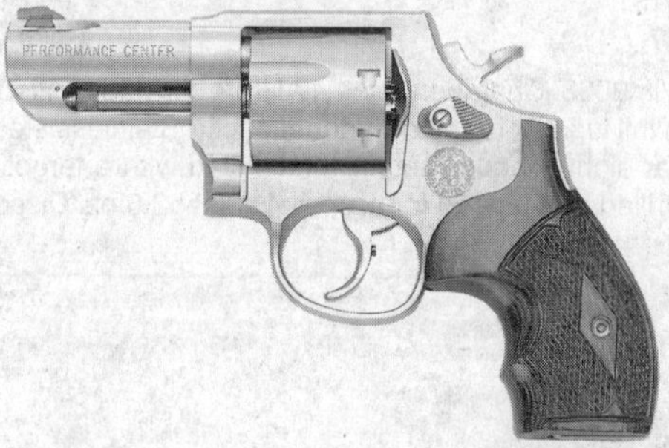

NIB	Exc.	V.G.	Good	Fair	Poor
2400	1900	1400	—	—	—

Model 686 (686, 686-1, 686-2, 686-3 1980-1993 Pre-Locks)

Six-/seven-shot double-action revolver (L-frame). Chambered for .357 Magnum cartridge. It will also chamber and fire .38 Special +P cartridges. Available with 2.5", 3", 4", 5", 6" and 8-3/8" barrel lengths. Stainless steel frame and cylinder, adjustable sights, walnut Magna or rubber grips. Introduced in 1980 to date in various configurations. Probably this model has more variations than any other S&W handgun. See Performance Center for additional limited editions. Add 25% for prelock. Seven engineering changes.

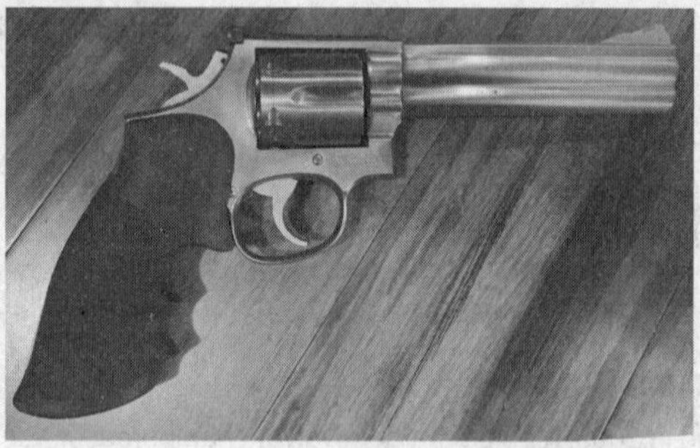

Courtesy Keith Kramis

NIB	Exc.	V.G.	Good	Fair	Poor
1600	1200	900	700	500	200

Model 686—5" Barrel

A .357 Magnum stainless steel model. Fitted with a 5" barrel, with HiViz front sight and adjustable rear. Cylinder holds 7 rounds. Cocobolo wood grips. Weight 41 oz. Introduced in 2004.

NIB	Exc.	V.G.	Good	Fair	Poor
800	650	500	350	280	200

Model 686-3 Hunter Performance Center

Limited edition Lew Horton revolver. Similar to Model 686 Competitor. Chambered for .357 Magnum. Features under barrel weight system, internal scope mount and custom tuned action. Special serial numbers. Pre-lock version.

NIB	Exc.	V.G.	Good	Fair	Poor
2200	1800	1500	—	—	—

Model 686-3 Carry Comp 6 Performance Center

Offered in limited quantities by Lew Horton and Performance Center in 1992. This new design features unique single-chamber integral barrel compensator. Front is windage adjustable and action is custom tuned. Chambered for .357 Magnum cartridge. Special serial numbers. Pre-lock version.

NIB	Exc.	V.G.	Good	Fair	Poor
1200	1000	800	—	—	—

Model 686-4 Powerport 6" (1995 Prelock)

NIB	Exc.	V.G.	Good	Fair	Poor
1500	1150	950	800	600	250

Model 686-4

30% Premium for 7-shot, 50% premium for 2.5"/3" (2.5" Fine 1530).

NIB	Exc.	V.G.	Good	Fair	Poor
1300	1000	800	700	500	250

Model 686-4 Competitor Performance Center

Introduced by Lew Horton and Performance Center for 1993. Limited edition revolver features a match-grade barrel and unique under-barrel weight system. Action has been custom-tuned and the receiver is drilled and tapped for scope mounts. Charge holes are chambered, ejector rod housing is enclosed and the grip is an extended competition type. Special serial numbers. Pre-lock version.

NIB	Exc.	V.G.	Good	Fair	Poor
2000	1700	1400	—	—	—

Model 686-4 Light Hunter Performance Center

Features 6" slabside barrel, ported, full-length rail, 7-shot unfluted cylinder.

NIB	Exc.	V.G.	Good	Fair	Poor
2500	2000	1500	—	—	—

Model 686 Carry Comp 3" Performance Center

The 1993 Lew Horton limited edition version of Model 686 Carry Comp 4" model, with a 3" barrel. Same features apply to both models. Pre-lock version.

NIB	Exc.	V.G.	Good	Fair	Poor
1200	1000	800	—	—	—

Model 686-4 Plus Performance Center

This Lew Horton model features a 7-round cylinder, with chamfered charge holes for use with full moon clips for both .38 Special and .357 Magnum cartridges. Fitted with a tapered 6" barrel, with countersunk muzzle. Gold bead front sight and adjustable rear. Altamont wood grips are standard. Stainless steel finish. Weight 44 oz. Pre-lock version.

NIB	Exc.	V.G.	Good	Fair	Poor
1400	1150	1000	—	—	—

Model 686-4 Magnum Plus (1993 Pre-Lock)

Offered for the first time in 1996. Features a 7-shot cylinder and available with 2-1/2", 4" or 6" barrel lengths. Fitted with red ramp front sight and fully adjustable rear. Frame drilled and tapped for scope mounts. Hogue synthetic grips are standard. Stainless steel is satin finished. Weight 45 oz. Add 50% for pre-lock guns in VG or better.

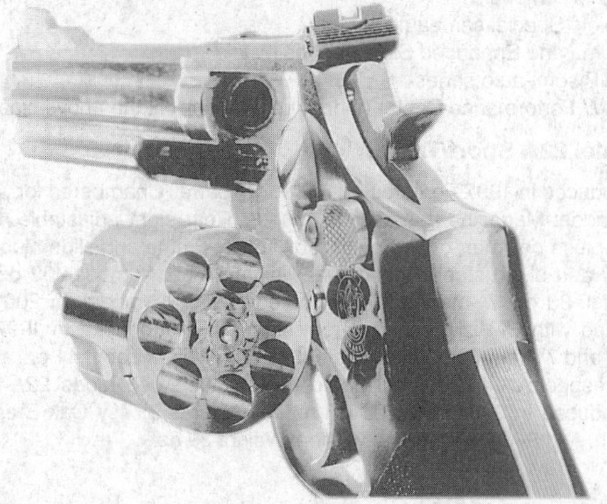

NIB	Exc.	V.G.	Good	Fair	Poor
1800	1400	1100	800	600	250

Model 686-5 5" (Hi-Viz 7-shot)

NIB	Exc.	V.G.	Good	Fair	Poor
800	650	500	350	280	200

686-5 6- and 7-Shot

NIB	Exc.	V.G.	Good	Fair	Poor
1000	900	800	700	500	250

Model 686-5 Plus Mountain Gun 4" (1998 Pre-Lock)

Fitted with 4" tapered barrel and chambered for .357 Magnum cartridge. Has adjustable rear sights. Hogue rubber grips are standard. Stainless steel finish. Weight 44 oz.

NIB	Exc.	V.G.	Good	Fair	Poor
1700	1400	1100	800	600	250

Model 686-6 VR UF

NIB	Exc.	V.G.	Good	Fair	Poor
1130					

Model 686-7 .38 Super Performance Center

Introduced in 2003. This 6-round revolver chambered for .38 Super cartridge. Fitted with a 4" barrel, with tapered lug. Interchangeable red ramp front sight and adjustable rear. Stainless steel, with glass bead finish. Cocobolo grips. Weight about 37 oz. Distributed by Bangers.

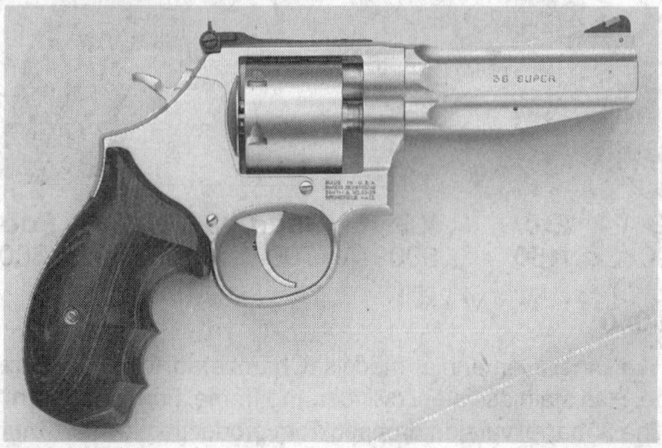

NIB	Exc.	V.G.	Good	Fair	Poor
1400	1150	1000	—	—	—

Model 686 Plus (With Lock)

Single-/double-action L-frame revolver in .38/.357 Magnum. 7-shot cylinder, 3" barrel, Patridge front sight, adjustable rear, stainless finish, rubber grips. Introduced 2007.

NIB	Exc.	V.G.	Good	Fair	Poor
800	660	450	400	300	200

Model 686 Plus Pro Series

Single-/double-action L-frame revolver chambered in .357 Magnum. Features include 5" barrel, with tapered underlug, 7-round cylinder, satin stainless steel frame and cylinder, synthetic grips, interchangeable and adjustable sights. From S&W Performance Center.

NIB	Exc.	V.G.	Good	Fair	Poor
800	650	500	400	300	200

Model 686 CS1 U.S. Customs Service

NIB	Exc.	V.G.	Good	Fair	Poor
1290					

Model 686 SSR PRO

NIB	Exc.	V.G.	Good	Fair	Poor
920					

Model 696 3"

An L-frame model chambered in .44 Special with 5-shot cylinder, 3" fully-shrouded barrel, adjustable rear sight. Discontinued.

NIB	Exc.	V.G.	Good	Fair	Poor
1900	1300	1000	800	500	300

Model 929

Built on the N-frame, this is an 8-shot 9mm revolver. Used by Smith & Wesson competitive shooter Jerry Miculek. Barrel length 6.5". Adjustable rear and Patridge front sight. From S&W Performance Center.

NIB	Exc.	V.G.	Good	Fair	Poor
1300	1150	900	700	500	300

Model 940

Styled like other Centennial models. Chambered for 9mm Parabellum cartridge. Has stainless steel cylinder and frame. Furnished with 2" or 3" barrel. The 3" barrel version dropped from production in 1993. Introduced 1991, discontinued 1998. Two engineering changes.

NIB	Exc.	V.G.	Good	Fair	Poor
1200	900	700	500	400	300

Model 940 Centennial .356 TSW Performance Center

Offered exclusively from Lew Horton. This J-frame revolver chambered for new .356 cartridge. Has a 2" compensated barrel. It will also fire 9mm cartridge. Features a tuned action, radius hammer and trigger. Special serial numbers.

NIB	Exc.	V.G.	Good	Fair	Poor
3000	1600	1200	—	—	—

Model 986

From S&W Performance Center, this 9mm is built on the L-frame, with 7-shot cylinder. Designed for use with moon clips. Barrel length 5". Sights are adjustable rear and Patridge-style front.

NIB	Exc.	V.G.	Good	Fair	Poor
1100	1000	850	700	—	—

Governor Matte Black or Stainless

Built on S&W L-frame. This 6-shot revolver can fire .410 shotshells, .45 Colt and .45 ACP (with moon clips) ammunition. Scandium alloy frame, stainless steel cylinder, Tritium night sight, internal security lock and Hogue synthetic grips. Barrel length 2.75"; weight 29.6 oz.; overall length 8.5". Matte black finish. Available with Crimson Trace Lasergrips. Introduced in 2011. Note: Add $200 for Crimson Trace Lasergrips.

NIB	Exc.	V.G.	Good	Fair	Poor
900	830	750	—	—	—

SEMI-AUTOMATIC PISTOLS

Note: Pistols with S&W factory-installed night sights add $100 to NIB and Exc. prices; S&W factory engraving add $1,000 for Class C (1/3 coverage); $1,250 for Class B (2/3 coverage); $1,500 for Class A (full coverage). This section is listed in the following order:

- .22 rimfire pistols
- Numbered model centerfire pistols, in model number order
- SW1911 models
- Chiefs Special semi-auto series
- Sigma and Enhanced Sigma series pistols
- M&P semi-auto series
- S&W Performance Center handguns (that don't fit the above classes)

Model 22A Sport/Target

Introduced in 1997. Features 4", 5.5", or 7" barrel. Chambered for .22 LR cartridge. Magazine capacity 10 rounds. Rear sight adjustable. Grips: two-piece polymer; or two-piece Soft Touch. Frame and slide aluminum alloy and blued steel. Finish blue. Weight 28 oz. 4" model; 32 oz. 5.5" model; 33 oz. 7" model. Prices quoted are for 4" model. In 2001, furnished with Hi-Viz green dot front sight. Also introduced in 1997 with 5.5" and 7" barrel on stainless steel frames. Weight about 41 oz. and 42 oz. respectively. In 2008, full-camo version introduced. Model 22A Camo Introduced in 2004. This .22 LR model features Mossy Oak Break-Up finish. Add $40 for full-camo version. Weight 39 oz.

NIB	Exc.	V.G.	Good	Fair	Poor
350	300	250	180	130	80

Model 22S Sport/Target

Identical to the Model 22A except with stainless finish and components.

NIB	Exc.	V.G.	Good	Fair	Poor
400	350	300	250	200	130

Model 41

Note: Add up to $500 (depending on condition) for full set of steel and aluminum barrel weights; $750 (depending on condition) for .22 Short conversion kit; 400% for military-marked pistols.

NIB	Exc.	V.G.	Good	Fair	Poor
2500	1800	1400	850	600	350

Model 41 (New Model 5.5" or 7" and Compliance Models)

Restyled in 1994. Featuring recontoured hardwood stocks, Millet adjustable rear sight, drilled and tapped barrel for scope mounting.

NIB	Exc.	V.G.	Good	Fair	Poor
1200	1100	900	700	500	300

Model 41-1 (.22 Short)

Introduced in 1960. Chambered for .22 Short rimfire only. Developed for International Rapid Fire competition. In appearance quite similar to Model 41, except slide and frame made of aluminum alloy in order to lighten it to function with .22 Short cartridge. Not a commercial success like Model 41, so it was discontinued after fewer than 1,000 were manufactured.

Courtesy John J. Stimson, Jr.

Model 41-1 .22 Short with optional weights.

NIB	Exc.	V.G.	Good	Fair	Poor
3000	2500	2000	1400	700	400

Model 41 50th Anniversary Edition

Similar to original Model 41, but machine-engraved with Class A+ coverage. Gold-plated borders. Glass-topped presentation case. Introduced 2008. Serial Number Range: FYA0001-FYA0500.

NIB	Exc.	V.G.	Good	Fair	Poor
2000	1500	—	—	—	—

Model 46

Lower-cost version of Model 41. Developed for the Air Force in 1959. Appearance essentially same as Model 41, with 7" barrel. Later a 5" barrel introduced and finally in 1964, a heavy 5.5" barrel. This economy target pistol never had the popularity the more expensive Model 41 had. Discontinued in 1968, after approximately 4,000 were manufactured.

Courtesy Mike Stuckslager

NIB	Exc.	V.G.	Good	Fair	Poor
2500	1300	900	600	500	300

Model 61 Escort

In 1970, Model 61 was introduced as the only true pocket automatic that S&W produced. Chambered for .22 LR cartridge, with 2.5" barrel and 5-round magazine. Offered blued or nickel finish, with black checkered plastic grips. Dropped from product line in 1974.

NIB	Exc.	V.G.	Good	Fair	Poor
600	500	400	300	200	150

SW22 Victory

A new .22 LR target pistol design, with removable and interchangeable match barrel, fiber-optic adjustable sights, Picatinny rail, textured grips with finger grooves and all stainless construction. Magazine capacity 10 rounds. Two magazines are included. Optional Kryptek Highlander camo finish brings $50 premium. Available with threaded barrel. Introduced 2016.

NIB	Exc.	V.G.	Good	Fair	Poor
360	320	290	270	230	200

S&W .32 Automatic Pistol

In 1921, it became apparent to the powers that controlled S&W that .35-caliber automatic was never going to be a commercial success. Harold Wesson, the new president, began to redesign the pistol to accept the .32 ACP, a commercially accepted cartridge, and to streamline the appearance to be more competitive with other pistols on the market, notably Colt's. This new pistol used as many parts from older models as possible for economy's sake. Pivoting barrel was discontinued, as was the cam-type safety in the rear grip strap. A magazine disconnector and a reduced-strength recoil spring to ease cocking were employed. Barrel length kept at 3.5" and 7-shot magazine was retained. Finish is blued only and grips are smooth walnut. Manufactured only 957, between 1924 and 1936. They are eagerly sought by collectors.

Courtesy James Rankin

NIB	Exc.	V.G.	Good	Fair	Poor
—	3000	2000	1200	700	500

S&W .35 Automatic Pistol

Production of the .35 Automatic was S&W's first attempt at an auto-loading pistol. Has a 3.5" barrel and 7-shot detachable magazine. Chambered in .35 S&W Automatic, a one-time-only cartridge, that eventually proved to be the major downfall of this pistol from a commercial standpoint. There were two separate safety devices — a revolving cam on the backstrap and a grip safety on the frontstrap that had to be fully depressed simultaneously while squeezing the trigger. Finish blued or nickel-plated; grips are walnut, with S&W inlaid medallions. Magazine release slides from side to side and is checkered, expensive to manufacture, and destined to be modified. Approximately 8,350 manufactured.

NIB	Exc.	V.G.	Good	Fair	Poor
—	1000	500	400	300	200

Model 39

First double-action semi-automatic pistol produced in the United States. Introduced in 1957. Had an alloy frame and chambered for 9mm Parabellum or .30 Luger. Barrel was 4". Finish blued or nickel, with checkered walnut grips. Rear sight was adjustable. Magazine capacity 8 rounds. Discontinued in 1982. The .30 Luger model is very rare and was mostly sold in Europe. Note: Add 150% for .30 Luger; 200% for early production—serial number 1001-2600. (100% premium for Pre-model 39.)

NIB	Exc.	V.G.	Good	Fair	Poor
1250	1000	700	500	400	300

Model 39 Steel Frame

A total of 927 steel frame Model 39s produced. Rare. Use caution.

NIB	Exc.	V.G.	Good	Fair	Poor
4000	3000	2500	1700	1200	700

Model 59 Blue or Nickel

Introduced in 1971. Similar to Model 39, with a wide grip to hold a double column magazine of 14 rounds. Furnished with black checkered plastic grips. Discontinued in 1982.

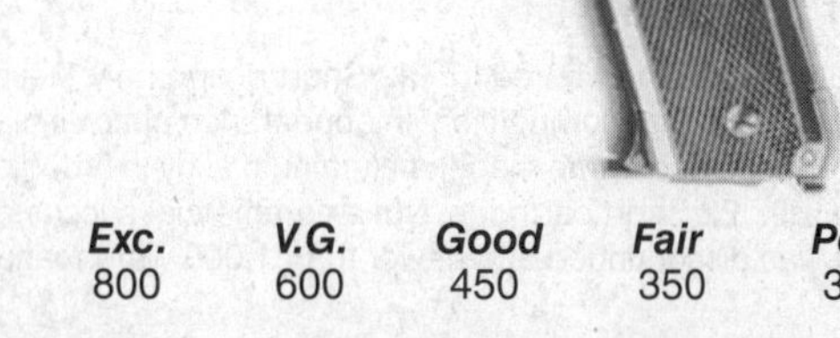

NIB	Exc.	V.G.	Good	Fair	Poor
1100	800	600	450	350	300

Model 44 Single Action 9mm

Introduced 1958. Chambered 9mm caliber. Reported that only 10 were made. Rare. Use caution. Sales reported over $20,000.

Model 52A .38 AMU (Rare)

Introduced in 1961. Chambered in .38 AMU caliber for Army marksmanship training. Army rejected the 87 pistols built, so they were released to the public. Letter "A" stamped behind model designation. Rare. Use caution.

NIB	Exc.	V.G.	Good	Fair	Poor
10000	7000	5000	2500	1500	1000

Model 52 (.38 Master)

Introduced in 1961 as a target pistol. Chambered for .38 Special mid-range wadcutter cartridge. Similar in appearance to the Model 39, but single-action-only by virtue of a set screw. Fitted with 5" barrel and 5-round magazine. Blued finish, with checkered walnut grips. About 3,500 produced in this configuration. Discontinued in 1963.

NIB	Exc.	V.G.	Good	Fair	Poor
2500	2000	1500	900	700	400

Model 52-1

In 1963, this variation featured a true single-action design. Produced until 1971.

NIB	Exc.	V.G.	Good	Fair	Poor
2000	1500	1000	750	500	400

Model 52-2

Introduced in 1971, with a coil spring-style extractor. Discontinued in 1993.

NIB	Exc.	V.G.	Good	Fair	Poor
1800	1200	1000	700	450	400

Model 147A

Introduced 1979, 130 made, chambered 9mm. Rare. Use caution.

NIB	Exc.	V.G.	Good	Fair	Poor
3800	3300	2500	2000	—	—

Model 410

First introduced in 1996. Features an alloy frame, with carbon steel slide. Chambered for .40 S&W cartridge. Barrel length 4". Magazine capacity 10 rounds. Overall length 7.5". Weight about 29 oz.

NIB	Exc.	V.G.	Good	Fair	Poor
500	450	350	300	250	200

Model 410 Two-Tone

Same as Model 410, with alloy finish frame and black slide. Limited edition.

NIB	Exc.	V.G.	Good	Fair	Poor
530	480	400	350	280	250

Model 410S

Introduced in 2003. Stainless steel version of Model 410. Weight 28 oz.

NIB	Exc.	V.G.	Good	Fair	Poor
550	500	450	400	300	280

Model 411

Introduced in 1993 as a no frills model. Features alloy frame, 4" barrel, matte blue finish, fixed sights and wrap-around rubber grips. Chambered for .40 S&W cartridge, with 11-round magazine. Overall length 7.5"; weight about 29 oz.

NIB	Exc.	V.G.	Good	Fair	Poor
550	450	400	350	280	250

These 422 models, as well as 622, 2206, and 2214, have a threaded nut on the muzzle which can be removed and replaced with a thread adapter to accommodate suppressors.

Model 422 Field

Introduced in 1987. This .22 LR pistol has 4.5" or 6" barrel, with an alloy frame and steel slide. Magazine capacity 10 rounds. Fixed sights and black plastic grips. Finish matte blue.

NIB	*Exc.*	*V.G.*	*Good*	*Fair*	*Poor*
500	450	400	300	200	150

Model 422 Target

Same as Field model, with adjustable sights and checkered walnut grips.

NIB	*Exc.*	*V.G.*	*Good*	*Fair*	*Poor*
600	500	450	350	250	200

Model 439

Introduced in 1979. Improved version of Model 39. Furnished with adjustable rear sight. Discontinued in 1988.

NIB	*Exc.*	*V.G.*	*Good*	*Fair*	*Poor*
1000	750	600	500	350	300

Model 457

Introduced in 1996. This .45 ACP model features 3.75" barrel, with rounded triggerguard and double-action. Fitted with single side decocker. Magazine capacity 7 rounds. Overall length 7.25"; weight 29 oz. Frame is alloy and slide carbon steel. Finish matte black.

NIB	*Exc.*	*V.G.*	*Good*	*Fair*	*Poor*
600	550	500	450	350	300

Model 457S

Same as Model 457, only in stainless steel. Weight 29 oz. Introduced in 2003.

NIB	*Exc.*	*V.G.*	*Good*	*Fair*	*Poor*
1000	700	500	450	350	300

Model 459

Improved-sight version of 15-shot Model 59 9mm pistol. Introduced in 1979; discontinued 1987.

NIB	*Exc.*	*V.G.*	*Good*	*Fair*	*Poor*
800	700	600	500	400	300

Model 469

The Model 469 answered the need for a more concealable high-capacity pistol. Essentially a "Mini" version of Model 459. Chambered for 9mm Parabellum. Detachable 12-round magazine, with finger grip extension and shortened frame. Barrel 3.5" long; hammer bobbed and does not protrude; safety ambidextrous. Finish matte blue, with black plastic grips. Introduced in 1983; discontinued 1988.

NIB	*Exc.*	*V.G.*	*Good*	*Fair*	*Poor*
650	500	450	380	330	280

Model 539

Another version of Model 439 9mm pistol. Incorporates all features of Model 439, with a steel frame instead of aluminum alloy. Introduced in 1980; discontinued 1983.

NIB	*Exc.*	*V.G.*	*Good*	*Fair*	*Poor*
1300	1000	800	700	400	300

Model 559

This variation of Model 459 9mm pistol, has a steel frame instead of aluminum alloy. Identical in all other respects. 25% premium for nickel.

NIB	Exc.	V.G.	Good	Fair	Poor
1300	900	600	500	400	300

Model 622 Target

Stainless steel version of Model 422 Target. Alloy frame.

NIB	Exc.	V.G.	Good	Fair	Poor
750	600	500	350	250	200

Model 622 Field

Stainless steel version of Model 422 Field. Alloy frame.

NIB	Exc.	V.G.	Good	Fair	Poor
700	600	500	400	250	200

Model 622VR

Redesigned in 1996. This .22-caliber model features 6" ventilated rib barrel. Fitted with matte black trigger and new triggerguard. Front sight serrated ramp style, with adjustable rear. Weight 23 oz. Grips are black polymer.

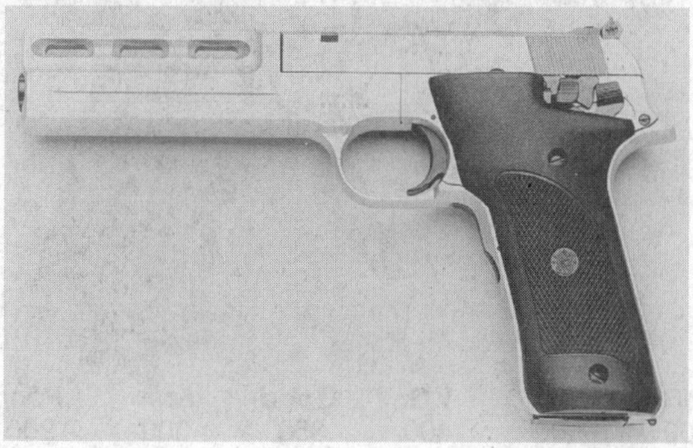

NIB	Exc.	V.G.	Good	Fair	Poor
800	700	550	400	300	250

Model 639

Stainless steel version of Model 439. Introduced in 1984; discontinued 1988.

NIB	Exc.	V.G.	Good	Fair	Poor
1000	900	800	600	400	300

Model 645

Model 645 is a large-framed, stainless steel double-action pistol. Chambered for .45 ACP cartridge. Has a 5" barrel, adjustable sights and detachable 8-shot magazine. Offered with fixed or adjustable sights. Ambidextrous safety. Grips are molded black nylon. Manufactured between 1985 and 1988.

NIB	Exc.	V.G.	Good	Fair	Poor
1200	950	850	700	500	350

Model 659

Stainless steel version of Model 459 9mm pistol. Features ambidextrous safety and all other options of Model 459. Introduced in 1982; discontinued 1988.

NIB	Exc.	V.G.	Good	Fair	Poor
1000	750	650	550	400	350

Model 669

Stainless steel version of Model 469 9mm pistol. All features of Model 469 are incorporated. Model 669 manufactured from 1986 to 1988.

NIB	Exc.	V.G.	Good	Fair	Poor
500	450	400	350	300	250

Model 745—IPSC

Similar in outward appearance to Model 645, but quite a different pistol. A single-action semi-automatic chambered for .45 ACP cartridge. Frame made of stainless steel. Slide of blued carbon steel. Barrel 5". Detachable magazine holds 8 rounds. Sights are fully adjustable target types. Grips checkered walnut. Introduced in 1986; discontinued 1990.

NIB	Exc.	V.G.	Good	Fair	Poor
900	730	600	400	270	220

Model 745 IPSC Commemorative

Introduced in 1986. Limited to 5362 guns. Serial numbers DVC0000-DVC5362.

NIB	Exc.	V.G.	Good	Fair	Poor
1100	—	—	—	—	—

Model 845 Single-Action Performance Center

Offered by Lew Horton. Chambered for .45 ACP. Designed for the competitive shooter. Adjustable reach trigger precision fitted slide, frame and barrel are some of the special features. Barrel bushing spherical and front sight dovetailed. Magazine well extended as is magazine release and safety. Both front and rear sight are adjustable.

NIB	Exc.	V.G.	Good	Fair	Poor
2000	1700	1400	—	—	—

Model 908

Introduced in 1996. An economy compact pistol. Chambered for 9mm cartridge. Fitted with 3.5" barrel. Traditional double-action. Fixed rear sight. Magazine capacity 8 rounds. Overall length 6.875"; weight 26 oz.

NIB	Exc.	V.G.	Good	Fair	Poor
500	450	400	350	300	250

Model 908S

Same as Model 908 in stainless steel. Weight 24 oz. Introduced in 2003.

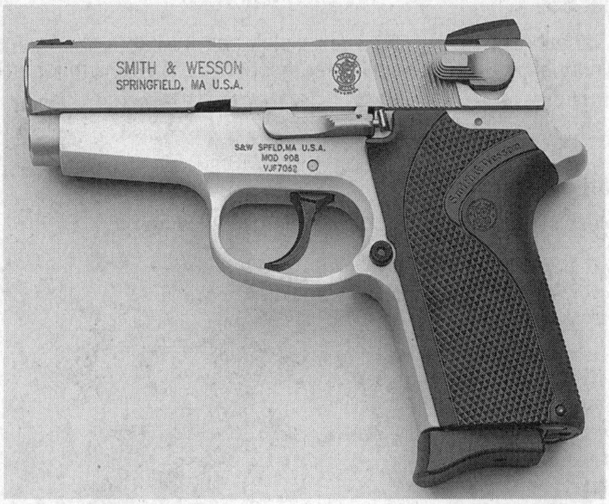

NIB	Exc.	V.G.	Good	Fair	Poor
600	550	500	430	350	300

Model 909

Introduced in 1995. Chambered for 9mm cartridge. Blue carbon steel slide, aluminum alloy frame and double-action. Single-column magazine and curved backstrap.

NIB	Exc.	V.G.	Good	Fair	Poor
600	500	400	350	300	200

Model 910

Also introduced in 1995. Same as above, with double-column magazine and straight backstrap.

NIB	Exc.	V.G.	Good	Fair	Poor
600	500	400	350	300	200

Model 910S

Introduced in 2003. Stainless steel version of Model 910. Weight 28 oz.

NIB	Exc.	V.G.	Good	Fair	Poor
700	600	500	400	350	250

Model 915

Introduced in 1993. Chambered for 9mm cartridge. Features 4" barrel, matte blue finish, fixed rear sight and wrap-around rubber grips. Overall length 7.5"; weight about 28 oz.

NIB	Exc.	V.G.	Good	Fair	Poor
650	550	450	400	350	300

Model 945

See—Performance Center

NIB	Exc.	V.G.	Good	Fair	Poor
1800	1500	1300	—	—	—

Model 945 Performance Center 5"

A single-action-only pistol chambered for .45 ACP cartridge. Fitted with a 5" match-grade barrel and Bomar adjustable rear sight. Grips checkered black/silver wood laminate, with matte stainless steel slide and frame. Magazine capacity 8 rounds. Empty weight 44 oz. Introduced in 1998.

NIB	Exc.	V.G.	Good	Fair	Poor
2500	2000	1600	—	—	—

Model 945-1 Black Model Performance Center 4"

Performance Center Model features 3.25" barrel, with black stainless steel slide. Frame aluminum. Novak Lo-Mount sights. Hogue checkered wood laminate grips. Furnished with two 6-round magazines and locking aluminum gun case. Weight 24 oz. Exclusive with RSR.

NIB	Exc.	V.G.	Good	Fair	Poor
2300	1800	1200	—	—	—

Model 945-40 Performance Center 3-3/4"

This PC model fitted with a 3.75" barrel chambered for .40 S&W cartridge. Novak Lo-Mount sights and Hogue checkered wood laminate grips are standard. Furnished with two 7-round magazines and locking aluminum case. Clear glass bead finish. Exclusive with Sports South.

NIB	Exc.	V.G.	Good	Fair	Poor
2400	2000	1300	—	—	—

Model 945 Micro Black Performance Center 3-1/4"

Similar to Model 945 Black Model, with stainless steel finish. Exclusive with Camfour Distributor.

NIB	Exc.	V.G.	Good	Fair	Poor
3000	2200	1800	—	—	—

Model 952 Performance Center

NIB	Exc.	V.G.	Good	Fair	Poor
2800	2300	2000	—	—	—

Model 1006

Full-size 10mm pistol, with 5" barrel and 9-round magazine. Choice of fixed or adjustable sights. Both slide and frame are stainless steel.

NIB	Exc.	V.G.	Good	Fair	Poor
1600	1200	900	800	500	300

Model 1026

Similar to Model 1006, with 5" barrel and frame-mounted decocking lever.

NIB	Exc.	V.G.	Good	Fair	Poor
2000	1600	1100	800	500	300

Model 1046

Limited production of approx. 150 in 1991. Rare.

NIB	Exc.	V.G.	Good	Fair	Poor
3500	3000	2500	—	—	—

Model 1066

Slightly smaller version of Model 1006. Furnished with 4.25" barrel. Discontinued in 1993.

NIB	Exc.	V.G.	Good	Fair	Poor
2500	2000	1500	1000	500	300

Model 1076

Identical to Model 1066, except for frame-mounted decocking lever. Limited Sales to FBI in 1990. Be cautious.

NIB	Exc.	V.G.	Good	Fair	Poor
1800	1500	1200	1000	500	300

Model 1086

Similar to Model 1066, but offered in double-action-only. Discontinued in 1993.

NIB	Exc.	V.G.	Good	Fair	Poor
1500	1100	800	500	400	300

Model 2206

This .22 LR pistol offered with 4.5" or 6" barrel. Magazine capacity 12 rounds. Adjustable rear sight. Stainless steel frame and slide.

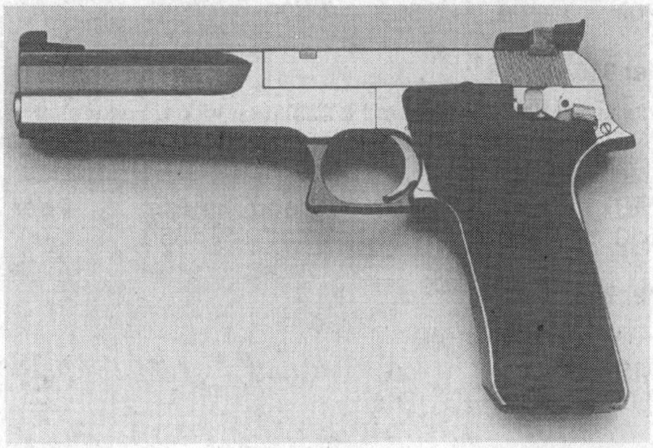

NIB	Exc.	V.G.	Good	Fair	Poor
800	600	500	400	300	250

Model 2206 TGT (Target)

Introduced in 1995. Features selected 6" barrel, bead blasted sighting plane and polished flat side surfaces. Patridge front sight and Millet adjustable rear are standard. Serrated trigger, with adjustable trigger stop and 10-round magazine.

NIB	Exc.	V.G.	Good	Fair	Poor
1200	900	600	500	400	300

Model 2214 (The Sportsman)

Semi-automatic pistol chambered for .22 LR. Designed for casual use. Fitted with a 3" barrel. Magazine capacity 8 rounds. Slide blued carbon steel. Frame is alloy. Introduced in 1990; discontinued 1997.

NIB	Exc.	V.G.	Good	Fair	Poor
650	550	450	400	300	250

Model 2213 (The Sportsman Stainless)

Identical to the Model 2214 except with stainless components.

NIB	Exc.	V.G.	Good	Fair	Poor
700	600	550	400	300	250

Model 3904

In 1989, S&W redesigned the entire line of 9mm semi-automatic handguns. The 3904 is chambered for 9mm Parabellum. Has an 8-shot detachable magazine and 4" barrel with a fixed bushing. Frame is alloy. Triggerguard squared for two-hand hold. Magazine well beveled and grips are one-piece wrap-around made of Delrin. Three-dot sighting system is employed. Discontinued.

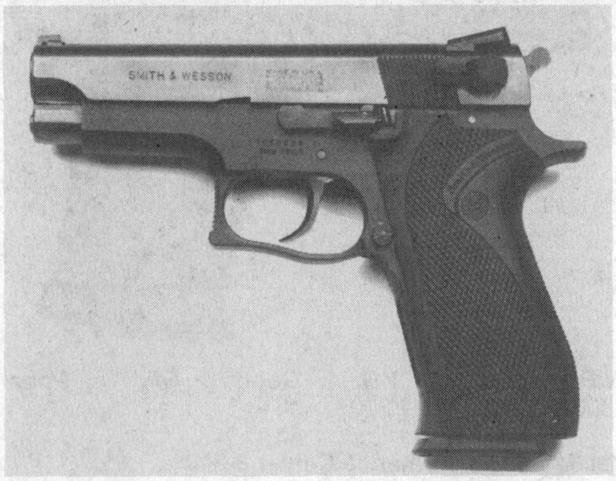

NIB	Exc.	V.G.	Good	Fair	Poor
1000	700	400	350	250	200

Model 3906

Stainless steel version of Model 3904. Features are the same. Introduced in 1989; discontinued.

NIB	*Exc.*	*V.G.*	*Good*	*Fair*	*Poor*
900	700	550	400	300	200

Model 3913

Similar to Model 3914, but features a stainless steel slide and alloy frame.

NIB	*Exc.*	*V.G.*	*Good*	*Fair*	*Poor*
700	600	500	400	300	200

3913/3914/3953 TSW

Chambered for 9mm cartridge. Fitted with 3.5" barrel. White dot front sight and Novak Lo-Mount rear. Aluminum alloy frame. Magazine capacity 7 rounds. Weight 25 oz. Stainless steel finish. The 3913 is traditional double-action; while 3953 double-action-only.

NIB	*Exc.*	*V.G.*	*Good*	*Fair*	*Poor*
900	700	500	400	300	200

Model 3913LS

Identical to Model 3914LS, with exception of stainless steel slide.

NIB	*Exc.*	*V.G.*	*Good*	*Fair*	*Poor*
850	700	500	400	300	200

Model 3914

Offered as a slightly smaller alternative to Model 3904. This 9mm pistol has 3.5" barrel, 8-round magazine, blued carbon steel slide and alloy frame.

NIB	*Exc.*	*V.G.*	*Good*	*Fair*	*Poor*
800	700	500	400	300	200

Model 3914LS

Redesigned Model 3914 that has a more modern appearance. LS refers to LadySmith. Chambered for 9mm cartridge. All other features same as Model 3914, including blued carbon slide and alloy frame.

NIB	*Exc.*	*V.G.*	*Good*	*Fair*	*Poor*
800	700	500	400	300	200

Model 3954

Similar to Model 3914, but offered in double-action-only. Discontinued in 1993.

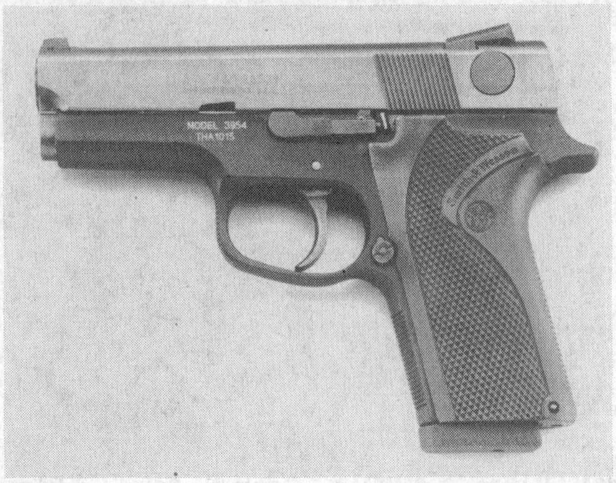

NIB	Exc.	V.G.	Good	Fair	Poor
800	700	500	400	300	200

Model 4003

Chambered for .40 S&W cartridge. Fitted with 4" barrel, 11-round magazine, serrated hammer. Stainless steel slide and alloy frame.

NIB	Exc.	V.G.	Good	Fair	Poor
800	700	500	400	300	200

Model 4003/4006/4043/4046 TSW

These models come in the same configurations as 5903 group, except chambered for .40 S&W cartridge. Magazine capacity 10 rounds. Weight 28 oz. Note: Add $100 for night sights.

NIB	Exc.	V.G.	Good	Fair	Poor
900	700	500	400	300	200

Model 4004

Identical to Model 4003, except for blue carbon steel slide and alloy frame. Discontinued in 1993.

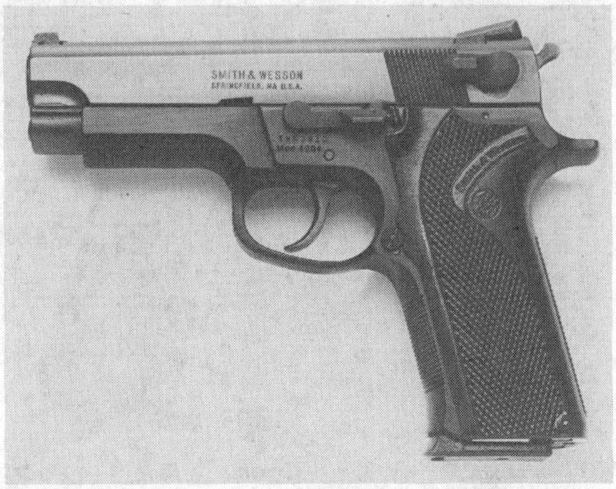

NIB	Exc.	V.G.	Good	Fair	Poor
800	700	500	400	300	200

Model 4006

Identical to Model 4003, except both slide and frame are stainless steel. This adds 8 oz. to weight of pistol.

NIB	Exc.	V.G.	Good	Fair	Poor
660	550	410	300	250	220

Model 4013

Compact version of 4000 series. This .40-caliber model features 3.5" barrel, 8-round magazine, stainless steel slide and alloy frame.

NIB	Exc.	V.G.	Good	Fair	Poor
700	600	500	400	300	200

4013/4053 TSW

Chambered for .40 S&W cartridge. Fitted with 3.5" barrel. White dot front sight and Novak Lo-Mount rear sight. Aluminum alloy frame and stainless steel slide. Magazine capacity 9 rounds. Weight 27 oz. The 4013 is traditional double-action; while 4053 double-action-only.

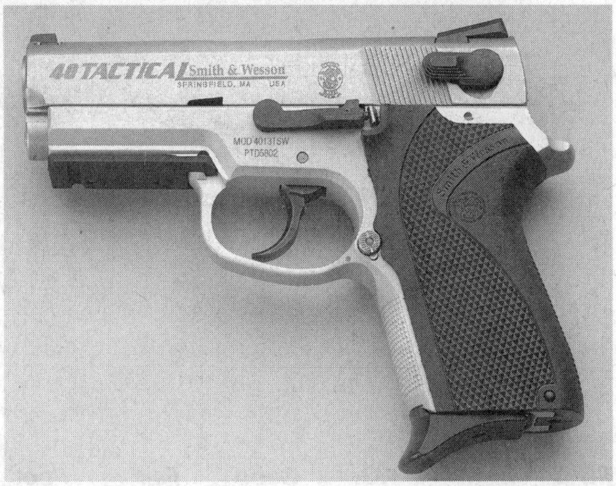

NIB	*Exc.*	*V.G.*	*Good*	*Fair*	*Poor*
800	700	550	400	300	200

Model 4014

Identical to Model 4013, except for a blued carbon steel slide and alloy frame. Scarce.

NIB	*Exc.*	*V.G.*	*Good*	*Fair*	*Poor*
1750	1000	—	—	—	—

Model 4026

Similar to Model 4006, except has a frame-mounted decocking lever.

NIB	*Exc.*	*V.G.*	*Good*	*Fair*	*Poor*
700	600	500	400	300	200

Model 4040PD Airlite

When introduced in 2003, this was the first Scandium-frame S&W pistol. Chambered for the .40 S&W cartridge. Fitted with 3.5" barrel. White-dot front sight, with Novak Lo Mount rear. Matte black finish. Magazine capacity 7 rounds. Soft rubber grips. Weight 25.6 oz.

NIB	*Exc.*	*V.G.*	*Good*	*Fair*	*Poor*
800	700	500	400	300	200

Model 4046/4046 NS

Similar to Model 4006, with double-action-only configuration.

NIB	*Exc.*	*V.G.*	*Good*	*Fair*	*Poor*
600	450	350	300	250	200

Model 4053

Identical to Model 4013, except offered in double-action-only configuration.

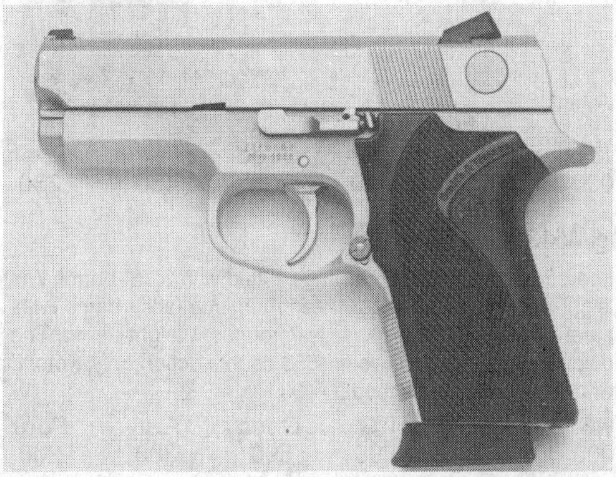

NIB	*Exc.*	*V.G.*	*Good*	*Fair*	*Poor*
700	600	500	400	300	200

Model 4054

Same as Model 4053, except for a blued carbon steel slide and alloy frame. Dropped from S&W product line in 1992.

NIB	Exc.	V.G.	Good	Fair	Poor
2500	2000	—	—	—	—

Model 4056 TSW

A double-action-only pistol chambered for .40 S&W cartridge. Fitted with 3.5" barrel, with white dot sights. Curved backstrap. Stainless steel. Magazine capacity 9 rounds. Introduced in 1997. Weight 36 oz.

NIB	Exc.	V.G.	Good	Fair	Poor
1000	750	550	400	300	200

Model 4505

Identical to Model 4506, except with blued slide and frame.

NIB	Exc.	V.G.	Good	Fair	Poor
1500	1000	750	600	350	250

Model 4506

Double-action .45 ACP pistol. All stainless steel. Has 5" barrel, 8-shot detachable magazine and wrap-around black Delrin grips. Discontinued.

NIB	Exc.	V.G.	Good	Fair	Poor
2000	1600	1100	800	450	250

Model 4513/4553 TSW

Chambered for the .45 ACP cartridge. Fitted with 3.75" barrel. White-dot front sight and Novak Lo-Mount rear. Aluminum-alloy frame with stainless steel slide. Magazine capacity 7 rounds. Weight 29 oz. The 4513 is traditional double-action; while 4553 double-action-only. Note: Deduct $50 for double-action-only model 4553.

NIB	Exc.	V.G.	Good	Fair	Poor
1000	900	800	500	300	200

Model 4516

Compact version of full-size .45-caliber S&W automatics. Furnished with 3.75" barrel and 7-round magazine. Chambered in .45-caliber. Has stainless slide and frame. Discontinued in 1991; reintroduced in 1994.

NIB	Exc.	V.G.	Good	Fair	Poor
1000	900	800	700	500	200

Model 4536

Compact version and similar to Model 4616. Offered with decock lever on frame.

NIB	Exc.	V.G.	Good	Fair	Poor
1200	900	600	400	300	200

Model 4546

Full-size version of Model 4506. Offered in double-action-only.

NIB	Exc.	V.G.	Good	Fair	Poor
900	700	500	400	300	200

Models 4553/4556/4566/4567/4576/4583/4586/4596

All these .45 ACP pistols were introduced in the early 1990s during S&W's "gun of the week" period, when a proliferation of models was added to the line with variations in features. The basic mechanical design is similar, with variations in finish, barrel length, sights, type of action, etc. Values will be generally similar but be aware that some of these may be rare and could bring significant premiums — for example very few Model 4556s were produced. A collector market has yet to fully emerge. See Standard Catalog of Smith & Wesson available at GunDigestStore.com for more information. These listings may be expanded in future editions, reader input is invited.

NIB	*Exc.*	*V.G.*	*Good*	*Fair*	*Poor*
1000	750	500	400	300	200

Model 4553/4563/4566/4583/4586 TSW

Tactical S&W configuration .45 ACP. 4.25" barrel; 31 oz. Add $100 for night sights.

NIB	*Exc.*	*V.G.*	*Good*	*Fair*	*Poor*
1000	800	700	500	350	200

Model 5903

Same caliber and features as Model 5904 and Model 5906, but furnished with stainless steel slide and alloy frame.

NIB	*Exc.*	*V.G.*	*Good*	*Fair*	*Poor*
650	500	400	350	300	200

Model 5903/5906/5943/5946 TSW

These pistols chambered for 9mm cartridge. Fitted with 4" barrel. Fixed sights standard (5903, 5906, 5943, 5946); optional, adjustable and night sights (5906). Offered in traditional double-action (5903, 5906); while double-action-only (5943, 5946). Magazine capacity 10 rounds. Weight 38 oz. Stainless steel finish. Note: Add $100 for night sights; $50 for adjustable sights.

NIB	*Exc.*	*V.G.*	*Good*	*Fair*	*Poor*
700	550	450	350	300	200

Model 5904

A full high-capacity 15-shot version of Model 3904. Introduced in 1989. Features slide mounted decocking lever and 4" barrel. Blued carbon steel slide and alloy frame. Discontinued.

NIB	*Exc.*	*V.G.*	*Good*	*Fair*	*Poor*
700	600	500	450	350	200

Model 5906/5906NS

Stainless steel version of Model 5904. Both slide and frame are stainless steel.

NIB	*Exc.*	*V.G.*	*Good*	*Fair*	*Poor*
1000	650	550	400	300	200

Model 5906 Special Edition

Double-action semi-automatic pistol chambered for 9mm, with 15-round magazine. Frame and slide have a special machine finish. Grips are one-piece wrap-around Xenoy. Front sight is a white dot post. Rear sight a Novak L-Mount Carry, with two white dots. Manual safety/decocking lever and firing pin safety. Introduced in 1993.

NIB	*Exc.*	*V.G.*	*Good*	*Fair*	*Poor*
700	600	450	350	250	200

Model 5906 Performance Center

Introduced in 1998. This 9mm pistol features front slide serrations, ambidextrous decocker, titanium coated barrel bushing, match-grade barrel and Novak Lo-Mount sights. Sold with one 15- and 10-round magazine. Stainless steel finish.

NIB	*Exc.*	*V.G.*	*Good*	*Fair*	*Poor*
1500	1250	1000	—	—	—

Model 5926

S&W offers a 9mm pistol similar to 5906, with frame mounted decocking lever. Both slide and frame are stainless steel. Discontinued in 1993.

NIB	Exc.	V.G.	Good	Fair	Poor
1000	750	500	400	300	200

Model 5946

This 9mm pistol offers the same features as Model 5926, but in a double-action-only model. Hammer configuration is semi-bobbed instead of serrated.

NIB	Exc.	V.G.	Good	Fair	Poor
700	550	450	350	300	200

Model 5967

A 9mm model with M5906 frame and M3914 slide. Has stainless steel frame and blued slide. Novak Lo-Mount fixed sights. Introduced in 1990 and sold through Lew Horton. Scarce.

NIB	Exc.	V.G.	Good	Fair	Poor
1200	1000	800	500	300	200

Model 6904

Concealable shortened version of Model 5904. Has 12-shot magazine, fixed sights, bobbed hammer and 3.5" barrel.

NIB	Exc.	V.G.	Good	Fair	Poor
550	500	400	300	250	200

Model 6906/6906NS

Stainless steel slide and alloy frame, but otherwise similar to M6904.

NIB	Exc.	V.G.	Good	Fair	Poor
700	550	450	400	300	200

Model 6946

Double-action version of Model 6906.

NIB	Exc.	V.G.	Good	Fair	Poor
600	500	450	350	300	200

1911 SERIES

Model SW1911

Introduced in 2003. Full-size pistol chambered for .45 ACP and 9mm Parabelluum cartridges. Fitted with 5" barrel. White dot front sight and Novak Lo-Mount rear. Stainless steel frame and slide. Checkered black rubber grips. Magazine capacity 8 rounds (9 in 9mm). Weight 39 oz. In 2005, offered with wood grips and black oxide finish.

NIB	Exc.	V.G.	Good	Fair	Poor
1300	1000	800	700	400	250

Model SW1911 Adjustable

Like the Model SW1911 only fitted with adjustable sights. Introduced in 2004.

NIB	Exc.	V.G.	Good	Fair	Poor
1500	1200	900	800	400	250

Model SW1911Sc

This .45 ACP model fitted with Commander size slide and Scandium frame. Fixed sights. Checkered wood grips. Black oxide finish. Weight 28 oz. Introduced in 2004.

NIB	Exc.	V.G.	Good	Fair	Poor
1500	1200	900	700	400	250

Model 1911 PD

This .45 ACP model offered with 4.25" or 5" barrel, with Novak low mount sights. Wood grips. Frame alloy, with black finish. Magazine capacity 8 rounds. Weight 28 oz. 4.25" model; 29.5 oz. 5" model.

NIB	Exc.	V.G.	Good	Fair	Poor
1350	1100	950	750	400	250

Model SW1911E Series

Full-size 1911-style pistol in .45 ACP caliber. Stainless steel frame and slide, with "fish scale" scalloped slide serrations front and rear. Other features include checkered frontstrap, mainspring housing, oversized extractor, enlarged ejection port, titanium firing pin and laminated textured wood grips. Available with Crimson Trace Lasergrips. Introduced in 2011. Note: Add 20% for Crimson Trace Lasergrips; 30% for integral accessory rail.

NIB	Exc.	V.G.	Good	Fair	Poor
1300	1000	900	800	400	250

Model SW1911 DK (Doug Koenig)

Introduced in 2005. This .45 ACP model fitted with 5" stainless steel barrel. Adjustable rear sight, with black blade front. Frame stainless steel, with black carbon steel slide. Wood grips. Magazine capacity 8 rounds. Weight 41 oz.

NIB	Exc.	V.G.	Good	Fair	Poor
1400	1200	1000	800	400	250

Model SW1911 Pro Series

Similar to Model SW1911, with Novak fiber optic sights, skeletonized trigger and various tactical/performance enhancements. Introduced 2008. Available in .45 ACP or 9mm.

NIB	Exc.	V.G.	Good	Fair	Poor
1400	1100	900	750	400	250

Model SW1911 Pro Sub-Compact

Chopped 1911-style semi-automatic pistol. Chambered for .45 ACP. 7+1 capacity, 3" barrel. Wood grips, Scandium frame with stainless steel slide, matte black finish throughout. Overall length 6.9"; weight 26.5 oz.

NIB	Exc.	V.G.	Good	Fair	Poor
1200	1000	900	800	400	250

Model SW1911 Performance Center

This .45 ACP PC model features a 5" barrel, micro-click adjustable black rear sight and dovetail black front. Checkered wine laminate grips. Stainless steel frame and slide, with black oxide finish. Magazine capacity 8 rounds. Weight 41 oz. Introduced in 2004.

NIB	Exc.	V.G.	Good	Fair	Poor
1500	1100	900	800	—	—

Model SW1911 Tactical Rail Performance Center

One of Tactical Rail Series for SWAT Teams and tactical applications. Picatinny rail and fixed sights. Blued or stainless. Single-action .45 ACP, with 5" barrel and 8+1 capacity. Weight 39 oz. Introduced 2006.

NIB	Exc.	V.G.	Good	Fair	Poor
1200	1000	900	800	—	—

Model SW1911 PD Gunsite

Honors Lt. Col. Jeff Cooper's Gunsite Training Academy. Scandium alloy single-action .45 ACP, with 4.25" barrel and 8+1 capacity. Fixed sights. 28 oz. Introduced 2006.

NIB	Exc.	V.G.	Good	Fair	Poor
1400	1200	1000	900	—	—

Model SW1911 Rolling Thunder

Limited edition commemorates American POW-MIAs. Rolling Thunder and POW-MIA logos in imitation bonded ivory grips. Chambered for .45 ACP. Blued, 8+1 capacity, 5" barrel, 38.5 oz. Introduced 2006.

NIB	Exc.	V.G.	Good	Fair	Poor
1200	1000	900	—	—	—

CHIEF'S SPECIAL SERIES

CS9

Chambered for 9mm cartridge. Fitted with 3" barrel. Has stainless steel slide and aluminum alloy frame. Also available in blued finish. Hogue wrap-around grips standard. Fixed sights. Magazine capacity 7 rounds. Weight 21 oz.

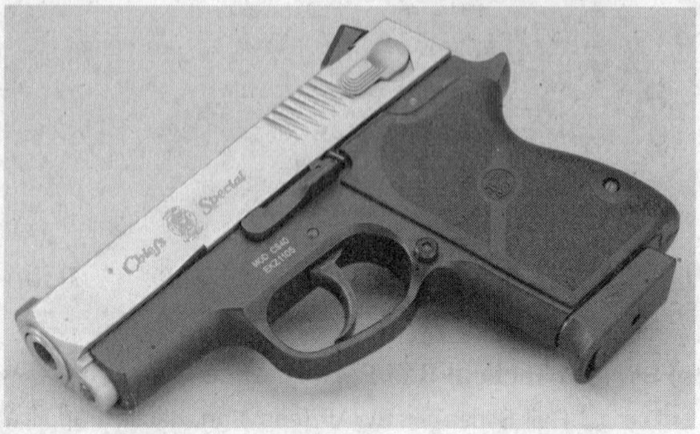

NIB	Exc.	V.G.	Good	Fair	Poor
700	500	400	300	—	—

CS40

This Chief's Special model chambered for .40 S&W cartridge. Barrel length 3.25". Magazine capacity 7 rounds. Weight 24 oz.

NIB	Exc.	V.G.	Good	Fair	Poor
900	700	500	400	300	250

CS40 Two-Tone

Same as CS40, with alloy frame and black slide. Limited edition. Introduced in 2000.

NIB	Exc.	V.G.	Good	Fair	Poor
1000	800	700	600	400	250

CS45

Similar to Model CS9 but chambered for .45 ACP cartridge. Barrel length 3.25". Magazine capacity 6 rounds. Weight 24 oz.

NIB	Exc.	V.G.	Good	Fair	Poor
1000	850	700	550	400	250

SD SERIES

SD9

NIB	Exc.	V.G.	Good	Fair	Poor
350	300	280	250	200	150

SD9VE

NIB	Exc.	V.G.	Good	Fair	Poor
250	200	180	150	130	100

SD40

NIB	Exc.	V.G.	Good	Fair	Poor
230	200	180	150	130	100

SIGMA SERIES

SW40F

New pistol introduced in 1994. A departure from traditional S&W pistol. Features stainless steel barrel, carbon steel slide and polymer frame. Offered in .40 S&W and 9mm calibers, with 15- and 17-round capacities.

NIB	Exc.	V.G.	Good	Fair	Poor
400	350	300	230	200	150

SW9C

Same as SW40F, with barrel and slide .5" shorter than full-size Sigma. Offered in both .40 S&W and 9mm.

NIB	Exc.	V.G.	Good	Fair	Poor
330	300	280	250	200	150

SW9M

Introduced in 1996. Chambered for 9mm cartridge. Fitted with 3.25" barrel. Magazine capacity 7 rounds. Frame is polymer and slide carbon steel. Height 4.5"; overall length 6.25"; weight 18 oz.

NIB	Exc.	V.G.	Good	Fair	Poor
400	250	220	200	180	150

SW9V

Chambered for 9mm cartridge. Fitted with 4" barrel and 10-round magazine. A traditional double-action. White dot sights are standard. Grips integral to the frame. Stainless steel slide. Satin stainless finish, with gray or black frame. Weight 25 oz. Introduced in 1997.

NIB	Exc.	V.G.	Good	Fair	Poor
450	400	350	300	250	200

SW9P

Same as Model SW9V, with a ported barrel. Introduced in 2001.

NIB	Exc.	V.G.	Good	Fair	Poor
330	300	250	200	180	150

SW9G

Same as standard SW9, with black Melonite stainless steel slide and NATO green polymer frame. Introduced in 2001.

NIB	Exc.	V.G.	Good	Fair	Poor
330	300	250	200	180	150

SW40V

Same as SW9G but chambered for .40 S&W cartridge. Weight 25 oz. Introduced in 1997.

NIB	Exc.	V.G.	Good	Fair	Poor
450	400	350	300	250	200

SW40P

Same as Model SW40V, with a ported barrel. Introduced in 2001.

NIB	Exc.	V.G.	Good	Fair	Poor
350	300	250	200	180	150

SW40G

Same as standard SW40, with black Melonite stainless steel slide and NATO green polymer frame. Introduced in 2001.

NIB	Exc.	V.G.	Good	Fair	Poor
330	300	250	200	180	150

SW380

Introduced in 1995. Chambered for .380 ACP cartridge. Barrel length 3"; overall length 5.8"; weight 14 oz. Magazine capacity 6 rounds.

NIB	Exc.	V.G.	Good	Fair	Poor
280	250	230	200	150	100

SW9E

Chambered for 9mm cartridge. Has a 4" barrel, with Tritium sights. Stainless steel slide, with black Melonite finish. Magazine capacity 10 rounds. Weight 25 oz.

NIB	Exc.	V.G.	Good	Fair	Poor
380	250	230	200	150	100

SW40E

Similar to above, but chambered for .40 S&W cartridge. Weight 24 oz.

NIB	Exc.	V.G.	Good	Fair	Poor
280	250	230	200	150	100

SW9VE

Chambered for 9mm cartridge. Fitted with a 4" barrel. Fixed sights and stainless steel slide. Weight 25 oz.

NIB	Exc.	V.G.	Good	Fair	Poor
300	280	250	230	180	100

SW40VE

Similar to above, but chambered for .40 S&W cartridge. Weight 24 oz.

NIB	Exc.	V.G.	Good	Fair	Poor
350	300	250	230	180	100

SW99

Features a polymer frame designed and manufactured in Germany by Walther. Slide and barrel manufactured by S&W in the U.S. Chambered for 9mm or .40 S&W cartridge. Fitted with 4" barrel on 9mm; 4.125" barrel on .40 S&W. Adjustable rear sights. Decocking slide-mounted lever. Barrel and slide stainless steel, with black Melonite finish. Trigger traditional double-action. Magazine capacity 10 rounds. Weight 25 oz. Introduced in 1999.

NIB	Exc.	V.G.	Good	Fair	Poor
650	600	550	400	250	150

SW99 Compact

Introduced in 2003. Similar to full size SW99, with 3.5" barrel and shorter grip frame. Chambered for both 9mm or .40 S&W cartridge. Stainless steel barrel and slide, with polymer frame. Magazine capacity: 10 rounds 9mm; 8 rounds .40 S&W. Weight 23 oz.

NIB	Exc.	V.G.	Good	Fair	Poor
600	550	500	400	250	150

SW99 .45 ACP

Same as SW99, but chambered for .45 ACP cartridge. Magazine capacity 9 rounds. Weight 26 oz. Introduced in 2003.

NIB	Exc.	V.G.	Good	Fair	Poor
500	450	400	350	250	150

SW990L Compact

Introduced in 2005. Chambered for 9mm or .40 S&W cartridge. Barrel length 3.5". Adjustable rear sight, with dot front. Polymer frame. Stainless steel slide, with Melonite finish. Plastic grips. Magazine capacity: 10 rounds 9mm; 8 rounds .40 S&W. Weight 23 oz.

NIB	Exc.	V.G.	Good	Fair	Poor
600	550	500	400	250	150

SW990L Full Size

Similar to SW990L Compact but chambered for 9mm, .40 S&W and .45 ACP cartridges. Barrel lengths: 4" for 9mm; 4.125" for .40 S&W model; 4.25" for .45 ACP. Magazine capacity: 16 rounds 9mm; 12 rounds .40 S&W. Weight 25 oz. Introduced in 2005. Note: Add $40 for .45 ACP model.

NIB	Exc.	V.G.	Good	Fair	Poor
500	450	400	350	250	150

MILITARY & POLICE (M&P) SEMI-AUTO SERIES

Model M&P 15/22P Original Quad Rail

.22 LR, no stock 6" threaded barrel pistol version of M&P 15-22 rifle, made one year only, 2010. Discontinued 2011. Scarce.

NIB	Exc.	V.G.	Good	Fair	Poor
500	400	300	—	—	—

M&P 9mm

Full-size (M&P) semi-automatic chambered in 9mm. Double-action-only (DAO), striker-fired operation. Capacity 17+1, 4.25" barrel, 6.5 lb. trigger, weight 24.25 oz. Picatinny rail and polymer frame. Optional Tritium low-light sights. Introduced 2006.

NIB	Exc.	V.G.	Good	Fair	Poor
500	420	300	220	150	80

M&P 9-JG

Similar to M&P 9mm with interchangeable palmswell grip panels, including two pink ones. Dealer sets pricing. Introduced 2008.

NIB	Exc.	V.G.	Good	Fair	Poor
480	420	300	220	150	80

M&P 9 Pro Series

Similar to M&P9 and M&P40, with green fiber-optic sights and interchangeable palmswell grip panels. Black Melonite finish. Introduced 2008.

NIB	Exc.	V.G.	Good	Fair	Poor
600	480	350	250	150	80

M&P 9L

Similar to M&P9, with 5" barrel. Introduced 2008.

NIB	Exc.	V.G.	Good	Fair	Poor
580	420	300	220	150	80

M&P 40

Full-size semi-automatic chambered in .40 S&W. First of new M&P series. Capacity 15+1, 4.25" barrel, .5 lb. trigger, weight 24.25 oz. Polymer frame and Picatinny rail. Optional Tritium low-light sights. Introduced 2006.

NIB	Exc.	V.G.	Good	Fair	Poor
500	430	300	230	150	80

M&P .357 SIG

Full-size (M&P) semi-automatic chambered in .357 Magnum. Capacity 15+1, 4.25" barrel, 6.5 lb. trigger, weight 24.25 oz. Polymer frame and Picatinny rail. Optional Tritium low-light sights. Introduced 2006.

NIB	Exc.	V.G.	Good	Fair	Poor
600	450	300	230	150	80

M&P 45

Semi-automatic similar to M&P40 in .45 ACP. Black or Dark Earth Brown finish. Introduced 2007.

NIB	Exc.	V.G.	Good	Fair	Poor
500	400	300	230	150	80

M&P 45 with Thumb Safety

Similar to above, with ambidextrous thumb safety. Introduced 2008.

NIB	Exc.	V.G.	Good	Fair	Poor
500	400	310	240	160	80

M&P 9c

Semi-automatic compact similar to M&P9, with 3.5" barrel, short grip frame and 10+1 or 12+1 capacity. Black Melonite finish. Introduced 2007.

NIB	Exc.	V.G.	Good	Fair	Poor
480	420	300	220	150	80

M&P 40c

Semi-automatic compact similar to M&P9c in .40 S&W. Black Melonite finish. Introduced 2007.

NIB	Exc.	V.G.	Good	Fair	Poor
480	420	300	220	150	80

M&P 357c

Semi-automatic compact similar to M&P40c in .357 SIG. Black Melonite finish. Introduced 2007.

NIB	Exc.	V.G.	Good	Fair	Poor
580	420	300	220	150	80

M&P Shield

Sub-compact version of M&P series in 9mm or .40 S&W. Barrel 3.1", weight 19 oz. Available in two grip lengths, with one additional round in longer magazine. Capacity: 7 or 8 rounds 9mm; 6 or 7 rounds .40 S&W. Introduced in 2012

NIB	Exc.	V.G.	Good	Fair	Poor
350	330	250	—	—	—

M&P 45 Shield

.45 ACP model of the Shield. Has all features of 9mm and .40 S&W versions, plus a more aggressive grip texture, front cocking serrations, 3.3" barrel, weight about 1.5 oz. more - 20.5 oz. Magazine capacity 6+1 or 7+1, with both magazines provided. Available with/without thumb safety. Introduced in 2016. Note: Add $70 for ported model.

NIB	Exc.	V.G.	Good	Fair	Poor
450	380	350	300	230	210

M&P C.O.R.E.

Similar to above. 9mm or .40 S&W, 10- or 17-round magazine. 5" barrel. Striker-fire trigger. 3-dot sights and optics ready. Weight 24 oz. Armornite finish. Manufactured 2013 to 2017.

NIB	Exc.	V.G.	Good	Fair	Poor
550	480	400	330	250	180

M&P BG380

Sub-compact, hammer-fired model chambered for .380 ACP cartridge. (BG) stands for Bodyguard, which should not be confused with Bodyguard .38 S&W J-frame revolver. Barrel length 2.75"; overall length 5.25"; unloaded weight listed at 12.3 oz. Available with/without thumb safety. Also offered with integrated Crimson Trace Red Laser or Crimson Trace Green Laserguard. Note: Add $80 for Red Laser; $140 for Green Laserguard.

NIB	Exc.	V.G.	Good	Fair	Poor
340	300	260	220	200	180

M&P VTAC

Caliber 9mm Parabellum/.40 S&W. Magazine capacity: 19 (9mm); 17 (.40). Stainless steel slide. Polymer frame, with Flat Dark Earth finish. Striker fired double-action-only ambidextrous slide release. Reversible magazine catch. Weight 24 oz. Barrel 4.25", with VTAC Warrior night sights.

NIB	Exc.	V.G.	Good	Fair	Poor
660	550	480	400	300	150

M&P 22

Rimfire version of M&P pistol. Striker-fired, with aluminum alloy slide and polymer frame. Magazine capacity 10 or 12 rounds. Ambidextrous thumb safety and slide release. Reversible magazine catch. Weight 24 oz. Barrel length 4.1". Introduced in 2011.

NIB	Exc.	V.G.	Good	Fair	Poor
500	450	400	300	230	150

M&P M2.0 SERIES

Calibers: 9mm, .40 S&W, .45 Auto, and 10mm. Capacities, full-size models: 17 rounds (9mm), 15 rounds (.40). Compact models: 12 (9mm), 10 (.40). Barrels: 3.6", 4.25", 5" or 5.6". Weights: 22-24 oz. Lengths: 7.6", 6.7". Grips: Polymer with three interchangeable palm swell grip sizes. Sights: Three-dot system with low-profile rear or fiber optic. Finishes: Armornite Black or Flat Dark Earth. Features: Polymer frame with a stainless steel slide, barrel, and structural components. Numerous options for finishes, sights, and operating controls.

NIB	Exc.	V.G.	Good	Fair	Poor
560	540	480	400	370	—

M&P M2.0 Compact

NIB	Exc.	V.G.	Good	Fair	Poor
520	460	390	370	330	—

M&P M2.0 Subcompact

NIB	Exc.	V.G.	Good	Fair	Poor
520	500	460	390	340	—

M&P SHIELD M2.0

Calibers: 9mm, .40 S&W, .45 Auto. Capacities: seven and eight rounds (9mm), six and seven rounds (.40). Barrel: 3.1". Weights: 18.3 oz. Lengths: 6.1". Grips: Polymer. Sights: Three-dot system with a low-profile rear. Finishes: Armornite Black. Features: Polymer frame, micro-compact size.

NIB	Exc.	V.G.	Good	Fair	Poor
430	380	330	300	240	—

M&P 380 Shield EZ

.380 ACP, 8-round magazine. 3.7" barrel. Striker-fire trigger. 3-dot sights. Grip safety. Weight 18.5 oz. Armornite finish. Introduced 2019.

NIB	Exc.	V.G.	Good	Fair	Poor
400	340	290	—	—	—

PERFORMANCE CENTER HANDGUNS

The role of Smith & Wesson's Performance Center has changed, since it was established in 1990. What was once a specialized tune-up and competition one-off production department, has now become a separate facility in providing specialized and limited handguns to the public, often with distributors participation. Change came about 1991, when Performance Center initiated its own limited edition designs. These editions are generally limited between 100 and 600 pistols for each model. Performance Center, in fact, has its own distinct product line. Performance Center pistols are made in its own shop using its own designers. One of these distributors that has played a major role in offering these special guns to the public is Lew Horton Distribution Company. This is a list of a few of the PC guns, with the suggested retail introductory price, and an estimate of the current New In Box value. Generally, for the same model, a pre-lock gun will bring more than one with an integral lock. Performance Center guns based on standard models are listed with those models in the preceding sections. The PC models listed below have model designations that do not conform to the usual S&W model name conventions.

Performance Center M&P380 Shield EZ

Caliber: .380 ACP. Capacity: 8-round magazine. Barrel: 3.67". Grips: Textured polymer. Sights: Fixed, HI-VIZ Litewave H3 Tritium/Litepipe. Length: 6.8" overall. Weight: 23 oz. unloaded. Finish: Black Armornite frame and black, silver or gold accents. Features: Easy to rack slide, grip safety, manual thumb safety, accessory rail, reversible magazine release, ported barrel and lightening cuts in slide.

NIB	Exc.	V.G.	Good	Fair	Poor
450	380	330	—	—	—

Performance Center M&P9 Shield EZ M2.0

Caliber: 9mm. Capacity: 8-round magazine. Barrel: 3.67". Grips: Textured polymer. Sights: Fixed, 3-dot. Length: 6.8" overall. Weight: 23.2 oz. unloaded. Finish: Black Armornite. Features: Accessory rail and reversible magazine release, with or without manual thumb safety.

NIB	Exc.	V.G.	Good	Fair	Poor
370	330	280	—	—	—

Performance Center M&P9 M2.0 C.O.R.E. Pro

Calibers: 9mm. Capacity: 17-round (9mm) magazine. Barrel: 4.25" or 5". Grips: Four interchangeable palm-swell inserts. Sights: Fixed, tall 3-dot/ C.O.R.E. optics-ready system. Length: 7.5"-8.5" overall. Weight: 23-27.2 oz. unloaded. Finish: Black Armornite. Features: Accessory rail, reversible magazine release and tuned action with audible trigger reset.

NIB	Exc.	V.G.	Good	Fair	Poor
640	550	450	—	—	—

Performance Center M&P9 M2.0 Ported

Calibers: 9mm. Capacity: 17-round (9mm) magazine. Barrel: 4.25" or 5". Grips: Four interchangeable palm-swell inserts. Sights: Fixed, fiber-optic front and rear. Length: 8.5" overall. Weight: 23 oz. unloaded. Finish: Black Armornite. Features: Accessory rail, reversible magazine release, ported barrel and slide and tuned action with audible trigger reset.

NIB	Exc.	V.G.	Good	Fair	Poor
640	550	450	—	—	—

Performance Center M&P9 M2.0 Ported C.O.R.E.

Calibers: 9mm. Capacity: 17-round (9mm) magazine. Barrel: 4.25" or 5". Grips: Four interchangeable palm-swell inserts. Sights: Fixed, tall 3-dot/C.O.R.E. optics-ready system. Length: 8.5" overall. Weight: 23 oz. unloaded. Finish: Black Armornite. Features: Accessory rail, reversible magazine release, oversized slide release, ported barrel and slide, and tuned action with audible trigger reset.

NIB	Exc.	V.G.	Good	Fair	Poor
650	550	450	—	—	—

Performance Center M&P9 M2.0 Compact

Caliber: 9mm. Capacity: 15-round magazine. Barrel: 4". Grips: Four interchangeable palm-swell inserts. Sights: Fixed, steel 3-dot. Length: 7.3" overall. Weight: 26.6 oz. unloaded. Finish: FDE. Features: Accessory rail, with or without manual thumb safety.

NIB	Exc.	V.G.	Good	Fair	Poor
500	400	300	—	—	—

Performance Center M&P40 M2.0 Ported

Calibers: .40 S&W. Capacity: 15-round (.40 S&W) magazine. Barrel: 4.25" or 5". Grips: Four interchangeable palm-swell inserts. Sights: Fixed, fiber-optic front and rear. Length: 8.5" overall. Weight: 23 oz. unloaded. Finish: Black Armornite. Features: Accessory rail, reversible magazine release, ported barrel and slide and tuned action with audible trigger reset.

NIB	Exc.	V.G.	Good	Fair	Poor
640	550	450	—	—	—

Performance Center M&P40 M2.0 Ported C.O.R.E.

Calibers: .40 S&W. Capacity: 15-round (.40 S&W) magazine. Barrel: 4.25" or 5". Grips: Four interchangeable palm-swell inserts. Sights: Fixed, tall 3-dot/C.O.R.E. optics-ready system. Length: 8.5" overall. Weight: 23 oz. unloaded. Finish: Black Armornite. Features: Accessory rail, reversible magazine release, oversized slide release, ported barrel and slide, and tuned action with audible trigger reset.

NIB	Exc.	V.G.	Good	Fair	Poor
650	550	450	—	—	—

Performance Center M&P40 M2.0 C.O.R.E. Pro

Calibers: .40 S&W. Capacity: 15-round (.40 S&W) magazine. Barrel: 4.25" or 5". Grips: Four interchangeable palm-swell inserts. Sights: Fixed, tall 3-dot/C.O.R.E. optics-ready system. Length: 7.5"-8.5" overall. Weight: 23-27.2 oz. unloaded. Finish: Black Armornite. Features: Accessory rail, reversible magazine release and tuned action with audible trigger reset.

NIB	Exc.	V.G.	Good	Fair	Poor
640	550	450	—	—	—

.40 S&W Tactical Performance Center

Limited edition semi-automatic handgun offered exclusively by Lew Horton through Performance Center. Special pistol fitted with 5" match-grade barrel, hand-fit spherical barrel bushing, custom-tuned action, special trigger job, oversized frame and slide rails, wrap-around straight backstrap grip. Replaceable front and Novak rear sights. Special serial numbers. Offered in 1992. Limited to 200 units.

NIB	Exc.	V.G.	Good	Fair	Poor
2500	2100	1800	—	—	—

.40 S&W Compensated Performance Center

Similar to .40 S&W Tactical, but furnished with 4.625" barrel and single chamber compensator. Also a Lew Horton/Performance pistol. Production of 250 units. Offered in 1992.

NIB	Exc.	V.G.	Good	Fair	Poor
2700	2300	1950	—	—	—

.40 S&W Performance Action Pistol Performance Center

Offered in limited quantities in 1990. This Performance Center .40 S&W semi-automatic pistol was used by the Smith & Wesson shooting team. Frame and barrel are stainless steel with blued carbon steel slide, two port compensator, two fitted and numbered 13-round magazines, 5.25" match-grade barrel, extended frame beavertail, square combat triggerguard, oversize magazine release button, spherical barrel bushing, wrap-around straight backstrap grip, extended magazine funnel and BoMar adjustable rear sight. Action is tuned for accuracy and precision.

NIB	Exc.	V.G.	Good	Fair	Poor
2700	2300	1950	—	—	—

SHORTY SERIES

The Shorty models have recently been offered at online sources at significantly higher values, sometimes more than $2,000. They had languished for years at or below original MSRP, but recently sellers have latched on to the low production numbers and asking prices may reflect that perception. NIB values listed are our best guess at current market value.

"Shorty-Forty" .40 S&W Performance Center

Introduced in 1992. Available exclusively from Lew Horton. Limited edition Performance Center pistol features light alloy frame, oversize slide rails and spherical barrel bushing. Match-grade barrel is joined to a custom tuned action. Special serial numbers.

NIB	Exc.	V.G.	Good	Fair	Poor
1600	1350	1150	—	—	—

"Shorty Forty" Mark III Performance Center

Offered in 1995. A Lew Horton exclusive features low-mount adjustable sights, hand-fitted titanium barrel bushing, checkered front strap. Action has been hand honed. Sold with two magazines: one 11 rounds; other 9 rounds.

NIB	Exc.	V.G.	Good	Fair	Poor
1500	1300	1100	—	—	—

Shorty .45 Performance Center

Introduced by Lew Horton in 1996. This .45 ACP pistol has a hand-fitted titanium barrel bushing, oversize frame and slide rails, match-grade barrel, checkered front strap, hand-honed double-action and special serial numbers.

NIB	Exc.	V.G.	Good	Fair	Poor
1500	1300	1100	—	—	—

Shorty Nine Performance Center

Lew Horton exclusive limited to 100 units. Features hand-fitted titanium barrel bushing, oversize slide rails, action job, low mount adjustable sights, checkered front strap, match-grade barrel and two-tone finish. Furnished with two 12-round magazines.

NIB	Exc.	V.G.	Good	Fair	Poor
1500	1300	1100	—	—	—

9 Recon Performance Center

A RSR exclusive introduced in 1999. Chambered for 9mm cartridge. Fitted with 3.5" barrel. Rear sight Novak Lo-Mount. Hogue wrap-around rubber grips. Slide black carbon steel, with alloy frame. Magazine capacity 12 rounds. Weight 27 oz.

NIB	Exc.	V.G.	Good	Fair	Poor
3000	2500	2000	1500	—	—

Performance Center .45 Limited

A Lew Horton full-size single-action pistol. Hand-fitted titanium barrel bushing, fitted slide lock, match-grade barrel, adjustable sights, oversize magazine well, tuned action and checkered front strap.

45 Recon Performance Center

Another RSR pistol. Chambered for .45 ACP cartridge. An enhanced version of "Shorty 45". The 4.25" barrel is ported, with Novak Lo-Mount sights. Hogue wrap-around rubber grips. Stainless steel slide and barrel, with aluminum frame. Weight 28 oz. Magazine capacity 7 rounds. Matte black finish. Furnished with aluminum case.

NIB	Exc.	V.G.	Good	Fair	Poor
1500	1300	1100	—	—	—

Shorty .356 TSW Performance Center

This new cartridge also available in another Lew Horton/Performance Center limited edition pistol with 4" barrel. Features a steel frame and hand-fitted slide, with spherical barrel bushing. Double-action custom tuned by Performance Center. Magazine holds 12 rounds. Similar in appearance to "Shorty-Forty". Offered in 1993. Special serial numbers.

NIB	Exc.	V.G.	Good	Fair	Poor
2200	1600	1350	—	—	—

Model .356 TSW "Limited Series" Performance Center

A Lew Horton gun. Chambered for new .356 TSW caliber (TSW stands for Team Smith & Wesson). A new caliber, actually 9mm x 21.5mm cartridge, with ballistics of around 1,235 fps with 147-grain bullet. Designed as a low-end .357 competition pistol. Built for the competitive shooter (IPSC) it features a 15-round magazine and distinctive profile and markings. Single-action trigger is adjustable for reach while slide, frame and barrel are custom fitted. Comes with a spherical barrel bushing and adjustable BoMar sights. Frame grip is checked 20 lpi. Magazine well is extended as is magazine release. Magazine is fitted with a pad.

NIB	Exc.	V.G.	Good	Fair	Poor
2700	1900	1600	—	—	—

Model .45 CQB Combat Performance Center

Introduced in 1998. This Lew Horton model features a 4" match-grade barrel. Novak Lo-Mount sights. Double-action trigger, with ambidextrous decocker. Available in both matte black and stainless steel finish. Matte black model has alloy frame; weight about 30 oz. Stainless steel version has stainless frame; weight 38 oz.

NIB	Exc.	V.G.	Good	Fair	Poor
1800	1500	1250	—	—	—

Schofield Model of 2000

Reintroduction in 2000 by S&W Performance Center of the famous Schofield revolver. Single-action top-break model chambered for .45 Colt cartridge. Barrel length 7". Frame and barrel are blue, hammer and trigger are casehardened. Sights are fixed rear notch and half-moon post front. Walnut grips. Weight 40 oz. In 2002, offered in 7" nickel version as well as 5" blue and 5" nickel configuration.

NIB	Exc.	V.G.	Good	Fair	Poor
1050	800	650	500	300	210

SMITH & WESSON LONG ARMS

.320 Revolving Rifle (Antique)

Model is a rare and unique prize to a S&W collector. Revolving Rifle chambered for .320 S&W Revolving Rifle cartridge. Has a 6-shot fluted cylinder. Offered with 16", 18" and 20" barrel. Only 76 rifles are nickel plated and remainder of production are blued. Butt rounded, with mottled red hard rubber checkered grips and forearm of the same material. Detachable shoulder stock, with black hard rubber buttplate featuring S&W logo. Rifle furnished in a leather carrying case, with accessories. As fine a firearm as this was, it was a commercial failure for S&W, which finally came to the realization the public did not want a revolving rifle. It manufactured only 977 of them between 1879 and 1887. Note: Values are for a complete unit. Deduct 40% without stock. Add 10% for 16" or 20" barrels.

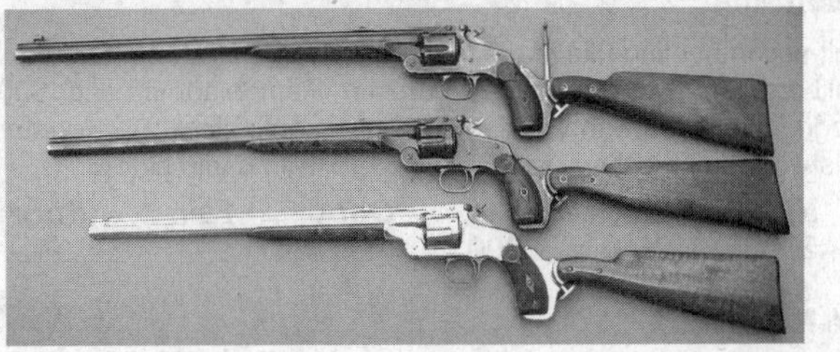

Jim Supica photo

Exc.	Fine	V.G.	Good	Fair	Poor
17000	9000	6500	4000	2500	1200

Model A Rifle

Bolt-action with 23.75" barrel, chambered for .22-250, .243, .270, .308, .30-06, 7mm Magnum and .300 Win. Magnum. Folding rear sight. Checkered Monte Carlo stock, with contrasting rosewood forend tip. Pistol grip cap. Manufactured for S&W by Husqvarna of Sweden, from 1969 to 1972.

NIB	Exc.	V.G.	Good	Fair	Poor
750	700	500	350	250	150

Model B

Similar to Model A Rifle, with Schnabel forend and 20.75" barrel.

NIB	Exc.	V.G.	Good	Fair	Poor
800	750	600	350	250	150

Model C

Similar to Model B Rifle, with cheekpiece.

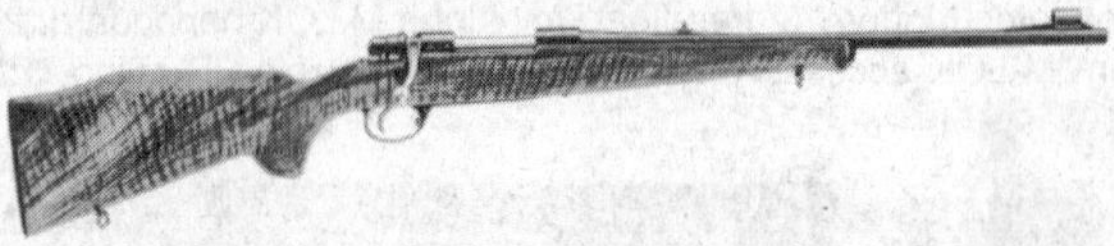

NIB	Exc.	V.G.	Good	Fair	Poor
800	650	500	350	250	150

Model D

Similar to Model C Rifle, with Mannlicher-style stock.

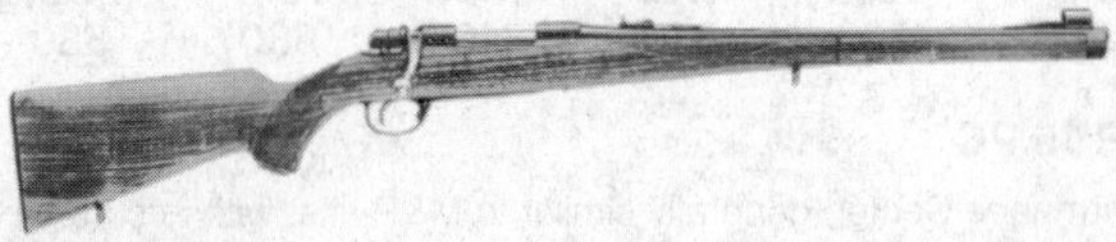

NIB	Exc.	V.G.	Good	Fair	Poor
1200	900	600	400	300	200

Model 1500 Series

Bolt-action series of hunting rifles made for S&W by Howa of Japan in 1983 and 1984. Calibers included .222 Rem., .223 Rem., .22-250 Rem., .243 Win., .25-06 Rem., .270 Win., 7mm Rem. Magnum, .308 Win., .30-06 and .300 Win. Magnum. Offered in several variations with blue or stainless receiver, plain or checkered wood stock (Deluxe model). Barrel lengths 22", except 24" for Magnum calibers. Heavy barrel varmint version was available. Model 1700 Classic Hunter was similar, except for a removable magazine and schnabel forend. Note: Add 10% for Deluxe or Varmint model; 15% for Model 1700. Premium for deluxe varmint heavy barrel.

NIB	Exc.	V.G.	Good	Fair	Poor
800	700	600	500	250	200

I-Bolt Rifle

Bolt-action hunting rifle made in the U.S.A. by S&W, from 2008 to 2009. Calibers .25-06, .270 Win., .30-06, 7mm Rem. Magnum and .300 Win. Magnum. Offered with wood, synthetic or camo stock. Blue or stainless finish. Integral Picatinny rail. Note: Add 10% for camo stock.

NIB	Exc.	V.G.	Good	Fair	Poor
300	250	200	—	—	—

M&P SERIES

M&P 15 Military & Police Tactical Rifle/Modern Sporting Rifle

Gas-operated semi-automatic built along lines of AR-15. Caliber 5.56mm NATO. Magazine capacity 30. Barrel 16". 1:9. Stock 6-position telescoping composite. Weight 6.74 lbs. unloaded. Sights, adjustable front and rear. Many other variations in addition to those listed below. Introduced 2006.

M&P15

Carry handle/rear sight adjustable up to 600 meters; chrome-lined bore and chamber.

NIB	Exc.	V.G.	Good	Fair	Poor
1000	850	720	610	520	440

M&P15A

No longer in production. Flattop receiver.

NIB	Exc.	V.G.	Good	Fair	Poor
1000	850	720	610	520	440

M&P15 Competition

Performance Center build. Has Performance Center muzzle brake, two-stage match trigger, 15" free-float Troy Alpha M-LOK handguard, 2" aluminum M-LOK accessory rail, VLTOR I-Mod stock, 5R rifling, 1:8 RH twist.

NIB	Exc.	V.G.	Good	Fair	Poor
1200	1020	870	740	630	530

M&P 15 PC

Performance Center, generally similar to M&P rifle, with accurized tubular floated barrel, 2-stage match trigger, 20" matte stainless barrel. Advantage MAX-1 camouflage, no sights. Introduced 2007. Early variation as pictured worth 50% premium.

NIB	Exc.	V.G.	Good	Fair	Poor
1200	1020	870	740	630	530

M&P 15 Sport

More economical addition to M&P rifle line. Chambered for 5.56 NATO, with black-anodized upper and lower receiver of 7075 T6 aluminum. Polymer handguard, 16" 4140 steel barrel, 1:8 rate of twist. Adjustable sights, single-stage trigger, chrome-lined gas key and bolt carrier. Flash suppressor compensator. Introduced in 2011.

NIB	Exc.	V.G.	Good	Fair	Poor
550	470	400	340	290	240

M&P15 SPORT II SERIES

M&P15T

No carry handle; folding battle sight. Production gun in 2019 has 13" M&P Slim Modular Free-Float Rail System with Magpul M-LOK capability, 2" M-LOK Picatinny-Style Rail Panels, and Magpul MBUS Sights.

NIB	Exc.	V.G.	Good	Fair	Poor
1000	850	720	610	520	440

Caliber: 5.56mm NATO/.223. Capacity: 30-shot steel magazine. Barrel: 16", 1:9" twist. Weight: 6.74 lbs., w/o magazine. Lengths: 32" to 35". overall. Stock: Black synthetic. Sights: Adjustable post front sight, adjustable dual aperture rear sight. Features: six-position telescopic stock, thermo-set M4 handguard. 14.75" sight radius. 7-lb. (approx.) trigger pull. 7075 T6 aluminum upper, 4140 steel barrel. OR (Optics Ready) model has Crimson Trace CTS-103 Red/Green Dot Electronic Sight. Hardcoat black-anodized receiver and barrel finish. Made in USA. SEE POLITICAL PANIC PRICING.

M&P15 Sport II

Caliber: 5.56mm NATO/.223. Capacity: 30-shot steel magazine. Barrel: 16", 1:9 twist. Weight: 6.74 lbs., w/o magazine. Lengths: 32" to 35" overall. Stock: Black synthetic. Sights: Adjustable post front sight, adjustable dual aperture rear sight. Features: 6-position telescopic stock, thermo-set M4 handguard. 14.75" sight radius. 7-lb. (approx.) trigger pull. 7075 T6 aluminum upper, 4140 steel barrel. OR (Optics Ready) model has Crimson Trace CTS-103 Red/Green Dot Electronic Sight. Hardcoat black-anodized receiver and barrel finish. Made in USA.

NIB	Exc.	V.G.	Good	Fair	Poor
700	600	480	—	—	—

M&P15 Sport II 12938

Fixed stock, CA compliant. Crimson Trace CTS-103 Red/Green Dot Electronic Sight. Similar No. 12055 lacks the optic.

NIB	Exc.	V.G.	Good	Fair	Poor
700	600	500	—	—	—

M&P15 Sport II 12024

Supplied with Magpul MOE M-LOK Carbine-Length Handguard and 2" M-LOK Picatinny-style rail panel.

NIB	Exc.	V.G.	Good	Fair	Poor
680	550	480	—	—	—

M&P15 Sport II 12937

10-round magazine. Crimson Trace CTS-103 Red/Green Dot Electronic Sight.

NIB	Exc.	V.G.	Good	Fair	Poor
800	650	550	—	—	—

M&P15 Sport II Optics Ready Promo Kit

Comes with Caldwell Mag Charger TAC-30 (397493), Duty Series Gun Case 110014, and Crimson Trace CTS-103 Red/Green Dot Electronic Sight. Model 12096 is similar but has 10-round magazine and lacks optic.

Model 12095 is similar but lacks optic.

NIB	Exc.	V.G.	Good	Fair	Poor
750	620	500	—	—	—

M&P 15VTAC Viking Tactics

AR-style semi-automatic rifle chambered in .223 Rem./5.56 NATO. Six-position CAR stock. 16" barrel. Surefire flash-hider and G2 light with VTAC light mount; VTAC/JP handguard; JP single-stage match trigger and speed hammer; three adjustable Picatinny rails; VTAC padded two-point adjustable sling. Overall length 35" extended; 32" collapsed. Weight 6.5 lbs. 30-round magazine.

NIB	Exc.	V.G.	Good	Fair	Poor
1450	1320	1120	950	810	690

M&P15 VTAC II Viking Tactics

No. 811025.5R Rifling, VTAC/Troy 13" Battlerail Alpha Handguard, Smith & Wesson Flash Suppressor, Geissele Super-V Trigger, Viking Tactics Light Mount, Tactical Sling, LPSM Low-Profile Sling Mount. Discontinued.

NIB	Exc.	V.G.	Good	Fair	Poor
1500	1280	1080	920	780	670

M&P15PS (Piston)

Introduced 2009. Similar to AR-derived M&P15, with gas piston. Chambered in 5.56 NATO. Features adjustable gas port, optional Troy quad mount handguard, chromed bore/gas key/bolt carrier/chamber, 6-position telescoping or MagPul MOE stock, flattop or folding MBUS sights, aluminum receiver, alloy upper and lower, black anodized finish, 30-round magazine,16" barrel with birdcage. No. 812006 has standard handguard); PSX had Troy quad mount handguard.

M&P15 PS 812006

NIB	Exc.	V.G.	Good	Fair	Poor
1030	880	740	630	540	460

M&P15 PSX 811023

NIB	Exc.	V.G.	Good	Fair	Poor
1150	980	830	710	600	510

M&P15 300 Whisper

Chambered for .300 Whisper cartridge. Comes with/without suppressor. Stock and forend in Realtree APG camo. No. 811302 (black) and No. 811300 (camo). Discontinued.

NIB	Exc.	V.G.	Good	Fair	Poor
880	740	630	540	460	390

M&P15X 11535

New, M&P slim, aluminum carbine-length handguard with Magpul M-LOK.

NIB	Exc.	V.G.	Good	Fair	Poor
1100	940	800	680	570	490

M&P15X 811008

Troy carbine-length handguard and Troy rear folding battle sight.

NIB	Exc.	V.G.	Good	Fair	Poor
1030	880	740	630	540	460

M&P15R

This variation chambered for Russian 5.45x39mm cartridge. Made from 2008 to 2011.

NIB	Exc.	V.G.	Good	Fair	Poor
850	720	610	520	440	380

M&P15P

NIB	Exc.	V.G.	Good	Fair	Poor
700	600	500	—	—	—

M&P15-22

.22 LR rimfire verson of AR-derived M&P tactical autoloader. Features include blowback action, 15.5" or 16" barrel, 6-position telescoping or fixed stock, quad mount Picatinny rails, plain barrel or compensator, alloy upper and lower, matte black finish, 10- or 25-round magazine.

NIB	Exc.	V.G.	Good	Fair	Poor
430	350	300	—	—	—

M&P15 VOLUNTEER XV SERIES

Caliber: 5.56mm NATO/.223. Capacity: 30-shot steel magazine. Barrel: 16" 4140 steel, 1:8" twist. Flat-faced trigger. BCM Gunfighter forend with M-LOK attachments. Gas block with integral Picatinny-style rail. B5 Systems Bravo Stock and P-Grip 23 pistol grip. Chromed firing pin. Forward assist. A2 flash suppressor. Adjustable A2 front sight post. Forged integral triggerguard. Armornite finish on barrel (internal and external). Weight: 8.8 lbs. Length: 36.25" No. 13507. Introduced 2022. SEE POLITICAL PANIC PRICING.

NIB	Exc.	V.G.	Good	Fair	Poor
970	850	700	500	—	—

M&P15 Volunteer XV Optics Ready

Caliber: 5.56mm NATO/.223. Similar to Volunteer XV except has a gas block with integral Picatinny-style rail. Weight: 9 lbs. Length: 36.25". No. 13510. Introduced 2022. SEE POLITICAL PANIC PRICING.

NIB	Exc.	V.G.	Good	Fair	Poor
970	850	700	500	—	—

M&P15 Volunteer XV Red Dot Sight

Caliber: 5.56mm NATO/.223. Similar to Volunteer XV except has a gas block with integral Picatinny-style rail and includes Crimson Trace red-dot sight. Weight: 9.375 lbs. Length: 36.25". No. 13513. Introduced 2022. SEE POLITICAL PANIC PRICING.

NIB	Exc.	V.G.	Good	Fair	Poor
1050	900	700	—	—	—

M&P15 Volunteer XV Pro

Caliber: 5.56mm NATO/.223. Similar to Volunteer XV except has a gas block with integral Picatinny-style rail, B5 SOPMOD stock, and upright B5 grip. Mid-length gas system, 15-in. aluminum S&W M-LOK forend. Primary Weapons Systems muzzle brake, and 5R rifling. Sights: WGS Tactical Folding Sight front and rear. 16" target crowned, threaded barrel (No. 13515) or 14.5" (No. 13516), the latter with a pinned flash hider. Weight: 6.8 lbs. Length: 36.75". Introduced 2022. SEE POLITICAL PANIC PRICING.

NIB	*Exc.*	*V.G.*	*Good*	*Fair*	*Poor*
1400	1250	1000	730	—	—

M&P15 Volunteer XV DMR

Caliber: 5.56mm NATO/.223. Similar to Volunteer XV Pro except rifle-length gas system and 20" barrel (No. 13517). Weight: 8.125 lbs. Length: 40.7" Introduced 2022. SEE POLITICAL PANIC PRICING.

NIB	*Exc.*	*V.G.*	*Good*	*Fair*	*Poor*
1450	1300	1120	950	—	—

M&P10 SPORT SERIES

M&P10

Caliber: .308 Win., 6.5 Creedmoor. Capacity: 10 rounds. Barrel: 18" to 20". Weight: 7.7 pounds. Features: Magpul MOE stock with MOE Plus grip, 15-in. free-float Troy M-LOK handguard, black hard anodized finish. Camo-finish hunting model available w/5-round magazine. Add 18% for 6.5 Creedmoor version.

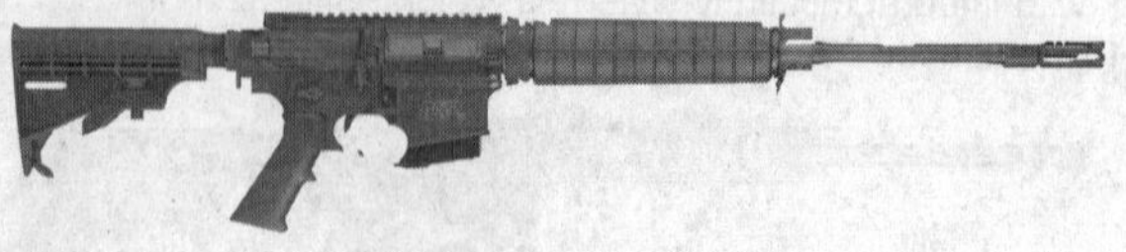

NIB	*Exc.*	*V.G.*	*Good*	*Fair*	*Poor*
1300	1060	900	770	650	560

M&P10 PC 6.5 Creedmoor

NIB	*Exc.*	*V.G.*	*Good*	*Fair*	*Poor*
2000	1850	1600	1250	—	—

M&P10 Sport Optics Ready

Caliber: .308 Win., 6.5 Creedmoor. Capacity: 10 rounds. Barrel: 18" to 20". Weight: 7.7 pounds. Features: Magpul MOE stock with MOE Plus grip, 15" free-float Troy M-LOK handguard, black hard-anodized finish. Camo-finish hunting model available w/five-round magazine. SEE POLITICAL PANIC PRICING.

NIB	*Exc.*	*V.G.*	*Good*	*Fair*	*Poor*
1060	900	720	500	—	—

SHOTGUNS

Model 916

Series of slide-action shotguns made in U.S.A. by S&W, from 1972 to 1981. Made in 12-, 16- and 20-gauge in various barrel lengths, with Fixed chokes. Ventilated rib or plain barrel. Offered in both solid-frame and take-down versions. Note: Add 10% for ventilated rib; 10% for takedown model.

NIB	*Exc.*	*V.G.*	*Good*	*Fair*	*Poor*
500	400	300	250	180	150

Model 3000

Slide-action shotgun made in Japan by Howa, for S&W. Imported from 1982 to about 1989. In 12- or 20-gauge, with 3" chamber, checkered wood stock and forend. Fixed chokes or choke tubes. Standard barrel lengths 26", 28" or 30". Also offered in 18" or 20" in police model; 22" in a slug gun with rifle sights. Note: Add 10% for choke tubes.

NIB	*Exc.*	*V.G.*	*Good*	*Fair*	*Poor*
600	500	400	300	200	150

Model 1000

Series of gas-operated semi-automatic shotguns patterned after Rem. Model 1100. Offered in 12- or 20-gauge, with barrel lengths from 22" to 30" with Fixed chokes or interchangeable tubes. Checkered walnut stock and forend. Engraved aluminum receiver. Available in several variations including waterfowl, trap and skeet models. Note: Add 25% for waterfowl; 50% for trap. Premium for 20 gauge.

NIB	*Exc.*	*V.G.*	*Good*	*Fair*	*Poor*
600	500	400	300	200	150

Model 1012/1020

Series of gas-operated semi-automatics imported by S&W from Turkey, from 2007 to 2009. Available in 12-gauge (1012) or 20-gauge (1020), with barrel lengths from 24" to 30" and five choke tubes. Stock adjustable for length and drop. Satin-finished walnut or black synthetic stock or total camo coverage. Note: Add 20% for camo coverage; 30% for 3.5" 12-gauge model.

NIB	*Exc.*	*V.G.*	*Good*	*Fair*	*Poor*
500	400	300	250	200	150

Elite Gold & Silver Series

Elite Gold side-by-side in 20-gauge only, with quality double-gun features. Grade III checkered walnut stock, with English-style straight-/pistol grip. Choice of single/double triggers. Automatic ejectors, color case-hardened frame, Fixed chokes of IC/M or M/F. Barrel lengths 26" or 28". Weight about 6.5 lbs. Elite Silver an over/under in 12-gauge only. Features similar to Elite Gold, except has five choke tubes, single trigger and recoil pad. Weight about 7.5 lbs. Both of these models imported from Turkey, from 2007 to 2010.

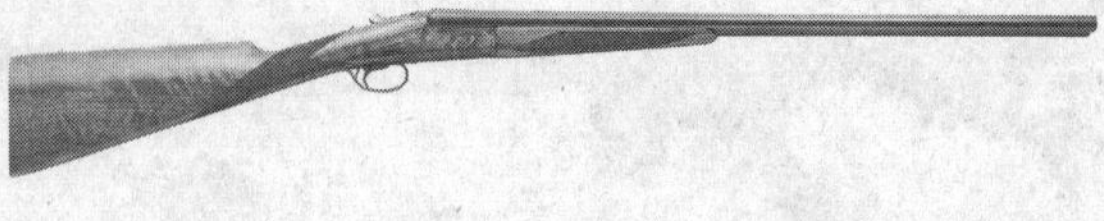

NIB	*Exc.*	*V.G.*	*Good*	*Fair*	*Poor*
2500	1800	1500	—	—	—

M&P-12

Gauge: 12 ga. 3". Barrel: 19". Length: 27.8". Weight: 8.3 lbs. Stock: Black synthetic with fixed stock. Features: Single barrel pump-action shotgun with two independent magazine tubes. Capacity of seven rounds of 2-3/4" shells or six rounds of 3" shells per tube. Vertical foregrip, action lock lever button, and push button mag tube selector. Ships with four interchangeable pistol grip palm swell inserts. Picatinny top rail, M-LOK barrel slots. Includes Rem-Choke-style choke tubes (M, C), choke wrench, and foam-lined hard gun case.

NIB	Exc.	V.G.	Good	Fair	Poor
1030	—	—	—	—	—

SNAKE CHARMER

Sporting Arms Manufacturing, Inc.
Little Field, Texas

Snake Charmer

A .410 bore single-shot shotgun, with 18.5" barrel. Stainless steel, with composition stock.

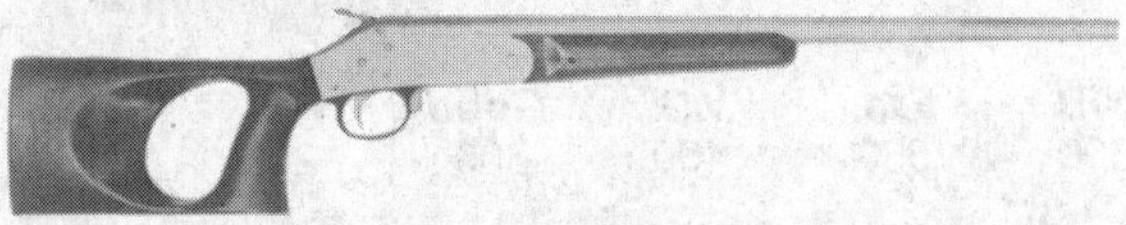

NIB	Exc.	V.G.	Good	Fair	Poor
200	120	100	80	50	20

SNEIDER, CHARLES E.

Baltimore, Maryland

Two-Cylinder Revolver Antique

A .22-caliber spur trigger revolver, with 2.75" octagonal barrel and twin 7-shot cylinders that can be pivoted. Barrel marked "E. Sneider Pat. March 1862". Produced in limited quantities during 1860s. Too rare to estimate values, no recent sales found. Value might be in $5000-$25,000 range.

SODIA, FRANZ

Ferlach, Austria

A wide variety of double-barrel shotguns, drillings and combination shotgun/rifles are made by this maker.

SOKOLOVSKY CORP. SPORT ARMS

Sunnyvale, California

.45 Automaster

A .45-caliber stainless steel semi-automatic pistol, with 6" barrel fitted with Millet adjustable sights and 6-shot magazine. Approximately 50 pistols have been made since 1984.

NIB	Exc.	V.G.	Good	Fair	Poor
4850	3800	2750	2000	1500	500

SPALDING & FISHER

Worcester, Massachusetts

Double Barreled Pistol Antique

A .36-caliber percussion double-barrel pocket pistol, with 5.5" barrels, blued iron frame and walnut grips. Top of barrels marked "Spalding & Fisher". Produced during 1850s.

Exc.	Fine	V.G.	Good	Fair	Poor
1350	920	660	400	100	70

SPANG & WALLACE

Philadelphia, Pennsylvania

Pocket Pistol Antique

A .36-caliber percussion pocket pistol, with 2.5" to 6" barrel, German silver furniture and checkered walnut stock. Barrel marked "Spang & Wallace/Phila.". Manufactured during late 1840s and early 1850s.

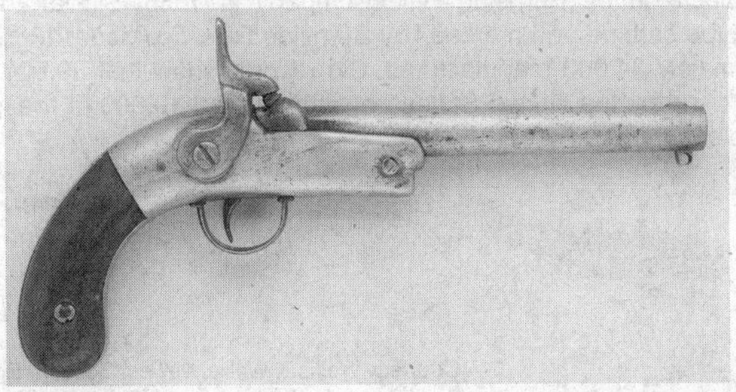

Courtesy Bonhams & Butterfields

Exc.	Fine	V.G.	Good	Fair	Poor
2850	1500	1120	750	200	140

SPENCER

Boston, Massachusetts

Spencer Model 1860 Carbine Antique

One of the most popular firearms used by Union forces during the Civil War. Chambered for a metallic rimfire cartridge known as "No. 56". It's actually a .52-caliber and made with a copper case. Barrel is 22" in length. Finish blued, with a carbine-length walnut stock held on by one barrel band. There is a sling swivel at the butt. Approximately 50,000 manufactured between 1863 and 1865.

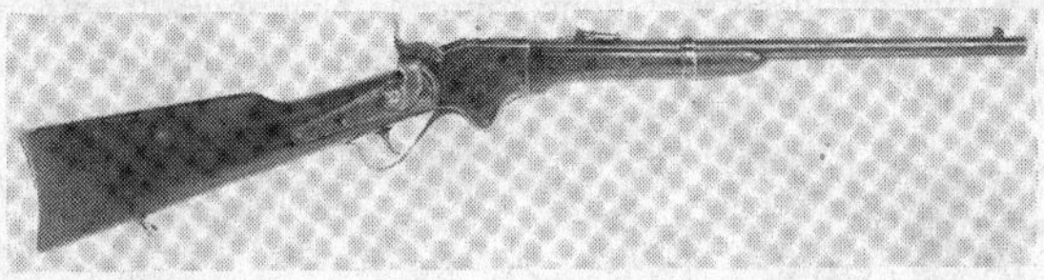

Exc.	Fine	V.G.	Good	Fair	Poor
7500	5000	3750	2500	750	350

Military Rifle—Navy Model Antique

Similar to the carbine, with 30" round barrel and full-length walnut stock held on by three barrel bands. Features an iron forend tip and sling swivels. Civil War production consisted of two models. A Navy model manufactured between 1862 and 1864 (approximately 1,000 of these so marked).

Exc.	Fine	V.G.	Good	Fair	Poor
10000	7500	6250	5000	1000	700

Military Rifle—Army Model Antique

Approximately 11,450 produced for the Army during the Civil War. Similar to Navy model, except front sight doubles as a bayonet lug. Manufactured in 1863 and 1864.

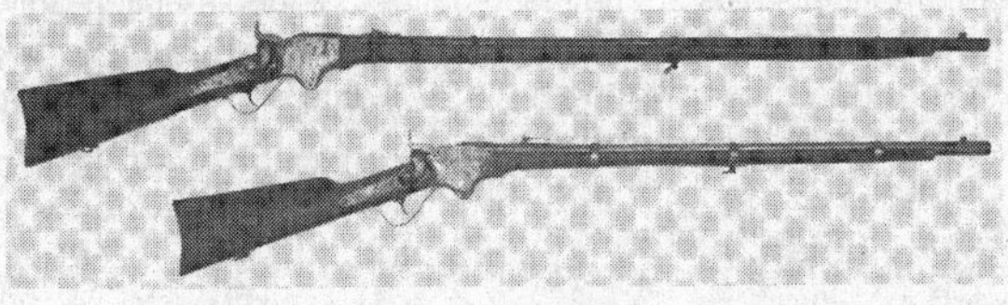

Courtesy Milwaukee Public Museum, Milwaukee, Wisconsin

Exc.	Fine	V.G.	Good	Fair	Poor
8000	6000	4250	2500	600	420

Springfield Armory Post-war Alteration (Antique)

After conclusion of the Civil War, approximately 11,000 carbines were refurbished and rechambered for .50-caliber rimfire. Barrels were sleeved and a device known as "Stabler cut-off" was added to convert the arm to single-shot function. Often they were refinished and restocked. Inspector's marks "ESA" will be found in an oval cartouche on left side of the stock. These alterations took place in 1867 and 1868.

Exc.	*Fine*	*V.G.*	*Good*	*Fair*	*Poor*
5250	3950	2820	1700	500	350

Model 1865 Carbine (Antique)

Manufactured by Burnside Rifle Company in 1865. Similar to Civil War-type carbine and marked "By Burnside Rifle Co./Model 1865". Approximately 34,000 manufactured. Old records show that 30,500 were purchased by the United States government and 19,000 of these had "Stabler cut-off" device.

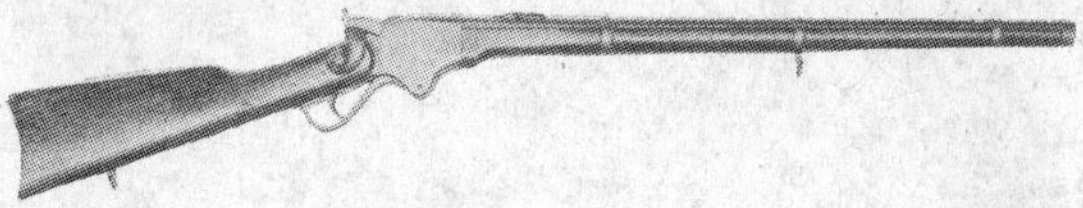

Courtesy Wallis & Wallis, Lewes, Sussex, England

Exc.	*Fine*	*V.G.*	*Good*	*Fair*	*Poor*
7000	4000	3000	2000	700	350

SPENCER ARMS CO.
Windsor, Connecticut

Slide-Action Shotgun (Antique)

From 1882 to 1889, they manufactured the first successful slide action repeating shotgun. Designed by Christopher M. Spencer, who also designed Civil War era Spencer military carbines. Shotgun came in both solid and take-down, in 10- and 12-gauge. In 1890, Francis Bannerman & Sons of New York, bought patents and machinery and moved the operation to Brooklyn, New York. They produced what is known as Spencer Bannerman models from 1890 to 1907. Later Bannerman models are worth 50 percent less than Spencer models. Note: Add 20 percent premium for take-down model; 10 percent premium for 10-gauge models.

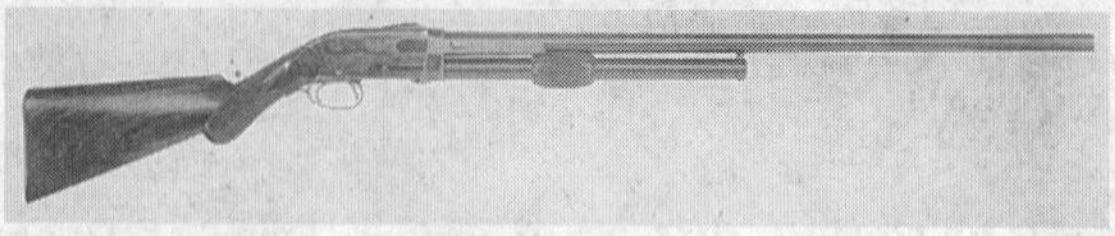

Exc.	*Fine*	*V.G.*	*Good*	*Fair*	*Poor*
2000	1200	700	500	300	150

SPENCER REVOLVER
Maltby, Henley & Company
New York, New York

Safety Hammerless Revolver (Antique)

See SMITH, OTIS A.

SPHINX
Sphinx Engineering SA
Porrentru, Switzerland
Imported by Sile Distributors Inc.

AT-380

Semi-automatic pistol is a small .380-caliber in double-action-only. Magazine capacity 11 rounds. Offered in stainless steel, blued or two-tone finish. Barrel 3.27"; overall length 6.03". Sights are fixed and grips are black checkered plastic. Weight 25 oz.

NIB	*Exc.*	*V.G.*	*Good*	*Fair*	*Poor*
600	550	400	300	200	100

AT-2000 SERIES PISTOLS

A series number applied to several different variations of the same basic design. Based on CZ 75 pistol. AT-2000 is a semi-automatic pistol, offered in 9mm and .40 S&W. Barrel lengths are different depending on variation, but AT-2000 can be converted from double-action to double only in just a matter of minutes.

AT-2000S/SDA

Chambered for 9mm or .40 S&W cartridge. Barrel length 4.53". Overall length 8.12". Magazine capacity: 15 rounds for 9mm; 13 rounds for .40 S&W. Available in double-action (S) or double-action-only (SDA). Offered with two-tone or all blued finish. Weight 35 oz.

NIB	*Exc.*	*V.G.*	*Good*	*Fair*	*Poor*
1500	1150	880	680	600	300

AT-2000P/PDA

Slightly smaller of the AT-2000S. Magazine capacity: 13 rounds for 9mm; 11 rounds for .40 S&W. Features the same, except barrel length 3.66". Overall length 7.25"; weight 31 oz.

NIB	*Exc.*	*V.G.*	*Good*	*Fair*	*Poor*
1500	1150	880	680	600	300

AT-2000PS

This version, sometimes referred to as Police Special, features shorter barrel of AT-2000P model on the larger AT-2000S frame. Barrel length 3.66". Magazine capacity: 15 rounds for 9mm; 13 rounds for .40 S&W.

NIB	*Exc.*	*V.G.*	*Good*	*Fair*	*Poor*
1500	1150	880	680	600	300

AT-2000H/HDA

Smallest version of AT-2000 series. Magazine capacity: 10 rounds for 9mm; 8 rounds for .40 S&W. Barrel length 3.34"; overall length 6.78"; weight 26 oz.

NIB	*Exc.*	*V.G.*	*Good*	*Fair*	*Poor*
1500	1150	880	680	600	300

AT-2000C

This is the competitor model. Features a competition slide, dual port compensator, match barrel and Sphinx scope mount. Offered in double-/single-action. Available in 9mm, 9x21 and .40 S&W.

NIB	*Exc.*	*V.G.*	*Good*	*Fair*	*Poor*
2200	1600	1200	800	600	400

AT-2000CS

Same as above model. Fitted with BoMar adjustable sights.

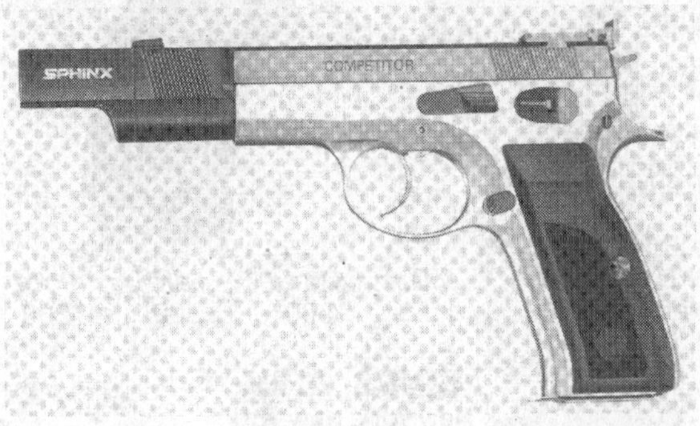

NIB	*Exc.*	*V.G.*	*Good*	*Fair*	*Poor*
2250	1650	1250	850	650	420

AT-2000GM

Grand Master model. Features are similar to AT-2000C. Offered in single-action-only.

NIB	*Exc.*	*V.G.*	*Good*	*Fair*	*Poor*
3000	2550	2100	1750	1250	500

AT-2000GMS

Same as above. Fitted with BoMar adjustable sights.

NIB	Exc.	V.G.	Good	Fair	Poor
3050	2600	2150	1800	1300	520

3000

16+1 autoloader chambered in 9mm or .45 ACP. Stainless steel frame and slide, manual safety, single/double/decocking action. Weight 40.56 oz. Also available in compact version.

NIB	Exc.	V.G.	Good	Fair	Poor
2000	1650	1150	500	300	200

SPIES, A. W.
New York, New York

Pocket Pistol

A .41-caliber percussion pocket pistol, with 2.5" barrel, German silver furniture and checkered walnut stock. Produced during 1850s.

NIB	Exc.	V.G.	Good	Fair	Poor
—	—	1950	1780	900	300

SPILLER & BURR
Atlanta, Georgia

Navy Revolver (Antique)

A .36-caliber percussion revolver, with 6" or 6.5" octagonal barrel and 6-shot cylinder. Barrel and cylinder blued. Frame of brass, with walnut grips. Some pistols are marked "Spiller & Burr" while others are simply marked "C.S.". Approximately 1,450 made between 1862 and 1865. Expert evaluation highly recommended.

Exc.	Fine	V.G.	Good	Fair	Poor
45000	22500	19000	15500	5000	3500

SPITFIRE
JSL (Hereford) Ltd.
Hereford, England

Semi-automatic pistol is a design based on CZ 75. This is a hand-built pistol designed by John Slough and built from a solid block of steel. Stainless steel frame and slide are cut with spark erosion and diamond grinding. Barrels are built and bored in the same factory. This is primarily a competition pistol. Manufactured 1992-1994.

Standard Model (G1)

Chambered for 9x21, 9mm Parabellum or .40 S&W cartridges. Uses locked breech concept. Trigger system single-/double-action. Fitted with an ambidextrous safety. Barrel 3.7"; overall length 7.1". Magazine capacity 9mm is 15 rounds. Sights are fixed. Empty weight 35 oz. Finish stainless steel. Comes supplied with presentation box, two magazines and allen key. Discontinued.

NIB	Exc.	V.G.	Good	Fair	Poor
1300	900	700	500	300	200

Master Model

Similar to Standard Model, without sights. Fitted with a stainless steel bridge mount to take an Aimpoint sight. Also has a dual port compensator. Supplied with presentation box and two magazines. Discontinued.

NIB	Exc.	V.G.	Good	Fair	Poor
2100	1750	1250	800	400	200

Squadron Model

This model has a Standard Model frame, adjustable rear sight slide, adjustable rear sight slide with compensator, Master Model slide and barrel with stainless steel bridge mount and Aimpoint sight, four magazines, screwdriver, allen key, oil bottle, spare springs, cleaning kit, and fitted leather case. Discontinued.

NIB	Exc.	V.G.	Good	Fair	Poor
6000	4800	2100	900	450	200

Sterling Model (G2)

Chambered for 9x21, 9mm Parabellum or .40 S&W cartridges. Features same as Standard Model, except it has adjustable sights. Discontinued.

NIB	Exc.	V.G.	Good	Fair	Poor
1400	1000	800	600	300	200

Super Sterling (G7)

Also chambered for 9x21, 9mm Parabellum and .40 S&W. Features single port compensator and 4.3" barrel. Overall length 8.25". Weight about 36 oz. Discontinued.

NIB	Exc.	V.G.	Good	Fair	Poor
1600	1200	900	700	350	200

Competition Model (G3)

Chambered for 9x21, 9mm Parabellum or .40 S&W cartridge. Features tapered slide rib, adjustable rear sight, dual pod compensator, match hammer, adjustable trigger stop with presentation box. Barrel 5.27", with compensator. Weight 40 oz. Discontinued.

NIB	Exc.	V.G.	Good	Fair	Poor
1800	1400	1000	800	400	200

Battle of Britain Commemorative

A limited edition of 1,056 Spitfires in 9mm Parabellum. Each one represents one of the Spitfire aircraft. Stainless steel slide has inscription "Battle of Britain-50th Anniversary". Grips are checkered walnut, log book of history of that particular aircraft and a wooden presentation box with engraved plaque. Discontinued.

NIB	Exc.	V.G.	Good	Fair	Poor
1950	1400	1000	800	400	200

Westlake Britarms

This is a .22 LR Match pistol. Barrel length 5.77", sight base 8.42", magazine capacity 5 rounds. Weight about 47 oz. Trigger adjustable for length, front and rear trigger stops, adjustable palm rest on contoured wood grips, take-down barrel design with removable weight. Limited importation.

NIB	Exc.	V.G.	Good	Fair	Poor
1850	1400	1000	800	400	200

SPRINGFIELD ARMORY

Springfield Armory was our country's first federal armory begun in 1777 in Springfield, Massachusetts, at a site chosen by George Washington. For almost two centuries, it was the primary facility for the manufacturer of firearms for the armed forces of the United States, until its closing in 1968. For information on the many models made at Springfield Armory, please refer to the Standard Catalog of Military Firearms, available at GunDigestStore.com. Current manufacturer and importer of modern rifles and handguns, Springfield Armory, Inc. of Geneseo, Illinois, is not associated with the historic military armory of the same name.

SPRINGFIELD ARMORY INC.

Geneseo, Illinois

Springfield Armory, Inc., is a manufacturer and importer of rifles and handguns for self-defense and competition located in Geneseo, Illinois. Begun by the Reese family in 1974, the name "Springfield Armory" was registered and the firm began by resurrecting historically significant designs produced by the National Armory such as the M1 Garand, M1911-A1 and a semi-auto only version of the M14 called the M1A. Currently the firm produces an extensive line of Modern Sporting Rifles, polymer-framed pistols and micro-compact pistols in addition to its signature lines of the M1A and M1911. SEE POLITICAL PANIC PRICING.

RIFLES

M1 Garand Rifle

A .270 (discontinued), .308 or .30-06 caliber semi-automatic rifle, with 24" barrel and 8-shot magazine. Patterned directly after U.S. M1 Rifle. Discontinued.

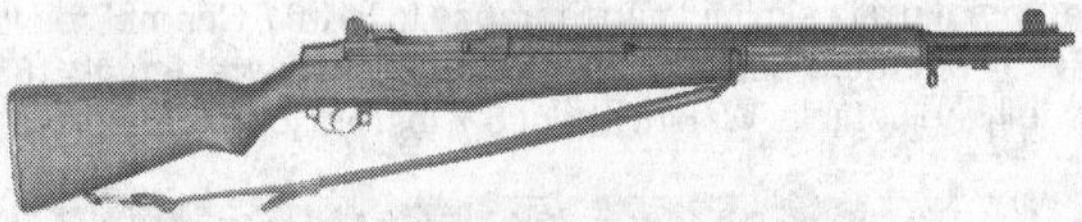

Courtesy Milwaukee Public Museum, Milwaukee, Wisconsin

NIB	Exc.	V.G.	Good	Fair	Poor
—	1000	820	550	400	300

Iwo Jima M1 Garand

Similar to standard M1 Model, but shipped in reproduction WWII-era crate with signed decorative lithograph. Introduced 2006. Discontinued.

NIB	Exc.	V.G.	Good	Fair	Poor
1600	1300	1000	800	400	200

D-Day M1 Garand Limited Edition

Introduced in 2005. Chambered for .30-06 cartridge. Fitted with 24" barrel. Military-style sights. Two-stage military trigger. Limited to 1,944 rifles, each with a military-style wooden crate. Each side of the buttstock has stamped memorials to D-Day. Discontinued.

NIB	Exc.	V.G.	Good	Fair	Poor
1600	1200	920	680	420	250

M1A Basic Rifle

Chambered for .308 Win. Fitted with a painted black fiberglass stock. Barrel length 22", without flash suppressor. Front sights are military square post and rear military aperture (battle sights). Magazine capacity 5, 10 or 20 box. Weight 9 lbs.

NIB	Exc.	V.G.	Good	Fair	Poor
1400	1200	950	750	500	300

M1A Standard Rifle

Long in the catalog, this M1A is chambered for .308 Win. or .243 (discontinued) cartridge. Fitted with 22" barrel with flash suppressor, adjustable rear sight and FDE synthetic, black synthetic or walnut stock, with fiberglass handguard. Previously with one 20-round box magazine; currently with one 10-round mag. Weight about 9 lbs. Note: Add about $75 for walnut stock.

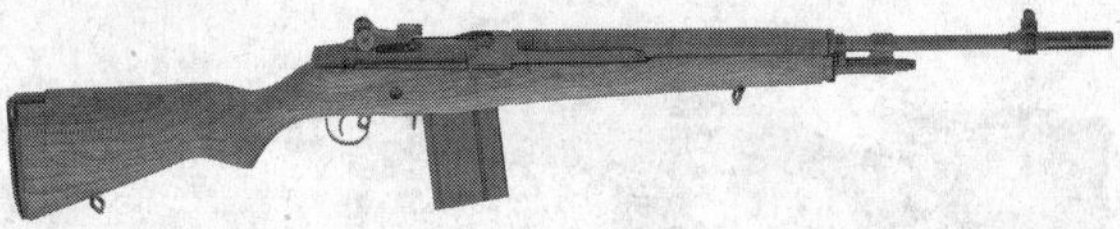

NIB	Exc.	V.G.	Good	Fair	Poor
1700	1500	1200	900	500	300

M1A-A1 Bush Rifle

Chambered for .308 or .243. Choice of walnut stock, black fiberglass or folding stock (no longer produced). Fitted with 18.25" barrel. Weight 8.75 lbs. Note: Add $250 for folding stock. Discontinued.

NIB	Exc.	V.G.	Good	Fair	Poor
1400	1100	850	650	400	250

M1A Scout Squad Rifle

This version has an 18" barrel with muzzle brake, National Match front sight blade, standard military aperture rear and forward-mounted scout-style scope rail in black composite or walnut stock. Weight of 8 lbs., 8 oz., with one 10-round magazine. Note: Add $75 for walnut stock.

NIB	Exc.	V.G.	Good	Fair	Poor
1700	1500	1100	950	550	350

M1A National Match

Springfield's match-grade rifle chambered for .308. Fitted with medium weight Match-grade barrel with tuned gas cylinder, glass bedded walnut stock, tuned 2-stage trigger Match-grade front and rear sights, one 10-round mag and a weight of 9 lbs, 8 oz. Note: Add $50 for stainless steel barrel.

NIB	Exc.	V.G.	Good	Fair	Poor
2400	2000	1700	1400	800	450

M1A Super Match

This is Springfield's best match-grade rifle. Chambered for .308 as standard and also .243 cartridge. Fitted with special oversize heavy walnut stock, heavy Douglas match glass bedded barrel and special rear lugged receiver. Special rear adjustable sight. Weight 10.125 lbs. Note: Add $165 for walnut stock and Douglas barrel; $600 for black McMillan stock and Douglas stainless steel barrel; $600 for Marine Corp. camo stock and Douglas stainless steel barrel; $535 for adjustable walnut stock and Douglas barrel; $900 for adjustable walnut stock and Krieger barrel. Add $150-$250 for walnut stock and Douglas barrel; McMillan stock and Douglas stainless steel barrel; a Marine Corp. camo stock or Krieger barrel. Discontinued.

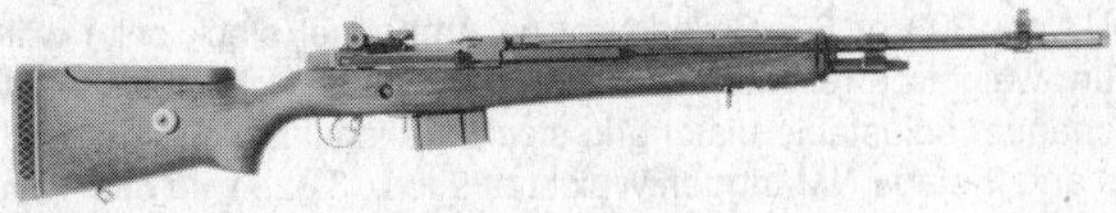

NIB	Exc.	V.G.	Good	Fair	Poor
3000	2250	1750	1000	700	350

M1A Model 25 Carlos Hathcock

Introduced in 2001. Features match trigger, stainless steel heavy match barrel, McMillan synthetic stock with adjustable cheek pad, Harris Bi-pod and other special features. Chambered for .308. Weight 12.75 lbs. A special logo bears his signature. Discontinued.

NIB	Exc.	V.G.	Good	Fair	Poor
4650	3450	2500	1750	800	400

M21 Law Enforcement/Tactical Rifle

Similar to Super Match. Addition of a special stock, with rubber recoil pad and height adjustable cheekpiece. Available as a special order only. Weight 11.875 lbs. Discontinued.

NIB	Exc.	V.G.	Good	Fair	Poor
3000	2600	2000	1500	650	350

M1A SOCOM 16

This M1A1 rifle features 16.25" barrel, with muzzle brake. Black fiberglass stock, with steel buttplate. Forward scout-style scope mount. Front sight post has Tritium insert. Weight about 9 lbs. Introduced in 2004.

NIB	Exc.	V.G.	Good	Fair	Poor
2000	1500	1000	650	400	250

M1A SOCOM II

Introduced in 2005. Features full-length top rail and short bottom rail for accessories. Weight 11 lbs. Discontinued.

NIB	Exc.	V.G.	Good	Fair	Poor
2000	1500	1000	700	450	300

M1A SOCOM Urban Rifle

Similar to SOCOM, with black and white camo stock. Introduced in 2005. Discontinued.

NIB	Exc.	V.G.	Good	Fair	Poor
2000	1500	1000	700	450	300

M1A Loaded Precision Rifle

An M1A in .308 or 6.5 Creedmoor (in Archangel stock only) with 22" medium weight barrel with flash suppressor in black composite, walnut or Archangel adjustable pistol grip stock. National Match front and rear sights and 2-stage NM trigger. Weight of 9 lbs., 3 oz., with one 10-round mag. Add $75 for walnut stock; Add $125 for Archangel stock; Add $175 for 6.5 Creedmoor in Archangel stock.

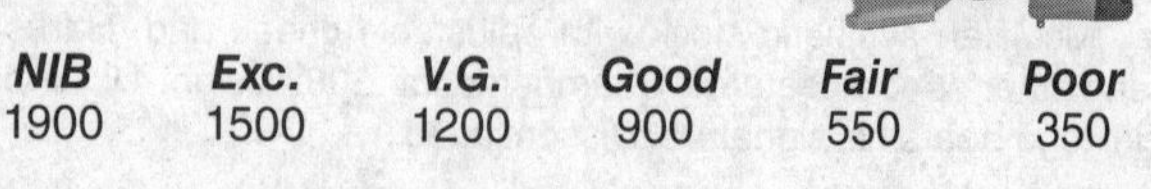

NIB	Exc.	V.G.	Good	Fair	Poor
1900	1500	1200	900	550	350

M1A SOCOM 16/CQB/Tanker

Shortened M1A rifle with 16.25" barrel and muzzle brake. Black fiberglass or walnut (Tanker) stock, with steel buttplate. Forward scout-style scope mount (except Tanker). Ghost ring rear sight, front VS sight post has Tritium insert. Weight about 9 lbs. with one 10-round mag. Introduced in 2004. Note: Add $150 for CQB pistol grip synthetic stock with accessory rails; Add $400 for CQB with Vortex Venom Reflex sight.

NIB	Exc.	V.G.	Good	Fair	Poor
1700	1350	1080	930	550	350

IDF Mauser Rifle Model 66SP

Bolt-action rifle chambered for .308 Win. cartridge. Adjustable trigger for pull and travel. Barrel length 27". Specially designed stock has broad forend and thumbhole pistol grip. Cheekpiece adjustable as is recoil pad. Supplied with case. Rifle is military-issue. Fewer than 100 imported into the U.S. Discontinued.

NIB	Exc.	V.G.	Good	Fair	Poor
2200	1750	950	700	450	300

SAR-48

This is a pre-ban version of the SAR-4800. Discontinued.

NIB	Exc.	V.G.	Good	Fair	Poor
3000	2500	1400	1000	600	300

SAR-4800

Semi-automatic gas-operated rifle, similar in appearance to FN-FAL/LAR rifle. Chambered for .308 Win. cartridge. Fitted with 21" barrel. Has a fully adjustable rear sight. Weight 9.5 lbs. No longer imported.

NIB	Exc.	V.G.	Good	Fair	Poor
2500	1800	1200	800	500	300

SAR-8

Semi-automatic rifle similar in appearance to HK-91. Chambered for .308 Win. Recoil operated delayed roller-lock design. Barrel length 18". Rear sight is fully adjustable. Weight about 8.7 lbs. No longer imported.

NIB	Exc.	V.G.	Good	Fair	Poor
1500	1100	750	500	300	200

SAR-8 Tactical

Similar to above model. Fitted with a heavy barrel. Introduced in 1996. No longer imported. Fewer than 100 imported into U.S. Discontinued.

NIB	Exc.	V.G.	Good	Fair	Poor
2000	1600	1000	750	400	300

SAINT AR-15 SERIES

Caliber: 5.56 NATO. Introduced 2016. Springfield Armory's first entry into AR category. Capacity: 30-round magazine. Barrel: 16", 1:8 twist. Weight: 6 lbs., 11 oz. Sights: A2-style fixed post front or gas block with Pic rail, flip-up aperture rear. Features: Mid-length gas system, BCM 6-position stock, Mod 3 grip PMT KeyMod handguard 7075 T6 aluminum receivers. In 2020, several models with M-LOK handguards were added. The Bravo Company handguards have an internal aluminum heat shield.

NIB	Exc.	V.G.	Good	Fair	Poor
1000	—	—	—	—	—

SAINT AR-15 Rifle 16" 5.56 A2 Front

As above, but with a fixed A2 front sight on the gas block. Can be had with B5 Systems furniture and triggerguard at same price, giving a reduced weight of 6 lbs, 4 oz.

NIB	Exc.	V.G.	Good	Fair	Poor
1250	1070	900	770	650	560

SAINT AR-15 Rifle 16" 5.56 ST916556BM

BCMGUNFIGHTER PKMR, M-Lok handguard, BCMGUNFIGHTER triggerguard, BCMGUNFIGHTER Mod 3 pistol grip, BCMGUNFIGHTER Mod 0 butt stock. (1) 30-Round Magpul PMAG Gen M3. Pinned Picatinny railed gas block.

NIB	Exc.	V.G.	Good	Fair	Poor
1250	1060	900	770	650	560

SAINT AR-15 Rifle 16" 5.56 ST916556BMA

Similar to item above, but with A2-style front sight and pinned gas block.

NIB	Exc.	V.G.	Good	Fair	Poor
1000	850	720	610	520	440

SAINT State Compliant Versions

As various states impose legislation to restrict AR-style rifles, Springfield Armory creates models to satisfy the requirements. This can be as simple as coming with a 10-round magazine or as onerous as the "California" version with a fixed stock, Strike Ind. Compliant Pistol Grip and muzzle brake instead of a flash hider. Note: Add $20 for Picatinny gas block. Model shown is SAINT AR-15 Rifle 16" 5.56 ST916556BMACA-S.

NIB	Exc.	V.G.	Good	Fair	Poor
1000	850	720	610	520	440

SAINT AR-15 Rifle 16" 5.56 ST916556BMCA-S

Magpul fixed buttstock, Strike Industries pistol grip, (1) 10-Round Magpul PMAG Gen M3. Pinned Picatinny railed gas block.

NIB	Exc.	V.G.	Good	Fair	Poor
820	700	590	500	430	360

SAINT AR-15 Rifle 16" 5.56 w/Free Float Handguard

Comes with free-float M-Lok handguard system, pinned low-profile gas block. SA low profile flip-up, dual aperture rear 1/2 moa windage adj, flip-up front 1/2 moa elevation adjustment. ST916556FDEFFH is Desert FDE; ST916556GRYFFH is Tactical Gray; ST916556ODGFFH is OD Green. 32.25" to 35.5" long, 6.75 lbs.

NIB	Exc.	V.G.	Good	Fair	Poor
850	720	610	520	440	380

SAINT AR-15 Rifle PIC Gas Block

Carbine-length forearm with Picatinny rail gas block and fold-down front sight. Bravo Co. Mfg. Gunfighter Model 0 stock, Mod 3 grip and M-LOK forend with one 30-round Magpul P-mag. Overall length of 32.5" to 35.75". Weight 6 lbs, 11 oz.

NIB	Exc.	V.G.	Good	Fair	Poor
700	600	510	430	370	310

SAINT AR-15 SBR 11.5" 5.56 ST9115556B

11.5" CMV, Melonite-coated internally and externally, A2 flash hider, 1:8 twist. Full-length aluminum free-float handguard w/M-Lok attachment points. 27.5" to 30.75" length. 5.75 lbs. SA proprietary low-profile carbine length adjustable gas block. Bravo Company triggerguard.

NIB	Exc.	V.G.	Good	Fair	Poor
900	770	650	550	470	400

SAINT AR-15 Pistol

A handgun version of the SAINT, it has a 9.6" 5.56 chrome moly vanadium barrel, A2 flash hider, adjustable Trinity Force Breach Pistol Brace 1.0 stock, BCM Gunfighter PMCR, Forward Handstop, M-Lok and Mod 3 grip. Overall length 25.8" to 28.3". Weight 5 lbs, 8 oz. (Weight 2 oz less with B5 Systems forend and Type 23 pistol grip.) One 30-round Magpul P-Mag. A state-compliant version is available, and one chambered in .300 BLK.

NIB	Exc.	V.G.	Good	Fair	Poor
730	620	520	450	270	160

SAINT AR-15 Pistol 9.6" 5.56

5.56 NATO. Features an SB Tactical SBX-K forearm brace, 7.5" 416R stainless-steel barrel, Melonite treated, 1:7 twist. ST975556FDE is Desert FDE; ST975556GRY is Tactical Gray; ST975556ODG is OD Green.

NIB	Exc.	V.G.	Good	Fair	Poor
740	630	530	450	380	330

SAINT AR-15 Pistol 9" 300 BLK

NIB	Exc.	V.G.	Good	Fair	Poor
870	740	630	530	450	380

SAINT VICTOR SERIES

Caliber: 5.56 NATO. Capacity: Includes one 30-round Magpul PMAG Gen M3. Barrel: 16", CMV, 1:8 twist, Melonite-finished barrels, Springfield Armory proprietary muzzle brake. Upper/Lower Receivers: Lowers are Accu-Tite tension-bonded to a flat-top forged upper receiver with Melonite finish. Stock: BCMGUNFIGHTER Mod 0. Pistol Grip: BCMGUNFIGHTER Mod 3. Sights: Spring-loaded, flip-up iron sights adjustable for windage and elevation. Weight: 6.9 lbs. Trigger: Enhanced nickel-boron-coated, single-stage flat trigger. Overall Length: 32.25 to 35.5 in. Features: Direct-impingement mid-length gas system. M16 bolt carrier Melonite finished, HPT/MPI tested, shot-peened, and houses a 9310 steel bolt. 15-in. M-LOK free-float handguard, pinned, low-profile gas block. QD mounts are built into the endplate and stock. Desert FDE color approx. $60 extra. Introduced 2019.

NIB	Exc.	V.G.	Good	Fair	Poor
1130	910	780	660	560	480

SAINT Victor SBR AR-15 Rifle

A Short-Barreled Rifle version requiring NFA transfer compliance, the SBR has an 11.5" 5.56 barrel, A2 flash hider, BCM Mod 0 stock, Mod 3 pistol grip, one 30-round Magpul P-mag. Overall length of 27.5" to 30.75". Weight 5 lbs., 9 oz.

NIB	Exc.	V.G.	Good	Fair	Poor
900	780	650	560	340	200

SAINT Victor AR-15 Pistol

A handgun version of the Victor with 7.5-in. 416R stainless barrel with SA forward blast diverter in 5.56 (also .300 BLK), Melonite coated, SA locking tab forearm with handstop, SB Tactical SBA3 Pistol Brace, BCM Mod 3 grip. Overall length of 26.5 in. Weight 5 lbs., 8 oz. Note: Add $20 for FDE, OD Green or Grey finish with matching color Magpul grip.

NIB	Exc.	V.G.	Good	Fair	Poor
890	760	650	550	330	200

SAINT Victor AR-15 Rifle 16" 5.56 B5 Stock

Same as above, but with B5 Systems SOPMOD stock, B5 Type 23 grip and B5 polymer triggerguard. Weight 6 lbs, 11 oz.

NIB	Exc.	V.G.	Good	Fair	Poor
1080	910	780	660	560	480

SAINT Victor AR-15 Rifle 16" 5.56 State Compliant

A SAINT Victor with modifications to satisfy various state compliance mandates. May be as simple as a 10-shot magazine or with Strike Industries California-compliant pistol grip and Magpul fixed stock.

NIB	Exc.	V.G.	Good	Fair	Poor
1080	910	780	660	560	480

SAINT Victor AR-15 Rifle 16" 5.56

Caliber: 5.56 NATO. Capacity: Includes one 30-round Magpul PMAG Gen M3. Barrel: 16", CMV, 1:8" twist, Melonite-finished barrels, Springfield Armory proprietary muzzle brake. Upper/Lower Receivers: Lowers are Accu-Tite tension-bonded to a flat-top forged upper receiver with Melonite finish. Stock: BCMGUNFIGHTER Mod 0. Pistol Grip: BCMGUNFIGHTER Mod 3. Sights: Spring-loaded, flip-up iron sights adjustable for windage and elevation. Weight: 6.9 lbs. Trigger: Enhanced nickel-boron-coated, single-stage flat trigger. Overall length: 32.25" to 35.5". Features: Direct-impingement mid-length gas system. M16 bolt carrier Melonite finished, HPT/MPI tested, shot peened, and houses a 9310 steel bolt. 15" M-LOK free-float handguard, pinned, low-profile gas block. QD mounts built into the end plate and stock. Desert FDE color approx. $60 extra. Introduced 2019. Saint Victor Carbine 9mm (add $150) introduced December 2022. SEE POLITICAL PANIC PRICING.

NIB	Exc.	V.G.	Good	Fair	Poor
1030	900	770	600	—	—

SAINT Victor AR-15 Rifle SBR 11" 5.56

NIB	Exc.	V.G.	Good	Fair	Poor
1250	1060	900	770	650	560

SAINT Victor AR-10 Rifle 16" .308

NIB	Exc.	V.G.	Good	Fair	Poor
1300	1110	940	800	680	580

SAINT Victor Pistol

Similar to other Victor products, but with 7.5" 416R stainless steel barrel, 1:7 twist, Melonite finished. Muzzle device is a SA Forward Blast Diverter, the forearm brace and SB Tactical SBX-K. Gas system is direct impingement pistol-length unit. Comes with (1) 30-Round Magpul Gen M3 magazine. 5.56 NATO length is 26.5", weight is 5.5 lbs. .300 Blackout chambering is 27.75" long and weight 5.75 lbs.

NIB	Exc.	V.G.	Good	Fair	Poor
990	840	710	610	510	440

SAINT Victor AR-15 Pistol .300 BLK

NIB	Exc.	V.G.	Good	Fair	Poor
800	680	580	490	420	360

SAINT Victor AR-10

Caliber: .308 Win. Capacity: One 20-round Magpul Gen M3. Barrel: 16", 1:10" twist, lightweight profile, CMV Melonite finish, SA muzzle brake. Upper/Lower Receivers: Forged Type III hardcoat anodized, 7075 T6 Aluminum. Lower has Accu-Tite Tension System. Stock: Bravo Company six-position. Pistol grip: Bravo Company Mod. 3. Sights: Spring-loaded, flip-ups. Weight: 7.8 lbs. Trigger: Enhanced nickel boron-coated, single-stage flat trigger. Overall length: 34.5" to 37.5". Features: Gas system is direct impingement, mid-length, pinned gas block. Bolt carrier group is MPT, Melonite finish with a 9310 steel bolt; handguard is 15" M-LOK aluminum free-float with SA locking tabs. Introduced 2019. SEE POLITICAL PANIC PRICING.

NIB	Exc.	V.G.	Good	Fair	Poor
1300	1150	970	810	—	—

SAINT Victor .308 Pistol 10.3"

A handgun version of the Victor in .308 Winchester with 10.3" chrome moly vanadium barrel with SA 2-piece forward blast diverter, Melonite coated, SA locking tab forearm with handstop, SB Tactical SBA3 Pistol Brace, BCM Mod 3 grip. Overall length of 28.25" to 30.5". Weight 8 lbs, 6 oz. One 20-round Magpul P-Mag.

NIB	Exc.	V.G.	Good	Fair	Poor
1000	850	720	610	520	440

SAINT EDGE SERIES

Contains rifle, SBR, and pistol models in 5.56 NATO. Rifle line, at just over 6 lbs. is one of the lightest AR-15s on the market. Patent-pending free float handguard and billet receiver with lightening cuts, SA proprietary muzzle brake, Melonite-treated trigger. Accu-Tite tension system removes rattle between the upper and lower receivers. Premium M16 BCG has been shot peened and MPI tested for reliability. Adjustable pinned gas block, 16" barrel with 1:8 twist and lightweight profile, flared mag well, metal flip-up sights and Bravo Company Mod 2 pistol grip and six-position Bravo Mod 0 SopMod buttstock.

SAINT Edge SBR

A Short-Barreled Rifle version as above requiring NFA transfer compliance with an 11.5" 5.56 barrel, A2 flash hider, one 30-round Magpul P-mag. Overall length of 27.5" to 30.75" Weight 5 lbs., 10 oz.

NIB	Exc.	V.G.	Good	Fair	Poor
1100	840	720	600	370	220

SAINT Edge AR-15 Rifle 16" 5.56

The Edge series are the top tier models based on all premium components. Key Edge features are a forged 7075 T6 upper with a lower machined from a 7075 T6 billet with lightening cuts and flared magazine well. Chambered in 5.56 with a 16" barrel, SA ported muzzle brake, match-grade, short-reset, and Melonite treated single-stage trigger. Carbine-length aluminum handguard with SA Locking Tabs, BCM Mod 0 stock, Mod 3 grip, ambi safety, adjustable folding front and rear sights, one 30-round Magpul P-mag. Overall length of 32.5" to 35.75". Weight 6 lbs., 3 oz.

NIB	Exc.	V.G.	Good	Fair	Poor
1100	940	800	680	570	490

SAINT Edge SBR AR-15 Rifle 10.3" 5.56

The Edge Pistol in 5.56 with 10.3" chrome moly vanadium barrel, A2 flash hider, free-floated aluminum handgun with SA locking tabs, hand stop. No sights. The billet-cut 7075 T6 aluminum lower offers stiffness and minimal weight. Maxim Defense 4-position arm brace, BCM Mod 3 grip. Overall length of 24.6" to 28.5". Weight 5 lbs, 11 oz. A PDW and EVAC Models should be available in late 2020. Note: Deduct $50 for PDW or EVAC models.

NIB	Exc.	V.G.	Good	Fair	Poor
1400	1190	1010	860	730	620

SAINT Edge PDW AR-15 Pistol 5.5" 5.56

NIB	Exc.	V.G.	Good	Fair	Poor
1700	1450	1230	1040	890	750

SAINT Edge EVAC AR-15 Pistol 7.5" 5.56

Caliber: 5.56 NATO. Capacity: 30-round magazine. Barrel: 7.5". Grips: Reptilla CQG. Sights: Low-profile, spring-loaded adjustable flip-up. Length: 18"-26.5" overall. Weight: 7.1 lbs. unloaded. Finish: Matte black. Features: Takedown, linear compensator, single-stage flat trigger, M-LOK handguard, Edge forward hand stop, and side-folding Gear Head Works Mod 1 Tailhook brace.

NIB	Exc.	V.G.	Good	Fair	Poor
1580	1340	1140	970	820	700

SAINT Edge ATC Rifle

Chamber: .223 Wylde. Accurized Tactical Chassis rifles comes with guaranteed sub-MOA accuracy for three shots with match-grade ammunition and a skilled shooter. Features: Chassis system of a one-piece monolithic lower machined from 6061 T6 aluminum. Free-floated design keeps the barrel, barrel nut, and gas system from contacting the lower chassis. Also includes Accu-Tite Plus tensioning system, conical set screws in the lower that eliminate play between the upper receiver and lower chassis. Barrel: 18-in. Ballistic Advantage, 1:7" rate of twist, Melonite coating. Comes with B5 Systems Enhanced SOPMOD collapsible stock, flat modular match trigger, B5 Systems Type 23 P-Grip, 20-round Magpul PMAG. Weight: 9.5 lbs. Length: 35.5" to 38.25". Introduced December 2021. SEE POLITICAL PANIC PRICING.

NIB	Exc.	V.G.	Good	Fair	Poor
1200	1000	850	690	—	—

SAINT Edge ATC Elite

Chamber: .223 Wylde. Introduced December 2021. Similar to Standard model. Elite variant features LaRue two-stage trigger and collapsible B5 Systems Precision Stock. Weight: 10.1 lbs. Length: 36.5" to 39.75". Model No. STAE918223CB.

NIB	Exc.	V.G.	Good	Fair	Poor
1800	—	—	—	—	—

HELLION SERIES

Hellion Bullpup

Caliber: 5.56 NATO. Ambidextrous controls, including the safety, charging handle, magazine, and bolt releases. Reversible case ejection system. Barrel: 16", 1:7" rate of twist, Melonite coating. Picatinny top rail, flip-up iron sights. Bravo Company USA BCMGUNFIGHTER Mod 3 grip. Five-position adjustable buttstock. Polymer handguard with nine M-LOK slots, three each at 3, 6 and 9 o'clock positions. Two-position adjustable gas block with "S" suppressed and "N" normal modes. Magazine: 30-round Magpul PMAG. Weight: 8 lbs. Length: 28.25". Introduced January 2023. SEE POLITICAL PANIC PRICING.

NIB	Exc.	V.G.	Good	Fair	Poor
1750	—	—	—	—	—

M6 SERIES

M6 Scout

A .22, .22 Magnum or .22 Hornet and .410 bore over/under combination shotgun/rifle, with 18" barrel. Black anodized finish, with synthetic stock. Discontinued. U.S.-made version commands a premium over Czech-made. Values shown are for U.S.-made version. Note: Add 30% for Hornet.

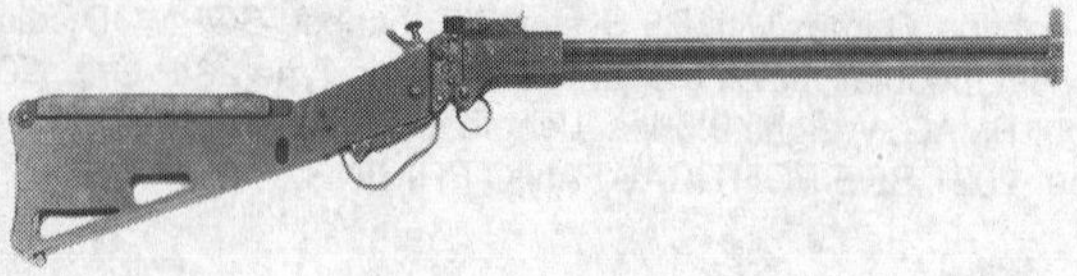

NIB	Exc.	V.G.	Good	Fair	Poor
600	450	300	200	100	50

M6 Scout—Stainless Steel

Same as above in stainless steel. First introduced in 1996; discontinued.

NIB	Exc.	V.G.	Good	Fair	Poor
620	480	320	220	150	80

M6 Scout Pistol

As above, with 10" barrel and no folding stock. Parkerized or stainless steel finish. Weight about 28 oz. Introduced in 2002; discontinued. Note: Add $30 for stainless steel. Discontinued.

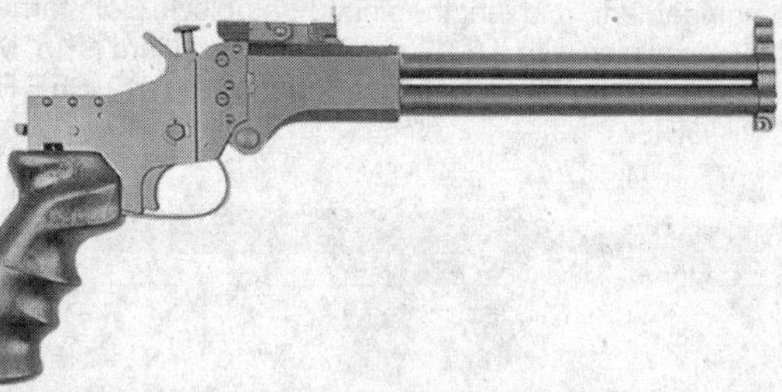

NIB	Exc.	V.G.	Good	Fair	Poor
580	420	300	200	100	50

PISTOLS

P9 SERIES

A double-action 9mm, .45 ACP or .40 S&W pistol based on Czech CZ 75 design. Incorporates several design features including: stainless steel trigger, sear safety mechanism, extended sear safety lever, redesigned backstrap, lengthened beavertail grip area and new high strength slide stop. Discontinued in 1993.

P9 Standard

Standard pistol fitted with 4.7" barrel, low profile target sights and ribbed slide. Magazine capacity: 9mm 16 rounds; .45 ACP 10 rounds; .40 S&W 12 rounds. Offered in blue or stainless finish. Weight 35 oz. Discontinued.

NIB	Exc.	V.G.	Good	Fair	Poor
600	500	420	380	300	180

P9 Factory Comp.

Competition pistol fitted with triple port compensator, extended magazine release, adjustable rear sight, slim competition wood grips and bi-tone finish. Weight 34 oz. Dropped from Springfield product line in 1993.

NIB	Exc.	V.G.	Good	Fair	Poor
700	600	400	350	220	120

P9 Ultra (IPSC Approved)

Competition pistol features longer slide and barrel, 5" Special target sights, rubberized competition grips. Engraved with IPSC logo. Available in bi-tone finish only. Weight 34.5 oz. Dropped from production in 1993.

NIB	Exc.	V.G.	Good	Fair	Poor
780	580	420	350	250	200

M1911 SERIES

Springfield Armory has long made M1911 pistols carefully tailored to market demands in a wide range of configurations for target and self-defense. Beginning with a Mil-Spec Parkerized GI-style 1911 with forged frame and slide, models have constantly evolved and improved over the years including a long-barreled single-shot conversion. The wide range of models and sub models provides a challenge for the collector. Below are a sampling of the types of M1911s offered over the decades and should not be considered complete. The Springfield Armory has also been the basis for many a custom pistol, and Springfield Armory maintains a Custom Shop dedicated to high-end pistols. Current production models are at the end of this section.

1911-A1 GI

Long cataloged, this 1911 was originally a mil-spec WWII-style M1911 chambered in .45 ACP cartridge, 5" barrel, old-style fixed sights, standard checkered brown plastic grips, lanyard loop on mainspring housing, and traditional 7-round magazine. Currently chambered only in .45 ACP, this model has also been offered in 9mm and .38 Super. Weight about 38 oz. One of the arms evolving over the years, early versions had a GI ejection port, while modern ones have a lowered, flared port and modern high-profile sights. Originally offered Parkerized only, blued and stainless steel have been offered. The "Legacy" is the new entry-level model (Parkerized only). Mil-Spec or stainless steel are upgrades. Note: Add $175 for Mil-Spec; Add $275 for stainless steel.

NIB	Exc.	V.G.	Good	Fair	Poor
470	400	340	290	170	100

Model 1911-A1 Service Model

Introduced in 2003. This .45 ACP pistol has a 5" barrel, with Bo-Mar adjustable three-dot rear sight. Also a number of special features such as extended mag well, titanium firing pin and beavertail grip safety. Stainless steel magazine capacity 7 rounds. Black stainless steel finish. Weight about 35 oz. Discontinued.

NIB	Exc.	V.G.	Good	Fair	Poor
920	750	600	500	400	200

Model 1911-A1 Service Mil-Spec

Chambered for .45 ACP cartridge. Fitted with a 5" barrel. Fixed sights. Matte stainless steel finish. Black plastic grips. Weight 36 oz. Introduced in 2003.

NIB	Exc.	V.G.	Good	Fair	Poor
610	480	380	350	300	250

Model 1911-A1 Service Model Lightweight

This .45 ACP pistol has a 5" barrel, with lightweight alloy frame and bi-tone finish. Novak Lo-Mount sights. A large number of special features. Checkered Cocobolo grips. Magazine capacity 7 rounds. Weight 30 oz. Introduced in 2003. Discontinued.

NIB	Exc.	V.G.	Good	Fair	Poor
880	700	600	500	400	200

Model 1911-A1 Stainless

Similar to standard Model 1911, but chambered for .45 ACP cartridge. Offered in stainless steel. Equipped with three-dot sights, beveled magazine well and checkered walnut grips. Weight about 39.2 oz. Note Add $50 for Bomar sights.

NIB	Exc.	V.G.	Good	Fair	Poor
900	750	620	400	350	200

Model 1911-A1 Factory Comp

Chambered for .45 ACP or .38 Super. Fitted with a three-chamber compensator. Rear sight is adjustable. Extended thumb safety and Videcki speed trigger are standard features. Also, checkered walnut grips, beveled magazine well, and Commander hammer are standard. Weight 40 oz. Note: Factory Comp pistols chambered for .38 Super may bring a small premium. Discontinued.

NIB	Exc.	V.G.	Good	Fair	Poor
1050	920	750	600	500	300

Model 1911-A1 Factory Comp High Capacity

Same as above, with 13-round magazine. Discontinued.

NIB	Exc.	V.G.	Good	Fair	Poor
1050	920	750	600	500	300

Model 1911-A2 S.A.S.S.

Single-shot pistol built on Model 1911 frame. Available in two barrel lengths; 10.75" and 14.9". Offered in .22 LR, .223, 7mm-08, 7mmBR, .357 Magnum, .308 and .44 Magnum calibers. This conversion kit is available for those wishing to use it on their own Model 1911 pistol frames. Discontinued.

NIB	Exc.	V.G.	Good	Fair	Poor
500	400	320	280	200	100

Model 1911-A1 Defender

Chambered for .45 ACP cartridge. Fitted with a tapered cone dual port compensator, reversed recoil plug, full-length recoil spring guide, fully adjustable rear sight, serrated front strap, rubberized grips and Commander-style hammer. Capacity 8-round magazine. Finish is bi-tone. Weight 40.16 oz. Discontinued.

NIB	Exc.	V.G.	Good	Fair	Poor
880	700	600	500	400	200

Model 1911-A1 Loaded Defender Lightweight

As above, with loaded features: precision fit frames, slides and barrels, flat serrated mainspring housing, lowered and flared ejection port, Delta lightweight hammer, loaded chamber indicator, titanium firing pin, carry bevel treatment, ambidextrous thumb safety, high hand beavertail grip safety, dovetail front sight, Novak or adjustable rear sight and adjustable speed trigger. Discontinued.

NIB	Exc.	V.G.	Good	Fair	Poor
950	780	680	550	450	250

Model 1911-A1 Compact

Available in blue or bi-tone, this .45 ACP fitted with 4.5" barrel and compact compensator. Equipped with Commander-style hammer and three-dot sights. Walnut grips are standard. Comes with 7-round magazine. Weight 37.2 oz. Note: Add $40 for stainless steel. Deduct $50 for Parkerized. Discontinued.

NIB	Exc.	V.G.	Good	Fair	Poor
900	750	620	400	350	200

Lightweight Compact Comp

Fitted with 4.5" barrel and single port compensator. Magazine holds 8 rounds of .45 ACP. Frame is alloy. Weight 30 oz. Discontinued.

NIB	Exc.	V.G.	Good	Fair	Poor
900	750	620	400	350	200

Model 1911-A1 Compact Mil-Spec

Same as standard blued steel Compact model, with Parkerized finish.

NIB	Exc.	V.G.	Good	Fair	Poor
850	700	580	350	300	200

Model 1911-A1 Long Slide

Features 6" barrel, 3-dot fixed sights, checkered wooden grips and 8-round magazine capacity. Finish stainless steel. Weight 38 oz. Introduced in 1997. Discontinued.

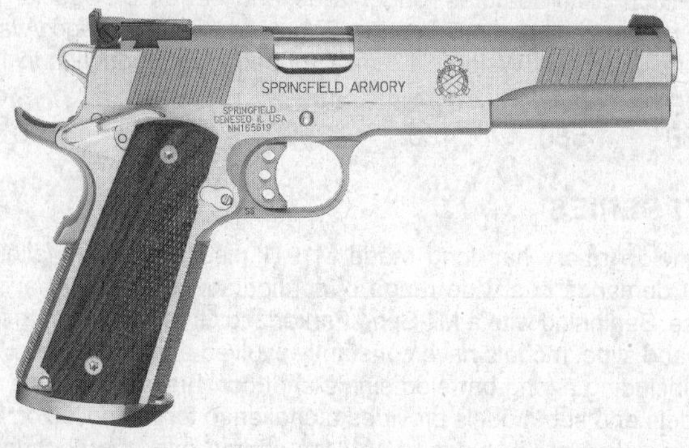

NIB	Exc.	V.G.	Good	Fair	Poor
950	780	680	550	450	250

Model 1911-A1 Loaded Long Slide

As above, with loaded features: precision fit frames, slides and barrels, flat serrated mainspring housing, lowered and flared ejection port, Delta lightweight hammer, loaded chamber indicator, titanium firing pin, carry bevel treatment, ambidextrous thumb safety, high hand beavertail grip safety, dovetail front sight, Novak or adjustable rear sight and adjustable speed trigger. Discontinued.

NIB	Exc.	V.G.	Good	Fair	Poor
1100	950	780	600	480	350

Model 1911-A1 Champion

This .45 ACP pistol has a shortened slide, barrel and reduced size frame. Fitted with 4" barrel, 8-round magazine, Commander hammer, checkered walnut grips and special 3-dot sights. Weight 33.4 oz.

NIB	Exc.	V.G.	Good	Fair	Poor
800	650	500	400	300	150

Model 1911-A1 Champion Mil-Spec

Same as above, with Parkerized finish.

NIB	Exc.	V.G.	Good	Fair	Poor
700	600	400	350	220	120

Model 1911-A1 Stainless Champion

Same as above, but offered in stainless steel. Weight 33.4 oz.

NIB	Exc.	V.G.	Good	Fair	Poor
850	700	580	350	300	200

Model 1911-A1 Loaded Champion Stainless

As above, with loaded features: precision fit frames, slides and barrels, flat serrated mainspring housing, lowered and flared ejection port, Delta lightweight hammer, loaded chamber indicator, titanium firing pin, carry bevel treatment, ambidextrous thumb safety, high hand beavertail grip safety, dovetail front sight, Novak or adjustable rear sight and adjustable speed trigger. Discontinued.

NIB	Exc.	V.G.	Good	Fair	Poor
1000	880	700	580	500	300

Champion Compact

Includes same features as Champion, with shortened grip frame length. Discontinued.

NIB	Exc.	V.G.	Good	Fair	Poor
850	700	580	350	300	200

Model 1911 Loaded Champion Lightweight

A lightweight aluminum frame, with Novak night sights. Checkered rubber grips. Finish OD Green and Black Armory Kote. Weight 28 oz. Introduced in 2004. Discontinued.

NIB	Exc.	V.G.	Good	Fair	Poor
850	700	580	350	300	200

Ultra Compact 1911-A1

Features a 3.5" .45 ACP barrel, with 7.125" overall length. Has a stainless steel frame, beveled mag well, speed trigger, match-grade barrel and walnut grips. Weight 31 oz. Note: Deduct $100 for blue or Parkerized finish. Discontinued.

NIB	Exc.	V.G.	Good	Fair	Poor
850	700	580	350	300	200

Ultra Compact Lightweight MD-1

Same as above in .380-caliber, with alloy frame. Weight 24 oz. Discontinued.

NIB	Exc.	V.G.	Good	Fair	Poor
700	600	400	350	220	120

Ultra Compact 1911-A1 Mil-Spec

Same as Ultra Compact Model, with Parkerized or blued finish.

NIB	Exc.	V.G.	Good	Fair	Poor
750	650	450	350	220	120

V10 Ultra Compact 1911-A1

Same as Ultra Compact 1911-A1, but fitted with a compensator built into barrel and slide.

NIB	Exc.	V.G.	Good	Fair	Poor
900	750	620	400	350	200

V10 Ultra Compact 1911-A1 Mil-Spec

Same as above, with Parkerized finish.

NIB	Exc.	V.G.	Good	Fair	Poor
850	700	580	350	300	200

Model 1911-A1 High Capacity

Chambered in .45 ACP (10- or 13-rounds) or 9mm (16-rounds). Standard features include Commander hammer, walnut grips and beveled magazine well. Blued finish. Weight 42 oz. In 1997, offered in stainless steel and Parkerized finish. Note: Add $40 for stainless steel. Deduct $50 for Parkerized finish. Discontinued.

NIB	Exc.	V.G.	Good	Fair	Poor
650	520	400	300	200	100

Compact High Capacity

Same as above, with 11-round magazine. Discontinued.

NIB	Exc.	V.G.	Good	Fair	Poor
650	520	400	300	200	150

Ultra Compact High Capacity

This .45 ACP model offered in three different 3.5" barrel variations: stainless steel, Parkerized and ported. Standard magazine capacity 10 rounds. Weight about 31 oz. Note: Add $60 for stainless steel; $100 for ported models. Discontinued.

NIB	Exc.	V.G.	Good	Fair	Poor
700	600	400	350	220	120

Micro Compact—Parkerized

Chambered for .45 ACP cartridge. Fitted with 3" bull barrel. Aluminum frame, with steel slide. Novak night sights. Cocobolo grips. Offered with Parkerized finish. Weight about 24 oz. Magazine capacity 6 rounds. Introduced in 2002. Note: Add about $50 for stainless steel, O.D. Green Armory Kote, or black stainless. Discontinued.

NIB	Exc.	V.G.	Good	Fair	Poor
850	700	580	350	300	200

Micro Compact—Stainless

As above, with stainless steel frame and slide. Novak Tritium night sights. Weight about 24 oz. Introduced in 2003.

NIB	Exc.	V.G.	Good	Fair	Poor
900	750	620	400	350	200

Micro Compact—O.D. Green

As above, with Armory Kote Green finish. Pearce grips. Introduced in 2003.

NIB	Exc.	V.G.	Good	Fair	Poor
900	750	620	400	350	200

Micro Compact—Black Stainless

As above, with black stainless steel finish and Slimline Cocobolo grips. Weight about 32 oz. Introduced in 2003.

NIB	Exc.	V.G.	Good	Fair	Poor
900	750	620	400	350	200

Micro Compact Lightweight

Similar to other Micro models, but fitted with an aluminum frame and Novak night sights. Cocobolo wood grips. Bi-Tone finish. Equipped with XML Mini Light. Introduced in 2004. Weight 24 oz. Discontinued.

NIB	Exc.	V.G.	Good	Fair	Poor
900	750	620	400	350	200

Loaded Micro Compact Lightweight

As above, with loaded features: precision fit frames, slides and barrels, flat serrated mainspring housing, lowered and flared ejection port, Delta lightweight hammer, loaded chamber indicator, titanium firing pin, carry bevel treatment, ambidextrous thumb safety, high hand beavertail grip safety, dovetail front sight, Novak or adjustable rear sight and adjustable speed trigger. Introduced in 2005. Discontinued.

NIB	Exc.	V.G.	Good	Fair	Poor
1000	980	780	600	480	300

Model 1911-A1 Mil-Spec Operator

Chambered for .45 ACP. Fitted with 5" barrel. Features Picatinny rail system on frame. Fixed sights. Magazine capacity 7 rounds. Parkerized finish. Discontinued.

NIB	Exc.	V.G.	Good	Fair	Poor
900	750	620	400	350	200

Model 1911-A1 Loaded Operator

Introduced in 2002. Features an integral Picatinny rail on the frame. Chambered for .45 ACP cartridge. Fitted with a 5" barrel. Novak night sights. Parkerized finish. Magazine capacity 7 rounds. Discontinued.

NIB	Exc.	V.G.	Good	Fair	Poor
1150	950	700	500	380	250

Combat Commander

Copy of Colt Model 1911-A1 Combat Commander. Chambered for .45 ACP only. Introduced in 1988.

NIB	Exc.	V.G.	Good	Fair	Poor
600	500	400	350	220	120

Trophy Match

This model has special features such as fully adjustable target sights, match-grade 5" barrel and special wide trigger. Weight about 36 oz. Available in blue, stainless steel or bi-tone finish. In 1997, offered chambered for 9mm cartridge. Values would be the same for both .45 ACP and 9mm models. Note: Add $40 for stainless steel. Discontinued.

NIB	Exc.	V.G.	Good	Fair	Poor
1000	980	780	600	480	300

Loaded Leatham Trophy Match

Introduced in 2005. This .40 S&W pistol fitted with a 5" barrel, with fully adjustable target sights. Black Polymer grips. Dawson magazine well, tuned trigger, match barrel and bushing, checkered frontstrap and other special features. Black finish. Weight about 39 oz. Discontinued.

NIB	Exc.	V.G.	Good	Fair	Poor
1200	1080	900	700	580	300

1911 Emissary

Calibers: 9mm or .45 ACP. Capacity: seven- (.45 ACP) or nine-round (9mm) magazine. Barrel: 4.25" or 5". Grips: Textured G10. Sights: Tactical rack rear/tritium front sights. Length: 8.4" overall. Weight: 40 oz. unloaded. Finish: Two-tone, black slide/stainless frame. Features: Square triggerguard, custom milled slide, flat trigger.

NIB	Exc.	V.G.	Good	Fair	Poor
1230	1150	1100	950	800	—

1911 Garrison

Calibers:.45 ACP. Capacity: seven-round magazine. Barrel: 5". Grips: Thinline checkered wood. Sights: Low profile, three-dot. Length: 8.4" overall. Weight: 37 oz. unloaded. Finish: Blued or stainless. Features: Heirloom-quality 1911.

NIB	Exc.	V.G.	Good	Fair	Poor
800	750	700	680	600	—

1911 GI SERIES

Full Size

Chambered for .45 ACP cartridge. Fitted with a 5" barrel. Old-style fixed sights. Standard checkered brown plastic grips. Lanyard loop on mainspring housing. Stainless steel frame and slide. Magazine capacity 7 rounds. Weight 36 oz. Introduced in 2004. Also offered with Parkerized, OD Green or stainless steel finish. Note: Add $30 for stainless steel. Deduct $45 for Parkerized or OD finish.

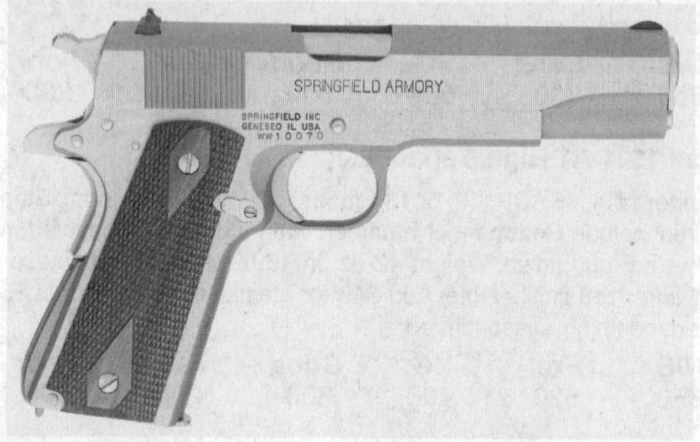

NIB	Exc.	V.G.	Good	Fair	Poor
560	450	380	320	250	120

Full Size High-Capacity

As above, with 10-round magazine. Weight about 38 oz. Introduced in 2005.

NIB	Exc.	V.G.	Good	Fair	Poor
600	500	420	380	300	180

Champion

A scaled-down version of full-size model above. Fitted with 4" fully supported barrel and low-profile military sights. Also has double diamond walnut grips. Black or Parkerized finish. Weight about 34 oz. Introduced in 2004. Discontinued.

NIB	Exc.	V.G.	Good	Fair	Poor
600	500	420	380	300	180

Champion Lightweight

Introduced in 2005. This .45 ACP model fitted with a 4" barrel, with fully supported ramp. Low-profile military sights. Checkered walnut grips. Weight about 28 oz. Discontinued.

NIB	Exc.	V.G.	Good	Fair	Poor
600	500	420	380	300	180

Micro-Compact

As above, but fitted with a 3" fully supported and ramped barrel. Magazine capacity 6 rounds. Weight about 32 oz. Introduced in 2004. Discontinued.

NIB	Exc.	V.G.	Good	Fair	Poor
600	500	420	380	300	180

Super Tuned Champion

Introduced in 1997. Features 4" barrel chambered for .45 ACP cartridge and Novak fixed Lo-Mount sights. Tuned and polished extractor and ejector. Polished feed ramp and barrel throat. Magazine capacity 7 rounds. Choice of blued or Parkerized finish. Weight about 36 oz. Discontinued.

NIB	Exc.	V.G.	Good	Fair	Poor
850	700	580	350	300	200

Super Tuned V10

Similar to model above, with 3.5" barrel. Finish is bi-tone or stainless steel. Weight about 33 oz. Introduced in 1997. Note: Add $100 for stainless steel. Discontinued.

NIB	Exc.	V.G.	Good	Fair	Poor
1000	900	700	600	400	250

Super Tuned Standard

Features a 5" barrel, with stainless steel finish. Weight 39 oz. Has all other super tune features. Introduced in 1997. Discontinued.

NIB	Exc.	V.G.	Good	Fair	Poor
1000	900	700	600	400	250

Range Officer

A 1911 pistol ready to compete out of the box. Caliber: .45 ACP and 9mm. Barrel 5" with blue finish, forged steel slide and frame, 7-round magazine. Other features include adjustable rear sight, match-grade barrel and bushing, checkered mainspring housing, lightweight Delta hammer, extended thumb safety and beavertail grip tang. Weight 40 oz. Discontinued.

NIB	Exc.	V.G.	Good	Fair	Poor
800	680	550	450	350	200

Range Officer Champion

Similar as above. 9mm or .45 ACP single-stack, with 4" barrel. Sights are fiber-optic front and low-profile rear. Lightweight aluminum frame.

NIB	Exc.	V.G.	Good	Fair	Poor
920	790	690	500	360	300

Range Officer Operator

Similar as above. 9mm or .45 ACP single-stack, with 5" barrel. Sights are fiber-optic front and low-profile rear. Parkerized finish. Cocobolo grips.

NIB	Exc.	V.G.	Good	Fair	Poor
1040	900	830	730	400	330

Range Officer Elite Series

Single-stack 1911 like RO Series but with Gen 2 trigger, forward slide serrations, fiber optic front sight, and accessory rail in 9mm, 10mm (new for 2020) or .45 ACP. Introduced 2017. Note: Add $100 for Operator model.

NIB	Exc.	V.G.	Good	Fair	Poor
1030	900	830	730	400	330

Range Officer Compact

Similar as above. 9mm or .45 ACP single-stack, with 4" barrel. Sights are fiber-optic front and low profile rear. Weight 28.5 oz.

NIB	*Exc.*	*V.G.*	*Good*	*Fair*	*Poor*
920	790	690	500	360	300

Tactical Response Pistol (TRP)

Caliber: .45 ACP. Features: Similar to the 1911A1, except checkered frontstrap and mainspring housing, Novak Night Sight combat rear sight and matching dovetailed front sight, tuned, polished extractor, oversize barrel link; lightweight speed trigger and combat action job, match barrel and bushing, extended ambidextrous thumb safety and fitted beavertail grip safety. Textured G10 grips. Finish: Blued or stainless.

NIB	*Exc.*	*V.G.*	*Good*	*Fair*	*Poor*
1450	1260	1030	930	780	—

TRP Champion

Same as above, with 3.9" barrel and Black Armory Kote finish. Weight 33 oz.

NIB	*Exc.*	*V.G.*	*Good*	*Fair*	*Poor*
1180	950	800	600	400	200

TRP Pro

Fitted with a 5" barrel and many special features including Novak Lo-Mount Tritium sights. Magazine capacity 7 rounds. Meets specifications for FBI SWAT team. Weight 36 oz.

NIB	*Exc.*	*V.G.*	*Good*	*Fair*	*Poor*
2000	1750	1200	900	680	300

TRP Operator

This model has all the features of TRP series, with addition of an integral light rail on the frame. Fitted with a 5" barrel. Adjustable night sights. Introduced in 2002. Note: Add $60 for night sights; $100 for OD Green frame and slide.

NIB	*Exc.*	*V.G.*	*Good*	*Fair*	*Poor*
1350	1020	800	600	400	250

1911 Loaded

These Government Models with 5-in. 9mm or .45 ACP match-grade barrels have the features most requested on a custom gun including front and back slide serrations, beavertail grip safety with memory pad, fixed tritium night sights, ambi extended safety, crisp speed trigger, flat mainspring housing. Note: Add $30 for stainless steel; Add $300 for Marine Corps with light rail on frame; Add $400 for light rail and fitted barrel and bushing.

NIB	*Exc.*	*V.G.*	*Good*	*Fair*	*Poor*
800	690	590	500	300	180

Vickers Tactical

Calibers: .45 ACP. Capacity: Eight-round magazine. Barrel: 5" match grade. Grips: Textured G10. Sights: Tritium/Luminescent front, Vickers Elite Battle U-Notch rear. Length: 8.6" overall. Weight: 41.5 oz. unloaded. Finish: Black Cerakote. Features: Solid aluminum match trigger, woven slide serrations, two Vickers Duty magazines, Wilson Combat hammer and safety.

NIB	*Exc.*	*V.G.*	*Good*	*Fair*	*Poor*
1280	1100	960	860	710	—

Lightweight Operator

Blued semi-automatic .45 ACP, with 5" bull barrel. Fixed sights, 5 to 6 lb. trigger pull, Cocobolo grips. Weight 31 oz. Picatinny rail. Introduced 2006. Discontinued.

NIB	*Exc.*	*V.G.*	*Good*	*Fair*	*Poor*
850	700	580	350	300	200

Lightweight Champion Operator

Similar to above, with 4" bull barrel. Introduced 2006. Discontinued.

NIB	*Exc.*	*V.G.*	*Good*	*Fair*	*Poor*
850	700	580	350	300	200

Ronin

Calibers: 9mm, 10mm, or .45 ACP. Capacity: seven- (.45 ACP) or nine-round (9mm) magazine. Barrel: 3", 4", 4.25", or 5". Grips: Checkered wood. Sights: Fiber-optic front, tactical rack, white-dot rear. Length: 8.6" overall. Weight: 40 oz. unloaded. Finish: Two-tone, black slide/stainless frame.

NIB	Exc.	V.G.	Good	Fair	Poor
790	750	720	700	600	—

Ronin Operator

Calibers: 9mm, .45 ACP. Capacity: 7-round (.45 ACP) or 9-round (9mm) magazine. Barrel: 5". Grips: Checkered wood. Sights: Fiber-optic front, tactical-rack, white-dot rear. Length: 8.6". overall. Weight: 40 oz. unloaded. Finish: Two-tone, black slide/stainless frame.

NIB	Exc.	V.G.	Good	Fair	Poor
710	—	—	—	—	—

Enhanced Micro Pistol (EMP)

Compact small-frame 1911-style semi-automatic chambered in 9mm Parabellum or .40 S&W (discontinued), 3" bull barrel, fixed sights. The aluminum frame is reduced .125" just for 9mm-overall-length rounds, thus using only EMP 9-round magazines. Weight is 27 oz, overall length 6.6", height 5". Comes with fixed low profile sights with fiber optic front, double-diamond cocobolo grips. Note: Add $100 for stainless slide.

NIB	Exc.	V.G.	Good	Fair	Poor
1100	960	830	690	520	410

EMP Champion

Longer-slide version with has 4" 9mm barrel, bi-tone finish (stainless steel slide with black aluminum frame), textured frontstrap, low profile fixed sights with fiber-optic front, and comes with three 10-shot magazines. Weight is 31 oz. Thin double-diamond cocobolo grips. Note: Add $40 for bobbed (rounded) mainspring housing in bi-tone or FDE Cerakote.

NIB	Exc.	V.G.	Good	Fair	Poor
1030	910	680	580	480	410

Model 911 .380 ACP

A locked-breech mini-compact .380 ACP with 2.7" barrel, black or stainless slide, aluminum frame, textured front strap and rear mainspring housing, grip safety, polymer grips, and extended thumb safety. One 6-round magazine. Smallest Springfield Armory model. Weight is 12.6 oz. Introduced in 2018. Note: Add $100 for 3-dot tritium night sights and 7-round extra magazine, G-10 grips; Add about $200 for all those extras and FDE, titanium nitride finish; Add about $250 for high-polish stainless slide, vintage blue with ivory-style grips.

NIB	Exc.	V.G.	Good	Fair	Poor
370	300	270	230	140	80

Model 911 9mm

A locked breech mini-compact with 3-in. 9mm barrel, stainless slide and (brushed or nitride finish), one 6-round mag and one 7-round extended mag, tritium night sights, rubber wraparound grips. Weight is 15.3 oz. Introduced in 2019. Note: Add $20 for G10 grips; Add $200 for Viridian Laser Grip.

NIB	Exc.	V.G.	Good	Fair	Poor
470	400	340	290	180	100

XD PISTOLS

Introduced in 2001, Springfield Armory's XD series built in Croatia redefined polymer pistol ergonomics with features such as the grip safety, Ultra Safety Assurance (USA) Action Trigger System, and firing pin block safety. The standard XD is built with a forged slide and hammer-forged barrel, a Melonite finish and a set of steel white dot sights. From these basics come a wide and growing array of pistols in many sizes for sport, target and self-defense. Grip texturing and styles have changed over the years as have other ergonomic features. Calibers .357 Sig and .45 GAP are discontinued. Current models are listed at the end of this section.

XD 4"

Chambered for 9mm, .40 S&W, .357 SIG or .45 GAP cartridges. Barrel length 4". Magazine capacity: 9mm 15 rounds; .40 S&W 12 rounds; .357 SIG 12 rounds; .45 GAP 9 rounds. Weight 23 oz. Note: Add $60 for night sights. Discontinued. The .357 SIG and .45 GAP are discontinued.

NIB	Exc.	V.G.	Good	Fair	Poor
550	450	350	250	180	120

XD 4" Bi-Tone

Offered in 9mm or .40 S&W. This 4" pistol has a black polymer frame and stainless steel slide. Magazine capacity 10 rounds. Weight about 26 oz. Introduced in 2003. Discontinued.

NIB	Exc.	V.G.	Good	Fair	Poor
480	420	320	280	200	150

XD V-10 Ported 4"

Similar to XD, with 4" ported barrel chambered for 9mm, .40 S&W or .357 SIG. Black finish. Weight about 26 oz. Discontinued.

NIB	Exc.	V.G.	Good	Fair	Poor
550	450	350	250	180	120

XD 5" Tactical

Fitted with 5" barrel. Chambered for 9mm, .40 S&W, .357 SIG and .45 ACP. From 2005 to 2007, also offered .45 GAP. Magazine capacity: 9mm 15 rounds; .40 S&W or .357 SIG 12 rounds; .45 ACP 10 rounds; .45 GAP 9 rounds. Weight from 26 to 31 oz. Offered in black or O.D. Green finish. Discontinued.

NIB	Exc.	V.G.	Good	Fair	Poor
500	400	350	250	200	150

XD 5" Tactical Pro

Introduced in 2003. Features Robar NP3 finish, fiber-optic front sight and fixed rear. Frame built with an oversized beavertail frame extension of a higher grip. Chambered for 9mm, .357 SIG., 40 S&W and .45 GAP cartridge. Magazine capacity: 9mm 15 rounds; .40 S&W and .357 SIG 12 rounds; .45 GAP 9 rounds. Weight 31 oz. Discontinued.

NIB	Exc.	V.G.	Good	Fair	Poor
880	750	600	500	380	250

XD 5" Bi-Tone Tactical

Introduced in 2005. Chambered for .45 GAP cartridge. Fitted with a 5" barrel. Black polymer frame and stainless steel slide. Magazine capacity 9 rounds. Weight 31 oz. Discontinued.

NIB	Exc.	V.G.	Good	Fair	Poor
500	400	350	300	200	120

XD Sub-Compact

Introduced in 2003. This polymer pistol chambered for 9mm or .40 S&W cartridge. Fitted with a 3" barrel, with light rail on the dust cover. Grip safety and safe action trigger. Magazine capacity 10 rounds. Weight about 20 oz. Fixed sights. Note: Add $60 for night sights; $70 for XML Mini light. Discontinued.

NIB	Exc.	V.G.	Good	Fair	Poor
450	400	300	250	180	120

XD 45 ACP

Polymer semi-automatic in black, green or bi-tone. Holds 13+1 .45 ACP. Imported from Croatia. Fixed sights. Service model: 4" barrel, weight 30 oz. Tactical model: 5" barrel, weight 32 oz. Picatinny rail. Introduced 2006. Discontinued.

NIB	Exc.	V.G.	Good	Fair	Poor
580	500	380	280	200	150

XD(M)

Enhanced variation of XD series, with interchangeable backstraps, improved magazine release and disassembly design. Offered in 9mm, .40 S&W or .45 ACP, with 4.5" barrel. Three-dot sights with night sights available. Black or two-tone polymer frame, Ultra Safety Assurance trigger, striker fired, grip safety, ambidextrous magazine releases, accessory rail, loaded chamber and cocked striker indicators. Weight 27 oz. empty. Also available in Competition model (9mm only), with 5.25" barrel with lightening cut on top of slide. Discontinued.

NIB	Exc.	V.G.	Good	Fair	Poor
550	480	420	300	200	100

XDM-3.8

Sub-compact model chambered in 9mm Parabellum (19+1) and .40

S&W (16+1). Features include 3.8" steel full-ramp barrel; dovetail front and rear 3-dot sights (Tritium and fiber-optics sights available); polymer frame; stainless steel slide with slip-resistant slide serrations; loaded chamber indicator; grip safety. Black, bi-tone or stainless steel finish. Overall length 7", weight 27.5 oz. (9mm). Discontinued.

NIB	Exc.	V.G.	Good	Fair	Poor
550	480	420	300	200	100

XD-E

Polymer-frame with exposed hammer, DA/SA trigger. 9mm or .45 ACP single-stack, with 3.3", 3.8" or 4". barrel. Sights are fiber-optic front and dovetail rear. Extended magazine grip and flush magazine.

NIB	Exc.	V.G.	Good	Fair	Poor
540	480	400	340	340	200

XD-S

Designed for concealed carry, this member of XD polymer-frame series is a single-stack 9mm or .45 ACP, with 3.3" or 4" barrel. Sights are fiber-optic front and dovetail rear. Magazine capacity: 9mm 7 rounds; .45 ACP 5 rounds. Discontinued.

NIB	Exc.	V.G.	Good	Fair	Poor
500	440	350	300	250	200

XD Mod. 2

This model has the same features as other XD models, with several enhancements. These include improved gripping textures, re-contoured slimmer frame and slide, higher position grip safety and no-snag trigger-guard. In 9mm, .40 S&W or .45 ACP, with 3", 3.3", 4", or 5" barrel. Add $25 for .45-caliber, available only with 3.3" barrel. Discontinued.

NIB	Exc.	V.G.	Good	Fair	Poor
500	420	350	280	220	200

LEATHAM LEGEND SERIES

This series introduced in 2003. Identified with a unique series marking, serial number and certificate of authenticity. Two sets of grips will come with each pistol: one Cocobolo with laser engraved signature of Rob Leatham; the other a black micarta double diamond slimline grip. Custom aluminum case is standard for this series. Discontinued.

TGO 1

Full custom pistol from Springfield Custom Shop, with Nowlin Match-Grade throated barrel and bushing. Robar bi-tone finish, Bomar low-mount adjustable sights and a number of other custom features. Chambered for .45 ACP cartridge. Weight 38 oz. Four magazines are standard. Discontinued.

NIB	Exc.	V.G.	Good	Fair	Poor
2400	1880	1500	—	—	—

TGO 2

Similar to TGO 1, but hand-built by Springfield Armory. Discontinued.

NIB	Exc.	V.G.	Good	Fair	Poor
1900	1500	1200	—	—	—

TGO 3

An enhanced high-end production model, with lightweight aluminum slide. Bi-tone finish. Weight 30 oz. Discontinued.

NIB	Exc.	V.G.	Good	Fair	Poor
1300	1020	800	—	—	—

SPRINGFIELD CUSTOM SHOP

Springfield Armory's Custom Shop currently offers 20 models of 1911 ranging from $2,395 to $3,995 for a variety of shooting competitions and disciplines including premium self-defense models. All are hand built from select components by the Shop's craftsmen and many options are available. Values should be judged by individual model and options selected. When these one-of-a-kind pistols are encountered, it is advisable for shooter or collector to get an independent appraisal. Firearm styles below become "discontinued" as the shooting disciplines and firearm design have evolved.

Custom Carry

The basic Custom Shop 1911. Previously, it may be encountered chambered for the following cartridges: .45 ACP, 9mm Parabellum, .38 Super, 10mm, .40 S&W, 9mmx21. Currently in .45 ACP only. Fitted with Novak low profile 3-dot sights, speed trigger, match barrel and bushing, extended thumb safety, beveled magazine well, Commander hammer, polished feed ramp and throated barrel, tuned extractor, lowered and flared ejection port, fitted slide to frame, full-length spring guide rod and cocobolo grips. Supplied with two magazines and plastic carrying case. Note: Add $1,000 for Ultimate Carry in 9mm or .45; Add $1,100 for compact carry in 9mm or .45.

NIB	Exc.	V.G.	Good	Fair	Poor
2050	1730	1480	1250	750	450

Basic Competition Model

Chambered for .45 ACP. Features a variety of special options for the competition shooter. Special BoMar sights, match trigger, custom slide to frame fit, polished feed-ramp and throated barrel are just some of the features.

NIB	Exc.	V.G.	Good	Fair	Poor
1800	1600	1280	1050	650	400

N.R.A. PPC

Designed to comply with NRA rules for PPC competition. Chambered for .45 ACP cartridge, with match-grade barrel and chamber. Polished feedramp, throated barrel, recoil buffer system, walnut grips and fully adjustable sights. Sold with a custom carrying case. Discontinued.

NIB	Exc.	V.G.	Good	Fair	Poor
1600	1450	1080	800	500	300

Trophy Master Expert Limited Class

Chambered for .45 ACP. Adjustable BoMar rear sight, match barrel, polished ramp and throated barrel, extended ambidextrous thumb safety, beveled and polished magazine well, full-length recoil spring guide, match trigger, Commander hammer, lowered and flared ejection port, tuned extractor, fitted slide to frame, extended slide release, flat mainspring housing, Pachmayr wrap-around grips, two magazines with slam pads and plastic carrying case. Discontinued.

NIB	Exc.	V.G.	Good	Fair	Poor
2100	1750	1300	950	600	400

Expert Pistol

Similar to above model, with progressive triple port compensator. Discontinued.

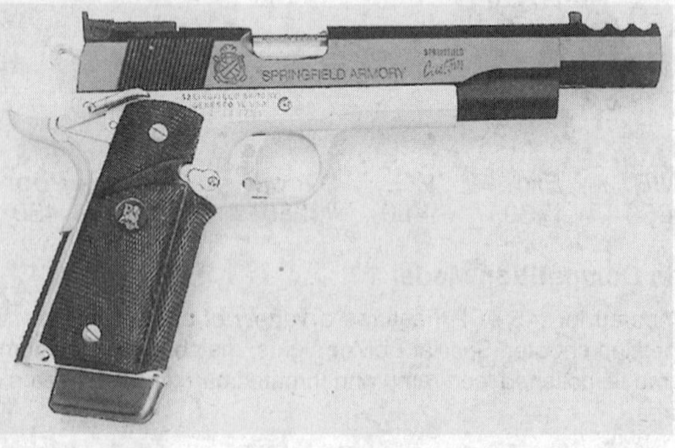

NIB	Exc.	V.G.	Good	Fair	Poor
2200	1850	1400	1000	650	400

Bureau Model 1911-A1

Introduced in 1998. Features 5" match barrel, speed trigger, lowered and flared ejection port, beavertail grip safety, Lo-Mount Novak night sights, frontstrap checkering, Black T finish and special serial numbers with FBI prefix. Bureau Model markings on slide. Discontinued.

NIB	Exc.	V.G.	Good	Fair	Poor
2100	1750	1300	950	600	400

Springfield Formula "Squirtgun"

Chambered for .45 ACP, .38 Super, 9mmx19, 9mmx21, 9mmx23. Fitted with a high capacity 20-round frame, customer specifications sights, hard chrome frame and slide, triple chambered tapered cone compensator, full recoil spring guide and reverse plug, shock butt, lowered and flared ejection port, fitted trigger, Commander hammer, polished feed ramp and throated barrel, flat checkered mainspring housing, extended ambidextrous thumb safety, tuned extractor, checkered front strap, bottom of triggerguard checkered, rear of slide serrated, cocking sensations on front of slide, built in beveled magazine well and checkered wood grips. Discontinued.

NIB	Exc.	V.G.	Good	Fair	Poor
3500	2950	2500	2000	1400	700

Bullseye Wadcutter

Chambered for .45 ACP, .38 Super, 10mm and .40 S&W. Slide fitted with BoMar rib. Standard features include full-length recoil spring guide rod, speed trigger, Commander hammer, lowered and flared ejection port, tuned extractor, fitted slide to frame, beveled magazine well, checkered front strap, checkered main spring housing, removable grip scope mount, match barrel and bushing, polished feed ramp and throated barrel, walnut grips and two magazines with slam pads. Discontinued.

NIB	Exc.	V.G.	Good	Fair	Poor
1800	1600	1280	1050	650	400

Trophy Master Distinguished Pistol

Chambered for the following cartridges: .45 ACP, .38 Super, 10mm, .40 S&W, 9mmx21. Special BoMar adjustable rear sight with hidden rear leaf, triple port compensator on match barrel, full-length recoil spring guide rod and recoil spring retainer, shock butt, lowered and flared ejection port, fitted speed trigger, Commander hammer, polished feed ramp and throated barrel, flat checkered magazine well and mainspring housing matched to beveled magazine well, extended ambidextrous thumb safety, tuned extractor, checkered front strap, flattened and checkered triggerguard, serrated slide top and compensator, cocking sensations on front of slide, checkered walnut grips, two magazines with slam pads and carrying case. Discontinued.

NIB	Exc.	V.G.	Good	Fair	Poor
2450	1900	1350	1000	650	500

Distinguished Limited Class

Similar to above model, but built to comply with USPSA "Limited Class" competition rules. This model has no compensator. Discontinued.

NIB	Exc.	V.G.	Good	Fair	Poor
2700	2000	1500	1000	650	500

National Match Hardball & Bullseye

Government Model 1911 with custom fitted frame and slide with fitted 9mm or .45 ACP barrel and bushing, fully adjustable target sights, fitted trigger with 4-lb. pull, overall tuned with parts polished for reliability and accuracy. Checkered frontstrap. Weight of 40 oz. Also available in a Bullseye Wadcutter model in same calibers with slide mounted scope rail. First introduced in 1988.

NIB	Exc.	V.G.	Good	Fair	Poor
2200	1880	1500	1200	730	440

CMC Formula "Squirtgun"

Chambered for .45 ACP, .38 Super, 9mmx19, 9mmx21, 9mmx23. Has a 20-round magazine and modular frame. All other features same as Trophy Master.

NIB	Exc.	V.G.	Good	Fair	Poor
2750	2000	1200	800	400	200

National Match Model

As above, with National Match barrel and bushing, adjustable sights and checkered walnut grips. Introduced in 1988.

NIB	Exc.	V.G.	Good	Fair	Poor
1540	1150	850	600	400	300

Competition Grade

Hand-tuned match-grade trigger, low-profile combat sights, ambidextrous safety and Commander-type hammer. Furnished with Pachmayr grips. Introduced in 1988. Discontinued.

NIB	Exc.	V.G.	Good	Fair	Poor
1600	1200	900	650	400	350

A Model Master Grade Competition Pistol

Similar to Custom Carry Gun, with National Match barrel and bushing. Introduced in 1988. Discontinued.

NIB	Exc.	V.G.	Good	Fair	Poor
1700	1500	1250	850	400	350

Model B-1 Master Grade Competition Pistol

Specially designed for USPSA/IPSC competition. Introduced in 1988. Discontinued.

NIB	Exc.	V.G.	Good	Fair	Poor
2000	1750	1250	850	400	350

High Capacity Full-House Race Gun

Built with all available Racegun options. Offered in .45 ACP, 9x25 Dillon, .38 Super and custom calibers on request. Discontinued.

Night Light Standard

Introduced in 1996. Limited edition from Springfield, distributor Lew Horton. Full-size Model 1911A1 pistol chambered for .45 ACP. Has a lightweight frame and slide, with Millett night sights with Hogue rubber wrap-around grips. Fitted with extended beavertail safety. Weight 29 oz. Discontinued.

NIB	Exc.	V.G.	Good	Fair	Poor
620	500	400	300	200	100

Night Light Compact

This model also introduced by Lew Horton in 1996. Similar to above model, but fitted with 4.25" barrel and lightweight frame and slide. Weight 27 oz. Discontinued.

NIB	Exc.	V.G.	Good	Fair	Poor
620	500	400	300	200	100

Night Compact

Same as above, with steel frame and slide. Discontinued.

NIB	Exc.	V.G.	Good	Fair	Poor
620	500	400	300	200	100

Omega

A .38 Super, 10mm Norma or .45-caliber semi-automatic pistol, with 5" or 6" polygon rifled barrel, ported or unported, adjustable sights and Pachmayr grips. Patterned somewhat after Colt Model 1911. Introduced in 1987. Note: Add $400 for Caliber Conversion Units. Discontinued.

NIB	Exc.	V.G.	Good	Fair	Poor
650	500	350	250	200	120

XD Custom Pro

This pistol was built in the Custom Shop and available in service and tactical sizes. Calibers offered include 9mm, .357 SIG, .40 S&W, .40 GAP and .45 ACP. Among some of the special features are high hand frame relief, overtravel stop, low-mount Bomar sights, extended magazine release, National Match barrel and special finish. Discontinued.

NIB	Exc.	V.G.	Good	Fair	Poor
1500	1100	820	680	500	300

XD Carry Pro

This model offered in sub-compact, service and tactical sizes. In sub-compact size the following calibers are offered: 9mm and .40 S&W. Many special features as listed above. Discontinued.

NIB	Exc.	V.G.	Good	Fair	Poor
750	550	400	300	200	100

NEW PRODUCTION

XD Legacy Service

The basic XD that started it all. A 4" barreled service-size belt pistol in 9mm, 7.3" long, 5.5" high and a weight of 28 oz. Comes with one 16-round magazine. Black Melonite finish.

NIB	Exc.	V.G.	Good	Fair	Poor
290	250	210	180	100	70

XD Legacy Defender Sub-Compact

A 3"-barreled 9mm designed for CCW with one 13-round magazine, a height of 4.75", length of 6.25" and a weight of 26 oz.

NIB	Exc.	V.G.	Good	Fair	Poor
290	240	210	180	100	60

XD-M

A large-frame in .45 ACP or 10mm with 4.5" barrel, 7.7" long, 5.75" high and a weight of 31 or 32 oz. Two 13-round magazines (.45); 15-round (19mm). Fiber-optic front sight and white dot rear. Black Melonite finish. Note: Add 30% for .578x28 threaded 5.28-in. barrel and suppressor-height sights.

NIB	Exc.	V.G.	Good	Fair	Poor
550	470	400	340	200	130

XD-M Competition

A competition model in .45 ACP or 10mm with 5.25" barrel, 8.3" long, 5.75" high and weight of 32 oz., fully adjustable rear sight and fiber-optic front. Black Melonite finish. Comes with three magazines.

NIB	Exc.	V.G.	Good	Fair	Poor
660	560	480	400	250	150

XD-M Elite

A 9mm XD with barrel lengths of 3.8", 4.4" (20-round magazine), 5.28" (threaded .5x28) or 5.25". barrel (22-round). Short barrel models come with Tactical Rack sights; threaded model with suppressor height sights, target model with fully adjustable sights. Weights of 28 to 30 oz. Note: Add $125 for threaded model in FDE Cerakote; Add $75 for 5.25" barrel with fully adjustable target sights.

NIB	Exc.	V.G.	Good	Fair	Poor
480	400	350	290	180	100

XD-M Elite 3.8" Compact

Caliber: .45 ACP or 10mm. Capacity: 10-round magazine. Barrel: 3.8". Grip: Textured polymer. Sights: Fixed, fiber-optic front, low profile U-Notch rear. Length: 6.75" overall. Weight: 25 oz. unloaded. Finish: Melonite. Features: Removable magwell.

NIB	Exc.	V.G.	Good	Fair	Poor
600	590	570	510	500	—

XD-M Elite 3.8" Compact Hex Dragonfly Optic

NIB	Exc.	V.G.	Good	Fair	Poor
690	630	600	580	540	—

XD-S Mod.2 Single Stack

Caliber: .45 ACP or 9mm. Capacity: 10-round magazine. Barrel: 3.3" or 4". Grip: Textured polymer. Sights: Fixed, fiber-optic front, low-profile U-Notch rear. Length: 6.3" overall with 3.3" barrel. Weight: 23 oz. unloaded with a flush-mount magazine. Finish: Melonite. Features: Removable magwell.

NIB	Exc.	V.G.	Good	Fair	Poor
400	390	330	280	250	—

XD-S Mod.2 Single Stack OSP Crimson Trace Optic

NIB	Exc.	V.G.	Good	Fair	Poor
510	490	430	380	350	—

XD-E

A single-stack, conventional double-single-action pistol with exposed hammer and ambi safety/decocker with 3.3" (9mm or .45 ACP), 3.8" or 4.5" barrel in 9mm. Features include low cocking effort slide, fiber optic front sight and white dot rear, grip width of 1", height of 5" and a weight of 24.8 to 28 oz., length 6.75" to 7.87" depending on barrel length. Note: Add 30% for .45 ACP.

NIB	Exc.	V.G.	Good	Fair	Poor
460	390	330	280	170	100

Hellcat

A high-capacity micro-compact 9mm with 3" barrel, width of 1" and weight of 18.3 oz. One flush-fit 11-round, one extended 13-round magazine. Fiber-optic front sight and Tactical Rack U-notch rear. Black frame and Melonite finished slide. Note: Add $20 for optics ready; Add $40 for FDE Cerakote finish; Add $100 for optics ready slide and FDE Cerakote finish.

NIB	Exc.	V.G.	Good	Fair	Poor
490	410	350	300	180	100

Hellcat 3" Micro Compact

Caliber: 9mm. Capacity: 11- and 13-round magazine. Barrel: 3". Grip: Textured polymer. Sights: Fixed, Tritium/Luminescent front, Tactical Rack U-Notch rear. Length: 6" overall. Weight: 18.3 oz. unloaded with flush magazine. Finish: Matte black or Desert FDE. Features: Dual captive recoil spring w/ full-length guide rod. With or without a manual thumb safety.

NIB	Exc.	V.G.	Good	Fair	Poor
580	450	410	420	400	—

Hellcat Micro Compact OSP with optical sight mount

NIB	Exc.	V.G.	Good	Fair	Poor
590	460	450	410	390	—

Hellcat RDP (Rapid Defense Package)

Caliber: 9mm. Capacity: 11- and 13-round magazine. Barrel: 3.8". Grip: Textured polymer. Sights: Fixed, Springfield Armory HEX micro red dot. Length: 7" overall. Weight: 19.3 oz. unloaded with a flush magazine. Finish: Matte black. Features: Self-indexing single port compensator, with or without a manual thumb safety.

NIB	Exc.	V.G.	Good	Fair	Poor
870	800	750	660	560	—

1911 PPC

A long-slide version in 9mm or .45 ACP with 6" barrel, low mount Aristocrat T5-45 fully adjustable target sights, undercut front, G10 grips, 3.5-lb trigger, checkered frontstrap and mainspring housing.

NIB	Exc.	V.G.	Good	Fair	Poor
3100	2650	2250	1900	1150	690

1911 Single Stack Classic & Distinguished

Standard 5" 9mm or .45 ACP hand fitted with 3.5-lb. trigger pull, Tech Well mag well and grips, two 7-round magazines (10-round in 9mm). fully adjustable rear, fiber-optic front. Note: Add $500 for Distinguished Classic with Octo-Grip front strap and mainspring housing texturing, a charcoal-blued finish, French border on slide, and gold bead front sight.

NIB	Exc.	V.G.	Good	Fair	Poor
2850	2430	2050	1750	1050	650

1911 TGO

Designed by Rob Leatham and with his signature grips, 5" .45 ACP barrel, two-tone with blue slide over stainless frame, fully adjustable target sights and fiber-optic front. Two 7-round magazines.

NIB	Exc.	V.G.	Good	Fair	Poor
3370	2860	2430	2070	1240	750

1911 Professional

Has the same features as the older "FBI HRT" model with 5" barrel in 9mm or .45 ACP, fitted and tuned for reliability with 4.5-lb trigger, low mount Novak sights with tritium inserts, hand checkered frontstrap, cocobolo grips and six 7-round magazines (six 9-round mags in 9mm). Comes with or without underframe accessory rail.

NIB	Exc.	V.G.	Good	Fair	Poor
2850	2430	2050	1750	1050	650

SA-35

Calibers: 9mm. Capacity: 13-round magazine. Barrel: 4.7". Grips: Checkered walnut. Sights: White dot front, tactical rack rear. Length: 7.8" overall. Weight: 31.5 oz. unloaded. Finish: Matte blued. Features: Clone of the iconic Hi Power pistol.

NIB	Exc.	V.G.	Good	Fair	Poor
670	650	600	500	400	—

SPRINGFIELD ARMS COMPANY

Springfield, Massachusetts

Belt Model (Antique)

A .31-caliber percussion revolver, with 4", 5" or 6" round barrels, centrally mounted hammer and etched 6-shot cylinder. Made with/without a loading lever. Early production versions marked "Jaquith's Patent 1838" on frame; later production marked "Springfield Arms" on top strap. Approximately 150 made.

Exc.	Fine	V.G.	Good	Fair	Poor
2600	1920	1400	880	400	250

Warner Model (Antique)

As above, but marked "Warner's Patent Jan. 1851". Approximately 150 made.

Exc.	Fine	V.G.	Good	Fair	Poor
5000	3000	2000	1000	500	300

Double Trigger Belt Model (Antique)

As above, with two triggers set within a conventional triggerguard. Forward trigger revolves the cylinder. Approximately 350 made in 1851.

Exc.	Fine	V.G.	Good	Fair	Poor
1620	1280	910	550	200	140

Pocket Model Revolver (Antique)

A .28-caliber percussion revolver with 2.5" round barrel, centrally mounted hammer, no loading lever and etched 6-shot cylinder. Marked "Warner's Patent Jan. 1851" and "Springfield Arms Company". Blued case-hardened, with walnut grips. Early production examples do not have a groove on cylinder and have a rounded frame. Approximately 525 made in 1851.

Courtesy Milwaukee Public Museum, Milwaukee, Wisconsin

Exc.	Fine	V.G.	Good	Fair	Poor
1750	1250	910	580	150	100

Ring Trigger Pocket Model (Antique)

As above, fitted with a ring trigger that revolved the cylinder. Approximately 150 made in 1851.

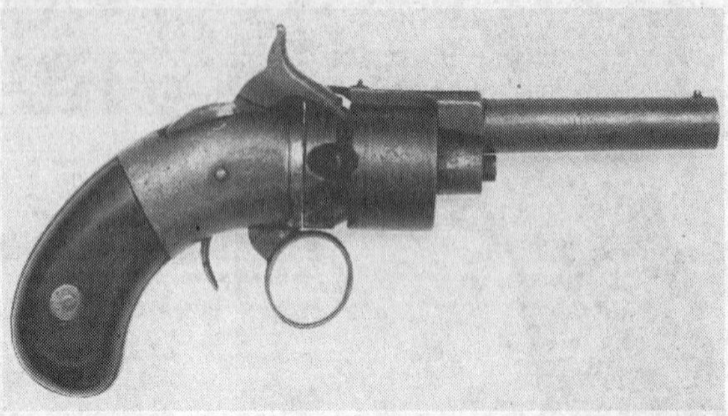

Courtesy Milwaukee Public Museum, Milwaukee, Wisconsin

Exc.	Fine	V.G.	Good	Fair	Poor
1720	1280	910	550	200	140

Double Trigger Pocket Model (Antique)

As above, with two triggers, one which locks the cylinder. Approximately 100 made in 1851.

Exc.	Fine	V.G.	Good	Fair	Poor
2750	2200	1540	880	200	140

Late Pocket Model (Antique)

As above, except cylinder is automatically turned when hammer is cocked. Top strap marked "Warner's Patent/James Warner, Springfield, Mass.". Approximately 500 made in 1851.

Exc.	Fine	V.G.	Good	Fair	Poor
1300	880	600	320	100	70

Dragoon Model (Antique)

A .40-caliber percussion revolver with 6" or 7.5" round barrel. Some fitted with/without loading levers. Top strap marked "Springfield Arms Company". Blued with walnut grips. Approximately 110 made in 1851. Values are speculative due to rarity.

Exc.	Fine	V.G.	Good	Fair	Poor
—	—	9000	6000	3000	1500

Navy Model (Antique)

A .36-caliber percussion revolver with 6" round barrel, centrally mounted hammer and 6-shot etched cylinder. Top strap marked "Springfield Arms Company". Blued case-hardened, with walnut grips. This model manufactured in two variations: one with a single trigger; other with a double trigger, the forward one which locks the cylinder. Both variations had loading levers. Approximately 250 made in 1851.

Exc.	Fine	V.G.	Good	Fair	Poor
6000	4250	2950	1650	500	350

Double-Barrel Shotguns

Springfield Arms Co. was bought by Stevens, who used the Springfield brand name on many good quality single-/double-barrel shotguns. Values range from $100 to $1,600 depending on model, gauge and condition. See also Stevens.

S.P.S. (Eagle Imports)
Spain

Manufacturer of high-end competition firearms, imported by Eagle Imports.

Vista

Calibers: 9mm, .38 Super. Capacity: 17-round magazine. Barrels: 5- or 5.5-in., match-grade with compensator. Sights: Optic ready. Weight: 43 oz. Finish: Black chrome. Grips: Aluminum. Features: Polymer frame, checkered frontstrap serrations, skeletonized trigger and hammer, flared and lowered ejection port, ambidextrous safety, wide mag well. Imported from Spain by Eagle Imports.

NIB	Exc.	V.G.	Good	Fair	Poor
2450	—	—	—	—	—

Pantera

Calibers: 9mm, .40 S&W, .45 ACP. Capacity: 12-, 16- or 18-round magazine. Barrel: 5-in., match-grade. Sights: Bomar-type, fully adjustable rear, fiber-optic front. Weight: 36.6 oz. Finish: Black, black chrome, chrome. Grips: Polymer. Features: Polymer frame, checkered frontstrap serrations, skeletonized trigger and hammer, flared and lowered ejection port, ambidextrous safety, wide mag well, full dust cover. Imported from Spain by Eagle Imports.

NIB	Exc.	V.G.	Good	Fair	Poor
1700	—	—	—	—	—

SPS
Spain

Manufacturer of competition 1911 pistols imported by Eagle Imports and RSA Enterprises.

Vista

1911-style semi-auto pistol designed for IPSC and USPSA competition available in 9mm with 5" barrel or .38 Super with 5.5" barrel.

NIB	Exc.	V.G.	Good	Fair	Poor
1950	1750	—	—	—	—

Pantera

1911-style semi-auto pistol with custom features. 5" barrel in calibers .45 ACP, .40 S&W, or 9mm.

NIB	Exc.	V.G.	Good	Fair	Poor
1500	1300	—	—	—	—

SQUIBBMAN

See—SQUIRES BINGHAM MFG. CO., INC.

SQUIRES BINGHAM MFG. CO., INC.

Rizal, Philippine Islands

Firearms produced by this company are marketed under the trademark Squibbman.

Model 100D

A .38 Special caliber double-action swingout cylinder revolver, with 3", 4" or 6" ventilated rib barrel, adjustable sights, matte black finish and walnut grips.

NIB	Exc.	V.G.	Good	Fair	Poor
—	180	100	80	60	40

Model 100DC

As above, without ventilated rib.

NIB	Exc.	V.G.	Good	Fair	Poor
—	200	100	80	60	40

Model 100

As above, with tapered barrel and uncheckered walnut grips.

NIB	Exc.	V.G.	Good	Fair	Poor
—	200	100	80	60	40

Thunder Chief

As above in .22 or .22 Magnum caliber with heavier ventilated rib barrel, shrouded ejector and ebony grips.

NIB	Exc.	V.G.	Good	Fair	Poor
—	220	120	100	80	60

SSK INDUSTRIES

Bloomingdale, Ohio

SSK-Contender

Custom-made pistol available in 74 different calibers from .178 Bee to .588 JDJ. Built on Thompson/Center action.

NIB	Exc.	V.G.	Good	Fair	Poor
1250	1050	880	600	550	300

SSK-XP100

Custom-made pistol utilizing Rem. XP100 action. Available in a variety of calibers and sight configurations.

NIB	Exc.	V.G.	Good	Fair	Poor
1400	1220	900	620	580	400

.50 Caliber XP100

As above, with integral muzzle brake and reinforced composition stock.

NIB	Exc.	V.G.	Good	Fair	Poor
1750	1500	1250	1000	750	450

STACATTO (STI INTERNATIONAL)

See—STI INTERNATIONAL

STACCATO 2011 SERIES

Calibers: 9mm, .40 S&W, .38 Super. Capacity: Nine-, 17- or 21-round magazine. Barrels: 3.9" or 5" match-grade. Sights: Optic-ready, Dawson Precision Perfect Impact. Weight: 38–46.5 oz. Finish: Carbon black. Grips: Textured polymer. Features: 4-lb. trigger pull, ambidextrous safety levers, single- or double-stack magazine.

Staccato-P

9mm, 4.4" barrel, double-stack magazine. Weight 33 oz. Add $500 for Model P Tactical with DUO optical sight, as pictured.

NIB	Exc.	V.G.	Good	Fair	Poor
1790	1560	1330	1210	960	—

Staccato-C2

Compact version of Model P above, with 3.9" barrel, 9mm double-stack 16-round magazines. Weight 25 oz. Add $500 for DUO optical sight.

NIB	Exc.	V.G.	Good	Fair	Poor
1710	1510	1310	1160	960	—

Staccato-C

Similar to Model C2 except with a single-stack magazine.

NIB	Exc.	V.G.	Good	Fair	Poor
1620	1420	1220	1120	900	—

Stacatto R

9mm or .45ACP single stack magazine, 5" barrel, 35 oz.

NIB	Exc.	V.G.	Good	Fair	Poor
2000	—	—	—	—	—

Staccato-XC

9mm, 5" barrel, 39 oz. Integrated compensator, DUO optical sight.

NIB	Exc.	V.G.	Good	Fair	Poor
3660	3220	2760	2500	1660	—

Staccato-XL

9mm or .40 S&W double-stack magazine, 5.4" barrel, 38 oz. Add $400 for chrome finish version.

NIB	Exc.	V.G.	Good	Fair	Poor
2910	2560	2160	1960	1610	—

STAFFORD, T. J.

New Haven, Connecticut

Pocket Pistol (Antique)

A .22-caliber single-shot spur trigger pistol, with 3.5" octagonal barrel marked "T.J. Stafford New Haven Ct.". Silver-plated brass frame. Walnut or rosewood grips. Values are for engraved specimens, as those are the most often encountered.

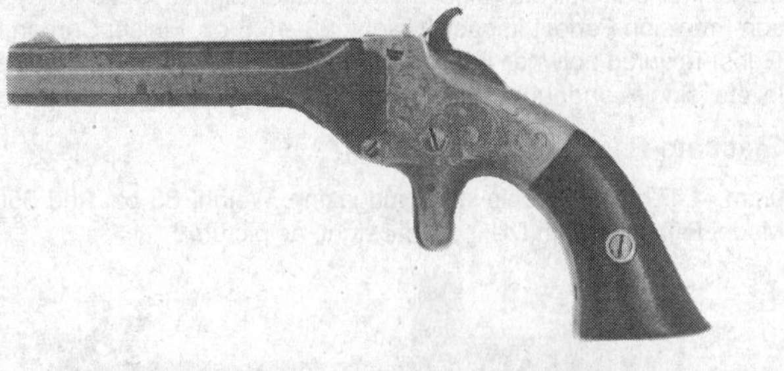

Courtesy W.P. Hallstein III and son Chip

Exc.	*Fine*	*V.G.*	*Good*	*Fair*	*Poor*
1700	1200	800	600	350	200

Large Frame Model Antique

As above in .38 rimfire caliber, with 6" barrel. Values are speculative due to rarity.

Exc.	*Fine*	*V.G.*	*Good*	*Fair*	*Poor*
—	2000	1200	750	500	300

STAG ARMS
New Britain, Connecticut

NOTE: All Stag rifles are available in left-hand configuration. Prices are approximately $25 - $40 higher than right-handed models listed here. SEE POLITICAL PANIC PRICING.

STAG 15 SERIES

Calibers: 5.56 NATO/.223, 6mm ARC, 6.8 SPC II. Capacities: 20- or 30-round magazine. Features: This manufacturer offers many AR-style rifles or carbines with many optional features including barrel length and configurations, stocks, sights, rail systems, and both direct-impingement and gas-piston operating systems. Left-hand models are available on some products. Tactical line added 2022. SEE POLITICAL PANIC PRICING.

Stag 15 Tactical 16

NIB	*Exc.*	*V.G.*	*Good*	*Fair*	*Poor*
900	790	630	500	—	—

Stag 15 Model 1

Basic M-4 Carbine pattern. Cal. 5.56mm/.223. 16" M-4 barrel, with flash hider and bayonet lug. A2 upper receiver, with adjustable rear sight. Six-position collapsible buttstock.

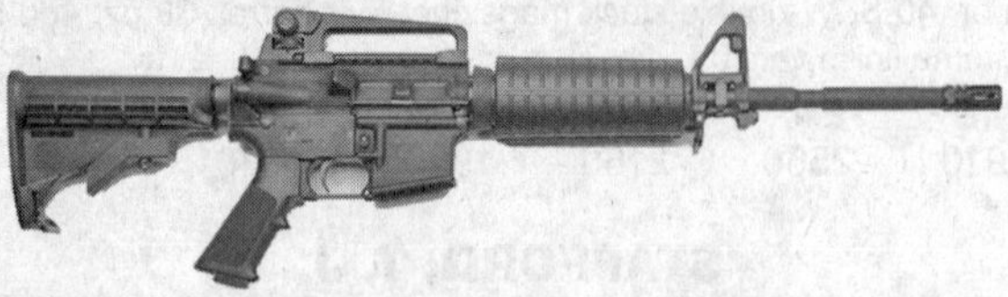

NIB	*Exc.*	*V.G.*	*Good*	*Fair*	*Poor*
950	800	680	500	350	200

Stag 15 Model 2

As above, with flattop upper receiver. Includes MI ERS flip type rear sight assembly.

NIB	*Exc.*	*V.G.*	*Good*	*Fair*	*Poor*
950	800	680	500	350	200

Stag 15 Model 2 T

As above, with A.R.M.S. sight system and Samson MRFS-C four sided handguard.

NIB	*Exc.*	*V.G.*	*Good*	*Fair*	*Poor*
1050	900	780	600	400	250

Stag 15 Model 3

M4-type carbine featuring flattop receiver and gas block, with Picatinny rails. Six-position collapsible buttstock.

NIB	*Exc.*	*V.G.*	*Good*	*Fair*	*Poor*
950	800	680	500	350	200

Stag 15 Model 4

An A2-type rifle featuring 20" barrel. Flash hider and bayonet lug.

NIB	*Exc.*	*V.G.*	*Good*	*Fair*	*Poor*
950	800	680	500	350	200

Stag 6.8 Model 5

Cal. 6.8 SPC. 16" barrel. Flattop receiver, with Picatinny rail. Six-position collapsible buttstock. 25-round magazine.

NIB	*Exc.*	*V.G.*	*Good*	*Fair*	*Poor*
1050	900	780	600	400	250

Stag 15 Model 6 Super Varminter

24" heavy barrel. No flash hider. Flattop receiver, with Picatinny rail. Two-stage trigger. Free-float round handguard. A2-type fixed stock.

NIB	Exc.	V.G.	Good	Fair	Poor
1050	900	780	600	400	250

Stag 8T

AR/M4-style in .223 Rem./5.56 NATO, with 16" chrome-lined barrel. Adjustable gas piston action, synthetic pistol grip, Diamondhead VRS-T aluminum handguard and flip-up front and rear sights.

NIB	Exc.	V.G.	Good	Fair	Poor
1000	900	800	500	400	300

Stag 15 Pistol

Features 7.5" 5.56 barrel, with QPQ finish and Low Pro Gas Block. Magazine capacity 30 rounds (10 where required). Features include 4" free-float handguard, Magpul MOE pistol grip and triggerguard, compensator and pistol length buffer tube, with 3" foam cover. Length 22.5"; weight 4.8 lbs.

NIB	Exc.	V.G.	Good	Fair	Poor
850	700	500	400	250	180

Stag 15 M4

NIB	Exc.	V.G.	Good	Fair	Poor
900	780	600	490	—	—

Stag 15 Retro

NIB	Exc.	V.G.	Good	Fair	Poor
1040	920	800	650	—	—

Stag 15 Bones

NIB	Exc.	V.G.	Good	Fair	Poor
800	—	—	—	—	—

Stag 15 O.R.C.

NIB	Exc.	V.G.	Good	Fair	Poor
800	—	—	—	—	—

Stag 15 Super Varminter (6.8)

NIB	Exc.	V.G.	Good	Fair	Poor
1100	980	800	610	—	—

Stag 15 LEO

NIB	Exc.	V.G.	Good	Fair	Poor
1150	1000	820	600	—	—

Stag 15 Tactical SBR 10.5

NIB	Exc.	V.G.	Good	Fair	Poor
1000	—	—	—	—	—

Stag 15 3-Gun Elite

NIB	Exc.	V.G.	Good	Fair	Poor
1600	1500	1300	1000	—	—

Stag 15 Pursuit

Caliber: .350 Legend. 16" stainless-steel nitride-coated barrel, mid-length gas systems, 13.5" slim handrails. Weight: 6.2 lbs. Caliber: 6.5 Grendel, 18" barrel, rifle-length gas system, 16.5" slim handguards. Steel 10-round magazines. 8.2 lbs. Left-hand models available; add $50. Midnight bronze Cerakote. Magpul CTR stock with custom leather stock, ambi safety levers with 60- or 90-degree throw, large charging handle, Magpul K2+ grip, VG6 muzzle brake, Timney two-stage triggers. Lifetime Transferable Warranty and Infinite Shot Barrel Guarantee. Initial rifles are built to order. Made in USA. Introduced 2023. SEE POLITICAL PANIC PRICING.

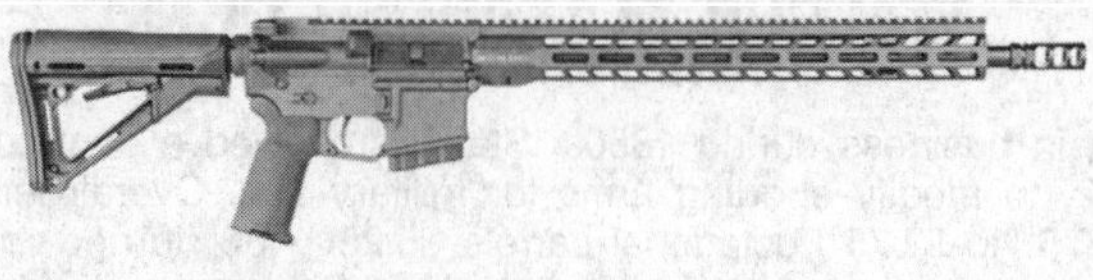

NIB	Exc.	V.G.	Good	Fair	Poor
1300	—	—	—	—	—

STAG 10 SERIES

Similar to AR-15 models but chambered in .308 Win. or 6.5 Creedmoor.

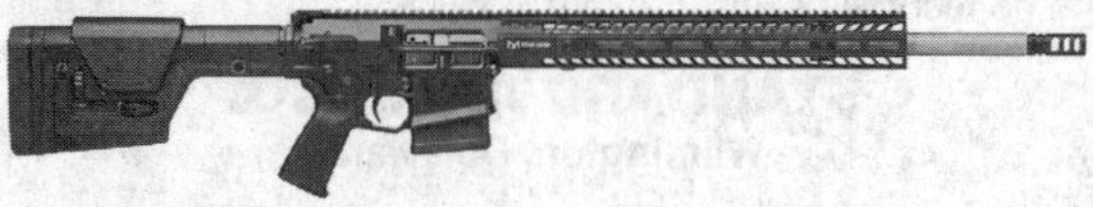

Stag 10 Creedmoor Bones

NIB	Exc.	V.G.	Good	Fair	Poor
1600	1200	800	—	—	—

Stag 10 Long Range 20 in.

NIB	Exc.	V.G.	Good	Fair	Poor
2100	1500	1000	—	—	—

Stag 10 Creedmoor S

NIB	Exc.	V.G.	Good	Fair	Poor
2000	1500	1000	—	—	—

Stag 10 .308 M-LOK

NIB	Exc.	V.G.	Good	Fair	Poor
1800	1350	900	—	—	—

Stag 10 Creedmoor

NIB	Exc.	V.G.	Good	Fair	Poor
2200	1600	1100	—	—	—

Stag 10 Tactical 16 in.

NIB	Exc.	V.G.	Good	Fair	Poor
1460	—	—	—	—	—

Stag 10 Classic 18 in.

NIB	Exc.	V.G.	Good	Fair	Poor
1270	—	—	—	—	—

Stag 10 Classic 20 in.

NIB	Exc.	V.G.	Good	Fair	Poor
1270	—	—	—	—	—

Stag 10 Marksman 18 in. LH

NIB	Exc.	V.G.	Good	Fair	Poor
1520	—	—	—	—	—

Stag 10 Long Range 24 in.

NIB	Exc.	V.G.	Good	Fair	Poor
1830	—	—	—	—	—

Stag 10 Pursuit

Similar to AR-15 Pursuit Rifles. Caliber: .308 Win. 16" stainless steel barrel. Caliber: 6.5 Creedmoor, 18" barrel. Weight: 7.8 lbs. Magpul magazines. SEE POLITICAL PANIC PRICING.

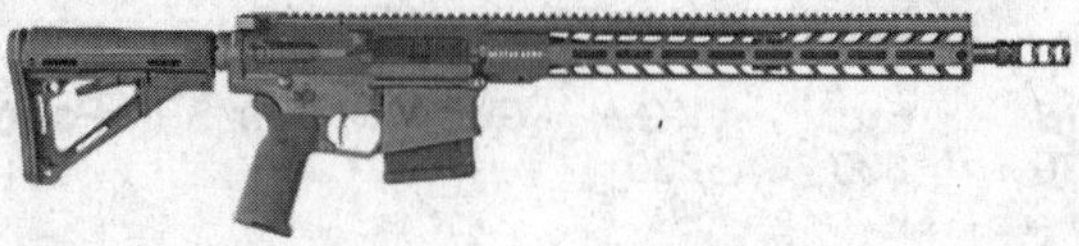

NIB	Exc.	V.G.	Good	Fair	Poor
1900	—	—	—	—	—

STALCUP, ALEXANDER T.F.M.
Nashville, Tennessee

First in business during 1850s, Stalcup received a contract in 1862, to modify sporting arms for military use. Overall length 50.875" to 51.75"; octagonal barrels 35.25" - 36" turned round at muzzle for socket bayonets; .54-caliber. Rifles assembled with sporting locks, new stocks and brass furniture. At least 102 rifles were delivered in 1862. These arms are unmarked.

Modified Confederate Rifle (Antique)

One source reports that only 3 specimens are known to survive, and we can find no recorded sales. Too rare to value.

STANDARD ARMS CO.
Wilmington, Delaware

Model G

Chambered for .25 Rem., .30 Rem. and .35 Rem., with 22" barrel. Open sights. Integral box magazine and closable gas port that allowed rifle to be used as a slide action. Blued, with walnut stock. Produced in limited quantities, circa 1910. A notorious jamamatic. Bronze alloy buttplate and forend.

NIB	*Exc.*	*V.G.*	*Good*	*Fair*	*Poor*
—	750	600	450	250	150

Model M

Manually-operated pump-only version of Model G.

NIB	*Exc.*	*V.G.*	*Good*	*Fair*	*Poor*
—	900	720	550	300	150

STANDARD MANUFACTURING
New Britain, Connecticut

Standard Manufacturing is based in New Britain, Connecticut. The company is best known for its DP-12, a 12-gauge double-barreled pump shotgun.

S333 Thunderstruck

Caliber: .22 Magnum. Capacity: 8 rounds. Barrel: 1.25 in. Grip: Polymer. Sights: Fixed front and rear. Weight: 18 oz. Features: Designed to be the ultimate in personal protection and featuring two-barrels that fire simultaneously with each trigger pull. The DA revolver has an 8-round, .22 Magnum capacity. Frame is constructed of 7075 aircraft-grade aluminum with anodized finish.

NIB	*Exc.*	*V.G.*	*Good*	*Fair*	*Poor*
370	300	230	—	—	—

Nickel Single Action

Caliber: .38 Special, .45 Colt. Capacity: 6 rounds. Barrel: 4.75, 5.5, 7.5 in. Grip: Walnut. Sights: Fixed front and rear. Weight: 40 oz. Features: This is one of the finest Single Action Army reproductions ever built, with great attention to detail. Made entirely from 4140 steel, the new nickel-plated revolvers are available in .38 special and the iconic .45 Colt. You can also opt for C-coverage engraving, making for a truly remarkable firearm. One- or two-piece walnut grips available.

NIB	*Exc.*	*V.G.*	*Good*	*Fair*	*Poor*
2000	1500	1000	—	—	—

1911 SERIES

1911

Caliber: .45 ACP. Capacity: 7-round magazine. Barrel: 5-inch stainless steel match grade. Weight: 38.4 oz. Length: 8.6 in. Grips: Checkered rosewood double diamond. Sights: Fixed, Warren Tactical blade front/U-notch rear. Finish: Blued, case color, or nickel. Features: Forged frame and slide, beavertail grip safety, extended magazine release and thumb safety, checkered mainspring housing and front grip strap.

NIB	*Exc.*	*V.G.*	*Good*	*Fair*	*Poor*
1180	900	750	—	—	—

SKO-12

Gauge: 12 ga., 3 in. Capacity: 5-round magazine. Barrel: 18-7/8-in. Weight: 7 lbs., 10 oz. Length: 38 in. Stock: Synthetic with six-position buttstock and will accept any Mil-Spec buttstock. Features: Gas-operated semi-automatic. Receivers machined from aircraft-grade aluminum and Mil-Spec hard anodized. Extended 22-inch Picatinny rail. Ambidextrous safety, AR-style mag and bolt release. MOE slots on forend. Tru-Choke thread pattern.

NIB	*Exc.*	*V.G.*	*Good*	*Fair*	*Poor*
980	700	500	—	—	—

SKO Shorty

Gauge: 12 ga., 3 in. Capacity: 5-round magazine. Barrel: 18-7/8-in. Weight: 7.14 lbs. Length: 28.75 in. Stock: Black synthetic with forward vertical grip, but without a buttstock. Features: Gas-operated semi-automatic. Receivers machined from aircraft-grade aluminum and Mil-Spec hard anodized. Ambidextrous safety, AR-style mag and bolt release. MOE slots on forend. No sights or top rail. Tru-Choke thread pattern. Buttstock conversion kit available from manufacturer.

NIB	*Exc.*	*V.G.*	*Good*	*Fair*	*Poor*
530	400	300	—	—	—

DP-12

Gauge: 12 ga., 3 in. Capacity: 14+2. Barrels: 18-7/8 in. Weight: 9 lbs., 12oz. Length: 29.5 in. Stock: Black synthetic. Features: Double-barrel bullpup pump design. Single trigger, inline shell feeding. Machined from aircraft-grade aluminum with thermal-coated receiver. Ambidextrous safety and pump-slide release. Composite front vertical grip, sling attachments, forend MOE rails. Rubber recoil pad with dual-spring shock absorbing mechanism. Includes spreader choke tubes with Tru-Choke thread pattern.

NIB	*Exc.*	*V.G.*	*Good*	*Fair*	*Poor*
1200	900	700	—	—	—

DP-12 Professional

Gauge: 12 ga. 3 in. Barrels: 18-7/8 in. Length: 29.5 in. Weight: 9 lb. 12 oz. Stock: Synthetic with anodized aluminum. Features: Upgraded

Professional version of the pump-action DP-12 high-capacity defense shotgun. Additions include an aluminum rail with front grip, which wears an integral laser and flashlight. Precision-honed bores and chambers finished with hand-lapping. PVD coating on all critical wear areas. Mil-spec hard anodized finish with accents in either Blue or OD Green. Includes Reflex Sight with multiple brightness levels. Ships with both soft and hard cases.

NIB	Exc.	V.G.	Good	Fair	Poor
2850	2000	1500	—	—	—

STAR, BONIFACIO ECHEVERRIA

Eibar, Spain

See—ECHEVERRIA

STARR, EBAN T.

New York, New York

Single-Shot Derringer Antique

A .41-caliber single-shot pistol, with pivoted 2.75" round barrel. Hammer mounted on right side of frame. Trigger formed in the shape of a button located at front of the frame. Frame marked "Starr's Pat's May 10, 1864". Brass frame silver-plated. Barrel blued or silver-plated, with checkered walnut grips. Manufactured from 1864 to 1869.

Courtesy Milwaukee Public Museum, Milwaukee, Wisconsin

Exc.	Fine	V.G.	Good	Fair	Poor
2300	1850	1330	820	200	140

Four Barreled Pepperbox

A .32-caliber 4 barreled pocket pistol, with 2.75" to 3.25" barrels. Frame marked "Starr's Pat's May 10, 1864". Brass frames, silver-plated. Barrel blued, with plain walnut grips. Produced in six variations.

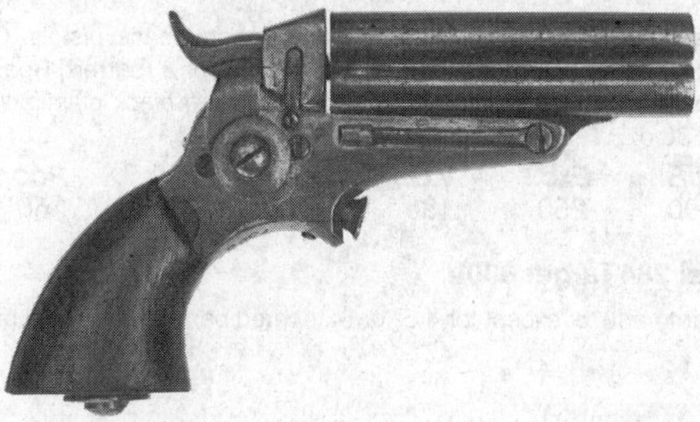

Courtesy Milwaukee Public Museum, Milwaukee, Wisconsin

First Model Antique

Exc.	Fine	V.G.	Good	Fair	Poor
3900	2750	1810	880	200	140

Second Model Antique

Exc.	Fine	V.G.	Good	Fair	Poor
2500	1920	1280	650	200	140

Third Model Antique

Exc.	Fine	V.G.	Good	Fair	Poor
2350	1650	1100	550	150	100

Fourth Model Antique

Exc.	Fine	V.G.	Good	Fair	Poor
2100	1650	1100	550	150	100

Fifth Model Antique

Exc.	Fine	V.G.	Good	Fair	Poor
1950	1400	920	450	150	100

Sixth Model Antique

Exc.	Fine	V.G.	Good	Fair	Poor
2100	1650	1100	550	150	100

STARR ARMS COMPANY

New York, New York

1858 Navy Revolver

A .36-caliber double-action percussion revolver, with 6" barrel and 6-shot cylinder. Blued case-hardened, with walnut grips. Frame marked "Starr Arms Co. New York". Approximately 3,000 made between 1858 and 1860.

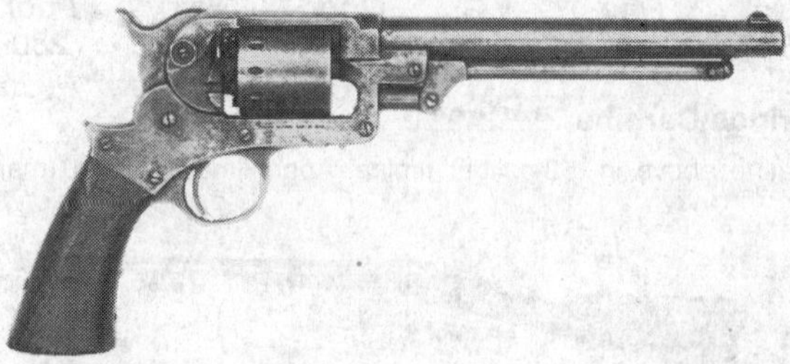

Courtesy Milwaukee Public Museum, Milwaukee, Wisconsin

Standard Model Antique

Exc.	Fine	V.G.	Good	Fair	Poor
4100	3250	2170	1100	350	240

Martially Marked (JT) Antique

Exc.	Fine	V.G.	Good	Fair	Poor
9000	7500	3000	1750	700	480

1858 Army Revolver Antique

A .44-caliber double-action percussion revolver, with 6" barrel and 6-shot cylinder. Blued case-hardened, with walnut grips. Frame marked "Starr Arms Co. New York". Approximately 23,000 manufactured.

Exc.	Fine	V.G.	Good	Fair	Poor
4300	2500	1800	1100	300	210

1863 Army Revolver (Antique)

Similar to above, but single-action with 8" round barrel. Approximately 32,000 manufactured between 1863 and 1865.

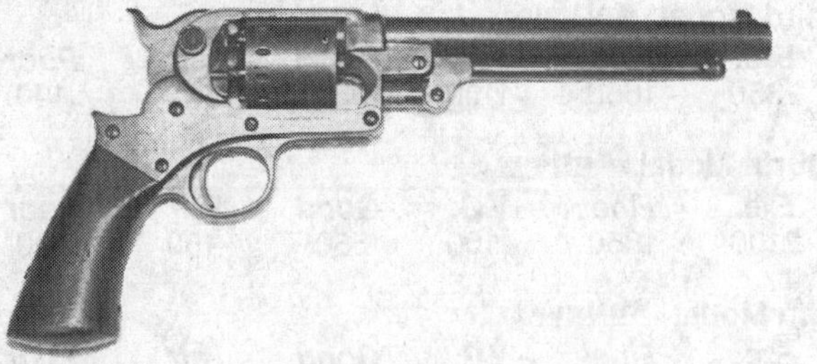

Courtesy Milwaukee Public Museum, Milwaukee, Wisconsin

Exc.	Fine	V.G.	Good	Fair	Poor
7000	3500	2370	1500	350	240

Percussion Carbine (Antique)

A .54-caliber breech-loading percussion carbine, with 21" round barrel secured by one barrel band. Blued case-hardened, with walnut stock. Lock marked "Starr Arms Co./Yonkers, N.Y.".

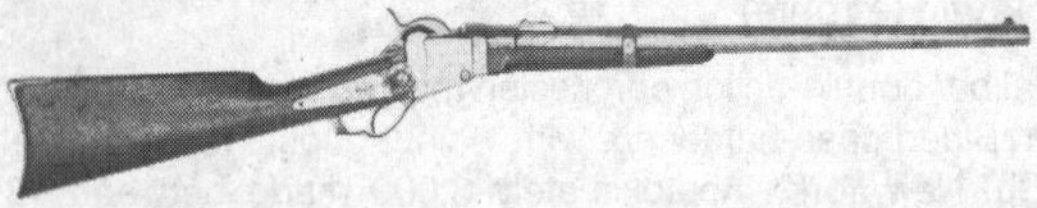

Courtesy Milwaukee Public Museum, Milwaukee, Wisconsin

Exc.	Fine	V.G.	Good	Fair	Poor
3500	2750	2000	1250	400	280

Cartridge Carbine (Antique)

Similar to above in .52-caliber rimfire. Approximately 5,000 manufactured.

Courtesy Milwaukee Public Museum, Milwaukee, Wisconsin

Exc.	Fine	V.G.	Good	Fair	Poor
3750	2500	1750	1000	350	240

STEEL CITY ARMS, INC.
Pittsburgh, Pennsylvania

Double Deuce

A .22-caliber stainless steel double-action semi-automatic pistol, with 2.5" barrel, 7-shot magazine and plain rosewood grips. Introduced in 1984.

Courtesy J.B. Wood

NIB	Exc.	V.G.	Good	Fair	Poor
—	300	250	200	150	100

STENDA WAFFENFABRIK
Suhl, Germany

Pocket Pistol

A 7.65mm semi-automatic pistol similar to "Beholla", "Leonhardt" and "Menta". Stenda took over production of Beholla pistol design at the end of WWI. Only major difference in Stenda design was elimination of Beholla's worst feature, the pin that went through slide and retained the barrel. Replaced by a sliding catch that anchored it in place and unlocked the slide so barrel could be removed without the need of a vise and drift pin. Stenda pistol can be identified by the fact there are no holes through the slide and there is a catch on the frame above the trigger. Finish blued with plastic grips; slide marked "Waffenfabrik Stendawerke Suhl". Approximately 25,000 made before production ceased in 1926.

NIB	Exc.	V.G.	Good	Fair	Poor
—	450	280	220	160	100

STERLING ARMAMENT LTD.
London, England

Parapistol MK 7 C4

A 9mm semi-automatic pistol, with 4" barrel. Detachable 10-round magazine. Black wrinkled paint finish, with plastic grips.

NIB	Exc.	V.G.	Good	Fair	Poor
600	480	400	300	200	100

Parapistol MK 7 C8

As above, with 7.8" barrel.

NIB	Exc.	V.G.	Good	Fair	Poor
620	500	400	300	200	100

Sterling MK 6

A semi-automatic copy of Sterling submachine gun, with 16.1" barrel, folding metal stock and side mounted magazine. Finished as above.

NIB	Exc.	V.G.	Good	Fair	Poor
1500	950	750	500	300	200

Sterling AR 180

Copy of Armalite Model AR18, 5.56mm rifle. Finished with black wrinkled paint, or more rarely, blued.

NIB	Exc.	V.G.	Good	Fair	Poor
1500	1250	900	750	—	—

STERLING ARMS CORPORATION
Gasport, New York

Model 283 Target 300

Similar in appearance to Hi-Standard semi-automatic pistols. Chambered for .22 LR cartridge. Offered with 4", 4.5" or 8" barrels. Rear sight adjustable. Magazine holds 10 rounds. Grips are black plastic. Weight about 36 oz.

NIB	Exc.	V.G.	Good	Fair	Poor
300	250	180	100	80	60

Model 284 Target 300L

Similar to above, except for 4.5" or 6" tapered barrel, with barrel band.

Courtesy John J. Stimson, Jr.

NIB	Exc.	V.G.	Good	Fair	Poor
320	280	180	100	80	60

Model 285 Husky

Similar to Model 283, with fixed sights. Offered with 4.5" barrel only.

NIB	Exc.	V.G.	Good	Fair	Poor
300	250	180	100	80	60

Model 286 Trapper

Similar to Model 284, except for fixed sights.

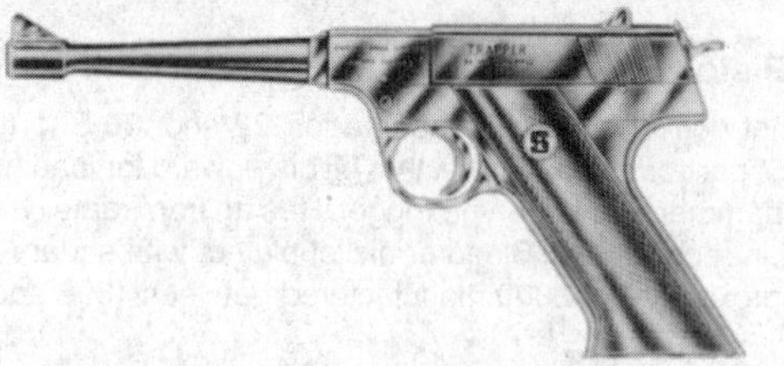

NIB	Exc.	V.G.	Good	Fair	Poor
300	250	180	100	80	60

Model 287 PPL .380

Pocket-size semi-automatic pistol, chambered for .380 ACP cartridge. Fitted with a 1" barrel. Overall length 5.25". Magazine holds 6 rounds. Weight about 22 oz.

NIB	Exc.	V.G.	Good	Fair	Poor
220	180	120	80	50	20

Model PPL .22

Small pocket pistol similar to Model 287. Chambered for .22 LR cartridge. Barrel 1" long. Weight about 24 oz.

NIB	Exc.	V.G.	Good	Fair	Poor
280	220	150	80	60	50

Model 300

Similar to Model 287, but chambered for .25 ACP cartridge. Has a 2.25" barrel, with 6-round magazine. Overall length 5". Weight about 14 oz.

NIB	Exc.	V.G.	Good	Fair	Poor
250	220	150	80	50	40

Model 300S

Stainless steel version of Model 300.

NIB	Exc.	V.G.	Good	Fair	Poor
260	240	160	80	50	40

Model 302

Identical to Model 300, except chambered for .22 LR cartridge.

NIB	Exc.	V.G.	Good	Fair	Poor
250	220	150	80	50	40

Model 302S

Same as above in stainless steel.

NIB	Exc.	V.G.	Good	Fair	Poor
260	240	160	80	60	50

Model 400

Double-action semi-automatic pistol. Chambered for .380 ACP cartridge, with 3.5" barrel. Magazine holds 7 rounds. Overall length 6.5". Weight about 24 oz.

NIB	Exc.	V.G.	Good	Fair	Poor
300	280	200	120	100	80

Model 400S

Stainless steel version of Model 400.

NIB	Exc.	V.G.	Good	Fair	Poor
320	300	2260	120	100	80

Model 402

Similar to Model 400, except chambered for .22 LR cartridge.

NIB	Exc.	V.G.	Good	Fair	Poor
250	220	150	80	60	40

Model X-Caliber

Single-shot .22 LR, .22 WMR, .357 Magnum or .44 Magnum pistol. Interchangeable barrels from 8" and 10". Adjustable rear sight. Finger groove grips. Note: Deduct 50 percent for rimfire.

NIB	Exc.	V.G.	Good	Fair	Poor
450	400	300	220	150	100

STEVENS ARMS CO., J.

Chicopee Falls, Massachusetts

In 1864, this firm began doing business as J. Stevens & Company. In 1888, it was incorporated as J. Stevens Arms & Tool Company. It operated as such until 1920, when it was taken over by Savage Arms Company. It has operated as an independent division in this organization since. This company produced a great many firearms—most that were of an affordable nature. They are widely collected. One interested in them should take advantage of literature available on the subject.

Vest Pocket Pistol (Antique)

Single-shot pocket pistol. Chambered for .22 and .30 rimfire cartridges. The .22-caliber version is rarely encountered and would be worth approximately 25 percent more than values illustrated. Has a 2.75" part-octagonal barrel that pivots upward for loading, external hammer and spur-type trigger. Frame nickel-plated or blued, with blued barrel. Odd shaped flared-grips are made of rosewood. First models marked "Vest Pocket Pistol" only. Later models have barrels marked "J. Stevens & Co. Chicopee Falls, Mass.". Approximately 1,000 manufactured between 1864 and 1876.

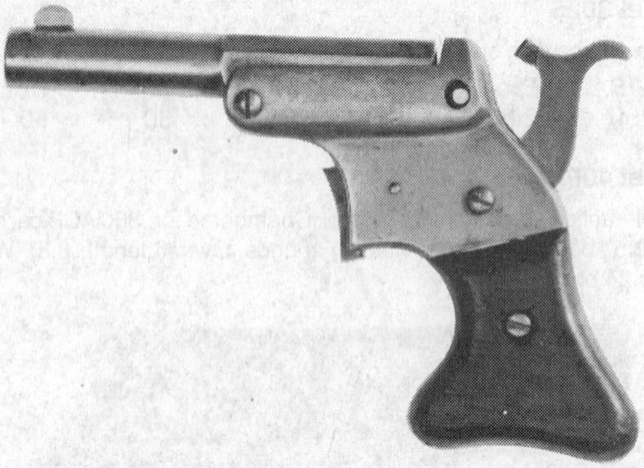

Courtesy Milwaukee Public Museum, Milwaukee, Wisconsin

Exc.	Fine	V.G.	Good	Fair	Poor
3450	2300	1800	1300	1000	700

Old Model Pocket Pistol (Antique)

A more conventional-appearing single-shot pocket pistol. Chambered for .22 or .30 rimfire cartridges. Has a 3.5" part-octagonal barrel that pivots upward for loading. Features plated brass frame, with blued or nickel-plated barrel and rosewood two-piece grips. Barrel marked "J. Stevens & Co. Chicopee Falls, Mass.". Approximately 15,000 manufactured between 1864 and 1886.

Courtesy Milwaukee Public Museum, Milwaukee, Wisconsin

Exc.	Fine	V.G.	Good	Fair	Poor
700	500	350	200	125	75

Gem Pocket Pistol (Antique)

Single-shot derringer-type pocket pistol. Chambered for .22 or .30 rimfire cartridges. Has a 3" part-octagonal barrel that pivots to side for loading, nickel-plated brass frame, with blued or plated barrel and bird's-head grips made of walnut or rosewood. Barrel marked "Gem". Stevens name or address does not appear on this firearm. Approximately 4,000 manufactured between 1872 and 1890.

Exc.	Fine	V.G.	Good	Fair	Poor
900	600	510	420	300	210

.22 or .41 Caliber Derringer (Antique)

Single-shot pocket pistol. Chambered for .22- or .41-caliber rimfire cartridge. Has a 4" part-octagonal barrel that pivots upward for loading, spur trigger and external hammer. Frame plated brass, with blued barrel. Walnut bird's-head grips. Firearm completely unmarked except for serial number. Approximately 100 manufactured in 1875.

.22 Caliber (Antique)

Exc.	Fine	V.G.	Good	Fair	Poor
6000	5000	4000	3000	1500	1050

.41 Caliber (Antique)

Exc.	Fine	V.G.	Good	Fair	Poor
5600	4000	3250	2500	1400	970

No. 41 Pistol

Single-shot pocket pistol. Chambered for .22 and .30 Short cartridges. Has a 3.5" part-octagonal barrel that pivots upward for loading. Features external hammer and spur-type trigger. Has an iron frame, with firing pin mounted in recoil shield. Blued or nickel-plated, with square-butt walnut grips. Approximately 90,000 manufactured between 1896 and 1916.

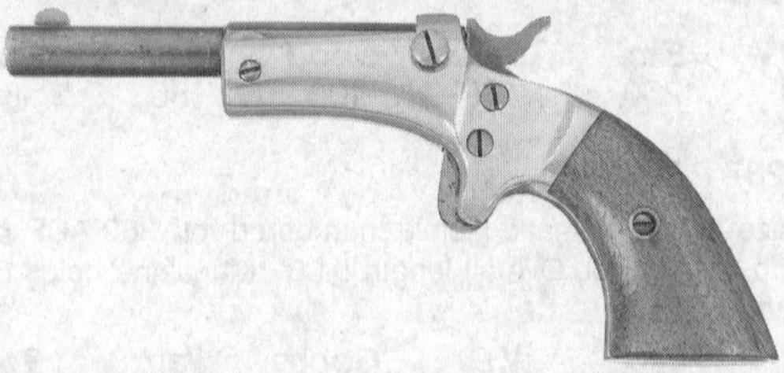

Courtesy Rock Island Auction Company

NIB	Exc.	V.G.	Good	Fair	Poor
—	500	420	300	250	140

Single-Shot Pistol (Antique)

Single-shot pistol chambered for .22 or .30 rimfire cartridges. Has a 3.5" part-octagonal barrel that pivots upward for loading. Quite similar in appearance to original pocket pistol. Plated brass frame and blued or nickel-plated barrel, with walnut square-butt grips. Barrel marked "J. Stevens A&T Co.". Approximately 10,000 manufactured between 1886 and 1896.

Exc.	Fine	V.G.	Good	Fair	Poor
400	300	250	200	150	100

Tip Up Rifles (Antique)

Series of rifles produced by Stevens beginning in 1870s through 1895. There are a number of variations, but are all quite similar in appearance. They feature a distinctive sloped frame made of iron and nickel-plated. Most frames are similar in size, but there is a slightly lighter frame used on "Ladies Model" rifles. These Tip Up rifles are chambered for various calibers from .22 rimfire to .44 centerfire cartridges. Offered barrel lengths of 24", 26", 28" or 30". Actions are nickel-plated, as well as triggerguards and buttplates. Barrels blued, and two-piece stocks are of walnut. Offered with various buttplates and sights. A shotgun version is also offered. There are a number of variations that differ only slightly. Model numbers are not marked on rifles. We suggest securing a qualified appraisal if in doubt. Major variations and their values are as follows:

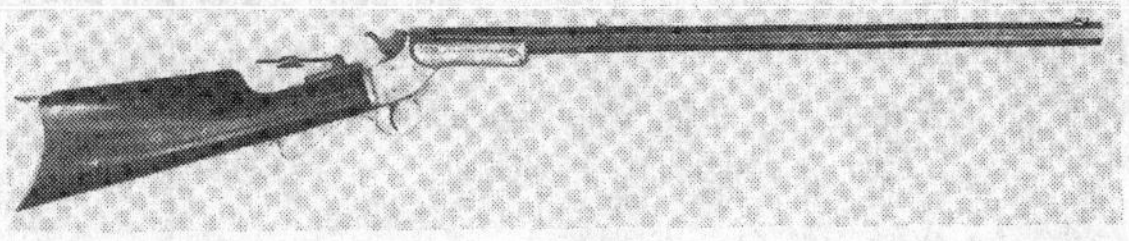

Courtesy Milwaukee Public Museum, Milwaukee, Wisconsin

Ladies Model—.22 or .25 Rimfire Only, 24" or 26" Barrel Antique

Exc.	Fine	V.G.	Good	Fair	Poor
2500	1500	900	650	400	250

Tip Up Rifle—Without Forend Antique

Exc.	Fine	V.G.	Good	Fair	Poor
650	500	370	250	200	140

Tip Up Rifle—With Forend, Swiss-Type Buttplate Antique

Exc.	Fine	V.G.	Good	Fair	Poor
1000	600	500	400	250	170

Tip Up Shotgun—All Gauges, 30" or 32" Barrel Antique

Exc.	Fine	V.G.	Good	Fair	Poor
500	300	220	150	100	70

Ideal Single-Shot Rifle Antique

This excellent rifle manufactured by Stevens between 1896 and 1933. A single-shot falling-block type action that is activated by a triggerguard action lever. Produced in many popular calibers from .22 rimfire up to .30-40. Also manufactured in a number of special Stevens calibers. Offered with various barrel lengths in many different grades, from plain Spartan starter rifles up to some extremely high-grade Schuetzen-type target rifles, with all available options. In 1901, Harry Pope of Hartford, Connecticut, went to work for Stevens and brought his highly respected barrel to Stevens Company. He remained an employee for only two years and firearms produced during this period have the name "Stevens-Pope" stamped on top of barrel in addition to other factory markings. Rifles marked in this manner and authenticated, would be worth an approximate 50 percent premium if they are in very good to excellent condition. Due to numerous variations and options offered, we strongly recommend securing a qualified appraisal, especially on higher-grade Ideal series rifles, before a purchase.

No. 44

This version chambered for various calibers. Offered with 24" or 26" barrel. Has an open rear sight, with Rocky Mountain-type front sight. Finish blued and case colored, with walnut stock. Approximately 100,000 manufactured between 1896 and 1933. Premium for pre-1899 antique specimens.

NIB	Exc.	V.G.	Good	Fair	Poor
1080	700	550	400	220	150

No. 44-1/2

Similar in appearance to No. 44, but features an improved action. Barrel lengths up to 34" and will be found with Stevens-Pope barrel. Manufactured between 1903 and 1916.

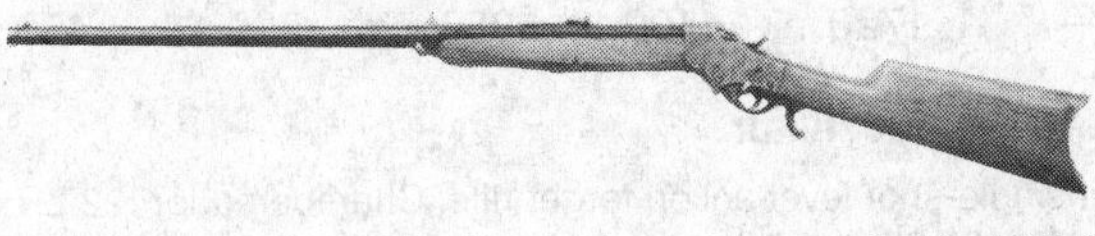

Courtesy J.B. Barnes

NIB	Exc.	V.G.	Good	Fair	Poor
—	2180	1950	1500	1000	720

No. 044-1/2

This version also known as "English Model" rifle. Similar to No. 44-1/2, except it has a shotgun butt and tapered barrel. There were a number of options offered that would affect the value. Manufactured between 1903 and 1916.

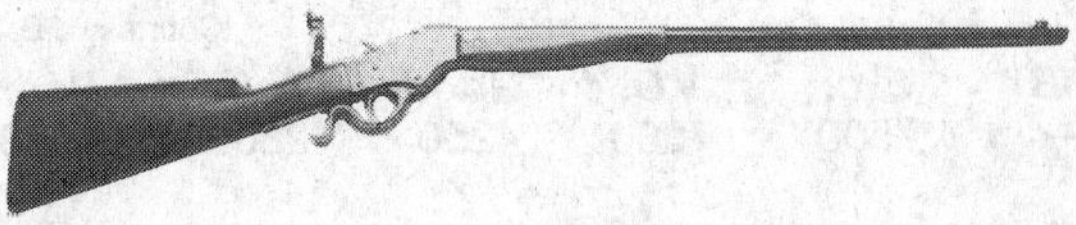

Courtesy Mike Stuckslager

NIB	Exc.	V.G.	Good	Fair	Poor
—	2180	1950	1500	1000	720

No. 45

This version also known as "Range Rifle". Chambered for various calibers from .22 rimfire to .44-40. Identifying features are Beach sights, with additional vernier tang sight and Swiss-type buttstock. Offered with 26" or 28" part-octagonal barrel. Manufactured between 1896 and 1916. Values listed are for standard version. Note: Deduct 25 percent for .44 action.

NIB	Exc.	V.G.	Good	Fair	Poor
—	2380	2150	1600	1100	820

No. 46

Same as No. 45, with fancy wood stock. Manufactured from 1896 to 1902. Built in No. 44 action-only.

NIB	Exc.	V.G.	Good	Fair	Poor
—	2700	2380	1900	1500	1100

No. 47

This version similar to No. 45, with pistol grip buttstock. Note: Deduct 25 percent for .44 action.

NIB	Exc.	V.G.	Good	Fair	Poor
—	4500	3800	3000	2400	900

No. 48

Same as No. 47, with fancy wood checkered stock. Manufactured from 1896 to 1902. Built in No. 44 action-only. A very rare model.

NIB	Exc.	V.G.	Good	Fair	Poor
—	5000	4000	3500	2500	1500

No. 49

Also known as "Walnut Hill Rifle". A high grade target rifle chambered for many calibers between .22 rimfire and .44-40. Offered with 28" or 30" part-octagonal barrel that is medium-/heavy-weight. Furnished with globe front sight and vernier tang sight. Blued, with case colored frame. Has a high-grade checkered varnished walnut stock, that has a high comb. Features a pistol grip, cheekpiece, Swiss-type buttplate and loop-type triggerguard lever that resembles that of a lever-action rifle. Receiver engraved. There were a number of options available that would increase value when present. We recommend an appraisal when in doubt. Manufactured between 1896 and 1916.

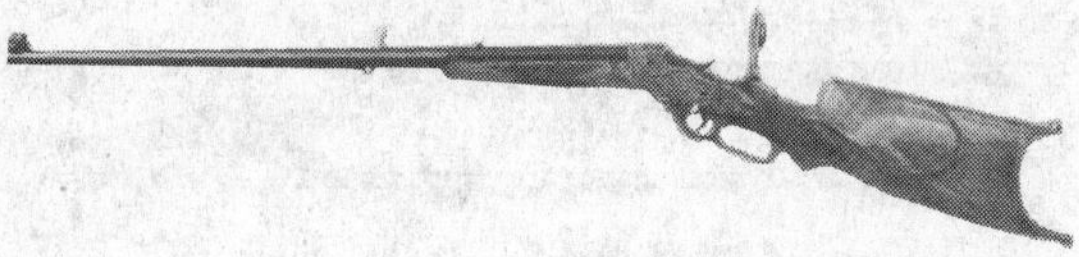

Courtesy J.B. Barnes

NIB	Exc.	V.G.	Good	Fair	Poor
—	6500	6000	3500	2500	1500

Model 50

Identical to Model 49, but offered with higher-grade walnut stock. A very rare model.

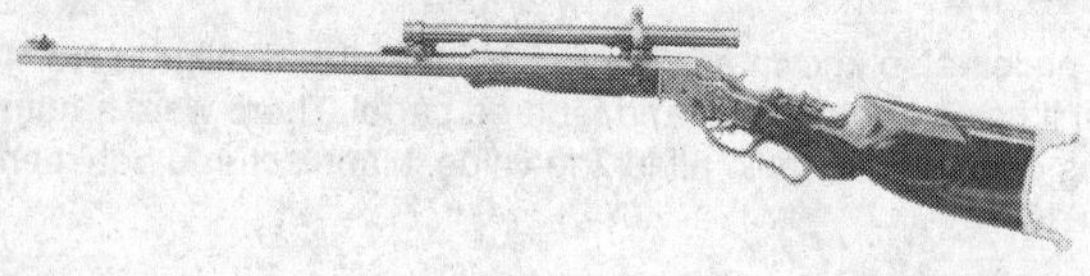

Courtesy J.B. Barnes

NIB	Exc.	V.G.	Good	Fair	Poor
—	7500	7000	4250	2800	1900

Model 51

This version also known as "Schuetzen Rifle". Quite similar to No. 49, except it features double-set triggers, higher-grade walnut stock, wooden insert in triggerguard action lever and heavy Schuetzen-type buttplate. There were many options available on this model. We recommend securing an appraisal when in doubt. Manufactured between 1896 and 1916.

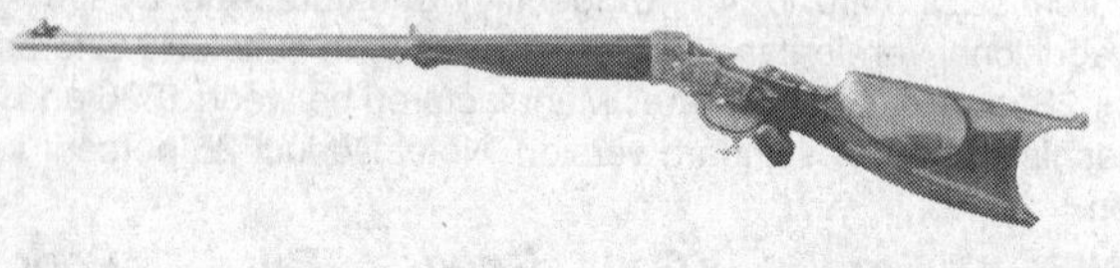

Courtesy J.B. Barnes

NIB	Exc.	V.G.	Good	Fair	Poor
—	12000	10000	6500	4000	2000

No. 52

Also known as "Schuetzen Junior". Similar to No. 51, except it features more engraving and higher-grade walnut stock. Manufactured between 1897 and 1916.

Courtesy J.B. Barnes

NIB	Exc.	V.G.	Good	Fair	Poor
—	12000	10000	6500	4000	2000

No. 53

Same as No. 51, except for addition of a fancy wood stock and palm rest. Produced from 1896 to 1902. Offered only with No. 44 action. A rare rifle.

NIB	Exc.	V.G.	Good	Fair	Poor
—	11000	8000	6500	4000	2000

No. 54

Similar to No. 52, except it has double-set triggers, palm rest and heavy Swiss-style buttplate. Offered with 30" or 32" part-octagonal heavy barrel. This was Stevens' top-of-the-line rifle. Offered with many options. An appraisal should be secured if in doubt. Manufactured between 1897 and 1916. Note: Prices are based on No. 44-1/2 action. A No. 44 action will bring 20 percent less than the prices listed.

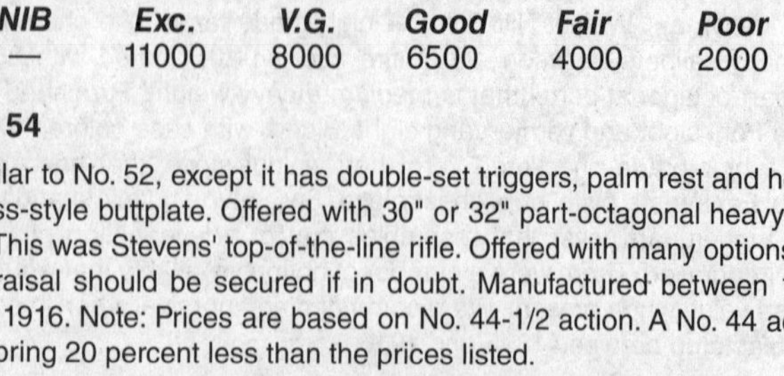

NIB	Exc.	V.G.	Good	Fair	Poor
—	16000	14000	10000	7250	4500

No. 55

This version is one of Stevens' Ideal Ladies Models. Chambered for smaller rimfire calibers between .22 Short and .32 Long rimfire. Features 24" or 26" part-octagonal barrel, with vernier tang sight. Finish blued and case colored, with checkered pistol grip walnut stock that features Swiss-type buttplate. Lighter weight rifle manufactured between 1897 and 1916.

NIB	Exc.	V.G.	Good	Fair	Poor
—	5750	4500	3000	1750	850

No. 56

Ladies' Model rifle similar to No. 55, except chambered for centerfire cartridges. Has a higher-grade walnut stock. It was made on improved No. 44-1/2 action. Manufactured between 1906 and 1916.

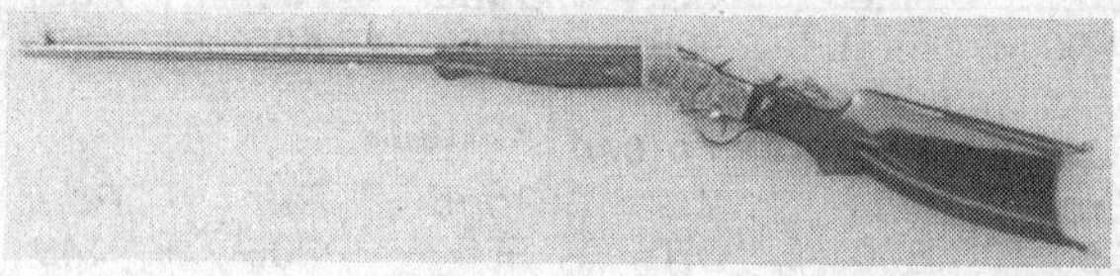

Courtesy J.B. Barnes

NIB	Exc.	V.G.	Good	Fair	Poor
—	6000	5000	3500	2000	950

No. 404

This version chambered for .22 rimfire cartridge only. Features 28" round barrel, with globe front sight and Lyman No. 42 receiver sight. Finish blued and case colored. Walnut straight-grip stock, with semi-beavertail forend. Features shotgun-type buttplate. Manufactured between 1910 and 1916.

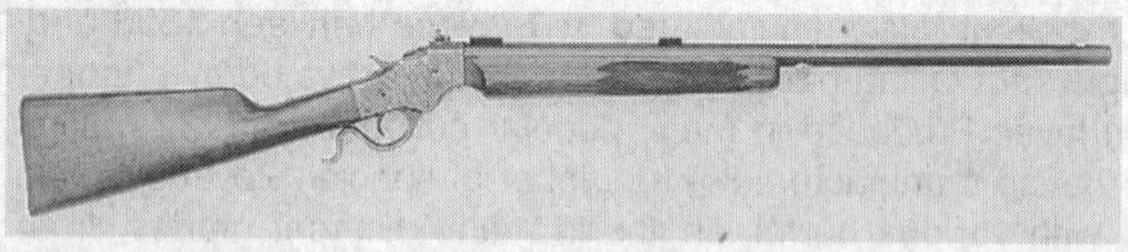

NIB	Exc.	V.G.	Good	Fair	Poor
—	1300	1080	880	750	600

No. 414

Also known as "Armory Model". Chambered for .22 LR cartridge only. Built on No. 44 action. Features 26" round barrel. Has Rocky Mountain front sight, with Lyman receiver sight at rear. Finish blued and case colored, with straight-grip walnut stock. Forend held on by single barrel band. Manufactured between 1912 and 1932.

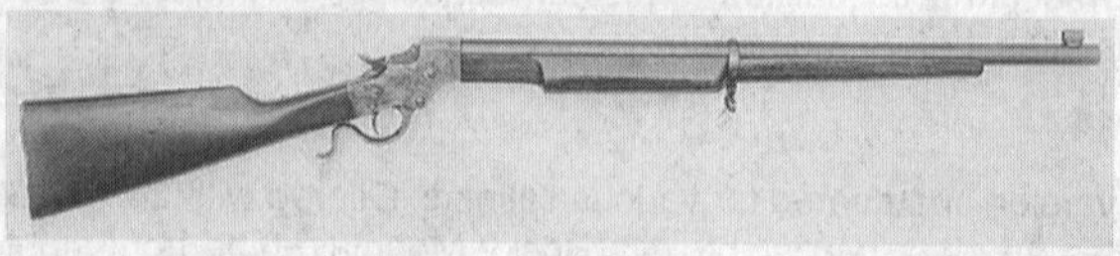

Courtesy Mike Stuckslager

NIB	Exc.	V.G.	Good	Fair	Poor
—	1000	750	550	300	280

No. 417 Walnut Hill Model

Heavy single-shot lever-action target rifle. Chambered for .22 LR, .22 Short or .22 Hornet cartridges. Weight about 10.5 lbs. Produced from 1932 to 1940.

NIB	Exc.	V.G.	Good	Fair	Poor
—	1620	1300	850	600	400

No. 417 1/2 Walnut Hill Model

A sporting version of Model 417. Weight about 8.5 lbs. Manufactured from 1932 to 1940.

NIB	Exc.	V.G.	Good	Fair	Poor
—	1720	1400	950	700	450

No. 418 Walnut Hill Jr.

A light single-shot lever-action target rifle. Chambered for .22 LR or .22 Short. Weight about 6.5 lbs. Manufactured from 1932 to 1940.

NIB	Exc.	V.G.	Good	Fair	Poor
—	980	800	550	300	200

No. 418 1/2 Walnut Hill Jr.

Similar to Model 418, but chambered for .25 rimfire or .22 WRF cartridges. Also fitted with sporting sights. Manufactured from 1932 to 1940.

NIB	Exc.	V.G.	Good	Fair	Poor
—	980	800	550	300	200

BOY'S RIFLES

Stevens Company produced an extensive line of smaller, single-shot rifles chambered for small calibers. Intended primarily for use by young shooters. These firearms have become quite collectible and are considered a field of specialty by many modern collectors. Note: There are many variations that were available with a number of options that would affect their value. We supply information and values for the major variations, but would recommend securing a qualified appraisal if in doubt.

"FAVORITE" RIFLES""

This series of rifles chambered for .22, .25 and .32 rimfire. Has a 22 blued part-octagonal barrel, with case colored frame. A take-down type action, with interchangeable barrel feature. Available with optional sights and buttplates. Approximately 1,000,000 manufactured between 1893 and 1939. The variations are listed.

Courtesy Buffalo Bill Historical Center, Cody, Wyoming

1st Model Favorite Antique

This version chambered for .22 or .25 rimfire cartridge. Has a removable sideplate on right side of receiver, not found on any other variation. Approximately 1,000 manufactured between 1893 and 1894.

Exc.	Fine	V.G.	Good	Fair	Poor
880	700	600	500	350	240

No. 17

This is standard plain version, with open sights.

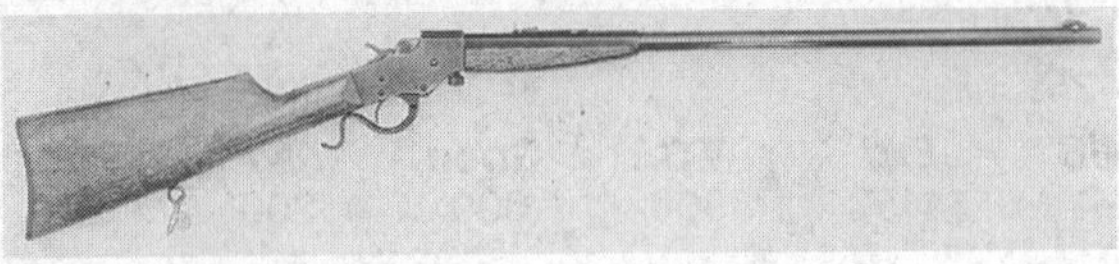

NIB	Exc.	V.G.	Good	Fair	Poor
—	600	440	320	180	120

No. 20

This version chambered for .22 or .32 rimfire shot cartridges. Has a smoothbore barrel and no rear sight.

NIB	Exc.	V.G.	Good	Fair	Poor
—	650	480	350	180	120

No. 21

Known as "Bicycle Rifle". Features 20" barrel, with open sights standard. Furnished with canvas carrying case that would be worth approximately a 30 percent premium. Manufactured between 1898 and 1903.

NIB	Exc.	V.G.	Good	Fair	Poor
—	800	620	380	170	110

No. 21 Ladies Model

This version bears same model number as "Bicycle Rifle", but has 24" barrel and high grade checkered walnut stock, with Swiss buttplate. Features vernier tang sight. Manufactured between 1910 and 1916.

NIB	Exc.	V.G.	Good	Fair	Poor
—	7000	5500	3750	2200	1100

No. 16

This version known as "Crack Shot". Chambered for .22 or .32 rimfire cartridges, with 20" round barrel. Rolling-block-type action, with thumb lever on side. Utility-type rifle with open sights. Blued and case colored finish. Plain two-piece walnut stock, with rubber buttplate. Barrel marked "Crack Shot" along with standard Stevens' barrel address markings. Manufactured between 1900 and 1913.

NIB	Exc.	V.G.	Good	Fair	Poor
—	600	500	350	220	100

No. 16-1/2

Similar to No. 16, except chambered for .32 rimfire shot cartridge, with smoothbore barrel. Manufactured between 1900 and 1913.

NIB	Exc.	V.G.	Good	Fair	Poor
—	620	520	380	250	120

No. 23—Sure Shot

This version chambered for .22 rimfire cartridge. Has a 20" round barrel that pivots to right for loading and a barrel release on the frame. Blued and case colored, with plain walnut buttstock and no forend. Manufactured between 1894 and 1897.

NIB	Exc.	V.G.	Good	Fair	Poor
—	2700	2380	1500	1000	600

No. 15

Also known as "Maynard Junior". Chambered for .22 rimfire cartridge. Has an 18" part-octagonal barrel. Action similar to Civil War Maynard rifle, with triggerguard activating lever. Finish all blued, with board-type buttstock and no forearm. Barrel marked "Stevens Maynard, J. R." in addition to standard Stevens' barrel address. Manufactured between 1902 and 1912.

Courtesy Mike Stuckslager

NIB	Exc.	V.G.	Good	Fair	Poor
—	600	500	350	220	100

No. 15-1/2

A smoothbore version of No. 15.

NIB	Exc.	V.G.	Good	Fair	Poor
—	620	520	380	250	120

No. 14

Also known as "Little Scout". Utility take-down rifle. Blued, with one-piece board-type stock. Features rolling-block-type action. Manufactured between 1906 and 1910.

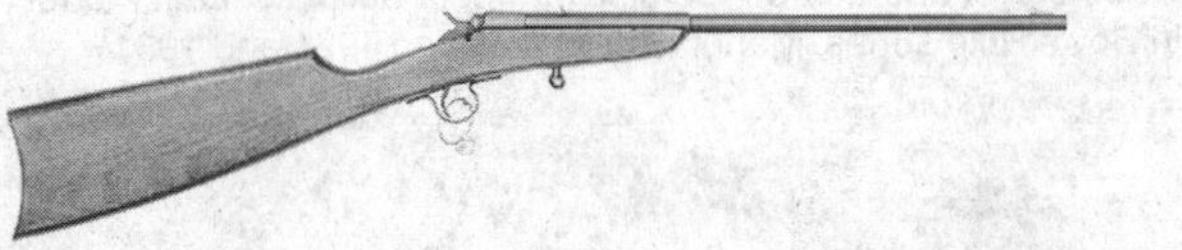

NIB	Exc.	V.G.	Good	Fair	Poor
—	550	420	300	220	100

No. 14-1/2

Similar to No. 14, except has a two-piece stock. Also marked "Little Scout". Manufactured between 1911 and 1941.

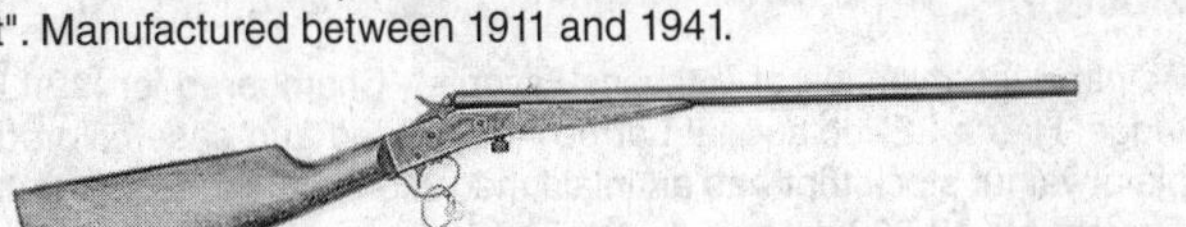

NIB	Exc.	V.G.	Good	Fair	Poor
—	500	380	200	150	100

No. 65

Also known as "Little Krag". Single-shot bolt-action rifle chambered for .22 rimfire cartridge. One-piece stock and 20" round barrel marked "Little Krag". Quite scarce. Manufactured between 1903 and 1910.

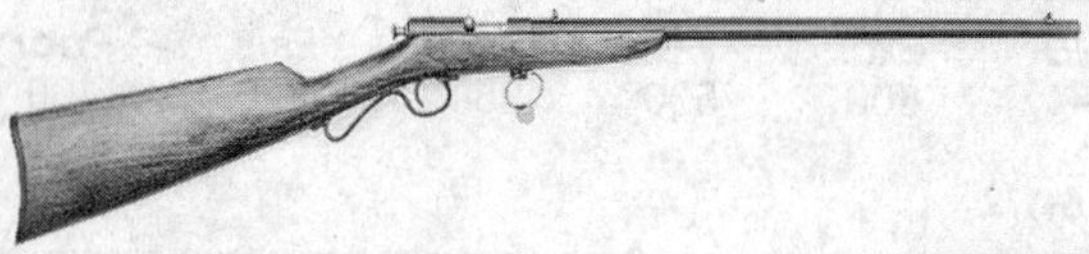

NIB	Exc.	V.G.	Good	Fair	Poor
—	600	500	350	200	100

No. 12

Also known as "Marksman". Chambered for .22, .25 and .32 rimfire cartridges. Has a 22" barrel that pivots upward for loading. Activated by an S-shaped triggerguard lever. Manufactured between 1911 and 1930.

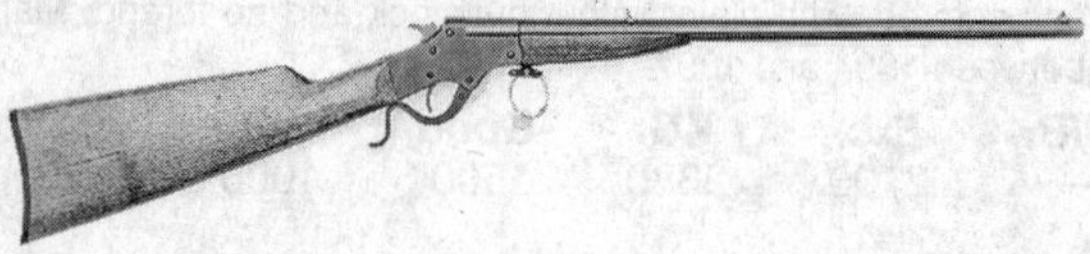

Courtesy Mike Stuckslager

NIB	Exc.	V.G.	Good	Fair	Poor
—	550	420	300	220	100

No. 26

Also known as "Crack Shot". Has a rolling-block-type action. Chambered for .22 or .32 rimfire cartridges. Offered with 18" or 20" round barrel. Blued and has a two-piece stock. Manufactured between 1912 and 1939.

Courtesy Mike Stuckslager

NIB	Exc.	V.G.	Good	Fair	Poor
—	550	420	300	220	100

No. 26-1/2

Smoothbore version of No. 26.

NIB	Exc.	V.G.	Good	Fair	Poor
—	550	500	350	250	100

No. 11—Junior

Single-shot rolling block rifle chambered for .22 rimfire cartridge. Has 20" blued barrel and board-type stock, without buttplate. Last model offered in Boy's Rifle series. Manufactured between 1924 and 1931.

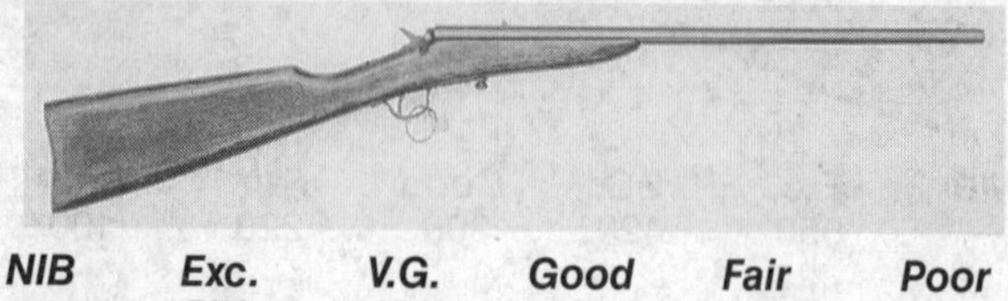

NIB	Exc.	V.G.	Good	Fair	Poor
—	550	420	300	220	100

Model 71

Reintroduced version of "Stevens Favorite". Chambered for .22 LR cartridge. Has a 22" octagonal barrel. Finish blued and case colored, with plain walnut stock that has an inlaid medallion and a crescent buttplate. There were 10,000 manufactured in 1971.

NIB	Exc.	V.G.	Good	Fair	Poor
400	300	180	120	100	80

Model 72

Reintroduced version of "Crack Shot". Features single-shot, falling-block action. Chambered for .22 rimfire cartridge. Has 22" octagon barrel, with open sights. Blued and case colored, with straight walnut stock. Introduced in 1972.

NIB	Exc.	V.G.	Good	Fair	Poor
400	300	180	120	100	80

Model 70

Slide-action rifle chambered for .22 rimfire cartridge. Also known as "Visible Loading Rifle". Features 20" round barrel, with 3/4-length tubular magazine. Finish blued and case colored, with walnut stock. Features open sights, but available with other options. Offered as No. 70-1/2, 71, 71-1/2, 72 and 72-1/2. These different model numbers denote various sight combinations. Otherwise, they are identical. Manufactured between 1907 and 1932.

NIB	Exc.	V.G.	Good	Fair	Poor
—	450	350	220	100	80

No. 80

Slide-action repeating rifle chambered for .22 rimfire cartridge. Has 24" round barrel, with tubular magazine. Features open sights and blued, with walnut stock. Manufactured between 1906 and 1910.

NIB	Exc.	V.G.	Good	Fair	Poor
—	500	350	220	180	100

High Power Rifle

A series of lever-action hunting rifles chambered for .25, .300, .32 and .35 Rem. centerfire cartridges. Features 22" round barrel, with tubular magazine. Finish blued, with walnut stock. Available in four variations: No. 425, No. 430, No. 435 and No. 440. These designations denote increased ornamentation and high quality materials and workmanship used in construction. Approximately 26,000 manufactured between 1910 and 1917.

No. 425

NIB	Exc.	V.G.	Good	Fair	Poor
—	1150	900	600	300	200

No. 430

NIB	Exc.	V.G.	Good	Fair	Poor
—	1300	1000	650	400	300

No. 435

NIB	Exc.	V.G.	Good	Fair	Poor
—	1750	1400	1000	600	400

No. 440

NIB	Exc.	V.G.	Good	Fair	Poor
—	3350	3000	2400	1600	850

SPORTING PISTOLS

Beginning in 1869, Stevens Company produced a series of single-shot break-open target and sporting pistols that pivot upward for loading. Chambered for .22 and .25 rimfire cartridges, as well as various centerfire cartridges from .32 Short Colt to .44 Russian. These pistols were made with various barrel lengths and have spur trigger or conventional trigger with a guard. They are all single-actions, with exposed hammers. Finishes are nickel-plated frames, with blued barrels and walnut grips. Variations and their values are listed.

Six-inch Pocket Rifle (Antique)

This version chambered for .22 rimfire cartridge. Has a 6" part-octagonal barrel, with open sights. Barrel marked "J. Stevens & Co. Chicopee Falls,

Mass.". Approximately 1,000 manufactured between 1869 and 1886.

Exc.	Fine	V.G.	Good	Fair	Poor
500	400	370	350	200	140

No. 36 Antique

This version known as "Stevens-Lord" pistol. Chambered for various rimfire and centerfire calibers up to .44 Russian. Offered with 10" or 12" part-octagonal barrel. Features a firing pin in the frame, with a bushing. Has a conventional trigger, with spurred triggerguard. Features standard Stevens barrel address. Named after Frank Lord, a target shooter well-known at this time. Approximately 3,500 manufactured from 1880 to 1911.

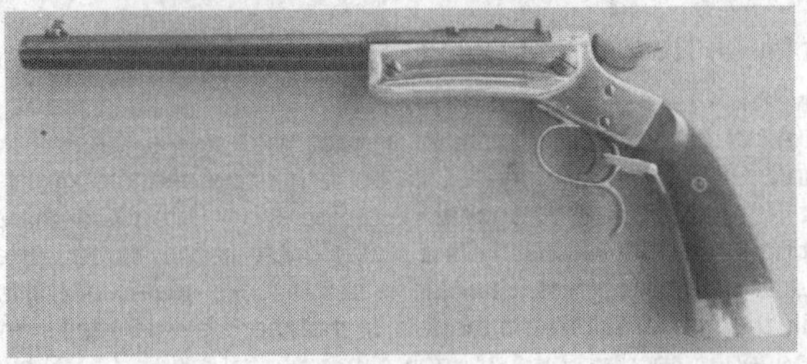

Courtesy J.B. Barnes

Exc.	Fine	V.G.	Good	Fair	Poor
1200	800	600	400	300	150

First Issue Stevens-Conlin Antique

Chambered for .22 or.32 rimfire cartridges. Has a 10" or 12" part-octagonal barrel. Features a plated brass frame, with blued barrel and checkered walnut grips with a weighted buttcap. Has a spur trigger with/without a triggerguard. Named after James Conlin, owner of a shooting gallery located in New York City. Approximately 500 manufactured between 1880 and 1884.

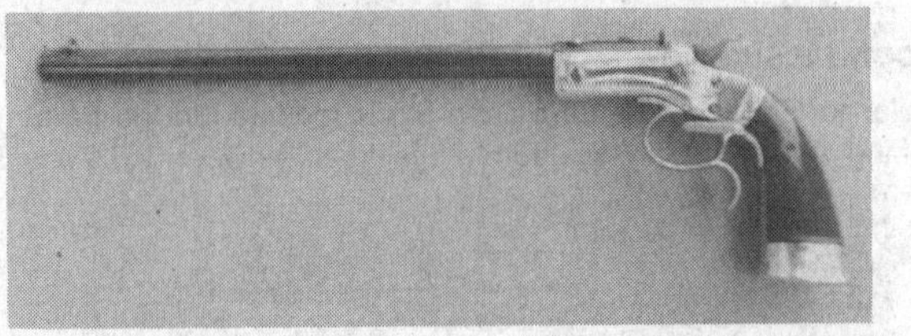

Courtesy J.B. Barnes

Exc.	Fine	V.G.	Good	Fair	Poor
2000	1200	700	400	300	150

Second Issue Stevens-Conlin No. 38 Antique

Similar to First Issue, with conventional trigger, spurred triggerguard and fully adjustable rear sight. Approximately 6,000 manufactured between 1884 and 1903.

Exc.	Fine	V.G.	Good	Fair	Poor
1800	1000	700	400	300	150

No. 37 Antique

Also known as "Stevens-Gould". Named after a 19th century firearms writer. Resembles No. 38, without spur on the triggerguard. Approximately 1,000 manufactured between 1889 and 1903.

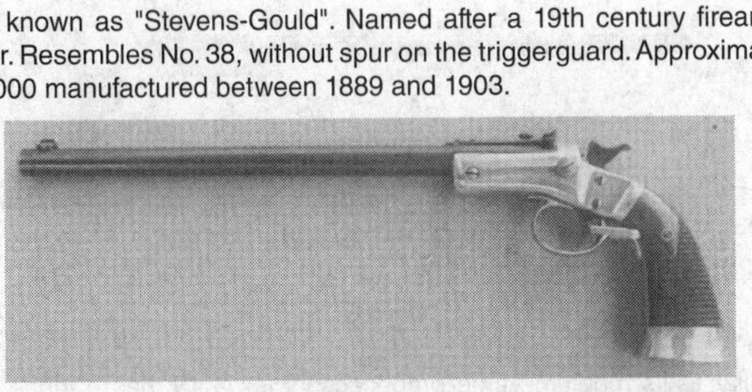

Courtesy J.B. Barnes

Exc.	Fine	V.G.	Good	Fair	Poor
1250	900	650	400	300	150

No. 35

Chambered for .22 rimfire, .22 Stevens-Pope and .25 Stevens cartridges. Offered with 6", 8", 10" or 12.25" part-octagonal barrel. Firing pin has no bushing. Features an iron frame that is blued or plated, with a blued barrel. Plain walnut grips, with a weighted buttcap. Featured open sights. Approximately 43,000 manufactured between 1923 and 1942. Note: Longer barrels worth a premium.

NIB	Exc.	V.G.	Good	Fair	Poor
—	450	320	280	180	100

No. 35 Target

Similar to No. 35, but has a better quality triggerguard and sights. Approximately 35,000 manufactured between 1907 and 1916.

NIB	Exc.	V.G.	Good	Fair	Poor
—	500	400	320	200	100

No. 35 Off-Hand/Auto-Shot Shot Gun

Stevens No. 35 is a .410 bore pistol manufactured by J. Stevens Arms Co., Chicopee Falls, Massachusetts. It was available with an 8" or 12.25" smoothbore barrel, for 2.5" shells only. In two variations: Off-Hand Shot Gun (1923 to 1929); and Auto-Shot (1929 to 1934). Total production is unknown because the .410 and .22 rimfire variations of No. 35 share the same serial number range. Researcher Ken Cope estimates total Auto-Shot production was approximately 2,000, and Off-Hand production at 20,000 to 25,000. Production was halted after the government ruled the .410 Stevens to be a "firearm" in the "any other weapon" category under the NFA in 1934, when its retail price was about $12. Stevens does not possess the same collector appeal as other .410 smoothbore pistols, because (1) its relatively light weight makes it an uncomfortable shooter, and (2) the gun is not well made. Note: 8" barrel commands a 25 to 50 percent premium. These are considered Class III firearms under NFA. Possession is illegal unless registered with BATFE.

No. 35 Off-Hand Shot Gun

Serial range from 1 to 43357.

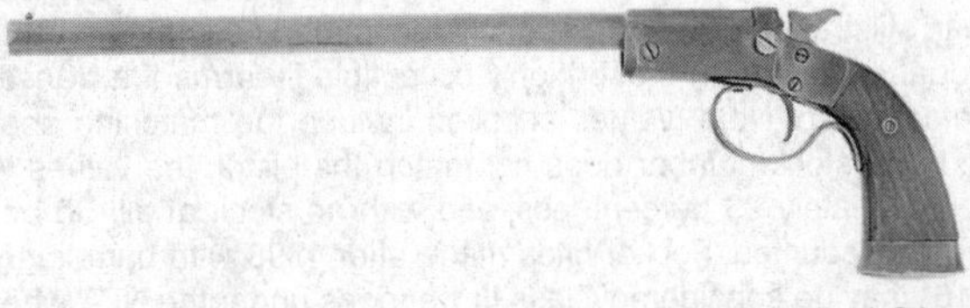

Courtesy John J. Stimson, Jr.

NIB	Exc.	V.G.	Good	Fair	Poor
—	400	250	200	100	80

No. 35 Auto-Shot

NIB	Exc.	V.G.	Good	Fair	Poor
—	450	300	200	120	100

No. 43

This version also called "Diamond." Produced in two distinct variations called First Issue and Second Issue. First Issue has a brass frame; Second Issue an iron frame and no firing pin bushing. Otherwise, they are quite similar and would be valued the same. They are chambered for .22 rimfire cartridge. Offered with 6" or 10" part-octagonal barrel. Frames nickel-plated or blued, with blued barrels and square-butt walnut grips. Approximately 95,000 manufactured between 1886 and 1916. Note: Add 25 percent premium for 10" barrels.

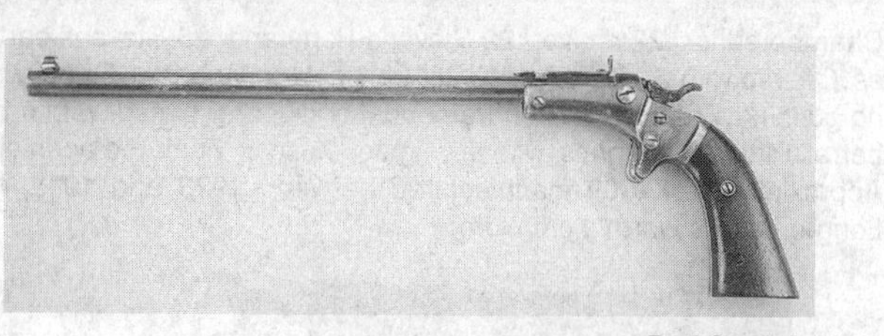

Paul Goodwin photo

NIB	Exc.	V.G.	Good	Fair	Poor
—	600	400	250	150	80

No. 10 Target Pistol

This version was a departure from its predecessors. Very much resembles a semi-automatic pistol, but in reality a single-shot. Chambered for .22 rimfire cartridge. Has an 8" round barrel that pivots upward for loading and a blued steel frame, with checkered rubber grips. Instead of the usual exposed hammer, this version has a knurled cocking piece that extends through rear of the frame. Approximately 7,000 manufactured between 1919 and 1933.

Courtesy John J. Stimson, Jr.

NIB	Exc.	V.G.	Good	Fair	Poor
—	400	300	200	150	100

POCKET RIFLES

This series of pistols is similar to target and sporting pistols, except that these were produced with detachable shoulder stocks that bear the same serial number as the pistol with which they were sold. They are sometimes referred to as "Bicycle Rifles". The collector interest in these weapons is quite high; but it would behoove one to be familiar with the provisions of the Gun Control Act of 1968 when dealing in or collecting this variation—as when the stock is attached, they can fall into the category of a short-barreled rifle. Some are considered to be curios and relics, and others have been totally declassified; but some models may still be restricted. We strongly recommend securing a qualified, individual appraisal on these highly collectible firearms if a transaction is contemplated. Note: Values supplied include the matching shoulder stock. If the stock number does not match the pistol, the values would be approximately 25 percent less; and with no stock at all, 50 percent should be deducted. Pocket rifles made after 1898 with barrels shorter than 16" may be considered Class III weapons under the NFA when accompanied by a stock.

Old Model Pocket Rifle (Antique)

Chambered for .22 rimfire cartridge. Has an 8" or 10" part-octagonal barrel, a spur trigger and an external hammer on which the firing pin is mounted. Extractor is spring-loaded. A plated brass frame, blued barrel and walnut or rosewood grips. Shoulder stock nickel-plated or black. Barrel marked "J. Stevens & Co. Chicopee Falls, Mass.". Approximately 4,000 manufactured between 1869 and 1886.

Exc.	Fine	V.G.	Good	Fair	Poor
700	550	430	320	200	140

Reliable Pocket Rifle

Chambered for .22 rimfire cartridge. Appearance is quite similar to Old Model. Basic difference is the extractor operates as part of the pivoting barrel mechanism instead of being spring-loaded. Barrel marked "J. Stevens A&T Co.". Approximately 4,000 manufactured between 1886 and 1896. Premium for pre-1899 antique specimens.

NIB	Exc.	V.G.	Good	Fair	Poor
620	500	450	400	300	210

No. 42 Reliable Pocket Rifle

Similar to first issue Reliable, except it has an iron frame, with the firing pin mounted in it without a bushing. Shoulder stock is shaped differently. Approximately 8,000 manufactured between 1896 and 1916.

NIB	Exc.	V.G.	Good	Fair	Poor
—	700	580	480	350	250

First Issue New Model Pocket Rifle (Antique)

This version is first of the medium-frame models, with a frame width of 1". All of its predecessors have a .625" wide frame. Chambered for .22 and .32 rimfire cartridges. Offered with barrel lengths of 10", 12", 15" or 18" that are part-octagonal in configuration. External hammer has the firing pin mounted on it. Has a plated brass frame, blued barrel and walnut or rosewood grips. Shoulder stock is nickel-plated and fitted differently than the small-frame models, in that there is a dovetail in the butt and top leg is secured by a knurled screw. Barrel marked "J. Stevens & Co. Chicopee Falls, Mass.". Approximately 8,000 manufactured between 1872 and 1875.

Courtesy Mike Stuckslager

Exc.	Fine	V.G.	Good	Fair	Poor
1000	650	570	500	400	280

Second Issue New Model Pocket Rifle (Antique)

Similar to First Issue, except firing pin is mounted in the frame with a bushing. Approximately 15,000 manufactured between 1875 and 1896.

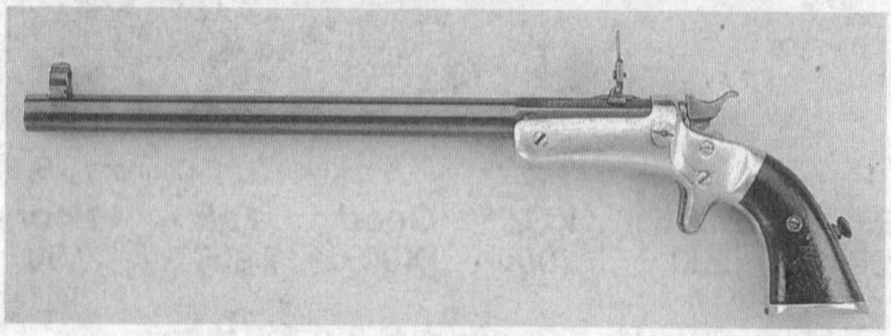

Paul Goodwin photo

Exc.	Fine	V.G.	Good	Fair	Poor
950	600	550	500	350	240

Vernier Model (Antique)

Similar to Second Issue, except it features a vernier tang sight located on backstrap. Approximately 1,500 manufactured between 1884 and 1896.

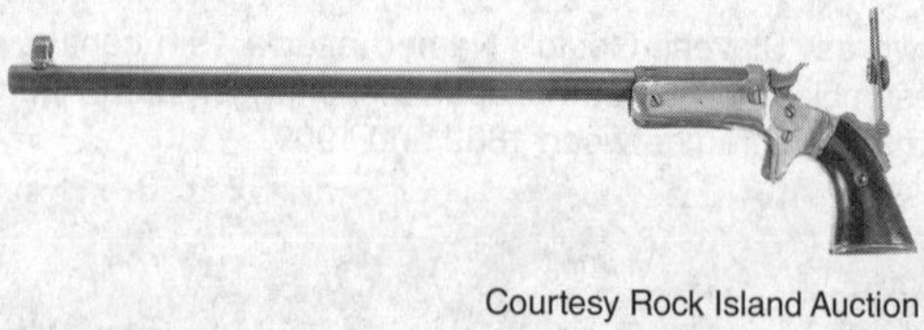

Courtesy Rock Island Auction Company

Exc.	Fine	V.G.	Good	Fair	Poor
2000	1400	700	500	300	200

No. 40

Similar to its medium-frame predecessors, except it has a longer grip frame and a conventional trigger, with triggerguard. Approximately 15,000 manufactured between 1896 and 1916.

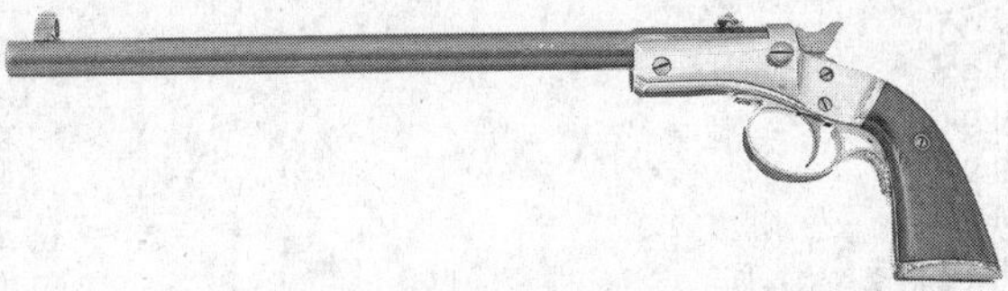

Courtesy Rock Island Auction Company

NIB	Exc.	V.G.	Good	Fair	Poor
—	980	850	650	400	300

No. 40-1/2

Similar to No. 40, with a vernier tang sight mounted on the backstrap. Approximately 2,500 manufactured between 1896 and 1915.

NIB	Exc.	V.G.	Good	Fair	Poor
—	1100	980	700	550	400

No. 34 (Hunter's Pet) Antique

This is first of the heavy-frame pocket rifles that featured a 1.25" wide frame. Also known as "Hunter's Pet". Chambered for many popular cartridges from .22 rimfire to .44-40 centerfire. Offered with part-octagonal 18", 20", 22" or 24" barrel. Has a nickel-plated iron frame and blued barrel. Detachable stock is nickel-plated and grips are walnut. Few produced with a brass frame; and if located, these would be worth twice the value indicated. Firing pin mounted in the frame, with the bushing and features a spur trigger. Approximately 4,000 manufactured between 1872 and 1900.

Exc.	Fine	V.G.	Good	Fair	Poor
1050	700	570	450	350	240

No. 34-1/2 Antique

Similar to No. 34, except it features a vernier tang sight mounted on the backstrap. Approximately 1,200 manufactured between 1884 and 1900.

Exc.	Fine	V.G.	Good	Fair	Poor
1250	900	770	650	450	310

BOLT-ACTION UTILITY RIFLES

Stevens Company produced a number of inexpensive, utilitarian, bolt-action rifles. These were both single-shot and repeaters. They have been popular over the years as starter rifles for young shooters. Their values are quite similar and are listed for reference purposes only.

Model 053—Single-Shot
Model 056—5-Shot Magazine
Model 066—Tube Magazine
Model 083—Single-Shot
Model 084—5-Shot Magazine
Model 086—Tube Magazine
Model 15—Single-Shot
Model 15Y—Single-Shot
Model 419—Single-Shot
Model 48—Single-Shot
Model 49—Single-Shot
Model 50—Single-Shot
Model 51—Single-Shot
Model 52—Single-Shot
Model 53—Single-Shot
Model 56—5-Shot Magazine
Model 66—Tube Magazine

NIB	Exc.	V.G.	Good	Fair	Poor
—	—	200	100	70	50

Model 416

Target rifle chambered for .22 LR cartridge. Has 24" heavy barrel, with aperture sights. Features 5-round detachable magazine. Blued, with target-type walnut stock.

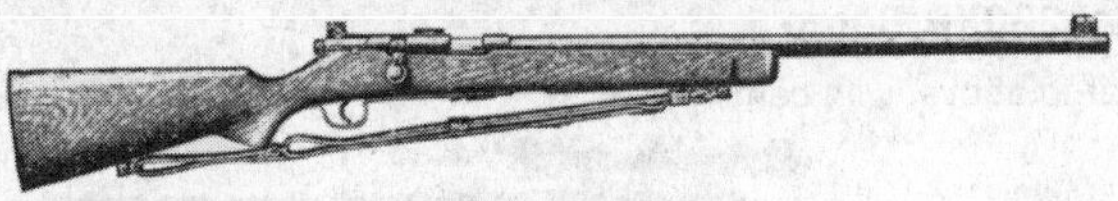

NIB	Exc.	V.G.	Good	Fair	Poor
—	450	350	200	150	100

Model 322

Bolt-action sporting rifle chambered for .22 Hornet cartridge. Has a 20" barrel, with open sights and detachable box magazine. Finish blued, with plain walnut stock.

NIB	Exc.	V.G.	Good	Fair	Poor
—	180	120	100	80	50

Model 322-S

This version features an aperture rear sight.

NIB	Exc.	V.G.	Good	Fair	Poor
—	220	120	100	80	50

Model 89

Single-shot Martini-type falling-block rifle, chambered for .22 LR cartridge. Has an 18.5" barrel and triggerguard loop-lever activator. Finish blued, with straight walnut stock. Introduced in 1976; discontinued.

NIB	Exc.	V.G.	Good	Fair	Poor
—	120	80	70	60	40

Model 87M

Designed to look like the M1 Garand. Chambered for .22 rimfire cartridge.

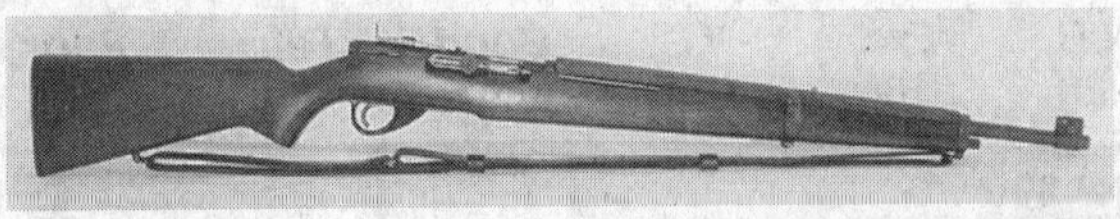

Courtesy Richard M. Kumor, Sr.

NIB	Exc.	V.G.	Good	Fair	Poor
—	600	500	380	220	150

Model 987

Blowback-operated semi-automatic rifle, chambered for .22 LR cartridge. Has a 20" barrel, with 15-round tubular magazine. Finish blued, with hardwood stock.

NIB	Exc.	V.G.	Good	Fair	Poor
—	150	100	80	50	20

ECONOMY LINE (SAVAGE, 2006)

Model 200

Long-/short-action bolt rifle, chambered in .223, .22-250, .243, 7MM-08, .308, .25-06, .270, .30-06, 7mm RM or .300 WM. Gray checkered synthetic stock and 22" (short-action) or 24" (long-action) blued sightless barrel. Introduced 2006.

NIB	Exc.	V.G.	Good	Fair	Poor
320	280	220	180	120	100

Model 200XP Long or Short Action Package Rifle

Similar to above, with 4x12 scope.

NIB	Exc.	V.G.	Good	Fair	Poor
380	300	250	200	150	120

Model 200XP Camo

Similar to above, with camo stock.

NIB	Exc.	V.G.	Good	Fair	Poor
400	320	280	220	180	150

Cadet Mini-Youth

Similar to Savage Cub .22 rimfire. Introduced 2006.

NIB	Exc.	V.G.	Good	Fair	Poor
200	150	120	100	80	50

Model 315 Youth

Similar to Cadet Mini-Youth, with sightless barrel. Introduced 2006.

NIB	Exc.	V.G.	Good	Fair	Poor
200	150	120	100	80	50

Model 310

Five-shot bolt-action repeater chambered for .17 HMR. Detachable box magazine, synthetic stock, blued 20.75" sightless barrel. Introduced 2006.

NIB	Exc.	V.G.	Good	Fair	Poor
200	150	120	100	80	50

Model 310 Heavy Barrel

Similar to Stevens Model 310, with 21" bull barrel. Introduced 2006.

NIB	Exc.	V.G.	Good	Fair	Poor
220	180	150	120	80	50

Model 300

Clip-fed bolt-action repeater chambered for .22 rimfire. Gray synthetic stock and 20.75" blued barrel. Also available with scope package (add 10 percent). Introduced 2006.

NIB	Exc.	V.G.	Good	Fair	Poor
200	150	120	100	80	50

Model 305

Similar to Model 310. Chambered in .22 WMR. Introduced 2006.

NIB	Exc.	V.G.	Good	Fair	Poor
220	180	150	120	80	50

Model 334

Calibers: .243 Win., .308 Win., 6.5 Creedmoor. Barrel: 20" free-floating button rifled. Stock: Walnut or black synthetic. Features: The first centerfire rifle under the Stevens by Savage name in decades. Budget bolt action built completely in Turkey. Two-stage trigger, 60-degree bolt throw, three-position safety. Three-round box magazine. Drilled and tapped with Savage 110 spacing.

NIB	Exc.	V.G.	Good	Fair	Poor
330	—	—	—	—	—

MISCELLANEOUS SINGLE-SHOT SHOTGUNS

This company manufactured a number of single-barrel break-open single-shot shotguns. They were chambered for various gauges, with various length barrels and chokes. They are quite similar in appearance and were designed as inexpensive utility-grade weapons. There is little or no collector interest in them at this time and their values are similar. They are listed for reference purposes only.

Model 89
Model 90
Model 93
Model 94
Model 94A
Model 94C
Model 95
Model 97
Model 100
Model 102
Model 104
Model 105
Model 106
Model 107
Model 108
Model 110
Model 120
Model 125
Model 140
Model 160
Model 165
Model 170
Model 180
Model 944
Model 958
Model 970

Model 107

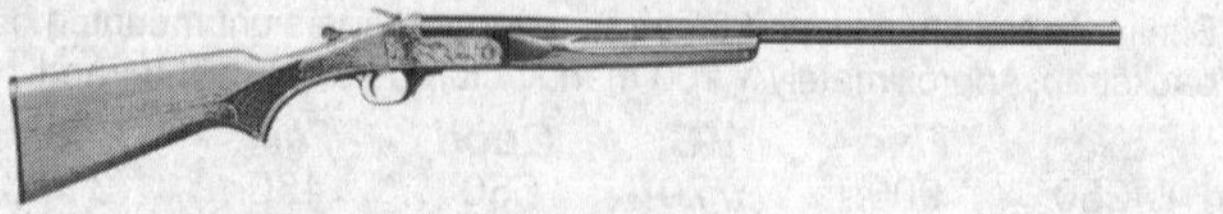

NIB	Exc.	V.G.	Good	Fair	Poor
—	150	100	80	50	20

MISCELLANEOUS SINGLE-SHOT SHOTGUNS

Model 182

Single-shot break-open shotgun, chambered for 12-gauge. Offered with 30" or 32" trap choked barrels. Features hammerless action, with an automatic ejector and lightly engraved receiver. Finish blued, with checkered trap-grade stock.

NIB	Exc.	V.G.	Good	Fair	Poor
—	180	120	100	80	50

Model 185

This version features a half-octagonal barrel, with automatic ejector and checkered walnut stock. Note: Deduct 25 percent for Damascus barrel.

NIB	Exc.	V.G.	Good	Fair	Poor
—	180	120	100	80	50

Model 190

A 12-gauge hammerless gun, with an automatic ejector. Lightly engraved, with a half-octagonal barrel. Note: Deduct 25 percent for Damascus barrel.

NIB	Exc.	V.G.	Good	Fair	Poor
—	180	120	100	80	50

Model 195

Another deluxe version that features engraving, half-octagonal barrel and high-grade checkered walnut stock. Note: Deduct 25 percent for Damascus barrel.

NIB	Exc.	V.G.	Good	Fair	Poor
—	350	250	200	150	100

Model 240

Over/under model features a boxlock frame, with exposed hammers.

NIB	Exc.	V.G.	Good	Fair	Poor
—	400	300	250	200	150

Model .22/.410

Over/under .22/.410 combo gun, with Tenite stock. Manufactured 1939-1950.

NIB	Exc.	V.G.	Good	Fair	Poor
—	350	300	250	180	100

Model 301 Turkey XP

Gauges: 20 ga., 3 in., .410 bore, 3 in. Barrel: 26 in., black matte. Weight: 5.07 lbs. Length: 41.5 in. Stock: Camouflage synthetic stock and forend with either Mossy Oak Obsession or Mossy Oak Bottomland pattern. Features: Single-shot break action with removable one-piece rail. XP variant includes mounted and bore-sighted 1x30 red-dot optic. Barrel optimized for Federal Premium TSS Heavyweight turkey loads. Swivel studs, front bead, manual hammer block safety, rubber recoil pad. Includes Winchoke pattern Extra Full turkey choke.

NIB	Exc.	V.G.	Good	Fair	Poor
190	—	—	—	—	—

DOUBLE-BARREL SHOTGUNS

STEVENS BRAND

Firm of J. Stevens and its successors, produced a number of utility-grade side-by-side double-barrel shotguns, between 1877 and 1988. Chambered for 10-, 12-, 16- or 20-gauge and .410 bore. Stevens shotguns in 10-gauge and .410 bore will normally bring a premium as do guns with single triggers and ejectors. They have various-length barrels and choke combinations. Feature double triggers and extractors, except where noted. A complete list of Stevens brand models, including the three in-house brands, Riverside, Springfield and Super Value, are listed.

Model 1877—Hammer Boxlock

NIB	Exc.	V.G.	Good	Fair	Poor
—	580	450	350	250	200

Model 250—Hammer Sidelock

NIB	Exc.	V.G.	Good	Fair	Poor
—	580	450	350	250	200

Model 225—Hammer Boxlock

Courtesy Nick Niles, Paul Goodwin photo

NIB	Exc.	V.G.	Good	Fair	Poor
—	580	450	350	250	200

Model 260—Hammer Sidelock

NIB	Exc.	V.G.	Good	Fair	Poor
—	580	450	350	250	200

Model 270—Hammer Sidelock

NIB	Exc.	V.G.	Good	Fair	Poor
—	580	450	350	250	200

Model 280—Hammer Sidelock

NIB	Exc.	V.G.	Good	Fair	Poor
—	580	450	350	250	200

Model 325—Hammerless Boxlock

NIB	Exc.	V.G.	Good	Fair	Poor
—	450	400	350	250	200

Model 350—Hammerless Boxlock

NIB	Exc.	V.G.	Good	Fair	Poor
—	450	400	350	250	200

Model 360—Hammerless Boxlock

NIB	Exc.	V.G.	Good	Fair	Poor
—	450	400	350	250	200

Model 370—Hammerless Boxlock

NIB	Exc.	V.G.	Good	Fair	Poor
—	450	400	350	250	200

Model 380—Hammerless Boxlock

NIB	Exc.	V.G.	Good	Fair	Poor
—	580	450	350	250	200

Model 235—Hammer Boxlock

NIB	Exc.	V.G.	Good	Fair	Poor
—	450	400	350	250	200

Model 335 (Early)—Hammerless Boxlock

Courtesy Nick Niles, Paul Goodwin photo

NIB	Exc.	V.G.	Good	Fair	Poor
—	450	400	350	250	200

Model 335 (Late)—Hammerless Boxlock

NIB	Exc.	V.G.	Good	Fair	Poor
—	450	400	350	250	200

Model 255—Hammer Sidelock

NIB	Exc.	V.G.	Good	Fair	Poor
—	450	400	350	250	200

Model 265—Hammer Sidelock

Courtesy Nick Niles, Paul Goodwin photo

NIB	Exc.	V.G.	Good	Fair	Poor
—	450	400	350	250	200

Model 355—Hammerless Boxlock

NIB	Exc.	V.G.	Good	Fair	Poor
—	800	580	450	350	250

Model 365—Hammerless Boxlock

Courtesy Nick Niles, Paul Goodwin photo

NIB	Exc.	V.G.	Good	Fair	Poor
—	920	620	500	400	300

Model 375 (London Proofs)—Hammerless Boxlock

NIB	Exc.	V.G.	Good	Fair	Poor
—	1500	950	700	450	350

Model 375 (U.S.)—Hammerless Boxlock

NIB	Exc.	V.G.	Good	Fair	Poor
—	1100	700	580	400	300

Model 385 (London Proofs)—Hammerless Boxlock

NIB	Exc.	V.G.	Good	Fair	Poor
—	1650	1050	700	450	350

Model 385 (U.S.)—Hammerless Boxlock

NIB	Exc.	V.G.	Good	Fair	Poor
—	1200	850	580	450	300

Model 345—Hammerless Boxlock

Courtesy Nick Niles, Paul Goodwin photo

NIB	Exc.	V.G.	Good	Fair	Poor
—	580	450	350	250	200

Model 330—Hammerless Boxlock

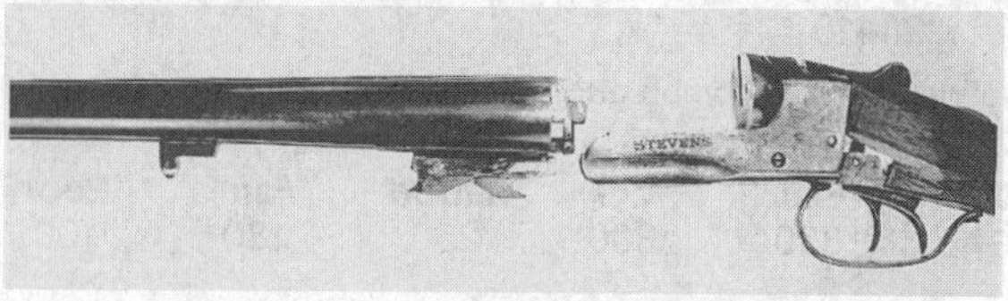

Stevens Model 330 early fork-type cocking lever

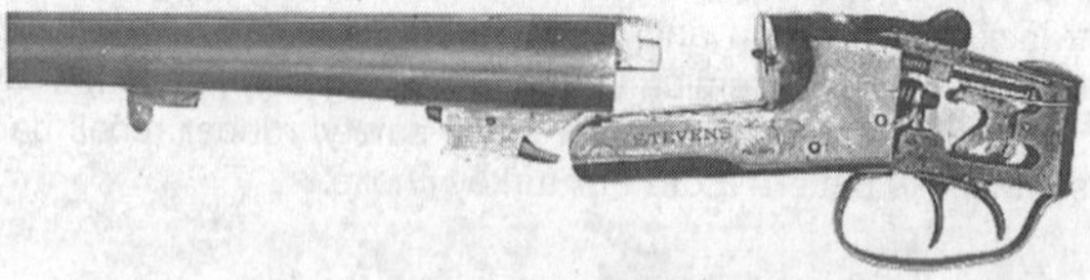

NIB	Exc.	V.G.	Good	Fair	Poor
—	450	400	350	250	200

Model 515—Hammerless Boxlock

NIB	Exc.	V.G.	Good	Fair	Poor
—	620	520	450	350	300

Model 515—Single Trigger Hammerless Boxlock

NIB	Exc.	V.G.	Good	Fair	Poor
—	750	580	450	350	300

Model 500—Skeet Hammerless Boxlock

Courtesy Nick Niles, Paul Goodwin photo

NIB	Exc.	V.G.	Good	Fair	Poor
—	1250	920	800	700	400

Model 530—Hammerless Boxlock

NIB	Exc.	V.G.	Good	Fair	Poor
—	450	400	350	250	200

Model 530M—Tenite Hammerless Boxlock

NIB	Exc.	V.G.	Good	Fair	Poor
—	450	400	350	250	200

Model 530M—Tenite Single Trigger Hammerless Boxlock

NIB	Exc.	V.G.	Good	Fair	Poor
—	750	580	450	350	300

Model 530A—Hammerless Boxlock

Courtesy Nick Niles, Paul Goodwin photo

NIB	Exc.	V.G.	Good	Fair	Poor
—	450	400	350	250	200

Model 530A—Single Trigger Hammerless Boxlock

NIB	Exc.	V.G.	Good	Fair	Poor
—	520	450	350	300	250

Model 311—Tenite Hammerless Boxlock

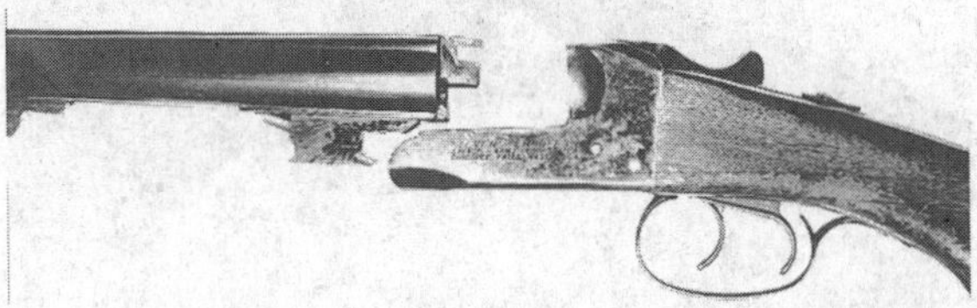

Courtesy Nick Niles

Stevens Model 311

NIB	Exc.	V.G.	Good	Fair	Poor
—	450	400	350	250	200

Model 331—Single Trigger Hammerless Boxlock

NIB	Exc.	V.G.	Good	Fair	Poor
—	520	400	300	250	200

Model 311—Tenite Single Trigger Hammerless Boxlock

NIB	Exc.	V.G.	Good	Fair	Poor
—	580	500	450	350	300

Model 311A—Hammerless Boxlock

NIB	Exc.	V.G.	Good	Fair	Poor
—	520	450	350	250	200

Model 311C—Hammerless Boxlock

Courtesy Nick Niles, Paul Goodwin photo

NIB	Exc.	V.G.	Good	Fair	Poor
—	400	350	250	200	150

Model 311D—Hammerless Boxlock

Courtesy Nick Niles, Paul Goodwin photo

NIB	Exc.	V.G.	Good	Fair	Poor
—	450	400	350	250	200

Model 311E—Hammerless Boxlock

NIB	Exc.	V.G.	Good	Fair	Poor
—	600	450	400	300	250

Model 311F—Hammerless Boxlock

NIB	Exc.	V.G.	Good	Fair	Poor
—	450	400	350	250	200

Model 311H—Hammerless Boxlock

NIB	Exc.	V.G.	Good	Fair	Poor
—	450	400	350	250	200

Model 311H—Vent Rib Hammerless Boxlock

Courtesy Nick Niles, Paul Goodwin photo

NIB	Exc.	V.G.	Good	Fair	Poor
—	500	450	350	300	250

Model 311J/R—Hammerless Boxlock

Courtesy Nick Niles, Paul Goodwin photo

NIB	Exc.	V.G.	Good	Fair	Poor
—	400	350	250	200	150

Model 311J/R—Solid Rib Hammerless Boxlock

NIB	Exc.	V.G.	Good	Fair	Poor
—	400	350	250	200	150

Model 311H—Waterfowler Hammerless Boxlock

NIB	Exc.	V.G.	Good	Fair	Poor
—	700	580	450	350	250

Model 240—.410 Over/Under Hammer Tenite

NIB	Exc.	V.G.	Good	Fair	Poor
—	580	450	350	250	200

RIVERSIDE BRAND

Model 215—Hammer Boxlock

Courtesy Nick Niles, Paul Goodwin photo

NIB	Exc.	V.G.	Good	Fair	Poor
—	750	520	400	250	200

Model 315 (Early)—Hammerless Boxlock

NIB	Exc.	V.G.	Good	Fair	Poor
—	580	450	350	250	200

Model 315 (Late)—Hammerless Boxlock

NIB	Exc.	V.G.	Good	Fair	Poor
—	580	450	350	250	200

SUPER VALUE BRAND

Model 511—Hammerless Boxlock

NIB	Exc.	V.G.	Good	Fair	Poor
—	520	400	300	200	150

Model 511—Sunken Rib Hammerless Boxlock

NIB	Exc.	V.G.	Good	Fair	Poor
—	580	450	350	200	150

SPRINGFIELD BRAND

Model 215—Hammer Boxlock

NIB	Exc.	V.G.	Good	Fair	Poor
—	580	450	350	250	150

Model 311—Hammerless Boxlock

Courtesy Nick Niles, Paul Goodwin photo

NIB	Exc.	V.G.	Good	Fair	Poor
—	580	450	350	250	150

Model 315—Hammerless Boxlock

Courtesy Nick Niles, Paul Goodwin photo

NIB	Exc.	V.G.	Good	Fair	Poor
—	580	450	350	250	200

Model 3150—Hammerless Boxlock

NIB	Exc.	V.G.	Good	Fair	Poor
—	700	580	400	250	200

Model 3151—Hammerless Boxlock

NIB	Exc.	V.G.	Good	Fair	Poor
—	850	700	450	350	250

Model 3151—Single Trigger Hammerless Boxlock

NIB	Exc.	V.G.	Good	Fair	Poor
—	950	800	580	450	300

Model 311—Single Trigger Hammerless Boxlock

NIB	Exc.	V.G.	Good	Fair	Poor
—	800	700	580	450	300

Model 5151—Hammerless Boxlock

Courtesy Nick Niles, Paul Goodwin photo

NIB	Exc.	V.G.	Good	Fair	Poor
—	580	450	350	250	200

Model 5151—Single Trigger Hammerless Boxlock

NIB	Exc.	V.G.	Good	Fair	Poor
—	700	520	400	300	200

Model 311—New Style Hammerless Boxlock

Courtesy Nick Niles, Paul Goodwin photo

NIB	Exc.	V.G.	Good	Fair	Poor
—	580	450	350	250	150

Model 311—New Style Tenite Hammerless Boxlock

NIB	Exc.	V.G.	Good	Fair	Poor
—	580	450	350	250	150

Model 511—Sunken Rib Hammerless Boxlock

NIB	Exc.	V.G.	Good	Fair	Poor
—	580	450	350	250	150

Model 511—Hammerless Boxlock

NIB	Exc.	V.G.	Good	Fair	Poor
—	520	400	300	200	150

Model 511A—Hammerless Boxlock

NIB	Exc.	V.G.	Good	Fair	Poor
—	520	400	300	200	150

STEVENS/SAVAGE SHOTGUNS

Model 411 Upland Sporter

Introduced in 2003. Side-by-side shotgun chambered for 12- or 20-gauge and .410 bore. The 12-gauge fitted with 28" barrels; 20-gauge and .410 have 26" barrels. Single trigger with ejectors. False sideplates are laser engraved. European walnut stock, with pistol grip and splinter forend. Weight about 6.75 to 6.5 lbs. depending on gauge. Note: Add 50 percent for 20-gauge and .410 bore models.

NIB	***Exc.***	***V.G.***	***Good***	***Fair***	***Poor***
380	320	270	230	200	170

Model 555

This over/under model offered in 12-, 20-, 28-gauge or .410 bore, with 24", 26" or 28" barrels. Has five choke tubes, aluminum receiver, single-selective trigger, manual extractors and a Turkish walnut stock. Enhanced model has automatic ejectors, engraved receiver, Imperial-grade walnut stock. Note: Add $150 for Enhanced model.

NIB	***Exc.***	***V.G.***	***Good***	***Fair***	***Poor***
600	500	400	300	180	120

Model 555 Trap

Gauges: 12 ga., 3 in., 20 ga., 3 in. Barrel: 30 in., raised ventilated rib. Weight: 6.6-6.8 lbs. Length: 47.5 in. Stock: Turkish walnut stock and forend with adjustable comb and oil finish. Features: Lightweight silver aluminum receiver scaled to gauge with steel breech reinforcement. Top single barrel with shell extractor. Manual tang safety, front bead, chrome-lined barrel, semi-gloss metalwork finish. Includes three chokes.

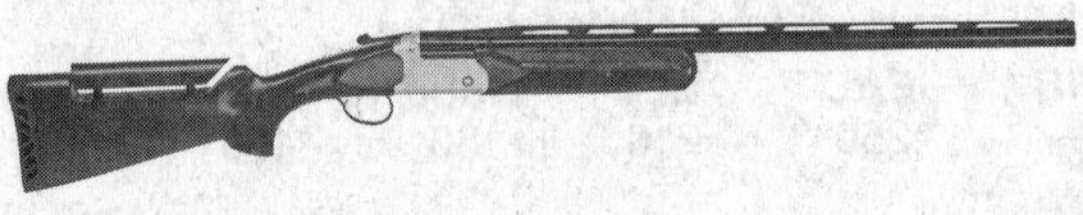

NIB	***Exc.***	***V.G.***	***Good***	***Fair***	***Poor***
620	530	450	—	—	—

Model 555 Trap Compact

Gauges: 12 ga., 3 in., 20 ga., 3 in. Barrel: 26 in., raised ventilated rib. Weight: 7.3-7.5 lbs. Length: 42.5 in. Stock: Turkish walnut stock and forend with adjustable comb and oil finish. Features: Lightweight silver aluminum receiver scaled to gauge with steel breech reinforcement. Top single barrel with shell extractor. Manual tang safety, front bead, chrome-lined barrel, semi-gloss metalwork finish. Compact 13.5 in. length of pull. Includes three chokes.

NIB	***Exc.***	***V.G.***	***Good***	***Fair***	***Poor***
620	530	450	—	—	—

Model 560

Gauges: 12 ga. Barrels: 28" black matte. Stock: Turkish Walnut, checkered with a satin finish. Features: New budget autoloader built in Turkey for Stevens by Savage. Gas operated with a 3" chamber and aluminum alloy receiver. Hard chrome-lined barrel. Oversized controls. Fiber-optic front sight. Available in both standard and compact variants at the same price. Ships with three flush choke tubes.

NIB	***Exc.***	***V.G.***	***Good***	***Fair***	***Poor***
430	370	—	—	—	—

320 Security Thumbhole

Gauge: 12 ga. 3 in., or 20 ga. 3in. Barrel: 18.5-in. chrome alloy steel matte black. Weight: 7.0–7.3 lbs. Length: 39.1 in. Stock: Black matte synthetic with thumbhole cutout. Features: Pump action with dual slide bars and rotary bolt. Thumbhole stock design with ambidextrous cheek riser and grip texture. Swivel studs. Bottom-loading tubular magazine with 5+1-round capacity. Black rubber recoil pad. Ghost Ring Sight or Front Bead Sight models available in both chamberings.

NIB	***Exc.***	***V.G.***	***Good***	***Fair***	***Poor***
240	200	170	—	—	—

320 Turkey Thumbhole

Gauge: 12 ga. 3 in., or 20 ga. 3 in. Barrel: 22-in. chrome alloy steel matte black with ventilated rib. Weight: 7.6 lbs. Length: 43.4 in. Stock: Olive drab green matte synthetic with thumbhole cutout. Features: Pump action with dual slide bars and rotary bolt. Thumbhole stock design with ambidextrous cheek riser and grip texture. Swivel studs. Bottom-loading tubular magazine with 5+1-round capacity. Black rubber recoil pad. Adjustable fiber-optic turkey sights. Extended Win-Choke-style Extra Full choke tube.

NIB	***Exc.***	***V.G.***	***Good***	***Fair***	***Poor***
280	240	200	—	—	—

301 Turkey Thumbhole

Gauge: .410 bore 3 in. Barrel: 26 in. chrome alloy steel black matte. Weight: 5.07 lbs. Length: 41.5 in. Stock: Olive drab green matte synthetic thumbhole style. Features: Continuation of the 301 single-shot break-action line with a removeable one-piece rail and gobbler-specific features. Ambidextrous cheek riser. Barrel optimized for Federal Premium Heavyweight TSS turkey loads. Swivel studs, front bead sight, manual hammer block safety, rubber recoil pad. Includes Win-Choke pattern Extra Full turkey choke.

NIB	***Exc.***	***V.G.***	***Good***	***Fair***	***Poor***
190	160	140	—	—	—

STEVENS DATE CODE

Collectors will find a date code stamped on every double-barrel shotgun in Stevens brands, produced between March 1949 and December 1968. Usually, it's behind the hinge pin or ahead of triggerguard on bottom of the frame. It will appear as a small circle containing a number and letter. Letters correspond to years shown in the following table. Significance of the numbers is not known.

BOLT-ACTION SHOTGUNS

Stevens Company produced a number of bolt-action shotguns that are single-shot or repeaters. Chambered for 20-gauge or .410 bore. Blued, with walnut stocks. Values for these utility-grade shotguns are similar.

Model 237—Single-Shot
Model 258—Clip Fed
Model 37—Single-Shot
Model 38—Clip Fed
Model 39—Tube Magazine
Model 58—Clip Fed
Model 59—Tube Magazine

Model 58

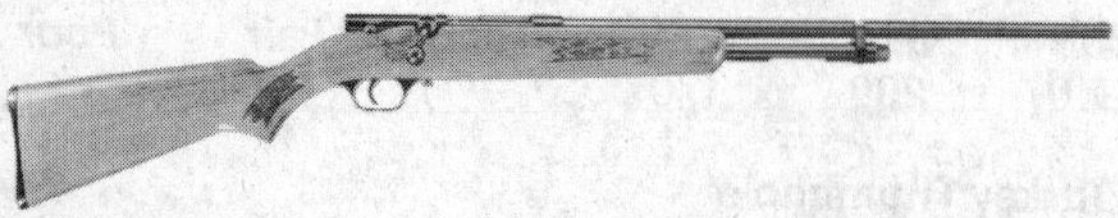

Model 59

NIB	Exc.	V.G.	Good	Fair	Poor
—	120	100	80	50	40

SLIDE-ACTION UTILITY-GRADE SHOTGUNS

J. Stevens Arms Company also produced a series of utility-grade slide-action shotguns. Chambered for various gauges, barrel lengths and chokes. Finishes blued, with walnut stocks. Values are similar and listed for reference purposes.

Model 67
Model 67-VR
Model 77
Model 77-AC
Model 77-M
Model 77-SC
Model 520
Model 522
Model 620
Model 621
Model 820

NIB	Exc.	V.G.	Good	Fair	Poor
—	220	150	120	100	80

Model 620

NIB	Exc.	V.G.	Good	Fair	Poor
—	180	150	130	110	91

Model 620 U.S. Marked Trench Gun

Note: Add $150 for bayonet.

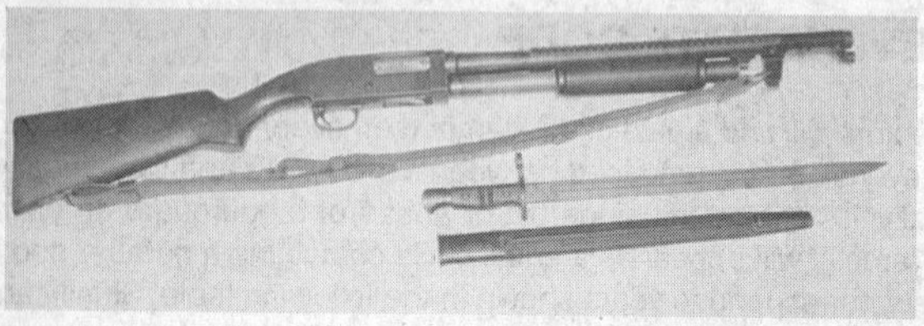

Courtesy Richard M. Kumor Sr.

NIB	Exc.	V.G.	Good	Fair	Poor
2900	2460	2100	1780	1510	1290

SLIDE-ACTION UTILITY-GRADE SHOTGUNS

Model 124

Manually-operated bolt-action shotgun, chambered for 12-gauge. Has 28" barrel, with various chokes. Blued and brown plastic Tenite stock. An odd duck: looks like a semi-automatic and is often mistaken for such.

NIB	Exc.	V.G.	Good	Fair	Poor
—	220	180	80	60	50

Model 67

Slide-action shotgun chambered for 12- or 20-gauge and .410 bore. Has 3" chambers. Offered with various barrel lengths and choke tubes, with 5-shot tube magazine. Features blued steel receiver, with walnut stock. Discontinued in 1989.

NIB	Exc.	V.G.	Good	Fair	Poor
—	250	210	180	150	130

Model 675

Slide-action shotgun chambered for 12-gauge, with 24" ventilated rib barrel and iron sights. Finish blued, with hardwood stock and recoil pad. Manufactured in 1987 and 1988.

NIB	Exc.	V.G.	Good	Fair	Poor
—	280	240	200	150	100

Model 69-RXL

Matte-finished riot version of Model 67 series slide-action shotgun. Has 18.25" cylinder-bore barrel and furnished with a recoil pad. Discontinued in 1989.

NIB	Exc.	V.G.	Good	Fair	Poor
—	200	170	140	120	100

Model 350 Pump Shotgun

Pump-action shotgun chambered for 2.75" and 3" 12-gauge. Features include all-steel barrel and receiver; bottom-load and -eject design; black synthetic stock; 5+1 capacity. Price: $267 (Field Model w/28" barrel, screw-in choke); $241 (Security Model w/18" barrel, fixed choke); $307 (Combo Model with Field and Security barrels); $254 (Security Model with 18.25" barrel w/ghost ring rear sight).

NIB	Exc.	V.G.	Good	Fair	Poor
—	250	210	180	150	130

Model 77

NIB	Exc.	V.G.	Good	Fair	Poor
—	180	150	130	110	90

Model 77-SC

NIB	Exc.	V.G.	Good	Fair	Poor
—	180	150	130	110	90

STEYR
Steyr, Austria

STEYR & MANNLICHER PISTOLS

By: Joseph Schroeder: Not all Mannlicher pistols made by Steyr. Many pistols made by Steyr were not designed by Mannlicher. However, since by far greatest number of Mannlicher's pistols were made by Steyr we believe it will be appropriate to include all of Ferdinand Ritter von Mannlicher's pistols along with other Steyr designs under this heading.

Schoenberger

Considered by many to be first "commercial" semi-automatic pistol. Only about two dozen were made in 1892. Steyr-made 8mm Schoenberger was based on patents granted to Laumann in 1890-91. Had a magazine in front of triggerguard. Too rare to price.

Mannlicher Model 1894 (Antique)

Mannlicher's first "successful" self-loading pistol. Model 1894 had a blow-forward action and double-action lockwork. Earliest examples were made in Austria, probably by Steyr, in 7.6mm. Greatest number made by SIG in 1896-97 for Swiss army tests. These 100 pistols had shorter barrel, smaller frame and in 6.5mm. Prices are for Swiss examples. Note: Add 20% for 7.6mm pistols. Values are speculative due to rarity.

Courtesy Rock Island Auction Company

Exc.	Fine	V.G.	Good	Fair	Poor
20000	8000	6000	5500	3000	2100

Mannlicher Model 1896/03

Most confusing of Mannlicher's pistols. Earliest examples, which have fixed magazine and ribbed barrel, may have been made by Steyr and are very rare. Later versions, with removable box magazine, have been called "Model 1896/03" and "Model 1901", and made as both pistol and pistol-carbine, possibly in Switzerland. Chambered for 7.65mm Mannlicher cartridge, which is really a 7.65mm Borchardt. Prices listed are for standard later model pistol or pistol-carbine (12" barrel, tangent sight); double prices for early pistol or late model pistol with detachable holster stock.

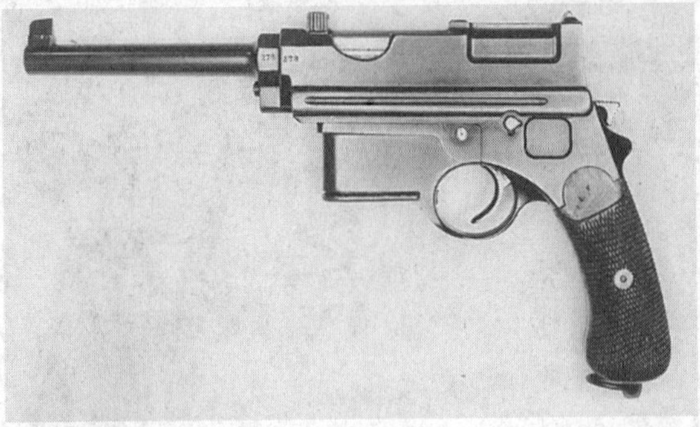

Courtesy Joseph Schroeder

NIB	Exc.	V.G.	Good	Fair	Poor
—	8250	5500	3850	2750	1500

Mannlicher Model 1899

Earliest version of Mannlicher's final semi-automatic pistol design. Only about 250 made by Dreyse in Soemmerda, Germany. Chambered for tapered case 7.63mm Mannlicher cartridge. Distinguished by large safety lever on left side, take-down screw under barrel and Dreyse markings.

Courtesy Joseph Schroeder

NIB	Exc.	V.G.	Good	Fair	Poor
—	9400	7150	4950	3850	2000

Mannlicher Model 1901

Marked "WAFFENFABRIK Steyr" on left side and "SYSTEM MANNLICHER" on right. Model 1901 distinguished by its checkered grips, rear sight located on rear of barrel, 8-round fixed magazine. Serial numbers to little over 1000.

Courtesy Joseph Schroeder

NIB	Exc.	V.G.	Good	Fair	Poor
—	4000	3500	1750	900	700

Mannlicher Model 1905

Improved version of Model 1901. Longer grip holding 10 rounds, grooved wooden grips, rear sight on rear of breech-block and "MODEL 1905" added to right side. Later production moved all markings to left side so Argentine crest could be placed on right side. Prices listed for original commercial Model 1905, NOT a re-blued Argentine contract with crest ground off. Note: Deduct 60% for reworked examples.

Courtesy Joseph Schroeder

NIB	Exc.	V.G.	Good	Fair	Poor
—	2420	1880	1350	800	400

Argentine Contract

NIB	Exc.	V.G.	Good	Fair	Poor
—	2750	2250	1650	900	500

Roth Steyr Model 1907

Based on patents granted to Karel Krnka and Georg Roth. The 8mm Model 1907 had rotating barrel locking system and was first self-loading pistol adopted by Austro-Hungarian Army. Note: Add 20% for early Steyr examples without large pin visible on right side of frame, or for those made in Budapest instead of Steyr. Slight premium for correct stripper clips.

Courtesy Joseph Schroeder

NIB	Exc.	V.G.	Good	Fair	Poor
—	1250	750	600	350	250

Steyr Model 1908 Pocket Pistol

Based on Belgian patents of Nicholas Pieper. These .25- and .32-caliber pocket pistols featured tipping barrels built by Steyr under license from Pieper in Liege. Production suspended during WWI, but may have resumed after war ended. Prices for either caliber.

NIB	Exc.	V.G.	Good	Fair	Poor
—	380	280	160	100	80

Steyr Hahn Model 1911 Commercially Marked

Note: Military versions of this model see Standard Catalog of Military Firearms at GunDigestStore.com.

NIB	Exc.	V.G.	Good	Fair	Poor
—	2200	1650	1220	880	450

Steyr Hahn Model 1912

NIB	Exc.	V.G.	Good	Fair	Poor
—	900	700	450	300	150

Steyr Model SP

Steyr's first post WWII pistol. Model SP was a beautifully made .32 ACP. Being double-action-only and more expensive than most of its contemporaries, was not competitive and discontinued in early 1960s. Fewer than 1,000 made. Slide marked "STEYR-DAIMLER-PUCH A.G. MOD. SP KAL. 7.65mm".

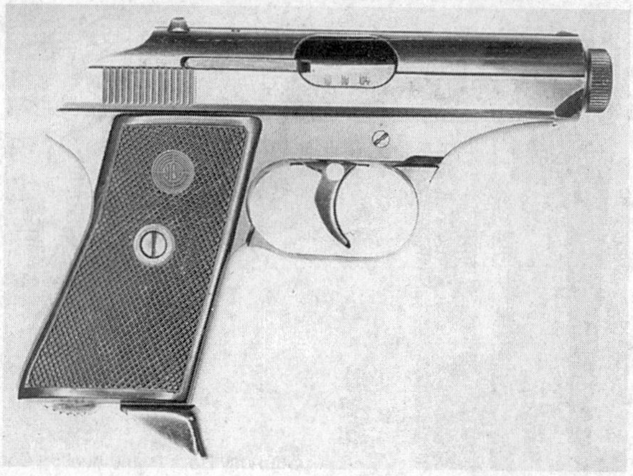

Courtesy Joseph Schroeder

NIB	Exc.	V.G.	Good	Fair	Poor
—	950	820	550	380	200

Steyr Model GB

GB introduced in mid-1970s as a 9mm Parabellum military pistol. Large in size, with 18-round magazine capacity. Other features included polygon rifling and gas trap around barrel to delay breech opening. Initially produced as Rogak P-18 by L.E.S. of Morton Grove, Illinois. Discontinued due in part to quality control problems. Just over 2,000 made. Later production by Steyr as GB was to much higher standards, but GB never achieved much popularity and discontinued in 1988.

Rogak P-18

NIB	Exc.	V.G.	Good	Fair	Poor
—	420	350	250	180	120

Steyr GB

NIB	Exc.	V.G.	Good	Fair	Poor
—	800	680	520	400	200

RIFLES

Headquartered in Austria, Steyr/Mannlicher guns were imported by GSI Inc. Trussville, Alabama. Steyr currently manufactures the AUG in the United States and bolt actions are imported from Austria by Steyr Arms, USA located in Bessemer, Alabama. Note: For earlier models see Mannlicher Schoenauer.

SPORTER SERIES

Series includes rifles that are lightweight and have reduced overall length. All Sporter models have interchangeable 5-round rotary magazine. Stock is oil-finished walnut in Mannlicher full stock design or half stock version. In both stock configurations an oval European cheekpiece is standard. Rifles offered in four different action lengths: SL (super light), L (light), M (medium) or S (Magnum). Also available with single-/double-set triggers.

CL II

Based on the Pro Hunter, the CL II comes with the SBS (Safe Bolt System) in half stock with contrasting forend tip, direct or set trigger, detachable magazine and cold hammer-forged 22" barrel in .222, .223, .243, .25-06, 6.5x55, .270, 7mm-08, .308, .30-06, 8x57 or 9.3x62. Magnums with 25" barrel in .270 WSM, 7mm Rem Mag, .300 WSM, .300 Win Mag, .300 Wby., 8x68 S, .375 H&H or .458 Win. Mag. Mountain and Mannlicher stock versions in standard calibers with 20" barrel. Note: Add about $275 for magnums ($1,100 for .375 and .458); Add $200 for Mannlicher stock. Metal has Steyr's moisture and corrosion-resistant Mannox matte finish. Weight about 7.5 lbs. (magnums 8 lbs.).

NIB	Exc.	V.G.	Good	Fair	Poor
2170	1850	1570	1350	1000	750

CL II SX

Calibers and finish as above in green synthetic stock with aluminum bedding block. Note: Add about $275 for magnums ($1,050 for .375 and .458). Half stock only in standard, magnum or mountain. Weight 7.5 lbs.

NIB	Exc.	V.G.	Good	Fair	Poor
1600	1350	1150	980	750	550

CL II Carbon

CL II action housed in Fine Ballistic Tools carbon fiber stock offering the quiet acoustic characteristic of a wooden stock. Comes with Combi trigger. Comes with barrel threaded 5/8x24 in .308 (20", weight: 6.7 lbs.), 6.5 C (25", 7.5 lbs.) or .338 Lapua (25.5", 7.7 lbs.). Note: Add $300 for 6.5 C; Add $400 for .338 Lapua.

NIB	Exc.	V.G.	Good	Fair	Poor
3870	3280	2800	2380	1750	1350

SM 12

Similar to the CL II but includes Steyr's "hand cocking system" and "Combi" trigger with 1.5-lb pull weight can be configured as direct or set trigger. Calibers include: .243, 6.5x55, .270, 7mm-08, 7x64, .308, .30-06, 8x57 or 9.3x62. Magnums with 25" barrel in .270 WSM, 7mm Rem Mag, .300 WSM, .300 Win Mag, .300 Wby or 8x68 S. Mountain and Mannlicher stock versions in standard calibers with 20" barrel. Note: Add about $275 for magnums; Add $200 for Mannlicher stock. Metal has Steyr's moisture and corrosion-resistant Mannox matte finish. Weight 7.7 lbs. (magnums 7.9 lbs.).

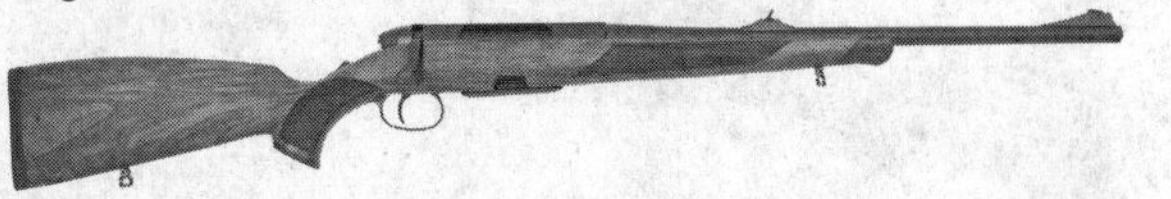

NIB	Exc.	V.G.	Good	Fair	Poor
2350	2000	1700	1450	1050	820

SM 12 SX

As SM 12 above but in green synthetic stock with an aluminum bedding block. Note: Add $275 for magnums. Metal has Steyr's moisture and corrosion-resistant Mannox matte finish. Weight 7.5 lbs. (magnums 7.7 lbs.).

NIB	Exc.	V.G.	Good	Fair	Poor
1880	1600	1350	1150	870	650

Monobloc

Featuring a unique hunting rifle with a barreled action cold hammer forged from a single piece of steel then milled to form the chamber and action. Fitted into a distinctive synthetic stock (five color options) with leather inlays, aluminum bedding block and detachable magazine. Has the Hand Cocking System and a detachable trigger group which can be housed in the buttstock. Available with 22" barrel in .308 or .30-06 only.

NIB	Exc.	V.G.	Good	Fair	Poor
4680	3980	3350	2880	—	—

Model M72 L/M

Bolt-action rifle, with 23" fluted barrel and single-/double-set triggers. 243, .270, 7x57mm, 7x64mm, .308 or .30-06 caliber. Blued, checkered walnut stock. Manufactured from 1972 to 1980.

NIB	Exc.	V.G.	Good	Fair	Poor
—	1320	1020	750	550	450

Model SL

Features super light action. Offered with 20" barrel in full stock version or 23" barrel in half stock version. Rubber buttpad standard. Model does not have forend tip on its half stock variation. Offered in following calibers: .222 Rem., .222 Rem. Magnum, .223 and 5.6x50 Magnum. Weight about: 6.2 lbs. full stock; 6.3 lbs. half stock. Also came in an "L" Model and "SL Carbine" with 20" barrel in Mannlicher stock. Discontinued.

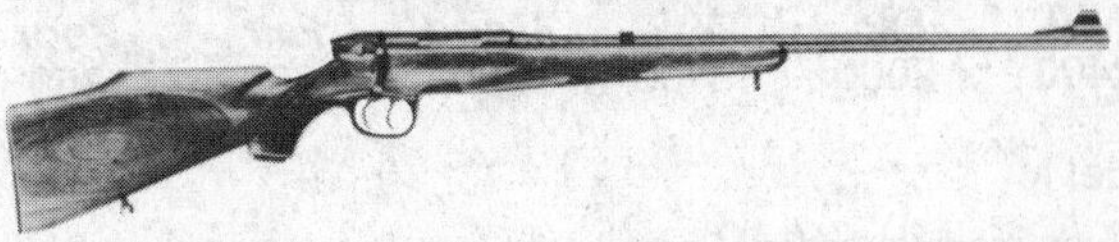

NIB	Exc.	V.G.	Good	Fair	Poor
2000	1650	1000	750	500	300

Model SL Carbine

As above, with 20" fluted barrel. Mannlicher-style stock.

NIB	Exc.	V.G.	Good	Fair	Poor
1950	1750	1050	800	550	350

Varmint Model

Features heavy 26" barrel. Chambered for .222 Rem., .223, 5.6x57, .243 Win., .308 Win. and .22-250. Forend of stock is ventilated. Grip enlarged and textured. Choice of single-/double-set triggers. Recoil pad standard. Weight about 8 lbs. Discontinued.

NIB	Exc.	V.G.	Good	Fair	Poor
1950	1750	1050	800	550	350

Model L

Rifle has light action. Offered in same stock configuration and barrel lengths as Model SL. Calibers are: 5.6x57, .243 Win., .308, .22-250 and 6mm Rem. Weight about: 6.3 lbs. full stock; 6.4 lbs. half stock.

NIB	Exc.	V.G.	Good	Fair	Poor
1850	1650	1000	750	500	300

Luxus Series

Luxury model offers choice of full or half-stock variations in select walnut, with fine-line checkering. Pistol grip is steeply angled. Luxus rifles fitted with swept back European cheekpiece. Single-set trigger standard. Box magazine holds 3 rounds. Luxus rifles available with light (L), medium (M) or magnum (S) length actions. "L" available in 5.6x57, .243, .308, .22-250 and 6mm Rem; "M" in 6.5x57, .270, 7x64, .30-06, 9.3x62, 6.5x55, 7.5 Swiss, 7x57 and 8x57JS; "S" in 6.5x68, 7mm Rem Mag, .300 Win Mag and 8x68S. Note: Optional engraving and stock carving may be encountered on these models, that will dramatically affect price. Currently, high end models are handled by the Steyr Custom Shop on an individual basis.

Luxus Model L

Same dimensions and barrel lengths as Sporter version. Calibers are: 5.6x57, .243 Win., .308, .22-250 and 6mm Rem.

NIB	Exc.	V.G.	Good	Fair	Poor
2400	2000	1100	800	600	350

Luxus Model M

Same dimensions and barrel lengths as Sporter Model M. Available in these calibers: 6.5x57, .270 Win., 7x64, .30-06, 9.3x 62, 6.5x55, 7.5 Swiss, 7x57 and 8x57JS.

NIB	Exc.	V.G.	Good	Fair	Poor
2400	2000	1100	800	600	350

Luxus Model S

Same as Sporter Model S. Offered in following calibers: 6.5x68, 7mm Rem. Magnum, .300 Win. Magnum and 8x68S.

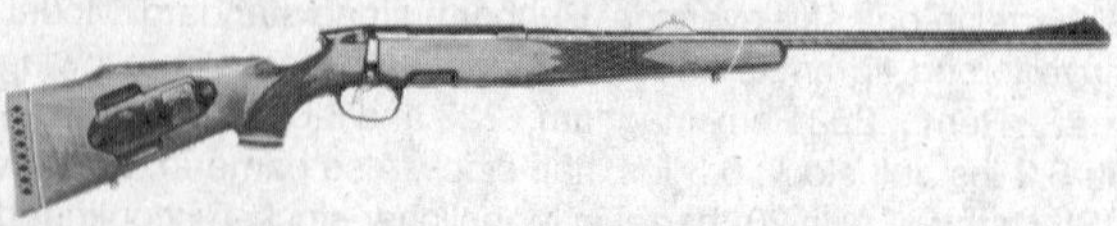

NIB	Exc.	V.G.	Good	Fair	Poor
2400	2000	1100	800	600	350

Model M

Features medium action. Same barrel and stock configurations as SL above. Exception, has no buttpad and does have forend tip on its half-stock variation. Available in these calibers: 6.5x57, .270 Win., 7x64, .30-06, 9.3x62, 6.5x55, 7.5 Swiss, 7x57 and 8x57JS. Weight about: 6.8 lbs. full stock; 7 lbs. half stock. Note: Deduct $1,000 for Professional Model M in black synthetic stock. Discontinued.

NIB	Exc.	V.G.	Good	Fair	Poor
2500	2100	1200	900	600	300

Professional Model M

Fitted with medium-weight action. Features black synthetic checkered stock. Comes fitted with ventilated rubber recoil pad. Offered with 20" or 23.6" barrel. Available with single-/double-set trigger. Available in these calibers: 6.5x57, .270 Win., 7x64, .30-06, 9.3x62, 6.5x55, 7.5 Swiss, 7x57 and 8x57JS. Weight 7.25 lbs.

NIB	Exc.	V.G.	Good	Fair	Poor
1500	1200	950	700	600	300

Model S/T

Similar to above in heavy-barreled version. Offered in these calibers: 9.3x64, .375 H&H and .458 Win. Magnum. Optional buttstock magazine available. Weight 9 lbs. Discontinued.

NIB	Exc.	V.G.	Good	Fair	Poor
2100	1900	1400	1100	800	500

Tropical Rifle

As above, with 26" heavy barrel. Chambered for .375 H&H and .458 Win. Magnum. Not imported after 1985.

NIB	Exc.	V.G.	Good	Fair	Poor
—	2000	1750	1100	650	450

Model MIII Professional

Introduced in 1995. Economy version of Model M Professional. Fitted with 23.5" barrel, black synthetic stock and choice of single-/double-set triggers. Offered in .25-06, .270 Win., .30-06 and 7x64 calibers. Weight 7.5 lbs. Note: Add $100 for checkered walnut stock. Discontinued.

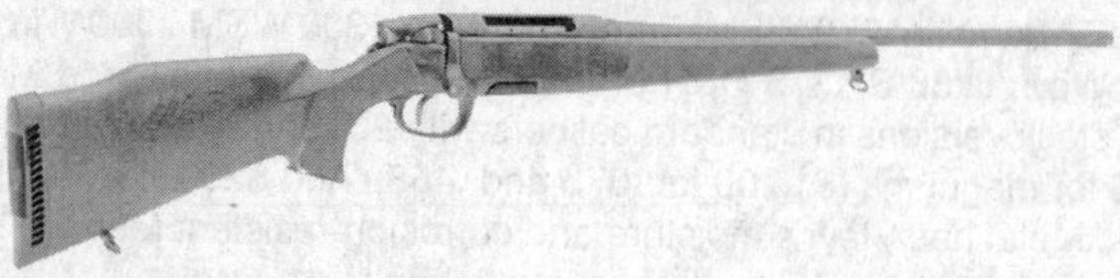

NIB	Exc.	V.G.	Good	Fair	Poor
1000	800	600	400	300	200

STEYR SBS (SAFE BOLT SYSTEM)

Series introduced in 1997. Features a newly designed bolt. Offered in two distinct models: SBS Forester and SBS ProHunter.

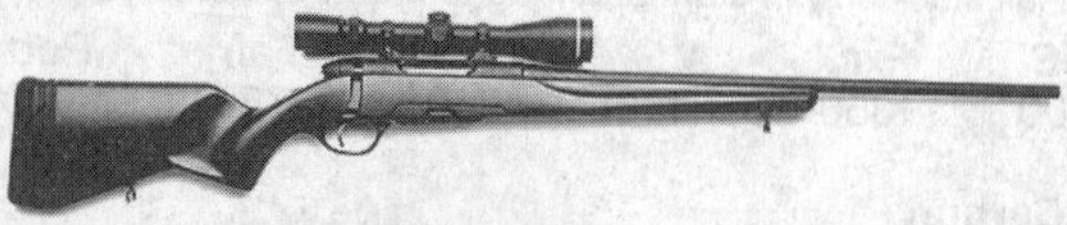

SBS ProHunter

Standard model has 23.6" barrel, 4-round magazine and single adjustable trigger. Offered in .243 Win., .25-06, .270 Win., 7mm-08, .308 Win., .30-06, 7mm Rem Mag, .300 Win Mag and several European calibers. Weight about 7.5 lbs. Furnished with black synthetic stock, recoil pad and buttspacers. Introduced in 1999. Note: Add $150–$300 for custom metric calibers; $30 for 7mm Magnum and .300 Win. Magnum calibers. Add $150 for stainless steel; $250 for camo stock and $50 more for stainless. Discontinued.

NIB	Exc.	V.G.	Good	Fair	Poor
750	650	580	400	300	150

SBS ProHunter Stainless Steel

Same as ProHunter model, with stainless steel action and barrel. Introduced in 2000. Note: Add $150-$300 for custom metric calibers; $30 for 7mm Magnum and .300 Win. Magnum calibers.

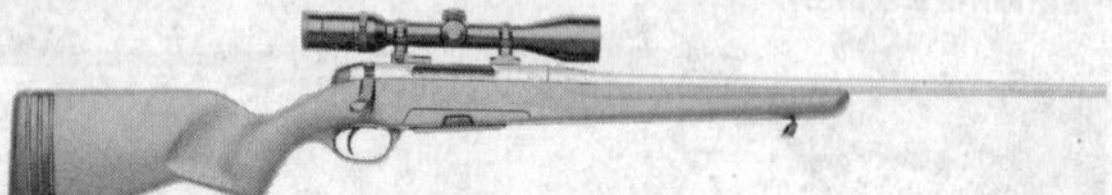

NIB	Exc.	V.G.	Good	Fair	Poor
900	750	680	500	400	250

SBS ProHunter Camo

Same as standard ProHunter, with camo synthetic stock. Note: Add $150-$300 for custom metric calibers; $30 for 7mm Magnum and .300 Win. Magnum calibers.

NIB	Exc.	V.G.	Good	Fair	Poor
1000	850	700	580	400	200

SBS ProHunter Camo Stainless Steel

Same as above, with stainless steel action and barrel. Note: Add $150-$300 for custom metric calibers; $30 for 7mm Magnum and .300 Win. Magnum calibers.

NIB	Exc.	V.G.	Good	Fair	Poor
1050	900	750	600	480	250

SBS ProHunter Mountain Rifle

Chambered for .243, .25-06, .270 and 7mm-08 calibers. Fitted with 20" barrel and no sights. Receiver engraved "Mountain Rifle". Synthetic stock with recoil pad standard. Weight 7.25 lbs. Introduced in 1999. Note: Add $50 for stainless steel; $100 for camo stock. Discontinued.

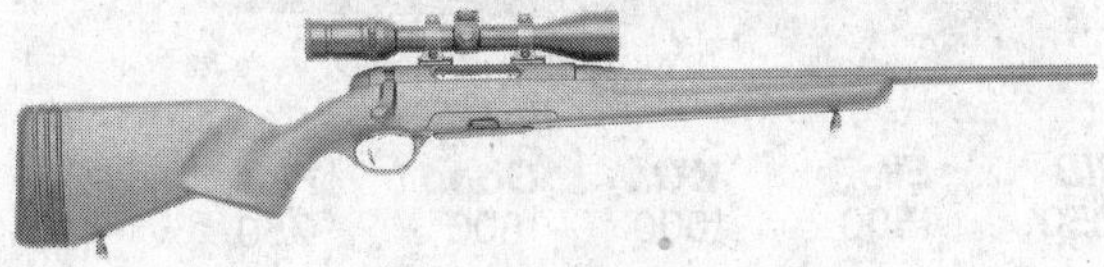

NIB	Exc.	V.G.	Good	Fair	Poor
1000	850	700	580	400	200

SBS ProHunter Mountain Stainless Steel

Same as ProHunter Mountain, with stainless steel action and barrel. Introduced in 2000.

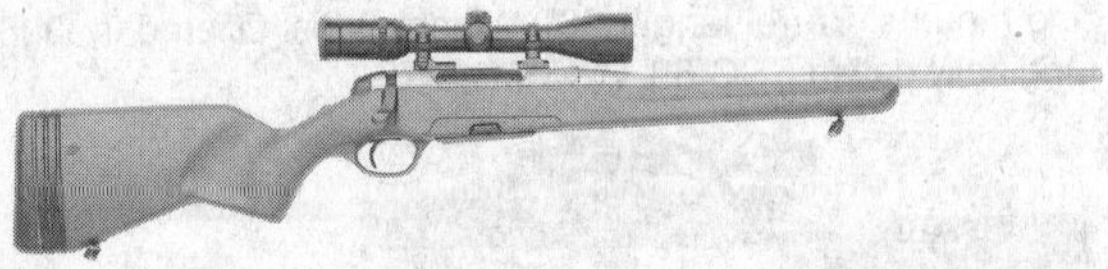

NIB	Exc.	V.G.	Good	Fair	Poor
1050	900	750	600	420	200

SBS ProHunter Mountain Camo

Same as ProHunter, with camo synthetic stock. Introduced in 2000.

NIB	Exc.	V.G.	Good	Fair	Poor
1150	1000	850	700	480	250

SBS ProHunter Mountain Camo Stainless Steel

Same as above, with stainless steel action and barrel. Introduced in 2000.

NIB	Exc.	V.G.	Good	Fair	Poor
1150	1000	850	700	480	250

SBS ProHunter (Youth/Ladies)

Fitted with walnut stock and buttspacers (to create shorter length of pull). Extra thick recoil pad. Chambered for .243, 7mm-08 and .308. Weight 7.25 lbs. Introduced in 1999 and as a Compact Model with black synthetic stock. Discontinued.

NIB	Exc.	V.G.	Good	Fair	Poor
1000	850	700	580	400	200

SBS ProHunter Compact

Same as above, with black synthetic stock. Offered with stainless steel action and barrel. Note: Add $80 for stainless steel.

NIB	Exc.	V.G.	Good	Fair	Poor
1000	850	700	580	400	200

SBS ProHunter 376 Steyr

Chambered for .376 Steyr cartridge. Fitted with 20" barrel and iron sights. Synthetic stock, with special thick pad. Weight 8 lbs. Introduced in 1999. Discontinued.

NIB	Exc.	V.G.	Good	Fair	Poor
1200	950	800	680	400	200

Pro Hunter II

Calibers: .223 Rem., 7mm-08 Rem., 6.5 Creedmoor, .308 Win. Capacity: 4 to 5. Barrel: 20", hammer-forged stainless steel. Stock: Wood laminate, Boyds. Sights: None, drilled and tapped. Weight: 7 lbs. Features: Three-position safety, crisp 3-lb. trigger.

NIB	Exc.	V.G.	Good	Fair	Poor
1100	—	—	—	—	—

SBS Forester

Same as Pro Hunter model. Furnished with walnut stock and recoil pad. Note: Add $150-$300 for custom metric calibers; $30 for 7mm Rem. Magnum and .300 Win. Magnum. The SBS Forester Mountain Rifle with 20" barrel came in standard calibers only. Discontinued.

NIB	Exc.	V.G.	Good	Fair	Poor
850	720	620	500	400	200

SBS Classic American

Features 23.6" barrel, single adjustable trigger, stain finish walnut stock with recoil pad. Offered in calibers from .243 to .300 Win. Magnum. Weight about 7.2 lbs. Introduced in 2000. Note: Add $150-$300 for custom metric calibers; $30 for 7mm Magnum and .300 Win. Magnum calibers. Note: Add $700 for Mannlicher stock in standard calibers only. Discontinued.

NIB	Exc.	V.G.	Good	Fair	Poor
1500	1100	850	650	500	300

SBS Classic Mannlicher

Offered in same calibers as above, except for 7mm Rem. Magnum and .300 Win. Magnum. Fitted with 25.6" barrel. Walnut stock is full Mannlicher style, with recoil pad. Fitted with open sights. Weight 7.2 lbs. Introduced in 2000.

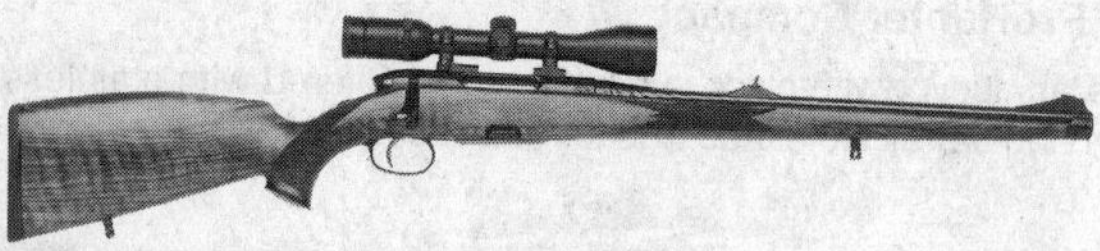

NIB	Exc.	V.G.	Good	Fair	Poor
2300	2000	1600	1000	680	400

SBS Forester Mountain Rifle

Walnut stock with 20" barrel and no sights. Chambered for a variety of calibers including .243, .25-06, .270, 7mm-08, .308, .30-06 and 6.5x55. Receiver engraved "Mountain Rifle". Introduced in 1999.

NIB	Exc.	V.G.	Good	Fair	Poor
850	720	620	500	400	200

Mannlicher SBS European

Fitted with 23.6" barrel and iron sights. Chambered for wide variety of American and European calibers from .243 to 9.3x62. European-style figured walnut stock. Adjustable trigger. Recoil pad. Weight 7.5 lbs. Note: A 20" Carbine is available; Add $100 for Mannlicher stock. Discontinued.

NIB	Exc.	V.G.	Good	Fair	Poor
2800	2200	1750	1200	700	400

Mannlicher SBS European—Half Stock Carbine

Same as above, with 20" barrel.

NIB	Exc.	V.G.	Good	Fair	Poor
2800	2200	1750	1200	700	400

Mannlicher SBS European—Full Stock

Same as above, with full European stock covering 20" barrel.

NIB	Exc.	V.G.	Good	Fair	Poor
2900	2300	1800	1250	750	450

Mannlicher SBS Magnum European—Half Stock

Chambered for 7mm Rem. Magnum, .300 Win. Magnum, 6.5x68 and 8x68S calibers. Fitted with 25.6" barrel and iron sights. Walnut stock. Weight 7.75 lbs. Discontinued.

NIB	Exc.	V.G.	Good	Fair	Poor
2900	2300	1800	1250	750	450

Steyr Scout—Jeff Cooper Package

Developed by Col. Jeff Cooper. Chambered for .308 Win. cartridge. Fitted with 19" fluted barrel. Stock is gray synthetic, with removable butt-spacers and folding bi-pod. Magazine capacity 5 rounds, with optional 10-round magazines available. Weight about: 7 lbs. w/scope; 6.3 lbs. w/o scope. Adjustable single trigger. Factory-installed Leupold M8 2.5x28mm scope. Introduced in 1998. Discontinued.

NIB	Exc.	V.G.	Good	Fair	Poor
2600	2000	1600	1100	650	400

Steyr Scout

Current version of the Jeff Cooper Scout has 19" fluted or 22" smooth threaded barrel, tactical bolt, black, green or mud synthetic stock with integral bipod and spare magazine housed in the butt. Offered in .223, .243, 6.5 C, 7mm-08 and .308. Weight 6.6 - 7 lbs.

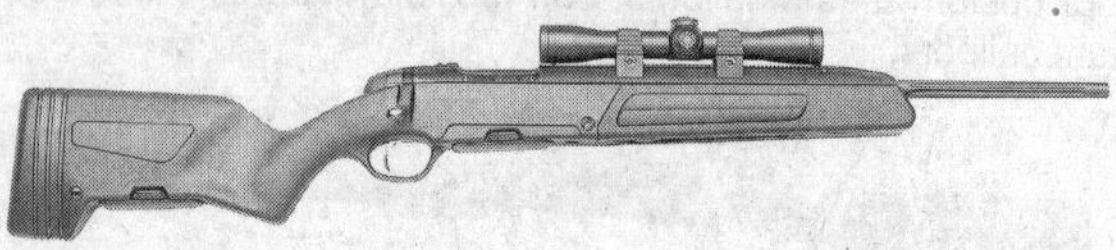

NIB	Exc.	V.G.	Good	Fair	Poor
1600	1380	1150	990	750	550

Steyr Scout Tactical

Model has 19.25" fluted barrel. Chambered for .223 or .308 Win. cartridge. Integral bipod. Emergency ghost ring sights. Note: Add $100 for stainless steel.

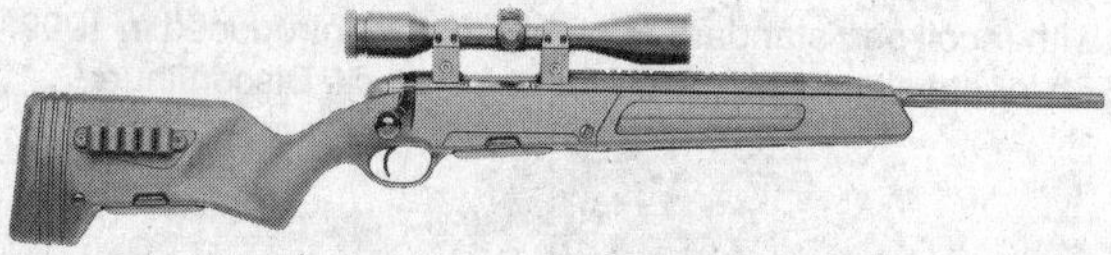

NIB	Exc.	V.G.	Good	Fair	Poor
2050	1500	1000	800	750	420

PRECISION/TACTICAL RIFLES

Model SSG-PI

Features black synthetic stock. Originally designed as a military sniper rifle. Fitted with cocking indicator, single-/double-set trigger, 5-round rotary magazine or 10-round. Receiver milled to NATO specifications for Steyr ring mounts. Barrel length 26". Weight 9 lbs. Offered in .308 Win. Note: Originally called SSG 69. Discontinued.

NIB	Exc.	V.G.	Good	Fair	Poor
1700	1300	1000	800	600	400

SSG-PII Police Rifle

Version of SSG, with heavier 26" barrel. Larger knob-style bolt handle. Weight 10.11 lbs. SSG-PIIK Police Kurz has a 20" barrel. Discontinued.

NIB	Exc.	V.G.	Good	Fair	Poor
1700	1300	1000	800	600	400

SSK-PIIK Police Kurz

Similar to above, with 20" heavy barrel. Weight 10 lbs.

NIB	Exc.	V.G.	Good	Fair	Poor
1700	1300	1000	800	600	400

SSG-PII & PIIK McMillan

Fitted with McMillan A-3 stock, adjustable cheekpiece and removable buttspacers. Special forearm rail. Add $200 for PIV with 16.75" barrel. Discontinued.

NIB	Exc.	V.G.	Good	Fair	Poor
2300	1750	1350	950	750	500

SSG-PIV

Similar to PIIK, with 16.75" heavy barrel and removable flash hider. Barrel is threaded. Weight 9.11 lbs.

NIB	Exc.	V.G.	Good	Fair	Poor
2500	2000	1500	1000	750	500

Match

NIB	Exc.	V.G.	Good	Fair	Poor
3000	2500	2000	1500	800	500

SSG 08

Bolt-action chambered in .308 Win., .300 Win. Magnum and .338 Lapua Magnum. Barrel length 20" to 23.6", with muzzle brake. Fully adjustable aluminum folding stock and pistol grip, Versa-Pod and optics rail.

NIB	Exc.	V.G.	Good	Fair	Poor
5000	4000	3200	2500	2000	500

SSG Carbon Fiber

Features an innovative carbon-fi ber stock made from a chipped-carbon sheet molding compound similar to that used in Formula One cars and jet fighters. Material is lighter and much stronger than steel. Stock has an adjustable cheekpiece and buttplate, heavy bipod and integral adjustable rear elevation pod. Barreled action with 20" barrel and muzzle brake. Safe Bolt system are the same as on other SSG rifl es. Introduced in 2015. Discontinued.

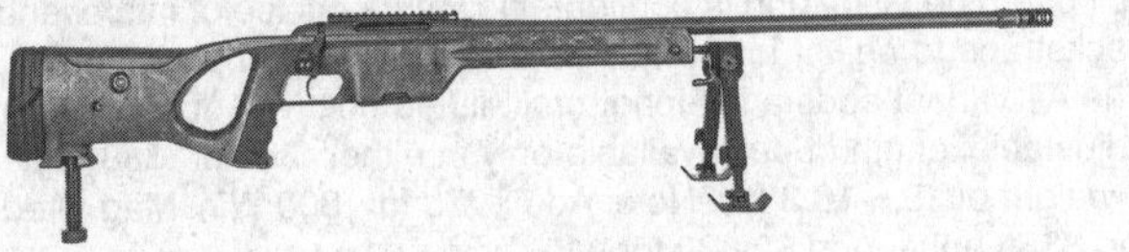

NIB	Exc.	V.G.	Good	Fair	Poor
3300	3000	—	—	—	—

Match UIT

Designed as an international target rifle. Features special shaped pistol grip, adjustable trigger for length of pull and pressure. Enlarged bolt handle and non-glare barrel. Chambered for .308 Win. cartridge. Discontinued.

NIB	Exc.	V.G.	Good	Fair	Poor
3900	3500	3000	2000	1500	1000

JAGD Match

Introduced in 1995. Features 20" or 23.5" barrel with sights. Stock is laminated. Full stock version offered on 20" barrel; half stock on 23.5" barrel. Available in a variety of configurations, with calibers from .222 Rem. to .458 Win. Magnum. Discontinued.

NIB	Exc.	V.G.	Good	Fair	Poor
1750	1250	900	500	350	200

SBS TACTICAL SERIES

SBS Tactical

Fitted with black synthetic stock, 20" barrel with no sights. Chambered for .308 cartridge. Removable buttspacers. Black bolt body. Receiver engraved "SBS Tactical". Introduced in 1999. Weight 7.25 lbs. Available as a carbine. Note: Add $100 for stainless steel (introduced 2000), Add $100 for 26" Heavy Barrel; Add $450 for McMillan A-3 stock. Discontinued.

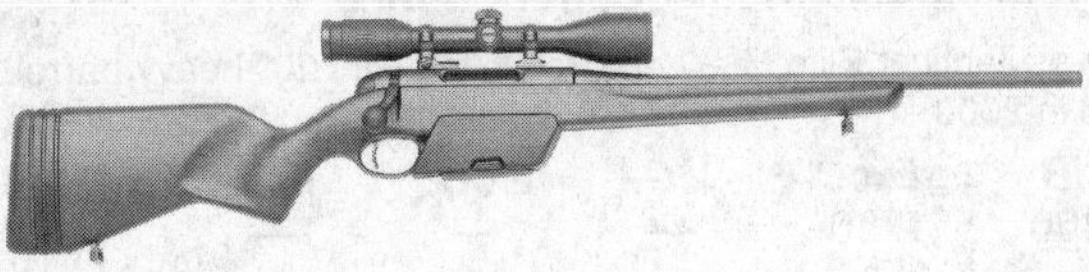

NIB	Exc.	V.G.	Good	Fair	Poor
1150	950	700	550	300	200

SBS Tactical Heavy Barrel

Also has black synthetic stock. Fitted with 26" heavy barrel and no sights. Black bolt body. Receiver engraved "SBS Tactical HB". Weight 8 lbs. Introduced in 1999. Offered with 20" barrel called "HBC". Both barrel lengths chambered for .308 cartridge.

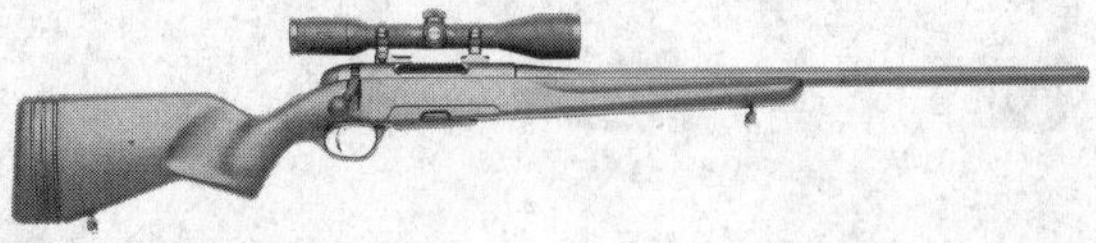

NIB	Exc.	V.G.	Good	Fair	Poor
1250	1050	800	650	300	200

SBS Tactical Heavy Barrel Carbine

Features 20" heavy barrel, no sights, matte blue finish. Chambered for .308 caliber. Introduced in 2000.

NIB	Exc.	V.G.	Good	Fair	Poor
1150	950	700	550	300	200

SBS Tactical McMillan

Fitted with 26" barrel chambered for .308 cartridge. Has McMillan A-3 stock. Oversize bolt handle. Weight 9.8 lbs. Introduced in 1999.

NIB	Exc.	V.G.	Good	Fair	Poor
1600	1250	950	750	60	400

SBS CISM Rifle

Chambered for .308 cartridge and fi tted with 19.7" heavy barrel. Stock is laminated wood, with black lacquer finish. Stock has forearm rail, with handstop adjustable buttplate and cheekpiece. Trigger is adjustable. Weight 10.25 lbs. Introduced in 1999. Discontinued.

NIB	Exc.	V.G.	Good	Fair	Poor
3300	2500	1950	1600	1200	700

SBS Tactical Elite Heavy Barrel

Introduced in 2000. Features 26" heavy barrel, no sights, matte blue finish, Zytel stock with adjustable cheekpiece and buttplate. Full-length Picatinny mounting rail. Magazine capacity 5 or 10 rounds. Chambered for .308 cartridge. Note: Add $100 for stainless steel; $1,000 for ZF optics. Note: Also available as a Carbine with 20" barrel. Discontinued.

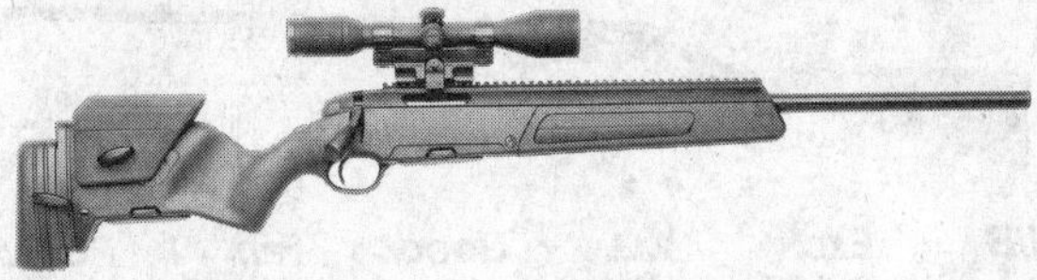

NIB	Exc.	V.G.	Good	Fair	Poor
2400	1750	1400	1000	700	400

SBS Tactical Elite Heavy Barrel Carbine

Same as Tactical Elite Heavy Barrel. Fitted with 20" heavy barrel. Introduced in 2000.

NIB	Exc.	V.G.	Good	Fair	Poor
2400	1750	—	—	—	—

Steyr AUG

5.56mm semi-automatic bullpup rifle, with 20" barrel incorporating Swarovski 1.5x telescopic sight. Green carbon composite stock. Weight 8.5 lbs. Recommend independent local appraisals.

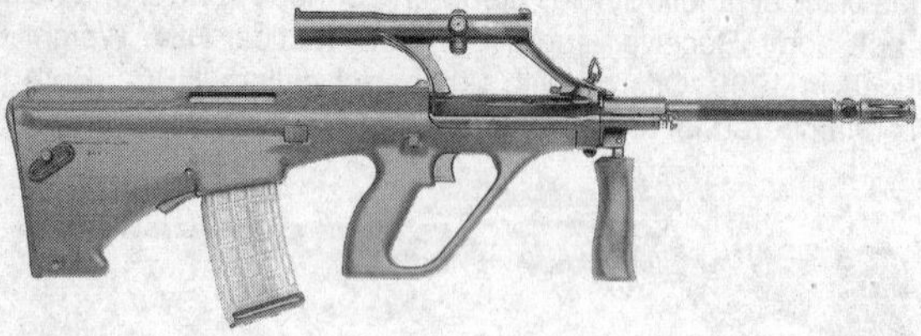

NIB	Exc.	V.G.	Good	Fair	Poor
2000	1700	1500	—	—	—

Steyr AUG—Police Model

Same as above, with black stock and 16" barrel.

NIB	Exc.	V.G.	Good	Fair	Poor
2000	1700	1200	—	—	—

Steyr USR

Post-ban version of AUG. Fitted with Swarovski 1.5x scope and gray synthetic stock.

NIB	Exc.	V.G.	Good	Fair	Poor
2000	1700	1200	—	—	—

RIMFIRE SERIES

Zephyr II

A rebirth of the original Zephyr rifle, the Zephyr II comes in a European walnut stock with fish-scale checkering, detachable 5-round magazine and top tang safety. The cold hammer-forged 19.7" barrel is threaded 1/2x28 in .17 HMR, .22 LR and .22 WMR. Weight 5.8 lbs. Note: Add $25 for threaded barrel.

NIB	Exc.	V.G.	Good	Fair	Poor
970	820	700	600	450	350

Steyr Zephyr

The half-stock Zephyr in .22 LR was made from 1955 to 1971. It offered many upscale extras including Mannlicher full stock with checkering, single or double-set triggers, sling swivels and iron sights. Less than 4,000 were ever made. Mannlichers with the extras will bring a substantial premium.

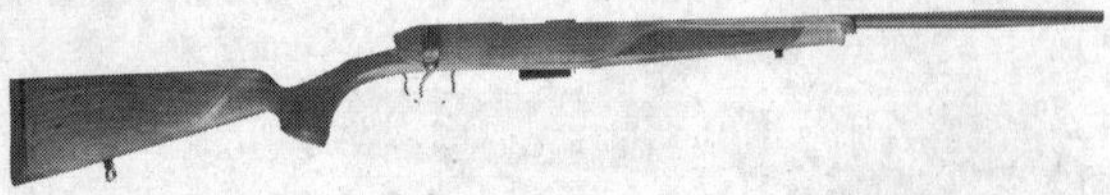

NIB	Exc.	V.G.	Good	Fair	Poor
—	1400	1190	1000	850	780

CURRENT TACTICAL MODELS

PRO THB

An entry-level precision rifle with SBS action, 16", 20", 25" (6.5 C only) or 26" cold hammer-forged barrel threaded 5/8-24 in .308 or 6.5 C. Metal given the Mannox finish. A black or green synthetic stock with interchangeable buttstock spacers and 4-round detachable magazine. Note: Add $240 for 6.5 Creedmoor; Add $375 for A-1 with full-length Picatinny rail, Add about $600 for McMillan or Manners stock. Weight 8 lbs.

NIB	Exc.	V.G.	Good	Fair	Poor
1350	1150	980	820	620	480

SSG 04

Action and barrel as above, with 20" or 23.6" barrel with muzzle brake in .243, .308 or .300 Win Mag, with 10-shot (8 in .300 Win Mag) detachable magazine. Fiberglass reinforced stock is fully adjustable for comb height and LOP. Note: Add $275 for magnum; Add $500 for A-1 with full-length Picatinny rail. Weight 11 lbs.

NIB	Exc.	V.G.	Good	Fair	Poor
2180	1850	1480	1250	950	700

SSG 08

Action and barrel as above, with barrel lengths of 20", 23.6" or 25.6" in .243, .308, .300 Win. Mag. or .338 Lapua. Comes fitted with muzzle brake. Features include detachable magazine holding 10 (.243, .308), 8 (.300 Win Mag) or 6 (.338 Lapua) in a folding Eloxal-coated aircraft aluminum stock with an adjustable rear monopod, cheekpiece and recoil pad. The pistol grip is configurable with a choice of interchangeable backstraps to adjust for hand size and optimized grip. Weight 12.5 lbs. The A1 variant adds a full-length rail, fluted bolt with dust cover, and an adjustable length of pull available only in either .308 or .338 Lapua and a weight of 15.5-16.3 lbs. Note: Add $275 for .300 Win. Mag.; Add $950 for .338 Lapua, Add $2,800 for A1.

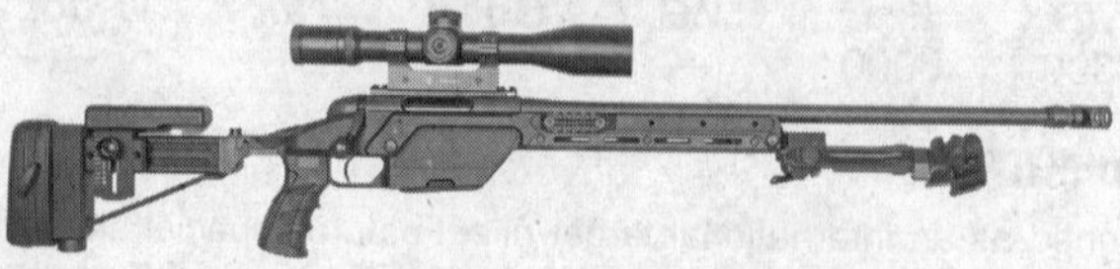

NIB	Exc.	V.G.	Good	Fair	Poor
5580	4750	4000	3420	—	—

SSG M1

New for 2019, the M1 is a configurable sniper rifle built on the SBS bolt action with a new ambidextrous safety selector. The barrels and calibers can be switched with ease and come in 6.5 Creedmoor, .308 or .338 Lapua in lengths of 20", 25" (6.5, .308) or 27.2 (.338 Lapua) and an attached muzzle brake. The receiver includes a built-in Picatinny optical base, fluted bolt, and dust cover, an adjustable two-stage, three-position trigger. The pistol grip comes with interchangeable backstraps and is replaceable with most AR-15 pattern grips. The rifle chassis features a forend available in M-LOK or Key Mod. The right-side folding stock has a fully adjustable comb, length of pull, and recoil pad. Weight 14-15 lbs. Note: Add $2100 for Performance Edition.

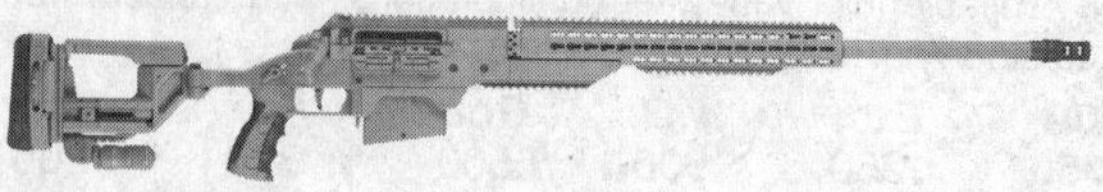

NIB	Exc.	V.G.	Good	Fair	Poor
9450	8000	6820	—	—	—

HS .50-M1

A bolt-action rifle chambered in .460 or .50 BMG as a single shot or with a 5-shot side-loading magazine (.50 only), adjustable cheekpiece and buttpad, monopod and folding bipod. Barrel lengths 24" or 33" (5-shot version) ending in a muzzle brake, weight 26-30 lbs.

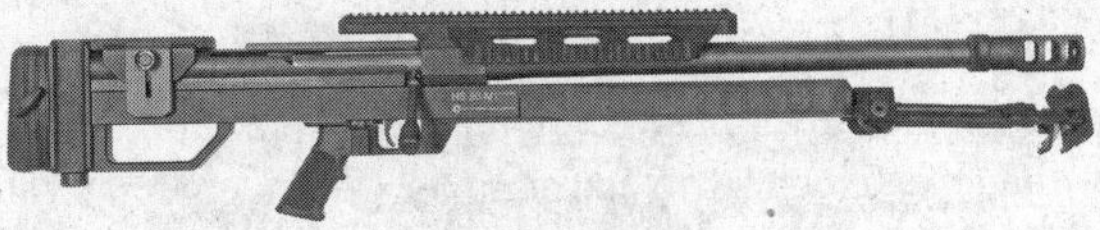

NIB	Exc.	V.G.	Good	Fair	Poor
7280	6180	5250	—	—	—

PISTOLS

Model SPP

Introduced in 1993, this is a 9mm semi-automatic pistol. Made from synthetic materials and operates on a delayed blowback rotating barrel system. Magazine capacity 15 or 30 rounds. Barrel length 5.9"; overall length 12.75"; weight 42 oz. Due to its appearance and design, this pistol was banned from importation into U.S. shortly after its introduction. Because of this circumstance, price of this pistol may fluctuate widely.

NIB	Exc.	V.G.	Good	Fair	Poor
1000	900	750	600	500	400

Model M

Chambered for .40 S&W, 9mm or .357 SIG cartridge. Semi-automatic pistol has polymer frame and three user-selectable safety systems. Loaded chambered indicator. Triangle/Trapezoid sights. Limited access lock with key. Weight 28 oz. Magazine capacity 10 rounds. Introduced in 1999.

NIB	Exc.	V.G.	Good	Fair	Poor
500	400	320	280	240	200

Model M-A1

Updated version of Model M, with redesigned grip frame and Picatinny rail. Striker-fired DA-only pistol in 9mm, .357 SIG and .40 S&W. Magazine capacity: 15 for 9mm, 12 for .40 and .357 SIG. 3.5" or 4" barrel (S-A1).

NIB	Exc.	V.G.	Good	Fair	Poor
500	400	320	280	240	200

Model C-A1

Similar to above. Compact variant with 3.6" or 3.8" barrel. 12- or 17-round magazine.

NIB	Exc.	V.G.	Good	Fair	Poor
580	500	460	360	280	260

Model L-A1

Similar to above. Full-size variant with 4.5" or 5" barrel. 12- or 17-round magazine. Adjustable sights. Introduced 2014. Note: Add $50 for 5" threaded barrel and $170 for TFX optic mount variant.

NIB	Exc.	V.G.	Good	Fair	Poor
580	500	460	360	280	260

Model S-A1

Similar to above. Compact variant. 10-round magazine. Adjustable sights.

NIB	Exc.	V.G.	Good	Fair	Poor
580	500	460	360	280	260

Model A2 MF

Full-size frame 9mm caliber 4.5" barrel. 10- or 17-round magazine. Fixed sights. Flared magazine well. Introduced 2019.

NIB	Exc.	V.G.	Good	Fair	Poor
680	600	560	—	—	—

L9-A2 MF

Calibers: 9mm. Capacities: 10 or 17 round. Barrels: 4.5". Weight: 27.2 oz. Sights: Trapizoid. Grips: Polymer, textured grip modules. Features: DAO striker-fired operation.

NIB	Exc.	V.G.	Good	Fair	Poor
660	610	510	460	380	—

STEYR HAHN

See—STEYR

STEYR MANNLICHER

See—STEYR

STI INTERNATIONAL

Georgetown, Texas

In 2020, STI International became Stacatto. STI was founded in 1980. In the 1990s it developed high-capacity modular-frame 1911-style competition pistols. Current Stacatto production consists of variations of Model 2011 modular frame 1911 system semi-auto pistols.

LS9 & LS40

Single-stack pistol chambered for 9mm or .40 S&W cartridge. Fitted with 3.4" barrel and short grip. Heine Low Mount sights. Rosewood grips. Matte blue finish. Magazine capacity: 7 rounds 9mm; 6 rounds .40 S&W. Weight about 28 oz.

NIB	Exc.	V.G.	Good	Fair	Poor
750	680	550	400	300	200

BLS9 & BLS40

Same as above, with full-length grip. Magazine capacity: 9 rounds 9mm; 8 rounds .40 S&W.

NIB	Exc.	V.G.	Good	Fair	Poor
720	650	520	380	280	200

Ranger

Chambered for .45 ACP cartridge. Fitted with 3.9" barrel, with a short grip. Fixed STI sights. Blued frame, with stainless steel slide. Weight about 29 oz.

NIB	Exc.	V.G.	Good	Fair	Poor
950	780	600	500	400	200

Ranger II

Chambered for .45 ACP cartridge. Fitted with 4.15" ramped bull barrel. Slide is flattop, with rear serrations and chamfered forend. Ambidextrous safety and high rise grip safety. Adjustable rear sight. Blued lower frame. Weight about 39 oz.

NIB	Exc.	V.G.	Good	Fair	Poor
920	800	680	520	400	200

Trojan

Chambered for .45 ACP, .40 Super, .40 S&W and 9mm cartridge. Fitted with a 5" barrel. Rosewood grips. Matte blue finish. 8-round magazine capacity. Weight about 36 oz. Note: Add $275 for .40 Super with .45 ACP conversion; $250 for Trojan with 6" slide.

NIB	Exc.	V.G.	Good	Fair	Poor
1150	920	750	600	500	300

Tactical 4.15

Chambered for 9mm, .40 S&W or .45 ACP cartridge. Fully supported ramped 4.15" bull barrel. Frame has tactical rail. Slide has rear serrations. Fixed rear sight. Aluminum magazine well. Black polycoat finish. Weight about 34.5 oz.

Tactical

As above, with 5" barrel. Flat blue finish. Weight about 39 oz.

NIB	Exc.	V.G.	Good	Fair	Poor
1750	1480	1150	900	650	350

Trubor

Chambered for 9mm "major", 9x23 or .38 Super cartridges. Steel frame fully supported and ramped one piece, with bull barrel and integral compensator. Slide has front and rear serrations. Sights are C-More or OK Red Dot reflix. Blued finish. Weight about 42.5 oz. with scope.

NIB	Exc.	V.G.	Good	Fair	Poor
2500	2100	1600	1200	900	500

Lawman

This model comes in 9mm or .45 ACP, with 5" ramped barrel and match-grade bushing. Other features include aluminum trigger, Series 70 grip safety, Novak 3-dot sights and walnut grips. Polymer finish, with brown slide over tan frame. Weight about 36 oz. Also available with 3" or 4" barrel.

NIB	Exc.	V.G.	Good	Fair	Poor
1200	980	820	680	500	250

Xcaliber Single Stack

Chambered for .450 SMC cartridge. Fitted with a 6" slide. Adjustable rear sight. Weight about 38 oz. Blue finish. Single-stack magazine. Discontinued.

NIB	Exc.	V.G.	Good	Fair	Poor
1480	1280	1050	780	500	350

Xcaliber Double Stack

Same as Xcaliber Single Stack, except it has a double-stack magazine. Discontinued.

NIB	Exc.	V.G.	Good	Fair	Poor
1800	1600	1180	900	600	400

Executive

Chambered for .40 S&W cartridge. Fitted with a 5" ramped bull barrel. Adjustable rear sight. Gray synthetic grip and hard chrome slide. Weight about 39 oz. Double-stack magazine.

NIB	Exc.	V.G.	Good	Fair	Poor
2350	2000	1650	1100	720	400

VIP

Chambered for .45 ACP cartridge. Fitted with a 3.9" ramped bull barrel. Stainless steel flattop slide. Fixed rear sight. 10-round magazine capacity. Weight about 25 oz.

NIB	Exc.	V.G.	Good	Fair	Poor
1400	1100	800	650	400	250

Edge

Chambered for 9mm, 10mm, .40 S&W and .45 ACP cartridge, with 5" ramped bull barrel. Dual-stack magazine. Bomar style sights. Blue finish. Weight about 39 oz.

NIB	Exc.	V.G.	Good	Fair	Poor
1800	1400	1000	700	500	300

Eagle

Chambered for customer's choice of caliber. Fitted with 5" ramped bull barrel. Fixed sights. Blued frame and stainless steel slide. Weight about 30 oz.

NIB	Exc.	V.G.	Good	Fair	Poor
1700	1200	900	600	400	250

Duty One

Chambered for 9mm, .40 S&W or .45 ACP cartridges. 5" bull barrel is fully supported and ramped. Steel frame, with single-stack magazine. Front strap checkering and tactical rail. Grips are rosewood. Slide has front and rear serrations. Adjustable sights. Finish flat blue. Weight about 38 oz.

NIB	Exc.	V.G.	Good	Fair	Poor
1100	900	750	500	400	250

Duty CT

1911-style steel frame single-stack, with integral tactical rail and rosewood grips. 5" slide/barrel, fixed 2-dot Tritium rear sight. Weight 36.6 oz. Also available in 4.15" Commander size. Blued.

NIB	Exc.	V.G.	Good	Fair	Poor
1100	900	750	500	400	250

Competitor

Chambered for .38 Super cartridge. Fitted with 5.5" ramped bull barrel, with compensator and C-More scope. Stainless steel slide. Weight about

44 oz. with scope and mount. Discontinued.

NIB	Exc.	V.G.	Good	Fair	Poor
2350	2000	1650	1100	720	400

Grandmaster

Custom built to customer's specifications in 9mm "major", 9x23 and .38 Super.

NIB	Exc.	V.G.	Good	Fair	Poor
2800	2500	2000	1500	850	500

Rangemaster

Fitted with 5" fully supported and ramped bull barrel. Chambered for 9mm or .45 ACP cartridge. Has a full-length dust cover, checkered front strap, mainspring housing and square triggerguard. Front and rear slide serrations. Adjustable sights. Rose grips. Polished blue finish. Weight about 38 oz.

NIB	Exc.	V.G.	Good	Fair	Poor
1500	1350	1100	800	500	250

Rangemaster II

Single-stack blued variation of Rangemaster. Chambered for 9mm, .40 S&W, .45 ACP. 5" slide/barrel. Weight 37 oz. Introduced 2006.

NIB	Exc.	V.G.	Good	Fair	Poor
1300	1120	900	600	400	200

Targetmaster

As above, with 6" barrel.

NIB	Exc.	V.G.	Good	Fair	Poor
1650	1250	900	650	400	250

Stinger

Chambered for 9mm or .38 Super cartridge. Fitted with 3.9" barrel, with compensator. Sights are OKO or C-More on STI mount. Blued finish. Weight about 38 oz.

NIB	Exc.	V.G.	Good	Fair	Poor
2780	2280	1850	1450	900	500

Hawk 4.3

This pistol modeled on 1911 design. Equipped with 4.3" barrel, with steel slide. Frame made from polymer. Features an increased magazine capacity while retaining the 1911 grip thickness. Chambered for .38 Super, .45 ACP, .40 S&W, 10mm and 9x25 calibers. Built primarily for competition shooting. Discontinued.

NIB	Exc.	V.G.	Good	Fair	Poor
1700	1200	900	600	400	250

Night Hawk 4.3

Chambered for .45 ACP only, with 4.3" bull barrel. A host of special features: narrow tactical safety, front and rear slide serrations and extended dust cover. Tritium sights optional. Blued finish. Weight 33 oz. Discontinued.

NIB	Exc.	V.G.	Good	Fair	Poor
1920	1600	1300	1050	750	400

Falcon 3.9

Similar to above model. Fitted with 3.9" barrel. Weight about: 30 oz. w/ steel frame; 25 oz. w/aluminum frame. Discontinued.

NIB	Exc.	V.G.	Good	Fair	Poor
1920	1600	1300	1050	750	400

Sparrow 5.0

Chambered for .22 LR cartridge only. Fitted with 5" bull barrel, with fixed sights. Weight about 30 oz. Discontinued.

NIB	Exc.	V.G.	Good	Fair	Poor
920	800	680	520	400	200

Edge 5.1

Chambered for .40 S&W only, with 5" bull barrel and many special features. BoMar front and rear sights. Weight 39 oz.

NIB	Exc.	V.G.	Good	Fair	Poor
1800	1400	1000	700	500	300

Eagle 5.1

Similar to Model 2011 Hawk, but furnished with 5" barrel. Comes standard with BoMar adjustable sights.

NIB	Exc.	V.G.	Good	Fair	Poor
1920	1600	1300	1050	750	400

Eagle 5.5

Similar to above model. Furnished with 5.5" barrel, with compensator.

NIB	Exc.	V.G.	Good	Fair	Poor
2400	1950	1600	1200	850	500

Eagle 6.0

Chambered for 9mm, .38 Super, .40 S&W or .45 ACP cartridges. Fitted with a 6" bull barrel. Many special features. BoMar front and rear sights. Blued finish. Weight about 42 oz.

NIB	Exc.	V.G.	Good	Fair	Poor
1920	1600	1300	1050	750	400

Hunter 6.0

Chambered for 10mm cartridge only. Fitted with a 6" bull barrel. Heavy extended frame. Many special features. Leupold 2x scope. Blued finish. Weight with scope 51 oz.

NIB	Exc.	V.G.	Good	Fair	Poor
2350	1900	1600	1200	850	500

Special Edition

Chambered for 9mm, .40 S&W or .45 ACP cartridge. Fitted with a fully supported and ramped 5" bull barrel. Hi-Rise grip. Sights are Dawson fiber optic, with adjustable rear. Slide has Saber Tooth serrations and custom engraving. Finish is 24 karat gold on all steel parts except barrel. Weight about 38 oz.

NIB	Exc.	V.G.	Good	Fair	Poor
2900	2500	1980	1600	1200	500

I.P.S.C. 30th Anniversary

Similar to Special Edition. Hard chrome upper, with color inlays and blued lower.

NIB	Exc.	V.G.	Good	Fair	Poor
2780	2400	1700	1400	950	450

TruSight

Semi-automatic pistol chambered for 9mm, .40 S&W, .45 ACP. Double-stack magazine. Steel frame, 4.15" slide/barrel. Dawson fiber optic front sight, adjustable rear. Weight 36.1 oz. Blued, with multiple options. IPSC, USPSA approved. Introduced 2006.

NIB	Exc.	V.G.	Good	Fair	Poor
1800	1580	1200	900	600	350

Legacy

Chambered for .45 ACP single-stack. 5" slide/barrel, LOA 8.5", weight 38 oz. with adjustable rear sight. Cocobola smooth grips. IDPA, USPSA approved. Introduced 2006.

NIB	Exc.	V.G.	Good	Fair	Poor
1500	1300	1050	750	600	300

GP6

Polymer framed single-/double-action pistol, with ambidextrous safeties and fixed three-dot sight system. Chambered in 9mm Parabellum.

NIB	Exc.	V.G.	Good	Fair	Poor
650	500	380	250	180	80

Sentinel Premier

Top-of-the-line ISPC and IDPA competition 1911, with Dawson Precision/ STI "Perfect Impact" style white outline Tritium adjustable sights and STI Tritium competition front; forged steel government length standard-width frame; and many other refinements. Sentinel Premier comes standard with case, owner's manual and one Wilson Combat Elite Tactical magazine.

NIB	Exc.	V.G.	Good	Fair	Poor
1700	1500	1300	1000	800	450

Limited Edition 20th Anniversary

1911-style semi-automatic pistol. Chambered in 9x19, .38 Super, .40 S&W and .45 ACP to commemorate 20th Anniversary. Features include ambidextrous thumb safeties and knuckle relief high-rise beavertail grip safety; gold TiN (or Titanium Nitride) coating; full-length steel bar stock slide, with custom serrations specific to this model; 5" fully ramped and supported bull barrel; STI adjustable rear sight and Dawson fiber optic front sight. STI will only build 200 of these pistols and serial numbers reflect this (1 of 200, 2 of 200, etc.)

NIB	Exc.	V.G.	Good	Fair	Poor
3200	2900	2600	—	—	—

Duty One

1911-style semi-automatic pistol. Chambered in .45 ACP. Features include government size frame, with integral tactical rail and 30 lpi checkered front strap; milled tactical rail on dust cover of the frame; ambidextrous thumb safeties; high rise beavertail grip safety; lowered and flared ejection port; fixed rear sight; front and rear cocking serrations; 5" fully supported STI International ramped bull barrel.

NIB	Exc.	V.G.	Good	Fair	Poor
1300	1100	850	700	300	200

Apeiro

1911-style semi-automatic pistol. Chambered in 9x19, .40 S&W and .45 ACP. Features include Schuemann "Island" barrel; patented modular steel frame, with polymer grip; high capacity double-stack magazine; stainless steel ambidextrous thumb safeties and knuckle relief high-rise beavertail grip safety; unique sabertooth rear cocking serrations; 5" fully ramped fully supported "island" bull barrel, with sight milled in to allow faster recovery to point of aim; custom engraving on polished sides of (blued) stainless steel slide; stainless steel magwell; STI adjustable rear sight and Dawson fiber optic front sight; blued frame.

NIB	Exc.	V.G.	Good	Fair	Poor
2200	1850	1500	1200	800	400

Eclipse

Compact 1911-style semi-automatic pistol. Chambered in 9x19, .40 S&W

and .45 ACP. Features include slide with rear cocking serrations, oversized ejection port; 2-dot Tritium night sights recessed into the slide; high-capacity polymer grip; single sided blued thumb safety; bobbed high-rise blued knuckle relief beavertail grip safety; 3" barrel. Also comes with alloy frame as Escort model.

NIB	Exc.	V.G.	Good	Fair	Poor
1620	1400	1180	900	600	300

DVC Open

Top-of-the-line competition pistol, with slide cuts to decrease weight, increase cycle rate and alleviate muzzle jump. Titanium Nitride finished barrel and improved compensator, new sear and trigger mechanism, special texturing and improved ergonomics. In .38 Super or 9mm, with 10- or 20-round magazine, 5" barrel, polished hard chrome finish, C-More 6 MOA dot sight. Weight 48 oz. Introduced in 2015.

NIB	Exc.	V.G.	Good	Fair	Poor
3600	3200	2700	—	—	—

DVC 3-Gun

Designed for 3-Gun competition. In 9mm with two 21-shot magazines, 5.4-inch barrel, adjustable rear and fiber optic front sights, accessory rail, DVS 2011 black grips. Dawson Precision special features include Tool-less guide rod and Lo-Pro mag release button.

NIB	Exc.	V.G.	Good	Fair	Poor
2500	2150	1700	1200	800	400

DVC Tactical

Designed for extreme environments with DLC (diamond-like carbon) finish, tree bark texture grips, fixed tritium ledge rear and front sights. Chambered in .45 ACP or 9mm with 10, 13 or 21-shot capacity. Two magazines provided. Barrel is 4.15-inch bull contour. Other features include Recoil Master, Tactical Slim magwell and Picatinny rail.

NIB	Exc.	V.G.	Good	Fair	Poor
1700	1400	1100	900	700	400

DVC Steel

Similar to DVC Open in 9mm or .38 Super. Has 4.15" TX1 Compensated barrel, with C-More dot sight, hard chrome finish and stippled black grips. Magazine capacity 10, 21 or 27 rounds. Introduced 2017.

NIB	Exc.	V.G.	Good	Fair	Poor
3400	3000	2400	—	—	—

DVC Classic

Designed for USPSA Single-Stack Division in 9mm, .40 S&W or .45 ACP. Has 5.4" bushing barrel, hard chrome finish, adjustable rear and fiber optic front sights. Other features include extended mag well and base pads, VZ Operator II black grips, 2.5 lb. trigger, ambidextrous safety lever. Introduced 2016.

NIB	Exc.	V.G.	Good	Fair	Poor
2400	1800	1200	1000	500	300

H.O.S.T. SS/DS

Designed to "host" (Holographic Optic Slide Top) an optic, light or suppressor in 9mm, 10mm or .45 ACP, with 4.15" or 5" barrel with threaded bushing. SS model is single-stack; DS double-stack. Magazines have extended base pads, capacity 8 or 10 rounds (SS); 9 or 15 rounds (DS). Introduced in 2017.

SS Model

NIB	Exc.	V.G.	Good	Fair	Poor
2200	1800	1350	—	—	—

DS Model

NIB	Exc.	V.G.	Good	Fair	Poor
2800	2200	1750	—	—	—

DVC Limited

Competition model designed for Limited Division. Similar to DVC Open model, with fiber optic front and adjustable rear sights. Chambered in 9mm or .40 S&W. Introduced in 2015

NIB	Exc.	V.G.	Good	Fair	Poor
2700	2200	1800	—	—	—

STACCATO 2011 SERIES

Calibers: 9mm, .40 S&W, .38 Super. Capacity: 9-, 17- or 21-round magazine. Barrels: 3.9- or 5-in., match-grade. Sights: Optics-ready, Dawson Precision Perfect Impact. Weight: 38–46.5 oz. Finish: Carbon black. Grips: Textured polymer. Features: 4-lb. trigger pull, ambidextrous safety levers, single- or double-stack magazine.

NIB	Exc.	V.G.	Good	Fair	Poor
1600	1350	1100	—	—	—

Texican Single Action Revolver

SAA-styled revolver chambered in .38 Special and .45 Colt. Features include 4.75" or 6.5" (.45) or 5.25" barrel (.38), competition sights, springs, triggers and hammers; color case-harden and blued finish standard.

NIB	Exc.	V.G.	Good	Fair	Poor
1100	940	780	600	300	200

FPI 2260 Rifle

Chambered for .22 Long rifle cartridge. Aluminum receiver, with adjustable trigger and quick magazine release. Integral scope mount.

NIB	Exc.	V.G.	Good	Fair	Poor
1000	850	680	500	300	150

Sporting Competition Rifle

AR-style semi-automatic rifle. Chambered in 5.56 NATO. Features include 16" 410 stainless 1:8 barrel; mid-length gas system; Nordic Tactical Compensator and JP Trigger group; custom STI Valkyrie handguard and gas block; flattop design with Picatinny rail; anodized finish with black Teflon coating. Also available in Tactical configuration.

NIB	Exc.	V.G.	Good	Fair	Poor
1180	1000	820	650	350	250

STOCK, FRANZ
Berlin, Germany

Stock

A .22, 6.35mm or 7.65mm semi-automatic pistol, with an open topped slide. Frame marked "Franz Stock Berlin". Blued, with black composition grips impressed with the name "Stock" at the top. Manufactured from 1918 to early 1930s.

Courtesy J.B. Wood

NIB	Exc.	V.G.	Good	Fair	Poor
—	520	400	300	250	150

STOCKING & CO.
Worcester, Massachusetts

Pepperbox Antique

A .28 or .316 barreled percussion pepperbox revolver, with barrel lengths from 4" to 6". Hammer fitted with a long cocking piece at the rear and triggerguard may or may not be made with a spur at the rear. Blued, with walnut grips. Barrel group marked "Stocking & Co., Worcester". Manufactured between 1846 and 1854.

Exc.	Fine	V.G.	Good	Fair	Poor
1950	1650	1120	600	200	140

Single-Shot Pistol Antique

A .36-caliber single-shot percussion pistol. Same pattern as Pepperbox, with 4" half octagonal barrel. Marked as above. Manufactured from 1849 to 1852.

Exc.	Fine	V.G.	Good	Fair	Poor
1200	850	600	350	100	70

STOEGER, A. F./STOEGER INDUSTRIES

First guns shown, pistols, were imported many years ago to South Hackensack, New Jersey. All the rest have been imported by Stoeger Industries in: Accokeek, Maryland

HANDGUNS

.22 Luger

A .22-caliber simplified copy of German Model P.08 semi-automatic pistol, with 4.5" or 5.5" barrel and aluminum frame. Word "Luger" is roll engraved on right side of the frame. Blued, with checkered brown plastic grips. Made by Erma.

NIB	Exc.	V.G.	Good	Fair	Poor
—	350	280	200	150	100

Target Luger

As above, with adjustable target sights. Made by Erma.

NIB	Exc.	V.G.	Good	Fair	Poor
—	380	300	220	180	120

Luger Carbine

As above, with an 11" barrel, walnut forend and checkered walnut grips. Furnished with a red velvet lined black leatherette case. Manufactured during 1970s. Made by Erma.

NIB	Exc.	V.G.	Good	Fair	Poor
—	1100	780	500	350	150

American Eagle Luger

Identical to German design. Chambered for 9mm, with 7-round magazine and fitted with a 4" barrel. Checkered walnut grips. Stainless steel. Weight 32 oz.

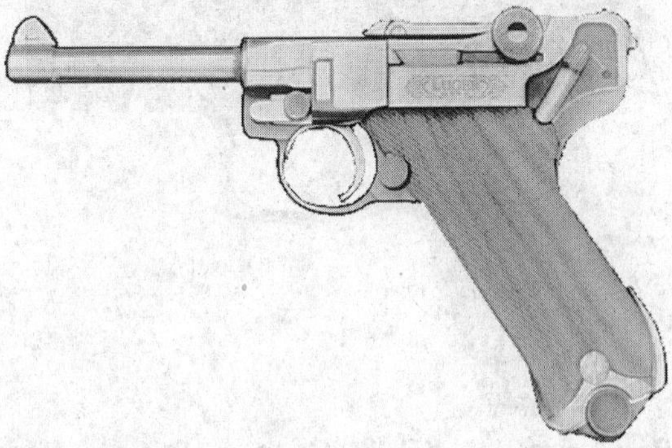

NIB	Exc.	V.G.	Good	Fair	Poor
1100	980	650	450	300	100

American Eagle Navy Model

Same as above, with a 6" barrel.

NIB	Exc.	V.G.	Good	Fair	Poor
1200	1080	700	450	300	100

Cougar

Double-action semi-automatic offered in 9mm. .40 S&W or .45 ACP. Manufactured in Turkey and based on Beretta model of the same name. Traditional DA/SA design, with ambidextrous safety/decocking lever, white dot sights and Picatinny rail (.45 only). Also made in compact variation. Discontinued.

NIB	Exc.	V.G.	Good	Fair	Poor
420	380	320	280	200	150

Pro Series 95

Target pistol in .22 LR, with 5.5" or 7.25" barrel, adjustable trigger and sights. Imported by Stoeger in 1995 and 1996. Note: Add $75 for bull barrel.

NIB	Exc.	V.G.	Good	Fair	Poor
450	400	350	300	250	150

STR-9

9mm synthetic frame semi-auto pistol, 4.17" barrel. Available options at extra cost include optics-ready, interchangeable backstraps, and tritium night sights.

NIB	Exc.	V.G.	Good	Fair	Poor
330	280	230	—	—	—

STR-9 Compact

Caliber: 9mm. Capacity: 13-round magazine. Barrel: 3.8". Grips: Three interchangeable backstraps. Sights: 3-dot sights or tritium night sights. Length: 6.9". overall. Weight: 24 oz. unloaded. Finish: Matte black. Features: Compact version of the STR-9 striker-fire pistol. Aggressive forward and rear slide serrations and accessory rail. Made in Turkey.

NIB	Exc.	V.G.	Good	Fair	Poor
300	250	200	—	—	—

STR-9SC Subcompact

NIB	Exc.	V.G.	Good	Fair	Poor
290	250	220	200	160	—

STR-9S Combat

Compact version of the above, 10-round magazine and optics-ready.

NIB	Exc.	V.G.	Good	Fair	Poor
520	460	390	350	280	—

STR-9 Optics-Ready

NIB	Exc.	V.G.	Good	Fair	Poor
350	310	260	240	190	—

STR-9F Full-Size

NIB	Exc.	V.G.	Good	Fair	Poor
280	250	220	200	160	—

SHOTGUNS

Model 2000

Semi-automatic shotgun chambered for 12-gauge shell. Fitted with 26", 28" or 30" ventilated rib barrel. Single trigger, with screw-in chokes. Weight 7 lbs. Introduced in 2001.

NIB	Exc.	V.G.	Good	Fair	Poor
500	400	300	200	150	80

Model 2000 Deluxe

Same as above, with high grade walnut stock and etched receiver. Gold trigger.

NIB	Exc.	V.G.	Good	Fair	Poor
620	500	400	300	250	120

Model 2000 Camo

As above, with Advantage Timber HD camo stock.

NIB	Exc.	V.G.	Good	Fair	Poor
500	400	300	200	150	80

Model 2000 Slug

Chambered for 12-gauge shell, with 3" chamber. Barrel length 24". Fitted with a black synthetic stock. Smoothbore barrel. Adjustable rifle-type sights. Optional field-style barrels in 24", 26" or 28". Weight 6.7 lbs. Introduced in 2003.

NIB	Exc.	V.G.	Good	Fair	Poor
450	350	250	180	120	50

Model 2000 Synthetic

As above, with 24", 26" or 28" ventilated rib barrel. Black synthetic stock. Weight 6.8 lbs. Introduced in 2003.

NIB	Exc.	V.G.	Good	Fair	Poor
500	400	300	200	150	80

Model 3000

Gauges: 12 ga. Barrels: 24", 26", 28". Stock: Black synthetic, Camo, Walnut. Features: Redesigned in 2023 as a 3" chambered 12-gauge semi-auto. New recoil pad and removable cheek pieces on all except satin walnut models. Stock grip areas are trimmer with an overall less boxy look. Oversized controls, slimmer magazine cap, and beveled loading port. Red fiber-optic front sight. Ships with three choke tubes.

NIB	Exc.	V.G.	Good	Fair	Poor
500	450	400	300	200	—

M3K

Gauges: 12 ga. Barrels: 24". Stock: Black synthetic. Features: Race-ready factory semi-automatic build for 3-Gun competitors. Oversized controls with contrasting blue anodizing. Enlarged loading port and elongated carrier. A 3" chamber and 4+1-round capacity. Uses the Inertia-Drive system. Upgraded recoil pad and integrated cheek pad. Ships with three choke tubes.

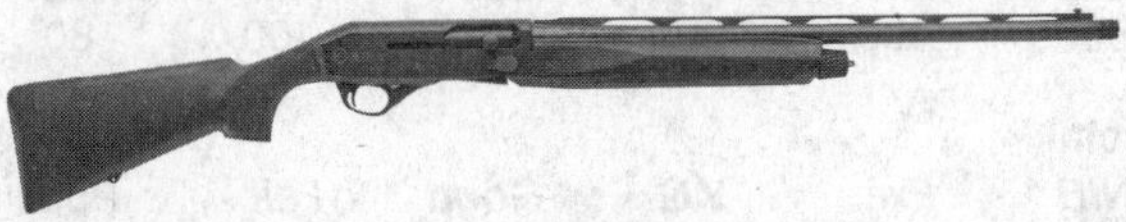

NIB	Exc.	V.G.	Good	Fair	Poor
610	520	—	—	—	—

Model 3020

Gauges: 20 ga. Barrels: 18.5", 24", 26", 28". Stock: Black synthetic, Gloss Walnut, Camo. Features: Inertia-driven semi-automatic 20-gauge family chambered for 2.75" and 3" shells. Fiber-optic front sight. Includes numerous model variants and styles. A shim kit comes standard.

NIB	Exc.	V.G.	Good	Fair	Poor
500	450	400	300	200	—

Model 3500

Redesigned for 2023 with slimmer stock dimensions, oversized controls, and an easy-grip magazine cap. View from receiver to rib is lower. Upgraded recoil pad. Addition of cheek pad on all but walnut models.

NIB	Exc.	V.G.	Good	Fair	Poor
600	540	450	300	200	—

Model 3500 Predator/Turkey

Gauge: 12 ga., 3.5". Capacity: 4+1. Barrel: 24", ventilated rib. Length: 46". Weight: 7.5 lbs. Stock: Synthetic Mossy Oak Overwatch. Features: Inertia-driven autoloader model with a shorter barrel and rubber pistol grip. Red bar fiber-optic front sight. Receiver drilled and tapped for optics mounting. Ships with a paracord sling and five extended chokes, including MOJO Predator and MOJO Turkey tubes.

NIB	Exc.	V.G.	Good	Fair	Poor
850	730	600	—	—	—

Model 3500 Waterfowl

Gauge: 12 ga., 3.5". Barrel: 28", ventilated rib. Length: 50". Weight: 7.8 lbs. Stock: Synthetic Realtree Max-5, Mossy Oak Shadow Grass Blades, or True Timber DRT. Features: Inertia-driven autoloader. Red bar fiber-optic front sight. Flat Dark Earth Cerakote finish, enlarged triggerguard, drilled and tapped for optics mounting. Ships with a paracord sling and five extended chokes.

NIB	Exc.	V.G.	Good	Fair	Poor
780	650	550	—	—	—

Model 3500 Snow Goose

Gauge: 12 ga. 3.5". Barrel: 28". ventilated rib. Length: 50". Weight: 8.2 lbs. Stock: Synthetic with distressed white Cerakote finish. Features: Stoeger combined the M3500 Waterfowl semi-auto with the 922R-compliant extended magazine Freedom Series to create the higher-capacity M3500 Snow Goose. Full 10+1 capacity. Inertia-driven autoloader with oversized controls. Beveled loading port. Distressed white Cerakote finish on stock, forend, receiver, and barrel act as winter camo. Red bar front sight. Includes paracord sling and shim kit for adjusting drop and cast. Ships with five extended choke tubes (IC, M, XFT, Close Range, Mid Range).

NIB	Exc.	V.G.	Good	Fair	Poor
790	650	550	—	—	—

Coach Gun

Side-by-side gun chambered for 12- or 20-gauge and .410 shell. Fitted with 20" barrels, with double triggers. Improved Cylinder and Modified fixed chokes. Weight 7 lbs. Note: Add $50 for nickel finish.

NIB	Exc.	V.G.	Good	Fair	Poor
390	280	220	180	120	80

Silverado Coach Gun

Offered in 12-, 20-gauge and .410 bore, with straight-/pistol grip stock. Matte nickel finish. Straight stock version offered in 12- and 20-gauge only. Weight 6.5 lbs.

NIB	Exc.	V.G.	Good	Fair	Poor
450	320	250	180	120	80

Coach Gun Supreme

Similar to above, but offered with blue, stainless or nickel receiver. Introduced in 2004. Note: Add $10 for stainless; $30 for nickel.

NIB	Exc.	V.G.	Good	Fair	Poor
450	320	250	180	120	80

Coach Gun .410 Bore

.410 bore. 3" chamber, 20" barrel.

NIB	Exc.	V.G.	Good	Fair	Poor
390	330	280	—	—	—

Coach Gun Black-Finished Hardwood/Polished-Nickel Model

NIB	Exc.	V.G.	Good	Fair	Poor
490	400	350	—	—	—

Uplander

Side-by-side shotgun chambered for 12-, 16-, 20-, 28-gauge and .410 bore. Choice of 26" or 28" barrels. Fixed chokes. Double triggers. Weight 7.25 lbs.

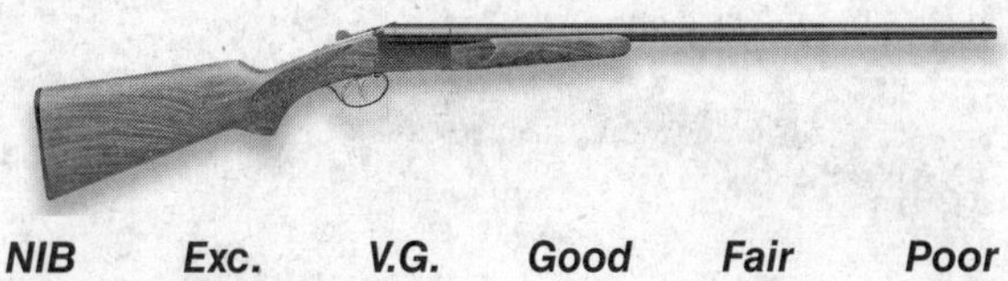

NIB	Exc.	V.G.	Good	Fair	Poor
380	280	180	120	100	80

Uplander Special

As above, with straight-grip and oil-finish stock. Offered in 12-, 20- or 28-gauge. Weight 7.3 lbs.

NIB	Exc.	V.G.	Good	Fair	Poor
400	300	200	150	100	80

Uplander Supreme

Same as above, with select wood and screw-in chokes.

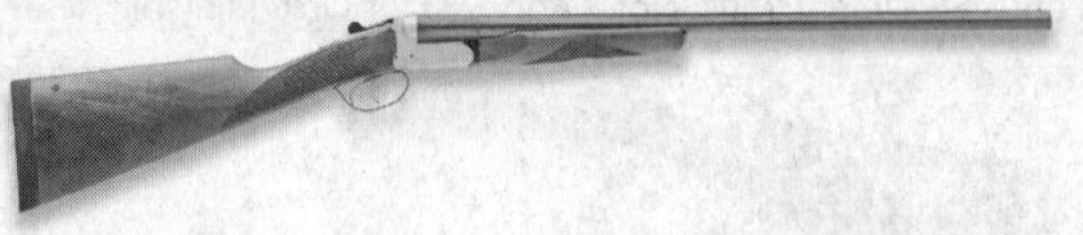

NIB	Exc.	V.G.	Good	Fair	Poor
420	350	250	180	120	100

Uplander English

This variation fitted with a straight-grip stock. Chambered for 20 gauge or .410 bore. Fitted with 24" barrels. Weight 7 lbs. Also available with a short stock.

NIB	Exc.	V.G.	Good	Fair	Poor
400	300	200	150	100	80

Uplander Youth

Offered in 20-gauge or .410 bore. Features 13" LOP, with 22" barrels choked Improved Modified and Modified. Weight 6.75 lbs.

NIB	Exc.	V.G.	Good	Fair	Poor
380	280	180	120	100	80

Condor

Over/under shotgun chambered in 12-, 16-, 20-gauge and .410 bore. Available with 26" and 28" barrels in all gauges; 26" barrel in .410 bore. Single trigger. Blued finish. 16-gauge chambered for 2.75" shells; all others have 3" chambers. Weights run from 6 lbs. to 7.4 lbs. depending on bore.

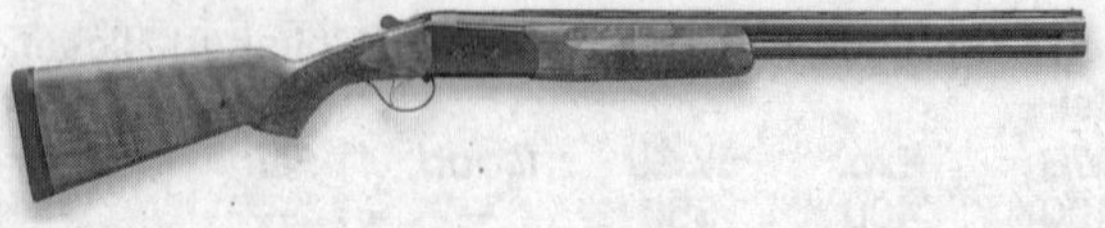

NIB	Exc.	V.G.	Good	Fair	Poor
380	280	180	120	100	80

Condor Special

Similar to standard Condor, with matte stainless receiver. Rubbed oil-finish stock. Introduced in 2003.

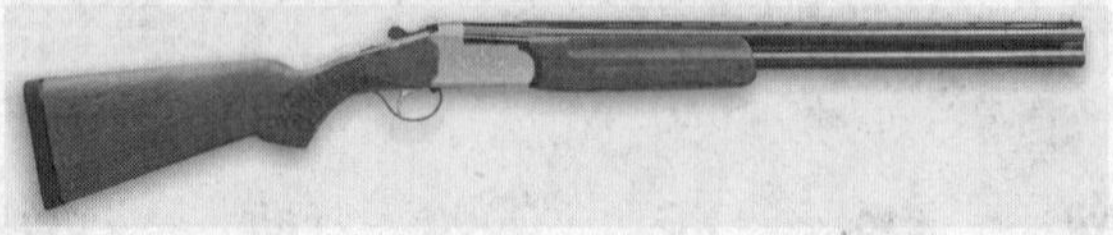

NIB	Exc.	V.G.	Good	Fair	Poor
480	380	300	200	120	100

Condor Combo

Introduced in 2004. Features a two-barrel set of 12 and 20 gauge. Barrel length: 12-gauge 28"; 20-gauge 26". Choke tubes. Offered in 3 grades: Field, Special and Supreme.

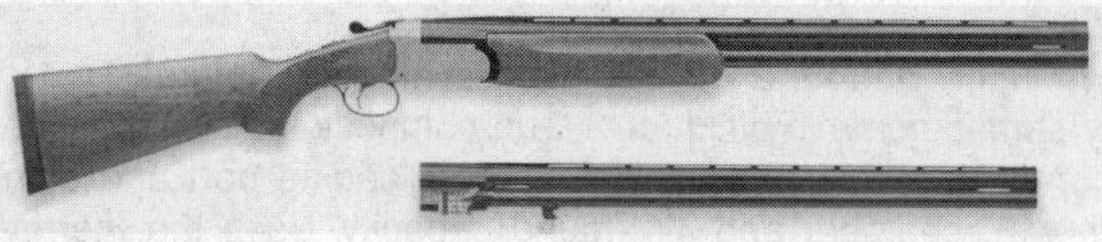

Field

NIB	Exc.	V.G.	Good	Fair	Poor
500	400	300	200	100	80

Special

NIB	Exc.	V.G.	Good	Fair	Poor
650	500	400	280	180	120

Supreme

NIB	Exc.	V.G.	Good	Fair	Poor
780	650	500	300	200	150

Condor Supreme Deluxe

Similar to above model, with cut checkering and high polish blue. Offered in 12 and 20 ga., with 26" or 28" barrels as well as 24" barrels for 20 ga. Automatic ejectors.

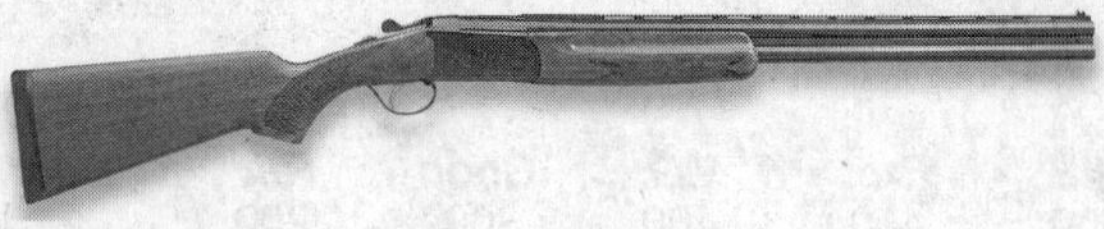

NIB	Exc.	V.G.	Good	Fair	Poor
500	400	300	200	100	80

Condor Competition

These 3" 12- and 20-gauge over/unders feature 30" barrels, AA Grade wood and adjustable combs. Three choke tubes. Weight 7.3 lbs. 20 ga.; 7.8 lbs. 12-ga.

NIB	Exc.	V.G.	Good	Fair	Poor
650	500	400	280	180	120

Condor Competition Combo

As above, with 12- and 20-gauge barrels.

NIB	Exc.	V.G.	Good	Fair	Poor
780	650	500	300	200	150

Condor Outback

New in 2007. Outback comes in 12 and 20 ga. Chambered for 3" shells. Finish A Grade satin walnut stock, with blued barrels and receiver or matte black walnut stock, with polished barrels and receiver. Barrels are 20", with rifle sights. Includes two choke tubes. Note: Add $40 for black/nickel finish.

NIB	Exc.	V.G.	Good	Fair	Poor
380	280	180	120	100	80

Single Barrel Classic Youth

Available in 20 ga. or .410 bore, with 13" length of pull and 22" ventilated rib barrel. Straight-grip stock. Weight 5 lbs.

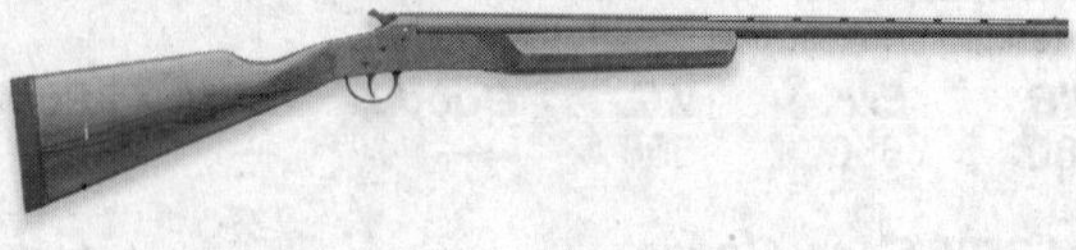

NIB	Exc.	V.G.	Good	Fair	Poor
120	100	80	50	20	10

Single Barrel Classic

As above, with standard length of pull. Available in 12, 20 ga. or .410 bore. Barrel length: 12-ga. 26" or 28"; 20-ga. 26"; .410 bore 24". Open pistol grip. Weight 5.5 lbs.

NIB	Exc.	V.G.	Good	Fair	Poor
120	100	80	50	20	10

Single Barrel Special

As above, with stainless steel frame. Offered in 12 and 20 ga. or .410 bore. Weight 5.5 lbs.

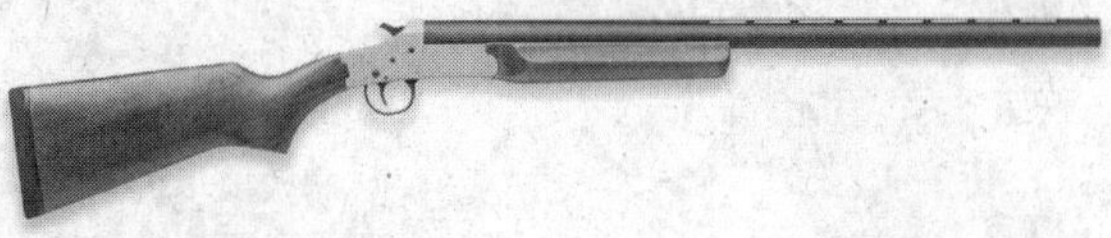

NIB	Exc.	V.G.	Good	Fair	Poor
120	100	80	50	20	10

P-350

Pump-action 12-ga. shotgun introduced in 2005. All versions are chambered for 3.5" shells. Available with 24", 26" or 28" barrels in matte black synthetic or Advantage Timber camo finish; 26" or 28" barrel in Max-4 camo finish. Comes with 5 choke tubes. Weight 6.8 lbs. Also available is a Defense model with 18.5" barrel and fixed cylinder bore. Note: Add 15% for camo models.

NIB	Exc.	V.G.	Good	Fair	Poor
280	220	180	120	100	50

P-350 Camo

Pump-action 12-ga. chambered for 3.5" shells. Has a 24", 26" or 28" barrel and matte black, Max-4, Timber or APG finish. Also some pistol grip stock offerings with 24" barrels. Includes five choke tubes. Weight 6.8 lbs. Note: Add $20 for pistol grip stock; $75 for camo finish.

NIB	Exc.	V.G.	Good	Fair	Poor
350	280	220	150	120	80

P-350 Defense

Same as above in matte black finish, with 18.5" fixed cylinder choke barrel. Note: Add $20 for pistol grip stock.

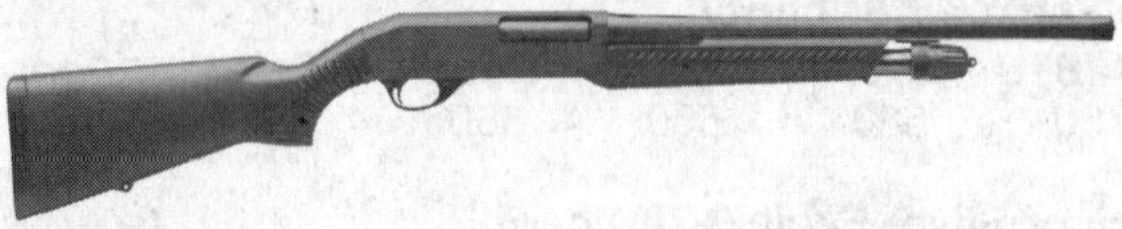

NIB	Exc.	V.G.	Good	Fair	Poor
300	220	180	120	100	50

Model P3000

Gauges: 12 ga. Barrels: 28". Stock: Synthetic in Realtree Max-7 camo Features: Redesigned in 2023 as a 3" chambered 12-gauge pump action. Improved ergonomics. Barrel extension reaches deeper into the receiver for greater longevity of the action. Pistol grip inset with Stoeger logo cap. Integrated swivel studs.

NIB	Exc.	V.G.	Good	Fair	Poor
320	280	—	—	—	—

P3500

Gauges: 12 ga. Barrels: 26", 28". Stock: Synthetic in Realtree Max-7 camo. Features: Redesigned in 2023 as a hunting gun with checkered synthetic stocks, integrated swivel studs, and slimmer stock lines. Twin steel action bars, no-stick pump action, and rotating bolt head. Cycles 2.75", 3", and 3.5" shells.

NIB	Exc.	V.G.	Good	Fair	Poor
400	320	—	—	—	—

STONER TACTICAL ORDNANCE

Manufacturer of AR-style rifles by the family of Eugene Stoner.

SR-15 SERIES

SR-15 MOD 2 Rifle

Caliber: 5.56mm NATO. Capacity: 30-round magazine. Barrel: 16" 1:7" twist, free-floated inside M-LOK URX handguard. Weight: 6.3 lbs. Length: 32" to 35" overall. Stock: Magpul MOE. Sights: Post front, fully adjustable rear (300m sight). Features: URX-4 upper receiver; two-stage trigger, 30-round magazine. Black finish. Made in USA by Knight's Armament Co. SEE POLITICAL PANIC PRICING.

NIB	Exc.	V.G.	Good	Fair	Poor
2750	—	—	—	—	—

SR-15 LPR MOD 2

Caliber: .223. Capacity: 30-round magazine. Barrel: 18", free-floated inside M-LOK URSx handguard. Weight: 7.6 lbs. Length: 38" overall. Stock: Mag-Pul MOE. Sights: Post front, fully adjustable rear (300m sight). Features: URX-4 upper receiver; two-stage trigger, 30-round magazine. Black finish. Made in USA by Knight's Armament Co. SEE POLITICAL PANIC PRICING.

NIB	Exc.	V.G.	Good	Fair	Poor
3050	—	—	—	—	—

SR-25 SERIES

SR-25 Rifle

Caliber: 7.62 NATO. Capacity: 10- or 20-shot steel magazine. Barrel: 16" with flash hider. Weight: 8.5 lbs. APC (Carbine) features: Shortened, non-slip handguard; drop-in two-stage match trigger, removable carrying handle, ambidextrous controls, matte-black finish. APR (Rifle) has 20" heavy barrel. Made in USA by Knight's Armament Co. SEE POLITICAL PANIC PRICING.

NIB	Exc.	V.G.	Good	Fair	Poor
5700	—	—	—	—	—

STRASSER

Eugendorf, Austria

Strasser (Waffenmanufaktur HMS Präzisionstechnik GmbH) is an Austrian firearms manufacturer known for making high-end sporting rifles.

RS 14 Evolution Standard

Calibers: .222 Rem., .223 Rem., .300 AAC Blackout, .22-250 Rem., .243 Win., 6 XC, 6.5 Creedmoor, .284 Norma, 6.5x55SE, 6.5x65RWS, .270 Win., 7x64, 7mm-08 Rem, .308 Win., .30-06, 8x57 IS, 8.5x63, 9.3x62, 9.3x57, 7mm Rem. Mag., .300 Win. Mag., .375 Ruger, .338 Win. Mag., .458 Win. Mag., 10.3x68. Capacity: 3 to 7. Barrel: 22 to 24 in., blued. Stock: Grade-1 wood, grade-2 wood, standard or thumbhole. Sights: Integrated Picatinny rail. Weight: 6.75 to 7.725 lbs. Features: Barrel-exchange system, adjustable trigger with trigger set, plasma-hardened bolt.

NIB	Exc.	V.G.	Good	Fair	Poor
3400	2900	2500	—	—	—

RS 14 Evolution TAHR

Calibers: .222 Rem., .223 Rem., .300 AAC Blackout, .22-250 Rem., .243 Win., 6 XC, 6.5 Creedmoor, .284 Norma, 6.5x55SE, 6.5x65RWS, .270 Win., 7x64, 7mm-08 Rem., .308 Win., .30-06, 8x57 IS, 8.5x63, 9.3x62, 9.3x57, 7mm Rem. Mag., .300 Win. Mag., .375 Ruger, .338 Win. Mag., .458 Win. Mag., 10.3x68. Capacity: 3 to7. Barrel: 22 to 24 in., blued. Stock: Laminate, standard or thumbhole. Sights: Integrated Picatinny rail. Weight: 6.75 to 7.725 lbs. Features: Barrel-exchange system, adjustable trigger with trigger set, plasma-hardened bolt.

NIB	Exc.	V.G.	Good	Fair	Poor
3400	2900	2500	—	—	—

STREET SWEEPER
Atlanta, Georgia

Street Sweeper

A 12-gauge semi-automatic double-action shotgun, with 18" barrel and 12-shot rotary drum magazine. Matte black finish. Introduced in 1989. Note: This firearm is now on the restricted list as a Class III weapon and subject to NFA rules. This model requires registration with BATFE to avoid federal penalties. Make sure the shotgun is transferable prior to sale.

NIB	Exc.	V.G.	Good	Fair	Poor
2200	1850	1600	—	—	—

STURDIVANT, LEWIS G.
Talladega, Alabama

Received contract from the state of Alabama for 2,000 "Mississippi" or "Enfield" rifles. Two hundred and eighty were received on this contract. These arms resemble U.S. Model 1841 Rifles without patchboxes. Overall length 48.5"; barrel length 33"; .577-caliber. Unmarked.

STURM, RUGER & CO.
Southport, Connecticut

Sturm, Ruger & Company, Inc., better known today as simply Ruger, is based in Southport, Connecticut, with plants in Newport, New Hampshire; Mayodan, North Carolina; and Prescott, Arizona. Alexander M. Sturm and William B. Ruger founded the company in 1949. The now-publicly traded gun manufacturer makes bolt action, semi-automatic, and single-shot rifles, semi-automatic pistols, and single- and double-action revolvers. SEE POLITICAL PANIC PRICING.

SEMI-AUTOMATIC RIMFIRE PISTOLS

Standard Model "Red Eagle Grips"

Blowback semi-automatic, with fixed exposed 4.75" barrel. Receiver tubular, with round bolt. There is a 9-shot detachable magazine. Sights are fixed. Finish blued. Black hard rubber grips on this first model feature a red Ruger eagle or hawk medallion on the left side. Approximately 25,600 manufactured before Alexander Sturm's death in 1951, but this model may be seen as high as 35000 serial number range. Because variations of this model exist, an expert opinion should be sought before a final price is established. Note: Factory verified plated pistols will bring between $2,500 and $5,000 depending on condition. Approximately 890 pistols were shipped in a wooden "salt cod" box. Add a premium of $3,000 if NIB; $1,000 to $2,000 if good to excellent condition.

NIB	Exc.	V.G.	Good	Fair	Poor
980	610	460	370	240	180

Standard Model

Identical to Red Eagle, except after Sturm's death grip medallions were changed from red to black. Produced from 1952-1982 in 4.75" and 6" barrels. There are a great many variations of this pistol, but a book dealing with this pistol alone should be consulted as differences in variations are subtle and valuation of these variations is definitely a matter for individual appraisal.

NIB	Exc.	V.G.	Good	Fair	Poor
560	410	360	270	200	110

Standard Model—Marked "Hecho en Mexico"

Early in 1957, Ruger shipped 250 sets of parts to Armanex in Mexico. Armanex fabricated barrels for the sets of parts and then finished and assembled 250 pistols — 200 with 4.75" barrels and 50 with 6.5" barrels. Due to the rarity of these pistols, an expert examination and appraisal is recommended.

NIB	Exc.	V.G.	Good	Fair	Poor
1750	1500	1200	850	600	400

Mark I Target Model

Success of Ruger Standard Model, led quite naturally to a demand for a more accurate target model. In 1951, a pistol that utilized the same frame and receiver with a 6.875" target-type barrel and adjustable sights was introduced. Early target models number 15000 to 16999 and 25000 to 25300 have Red Eagle grips. In 1952, a 5.25" tapered barrel model was introduced, but was soon discontinued. In 1963, popular 5.5" bull barrel model was introduced. These models enjoyed well-deserved success. Manufactured from 1951-1982.

NIB	Exc.	V.G.	Good	Fair	Poor
960	810	660	440	260	200

Red Eagle 6-7/8" barrel

NIB	Exc.	V.G.	Good	Fair	Poor
750	680	500	350	250	150

Black or Silver Eagle 6-7/8" barrel

Note: Add 35% for original hinged box; $75-$100 with factory-supplied muzzle brake; add 50% for other Mark I Target models under serial number 72500 in original hinged box.

NIB	Exc.	V.G.	Good	Fair	Poor
630	460	380	300	180	160

5-1/4" Tapered Barrel Model

Note: Add 50% if in original 5.25"-marked hinged box.

NIB	Exc.	V.G.	Good	Fair	Poor
960	800	660	480	260	200

5-1/2" Bull Barrel Model

NIB	Exc.	V.G.	Good	Fair	Poor
530	400	330	280	180	160

Rollmarked with U.S. on Top of Frame

These pistols will have .0625" or .125" high serial numbers. Note: Add 25% if pistol has .125" high serial numbers.

NIB	Exc.	V.G.	Good	Fair	Poor
—	1200	960	700	500	360

Stainless Steel 1 of 5,000

This model is a special commemorative version of first standard with "Red Eagle" grips. Made of stainless steel and rollmarked with Bill Ruger's signature on it. Pistol is encased in a wood "salt cod" case.

NIB	Exc.	V.G.	Good	Fair	Poor
500	380	330	230	180	130

MARK II SERIES

Supplied in .22 LR, with various barrel weights and lengths. Magazine capacity 10 rounds. Trigger grooved, with curved finger surface. High-speed hammer provides fast lock time. Grips are sharply checkered and made of black gloss Delrin material. Stainless steel models have a brushed satin finish. Note: Beginning in 2004, all Ruger adjustable sight .22 pistols were drilled and tapped for an included Weaver-type scope base adapter.

Standard Model

Generally an improved version of first Ruger pistol. There is a hold-open device. Magazine holds 10 rounds. Introduced in 1982.

NIB	Exc.	V.G.	Good	Fair	Poor
350	250	150	120	100	80

Model MK450

Introduced in 1999, to commemorate 50th Anniversary of first Ruger rimfire pistol. Fitted with 4.75" barrel, with fixed sights. Chambered for .22 LR cartridge. Pistol grips have a red Ruger medallion and Ruger crest on the barrel. Furnished in a red case. Weight 35 oz. Production limited to one year.

NIB	Exc.	V.G.	Good	Fair	Poor
380	350	250	180	120	80

Model MK6

Same as above, with 6" barrel. Weight 37 oz.

NIB	Exc.	V.G.	Good	Fair	Poor
350	280	220	120	100	80

Model KMK4

Same as Mark II Standard, except made of stainless steel.

NIB	Exc.	V.G.	Good	Fair	Poor
380	300	200	150	120	100

Model KMK6

Same as above, with 6" barrel. Weight 37 oz. Note: In 1997, Ruger produced 650 of Model MK6, with special features for "Friends of the NRA" auction of the same year. These guns have high polish bluing, faux ivory grip panels, gold inlaid National Rifle Association inscription and gold inlaid number of "1 of 650" to "650 of 650".

NIB	Exc.	V.G.	Good	Fair	Poor
380	300	200	150	120	100

Target Model

Model incorporates the same improvements as Mark II Standard. Offered with 5.5" bull, 6.875" tapered and 10" heavy barrel. A 5.25" tapered barrel was added in 1990, but discontinued in 1994. Blued finish. This model has adjustable target sights. Introduced in 1982. Note: In 1989, approximately 2,000 5.5" bull barrel Mark II pistols, with blue barreled receivers and stainless steel grip frames were produced by Ruger on order from a Ruger distributor. They exist in the 215-25xxx to 215-43xxx serial number range.

NIB	Exc.	V.G.	Good	Fair	Poor
400	350	300	220	180	120

Stainless Steel Target Model

Same as blued version, but made of stainless steel.

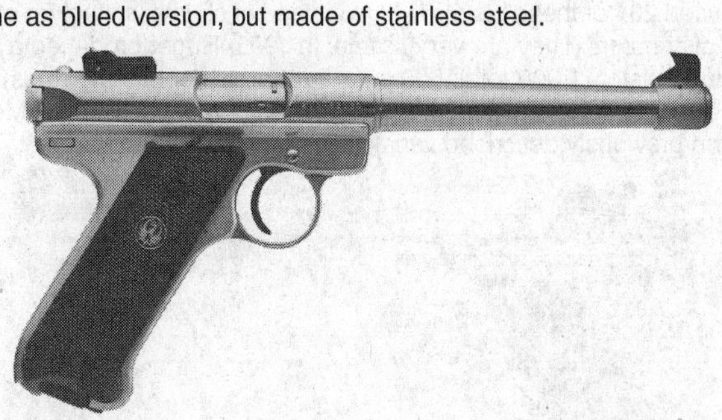

NIB	Exc.	V.G.	Good	Fair	Poor
450	400	350	300	250	200

Government Model

Similar to blue Mark II Target, with 6.875" bull barrel. Civilian version of a training pistol that the military is purchasing from Ruger. Only difference is this model does not have U.S. markings. Note: Add 150% to 175% premium for models with "U.S." marking. An expert examination and appraisal is suggested.

NIB	*Exc.*	*V.G.*	*Good*	*Fair*	*Poor*
480	360	280	200	150	100

Stainless Steel Government Model

Stainless steel version of Government Model. Note: Same with U.S. markings. These are found in serial number range of 210-00001 to 210-18600. Only a couple dozen are in civilian hands.

NIB	*Exc.*	*V.G.*	*Good*	*Fair*	*Poor*
480	350	250	220	180	120

Competition Model KMK678GC

Competition model features a stainless steel frame, with checkered laminated hardwood thumbrest grips, heavy 6.875" bull barrel factory drilled and tapped for scope mount, Partridge type front sight undercut to prevent glare and adjustable rear sight. Weight 45 oz. Note: In 1997, Ruger produced 204 of these pistols in blue instead of stainless steel for one of their distributors. They are very scarce. In 1995, Ruger produced a similar blued pistol (1,000 total: 500 each with or without scope rings) with 5.5" slabside barrels. These are not marked "Competition Target Model" like the previously described variation.

NIB	*Exc.*	*V.G.*	*Good*	*Fair*	*Poor*
400	320	280	200	120	100

Bull Barrel Model MK4B

Introduced in 1996. This bull-barrel variation has a blued finish, with 4" barrel. Grips are checkered composition. Weight 38 oz.

NIB	*Exc.*	*V.G.*	*Good*	*Fair*	*Poor*
400	320	280	200	120	100

RUGER 22/45 MODEL

This .22 LR caliber pistol has same grip angle and magazine latch as Model 1911 .45 ACP. Semi-automatic action is stainless steel and grip frame is made from Zytel, a fiberglass reinforced lightweight composite material. Front sight Patridge-type. Available in several different configurations. A 4" tapered barrel and standard model sights; 5.25" tapered barrel with target sights; 5.5" bull barrel with target sights. The 5.25" barrel was discontinued in 1994.

KP4

Features 4.75" standard weight barrel, with fixed sights. Weight 28 oz.

NIB	*Exc.*	*V.G.*	*Good*	*Fair*	*Poor*
300	280	250	200	120	80

KP514

Furnished with a target tapered barrel 5.25" in length. Comes with adjustable sights. Weight 38 oz. Discontinued.

NIB	*Exc.*	*V.G.*	*Good*	*Fair*	*Poor*
300	200	180	150	100	80

KP512

Equipped with 5.5" bull barrel, with adjustable sights. Weight 42 oz. Note: In 1995, Ruger produced 500 22/45s with stainless steel 6.875" Government type barreled receivers for one of their distributors. They appear around 220-59xxx serial number range. In 1997, another Ruger distributor succeeded in contracting Ruger to make a similar 22/45 only in blue, with 6.875" slabside bull barrels. Approximately 1,000 were produced, with serial numbers extending to 220-87xxx serial number range.

NIB	Exc.	V.G.	Good	Fair	Poor
300	200	180	150	100	80

P4

A limited number, about 1,000, of this variation were produced in 1995. A 4" bull barrel on a P frame. Introduced into the product line as a production pistol in 1997. Weight 31 oz.

NIB	Exc.	V.G.	Good	Fair	Poor
350	200	150	100	80	50

22/45 Threaded Barrel

Variation of Model 22/45 Mark III action, with muzzle threaded to accept various accessories. Muzzle capped to protect threads, receiver and barrel drilled and tapped to accept accessory rails. Weight 32 oz.; 4.5" barrel, with blue finish.

NIB	Exc.	V.G.	Good	Fair	Poor
430	380	320	300	200	150

P512

This variation of the stainless steel version has a blued receiver, with P-style frame.

NIB	Exc.	V.G.	Good	Fair	Poor
350	250	150	100	80	60

22/45 Lite

Lightened version of standard 22/45 Mark III model, with 4.4" barrel. Weight 23 oz. Manufactured 2012-2016.

NIB	Exc.	V.G.	Good	Fair	Poor
470	370	340	300	260	230

MARK III SERIES

Mark III series was introduced in 2004. Series features a newly designed magazine release button located on left side of the frame. Mark III pistols also have a visible loaded chamber indicator, an internal lock, magazine disconnect, re-contoured sights and ejection port.

Standard Pistol

Introduced in 2005. This .22-caliber pistol with 4.75" or 6" barrel. Fixed rear sight. Blued finish. Magazine capacity 10 rounds. Black checkered grips. Weight 35 oz.

NIB	Exc.	V.G.	Good	Fair	Poor
370	310	260	230	200	170

Hunter

This .22-caliber pistol fitted with 6.88" target crowned fluted stainless steel barrel. Adjustable rear sight, with Hi-Viz front. Checkered Cocobolo grips. Drilled and tapped for scope mount. Supplied with green case, scope base adapter and six interchangeable LitePipes for front sight. Weight 41 oz. Introduced in 2005. Note: Add 50% for Crimson Trace Lasergrips (limited edition for 2008).

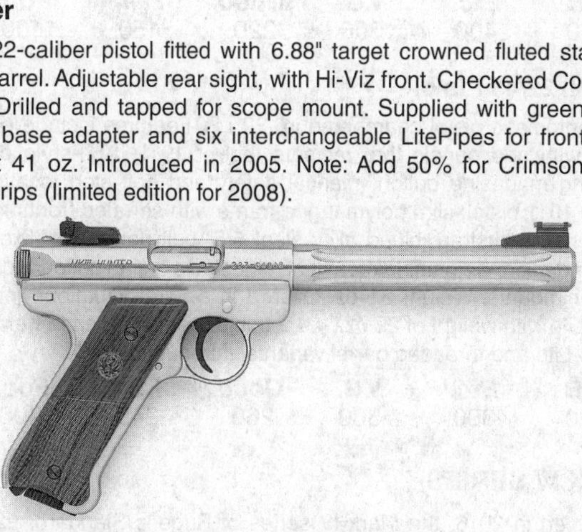

NIB	Exc.	V.G.	Good	Fair	Poor
580	500	400	320	220	120

Competition

This .22-caliber model features 6.88" flat-sided heavy barrel, with adjustable rear sight and Patridge front. Stainless steel finish. Checkered wood grips. Weight 45 oz. Introduced in 2005.

NIB	Exc.	V.G.	Good	Fair	Poor
580	470	390	280	240	200

Mark III 22/45 Standard Pistol

This .22-caliber pistol has a grip frame similar to Colt 1911 pistol. The 4" bull barrel is flat-sided. Blued steel frame. Fixed sights. Magazine capacity 10 rounds. Grips are checkered black polymer. Weight 29 oz.

NIB	Exc.	V.G.	Good	Fair	Poor
350	290	260	180	160	120

Mark III 22/45 Stainless

Similar to above, with stainless barrel, aluminum upper receiver, Zytel polymer frame.

NIB	Exc.	V.G.	Good	Fair	Poor
420	380	320	250	180	120

Mark III 512 Pistol

This .22 LR pistol has 5.5" bull barrel and adjustable rear sight. Steel frame blued. Checkered black synthetic grips. Weaver-style scope base adapter included. Magazine capacity 10 rounds. Weight 41 oz.

NIB	Exc.	V.G.	Good	Fair	Poor
350	300	220	180	120	100

Mark III 22/45 Hunter

Similar to 22/45 .22 pistol, with Mark III-style improvements. 6.875" or 4.5" fluted barrel, HiViz front sight, with six interchangeable inserts. Blued or stainless finish. Pricing is for stainless model. Introduced in 2007.

NIB	Exc.	V.G.	Good	Fair	Poor
460	400	300	220	150	100

Mark III 22/45 Pistol

Semi-automatic pistol chambered in .22 LR. Features include polymer frame with grip panels that recreate feel of 1911; 1911-style controls including magazine button, manual safety and bolt stop locations as classic 1911 pistol; slim polymer grip frame with serrated frontstrap and checkered backstrap; blued alloy steel 5.5" bull barrel with fixed front sight and micro-adjustable rear sight; adjustable sights drilled/tapped for Weaver mounts. Weight 31 oz. Offered in several variations including 22/45 Lite with weight of 23 oz., 4.4" stainless steel threaded barrel. Add $25 for Lite and threaded barrel variants. Introduced in 2013.

NIB	Exc.	V.G.	Good	Fair	Poor
420	380	300	260	240	200

MARK IV SERIES

Introduced in 2016, the Mark IV series of Ruger's Standard .22 pistol involved a significant design change, which made takedown and reassembly quick and easy, via a hinged connection between the upper receiver and grip frame.

MK IV Standard

Similar to the Mark III but with the improved hinged design and quick push-button takedown. 4.75" or 6" tapered barrel. Weight 28.2-30.1 oz. Blued finish.

NIB	Exc.	V.G.	Good	Fair	Poor
450	380	300	280	200	180

MK IV Target

Latest evolution of Standard Model and successor of Mark III series. Major difference is an improved take-down system. A button on rear of grip frame just below the receiver is pressed and barrel/receiver assembly tilts downward at muzzle until bolt stop pin is cleared. Barrel/receiver assembly can then be lifted away from grip frame and bolt can be removed. Most other features of Mark IV are the same as Mark III. Introduced in 2016.

NIB	Exc.	V.G.	Good	Fair	Poor
530	460	400	340	280	260

MK IV Competition

This variant has a 6.88" slabsided bull barrel, adjustable rear sight, satin stainless finish and checkered laminate grips with thumbrest. Introduced in 2017. Hunter model has 6.88" fluted barrel, fiber-optic sight. Note: Add $50 for Hunter model.

NIB	Exc.	V.G.	Good	Fair	Poor
750	640	560	490	440	300

MK IV Hunter

Similar to the Mark IV Competition model. 6.75" fluted barrel. Weight 44 oz. Satin stainless finish.

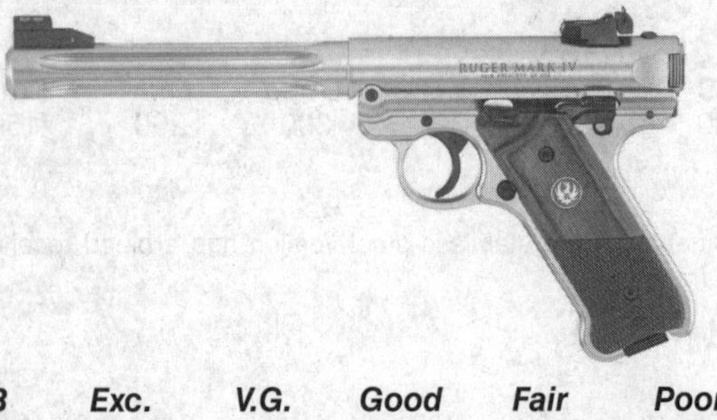

NIB	Exc.	V.G.	Good	Fair	Poor
770	660	580	500	300	260

MK IV Tactical

Similar to the Mark IV Hunter. 4.4" threaded barrel. Weight 34.6 oz. Blued finish.

NIB	Exc.	V.G.	Good	Fair	Poor
570	490	430	370	260	240

MK IV 22/45 Lite

Polymer grip frame with 1911-style grip, 4.5" threaded bull barrel, adjustable rear sight. Receiver is ventilated for lighter weight and made of aerospace-grade aluminum, with bronze or black anodized finish. Standard 22/45 model has 5.5" barrel, alloy steel receiver. Introduced in 2017. Note: Deduct $100 for Standard 22/45 model.

NIB	Exc.	V.G.	Good	Fair	Poor
560	480	420	360	300	240

MK IV 22/45 Tactical

Similar to above. 4.4" threaded barrel. Weight 33.3 oz. Blued finish.

NIB	Exc.	V.G.	Good	Fair	Poor
540	460	400	340	280	230

CHARGER SERIES

Charger

A 10" barrel pistol version of 10/22 .22 LR rifle. Black matte finish, black laminated stock (other colors available), bipod and Weaver-style mounts. Includes one 10-round magazine. Introduced in 2008; discontinued 2012.

NIB	Exc.	V.G.	Good	Fair	Poor
380	300	220	180	120	100

Charger — New Model

New variation of Charger design offers improved ergonomics, new features and new BX-15 magazine. Take-down model has all features of standard model plus quick disconnect feature found on 10/22 Take-down rifle. Choice of brown or Green Mountain laminate stock. Introduced in 2015. Note: Add $100 for Green Mountain.

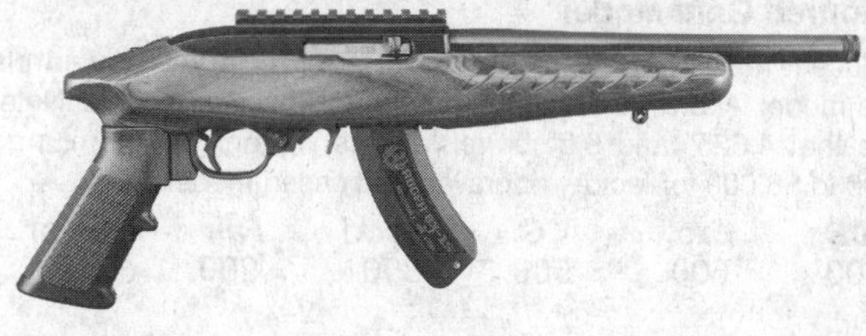

NIB	Exc.	V.G.	Good	Fair	Poor
310	270	240	200	150	100

PC Charger

Caliber: 9mm. Capacity: 17-round magazine. Barrel: Threaded 6.5". Grips: AR-15 A2 style. Sights: Optic-ready, Picatinny-style rail. Length: 16.5" overall. Weight: 5.2 lbs. unloaded. Finish: Blued. Features: Pistol version of the Ruger PC Carbine with a glass-filled polymer chassis system and M-LOK rail. Easy takedown system separates barrel/forend assembly from the action, and interchangeable magazine wells for Ruger American, Ruger Security-9 or Glock magazines. Made in the USA.

NIB	Exc.	V.G.	Good	Fair	Poor
650	530	450	—	—	—

OLD MODEL SINGLE-ACTION REVOLVERS (PRE-TRANSFER BAR)

Single Six Revolver

A .22 rimfire 6-shot single-action revolver. First offered with 5.5" barrel length and fixed sight. In 1959, additional barrel lengths were offered in 4.625", 6.5" and 9.5". Based in appearance on Colt Single-Action Army, but internally a new design that features coil springs instead of old-style flat leaf springs. Also features a floating firing pin and is generally a stronger action than what was previously available. Early model had a flat loading gate and was made this way from 1953-1957, when the contoured gate became standard. Early models had checkered hard rubber grips; changed to smooth varnished walnut by 1962. Black eagle grip medallions were used from the beginning of production to 1971, when a silver eagle grip medallion replaced it. No "Red Eagle" single-sixes were ever produced. Manufactured from 1953-1972.

Flat Gate Model

60,000 produced. Be aware that revolvers serial numbered under 2000 will bring a premium of 25% to 125% depending on condition, low serial number, and color of cylinder frame — bright reddish-purple is the most desirable. Values cited below are for unconverted examples and for converted examples with original parts present.

Courtesy John C. Dougan

NIB	Exc.	V.G.	Good	Fair	Poor
900	700	500	450	220	150

Contoured Gate Model

Introduced 1957. There were 258 5.5" barrel factory engraved pistols in this model. Add a 25 percent premium for 3-screw models. Note: Be aware that 4.625" and 9.5" barrel lengths will bring a premium. Add $3,500 to $6,000 for factory engraved and cased models.

NIB	Exc.	V.G.	Good	Fair	Poor
700	600	500	350	200	120

Single Six Convertible

Similar to Single Six, but furnished with an extra .22 rimfire Magnum cylinder. Barrel lengths in 4.625" and 9.5" will bring a premium.

NIB	Exc.	V.G.	Good	Fair	Poor
650	550	450	380	220	150

Single Six .22 Magnum Model

Similar to Single Six, except chambered for .22 rimfire Magnum and frame was so marked. Offered in 6.5" barrel length only. Manufactured for three years. An extra long rifle cylinder was added later in production. Serial numbers are in 300000-340000 range.

NIB	Exc.	V.G.	Good	Fair	Poor
600	500	400	350	200	120

Lightweight Single Six

Similar to Single Six, with aluminum alloy frame and 4.625" barrel. Variation produced between 1956 and 1958. Serial number range 200000-212000. Approximately first 6,500 produced with alloy cylinders and steel chamber inserts. Note: An "S" will be found following the serial number or on bottom of frame. Individual evaluation and appraisal recommended. These are factory seconds and are verifiable. Add 25% to 40% for original Lightweight Single Six boxes.

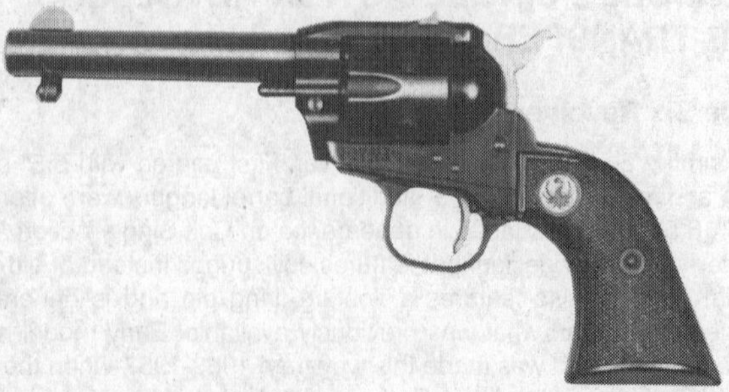

Courtesy Know Your Ruger Single-Action Revolvers 1953-63, Blacksmith Corp.

Silver Anodized Frame with Aluminum Cylinder Model with Martin Hardcoat Finish

NIB	Exc.	V.G.	Good	Fair	Poor
1500	1100	900	750	500	300

Black Anodized Aluminum Frame and Cylinder Model

NIB	Exc.	V.G.	Good	Fair	Poor
1100	950	700	600	350	250

Black Anodized Frame with Blue Steel Cylinder Model

NIB	Exc.	V.G.	Good	Fair	Poor
950	800	600	500	300	200

Silver Anodized Aluminum Frame with Blue Steel Cylinder and "S" Marking

Only a few hundred pistols, in this variation, were produced by the factory with an S" suffix.

NIB	Exc.	V.G.	Good	Fair	Poor
1600	1200	900	750	500	300

Super Single Six

Introduced in 1964. Single Six with adjustable sights. Prices listed for pistols with 5.5" and 6.5" barrels. Listed models are factory verifiable.

Courtesy Know Your Ruger Single-Actions: The Second Decade. Blacksmith Corp.

NIB	Exc.	V.G.	Good	Fair	Poor
600	500	400	350	200	120

4-5/8" Barrel

200 built.

NIB	Exc.	V.G.	Good	Fair	Poor
1750	1500	1200	900	500	250

Nickel-Plated Model

Approximately 100 built.

NIB	Exc.	V.G.	Good	Fair	Poor
2350	1900	1600	1200	600	300

Bearcat (Old Model)

Scaled-down version of single-action. Chambered for .22 rimfire. Has 4" barrel and unfluted roll engraved cylinder. Frame is alloy and has a brass colored anodized alloy triggerguard. Finish is blue and grips are plastic impregnated wood until 1963, thereafter, walnut with eagle medallions were used. Manufactured from 1958-1970. Note: Add $150 to $200 premium for a serial number under 30000; $350 for black anodized triggerguard; 20% for alphabet prefix serial number.

Courtesy Know Your Ruger Single-Actions: The Second Decade. Blacksmith Corp.

NIB	Exc.	V.G.	Good	Fair	Poor
450	350	300	260	220	180

Super Bearcat (Old Model)

Similar to Bearcat, with a steel frame. Later models a blued steel triggerguard and grip frame. Early examples still used brass. Manufactured from 1971 to 1974.

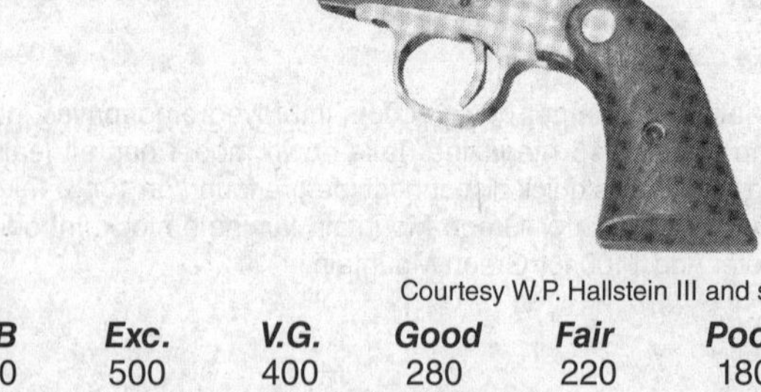

Courtesy W.P. Hallstein III and son Chip

NIB	Exc.	V.G.	Good	Fair	Poor
580	500	400	280	220	180

Flattop—.357 Magnum

Success of Single Six led to production of a larger version chambered for .357 Magnum cartridge. This model is a single-action, with 6-shot fluted cylinder and flattop strap with adjustable "Micro sight". Barrel length 4.625", 6.5" and 10". Finish blue, with checkered hard rubber grips on early examples and smooth walnut on later ones. Approximately 42,600 manufactured between 1955 and 1962.

4-5/8" Barrel

NIB	*Exc.*	*V.G.*	*Good*	*Fair*	*Poor*
1200	1000	600	350	250	200

6-1/2" Barrel

NIB	*Exc.*	*V.G.*	*Good*	*Fair*	*Poor*
1000	850	600	450	350	250

10" Barrel

NIB	*Exc.*	*V.G.*	*Good*	*Fair*	*Poor*
2800	2500	1000	850	750	600

Blackhawk Flattop .44 Magnum

In 1956, the .44 Magnum was introduced and Ruger jumped on the bandwagon. Similar in appearance to .357, but has a slightly heavier frame and larger cylinder. Available in 6.5", 7.5" and 10" barrel. Manufactured from 1956-1963. Approximately 29,700 manufactured.

6-1/2" Barrel

NIB	*Exc.*	*V.G.*	*Good*	*Fair*	*Poor*
1500	1100	850	450	350	250

7-1/2" Barrel

NIB	*Exc.*	*V.G.*	*Good*	*Fair*	*Poor*
2400	1700	1100	600	450	300

10" Barrel

NIB	*Exc.*	*V.G.*	*Good*	*Fair*	*Poor*
3200	2500	1500	800	700	400

Blackhawk

Similar to "Flattop", but rear sight is protected by two raised protrusions — one on each side. Available chambered for .30 Carbine, .357 Magnum, .41 Magnum or .45 Colt cartridge. Barrel lengths: 4.625" or 6.5" in .357 Magnum and .41 Magnum; 4.625" or 7.5" in .45 Colt; 7.5" only in .30 Carbine. Finish blue and grips are walnut, with Ruger medallions. Produced from 1962 to 1972. Note that "Old Style" Blackhawk (i.e., pre-transfer bar) is a popular platform for custom revolvers, so prices may exceed those shown depending on circumstances. Note: Add 20% for .41 Magnum; 50% for .45 Colt; 35% for .30 Carbine. Original verified factory brass grip frame will add at least $1,000 to prices below. It was available chambered for .357 Magnum or .41 Magnum (4.625" or 6.5" barrel), or .45 Colt (4.625" or 7.5" barrel). The .41 Magnum with factory brass frame and 6 1/2-inch barrel will bring $2,000 to $3,000. With a 4 5/8-inch barrel, it could bring $4,000 to $5,000. These values assume excellent or NIB condition.

Courtesy Know Your Ruger Single-Action Revolvers 1953-63. Blacksmith Corp.

NIB	*Exc.*	*V.G.*	*Good*	*Fair*	*Poor*
700	500	350	200	150	120

Blackhawk Convertible

Same as Blackhawk, with an extra cylinder to change or convert calibers. The .357 Magnum has a 9mm cylinder; .45 Colt a .45 ACP cylinder. Note: The 4.625" barrel will bring a slight premium. Non-prefix serial numbered .357/9mm Blackhawks will bring a premium.

.357/9mm

NIB	*Exc.*	*V.G.*	*Good*	*Fair*	*Poor*
750	650	450	300	200	150

.45 L.C./.45 ACP

NIB	*Exc.*	*V.G.*	*Good*	*Fair*	*Poor*
1250	1100	800	600	400	200

Super Blackhawk Old Model

The formidable recoil of .44 Magnum cartridge was difficult to handle in a revolver, with a small grip such as found on Blackhawk. So, it was decided to produce a larger-framed revolver, with increased size in grip. Rear of triggerguard was squared off and cylinder was left unfluted to increase mass. Offered with 7.5" barrel; 600 6.5" barrel Super Blackhawks were produced by factory error. This model is blued and has smooth walnut grips with medallions. First of these revolvers were offered in a fitted wood case and are rare today. Super Blackhawk was made from 1959-1972. Note: Pistols with verified factory-installed brass grip frame, each example should be appraised. Add $250 for pistols with brass grip frames.

NIB	*Exc.*	*V.G.*	*Good*	*Fair*	*Poor*
800	600	400	300	200	150

Early Model in Wood Presentation Case

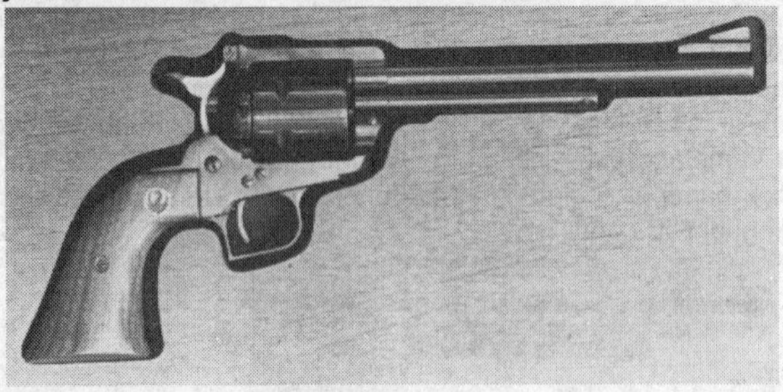

NIB	Exc.	V.G.	Good	Fair	Poor
1200	1000	750	480	400	300

In Fitted White Cardboard Case

NIB	Exc.	V.G.	Good	Fair	Poor
1800	1600	1000	950	880	680

Long Grip Frame in Wood Case

300 guns built.

NIB	Exc.	V.G.	Good	Fair	Poor
2000	1800	1150	1050	800	680

Factory Verified 6-1/2" Barrel

Approximately 600 guns built in 23000-25000 serial number range.

NIB	Exc.	V.G.	Good	Fair	Poor
1500	1300	950	700	450	380

Hawkeye Single-Shot

Shooting public wanted a small-caliber high-velocity handgun. Smith & Wesson Model 53, chambered for .22 Jet, appeared in 1961; cartridge created extraction problems for a revolver. Ruger solved this problem with introduction of Hawkeye — a single-shot that looked like a six shooter. In place of the cylinder was a breech-block that cammed to the side for loading. This pistol was excellent from an engineering and performance standpoint, but was not a commercial success. Hawkeye chambered for .256 Magnum, a bottleneck cartridge and 8.5" barrel and adjustable sights. Finish blued, with walnut medallion grips. Barrel tapped at the factory for a 1" scope base. Pistol is quite rare as only 3,300 were produced in 1963 and 1964.

Courtesy John C. Dougan

NIB	Exc.	V.G.	Good	Fair	Poor
2500	1900	1400	850	600	500

NEW MODEL SINGLE-ACTION REVOLVERS

In 1973, Ruger completely modified its single-action lockwork to accommodate a hammer block or transfer bar. This hammer block or transfer bar prevented accidental discharge, should a revolver be dropped. In doing so, the company circumvented a great deal of potential legal problems and made collectibles out of previous models.

SINGLE-SIX SERIES

Super Single Six Convertible (New Model)

Similar in appearance to old model, but has the new hammer block safety system. Frame has two pins instead of three screws. Opening the loading gate frees cylinder stop for loading. Barrel lengths are 4.625", 5.5", 6.5" and 9.5". Sights are adjustable and finish blued. Grips are walnut, with a medallion. An interchangeable .22 Magnum cylinder is supplied. Introduced in 1973 and currently in production.

NIB	Exc.	V.G.	Good	Fair	Poor
450	350	250	200	180	120

Stainless Steel Single Six Convertible

Same as standard blued model, but made from stainless steel. Offered with 4.625", 6.5" and 9.5" barrel. Note: Add 40% premium for pre-warning pistols (1973-1976) with 4.625" or 9.5" barrel; 100% premium, at least, to NIB prices for pistols with 4.625" barrels with "made in the 200th year of American Liberty" rollmark on the barrel.

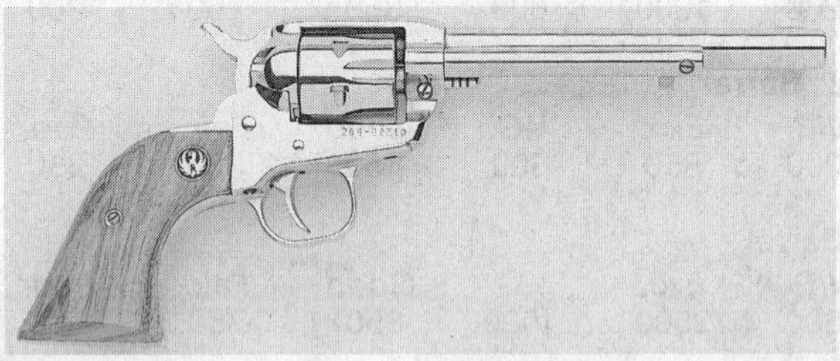

NIB	Exc.	V.G.	Good	Fair	Poor
480	400	300	250	220	180

New Model Single Six (.22 LR only) "Star" Model

Produced in blue and stainless for one year only in 4.625, 5.5", 6.5" and 9.5" barrel lengths. Very low production on this model.

Blue Variation 5.5" or 6.5" Barrel

NIB	Exc.	V.G.	Good	Fair	Poor
450	400	350	300	280	200

9.5" Barrel—Rare

NIB	Exc.	V.G.	Good	Fair	Poor
550	500	450	400	350	250

4.62" Barrel—Very Rare

NIB	Exc.	V.G.	Good	Fair	Poor
800	750	450	400	350	250

Stainless Variation 5.5" or 6.5" Barrel

NIB	Exc.	V.G.	Good	Fair	Poor
450	350	280	220	180	150

9.5" Barrel

NIB	Exc.	V.G.	Good	Fair	Poor
600	500	400	300	220	180

4.62" Barrel—Rare

NIB	Exc.	V.G.	Good	Fair	Poor
650	550	500	400	300	200

Fixed Sight New Model Single Six

First made as drift adjustable rear sight (500 each in 4.625", 5.5" and 6.5" blue); and now a catalogued item as a pinched frame style fixed rear sight. Barrel lengths offered in 5.5" and 6.5" lengths. Finish blued or glossy stainless steel. Rear sight fixed. Weights between 32 and 38 oz. depending on barrel length and cylinder.

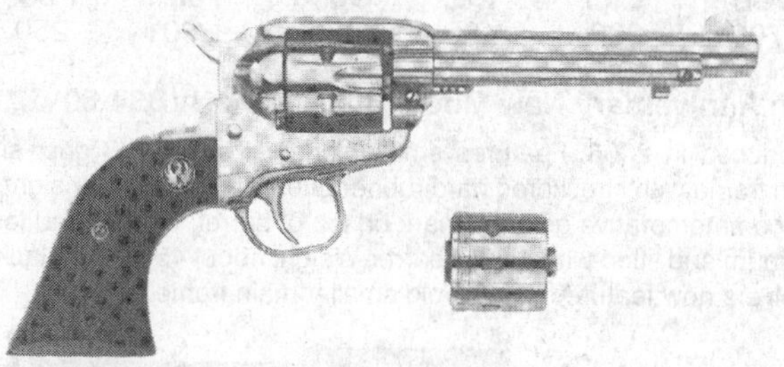

Blued Finish

NIB	Exc.	V.G.	Good	Fair	Poor
580	450	350	160	120	100

Stainless Steel

NIB	Exc.	V.G.	Good	Fair	Poor
500	400	300	200	150	120

Colorado Centennial Single Six

A stainless steel grip frame and balance blued. Walnut grips, with medallion insert. Barrel 6.5". Furnished with a walnut case with a centennial medal insert. Manufactured 15,000 in 1975.

NIB	Exc.	V.G.	Good	Fair	Poor
500	400	300	200	120	100

Model "SSM" Single Six

Single Six chambered for .32 H&R Magnum cartridge. First 800 pistols marked with SSM" on cylinder frame and will bring a slight premium. Sold from 1984 to 1997. Adjustable sights.

NIB	Exc.	V.G.	Good	Fair	Poor
700	520	380	220	150	120

New Model Single Six .32 H&R

Introduced in 2000. Revolver chambered for .32 H&R Magnum cartridge. Fitted with 4.625" barrel. Offered in blue or stainless steel. Short (.250" shorter) simulated ivory grips. Vaquero-style frame, with fixed sights. Values shown are for stainless. Note: Deduct 25% for blued.

NIB	Exc.	V.G.	Good	Fair	Poor
520	400	300	220	180	120

New Model Single Six 50th Anniversary Model

Introduced in 2003. Features 4.625" barrel, with blued finish. Top of barrel rollmarked "50 YEARS OF SINGLE SIX 1953 TO 2003". Comes standard with both .22 LR and .22 WMR cylinders. Cocobolo grips, with red Ruger medallion. Packaged in a red plastic case, with special "50 Year" label. Offered only in 2003.

NIB	Exc.	V.G.	Good	Fair	Poor
420	350	300	220	180	120

New Model Super Single Six

Chambered for .22 LR and a separate cylinder for .22 WMR cartridge. Barrel lengths 4.625", 5.5", 6.5" and 9.5". Rosewood grips. Adjustable or fixed sights. Blued finish, except optional stainless steel on 5.5" or 6.5" revolvers. Weight 35 oz. depending on barrel length. Note: Add $80 for stainless steel model.

NIB	Exc.	V.G.	Good	Fair	Poor
380	320	280	220	180	120

New Model Super Single Six, .17 HMR

As above, with 6.5" barrel. Chambered for .17 HMR cartridge. Weight 35 oz. Introduced in 2003.

NIB	Exc.	V.G.	Good	Fair	Poor
400	350	280	220	180	120

New Model Single Six Hunter Convertible

Chambered for .17 HMR/.17 Mach 2. Fitted with 7.5" barrel, with adjustable rear sight. Stainless steel finish, with black laminate grips. Integral barrel rib machined for scope rings. Weight 45 oz. Introduced in 2005.

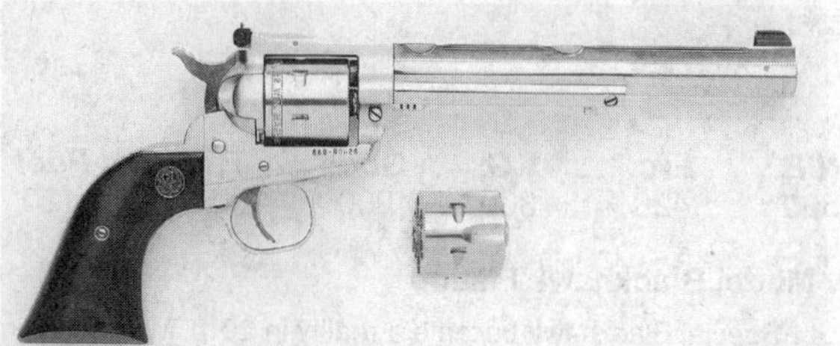

NIB	Exc.	V.G.	Good	Fair	Poor
680	500	400	300	250	180

Single-Ten

10-shot version of Single Six, with 5.5" barrel and walnut Gunfighter grips. Other features include satin stainless finish and Williams adjustable fiber-optic sights. Introduced in late 2011. A 9-shot variation with 6.5" barrel introduced in 2013 as Single-Nine.

NIB	Exc.	V.G.	Good	Fair	Poor
520	450	380	300	220	150

Single-Nine

Identical to Single-Ten, except chambered for .22 Win. Magnum rimfire. Has 9-round cylinder.

NIB	Exc.	V.G.	Good	Fair	Poor
520	450	380	300	220	150

Single Seven

Distributor exclusive model (from Lipsey's) is chambered for .327 Federal Magnum cartridge, with a 7-round cylinder. Stainless revolver has 5.5" barrel, adjustable sights and wood grips. Introduced in 2015.

NIB	Exc.	V.G.	Good	Fair	Poor
560	500	420	—	—	—

Buckeye Special

Built in 1989 and 1990. Chambered for .38-40, 10mm, .32-20 or .32 H&R cartridges.

NIB	Exc.	V.G.	Good	Fair	Poor
750	600	400	280	200	120

NEW MODEL BLACKHAWK SERIES

New Model Blackhawk

Similar in appearance to old model Blackhawk. Offered in same calibers and barrel lengths. Has transfer bar safety device. Introduced in 1973. Chambered in .30 Carbine, .357 Magnum, .41 Magnum and .45 Colt. Various barrel lengths.

NIB	Exc.	V.G.	Good	Fair	Poor
500	420	300	200	150	120

New Model Blackhawk Flattop

The .44 Special Blackhawk became a reality in 2010. Made only in Flattop design, with blue finish and 4.625" or 5.5" barrel.

NIB	Exc.	V.G.	Good	Fair	Poor
500	420	300	200	150	120

New Model Blackhawk Bisley

Based on Colt Bisley frame, with adjustable sights and longer grip frame. Chambered in .44 Magnum or .45 Colt, with 7.5" barrel, blue finish, alloy frame and hardwood grips.

NIB	Exc.	V.G.	Good	Fair	Poor
700	600	480	380	300	250

50th Anniversary New Model Blackhawk NVB34-50

Introduced in 2005. Features smaller original size XR-3 grip, smaller main frame with checkered hard rubber grips. Adjustable rear sight. Special commemorative gold roll mark on top of barrel. Chambered for .357 Magnum and fitted with 4.625" barrel. Weight about 45 oz. All Blackhawk revolvers now feature this new/old smaller main frame.

NIB	Exc.	V.G.	Good	Fair	Poor
580	420	300	200	150	120

Stainless Steel Blackhawk (New Model)

New Model Blackhawk made from stainless steel. To date offered in .357, .44, .45 L.C. and .327 Federal calibers.

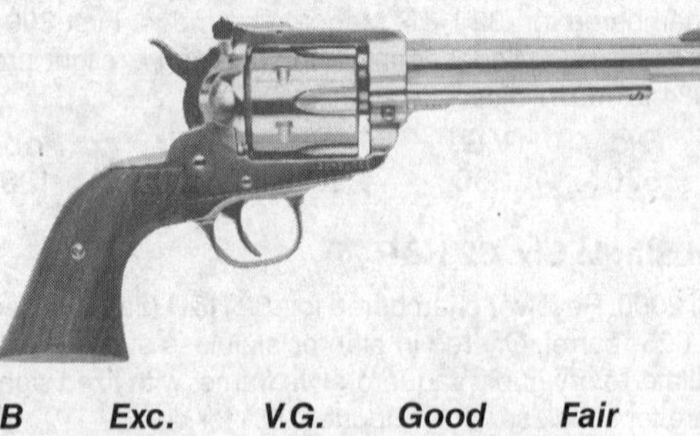

NIB	Exc.	V.G.	Good	Fair	Poor
600	500	420	300	200	150

Blackhawk Convertible (New Model)

Same as Blackhawk, with interchangeable conversion cylinders — .357 Magnum/9mm and .45 Colt/.45 ACP. Prices listed are for blued model.

NIB	Exc.	V.G.	Good	Fair	Poor
460	350	250	180	150	120

.45 ACP & .45 Long Colt Convertible (1998)

NIB	Exc.	V.G.	Good	Fair	Poor
550	450	350	280	220	150

Stainless Model .357/9mm

300 guns built.

NIB	Exc.	V.G.	Good	Fair	Poor
920	700	600	500	380	250

Fiftieth Anniversary .44 Magnum Flattop New Model Blackhawk

Six-shot single-action .44 Magnum (also accepts .44 Special), with 6.5" barrel and adjustable rear sight. Weight 47 oz. Recreation of original .44 Flattop Blackhawk. Blued, with checkered rubber grips. Gold color-filled rollmark on top of barrel. Introduced 2006.

NIB	Exc.	V.G.	Good	Fair	Poor
750	620	520	400	350	300

Model SRM Blackhawk .357 Maximum

This is the New Model Blackhawk, with 7.5" or 10.5" barrel. Chambered for .357 Maximum and intended for silhouette shooting. This model experienced problems with gas erosion in the forcing cone and under the top strap and was removed from production in 1984. Approximately 9200 were manufactured.

NIB	Exc.	V.G.	Good	Fair	Poor
—	680	580	400	280	250

50th Anniversary Matched Set .357 and .44 Magnum

Matched pair of Ruger New Blackhawks, one in .44 and the other in .357, commemorating 50th Anniversary of Ruger Blackhawk revolver. Gold-filled rollmarked 6.5" and 4.625" barrels, respectively. Includes presentation case. Production limited. Introduced 2007.

NIB	Exc.	V.G.	Good	Fair	Poor
1350	1150	900	780	600	400

NEW MODEL SUPER BLACKHAWK SERIES

Super Blackhawk (New Model)

Similar in appearance to Old Model, but has the transfer bar safety device. Manufactured from 1973 to present. Commenced at serial number 81-00001.

NIB	Exc.	V.G.	Good	Fair	Poor
600	550	450	320	250	180

Super Blackhawk Stainless Steel

Same as blued version, but made of stainless steel. In 1998, offered in 4.625" or 7.5" barrels, with hunter grip frame. Laminated grip panels. Note: Add $50 for hunter grip frame and laminated grip panels.

NIB	Exc.	V.G.	Good	Fair	Poor
650	600	500	350	250	180

Super Blackhawk Hunter

Introduced in 2002. This .44 or .41 Magnum features 7.5" barrel, with integral full-length solid rib for scope mounts. Stainless steel. Adjustable rear sight. Scope rings included. Weight 52 oz.

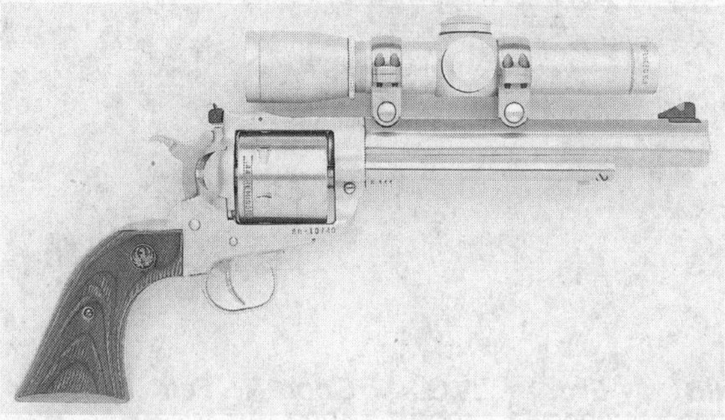

NIB	Exc.	V.G.	Good	Fair	Poor
800	700	500	350	250	180

Bisley Model

This model has the modified features found on famous old Colt Bisley Target model — the flattop frame, fixed or adjustable sights and longer grip frame that has become the Bisley trademark. Bisley is available chambered for .22 LR, .32 H&R Magnum, .357 Magnum, .41 Magnum, .44 Magnum and .45 Long Colt. Barrel lengths 6.5" and 7.5"; cylinders fluted or unfluted and roll engraved. Finish a satin blue, and grips are smooth Goncalo Alves with medallions. Bisley was introduced in 1986. Note: Approximately 750 stainless grip frame .22-caliber Bisleys were made. These will demand a premium. Add $100 for stainless; $125 for convertible stainless.

The Ruger New Model Super Blackhawk Bisley Hunter.

.22 LR and .32 H&R Magnum

Note: Add $100 for .32 Magnum Bisley.

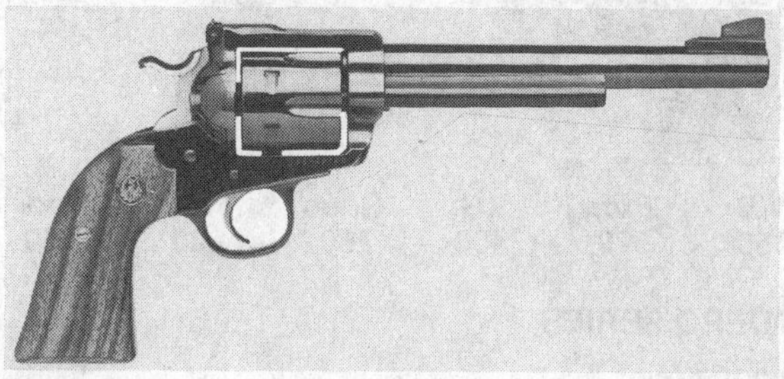

NIB	Exc.	V.G.	Good	Fair	Poor
420	380	220	200	150	120

.357 Magnum, .41 Magnum, .44 Magnum, .45 Colt

NIB	Exc.	V.G.	Good	Fair	Poor
700	600	480	300	200	120

Shootists Bisley

Produced in 1994, for Shootist organization in memory of Tom Ruger. Chambered for .22 cartridge, these revolvers were limited to 52 total produced. Stainless steel and fitted with 4.625" barrels. Barrels marked, "IN MEMORY OF OUR FRIEND TOM RUGER THE SHOOTIST 1994" .

Some of these revolvers, but not all, have name of the owner engraved on backstrap. Due to this model's rarity, values are speculative.

Courtesy Jim Taylor

NIB	Exc.	V.G.	Good	Fair	Poor
2500	2000	1200	1000	—	—

PERCUSSION REVOLVER SERIES

Old Army Percussion Revolver

A .45-caliber percussion revolver, with 5" or 7.5" barrel. Has 6-shot cylinder, with blued finish and walnut grips. Beginning in 1994, this model offered with fixed sights. Weight about 46 oz. All models now discontinued. Note: Add $450 for pistols with original factory-installed brass grip frame; add 20% for 5.5" model.

NIB	Exc.	V.G.	Good	Fair	Poor
580	480	380	250	180	150

Old Army Stainless Steel

Same as blued version, except made of stainless steel. Note: Add 200% for stainless 200th Year model.

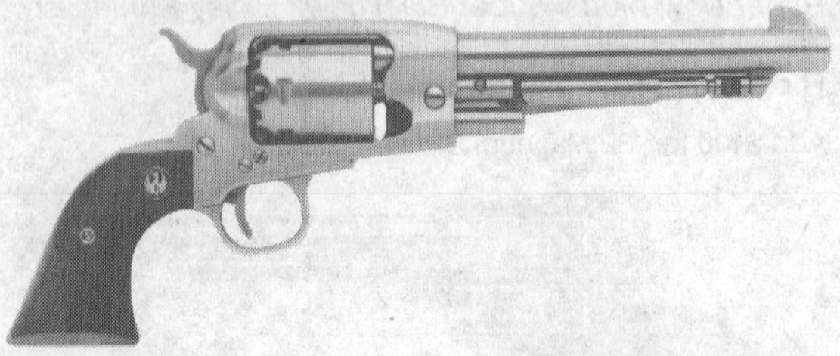

NIB	Exc.	V.G.	Good	Fair	Poor
650	520	400	280	220	150

VAQUERO SERIES

Ruger Vaquero

Single-action pistol introduced in 1993. Voted handgun of the year by the shooting industry. Fixed sight version of New Model Blackhawk. Available in stainless steel or blued, with case-colored frame. Offered in three different barrel lengths: 4.62", 5.5" and 7.5". Chambered for .45 Long Colt. In 1994, .44-40 and .44 Magnum calibers were added to Vaquero line. Capacity 6 rounds. Weight between 39 and 41 oz. depending on barrel length. Discontinued; superseded by New Vaquero. Note: Add 25% for Vaqueros with 4.625" barrel chambered for .44 Magnum in both blue and stainless are un-cataloged.

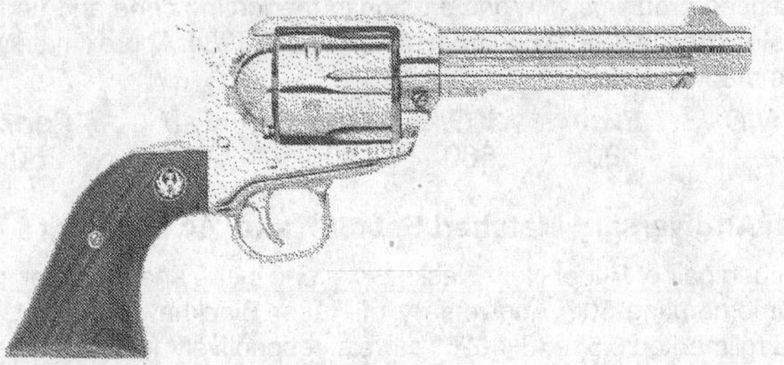

NIB	Exc.	V.G.	Good	Fair	Poor
500	420	320	200	150	100

Ruger Bisley Vaquero

Introduced in 1997. Features 5.5" barrel chambered for .44 Magnum or .45 Long Colt. Grips are smooth rosewood. Finish blued, with case colored frame. Blade front sight and notch rear. Weight 40 oz. Discontinued.

NIB	Exc.	V.G.	Good	Fair	Poor
600	500	420	320	220	150

Ruger Vaquero Birdshead

Introduced in 2001. Features bird's-head grip. Chambered for .45 Long Colt cartridge. Fitted with 5.5" barrel. Offered in stainless steel and blued finish. Weight 40 oz. Discontinued. In 2002, offered with 3.75" barrel and black Micarta grips. In 2003, offered chambered for .357 Magnum cartridge. Simulated ivory grips also offered.

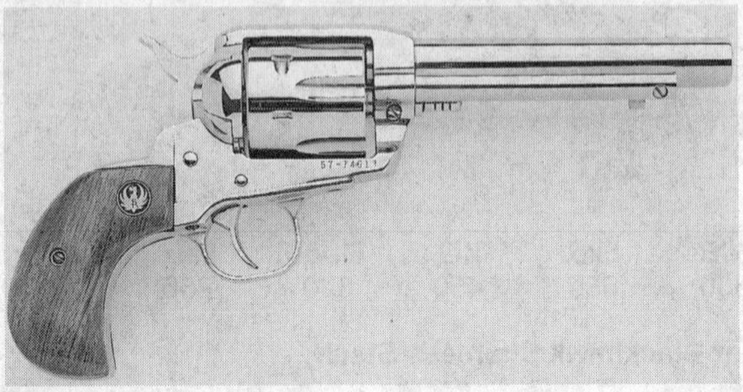

NIB	Exc.	V.G.	Good	Fair	Poor
650	550	400	300	180	120

"Cowboy Pair" Vaqueros

Matched pair of engraved and consecutively serial-numbered New Vaquero revolvers in .45 Colt. Includes lined wood collector case. Production limited to 500 sets. Introduced 2007.

NIB	Exc.	V.G.	Good	Fair	Poor
3500	3000	2500	1350	1000	600

Ruger New Vaquero

Introduced in 2005. Features slimmer pre-1962 XR-3 style grip frame, with color-case finish. Cylinder frame is mid-size. Cylinder is beveled. Ejector rod head is crescent-shaped. Chambered for .357 Magnum or .45 Colt. Barrel lengths 4.625", 5.5" and 7.5" (not in .357). Choice of case-colored finish or stainless steel. Black checkered grips. Weight 37 oz.

NIB	Exc.	V.G.	Good	Fair	Poor
580	480	400	300	200	100

SASS Vaquero Set

Two high-gloss stainless Vaqueros in .357 and/or .45 Colt, with consecutive serial numbers. SASS (Single Action Shooting Society) prefixes.

NIB	Exc.	V.G.	Good	Fair	Poor
1500	1400	1250	1000	—	—

Ruger New Model Bisley Vaquero

Similar to New Vaquero, with Bisley-style hammer and grip frame. Chambered in .357 and .45 Colt. Features include 5.5" barrel, simulated ivory grips, fixed sights, 6-shot cylinder. Overall length 11.12". Weight: 45 oz. Note: Add 15% for stainless steel finish.

NIB	Exc.	V.G.	Good	Fair	Poor
560	420	320	220	160	150

BEARCAT SERIES

New Ruger Bearcat (Super Bearcat)

This old favorite was reintroduced in 1994. Furnished with .22 LR and .22 WMR cylinder. Barrel length 4", with fixed sights. Grips walnut. Offered with blued finish. Note: There was a factory recall on Magnum cylinders. Bearcats with both cylinders are very rare.

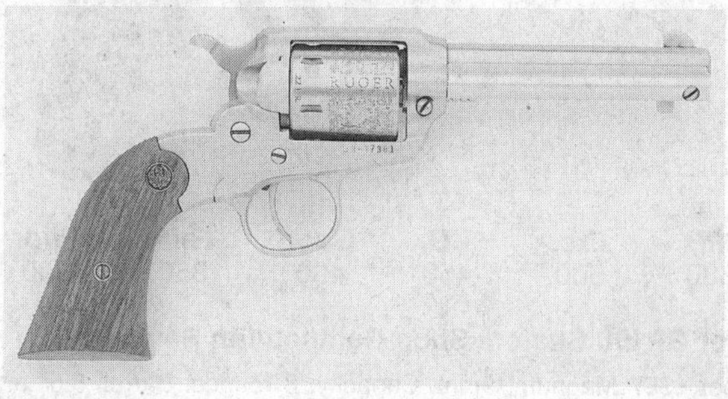

Blue

NIB	Exc.	V.G.	Good	Fair	Poor
420	320	250	180	120	100

Stainless Steel

NIB	Exc.	V.G.	Good	Fair	Poor
450	350	280	200	150	120

Convertible (Recalled)

NIB	Exc.	V.G.	Good	Fair	Poor
1100	1000	900	650	400	200

Adjustable Sights (Lipsey's Exclusive)

NIB	Exc.	V.G.	Good	Fair	Poor
560	500	420	380	320	280

New Model Super Bearcat

Reintroduced in 2002, this .22-caliber features stainless steel or blued finish, 4" barrel with fixed sights and rosewood grips. Weight about 24 oz. Note: Add $50 for stainless steel.

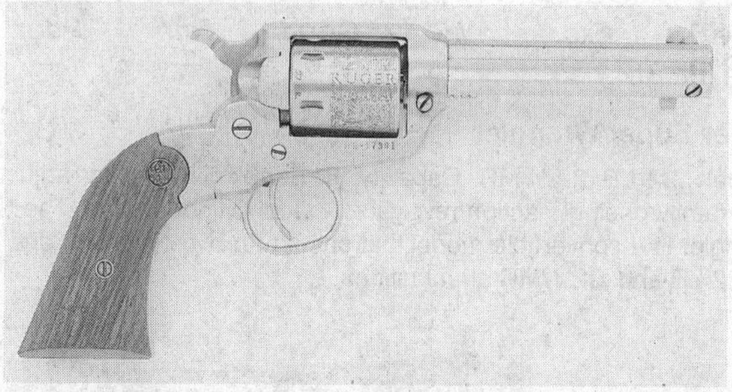

NIB	Exc.	V.G.	Good	Fair	Poor
420	320	250	180	120	100

50th Anniversary New Bearcat

Gussied-up version of New Bearcat (.22 LR only). Commemorating 50th Anniversary of original Bearcat. Blued finish, with gold-filled anniversary script, gold-colored triggerguard. Special box with anniversary booklet. Manufactured in 2008 only.

NIB	Exc.	V.G.	Good	Fair	Poor
700	600	500	—	—	—

WRANGLER SERIES

Wrangler

Caliber: .22 LR. Capacity: 6-round cylinder. Barrel: 3.75", 4.62", 6.5", and 7.5" Grips: Checkered synthetic. Sights: Fixed front and rear. Weight: 30 oz. Features: Inexpensive to own and shoot, this SA revolver is built on an aluminum alloy frame and fitted with a cold hammer-forged barrel. Available in three models with three different Cerakote finishes: Black, silver, or burnt bronze. Equipped with a transfer-bar mechanism and a freewheeling pawl, allowing for easy loading and unloading.

NIB	Exc.	V.G.	Good	Fair	Poor
200	180	150	—	—	—

Wrangler Birdshead

.22 LR, Grips: Birdshead synthetic. Capacity: 6. Front sight: Blade. Barrel length: 3.75". Overall length: 8.62". Weight: 28 oz. Finish: Black Cerakote, silver Cerakote, burnt bronze Cerakote. Cylinder frame material: aluminum alloy. Rear sight: integral. Twist 1:14 in. RH. Grooves: 6.

NIB	Exc.	V.G.	Good	Fair	Poor
210	—	—	—	—	—

Ruger Super Wrangler

Caliber: .22 LR/.22 WMR. Capacity: 6. Barrel: 5.5" Sights: adjustable. New family of single-action revolvers. A steel cylinder frame. The Super Wrangler is a convertible model that ships with two cylinders, one each for .22 LR and .22 WMR ammunition.

NIB	Exc.	V.G.	Good	Fair	Poor
290	—	—	—	—	—

DOUBLE-ACTION REVOLVERS

Security Six

This revolver, also known as Model 117, chambered for .357 Magnum cartridge. Has 2.75", 4", or 6" barrel. Features adjustable sights, with blue or stainless finish and a square butt, with checkered walnut grips. Manufactured between 1970 and 1985. Early guns with fixed sights and square butt were also marked "Security-Six". Later termed "Service-Six" and so marked. Prices listed only for adjustable sight and square butt "Security-Six" models. Note: Fixed sight guns marked "Security-Six" and round butt "Security-Sixes" with adjustable sights worth a premium.

NIB	Exc.	V.G.	Good	Fair	Poor
450	400	350	300	200	150

Speed Six

Known as: Model 207 chambered for .357 Magnum; Model 208 chambered for .38 Special; Model 209 chambered for 9mm. Has 2.75" or 4" barrel, fixed sights, round butt with checkered walnut grips and was blued. Some with factory bobbed hammers. Introduced in 1973; discontinued. Note: Add 200% for military (lanyard ring) and .38 S&W (not .38 Special) marked models.

NIB	Exc.	V.G.	Good	Fair	Poor
400	350	300	250	200	150

Models 737, 738, 739

These are designations for stainless steel versions of Speed Six. Same revolver except for material used in manufacture. Note: Add $150 for 739.

NIB	Exc.	V.G.	Good	Fair	Poor
500	420	350	300	220	120

GP-100

Chambered for .327 Federal or .357 Magnum/.38 Special. Available with fixed or adjustable sights. Barrel lengths 3", 4", or 6". Frame designed for constant use of heavy magnum loads. Rear sight has a white outline. Front sight features interchangeable colored inserts. Finish blued. Grips are a new design made of rubber, with smooth Goncalo Alves inserts. Introduced in 1986.

NIB	Exc.	V.G.	Good	Fair	Poor
650	500	350	250	150	100

GP-100 Stainless

Same as GP-100, except material used is stainless steel. A .44 Special model with 3" barrel, fixed sights, 5-round cylinder was introduced in 2017. A 10-shot model in .22 LR was introduced in 2016. Seven-round .327 and .357 models were introduced in 2018. Add $100 for 7-round models. Add $25 for .44 Special model.

NIB	Exc.	V.G.	Good	Fair	Poor
700	600	500	400	300	250

GP-100 Match Champion

This .357 Magnum has a slab-sided half-lug 4.2" barrel. Novak Lo-Mount rear and green fiber-optic front sights. Stainless finish. Hogue hardwood grips, with stippled sides. Introduced in 2014. Note: Add $40 for fixed sights.

NIB	Exc.	V.G.	Good	Fair	Poor
580	500	450	400	350	300

Super GP100 Custom Shop Competition Revolver

Caliber: .357 Magnum, 9mm. Capacity: 8 rounds. Barrel: 5.5" and 6". Grip: Hogue hand-finished hardwood. Sights: Adjustable rear, fiber-optic front. Weight: 47 oz., 45.6 oz. Features: Designed for competition, the new Super GP100 is essentially a Super Redhawk with the frame extension removed and replaced by a shrouded, cold hammer-forged barrel. The Super GP utilizes the superior action of the Super Redhawk. The high-strength stainless steel cylinder has a PVD finish and is extensively fluted for weight reduction. Comes with high-quality, impact-resistant case.

NIB	Exc.	V.G.	Good	Fair	Poor
1160	—	—	—	—	—

SP-101

Similar in appearance to GP-100, but has a smaller frame. Chambered for .22 LR (6-shot), .38 Special (5-shot), .357 Magnum (5-shot), 9mm (5-shot). Grips are all black synthetic. Sights adjustable for windage. Barrel lengths 2" or 3". Construction of stainless steel. Introduced in 1989. 6" barrel available for .22 caliber. .327 Federal Magnum chambering added 2008. Note: Add $100 for Crimson Trace Lasergrips (limited edition for 2008).

NIB	Exc.	V.G.	Good	Fair	Poor
520	420	300	200	150	120

SP-101 Spurless-Hammer

Introduced in 1993. Features SP-101, without exposed hammer spur. Available in two calibers: .38 Special; .357 Magnum, with 2.25" barrel. Double-action revolver has fixed sights. Holds 5 rounds. Weight 26 oz.

NIB	Exc.	V.G.	Good	Fair	Poor
550	450	320	220	150	120

Redhawk

Large frame double-action revolver. Chambered for .357 and .41 Magnums until 1992; .44 Magnum until discontinued in 2009. Barrel lengths 5.5" and 7.5". Finish blued and grips are smooth walnut. Redhawk introduced in 1979. Note: Add 100% for .357 mag.; add 50% for .41 mag.

NIB	Exc.	V.G.	Good	Fair	Poor
650	500	420	350	250	150

Redhawk Stainless Steel

Same as blued version, except constructed of stainless steel. Chambered for .357 Magnum until 1985; .41 Magnum until 1992; and currently for .44 Magnum. In 1998, offered chambered for .45 Long Colt cartridge. Barrel lengths 4", 5.5", and 7.5". Temporarily discontinued in 2013, but back in production in 2014. Note: Add 100% for .357 mag.; add 50% for .41 mag.

NIB	Exc.	V.G.	Good	Fair	Poor
800	680	520	400	300	200

Redhawk 4" .45 Colt (2008)

Similar to original stainless Redhawk, but in .45 Colt only, with 4" barrel. Hogue molded grips.

NIB	Exc.	V.G.	Good	Fair	Poor
800	700	600	450	300	200

Redhawk .45 ACP/.45 Colt

An all stainless steel model, with 4.2" barrel, checkered hardwood grips, adjustable rear and red ramp front sights. Chambered for both .45 ACP and .45 Colt ammunition. Uses half-moon clips, three included. Introduced in 2016.

NIB	Exc.	V.G.	Good	Fair	Poor
950	800	700	—	—	—

Redhawk .357 Magnum

An 8-shot .357 Magnum, with stainless finish, cylinder relieved for full-moon clips (three included), round butt frame, smooth hardwood grips and fixed sights. Introduced in 2017.

NIB	*Exc.*	*V.G.*	*Good*	*Fair*	*Poor*
900	800	700	—	—	—

Super Redhawk

A larger version of the Redhawk. Weight 53 oz. Offered with 7.5" or 9.5" barrel. Made of stainless steel, with brushed or dull gray finish. Barrel rib milled to accept Ruger scope-ring system. Grips are combination rubber and Goncalo Alves-type found on GP-100. Introduced in 1987. In 1999, offered in .454 Casull cartridge, with 7.5" or 9.5" barrel. In 2001, offered in .480 Ruger caliber in 7.5" or 9.5" barrel. Also available in .44 Magnum. Note: Add $200 for .454 Casull or .480 Ruger caliber. Revolvers chambered for .454 Casull also accept .45 Long Colt cartridges.

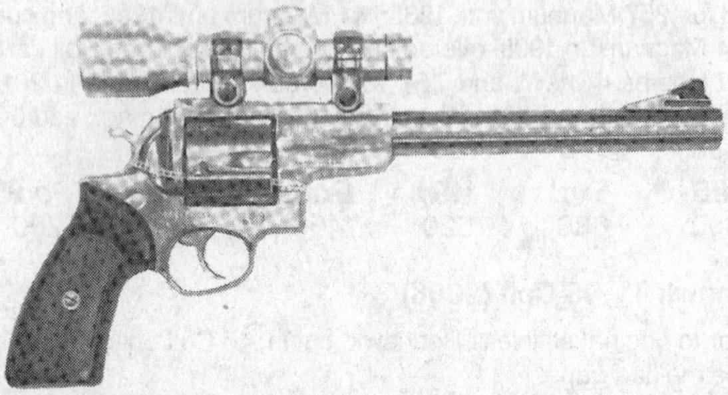

NIB	*Exc.*	*V.G.*	*Good*	*Fair*	*Poor*
740	550	400	280	200	150

Super Redhawk Alaskan

Chambered for .454 Casull and .45 Colt interchangeable or .480 Ruger cartridge. Barrel length 2.5", with adjustable rear sight. Cylinder capacity 6 rounds. Stainless steel finish. Hogue Tamer rubber grips. Weight about 42 oz. Introduced in 2005. .44 Magnum chambering added 2007.

NIB	*Exc.*	*V.G.*	*Good*	*Fair*	*Poor*
850	700	500	380	250	200

Police Service-Six

Also known as: Model 107 chambered for .357 Magnum; Model 108 chambered for .38 Special; Model 109 chambered for 9mm. Barrel 2.75", or 4". A few 6" barrel Service-Sixes also produced and these are worth a premium. Has fixed sights and square butt, with checkered walnut grips. Finish blued. 9mm discontinued in 1984; other two calibers in 1988. Note: Add 60% for 9mm.

NIB	*Exc.*	*V.G.*	*Good*	*Fair*	*Poor*
420	350	300	200	150	100

Model 707 and 708

Designation for stainless versions of Police Service-Six. Not produced in 9mm and only 4" barrel offered. Discontinued in 1988.

NIB	*Exc.*	*V.G.*	*Good*	*Fair*	*Poor*
450	380	300	200	150	100

LCR Lightweight Compact Revolver

Polymer-frame compact revolver chambered in .22 LR, 9mm, .38 Special and .357 Magnum. Features include 5-shot stainless steel cylinder finished in Advanced Target Gray, 1.875" stainless steel barrel, fixed sights, Hogue or Crimson Trace grips, matte black frame. Overall length 6.5". Weight 13 oz. Note: Add $75 for .357 Magnum; $200 for Crimson Trace Lasergrips.

NIB	*Exc.*	*V.G.*	*Good*	*Fair*	*Poor*
420	350	250	200	150	100

LCRX

Same basic design as LCR model, except for visible external hammer. Available with 1.875" or 3" barrel (shown), with Crimson Trace Lasergrips. Note: Add $60 for 9mm or .357; add $280 for Lasergrips.

NIB	*Exc.*	*V.G.*	*Good*	*Fair*	*Poor*
460	400	350	300	250	180

SEMI-AUTOMATIC CENTERFIRE HANDGUNS

P-85

Ruger's entry into the "wonder-nine" market. While it was announced in 1985, it was 1987 before it went into production. The first of a series of "P" model Ruger pistols, which remained in production through 2013. Also, first Ruger firearm manufactured at Prescott, Arizona plant. A very successful moderately priced double-action high-capacity 9mm pistol, at a time when law enforcement and much of the civilian market was embracing this type of pistol. Original model had a matte black finish, black synthetic grips, alloy frame and steel slide. Other features were 4.5" barrel, fixed three-dot sights and ambidextrous safety. Note: As of 2013, all P-series pistols had been discontinued.

NIB	Exc.	V.G.	Good	Fair	Poor
400	360	300	280	200	150

KP85

Same as matte black version, except receiver assembly made of stainless steel.

NIB	Exc.	V.G.	Good	Fair	Poor
420	380	320	300	200	150

KP89X

Introduced in 1993. Features stainless steel convertible safety model, which comes with both 9mm and .30 Luger barrels. Barrels are interchangeable, without the use of tools. Magazine capacity 15 rounds. Fewer than 6,000 produced.

NIB	Exc.	V.G.	Good	Fair	Poor
500	400	340	240	200	150

P89

Introduced in 1991. Semi-automatic pistol chambered for 9mm cartridge. Blued finish and 15-round magazine. Safety is a manual ambidextrous lever type. Barrel 4.5". Empty weight 36 oz.

NIB	Exc.	V.G.	Good	Fair	Poor
420	350	300	220	150	100

KP89

Same configuration as P89, but furnished with stainless steel finish. Introduced in 1991.

NIB	Exc.	V.G.	Good	Fair	Poor
450	380	320	250	150	100

P89DC

Features a blued finish. Chambered for 9mm Parabellum cartridge. Fitted with a decock-only lever (no manual safety). After decocking, the gun can be fired by a double-action pull of the trigger.

NIB	Exc.	V.G.	Good	Fair	Poor
420	380	350	250	200	150

KP89DC

Stainless steel version of P89DC, with decock-only.

NIB	Exc.	V.G.	Good	Fair	Poor
450	380	320	250	150	100

KP89DAO

Chambered for 9mm cartridge. Stainless steel double-action-only version of above model.

NIB	Exc.	V.G.	Good	Fair	Poor
450	380	320	250	150	100

KP90

Chambered for .45 ACP cartridge. Stainless steel. Magazine holds 7 rounds. Fitted with a manual safety. Introduced in 1991.

NIB	Exc.	V.G.	Good	Fair	Poor
500	450	380	280	220	150

KP90DC

Stainless steel version of KP90, with decock-only system. Chambered for .45 ACP cartridge.

NIB	Exc.	V.G.	Good	Fair	Poor
500	450	380	280	220	150

P90

Same as above model, with blued finish. Introduced in 1998.

NIB	Exc.	V.G.	Good	Fair	Poor
480	420	350	280	220	150

KP91DC

Features stainless steel finish. Chambered for .40 S&W cartridge. Magazine capacity 11 rounds. Has a decock-only system. Introduced in 1992; discontinued.

NIB	Exc.	V.G.	Good	Fair	Poor
480	380	320	300	200	150

KP91DAO

Chambered for .40 S&W, with stainless steel finish. Features double-action-only system. Discontinued.

NIB	Exc.	V.G.	Good	Fair	Poor
480	380	320	300	200	150

P93D

Blued version, with ambidextrous decocker and 3.9" barrel. Introduced in 1998.

NIB	Exc.	V.G.	Good	Fair	Poor
400	300	250	200	150	100

KP93DC

Introduced in 1993, as a compact stainless steel model. Chambered for 9mm cartridge. Magazine capacity 15 rounds. Available in decock-only configuration. Barrel length 3.9". Weight 24 oz. empty.

NIB	Exc.	V.G.	Good	Fair	Poor
480	420	350	280	220	150

KP93DAO

Double-action-only version of KP93 compact series.

NIB	Exc.	V.G.	Good	Fair	Poor
480	420	350	280	220	150

KP94

Introduced in 1994. This model is smaller than full-size "P" series and compact P93 pistols. Offered in 9mm or .40 S&W calibers. Has an aluminum alloy frame and stainless steel slide. Barrel length 4.25". Magazine capacity: 9mm 15 rounds; .40 S&W 11 rounds. Weight 33 oz. Offered in double-action-only and traditional double-action. Decock-only model also available.

NIB	Exc.	V.G.	Good	Fair	Poor
420	350	300	250	200	150

KP94DC

Similar to model above in decock-only.

NIB	Exc.	V.G.	Good	Fair	Poor
420	350	300	250	200	150

P94

Blued version of KP94. Introduced in 1998.

NIB	Exc.	V.G.	Good	Fair	Poor
400	300	250	200	150	100

KP94DAO

Same as KP94, but in double-action-only.

NIB	Exc.	V.G.	Good	Fair	Poor
400	350	300	250	200	150

KP944

Chambered for .40 S&W cartridge. Has a stainless steel tapered slide, 11-round magazine and manual safety. Models made after September, 1994 have a 10-round magazine.

NIB	Exc.	V.G.	Good	Fair	Poor
450	400	350	280	220	150

KP944DC

Same as above, with decock-only system.

NIB	Exc.	V.G.	Good	Fair	Poor
450	400	350	280	220	150

KP944DAO

Same as model above in double-action-only.

NIB	Exc.	V.G.	Good	Fair	Poor
450	400	350	280	220	150

P95

Introduced in 1996. This 9mm pistol features 3.9" barrel, polymer frame and stainless steel slide. Decocker-only. Fixed 3-dot sights are standard. Overall length 7.3". Empty weight about 29 oz. In 2001, offered with a manual safety and blued finish.

NIB	Exc.	V.G.	Good	Fair	Poor
450	350	300	220	150	100

KP95DC

Same as matte black version of P95, only in stainless steel. Has a decock-only lever.

NIB	Exc.	V.G.	Good	Fair	Poor
450	350	300	220	150	100

P95DAO

Same as above in double-action-only.

NIB	Exc.	V.G.	Good	Fair	Poor
450	350	300	220	150	100

KP95DAO

Same as model above in double-action-only. In 2001, offered with a manual safety and blued finish.

NIB	Exc.	V.G.	Good	Fair	Poor
450	350	300	220	150	100

KP97D

Introduced in 1999. Decock-only model chambered for .45 ACP cartridge. Has a stainless steel slide. Magazine capacity 7 rounds. Fixed sights. Weight 27 oz.

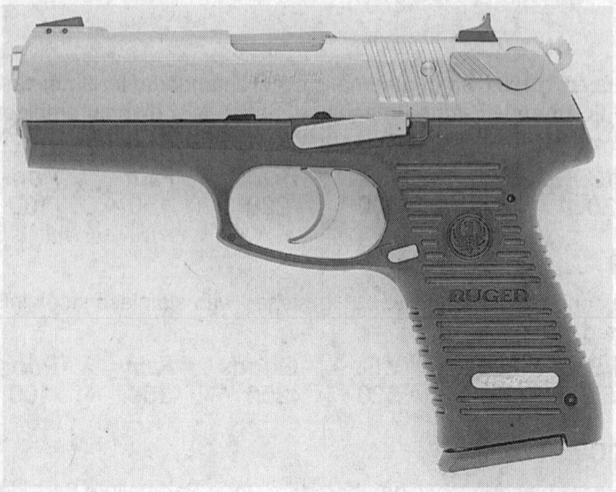

NIB	Exc.	V.G.	Good	Fair	Poor
450	350	300	220	150	100

KP97DAO

Same specifications as model above in double-action-only. Introduced in 1999.

NIB	Exc.	V.G.	Good	Fair	Poor
450	350	300	220	150	100

KP345

Introduced in 2004. This .45 ACP model features 4.2" stainless steel barrel and slide, fixed sights, internal lock, loaded chamber indicator, magazine disconnect and new cam block design to reduce recoil. Black polymer checkered grips. Magazine capacity 8 rounds. Weight 29 oz. Available with ambidextrous safety or decocker.

NIB	*Exc.*	*V.G.*	*Good*	*Fair*	*Poor*
550	420	300	250	180	120

KP345PR

Similar to model above, but fitted with Picatinny-style rail under forward portion of the frame. Introduced in 2004.

NIB	*Exc.*	*V.G.*	*Good*	*Fair*	*Poor*
550	420	300	250	180	120

SR9/SR40

Introduced in 2008. Ruger's first striker-fired semi-automatic pistol. Chambered in 9mm Parabellum or .40 S&W. Double-action-only, with 4.14" barrel, 17+1 capacity. Available in three finish configurations: stainless steel slide with matte black frame; blackened stainless slide with matte black frame; blackened stainless slide with matte black frame. Also available in compact version, with 3.5" barrel (SR9c, SR40c). Note: Ruger recalled all early-production SR9 pistols with a "330" serial number prefix because of a potential safety issue. SR40 has a 15-round magazine.

NIB	*Exc.*	*V.G.*	*Good*	*Fair*	*Poor*
450	350	300	220	150	100

SR22

Polymer-frame semi-automatic in .22 LR. Barrel length 3.5", overall length 6.4". Weight unloaded 17.5 oz. Features include Picatinny accessory rail, interchangeable grips and adjustable sights. Thumb safety/decocking lever and magazine release are all ambidextrous. Note: Add $25 for threaded barrel or silver anodized finish.

NIB	*Exc.*	*V.G.*	*Good*	*Fair*	*Poor*
350	300	280	220	150	100

SR45

Slightly larger variation of SR40. Chambered for .45 ACP, with 10-round magazine, 4.5" barrel.

NIB	*Exc.*	*V.G.*	*Good*	*Fair*	*Poor*
480	420	380	300	250	200

9E

An economy priced variation of SR9, with fixed (drift adjustable) sights.

NIB	*Exc.*	*V.G.*	*Good*	*Fair*	*Poor*
380	350	300	260	220	150

LCP (Lightweight Compact Pistol)

Introduced in 2008. Ruger's first true pocket pistol. Chambered in .380 (6+1 capacity), with 2.75" barrel. Double-action-only. Glass-filled nylon frame, with steel barrel. Black matte finish.

NIB	*Exc.*	*V.G.*	*Good*	*Fair*	*Poor*
320	280	240	180	120	100

LCP Crimson Trace

Similar to above, with Crimson Trace Lasergrips.

NIB	*Exc.*	*V.G.*	*Good*	*Fair*	*Poor*
480	420	350	280	220	150

Lite Rack LCP II

Caliber: .22 LR. Capacity: 10-round magazine. Barrel: 2.75":. Grips: Textured polymer. Sights: Integral-notch rear/post front. Length: 5.2". overall. Weight: 11.2 oz. unloaded. Finish: Black. Features: Lite Rack system with refined slide serrations, cocking ears and lighter recoil spring. Made in the USA.

NIB	*Exc.*	*V.G.*	*Good*	*Fair*	*Poor*
230	200	160	—	—	—

LC9

Sub-compact 9mm pistol designed for concealed carry. Magazine capacity 7 rounds; barrel length 3.12"; weight 17.1 oz. Steel slide, glass-filled nylon receiver, double-action-only trigger, hammer-fired operation. Three-dot sights, loaded-chamber indicator, manual safety, magazine disconnect and slide stop. Note: Add $100 for Crimson Trace LG-431 laser sight.

NIB	Exc.	V.G.	Good	Fair	Poor
380	340	280	200	150	100

LC380

Variation of LC9. Chambered for .380 ACP cartridge. Dimensions identical to LC9. New 2013.

NIB	Exc.	V.G.	Good	Fair	Poor
460	400	340	300	260	230

American Pistol

This is a full-size semi-automatic striker-fired pistol. Chambered in 9mm or .45 ACP, with a Browning-type locked-breech action. A patent-pending barrel cam controls rearward movement of the slide, reducing felt recoil and muzzle flip. The frame is glass-filled nylon, with integral grips and three grip inserts to adjust to the shooter's preference. The slide is stainless steel, with a black nitride finish. Magazine capacity (17 rounds) 9mm; (10) .45 ACP. In addition to the central trigger safety, which is depressed when trigger is pulled, the pistol is available with/without an external thumb safety. Weight 31 oz. unloaded. Sights are Novak three-dots and are adjustable for windage. Introduced in 2016. Compact model available with 3.5" barrel.

NIB	Exc.	V.G.	Good	Fair	Poor
580	480	360	280	240	220

American Competition

Caliber: 9mm. Capacity: 17-round magazine. Barrel: 5". Grips: Three interchangeable grip inserts. Sights: Adjustable rear, fiber-optic front, optic ready. Length: 8.3". overall. Weight: 34.1 oz. unloaded. Finish: Black Nitrite. Features: Slide is drilled and tapped for mounting red-dot reflex optics, ported stainless steel slide. Made in the USA.

NIB	Exc.	V.G.	Good	Fair	Poor
580	—	—	—	—	—

Security-9

Compact 9mm with textured glass-filled nylon grip frame and blue alloy steel slide. Features include hammer-fired LCP control system, high visibility fixed sights, 4" barrel, bladed trigger safety, and manual safety. Introduced in 2018.

NIB	Exc.	V.G.	Good	Fair	Poor
380	320	280	220	150	120

Security-9 Pro

Caliber: 9mm. Capacity: 15-round magazine. Barrel: 4". Grips: Textured polymer. Sights: Fixed-steel tritium. Length: 7.24" overall. Weight: 23.8 oz. unloaded. Finish: Black oxide. Features: Rugged construction with black oxide, through-hardened, alloy-steel slide and barrel and high-performance, glass-filled nylon grip frame. Made in the USA.

NIB	Exc.	V.G.	Good	Fair	Poor
480	—	—	—	—	—

Security-9 Compact Pro

Caliber: 9mm. Capacity: 10-round magazine. Barrel: 3.42". Grips: Textured polymer. Sights: Fixed-steel tritium. Length: 6.52" overall. Weight: 21.9 oz. unloaded. Finish: Black oxide. Features: Similar to Ruger Security-9 Pro. Precision-machined, hard-coat, anodized-aluminum chassis with full-length guide rails. Made in the USA.

NIB	Exc.	V.G.	Good	Fair	Poor
480	—	—	—	—	—

SR 1911

Caliber .45 ACP, stainless steel slide and frame, 8-round magazine, extended thumb safety, grip tang and magazine release, Novak Lo-Mount 3-dot sights, checkered mainspring housing and hardwood grips. Standard 1911 dimensions and controls. Introduced in 2011. A Commander-size model with 4.25" barrel introduced in 2013.

NIB	Exc.	V.G.	Good	Fair	Poor
940	790	500	390	360	280

SR 1911 Competition

Similar to above. 9mm 10-round magazine. 5" barrel. Weight 41 oz. Two-tone finish.

NIB	Exc.	V.G.	Good	Fair	Poor
2500	2260	1700	1530	1030	800

SR 1911 LW Cmdr.

Lightweight version of Commander-size SR 1911. A two-tone model, with black matte anodized aluminum frame and stainless slide. Introduced in 2015.

NIB	Exc.	V.G.	Good	Fair	Poor
980	830	720	560	380	300

SR 1911 Officer Style

Same features as SR 1911 LW Cmdr. with compact frame and slide, 3.6" barrel. Introduced in 2018.

NIB	Exc.	V.G.	Good	Fair	Poor
980	830	720	560	380	300

SR 1911 Target

Similar to above. 9mm, 10mm or .45 ACP. 5" barrel. Weight 41 oz. Adjustable Bomar-style sights. Satin stainless finish.

NIB	Exc.	V.G.	Good	Fair	Poor
1020	870	660	480	400	330

Ruger-57

Caliber: 5.7x28mm. Capacity: 20-round magazine. Barrel: 4.94". Grips: Textured polymer. Sights: Adjustable rear/fiber-optic front, optic ready. Length: 8.65". overall. Weight: 24.5 oz. unloaded. Finish: Black oxide. Features: 1911-style ambidextrous manual safety, Picatinny-style accessory rail, drilled and tapped for optics with optic-adapter plate. Made in the USA.

NIB	Exc.	V.G.	Good	Fair	Poor
900	—	—	—	—	—

SEMI-AUTOMATIC RIFLES

10/22 SERIES

10/22 Standard Carbine With Walnut Stock

This model has an 18.5" barrel and chambered for .22 LR. A 10-shot detachable rotary magazine and folding rear sight. Stock is smooth walnut, with a barrel band and carbine-style buttplate. Rifle enjoys a fine reputation for accuracy and dependability and considered an excellent value. Introduced in 1964. Note: Deduct $20 for birch stock.

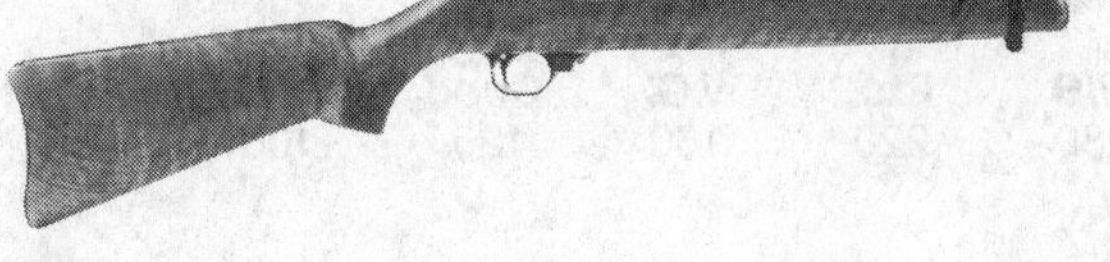

NIB	Exc.	V.G.	Good	Fair	Poor
280	220	120	100	80	50

10/22 Standard Carbine Stainless Steel

Same as above, with stainless steel barrel and receiver.

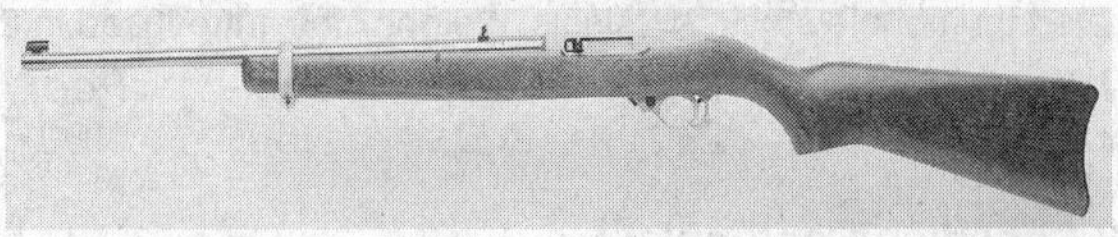

NIB	Exc.	V.G.	Good	Fair	Poor
300	250	150	120	100	80

10/22 Magnum

Introduced in 1999. Chambered for .22 Magnum cartridge. Barrel length 18.5". Folding rear sight and gold bead front. Hardwood stock. Weight 5.5 lbs. Discontinued.

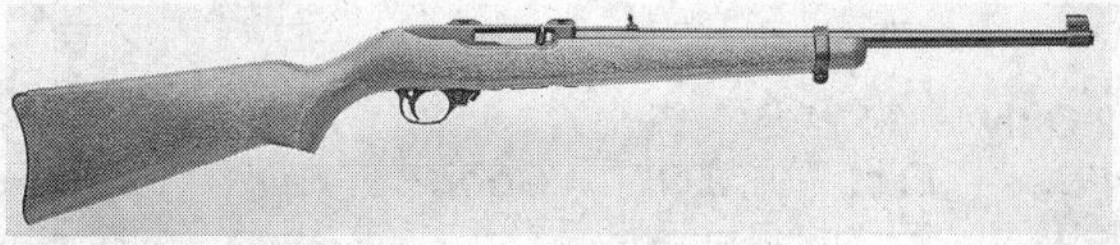

NIB	Exc.	V.G.	Good	Fair	Poor
950	800	700	500	350	200

10/22 Sporter (Finger Groove Old Model)

Similar to Standard Carbine, except it has a Monte Carlo stock, finger-groove forend and no barrel band. Manufactured between 1966 and 1971. Note: Add 300% for factory hand-checkering.

NIB	Exc.	V.G.	Good	Fair	Poor
650	580	450	350	250	200

10/22 Deluxe Sporter

Same as Sporter, with checkered stock and better buttplate. Introduced in 1971.

NIB	Exc.	V.G.	Good	Fair	Poor
320	250	150	120	100	80

10/22 International Carbine

Similar to Standard Carbine, with full-length Mannlicher-style stock. Manufactured between 1966-1971. Fairly rare in today's market. Note: Add 50% for factory hand-checkering.

NIB	Exc.	V.G.	Good	Fair	Poor
—	1100	620	450	300	250

10/22 International Carbine (New Model)

This 1994 model is a reintroduction of older version. Offered in blued or stainless steel finish. Barrel length 18.5". Magazine capacity 10 rounds. Hardwood stock had no checkering when first introduced. Shortly afterward factory began checkering these stocks. Weight 5.2 lbs. Discontinued.

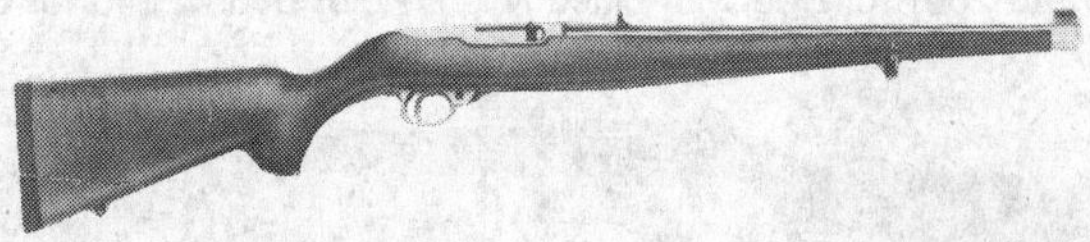

NIB	Exc.	V.G.	Good	Fair	Poor
460	300	220	—	—	—

10/22T

Introduced in 1996. Target version of 10/22 line. Has laminated American hardwood stock, with blued heavy barrel and hammer-forged spiral finish. Comes standard without sights. Barrel length 20". Weight 7.25 lbs.

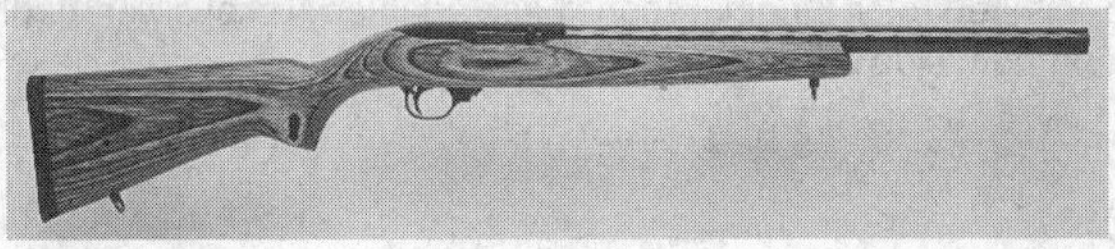

NIB	Exc.	V.G.	Good	Fair	Poor
450	350	280	200	150	100

10/22TNZ

This target model features 20" stainless steel barrel and receiver, with laminated thumbhole stock. No sights. Weight 7 lbs. Introduced in 2001.

NIB	Exc.	V.G.	Good	Fair	Poor
500	380	280	200	150	100

10/22 Canadian Centennial

In 1966 and 1967, approximately 4,500 10/22 Sporters were built for the Canadian Centennial. First 2,000 sold with Rem. Model 742 in .308-caliber, with matching serial numbers. Ruger Sporter may be checkered or uncheckered. Two-gun set boxed separately or together.

Two Gun Set

NIB	Exc.	V.G.	Good	Fair	Poor
700	—	—	—	—	—

10/22 Only

NIB	Exc.	V.G.	Good	Fair	Poor
450	—	—	—	—	—

10/22 Laminated Stock Carbine

Produced in varying quantities since 1986, these models are becoming quite collectible. Stocks range in color from dark green to gray and various shades of brown. Because there are so many different variations, each should be individually appraised. Prices listed are for blued carbine models. Note: Add about $40 to NIB price for stainless steel.

NIB	Exc.	V.G.	Good	Fair	Poor
250	200	180	150	120	100

10/22 Laminated Stock Sporter

This model has a tree bark laminated stock.

NIB	Exc.	V.G.	Good	Fair	Poor
320	280	220	180	150	100

10/22 Laminated Stock International

Stainless steel model was an exclusive Walmart product. A few of these models were produced in blue.

Blue

NIB	Exc.	V.G.	Good	Fair	Poor
400	320	250	200	150	100

Stainless Steel

NIB	Exc.	V.G.	Good	Fair	Poor
350	280	220	180	120	100

10/22 All Weather

Fitted with stainless steel barrel, action and synthetic stock. Introduced in 1997. In 2001, offered with blued finish. Note: Deduct $40 for blued model.

NIB	Exc.	V.G.	Good	Fair	Poor
300	220	180	120	100	70

10/22 Carbine 40th Anniversary

Blued, with hardwood stock. Equipped with 40th Anniversary clear magazine, with red rotor. Original scope base adapter. Nickel-silver medallion inlaid on right side of buttstock.

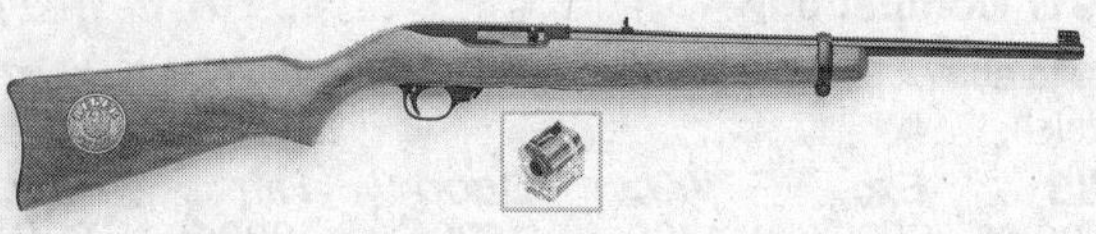

NIB	Exc.	V.G.	Good	Fair	Poor
280	220	180	120	100	80

10/22 50th Anniversary

In 2013 early 2014, Ruger staged a contest for 10/22 fans to design a 50th Anniversary Model. Winning entry became a production model in mid 2014. Has 18.5" stainless barrel, black composite stock with adjustable comb and length of pull, ghost ring adjustable sights and grooved forend.

NIB	Exc.	V.G.	Good	Fair	Poor
300	280	—	—	—	—

10/22 Compact Rifle 10/22 CRR

Similar to 10/22 standard rifle, with 16.25" blued barrel, shorter hardwood stock, fiber optic sights and 34.5" overall length. Introduced 2006.

NIB	Exc.	V.G.	Good	Fair	Poor
280	220	180	120	100	80

K10/22T Ruger 10/22 Target Stainless

Similar to 10/22 Target, with stainless steel barrel and laminated stock.

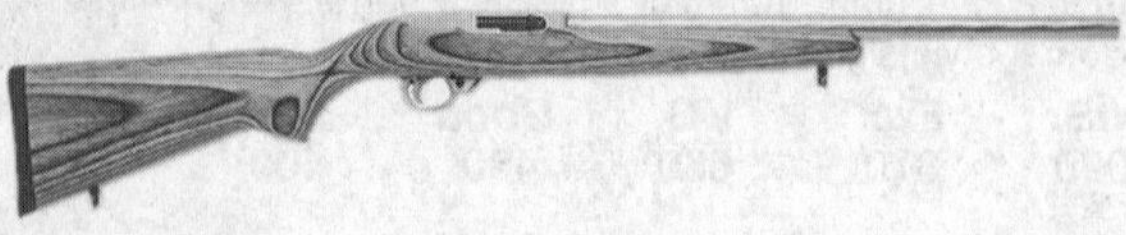

NIB	Exc.	V.G.	Good	Fair	Poor
500	420	350	280	200	150

10/22-T

Similar to 100/22 Target Stainless, with blued steel barrel and receiver. Introduced in 2007.

NIB	Exc.	V.G.	Good	Fair	Poor
450	350	280	200	150	100

10/22RPFCARH (Lipsey's Distributor's Special)

Similar to 10/22, but covered throughout with Realtree Hardwoods HD camo finish. Introduced 2008.

NIB	Exc.	V.G.	Good	Fair	Poor
280	220	180	120	100	80

10/22VLEH Target Tactical

Semi-automatic rimfire chambered in .22 LR. Features include precision-rifled cold hammer-forged spiral-finished 16.125" crowned match barrel; Hogue OverMolded stock; 10/22T target trigger; precision-adjustable bipod for steady shooting from bench; 10-round rotary magazine. Weight 6.875 lbs.

NIB	Exc.	V.G.	Good	Fair	Poor
480	400	350	300	220	150

10/22 Takedown

Barrel and forend separate from rest of rifle. Features same as other 10/22 models. Comes with nylon carry bag. Note: Add $20 for threaded 16.6" barrel and flash suppressor.

NIB	Exc.	V.G.	Good	Fair	Poor
360	320	280	240	220	200

Model 10/17

Introduced in 2004. Chambered for .17 HMR cartridge. Fitted with 20" barrel. Magazine capacity 9 rounds. Weight 6.5 lbs. Discontinued.

NIB	Exc.	V.G.	Good	Fair	Poor
600	480	300	200	150	100

MODEL 44 SERIES

Model 44 Carbine

A short 18.5" barreled gas-operated carbine. Chambered for .44 Magnum cartridge. Has a 4-shot non-detachable magazine, folding rear sight and plain walnut stock. Handy deer hunting carbine. Manufactured from 1961-1985.

NIB	Exc.	V.G.	Good	Fair	Poor
750	600	500	380	300	200

Deerstalker Model

Same as Model 44 Carbine, with "Deerstalker" stamped on it. Manufactured 1961-1962 only.

NIB	Exc.	V.G.	Good	Fair	Poor
1100	900	700	400	300	200

Model 44 RS

This is Model 44, with sling swivels and aperture sight. Note: "Liberty"-marked 44RS carbines are extremely rare and will bring a premium.

NIB	Exc.	V.G.	Good	Fair	Poor
800	600	550	350	200	150

Model 44 Sporter (Finger Groove Old Model)

This version has Monte Carlo stock, finger-groove forend and no barrel band. Manufactured until 1971. Note: Factory hand-checkered models will bring at least 75% premium.

NIB	Exc.	V.G.	Good	Fair	Poor
950	750	600	400	250	200

Model 44 International Carbine

This version features a full-length Mannlicher-style stock. Discontinued in 1971 and quite collectible. Note: Factory hand-checkered models will bring at least 50% premium.

NIB	Exc.	V.G.	Good	Fair	Poor
1000	800	600	420	350	280

Model 44 25th Anniversary Model

This version lightly engraved. Has a medallion in the stock. Only made in 1985, the last year of production.

NIB	Exc.	V.G.	Good	Fair	Poor
550	400	350	300	250	200

Model 99/44 Deerfield Carbine

While chambered in .44 Magnum, this model is not related to .44 Carbine, but a variation of Mini-14. In production from 2000 to 2006. Fitted with 18.5" barrel, this gas-operated rifle has a hardwood stock and 4-round magazine. Adjustable rear sight. Blued finish. Weight 6.2 lbs. This rifle will not cycle .44 Special ammo. Discontinued.

NIB	Exc.	V.G.	Good	Fair	Poor
700	520	400	280	200	150

AR-556 SERIES

AR-556 Standard

Caliber: 5.56 NATO. Capacity: 30-round magazine. 16.1" barrel, 1:8" RH twist, 1/2x28 muzzle thread pattern. Features: Basic AR M4-style Modern Sporting Rifle with direct impingement operation, forged aluminum upper and lower receivers, and cold hammer-forged chrome-moly steel barrel with M4 feed ramp cuts. Other features include Ruger Rapid Deploy folding rear sight, milled F-height gas block with post front sight, telescoping six-position stock, and one 30-round Magpul magazine. Weight: 6.5 lb. Overall Length: 32.25" to 35.50". Introduced 2015. Add $50 for Magpul MOE furniture. SEE POLITICAL PANIC PRICING.

NIB	Exc.	V.G.	Good	Fair	Poor
760	670	590	450	—	—

AR-556 Model 8502 16.1"

Fixed M4-style buttstock and Mil-Spec buffer tube. No muzzle threads. 10-round metal magazine.

NIB	Exc.	V.G.	Good	Fair	Poor
800	680	580	490	420	360

AR-556 Model 8511 16.1"

10-round metal magazine to meet state capacity restrictions.

NIB	Exc.	V.G.	Good	Fair	Poor
800	680	580	490	420	360

AR-556 Model 8513 16.1"

Fixed A2 Stock, MonsterMan Grip, 10-round magazine to meet state restrictions.

NIB	Exc.	V.G.	Good	Fair	Poor
830	710	600	510	430	370

AR-556 Model 8515 16.1"

Magpul MOE M-LOK handguard, 6-position telescoping Magpul MOE Carbine buttstock, Mil-Spec buffer tube, medium contour barrel, (1)

30-round Magpul PMAG magazine. Introduced 2019, Model 8537 is similarly equipped, except it comes with 10-round metal magazine.

NIB	Exc.	V.G.	Good	Fair	Poor
950	810	690	580	500	420

AR-556 Model 8525 16.1"

Flattop upper receiver and same-plane Picatinny gas block for easy attachment of magnified optic, red dot or open sights. 30-round magazine. Model 8536 is the same except 10-round magazine.

NIB	Exc.	V.G.	Good	Fair	Poor
820	700	590	500	430	360

AR-556 Model 8523 16.1"

Introduced 2019. Includes Juggernaut Tactical's fixed magazine kit, which disables the magazine release. Quick-release takedown pin allows for convenient separation of the upper and lower receivers for reloading.

NIB	Exc.	V.G.	Good	Fair	Poor
680	570	490	420	350	300

AR-556 Model 8529 16.1"

Introduced 2019. 11" free-float aluminum handguard, Magpul M-LOK accessory attachment slots along the 3 'o clock, 6 'o clock, and 9 'o clock positions with additional slots on the angled faces near the muzzle. Flat top upper receiver features a Picatinny rail.

NIB	Exc.	V.G.	Good	Fair	Poor
900	770	650	550	470	400

AR-556 Model 8503 Davidson's Exclusive

Barrett Brown synthetic collapsible rear stock, Barrett Brown glass-filled nylon handguard, Barrett Brown Cerakote receiver finish.

NIB	Exc.	V.G.	Good	Fair	Poor
950	810	690	580	500	420

AR-556 Model 8504 Lipsey's Exclusive

OD Green furniture, OD Green Cerakote.

NIB	Exc.	V.G.	Good	Fair	Poor
700	600	510	430	370	310

AR-556 Model 8507 United Sporting Companies Exclusive

Flat Dark Earth Magpul Synthetic Collapsible buttstock, Flat Dark Earth Magpul MOE M-LOK handguard.

NIB	Exc.	V.G.	Good	Fair	Poor
970	830	700	600	510	430

AR-556 Model 8517 Talo Exclusive

Turquoise furniture and turquoise Cerakote receiver finish.

NIB	Exc.	V.G.	Good	Fair	Poor
820	700	590	500	430	360

AR-556 Model 8519 Talo Exclusive

White furniture and white Cerakote receiver finish.

NIB	Exc.	V.G.	Good	Fair	Poor
950	810	690	580	500	420

AR-556 Pistol

Calibers: 5.56 NATO, .350 Legend, .300 BLK. Capacity: .350 Legend (5-round magazine), 5.56 NATO or .300 BLK (30-round magazine). Barrels: 9.5" - 10.5" Weight: 6.2 lbs. Sights: Optic-ready, Picatinny rail. Grips: AR15 A2 style. Features: SB Tactical SBA3 brace.

NIB	Exc.	V.G.	Good	Fair	Poor
800	—	—	—	—	—

AR-556 MPR (MULTI-PURPOSE RIFLE) SERIES

Caliber: 5.56 NATO, .350 Legend, .450 Bushmaster. MPR model has 16.1", 18", 18.38", and 18.63" barrels with muzzle brake, flat-top upper, 15" free-floating handguard with Magpul M-LOK accessory slots, Magpul MOE SL collapsible buttstock and MOE grip. Add $920 for Proof Research carbon-fiber barrel, added December 2022. SEE POLITICAL PANIC PRICING.

NIB	Exc.	V.G.	Good	Fair	Poor
900	850	720	610	520	440

5.56

NIB	Exc.	V.G.	Good	Fair	Poor
1000	—	—	—	—	—

AR-556 MPR Model 8535 5.56 18"

Introduced 2019 with 15" free-float handguard.

NIB	Exc.	V.G.	Good	Fair	Poor
740	630	540	450	390	330

AR-556 MPR Model 8522 .450 Bushmaster 18.63"

NIB	Exc.	V.G.	Good	Fair	Poor
1070	910	770	660	560	480

AR-556 MPR Model 8532 .350 Legend 16.38"

Chambering for new cartridge introduced 2019.

NIB	Exc.	V.G.	Good	Fair	Poor
1000	850	720	610	520	440

AR-556 Free-Float Handguard Model

Caliber: 5.56 NATO, .300 BLK. 16.1" barrel. Similar to the MPR model, with an 11" aluminum free-floated handguard. Magpul M-LOK accessory attachment slots at the 3, 6, and 9 o'clock positions with additional slots on the angled faces near the muzzle. Introduced 2016. .300 BLK chambering added in 2019. SEE POLITICAL PANIC PRICING.

NIB	Exc.	V.G.	Good	Fair	Poor
830	700	570	450	—	—

SR SERIES

SR-556

Introduced 2009. AR-style semi-automatic chambered in 5.56 NATO. Features include two-stage piston; quad rail handguard; Troy Industries sights; black synthetic fixed or telescoping buttstock; 16.12" 1:9 steel barrel with birdcage; 10- or 30-round detachable box magazine; black matte finish overall. The 6.8 PPC was added in 2010, but discontinued after one year. Discontinued 2016. In 2019, only the Takedown model 5924 was still listed on the company website. Replaceable barrel kits chambered in .300 AAC Blackout (90455) are available on ShopRuger.com, $450.

NIB	Exc.	V.G.	Good	Fair	Poor
1200	950	800	700	500	250

SR-556 Takedown

Barrel is removed from the upper receiver by moving the slider bar towards the breech, rotating the barrel and pulling it free (no tools required).

NIB	Exc.	V.G.	Good	Fair	Poor
1250	1000	850	700	500	250

SR-762

Same basic AR-style design of SR-556, but modified to handle 7.62 NATO (.308 Win.) cartridge.

NIB	Exc.	V.G.	Good	Fair	Poor
1780	1510	1280	1090	930	790

SR-22 Rifle

AR-style semi-automatic rifle. Chambered in .22 LR, based on 10/22 action. Features include all-aluminum chassis replicating AR-platform dimensions between sighting plane; buttstock height and grip; Picatinny rail optic mount includes 6-position telescoping M4-style buttstock (on Mil-Spec diameter tube); Hogue Monogrip pistol grip; buttstocks and grips interchangeable with any AR-style compatible option; round mid-length handguard mounted on a standard-thread AR-style barrel nut; precision-rifled cold hammer forged 16.125" alloy steel barrel capped with an SR-556/Mini-14 flash suppressor.

NIB	Exc.	V.G.	Good	Fair	Poor
540	460	380	320	250	150

SMALL FRAME SERIES

Small-Frame Autoloading Rifle

Chambering: 7.62 NATO/.308 Win. The SFAR combines the ballistic advantages of .308 Win. in the size of a traditional MSR. Barrel: 16" cold hammer-forged, 5R rifling, 5/8x24 muzzle thread, tapered lugs, black-nitride finish. Trigger: Ruger Elite 452. Receivers: CNC-machined from 7075-T6 forgings, oversized magazine well, forward assist, dust cover and brass deflector. Four-position regulated gas block, included 3/16" ball-end wrench for regulator adjustment, two-port Boomer muzzle brake. Handguard: Magpul M-LOK accessory attachment slots at the 3:00, 6:00, and 9:00 positions, sockets for QD sling swivels. Model 5610: 16" barrel, mid-length gas system, 15" Lite free-float handguard. Model 5611: 20" barrel, rifle-length gas system, 15" handguard with a full Picatinny top rail. Magpul MOE SL stock, MOE grip and one 20-rd. Magpul PMAG magazine. Weight: 6.8 pounds unloaded. Introduced 2022. State-compliant models with 10-rd. magazines added 2023. SEE POLITICAL PANIC PRICING.

NIB	Exc.	V.G.	Good	Fair	Poor
1100	—	—	—	—	—

MINI SERIES

Mini-14

Paramilitary-style carbine chambered for .223 Rem. and on a limited basis for .222 cartridge. Has an 18.5" barrel and gas-operated. Detachable magazines originally offered held 5, 10 or 20 rounds. High-capacity magazines are now discontinued. Prices for them are what the market will bear. Mini-14 has a military-style stock and aperture sight. Introduced in 1975. 20-round magazine added 2009.

NIB	Exc.	V.G.	Good	Fair	Poor
900	750	650	500	400	200

Mini-14 Stainless Steel

Same as Mini-14, except constructed of stainless steel.

NIB	Exc.	V.G.	Good	Fair	Poor
950	800	700	500	400	200

Mini-14 Target

Accurized version of Mini-14, with matte stainless barrel and receiver, black laminated thumbhole stock, adjustable harmonic dampener. No sights. Also available with non-thumbhole synthetic stock. Introduced in 2007.

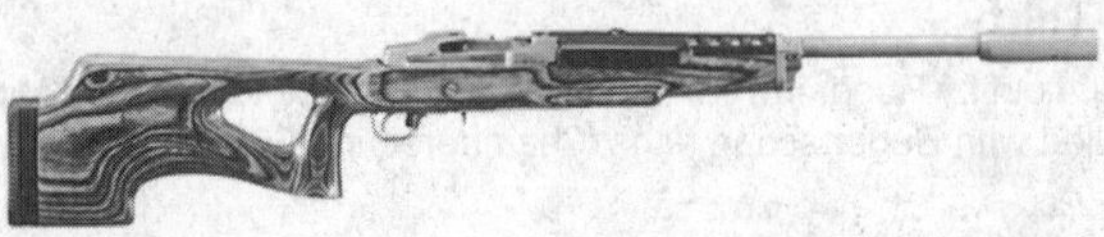

NIB	Exc.	V.G.	Good	Fair	Poor
1020	900	780	600	400	250

Mini-14 Ranch

Similar to standard Mini-14, with folding rear sight and receiver milled to accept Ruger scope-ring system. Rings are supplied with rifle. 6.8 Rem. chambering also available. Note: Models chambered in .222-caliber will bring a premium.

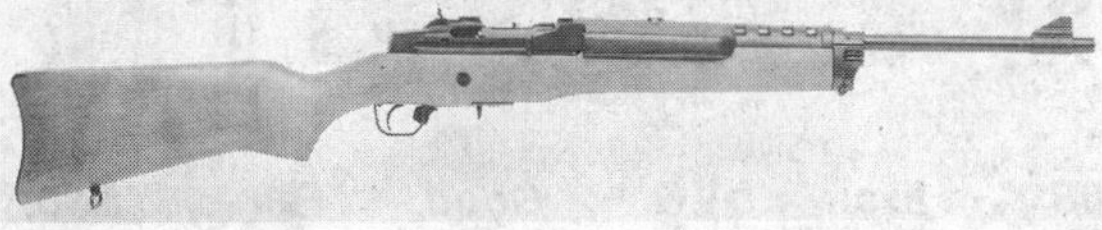

NIB	Exc.	V.G.	Good	Fair	Poor
900	750	650	500	400	200

Mini-14 Stainless All-Weather Ranch

Introduced in 1999. Has all the features of stainless steel Ranch, with addition of black polymer stock. Weight 6.5 lbs.

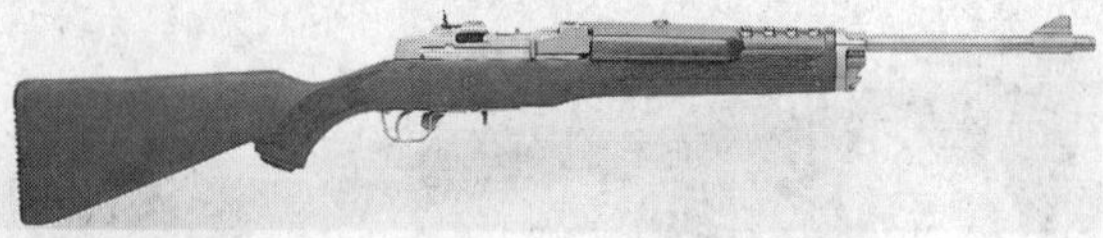

NIB	Exc.	V.G.	Good	Fair	Poor
950	800	700	500	400	200

Mini-14 NRA

Ruger Mini-14 NRA, with two 20-round magazines, gold-tone medallion in grip cap and special serial number sequence (NRA8XXXXX). Produced in 2008 only. Also available with 5-round magazine.

NIB	Exc.	V.G.	Good	Fair	Poor
1000	700	580	—	—	—

Mini-14 ATI Stock

Tactical version of Mini-14, with 6-position collapsible stock or folding stock, grooved pistol grip, multiple Picatinny optics/accessories rails.

NIB	Exc.	V.G.	Good	Fair	Poor
1000	850	750	500	400	200

Mini-14 Tactical

Similar to Mini-14, with 16.12" barrel with flash hider, black synthetic stock, adjustable sights. Also chambered for .300 Blackout.

NIB	Exc.	V.G.	Good	Fair	Poor
1100	900	800	600	450	250

Mini-Thirty

Brought out by Ruger in 1987. Similar in appearance to standard Mini-14. Supplied with Ruger scope rings. Chambered in 7.63x39; 6.8mm added in 2007.

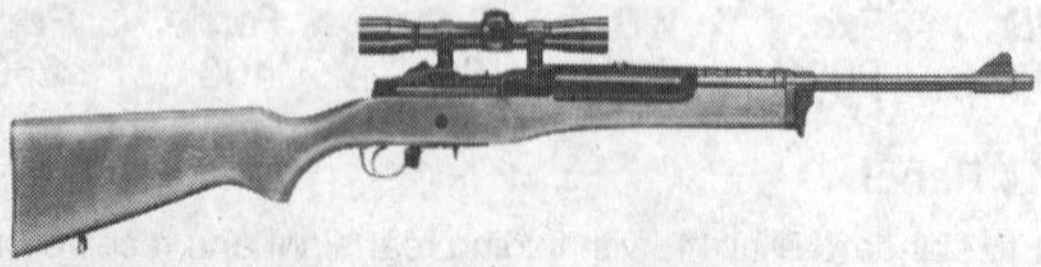

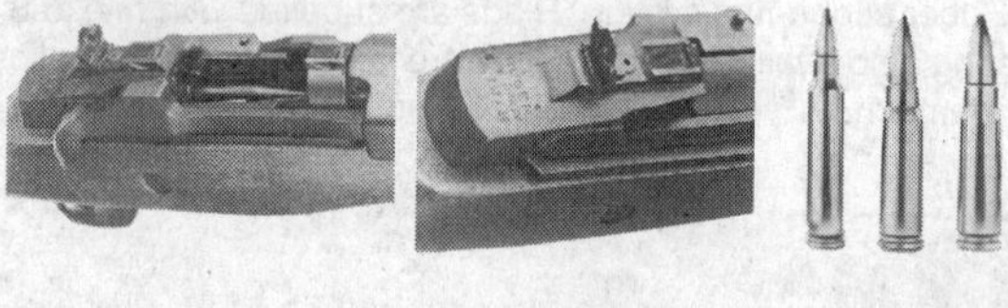

NIB	Exc.	V.G.	Good	Fair	Poor
900	750	650	500	400	200

Mini-Thirty Stainless with Synthetic Stock

NIB	Exc.	V.G.	Good	Fair	Poor
1100	900	700	550	400	200

GB Model

This model has a factory-installed folding stock, flash suppressor and bayonet lug. Designed and sold by Ruger to law enforcement agencies. A number have come on the civilian market through surplus sales and police trade-ins. With the assault rifle hysteria, prices of this model have fluctuated wildly in some areas. Now that Ruger has discontinued the folding stock and high-capacity magazines, this could become even less predictable. Note that this is a semi-automatic and totally different than the full-auto version of this weapon available only through Class 3 dealers.

NIB	Exc.	V.G.	Good	Fair	Poor
—	1350	1100	650	400	300

PC4/PC9 Carbine

Semi-automatic carbine chambered for 9mm (PC9) or .40 S&W (PC4) cartridges. Fitted with 16.25" barrel and black synthetic stock. Post front sight, with adjustable rear. Receiver sight is also offered. Detachable magazine has 10-round capacity. Weight about 6.4 lbs. Introduced in 1998; discontinued. Note: Add $30 for receiver sight.

NIB	Exc.	V.G.	Good	Fair	Poor
620	450	320	220	150	100

PC Carbine

Improved variation of PC4/PC9 in 9mm only with threaded, fluted 16.12" barrel, adjustable ghost ring rear sight. Stock is black synthetic with top and bottom accessory rails. Operates with Ruger or Glock magazines. Introduced in 2018.

NIB	Exc.	V.G.	Good	Fair	Poor
550	500	400	–	–	–

SINGLE-SHOT RIFLES

In 2013 Ruger announced that beginning in 2014, each variation of No. 1 rifle would be chambered in a different caliber each year. In 2014, Light Sporter was made only in .280 Rem., Varminter in .220 Swift, RSI International in .257 Roberts, Medium Sporter in 9.3x62 and Tropical in .450/400 Nitro Express 3". In 2015, Light Sporter chambered in 7mm-08 Rem., Varminter in .223 Rem., RSI International 6.5x55, Standard in .257 Wby., Tropical in .375 H&H and Medium Sporter in .30-06. Firearms distributor Lipsey's is the exclusive source for all currently manufactured No. 1 rifles. It is unknown how this limiting of caliber choices will affect values of Ruger No. 1s in the future. In 2016, Lipsey's announced these variations of Ruger No. 1: Light Sporter (1-A) .275 Rigby (7x57 Mauser), 24" bbl.; Standard Rifle (1-B) .257 Wby. or 6.5 Creedmoor, 28" bbl.; Medium Sporter (1-S) .35 Whelen, 24" bbl. or .44 Magnum, 20" bbl.; Varmint (1-V) .243 Win., 26" bbl. In 2017, Lipsey's announced for Standard No. 1: .22-250, .270 Win., .450 Bushmaster; Medium Sporter: .35 Whelen, .44 Magnum; Light Sporter: .30-06; Varminter: .204 Ruger. For 2018, two chamberings were offered: .450 Bushmaster and .450 Marlin. Features include a 20" barrel with muzzle brake, no sights, and a black laminate stock. In 2019, Lipsey's announced the Mannlicher-stocked No. 1 International in stainless steel and walnut in 6.5x55 or .308.

NO.1 SERIES

No. 1 Light Sporter (1-A)

Features open sights, barrel band on lightweight barrel and Alexander Henry-style forearm. Offered with 22" barrel in many popular calibers. Weight 7.25 lbs.

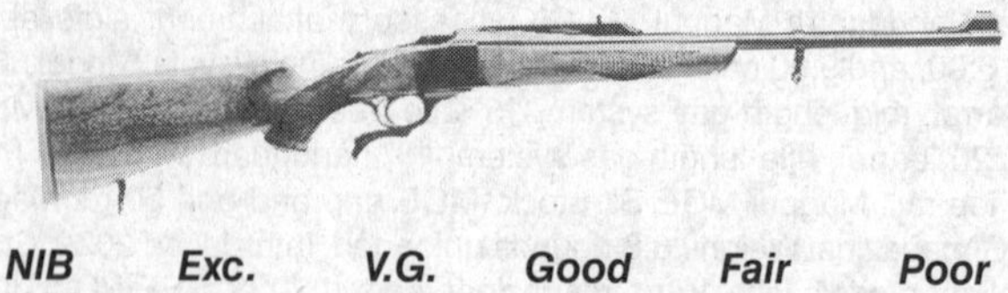

NIB	Exc.	V.G.	Good	Fair	Poor
1050	900	750	550	350	200

No, 1 Light Standard (1-AB)

Similar to Light Sporter 1-A, with 22" sightless blued barrel.

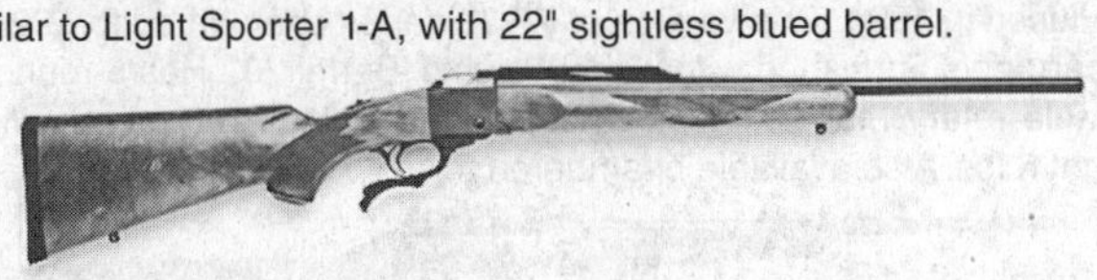

NIB	Exc.	V.G.	Good	Fair	Poor
900	800	650	450	300	200

No. 1 Standard (1-B)

Furnished with no sights, medium barrel, semi-beavertail forearm and quarter rib with 1" Ruger scope rings. Weight 8 lbs. Introduced in 1966. Chambered in most popular calibers at various times. Note: Add 25% to 50% premium for rare calibers like .257 Roberts, 6.5 Rem. Magnum, 7x57 Mauser.

NIB	Exc.	V.G.	Good	Fair	Poor
960	720	550	380	250	200

No. 1 Standard Stainless (1-B-BBZ)

In production from 2000 to 2010. Chambered in most popular calibers from .204 Ruger to .458 Win. Gray laminate stock. Barrel lengths from 22" to 26".

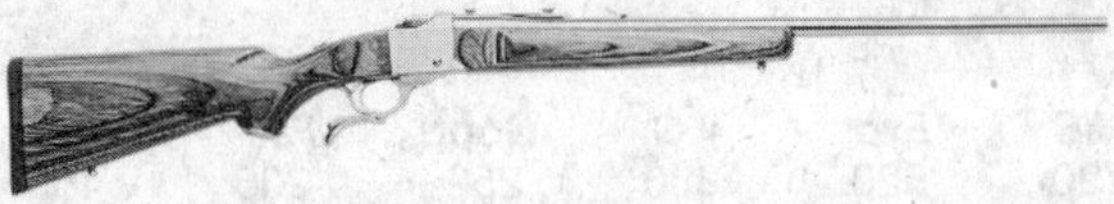

NIB	Exc.	V.G.	Good	Fair	Poor
1000	750	550	380	250	200

No. 1 Tropical (1-H)

Fitted with open sights. Barrel band on heavy barrel, with Alexander Henry-style forearm. Weight 9 lbs. In 2001: offered with stainless steel finish and black laminated stock in .375 H&H. Added in 2003: .458 Lott and .405 Win. cartridges; In 2008: .450/.400 Nitro Express; In 2009: .416 Ruger. Few 24" heavy barrel 1-H rifles chambered for .45-70 Government cartridge up to 1976. These bring substantial premium and should be appraised individually. Note: Add 100% for .404 Jeffery caliber; add 250% for .45-70.

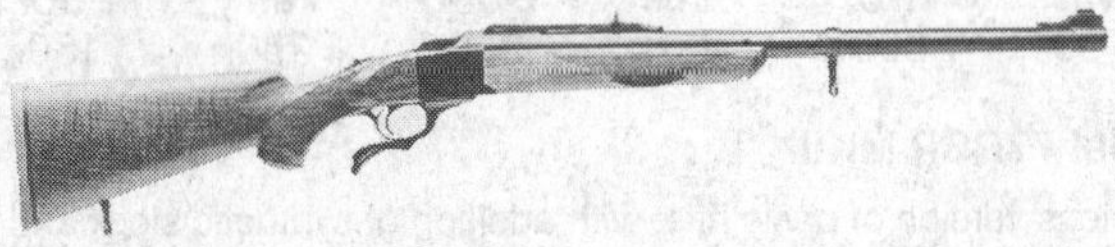

NIB	Exc.	V.G.	Good	Fair	Poor
1050	900	750	550	350	200

No. 1 International (1-RSI)

This No. 1 rifle features a lightweight barrel, with full-length forearm and open sights. Weight 7.25 lbs.

NIB	Exc.	V.G.	Good	Fair	Poor
1100	950	800	600	400	250

No. 1 Medium Sporter (1-S)

Equipped with open sights, barrel band on medium weight barrel and Alexander Henry-style forearm. Weight 8 lbs. In 2001, offered in stainless steel and black laminated stock in .45-70 caliber. Chambered in a wide range of calibers including .218 Bee to .480 Ruger. Added in 2009, .300 H&H, .338 Ruger Compact Magnum, .375 Ruger, .460 S&W Magnum, .480Ruger/.475 Linebaugh. Note: In 1999, a 50th Anniversary No. 1 Medium Sporter Model in .45-70 with engraving and high grade walnut stock offered. Add 100% premium for this model.

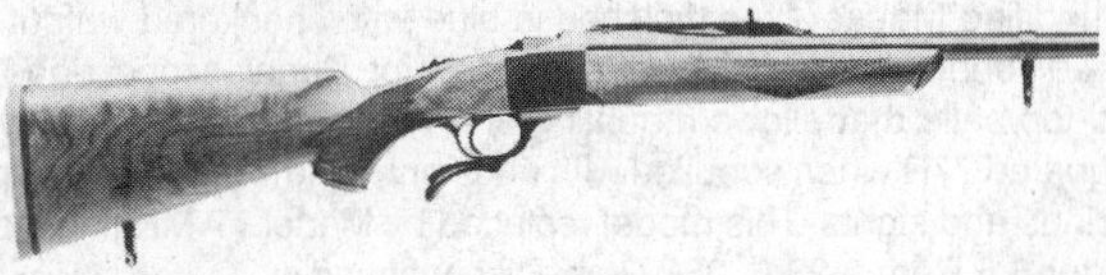

NIB	Exc.	V.G.	Good	Fair	Poor
1000	850	700	500	300	200

No. 1 Special Varminter (1-V)

Model furnished with no sights, heavy barrel, target scope blocks with 1" Ruger scope rings and semi-beavertail forearm. Weight 9 lbs.

NIB	Exc.	V.G.	Good	Fair	Poor
1100	950	800	600	400	250

No. 1 Stainless Varminter (1-V-BBZ)

Introduced in 2000. Features laminated wood stock and stainless steel finish. Chambered for .22-250. Fitted with 24" barrel. Weight 9 lbs.

NIB	Exc.	V.G.	Good	Fair	Poor
1000	750	550	380	250	200

No. 1 50th Anniversary

Limited edition in .308 Winchester with high grade American walnut stock, satin blued finish, custom engravings on either side of action commemorating the 50th anniversary of the No. 1 rifle.

NIB	Exc.	V.G.	Good	Fair	Poor
2000	1850	1700	—	—	—

No. 3 Carbine

A less elaborate inexpensive version of No.1. Action the same, except lever is less ornate in appearance and lacks the locking bar. Uncheckered stock is a military carbine style, with barrel band. Similar in appearance to Model 44 and 10/22. This serviceable rifle chambered for .45-70, when released in 1972. Later chamberings added .22 Hornet, .30-40 Krag, .223, .44 Magnum and .375 Win. Barrel 22" long. Folding rear sight. Discontinued in 1987. Note: Add 25% premium for .44 Magnum or .375 Win.

NIB	Exc.	V.G.	Good	Fair	Poor
750	620	500	300	200	120

BOLT-ACTION RIFLES

Ruger introduced the Model 77R in 1968 filling the need for a good quality reasonably priced bolt-action hunting rifle, and it has been a commercial success. There are certain variations of this rifle that collectors actively seek. One should avail oneself of specialized literature on this model and secure individual appraisals on rare variations, as differences are slight and beyond the scope of this book. The new Model 77 Hawkeye replaces the Model 77 Mk II. The Ruger American Rifle introduced in 2014 is an entry-level bolt-action hunting rifle selling well below the premium Model 77. It is now a fast-growing segment of the Ruger Rifle family with many new models currently. Distributor exclusives are often encountered with features like a camo stock or special caliber.

MODEL 77 SERIES

Model 77-R/RS

Introduced in 1968. Offered with 22", 24" or 26" barrel. Model 77 chambered for most calibers from .22-250 through .458 Win. Magnum. Action is a modified Mauser-type, finished in blue with checkered walnut stock and red rubber buttplate. Available milled for Ruger scope rings or in round-top style that allows mounting of any popular scope ring system. Designated 77R when supplied with rings only; and 77RS when supplied with rings and sights. This model replaced by Model 77 MK II. Note: Add $400 for 6.5 Rem., .284, .350 Rem. Discontinued.

NIB	Exc.	V.G.	Good	Fair	Poor
550	450	400	300	250	200

Model 77 Flat Bolt

This is an example of the slight variations that make this model collectible. Essentially same rifle, with knob on bolt handle flattened. Only produced in this configuration until 1972. Watch for fakes and read specialized material. Calibers such as 6.5 Rem. Magnum, .284 and .350 Rem. Magnum will bring a premium especially in RS model. Non-prefixed rifles exist in calibers and configurations other than those advertised by Ruger These should be individually appraised. Note: Add $400 for 6.5. Rem., .284, .350 Rem. Discontinued.

NIB	Exc.	V.G.	Good	Fair	Poor
—	650	500	400	350	280

Model 77 RL & RLS

This variation similar to standard model, except it features an ultralight 20" barrel and black forearm tip. Also available in 18.5" carbine version, with sights designated RLS. Chambered for .22-250, .243, .257, .270, .250-3000, .308 and .30-06. Weight 6 lbs. Discontinued.

NIB	Exc.	V.G.	Good	Fair	Poor
550	450	380	320	280	220

Model 77V Varmint

Similar to standard Model 77, except it has a 24" heavy barrel that is drilled and tapped for target-scope bases and wider beavertail forearm. Chambered for .22-250, .243, 6mm, .25-06, .280 and .308. Also chambered for .220 Swift in a 26" heavy weight barrel. Discontinued.

NIB	Exc.	V.G.	Good	Fair	Poor
500	400	350	300	250	200

Model 77 RSI

This version of Model 77 has a full-length Mannlicher-style stock. Was chambered for .22-250, .250-3000, .243, .270, 7mm-08, .308 and .30-06. Discontinued.

NIB	Exc.	V.G.	Good	Fair	Poor
700	600	500	300	280	200

Model 77 RS African

A heavier-barreled version, with steel triggerguard and floorplate. Earlier versions were stocked with fine-quality Circassian walnut. Chambered for .458 Win. Magnum. Fewer than 50 rifles chambered for .416 Taylor cartridge and produced up to 1976. Selling prices range from $3,000 to $5,000 and should be individually appraised. Note: Add $100 for early models with Circassian walnut stocks. Discontinued.

NIB	Exc.	V.G.	Good	Fair	Poor
700	550	400	350	300	—

Model 77/22—.22 Hornet

Introduced in 1994. This version of 77/22 series chambered for .22 Hornet cartridge. Furnished with/without sights. Barrel 20". Has 6-round detachable rotary magazine. Stock checkered walnut, with sling swivels. Weight 6 lbs. Also available chambered for .17 Hornet.

NIB	Exc.	V.G.	Good	Fair	Poor
720	620	500	380	250	150

Model K77/22VHZ

Introduced in 1995. This .22 Hornet variation features stainless steel heavy weight barrel and laminated American hardwood stock. Offered without sights.

NIB	Exc.	V.G.	Good	Fair	Poor
680	520	420	300	250	150

Model 77R MKII

Introduced in 1992. A basic Model 77 rifle. Features blued metal parts and no sights. Available in 15 different calibers from .223 to .338 Win. Magnum. Barrel lengths from 22" to 24" depending on caliber. Comes from factory with scope bases and rings. Weight 7 lbs. Discontinued.

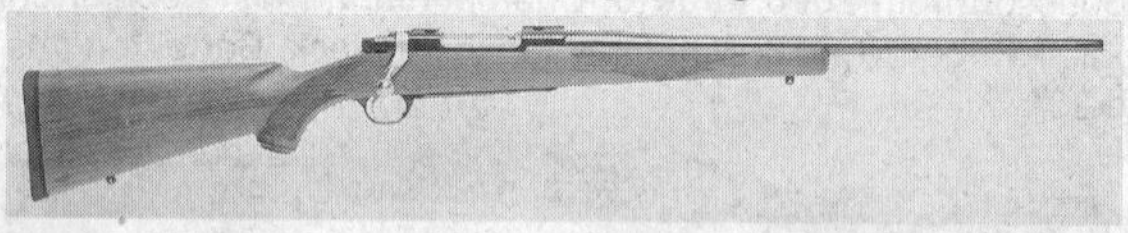

NIB	Exc.	V.G.	Good	Fair	Poor
720	520	380	250	200	150

Model 77RP MKII

Also introduced in 1992 and differs from Model 77R. Added stainless steel barrel, receiver and synthetic stock. Available in 10 calibers. In 1998, added the .25-06 caliber. Discontinued.

NIB	Exc.	V.G.	Good	Fair	Poor
720	520	380	250	200	150

Model 77RS MKII

Blued version of basic rifle, with addition of open sights. Available in nine calibers from .243 Win. to .458 Win. Magnum. Discontinued.

NIB	Exc.	V.G.	Good	Fair	Poor
760	600	450	350	250	180

Model 77RSP MKII

Stainless version of basic rifle, with addition of synthetic stock and open sights. Available in six calibers: .243, .270, 7MM Rem. Magnum, .30-06, .300 Win. Magnum, .338 Win. Magnum. Introduced in 1993. Discontinued.

NIB	Exc.	V.G.	Good	Fair	Poor
500	400	350	300	250	180

Model 77RSI MKII

Also introduced in 1993. Features blued barrel and full-length walnut stock. Offered in .243-, .270-, .30-06-, .308-calibers, all with 18" barrel.

NIB	Exc.	V.G.	Good	Fair	Poor
820	600	450	350	250	180

Model 77RL MKII

This model features a short-action in six calibers from .223 to .308, all with 20" barrel. Weight 6 lbs. Introduced in 1992. Discontinued.

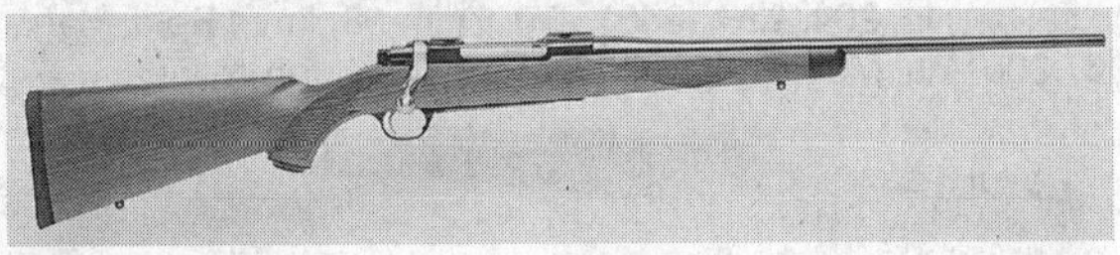

NIB	Exc.	V.G.	Good	Fair	Poor
770	580	420	300	200	150

Model 77LR MKII

A left-handed rifle furnished in long-action calibers: .270, 7mm Rem. Magnum, .30-06, .300 Win. Magnum. Introduced in 1992. Discontinued.

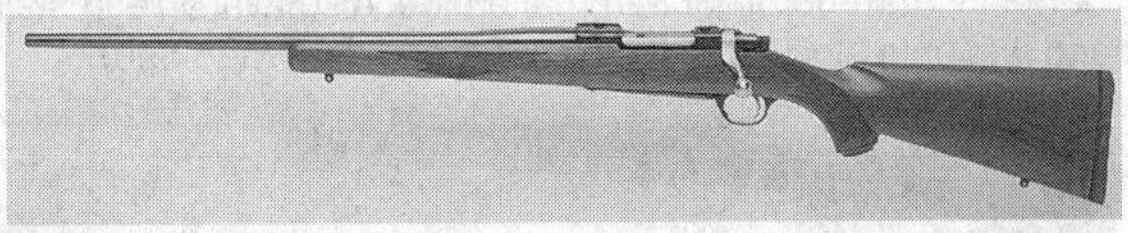

NIB	Exc.	V.G.	Good	Fair	Poor
770	580	420	300	200	150

Model 77RLP MKII

Introduced in 1999. Similar to RL model above, with all-weather synthetic stock. Weight 6.5 lbs. Discontinued.

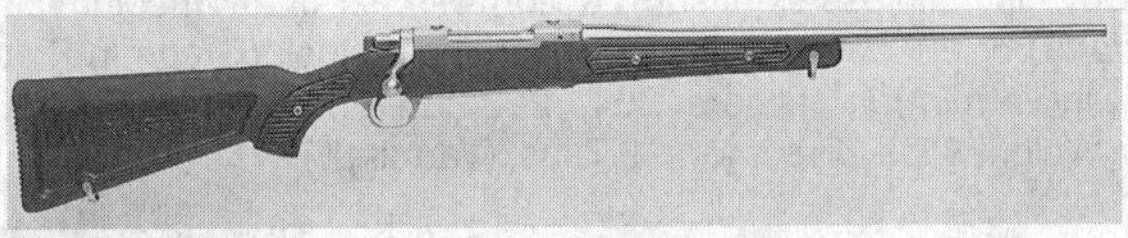

NIB	Exc.	V.G.	Good	Fair	Poor
720	520	400	280	200	150

Model 77VT MKII

A target rifle introduced in 1993. Furnished with no sights, heavy laminated wood stock with beavertail forend and adjustable trigger. Barrel, bolt, and action are stainless steel. Weight 9.75 lbs. Furnished in eight calibers from .223 to .308. Discontinued.

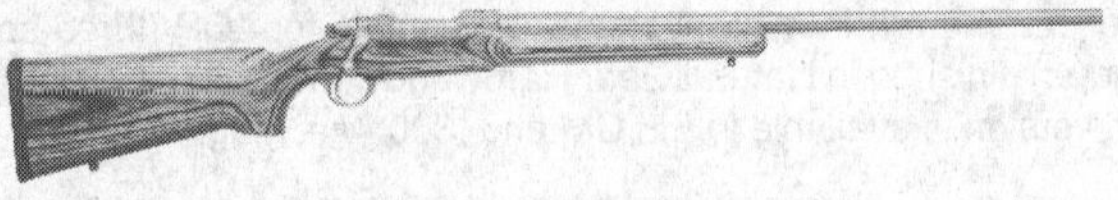

NIB	Exc.	V.G.	Good	Fair	Poor
820	650	480	350	250	180

Model 77RBZ MKII

Features a stainless steel barrel and action. Fitted with laminated hardwood stock. No sights. Weight 7.25 lbs. Offered in a wide variety of calibers from .223 to .338 Win. Magnum. Introduced in 1997. Discontinued.

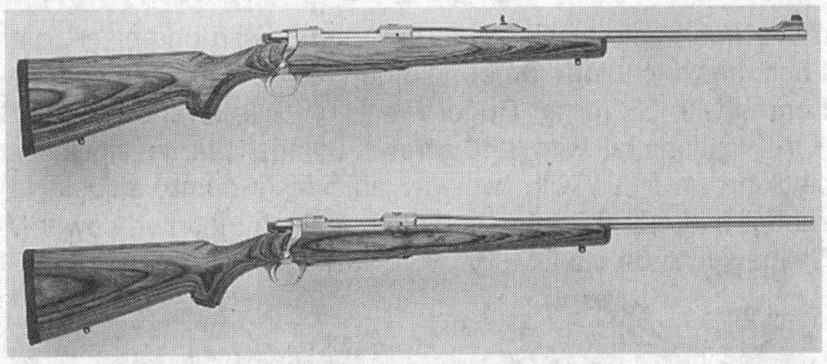

NIB	Exc.	V.G.	Good	Fair	Poor
600	500	400	300	220	180

Model 77RSBZ MKII

Same as above, but fitted with open sights. Introduced in 1997. Discontinued.

NIB	Exc.	V.G.	Good	Fair	Poor
800	650	480	350	250	120

Model 77CR MKII Compact Rifle

Introduced in 2001. Features 16.5" barrel, with 4-round magazine. Chambered for .223 Rem., .243 Win., .260 Rem. and .308 Win. cartridges. Blued model fitted with walnut stock; stainless steel model with black laminated stock. Weight 5.75 lbs. Note: Add $50 for stainless steel model (M77CRBBZ). Discontinued.

NIB	Exc.	V.G.	Good	Fair	Poor
650	550	400	280	200	150

Model 77 Express MKII

Introduced in 1992. Features select Circassian walnut straight comb checkered (22 lpi) stock. Buttstock fitted with a rubber recoil pad; pistol-grip with metal grip cap. Barrel length 22" features blade front sight and V-notch rear express. Receiver machined for scope mounts, which are included. Available in these calibers: .270, .30-06, 7mm Rem. Magnum, .300 Win. Magnum, .338 Win. Magnum. Weight 7.5 lbs. Discontinued.

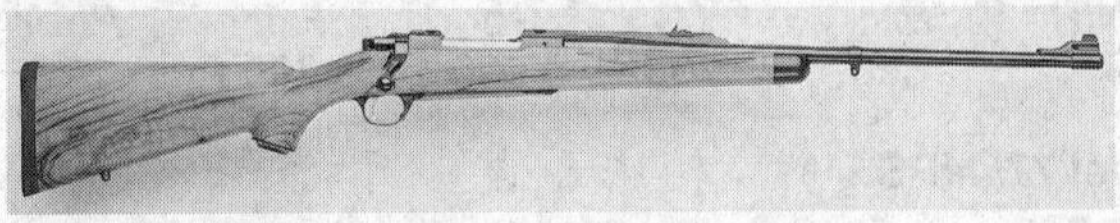

NIB	Exc.	V.G.	Good	Fair	Poor
1200	850	650	550	400	200

Model 77 Magnum MKII RSM

Similar in all respects to Model 77 Express MKII, except offered in these calibers: .375 H&H, .416 Rigby, and .458 Lott. Weight 9.25 lbs. for .375; 10.25 lbs. for.416 and .458 Lott. Discontinued.

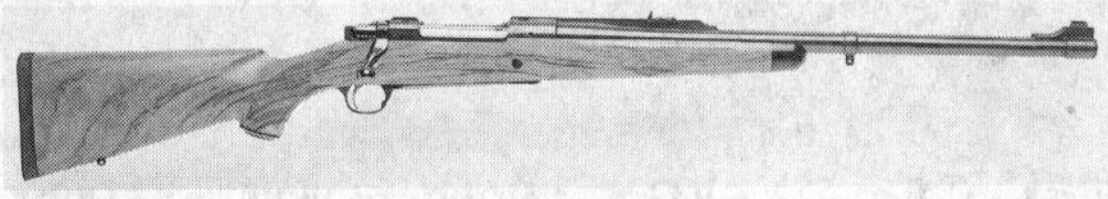

NIB	Exc.	V.G.	Good	Fair	Poor
1980	1500	1100	750	520	350

Model 77 MKII Frontier Rifle

Bolt-action rifle based on M77 MKII chassis. Introduced in 2005, this variation is configured for scout-style scope mount system. Chambered in .243, .308, 7mm-08, .300 WSM, .325 WSM, .338 Federal. Gray laminated stock, 16.5" blued or stainless barrel. Stainless barrel and action model introduced 2006. In 2008, added .338 Federal and .358 Win. Frontier Rifle discontinued in 2008. Note: Add 15% for stainless barrel; add 10% for stainless barrel and action. Discontinued.

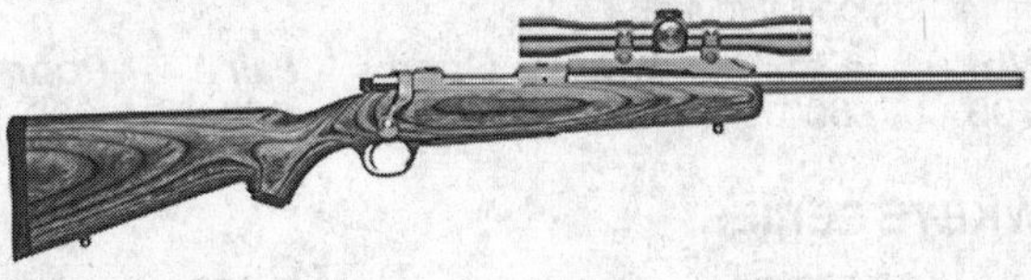

NIB	Exc.	V.G.	Good	Fair	Poor
600	500	400	300	220	180

Model 77 Guide Gun

Like Hawkeye in stainless steel with Green Mountain laminate stock, 20" barrel, in calibers .30-06, .300 Win. Mag., .338 Win. Mag. and .375 Ruger. Fitted with shallow "express-style" windage-adjustable V-notch rear sight and large white bead front sight; barrel band-mounted swivel stud, optional forend swivel stud; Ruger Muzzle Brake System with removable, radial-port muzzle brake and dynamically-matched muzzle weight (eliminates point-of-impact shift) or thread protector (all three included). Left-hand version in .375 Ruger only.

NIB	Exc.	V.G.	Good	Fair	Poor
1090	920	740	620	380	220

Model 77 Scout Rifle

Introduced in 2011 as the Gunsite Scout in honor of Jeff Cooper, today's Scout is in Hawkeye series with a 16.1" barrel in black laminate or synthetic stock, built-in adjustable ghost ring rear aperture sight and protected blade front sight, flash suppressor or muzzle brake, forward-mounted Picatinny rail for intermediate eye relief scopes, detachable box magazine with push-forward magazine release. Caliber .308 (a left-hand model available) or .450 Bushmaster (in matte blue with walnut stock or stainless steel and synthetic stock). Weight 7 lbs. Note: Add $60 for stainless steel or .450 Bushmaster.

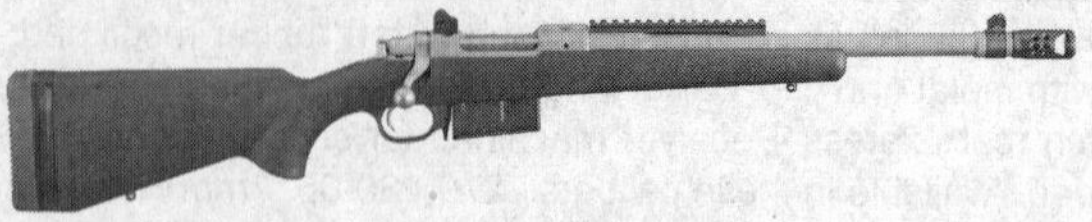

NIB	Exc.	V.G.	Good	Fair	Poor
970	820	700	600	360	220

Model 77/44RS

Bolt-action chambered for .44 Magnum cartridge. Features 18.5" barrel, with open sights. Stock American walnut, with rubber buttpad and checkering on forearm and pistol grip. Detachable rotary magazine has 4 round capacity. Weight 6 lbs. Introduced in mid-1997. Discontinued in 2004, reintroduced in 2009, with synthetic or Next GI Vista camo stock. Note: Deduct $100 for older model with wood stock.

NIB	Exc.	V.G.	Good	Fair	Poor
750	650	500	400	280	150

Model 77/44RSP

Introduced in 1999. Has matte stainless steel barrel and action. Black synthetic stock. Chambered for .44 Magnum cartridge. Weight 6 lbs.

NIB	Exc.	V.G.	Good	Fair	Poor
580	460	380	250	180	120

Model 77/357

Rotary magazine rifle similar to 77/44RS, except chambered for .357 Magnum/.38 Special rounds.

NIB	Exc.	V.G.	Good	Fair	Poor
700	600	450	380	250	200

HAWKEYE SERIES

Introduced in 2007, the Hawkeye replaced the Model 77 Mk II bolt-action rifle. Common features in the Hawkeye include short or long bolt action with 1-piece stainless steel bolt in both blue and stainless actions, non-rotating, Mauser-type controlled-round-feed extractor, fixed blade-type ejector, cold hammer-forged barrel, hinged, steel floorplate with latch flush with the triggerguard, three-position safety, LC-6 trigger and integral scope mounts (rings included).

Model 77 Hawkeye Standard

As above, with matte blue barrel and action in checkered American walnut stock. No iron sights. Cold hammer-forged 22" or 24" barrel (depending on caliber) in .204, 223, .243, .270, 7mm-08, 7mm Rem. Mag., .308, .30-06, .300 Win. Mag. Weight 7.5 lbs. depending on caliber.

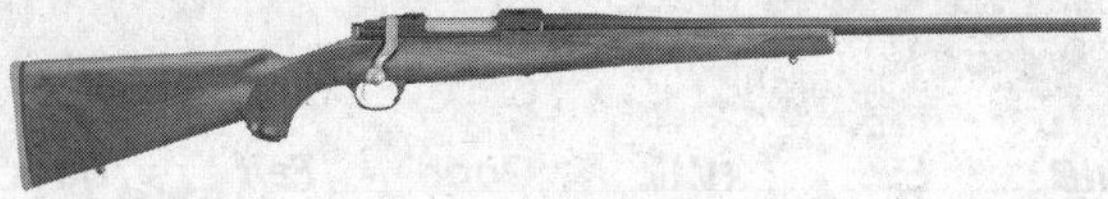

NIB	Exc.	V.G.	Good	Fair	Poor
830	700	600	510	300	180

M77 Hawkeye Compact

16.5" barrel in 7mm-08 or .308 in matte blue. Also available in stainless steel and laminate stock in .243, 7mm-08 and .308 (add $90).

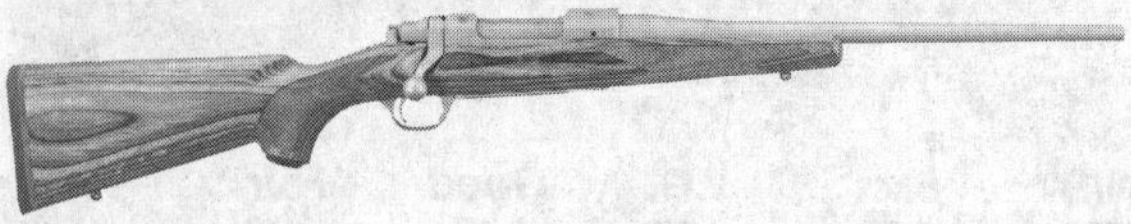

NIB	Exc.	V.G.	Good	Fair	Poor
830	700	600	510	300	180

Model 77 Hawkeye Predator or Varmint Target

As above in stainless steel short action with 22" or 24" medium contour (Predator) or 26" heavy (varmint) in laminate stock (Green in Predator; Black in Varmint) in calibers .204, .223, .22-250, 6.5 C, .308 (Varmint only). Weight 8 lbs. (Predator); 9.7 lbs. (Varmint).

NIB	Exc.	V.G.	Good	Fair	Poor
970	820	700	600	360	220

Model 77 Hawkeye FTW Hunter

Stainless steel action and 24" barrel in 6.5 CM, .300 Win. Mag. and .375 Ruger (22" barrel) in synthetic stock adjustable for LOP (three spacers included), finished in Natural Gear Hardwood camo, weight 7.5 lbs. A left-hand version is available in 6.5 CM and .300 Win. Mag.

NIB	Exc.	V.G.	Good	Fair	Poor
1090	920	740	620	380	220

Model 77 Hawkeye Long Range Target

As above with matte black action and barrel, with one-piece, stainless steel bolt, heavy-contour target cold hammer-forged 4140 chrome-moly steel barrel with 5R rifling, Ruger Precision Rifle Hybrid Muzzle Brake, 20 MOA Picatinny rail with 8-40 screws. Synthetic target stock in speckled black/brown finish with two-way adjustable comb, adjustable LOP, soft rubber buttpad, QD attach points and flush mounted Lower M-LOK rail. Calibers include 6.5 CM, 6.5 PRC and .300 Win. Mag.

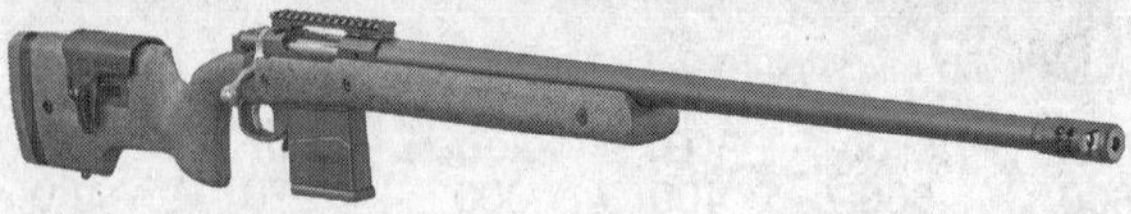

NIB	Exc.	V.G.	Good	Fair	Poor
1090	920	740	620	380	220

M77 Hawkeye Ultra-Light

Hawkeye with lightweight 20" blued barrel. Chambered in .223, .243 Win., .257 Roberts, .270 Win., .308 Win., and .30-06. Discontinued.

NIB	Exc.	V.G.	Good	Fair	Poor
700	600	450	300	220	180

M77 Hawkeye All-Weather Ultra-Light

Similar to above, with black synthetic stock. Matte stainless barrel and receiver. Chambered in .204, .223, .243 Win., .270 Win., and .30-06. Discontinued.

NIB	Exc.	V.G.	Good	Fair	Poor
600	500	400	300	220	180

M77 Hawkeye All-Weather

All-weather version of HM77R Hawkeye, with synthetic stock and stainless barrel. Same chamberings as HM77R, with .338 Federal and .358 Win. as well. Introduced 2007. Left-hand introduced 2008. Discontinued.

NIB	Exc.	V.G.	Good	Fair	Poor
700	550	420	300	220	150

M77PRCM Hawkeye Compact Magnum

Blued barrel and walnut stock. Introduced 2008. Discontinued.

NIB	Exc.	V.G.	Good	Fair	Poor
800	700	580	480	350	200

M77RCM Hawkeye Compact Magnum

Blued barrel and walnut stock. Introduced 2008.

NIB	Exc.	V.G.	Good	Fair	Poor
800	700	580	480	350	200

M77 Hawkeye Magnum Hunter

Stainless model offered only in .300 Win. Mag. Features include Green Hogue stock, 24" barrel with removable muzzle brake, and LC6 trigger. Discontinued.

NIB	Exc.	V.G.	Good	Fair	Poor
950	800	600	400	250	150

Model 77 Hawkeye Alaskan

Stainless steel with black synthetic Hogue Overmolded stock, 20" barrel. Calibers include .300 Win. Mag., .338 Win. Mag. and .375 Ruger. Fitted with shallow "express-style" windage-adjustable V-notch rear sight and large white bead front sight; barrel band mounted swivel stud, optional forend swivel stud; Ruger Muzzle Brake System with removable, radial-port muzzle brake and dynamically matched muzzle weight (eliminates point-of-impact shift) or thread protector (all three included).

NIB	Exc.	V.G.	Good	Fair	Poor
1090	920	740	620	380	220

Model 77 Hawkeye African

As above, with matte blue action in checkered American walnut stock with ebony forend cap, 23" barrel in .300 Win. Mag., .338 Win. Mag., .375 Ruger, and .416 Ruger. Fitted with shallow "express-style" windage-adjustable V-notch rear sight and large white bead front sight; barrel band mounted swivel stud, optional forend swivel stud; Ruger Muzzle Brake System with removable, radial-port muzzle brake and dynamically matched muzzle weight (eliminates point-of-impact shift) or thread protector (all three included). Left-hand version in .375 Ruger only.

NIB	Exc.	V.G.	Good	Fair	Poor
1090	920	740	620	380	220

M77 Hawkeye Tactical

Similar to the M77 Hawkeye, with 20" matte blue heavy barrel, overmolded Hogue synthetic stock. Chambered in .223, .243 Win. and .308 Win. Discontinued.

NIB	Exc.	V.G.	Good	Fair	Poor
880	750	620	500	300	200

M77 Hawkeye International

Similar to Hawkeye, with 18.5" barrel and full-length Mannlicher-style stock. Chambered in .243, .270, .308 Win., and .30-06. Discontinued.

NIB	Exc.	V.G.	Good	Fair	Poor
820	720	600	480	350	220

M77 Hawkeye Varmint Target

Chambered in .204 Ruger, .223 Rem., 22-250, 6.5 Creedmoor and .308 Win. Features heavy contour 26" barrel, black laminate target-type stock and adjustable two-stage trigger.

NIB	Exc.	V.G.	Good	Fair	Poor
850	700	550	400	250	150

Hawkeye Long-Range Hunter

Calibers: 6.5 Creedmoor, 6.5 PRC. Capacity: 3 to 5. Barrel: 22", stainless steel, threaded. Stock: Speckled wood laminate. Sights: 20 MOA Picatinny rail. Weight: 7.2 lbs. Features: Three-position safety, non-rotating Mauser-type controlled-round-feed extractor.

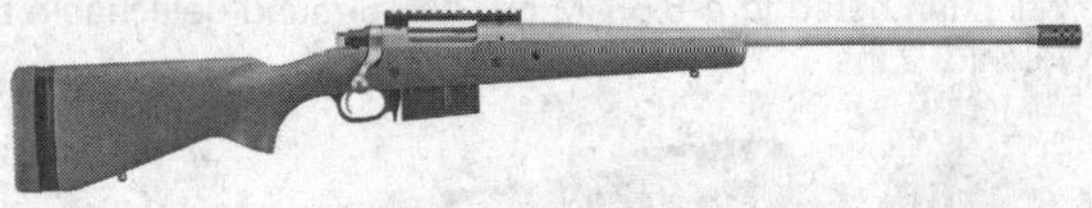

NIB	Exc.	V.G.	Good	Fair	Poor
1150	—	—	—	—	—

AMERICAN SERIES

American Standard

A bolt-action rifle with one-piece, three-lug bolt with 70-deg. lift, tang safety, Marksman Adjustable trigger, cold hammer-forged 22" barrel in black synthetic stock with integral bedding block system, soft rubber buttpad, one magazine and sling swivel studs. Weight 6.5 lbs. Calibers include .243, 7mm-08, .270, .308, .30-06.

NIB	Exc.	V.G.	Good	Fair	Poor
420	350	300	250	150	100

Ruger American Compact

In short-action with 18" barrel calibers include .243, 7mm-08, and .308. Weight 6 lbs.

NIB	Exc.	V.G.	Good	Fair	Poor
420	350	300	250	150	100

American Go Wild Camo

As above, with Cerakote Bronze metal, Go Wild Brush camo stock, Picatinny scope rail, factory-installed 5/8"-24 muzzle break. Additional calibers include 6.5 CM, .300 Win. Mag. and .450 Bushmaster.

NIB	Exc.	V.G.	Good	Fair	Poor
540	450	360	300	180	120

American Vortex Crossfire II

As above, with factory installed Vortex 3-9X. Additional calibers include .223 and 6.5 CM. Also available in Moss Green synthetic stock with factory-installed Vortex 4-12X scope (add $60) in calibers above plus .204 as well.

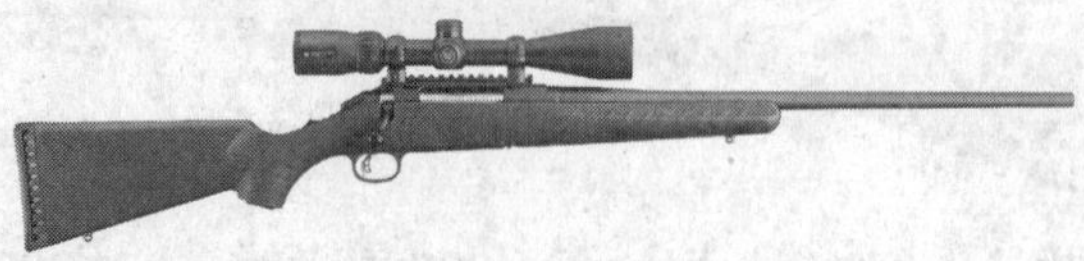

NIB	Exc.	V.G.	Good	Fair	Poor
540	470	400	300	200	100

American Predator

As above, in short-action calibers including .204, .223, .22-250, 6mm CM, 6.5 Grendel, 6.5 C, 7mm-08, .308 in Moss Green synthetic stock, heavier tapered, threaded barrel with factory-installed thread protector and scope rail. Left-hand versions (add $40) available in some calibers.

NIB	Exc.	V.G.	Good	Fair	Poor
450	360	300	260	150	100

American Hunter

New in 2019, American short action in gray Magpul Hunter American stock, heavy 20" barrel with factory installed muzzle brake and Picatinny scope rail chambered in a 6.5 CM or .308, 5-round detachable magazine. Weight 9.2 lbs.

NIB	Exc.	V.G.	Good	Fair	Poor
680	580	490	420	250	150

American Magnum

Stainless steel action and 24" barrel threaded for muzzle brake in .300 Win. Mag., black synthetic stock, Picatinny scope rail. Weight 7.5 lbs.

NIB	Exc.	V.G.	Good	Fair	Poor
600	500	430	360	220	140

American Ranch Rifle

In short actions only with compact, 16.12" threaded barrel with factory-installed thread protector or Ruger Hybrid muzzle brake, one-piece Picatinny scope base. Calibers include 5.56 NATO, 7.62x39, .300 Blk, .350 Legend, .450 Bushmaster. Weight 6.1 lbs.

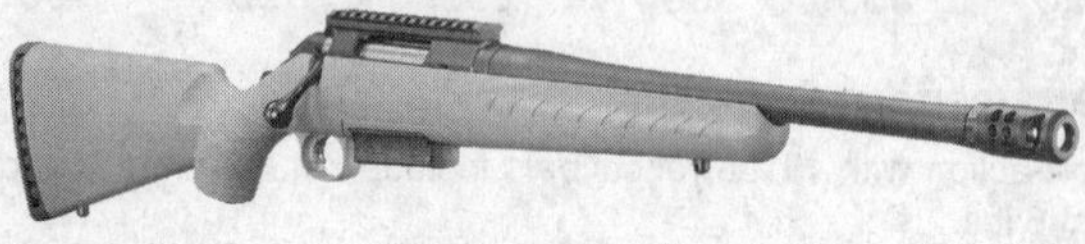

NIB	Exc.	V.G.	Good	Fair	Poor
460	400	340	280	160	100

American Rifle All-Weather Stainless

Same features as standard model, with stainless steel barrel and action. Also offered in Compact model. Introduced in 2014.

NIB	Exc.	V.G.	Good	Fair	Poor
500	420	350	300	220	150

American Rimfire Rifle

In 2014, a rimfire version of American Rifle was introduced. Similar features as centerfire model. Available in full-size version, with 22" barrel; compact model, with 18" barrel.

NIB	Exc.	V.G.	Good	Fair	Poor
280	240	200	180	150	120

Ruger Precision Rifle

A precision bolt-action target rifle built using an "upper" receiver with one-piece bolt CNC-machined from pre-hardened 4140 chrome-moly steel, and oversized bolt handle. Cold hammer-forged, chrome-moly steel barrel with 5R rifling in lengths of 20", 24", or 26" depending on caliber. Calibers include .223 (discontinued), 6mm C, 6.5 CM, 6.5 PRC, .308, .300 Win. Mag., .300 PRC, and .338 Lapua all with a Ruger Precision Rifle Hybrid Muzzle Brake. 20 or 30 MOA Picatinny rail secured with 8-40 screws for increased long-range elevation capabilities, depending on caliber. "Lower" magazine well halves are precision machined from 7075-T6 aluminum Type III hard-coat anodized. Externally adjustable Ruger Marksman trigger with a pull range of 2.25 to 5 pounds. Extended trigger-reach AR-style grip and 45-deg ambidextrous safety selector. May be configured with any AR-style grip and selector. Ruger Precision MSR stock is fully adjustable for comb height and LOP, has QD sling and bottom Picatinny rail with soft rubber buttpad; a left-folding stock hinge attached to an AR-style buffer tube (accepts any AR-style stock). Aluminum free-float handguard is black hard-coat anodized aluminum with Magpul M-LOK slots on all four sides. Note: Add $500 for .300 Win. Mag., .300 PRC and .338 Lapua.

NIB	Exc.	V.G.	Good	Fair	Poor
1340	1150	980	840	500	300

MODEL 77 PISTOL-CALIBER SERIES

A small bolt action for revolver-size cartridges in blue or stainless steel, stainless steel bolt with 90° bolt throw, detachable flush-mount rotary magazine, cold hammer-forged barrel, integral scope mounts, three-position safety, sling swivel studs. (See Rimfire section for 77/17 in .17 WSM).

Model 77/17

Chambered for the .17 Hornet with stainless steel action, 20" barrel, 6-shot magazine in Green Mountain laminate stock.

NIB	Exc.	V.G.	Good	Fair	Poor
900	780	650	560	340	200

Model 77/22

Chambered for the .22 Hornet with blued action and barrel (American walnut) or stainless steel (Green Mountain laminate stock), 24" barrel, 6-shot magazine. Note: Add $70 for stainless/laminate.

NIB	Exc.	V.G.	Good	Fair	Poor
850	720	620	520	320	180

Model 77/357

Chambered for .357 Magnum/.38 Special with 18.5" stainless steel barrel and action in black synthetic stock.

NIB	Exc.	V.G.	Good	Fair	Poor
850	720	620	520	320	180

Model 77/44RS & 77/44RSP

Chambered for .44 Magnum cartridge with 18.5" barrel, open sights. Synthetic or American walnut, with rubber buttpad and checkering on forearm and pistol grip. Detachable rotary magazine has 4-round capacity. Weight about 6 lbs. Introduced in mid-1997. Discontinued in 2004, re-introduced in 2009. Add $60 for current model with wood stock or stainless steel in synthetic stock.

NIB	Exc.	V.G.	Good	Fair	Poor
800	680	580	490	300	180

RIMFIRE BOLT ACTION RIFLES

AMERICAN SERIES

American Series Rimfire have many upscale features in a budget-priced rifle. Cold hammer-forged barrel, a 60-deg. bolt lift, receiver-mounted bolt release, Ruger Marksman Adjustable trigger, a 3/8" rimfire scope base machined into the receiver, which is also drilled and tapped for Weaver No. 12 bases. Long Rifle models accept Ruger BX-1 10/22 magazines, and magnums take the JMX-1 flush-fit 9-round mags. Power Bedding integral bedding block system positively locates the receiver and free-floats the barrel, and synthetic stocks offer comb height adjustment for scope or Williams fiber optic front sight and adjustable, V-slot, folding-leaf rear iron sights. Begun in the 1990s with the 77/22, only the hot .17 WSM remains of the an extensive premium line of standard and magnum rimfires.

American Rimfire Standard

As above, in black synthetic stock, matte blue metal, 22" barrel in .22 LR, .17 HMR, and .22 WMR; weight 6 lbs. Add $30 for 18" barreled carbine in all calibers. Add $100 for wood stock in .22 LR.

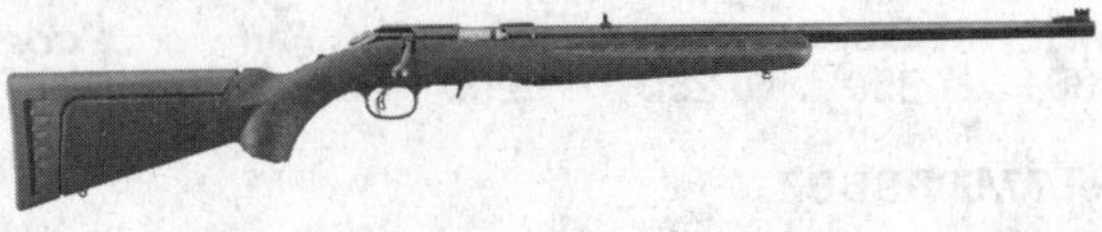

NIB	Exc.	V.G.	Good	Fair	Poor
300	260	220	180	120	70

American Rimfire Standard Stainless

As above, with stainless steel action and 18" barrel in .22 LR, .17 HMR or .22 WMR. Has factory-installed aluminum scope rail, no sights and barrel is threaded 1/2-28 for a suppressor.

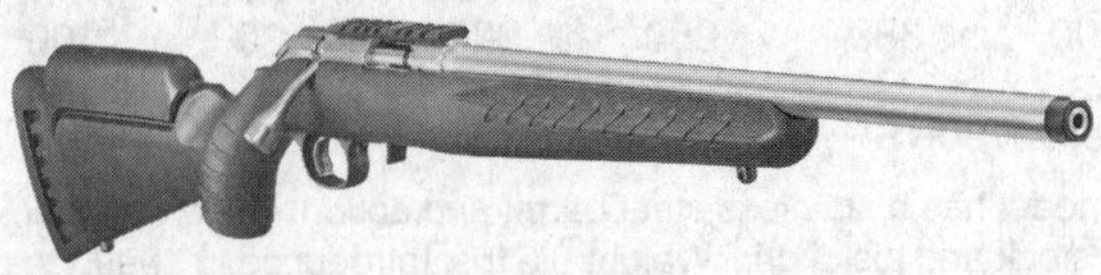

NIB	Exc.	V.G.	Good	Fair	Poor
360	300	260	220	140	80

American Rimfire Compact

As above, in black synthetic stock with 12.5" LOP, matte blue metal, 18" barrel in .22 LR, .17 HMR, and .22 WMR; weight 5.3 lbs. Add $30 for 1/2-28 threaded barrel carbine in .22 LR.

NIB	Exc.	V.G.	Good	Fair	Poor
300	260	220	180	120	70

American Rimfire Target

As above, in matte blue or stainless steel with 18" heavy barrel, threaded 1/2-28, in .22 LR, .17 HMR or .22 WMR. Has black laminate stock, scope base installed (no sights), weight 6.7 lbs. Add $30 for stainless steel; add $60 for black laminate thumbhole stock (.22 LR only).

NIB	Exc.	V.G.	Good	Fair	Poor
420	360	300	260	150	100

Ruger Precision Rimfire

A rimfire version of the Ruger Precision Rifle in a molded, 1-piece chassis of glass-filled nylon with adjustable buttstock and flat Picatinny bag rider for rear monopod. A molded-in window provides a tether point for your squeeze bag and a metal QD pocket to secure a sling. AR-Pattern pistol grip and reversible safety selector. Compatible with most AR-style grips and selectors. The 18" target barrel in .22 LR, .17 HMR or .22 WMR is cold hammer-forged from 1137 alloy steel threaded 1/2"-28. Oversized bolt handle (same as the Ruger Precision Rifle). Big-Gun bolt throw adjustment enables shooters to change from a rimfire 1-1/2" bolt throw to a short-action centerfire 3" bolt throw, reducing the chance of short-stroking your bolt in competition. Ruger Marksman Adjustable trigger is externally adjustable, with a trigger pull range of 2.25 to 5 pounds. A 15" aluminum free-float handguard is black hard-coat anodized with M-LOK slots on all four sides. Use Ruger BX-1 and JMX-1 magazines.

NIB	Exc.	V.G.	Good	Fair	Poor
450	380	320	280	160	100

MODEL 77 RIMFIRE SERIES

Ruger 77/17

Chambered for the .17 WSM with matte blue action and 20" barrel in American walnut stock or stainless steel action and 18.5" barrel in Green Mountain laminate stock. No sights, integral scope mounts (rings included) and 6-shot magazine. Weight 5.7 lbs. Add $70 for stainless/laminate.

NIB	Exc.	V.G.	Good	Fair	Poor
850	720	620	520	320	180

Model 77/17

Introduced in 2003. Chambered for .17 HMR cartridge. Fitted with 22" barrel, with no sights. Walnut stock, with blued finish. Magazine capacity 9 rounds. Weight 6 lbs. Discontinued.

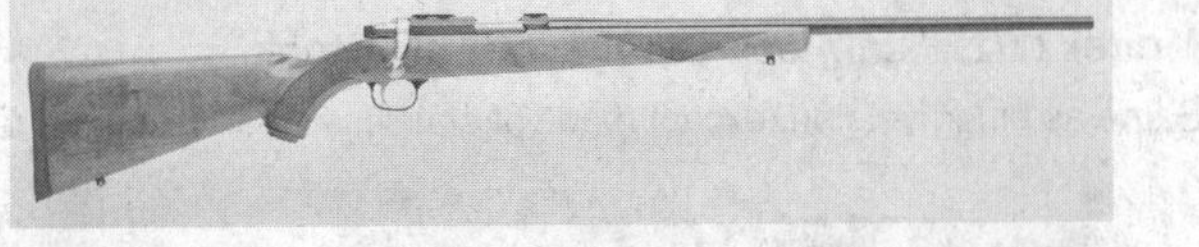

NIB	Exc.	V.G.	Good	Fair	Poor
700	600	480	380	250	150

Model 77/17 Synthetic

As above, with black synthetic stock and blued finish. Discontinued.

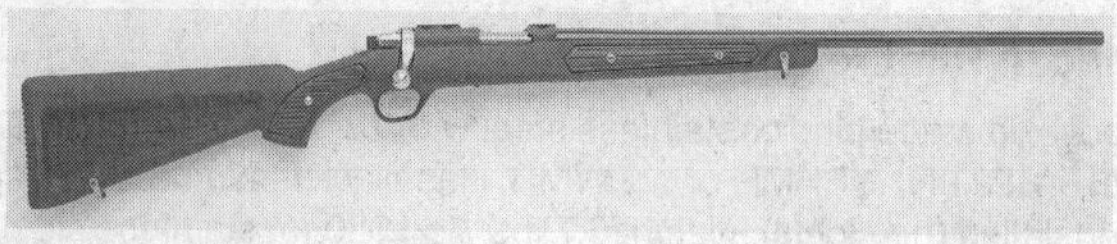

NIB	Exc.	V.G.	Good	Fair	Poor
620	480	350	250	180	120

Model 77/17 Varmint

As above, with black laminate stock and 24" stainless steel heavy barrel, with no sights. Weight 7 lbs. Discontinued.

NIB	Exc.	V.G.	Good	Fair	Poor
680	500	380	260	200	140

Model 77/17RM2

Introduced in 2005. Chambered for .17 Mach 2 caliber. Fitted with 20" barrel, with no sights. Walnut stock, with checkering. Blued finish. Weight 6.5 lbs. Discontinued.

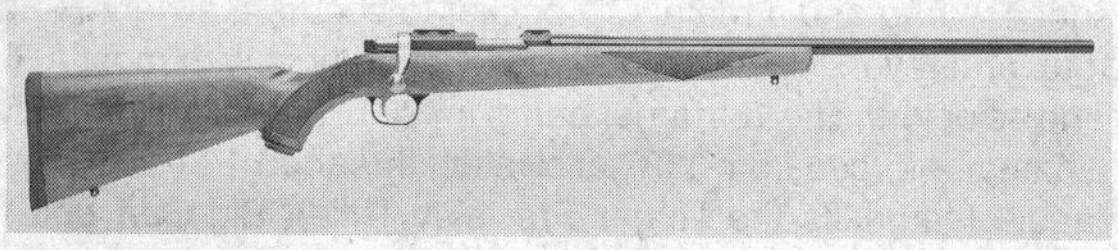

NIB	Exc.	V.G.	Good	Fair	Poor
620	480	350	250	180	120

Model 77/17RM2 Stainless Steel

As above, with stainless steel finish and black laminate stock. Weight 7.25 lbs. Introduced in 2005. Discontinued.

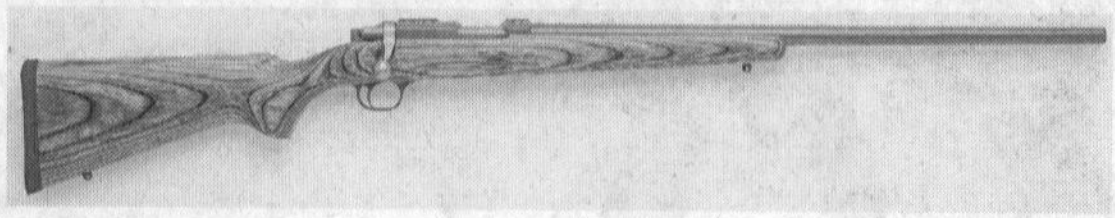

NIB	Exc.	V.G.	Good	Fair	Poor
740	620	500	400	280	150

Model 77/22

A high quality, .22 rimfire (LR and WMR) rifle designed for the serious shooter. Has a 20" barrel and 9- or 10-shot detachable rotary magazine. Made of steel and stock with checkered walnut. Available with sights, scope rings or both as an extra-cost ($20) option. Introduced in 1984. Early guns without 77/22 rollmark on the receiver will bring a premium. Discontinued.

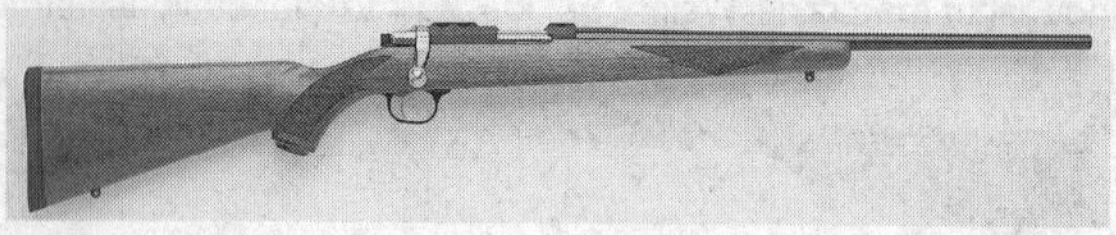

NIB	Exc.	V.G.	Good	Fair	Poor
700	600	480	380	250	150

Model 77/22 Synthetic Stock

This version is quite similar to standard 77/22, with black matte-finished synthetic stock. Discontinued.

NIB	Exc.	V.G.	Good	Fair	Poor
620	450	350	250	200	150

Model 77/22 Stainless Steel/Synthetic Stock

Same as blued version, except made of stainless steel. Discontinued.

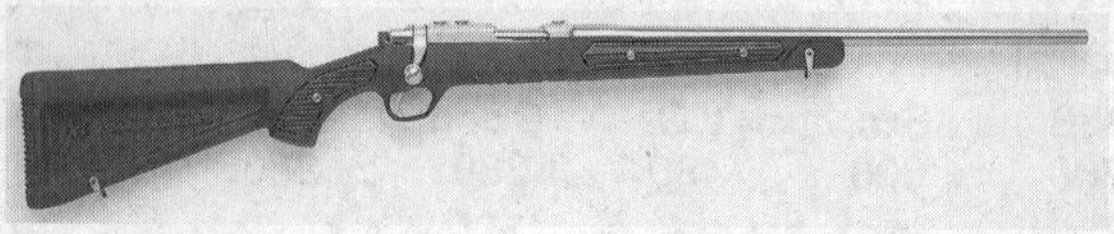

NIB	Exc.	V.G.	Good	Fair	Poor
750	650	500	400	280	150

Model 77/22 Varmint

Introduced in 1993. Features stainless steel finish, laminated wood stock, heavy 20" varmint barrel with no sights. Scope rings are included as standard. Chambered for .22 LR or Win. Magnum rimfire. Discontinued.

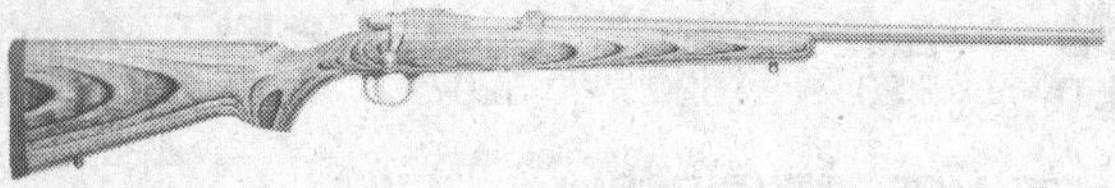

NIB	Exc.	V.G.	Good	Fair	Poor
650	520	420	300	250	150

Model 77/22M

Simply 77/22 chambered for .22 Magnum cartridge. Finish is blue. Magazine capacity 9 rounds. Discontinued.

NIB	Exc.	V.G.	Good	Fair	Poor
700	600	480	380	250	150

Model 77/22M Stainless Steel

Same as blued 77/22M, only constructed of stainless steel. Discontinued.

NIB	Exc.	V.G.	Good	Fair	Poor
750	650	500	400	280	150

BOLT-ACTION RIFLES

MUZZLELOADERS

Model 77/50RS

An inline percussion rifle chambered for .50-caliber. Fitted with a 22" barrel and open sights. Stock is birch, with rubber buttplate and no checkering. Blued finish. Weight 6.5 lbs. Introduced in mid-1997; discontinued.

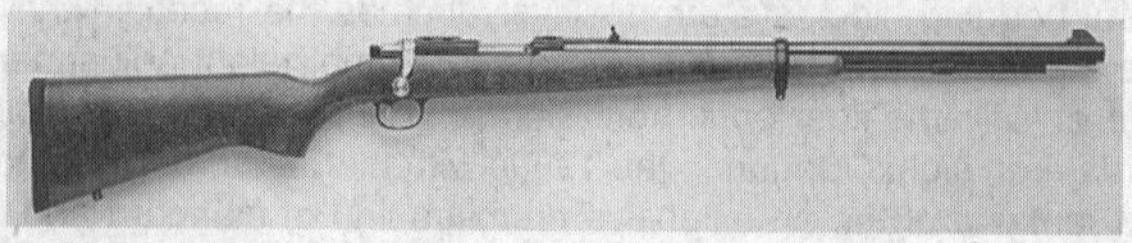

NIB	Exc.	V.G.	Good	Fair	Poor
420	320	220	180	120	100

Model 77/50RSO

Similar to model above, with straight-grip checkered walnut stock and curved buttplate. Introduced in 1998.

NIB	Exc.	V.G.	Good	Fair	Poor
480	350	250	200	120	100

Model 77/50RSBBZ

Introduced in 1998. Features all specifications of Model 77/50RS, with addition of black/gray laminated stock and stainless steel finish.

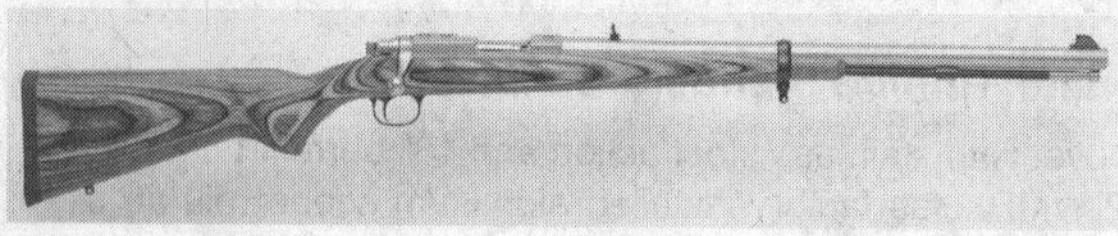

NIB	Exc.	V.G.	Good	Fair	Poor
500	380	280	220	120	100

Model 77/50RSP

This model has a stainless steel barrel and action. Fitted with black synthetic stock and pistol grip. Weight 6.5 lbs. Introduced in 1999.

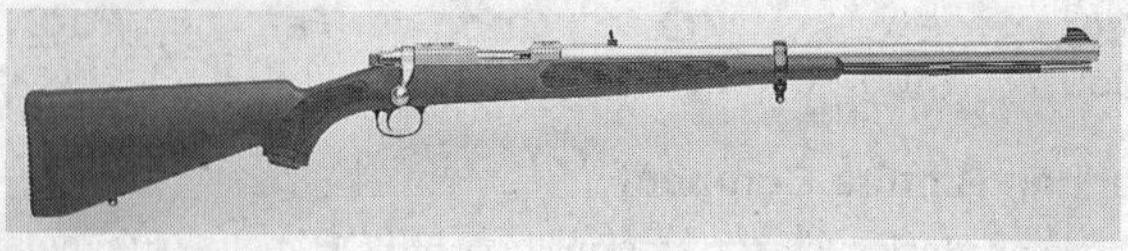

NIB	Exc.	V.G.	Good	Fair	Poor
580	400	300	200	120	100

LEVER-ACTION RIFLES

Model 96/17

Introduced in 2003. Chambered for .17 HMR cartridge. Fitted with an 18.5" barrel. Magazine capacity 9 rounds. Hardwood stock and open sights. Weight 5.25 lbs. Discontinued.

NIB	Exc.	V.G.	Good	Fair	Poor
600	500	400	300	150	120

Model 96/22

Introduced into Ruger line in 1996. Chambered for .22 LR. Stock American hardwood. Barrel length 18.5". Magazine capacity 10 rounds. Open sights are standard. Weight 5.25 lbs. Discontinued.

NIB	Exc.	V.G.	Good	Fair	Poor
500	400	320	200	150	120

Model 96/22M

Chambered for .22 WMR cartridge. Magazine capacity 9 rounds. Discontinued.

NIB	Exc.	V.G.	Good	Fair	Poor
600	500	400	300	200	120

Model 96/44

Same as .22 caliber, except chambered for .44 Magnum cartridge. Magazine capacity 4 rounds. Weight 5.875 lbs. Discontinued.

NIB	Exc.	V.G.	Good	Fair	Poor
750	600	500	300	200	120

SHOTGUNS

Red Label Early Production

Red Label over/under shotgun introduced in 1977. Only in 20 gauge, with 12-gauge version added in 1982; 28 gauge in 1995. Original Red Label had blue finish on both receiver and barrels. Fixed chokes, with 26" or 28" ventilated rib barrels and bead front sight. Interchangeable choke tubes were offered as an option in 1988 and became standard in 1990. Stainless receiver with blued barrel became optional in 1985 and then standard starting in 1989. General features include single selective mechanical trigger, selective automatic ejectors and checkered American walnut stock, with pistol grip or English-type straight-grip. Streamlined boxlock action has no exposed pins or screws. Weights ranged from 7 to 8 lbs. Red label was in production through 2011. After a hiatus of a couple years and a few minor changes, it returned to Ruger catalog in 2014.

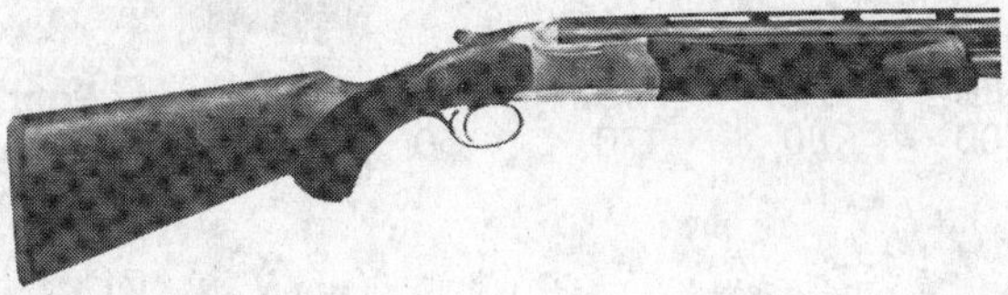

NIB	Exc.	V.G.	Good	Fair	Poor
—	1200	1020	870	740	630

Red Label 2014 Model

This model returned to Ruger line in 2014 with a few changes, mostly on the inside. The 2014 model, in 12-gauge only, has a one-piece cast receiver, compared to two pieces welded together in older version. Locking lugs do not protrude through receiver and there are no side ribs between barrels. After being back in production for only about a year, at the end of 2014 Red Label was discontinued for the second time, and perhaps forever.

NIB	Exc.	V.G.	Good	Fair	Poor
1250	1060	900	770	650	560

Red Label Sporting Clays

Introduced in 1994. Offered in 20 gauge, with 3" chambers and 30" barrels. Walnut stock has checkering and pistol grip. Weight 7 lbs.

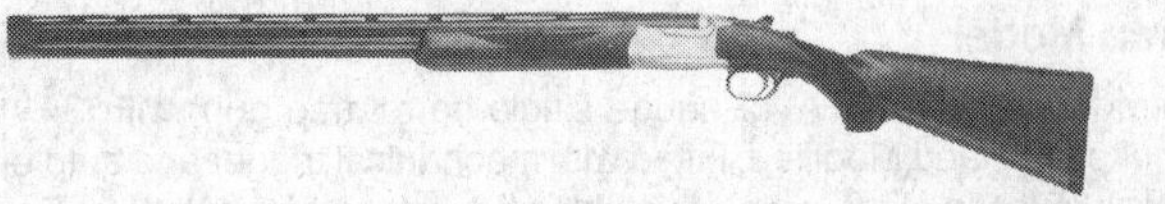

Courtesy compliments of Bill Ruger, John C. Dougan

NIB	Exc.	V.G.	Good	Fair	Poor
1580	1340	1140	970	820	700

Red Label All-Weather

Offered in 12-gauge only, with 26", 28" or 30" barrels. Fitted with black synthetic stock and pistol grip. Weight 7.5 lbs. Introduced in 1999.

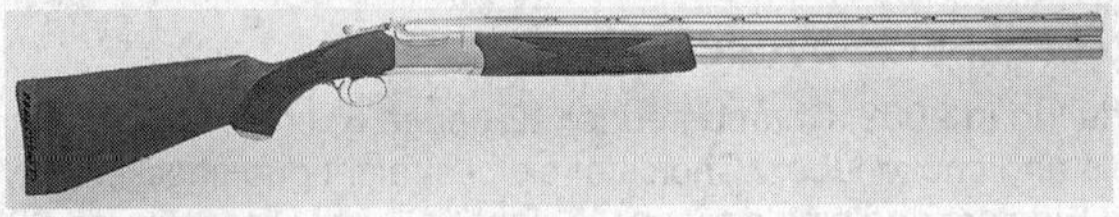

NIB	Exc.	V.G.	Good	Fair	Poor
1350	1150	980	830	700	600

Red Label Series — Hand Engraved

This series of hand-engraved Red Labels was first catalogued in 1996, with three different engraving coverages. A total of 375 were produced by several prominent engravers, between 1997 and 2000.

Grade 1

NIB	Exc.	V.G.	Good	Fair	Poor
2400	2000	1500	1200	—	—

Grade 2 (1/3 coverage)

NIB	Exc.	V.G.	Good	Fair	Poor
2600	2200	1700	1400	—	—

Grade 3 (2/3 coverage)

NIB	Exc.	V.G.	Good	Fair	Poor
3000	2500	2000	1700	—	—

Red Label Engraved

Features scroll engraved receiver, with gold inlaid game bird appropriate to gauge. 12-gauge pheasant; 20-gauge grouse; 28-gauge woodcock. Walnut stock. Other specifications same as standard Red Label shotguns. Introduced in 2000 and made until 2011. Premium for 28-gauge.

NIB	Exc.	V.G.	Good	Fair	Poor
1800	1500	1200	900	500	300

Red Label All-Weather Engraved

Introduced in 2000. Features scroll engraved receiver, with gold inlaid duck. Offered in 12-gauge only, with 26", 28" or 30" barrel.

NIB	Exc.	V.G.	Good	Fair	Poor
1680	1320	1080	750	500	300

Woodside Over/Under

Introduced in 1995. Features Circassian walnut stock, with pistol/straight grip. Available in 12 or 20 gauge, with barrel lengths 26", 28" or 30". Screw-in chokes are standard. Note: Woodside shotgun also available in three different engraving patterns. Discontinued 2002.

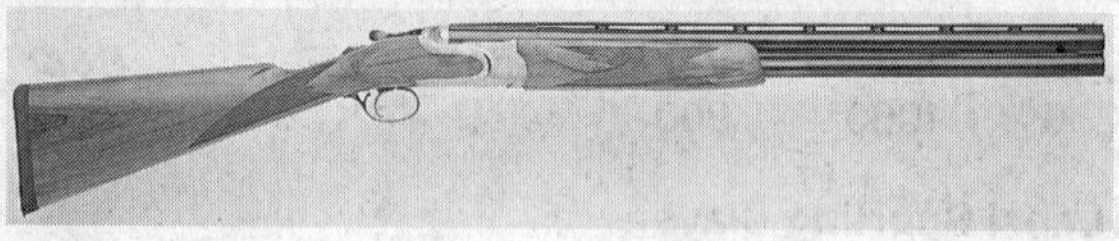

NIB	Exc.	V.G.	Good	Fair	Poor
—	1550	1320	1120	950	810

Trap Model

Introduced in 2000. A 12-gauge single-barrel trap gun, with 34" barrel choked Full and Modified. Fitted with mechanical trigger and auto ejector. Stock select walnut, with adjustable cheekpiece and buttplate. Receiver engraved. Weight 9 lbs.

NIB	Exc.	V.G.	Good	Fair	Poor
—	3200	2720	2310	1960	1670

Gold Label Side-by-Side

Introduced in 2002. Chambered for 12-gauge 3" shell. Offered with 28" barrels and choke tubes. Choice of pistol/straight grip checkered walnut stock. Ejectors and single trigger. Weight 6.33 lbs. Discontinued 2008.

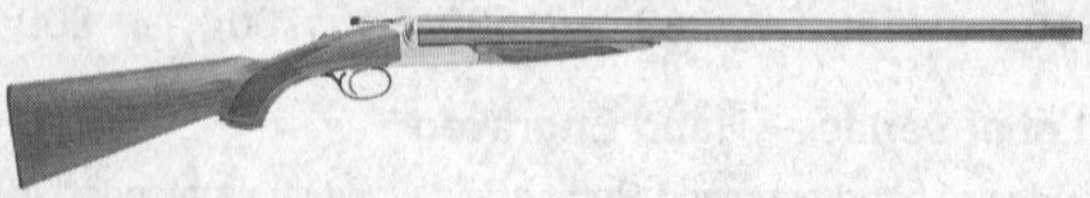

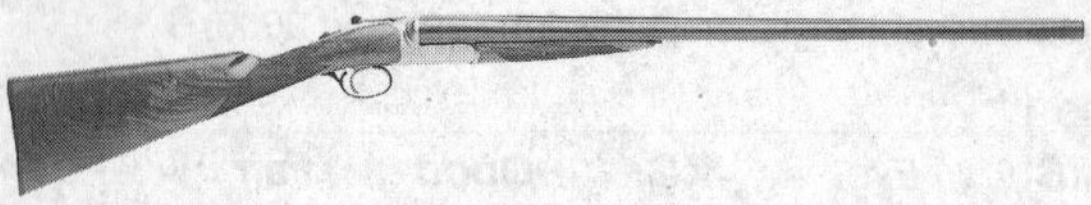

NIB	Exc.	V.G.	Good	Fair	Poor
—	2850	2420	2060	1750	1490

Introduced in 2002. Chambered for 12-gauge 3" shell. Offered with 28" barrels and choke tubes. Choice of pistol/straight grip checkered walnut stock. Ejectors and single trigger. Weight 6.33 lbs. Discontinued 2008.

SUNDANCE INDUSTRIES, INC.

North Hollywood, California

This company was in business from 1989 to 2002.

Model D-22M

A .22 or .22 Magnum caliber double-barrel over/under pocket pistol, with 2.5" barrels and aluminum alloy frame. Blackened finish or chrome-plated, with simulated pearl or black grips. Introduced in 1989.

NIB	Exc.	V.G.	Good	Fair	Poor
—	220	180	120	100	80

Model BOA

Introduced in 1991. Semi-automatic pistol chambered for .25 ACP cartridge. Fitted with 2.5" barrel, with fixed sights. Grip safety. Choice of black or chrome finish. Magazine capacity 7 rounds. Weight about 16 oz.

NIB	Exc.	V.G.	Good	Fair	Poor
120	100	80	70	50	20

Model A-25

Similar to BOA, without grip safety.

NIB	Exc.	V.G.	Good	Fair	Poor
120	100	80	70	50	20

Model Laser 25

Similar to Model BOA, with grip safety. Equipped with a laser sight. Laser activated by squeezing grip safety. Weight with laser 18 oz. Introduced in 1995.

NIB	Exc.	V.G.	Good	Fair	Poor
220	180	120	100	80	50

Sundance Point Blank

An over/under derringer chambered for .22 LR cartridge. Fitted with 3" barrel and double-action trigger. Enclosed hammer. Matte black finish. Weight about 8 oz. Introduced in 1994.

NIB	Exc.	V.G.	Good	Fair	Poor
100	80	70	50	20	10

SUPER SIX LTD.
Fort Atkinson, Wisconsin

Bison Bull

Massive single-action .45-70 revolver, with blued carbon steel (Bison Bull) or engraved molybdenum bronze (Golden Bison Bull) frame. Adjustable sights, 10.5" barrel, 17.5" overall length, weight 6 lbs. Introduced in 2006. Value shown for blued version. Note: Add 350 percent for engraved version.

NIB	Exc.	V.G.	Good	Fair	Poor
1200	1050	900	780	600	500

SUTHERLAND, S.
Richmond, Virginia

Pocket Pistol (Antique)

A .41-caliber percussion single-shot pistol, with round barrels of 2.5" to 4" in length. German silver mounts and walnut stock. Lock normally marked "S. Sutherland" or "S. Sutherland/Richmond". Manufactured during 1850s.

Exc.	Fine	V.G.	Good	Fair	Poor
2950	2200	1500	800	300	210

SYMS, J. G.
New York, New York

Pocket Pistol (Antique)

A .41-caliber single-shot percussion pistol, with 1.5" to 3.5" barrels. German silver mounts and walnut stock. Lock normally marked "Syms/New York". Manufactured during 1850s.

Exc.	Fine	V.G.	Good	Fair	Poor
2600	2150	1480	820	300	210

SYREN SHOTGUNS
Cambridge, Maryland

Syren Tempio

These shotguns are marketed primarily to women. Made by Caesar Guerini and Fabarm in Italy and have features that are found on better grades of over/unders. Gauges are 12, 20 and 28, with .410 available in a combo with 28- or 20-/28-gauges. Barrel lengths are 28", 30" or 32" (Sporting), with choke tubes, choice of manual or automatic safety, deluxe grade walnut stock, coin finished receiver with roses and scroll engraving. Field and Light model weight 5.25 to 6 lbs.; Sporting model from 7.5 to 8 lbs. Introduced in 2015. Note: Add $300 for Sporting model.

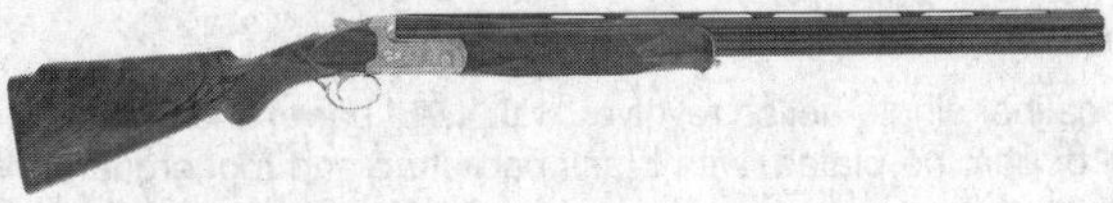

NIB	Exc.	V.G.	Good	Fair	Poor
3300	2800	2500	1600	800	300

XLR5 Sporter

Semi-automatic designed for lighter target loads. Stock designed for female anatomy, with smaller pistol grip, Monte Carlo comb, optimized cast, pitch and length of pull. Made by Fabarm. Introduced in 2014.

NIB	Exc.	V.G.	Good	Fair	Poor
1750	1400	1000	800	400	200

Julia Field

Gauges: 20 ga., 28 ga. Barrels: 28". Stock: Deluxe-grade Turkish Walnut with semi-gloss oil finish. Features: Designed specifically for women as part of Caesar Guerini's Syren division is built as a field gun. Side plate action with fantasy-style engraving depicting a woman's face evolving from a floral scroll. Color-casehardened finish. Single selective trigger, silver front bead, and manual safety. Left-hand stock option and 20/28 combo sets available by special order. Ships with a hard case, velvet sleeves, and five flush choke tubes.

NIB	Exc.	V.G.	Good	Fair	Poor
6080	5300	4200	3000	—	—

T

TACONIC FIREARMS LTD.
Cambridge, New York

M98 Ultimate Hunter

Bolt-action rifle based on M98 Mauser action. Available in calibers from .22-250 to .358 Win. Stainless steel and barrel length 22". Titanium grip cap. Stock is XXX English walnut, with cheekpiece and oil-finish. Ebony forend tip. Scope bases are integral to receiver. Prices listed are for standard rifle. There is an extensive list of options which will greatly affect price. For example, an optional quarter rib will add $1000 to the base price of gun. Value speculative.

NIB	Exc.	V.G.	Good	Fair	Poor
6000					

TALLASSEE
Tallassee, Alabama

Carbine (Antique)

A .58-caliber single-shot percussion carbine, with 25" round barrel and full-length stock secured by two barrel bands. Fitted with sling swivels. Barrel and lock finished in bright brass furniture and walnut stock. Lock marked "C.S./Tallassee/ Ala.". Approximately 500 of these carbines manufactured in 1864. One of the rarest Confederate arms, expert authentication is essential. Too rare to estimate values. The last public sale was in 2012 at Julia Auction of a gun described as good with brown patina and pitting. It sold for $17,500.

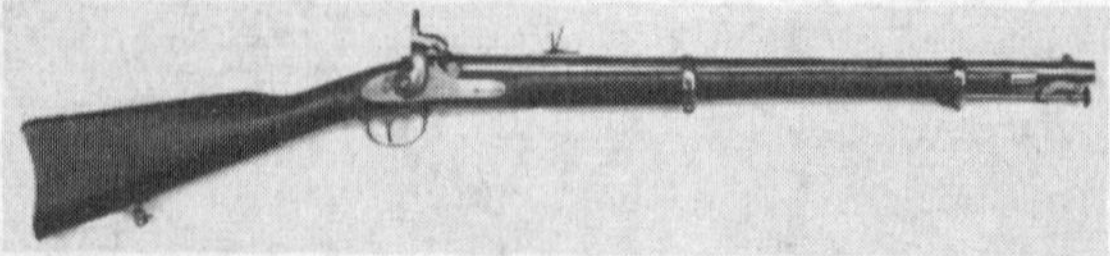

Courtesy Milwaukee Public Museum, Milwaukee, Wisconsin

Exc.	Fine	V.G.	Good	Fair	Poor
—	—	—	—	—	—

TANFOGLIO
Valtrompia, Italy

Products of this company, which was established in late 1940s, have been imported into the United States by various companies including Eig Corporation, F.I.E. of Hialeah, Florida and Excam. Current importer is European American Armory, see listings.

Sata

A .22 or 6.35mm caliber semi-automatic pistol, with 3" barrel. Slide marked "Pistola SATA Made in Italy"; grips "SATA". Blued, with black plastic grips.

NIB	Exc.	V.G.	Good	Fair	Poor
—	250	180	120	90	80

Titan

A 6.35mm caliber semi-automatic pistol, with 2.5" barrel and external hammer. Slide marked "Titan 6.35"; on U.S. imported examples "EIG". Blued, with plastic grips.

NIB	Exc.	V.G.	Good	Fair	Poor
—	250	180	120	90	80

Super Titan

Similar in design to above, with larger frame. In .380 ACP. Walnut grips.

NIB	Exc.	V.G.	Good	Fair	Poor
—	260	200	150	120	100

TA 90 or TZ-75

A 9mm caliber semi-automatic pistol, with 4.75" barrel and 15-shot magazine. Blued or chrome-plated, with walnut or rubber grips. Those imported by Excam were known as Model TA 90, while those imported by F.I.E. are known as Model TZ-75.

NIB	Exc.	V.G.	Good	Fair	Poor
450	400	350	300	250	200

TA 90B

As above, with a 3.5" barrel, 12-shot magazine and Neoprene grips. Introduced in 1986.

NIB	Exc.	V.G.	Good	Fair	Poor
450	400	350	300	250	200

TA 90 SS

As above, with a ported 5" barrel, adjustable sights and two-tone finish. Introduced in 1989.

NIB	Exc.	V.G.	Good	Fair	Poor
650	600	500	450	400	300

TA 41 AE

As above, in .41 Action Express caliber. Introduced in 1989.

NIB	Exc.	V.G.	Good	Fair	Poor
500	450	400	350	300	250

TA 41 SS

As above, with ported 5" barrel, adjustable sights and two-tone finish. Introduced in 1989.

NIB	Exc.	V.G.	Good	Fair	Poor
650	600	500	450	400	300

TA 76

A .22-caliber single-action revolver, with 4.75" barrel and 6-shot cylinder. Blued or chrome-plated, with brass backstrap and triggerguard. Walnut grips.

NIB	Exc.	V.G.	Good	Fair	Poor
100	90	80	60	50	20

TA 76M Combo

As above, with 6" or 9" barrel. Interchangeable .22 Magnum caliber cylinder.

NIB	Exc.	V.G.	Good	Fair	Poor
110	100	90	80	60	40

TA 38SB

A .38 Special caliber over/under double-barrel pocket pistol, with 3" barrels and hammer block safety. Blued, with checkered nylon grips. Discontinued in 1985.

NIB	Exc.	V.G.	Good	Fair	Poor
—	100	90	80	60	40

TANNER, ANDRE
Switzerland

Model 300 Free Rifle

A 7.5mm Swiss or .308-caliber single-shot rifle. Varying length barrels having adjustable target sights and adjustable trigger. Walnut stock fitted with palm rest and adjustable cheekpiece. Blued.

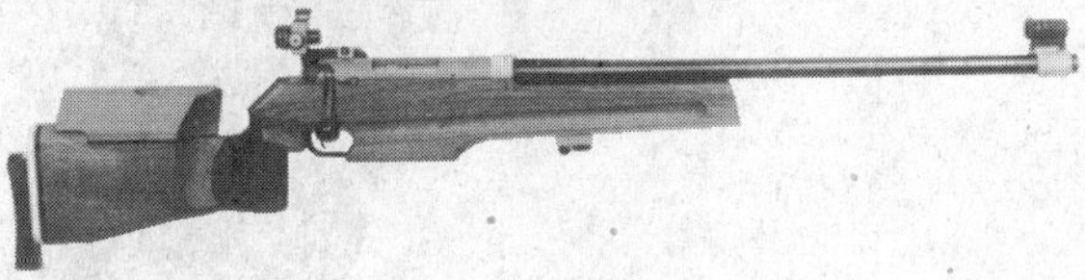

NIB	Exc.	V.G.	Good	Fair	Poor
4750	3750	3000	2500	1500	750

Model 300S

As above, with 10-shot magazine. Not fitted with a palm rest. Discontinued in 1988.

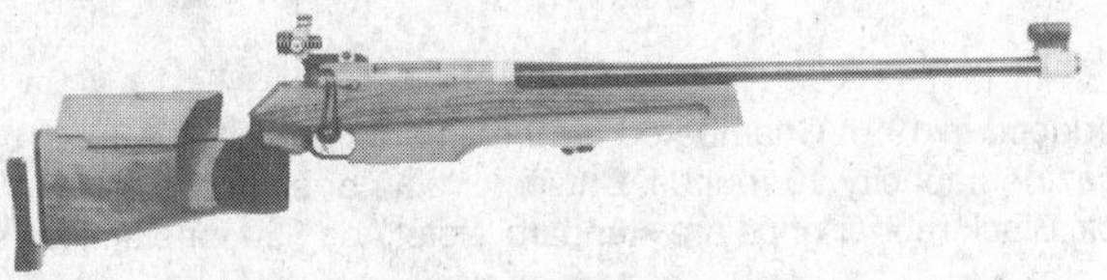

NIB	Exc.	V.G.	Good	Fair	Poor
4500	3500	2750	2250	1250	750

Model 50F

As above in .22-caliber, with thumbhole stock. Discontinued in 1988.

NIB	Exc.	V.G.	Good	Fair	Poor
3750	3000	2500	1750	900	500

TARPLEY J. & F. AND E. T. GARRETT & CO.
Greensboro, North Carolina

Carbine (Antique)

A .52-caliber breech-loading single-shot percussion carbine, with 22" round barrel and plain walnut buttstock. Blued, with case-hardened frame. Tang marked "J H Tarpley's./Pat Feb 14./1863". Over 400 of these carbines manufactured. Exceedingly rare Confederate arm, expert evaluation recommended. Estimated values are speculative. A Tarpley carbine with historic attribution described as the "finest known" sold at Cowan's Auction in 2016 for $93,125. Catalog states that 20 are known to exist, and nine of these are in private collections. Previously, in 2006, one sold at Julia Auction for $80,500.

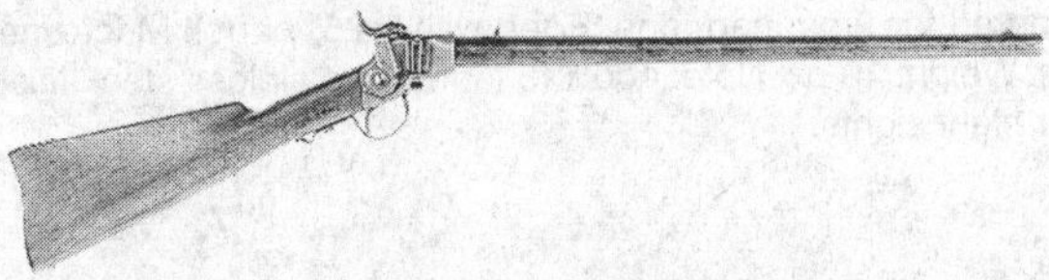

Exc.	Fine	V.G.	Good	Fair	Poor
—	—	70000	—	—	—

TAURUS INTERNATIONAL MFG. CO.
Porto Alegre, Brazil

PISTOLS

PT-92C

This 9mm model is a large capacity semi-automatic pistol, with 4.25" barrel. Drift adjustable 3-dot combat rear sight. Magazine holds 13 rounds in a double column. Choice of blued, satin nickel or stainless steel finish. Brazilian hardwood grips are standard. Weight 31 oz.

NIB	Exc.	V.G.	Good	Fair	Poor
450	400	350	300	200	180

PT-92

Slightly larger and heavier version of PT-92C. Has 5" barrel, with drift adjustable 3-dot combat rear sight. Magazine capacity 15 rounds. Model is 1" longer overall than above model. Weight 34 oz. Also available in blued, nickel and stainless steel. Note: Add $20 for stainless steel; $50 for blue with gold finish; $60 for stainless steel with gold accents; $250 for blued or stainless steel .22 LR conversion kit.

NIB	Exc.	V.G.	Good	Fair	Poor
530	460	390	330	240	190

PT-99

Similar in appearance and specifications to PT-92. This version has additional feature of fully adjustable 3-dot rear sight. Note: Add $20 for stainless steel finish.

NIB	Exc.	V.G.	Good	Fair	Poor
420	320	250	150	100	80

PT-92AF

A 9mm caliber double-action semi-automatic pistol, with 4.92" barrel, exposed hammer and 15-shot magazine. Blued or nickel-plated, with plain walnut grips.

NIB	Exc.	V.G.	Good	Fair	Poor
400	350	300	250	200	150

PT-100

Similar to other full-size Taurus semi-automatics, except chambered for .40 S&W cartridge. Supplied with 5" barrel, with drift adjustable rear sight. Magazine capacity 11 rounds. Also available in blued, nickel or stainless steel. Weight 34 oz. Note: Add $50 for Special Edition, blued steel with gold fixtures and rosewood grips; $110 for blued steel with gold fixtures and pearl grips.

NIB	*Exc.*	*V.G.*	*Good*	*Fair*	*Poor*
500	400	300	200	150	100

PT-101

Same as PT-100, but furnished with fully adjustable rear 3-dot combat sight.

NIB	*Exc.*	*V.G.*	*Good*	*Fair*	*Poor*
450	350	300	250	150	100

Deluxe Shooter's Pak

Offered by Taurus as a special package. Consists of pistol, with extra magazine in a fitted custom hard case. Available for these models: PT-92, PT-99, PT-100, and PT-101. Note: Add 10% for this special feature.

PT-138

Introduced in 1998. This polymer frame pistol chambered for .380 cartridge. Fitted with 4" barrel in blue or stainless steel. Weight 16 oz. Magazine capacity 10 rounds.

Blue

NIB	*Exc.*	*V.G.*	*Good*	*Fair*	*Poor*
350	250	200	180	120	100

Stainless Steel

NIB	*Exc.*	*V.G.*	*Good*	*Fair*	*Poor*
380	280	220	180	120	100

PT-908

Semi-automatic double-action pistol chambered for 9mm Parabellum cartridge. Fitted with 3.8" barrel, with drift adjustable rear 3-dot combat sight. Magazine capacity 8 rounds in a single column. Available in blued, satin nickel or stainless steel. Stocks are black rubber. Weight 30 oz. Introduced in 1993.

NIB	*Exc.*	*V.G.*	*Good*	*Fair*	*Poor*
380	320	280	220	150	100

PT-911

Introduced in 1997. Chambered for 9mm cartridge. Fitted with 4" barrel. Magazine capacity 10 rounds. Choice of blue or stainless steel. Weight 28 oz. Black rubber grips are standard. Note: Add $20 for stainless steel.

NIB	*Exc.*	*V.G.*	*Good*	*Fair*	*Poor*
450	350	280	220	180	120

PT-111

Chambered for 9mm cartridge. Fitted with 3.25" barrel. Magazine is 10 rounds. Weight 19 oz. Note: Add $15 for matte stainless steel finish; add $80 for night sights.

NIB	*Exc.*	*V.G.*	*Good*	*Fair*	*Poor*
380	300	250	180	120	100

PT-140

Chambered for .40 S&W cartridge. Fitted with 3.25" barrel. Magazine capacity 10 rounds. Weight 19 oz. Note: Add $15 for matte stainless steel finish; add $80 for night sights.

NIB	Exc.	V.G.	Good	Fair	Poor
350	300	260	180	120	100

PT-140 Millennium

Chambered for .40 S&W cartridge. Fitted with 3.25" barrel. Features polymer frame and blue or stainless steel slide. Fixed sights. Magazine capacity 10 rounds. Weight 19 oz. Note: Add $75 for night sights.

Blue

NIB	Exc.	V.G.	Good	Fair	Poor
340	320	220	150	100	80

Stainless Steel

NIB	Exc.	V.G.	Good	Fair	Poor
380	320	250	180	100	80

PT-145 Millennium

Similar to PT-140. Chambered for .45 ACP cartridge. Barrel length 3.27". Weight 23 oz. Magazine capacity 10 rounds. Note: Add $75 for night sights.

Blue

NIB	Exc.	V.G.	Good	Fair	Poor
340	320	220	150	100	80

Stainless Steel

NIB	Exc.	V.G.	Good	Fair	Poor
380	320	250	180	100	80

Millennium Pro

Introduced in 2003. This pistol is third generation series in Millennium line. Features captured dual spring and guide assembly, re-engineered magazine release and internal firing pin lock. Larger 3-dot sighting system, positive slide serrations, internal magazine base extension and enlarged external safety with positive click are other improvements.

NIB	Exc.	V.G.	Good	Fair	Poor
360	300	200	150	100	80

Millennium G2

Moderately priced concealed-carry 9mm model, with thin profile and melted edges. Available in two compact models, PT111 and PT140. Features include high profile sights, accessory rail and textured grips. Double-/single-action operation. Introduced in 2014.

NIB	Exc.	V.G.	Good	Fair	Poor
280	250	220	200	150	120

G3

Caliber: 9mm. Capacity: 17-round magazine. Barrel: 4.0-in. Grip: Textured polymer. Sights: White dot front, notch rear. Length: 7.28 in. overall. Weight: 24.8 oz. unloaded. Finish: Matte black, gray, tan. Features: Restrike trigger, accessory rail.

NIB	Exc.	V.G.	Good	Fair	Poor
270	250	220	200	180	—

G3c Compact

New 2020 version of the G series compact 9mm personal defense semi-auto pistol. Striker-fired, polymer frame, 10- or 12-round capacity, 3.2" barrel, 22 oz.

NIB	Exc.	V.G.	Good	Fair	Poor
270	250	220	200	170	—

G3X

NIB	Exc.	V.G.	Good	Fair	Poor
290	270	230	200	170	—

GX4

Caliber: 9mm. Capacity: 11-round magazine. Barrel: 3.06". Grip: Textured polymer, modular back straps. Sights: White-dot front, notch rear. Length: 5.8" overall with a small backstrap. Weight: 18.7 oz. unloaded. Finish: Matte black. Features: T.O.R.O. model is optics-ready with mounting plates.

NIB	Exc.	V.G.	Good	Fair	Poor
330	300	260	230	180	—

GX4 T.O.R.O.

NIB	Exc.	V.G.	Good	Fair	Poor
410	360	310	280	230	—

Model 609TI-PRO

Similar to Millennium Pro, with titanium slide. Chambered in 9mm Parabellum. Features include 13+1 capacity, 3.25" barrel, checkered polymer grips, Heinie Straight-8 sights. Overall length 6.125"; weight 19.7 oz.

NIB	Exc.	V.G.	Good	Fair	Poor
500	450	320	220	180	120

PT-400/400SS

Chambered for .400 CorBon cartridge. Fitted with 4.25" ported barrel, with fixed sights. Magazine capacity 8 rounds. Offered in blue or stainless steel. Rubber grips. Weight 30 oz.

Blue

NIB	Exc.	V.G.	Good	Fair	Poor
380	300	200	150	100	80

Stainless Steel

NIB	Exc.	V.G.	Good	Fair	Poor
420	320	220	150	100	80

PT-132

Chambered for .32 ACP cartridge. Fitted with 3.25" barrel. Magazine capacity 10 rounds. Weight 20 oz. Note: Add $15 for matte stainless steel finish.

NIB	Exc.	V.G.	Good	Fair	Poor
320	280	200	150	100	80

PT-58

Introduced in 1988. Chambered for .380 ACP cartridge. Fitted with 4" barrel, with drift adjustable rear sight. Conventional double-action design. Available in blued, satin nickel or stainless steel. Fitted with Brazilian hardwood grips. Weight 30 oz.

NIB	Exc.	V.G.	Good	Fair	Poor
300	250	200	150	100	80

PT-145

Chambered for .45 ACP cartridge. Fitted with 3.25" barrel. Magazine capacity 10 rounds. Weight 23 oz. Note: Add $15 for matte stainless steel finish; $80 for night sights.

NIB	Exc.	V.G.	Good	Fair	Poor
320	280	250	200	150	100

PT-45

Introduced in 1994. Semi-automatic double-action pistol. Chambered for .45 ACP cartridge. Barrel is 3.75" in length. Magazine capacity 8 rounds. Offered in blued or stainless steel, with grips of Brazilian hardwood. Fixed sights are standard. Overall length 7.1"; weight 30 oz.

Blue

NIB	Exc.	V.G.	Good	Fair	Poor
350	280	200	150	100	80

Stainless Steel

NIB	Exc.	V.G.	Good	Fair	Poor
400	320	250	200	150	100

PT-745B/SS

Chambered for .45 ACP cartridge. Fitted with 3.25" barrel. Fixed sights. Polymer grips. Blue or stainless steel. Magazine capacity 6 rounds. Weight 21 oz. Introduced in 2004. Note: Add $15 for stainless steel.

NIB	Exc.	V.G.	Good	Fair	Poor
380	320	280	220	120	180

PT-640B/SS

Similar to above. Chambered for .40 S&W cartridge. Magazine capacity 10 rounds. Weight 24 oz. Introduced in 2004. Note: Add $15 for stainless steel.

NIB	Exc.	V.G.	Good	Fair	Poor
380	320	280	220	120	180

PT-24/7-45B

This .45 ACP pistol fitted with 4.25" barrel and fixed sights. Ribbed grips. Blued receiver. Magazine capacity 12 rounds. Weight 27 oz. Introduced in 2004. Note: Add $15 for stainless steel slide.

NIB	Exc.	V.G.	Good	Fair	Poor
400	300	280	220	150	100

PT-24/7 G2

Double-/single-action semi-automatic pistol. Chambered in 9mm Parabellum (15+1), .40 S&W (13+1), and .45 ACP (10+1). Features include blued or stainless finish; "Strike Two" capability; new trigger safety; low-profile adjustable rear sights for windage and elevation; ambidextrous magazine release; 4.2" barrel; Picatinny rail; polymer frame; polymer grip with metallic inserts and three interchangeable backstraps. Also offered in compact model, with shorter grip frame and 3.5" barrel.

NIB	Exc.	V.G.	Good	Fair	Poor
420	350	300	250	180	120

PT-24/7-PRO Standard

4" barrel; stainless, duotone or blued finish.

NIB	Exc.	V.G.	Good	Fair	Poor
400	300	280	220	150	100

PT-24/7-PRO Compact

3.2" barrel; stainless, titanium or blued finish.

NIB	Exc.	V.G.	Good	Fair	Poor
400	300	280	220	150	100

PT-24/7-PRO Long Slide

5.2" barrel; matte stainless, blued or stainless finish.

NIB	Exc.	V.G.	Good	Fair	Poor
400	300	280	220	150	100

PT-24/7-9B

As above, but chambered for 9mm cartridge. Magazine capacity 17 rounds. Weight 27 oz. Introduced in 2005. Note: Add $15 for stainless steel slide.

NIB	Exc.	V.G.	Good	Fair	Poor
400	300	280	220	150	100

PT-24/7-40B

As above, but chambered for .40 S&W cartridge. Magazine capacity 15 rounds. Weight 27 oz. Introduced in 2005. Note: Add $15 for stainless steel slide.

NIB	Exc.	V.G.	Good	Fair	Poor
400	300	280	220	150	100

PT-24/7LS-9SS-17

Full-size stainless semi-automatic chambered for 9mm. Long grip and slide. Capacity 17+1. Single-/double-action. 5" barrel. Weight 27.2 oz. Fixed 2-dot rear sight. In short grip 10+1 capacity. Introduced in 2006; discontinued 2010.

NIB	Exc.	V.G.	Good	Fair	Poor
420	340	300	240	180	120

PT-24/79SSC-17

Compact stainless semi-automatic chambered for 9mm. Short grip and slide. Capacity 15+1. Single-/double-action. 3.5" barrel. Weight 27.2 oz. Fixed 2-dot rear sight. In short grip 10+1 capacity. Introduced in 2006; discontinued 2010.

NIB	Exc.	V.G.	Good	Fair	Poor
400	300	280	220	150	100

PT-24/7PLS-9SSPTi-17

Full-size semi-automatic chambered for 9mm. Capacity 17+1 or 10+1. Single-/double-action. Titanium slide, 4" barrel. Weight 27.2 oz. Introduced in 2006.

NIB	Exc.	V.G.	Good	Fair	Poor
400	300	280	220	150	100

PT-24/7 OSS

Introduced in 2007. Available in .45 ACP, .40 S&W and 9mm Parabellum. 12+1 capacity (.45), single-/double-action. Ambidextrous decock and safety, match-grade barrel, polymer frame with steel upper. Claimed to exceed all requirements set by United States Special Operations Command. Developed to compete in SOCOM pistol trials. Note: Add 5 percent for stainless.

NIB	Exc.	V.G.	Good	Fair	Poor
420	340	300	240	180	120

PT-24/7PLS-9SSCTi-17

Compact semi-automatic chambered for 9mm. Capacity 17+1. Single-/double-action. Titanium slide, 3.3" barrel. Weight 25.4 oz. Introduced in 2006.

NIB	Exc.	V.G.	Good	Fair	Poor
420	340	300	240	180	120

PT-24/7PLS

Similar to above, with 5" barrel. Chambered in 9mm Parabellum, .38 Super and .40 S&W.

NIB	Exc.	V.G.	Good	Fair	Poor
420	340	300	240	180	120

2045 Large Frame Pistol

Similar to Taurus Model 24/7, but chambered in .45 ACP only. Features include polymer frame, blued or matte stainless steel slide, 4.2" barrel, ambidextrous "memory pads" to promote safe finger position during loading, ambi three-position safety/decocker. Picatinny rail system, fixed sights. Overall length 7.34". Weight 31.5 oz.

NIB	Exc.	V.G.	Good	Fair	Poor
450	380	320	250	180	120

809-B 9mm

Introduced in 2008. Basically a Model 24/7 OSS, with an exposed hammer. 17+1 capacity, black Tenifer finish.

NIB	Exc.	V.G.	Good	Fair	Poor
550	420	350	280	200	150

800 Series Compact

Compact double-/single-action semi-automatic pistol chambered in 9mm (12+1), .357 SIG (10+1) and .40 cal. (10+1). Features include 3.5" barrel; external hammer; loaded chamber indicator; polymer frame; blued or stainless slide.

NIB	Exc.	V.G.	Good	Fair	Poor
480	410	350	280	200	150

PT191140B

1911-style .40-caliber semi-automatic. Blued steel. 5" barrel, 8+1 capacity. Weight 32 oz. Fixed Heinie two-dot straight-eight sight. Blue or stainless. Introduced in 2006. Note: Add 10% for stainless.

NIB	Exc.	V.G.	Good	Fair	Poor
680	550	420	300	200	120

PT1911

Blued or stainless 1911-style single-action in .45 ACP. 8+1 capacity. LOA 8.5". Weight 32 oz. 5" barrel, fixed Heinie two-dot straight-eight sight. Numerous options. Introduced in 2006. Note: Add 10% for alloy frame and Picatinny rail versions (added 2007); 10% for stainless.

NIB	Exc.	V.G.	Good	Fair	Poor
680	550	420	300	200	120

Model 1911B-9

Similar to above, but chambered in 9mm Parabellum (9+1).

NIB	Exc.	V.G.	Good	Fair	Poor
680	550	420	300	200	120

Model 1911B-38

Similar to above, but chambered in .38 Super.

NIB	Exc.	V.G.	Good	Fair	Poor
680	550	420	300	200	120

Model 1911 Commander

Similar to above. Commander variant. 4.25" barrel .45 ACP 8-round magazine. Novak adjustable sights. Introduced 2018.

NIB	Exc.	V.G.	Good	Fair	Poor
620	540	460	360	240	180

Model 1911 Officer

Similar to above. Officer variant. 3.5" barrel. .45 ACP 8-round magazine. Novak adjustable sights. Introduced 2018.

NIB	Exc.	V.G.	Good	Fair	Poor
640	540	470	360	240	180

Model 1911HC

Similar to Taurus Model 1911, with 12+1 capacity; .45 ACP only.

NIB	Exc.	V.G.	Good	Fair	Poor
720	600	480	380	250	150

PT-745GB

Blued semi-automatic in .45 GAP, with 7+1 capacity. 3.25" barrel, fixed sights, weight 22 oz., polymer grip plates. Introduced in 2006.

NIB	Exc.	V.G.	Good	Fair	Poor
380	300	220	180	120	100

PT745B/SS-LS

Blued or stainless semi-automatic in .45 ACP. 4.25" barrel, weight 23.3 oz. 7+1 capacity, polymer grip plates. Introduced in 2006.

NIB	Exc.	V.G.	Good	Fair	Poor
380	300	220	180	120	100

PT917B20

9mm blued or stainless semi-automatic, with 20+1 capacity. Fixed sights, 4" barrel, weight 31.8 oz. Introduced in 2006.

NIB	Exc.	V.G.	Good	Fair	Poor
380	300	220	180	120	100

PT609Ti-13

This 9mm semi-automatic has titanium finish plus 13+1 capacity, 3.25" barrel. Fixed sights, weight 19.2 oz. Introduced in 2006.

NIB	Exc.	V.G.	Good	Fair	Poor
500	420	300	220	150	100

PT138BP12 Millennium Pro

Blued or stainless SA/DA semi-automatic in .380 ACP, with 12+1 capacity. Fixed sights, 3.25" barrel, weight 18.7 oz. Introduced in 2006. Also available in .32 ACP and .40 S&W.

NIB	Exc.	V.G.	Good	Fair	Poor
400	300	280	220	150	100

PT-38B/SS

Chambered for .38 Super cartridge. Fitted with 4.25" barrel, with fixed sights. Grips are checkered rubber. Blued or stainless steel. Magazine capacity 10 rounds. Weight 30 oz. Introduced in 2004. Note: Add $15 for stainless steel.

NIB	Exc.	V.G.	Good	Fair	Poor
420	340	300	240	180	120

PT-38SSSPRL

Introduced in 2005. Chambered for .38 Super cartridge. Fitted with 4.25" barrel. Magazine capacity 10 rounds. Finish is stainless steel and gold. Weight 30 oz. Note: Deduct $60 for stainless steel only.

NIB	Exc.	V.G.	Good	Fair	Poor
480	400	300	220	150	100

738 TCP Compact Pistol

Lightweight DAO semi-automatic pistol. Chambered for .380 ACP. Features include 3.35" barrel; polymer frame; blued (738B), stainless (738SS) or titanium (738Ti) slide; concealed hammer; low-profile fixed sight; ambi safety; loaded chamber indicator. Capacity 6+1 (standard magazine) or 8+1 (extended magazine). Overall length 5.195". Weight 9 oz. (titanium slide) to 10.2 oz.

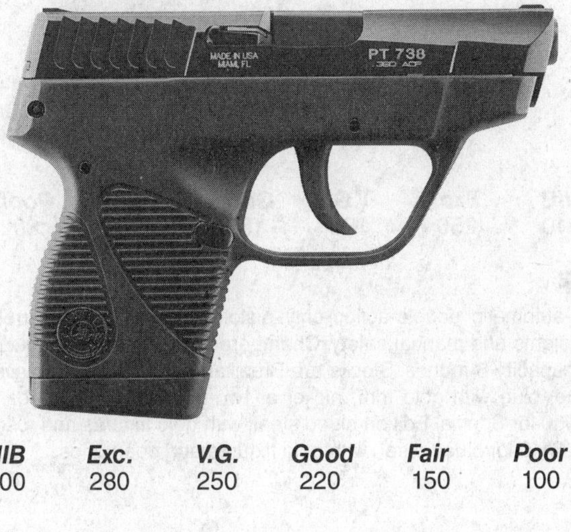

NIB	Exc.	V.G.	Good	Fair	Poor
300	280	250	220	150	100

709 "Slim"

Semi-automatic pistol chambered in 9mm Parabellum. Features include streamlined profile, 3.25" barrel, 7+1 capacity, fixed sights, checkered polymer grips, choice of blued (709B) or stainless (709SS) slide. Single/double action. Overall length 6.25". Weight 10 oz.

NIB	Exc.	V.G.	Good	Fair	Poor
400	300	280	220	150	100

638 Pro Compact

Caliber .380 ACP, steel slide, polymer frame, 15-round magazine. Barrel length 3.2". Single-action trigger has integral safety. Other features include ambidextrous thumb safety, accessory rail, adjustable rear sight and loaded chamber and cocked striker indicators. Taurus Security System. Weight 28 oz. Blue or matte stainless finish.

NIB	Exc.	V.G.	Good	Fair	Poor
410	350	300	250	200	150

DT Hybrid

Caliber 9mm Parabellum/.40 S&W, steel slide, polymer/steel frame, 3.2" barrel. Magazine capacity 13 rounds, 11 for .40. Single-action trigger has Strike Two capability. Integral trigger safety, manual safety and Taurus Security System. Ambidextrous magazine release, adjustable rear sight and loaded-chamber indicator. Weight 24 oz. Finish blue or matte stainless.

NIB	Exc.	V.G.	Good	Fair	Poor
460	400	350	280	200	150

917

Lightweight compact semi-automatic chambered in 9mm Parabellum. Matte blue or stainless finish, 17+1 or 20+1 capacity. Introduced in 2007.

NIB	Exc.	V.G.	Good	Fair	Poor
400	300	280	220	150	100

PT-945C

Introduced in 1995. This .45 ACP double-action pistol features 4" barrel, with 8-round magazine. Grips are black rubber. Sights are drift adjustable 3-dot combat style. Weight 30 oz. Offered in blue or stainless steel, with or without ported barrel.

Blue

Note: Add $45 for blued finish with gold accents and ported barrel; $35 for ported barrel and blue finish; $40 for ported barrel.

NIB	Exc.	V.G.	Good	Fair	Poor
450	350	250	200	150	100

Stainless Steel

Note: Add $40 for ported barrel with stainless steel finish or stainless steel finish with gold accents.

NIB	Exc.	V.G.	Good	Fair	Poor
480	400	300	250	150	100

PT-945S

Same as above, but chambered for .45 Super cartridge. Introduced in 1998.

Blue

NIB	Exc.	V.G.	Good	Fair	Poor
450	350	250	200	150	100

Stainless Steel

NIB	Exc.	V.G.	Good	Fair	Poor
480	380	280	220	150	100

PT-940

Similar to PT-945, except chambered for .40 S&W cartridge. Fitted with a 4" barrel. Magazine capacity 10 rounds. Choice of blue or stainless steel. Black rubber grips. Weight 28 oz. Introduced in 1997. Note: Add $20 for stainless steel.

NIB	Exc.	V.G.	Good	Fair	Poor
420	320	260	200	120	80

PT-938

Chambered for .380 ACP cartridge. Fitted with 3" barrel. Black rubber grips. Choice of blue or stainless steel. Weight 27 oz. Introduced in 1997.

NIB	Exc.	V.G.	Good	Fair	Poor
360	300	240	180	80	50

922 Sport

Introduced in 2003. Semi-automatic .22-caliber pistol features lightweight polymer frame. Single-/double-action trigger. Barrel length 6". Magazine capacity 10 rounds. Adjustable sights. Weight about 25 oz. Note: Add $15 for matte stainless steel finish.

NIB	Exc.	V.G.	Good	Fair	Poor
310	250	180	150	100	80

PT-22

Semi-automatic double-action-only pistol. Features 2.75" barrel, with fixed sights and manual safety. Chambered for .22 LR cartridge. Magazine capacity 8 rounds. Stocks are Brazilian hardwood. Finish available in blue, blue with gold trim, nickel or two-tone. Weight 12.3 oz. Note: Add $50 for Special Edition blued steel, with gold fixtures and rosewood grips; $110 for blued steel, with gold fixtures and pearl grips.

NIB	*Exc.*	*V.G.*	*Good*	*Fair*	*Poor*
250	180	250	80	60	50

PT-922

.22-caliber pistol has 6" barrel, with fiber optic adjustable sights. Polymer grips. 10-round magazine. Blued finish. Weight 29 oz. Introduced in 2004.

NIB	*Exc.*	*V.G.*	*Good*	*Fair*	*Poor*
360	300	240	180	80	50

PT-25

Similar in appearance to PT-22. Chambered for .25 ACP cartridge. Magazine capacity 9 rounds. Fitted with 2.75" barrel. Offered in blue, blue with gold trim, two-tone finish or nickel. Note: Add $50 for Special Edition blued steel, with gold fixtures and rosewood grips; $110 for blued steel, with gold fixtures and pearl grips.

NIB	*Exc.*	*V.G.*	*Good*	*Fair*	*Poor*
250	180	120	80	60	50

22PLY/25PLY Small Polymer Frame Pistols

Caliber: .22 LR. Capacity: Eight-round magazine. Barrel: 2.34". Grip: Textured polymer. Sights: Integrated, fixed. Length: 4.9" overall. Weight: 11 oz. unloaded. Finish: Matte black, two-tone. Features: DAO trigger, tip-up barrel.

NIB	*Exc.*	*V.G.*	*Good*	*Fair*	*Poor*
260	210	200	150	100	—

Taurus Curve

Unique .380 semi-automatic, designed to fit contours of the body for more confort and security when carry concealed. Magazine capacity 6+1, weight 10.2 oz., barrel length 2.5". Other dimensions: overall length 5.2 in.; height 3.7 in.; width 1.18 in. Introduced in 2015. Discontinued.

NIB	*Exc.*	*V.G.*	*Good*	*Fair*	*Poor*
340	300	250	200	180	150

Spectrum

A .380-caliber sub-compact semi-automatic. Double-action only, striker-fire operation. Insert panels of various colors attach to grip and slide. Introduced in 2017.

NIB	*Exc.*	*V.G.*	*Good*	*Fair*	*Poor*
250	230	200	170	130	100

Model TH Series

Hammer fired. Full and compact polymer frame models. 3.5" or 4.25" barrel. 9mm or .40 S&W 11-, 13-, 15- or 17-round magazine. Novak adjustable sights. Introduced 2019.

NIB	*Exc.*	*V.G.*	*Good*	*Fair*	*Poor*
340	300	280	230	210	190

Model TX22

Caliber: .22 LR. Capacity: 10- or 16-round magazine. Barrel: 4.1". Grip: Textured polymer, wrap around. Sights: Adjustable rear, white dot front. Length: 7.06" overall. Weight: 17.3 oz. unloaded. Finish: Matte black to tan.

NIB	Exc.	V.G.	Good	Fair	Poor
300	280	250	230	200	—

TX22 Competition

Caliber: .22 LR. Capacity: 10- or 16-round magazine. Barrel: 5.25". Grip: Textured polymer, wrap around. Sights: Adjustable rear, optics-ready. Length: 8.21" overall. Weight: 17.3 oz. unloaded. Finish: Matte black. Features: Red-dot optics-ready with mounting plates.

NIB	Exc.	V.G.	Good	Fair	Poor
420	380	310	280	190	—

TX22 Competition SCR

NIB	Exc.	V.G.	Good	Fair	Poor
460	430	360	330	240	—

REVOLVERS

Model 17MB2/MSS2

This 8-shot revolver chambered for .17 HMR cartridge. Fitted with 1.75" barrel, with fixed sights. Blued or stainless steel. Hard rubber grips. Weight 22 oz. Introduced in 2004. Note: Add $45 for stainless steel.

NIB	Exc.	V.G.	Good	Fair	Poor
360	280	220	180	150	100

Model 327

The new Taurus 327 is a double-action/single-action revolver, available with a 2" or 3" barrel that is multi-cartridge compatible, can accept .32 H&R Magnum and .32 S&W Long cartridges. The matte black carbon steel or stainless steel barrel, cylinder and frame are backed by a recoil-absorbing rubber grip that is comfortable and provides excellent retention in a compact handgun platform. The Taurus 327's front serrated ramp sight and no-snag rear sight channel provide quick and clear target acquisition.

NIB	Exc.	V.G.	Good	Fair	Poor
280	—	—	—	—	—

Model 73

A .32 S&W Long double-action swing-out cylinder revolver, with 3" barrel and 6-shot cylinder. Blued or nickel plated, with walnut grips.

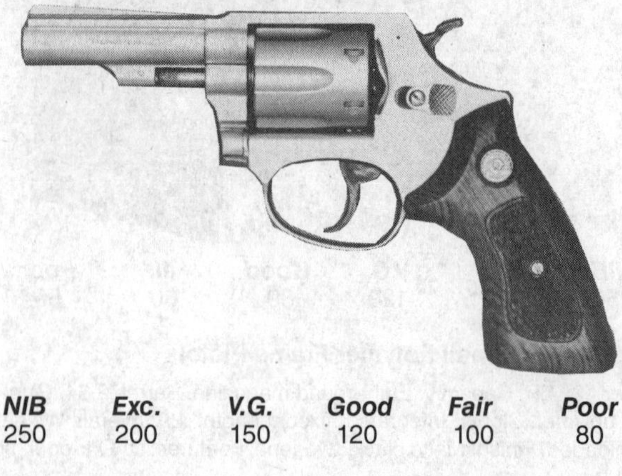

NIB	Exc.	V.G.	Good	Fair	Poor
250	200	150	120	100	80

Model 80

Full-size 6-round .38 Special. with 3" or 4" heavy tapered barrel. Supplied with fixed sights. Offered with blued or stainless steel (offered new in 1993) finish. Brazilian hardwood grips are standard. Weight 30 oz. Note: Add $45 for stainless steel

NIB	Exc.	V.G.	Good	Fair	Poor
280	200	140	110	80	700

Model 82

Nearly identical to Model 80. Has 3" or 4" heavy solid rib barrel in place of heavy tapered barrel. Weight 34 oz. Note: Add $40 for stainless steel.

NIB	Exc.	V.G.	Good	Fair	Poor
280	200	140	110	80	70

Model 82B4

Chambered for .38 Special +P cartridge. Fitted with 4" heavy solid rib barrel. Cylinder holds 6 rounds. Rubber grips. Fixed sights. Blue finish. Weight 37 oz.

NIB	Exc.	V.G.	Good	Fair	Poor
300	250	200	120	100	80

Model 82SS4

Same as above, with stainless steel finish. Weight 37 oz.

NIB	Exc.	V.G.	Good	Fair	Poor
320	260	180	120	100	80

Model 827B4

Chambered for .38 Special +P cartridge. Fitted with 4" heavy barrel, with solid rib. Cylinder is 7 shots. Rubber grips. Blued finish. Weight 37 oz. Fixed sights.

NIB	Exc.	V.G.	Good	Fair	Poor
300	250	200	150	100	80

Model 827SS4

Same as above, with stainless steel finish. Weight 35 oz.

NIB	Exc.	V.G.	Good	Fair	Poor
350	300	250	180	120	80

Model 83

Similar to Model 82, except for fully adjustable rear sight and Patridge-type front sight. Offered with 4" barrel only, with blued or stainless steel (new for 1993) finish. Weight 34 oz.

NIB	Exc.	V.G.	Good	Fair	Poor
300	250	200	150	100	80

Model 86

Similar to Model 83, with exception of 6" barrel, target hammer, adjustable trigger and blue-only finish. Weight 34 oz.

NIB	Exc.	V.G.	Good	Fair	Poor
320	280	220	180	120	80

Model 85

Double-action revolver chambered for .38 Special. Available in 2" or 3" heavy solid rib barrel fitted with ejector shroud. Sights are fixed. Blued finish and stainless steel (new for 1993) are offered, with Brazilian hardwood grips. Weight 21 oz. with 2" barrel. Beginning in 1996, model was furnished with Uncle Mike's Boot Grips. Note: Add $50 for Special Edition blued steel, with gold fixtures and rosewood grips; $110 for blued steel, with gold fixtures and pearl grips.

NIB	Exc.	V.G.	Good	Fair	Poor
300	220	180	120	100	80

Model 85 Stainless

As above in stainless steel. Beginning in 1996, furnished with Uncle Mike's Boot Grips.

NIB	Exc.	V.G.	Good	Fair	Poor
350	280	220	200	150	100

Model 85CH

Same as above, but offered in 2" or 3" barrel with shrouded hammer. Double-action-only. Note: Add $50 for stainless steel; $25 for ported barrel on 2" models.

NIB	Exc.	V.G.	Good	Fair	Poor
300	220	180	120	100	80

Model 85 UL

Double-action revolver built on small aluminum frame. Chambered for .38 Special cartridge. Fitted with 2" barrel. Choice of blue or stainless steel finish. Weight 17 oz. Introduced in 1997. Note: Add $50 for Special Edition blued steel, with gold fixtures and rosewood grips; $110 for blued steel, with gold fixtures and pearl grips; $30 for stainless steel.

NIB	Exc.	V.G.	Good	Fair	Poor
320	250	200	150	120	100

Model 85 Hy-Lite Magnesium

Similar to Model 85. Weight 13.8 oz. Gray alloy frame and Hy-Lite sights. Introduced in 2007.

NIB	Exc.	V.G.	Good	Fair	Poor
380	300	250	200	180	120

Model 85 Ultra-Lite Gray

Similar to Model 85, with lightweight magnesium frame. Fixed or fiber-optic front sight. Introduced in 2007.

NIB	Exc.	V.G.	Good	Fair	Poor
380	300	250	200	180	120

Model 85 Ultra-Lite Titanium

Similar to Model 85, with titanium cylinder and barrel shroud. Introduced in 2007.

NIB	Exc.	V.G.	Good	Fair	Poor
480	400	280	200	180	120

Model 85 View

Variant of Model 85 series of 5-shot .38-Special revolvers. Sideplate on right side of frame made of clear Lexan polycarbon thermoplastic, showing inner working's of the revolver's mechanism. Rest of frame is aluminum, with silver or pink finish. Cylinder and barrel are of titanium. Introduced in 2014, but sales were poor, production was limited and model was discontinued. It was announced in 2015, that the View would be replaced by Moded 85 "No-View", same design but with a blue aluminum sideplate. Values shown apply to either model. Discontinued in 2016.

NIB	Exc.	V.G.	Good	Fair	Poor
500	420	380	—	—	—

Model 850

Chambered for .38 Special cartridge. Fitted with 2" barrel, with fixed sights. Hammerless with 5-round cylinder. Rubber grips. Weight 23 oz. Choice of blue or stainless steel. Note: Add $50 for stainless steel.

NIB	*Exc.*	*V.G.*	*Good*	*Fair*	*Poor*
380	300	250	200	180	120

Model 850 Ultra-Lite Blue

Similar to Model 850, with lightweight alloy frame. Introduced 2007.

NIB	*Exc.*	*V.G.*	*Good*	*Fair*	*Poor*
380	300	250	200	180	120

Model 850 Ultra-Lite Stainless Steel

Similar to Model 850 Ultra-Lite Blue, with stainless finish. Introduced in 2007.

NIB	*Exc.*	*V.G.*	*Good*	*Fair*	*Poor*
380	300	250	200	180	120

Model 605

Introduced in 1995. Revolver chambered for .357 Magnum cartridge. Fitted with 2.25" or 3" heavy barrel. Offered in blue or stainless steel. Weight 25 oz.

NIB	*Exc.*	*V.G.*	*Good*	*Fair*	*Poor*
380	300	250	200	180	120

Model 605 Defender

Capacity: 5 rounds, Action Type: Double-Action/Single-Action, Firing System: Hammer, Front Sight: Night sight with orange outline, Rear Sight: Fixed, Grip: Hogue rubber grips, VZ, Altamont. Caliber: .38 Spl. +P, .357 Mag, Frame Size: Small, Barrel Length: 3", Overall Length: 7.50", Overall Height: 4.80", Overall Width: 1.41". Weights: 23.52–25.52 oz., Features: Extended ejector rod, night sights, Safety: Transfer Bar. Finishes: Matte black oxide, matte stainless steel, tungsten Cerakote.

NIB	*Exc.*	*V.G.*	*Good*	*Fair*	*Poor*
410	—	—	—	—	—

Taurus Polymer Protector

Single-/double-action revolver chambered in .38 Special +P. Features include 5-round cylinder; polymer frame; faux wood rubber-feel grips; fixed sights; shrouded hammer with cocking spur; blued finish; 2.5" barrel. Weight 18.2 oz.

NIB	*Exc.*	*V.G.*	*Good*	*Fair*	*Poor*
380	320	280	230	200	150

Model 650

Same as Model 850, but chambered for .357 Magnum cartridge. Note: Add $50 for stainless steel.

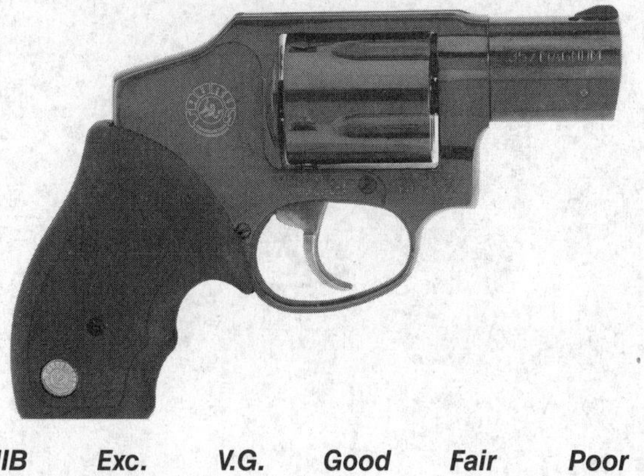

NIB	*Exc.*	*V.G.*	*Good*	*Fair*	*Poor*
380	300	250	200	180	120

Taurus 405 Revolver

Chambered for .40 S&W, with steel cylinder, alloy frame, 5-round capacity, 2" barrel. Taurus Security System and Ribber (ribbed) grips. Weight 29 oz. Blue or matte stainless finish. Available in .44 Special as Model 445, with weight of 22 oz. Note: Add 15% for stainless finish.

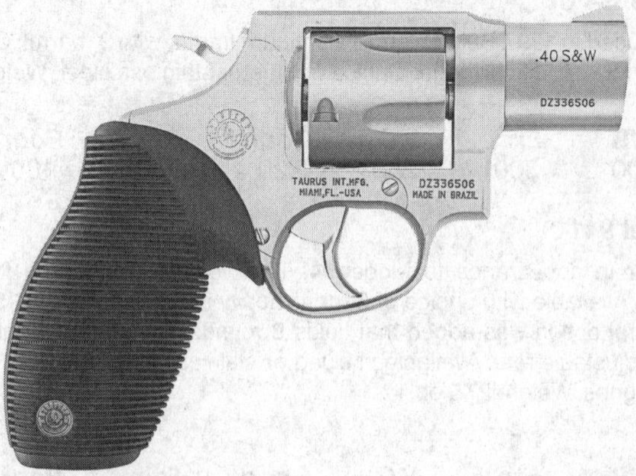

NIB	*Exc.*	*V.G.*	*Good*	*Fair*	*Poor*
380	320	280	240	200	150

Model 851 and 651 Revolvers

Small-frame SA/DA revolvers similar to Taurus Model 85, with Centennial-style concealed-hammer frame. Chambered in .38 Special +P (Model 851) or .357 Magnum (Model 651). Features include five-shot cylinder; 2" barrel; fixed sights; blue, matte blue, titanium or stainless finish; Taurus security lock. Overall length 6.5". Weight 15.5 oz. (titanium) to 25 oz. (blued and stainless).

NIB	*Exc.*	*V.G.*	*Good*	*Fair*	*Poor*
400	300	280	220	150	100

Model 94

Double-action revolver chambered for .22 LR cartridge. Swing-out cylinder holds 9 rounds. Available with heavy solid rib, 3" or 4" barrel. In 1996, a 5" barrel option was added in both blue and stainless steel. Ramp front sight with fully adjustable rear. Offered in blued or stainless steel, with Brazilian hardwood grips. Weight 25 oz. with 4" barrel.

Blue

NIB	Exc.	V.G.	Good	Fair	Poor
350	280	220	200	150	100

Stainless Steel

NIB	Exc.	V.G.	Good	Fair	Poor
380	300	250	220	180	120

Model 94 UL

Introduced in 1997. Built on small aluminum frame, with 2" barrel. Chambered for .22 LR cartridge. Choice of blue or stainless steel. Weight 14 oz.

NIB	Exc.	V.G.	Good	Fair	Poor
400	300	280	220	150	100

Model 941

Similar in appearance to Model 94. This version chambered for .22 WMR. Available with choice of 3" or 4" heavy solid rib barrel. In 1996, a 5" barrel option was added that holds 8 rounds. Ramp front sight, with fully adjustable rear. Available in blued or stainless steel. Brazilian hardwood grips. Weight 27.5 oz.

Blue

NIB	Exc.	V.G.	Good	Fair	Poor
350	250	180	120	100	80

Stainless Steel

NIB	Exc.	V.G.	Good	Fair	Poor
380	280	200	150	100	80

Model 941 UL

Same as standard Model 941, with aluminum frame and 2" barrel. Weight 18 oz. Introduced in 1997.

NIB	Exc.	V.G.	Good	Fair	Poor
400	300	280	220	150	100

Model 942

Eight-shot .22 LR or .22 WMR double-action revolver, 2" or 3" barrel, matte black or matte stainless ($20 premium), weighs 18 to 24 oz. Introduced 2020.

NIB	Exc.	V.G.	Good	Fair	Poor
320	280	—	—	—	—

Model 96

Full-size .22 LR revolver, with 6" heavy solid rib barrel. Fully adjustable rear sight, with target hammer and adjustable target trigger. Cylinder holds 6 rounds. Available in blued only, with Brazilian hardwood grips. Weight 34 oz.

NIB	Exc.	V.G.	Good	Fair	Poor
300	250	200	150	120	100

Model 741

Double-action revolver chambered for .32 H&R Magnum cartridge. Features 3" or 4" heavy solid rib barrel, with fully adjustable rear sight. Swing-out cylinder holds 6 rounds. Available in blued or stainless steel (introduced in 1993), with Brazilian hardwood grips. Weight 30 oz. Note: Add $40 for stainless steel.

NIB	Exc.	V.G.	Good	Fair	Poor
200	180	150	120	100	80

Model 761

Similar to Model 741. This version has 6" barrel, target hammer and adjustable target trigger. Available blued only. Weight 34 oz.

NIB	Exc.	V.G.	Good	Fair	Poor
350	250	180	120	100	80

Model 65

Double-action revolver chambered for .357 Magnum cartridge. Offered with 2.5" (introduced in 1993) or 4" heavy solid rib barrel, with ejector shroud. Fitted with fixed sights. Brazilian hardwood grips. Available blued or stainless steel. Weight 34 oz. with 4" barrel. Note: Add $40 for stainless steel.

NIB	Exc.	V.G.	Good	Fair	Poor
320	220	150	120	100	80

Defender 856

Six-shot .38 Special double-action revolver, 3" barrel, night sight, 35 oz. Available in matte stainless, matte black, anodized black or Cerakote — special finishes can add up to $50 to price. Introduced 2020.

NIB	Exc.	V.G.	Good	Fair	Poor
320	280	—	—	—	—

Taurus Defender 856 T.O.R.O

Caliber: .38 Special (+P) Capacity: 6 rounds. Barrel length: 3" Finish: Stainless steel matte. Optics-ready, accepts compact red-dot sights that fit the Holosun K-footprint. Front Sight: Removable. Rear Sight: Fixed. Small frame. Overall Length 7.50" Overall Height: 4.80" Overall Width: 1.40" Overall Weight: 23.50 oz. (unloaded).

NIB	Exc.	V.G.	Good	Fair	Poor
350	—	—	—	—	—

Model 605

Introduced in 1995. Revolver chambered for .357 Magnum cartridge. Fitted with 2.25 or 3" heavy barrel. Offered in blue or stainless steel. Weight 25 oz.

Blue

NIB	Exc.	V.G.	Good	Fair	Poor
320	220	150	120	100	80

Stainless Steel

NIB	Exc.	V.G.	Good	Fair	Poor
380	280	200	150	100	80

Model 605 Custom (B2C)

Same as above. Offered with 2.25" compensated barrel.

Blue

NIB	Exc.	V.G.	Good	Fair	Poor
400	300	280	220	150	100

Stainless Steel

NIB	Exc.	V.G.	Good	Fair	Poor
450	350	300	250	150	100

Model 605CHB2/SS2

Chambered for .357 Magnum cartridge. Fitted with 2.25" solid rib barrel and 5-shot cylinder. Offered with concealed hammer. Weight 24 oz.

Blue

NIB	Exc.	V.G.	Good	Fair	Poor
350	250	180	120	100	80

Stainless Steel

NIB	Exc.	V.G.	Good	Fair	Poor
380	280	200	150	100	80

Model 605CHB2C/SS2C

Same as above, with concealed hammer and ported barrels.

Blue

NIB	Exc.	V.G.	Good	Fair	Poor
350	250	180	120	100	80

Taurus 605 T.O.R.O

Caliber: .357 Mag. Capacity: 5 rounds. Otherwise nearly identical to the 856.

NIB	Exc.	V.G.	Good	Fair	Poor
350	—	—	—	—	—

Model 605CHB2C/SS2CStainless Steel

NIB	Exc.	V.G.	Good	Fair	Poor
380	280	200	150	100	80

Model 66

Similar to Model 65. Offered with 2.5", 4" or 6" barrel, with fully adjustable rear sight. Blued or stainless steel. Weight 35 oz. with 4" barrel. The 2.5" barrel introduced in 1993.

NIB	Exc.	V.G.	Good	Fair	Poor
220	200	180	150	120	100

Model 66CP

Similar to Model 66. Features compensated heavy solid rib 4" or 6" ejector shroud barrel. Introduced in 1993. Weight 35 oz.

NIB	Exc.	V.G.	Good	Fair	Poor
250	220	200	150	120	100

Model 66B4/SS4

Chambered for .357 Magnum cartridge, with 4" solid rib barrel and 7-shot cylinder. Adjustable sights. Rubber grips. Weight 38 oz.

Blue

NIB	Exc.	V.G.	Good	Fair	Poor
350	280	220	150	120	100

Stainless Steel

NIB	Exc.	V.G.	Good	Fair	Poor
400	320	280	220	150	100

Model 606

Introduced in 1997. This 6-round model chambered for .357 Magnum cartridge. Fitted with 2" solid rib barrel, with ramp front sight and notched rear. Available in double-/single-action or double-action-only. Offered in blue or stainless steel. Rubber grips are standard. Weight 29 oz. A number of variations offered on this model. Note: Add $50 for stainless steel.

NIB	Exc.	V.G.	Good	Fair	Poor
380	280	200	150	100	80

Model 607

Introduced in 1995. This .357 Magnum features 4" or 6.5" integral compensated barrel in blue or stainless steel. The 6.5" barrel fitted with a ventilated rib.

Blue

NIB	Exc.	V.G.	Good	Fair	Poor
320	280	220	200	150	100

Stainless Steel

NIB	Exc.	V.G.	Good	Fair	Poor
400	350	300	200	150	100

Model 608

Introduced in 1996. Revolver chambered for .357 Magnum cartridge. Cylinder bored for 8 rounds. Offered in 4" and 6.5" barrel lengths, with integral compensator. Front sight serrated ramp, with red insert and rear is adjustable. Offered in both blued and stainless steel versions. Weight 51.5 oz. with 6.5" barrel.

Blue

NIB	Exc.	V.G.	Good	Fair	Poor
420	320	250	200	150	100

Stainless Steel

NIB	Exc.	V.G.	Good	Fair	Poor
450	350	300	200	150	100

Model 689

Chambered for .357 Magnum cartridge. Features heavy ventilated rib barrel in 4" or 6" lengths. Fully adjustable rear sight is standard. Offered in blued or stainless steel. Weight 37 oz. In 1998, fitted with 7-round cylinder.

NIB	Exc.	V.G.	Good	Fair	Poor
380	280	200	150	100	80

Model 617

Chambered for .357 Magnum cartridge, with 7-round cylinder. Fitted with 2" barrel. Choice of blue or stainless steel finish. Some variations offered a ported barrel. Introduced in 1998.

Blue

NIB	Exc.	V.G.	Good	Fair	Poor
400	320	280	220	180	120

Stainless Steel

NIB	Exc.	V.G.	Good	Fair	Poor
400	320	280	220	180	120

Ported Barrel

NIB	Exc.	V.G.	Good	Fair	Poor
420	320	250	200	150	100

Model 617 CHB2/SS2

Chambered for .357 Magnum cartridge. Features concealed hammer, 2" solid rib barrel and fixed sights.

Blue

NIB	Exc.	V.G.	Good	Fair	Poor
350	280	220	180	120	100

Stainless Steel

NIB	Exc.	V.G.	Good	Fair	Poor
420	320	250	200	150	100

Model 627 Tracker

Chambered for .357 Magnum cartridge. Has 7-round cylinder. The 4" barrel is ported, with heavy underlug. Adjustable rear sight. Matte stainless steel finish. Introduced in 2000.

NIB	Exc.	V.G.	Good	Fair	Poor
450	320	280	220	180	120

Model 669

Chambered for .357 Magnum cartridge. Features 4" or 6" heavy solid rib barrel, with full shroud. Fully adjustable rear sight. Available with blued or stainless steel finish. Brazilian hardwood grips are standard. Weight 37 oz. with 4" barrel. Note: Add $60 for stainless steel.

NIB	Exc.	V.G.	Good	Fair	Poor
380	280	200	150	100	80

Model 669CP

Variation of Model 669 was introduced in 1993. Features 4" or 6" compensated barrel. Fully adjustable rear sights are standard. Offered with blue or stainless steel finish. Weight 37 oz. In 1998, fitted with 7-round cylinder. Note: Add $60 for stainless steel.

NIB	Exc.	V.G.	Good	Fair	Poor
420	320	250	200	150	100

Model 692

A seven-shot mid-size revolver chambered for .357/.38 Special or for 9mm. Double/single action design with spur hammer, adjustable sights, non-fluted cylinder, Taurus Ribber grips. Choice of 3" or 6.5" barrel. Introduced in 2018.

NIB	Exc.	V.G.	Good	Fair	Poor
600	520	480	—	—	—

Model 415

Chambered for .41 Magnum cartridge. Fitted with 2.5" ported barrel. Fixed sights. Rubber grips. Matte stainless steel finish. Weight 30 oz.

NIB	Exc.	V.G.	Good	Fair	Poor
450	350	300	200	150	100

Model 431

Chambered for .44 Special cartridge. This double-action revolver furnished with 3" or 4" heavy solid rib barrel, with ejector shroud. Cylinder capacity 5 rounds. Fixed sights are standard. Choice of blued or stainless steel finish. Weight 35 oz. Note: Add $60 for stainless steel.

NIB	Exc.	V.G.	Good	Fair	Poor
450	350	300	200	150	100

Model 817 (Ultra-Lite)

Chambered for .357 Magnum cartridge. Fitted with 7-shot cylinder and 2" solid rib barrel. Features an alloy frame. Stainless steel or blued finish. Some models are ported. Weight 21 oz. Note: Add $20 for ported barrels.

Blue

NIB	Exc.	V.G.	Good	Fair	Poor
350	280	220	180	120	100

Stainless Steel

NIB	Exc.	V.G.	Good	Fair	Poor
390	320	280	220	180	100

Model 942

Caliber: .22 LR. Capacity: 8 rounds. Barrel: 2", 3". Grip: Soft rubber. Sights: Drift-adjustable rear, serrated-ramp front. Weight: 17.8, 25 oz. Features: The 942 is based closely on the Taurus 856 revolver but chambered in .22 LR with an 8-shot cylinder. Eight models are available: 2" and 3"-barrel models with a steel-alloy frame and cylinder in matte-black finish, 2" and 3"-barrel models with an ultralight aluminum-alloy frame in hardcoat, black-anodized finish, 2" and 3"-barrel models with a stainless steel frame and cylinder in a matte finish, and 2" and 3"-barrel models with an ultralight aluminum-alloy frame in a stainless-matte finish. Imported by Taurus International.

NIB	Exc.	V.G.	Good	Fair	Poor
300	—	—	—	—	—

Model 441

Similar to Model 431. Furnished with 3" or 4" plus 6" barrel. Comes standard with fully adjustable rear sight. Cylinder capacity 5 rounds. Blued or stainless steel finish. Weight 40.25 oz. with 6" barrel. Note: Add $60 for stainless steel.

NIB	Exc.	V.G.	Good	Fair	Poor
400	300	240	150	120	100

Model 444 Multi

Features 4" barrel, with adjustable sights. Chambered for .44 Magnum cartridge. Cylinder holds 6 rounds. Frame is alloy, with titanium cylinder. Grips have cushion inset. Weight 28 oz. Introduced in 2004.

NIB	Exc.	V.G.	Good	Fair	Poor
580	480	380	300	280	200

Model 905I-B1/SS1

Introduced in 2003. Revolver chambered for 9mm pistol cartridge. Barrel length 2". Cylinder capacity 5 rounds. Weight 21 oz. Blue or stainless steel finish. Note: Add $45 for matte stainless steel finish.

NIB	Exc.	V.G.	Good	Fair	Poor
380	320	250	180	100	80

Model 951SH2

Chambered for 9mm cartridge. Fitted with 2" barrel, with adjustable sights. Cylinder holds 5 rounds. Titanium frame and finish. Rubber grips. Weight 16 oz.

NIB	Exc.	V.G.	Good	Fair	Poor
480	350	260	200	150	100

Model 907SH2

9mm revolver has 7-shot cylinder, 2" barrel, with fixed sights and rubber grips. Titanium frame and finish. Weight about 17 oz. Introduced in 2004.

NIB	Exc.	V.G.	Good	Fair	Poor
480	350	260	200	150	100

Model 907B2/SS2

Chambered for 9mm cartridge. Fitted with 2" barrel, with fixed sights. Rubber grips. Ultra light alloy frame in blue or stainless steel. Weight 18.5 oz. Introduced in 2004. Note: Add $45 for stainless steel.

NIB	Exc.	V.G.	Good	Fair	Poor
390	300	250	200	150	100

RAGING BULL SERIES

Model 218 Raging Bee

Introduced in 2002. Chambered for .218 Bee cartridge. Fitted with 10" ventilated rib barrel, with adjustable sights. Cylinder holds 8 rounds. Matte stainless steel finish.

NIB	Exc.	V.G.	Good	Fair	Poor
900	780	600	480	350	200

Model 22H Raging Hornet

Chambered for .22 Hornet cartridge. Has 10" barrel, with base mount and adjustable sights. Matte stainless steel finish. Cylinder holds 8 rounds. Rubber grips.

NIB	Exc.	V.G.	Good	Fair	Poor
750	680	550	400	300	200

Model 30C Raging Thirty

Chambered for .30 Carbine cartridge. Fitted with 10" ventilated rib barrel, with adjustable sights. Cylinder holds 8 rounds. Supplied with full-moon clips. Matte stainless steel finish. Introduced in 2002.

NIB	Exc.	V.G.	Good	Fair	Poor
750	680	550	400	300	200

Model 416 Raging Bull

Model has 6.5" ventilated rib ported barrel, with adjustable sights. Chambered for .41 Magnum cartridge. Matte stainless steel finish. Introduced in 2002. Cylinder holds 6 rounds.

NIB	Exc.	V.G.	Good	Fair	Poor
620	500	400	300	220	100

Model 454 Raging Bull

Chambered for .454 Casull. Built on a large frame, with 5-round capacity. Barrel lengths 5", 6.5" or 8.375"; fitted with ventilated rib and integral compensator. Sights are adjustable. Finish blue or stainless steel. Black rubber or walnut grips. Weight 53 oz. with 6.5" barrel.

Blue

NIB	Exc.	V.G.	Good	Fair	Poor
700	650	580	450	320	180

Stainless Steel

NIB	Exc.	V.G.	Good	Fair	Poor
750	680	550	400	300	200

Black Stainless Steel

NIB	Exc.	V.G.	Good	Fair	Poor
750	680	550	400	300	200

Model 500 Magnum Raging Bull

Introduced in 2004. Chambered for .500 Magnum cartridge. Ventilated barrel length 10", with adjustable sights. Cushion inset grips. Stainless steel finish. Weight 72 oz.

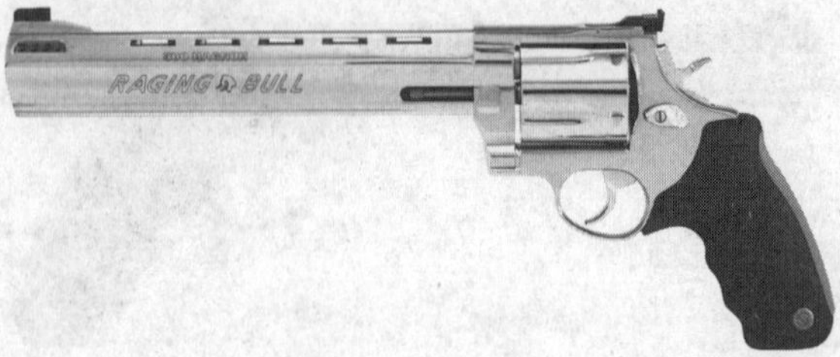

NIB	Exc.	V.G.	Good	Fair	Poor
900	780	600	480	350	200

Model 500MSS2 Raging Bull

Stainless .500 S&W Magnum, with 5-shot capacity, 2.25" barrel, soft rubber grips. Weight 68 oz. Adjustable rear sight, single/double action. Introduced in 2006.

NIB	Exc.	V.G.	Good	Fair	Poor
900	780	600	480	350	200

Raging Hunter

Calibers: .357 Magnum, .44 Magnum, .454 Casull. Capacity: 7 (.357), 6 (.44) and 5 (.454) rounds. Barrel: 5.12", 6.75", 8.37". Grips: Cushioned rubber. Sights: Adjustable rear, fixed front. Weight: 49 - 59.2 oz. Features: This is a DA/SA big-game-hunting revolver, available in three calibers and three barrel lengths, each featuring a Picatinny rail for easy optic mounting without removing the iron sights. All Raging Hunter models come with factory porting and cushioned rubber grips. Two finishes are available: matte black and two-tone matte stainless. Imported by Taurus International.

NIB	Exc.	V.G.	Good	Fair	Poor
680	—	—	—	—	—

Taurus Raging Hunter Two Tone

Caliber: .460 S&W. Barrel: 10.5" w/ compensator. Capacity: 5 rounds. Lower Picatinny rail to attach bipods and shooting sticks. A top rail allows for additional sight/scope options. Fixed front sight, fully adjustable rear. Frame Size: Large. Overall length: 16.22" Overall height: 6.40" Overall width: 1.80" Weight: 71.26 oz. (unloaded).

NIB	Exc.	V.G.	Good	Fair	Poor
950	—	—	—	—	—

Taurus Raging Hunter 500

Caliber: .500 S&W Magnum. Capacity: 5 rounds. Barrel Length: 5.12", 6.75", and 8.37" Finish: Matte black or two-tone. Picatinny rail, ported barrel. Sights: Fixed front. Fully adjustable rear.

NIB	Exc.	V.G.	Good	Fair	Poor
800	—	—	—	—	—

Model 44/444

Introduced in 1994. Heavy frame revolver chambered for .44 Magnum cartridge. Choice of three barrel lengths: 4" with solid rib; 6.5" and 8.375" with ventilated rib. All Model 44s have a built in compensator. Front sight is a serrated ramp, with adjustable rear. Blued or stainless finish. Weight 53 oz. for 6.5" barrel.

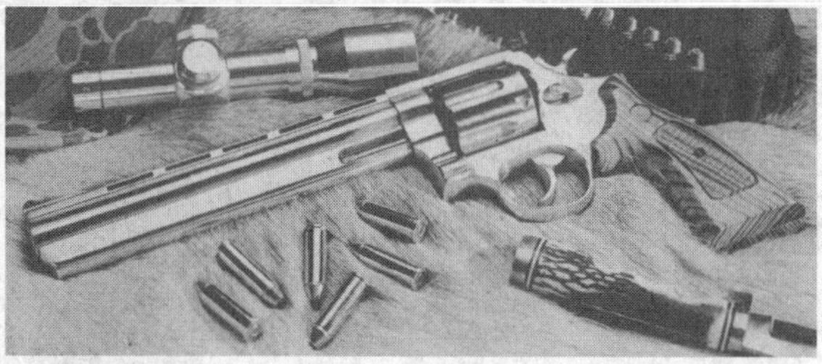

Blue

NIB	Exc.	V.G.	Good	Fair	Poor
—	420	300	200	150	100

Stainless Steel

NIB	Exc.	V.G.	Good	Fair	Poor
600	480	380	250	200	120

TRACKER SERIES

Model 17

Introduced in 2002. Features 6.5" or 12" ventilated rib barrel. Chambered for .17 HMR cartridge. Adjustable sights. Matte stainless steel finish. Cylinder holds 7 rounds. Weight 41 oz. for 6.5"; 50 oz. for 12".

NIB	Exc.	V.G.	Good	Fair	Poor
380	300	220	180	120	100

Model 970

Chambered for .22 LR cartridge. Fitted with 6.5" ventilated rib heavy barrel, with adjustable sights. Matte stainless steel finish. Rubber grips. Cylinder holds 7 rounds. Introduced in 2002.

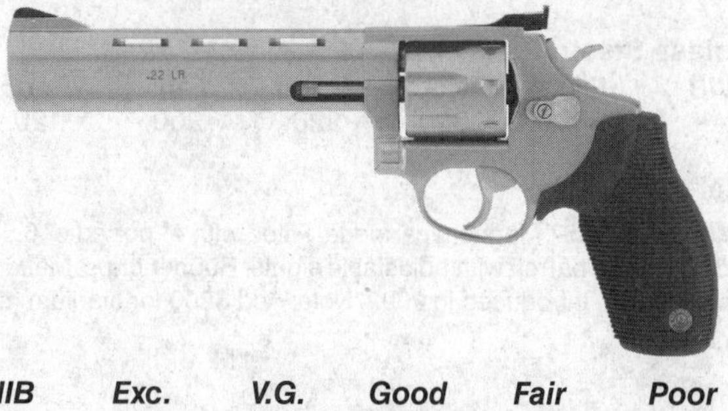

NIB	Exc.	V.G.	Good	Fair	Poor
300	200	160	120	100	80

Model 971

Same as Model 970, but chambered for .22 Magnum cartridge. Introduced in 2002.

NIB	Exc.	V.G.	Good	Fair	Poor
300	200	160	120	100	80

Tracker .22/.22 Mag.

Same as Model 971, except chambered for .22 LR, with interchangeable .22 WMR cylinder. Both cylinders hold 9 rounds. Weight: 38 to 44 oz., with 4.5" or 6" barrel. Blue or matte stainless finish. Note: Add 10% for stainless.

NIB	Exc.	V.G.	Good	Fair	Poor
460	400	350	280	200	150

Model 425 Tracker

Chambered for .41 Magnum cartridge. Features 4" heavy underlug ported barrel. Adjustable rear sight. Cylinder chambered for 5 rounds. Matte stainless steel finish. Introduced in 2000.

NIB	Exc.	V.G.	Good	Fair	Poor
420	320	250	200	150	100

Model 44 Tracker

.44 Magnum revolver has 4" barrel, with adjustable sights and Ribber (ribbed) grips. 5-shot cylinder. Stainless steel finish. Weight 34 oz. Introduced in 2004.

NIB	Exc.	V.G.	Good	Fair	Poor
420	320	250	200	150	100

Tracker .45

Similar to other Tracker models, but chambered in .45 ACP (via full-moon clips), with 5-shot cylinder. 4" barrel, with Picatinny rail. Stainless steel frame and cylinder. Introduced in 2007.

NIB	Exc.	V.G.	Good	Fair	Poor
450	350	280	220	180	120

Model 445

Small frame revolver chambered for .44 Special cartridge. Fitted with 2" barrel, with ramp front sight and notched rear. Cylinder holds 5 rounds. Black rubber grips. Offered in blue or stainless steel. Weight 28 oz. Factory barrel porting, add $20, is optional. Introduced in 1997. Note: Add $50 for stainless steel.

NIB	Exc.	V.G.	Good	Fair	Poor
420	320	250	200	150	100

Model 450

Chambered for .45 Long Colt cartridge. Features 2" heavy solid rib barrel, with 5-shot cylinder and fixed sights. Ported barrel. Rubber grips. Stainless steel finish. Weight about 28 oz. Note: Add $30 for Ultra Lite model.

NIB	Exc.	V.G.	Good	Fair	Poor
450	350	280	220	180	120

Model 455

Introduced in 2002. Chambered for .45 ACP cartridge. Choice of 2", 4" or 6.5" barrels. Adjustable sights on 4" and 6.5" barrels. Matte stainless steel finish. Rubber grips. Supplied with full-moon clips.

NIB	Exc.	V.G.	Good	Fair	Poor
450	350	280	220	180	120

Model 460

Chambered for .45 Long Colt cartridge. Fitted with 4" or 6.5" ventilated rib barrel, with adjustable sights. Matte stainless steel finish. Introduced in 2002.

NIB	Exc.	V.G.	Good	Fair	Poor
450	350	280	220	180	120

Model 45

Chambered for .45 Long Colt. Fitted with choice of 6.5" or 8.375" heavy ventilated rib barrels. Cylinder holds 6 rounds. Rubber grips, ported barrels and adjustable sights are standard. Weight 53 oz. with 6.5" barrel.

Blue

NIB	Exc.	V.G.	Good	Fair	Poor
450	350	280	220	180	120

Stainless Steel

NIB	Exc.	V.G.	Good	Fair	Poor
—	380	300	220	200	120

Model 627

Chambered for .357 Magnum cartridge. Fitted with 4" ported or 6.5" ventilated rib ported barrel, with adjustable sights. Rubber grips. Matte stainless steel finish. Introduced in 2002. Note: Add $200 for titanium model.

NIB	Exc.	V.G.	Good	Fair	Poor
420	350	280	220	150	100

Tracker 10mm 10TSS4

Matte stainless 10mm, with 4" barrel and fixed sights. Five-shot, rubber grip. Weight 34.8 oz. Introduced in 2006.

NIB	Exc.	V.G.	Good	Fair	Poor
500	400	300	250	180	120

Tracker 10SS8

10mm 6-shot matte stainless, with 6.5" (54.5 oz.) or 8.375" (59.5 oz.) barrel. Fixed sights, rubber grips. Introduced in 2006.

NIB	Exc.	V.G.	Good	Fair	Poor
500	400	300	250	180	120

Tracker 4510TKR

Shoots 2.5" .410 bore shells or .45 Colt. Holds 5 shots. Stainless or blued, 2.25" or 6.5" barrel, rubber grip. Single-/double-action, 9.1" LOA. Weight 32 oz. Introduced in 2006.

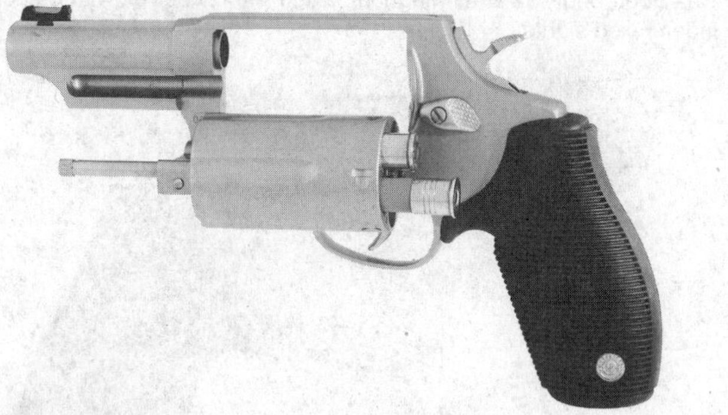

NIB	Exc.	V.G.	Good	Fair	Poor
500	400	300	250	180	120

Tracker 590 5mm

Double-action 9-shot stainless steel revolver. Chambered in 5mm Rem. Magnum rimfire. Introduced in 2008; discontinued 2011.

NIB	Exc.	V.G.	Good	Fair	Poor
400	350	300	220	200	150

JUDGE SERIES

Judge

Stainless steel or lightweight alloy-frame version of Tracker Model 4410. Chambered in 3" .410/.45 Colt (4510TKR-3MAG) or 2.5" .410/.45 Colt (4510TKR-3UL) with 3" (3" Magnum) or 2.5" barrel (2.5"). Introduced in 2007.

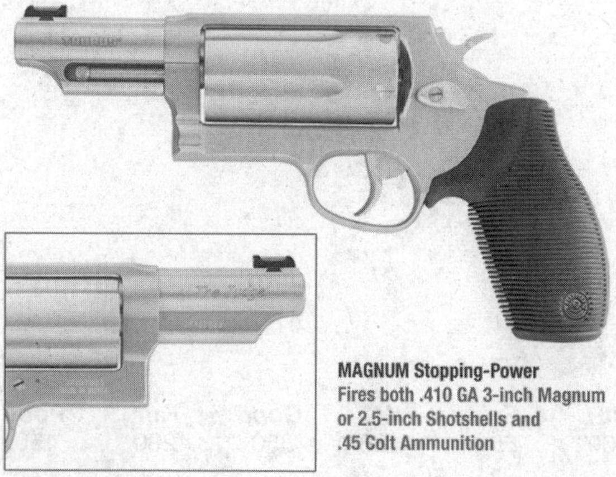

NIB	Exc.	V.G.	Good	Fair	Poor
520	420	300	260	200	150

Model 4510TKR-SSR

Similar to Judge, with ported barrel and tactical rail.

NIB	Exc.	V.G.	Good	Fair	Poor
600	520	420	300	260	180

Judge Public Defender Polymer

Single-/double-action revolver chambered in .45 Colt/.410. Features include 5-round cylinder; polymer frame; Ribber rubber-feel grips; fiber-optic front sight; adjustable rear sight; blued or stainless cylinder; shrouded hammer with cocking spur; blued finish; 2.5" barrel. Weight 27 oz.

NIB	Exc.	V.G.	Good	Fair	Poor
550	450	380	300	250	150

Judge Public Defender Ultra-Lite

Single-/double-action revolver chambered in .45 Colt/.410. Features include 5-round cylinder; lightweight aluminum frame; Ribber rubber-feel grips; fiber-optic front sight; adjustable rear sight; blued or stainless cylinder; shrouded hammer with cocking spur; blued finish; 2.5" barrel. Weight 20.7 oz.

NIB	Exc.	V.G.	Good	Fair	Poor
600	500	420	320	250	150

Raging Judge Magnum

Single-/double-action revolver chambered for .454 Casull, .45 Colt, 2.5" and 3" .410. Features include 3" or 6" barrel; fixed sights with fiber-optic front; blued or stainless steel finish; ventilated rib for scope mounting (6" only); cushioned Raging Bull grips.

NIB	Exc.	V.G.	Good	Fair	Poor
820	700	550	400	350	200

Raging Judge Magnum Ultra-Lite

Single-/double-action revolver chambered for .454 Casull, .45 Colt, 2.5" and 3" .410. Features include 3" or 6" barrel; aluminum alloy frame; fixed sights with fiber-optic front; blued or stainless steel finish; cushioned Raging Bull grips. Weight: 41.4 oz. (3" barrel).

NIB	Exc.	V.G.	Good	Fair	Poor
880	720	580	420	350	200

Taurus Executive Grade Judge

Caliber: .45 Colt/.410 Capacity: 5 Rounds. Finish: Hand-polished Stainless steel satin. Tuned action. Presentation-grade wood grips and brass bead front sight on a 3" barrel. Frame Size: Tracker. Overall Length: 9.50" Overall Height: 5.10" Overall Width: 1.50" Weight: 36 oz. (unloaded). Transfer bar safety.

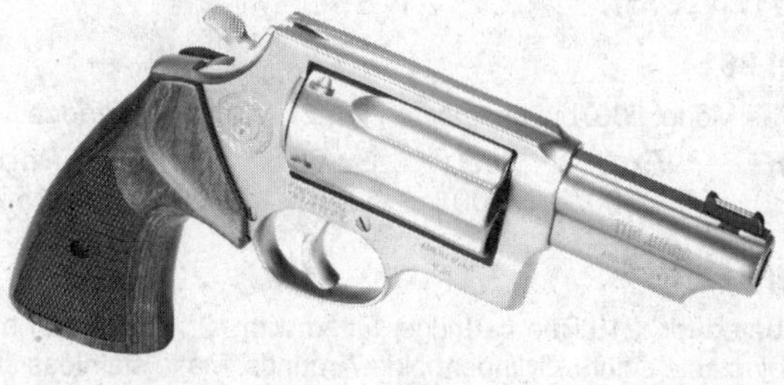

NIB	Exc.	V.G.	Good	Fair	Poor
710	—	—	—	—	—

SILHOUETTE SERIES

Model 17-12

Chambered for .17 HMR cartridge. Fitted with 12" ventilated rib silhouette barrel. Adjustable sights. Cylinder holds 7 rounds. Matte stainless steel finish. Introduced in 2002.

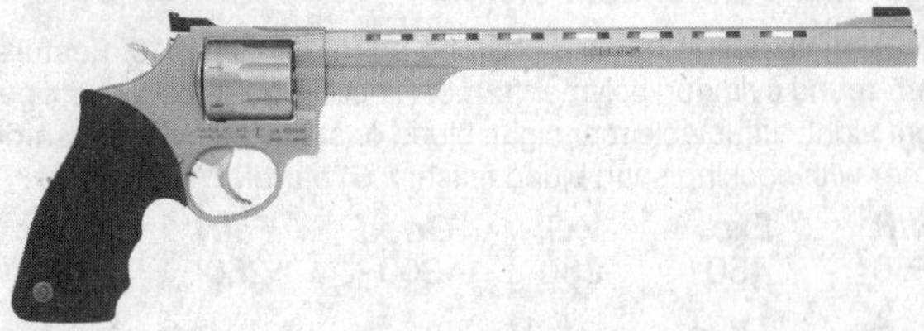

NIB	Exc.	V.G.	Good	Fair	Poor
700	600	480	350	200	150

Model 66

Chambered for .357 Magnum cartridge. Fitted with 12" barrel, with adjustable sights. Choice of blue or stainless steel finish. Rubber grips. Introduced in 2002. Note: Add $60 for stainless steel.

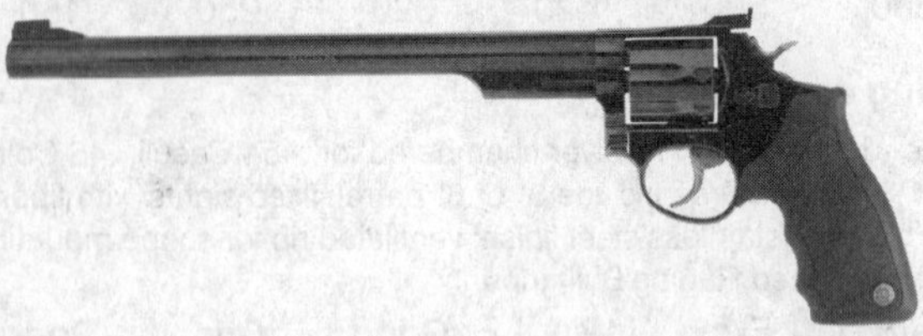

NIB	Exc.	V.G.	Good	Fair	Poor
520	420	300	260	200	150

Model 980

Chambered for .22 LR cartridge. Fitted with 12" target barrel, with adjustable sights. Cylinder holds 7 rounds. Matted stainless steel finish. Rubber grips. Introduced in 2002.

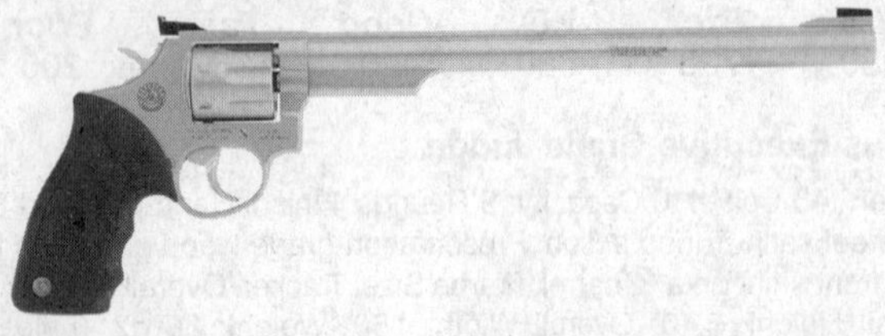

NIB	Exc.	V.G.	Good	Fair	Poor
380	350	300	250	200	150

Model 981

Same as Model 980, but chambered for .22 Magnum cartridge.

NIB	Exc.	V.G.	Good	Fair	Poor
380	350	300	250	200	150

Model 217

Chambered for .218 Bee cartridge. Fitted with 12" ventilated rib barrel, with adjustable sights. Cylinder holds 7 rounds. Matte stainless steel finish. Introduced in 2002.

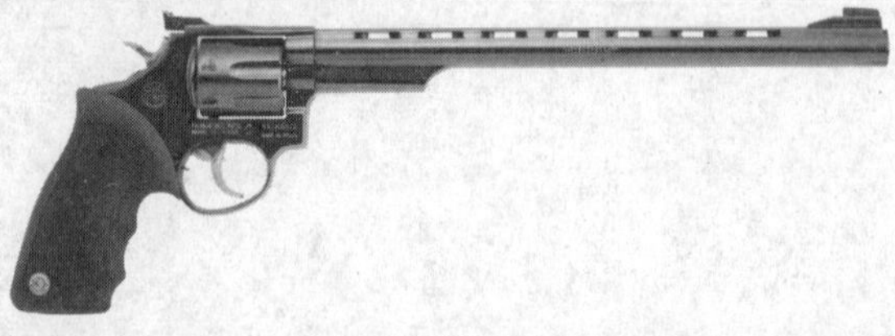

NIB	Exc.	V.G.	Good	Fair	Poor
900	780	600	480	350	200

TITANIUM SERIES

Introduced in 1999. This series of revolvers features titanium barrels, with stainless steel bore liners, titanium frames and cylinders. Hammers, triggers, latches, ejector rod and other small parts are made from case-hardened chrome moly steel. All Taurus Titanium revolvers have factory porting and rated for +P ammunition. Rubber grips are standard. Three different finishes are offered: Bright Spectrum blue, Matte Spectrum blue and Matte Spectrum gold.

Model 85Ti

Chambered for .38 Special. Fitted with 2" barrel, with 5-shot cylinder. Fixed sights.

NIB	Exc.	V.G.	Good	Fair	Poor
520	420	300	200	150	100

Model 731Ti

Chambered for .32 H&R Magnum. Fitted with 2" barrel, with 6-shot cylinder. Fixed sights.

NIB	Exc.	V.G.	Good	Fair	Poor
520	420	300	200	150	100

Model 617Ti

Chambered for .357 Magnum. Fitted with 2" barrel and 7-shot cylinder. Fixed sights. Weight 20 oz.

NIB	Exc.	V.G.	Good	Fair	Poor
600	520	420	300	260	180

Model 627Ti

Features 7-round cylinder chambered for .357 Magnum cartridge. Fitted with ported 4" barrel, with adjustable sights. Gray finish. Weight 28 oz. depending on barrel length.

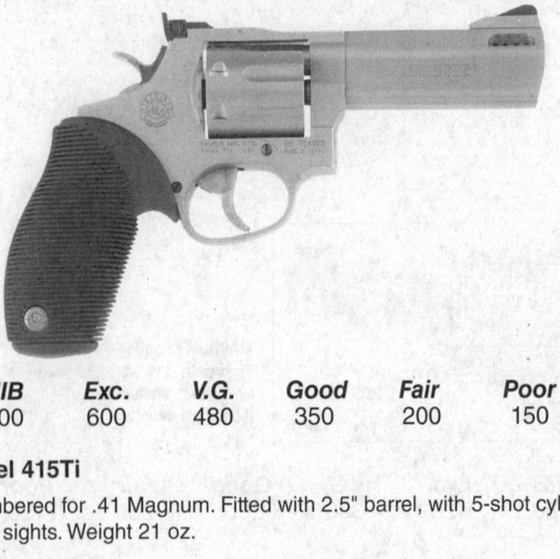

NIB	Exc.	V.G.	Good	Fair	Poor
700	600	480	350	200	150

Model 415Ti

Chambered for .41 Magnum. Fitted with 2.5" barrel, with 5-shot cylinder. Fixed sights. Weight 21 oz.

NIB	Exc.	V.G.	Good	Fair	Poor
600	480	350	250	150	120

Model 425Ti

Chambered for .41 Magnum cartridge. Has a 5-round cylinder, ported 4" barrel, with adjustable rear sight. Gray finish. Introduced in 2000.

NIB	Exc.	V.G.	Good	Fair	Poor
600	480	350	250	150	120

Model 450Ti

Chambered for .45 Long Colt. Fitted with 2" barrel, with 5-shot cylinder. Fixed sights. Weight 19 oz.

NIB	Exc.	V.G.	Good	Fair	Poor
600	480	350	250	150	120

Model 445Ti

Chambered for .44 Special. Fitted with 2" barrel, with 5-shot cylinder. Fixed sights. Weight 20 oz.

NIB	Exc.	V.G.	Good	Fair	Poor
600	480	350	250	150	120

Model UL/Ti

Chambered for .38 Special. Has Titanium cylinder and alloy frame. Fitted with 2" unported barrel. Cylinder is 5 shot. Fixed sights.

NIB	Exc.	V.G.	Good	Fair	Poor
520	420	300	200	150	100

GAUCHO SERIES

S/A-45, B/S/SM

Chambered for .45 Colt cartridge. Fitted with 5.5" barrel, with fixed sights. Checkered wood grips. Blued or stainless steel finish. Weight 37 oz. Introduced in 2004; discontinued. Note: Add $15 for stainless steel.

NIB	Exc.	V.G.	Good	Fair	Poor
400	320	280	220	180	120

S/A-45, S/S/CH

Chambered for .45 Colt cartridge. Fitted with 5.5" barrel, with fixed sights. Choice of Sundance stainless steel finish or case-hardened blued finish. Weight 37 oz. Introduced in 2004; discontinued.

NIB	Exc.	V.G.	Good	Fair	Poor
400	320	280	220	180	120

S/A-357-B, S/SM, S/S, CHSA

Single-action 6-shot chambered for .357/.38-caliber. Barrel lengths 4.75" (36.2 oz.), 5.5" (36.7 oz.), 7.5" (37.7 oz.). Fixed sights. Blued matte stainless, polished stainless or blued/case-hardened receiver. Introduced in 2006; discontinued. Note: Add $15 for stainless steel.

NIB	Exc.	V.G.	Good	Fair	Poor
400	320	280	220	180	120

S/A-44-40-B, S/SM, S/S, CHSA

Single-action 6-shot chambered for .44-40 caliber. Barrel lengths 4.75" (36.2 oz.), 5.5" (36.7 oz.), 7.5" (37.7 oz.). Fixed sights. Blued matte stainless, polished stainless or blued/case-hardened receiver. Introduced in 2006; discontinued.

NIB	Exc.	V.G.	Good	Fair	Poor
450	380	300	220	180	120

S/A-45-B12, S/SM12, S/S12, CHSA12

Single-action Buntline-style 6-shot revolver chambered for .45 Colt. Barrel length 12" (41.5 oz.). Fixed sights. Blued matte stainless, polished stainless or blued/case-hardened receiver. Introduced in 2006; discontinued. Note: Add $15 for stainless steel.

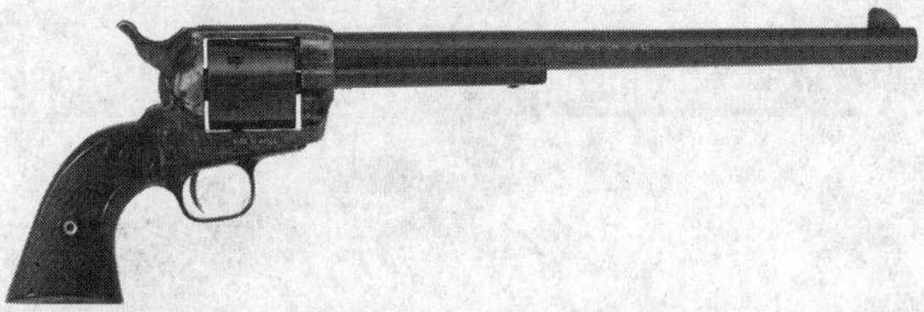

NIB	Exc.	V.G.	Good	Fair	Poor
450	380	300	250	200	100

RIFLES

Model 62

Introduced in 2000. Replica of Winchester Model 62 .22-caliber rifle. Fitted with 23" barrel and adjustable rear sight. Magazine capacity 13 rounds. Weight 5 lbs. Hardwood stock. In 2003, offered in .22 WMR and .17 HMR calibers. Discontinued. Note: Add 15% for stainless.

NIB	Exc.	V.G.	Good	Fair	Poor
350	300	220	180	120	80

Model 62 Carbine

Same as above, with 16.5" barrel. Magazine capacity 12 rounds. Weight 4.5 lbs. Introduced in 2000. In 2003, offered in .22 WMR and .17 HMR calibers. Discontinued. Note: Add 10% for stainless.

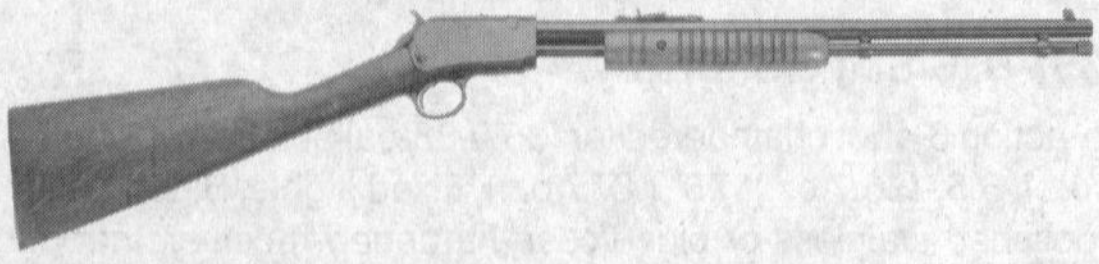

NIB	Exc.	V.G.	Good	Fair	Poor
350	300	220	180	120	80

Model 62 Upstart

Similar to Model 62 above, with shorter buttstock. Introduced in 2002; discontinued.

NIB	Exc.	V.G.	Good	Fair	Poor
350	300	220	180	120	80

Model 72

Same as Model 62, but chambered for .22 Magnum cartridge. Discontinued. Note: Add $15 for stainless steel.

NIB	Exc.	V.G.	Good	Fair	Poor
350	300	220	180	120	80

Model 72 Carbine

Same as Model 62 Carbine, but chambered for .22 Magnum cartridge. Discontinued. Note: Add $15 for stainless steel.

NIB	Exc.	V.G.	Good	Fair	Poor
350	300	220	180	120	80

Model 63

Copy of Winchester Model 63 in take-down. Chambered for .22 LR cartridge. Fitted with 23" round barrel, with adjustable rear sight. Offered in blue or stainless steel. Introduced in 2002. In 2003, offered chambered for .17 HMR and .22 WMR. Discontinued.

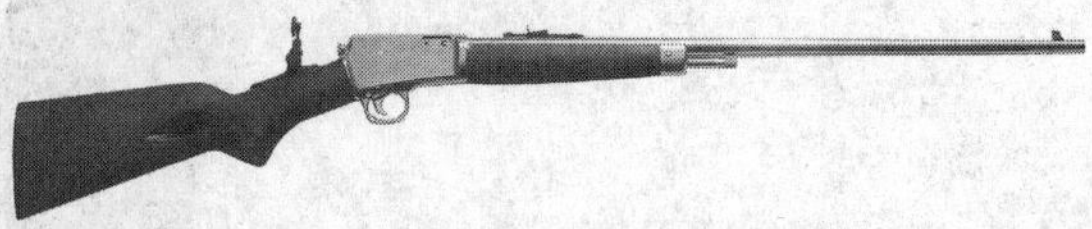

NIB	Exc.	V.G.	Good	Fair	Poor
300	240	200	150	100	80

Model 62LAR Lever Rifle

Lever-action rifle chambered in .22 LR. 23" blued barrel, walnut-finish hardwood stock. Introduced 2006; discontinued.

NIB	Exc.	V.G.	Good	Fair	Poor
300	250	200	150	120	100

Model 62LAR-SS

Similar to Model 62LAR in stainless steel. Introduced 2006; discontinued.

NIB	Exc.	V.G.	Good	Fair	Poor
350	300	220	180	150	120

Thunderbolt

Slide-action rifle a knockoff of Colt Lightning rifle. Chambered for .45 Colt cartridge and .38/.357 Magnum. Fitted with 26" barrel, with adjustable sights. Blued or stainless steel finish. Stocks are hardwood. Weight 8.125 lbs. Introduced in 2004; discontinued. Note: Add $50 for stainless steel or bright "Sundance" stainless finish.

NIB	Exc.	V.G.	Good	Fair	Poor
550	450	320	250	180	150

CT9G2

Semi-automatic carbine, with hybrid aluminum/polymer construction. Reinforced steel frame. Lower receiver made with high-strength polymer reinforced with steel. Upper receiver has flattop Picatinny rail. Two-position safety lever. Adjustable rear sight, fixed front. Ambidextrous slide catch. Available in 9mm, .40 S&W, .45 ACP. Taurus Security System installed. Introduced in 2011; discontinued.

NIB	Exc.	V.G.	Good	Fair	Poor
600	500	400	—	—	—

TAVOR

See—ISRAEL WEAPON INDUSTRIES

TAYLOR'S & CO., INC.

Winchester, Virginia

HANDGUNS

Napoleon Le Page Pistol (Model 551)

Percussion French-style duelling pistol. Chambered for .45-caliber. Fitted with 10" octagon barrel. Walnut stock, silver plated buttcap and triggerguard. Double-set triggers. Made by Uberti.

NIB	Exc.	V.G.	Good	Fair	Poor
450	380	300	250	200	100

Kentucky Pistol (Model 550)

Chambered for .45-caliber ball. Fitted with 10" barrel. Bird's-head grip, with brass ramrod thimbles and case-hardened sidelock. Made by Uberti.

NIB	Exc.	V.G.	Good	Fair	Poor
300	220	200	120	80	60

Colt Model 1847 Walker (Model 500A)

Fitted with 9" round barrel. Chambered for .44-caliber. Has 6-round engraved cylinder. Steel frame and backstrap. Brass triggerguard. One-piece walnut grips. Made by Uberti.

NIB	Exc.	V.G.	Good	Fair	Poor
400	320	280	250	200	100

Colt Model 1851 Navy

Offered with brass or steel frame. Brass backstrap and triggerguard. Chambered for .36-caliber. Fitted with 7.5" barrel. Cylinder holds 6 rounds. One-piece walnut grip. Brass frame model made by Armi San Marco; steel frame by F.LLI Pietta.

Brass Frame (Model 210)

NIB	Exc.	V.G.	Good	Fair	Poor
300	220	200	120	80	60

Steel Frame (Model 245)

NIB	Exc.	V.G.	Good	Fair	Poor
350	250	200	150	100	80

Remington Model 1858

A .44-caliber brass or steel frame. Brass triggerguard model, with 8" octagon barrel. Cylinder holds 6 rounds. Two-piece walnut grips. Brass frame made by F. LLI Pietta; steel frame by Armi San Marco.

Brass Frame (Model 410)

NIB	Exc.	V.G.	Good	Fair	Poor
300	220	200	120	80	60

Steel Frame (Model 430)

NIB	Exc.	V.G.	Good	Fair	Poor
350	250	200	150	100	80

Colt Model 1848 Baby Dragoon (Models 470, 471, 472)

Chambered for .31-caliber. Fitted with 5-round cylinder. Barrel length 4". Choice of blued or white steel frame. Brass backstrap and triggerguard. One-piece walnut grip. Made by Uberti.

NIB	Exc.	V.G.	Good	Fair	Poor
350	250	200	150	100	80

Starr Model 1858 (Model 510, 511)

Offered in double/single action. Chambered for .44-caliber. Fitted with 6" round barrel. Made by F. LLI Pietta.

NIB	Exc.	V.G.	Good	Fair	Poor
350	250	200	150	100	80

Colt Model 1860 Army

Features 8" round barrel except for Sheriff's model which is 5.5". Choice of brass or steel frame. Brass backstrap and triggerguard. Chambered for .44-caliber. One-piece walnut grip. Brass frame model made by Armi San Marco; steel frame by Uberti. Note: Half-fluted cylinder model also offered.

Brass Frame (Model 300)

NIB	Exc.	V.G.	Good	Fair	Poor
300	220	200	120	80	60

Steel Frame (Model 310, 312, 315)

NIB	Exc.	V.G.	Good	Fair	Poor
350	250	200	150	100	80

Colt Dragoon (Models 485A, 490A, 495A)

Offered in 1st, 2nd and 3rd models each. Fitted with 7.5" barrel. Chambered for .44-caliber. Steel frame, brass backstrap and triggerguard. The 2nd and 3rd models have square cylinder stop. Loading lever inverted on 3rd model. All have one-piece walnut grip. Made by Uberti. Note: Add $15 for 3rd model.

NIB	Exc.	V.G.	Good	Fair	Poor
350	250	200	150	100	80

Colt Model 1861 Navy (Model 210)

Chambered for .36-caliber. Fitted with 7.5" round barrel. Cylinder 6 rounds. Brass frame, backstrap and triggerguard. One-piece walnut grip. Made by Uberti.

NIB	Exc.	V.G.	Good	Fair	Poor
300	220	200	120	80	60

Colt Model 1862 Police (Model 315B)

Fitted with 6.5" round barrel. Chambered for .36-caliber. Case-hardened frame, with brass backstrap and triggerguard. Made by Uberti.

NIB	Exc.	V.G.	Good	Fair	Poor
350	250	200	150	100	80

Colt Model 1862 Pocket (Model 315C)

Similar to above model, but fitted with 6.5" octagonal barrel. Made by Uberti.

NIB	Exc.	V.G.	Good	Fair	Poor
350	250	200	150	100	80

Remington Model 1863 Pocket (Model 435)

Chambered for .31-caliber ball. Fitted with 3.5" barrel. Cylinder 5 rounds. Frame, backstrap and triggerguard are brass. Walnut grip. Made by Armi San Marco.

NIB	Exc.	V.G.	Good	Fair	Poor
300	220	200	120	80	60

Colt Model 1873 Cattleman (Models 700, 701, 702)

Famous replica made in several different configurations. Offered in barrel lengths of 4.75", 5.5" and 7.5". Calibers are: .45 Colt, .44-40, .44 Special, .38-40, .357 Magnum and .45 ACP. Frame case-hardened, with steel backstrap. One-piece walnut grip. Made by Uberti. Note: Add $80 for dual cylinder; add $80 for nickel finish; add $75 for laser engraving.

NIB	Exc.	V.G.	Good	Fair	Poor
650	500	350	200	150	120

Colt Model 1873 Bird's-head (Models 703A, 703B, 703C)

Same as above. Offered with bird's-head grip.

NIB	Exc.	V.G.	Good	Fair	Poor
500	380	220	180	150	120

Colt Model 1873 "Outfitter"

Chambered for .45 Colt or .357 Magnum cartridge. Fitted with 4.75, 5.5" or 7.5" barrel. Stainless steel finish. Walnut grips.

NIB	Exc.	V.G.	Good	Fair	Poor
500	380	220	180	150	120

Gunfighter Defender

Caliber: .357 Mag., .45 LC Capacity: 6. Weight: 4.75" 2.45 lb., 5.5" 2.50 lb. Finish: Blue with casehardened frame. Grip/Stock: Checkered walnut. Manufacturer: Uberti. Sights: Fixed front blade. Rear Frame Notch. Overall Length: 4.75" (10.35"), 5.5" (11.10"), Action: Taylor tuning available. The Gunfighter Defender with lowered Runnin' Iron hammer, 1860 Army grip is longer and slightly wider than the smaller Navy grip usually found on 1873 single-action models.

NIB	Exc.	V.G.	Good	Fair	Poor
530	—	—	—	—	—

TC9 1873 Cattleman

Caliber: 9mm. Barrel: 4.74" and 5.5" barrel lengths. The TC9 9mm pistol is offered in two styles; a large Army-size, walnut checkered grip and a black checkered standard-size grip. The 9mm revolver clone has a steel frame with a rear frame notch and fixed front blade sight. This iconic 9mm 1873 Cattleman revolver is offered in a black checkered grip, casehardened frame, with a blued steel finish. Add 7% for the color-casehardened version.

NIB	Exc.	V.G.	Good	Fair	Poor
410	—	—	—	—	—

HARTFORD ARMORY MODELS

Introduced to Taylor product line in 2004. Company produces revolvers made entirely in U.S. Each gun comes with a lifetime warranty. All Hartford Armory revolvers come in a numbered wooden case, with brass snap caps and plaque.

Remington Model 1875

Offered in these calibers: .38/.357, .44-40, .44 Special/Magnum or .45 Colt. Barrel lengths 5.75" or 7.5". Walnut grips. Armory dark blue finish.

NIB	Exc.	V.G.	Good	Fair	Poor
900	800	700	600	450	300

Remington Model 1890

Offered in .38/.357, .44-40, .44 Special/Magnum or .45 Colt. Choice of 5.5" or 7.5" barrel. Armory dark blue finish. Walnut grips.

NIB	Exc.	V.G.	Good	Fair	Poor
900	800	700	600	450	300

1911-A1 Model

Replica of famous 1911-A1 .45 ACP semi-automatic. Imported by Taylor's from Armscor in the Phillippines. Basic model has 5" barrel, blue finish, flat or arched mainspring housing and several optional grip choices: checkered or smooth walnut; Cocobolo wood with/without diamond design. There is also a Tactical model in 9mm, 10mm or .45 ACP, with Picatinny rail, fiber optic front sight, extended beavertail, ambidextrous safety and combat hammer. Compact Tactical also offered with 3.625" barrel. Note: Add $20 to $40 for Tactical models, based on overall condition.

NIB	Exc.	V.G.	Good	Fair	Poor
440	400	350	200	150	100

RIFLES

Kentucky Rifle

Offered in flintlock or percussion. Rifle is .40-caliber. Fitted with 3.5" barrel. One-piece stock, with brass fixtures.

Flintlock (Model 183)

NIB	Exc.	V.G.	Good	Fair	Poor
500	340	220	150	100	80

Percussion (Model 182)

NIB	Exc.	V.G.	Good	Fair	Poor
480	320	200	150	100	80

Model 1842 U.S. Percussion Musket (Model 125)

Offered as a smoothbore or rifled musket, with 42" .69-caliber barrel. Finish is white. One-piece walnut stock.

Smoothbore

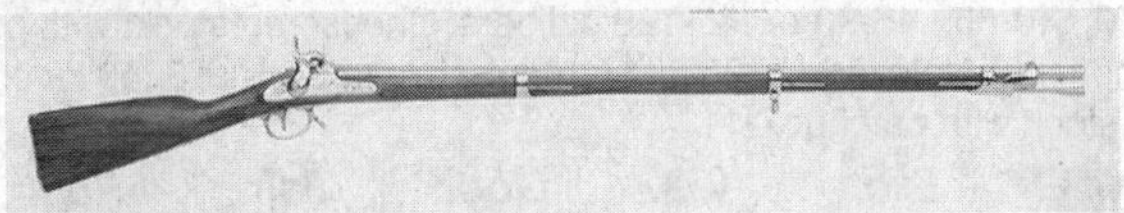

NIB	Exc.	V.G.	Good	Fair	Poor
450	320	250	200	150	100

Rifled with Rear Sight (Model 126)

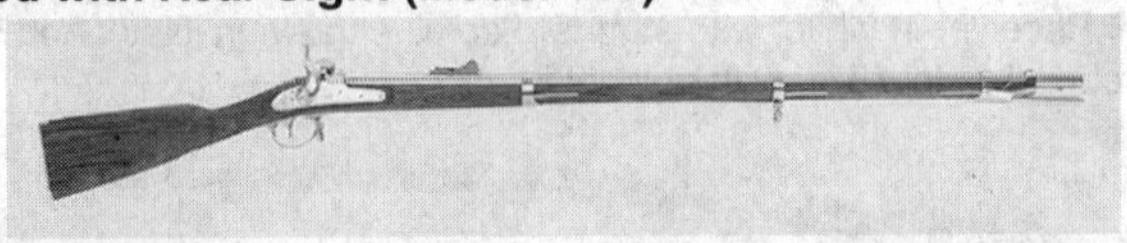

NIB	Exc.	V.G.	Good	Fair	Poor
450	320	250	200	150	100

Model 1855 U.S. Percussion Musket (Model 116)

Has .58-caliber 40" barrel, with rear sight. One-piece walnut stock. White satin finish.

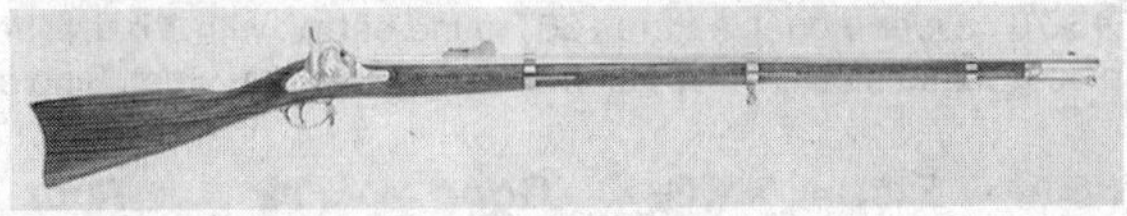

NIB	Exc.	V.G.	Good	Fair	Poor
500	380	220	180	150	120

Model 1853 3-Band Enfield Musket (Model 120)

Rifled musket has 39" .58-caliber barrel. Blued finish. One-piece walnut stock. Brass buttplate, nosecap and triggerguard.

NIB	Exc.	V.G.	Good	Fair	Poor
480	350	300	250	200	100

Model 1858 2-Band Enfield Musket (Model 121)

Similar to above, with .58-caliber 33" barrel.

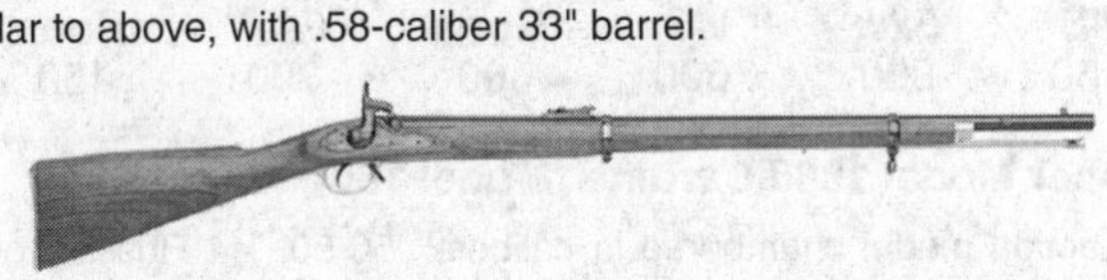

NIB	Exc.	V.G.	Good	Fair	Poor
480	350	300	250	200	100

Model 1861 Springfield Musket (Model 110)

Has 40" .58-caliber barrel, with one-piece walnut stock. White satin finish.

NIB	Exc.	V.G.	Good	Fair	Poor
550	420	350	300	200	100

Model 1862 C.S. Richmond Musket (Model 115)

Fitted with 40" .58-caliber barrel, with three barrel bands. Brass buttplate and nosecap. White satin finish. One-piece walnut stock.

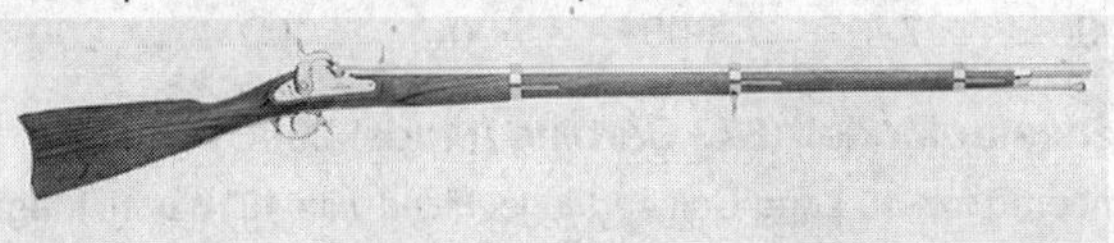

NIB	Exc.	V.G.	Good	Fair	Poor
550	420	350	300	200	100

Model 1863 Remington Zouave (Model 140)

Fitted with 33" barrel. Chambered for .58-caliber ball. One-piece walnut stock. Blued finish, brass buttplate, nosecap, triggerguard, patchbox and barrel bands.

NIB	Exc.	V.G.	Good	Fair	Poor
450	320	250	200	150	100

Henry Rifle

Lever-action rifle chambered for .44-40 or .45 Colt cartridge. Fitted with 24.25" octagon barrel. Walnut stock. Open sights.

Brass Frame (Model 198)

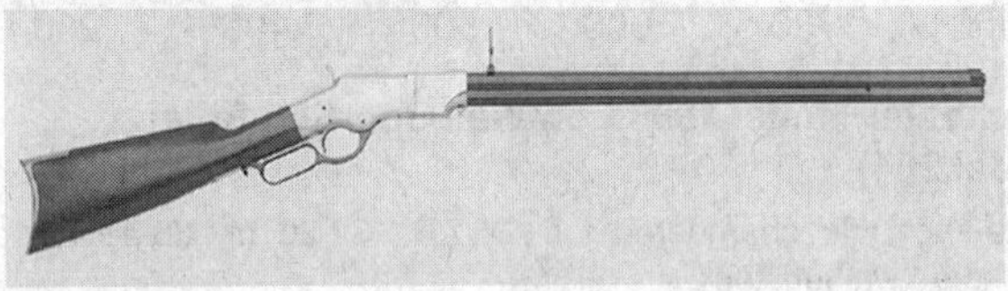

NIB	Exc.	V.G.	Good	Fair	Poor
1200	900	750	600	400	200

Iron Frame (Model 199)

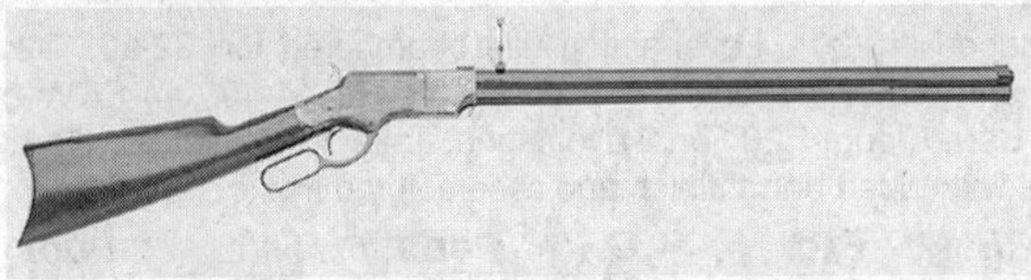

NIB	Exc.	V.G.	Good	Fair	Poor
1280	980	800	650	400	200

Winchester Model 1866 (Model 201)

Chambered for .44-40 or .45 Colt cartridge. Fitted with 24.25" octagon barrel. Brass frame. Open sights. Made by Uberti.

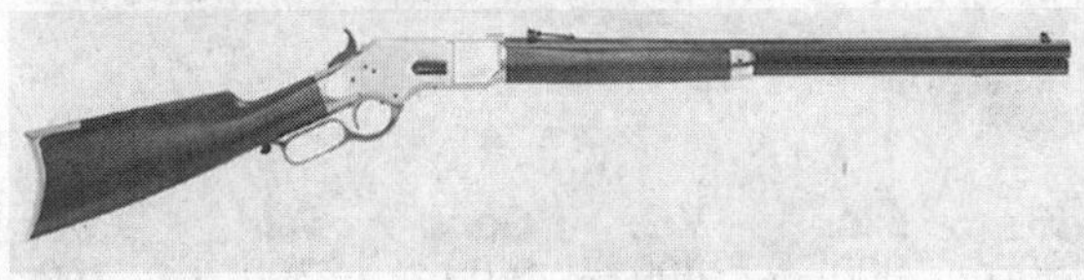

NIB	Exc.	V.G.	Good	Fair	Poor
900	700	580	400	300	180

Winchester Model 1866 Yellowboy Carbine (Model 202)

Same as above, with 19" round barrel and additional .38 Special caliber. Made by Uberti.

NIB	Exc.	V.G.	Good	Fair	Poor
950	700	520	450	300	150

Winchester Model 1873 (Model 200)

Lever-action chambered for .44-40 or .45 Colt cartridge. Fitted with 24.25" octagon barrel. Made by Uberti.

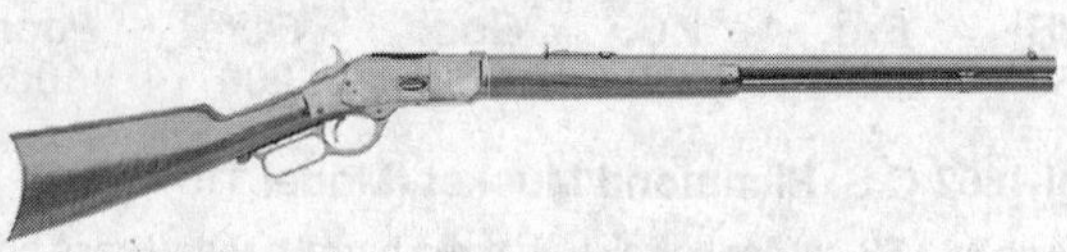

NIB	Exc.	V.G.	Good	Fair	Poor
900	720	600	500	400	200

Winchester Model 1873 Carbine (Model 200B)

Chambered for .45 Long Colt cartridge. Fitted with 19" barrel. Magazine capacity 10 rounds. Walnut stock. Case colored frame.

NIB	Exc.	V.G.	Good	Fair	Poor
900	720	600	500	400	200

Winchester Model 1873 Sporting Rifle (Model 200C)

Chambered for .45 Long Colt cartridge. Fitted with 30" octagon barrel. Checkered walnut stock, with pistol grip. Case colored frame. Blued barrel.

NIB	Exc.	V.G.	Good	Fair	Poor
900	720	600	500	400	200

Winchester Model 1885 High Wall (Model 203)

Offered with 30" or 32" barrels. Chambered for .45-70 cartridge. Walnut stock.

NIB	Exc.	V.G.	Good	Fair	Poor
900	720	600	500	400	200

Winchester Model 1885 Low Wall Sporting Rifle (Model 204)

Single-shot rifle chambered for .22 LR, .32-20 or .38-40 cartridge. Checkered walnut stock.

NIB	Exc.	V.G.	Good	Fair	Poor
900	720	600	500	400	200

Winchester Model 92

Introduced in 2004. Lever-action rifle chambered for .32-20, .32 H&R Magnum, .357 Magnum, .38 Special, .38-40, .44-40, .44 S&W or .45 Colt. Barrel length 20" or 24" octagon. Take-down feature. Hardwood stock, with blued barrel finish and case colored frame.

NIB	Exc.	V.G.	Good	Fair	Poor
720	620	450	300	250	200

Sharps Model 1859 Infantry (Model 151)

Rifle fitted with 30" round barrel. Chambered for .54-caliber cartridge. One-piece walnut, with 3 barrel bands. Adjustable rear sight.

NIB	Exc.	V.G.	Good	Fair	Poor
1150	800	600	400	300	150

Sharps Model 1859 Berdan Military (Model 152)

.54-caliber rifle fitted with 30" round barrel. One-piece walnut stock, with 3 barrel bands. Adjustable rear sight. Fitted with double-set triggers.

NIB	Exc.	V.G.	Good	Fair	Poor
1150	800	600	400	300	150

Sharps Model 1859 Cavalry (Model 153)

Model has 22" round barrel, with adjustable rear sight. Chambered for .54 caliber. Walnut stock fitted with patchbox.

NIB	Exc.	V.G.	Good	Fair	Poor
1150	800	600	400	300	150

Sharps Model 1863 Cavalry (Model 154)

Similar to Model 1859 Cavalry, without patchbox.

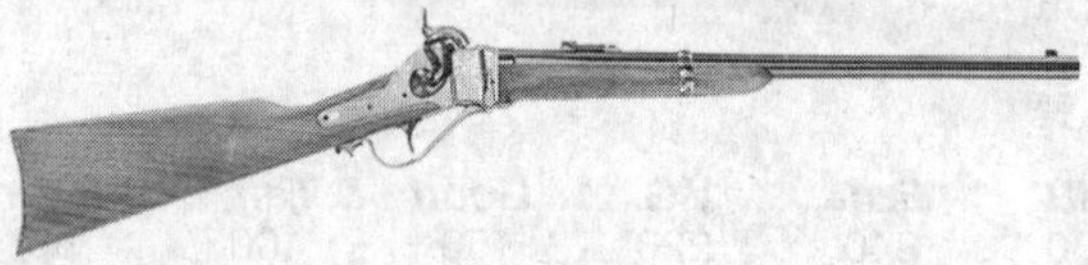

NIB	Exc.	V.G.	Good	Fair	Poor
1150	800	600	400	300	150

Sharps Model 1863 Sporting Rifle (Model 131)

.54-caliber model offered with 30" or 32" octagon barrel. Single-/double-set triggers. Walnut stock. Note: Add $20 for double-set trigger.

NIB	Exc.	V.G.	Good	Fair	Poor
1150	800	600	400	300	150

Sharps Model 1874 Sporting Rifle (Model 138)

Offered with a variety of features. Available in .45-70 with choice of: 30" or 32" octagon barrel; single trigger or double-set triggers. Also available with Hartford-style pewter forend tip. In this configuration, available in .45-70, .40-65, .45-90 or .45-120 calibers. Checkered stock, with patchbox optional. Note: Add $125 for Hartford-style forend tip; $250 for checkered stock with patchbox.

NIB	Exc.	V.G.	Good	Fair	Poor
900	700	540	400	320	180

Sharps Model 1874 Deluxe Sporting Rifle (Model 155)

This .45-70 caliber model features hand-checkered walnut stock, with oil finish. Receiver in white, with standard scroll engraving. Note: Add $800 for Deluxe Model 1874, with gold inlay.

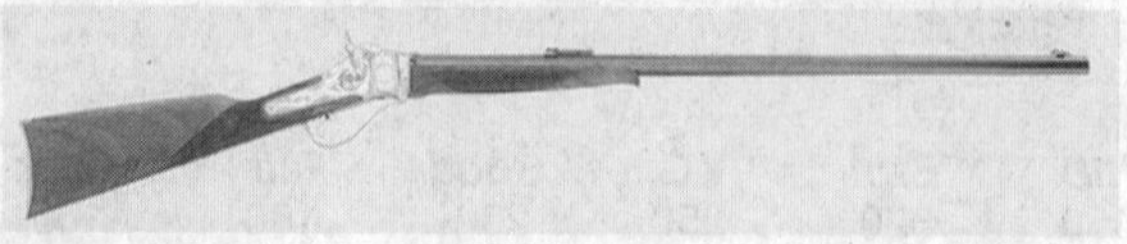

NIB	Exc.	V.G.	Good	Fair	Poor
1800	1350	1050	780	600	200

Sharps Model 1874 Infantry Rifle (Model 157)

This .45-70 caliber model features 30" round barrel, with 3 barrel bands. One-piece walnut stock, with patchbox. Adjustable rear sight. Single trigger.

NIB	Exc.	V.G.	Good	Fair	Poor
1320	1000	750	550	380	200

Sharps Model 1874 Berdan Rifle (Model 158)

Similar to above, with double-set trigger.

NIB	Exc.	V.G.	Good	Fair	Poor
1320	1000	750	550	380	200

Sharps Model 1874 Cavalry (Model 159)

This .45-70 caliber model fitted with 22" round barrel. Adjustable rear sight.

NIB	Exc.	V.G.	Good	Fair	Poor
1150	800	600	400	300	150

Spencer Model 1865 Carbine (Model 160)

Lever-action model chambered in calibers: .56-50, .44 Russian or .45 Schofield. Fitted with 20" round barrel. Walnut stock. Case-hardened receiver. Blued barrel. Made by Armi Sport.

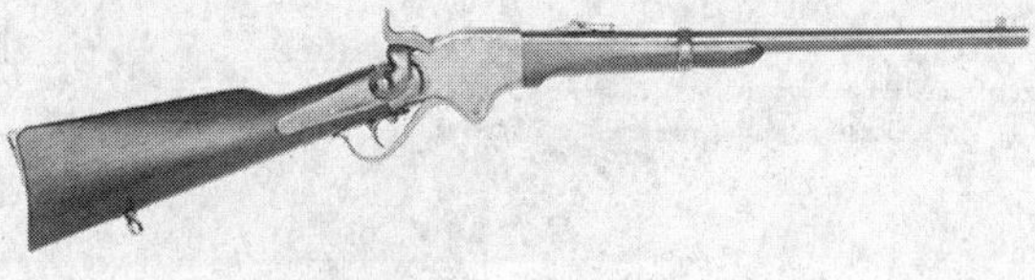

NIB	Exc.	V.G.	Good	Fair	Poor
1200	1050	880	750	500	400

Spencer Model 1865 Rifle

As above, with 30" barrel and three barrel bands. Chambered for .56-50 cartridge.

NIB	Exc.	V.G.	Good	Fair	Poor
1200	1050	880	750	500	400

SHOTGUNS

1878 Coach Gun

Classic side-by-side hammer gun, with double triggers and 20" barrels. Chambered for 3" 12-gauge shells. Features include checkered stock, with pistol grip and color case-hardened frame.

NIB	Exc.	V.G.	Good	Fair	Poor
800	700	550	400	250	150

1887 Lever Action

Replica of Winchester lever-action 12-gauge Model 1887 shotgun. Made with 18.5", 22" or 28" barrel. Color case-hardened frame.

NIB	Exc.	V.G.	Good	Fair	Poor
1000	820	650	500	250	150

TAYLOR, L.B.
Chicopee, Massachusetts

Pocket Pistol (Antique)

A .32-caliber spur trigger single-shot pocket pistol, with 3.5" octagonal barrel marked "L. B. Taylor & Co. Chicopee Mass.". Silver-plated brass frame, blued barrel and walnut grips. Manufactured during late 1860s and early 1870s.

Exc.	Fine	V.G.	Good	Fair	Poor
1150	880	630	380	100	70

TERRIER ONE

Terrier One

A .32-caliber double-action swing-out cylinder revolver, with 2.25" barrel and 5-shot cylinder. Nickel-plated, with checkered walnut grips. Manufactured from 1984 to 1987.

NIB	Exc.	V.G.	Good	Fair	Poor
—	100	80	50	30	20

TERRY, J. C.
New York City, New York

Pocket Pistol (Antique)

A .22-caliber spur trigger single-shot pocket pistol, with 3.75" round barrel. Backstrap marked "J.C. Terry/Patent Pending". Silver-plated brass frame, blued barrel and rosewood or walnut grips. Manufactured in late 1860s.

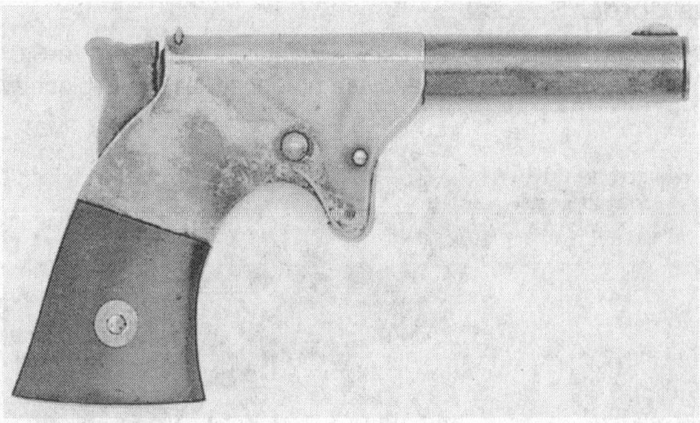

Exc.	Fine	V.G.	Good	Fair	Poor
2000	1500	1000	750	400	250

TEXAS CONTRACT RIFLES

Three contractors produced rifles for the State of Texas during 1862 and 1863. One of these patterns has a sporting back-action lock, Enfield barrel bands, an overall length of 47.375", heavy 32" long barrel of .58-caliber. Total deliveries by all contractors amounted to 1,464 rifles. Quality of these arms was decidedly inferior and often complained about. Contracting makers included Short Biscoe & Co. (only one rifle completed), Whitescarver Campbell & Co., Billups & Hassall, Tyler Ordnance Works (see separate listing) and N.B. Tanner & Co. As with all Confederate arms, expert authentication is essential. Sales are so rare as to make value estimates impractical. Burley Auction reported the sale of a Billups & Hassall for $9,000 in 2019.

TEXAS GUNFIGHTERS
Ponte Zanano, Italy

Shootist Single-Action

A .45 Long Colt caliber single-action revolver, with 4.75" barrel. Nickel-plated, with one-piece walnut grips. Made by Aldo Uberti. Introduced in 1988.

NIB	Exc.	V.G.	Good	Fair	Poor
400	350	250	200	150	80

1-of-100 Edition

As above, with one-piece mother-of-pearl grips. Fitted in a case, with an additional set of walnut grips. 100 were made in 1988.

NIB	Exc.	V.G.	Good	Fair	Poor
450	380	300	220	180	100

TEXAS LONGHORN ARMS, INC.
Richmond, Texas

Jezebel

A .22 or .22 Magnum single-shot pistol, with 6" barrel. Stainless steel, with walnut stock and forend. Introduced in 1987.

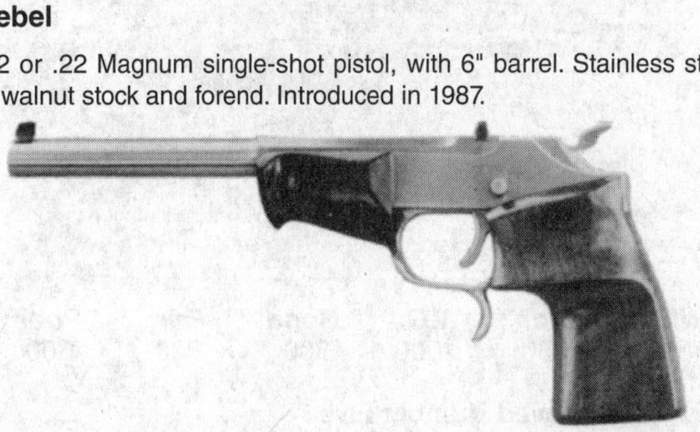

NIB	Exc.	V.G.	Good	Fair	Poor
750	680	600	550	500	350

Texas Border Special

A .44 Special or .45 Colt caliber single-action revolver, with 3.5" barrel and Pope-style rifling. Blued case-hardened, with one-piece walnut grips.

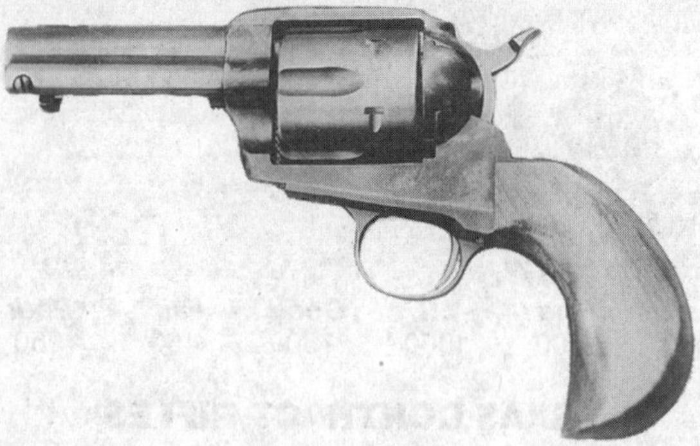

NIB	Exc.	V.G.	Good	Fair	Poor
1500	1250	1000	800	600	300

Mason Commemorative

As above in .45 Colt, with 4.75" barrel and Mason's insignia. Gold inlaid. Introduced in 1987.

NIB	Exc.	V.G.	Good	Fair	Poor
1500	1250	1000	800	600	300

South Texas Army

As above, with 4.75" barrel. Chambered for .357 Magnum cartridge. Fitted with conventional one-piece walnut grips.

NIB	Exc.	V.G.	Good	Fair	Poor
1500	1250	1000	800	600	300

West Texas Target

As above, with 7.5" barrel and flattop frame. Caliber .32-20, in addition to calibers noted above.

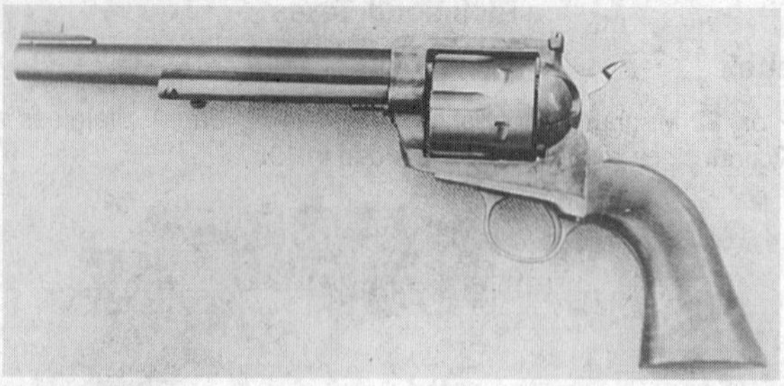

NIB	Exc.	V.G.	Good	Fair	Poor
1500	1250	1000	800	600	300

Grover's Improved Number Five

Similar to above in .44 Magnum, with 5.5" barrel. Serial Numbered K1 to K1200. Introduced in 1988.

NIB	Exc.	V.G.	Good	Fair	Poor
2300	1350	800	—	—	—

Texas Sesquicentennial Commemorative

As above, engraved in style of Louis D. Nimschke. One-piece ivory grips and fitted case.

NIB	Exc.	V.G.	Good	Fair	Poor
2500	2000	1500	900	750	400

THAMES ARMS CO.
Norwich, Connecticut

A .22-, .32- or .38-caliber double-action top-break revolver, with varying barrels lengths. Normally marked ?Automatic Revolver", which refers to cartridge ejector. Nickel-plated, with walnut grips.

NIB	Exc.	V.G.	Good	Fair	Poor
—	500	200	100	80	50

THIEME & EDELER
Eibar, Spain

Pocket Pistol

A 7.65mm caliber semi-automatic pistol, with 3" barrel marked "T E". Blued, with black plastic grips. Manufactured prior to 1936.

NIB	Exc.	V.G.	Good	Fair	Poor
—	250	150	100	80	50

THOMPSON
See—AUTO ORDNANCE CORP.

THOMPSON/CENTER ARMS
Springfield, Massachusetts

Thompson/Center Arms Co. was founded in Rochester, New York in 1965 by K.W. Thompson and Warren Center. Company's first gun was a break-open, single-shot pistol, known as Contender. More than 400,000 were produced between 1967 and 2000, when the original model was discontinued. In 2007, Thompson/Center became a division of Smith & Wesson and production was moved to Springfield, Massachusetts.

CONTENDER

Standard version offered with 10" octagon barrel. Later with 10" Bull barrel, 10" ventilated rib barrel, 14" Super models, 14" Super with ventilated rib, 16" Super models and 16" Super models with ventilated rib. Stainless steel finish available on all models except 10" octagon barrel. Action on these handguns is a single-shot break-open design. Unless otherwise stated, barrels are blued. Competitor grip is walnut, with rubber insert mounted on back of grip. Finger groove grip is also available made from walnut, with finger notching and thumbrest. Forend is American black walnut in various lengths and designs depending on barrel size. Stainless steel models have rubber grips, with finger grooves. Standard sights are Patridge rear, with ramp front. An adjustable rear sight was offered as an option. Barrels with ventilated ribs were furnished with fixed rear sight and bead front. Note: Early frames with no engraving, called flatsides, and those with eagle engraving bring between $2,000 and $2,500 on collector market.

Note: Barrel interchangeability is acceptable for blued barrels and frames, with stainless steel barrels and frames. DO NOT interchange Alloy II barrels and frames with blued or stainless steel components.

10" Octagon Barrel Model

First Contender design. Offered in .22 LR only. Supplied with adjustable rear sight and mounting holes for scope. Grips are Competitor or rubber. Weight about 44 oz.

NIB	*Exc.*	*V.G.*	*Good*	*Fair*	*Poor*
380	300	250	200	150	100

10" Bull Barrel Model

Comes standard with adjustable rear sight, mounting holes for scope mounts and Competitor grips for blued models; rubber grips on stainless steel. Offered in these calibers as complete pistols: .22 LR, .22 LR Match, .22 Win. Magnum (blued only), .22 Hornet, .223, 7mm T.C.U. (blued only), .30-30, .32-20 (blued only), .357 Magnum, .357 Rem. Max (blued only), .44 Magnum, .45 Colt, .410 bore. In 1994, Thompson/Center introduced .300 Whisper cartridge to its Contender product line. Weight about 50 oz.

NIB	*Exc.*	*V.G.*	*Good*	*Fair*	*Poor*
380	300	250	200	150	100

10" Vent Rib Model

Features a raised ventilated rib. Chambered for .45 Long Colt/.410 bore. Fixed rear sight and bead front. Detachable choke screws into the muzzle for use with .410 shell. Furnished with Competitor or rubber grips.

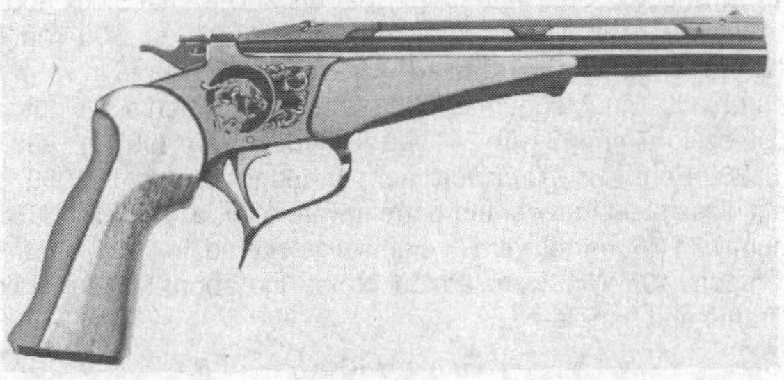

NIB	*Exc.*	*V.G.*	*Good*	*Fair*	*Poor*
370	320	270	220	150	100

Super 14" Model

Features a 14 bull barrel. Furnished with adjustable rear sight and ramp front. Drilled and tapped for scope mounts. Competitor or rubber grips offered. Available in blued or stainless steel finish. Furnished in these calibers in a complete pistol only: .22 LR, .22 LR Match, .17 Rem. (blued only), .22 Hornet, .222 Rem. (blued only), .223 Rem., 7mm T.C.U. (blued only), 7-30 Waters, .30-30, .357 Rem. Max (blued only), .35 Rem., .375 Win. (blued only), .44 Magnum (blued only). Weight about 56 oz.

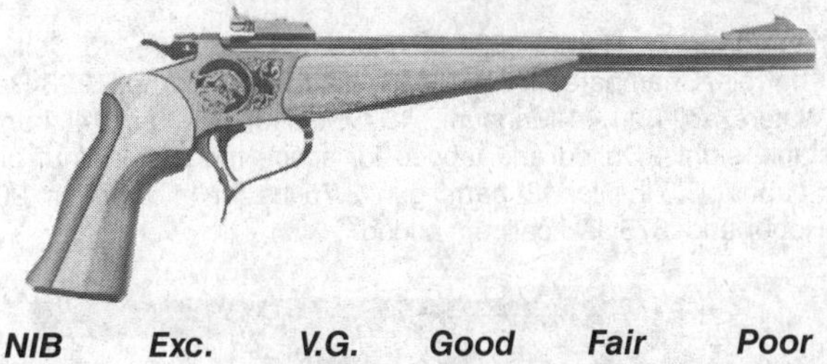

NIB	*Exc.*	*V.G.*	*Good*	*Fair*	*Poor*
400	360	300	250	200	150

Super 14" Vent Rib Model

Similar to 10 ventilated rib model. Chambered for .45 Long Colt/.410 bore. Furnished with 14" ventilated rib barrel.

NIB	*Exc.*	*V.G.*	*Good*	*Fair*	*Poor*
480	380	320	280	220	150

Super 16" Model

Fitted with 16.25 tapered barrel and two position adjustable rear sight. Drilled and tapped for scope mount. Furnished with Competitor or rubber grips. Choice of blued or stainless steel finish. Available in these calibers as complete pistols only: .22 LR, .22 Hornet, .223 Rem., 7-30 Waters, .30-30, .35 Rem., .45-70 Government. Weight about 56 oz.

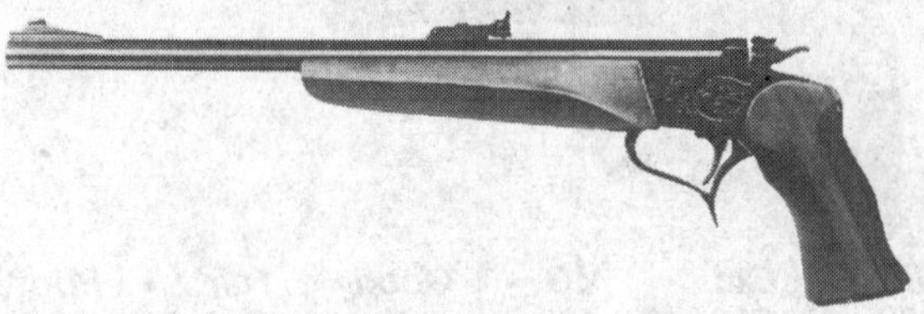

NIB	*Exc.*	*V.G.*	*Good*	*Fair*	*Poor*
370	320	280	220	150	100

Super 16" Vent Rib Model

Chambered for .45 Long Colt/.410 bore. Offered for the first time in 1993. All other features same as other Contender .45/.410 bore pistols.

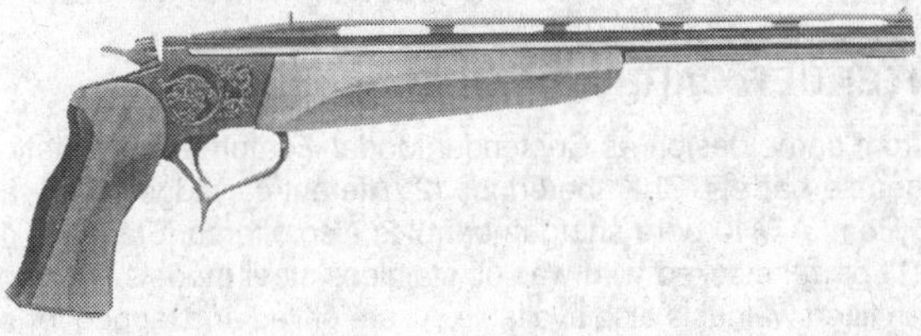

NIB	*Exc.*	*V.G.*	*Good*	*Fair*	*Poor*
390	350	300	250	180	120

Contender Hunter Model

Designed for handgun hunting. Offered in two barrel lengths 12" and 14", fitted with compensator and 2.5 power scope. There are no iron sights fitted. Nylon carrying sling and soft leather carrying case are standard. Offered in these calibers: 7-30 Waters, .30-30 Win., .35 Rem., .45-70 Government, .44 Magnum, .223 Rem. and .375 Win. Fitted with Competitor grips. Offered in blued or stainless steel finish. Weight about 64 oz.

NIB	*Exc.*	*V.G.*	*Good*	*Fair*	*Poor*
580	500	400	300	200	100

G2 CONTENDER SERIES

Introduced in 2003. A second generation Contender that features a slightly different look: simplified internal design that allows re-cocking the hammer, without having to break-open the action; different shaped grips that give more clearance between grip and finger guard. These G2 firearms will accept previously manufactured Contender barrels and forends, but not grips.

G2 Contender

Chambered for .22 Hornet, .357 Magnum, .44 Magnum, .45 Colt/.410 in 12" barrels. Chambered for .17 HMR, .22 LR, .22 Hornet, .223 Rem., 7-30 Waters, .30-30, .44 Magnum, .45 Colt/.410, .45-70 in 14" barrels. Adjustable sights. Drilled and tapped for scope mounts. Walnut grips. Weight about: 3.5 lbs. for 12" barrel gun; 3.75 lbs. for 14" barrel. In 2004, .204 Ruger and .375 JDJ calibers added.

NIB	Exc.	V.G.	Good	Fair	Poor
560	450	380	300	250	180

G2 Contender Rifle

Fitted with 23" barrel, with no sights. Chambered for .17 HMR, .22 LR, .223 Rem., .30-30, .45-70. Walnut stock, with blued finish. Weight about 5.4 lbs. In 2004, .375 JDJ and .204 Ruger calibers added.

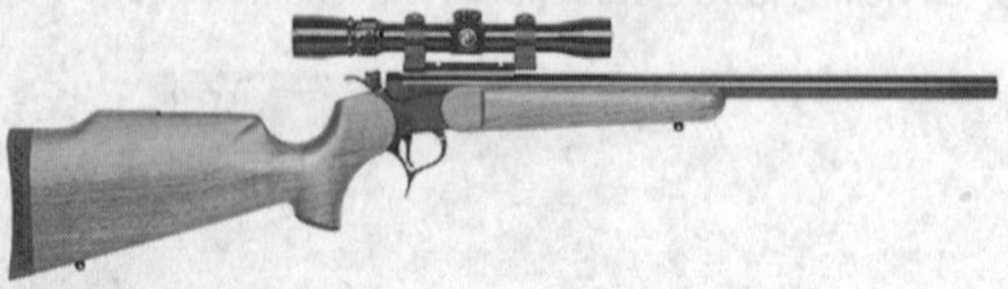

NIB	Exc.	V.G.	Good	Fair	Poor
600	500	400	320	280	200

G2 Contender Shotgun

Chambered for .410 bore shell. Fitted with 24" ventilated rib barrel. Walnut stock. Weight about 5.4 lbs. Introduced in 2004.

NIB	Exc.	V.G.	Good	Fair	Poor
600	500	400	320	280	200

CONTENDER CARBINE MODEL

Built from same design as Contender Model. Features completely interchangeable barrels. Chambered for 12 different cartridges from .22 LR to .35 Rem. A .410 bore shotgun barrel is also offered. Standard model has 21" barrel stocked with walnut; stainless steel models a composite stock in fitted walnut is also available. All are drilled and tapped for scope mounts. Available in blued or stainless steel.

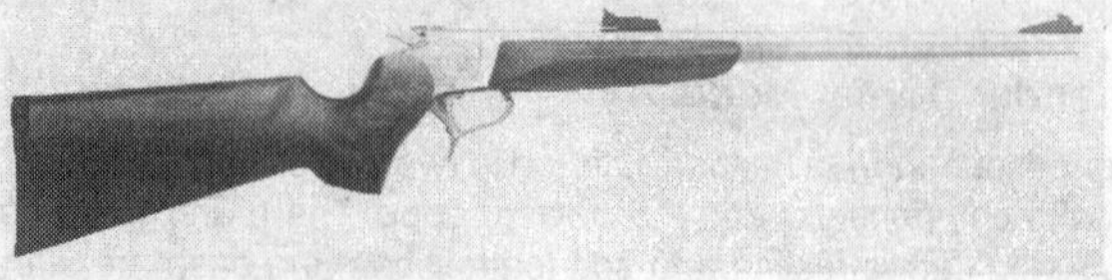

Standard 21" Carbine

Fitted with 21 plain barrel and walnut stocks. Offered in these calibers as a complete gun only: .22 LR, .22 LR Match (blued only), .17 Rem. (blued only), .22 Hornet, .223 Rem., 7-30 Waters, .30-30, .35 Rem. (blued only), .375 Win. (blued only). Weight 5.3 lbs.

NIB	Exc.	V.G.	Good	Fair	Poor
500	400	350	300	250	200

21" Carbine .410 Bore

Same as above, with ventilated rib barrel and screw-in choke.

NIB	Exc.	V.G.	Good	Fair	Poor
480	380	300	250	200	100

16" Youth Model Carbine

Special walnut buttstock, with 12 length of pull and 16.25" barrel. Short buttstock can be replaced with standard buttstock. Blued or stainless steel finish. Complete guns offered in same calibers as 21" Carbine, with exception of .375 Win. and addition of .45 Long Colt/.410 bore with ventilated rib barrel.

NIB	Exc.	V.G.	Good	Fair	Poor
480	380	300	250	200	100

ENCORE SERIES

Encore Pistol

Introduced in 1996. Single-shot pistol will feature 10.625", 15" or 24" barrels chambered for .30-06, .308 Win., 7mm-08 Rem., .223 Rem., .22-250 Rem., .44 Magnum, 7mmBR. This new handgun is designed for use with higher pressure cartridges. Barrels will not interchange with Contender. Weight about: 56 oz. for 10.625" barrel gun; 4 lbs. 15" barrel; 6.75 lbs. 24" barrel. Note: Add $60 for stainless steel frame and barrels.

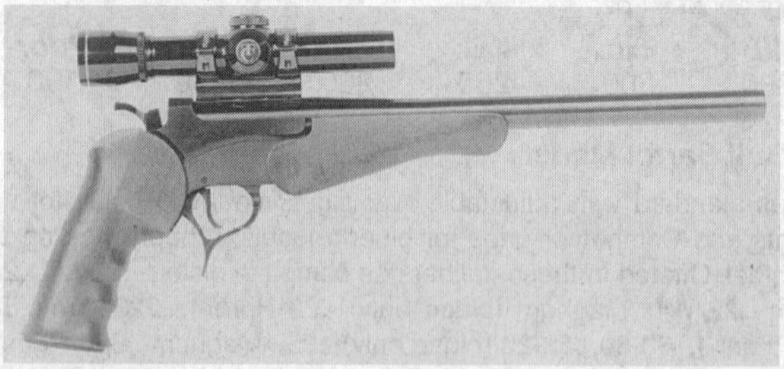

NIB	Exc.	V.G.	Good	Fair	Poor
550	450	380	300	250	180

HotShot Youth Rifle

Single-shot dropping-barrel rifle chambered in .22 LR. Features include crowned 19" steel barrel, exposed hammer, synthetic forend and buttstock, peep sight (receiver drilled and tapped for optics), three stock pattern options (black, Realtree AP and pink AP). Overall weight 3 lbs., 11.5" length of pull.

NIB	Exc.	V.G.	Good	Fair	Poor
200	160	120	100	80	50

Encore Rifle

Similar to Encore pistol, with longer barrels and walnut stock and forearm. A wide variety of calibers offered from .22-250 to .300 Win. Magnum. Barrel lengths from 24" to 26". Heavy barrels offered in 7mm Rem. Magnum, .300 Win. Magnum and .22-250, with no sights. Weight about: 6 lbs. 12 oz. for 7mm-08 with 24" barrel. Introduced in 1997. In 1998, .260 Rem., .280 Rem., .45-70 Government cartridges added. In 1999, blued and stainless steel frames and barrels were offered. In 2003, .375 H&H Magnum with 26" barrel without sights was offered. In 2004, .280 Rem., .204 Ruger, .405 Win. were added. Note: Add about $60 for stainless steel frame and barrels.

NIB	Exc.	V.G.	Good	Fair	Poor
650	550	420	300	220	180

Encore Katahdin Carbine

Fitted with heavy 18" barrel, with integral muzzle brake. Offered in .444

Marlin, .450 Marlin and .45-70 Government calibers. Blued finish, with composite stock and adjustable fiber optic sights. Weight about 6.75 lbs. Introduced in 2002.

NIB	Exc.	V.G.	Good	Fair	Poor
650	550	420	300	220	180

Encore Katahdin Turkey Gun

A 12-gauge 3" chamber gun, with 20" barrel and screw-in Turkey Chokes. Open sights. Realtree Hardwoods HD camo composite stock. Weight about 6 lbs. Introduced in 2005.

NIB	Exc.	V.G.	Good	Fair	Poor
750	580	450	320	220	200

Encore Shotgun 20 Gauge

Introduced in 1998. Fitted with 26" 20-gauge ventilated rib barrel. Walnut stock and forend. Choke tubes are standard.

NIB	Exc.	V.G.	Good	Fair	Poor
650	550	420	300	220	180

Encore Camo Shotgun 12 Gauge

Features 24" smoothbore barrel, with screw-in Turkey Choke, camo stock and metal pattern. Blued frame, with composite stock. Introduced in 2002.

NIB	Exc.	V.G.	Good	Fair	Poor
750	580	450	320	220	200

Encore Shotgun 12 Gauge

Features 3" chamber and 26" ventilated rib barrel, with bead front sight. Blued, with walnut stock. Weight about 6.6 lbs. Introduced in 2004.

NIB	Exc.	V.G.	Good	Fair	Poor
750	580	450	320	220	200

Encore Rifled Shotgun 20 Gauge

Introduced in 2000. Features 26" rifled shotgun barrel chambered for 20-gauge shell. Adjustable rear sight. Walnut stock and blued finish.

NIB	Exc.	V.G.	Good	Fair	Poor
650	550	420	300	220	180

Encore Rifled Shotgun 12 Gauge

Introduced in 2002. Fitted with 24" rifled barrel, with adjustable fiber optic sights. Blued, with walnut stock.

NIB	Exc.	V.G.	Good	Fair	Poor
650	550	420	300	220	180

Encore Turkey Gun

Introduced in 2005. Chambered for 20-gauge shell, with 3" chamber. Barrel 26", with open sights and screw-in Turkey Chokes. Realtree Hardwoods HD camo composite stock.

NIB	Exc.	V.G.	Good	Fair	Poor
650	550	420	300	220	180

PRO HUNTER SERIES

Pro Hunter

Similar to Encore rifle, with plain or fluted barrel. Various finish and stock options. Barrels interchange with standard Encore barrels. Muzzleloading and pistol versions available. Introduced 2007. Current muzzleloading rifle iteration is FX designation in .50-cal. only, 26" barrel, with black or camo FlexTech stock (28205800 and 28205799, respectively.)

NIB	Exc.	V.G.	Good	Fair	Poor
590	500	430	360	310	260

Pro Hunter XT

.50 caliber, 28" barrels. Quick Load Accurizor with reduced rifling at the tip for easy loading, Weather Shield coating, ambidextrous Swing Hammer. Configurations and model numbers are Stainless Steel/Black Stock, 28205722; Stainless Steel/AP Camo Stock, 28205724; Weather Shield/Black FlexTech Stock, 28205744; Weather Shield/FlexTech Camo, 28205743, price for which is shown below.

NIB	Exc.	V.G.	Good	Fair	Poor
770	660	560	470	400	340

Pro Hunter Predator Rifle

Contender-style break-action single-shot rifle. Chambered in .204 Ruger, .223 Rem., .22-250, .308 Win. Features include 28" deep-fluted interchangeable barrel, composite buttstock and forend with non-slip inserts in cheekpiece, pistol grip and forend. Max 1 camo finish overall. Overall length 42.5". Weight 7.75 lbs.

NIB	Exc.	V.G.	Good	Fair	Poor
750	650	500	400	300	250

Pro Hunter Turkey Gun

Contender-style break-action single-shot shotgun. Chambered in 12- or 20-gauge and 3" shells. Features include 24" barrel, with interchangeable choke tubes (Extra Full supplied), composite buttstock and forend with non-slip inserts in cheekpiece, pistol grip and forend. Adjustable fiber-optic sights, Sims recoil pad, AP camo finish overall. Overall length 40.5". Weight 6.5 lbs.

NIB	Exc.	V.G.	Good	Fair	Poor
750	650	520	400	250	150

Pro Hunter Katahdin

Chambered in .45-70, .460 S&W or .500 S&W. This break-action single-shot has 20" interchangeable fluted barrel, Flex-Tech stock with textured and grooved grip surfaces. Adjustable rear and fiber optic front sights.

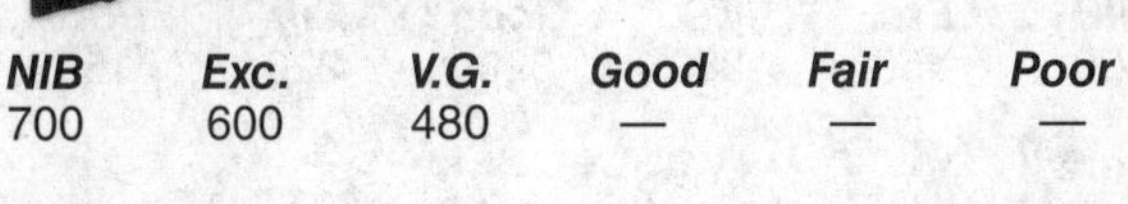

NIB	Exc.	V.G.	Good	Fair	Poor
700	600	480	—	—	—

ICON SERIES

Icon

Bolt-action centerfire rifle chambered in .22-250, .243, .308, .30 Thompson-Center. Barrel length 22" (iron sight) or 24" (sightless). Detachable box magazine, Introduced in 2007.

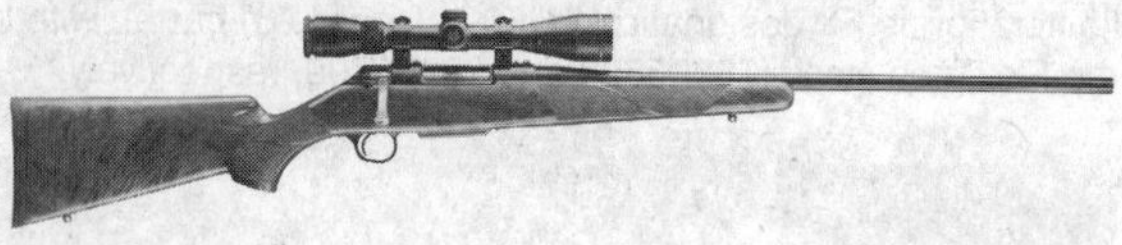

NIB	Exc.	V.G.	Good	Fair	Poor
900	800	680	520	300	200

Icon Classic Long Action Rifle

Similar to Icon, with long-action design. Chambered for .270, .30-06, .300 Win. Magnum and 7mm Rem. Magnum.

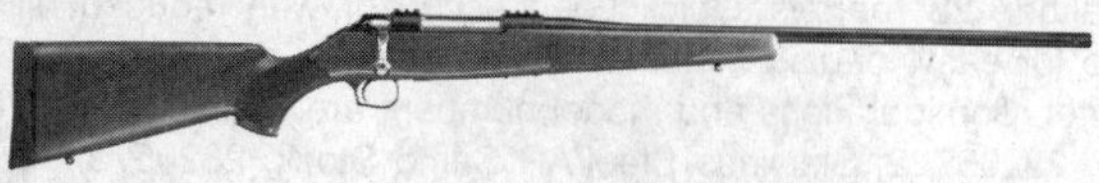

NIB	Exc.	V.G.	Good	Fair	Poor
1000	850	700	600	400	200

Icon Weathershield Medium Action Rifle

Similar to Icon, with stainless steel barrel and receiver. Black synthetic or Realtree AP Camo stock.

NIB	Exc.	V.G.	Good	Fair	Poor
1000	850	700	600	400	200

VENTURE SERIES

Venture Medium Action Rifle

Bolt-action rifle chambered in .204, .22-250, .223, .243, 7mm-08, .308 and 30TC. Features include 24" crowned medium weight barrel, classic styled composite stock with inlaid traction grip panels, adjustable 3.5 to 5 lb. trigger along with drilled and tapped receiver (bases included). 3+1 detachable nylon box magazine. Overall length 43.5". Weight 7 lbs.

NIB	Exc.	V.G.	Good	Fair	Poor
500	400	320	250	180	100

Venture Predator PDX Rifle

Bolt-action rifle chambered in .204, .22-250, .223, .243, .308. Similar to Venture Medium action, with heavy deep-fluted 22" barrel and Max-1 camo finish overall. Overall length 41.5". Weight 8 lbs.

NIB	Exc.	V.G.	Good	Fair	Poor
600	500	420	350	280	200

Venture Weather Shield

Advanced Weather Shield finish for durability. Classic styled composite stock, with Hogue Overmolded Grip panels. T/C large bolt design for smooth operation. 60 degree bolt lift. Receiver drilled and tapped, with bases included. Magazine capacity, 3+1. Available in short-/long-action models for most standard, Magnum and WSM cartridges.

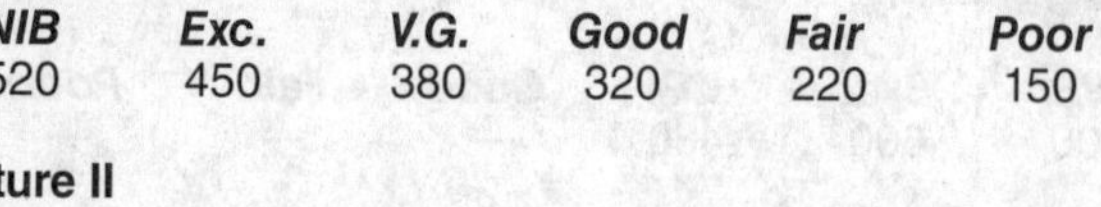

NIB	Exc.	V.G.	Good	Fair	Poor
520	450	380	320	220	150

Venture II

Bolt-action hunting rifle with Generation II trigger. .243 Win, .270 Win, .300 Win Mag, .308 Win, .223, .30-06, .350 Legend, or 6.5 Creedmoor with 22" or 24" barrel depending on caliber. Black composite stock, 7.5 lbs.

NIB	Exc.	V.G.	Good	Fair	Poor
530	450	—	—	—	—

Dimension

Bolt-action rifle available in 10 calibers from .204 Ruger to .300 Win. Magnum. Barrel lengths 22" or 24". Synthetic stock has competition cheekpiece. Other features are an aluminum receiver, free-floated barrel and choice of right-/left-hand action. Introduced in 2012.

NIB	Exc.	V.G.	Good	Fair	Poor
600	520	450	400	350	200

OTHER RIFLES

Compass Utility

No-frills bolt-action rifle in .243, .270, .308, .223, .30-06 or 6.5 Creedmoor 21.6" barrel. Available with T/C scope combo at $100 premium.

NIB	Exc.	V.G.	Good	Fair	Poor
350	300	—	—	—	—

Compass II

Bolt-action rifle in above calibers plus .30-06, .300 Win. Mag., or 7mm Rem Mag. 21.6" to 24" barrel depending on caliber. Available with Crimson Trace scope combo at $175 premium.

NIB	Exc.	V.G.	Good	Fair	Poor
450	400	—	—	—	—

Compass II Compact

As above in .223, .243, .308, or 6.5 Creedmoor with a shorter 16.5" barrel.

NIB	Exc.	V.G.	Good	Fair	Poor
450	400	—	—	—	—

LRR

Performance Center Long Range Rifle, precision bolt action. .243 Win., .308 Win., or 6.5 Creedmoor. 20", 21.5", 26", or 27.5" barrel, 10-round box magazine, 12 lbs. Available with Diamondback 4-12x40 scope for $300 premium.

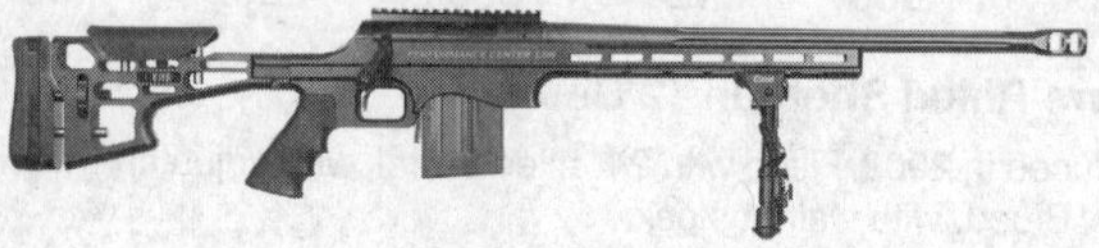

NIB	Exc.	V.G.	Good	Fair	Poor
1200	1000	—	—	—	—

Model R55

Semi-automatic rifle chambered for .17 Mach 2 cartridge. Fitted with 20" match-grade barrel, with adjustable sights. Black composite or laminated hardwood stock. Receiver blued or stainless steel. Magazine capacity 5 rounds. Weight 5.5 lbs. Introduced in 2005. Note: Add $65 for black composite stock.

NIB	Exc.	V.G.	Good	Fair	Poor
550	450	380	300	250	180

TCR 87 Hunter Model

Single-shot toplever rifle. Chambered for cartridges from .22 LR to .308 Win. Fitted with 23" barrel. Finish blue, with walnut stock. Discontinued as a regular production rifle in 1993.

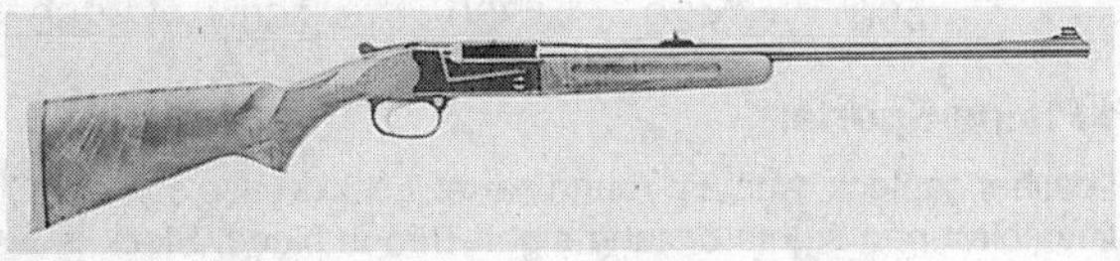

NIB	Exc.	V.G.	Good	Fair	Poor
650	550	420	300	220	180

T/C 22 LR Classic

Introduced in 2000. A semi-automatic rifle chambered for .22 LR cartridge. Fitted with 22" match-grade barrel. Walnut stock, with Monte Carlo comb. Adjustable rear sight. Magazine capacity 8 rounds. Weight 5.5 lbs.

NIB	Exc.	V.G.	Good	Fair	Poor
450	350	280	220	180	100

.22 Classic Benchmark

An updated version of Classic, with 18" heavy barrel and no sights. Wood laminated target stock. Magazine capacity 10 rounds. Weight 6.8 lbs. Introduced in 2003.

NIB	Exc.	V.G.	Good	Fair	Poor
480	380	300	250	200	100

Silver Lynx

This .22-caliber semi-automatic rifle introduced in 2004. Fitted with a 20" stainless steel barrel. Black composite stock, with Monte Carlo comb. Magazine capacity 5 rounds. Weight 5.5 lbs.

NIB	Exc.	V.G.	Good	Fair	Poor
400	300	220	150	100	80

R22

.22 LR semi-auto rifle, 10-round rotary magazine, aluminum receiver, stainless steel barrel, Magpul stock. Green fiber front and rear peep sight with picatinny rail. 17" barrel, 4.4 lbs. Variety of stock options include PC Hogue thumbhole stock ($100 premium) and PC Altamont laminated thumbhole stock ($215 premium).

NIB	Exc.	V.G.	Good	Fair	Poor
380	330	—	—	—	—

Performance Center R22 Carbon Fiber Barrel

As above with carbon-fiber barrel and laminated thumbhole stock.

NIB	Exc.	V.G.	Good	Fair	Poor
630	550	—	—	—	—

BLACKPOWDER FIREARMS

System 1

Introduced in 1997. This concept features complete muzzleloading system, with interchangeable barrels. Offered with .32-, .50-, .54-, .58-caliber and 12-gauge shotgun barrels, with walnut stock and blued finish; or stainless steel, with synthetic stock. Barrel lengths 26". Weight 7.5 lbs. Sights adjustable. Note: Add $30 for synthetic stock and stainless steel.

NIB	Exc.	V.G.	Good	Fair	Poor
—	300	220	180	120	80

Thunder Hawk

Introduced in 1993. Features .50-caliber caplock inline ignition, with 21" round barrel. Rear sight adjustable and ramp front. Stock is plain American black walnut, with rubber recoil pad. Trigger adjustable. In 1994, available in stainless steel. Weight 6.75 lbs.

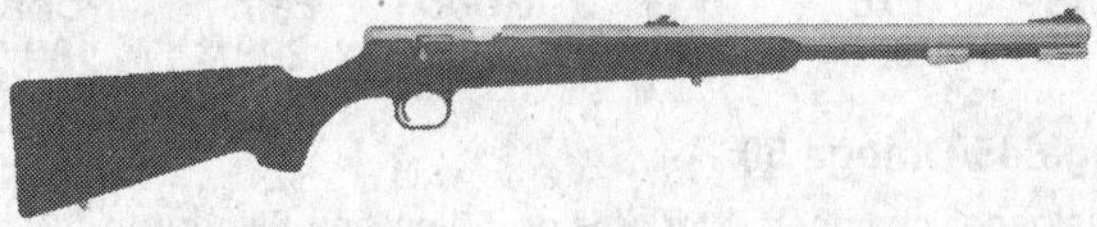

NIB	Exc.	V.G.	Good	Fair	Poor
—	320	280	240	200	170

Thunder Hawk Shadow

Introduced in 1996. Features inline ignition in .50- or .54-caliber, with 24" round barrel. Comes standard with black checkered composite stock. Weight 7 lbs. In 1997, offered with camouflage stock and blued finish.

NIB	Exc.	V.G.	Good	Fair	Poor
—	320	280	240	200	170

Grey Hawk

Stainless steel composite stock rifle is a .50-caliber caplock, with 24" round barrel. Utilizes a hooked breech system. Lock is a heavy-duty coil spring, with floral engraving pattern. Adjustable rear sight and bead front are standard. Weight 7 lbs.

NIB	Exc.	V.G.	Good	Fair	Poor
—	200	170	140	120	100

Hawken Caplock Rifle

Available in .45-, .50- and .54-caliber. Rifle has 28" octagonal barrel and hooked breech system. Triggers are fully adjustable and can function as double-set or single-stage. Adjustable sights, with bead front are standard. Trim is solid brass. Stock select American walnut, with cheekpiece. Weight 8.5 lbs.

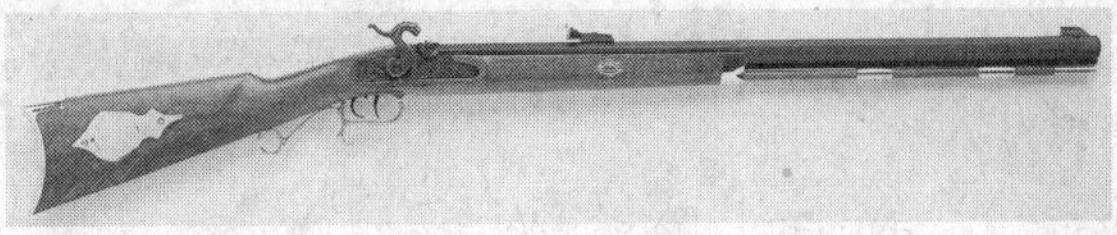

NIB	Exc.	V.G.	Good	Fair	Poor
—	490	420	350	300	260

Hawken Flintlock Rifle

Offered in .50-caliber, with 28" octagonal barrel. All other features same as above.

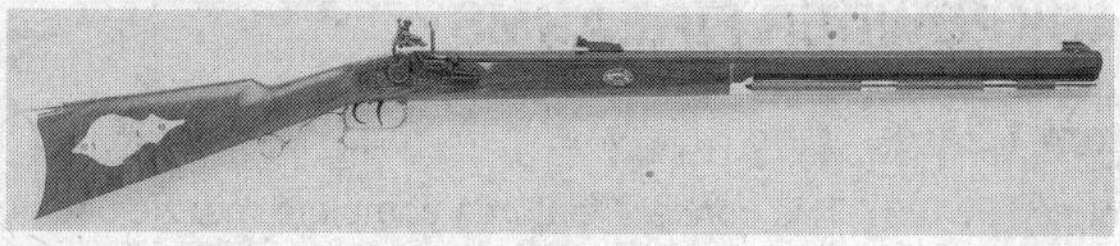

NIB	Exc.	V.G.	Good	Fair	Poor
—	350	300	250	220	180

Hawken Custom/Elite

Introduced in 1994. Model is .50-caliber traditional caplock rifle, with double-set triggers and crescent butt. Select American walnut stock, with no patchbox. Finish is high luster blue.

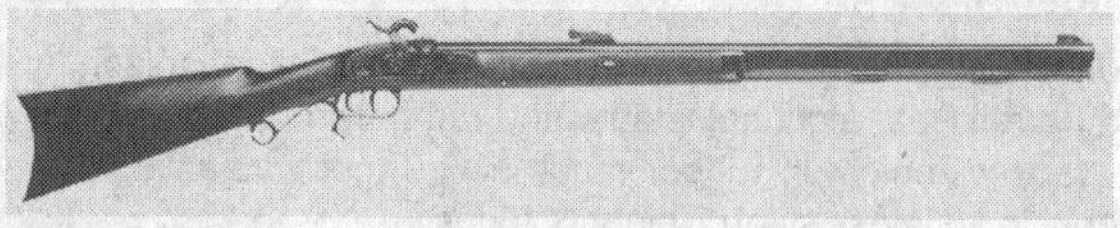

NIB	Exc.	V.G.	Good	Fair	Poor
—	350	300	250	220	180

Omega 45/Omega 50

Muzzleloader chambered for .45- or .50-caliber. Fitted with 28" round barrel. Adjustable sights. Composite or laminated stock. Weight 7 lbs. Introduced in 2002. Note: Add $50 for stainless steel; $60 for Realtree camo stock.

NIB	Exc.	V.G.	Good	Fair	Poor
380	320	270	230	200	170

Omega Pivoting Breech Rifle

Introduced in 2004. Rifle has 28" stainless steel fluted barrel bored for .50-caliber slug. Laminated wood thumbhole stock. Fiber-optic sights. Weight 7 lbs.

NIB	Exc.	V.G.	Good	Fair	Poor
380	320	270	230	200	170

Renegade Caplock Rifle

Offered in .50- or .54-caliber, with 26" octagonal barrel. Adjustable triggers can function as double-set or single-stage. Adjustable sights, with blued trim. Walnut stock. Offered in right-/left-hand models. Weight 8 lbs.

NIB	Exc.	V.G.	Good	Fair	Poor
550	470	400	340	290	240

Renegade Flintlock

Available in .50-caliber and right-hand only. Other features same as Caplock model.

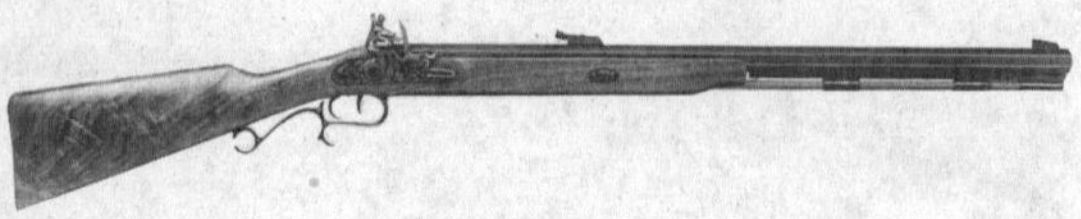

NIB	Exc.	V.G.	Good	Fair	Poor
550	470	400	340	290	240

Big Boar Rifle

Hooked breech model features .58-caliber, with 26" octagonal barrel. Single trigger and adjustable sights are standard. Trim is blued steel. American walnut stock, with rubber pad. Weight 7.75 lbs.

NIB	Exc.	V.G.	Good	Fair	Poor
—	500	420	360	200	260

High Plains Sporter

A .50-caliber caplock, with 24" round barrel. Lock is case colored. Choice of adjustable open sights or tang sight. Trim is blued. Stock is walnut, with rubber recoil pad, pistol grip and sling swivel studs. Weight 7 lbs.

NIB	Exc.	V.G.	Good	Fair	Poor
—	400	340	290	250	210

Tree Hawk

Available in caplock .50 caliber or 12 gauge. .50-caliber carbine has 21" barrel and offered in camo colors; 12-gauge shotgun fitted with 27" barrel and also comes in camo colors. Weight 6.75 lbs.

Rifle

NIB	Exc.	V.G.	Good	Fair	Poor
—	200	170	140	120	100

Shotgun

NIB	Exc.	V.G.	Good	Fair	Poor
—	200	170	140	120	100

White Mountain Carbine

Available in .45-, .50- or .54-caliber caplock or .50 flintlock. Fitted with 20.5" octagon barrel. Lock is case colored and trim blued. Stock is walnut, with rubber recoil pad. Weight 6.5 lbs. Discontinued.

NIB	Exc.	V.G.	Good	Fair	Poor
—	420	360	310	260	220

Black Mountain Magnum

Introduced in 1999. Features 26" round barrel, with walnut or composite stock. Chambered for .50-, .54-caliber or 12 gauge, with 27" round barrel. All models are caplock. Blued finish. Discontinued.

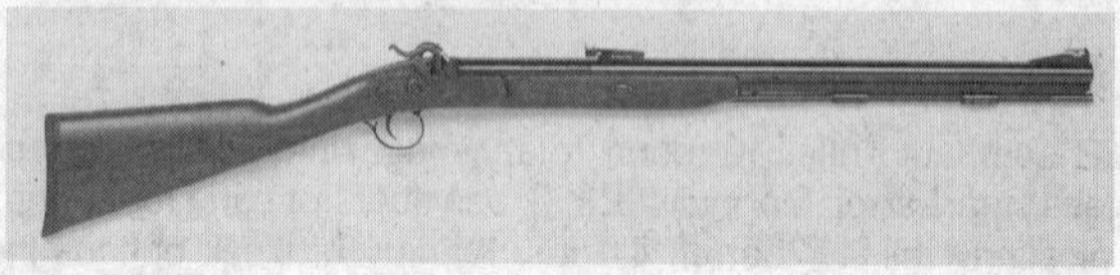

NIB	Exc.	V.G.	Good	Fair	Poor
—	420	360	310	260	220

Pennsylvania Hunter

Offered in .50-caliber caplock or flintlock. Fitted with octagon/round barrel in 31.5" or 21.5". Fully adjustable sights, walnut stock and blued trim are standard. Rifle weight about 7.5 lbs.; carbine 6.5 lbs. Discontinued.

Rifle

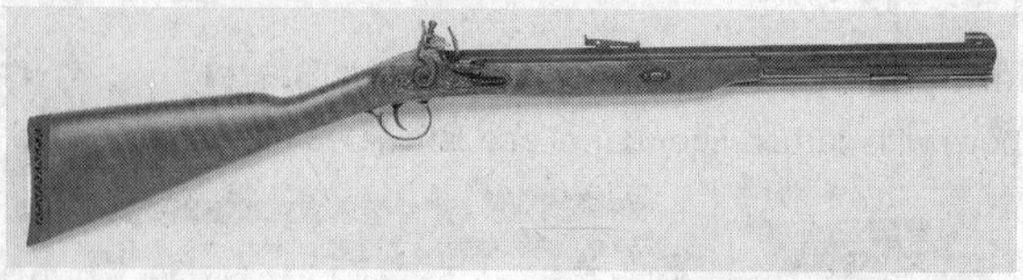

NIB	Exc.	V.G.	Good	Fair	Poor
—	320	280	240	200	170

Carbine

NIB	Exc.	V.G.	Good	Fair	Poor
—	320	280	240	200	170

Pennsylvania Match Rifle

Similar to Pennsylvania Hunter Rifle, except equipped with tang peep sight and globe front sight. Discontinued.

NIB	Exc.	V.G.	Good	Fair	Poor
—	380	320	270	230	200

New Englander Rifle

Offered in .50- or .54-caliber caplock, with walnut stock and 26" round barrel. Adjustable sights. Weight 7 lbs. 15 oz. A 12" barrel is optional. Discontinued. Note: Add $150 for interchangeable shotgun barrel.

NIB	Exc.	V.G.	Good	Fair	Poor
—	280	230	200	170	140

New Englander Shotgun

Same as above, with 27" barrel in 12 gauge, with screw-in Full choke. Weight 6 lbs. 8 oz. Discontinued.

NIB	Exc.	V.G.	Good	Fair	Poor
—	280	230	200	170	140

New Englander Composite

Offered with composite stock. The .50- or .54-caliber rifle has 24" barrel and 12-gauge shotgun has 27" barrel. Discontinued.

Rifle

NIB	Exc.	V.G.	Good	Fair	Poor
—	280	230	200	170	140

Shotgun

NIB	Exc.	V.G.	Good	Fair	Poor
—	280	230	200	170	140

Scout Carbine

Muzzleloading carbine of .50- or .54-caliber, with inline ignition system. Offered with walnut or composite stock (first offered in 1993). Fitted with 21" round barrel. Adjustable rear sight and fixed blade front. Brass barrel band and triggerguard on walnut stock; blued barrel band and triggerguard on composite stock. Weight 7 lbs. 4 oz. Discontinued.

Walnut Stock

NIB	Exc.	V.G.	Good	Fair	Poor
—	280	230	200	170	140

Composite Stock

NIB	Exc.	V.G.	Good	Fair	Poor
—	220	190	160	140	120

Scout Rifle

Similar to Scout Carbine, with 24" stepped half-round, half-octagonal barrel. Weight about 8 lbs. Discontinued.

Walnut Stock

NIB	Exc.	V.G.	Good	Fair	Poor
—	350	300	250	220	180

Composite Stock

NIB	Exc.	V.G.	Good	Fair	Poor
—	320	280	240	200	170

Scout Pistol

Same design as Scout carbine. Single-action pistol available in .45-, .50- or .54-caliber. Fitted with 12" barrel, adjustable rear sight and blued finish, with brass triggerguard. Black walnut grips. Weight 4 lbs. 6 oz. Discontinued.

NIB	Exc.	V.G.	Good	Fair	Poor
—	200	170	140	120	100

Fire Hawk Deluxe

Introduced in 1996. An inline muzzleloader. Offered in .50 or .54 caliber, with blued or stainless steel barrel. Semi-fancy checkered walnut stock has a cheekpiece. Round barrel is 24" long. Adjustable rear leaf sight, with ramp-style front bead. Weight 7 lbs.

NIB	Exc.	V.G.	Good	Fair	Poor
—	320	280	240	200	170

Fire Hawk

Similar to Deluxe Fire Hawk, with standard American walnut stock or composition stock.

NIB	Exc.	V.G.	Good	Fair	Poor
—	250	210	180	150	130

Thumbhole Stock

NIB	Exc.	V.G.	Good	Fair	Poor
—	280	230	200	170	140

Camo Stock

NIB	Exc.	V.G.	Good	Fair	Poor
—	280	230	200	170	140

Bantam

NIB	Exc.	V.G.	Good	Fair	Poor
—	220	190	160	140	120

.32- & .58-Caliber Models

NIB	Exc.	V.G.	Good	Fair	Poor
—	250	210	180	150	130

Fire Storm

Offered as a percussion or flintlock. Fitted with 26" barrel chambered for .50 caliber. Black composite stock. Adjustable fiber-optic rear sight. Weight 7 lbs. Introduced in 2000.

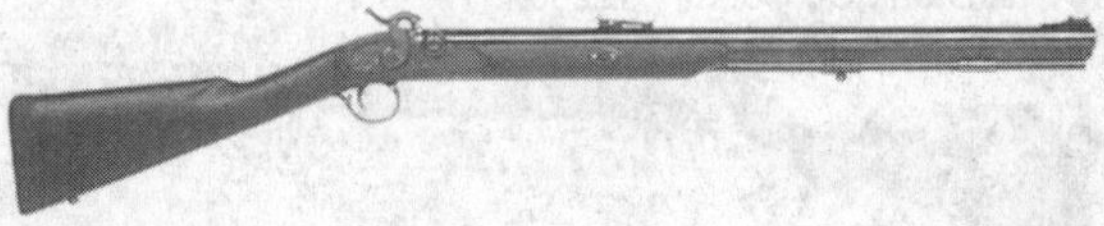

NIB	Exc.	V.G.	Good	Fair	Poor
—	300	260	220	180	160

Black Diamond

An inline muzzleloading rifle, with removable breech plug. Fitted with 22.5" .50-caliber barrel. Stock is Rynite. Choice of blue or stainless steel. Introduced in 1998; discontinued. Note: Add $50 for stainless steel.

NIB	Exc.	V.G.	Good	Fair	Poor
—	220	190	160	140	120

Black Diamond XR

This .45- or .50-caliber muzzleloader is fitted with 26" round barrel. Offered with blued finish, camo or stainless steel. Weight 6.75 lbs. Introduced in 2002; discontinued.

NIB	Exc.	V.G.	Good	Fair	Poor
—	300	260	220	180	160

Triumph

.50-caliber toggle-breech inline muzzleloader, with only four moving parts. Blued/synthetic, Weathershield/synthetic or Weathershield/stainless finish. Introduced 2007.

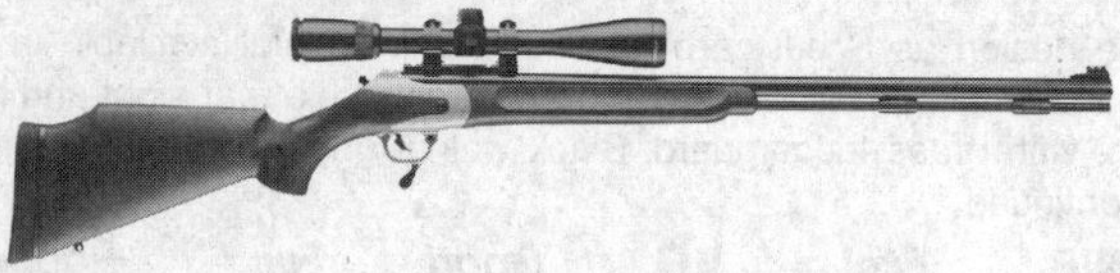

NIB	Exc.	V.G.	Good	Fair	Poor
—	320	280	240	200	170

Triumph Bone Collector

.50 caliber, 28" barrels. Ultra-light aircraft-grade aluminum frame. Accepts magnum charges of up to 150 grains of FFG blackpowder, or equivalent blackpowder substitute. Breech plugs are Speed Breech XT. Metal finish and stock configurations and model numbers are Weather Shield Silver/Black, 10168526; Weather Shield Black/Realtree Edge Stock, 12275; Realtree Edge Full Coverage, 12274; and Weather Shield Black/Realtree Original, 12277.

NIB	Exc.	V.G.	Good	Fair	Poor
600	510	430	370	310	270

Impact Muzzleloading Rifle

.50-caliber single-shot rifle. Features include 209 primer ignition, sliding hood to expose removable breech plug, synthetic stock adjustable from 12.5" to 13.5", 26" blued 1:28 rifled barrel, adjustable fiber-optic sights, aluminum ramrod, camo composite stock, QLA muzzle system. Weight 6.5 lbs. Note: Add $20 for camo stock.

NIB	Exc.	V.G.	Good	Fair	Poor
—	180	150	130	110	90

IMPACT!SB

.50 caliber, 26" barrels. Offered in both a blued and Weather Shield corrosion-resistant finish. Also includes a 1" removable buttstock spacer, allowing the user to adjust the length of pull to best suit clothing choice and weather conditions in the field. Metal finish and stock configurations and model numbers are Blued/Black Composite, 12065; Silver Weather Shield/Realtree Edge, 12282; Silver Weather Shield/Black Composite, 12283; Blued/Mossy Oak Bottomland, 12285; and Silver Weather Shield/Mossy Oak Break-Up Country 12286.

NIB	Exc.	V.G.	Good	Fair	Poor
250	210	180	150	130	110

Strike

.50 caliber, 24" barrels. Striker-fired muzzleloader with the Adapt breech system, Armornite barrel coating, 24" barrel with 1:28" twist. Stealth Striker ambidextrous cocking system, match-grade trigger, adjustable sights with fiber optics, Weaver-style scope mount base. Introduced 2015. Metal finish and stock configurations and model numbers are Black Stock, 10291; G2 Camo, 10292; Walnut, 10293.

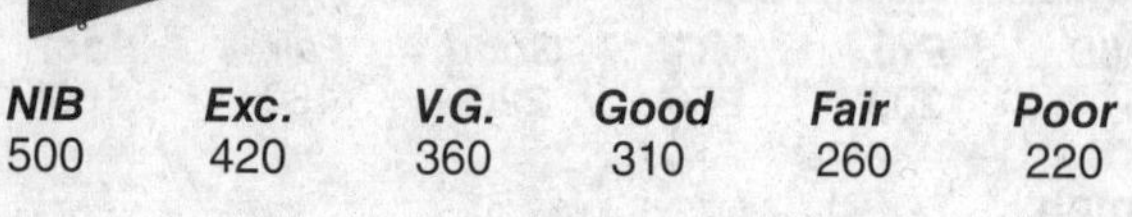

NIB	Exc.	V.G.	Good	Fair	Poor
500	420	360	310	260	220

NorthWest Explorer Muzzleloading Rifle

.50-caliber single-shot rifle. Features include dropping block action, #11 percussion cap ignition, 28" blued or Weathershield 1:48 rifled barrel, adjustable fiber optic sights, aluminum ramrod, black or camo composite stock with recoil pad, QLA muzzle system. Weight 7 lbs. Note: Add $60 for Realtree Hardwoods camo stock.

NIB	Exc.	V.G.	Good	Fair	Poor
—	220	190	160	140	120

G2 Contender Muzzleloader Barrel

A 209x45 24" muzzleloader barrel. Will interchange with G2 Contender rifle barrels. Weight 5.5 lbs.

NIB	Exc.	V.G.	Good	Fair	Poor
300	260	220	180	160	130

G2 Contender Muzzleloader .50 caliber

In .50-caliber, with 24" barrel. Weight 6.5 lbs. Introduced in 2005.

NIB	Exc.	V.G.	Good	Fair	Poor
580	490	420	350	300	260

Encore 209x50 Mag Rifle

Muzzleloading rifle chambered for .50-caliber. Fitted with 26" barrel. Designed to handle Magnum loads up to 150 grains of FFG blackpowder. Blued or stainless steel finish. Introduced in 1998. Note: Add $75 for stainless steel; $140 for Realtree camo stock

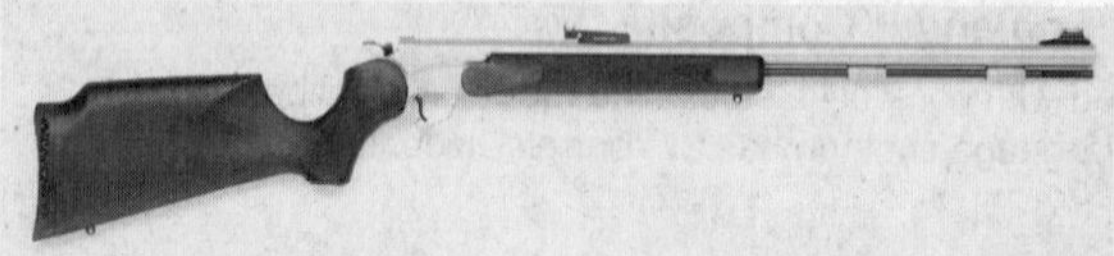

NIB	Exc.	V.G.	Good	Fair	Poor
520	450	380	320	270	230

Encore 209x50 Mag Carbine

Similar to above model. Fitted with 20" ported barrel. Realtree camo stock. Weight 6.75 lbs. Introduced in 2004.

NIB	Exc.	V.G.	Good	Fair	Poor
520	450	380	320	270	230

Encore 209x50 Pistol

Model features 15" barrel chambered for .50 caliber. Walnut stock and blued finish. Weight 16 oz. Introduced in 2000.

NIB	Exc.	V.G.	Good	Fair	Poor
550	470	400	340	290	240

THUNDER FIVE

MIL Inc.
Piney Flats, Tennessee

Thunder-Five

Five shot double-action revolver, with 2" rifled barrel, matte finish, ambidextrous hammer block safety, Pachmayr grips, chambered in .45 Long Colt/.410 shotgun.

NIB	Exc.	V.G.	Good	Fair	Poor
580	420	340	250	200	150

TIKKA
Tikkakoski, Finland

RIFLES

Whitetail Hunter

Features hand-checkered walnut stock, with matte lacquer finish. Furnished without sights, but receiver is grooved. Magazine is detachable box type. Three action lengths are offered: short, medium and long. In short-action caliber choices are: .17 Rem., .223, .22-250, .243 and .308 with 22.4" barrels and weight 7 lbs.; medium-action: .270 and .30-06 with 22.4" barrels and weight 7.3 lbs.; long-action: 7mm Rem. Magnum, .300 and .338 Win. Magnum with 24.4" barrel and weight 7.5 lbs.

NIB	Exc.	V.G.	Good	Fair	Poor
720	600	500	400	200	150

Whitetail Hunter Deluxe

Similar to standard model above, but furnished with cheekpiece, select walnut stock, rosewood pistol grip cap and forend tip. Metal surfaces are a highly polished blue. Same calibers as offered above.

Whitetail/Battue Rifle

Rifle originally designed for the French market. Barrel 20.5" long and fitted with a raised quarter rib. Walnut is checkered, with rubber recoil pad standard. Black fiberglass stock is offered as an option. In a medium-action only caliber is .308. In a long-action calibers are: .270, .30-06, 7mm Rem. Magnum, .300 and .338 Win. Magnum. All models weigh about 7 lbs. In 2000, offered in a left-hand model. Note: Add $50 for stainless steel finish; $20 for Magnum calibers; $60 for left-hand model.

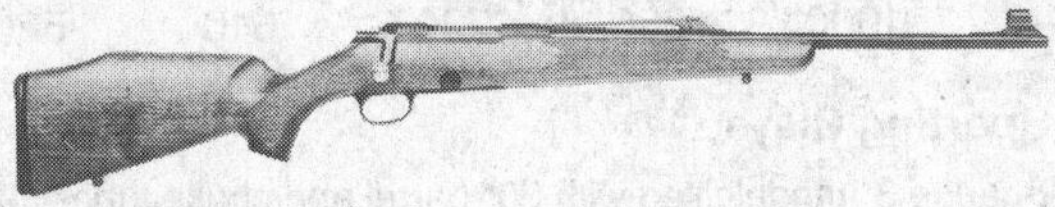

NIB	Exc.	V.G.	Good	Fair	Poor
650	500	400	280	200	100

Varmint/Continental Rifle

Features 23.5" heavy barrel, without sights. Checkered walnut stock has a wide forend. Offered in .17 Rem., .223, .22-250, .243 and .308. Weight about 8.5 lbs.

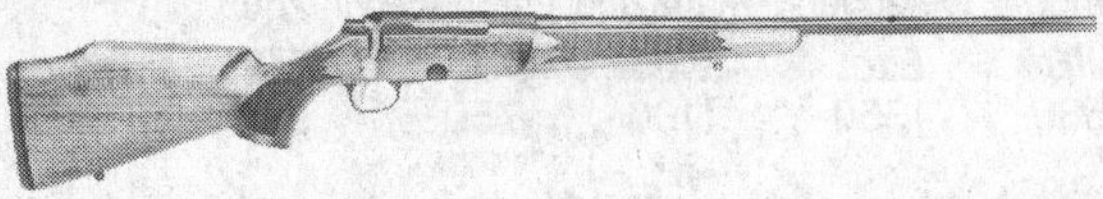

NIB	Exc.	V.G.	Good	Fair	Poor
720	600	500	400	200	150

Long Range Hunting

Same as above in .25-06, .270, .7mm Magnum and .300 Win. Magnum. Fitted with 26" heavy barrel.

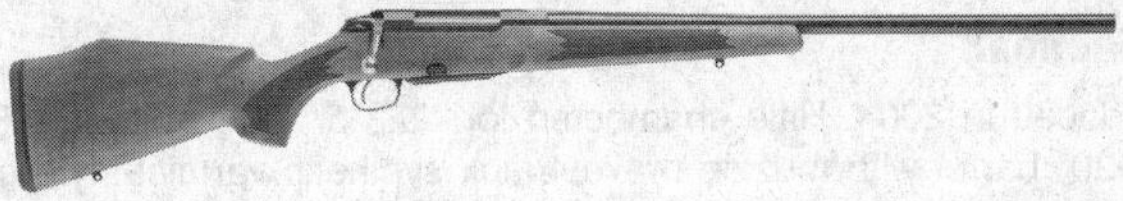

NIB	Exc.	V.G.	Good	Fair	Poor
720	600	500	400	200	150

Sporter

Introduced in 1998. Features a select walnut stock, adjustable cheekpiece, adjustable buttplate, adjustable trigger. Comes without open sights. Detachable 5-round magazine. Chambered for .223, .22-250 and .308-calibers.

NIB	Exc.	V.G.	Good	Fair	Poor
950	820	680	500	400	200

T3 Hunter

Introduced in 2003. This bolt-action rifle features a hand-forged barrel and adjustable trigger. Offered in standard and Magnum calibers from .223 to .338 Win. Magnum. Walnut stock with recoil pad. Detachable magazine holds three rounds for all calibers except .223 (four). No sights. Barrel lengths are 22.5" and 24.25" for standard and Magnum calibers respectively. Weight about 6.75 lbs.

NIB	Exc.	V.G.	Good	Fair	Poor
750	620	500	400	200	150

T3 Lite

As above, with a black synthetic stock and blued finish. Introduced in 2003.

NIB	Exc.	V.G.	Good	Fair	Poor
680	550	420	320	150	100

T3 Lite Stainless

As above, with stainless steel barrel and synthetic stock.

NIB	Exc.	V.G.	Good	Fair	Poor
720	600	500	400	200	150

T3 Big Boar

Bolt-action rifle chambered for .308, .30-06 or .300 WSM cartridges. Fitted with 19" barrel with no sights. Black synthetic stock, with recoil pad. Blued finish. Magazine capacity 3 rounds. Weight about 6 lbs. Introduced in 2005.

NIB	Exc.	V.G.	Good	Fair	Poor
720	600	500	400	200	150

T3 Super Varmint

Bolt-action model chambered for .223 Rem., .22-250 Rem. or .308 cartridge. Stainless steel receiver and barrel, with Picatinny rail on receiver. Barrel length 23.3". Black synthetic stock has adjustable comb. Adjustable trigger. Detachable magazine. Introduced in 2005.

NIB	Exc.	V.G.	Good	Fair	Poor
1580	1350	1100	750	580	300

T3 Varmint

Chambered for .223, .22-250 and .308 cartridges. Fitted with 23.3" barrel with no sights. Synthetic stock, with blued finish. Adjustable trigger. Rubber recoil pad. Note: Add $70 for stainless steel version.

NIB	Exc.	V.G.	Good	Fair	Poor
850	720	580	400	300	150

T3 Tactical

Introduced in 2004. Rifle chambered for .223 or .308 cartridge. Fitted with 20" barrel with muzzle brake. Black synthetic varmint-style stock, with adjustable cheekpiece. Detachable magazine capacity 5 rounds. Picatinny rail on receiver top.

NIB	Exc.	V.G.	Good	Fair	Poor
1500	1350	1050	850	580	350

T3X

An improved variant of the T3 series. Offered with choice of a wood, laminate, or synthetic modular stock, the latter with interchangeable pistol grips, a new recoil pad, and butt plate spacers to adjust the length of pull. The forend width is also adjustable. Other changes include a redesigned ejection port, improved bolt shroud and rail attachment. Offered in virtually any popular chambering from .204 Ruger to .300 WSM. There are several variations including Forest, Hunter, Varmint, Lite and Tactical models; all are guaranteed to deliver one minute-of-angle accuracy. Left-hand models are available. Prices shown are for Forest Model (shown). Add 10 percent for Varmint version, 20 percent for Laminate Stainless, 35 percent for Tactical Compact model.

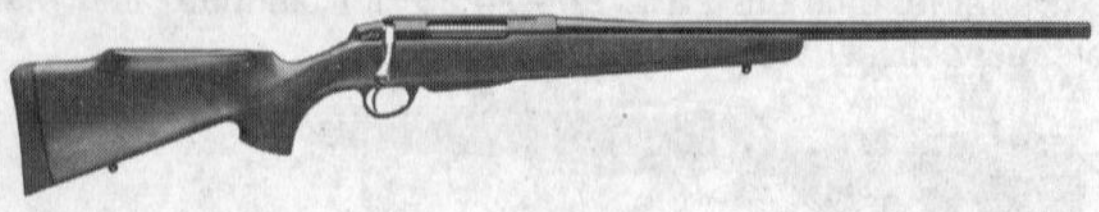

NIB	Exc.	V.G.	Good	Fair	Poor
850	750	600	450	300	200

T3X TAC A1

Model designed for outstanding long range shooting. Chambered for .223 Rem., .260 Rem., 6.5 Creedmoor, .308 Win., .300 Win. Mag., 5 or 6-shot detachable magazine. Semi-heavy 16, 20 or 24-inch barrel. Modular chassis built to meet Military and Law Enforcement specifications. Bolt action with AR butt stock, pistol grip and forend interface. Adjustable cheek piece, length of pull and butt stock angle. Other features include pistol grip with textured surface, full-length top Picatinny rail, height adjustable soft recoil pad, and M-Lok forend.

NIB	Exc.	V.G.	Good	Fair	Poor
1750	1450	1000	800	700	500

Tikka Target

Bolt-action rifle chambered for .223, .22-250, 7mm-08 Rem., .308 Win. and 6.5x55 Swedish Mauser cartridge. Fitted with 23.25" barrel. Adjustable walnut target stock. Trigger is adjustable for weight. No sights. Weight about 9 lbs.

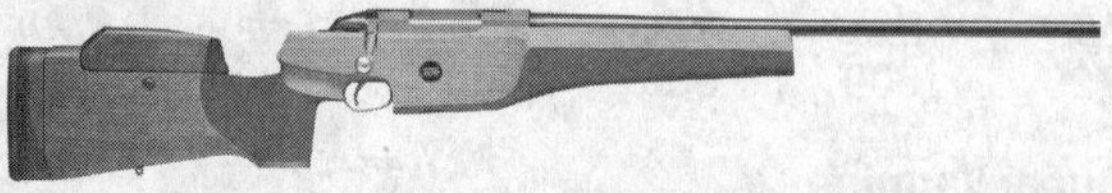

NIB	Exc.	V.G.	Good	Fair	Poor
950	820	680	500	400	200

SHOTGUNS/DOUBLE RIFLES (FORMERLY VALMET)

Tikka, Valmet and Sako have been merged into one company, SAKO Ltd. These firearms are now manufactured in Italy under the brand name Tikka. Parts are interchangeable between Valmet guns made in Finland and Tikka guns made in Italy.

412S Shotgun

Over/under shotgun available in 12-gauge only, with 26" or 28" barrels. Stock is checkered European walnut. Weight about 7.25 lbs.

NIB	Exc.	V.G.	Good	Fair	Poor
—	1050	890	760	640	550

412S Shotgun/Rifle

Same as above, with 12-gauge barrel and choice of .222 or .308 barrel. Barrel length 24". Weight 8 lbs.

NIB	Exc.	V.G.	Good	Fair	Poor
—	900	760	650	550	470

412S Double Rifle

Same as above, with 24" over/under rifle barrel in 9.3x74R. Weight about 8.5 lbs.

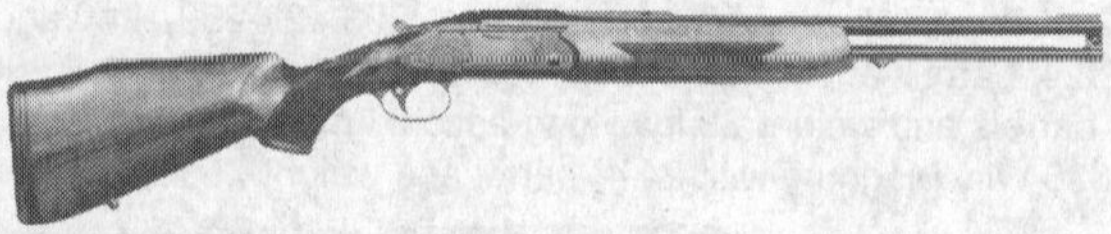

NIB	Exc.	V.G.	Good	Fair	Poor
—	900	760	650	550	470

412S Sporting Clays

Introduced in 1993. Offered in 12-gauge, with 28" barrels and choke tubes.

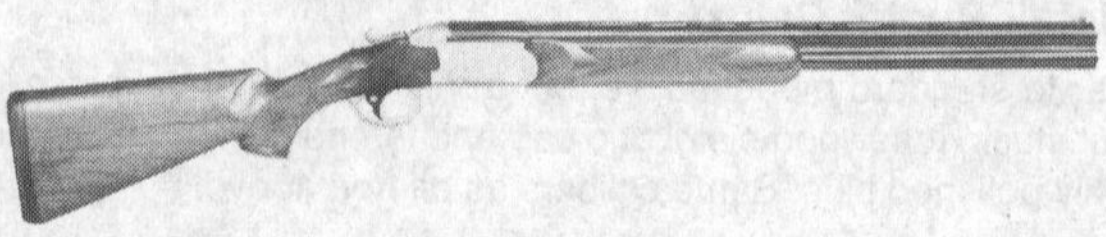

NIB	Exc.	V.G.	Good	Fair	Poor
—	900	760	650	550	470

512S Field Grade

Introduced in 2000. Over/under gun chambered for 12-gauge 3" shell. Fitted with 26" or 28" choke tube barrels. Note: Add $650 per set for shotgun/rifle barrel sets.

NIB	Exc.	V.G.	Good	Fair	Poor
—	1000	850	720	610	520

512S Sporting Clays

This 12-gauge 3" model fitted with 30" barrel and choke tubes.

NIB	Exc.	V.G.	Good	Fair	Poor
—	1150	980	830	710	600

TIMBER WOLF

See—ACTION ARMS LTD.

TIPPING & LAWDEN
Birmingham, England

Thomas Revolver (Antique)

A .320, .380 or .450 double-action revolver, with 4.5" barrel and 5-shot cylinder. Utilizing a cartridge extraction system, designed by J. Thomas of Birmingham. in which barrel and cylinder may be moved forward. Manufactured from 1870 to 1877.

Exc.	Fine	V.G.	Good	Fair	Poor
2000	1200	700	400	200	125

TIPPMANN ARMS
Fort Wayne, Indiana

Model 1917

A .22-caliber semi-automatic one-half scale reproduction of Browning Model 1917 water-cooled machine gun. Barrel length 10". A tripod was sold with this model. Manufactured in 1986 and 1987.

NIB	Exc.	V.G.	Good	Fair	Poor
5750	5250	—	—	—	—

Model 1919 A-4

A .22-caliber semi-automatic one-half scale reproduction of Browning Model 1919 A-4 machine gun. Barrel length 11". Furnished with a tripod. Manufactured in 1986 and 1987.

NIB	Exc.	V.G.	Good	Fair	Poor
3000	2750	—	—	—	—

Model .50 HB

A .22 Magnum caliber semi-automatic one-half scale reproduction of Browning .50-caliber machine gun. Barrel length 18.25". Furnished with a tripod. Manufactured in 1986 and 1987.

NIB	Exc.	V.G.	Good	Fair	Poor
6000	5500	—	—	—	—

M4-22 Rifle

Semi-auto .22 LR rifle patterned on the M4, 16" barrel, adjustable stock. Base model is the M4-22 Pro. Available upgraded models include M4-22 Elite (add $40 premium to NIB value), M4-22 Sharpshooter with scope (add $220), M4-22 MMSSA (add $200), and M4-22 MMSSA Competition (add $380).

NIB	Exc.	V.G.	Good	Fair	Poor
530	450	380	—	—	—

M4-22 Pistol

Similar to above in pistol configuration with arm brace, 11" barrel. Base model is Pro. Available upgraded models include Elite (add $40), and Micro Elite with shorter 7" barrel (add $20).

NIB	Exc.	V.G.	Good	Fair	Poor
550	480	380	—	—	—

TISAS (TRABZON GUN INDUSTRY CORP.)
Trabzon, Turkey

This Turkish manufacturer offers a wide number of models of inexpensive semi-auto pistols. Most are retailed in the $300 to $500 range. Models in 9mm not covered in this edition include Zigana P9L series, Zigana FC series, additional Zigana K models, additional Zigana M16 models, and Zigana PX-9 V2 series.

Fatih 13

Beretta-style auto-pistol clone chambered in .32 ACP or .380 ACP. Introduced 1994.

NIB	Exc.	V.G.	Good	Fair	Poor
350	310	260	190	160	130

Kanuni 16

Single-/double-action autopistol chambered in 9mm Parabellum, with 15- or 17-shot capacity. Black, chrome or chrome/gold finish. Introduced 1999.

NIB	Exc.	V.G.	Good	Fair	Poor
320	220	150	120	80	50

Kanuni S

Lightweight version of Kanuni 16. Black, chrome or chrome/black finish. Introduced 2000.

NIB	Exc.	V.G.	Good	Fair	Poor
320	220	150	120	80	50

Zigana M16

Single-/double-action autopistol chambered in 9mm Parabellum, with 15- or 17-shot capacity and 5" barrel. Introduced 2000.

NIB	Exc.	V.G.	Good	Fair	Poor
400	300	220	200	150	80

Zigana K

Compact version of Zigana M16, with 4" barrel. Introduced 2002.

NIB	Exc.	V.G.	Good	Fair	Poor
400	300	220	200	150	80

Zigana T

Longer (5.5") barrel version of Zigana M16. Introduced 2002.

NIB	Exc.	V.G.	Good	Fair	Poor
400	300	220	200	150	80

Zigana Sport

Compensated version of Zigana K, with 4.5" barrel. Introduced 2005.

NIB	Exc.	V.G.	Good	Fair	Poor
400	300	220	200	150	80

Zigana C45

Similar to Zigana M16. Chambered in .45 ACP, with 4.75" barrel. Introduced 2005.

NIB	Exc.	V.G.	Good	Fair	Poor
400	300	220	200	150	80

Zigana F

"Meltdown" version of Zigana M16, with radiused edges and improved ergonomics. Introduced 2007.

NIB	Exc.	V.G.	Good	Fair	Poor
400	300	220	200	150	80

ZIG 1911 Pattern Pistols

As of 2020, Tisas lists several versions of 1911 pistols in 9mm or .45 ACP, including full size and compact versions with stainless or black finishes. ZIG Model designations include M1A1 (original 1911 style sights), M1 (full size .45), M9 (compact 9mm), and PC9 (full size 9mm). Values for most models are similar. Most retail new in the $400 to $550 range.

NIB	Exc.	V.G.	Good	Fair	Poor
450	380	300	—	—	—

ZIG 14

Browning Hi-Power clones. Offered in black or stainless finish. 9mm, 13-15 rounds.

NIB	Exc.	V.G.	Good	Fair	Poor
480	400	300	—	—	—

TOBIN ARMS MANUFACTURING CO.

Norwich, Connecticut and Windsor, Ontario, Canada

Tobin Arms Manufacturing Co. operated from about 1905 to 1925 making an exposed hammer double and two hammerless models in four grades. The ?Simplex? was cleverly designed (based on a patent by C.M. Wollam) side plated double-barrel internal hammer shotgun which resembled the Hopkins and Allen guns of that time. Some may have been private branded. Most of the Tobin doubles were made in Norwich, Conn. and are so marked. After 1909, operations were transferred to Windsor, Ont., Canada. Some guns will be found with that address. Tobin guns are not often seen by collectors and are highly prized because of their relative rarity and they were considered good guns by top dealers such as C.J. Godfrey Co. of New York City and Iver Johnson Sporting Goods of Boston. Values depend on condition and range from $200 in poor condition to $1000 and up for engraved versions in good to very good condition.

NOTE: Tobin also manufactured a .22 rimfire single-shot rifle apparently during the period 1910-1925. These are rather scarce and their value is estimated to be in the $500 - $700 range, depending on condition.

A rough timeline of Tobin Arms Manufacturing Company follows:

1903: founded by Frank M. Tobin in Norwich, CT.
1904-1909: manufactured hammer and hammerless sidelock shotguns (12ga. and 16ga.) in Norwich, Connecticut, USA
1909: purchased by a group of Canadian Investors and moved to Woodstock, ON, CAN
1910-1923/25: manufactured shotguns and rifles (entire product list unknown)
1923/25: purchased by sporting goods distributor G.B.Crandall
1923/25-1951: G.B.Crandall continued production until 1951 (possibly under the name GB Crandall)
Thanks to Jack of Florida for furnishing us with this information!

TODD, GEORGE H.

Montgomery, Alabama

Rifled Musket

A .58-caliber single-shot percussion rifle, with 40" barrel and full-length stock secured by three barrel bands. Barrel and lock finished in bright brass furniture and walnut stock. Lock marked "George H. Todd/ Montgomery, Ala." TOO RARE TO PRICE.

Percussion Revolver

Colt 1851 Navy pattern, .36 caliber. This has been called "the rarest confederate revolver." As with all CSA arms, expert authentication is essential. Too rare to estimate values. The only sale we could find was Heritage Auctions in 2007, reporting a price of $59,750.

TOKAREV

USSR

Russian Tokarev

Russian Tula Tokarev or TT-33, replaced earlier TT-30 in 1934 and remained in service into the late 1950s, despite its supposed replacement by the Makarov in 1951. An 8-shot semi-automatic pistol in 7.62x25mm caliber. Has a 4.6" barrel, with a short-recoil tilting barrel system. Tokarev was manufactured at Izshevsk arsenal until 1952. Probably has seen service with more countries, both communist and third world, than any other military handgun. Only safety feature on this pistol is placing the hammer at half-cock. Blued finish, hard rubber lined grips with communist star and CCCP (USSR) marked between the star points. Serial number with star and year of production is found on rear left frame. Top of slide also numbered. Take-down latch located on right frame. Russian Tokarev has recently become highly collectible, especially WWII dated examples. Note: Add 40 percent premium for pistols with wartime wooden grips.

NIB	Exc.	V.G.	Good	Fair	Poor
—	950	800	680	580	300

Chinese Licenses Tokarev

China received tooling to manufacture the Tokarev in 1950, and began production of their own copy at Number 66 Shenyang factory. Introduced as Type 51, which used a combination of Russian and Chinese made parts, it was practically identical to its Russian Counterpart. Replaced by Type 54 (in 1954), it differed by virtue that its construction was completely indigenous without borrowed Russian components. Markings on Type 51 and 54 have serial number, a star and production year on rear left frame, with Chinese written model number on right side, as well as stamped on upper top rear of the slide. As with the Russian version, they have become highly collectible in recent times given their affiliation with both Korean and Vietnam wars. Surviving Type 51 pistols are normally in very rough shape, but reap high prices, as much as 50 percent over those shown, which represent the more common Type 54. These were never imported into the United States and the majority are war-time bring backs. Again, the presence of capture papers greatly enhance values.

NIB	Exc.	V.G.	Good	Fair	Poor
—	750	680	600	480	300

Polish Licensed Tokarev

From 1947 to 1959, Poland manufactured the PW wz.33 at FB factory Number 11 in Radom. This was their copy of Russian Tokarev built under Soviet license. Mechanically identical to TT-33, its hard rubber grips do not have the star in a circle and are straight lined. Production year and Number 11 in a circle are marked on slide top, with serial number and year marked on left frame. Imported to United States in the 1990s, BATF demanded that all Tokarev-type imports be installed with a trigger block safety. Thus, importers were responsible in assuring installation of this prior to the pistols entering U.S. Most import outlets have since sold out of these pistols. Collectors feel it destroys originality, which is true, not to mention the addition of import markings which reduce value as well. Polish Tokarev imports have a rotating thumb or bar safety on left frame (depending on the importer), which some owners have removed and replaced with a dummy pin to restore originality. Those Polish Takarev variants picked up in Vietnam or elsewhere, without this feature, will increase prices 50 to 60 percent higher.

NIB	Exc.	V.G.	Good	Fair	Poor
—	400	320	300	220	200

M48 Hungarian Tokarev

Perhaps the rarest of all Eastern European Tokarev pistols is the Hungarian Model 48. Manufactured at the Femaru factory in Budapest from 1949 to about 1958. Never imported to United States and very few have been found on the world market making it quite scarce. Those made from 1949 to 1956 have "Rakosi" crest (the Hungarian premier at the time); those from late 1956 to possibly 1958 having "Kadar" crest. Lined hard rubber grips on M48 have Hungarian communist emblem in the center. Serial numbers and manufacture year on left frame.

NIB	Exc.	V.G.	Good	Fair	Poor
—	2500	1850	1500	1200	600

Romanian Licensed Tokarev

Manufactured at Cugir Romania arms factory, TTC or Tulskiye Tokarev Cugir was produced from 1952 to 1959. Remained the standard Romanian service pistol until the Romanian revolution of 1989. Huge quantities of TTC have been imported to United States in the last 15 years and are still available from distributors as of this writing. Lined hard rubber grips have "RPR" between the star points which is *Republika Populus Romana* or Peoples Republic of Romania. Much like the Polish version, TTC has BATF-required supplemental trigger safety. It is believed none were ever exported to other nations such as North Vietnan, thus their appearance in the United States was an all time first. However, an example found without the import safety or markings would yield a great price. Serial number located on left frame and upper slide. Interestingly, the narrow finger grips at the slide's rear are similar to a Colt 1911, and not the line and oval type of Russian TT-33. Most offered for sale from dealers at the present include a brown leather holster. Romanian TTC Tokarev imports that are encountered with a Wreath, Hammer and Sickle on the rear of the upper slide between the rear sight and serial number are very scarce. These pistols were specially stamped for issue to Communist Party Apparatchiks or high level members of the Romanian communist party. This marking is found thus far on pistols dated 1952 and 1953, and less than 2,500 were stamped. Very few have been imported and the markings should add 200 percent to the below listed prices. Condition of pistols with such emblems are not affected by this increase given their extreme scarcity.

NIB	Exc.	V.G.	Good	Fair	Poor
—	300	250	200	150	100

Pakistani TT-33 Tokarev

Since 1941, Badar & Brother have produced sporting arms and some military ordnance as well. Though not a Com Bloc country, Pakistan used the Tokarev until sometime in the recent 15 years. B&B manufactured a very high quality copy of which a thousand or more were imported to United States through TGI in Knoxville, Tennessee from 2008 to 2009 time frame. They have since sold out from distributors and are identical to Russian version. This model likely holds the distinction of being the newest Tokarev manufactured. Those imported were available in original 7.62x25 or 9mm Luger. Finished in a matte-like blue finish, they were neatly boxed and came with a manual and spare magazine. Regarding the required BATF supplemental safety, the B&B Tokarev has a very efficient thumb safety installed on rear left side of frame. Far more efficient and cosmetically appealing than those installed on aforementioned Polish and Romanian import.

NIB	Exc.	V.G.	Good	Fair	Poor
—	550	500	350	250	150

Yugoslavian M-57A Licensed Tokarev

This version of Tokarev was manufactured by Crvena Zastava in Serbia from 1957 to 1992. A redesigned variant of the Tokarev. Frame was extended with a longer grip to allow use of a 9-shot magazine. Has a clamp-retained firing pin assembly versus cross pin retainer found on standard Tokarev design. A matted sight ramp on the slide top was also added to reduce glare. M-57 Tokarev pistols began to be imported to United States in the 1990s. Listed as M-57A, because of the addition to U.S.-required supplemental safety, which is a flat, frame mounted type that slides along the upper left grip. Those that have the communist crest, with six pointed flame and Roman numerals, are of interest to collectors as they are pre-1980s production and will enhance values up to 40 percent. Serial number is located on right frame and slide flat, with M-57 marked on left slide. Zastava continues to produce this pistol in 9mm Luger and lists as M-70A. Any of the current military surplus M-57A Licensed Tokarev pistols with an A or B suffix following the serial number and a Five Torch Crest on the upper slide, should have 70 percent added to below prices. M-57A pistols produced from 1961 through 1974 will have a prefix in lieu of a suffix and will be marked C through P with a Six Torch Crest. The latter became standard in 1964 following the change of the Yugoslavian Republic from Federated National Republic of Jugoslavia to Socialist Federated Republic of Jugoslavia. Prices for the latter remain as indicated below.

NIB	Exc.	V.G.	Good	Fair	Poor
—	400	250	200	180	130

TOMISKA, ALOIS
Pilsen, Czechoslovakia

Little Tom

A 6.35mm or 7.65mm caliber semi-automatic pistol, with 2.5" barrel. Slide marked "Alois Tomiska Plzen Patent Little Tom". Grips inlaid with a medallion bearing the monogram "AT". Blued, with checkered walnut grips. Manufactured from 1908 to 1918. Subsequently produced by Wiener Waffenfabrik.

NIB	Exc.	V.G.	Good	Fair	Poor
—	550	420	350	250	120

TORKELSON ARMS CO.
Harfield, Warren, and Worcester, Massachusetts

Double-Barrel Shotguns

Reinhard T. Torkelson's company made double-barrel boxlock side-by-side hammerless shotguns, in four models at several locations between 1885 and 1910. He worked with Iver Johnson at Fitchburg, Mass. and also built guns carrying Lovell (Boston) name. His "New Worcester" marked guns are quite common. They were sold by Sears and other large and well known houses.

NIB	Exc.	V.G.	Good	Fair	Poor
—	600	300	200	150	100

TRADEWINDS
Tacoma, Washington

Model H-170

A 12-gauge semi-automatic shotgun, with 26" or 28" ventilated rib barrel and 5-shot tubular magazine. Blued anodized alloy receiver and walnut stock.

NIB	Exc.	V.G.	Good	Fair	Poor
—	300	250	220	150	100

Model 260-A

A .22-caliber semi-automatic rifle, with 22.5" barrel, open sights and 5-shot magazine. Blued, with walnut stock.

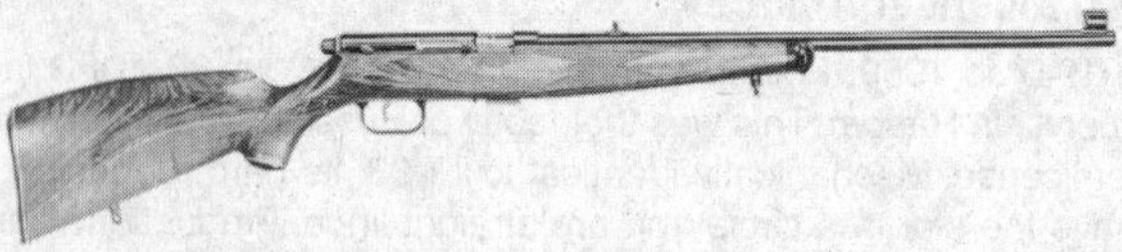

NIB	Exc.	V.G.	Good	Fair	Poor
—	200	180	120	100	80

Model 311-A

A .22-caliber bolt-action rifle, with 22.5" barrel, open sights and 5-shot magazine. Blued, with walnut stock.

NIB	Exc.	V.G.	Good	Fair	Poor
—	180	150	100	80	50

Model 5000 "Husky"

A centerfire bolt-action rifle, with 24 barrel, adjustable sights and 4-shot magazine. Blued, with walnut stock.

NIB	Exc.	V.G.	Good	Fair	Poor
—	350	300	280	200	100

TRADITIONS
Old Saybrook, Connecticut

These shotguns were imported from Italy until 2007. They were made by Stefano Fausti and Emil Rizzini. Traditions also offers percussion revolvers and Peacemaker pattern cartridge revolver by Pietta.

OVER/UNDER SHOTGUNS

Hunter

Introduced in 2001. Features 12- or 20-gauge chambers, 26" or 28" ventilated rib barrels with fixed chokes. Single-selective trigger. Extractors. Checkered walnut stock. Blued frame and barrels. Black rubber recoil pad. Weight about: 7.25 lbs. 12-gauge; 6.75 lbs. 20-gauge.

NIB	Exc.	V.G.	Good	Fair	Poor
—	550	470	400	340	290

Field I

Offered in 12-, 20-, 28-gauge and.410 bore. Barrel lengths 26". Fixed chokes. Single-selective trigger and extractors. Coin finish engraved receiver. Checkered walnut stock. Black rubber recoil pad. Weight similar to Hunter model; .410 bore about 6.5 lbs.

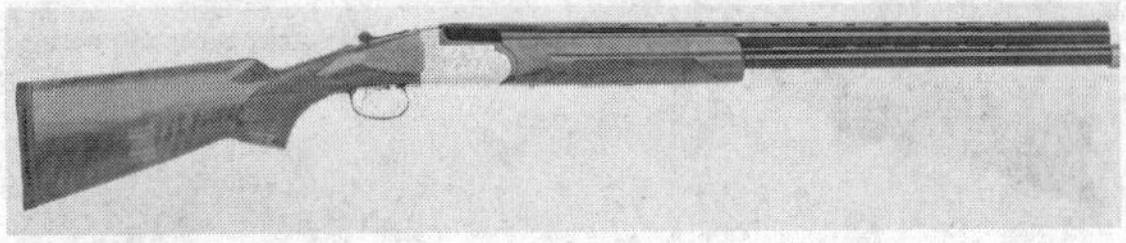

NIB	Exc.	V.G.	Good	Fair	Poor
—	480	400	340	290	250

Field II

Similar to Field I, with additional choice of 16-gauge with 28" barrels. Also features screw-in chokes and automatic ejectors.

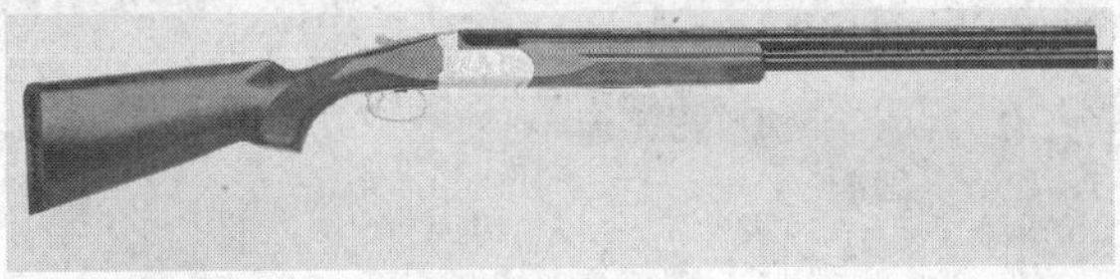

NIB	Exc.	V.G.	Good	Fair	Poor
—	650	550	470	400	340

Field II Combo

Features 20-gauge and .410 bore two barrel set. Both barrels are 26", with fixed chokes. Checkered walnut stock. Weight about 6 lbs. Introduced in 2004.

NIB	Exc.	V.G.	Good	Fair	Poor
—	1300	1100	940	800	680

Field III Gold

Similar to other Field series of guns, but offered in 12-gauge only with 26" or 28" barrels. Select oil-finish walnut stock. Engraved receiver, with gold pheasants and woodcock.

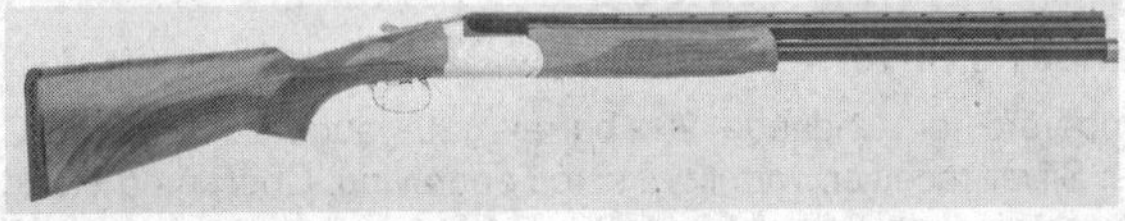

NIB	Exc.	V.G.	Good	Fair	Poor
—	1100	940	800	680	570

Upland II

Offered in both 12- and 20-gauge, with 26" barrels in 12-gauge; 24" or 26" barrels in 20-gauge. Straight-grip walnut stock. Engraved blued receiver. Schnabel forend. Choke tubes. Single-selective trigger and auto ejectors. Weight about: 12-gauge 7.25 lbs.; 20-gauge 6.25 lbs.

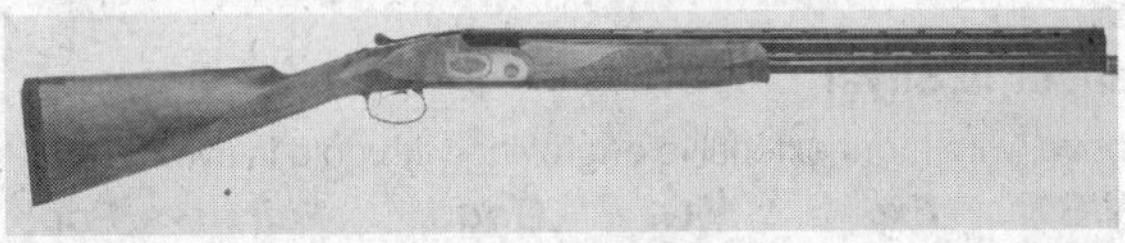

NIB	Exc.	V.G.	Good	Fair	Poor
—	700	600	510	430	360

Upland III

Introduced in 2001. Features 12-gauge, with 26" ventilated rib barrels. High-grade checkered walnut stock, with hand-engraved gold receiver. Schnabel forend. Single-selective trigger and auto ejectors standard. Screw-in chokes. Black rubber recoil pad. Weight about 7.25 lbs.

NIB	Exc.	V.G.	Good	Fair	Poor
—	1200	1020	870	740	630

Sporting Clay II

This 12-gauge gas-operated model has 28" or 30" ventilated rib ported barrels. Screw-in extended choke tubes. Checkered walnut stock, with blued receiver and barrels. Weight about 8 lbs.

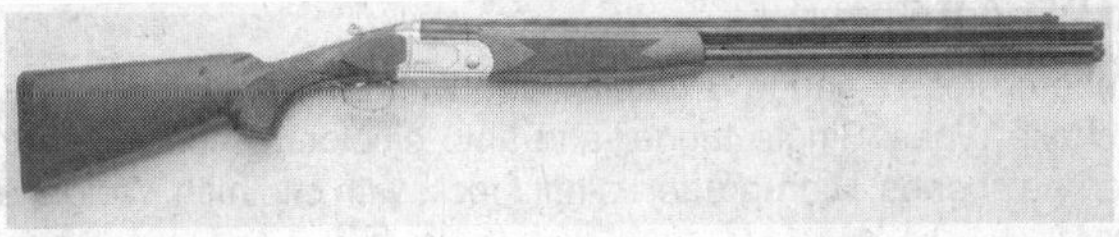

NIB	Exc.	V.G.	Good	Fair	Poor
—	780	660	560	480	400

Sporting Clay III

Features 12- or 20-gauge, with 28" or 30" ventilated rib barrels. High-grade checkered walnut stock. Choke tubes. Weight about: 8.5 lbs. 12-gauge; 8.25 lbs. 20-gauge. Note: Add $200 for 20-gauge.

NIB	Exc.	V.G.	Good	Fair	Poor
—	1200	1020	870	740	630

Waterfowl II

Introduced in 2001. This 12-gauge fitted with 28" ventilated rib barrels and 3.5" chambers. Finish on stock and barrels is Advantage Wetlands camo. Blued engraved receiver. Recoil pad. Single-selective trigger, with auto ejectors. Weight about 7.25 lbs.

NIB	Exc.	V.G.	Good	Fair	Poor
—	650	550	470	400	340

Turkey II

Offered in 12-gauge, with choice of 24" or 26" ventilated rib barrels. Mossy Oak Break-Up camo finish, with blued receiver. X-Full choke. Single-selective trigger and auto ejectors. Weight about 7 lbs.

NIB	Exc.	V.G.	Good	Fair	Poor
—	650	550	470	400	340

Mag Hunter II

This 12-gauge features 28" barrels, with 3.5" chambers. Engraved blued receiver, with walnut stock or blued receiver, with Realtree Max-4 finish. Rubber recoil pad. Single-selective trigger, with auto ejectors. Screw-in chokes. Weight about 7 lbs. Note: Add 10 percent for camo model.

NIB	Exc.	V.G.	Good	Fair	Poor
—	650	550	470	400	340

Real 16

16-gauge gun fitted with 26" ventilated rib barrels. Checkered walnut stock. Choke tubes. Single trigger, with auto ejectors. Receiver is game scene engraved. Weight about 6.75 lbs. Introduced in 2004.

NIB	Exc.	V.G.	Good	Fair	Poor
—	800	680	580	490	420

Real 16 Gold

As above, with gold-filled birds on receiver.

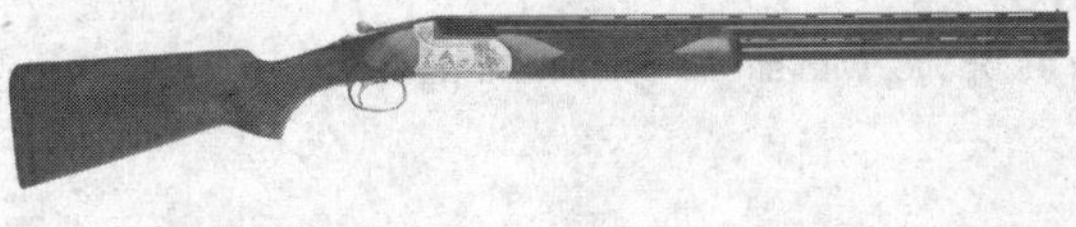

NIB	Exc.	V.G.	Good	Fair	Poor
—	950	810	690	580	500

Gold Wing II Silver

Chambered for 12-gauge 3" shell. Fitted with 28" ventilated rib barrels, with choke tubes. Single trigger and auto ejectors. Receiver engraved with game scenes. High-grade walnut stock, with oil-finish. Weight about 7.5 lbs.

NIB	Exc.	V.G.	Good	Fair	Poor
—	1100	940	800	680	570

Gold Wing III

As above, with case colored receiver with gold inlays.

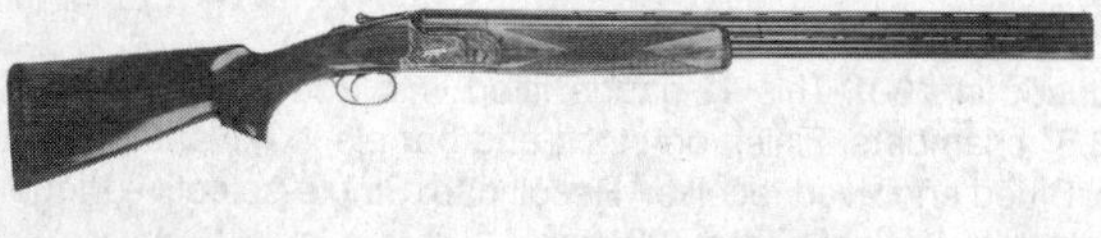

NIB	Exc.	V.G.	Good	Fair	Poor
—	1400	1190	1010	860	730

Gold Wing III Silver

As above, with silver receiver with gold inlays.

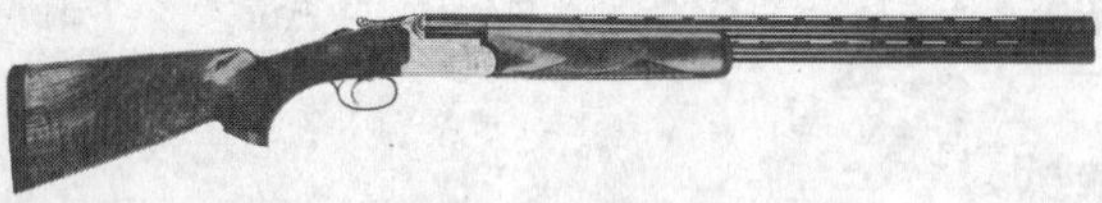

NIB	Exc.	V.G.	Good	Fair	Poor
—	1500	1280	1080	920	780

Gold Wing SL III

As above, with case colored side plates and gold inlays.

NIB	Exc.	V.G.	Good	Fair	Poor
—	1580	1340	1140	970	820

Gold Wing SL III Silver

As above, with silver side plates and gold inlays.

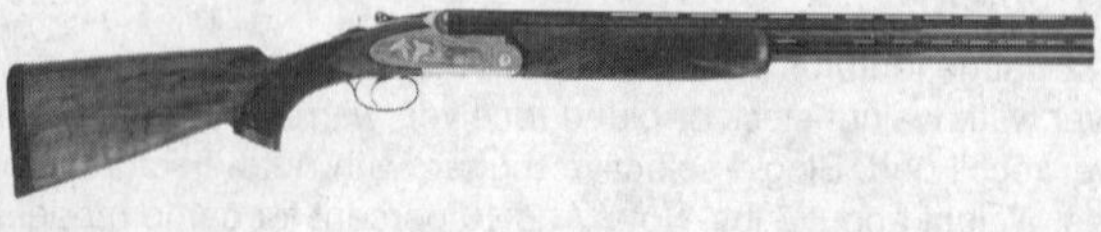

NIB	Exc.	V.G.	Good	Fair	Poor
—	1680	1420	1210	1030	870

SIDE-BY-SIDE SHOTGUNS

Elite I DT

Offered in 12-, 20-, 28-gauge and.410 bore. All gauges fitted with 26" barrels, with fixed chokes. Double triggers and extractors. Walnut stock. Weight about 6 lbs. Note: Add $60 for 28-gauge and .410 bore models.

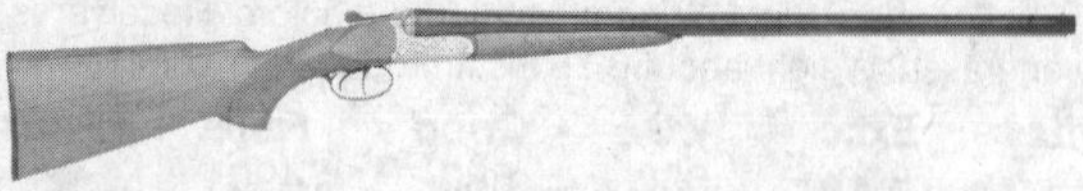

NIB	Exc.	V.G.	Good	Fair	Poor
—	600	510	430	370	310

Elite I ST

Same as above, with single-selective trigger.

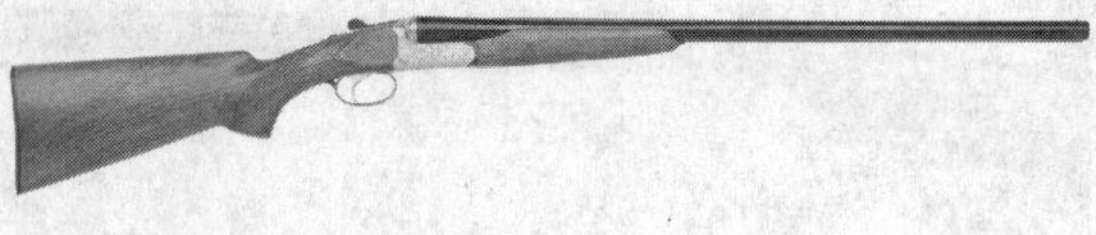

NIB	Exc.	V.G.	Good	Fair	Poor
—	750	640	540	460	390

Elite Hunter

Introduced in 2001. Features 12- or 20-gauge, with 26" barrels with screw-in chokes. Walnut stock, with beavertail forend. Single non-selective trigger. Weight about 6.5 lbs.

NIB	Exc.	V.G.	Good	Fair	Poor
—	800	680	580	490	420

Elite Field III ST

Introduced in 2001. Offered in 28-gauge or .410 bore, with 26" barrels. High-grade walnut stock, with straight-grip. Fixed chokes. Engraved receiver with gold. Weight about 6.25 lbs.

NIB	Exc.	V.G.	Good	Fair	Poor
—	1400	1190	1010	860	730

Uplander II Silver

Chambererd for 12-gauge 28" barrels; 20-gauge 26" barrels. Choke tubes. Silver receiver, with light scroll engraving. Checkered stock, with high-grade walnut. Straight-grip. Single trigger and auto ejectors. Weight about 6.75 lbs.

NIB	Exc.	V.G.	Good	Fair	Poor
—	1850	1570	1340	1140	970

Uplander III Silver

As above, with more extensive engraving with gold inlays.

NIB	Exc.	V.G.	Good	Fair	Poor
—	2150	1830	1550	1320	1120

Uplander V Silver

As above, with sideplates, extensive engraving and gold inlays.

NIB	Exc.	V.G.	Good	Fair	Poor
—	2650	2120	1700	1360	1080

SEMI-AUTOMATIC SHOTGUNS

ALS Field

Introduced in 2001. Offered in both 12- and 20-gauge, with 24", 26" or 28" ventilated rib barrels. Walnut stock, with black pad. Blued receiver and barrels. Screw-in chokes. Weight about 6.25 lbs.

NIB	Exc.	V.G.	Good	Fair	Poor
—	350	280	220	180	140

ALS Hunter

Same as above, with synthetic stock with 26" or 28" barrels.

NIB	Exc.	V.G.	Good	Fair	Poor
—	350	280	220	180	140

ALS Waterfowl

This 12-gauge has Advantage Wetlands camo. Fitted with 28" barrel, with screw-in chokes. Weight about 6.5 lbs.

NIB	Exc.	V.G.	Good	Fair	Poor
—	400	320	260	200	160

ALS Turkey

Same as above, with 21" barrel and Mossy Oak Break-up camo. Weight about 6 lbs.

NIB	Exc.	V.G.	Good	Fair	Poor
—	400	320	260	200	160

CENTERFIRE & RIMFIRE RIFLES

Outfitter G3

Single-shot break-action centerfire rifle, 22" barrel, 6.5 lbs. .350 Legend, .450 Bushmaster, .45-70, .35 Rem, .44 Mag., .357 Mag. and .35 Whelen. A Youth Model with 16" barrel and 13" length of pull is available in .300 AAC Blackout. Add $100 for 3-9x40 scope.

NIB	Exc.	V.G.	Good	Fair	Poor
450	400	350	—	—	—

Crackshot

Single-shot rimfire rifle in similar configuration to G3 above, 16.5" barrel. .22 LR or .17 HMR. Youth Model available. And $45 for 4X scope.

NIB	Exc.	V.G.	Good	Fair	Poor
220	180	140	—	—	—

Crackshot XBR

A .22 Crackshot that can be converted to fire arrows. Swapping the rifle barrel for an XBR barrel allows shooting arrows using Powerload .27 caliber blanks.

NIB	Exc.	V.G.	Good	Fair	Poor
550	480	400	—	—	—

MUZZLELOADING FIREARMS

VORTEK SERIES

Rifles are .50-cal. strikerfire models in several variations and packages, as listed below.

Kentucky Deluxe

Caliber: .50. Barrel: 33.5 in., blued octagon. Stock: Walnut-finished select hardwood. Sights: Fixed blade. Weight: 7 lbs. Features: Double set trigger, brass patch box, available as a kit, authentic wooden ramrod.

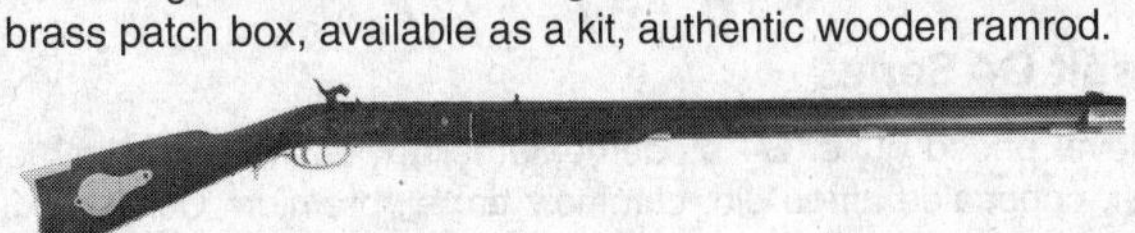

NIB	Exc.	V.G.	Good	Fair	Poor
380	—	—	—	—	—

Nitrofire

Caliber: .50. Barrel: 26 in., ultralight chromoly steel, tapered and fluted, premium Cerakote finish. Stock: Synthetic black or camo. Sights: Drilled and tapped, optional 3-9x40 scope. Weight: 6.5 lbs. Features: Several stock color options, Federal FireStick ignition system, no breech plug required, aluminum ramrod, sling swivel studs.

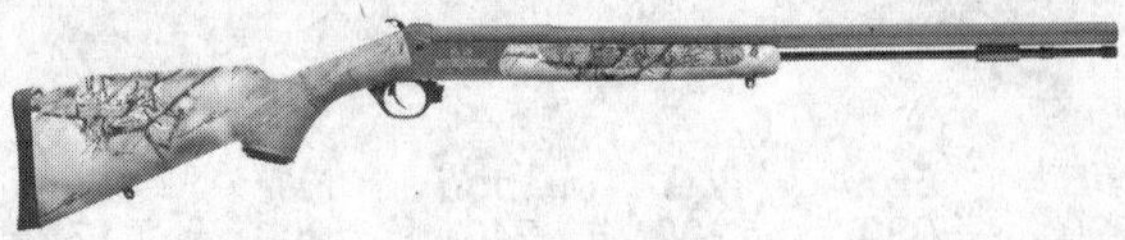

NIB	Exc.	V.G.	Good	Fair	Poor
550	—	—	—	—	—

Vortek StrikerFire LDR .50 Cal 30" Barrel Black/CeraKote

Baseline rifle has 30" Chromoly barrel, TAC2™ Trigger System, a two-stage competition-style trigger set at 2 pounds, Stow-N-Go Removable Butt Pad, 1-piece Accelerator Breech Plug, Dual Safety System, Premium CeraKote Finish, and Speed Load System. Also comes with the Quick-T Ramrod Handle, which has a t-shaped piece with brass jag that screws in, allowing ramrod to function like a work or cleaning rod. 6.8 lbs., no sights. No. R591140NS.

NIB	Exc.	V.G.	Good	Fair	Poor
370	320	270	230	190	160

Vortek StrikerFire LDR .50 Cal 30" R5-5992621DC

Rifle similar to above, but package comes with Realtree Edge camo, 3-9x40 duplex scope, deluxe case.

NIB	Exc.	V.G.	Good	Fair	Poor
530	450	380	320	280	240

Vortek StrikerFire LDR .50 cal 30" R67-5944621

Comes with a 3-9x40 Rangefinding Realtree Edge Scope mounted and boresighted. No sights.

NIB	Exc.	V.G.	Good	Fair	Poor
580	490	420	350	300	260

Vortek StrikerFire LDR .50 cal 30" R29-594446

Full Realtree Xtra Camo with a 3-9x40 RangeFinding Traditions riflescope.

NIB	Exc.	V.G.	Good	Fair	Poor
650	550	470	400	340	290

Pursuit G4 Series

Mid-level priced guns. G4 model features a wider forend, slimmer receiver, concealed hinge pin, chromoly barrel, premium CeraKote finish on barrel and receiver. LT-1 Alloy Frame. Accelerator Breech Plug allows firing both loose or pelletized powders. Dual Safety System with internal hammer block safety and trigger block safety.

Pursuit G4 Ultralight .50 Cal Select Hardwoods/CeraKote

No. R741101NS. 5.75 lbs., 26" ultralight chromoly tapered, fluted barrel, select hardwoods stock. Add factory-mounted and bore-sighted 3-9x40mm range finding scope and carrying case, $400, R5-741101MZ.

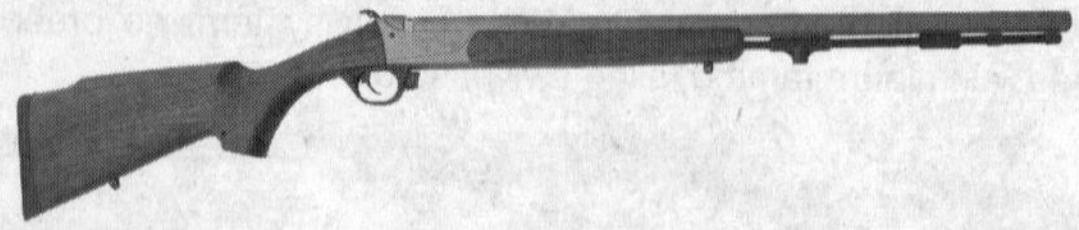

NIB	Exc.	V.G.	Good	Fair	Poor
390	330	280	240	200	170

Pursuit G4 Limited Edition Lady Whitetail Youth Model

.50 cal 24" Barrel Hot Leaf Camo/Tactical Grey CeraKote RY22-7255418 G4 Ultralight platform in in Hot Leaf Camo. Released 2016.

NIB	Exc.	V.G.	Good	Fair	Poor
300	260	220	180	160	130

Pursuit G4 Ultralight R7492421NS

.50 cal., nitride finish, Realtree Edge camo. Add factory-mounted and bore-sighted 3-9x40mm range finding scope and carrying case, +$110, No. R5-7411416DC.

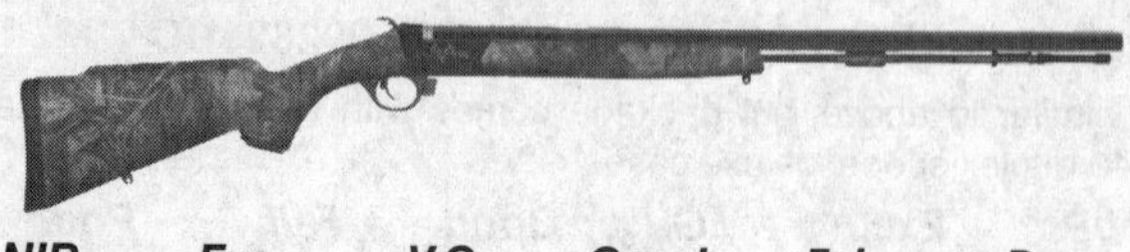

NIB	Exc.	V.G.	Good	Fair	Poor
340	290	250	210	180	150

Pursuit G4 Ultralight Northwest Magnum .50 cal Black/CeraKote

Designed for hunters in the Northwestern part of the United States. Exposed musket nipple and Williams metal fiber optic sights to meet state-specific regulations. No. R741140WA. Realtree Edge camo, +$60, R7492421WA.

NIB	Exc.	V.G.	Good	Fair	Poor
280	240	200	170	150	120

Buckstalker Series

24" 50-cal. Finishes include Black/Blued (R72003540), Black/CeraKote (R72103540, add $35), Vista Camo/CeraKote (R72103547, add $60). Scope packages also available, add $40. Northwest package (R72113547WA), +80.

NIB	Exc.	V.G.	Good	Fair	Poor
190	160	140	120	100	80

Evolution Series

24" 50-cal. inline slide bolt-action muzzleloader, fluted barrel, CeraKote finish. Comes with both 209 and musket ignition systems. Finishes include Black/Blued (R44003470), Black/CeraKote (R67113350), and Realtree AP Camo/CeraKote R67113353.

NIB	Exc.	V.G.	Good	Fair	Poor
170	140	120	100	80	70

SIDELOCKS

Classic line includes Hawken Woodsman, Kentucky Rifle, Pennsylvania Rifle, Crockett Rifle, Mountain Rifle, Prairie Hawken Rifle, and Classic Musket.

Hawken Woodsman

.50-cal., 28" octagonal blued barrel, Percussion and flintlock models, hooked breech, click-adjustable rear hunting sight, double-set triggers, oversized glove-fitting triggerguard with finger rest, inletted solid brass patch box. 44.5" in length, 7.9 lbs. Select hardwood stock, No. R24008. Add $30 for flintlock, No. R2390801.

NIB	Exc.	V.G.	Good	Fair	Poor
400	340	290	250	210	180

Kentucky Rifle

50-cal., 33.5" blued barrel with percussion or flintlock ignition system. 1:66" twist, single trigger, fixed/blade sights, select hardwood stock. Percussion select hardwood/blued No. R2020; Add $40 for flintlock, No. R2010.

NIB	Exc.	V.G.	Good	Fair	Poor
370	320	270	230	190	160

Pennsylvania Rifle

.50-cal., 40.25" blued barrel with percussion ignition system, 1:66" twist. Authentic for re-enactment use per the American Revolutionary Brigade. Full-length walnut stock with cheekpiece, solid brass patch box, stock inlay ornamentation and toe plate. Double-set triggers. Adjustable primitive style rear sight. Percussion No. R2100; flintlock, No. R2090.

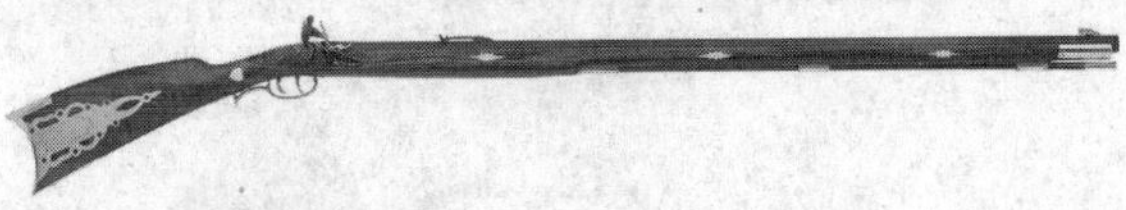

NIB	Exc.	V.G.	Good	Fair	Poor
750	640	540	460	390	330

Crockett Rifle Hardwood/Blued R26128101

.32 cal., 32" blued barrel with percussion ignition system, 1:48" twist. Based off "Old Betsy." Small game gun, half-stocked .32 caliber. Brass inlays, percussion lock and octagonal barrel.

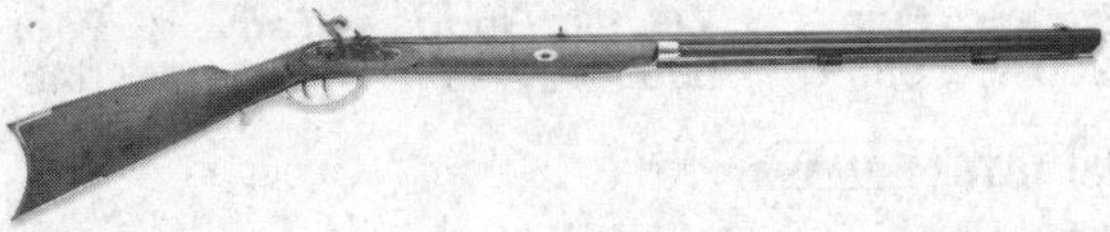

NIB	Exc.	V.G.	Good	Fair	Poor
410	350	300	250	210	180

Mountain Rifle

Caliber: .50. Barrel: 32 in., octagon with brown Cerakote finish. Stock: Select hardwoods. Sights: Primitive, adjustable rear. Weight: 8.25 lbs. Features: Available in percussion or flintlock, case-hardened lock, wooden ramrod, available as a kit.

NIB	Exc.	V.G.	Good	Fair	Poor
500	420	350	300	260	220

Prairie Hawken Rifle R2190

.50-cal. 28" blued barrel, 1:48" twist. Based on rifles used during the Rocky Mountain Fur Trading era. Two-Tenon sidelock rifle, double-set trigger, black chrome finish on silver furniture, blued finish on steel furniture. Custom two-piece forend cap and silver inlays on mortise area and buttstock. 14.5" LOP. No. R2170 is percussion ignition, price below; R2190 is flintlock (+$50).

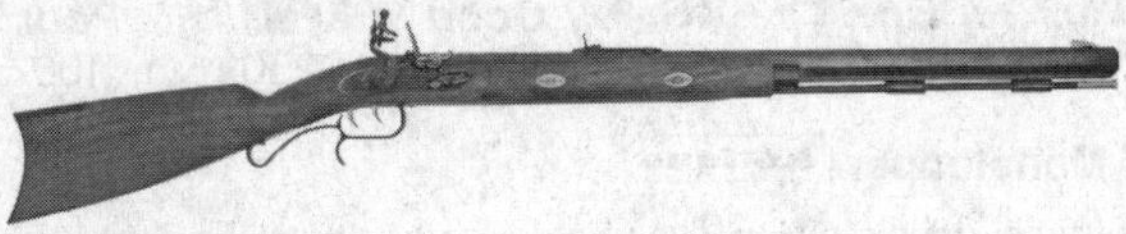

MUSKET RIFLES

Premium metal and wood finishes, including hand-oiled wood stocks. These muzzleloaders are authentic, true reproductions. Available in .58 or .69 calibers and approved by the North-South Skirmish Association (N-SSA).

1863 Zouave Musket Rifle .58 Cal Rifled R186306

1863 Zouave Musket Rifle .58 Cal Rifled R186306

NIB	Exc.	V.G.	Good	Fair	Poor
1020	870	740	630	540	460

1861 Springfield Musket .58 cal Rifled R186100

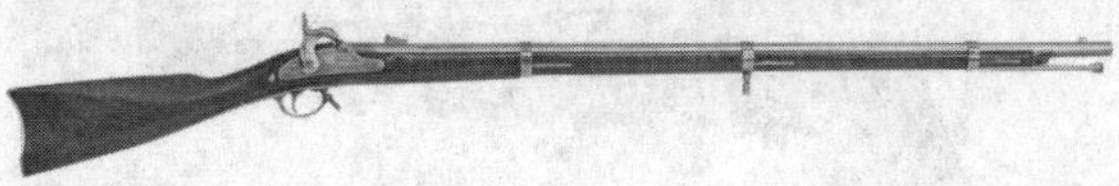

NIB	Exc.	V.G.	Good	Fair	Poor
800	680	580	490	420	360

1853 Enfield Musket Rifle .58 Cal Rifled R185303

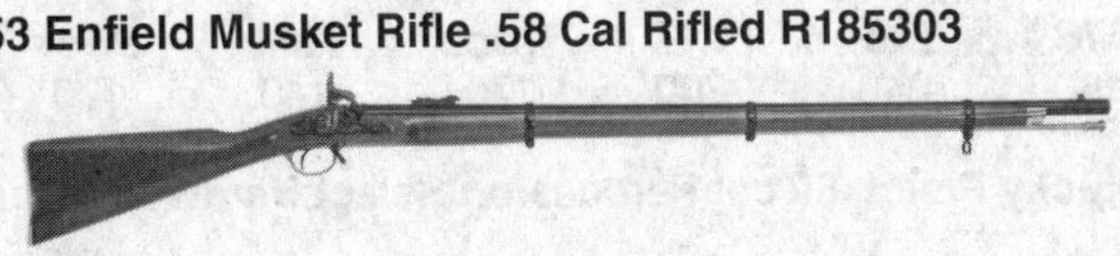

NIB	Exc.	V.G.	Good	Fair	Poor
900	760	650	550	470	400

1842 Springfield Musket .69 Cal Rifled R184205

NIB	Exc.	V.G.	Good	Fair	Poor
1020	870	740	630	540	460

PISTOLS

Vest Pocket Derringer .31 cal. Simulated Ivory/Brass P1381

.31-Cal., 2.25" round brass barrel. Percussion cap ignition system, simulated ivory stock. Weighs 0.75 pounds, 4.75" long. Bead sights.

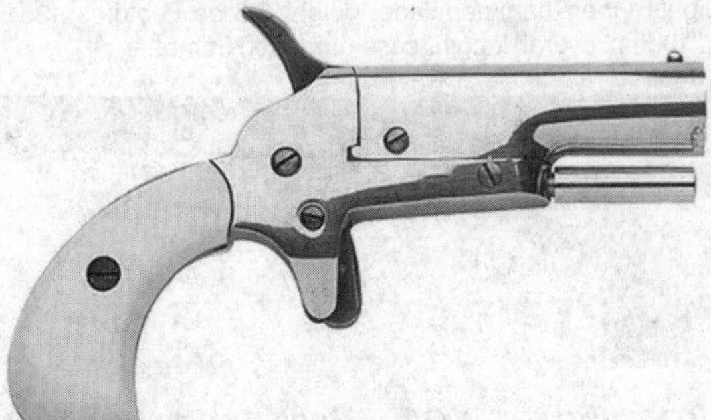

NIB	Exc.	V.G.	Good	Fair	Poor
180	150	130	110	90	80

Trapper Pistol .50 cal Select Hardwood/Blued

.50-cal, 9.75" blued octagonal barrel. Percussion and Flintlock models. Primitive-style adjustable rear sight, double-set triggers capable of firing set or unset. 15.5" in length. Percussion model is P1100, price below. Flintlock is No. P1090, +$35.

NIB	Exc.	V.G.	Good	Fair	Poor
280	240	200	170	140	120

Kentucky Pistol .50 cal Percussion Select Hardwood/Blued P1060

.50-cal, 10" blued octagonal barrel, 1:20 twist. Made famous by the battle of New Orleans and favored by Davey Crockett. Bird's head grip, engraved lock plate, fixed sight, case colored sidelock and brass ramrod thimbles. 15" in length. 2.4 lbs.

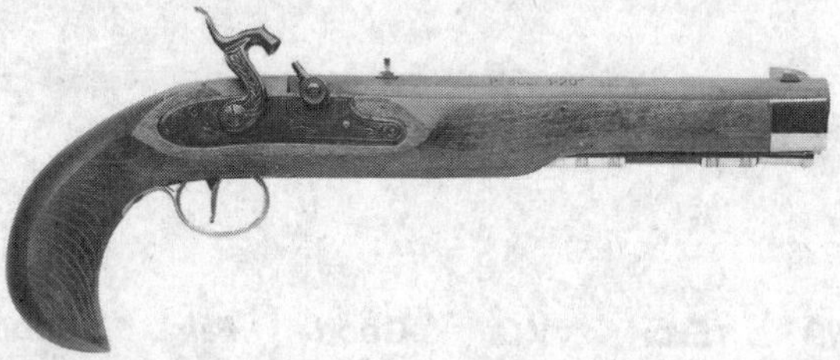

NIB	Exc.	V.G.	Good	Fair	Poor
210	180	150	130	110	90

U.S. Marshal

Caliber: .36, 6-shot. Barrel: 8 in., blued. Grips: One-piece walnut. Sights: Open, hammer/blade. Weight: 2.61 lbs. Features: Case-hardened frame, single action, U.S. Marshal logo on grips.

NIB	Exc.	V.G.	Good	Fair	Poor
350	—	—	—	—	—

Wildcard

Caliber: .36, 6-shot. Barrel: 7.375 in., blued octagon. Grips: Simulated stag. Sights: Open, hammer/blade. Weight: 2.5 lbs. Features: 1851 "Gunfighter," 13.5-in. overall length, case-hardened frame.

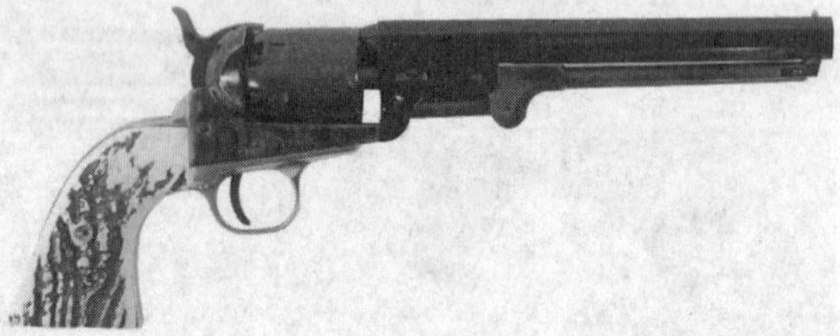

NIB	Exc.	V.G.	Good	Fair	Poor
400	—	—	—	—	—

TRANTER, WILLIAM

Birmingham, England

William Tranter produced a variety of revolvers on his own. A number of other makers produced revolvers based upon his designs. Consequently, "Tranter's Patent" is to be found on revolvers made by such firms as Deane, Adams and Deane, etc. Tranter was a significant and influential gunmaker. With the British practice of including patent markings and distributor names on guns in addition to (or instead of) the actual manufacturer, identification can be confusing. We have attempted to expand the Tranter listings to include some important and interesting Tranter-marked products. Values on these new listings are generally speculative. Reader input, corrections, and suggestions are most welcome. Also see DEANE, ADAMS, & DEANE listings.

Model 1872 Antique

A .38-caliber double-action revolver, with 6" octagonal barrel and 6-shot cylinder. Blued, with walnut grips.

Courtesy Wallis & Wallis, Lewes, Sussex, England

Exc.	Fine	V.G.	Good	Fair	Poor
2200	980	690	400	200	140

Model 1878 Antique

A .450-caliber double-action revolver, with 6" octagonal barrel. Blued, with walnut grip, solid-frame. Manufactured from 1878 to 1887.

Exc.	Fine	V.G.	Good	Fair	Poor
3000	2250	1700	1200	500	250

Double-trigger percussion revolver Antique

Unusual design with one trigger to rotate the cylinder and cock the hammer and a second to fire the revolver, with the cocking trigger extending below the triggerguard. Various sizes, calibers, and configurations are known, including models with and without hammer spurs. Generally larger calibers bring more than smaller. Premium for New Orleans distributor markings or other indications of possible confederate use.

Exc.	Fine	V.G.	Good	Fair	Poor
7000	4000	3000	2000	900	400

54 Bore Percussion Revolver

Double-action single-trigger five-shot percussion revolver, .443 caliber, 6" oct. barrel.

NIB	Exc.	V.G.	Good	Fair	Poor
4000	2000	1200	750	400	200

Spur-trigger Pocket Revolver Antique

Solid-frame single-action brass-frame .23 cal. revolver.

Exc.	Fine	V.G.	Good	Fair	Poor
2000	1000	700	400	250	100

.577 Manstopper Antique

Solid-frame double-action five-shot revolver chambered for the .577 Manstopper cartridge with removable backing plate at the rear of the cylinder to support the massive cartridge. Rare, few sales, values very speculative. In 2020, Rock Island Auction sold one in excellent condition for $34,500.

Exc.	Fine	V.G.	Good	Fair	Poor
—	—	10000	—	—	—

Double-action Army & Navy revolver Antique

Large-frame top-break revolver caliber .450/455 manufactured 1878-1887.

Exc.	Fine	V.G.	Good	Fair	Poor
2000	1000	750	500	350	200

TRIPLETT & SCOTT/MERIDEN MANUFACTURING COMPANY

Meriden, Connecticut

Repeating Carbine (Antique)

A .50-caliber carbine, with 22" or 30" round barrel and 7-shot magazine located in the butt. Loaded by turning barrel until it comes in line with the magazine. Blued case-hardened, with walnut stock. Approximately 5,000 made in 1864 and 1865. Note: Add 20 percent for even scarcer 22" barrel version.

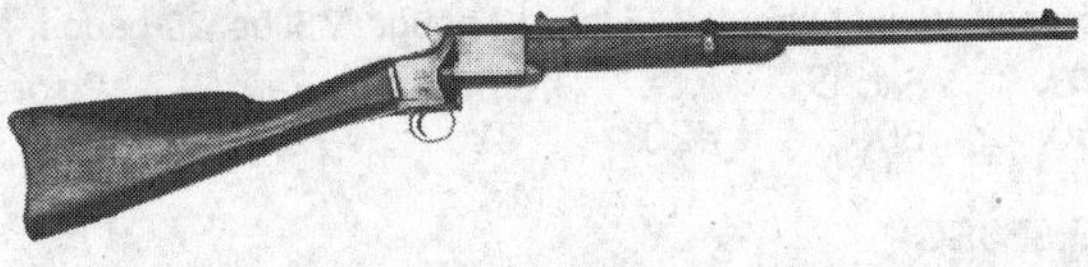

Courtesy Milwaukee Public Museum, Milwaukee, Wisconsin

Exc.	Fine	V.G.	Good	Fair	Poor
3500	1500	1000	500	200	140

TRISTAR SPORTING ARMS

N. Kansas City, Missouri

In 2000, Tristar bought American Arms. American Arms no longer exists, but some of its models will appear under Tristar name. For American Arms firearms built prior to sale, see that section.

SILVER SERIES

Series of over/under guns that were produced by Spanish company Zabala.

Silver Sporting

Offered in 12-gauge, with 28" or 30" barrels. Single-selective trigger, auto ejectors, choke tubes, ported barrels with target rib. Checkered walnut stock, with pistol grip and recoil pad.

NIB	Exc.	V.G.	Good	Fair	Poor
800	680	520	400	200	120

Specialty Magnums

A 12-gauge Magnum chambered for 3.5" shell. Fitted with 28" barrel. Choke tubes. Checkered black walnut stock, with pistol grip. In 2003, a camo finish was offered. Note: Add $85 for camo finish.

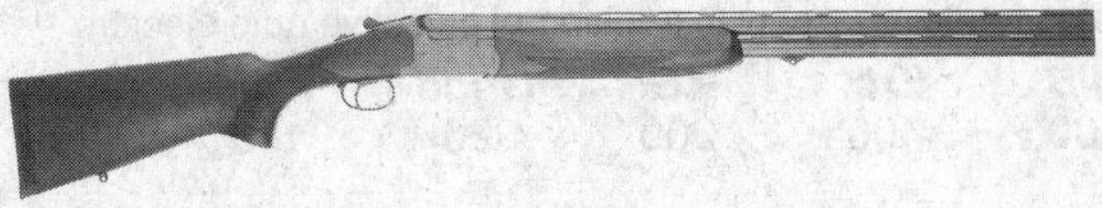

NIB	Exc.	V.G.	Good	Fair	Poor
640	500	400	300	200	100

Silver Hunter

Offered in both 12- and 20-gauge, with 26" or 28" ventilated rib barrels. Single-selective trigger, choke tubes, engraved receiver with silver finish. Checkered walnut stock, with pistol grip.

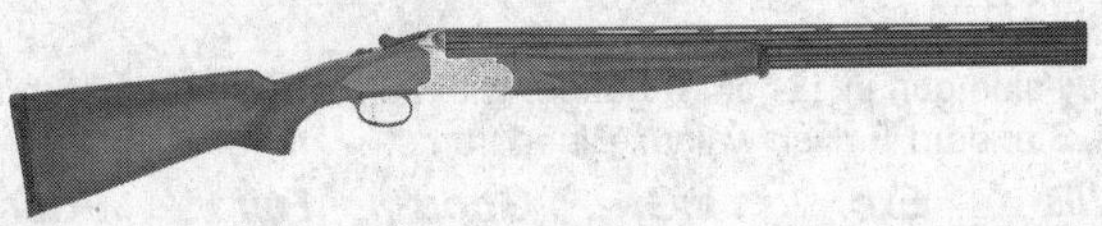

NIB	Exc.	V.G.	Good	Fair	Poor
620	500	400	300	200	100

Silver II

As above, with fixed chokes for 16-, 28-gauge and.410 bore models.

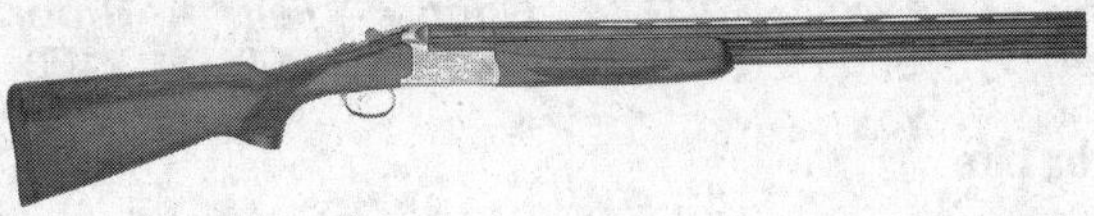

NIB	Exc.	V.G.	Good	Fair	Poor
670	520	420	320	220	120

Silver Classic

Offered in 12- and 20-gauge, with 28" ventilated rib barrels and choke tubes. Frame case colored and scroll engraved. Single-selective trigger and ejectors. Weight about 6.75 lbs.

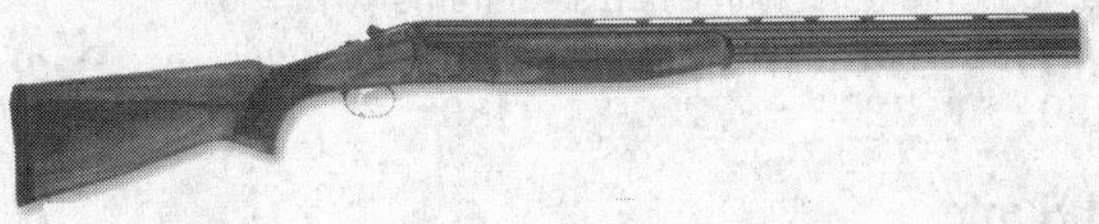

NIB	Exc.	V.G.	Good	Fair	Poor
800	650	500	400	300	180

BASQUE SERIES

Series of side-by-side shotguns. Introduced in 2003. Produced in Spain by Zabala.

Brittany Sporting

Offered in 12- and 20-gauge, with 28" barrels, 3" chambers and choke tubes. Action is boxlock, with sideplates scroll engraved with case coloring. Semi-fancy checkered walnut stock, with oil-finish and pistol grip. Semi-beavertail forend. Single-selective trigger and ejectors. Weight about 6.75 lbs.

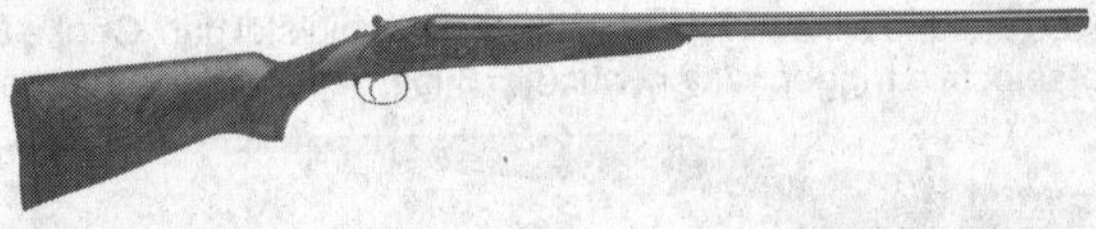

NIB	Exc.	V.G.	Good	Fair	Poor
850	750	600	400	300	150

Brittany

Features boxlock action, with case colored frame with scroll engraving. Straight-grip walnut stock, with semi-beavertail forend. Offered in 12-, 16-, 20-, 28-gauge and .410 bore, with 3" chambers and choke tubes. Weight 6.2 - 7.4 lbs. depending on gauge.

NIB	Exc.	V.G.	Good	Fair	Poor
900	800	650	450	300	200

Brittany Classic

Enhanced Brittany model. Features fancy walnut wood and rounded pistol grip, cut checkering, engraved case colored frame and auto selective ejectors. Available in 12-, 16-, 20-, 28-gauge and .410 bore, all with 3" chambers and 27" barrels. Weight about 6.7 lbs. in 12-gauge and slightly less in sub-gauges.

NIB	Exc.	V.G.	Good	Fair	Poor
1050	880	700	580	400	200

York

Side-by-side, with blued engraved receiver and 3" chambers. Comes in 12- and 20-gauge, with 26" or 28" barrels. Walnut pistol grip stock and rubber recoil pad.

NIB	Exc.	V.G.	Good	Fair	Poor
620	500	400	300	200	100

Hunter Lite

Over/under with silver alloy engraved frame, 3" chambers, extractors, choke tubes and walnut pistol grip stock and forearm. Weight: 20-gauge with 26" barrels 5.4 lbs.; 12-gauge with 28" barrels 6 lbs.

NIB	Exc.	V.G.	Good	Fair	Poor
450	320	220	180	100	80

Hunter

Similar to Hunter Lite, with blued steel frame.

NIB	Exc.	V.G.	Good	Fair	Poor
450	320	220	180	100	80

Field Hunter

Based on Hunter, this model includes selective auto ejectors and five choke tubes.

NIB	Exc.	V.G.	Good	Fair	Poor
580	450	320	250	150	100

Gentry/Gentry Coach

Offered in 12-, 16-, 20-, 28-gauge and .410 bore in Gentry and 12- and 20-gauge in Gentry Coach. Barrel lengths are 28" for Gentry (26" for 28-gauge and .410 bore) and 20" for Gentry Coach. Boxlock action, with engraved antique silver finish. Walnut stock, with pistol grip. Choke tubes. Single-selective trigger. Weight about 6.5 lbs. depending on gauge.

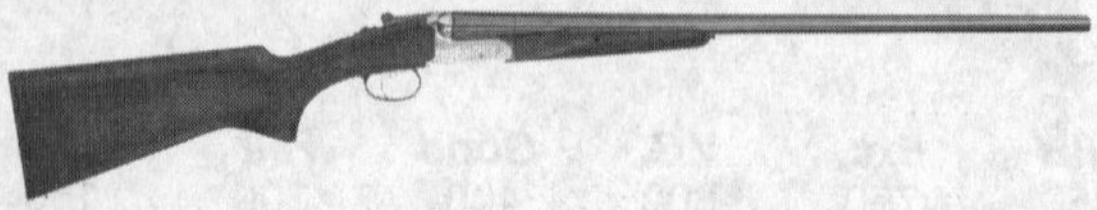

NIB	Exc.	V.G.	Good	Fair	Poor
750	620	500	400	250	100

Derby Classic

Features sidelock frame and action that is engraved and case colored. Offered in 12-gauge, with fixed chokes in Modified and Full. Fitted with 28" barrel. Double trigger and automatic ejectors. Weight about 7.75 lbs.

NIB	Exc.	V.G.	Good	Fair	Poor
1200	1000	800	650	450	200

TSA SERIES

These gas-operated semi-automatics are available in 12- and 20-gauge, with barrels from 24" to 26" depending on model.

TSA Field

Walnut forend and pistol grip stock, 3" chamber, 3 choke tubes and magazine-cut-off feature. Weight about 5.7 lbs. in 20-gauge; 6.5 lbs. in 12-gauge depending on barrel length. 20-gauge available in youth model.

NIB	Exc.	V.G.	Good	Fair	Poor
380	320	280	180	120	80

TSA Synthetic and Synthetic Mag

Same features as TSA Field Model, with non-glare black synthetic stock and forend. Also available with complete Realtree Max-4 coverage. Mag model has 3.5" chamber.

NIB	Exc.	V.G.	Good	Fair	Poor
380	320	280	180	120	80

300 SERIES

Tristar 300 series over/under guns were imported from Turkey.

Model 333

This over/under gun available in 12- or 20-gauge, with 26", 28" or 30" barrels in 12-gauge. Hand engraved frame. Fitted with 3" chambers and choke tubes. Single-selective triggers and auto ejectors. Fancy Turkish walnut stock. Weight about: 7.75 lbs. 12-gauge; 7.5 lbs. 20-gauge.

NIB	Exc.	V.G.	Good	Fair	Poor
650	600	420	320	220	150

Model 333SC

Similar to above model, with addition of 11mm sporting rib, recoil pad, forcing cones and ported barrels. Extended choke tubes.

NIB	Exc.	V.G.	Good	Fair	Poor
700	650	480	380	250	180

Model 333SCL

Same features as Model 333SC, with special stock.

NIB	Exc.	V.G.	Good	Fair	Poor
700	650	480	380	250	180

Model 333L

Same features as Model 333, with a special stock designed for women. Length of pull shorter, with special Monte Carlo comb.

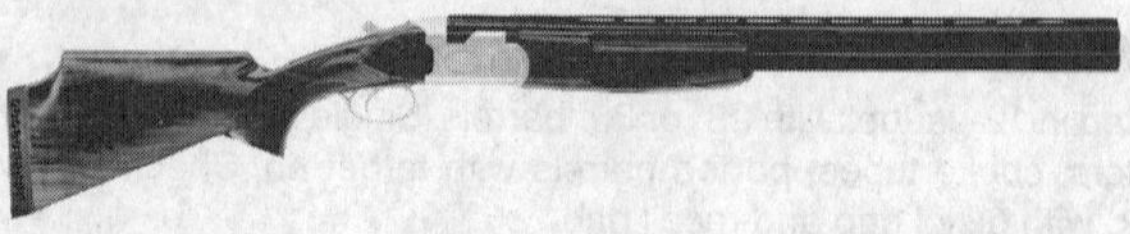

NIB	Exc.	V.G.	Good	Fair	Poor
650	600	420	320	220	150

Model 330

This over/under has a standard Turkish walnut stock, with etched engraved frame. Offered in 12- and 20-gauge. Single trigger, with extractors and fixed chokes.

NIB	Exc.	V.G.	Good	Fair	Poor
450	320	220	180	100	80

Model 330D

Same as model above, with addition of selective auto ejectors.

NIB	Exc.	V.G.	Good	Fair	Poor
500	400	300	220	180	100

Model 300

Features an underlug action lock, with double triggers and extractors. Frame is etched. Offered in 12-gauge only, with 26" or 28" barrels with fixed chokes.

NIB	Exc.	V.G.	Good	Fair	Poor
450	320	220	180	100	80

Model 311

Side-by-side gun in 12- or 20-gauge, with 26" or 28" barrels with choke tubes. Standard Turkish walnut. Blued frame.

NIB	Exc.	V.G.	Good	Fair	Poor
500	400	300	220	180	100

Model 311R

Same as above, with 20" barrel choked Cylinder and Cylinder.

NIB	Exc.	V.G.	Good	Fair	Poor
500	400	300	220	180	100

EMILIO RIZZINI (Old Nova Series)

Gun line no longer imported. Tristar Nova series were imported from Italy.

TR-L

Offered in 12- or 20-gauge, with choice of 28" or 30" ventilated rib barrels. Choke tubes standard. Standard grade walnut, with pistol grip. Action is silver finish boxlock, with auto ejectors and single-selective trigger. Weight about 7.5 lbs. Stock dimensions are made for a smaller shooter. Introduced in 1998.

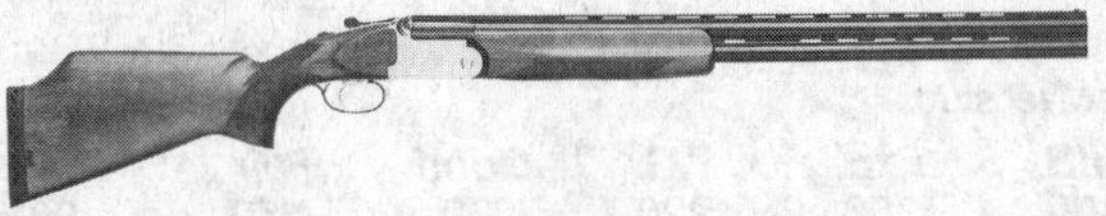

NIB	Exc.	V.G.	Good	Fair	Poor
1000	850	700	580	400	200

TR-SC

Similar to Nova L. Offered in 12-gauge only, with standard stock dimensions. Semi-fancy walnut stock, with pistol grip. Black sporting clays-style recoil pad. Weight between 7.5 and 8 lbs. depending on barrel length. Introduced in 1998.

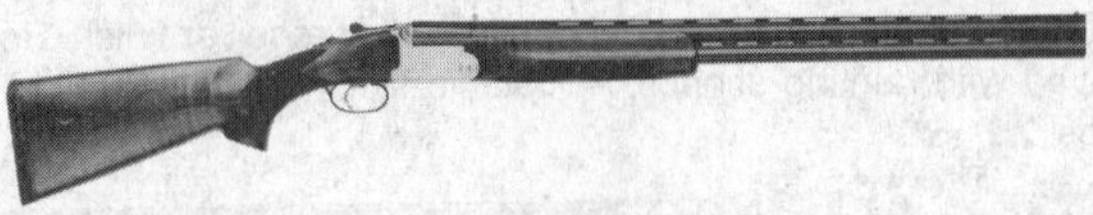

NIB	Exc.	V.G.	Good	Fair	Poor
1000	850	700	580	400	200

TR-I

Offered in 12- and 20-gauge, with 26" or 28" barrels with fixed chokes. Walnut stock, with hand-checkering and pistol grip. Beavertail forend. Boxlock action is blue, with single-selective trigger and extractors. Weight about 7.5 lbs. Introduced in 1998.

NIB	Exc.	V.G.	Good	Fair	Poor
650	600	420	320	220	150

TR-II (Nova II)

Same as above, but fitted with automatic ejectors.

NIB	Exc.	V.G.	Good	Fair	Poor
700	650	480	380	250	180

TR-Mag

Similar to the Nova I. Chambered for 10- and 12-gauge with 3.5" shell. Choice of 24" or 28" ventilated rib barrels, with choke tubes. Non-reflective non-glare blue finish. Introduced in 1998. Note: Add $175 for 12-gauge with ejectors; $350 for 10-gauge gun.

NIB	Exc.	V.G.	Good	Fair	Poor
750	650	480	380	250	180

TTR-Royal

Offered in 12-, 20- or 28-gauge, with 28" ported choke tube barrels, straight-grip semi-fancy walnut stock and auto ejectors. Silver receiver, with gold engraving.

NIB	Exc.	V.G.	Good	Fair	Poor
1300	1250	1100	880	600	300

TR-Class SL

Top-of-the-line model, with sculptured frame and engraved side plates. Offered in 12-gauge only.

NIB	Exc.	V.G.	Good	Fair	Poor
1780	1500	1250	1000	750	500

TT-15 Field & Sporting Models

Over-Under shotgun, 12 or 20 ga., available in 28 ga. or .410 ga. for $30 premium. Five choke tubes, top-tang selector and safety, ejectors, fiber-optic front sight, single selective trigger. Pricing is for TT-15 Field Model, add $75 for TT-15 Sporting Model.

NIB	Exc.	V.G.	Good	Fair	Poor
830	730	630	—	—	—

TT-15 Trap Models

Over-Under or single-barrel trap models with vent-rib barrels and adjustable stocks. Pricing is for Mono Trap base model. Available upgraded models, with premium to add to MSRP base price: Top Single, add $175; Unsingle, add $250; DT Adjustable double, add $325; CTA Double, add $750; CTA Deluxe double, add $1,135.

NIB	Exc.	V.G.	Good	Fair	Poor
1180	1000	850	—	—	—

Hunter Mag Camo

Gauge: 12 ga., 3.5 in. Barrels: 26 in., 28 in., 30 in., ventilated rib. Length: 44-48 in. Weight: 7.3-7.9 lbs. Stock: Synthetic, with choice of black or numerous Mossy Oak patterns. Features: The 3.5-inch magnum chambered Hunter Mag O/U expands with the addition of Cerakote/Mossy Oak combination models. Steel mono-block construction, extractors, rubber recoil pad, fiber-optic front sight, single selective trigger, chrome-lined barrel, swivel studs. Includes five Mobil-style choke tubes (SK, IC, M, IM, F).

NIB	Exc.	V.G.	Good	Fair	Poor
600	—	—	—	—	—

Trinity

Gauges: 12 ga., 3 in., 16 ga., 2.75 in., 20 ga., 3 in. Barrels: 26 in., 28 in., steel ventilated rib. Weight: 6.3-6.9 lbs. Length: 43.5-45.5 in. Stock: Oil-finished Turkish walnut with checkering. Features: The CNC-machined all-steel receiver Trinity wears 24-karat gold inlay on the silver-finish engraved receiver. Barrels are blued steel. Single selective trigger, red fiber-optic front sight, rubber buttpad, dual extractors. Includes five Beretta Mobil-style chokes (SK, IC, M, IM, F).

NIB	Exc.	V.G.	Good	Fair	Poor
620	—	—	—	—	—

Trinity LT

Gauges: 12 ga., 3 in., 20 ga., 3 in., 28 ga., 2.75 in., .410 bore, 3 in. Barrels: 26 in., 28 in, ventilated rib. Weight: 5.3-6.3 lbs. Length: 43.5-45.5 in. Stock: Oil-finished Turkish walnut with checkering. Features: The CNC-machined lightweight aluminum-alloy receiver Trinity LT is engraved and wears a silver finish. Barrels are blued steel. Single selective trigger, red fiber-optic front sight, rubber buttpad, dual extractors. Includes five Beretta Mobil-style chokes (SK, IC, M, IM, F).

NIB	Exc.	V.G.	Good	Fair	Poor
640	—	—	—	—	—

Setter

Over-Under shotgun, 12 or 20 ga., available in 28 ga. or .410 ga. for $30 premium. Five choke tubes, top-tang selector and safety, extractors, fiber-optic sight, single selective trigger.

NIB	Exc.	V.G.	Good	Fair	Poor
530	450	380	—	—	—

411 SERIES

Shotguns are made in Italy by R.F.M. Luciano Rota.

Model 411

Side-by-side double imported from Italy. Introduced in 1998. Chambered for 12-, 20-gauge and .410 bore, with choice of 26" or 28" barrels with choke tubes or fixed chokes. Boxlock action, with engraving and case coloring. Double triggers and extractors. Standard walnut stock, with pistol grip and splinter forearm. Weight between 6 and 6.5 lbs.

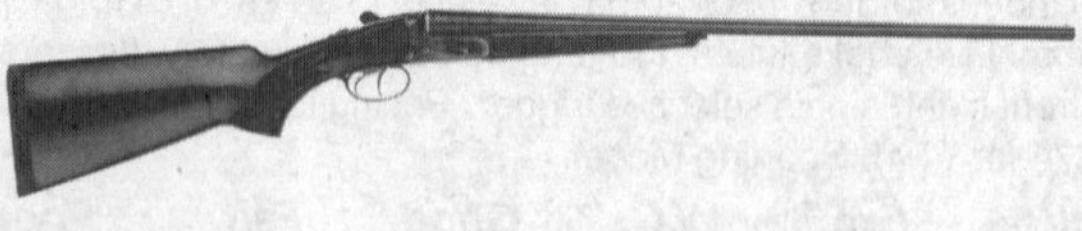

NIB	Exc.	V.G.	Good	Fair	Poor
850	680	500	380	250	150

Model 411R

Offered in 12- or 20-gauge, with 20" barrel. Fixed cylinder chokes. Extractors. Weight about: 6.5 lbs. 12-gauge; 6 lbs. 20-gauge.

NIB	Exc.	V.G.	Good	Fair	Poor
750	650	480	380	250	180

Model 411D

Similar to Model 411, with engraved case colored finish on receiver, auto ejectors, single trigger and straight-grip stock. Weight about: 28-gauge 6.25 lbs.; 12-gauge 7 lbs.

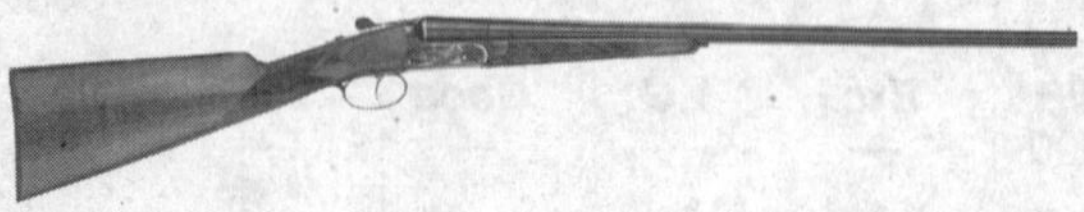

NIB	Exc.	V.G.	Good	Fair	Poor
1050	880	700	580	400	200

Model 411F

Same as Model 411D, with silver engraved receiver.

NIB	Exc.	V.G.	Good	Fair	Poor
1600	1400	1050	800	600	400

PHANTOM SERIES

Shotguns made in Turkey by Eqsilah. Discontinued in favor of new redesigned gun found under Diana Series.

Phantom Field

Gas-operated semi-automatic shotgun. Chambered for 12-gauge and 2.75" or 3" shell. Fitted with 24", 26" or 28" barrel. Checkered walnut stock, with pistol grip. Screw-in chokes. Five-round magazine. Note: Add $75 for Magnum models.

NIB	Exc.	V.G.	Good	Fair	Poor
420	320	280	200	150	100

Phantom Synthetic

Same as above, with synthetic stock. Note: Add $75 for Magnum models.

NIB	Exc.	V.G.	Good	Fair	Poor
400	300	220	200	150	80

Phantom HP

Same features as Phantom Field, except with synthetic stock, 19" barrel and swivel studs.

NIB	Exc.	V.G.	Good	Fair	Poor
400	300	220	200	150	80

BREDA SERIES

Semi-automatic shotguns are made in Italy by Breda. Guns first imported by Tristar in 2003.

Ermes

Chambered for 12-gauge 3" shell. Fitted with 26" or 28" ventilated rib barrel. Inertia operated recoil system. Checkered walnut stock, with pistol grip. Choice of black, nickel, gold or silver alloy receiver finish. Receiver engraved with hunting scenes. Adjustable stock spacers. Weight about 7.75 lbs.

Gold

NIB	Exc.	V.G.	Good	Fair	Poor
1940	1500	1250	1080	800	400

Silver

NIB	Exc.	V.G.	Good	Fair	Poor
1720	1350	1100	900	650	300

Nickel

NIB	Exc.	V.G.	Good	Fair	Poor
1650	1200	1050	750	500	300

Black

NIB	Exc.	V.G.	Good	Fair	Poor
1260	980	750	600	500	250

Astra 20

A 20-gauge, with 26" ventilated rib barrel. Black receiver. Walnut with pistol grip and solid rubber recoil pad. Furnished with five choke tubes. Weight about 6 lbs.

NIB	Exc.	V.G.	Good	Fair	Poor
1140	900	750	600	460	200

Mira Sporting

Semi-automatic shotgun is gas-operated. Chambered for 12-gauge shell, with 3" chamber. Fitted with 30" ventilated rib barrel, with 10mm wide rib. Checkered walnut stock, with pistol grip. Weight about 7 lbs.

NIB	Exc.	V.G.	Good	Fair	Poor
880	700	550	400	300	200

Mira Camo

As above, with 28" barrel and camo finish.

NIB	Exc.	V.G.	Good	Fair	Poor
880	700	550	400	300	200

Raptor

Semi-automatic line of 12 and 20-gauge shotguns. Gas-operated actions with 3-inch chambers. Field grade comes with three Beretta-style choke tubes, fiber optic front sight, molded stock with ventilated recoil pad. Camo stock available. Magazine capacity five rounds. Magazine cut-off allows shooter to clear chamber without loading another round. Add $80 for camo stock.

NIB	Exc.	V.G.	Good	Fair	Poor
350	300	260	220	200	150

Viper G2 Series

Gas-operated semi-auto series in 12, 20, 28 gauge or .410 bore. Offered in several model variations with synthetic or high-grade select Turkish walnut stock with cut checkering and high gloss finish. Choices for metal finish are blued, bronze (shown), silver or camo. Chrome-lined barrel has ventilated rib and five Beretta-style extended choke tubes. Five-shot magazine has manual cut-off to allow clearing chamber without loading another round. Prices shown are for synthetic stock model. Add $60 for wood or camo stock, $100 for silver finish, $225 for bronze, $275 for Sporting Model with adjustable stock. Add $25 to $35 for 28 gauge or .410 bore.

NIB	Exc.	V.G.	Good	Fair	Poor
450	400	380	320	280	220

Viper G2 Pro

Gauges: 12 ga., 20 ga., 28 ga., .410 bore. Barrels: 26", 28", (30" Snow Camo only). Stock: Depending on model, premium-select walnut (Pro Bronze), select walnut (Silver), synthetic (Camo). Features: Gas-operated autoloader with 3" chambers. Last shot bolt hold open. Rubber recoil pad. Chrome-lined chamber. Shim kits included. Fiber-optic front sight. Manual E-Z load magazine cutoff. Oversized controls. Triangular safety. Enlarged mag well. Ships with three Beretta/Benelli Mobil choke tubes.

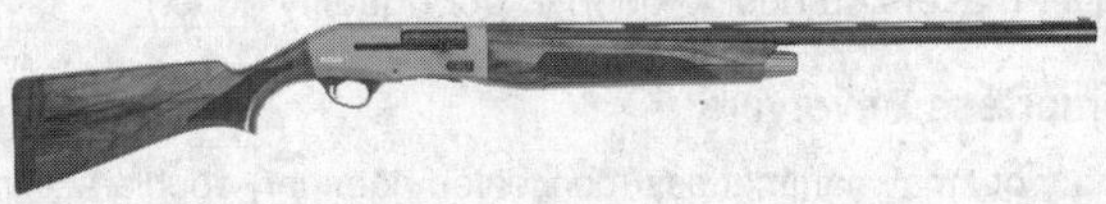

NIB	Exc.	V.G.	Good	Fair	Poor
800	720	—	—	—	—

COBRA PUMP-ACTION SHOTGUN SERIES

Pump shotguns in 12 or 20 ga. Values shown are for base Field or Tactical model with black synthetic stock. Field Model hunting upgrades, with additional price over base MSRP include: Max 5, add $60; Timber Turkey, camo, pistol grip, add $90; Walnut stock, add $30; Tactical model upgrades, with additional price over base MSRP include: Force with pistol grip, fiber optic, ghost ring, add $40; Marine, add $10.

NIB	Exc.	V.G.	Good	Fair	Poor
290	250	200	—	—	—

Cobra III Camo

Gauges: 12 ga., 3 in., 20 ga., 3 in. Barrels: 24 in., 26 in., 28 in., ventilated rib. Weight: 6.7-6.9 lbs. Length: 44.5-48.5 in. Stock: Synthetic camo with either Realtree Max-5 or Realtree Advantage Timber. Features: Third model upgrade to the Cobra pump action with extended forend. Solid rubber buttpad, cross-bolt safety, chrome-lined barrel, sling studs. Realtree camo coverage. Includes three Beretta Mobil-style choke tubes (IC, M, F).

NIB	Exc.	V.G.	Good	Fair	Poor
320	280	230	—	—	—

Cobra III Field

Gauges: 12 ga., 3 in., 20 ga., 3 in. Barrels: 26 in., 28 in., ventilated rib. Weight: 6.7-7.0 lbs. Length: 46.5-48.5 in. Stock: Field models available with either Turkish walnut or black synthetic furniture. Features: Third model upgrade to the Cobra pump-action line with extended forend. Rubber buttpad, cross-bolt safety, chrome-lined barrel, high-polish blue metalwork, sling studs. Includes three Beretta Mobil-style choke tubes (IC, M, F).

NIB	Exc.	V.G.	Good	Fair	Poor
280	240	200	—	—	—

Cobra III Youth

Gauge: 20 ga., 3 in. Barrel: 24 in., ventilated rib. Weight: 5.4-6.5 lbs. Length: 37.7 in. Stock: Version III youth models available with black synthetic, Realtree Max-5 camo or Turkish-walnut furniture. Features: Third iteration of the Cobra pump-action with extended forend. Ventilated rubber buttpad, cross-bolt safety, chrome-lined barrel, sling studs. Shorter length of pull on Youth model. Includes three Beretta Mobil-style choke tubes (IC, M, F).

NIB	Exc.	V.G.	Good	Fair	Poor
280	230	200	—	—	—

CD DIANA SERIES

Shotguns made in Turkey by Eqsilah. This line replaced Phantom Series. First imported by Tristar in 2003.

CD Diana Field

Gas-operated semi-automatic shotgun. Chambered for 12-gauge 3" shell. Fitted with 26", 28" or 30" ventilated rib barrel. Checkered walnut stock, with pistol grip. Choke tubes. Magazine cutoff. Weight about 7 lbs. depending on barrel length.

NIB	Exc.	V.G.	Good	Fair	Poor
420	320	280	200	150	100

CD Diana Synthetic

As above, with black synthetic stock. Also offered with 3.5" chamber. Weight about 6.75 lbs. Note: Add $90 for 3.5" Magnum model.

NIB	Exc.	V.G.	Good	Fair	Poor
400	300	250	200	150	100

CD Diana Slug

12-gauge gun fitted with 24" rifled slug barrel, with open adjustable sights. Black synthetic stock. Weight about 6.75 lbs.

NIB	Exc.	V.G.	Good	Fair	Poor
420	320	280	200	150	100

CD Diana Camo Mag

Similar to models above, with camo stock and barrel. Choice of 24" or 28" barrel, with 3.5" chamber. Weight about 6.75 lbs.

NIB	Exc.	V.G.	Good	Fair	Poor
580	450	350	220	180	100

Pee Wee

Single-shot bolt-action rifle chambered for .22 LR cartridges. Stock is walnut and about 1/2 the size of an adult rifle. Weight about 2.75 lbs. Open sights. Finish is blue.

NIB	Exc.	V.G.	Good	Fair	Poor
200	150	100	80	50	20

KRX Tactical

Semi-auto five-round box-fed 12-ga. shotgun in AR configuration, 20" barrel, 7.4 lbs.

NIB	Exc.	V.G.	Good	Fair	Poor
500	430	380	—	—	—

Compact Tactical

Similar to above, but in bullpup configuration, 8.6 lbs.

NIB	Exc.	V.G.	Good	Fair	Poor
700	630	580	—	—	—

Bristol

Gauge: 12 ga. 3 in., 16 ga., 20 ga. 3 in., 28 ga. 2.75 in., .410 bore 3 in. Barrels: 28 in. Weight: 5.08–6.74 lbs. Stock: Select Turkish Walnut with oil finish, English style. Features: Side-by-side double available in four gauges, each built on a true steel frame. Laser engraved detail. Features an English-style straight stock paired with case colored receiver. Dual purpose tang safety/barrel selector. Auto-ejectors, brass front sight, single selective trigger. Chrome-lined chamber and barrel. Includes five Beretta-style choke tubes (SK, IC, M, IM, F).

NIB	Exc.	V.G.	Good	Fair	Poor
930	800	680	—	—	—

Bristol Silver

Gauge: 12 ga. 3 in., 16 ga., 20 ga. 3 in., 28 ga. 2.75 in., .410 bore 3 in. Barrels: 28 in. Weight: 5.08–6.74 lbs. Stock: Select Turkish Walnut with oil finish, English style. Features: Side-by-side double available in four gauges, each built on a true steel frame. Laser engraved detail. Features an English-style straight stock paired with case colored receiver. Dual purpose tang safety/barrel selector. Auto-ejectors, brass front sight, single selective trigger. Chrome-lined chamber and barrel. Includes five Beretta-style choke tubes (SK, IC, M, IM, F).

NIB	Exc.	V.G.	Good	Fair	Poor
890	750	650	—	—	—

LEVER-ACTION SERIES

LR94

Gauges: .410 bore. Barrels: 22", 24". Stock: Turkish Walnut, checkered and oil finished. Features: The company's first lever-action firearm. Top safety, blade/bead front sight and rifle-style rear sight. 2.5" chamber. Side-loading gate and tubular magazine. Leather-wrapped lever. Accepts CT-1 interchangeable choke tubes. Choice of three finish options. Add 10% for case color/walnut, and 7.5% for nickel/walnut.

NIB	Exc.	V.G.	Good	Fair	Poor
920	800	—	—	—	—

HANDGUNS

C, P, S, & T Series Pistols

TriStar offers a diverse series of semi-auto traditional double-action pistol models based on the CZ 75 design. TriStar reports that they produce for 25 militaries across the world. Pricing is similar for most models. Add $20 to $40 for finishes other than black. Models: C100 – 9mm, 3.9" barrel, 1.7 lbs., 15 rounds; P100 – 9mm or .40 S&W, 3.9", 2.3 lbs., 15 rds.; P120 – 9mm, 4.7", 2.5 lbs., 19 rds.; S120 – 9mm, 4.7", 2.3 lbs., 17 rds.; T100 – 9mm, 3.9", 1.6 lbs., 15 rds.; T120 – 9mm, 4.7", 1.8 lbs, 17 rds.

NIB	Exc.	V.G.	Good	Fair	Poor
430	380	330	—	—	—

American Classic II 1911

Calibers: 9mm, 10mm, or .45 ACP. Capacity: 7-round (.45 ACP) or 9-round (9mm) magazine. Barrel: 4.25 or 5 in. Grips: Checkered wood. Sights: Ramp front, low-profile rear. Length: 8.5 in. overall. Weight: 39.5 oz. unloaded. Finish: Hard chrome or blued.

NIB	Exc.	V.G.	Good	Fair	Poor
800	—	—	—	—	—

TROCALOA ARANZABAL y CIA (TAC)

Eibar, Spain

The Aranzabals began arms production around 1883, continuing as Trocaloa, Aranzabal y Cia from 1895 to 1937. Along with Orbea Hermanos and Garate Anitua, TAC was a maker of quality copies of American revolver design in the Eibar region (along with many smaller makers producing good to poor quality guns.)

Hammerless Revolvers

A variety of small hammerless (concealed hammer) double-action-only revolvers with manual safety levers on the left side of frame. Most common configuration for TAC is probably top-break in 6mm with an 8- to 10-round capacity and a fixed triggerguard (contrasting to most velo-dog revolvers which typically had folding triggers.) TAC model markings included Velomith and Velo Smith among others, usually with intertwined TA logo hard rubber grips.

NIB	Exc.	V.G.	Good	Fair	Poor
—	500	250	200	100	50

Russian Model

Copy of the S&W Russian Model 6-shot top-break single-action in .44 Russian. Most TAC Russians have a shorter ejector housing than the S&W originals, more like the New Model No. 3. They retain the trigger-guard spur and the extreme knuckle backstrap of the S&W originals.

NIB	Exc.	V.G.	Good	Fair	Poor
—	2000	650	1000	350	200

Double Action Top-Break

Like the S&W .44 DA model, most chambered for .44 Russian, but also manufactured in .455 for England during WWI (worth premium). Values shown are for the large-frame .44 size revolvers. These are also reported in smaller frame .32- and .38-caliber sizes, and values for those might be about half of what the large revolvers bring.

NIB	Exc.	V.G.	Good	Fair	Poor
—	1000	700	500	250	100

Hand Ejector Revolvers

Also marketed as "Imitacion S&W y Colt," these are medium-frame double-action swing-out cylinder revolvers based on early 20th-century contemporary models by Smith & Wesson and Colt. They are often found with a circular thumb latch. Most common caliber is .32 S&W. Also made in 8mm Lebel for France during WWI, sometimes called "Model 92s" or "Spanish 92s" after the Lebel Model 92 revolver and nicknamed "Marcel." These military models are worth a premium.

NIB	Exc.	V.G.	Good	Fair	Poor
—	500	230	150	80	50

TRYON, EDWARD K. & COMPANY

Philadelphia, Pennsylvania

Pocket Pistol (Antique)

A .41-caliber single-shot percussion pocket pistol, with 2" or 4" barrel, German silver mounts and walnut stock. Lock marked "Tryon/Philada". Manufactured during 1860s and 1870s.

Exc.	Fine	V.G.	Good	Fair	Poor
2550	1900	1320	750	200	140

TUCKER SHERRARD & COMPANY

Lancaster, Texas

Dragoon (Antique)

A .44-caliber percussion revolver, with 7.75" round barrel. Fitted with loading lever and 6-shot cylinder. Barrel marked "Clark, Sherard & Co., Lancaster, Texas". Cylinder etched in two panels, with crossed cannons and legend "Texas Arms". Approximately 400 revolvers of this type were made between 1862 and 1867. Prospective purchasers are advised to secure a qualified appraisal prior to acquisition. Some sources report that there are only four known surviving examples. Values are extremely speculative.

Exc.	Fine	V.G.	Good	Fair	Poor
100000	—	70000	—	—	—

TUFTS & COLLEY

New York, New York

Pocket Pistol (Antique)

A .44-caliber single-shot percussion pocket pistol, with 3.5" barrel, German silver mounts and walnut stock. Lock marked "Tufts & Colley"; barrel "Deringer/Pattn.". Manufactured during 1860s. Seldom sold; values are very speculative. Only recently reported sale was an excellent example for $625, which seems low for the type.

Exc.	Fine	V.G.	Good	Fair	Poor
—	—	500	—	—	—

TURBIAUX, JACQUES

Paris, France

See—AMES

TURNER, THOMAS

Redding, England

Pepperbox (Antique)

A .476 double-action percussion pepperbox having 6 barrels. Blued case-hardened, with walnut grips. Left side of frame engraved in an oval "Thomas Turner, Redding". Turner was probably better known as a maker of double shotguns. His pepperboxes rarely come on the market, values are very speculative.

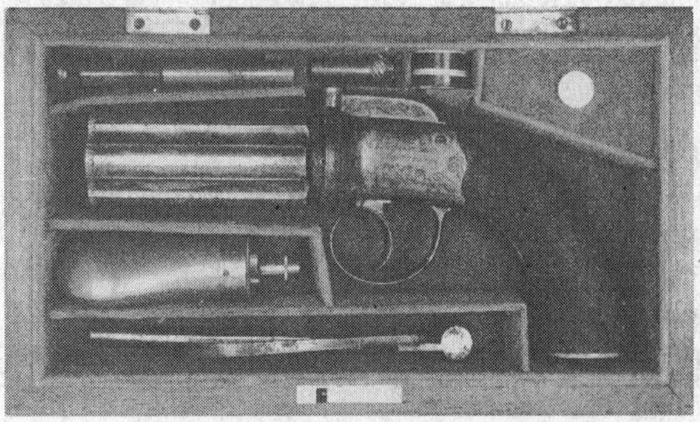

Courtesy Bonhams & Butterfields, San Francisco, California

Exc.	Fine	V.G.	Good	Fair	Poor
5500	1900	1440	980	400	280

TYLER ORDNANCE WORKS

Tyler, Texas

This company produced 56 Austrian rifles, 508 Enfield rifles, 423 Hill rifles and 1,009 Texas rifles during the Civil War. NOTE: These rifles are very rare. Expert evaluation recommended, values listed are speculative.

Tyler Texas Rifle (Antique)

A .57-caliber single-shot rifle, with 27" barrel and full stock secured by two barrel bands. Lock marked "Texas Rifle/Tyler/Cal. .57".

Exc.	Fine	V.G.	Good	Fair	Poor
—	—	25000	—	—	—

Hill Rifle (Antique)

A .54-caliber single-shot percussion rifle, with 27" barrel and full stock secured by two brass barrel bands. Iron triggerguard and buttplate. Lock marked "Hill Rifle/Tyler/Tex/ Cal. .54".

Exc.	Fine	V.G.	Good	Fair	Poor
—	—	20000	—	—	—

U

U.S. ARMS CO.

Riverhead, New York

See—UNITED SPORTING ARMS, INC.

U.S. M1 CARBINE

Various Manufacturers

For history, technical data, descriptions, photos and prices, see *Standard Catalog of Military Firearms* under United States Rifles. Prices listed are for rifles in original, unaltered condition. NOTE: Rifles that have been refinished or restored deduct about 50 percent.

M1 Carbine

For M1 Carbine copies and rebuilds, also see: Arlington Ordnance, Auto Ordnance, IAI, Iver Johnson, Miltech, Plainfield Machine Co. and United States Small Arms Company.

Inland

NIB	Exc.	V.G.	Good	Fair	Poor
2000	1800	1200	600	420	350

Underwood

NIB	Exc.	V.G.	Good	Fair	Poor
2000	1800	1250	550	400	280

S.G. Saginaw

NIB	Exc.	V.G.	Good	Fair	Poor
2000	1800	1400	700	450	380

IBM

NIB	Exc.	V.G.	Good	Fair	Poor
2200	1900	1500	1000	500	250

Quality Hardware

NIB	Exc.	V.G.	Good	Fair	Poor
2000	1700	1100	520	380	250

National Postal Meter

NIB	Exc.	V.G.	Good	Fair	Poor
2100	1800	1100	580	380	250

Standard Products

NIB	Exc.	V.G.	Good	Fair	Poor
2150	1900	1200	600	420	250

Rockola

NIB	Exc.	V.G.	Good	Fair	Poor
2400	2000	1400	750	480	350

SG Grand Rapids

NIB	Exc.	V.G.	Good	Fair	Poor
2400	2000	1400	600	420	350

Winchester

NIB	Exc.	V.G.	Good	Fair	Poor
2500	2200	1700	1100	600	380

Irwin Pedersen

NIB	Exc.	V.G.	Good	Fair	Poor
4200	3500	2500	1300	800	500

M1 Carbine Cutaway

NIB	Exc.	V.G.	Good	Fair	Poor
—	2500	1500	900	600	500

M1 Carbine Sniper with infra red conversion

NIB	Exc.	V.G.	Good	Fair	Poor
—	1450	1000	800	400	300

U.S. M1 A1 Paratrooper Model

NIB	Exc.	V.G.	Good	Fair	Poor
—	4500	3500	2500	1250	750

U.S. ORDNANCE

Reno, Nevada

Models listed are machined to military specifications and semi-automatic only.

M-60

7.62mm belt-fed semi-automatic weapon. Modeled after famous machine gun used in Vietnam. Fitted with 22" barrel. Weight about 24 lbs.

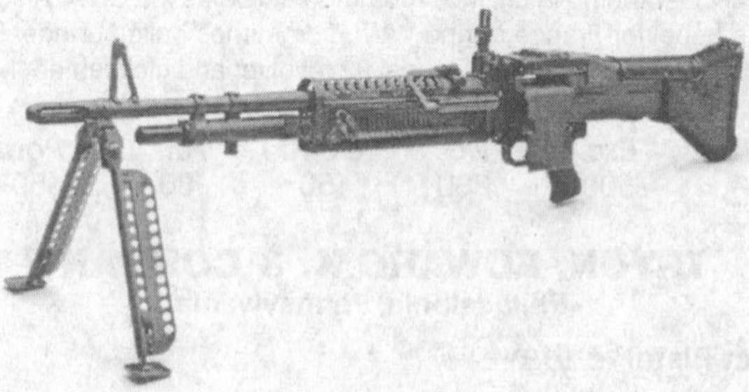

NIB	Exc.	V.G.	Good	Fair	Poor
10000	8900	7000	5500	4000	2500

M-60E3

Shorter more lightweight version of standard M-60. Fitted with 17" barrel. Weight about 18 lbs.

NIB	Exc.	V.G.	Good	Fair	Poor
8900	7000	5500	4000	3000	1750

Browning Model 1919

Belt-fed model chambered for 7.62mm/.30-06 cartridges. Fitted with 23" barrel. Weight about 30 lbs. Prices listed are for gun only. Note: Add $125 for A6 stock, bipod and carry handle; $450 for A4 tripod.

Model 1919 with A4 tripod

NIB	Exc.	V.G.	Good	Fair	Poor
2800	2400	1900	1500	1200	900

Vickers

Chambered for .303 cartridge and belt-fed. Weight about 40 lbs. Prices listed are for gun only. Note: Add $500 for tripod.

NIB	Exc.	V.G.	Good	Fair	Poor
4800	4000	3000	2200	1700	900

U.S. REPEATING ARMS CO.

See—WINCHESTER

U.S. REVOLVER CO.

See—IVER JOHNSON

UBERTI, ALDO/UBERTI USA

Ponte Zanano, Italy

Company manufactures high-grade reproductions of famous Western-style American firearms. Their products have been imported over the years by a number of different companies. They produce both blackpowder guns and cartridge firearms that are included in this section. This Italian manufacturer builds high quality firearms of the American West. Featured are Colt, Winchester and Remington. Each importer stamps its name on the firearm in addition to Uberti address. In 2000, Beretta Holding Company purchased Uberti.

Paterson Revolver

Exact copy of famous and rare Colt pistol. Offered in .36-caliber, with engraved 5-shot cylinder. Barrel is 7.5" long and octagonal forward of lug. Frame and backstrap are case-hardened steel. Grips are one-piece walnut. Overall length 11.5"; weight about 2.5 lbs.

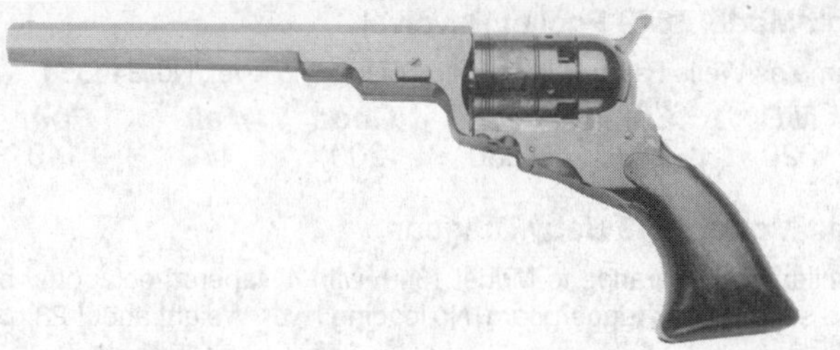

NIB	Exc.	V.G.	Good	Fair	Poor
500	420	360	310	260	220

1847 Walker Colt Revolver

Faithful reproduction of famous and highly sought-after Colts. Caliber .44; round barrel 9" long. Frame case-hardened steel. Triggerguard brass. 6-shot cylinder engraved with fighting dragoon scene. Grip, one-piece walnut. Overall length 15.75"; weight a hefty 70 oz. Uberti Model No. 340200.

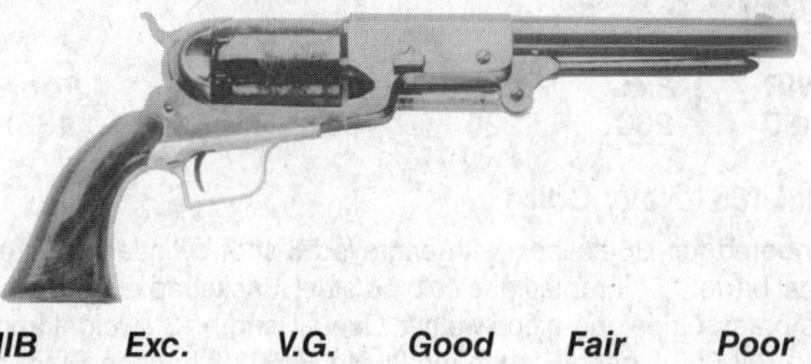

NIB	Exc.	V.G.	Good	Fair	Poor
370	320	270	230	190	160

Colt Whitneyville Dragoon

Transition Walker, reduced version of Model 1847 Walker. Fitted with 7.5" barrel. Chambered for .44-caliber. No. 340830.

NIB	Exc.	V.G.	Good	Fair	Poor
420	360	300	260	220	190

Colt 1st Model Dragoon Revolver

Shorter version of Walker. Evolved directly from that original design. A 6-shot .44-caliber, with 7.5" barrel. Frame color case-hardened steel. Backstrap and triggerguard brass. Grips one-piece walnut. Overall length 13.5"; weight about 63 oz. No. 340800.

NIB	Exc.	V.G.	Good	Fair	Poor
400	340	290	250	210	180

Colt 2nd Model Dragoon Revolver

Differs from 1st model in that cylinder bolt slot is square instead of oval. No. 340810.

NIB	Exc.	V.G.	Good	Fair	Poor
360	310	260	220	190	160

Colt 3rd Model Dragoon Revolver

Model varies from 2nd model as follows. No. 340860. Loading lever taper is inverted; loading lever latch hook is different shape; loading lever latch; backstrap steel and triggerguard brass oval; and frame is cut for shoulder stock.

NIB	Exc.	V.G.	Good	Fair	Poor
360	310	260	220	190	160

Colt Model 1849 Wells Fargo

No loading lever. Chambered for .31-caliber cartridge. Barrel is octagonal. Frame colored case-hardened steel. Backstrap and triggerguard brass. Cylinder engraved and holds 5 rounds. Grip one-piece walnut. Overall length 9.5"; weight 34 oz. No. 340380.

NIB	Exc.	V.G.	Good	Fair	Poor
350	300	250	220	180	160

Colt Model 1849 Pocket Revolver

Same as Wells Fargo, with addition of loading lever. No. 340350.

NIB	Exc.	V.G.	Good	Fair	Poor
320	270	230	200	170	140

Colt Model 1848 Baby Dragoon

Similar is appearance to Model 1849, with 4" tapered octagonal barrel and square back triggerguard. No loading lever. Weight about 23 oz.

NIB	Exc.	V.G.	Good	Fair	Poor
300	260	220	180	160	130

Model 1851 Navy Colt

Chambered for .36-caliber, with engraved 6-shot cylinder. Tapered octagonal barrel 7.5". Frame case colored steel. Backstrap and oval triggerguard brass. Grips one-piece walnut. Overall length 13"; weight about 44 oz. No. 340000. Leech-Rigdon model No. 340030; London Steel model No. 340050.

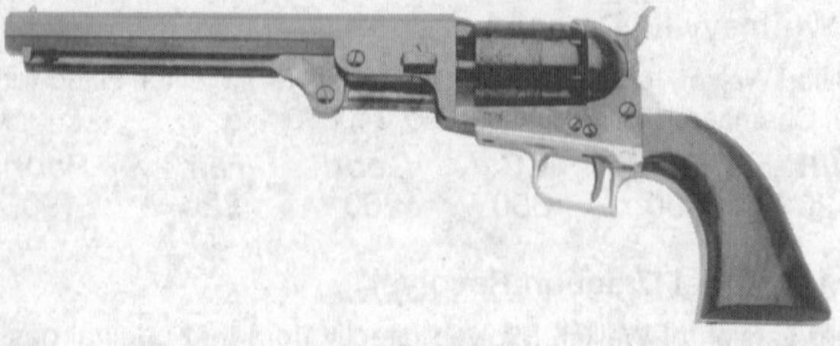

NIB	Exc.	V.G.	Good	Fair	Poor
310	260	220	190	160	140

Model 1861 Navy Colt

Sometimes referred to as "New Navy". Similar in appearance to Model 1851. Offered in two variations: military version has steel backstrap, triggerguard and cut for shoulder stock; civilian version has brass backstrap, triggerguard and not cut for shoulder stock.

Military Model 340500

NIB	Exc.	V.G.	Good	Fair	Poor
320	270	230	200	170	140

Civilian Model 340630

NIB	Exc.	V.G.	Good	Fair	Poor
310	260	220	190	160	140

Colt Model 1860 Army

Chambered for .44-caliber ball. Fitted with round tapered 8" barrel. Revolver has 6-shot engraved cylinder. Grips one-piece walnut. Overall length 13.75"; weight about 42 oz.

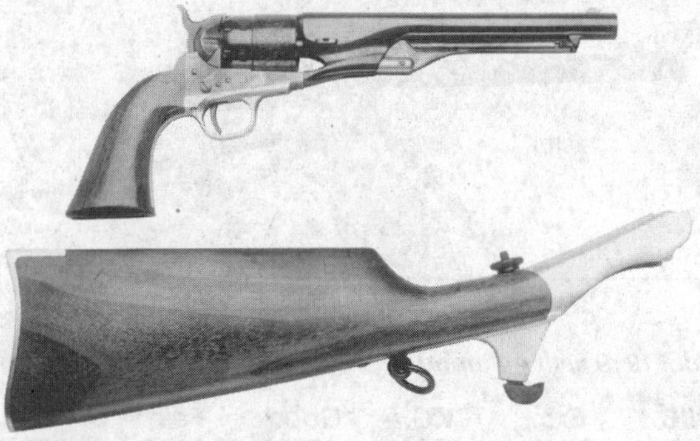

Military 340400

Steel backstrap, brass triggerguard and cut for shoulder stock.

NIB	Exc.	V.G.	Good	Fair	Poor
310	260	220	190	160	140

Fluted Cylinder Military 340410

NIB	Exc.	V.G.	Good	Fair	Poor
320	270	230	200	170	140

Civilian 340480

Brass backstrap and triggerguard. Not cut for shoulder stock.

NIB	Exc.	V.G.	Good	Fair	Poor
370	320	270	230	190	160

Colt Model 1862 Police Revolvers

Chambered for .36-caliber. Fitted with round tapered barrel in 4.5", 5.5" (340710) or 6.5" (340700) and 5-shot fluted cylinder. Frame color case-hardened steel. Backstrap and triggerguard brass. Grips one-piece walnut. Weight about 25 oz.

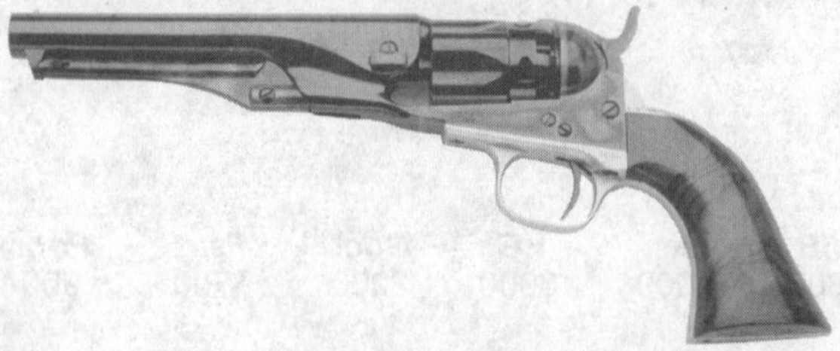

NIB	Exc.	V.G.	Good	Fair	Poor
300	260	220	180	160	130

Colt Model 1862 Pocket Navy Revolver

Similar to Model 1862 Police. Fitted with 5-shot engraved non-fluted cylinder. Barrel lengths 4.5", 5.5" (340760) and 6.5" (340750). Weight about 27 oz.

NIB	Exc.	V.G.	Good	Fair	Poor
320	270	230	190	160	140

Colt Model 1868 Army Thuer Conversion 341001

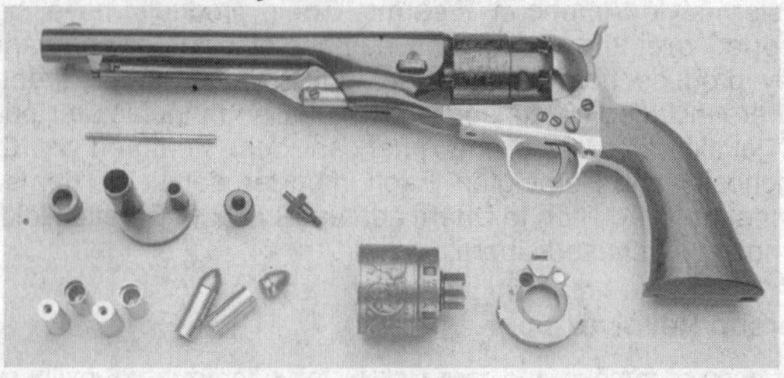

NIB	Exc.	V.G.	Good	Fair	Poor
450	380	320	280	240	200

Colt Model 1873 Cattleman Series

Many variants of Colt Single Action Army revolver. Offered in virtually all popular western sixgun calibers and barrel lengths. Add $50 for stainless finish, $100 for nickel, $300 for engraved model.

NIB	Exc.	V.G.	Good	Fair	Poor
500	450	420	380	300	200

1873 Cattleman Brass 9mm

This replica set the standard for the style and performance of the modern-era single-action shooter. The 1873 Cattleman Brass blends a sleek walnut grip, casehardened frame, and blued steel barrel and cylinder with brass backstrap and triggerguard.

NIB	Exc.	V.G.	Good	Fair	Poor
450	—	—	—	—	—

1873 Cattleman Brass Dual Cylinder 9mm/.357 Magnum

1873 Cattleman Brass Dual Cylinder 9mm/.357 Magnum Delivering the same performance and standout features as the 1873 Cattleman Brass 9mm, the 1873 Cattleman Brass Dual Cylinder ups the ante with two included cylinders — one chambered in 9mm Luger and the other in .357 Magnum.

NIB	Exc.	V.G.	Good	Fair	Poor
560	—	—	—	—	—

Remington Model 1858 New Army .44 Caliber

Chambered for .44-caliber and fitted with tapered octagonal 8" barrel. Cylinder holds 6-shots. Frame blued steel. Triggerguard brass. Grips two-piece walnut. Overall length 13.75"; weight about 42 oz. No. 341000.

NIB	Exc.	V.G.	Good	Fair	Poor
300	260	220	180	160	130

Remington Model 1858 New Army .36 Caliber

Similar to above. Fitted with 7.375" tapered octagonal barrel. Weight about 40 oz.

NIB	Exc.	V.G.	Good	Fair	Poor
300	260	220	180	160	130

Remington Model 1858 New Army .44 Caliber Target

Version fitted with fully adjustable rear sight and ramp front.

NIB	Exc.	V.G.	Good	Fair	Poor
320	270	230	200	170	140

Remington Model 1858 New Army .44 Caliber Stainless Steel

All parts stainless steel. No. 341020.

NIB	Exc.	V.G.	Good	Fair	Poor
380	320	270	230	200	170

Remington Model 1858 New Army .44 Cal. SS Target

Same as Target Model. All parts stainless steel. Discontinued.

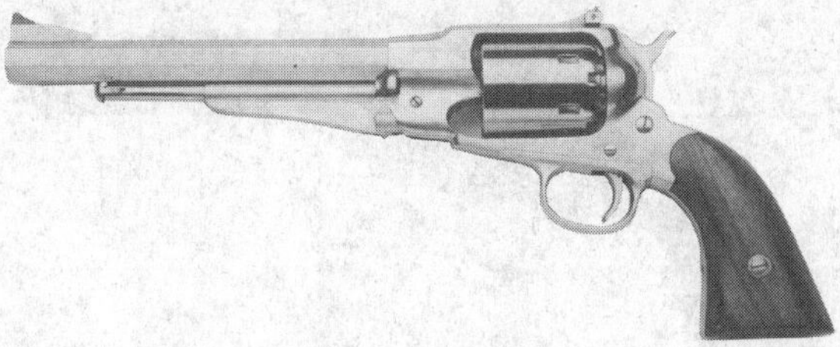

NIB	Exc.	V.G.	Good	Fair	Poor
430	370	310	260	220	190

Remington Model 1858 Target Revolving Carbine

Chambered for .44-caliber and fitted with 18" octagon barrel. Frame blued steel. Triggerguard brass. Stock select walnut. Overall length 35"; weight about 4.4 lbs. No. 341200.

NIB	Exc.	V.G.	Good	Fair	Poor
490	420	350	300	260	220

1875 Remington "Outlaw"

Replica of original Remington cartridge pistol. Chambered for .357 Magnum, .44-40, .45 ACP, .45 ACP/.45 L.C. conversion and .45 Colt. Frame case colored steel. Triggerguard brass. Offered with 7.5 round barrel blued or nickel-plated. Two-piece walnut grips. Overall length 13.75"; weight about 44 oz.

NIB	Exc.	V.G.	Good	Fair	Poor
450	320	250	200	120	80

Remington Model 1875 Frontier

Introduced in 2005. Features 5.5" barrel chambered for .45 Colt cartridge. Case colored frame with blued barrel, backstrap and triggerguard. Two-piece walnut grips. Weight about 40 oz.

NIB	Exc.	V.G.	Good	Fair	Poor
500	380	250	180	150	100

Remington Model 1890 Police

A 5.5"-barreled replica of original Remington Pistol. Chambered for .357 Magnum, .44-40, .45 ACP, .45 ACP/.45 L.C. conversion and .45 Colt. Frame case colored steel. Triggerguard brass. Available blued or nickel-plate. Grips two-piece walnut and fitted with grip ring. Overall length 11.75"; weight about 41 oz.

NIB	Exc.	V.G.	Good	Fair	Poor
500	380	250	180	150	100

Model 1871 Rolling Block Pistol

Single-shot target pistol chambered for .22 LR, .22 Magnum, .22 Hornet, .222 Rem., 223 Rem., .45 Long Colt or .357 Magnum. Has blued 9.5" half-octagonal half-round barrel. Case colored receiver. Walnut grip and forearm. Triggerguard brass. Overall length 14"; weight about 44 oz.

NIB	Exc.	V.G.	Good	Fair	Poor
500	380	250	180	150	100

Model 1871 Rolling Block Carbine

Similar to pistol, with 22.5" half-octagonal half-round barrel. Full-length walnut stock. Triggerguard and buttplate brass. Overall length 35.5"; weight about 4.8 lbs.

NIB	Exc.	V.G.	Good	Fair	Poor
650	520	400	280	200	120

Henry Rifle

Brass-framed reproduction of famous Winchester/Henry Rifle. Chambered for .44-40 or .45 Colt cartridge and basically only departure from being a true and faithful copy. Octagonal barrel 24.25" on rifle model; 22.25" on carbine model. Also two Trapper models offered: 18.5" barrel and 16.5" version. High-quality rifle and amazingly close to original in configuration. Three grades of engraving available. Weights are rifle 9.2 lbs.; carbine 9 lbs.; 18.5" trapper 7.9 lbs.; 16.5" trapper 7.4 lbs. Finish can be steel, standard blued or charcoal blue. Note: Add $350 Grade A; $450 Grade B; $600 Grade C.

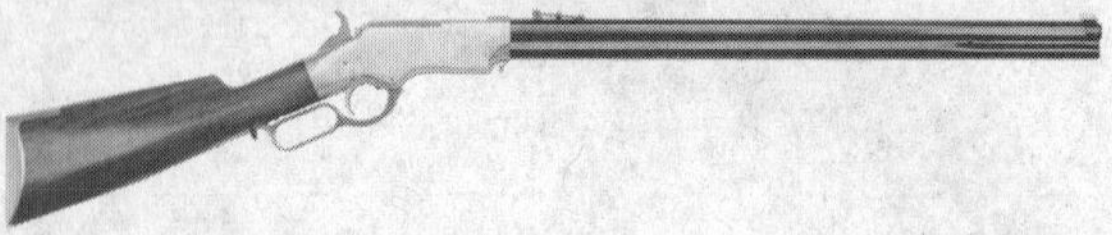

NIB	Exc.	V.G.	Good	Fair	Poor
900	700	550	450	350	200

Winchester Model 1866

Faithful replica of Winchester 1866. Chambered for .22 LR, .22 Magnum, .38 Special, .44-40 and .45 Long Colt. Rifle version has brass frame and 24.25" tapered octagon barrel. Frame finish brass, with walnut stock. Weight about 8 lbs.

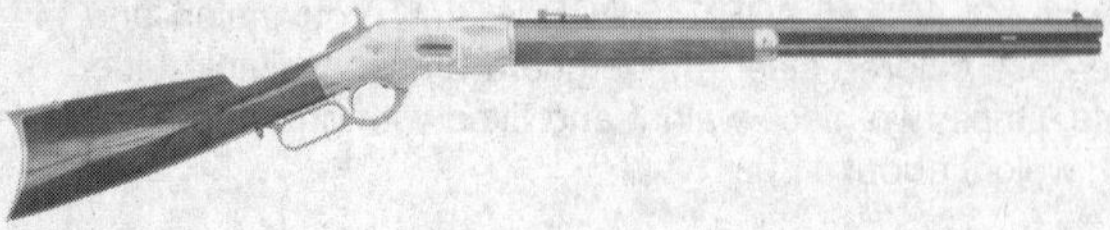

NIB	Exc.	V.G.	Good	Fair	Poor
800	650	550	450	350	200

1866 Yellowboy Carbine

Similar to standard rifle. Offered with 19" round tapered barrel.

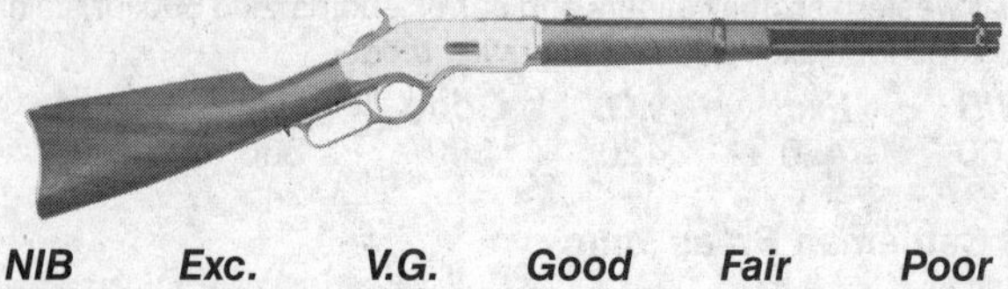

NIB	Exc.	V.G.	Good	Fair	Poor
700	600	500	450	350	200

1866 Yellowboy Deluxe

Caliber: .45 Colt. Barrel: 20" blued octagonal. Weight: 8.2 lbs. Stock: A-Grade walnut. Brass crescent buttplate. Blued barrel band. Casehardened lever. Iron sights. Features: Remake of Winchester's famed 1866 Yellowboy. Polished brass frame with classically inspired engraving pattern, including a bugling elk. The blank area on the right escutcheon is intended for the owner's custom engraving.

NIB	Exc.	V.G.	Good	Fair	Poor
1620	—	—	—	—	—

Winchester Model 1873 Carbine

Reproduction of Winchester 1873. Chambered for .357 Magnum, .45 Long Colt and .44-40. Case colored steel receiver, lever and round 19" tapered barrel. Stock and forearm walnut. Overall length 38.25"; weight about 7.4 lbs.

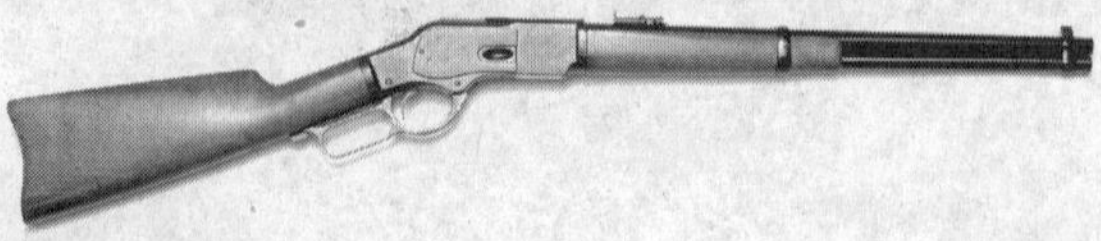

NIB	Exc.	V.G.	Good	Fair	Poor
900	700	500	450	350	200

Winchester Model 1873 Rifle

Similar to Carbine, with 24.25" octagonal barrel. Overall length 43.25"; weight about 8.2 lbs. Note: Extra barrel lengths from 20" to 30" in .45 L.C. and .44-40 also offered at extra cost.

NIB	Exc.	V.G.	Good	Fair	Poor
950	750	600	450	350	200

Winchester 1873 Short Sporting Rifle

As above fitted with 20" octagon barrel.

NIB	Exc.	V.G.	Good	Fair	Poor
950	800	600	450	350	200

Winchester 1873 Half-Octagon Rifle

Same as above, with 24.25" half octagon barrel. Stock has checkered pistol grip.

NIB	Exc.	V.G.	Good	Fair	Poor
1000	800	600	450	350	200

Winchester 1873 Musket

Chambered for .44-40 or .45 Long Colt cartridge. Fitted with 30" barrel, full stock and three barrel bands. Magazine capacity 14 rounds. Weight about 9 lbs.

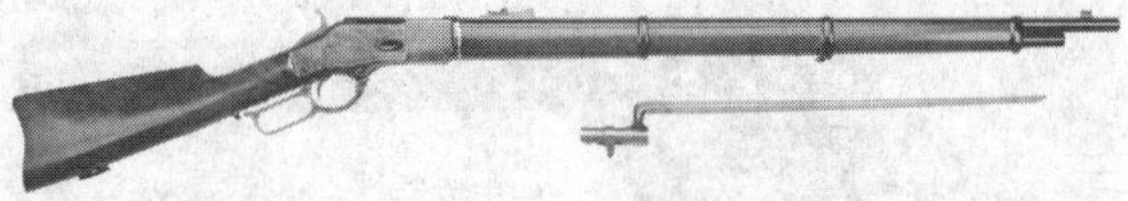

NIB	Exc.	V.G.	Good	Fair	Poor
1000	800	600	450	350	200

150TH Anniversary 1873 Rifle

Caliber: .45 Colt, .357 Mag. Capacity: 10+1 rounds. Barrel: 20" blued octagonal. Weight: 8.2 lbs. Stock: A-Grade satin walnut. Iron sights. Blued crescent buttplate. Features: Special anniversary remake of Winchester's Model 1873 "The gun that won the West." Casehardened receiver finish. Sideplate engraving reproduced from an original Winchester by Atelier Giovanelli of Italy.

NIB	Exc.	V.G.	Good	Fair	Poor
1680	—	—	—	—	—

Model 1886 Lite

Faithful reproduction of Winchester Model 1886, chambered in .45-70. Features a case-hardened blued frame, 22" round barrel with step-adjustable rear sight, A-grade walnut checkered stock with black recoil pad and forend cap. Magazine capacity 8+1. Sporting Rifle version has 26" barrel. Introduced in 2017.

NIB	Exc.	V.G.	Good	Fair	Poor
1700	1500	1200	—	—	—

Model 1885 High Wall Single-Shot Carbine

Chambered for .38-55, .30-30, .44-40, .45 Colt, .40-65 or .45-70, with 28" barrel. Walnut stock.

NIB	Exc.	V.G.	Good	Fair	Poor
820	600	450	350	250	200

Model 1885 High Wall Single-Shot Rifle

Same as above, with 30" barrel.

NIB	Exc.	V.G.	Good	Fair	Poor
900	680	500	400	300	200

Model 1885 High Wall Single-Shot Rifle Pistol Grip

Fitted with 30" or 32" barrel and checkered pistol grip stock. Same calibers as above.

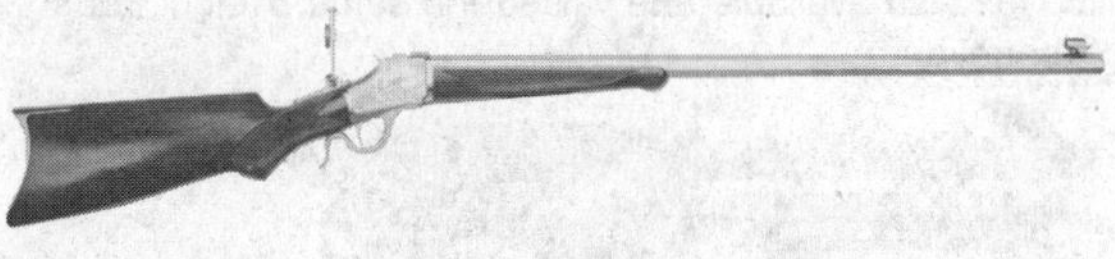

NIB	Exc.	V.G.	Good	Fair	Poor
1000	800	600	450	350	200

Winchester 1885 Low Wall Sporting Rifle

Version of Low Wall Winchester. Chambered for .22 Hornet, .30-30, .44 Magnum or .45 Colt cartridges. Fitted with 30" octagon barrel. Walnut stock with pistol grip. Weight about 7.5 lbs. Introduced in 2004.

NIB	Exc.	V.G.	Good	Fair	Poor
950	800	600	450	350	200

Winchester 1885 Low Wall Schuetzen

As above chambered for .45 Colt cartridge. Fitted with palm rest and Swiss butt. Weight about 7.75 lbs. Introduced in 2004.

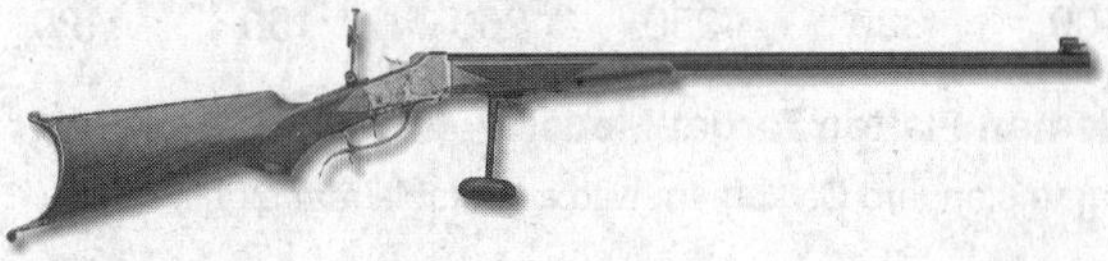

NIB	Exc.	V.G.	Good	Fair	Poor
1200	950	800	600	450	350

1885 Courteney Stalking Rifle

Caliber: .303 British. Barrel: 24 in., round blue steel. Stock: A-grade walnut, Prince of Wales. Sights: Hooded front, V-style express rear. Weight: 7.1 lbs. Features: Casehardened receiver, checkered pistol grip, rubber buttpad.

NIB	Exc.	V.G.	Good	Fair	Poor
1680	—	—	—	—	—

Hawken Santa Fe

Based on famous original rifle. Reproduction bored for .54-caliber. Fitted with 32" octagon barrel, double-set trigger and case-hardened lock plate standard. Stock ferrule and wedge plates are German silver. Walnut stock with cheekpiece. Overall length 50"; weight about 9.5 lbs. Available in kit form.

NIB	Exc.	V.G.	Good	Fair	Poor
350	300	250	200	150	100

Cattleman

Single-action revolver patterned closely after Colt Single-Action Army. Chambered in various popular calibers: .357 Magnum, .44-40, .44 Special, .45 ACP, .45 L.C./.45 ACP convertible and .45 Colt. Offered with barrel lengths of 4.75", 5.5" and 7.5". Also with modern or blackpowder-type frame. Brass or steel backstraps. Finish blued, with walnut grips. Sheriff's Model with 3" barrel and no ejector rod. Chambered for .44-40 and .45 Colt also available and valued the same. Weight about 38 oz. for 5.5" barrel gun.

NIB	Exc.	V.G.	Good	Fair	Poor
400	280	220	150	100	80

Cattleman .22

Rimfire model chambered for .22 LR, with cylinder capacity of 6 or 12 rounds. Traditional SAA barrel lengths of 4.75", 5.5" or 7". Blue finish, with color case-hardened frame. Choice of steel or brass triggerguard and backstrap. Note: Add $50 for 12-round cylinder capacity.

NIB	Exc.	V.G.	Good	Fair	Poor
400	320	280	200	150	120

Cattleman Flattop Target Model

Similar to standard Cattleman, with adjustable rear sight.

NIB	Exc.	V.G.	Good	Fair	Poor
440	350	280	220	180	120

Cattleman Gunfighter NM

Chambered for .45 Colt cartridge. Fitted with 4.75", 5.5" or 7.5" barrel. Black checkered grip, with matte blued finish. Weight about 37 oz. Introduced in 2005.

NIB	Exc.	V.G.	Good	Fair	Poor
400	280	220	150	100	80

Cattleman Cody NM

As above, with nickel finish and ivory-style grips.

NIB	Exc.	V.G.	Good	Fair	Poor
500	380	250	180	150	100

Cattleman Frisco NM

As above, with charcoal blued barrel and case colored frame. Pearl grips.

NIB	Exc.	V.G.	Good	Fair	Poor
500	380	250	180	150	100

Cattleman El Patron CMS

Designed for Cowboy Mounted Shooter (CMS) competition. Caliber .357 Magnum or .45 Colt. Steel cylinder, frame and barrel, 6-round capacity, single-action trigger, low profile hammer, fixed sights and wood grips. Weight 36.8 oz. Barrel 3.5" or 4", with blue/case-hardened or stainless finish. Note: Add 25 percent for stainless finish.

NIB	Exc.	V.G.	Good	Fair	Poor
520	420	350	300	220	150

Bisley

Chambered for .32-20, .38 Special, .357 Magnum, .38-40, .44-40 and .44 Special. Fitted with 4.75", 5.5" or 7.5" barrel. Case-hardened frame, with two-piece walnut grips.

NIB	Exc.	V.G.	Good	Fair	Poor
440	350	280	220	180	120

Flattop

As above, with adjustable rear sight.

NIB	Exc.	V.G.	Good	Fair	Poor
440	350	280	220	180	120

Buntline Carbine

Version has 18" barrel. Fitted with permanently mounted shoulder stock, with brass buttplate and sling swivel. Chambered for .44-40, .45 Long Colt, .357 Magnum and .44 Magnum. Offered with fixed or adjustable sights.

NIB	Exc.	V.G.	Good	Fair	Poor
450	400	350	300	250	200

Buckhorn Buntline

Version chambered for .44 Magnum. Has 18" round barrel and cut for attaching shoulder stock. Steel backstrap and triggerguard. Overall length 23"; weight about 57 oz. Note: Add 25 percent for detachable shoulder stock.

NIB	Exc.	V.G.	Good	Fair	Poor
400	320	300	250	200	100

Buckhorn Target

Same as above. Fitted with adjustable rear sight and ramp front. Has flat upper frame.

NIB	Exc.	V.G.	Good	Fair	Poor
450	350	300	250	200	100

Phantom

Similar to Buckhorn. Chambered for .44 and .357 Magnum. Round 10.5" barrel. Frame blued, with blued steel backstrap. One-piece walnut grips, with anatomic profile. Adjustable sight. Weight about 53 oz.

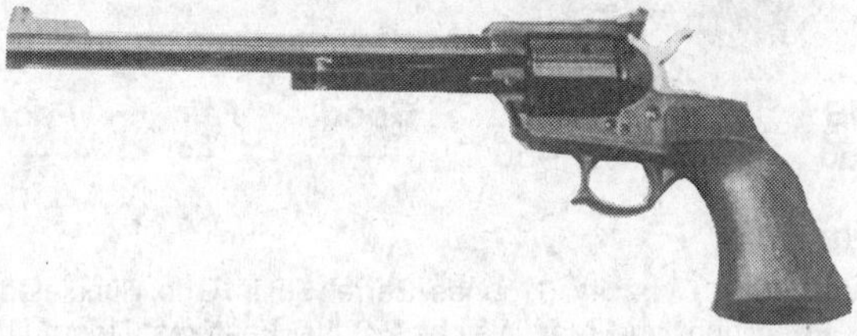

NIB	Exc.	V.G.	Good	Fair	Poor
400	280	220	150	100	80

New Thunderer Model

Designed and imported exclusively by Cimarron Arms, for single-action shooting competition. Fitted with bird's-head grip with hard rubber. Chambered for .357 Magnum, .44 Special, .44 WCF and .45 Colt. Offered in barrel lengths of 3.5" and 4.75". Finish in nickel or blued, with case colored frame.

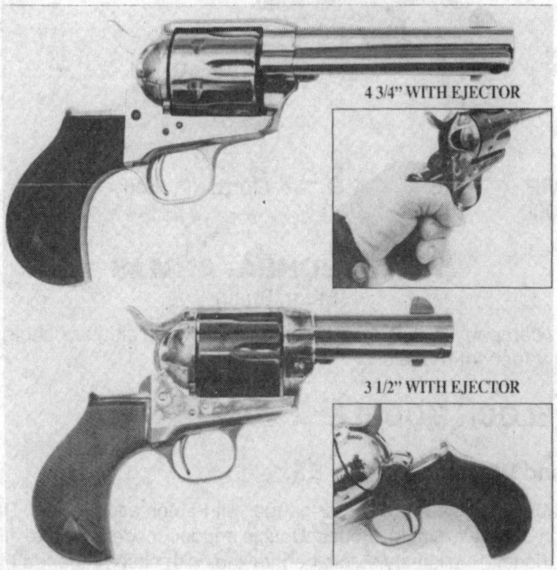

NIB	Exc.	V.G.	Good	Fair	Poor
450	350	300	250	200	100

1873 Stallion

Scaled-down version chambered for .22 LR/.22 Magnum. Blued, with case colored frame. Features one-piece walnut grips.

NIB	Exc.	V.G.	Good	Fair	Poor
350	300	250	200	150	100

1873 El Patrón 9mm

Presented with checkered walnut grips, casehardened frame, 5.5-in. blued barrel, numbered cylinder, and EasyView sights, the El Patrón has the classic profile of the Old West SAA revolvers.

NIB	Exc.	V.G.	Good	Fair	Poor
550	—	—	—	—	—

Tornado

Five-shot revolver chambered for .454 Casull. Fitted with 4.75", 5.5" or 7.5" with ported barrel. Sandblasted nickel finish. Weight about 47 oz.

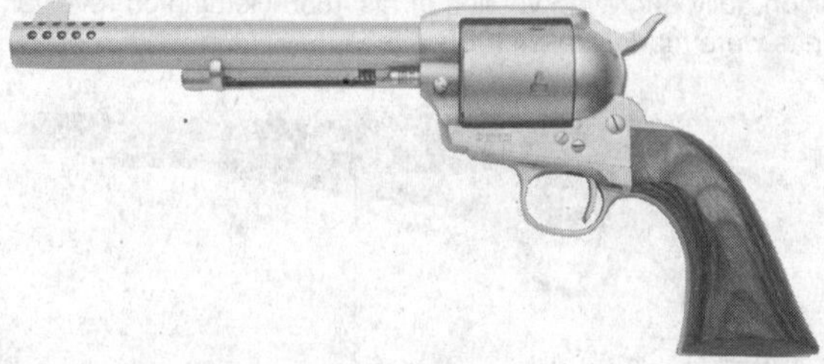

NIB	Exc.	V.G.	Good	Fair	Poor
1000	900	750	600	500	400

No. 3 Schofield Revolver

Patterned after original S&W revolver. Chambered for .44-40 or .45 Colt cartridge. Fitted with 3.5", 5" or 7" barrel. Weight with 7" barrel about 40 oz.

NIB	Exc.	V.G.	Good	Fair	Poor
800	700	600	480	320	200

No. 3 New Model Russian

Chambered for .44 Russian cartridge. Fitted with 6" or 7" barrel.

NIB	Exc.	V.G.	Good	Fair	Poor
900	800	700	580	400	300

Inspector Model

Double-action revolver built on same general lines as Colt Detective. Cylinder holds 6 cartridges. Chambered for .38 Special. Offered in barrel lengths with fixed sights: 2", 2.125", 2.5", 3", 4", 6". Also offered in 4" or 6" barrel lengths with adjustable sights. Grips are walnut. Finish blued or chrome. With 3" barrel weight about 24 oz.

NIB	Exc.	V.G.	Good	Fair	Poor
280	200	150	120	100	80

1858 Buffalo Bill Centennial

Introduced 2017. To honor Buffalo Bill's centennial, Uberti offered a limited-edition, fully engraved version of his 1858 Remington revolver. Only 500 units were made. No. 3410BB.

NIB	Exc.	V.G.	Good	Fair	Poor
850	720	610	520	440	380

Stainless Steel Short Stroke CMS Pro

Caliber: .45 Colt. Capacity: 6 rounds. Barrel: 3.5 in. Grip: Synthetic traditional. Sights: Fixed front and rear. Weight: 2.1 lbs. Features: Made specifically for the rigors of Cowboy Mounted Shooting competition, and built entirely of stainless steel. Good for quick, one-handed shooting while riding a horse. Features low-profile, short-stroke hammer with 20-percent less travel. Extra-wide, deeply grooved hammer, and chambered in the classic .45 Colt.

NIB	Exc.	V.G.	Good	Fair	Poor
750	650	550	—	—	—

Stainless Steel Short Stroke CMS KL Pro

Caliber: .45 Colt. Capacity: 6 rounds. Barrel: 3.5 in. Grip: Synthetic bird's head. Sights: Fixed front and rear. Weight: 2.1 lbs. Features: Made specifically for the rigors of Cowboy Mounted Shooting competition, and built entirely of stainless steel. This model is the result of the partnership between Uberti USA and legendary Cowboy Mounted Shooter competitor Kenda Lenseigne, winner of multiple world and national mounted shooting championships. It features a modified bird's-head grip with Lenseigne's brand on the grip and her signature engraved on the barrel. Features low-profile, short-stroke hammer with 20-percent less travel. Extra-wide, deeply grooved hammer, and chambered in the classic .45 Colt.

NIB	Exc.	V.G.	Good	Fair	Poor
650	550	450	—	—	—

Dalton

Caliber: .45 Colt. Capacity: 6 rounds. Barrel: 5.5 in. Grip: Simulated pearl. Sights: Fixed front and rear. Weight: 2.3 lbs. Features: Uberti USA expands its Outlaws & Lawmen Series of revolvers with the addition of the Dalton Revolver, a faithful reproduction of the Colt Single Action Army revolver used by Dalton Gang leader Bob Dalton. Features hand-chased engraving from famed Italian engraving company, Atelier Giovanelli, on the receiver, grip frame and cylinder.

NIB	Exc.	V.G.	Good	Fair	Poor
1000	850	700	—	—	—

UGARTECHEA, ARMAS

Eibar, Spain

This company makes side-by-side boxlock and sidelock shotguns in a variety of models.

SIDELOCK MODELS

Upland Classic Model 75 EX

Available in 12-, 16-, 20- or 28-gauge, with automatic ejectors. Double or non-selective single trigger. Double trigger models feature hinged front trigger. English-style scroll engraving, with case-hardened or coin finished receiver. Note: Add $300 for 28-gauge; $800 for higher grade hand-rubbed wood.

NIB	Exc.	V.G.	Good	Fair	Poor
3100	2750	2000	1800	1200	800

Upland Classic Model 110

Available in 12-, 16-, 20- or 28-gauge and .410 bore. Round body design, with other features similar to Model 75 EX. Note: Add $300 for 28-gauge; $400 for .410 bore.

NIB	Exc.	V.G.	Good	Fair	Poor
4000	3400	2500	2000	1500	1000

Custom Grade Models

This series of sidelock guns are made on special order. Many custom options including barrel lengths, stock dimensions and upgraded wood. Higher grades feature increasing levels of engraving. Values for excellent condition models range from $4,000 to $10,000.

BOXLOCK MODELS

Upland Classic Grade I Model 30

Basic boxlock model offered in all gauges, with double triggers, extractors, splinter forend and straight-grip stock. Note: Add $200 for 28-gauge; $300 for .410 bore.

NIB	Exc.	V.G.	Good	Fair	Poor
1700	1300	1000	800	500	300

Upland Classic Grade III Model 40 NEX

Similar to Model 30, with automatic ejectors, double or non-selective single trigger, engraved receiver. Note: Add $300 for 28-gauge; $500 for .410 bore.

NIB	Exc.	V.G.	Good	Fair	Poor
2400	2000	1400	1200	900	500

UHLINGER, WILLIAM P.
Philadelphia, Pennsylvania

Pocket Revolver (Antique)

Spur trigger revolver, with 2.75" or 3" octagonal barrel and unfluted 6-shot cylinder. Blued, with rosewood or walnut grips. Manufactured during late 1860s early 1870s. Uhlinger-manufactured pistols will often be found with retailer's names on them, such as D.D. Cone, Washington, D.C.; J.P. Lower; W.L. Grant.

.22 Rimfire Long Cylinder (1-3/16") (Antique)

Exc.	Fine	V.G.	Good	Fair	Poor
800	600	420	250	100	70

.22 Rimfire Short Cylinder (1") (Antique)

Exc.	Fine	V.G.	Good	Fair	Poor
650	420	300	180	80	50

.32 Rimfire Model (5", 6", or 7" Barrel) (Antique)

Exc.	Fine	V.G.	Good	Fair	Poor
800	600	420	250	100	70

ULTIMATE
See—CAMEX-BLASER USA, INC.

ULTRA LIGHT ARMS
See—NEW ULTRA LIGHT ARMS

UMAREX USA
Fort Smith, Arkansas

Umarex Colt Tactical Rimfire M4 Ops Carbine

Blowback semi-automatic rifle styled to resemble Colt M16. Chambered in .22 LR. Features include 16.2" barrel; front sight adjustable for elevation; adjustable rear sight; alloy lower; adjustable telestock; flattop receiver with removable carry handle; 10- or 30-round detachable magazine.

NIB	Exc.	V.G.	Good	Fair	Poor
500	420	360	300	220	150

Umarex Colt Tactical Rimfire M4 Carbine

Blowback semi-automatic rifle styled to resemble Colt M4. Chambered in .22 LR. Features include 16.2" barrel; front sight adjustable for elevation; adjustable rear sight; alloy lower; adjustable telestock; flattop receiver with optics rail; 10- or 30-round detachable magazine.

NIB	Exc.	V.G.	Good	Fair	Poor
550	460	400	340	250	160

Umarex Colt Tactical Rimfire M16 Rifle

Blowback semi-automatic rifle styled to resemble Colt M16. Chambered in .22 LR. Features include 21.2" barrel; front sight adjustable for elevation; adjustable rear sight; alloy lower; fixed stock; flattop receiver; removable carry handle; 10- or 30-round detachable magazine.

NIB	Exc.	V.G.	Good	Fair	Poor
500	420	360	300	220	150

Umarex Colt Tactical Rimfire M16 SPR Rifle

Blowback semi-automatic rifle styled to resemble Colt M16 SPR. Chambered in .22 LR. Features include 21.2" barrel; front sight adjustable for elevation; adjustable rear sight; alloy lower; fixed stock; flattop receiver with optics rail; removable carry handle; 10- or 30-round detachable magazine.

NIB	Exc.	V.G.	Good	Fair	Poor
580	480	420	360	280	180

Umarex H&K 416-22

Blowback semi-automatic rifle styled to resemble H&K 416. Chambered in .22 LR. Features include metal upper and lower receivers; RIS - (rail interface system); retractable stock; pistol grip with storage compartment; on-rail sights; rear sight adjustable for wind and elevation; 16.1" barrel; 10- or 20-round magazine. Also available in pistol version with 9" barrel.

NIB	Exc.	V.G.	Good	Fair	Poor
580	480	420	360	280	180

Umarex H&K MP5 A5

Blowback semi-automatic rifle styled to resemble H&K MP5. Chambered in .22 LR. Features include metal receiver; compensator; bolt catch; NAVY pistol grip; on-rail sights; rear sight adjustable for wind and elevation; 16.1" barrel; 10- or 25-round magazine. Also available in pistol version with 9" barrel and SD-type forend.

NIB	Exc.	V.G.	Good	Fair	Poor
450	380	300	250	200	150

UNCETA
See—ASTRA-UNCETA SA

UNION

Pocket Pistol (Antique)

.22-caliber spur trigger single-shot pistol, with 2.75" barrel marked "Union". Nickel-plated, with walnut grips.

Exc.	Fine	V.G.	Good	Fair	Poor
650	400	250	100	80	50

UNION FIRE ARMS COMPANY
Toledo, Ohio

Company was incorporated in 1902 and used names of Union Fire Arms, Union Arms Company, Illinois Arms Company (made for Sears) and Bee Be Arms Company. In 1917, company was bought up or absorbed by Ithaca Gun Company. NOTE: Union Fire Arms Company (or Union Firearms Company, as it is sometimes known) slide action shotguns are not commonly seen. Though not widely collected, they seem to attract considerable interest as oddities, much as Spencer/Bannerman slide action shotguns do. Values given below are approximate; as always, true value lies in eyes of buyer, not seller.

Double Barrel Shotguns

Union's predecessor, Colton Manufacturing Co. (1894-1902), made a double for Sears. Cleverly designed with coil mainspring striker locks set into sideplates. Union double in 12- and 16-gauge, with steel or Damascus barrels derived from it, but was a traditional hammerless sidelock side-by-side well-made gun (1902-1913) and also sold by Sears. Values depend on grade and condition. Union also offered, about 1905, an unusual boxlock hammer gun Model 25 in 12-gauge only. Employs external hammers, but they are mounted within frame and spurs protrude in front of top-snap opener. These guns are hard to find and values range from $300 to $1,200 depending on condition. Produced with steel twist or Damascus barrels only in plain grade.

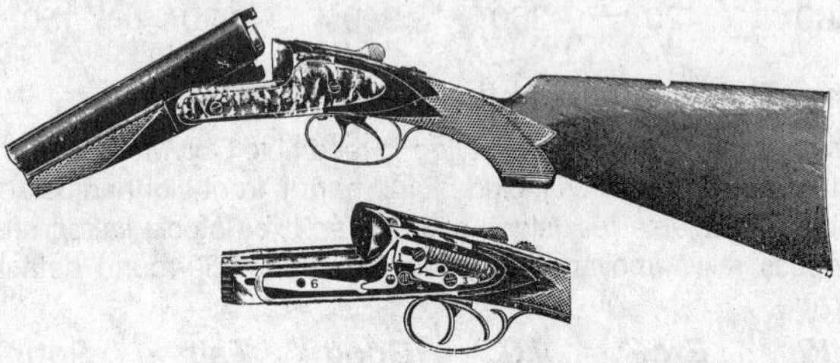

Courtesy Nick Niles

Model 24

Slide action Model 25 Peerless, was a fancy version of Model 24 and Model 25A, which was a trap model. Manufactured from 1902 to 1913 in 12- or 16-gauge, with 24", 26", 28" or 32" steel or Damascus barrels. Gun had unique double trigger. Front trigger cocked and decocked an internal firing pin and back trigger fired the gun. Gun is marked on left side of frame and pump release is on right side. Model had one serious drawback, the slide that extracted a spent shell extended back over comb of stock. This often hit shooter's thumb knuckle and caused injury. In 1907, Union redesigned their slide by reducing its length and shielding it behind a steel plate that covered rear half of opening. These are Model 24, 25 and 25A improved versions. Approximately 17,000 of all models combined were made.

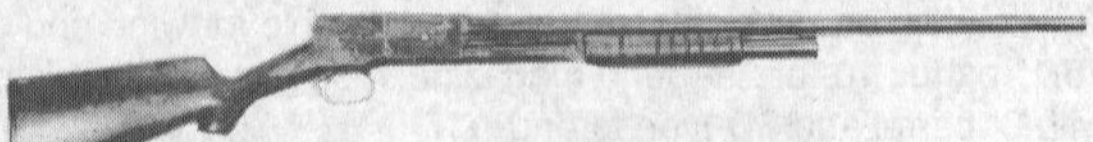

NIB	Exc.	V.G.	Good	Fair	Poor
—	—	750	300	200	100

Model 50

Manufactured 1911 to 1913. Basically redesign of Model 24. Main distinguishing feature of Model 50 was the frame sloped down to meet comb of stock. Double trigger system was replaced by single trigger. Came in 12- or 16-gauge, with 26", 28", 30" or 32" Krupp steel barrel. Fewer than 3,000 made.

NIB	Exc.	V.G.	Good	Fair	Poor
—	—	850	400	300	200

Model 22

Essentially a no frills Model 23. Same barrel length and steel options. Plain walnut stock and no engraving. Fewer than 10,000 Model 22 and 23s made.

NIB	Exc.	V.G.	Good	Fair	Poor
—	—	300	100	80	50

Model 23

Manufactured between 1902 and 1913. Hammerless double with-/without automatic ejectors. Some engraving, came in both single/double trigger models. This was their top grade gun. Came in 12- and 16-gauge, with 28", 30" or 32" steel twist or Damascus barrels.

NIB	Exc.	V.G.	Good	Fair	Poor
—	—	450	150	120	100

Diamond Grade

Manufactured between 1905 and 1910. Unique octagonal breech in 12-gauge only, with 30" steel laminated or Damascus barrel. Premium grade single-shot. Few were made.

NIB	Exc.	V.G.	Good	Fair	Poor
—	—	450	200	100	50

Model 18

Manufactured 1906 to 1913. Came in 12- or 16-gauge, with 30", 32", 34" or 36" steel barrel. Plain single-shot. Very few made.

NIB	Exc.	V.G.	Good	Fair	Poor
—	—	200	80	50	20

Reifngraber

.32 or .38 S&W caliber gas operated semi-automatic pistol, with 3" barrel. Blued, with walnut grips. Approximately 100 were manufactured.

NIB	Exc.	V.G.	Good	Fair	Poor
—	—	2250	1100	500	350

Automatic Revolver

.32 S&W caliber. Similar to Webley Fosbery semi-automatic revolver, with 3" barrel. Blued, with walnut or hard rubber grips. Cylinder has zigzag grooves.

NIB	Exc.	V.G.	Good	Fair	Poor
—	—	3250	1250	500	250

UNIQUE

Hendaye, France

See—PYRENEES

UNITED SPORTING ARMS, INC.

Tucson, Arizona

United Sporting Arms manufactured high-quality, heavy-duty single-action revolvers in several locations in NY, CT, ID, NC, and AZ from about 1972 to 1999. Initial production model was called the Abilene, offered in .357 or .44 Mag., and limited numbers of .45 Colt. The Abilene was acquired by Mossberg. Successor models by United Sporting Arms were the Seville and the El Dorado, both models produced in many variations. The El Dorado was the first all-stainless .44 Magnum single-action on the market. Associated firms producing these models included El Dorado Arms and Sporting Arms, Inc. Most common chambering is .44 Magnum, but a stretched frame variation was produced for longer cartridges such as the.357 Maximum. Other production is reported in .22 LR, .454. Mag, .41 Mag, .45 Win. Mag. and .357

Super Mag. Extremely rare chamberings reportedly include 9mm, .44-40, .32 H&R Mag, .22 K-Hornet, and .218 Mashburn Bee. Any chambering other than .44 Magnum brings a premium. Unusual configurations such as short Sheriff's Models, long Silhouette Models, birds-head grip, unusual factory finishes, and brass grip frame should also bring a premium. Guns made in Hauppauge, NY or Post Falls, ID may bring 10% to 20% less than those made in other locations. Packages including extra barrels and cylinders were offered as Quik-Kit guns, and a premium is added for these additional components.

Abilene or Seville

Single-action revolver. Pricing is for standard frame blued finish, and standard barrel lengths. Add $75 for stainless steel. Add 50% for long frame (.357 Max and other long cartridges). Add 25% for short-barrel Sheriff's model.

NIB	Exc.	V.G.	Good	Fair	Poor
550	480	430	350	—	—

Abilene Silhouette

As above with 10.5" barrel. Add $75 for stainless steel. Add 50% for long frame.

NIB	Exc.	V.G.	Good	Fair	Poor
550	450	400	330	—	—

El Dorado

Single-action revolver. Pricing is for standard frame and standard barrel lengths. Add 50% for long frame (.357 Max and other long cartridges, as pictured).

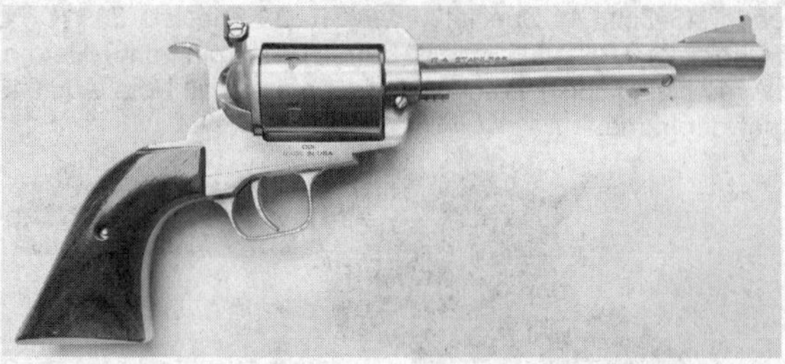

Jim Supica photo

NIB	Exc.	V.G.	Good	Fair	Poor
650	550	450	400	—	—

El Dorado Silhouette

As above with 10.5" barrel. Add 50% for long frame.

NIB	Exc.	V.G.	Good	Fair	Poor
680	580	480	380	—	—

Tombstone Commemorative

NIB	Exc.	V.G.	Good	Fair	Poor
1000	750	620	520	—	—

Quik-Kit Stainless Steel

Note: Add $200 for each barrel and cylinder for Quik-Kit guns with extra barrel and cylinder; 20 percent if El Dorado Arms (either N.Y. or N.C.); 10 percent for 1.5" barrel Sheriff's Model; 20 percent for 10.5" barrel; 20 percent for bird's-head grip frame; 20 percent if brass grip frame. Deduct 10 percent if United Sporting Arms, Hauppauge, N.Y.; 20 percent if United Sporting Arms, Post Falls, ID.

NIB	Exc.	V.G.	Good	Fair	Poor
1500	1250	800	—	—	—

Quik-Kit Blued

NIB	Exc.	V.G.	Good	Fair	Poor
1200	1000	650	—	—	—

UNITED STATES ARMS

Rockfall, Connecticut

See—SMITH, OTIS A

UNITED STATES FIRE ARMS MFG.

(Formerly United States Patent Firearms Mfg. Co.)
Hartford, Connecticut

Company produced a wide variety of high quality replica handguns and rifles from 1992 until 2012.

Single-Action Army Revolver

Offered in wide variety of calibers including .22 rimfire, .32 WCF, .38 S&W, .357 Magnum, .38-40, .41 Colt, .44 Russian, .44-40, .45 Colt and .45 ACP. Barrel lengths 4.75", 5.5", 7.5", with/without ejector. Modern cross pin frame available for additional $10. Prices listed for standard grips and finish, Armory bone case finish and Dome blue finish.

NIB	Exc.	V.G.	Good	Fair	Poor
980	900	800	680	520	300

Single-Action Army Revolver Pre-War

As above, with pre-war "P" frame.

NIB	Exc.	V.G.	Good	Fair	Poor
1400	1150	950	700	550	300

Shooting Master

Large-frame model in .357 Magnum, with 7.5" barrel, U.S. hard rubber grips, blue finish and enlarged triggerguard. Adjustable rear sight, 6-round cylinder. Introduced in 2011. Also available in .327 Federal, with 8-shot cylinder (Sparrowhawk model).

NIB	Exc.	V.G.	Good	Fair	Poor
1300	1100	950	800	520	250

Flattop Target Model

Offered with same calibers as Single-Action Army above. Barrel lengths 4.75", 5.5" and 7.5". Grips two-piece hard rubber. Prices listed for standard finish. Introduced in 1997.

NIB	Exc.	V.G.	Good	Fair	Poor
1660	1450	1200	900	680	400

Rodeo

Single-action revolver offered in .45 Colt, .44-40, .44 Special, .32-20, .38-40 and .38 Special calibers. Choice of 4.75" or 5.50" barrel. Satin blue finish, with bone case hammer. "US" hard rubber grips standard.

NIB	Exc.	V.G.	Good	Fair	Poor
620	550	450	350	250	180

Rodeo II

Similar to Rodeo, with matte nickel finish and burl wood grips.

NIB	Exc.	V.G.	Good	Fair	Poor
580	480	350	280	220	200

Buntline

Features all blued finish, with 16" barrel. Chambered for .45 Colt cartridge.

NIB	Exc.	V.G.	Good	Fair	Poor
2300	1750	1480	1100	700	450

Buntline Special

Fitted with 16" barrel. Chambered for .45 Colt cartridge. Supplied with nickel stock. Limited edition. Cased.

NIB	Exc.	V.G.	Good	Fair	Poor
2900	2250	1750	1480	1100	700

China Camp Cowboy Action Gun

Chambered for .45 Colt cartridge, but other calibers available from .32 WCF to .44 WCF. Barrel lengths 4.75", 5.5" and 7.5". Special action job. Two-piece hard rubber grips standard. Finish is silver steel.

NIB	Exc.	V.G.	Good	Fair	Poor
1400	1150	950	700	550	300

Henry Nettleton Revolver

Exact reproduction of U.S. Government inspector model, produced in Springfield Armory. Offered in 5.5" and 7.5" models. Introduced in 1997. Discontinued.

NIB	Exc.	V.G.	Good	Fair	Poor
1580	1450	1200	900	600	350

.22 Plinker

Chambered for .22 cartridge. Fitted with choice of barrel lengths: 4.75", 5.5" or 7.5". Extra .22 WMR cylinder included.

NIB	Exc.	V.G.	Good	Fair	Poor
980	880	720	550	300	150

.22 Target

As above, with adjustable rear sight and replaceable front sight blade.

NIB	Exc.	V.G.	Good	Fair	Poor
1660	1450	1200	900	680	400

Gunslinger

Offered in .45 Colt, .44 Special, .44 WCF, .38 Special, .38 WCF or .32 WCF. Choice of 4.75", .5.5" or 7.5" barrel. Cross pin frame. Hard rubber grips. Aged bluing finish. Black-style frame optional. Note: Add $135 for blackpowder frame.

NIB	Exc.	V.G.	Good	Fair	Poor
1140	1020	800	620	500	250

Custer Battlefield Gun

Replica of 1873 revolver used during height of Indian Wars, including Custer's Last Stand. Limited edition with cartouche of Ordnance Sub-inspector Orville W. Ainsworth; serial range 200 - 14,343. Six-shot 7.5" barrel. Antique Patina aged blue. One-piece walnut stock.

NIB	Exc.	V.G.	Good	Fair	Poor
1620	1450	1200	900	680	400

Hunter

Revolver chambered for .17 HMR cartridge. Fitted with 7.5" barrel, with adjustable rear sight and replaceable front sight blade. Finish matte blue. Discontinued.

NIB	Exc.	V.G.	Good	Fair	Poor
980	880	720	550	300	150

Sheriff's Model

Chambered for wide variety of calibers from .45 Colt to .32 WCF. Choice of 2.5", 3", 3.5" or 4" barrel. No ejector. Note: Add $250 for nickel finish.

NIB	Exc.	V.G.	Good	Fair	Poor
980	880	720	550	300	150

Omni-Potent Bird's-Head Model

Chambered for .45 Colt, .45 ACP, .44 Special, .44 WCF, .38 Special, .38 WCF or .32 WCF cartridges. Offered with bird's-head grips. Available with 3.5", 4" or 4.75" barrel lengths.

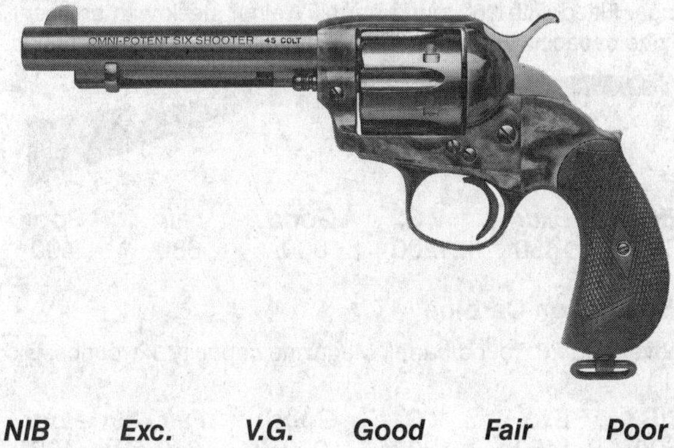

NIB	Exc.	V.G.	Good	Fair	Poor
1620	1450	1200	900	680	400

Omni-Potent Snubnose

As above, with 2", 3" or 4" barrel without ejector.

NIB	Exc.	V.G.	Good	Fair	Poor
1480	1300	1050	800	580	400

Omni-Potent Target

Choice of 4.75", 5.5" or 7.5" barrel, with adjustable rear sight and replaceable front blade sight.

NIB	Exc.	V.G.	Good	Fair	Poor
1400	1150	950	700	550	300

Bisley Model

Based on famous Bisley model. Reproduction features barrel lengths of 4.75", 5.5", 7.5" and 10". The .45 Colt caliber is standard, but .32 WCF, .38 S&W, .44 S&W, .41 Colt, .38 WCF, .44 WCF are optional. Introduced in 1997. Note: Add $60 for 10" models.

NIB	Exc.	V.G.	Good	Fair	Poor
1580	1450	1200	900	600	350

Target

As above, with adjustable rear sight and replaceable blade front sight.

NIB	Exc.	V.G.	Good	Fair	Poor
1620	1450	1200	900	680	400

Pony Express

Features 5.50" engraved barrel and frame, with special finish. Ivory grips etched with pony express rider. Custom gun.

NIB	Exc.	V.G.	Good	Fair	Poor
3900	3500	2950	2200	1500	700

Sears 1902 Colt

Replica of Sears 1902 Colt SAA. Fitted with 5.50" barrel, pearl grips, full coverage engraving with gold line work on cylinder and barrel. Custom gun.

NIB	Exc.	V.G.	Good	Fair	Poor
9000	7500	6000	500	4000	1000

Model 1910

Stylized version of early Colt Model 1910 .45 ACP pistol.

NIB	Exc.	V.G.	Good	Fair	Poor
1900	1700	1550	1200	900	500

Model 1911 Army or Navy

Faithful version of early Colt Model 1911 military model.

NIB	Exc.	V.G.	Good	Fair	Poor
1700	1500	1100	900	500	350

Ace .22 LR

Recreation of 1911-style Colt Ace .22 LR, with 10+1 capacity. Walnut grips. Introduced 2006.

NIB	Exc.	V.G.	Good	Fair	Poor
1850	1650	1100	900	500	350

Super .38

1911-style semi-automatic. Blued finish; chambered for .38 Super Automatic with 9+1 capacity. Walnut grips. Introduced 2006.

NIB	Exc.	V.G.	Good	Fair	Poor
1800	1600	1200	900	500	350

RIFLES

Cowboy Action Lightning

Copy of Colt Lightning rifle. Chambered for .44-40, .45 Colt or .38 WCF cartridge. Fitted with 26" round barrel. Walnut stock with crescent butt. Magazine capacity 15 rounds. Introduced fall of 2003; discontinued.

NIB	Exc.	V.G.	Good	Fair	Poor
1620	1450	1200	900	680	400

Cowboy Action Carbine

As above, with 20" round barrel. Magazine capacity 12 rounds. Discontinued.

NIB	Exc.	V.G.	Good	Fair	Poor
1620	1450	1200	900	680	400

Lightning Magazine Rifle

Premium version of Cowboy Action Lightning. Features choice of 26" round/half-round or octagon barrel. Checkered American walnut forearm, with non-checkered stock with oil-finish. Many extra cost options are offered for this model. Discontinued. Note: Add $200 for half round barrel. Fancy wood, pistol grip, finish and engraving offered for this rifle.

NIB	Exc.	V.G.	Good	Fair	Poor
1620	1450	1200	900	680	400

Lightning Magazine Carbine

As above, with 20" round barrel. Discontinued.

NIB	Exc.	V.G.	Good	Fair	Poor
1620	1450	1200	900	680	400

Lightning Baby Carbine

Fitted with 20" special round tapered barrel. Lightweight carbine forearm with border line. Discontinued.

NIB	Exc.	V.G.	Good	Fair	Poor
2000	1820	1600	1250	950	650

UNITED STATES REVOLVER ASSOCIATION

See—HARRINGTON & RICHARDSON ARMS CO.

UNITED STATES SMALL ARMS CO.

Chicago, Illinois

Huntsman Model Knife Pistol

Made from approximately 1918-1930.

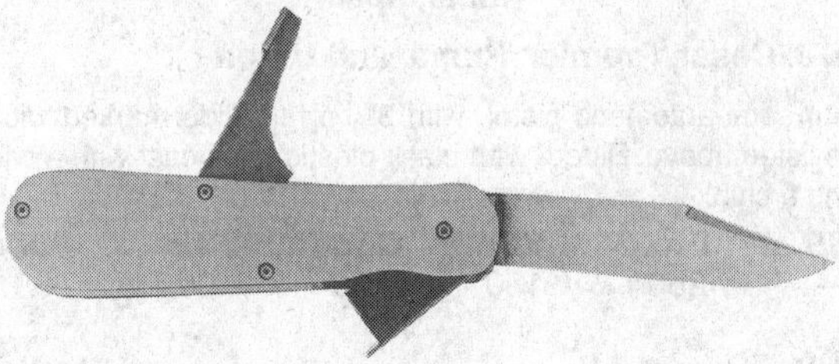

NIB	Exc.	V.G.	Good	Fair	Poor
—	1200	800	400	200	100

UNIVERSAL FIREARMS

Hialeah, Florida/Jacksonville, Arkansas

Universal merged with Iver-Johnson in 1985 and relocated to Arkansas in 1986. Universal operated out of Florida from late 1950s to 1985.

Model 7312

12-gauge over/under shotgun. Separated 30" ventilated rib barrels, single-selective trigger and automatic ejectors. Case-hardened receiver engraved. Blued, with walnut stock. Imported from Italy.

NIB	Exc.	V.G.	Good	Fair	Poor
—	1250	900	450	300	180

Model 7412

As above, with extractors. Imported from Italy.

NIB	Exc.	V.G.	Good	Fair	Poor
—	1000	750	400	250	150

Model 7712

As above, with 26" or 28" barrels, non-selective single trigger and extractors. Imported from Italy.

NIB	Exc.	V.G.	Good	Fair	Poor
—	550	400	350	250	100

Model 7812

As above, with more detailed engraving and automatic ejectors. Imported from Italy.

NIB	Exc.	V.G.	Good	Fair	Poor
—	700	550	450	350	150

Model 7912

As above, with gold wash frame and single-selective trigger. Imported from Italy.

NIB	Exc.	V.G.	Good	Fair	Poor
—	1350	1000	750	600	300

Model 7112

12-gauge double-barrel boxlock shotgun, with 26" or 28" barrels, double triggers and extractors. Blued case-hardened, with walnut stock. Imported from Italy.

NIB	Exc.	V.G.	Good	Fair	Poor
—	450	300	250	200	100

Double Wing

10-, 12-, 20-gauge or .410 bore boxlock double-barrel shotgun, with 26", 28" or 30" barrels, double triggers and extractors. Blued, with walnut stock. Imported from Italy. Premium for 10-gauge and .410 bore.

NIB	Exc.	V.G.	Good	Fair	Poor
—	450	300	250	200	100

Model 7212

12-gauge single-barrel trap shotgun, with 30" ventilated rib, ported barrel and automatic ejector. Engraved case-hardened receiver and walnut stock. Imported from Italy.

NIB	Exc.	V.G.	Good	Fair	Poor
—	1200	850	650	450	300

Model 1000 Military Carbine

Copy of U.S. M1 Carbine, with 18" barrel. Blued, with birchwood stock.

NIB	Exc.	V.G.	Good	Fair	Poor
600	500	400	300	150	80

Model 1003

As above, with 16", 18" or 20" barrel.

NIB	Exc.	V.G.	Good	Fair	Poor
550	450	300	250	100	80

Model 1010

As above but nickel-plated.

NIB	Exc.	V.G.	Good	Fair	Poor
550	450	300	250	130	100

Model 1015

As above but gold-plated.

NIB	Exc.	V.G.	Good	Fair	Poor
600	500	300	250	100	80

Model 1005 Deluxe

As above, with polished blue finish and Monte Carlo-style stock.

NIB	Exc.	V.G.	Good	Fair	Poor
550	450	300	250	130	80

Model 1006 Stainless

As Model 1000 in stainless steel.

NIB	Exc.	V.G.	Good	Fair	Poor
650	550	450	350	200	—

Model 1020 Teflon

As above, with black or gray Dupont Teflon-S finish.

NIB	Exc.	V.G.	Good	Fair	Poor
550	450	300	250	130	100

Model 1256 Ferret

Model 1000 in .256 Win. Magnum caliber.

NIB	Exc.	V.G.	Good	Fair	Poor
550	450	300	150	130	100

Model 3000 Enforcer

Pistol version of Model 1000, with 11.25" barrel and 15- or 30-shot magazines. Prices for blued models. Note: Add 20 percent nickel finish; 40 percent gold-plated; 30 percent stainless steel; 20 percent Teflon-S.

NIB	Exc.	V.G.	Good	Fair	Poor
650	500	400	300	200	100

Model 5000 Paratrooper

Model 1000, with 16" or 18" barrel and folding stock. In stainless steel known as Model 5006.

NIB	Exc.	V.G.	Good	Fair	Poor
650	550	450	350	250	150

1981 Commemorative Carbine

Limited production version of Model 1000 cased with accessories. Produced in 1981.

NIB	Exc.	V.G.	Good	Fair	Poor
650	500	400	300	150	80

Model 2200 Leatherneck

.22-caliber version of U.S. M1 Carbine, with 18" barrel and blowback action. Blued, with birchwood stock.

NIB	Exc.	V.G.	Good	Fair	Poor
400	300	180	150	100	80

UNWIN & RODGERS
Sheffield, England

Non-XLL Knife Pistol [Antique]

Two-blade folding pocketknife with pistol barrel, fold-down trigger and exposed hammer made during the mid- through late-19th century. Both .31 cal. percussion and .25 or .32 rimfire models are known. Percussion models have a trap door compartment to store spare lead balls, along with a ramrod and a folding scissor-style bullet mold that fit in slots in the scales like the tweezer and toothpick on a Swiss Army knife. Rare double-barrel mode is worth a premium.

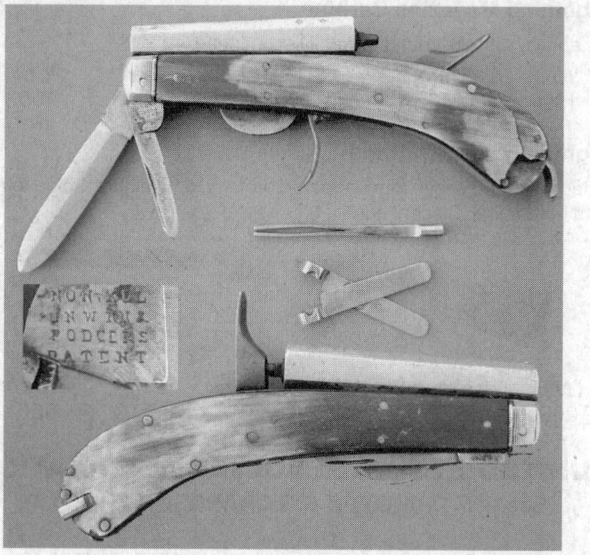

Jim Supica photo

Exc.	Fine	V.G.	Good	Fair	Poor
3000	2000	1500	1000	700	480

URIZAR, TOMAS
Eibar, Spain

Celta, J. Cesar, Premier, Puma, and Union

6.35mm semi-automatic pistol, with 3" barrel. Slide marked with trade names listed above. Blued, with black plastic grips cast with a wild man carrying a club.

NIB	Exc.	V.G.	Good	Fair	Poor
—	250	150	120	90	80

Dek-Du

5.5mm folding trigger double-action revolver, with 12-shot cylinder. Later versions made in 6.35mm. Manufactured from 1905 to 1912.

NIB	Exc.	V.G.	Good	Fair	Poor
—	400	250	180	130	50

Express

6.35mm semi-automatic pistol, with 2" barrel. Slide marked "The Best Automatic Pistol Express". Blued, with walnut grips. A 7.65mm variety exists with 4" barrel.

NIB	Exc.	V.G.	Good	Fair	Poor
—	220	120	100	80	50

Imperial

6.35mm caliber semi-automatic pistol, with 2.5" barrel. Model actually made by Aldazabal. Manufactured circa 1914.

NIB	Exc.	V.G.	Good	Fair	Poor
—	220	120	100	80	50

Le Secours or Phoenix

7.65mm semi-automatic pistol marked with trade names listed above.

NIB	Exc.	V.G.	Good	Fair	Poor
—	220	120	100	80	50

Princeps

6.35mm or 7.65mm semi-automatic pistol. Marked on slide "Made in Spain Princeps Patent".

NIB	Exc.	V.G.	Good	Fair	Poor
—	220	120	100	80	50

Venus

7.65mm semi-automatic pistol, with grips having trade name "Venus" cast in them.

NIB	Exc.	V.G.	Good	Fair	Poor
—	220	120	100	80	50

USAS 12 DAEWOO PRECISION IND., LTD.

South Korea

USAS 12

12-gauge semi-automatic shotgun, with 18.25" cylinder-bored barrel. 10-shot box or 20-shot drum magazine. Parkerized with composition stock. Model no longer imported. **WARNING:** As of May 1, 2001, this firearm must be registered with ATF and transfer tax of $200 paid. This firearm classified as a destructive device. Unregistered guns will be considered contraband after this date. Persons in possession will be in violation of federal law. Value speculative.

USELTON ARMS INC.

Goodlettsville, Tennessee

NOTE: Values shown for basic models. Sky's the limit.

Compact Classic

Chambered for .45 ACP cartridge, with 5" barrel. Checkered rosewood grips. Low-profile sights. Black and gray finish. Magazine capacity 7 rounds. Weight about 32 oz.

NIB	Exc.	V.G.	Good	Fair	Poor
2000	1700	1500	1100	800	500

Ultra Compact Classic

1911-style semi-automatic in .45-caliber, with fixed sights. Barrel 4.25", weight 34 oz., trigger pull 3-4 lb., 7+1 capacity. Rosewood or imitation ivory grips. Introduced 2006.

NIB	Exc.	V.G.	Good	Fair	Poor
2000	1700	1500	1100	800	500

Compact Classic Companion

Chambered for .357 Sig or .40 S&W cartridge. Fitted with 5" barrel. Low-profile sights. Black or polymer ivory grips. Stainless or gray finish. Magazine capacity 7 rounds. Weight about 32 oz.

NIB	Exc.	V.G.	Good	Fair	Poor
2250	1900	1700	1250	900	600

Carry Classic

Chambered for .45 ACP cartridge. Fitted with 4.25" barrel, with low-profile sights. Rosewood or polymer ivory grips. Gray and black finish. Magazine capacity 7 rounds. Weight about 34 oz.

NIB	Exc.	V.G.	Good	Fair	Poor
2000	1700	1500	1100	800	500

Ultra Carry

.45 ACP model features Damascus slide and titanium frame. Fitted with 3" barrel, with low-profile sights. Magazine capacity 7 rounds. Weight about 27 oz. Note: Also offered in titanium and stainless for $2350; stainless and black for $1850.

NIB	Exc.	V.G.	Good	Fair	Poor
3250	2900	2500	2000	1500	800

Tactical 1911

Chambered for .45 ACP cartridge. Fitted with 5" barrel, with Caspian adjustable sights. Rubber grips and moly coat finish. Magazine capacity 8 rounds. Weight about 40 oz.

NIB	Exc.	V.G.	Good	Fair	Poor
2200	1980	1600	1200	1000	500

Classic National Match

.45 ACP pistol has 5" barrel, with Caspian adjustable sights. Black aluma grips and finish. Magazine capacity 8 rounds. Weight about 40 oz. Note: Add $300 for compensator.

NIB	Exc.	V.G.	Good	Fair	Poor
2200	1980	1600	1200	1000	500

UZI

See—ISRAEL WEAPON INDUSTRIES/ISRAEL MILITARY INDUSTRIES

V

VALKYRIE ARMS, LTD.
Olympia, Washington

Valkyrie Arms filed for bankruptcy in early 2008.

Browning 1919 A4 .30 Caliber

Semi-automatic version of famous Browning machine gun. Chambered for .30-06 or .308 cartridge. Comes equipped with tripod, pintle, T&E, belly linker and 200 links. An A6 configuration available. Introduced in1996.

NIB	Exc.	V.G.	Good	Fair	Poor
2850	2000	1500	1100	750	600

U.S. M3-A1

Re-creation of famous "grease gun" in semi-automatic. Barrel length 16.5". Supplied with three 30-round magazines. Note: Add $50 for dummy suppressor; $300 plus transfer tax of $200 for real suppressor. All NFA rules and state laws must be followed for suppressors.

NIB	Exc.	V.G.	Good	Fair	Poor
2000	1500	1250	1000	500	300

DeLisle Carbine

Copy of famous World War II commando carbine used by British forces. Chambered for .45 ACP. Integral suppressor. All NFA rules must be followed. Only 167 original WWII carbines were produced. Note: Deduct $300 for dummy suppressor.

NIB	Exc.	V.G.	Good	Fair	Poor
2200	1700	1300	1000	500	300

VALMET, INC.
Jyvaskyla, Finland

M-62S

Semi-automatic copy of Finnish M-62 service rifle in 7.62x39 caliber. Patterned after Russian AK47. Fitted with walnut or tubular steel stock. Manufactured after 1962.

NIB	Exc.	V.G.	Good	Fair	Poor
7500	5000	4000	2500	1200	750

M-71S

As above in 5.56mm caliber. Available with composition stock.

NIB	Exc.	V.G.	Good	Fair	Poor
3000	2250	1700	1200	800	500

Model 76s

As above in 5.56mm, 7.62x39mm or 7.62x51mm. Barrel 16.75" or 20.5".

5.56mm

NIB	Exc.	V.G.	Good	Fair	Poor
3500	2500	2000	1500	850	600

7.62x39mm

NIB	Exc.	V.G.	Good	Fair	Poor
3800	3000	2750	2500	2000	1250

Model 78

As above in 7.62x51mm, 7.62x39 or .223, with 24.5" barrel, wood stock and integral bipod.

NIB	Exc.	V.G.	Good	Fair	Poor
5000	3500	2500	1750	1250	700

Model 212 Lion

12-gauge over/under shotgun, with 26", 28" or 30" barrels, single-selective trigger and extractors. Blued, with walnut stock. Manufactured from 1947 to 1968. Amazingly similar to Savage Model 330 over/under. Values shown for standard field grade.

NIB	Exc.	V.G.	Good	Fair	Poor
—	750	620	500	400	300

Model 412 Combination Gun

12-gauge .30-06 over/under combination gun. Built on frame of 12-gauge Lion shotgun. Discontinued.

NIB	Exc.	V.G.	Good	Fair	Poor
—	1900	1480	1200	1050	700

VALTRO
Italy

1998 A1

Model 1911 clone chambered for .45 ACP. Fitted with match-grade 5" barrel. Many special features include checkered front strap, beavertail grip safety, deluxe wood grips, serrated slide front and back, beveled magazine well. Weight about 40 oz. Introduced in 1998.

NIB	Exc.	V.G.	Good	Fair	Poor
2250	1950	1600	1280	800	500

Tactical 98 Shotgun

Chambered for 12-gauge. Fitted with 18.5" or 20" ported barrel. Pistol grip or standard stock. Extended magazine with 5- or 7-rounds. Ghost ring sights.

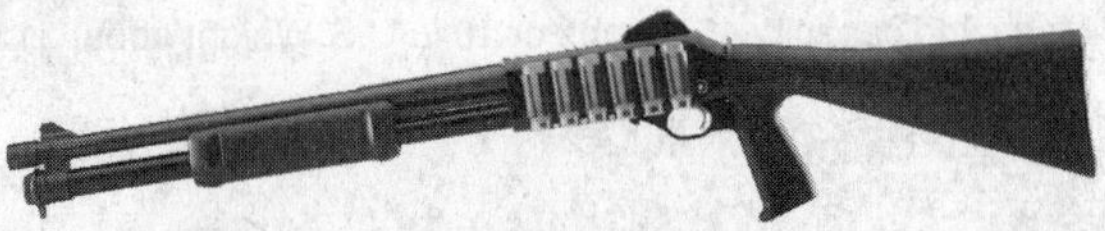

NIB	Exc.	V.G.	Good	Fair	Poor
—	900	750	680	500	320

PM5

Slide-action shotgun chambered for 12-gauge 3" shell. Barrel length 20" choked Cylinder. Box-fed magazine. Value shown for pre-ban model.

NIB	Exc.	V.G.	Good	Fair	Poor
—	500	430	350	—	—

VARNER SPORTING ARMS, INC.

Marietta, Georgia

Company made several over/under shotguns and rifle/shotgun combinations for Savage Company. These are no longer being imported into this country. Rifles listed are all patterned after Stevens Favorite model.

Hunter

.22-caliber single-shot rifle, with 21.5" half-octagonal take-down barrel fitted with an aperture rear sight. Blued, with well-figured walnut stocks. Introduced in 1988.

NIB	Exc.	V.G.	Good	Fair	Poor
380	300	250	200	150	100

Hunter Deluxe

As above, with case-hardened receiver and more finely figured stock.

NIB	Exc.	V.G.	Good	Fair	Poor
500	400	350	250	180	120

Presentation Grade

As above, with target hammer and trigger. Hand-checkered stock.

NIB	Exc.	V.G.	Good	Fair	Poor
580	480	420	350	250	200

No. 1 Grade

Engraved.

NIB	Exc.	V.G.	Good	Fair	Poor
650	550	500	450	350	200

No. 2 Grade

NIB	Exc.	V.G.	Good	Fair	Poor
780	650	600	500	400	200

No. 3 Grade

NIB	Exc.	V.G.	Good	Fair	Poor
1100	850	700	550	350	200

VECTOR ARMS, INC.

North Salt Lake, Utah

Mini Uzi

Smaller version of full size Uzi. Chambered for 9mm cartridge only. Fitted with 18" barrel.

Pre-Ban

NIB	Exc.	V.G.	Good	Fair	Poor
—	1500	1250	1000	—	—

Post-Ban

NIB	Exc.	V.G.	Good	Fair	Poor
—	1200	950	800	—	—

Uzi

Semi-automatic pre-ban Uzi carbine, with 18" barrel. Chambered for 9mm cartridge. Receiver built by Group Industries of Louisville, Kentucky, prior to May 1986. Receiver fixed parts manufacturing and receiver assembly by Vector Arms. Only 97 of these semi-automatic receivers manufactured. Note: Add $200 for .45 ACP or .22-caliber conversion kit.

Pre-Ban

NIB	Exc.	V.G.	Good	Fair	Poor
—	1300	1100	950	—	—

Post-Ban

NIB	Exc.	V.G.	Good	Fair	Poor
—	1000	850	700	—	—

VEKTOR

Pretoria, South Africa

Company made a variety of handguns and rifles for U.S. market until 2001. Now only manufactures firearms for South African military and law enforcement.

HANDGUNS

Model Z88

Semi-automatic pistol chambered for 9mm cartridge. Has 5" barrel and fixed sights. Weight about 35 oz. Blue finish. Magazine capacity 15 rounds or 10 in U.S. Clone of Beretta 92.

NIB	Exc.	V.G.	Good	Fair	Poor
600	480	350	250	180	100

Model SP1 Service Pistol

Chambered for 9mm cartridge. Fitted with 4.625" barrel. Fixed sights. Weight 35 oz. Blue finish. Magazine capacity 15 rounds or 10 in U.S. Note: Add $30 for anodized or nickel finish.

NIB	Exc.	V.G.	Good	Fair	Poor
600	480	350	250	180	100

Model SP1 Sport

Similar to SP1. Features 5" barrel, with three-chamber compensator. Blue finish. Weight about 38 oz.

NIB	Exc.	V.G.	Good	Fair	Poor
720	580	450	350	280	180

Model SP1 Tuned Sport

Model has three-chamber compensator on 5" barrel. Adjustable straight trigger and LPA 3-dot sighting system. Nickel finish. Weight about 38 oz.

NIB	Exc.	V.G.	Good	Fair	Poor
1200	950	800	580	400	300

Model SP1 Target

9mm model fitted with 6" barrel with adjustable straight trigger. LPA 3-dot sighting system. Weight about 40.5 oz. Two-tone finish.

NIB	Exc.	V.G.	Good	Fair	Poor
1200	950	800	580	400	300

Model SP1 Compact (General's Model)

Compact version of 9mm pistol fitted with 4" barrel. Fixed sights. Blue finish. Magazine capacity 15 rounds or 10 in U.S. Weight about 31.5 oz.

NIB	Exc.	V.G.	Good	Fair	Poor
650	520	400	300	200	80

Model SP2

Full-size service pistol chambered for .40 S&W cartridge. Fitted with 4.625" barrel. Fixed sights. Magazine capacity 11 rounds or 10 in U.S. Blued finish. Weight about 35 oz.

NIB	Exc.	V.G.	Good	Fair	Poor
650	520	400	300	200	80

Model SP2 Compact (General's Model)

Compact .40 S&W pistol, with 4" barrel. Magazine capacity 11 rounds or 10 in U.S. Weight about 31.5 oz. Blue finish. Fixed sights.

NIB	Exc.	V.G.	Good	Fair	Poor
650	520	400	300	200	80

Model SP2 Competition

Chambered for .40 S&W cartridge. Fitted with 5.875" barrel. Features enlarged safety levers and magazine catch. Frame has been thickened for scope mount. Beavertail grip and straight trigger. Weight about 42 oz.

NIB	Exc.	V.G.	Good	Fair	Poor
1000	750	600	450	320	200

Model SP1 Ultra Sport

Designed for IPSC open-class competition. Barrel length 6", with 3" chamber compensator. Chambered for 9mm cartridge. Optical scope mount, with Weaver rails. Magazine capacity 19 rounds or 10 in U.S. Weight about 41.5 oz. Priced with Lynx scope.

NIB	Exc.	V.G.	Good	Fair	Poor
2150	1800	1580	1200	800	500

Model SP2 Ultra Sport

Same as above chambered for .40 S&W cartridge. Magazine capacity 14 rounds or 10 in U.S.

NIB	Exc.	V.G.	Good	Fair	Poor
2150	1800	1580	1200	800	500

Model SP2 Conversion Kit

Made for SP2, this is a 9mm conversion kit that consists of 9mm barrel, recoil spring and 9mm magazine.

NIB	Exc.	V.G.	Good	Fair	Poor
200	150	100	80	50	20

Model CP-1 Compact

Chambered for 9mm cartridge. Fitted with 4" barrel. Polymer frame and fixed sights. Weight about 25 oz. Magazine capacity 13 rounds standard, 12 rounds compact or 10 rounds in U.S. Offered with black or nickel slide. Note: This model was recalled in 2000 due to safety concerns.

NIB	Exc.	V.G.	Good	Fair	Poor
480	380	250	150	100	50

RIFLES

Vektor H5 Pump-Action Rifle

Pump-action rifle chambered for .233 cartridge. Fitted with thumbhole stock and 22" barrel. Magazine capacity 5 rounds.

NIB	Exc.	V.G.	Good	Fair	Poor
850	720	600	480	300	200

Vektor 98

Built on Mauser action. Chambered for a variety of calibers from .243 to .375 H&H. Fitted with one-piece walnut stock, with hand-checkering. Magazine capacity 5 rounds. Open sights on Magnum calibers only.

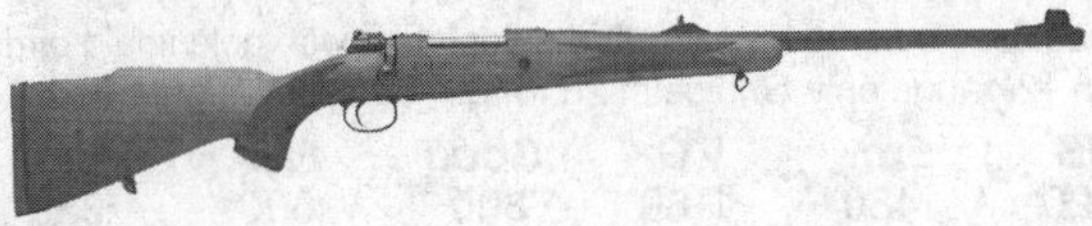

NIB	Exc.	V.G.	Good	Fair	Poor
1200	950	800	580	400	300

Vektor Lyttelton

Numerous special features. Fitted with classic walnut stock and wrap-around checkering. Fixed sights. Calibers offered from .243 to .375 H&H.

NIB	Exc.	V.G.	Good	Fair	Poor
1600	1400	1100	800	580	300

VENUS WAFFENWERKE
Zella Mehlis, Germany

Venus

6.35mm, 7.65mm or 9mm semi-automatic pistol, with 3.5" barrel. Slide marked "Original Venus Patent"; grips bear monogram "OW". Designed by Oskar Will. Blued plastic grips. Manufactured from 1912 to 1914.

NIB	Exc.	V.G.	Good	Fair	Poor
—	700	550	400	250	100

VERNEY-CARRON
St. Etienne, France

Concours

12-gauge over/under boxlock shotgun, with 26" or 28" ventilated rib barrels, single-selective triggers, automatic ejectors and profuse engraving. Blued French case-hardened, with checkered walnut stock. First imported in 1978.

NIB	Exc.	V.G.	Good	Fair	Poor
—	1450	900	700	600	300

Skeet Model

As above, with 28" Skeet-choked barrel and pistol grip stock.

NIB	Exc.	V.G.	Good	Fair	Poor
—	1600	1050	700	600	300

Snake Charmer II

.410 single-barrel break-action shotgun, with stainless steel barrel and receiver. Black ABS stock. Overall length 29".

NIB	Exc.	V.G.	Good	Fair	Poor
—	180	150	100	80	50

VERONA
Italy

HUNTING SHOTGUNS

Model SX401/S

12- or 20-gauge 3" semi-automatic. Offered with 26" or 28" ventilated rib barrel, with choke tubes. Checkered Turkish walnut stock. Weight about 6.75 lbs.

NIB	Exc.	V.G.	Good	Fair	Poor
800	600	480	350	150	100

Model SX405/S/L

As above, with black composite stock. Weight about 6.5 lbs.

NIB	Exc.	V.G.	Good	Fair	Poor
700	600	550	300	100	80

Model SX405W/H/SW/SH

12-gauge 3" Magnum semi-automatic gun. Choice of 26" or 28" ventilated rib barrel, with wetland or hardwood camo pattern. Weight about 6.5 lbs.

NIB	Exc.	V.G.	Good	Fair	Poor
800	600	480	350	150	100

LX501

Over/under shotgun chambered for 12-, 20-, 28-gauge and .410 bore. Single-selective trigger. Ejectors. Blued steel receiver. Walnut stock, with machine checkering. Offered with 28" ventilated rib barrels. Screw-in chokes for 12- and 20-gauge. Fixed chokes for 28-gauge and .410 bore. Chambers are 3" for all gauges except 28-gauge. Weight between 6.25 lbs. and 6.75 lbs. depending on gauge. Note: Add $30 for 28-gauge and .410 bore.

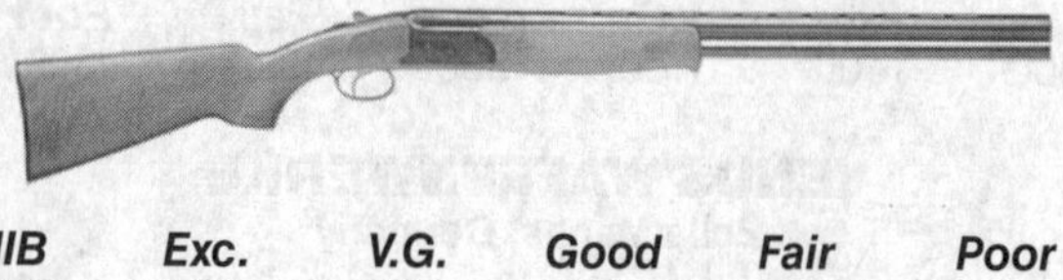

NIB	*Exc.*	*V.G.*	*Good*	*Fair*	*Poor*
1000	880	600	400	300	220

LX692G

Also offered in 12-, 20-, 28-gauge and .410 bore, with 28" ventilated rib barrels. Receiver fitted with sideplate. Gold inlaid hunting scenes on three sides. Matte finish walnut stock, with schnabel forearm, hand-cut checkering. Weight between 7.25 lbs. and 7.75 lbs. depending on gauge. Note: Add $40 for 28-gauge; $25 for .410 bore.

NIB	*Exc.*	*V.G.*	*Good*	*Fair*	*Poor*
1250	1100	880	720	500	300

LX692G-20/28

Same as above. Features 20-gauge, with extra set of 28-gauge barrels. Choke tubes standard. Weight about 7.5 lbs. with 20-gauge barrels.

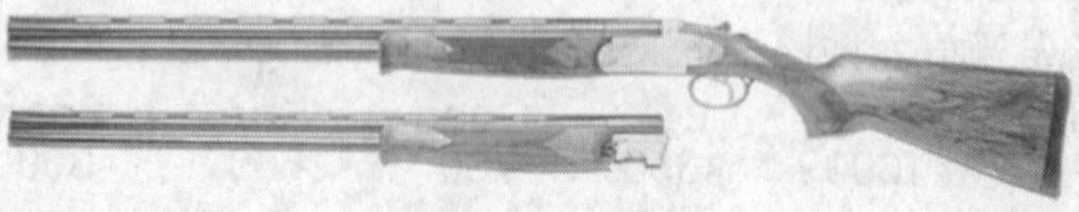

NIB	*Exc.*	*V.G.*	*Good*	*Fair*	*Poor*
2000	1800	1500	1200	900	500

Model LX1001 Express Combo

Over/under gun features two sets of barrels; one for 20-gauge 2.75"; other .223, .243, .270, .308 or .30-06. The 20-gauge barrels are 28" ventilated rib and rifle are 22". Checkered walnut stock, with oil-finish. Engraved receiver.

NIB	*Exc.*	*V.G.*	*Good*	*Fair*	*Poor*
2580	2300	1980	1600	900	600

LX702G

Offered in 12- or 20-gauge, with 28" barrel chambered for 3" shells. Features case colored receiver, with side plates. Receiver engraved on three sides with gold inlaid upland bird hunting scenes. Full-figured Turkish walnut, with hand-checkering and oil-finish. Single-selective trigger, black recoil pad, ejectors and schnabel forearm. Weight about: 12-gauge 7 lbs.; 20-gauge 6 lbs.

NIB	*Exc.*	*V.G.*	*Good*	*Fair*	*Poor*
1380	1200	950	700	500	350

SIDE-BY-SIDE SHOTGUNS

Model SS662GL

Side-by-side offered in 20- or 28-gauge, with 28" barrels choked Modified and Full. Double triggers. Engraved receiver. Checkered walnut stock, with straight-grip. Weight about 6 lbs. Made by Bernardelli. Note: Add 20 percent for 28-gauge.

NIB	*Exc.*	*V.G.*	*Good*	*Fair*	*Poor*
2200	2000	1750	1400	1000	500

Model SS772GL

As above, with slightly more engraving. Note: Add 20 percent for 28-gauge.

NIB	*Exc.*	*V.G.*	*Good*	*Fair*	*Poor*
2450	2200	1850	1550	1180	550

SPORTING/COMPETITION SHOTGUNS

LX680

Chambered for 12- or 20-gauge shells, with 2.75" chambers. Single-selective trigger, ejectors, lightly engraved steel receiver. Walnut stock, with beavertail firearm and hand-cut checkering. Ventilated recoil pad standard. Fitted with 28" barrels, with ventilated rib between barrels. Choke tubes. Weight about 6.5 lbs. depending on gauge.

NIB	*Exc.*	*V.G.*	*Good*	*Fair*	*Poor*
1080	900	700	520	380	250

LX692GS

Similar to above, with sideplates and gold inlaid hunting scenes.

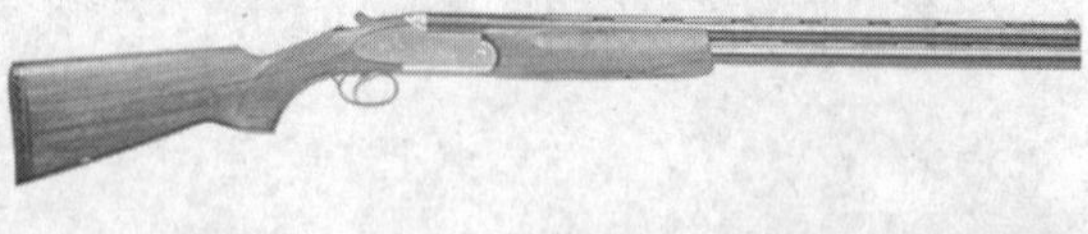

NIB	*Exc.*	*V.G.*	*Good*	*Fair*	*Poor*
1420	1300	1050	750	500	350

LX680C S&T

Over/under features 28" or 30" 11mm ventilated rib barrels on 12-gauge frame. Single-selective trigger, ejectors. Matte finish Turkish walnut stock, with hand-cut checkering, beavertail forearm, wider comb. Lightly engraved steel receiver. Ventilated rib between barrels. Choke tubes. Weight about 7.75 lbs. depending on barrel length. 28" barrel designated as Skeet/Sporting; 30" Trap.

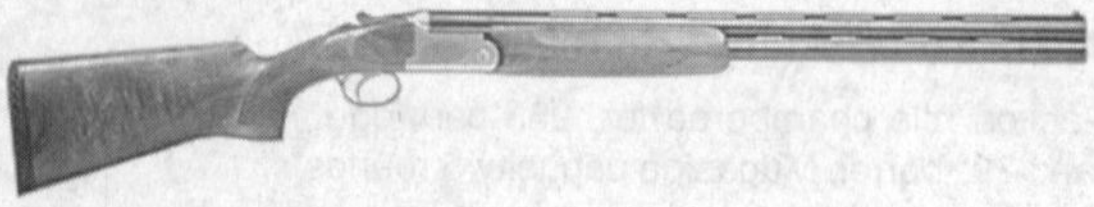

NIB	*Exc.*	*V.G.*	*Good*	*Fair*	*Poor*
1180	1000	800	600	420	280

LX692GC S&T

Same as above, with sideplates and gold inlaid game scenes.

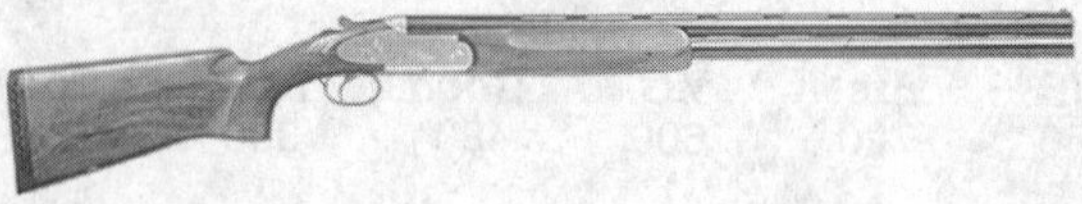

NIB	*Exc.*	*V.G.*	*Good*	*Fair*	*Poor*
1550	1400	1150	850	600	350

LX702GC S&T

Features case colored receiver and sideplates, with gold inlaid birds. Offered in 12-gauge only. Choice of 28" or 30" barrels. Weight about 7.5 lbs.

NIB	*Exc.*	*V.G.*	*Good*	*Fair*	*Poor*
1620	1480	1180	800	600	350

Model SX801/L

Semi-automatic 12-gauge 2.75" shotgun. Fitted with 28" or 30" ventilated rib ported barrels, with choke tubes and Hi-Viz sights. Walnut stock, with Monte Carlo or adjustable comb. Weight about 6.75 lbs.

NIB	Exc.	V.G.	Good	Fair	Poor
860	700	580	400	280	200

Model SX801G/GL

As above, with higher grade walnut stock.

NIB	Exc.	V.G.	Good	Fair	Poor
1060	900	720	600	450	200

Model LX980CS

12-gauge 2.75" over/under gun. Fitted with 30" ported barrels, with extended choke tubes. Removable trigger assembly. Black receiver. Checkered select walnut stock. Weight about 7.5 lbs.

NIB	Exc.	V.G.	Good	Fair	Poor
3520	3200	2500	2000	1550	600

Model LX980GCS/GCT

As above, with 30" or 32" ported barrels. Select walnut stock has adjustable comb. Weight about 7.5 lbs.

NIB	Exc.	V.G.	Good	Fair	Poor
3780	3400	2800	2250	1700	650

VICKERS, LTD.

Crayford/Kent, England

Jubilee

.22-caliber single-shot Martini-action rifle, with 28" barrel, adjustable sights and pistol grip walnut stock. Blued. Manufactured prior to WWII.

NIB	Exc.	V.G.	Good	Fair	Poor
—	1000	700	550	380	200

Empire

As above, with 27" or 30" barrel and straight stock.

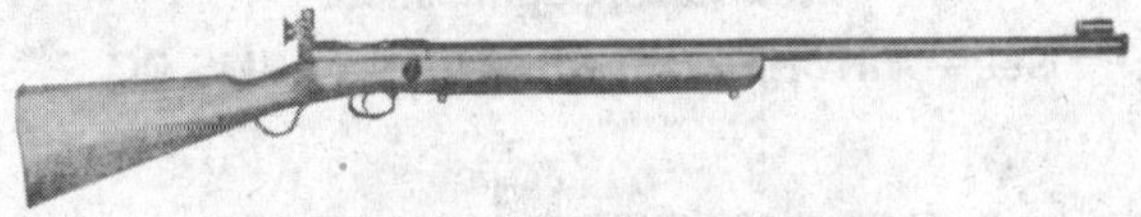

NIB	Exc.	V.G.	Good	Fair	Poor
—	1000	700	550	380	200

VICTOR EJECTOR

See—CRESCENT F. A. CO.

VICTORY ARMS CO., LTD.

Northhampton, England

Model MC5

9mm, .38 Super, .41 Action Express, 10mm or .45-caliber semi-automatic pistol, with 4.25", 5.75" or 7.5" barrel, 10-, 12- or 17-shot magazine, decocking lever and Millett sights. Interchangeable barrels were available. Introduced in 1989.

NIB	Exc.	V.G.	Good	Fair	Poor
500	400	300	250	200	150

VIRGINIAN

See—INTERARMS

VOERE

Kufstein, Austria

In 1987, this company was purchased by Mauser-Werke. Voere actions are used in rifles made and sold by KDF, Inc. (Kleinguenther), of Seguin, Texas. Values for older-production rifles are listed.

Model 1007

Bolt-action rifle chambered for .22 LR cartridge. Fitted with 18" barrel, open sights, beechwood stock. Introduced in 1984; discontinued 1991.

NIB	Exc.	V.G.	Good	Fair	Poor
450	380	300	200	150	80

Model 1013

Bolt-action rifle chambered for .22 WMR cartridge. Fitted with 18" barrel. Magazine capacity 8 rounds. Open sight with adjustable rear. Military-style stock oil-finished. Double-set triggers.

NIB	Exc.	V.G.	Good	Fair	Poor
650	580	500	380	250	120

Model 2107

.22 LR bolt-action rifle has 19.5" barrel, with Monte Carlo stock. 8-round magazine. Weight about 6 lbs.

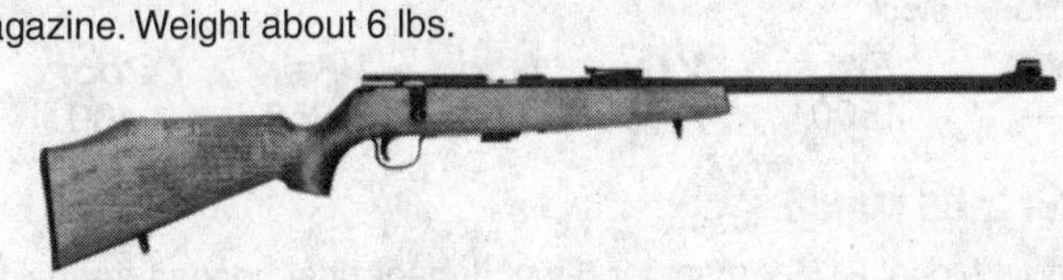

NIB	Exc.	V.G.	Good	Fair	Poor
650	580	500	380	250	120

Model 2107 Deluxe

Bolt-action rifle chambered for .22 LR cartridge. Checkered stock, with raised cheekpiece. Discontinued in 1988.

NIB	Exc.	V.G.	Good	Fair	Poor
650	580	500	380	250	120

Model 2114S

Semi-automatic rifle chambered for .22 LR cartridge. Fitted with 18" barrel. Magazine capacity 15 rounds. Open sight. Stock is beechwood. Single-stage trigger. No longer in production.

NIB	Exc.	V.G.	Good	Fair	Poor
450	380	300	200	150	80

Model 2115

Similar to above, with checkered stock. Weight about 5.75 lbs. Discontinued in 1995.

NIB	Exc.	V.G.	Good	Fair	Poor
500	420	350	250	200	100

Model 2150

Bolt-action centerfire rifle chambered for calibers from .22-250 to .338 Win. Magnum. Fitted with 22" barrels (24" on Magnums). Open sights with adjustable rear. Checkered walnut stock with oil-finish. Built on M98 Mauser action. Weight about 8 lbs. depending on caliber. Discontinued in 1995.

NIB	Exc.	V.G.	Good	Fair	Poor
—	1500	1200	850	550	300

Model 2155

Similar to Model 2150, with no sights and double-set triggers. Discontinued in 1995.

NIB	Exc.	V.G.	Good	Fair	Poor
—	1650	1350	1000	700	220

Model 2165

Similar to above, with open sights, walnut stock with Bavarian cheekpiece and schnabel forearm. Rosewood grip cap. Discontinued.

NIB	Exc.	V.G.	Good	Fair	Poor
—	1650	1350	1000	700	220

Model 2185

Semi-automatic centerfire rifle chambered for 7x64, .308 and .30-06 cartridges. Fitted with 20" barrel, open sights and adjustable rear. Checkered walnut stock. Available with full stock as well. Note: Add $100 for Mannlicher stock.

NIB	Exc.	V.G.	Good	Fair	Poor
—	1500	1200	950	850	400

Model 2185 Match

Same as Model 2185 except for 5-round magazine, hooded front sight, laminated stock with adjustable cheekpiece. Discontinued in 1994.

NIB	Exc.	V.G.	Good	Fair	Poor
4000	3400	2750	1150	650	400

Model Titan

Centerfire bolt-action rifle chambered in calibers from .243 to .375 H&H. Fitted with 24" or 26" barrels depending on caliber. No sights. Checkered Monte Carlo walnut stock with oil-finish. Discontinued in 1988.

NIB	Exc.	V.G.	Good	Fair	Poor
—	1200	1000	780	500	350

Model Titan Menor

Bolt-action rifle chambered for .222 Rem. and .223 Rem. Fitted with 23.5" barrel and 3-round magazine. No sights. Checkered Monte Carlo walnut stock, with rosewood grip cap. Introduced in 1986; dropped 1988.

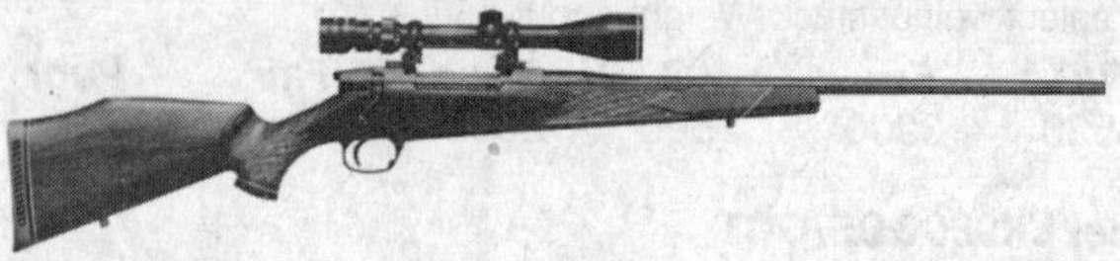

NIB	Exc.	V.G.	Good	Fair	Poor
—	1000	800	600	400	250

Model VEC-91 Series

Bolt-action rifle that fires caseless 5.7mm ammo. Adjustable rear sight on 20" barrel. Checkered walnut stock with cheekpiece. Electronic trigger. Limited importation into U.S. from 1991 to about 2008. Seldom seen for sale on used gun market, in part due to expensive case-less ammunition.

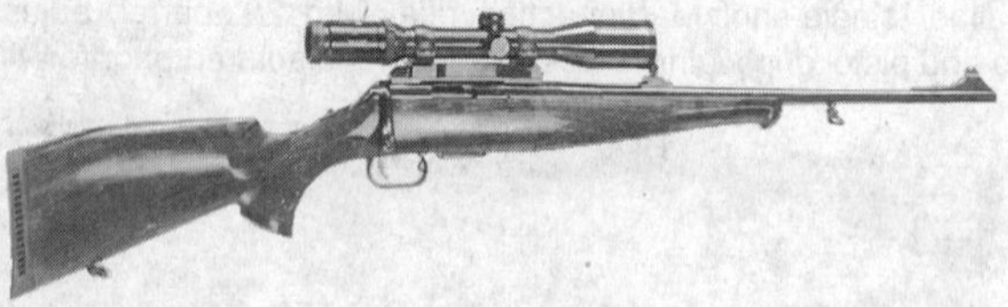

NIB	Exc.	V.G.	Good	Fair	Poor
2000	1600	1450	1000	—	—

VOLCANIC ARMS COMPANY

New Haven, Connecticut

See—WINCHESTER REPEATING ARMS CO.

VOLQUARTSEN CUSTOM

Carroll, Iowa

Company started in 1973 and began specializing in Ruger 10/22 aftermarket conversions. In 1997, the company began producing its own receivers. NOTE: Volquartsen offers beaucoup options on a wide variety of rifles. Values shown below are for more-or-less base models.

SEMI-AUTO RIFLES

Rifles are based on Ruger 10/22 design. Chambered for .22 LR or .22 WMR cartridge.

Standard

Fitted with 18.5" stainless steel barrel. Hogue rubber stock or brown laminated. No sights. Integral Weaver rail.

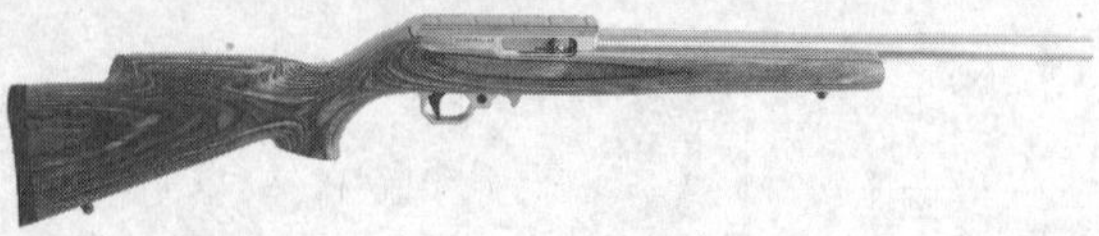

NIB	Exc.	V.G.	Good	Fair	Poor
1350	1200	950	700	550	300

Lightweight

Has 16.5" carbon-fiber barrel. Rubber or laminated stock. Integral Weaver rail.

NIB	Exc.	V.G.	Good	Fair	Poor
1370	1220	980	720	550	300

Deluxe

Has 20" stainless steel fluted and compensated barrel. Laminated or rubber stock.

NIB	Exc.	V.G.	Good	Fair	Poor
1360	1200	950	700	550	300

VT2

Caliber: .22 LR, .22 WMR, .17 HMR. Capacity: 9-shot detachable magazine. Barrel: 16.5" carbon-fiber tensioned with flush-fitting blow-forward compensator and aluminum thread protector. Stock: Magpul Milspec stock and MOE-K grip. Available in both 6" and 12" handguard lengths with M-LOK on both. Sights: Integral 0 MOA Picatinny rail. Features: VT2 semi-automatic takedown design utilizes a unique button and lever combination to slide the barrel out of the receiver for easy stowing. Unique new design VT2 rifles built for either .22 WMR and .17 HMR to swap calibers simply by changing the barrel. TG2000 trigger set at 2.5 lbs. Made in the USA.

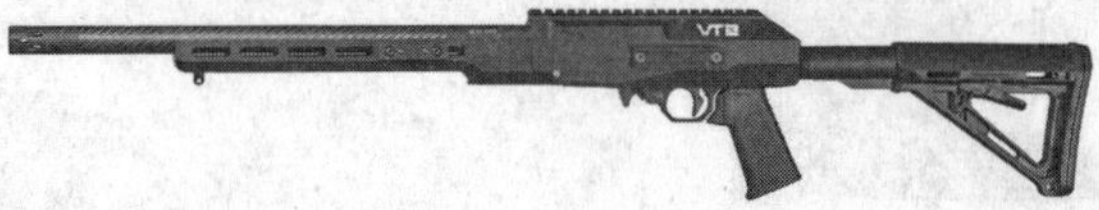

NIB	Exc.	V.G.	Good	Fair	Poor
2040	—	—	—	—	—

SIGNATURE SERIES

Fitted with 20" stainless steel fluted and compensated barrel. Engraved receiver, triggerguard and rings. Comes with Nikon 3.3x10 Titanium scope. Fancy walnut stock.

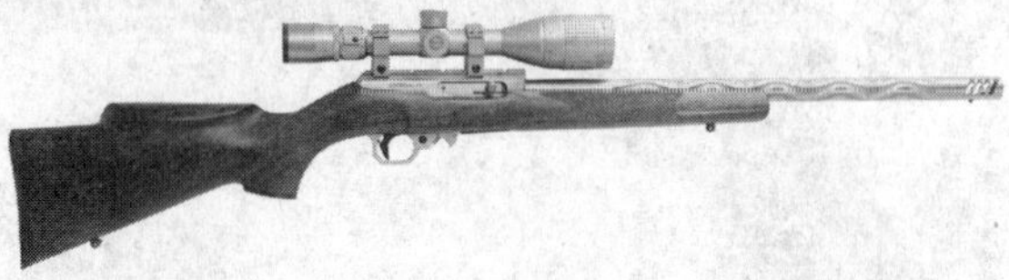

NIB	Exc.	V.G.	Good	Fair	Poor
2500	2200	1650	1200	600	300

VG-1

Has 20" stainless steel fluted and compensated barrel. Fitted with green McMillan fiberglass stock. Finish is black epoxy powder coating. Offered in .22 WMR only.

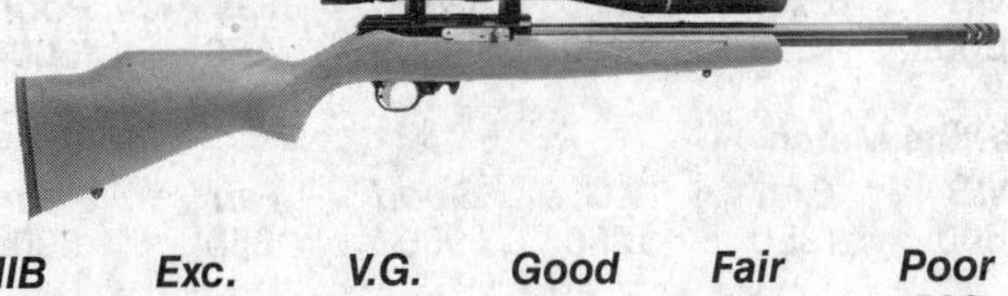

NIB	Exc.	V.G.	Good	Fair	Poor
1900	1700	1400	1150	900	500

Fusion Takedown Model

This semi-automatic has quick-change barrels in three different calibers: .17 HMR, .22 WMR and .22 LR.

One Barrel: .22 LR

NIB	Exc.	V.G.	Good	Fair	Poor
1380	1120	950	700	350	150

One Barrel: .17 WMR or .22 WMR

NIB	Exc.	V.G.	Good	Fair	Poor
1580	1260	1050	800	400	200

All Three Barrels Included

NIB	Exc.	V.G.	Good	Fair	Poor
1780	1450	1100	900	450	250

Evolution Model

Centerfire model in .204 Ruger or .223 Rem. Gas-operated action. Stainless steel receiver has integral Picatinny rail. Laminate or laminate thumbhole stock in gray or brown. Note: Add $100 for thumbhole stock.

NIB	Exc.	V.G.	Good	Fair	Poor
2200	1820	1350	1100	500	300

VX-2500

Features 20" stainless steel fluted and compensated barrel. Fitted with VX-2500 stock, with aluminum forearm. Designed for benchrest shooting.

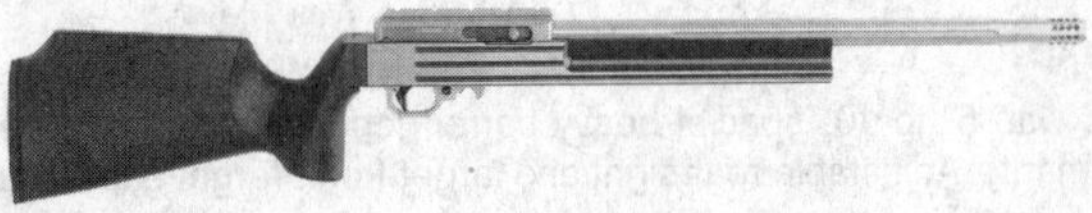

NIB	Exc.	V.G.	Good	Fair	Poor
2000	1750	1500	1200	900	500

VX-5000

Fitted with 18" carbon-fiber lightweight barrel, with compensator. Comes standard with VX-5000 stock, with aluminum forend.

NIB	Exc.	V.G.	Good	Fair	Poor
2200	1950	1700	1400	1000	600

Ultralite Modshot

Caliber: .22 LR. Capacity: 10. Barrel: Forward blow comp, anodized aluminum. Stock: Modshot. Sights: Picatinny rail. Weight: 3.8 lbs. Features: Ultralight design, 2.25-lb. trigger pull, uses Ruger magazines, made in the USA.

NIB	Exc.	V.G.	Good	Fair	Poor
1700	1450	1200	—	—	—

Summit 17 WSM

Caliber: .17 WSM. Capacity: 6. Barrel: 20" threaded heavy. Stock: Laminated wood, sporter style. Sights: Picatinny rail. Weight: 7.7 lbs. Features: 1.75-lb. trigger pull, made in the USA, stainless steel receiver.

NIB	Exc.	V.G.	Good	Fair	Poor
1500	1250	1100	—	—	—

PISTOLS

Pistols based on Ruger MK II design.

Black Cheetah Pistol

Special order only.

Compact

Fitted with 3.5" bull barrel and Hogue Monogrip. Adjustable rear sight and target front. Stainless steel finish. Weight 42 oz.

NIB	Exc.	V.G.	Good	Fair	Poor
1000	850	700	520	400	300

Deluxe

Fitted with 5" to 10" special heavy barrel depending on customer's requirements. Adjustable rear sight and target front. Target grips. Stainless steel finish.

NIB	Exc.	V.G.	Good	Fair	Poor
1250	1000	900	700	580	450

Masters

Features 6.5" barrel, with aluminum alloy-finned underlug. Top rib has front blade sight with an adjustable rear. Rib cut to accommodate optics. Integral compensator. Weight 56 oz.

NIB	Exc.	V.G.	Good	Fair	Poor
1600	1350	1200	900	650	500

Olympic

Designed for NRA or UIT competitive shooting. Has 7.5" match barrel, with unique gas chamber for recoil-free shooting. Target front sight and adjustable rear. Weight 36 oz.

NIB	Exc.	V.G.	Good	Fair	Poor
1750	1450	1300	1000	650	500

Stingray

Fitted with 7.5" match-grade barrel, with radial flutes. Compensator standard. Supplied with Ultra Dot red-dot optic or TL rear. Weight 56 oz.

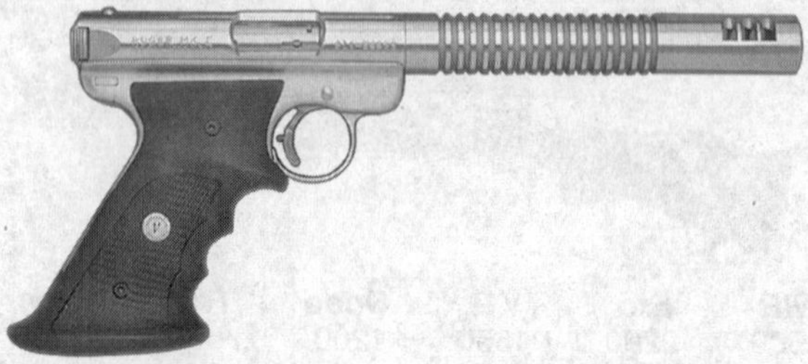

NIB	Exc.	V.G.	Good	Fair	Poor
1600	1350	1200	900	650	500

Terminator

Fitted with 7.5" match barrel, with integral compensator. Weaver-style or .375" tip-off scope mounting system. Note: Add $150 for Ultra Dot optics.

NIB	Exc.	V.G.	Good	Fair	Poor
1600	1350	1200	900	650	500

Ultra-Lite Match

NIB	Exc.	V.G.	Good	Fair	Poor
1600	1350	1200	900	650	500

V-6

V-6 has 6" ventilated rib triangular-shaped match barrel, with full-length underlug. Adjustable rear sight and target front. Rubber target grips. Weight 36 oz.

NIB	Exc.	V.G.	Good	Fair	Poor
1350	1200	950	700	550	300

V-2000

Fitted with 6" match barrel. Alloy-finned underlug. Rubber target grips. Adjustable rear sight with target front. Weight 37 oz.

NIB	Exc.	V.G.	Good	Fair	Poor
1350	1200	950	700	550	300

V-Magic II

Has 8" fluted match barrel, with integral compensator. Rubber target grips and Ultra Dot red-dot optic. No open sights. Weight 46 oz.

NIB	Exc.	V.G.	Good	Fair	Poor
1350	1200	950	700	550	300

VOLUNTEER ENTERPRISES

Knoxville, Tennessee

See—COMMANDO ARMS

VOUZELAUD

Paris, France

Model 315 E

12-, 16-, or 20-gauge boxlock shotgun, with 20" barrels, double triggers and straight-grip stock. Blued case-hardened. Imported prior to 1988.

NIB	Exc.	V.G.	Good	Fair	Poor
—	7500	6000	4000	2000	900

Model 315 EL

As above, with more engraving. Available in 28-gauge or .410 bore, which are worth approximately $1,000 more than values listed.

NIB	Exc.	V.G.	Good	Fair	Poor
—	10000	8000	5000	2500	1100

Model 315 EGL

As above, with French case-hardened receiver. Discontinued in 1987.

NIB	Exc.	V.G.	Good	Fair	Poor
—	15000	12000	8500	4000	1500

Model 315 EGL-S

As above, with engraved hunting scenes. Discontinued in 1987.

NIB	Exc.	V.G.	Good	Fair	Poor
—	5500	4500	3500	2000	1000

W

WALCH, JOHN
New York, New York

Navy Revolver (Antique)

A .36-caliber superimposed load percussion revolver, with 6" octagonal barrel and 6-shot cylinder. Fitted with 12 nipples, two hammers and two triggers. Barrel marked "Walch Firearms Co. NY." and "Patented Feb. 8, 1859". Blued, with walnut grips.

Exc.	Fine	V.G.	Good	Fair	Poor
13000	9000	6500	4000	950	660

Pocket Revolver (Antique)

A spur trigger .31-caliber 10-shot percussion revolver, with brass or iron frame and walnut grips. Iron frame version worth approximately 50 percent more than brass variety.

Courtesy Greg Martin Auctions

Exc.	Fine	V.G.	Good	Fair	Poor
5000	2750	1870	1000	300	210

WALDMAN
Germany

Waldman

A 7.65mm semi-automatic pistol, with 3.5" barrel and 8-shot magazine. Slide marked "1913 Model Automatic Pistol" and some examples are marked "American Automatic Pistol". Blued, with checkered walnut grips inlaid with a brass insert marked "Waldman".

NIB	Exc.	V.G.	Good	Fair	Poor
—	300	220	200	150	100

WALLIS & BIRCH
Philadelphia, Pennsylvania

Pocket Pistol

A .41-caliber single-shot percussion pocket pistol, with 2.5" or 3" barrel, German silver furniture and walnut stock. Barrel marked "Wallis & Birch Phila.". Produced during 1850s.

NIB	Exc.	V.G.	Good	Fair	Poor
—	—	4050	2250	800	250

WALTHER, CARL
Zella Mehilis and Ulm/Donau, Germany

Model 1

A 6.35mm semi-automatic pistol. Barrel lengths 2" to 6". Blued, with checkered hard rubber grips. Walther logo on each grip. Introduced in 1908.

NIB	Exc.	V.G.	Good	Fair	Poor
—	1200	1000	800	360	260

Model 2

A 6.35mm semi-automatic pistol, with a knurled bushing at the muzzle that retains the mainspring. There are two variations: fixed rear sight; pop-up rear sight. Blued, with checkered hard rubber grips. Walther logo on each grip. Introduced in 1909.

Fixed Sights

NIB	Exc.	V.G.	Good	Fair	Poor
—	800	600	300	200	150

Pop Up Sights

NIB	Exc.	V.G.	Good	Fair	Poor
—	3000	2500	2000	1000	760

Model 3

7.65mm semi-automatic pistol having a smooth barrel bushing. Blued, with checkered hard rubber grips. Walther logo on each grip. Introduced in 1910.

Courtesy James Rankin

NIB	Exc.	V.G.	Good	Fair	Poor
4500	3500	2500	2000	1000	760

Model 4

A 7.65mm semi-automatic pistol larger than preceding models. Many variations of this model produced. Blued, with checkered hard rubber grips. Walther logo on each grip. Introduced in 1910.

Courtesy James Rankin

NIB	Exc.	V.G.	Good	Fair	Poor
700	600	500	400	280	150

Model 5

A 6.35mm semi-automatic pistol that is almost identical to Model 2. Fixed sights. Blued, with checkered hard rubber grips. Walther logo on each grip.

Courtesy James Rankin

NIB	Exc.	V.G.	Good	Fair	Poor
600	500	400	300	200	150

Model 6

9mm semi-automatic pistol. Largest of Walther numbered pistols. Approximately 1,500 manufactured. Blued, with checkered hard rubber grips. Walther logo on each grip. Sometimes seen with plain checkered wood grips. Introduced in 1915.

NIB	Exc.	V.G.	Good	Fair	Poor
12000	10000	8000	4000	3000	2000

Model 7

A 6.35mm semi-automatic pistol in the same style as Model 4. Blued, with checkered hard rubber grips. Walther logo on each side. Introduced in 1917.

NIB	Exc.	V.G.	Good	Fair	Poor
800	700	500	300	200	150

Model 8

A 6.35mm semi-automatic pistol. Finish is blue, silver or gold. Most were unengraved, but three types of engraving coverage were available from the factory: slide only, slide and frame and complete coverage overall. Grips are checkered hard rubber, with WC logo on one grip and 6.35mm on opposite side. Ivory grips are seen with many of the engraved models. Introduced in 1920 and produced until 1944. Note: Add $500 for factory case.

Courtesy James Rankin

Blue, Silver or Gold Finish

NIB	Exc.	V.G.	Good	Fair	Poor
—	750	600	300	200	150

Engraved Slide

NIB	Exc.	V.G.	Good	Fair	Poor
—	1000	700	500	300	200

Engraved Slide and Frame

NIB	Exc.	V.G.	Good	Fair	Poor
—	2500	2000	1100	450	300

Engraved, Complete Coverage

NIB	Exc.	V.G.	Good	Fair	Poor
—	4000	3500	1400	500	300

Model 9

A 6.35mm semi-automatic pistol. Smaller than Model 8. Built as Model 1, with exposed barrel. Same finishes and engraving as Model 8. Introduced in 1921; produced until 1944. All values same as Model 8.

Courtesy James Rankin

Sport Model 1926/ Walther Hammerless Target 22/ Walther Standard Sport/ Walther 1932 Olympia/ Sport Model Target/ Special Stoeger Model

All of these .22 LR caliber semi-automatic pistols are the same target pistol. Introduced by Walther in 1926. A well-made pistol, with a barrel length between 6" to 16". Has one-piece checkered wrap-around wood grips. There was also a .22 Short version of Olympia model produced for rapid fire Olympic shooting. There was also a torpedo-shape target weight available for shooters. Note: Add $200 for target weight; $500 for case.

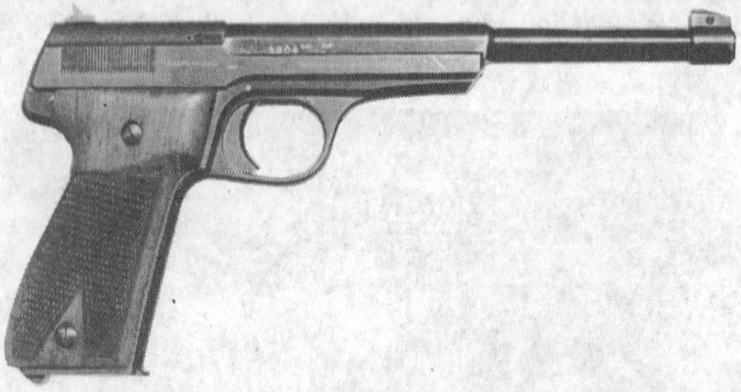

Courtesy Orvel Reichert

NIB	Exc.	V.G.	Good	Fair	Poor
—	1800	1300	900	500	300

Walther 1936 Olympia

Semi-automatic target pistol in .22-caliber resembled earlier 1932 Olympia, but with many improvements. There were four standard models produced with many variations of each one. These variations included many barrel lengths, both round and octagon. There were duraluminum slides, frames and triggers. Various weight configurations as many as four separate weights to one gun. One-piece wrap-around checkered wood grips in different configurations for the individual shooter. Produced until 1944. Note: Prices are for Standard Model. Add $500 for Pentathlon or Hunter; $300 for Rapid Fire; $750 for weights. The four models were:

1. Funfklamph Pentathlon
2. Jagerschafts—Hunter
3. Sport or Standard Model
4. Schnellfeur—Rapid Fire

Courtesy John J. Stimson, Jr.

Olympia without weights

NIB	Exc.	V.G.	Good	Fair	Poor
2000	1500	1300	750	480	250

Model MP

A 9mm semi-automatic pistol that was the forerunner of Model AP and P.38 series. Found in variations that resemble a large Model PP or P.38. Blued finish, with one-piece wrap-around checkered wood grips.

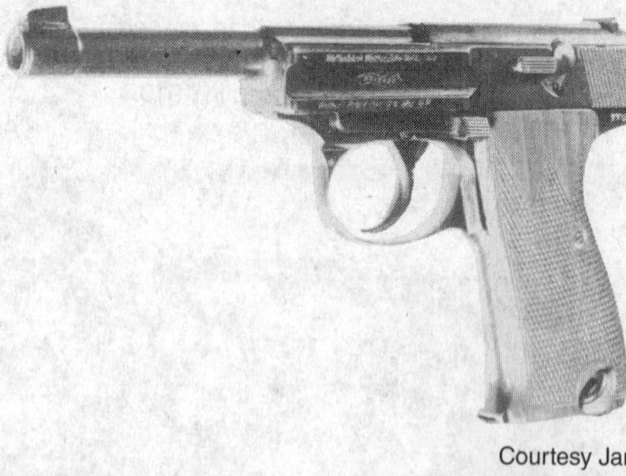

Courtesy James Rankin

NIB	Exc.	V.G.	Good	Fair	Poor
—	35000	30000	25000	20000	15000

Model AP

A 9mm semi-automatic pistol that was the forerunner of Model P.38. A hammerless pistol in various barrel lengths. Sometimes with duraluminum frames and some with stocks. Blued finish, with one-piece wrap-around checkered wood grips. Note: Add $4000 with stock.

NIB	Exc.	V.G.	Good	Fair	Poor
—	28000	25000	20000	15000	10000

Model PP

Semi-automatic pistol in .22-, .25-, .32- and .380-caliber. Introduced in 1928. First successful commercial double-action pistol. Manufactured in finishes of blue, silver and gold, with three different types of engraving. Grips generally two-piece black or white plastic, with Walther banner on each grip. Grips in wood or ivory are seen, but usually on engraved guns. Many variations of Model PP and numerous NSDAP markings seen on pre-1946 models that were produced during Nazi regime. All reflect various prices.

.22 Caliber

NIB	Exc.	V.G.	Good	Fair	Poor
1200	800	600	350	250	150

.25 Caliber

NIB	Exc.	V.G.	Good	Fair	Poor
8000	6500	5000	3000	1500	700

.32 Caliber, High Polished Finish

Courtesy James Rankin

NIB	Exc.	V.G.	Good	Fair	Poor
1000	850	650	320	220	180

.32 Caliber, Milled Finish

NIB	Exc.	V.G.	Good	Fair	Poor
800	700	500	250	200	120

.380 Caliber

NIB	Exc.	V.G.	Good	Fair	Poor
2000	1600	1300	800	480	350

.32 Caliber, with Duraluminum Frame

NIB	Exc.	V.G.	Good	Fair	Poor
1000	900	700	550	400	200

.32 Caliber, with Bottom Magazine Release

NIB	Exc.	V.G.	Good	Fair	Poor
1500	1400	1000	600	400	200

.32 Caliber, with Verchromt Finish

NIB	Exc.	V.G.	Good	Fair	Poor
3000	2800	2500	1200	700	400

.32 Caliber, Allemagne Marked

NIB	Exc.	V.G.	Good	Fair	Poor
950	850	700	550	320	250

.32 Caliber, A. F. Stoeger Contract

NIB	Exc.	V.G.	Good	Fair	Poor
2700	2500	1750	1050	700	400

.32 Caliber, with Waffenampt Proofs, High Polished Finish

NIB	Exc.	V.G.	Good	Fair	Poor
2500	1900	1500	900	280	150

.32 Caliber, with Waffenampt Proofs, Milled Finish

NIB	Exc.	V.G.	Good	Fair	Poor
1300	1000	750	400	250	150

.32 Caliber, in Blue Finish and Full Coverage Engraving

Note: Add $500 for ivory grips; $700 for leather presentation cases; $1000 for .380-caliber.

NIB	Exc.	V.G.	Good	Fair	Poor
—	5000	4000	3000	1200	700

.32 Caliber, in Silver Finish and Full Coverage Engraving

Note: Add $500 for ivory grips; $700 for leather presentation cases; $1000 for .380-caliber.

NIB	Exc.	V.G.	Good	Fair	Poor
—	5500	4500	3000	1200	700

.32 Caliber, in Gold Finish and Full Coverage Engraving

Note: Add $500 for ivory grips; $700 for leather presentation cases; $1000 for .380-caliber.

NIB	Exc.	V.G.	Good	Fair	Poor
—	5800	5000	3500	1500	700

.32 Caliber, Police Eagle/C Proofed, High Polished Finish

NIB	Exc.	V.G.	Good	Fair	Poor
1600	1200	800	380	250	150

.32 Caliber, Police Eagle/C and Police Eagle/F Proofed, Milled Finish

NIB	Exc.	V.G.	Good	Fair	Poor
1000	900	600	380	280	150

.32 Caliber, NSKK Marked on the Slide

Note: Add $1,000 with proper NSKK DRGM AKAH holster.

NIB	Exc.	V.G.	Good	Fair	Poor
5000	4000	3000	1200	550	300

.32 Caliber, NSDAP Gruppe Markings

Note: Add $1,000 with proper SA DRGM AKAH holster.

NIB	Exc.	V.G.	Good	Fair	Poor
2700	2500	2000	1000	500	300

.32 Caliber, PDM Marked with Bottom Magazine Release

NIB	Exc.	V.G.	Good	Fair	Poor
2400	2000	1500	1100	480	300

.32 Caliber, RJ Marked

NIB	Exc.	V.G.	Good	Fair	Poor
1400	900	700	480	400	150

.32 Caliber, RFV Marked, High Polished or Milled Finish

NIB	Exc.	V.G.	Good	Fair	Poor
1400	900	700	480	400	150

.32 Caliber, RBD Munster Marked

NIB	Exc.	V.G.	Good	Fair	Poor
2500	2200	1750	1200	650	400

.32 Caliber, RpLt Marked

NIB	Exc.	V.G.	Good	Fair	Poor
1650	1500	1200	700	380	200

.32 Caliber, Statens Vattenfallsverk Marked

NIB	Exc.	V.G.	Good	Fair	Poor
1650	1500	1200	700	380	200

.32 Caliber, AC Marked

NIB	Exc.	V.G.	Good	Fair	Poor
800	700	500	300	250	150

.32 Caliber, Duraluminum Frame

NIB	Exc.	V.G.	Good	Fair	Poor
1000	900	700	500	400	150

.380 Caliber, Bottom Magazine Release and Waffenampt Proofs

NIB	Exc.	V.G.	Good	Fair	Poor
2400	2000	1500	700	500	300

Model PPK

Semi-automatic pistol in .22-, .25-, .32- and .380-caliber. Introduced six months after Model PP in 1929. A more compact version of Model PP, with one less round in magazine. One-piece wrap-around checkered plastic grips in brown, black and white. Walther banner on each side of grips. Model PPK will be found with same types of finishes as Model PP, as well as same styles of engraving. Grips in wood or ivory are seen with some of the engraved models. As with Model PP, there are many variations of Model PPK and numerous NSDAP markings seen on pre-1946 models that were produced during the Nazi regime. All reflect various prices.

Courtesy James Rankin

.22 Caliber

NIB	Exc.	V.G.	Good	Fair	Poor
2400	1700	1500	750	320	180

.25 Caliber

NIB	Exc.	V.G.	Good	Fair	Poor
10000	6000	4000	1850	1000	500

.32 Caliber, High Polished Finish

NIB	Exc.	V.G.	Good	Fair	Poor
1700	950	750	450	250	150

.32 Caliber, Milled Finish

NIB	Exc.	V.G.	Good	Fair	Poor
1500	900	700	400	250	150

.380 Caliber

NIB	Exc.	V.G.	Good	Fair	Poor
4500	3000	2500	1600	750	380

.32 Caliber, with Duraluminum Frame

NIB	Exc.	V.G.	Good	Fair	Poor
2000	1500	1300	600	400	200

.32 Caliber, Marked Mod. PP on Slide

NIB	Exc.	V.G.	Good	Fair	Poor
6000	5000	4000	2500	1500	1000

.32 Caliber, with Panagraphed Slide

NIB	Exc.	V.G.	Good	Fair	Poor
2000	1200	750	450	300	200

.32 Caliber, with Verchromt Finish

NIB	Exc.	V.G.	Good	Fair	Poor
3800	2800	2500	1200	700	350

.32 Caliber, in Blue Finish and Full Coverage Engraving

Note: Add $1,000 for ivory grips; $1,000 for leather presentation cases; $1,000 for .380-caliber.

NIB	Exc.	V.G.	Good	Fair	Poor
—	5000	3500	2500	1200	700

.32 Caliber, in Silver Finish and Full Coverage Engraving

Note: Add $1,000 for ivory grips; $1,000 for leather presentation cases; $1,000 for .380-caliber.

NIB	Exc.	V.G.	Good	Fair	Poor
—	6000	4000	3000	1500	700

.32 Caliber, in Gold Finish and Full Coverage Engraving

Note: Add $1,000 for ivory grips; $1,000 for leather presentation cases; $1,000 for .380-caliber.

NIB	Exc.	V.G.	Good	Fair	Poor
—	6500	5500	3500	1500	700

.32 Caliber, Czechoslovakian Contract

NIB	Exc.	V.G.	Good	Fair	Poor
2000	1850	1500	1000	550	300

.32 Caliber, Allemagne Marked

NIB	Exc.	V.G.	Good	Fair	Poor
1150	1000	800	600	400	250

.32 Caliber, with Waffenampt Proofs and a High Polished Finish

NIB	Exc.	V.G.	Good	Fair	Poor
2400	1900	1600	900	400	250

.32 Caliber, with Waffenampt Proofs and a Milled Finish

NIB	Exc.	V.G.	Good	Fair	Poor
1700	1500	1300	750	300	180

.32 Caliber, Police Eagle/C Proofed, High Polished Finish

NIB	Exc.	V.G.	Good	Fair	Poor
1500	1200	1000	500	300	180

.32 Caliber, Police Eagle/C Proofed. Milled Finish

NIB	Exc.	V.G.	Good	Fair	Poor
1100	900	700	380	280	180

.32 Caliber, Police Eagle/F Proofed, Duraluminum Frame, Milled Finish

NIB	Exc.	V.G.	Good	Fair	Poor
1600	1300	1000	550	350	220

.22 Caliber, Late War, Black Grips

NIB	Exc.	V.G.	Good	Fair	Poor
2400	1800	1500	600	450	300

.32 Caliber, Party Leader Grips, Brown

NIB	Exc.	V.G.	Good	Fair	Poor
8000	6000	5500	3000	2250	2000

.32 Caliber, Party Leader Grips, Black

Note: Add $1,500 with proper Party Leader DRGM AKAH holster.

NIB	Exc.	V.G.	Good	Fair	Poor
8000	6000	5500	3200	2550	2500

.32 Caliber, RZM Marked

NIB	Exc.	V.G.	Good	Fair	Poor
3000	2400	1700	800	400	300

.32 Caliber, PDM Marked with Duraluminum Frame and Bottom Magazine Release

NIB	Exc.	V.G.	Good	Fair	Poor
3500	3200	2800	1300	750	450

.32 Caliber, RFV Marked

NIB	Exc.	V.G.	Good	Fair	Poor
3000	2500	2000	1150	650	400

.32 Caliber, DRP Marked

NIB	Exc.	V.G.	Good	Fair	Poor
2800	2400	1800	1200	450	280

.32 Caliber, Statens Vattenfallsverk

NIB	Exc.	V.G.	Good	Fair	Poor
1700	1500	1200	700	450	300

WALTHER POST-WORLD WAR II

Manufactured by the firm of: Manufacture de Machines du Haut Rhin at Mulhouse, France under license by Walther.

Model PP—Some with Duraluminum Frames

.22 Caliber

NIB	Exc.	V.G.	Good	Fair	Poor
850	750	600	400	280	180

.32 Caliber

NIB	Exc.	V.G.	Good	Fair	Poor
600	500	380	350	280	180

.380 Caliber

NIB	Exc.	V.G.	Good	Fair	Poor
850	750	600	400	280	180

Model PP—All Three Calibers Finished In Blue, Silver and Gold with Full Coverage EngravingBlue

NIB	Exc.	V.G.	Good	Fair	Poor
—	1900	1500	900	600	300

Silver

NIB	Exc.	V.G.	Good	Fair	Poor
—	1900	1500	900	600	300

Gold

NIB	Exc.	V.G.	Good	Fair	Poor
—	1900	1500	900	600	300

Model PP Mark II

These Walthers were manufactured under license by Walther and produced by Manurhin Company. Sold exclusively by Interarms, Alexandria, Virginia. Mark IIs were the same pistols as those above and have the same types of finish and engraving as well as the same value.

Model PP Manurhin

Manurhin Company manufactured with Manurhin logo and inscription. Usually "Licensed by Walther" somewhere on the pistol. Same pistols as those above. Bearing same types of finish and engraving and having the same values.

Model PP Sport, Manurhin

Same gun as Model PP, with different barrel lengths running from 5.75" to 7.75". Basically a target .22-caliber, with adjustable rear sights for elevation and windage. Front sight also adjustable. There is a barrel bushing at the muzzle that attaches front sight to the barrel. Grips are contoured checkered plastic and squared at the bottom of grips or in the shape of an inverted bird's-head.

NIB	Exc.	V.G.	Good	Fair	Poor
—	900	600	450	380	280

Model PP Sport C, Manurhin

Same gun as Model PP Sport, but in single-action with a spur hammer. Has front and rear adjustable sights and squared target grips in checkered black, brown and plastic. Blued and silver finish.

NIB	Exc.	V.G.	Good	Fair	Poor
—	900	600	450	380	280

Model PP Sport, Walther

A .22-caliber Sport was manufactured by Manurhin, but sold by Walther with Walther logo and inscription. Same gun as Model PP Sport, Manurhin. Only sold for a period of two years.

Courtesy John J. Stimson, Jr.

Walther PP Sport

NIB	Exc.	V.G.	Good	Fair	Poor
—	900	600	450	380	280

Model PP 50th Anniversary Commemorative Model

In .22 or .380 caliber. Blued, with gold inlays. Hand-carved grips, with oak leaves and acorns. Walther banner carved into each side of grips. Wood presentation case.

NIB	Exc.	V.G.	Good	Fair	Poor
—	1500	1000	750	500	300

Model PPK—Some with Duraluminum Frames

.22 Caliber

NIB	Exc.	V.G.	Good	Fair	Poor
—	750	600	400	280	180

.32 Caliber

NIB	Exc.	V.G.	Good	Fair	Poor
—	550	400	350	280	180

.380 Caliber

NIB	Exc.	V.G.	Good	Fair	Poor
—	750	600	400	280	180

Model PPK—All Three Calibers Finished In Blue, Silver and Gold With Full Coverage Engraving

Blue

NIB	Exc.	V.G.	Good	Fair	Poor
—	1900	1500	750	450	300

Silver

NIB	Exc.	V.G.	Good	Fair	Poor
—	1900	1500	750	450	300

Gold

NIB	Exc.	V.G.	Good	Fair	Poor
—	1900	1500	750	450	300

Model PPK Mark II

These Walthers were manufactured under license by Walther and produced by Manurhin Company. Sold exclusively by Interarms, Alexandria, Virginia. Mark IIs were the same pistols as those above and have the same types of finish and engraving as well as the same value.

Model PPK Manurhin

Manurhin Company manufactured with Manurhin logo and inscription. Usually "Licensed by Walther" somewhere on the pistol. Same pistols as above. Bearing same types of finish and engraving and having the same value.

Courtesy James Rankin

Model PPK 50th Anniversary Commemorative Model

In .22 or .380 caliber. Blued, with gold inlays. Hand-carved grips, with oak leaves and acorns. Walther banner carved into each side of grips. Wood presentation case.

NIB	Exc.	V.G.	Good	Fair	Poor
—	2100	1800	1250	1000	500

Model PPK American

In 1986, Model PPK was licensed by Walther Company to be manufactured in the United States. Finish stainless steel in .380 caliber.

NIB	Exc.	V.G.	Good	Fair	Poor
—	500	380	300	200	150

Model PPK/S

This Walther originally manufactured in Germany in .22, .32, and .380 caliber. For sale in U.S. market after introduction of United States Gun Control Act of 1968. Basically a Model PP, with cut-off muzzle and slide. Has two-piece black checkered plastic grips as seen on Model PP. Finished in blue, nickel, and dull gold. Prices shown for .380 model. Note: Add 25% for .22; add 10% for .32.

NIB	Exc.	V.G.	Good	Fair	Poor
600	520	450	400	350	250

Model PK380

Polymer compact frame. .380 ACP 8-round magazine. 3.6" barrel. DA/SA trigger. 3-dot sights. Black or two tone finish. Introduced 2009. Note: Add $50 for two tone.

NIB	Exc.	V.G.	Good	Fair	Poor
400	360	320	260	200	190

Model PPK/S American

Manufactured in United States. Same as German Model PPK/S. Caliber .380. Pistol finished in blue or stainless steel. Note: Add 50% for pre-2000 manufacture, with Alabama address.

NIB	Exc.	V.G.	Good	Fair	Poor
500	400	350	300	200	150

Model TP

A Walther-manufactured semi-automatic pistol in .22 and .25 calibers. Patterned after earlier Model 9. Finish is blue. Silver black plastic checkered grips, with Walther banner medallions in each grip.

NIB	Exc.	V.G.	Good	Fair	Poor
—	900	700	500	380	250

Model TPH

A Walther-manufactured semi-automatic pistol in .22 and .25 caliber. Double-action pistol, with Duraluminum frame. Finished in blue or silver. Two-piece black checkered plastic grips. Full coverage engraving available. Note: Add $300 for engraved model.

NIB	Exc.	V.G.	Good	Fair	Poor
—	650	500	450	350	250

Model TPH American

Double-action semi-automatic pistol produced in both .22 and .25 caliber. Licensed by Walther and manufactured in the United States. Produced in stainless steel. Has two-piece black plastic checkered grips.

NIB	Exc.	V.G.	Good	Fair	Poor
—	400	300	200	150	100

Model PP Super

A .380 and 9x18 caliber double-action semi-automatic manufactured by Walther. Similar in design to Model PP, with P.38 type of mechanism. Finish is blue. Grips are wrap-around black checkered plastic or a type of molded wood-colored plastic.

Courtesy Orvel Reichert

NIB	Exc.	V.G.	Good	Fair	Poor
—	750	500	350	250	150

Model P.38

Following WWII, P.38 was reintroduced in a variety of calibers, with 5" barrel and alloy or steel frame.

.22 Caliber

NIB	Exc.	V.G.	Good	Fair	Poor
1200	850	650	500	350	200

Other Calibers

NIB	Exc.	V.G.	Good	Fair	Poor
750	600	500	400	300	200

Steel-Framed (Introduced 1987)

Factory-engraved versions of P.38 pistol were blued, chrome, silver or gold-plated. We suggest that a qualified appraisal be secured when contemplating purchase.

NIB	Exc.	V.G.	Good	Fair	Poor
1400	1250	1000	750	500	400

Model P.38K

As above, with 2.8" barrel. Front sight mounted on the slide. Imported between 1974 and 1980.

NIB	Exc.	V.G.	Good	Fair	Poor
—	900	650	450	300	200

Model P.38 II

NIB	Exc.	V.G.	Good	Fair	Poor
—	800	550	350	250	200

Model P.38 IV

Redesigned version of above, with 4.5" barrel and 8-shot magazine. Fitted with a decocking lever and adjustable sights. Imported prior to 1983.

NIB	Exc.	V.G.	Good	Fair	Poor
—	900	650	450	300	200

RECENT AND CURRENT PRODUCTION

In 1999, Carl Walther Gmbh of Germany and Smith & Wesson entered into a joint agreement to manufacture and distribute Walther-branded firearms and accessories into U.S., beginning August 1, 1999. In 2012, Walther established Walther Arms, Inc. in Fort Smith, Arkansas to import and sell all Walther products in U.S.A., beginning in 2013.

Model PP Limited Edition

Introduced in 2000. Limited edition of 100 pistols: chambered in .380 ACP; 50 in .32 ACP. Finish high-polish blue. Slide marked "LAST EDITION 1929-1999". Supplied with a special case, with certificate and video of the history of Walther.

NIB	Exc.	V.G.	Good	Fair	Poor
1350	1100	900	700	500	300

Model PPK/E—Walther USA

Introduced in 2000. Chambered for .380 or .32 ACP cartridges. Later in that year .22 LR. Has a double-action trigger. Produced in Hungary by Walther. Barrel length 3.4". Magazine capacity: 7 rounds .380; 8 rounds for .32 ACP and .22 LR. Blued finish and plastic grips.

NIB	Exc.	V.G.	Good	Fair	Poor
530	470	440	360	340	300

Model PPK

Chambered for .380 ACP or .32 ACP cartridge. Fitted with 3.35" barrel. Offered in blue or stainless steel. Black plastic grips. Fixed red-dot sights. Magazine capacity: 6 rounds .380 ACP; 7 rounds .32 ACP. Weight 21 oz.

NIB	Exc.	V.G.	Good	Fair	Poor
550	420	300	250	180	80

Model PPK/S

Same as PPK, with .25" longer grip. Magazine capacity: 7 rounds .380 ACP; 8 rounds .32 ACP. Weight 23 oz. Offered in blue, stainless steel and two-tone finish. In 2013, .22 LR version reintroduced with magazine capacity of 10 rounds. Note: Deduct 15% for .22 LR.

NIB	Exc.	V.G.	Good	Fair	Poor
550	420	300	250	180	80

Model PPS

Striker-fired compact DAO semi-automatic pistol. Chambered in .40 S&W (6 rounds) or 9mm Parabellum (7 rounds). Features include polymer frame and grip, decocker button, loaded chamber indicator, 3.2" stainless steel barrel, integral Weaver-style accessory rail, black Tenifer finish overall. Discontinued.

NIB	Exc.	V.G.	Good	Fair	Poor
620	540	450	350	250	150

Model PPS M2

Similar to above. 9mm 6-, 7-, or 8-round magazine. 3.18" barrel. Striker-fire trigger. 3-dot sights. Black or two-tone finish. Introduced 2009. Note: Add $30 for LE model with night sights, add $150 for RMSC optic model.

NIB	Exc.	V.G.	Good	Fair	Poor
470	450	400	360	280	230

75th Anniversary PPK

Blued, with wood grips. Machine engraving. Available in .380 ACP with 6+1 capacity. Special SN beginning with 0000PPK. Shipped with glass-top display case. Single-/double-action 3.3" barrel. Weight 20.8 oz. Windage adjustable rear sight. Introduced 2006.

NIB	Exc.	V.G.	Good	Fair	Poor
800	700	600	400	—	—

Model P5

A 9mm semi-automatic pistol, with double-action firing mechanism. One of the first Walthers to have a decocker lever. Finish is a combination of black matte and high polish. Has black plastic checkered grips.

NIB	Exc.	V.G.	Good	Fair	Poor
1960	1500	1160	840	720	600

Model P5, Compact

A shorter version of standard Model P5.

NIB	Exc.	V.G.	Good	Fair	Poor
1450	1100	850	600	380	250

Model P5 100-Year Commemorative

Blued, with gold inlays. Hand-carved grips, with oak leaves and acorns. Walther banner carved into each side of grips.

NIB	Exc.	V.G.	Good	Fair	Poor
2750	1950	1600	1000	750	400

Model P88

A 9mm semi-automatic in double-action, with an ambidextrous decocking lever. 15-shot magazine and two-piece black checkered plastic grips. Combination of high polish and black matte finish.

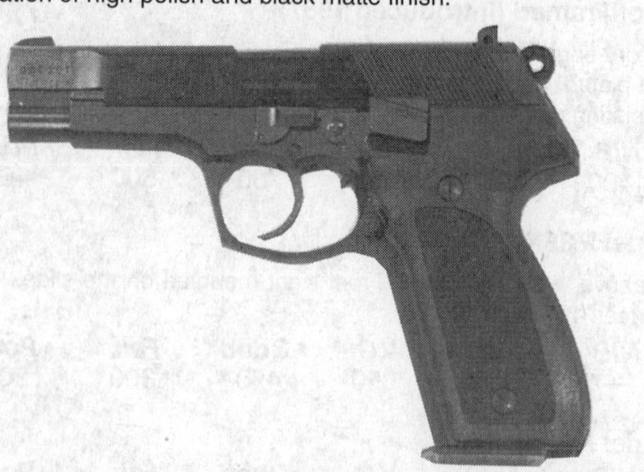

NIB	Exc.	V.G.	Good	Fair	Poor
1960	1500	1160	840	720	600

Model P88 Compact

Shorter version of standard Model P88.

NIB	Exc.	V.G.	Good	Fair	Poor
1600	1420	1140	850	600	400

Model P99

Introduced in 1997. Single-/double-action design, with 4" barrel and polymer frame. Chambered for 9mm or .40 S&W cartridge. Magazine capacity 10 rounds (16 rounds 9mm; 12 rounds .40 S&W for law enforcement). Front sight interchangeable. Rear sight windage adjustable. Finish blue Tenifer. Total length 7". Weight 25 oz.

NIB	Exc.	V.G.	Good	Fair	Poor
800	700	550	450	300	200

Model P99 Compact AS/QA

Chambered for 9mm or .40 S&W cartridges, with double-action trigger. Quick-action striker fired. Barrel length 3.5", with fixed sights. Magazine capacity: 10 rounds 9mm; 8 rounds .40 S&W. Weight 19 oz.

NIB	Exc.	V.G.	Good	Fair	Poor
680	580	400	320	200	180

Model P990

Double-action-only version of P99.

NIB	Exc.	V.G.	Good	Fair	Poor
680	550	400	320	200	180

Model P99 QPQ

Similar to P99, with silver Tenifer finish.

NIB	Exc.	V.G.	Good	Fair	Poor
750	620	480	380	280	250

Model P990 QPQ

Double-action-only version of P99 QPQ.

NIB	Exc.	V.G.	Good	Fair	Poor
750	620	480	380	280	250

Model P99 QA

Similar to P99, with constant short trigger pull of 6.5 lbs. Offered in both 9mm and .40 S&W calibers. Introduced in 2000.

NIB	Exc.	V.G.	Good	Fair	Poor
680	580	400	320	200	180

Model P99 Military

Similar to P99, with military finish.

NIB	Exc.	V.G.	Good	Fair	Poor
680	580	400	320	200	180

Model P99 La Chasse DU

Features laser-engraving on blue Tenifer slide.

NIB	Exc.	V.G.	Good	Fair	Poor
750	620	480	380	280	250

Model P99 La Chasse

Features hand-engraving on gray Tenifer slide.

NIB	Exc.	V.G.	Good	Fair	Poor
1680	1350	1100	750	500	300

Model P99 Commemorative

Limited edition P99 that features a high polish blue slide, with a special serial number and marking "COMMEMORATIVE FOR THE YEAR 2000". Offered in both 9mm and .40 S&W caliber. Each handgun comes with a special certificate and video of the history of Walther.

NIB	Exc.	V.G.	Good	Fair	Poor
750	620	480	380	280	250

PPQ

Caliber: 9mm Parabellum or .40 S&W. Steel slide polymer frame, with interchangeable backstraps. Magazine capacity: 15/12 (9mm); 17/14 (.40). Other features include front slide serrations, Quick Defense Trigger with integral safety, ambidextrous slide, magazine release, adjustable rear sight and loaded-chamber indicator. Finish matte black. Weight 24.5 oz., barrel length 4".

NIB	Exc.	V.G.	Good	Fair	Poor
520	480	420	380	320	200

Model PPQ Navy

Similar to above. 4.6" threaded barrel.

NIB	Exc.	V.G.	Good	Fair	Poor
700	600	500	460	300	280

Model PPQ SC

Similar to above. Subcompact frame. 9mm. 10- or 15-round magazine. 3.5" barrel.

NIB	Exc.	V.G.	Good	Fair	Poor
650	560	480	380	300	280

Model PPQ M2 Q4 TAC

Similar to above. Full-size frame. 9mm. 15- or 17-round magazine. 4.6" threaded barrel.

NIB	Exc.	V.G.	Good	Fair	Poor
750	630	580	400	320	290

Q4 Steel Frame

Caliber: 9mm. Capacity: 15-round magazine. Barrel: 4". Grips: Textured polymer, wrap around. Sights: 3-dot night. Length: 7.4" overall. Weight: 39.7 oz. unloaded. Finish: Matte black Tenifer. Features: Duty-optimized beaver tail, Quick Defense trigger, accessory rail, oversized controls.

NIB	Exc.	V.G.	Good	Fair	Poor
1260	—	—	—	—	—

PPQ .45

Similar to PPQ model, except chambered for .45 ACP. Has 4.25" barrel, polygonal rifling, ambidextrous controls, front and rear serrations on slide, combat 3-dot sights. Introduced in 2015.

NIB	Exc.	V.G.	Good	Fair	Poor
600	520	480	420	—	—

PPQ M2

Similar to PPQ model, with several improvements. Also available in .45 ACP.

NIB	Exc.	V.G.	Good	Fair	Poor
550	500	450	400	350	300

PPQ M2 Q5 Match

Caliber: 9mm. Capacity: 15-round magazine. Barrel: 5". Grips: Textured polymer. Sights: LPA fiber-optic front, adj. rear. Length: 8.1" overall. Weight: 27.9 oz. unloaded. Finish: Matte black. Features: Polymer frame, optics-ready, accessory rail.

NIB	Exc.	V.G.	Good	Fair	Poor
960	900	890	780	750	—

PPQ M2 Q5 Match Steel Frame

Caliber: 9mm. Capacity: 15-round magazine. Barrel: 5". Grips: Textured polymer. Sights: LPA fiber-optic front, adj. rear. Length: 8.7" overall. Weight: 41.6 oz. unloaded. Finish: Matte black. Features: Metal frame, optics-ready, accessory rail.

NIB	Exc.	V.G.	Good	Fair	Poor
1770	1270	1150	1110	900	—

Model PPX

Polymer frame hammer-fired DA-only pistol, in 9mm or .40 S&W. Features include loaded-chamber viewpoint, ambidextrous slide stop, reversible mag release, Picatinny rail, two drop safeties and firing pin block. Black or stainless finish. New 2013. Note: Add $50 for stainless.

NIB	Exc.	V.G.	Good	Fair	Poor
400	350	300	280	250	200

Model P22 Standard

Introduced in 2002. This .22-caliber pistol chambered for LR cartridge. Barrel length 3.4". Polymer frame, with double-action trigger. Adjustable rear sight. Magazine capacity 10 rounds. Weight 20 oz. Note: In 2003, offered with military black slide and green frame or silver slide with black frame. Carbon fiber-framed model also available at about same price as standard models. Barrels are interchangeable on both P22 pistols.

NIB	*Exc.*	*V.G.*	*Good*	*Fair*	*Poor*
400	320	250	200	150	80

Model P22 Target

Similar to standard P22 model, with 5" barrel and weight. Weight 21 oz.

NIB	*Exc.*	*V.G.*	*Good*	*Fair*	*Poor*
420	350	280	220	180	80

Creed

Polymer frame 9mm with 4" barrel, pre-cocked DA trigger system and bobbed hammer, front and rear cocking serrations and low profile 3-dot sights. Metal components have matte black Tenifer finish. Ergonomic non-slip grip, with cross-directional surface. Magazine capacity 10 or 16 rounds. Introduced in 2017. Discontinued.

NIB	*Exc.*	*V.G.*	*Good*	*Fair*	*Poor*
350	300	280	230	200	180

TARGET PISTOLS

Model FP

A .22 LR caliber single-shot target pistol that fires electrically. Has micro-adjustable electric firing system, with micrometer sights. Contoured wooden grips that are adjustable. Barrel 11.7". Finish blued.

NIB	*Exc.*	*V.G.*	*Good*	*Fair*	*Poor*
—	2000	1600	1000	500	400

Model GSP

Semi-automatic target pistol in .22 LR and .32 caliber. Has 4.5" barrel, 5-shot magazine and contoured wood target grips. Blued finish. Sold with attache-style extra-barrel case and accessories.

Courtesy John J. Stimson, Jr.

NIB	*Exc.*	*V.G.*	*Good*	*Fair*	*Poor*
1300	1000	650	500	400	200

Model GSP-C

Almost same pistol as Model GSP, but in .32-caliber S&W wadcutter.

NIB	*Exc.*	*V.G.*	*Good*	*Fair*	*Poor*
1300	1000	650	500	400	200

Model OSP

A .22 Short semi-automatic target pistol. Similar to Model GSP. Made for rapid fire target shooting. Blued finish, with contoured wood grips.

Custom engraved OSP

NIB	*Exc.*	*V.G.*	*Good*	*Fair*	*Poor*
1500	1100	750	500	400	200

Free Pistol

.22-caliber single-shot target pistol, with 11.7" barrel, micrometer sights, adjustable grips and electronic trigger. Blued.

NIB	*Exc.*	*V.G.*	*Good*	*Fair*	*Poor*
1900	1600	1200	900	700	550

Model R99

This 6-shot revolver chambered for .357 Magnum cartridge. Barrel length 3". Weight 28 oz. Offered in blue or stainless steel. Introduced in 1999. Said to be a close ringer for S&W M19, but with different grips.

NIB	*Exc.*	*V.G.*	*Good*	*Fair*	*Poor*
1500	1300	1100	950	700	500

Model SP22-M1

.22 LR autoloader, with aluminum frame and 4" barrel.

NIB	Exc.	V.G.	Good	Fair	Poor
400	320	350	150	100	80

Model SP22-M2

Similar to above, with 6" barrel.

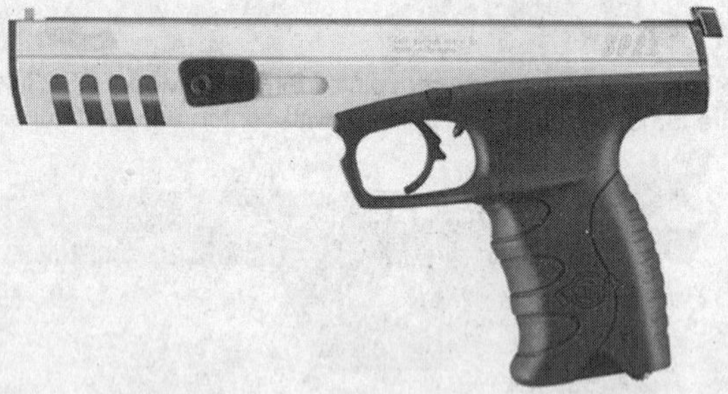

NIB	Exc.	V.G.	Good	Fair	Poor
400	320	250	150	100	80

Model SP22-M3

Similar to above, with match-grade barrel and adjustable trigger.

NIB	Exc.	V.G.	Good	Fair	Poor
480	400	320	200	150	100

Model SP22-M4

Similar to above, with wooden free-style grip assembly.

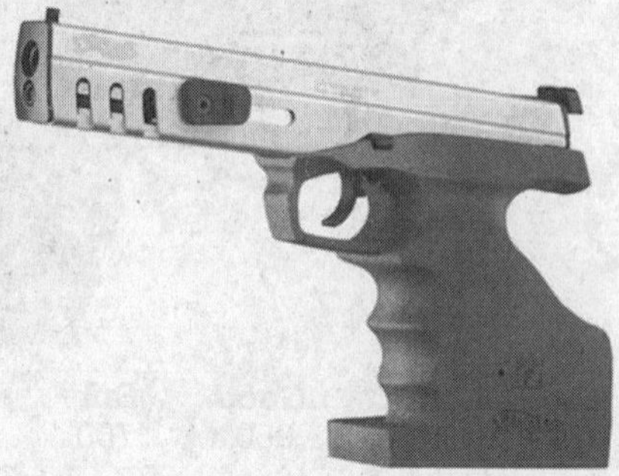

NIB	Exc.	V.G.	Good	Fair	Poor
750	680	550	400	250	150

RIFLES

Model B

A .30-06 caliber bolt-action rifle, with 22" barrel, 4-shot magazine and single/double-set triggers. Double-set triggers are worth approximately 20% more than values listed. Blued, with walnut stock.

NIB	Exc.	V.G.	Good	Fair	Poor
—	780	700	450	250	180

Olympic Single-Shot

A .22-caliber bolt-action rifle, with 26" barrel, adjustable target sights and walnut stock. Fitted with palm rest and adjustable buttplate. Blued.

NIB	Exc.	V.G.	Good	Fair	Poor
—	1150	950	800	500	400

Model V

A .22-caliber single-shot bolt-action rifle, with 26" barrel and adjustable sights. Blued, with plain walnut stock. Manufactured before WWII.

NIB	Exc.	V.G.	Good	Fair	Poor
—	550	450	300	200	150

Model V Champion

As above, with checkered walnut stock.

NIB	Exc.	V.G.	Good	Fair	Poor
—	600	500	350	250	200

Model KKM International Match

A .22-caliber single-shot bolt-action rifle, with 28" barrel and adjustable sights. Blued, with walnut stock. Fitted for palm rest and adjustable buttplate. Manufactured after WWII.

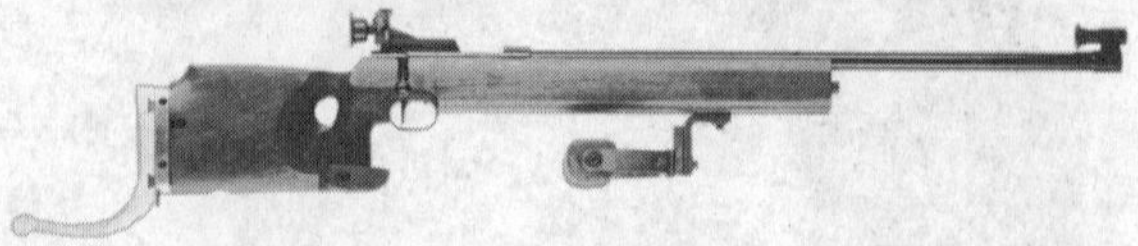

NIB	Exc.	V.G.	Good	Fair	Poor
—	1550	1280	850	450	350

Model KKM-S

As above, with adjustable cheekpiece.

NIB	Exc.	V.G.	Good	Fair	Poor
—	1620	1350	850	500	400

Model KKW

As above, with military-style stock.

NIB	Exc.	V.G.	Good	Fair	Poor
—	1250	980	600	250	180

Model KKJ Sporter

A .22-caliber bolt-action rifle, with 22.5" barrel and 5-shot magazine. Blued, with checkered walnut stock. Available with double-set triggers and their presence would add approximately 20% to values listed. Manufactured after WWII.

NIB	Exc.	V.G.	Good	Fair	Poor
—	900	800	550	350	300

Model KKJ-MA

As above, in .22 Magnum rimfire.

NIB	Exc.	V.G.	Good	Fair	Poor
—	850	750	550	350	300

Model KKJ-HO

As above, in .22 Hornet.

NIB	Exc.	V.G.	Good	Fair	Poor
—	950	850	650	450	350

Model SSV Varmint

A .22-caliber bolt-action single-shot rifle, with 25.5" barrel not fitted with sights. Monte Carlo-style stock. Blued. Manufactured after WWII.

NIB	Exc.	V.G.	Good	Fair	Poor
—	700	600	480	380	300

Model UIT BV Universal

As above, with adjustable target sights. Walnut stock fitted with a palm rest and adjustable buttplate.

NIB	Exc.	V.G.	Good	Fair	Poor
1750	1500	1250	900	650	500

Model UIT Match

As above, with stippled pistol grip and forend. Also available with an electronic trigger that would add approximately $50 to values listed.

NIB	Exc.	V.G.	Good	Fair	Poor
1350	1100	800	600	450	400

GX 1

As above, with adjustable Free Rifle stock.

NIB	Exc.	V.G.	Good	Fair	Poor
2250	2000	1750	1250	850	700

Prone Model 400

Target rifle in .22-caliber, with prone position stock.

NIB	Exc.	V.G.	Good	Fair	Poor
800	700	600	450	350	300

Model KK/MS Silhouette

A .22-caliber bolt-action rifle, with 25.5" front-weighted barrel furnished without sights. Thumbhole stock, with adjustable buttplate. Introduced in 1984.

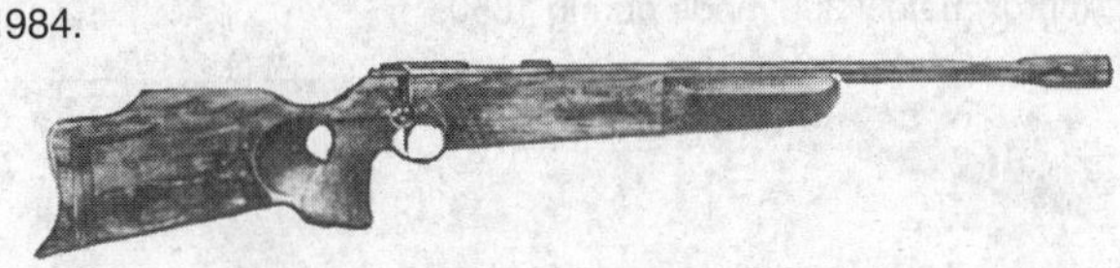

NIB	Exc.	V.G.	Good	Fair	Poor
1300	1100	850	700	550	400

Running Boar Model 500

As above, with 23.5" barrel.

NIB	Exc.	V.G.	Good	Fair	Poor
1550	1350	950	750	600	450

Model WA-2000

A .300 Win. Magnum or .308-caliber bolt-action sporting rifle. Produced on custom order. Imported prior to 1989.

NIB	Exc.	V.G.	Good	Fair	Poor
30000	25000	20000	—	—	—

Model G22

A .22-caliber rifle, with 20" barrel and adjustable sights. Features cocking indicator, integrated lock, slide safety and multi function rail. Black or green finish. Weight 6 lbs. Also sold as a package.

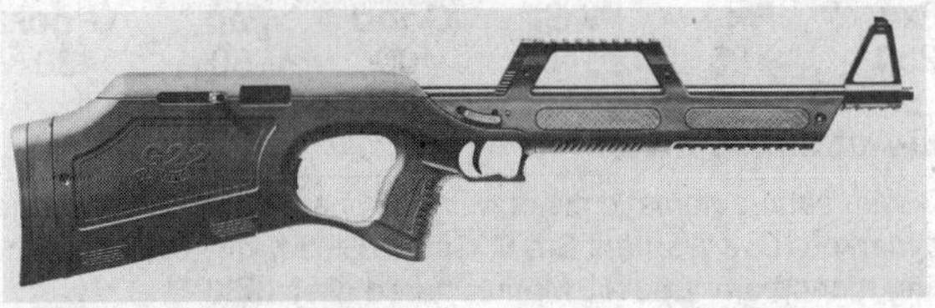

NIB	Exc.	V.G.	Good	Fair	Poor
450	350	220	180	120	100

Package A1 with Walther rifle scope

NIB	Exc.	V.G.	Good	Fair	Poor
500	400	280	220	180	150

Package A2 with laser

NIB	Exc.	V.G.	Good	Fair	Poor
500	400	280	220	180	150

Package A3 with Walther rifle scope & laser

NIB	Exc.	V.G.	Good	Fair	Poor
500	400	280	220	180	150

Package A4 with Walther PS22 red-dot sight

NIB	Exc.	V.G.	Good	Fair	Poor
500	400	280	220	180	150

SHOTGUNS

Model SF

A 12- or 16-gauge boxlock double-barrel shotgun. Fitted with double triggers and extractors. Blued, with checkered walnut stock fitted with sling swivels.

NIB	Exc.	V.G.	Good	Fair	Poor
—	1150	900	750	600	450

Model SFD

As above, with stock having a cheekpiece.

NIB	Exc.	V.G.	Good	Fair	Poor
—	1150	900	750	600	450

WALTHER MANURHIN

Mulhouse, France

Manurhin-manufactured Walther pistols are listed in Walther section under their respective model headings.

WARNANT, L. AND J.
Ognee, Belgium

Revolver (Antique)

Top-break double-action. Warnants produced a variety of revolvers in .32-, .38- or .45-caliber, between 1870 and 1890. Values are for the most commonly encountered large frame 11mm (.45) caliber revolvers. Smaller frame revolvers will bring less.

Exc.	Fine	V.G.	Good	Fair	Poor
250	180	140	100	50	30

Semi-Automatic Pistol

A 6.35mm semi-automatic pistol, with 2.5" barrel and 5-shot magazine. Slide marked "L&J Warnant Bte 6.35mm". Blued, with black plastic grips bearing monogram "L&JW". Manufactured after 1908.

NIB	Exc.	V.G.	Good	Fair	Poor
—	350	200	150	100	80

1912 Model

A 7.65mm caliber semi-automatic pistol, with 3" barrel and 7-shot magazine. Slide marked "L&J Warnant Brevetes Pist Auto 7.65mm". Manufactured prior to 1915.

NIB	Exc.	V.G.	Good	Fair	Poor
—	350	200	150	100	80

WARNER ARMS CORPORATION
Brooklyn, New York and Norwich, Connecticut

Established in 1912, this firm marketed revolvers, rifles, semi-automatic pistols and shotguns made for them by other companies (including N.R. Davis & Sons, Ithaca Gun Company and so forth). In 1917, the company was purchased by N.R. Davis & Company. See also Davis-Warner. The arms marketed by Warner prior to 1917 are listed.

SHOTGUNS

Single Trigger Hammerless Utica Special Double-Barrel

In 12-gauge, with 28", 30" or 32" barrels.

Double Trigger Hammerless Double-Barrel

In 12- or 16-gauge, with 28", 30" or 32" barrels.

Grade X, SF, XT, SFT, XD and XDF Hammer Guns

In 12-, 16- or 20-gauge, with 28", 30" or 32" barrels.

Field Grade Hammer Gun

In 12- or 16-gauge, with 28" or 30" barrels.

Boxlock Hammerless

In 12- or 16-gauge, with 28", 30" or 32" barrels.

RIFLES

Number 522

A .22-caliber single-shot rifle, with 18" barrel.

Number 532

A .32-caliber single-shot rifle, with 18" barrel.

REVOLVERS

Double-Action

.32- and .38-caliber, with 4" or 5" barrels.

Double-Action Hammerless

.32- and .38-caliber, with 4" or 5" barrels.

SEMI-AUTOMATIC PISTOLS

"Faultless": Warner-Schwarzlose Model C, .32 ACP

NIB	Exc.	V.G.	Good	Fair	Poor
—	—	500	300	200	100

WARNER, CHAS.
Windsor Locks, Connecticut

Pocket Revolver (Antique)

A .31-caliber percussion revolver, with 3" round barrel and 6-shot unfluted cylinder. Cylinder marked "Charles Warner. Windsor Locks, Conn.". Blued, with walnut grips. Approximately 600 made between 1857 and 1860.

Exc.	Fine	V.G.	Good	Fair	Poor
1620	1300	900	500	100	70

WARNER, JAMES
Springfield, Massachusetts

Revolving Carbines (Antique)

A variety of revolving carbines were made by this maker. Nearly all of which are .40-caliber, with octagonal barrels measuring 20" to 24" in length. Most commonly encountered variations are listed.

Manually Revolved Grooved Cylinder (Antique)

Fitted with two triggers, one of which is a release so that cylinder can be manually turned. Not fitted with a loading lever. Top strap marked "James Warner/Springfield, Mass.". Approximately 75 made in 1849.

Courtesy Milwaukee Public Museum, Milwaukee, Wisconsin

Exc.	Fine	V.G.	Good	Fair	Poor
7500	4700	3450	2200	500	350

Retractable Cylinder Model (Antique)

This version has a cylinder that fits over the breech and it must be retracted before it can be manually rotated. Cylinder release is a button located in front of the trigger. It is marked "James Warner/Springfield Mass" and with an eagle over letters "U.S.". Cylinder is etched and there is no loading lever. Has a walnut stock, with patchbox and no forearm. Approximately 25 manufactured in 1849.

Exc.	Fine	V.G.	Good	Fair	Poor
9500	6900	4950	3000	800	560

Automatic Revolving Cylinder (Antique)

Cylinder is automatically turned when hammer is cocked. Fitted with loading lever. Marked "Warner's Patent/Jan. 1851" and "Springfield Arms Co.". Approximately 200 made during 1850s.

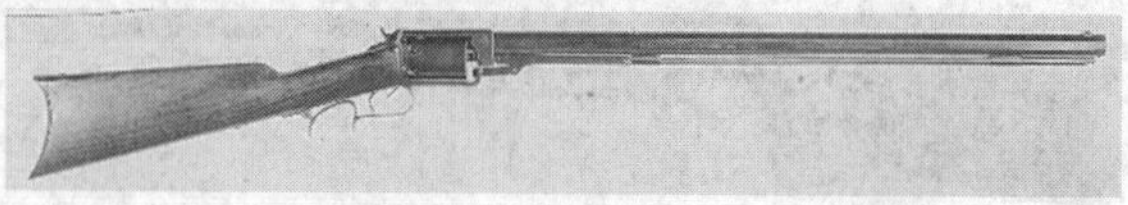

Courtesy Milwaukee Public Museum, Milwaukee, Wisconsin

Exc.	Fine	V.G.	Good	Fair	Poor
7500	4700	3300	1900	500	350

Belt Revolver (Antique)

A .31-caliber double-action percussion revolver, with 4" or 5" round barrel and 6-shot etched cylinder. Blued, with walnut grips. No markings appear on this model except serial number. Manufactured in 1851.

Courtesy Milwaukee Public Museum, Milwaukee, Wisconsin

Exc.	Fine	V.G.	Good	Fair	Poor
2100	1650	1160	680	100	70

Pocket Revolver Antique

A .28-caliber percussion revolver, with 3" octagonal barrel and 6-shot cylinder. Barrel marked "James Warner, Springfield, Mass., USA". Blued, with walnut grips. Approximately 500 were made.

Exc.	Fine	V.G.	Good	Fair	Poor
1050	720	500	280	100	70

Pocket Revolver Second Model Antique

As above, with 3" or 4" barrel marked "Warner's Patent 1857".

Courtesy Wallis & Wallis, Lewes, Sussex, England

Exc.	Fine	V.G.	Good	Fair	Poor
1100	750	530	320	100	70

Pocket Revolver Third Model Antique

As above, in .31-caliber.

Exc.	Fine	V.G.	Good	Fair	Poor
1000	650	470	300	100	70

Single-Shot Derringer Antique

A .41-caliber rimfire single-shot pocket pistol, with 2.75" round barrel, brass frame and walnut grips. As this model is unmarked, it can only be identified by the large breech-block which lifts upward and to the left for loading.

Exc.	Fine	V.G.	Good	Fair	Poor
22500	19000	13120	7250	1000	700

Pocket Revolver Antique

A .30-caliber rimfire revolver, with 3" barrel and 5-shot cylinder. Barrel marked "Warner's Patent 1857". Blued or nickel-plated, with walnut grips. Approximately 1,000 made during late 1860s.

Exc.	Fine	V.G.	Good	Fair	Poor
980	600	380	160	80	50

WEATHERBY

Sheridan, Wyoming

Founded by Roy Weatherby in 1945 in South Gate, California, the original rifles were custom guns made to order on Mauser actions. In 1956, he contracted with both Sako and Schultz & Larsen to manufacture complete rifles, while he continued to make custom guns in California. In 1958, Weatherby introduced his Mark V action, which was designed to handle the high pressures of his proprietary cartridges. Mark V action was made in U.S., with rifles assembled and finished at Weatherby shop in South Gate. Mark V featured a very modern stock design with glossy finish, high comb for scope use and contrasting grip and forend caps. Beginning in 1959, rifles were made in what was then West Germany. In 1972, production was moved to Japan, where rifles were made until 1995. Since that year, Weatherby rifles have been made in the U.S. Barreled actions for Mark V were made by ATEK in Brainerd, Minnesota. Mark V rifles are currently made in Sheridan, Wyoming. The action for Vanguard is made by Howa in Japan. For many years, Weatherby shotguns were made in Japan or Italy. Current models are made in Turkey. The family-run firm is currently run by Adam Weatherby, the 3rd generation Weatherby at the helm. Weatherby moved operations from Paso Robles, California, to Sheridan, Wyoming, in 2019. As of April 2019, Weatherby relocated its manufacturing and business operations to Sheridan, Wyoming.

RIFLES

OLDER MARK V RIFLES

Mark V

Deluxe bolt-action repeating rifle. Chambered for various popular standard calibers, as well as the full line of Weatherby cartridges from .240 Wby. Magnum to .300 Wby. Magnum. Furnished with 24" or 26" barrel, without sights. Has 3- or 5-round magazine, depending on caliber, deluxe high-polish blued finish, with select skip-line checkered walnut stock with rosewood forearm tip and pistol grip cap. Available with a left-hand action. Early pre-Japan-made Mark V rifles will command a 20% or 30% premium.

NIB	Exc.	V.G.	Good	Fair	Poor
1600	1380	1200	1050	800	600

Mark V Deluxe

Pillar bedded "AA" Claro Walnut, polished blue metal, Calibers: .240 Wby, .257 Wby, 6.5 CM, 6.5-300 Wby, .270 Win, .270 Wby, 7mm Wby, .308, .30-06, .300 Win, .300 Wby, .340 Wby, .378 Wby, .416 Wby, .460 Wby. Base price shown. Accubrake extra, standard (add 800) with .378, .416, .460.

NIB	Exc.	V.G.	Good	Fair	Poor
2700	2300	1950	1650	1000	600

Mark V Sporter

Introduced in 1993. Wood stock with matte blue metal, No. 2 contour 24" or 26", calibers: .257 Wby, .270 Wby, 7mm Rem, .300 Win. Mag., .300 Wby.

NIB	Exc.	V.G.	Good	Fair	Poor
1350	1100	850	650	500	300

Mark V .375 Weatherby Magnum

This version was manufactured in Germany only. Chambered for currently obsolete .375 Wby. Magnum cartridge. This version has become very collectible.

NIB	Exc.	V.G.	Good	Fair	Poor
5000	3500	3000	2500	2000	1500

Mark V .378 Weatherby Magnum

Chambered for .378 Wby. Magnum cartridge. Furnished with 26" barrel only. Note: Add 50% for German guns in this caliber.

NIB	Exc.	V.G.	Good	Fair	Poor
2300	1820	1550	1200	850	500

Mark V .416 Weatherby Magnum

Extremely powerful rifle suitable for hunting the biggest game. Introduced in 1989.

NIB	Exc.	V.G.	Good	Fair	Poor
2400	1820	1550	1200	850	500

Mark V .460 Weatherby Magnum

Said to be the most powerful commercial rifle available in the world, with the possible exception of some of the recently-reintroduced British nitro chamberings. Available with 24" or 26" heavy barrel, with an integral recoil-reducing muzzle brake. Has a custom reinforced stock. Note: Add 100% for German guns in this caliber.

NIB	Exc.	V.G.	Good	Fair	Poor
2500	2200	1850	1500	1000	600

Mark V Dangerous Game Rifle

Introduced in 2001. Composite stock, iron sights, No. 2, 3 or 4 contour barrel in 24" or 26" lengths, 8 3/4 pounds to 9 1/2 pounds. Calibers: .300 Wby, .340 Wby, .375 H&H, .375 Wby, .378 Wby, .416 Wby, .460 Wby. Base price shown. Accubrake extra (add 300-400). Accubrake extra and standard with .378, .416, .460.

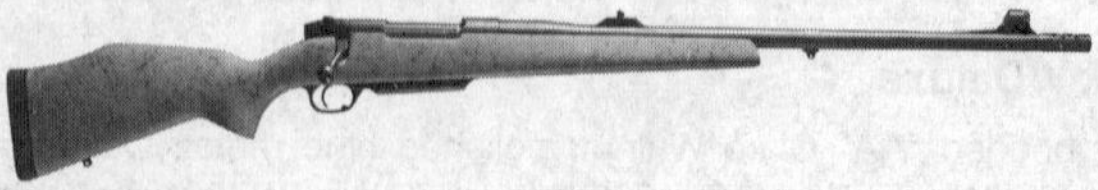

NIB	Exc.	V.G.	Good	Fair	Poor
3100	2700	2300	1800	—	—

Mark V Euromark

Features hand-checkered oil-finished Claro walnut stock, with ebony forend tip and pistol grip cap. Has satin blued finish. Introduced in 1986.

NIB	Exc.	V.G.	Good	Fair	Poor
1500	1300	1050	800	580	350

Mark V Fluted Stainless

Introduced late in 1996. Features a fluted stainless steel barrel. Chambered for .257 Wby. Magnum to .300 Wby. Magnum calibers as well as 7mm Rem. Magnum and .300 Win. Mag. Stock is synthetic, with raised comb and checkered stock. Weight varies depending on caliber.

NIB	Exc.	V.G.	Good	Fair	Poor
1200	1050	800	600	500	250

Mark V Fluted Synthetic

Similar to above model, with blued carbon steel action and barrel. Synthetic stock. Introduced late in 1996.

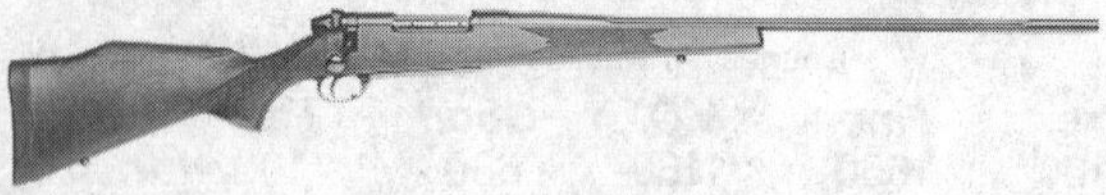

NIB	Exc.	V.G.	Good	Fair	Poor
1000	850	650	450	400	200

Mark V SLS

Features stainless steel barreled action, with laminated wood stock. Fitted with 1" black recoil pad. Chambered for calibers: .257 through .340 Wby. Magnum; 7mm Rem. Magnum, .300; .338 Win. Mag.; .375 H&H Magnum. Weight 8.25 lbs., varies by caliber. Introduced in late 1996.

NIB	Exc.	V.G.	Good	Fair	Poor
1200	1050	800	600	500	250

Mark V Varmint

Chambered for .22-250 and .224 Wby. cartridge. Offered with 24" or 26" heavy barrel. Note: Add 50% for German built.

NIB	Exc.	V.G.	Good	Fair	Poor
980	800	750	550	450	400

Mark V Lazermark

Pillar bedded "AA" Claro Walnut with laser carved oak-leaf pattern, polished blue metal, Calibers: .257 Wby, 6.5-300 Wby, .270 Win, .300 Wby. This version had a laser-carved pattern on the stock and forearm in place of usual checkering. Introduced in 1985.

NIB	Exc.	V.G.	Good	Fair	Poor
2450	2080	1700	1450	880	400

Mark V Fibermark Composite

This version has a matte blue finish. Furnished with synthetic black wrinkle-finished stock. Chambered for calibers .22-250 to .375 H&H. Barrel lengths 24" to 26" depending on caliber.

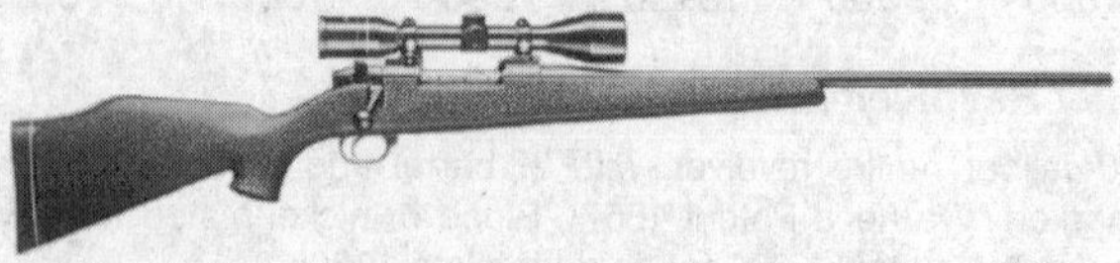

NIB	Exc.	V.G.	Good	Fair	Poor
1250	1000	800	550	400	250

Mark V Ultramark

Custom-finished version, with glass-bedded action and special high-polish blue. Action hand-honed. Walnut stock features basket weave checkering. Introduced in 1989.

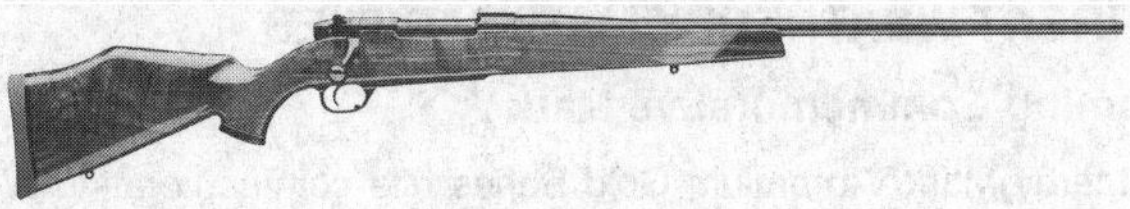

NIB	Exc.	V.G.	Good	Fair	Poor
2400	2000	1650	1200	800	500

Mark V Accumark

Introduced in 1995. Features Mark V Magnum action. Trigger preset at factory for 3.5 lbs. of pull. Fully adjustable for sear engagement at let-off weight. Action metal black oxide coated, with bead blast matte finish. Stainless steel barrel 26" in length, with low luster brushed finish. Weight 8 lbs. Offered in all Weatherby calibers from .240 to .340 Wby. Magnum, plus 7mm Rem. Magnum, 7mm STW and .300 Win. Magnum.

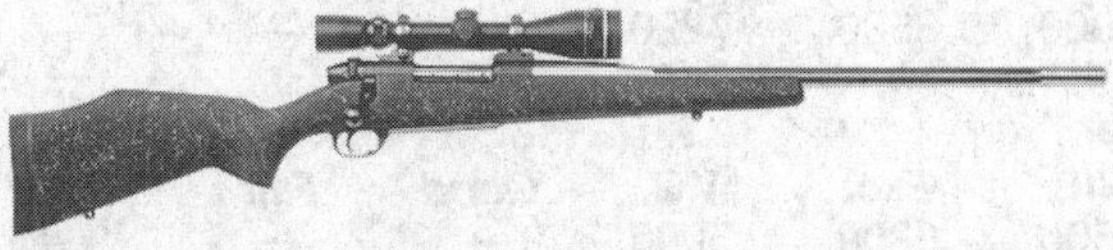

NIB	Exc.	V.G.	Good	Fair	Poor
1700	1100	950	800	500	300

Mark V Accumark RC

Upgraded model with Range Certified (RC) guarantee to deliver sub-MOA 3-shot groups with Weatherby ammo. Chambered in all Weatherby Magnums up to .340, plus .270 Win., 7mm Rem., .308 Win., .30-06, .300 Win. Magnum and .338 Lapua. Button rifled free-floated barrel, with target crown, T-6 bedding block, tuned/adjustable trigger.

NIB	Exc.	V.G.	Good	Fair	Poor
2100	1500	1250	1000	600	400

35th Anniversary Commemorative Mark V

Specially embellished rifle commemorated 35th Anniversary of the company. There were 1,000 produced in 1980. As with all commemoratives, it must be NIB with all furnished materials to be worth top dollar.

NIB	Exc.	V.G.	Good	Fair	Poor
1500	1300	1000	750	500	350

40th Anniversary Commemorative Mark V

Similar to 35th Anniversary model. Only 200 manufactured in 1985.

NIB	Exc.	V.G.	Good	Fair	Poor
1500	1300	1000	750	500	350

50th Anniversary Commemorative Mark V

Chambered only in .300 Wby. Magnum, with high-grade walnut Monte Carlo stock. Limited manufacture in 1995.

NIB	Exc.	V.G.	Good	Fair	Poor
2000	1500	1200	750	500	350

70th Anniversary Commemorative Mark V

Limited to 70 rifles in 2015. Chambered in .257 Wby. Magnum, with 24" barrel, high-grade checkered Claro walnut stock with rosewood grip and forend caps. Special engraved floorplate. Comes with custom leather case and commemorative knife.

NIB	Exc.	V.G.	Good	Fair	Poor
5400	4800	—	—	—	—

1984 Olympic Commemorative Mark V

Specially embellished Mark V rifle has gold-plated accents. Exhibition-grade walnut stock, with a star inlay. There were 1,000 manufactured in 1984. A commemorative rifle and must be NIB to bring premium value.

NIB	Exc.	V.G.	Good	Fair	Poor
1600	1300	1050	750	500	350

Crown Grade Mark V

Weatherby's best-grade rifle. Available on a custom-order basis only. Features an engraved receiver and barrel, with exhibition-grade hand-checkered walnut stock. Also furnished with an engraved scope mount.

NIB	Exc.	V.G.	Good	Fair	Poor
8000	7000	5500	4000	1500	500

Mark V Super Varmint Master (SVM)

Introduced in 2000. Features 26" stainless steel barrel. Stock is laminated, with Monte Carlo comb. Fully adjustable trigger. Chambered for .220 Swift, .223 Rem., .22-250, .243 Win., 7mm-08 and .308 Win. Also offered in single-shot configuration. Weight 8.5 lbs.

NIB	Exc.	V.G.	Good	Fair	Poor
1680	1400	1200	900	600	350

Mark V Special Varmint Rifle (SVR)

Introduced in 2003. Features 22" Krieger heavy barrel, Monte Carlo composite stock, black recoil pad and matte black finish. Adjustable trigger is standard. Available in .223 Rem. and .22-250. Weight 7.25 lbs.

NIB	Exc.	V.G.	Good	Fair	Poor
1100	1000	800	700	500	300

MARK V LIGHTWEIGHT RIFLES

Mark V Synthetic Lightweight

Chambered in calibers from .22-250 to .308 Win.. Fitted with 24" barrel. Synthetic stock, with Monte Carlo comb. Magazine capacity 5 rounds. Weight 6.5 lbs. Carbine version offered, with 20" barrel in .243, 7mm-08 and .308. Weight 6 lbs.

NIB	Exc.	V.G.	Good	Fair	Poor
900	750	600	480	350	250

Mark V Stainless Lightweight

Similar to model above, with stainless steel barrel and action. Weight 6.5 lbs. Carbine version also available.

NIB	Exc.	V.G.	Good	Fair	Poor
1100	950	800	650	520	300

Mark V Sporter Lightweight

Chambered for calibers ranging from .22-250 to .308 Win.. Fitted with 24" barrel. Stock is Claro walnut, with Monte Carlo comb. Weight 6.75 lbs.

NIB	Exc.	V.G.	Good	Fair	Poor
1050	900	750	600	480	250

Mark V Accumark Lightweight

Chambered for calibers from .22-250 to .300 Wby. Fitted with 24" barrel. Magazine capacity 5 rounds. Special laminated synthetic stock. Weight 7 lbs. Introduced in 1998.

NIB	Exc.	V.G.	Good	Fair	Poor
1250	1000	900	800	650	400

Mark V Ultra Lightweight

Similar to above model, with lightened components. Calibers begin with .243 and go to .300 Wby. Fitted with 24" or 26" barrel depending on caliber. Weight 5.75 lbs. Introduced in 1998. In 2000, offered in a left-hand version. In 2001, available chambered for .338-06 A-Square cartridge.

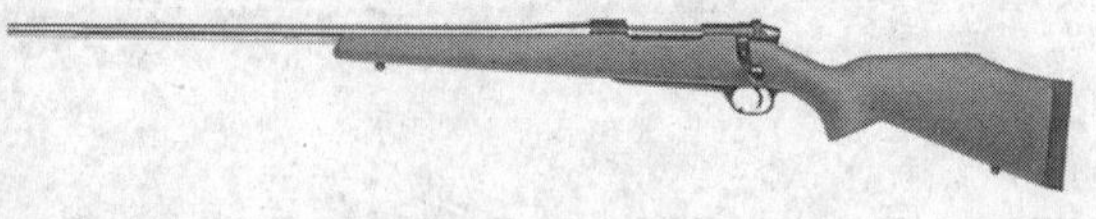

NIB	Exc.	V.G.	Good	Fair	Poor
1450	1200	950	700	450	300

Mark V Deluxe Lightweight

Offered in calibers from .22-250 to .30-06. Fitted with 24" barrel, hand-select walnut Monte Carlo stock, with rosewood forend tip and pistol grip cap. Fine line checkering. Weight 6.75 lbs. Introduced in 1999.

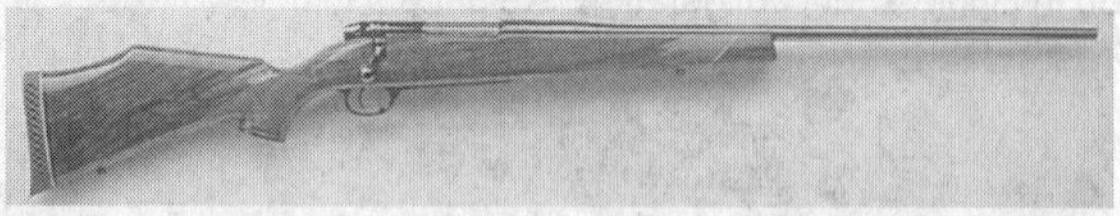

NIB	Exc.	V.G.	Good	Fair	Poor
1650	1250	1000	800	600	400

Mark V SPM (Super Predator Master)

Introduced in 2001. Features 24" blackened stainless steel fluted barrel. Chambered for .223 Rem., .22-250 Rem., .243 Win., 7mm-08 Rem. and .308 Win. cartridges. Fully adjustable trigger. Synthetic stock. Weight 6.5 lbs. Right-hand only.

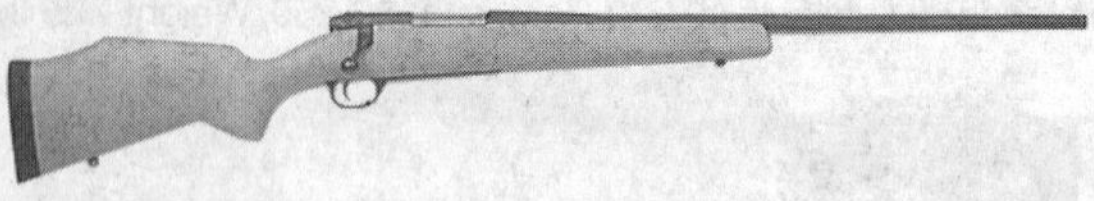

NIB	Exc.	V.G.	Good	Fair	Poor
1600	1300	1050	750	500	350

Mark V SBGM (Super Big Game Master)

Features 24" blackened stainless steel barrel Krieger fluted barrel (26" for Magnum calibers). Fully adjustable trigger. Tan composite stock, with raised comb Monte Carlo. Pachmayr Decelerator recoil pad. Offered in a wide variety of calibers from .240 Wby. Magnum to .300 Wby. Magnum. Weight 5.75 lbs.; 6.75 lbs. for Magnum rifles. Introduced in 2002. Note: Add $60 for Magnum calibers.

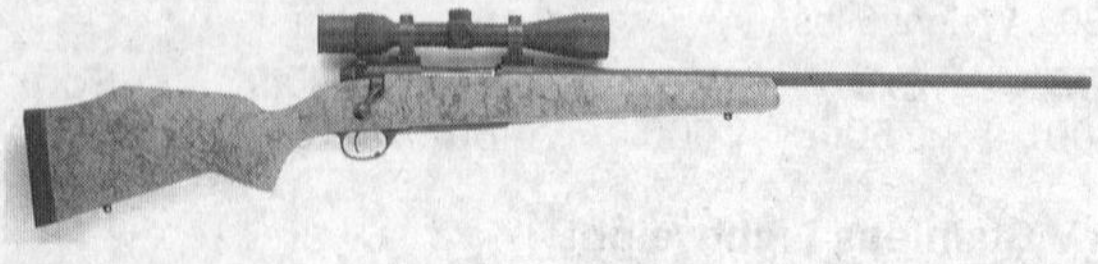

NIB	Exc.	V.G.	Good	Fair	Poor
1650	1250	1000	800	600	400

Mark V Arroyo

Offered in 15 calibers from .240 Wby. Magnum to .340 Wby. Magnum. Features include fully adjustable trigger, stainless fluted barrel (22", 24" 26" depending on caliber), composite stock with palm swell and laminate raised comb, KUIU Clas camo. Accubrake available on some calibers. From Weatherby Custom Shop. Introduced in 2015.

NIB	Exc.	V.G.	Good	Fair	Poor
2400	2000	1500	1200	600	300

Mark V Outfitter

Chambered in all Weatherby calibers from .240 to .300, including 6.5-300 Wby. Magnum plus .270 Win., .308 Win. and .30-06. Features similar to Arroyo, with lighter weight (5.5 to 6.75 lbs.). Carbon-fiber stock has High Desert camo finish. From Weatherby Custom Shop. Introduced in 2015.

NIB	Exc.	V.G.	Good	Fair	Poor
2400	2000	1500	1200	600	300

CURRENT WEATHERBY MARK V RIFLES

Wyoming Commemorative Mark V

Weatherby Mark V premium Gold Series rifle commemorating Weatherby's move to Sheridan, Wyoming. Fewer than 1,000 in a Gold and Silver Edition made starting with serial number WY000001. Stocked in exhibition grade walnut (Gold) or AAA Grade (Silver), chambered in .300 Wby with 26" barrel. Both are engraved.

Wyoming Commemorative Mark V Gold

NIB	Exc.	V.G.	Good	Fair	Poor
9000	8500	7220	—	—	—

Silver

NIB	Exc.	V.G.	Good	Fair	Poor
7500	6300	5000	—	—	—

Safari Grade Mark V

"AAA" fancy French walnut stock, iron sights, No. 2, 3 or 4 contour barrel in 24" or 26" lengths, 8 3/4 pounds to 10 pounds. Calibers: .257 Wby, .270 Win, 7mm Wby, .300 Wby, .340 Wby, .375 H&H, .375 Wby, .378 Wby, .416 Wby, .460 Wby. Base price shown. Accubrake extra (add $300-$400). Accubrake extra and standard with .378, .416, .460.

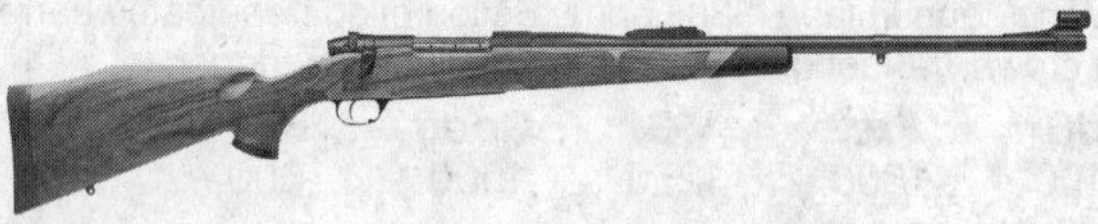

NIB	Exc.	V.G.	Good	Fair	Poor
6000	5000	4250	3500	—	—

Mark V Camilla Ultra Lightweight

Lightweight synthetic stocked rifle designed by women to fit a woman's form and named after the Weatherby Matriarch Camilla. The UL has a stainless steel, fluted barrel with 24" barrel, 5 3/4 pounds, 13" length of pull. Calibers: .240 Wby, 6.5 Creedmoor, .270 Win., .308 Win., .30-06.

NIB	Exc.	V.G.	Good	Fair	Poor
2000	1750	1450	1100	850	500

Mark V Camilla Subalpine

Lightweight synthetic stocked rifle with Gore Ultrafade camo designed by women to fit a woman's form and named after the Weatherby Matriarch Camilla. The Subalpine finished in FDE Cerakote, fluted barrel with 24" barrel, 5 3/4 pounds, 13" length of pull. Calibers: .240 Wby, 6.5 Creedmoor, .270 Win., .308 Win., .30-06.

NIB	Exc.	V.G.	Good	Fair	Poor
2350	2000	1750	1350	1000	600

Mark V Camilla Deluxe

Pillar bedded "AA" Claro Walnut, polished blue metal, designed by women to fit a woman's form and named after the Weatherby Matriarch Camilla. The Deluxe has a 24" barrel, weighs 5 3/4 pounds, 13" length of pull. Calibers: .240 Wby, 6.5 Creedmoor, .270 Win., .308 Win., .30-06.

NIB	Exc.	V.G.	Good	Fair	Poor
2350	2000	1750	1350	1000	600

Mark V Subalpine

Lightweight synthetic stocked rifle in subalpine camo with fluted 22" barrel, 5 3/4 pounds (standard calibers) or 26" barrel 6 3/4 pounds (magnum calibers), flat dark earth Cerakote finish. Calibers: .257 Wby, 6.5 C,

6.5-300 Wby, .270 Wby, .300 Wby. Base price shown. Accubrake add 200; Range Certified add $500 extra.

NIB	Exc.	V.G.	Good	Fair	Poor
2350	2000	1750	1350	1000	600

Mark V Kryptek Altitude

Synthetic stock with Kryptek camo, metal with tungsten Cerakote. No. 1 or No. 2 contour barrel in 22", 24" or 26" lengths, 5 3/4 to 6 3/4 pounds. Calibers: .240 Wby, .257 Wby, 6.5 Creedmoor, 6.5-300 Wby, .270 Win, .270 Wby, .308, .30-06, .300 Wby. Base price shown. Accubrake add 200; Range Certified add $500 extra.

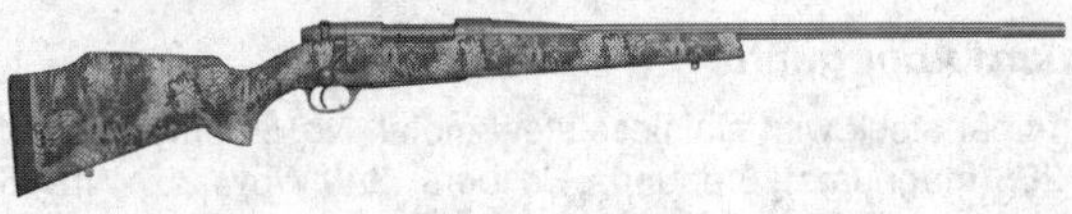

NIB	Exc.	V.G.	Good	Fair	Poor
3000	2550	2150	1850	1100	650

Mark V Outfitter FDE

High Desert-colored composite stock with spiderweb accents, metal with Flat Dark Earth Cerakote. No. 1 or No. 2 contour barrel in 22", 24" or 26" lengths, 5 3/4 to 6 3/4 pounds. Calibers: .240 Wby, .257 Wby, 6.5 Creedmoor, 6.5-300 Wby, .270 Win, .270 Wby, 7mm Wby, .308, .30-06, .300 Wby. Base price shown. Range Certified (add $500) extra.

NIB	Exc.	V.G.	Good	Fair	Poor
2200	1880	1600	950	580	350

Mark V Accumark

Composite stock, matte blue metal. No. 3 contour fluted barrel in 22", 24" or 26" lengths, 7 1/4 to 8 1/4 pounds. 8 1/2 pounds (.30-378 Wby). Calibers: .240 Wby, .257 Wby, 6.5 C, 6.5-300 Wby, .270 Win, .270 Wby, 7mm Rem, 7mm Wby, .308, .30-06, .300 Win, .300 Wby, .30-378, .338 Lapua, .338-378 Wby, .340 Wby. Base price shown. Accubrake add 200; Lapua add 300; Range Certified add 500 extra.

NIB	Exc.	V.G.	Good	Fair	Poor
2000	1750	1500	1100	850	500

Mark V Krieger Custom Rifle (KCR)

Composite stock, matte FDE/Black Cerakote metal. No. 3 contour fluted Krieger match-grade barrel, cryogenically stress relieved, in 22", 24" or 26" lengths, 7 1/4 to 8 1/4 pounds. 8 1/2 pounds (.30-378 Wby). Calibers: .257 Wby, 6.5-300 Wby, .300 Wby, .30-378. Base price shown. Accubrake add $200; Range Certified add $500 extra.

NIB	Exc.	V.G.	Good	Fair	Poor
3100	2600	2200	1320	600	300

Mark V Carbon Mark

Composite stock, 9-lug action, 26" Proof Research carbon-fiber barrel. Weight: 7 3/4 pounds. Calibers: .257 Wby, .300 Wby.

NIB	Exc.	V.G.	Good	Fair	Poor
3500	2950	2500	1500	900	450

Mark V Weathermark

Introduced in 1993. Composite stock, grey Cerakote metal. No. 1, 2 or 3 contour barrel in 24" or 26" lengths, 6 1/4 to 8 pounds (.375 H&H). Calibers: .240 Wby, .257 Wby, 6.5 Creedmoor, 6.5-300 Wby, .270 Win, .270 Wby, 7mm Rem, 7mm Wby, .308, .30-06, .300 Win, .300 Wby, .340 Wby, .375 H&H.

NIB	Exc.	V.G.	Good	Fair	Poor
1450	1220	1050	620	380	200

Mark V Tacmark

Fully adjustable stock with CNC machined aluminum bedding plate, detachable 5-round magazine, No. 3 contour fluted barrel up to 28" weighing 11 1/4 pounds. Calibers: 6.5-300 Wby, .300 Wby, .30-378 Wby, .338 Lapua, .338-378 Wby. Comes with Accubrake.

NIB	Exc.	V.G.	Good	Fair	Poor
3500	2950	2500	1500	—	—

Mark V Tacmark Elite

Fully adjustable stock with CNC machined aluminum bedding plate, detachable 5-round magazine, DD Ross bolt knob, No. 3 contour Krieger fluted barrel, cryogenically stress relieved up to 28" weighing 11 1/2 pounds. Calibers: 6.5-300 Wby, .300 Wby, .30-378 Wby, .338 Lapua, .338-378 Wby. Comes with Accubrake.

NIB	Exc.	V.G.	Good	Fair	Poor
5280	4480	3800	3000	—	—

Mark V Backcountry

Calibers: .240 Weatherby Mag., .257 Weatherby Mag., .270 Weatherby Mag., .280 AI, .300 Weatherby Mag., 6.5 Creedmoor, 6.5 Weatherby RPM, 6.5-300 Weatherby Mag., 6mm Creedmoor, 7mm Weatherby Mag. Capacity: 4 to 6. Barrel: 22 to 26 in. fluted, McMillan Cerakote. Stock: Carbon fiber. Sights: None, drilled and tapped. Weight: 5.3 lbs. Features: 3D HEX recoil reducer, Trigger Tech trigger, six-lug receiver.

NIB	Exc.	V.G.	Good	Fair	Poor
2280	—	—	—	—	—

Backcountry 2.0

Replaces the original Backcountry family. Upgraded with carbon-fiber Peak44 Blacktooth stock that weights under 20 oz. Other improvements include: second generation 3DHEX recoil pad, the first printed pad made. Deeper spiral fluting on the bolt and threaded bolt handle. Fit with Accubrake ST. Patriot Brown Cerakote finish. Weight 5.2 lbs. Carbon models include a carbon-fiber barrel. Ti models are built on a titanium action.

NIB	Exc.	V.G.	Good	Fair	Poor
2580	—	—	—	—	—

Mark V Apex

Calibers: .240 Weatherby Mag. to 338-378 Weatherby Mag. Barrel: 24" to 28" with a coyote tan Cerakote and fluting. Weight: 6.4 to 7.5 lbs. Stock: Peak 44 Bastion carbon fiber with a vertical grip. Features: The Apex is billed as a long-range hunting rifle. Introduced in 2023.

NIB	Exc.	V.G.	Good	Fair	Poor
2570	—	—	—	—	—

CURRENT VANGUARD RIFLES

Vanguard First Lite

Polymer stock with First Lite Fusion camo, FDE Cerakote metal, No. 2 contour fluted barrel with Accubrake, 24" or 26" (magnums), 7 to 7 1/4 pounds. Calibers: .240 Wby, .25-06, .257 Wby, 6.5 Creedmoor, 6.5-300 Wby, .270 Win, .308, .30-06, .300 Win, .300 Wby.

NIB	Exc.	V.G.	Good	Fair	Poor
920	800	680	400	350	200

Vanguard Stainless

Griptonite synthetic stock stainless steel barrel and action, No. 2 contour barrel 24" or 26" (magnums), 7 1/2 pounds. Calibers: .243, .257 Wby, .270 Win, 7mm Rem, .308, .30-06, .300 Win., .300 Wby.

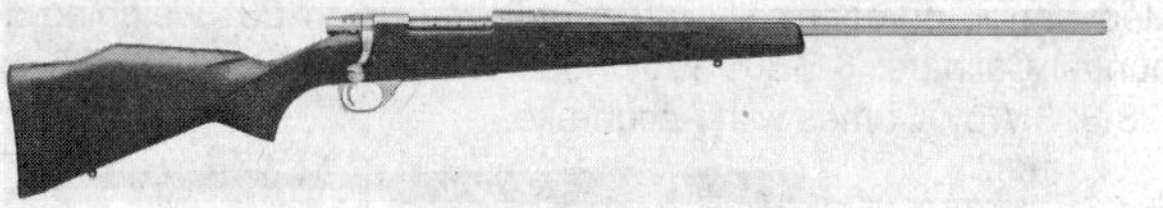

NIB	Exc.	V.G.	Good	Fair	Poor
680	580	500	350	280	150

Vanguard Badlands

Howa barreled action in Badlands Approach camo stock, Burnt Bronze Cerakote metal, No. 2 contour barrel 24" or 26" (magnums). Calibers: .25-06, .257 Wby, 6.5 C, 6.5-300 Wby, .270 Win, 7mm-08, 7mm Rem, .308, .30-06, .300 Win, .300 Wby.

NIB	Exc.	V.G.	Good	Fair	Poor
720	600	520	300	200	150

Vanguard Synthetic Compact

Composite stock, adjustable LOP from 12 1/2" to 13 5/8", matte blue metal, No. 1 contour 20" barrel. Calibers: .243, .240 Wby, 6.5 Creedmoor, 7mm-08, .308.

NIB	Exc.	V.G.	Good	Fair	Poor
500	420	380	250	180	120

Vanguard Select

Polymer stock with matte blue metal, No. 2 contour barrel, 24" or 26", 7 1/2 pounds. Calibers: .243, 6.5 Creedmoor, 6 .270 Win, 7mm Rem, .308 Win., .30-06, .300 Win.

NIB	Exc.	V.G.	Good	Fair	Poor
500	420	380	280	180	120

Vanguard Weatherguard

Griptonite synthetic stock with grey Cerakote metal, No. 2 contour barrel 24" or 26" (magnums), 7 1/4 to 7 1/2 pounds, standard or detachable magazine. Calibers: .223, .22-250, .243, .240 Wby, .25-06, .257 Wby, 6.5 Creedmoor, 6.5-300 Wby, .270 Win, 7mm-08, 7mm Rem, .308, .30-06, .300 Win, .300 Wby.

NIB	Exc.	V.G.	Good	Fair	Poor
650	550	450	280	160	120

Vanguard Wilderness

Carbon-fiber stock with matte blue metal, No. 2 contour barrel 24" or 26" (magnums), 7 1/4 to 7 1/2 pounds, standard or detachable magazine. Calibers: .223, .22-250, .243, .240 Wby, .25-06, .257 Wby, 6.5 C, 6.5-300 Wby, .270 Win, .308, .30-06, .300 Win, .300 Wby.

NIB	Exc.	V.G.	Good	Fair	Poor
850	720	600	400	300	200

Vanguard Backcountry

Carbon-fiber stock with grey Cerakote metal, No. 2 contour fluted barrel 24" or 26" (magnums), 6 3/4 pounds. Calibers: .223, .22-250, .243, .240 Wby, .257 Wby, 6.5 Creedmoor, .270 Win, .30-06, .300 Win, .300 Wby.

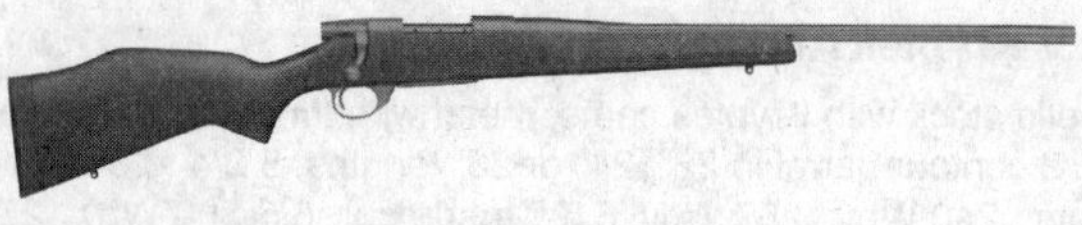

NIB	Exc.	V.G.	Good	Fair	Poor
1020	880	720	450	380	250

Vanguard Accuguard

Carbon-fiber stock with stainless steel metal, No. 3 contour fluted barrel 24" or 26" (magnums), 8 pounds. Calibers: .240 Wby, .257 Wby, 6.5-300 Wby, .30-06, .300 Win, .300 Wby.

NIB	Exc.	V.G.	Good	Fair	Poor
920	800	680	400	350	200

Vanguard Camilla

"A" grade Turkish walnut, matte blue metal, designed by women to fit a woman's form and named after the Weatherby Matriarch Camilla. The Deluxe has a No. 1 contour 20" barrel, weighs 6 1/2 pounds, 13" length of pull. Calibers: .243, 6.5 Creedmoor, 7mm-08, .308.

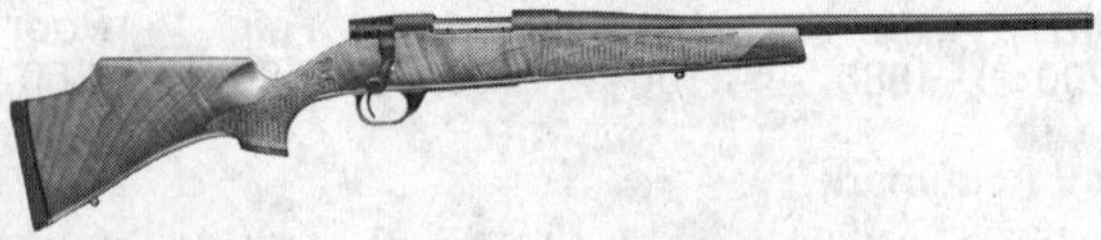

NIB	Exc.	V.G.	Good	Fair	Poor
720	600	520	350	200	100

Vanguard Deluxe

"AA" Claro walnut, polished blue metal. The Deluxe has a No. 2 contour 24" to 26" barrel, weighs 7 1/2 pounds. Calibers: .257 Wby, .270 Win, .30-06, .300 Wby.

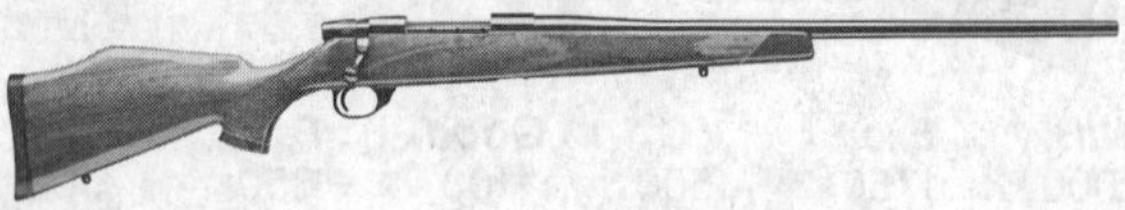

NIB	Exc.	V.G.	Good	Fair	Poor
980	820	700	420	250	180

Vanguard Lazerguard

"AA" Claro walnut with laser-carved oak leaf pattern, polished blue metal. The Lazerguard has a No. 2 contour 24" to 26" barrel, weighs 7 1/2 pounds. Calibers: .243, .257 Wby, .270 Win, .308, .30-06, .300 Win, .300 Wby.

NIB	Exc.	V.G.	Good	Fair	Poor
1020	850	720	450	280	200

Vanguard Sporter

"A" grade Turkish walnut stock, matte blue metal, No. 2 contour barrel in 24" or 26" length, optional DBM, weighs 7 1/4 to 7 1/2 pounds. Calibers: .223, .22-250, .243, .25-06, .257 Wby, .270 Win, 7mm-08, 7mm Rem, .308, .30-06, .300 Win, .300 Wby.

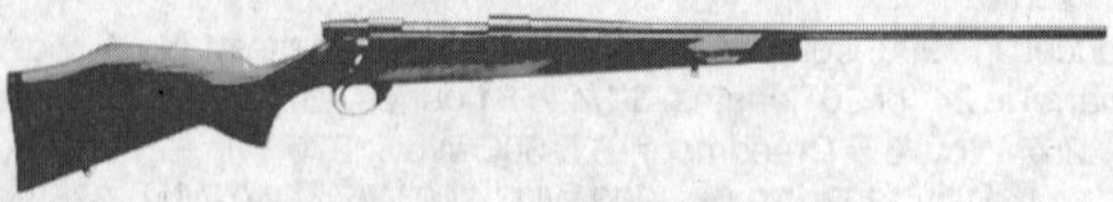

NIB	Exc.	V.G.	Good	Fair	Poor
720	600	520	300	180	150

Vanguard Safari

European walnut stock, matte blue metal, 24" No. 2 or 2.5 contour barrel, 7 3/4 pounds. NECG Iron sights .375 only. Calibers: .30-06, .300 Wby, .375 H&H (add $200).

NIB	Exc.	V.G.	Good	Fair	Poor
1020	850	720	450	300	200

Vanguard DGR

Carbon-fiber composite stock, matte blue metal, 24" No. 2.5 contour barrel with NECG iron sights, 7 3/4 pounds. Calibers: .375 H&H.

NIB	Exc.	V.G.	Good	Fair	Poor
1100	950	800	480	300	200

VANGUARD SERIES

Vanguard (early production)

This was Weatherby's Japanese-manufactured economy rifle. Chambered for various popular standard American cartridges from .22-50 to .300 Win. Magnum cartridge. Bolt-action repeater, with 24" barrel furnished without sights. Has 3- or 5-shot magazine; finish is polished blue, with select checkered walnut stock with rosewood forend tip and pistol grip cap. Discontinued in 1988.

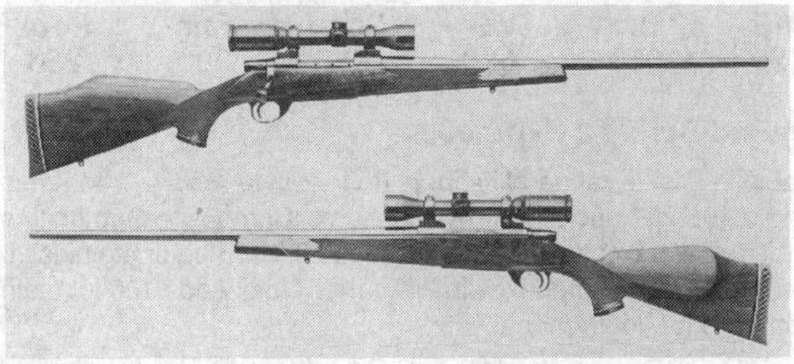

NIB	Exc.	V.G.	Good	Fair	Poor
—	1100	920	750	600	350

Vanguard VGS

Satin-finish version. Discontinued in 1988.

NIB	Exc.	V.G.	Good	Fair	Poor
—	1000	820	650	500	300

Vanguard VGL

Lightweight carbine version has 20" barrel. Discontinued in 1988.

NIB	Exc.	V.G.	Good	Fair	Poor
—	900	720	550	400	250

Fiberguard

This version has matte-blued finish, with green fiberglass stock. Discontinued in 1988.

NIB	Exc.	V.G.	Good	Fair	Poor
—	750	580	400	300	200

Vanguard Classic I

Chambered for various popular standard calibers. Has 24" barrel and 3- or 5-shot magazine. Satin blue finish. Select checkered oil-finished walnut stock. Introduced in 1989.

NIB	Exc.	V.G.	Good	Fair	Poor
700	600	500	400	300	200

Vanguard Classic II

A more deluxe version, with higher-grade walnut stock.

NIB	Exc.	V.G.	Good	Fair	Poor
720	620	520	420	320	220

Vanguard VGX Deluxe

This version has high-gloss Monte Carlo-type stock and high-polished blued finish. Introduced in 1989.

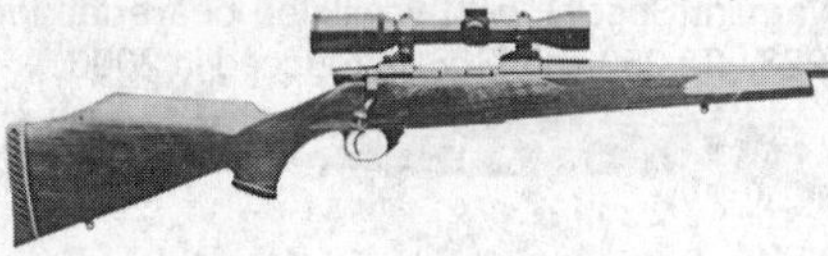

NIB	Exc.	V.G.	Good	Fair	Poor
800	700	600	500	400	300

Vanguard Synthetic

Features upgraded composite stock, with Monte Carlo comb, a ring/base scope mounting system and 24" barrel. Calibers from .223 Rem. to .338 Win. Magnum, including .257 Wby. Weight 7.75 lbs. Introduced in 2004.

NIB	Exc.	V.G.	Good	Fair	Poor
400	350	300	250	180	100

Vanguard Sporter SS

Similar to Vanguard Sporter, with stainless steel barrel and receiver.

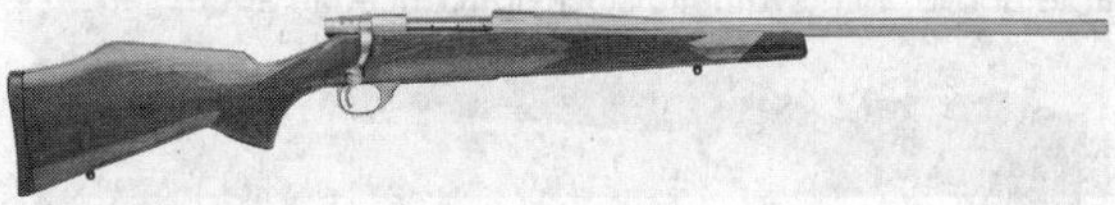

NIB	Exc.	V.G.	Good	Fair	Poor
680	580	480	380	280	120

Vanguard Varmint Special

Chambered in .223, .22-250 or .308. Blued No. 3 contour heavy crowned 22" barrel. Adjustable trigger. Synthetic tan composite stock, with black spiderweb pattern. Introduced in 2006.

NIB	Exc.	V.G.	Good	Fair	Poor
580	480	380	280	200	120

Vanguard Synthetic Package

Introduced in 2004. Features 24" barrel, with adjustable trigger. Chambered for a variety of calibers from .223 Rem. to .338 Win. Magnum. Supplied with Bushnell Banner 3-9x40 scope, sling and hard case. Weight 7.75 lbs.

NIB	Exc.	V.G.	Good	Fair	Poor
650	550	350	280	220	150

Vanguard Sub-MOA Matte or Stainless

Introduced in 2005. Features a guarantee to shoot .99" at 100 yards. Calibers from .223 Rem. to .338 Win. Magnum. Barrel length 24", with Monte Carlo Fiberguard stock. Adjustable trigger. Weight 7.75 lbs. Also available in stainless steel. Note: Add $120 for stainless steel.

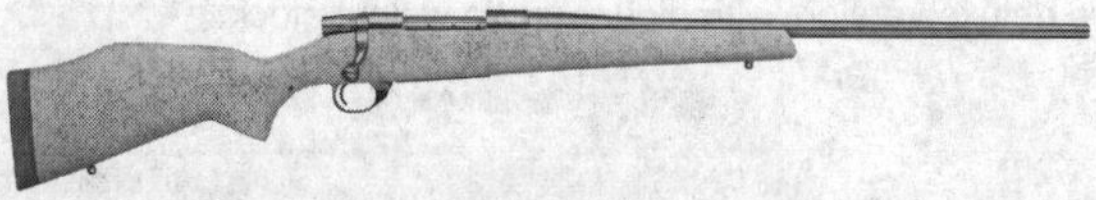

NIB	Exc.	V.G.	Good	Fair	Poor
800	700	600	500	300	200

Vanguard Sub-MOA Varmint

Similar to Vanguard Varmint Special, with ventilated beavertail forend. Chambered in .204, .223, .22-250 and .308. Introduced in 2006.

NIB	Exc.	V.G.	Good	Fair	Poor
920	800	650	500	300	200

Vanguard Compact

Chambered for ..223, 22-250, .243 or .308. Fitted with 20" barrel and scaled-down hardwood stock, with shorter length of pull. Also included is a full-size composite stock. Weight 6.75 lbs. Introduced in 2005.

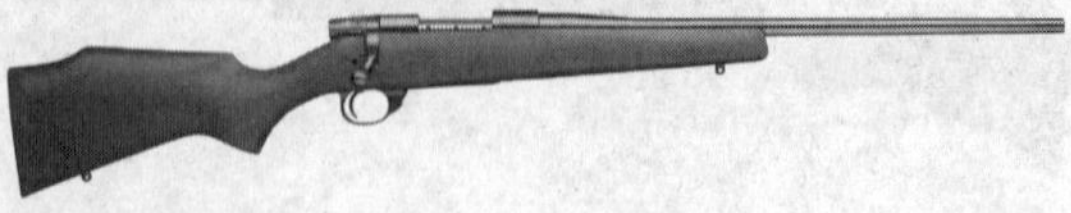

NIB	Exc.	V.G.	Good	Fair	Poor
550	450	350	250	180	100

Vanguard Youth Compact

Similar to above, with synthetic stock. Introduced in 2008.

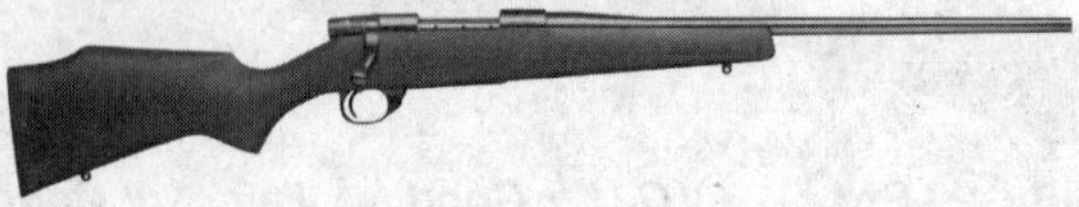

NIB	Exc.	V.G.	Good	Fair	Poor
550	450	350	250	180	100

Weathermark Alaskan

Similar to Weathermark, with checkered composite stock. Barreled action is electroless nickel, with non-glare finish. Muzzle brake optional. Available in same calibers as Weathermark. Weight 7.7 lbs.

NIB	Exc.	V.G.	Good	Fair	Poor
750	650	550	450	320	220

VANGUARD SERIES 2

Vanguard Series 2 Back Country

All Vanguard Series 2 rifles guaranteed to shoot 3-shot group of less than 1" at 100 yds. when used with specified Weatherby factory or premium ammunition. Available in .240, .257 and .300 Wby. Magnum, plus .270 Win., .30-06, .300 Win. Magnum. Features include match-grade adjustable trigger, fluted 24" barrel, pillar-bedded Monte Carlo composite stock, with spiderweb accents, Pachmayr Decelerator recoil pad, Cera-Kote Tactical Gray finish. Average weight 6.75 lbs.

NIB	Exc.	V.G.	Good	Fair	Poor
1250	1100	950	800	500	350

Vanguard Series 2 Sporter

Classic Weatherby look. Monte Carlo A-grade Turkish walnut stock, with raised comb, rosewood forend and fine-line diamond point checkering. Other features similar to Back Country model. Chambered in most popular calibers from .223 to .338 Win. Magnum, including .257 and .300 Wby. Magnums. Deluxe model has higher grade wood, with high-gloss finish. Note: Add $300 for deluxe model.

NIB	Exc.	V.G.	Good	Fair	Poor
750	650	520	400	300	250

Vanguard Series 2 Synthetic

Available in a wide range of calibers from .223 to .338 Win. Magnum, including .240, .257 and .300 Wby. Magnums. Composite Griptonite stock. Barrel is 24" No. 2 contour. Weight 7.25 to 7.5 lbs. Blue or stainless finish. Also offered in youth model, with 20" barrel. Note: Add $100 for stainless. Deduct 10% for youth model.

NIB	Exc.	V.G.	Good	Fair	Poor
600	520	450	380	300	250

Vanguard Series 2 Varmint Special

Similar to Synthetic model in .223, .22-250 and .308 Win., with semi-heavy No. 3 contour 20" barrel. Weight 8.75 lbs.

NIB	Exc.	V.G.	Good	Fair	Poor
750	650	520	400	300	250

Vanguard VAC

Vanguard Adaptive Composite (VAC) model comes with MOA accuracy guarantee of .99" or less at 100 yds. Target-style stock with wide forend, quick adjustments and rubberized grip panels. Hammer-forged 20" threaded bull barrel (suppressor not included). Introduced in 2017.

NIB	Exc.	V.G.	Good	Fair	Poor
1050	900	700	—	—	—

Vanguard RC

Range Certified (RC) model comes with printout of Oehler Ballistic Imaging System, with load/ballistic data and image of actual 3-shot group. Guaranteed .99" group or less at 100 yds., with Weatherby factory or other premium ammunition. Barrel 24", with bead blasted matte blue finish, composite Monte Carlo pillar-bedded stock. Available in .243 Win., .25-06 Rem., .257 Wby. Magnum, 6.5 Creedmoor, .270 Win., 7mm Rem. Magnum, .308 Win., .30-06, .300 Win. Magnum, .300 Wby. Magnum.

NIB	Exc.	V.G.	Good	Fair	Poor
950	800	650	500	400	200

WBY-X

Series of colorful and stylized bolt-actions built on Vanguard Series 2 design. Moderately priced and offer most of the features of other Weatherby rifles. All variations feature composite stocks, with camo finishes. Most models are offered in popular calibers from .223 Rem. to .300 Win. Magnum. Introduced in 2014.

NIB	Exc.	V.G.	Good	Fair	Poor
650	600	500	350	250	200

MARK XXII SERIES

Mark XXII

Semi-automatic rifle chambered for .22 LR cartridge. Two versions with: detachable magazine; tubular magazine. Has 24" barrel, with adjustable sights. Select checkered walnut stock, with rosewood forearm tip and pistol grip cap. Originally produced in Italy and later manufactured in Japan. Introduced in 1965; discontinued 1989. Note: Premium for Italian guns.

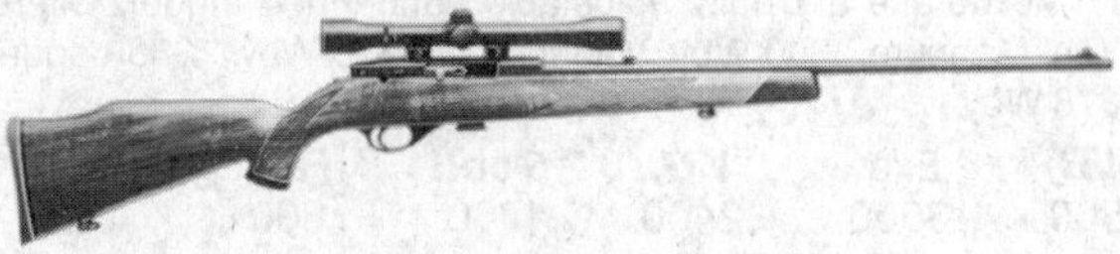

Mark XXII Clip Model

Mark XXII Tube Model

NIB	Exc.	V.G.	Good	Fair	Poor
800	650	500	350	220	200

Mark XXII Bolt Action

Based on Anschutz design. Available in .22 Long Rifle or .17 HMR. Classic Mark V-style high-gloss walnut Monte Carlo stock, with precision cut checkering, rosewood forend tip and grip cap. Target-grade barrel is 23", weight 6.5 lbs. Fully adjustable single-stage trigger. Introduced in 2007. Note: Add 10% for .17 HMR.

NIB	Exc.	V.G.	Good	Fair	Poor
1250	1000	800	600	400	300

CUSTOM RIFLES

Weatherby custom rifles offered with many different options that will affect price. Consult an expert prior to sale.

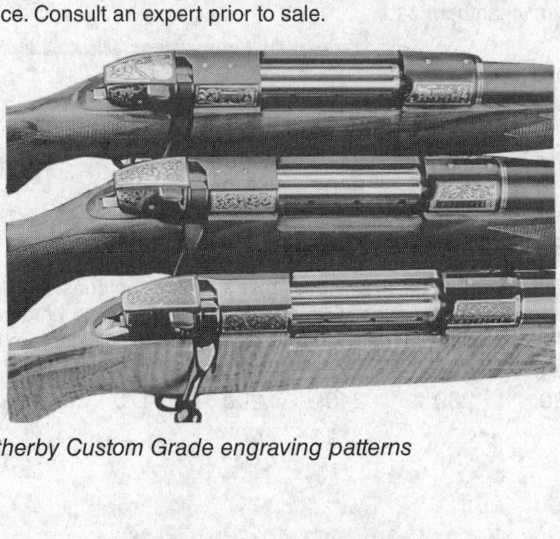

Weatherby Custom Grade engraving patterns

Vanguard Sage Country Custom

Introduced in 2008. Similar to Vanguard Synthetic, with injection-molded Desert Camo stock. Available in a variety of chamberings from .223 to .338 Win. Magnum.

NIB	Exc.	V.G.	Good	Fair	Poor
600	500	400	300	220	180

Vanguard Back Country Custom

Introduced in 2008. Lightweight version of Vanguard Synthetic, with fluted barrel, textured stock and overall weight of 6.75 lbs. Available in a variety of chamberings from .257 Wby. Magnum to .300 Wby. Magnum.

NIB	Exc.	V.G.	Good	Fair	Poor
950	850	720	620	420	200

Classic Custom

Features oil-finished French walnut stock, with 20 lpi checkering, ebony forend tip, metal grip cap and skeltonized steel buttplate. All metalwork is matte blue. Calibers are all Weatherby from .257 Wby. Magnum to .340 Wby. Magnum.

NIB	Exc.	V.G.	Good	Fair	Poor
5100	4600	3500	2250	900	500

Safari Grade Custom

Features oil-finish French walnut stock, with Monte Carlo comb and fleur-de-lis checkering. Ebony forend tip and pistol grip cap. Damascened bolt and follower, with checkered bolt handle. Quarter rib. Engraved floorplate "Safari Custom". Calibers from .257 Wby. Magnum to .460 Wby. Magnum.

NIB	Exc.	V.G.	Good	Fair	Poor
5300	4800	3700	2450	1050	550

Crown Custom

Features hand-carved walnut stock, with buttstock inlay, damascened bolt and follower with checkered bolt handle. Engraved barrel, receiver and triggerguard. Floorplate engraved with gold inlays.

NIB	Exc.	V.G.	Good	Fair	Poor
7500	6250	5000	3000	1500	750

Royal Custom

Introduced in 2002. Features Monte Carlo hand-checkered stock of fancy Claro walnut, with high-gloss finish. Engraved receiver, bolt sleeve and floorplate. Barrel length 26". Available in a wide variety of calibers.

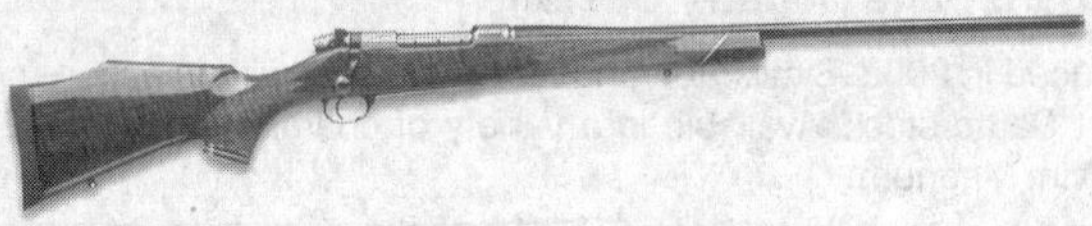

NIB	Exc.	V.G.	Good	Fair	Poor
5300	4800	3700	2450	1050	550

Outfitter Custom

Features Bell & Carlson synthetic stock, with custom camo and Pachmayr pad. Lightweight stainless steel fluted barrel. Titanium nitride finish on all metalwork.

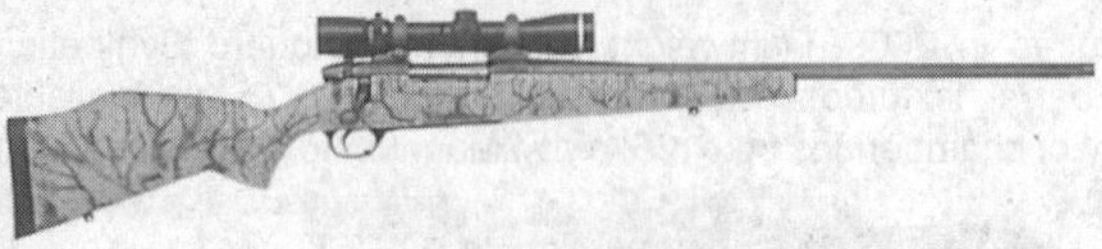

NIB	Exc.	V.G.	Good	Fair	Poor
2250	1700	1400	1100	700	400

Outfitter Krieger Custom

Features Bell & Carlson synthetic stock, with custom camo and Pachmayr pad. Custom Krieger stainless steel fluted barrel. Titanium nitride finish on all metalwork.

NIB	Exc.	V.G.	Good	Fair	Poor
3500	3000	2500	2000	1300	600

Chris Kyle Limited Edition

From Weatherby Custom Shop, this special limited edition rifle is in honor of Navy Seal Sniper Chris Kyle, who died in 2013. A portion of the proceeds from the sale of this rifle are donated to the Kyle family. Chambered in .300 Win. Magnum. Has a hand-laminated composite stock, with raised comb and Kryptek Highlander camo pattern. Other features include a fully adjustable trigger, fluted and free-floated stainless steel barrel, Pachmayr Decelerator pad and Chris Kyle frog logo on floorplate

NIB	Exc.	V.G.	Good	Fair	Poor
3500	3000	2700	2500	—	—

THREAT RESPONSE RIFLE SERIES

These rifles are based on the Mark V action.

TRR

Chambered for .223 or .308 Win. cartridge. Fitted with 22" heavy-contour black Krieger barrel. Black composite stock, with raised comb Monte Carlo. Flat-bottom forearm. Fully adjustable trigger. Recoil pad. Introduced in 2002.

NIB	Exc.	V.G.	Good	Fair	Poor
1250	1000	900	800	650	400

TRR Magnum

As above chambered for .300 Win. Magnum, .300 Wby. Magnum, .30-378 Wby. Magnum or .338-378 Wby. Magnum. Barrel length 26". Note: Add $150 for .30-378 and .338-378 calibers.

NIB	Exc.	V.G.	Good	Fair	Poor
1450	1200	950	700	450	300

TRR Magnum Custom

Has all the features of TRR Magnum, with addition of a fully adjustable stock. DO NOT use this model until company performs a safety upgrade to the bolt. Rifle can accidentally discharge without the bolt being fully engaged. Affected rifles bear serial numbers from one of these series on the receiver: 00001 through 03810; V00001 through V80966; VX00001 through VX44065; VS00001 through VS23699; VL00001 through VL46984; W00001 through W0099; NV0001 through NV0099. For more information contact Weatherby at 800-227-2018. Note: Add $150 for .30-378 or .338-378 calibers.

NIB	Exc.	V.G.	Good	Fair	Poor
2500	2200	1900	1600	1250	500

TRR RC (Range Certified)

Features laminated stock, with three-position buttstock, 26" Kreiger barrel with Accubrake and fully adjustable hand-tuned trigger. Offered in .300 Win. Magnum, .300 Wby. Magnum, .30-378 Wby., .338 Lapua and .338/378 Wby.

NIB	Exc.	V.G.	Good	Fair	Poor
3500	3000	2400	1700	800	350

SHOTGUNS

18i SERIES

Italian-made inertia-driven shotgun product line. The 18i Deluxe model is available in a 12-gauge 28" high-gloss-blued barrel with a 3" chamber. Deluxe has matte-finish European walnut stock and forearm, nickel-finished aluminum receiver metalwork with LaserTech engraving, 4+1 capacity, full-length ventilated top rib, and LPA Fiber sights. Five choke tubes and a wrench are included in a small plastic case. The 18i Synthetic model features a 12-gauge 28" barrel with a 3.5" chamber, Weatherby's first such chamber size. The 18i Waterfowler model is a 12-gauge 28" barrel 3.5" chamber with a Realtree Max 5 camo pattern or Mossy Oak Shadow Grass Blades camo.

18i Deluxe

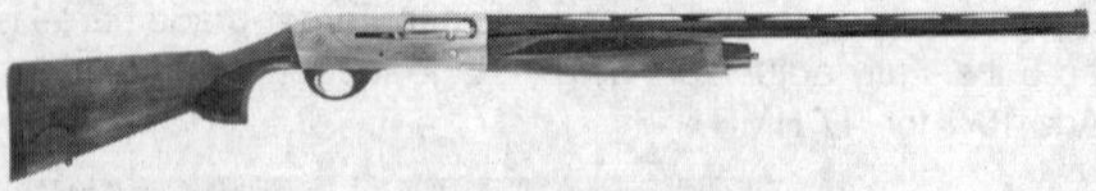

NIB	Exc.	V.G.	Good	Fair	Poor
1560	1330	1130	—	—	—

18i Synthetic

NIB	Exc.	V.G.	Good	Fair	Poor
920	790	680	—	—	—

18i Waterfowler

Gauges: 12 ga. Barrels: 28". Stock: Synthetic camo. Features: 3.5" "Super Magnum" chamber.

NIB	Exc.	V.G.	Good	Fair	Poor
1110	1000	850	700	—	—

PA-08 PUMP-ACTION SERIES

Weatherby introduced this line of pump-action shotguns in 2008. All models come in 12-gauge, with 3" chambers and have chrome-lined barrels. Knoxx stock models reduced recoil and are adjustable in length.

NIB	Exc.	V.G.	Good	Fair	Poor
320	280	240	200	170	140

PA-08 Upland

Has a walnut stock and forend, with low-luster finish. Matte black metalwork. Available with 26" or 28" barrel. Includes three choke tubes.

NIB	Exc.	V.G.	Good	Fair	Poor
320	280	220	180	120	80

PA-08 Knoxx Strutter X

Strutter models feature synthetic stock and 24" ventilated rib barrel. Three choke tubes included. Note: Add 15% for Apparition Excel camo pattern.

NIB	Exc.	V.G.	Good	Fair	Poor
420	360	310	260	220	190

PA-08 Knoxx HD

Home defense model. Features 18" non-ventilated rib barrel and cylinder choke.

NIB	Exc.	V.G.	Good	Fair	Poor
420	360	310	260	220	190

PA-08 Field/Slug Combo

Features both 28" field barrel for hunting birds and 24" rifled slug barrel for deer. Field barrel is chrome lined and has a ventilated rib. Integral choke system features Briley thread pattern and comes with Improved Cylinder, Modified and Full-choked tubes. The 8-groove Slug barrel has a Weaver-compatible cantilevered scope mount base. Matte black finish. Weight 6.75 lbs. Introduced in 2011.

NIB	Exc.	V.G.	Good	Fair	Poor
520	450	380	320	270	230

PA-459 Turkey Camo

Pump gun features Mothwing Camo's Spring Mimicry pattern on stock and forend. The 12-gauge gun has 19" barrel, 13.5" length of pull and overall length of 40". Weight 6.5 lbs. Integral Picatinny rail allows mounting optical sights or other accessories. Rail has a clamp-style LPA ghost ring rear sight adjustable for windage and elevation.

NIB	Exc.	V.G.	Good	Fair	Poor
360	310	260	220	190	160

Centurion

Gas-operated semi-automatic shotgun chambered for 12-gauge. Offered with various barrel lengths and chokes. Has a checkered walnut stock. Manufactured between 1972 and 1981.

NIB	Exc.	V.G.	Good	Fair	Poor
—	300	260	220	180	160

Centurion Deluxe

This version is slightly engraved. Features ventilated rib barrel and higher-grade wood.

NIB	Exc.	V.G.	Good	Fair	Poor
350	300	250	220	180	160

Model 82

Gas-operated semi-automatic shotgun. Chambered for 12-gauge, with 2.75" or 3" chambers. Has various barrel lengths, with ventilated ribs and screw-in choke tubes. Features an alloy receiver and deluxe checkered walnut stock. Also available as the Buckmaster, with 22" open-choked barrel. Introduced in 1983.

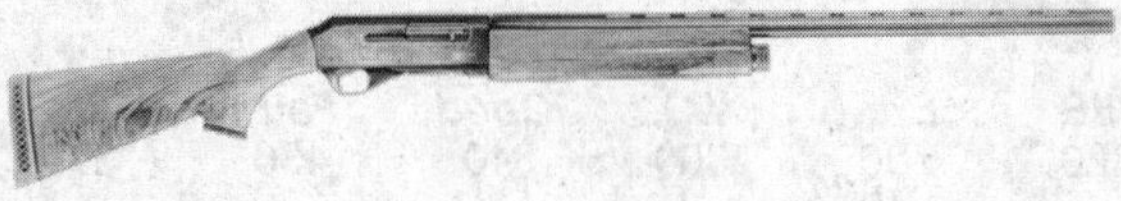

NIB	Exc.	V.G.	Good	Fair	Poor
400	340	290	250	210	180

SAS SERIES

Model SAS Field

Introduced in 1999. Gas-operated semi-automatic features high-grade Claro walnut stock, with black pistol grip cap. Fine-line checkering. Chambered for 12- or 20-gauge. Fitted with 26", 28" or 30" ventilated rib barrels in 12-gauge; 26" or 28" in 20-gauge. Weight: 7.5 lbs. 12-gauge; 7 lbs. 20-gauge, depending on barrel lengths., Fitted with Briley choke tubes.

NIB	Exc.	V.G.	Good	Fair	Poor
750	640	540	460	390	330

Model SAS Camo

Offered with Shadowgrass or Superflauge camo stocks. Available in 12-gauge only, with 3" chambers. Shadowgrass offered with 26" or 28" barrels; Superflauge with 24" or 26" barrels. Weight 7.5 lbs.

NIB	Exc.	V.G.	Good	Fair	Poor
800	680	580	490	420	360

Shadow Grass

NIB	Exc.	V.G.	Good	Fair	Poor
750	600	500	380	300	220

Superflauge

NIB	Exc.	V.G.	Good	Fair	Poor
780	660	560	480	400	340

Model SAS Slug Gun

Features 22" rifled barrel chambered for 3" 12-gauge shell. Barrel has cantilever base for scope mounts. Walnut stock has raised Monte Carlo comb. Sling swivel studs. Weight 7.25 lbs. Introduced in 2003.

NIB	Exc.	V.G.	Good	Fair	Poor
800	680	580	490	420	360

Model SAS Sporting Clays

This 12-gauge gun fitted with 28" or 30" ventilated rib ported barrel. Walnut stock, with pistol grip. Choke tubes standard. Weight 7.5 lbs. Introduced in 2002.

NIB	Exc.	V.G.	Good	Fair	Poor
820	700	600	510	430	370

Model SAS Synthetic

Features black synthetic stock chambered for 12- or 20-gauge barrels as above. Introduced in 2000.

NIB	Exc.	V.G.	Good	Fair	Poor
700	600	510	430	360	310

SA SERIES

SA-08 Upland

This semi-automatic was new in 2008. Features walnut stock, with oil-finish. Available in 12- and 20-gauge, with 3" chambers and 28" or 26" barrels. Three choke tubes included.

NIB	Exc.	V.G.	Good	Fair	Poor
700	600	510	430	360	310

SA-08 Deluxe

Current (2019) entries have select walnut stock with high-gloss finish, 22-lpi checkering on pistol grip and forend. Model numbers include 12-gauge 28" barrel, SA08D1228PGM and 26" barrel SA08D1226PGM; 20-gauge 28" barrel SA08D2028PGM and 26" barrel SA08D2026PGM; and 28-gauge SA08D2826PGM with 2.75" chamber.

NIB	Exc.	V.G.	Good	Fair	Poor
660	560	480	400	340	290

SA-08 Synthetic

NIB	Exc.	V.G.	Good	Fair	Poor
500	420	360	310	260	220

SA-08 Synthetic Compact

NIB	Exc.	V.G.	Good	Fair	Poor
500	420	360	310	260	220

SA-459 TR

NIB	Exc.	V.G.	Good	Fair	Poor
610	520	440	380	320	270

SA-08 Youth

As above in 20 gauge, with 26" barrel only. Shorter 12.5" length of pull.

NIB	Exc.	V.G.	Good	Fair	Poor
500	420	360	310	260	220

SA-08 Entre Rios

Entre Rios autoloader has a scaled-down frame for 28 gauge. Features include a select cut-checkered walnut stock and high-gloss finish on barrel and receiver. Comes equipped with Skeet Improved cylinder and Modified choke tubes. Weight 5.25 lbs. Available with 26" or 28" barrel.

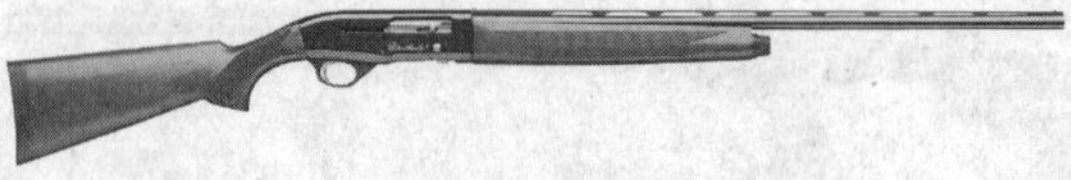

NIB	Exc.	V.G.	Good	Fair	Poor
600	510	430	370	310	270

ELEMENT SERIES

Element Upland 12 Gauge

NIB	Exc.	V.G.	Good	Fair	Poor
550	470	400	340	290	240

Element Deluxe

Introduced 2015. Originally available in 12, 20, or 28 gauge. Inertia-operated action, with chrome-plated bolt, drop-out trigger system, AA-grade American walnut stock. Barrel 26" or 28", with ventilated rib, fiber-optic front sight and three choke tubes. Also available as Element Synthetic with synthetic stock, rubberized pistol grip and forend inserts; Element Waterfowler with Realtree Max-5 camo pattern. Note: Add $50 for 28 gauge. This 28 gauge was not offered in 2019. In 2019, Element Upland had Turkish walnut furniture, in 12 gauge (EUP1228PGM and EUP-1226PGM) and 20 gauge (EUP2028PGM and EUP2026PGM). The Synthetic likewise was available in 12 gauge (ESN1226PGM or ESN-1228PGM) or 20 gauge (ESN2026PGM or ESN2028PGM). Element Waterfowler is a 12/20 with 28" barrels and Max-5 camo treatment. Also has drop and cast adjustments and Griptonite stock inserts at grip and forend.

NIB	Exc.	V.G.	Good	Fair	Poor
900	750	600	450	300	200

Element Waterfowler Max-5

NIB	Exc.	V.G.	Good	Fair	Poor
520	440	380	320	270	230

OLDER MODEL PUMP ACTIONS

Patrician

Slide-action shotgun chambered for 12-gauge. Offered with various barrel lengths and choke combinations. Has a ventilated rib barrel, blued finish and checkered walnut stock. Manufactured between 1972 and 1981.

NIB	Exc.	V.G.	Good	Fair	Poor
—	300	260	220	180	160

Patrician Deluxe

Slightly engraved version, with fancier-grade walnut.

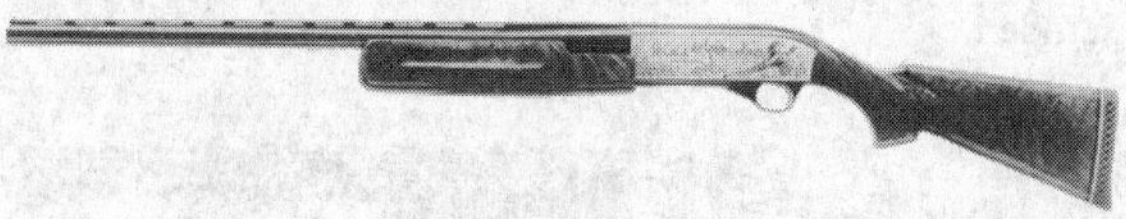

NIB	Exc.	V.G.	Good	Fair	Poor
—	350	300	250	220	180

Model 92

Slide-action shotgun chambered for 12-gauge, with 2.75" or 3" chambers. Offered with 26", 28" or 30" ventilated rib barrels, with screw-in choke tubes. Features a short twin-rail slide action and engraved alloy receiver. Finish is blued, with deluxe checkered walnut stock. A Buckmaster model with 22" open-choke barrel and rifle sights is also available.

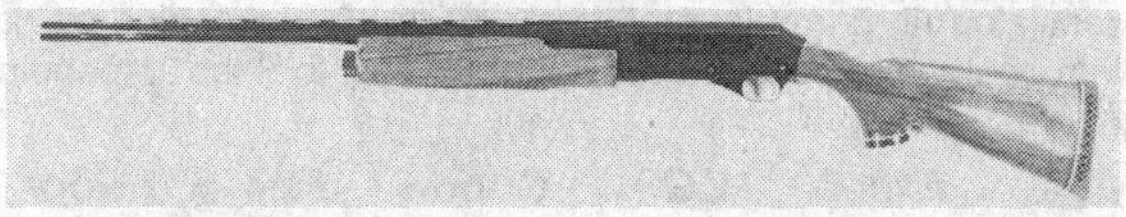

NIB	Exc.	V.G.	Good	Fair	Poor
—	350	300	250	220	180

SIDE-BY-SIDES

These shotguns are built in Spain.

Athena SBS

Introduced in 2002. Features a case colored boxlock receiver, with false sideplates with scroll engraving. Offered in 12 or 20 gauge, with 26" or 28" barrels. Choke tubes. Turkish walnut stock, with straight-grip and recoil pad. Checkering is 22 lpi. Single trigger and ejectors. Weight 7 lbs.

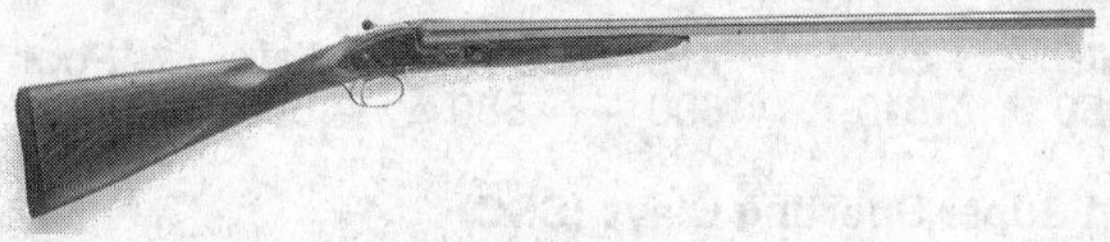

NIB	Exc.	V.G.	Good	Fair	Poor
1280	1080	920	780	670	570

Athena D'Italia

Introduced in 2005. Chambered for 12, 20, or 28 gauge. Fitted with 28" barrels for 12 gauge; 26" barrels for 20 and 28 gauge. Receiver has silver sideplates, with scroll engraving. Checkered walnut stock, with straight-grip. Weight 7 lbs. Add $135 for 28 gauge.

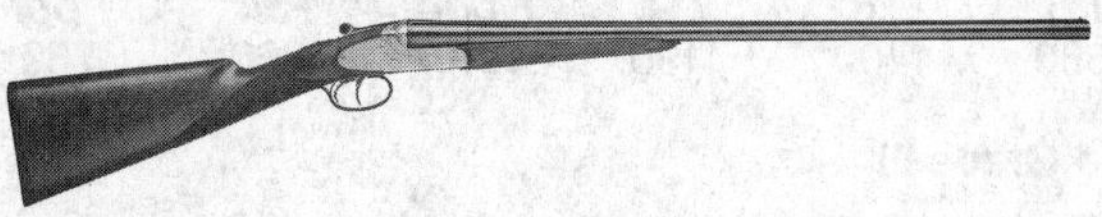

NIB	Exc.	V.G.	Good	Fair	Poor
2750	2340	1990	1690	1440	1220

Athena D'Italia PG

Introduced in 2006. Offered in same configurations as D'Italia. Identical in action and frame to D'Italia, with rounded pistol grip stock and single gold trigger. Laser-cut checkering at 20 lpi. Introduced 2006. Pricing is for 12 and 20 gauge. Note: Add $200 for 28 gauge.

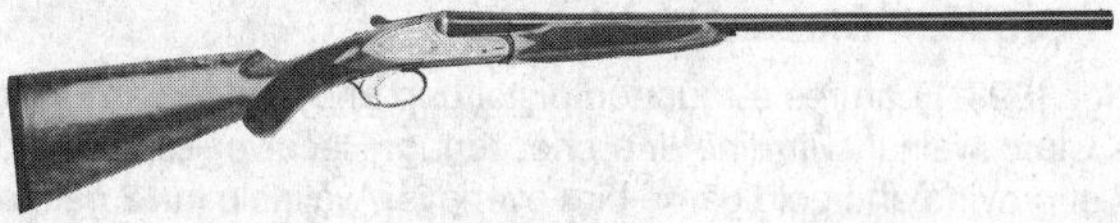

NIB	Exc.	V.G.	Good	Fair	Poor
3000	2550	2170	1840	1570	1330

Athena D'Italia Deluxe

Renaissance floral engraving, with Bolino-style game scene. AAA Fancy Turkish walnut, with 24 lpi hand-checkering adorn this straight-grip stock model. Available in 12, 20, and 28 gauge, with 26" or 28" barrels with fixed IC and Modified chokes. Single trigger. Introduced 2006.

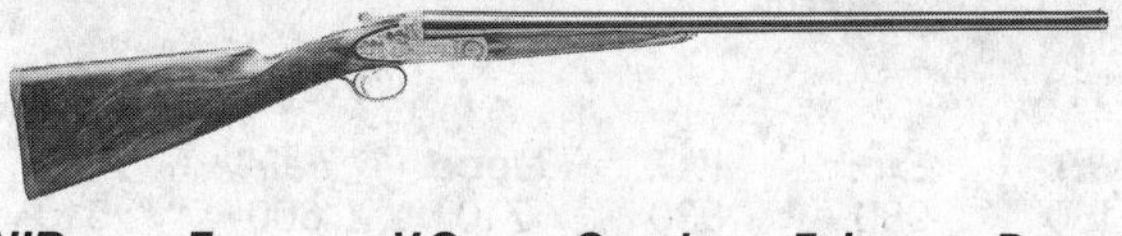

NIB	Exc.	V.G.	Good	Fair	Poor
6980	5930	5040	4280	3640	3100

Orion SBS

Lower cost alternative to Athena. Turkish walnut stock, with pistol grips and 18 lpi checkering. Case-colored boxlock receiver. Offered in 12, 20, 28 gauge, and .410 bore. Choke tubes except for .410 bore. Choice of 26" or 28" barrels. Weight 7 lbs. Introduced in 2002.

NIB	Exc.	V.G.	Good	Fair	Poor
1850	1570	1340	1140	970	820

OVER/UNDER GUNS

Regency Field Grade

This is an over/under double-barrel shotgun chambered for 12 or 20 gauge. Has various-length ventilated rib barrels and boxlock action, with engraved false sideplates. Features single-selective trigger and automatic ejectors. Finish blued, with checkered walnut stock. Imported from Italy between 1972 and 1980. Also offered as a trap grade with same value.

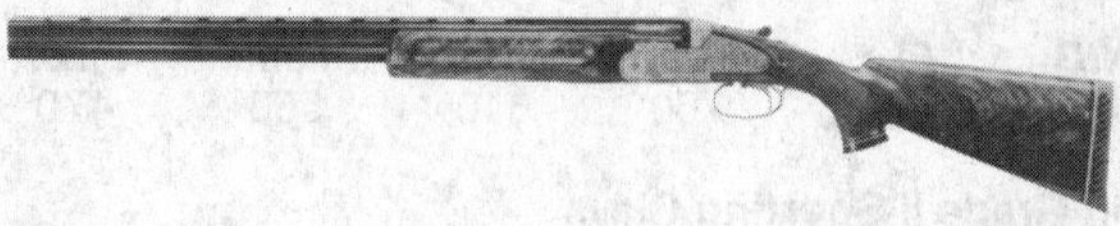

NIB	Exc.	V.G.	Good	Fair	Poor
1380	1170	990	840	720	610

Olympian

Similar to Regency, with less engraving. Not imported after 1980. Skeet and trap as well as a field-grade model were available. Values were similar.

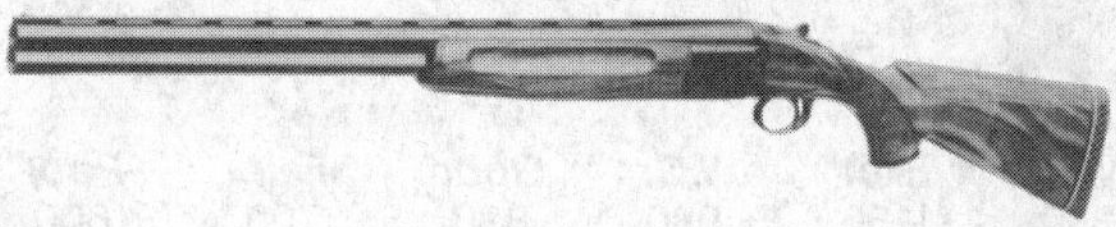

NIB	Exc.	V.G.	Good	Fair	Poor
900	760	650	550	470	400

Orion Upland

This 12 or 20 gauge features Claro walnut stock, with rounded pistol grip and slim forearm. Plain blued receiver. Choice of 26" or 28" ventilated rib barrel, with 3" chambers. Multi-choke system. Introduced in 1999.

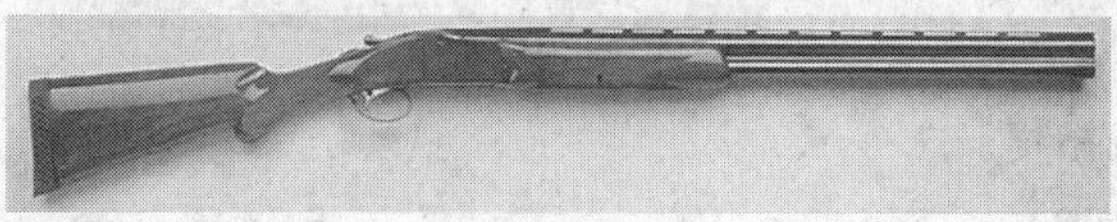

NIB	Exc.	V.G.	Good	Fair	Poor
1180	1000	850	720	610	520

Orion Grade I

An over/under double-barrel shotgun chambered for 12 or 20 gauge, with 3" chambers. Offered with 26" or 28" ventilated rib barrels, with screw-in chokes. Has single selective trigger and automatic ejectors. Boxlock action features no engraving. Finish blued, with checkered walnut stock. Introduced in 1989; discontinued in 2002; reintroduced in 2015.

(See New Production below.)

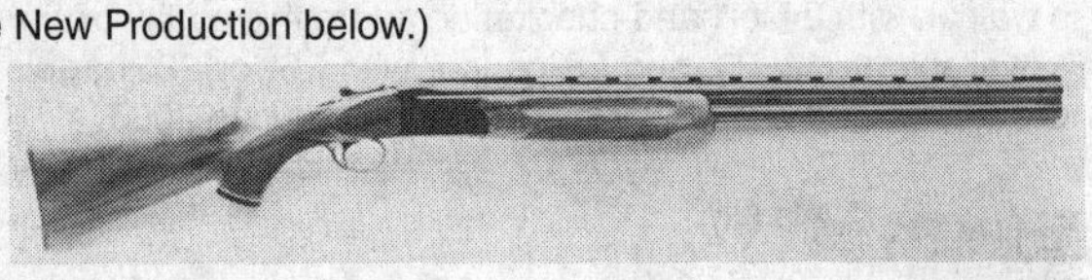

NIB	Exc.	V.G.	Good	Fair	Poor
1150	980	830	710	600	510

Orion Grade I — New Production

Current production in 2019 has the same specs as above, but only in 12 gauge 26"/28" (OR11226RGG and OR11228RGG, respectively). Prince of Wales grip, automatic ejectors, chrome-lined bores. In 2019, only the 30" barrel was offered in the Sporting variation (OSP1230PGG).

NIB	Exc.	V.G.	Good	Fair	Poor
670	570	480	410	350	300

Orion I Sporting

NIB	Exc.	V.G.	Good	Fair	Poor
850	720	610	520	440	380

Orion Grade II Skeet

Supplied with Claro walnut checkered stock, with full pistol grip and rosewood grip cap. Receiver matte blue, with scroll engraving. Barrel has matte ventilated rib, with side vents and mid-point head with white bead front sight. Special ventilated recoil pad. Offered in 12 and 20 gauge, with 26" barrels. Fixed Skeet chokes are standard. Weight: 12 gauge 7.5 lbs.; 20 gauge 7.25 lbs. This version was not cataloged in 2019.

NIB	Exc.	V.G.	Good	Fair	Poor
1050	890	760	640	550	470

Orion Grade II Sporting Clays

Similar to Classic model, with full pistol grip and rosewood grip cap. Receiver silver gray, with scroll engraving. Claro walnut stock is checkered with high-gloss finish. Offered in 12 gauge, with 28" to 30" ventilated rib barrels. Supplied with five screw-in choke tubes.

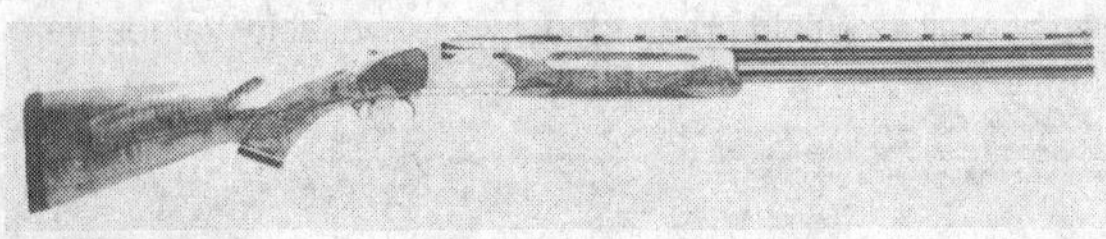

NIB	Exc.	V.G.	Good	Fair	Poor
1350	1150	980	830	700	600

Orion Grade II Double Trap

Features an integral multi-choke tube. Monte Carlo stock has rosewood pistol grip cap, with diamond-shaped inlay. Receiver blue, with scroll engraving. Available with 30" or 32" ventilated rib barrels. Weight 8 lbs. This version was not cataloged in 2019.

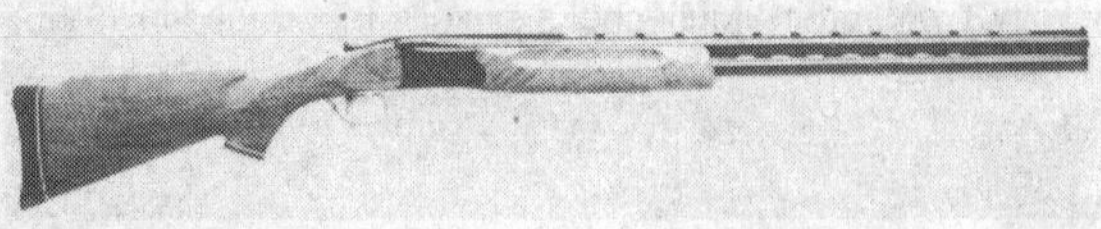

NIB	Exc.	V.G.	Good	Fair	Poor
900	760	650	550	470	400

Orion Grade II Single Trap

Similar to Double Trap. Furnished with single 32" barrel. Weight 8 lbs. This version was not cataloged in 2019.

NIB	Exc.	V.G.	Good	Fair	Poor
800	680	580	490	420	360

Orion Grade II

This version is lightly engraved. Has a high-gloss finish. Otherwise, similar to Grade I.

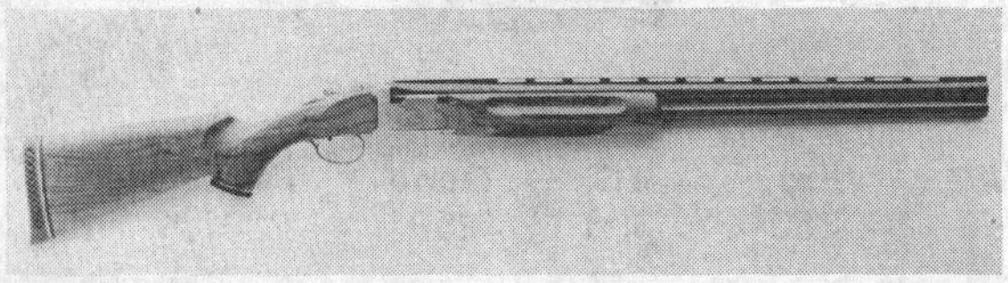

NIB	Exc.	V.G.	Good	Fair	Poor
1300	1100	940	800	680	580

Orion Grade II Classic Field

Introduced in 1993. Features rounded pistol grip and slim forearm design. Walnut stock is oil-finished. Receiver blued, with game scene engraving. Solid recoil pad is standard. Available in 12, 20, and 28 gauge, with ventilated rib barrel lengths from 26" to 30" depending on gauge. Screw-in choke tubes standard. Weight 6.5 lbs. to 8 lbs. depending on gauge.

NIB	Exc.	V.G.	Good	Fair	Poor
1000	850	720	610	520	440

Orion Grade II Classic Sporting Clays

Introduced in 1993. Has rounded pistol grip, with slender forearm and oil-finished stock. Receiver blued, with scroll engraving. A stepped competition matte ventilated rib, with additional side vents is supplied. Recoil pad has a special radius heel. Offered in 12 gauge with 28" barrel. Furnished with five screw-in choke tubes. Weight 7.5 lbs.

NIB	Exc.	V.G.	Good	Fair	Poor
950	810	690	580	500	420

Orion Super Sporting Clays (SSC)

Introduced in 1999. This 12 gauge features walnut stock, with sporter-style pistol grip and cast off. Barrel lengths 28", 30" or 32", with 3" chambers and 12mm grooved rib. Barrels are also ported and backbored. Comes with five choke tubes. Weight 8 lbs.

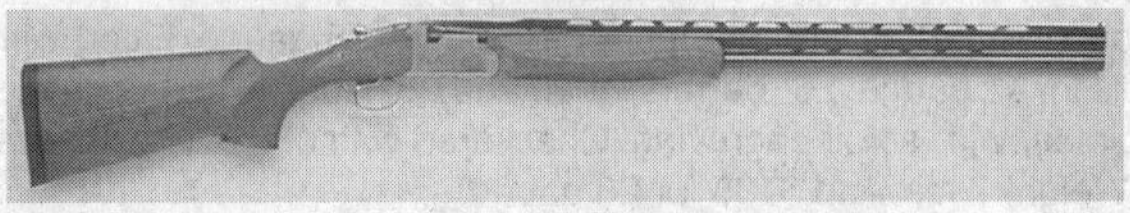

NIB	Exc.	V.G.	Good	Fair	Poor
1650	1400	1190	1010	860	730

Orion Grade III

This version has a game scene engraved coin-finished receiver and higher-grade walnut. Introduced in 1989.

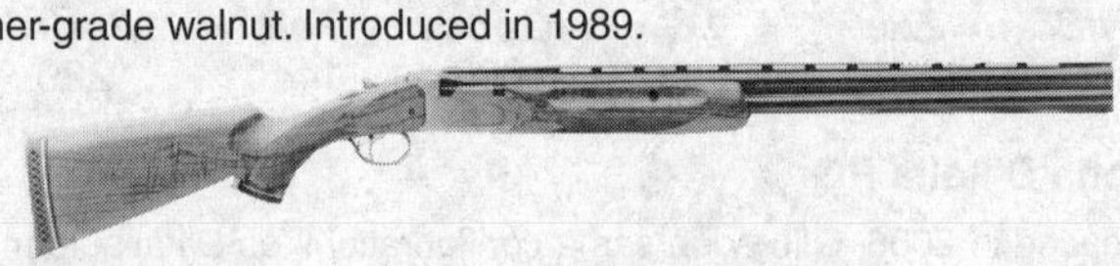

NIB	Exc.	V.G.	Good	Fair	Poor
1500	1280	1080	920	780	670

Orion Grade III Classic Field

New for 1993. Features a rounded pistol grip and slim forearm, with oil-finish Claro walnut with fine line checkering. Receiver silver gray, with scroll engraving and gold game bird overlays. Available in 12 gauge with 28" ventilated rib barrels; 20 gauge with 26" ventilated rib barrels. Screw-in choke tubes standard.

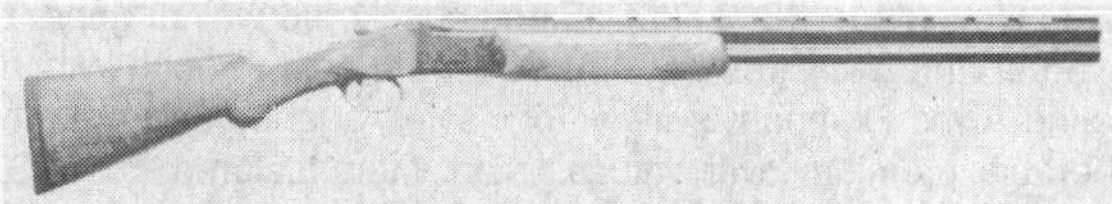

NIB	Exc.	V.G.	Good	Fair	Poor
1700	1440	1230	1040	890	750

Orion Grade III Classic English Field

Features English-style straight-grip stock. Choice of 12 gauge with 28" barrel; 20 gauge with 26" or 28" barrels. Receiver is engraved. Stock is oil-finished hand-checkered. Weight 12 gauge 7 lbs.; 20 gauge 6.5 lbs. Introduced in 1996.

NIB	Exc.	V.G.	Good	Fair	Poor
1600	1360	1160	980	840	710

Orion D'Italia

Engraved silver-finish metalwork and fine line 20 lpi checkering. Turkish walnut stock, with high-gloss finish. Available in 12 gauge with 28" barrel; 20 gauge with 26" barrel.

NIB	Exc.	V.G.	Good	Fair	Poor
1750	1500	1200	900	750	400

Orion D'Italia III

NIB	Exc.	V.G.	Good	Fair	Poor
1820	1550	1319	1121	953	810

Athena Grade III Classic Field

Offered in 12 or 20 gauge. Features hand-select Claro walnut stock, with oil-finish. Pistol grip is rounded. Silver/gray sideplates feature a rose and scroll engraving pattern, with gold overlaid hunting scenes. Available with 26" or 28" ventilated rib barrels, with multi-choke system. Weight 7.5 lbs. 12 gauge; 7 lbs. 20 gauge. Introduced in 1999. In 2001, a 28-gauge version offered with 26" or 28" barrels.

NIB	Exc.	V.G.	Good	Fair	Poor
2100	1780	1520	1290	1100	930

Athena Grade IV

An over/under double-barrel shotgun chambered for 12, 20, 28 gauge, and .410 bore. Has 3" chambers. Offered with various barrel lengths with ventilated ribs and screw-in choke tubes. Has a boxlock action, with Greener crossbolt single-selective trigger and automatic ejectors. Engraved false sideplates and satin nickel-plated action. Barrels blued, with select checkered walnut stock. Introduced in 1989.

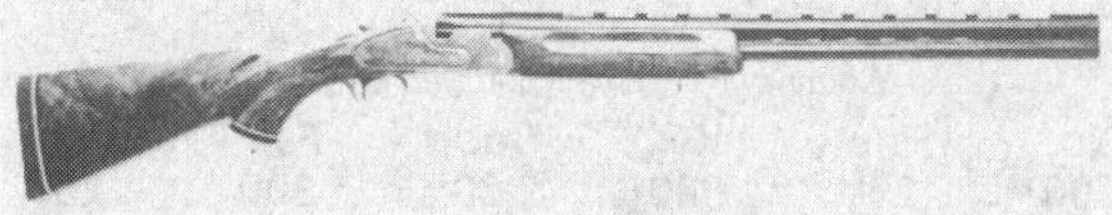

NIB	Exc.	V.G.	Good	Fair	Poor
2100	1780	1520	1290	1100	930

Athena Grade V Classic Field

Introduced in 1993. Features rounded pistol grip, with slender forearm. High-grade Claro walnut stock is oil-finished, with fine-line checkering. Receiver has a sideplate that is silver/gray, with rose and scroll engraving. Ventilated rib barrels also have side vents. An Old English recoil pad is supplied. Offered in 12 gauge with 26", 28" or 30" barrels; 20 gauge with 26" and 28" barrels. Choke tubes are standard. Weatherby Athena Master skeet tube set: 12 gauge 28" skeet shotgun, plus two each 20, 28 gauge and .410 bore fitted full-length Briley tubes with integral extractors. Packed in custom fitted aluminum case (not shown). Note: Add 50% for Master Skeet Set.

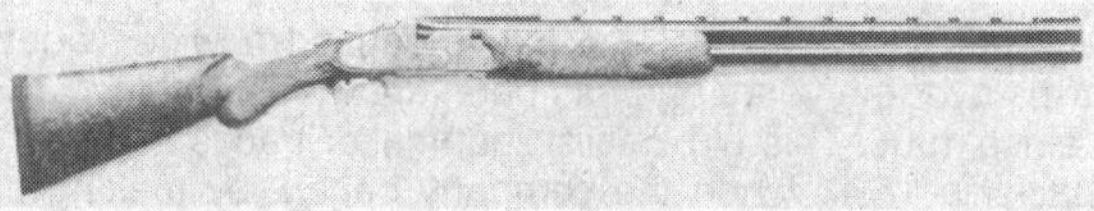

NIB	Exc.	V.G.	Good	Fair	Poor
2400	2040	1730	1470	1250	1060

Athena Competition Model

A trap or skeet version, with stock dimensions designed for skeet or trap. Competition-type ribs.

NIB	Exc.	V.G.	Good	Fair	Poor
1400	1190	1010	860	730	620

HANDGUNS

Mark V – CFP (Compact Firing Platform)

Bolt-action handgun, with 5+1 capacity. 16" barrel, adjustable trigger, composite stock. Available in .223, .22-250, .243 and 7mm-08. Weight 5.25 lbs. Introduced 2006.

NIB	Exc.	V.G.	Good	Fair	Poor
1300	1050	800	600	400	200

Mark V Accumark CFP

Similar to Accumark rifle. Features synthetic stock of Kevlar and fiberglass, with matte black gel-coat finish. Offered in .223 Rem., .22-250, .243 Win., 7mm-08 and .308 Win. calibers. Fluted barrel length is 15". Weight 5 lbs. Introduced in 2000.

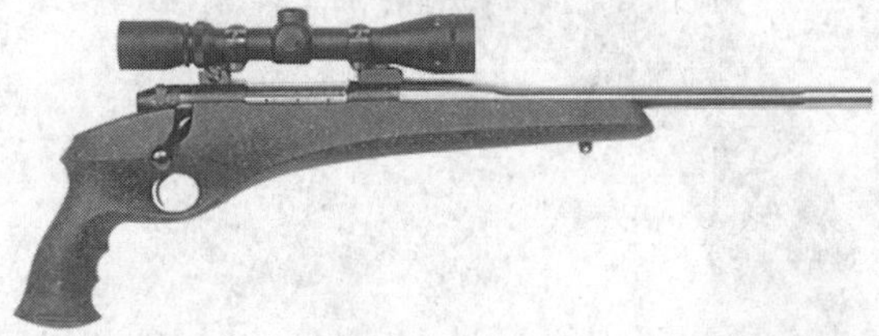

NIB	Exc.	V.G.	Good	Fair	Poor
1050	800	600	400	220	150

WEAVER ARMS

Escondido, California

Nighthawk Assault Pistol

A 9mm semi-automatic pistol, with 10" or 12" barrel, alloy receiver and ambidextrous safety. Blackened with plastic grips. Introduced in 1987.

NIB	Exc.	V.G.	Good	Fair	Poor
550	450	400	350	300	150

Nighthawk Carbine

As above, with 16.1" barrel, retractable shoulder stock, 25-, 32-, 40- or 50-shot magazine. Introduced in 1984.

NIB	Exc.	V.G.	Good	Fair	Poor
600	500	450	350	300	150

WEBLEY & SCOTT, LTD.

Birmingham, England

Established in 1860, this firm has produced a wide variety of firearms over the years and has been known as Webley & Scott, Ltd. since 1906. This old English gunmaker traces its history as far back as 1790, when the company began, by making bullet moulds. In 1878, the British Bulldog revolver was developed and in 1887, the Webley model became the official sidearm of the British Defense Forces until 1964. Webley & Scott's history with shotguns goes back to the 1860s, when the company patented the first successful sidelock. Currently the company imports a line of quality shotguns from Turkey.

Model 1872 Royal Irish Constabulary Antique

A .450 double-action revolver, with 3.25" barrel, 5-shot cylinder and rotating ejector. Also offered with 2.5" and 3.5" barrels. Blued, with checkered walnut grips.

Exc.	Fine	V.G.	Good	Fair	Poor
1250	750	500	375	250	175

Model 1880 Metropolitan Police Antique

As above, with 2.5" barrel and 6-shot cylinder.

Exc.	Fine	V.G.	Good	Fair	Poor
2000	1400	750	500	300	200

Model 1878 Webley-Pryse Antique

Chambered for .455 and .476 Eley cartridge. Note: Add 200 percent premium for revolvers chambered for .577. Deduct 50 percent for revolvers chambered for cartridges below .442.

Exc.	Fine	V.G.	Good	Fair	Poor
2500	1500	900	550	350	250

New Model 1883 R.I.C. Antique

Similar to Model 1880. Chambered in .455-caliber, with 4.5" barrel. Also made with 2.5" barrel.

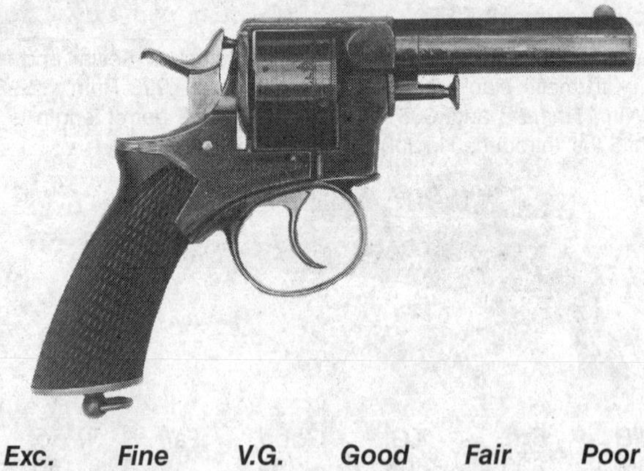

Exc.	Fine	V.G.	Good	Fair	Poor
1200	700	500	350	250	150

Model 1884 R.I.C. Naval Antique

As above, with brass frame and oxidized finish. Octagon barrel length 2.75".

Exc.	Fine	V.G.	Good	Fair	Poor
1650	1250	900	600	500	350

British Bulldog Antique

Similar to New Model 1883 R.I.C. Blued checkered walnut grips. Those engraved on the backstrap "W.R.A. Co." were sold through Winchester Repeating Arms Company's New York sales agency and are worth a considerable premium over values listed. Manufactured from 1878 to 1914. Note: Add a premium for U.S. dealer markings, see model description.

Exc.	Fine	V.G.	Good	Fair	Poor
1250	850	700	600	325	200

Pug Antique

Similar to British Bulldog, but somewhat smaller. Interesting in that it has a manual safety. Chambered in .450, .442, and possibly others as well.

Exc.	Fine	V.G.	Good	Fair	Poor
1250	750	600	400	250	150

Model 1878 Army Express Revolver Antique

A .455-caliber double-action revolver, with 6" barrel and integral ejector. Blued, with one-piece walnut grips. Note: Add 100 percent premium for single-action version; 25 percent for .45 Long (.45 Colt) markings.

Exc.	Fine	V.G.	Good	Fair	Poor
2500	1400	800	500	350	250

Webley Kaufmann Model 1880 Antique

Top-break hinged-frame double-action revolver. Chambered for .450 centerfire cartridge, with 5.75" barrel. Curved bird's-head butt. Blued, with walnut grips.

Exc.	Fine	V.G.	Good	Fair	Poor
2000	1500	1000	600	300	210

Webley-Green Model Antique

Double-action top-break revolver. Chambered for .455 cartridge, with 6" ribbed barrel and 6-shot cylinder. The cylinder flutes are angular and not rounded in shape. Blued, with checkered walnut squared butt grips with a lanyard ring on the butt. Introduced in 1882. Manufactured until 1896. Also known as "WG" model.

Exc.	Fine	V.G.	Good	Fair	Poor
1700	1200	800	500	250	150

Mark I Antique

A .442, .455 or .476 double-action top-break revolver, with 4" barrel and 6-shot cylinder. Blued, with checkered walnut grips. Manufactured from 1887 to 1894.

Courtesy Faintich Auction Services, Inc., Paul Goodwin photo

Exc.	Fine	V.G.	Good	Fair	Poor
1700	1250	900	500	300	200

Mark II

As above, with a larger hammer spur and improved barrel catch. Manufactured from 1894 to 1897.

NIB	Exc.	V.G.	Good	Fair	Poor
—	920	550	350	220	100

Mark III

As above, with internal improvements. Introduced in 1897.

NIB	Exc.	V.G.	Good	Fair	Poor
—	980	600	320	200	80

Mark IV

As above, with .455-caliber 3", 4", 5" or 6" barrel. Also available in: .22-caliber 6" barrel; .32-caliber 3" barrel; .38-caliber 3", 4" or 5" barrel.

Courtesy Faintich Auction Services, Inc., Paul Goodwin photo

NIB	Exc.	V.G.	Good	Fair	Poor
—	900	580	380	200	80

Mark IV Target

Chambered for .22-caliber cartridge. Fitted with 6" barrel, with target sights.

Courtesy Rock Island Auction Company

NIB	Exc.	V.G.	Good	Fair	Poor
—	1450	1000	800	500	300

Mark V

Similar to Mark IV, with 4" or 6" barrel. Manufactured from 1913 to 1915.

Courtesy Faintich Auction Services, Inc., Paul Goodwin photo

NIB	Exc.	V.G.	Good	Fair	Poor
—	1000	700	400	250	150

Mark VI

Similar to previous .455 models, but with a larger square butt and a longer 6" barrel. Adopted 1915 and produced through 1926. The most common of the .455 Webleys. Sometime found with the rear of the cylinder thinned to allow use of .45 AutoRim or .45 ACP moon clips. This reduces value 25%.

Courtesy Faintich Auction Services, Inc., Paul Goodwin photo

NIB	Exc.	V.G.	Good	Fair	Poor
—	800	600	380	220	150

Mark VI .22 Rimfire

Standard-size Mark VI. Chambered for .22 rimfire cartridge. Used as a training pistol. Manufactured in 1918. Quite scarce.

Courtesy Faintich Auction Services, Inc., Paul Goodwin photo

NIB	Exc.	V.G.	Good	Fair	Poor
—	850	650	450	350	200

Mark IV .38/200 Service Revolver

Similar to the Mark VI in design, with a smaller frame - 4- or 6-in. barrel. Chambered for .38/200 (.38 S&W). Introduced 1932 and in service through 1978.

NIB	Exc.	V.G.	Good	Fair	Poor
—	600	450	380	300	200

WEBLEY SEMI-AUTOMATIC PISTOLS

Webley-Fosbery Automatic Revolver

Recoil forces top half of this unusual pistol back to cock the hammer, while a stud in the frame cams the cylinder around to bring a fresh chamber into position. Early examples under serial number 75 or so, appear to be hand-made as no two seem to be identical; these bring a 100 percent premium over late-model pistols. Other low-number guns, under serial number 300 or so, also differ in appearance from later production and bring 25 percent premium. Early production was all in .455 Webley with 6-round cylinder; a .38 ACP version with 8-round cylinder was introduced about 1903, but is much scarcer than the .455.

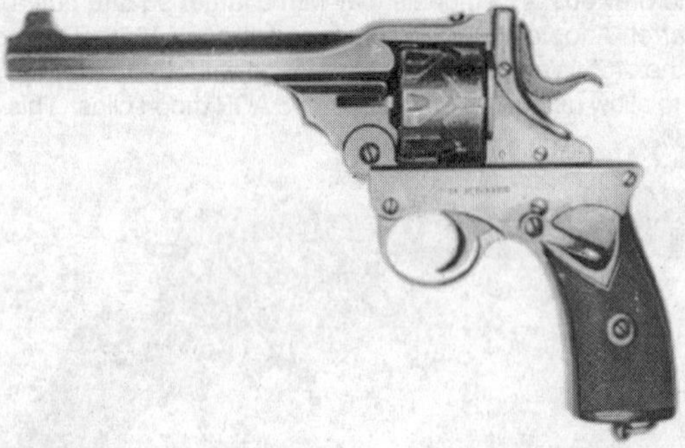

Courtesy Joseph Schroeder

.455 Caliber

NIB	Exc.	V.G.	Good	Fair	Poor
—	18000	10000	8000	6000	4000

.38 Caliber

NIB	Exc.	V.G.	Good	Fair	Poor
—	—	15000	10000	8000	4000

Model 1904

Made experimentally in both .38 ACP and .455-calibers. Highest serial numbered 1904 known in 30s. Very few seem to have survived. A later Webley experimental Model 1906 made in .45 for the U.S. Army trial, but apparently never submitted. Either model too rare to price.

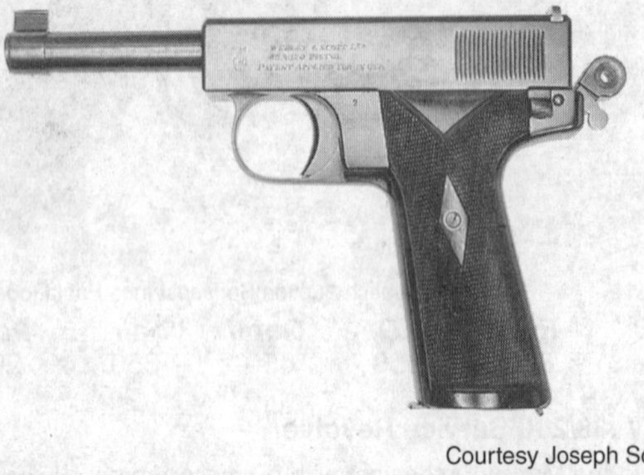

Courtesy Joseph Schroeder

Model 1905

Webley's first commercial semi-automatic pistol was this compact .32-caliber. Earliest Model 1905s have a diagonal machined flat on the slide and a hammer-mounted safety; these bring about 50 percent premium. Model 1905 was replaced by Model 1908, after about 20,000 were made.

Courtesy Joseph Schroeder

NIB	Exc.	V.G.	Good	Fair	Poor
—	1200	1000	750	400	250

Model 1907

The 1907 is a .25-caliber pistol, with an outside hammer. One of Webley's most popular handguns. Remained in production until WWII. Over 50,000 made.

Courtesy Joseph Schroeder

NIB	Exc.	V.G.	Good	Fair	Poor
—	800	600	400	200	100

Model 1908

Model 1908 is a slight redesign of Model 1905. Webley's most popular self-loading pistol. Remained in production until WWII. Examples bearing a crown and letters "MP" were made for Metropolitan Police and bring a slight premium.

NIB	Exc.	V.G.	Good	Fair	Poor
—	650	550	350	180	120

Model 1909

Model 1909 is a modified and enlarged version of Model 1908. Chambered for 9mm Browning Long cartridge. Never popular and manufacture ended in 1914, with just under 1,700 made. Its most unusual feature was the slide release on top of the slide.

Courtesy J.B. Wood

NIB	Exc.	V.G.	Good	Fair	Poor
—	1480	850	500	300	200

Model 1910 .380

Simply a Model 1908 modified to accept .380 cartridge. Never very popular. Under 2,000 sold.

Courtesy Joseph Schroeder

NIB	Exc.	V.G.	Good	Fair	Poor
—	1500	880	520	—	—

Model 1910 .38 ACP

Webley's first locked-breech pistol. Based closely on experimental Model 1906 design. Chambered for .38 ACP cartridge. There are two models, both with internal hammers; one with a grip safety and later without. Total production for both under 1,000, so both are rare.

Courtesy Joseph Schroeder

NIB	Exc.	V.G.	Good	Fair	Poor
—	2250	1500	900	500	350

Model 1911

Model 1911 is a single-shot .22-caliber training version of Model 1908. Developed specifically for Metropolitan Police. Features "blow open" action that ejects fired cartridge, but remains open for reloading. Bottom of frame is slotted for attaching a shoulder stock. Stocks are quite rare and will add more than 100 percent to value of the pistol.

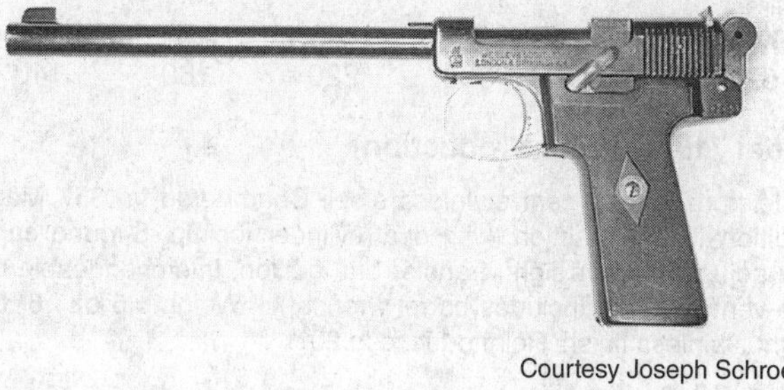

Courtesy Joseph Schroeder

NIB	Exc.	V.G.	Good	Fair	Poor
—	1750	1400	1100	800	300

Model 1912

A perceived need for a hammerless version of Model 1907, led to the introduction of Model 1912. It actually does have an internal hammer, but recoil spring is two coils in the slide instead of large V-spring under the right grip frame, found in all other Webley semi-automatic pistols. Not as popular as Model 1907. Production totaled almost 15,000 vs. over 50,000 for hammer model.

NIB	Exc.	V.G.	Good	Fair	Poor
—	1200	1000	750	400	200

Model 1913

Model 1913 was the result of years of development in conjunction with the British government. Finally adopted in 1913, as Model 1913 MK1N for Royal Navy issue. Same breech-locking system as Model 1910, but has an external hammer. Chambered for .455 Webley Self-Loading cartridge. About 1,000 Model 1913s were sold commercially and serial-numbered along with smaller-caliber pistols. In 1915, a variation of Model 1913, with butt slotted for a shoulder stock, adjustable rear sight and hammer safety adopted for use by Royal Horse Artillery. Shoulder stocks are very rare. Double values listed for RHA model. All militaries were numbered in their own series; about 10,000 made in both variations.

NIB	Exc.	V.G.	Good	Fair	Poor
—	1950	1200	800	500	300

(RHA model)

Courtesy Joseph Schroeder

NIB	Exc.	V.G.	Good	Fair	Poor
—	5000	4000	3000	1000	600

Model 1922

Model 1922 was a redesign of Model 1909, in hopes of military adoption. Grip safety was replaced by a manual safety mounted on the slide; grip angle was changed; lanyard ring added to the butt. Unfortunately for Webley, its only official use was by the Union Defense Force of South Africa (1,000 pistols). South African guns are marked with a large "U" with an arrow in it. Note: Add 20 percent premium for South African marked guns.

NIB	Exc.	V.G.	Good	Fair	Poor
—	3000	2500	2000	1000	600

Model 2000 O/U

This 12-gauge features 3" chambers, five choke tubes, select grade oil-finished Turkish walnut stock, color case-hardened receiver, automatic ejectors and single trigger.

NIB	Exc.	V.G.	Good	Fair	Poor
400	350	300	250	200	150

Model 2000 SxS

Side-by-side model, with similar features and quality as 2000 over/under.

NIB	Exc.	V.G.	Good	Fair	Poor
400	350	300	250	200	150

Model 3000 Sidelock Series

This higher grade model features true sidelocks. The 7-pin design and two independent firing mechanisms are mounted on the sideplate and carefully inletted into the stock and mated with the receiver. Stock is a grade 2.5 walnut hand-checkered and oil-finished. The 3000 series is made in over/under and side-by-side configurations.

NIB	Exc.	V.G.	Good	Fair	Poor
5000	4000	3200	2500	1200	500

WEIHRAUCH, HANS HERMANN
Melrichstadt, West Germany

Model HW 60M

A .22-caliber single-shot bolt-action rifle, with 26.75" barrel. Adjustable sights. Blued, with walnut stock.

NIB	Exc.	V.G.	Good	Fair	Poor
800	650	550	400	350	250

Model HW 66

A .22 Hornet or .222 Rem. bolt-action rifle, with stainless steel 26" barrel. Single-/double-set triggers. Blued, with walnut stock.

NIB	Exc.	V.G.	Good	Fair	Poor
700	550	500	350	300	200

Model HW-3

Double-action solid-frame swing-out cylinder revolver. Chambered for .22 LR or .32 S&W Long cartridge. Barrel length 2.75". Cylinder holds 7- or 8-cartridges. Blued, with walnut grips. In America, known as Dickson Bulldog; in Europe as Gecado.

NIB	Exc.	V.G.	Good	Fair	Poor
—	100	80	50	40	20

Model HW-5

As above, with 4" barrel. Sold in United States under trade name "Omega".

NIB	Exc.	V.G.	Good	Fair	Poor
—	100	80	50	40	20

Model HW-7

As above in .22-caliber, with 6" barrel and 8-shot cylinder. Sold in United States as "Herter's Guide Model". Also available with target sights and thumbrest grips as Model HW-7S.

NIB	Exc.	V.G.	Good	Fair	Poor
—	100	80	50	40	20

Model HW-9

These pistols all carry Arminius trademark: bearded head wearing a winged helmet. Model number will be found on cylinder crane; caliber on barrel; words "Made in Germany" on the frame.

NIB	Exc.	V.G.	Good	Fair	Poor
—	100	80	50	40	20

WEISBURGER, A.
Memphis, Tennessee

Pocket Pistol (Antique)

A .41-caliber percussion single-shot pocket pistol, with 2.5" barrel. German silver furniture and walnut stock. Manufactured during 1850s.

Exc.	Fine	V.G.	Good	Fair	Poor
6500	5100	4170	3250	1800	1260

WESSON FIREARMS, DAN
Norwich, New York

See—WESSON FIREARMS CO., INC., separate listing.

In 1996, assets of the Wesson Firearms Co. was purchased by New York International Corp. Full production of new models occurred in 1997. These firearms are laser marked on the barrel or frame with: "NYI" in an oval and below "DAN WESSON FIREARMS"; on the next line "NORWICH, NEW YORK USA". In April 2005, Dan Wesson Firearms was acquired by CZ-USA. Production continues at the Norwich, New York facility.

NEW GENERATION SMALL-FRAME SERIES

Note: The "7" prefix denotes stainless steel frame and barrel. For models listed, add between 4 and 9 percent depending on barrel length and for stainless steel.

Model 22/722

A 6-shot revolver chambered for .22-caliber cartridge. Interchangeable barrel lengths 2.5", 4", 5.6", 8" and 10". Adjustable rear sight and interchangeable front. Hogue finger groove rubber grips. Weight: 36 oz.—2.5" barrel; 58 oz.—10" barrel.

NIB	Exc.	V.G.	Good	Fair	Poor
480	380	300	250	200	140

Model 22M/722M

Same as above, but chambered for .22 Win. Magnum cartridge.

NIB	Exc.	V.G.	Good	Fair	Poor
520	400	300	220	180	140

Model 32/732

Same as above, but chambered for .32 H&R cartridge.

NIB	Exc.	V.G.	Good	Fair	Poor
550	420	320	250	200	160

Model 3220/73220

Same as above, but chambered for .32-20 cartridge.

NIB	Exc.	V.G.	Good	Fair	Poor
550	420	320	250	200	160

Model 15/715

Same as above, but chambered for .38 Special and .357 Magnum cartridges.

NIB	Exc.	V.G.	Good	Fair	Poor
520	400	300	220	180	140

Model 715 (Current Production)

Made from 100 percent stainless steel. Chambered in .357 Magnum. Traditional double-action, with dual cylinder lockup, 6-round capacity, fully adjustable rear sight, transfer bar ignition. Interchangeable barrel, with ventilated rib. Includes barrel wrench kit. Weight 46 oz., 6" barrel, bright stainless finish. Reintroduced in 2011.

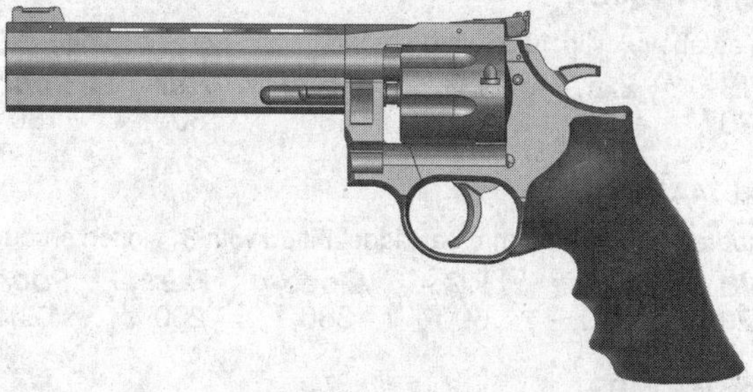

NIB	Exc.	V.G.	Good	Fair	Poor
980	850	700	500	350	200

NEW GENERATION LARGE-FRAME SERIES

Note: The "7" prefix denotes stainless steel frame and barrel. For models listed, add between 4 and 9 percent depending on barrel length and for stainless steel.

Model 41/741

A large-frame revolver, with 6-shot cylinder. Interchangeable barrels 4", 6", 8" and 10". Adjustable rear sight, with interchangeable front. Hogue finger groove rubber grips standard. Weight from 49 oz. for 4" barrel to 69 oz. for 10" barrel.

NIB	Exc.	V.G.	Good	Fair	Poor
580	480	350	220	180	120

Model 44/744

Same as above, but chambered for .44 Magnum cartridge.

NIB	Exc.	V.G.	Good	Fair	Poor
580	480	350	220	180	120

Model 45/745

Same as above, but chambered for .45 Colt cartridge.

NIB	Exc.	V.G.	Good	Fair	Poor
600	500	380	250	200	120

Model 360/7360

Same as above, but chambered for .357 Magnum cartridge.

NIB	Exc.	V.G.	Good	Fair	Poor
580	480	350	220	180	120

Model 460/7460

Same as above, but chambered for .45 ACP, .45 Auto Rim, .45 Super, .45 Win. Magnum or .460 Rowland cartridges.

NIB	Exc.	V.G.	Good	Fair	Poor
750	620	500	400	300	200

NEW GENERATION SUPERMAG-FRAME SERIES

Note: The "7" prefix denotes stainless steel frame and barrel. For models listed, add between 4 and 9 percent depending on barrel length and for stainless steel.

Model 40/740

A 6-shot revolver chambered for .357 Magnum, .357 Super Magnum/Maximum cartridges. Interchangeable barrels 4", 6", 8" or 10" lengths. Adjustable rear sight and interchangeable front. Hogue finger groove rubber grips standard. Weight from 51 oz. for 4" barrel to 76 oz. for 10" barrel.

NIB	Exc.	V.G.	Good	Fair	Poor
1300	1120	850	680	400	250

Model 414/7414

Same as above, but chambered for .414 Super Magnum cartridge.

NIB	Exc.	V.G.	Good	Fair	Poor
1300	1120	850	680	400	250

Model 445/7445

Same as above, but chambered for .445 Super Magnum cartridge.

NIB	Exc.	V.G.	Good	Fair	Poor
1500	1320	1050	880	550	350

NEW GENERATION COMPENSATED SERIES

Note: The "7" prefix denotes stainless steel frame and barrel. For models listed, add between 4 and 9 percent depending on barrel length and for stainless steel.

Model 15/715

A 6-shot revolver chambered for .357 Magnum cartridge. Interchangeable barrels 4", 6" or 10" lengths. Barrels have an integral compensator. Adjustable rear sight and interchangeable front. Hogue finger groove rubber grips.

NIB	Exc.	V.G.	Good	Fair	Poor
580	450	320	250	180	100

Model 41/741

Same as above, but chambered for .41 Magnum cartridge.

NIB	Exc.	V.G.	Good	Fair	Poor
680	550	420	350	250	120

Model 44/744

Same as above, but chambered for .44 Magnum cartridge.

NIB	Exc.	V.G.	Good	Fair	Poor
680	550	420	350	250	120

Model 45/745

Same as above, but chambered for .45 Colt cartridge.

NIB	Exc.	V.G.	Good	Fair	Poor
680	550	420	350	250	120

Model 360/7360

Same as above, but chambered for .357 Magnum on large frame.

NIB	Exc.	V.G.	Good	Fair	Poor
680	550	420	350	250	120

Model 445/7445 (Alaskan Guide)

Chambered for .445 Super Magnum cartridge. Fitted with 4" heavy ported barrel. Special matte black coating over stainless steel. Introduced in 2002.

NIB	Exc.	V.G.	Good	Fair	Poor
1000	800	680	500	380	250

Model 460/7460

Same as above, but chambered for .45 ACP, .45 Auto Rim, .45 Super, .45 Win. Magnum or .460 Rowland cartridges.

NIB	Exc.	V.G.	Good	Fair	Poor
820	650	500	380	200	120

STANDARD SILHOUETTE SERIES

Note: All Standard Silhouette series revolvers are stainless steel.

Model 722 VH10

A 6-shot revolver chambered for .22-caliber cartridge. Interchangeable barrel system. Choice of fluted or non-fluted cylinders. Patridge front sight and adjustable rear. Hogue finger groove rubber grips standard. Lightweight slotted 8" shroud.

NIB	Exc.	V.G.	Good	Fair	Poor
820	650	500	380	200	120

Model 7360 V8S

Same as above, but chambered for .357 Magnum cartridge.

NIB	Exc.	V.G.	Good	Fair	Poor
820	650	500	380	200	120

Model 741 V8S

Same as above, but chambered for .41 Magnum cartridge with 8" slotted shroud.

NIB	Exc.	V.G.	Good	Fair	Poor
820	650	500	380	200	120

Model 741 V10S

Same as above, with 10" slotted shroud.

NIB	Exc.	V.G.	Good	Fair	Poor
920	750	600	480	300	180

Model 744 V8S

Chambered for .44 Magnum cartridge. Fitted with 8" slotted shroud.

NIB	Exc.	V.G.	Good	Fair	Poor
820	650	500	380	200	120

Model 744 V10S

Same as above, but fitted with 10" slotted shroud.

NIB	Exc.	V.G.	Good	Fair	Poor
920	750	600	480	300	180

Model 740 V8S

Chambered for .357 Super Magnum. Fitted with 8" slotted shroud.

NIB	Exc.	V.G.	Good	Fair	Poor
920	750	600	480	300	180

Model 7414 V8S

Chambered for .414 Super Magnum. Fitted with 8" slotted shroud.

NIB	Exc.	V.G.	Good	Fair	Poor
920	750	600	480	300	180

Model 7445 V8S

Chambered for .445 Super Magnum. Fitted with 8" slotted shroud.

NIB	Exc.	V.G.	Good	Fair	Poor
920	750	600	480	300	180

Dan Wesson VH8

.445 Super Magnum revolver designed for barrel interchangeability. Also fires standard .44-caliber rounds. Stainless; 6-shot; 8" barrel; weight 4.1 lb. Single-/double-action. Introduced 2006.

NIB	Exc.	V.G.	Good	Fair	Poor
1100	950	780	600	450	280

SUPER RAM SILHOUETTE SERIES

Note: All Super Ram Silhouette series revolvers are stainless steel.

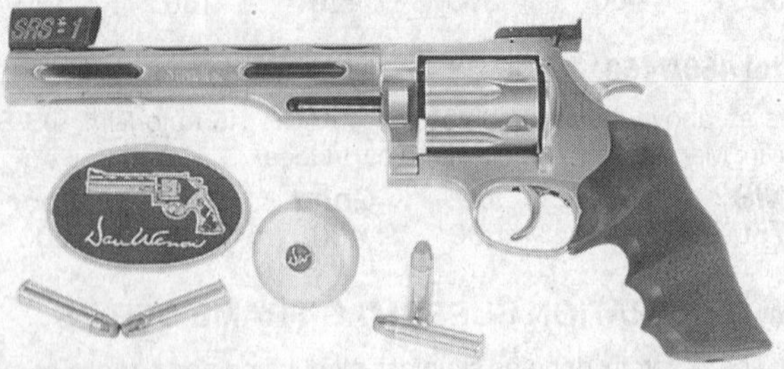

Model 722 VH10 SRS1

Chambered for .22-caliber cartridge. Fitted with 10" slotted shroud. Interchangeable barrel system. Adjustable Bomar rear sight; Bomar SRS-1 hood front sight. Fluted or non-fluted cylinders. Hogue finger groove rubber grips.

NIB	Exc.	V.G.	Good	Fair	Poor
920	750	600	480	300	180

Model 7360 V8S SRS1

Same as above, but chambered for .357 Magnum cartridge. Fitted with 8" slotted shroud.

NIB	Exc.	V.G.	Good	Fair	Poor
1100	950	780	600	450	280

Model 741 V8S SRS1

Same as above, but chambered for .41 Magnum cartridge. Fitted with 8" slotted shroud.

NIB	Exc.	V.G.	Good	Fair	Poor
1100	950	780	600	450	280

Model 741 V10S SRS1

Same as above, but fitted with 10" slotted shroud.

NIB	Exc.	V.G.	Good	Fair	Poor
1100	950	780	600	450	280

Model 744 V8S SRS1

Same as above, but chambered for .44 Magnum cartridge. Fitted with 8" slotted shroud.

NIB	Exc.	V.G.	Good	Fair	Poor
1100	950	780	600	450	280

Model 744 V10S SRS1

Same as above, but fitted with 10" slotted shroud.

NIB	Exc.	V.G.	Good	Fair	Poor
1100	950	780	600	450	280

Model 740 V8S SRS1

Same as above, but chambered for .357 Super Magnum. Fitted with 8" slotted shroud.

NIB	Exc.	V.G.	Good	Fair	Poor
1200	1050	880	700	550	300

Model 7414 V8S SRS1

Same as above, but chambered for .414 Super Magnum. Fitted with 8" slotted shroud.

NIB	Exc.	V.G.	Good	Fair	Poor
1200	1050	880	700	550	300

Model 7445 V8S SS1

Same as above, but chambered for .445 Super Magnum. Fitted with 8" slotted shroud.

NIB	Exc.	V.G.	Good	Fair	Poor
1200	1050	880	700	550	300

PISTOL PACK SERIES

This series consists of a Dan Wesson revolver of customer's choice, with adjustable rear sight and four barrel assemblies in small-frame calibers (2.5", 4", 6" and 8"); large frame and supermag frame have three barrel assemblies (4", 6" and 8"). Also included is a cleaning kit, wrench kit, extra exotic wood grips, instruction manual and fitted hard case. Choice of blue or stainless steel finish ("7" prefix).

Model 22/722

Chambered for .22 LR.

NIB	Exc.	V.G.	Good	Fair	Poor
1200	1050	880	700	550	300

Model 32/732

Chambered for .32 H&R Magnum.

NIB	Exc.	V.G.	Good	Fair	Poor
2000	1700	1300	1000	550	300

Model 3220/73220

Chambered for .32-20.

NIB	Exc.	V.G.	Good	Fair	Poor
2000	1700	1300	1000	550	300

Model 15/715

Chambered for .357 Magnum. Note: Add $500 for current production, 2016 and after.

NIB	Exc.	V.G.	Good	Fair	Poor
1200	1050	880	700	550	300

Model 41/741

Chambered for .41 Magnum.

NIB	Exc.	V.G.	Good	Fair	Poor
2000	1700	1300	1000	650	350

Model 44/744

Chambered for .44 Magnum.

NIB	Exc.	V.G.	Good	Fair	Poor
2000	1700	1300	1000	650	350

Model 45/745

Chambered for .45 Colt.

NIB	Exc.	V.G.	Good	Fair	Poor
2000	1700	1300	1000	650	350

Model 460/7460

Chambered for .45 ACP, .45 Auto Rim, .45 Super, .45 Win. Magnum, .460 Rowland cartridges.

NIB	Exc.	V.G.	Good	Fair	Poor
1450	1250	1050	850	650	350

Model 40/740

Chambered for .357 Maximum.

NIB	Exc.	V.G.	Good	Fair	Poor
1650	1300	1150	950	750	450

Model 414/7414

Chambered for .414 Super Magnum.

NIB	Exc.	V.G.	Good	Fair	Poor
1650	1300	1150	950	750	450

Model 445/7445

Chambered for .445 Super Magnum.

NIB	Exc.	V.G.	Good	Fair	Poor
1650	1300	1100	—	—	—

HUNTER PACK SERIES

Hunter Pack comes with a Dan Wesson revolver of customer's choice, with adjustable rear sight and two 8" barrel assemblies, one with open sights; one drilled and tapped with Burris or Weaver mount installed. Extra set of exotic wood grips, wrench kit, cleaning kit and manual. Offered in blue or stainless steel ("7" prefix).

Model 22/722

Chambered for .22 LR.

NIB	Exc.	V.G.	Good	Fair	Poor
1200	950	850	—	—	—

Model 32/732

Chambered for .32 H&R Magnum.

NIB	Exc.	V.G.	Good	Fair	Poor
1200	950	850	—	—	—

Model 3220/73220

Chambered for .32-20.

NIB	Exc.	V.G.	Good	Fair	Poor
1200	1050	880	700	550	300

Model 15/715

Chambered for .357 Magnum.

NIB	Exc.	V.G.	Good	Fair	Poor
1200	1050	880	700	550	300

Model 41/741

Chambered for .41 Magnum.

NIB	Exc.	V.G.	Good	Fair	Poor
1450	1250	1050	850	650	350

Model 44/744

Chambered for .44 Magnum.

NIB	Exc.	V.G.	Good	Fair	Poor
1450	1250	1050	850	650	350

Model 45/745

Chambered for .45 Colt.

NIB	Exc.	V.G.	Good	Fair	Poor
1450	1250	1050	850	650	350

Model 460/7460

Chambered for .45 ACP, .45 Auto Rim, .45 Super, .45 Win. Magnum, .460 Rowland cartridges

NIB	Exc.	V.G.	Good	Fair	Poor
1450	1250	1050	850	650	350

Model 40/740

Chambered for .357 Maximum.

NIB	Exc.	V.G.	Good	Fair	Poor
1650	1300	1150	950	750	450

Model 414/7414

Chambered for .414 Super Magnum.

NIB	Exc.	V.G.	Good	Fair	Poor
1650	1300	1150	950	750	450

Model 445/7445

Chambered for .445 Super Magnum.

NIB	Exc.	V.G.	Good	Fair	Poor
1650	1300	1150	950	750	450

PISTOLS

A2

Similar to a US Military 1911 A1, except match stainless barrel, fixed snag free sights, bead blast finish, and double diamond walnut grips. Introduced in 2017.

NIB	Exc.	V.G.	Good	Fair	Poor
1160	1000	880	780	560	460

A2 Commander

Similar to A2, except 4.25" barrel. Introduced in 2017.

NIB	Exc.	V.G.	Good	Fair	Poor
1160	1000	880	780	560	460

Bruin

Similar to Pointman series, except 6.03" barrel. Chambered in .45 ACP or 10mm. Adjustable sights. Introduced in 2016.

NIB	Exc.	V.G.	Good	Fair	Poor
1760	1530	1330	1200	830	660

Commander Classic

Similar to Pointman series, except 4.25" barrel. Stainless steel receiver and slide. Bobtail receiver. Chambered in .45 ACP. Fixed snag-free sights. Checkered wood grips. Produced 2005–09, and 2016.

NIB	Exc.	V.G.	Good	Fair	Poor
1460	1280	1100	990	690	560

Discretion

Similar to Pointman series, except 5.75" barrel suppressor ready. Stainless steel receiver with accessory rail and slide with relief cuts. Chambered in 9mm or .45 ACP. Fixed tall sights. Textured G10 grips. Introduced 2016.

NIB	Exc.	V.G.	Good	Fair	Poor
1830	1600	1380	1260	880	700

Discretion Commander

Similar to Discretion, except 4.25" barrel suppressor ready. Introduced 2018.

NIB	Exc.	V.G.	Good	Fair	Poor
1830	1600	1380	1260	880	700

ECP

Similar to ECO, except aluminum bobtail frame. 9mm or .45 ACP. 29

ounces. Introduced 2018.

NIB	Exc.	V.G.	Good	Fair	Poor
1360	1180	1020	930	630	530

Elite Series Chaos

1911-style platform but with double-stack 21-round magazine. Chambered 9mm. Steel frame with rail and slide. Adjustable sights. Ambidextrous thumb safety. Introduced 2014.

NIB	Exc.	V.G.	Good	Fair	Poor
3260	2860	2460	2220	1500	1330

Elite Series Fury

Similar to Elite Series Chaos, but in 9mm or 10mm and with 5.5" barrel. RMR optic and tall fixed sights. Introduced 2017.

NIB	Exc.	V.G.	Good	Fair	Poor
4180	3660	3160	2830	1960	1630

Elite Series Mayhem

Similar to Elite Series Chaos, but in .40 S&W and 6" barrel. Adjustable sights. Designed for competitive shooting. Introduced 2011.

NIB	Exc.	V.G.	Good	Fair	Poor
3330	2930	2500	2260	1500	1330

Elite Series Titan

Similar to Elite Series Chaos, but in 10mm and 4.75" barrel. Adjustable sights. Introduced 2011.

NIB	Exc.	V.G.	Good	Fair	Poor
3230	2860	2460	2220	1500	1330

Kodiak

Caliber: 10mm. Capacity: 8-round magazine. Barrel: 6.03" Grips: Textured G10. Sights: Fixed, fiber-optic front/adjustable rear. Length: 9.7" overall. Weight: 47.1 oz. unloaded. Finish: Black or tri-tone. Features: 1911 platform with coarse slide serrations, mag well and ambidextrous safety. Black version has bronzed controls and barrel, and tri-tone with a matte gray slide.

NIB	Exc.	V.G.	Good	Fair	Poor
2130	2000	1700	—	—	—

Pointman Major

Semi-automatic pistol chambered for .45 ACP cartridge. Many special features including interchangeable front sight and adjustable rear, Jarvis match barrel, beveled magazine well and others. Stainless steel slide and frame. Rosewood checkered grips. Slide serrations both front and rear. High sighting rib, with interchangeable sights. Introduced in 2000.

NIB	Exc.	V.G.	Good	Fair	Poor
1200	1050	800	620	500	300

Pointman Seven

Many of the same features as Pointman Major, with blued slide and frame. No sighting rib.

NIB	Exc.	V.G.	Good	Fair	Poor
1100	950	700	520	400	300

Pointman Seven Stainless

Same as above, with stainless steel frame and slide.

NIB	Exc.	V.G.	Good	Fair	Poor
1200	1050	800	620	500	300

Pointman Minor

Same as above, except blued slide and frame. No match barrel.

NIB	Exc.	V.G.	Good	Fair	Poor
1100	950	700	520	400	300

Pointman Nine

Full-size 1911-style in 9mm, with 9+1 capacity. Front and rear slide serrations, adjustable rear sight, fiber-optic front.

NIB	Exc.	V.G.	Good	Fair	Poor
1300	1100	850	600	450	300

Pointman Guardian

Fitted with 4.25" barrel and match trigger group. Adjustable rear sight, plus many other special features. Blued frame and slide, with sighting rib.

NIB	Exc.	V.G.	Good	Fair	Poor
1200	1050	800	620	500	300

Pointman Guardian Duce

Same as above, with blued steel slide and stainless steel frame.

NIB	Exc.	V.G.	Good	Fair	Poor
820	680	520	400	300	180

Pointman Major Australian

Introduced in 2002. Features fully adjustable Bomar-style target sight. Unique slide top configuration that features a rounded radius, with lengthwise sight serrations. Slide has Southern Cross engraved on right side. Chambered for .45 ACP cartridge only.

NIB	Exc.	V.G.	Good	Fair	Poor
1200	1050	800	620	500	300

Pointman Hi-Cap

This .45 ACP pistol fitted with 5" barrel. Blued carbon alloy wide-body frame, with 10-round magazine. Fixed rear target sight. Extended thumb safety as well as other special features.

NIB	Exc.	V.G.	Good	Fair	Poor
1100	950	700	520	400	300

Pointman Dave Pruitt Signature Series

Fitted with 5" match-grade barrel, with rounded top slide with bead blast matte finish. Chevron-style cocking serrations. Fixed rear sight, with tactical/target ramp front. Many special features.

NIB	Exc.	V.G.	Good	Fair	Poor
1100	950	700	520	400	300

RZ-10

10mm single-action semi-automatic, with 8+1 capacity, 5" barrel, fixed sights. Weight 2.4 lbs. Introduced 2006.

NIB	Exc.	V.G.	Good	Fair	Poor
1100	950	700	520	400	300

RZ-45 Heritage

Same as discontinued RZ-10, except in .45 ACP. The RZ refers to "Razorback", which is based on serrated Clark-style target rib machined onto top of the slide. Introduced in 2010.

NIB	Exc.	V.G.	Good	Fair	Poor
1100	950	700	520	400	200

Specialist

Similar to Razorback series but chambered in 9mm or .45 ACP with railed receiver, night sights, 5" barrel. matte stainless or duty finish. Introduced 2012.

NIB	Exc.	V.G.	Good	Fair	Poor
1460	1280	1100	990	680	530

Specialist Commander

Similar to Specialist, but with 4.25" barrel. Introduced 2017.

NIB	Exc.	V.G.	Good	Fair	Poor
1460	1280	1100	990	680	530

Specialist Distressed

Similar to Specialist but chambered in .45 ACP and with distressed finish. Introduced 2018.

NIB	Exc.	V.G.	Good	Fair	Poor
1720	1500	1290	1170	780	630

TCP

Similar to Specialist Commander but chambered in .45 ACP and with aluminum alloy frame. Introduced 2018.

NIB	Exc.	V.G.	Good	Fair	Poor
1460	1280	1100	990	680	530

Guardian

Designed for concealed carry, with Bobtail frame. Calibers .38 Super, 9mm or .45 ACP, with steel slide, alloy frame, Novak Lo-Mount night sights, extended thumb and grip safeties, 8- or 9-round magazine and stippled Shadow grips. Weight 28.8 ozs., 4.3" barrel and black Duty finish.

NIB	Exc.	V.G.	Good	Fair	Poor
1300	1100	850	600	450	300

Valkyrie

In .45 ACP. This model has what is essentially a 4.5" Commander size barrel, with an Officer's model slide. Features include Black Duty finish, fixed Tritium night sights and slim-line G-10 grips. Introduced in 2015.

NIB	Exc.	V.G.	Good	Fair	Poor
1750	1400	1000	850	400	250

ECO

Officer-size model, with 3.5" barrel in 9mm or .45 ACP. Features aluminum frame and steel slide, night sights, G-10 grips, Duty Black finish.

NIB	Exc.	V.G.	Good	Fair	Poor
1400	1100	900	700	450	350

Valor

Caliber: .45 ACP. Capacity: 8-round magazine. Barrel: 5" Grips: Textured G10. Sights: Fixed, night-sight front/U-notch rear. Length: 8.75" overall. Weight: 39.7 oz. unloaded. Finish: Matte stainless or black Duty Coat. Features: 1911 platform with GI-style slide serrations, Stan Chen SI mag well, tapered grip and tactical ambidextrous safety.

NIB	Exc.	V.G.	Good	Fair	Poor
1550	1350	1050	800	500	400

Vigil

Similar to Valor but chambered in 9mm or .45 ACP and with aluminum alloy frame. Introduced 2018.

NIB	Exc.	V.G.	Good	Fair	Poor
1100	980	830	760	500	400

Vigil Commander

Similar to Vigil but with 4.25" barrel. Introduced 2018.

NIB	Exc.	V.G.	Good	Fair	Poor
1100	980	830	760	500	400

Vigil CCO

Similar to Vigil Commander but with shorter frame. Introduced 2018.

NIB	Exc.	V.G.	Good	Fair	Poor
1100	980	830	760	500	400

Wraith

Similar to Specialist but no rail, suppressor ready, and distressed finish. Introduced 2018.

NIB	Exc.	V.G.	Good	Fair	Poor
1780	1560	1360	1200	830	660

Elite Series — Havoc

Designed for Open IPSC/USPSA competition. In .38 Super or 9mm, with 5" barrel with compensator and C-More red dot sights. A 4.5" barrel was previously offered.

NIB	Exc.	V.G.	Good	Fair	Poor
3500	3000	2500	1700	900	500

PATRIOT SERIES

Patriot Marksman

Introduced in 2002. This .45 ACP pistol has 5" match-grade barrel. Fixed sights. Many special features such as beveled mag well, lowered and flared ejection port, checkered wood grips. Magazine capacity 8 rounds. Weight 38 oz.

NIB	Exc.	V.G.	Good	Fair	Poor
800	650	520	400	300	180

Patriot Expert

As above, but fitted with Bomar target-style adjustable rear sight.

NIB	Exc.	V.G.	Good	Fair	Poor
900	750	620	500	400	220

DWX Full Size

Calibers: 9mm, .40 S&W. Capacity: 19-round magazine (9mm), 15-round magazine (.40 S&W). Barrel: 5" Grips: Checkered red aluminum. Sights: Fixed fiber-optic front/adjustable rear. Length: 8.52" overall. Weight: 43 oz. unloaded. Finish: Black Duty Coat. Features: Hybrid pistol built using the single-action fire control group of a Dan Wesson 1911 and frame of a CZ 75 pistol. Compatible with CZ P-09 and CZ P-10 F magazines. Bull barrel and full dust cover with accessory rail. Flat red aluminum trigger. Oversized controls.

NIB	Exc.	V.G.	Good	Fair	Poor
1720	1450	1250	—	—	—

DWX Compact

Caliber: 9mm. Capacity: 15-round magazine. Barrel: 5". Grips: Checkered red aluminum. Sights: Fixed, night-sight front/U-notch rear. Length: 7.47" overall. Weight: 28.5 oz. unloaded. Finish: Black Duty Coat. Features: Hybrid pistol built using the single-action fire control group of a Dan Wesson 1911 and frame of a CZ 75 pistol. With or without accessory rail. Full dust cover. Flat red aluminum trigger. Oversized controls.

NIB	Exc.	V.G.	Good	Fair	Poor
1720	1450	1250	—	—	—

RIFLES

Coyote Target

Chambered for .22 LR or .22 Magnum cartridge. Fitted with 18.375" heavy bull barrel. Receiver drilled and tapped for scope mount. Hardwood stock, with high comb and flat-bottom forend. Magazine capacity 6 or 10 rounds. Note: Unknown whether Dan Wesson Coyote rifles were ever actually produced; we suspect not. Values shown are based on 2002 suggested retail prices.

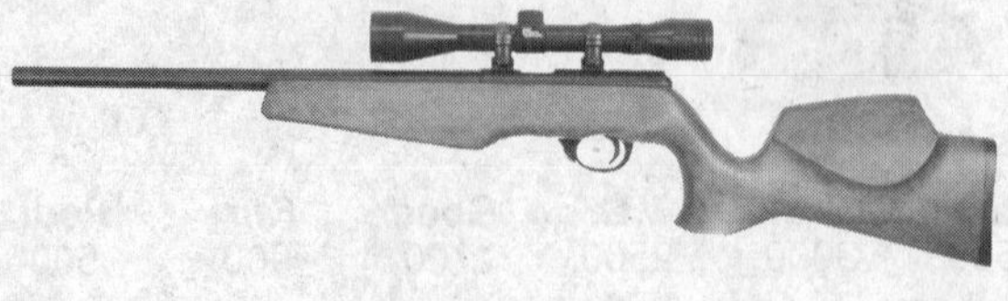

NIB	Exc.	V.G.	Good	Fair	Poor
280	230	200	—	—	—

Coyote Classic

Also chambered for .22 LR or .22 Magnum cartridge. Fitted with 22.75" barrel, with open sights. Drilled and tapped for scope mount. Checkered hardwood stock. Magazine capacity 6 or 10 rounds. Introduced in 2002.

NIB	Exc.	V.G.	Good	Fair	Poor
240	200	180	—	—	—

WESSON FIREARMS CO., INC.

Palmer, Massachusetts

Company was founded in 1968 by Daniel B. Wesson, great-grandson of D.B. Wesson co-founder of Smith & Wesson. This line of handguns is unique for its barrel/shroud interchangeability. Dan Wesson revolvers have established themselves as champion metallic silhouette competition guns. Company offers a comprehensive line of handguns for almost every use and will also custom build a handgun to customer specifications. Dan Wesson Arms was restructured on January 4, 1991 and identified as Wesson Firearms Company, Inc. Wesson handguns made after this date will be stamped with this new corporate name. In 1995, the company declared bankruptcy. (See WESSON FIREARMS, DAN)

Model 11

A .357 Magnum caliber double-action swing-out cylinder revolver, with interchangeable 2.5", 4" or 6" barrels. 6-shot cylinder. Blued, with walnut grips. Manufactured in 1970 and 1971. Note: Add 25 percent per barrel for extra barrels.

NIB	Exc.	V.G.	Good	Fair	Poor
300	280	150	120	100	80

Model 12

As above, with adjustable target sights.

NIB	Exc.	V.G.	Good	Fair	Poor
350	300	200	180	120	100

Model 14

As above, with recessed barrel locking nut. Furnished with a spanner wrench. Manufactured from 1971 to 1975.

NIB	Exc.	V.G.	Good	Fair	Poor
350	250	180	150	100	80

Model 15

As above, with adjustable target sights.

NIB	Exc.	V.G.	Good	Fair	Poor
380	280	200	180	120	100

Model 8

As above, in .38 Special caliber.

NIB	Exc.	V.G.	Good	Fair	Poor
320	220	150	120	100	80

Model 9

As Model 15, with adjustable sights. In .38 Special caliber. Manufactured from 1971 to 1975.

NIB	Exc.	V.G.	Good	Fair	Poor
350	280	200	180	120	100

.22 CALIBER REVOLVERS

Model 22

Double-action target revolver chambered for .22 LR cartridge. Available in 2", 4", 6" and 8" barrel length. Choice of shroud: standard rib; ventilated rib; ventilated heavy rib. All variations feature adjustable rear sight and red ramp interchangeable front. Target grips. Offered in bright blue or stainless steel finish. For revolvers with standard barrel assembly weights are: 2"—36 oz.; 4"—40 oz.; 6"—44 oz.; 8"—49 oz.

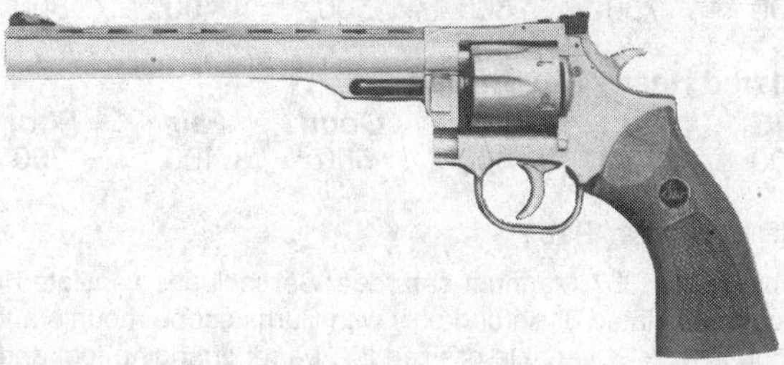

Model 722

Same as above, with stainless steel finish.

Model 22M

Same as above, but chambered for .22 Magnum with blued finish.

Model 722M

Same as above, but chambered for .22 Magnum. Stainless steel finish. Note: Add 10 percent for stainless steel finish.

Standard Rib Shroud

NIB	*Exc.*	*V.G.*	*Good*	*Fair*	*Poor*
380	300	200	150	100	80

Ventilated Rib Shroud

NIB	*Exc.*	*V.G.*	*Good*	*Fair*	*Poor*
400	320	220	150	100	80

Ventilated Heavy Rib Shroud

NIB	*Exc.*	*V.G.*	*Good*	*Fair*	*Poor*
420	330	240	200	120	100

P22 Pistol Pac

Also a target revolver similar to Model 22 and its variations. Chambered for .22 LR or .22 Magnum. Offered with three types of barrel shrouds: standard; ventilated; or ventilated heavy. Available in blued or stainless steel finish. Principal feature of Pistol Pac is the three barrel assemblies in 2.5", 4", 6" and 8", with extra grips, four additional front sights and a fitted carrying case. Note: Add 10 percent for stainless steel finish.

Standard Rib Shroud

NIB	*Exc.*	*V.G.*	*Good*	*Fair*	*Poor*
750	550	400	350	300	150

Ventilated Rib Shroud

NIB	*Exc.*	*V.G.*	*Good*	*Fair*	*Poor*
800	600	500	450	350	150

Ventilated Heavy Rib Shroud

NIB	*Exc.*	*V.G.*	*Good*	*Fair*	*Poor*
800	600	500	450	350	150

HP22 Hunter Pac

Chambered for .22 Magnum cartridge. Set includes ventilated heavy 8" shroud, ventilated 8" shroud only with Burris scope mounts and Burris scope in 1.5x4X variable or fixed 2X, barrel changing tool and fitted carrying case. Finish blued or stainless steel. Note: Hunter Pacs are a special order item and should be evaluated at the time of sale.

.32 CALIBER REVOLVERS

Model 32

A target revolver chambered for .32 H&R Magnum cartridge. Offered in 2", 4", 6" or 8" barrel lengths, with choice of rib shrouds. All variations are fitted with adjustable rear sight and red ramp interchangeable front. Target grips. Available in blued or stainless steel finish. Weights depend on barrel length and shroud type, but are between 35 and 53 oz.

Model 732

Same as above, with stainless steel finish.

Model 322

Same as above, but chambered for .32-20 cartridge with blued finish.

Model 7322

Same as above, but chambered for .32-20 cartridge. Stainless steel finish. Note: Add 10 percent for stainless steel finish.

Standard Rib Shroud

NIB	*Exc.*	*V.G.*	*Good*	*Fair*	*Poor*
480	320	200	150	100	80

Ventilated Rib Shroud

NIB	*Exc.*	*V.G.*	*Good*	*Fair*	*Poor*
500	350	220	150	100	80

Ventilated Heavy Rib Shroud

NIB	*Exc.*	*V.G.*	*Good*	*Fair*	*Poor*
520	380	250	150	100	80

P32 Pistol Pac

Offers same calibers, barrel shrouds and finishes as above models. In a set consisting of 2", 4", 6" and 8" barrels, extra grips, four additional sights and fitted case. Note: Add 10 percent for stainless steel finish.

Standard Rib Shroud

NIB	*Exc.*	*V.G.*	*Good*	*Fair*	*Poor*
1200	1000	650	500	400	300

Ventilated Rib Shroud

NIB	*Exc.*	*V.G.*	*Good*	*Fair*	*Poor*
1200	1000	650	500	400	300

Ventilated Heavy Rib Shroud

NIB	*Exc.*	*V.G.*	*Good*	*Fair*	*Poor*
1200	1000	650	500	400	300

329HP32 Hunter Pac

Chambered for .32 H&R Magnum or .32-20 cartridge. Set includes ventilated heavy 8" shroud, ventilated 8" shroud only with Burris scope mounts and Burris scope in 1.5x4X variable or fixed 2X, barrel changing tool and fitted carrying case. Finish blued or stainless steel. Note: Hunter Pacs are a special order item and should be evaluated at the time of sale.

.357 MAGNUM AND .38 CALIBER REVOLVERS

Model 14

Double-action service revolver chambered for .357 Magnum cartridge. Available with 2", 4" or 6" barrel, with service shroud. Has fixed sights, service grip. Offered in blued or stainless steel finish.

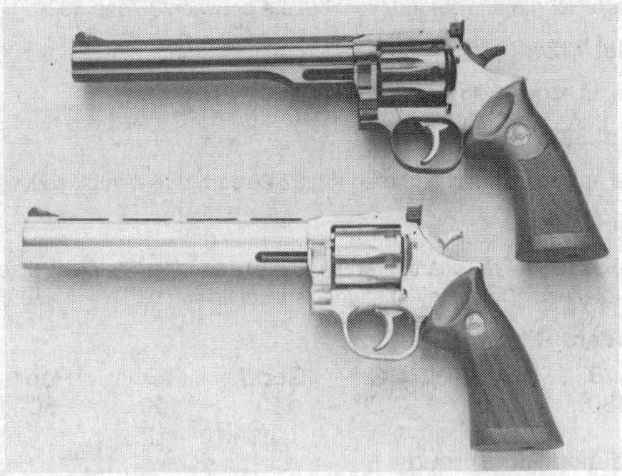

Model 714

Same as above, with stainless steel finish.

Model 8

Same as above, but chambered for .38 Special cartridge with blued finish.

Model 708

Same as above, but chambered for .38 Special. Stainless steel finish. Note: Add 10 percent for stainless steel finish.

NIB	Exc.	V.G.	Good	Fair	Poor
400	350	250	120	100	80

P14/8 Pistol Pac

This set consists of 2", 4" and 6" barrel, with service shroud and fixed sights. Has an extra grip, with fitted carrying case. P14 chambered for .357 Magnum; P8 chambered for .38 Special.

NIB	Exc.	V.G.	Good	Fair	Poor
800	700	600	500	400	300

Model 15

Designed as a double-action target revolver. Chambered for .357 Magnum cartridge. Available with 2", 4", 6", 8" and 10" barrel lengths, with standard rib shroud. Features adjustable rear sight and red ramp interchangeable front. Target grips. Offered with blued finish. Weights according to barrel length: 2"—32 oz.; 4"—36 oz.; 6"—40 oz.; 8"—44 oz.; 10"—50 oz.

Model 715

Same as above, with stainless steel finish.

Model 9

Same as above, but chambered for .38 Special cartridge. Blued finish.

Model 709

Same as above, with stainless steel finish. Note: Add 10 percent for stainless steel finish.

Standard Rib Shroud

NIB	Exc.	V.G.	Good	Fair	Poor
800	700	600	500	400	300

Ventilated Rib Shroud

NIB	Exc.	V.G.	Good	Fair	Poor
800	700	600	500	400	300

Ventilated Heavy Rib Shroud

NIB	Exc.	V.G.	Good	Fair	Poor
800	700	600	500	400	300

330HP15 Hunter Pac

Chambered for .357 Magnum cartridge. Set includes ventilated heavy 8" shroud, ventilated 8" shroud only with Burris scope mounts and Burris scope in 1.5x4X variable or fixed 2X, barrel changing tool and fitted carrying case. Finish blued or stainless steel. Note: Hunter Pacs are a special order item and should be evaluated at the time of sale.

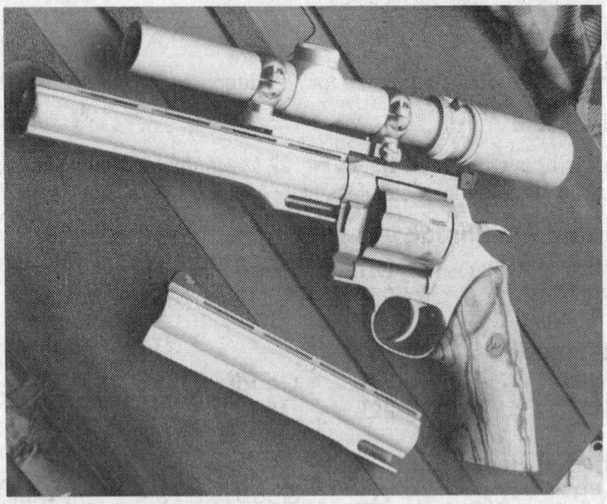

331Model 40/Supermag

Target revolver chambered for .357 Maximum cartridge. Has adjustable rear sight and red ramp interchangeable front, ventilated rib shroud and target grip. Barrel lengths 4", 6", 8" or 10". Ventilated slotted shroud available in 8" only. In 1993, a compensated barrel assembly "CBA" was added to product line as a complete gun. Finish blued. Weight about 64 oz. with ventilated rib shroud barrel. Note: Add 20 percent for Model 740 in stainless steel; 10 percent for stainless steel finish; $30 for .357 Supermag with compensated barrel assembly.

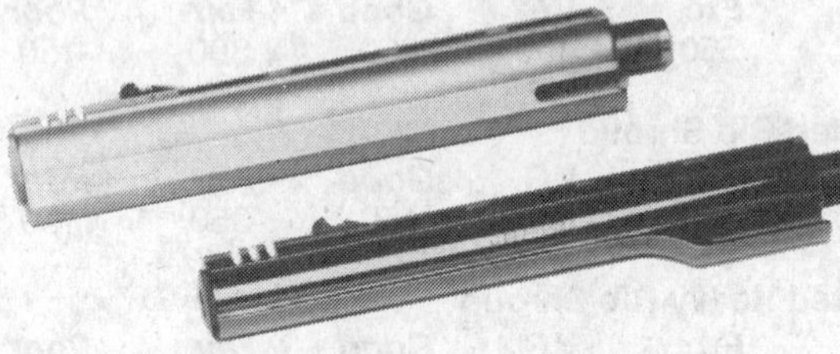

Ventilated Rib Shroud

NIB	Exc.	V.G.	Good	Fair	Poor
1100	950	750	600	450	300

Ventilated Slotted Shroud—8" barrel only

NIB	Exc.	V.G.	Good	Fair	Poor
1100	950	750	600	450	300

Ventilated Heavy Rib Shroud

NIB	Exc.	V.G.	Good	Fair	Poor
1100	950	750	600	450	300

332HP40 Hunter Pac

Chambered for .357 Supermag cartridge. Set includes ventilated heavy 8" shroud, ventilated 8" shroud only with Burris scope mounts and Burris scope in 1.5x4X variable or fixed 2X, barrel changing tool and fitted carrying case. Finish blued or stainless steel. Note: Hunter Pacs are a special order item and should be evaluated at the time of sale.

Model 375

Also known as .375 Supermag. Chambered for .357 Maximum cartridge based on .375 Win. cartridge. Offered in 6", 8", 10" ventilated, ventilated heavy or ventilated slotted rib barrels. Sights are interchangeable and adjustable. Available in bright blue finish only. Weight about 64 oz. with ventilated rib shroud barrel.

Ventilated Rib Shroud

NIB	Exc.	V.G.	Good	Fair	Poor
1100	950	750	600	450	300

Ventilated Heavy Rib Shroud

NIB	Exc.	V.G.	Good	Fair	Poor
1100	950	750	600	450	300

Ventilated Slotted Shroud—8" barrel only

NIB	Exc.	V.G.	Good	Fair	Poor
1100	950	750	600	450	300

P15/9 Pistol Pac

A set with 2", 4", 6" and 8" barrels. Chambered for .357 or .38 Special, with standard rib shroud, four additional sights, extra grip and carrying case. P15 chambered for .357 Magnum; P9 chambered for .38 Special. Note: Add 10 percent for stainless steel finish.

Standard Rib Shroud

NIB	Exc.	V.G.	Good	Fair	Poor
800	700	600	500	400	300

Ventilated Rib Shroud

NIB	Exc.	V.G.	Good	Fair	Poor
800	700	600	500	400	300

Ventilated Heavy Rib Shroud

NIB	Exc.	V.G.	Good	Fair	Poor
800	700	600	500	400	300

354HP375 Hunter Pac

Chambered for .375 Super Magnum cartridge. Set includes ventilated heavy 8" shroud, ventilated 8" shroud only with Burris scope mounts and Burris scope in 1.5x4X variable or fixed 2X, barrel changing tool and fitted carrying case. Finish blued or stainless steel. Note: Hunter Pacs are a special order item and should be evaluated at the time of sale.

.41, .44 MAGNUM AND .45 LONG COLT REVOLVERS

Model 44

A target double-action revolver chambered for .44 Magnum. Has 4", 6", 8" or 10" barrels, with ventilated rib shrouds. Other features include adjustable rear sight and red ramp interchangeable front. Target grips. Finish bright blue. Weights according to barrel length: 4"—40 oz.; 6"—56 oz.; 8"—64 oz.; 10"—69 oz.

Model 744

Same as above, with stainless steel finish.

301 Model 41

Same as above, but chambered for .41 Magnum with blued finish.

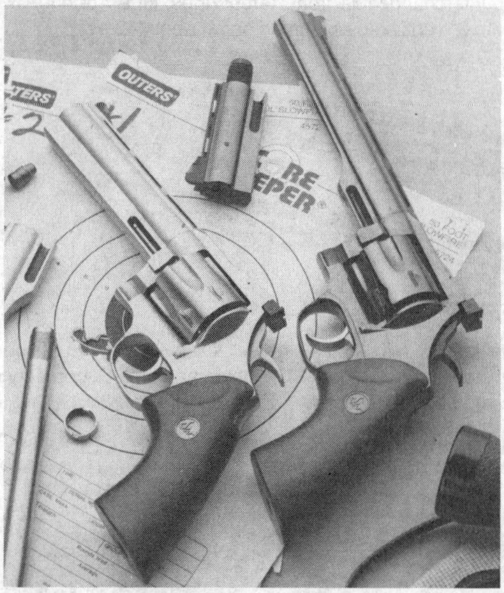

302 Model 741

Same as above, with stainless steel finish.

Model 45

Same as above, but chambered for .45 Long Colt with bright blue finish.

Model 745

Same as above, with stainless steel finish. Note: Add 10 percent for stainless steel finish.

Ventilated Rib Shroud

NIB	Exc.	V.G.	Good	Fair	Poor
1000	850	550	450	300	200

Ventilated Heavy Rib Shroud

NIB	Exc.	V.G.	Good	Fair	Poor
1000	850	550	450	300	200

P44/P41/P45 Pistol Pac

This set features 6" and 8" barrel assembly, with ventilated rib shroud, extra grip, two additional front sights and fitted carrying case. Chambered for .41 Magnum, .44 Magnum or .45 Long Colt. Note: Add 10 percent for stainless steel finish.

Ventilated Rib Shroud

NIB	Exc.	V.G.	Good	Fair	Poor
1000	850	550	450	300	200

Ventilated Heavy Rib Shroud

NIB	Exc.	V.G.	Good	Fair	Poor
1000	850	550	450	300	200

357HP41/44 Hunter Pac

Chambered for .41 or .44 Magnum cartridge. Set includes ventilated heavy 8" shroud, ventilated 8" shroud only with Burris scope mounts and Burris scope in 1.5x4X variable or fixed 2X, barrel changing tool and fitted carrying case. Finish blued or stainless steel. Note: Hunter Pacs are a special order item and should be evaluated at the time of sale.

359 Model 445

Double-action target revolver chambered for .445 Super Magnum cartridge. Barrel lengths and shrouds offered: 8" with ventilated slotted rib; 8" ventilated heavy slotted rib; 10" ventilated slotted rib. Barrel lengths also available in 4", 6", 8" and 10", with ventilated rib or ventilated heavy rib shrouds. In 1993, a compensated barrel assembly "CBA" was added to product line as a complete gun. Fitted with adjustable rear sights and red ramp interchangeable front. Target grips. Finish bright blue. Typical weight with 8" ventilated rib shroud barrel about 62 oz.

Model 7445

Same as above, with stainless steel finish. Note: Add 10 percent for stainless steel finish; $30 for .44 Magnum and .445 Super Magnum, with compensated barrel assembly.

Ventilated Rib Shroud

NIB	Exc.	V.G.	Good	Fair	Poor
1100	950	750	600	450	300

Ventilated Heavy Rib Shroud

NIB	Exc.	V.G.	Good	Fair	Poor
1100	950	750	600	450	300

Model 7445 Alaskan Guide Special

Limited edition model (only 500 produced). Chambered for .445 Super Magnum cartridge. Features 4" ventilated heavy compensated shroud barrel assembly, synthetic grips and matte black titanium nitride finish. Overall barrel length 5.5"; weight 56 oz.

NIB	Exc.	V.G.	Good	Fair	Poor
950	700	600	350	200	100

HP455 Hunter Pac

Chambered for .445 Super Magnum cartridge. Set includes ventilated heavy 8" shroud, ventilated 8" shroud only with Burris scope mounts and Burris scope in 1.5x4X variable or fixed 2X, barrel changing tool and fitted carrying case. Finish blued or stainless steel. Note: Hunter Pacs are a special order item and should be evaluated at the time of sale.

FIXED BARREL HANDGUNS

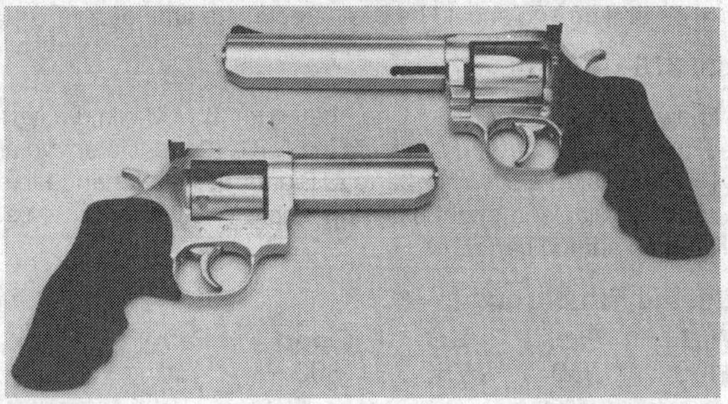

Model 38P

A 5-shot double-action revolver designed for .38 Special cartridge. Barrel 2.5", with fixed sights. Choice of wood or rubber grips. Finish is blued. Weight 24.6 oz.

NIB	Exc.	V.G.	Good	Fair	Poor
350	220	150	120	100	80

Wesson Firearms Silhouette .22

A 6-shot .22 LR single-action only revolver, with 10" barrel. Fitted with compact-style grips, narrow notch rear sight. Choice of ventilated or ventilated heavy rib shroud. Finish blued or stainless steel. Weight with shroud: 55 oz. ventilated rib; 62 oz. ventilated heavy rib. Note: Add 10 percent for stainless steel finish.

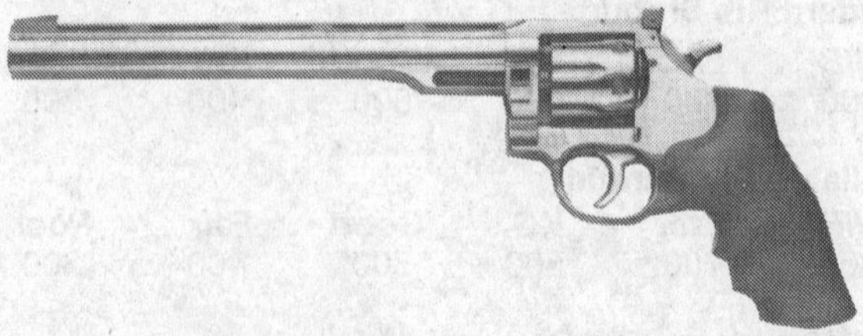

Ventilated Rib Shroud

NIB	Exc.	V.G.	Good	Fair	Poor
500	320	280	200	150	100

Ventilated Heavy Rib Shroud

NIB	Exc.	V.G.	Good	Fair	Poor
500	350	280	200	150	100

Model 738P

Same as above, with stainless steel finish.

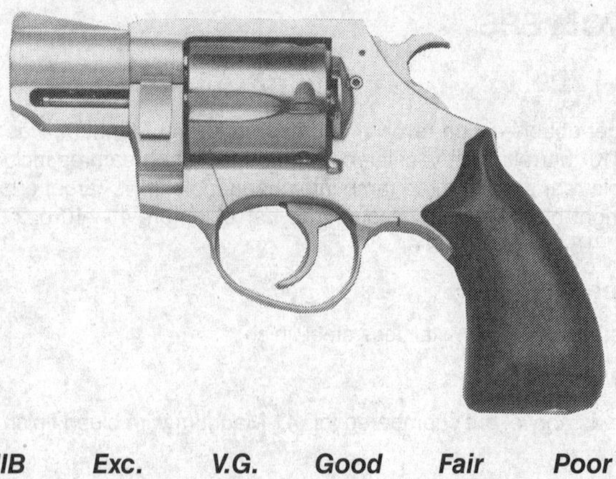

NIB	Exc.	V.G.	Good	Fair	Poor
520	350	280	200	150	100

Model 45/745 Pin Gun

This model uses a .44 Magnum frame, with 5" barrel and two-stage compensator. Choice of ventilated or ventilated heavy rib shroud. Chambered for .45 ACP, with/without half moon clips. Finish blued or stainless steel. Weight 54 oz. Note: Add 10 percent for stainless steel finish.

Ventilated Rib Shroud

NIB	Exc.	V.G.	Good	Fair	Poor
1100	950	750	600	450	300

Ventilated Heavy Rib Shroud

NIB	Exc.	V.G.	Good	Fair	Poor
1100	950	750	600	450	300

Model 14/714 Fixed Barrel Service

Same features as .357 Magnum Model 14, without interchangeable barrels. Barrel length 2.5" or 4", with fixed sights. Offered in blued or stainless steel. Weight with barrels: 2.5"—30 oz.; 4"—34 oz. Note: Add 10 percent for stainless steel finish.

NIB	Exc.	V.G.	Good	Fair	Poor
280	240	150	120	100	80

Model 15/715 Fixed Barrel Target

Same as .357 Magnum Model 15, with target sights and grips. Fixed barrel lengths 3" or 5". Available in blued or stainless steel. Weight with barrels: 3"—37 oz.; 5"—42 oz. Note: Add 10 percent for stainless steel finish.

NIB	Exc.	V.G.	Good	Fair	Poor
300	250	160	120	100	80

WESSON, EDWIN
Hartford, Connecticut

Dragoon Antique

A .45-caliber percussion revolver, with 7" round barrel and 6-shot unfluted cylinder. Barrel blued, frame case-hardened. Walnut grips fitted with a brass buttcap. Manufactured in 1848 and 1849. Edwin Wesson also produced many other types of firearms. This dragoon revolver is very rare; values are speculative.

Exc.	Fine	V.G.	Good	Fair	Poor
13500	9500	7250	5000	1750	1220

WESSON, FRANK
Worcester & Springfield, Massachusetts

Manual Extractor Model Pistol Antique

A .22-caliber spur trigger single-shot pistol, with 4" octagonal barrel and thin brass frame. Barrel release located in front of trigger. No markings. Approximately 200 made in 1856 and 1857.

Exc.	Fine	V.G.	Good	Fair	Poor
1400	950	670	400	100	70

First Model Small Frame Pistol Antique

As above, with 3", 3.5" or 6" half-octagonal barrel. Blued, with rosewood or walnut grips. Barrel marked "Frank Wesson Worcester Mass/Pat'd Oct. 25, 1859 & Nov. 11, 1862". Serial numbered from 1 to 2500.

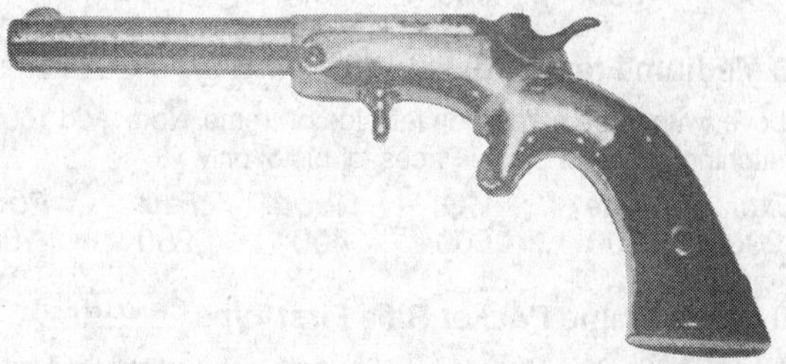

Exc.	Fine	V.G.	Good	Fair	Poor
900	580	400	220	80	50

Second Type Small Frame Pistol Antique

As above, with flat sighted frame and circular sideplate.

Exc.	Fine	V.G.	Good	Fair	Poor
900	580	400	220	80	50

First Model Medium Frame Pistol Antique

As above in .30 or .32 rimfire, with 4" half-octagonal barrel and iron frame. Approximately 1,000 made between 1859 and 1862.

Exc.	Fine	V.G.	Good	Fair	Poor
950	600	410	220	80	50

Medium Frame Second Model Pistol Antique

As above, with a longer spur trigger and slightly wider frame at the barrel hinge. Manufactured from 1862 to 1870.

Exc.	Fine	V.G.	Good	Fair	Poor
950	600	410	220	80	50

Small Frame Pocket Rifle Antique

A .22-caliber spur trigger single-shot pistol, with 6" half-octagonal barrel and narrow brass frame. Adopted for use with a detachable skeleton shoulder stock. Barrel marked "Frank Wesson Worcester, Mass.". Manufactured from 1865 to 1875, with approximately 5,000 made. Note: Add 100 percent for matching shoulder stock. Prices for pistol only.

Exc.	Fine	V.G.	Good	Fair	Poor
1500	920	630	350	100	70

Medium Frame Tip-up Pocket Rifle Antique

As above in .22, .30 or .32 rimfire, with 10" or 12" half-octagonal barrel. Approximately 1,000 made from 1862 to 1870. Note: Add 100 percent for matching shoulder stock. Prices for pistol only.

Exc.	Fine	V.G.	Good	Fair	Poor
1000	650	420	200	80	50

Model 1870 Small Frame Pocket Rifle Antique

As above in .22-caliber, with 10", 12", 15", 18" or 20" half-octagonal barrel that rotates to side for loading. Made with brass or iron frame. Has a half cocked notch on the hammer. Note: Add 100 percent for matching shoulder stock. Prices for pistol only.

Exc.	Fine	V.G.	Good	Fair	Poor
1000	650	420	200	80	50

1870 Medium Frame Pocket Rifle First Type Antique

As above, with slightly larger frame. Chambered for .32 rimfire. Approximately 5,000 made from 1870 to 1893. Note: Add 100 percent for matching shoulder stock. Prices for pistol only.

Exc.	Fine	V.G.	Good	Fair	Poor
1400	850	650	400	250	150

1870 Medium Frame Pocket Rifle Second Type Antique

As above, with an iron frame and push-button half cocked safety. Note: Add 100 percent for matching shoulder stock. Prices for pistol only

Exc.	Fine	V.G.	Good	Fair	Poor
1200	800	600	400	250	150

1870 Medium Frame Pocket Rifle Third Type Antique

As above, with three screws on left side of frame. Note: Add 100 percent for matching shoulder stock. Prices for pistol only.

Exc.	Fine	V.G.	Good	Fair	Poor
1200	800	600	400	250	150

1870 Large Frame Pocket Rifle First Type Antique

As above in .32, .38, .42 or .44 rimfire, with octagonal barrel from 15" to 24" in length. Barrel marked "Frank Wesson Worcester, Mass Patented May 31, 1870". Fewer than 250 made between 1870 and 1880. Note: Add 100 percent for matching shoulder stock. Prices for pistol only.

Exc.	Fine	V.G.	Good	Fair	Poor
2750	1500	1020	550	200	140

1870 Large Frame Pocket Rifle Second Type Antique

As above, with sliding extractor. Note: Add 100 percent for matching shoulder stock. Prices for pistol only.

Exc.	Fine	V.G.	Good	Fair	Poor
2750	1500	1020	550	200	140

Small Frame Superposed Pistol Antique

A .22-caliber spur trigger over/under pocket pistol, with 2" or 2.5" octagonal barrels that revolve. Approximately 3,500 made between 1868 and 1880. On occasion, found with a sliding knife blade mounted on side of the barrels. Note: Add 25 percent for sliding knife blade mounted.

Exc.	Fine	V.G.	Good	Fair	Poor
3000	1750	1300	850	250	170

Medium Frame Superposed Pistol Antique

As above in .32 rimfire, with 2.5" or 3.5" barrels. Like the smaller version, occasionally found with a sliding knife blade mounted on side of the barrels. Manufactured from 1868 to 1880. Note: Add 25 percent for sliding knife blade mounted.

First Type Marked "Patent Applied For" Superposed Pistol Antique

Exc.	Fine	V.G.	Good	Fair	Poor
2500	1250	820	400	100	70

Second Type Marked "Patent December 15, 1868" Superposed Pistol Antique

Exc.	Fine	V.G.	Good	Fair	Poor
2450	1200	800	400	100	70

Third Type Full-Length Fluted Barrels Superposed Pistol Antique

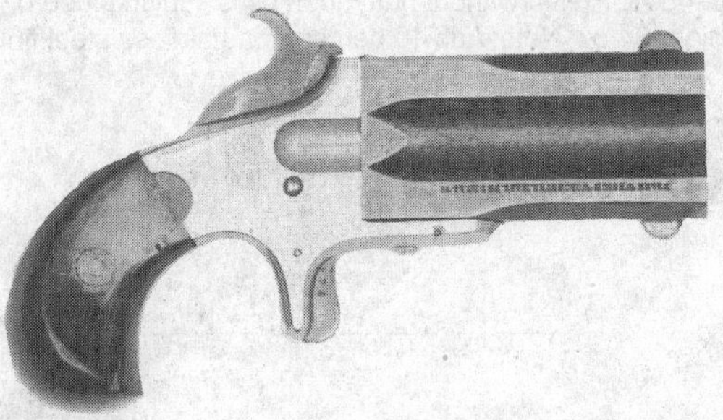

Courtesy W.P. Hallstein III and son Chip

Exc.	Fine	V.G.	Good	Fair	Poor
2750	1500	970	450	150	100

Large Frame Superposed Pistol Antique

As above in .41 rimfire, with 3" octagonal barrel. Fitted with a sliding knife blade. Approximately 2,000 made from 1868 to 1880.

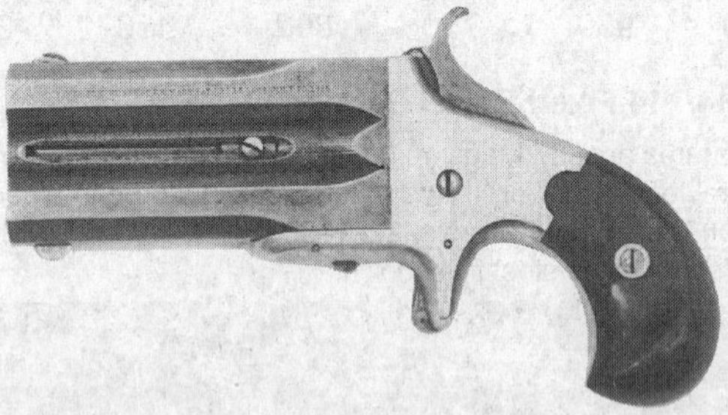

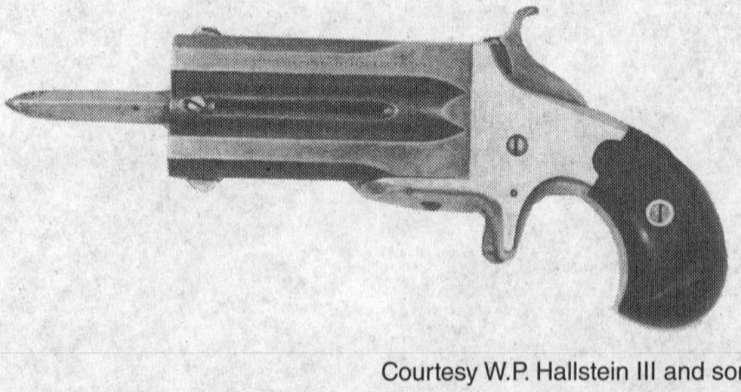

Courtesy W.P. Hallstein III and son Chip

Exc.	Fine	V.G.	Good	Fair	Poor
4200	2750	2000	1250	400	280

No. 1 Long Range Rifle Antique

A .44-100 or .45-100 caliber single-shot dropping block rifle, with 34" octagonal barrel. Blued, with checkered walnut stock. Barrel marked "F. Wesson Mfr. Worcester, Mass. Long Range Rifle Creedmoor". Manufactured in 1876.

Exc.	Fine	V.G.	Good	Fair	Poor
15000	7000	3250	2000	500	350

No. 2 Mid-Range or Hunting Rifle Antique

Similar to above, with firing pin located in a bolster on right side of the receiver. Triggerguard has a rear finger loop. Standard barrel lengths 28", 32" and 34"; and marked "F. Wesson Maker Worcester, Mass.". The 32" and 34" barrels are occasionally marked "Long Range Rifle Creedmoor". Approximately 100 made.

Courtesy Buffalo Bill Historical Center, Cody, Wyoming

Exc.	Fine	V.G.	Good	Fair	Poor
12000	5000	2750	1750	500	350

No. 2 Sporting Rifle Antique

A .38-100, .40-100 or .45-100 caliber single-shot dropping barrel-action rifle. Barrels ranging from 28" to 34" in length. Approximately 25 made.

Courtesy Buffalo Bill Historical Center, Cody, Wyoming

Exc.	*Fine*	*V.G.*	*Good*	*Fair*	*Poor*
8250	3750	2750	1750	500	350

Two-Trigger Military Carbine Antique

Fitted with 24" barrel, with sling swivels. Chambered for .44-caliber rimfire cartridge. Approximately 4,500 manufactured. Note: Add 100 percent for martially marked examples.

Exc.	*Fine*	*V.G.*	*Good*	*Fair*	*Poor*
4000	2000	1200	700	500	350

WESSON & LEAVITT

Chicopee Falls, Massachusetts

See MASSACHUSETTS ARMS CO.

WESTERN ARMS

See—BACON ARMS CO.

WESTERN ARMS CORPORATION

See—ITHACA GUN CO.

WESTERN FIELD

Montgomery Ward

Western Field is the trade name used by Montgomery Ward & Company on arms that they retail. See Firearms Trade Names list at the end of this book.

WESTLEY RICHARDS & CO., LTD.

Birmingham, England

A wide variety of firearms have been produced by this company since its founding. Presently, it produces boxlock and sidelock double-barrel shotguns of both side-by-side and over/under form, bolt-action rifles and double-barrel rifles. Prospective purchasers are advised to secure individual appraisals prior to acquisition.

B Model SxS Boxlock, Pre-WWII

Note: Add 50 percent for 20-gauge; 80 percent for 28-gauge.

NIB	*Exc.*	*V.G.*	*Good*	*Fair*	*Poor*
5000	4250	3500	2800	—	—

Best Quality Sidelock, Current Model

Deluxe Sidelock

NIB	*Exc.*	*V.G.*	*Good*	*Fair*	*Poor*
30000	26500	22500	17500	—	—

Magazine Rifle

NIB	*Exc.*	*V.G.*	*Good*	*Fair*	*Poor*
12500	10000	8500	7250	—	—

Boxlock Double Rifle

NIB	*Exc.*	*V.G.*	*Good*	*Fair*	*Poor*
39000	33000	26500	22000	—	—

Best Quality Over/Under Shotgun, Current Model

NIB	*Exc.*	*V.G.*	*Good*	*Fair*	*Poor*
55000	47500	40000	32000	—	—

WHITE, ROLLIN

Lowell, Massachusetts

Pocket Pistol Antique

A .32 or .38 rimfire spur trigger single-shot pistol, with 3" or 5" octagonal barrel. Brass or iron frames, with walnut grips. The .38-caliber version with 5" barrel was not produced in large quantities, therefore worth approximately 25 percent more than values listed. Barrels marked "Rollin White Arms Co., Lowell, Mass.".

Exc.	*Fine*	*V.G.*	*Good*	*Fair*	*Poor*
1500	750	550	350	150	100

Pocket Revolver Antique

A .22-caliber spur trigger revolver, with 3.25" octagonal barrel and 7-shot cylinder. Brass frame silver-plated, barrel blued and grips of walnut. Revolver marked in a variety of ways including: "Rollin White Arms Co., Lowell, Mass."; "Lowell Arms Co., Lowell, Mass."; or "Made for Smith & Wesson by Rollin White Arms Co., Lowell, Mass.". Approximately 10,000 made during late 1860s.

Exc.	*Fine*	*V.G.*	*Good*	*Fair*	*Poor*
780	600	420	250	80	50

WHITNEY ARMS COMPANY

ELI WHITNEY, SR./P. & E.W. BLAKE/ELI WHITNEY, JR.

As the United States' first major commercial arms maker, Eli Whitney's New Haven plant, which began production in 1798 and continued under family control for the next 90 years, was one of the more important American arms manufactories of the 19th century. Its products, accordingly, are eminently collectible. Moreover, during its 90 years of operation, Whitney clan produced a number of unusual arms, some exact copies of regulation U.S. martial longarms, other variations and derivatives of U.S. and foreign longarms, a variety of percussion revolvers and finally a variety of single-shot and repeating breech-loading rifles in an attempt to capture a portion of the burgeoning market in these cartridge arms during the post-Civil War period. Contrary to the prevailing myth, Eli Whitney Sr., who also invented the cotton gin, did NOT perfect a system of interchangeability of parts in the arms industry. His contributions in this line were more as a propagandist for the concept that was brought to fruition by others, notably Simeon North and John Hall.

Eli Whitney, Sr. Armory Muskets, 1798-1824. 1798 U.S. Contract Muskets, Types I-IV (Antique)

On January 14, 1798, Eli Whitney Sr., having convinced the U.S. War Department that he could mass-produce interchangeable musket parts, was awarded a contract for 10,000 muskets following the "Charlesville" (French M1766) pattern, then also being copied at the newly opened Springfield Armory and most of the U.S. musket contractors. Whitney's 1798 contract muskets measure between 58.875" and 57.75" in overall length, with longer arms delivered earlier. The .69-caliber smoothbore barrels measure approximately 44", though most are shy of that length by anywhere from .0625" to a maximum of 1.25". Lockplates are flat with a beveled edge and marked "U.STATES" in a curve on the pointed tail, with a perched eagle with down folded wings over "NEW HAVEN" forward of the cock. Four differences in material and manner of attachment of the pan distinguish subtypes: first delivery of 500 muskets in September, 1801 had an integral faceted iron pan (Type I); second delivery of 500 muskets in June, 1802 also had faceted iron pans, but were detachable (Type II); 1,000 muskets delivered in September, 1802 and March, 1803 had faceted detachable pans, but these were made of brass instead of iron (Type III); final 8,000 muskets delivered between 1803 and 1809, had detachable brass pans with a rounded bottom that Whitney copied from French M1777 musket (Type IV) and a rounded cock, also copied from French M1777 musket. Generally speaking, due to the limited production of Types I - III, they should command a higher price; prices are given for the more common Type IV 1798 contract musket. It should be noted however, that about 1804 Whitney delivered 112 Type IV muskets to Connecticut's "1st Company of Governor's Foot Guards". Although similar to Type IV musket, these 112 arms are distinguished by the absence of "U.STATES" on the tail of the lock and addition of the name "CONNECTICUT" to left sideplate. Such an arm should demand a considerable premium over usual Type IV musket.

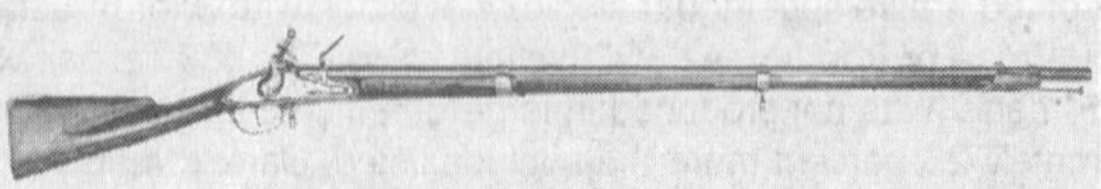

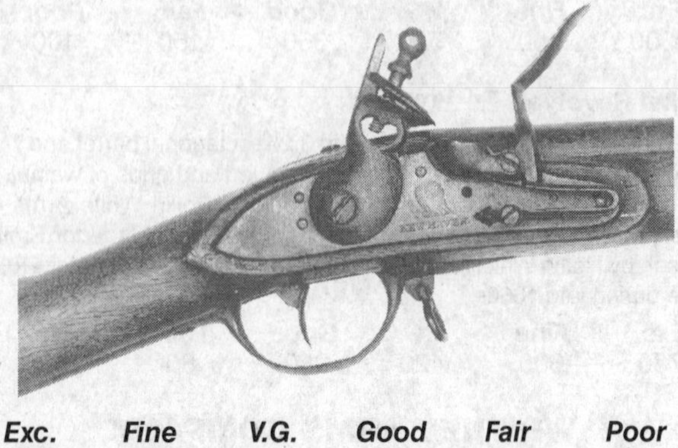

Exc.	Fine	V.G.	Good	Fair	Poor
7500	4500	3250	2000	1000	500

Whitney Connecticut, New York, and U.S. 1812 Contract Muskets (Antique)

In 1808, Whitney received a contract from the state of New York for 2,000 muskets. In 1810, he received a second contract from the same source for an additional 2,000 muskets, all of which were eventually delivered by mid-1813. In the interim, in 1809, state of Connecticut contracted with Whitney to deliver 700 muskets per year over the next three years. With the outbreak of the War of 1812, in July, 1812, a contract was let to Eli Whitney for 15,000 muskets (later extended by another 3,000 muskets), conforming to the pattern he had made for the state of New York, but with 42" long barrels. All of these contract muskets shared most of the same features. Overall length was 58". The .69-caliber smoothbore barrel was nominally 42", though the two state contracts did not rigidly enforce that dimension. Lockplate of these muskets bore inscription "NEW HAVEN" within a curving scroll forward of the cock. Like Type III 1798 U.S. contract muskets, lockplates incorporated a detachable round-bottomed brass pan and a round faced cock. Stock was distinguished by having a low, virtually nonexistent comb similar to that of 1816 musket pattern. New York state contract muskets are distinguished by having the state ownership mark "SNY" on axis of barrel near the breech. (It should be noted that first 1,000 muskets delivered under U.S. 1812 contract were also delivered to New York, but these have the mark across the breech at right angles to axis of the barrel). Connecticut contract muskets are distinguishable by having state-ownership mark "S.C." (for "state of Connecticut" on barrel and top of the comb of the stock). On Connecticut muskets in better condition, Connecticut coat of arms (a shield with three clusters of grape vines) should also be visible struck into the wood on left side of the musket opposite the lock. Verifiable Connecticut and New York contract muskets should bring a premium over U.S. contract muskets.

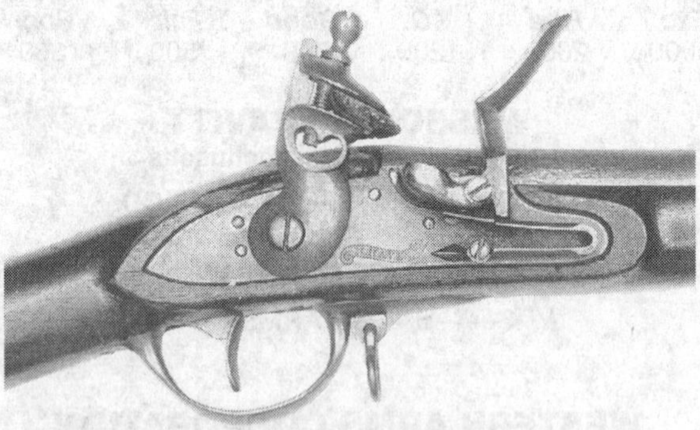

Exc.	Fine	V.G.	Good	Fair	Poor
6000	3250	2370	1500	500	350

Whitney (and P. & E.W. Blake) U.S. M1816/1822 Contract Muskets (Antique)

U.S. M1816/1822 muskets manufactured at Whitney's Armory were identical to those produced at U.S. Armories at Springfield and Harpers Ferry. Overall length was 57.75". The 42" long, .69-caliber smoothbore barrels were finished with a browning solution until 1831; after that date metal was left in polished "bright". Stock and lock reflect Whitney's earlier attempts to impart his design elements into the U.S. patterns. Stock had low comb of his M1812 musket and lock incorporated rounded cock and round bottomed brass pan that he had championed from French M1777 musket. Lock markings varied during the period that this arm was produced, though all were marked on the pointed tail with a vertical stamp: "NEW HAVEN" arced around date (1825-1830), or in three vertical lines: "NEW / HAVEN / (date: 1831-1842)". Those made between 1825 and 1830, under direct supervision of Whitney's nephews, bore two line mark "U.S. / P. & E.W. BLAKE" forward of cock; those made from 1830 to 1837 bear "U.S" over "E. WHITNEY" with a crossed arrow and olive branch between; after 1837, crossed arrow and olive branch motif was eliminated in favor of the simple two lines. In addition to Whitney Armory's federal contracts, Whitney executed at least one contract with the state of South Carolina in mid-1830s for an estimated 800 to 2,000 muskets. Basically identical in configuration to federal contract muskets, South Carolina muskets were distinguished by the substitution of "S.C." for "U.S." over "E. WHITNEY" stamp on the lockplate. They also bear state ownership mark "So. CAROLINA" on top of the barrel. Due to their relative rarity and Confederate usage (especially if altered to percussion by means of a brazed bolster), South Carolina contract arms should bring a considerable premium.

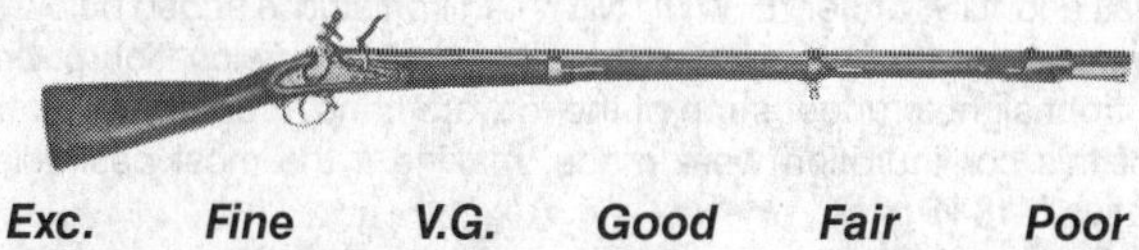

Exc.	Fine	V.G.	Good	Fair	Poor
6500	3500	2500	1500	500	350

Whitney Armory U.S. M1816/M1822 Muskets, Flintlock or Altered to Percussion and Adapted with "Sea Fencible" Heavy Buttplates (Antique)

A number of Whitney U.S. M1816/M1822 muskets were delivered to Commonwealth of Massachusetts under terms of the 1808 Militia Act. Many of these were subsequently altered to percussion at Watertown Arsenal near Boston for the state after 1850. At some time in their career, both flintlock arms and those that had been altered to percussion were adapted to a heavy brass buttplate, with a peculiar knob at its heel. In the process, buttstock was usually narrowed to conform to width of the new buttplate; because many of the muskets encountered with this buttplate bore the inspection mark of Samuel Fuller (SF/V" within a lozenge), these arms were initially considered to have been made for the Massachusetts "Sea Fencible" organizations formed during and after the War of 1812. That appellation, however, has been dismissed, although the exact purpose of the new buttplate and date of its application are not known. These buttplates are usually (but not necessarily) found on Whitney contract muskets and invariably are marked with Massachusetts state ownership mark "MS" on the barrel as well as rack numbers on tang of the buttplate itself. Despite the unknown purpose of these arms, they command a considerable premium over standard flintlock or altered to percussion Whitney muskets.

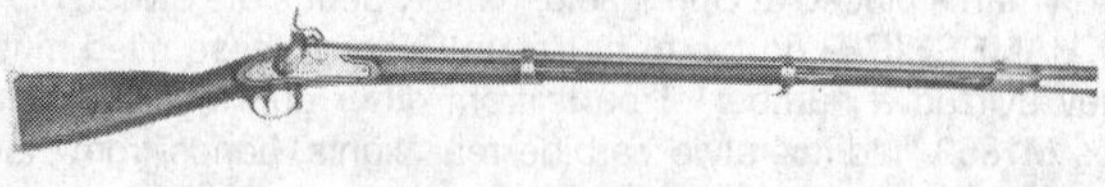

Exc.	Fine	V.G.	Good	Fair	Poor
6500	3500	2370	1250	400	280

Whitney Armory U.S. M1816/M1822 Muskets, Altered to Percussion

From 1850 through 1856, many of the contract muskets in store at U.S. arsenals were altered from flintlock to percussion by means of "Belgian" or "cone-in barrel" method. System of alteration involved removal of flintlock battery from the lock, filling in the screw holes from those parts, substituting a percussion hammer for the cock, plugging the vent, removing the breech plug so as to "upset" the upper right-hand side top of barrel, drilling and threading the "upset" section for a cone, reinserting breech plug and screwing in a new percussion cone. The percussion musket was effective, but the barrel was considerably weakened by this process. While some were rifled during the American Civil War, most saw service in that conflict as smoothbores. As a general rule, muskets so altered generally command about one-third the price of the arm in original flintlock. Exceptions are those with state ownership marks (e.g., "OHIO" in the stock), with regimental marks, or with so-called "Sea Fencible" buttplate.

Whitney Armory Muskets, 1825-1842

Eli Whitney died in 1825. Although he had a son destined to take over the family business, Eli Whitney Jr. was only 5 years old when his father passed away and could not assume legal possession until he turned 21 in 1842. In the interim, company was administered by senior Whitney's trustees, Henry Edwards and James Goodrich, while the plant itself was run by Whitney's nephews, Philo and Eli Whitney Blake. During their control of the factory, three contracts were fulfilled for the U.S. government: one awarded in August, 1822 for 15,000 muskets (delivered between 1826 and 1830); second awarded in March, 1830 for 8,750 muskets (delivered between 1831 and 1836); final contract in January, 1840 for 3,000 muskets (delivered between 1840 and 1842). An additional 6,750 were delivered under annual allotments granted by the War Department between 1835 and 1839, over and above contracts for distribution to states under the 1808 Militia Act. Although the 1840 contract had originally called for U.S. M1840 muskets, in April of that year, the contract was altered so that Whitney's plant could continue to deliver what it had delivered consistently from 1824, the U.S. M1816/1822 flintlock musket.

Eli Whitney, Jr. Armory Rifles and Rifle-Muskets, 1842-1865

Upon reaching the age of 21 in 1842, Eli Whitney Jr. assumed command of his late father's gun making empire. Although he realized that the armory required updating to meet improved tolerances adopted by the U.S. War Department, he also realized that a profit might be made in turning out arms of lesser standards for independent sale to militia or the states. As a result, younger Whitney's product line included not only several of the regulation U.S. longarms, but also a number of "good and serviceable" militia arms, including:

Whitney U.S. M1841 Contract Rifle (unaltered) (Antique)

Between 1842 and 1855, Eli Whitney Jr. received five contracts from the U.S. War Department to manufacture newly adopted U.S. M1841 percussion rifle: 7,500 in October, 1842 (delivered between 1844 and 1847); 7,500 in March, 1848, subsequently extended to 10,000 in January, 1849 (delivered between 1849 and 1853) 5,000 (previously contracted for by Edward K. Tryon) in October, 1848 (delivered contiguous with 1848 contract for 10,000); 5,000 in 1853 (delivered between 1853 and 1855); and 100 in 1855 (delivered that year). All except the final 1,100 delivered in 1855 conformed to the model made at Harpers Ferry, and of those 1,100, the only difference of 500 of them was the ramrod. This rifle was 49" in length overall, having a 33" long browned barrel, with .54-caliber rifled (7-groove) bore. Barrel bears stamp of inspection at the breech, usually "U S /(inspectors' initials) / P", while the left flat (after mid-1848 for Whitney rifles) should also bear stamping "STEEL" to indicate the barrel had been rolled from "cast steel". Furniture is brass, buttplate bearing stamped letters "U S". Lockplate is flat with a beveled edge and bears horizontal two line inscription "E. WHITNEY" / "U S" forward of the hammer and vertical two line inscription "N. HAVEN" / (date) on the tail. (Date also appears on breech plug tang). As originally made, M1841 rifle was not adapted for a bayonet, though several modifications were made to the rifle between 1855 and 1862 to affect that adaptation.

Exc.	Fine	V.G.	Good	Fair	Poor
7500	4750	3250	1750	500	350

Whitney U.S. M1841/1855 Contract Rifle, Adapted to Saber Bayonet and Long Range Sights (Antique)

Before the final 600 rifles (of 2,600 made in 1855) left the factory, U.S. War Department contracted with Whitney to bring them up to the standards of modified U.S. M1841 rifle then being produced or adapted at Harpers Ferry Armory. Adaptation was two fold. First, a long range rear "ladder" style rear sight having a 2..25" base was soldered to top of the barrel; then a .5" long bayonet lug with 1" guide was brazed to right side of the barrel, 2.5" from muzzle. To permit disassembly, old front band was removed and replaced with a shortened version. A new ramrod (also applied to 500 rifles without this adaptation) having an integral iron head cupped for newly adopted "Minie ball" replaced flat brass headed ramrod to complete the process; rifle remained in .54-caliber with 7-grooves. Neither was the front sight modified. Bayonets were furnished by Ames Manufacturing Company on a separate contract. Rifles so adapted at Whitney Armory are among the rarer variants of U.S. M1841 line and prices reflect that rarity.

Exc.	Fine	V.G.	Good	Fair	Poor
7500	4750	3250	1750	650	450

Whitney U.S. M1841 Contract Rifles, Adapted to Saber Bayonets and Long Range Rear Sights (Colt 1862 Adaptation) Antique

A large number of unaltered U.S. M1841 rifles remained on hand in U.S. Arsenals when the Civil War broke out. Primarily those of Whitney's and Robbins & Lawrence's manufacture. To upgrade these rifles, revolver maker, Samuel Colt arranged to purchase 10,500 and adapt them to bayonets and long-range sights. Sight that he affixed consisted of two leaf rear sight he had been using on his revolving rifles, with one leaf flopping forward and one flopping backward from the 100 yard block. Saber bayonet lug he attached consisted of a blued clamping ring with integral .5" long lug attached that could fasten to barrel so the lug projected from the right side. These lugs were numbered both to bayonet and rifle's barrel, the number appearing on lower surface of barrel just behind the location of clamping ring. Colt also bored the rifles up to .58-caliber, leaving some with 7-grooves but re-rifling others with 3 wide grooves. An estimated half of the 10,200 rifles so modified by Colt were of Whitney's earlier production. Due to the Colt association, rifles so modified usually command slightly higher prices than other Civil War adaptations for saber or socket bayonets.

Exc.	Fine	V.G.	Good	Fair	Poor
7500	4750	3250	1750	650	450

Whitney South Carolina Contract M1841 Rifle Antique

To meet perceived needs of South Carolina, during anti-slavery debates following Mexican War Annexation, Whitney produced a variant of U.S. M1841 rifle for that state, delivering only 274 in 1849. Markings of this rifle differed only in having letters "S C" on the plate beneath "E. WHITNEY" stamp. Because South Carolina had previously contracted for 1,000 variant M1841 rifles from William Glaze & Co. in 1853 which accepted a socket bayonet, Whitney provided 274, 1849 dated rifles with that provision also, although the lug was located under the barrel instead of atop it. Because the socket bayonet dominated the forward 3" of the barrel, front sight was relocated to top of upper strap of the front band. Rifles from this contract are exceedingly rare.

Exc.	Fine	V.G.	Good	Fair	Poor
10000	6500	4870	3250	950	660

Whitney "Good & Serviceable" M1841 Derivatives Antique

From parts or entire rifles rejected from his federal contracts for U.S. M1841 rifles, between 1848 and 1860, Eli Whitney Jr. assembled a number of rifles similar in overall characteristics to federal contract rifles, but differing both in quantity and number of minor details. At least four variations were produced between 1855 and 1862 and sold to various states or independent militia companies. Distinguishing characteristics of these four are:

Type I: M1841 rifle adapted to saber bayonet, but not to long range sights. A .5 long saber bayonet lug (with/without 1" guide) brazed to right side of the barrel; long front band replaced with short double strapped band left over from 1855 contract. Some of this type (without 1" guide) are known with "OHIO" state ownership marks and are thought to be from among 420 purchased by the state in 1861 from Schuyler, Hartley & Graham. Examples are known with lockplate dated 1855, without any date or "US" stamp below "E. WHITNEY".

Type II: M1841 rifle adapted to saber bayonet and Sharps long range sight. These rifles also bear .5" brazed saber bayonet lug (with 1" guide) and short front band, but they also have Sharps M1853 "ladder" rear sight added in lieu of standard notched iron block. Moreover, rifles in this configuration lack the brass patchbox lid and its underlying cavity for implements and greased patches.

Type III: M1841 rifle adapted to socket bayonet and Sharps long range sight. These late-production (1859-1860) derivatives of M1841 rifle are adapted to Sharps long-range sight used on Type II rifles but have a patchbox. Unlike standard production, however, it is covered with an iron lid and hinge. Triggerguard strap is also iron. Lock plates delete both date from tail and "US" under "E. WHITNEY". An iron stud is added below barrel near muzzle for a socket bayonet, necessitating relocation of brass blade front sight to upper strap of the forward band. Probably fewer than 100 of this configuration were made, making it the most desirable of derivative M1841 rifles.

Type IV: M1841 rifle unadapted using modified parts. Rifles of this configuration use same markings as Type III rifles, but delete entirely the patchbox and its lid (like Type II rifles). Triggerguard strap is iron and lock screws seem to be the same as Whitney used for his Whitney short Enfield derivative rifles. It is suspected that these rifles were purchased from New York dealers and sold to Georgia during the secession crisis of 1860-1861, thereby enhancing their collector's value, though in general Whitney M1841 derivative rifles are equal in pricing:

Exc.	Fine	V.G.	Good	Fair	Poor
6500	3250	2250	1250	500	350

Whitney M1842 Rifled Musket Derivative Antique

Using rejected U.S. M1842 barrels sold at auction by Springfield Armory, Whitney assembled approximately 2,000 .69-caliber rifled muskets that he exchanged with the state of New Hampshire in 1858 for a number of old flintlock muskets owned by that state. These rifled muskets exhibit a number of anomalies from U.S. M1842 musket, although overall length (57.75") and barrel length (42") remain the same as that musket, the bores are rifles with 7 narrow grooves. In addition to dates and inspection marks placed at Springfield, usually bear state ownership mark "NEW HAMPSHIRE" on top of barrel. In finishing these rifled muskets, Whitney utilized a number of parts from other gun makers, including Sharps M1853 "ladder" style carbine rear sights, bands from Robbins & Lawrence P1853 Enfield rifle-musket contract and internal lock parts remaining from his M1841 rifles. Parts that are unique to these arms include iron nosecap and flat lockplate. Lockplates are unmarked, but barrels usually show a letter/number code common to Whitney's production during this period. Despite a production of approximately 2,000 muskets, survival rate for this type of arm is quite low.

Exc.	Fine	V.G.	Good	Fair	Poor
6500	3250	2250	1250	400	280

Whitney P1853 "Long Enfield" Rifle-Musket Derivative Antique

Having secured a number of bands and other furniture from Robbins & Lawrence contract for P1853 Enfield rifle-muskets, about 1859 Whitney developed a derivative of that arm that combined those bands with a 40 barrel in .58-caliber and rifled with 7-grooves that basically resembled the configuration of U.S. M1855 rifle-musket, a copy of which Whitney was also making. The 56" long rifle-musket that resulted was sold to state militia companies and two states: Maryland purchasing 2,000; and Georgia contracting for 1,700 (of which 1,225 were delivered). Although several components of furniture were from Robbins & Lawrence contract, nosecap was pewter (Enfield style), iron buttplate and brass triggerguard (bow/iron strap) were of a style peculiar to Whitney' Enfield series. Rear sight resembled ladder pattern of U.S. M1855 rifle-musket. Unique flat and unbeveled lockplate simply bears one line stamp "E. WHITNEY" forward of the hammer.

Exc.	Fine	V.G.	Good	Fair	Poor
6500	3250	2250	1250	600	420

Whitney P1853 "Short Enfield" Rifle Derivative (Antique)

At the same time Whitney developed his Long Enfield" Rifle-Musket Derivative, he also prepared a short version of it, similar to British P1856 sergeant's rifle. Having an overall length of 49", rifle version had 33" long barrel in .58-caliber and rifled with 7-grooves like the rifle-musket. Furniture was basically same as rifle-musket as well, with a pewter nosecap, iron buttplate and combination brass bow and iron strap triggerguard (although some variants are known with all brass P1853 triggerguards). Two iron bands were from Robbins & Lawrence contract salvage, as were brass lock screw washers. Unique flat and unbeveled lockplate are same style used on "Long Enfield" Rifle-Musket Derivative and is similarly marked "E. WHITNEY" forward of the hammer. In manufacture of this rifle, four variants evolved as follows:

Type I: Buttstock incorporated an oval iron patchbox; front and rear sights were standard U.S. M1841 configuration and no provision was made for a saber bayonet.

Type II: Buttstock continued to incorporate an oval iron patchbox; rear sight was now the long range "ladder" type on a 2.3125" base as used on "Long Enfield" Rifle-Musket Derivative. Front sight was an iron block, with integral blade. A .5" long saber bayonet lug was added to right side of the barrel.

Type III: Oval iron patchbox was deleted from the buttstock. Front and rear sights remain as in Type II, as does bayonet lug.

Type IV. Identical to Type III, with a new single leaf rear sight on a 1.25" long base.

Total production of these rifles is estimated to have been between 800 and 1,000, with approximately half that number going to southern states. Prices should not vary between the four types; however, confirmed Confederate usage will increase the value significantly.

Exc.	Fine	V.G.	Good	Fair	Poor
8500	4250	3120	2000	600	420

Whitney M1855 Rifle Derivative (Antique)

At the same time Whitney advertised his Enfield derivative series of rifle-muskets and rifles, he also indicated the availability of a short rifle with saber bayonet. This rifle combined rejected barrels (made at Harpers Ferry in 1858 for U.S. M1855 rifles), with rejected unmilled Maynard tape primer lockplates that had been shaved of their top "hump", marked forward of hammer with single line stamp, "E. WHITNEY". Buttplate and triggerguard also conform to U.S. M1855 rifle, but bands are brass remaining from Whitney's M1841/1855 rifle contract. Early in production, these rifles used round brass lock screw washers following M1855 pattern; later production used winged brass lock screw washers that Whitney inherited from Robbins & Lawrence P1853 rifle-musket contract, which he used on his Enfield series derivatives. At least two patterns of saber bayonet were used on this rifle.

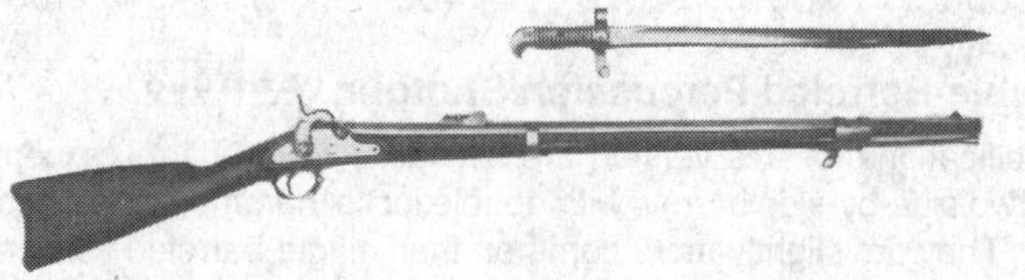

Exc.	Fine	V.G.	Good	Fair	Poor
7000	3500	2370	1250	500	350

Whitney M1855 Rifle-Musket Derivative (Antique)

In 1861, Whitney accepted a U.S. contract to produce 40,000 U.S. "M1855" rifle-muskets. What Whitney had in mind under this contract and what the War Department demanded were two different arms. Whitney's product was similar to U.S. M1855 rifle-musket, but differed in a number of respects. The 40" barrel was .58-caliber, but rifled with 7- rather than 3-grooves and adapted to English P1853 socket bayonet he had been using on his Enfield derivative rifle-muskets. Initial rear sight, while similar to U.S. M1855 type, was slightly shorter having a 2.3125" base. (On later production, Whitney substituted a shorter 1.25" long base, with a single pierced leaf sight). Nosecap was made of pewter and followed Enfield pattern rather than being malleable iron of U.S. M1855 pattern. On later production, Whitney also substituted brass winged lock screw washers from his Enfield derivative series. Lockplates for these arms were drawn from complete Maynard locks made at the federal armories in 1858 and 1859, but later rejected for flaws. Upon these plates Whitney stamped "E. WHITNEY / N. HAVEN", as on his early Connecticut contract M1861 derivative rifle-muskets. Except for the letter/number code, the barrels are unmarked. Examples are known whose stocks bear indications of issue to 8th Connecticut Infantry during the Civil War, suggesting Whitney may have sold the few made to Connecticut under his first state contract. Arms with these regimental marks should command a premium over unmarked arms.

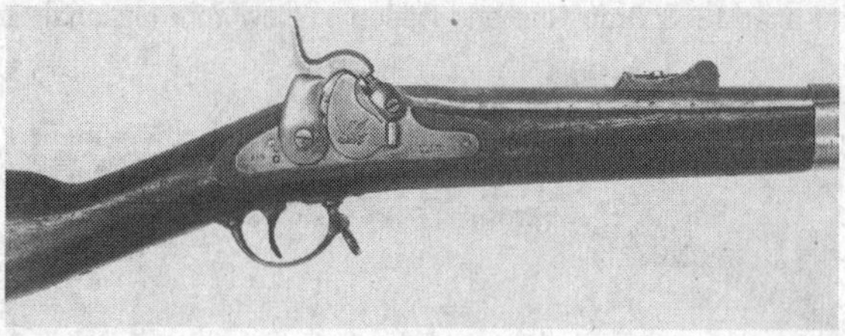

Exc.	Fine	V.G.	Good	Fair	Poor
7000	3500	2370	1250	500	350

Whitney M1861 Connecticut Contract Rifle-Musket Derivative (Antique)

In 1861 and 1862, Eli Whitney Jr. entered into two contracts with his home state of Connecticut for respectively 6,000 and 8,000 rifle-muskets, generally conforming to U.S. M1861 rifle-musket. A number of exceptions to U.S. model, however, were permitted. On the first contract, 40" barrels were in .58-caliber, but were made with 7-groove rifling instead of 3-groove; on the second contract, arms were made with 3-groove rifling. Nosecaps for both contracts were of U.S. M1855/1861 pattern, but were cast in pewter instead of malleable iron. An exception was also permitted in the rear sights, which initially were same 1.25" long base with pierced single leaf that Whitney had used on his Type IV short Enfield derivative rifles, though later the base was changed to conform to the pattern adopted for U.S. M1861 rifle-musket, but still retaining the single leaf. Lockplates were M1861-style marked forward of the hammer "E. WHITNEY / N. HAVEN" on early production and with an eagle surmounting a panoply of flags and trophies over "WHITNEYVILLE" on later production. Barrels bore typical Whitney letter/number code and were adapted to Enfield pattern socket bayonets rather than U.S. M1855 socket bayonets. Later production occasionally bears inspection letters "G.W.Q.".

Exc.	Fine	V.G.	Good	Fair	Poor
6000	2750	1950	1150	400	280

Whitney "High Humpback" Lockplate M1861 Rifle-Musket Derivative (Antique)

With the completion of his Connecticut contracts, Whitney combined excess parts from its production with some of the unmilled and unshaved lockplates that he still had on hand from his M1855 Rifle Derivatives. The 56 long rifle-muskets that resulted have 40" barrels in .58-caliber, with 3-groove rifling and a rear sight that conforms to U.S. M1861 pattern that Whitney began making in 1863. Flat beveled unmilled lockplates bear two line stamp "E. WHITNEY / N. HAVEN" that Whitney had used on his M1855 rifle-musket derivative and on early M1861 Connecticut contract rifle-muskets, but showing considerable wear, to the extent that the second line is often incomplete or missing entirely. Photograph evidence indicates that the 21st Connecticut Infantry received some of these rifle-muskets. They are often mistaken as a southern purchase, which artificially raises the asking prices.

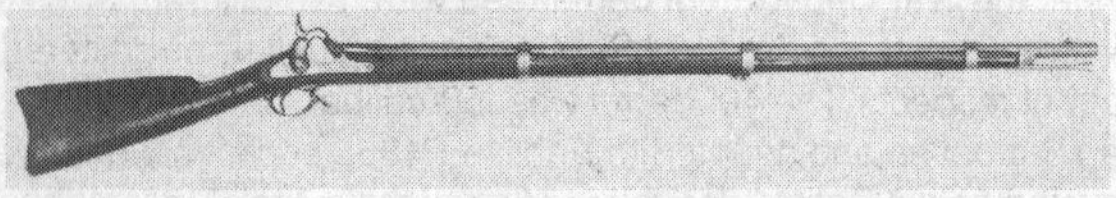

Exc.	Fine	V.G.	Good	Fair	Poor
7000	3250	2250	1250	500	350

Whitney "Manton" M1861 Rifle-Musket Derivative Antique

In order to dispose of some of his inferior arms from the second Connecticut state contract, Whitney assembled at least 1,300 bearing a fictitious Old English lock stamp Manton" forward of hammer and date "1862" on its tail. In most respects, this arm resembled U.S. M1861 rifle-musket complete with 3-groove rifling in .58-caliber 40" barrel with typical Whitney letter/number code near the muzzle (often marked "G.W.Q." on its left flat). Nosecaps, in typical Whitney style, were cast from pewter instead of being formed from malleable iron. Rear sight closely follows M1861 pattern, but lacks the step on its side walls since it utilized a simple pierced leaf instead of compound double leaf of M1861 rifle-musket. These arms were disposed of in the New York City market after 1863 Draft Riot and issued to New York National Guard.

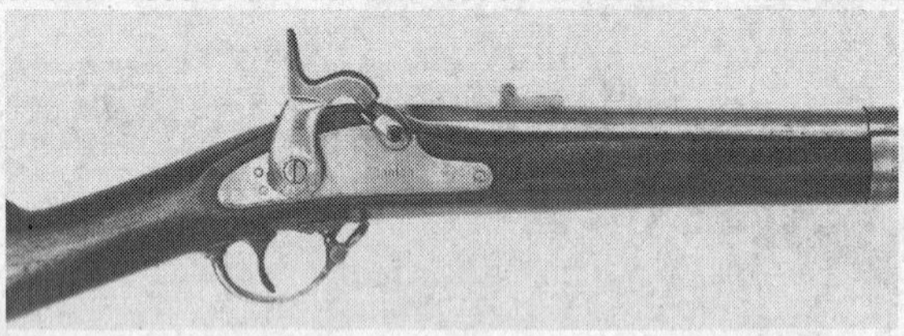

Exc.	Fine	V.G.	Good	Fair	Poor
8250	4250	3120	2000	600	420

Whitney "Direct Vent" M1861 Rifle-Musket Derivatives Antique

In his continued efforts to dispose of surplus and rejected parts from his Connecticut and federal contracts, Whitney devised in 1863 a rifle-musket generally conforming to M1861 rifle-musket except in two notable features. The bolster, instead of projecting considerably away from the barrel and having a clean-out screw was relatively short and flat faced. Process of making this bolster eliminated one production sequence, since it was not possible to drill the hole for the cone directly to the barrel. To accommodate the new cone position, lockplates were made flat without the bevel and in-letted flush with the stock. Lockplates bear eagle surmounting the panoply of flags and trophies over WHITNEYVILLE" stamp forward of hammer and are known with "1863" on the tail or without any date. Rear sight same as used on "Manton" rifle-musket derivative. Arms with barrels than 40", 39" and 30" exist, all in .58-caliber with 3-groove rifling; however, shortest of these may be post-war modifications for cadet use. Quantities made are not known, but surviving examples suggest limited production, probably to use faulty parts from 1863 federal contract.

Exc.	Fine	V.G.	Good	Fair	Poor
7000	3250	2250	1250	400	280

Whitney U.S. M1861 Contract Rifle-Musket Antique

In October 1863, Whitney secured a contract with U.S. War Department to produce 15,000 U.S. M1861 rifle-muskets. Arms manufactured under this contract conform in all respects to Springfield Model adopted in 1861. The 40" barrel in .58-caliber and rifled with 3-grooves; rear sight conforms to two-leaf model with stepped side walls. Nosecap is M1861 style and made of malleable iron. Socket bayonets furnished with them conform to U.S. M1855/M1861 pattern. Marks include "US" on buttplate and standard inspection marks on barrel and stock. Lockplate marked with eagle surmounting letters "US" forward of hammer and "WHITNEYVILLE" on forward projection of plate; date, "1863" or "1864" stamped on tail of plate.

Exc.	Fine	V.G.	Good	Fair	Poor
7000	3250	2250	1250	400	280

Whitney U.S. Navy Contract Rifle Antique

In July 1861, Whitney entered a contact with U.S. Navy to produce 10,000 rifles of "Plymouth Pattern". So called after U.S. Navy warship, whereupon the first Harpers Ferry trial rifles had been developed. New Navy rifle borrowed many of its characteristics from French M1846 "carbine a tige". Overall length 50" with 34" long barrel bearing a saber bayonet lug, with guide extending nearly to the muzzle on its right side. Bore was .69-caliber, rifled with 3 broad lands and grooves. Rear sight copied French M1846 and M1859 styles, i.e. it has an elevating ladder but no sidewalls. On early production, sights are serially numbered to rifle's serial number (appearing on breech plug tang). Barrels bear standard U.S. inspection marks on left quarter flat and production date ("1863" or "1864") on top of barrel near the breech. Two lock markings have been encountered. Earlier production uses flat beveled plate marked with date "1863" on its tail and an eagle surmounting a panoply of flags and trophies over name "WHITNEYVILLE". In later (after serial no. 3,000) lock's tail is marked "1864" and stamping forward of hammer matches that on U.S. M1861 Whitney contract rifle-muskets, i.e. a small eagle over "U S" and "WHITNEYVILLE" in forward projection of the plate. Inspector's initials (F.C.W.) appear on barrel and in a cartouche on the stock.

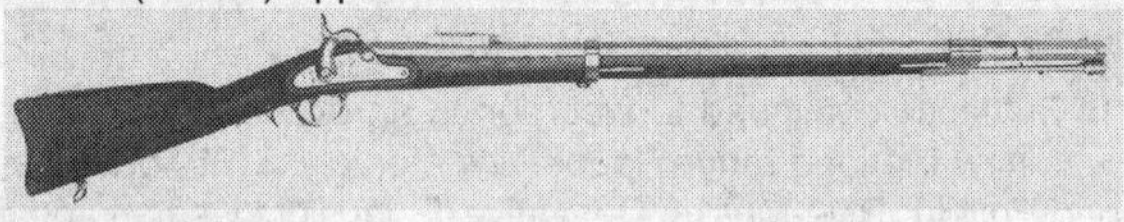

Exc.	Fine	V.G.	Good	Fair	Poor
8250	4250	3000	1750	600	420

The Whitney Arms Company, 1865-1888 Antique

With closing of the American Civil War, Eli Whitney Jr. again turned his eyes to manufacture inexpensive arms from parts remaining on hand from his Civil War contracts. Extra barrels were turned into inexpensive muzzleloading shotguns and a few breech-loading designs were toyed with. Following Remington's example, Whitney soon realized that a substantial profit could be made in the production of single-shot martial arms for foreign governments. The result was a series of breech-loading arms that copied many salient features of the Remington line, including a direct copy, after the expiration of Remington's patent, for "rolling block" mechanism. Not until late 1870s, did Whitney acquire the rights to several patents that led to the production of a lever-action repeating rifle. During the post-war period revolver production, which had begun with evasions of Colt's patents a decade prior to the Civil War, mushroomed with production of small spur-trigger rimfire cartridge revolvers. Despite the variety of arms produced, by 1883 Whitney was considering the sale of his company. Business reverses over the next five years necessitated the sale to Winchester in 1888. Primarily interested in securing patent rights for Whitney's lever-action series of rifles, Winchester closed the plant and moved its machinery to New Haven. After 90 years of production, Whitneyville Armory ceased to exist.

Single Barreled Percussion Shotgun Antique

Firearm manufactured by Whitney out of surplus .58-caliber rifle barrels that were opened up and converted to smoothbore .60-caliber shotgun barrels. Offered in lengths 28" to 36" and marked "Whitney Arms Co., Whitneyville, Conn. Homogeneous Wrought Steel". Finish blued, with varnished walnut stocks that are crudely checkered. Approximately 2,000 manufactured between 1866 and 1869. These guns are rarely encountered on today's market.

Exc.	Fine	V.G.	Good	Fair	Poor
1300	950	670	400	150	100

Double-Barreled Percussion Shotgun Antique

Specifications for this version are similar to single-barrel, except there are two side-by-side barrels with double locks, hammers and double triggers. They are slightly more common than single-barreled version.

Exc.	Fine	V.G.	Good	Fair	Poor
1300	950	670	400	150	100

Swing-Breech Carbine (Antique)

Single-shot breech-loading carbine chambered for .46-caliber rimfire cartridge. Has 22" round barrel, with button-released breech-block that swings to the side for loading. Finish blued, with walnut stock. Fewer than 50 manufactured in 1866.

Exc.	Fine	V.G.	Good	Fair	Poor
6000	3250	2500	1750	600	420

Whitney-Cochran Carbine (Antique)

Single-shot breech-loading carbine chambered for .44 rimfire cartridge. Has 28" round barrel, with lever-activated breech-block that raises upward for loading. Manufactured under license from J.W. Cochran. Finish blued, with walnut stock. There is a saddle ring on left side of the frame. Marked "Whitney Arms Co. - Whitneyville, Conn.". Produced for 1867 Government Carbine Trials. Fewer than 50 manufactured in 1866 and 1867.

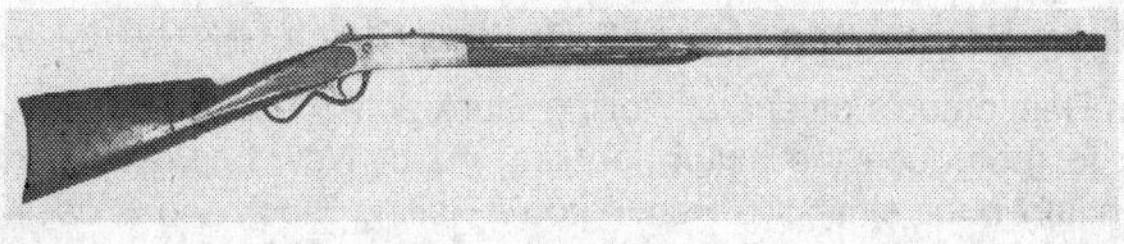

Courtesy Milwaukee Public Museum, Milwaukee, Wisconsin

Exc.	Fine	V.G.	Good	Fair	Poor
7000	3500	2500	1500	600	420

Excelsior (Antique)

Single-shot rifle chambered for .38, .44 or .50 rimfire cartridges. Found with various length octagonal or round barrels. Finish blued, with walnut stock. Forearm held on by one barrel band. Breech-block pivots downward for loading. There is a center-mounted hammer. Marked "Whitney Arms Co. Whitneyville Conn.". Shorter barreled carbine versions have a saddle ring on the frame. Approximately 200 manufactured between 1866 and 1870.

Exc.	Fine	V.G.	Good	Fair	Poor
6700	2750	1950	1150	400	280

Whitney-Howard Lever Action (Thunderbolt) (Antique)

Single-shot breech-loader chambered for .44 rimfire cartridge. Also been noted as a shotgun chambered for 20-gauge smoothbore, with barrels from 30" to 40" in length. Rifle version barrel lengths from 22" to 28". Breech-block opened by means of a combination lever and triggerguard. Also a carbine version with barrel lengths of 18.5" or 19". Approximately 2,000 manufactured totally between 1866 and 1870.

Whitney-Howard Lever Action (Thunderbolt) Shotgun (Antique)

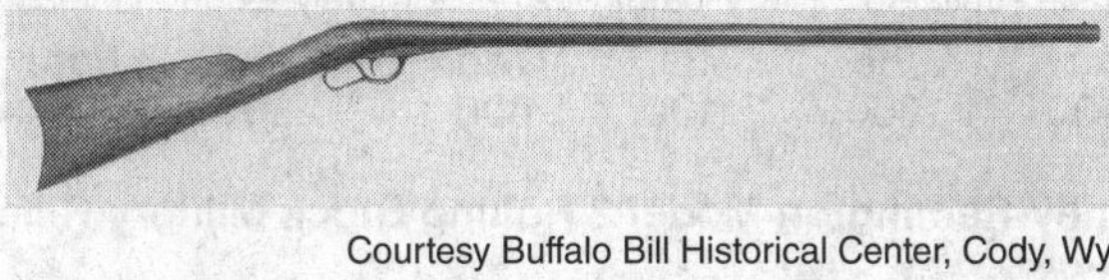

Courtesy Buffalo Bill Historical Center, Cody, Wyoming

Exc.	Fine	V.G.	Good	Fair	Poor
1400	650	470	300	100	70

Whitney-Howard Lever Action (Thunderbolt) Rifle (Antique)

Courtesy Milwaukee Public Museum, Milwaukee, Wisconsin

Exc.	Fine	V.G.	Good	Fair	Poor
2000	1000	800	600	300	150

Whitney-Howard Lever Action (Thunderbolt) Carbine (Antique)

Courtesy Milwaukee Public Museum, Milwaukee, Wisconsin

Exc.	Fine	V.G.	Good	Fair	Poor
2250	1250	870	600	300	150

Whitney Phoenix

Little is known about the origin of this model. Built on a patent issued to Whitney in 1874. There are a number of variations that are all marked "Phoenix, Patent May 24, 74". Whitney name is not marked on any of the versions. They are all single-shot breech-loaders, with breech-block that lifts to the right side and upward for loading. Barrels are all blued, with case colored or blued receivers and walnut stocks. Approximately 25,000 manufactured totally between 1867 and 1881. Models and values listed.

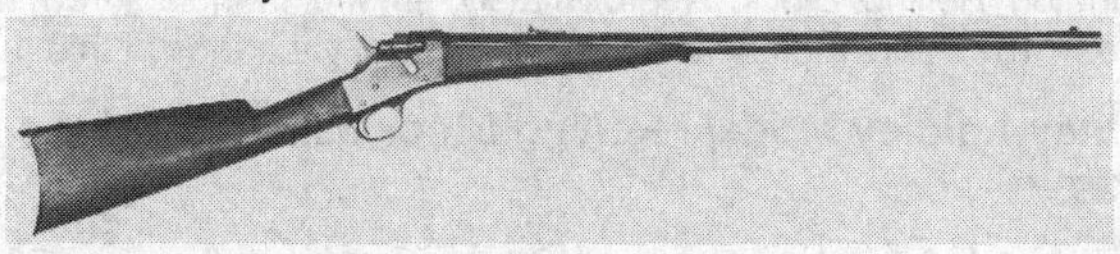

Courtesy Milwaukee Public Museum, Milwaukee, Wisconsin

Phoenix Gallery Rifle (Antique)

Chambered for .22 rimfire caliber. Has 24" half-octagonal barrel. Production quite limited.

Exc.	Fine	V.G.	Good	Fair	Poor
3250	1500	1050	600	200	140

Phoenix Shotgun (Antique)

Smoothbore version chambered for 10-, 12-, 14-, 16- or 22-gauge. Barrels between 26" and 32" in length. Approximately 5,000 manufactured.

Exc.	Fine	V.G.	Good	Fair	Poor
1100	600	420	250	100	70

Phoenix Military Rifle (Antique)

Chambered for .433-, .45- or .50-caliber centerfire cartridges. Has 35" round barrel, with full-length two-piece walnut stock held on by three barrel bands. Approximately 15,000 manufactured. Many were sent to Central or South America.

Exc.	Fine	V.G.	Good	Fair	Poor
5750	3000	2120	1250	400	280

Phoenix Schuetzen Rifle (Antique)

Target-shooting version chambered for .38, .40 or .44 centerfire cartridges. Has 30" or 32" octagonal barrel, with Schuetzen-type walnut stock; forearm features hand-checkering; nickel-plated Swiss-style buttplate; adjustable sights, with a spirit level. Model noted with double-set triggers. Few were manufactured.

Exc.	Fine	V.G.	Good	Fair	Poor
6000	3250	2250	1250	400	280

Phoenix Civilian Carbine (Antique)

Chambered for .44-caliber centerfire. Has 24" round barrel; finish blued, with case colored frame; walnut stock; forearm held on by one barrel band. Military-type sights, buttplate and saddle ring mounted on the frame. Approximately 500 manufactured.

Courtesy Milwaukee Public Museum, Milwaukee, Wisconsin

Exc.	Fine	V.G.	Good	Fair	Poor
4800	2500	1670	850	400	280

Phoenix Military Carbine (Antique)

Chambered for .433, .45 or .50 centerfire cartridges. Has 20.5" round barrel. Manufactured for Central and South America. Very rarely encountered on today's market.

Exc.	Fine	V.G.	Good	Fair	Poor
5000	2750	1870	1000	400	280

Whitney-Laidley Model I Rolling Block (Antique)

Whitney acquired manufacturing rights for this model from inventors T. Laidley and C.A. Emery, who had received the patent in 1866. Whitney immediately started modifying the action to become competitive with Remington Rolling Block. Approximately 50,000 manufactured totally between 1871 and 1881. There are a number of variations of this model.

Whitney-Laidley Model I Rolling Block Military Carbine (Antique)

Approximately 5,000 manufactured. Chambered for .433, .45 or .50 centerfire cartridges. Has 20.5" round barrel, with military-type sights. Saddle ring on receiver. Finish blued, with case colored frame and walnut stock. Most of them shipped to Central or South America.

Exc.	Fine	V.G.	Good	Fair	Poor
3500	1750	1220	700	250	170

Whitney-Laidley Model I Rolling Block Civilian Carbine (Antique)

Chambered for .44, .46 rimfire or .44 centerfire. Has 18.5" or 19.5" barrel. Blued, with case colored frame. Stock is walnut. Nickel-plated version also available. Approximately 1,000 manufactured.

Exc.	Fine	V.G.	Good	Fair	Poor
2800	1750	1220	700	250	170

Whitney-Laidley Model I Rolling Block Military Rifle (Antique)

Chambered the same as Military Carbine. Has 32.5" or 35" round barrel, with full-length two-piece stock held on by three barrel bands. Finish blued, with case colored receiver and walnut stock. Approximately 30,000 manufactured. Most of them shipped to Central or South America.

Courtesy Milwaukee Public Museum, Milwaukee, Wisconsin

Exc.	Fine	V.G.	Good	Fair	Poor
3950	2000	1400	800	300	210

Whitney-Laidley Model I Rolling Block Gallery Rifle (Antique)

A .22-caliber sporting-rifle version, with 24" octagonal barrel. Finish similar to Military Rifle. Approximately 500 manufactured.

Exc.	Fine	V.G.	Good	Fair	Poor
3400	1750	1220	700	250	170

Whitney-Laidley Model I Rolling Block Sporting Rifle (Antique)

Chambered for .38, .40, .44, .45 or .50 centerfire, as well as .32, .38 or .44 rimfire. Features barrel lengths from 24" to 30" in round or octagonal configurations. Finish similar to Military Rifle. Approximately 5,000 manufactured.

Exc.	Fine	V.G.	Good	Fair	Poor
6000	3000	1750	1000	500	300

Whitney-Laidley Model I Rolling Block Creedmoor No. 1 Rifle (Antique)

Chambered for .44-caliber cartridge. Has 32" or 34" round/octagonal barrel; blued finish, with case colored frame; hand-checkered select walnut stock and forearm. Features vernier adjustable sights, with a spirit level. Marked "Whitney Creedmoor". Fewer than 100 manufactured.

Exc.	Fine	V.G.	Good	Fair	Poor
11500	6250	4500	2750	850	590

Whitney-Laidley Model I Rolling Block Creedmoor No. 2 Rifle (Antique)

Similar to No. 1 Rifle, except chambered for .40-caliber cartridge, with 30" or 32" barrel.

Exc.	Fine	V.G.	Good	Fair	Poor
9500	4250	3000	1750	500	350

Whitney-Remington Model 2 Rolling Block (Antique)

When Remington's patent for Rolling Block action expired, Whitney was quick to reproduce the action labeling it his "New Improved System". Essentially quite similar to Remington's Rolling Block and is easily recognized when compared with Model 1 because it has only two parts — hammer and breech-block. Frame is also rounded. Tang on this model marked "Whitney Arms Company, New Haven Ct USA". Approximately 50,000 totally manufactured between 1881 and 1888. There are a number of variations listed.

Whitney-Remington Model 2 Rolling Block Shotgun (Antique)

Smoothbore version chambered for 12-, 14-, 16- or 20-gauge. Barrel lengths between 26" and 30", also 20" have been noted.

Exc.	Fine	V.G.	Good	Fair	Poor
1300	650	450	250	100	70

Whitney-Remington Model 2 Rolling Block Military Carbine (Antique)

Chambered for .433 and .45 centerfire cartridges. Has 20.5" barrel; blued, with case colored receiver; walnut stock. Approximately 5,000 manufactured. Most of them sent to South or Central America.

Exc.	Fine	V.G.	Good	Fair	Poor
3400	1750	1220	700	300	210

Whitney-Remington Model 2 Rolling Block Civilian Carbine (Antique)

Chambered for .44 rimfire or centerfire cartridge, with 18.5" round barrel. Finish similar to Military Carbine. Approximately 2,000 manufactured.

Exc.	Fine	V.G.	Good	Fair	Poor
3100	1600	1100	600	250	170

Whitney-Remington Model 2 Rolling Block Military Rifle (Antique)

Chambered for .433, .45 or .50 centerfire cartridge. Has 32.5" or 35" barrel. Finish similar to Military Carbine. Approximately 39,000 manufactured.

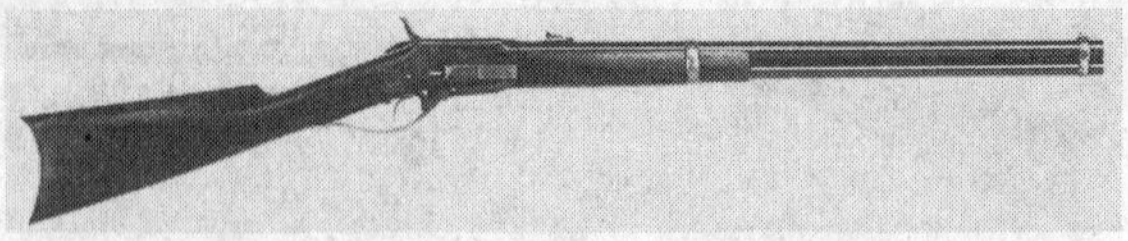

Courtesy Buffalo Bill Historical Center, Cody, Wyoming

Exc.	Fine	V.G.	Good	Fair	Poor
3950	2000	1370	750	300	210

Whitney-Remington Model 2 Rolling Block No. 1 Sporting Rifle (Antique)

Chambered for various popular sporting cartridges. Barrel lengths from

26" to 30" in round/octagonal configuration. Finish blued, with case colored receiver and varnished walnut stock. Many options available that could radically affect value. A qualified appraisal would be advisable. Approximately 3,000 manufactured.

Exc.	Fine	V.G.	Good	Fair	Poor
4850	2500	1750	1000	400	280

Whitney-Remington Model 2 Rolling Block No. 2 Sporting Rifle Antique

Smaller version of No. 1 Rifle. Chambered for .22 rimfire or .32, .38, .44-40 centerfire cartridges. Again, a qualified appraisal would be helpful as many options can affect value.

Exc.	Fine	V.G.	Good	Fair	Poor
3400	1750	1220	700	250	170

Whitney-Burgess-Morse Rifle

Lever-action repeating rifle chambered for .45-70 Government cartridge. There are three variations. All have a magazine tube mounted beneath the barrel. Blued finishes and walnut stocks. Barrels marked "G. W. Morse Patented Oct. 28th 1856". Tang marked "A. Burgess Patented Jan. 7th, 1873, Patented Oct 19th 1873". Approximately 3,000 totally manufactured between 1878 and 1882. Variations are listed.

Whitney-Burgess-Morse Sporting Rifle Antique

This version has 28" octagonal/round barrel; magazine tube holds 9 rounds. A number of options available that can increase value drastically. We recommend a competent individual appraisal. Value given is for a standard model.

Exc.	Fine	V.G.	Good	Fair	Poor
6500	3250	2250	1250	400	280

Whitney-Burgess-Morse Military Rifle Antique

Has 33" round barrel, with full-length forearm held on by two barrel bands; 11-round tubular magazine; bayonet lug and sling swivels. Features military sights. Also found chambered for .43 Spanish and .42 Russian cartridges. Approximately 1,000 manufactured.

Exc.	Fine	V.G.	Good	Fair	Poor
8000	4250	3120	2000	700	480

Whitney-Burgess-Morse Carbine Antique

Has 22" round barrel, with full-length forearm held on by one barrel band; 7-round tubular magazine; saddle ring attached to the frame. Approximately 500 manufactured.

Exc.	Fine	V.G.	Good	Fair	Poor
9000	4750	3500	2250	750	520

Whitney-Kennedy Rifle

Lever-action repeating rifle manufactured in two sizes. Has a magazine tube mounted under barrel; blued finish, with case colored lever; stock is walnut. Barrel marked "Whitney Arms Co New Haven, Conn. U.S.A.". Occasionally the word "Kennedy" is marked after the Whitney name. There are two major variations. One features a standard-type action lever; the other, same "S" shaped lever that is found on Burgess model. This version would be worth approximately 10 percent additional. As with many rifles of this era, there were many options available that will affect values. We strongly recommend securing a qualified appraisal for all, but the standard models, if a transaction is contemplated. Approximately 15,000 manufactured between 1879 and 1886. Variations of Whitney-Kennedy and their values are listed.

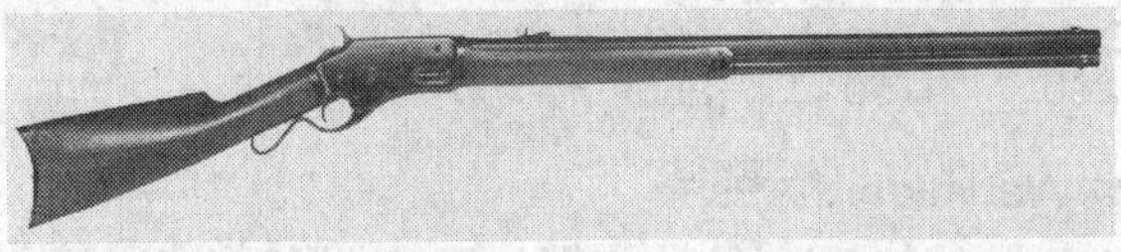

Courtesy Buffalo Bill Historical Center, Cody, Wyoming

Whitney-Kennedy Small Frame Sporting Rifle Antique

Chambered for .32-20, .38-40 and .40-40 cartridges. Has 24" round/octagonal barrel. Examples will be noted with full-/half-length tubular magazine.

Exc.	Fine	V.G.	Good	Fair	Poor
6000	3000	2500	1500	500	350

Whitney-Kennedy Large Frame Sporting Rifle Antique

Chambered for .40-60, .45-60, .45-75 and .50-90 cartridges. Barrel lengths 26" or 28". Note: Add 20 percent for uncommon .50-caliber version.

Exc.	Fine	V.G.	Good	Fair	Poor
6000	3000	2500	1500	500	350

Whitney-Kennedy Military Rifle Antique

Large-frame model chambered for .40-.60, .44-.40 and .45-60 cartridges. Has 32.25" round barrel; 11- or 16-round tubular magazine; full-length walnut forend held on by two barrel bands. Features bayonet lug and sling swivels. Approximately 1,000 manufactured. Most of them shipped to Central or South America.

Exc.	Fine	V.G.	Good	Fair	Poor
6400	3750	2750	1750	550	380

Whitney-Kennedy Military Carbine Antique

Built on small-/large-frame action. Chambered for .38-40, .44-40, .40-60 or .45-60 cartridges. Has 20" or 22" round barrel; 9- or 12-round tubular magazine, depending on caliber; short forend held on by a single barrel band. Approximately 1,000 manufactured. Most of them sent to Central or South America.

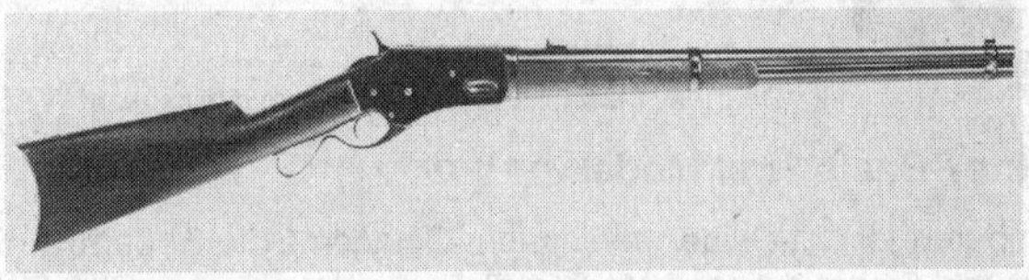

Courtesy Buffalo Bill Historical Center, Cody, Wyoming

Exc.	Fine	V.G.	Good	Fair	Poor
6400	3750	2750	1750	550	380

Hooded Cylinder Pocket Revolver Antique

An unusual revolver chambered for .28-caliber percussion. Has a manually rotated 6-shot hooded cylinder that has etched decorations. Octagonal barrel in lengths of 3" to 6". A button at the back of frame unlocks cylinder so it can be rotated. Finish blued, with brass frame and two-piece rounded walnut grips. Marked "E. Whitney N. Haven Ct.". Approximately 200 manufactured between 1850 and 1853.

Exc.	Fine	V.G.	Good	Fair	Poor
8000	5000	3000	1750	900	500

Two Trigger Pocket Revolver Antique

Conventional-appearing pocket revolver, with a manually rotated cylinder. A second trigger located in front of conventional triggerguard that releases the cylinder so it can be turned. Chambered for .32-caliber percussion. Has 3" to 6" octagonal barrel; 5-shot unfluted cylinder that is etched; brass frame and remainder blued, with squared walnut two-piece grips. Iron-frame version also available, but only 50 produced. Approximately 650 totally manufactured between 1852 and 1854. Note: Add 60 percent for iron-frame version.

Courtesy Milwaukee Public Museum, Milwaukee, Wisconsin

Exc.	Fine	V.G.	Good	Fair	Poor
2750	2000	1420	850	300	210

Whitney-Beals Patent Revolver

An unusual ring-trigger pocket pistol made in three basic variations. Also called "Walking-beam revolver."

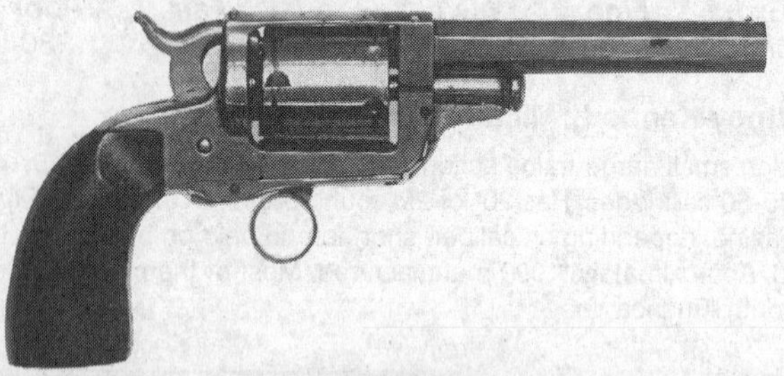

Courtesy Milwaukee Public Museum, Milwaukee, Wisconsin

Whitney-Beals First Model (Antique)

Chambered for .31-caliber percussion. Octagon 2" to 6" barrels. Brass frame and 6-shot cylinder. Marked "F. Beals/New Haven, Ct.". Only 50 manufactured.

Exc.	Fine	V.G.	Good	Fair	Poor
5000	3500	2500	1500	450	310

Whitney-Beals .31 Caliber Model (Antique)

Has an iron frame and 7-shot cylinder. Octagon 2" to 6" barrels. Marked "Address E. Whitney/Whitneyville, Ct.". Approximately 2,300 manufactured.

Exc.	Fine	V.G.	Good	Fair	Poor
2500	1500	1050	600	200	140

Whitney-Beals .28 Caliber Model (Antique)

Except for caliber, this model similar to .31 Caliber Model. Approximately 850 manufactured.

Exc.	Fine	V.G.	Good	Fair	Poor
2750	1750	1220	700	300	210

Whitney 1851 Navy (Antique)

A faithful copy of 1851 Colt Revolver. Virtually identical. There is a possibility that surplus Colt parts were utilized in construction of this revolver. Approximately 400 manufactured in 1857 and 1858.

Exc.	Fine	V.G.	Good	Fair	Poor
9000	4250	3000	1750	650	450

WHITNEY NAVY REVOLVER

Single-action revolver chambered for .36-caliber percussion. Has standard octagonal barrel length of 7.5"; iron frame; 6-shot unfluted cylinder that is roll engraved. Finish blued, with case colored loading lever. Two-piece walnut grips. Barrel marked "E. Whitney/N. Haven" or "Eagle Co.". There are a number of minor variations on this revolver. We strongly urge a competent appraisal if contemplating a transaction. There were 33,000 total manufactured between 1858 and 1862.

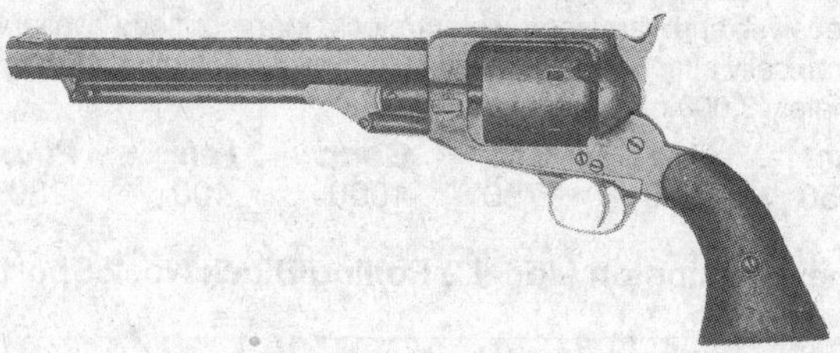

Courtesy Wallis & Wallis, Lewes, Sussex, England

First Model

Nearly entire production of First Model marked "Eagle Co.". Reason for this marking unknown. Four distinct variations of this model.

First Variation (Antique)

Has no integral loading-lever assembly. Has a thin top strap. Only 100 manufactured.

Exc.	Fine	V.G.	Good	Fair	Poor
5400	3750	2620	1500	550	380

Second Variation (Antique)

Similar to First Variation, with an integral loading lever. Approximately 200 manufactured.

Exc.	Fine	V.G.	Good	Fair	Poor
5000	3000	2100	1200	400	280

Third Variation (Antique)

Similar to Second Variation, with 3-screw frame instead of 4-screws. Loading lever also modified. Approximately 500 manufactured.

Exc.	Fine	V.G.	Good	Fair	Poor
4800	2500	1750	1000	300	210

Fourth Variation (Antique)

Has rounded frame and safety notch between nipples on rear of the cylinder. Examples noted marked "E. Whitney/N. Haven". Approximately 700 manufactured.

Exc.	Fine	V.G.	Good	Fair	Poor
4800	2500	1750	1000	300	210

Second Model

First Variation (Antique)

Features more robust frame, with brass triggerguard. Barrel marked "E. Whitney/N. Haven". Cylinder pin secured by a wing nut; has an integral loading lever. Approximately 1,200 manufactured.

Exc.	Fine	V.G.	Good	Fair	Poor
3750	2000	1450	900	300	210

Second Variation (Antique)

Has six improved safety notches on rear of cylinder. Approximately 10,000 manufactured.

Exc.	Fine	V.G.	Good	Fair	Poor
3200	1750	1250	750	250	170

Third Variation (Antique)

Improved Colt-type loading lever latch. Approximately 2,000 manufactured.

Exc.	Fine	V.G.	Good	Fair	Poor
3200	1750	1250	750	250	170

Fourth Variation (Antique)

Similar to Third Variation, except cylinder marked "Whitneyville". Approximately 10,000 manufactured.

Exc.	Fine	V.G.	Good	Fair	Poor
3200	1750	1250	750	250	170

Fifth Variation Antique

Has a larger triggerguard. Approximately 4,000 manufactured.

Exc.	Fine	V.G.	Good	Fair	Poor
3200	1750	1250	750	250	170

Sixth Variation Antique

Has larger triggerguard. 5-groove rifling instead of usual 7-groove. Approximately 2,500 manufactured.

Exc.	Fine	V.G.	Good	Fair	Poor
3200	1750	1250	750	250	170

WHITNEY POCKET REVOLVER

Single-action revolver chambered for .31-caliber percussion. Has 3" to 6" octagonal barrels; 5-shot unfluted cylinder that is roll engraved and marked "Whitneyville". Frame iron, with blued finish and case colored integral loading lever. Grips two-piece walnut. Development of this model, as far as models and variations go, is identical to that described in Navy Model designation. Values are different and we list them for reference. Again, we recommend securing a qualified appraisal if a transaction is contemplated. Approximately 32,500 manufactured from 1858 to 1862.

First Model

First Variation Antique

Exc.	Fine	V.G.	Good	Fair	Poor
3750	2000	1450	900	300	210

Second Variation Antique

Exc.	Fine	V.G.	Good	Fair	Poor
2200	1250	870	500	200	140

Third Variation Antique

Exc.	Fine	V.G.	Good	Fair	Poor
1900	1000	700	400	150	100

Fourth Variation Antique

Exc.	Fine	V.G.	Good	Fair	Poor
1900	1000	700	400	150	100

Fifth Variation Antique

Exc.	Fine	V.G.	Good	Fair	Poor
1900	1000	700	400	150	100

Second Model

First Variation Antique

Exc.	Fine	V.G.	Good	Fair	Poor
1700	900	650	400	100	70

Second Variation Antique

Exc.	Fine	V.G.	Good	Fair	Poor
1700	900	650	400	100	70

Third Variation Antique

Exc.	Fine	V.G.	Good	Fair	Poor
1700	900	650	400	100	70

Fourth Variation Antique

Exc.	Fine	V.G.	Good	Fair	Poor
1700	1000	710	420	120	80

New Model Pocket Revolver Antique

Single-action spur-triggered pocket revolver. Chambered for .28-caliber percussion. Has 3.5" octagonal barrel; 6-shot roll engraved cylinder. Features iron frame, with blued finish and two-piece walnut grips. Barrel marked "E. Whitney/N. Haven". Approximately 2,000 manufactured between 1860 and 1867.

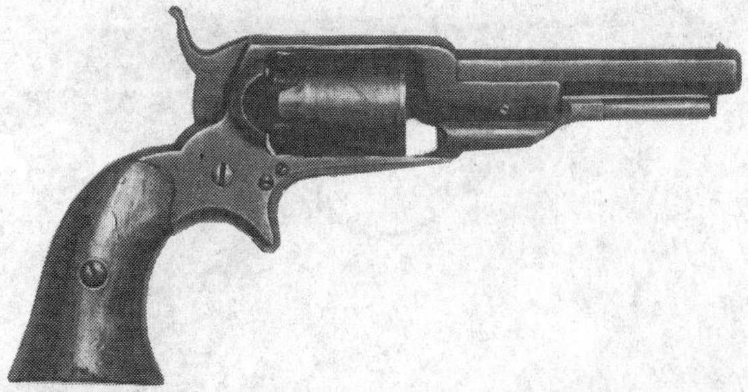

Courtesy Milwaukee Public Museum, Milwaukee, Wisconsin

Exc.	Fine	V.G.	Good	Fair	Poor
2000	1250	870	500	200	140

Rimfire Pocket Revolver Antique

Spur-trigger single-action solid-frame pocket revolver. Produced in three frame sizes, depending on caliber. Chambered for .22, .32 and .38 rimfire cartridges. Frame brass and found in a variety of finishes- nickel-plated or blued, or a combination thereof. Bird's-head grips are rosewood or hard rubber; ivory or pearl grips are sometimes encountered and will bring a slight premium in value. Octagon barrels 1.5" to 5" and marked "Whitneyville Armory Ct. USA". Also noted with trade names "Monitor", "Defender" or "Eagle". Commonly referred to as Model No. 1, No. 1.5, Model 2 or Model 2.5. Values for all are quite similar. Approximately 30,000 manufactured of all types between 1871 and 1879.

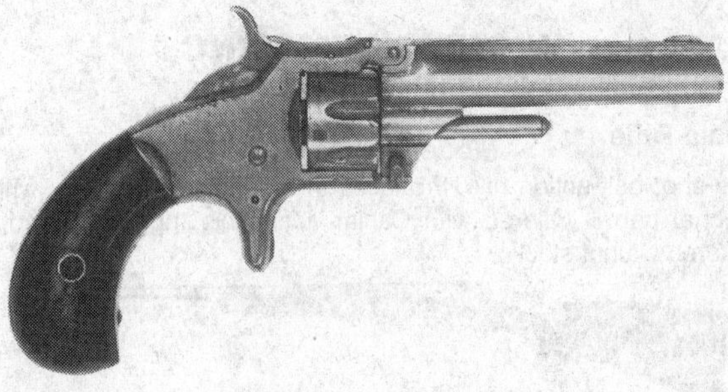

Courtesy Milwaukee Public Museum, Milwaukee, Wisconsin

Exc.	Fine	V.G.	Good	Fair	Poor
750	500	350	200	80	50

WHITNEY FIREARMS COMPANY

Hartford, Connecticut

Wolverine

A .22-caliber semi-automatic pistol, with 4.75" barrel. Blued or nickel-plated, with plastic grips and aluminum alloy frame. This pistol readily distinguishable by its streamlined form. Approximately 13,000 examples made with blue finish; 900 with nickel-plated finish. Some slides marked "Wolverine Whitney Firearms Inc., New Haven, Conn USA"; others "Whitney" only. Wolverine-marked pistols are considered more rare. Pistol produced in two locations: New Haven, Connecticut; and Hartford, Connecticut. Manufactured from 1955 to 1962. Now being reproduced by Olympic Arms. Pricing is for original version.

Blue Finish

Blued pistols most often have brown or black grips.

NIB	Exc.	V.G.	Good	Fair	Poor
750	550	400	350	250	200

Nickel-Plated

Nickeled pistols most often have white plastic grips.

NIB	Exc.	V.G.	Good	Fair	Poor
2000	1800	1500	1250	800	500

WHITWORTH

See—INTERARMS

WICHITA ARMS, INC.

Wichita, Kansas

Classic Rifle

Single-shot bolt-action rifle. Produced in a variety of calibers, with 21" octagonal barrel. Offered with Canjar adjustable triggers. Blued, with checkered walnut stock.

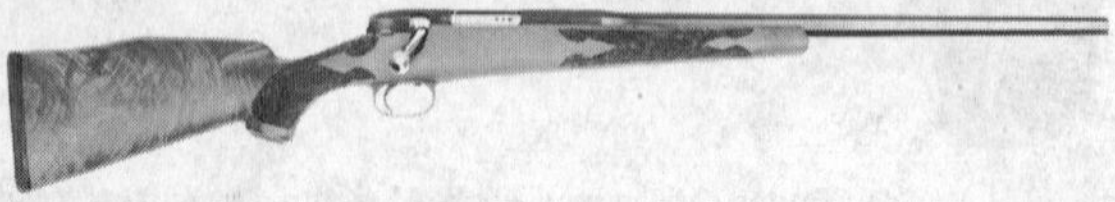

NIB	Exc.	V.G.	Good	Fair	Poor
3000	2500	2250	1850	1250	1000

Varmint Rifle

As above, with round barrel.

NIB	Exc.	V.G.	Good	Fair	Poor
2000	1750	1500	1250	1000	800

Silhouette Rifle

As above, with 24" heavy barrel, gray composition stock and 2-oz. Canjar trigger.

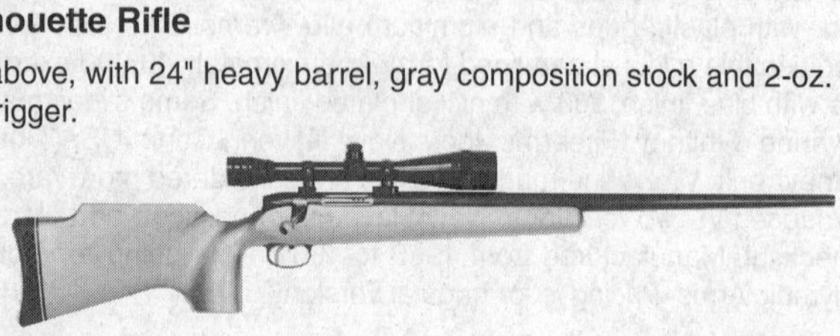

NIB	Exc.	V.G.	Good	Fair	Poor
2200	1900	1700	1000	850	650

Wichita International Pistol

Single-shot pivoted barrel target pistol. Produced in a variety of calibers from .22 to .357 Magnum, with 10.5" or 14" barrel. Fitted with adjustable sights or telescopic sight mounts. Stainless steel, with walnut fore-stock and grips.

NIB	Exc.	V.G.	Good	Fair	Poor
800	650	400	350	300	200

Wichita Classic Pistol

Bolt-action single-shot pistol. Chambered for a variety of calibers up to .308, with left-hand action and 11.25" barrel. Blued, with walnut stock.

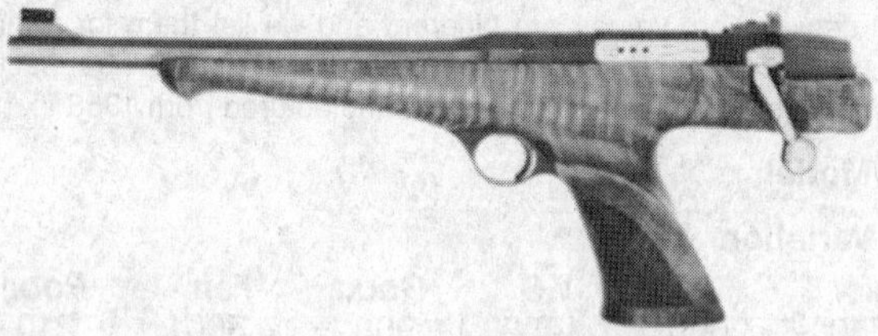

NIB	Exc.	V.G.	Good	Fair	Poor
3000	2500	2250	1850	1250	1000

Wichita Classic Engraved

As above, but embellished.

NIB	Exc.	V.G.	Good	Fair	Poor
5000	4250	3500	2500	2000	1500

Wichita Silhouette Pistol

As above in 7mm HMSA or .308, with 15" barrel. Walnut stock made so pistol grip is located beneath forward end of bolt.

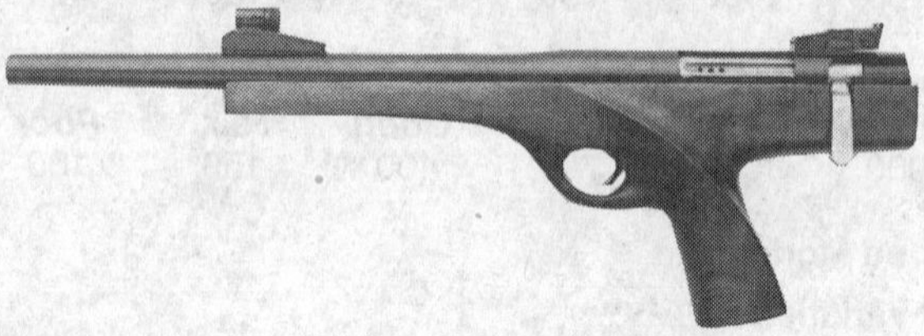

NIB	Exc.	V.G.	Good	Fair	Poor
1100	950	750	600	500	400

Wichita MK40

As above, with 13" barrel, multi-range sights and composition or walnut stock. Standard finish blued. Also made in stainless steel.

NIB	Exc.	V.G.	Good	Fair	Poor
1100	950	750	600	500	400

WICKLIFFE RIFLES

Triple S Development
Wickliffe, Ohio/Austinburg, Ohio

NOTE: Wickliffe Rifle Company has been reorganized as a maker of custom single-shot rifles. Values below are for original Wickliffe guns.

Model 76

Single-shot falling-block rifle. Produced in a variety of calibers from .22 Hornet to .45-70. Barrels: 22" lightweight; or 26" heavy weight. Blued, with walnut stock. Introduced in 1976; discontinued.

NIB	Exc.	V.G.	Good	Fair	Poor
—	1200	1000	750	550	300

Model 76 Deluxe

As above, with nickel-silver pistol grip cap, machine jeweled breechblock and more finely figured walnut stock. Introduced in 1976.

NIB	Exc.	V.G.	Good	Fair	Poor
—	1450	1250	900	700	450

Traditionalist

Model 76 in .30-06 or .45-70 caliber, with 24" barrel having open sights. Checkered walnut buttstock. Introduced in 1979.

NIB	Exc.	V.G.	Good	Fair	Poor
—	1200	1000	750	550	300

Stinger

Similar to Model 76. Chambered for .22 Hornet or .223 Rem., with 22" barrel. Fitted with Burris 6X power telescope. Blued, with checkered Monte Carlo-style stock. Introduced in 1979.

NIB	Exc.	V.G.	Good	Fair	Poor
—	1200	1000	750	550	300

Stinger Deluxe

As above, with a superior grade finish and more finely figured walnut stock.

NIB	Exc.	V.G.	Good	Fair	Poor
—	1250	1050	800	580	300

WIENER WAFFENFABRIK

Vienna, Austria

Little Tom

A 6.35mm or 7.65mm double-action semi-automatic pistol, with 2.5" barrel. Slide marked "Wiener Waffenfabrik Patent Little Tom" and caliber. Blued, with walnut or plastic grips inlaid with a medallion bearing company's trademark. Approximately 10,000 made from 1919 to 1925.

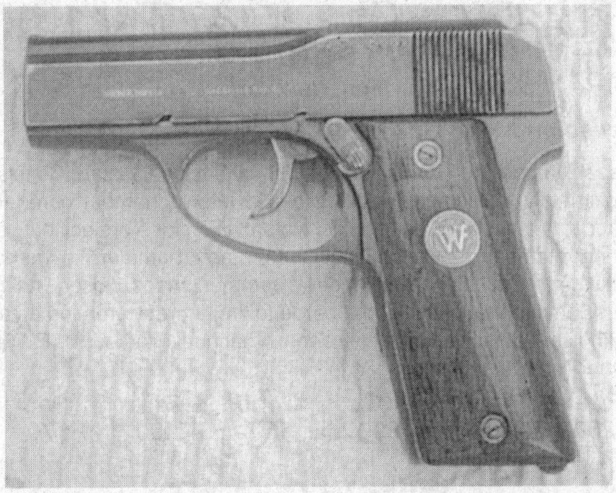

Paul Goodwin photo

Little Tom—7.65mm

NIB	Exc.	V.G.	Good	Fair	Poor
—	500	450	400	250	180

WILDEY FIREARMS CO., INC.

Cheshire, Connecticut
Newburg, New York
Warren, Connecticut

Wildey Auto Pistol

Gas-operated rotary-bolt double-action semi-automatic pistol. Chambered for .357 Peterbuilt, .45 Win. Magnum or .475 Wildey Magnum cartridges, with 5", 6", 7", 8" or 10" ventilated rib barrels. Gas-operated action is adjustable and features a single-shot cutoff. Rotary-bolt has three heavy locking lugs. Constructed of stainless steel, with adjustable sights and wood grips. Values of this rarely encountered pistol are based not only on condition, but caliber—as well as serial-number range. Earlier-numbered guns being worth a good deal more than later production models. All Wildey models are no longer in production.

Cheshire, Connecticut, Address

Produced in .45 Win. Magnum only. Serial numbered from No. 1 through 2489. Note: Serial numbers above 200 would be worth approximately $200 less respectively in each category of condition.

Serial No. 1 through 200

NIB	Exc.	V.G.	Good	Fair	Poor
2000	1500	1200	950	750	500

Survivor Model

Manufactured in Brookfield, Connecticut. Note: Add $100 for 12" barrel; $500 for 14" barrel; $1,100 for 18" Silhouette model.

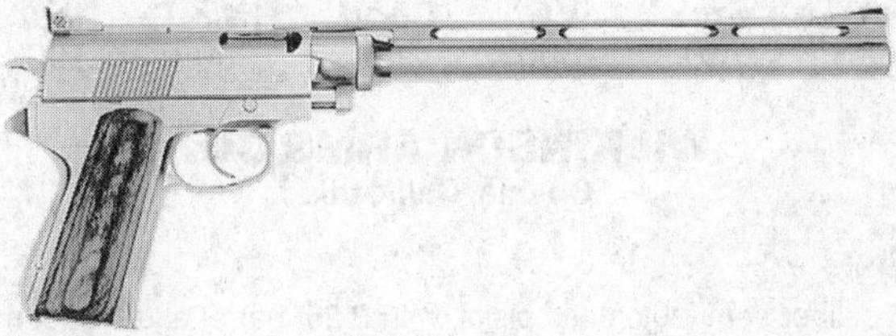

NIB	Exc.	V.G.	Good	Fair	Poor
1500	1000	750	550	450	300

Hunter Model

As above, with matte stainless steel finish.

NIB	Exc.	V.G.	Good	Fair	Poor
1780	1250	900	700	600	450

Pin Gun

Gas-operated auto-loading pistol for competition shooting. In polished or matte stainless, with muzzle brake. Variety of calibers and barrel lengths (7", 8", 10", 12", 14"). Weight 4.09 lb. (8" barrel).

NIB	Exc.	V.G.	Good	Fair	Poor
2000	1500	1200	950	750	500

Wildey Carbine

Features 18" barrel, with forearm. Calibers from .44 Auto Magnum to .475 Wildey Magnum. Choice of polished or matte stainless steel. Note: Add $225 for matte stainless finish.

NIB	Exc.	V.G.	Good	Fair	Poor
2500	2000	1550	1000	750	500

Presentation Model

As above, but engraved. Fitted with hand-checkered walnut grips.

NIB	Exc.	V.G.	Good	Fair	Poor
3000	2500	1950	1400	900	600

JAWS Viper

Jordanian Arms & Weapons System manufactured in Jordan. Semi-automatic chambered for 9mm, .40 S&W, 45 ACP. Barrels: 4.4" and 5". 10-round magazine. Stainless finish, with rubberized grip. .

NIB	Exc.	V.G.	Good	Fair	Poor
—	720	500	380	250	150

WILKINSON ARMS CO.
Covina, California

Diane

A .25-caliber semi-automatic pistol, with 2.25" barrel and 6-shot magazine. Blued, with plastic grips.

NIB	Exc.	V.G.	Good	Fair	Poor
—	400	320	200	150	100

Terry Carbine

A 9mm caliber semi-automatic carbine, with 16.25" barrel, adjustable sights and 30-shot magazine. Matte blued, with black composition or maple stock.

NIB	Exc.	V.G.	Good	Fair	Poor
—	680	450	320	200	120

WILLIAMSON
New York, New York

Derringer Antique

A single shot pistol adaptable to fire either .41 rimfire or .41 percussion rounds with 2.5" sliding barrel. Blued, with silver-plated furniture. Checkered walnut grip. Barrel marked "Williamson's Pat. Oct. 2, 1866 New York". Fitted with an auxiliary percussion cap chamber adaptor. Manufactured from 1866 to about 1870.

Exc.	Fine	V.G.	Good	Fair	Poor
1500	900	650	450	225	125

WILSON, J. P.
Ilion, New York

Percussion Alarm Gun Antique

Unusual little device chambered for .22-caliber percussion. Consists of approximately 1" rectangular brass block, with a chamber bored into it that accepts a blackpowder charge. No provision for a projectile. There is a spring retained arm on top, which works as a hammer. As the device is activated by a door or a window, hammer snaps closed striking a percussion cap that causes the charge to fire, thereby creating an alarm notifying that the perimeter has been breached. Marked "J. P. Wilson/ Patented Feb. 8, 1859/Ilion, NY".

Exc.	Fine	V.G.	Good	Fair	Poor
1200	850	600	350	100	70

WILSON COMBAT
Berryville, Arkansas

Wilson began making custom 1911-style pistols using Colt slides and frames in 1977. Company produces a wide range of quality components for 1911 pistols, such as slides, triggers, safeties, barrels, etc. Models listed are for complete factory-built-and-assembled guns. These factory-built pistols are sold with a lifetime warranty, even to subsequent buyers. Pistols listed are divided into two categories. Semi-custom pistols are off-the-shelf guns available through participating dealers. Custom pistols are special order guns. Models listed below are representative, not inclusive.

POLYMER FRAME PISTOLS

Tactical Carry (KZ-45)

Chambered for .45 ACP cartridge. Fitted with 5" stainless steel match barrel. Numerous special features such as night sights, front and rear slide serrations. Frame stainless steel and reinforced polymer. Magazine capacity 10 rounds. Finish black polymer. Weight about 31 oz. Introduced in 1999; discontinued.

NIB	Exc.	V.G.	Good	Fair	Poor
1050	900	750	600	500	300

KZ 9mm

Polymer frame 1911 chambered for 9mm. Full size 16+1 capacity, with 5" barrel; weight 33 oz. Compact size 14+1 capacity, with 4.1" barrel; weight 31 oz. Introduced 2006; discontinued.

NIB	Exc.	V.G.	Good	Fair	Poor
1500	1350	1200	900	750	300

Spec-Ops 9

An upgraded model based on discontinued KZ-9. Like KZ-9, it has a polymer frame and 16-round magazine. Chambering 9mm only. Barrel 4.5"; weight unloaded 29.6 oz.

NIB	Exc.	V.G.	Good	Fair	Poor
1950	1500	1200	900	450	200

ADP 9mm

Polymer frame. Capacity 11 rounds; weight 19.5 oz.; overall length 6.3"; barrel 3.75". Introduced 2006.

NIB	Exc.	V.G.	Good	Fair	Poor
680	520	400	300	200	120

SEMI-CUSTOM PISTOLS

Model 1996A2

Introduced in 1996. Offered in a number of different configurations which affect price. Base pistol chambered for .45 ACP cartridge. Has snag-free sights and blue finish. Barrel length 5"; magazine capacity 8 rounds; weight about 38 oz. There are numerous special features on the standard pistol. Note: Add $70 for Tritium night sights; $125 for Wilson adjustable sights; $275 for nights sights, ambi safety, hard chrome frame; $325 for Wilson adjustable sights, ambi safety, hard chrome frame.

NIB	Exc.	V.G.	Good	Fair	Poor
1450	1150	1000	800	620	300

Protector

Fitted to a 5" slide, with match barrel adjustable sights and numerous other special features. Weight about 38 oz. Black polymer finish on slide and frame. Introduced in 1996. Note: Add $100 for stainless steel.

NIB	Exc.	V.G.	Good	Fair	Poor
2100	1990	1790	1500	1200	—

Protector Compact

Same as above, with 4.25" match-grade barrel. Weight about 34 oz. Introduced in 1996.

NIB	Exc.	V.G.	Good	Fair	Poor
1800	1450	1150	900	650	400

Sentinel Ultra Compact

This .45 ACP pistol fitted with 3.6" heavy tapered cone hand-fitted barrel, night sights, high-ride beavertail and numerous special features. Magazine capacity 6 rounds. Weight about 29 oz. Finish black polymer.

NIB	Exc.	V.G.	Good	Fair	Poor
2100	1680	1300	950	700	450

Tactical

This .45 ACP pistol fitted with 5" tapered cone hand-fitted barrel. Cocking serrations on front and rear of slide. High-ride beavertail safety and other special features. Night sights are standard. Cocobolo grips. Weight about 38 oz. Finish is black polymer. Magazine capacity 8 rounds. Introduced in 1999.

NIB	Exc.	V.G.	Good	Fair	Poor
1820	1450	1100	900	700	400

Classic

This model has a 5" barrel, adjustable sights, hard chrome finish on frame and other special features. Weight about 38 oz. Introduced in 1996. Note: Add $100 for stainless steel.

NIB	Exc.	V.G.	Good	Fair	Poor
1900	1500	1200	900	700	400

Service Grade Target

Chambered for .45 ACP cartridge. Features 5" stainless steel match hand-fitted barrel, with full-length guide rod. Front and rear cocking serrations. Magazine well is beveled and grips are Cocobolo. Numerous other special features. Weight about 38 oz. Finish black polymer. Magazine capacity 8 rounds.

NIB	Exc.	V.G.	Good	Fair	Poor
1820	1450	1150	850	650	350

Beretta/Wilson 92G Brigadier Tactical

Limited production model features all-steel Beretta and Wilson Combat parts. These include steel ambidextrous decocker-only levers, enhanced slide, modified M9A1 style checkered frame, with accessory rail and rounded triggerguard. Other features are Wilson Combat G-10 grips, steel guide rod, Trijicon Tritium front sight and Wilson Combat rear. Chambered in 9m, with 15+1 round capacity. Weight empty 36 oz.; loaded 43 oz. Available only from Wilson Combat or its dealers.

NIB	Exc.	V.G.	Good	Fair	Poor
1050	800	650	550	400	350

Custom Carry Revolver

Built on Smith & Wesson .357 Magnum Model 66. Features 2.5" barrel, with adjustable night sights. Cylinder chambered and grip is black nylon, with smooth stainless steel finish. Weight about 30 oz.

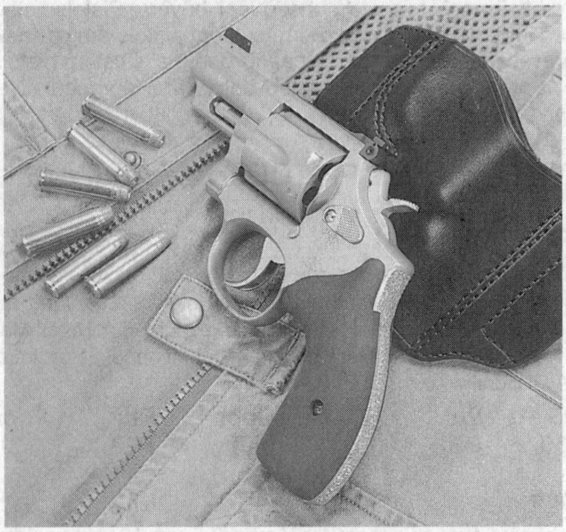

NIB	Exc.	V.G.	Good	Fair	Poor
1180	950	800	650	500	300

.22 Classic Rimfire Pistol

Chambered for .22-caliber rimfire cartridge. Fitted with 5" barrel. Hard chrome frame and black anodized slide. Weight less than standard .45-caliber pistol. Introduced in 1996.

NIB	Exc.	V.G.	Good	Fair	Poor
1120	980	800	620	500	250

CUSTOM-BUILT PISTOLS

Wilson Custom pistols bear Wilson Combat or Wilson Custom label on right side of frame on the dust cover. Full custom guns are typically built on a Colt, Springfield Armory, Norinco, STI, Strayer Voight or Wilson Combat gun.

Combat Classic Super Grade (Tactical Super Grade)

Fitted with 5" match-grade hand-fit stainless steel barrel. Adjustable sights, high ride beavertail safety, contoured magazine well and polymer slide with hard chrome frame. Weight about 45 oz. In 9mm, .38 Super, .40 S&W, 10mm and .45 ACP.

NIB	Exc.	V.G.	Good	Fair	Poor
3600	2850	2300	1900	1500	600

Tactical Super Grade Compact

Similar to above model, with 4.1" match-grade barrel. Magazine capacity 7 rounds. Weight about 40 oz. Introduced in 2003. Available in 9mm, .38 Super, .45 ACP.

NIB	Exc.	V.G.	Good	Fair	Poor
4480	3900	3200	2500	1850	650

Wilson X-TAC

Caliber .45 ACP, steel frame and slide, 8-round magazine, special XTAC-pattern slide serrations. Texturing on front strap and mainspring housing, stainless match-grade barrel and bushing, extended thumb safety, beavertail tang, G-10 grips and contoured mag well. Weight 38.1 oz., 5" barrel with black Parkerized finish.

NIB	Exc.	V.G.	Good	Fair	Poor
2000	1700	1450	1150	750	300

CQB Light-Rail Lightweight

Calibers: 9mm Parabellum, .38 Super, .45 ACP. Compact size with 4" barrel, steel slide, alloy round butt frame. Weight 27.34 oz. Comes with one 7- and two 8-round magazines, fiber optic front sight, integral accessory rail, G-10 grips, extended thumb safety, beavertail tang, checkered front strap and mainspring housing. Several other sizes and variations available in CQB series.

NIB	Exc.	V.G.	Good	Fair	Poor
2300	1980	1650	1300	850	300

Ultralight Carry Series

Full-size 1911, with aluminum frame and steel slide. Chambered in 9mm Parabellum, .38 Super or .45 ACP. Stainless fluted 5" barrel. Comes with one 7- and two 8-round magazines. Other features include countersunk slide stop, integral accessory rail, contoured mag well, G-10 grips, extended thumb safety, beavertail tang, checkered front strap and mainspring housing. Weight 26.5 oz. Several Armor-Tuff finish options including black, O.D., silver, tan or two-tone. Compact model has 4" barrel (all calibers), Sentinel 3.6" barrel (9mm only).

NIB	Exc.	V.G.	Good	Fair	Poor
3400	3000	2500	2000	1200	400

Stealth Defense System

Built with a 4.25" slide and match-grade stainless steel barrel. Features night sights, checkered front strap and mainspring housing, with numerous special features. Black polymer finish. Weight about 34 oz. Offered in 9mm, .38 Super, .40 S&W, .45 ACP.

NIB	Exc.	V.G.	Good	Fair	Poor
2900	2250	1700	1300	900	400

Defensive Combat Pistol

This .45 ACP pistol built with 5" match-grade stainless steel barrel, night sights and numerous special features. Finish black polymer. Weight 38 oz.

NIB	Exc.	V.G.	Good	Fair	Poor
2400	1850	1250	1000	600	300

Classic Master Grade

This .45 ACP pistol fitted with 5" stainless steel hand-fitted match-grade barrel. Numerous special features such as ultralight hammer, ambidextrous safety, etc. Finish stainless steel frame and black polymer slide. Weight about 38 oz. Magazine capacity 8 rounds.

NIB	Exc.	V.G.	Good	Fair	Poor
2900	2250	1700	1300	900	400

Tactical Elite

Similar to other Wilson pistols, with addition of a special tactical heavy tapered cone barrel.

NIB	Exc.	V.G.	Good	Fair	Poor
2900	2250	1700	1300	900	400

Defensive Combat Pistol Deluxe

Has 5" match-grade stainless steel barrel and numerous special features. Fitted with adjustable sights. Weight about 38 oz. Finish black polymer.

NIB	Exc.	V.G.	Good	Fair	Poor
2600	2000	1350	1050	700	300

Professional Model Pistol

Introduced in 2004. This .45 ACP pistol features 4.1" stainless steel match barrel, tactical combat sights with Tritium inserts. Many custom features. Magazine capacity 8 rounds. Offered in gray/black, green/black or all-black finish. Weight about 35 oz.

NIB	Exc.	V.G.	Good	Fair	Poor
1220	1650	1380	1100	750	450

Competition Pistols

Wilson Combat offers custom-built pistols to customer's specifications. An expert appraisal is recommended prior to sale.

TACTICAL RIFLES

AR-15 RIFLES

Caliber: .204 Ruger, .223 Rem./5.56mm NATO, .223 Wylde, 22 Nosler, .224 Valkyrie, 6mm ARC, 6.5 Grendel, 6.8 SPC, .300 Ham'r, .300 Blackout, .350 Legend, .375 SOCOM, .458 SOCOM, .450 Bushmaster. Capacity: Accepts all M-16/AR-15-style magazines, and includes one 20-round magazine. Barrel: 16.25", 1:9" twist, match-grade fluted. Weight: 6.9 lbs. Length: 36.25" overall. Stock: Fixed or collapsible. Features: Free-float ventilated aluminum quad-rail handguard, mil-spec Parkerized barrel and steel components, anodized receiver, precision CNC-machined upper and lower receivers, 7075 T6 aluminum forgings. Single-stage JP Trigger/Hammer Group, Wilson Combat Tactical muzzle brake, nylon tactical rifle case. Made in USA by Wilson Combat. SEE POLITICAL PANIC PRICING.

UT-15 Urban Tactical

Semi-automatic rifle fitted with 16.25" fluted barrel, with tactical muzzle brake. Flattop receiver. Aluminum handguard. Chambered for .223. Parkerized finish. Accepts all M-16/AR-15 magazines. Weight 6.5 lbs. Note: Add $100 for Armor-Tuff finish.

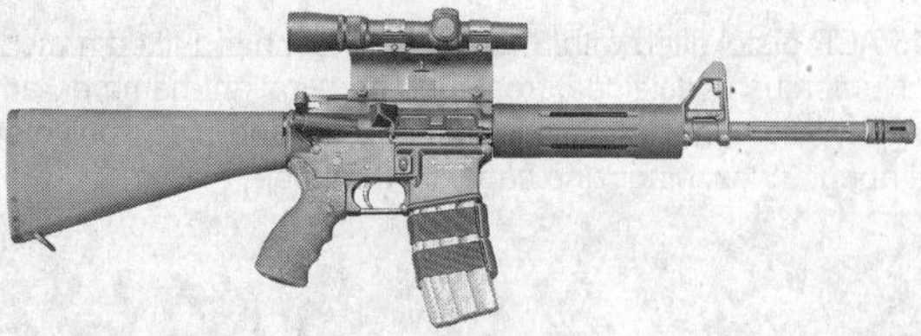

NIB	Exc.	V.G.	Good	Fair	Poor
1900	1700	1450	1100	900	500

Tactical Hunter LW 6.8

Chambered for Remington 6.8 SPC, with 15-round magazine. Stainless lightweight match-grade 16" or 18" barrel. Forged upper and lower receivers. Enhanced bolt and carrier, with NP3 coating. Wilson Combat Quadrail, Accu-Tac flash hider. Armor Tuff polymer finish in black, gray or tan. Collapsible stock.

NIB	Exc.	V.G.	Good	Fair	Poor
2000	1700	1450	1150	750	300

TPR-15 Tactical Precision Rifle

Fitted with match-grade 18" fluted barrel. Free-floating aluminum handguard. Chambered for .223. Weight 6.5 lbs. Parkerized finish. Note: Add $100 for Armor-Tuff finish.

NIB	Exc.	V.G.	Good	Fair	Poor
2500	2300	1950	1300	1100	600

M-4T Tactical Carbine

Features 16.25" M-4 style heavy barrel, with muzzle brake. Flattop receiver. Chambered for .223 cartridge. Parkerized finish. Weight 6.5 lbs. Note: Add $100 for Armor-Tuff finish.

NIB	Exc.	V.G.	Good	Fair	Poor
1900	1700	1450	1100	900	500

TL-15 Tactical Lightweight

Introduced in 2002. Flattop model features match-grade 16.25" lightweight barrel, with muzzle brake. Aluminum handguard and fixed buttstock. Chambered for .223. Black Mil-Spec finish. Note: Add $100 for Armor-Tuff finish.

NIB	Exc.	V.G.	Good	Fair	Poor
1900	1700	1450	1100	900	500

Super Sniper

Fitted with 20" stainless steel match-grade barrel, with 1:8 twist. Flattop receiver. Offered in Parkerized or Armor-Tuff finish. Note: Add $100 for Armor-Tuff finish.

NIB	Exc.	V.G.	Good	Fair	Poor
2700	2500	2100	1720	1390	—

Urban Super Sniper

NIB	Exc.	V.G.	Good	Fair	Poor
2800	2600	2280	1870	1450	—

Ranger

NIB	Exc.	V.G.	Good	Fair	Poor
1900	1800	1600	1350	1000	—

Ultralight Ranger

NIB	Exc.	V.G.	Good	Fair	Poor
2550	—	—	—	—	—

Recon Tactical

NIB	Exc.	V.G.	Good	Fair	Poor
2300	2150	1900	1550	1270	—

Protector

NIB	Exc.	V.G.	Good	Fair	Poor
2020	—	—	—	—	—

AR-10 RIFLES

Caliber: .243 Win., .260 Rem., 6.5 Creedmoor, 7mm-08 Rem., .308 Win., .338 Federal, .358 Win. Large-format BILLet-AR rifles with precision-machined match-grade barrels, M-LOK handguard rail, Tactical Trigger Units. Barrels: 14.7" barrel with pinned muzzle device on Recon Tactical. Also, 16", 18", and 20" fluted or standard Medium Recon-profile barrels. Receivers accept metal or polymer SR-25-pattern magazines. SEE POLITICAL PANIC PRICING.

Recon Tactical AR-10

NIB	Exc.	V.G.	Good	Fair	Poor
3200	2800	2450	1890	1550	—

Super Sniper AR-10

NIB	Exc.	V.G.	Good	Fair	Poor
3260	2870	2500	1900	1600	—

Tactical Hunter AR-10

NIB	Exc.	V.G.	Good	Fair	Poor
3000	2750	2300	1900	1650	—

Ranger AR-10

NIB	Exc.	V.G.	Good	Fair	Poor
3000	2750	2300	1900	1650	—

Ultralight Ranger

NIB	Exc.	V.G.	Good	Fair	Poor
3250	2960	2500	2000	1790	—

AR-9 Carbine

Caliber: 9mm Luger. AR-9 lower receivers with last-round bolt hold open compatible with 9mm service pistol magazines for Glock, Beretta, and Wilson Combat EDC X9. Accepts standard AR accessories. Integral triggerguard, flared magwell. Closed-bolt blowback operating system. Match-grade button-rifled 1:10" twist barrels. Introduced 2016. SEE POLITICAL PANIC PRICING.

NIB	Exc.	V.G.	Good	Fair	Poor
2000	1800	1590	1270	1000	—

WINCHESTER REPEATING ARMS

New Haven, Connecticut

Prices given here are, for the most part, standard guns without optional features that were so often furnished by the factory. These optional or extra-cost features are too numerous to list and can affect price of shotgun or rifle to an enormous degree. In some cases, these options are one of a kind. Collectors and those interested in Winchester firearms have the benefit of some original factory records. These records are now stored in Cody Firearms Museum, Buffalo Bill Historical Center, P.O. Box 1000, Cody, Wyoming (307) 587-4771. For a $25 fee, museum will provide factory letters containing original specifications of certain Winchester models using original factory records. CAUTION: Buyers should confirm by Cody letter any special-order feature on any Winchester within the Cody record range before paying a premium for a scarce feature.

Hunt Repeating Rifle

Walter Hunt described his repeating rifle as Volition Repeater. Hunt was granted U.S. patent #6663 in August 1849 for his repeating rifle. That paved the way for future generations of Winchester repeating rifles. Hunt's rifle design was unique and innovative as was his patent #5701 for a conical lead bullet that was to be fired in his rifle. This ingenious bullet had a hole in its base filled with powder and closed by a disc with an opening in the middle to expel the ignition from an independent priming source that used priming pellets made of fulminate of mercury. Rifle actually worked, but only the patent model was built; it is now in the Cody Firearms Museum.

Jennings

Second in the evolutionary line of Winchester rifles is the Jennings. Made by Robbins & Lawrence of Windsor, Vermont, this rifle incorporated the original concept of the Hunt design, with additional improvements utilized by Lewis Jennings. Jennings rifle is important not only as a link in the chain of repeating-rifle development, but also because it introduced Benjamin Tyler Henry to the concept of the tubular magazine lever-action repeating rifle. Jennings rifle was built in three separate and distinct models. While total production of the three types was contracted for 5,000 guns, it is probable that only about 1,000 were actually produced.

Jennings First Model (Antique)

First Model Jennings was built in .54-caliber breech-loading single-shot configuration, with ring trigger, oval triggerguard and 26" barrel. A ramrod was fixed to underside of barrel as well. This variation was made from 1850 to 1851.

Courtesy Milwaukee Public Museum, Milwaukee, Wisconsin

Exc.	Fine	V.G.	Good	Fair	Poor
35000	25000	16000	7000	1500	1050

Jennings Second Model (Antique)

Second Model Jennings was produced by adopting improvements made by Horace Smith. Second Model is a breech-loading repeating rifle, with an under barrel magazine tube and 26" barrel. Frame is sculpted, unlike First Model. Ring trigger is still present, but triggerguard was removed as part of the design change. Caliber remained .54 and rifle fitted with 25" barrel. Second Model produced in 1851 and 1852.

Courtesy Milwaukee Public Museum, Milwaukee, Wisconsin

Exc.	Fine	V.G.	Good	Fair	Poor
30000	20000	12500	5000	1200	840

Jennings Third Model (Antique)

Third Model represents an attempt by investors to use remaining parts and close out production. The .54-caliber Third Model was a muzzleloading rifle, with a ramrod mounted under the 26.5" barrel. Same frame as used on First Model, but trigger was more of the conventional type. Triggerguard had a bow in the middle giving this model a distinctive appearance. This variation was produced in 1852 and marks the end of early conceptual period in repeating rifle development.

Exc.	Fine	V.G.	Good	Fair	Poor
23500	9500	7000	4500	1500	1050

Smith & Wesson Volcanic Firearms

An interesting connection in the evolution of lever-action repeating firearm, is found in the production of a small group of pistols and rifles built in Norwich, Connecticut, by Horace Smith and Daniel Wesson under the firm name of Smith & Wesson. Company built two types of Volcanic pistols. One was a large-frame model, with 8" barrel chambered in .41-caliber. About 500 large-frames were built. The other was a small-frame version, with 4" barrel chambered in .31-caliber. About 700 small-frames were built. In both variations the barrel, magazine and frame were blued. Smith & Wesson also produced a lever-action repeating rifle. These rifles are exceedingly rare, with fewer than 10 having been built. They were chambered for .528-caliber and fitted with 23" barrels. Because of the small number of rifles built, no value is offered. The same Volcanic action was later used by Volcanic Repeating Arms Co. and Winchester predecessor New Haven Arms Co. (listed below). All Volcanics fired caseless self-contained ammo rounds called "rocket balls" consisting of a lead bullet with the power loaded in the hollow base, and a primer attached to the base. They are fed from a tube magazine mounted underneath the barrel.

Courtesy Buffalo Bill Historical Center, Cody, Wyoming

S&W Volcanic .31 caliber 4" Pistol (Antique)

Exc.	Fine	V.G.	Good	Fair	Poor
—	11000	7500	4000	1000	700

S&W Volcanic .41 caliber 8" Pistol (Antique)

Courtesy Buffalo Bill Historical Center, Cody, Wyoming

Exc.	Fine	V.G.	Good	Fair	Poor
—	13000	9500	6000	1500	1050

Volcanic Firearms (Volcanic Repeating Arms Company)

With the incorporation of Volcanic Repeating Arms Company, a new and important individual was introduced who would have an impact on the American arms industry for the next 100 years: Oliver F. Winchester. This new company introduced the Volcanic pistol using improvements made by Horace Smith and Daniel Wesson. Volcanic firearms are marked on the barrel, "THE VOLCANIC REPEATING ARMS CO. PATENT NEW HAVEN, CONN. FEB. 14, 1854". Volcanic was offered as a .38-caliber breech-loading tubular magazine repeater, with blued barrel and bronze frame. These pistols were available in three barrel lengths. Note: A few Volcanic pistols were produced with detachable shoulder stocks. These are considered quite rare. For original guns with this option, prices listed should be increased by 25 percent.

Courtesy Milwaukee Public Museum, Milwaukee, Wisconsin

Courtesy Buffalo Bill Historical Center, Cody, Wyoming

Volcanic 6" Barrel (Antique)

Exc.	Fine	V.G.	Good	Fair	Poor
—	7000	5250	3500	1500	1050

Volcanic Navy 8" Barrel (Antique)

Exc.	Fine	V.G.	Good	Fair	Poor
—	7000	5250	3500	1500	1050

16" Barrel (Antique)

Exc.	Fine	V.G.	Good	Fair	Poor
—	14000	9750	5500	2500	1750

Volcanic Firearms (New Haven Arms Company)

In 1857, New Haven Arms Company was formed to continue production of the former Volcanic Repeating Arms Company. Volcanic firearms continued to be built, but were now marked on the barrel, "NEW HAVEN, CONN. PATENT FEB. 14, 1854". New Haven produced a Number One model in .31 caliber with 3.5" barrel and a Model Two in .41 caliber with 6" barrel. Both were similar to the S&W and Volcanic Repeating Arms designs, and both had square butts.

No.1 Volcanic 3-1/2" Barrel (Antique)

Exc.	Fine	V.G.	Good	Fair	Poor
6500	5000	3750	2500	1500	1050

No. 2 Volcanic 6" Barrel (Antique)

Exc.	Fine	V.G.	Good	Fair	Poor
7500	5750	4370	3000	1500	1050

Volcanic Lever Action Carbine & Rifle

New Haven Arms introduced, for the first time, a Volcanic rifle that featured a full-length slotted magazine tube, with spring-activated thumb piece follower that moved along the entire length of the magazine tube. Rifles were chambered for .41 caliber and offered in 16", 20", 24" barrel lengths.

Courtesy Buffalo Bill Historical Center, Cody, Wyoming

Lever Action CarbineCarbine 16" Barrel (Antique)

Exc.	Fine	V.G.	Good	Fair	Poor
40000	25000	17000	12000	8000	4000

Rifle 20" Barrel (Antique)

Seldom sold; values are speculative.

Exc.	Fine	V.G.	Good	Fair	Poor
45000	30000	20000	15000	8000	4000

Rifle 24" Barrel (Antique)

Seldom sold; values are speculative.

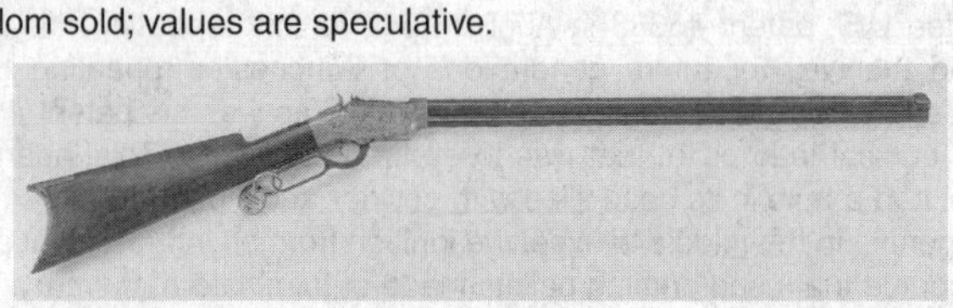

Courtesy Little John's Auction Service, Inc., Paul Goodwin photo

Exc.	Fine	V.G.	Good	Fair	Poor
60000	80000	30000	20000	—	5000

Henry Rifle

With the development of B. Tyler Henry's improvements in metallic rimfire cartridge and his additional improvements in Volcanic frame, direct predecessor to Winchester lever-action repeater was born. New cartridge was .44-caliber rimfire. Henry rifle featured 24" octagon barrel, with tubular magazine holding 15 shells. Rifle had no forearm. Furnished with walnut buttstock and two styles of buttplates: early rounded heel crescent shape seen on guns produced from 1860 to 1862; later sharper heel crescent butt found on guns built from 1863 to 1866. Early models produced from 1860 to 1861 were fitted with an iron frame; later models built from 1861 to 1866 were fitted with brass frames. About 14,000 Henry rifles were made during entire production period; only about 300 were iron frame rifles.

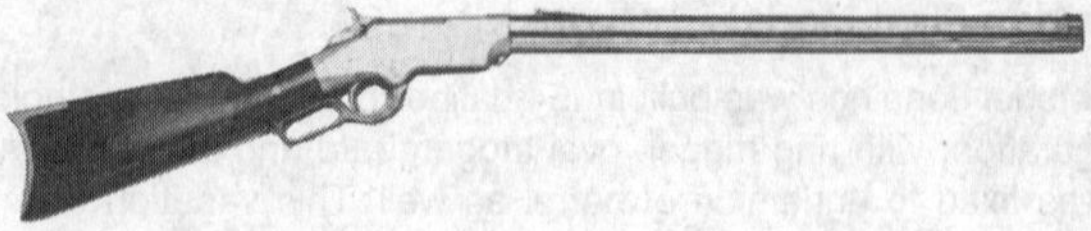

Courtesy Bonhams & Butterfields, San Francisco, California

Henry Iron Frame Rifle (Antique)

In 2013, Rock Island Auction sold an Iron Frame Henry described as "the finest in existence" for $603,750.

Courtesy Bonhams & Butterfields, San Francisco, California

Exc.	Fine	V.G.	Good	Fair	Poor
120000	80000	50000	30000	13000	9100

Henry Brass Frame Rifle (Antique)

Exc.	Fine	V.G.	Good	Fair	Poor
70000	37500	27500	17500	9000	6300

Martially Inspected Henry Rifles (Antique)

Beginning in 1863, Federal Government ordered 1,730 Henry Rifles for use in Civil War. Most of these government-inspected rifles fall into serial number range 3000 to 4000, while balance are close to this serial-number range. They are marked "C.G.C." for Charles G. Chapman, government inspector. These Henry rifles were used under actual combat conditions and for that reason it is doubtful there are any rifles that would fall into excellent condition category. Therefore, no price is given. Note: There are many counterfeit examples of these rifles. It is strongly advised that an expert in this field be consulted prior to sale.

Exc.	Fine	V.G.	Good	Fair	Poor
100000	60000	47500	35000	20000	14000

Winchester's Improvement Carbine (Antique)

Overall length 43.5"; barrel length 24"; caliber .44 rimfire. Walnut stock with brass buttplate; receiver and magazine cover/forend of brass; barrel and magazine tube blued. Magazine loading port is exposed by sliding the forend forward. This design was protected by O.F. Winchester's British Patent Number 3285 issued December 19, 1865. Unmarked except for internally located serial numbers. Approximately 700 manufactured in December 1865 and early 1866. The majority of these were sold to Maximilian of Mexico. Prospective purchasers are strongly advised to secure an expert appraisal prior to acquisition. Values are extremely speculative.

Exc.	Fine	V.G.	Good	Fair	Poor
27500	19500	16250	13000	9000	6300

Model 1866

In 1866, New Haven Arms Company changed its name to Winchester Repeating Arms Company. First firearm to be built under Winchester name was Model 1866. This first Winchester was a much-improved version of Henry. New magazine tube developed by Nelson King, Winchester's plant superintendent, was a vast improvement over slotted magazine tube used on Henry and its predecessor. Old tube allowed dirt to enter through slots and was weakened because of it. King's patent, assigned to Winchester, featured a solid tube that was much stronger and reliable. His patent also dealt with an improved loading system. Rifle now featured loading port on right side of receiver, with spring-loaded cover. Frame continued to be made from brass. Model 1866 was chambered for .44-caliber Flat Rimfire or .44-caliber Pointed Rimfire. Both cartridges could be used interchangeably.

Barrel on Model 1866 marked with two different markings. First, which is seen on early guns up to serial number 23000 reads, "HENRY'S PATENT-OCT. 16, 1860 KING'S PATENT-MARCH 29, 1866". Second marking reads, "WINCHESTER'S-REPEATING-ARMS. NEW HAVEN, CT. KING'S-IMPROVEMENT-PATENTED MARCH 29, 1866 OCTOBER 16, 1860". There are three basic variations of Model 1866:

1. Sporting Rifle: round or octagon barrel. Approximately 28,000 produced.
2. Carbine: round barrel. Approximately 127,000 produced.
3. Musket: round barrel. Approximately 14,000 produced.

Rifle and musket held 17 cartridges; carbine capacity 13. Unlike Henry, Model 1866s were fitted with walnut forearm. Model 1866 discontinued in 1898, with approximately 170,000 guns produced. Model 1866 sold in various special order configurations such as: barrels longer or shorter than standard, including engraved guns. Prices listed represent only standard-model 1866s. Guns with special-order features, an independent appraisal from an expert is highly recommended. Because of the bright brass frame, they were nicknamed the "Yellow Boy."

Courtesy Bonhams & Butterfields, San Francisco, California

1866 First Model Rifle (Antique)

First style has both Henry and King patent dates stamped on barrel. Flat-loading port cover and two-screw upper tang. Perhaps most distinctive feature of First Model is rapid drop at top rear of receiver near hammer. Often referred to as "Henry Drop", a reference to same receiver drop found on Henry rifle. The First Model is also called the "Flatside." First Models will be seen up through 15000 serial number range.

Exc.	Fine	V.G.	Good	Fair	Poor
80000	40000	20000	13000	4000	2800

1866 First Model Carbine (Antique)

Exc.	Fine	V.G.	Good	Fair	Poor
70000	30000	15000	11000	3000	2100

1866 Second Model Rifle

Second style differs from the first most noticeably in its single-screw upper tang and a flare at the front of receiver to meet the forearm. Second Model also has a more gradual drop at rear of the receiver than First Model. Second style Model 1866 appears through serial number 25000.

NIB	Exc.	V.G.	Good	Fair	Poor
25000	12500	10000	7500	4000	2500

1866 Second Model Carbine (Antique)

Exc.	Fine	V.G.	Good	Fair	Poor
20000	11000	8120	6750	3500	2000

1866 Third Model Rifle (Antique)

Third style's most noticeable characteristic is more moderately curved receiver shape at rear of frame. Serial number now stamped in block numerals behind trigger, thus allowing numbers to be seen for the first time without removing stock. Barrel marking stamped with Winchester address. Third Model found between serial numbers 25000 and 149000. For the first time, musket version was produced in this serial-number range.

Exc.	Fine	V.G.	Good	Fair	Poor
20000	12000	10000	7000	3500	2000

1866 Third Model Carbine (Antique)

Exc.	Fine	V.G.	Good	Fair	Poor
20000	9500	7500	5500	3500	2450

1866 Third Model Musket (Antique)

Exc.	Fine	V.G.	Good	Fair	Poor
20000	9500	7500	5500	3500	2450

1866 Fourth Model Rifle (Antique)

Fourth style has even less pronounced drop at top rear of frame. Serial number stamped in script on lower tang under lever. Fourth Model seen between serial number 149000 and 170100. Late guns having iron buttplate instead of brass.

Exc.	Fine	V.G.	Good	Fair	Poor
20000	9500	7500	5500	3500	2450

1866 Fourth Model Carbine (Antique)

Exc.	Fine	V.G.	Good	Fair	Poor
20000	9500	7500	5500	3500	2450

1866 Fourth Model Musket (Antique)

Exc.	Fine	V.G.	Good	Fair	Poor
20000	9500	7500	5500	3500	2450

Model 1866 Iron Frame Rifle Musket

Overall length 54.5"; barrel length 33.25"; caliber .45 centerfire. Walnut stock, with case-hardened furniture; barrel burnished bright; receiver case-hardened. Finger lever catch mounted within a large bolster at rear of the lever. Unmarked, except for serial numbers that appear externally on receiver and often buttplate tang. Approximately 25 made during early autumn of 1866. Value speculative.

Model 1866 Iron Frame Swiss Sharpshooters Rifle

As above, in .41-Swiss caliber. Fitted with Scheutzen-style stock supplied by the firm of Weber-Ruesch in Zurich. Marked Weber-Ruesch, Zurich on barrel and serial numbered externally. Approximately 400 to 450 manufactured in 1866 and 1867.

Model 1867 Iron Frame Carbine

Overall length 39.25"; barrel length 20"; caliber .44 rimfire. Walnut stock, with case-hardened furniture; barrel and magazine tube blued; receiver case-hardened. Finger lever catch mounted within rear curl of the lever. Unmarked, except for serial numbers that appear externally on receiver and often buttplate tang. Approximately 20 manufactured. Prospective purchasers are strongly advised to secure an expert appraisal prior to acquisition.

Model 1868 Iron Frame Rifle Musket

Calibers .45, .455 and .47 centerfire; overall length 49.5" (.455-cal.), 50.5" or 53" (.45- and .47-cal.); barrel length 29.5" (.455-cal.), 30.25" or 33" (.45- and .47-cal.). Walnut stock, with case-hardened or burnished bright furniture (.45- and .47-cal.); barrel burnished bright; receiver case-hardened or burnished bright (.45- and .47-cal.). Finger lever catch mounted on lower receiver tang. Rear of finger lever machined with a long flat extension on its upper surface. Unmarked, except for serial number. Approximately 30 examples made in .45- and .455-caliber; 250 in .47-caliber. In 2016 Rock Island Auction sold an iron frame musket made for British Trials in excellent condition for $28,750.

Model 1868 Iron Frame Carbine

Overall length 40"; barrel length 20"; caliber .44 centerfire. Walnut stock, with case-hardened furniture; barrel and magazine tube blued; receiver case-hardened. Finger lever catch as above. Unmarked, except for serial numbers (receiver and buttplate tang). Approximately 25 manufactured.

Model 1873

This Winchester rifle was one of the most popular lever-actions the company ever produced. This is the "gun that won the West" and with good reason. Chambered for the more powerful centerfire cartridge, .44-40. Compared to .44 Henry, this cartridge was twice as good. With the introduction of single-action Colt pistol in 1878, chambered for the same cartridge, the individual had the convenience of a pistol for protection and accuracy of the Winchester for food and protection. The .44-40 was the standard cartridge for Model 1873. Three additional cartridges were offered, but were not as popular as .44-40. The .38-40 first offered in 1879 and .32-20 introduced in 1882. In 1884, offered in .22-caliber rimfire, with a few special order guns built in .22 Extra Long rimfire. Approximately 19,552 .22-caliber Model 1873s were produced. Early model 1873s were fitted with an iron receiver until 1884, when a steel receiver was introduced.

Model 1873 was offered in three styles:
1. Sporting Rifle: 24" round, octagon or half-octagon barrel. Equipped standard with a crescent iron buttplate, straight-grip stock and capped forearm.
2. Carbine: 20" round barrel. Furnished standard with a rounded iron buttplate, straight-grip stock and carbine style forend fastened to barrel with a single barrel band.
3. Musket: 30" round barrel. Standard musket furnished with a nearly full-length forearm fastened to barrel with three barrel bands. Buttstock has a rounded buttplate.

Upper tang was marked with model designation and serial number was stamped on lower tang. Caliber stampings on Model 1873 are found on the bottom of the frame and on breech end of barrel. Winchester discontinued Model 1873 in 1919, after producing about 720,000 guns. Winchester Model 1873 was offered with a large number of extra-cost options that greatly affects the value of this gun. For example, Winchester built two sets of special Model 1873s: 1-of-100 and 1-of-1000. Winchester sold only eight 1-of-100 Model 1873s; and 136 of 1-of-1000 guns that were built. In recent years, some of these special guns were sold at auction and brought prices well in excess of $100,000. Prices listed here are for standard guns only. For Model 1873 with special features, it is best to secure an expert appraisal. Model 1873s with case colored receivers will bring a premium.

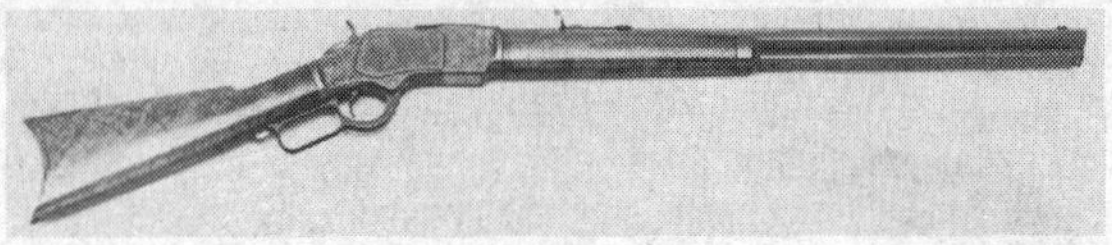

Courtesy Bonhams & Butterfields, San Francisco, California

1873 First Model Rifle Antique

Primary difference between the various styles of Model 1873, is found in appearance and construction of the dust cover. First Model has a dust cover held in place with grooved guides on either side. A checkered oval finger grip is found on top of the dust cover. Latch that holds lever firmly in place is anchored into the lower tang with visible threads. On later First Models, these threads are not visible. First Models appear from serial number 1 to about 31000.

Exc.	*Fine*	*V.G.*	*Good*	*Fair*	*Poor*
18000	10000	6500	3000	1400	970

1873 First Model Carbine Antique

Exc.	*Fine*	*V.G.*	*Good*	*Fair*	*Poor*
20000	12000	8000	4000	2500	1750

1873 First Model Musket Antique

Exc.	*Fine*	*V.G.*	*Good*	*Fair*	*Poor*
25000	15000	11250	7500	1800	1260

1873 Second Model Rifle Antique

Dust cover on Second Model operates on one central guide secured to receiver with two screws. Checkered oval finger grip is still used, but on later Second Models this is changed to a serrated finger grip on rear of the dust cover. Second Models are found in 31000 to 90000 serial number range.

Exc.	*Fine*	*V.G.*	*Good*	*Fair*	*Poor*
8000	4000	3000	2000	1250	870

1873 Second Model Carbine Antique

Exc.	*Fine*	*V.G.*	*Good*	*Fair*	*Poor*
13000	7000	5000	3000	1000	700

1873 Second Model Musket Antique

Few sales, values shown reflect two sales of Spanish muskets.

Exc.	*Fine*	*V.G.*	*Good*	*Fair*	*Poor*
—	17500	—	—	—	—

1873 Third Model Rifle Antique

Central guide rail is still present on Third Model, but is now integrally machined as part of the receiver. Serrated rear edges of dust cover are still present on Third Model.

Exc.	*Fine*	*V.G.*	*Good*	*Fair*	*Poor*
5000	3000	2000	1000	750	520

1873 Third Model Carbine Antique

Exc.	*Fine*	*V.G.*	*Good*	*Fair*	*Poor*
12000	5000	3500	2000	800	560

1873 Third Model Musket Antique

Exc.	*Fine*	*V.G.*	*Good*	*Fair*	*Poor*
8000	5000	3000	1500	700	500

Model 1873 .22 Rimfire Rifle (Antique)

Winchester's first .22-caliber rifle and first .22-caliber repeating rifle made in America, was introduced in 1884; discontinued in 1904. Its drawback was the small caliber. General preference during this period of time was for larger-caliber rifles. Winchester sold a little more than 19,000 .22-caliber Model 1873s.

Exc.	*Fine*	*V.G.*	*Good*	*Fair*	*Poor*
8500	5500	3500	2000	1200	600

Model 1876

Winchester's Model 1876, sometimes referred to as Centennial Model, was company's response to the public's demand for a repeater rifle capable of handling larger and more potent calibers. Many single-shot rifles were available at this time to shoot more powerful cartridges. Winchester redesigned earlier Model 1873 to answer this need. Principal changes made to Model 1873, were a larger and stronger receiver to handle more powerful cartridges. Both the carbine and musket had their forearms extended to cover the full-length of the magazine tube. Carbine barrel was increased in length from 20" to 22"; musket barrel from 30 to 32". Model 1876 was the first Winchester to be offered with a pistol grip stock on its special Sporting Rifle. Model 1876 was available in these calibers: .45-77 WCF, .50-95 Express, .45-60 WCF, .40-60 WCF.

Model 1876 was offered in four different styles:
1. Sporting Rifle: 28" round, octagon or half-octagon barrel. Fitted with a straight-grip stock, with crescent iron buttplate. A special sporting rifle was offered with a pistol grip stock.
2. Express Rifle: 26" round, octagon or half-octagon barrel. Same sporting rifle stock was used.
3. Carbine: 22" round barrel, with full-length forearm secured by one barrel band and straight-grip stock.
4. Musket: 32" round barrel, with full-length forearm secured by one barrel band and straight-grip stock.

Stamped on barrel is Winchester address with King's patent date. Caliber marking is stamped on bottom of receiver near magazine tube and breech end of barrel. Winchester also furnished Model 1876 in 1-of-100 and 1-of-1000 special guns. Only eight 1-of-100 1876s were built; and 54 1-of-1000 1876s. As with their Model 1873 counterparts, these rare guns often sell in the $75,000 range or more. Approximately 64,000 Model 1876s were built by Winchester between 1876 and 1897. As with other Winchesters prices given are for standard guns.

1876 First Model Rifle (Antique)

As with Model 1873, primary difference in model types lies in the dust cover. First Model has no dust cover. Seen between serial number 1 and 3000.

Exc.	*Fine*	*V.G.*	*Good*	*Fair*	*Poor*
25000	13000	9000	5000	1500	1050

1876 First Model Carbine (Antique)

Exc.	*Fine*	*V.G.*	*Good*	*Fair*	*Poor*
16000	10000	6250	2500	1000	700

1876 First Model Musket (Antique)

Exc.	*Fine*	*V.G.*	*Good*	*Fair*	*Poor*
20000	12000	8500	5000	1500	1050

1876 Second Model Rifle (Antique)

Second Model has a dust cover, with guide rail attached to receiver with two screws. On early Second Model, an oval finger guide is stamped on top of dust cover; while later models have a serrated finger guide along rear edge of dust cover. Second Models range from serial numbers 3000 to 30000.

Exc.	*Fine*	*V.G.*	*Good*	*Fair*	*Poor*
7500	4000	3000	2000	1000	700

1876 Second Model Carbine (Antique)

Exc.	*Fine*	*V.G.*	*Good*	*Fair*	*Poor*
15000	9000	6000	3000	1000	700

1876 Second Model Musket (Antique)

Exc.	*Fine*	*V.G.*	*Good*	*Fair*	*Poor*
15000	8000	4870	1750	1000	700

1876 Second Model Northwest Mounted Police Carbine (Antique)

Folding rear sight is graduated in meters instead of yards. Note: Deduct 50 percent from prices if factory records do not confirm NWMP use. A Model 1876 NWMP in excellent condition is very rare. Proceed with caution.

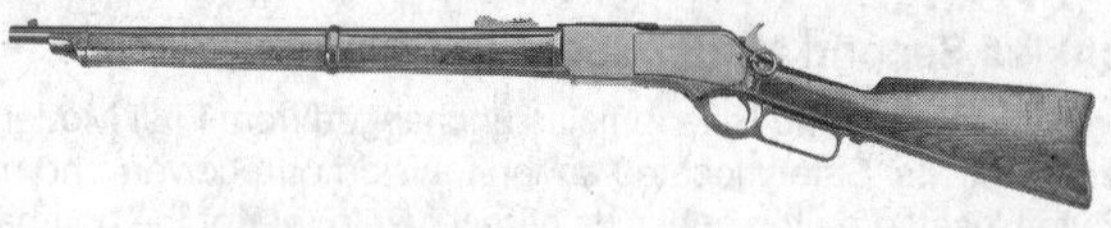

Courtesy Little John's Auction Service, Inc., Paul Goodwin photo

Exc.	*Fine*	*V.G.*	*Good*	*Fair*	*Poor*
17000	11000	7000	4000	1500	900

Third Model Rifle

Dust cover guide rail on Third Model is integrally machined as part of receiver, with serrated rear edge on dust cover. Third Model will be seen from serial numbers 30000 to 64000.

NIB	*Exc.*	*V.G.*	*Good*	*Fair*	*Poor*
—	14000	10000	6000	3000	1500

Third Model Carbine

NIB	*Exc.*	*V.G.*	*Good*	*Fair*	*Poor*
—	20000	17500	12000	6000	2000

Third Model Musket

NIB	*Exc.*	*V.G.*	*Good*	*Fair*	*Poor*
—	14000	10000	7500	4000	1000

Winchester Hotchkiss Bolt-Action Rifle

This model is also known as Hotchkiss Magazine Gun or Model 1883. Designed by Benjamin Hotchkiss in 1876. Winchester acquired manufacturing rights to this rifle in 1877. In 1879, the first guns were delivered for sale. Hotchkiss rifle was a bolt-action firearm designed for military and sporting use. First bolt-action rifle made by Winchester. Furnished in .45-70 Government, although the 1884 Winchester catalog lists a .40-65 Hotchkiss as being available. No evidence exists that such a chamber was ever actually furnished.

Model 1883 was available in three different styles:
1. Sporting Rifle: 26" round, octagon or half-octagon barrel. Fitted with a rifle-type stock that included a modified pistol grip or straight-grip stock.
2. Carbine: 24" or 22.5" round barrel, with military-style straight-grip stock.
3. Musket: 32" or 28" round barrel, with almost full-length military-style straight-grip stock.

Winchester produced Model 1883 until 1899, having built about 85,000 guns. U.S. Army or Navy marked specimens are rare and will bring a premium.

Courtesy Bonhams & Butterfields, San Francisco, California

Hotchkiss First Model Sporting Rifle (Antique)

This model has safety and turn button magazine cut-off located above triggerguard on the right side. Sporting Rifle furnished with 26" round or octagon barrel; carbine a 24" round barrel, with saddle ring on left side of stock; musket a 32" round barrel, with two barrel bands, steel forearm tip and bayonet attachment under the barrel. Serial number range between 1 and about 6419.

Exc.	Fine	V.G.	Good	Fair	Poor
4000	2000	1200	750	500	250

Hotchkiss First Model Carbine Antique

Exc.	Fine	V.G.	Good	Fair	Poor
4500	2250	1400	1000	500	350

Hotchkiss First Model Musket Antique

Exc.	Fine	V.G.	Good	Fair	Poor
3000	2000	1250	1000	500	350

Hotchkiss Second Model Sporting Rifle Antique

Second Model Sporting Rifle remains unchanged from First Model, with these exceptions. Safety located on top left side of receiver; and magazine cutoff located on top right side of receiver to rear of the bolt handle. Carbine has a 22.5" round barrel, with nickeled forearm cap; musket now a 28" barrel. Serial number range runs from 6420 to 22521.

Courtesy Milwaukee Public Museum, Milwaukee, Wisconsin

Exc.	Fine	V.G.	Good	Fair	Poor
2000	1500	1000	650	400	250

Hotchkiss Second Model Carbine Antique

Exc.	Fine	V.G.	Good	Fair	Poor
2500	1700	1200	800	400	250

Hotchkiss Second Model Musket Antique

Exc.	Fine	V.G.	Good	Fair	Poor
2700	2000	1400	900	400	250

Hotchkiss Third Model Sporting Rifle Antique

Third Model is easily identified by two-piece stock separated by the receiver. Specifications for sporting rifle remain the same as before; while carbine is now fitted with a 20" barrel, with saddle ring and bar on left side of the frame; and musket remains unchanged from Second Model, except with the two-piece stock. Serial numbers range from 22552 to 84555.

Exc.	Fine	V.G.	Good	Fair	Poor
2500	1250	900	700	500	250

Hotchkiss Third Model Carbine Antique

Very rare, values are speculative.

Exc.	Fine	V.G.	Good	Fair	Poor
10000	7000	4000	2000	1000	400

Hotchkiss Third Model Musket Antique

Exc.	Fine	V.G.	Good	Fair	Poor
4000	2500	1800	800	500	250

Model 1885 (Single-Shot)

Model 1885 marks an important development between Winchester and John M. Browning. The Single-Shot rifle was first, of many, Browning patents that Winchester would purchase and provide the company with opportunities to diversify its firearms line. Model 1885 was the first single-shot rifle built by Winchester. The company offered more calibers in this model than any other. A total of 45 centerfire calibers were offered from .22 Extra Long to .50-110 Express; as well as 14 rimfire calibers from .22 B.B. cap to .44 Flat Henry. Numerous barrel lengths, shapes and weights were available; as were stock configurations, sights and finishes. These rifles were also available in solid-frame and take-down styles. One could almost argue that each of the 139,725 Model 1885s built are unique. Model 1885 was manufactured between 1885 and 1920. Many collectors of Winchester Single-Shot specialize in nothing else. For this reason, it is difficult to provide pricing that will cover most of the Model 1885s that collectors will encounter. However, prices given here are for standard guns in standard configurations.

Model 1885 was offered in two basic frame types: A. High Wall was the first frame-type produced, and is so called because frame covers breech and hammer except for the hammer spur. B. Breech and hammer are visible on Low Wall frame, with its low sides. This frame-type was first introduced around 5000 serial number range.

Both High Wall and Low Wall were available in two type frame profiles; Thickside and Thinside. Thickside frame has flat sides that do not widen out to meet the stock. Thickside is more common on Low Wall rifle and rare on High Wall. Thinside frame has shallow milled sides that widen out to meet the stock. Thinside frames are common on High Wall rifle and rare on Low Wall.

1. Standard High Wall rifle was available with octagon or round barrel, with length determined by caliber. Buttstock and forearm were plain walnut, with crescent buttplate and blued frame.
2. Standard Low Wall rifle featured round or octagon barrel, with length determined by caliber. Plain walnut stock and forearm, with crescent buttplate.
3. High Wall musket most often had a 26" round barrel. Chambered for .22-caliber cartridge. Larger calibers were available as were different barrel lengths. Featured an almost full-length forearm fastened to barrel with a single barrel band and rounded buttplate.
4. Low Wall musket is most often referred to as Winder Musket, named after distinguished marksman, Colonel C.B. Winder. Features a Lyman receiver sight and made in .22-caliber.
5. High Wall Schuetzen rifle was designed for serious target shooting. Available with numerous extras, including 30" octagon barrel; medium weight without rear sight seat; fancy walnut checkered pistol grip Schuetzen-style buttplate; checkered forearm; double-set triggers; spur finger lever; adjustable palm rest.
6. Low Wall carbine was available in 15", 16", 18" and 20" round barrels. Carbine featured a saddle ring on left side of the frame and a rounded buttplate.
7. High Wall shotgun in 20-gauge, with 26" round barrel, straight-grip stock and shotgun style rubber buttplate.

Note: Add 25 percent premium for case colored frames over guns with blued frames. Calibers .50-110 and .50-100 will bring a premium depending on style and configuration.

CALIBER Note: As stated above, it is difficult to provide pricing on specific rifles, especially calibers, because of the wide range of variables. However, collectors may find it useful to know the most common rimfire calibers were .22 Short, .22 WCF and .22 Long in that order, with .22 Long Rifle a distant fourth. Most common centerfire calibers were .32 WCF and .32-40. Other popular centerfire calibers were .38-55, .25-20, .44 WCF, .32 Long WCF and .45-70. There were a number of chamberings that are extremely rare (one of each built). It is strongly recommended that research is done prior to a sale. Premium for antique specimens made prior to 1899 with serial numbers lower than approximately 84701.

Courtesy Bonhams & Butterfields, San Francisco, California

Standard High Wall Rifle

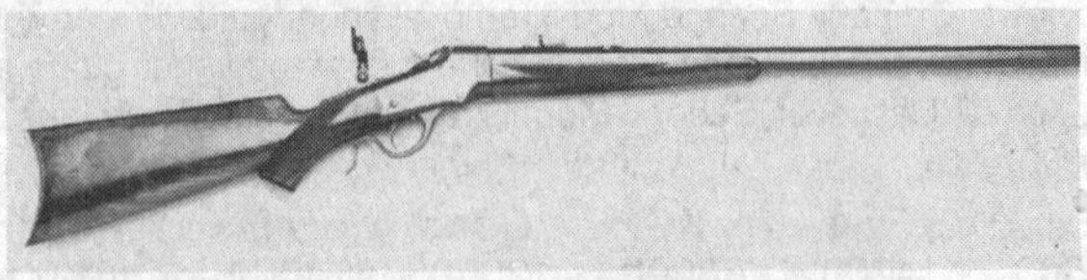

Courtesy Bonhams & Butterfields, San Francisco, California

Deluxe High Wall

NIB	Exc.	V.G.	Good	Fair	Poor
—	5000	3500	2200	1500	950

Standard Low Wall Rifle

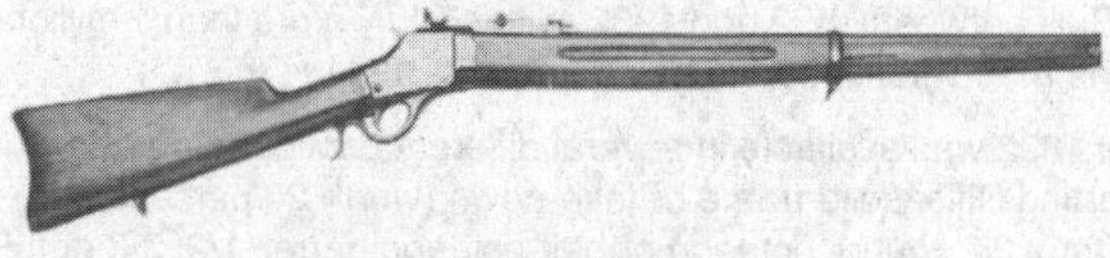

Courtesy Bonhams & Butterfields, San Francisco, California

NIB	Exc.	V.G.	Good	Fair	Poor
—	1800	1500	1400	1200	900

High Wall Musket

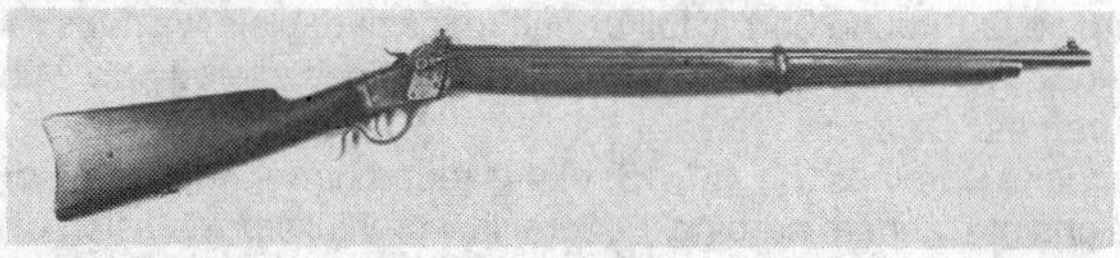

NIB	Exc.	V.G.	Good	Fair	Poor
—	1600	1300	1000	700	420

Low Wall Musket (Winder Musket)

Courtesy Buffalo Bill Historical Center, Cody, Wyoming

NIB	Exc.	V.G.	Good	Fair	Poor
—	1400	1200	800	500	300

High Wall Schuetzen Rifle

NIB	Exc.	V.G.	Good	Fair	Poor
—	10000	7000	3000	1850	1000

Low Wall Carbine

NIB	Exc.	V.G.	Good	Fair	Poor
—	7500	5000	3500	2750	1500

High Wall Shotgun

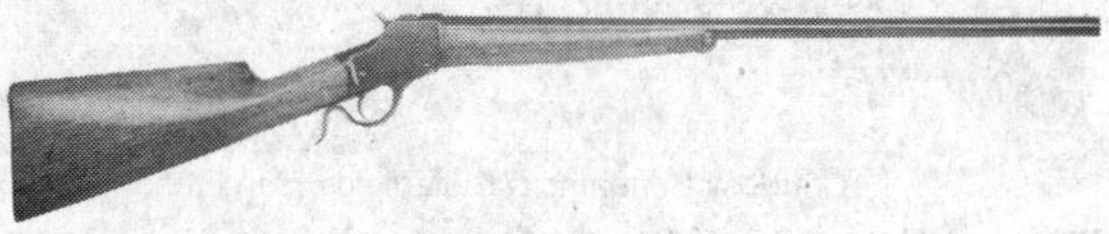

Courtesy Buffalo Bill Historical Center, Cody, Wyoming

NIB	Exc.	V.G.	Good	Fair	Poor
—	4500	3000	2250	1250	850

Model 1886

Based on a John Browning patent, Model 1886 was one of the finest and strongest lever-actions ever utilized in a Winchester rifle. Winchester introduced Model 1886, in order to take advantage of the more powerful centerfire cartridges of the time. Most popular caliber was .45-70 Government.

Model 1886 Rifles and Carbines were furnished with black walnut stocks, case-hardened frames, blued barrels and magazine tubes. In 1901, Winchester discontinued the use of case-hardened frames on all its rifles and used blued frames instead. For this reason, case-hardened rifles will bring a premium. Winchester provided a large selection of extra cost options on Model 1886. Rifles with these options, a separate evaluation should be made by a reliable source. Produced about 160,000 from 1886 to 1935. Note: A new record price for a single firearm was established in April 2016, when a very special Winchester Model 1886 rifle sold for $1.265 million. The historic rifle with serial number 1, had been presented to U.S. Army Captain Henry Lawton following his capture of Apache leader Geronimo in September of 1886. In near mint original condition, the rifle was sold at auction by Rock Island Auction Co. to an anonymous bidder.

Rifle was available in 10 different chambers:
.45-70 U.S. Government
.45-90 WCF
.40-82 WCF
.40-65 WCF
.38-56 WCF
.50-110 Express
.40-70 WCF
.38-70 WCF
.50-100-450
.33 WCF

Model 1886s were available in several different configurations:

1. Sporting Rifle: 26" round, octagon and half-octagon barrel; full or half magazine; straight-grip stock, with plain forearm.
2. Fancy Sporting Rifle: 26" round or octagon barrel; half or full magazine; fancy checkered walnut pistol grip, with checkered forearm.
3. Take-down Rifle: 24" round barrel; full or half magazine, with straight-grip stock fitted with shotgun rubber buttplate and plain forearm.
4. Extra Lightweight Take-down Rifle: 22" round barrel; full or half magazine, with straight-grip stock fitted with shotgun rubber buttplate and plain forearm.
5. Extra Lightweight Rifle: 22" round barrel; full or half magazine, with straight-grip stock fitted with a shotgun rubber buttplate and plain forearm.
6. Carbine: 22" round barrel; full or half magazine, with straight-grip stock and plain forearm.
7. Musket: 30" round barrel; musket-style forearm, with one barrel band. Military-style sights. About 350 Model 1886 Muskets were produced.

Note: Add 20 percent premium for .50 Express; 20 percent premium for case colored. Prices are influenced by caliber, with larger calibers bringing a premium. Premium for antique specimens made prior to 1899 with serial numbers lower than approximately 111193.

Sporting Rifle

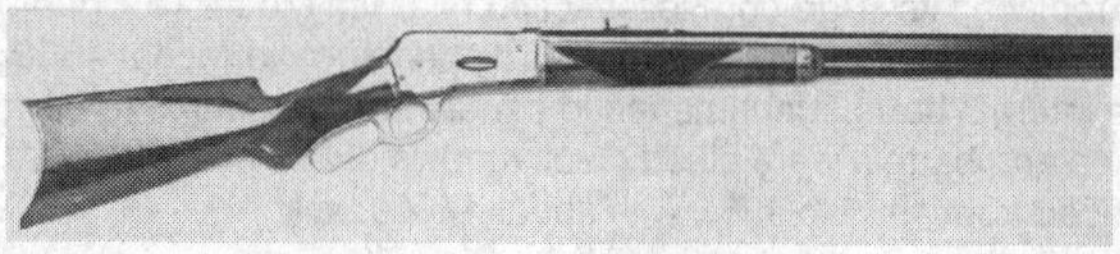

Courtesy Bonhams & Butterfields, San Francisco, California

NIB	Exc.	V.G.	Good	Fair	Poor
—	15000	15000	7500	5000	2500

Fancy Sporting Rifle

NIB	Exc.	V.G.	Good	Fair	Poor
—	25000	14500	8000	6000	3000

Takedown Rifle—Standard

NIB	Exc.	V.G.	Good	Fair	Poor
—	12500	900	4200	2000	700

Extra Lightweight Takedown Rifle—.33 caliber

NIB	Exc.	V.G.	Good	Fair	Poor
—	9000	5000	2000	750	400

Extra Lightweight Takedown Rifle—Other Calibers

NIB	Exc.	V.G.	Good	Fair	Poor
—	8750	6000	1800	1250	500

Extra Lightweight Rifle—.33 caliber

NIB	Exc.	V.G.	Good	Fair	Poor
—	6000	4000	1800	1000	500

Extra Lightweight Rifle—Other Calibers

NIB	Exc.	V.G.	Good	Fair	Poor
—	7000	5500	3000	950	500

Carbine

Carbine barrels are 22". Few were Trappers, with 20" barrels. Note: Add 50 percent if Trapper.

Courtesy Bonhams & Butterfields, San Francisco, California

NIB	Exc.	V.G.	Good	Fair	Poor
—	19000	11000	7500	4500	2000

Model 1886 Saddle Ring Carbine

Calibers: .45-70 Govt, .45-90 Win. Capacity: 7-round tubular magazine. Barrel: 22-in. round polished blued steel. Weight: 8 lbs. Length: 41 in. Stock: Grade I Black Walnut with straight grip and carbine-style forearm, oil finished. Sights: Carbine ladder-style rear and blade front. Features: Full-length magazine tube, steel barrel band. Drilled and tapped for receiver mount sight. Brushed polish receiver finish. Tang safety. Side saddle ring.

NIB	Exc.	V.G.	Good	Fair	Poor
1430	—	—	—	—	—

Model 1886Musket

NIB	Exc.	V.G.	Good	Fair	Poor
—	19000	15000	9000	3500	1500

Model 71

When Winchester dropped Model 1886 from its line in 1935, the company replaced its large-bore lever-action rifle with Model 71. Chambered for .348-caliber. Model 71 is similar in appearance to Model 1886, with some internal parts strengthened to handle the powerful .348 cartridge. Frames and barrels were blued on all models of this rifle. Model 71 was produced from 1935 to 1957, with about 47,000 built.

Model 71 was available in three basic configurations:
1. Standard Rifle: 24" round barrel; 3/4 magazine; plain walnut pistol grip stock; semi-beavertail forearm.
2. Standard Rifle (Carbine): 20" round barrel; 3/4 magazine; plain walnut pistol grip stock; semi-beavertail forearm.
3. Deluxe Rifle: 24" round barrel; 3/4 magazine; checkered walnut pistol grip stock; checkered semi-beavertail forearm.
4. Deluxe Rifle (Carbine): 20" round barrel; 3/4 magazine; checkered walnut pistol grip stock; checkered semi-beavertail forearm.

Note: Add 10 percent for bolt peep sight; 20 percent premium for pre-war models (pre-war Model 71s have a longer tang than post-war equivalent).

Standard Rifle

NIB	Exc.	V.G.	Good	Fair	Poor
—	1500	1200	800	400	300

Standard Rifle (Carbine)

NIB	Exc.	V.G.	Good	Fair	Poor
—	3250	2000	1600	1200	650

Deluxe Rifle

NIB	Exc.	V.G.	Good	Fair	Poor
—	3500	3050	800	520	420

Deluxe Rifle (Carbine)

NIB	Exc.	V.G.	Good	Fair	Poor
—	4100	3500	2000	1250	700

Model 1892

Model 1892 was an updated successor to Model 1873, using a scaled down version of Model 1886 action. Chambered for popular smaller cartridges of the day, namely .25-20, .32-20, .38-40, .44-40 and rare .218 Bee. Built between 1892 and 1932, with slightly more than 1 million sold. Carbine model continued to be offered until 1941.

Model 1892 was available in several different configurations:
1. Sporting Rifle: solid-frame or take-down (worth 20 percent extra premium); 24" round, octagon or half-octagon barrel; 1/2, 2/3 or full magazines; plain straight-grip walnut stock, with capped forearm.
2. Fancy Sporting Rifle: solid-frame or take-down (worth 20 percent extra premium); 24" round, octagon or half-octagon barrel; 1/2, 2/3 or full magazines; checkered walnut pistol grip stock; checkered capped forearm.
3. Carbine: 20" round barrel; full or half magazine; plain walnut straight-grip stock, with one barrel band forearm. Carbines offered only with solid-frames.
4. Trapper's Carbine: 18", 16", 15" or 14" round barrel, with same dimensions of standard carbine. Federal law prohibits possession of rifles with barrel lengths shorter then 16". Model 1892 Trapper's Carbine can be exempted from this law, as a curio and relic, with federal permit providing trapper is an original trapper and left the factory with the short trapper barrel.
5. Musket: 30" round barrel, with full magazine. Almost full-length forearm held by two barrel bands. Buttstock plain walnut, with straight-grip.

Note: Add 10 percent premium for Antique Winchester Model 1892s (pre-1898 manufacture). Premium for antique specimens made prior to 1899 with serial numbers lower than approximately 165432.

Sporting Rifle

Courtesy Bonhams & Butterfields, San Francisco, California

NIB	Exc.	V.G.	Good	Fair	Poor
—	5000	3500	1250	700	350

Fancy Sporting Rifle

Courtesy Bonhams & Butterfields, San Francisco, California

NIB	Exc.	V.G.	Good	Fair	Poor
—	12000	7500	4000	2500	1000

Carbine

Courtesy Bonhams & Butterfields, San Francisco, California

NIB	Exc.	V.G.	Good	Fair	Poor
—	5000	3500	2500	1200	600

Trapper's Carbine

Note: Add 20 percent for 15" barrel; 50 percent for carbines chambered for .25-20 cartridge.

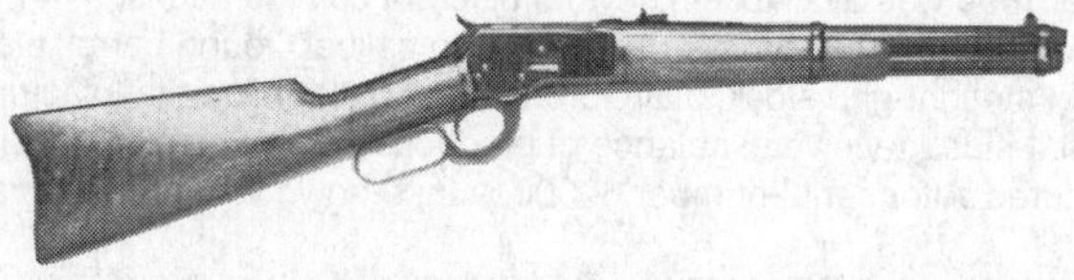

Courtesy Bonhams & Butterfields, San Francisco, California

NIB	Exc.	V.G.	Good	Fair	Poor
—	12000	8500	4000	2500	1250

Musket

NIB	Exc.	V.G.	Good	Fair	Poor
—	18500	12500	7500	2500	1500

Model 1894

Based on a John M. Browning patent, Model 1894 was the most successful centerfire rifle Winchester ever produced. This model is still in production. Values given here reflect those rifles produced before 1964, or around serial number 2550000. Model 1894 was the first Winchester developed especially for the smokeless powder. Chambered for these cartridges: .32-40, .38-55, .25-35 Win., .30-30 Win. and .32 Win. Special. All Model 1894s were furnished with blued frames and barrels. Case-hardened frames were available as an extra-cost option. Case colored Model 1894s are rare and worth a considerable premium, perhaps as much as 1,000 percent. Guns with extra-cost options should be evaluated by an expert to determine proper value. Between 1894 and 1963, approximately 2,550,000 Model 1894s were sold.

Model 1894s were available in several different configurations:

1. Sporting Rifle: 26" round, octagon or half-octagon barrel; solid-frame or take-down; full, 2/3 or 1/2 magazines; plain walnut straight-/pistol grip stock; crescent buttplate; plain capped forearm.
2. Fancy Sporting Rifle: 26" round, octagon or half-octagon barrel; solid-frame or take-down; full, 2/3 or 1/2 magazines; fancy walnut checkered straight-/pistol grip stock; crescent buttplate; checkered fancy capped forearm.
3. Extra Lightweight Rifle: 22" or 26" round barrel; half magazine; plain walnut straight-grip stock; shotgun buttplate; plain capped forearm.
4. Carbine: 20" round barrel; plain walnut straight-grip stock; carbine style buttplate; forearm was plain walnut uncapped, with one barrel band; solid-frame only. Carbines made prior to 1925, were fitted with a saddle ring on left side of receiver. Worth a premium over carbines without a saddle ring.
5. Trappers Carbine: 18", 16", 15" or 14" round barrel. Buttstock, forearm and saddle ring specifications same as standard carbine.

Note: Add 10 percent premium for Antique Winchester Model 1894s (pre-1898 manufacture); 100 percent premium for First year production guns, October 1894 to December 1894, documented by the Cody Museum; 25 percent for carbines chambered .25-35 or .38-55 cartridge. Deduct 35 percent for carbines without saddle rings. Values are for guns with saddle rings. Premium for antique specimens made prior to 1899 with serial numbers lower than approximately 147685.

First Model Sporting Rifle

Very early model. Incorporates a screw entering receiver over the loading port from outside. RARE.

NIB	Exc.	V.G.	Good	Fair	Poor
—	7000	4000	2000	1250	500

Sporting Rifle

Note: Add 20 percent for take-down versions.

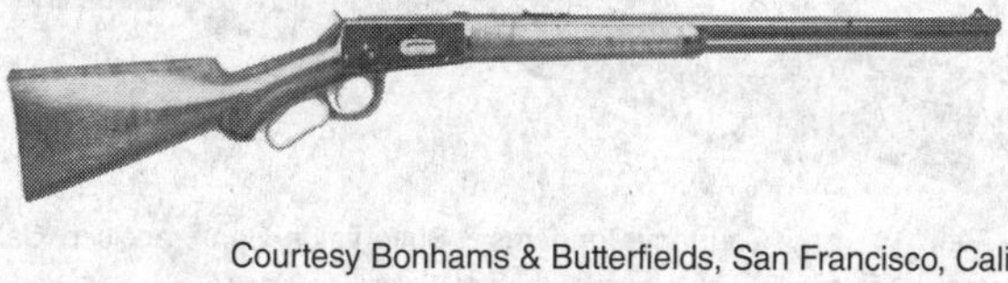

Courtesy Bonhams & Butterfields, San Francisco, California

NIB	Exc.	V.G.	Good	Fair	Poor
—	4000	3000	1500	850	450

Fancy Sporting Rifle

Note: Add 20 percent for take-down versions. Fancy Sporting Rifles were also engraved at customer's request. Check factory where possible and proceed with caution. Factory engraved Model 1894s are extremely valuable.

Courtesy Bonhams & Butterfields, San Francisco, California

NIB	Exc.	V.G.	Good	Fair	Poor
—	12000	7500	3500	2000	900

Extra Lightweight Rifle

Courtesy Bonhams & Butterfields, San Francisco, California

NIB	Exc.	V.G.	Good	Fair	Poor
—	5000	3500	1500	1000	450

Carbine

NIB	Exc.	V.G.	Good	Fair	Poor
—	3000	2000	600	400	200

Trapper's Carbine

Note: Add 30 percent for carbines chambered .25-35 or .38-55 calibers.

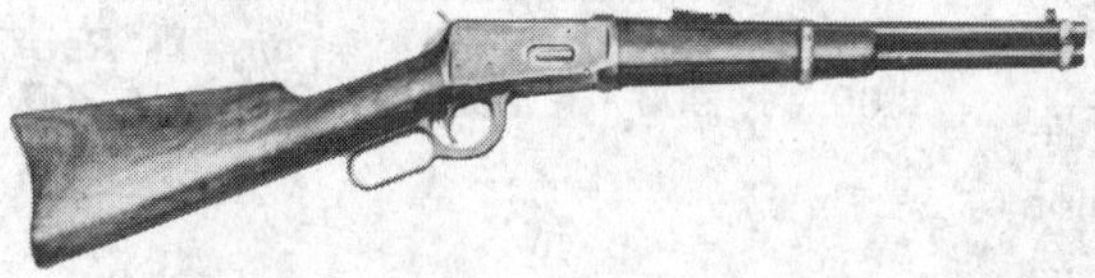

Courtesy Bonhams & Butterfields, San Francisco, California

NIB	Exc.	V.G.	Good	Fair	Poor
—	6500	4250	2500	1500	700

Model 53

A slightly more modern version of Model 1892. Offered in these calibers: .25-20, .32-20 and .44-40. Available in only one style: Sporting Rifle; 22" round barrel; half magazine; straight-/pistol grip plain walnut stock, with shotgun butt. Available in solid-frame or take-down, with blued frame and barrel. Produced from 1924 to 1932, with about 25,000 built. Note: Add 25 percent for take-down model; 60 percent for rifles chambered for .44-40 cartridge. Deluxe model was made with high-grade checkered stock. A few of these rifles were fitted with stainless steel barrels in early 1930s. If the black paint on these barrels is in good condition, they will bring a substantial premium.

NIB	Exc.	V.G.	Good	Fair	Poor
—	3000	2000	1000	500	300

Deluxe Model

NIB	Exc.	V.G.	Good	Fair	Poor
—	4000	3200	2400	1500	750

Model 55

A continuation of Model 1894, except in a simplified version. Available in same calibers as Model 1894. This rifle could be ordered only with a 24" round barrel; plain walnut straight-grip stock, with plain forend and shotgun butt. Frame and barrel were blued, with solid or take-down features. Produced between 1924 and 1932, with about 21,000 sold. Serial numbers were numbered separately until about serial number 4500; then numbered in Model 1894 sequence. Note: .25-35 calibers will bring up to 100 percent premium in V.G. or better condition. Add 20 percent premium for models with solid-frames.

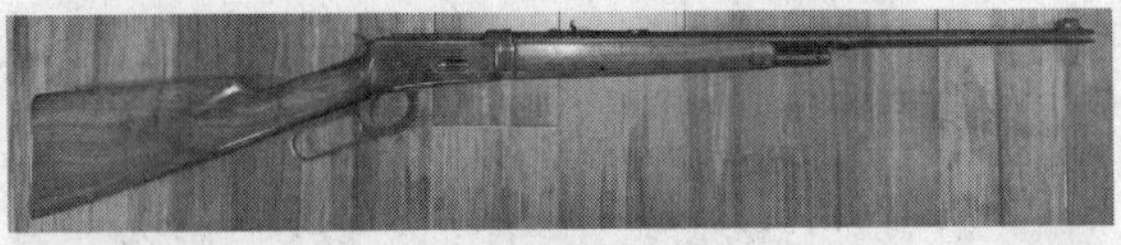

Courtesy Keith Kramis

Winchester Model 55 .30 WCF.

NIB	Exc.	V.G.	Good	Fair	Poor
—	2250	1500	900	500	300

Model 64

An improved version of Model 55. Features larger magazine, pistol grip stock and forged front sight ramp. Trigger pull was also improved. Frame and barrel were blued. Chambered for .25-35 Win., .30-30 Win., .32 Win. Special and .219 Zipper added in 1938 (discontinued in Model 64 in 1941). Serial numbers were concurrent with Model 1894. Built between 1933 and 1957. Approximately 67,000 were sold. Reintroduced in 1972; discontinued in 1973. Values listed are for early version only. For 1972 model, see POST-1963 RIFLES section. Note: Add 150 percent for Deluxe model. Rifles chambered in .219 Zipper or .25-35 calibers are very rare. Add 400 percent for .219 Zipper; 200 percent for .25-35; 10 percent for bolt peep sight. Model 64s in .219 Zipper left factory with these sights as original equipment.

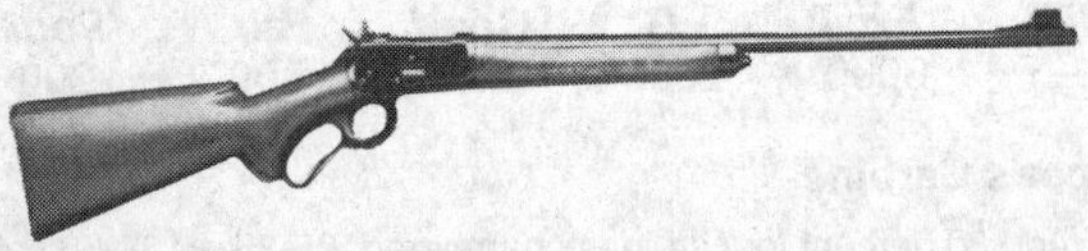

Bonhams & Butterfields, San Francisco, California

NIB	Exc.	V.G.	Good	Fair	Poor
—	1200	900	500	300	200

Carbine

20" barrel.

NIB	Exc.	V.G.	Good	Fair	Poor
—	2800	2000	1200	800	500

Model 65

Continuation of Model 53. Offered in three calibers: .25-20, .32-20 and .218 Bee. Had several improvements over Model 53, namely magazine capacity increased to 7 cartridges, forged ramp for front sight and lighter trigger pull. Available only in solid blued frame, with blued barrel and plain walnut pistol grip stock. About 5,700 built between 1933 and 1947. Note: Add 50 percent for Deluxe model with high-grade checkered walnut stock; 10 percent for bolt peep sight. Model 65s in .218 Bee left factory with bolt peep sights as original equipment.

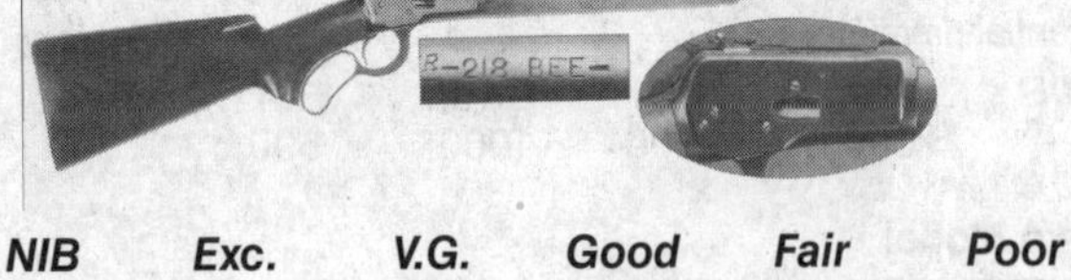

NIB	Exc.	V.G.	Good	Fair	Poor
—	5000	4000	2000	1000	500

Model 1895

Model 1895 was the first non-detachable box magazine rifle offered by Winchester. Built on a John M. Browning patent. Introduced by Winchester to meet the demand for a rifle that could handle new high-power, smokeless hunting cartridges of the period. Model 1895 was available in these calibers: .30-40 Krag, .38-72 Win., .40-72 Win., .303 British, .35 Win., .405 Government, 7.62 Russian, .30-03 and .30-06. Rifle gained fame as a favorite hunting rifle of Theodore Roosevelt. Because of its box magazine, Model 1895 has a distinctive look like no other Winchester lever-action rifle. Model 1895 was produced from 1895 to 1931, with about 426,000 sold.

Model 1895 was available in several different configurations:

1. Sporting Rifle: 28" or 24" (depending on caliber) round barrel; plain walnut straight-grip stock; plain forend. First 5,000 rifles manufactured with flat-sided receivers; balance of production built with receiver sides contoured. After serial-number 60000, a take-down version was available.
2. Fancy Sporting Rifle: 28" round barrel; fancy walnut checkered straight-grip stock and forearm. Rifles with serial numbers below 5000 had flat-sided frames.
3. Carbine: 22" round barrel; plain walnut straight-grip stock; military-style handguard forend. Some carbines furnished with saddle rings on left side of receiver.
4. Musket:

A. Standard Musket - 28" round barrel; plain walnut straight-grip stock; musket-style forend; two barrel bands.
B. U.S. Army N.R.A. Musket - 30" round barrel; Model 1901 Krag-Jorgensen rear sight; stock similar to standard musket. This musket could be used for "Any Military Arm" matches under the rules of National Rifle Association.
C. N.R.A. Musket Models 1903 and 1906 - 24" round barrel; special buttplate. Also eligible for all matches under "Any Military Arm" sponsored by NRA. This musket was fitted with the same stock as listed above.
D. U.S. Army Musket - 28" round barrel; chambered for .30-40 Krag; equipped with-/without knife bayonet. These muskets were furnished to U.S. Army for use during Spanish-American War and are "US" marked on receiver.
E. Russian Musket - similar to standard musket, but fitted with clip guides in top of receiver, with bayonet. Approximately 294,000 Model 1895 Muskets were sold to Imperial Russian Government between 1915 and 1916. First 15,000 Russian Muskets had 8" knife bayonets, balance fitted with 16" bayonets.

Note: Add 10 percent premium for rifles built before 1898. Premium for antique specimens made prior to 1899 with serial numbers lower than approximately 19872.

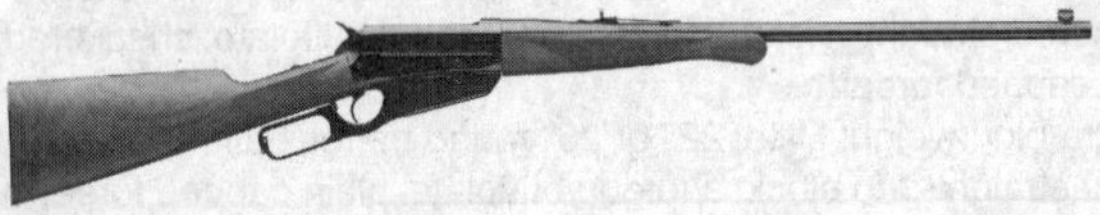

NIB	Exc.	V.G.	Good	Fair	Poor
1260	—	—	—	—	—

Sporting Rifle

Note: Add 100 percent premium for flat-side rifles; additional 15 percent for take-down rifles.

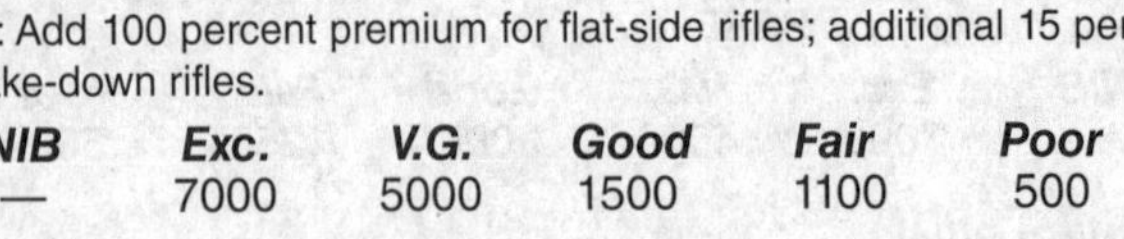

Flat-side rifle.

NIB	Exc.	V.G.	Good	Fair	Poor
—	5000	3000	1200	700	300

Fancy Sporting Rifles

Note: Add 100 percent premium for flat-side rifles; additional 15 percent for take-down rifles.

NIB	Exc.	V.G.	Good	Fair	Poor
—	7000	5000	1500	1100	500

Carbine

Courtesy Bonhams & Butterfields, San Francisco, California

NIB	Exc.	V.G.	Good	Fair	Poor
—	5500	3250	1550	900	300

Standard Musket

NIB	Exc.	V.G.	Good	Fair	Poor
—	3200	1800	1000	600	300

U.S. Army N.R.A. Musket

NIB	Exc.	V.G.	Good	Fair	Poor
—	4500	2000	1200	800	400

N.R.A. Musket, Model 1903 and 1906

NIB	Exc.	V.G.	Good	Fair	Poor
—	5500	2500	1200	800	400

U.S. Army Musket

NIB	Exc.	V.G.	Good	Fair	Poor
—	5000	3000	1500	850	450

Russian Musket

NIB	Exc.	V.G.	Good	Fair	Poor
—	4000	2500	1000	500	250

Breechloading Double-Barrel Shotgun

Winchester imported an English-made shotgun sold under the Winchester name between 1879 and 1884. Available in 10- and 12-gauge, with 30" or 32" Damascus barrels. Sold in five separate grades referred to as "classes". Lowest grade was "D" and best grade called "Match Grade". They were marked on the sidelocks. Center rib was stamped "Winchester Repeating Arms Co., New Haven, Connecticut, U.S.A.". Prices shown are for "D" grade. About 10,000 of these guns were imported by Winchester. Note: Add 10 percent for "C" grade; 20 percent for "B" grade; 30 percent for "A" grade.

Class A, B, C, and D Antique

Exc.	Fine	V.G.	Good	Fair	Poor
2250	1250	1050	850	500	350

Match Gun Antique

Exc.	Fine	V.G.	Good	Fair	Poor
4000	1800	1320	850	500	350

Model 1887 Shotgun

Winchester enjoyed a great deal of success with its imported English shotgun, so the company decided to manufacture a shotgun of its own. In 1885, Winchester purchased the patent for a lever-action shotgun designed by John M. Browning. By 1887, Winchester had delivered the first Model 1887 Shotgun in 12-gauge. Shortly thereafter, in 10-gauge. Both gauges offered with 30" or 32" Full choked barrels, with 30" standard on 12-gauge; 32" on 10-gauge. In 1898, a Riot Gun was offered in 10- and 12-gauge, with 20" barrels choked Cylinder. Both variations offered with plain walnut pistol grip stocks and forend. Frame was case-hardened and barrel blued. Between 1887 and 1901, Winchester sold approximately 65,000 Model 1887 shotguns.

1887 Standard Shotgun Antique

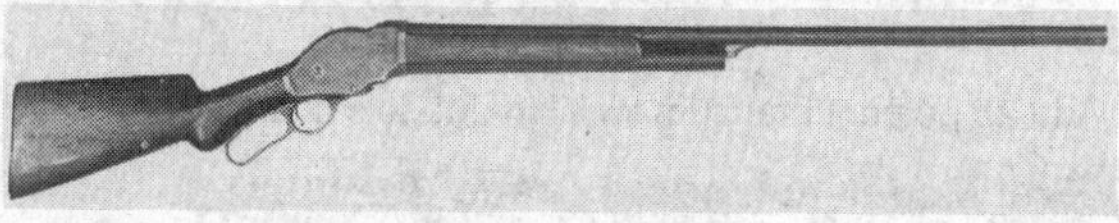

Courtesy Milwaukee Public Museum, Milwaukee, Wisconsin

Exc.	Fine	V.G.	Good	Fair	Poor
2500	1500	1000	750	500	250

1887 Riot Shotgun Antique

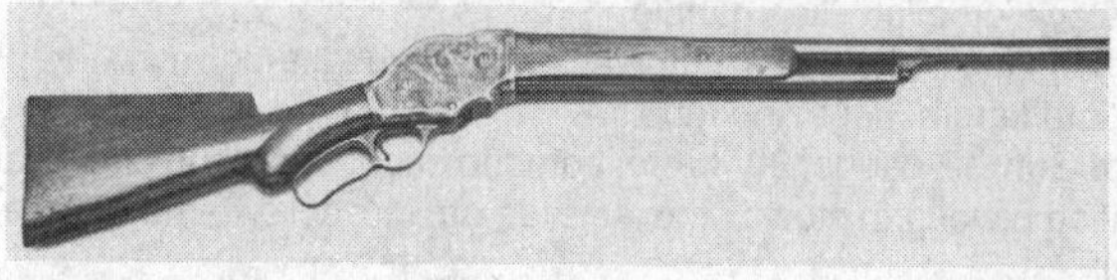

Courtesy Bonhams & Butterfields, San Francisco, California

Exc.	Fine	V.G.	Good	Fair	Poor
3000	2000	1200	900	600	300

Model 1901 Shotgun

A redesign of Model 1887 Shotgun. Offered in 10-gauge only, with 32" barrel choked Full, Modified or Cylinder. Barrel was reinforced to withstand the new smokeless powder loads. Frame blued instead of case-hardened. Stock was plain walnut, with a modified pistol and plain forearm. Built between 1901 and 1920. About 65,000 guns sold.

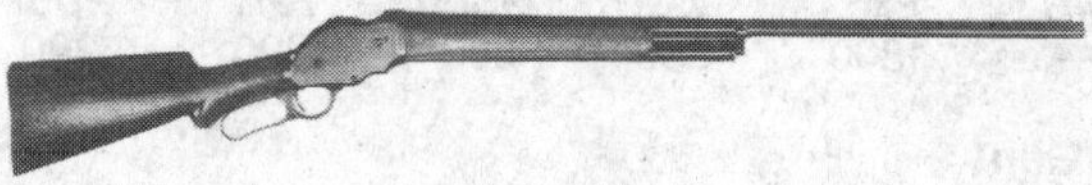

NIB	Exc.	V.G.	Good	Fair	Poor
—	3000	2200	1200	400	250

Model 1893 Shotgun Antique

First slide-action repeating shotgun built by Winchester. Featured an exposed hammer and side ejection. Based on a John M. Browning patent, this model was not altogether satisfactory. Action proved to be too weak to handle smokeless loads, even though the gun was designed for blackpowder. Offered in 12-gauge, with 30" or 32" barrels choked Full. Other chokes were available on special order and will command a premium. Stock was plain walnut, with a modified pistol grip grooved slide handle and hard rubber buttplate. Receiver and barrel blued. Produced between 1893 and 1897, selling about 31000 guns. Premium for antique specimens made prior to 1899 with serial numbers lower than approximately 34204.

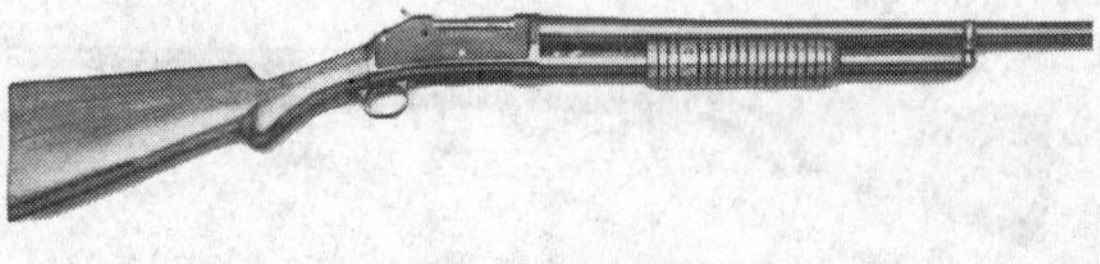

Courtesy Bonhams & Butterfields, San Francisco, California

Exc.	Fine	V.G.	Good	Fair	Poor
2000	1200	700	500	300	200

Model 1897

Model 1897 replaced Model 1893. Similar to Model 1893, the new model had several improvements such as stronger frame, chamber made longer to handle 2.75" shells, frame top was covered to force complete side ejection, stock made longer and with less drop. Available in 12- or 16-gauge, with 12-gauge in solid or take-down styles; 16-gauge in take-down only. Available with barrel lengths of 20", 26", 28", 30" and 32" in practically all choke options from Full to Cylinder. Model 1897 was a great seller for Winchester. During its 60-year production span, 1,025,000 guns were sold.

Model 1897 could be ordered in several different configurations:

1. Standard Gun: 12- or 16-gauge; 30" barrel 12-gauge and 28" barrel 16-gauge; plain walnut modified pistol grip stock; grooved slide handle; steel buttplate standard.
2. Trap Gun: 12- or 16-gauge; 30" barrel 12-gauge and 28" barrel 16-gauge; fancy walnut stock; oil-finish checkered pistol-/straight-grip stock; checkered slide handle. Marked "TRAP" on bottom of frame.
3. Pigeon Gun: 12- or 16-gauge; 28" barrel on both gauges; straight-/pistol grip stock; receiver hand-engraved.
4. Tournament Gun: 12-gauge only; 30" barrel; select walnut checkered straight-grip stock; checkered slide handle; top of receiver matted to reduce glare.
5. Brush Gun: 12- or 16-gauge; 26" barrel; cylinder choke has a slightly shorter magazine tube than standard gun; plain walnut modified pistol

grip stock; grooved slide handle.
6. Brush Gun, Take-down: same as above with take-down feature; standard length magazine tube.
7. Riot Gun: 12-gauge; 20" barrel bored to shoot buckshot; plain walnut modified pistol grip stock; grooved slide handle; solid-frame or take-down.
8. Trench Gun: same as Riot Gun, but fitted with barrel handguard and bayonet. Note: Add 100 percent for 16-gauge guns in excellent, very good and good condition.

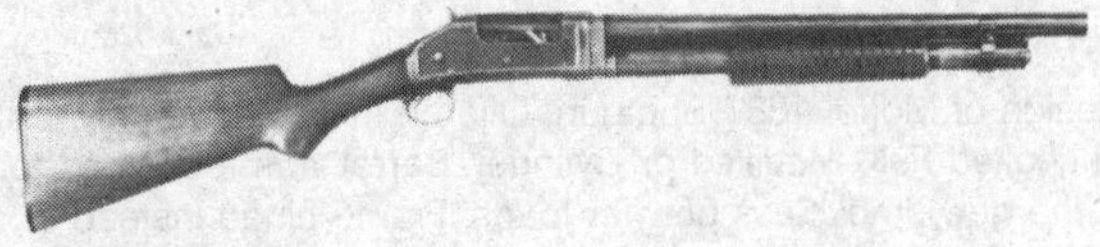

Standard Gun

NIB	Exc.	V.G.	Good	Fair	Poor
—	1300	850	650	300	200

Trap Gun

NIB	Exc.	V.G.	Good	Fair	Poor
—	1500	1200	800	500	400

Pigeon Gun/High Grade

NIB	Exc.	V.G.	Good	Fair	Poor
—	8000	6000	5000	4000	500

Tournament Gun

NIB	Exc.	V.G.	Good	Fair	Poor
—	2000	1700	900	750	400

Brush Gun

NIB	Exc.	V.G.	Good	Fair	Poor
—	950	750	600	500	400

Riot Gun

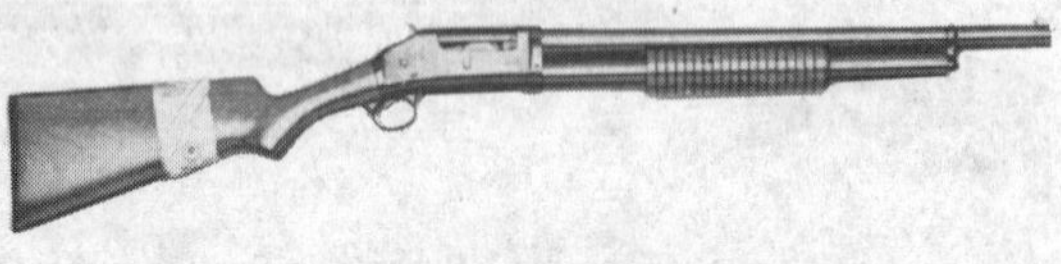

Courtesy Bonhams & Butterfields, San Francisco, California

NIB	Exc.	V.G.	Good	Fair	Poor
—	2500	1750	1000	600	400

Trench Gun

Note: Add 100 percent for 16-gauge in excellent, very good and good condition; 100 percent for military markings.

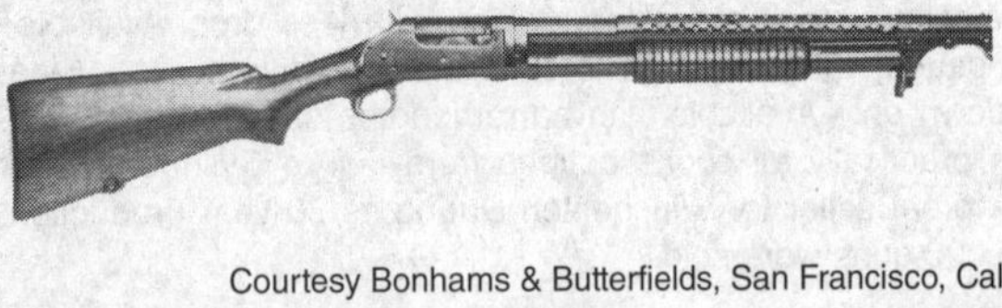

Courtesy Bonhams & Butterfields, San Francisco, California

NIB	Exc.	V.G.	Good	Fair	Poor
—	7500	4000	2000	1200	600

Winchester-Lee Straight Pull Rifle

Premium for antique specimens made prior to 1899 with serial numbers lower than approximately 13390.

U.S. Navy Musket

NIB	Exc.	V.G.	Good	Fair	Poor
—	2500	2000	1500	700	500

Commercial Musket

NIB	Exc.	V.G.	Good	Fair	Poor
—	2500	2000	1500	700	500

Sporting Rifle

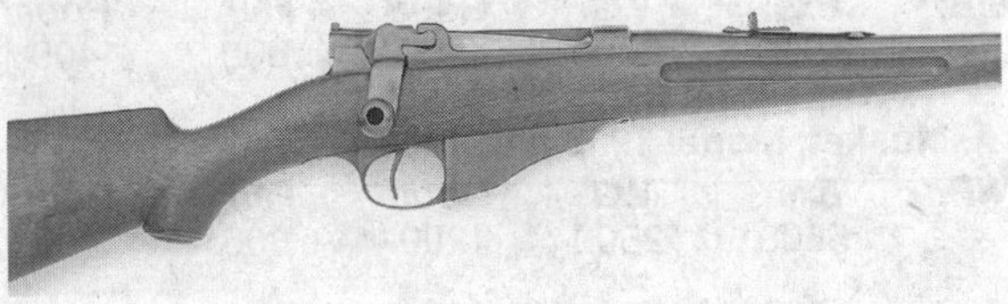

Courtesy Amoskeag Auction Company

NIB	Exc.	V.G.	Good	Fair	Poor
—	2500	2000	1500	700	500

Model 1890

Model 1890 was the first slide-action rifle ever produced by Winchester. Designed by John and Matthew Browning. Chambered for .22 Short, Long and Winchester Rimfire cartridges (WRF cartridge was developed by Winchester specifically for Model 1890) not on an interchangeable basis. In 1919, .22 LR cartridge was offered as well. This rifle was slide-action top ejecting, with an 18" under barrel magazine tube. All Model 1890s were furnished standard with plain walnut straight stocks, with crescent buttplate and 12-groove slide handle. One of Winchester's best selling small caliber firearms and in worldwide use. Winchester offered many extra-cost options for this rifle that will greatly affect value. Secure an expert appraisal before proceeding. Produced from 1890 to 1932, with approximately 775,000 guns sold.

Model 1890 came in three separate and distinct variations that greatly affect value:
1. First Model: solid-frame; 24" octagon barrel; case-hardened frame; fixed rear sight. Approximately 15,552 First Model guns produced. Their distinctive feature is concealed locking lugs and solid-frame. Serial numbered on lower tang only. Built from 1890 to 1892.
2. Second Model (Take-down): 24" octagon barrel; case-hardened frame; adjustable rear sight. Serial numbered from 15553 to 112970 (on lower tang only). These Second Model guns feature same concealed locking lugs, with added take-down feature. A Deluxe version was offered, with fancy walnut checkered straight-/pistol grip stock and grooved slide handle.
2A. Second Model (Blued Frame Variation): same as above, with blued frame. Serial numbered from 112971 to 325250 (on lower tang until 232328, then on bottom front end of receiver). These blued frame Second Models are much more numerous than case-hardened variety. A Deluxe version was offered, with fancy walnut checkered straight-/pistol grip stock and grooved slide handle.
3. Third Model (Take-down): 24" octagon barrel; blued frame; adjustable rear sight. Serial numbered from 325251 to as high as 853000 (numbered on both lower tang and bottom front of receiver). Distinctive feature of Third Model is locking cut made on the front top of receiver to allow breech-bolt to lock externally. A Deluxe version was offered, with fancy walnut checkered stock, straight-/pistol grip with grooved slide handle.

Note: Add 25 percent premium for Third Models chambered for .22 LR.

1890 First Model—Standard Grade (Antique)

Exc.	Fine	V.G.	Good	Fair	Poor
10000	5000	3120	1250	750	520

Second Model—Case Hardened Frame Standard

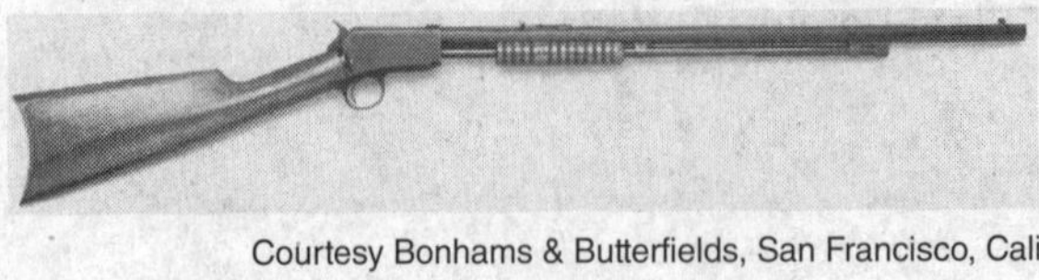

Courtesy Bonhams & Butterfields, San Francisco, California

NIB	Exc.	V.G.	Good	Fair	Poor
—	6000	3500	2000	1000	500

Deluxe

NIB	Exc.	V.G.	Good	Fair	Poor
—	10000	7000	3500	2000	1000

Second Model—Blued Frame Standard

NIB	Exc.	V.G.	Good	Fair	Poor
—	2500	1700	1500	750	250

Deluxe

NIB	Exc.	V.G.	Good	Fair	Poor
—	7500	5500	3000	1500	750

Third Model Standard

NIB	Exc.	V.G.	Good	Fair	Poor
—	2000	1400	900	450	250

Deluxe

NIB	Exc.	V.G.	Good	Fair	Poor
—	6500	4000	2000	1000	750

Model 1906

In 1906, Winchester decided to offer a lower-cost version of Model 1890. Model 1906 used same receiver, but fitted with 20" round barrel and plain gumwood straight-grip stock. When first introduced, it sold for two-thirds the price of Model 1890. For the first two years, it was chambered for .22 Short cartridge only. In 1908, it was modified to shoot .22 Short, Long and LR cartridges interchangeably. This modification ensured Model 1906's success. Between 1906 and 1932, about 800,000 were sold. All Model 1906s were take-down variety.

Model 1906 available in three important variations:
1. .22 Short Only: 20" round barrel; straight-grip gumwood stock; smooth slide handle. These were built from serial number 1 to around 113000.
2. Standard Model 1906: 20" round barrel; straight-grip gumwood stock; 12 groove slide handle. Serial numbered from 113000 to 852000.
3. Model 1906 Expert: 20" round barrel; pistol grip gumwood stock; fluted smooth slide handle. Expert was available from 1918 to 1924. Offered in three different finishes: regular blued; half nickel (receiver, guard and bolt); full nickel (receiver, guard, bolt and barrel).

.22 Short Only

Courtesy Bonhams & Butterfields, San Francisco, California

NIB	Exc.	V.G.	Good	Fair	Poor
—	3500	2500	1200	500	200

Standard

Courtesy Bonhams & Butterfields, San Francisco, California

NIB	Exc.	V.G.	Good	Fair	Poor
—	3000	2000	1000	400	200

Expert

Prices are for half nickel. Note: Add 10 percent for blued guns; 100 percent for full nickel.

Courtesy Bonhams & Butterfields, San Francisco, California

NIB	Exc.	V.G.	Good	Fair	Poor
—	3500	2500	1200	500	300

Model 61

Winchester developed Model 61 in an attempt to keep pace with its competitors' hammerless .22 rifles. Featured 24" round or octagonal barrel and could be ordered by customer in a variety of configurations. Collector interest is high, because of the fairly large number of variations. Model 61 is often considered a companion to Winchester Model 12 and Model 42 shotguns. Model 61 was fitted with plain walnut pistol grip stock, with grooved slide handle. All Model 61s were take-down variety. Pre-war models will have a short slide handle. Manufactured between 1932 and 1963. Approximately 342,000 guns were sold.

Following is a list of chamber and barrel variations found in this model:
1. 24" round barrel; .22 Short, Long, LR.
2. 24" octagonal barrel; .22 Short only; add 150 percent.
3. 24" octagonal barrel; .22 LR only; add 150 percent.
4. 24" octagonal barrel; .22 WRF only; add 100 percent.
5. 24" round barrel; .22 LR shot only; add 200 percent.
5A.24" round barrel; shot only Routledge bore; add 200 percent.
6. 24" round barrel; .22 WRF only; add 125 percent.
7. 24" round barrel; .22 LR only; add 50 percent.
8. 24" round barrel; .22 Win. Magnum; add 50 percent.
9. 24" round barrel; .22 Short only; add 100 percent.

Pre-war

Note: Add 50 percent premium (depending on caliber) for single caliber; 75 percent premium for octagon barrel; 250 percent premium for .22 LR shot only.

NIB	Exc.	V.G.	Good	Fair	Poor
3000	2200	1600	800	400	200

Post-war

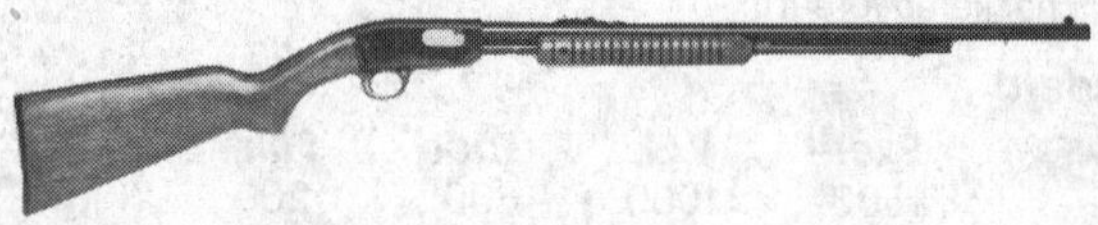

Courtesy Bonhams & Butterfields, San Francisco, California

NIB	Exc.	V.G.	Good	Fair	Poor
2000	1400	1200	600	300	250

Magnum

Note: This variation produced from 1960 to 1963.

NIB	Exc.	V.G.	Good	Fair	Poor
2800	2400	1600	780	600	400

Model 62 and 62A

Model 1890 and Model 1906 were dropped from the Winchester product line in 1932. Model 62 was introduced to take their place. An updated version of earlier slide-action .22 rifles. Fitted with 23" round barrel and capable of shooting .22 Short, Long and LR cartridges interchangeably. Winchester offered a Gallery version of Model 62, that was chambered for .22 Short only. Some of these Gallery guns have "Winchester" stamped on left side of receiver. Model 62 Gallery rifles have a triangular loading port on the loading tube that standard models did not have. A change in the breech-bolt mechanism brought about a change in the name designation from Model 62 to Model 62A. This occurred around serial number 98000. Letter "A" now appears behind the serial number. This model stayed in production until 1958. Collectors will concede a premium for guns built prior to WWII, with small slide handles. Stock was plain walnut, with straight-grip and grooved slide handle. Both receiver and barrel were blued. All Model 62 and 62As were take-down. Approximately 409,000 guns were sold.

Pre-war

Note: Barrels marked with Model 62 are worth more than barrels marked with Model 62A by approximately 15 percent. Gallery models will bring a premium of 300 percent.

NIB	Exc.	V.G.	Good	Fair	Poor
2200	1500	850	400	250	150

Post-war

Courtesy Bonhams & Butterfields, San Francisco, California

NIB	Exc.	V.G.	Good	Fair	Poor
1500	1100	600	500	220	120

Model 62 Gallery

.22 Short only, with triangular loading port & "WINCHESTER" stamped on side of receiver. Note: Model 62 with "WINCHESTER" stamped on side of receiver is more desirable than one without this stamping. Deduct 10 percent for Gallery rifles without this stamping.

NIB	Exc.	V.G.	Good	Fair	Poor
3200	2000	1000	650	400	200

Model 1903

First semi-automatic rifle produced by Winchester was designed by T.C. Johnson. Offered in a take-down version only. Available in a 20" round barrel. Chambered for .22 Win. Automatic Rimfire. This ammunition is no longer produced, and when found is very expensive. Tubular magazine located in buttstock and holds 10-cartridges. Manufactured from 1903 to 1932, with about 126,000 sold.

Available in two different configurations:
1. Standard Rifle: 20" round barrel; plain walnut straight-grip stock; plain forend; steel crescent butt standard.
2. Deluxe Rifle: 20" round barrel; fancy checkered walnut pistol grip stock; checkered forearm.

Standard

NIB	Exc.	V.G.	Good	Fair	Poor
—	1500	1000	600	200	100

Deluxe

Note: First 5,000 guns built without safeties; first 15,000 guns furnished with bronze firing pins instead of steel. Add 30 percent premium for early Model 1903s.

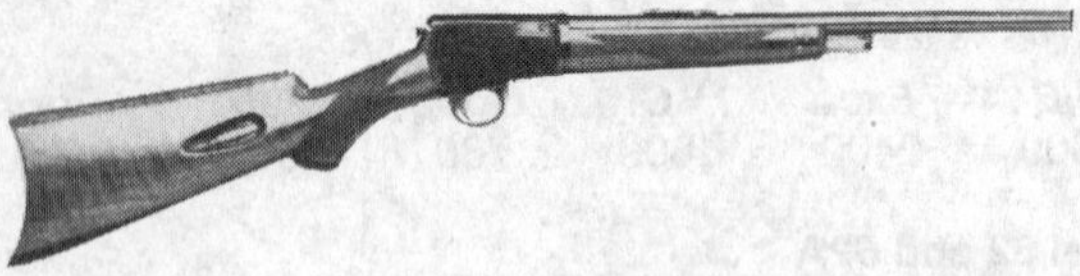

Courtesy Bonhams & Butterfields, San Francisco, California

NIB	Exc.	V.G.	Good	Fair	Poor
—	2500	2000	1200	500	250

Model 63

Model 63 took the place of Model 1903. In 1933, Winchester attempted to solve the problem of having to use a special .22-caliber cartridge to operate the blowback system. It is a very high quality semi-automatic rifle. Many collectors and shooters considered it the best rimfire semi-automatic rifle ever produced. Chambered for .22 LR cartridge. Available in a 20" barrel for the first four years or until about serial number 9800. Thereafter, offered with a 23" round barrel for remainder of the production period. Fitted with a plain walnut pistol grip stock and forearm. Tubular magazine was located in the buttstock that came with a steel buttplate. Last 10,000 Model 63s were sold with a grooved receiver top to make the addition of a scope easier. Manufactured between 1933 and 1958, with about 175,000 guns sold. Note: Add 20 percent premium for grooved top receivers.

20" Barrel

Courtesy Bonhams & Butterfields, San Francisco, California

NIB	Exc.	V.G.	Good	Fair	Poor
2750	1400	800	500	400	250

23" Barrel

Courtesy Bonhams & Butterfields, San Francisco, California

NIB	Exc.	V.G.	Good	Fair	Poor
2200	1600	900	600	400	200

Model 1905

Model 1905 was a larger version of Model 1903. Developed by T.C. Johnson to handle more powerful centerfire cartridges. Chambered for .32 Win. Self-Loading and .35 Self-Loading cartridges. Loading by means of a detachable box magazine. Available in take-down only. First Winchester semi-automatic rifle to fire centerfire cartridges. Produced from 1905 to 1920, with about 30,000 rifles sold.

Offered in two different styles:
1. Sporting Rifle: 22" round barrel; plain walnut straight-grip (changed to pistol grip in 1908) stock; plain forend.
2. Fancy Sporting Rifle: 22" round barrel; fancy walnut checkered pistol grip stock; checkered forend.

Sporting

NIB	Exc.	V.G.	Good	Fair	Poor
—	700	550	350	180	120

Fancy Sporting

NIB	Exc.	V.G.	Good	Fair	Poor
—	900	750	500	200	150

Model 1907

Model 1907 was an improved version of Model 1905. Chambered for new .351 Win. Self-Loading cartridge. Outward appearance same as Model 1905, except for 20" round barrel. First introduced in 1937. Discontinued in 1957, after selling about 59,000 guns. Note: Post-WWII Model 1907s command a premium over values shown below.

Available in three different styles:
1. Sporting Rifle: 20" round barrel; plain walnut pistol grip stock; plain forend. Discontinued in 1937.
2. Fancy Sporting Rifle: 20" round barrel; fancy walnut checkered pistol grip stock; checkered forend.
3. Police Rifle: 20" round barrel; plain walnut pistol grip stock; beavertail forend. This version fitted with a leather sling, with/without knife bayonet.

Sporting

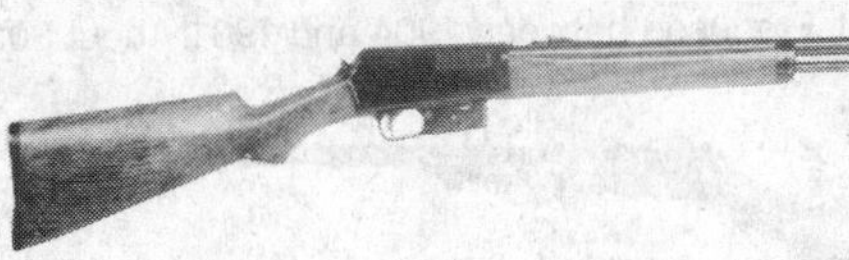

NIB	Exc.	V.G.	Good	Fair	Poor
—	750	500	350	180	120

Fancy Sporting

NIB	Exc.	V.G.	Good	Fair	Poor
—	850	650	450	200	150

Police

NIB	Exc.	V.G.	Good	Fair	Poor
—	950	750	580	300	250

Model 1910

Similar to Model 1907, but action made stronger to handle new Winchester .401 Self-Loading cartridge. Specifications for this model same as Model 1907. Built between 1907 and 1936. About 21,000 sold.

Sporting

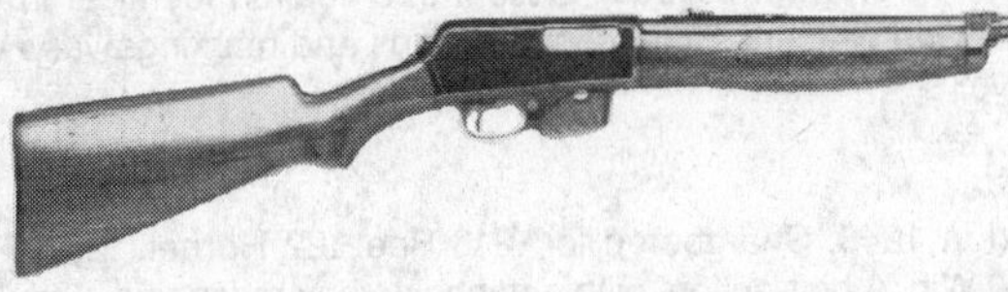

Courtesy Bonhams & Butterfields, San Francisco, California

NIB	Exc.	V.G.	Good	Fair	Poor
—	900	750	550	400	200

Fancy Sporting

NIB	Exc.	V.G.	Good	Fair	Poor
—	1000	800	600	450	250

Model 55 (Rimfire Rifle)

Not to be confused with lever-action model. This .22-caliber rifle was a semi-automatic (auto-ejecting, actually) single-shot, with 22" round barrel. Fitted with plain walnut pistol grip one-piece stock and forend. Safety goes on when each cartridge is inserted into chamber. This model was not serial numbered. Produced from 1957 to 1961. About 45,000 sold.

NIB	Exc.	V.G.	Good	Fair	Poor
—	400	350	220	150	80

Model 74

Semi-automatic chambered for .22 Short or .22 LR. Has a tubular magazine in the buttstock and a 24" round barrel. Bolt on this rifle was designed to be easily removed for cleaning or repair. Stock was plain walnut pistol grip, with semi-beavertail forend. Gallery Special was offered, chambered for .22 Short and fitted with a steel shell deflector. This Gallery model was also available with chrome trimmings, at extra cost.

Sporting

Courtesy C.H. Wolfersberger

NIB	Exc.	V.G.	Good	Fair	Poor
—	400	300	220	150	100

Gallery Special—.22 Short Only

Note: Add 50 percent premium for Gallery models with chrome trimmings.

NIB	Exc.	V.G.	Good	Fair	Poor
—	800	600	320	220	150

Model 77

Built on blow-back design for semi-automatic rifles. Chambered for .22 LR. Features 22" round barrel, detachable box magazine or under barrel tubular magazine. Has a triggerguard made of nylon, plain walnut pistol grip stock, with semi-beavertail forend and composition buttplate. Built between 1955 and 1963. Winchester sold about 217,000 of these rifles. Note: Add 10 to 20 percent premium for Models with tubular magazines.

NIB	Exc.	V.G.	Good	Fair	Poor
—	500	380	250	180	80

Model 100

Gas-operated semi-automatic chambered for .243-, .308- and .284-caliber cartridges. First commercial Winchester self-loading centerfire rifle made since Winchester Model 1905, Model 1907 and Model 1910. These models were produced until 1936-37. Winchester did produce the M1 Carbine during WWII. Available in a rifle version, with 22" round barrel; carbine version, with 19" barrel. Both furnished with a detachable box magazine. Stock was a one-piece design, with pistol grip offered in hand-cut checkering or pressed basket weave checkering. Rifles introduced in 1960; carbine in 1967. Model 100 last produced in 1973. About 263,000 sold.

Rifle

Note: Prices given are for .308-caliber; add 15 percent for .243; 20 percent for .284; 15 percent premium for Pre-1964 models.

NIB	Exc.	V.G.	Good	Fair	Poor
—	600	480	350	250	200

Carbine

Only about 53,000 carbines made; about 1 for every 5 rifles. Note: Add 25 percent premium for .243; 100 percent for .284.

NIB	Exc.	V.G.	Good	Fair	Poor
—	680	520	400	320	220

Model 88

A modern short-stroke lever-action chambered for .243-, .308-, 284- and .358-calibers. Available in a rifle version, with 22" round barrel; carbine version, with 19" round barrel. Carbine model was not chambered for .358 cartridge. Both furnished with a detachable box magazine. Stock was a one-piece design, with pistol grip offered in hand-cut checkering or pressed basket weave checkering after 1964. Rifle introduced in 1955; carbine in 1968. Both versions discontinued in 1973, with about 283,000 sold.

Rifle

Note: Add 50 percent for .243; 100 percent for .284; 300 percent for .358 Win.

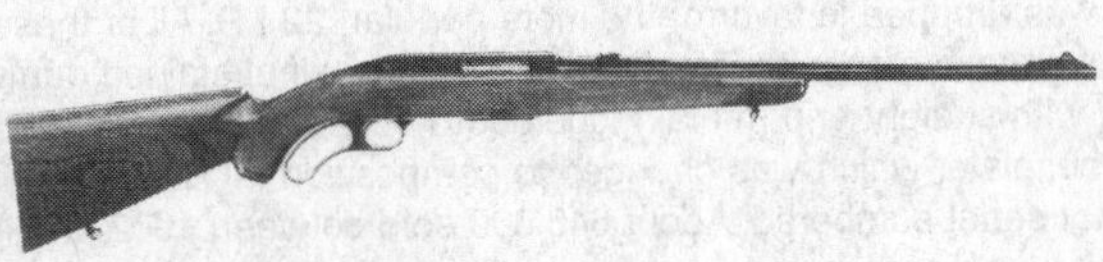

1955-1963 Rifle Production

NIB	Exc.	V.G.	Good	Fair	Poor
1200	1000	800	600	400	350

1964-1973 Rifle Production

NIB	Exc.	V.G.	Good	Fair	Poor
1000	900	700	500	300	250

Carbine

Only 28,000 carbines built; about 1 for every 10 rifles. Rarely encountered. Note: Add 25 percent for .243; 100 percent for .284.

NIB	Exc.	V.G.	Good	Fair	Poor
—	1300	1150	900	650	300

Model 99 or Thumb Trigger

A modification of Model 1902, without a traditional trigger. Rifle was fired by depressing trigger with the thumb, which was part of the sear and extractor located behind the bolt. Chambered for .22 Short and Long until 1914, when it was also chambered for .22 Extra Long. All cartridges could be shot interchangeably. Stock was same as Model 1902, walnut stained gumwood, without trigger or triggerguard. This model was not serial numbered. Built between 1904 and 1923. Winchester sold about 76,000 rifles.

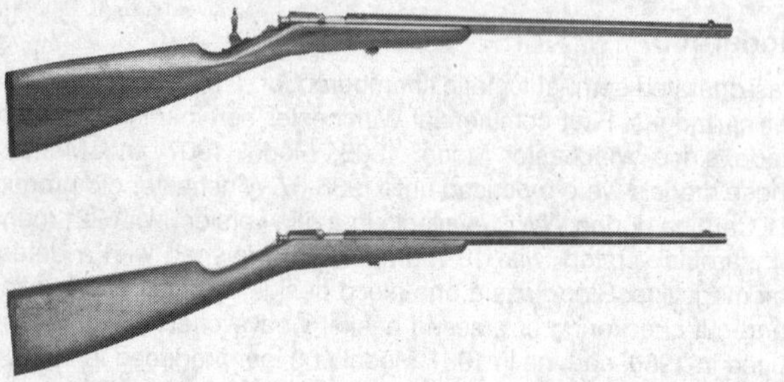

Courtesy Bonhams & Butterfields, San Francisco, California

NIB	Exc.	V.G.	Good	Fair	Poor
—	2400	2000	1000	700	500

Model 1900

Single-shot bolt-action .22-caliber rifle based on a John M. Browning design. Furnished with an 18" round barrel. Chambered for .22 Short and Long interchangeably. One-piece plain gumwood straight-grip stock, without a buttplate. Rifle was not serial numbered. Produced from 1899 to 1902. About 105,000 sold.

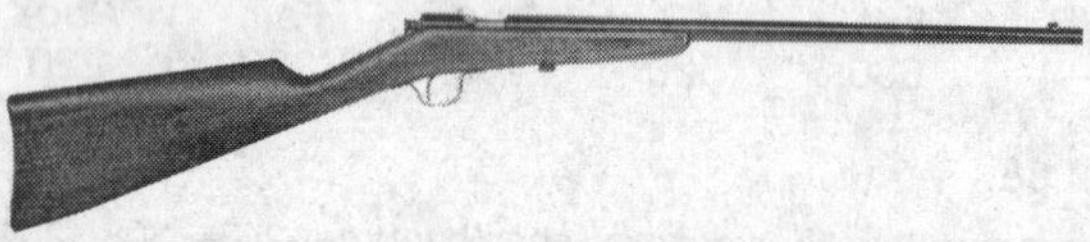

Courtesy Buffalo Bill Historical Center, Cody, Wyoming

NIB	Exc.	V.G.	Good	Fair	Poor
—	2000	1000	450	300	200

Model 1902

Also a single-shot, this model was the same general design as Model 1900, with several improvements. Special shaped metal triggerguard was added; shorter trigger pull; steel buttplate; rear peep sight; barrel was made heavier at the muzzle. Chambered for .22 Short and Long cartridges until 1914, when .22 Extra Long was added. In 1927, .22 Extra Long was dropped in favor of the more popular .22 LR. All of these cartridges were interchangeable. One-piece plain walnut stained gumwood stock, with straight-grip (metal triggerguard added a pistol grip feel) and steel buttplate, which was changed to composition in 1907. This model was not serial numbered. About 640,000 sold between 1902 and 1931, when it was discontinued.

NIB	Exc.	V.G.	Good	Fair	Poor
—	1000	750	400	220	120

Model 1904

A slightly more expensive version of Model 1902. Featured 21" round barrel, one-piece plain gumwood straight-grip stock (metal triggerguard added a pistol grip feel), with a small lip on the forend. Chambered for .22 Short and Long until 1914, when .22 Extra Long was added. In 1927, .22 LR cartridge was added in place of Extra Long. This model was not serial numbered. Produced between 1904 and 1931. About 303,000 rifles were sold.

NIB	Exc.	V.G.	Good	Fair	Poor
—	900	680	350	200	100

Model D Military Rifle

Overall length 46.375"; barrel length 26"; caliber 7.62mm. Walnut stock with blued barrel, receiver, magazine housing and furniture. Receiver ring over barrel breech stamped with serial number and Winchester proofmark. Total of 500 Model D rifles shipped to Russia for trial in March 1917. Value Speculative.

Imperial Bolt-Action Magazine Rifle (Model 51)

Designed by T.C. Johnson. Approximately 25 of these rifles made during 1919 and 1920, in two different styles and three calibers. Take-down variation has an overall length 42.25"; barrel length 22" and made in .27, .30-06 and .35 Newton calibers. Solid-frame version identical in form, dimensions and calibers. Sight configurations and markings vary. Value Speculative.

Model 43

Introduced in 1949. Chambered for .218 Bee, .22 Hornet, .25-20 Win. and .32-20 Win. A bolt-action, with detachable box magazine. Fitted with 24" round barrel and front sight ramp forged integrally with barrel. Not drilled and tapped for scope blocks except for a few late rifles. Produced from 1949 to 1957, with about 63,000 sold. Note: Add 50 percent premium for rifles chambered .25-20 and .32-20. Deduct 40 percent for rifles with non-factory drilled and tapped scope holes.

Available in two styles:
1. Standard Rifle: 24" round barrel; plain walnut pistol grip stock and forend; 1" sling swivels are standard.
2. Special Rifle: 24" round barrel; select walnut checkered pistol grip stock and forend. Furnished with open sporting rear sight or Lyman 57A micrometer receiver sight.

Standard

NIB	Exc.	V.G.	Good	Fair	Poor
—	800	700	550	300	200

Special or Deluxe

NIB	Exc.	V.G.	Good	Fair	Poor
—	1500	1200	800	450	180

Model 47

Single-shot bolt-action rifle chambered for .22 Short, Long and LR interchangeably. Furnished with 25" round barrel, plain walnut pistol grip stock and forend. Bolt, bolt handle and trigger are chrome plated. Has a special bolt, with a post on the underside. This moves into the safety position when bolt is closed. This model was not serial numbered. Produced between 1948 and 1954. About 43,000 sold. Note: Add 10 percent premium for factory peep sight.

Courtesy Buffalo Bill Historical Center, Cody, Wyoming

NIB	Exc.	V.G.	Good	Fair	Poor
—	450	350	250	200	150

Target Rifle

Fitted with 28" round standard weight or heavy weight barrel. Plain walnut modified pistol grip stock, with correct bolt.

NIB	Exc.	V.G.	Good	Fair	Poor
—	750	600	450	250	150

Model 52

One of the finest small-caliber well-made quality-built bolt-action rifles ever built. Model 52 was Winchester's answer to the increased demand for a military-style target rifle following WWI. Chambered for .22 LR cartridge. Designed by T.C. Johnson. Model 52 was built in several different configurations over its production life:

1. Model 52: with finger-groove in forend; one barrel band. Produced from 1920 to 1929.
2. Model 52 Target Rifle: same as above, without finger-groove in forend; has first speed lock. Made from 1929 to 1932.
3. Model 52A Target Rifle: same as above, with addition of reinforced receiver and locking lug. Made from 1932 to 1935.
4. Model 52B Target Rifle: same as above, with addition of adjustable sling swivel and single-shot adapter. Made from 1935 to 1947.
5. Model 52C Target Rifle: same as above, with addition of an easily adjustable vibration-free trigger mechanism. Made from 1947 to 1961.
6. Model 52D Target Rifle: single-shot, with free-floating barrel; new design stock, with adjustable hand-stop channel.
7. Model 52 Bull Gun: same as target rifle; fitted with extra-heavy weight barrel. Made from 1939 to 1960. Bull barrel measures 1.125" at receiver juncture; heavy weight measures 1". Both barrels measure .875" at muzzle.
8. Model 52 International Match: free-style stock, with thumbhole; adjustable buttstock and forend; introduced in 1969. International Prone model, with no thumbhole or adjustable buttplate and forend; introduced in 1975. Both discontinued in 1980.
9. Model 52 Sporter: 24" round barrel; select walnut checkered pistol grip stock, with cheekpiece; forend, with black plastic tip; pistol grip furnished with hard rubber grip cap. Model 52 Sporter introduced in 1934; discontinued in 1958. It went through same improvements as Target Rifle, thus designation Model 52A Sporter, etc.

Standard

NIB	Exc.	V.G.	Good	Fair	Poor
—	1250	1000	750	250	300

Target

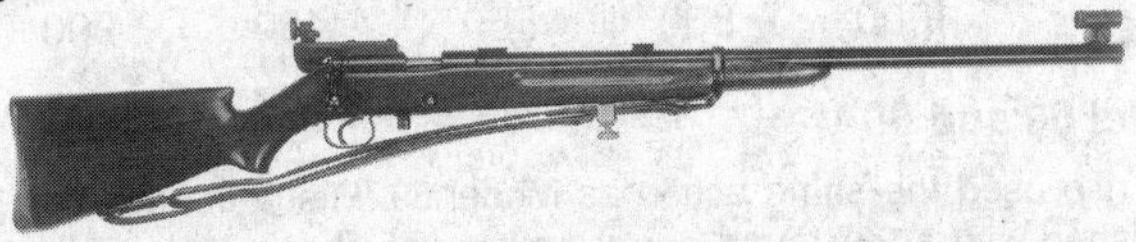

Courtesy Rock Island Auction Company

NIB	Exc.	V.G.	Good	Fair	Poor
—	1750	1500	1150	900	350

Target—Speed Lock

NIB	Exc.	V.G.	Good	Fair	Poor
—	1700	1400	1050	900	350

Model 52A Target Heavy Barrel—Rare

NIB	Exc.	V.G.	Good	Fair	Poor
—	1700	1400	1050	900	350

Model 52B Target Heavy & Standard Barrel

NIB	Exc.	V.G.	Good	Fair	Poor
—	1500	1300	950	700	300

Model 52B Target Bull Barrel

NIB	Exc.	V.G.	Good	Fair	Poor
—	1700	1400	1050	900	350

Model 52C Target

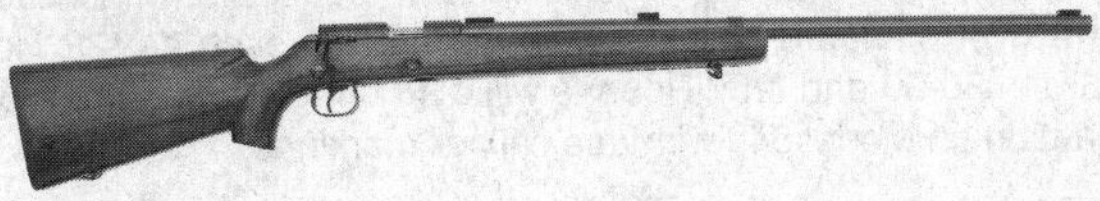

Courtesy Amoskeag Auction Company

NIB	Exc.	V.G.	Good	Fair	Poor
—	1700	1400	1050	800	500

Model 52D Target

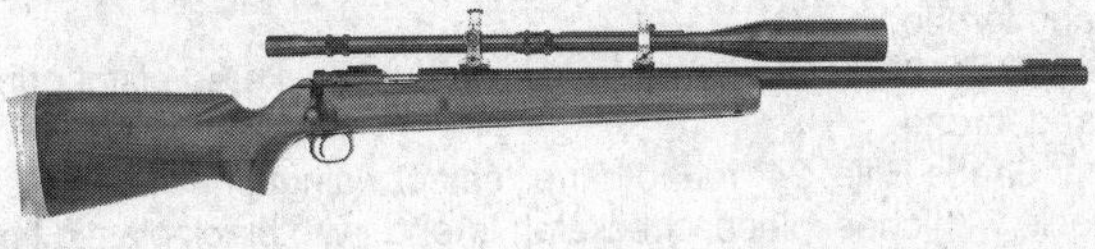

Courtesy Amoskeag Auction Company

NIB	Exc.	V.G.	Good	Fair	Poor
—	1800	1500	1300	1050	500

Model 52B Bull Gun

NIB	Exc.	V.G.	Good	Fair	Poor
—	1800	1500	1300	1050	500

Model 52C Bull Gun

NIB	Exc.	V.G.	Good	Fair	Poor
—	1800	1500	1300	1050	500

International Match - Free Style

Approximately 300 manufactured.

NIB	Exc.	V.G.	Good	Fair	Poor
—	3550	2900	2050	1200	600

International Match - Prone

Note: Post-WWII Model 1907s command a premium over values shown below.

NIB	Exc.	V.G.	Good	Fair	Poor
—	1600	1350	1150	800	600

Model 52A Sporter

NIB	Exc.	V.G.	Good	Fair	Poor
5800	5000	4000	3000	1500	500

Model 52B Sporter

NIB	Exc.	V.G.	Good	Fair	Poor
4500	3900	3200	2400	1850	600

Model 52C Sporter

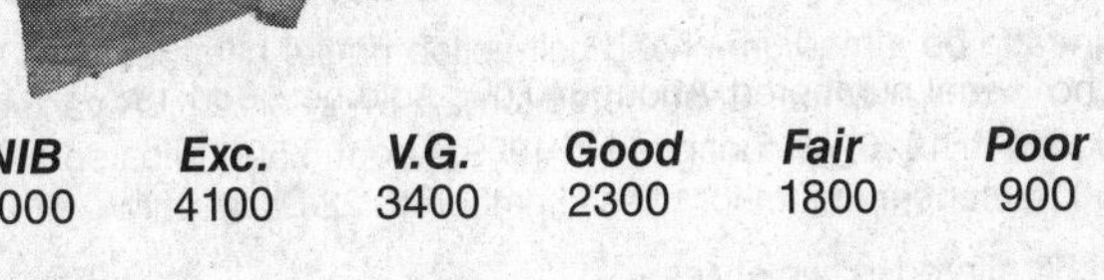

NIB	Exc.	V.G.	Good	Fair	Poor
5000	4100	3400	2300	1800	900

Model 54

Model 54 was to centerfire cartridges what Model 52 was to rimfire cartridges. Model 54 was also a quality-made bolt-action rifle, with non-detachable box magazine. Chambered for a variety of calibers: .270, .30-06, .30-30, 7mm, 7.65mm, 9mm, .250-3000, .22 Hornet, .220 Swift and .257 Roberts. This was Winchester's first bolt-action rifle built for heavy, high velocity ammunition. Introduced in 1925; discontinued in 1936.

About 50,000 sold. Note: Rare calibers are 7mm, 7.65mm and 9mm, which bring considerable premiums (in some cases as much as 250 percent) over standard calibers. Popular calibers such as .22 Hornet, .220 Swift, .30-30 and .257 Roberts will also bring a premium. Proceed with caution on Model 54s with rare caliber markings.

Model 54 was available in several different styles:
1. Standard Rifle: 24" or 20" round barrel (except .220 Swift which was 26"); plain walnut checkered pistol grip stock and forend.
2. Carbine: 20" round barrel; plain walnut pistol grip stock, with finger-groove on each side of forend.
3. Sniper's Rifle: 26" round heavy weight barrel; plain walnut pistol grip stock and forend.
4. N.R.A. Rifle: 24" round barrel; select walnut checkered pistol grip stock and forend.
5. Super Grade Rifle: 24" round barrel; select walnut checkered pistol grip stock, with cheekpiece; checkered forend, with black plastic tip; pistol grip capped with hard rubber cap; Super Grade was equipped with 1" detachable sling swivels.
6. Target Rifle: 24" round heavy weight barrel; plain walnut checkered pistol grip stock and forend.
7. National Match Rifle: 24" round barrel; plain walnut special target stock and forend.

Standard

NIB	Exc.	V.G.	Good	Fair	Poor
—	1300	1100	800	600	420

Carbine

NIB	Exc.	V.G.	Good	Fair	Poor
—	1400	1200	900	700	480

Sniper's Rifle

NIB	Exc.	V.G.	Good	Fair	Poor
—	1800	1500	1200	1000	550

N.R.A.

NIB	Exc.	V.G.	Good	Fair	Poor
—	1800	1500	1200	1000	550

Super Grade

NIB	Exc.	V.G.	Good	Fair	Poor
—	2400	1950	1600	1350	600

Target

NIB	Exc.	V.G.	Good	Fair	Poor
—	1800	1500	1200	1000	550

National Match

NIB	Exc.	V.G.	Good	Fair	Poor
—	1800	1500	1200	1000	550

Model 56

Designed to be a medium-priced bolt-action rimfire rifle. Featured a detachable box magazine. Chambered for .22 Short or .22 LR cartridges. Introduced in 1926; discontinued in 1929. About 8,500 rifles sold. Note: Add 50 percent premium for rifles chambered .22 Short only.

Model 56 offered in two styles:
1. Sporting Rifle: 22" round barrel; plain walnut pistol grip stock and forend. Both styles had a distinctive lip on forend tip
2. Fancy Sporting Rifle: 22" round barrel; fancy walnut checkered pistol grip stock and forend.

Sporting

NIB	Exc.	V.G.	Good	Fair	Poor
—	1500	1000	750	520	400

Fancy Sporting

Very rare, use caution.

NIB	Exc.	V.G.	Good	Fair	Poor
—	3000	2000	1500	900	750

Model 57

Model 57 was close in appearance to Model 56, with addition of a heavier stock, target sights and swivel bows attached to stock. Chambered for .22 Short or .22 LR. Featured 22" round barrel, with detachable box magazine. Stock was plain walnut pistol grip and forend. Introduced in 1927; discontinued in 1936. About 19,000 sold. Note: Add 20 percent premium for web sling.

NIB	Exc.	V.G.	Good	Fair	Poor
—	950	700	450	320	250

Model 58

This model was an attempt by Winchester to market a low-priced .22-caliber rimfire rifle in place of its Models 1902 and 1904. Single-shot bolt-action cocked by pulling firing pin head to the rear. Had an 18" round barrel. Chambered for .22 Short, Long and LR interchangeably. One-piece plain wood stock, with straight-grip. This model was not serial numbered. Introduced in 1928; discontinued in 1931. About 39,000 sold.

NIB	Exc.	V.G.	Good	Fair	Poor
—	800	700	450	300	200

Model 59

Essentially a Model 58, with addition of a pistol grip stock and 23" round barrel. Introduced in 1930 and dropped the same year. Total sales about 9,000 guns.

NIB	Exc.	V.G.	Good	Fair	Poor
—	1000	800	550	400	200

Model 60 and 60A

This rifle used the same action as Model 59. First introduced in 1931. Furnished with a 23" round barrel, which was changed to 27" in 1933. Several other mechanical improvements were included; perhaps most noticeable were the chrome-plated bolt, bolt handle and trigger. Plain wood stock, with pistol grip. In 1933, Model 60A was added which was the same rifle but in a target configuration. Front sight was a square top military blade, with Lyman 55W receiver sight. Model 60 discontinued in 1934: about 166,000 sold. Model 60A dropped in 1939: about 6,100 sold.

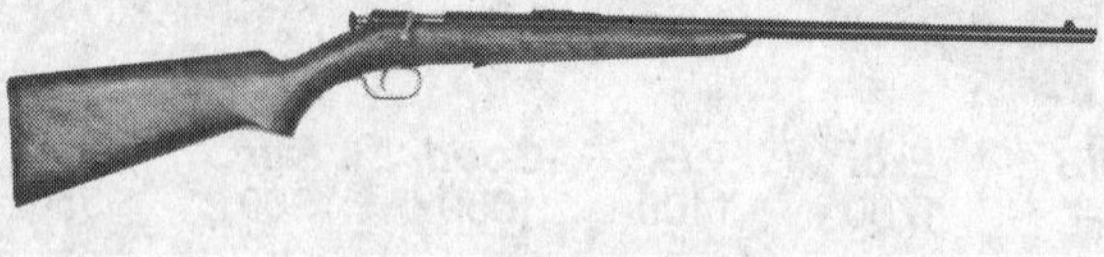

Courtesy Buffalo Bill Historical Center, Cody, Wyoming

Model 60

NIB	Exc.	V.G.	Good	Fair	Poor
—	380	250	200	150	100

Model 60A

NIB	Exc.	V.G.	Good	Fair	Poor
—	500	420	300	200	100

Model 67

Winchester again upgraded and improved Model 60, with an expansion of styles offered to the shooting public. Standard chamber was .22 Short, Long and LR interchangeably, with WRF added in 1935. Model 67s were not serial numbered for domestic sales, but numbered for foreign sales. Introduced in 1934; discontinued in 1963. About 384,000 sold. Many were fitted at the factory with telescopes. Bases were mounted on the rifle and scope was packed separately.

Model 67 was available in several different styles:
1. Sporting Rifle: 27" round barrel; stock similar to Model 60.
2. Smoothbore Rifle: 27" barrel; chambered for .22 Long shot or .22 LR shot.
3. Junior Rifle: 20" round barrel; shorter stock.
4. Rifle with miniature target boring: 24" round barrel; chambered for .22 LR shot.

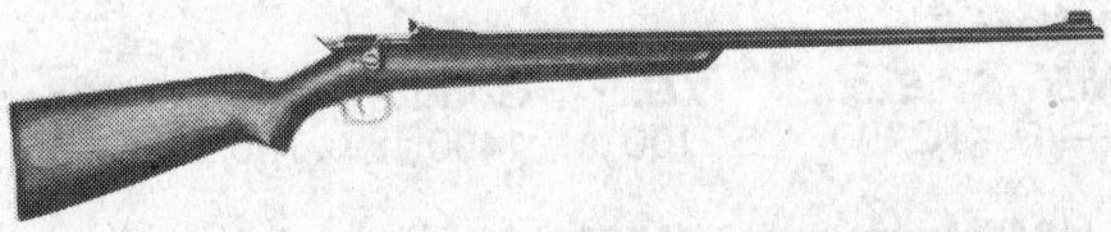

Courtesy Buffalo Bill Historical Center, Cody, Wyoming

Sporting

NIB	Exc.	V.G.	Good	Fair	Poor
—	450	350	250	180	100

Smoothbore

Courtesy Buffalo Bill Historical Center, Cody, Wyoming

NIB	Exc.	V.G.	Good	Fair	Poor
—	800	600	400	250	200

Junior

NIB	Exc.	V.G.	Good	Fair	Poor
—	500	350	280	200	120

Miniature Target

Marked "for shot only". Has beads instead of standard iron rifle sights.

NIB	Exc.	V.G.	Good	Fair	Poor
—	1200	900	700	400	300

Model 677

Looked the same as Model 67, but manufactured without iron sights. Therefore, will have no sight cuts in the barrel. Furnished with 2.75 power scopes or 5-power scopes. This model was not serial numbered. Introduced in 1937; discontinued in 1939. Note: Add 100 percent premium for rifles chambered .22 WRF.

NIB	Exc.	V.G.	Good	Fair	Poor
—	2400	1800	1100	600	300

Model 68

Another takeoff on Model 67. Differed only in sight equipment offered. Fitted with a peep sight. First sold in 1934; discontinued in 1946. Sales about 101,000. Note: Add 50 percent for factory scopes and no sights; 400 percent for factory scopes and no sights chambered .22 WRF.

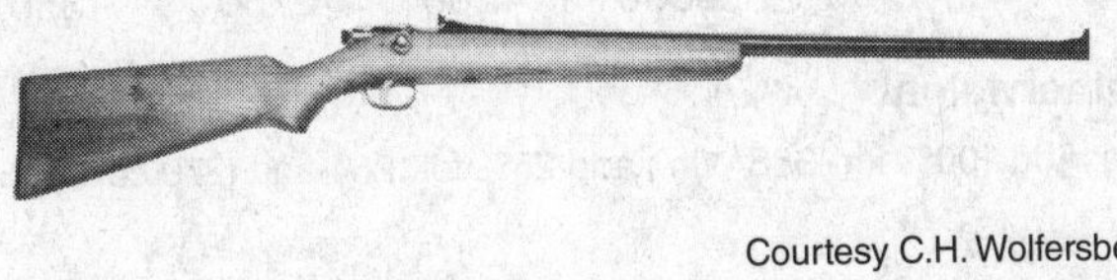

Courtesy C.H. Wolfersberger

With Scope

NIB	Exc.	V.G.	Good	Fair	Poor
—	900	780	450	300	200

Without Scope

NIB	Exc.	V.G.	Good	Fair	Poor
—	300	220	150	100	80

Model 69 and 69A

Designed by Winchester to answer the demand for a medium-priced hunting and target .22 rimfire bolt-action rifle. Had a detachable box magazine. Many offered with factory-installed telescopes in 2.75 and 5-power. Plain walnut pistol grip stock and forend. This model was not serial numbered. Model 69A introduced in 1937. Featured an improved cocking mechanism. Model 69 Introduced in 1935; discontinued in 1963. About 355,000 sold. Note: Add 25 percent for Target Model; 35 percent for grooved receiver.

NIB	Exc.	V.G.	Good	Fair	Poor
—	480	400	350	200	100

Model 697

Similar in appearance to Model 69, except equipped exclusively for a telescope. Winchester offered 2.75 or 5-power scope, with bases attached at the factory and scope packed separately. Built between 1937 and 1941, with small sales. This model was not serial numbered. Note: Add 50 percent for factory scopes with no sights.

NIB	Exc.	V.G.	Good	Fair	Poor
—	2000	1200	800	600	400

RIFLES

PRE-1964 MODEL 70

Model 70

Considered by many to be the finest bolt-action rifle ever built in the United States. Pre-1964 Model 70 is highly sought after by shooters and collectors alike. Its smooth strong action has no peer. Often referred to as "The Riflemen's Rifle." Model 70 is an updated and improved version of Model 54. Features a hinged floorplate, new speed locks, new safety design that does not interfere with telescope, manually releasable bolt stop, forged steel triggerguard, more attractive buttstock, and forend. Like many Winchesters, Model 70 was available with several extra-cost options that should be evaluated by an expert. Values listed are given for pre-1964 Model 70s, with serial numbers from 1 to 581471. Standard calibers offered for Model 70 are these in order of rarity: .300 Savage, .35 Rem., .458 Win Magnum, 7mm, .358 Win., .250-3000 Savage, .300 Win Magnum, .338 Win. Magnum, .375 H&H Magnum, .257 Roberts, .220 Swift, .22 Hornet, .264 Win. Magnum, .300 H&H Magnum, .308 Win., .243 Win., .270 WCF, .30-06. Model 70 was available in several different styles: 1. Standard Grade: 24" round barrel (except 26" round barrel for .220 Swift and .300 H&H Magnum—25" round barrel for .375 H&H Magnum after 1937); plain walnut checkered pistol stock and forend. Built from 1936 to 1963. 2. Standard Grade Carbine: 20" round barrel; chambered for .22 Hornet, .250-3000, .257 Roberts, .270, 7mm and .30-06; same stock as Standard Grade. Built from 1936 to 1946. 3. Super Grade Rifle: same barrel and calibers as Standard Grade; select checkered walnut capped pistol grip stock, with cheekpiece; checkered forend, with plastic tip. Built from 1936 to 1960. 4. Featherweight: 22" round barrel; chambered for .243, .264, .270, .308, .30-06 and .358; fitted with aluminum triggerguard, buttplate and floorplate. Later versions with plastic buttplate. Built from 1952 to 1963. 5. Featherweight Super Grade: same as above, except not chambered for .358 cartridge; fitted with Super Grade stock. Built from 1952 to 1963. 6. National Match: same as Standard Grade, but fitted with target-type stock and telescope bases; chambered for .30-06 only. Discontinued in 1960. 7. Target: 24" round medium-weight barrel; same stock as National Match; in .243 and .30-06 calibers. Discontinued in 1963. 8. Varmint: 26" round heavy barrel; heavier varmint stock; chambered for .243 and rare .220 Swift. Built from 1956 to 1963. 9. Westerner: 26" round barrel; Standard Grade stock; chambered for .264 Win. Magnum. Built from 1960 to 1963. Fitted with solid rubber pad for early production; vented pad for later guns. 10. Alaskan: 25" round barrel; Standard Grade stock; chambered for .338 Win. Magnum and .375 H&H Magnum. Built from 1960 to 1963. Fitted with solid rubber pad marked Winchester for early production; vented pad marked Winchester for later guns. 11. Bull Gun: 28" round barrel; same stock as National Match; chambered for .30-06 and .300 H&H Magnum. Built from 1936 to 1963. Prices for Model 70 are, in many cases, based on caliber of rifle; more rare the caliber, more premium the gun will command. Beware of fakes. There are some unscrupulous individuals who specialize in faking Model 70s, including chambering them to rare calibers. Many pre-1964 Model 70s are still available in new condition in original box, with all the papers. Note: Add 25% to 50% if box is serial numbered to gun. Use caution prior to purchase of NIB guns due to fake boxes and papers. Pricing Note: Asterisk (*) signifies value of rifle with respect to usable action. Model 70 unaltered receivers bring $500 regardless of condition of barrel and stock. If receiver is un-usable then rifle is worth the value of its usable parts, i.e. less than $500.For Model 70s with "X" or "D" prefix, add a collector premium of 10%. These letters indicate that there were two rifles mistakenly stamped with the same serial number.

Standard Rifle .30-06 Springfield (1937-1963)

Pre-War

NIB	Exc.	V.G.	Good	Fair	Poor
—	2200	1600	1100	500*	500*

Post-War

NIB	Exc.	V.G.	Good	Fair	Poor
—	1450	1200	800	500*	500*

.270 Win. (1937-1963)

Pre-War

NIB	Exc.	V.G.	Good	Fair	Poor
—	2200	1900	1000	500*	500*

Post-War

NIB	Exc.	V.G.	Good	Fair	Poor
—	1550	1400	900	500*	500*

.243 Win. (1955-1963)

NIB	Exc.	V.G.	Good	Fair	Poor
—	2750	2200	1100	500*	500*

.300 H&H Magnum (1937-1963)

Pre-War

NIB	Exc.	V.G.	Good	Fair	Poor
—	3100	2500	1700	1000	500*

Post-War

NIB	Exc.	V.G.	Good	Fair	Poor
—	2650	2000	1400	850	500*

.264 Win. Magnum (1959-1963)

NIB	Exc.	V.G.	Good	Fair	Poor
—	2500	2000	1400	850	500*

.22 Hornet (1937-1958)

Pre-War

NIB	Exc.	V.G.	Good	Fair	Poor
—	3000	2400	2000	1000	500*

Post-War

NIB	Exc.	V.G.	Good	Fair	Poor
—	2750	2000	1500	750	500*

.220 Swift (1937-1963)

Pre-War

NIB	Exc.	V.G.	Good	Fair	Poor
—	3000	2400	1750	900	500*

Post-War

NIB	Exc.	V.G.	Good	Fair	Poor
—	2500	1750	1200	650	500*

.257 Roberts (1937-1959)

Pre-War

NIB	Exc.	V.G.	Good	Fair	Poor
—	3200	2500	1500	950	500*

Post-War

NIB	Exc.	V.G.	Good	Fair	Poor
—	2900	2100	1400	750	500*

.375 H&H Magnum (1937-1963)

Pre-War

NIB	Exc.	V.G.	Good	Fair	Poor
—	4300	3700	2200	1350	500*

Post-War

NIB	Exc.	V.G.	Good	Fair	Poor
—	3200	2500	1800	1000	500*

.338 Win. Magnum (1959-1963)

NIB	Exc.	V.G.	Good	Fair	Poor
—	3150	2550	1550	900	500*

.300 Win. Magnum (1962-1963)

NIB	Exc.	V.G.	Good	Fair	Poor
—	2650	2250	1200	750	500*

.250-3000 Savage (1937-1949)

NIB	Exc.	V.G.	Good	Fair	Poor
—	4750	3500	2500	1200	500*

7mm (1937-1949)

NIB	Exc.	V.G.	Good	Fair	Poor
—	5900	4800	2700	1700	700

.35 Rem. (1944-1947)

Note: Very rare. Only 404 manufactured.

NIB	Exc.	V.G.	Good	Fair	Poor
—	12000	10000	5000	3000	2000

.300 Savage (1944-1954)

Note: Very rare. Only 362 manufactured.

NIB	Exc.	V.G.	Good	Fair	Poor
—	12500	10500	5000	3000	2000

.458 Win. Magnum African

Built in Supergrade only, 1956-1963.

NIB	Exc.	V.G.	Good	Fair	Poor
—	7400	5350	4200	2750	1350

Featherweight

Note: Add 100% for .358 Win.; add 25% for .264 and .270 calibers.

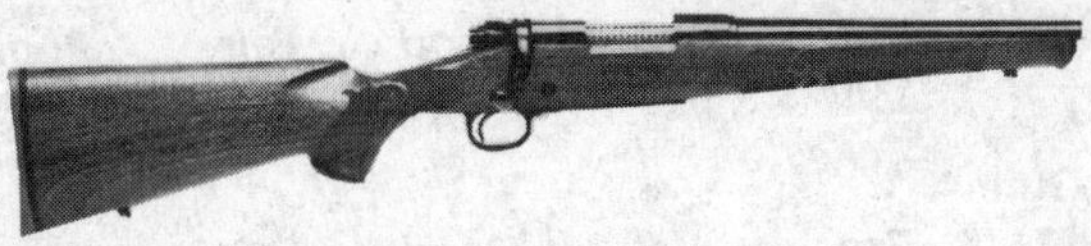

NIB	Exc.	V.G.	Good	Fair	Poor
—	2200	1450	1080	700	450

Super Grade

Features higher grade wood, with black forend tip, grip cap, cheekpiece, and hand-checkering. Made from 1937 to 1960 in all calibers. Prices shown are for standard calibers; .30-06 and .270 Win. Note: Add 50% to 100% for other chamberings (depending on condition) to prices listed by caliber.

NIB	Exc.	V.G.	Good	Fair	Poor
—	4400	3800	2200	1000*	1000*

Featherweight Super Grade

NIB	Exc.	V.G.	Good	Fair	Poor
—	5400	4300	3200	1650	1000

Standard Grade Carbine

Note: Add 100% for Super Grade rifles.

NIB	Exc.	V.G.	Good	Fair	Poor
—	2900	2000	1400	950	650

National Match

NIB	Exc.	V.G.	Good	Fair	Poor
—	3400	2550	1850	950	600

Target

NIB	Exc.	V.G.	Good	Fair	Poor
—	2450	2100	1150	750	550

Varmint

Note: Add 40% premium for .220 Swift.

NIB	Exc.	V.G.	Good	Fair	Poor
—	2350	1950	950	600	375*

Bull Gun

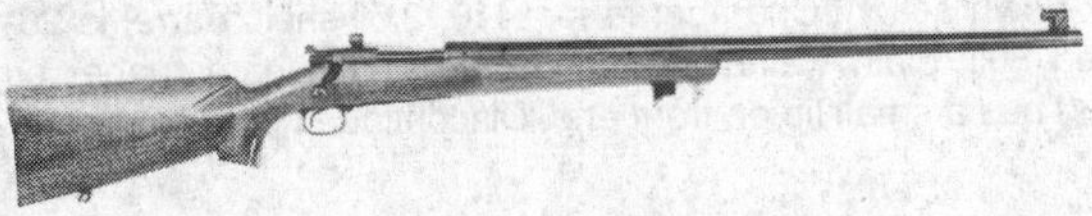

NIB	Exc.	V.G.	Good	Fair	Poor
—	3900	3200	2450	850	600

POST-1963 RIFLES

Model 71

A true reproduction of the original. Drilled and tapped for a receiver sight. Polished blue 24" round barrel. Oil-finished American walnut stock, forend cap, no checkering. Marble gold bead front sight and buckhorn rear. Chambered for original .348 WCF caliber only. Introduced in 2011.

NIB	Exc.	V.G.	Good	Fair	Poor
1300	1100	—	—	—	—

Model 72

Bolt-action rifle with tubular magazine. Chambered for .22 Short, Long and LR cartridges interchangeably. Early rifles available with 2.75x or 5x telescopes, but majority furnished with open or peep sights. This model was not serial numbered. Built between 1938 and 1959. About 161,000 sold. Note: Add 100% premium for Gallery Special: 200% for factory scopes and no sights (depending on condition); 25% premium for peep sights; 20% for Model 72A with grooved receiver. Available in two different configurations: 1. Sporting Rifle: 25" round barrel; chambered for .22 Short, Long and LR cartridges; one-piece plain walnut pistol grip stock and forend. 2. Gallery Special: 25" round barrel; chambered for .22 Short only; stock same as Sporting Rifle.

Courtesy C.H. Wolfersberger

NIB	Exc.	V.G.	Good	Fair	Poor
—	420	350	280	200	120

Model 75

This model discontinued in 1958, with about 89,000 sold. Available in two styles: 1. Sporting Rifle: 24" round barrel; chambered for .22 LR; select walnut checkered pistol grip stock and forend; furnished with open rear sights or Lyman 57E receiver sight. 2. Target Rifle: 28" round barrel; chambered for .22 LR; plain walnut pistol grip stock and forend; furnished with Winchester 8x telescope or a variety of target sights.

Sporter

NIB	Exc.	V.G.	Good	Fair	Poor
—	1500	1000	800	500	350

Target

NIB	Exc.	V.G.	Good	Fair	Poor
—	900	700	600	500	200

Model SXR Super X Rifle

Gas-operated semi-automatic patterned after Browning BAR ShortTrac and LongTrac. Caliber and capacity: .30-06 (4), .300WM (3), .270 WSM (3), .300 WSM (3). Barrel: 22" (.30-06), 24" Magnum calibers. Weight 7.25 lbs. Stock two-piece checkered walnut. Introduced 2006.

NIB	Exc.	V.G.	Good	Fair	Poor
600	500	400	320	250	120

Express Rifle

Over/under double-barreled rifle. Chambered for .257 Roberts, .270, 7.7x65R, .30-06 and 9.3x74R cartridges. Features 23.5" barrels, with solid rib and express sights. Engraved with game scenes. Has a satin-finished receiver. Stock checkered select walnut. Manufactured in 1984 and 1985.

NIB	Exc.	V.G.	Good	Fair	Poor
—	3500	3000	2100	1700	900

SHOTGUNS

Model 12

Designed by T.C. Johnson. First slide-action hammerless shotgun built by Winchester. Model 12 enjoyed great success in its 68-year history, with over two million sold. A high quality, well-made shotgun that is still in use in the hunting and shooting fields across the country. All Model 12s were of take-down variety. Dropped from regular product line in 1963, but a special model was produced in the Custom Shop until 1979. In 1972, Winchester resurrected Model 12 in its regular production line in 12-gauge only, with ventilated rib. This reintroduced Model 12 was dropped in 1980. Prices listed are for guns made prior to 1964 or with serial numbers below 1968307. Shotgun will be seen in many different combinations of gauges, barrel lengths, ribs and stocks, all of which determine value. The more rare a particular combination, higher the price. Buyer is urged to be extremely cautious before purchasing the more rare combinations, such as 28 gauge. Best advice is to seek assistance from an expert and get as many opinions as possible. Prices listed are for guns in standard configurations. Note: Following applies to all Model 12s: Add 10% for 16 ga.; add 50% for 20 ga.; add 60% for 28 ga.; add 20% for solid rib; add 30% for Winchester Special ventilated rib; add 40% for milled rib; add 20% for 32" barrels; add 30% premium for original box and papers.

Model 12 was offered in several different styles:
1. Standard Grade: 12-, 16-, 20- and 28-gauge; plain, solid or ventilated rib round barrels; standard lengths 26", 28", 30", 32"; plain walnut pistol grip stock; grooved slide handle. Built from 1912 to 1963.
2. Featherweight: same as above; lightweight alloy triggerguard. Built between 1959 and 1962.
3. Riot Gun: 12-gauge only; 20" round choked Cylinder; stock same as Standard Grade. Built between 1918 and 1963.
4. Trench Gun: chambered for 12-gauge only; 20" round barrel; ventilated handguard over barrel; fitted with bayonet lug; all metal surfaces "Parkerized"; these shotguns should be U.S. marked as a military firearm. Introduced in 1918 and built for U.S. Armed Forces on special order.
5. Skeet Grade: chambered for 12, 16, 20, and 28 ga.; 26" round barrel; solid or ventilated rib; select walnut checkered pistol stock; special checkered extension slide handle (longer than standard). Built from 1933 to 1963.
6. Trap Grade: chambered for 12-gauge only; 30" round barrel; solid or ventilated rib; select walnut pistol-/straight-grip stock; checkered extension slide handle. Built from 1914 to 1963.
7. Heavy Duck Gun: chambered in 12-gauge only; 30" or 32" round barrel; plain, solid or ventilated rib; plain walnut pistol grip stock; fitted with Winchester solid red rubber recoil pad; plain grooved slide handle. Built from 1935 to 1963.
8. Pigeon Grade: chambered for 12, 16, 20, and 28 ga.; standard barrel lengths; choice of ribs; special order shotgun; will be seen in many different variations; most were factory engraved. Built from 1914 to 1963.

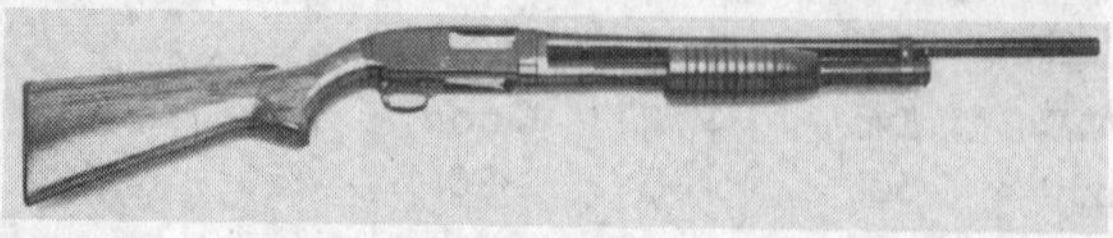

Courtesy Bonhams & Butterfields, San Francisco, California

Standard Grade—12 gauge

NIB	Exc.	V.G.	Good	Fair	Poor
950	650	500	380	300	250

Featherweight

NIB	Exc.	V.G.	Good	Fair	Poor
—	800	700	600	580	200

Riot Gun

NIB	Exc.	V.G.	Good	Fair	Poor
—	2400	1700	900	700	250

Trench Gun

NIB	Exc.	V.G.	Good	Fair	Poor
—	7500	6000	4000	1500	1000

Skeet Grade

NIB	Exc.	V.G.	Good	Fair	Poor
—	2200	1700	900	600	350

Trap Grade

NIB	Exc.	V.G.	Good	Fair	Poor
—	2000	1500	800	550	400

Heavy Duck Gun

Note: Add 25 percent premium for solid ribs.

NIB	Exc.	V.G.	Good	Fair	Poor
—	1150	900	350	420	300

Pigeon Grade

NIB	Exc.	V.G.	Good	Fair	Poor
—	3750	2300	1600	750	500

Model 25

Similar in appearance to Model 12. Does not have take-down feature. All guns were solid-frame. Furnished in 12-gauge, with 26" or 28" plain round barrel, walnut pistol grip stock and grooved slide handle. This was an attempt by Winchester to introduce a less expensive version of Model 12. Introduced in 1949; discontinued in 1954. About 88,000 sold.

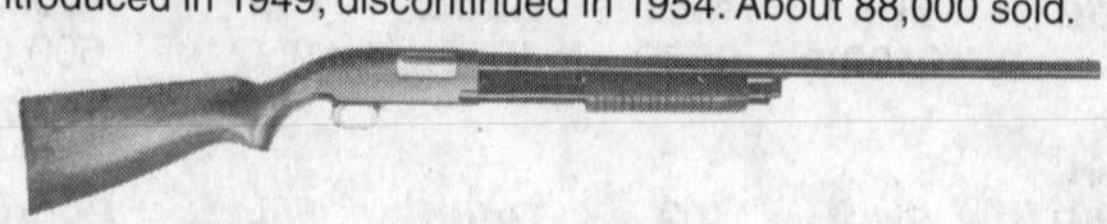

NIB	Exc.	V.G.	Good	Fair	Poor
—	700	550	400	250	100

Model 20

In order to utilize the expanded production facilities left over from WWI, Winchester introduced a series of three different models of single-shot shotguns; Model 20 was the first of three introduced in 1920. Has a visible hammer and toplever frame. First Winchester to have this type of break-down action. Chambered for .410, 2.5" shell. Barrel is 26" round choked Full, plain walnut pistol grip stock with hard rubber buttplate. Forend has a small lip on front end. Discontinued in 1924. About 24,000 sold.

Courtesy C.H. Wolfersberger

NIB	Exc.	V.G.	Good	Fair	Poor
—	750	500	350	200	150

Model 36

Second of the single-shot shotguns to be introduced in 1920. Features a bolt-action that is cocked by pulling firing pin head to the rear. Fitted with an 18" round barrel. Chambered for 9mm Long Shot, Short Shot and Ball interchangeably. Plain gumwood straight-grip stock, with special metal pistol grip triggerguard. Winchester referred to this model as "Garden Gun" for use against birds and pests around the house and barn. This model was not serial numbered. Discontinued in 1927. About

20,000 sold.

NIB	Exc.	V.G.	Good	Fair	Poor
—	1000	780	480	300	220

Model 41

Third of the low-priced single-shot shotguns to be introduced in 1920. Like Model 36, Model 41 was a bolt-action arrangement, but of much stronger construction and design. Features a 24" round barrel. Chambered for .410, 2.5" shell. Plain walnut pistol grip stock and forend. Straight-grip stock furnished at no extra charge. This model was not serial numbered. Discontinued in 1934. About 22,000 sold.

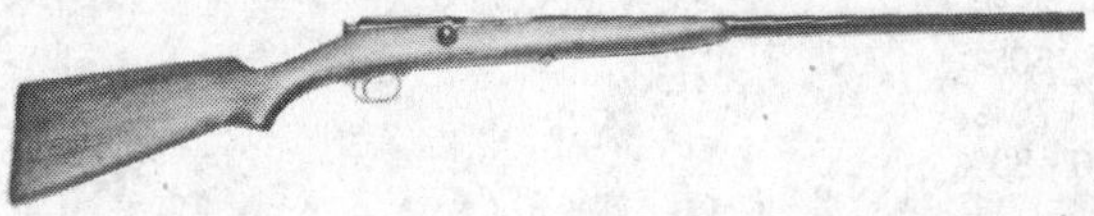

Courtesy C.H. Wolfersberger

NIB	Exc.	V.G.	Good	Fair	Poor
—	600	500	350	300	200

MODEL 21

Winchester's finest effort with regard to quality, reliability and strength. Developed in late 1920s, introduction of this fine side-by-side shotgun was delayed by the company's financial troubles. When Winchester was purchased by the Olin family, Model 21 was assured the attention it richly deserved due to John M. Olin's love for the gun. Despite Model 21 being offered as a production gun it was, in fact, a hand-built custom-made shotgun. Almost each Model 21 built has a personality of its own, because each shotgun is slightly different with regard to chokes, barrel lengths, stock dimensions and embellishments. Introduced in 1931. From 1931 to 1959, Model 21 was considered a production line gun. About 30,000 were sold. In 1960, when Custom Shop was opened, Model 21 was built there using the same procedures. Sales during Custom Shop era were about 1,000 guns. Winchester changed the name of some Model 21 styles, but production methods stayed the same. In 1981, Winchester sold its firearms division to U.S. Repeating Arms Company, including the right to build Model 21. Again, production procedures stayed the same as did many of the former employees. U.S. Repeating Arms expanded and changed some of the style designations for Model 21. Production discontinued in about 1991. No sales figures are available for this time period. Collectors and shooters will be given the price breakdown for all three eras of production separately. Note: Fewer than 50 .410 Model 21s were built between 1931 and 1959 in all grades. Number of 28-gauge Model 21s built is unknown, but probably no greater than .410 bore.

Model 21--1931 to 1959

Model 21 was available in several different styles and configurations:

1. Standard Grade: chambered in 12-, 16-, 20-gauge; barrel lengths 26", 28", 30", 32"; matted or ventilated rib; select walnut checkered pistol-/straight-grip stock; checkered beavertail forend. Built from 1931 to 1959.
2. Tournament Grade: same as above; special dimension stock; marked "TOURNAMENT" on bottom of trigger plate. Built from 1933 to 1934.
3. Trap Grade: same as above; slightly better-grade wood; stock made to customers' dimensions; marked "TRAP" on trigger plate. Built from 1932 to 1959.
4. Skeet Grade: same as above; addition of 28-gauge; stock furnished with checkered butt; marked "SKEET" on trigger plate. Built from 1936 to 1959.
5. Duck Gun: chambered for 12-gauge; 3" Magnum shells; 30" or 32" barrels; Standard Grade stock, except for shorter length of pull; marked "DUCK" on trigger plate. Built from 1940 to 1952.
6. Magnum Gun: chambered for 12- or 20-gauge; 3" Magnum shells; same stock as Duck Gun; not marked on trigger plate. Built from 1953 to 1959.
7. Custom Built/Deluxe Grade: chambered for 12-, 16-, 20-, 28-gauge and .410 bore; barrel lengths from 26" to 32"; stock built to customers specifications using fancy walnut; marked "CUSTOM BUILT" on top of rib or "DELUXE" on trigger plate; these grades are frequently, but not always engraved. Built from 1933 to 1959.

Note: Some early Model 21s furnished with double triggers, extractors and splinter forends. This combination reduces price of the gun regardless of grade. Deduct about 25 percent.

Standard Grade - 12 gauge

NIB	Exc.	V.G.	Good	Fair	Poor
7500	6000	5000	3750	2400	2000

Standard Grade - 16 gauge

NIB	Exc.	V.G.	Good	Fair	Poor
10000	8500	6700	5650	4700	4200

Standard Grade - 20 gauge

NIB	Exc.	V.G.	Good	Fair	Poor
11000	9500	7500	6500	5100	4700

Tournament Grade - 12 gauge

NIB	Exc.	V.G.	Good	Fair	Poor
—	6500	5200	4150	3500	3300

Tournament Grade - 16 gauge

NIB	Exc.	V.G.	Good	Fair	Poor
—	8500	7200	6000	5000	4500

Tournament Grade - 20 gauge

NIB	Exc.	V.G.	Good	Fair	Poor
—	10000	8200	7200	6000	4800

Trap Grade - 12 gauge

NIB	Exc.	V.G.	Good	Fair	Poor
—	6800	5300	4250	3800	3600

Trap Grade - 16 gauge

NIB	Exc.	V.G.	Good	Fair	Poor
—	8500	7300	6100	5300	4900

Trap Grade - 20 gauge

NIB	Exc.	V.G.	Good	Fair	Poor
—	9000	7500	6550	5800	5300

Skeet Grade - 12 gauge

NIB	Exc.	V.G.	Good	Fair	Poor
—	6500	5000	3950	3400	3200

Skeet Grade - 16 gauge

NIB	Exc.	V.G.	Good	Fair	Poor
—	8200	7200	6000	4900	4400

Skeet Grade - 20 gauge

NIB	Exc.	V.G.	Good	Fair	Poor
—	9500	7800	6600	5000	4500

Duck/Magnum Gun

Note: Add 30 percent for 20-gauge Magnum. Factory ventilated ribs command a premium of about $1,800 on 12-gauge; $2,500 on 16- and 20-gauge. Model 21s with factory furnished extra barrels will bring an additional premium of about $2,500. Refinished and restored Model 21s are in a somewhat unique category of American-made collectible shotguns. A gun that has been professionally refinished by a master craftsman will bring approximately 90 percent value of factory original guns.

NIB	Exc.	V.G.	Good	Fair	Poor
—	6500	5100	4450	4000	3800

Custom Built/Deluxe Grade

Prices paid for guns of this grade are determined by gauge, barrel and choke combinations, rib type, stock specifications and engraving. Expert appraisal is recommended. It is best to secure a factory letter from Cody Firearms Museum. With respect to such a letter, it is important to note that these records are incomplete and may be inaccurate in a few cases. Records for Model 21s built during 1930s may be missing. Special-order guns may have incomplete records. In such cases, a written appraisal from an authoritative collector or dealer may be helpful.

12 gauge

NIB	Exc.	V.G.	Good	Fair	Poor
—	8000	7000	5750	4500	4000

16 gauge

NIB	Exc.	V.G.	Good	Fair	Poor
—	9000	8000	6750	5500	4500

20 gauge

NIB	Exc.	V.G.	Good	Fair	Poor
—	10500	8500	7250	6000	5000

.410 Bore

NIB	Exc.	V.G.	Good	Fair	Poor
—	50000	40000	31000	26000	22000

Custom Shop Model 21s—1960 to 1981

When Winchester moved production of Model 21 into the Custom Shop, a number of styles were greatly reduced.

There were now three distinct styles:

1. Custom Grade: chambered in 12-, 16-, 20-, 28-gauge and .410 bore; barrel lengths 26" to 32"; matted rib; fancy walnut checkered pistol-/straight-grip stock; checkered forend; pistol grip guns furnished with steel grip cap; a small amount of scroll engraving was provided on frame of this grade.
2. Pigeon Grade: same chambers and barrel lengths as above; choice of matted or ventilated rib; leather-covered recoil pad; style "A" carving on stock and forend; gold engraved pistol grip cap; frame engraved with 21-6 engraving pattern.
3. Grand American Grade: same chambers and barrel lengths as Pigeon Grade; addition of "B" carving on stock and forend; 21-6 engraving with gold inlays; extra set of interchangeable barrels with extra forend; all enclosed in a leather trunk case.

EDITOR'S COMMENT: According to Ned Schwing's excellent book, "Winchester's Finest, The Model 21", there were only eight 28-gauge and five .410 bore models made during the Custom Shop production era from 1960 to 1981. Any price estimates would be highly speculative.

Custom Grade—12 Gauge

Note: Add $4,000 for 16-gauge; $5,000 for 20-gauge.

NIB	Exc.	V.G.	Good	Fair	Poor
—	10000	8500	7300	6000	5200

Pigeon Grade—12 Gauge

Note: Add $6,000 for 16-gauge; $5,000 for 20-gauge.

NIB	Exc.	V.G.	Good	Fair	Poor
—	19000	16500	12500	10000	8000

Grand American—12 Gauge

Note: Add $15,000 for 16-gauge (extremely rare); $5,000 for 20-gauge.

NIB	Exc.	V.G.	Good	Fair	Poor
—	32000	25000	17500	14000	13000

ENGRAVED MODEL 21s

Winchester catalogued a number of special-order engraving patterns which ranged from a small amount of scroll (#1) to full-coverage game scene and scroll (#6). In addition, there were a few guns engraved on special order to the customer's request. Engraved guns are extremely rare. Value added will vary with rarity of gauge and date of manufacture. The following table represents value added for various standard engraving patterns on 12-gauge guns for "Custom Shop" (1960-1982) and "Pre-Custom Shop" (1932-1959) periods. However, it is advisable to seek the opinion of an authorative collector or dealer prior to a sale.

Engraving Pattern Pre-Custom Shop Custom Shop
#130 - 20%
#240 - 30%
#360 - 45%
#470 - 50%
#590 - 70%
#6100 - 80%

Custom Shop Model 21s—1982 to 1993

When U.S. Repeating Arms Company took over production of Model 21, Pigeon Grade was dropped from the line. Grand American Grade was retained with all the features of its predecessor, with the addition of a small-bore set featuring 28-gauge and .410 bore set of barrels. Two new grades were introduced in 1983: Standard Custom Grade and Special Custom Built. In addition to these grades, the factory would undertake to build for its customers whatever was desired. Due to the unique nature of these guns, it is advised that an expert appraisal be sought to establish a value. While the changeover from Winchester to U.S. Repeating Arms was a transfer of business assets, craftsmen and personnel remained the same. Collectors are reluctant to assign the same values to U.S. Repeating Arms Model 21s as those produced by Winchester. No official production figures are available for U.S.R.A. Model 21s, but the number is most likely small, perhaps around 200 guns.

Standard Custom Built

NIB	Exc.	V.G.	Good	Fair	Poor
9000	7000	6000	5000	4500	4000

Grand American

NIB	Exc.	V.G.	Good	Fair	Poor
19000	14000	10500	8500	6000	5000

Grand American Small Gauge Set—28 or .410 bore

NIB	Exc.	V.G.	Good	Fair	Poor
62500	46500	37500	27000	22000	20000

CURRENT MODEL 21 PRODUCTION

In 1995, Connecticut Shotgun Mfg. Co. purchased the assets of Winchester Model 21 Custom Shop. Beginning in 2002, Winchester licensed CSMC to build Model 21s on a custom-order basis in a wide variety of grades and models, made to the buyer's specifications. For more information, see listing for Connecticut Shotgun Mfg. Co. in this edition.

Model 24

Model 24 was Winchester's attempt to develop a medium-priced double-barrel shotgun. Like Model 21, it was a toplever break-down model available in 12-, 16-, 20-gauge and in various barrel lengths from 26" to 30". Offered in Standard model only, with double triggers, raised matted rib, plain walnut pistol-/straight-grip stock with semi-beavertail forend. Introduced in 1939; discontinued in 1957. About 116,000 sold. Note: Add 10 percent for 16-gauge; 25 percent for 20-gauge.

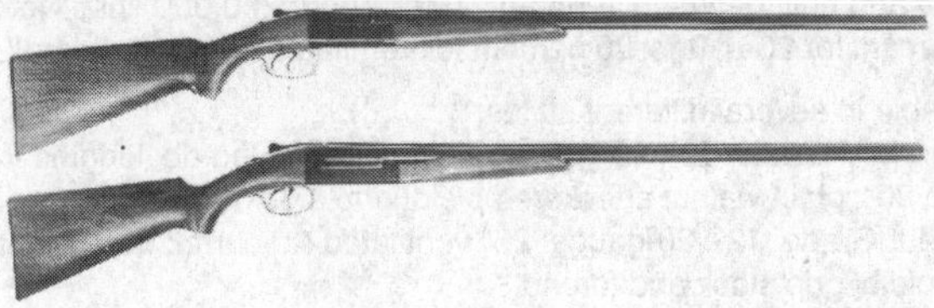

NIB	Exc.	V.G.	Good	Fair	Poor
—	750	500	400	250	200

Model 37

Developed to keep pace with Winchester's competitors in the low-price single-barrel exposed-hammer shotgun market. Available in 12-, 16-, 20-, 28-gauge and .410 bore, with barrel lengths from 26" to 30". Stock was plain walnut, with pistol grip and semi-beavertail forend. This model was not serial numbered. Introduced in 1936, it stayed in the company line until 1963. Sold slightly over 1,000,000 guns. Note: Add 15 percent premium for so-called "red letter" (red-filled "W" on bottom of receiver).

Courtesy C.H. Wolfersberger

12 gauge

NIB	Exc.	V.G.	Good	Fair	Poor
—	400	350	300	250	100

16 gauge

NIB	Exc.	V.G.	Good	Fair	Poor
—	450	400	350	300	80

20 gauge

NIB	Exc.	V.G.	Good	Fair	Poor
—	600	520	500	420	100

28 gauge

NIB	Exc.	V.G.	Good	Fair	Poor
—	2000	1600	1150	850	450

.410 bore

Note: Add 50 percent premium for 32" barrels in 12- and 16-gauge. Use caution for 28-gauge. Many fakes are seen for sale.

NIB	Exc.	V.G.	Good	Fair	Poor
—	1000	850	500	300	100

Youth Model

26" Modified choke barrel. Win. red factory pad. 20-gauge only.

NIB	Exc.	V.G.	Good	Fair	Poor
—	600	550	450	350	120

Model 42

Commentary and values by Bud Bugni.

First slide-action shotgun ever developed exclusively for .410 bore. Invented by William Roemer. It was in effect, at least in outward appearance, a miniature Model 12. This shotgun was quality-built, fast-handling, racy looking that many refer to as "Everybody's Sweetheart". First American .410 bore chambered for new 3" shell as well as 2.5". Offered in several different configurations throughout its production. These configurations will greatly influence value:

1. Standard Grade: 26" or 28" plain or solid rib barrel; plain walnut pistol grip stock; grooved slide handle; fitted with composition buttplate; straight-grip offered on special order basis, but is extremely rare. Built from 1933 to 1963.
2. Skeet Grade: 26" or 28" plain, solid or ventilated rib barrel; select walnut checkered pistol-/straight-grip stock; checkered extension slide handle; offered in Full, Modified, Improved Cylinder, Cylinder as well as Skeet chokes. Built from 1933 to 1963.
3. Trap Grade: 26" or 28" plain or solid rib barrel; fancy walnut special checkered pistol-/straight-grip stock; special checkered extension slide handle; checkering pattern has one closed diamond on each side of pistol grip; straight-grip diamond located on underside of grip; extension slide handle has two uncut diamonds on each side. Most were stamped "TRAP" on bottom of receiver under serial number. Built from 1934 to 1939.
4. Deluxe Grade: continuation of Trap Grade; available with ventilated rib in 1954; some early models stamped "DELUXE" on bottom of receiver. This stamping is seldom seen and probably discontinued around 1949. Built from 1940 to 1963.
5. Pigeon Grade: same as Deluxe Grade, but engraved with pigeon on lower magazine tube. Very few of this grade built by Winchester and majority were done in late 1940s. Authentic Pigeon Grade 42s appear to have been built between 1945 and 1949. Some estimate less than 50 produced. Rare Model 42. Seek an expert opinion before sale.

As of late, I have heard horror stories from sincere, honest, decent folks who have purchased mis-represented guns from unscrupulous sellers or sellers who simply do not know their products. In some cases there are no return privileges, or buyer was unable to authenticate his purchase in a timely manner. This often has resulted in a heavy financial loss and that's a dish served cold. Contributors are listed in Standard Catalog of Firearms. These knowledgeable and dedicated people are eager to assist readers, or refer them to sources who can.—Bud Bugni

Note: Engraved Model 42s will occasionally be seen. Collectors are urged to seek expert advice on these rare and expensive guns. Model 42 produced from 1933 to 1963. About 164,000 were sold. Factory service and repair for this model was discontinued in February of 1972.

EXTRA BARRELS: Winchester offered extra interchangeable barrels for its Model 42s, at customer's request beginning in 1934. These extra sets of barrels are a rare option. Both barrels should have same barrel markings and matching serial numbers before originality can be considered. Values are difficult to determine, but as a general rule, add 60 percent to price of a Model 42 if it has factory-original extra barrel sets.

EDITOR'S COMMENT: Contrary to traditional views, Winchester did install factory ventilated ribs on its Model 42. Former employees and factory drawings substantiate this fact. However, subject of what is a factory rib and what is not has been covered in great detail in an excellent book on Model 42. Seek expert advice before selling or purchasing any Model 42 with ventilated rib.

Note: Pigeon Grade Model 42s, with documentation on expert authentication, add 100 percent. Must be individually appraised. Proceed with caution.

CUTTS COMPENSATOR GUNS: Approximately 66 original Cutts Compensator guns were produced in the Winchester factory, making this one of the rarest options on Model 42. New information reveals that Cutts Compensators were available on Model 42 as early as 1950. This offering appeared in Winchester retail price list dated December 15, 1950. Considering this, since ventilated ribs were not offered on M42 until 1954, one may see an original "Cutts Gun" with plain or solid rib barrel minus a choke mark. Note: Add 25 percent for original Cutts guns; deduct 50 percent for non-original Cutts guns.

Standard Grade

Note: Add 50 percent for Standard Grade with solid ribs; 25 percent for pre-war.

NIB	Exc.	V.G.	Good	Fair	Poor
3250	2000	1450	1000	850	500

Skeet Grade—Solid Rib

Note: Add 25 percent for 2.5" chamber. Deduct 25 percent for no rib.

NIB	Exc.	V.G.	Good	Fair	Poor
6950	5450	4750	3950	2000	1250

Skeet Grade—Ventilated Rib

Note: Add 25 percent for 2.5" chamber.

NIB	Exc.	V.G.	Good	Fair	Poor
7950	6450	4950	3500	2200	1250

Trap Grade - Plain or Solid Rib

NIB	Exc.	V.G.	Good	Fair	Poor
—	12950	11500	9500	5500	3000

Deluxe Grade—Solid Rib

NIB	Exc.	V.G.	Good	Fair	Poor
12950	10500	8750	6450	3600	1280

Deluxe Grade—Ventilated Rib (must be factory)

NIB	Exc.	V.G.	Good	Fair	Poor
14500	12950	11000	7500	4750	2400

Model 1911

Winchester's first self-loading shotgun developed by T.C. Johnson, in order to keep pace with Remington Auto-Loading Shotgun Model 11, which was developed by John M. Browning with help from T.C. Johnson. Because of the delays involved in developing a brand new design, Model 1911 was introduced on October 7, 1911. This shotgun was a recoil operated mechanism, had a tubular magazine and take-down feature. Available in two styles:

1. Plain Model 1911: 26" or 28" barrel; 12-gauge; choked Full, Modified or Cylinder; plain birch laminated pistol grip stock and forend; hard rubber buttplate.
2. Fancy Model 1911: same as above, with fancy birch laminated stock.

Because of the hurry in getting this model ready for production, the shotgun demonstrated design weakness and never proved satisfactory. Discontinued in 1925. About 83,000 sold.

Plain

NIB	Exc.	V.G.	Good	Fair	Poor
—	650	380	300	250	200

Fancy

NIB	Exc.	V.G.	Good	Fair	Poor
—	800	500	400	300	250

Model 40

Represents Winchester's second attempt to build a self-loading long recoil-operated repeating shotgun. This shotgun was a hammerless tubular magazine gun, without the hump at rear of the receiver. Available in 12-gauge only, with barrel lengths from 28" to 30". Standard Grade had plain walnut pistol grip stock and forend; Skeet Grade fitted with select walnut checkered pistol grip stock and checkered forend. Model 40 suffered from the same design problems as Model 11. Introduced in 1940; discontinued in 1941. About 12,000 sold.

Standard Grade

NIB	Exc.	V.G.	Good	Fair	Poor
—	650	500	400	280	200

Skeet Grade

NIB	Exc.	V.G.	Good	Fair	Poor
—	950	600	500	300	250

Model 50

Company's third attempt to produce a satisfactory self-loading repeating shotgun. Winchester went to the short recoil system, utilizing a floating chamber design. This model begins with serial number 1000. Successful model and built between 1954 and 1961. About 200,000 sold. Note: Add 10 percent for 20-gauge; 20 percent for ventilated rib on Standard Grade.

Available in several different styles:
1. Standard Grade: 12-, 20-gauge; plain or ventilated rib; lengths from 26" to 30"; plain walnut checkered pistol grip stock and forend.
2. Skeet Grade: 12-, 20-gauge; 26" ventilated rib barrel; walnut checkered pistol grip stock and forend.
3. Trap Grade: 12-gauge; 30" ventilated rib barrel; walnut checkered Monte Carlo stock and forend.
4. Pigeon Grade: 12-, 20-gauge; barrel lengths to customers' specifications; fancy walnut checkered stock and forend; made on special orders only.
5. Featherweight: lighter version of all the above, except Trap Grade.

Standard Grade

NIB	Exc.	V.G.	Good	Fair	Poor
—	550	400	300	200	150

Skeet Grade

NIB	Exc.	V.G.	Good	Fair	Poor
—	600	500	350	250	200

Trap Grade

NIB	Exc.	V.G.	Good	Fair	Poor
—	600	500	350	250	200

Pigeon Grade

NIB	Exc.	V.G.	Good	Fair	Poor
—	1800	1200	750	450	250

Featherweight

NIB	Exc.	V.G.	Good	Fair	Poor
—	600	500	350	250	200

Model 59

Fourth and final pre-1964 Winchester self-loading shotgun. Featured a steel and fiberglass barrel, with aluminum alloy receiver. Available in 12-gauge only. Barrel lengths from 26" to 30", with a variety of chokes. In 1961, Winchester introduced "Versalite" choke tube. This gave shooter a choice of Full, Modified or Improved Cylinder chokes in the same barrel. Sold about 82,000 Model 59s between 1960 and 1965. Note: Also made in 10-gauge (very rare), 20-gauge and 14-gauge. If any of these very low production or prototype guns are encountered, use extreme caution and seek an expert appraisal. Add 40 percent premium for barrels with three Versalite chokes and wrench; 20 percent premium for original box and papers.

Available in two different styles:
1. Standard Grade: plain walnut checkered pistol grip stock and forend.
2. Pigeon Grade: select walnut checkered pistol grip and forend.

Standard Grade

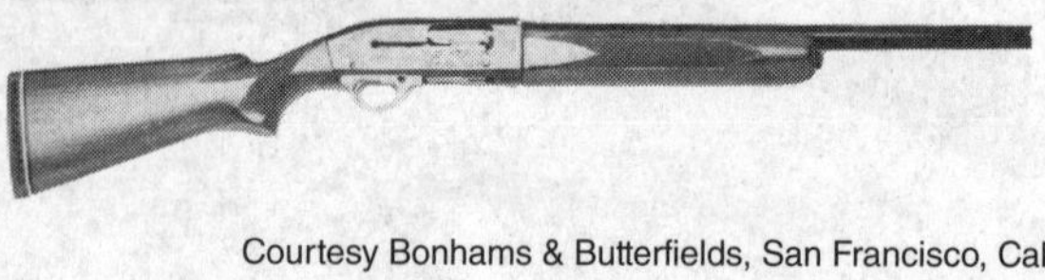

Courtesy Bonhams & Butterfields, San Francisco, California

NIB	Exc.	V.G.	Good	Fair	Poor
—	650	550	450	350	250

Pigeon Grade

NIB	Exc.	V.G.	Good	Fair	Poor
—	2500	2000	1200	600	300

POST-1963 RIFLES

Also see WINCHESTER COMMEMORATIVES listed before WINCHESTER CUSTOM GUN SHOP.

Model 52B Sporting Rifle: 1993-1997 Production

A 1993 limited-edition rifle (6,000 guns). Faithful reproduction of famous Winchester Model 52 Sporter. Equipped with 24" barrel, adjustable trigger and "B" style cheekpiece. Reissued in 1997. Limited to 3,000 rifles. Made by Miroku in Japan.

NIB	*Exc.*	*V.G.*	*Good*	*Fair*	*Poor*
1000	850	700	500	350	300

Model 121

A single-shot bolt-action rifle chambered for .22 rimfire cartridge. Has a 20.75" barrel, with open sights. Finish blued, with plain walnut stock. Manufactured between 1967 and 1973. A youth model, with a shorter stock was designated 121Y and valued the same.

Courtesy Buffalo Bill Historical Center, Cody, Wyoming

NIB	*Exc.*	*V.G.*	*Good*	*Fair*	*Poor*
—	220	150	100	60	40

Model 131

Bolt-action repeater chambered for .22 rimfire cartridge. Has a 20.75" barrel, with open sights and 7-round detachable magazine. Finish blued, with plain walnut stock. Manufactured between 1967 and 1973. A tubular magazine version was designated Model 141 and valued the same.

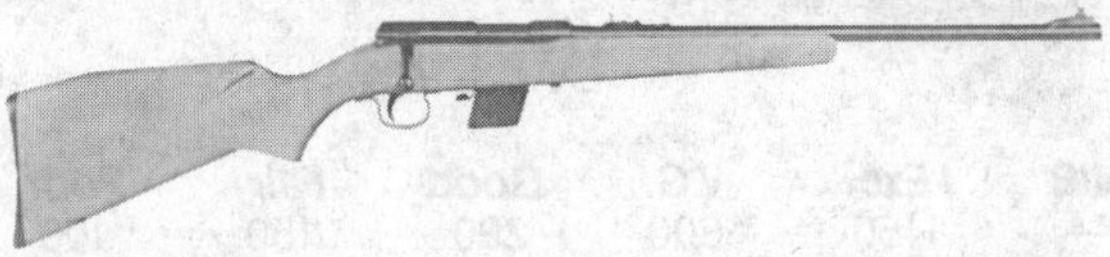

NIB	*Exc.*	*V.G.*	*Good*	*Fair*	*Poor*
—	250	180	100	60	40

Model 310

Single-shot bolt-action rifle chambered for .22 rimfire cartridge. Features 22" barrel, with open sights. Finish blued, with checkered walnut stock. Manufactured between 1972 and 1975.

Courtesy Buffalo Bill Historical Center, Cody, Wyoming

NIB	*Exc.*	*V.G.*	*Good*	*Fair*	*Poor*
—	250	150	120	100	80

Model 320

Bolt-action repeating rifle. Similar in configuration to Model 310 single-shot. Has a 5-round detachable box magazine. Manufactured between 1972 and 1974.

NIB	*Exc.*	*V.G.*	*Good*	*Fair*	*Poor*
—	400	300	250	180	120

Model 250

Lever-action repeating rifle, with a hammerless action. Chambered for .22 rimfire cartridge. Has a 20.5" barrel, with open sights and tubular magazine. Finish blued, with checkered pistol grip stock. Manufactured between 1963 and 1973.

NIB	*Exc.*	*V.G.*	*Good*	*Fair*	*Poor*
—	200	120	80	60	40

Model 250 Deluxe

This version similar to Model 250. Furnished with select walnut and sling swivels. Manufactured between 1965 and 1971.

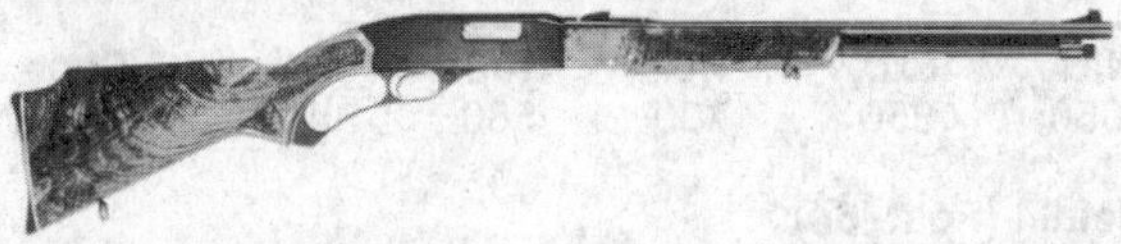

NIB	*Exc.*	*V.G.*	*Good*	*Fair*	*Poor*
—	280	200	120	100	80

Model 255

Simply Model 250 chambered for .22 WMR cartridge. Manufactured between 1964 and 1970.

NIB	*Exc.*	*V.G.*	*Good*	*Fair*	*Poor*
—	220	150	100	70	50

Model 255 Deluxe

This version offered with select walnut and sling swivels. Manufactured between 1965 and 1973.

NIB	*Exc.*	*V.G.*	*Good*	*Fair*	*Poor*
—	380	250	180	120	80

Model 490

A blowback-operated semi-automatic rifle chambered for .22 LR cartridge. Has a 22" barrel, with open sights and 5-round detachable magazine. Finish blued, with checkered stock. Manufactured between 1975 and 1980.

NIB	*Exc.*	*V.G.*	*Good*	*Fair*	*Poor*
—	350	220	160	100	80

Model 270

Slide-action rifle chambered for .22 rimfire cartridge. Has a 20.5" barrel and tubular magazine. Finish blued, with checkered walnut stock. Manufactured between 1963 and 1973.

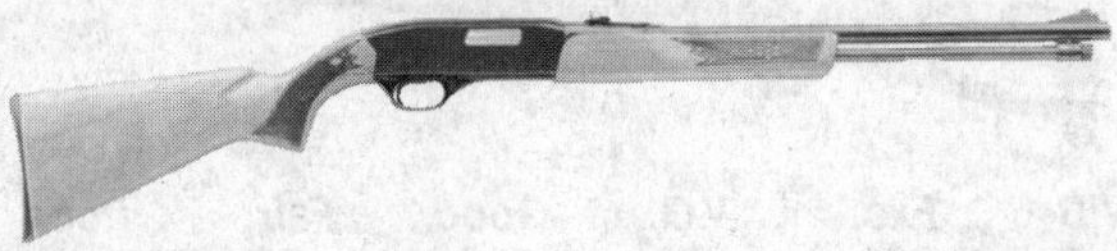

NIB	*Exc.*	*V.G.*	*Good*	*Fair*	*Poor*
—	350	220	160	100	80

Model 63 (1997)

Introduced in 1997. A re-creation of famous Model 63 .22-caliber automatic. Fitted with a 23" barrel and 10-round tubular magazine. Receiver top grooved for scope mounting.

Grade I

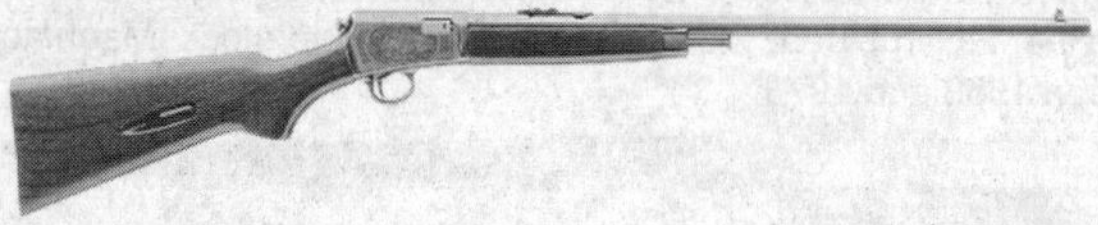

NIB	Exc.	V.G.	Good	Fair	Poor
800	520	—	—	—	—

High Grade

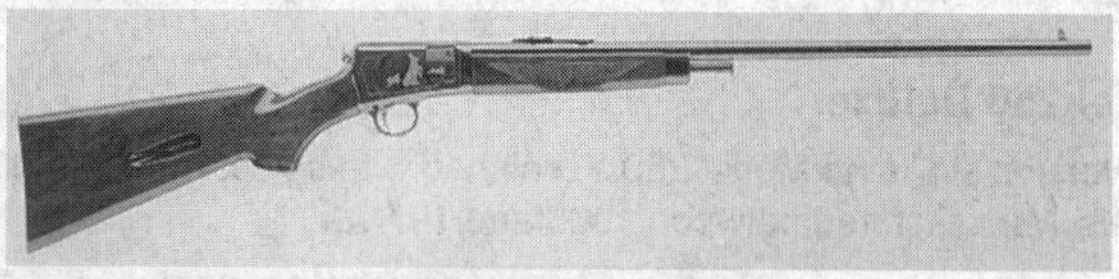

NIB	Exc.	V.G.	Good	Fair	Poor
1050	850	700	580	400	300

Model 64 (Post-'64)

A post-1964 version of lever-action Model 64. Chambered for .30-30 cartridge. Has 24" round barrel, with open sights and 5-round 2/3-length tubular magazine. Finish blued, with plain walnut pistol grip stock. Manufactured between 1972 and 1974.

NIB	Exc.	V.G.	Good	Fair	Poor
—	800	650	550	380	250

Wildcat

Bolt-action repeater styled after Mosin-Nagant military sporter. Caliber: .22 LR. Magazine: 5- and 10-round detachable. Stock: checkered walnut with schnabel. Barrel: 21" blued. Weight: 4.5 lbs. Imported. Introduced 2006. Sporter and Target/Varmint versions available. Note: Add 5% for Target/Varmint.

NIB	Exc.	V.G.	Good	Fair	Poor
240	180	150	120	100	50

Xpert

Calibers: .22 LR. Capacity: 10-round rotary detachable magazine, interchangeable with both Wildcat and Ruger 10/22. Barrel: 18" precision button rifled with recessed target crown. Weight: 4 lbs. 8 oz. Length: 36.25" Stock: Gray Synthetic skeletonized with optional LOP spacers and cheek riser. Sights: Adjustable rear and ramped post front. Drilled and tapped. Features: Bolt-action precision cousin to the Wildcat line of semi-auto rimfires. Xpert uses a rimfire version of the M.O.A. trigger found on Model 70 and XPR rifles. Semi-match Bentz chamber and hemispherical firing pin. Extended bolt handle. Ambidextrous side-mounted mag releases. Plastic butt plate.

NIB	Exc.	V.G.	Good	Fair	Poor
340	300	260	200	150	—

Wildcat 22 SR (Suppressor Ready)

NIB	Exc.	V.G.	Good	Fair	Poor
280	240	200	—	—	—

MODEL 94 SERIES

Model 94

Post-1964 lever-action carbine. Chambered for .30-30, 7-30 Waters and .44 Magnum cartridges. Offered with 20" or 24" barrel. Has a 6- or 7-round tubular magazine, depending on barrel length. Round barrel offered with open sights. Forearm held on by a single-barrel band. Finish blued, with straight-grip walnut stock. In 1982, modified to angle ejection to simplify scope mounting. Introduced as a continuation of Model 94 line, in 1964. In 2003, a top-tang safety was installed and .480 Ruger caliber was added. Model 94 series discontinued in 2006. Premium for unusual chamberings such as 7-30 Waters, etc.

NIB	Exc.	V.G.	Good	Fair	Poor
800	600	420	300	200	100

Model 94 Traditional—CW

As above, with checkered walnut stock. Chambered for .30-30, .44 Magnum and .480 Ruger cartridge. Note: Add $20 for .44 Magnum; $70 for .480 Ruger.

NIB	Exc.	V.G.	Good	Fair	Poor
850	580	450	320	220	120

Model 94 Ranger

Chambered for .30-30 cartridge. Fitted with a 20" barrel. Weight about 6.25 lbs. In 2003, a top-tang safety was installed.

NIB	Exc.	V.G.	Good	Fair	Poor
—	450	300	220	150	100

Model 94 Ranger Compact

Introduced in 1998. Features 16" barrel, with 12.5" lop. Chambered for .30-30 or .357 Magnum. Furnished with black recoil pad. Post-style front sight, with adjustable rear sight. Hardwood stock. Weight 5.87 lbs

NIB	Exc.	V.G.	Good	Fair	Poor
—	480	320	250	150	100

Model 94 Black Shadow

Features black synthetic stock, with non-glare finish and black recoil pad. Offered in .30-30, .44 Magnum or .444 Marlin. Fitted with a 20" barrel. Weight 6.5 lbs. Introduced in 1998.

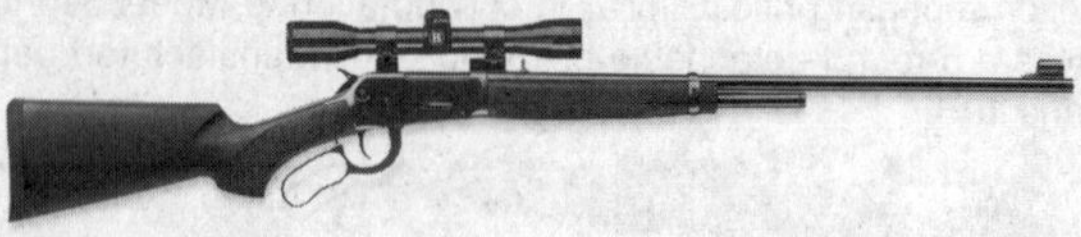

NIB	Exc.	V.G.	Good	Fair	Poor
600	480	380	250	220	180

Model 94 Deluxe

Checkered stock.

NIB	Exc.	V.G.	Good	Fair	Poor
850	680	550	400	300	200

Model 94 Win-Tuff

Laminated stock.

NIB	Exc.	V.G.	Good	Fair	Poor
500	400	280	220	160	120

Model 94 XTR

Select checkered walnut stock. Discontinued 1988.

NIB	Exc.	V.G.	Good	Fair	Poor
—	700	450	350	250	180

Model 94 XTR Deluxe

Fancy checkering.

NIB	Exc.	V.G.	Good	Fair	Poor
—	720	480	380	280	200

Model 94 Trapper

Chambered for .30-30, .357 Magnum, .44 Magnum or .45 Colt cartridge. Barrel 16". In 2003, a top-tang safety was installed. As of 2023, .357 Magnum brings a significant premium in all Model 94 variations. This may be a temporary market trend due to lack of availability.

NIB	Exc.	V.G.	Good	Fair	Poor
750	580	450	350	250	150

Model 94 Antique Carbine

Gold-plated saddle ring.

NIB	Exc.	V.G.	Good	Fair	Poor
—	800	600	480	350	200

Model 94 Wrangler

.32 Win. Special.

NIB	Exc.	V.G.	Good	Fair	Poor
—	900	720	520	400	250

Model 94 Wrangler II

Loop lever.

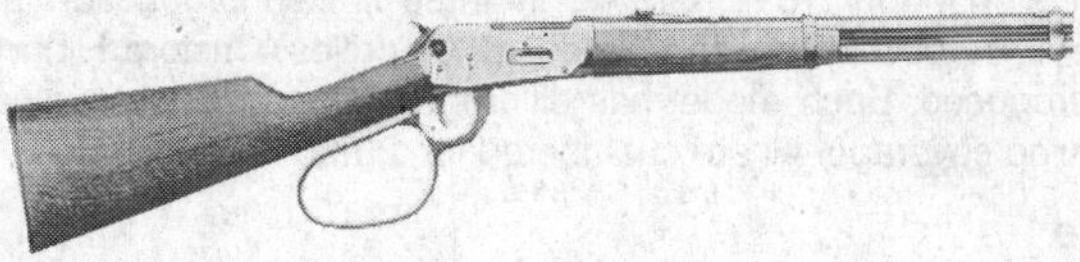

NIB	Exc.	V.G.	Good	Fair	Poor
700	520	420	300	150	—

Model 94 Legacy 20"

Chambered for .30-30 Win. Fitted with a 20" barrel and half pistol grip stock. Walnut buttstock and forearm are cut checkered. Weight 6.5 lbs. In 2003, a top-tang safety was installed.

NIB	Exc.	V.G.	Good	Fair	Poor
900	750	600	480	300	200

Model 94 Legacy 24"

Introduced in 2005. Features 24" round barrel, with full-length magazine. Checkered walnut stock, with semi-pistol grip. Chambered for .30-30, .357 Magnum, .44 Rem. Magnum or .45 Colt cartridge. Drilled and tapped for scope mount. Blued finish. Weight 6.75 lbs.

NIB	Exc.	V.G.	Good	Fair	Poor
900	750	600	480	300	200

Model 94 Legacy 26"

Similar to model above, but offered in both round and octagon barrel; blue or case colored receiver. Marbles' tang sight. Chambered for .30-30 or .38-55 calibers. Weight 7 lbs. Introduced in 2005. Premium for .38-55. Note: Add $55 for case-colored receiver; $100 for octagon barrel.

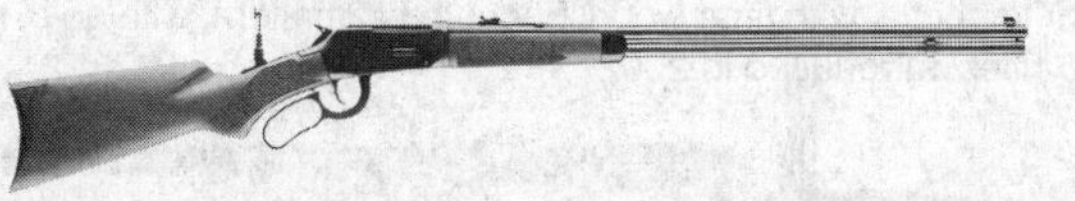

NIB	Exc.	V.G.	Good	Fair	Poor
1100	880	750	580	400	300

Model 94 XTR Big Bore

This version chambered for .307, .356 or .375 Win. cartridges. Features angle-ejection; blued, with walnut Monte Carlo-type stock; recoil pad. Round barrel length 20". Has 6-round tubular magazine. Introduced in 1978. Note: Deduct 12.5% for .375 Win.

NIB	Exc.	V.G.	Good	Fair	Poor
1050	900	780	580	400	300

Model 94 Centennial Limited Editions

Introduced in 1994. These models celebrate 100-year Anniversary of

Winchester Model 1894. Offered in three limited production grades: Grade 1 -12,000 rifles; High Grade - 3,000 rifles; Custom High Grade - 94 produced. Each model has different grades of select walnut and engraving coverage. All are chambered for .30-30 Win. cartridge.

Grade I

NIB	Exc.	V.G.	Good	Fair	Poor
1200	1000	900	700	580	400

High Grade

NIB	Exc.	V.G.	Good	Fair	Poor
1900	1300	1080	900	750	600

Custom High Grade

NIB	Exc.	V.G.	Good	Fair	Poor
4750	3900	2500	1000	750	450

Model 94 Heritage—Limited 1 of 1,000

Introduced in 2002. Limited to 1,000 rifles. Fitted with half round/half octagon 26" barrel. Engraved #3 pattern, with gold plate. Fancy walnut stock. Chambered for .38-55 cartridge.

NIB	Exc.	V.G.	Good	Fair	Poor
5000	4000	3000	1750	1200	600

Model 94 Heritage—Custom 1 of 100

Similar to above, with finer wood. Engraved #2 pattern, with gold. Limited to 100 rifles. Introduced in 2002.

NIB	Exc.	V.G.	Good	Fair	Poor
7500	—	—	—	—	—

Model 94 Trails End

Chambered for .357 Magnum, .44 Magnum, and .45 Colt. Offered with standard-size loop lever or Wrangler-style loop. Introduced in 1997. Note: Add $500 to NIB for .25-35 Win.

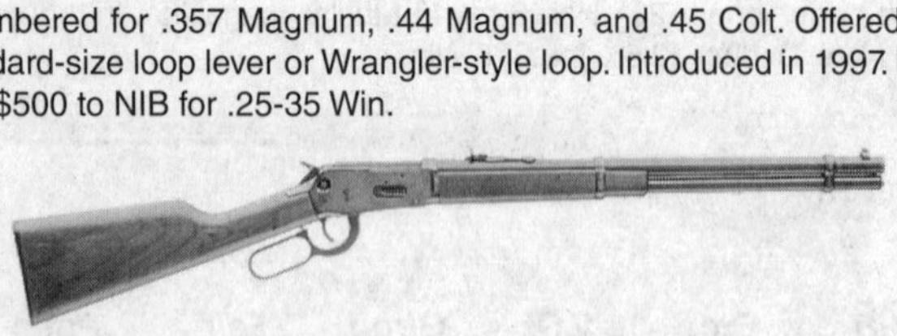

NIB	Exc.	V.G.	Good	Fair	Poor
1380	1050	820	600	450	300

Model 94 Trails End Octagon

As above, with 20" octagon barrel. Choice of blued or case-colored receiver. Crescent butt. Weight 6.75 lbs. Introduced in 2004. Note: Add $60 for case-colored receiver.

NIB	Exc.	V.G.	Good	Fair	Poor
1400	1100	850	600	450	300

Model 94 Trails End Hunter

Offered in .25-35 Win., .30-30 Win. or .38-55 Win. Fitted with 20" round or octagon barrel. Plain walnut stock. Blued finish on round barrel; case colored on octagon barrel. Weight 6.5 lbs. Introduced in 2005. Note: Add $290 for octagon barrel.

NIB	Exc.	V.G.	Good	Fair	Poor
1380	1050	820	600	450	300

Model 94 Timber Carbine

Introduced in 1999. Chambered for .444 Marlin. Barrel is 17.75" long and ported. Hooded front sight. Magazine capacity 5 rounds. Weight 6 lbs. Finish blue. Walnut stock. In 2004, chambered for .450 Marlin.

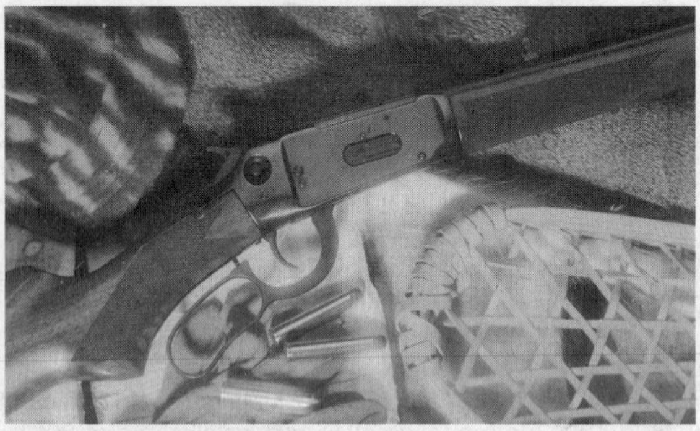

NIB	Exc.	V.G.	Good	Fair	Poor
1000	850	700	600	400	300

Model 94 Timber Scout

Introduced in 2005. Features an 18" barrel. Chambered for .30-30 Win. or .44 Rem. Magnum cartridges. Quick detachable scope mount attached to barrel for long eye relief. Plain walnut stock, with pistol grip. Blued finish. Weight 6 lbs. Scope not included.

NIB	Exc.	V.G.	Good	Fair	Poor
900	750	600	480	300	200

Model 94 Pack Rifle

Lever-action model features an 18" barrel. Chambered for .30-30 or .44 Magnum. Has a plain walnut stock, with pistol grip. Magazine is 3/4-style; 4-round capacity for .30-30; 5-round for .44 Magnum. Open sights. Weight 6.25 lbs. Introduced in 2000.

NIB	Exc.	V.G.	Good	Fair	Poor
900	750	600	480	300	200

Model 1894 Custom Grade

Lever-action rifle chambered in .30-30. Features include 24" half round/half octagon deeply blued barrel; buckhorn rear sight with Marbles gold bead front; Grade IV/V walnut stock and forend with a rich high-gloss finish; deep scroll engraving on both sides of blued receiver. Commemorates 200th Anniversary of Oliver F. Winchester's birth. An early Winchester Repeating Arms crest graces left side of receiver, with right side bearing the words "Two Hundred Years, Oliver F. Winchester" and dates "1810 - 2010" in gold. Barrel is deeply polished, with signature of Oliver F. Winchester in gold on top of the bolt. Sold individually in limited quantities and in 500 sets with High Grade.

NIB	*Exc.*	*V.G.*	*Good*	*Fair*	*Poor*
1800	1550	1300	—	—	—

Model 1894 High Grade

Lever-action rifle chambered in .30-30. Features include 24" half round/half octagon deeply blued barrel; buckhorn rear sight with Marbles gold bead front; silver nitride receiver; Grade II/III high gloss walnut stock and forend with a rich high-gloss finish; delicate scroll work, with Oliver F. Winchester's signature in gold on top of the bolt. Left side of receiver bears an early Winchester Repeating Arms crest; on right side are the words "Two Hundred Years, Oliver F. Winchester" and dates "1810 - 2010". Sold individually in limited quantities and in 500 sets with the Custom Grade.

NIB	*Exc.*	*V.G.*	*Good*	*Fair*	*Poor*
1300	1100	900	—	—	—

Model 94 Short Rifle

Latest incarnation of famous Model 94 Carbine, with 20" round barrel and straight-grip walnut stock. Rifle-styled forend has black grip cap and full-length magazine. Receiver drilled and tapped for scope mounts, with hammer extension included. Marble gold bead front sight, semi-buckhorn rear. Overall length 38"; weight 6.75 lbs. Chambered in .30-30 or .38-55.

NIB	*Exc.*	*V.G.*	*Good*	*Fair*	*Poor*
1150	1000	800	500	300	250

Model 94 Sporter

Reminiscent of original Model 1894 Rifle. This new model for 2011, has a 24" half round/half octagon blued barrel; satin oil-finished American walnut stock; steel crescent buttplate; double-line border checkering pattern. Blue receiver drilled and tapped for optical sights. Gold bead front sight and buckhorn rear. Hammer extension included. Available in .30-30 or .38-55 Win.

NIB	*Exc.*	*V.G.*	*Good*	*Fair*	*Poor*
1180	1000	850	—	—	—

Model 94 150th Commemorative

To commemorate 150 years of Winchester, this classic lever-action rifle features a 24" octagon barrel, with gold band and Winchester 150th Anniversary gold script engraving. Other special features are Ulrich-style engraved silver nitride receiver sideplates, crescent buttplate and forend cap. Iron sights are semi-buckhorn adjustable rear and Marble's gold bead front. Straight-grip stock has classic cut spade-style checkering and high polish oil-finish. Chambered for classic .30-30 Win., with 8-round magazine. Introduced in 2016.

NIB	*Exc.*	*V.G.*	*Good*	*Fair*	*Poor*
2500	2000	—	—	—	—

MODEL 9400 SERIES

Model 9410

Variation of Model 94 lever-action rifle. Chambered for .410 bore shotgun. Available in several versions. SEE: Model 9400 Series in lever-action rifle section.

NIB	*Exc.*	*V.G.*	*Good*	*Fair*	*Poor*
1450	1100	900	750	600	400

Model 9410 Semi-Fancy

As above, with semi-fancy walnut stock and checkering. Introduced in 2004.

NIB	*Exc.*	*V.G.*	*Good*	*Fair*	*Poor*
1600	1200	980	820	650	400

Model 9410 Packer

Introduced in 2002. Features 20" barrel, with 3/4 magazine and pistol grip stock. Weight 6.5 lbs.

NIB	*Exc.*	*V.G.*	*Good*	*Fair*	*Poor*
1000	850	700	600	400	300

Model 9410 Packer Compact

Introduced in 2003. Features reduced length of pull to 12.5". Fitted with Invector chokes. Weight 6.25 lbs.

NIB	*Exc.*	*V.G.*	*Good*	*Fair*	*Poor*
1000	850	700	600	400	300

Model 9410 Ranger

Same as standard or traditional Model 9410, with hardwood stock without checkering. Weight 6.75 lbs. Fitted with top-tang safety. Introduced in 2003.

NIB	*Exc.*	*V.G.*	*Good*	*Fair*	*Poor*
900	750	580	450	300	250

Model 9422

Introduced in 1972. Chambered for .22 rimfire and .22 rimfire Magnum cartridges. Fitted with a 20.5" barrel, front ramp sight with hood and adjustable semi-buckhorn rear. Tubular magazine holds 21 Shorts, 17 Longs and 15 LR cartridges. Magnum version holds 11 cartridges. Weight 6.25 lbs. Two-piece American walnut stock, with no checkering. Between 1972 and 1992, approximately 750,000 were produced.

NIB	Exc.	V.G.	Good	Fair	Poor
850	680	520	380	220	120

Model 9422 XTR

Deluxe lever-action take-down rifle chambered for .22 rimfire cartridge. Round 20.5" barrel and tubular magazine. Finish blued, with checkered high-gloss straight-grip walnut stock. Introduced in 1978. Note: Add $100 for .22 Magnum version.

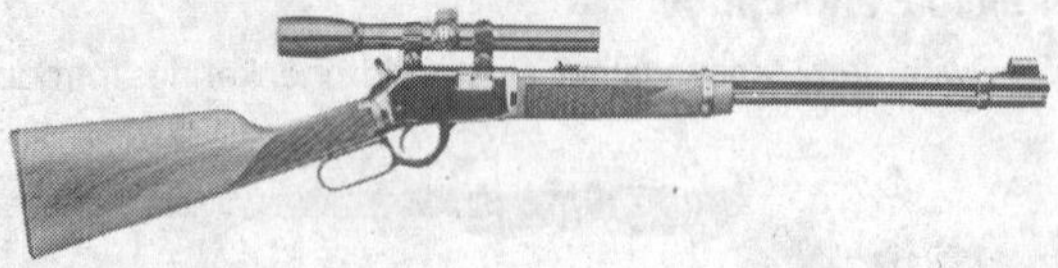

NIB	Exc.	V.G.	Good	Fair	Poor
1000	850	700	600	400	300

Model 9422 XTR Classic

Similar to standard Model 9422 XTR. Features 22.5" barrel; satin-finished plain pistol grip walnut stock. Manufactured between 1985 and 1987.

NIB	Exc.	V.G.	Good	Fair	Poor
1100	920	750	650	450	320

Model 9422 WinTuff

Features uncheckered laminated wood stock that is brown in color. Chambered for .22 rimfire and .22 Win. Magnum rimfire. Weight 6.25 lbs. Other features same as standard Model 9422.

NIB	Exc.	V.G.	Good	Fair	Poor
850	680	520	380	220	120

Model 9422 WinCam

Chambered only for .22 Win. Magnum rimfire. Laminated stock is a green color. Weight 6.25 lbs.

NIB	Exc.	V.G.	Good	Fair	Poor
850	680	520	380	220	120

Model 9422 Trapper

Introduced in 1996. Features 16.5" barrel. Overall length 33"; weight 5.5 lbs.

NIB	Exc.	V.G.	Good	Fair	Poor
850	680	520	380	220	120

Model 9422 High Grade

This variation features a specially engraved receiver and fancy wood stock. Barrel length 20.5"; weight 6 lbs.

NIB	Exc.	V.G.	Good	Fair	Poor
1000	850	700	600	400	300

Model 9422 25th Anniversary Rifle

Introduced in 1997. Features 20.5" barrel. Limited quantities.

Grade I

Engraved receiver.

NIB	Exc.	V.G.	Good	Fair	Poor
1000	850	700	600	400	300

High Grade

Engraved receiver, with silver border.

NIB	Exc.	V.G.	Good	Fair	Poor
1450	1100	900	750	600	400

Model 9422 Legacy

Has a checkered walnut semi-pistol grip stock. Shoots .22-caliber LR, L or S cartridges. Fitted with a 16" barrel. Weight 6 lbs. Introduced in 1998.

NIB	Exc.	V.G.	Good	Fair	Poor
850	680	520	380	220	120

Model 9422 Large Loop & Walnut

Introduced in 1998. Features walnut stock, with a large loop lever. Large loop offered on .22 LR, L or S. Standard lever on .22 WMR. Fitted with 16" barrel. Weight 6 lbs.

NIB	Exc.	V.G.	Good	Fair	Poor
900	750	580	450	300	250

Model 9422 High Grade Series II

Features high-grade walnut stock, with cut checkering. Receiver engraved with dogs and squirrels. 16" barrel. Weight 6 lbs. Introduced in 1998.

NIB	Exc.	V.G.	Good	Fair	Poor
1450	1100	900	750	600	400

Model 9417 Traditional

Introduced in 2003. Chambered for .17 HMR cartridge. Fitted with 20.5" barrel. Adjustable sights. Checkered walnut stock, with straight-grip. Weight 6 lbs.

NIB	Exc.	V.G.	Good	Fair	Poor
1200	980	850	680	400	300

Model 9417 Legacy

Similar to model above. 22.5" barrel. Plain walnut stock, with checkered pistol grip. Weight 6 lbs. Introduced in 2003.

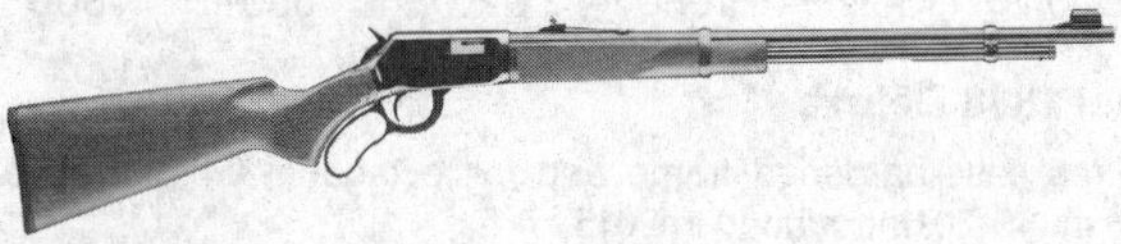

NIB	Exc.	V.G.	Good	Fair	Poor
1200	980	850	680	400	300

MODEL 9422 TRIBUTE SERIES

As of 2005, Model 9422 production ended. Model 9422s were limited to a total production of 9,422 rifles. Each rifle has Winchester Horse and Rider on one side and Model 9422 tribute logo on the other side.

Traditional Tribute

Features 20.5" barrel, with high-grade checkered walnut stock. Blued receiver, with high-relief silver inlay on both sides of receiver.

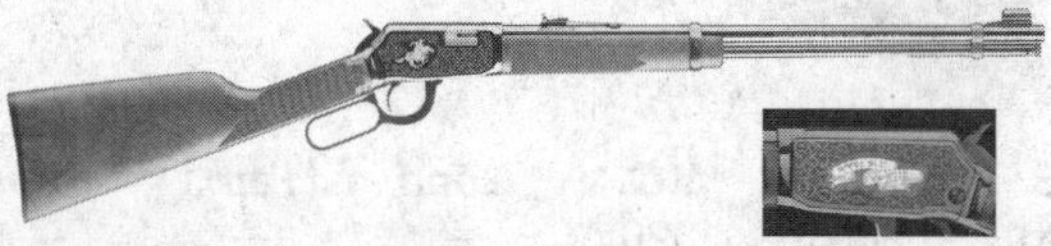

NIB	Exc.	V.G.	Good	Fair	Poor
1400	1200	980	820	650	300

Legacy Tribute

Similar to model above, with semi-pistol grip. Barrel 22.5".

NIB	Exc.	V.G.	Good	Fair	Poor
1500	1300	1080	920	650	300

Custom Traditional Tribute

Fitted with 20.5" barrel and high-grade checkered walnut stock. High-relief scroll engraved receiver, with gold logos on both sides. Limited to 222 rifles.

NIB	Exc.	V.G.	Good	Fair	Poor
2600	2200	1650	1200	800	500

Special Edition Traditional Tribute

Has checkered walnut straight-grip stock. Engraved blued receiver. Barrel 20.5". Engraved logos on both sides of receiver.

NIB	Exc.	V.G.	Good	Fair	Poor
1200	980	850	680	400	300

Special Edition Legacy Tribute

Checkered semi-pistol grip stock. Blued receiver, with engraved logos on both sides. Barrel 22.5".

NIB	Exc.	V.G.	Good	Fair	Poor
1200	980	850	680	400	300

MODEL 1885 SERIES

Today's single-shot Winchester 1885 rifles are modern versions of John M. Browning's classic put into production by Winchester in 1885. Revived by Browning Arms, (see Browning for earlier versions) they are now marked "Winchester" since both firms are owned by FN. Currently, they are offered in the "High Wall" for modern centerfire cartridges and "Low Wall" for rimfire.

Model 1885 High Wall Hunter

Single shot patterned after original Model 1885, designed by John Browning. Over the years, the Hunter has been offered in most modern centerfire rimless calibers from .223, to .45-70 including most belted magnums and WSMs. Stock is checkered walnut. Blued, sightless 28" octagon barrel, with Pachmayr pad. Weight 8.5 lbs. Versions will be encountered with blued or case-hardened receivers. Note: Add $270 for Traditional High Wall Hunter with tang sights, case hardened receiver in .45-70 or .38-55.

NIB	Exc.	V.G.	Good	Fair	Poor
1450	1220	1050	880	550	320

Model 1885 Low Wall

Introduced in 1999 in .22 LR and .17 Mach 2, today's Hunter Rimfire is chambered in .17 HMR, .17 WSM, .22 LR and .22 WMR. Fitted with 24" octagon barrel, with iron sights, drilled and tapped for tang sight and scope mounts. Blued metal, walnut stock. Weight 7.5 lbs. Grade I and High Grade versions were offered from 1999-2001. Note: Deduct about half for earlier Grade I and 25% for High Grade from prices below. Past centerfire Low Wall versions offered in select calibers from .204 to 6.5x55 including .22 Hornet.

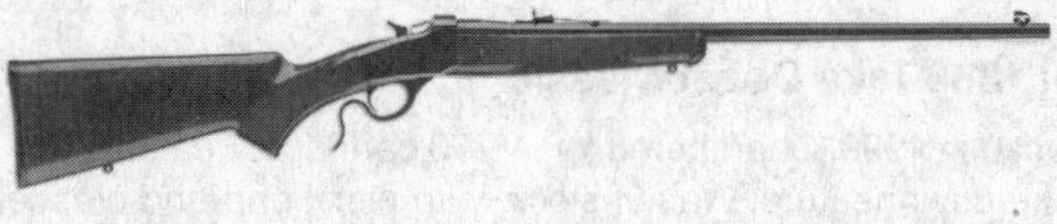

NIB	Exc.	V.G.	Good	Fair	Poor
1320	1120	950	820	500	300

Grade I

NIB	Exc.	V.G.	Good	Fair	Poor
1050	900	750	600	500	300

High Grade

NIB	Exc.	V.G.	Good	Fair	Poor
1300	1050	880	750	600	400

Model 1885 BPCR

High Wall with case-colored receiver, blued Badger half round, half octagon 30" barrel in .45-70, oil-finished Grade III/IV walnut Creedmoor-style stock and Schnabel forearm. Sights included Soule windage-style Creedmoor vernier rear sight and spirit level front sight with multiple apertures. Offered in 2009. Add $400 if sights are present. (See Browning Arms section for earlier versions.)

NIB	Exc.	V.G.	Good	Fair	Poor
1500	1280	1100	920	550	350

Model 1885 .30-06 Centennial High Wall Hunter

Similar to Model 1885 High Wall Hunter, with premium wood and gold inlay on receiver. Commemorates centennial of .30-06 cartridge. Introduced 2006.

NIB	Exc.	V.G.	Good	Fair	Poor
1300	1120	880	750	550	320

MODEL 1886 SERIES

Model 1886

Introduced to Winchester line in 1997. This was a non-cataloged item. Features 26" octagon barrel, semi-pistol grip and crescent buttplate.

Grade I

2,500 rifles, with blued receiver.

NIB	Exc.	V.G.	Good	Fair	Poor
1050	900	750	600	500	300

High Grade

1,000 rifles, with gold accents on receiver.

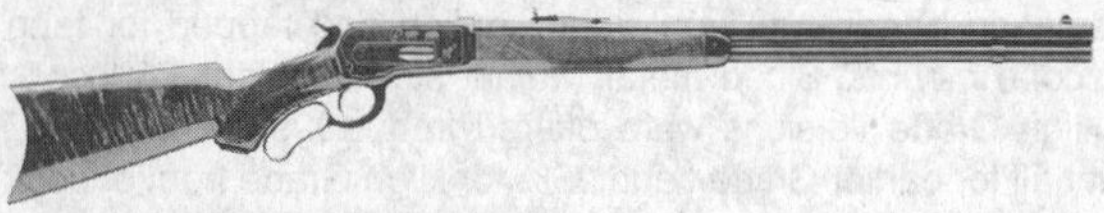

NIB	Exc.	V.G.	Good	Fair	Poor
1500	1300	1080	920	650	300

Model 1886 Take Down Classic

Introduced in 1999. Chambered for .45-70 cartridge. Features 26" barrel, with take-down feature. Walnut stock, with pistol grip and crescent butt. Magazine capacity 8 rounds. Weight 9.25 lbs.

NIB	Exc.	V.G.	Good	Fair	Poor
1300	1120	880	750	550	320

Model 1886 Extra Light

Similar to Model 1886 Classic. Fitted with 22" round tapered barrel and half magazine. Chambered for .45-70 cartridge. Shotgun butt. Weight 7.25 lbs. Limited edition. Introduced in 2000.

Grade I (3,500)

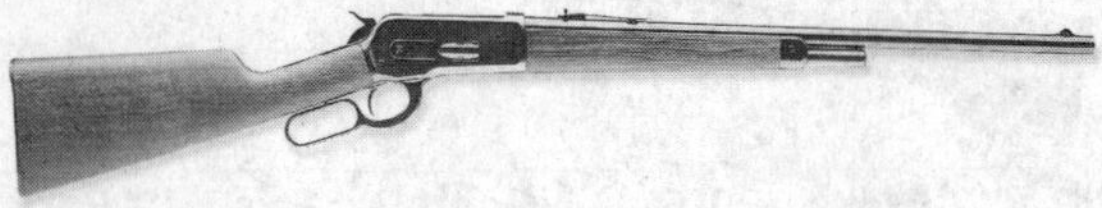

NIB	Exc.	V.G.	Good	Fair	Poor
1100	920	750	650	450	320

High Grade (1,000)

NIB	Exc.	V.G.	Good	Fair	Poor
1500	1300	1080	920	650	300

Model 1886 Deluxe

Features case-hardened frame and full octagonal 24" barrel. Chambered in .45-70. Introduced in 2015.

NIB	Exc.	V.G.	Good	Fair	Poor
1500	1380	1000	—	—	—

Model 1886 Short Rifle

Reintroduced version of famed Model 1886, with Grade I American walnut stock. Blue steel forend cap; crescent buttplate; barrel 24"; full-length tubular magazine holds six cartridges. Chambered in .45-70 Government. Elegant satin finish on all wood and no checkering. Deep blue receiver, barrel, and lever. Top-tang safety. Adjustable rear buckhorn sight and fine gold Marble front.

NIB	Exc.	V.G.	Good	Fair	Poor
1120	980	820	—	—	—

Model 1866 150th Commemorative

Only a limited number will be made to commemorate 150th Anniversary of the founding of Winchester Repeating Arms. Among the features are a Custom Grade V/VI walnut straight-grip stock, with satin finish and crescent buttplate. Full octagon 24" barrel, with gold band and special 150th Anniversary script and scroll engraving. Sights are ladder-style rear, with blade front. Chambered for .44-40 (WCF) caliber, with 13-round magazine. Introduced in 2016.

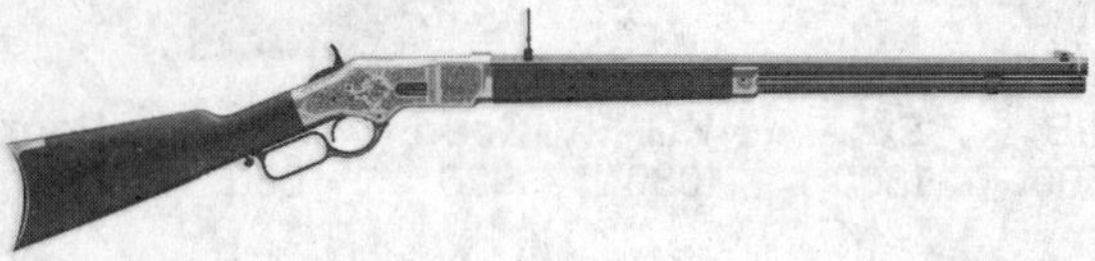

NIB	Exc.	V.G.	Good	Fair	Poor
3000	2600	—	—	—	—

MODEL 1892 SERIES

Model 1892

Introduced in mid-1997. Chambered for .357 Magnum, .44-40 and .45 Colt cartridges. Features straight-grip, full magazine and crescent buttplate.

Grade I

2,500 rifles, with engraved receiver.

NIB	Exc.	V.G.	Good	Fair	Poor
900	800	700	550	450	320

High Grade

1,000 rifles, with gold accents.

NIB	Exc.	V.G.	Good	Fair	Poor
1500	1300	1080	920	650	300

Model 1892 Carbine

Similar to 1892 Short Rifle, with satin-finished stock, full-length 10-shot magazine with barrel band. Introduced in 2011. Also available with large loop lever.

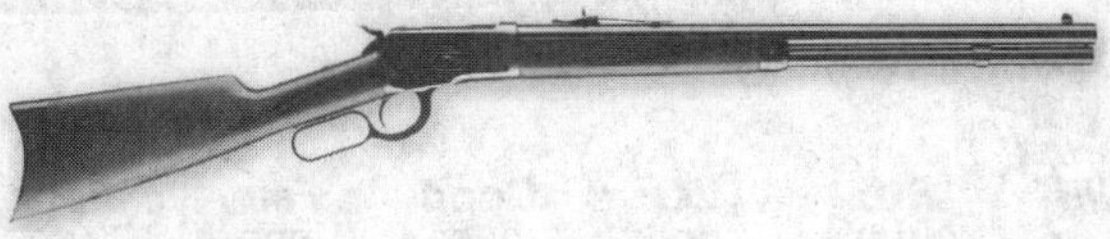

NIB	Exc.	V.G.	Good	Fair	Poor
950	800	700	—	—	—

Model 1892 Short Rifle

Fitted with 20" barrel. Chambered for .45 Colt, .357 Magnum, .44 Magnum and .44-40 cartridges. Walnut stock, with blued barrel and receiver. Weight 6.25 lbs. Introduced in 1999.

NIB	Exc.	V.G.	Good	Fair	Poor
1200	980	850	680	400	300

John Wayne Model 1892 High Grade

Features silver-nickel receiver, with engraved portrait of actor on receiver. Banners on sides of receiver have silver-nickel engraving "John Wayne-American 1907-2007" and "Courage, Strength, Grit". In .44-40 caliber, with 18.5" barrel, large loop lever, adjustable rear sight, blue hammer and trigger. Custom Grade has checkered stock, gold engraving, blue receiver. Limited editions with 4,000 High Grade and 1,000 Custom Grade. Manufactured 2007-2009. Note: Add $1,000 for Custom Grade.

NIB	Exc.	V.G.	Good	Fair	Poor
1750	1650	1550	—	—	—

MODEL 1895 SERIES

Model 1895 Limited Edition

Introduced in 1995. Reproduction of famous Model 1895. Offered in .30-06 caliber, with 24" barrel. Magazine capacity 4 rounds. Weight 8 lbs. Available in two grades, each limited to 4,000 rifles. Reintroduced in 2010, in .30-40 Krag caliber.

Grade I

NIB	Exc.	V.G.	Good	Fair	Poor
1050	900	750	600	500	300

High Grade

NIB	Exc.	V.G.	Good	Fair	Poor
1500	1300	1080	920	650	300

Model 1895—Limited Edition for the Year 2000

Same as above, but chambered for .405 Win. cartridge. Introduced in 2000.

Grade I

NIB	Exc.	V.G.	Good	Fair	Poor
1100	920	750	650	450	320

High Grade

NIB	Exc.	V.G.	Good	Fair	Poor
1500	1300	1080	920	650	300

Model 1895 Saddle Ring Carbine

Patterned after original Model 1895 carbine. Features include blued 22" barrel, ladder-style rear sight, D&T for Lyman side mount, saddle ring on left side of receiver, rollmarked .30 Gov't 06. Chambered in .30-06 only. Commemorates centennial of .30-06 cartridge. Introduced 2006. No longer in production.

NIB	Exc.	V.G.	Good	Fair	Poor
1200	980	850	680	400	300

Model 1895 Theodore Roosevelt Safari Centennial High Grade

Lever-action rifle patterned after original Winchester Model 1895. Chambered in .405 Win. Commemorates Theodore Roosevelt's 1909 African Safari. Blued round 24" barrel, 4-round box magazine, checkered walnut forend and buttstock, with inlaid "TR" medallion. Engraved and silvered receiver. Weight 8 lbs.

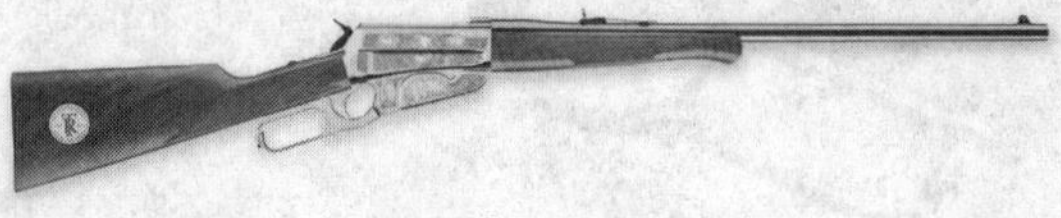

NIB	Exc.	V.G.	Good	Fair	Poor
1600	1380	1080	920	650	300

Custom Grade

Similar to above, with jeweled hammer, fancier wood and engraving, gold-filled highlights and numerous accessories. Production limited to 1,000 sets.

NIB	Exc.	V.G.	Good	Fair	Poor
3000	2500	1950	1580	1200	700

MODEL 1873 SERIES

Model 73

Winchester's latest incarnation of what some historians call "The Gun That Won the West". Offered in several variations. Chambered in .357 Magnum, .44-40 or .45 Colt. Short Rifle has 20" barrel, straight-grip stock; Sporter 24" round/octagonal barrel, with/without pistol grip (shown). Reintroduced in 2015. Note: Add $250 for color case-hardened receiver.

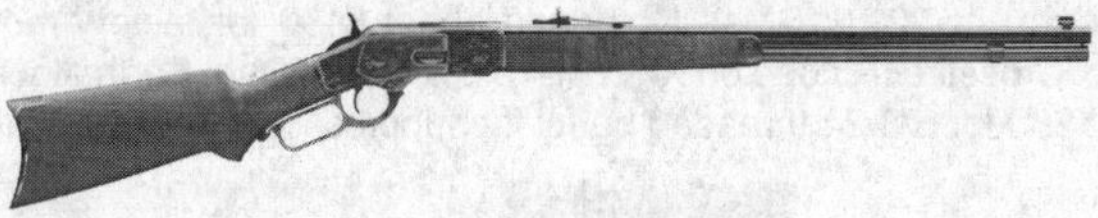

Short Rifle

NIB	Exc.	V.G.	Good	Fair	Poor
1100	950	800	—	—	—

Sporter

NIB	Exc.	V.G.	Good	Fair	Poor
1550	1400	1250	—	—	—

Model 1873 150th Commemorative

This "Gun That Won the West" commemorates 150-years of Winchester. Features include Grade V/VI walnut stock, scroll engraving with gold accents, adjustable tang sight, crescent buttplate and forend cap. Full octagon 24" barrel, with gold band and special 150th Anniversary script. Sights are tang-mounted rear peep and adjustable semi-buckhorn, with gold bead front. Chambered for .44-40 (WCF) caliber, with 13-round magazine. Introduced in 2016.

NIB	Exc.	V.G.	Good	Fair	Poor
3000	2600	—	—	—	—

1873 150TH Anniversary

Caliber: .44-40 Win. Barrel: 24" octagon. Weight: 8.0 lbs. Stock: Grade V/VI Black Walnut straight grip with laser-cut 20-LPI checkering. Features: Special anniversary edition of "The gun that won the West." High-gloss blued steel metalwork. Gold-filled 150th-anniversary engraving. Crescent buttplate with engraving detail. Semi buckhorn rear sight with Marble's gold bead front. The receiver is drilled and tapped for a tang-mounted sight. Introduced 2023.

NIB	Exc.	V.G.	Good	Fair	Poor
3530	—	—	—	—	—

XPR SERIES

New bolt-action rifle introduced in 2015, and made with modern manufacturing methods for a more affordable price. Key features include a bolt and receiver machined from chrome-moly bar stock and through-hardened, 1-piece nickel-Teflon-coated bolt, scope-base holes tapped 8-40, M.O.A. trigger system, bolt unlock button, free-floated button-rifled barrel with precision crown, detachable box magazine, Inflex Technology recoil pad and matte finish metal. Weight 6 lbs., 12 oz. Currently offered in a wide range of calibers in short or long actions. Calibers include, .243, 6.5 CM, .270 Win, .270 WSM, 7mm-08, 7mm Rem Mag, .308, .30-06, .300 WSM, .300 Win. Mag., .325 WSM, .338 Win. Mag., and .350 Legend.

XPR and XPR Compact

As above, in black polymer stock, matte blue finish, in barrel lengths of 22" (standard calibers), 24" (WSMs), or 26" (Magnums). An XPR Compact model in short actions (including WSMs) is also available with 20" (standard) or 22" (WSMs). Note: Add about $150 for factory-mounted Vortex Crossfire II scope on XPR with black or Flat Dark Earth stock. Add about $80 for 5/8-24 threaded barrel for suppressor or muzzle brake.

NIB	Exc.	V.G.	Good	Fair	Poor
500	420	350	300	180	120

XPR Hunter and Hunter Compact

As above, with dipped camo stock, Perma-cote action and barrel in black or brown. Camo patterns vary on the Hunter by year and have included Mossy Oak Break-Up Country or Mountain Country Range, True Timber Strata; Kuiu Vias or Verde 2.0; Kryptec Highlander. Patterns on Hunter Compact include Break-Up, Strata or Muddy Girl. Note: Add about $150 for factory-mounted Vortex Crossfire II scope on Hunter with True Timber Strata camo stock.

NIB	Exc.	V.G.	Good	Fair	Poor
540	460	390	330	200	120

XPR Thumbhole Varmint

As above in gray laminate thumbhole stock with raised cheekpiece, matte blued steel finish, in short action calibers. Barrel threaded 5/8-24 for suppressor or muzzle brake.

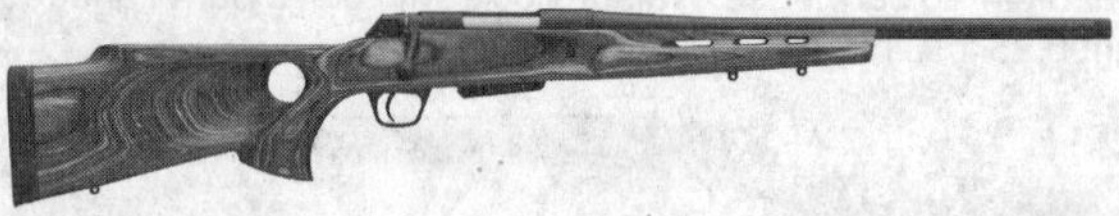

NIB	Exc.	V.G.	Good	Fair	Poor
720	620	520	450	260	160

XPR Sporter

As above, with walnut stock in barrel lengths of 22" (standard calibers), 24" (WSMs), or 26" (Magnums).

NIB	Exc.	V.G.	Good	Fair	Poor
540	460	390	330	200	120

XPR Renegade Long Range SR

Calibers: .243 Win., 6.5 Creedmoor, 7mm-08 Rem, .308 Win., .270 WSM, .300 WSM, 6.5 PRC. Capacity: 3. Barrel: 22 to 24 in., stainless steel, sporter. Stock: Composite Grayboe. Sights: None, drilled and tapped. Weight: 8.5 lbs. Features: Recessed target crown, Inflex Technology recoil pad, enlarged bolt knob.

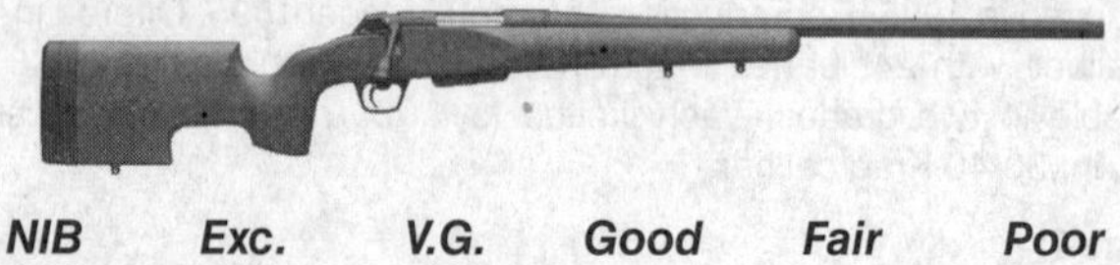

NIB	Exc.	V.G.	Good	Fair	Poor
980	830	700	—	—	—

XPR Hunter True Timber Strata

Calibers: .243 Win., 6.5 Creedmoor, 7mm-08 Rem., .308 Win., .270 WSM, .300 WSM, .325 WSM, .270 Win., .30-06, 7mm Rem. Mag., .300 Win. Mag., .338 Win. Mag., .350 Legend, .223 Rem., 6.5 PRC. Capacity: 3 to 5. Barrel: 22 to 26 in., steel sporter, with Permacote finish. Stock: Composite, True Timber Strata camo. Sights: None, drilled and tapped. Weight: 6.75 to 7 lbs. Features: Inflex Technology recoil pad, sling swivel studs.

NIB	Exc.	V.G.	Good	Fair	Poor
530	450	380	—	—	—

POST-1964 MODEL 70

These post-Model 70 rifles were fitted with: redesigned actions; bolt with free-floating barrels; new style stocks with impressed checkering. In 1994, U.S. Repeating Arms reintroduced pre-1964 Model 70 action on many of its Model 70 rifles. At the present time, this new action does not affect values but may do so in the future depending on shooter reaction.

In October of 2007, Winchester Repeating Arms announced that pre-'64-style Model 70 would once again be produced – this time at the FN plant in Columbia, South Carolina.

Model 70—Standard Grade

Bolt-action sporting rifle chambered for various popular calibers such as .22-250, .222 Rem., .243 Win., .270 Win., .30-06 and .308 Win. Features 22" barrel, with open sights and 5-round integral box magazine. Finish blued, with Monte Carlo-type stock furnished with sling swivels. Manufactured between 1964 and 1971.

NIB	*Exc.*	*V.G.*	*Good*	*Fair*	*Poor*
—	600	480	320	180	110

Model 70 Varmint

Chambered for .22-25, .222 Rem. and .243 Win. cartridges. Fitted with 24" heavy-weight barrel, with no sights. Magazine capacity 5 rounds. Weight 9.75 lbs. Built from 1964 to 1971.

NIB	*Exc.*	*V.G.*	*Good*	*Fair*	*Poor*
—	600	450	300	150	100

Model 70 Westerner

Chambered for .264 Win. Magnum and .300 Win. Magnum cartridges. Open sights; 24" barrel; ventilated recoil pad. Weight 7.25 lbs. Built from 1964 to 1971.

NIB	*Exc.*	*V.G.*	*Good*	*Fair*	*Poor*
—	650	480	320	180	110

Model 70 African

Chambered for .458 Win. Magnum cartridge. Fitted with 22" barrel, with open sights. Magazine capacity 3 rounds. Weight 8.5 lbs. Built from 1964 to 1971.

NIB	*Exc.*	*V.G.*	*Good*	*Fair*	*Poor*
—	920	750	480	280	180

Model 70 Magnum

Chambered for 7mm Rem. Magnum, .300 Win. Magnum and .375 H&H cartridges. Barrel length 24"; weight 7.75 lbs. Built from 1964 to 1971.

NIB	*Exc.*	*V.G.*	*Good*	*Fair*	*Poor*
—	750	580	380	220	180

Model 70 Deluxe

Built from 1964 to 1971. Features Monte Carlo stock, with hand-checkering and ebony forend tip. Offered in .243, .270, .30-06, .300 Win. Magnum. Barrel 22"; Magnum 24". Weight 7.5 lbs.

NIB	*Exc.*	*V.G.*	*Good*	*Fair*	*Poor*
—	750	580	350	180	120

Model 70 Mannlicher

Full-length Mannlicher-type stocked version of Model 70 bolt-action rifle. Chambered for .243, .270, .308 and .30-06 cartridges. Introduced in 1969. Features 19" barrel, with open sights. Finish blued. Discontinued in 1972. Only 2,401 produced. Excellent quality.

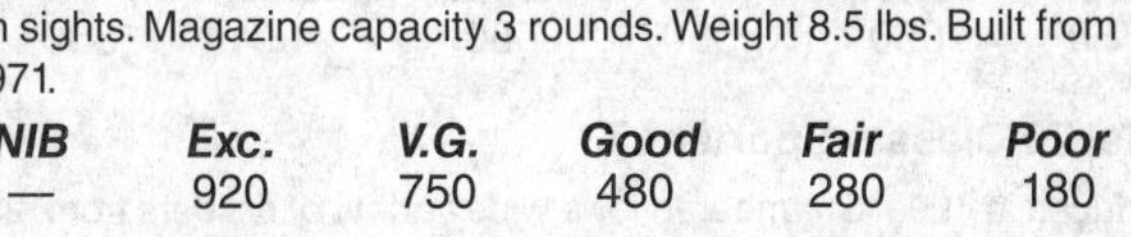

NIB	*Exc.*	*V.G.*	*Good*	*Fair*	*Poor*
—	980	820	620	420	310

Model 70 Target Rifle

Chambered for .308 or .30-06 cartridges. Offered with 24" heavy barrel, without sights. Furnished with bases for a target scope. Finish blued, with heavy walnut target stock and palm rest. Weight 10.25 lbs.

NIB	*Exc.*	*V.G.*	*Good*	*Fair*	*Poor*
—	880	780	580	380	260

Model 70 International Match Army

Chambered for .308 cartridge. Has 24" heavy barrel furnished without sights and adjustable trigger. Blued, with target-type heavy stock that has an accessory rail and adjustable butt.

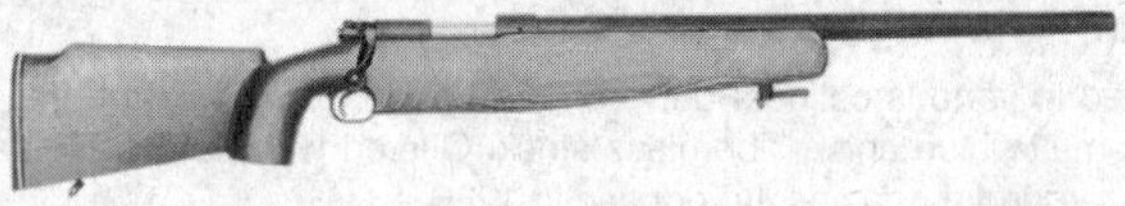

NIB	*Exc.*	*V.G.*	*Good*	*Fair*	*Poor*
—	950	850	600	400	300

Model 70A

Utility version of bolt-action post-1963 Model 70. Furnished without a hinged floorplate. Finish blued, with walnut stock. Manufactured between 1972 and 1978.

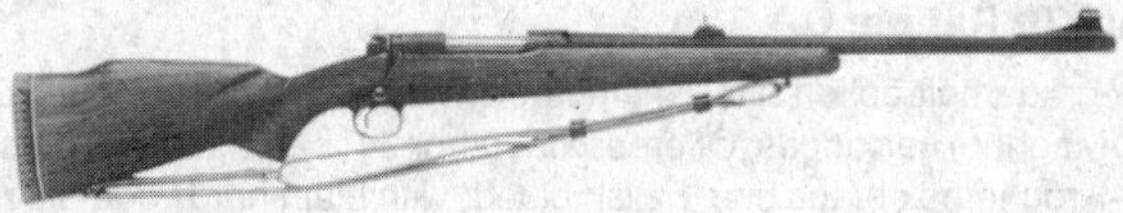

NIB	*Exc.*	*V.G.*	*Good*	*Fair*	*Poor*
—	500	400	350	300	120

Model 70 XTR Featherweight

Built after the takeover by U.S.R.A. Company. Bolt-action sporting rifle chambered for various calibers from .22-250 up to .30-06 cartridges. Has 22" barrel that is furnished without sights and 5-round integral magazine. Features short-/medium-length action. Finish blued, with checkered walnut stock. Introduced in 1981.

NIB	*Exc.*	*V.G.*	*Good*	*Fair*	*Poor*
—	720	620	450	320	260

Model 70 50th Anniversary

Commemorative version of post-1963 Model 70 bolt-action rifle. Chambered for .300 Win. Magnum. Offered with 24" barrel; engraved; high-gloss blued; deluxe checkered walnut stock. There were 500 manufactured in 1987. To realize collector potential, it must be NIB with all supplied materials.

NIB	*Exc.*	*V.G.*	*Good*	*Fair*	*Poor*
1500	1400	1200	900	500	300

Model 70 XTR Super Express

Heavy-duty version of post-1963 Model 70. Chambered for .375 H&H and .458 Win. Magnum cartridges. Offered with 22" or 24" heavy barrel and 3-round integral box magazine. Has extra recoil lugs mounted in the stock. Blued, with select straight-grain walnut stock. Recoil pad standard.

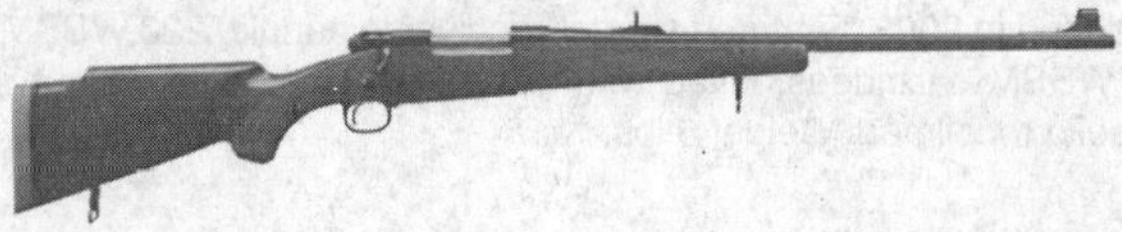

NIB	*Exc.*	*V.G.*	*Good*	*Fair*	*Poor*
1100	920	750	650	450	320

Model 70 XTR Varmint

Chambered for .22-250, .223 and .243 cartridges. Has 24" heavy barrel furnished without sights and 5-round magazine. Blued, with heavy walnut stock. Introduced in 1972.

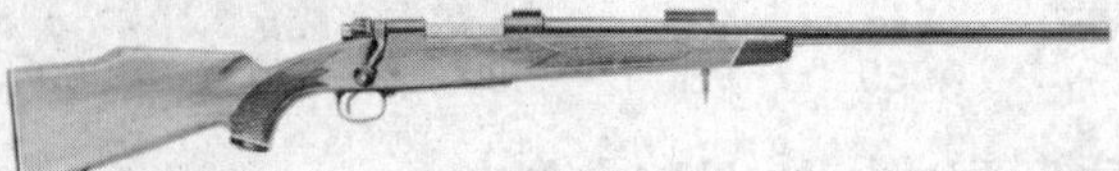

NIB	*Exc.*	*V.G.*	*Good*	*Fair*	*Poor*
650	550	400	250	200	100

Model 70 Winlight

Offered in various calibers between .270 and .338 Win. Magnum. Features matte blue finish; fiberglass stock. Offered with 22" or 24" barrel; 3- or 4-round magazine. Introduced in 1986.

NIB	*Exc.*	*V.G.*	*Good*	*Fair*	*Poor*
700	550	400	250	200	100

Model 70 Ranger

Utility-grade bolt-action rifle. Chambered for .270 Win., .30-06 and 7mm Rem. Magnum cartridges. Offered with 22" or 24" barrel, open sights and 3- or 4-round box magazine. Finish blued, with plain hardwood stock.

NIB	*Exc.*	*V.G.*	*Good*	*Fair*	*Poor*
450	300	280	220	150	100

Model 70 Featherweight

Bolt-action rifle chambered in .22-250, .243, 7mm-08, .308, .270 WSM, 7mm WSM, .300 WSM, .325 WSM, .25-06, .270, .30-06, 7mm Rem. Magnum, .300 Win. Magnum, .338 Win. Magnum. Blued 22" barrel (24" Magnum), satin-finished checkered Grade I walnut stock, controlled round feeding. Capacity five rounds (short action); three rounds (long action). Weight 6.5 to 7.25 lbs. Pachmayr Decelerator pad. No sights, but drilled and tapped for scope mounts. Values shown are for long action. In 2003, a left-hand model offered. Note: Add $35 for left-hand; $60 for stainless steel. Deduct 15% for short action.

NIB	*Exc.*	*V.G.*	*Good*	*Fair*	*Poor*
850	650	450	380	220	120

Model 70 Featherweight Classic All-Terrain

Introduced in 1996. Features weather-resistant stainless steel barrel and action, with fiberglass/graphite black synthetic stock. Offered in .270 Win., .30-06, 7mm Rem. Magnum, .330 Win. Magnum. Weight 7.25 lbs. Also offered with BOSS system. Note: Add $100 for BOSS.

NIB	*Exc.*	*V.G.*	*Good*	*Fair*	*Poor*
950	650	450	320	220	120

Model 70 Featherweight Super Short

Introduced in 2003. Features shorter receiver to handle .223 WSSM and .243 WSSM cartridges. Fitted with 22" barrel, checkered walnut stock and solid recoil pad. Weight 6 lbs.

NIB	*Exc.*	*V.G.*	*Good*	*Fair*	*Poor*
770	600	500	400	300	200

Model 70 Classic Laredo

First offered in 1996. Features heavy 26" barrel, with pre-1964 action on a gray synthetic stock. Chambered for 7mm Rem. Magnum and .300 Win. Magnum. Beavertail forearm. Finish matte blue. In 1997, offered chambered for 7mm STW cartridge. In 1998, offered with fluted barrel. Note: Add $100 for BOSS; add $125 for fluted barrel.

NIB	*Exc.*	*V.G.*	*Good*	*Fair*	*Poor*
750	650	550	500	400	300

Model 70 Classic Compact

Introduced in 1998. Scaled-down version of Featherweight. Length-of-pull 12.5"; 20" barrel. Chambered for .243, .308 and 7mm-08 calibers. Checkered walnut stock. Weight 6.5 lbs.

NIB	*Exc.*	*V.G.*	*Good*	*Fair*	*Poor*
750	650	550	500	400	300

Model 70 Classic Sporter LT

Introduced in 1999. Chambered for a wide variety of calibers from .25-06 to .338 Win. Magnum. Fitted with 24" or 26" barrel, depending on caliber and no sights. Walnut stock, with buttpad. Blued finish. Offered in left-hand models from .270 to .338 Win. Magnum. Weight 8 lbs. Note: Add $30 for left-hand models.

NIB	*Exc.*	*V.G.*	*Good*	*Fair*	*Poor*
750	650	550	500	400	300

Model 70 Classic Safari Express

Chambered for .375 H&H Magnum, .416 Rem. Magnum and .458 Win. Magnum. Fitted with 24" barrel. Magazine capacity 4 rounds. Walnut stock, with open sights. Left-hand model offered in .375 H&H. Weight 8.5 lbs. Introduced in 1999. Note: Add $30 for .375 H&H left-hand.

NIB	*Exc.*	*V.G.*	*Good*	*Fair*	*Poor*
1350	1100	900	650	500	300

Model 70 Super Grade

Another U.S.R.A. rifle that features select walnut stock, claw-controlled round feed, single reinforced cross bolt, 24" barrel shipped with bases and rings. Buttstock has a straight comb, with classic cheekpiece and deep-cut checkering. Available in .270, .30-06, 7mm Rem. Magnum, .300 Win. Magnum, .338 Win. Magnum, .270 WSM, .300 WSM. Weight 7.75 lbs.

NIB	Exc.	V.G.	Good	Fair	Poor
1500	1300	1080	920	650	300

Model 70 RMEF Super Grade

As above, with stainless steel action and barrel. Chambered for .300 Win. Magnum cartridge. Fitted with 26" barrel. Checkered walnut stock, with solid recoil pad. Weight 8 lbs. Introduced in 2003. Special RMEF (Rocky Mountain Elk Foundation) emblem on grip cap. Limited production.

NIB	Exc.	V.G.	Good	Fair	Poor
1600	1400	1180	980	650	300

Model 70 RMEF Super Grade III

Chambered for .325 WSM or .300 WSM calibers. Fitted with 24" stainless steel barrel, without sights. Super Grade walnut checkered stock, with shadowline cheekpiece. Weight 7.75 lbs. RMEF grip cap medallion. Introduced in 2005.

NIB	Exc.	V.G.	Good	Fair	Poor
1200	950	880	650	500	300

Model 70 Classic Super Grade III

Similar to above, but chambered for a variety of short-action calibers including WSM. Fitted with 24" barrel, except .300 Win. Magnum and .338 Win. Magnum have 26" barrels. No sights. Weight 7.75 to 8 lbs., depending on caliber. Introduced in 2005.

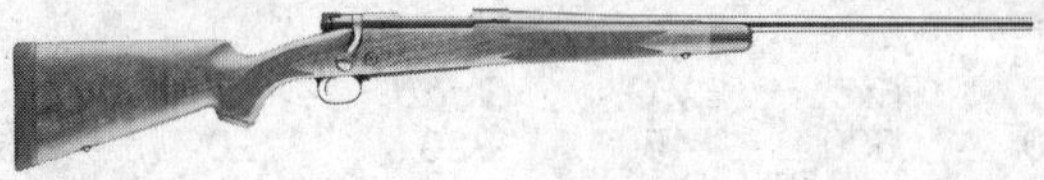

NIB	Exc.	V.G.	Good	Fair	Poor
1400	1100	880	650	500	300

Model 70 Super Express

A U.S.R.A. version of post-1963 XTR Super Express. Specifications same as earlier model. Weight 8.5 lbs. Introduced in 1993.

NIB	Exc.	V.G.	Good	Fair	Poor
1500	1200	1080	980	650	300

Model 70 Heavy Varmint

Introduced by U.S.R.A. in 1993. Features fiberglass/graphite stock, with heavy 26" stainless steel barrel. Offered in .223, .22-250, .243 and .308. In 1997, offered in .222 Rem. cartridge. Weight 10.75 lbs.

NIB	Exc.	V.G.	Good	Fair	Poor
750	580	500	420	380	200

Model 70 Heavy Varmint—Fluted Barrel

Introduced in 1997. Similar to above Varmint, with addition of fluted barrel. Calibers same as Heavy Varmint.

NIB	Exc.	V.G.	Good	Fair	Poor
820	620	500	480	350	250

Model 70 Stainless

All-metal parts are stainless steel, including barrel, with synthetic stock. Available with 24" barrel. Chambered for .270, .30-06, 7mm Rem. Magnum, .300 Win. Magnum and .338 Win. Magnum. Weight 7.5 lbs. Currently in production. In 2001, offered in .300 Win. Short Magnum (WSM).

NIB	Exc.	V.G.	Good	Fair	Poor
850	650	450	380	220	120

Model 70 Classic Laminated Stainless

Introduced in 1998. Features laminated stock, with stainless steel barrel and action. Offered in .270, .30-06, 7mm Rem. Magnum, .300 Win. Magnum and .338 Win. Magnum. Pre-1964 action. Bolt is jeweled and bolt handle knurled. Barrel lengths 24" and 26", depending on caliber. Weight 8 lbs. In 2001, offered in .300 Win. Short Magnum (WSM).

NIB	Exc.	V.G.	Good	Fair	Poor
850	650	450	380	220	120

Model 70 Classic Camo Stainless

Features Sporter-style Mossy Oak Treestand camo stock, with 24" or 26" barrel. Chambered for .270 Win., .30-06, 7mm Rem. Magnum and .300 Win Magnum. Magazine capacity five rounds. Weight 7.5 lbs. Introduced in 1998.

NIB	Exc.	V.G.	Good	Fair	Poor
850	650	450	380	220	120

Model 70 SM

Features synthetic stock, with black matte finish. Barrel length 24". Available in 10 calibers from .223 Rem. to .375 H&H Magnum. Weight between 7 and 8 lbs., depending on caliber.

NIB	Exc.	V.G.	Good	Fair	Poor
850	650	450	380	220	120

Model 70 DBM

DBM stands for (detachable box magazine). Fitted with straight-comb walnut stock. Jeweled bolt, with blued receiver. Shipped with scope bases and rings or open sights. Offered in 8 calibers from .223 Rem. to .300 Win. Magnum. Weight 7.35 lbs., depending on caliber. Introduced in 1993.

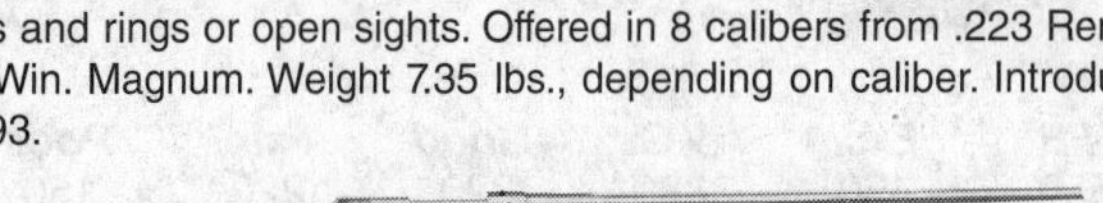

NIB	Exc.	V.G.	Good	Fair	Poor
700	600	450	320	220	150

Model 70 DBM-S

Similar to Model 70 SM, but fitted with detachable box magazine. Metal parts are blued; stock synthetic. Offered in 8 calibers from .223 Rem. to .338 Win. Magnum. Furnished with scope bases; rings are open sights. Weight 7.25 lbs., depending on caliber. Introduced in 1993.

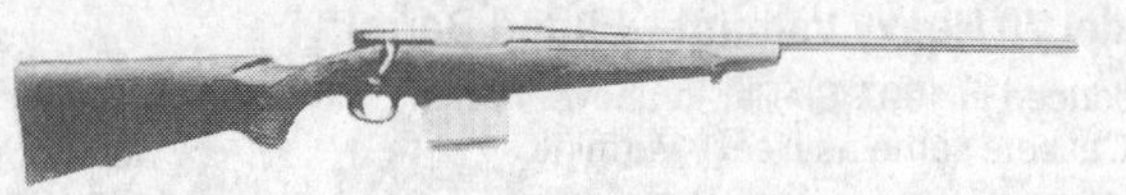

NIB	Exc.	V.G.	Good	Fair	Poor
650	550	450	380	220	120

Model 70 Varmint

Similar to Model 70 Heavy Varmint, but furnished with traditional walnut stock and 26" medium-heavy barrel. Offered in .223 Rem., .22-250, .243 and .308. Weight 9 lbs.

NIB	Exc.	V.G.	Good	Fair	Poor
700	600	450	320	220	150

Model 70 Sporter

U.S.R.A.'s basic Model 70. Standard offerings: straight-comb walnut stock, with checkering; jeweled bolt; blued receiver and barrel. Available in 12 calibers from .223 Rem. to .338 Win. Magnum, including .270 Wby. Magnum and .300 Wby. Magnum. Barrel length 24". Available with scope bases and rings or open sights. Weight 7.5 lbs.

NIB	Exc.	V.G.	Good	Fair	Poor
700	600	450	320	220	150

Model 70 WinTuff

Similar to Sporter, except fitted with laminated hardwood straight-comb stock, with cheekpiece. Barrel length 24". Choice of 6 calibers from .270 Win. to .338 Win. Magnum. Furnished with scope bases and rings. Weight 7.65 lbs., depending on caliber.

NIB	Exc.	V.G.	Good	Fair	Poor
700	600	450	320	220	150

Model 70 Lightweight

Similar to Model 70 Winlight. Offered with straight-comb checkered walnut stock, with knurled bolt. Blued 22" barrel and receiver. No sights. Offered in 5 calibers: .223, .243, .270, .308 and .30-06. Weight 7 lbs., depending on caliber.

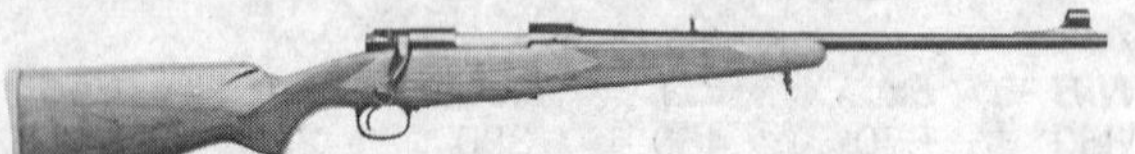

NIB	Exc.	V.G.	Good	Fair	Poor
700	600	450	320	220	150

Model 70 Black Shadow

Chambered for .270, .30-06, 7mm Rem. Magnum and .300 Win. Magnum. Fitted with 22" or 24" barrel, depending on caliber. Finish matte black, with composite stock. Push-feed action. Weight 7.25 lbs. Introduced in 1998.

NIB	Exc.	V.G.	Good	Fair	Poor
550	450	380	320	220	150

Model 70 Ultimate Shadow

Introduced in 2003. Bolt-action model features new black synthetic stock design, with improved gripping surfaces and soft recoil pad. Has blued action and barrel. Chambered for .300 WSM, .270 WSM or 7mm WSM cartridges. Fitted with 24" barrel. Weight about 6.75 lbs. Offered with stainless action and barrel. Note: Add $45 for stainless steel.

NIB	Exc.	V.G.	Good	Fair	Poor
800	700	420	350	280	120

Model 70 Ultimate Shadow Camo

As above, with Mossy Oak New Break-Up camo. Introduced in 2004.

NIB	Exc.	V.G.	Good	Fair	Poor
900	800	520	450	380	150

Model 70 Super Shadow Super Short

Similar to above model, but chambered for .223 WSM or .243 WSM cartridge. Fitted with 22" barrel and blind magazine. Weight 6 lbs. Introduced in 2003.

NIB	Exc.	V.G.	Good	Fair	Poor
700	600	450	320	220	150

Model 70 Super Shadow

Similar to Ultimate Shadow, but fitted with controlled round push-feed bolt. Chambered for .300 WSM, .270 WSM or 7mm WSM cartridge. Fitted with 22" barrel, composite stock and blind magazine. Weight 6.75 lbs. Introduced in 2003. In 2006, new calibers .243, .308, .270, .30-06, .300WM. Model discontinued in 2007.

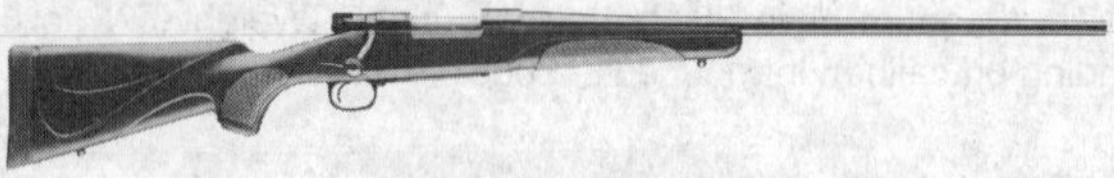

NIB	Exc.	V.G.	Good	Fair	Poor
700	600	450	320	220	150

Model 70 Stealth

Varmint model, with 26" heavy barrel. Chambered for .223 Rem., .22-250 or .308 Win. Has push-feed bolt-action. Black synthetic stock. Matte black finish. Weight 10.85 lbs. In 2004, .223 WSSM, .243 WSSM, and .25 WSSM calibers added.

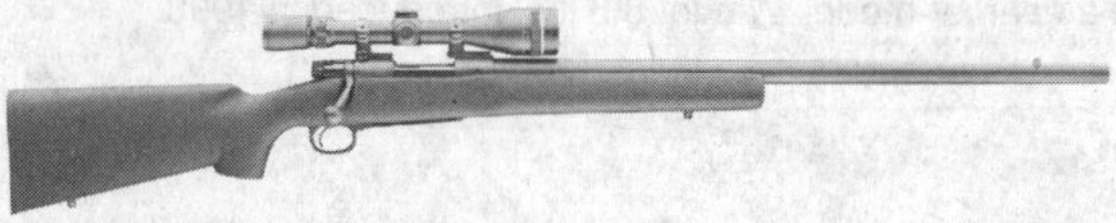

NIB	Exc.	V.G.	Good	Fair	Poor
850	650	450	380	220	120

Model 70 Coyote

Introduced in 2000. Has push-feed bolt-action. Chambered for .223 Rem, .22-250 and .243 Win. Fitted with medium-heavy 24" stainless steel barrel, with laminated stock and large forend. Weight 9 lbs. In 2002, offered in .270 WSM, 7mm WSM and .300 WSM. In 2005, .325 WSM was added. Discontinued 2006.

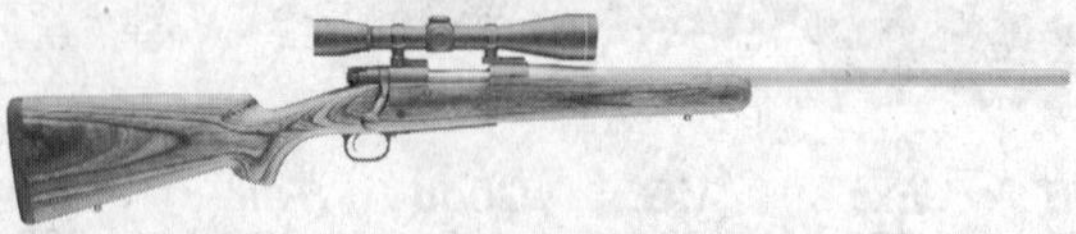

NIB	Exc.	V.G.	Good	Fair	Poor
750	650	450	380	220	120

Model 70 Coyote Lite

Introduced in 2005. Features lightweight composite stock, with skeletonized aluminum block bedding. Recoil pad. Fluted 24" medium-heavy barrel, with no sights. Offered in .223 Rem and all WSSM and WSM calibers. New calibers: .22-250, .243, .308. Note: Add $40 for stainless steel.

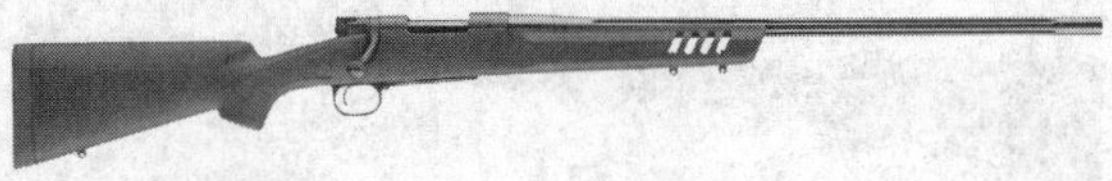

NIB	*Exc.*	*V.G.*	*Good*	*Fair*	*Poor*
850	650	450	380	220	120

Model 70 Ladies/Youth Ranger

Scaled-down version of Ranger. Length of pull 1" shorter than standard. Weight 6.5 lbs. Chambered in .243 and .308. In 1997, offered in .223 Rem. and 7mm-08 Rem.

NIB	*Exc.*	*V.G.*	*Good*	*Fair*	*Poor*
450	300	280	220	150	100

Model 70 Shadow Elite Stainless

Bolt-action rifle. Calibers: .22-250, .243, .308, .270, .30-06, .300 WM, .338 WM, .375 H&H, .270 WSM, 7mm WSM, .300 WSM, .325 WSM. Barrel stainless steel 24" or 26" (.300, .338 WM). Stock overmolded composite. Weight 6.5 to 7.75 lbs. Magazine capacity 3 or 5 rounds (.22-250, .243, .308, .270, .30-06). Introduced 2006.

NIB	*Exc.*	*V.G.*	*Good*	*Fair*	*Poor*
800	700	420	350	280	120

Model 70 Shadow Elite Camo Stainless

Similar to Shadow Elite Stainless, with Mossy Oak New Break Up camo synthetic stock.

NIB	*Exc.*	*V.G.*	*Good*	*Fair*	*Poor*
850	750	480	350	280	120

Model 70 Pro Shadow Blued

Bolt-action rifle. Calibers: .22-250, .243, .308, .270, .30-06, 7mm Rem. Magnum, .300 WM, .270 WSM, 7mm WSM, .300 WSM, .325 WSM. Barrel blued steel 22" (standard); 24" (Magnum). Stock over-molded composite. Weight 6.5 to 7 lbs. Magazine capacity 3 rounds (Magnum); 5 (standard). Introduced 2006.

NIB	*Exc.*	*V.G.*	*Good*	*Fair*	*Poor*
650	550	380	250	180	120

Model 70 Pro Shadow Stainless

Similar to Pro Shadow Blued, with stainless steel barrel. Chamberings .338 WM and .375 H&H.

NIB	*Exc.*	*V.G.*	*Good*	*Fair*	*Poor*
700	600	450	320	220	150

Model 70 Laminated Coyote Outback Stainless

Similar to Model 70 Coyote Lite, with skeletonized laminated stock and stainless steel only. Calibers: .22-250, .243, .308, .270, .30-06, 7mm Rem. Magnum, .300 WM, .270 WSM, 7mm WSM, .300 WSM, .325 WSM. Weight 7.75 lbs. Introduced 2006.

NIB	*Exc.*	*V.G.*	*Good*	*Fair*	*Poor*
750	650	450	380	220	120

Model 70 Laminated Coyote Gray or Brown Stainless

Similar to Model 70 Laminated Coyote Outback, with non-fluted barrel. Choice of brown or gray laminated stock.

NIB	*Exc.*	*V.G.*	*Good*	*Fair*	*Poor*
700	600	450	320	220	150

Model 670

Economy variation of Model 70 introduced in 1967; out of production in 1970. Features hardwood stock and blind magazine. Calibers .225 Win., .243 Win., .270 Win., .308 Win., .30-06 Springfield; Magnum: .264 Win., 7mm Rem., .300 Win. Note: Add 10% for Magnum calibers and .225 Win.

NIB	*Exc.*	*V.G.*	*Good*	*Fair*	*Poor*
350	300	250	200	180	150

POST-2007 MODEL 70

In 2006, Winchester closed its factory in New Haven, CT. and discontinued production of Model 70 and Model 94 rifles. Late in 2007, it was announced that production of Model 70 would resume at FN plant in Columbia, SC. FN (Fabrique Nationale of Belgium) is parent company of Winchester. Following models are produced at South Carolina plant. Features include Pre-64 Model 70 controlled-round feed in receivers machined from steel forgings with integral recoil lug, blade-type extractor, 3-position bolt-mounted safety, M.O.A. trigger, 1-piece bottom metal with hinged floorplate, free-floated barrel and Pachmayr Decelerator pad. Depending on model, current calibers include, .22-250, .243, .25-06, 6.5 C, .264 Win Mag, .270 Win, .270 WSM, 7mm-08, 7mm Rem Mag, .308, .30-06, .300 WSM, .300 Win Mag, .325 WSM, and .338 Win Mag.

Model 70 Featherweight Deluxe

As above with 22" or 24" barrel, depending on caliber. Weight 6.75 to 7.25 lbs. Introduced in 2008. Compact with 20" barrel, 13" LOP in short action and standard calibers only. Weight 6.5 lbs. Note: Add $50 for magnum calibers.

NIB	*Exc.*	*V.G.*	*Good*	*Fair*	*Poor*
900	780	660	560	340	200

Model 70 Sporter

As above, in WSMs and long action calibers, stock with non-Schnabel forend and cheekpiece. Note: Add $50 for Magnum calibers.

NIB	*Exc.*	*V.G.*	*Good*	*Fair*	*Poor*
900	780	660	560	340	200

Model 70 Super Grade

As above, in 6.5 CM (22") select WSM and long-action calibers (24" or 26" barrel), fancy stock with ebony forend and shadowline cheekpiece. Note: Add $50 for Magnum calibers.

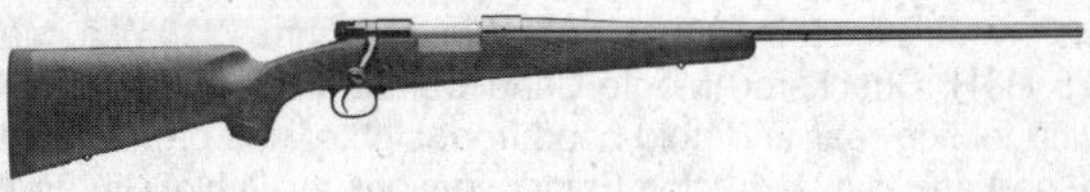

NIB	*Exc.*	*V.G.*	*Good*	*Fair*	*Poor*
1300	1100	940	800	480	290

New Model 70 Super Grade Special Limited Edition

Very fancy version of Model 70. Featuring post-'64 action, ultra-premium walnut, gold-filled engraving, black forend cap, steel grip cap, shadowline cheekpiece. Only 250 produced in 2008. Chambered in .300 Win. Magnum only.

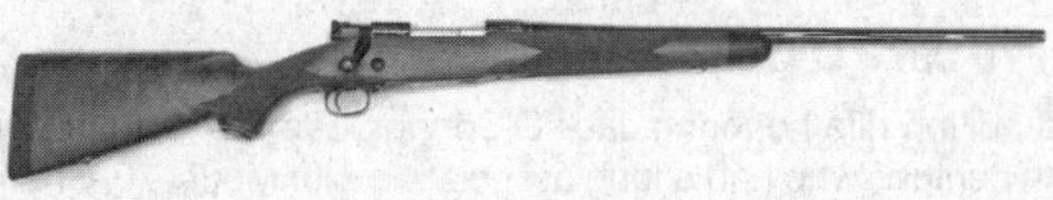

NIB	*Exc.*	*V.G.*	*Good*	*Fair*	*Poor*
2400	2000	1650	1300	900	500

Model 70 Extreme Weather SS

As above, with 22", 24" or 26" barrel, depending on chambering. Three-position safety, fluted stainless barrel and Bell & Carlson composite stock with 1-piece bedding block.

NIB	Exc.	V.G.	Good	Fair	Poor
1150	900	750	550	420	280

Model 70 Coyote Light SR

As above, with matte blue receiver with 24" medium-heavy fluted stainless steel barrel in Bell & Carlson stock with vented forend. Limited selection of short-action calibers including WSMs (add $40).

NIB	Exc.	V.G.	Good	Fair	Poor
1150	980	820	700	420	250

Model 70 Safari Express

Designed for dangerous game with controlled-round feed Pre-64 action. Calibers .375 H&H, .416 Rem. Magnum, .458 Win. Magnum. Express sights, 24" barrel, satin finished, checkered straight-comb walnut stock. Other features include iron barrel sights, reinforced crossbolts, dual recoil lugs and Pachmayr Decelerator recoil pad. Weight 9 lbs.

NIB	Exc.	V.G.	Good	Fair	Poor
1400	1200	1000	850	520	320

Model 70 75th Anniversary Super Grade

Commemorates 75th Anniversary of rifle. Introduced in 2012, this special edition in .30-06 caliber. Grade IV/V Full Fancy walnut stock. One-piece bottom metal has engraving, with scroll pattern of 75th Model 70 emblem. Other features include pre-64 style controlled round feed, with claw extractor and Pachmayr Decelerator recoil pad.

NIB	Exc.	V.G.	Good	Fair	Poor
1780	1500	1250	—	—	—

Model 70 Alaskan

Classic pre-64 Model in .30-06, .300 Win. Magnum, .338 Win. Magnum or .375 H&H. Checkered Monte Carlo walnut stock and forend. Barrel 25", with folding rear and gold bead front sights. Has pre-'64 controlled round feed and claw extractor. Earlier versions available with gray laminate stock and stainless steel barrel. Note: Add $200 for laminate/stainless model; add $40 for .375 H&H.

NIB	Exc.	V.G.	Good	Fair	Poor
1260	1050	900	780	460	280

Model 70 Jack O'Connor Tribute

Limited edition rifle honoring Jack O'Connor, dean of outdoor writers of the 20th century, who had a long association with Model 70. Chambered in his favorite caliber, .270 Win., with 22" hammer-forged barrel. Pre-64 style action, with controlled round feed; claw extractor; AA-grade French walnut stock, with shadowline cheekpiece; ebony forend tip. Other features include engraved pistol grip cap and floorplate. O'Connor's signature in nickel on triggerguard. Offered in two grades, with higher-grade version having AAA-grade French walnut stock and checkered metal buttplate. Introduced in 2012, with limited production only in that year. Note: Add $500 for higher-grade model.

NIB	Exc.	V.G.	Good	Fair	Poor
1700	1450	1220	—	—	—

Model 70 150th Commemorative

To commemorate company's 150th Anniversary. Features Super Grade styling, with Grade V/VI checkered walnut stock, shadowline cheekpiece, satin finish, black forend tip and special 150th grip cap. Deep relief scroll engraving, with gold embellishments highlight receiver, barrel, triggerguard and floorplate. Chambered for classic .270 Win., with 24" barrel. Introduced in 2016.

NIB	Exc.	V.G.	Good	Fair	Poor
1950	1800	—	—	—	—

Model 70 Extreme Hunter Strata MB

Calibers: .243 Win., 6.5 Creedmoor, 7mm-08 Rem., .308 Win., 6.5 PRC, 6.8 Western, .270 WSM, .300 WSM, .25-06 Rem., .270 Win., .30-06 Spfld., .264 Win. Mag., 7mm Rem. Mag., .300 Win. Mag. Capacity: 3-, 4-, or 5-round internal magazine with hinged floorplate. Barrel: 22-, 24-, or 26-in. sporter contour stainless, free-floating, fluted, with muzzle brake. Weight: 6 lb. 12 oz–7 lb. 4 oz. Length: 42.25–46.75 in. Stock: Bell & Carlson synthetic with True Timber Strata camo and sculpted cheekpiece. Sights: Drilled and tapped. Features: Bolt-action hunting rifle designed for adverse conditions. Controlled round feed with claw extractor. Jeweled bolt. Three-position safety. Sling studs. Pachmayr Decelerator recoil pad. FDE Cerakote metal finish.

NIB	Exc.	V.G.	Good	Fair	Poor
1550	—	—	—	—	—

WINCHESTER CUSTOM GUN SHOP

There were a number of special order options offered by the Custom Shop, that greatly affect price, including special-order engraving, stock carving, wood, sights, etc. Strongly suggest that an independent appraisal be secured prior to sale. NIB values listed are estimates of original manufacturer's price for these variations. Current values will vary.

Model 94 Custom Limited Edition New Generation

Lever-action rifle stocked with fancy checkered walnut, with pistol grip and long nose forend. Custom engraved, with gold inlaid moose on right side and gold inlaid buck and doe on left. Fitted with tang safety. Barrel 20". Chambered for .30-30 cartridge. Introduced in 2003. Weight 6.25 lbs.

NIB	Exc.	V.G.	Good	Fair	Poor
3000	—	—	—	—	—

Model 70 Featherweight Ultra Grade

Limited to 1,000 rifles. Profusely engraved with game scene and gold line inlaid. Serial number inlaid in gold. Offered in .270 caliber. Very fine-figured walnut stock, with fine-line checkering. Mahogany fitted case. Strongly suggest a qualified appraisal before sale.

NIB	Exc.	V.G.	Good	Fair	Poor
4000	—	—	—	—	—

Model 70 Custom Featherweight

Introduced in 2003. Chambered for .270, 7mm Win. Magnum or .30-06. Fitted with 22" barrel. Semi-fancy walnut stock, with Schnabel forend. Offered in blued or stainless steel finish in right-/left-hand models. Weight 7.25 lbs.

NIB	Exc.	V.G.	Good	Fair	Poor
3500	—	—	—	—	—

Model 70 Custom Carbon

Features stainless steel action, with Shilen barrel wrapped in graphite epoxy. Fitted with black composite stock. Chambered for .270 WSM, 7mm WSM, .300 WSM, .25-06 Rem. or .338 Win. Magnum cartridge. Fitted with 24" barrel on all calibers, except .338 (26"). Weight about 6.5 lbs. on WSM calibers; 7 lbs. on others. Magazine capacity 3 rounds. Introduced in 2003.

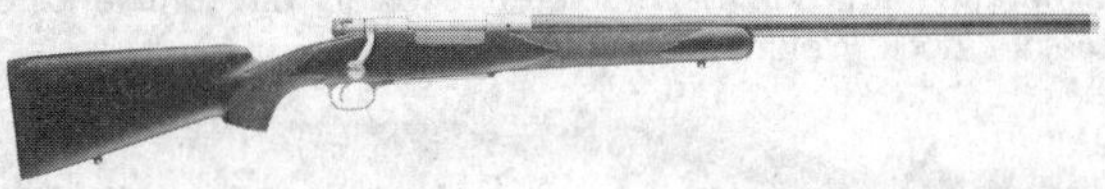

NIB	Exc.	V.G.	Good	Fair	Poor
3200	—	—	—	—	—

Model 70 Custom Sharpshooter

A U.S.R.A. Custom Shop gun. Fitted with stainless steel Schneider barrel, with hand-honed action and hand-fitted custom McMillan A-2 glass bedded stock. Offered in .223 Rem., .22-250 Rem., .308 Win. and .300 Win. Magnum. Comes from factory with a hard case. Currently in production.

NIB	Exc.	V.G.	Good	Fair	Poor
2500	—	—	—	—	—

Model 70 Custom Classic Sharpshooter II

Same as above, with H-S heavy target stock, pre-1964 action and stainless steel H-S barrel. Weight 11 lbs. Offered in .22-250, .308, .30-06 and .300 Win. Magnum. Introduced in 1996.

NIB	Exc.	V.G.	Good	Fair	Poor
2250	—	—	—	—	—

Model 70 Custom Sporting Sharpshooter

Essentially a take-off on Custom Sharpshooter, but configured for hunting. Fitted with McMillan sporter-style gray stock and Schneider stainless steel barrel. Offered in .270 Win., .300 Win. and 7mm STW. Introduced in 1993.

NIB	Exc.	V.G.	Good	Fair	Poor
2000	1700	1400	—	—	—

Model 70 Custom Classic Sporting Sharpshooter II

Introduced in 1996. Updated version of model above. Features pre-1964 action, with H-S special fiberglass stock and stainless steel barrel. Available in 7mm STW, .300 Win. Magnum. Weight 8.5 lbs.

NIB	Exc.	V.G.	Good	Fair	Poor
2500	—	—	—	—	—

Model 70 Custom Grade

Custom built Model 70 is hand-finished, polished and fitted in Custom Shop. Internal parts are hand-honed, while barrel is lead lapped. Customer can order individual items to his/her own taste, including engraving, special stock dimensions, carvings, etc. Each Custom Grade Model 70 should be priced on an individual basis.

Model 70 Custom Express

Also built in Custom Shop. Features figured walnut, hand-honed internal parts, bolt and follower are engine turned. Special 3-leaf rear sight also furnished. Offered in .375 H&H Magnum, .375 JRS, .416 Rem. Magnum, .458 Win. Magnum and .470 Capstick.

NIB	Exc.	V.G.	Good	Fair	Poor
3000	—	—	—	—	—

Model 70 Custom African Express

Introduced in 1999. Chambered for .340 Wby., .358 STA, .375 H&H, .416 Rem. Magnum and .458 Win. Magnum. Fitted with 24" barrel, select walnut stock and ebony pistol grip cap. Magazine capacity 4 rounds. Express sights. Weight 9.75 lbs.

NIB	Exc.	V.G.	Good	Fair	Poor
3850	—	—	—	—	—

Model 70 Custom Safari Express

Has a figured walnut stock, with bolt and follower engine turned. Express sights. Chambered in .340 Wby., .358 STA, .375 H&H, .416 Rem. Magnum and .458 Win. Magnum. Barrel length 24"; weight 9.5 lbs. Introduced in 1999.

NIB	Exc.	V.G.	Good	Fair	Poor
2500	—	—	—	—	—

Model 70 Custom "Ultra Light" Mannlicher

Features full-length stock of figured walnut, with smooth tapered barrel and blued action. Chambered for .260 Rem., .308 Win. and 7mm-08. Fitted with 19 barrel and optional open sights. Weight 6.75 lbs. Introduced in 1999.

NIB	Exc.	V.G.	Good	Fair	Poor
2500	—	—	—	—	—

Model 70 Ultimate Classic

Features a number of special options as standard. Included: pre-1964 action; choice of round, round fluted, half octagon half round, full tapered octagon, blued or stainless steel barrel actions; fancy American walnut stock; special Custom Shop serial numbers and proof stamp; inletted swivel bases; red recoil pad; fine cut checkering; hard case. Offered in a wide variety of calibers from .25-06 to .338 Win. Magnum. Weight 7.5 to 7.75 lbs., depending on caliber. Available in stainless steel. In 1997, introduced in left-hand version.

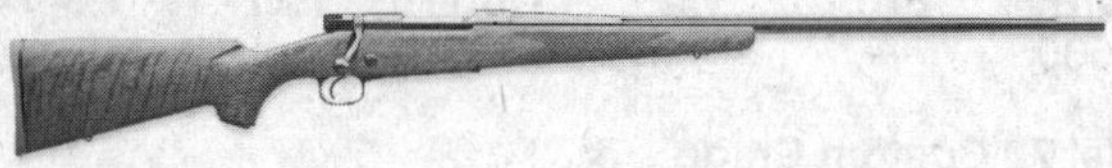

NIB	Exc.	V.G.	Good	Fair	Poor
2450	—	—	—	—	—

Model 70 Custom Short Action

Custom Shop model fitted with 22" match-grade barrel controlled feed. Chambered for short-action calibers from .243 to .358. Semi-fancy walnut stock. Hand-cut checkering. Supplied with hard case. Weight 7.5 lbs. Introduced in 2000. In 2003, offered in left-hand version.

NIB	Exc.	V.G.	Good	Fair	Poor
2700	—	—	—	—	—

Model 70 Custom Extreme Weather

Custom Shop model fitted with round or fluted 24" match-grade barrel. Both barrel and action are stainless steel. McMillan fiberglass stock, with cheekpiece. Chambered in calibers from .25-06 to .338 Win. Magnum. Weight 7.5 lbs. Introduced in 2000. Lightweight Extreme Weather II model, introduced in 2006 (6.25 to 7 lbs.). MSRP: $2,800.

NIB	Exc.	V.G.	Good	Fair	Poor
1950	—	—	—	—	—

Model 70 Custom Take Down

Introduced in 1998. This composite stock rifle has a special take-down feature. Chambered for .375 H&H, .416 Rem. Magnum, .300 Win Magnum, 7mm STW. Magazine capacity 3 rounds. Barrel length 26". Weight 8.5 to 9 lbs. Offered with fluted barrel in .300 Win. Magnum and 7mm STW.

NIB	Exc.	V.G.	Good	Fair	Poor
3300	—	—	—	—	—

Model 70 Custom 100th Anniversary .30-06

Semi-fancy walnut Featherweight stock, with single steel crossbolt, one-piece engraved floorplate, high-lustre blued and engraved 22" barrel. Commemorates centennial of .30-06 cartridge. Introduced 2006; only 100 manufactured.

NIB	Exc.	V.G.	Good	Fair	Poor
2700	—	—	—	—	—

Model 70 Custom Special "70 Years of the Model 70"

Calibers: .270, .30-06 Springfield, .300 WM. Barrel 24 or 26" (.300 WM), blued sightless. Engraved floorplate and barrel. Stock semi-fancy checkered walnut. Introduced 2006. Only 70 manufactured per caliber.

NIB	Exc.	V.G.	Good	Fair	Poor
2800	—	—	—	—	—

Model 70 Custom Maple

Calibers: .284, .270, .308, .30-06. Blued 24" barrel. Weight 7.75 lbs. Stocked in fiddleback maple, with pre-'64 pattern checkering. Quantities "very limited". Introduced 2006.

NIB	Exc.	V.G.	Good	Fair	Poor
4400	—	—	—	—	—

Model 70 Custom Continental Hunter

Calibers: .284, .270, .308, .30-06. Barrel 22" blued or stainless Krieger. Stock glossy claro walnut, round knob pistol grip, Schnabel forend.

NIB	Exc.	V.G.	Good	Fair	Poor
5300	—	—	—	—	—

Model 70 Custom Stainless Laminate

Calibers: .270 WSM, 7mm WSM, .300 WSM, .325 WSM. Barrel 24" stainless sporter. Stock black/gray or brown Featherweight laminated, with Schnabel and Pachmayr pad.

NIB	Exc.	V.G.	Good	Fair	Poor
2300	—	—	—	—	—

Model 94 Custom Limited Edition

Essentially a special order Model 94, with choice of engraving and stock carving. Chambered for .44-40. Fitted with 24" octagonal barrel. Fancy walnut stock. Limited to 75 rifles. Weight 7.75 lbs. Suggest an appraisal prior to sale.

NIB	Exc.	V.G.	Good	Fair	Poor
2300	—	—	—	—	—

Model 9410 Custom

Introduced in 2005. This .410 bore shotgun fitted with 24" round barrel and full-length magazine. Case-colored receiver, with semi-fancy checkered walnut stock. Weight 7 lbs.

NIB	Exc.	V.G.	Good	Fair	Poor
2300	—	—	—	—	—

POST-1963 SHOTGUNS

MODEL 12 "Y" SERIES SLIDE ACTIONS

Model 12 Field Grade

Later version of slide-action Model 12. Chambered for 12-gauge only. Offered with 26", 28" or 30" ventilated rib barrel and various chokes. Finish blued, with jeweled bolt and hand-checkered select walnut stock. This version easily recognizable as it has letter "Y" serial number prefix. Manufactured between 1972 and 1976.

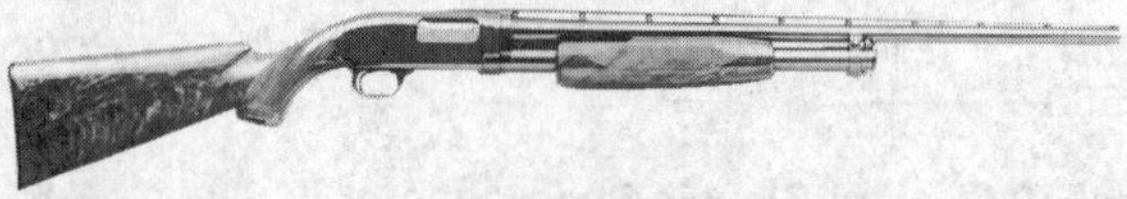

NIB	Exc.	V.G.	Good	Fair	Poor
—	680	570	490	420	350

Model 12 Super Pigeon Grade

Deluxe version that features extensive engraving and fancy checkering. Offered with turned action and select fancy-grade walnut. Limited production item produced between 1964 and 1972. Briefly reintroduced in 1984; discontinued again in 1985.

NIB	Exc.	V.G.	Good	Fair	Poor
—	3500	2800	2240	1790	1430

Model 12 Skeet

Similar to Field Grade, but offered with 26" ventilated rib and skeet-bored barrel. Finish blued, with skeet-type stock and recoil pad. Manufactured between 1972 and 1975.

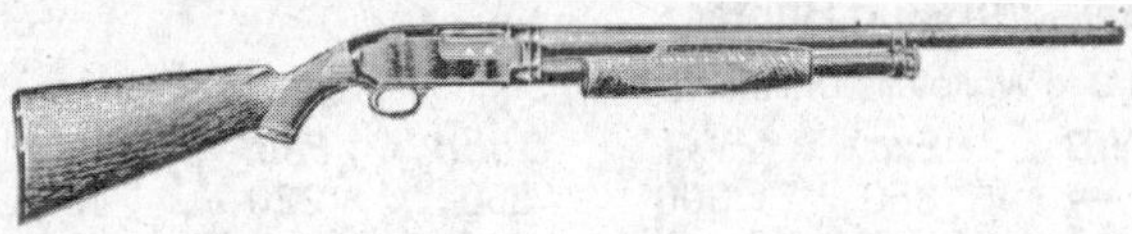

NIB	Exc.	V.G.	Good	Fair	Poor
—	1950	1560	1250	1000	800

Model 12 Trap Grade

Features 30" ventilated rib barrel, with Full choke. Blued, with standard or Monte Carlo trap-style stock and recoil pad. Manufactured between 1972 and 1980.

NIB	Exc.	V.G.	Good	Fair	Poor
—	1940	1640	1400	1190	1010

Model 12 (Limited Edition)

Available in 20-gauge only. Furnished with 26" ventilated rib barrel choked Improved Cylinder. Walnut stock checkered, with pistol grip. Introduced in 1993. Available in three different grades.

NIB	Exc.	V.G.	Good	Fair	Poor
—	1000	800	640	510	410

Grade I

4,000 guns.

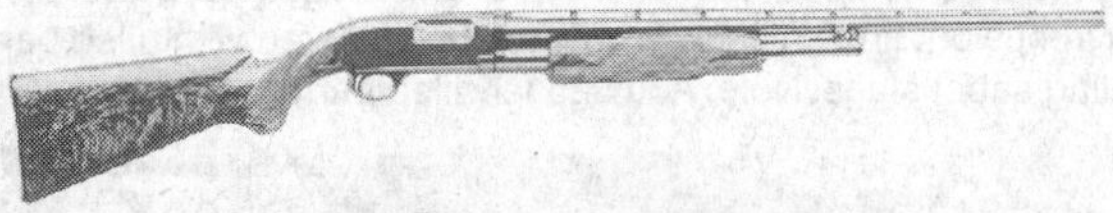

NIB	Exc.	V.G.	Good	Fair	Poor
1000	800	650	450	200	100

Grade IV

1,000 guns; gold highlights.

NIB	Exc.	V.G.	Good	Fair	Poor
—	1400	1260	1130	1020	920

Model 42 (Limited Edition)

Reproduction of famous Winchester Model 42, .410 bore slide-action shotgun. Furnished with 26" ventilated rib barrel choked Full. Receiver engraved with gold border. Introduced in 1993. Limited to 850 guns.

NIB	Exc.	V.G.	Good	Fair	Poor
—	1800	1530	1300	1100	940

Model 1200

Slide-action shotgun chambered for 12, 16, or 20 gauge. Offered with 26", 28" or 30" ventilated rib barrel, with various chokes. Has a blued alloy receiver. Checkered walnut stock and recoil pad. Manufactured between 1964 and 1981. Offered with plastic Hydrocoil stock. Note: Add 35% for plastic Hydrocoil stock.

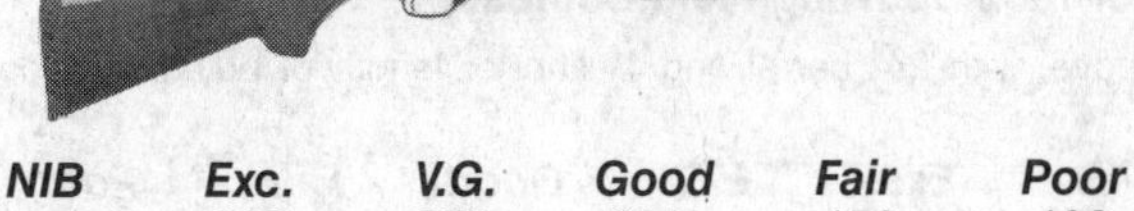

NIB	Exc.	V.G.	Good	Fair	Poor
—	300	250	200	150	100

Ducks Unlimited Model

Available through Ducks Unlimited chapters. An independent appraisal is suggested.

MODEL 1300 SERIES

Discontinued in 2006.

Model 1300 XTR

Chambered for 12 and 20 gauge, with 3" chambers. Take-down gun offered with various length ventilated rib barrels, with screw-in choke tubes. Has blued alloy frame, with walnut stock. Introduced in 1978.

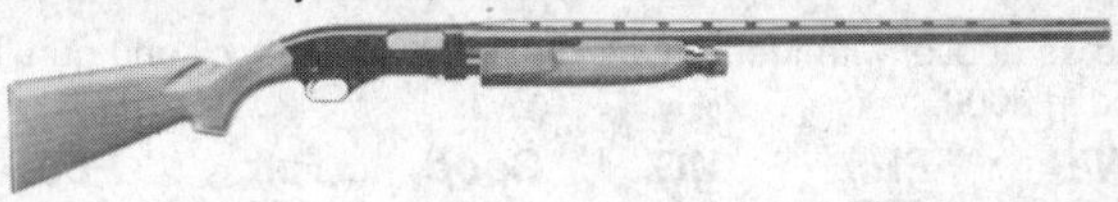

NIB	Exc.	V.G.	Good	Fair	Poor
—	300	260	220	180	160

Model 1300 Waterfowl

Chambered for 12-gauge 3" only. Has 30" ventilated rib barrel, with screw-in choke tubes. Matte-blued, with satin-finished walnut stock and recoil pad. Introduced in 1984. Laminated WinTuff stock made available in 1988. Note: Add $10 for laminated WinTuff stock.

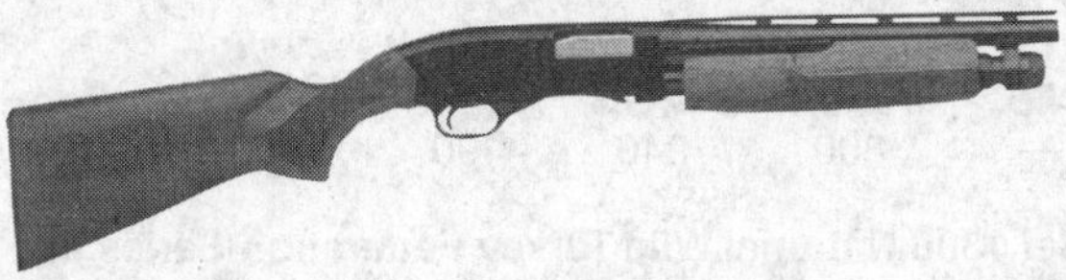

NIB	Exc.	V.G.	Good	Fair	Poor
—	300	260	220	180	160

Model 1300 New Shadow Grass

Introduced in 2004. This 12-gauge 3" gun fitted with 26" or 28" ventilated rib barrel, with choke tubes. Composite stock has New Shadow Grass camo pattern. Weight 7 lbs.

NIB	Exc.	V.G.	Good	Fair	Poor
—	370	320	270	230	190

Model 1300 WinCam Turkey Gun

Similar to Model 1300 Turkey Gun, with green laminated hardwood stock. Introduced in 1987. WinTuff version available. Note: Add $20 for WinTuff version.

NIB	Exc.	V.G.	Good	Fair	Poor
—	350	300	250	220	180

Model 1300 Stainless Security

Chambered for 12 or 20 gauge. Constructed of stainless steel. Has an 18" cylinder-bore barrel; 7- or 8-shot tubular magazine. Available with pistol grip stock. Note: Add 50% for pistol grip stock.

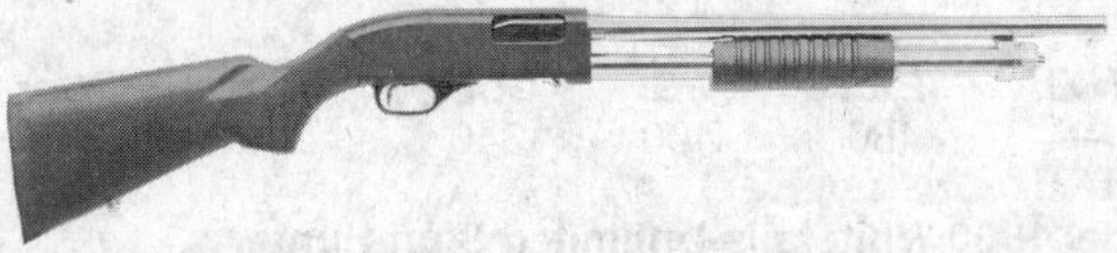

NIB	Exc.	V.G.	Good	Fair	Poor
—	760	650	550	470	400

Model 1300 Turkey

Slide-action model features 22" ventilated rib barrel. Chambered for 3" 12-gauge shells. Supplied with choke tubes. Weight 7.25 lbs.

NIB	Exc.	V.G.	Good	Fair	Poor
—	280	220	180	140	110

Model 1300 Realtree Turkey

Introduced in 1994. Features synthetic stock camouflaged with Realtree. Receiver and 22" barrel are matte finish.

NIB	Exc.	V.G.	Good	Fair	Poor
—	300	240	190	150	120

Model 1300 Mossy Oak Break-Up Turkey

Same as above, with Mossy Oak Break-Up camo stock and gun. Introduced in 2000.

NIB	Exc.	V.G.	Good	Fair	Poor
—	300	240	190	150	120

Model 1300 Black Shadow Turkey

Introduced in 1994. Features black composite stock, with non-glare finish on barrel, receiver, bolt and magazine. Barrel has 22" ventilated rib.

NIB	Exc.	V.G.	Good	Fair	Poor
—	300	240	190	150	120

Model 1300 National Wild Turkey Federation Series III

Engraved receiver, camo stock, open sights on a 22" plain barrel. All metal and wood parts are non-glare. Comes with quick detachable sling. Offered in 12-gauge only. Weight 7.25 lbs.

NIB	Exc.	V.G.	Good	Fair	Poor
—	420	360	300	260	220

Model 1300 National Wild Turkey Federation Series IV

Introduced in 1993. Similar to Series II, with addition of 22" ventilated rib barrel. Stock is black laminated. Comes with quick detachable sling. Weight 7 lbs.

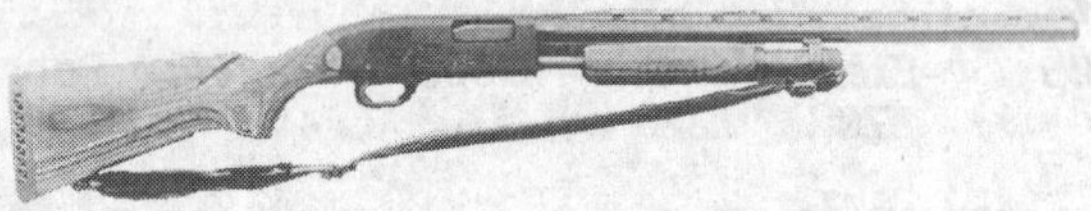

NIB	Exc.	V.G.	Good	Fair	Poor
—	520	440	380	320	270

Model 1300 NWTF Short Turkey

This 12 gauge fitted with an 18" barrel and extended choke tubes. Fiber-optic sights. Mossy Oak camo stock. NWTF medallion on pistol grip cap. Weight 6.5 lbs. Introduced in 2005.

NIB	Exc.	V.G.	Good	Fair	Poor
—	480	400	340	290	250

Model 1300 Whitetails Unlimited Slug Hunter

Slide-action model features full-length rifle barrel. Chambered for 3" 12-gauge shells. Barrel choked Cylinder. Fitted with checkered walnut stock. Engraved receiver drilled and tapped for bases and rings, which are included. Comes equipped with camo sling. Weight 7.25 lbs.

NIB	Exc.	V.G.	Good	Fair	Poor
—	350	300	250	220	180

Model 1300 Slug Hunter

Similar to Whitetails Unlimited model, without engraved receiver.

NIB	Exc.	V.G.	Good	Fair	Poor
—	350	300	250	220	180

Model 1300 Buck and Tom

Introduced in 2002. Camo stock fitted with 22" barrel and choke tubes for deer and turkey. Receiver drilled and tapped for scope mount. Weight 6.75 lbs.

NIB	Exc.	V.G.	Good	Fair	Poor
520	400	320	250	180	120

Model 1300 Universal Hunter

Introduced in 2002. Features camo stock, with 26" ventilated rib barrel. Choke tubes. Weight 7 lbs.

NIB	Exc.	V.G.	Good	Fair	Poor
—	420	360	310	260	220

Model 1300 Black Shadow Deer

Introduced in 1994. This 12 gauge features black composite stock, with non-glare finish on bolt, barrel, receiver and magazine. Barrel 22", with ramp front sight and adjustable rear. In 2000, offered with rifled barrel for shooting sabot slugs. Note: Add $25 for rifled barrel.

NIB	Exc.	V.G.	Good	Fair	Poor
—	350	300	250	220	180

Model 1300 Black Shadow Field

Same as above, but fitted with 26" or 28" ventilated rib barrel. Chambered for 3" Magnum shells. Weight 7 lbs.

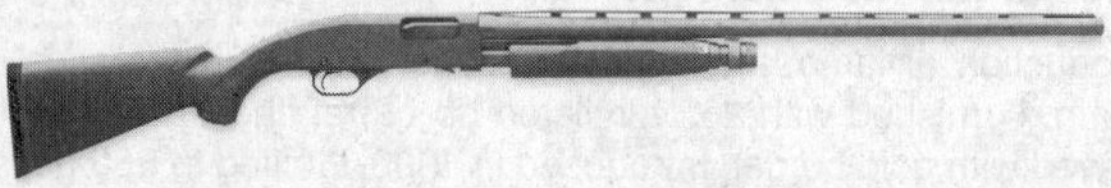

NIB	Exc.	V.G.	Good	Fair	Poor
—	280	220	180	140	120

Model 1300 Sporting/Field

This 12 gauge has 28" ventilated rib barrel, with five choke tubes. Checkered walnut stock. Black recoil pad. Weight 7.5 lbs. Introduced in 2002.

NIB	Exc.	V.G.	Good	Fair	Poor
—	350	280	220	180	140

Model 1300 Sporting/Field Compact

As above, with 24" barrel and 1" shorter length of pull. Introduced in 2002.

NIB	Exc.	V.G.	Good	Fair	Poor
—	350	280	220	180	140

Model 1300 Walnut Field

This 12-gauge 3" gun fitted with 26" or 28" ventilated rib barrels, with choke tubes. Checkered walnut stock, with recoil pad. Weight 7.25 lbs. Introduced in 2004.

NIB	Exc.	V.G.	Good	Fair	Poor
—	400	340	290	250	210

Model 1300 Slug Hunter Sabot (Smoothbore)

Similar to Slug Hunter, but furnished with smoothbore barrel. Special extended screw-in choke tube that is rifled.

NIB	Exc.	V.G.	Good	Fair	Poor
—	300	240	190	150	120

Model 1300 Upland Special

This 12-gauge slide-action shotgun fitted with 24" ventilated rib barrel. Straight-grip walnut stock. Weight 7 lbs. Introduced in 1999. In 2000, offered in 20 gauge.

NIB	Exc.	V.G.	Good	Fair	Poor
—	500	420	360	310	260

Model 1300 Upland Special Field

Introduced in 2004. Features 12- or 20-gauge 3" guns, with 24" ventilated rib barrel and choke tube. Checkered walnut stock, with straight-grip. Weight 6.75 lbs.

NIB	Exc.	V.G.	Good	Fair	Poor
—	500	420	360	310	260

Model 1300 Ranger

Slide-action shotgun is a lower-cost version of Model 1300. Furnished with hardwood stock. Available in 12 or 20 gauge, with 26" or 28" ventilated rib barrel. WinChokes are included.

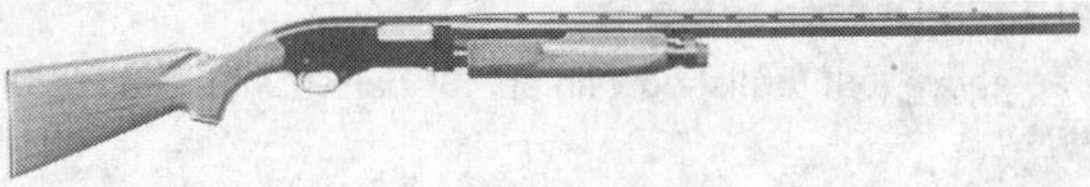

NIB	Exc.	V.G.	Good	Fair	Poor
—	280	230	180	150	120

Model 1300 Ranger Ladies/Youth-Compact

Available in 20-gauge only. Has 1" shorter than standard length of pull and 22" ventilated rib barrel. Choke tubes are included. Weight 6.75 lbs.

NIB	Exc.	V.G.	Good	Fair	Poor
—	220	190	160	140	120

Model 1300 Ranger Deer Slug

Comes in two principal configurations: 12-gauge 22" smooth barrel, with Cylinder choke; 12-gauge 22" rifled barrel. Both chambered for 3" shells. Weight 6.75 lbs.

NIB	Exc.	V.G.	Good	Fair	Poor
—	200	160	130	100	80

Model 1300 Ranger Deer Combo

Available in three different configurations. 12-gauge 22" smooth barrel, 12-gauge 22" rifled barrel, 20-gauge 22" smooth barrel. All configurations come with 28" ventilated rib barrel and WinChokes.

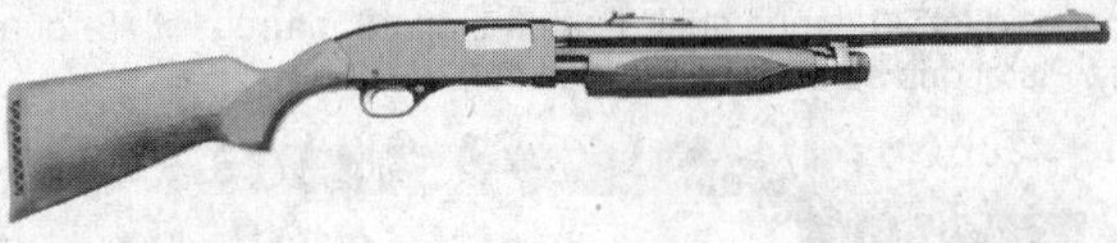

12 Gauge Combo

NIB	Exc.	V.G.	Good	Fair	Poor
—	280	220	190	160	100

20 Gauge Combo

NIB	Exc.	V.G.	Good	Fair	Poor
—	280	220	190	160	100

Model 1300 Defender Combo

Personal defense slide-action shotgun. Features 18" Cylinder choked barrel and 28" ventilated rib barrel, with modified WinChoke. Hardwood stock comes fitted to gun, with accessory pistol grip.

NIB	Exc.	V.G.	Good	Fair	Poor
—	300	270	240	220	200

Model 1300 Defender 5-Shot

Same as above, but furnished with hardwood stock only and 18" barrel.

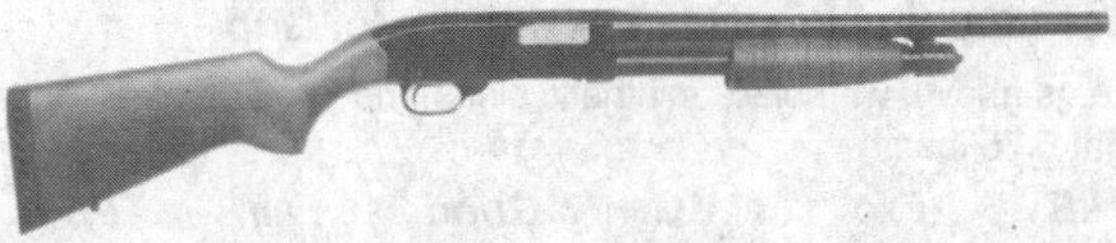

NIB	Exc.	V.G.	Good	Fair	Poor
—	300	260	220	180	160

Model 1300 Camp Defender

Introduced in 1999. This 12-gauge features a 22" barrel, with walnut stock. Magazine capacity 5 rounds. Barrel fitted with rifle sights. Weight 7 lbs. Comes with Cylinder choke tube.

NIB	Exc.	V.G.	Good	Fair	Poor
—	300	260	220	180	160

Model 1300 Defender 8-Shot

Same as above, but furnished with an 18" barrel, with extended magazine tube.

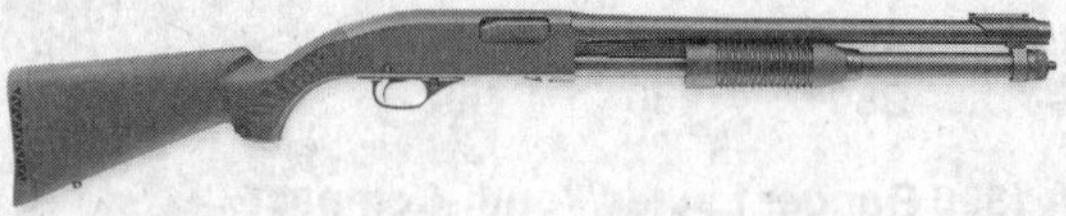

NIB	Exc.	V.G.	Good	Fair	Poor
—	320	280	240	200	170

Model 1300 Defender Synthetic Stock

Same as above. Fitted with black synthetic full stock. Available in 12 or 20 gauge.

NIB	Exc.	V.G.	Good	Fair	Poor
—	300	260	220	180	160

Model 1300 Defender Pistol Grip

Same as above. Fitted with black synthetic pistol grip and extended magazine tube.

NIB	Exc.	V.G.	Good	Fair	Poor
—	320	280	240	200	170

Model 1300 Lady Defender

Chambered for 20-gauge shell. Features an 18" barrel, with 8-round capacity. Pistol grip stock. Introduced in 1997.

NIB	Exc.	V.G.	Good	Fair	Poor
—	300	260	220	180	160

Model 1300 Stainless Marine

This 12-gauge slide-action shotgun comes with a black synthetic full stock. All metal parts chrome plated. Barrel 18". Magazine tube holds 7 rounds. Weight 6.75 lbs.

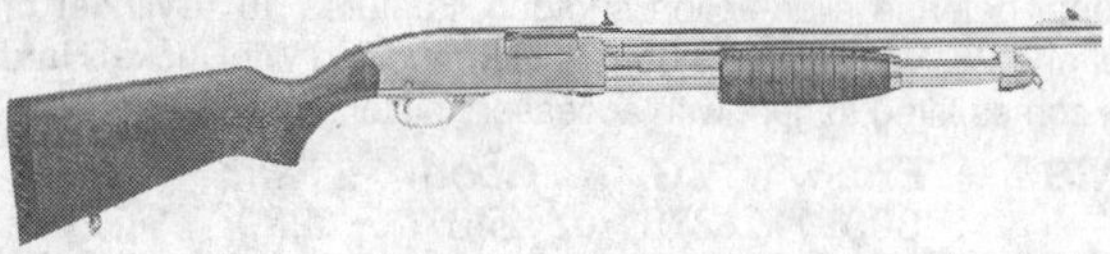

NIB	Exc.	V.G.	Good	Fair	Poor
—	500	420	360	310	260

Model 1300 Stainless Marine with Pistol Grip

Same as above, with black synthetic pistol grip in place of full buttstock. Weight 5.75 lbs.

NIB	Exc.	V.G.	Good	Fair	Poor
—	520	450	380	320	270

SPEED PUMP SERIES

This family of inertia-assisted slide-action shotguns was introduced in 2008. They took the place of discontinued Model 1300. The 3" 12 gauge available with 26" or 28" barrel. Three choke tubes included. Weight 7 to 7.25 lbs.

Speed Pump Walnut Field

High-gloss walnut, with traditional checkering.

NIB	Exc.	V.G.	Good	Fair	Poor
—	300	260	220	180	160

Speed Pump Black Shadow Field

Synthetic stock and forend, with matte black metal.

NIB	Exc.	V.G.	Good	Fair	Poor
—	320	280	240	200	170

Speed Pump Defender

This home-security 12 ga. has an 18" Cylinder choke barrel and 5-round magazine tube. Weight 6.5 lbs.

NIB	Exc.	V.G.	Good	Fair	Poor
—	220	190	160	140	120

MODEL SXP SERIES

Super X Pump is successor to Speed Pump series. Features same inertia-assisted action. Comes in 12-gauge only, with 3" chamber, 26" or 28" back-bored barrel with Invector choke tubes. Weight 6.8 lbs. Field grade model has Black Shadow composite stock. Waterfowl variation (shown) has full coverage Mossy Oak Duck Blind camo. Also available with 18" straight cylinder barrel as Defender model. Prices are for Black Shadow field model. Note: Add 20% for Waterfowl; 30% for Extreme Deer Hunter; 30% for Shadow Defender Marine.

NIB	Exc.	V.G.	Good	Fair	Poor
370	320	270	230	190	160

SXP Defender Shotgun

NIB	Exc.	V.G.	Good	Fair	Poor
320	280	230	200	170	—

SXP Defender Shotgun Desert Tan Synthetic Stock

Gauge: 12 ga., 3". Barrel: 18" with Heat Shield. Length: 38.5". Weight: 7.0 lbs. Stock: Flat Dark Earth composite with textured grip panels and pistol grip. Features: Aluminum-alloy receiver, hard-chrome chamber and bore, Picatinny rail with ghost-ring sight, blade front sight. Two interchangeable comb pieces and two quarter-inch length-of-pull spacers for custom fit. Side-mounted Picatinny accessory rails, sling studs, Inflex recoil pad. Includes one Invector Plus cylinder choke and one Door Breacher choke.

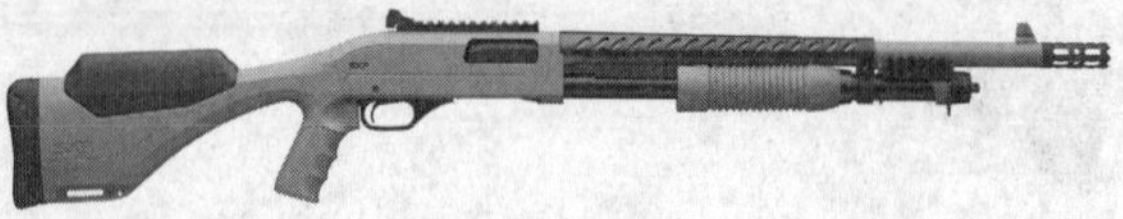

NIB	Exc.	V.G.	Good	Fair	Poor
460	300	250	220	180	160

Winchester SXP Black Shadow Black Synthetic Stock

NIB	Exc.	V.G.	Good	Fair	Poor
350	300	250	220	180	160

Winchester SXP Compact Field Shotgun Black Synthetic

Stock

NIB	Exc.	V.G.	Good	Fair	Poor
360	300	260	220	190	160

SXP Waterfowl/Turkey Combo (2019)

Waterfowl barrel w/sight + turkey barrel w/adjustable sights, Mossy Oak Bottomlands camouflage finish, chrome-plated chamber and bore, ventilated rib.

NIB	Exc.	V.G.	Good	Fair	Poor
500	430	360	—	—	—

SXP Waterfowl Hunter Realtree Timber (2019)

NIB	Exc.	V.G.	Good	Fair	Poor
390	330	280	—	—	—

SXP Hybrid Hunter Realtree Timber (2019)

NIB	Exc.	V.G.	Good	Fair	Poor
380	330	280	—	—	—

MODEL SXP SERIES

SXP Black Shadow

Black synthetic stock with textured gripping surfaces, back-bored barrel, Invector-Plus choke system, hard chrome-plated chamber and bore, black chrome bolt.

NIB	Exc.	V.G.	Good	Fair	Poor
340	290	250	210	180	150

SXP Waterfowl Hunter

Dipped Mossy Oak Shadow Grass Blades camo.

NIB	Exc.	V.G.	Good	Fair	Poor
420	350	300	260	220	180

SXP Waterfowl Hunter (2018)

Realtree Max-5 composite finish.

NIB	Exc.	V.G.	Good	Fair	Poor
380	320	270	230	200	170

SXP Hybrid Hunter True Timber Strata (2018)

Dipped camo stock, Permacote FDE finish on barrel and receiver, back-bored, Invector-Plus, hard chrome barrel and chamber, TRUGLO front fiber optic.

NIB	Exc.	V.G.	Good	Fair	Poor
380	320	270	230	200	170

SXP Universal Hunter

Mossy Oak Break-Up Country camo in 12/3.5"/24" and with receiver drilled and tapped for optional scope bases.

NIB	Exc.	V.G.	Good	Fair	Poor
420	360	300	260	220	190

SXP Muddy Girl

Dipped Muddy Girl camo, discontinued 2019.

NIB	Exc.	V.G.	Good	Fair	Poor
370	310	270	230	190	160

SXP Youth Field (2019)

Short length of pull and barrel, satin-finished stock, back-bored barrel, 3" chamber, Invector-Plus choke system, hard chrome-plated chamber and bore, black chrome bolt.

NIB	Exc.	V.G.	Good	Fair	Poor
320	270	230	190	160	140

SXP Buck/Bird Combo (2018)

The Winchester SXP Buck/Bird combo expands on the Super-X pump lineup with options in both 12 and 20 gauge. Choice of vent-rib bird barrel in either 26" or 28", along with a 22" rifled deer barrel with sights. Black synthetic stock, matte-finish metalwork.

NIB	Exc.	V.G.	Good	Fair	Poor
590	390	330	280	240	200

SXP Dark Earth Defender (2019)

Defender model in a dark earth finish, uses interchangeable Invector-Plus chokes, detachable TRUGLO fiber-optic bead. Chrome-plated bore and chamber, matte black chrome bolt.

NIB	Exc.	V.G.	Good	Fair	Poor
310	260	220	190	160	140

SXP Marine Defender

Hard chrome-plated barrel, magazine tube and other components. TRUGLO front sight, ribbed forearm.

NIB	Exc.	V.G.	Good	Fair	Poor
330	280	240	200	170	150

SXP Shadow Marine Defender

Dipped Kryptek Typhon camo, pistol grip stock with interchangeable height cheek pieces, spacers to adjust length of pull, back-bored, Invector Plus, hard chrome barrel and chamber, quick detach TRUGLO front fiber-optic sight.

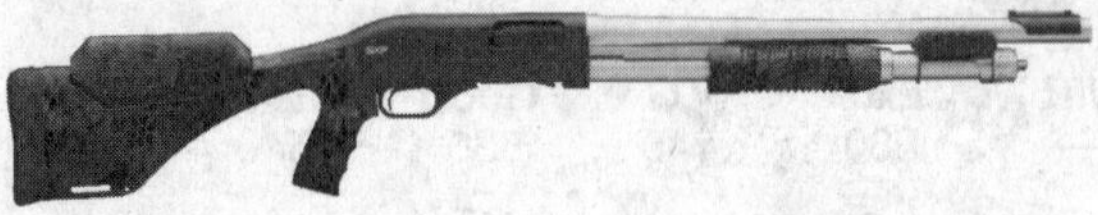

NIB	Exc.	V.G.	Good	Fair	Poor
410	350	300	250	220	180

Model 9410

Variation of Model 94 lever-action rifle. Chambered for .410 bore shotgun. Available in several versions. SEE: Model 9400 Series in lever-action rifle section.

Model 1500 XTR

Gas-operated semi-automatic shotgun. Chambered for 12 or 20 gauge, with 28" ventilated rib barrel with screw-in chokes. Finish blued, with walnut stock. Manufactured between 1978 and 1982.

NIB	Exc.	V.G.	Good	Fair	Poor
550	420	320	220	180	150

Super X Model 1

Self-compensating gas-operated semi-automatic shotgun. Chambered for 12 gauge. Offered with 26", 28" or 30" ventilated rib barrel, with various chokes. Features all-steel construction. Blued, with checkered walnut stock. Manufactured between 1974 and 1981.

NIB	Exc.	V.G.	Good	Fair	Poor
—	520	450	380	320	270

Super X Model 1 Custom Competition

Custom-order trap or skeet gun. Features self-compensating gas-operated action. Available in 12-gauge only from Custom Shop. Offered with a heavy degree of engraving on receiver. Fancy checkered walnut stock. Gold inlays are available. Add approximately 50% to values given. Introduced in 1987.

NIB	Exc.	V.G.	Good	Fair	Poor
—	1300	1040	830	670	530

SUPER X2 SERIES

Super X2 3.5" Magnum

Introduced in 1999. Gas-operated design chambered for 3.5" 12-gauge shells. Fitted with black synthetic stock. Choice of 24", 26" or 28" ventilated rib barrels. Invector chokes. Magazine capacity 5 rounds. Weight 7.5 lbs., depending on barrel length. Matte black finish.

NIB	Exc.	V.G.	Good	Fair	Poor
—	880	740	630	540	460

Super X2 Turkey

Similar to X2 Magnum, with 24" ventilated rib barrel with TruGlo sights. Extra-Full choke. Weight 7.25 lbs. Black synthetic stock. Introduced in 1999.

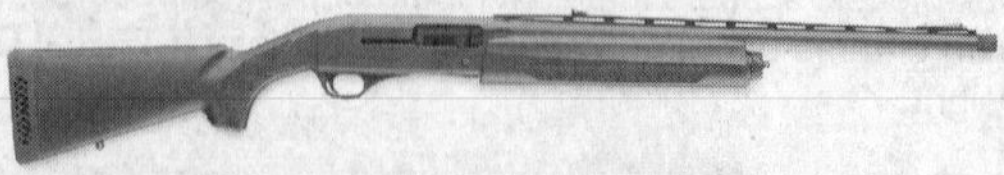

NIB	Exc.	V.G.	Good	Fair	Poor
—	880	740	630	540	460

Super X2 Turkey Mossy Oak Break-Up

Same as above, with Mossy Oak Break-Up camo on stock and gun. Introduced in 2000.

NIB	Exc.	V.G.	Good	Fair	Poor
—	900	760	650	550	470

Super X2 NWTF Turkey

Introduced in 2005. 3.5" 12 gauge fitted with 24" ventilated rib barrel, with Extra Full extended choke tubes. Three dot TruGlo sights. Mossy Oak camo stock. Brass NWTF medallion on pistol grip cap. Weight 7.5 lbs.

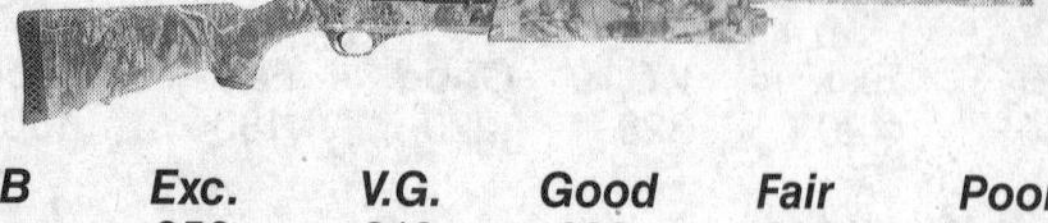

NIB	Exc.	V.G.	Good	Fair	Poor
—	950	810	690	580	500

Super X2 Universal Hunter

Similar to Super X2 Turkey, with 26" barrel with Extra Full choke tube. Weight 7.75 lbs. Introduced in 2002.

NIB	Exc.	V.G.	Good	Fair	Poor
—	810	690	580	500	420

Super X2 Camo Waterfowl

Chambered for 12-gauge 3.5" shells. Fitted with 28" ventilated rib barrel. Features Mossy Oak camo finish. Weight 8 lbs. Introduced in 1999. In 2004, New Shadow Grass camo pattern was added.

NIB	Exc.	V.G.	Good	Fair	Poor
—	900	760	650	550	470

Super X2 Magnum Greenhead

Introduced in 2002. Chambered for 12-gauge 3.5" shell. Has composite stock that is green in color. Fitted with 28" barrel. Weight 8 lbs.

NIB	Exc.	V.G.	Good	Fair	Poor
—	900	760	650	550	470

Super X2 Magnum Field

Chambered for 12-gauge 3" shell. Offered with walnut or black synthetic stock. Choice of 26" or 28" ventilated rib barrel, with Invector chokes. Weight 7.25 lbs. Introduced in 1999.

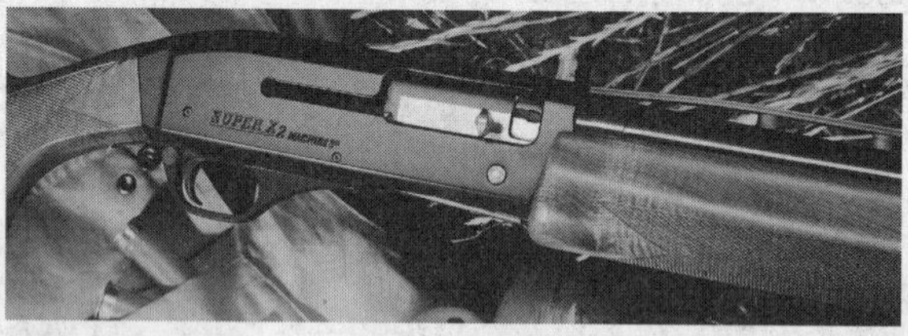

NIB	Exc.	V.G.	Good	Fair	Poor
—	880	740	630	540	460

Super X2 Light Field

Checkered walnut stock. Choice of 26" or 28" ventilated rib barrel, with choke tubes. Chambered for 12 gauge. Weight 6.5 lbs. Introduced in 2005.

Super X2 Cantilever Deer

This 12 gauge has 22" fully rifled barrel, with fold-down rear sight and scope mount. Black composite stock. Weight 7.25 lbs. Introduced in 2002.

NIB	Exc.	V.G.	Good	Fair	Poor
—	900	760	650	550	470

Super X2 Practical

Introduced in 2002. Designed for competition shooting. Fitted with a 22" barrel, with ghost ring sight and 8-round magazine. Black composite stock. Weight 8 lbs.

NIB	Exc.	V.G.	Good	Fair	Poor
1020	900	700	520	450	350

Super X2 Sporting Clays

Introduced in 2001. 12 gauge. Choice of 28" or 30" barrels, with high post rib. Barrels are back-bored, with Invector chokes. Adjustable comb. Weight 8 lbs.

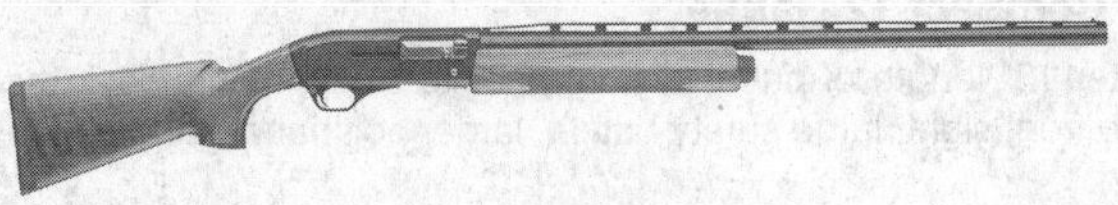

NIB	Exc.	V.G.	Good	Fair	Poor
950	810	690	580	500	420

Super X2 Sporting Clays Signature II

This 3" 12 gauge fitted with a 30" barrel, with choke tubes. Hardwood stock painted black metallic. Receiver a red-anodized alloy. Weight 8.25 lbs. Introduced in 2005.

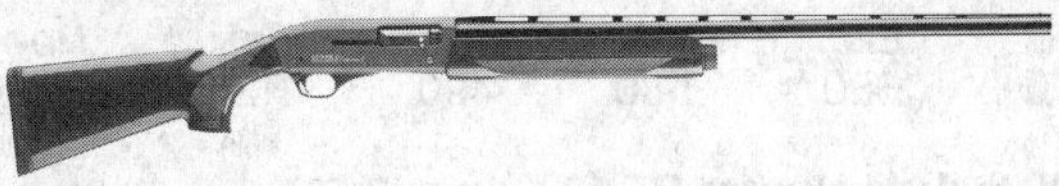

NIB	Exc.	V.G.	Good	Fair	Poor
880	740	630	540	460	390

Super X2 Signature Red Sporting

This 12-gauge 3" shell model features hardwood stock, with red Dura-Touch coating. Fitted with a 30" ventilated rib barrel, with five choke tubes. Weight 8 lbs. Introduced in 2003.

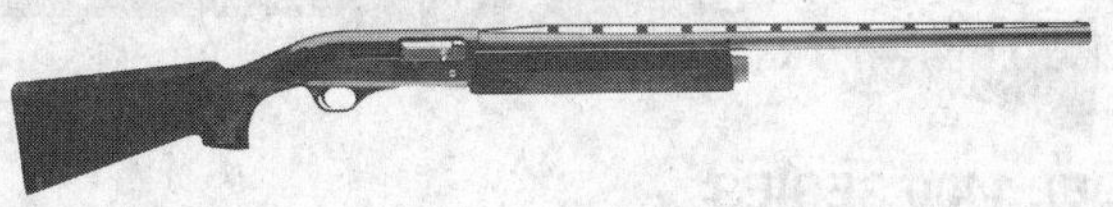

NIB	Exc.	V.G.	Good	Fair	Poor
950	880	700	520	450	300

SUPER X3 (SX3) SERIES

Introduced in 2006. Super X3 12-gauge features weight and recoil reducing features and .742" back-bored barrel. Available in a variety of configurations. Weight under 7 lbs. in 3" Field model; 7.5 lbs. in Composite, Camo and 3.5" models. All models, except Cantilever Deer, included three choke tubes.

NIB	Exc.	V.G.	Good	Fair	Poor
1020	870	740	630	530	450

Super X3 Field

Walnut stock and 26" or 28" barrel.

NIB	Exc.	V.G.	Good	Fair	Poor
1200	950	750	580	500	350

Super X3 Composite

Matte black stock and forend. Available in 26" or 28" barrel. Chambered 3" or 3.5". Note: Add $100 for 3.5" model.

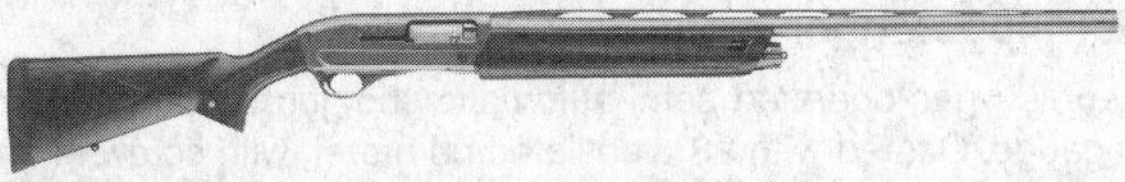

NIB	Exc.	V.G.	Good	Fair	Poor
950	810	690	580	500	420

Super X3 Camo

Composite camo stock, with 3.5" chamber. Available in various camo patterns, with 26" or 28" barrel.

NIB	Exc.	V.G.	Good	Fair	Poor
1000	850	720	610	520	440

Super X3 Cantilever Deer

Slug gun, with 22" barrel. Cantilever scope mount and 3" chamber.

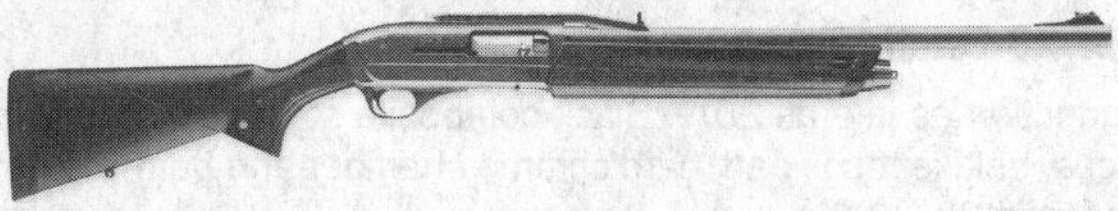

NIB	Exc.	V.G.	Good	Fair	Poor
1000	850	720	610	520	440

Super X3 "Flanigun" Exhibition/Sporting

With red receiver and forend cap, this is a duplicate of gun used by exhibition shooter Patrick Flanigan, with a shorter magazine tube. Has a 3" chamber and 28" barrel.

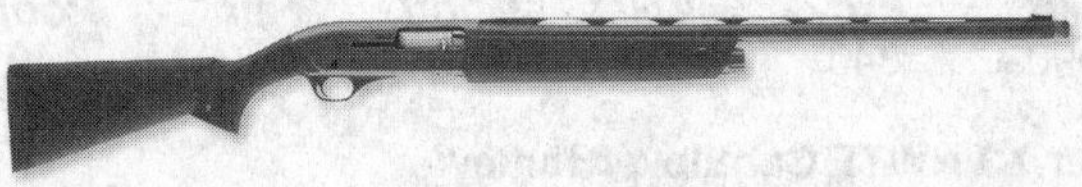

NIB	Exc.	V.G.	Good	Fair	Poor
1150	980	830	710	600	510

Super X3 Classic Field

Introduced in 2008. Similar to Super X3 Field, with traditional sharp checkering on pistol grip and forend. Barrel length 26" or 28".

NIB	Exc.	V.G.	Good	Fair	Poor
960	820	690	590	500	430

Super X3 Turkey

New in 2008. Dedicated turkey model has a 3.5" chamber, 24" barrel, Extra Full choke tube. Complete coverage in Mossy Oak New Breakup camo. Price includes TruGlo red-dot scope. Weight 7.5 lbs.

NIB	Exc.	V.G.	Good	Fair	Poor
1200	950	750	580	500	350

Super X3 Universal Hunter

In production as late as 2019. Mossy Oak Break-Up Country camo synthetic stock, back-bored barrel, Invector-Plus choke system, hard-chrome bore and barrel, TruGlo Long Bead fiber-optic sight. This model number is a 20/3"/28".

NIB	Exc.	V.G.	Good	Fair	Poor
910	780	660	560	480	400

Super X3 Ultimate Sporting Adjustable

In production as late as 2019. Satin oil finish grade II/III walnut, adjustable comb, sporting choke tube package, red stylized ergonomic operating hardware. This model number is a 12/2.75"/30".

NIB	Exc.	V.G.	Good	Fair	Poor
1440	1220	1040	880	750	640

Super X3 Composite Sporting Carbon Fiber

In production as late as 2019. Composite stock with carbon-fiber-dipped finish, sporting clays choke tube performance package, ported, red stylized ergonomic operating hardware, fiber-optic front sight. This model number is a 12/2.75"/28".

NIB	Exc.	V.G.	Good	Fair	Poor
1440	1220	1040	880	750	640

Super X3 Black Shadow

In production as late as 2019. Black composite stock, textured gripping surfaces, deluxe recoil pad, hard chrome chamber and bore. This model number is a 20/3"/26".

NIB	Exc.	V.G.	Good	Fair	Poor
890	750	640	540	460	390

Super X3 Waterfowl Hunter

In production as late as 2019. Mossy Oak Shadow Grass Blades camo. This model number is a 20/3"/26".

NIB	Exc.	V.G.	Good	Fair	Poor
990	840	720	610	520	440

Super X3 NWTF Cantilever Turkey

In production as late as 2019. Mossy Oak Break-Up Country camo synthetic stock, cantilever scope mount, TruGlo fiber-optic sight and adjustable rear sight, Extra-Full Turkey extended choke tube. This model number is a 12/3.5"/24".

NIB	Exc.	V.G.	Good	Fair	Poor
1020	860	730	620	530	450

Super X3 Long Beard 511168290

In production as late as 2019. Available in 20 gauge. Mossy Oak Break-Up Country camo synthetic stock with pistol grip, cantilever scope mount, cast and drop shims, TruGlo fiber-optic sight, Briley Extra-Full Long Beard extended choke tube. This model number is a 12/3.5"/24".

NIB	Exc.	V.G.	Good	Fair	Poor
1080	920	780	660	560	480

SUPER X4 (SX4) SERIES

SX-4

Introduced 2017 in 12-gauge only. Supersedes Super X3 (SX3) series. Among its features are larger controls that are easier to operate, synthetic stock with improved ergonomics, including a smaller pistol grip and textured gripping surfaces. Operates with self-adjusting system that cycles a variety of loads while reducing felt recoil. Back-bored, drop-out trigger group, length-of-pull spacers. Offered in several variants including Field and Field Compact, both with walnut stocks, synthetic stock model and Waterfowl Hunter (shown). In 2019, SX4 Waterfowl Hunter Realtree Timber, SX4 Hybrid Hunter Realtree Timber, SX4 Hybrid were released as SHOT Show specials and with 20-gauge models. Also, in 2019, the SX4 Compact 511230392 in 12/3"/28" was released, along with 20-gauge 3" chamber models with 24" barrels (511230690), 26" barrels (511230691), and 28" barrels (511230692).

NIB	Exc.	V.G.	Good	Fair	Poor
880	680	580	—	—	—

Super X4 20-Gauge 3"

NIB	Exc.	V.G.	Good	Fair	Poor
870	750	630	—	—	—

Super X4 Universal Hunter MOBU Camo

NIB	Exc.	V.G.	Good	Fair	Poor
990	—	—	—	—	—

SX4 Compact 12 Gauge 3"

Shorter 13" length of pull, black composite stock, matte black receiver, Truglo front sight, large safety button, larger bolt handle and bolt release button.

NIB	Exc.	V.G.	Good	Fair	Poor
650	580	530	—	—	—

SX4 Matte Black Synthetic 12 Gauge 3.5"

NIB	Exc.	V.G.	Good	Fair	Poor
800	680	580	490	420	360

SX4 Waterfowl Hunter RT 12 Gauge 3.5"

NIB	Exc.	V.G.	Good	Fair	Poor
890	760	640	550	470	400

SX4 Upland Field (2019)

Satin varnish finish grade II/III walnut stock, matte nickel finish alloy receiver, Truglo front sight.

MODEL 1400 SERIES

Model 1400

Gas-operated semi-automatic shotgun. Chambered for 12, 16 or 20 gauge. Offered with 26", 28" or 30" ventilated rib barrel, with various chokes. Finish blued, with checkered walnut stock. Manufactured between 1964 and 1981. Hydrocoil plastic stock available. Add approximately 35% to values given.

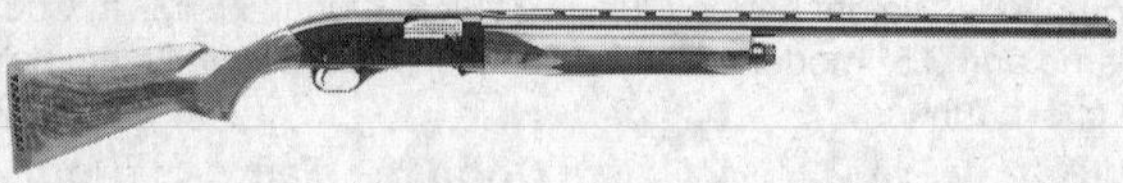

NIB	Exc.	V.G.	Good	Fair	Poor
450	350	300	250	200	120

New Model 1400

Gas-operated semi-automatic shotgun. Chambered for 12 or 20 gauge. Offered with 22" or 28" ventilated rib barrel, with screw-in chokes. Finish blued, with checkered walnut stock. Introduced in 1989.

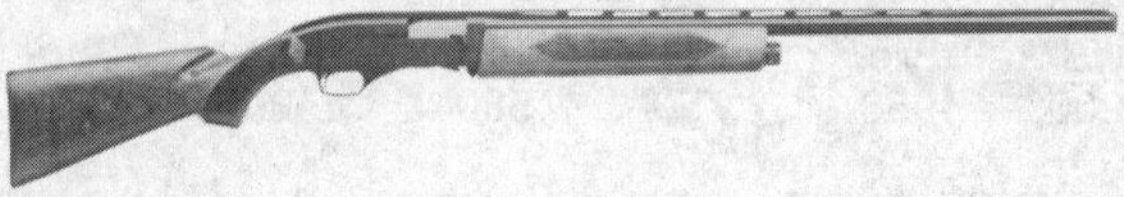

NIB	Exc.	V.G.	Good	Fair	Poor
450	350	300	250	200	120

Model 1400 Ranger

Utility-grade gas-operated semi-automatic shotgun. Chambered for 12 or 20 gauge. Offered with 28" ventilated rib barrel, with screw-in chokes or 24" slug barrel, with rifle sights. Finish blued, with checkered stock. Combination two-barrel set includes deer barrel - add 20% for set. Introduced in 1983.

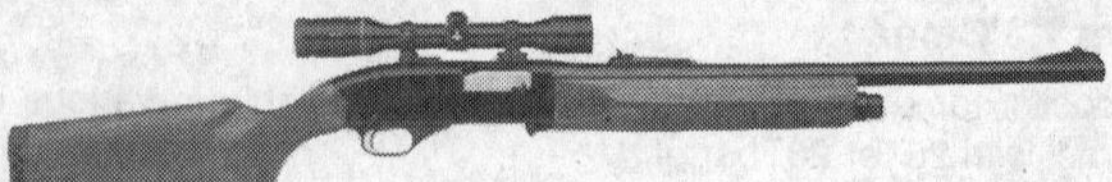

NIB	Exc.	V.G.	Good	Fair	Poor
400	300	250	200	150	100

Model 1400 Quail Unlimited

This 12-gauge semi-automatic shotgun introduced in 1993. Features compact engraved receiver, with 26" ventilated rib barrel supplied with WinChoke tubes. Stock checkered walnut. Weight 7.25 lbs.

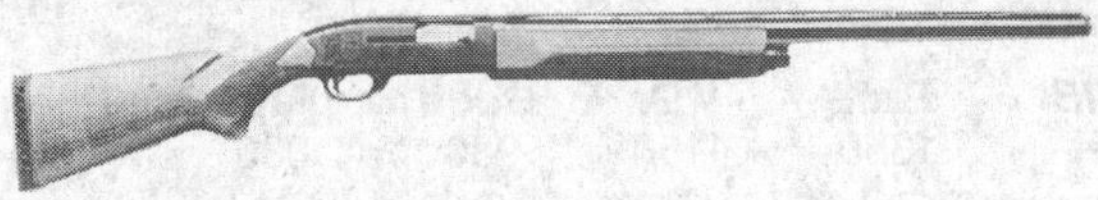

NIB	Exc.	V.G.	Good	Fair	Poor
400	300	250	200	150	100

Model 1400 Ranger Deer Combo

Features 12-gauge 22" smooth barrel and 28" ventilated rib barrel, with three WinChokes.

NIB	Exc.	V.G.	Good	Fair	Poor
400	300	250	200	150	100

Model 37A

Introduced in 1973. Single-shot shotgun, with exposed hammer. Offered in 12, 16, 20, 28 gauge and .410 bore. All guns choked Full, except youth model choked Modified. Walnut finish on hardwood stock. Pistol grip cap, with white spacer. Weight 6 lbs. About 395,000 produced until 1980.

NIB	Exc.	V.G.	Good	Fair	Poor
—	350	250	220	180	120

Model 22

Introduced in 1975. Side-by-side shotgun manufactured by Laurona in Spain, to Winchester's specifications for European market. Had an oil-finished stock, with checkered pistol grip semi-beavertail forearm and hand-engraved receiver. Finish black chrome. Fitted with double triggers and matted rib. Offered in 12-gauge only, with 28" barrels. Weight 6.75 lbs. Rare.

NIB	Exc.	V.G.	Good	Fair	Poor
1250	950	700	550	400	200

Model 91

Over/under shotgun built for Winchester by Laurona for its European markets. Offered in 12-gauge only, with 28" ventilated rib barrels and single/double triggers. Hand-checkered oil-finished walnut stock, with hand-engraved receiver. Finish was black chrome. Weight 7.5 lbs. Rare.

NIB	Exc.	V.G.	Good	Fair	Poor
1100	800	600	500	400	200

Supreme Field

Introduced in 2000. Over/under shotgun chambered for 12-gauge 3" shell. Fitted with 28" ventilated rib barrels, with Invector chokes. Walnut stock, with pistol grip. Blued engraved receiver. Weight 7.5 lbs.

NIB	Exc.	V.G.	Good	Fair	Poor
1020	900	700	520	450	350

Supreme Sporting

Similar to above model. Fitted with 28" or 30" blued ported barrels. Chambered for 12-gauge 2.75" shells. Polished silver receiver and adjustable trigger. Weight 7.5 lbs. Introduced in 2000.

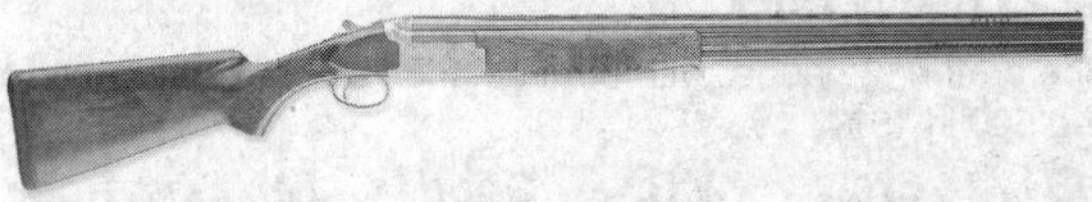

NIB	Exc.	V.G.	Good	Fair	Poor
1200	950	750	580	500	350

Supreme Elegance

Introduced in 2003. Over/under shotgun chambered for 12-gauge 3" shell. Choice of 26" or 28" ventilated rib barrels, with three choke tubes. Grayed receiver, with scroll and bird scenes. Weight 7 lbs., depending on barrel length.

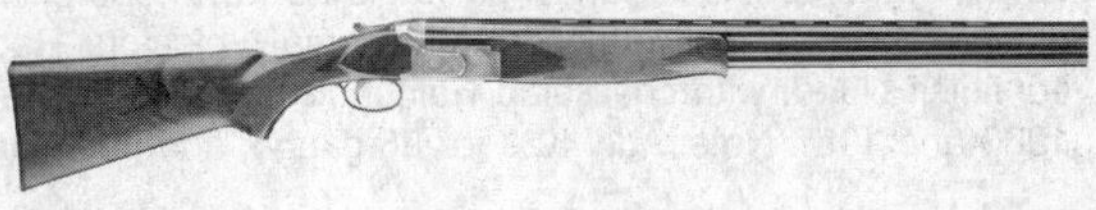

NIB	Exc.	V.G.	Good	Fair	Poor
1400	1100	850	500	200	100

MODEL 23 SERIES

Model 23 XTR

Side-by-side boxlock double-barrel shotgun. Chambered for 12 or 20 gauge. Offered with 25.5", 26", 28" or 30" ventilated rib barrels, with 3" chambers. Various choke combinations. Features single trigger and automatic ejectors. Scroll-engraved, with coin-finished receiver, blued barrels and checkered select walnut stock. Introduced in 1978. Available in a number of configurations. Differ in amount of ornamentation, quality of materials and workmanship utilized in their construction. Models and values listed. Discontinued.

NIB	Exc.	V.G.	Good	Fair	Poor
2000	1800	1400	1050	850	500

Pigeon Grade

With WinChokes.

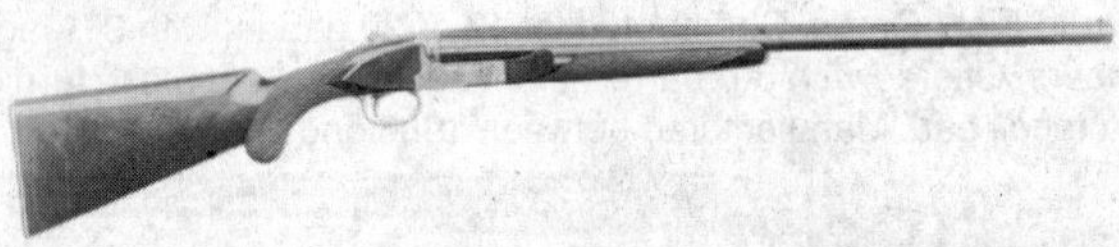

NIB	Exc.	V.G.	Good	Fair	Poor
—	2300	1950	1600	1300	500

Pigeon Grade Lightweight

Straight stock.

NIB	Exc.	V.G.	Good	Fair	Poor
—	2450	2100	1750	1400	500

Model 23 Golden Quail

This series available in 12, 20, 28 gauge and .410 bore. Features 25.5" barrels that are choked Improved Cylinder/Modified and straight-grip English-style stock, with recoil pad. Series discontinued in 1987. Note: Add 20% for 20 gauge; add 50% for 28 gauge or .410 bore.

NIB	Exc.	V.G.	Good	Fair	Poor
3000	2700	2400	2000	1200	500

Model 23 Light Duck

Chambered for 20 gauge. Offered with 28" Full and Full-choked barrel.

Manufactured 500 in 1985.

NIB	Exc.	V.G.	Good	Fair	Poor
3100	2900	2600	1800	800	500

Model 23 Heavy Duck

Chambered for 12 gauge, with 30" Full and Full-choked barrels. Manufactured 500 in 1984.

NIB	Exc.	V.G.	Good	Fair	Poor
3200	3000	2600	1800	800	500

MODEL 101 SERIES

Model 101 Field Grade

Over/under boxlock double-barrel shotgun. Chambered for 12, 20, 28 gauge, and .410 bore. Offered with 26", 28" or 30" ventilated rib barrels, with various choke combinations. Since 1983, screw-in chokes have been standard and models so furnished would be worth approximately $50 additional. Single-selective trigger and automatic ejectors. Receiver engraved; finish blued, with checkered walnut stock. Manufactured between 1963 and 1987. Note: Add 40% for 28-gauge; add 50% for .410 bore.

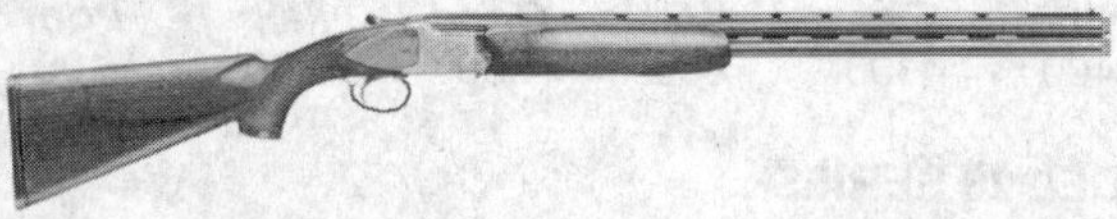

NIB	Exc.	V.G.	Good	Fair	Poor
—	1000	850	720	610	520

Model 101 Waterfowl

Chambered for 12-gauge 3" shell. Has 30" or 32" ventilated rib barrels and matte finish.

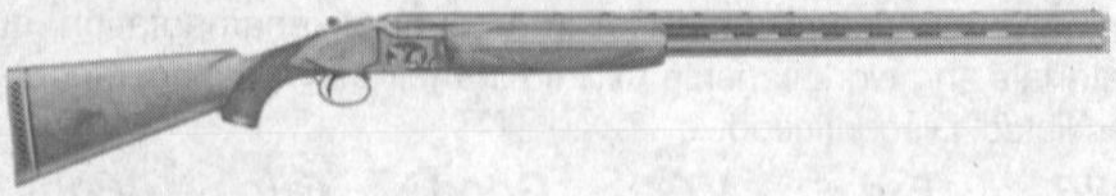

NIB	Exc.	V.G.	Good	Fair	Poor
—	1880	1590	1360	1150	980

Model 101 Magnum

Similar to Field Grade. Chambered for 12 or 20 gauge, with 3" Magnum chambers. Offered with 30" barrels and various chokes. Stock furnished with a recoil pad. Manufactured between 1966 and 1981.

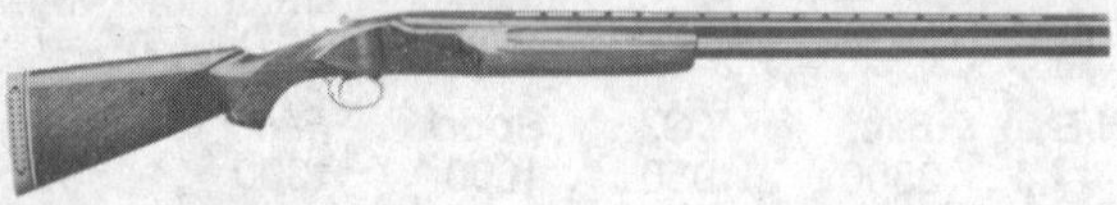

NIB	Exc.	V.G.	Good	Fair	Poor
—	1300	1100	940	800	680

Model 101 Skeet Grade

Offered with 26" skeet-bored barrels, with competition rib and skeet-type walnut stock. Manufactured between 1966 and 1984.

NIB	Exc.	V.G.	Good	Fair	Poor
—	1500	1250	1050	850	500

Model 101 Three-Gauge Skeet Set

Combination set offered with three barrels. Chambered for 20 gauge, 28 gauge, and .410 bore. Furnished with a fitted case. Manufactured between 1974 and 1984.

NIB	Exc.	V.G.	Good	Fair	Poor
—	3700	3140	2670	2270	1930

Model 101 Trap Grade

Chambered for 12-gauge only. Offered with 30" or 32" competition ribbed barrels choked for trap shooting. Furnished with competition-type stock. Manufactured between 1966 and 1984.

NIB	Exc.	V.G.	Good	Fair	Poor
—	1350	1150	980	830	700

Model 101 Pigeon Grade

More deluxe-engraved version of Model 101. Chambered for 12, 20, 28 gauge, and .410 bore. Features coin-finished receiver, with fancy checkered walnut stock. Introduced in 1974.

NIB	Exc.	V.G.	Good	Fair	Poor
—	2200	1870	1590	1350	1150

Model 101 Super Pigeon Grade

Deluxe version of Model 101. Chambered for 12 gauge. Heavily engraved, with several gold inlays. Receiver blued. Features high-grade walnut stock, with fleur-de-lis checkering. Imported between 1985 and 1987.

NIB	Exc.	V.G.	Good	Fair	Poor
—	5050	4290	3650	3100	2640

Model 101 Diamond Grade

Competition model chambered for all four gauges. Offered in trap or skeet configuration, with screw-in chokes. Engraved matte-finished receiver. Select checkered walnut stock. Skeet model features recoil-reducing muzzle vents.

NIB	Exc.	V.G.	Good	Fair	Poor
—	1750	1490	1260	1080	910

Model 101 Pigeon Grade Trap

Deluxe dedicated trap gun introduced in 2008. Features Grade III/IV walnut stock, with high-gloss finish and raised comb. Barrels are 30" or 32". Three choke tubes included. Weight 7.5 to 7.75 lbs. Note: Add 5% for adjustable comb stock.

NIB	Exc.	V.G.	Good	Fair	Poor
2400	2040	1730	1470	1250	1060

Model 101 Light

Gauge: 12 ga., 3". Barrels: 26", 28", ventilated rib. Length: 43 to 45". Weight: 6 lbs. to 6 lbs., 4 oz. Stock: Grade II/III Turkish walnut. Features: Similar to the Model 101, but weighs 1 pound less with its aluminum-alloy receiver; adorned with quail on the right and flushing pheasants on the left. Pachmayr Decelerator buttpad with white-line spacer, chrome-plated back-bored barrels, cut checkering, steel grip cap, brass front bead. Includes three Invector Plus chokes (F, M, IC).

NIB	Exc.	V.G.	Good	Fair	Poor
1700	1300	1100	940	800	680

Model 101 Field

In production as late as 2019. Pachmayr White Line Pad. Grade II/III walnut stock, Invector Plus chokes. This model number is a 12/3"/28".

NIB	Exc.	V.G.	Good	Fair	Poor
1350	1150	980	830	710	600

Model 101 Deluxe Field

Gauge: 12 ga., 3". Barrels: 26", 28", ventilated rib. Length: 43" to 45".

Weight: 6 lbs., 12 oz. Stock: Grade III European walnut. Features: Classic field gun design on the proven 101 line of O/U shotguns. Detailed engraving on the sides of the steel receiver. Blued metalwork. Pachmayr Decelerator recoil pad, hard-chrome-plated chamber and bore, steel grip cap, brass bead front, white mid-bead. Includes three Invector Plus chokes (F, M, IC).

NIB	*Exc.*	*V.G.*	*Good*	*Fair*	*Poor*
1750	1500	1280	1090	920	780

Model 101 Deluxe Field Maple

In production as late as 2019. AAA Maple and intricate receiver engraving. This model number is a 12/3"/26".

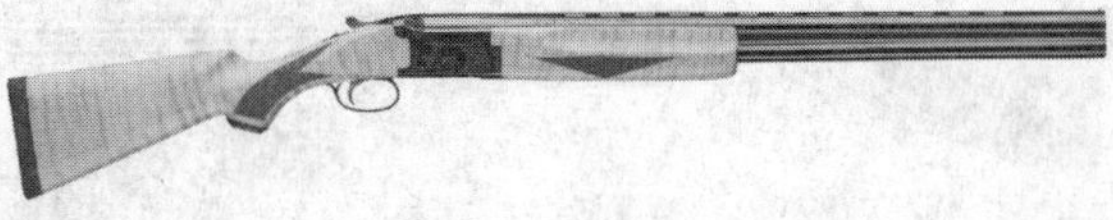

NIB	*Exc.*	*V.G.*	*Good*	*Fair*	*Poor*
1750	1390	1180	1010	860	730

Model 101 Sporting

In production as late as 2019. Ported, extended tubes, II/III walnut. This model number is a 12/2.75"/28".

NIB	*Exc.*	*V.G.*	*Good*	*Fair*	*Poor*
1800	1530	1300	1100	940	800

Model 101 Pigeon Trap

In production as late as 2019. Monte Carlo grade II/III stock, fine cut checkering, engraved receiver, ported barrel, TRUGLO front sight. This model number is a 12/2.75"/30".

NIB	*Exc.*	*V.G.*	*Good*	*Fair*	*Poor*
2180	1860	1580	1340	1140	970

Model 101 Pigeon Trap (Adjustable Comb)

In production as late as 2019. Original Pigeon Grade styling, grade II/III walnut, adjustable Monte Carlo comb, nickel-plated receiver, deep engraving. This model number is a 12/2.75"/30".

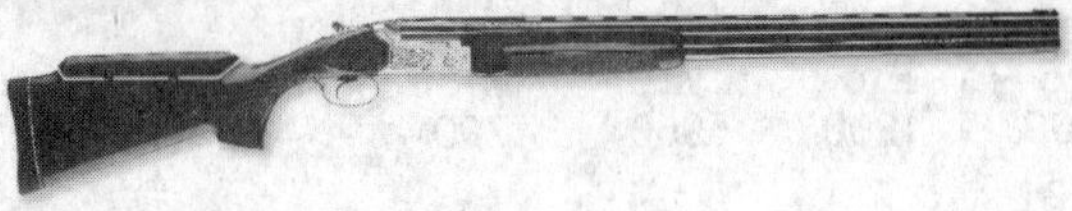

NIB	*Exc.*	*V.G.*	*Good*	*Fair*	*Poor*
1920	1630	1380	1180	1000	850

MODEL 101 SERIES

In production as late as 2019. Original Pigeon Grade styling, grade II/III walnut, adjustable Monte Carlo comb, nickel-plated receiver, deep engraving. This model number is a 12/2.75"/30".

NIB	*Exc.*	*V.G.*	*Good*	*Fair*	*Poor*
1920	1630	1380	1180	1000	850

Model 101 150th Anniversary Commemorative

In 12 gauge, with deep relief scroll engraving, gold inlays, silver nitride receiver, triggerguard, safety, and Winchester trademark. Barrels 28", with ventilated rib, ivory bead front sight and Winchester's Invector-Plus choke tubes. Grade IV/V walnut stock has 24 lpi checkering. Introduced in 2016.

NIB	*Exc.*	*V.G.*	*Good*	*Fair*	*Poor*
2800	2400	—	—	—	—

Select Model 101 Field

Belgian-made version of Winchesters popular Model 101. Features Grade II/III walnut; 26" or 28" barrels; deep-relief engraving; blued receiver that mimics original 101. Classic white line spacer and vented recoil pad. Three choke tubes. Weight 7.2 lbs. Introduced in 2007.

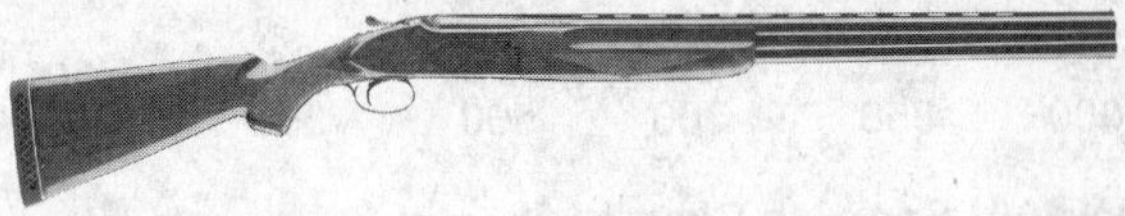

NIB	*Exc.*	*V.G.*	*Good*	*Fair*	*Poor*
1600	1400	1150	900	650	400

Select Model 101 Sporting

Similar to Field model plus competition features, such as, wider rib, adjustable trigger, white mid-bead and five extended Signature choke tubes. Ported barrels are 28", 30" or 32".

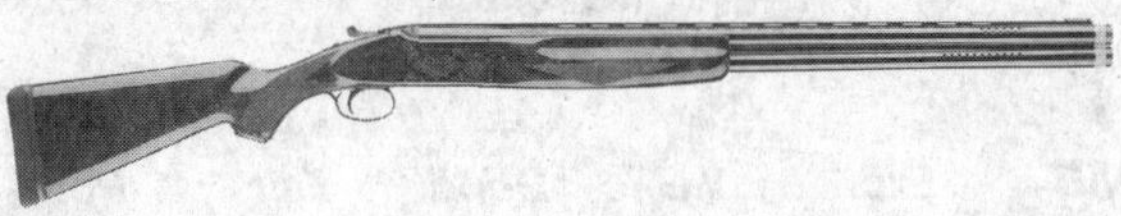

NIB	*Exc.*	*V.G.*	*Good*	*Fair*	*Poor*
1680	1480	1220	1050	780	450

Model 501 Grand European

Over/under double-barrel shotgun. Chambered for 12 or 20 gauge. Available in trap or skeet configurations. Offered with 27", 30" or 32" ventilated rib barrels. Heavily engraved and matte finish, with select checkered walnut stock. Manufactured between 1981 and 1986.

NIB	*Exc.*	*V.G.*	*Good*	*Fair*	*Poor*
—	2700	2100	1700	1300	500

Model 501 Presentation Grade

Deluxe version chambered in 12-gauge only. Ornately engraved and gold-inlaid. Stock made out of presentation-grade walnut. Furnished with a fitted case. Manufactured between 1984 and 1987.

NIB	*Exc.*	*V.G.*	*Good*	*Fair*	*Poor*
—	3400	2750	2200	1600	500

Combination Gun

Over/under rifle/shotgun combination. Chambered for 12-gauge over .222, .223, .30-06 and 9.3x74R cartridges. Features 25" barrels and select checkered walnut stock. Shotgun tube has screw-in choke. Engraved in fashion of Model 501 Grand European. Manufactured between 1983 and 1985.

NIB	*Exc.*	*V.G.*	*Good*	*Fair*	*Poor*
—	3000	2500	1600	1200	700

Model 96 Xpert

Utility-grade over/under double-barrel shotgun. Mechanically similar to Model 101. Chambered for 12 or 20 gauge. Offered with various barrel lengths and choke combinations. Boxlock action, with single-selective trigger and automatic ejectors. Plain receiver blued, with checkered walnut stock. Manufactured between 1976 and 1982. Competition-grade model for trap or skeet was also available. Would be worth approximately the same amount.

NIB	*Exc.*	*V.G.*	*Good*	*Fair*	*Poor*
—	1020	900	700	520	350

Model 1001 Field

New addition to U.S.R.A. product line for 1993. Over/under shotgun available in 12-gauge only, with 28" ventilated rib barrel. Furnished with WinPlus choke tubes. Walnut checkered pistol grip stock standard. Finish blued, with scroll engraving on receiver. Matte finish on receiver top. Weight 7 lbs. Subject to a 1995 recall.

NIB	Exc.	V.G.	Good	Fair	Poor
1000	850	700	500	350	200

Model 1001 Sporting Clays I & II

This model features: different stock dimensions; fuller pistol grip; radiused recoil pad; wider ventilated rib. Fitted on 28" barrel (Sporting Clays I); 30" (Sporting Clays II). Comes complete with choke tubes. Frame has silver nitrate finish. Special engraving features a flying clay target. Introduced in 1993. Weight 7.75 lbs. Subject to a 1995 recall.

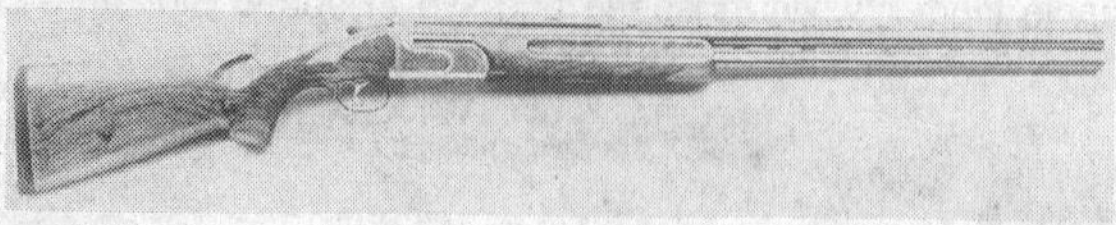

NIB	Exc.	V.G.	Good	Fair	Poor
1100	950	800	600	350	200

SELECT OVER/UNDER SERIES

This series of over/under shotguns was introduced into Winchester line in 2004. Series features a low-profile receiver, with unique engraving and lightweight barrels. Contoured walnut stocks, with distinctive checkering patterns.

Select Midnight

High-gloss bluing on receiver. Barrels with gold accent game bird pattern on both sides and bottom of receiver. Satin finished Grade II/III walnut. Oval checkering pattern. Choke tubes. Introduced 2006. Available in 26" and 28" barrels.

NIB	Exc.	V.G.	Good	Fair	Poor
1600	1400	1150	900	650	400

Select White Field

An engraved silver nitride receiver featured on both versions of White Field. Traditional Model: has traditional checkering; Extreme Model: features Select Series' unique oval checkering pattern. Both versions have choke tubes. Available in 26" and 28" barrels. Introduced 2006.

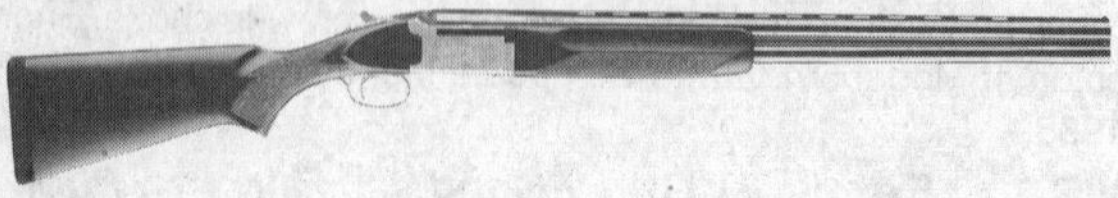

NIB	Exc.	V.G.	Good	Fair	Poor
1300	1200	1100	900	650	400

Select Energy Sporting

Chambered for 12-gauge 2.75" shell. Choice of 28", 30" or 32" ventilated rib barrels, with choke tubes and porting. TruGlo front sight. Adjustable trigger shoe. Walnut stock, with recoil pad. Weight 7.62 lbs. Adjustable comb available. Note: Add $150 for adjustable comb.

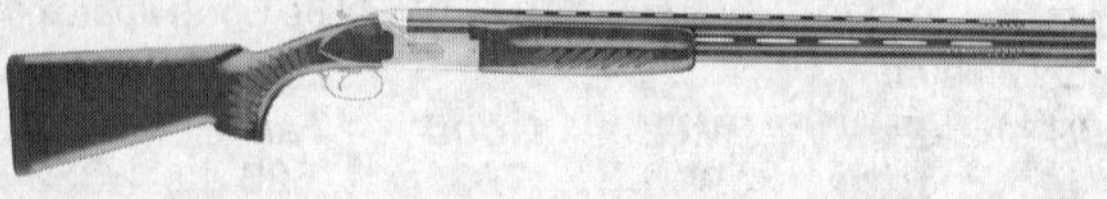

NIB	Exc.	V.G.	Good	Fair	Poor
1600	1400	1150	900	650	400

Select Energy Trap

This 12-gauge model fitted with choice of 30" or 32" back-bored ported barrels. Wide ventilated rib. Choke tubes. Walnut stock, with Monte Carlo comb. Weight 7.8 lbs. Adjustable comb available. Note: Add $150 for adjustable comb.

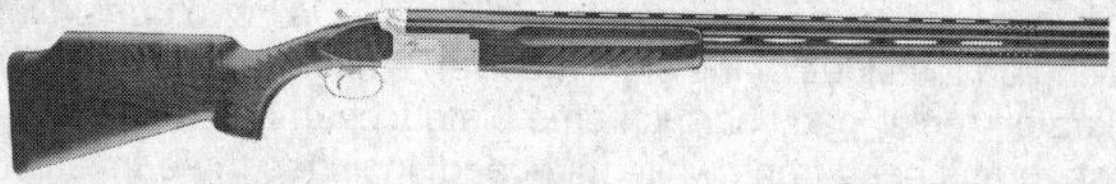

NIB	Exc.	V.G.	Good	Fair	Poor
1600	1400	1150	900	650	400

Select Elegance (Supreme)

This 12 gauge features full coverage engraving, with game scenes. Choice of 26" or 28" ventilated rib barrels, with choke tubes. Walnut stock, with unique checkering pattern. Weight 7 lbs.

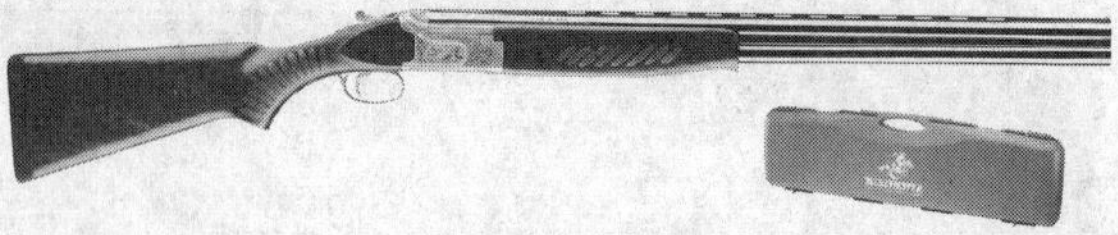

NIB	Exc.	V.G.	Good	Fair	Poor
1800	1400	1150	900	650	400

Select Field

This 12-gauge 3" gun fitted with choice of 26" or 28" ventilated rib barrels, with choke tubes. Engraved receiver, with oval checkering pattern. Weight 7 lbs.

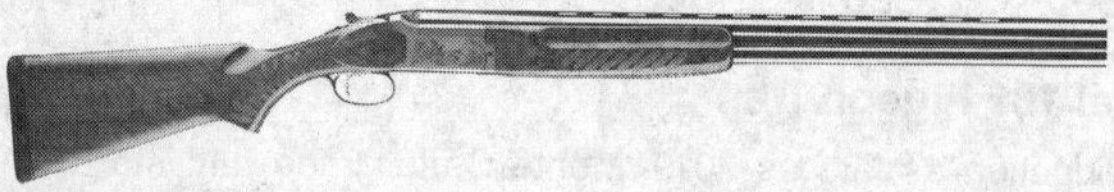

NIB	Exc.	V.G.	Good	Fair	Poor
1400	1200	950	700	450	300

Select Traditional Elegance

Similar to Select Elegance, with traditional checkering pattern.

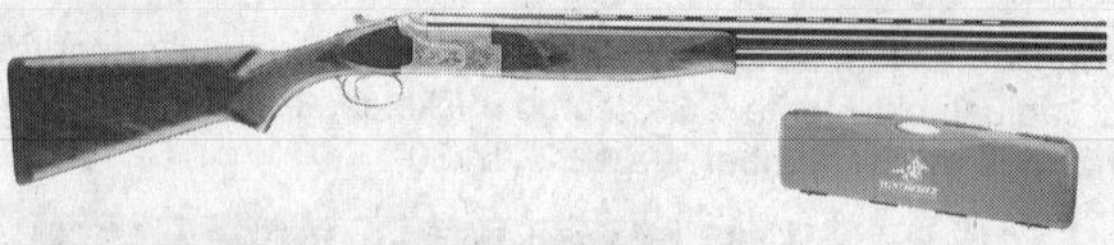

NIB	Exc.	V.G.	Good	Fair	Poor
1400	1200	950	700	450	300

Select Deluxe Field

New in 2007. Belgian-made 3" 12 gauge features engraved steel receiver, with silver nitride finish and Grade II walnut. Barrels are 26", 28" or 30". Three chokes included. Weight 7.25 lbs.

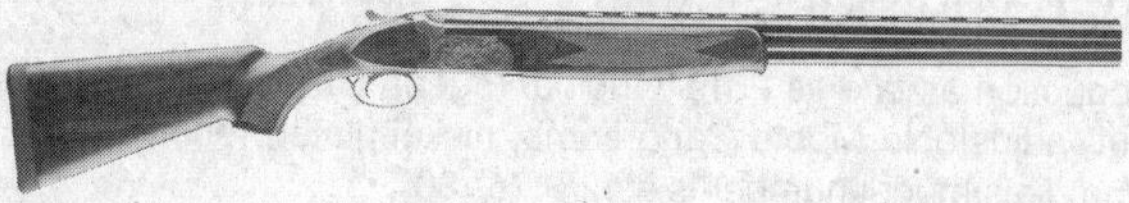

NIB	Exc.	V.G.	Good	Fair	Poor
1600	1400	1150	900	650	400

Select Platinum Field

This 3" 12 gauge introduced in 2007. Belgian-made and comes with 28" or 30" barrels, Grade II/III walnut and deep relief engraving. Includes three Signature extended choke tubes and hard case.

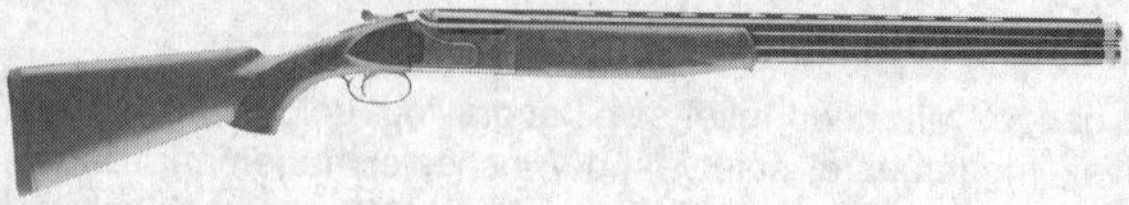

NIB	Exc.	V.G.	Good	Fair	Poor
2050	1800	1580	1200	900	500

Select Platinum Sporting

Similar to Platinum Field, with 28", 30" or 32" ported barrels, wide rib and adjustable trigger shoe. Five Signature extended choke tubes and hard case.

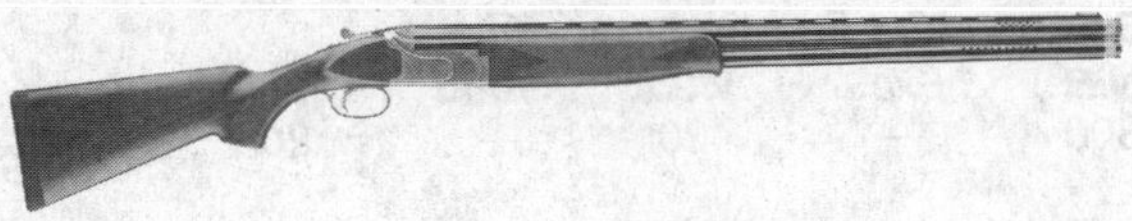

NIB	Exc.	V.G.	Good	Fair	Poor
2200	1950	1720	1380	1080	500

WINCHESTER COMMEMORATIVE RIFLES

Beginning 1964, Winchester began producing various limited edition "Commemorative" firearms. Most were based on the Model 94. These guns would have special decoration which celebrated an historic event or individual or organization, often associated with the Old West. Around 90 different commemorative models were introduced through 1990. In those years they found a market with some collectors, and the value of these guns tended to increase after production ended. Their popularity waned in more recent decades. Commemoratives that are As New in Box will still generally bring a premium over plain versions of the same model. The premium usually depends on how many were made (the fewer, the more value) and the quality and elaborateness of the decoration. However, once a commemorative begins to show use or wear, the value drops rapidly towards the value of a plain model.

1964 Wyoming Diamond Jubilee—Carbine

NIB	Exc.	V.G.	Good	Fair	Poor
1200	—	100	—	—	—

1966 Centennial—Rifle

NIB	Exc.	V.G.	Good	Fair	Poor
700	—	120	—	100	—

1966 Centennial—Carbine

NIB	Exc.	V.G.	Good	Fair	Poor
700	—	120	—	100	—

1966 Nebraska Centennial—Rifle

NIB	Exc.	V.G.	Good	Fair	Poor
1200	—	100	—	0	—

1967 Canadian Centennial—Rifle

NIB	Exc.	V.G.	Good	Fair	Poor
650	—	120	—	—	—

1967 Canadian Centennial—Carbine

NIB	Exc.	V.G.	Good	Fair	Poor
650	—	120	—	90	—

1967 Alaskan Purchase Centennial—Carbine

NIB	Exc.	V.G.	Good	Fair	Poor
1250	—	120	—	—	—

1968 Illinois Sesquicentennial—Carbine

NIB	Exc.	V.G.	Good	Fair	Poor
600	—	110	—	40	—

1968 Buffalo Bill—Carbine

NIB	Exc.	V.G.	Good	Fair	Poor
700	—	130	—	110	—

1968 Buffalo Bill—Rifle

NIB	Exc.	V.G.	Good	Fair	Poor
700	—	130	—	—	—

1968 Buffalo Bill "1 of 300" —Rifle

NIB	Exc.	V.G.	Good	Fair	Poor
3500	—	1000	—	300	—

1969 Theodore Roosevelt—Rifle

NIB	Exc.	V.G.	Good	Fair	Poor
700	—	140	—	—	—

1969 Theodore Roosevelt—Carbine

NIB	Exc.	V.G.	Good	Fair	Poor
700	—	140	—	50	—

1969 Golden Spike Carbine

NIB	Exc.	V.G.	Good	Fair	Poor
700	—	120	—	70	—

1970 Cowboy Commemorative Carbine

NIB	Exc.	V.G.	Good	Fair	Poor
750	—	120	—	30	—

1970 Cowboy Carbine "1 of 300"

NIB	Exc.	V.G.	Good	Fair	Poor
3500	—	1000	—	300	—

1970 Northwest Territories (Canadian)

NIB	Exc.	V.G.	Good	Fair	Poor
1000	—	150	—	—	—

1970 Northwest Territories Deluxe (Canadian)

NIB	Exc.	V.G.	Good	Fair	Poor
1300	—	500	—	250	—

1970 Lone Star—Rifle

NIB	Exc.	V.G.	Good	Fair	Poor
700	—	140	—	—	—

1970 Lone Star—Carbine

NIB	Exc.	V.G.	Good	Fair	Poor
700	—	140	—	40	—

1971 NRA Centennial—Rifle

NIB	Exc.	V.G.	Good	Fair	Poor
700	—	150	—	20	—

1971 NRA Centennial—Musket

NIB	Exc.	V.G.	Good	Fair	Poor
700	—	150	—	20	—

1971 Yellow Boy

NIB	Exc.	V.G.	Good	Fair	Poor
1300	—	250	—	—	—

1971 Royal Canadian Mounted Police (Canadian)

NIB	Exc.	V.G.	Good	Fair	Poor
900	—	190	—	10	—

1971 Mounted Police (Canadian)

NIB	Exc.	V.G.	Good	Fair	Poor
1000	—	190	—	—	—

1971 Mounted Police, Presentation

NIB	Exc.	V.G.	Good	Fair	Poor
10000	—	—	—	10	—

1974 Texas Ranger—Carbine

NIB	Exc.	V.G.	Good	Fair	Poor
800	—	140	—	—	—

1974 Texas Ranger Presentation Model

NIB	Exc.	V.G.	Good	Fair	Poor
3500	—	1000	—	150	—

1974 Apache (Canadian)

NIB	Exc.	V.G.	Good	Fair	Poor
900	—	150	—	10	—

1974 Commanche (Canadian)

NIB	Exc.	V.G.	Good	Fair	Poor
900	—	230	—	10	—

1974 Klondike Gold Rush (Canadian)

NIB	Exc.	V.G.	Good	Fair	Poor
900	—	240	—	10	—

1975 Klondike Gold Rush—Dawson City Issue (Canadian)

NIB	Exc.	V.G.	Good	Fair	Poor
8500	—	—	—	20	—

1976 Sioux (Canadian)

NIB	Exc.	V.G.	Good	Fair	Poor
900	—	280	—	10	—

1976 Little Bighorn (Canadian)

NIB	Exc.	V.G.	Good	Fair	Poor
1000	—	300	—	10	—

1976 U.S. Bicentennial Carbine

NIB	Exc.	V.G.	Good	Fair	Poor
800	—	320	—	20	—

1977 Wells Fargo

NIB	Exc.	V.G.	Good	Fair	Poor
800	—	350	—	20	—

1977 Legendary Lawman

NIB	Exc.	V.G.	Good	Fair	Poor
800	—	380	—	20	—

1977 Limited Edition I

NIB	Exc.	V.G.	Good	Fair	Poor
1600	—	1500	—	—	—

1977 Cheyenne—.22 Cal. (Canadian)

NIB	Exc.	V.G.	Good	Fair	Poor
1100	—	320	—	—	—

1977 Cheyenne—.44-40 Cal. (Canadian)

NIB	Exc.	V.G.	Good	Fair	Poor
900	—	300	—	10	—

1977 Cherokee—.22 Cal. (Canadian)

NIB	Exc.	V.G.	Good	Fair	Poor
1100	—	380	—	—	—

1977 Cherokee—.30-30 Cal. (Canadian)

NIB	Exc.	V.G.	Good	Fair	Poor
900	—	380	—	10	—

1978 "One of One Thousand" (European)

NIB	Exc.	V.G.	Good	Fair	Poor
8250	—	5000	—	250	—

1978 Antler Game Carbine

NIB	Exc.	V.G.	Good	Fair	Poor
800	—	380	—	20	—

1979 Limited Edition II

NIB	Exc.	V.G.	Good	Fair	Poor
1600	—	1500	—	—	—

1979 Legendary Frontiersman Rifle

NIB	Exc.	V.G.	Good	Fair	Poor
800	—	420	—	20	—

1979 Matched Set of 1,000

NIB	Exc.	V.G.	Good	Fair	Poor
3000	—	2800	—	—	—

1979 Bat Masterson (Canadian)

NIB	Exc.	V.G.	Good	Fair	Poor
900	—	650	—	10	—

1980 Alberta Diamond Jubilee (Canadian)

NIB	Exc.	V.G.	Good	Fair	Poor
1000	—	650			—

1980 Alberta Diamond Jubilee Deluxe (Canadian)

NIB	Exc.	V.G.	Good	Fair	Poor
1900	—	1800	—	300	—

1980 Saskatchewan Diamond Jubilee (Canadian)

NIB	Exc.	V.G.	Good	Fair	Poor
1000	—	700	—	—	—

1980 Saskatchewan Diamond Jubilee Deluxe (Canadian)

NIB	Exc.	V.G.	Good	Fair	Poor
2000	—	1800	—	300	—

1980 Oliver Winchester

NIB	Exc.	V.G.	Good	Fair	Poor
900	—	380	—	20	—

1981 U.S. Border Patrol

NIB	Exc.	V.G.	Good	Fair	Poor
1200	—	1000	—	—	—

1981 U.S. Border Patrol—Member's Model

NIB	Exc.	V.G.	Good	Fair	Poor
1000	—	800	—	700	—

1981 Calgary Stampede (Canadian)

NIB	Exc.	V.G.	Good	Fair	Poor
2200	—	1800	—	—	—

1981 Canadian Pacific Centennial (Canadian)

NIB	Exc.	V.G.	Good	Fair	Poor
900	—	800	—	—	—

1981 Canadian Pacific Centennial Presentation (Canadian)

NIB	Exc.	V.G.	Good	Fair	Poor
2200	—	1800	—	300	—

1981 Canadian Pacific Employee's Model (Canadian)

NIB	Exc.	V.G.	Good	Fair	Poor
900	—	800	—	—	—

1981 John Wayne (Canadian)

NIB	Exc.	V.G.	Good	Fair	Poor
1600	—	600	—	—	—

1981 John Wayne

NIB	Exc.	V.G.	Good	Fair	Poor
1600		600	50		

1981 Duke

NIB	Exc.	V.G.	Good	Fair	Poor
3750	—	2250	—	—	—

1981 John Wayne "1 of 300" Set

NIB	Exc.	V.G.	Good	Fair	Poor
10000	—	7500	—	300	—

1982 Great Western Artist I

NIB	Exc.	V.G.	Good	Fair	Poor
2200	—	1550	—	1000	—

1982 Great Western Artist II

NIB	Exc.	V.G.	Good	Fair	Poor
2200	—	1500	—	1000	—

1982 Annie Oakley

NIB	Exc.	V.G.	Good	Fair	Poor
1300	—	700	—	10	—

1983 Chief Crazy Horse

NIB	Exc.	V.G.	Good	Fair	Poor
800	—	600	—	200	—

1983 American Bald Eagle

NIB	Exc.	V.G.	Good	Fair	Poor
900	—	800	—	—	—

1983 American Bald Eagle—Deluxe

NIB	Exc.	V.G.	Good	Fair	Poor
4000	—	3000	—	200	—

1983 Oklahoma Diamond Jubilee

NIB	Exc.	V.G.	Good	Fair	Poor
2250	—	1750	—	—	—

1984 Winchester—Colt Commemorative Set

NIB	Exc.	V.G.	Good	Fair	Poor
4000	—	2250	—	—	—

1985 Boy Scout 75th Anniversary .22 Cal.

NIB	Exc.	V.G.	Good	Fair	Poor
1100	—	620	—	20	—

1985 Boy Scout 75th Anniversary—Eagle Scout

NIB	Exc.	V.G.	Good	Fair	Poor
6000	—	2140	—	—	—

Texas Sesquicentennial Model—Rifle .38-55 Cal.

NIB	Exc.	V.G.	Good	Fair	Poor
3000	—	2750	—	—	—

Texas Sesquicentennial Model—Carbine .38-55 Cal.

NIB	Exc.	V.G.	Good	Fair	Poor
1000	—	700	—	20	—

Texas Sesquicentennial Model Set with Bowie Knife

NIB	Exc.	V.G.	Good	Fair	Poor
8000	—	6500	—	150	—

1986 Model 94 Ducks Unlimited

NIB	Exc.	V.G.	Good	Fair	Poor
900	—	—	—	—	—

1986 Statue of Liberty

NIB	Exc.	V.G.	Good	Fair	Poor
9000	—	6500	—	100	—

1986 120th Anniversary Model—Carbine .44-40 Cal.

NIB	Exc.	V.G.	Good	Fair	Poor
1000	—	950	—	—	—

1986 European 1 of 1,000 Second Series (European)

NIB	Exc.	V.G.	Good	Fair	Poor
6000	—	1000	—	150	—

1987 U.S. Constitution 200th Anniversary .44-40

NIB	Exc.	V.G.	Good	Fair	Poor
15000	—	12000	—	200	—

1990 Wyoming Centennial—30-30

NIB	Exc.	V.G.	Good	Fair	Poor
1600	—	900	—	500	—

1991 Winchester 125th Anniversary

NIB	Exc.	V.G.	Good	Fair	Poor
6500	—	5000	—	60	—

1992 Arapaho—30-30

NIB	Exc.	V.G.	Good	Fair	Poor
1600	—	900	—	500	—

1992 Ontario Conservation—30-30

NIB	Exc.	V.G.	Good	Fair	Poor
1600	—	1200	—	400	—

1992 Kentucky Bicentennial—30-30

NIB	Exc.	V.G.	Good	Fair	Poor
1600	—	1000	—	500	—

1993 Nez Perce—30-30

NIB	Exc.	V.G.	Good	Fair	Poor
1600	—	1000	—	600	—

1995 Florida Sesquicentennial Carbine

NIB	Exc.	V.G.	Good	Fair	Poor
1600	—	1200	—	360	—

1996 Wild Bill Hickok Carbine

NIB	Exc.	V.G.	Good	Fair	Poor
1600	—	1200	—	350	—

2008 John Wayne 1892 .44-40

NIB	Exc.	V.G.	Good	Fair	Poor
2000	—	1000	—	—	—

WINDHAM WEAPONRY

Windham, Maine

Restart company from the original founder of Bushmaster, this mainly AR-15 manufacturer is based in Maine and is known for quality and value.

VEX-SS Wood Stock Series

Caliber: .223 Rem. Capacity: 5+1, ships with one 5-round magazine (accepts all standard AR-15 sizes). Barrel: 20", 1:8" RH twist, fluted 416R stainless steel, matte finish. Upper/Lower Receivers: A4-type flat-top upper receiver with optics riser blocks, forged 7075 T6 aircraft aluminum with aluminum triggerguard. Electroless nickel-plated finish. Stock/Forend: laminated wood. Pistol Grip: Hogue OverMolded rubber pistol grip. Sights: None, optics-ready, Picatinny rail partial top rail. Weight: 8.35 lbs. Length: 38.188". Features: Gas-impingement system, Carpenter 158 steel bolt. Compass Lake chamber specification with matched bolt. Wood stock series includes pepper and nutmeg. SEE POLITICAL PANIC PRICING.

NIB	Exc.	V.G.	Good	Fair	Poor
1200	1000	750	600	500	—

Model 20 Varmint

Caliber: .223 Rem./5.56mm NATO. Capacity: 5+1, ships with one 5-round magazine (accepts all standard AR-15 sizes). Barrel: 20", 1:8" RH twist, fluted 416R stainless steel, matte finish. Upper/Lower Receivers: A4-type flattop upper receiver, forged 7075 T6 aircraft aluminum with aluminum triggerguard. Electroless nickel-plated finish. Forend: 15 in. Windham Weaponry aluminum M-LOK free-float. Pistol Grip: Hogue OverMolded rubber pistol grip. Sights: None, optics-ready, Picatinny top rail. Weight: 8.4 lbs. Length: 38.1". Features: Gas-impingement system, Carpenter 158 steel bolt. Compass Lake chamber specification with a matched bolt. LUTH MBA-1 stock. Comes with a hard-plastic case and a black web sling. SEE POLITICAL PANIC PRICING.

NIB	Exc.	V.G.	Good	Fair	Poor
940	800	680	500	400	—

A1 Government

Caliber: .223 Rem./5.56mm NATO. Capacity: 30+1, ships with one 30-round magazine (accepts all standard AR-15 sizes). Barrel: 20", A2 profile, chrome-lined with A1 flash suppressor, 4150 chrome-moly Vanadium 11595E steel with M4 feed ramps. Rifling: 1:7" RH twist. Receivers: A1 upper with brass deflector and teardrop forward assist. Forend: Rifle-length triangular handguard with A1 Delta Ring. Pistol Grip: A1 Black Plastic Grip. Rear Sight: A1 dual aperture rear sight. Front Sight: Adjustable-height square post in A2 standard base. Trigger: Standard mil-spec trigger. Stock: A2 Solid Stock with Trapdoor Storage Compartment. Weight: 7.45 lbs. Length: 39.5". SEE POLITICAL PANIC PRICING.

NIB	Exc.	V.G.	Good	Fair	Poor
1100	1000	830	690	570	—

.223 Superlight SRC

Caliber: .223 Rem./5.56mm NATO. Similar to A1 Government internally. Barrel: 16 in., Superlight with Melonite QPQ Finish and A2 flash suppressor, M4 Feed Ramps, 1:9 rifling. Flattop-type upper receiver. Forend: Single-layer Heat Shield Handguard, A2 black plastic grip. Sights: None, optics ready. Six-position telescoping buttstock. Weight: 5.85 lbs. Length: 32.5-36.25 in.

NIB	Exc.	V.G.	Good	Fair	Poor
750	650	550	—	—	—

Dissipator M4

Caliber: .223 Rem./5.56mm NATO. Similar to Superlight SRC. Barrel: 16", M4 profile, chrome-lined with A2 flash suppressor. Flattop-type upper receiver with A4 detachable carry handle. Rifle-length heat-shielded handguards. A2 black plastic grip. Rear Sight: A4 dual-aperture elevation and windage adjustable for 300m–600m. Front Sight: adjustable-height square post in A2 standard base. Six-position telescoping buttstock. Weight: 7.2 lbs. Length: 32.375" to 36.125". SEE POLITICAL PANIC PRICING.

NIB	Exc.	V.G.	Good	Fair	Poor
960	800	630	500	—	—

SRC-308

Caliber: .308 Win. Capacity: 20+1, ships with one 20-round Magpul PMag magazine. Barrel: 16.5", medium-profile, chrome-lined with A2 flash suppressor; 4150M chrome-moly Vanadium 11595E steel; 1:10" right-hand-twist rifling, six lands and grooves. Upper/Lower Receivers: A4-type flattop upper receiver, forged 7075 T6 aircraft aluminum with aluminum triggerguard. Forend: Mid-length tapered shielded handguards. Pistol Grip: Hogue OverMolded rubber pistol grip. Sights: None, optics-ready, Picatinny top rail. Weight: 7.55 lbs. Length: 34.188" to 38". Features: Gas-impingement system, Carpenter 158 steel bolt. Compass Lake chamber specification with a matched bolt. Six-position telescoping buttstock. Comes with a hard-plastic case and a black web sling. Separate models available in .300 BLK and 7.62x39. SEE POLITICAL PANIC PRICING.

NIB	Exc.	V.G.	Good	Fair	Poor
1200	1070	890	700	590	—

.300 Blackout SRC

Caliber: .300 Blackout. Similar to SRC-308. Weight: 6.15 lbs. Length: 32.375 to 36.125 in.

NIB	Exc.	V.G.	Good	Fair	Poor
1200	1070	890	700	590	—

7.62x39 SRC

Caliber: 7.62x39. Similar to SRC-308. Weight: 6.15 lbs. Length: 32.375 to 36.125 in.

NIB	Exc.	V.G.	Good	Fair	Poor
1200	1070	890	700	590	—

WINDSOR

Windsor, Vermont
Robbins & Lawrence
Hartford, Connecticut

Windsor Rifle-Musket (Antique)

A .577-caliber single-shot percussion rifle, with 39" round barrel secured by three barrel bands. Lock marked "Windsor". Rifles of this pattern were contracted for/by the British Government. Lock and barrel finished in white brass furniture and walnut stock. Approximately 16,000 made from 1855 to 1858.

Exc.	Fine	V.G.	Good	Fair	Poor
3750	3000	1970	950	300	210

WINSLOW ARMS CO.

Camden, South Carolina

Bolt Action Rifle

High-grade semi-custom sporting rifle built upon a number of actions. Offered in all popular calibers from .17 Rem. to .458 Win. Magnum, with

24" barrel and 3-shot magazine. Larger Magnum models have 26" barrel and 2-shot magazine. Two basic stocks are offered—Conventional Bushmaster, which features a standard pistol grip and beavertail forearm; Plainsmaster, which has a full curled hooked pistol grip and wide flat beavertail forearm. Both have Monte Carlo-style stocks, with recoil pads and sling swivels. Offered in a choice of popular woods, with rosewood forend tips and pistol grip caps. Eight different grades of this rifle are available. Following lists the values applicable for each.

Commander Grade

Figured walnut stock. Rosewood forearm tip and grip cap. White line recoil pad. FN Supreme action.

NIB	Exc.	V.G.	Good	Fair	Poor
—	1450	1050	920	700	550

Regal Grade

All features of Commander Grade plus ivory and ebony inlay on stock, French-style checkering, jeweled bolt.

NIB	Exc.	V.G.	Good	Fair	Poor
—	2200	1800	1220	900	600

Regent Grade

As above, with addition of hand-carved checkering.

NIB	Exc.	V.G.	Good	Fair	Poor
—	2380	1850	1250	900	600

Regimental Grade

As above, with addition of basket weave carving, two ivory stock inlays and large ivory and ebony inlay on both sides of buttstock with animal silhouette.

NIB	Exc.	V.G.	Good	Fair	Poor
—	3000	2200	1500	1200	650

Crown Grade

As above, with more elaborate ivory inlays on stock.

NIB	Exc.	V.G.	Good	Fair	Poor
—	3700	2550	1800	1500	650

Royal Grade

As above, with addition of even more elaborate stock carving and ivory and ebony inlay.

NIB	Exc.	V.G.	Good	Fair	Poor
—	4500	3250	2000	1600	650

Imperial Grade

As above, with addition of engraved barrel from receiver to 11" forward. Engraved receiver ring, bolt handle and triggerguard. Engraved scope mounts and rings.

NIB	Exc.	V.G.	Good	Fair	Poor
—	5000	3750	2500	2000	700

Emperor Grade

As above, with addition of gold raised relief animals, engraved receiver and forward part of barrel with muzzle tip engraved as well. Highest Winslow grade.

NIB	Exc.	V.G.	Good	Fair	Poor
—	6250	5000	4000	3000	700

WISEMAN, BILL & CO.

Bryan, Texas

Rifle

Custom order bolt-action rifle utilizing a Sako action. McMillan stainless steel barrel and laminated stock. Action components are Teflon coated. Made in four styles: Hunter, Hunter Deluxe, Maverick and Varminter.

NIB	Exc.	V.G.	Good	Fair	Poor
—	2500	2150	1750	1500	600

Silhouette Pistol

Custom made single-shot pistol produced in a variety of calibers, with 14" fluted stainless steel barrel and laminated pistol grip stock. Furnished without sights. Introduced in 1989.

NIB	Exc.	V.G.	Good	Fair	Poor
—	1750	1450	1100	800	600

WITNESS

See—EUROPEAN AMERICAN ARMORY

WOLF SPORTING PISTOLS

Importer—Handgunner Gunshop
Topton, Pennsylvania

Wolf SV Target

Chambered for 9x19, 9x21, 9x23, .38 Super, .40 S&W or .45 ACP. Barrel 4.5" long. Weight 44 oz. Many special features. Built in Austria. Price listed for basic pistol. A number of special order items are offered. Check with importer before a sale. First imported in 1998.

NIB	Exc.	V.G.	Good	Fair	Poor
2000	1600	1250	1000	750	600

Wolf SV Match

Chambered for 9x19, 9x21, 9x23, .38 Super, .40 S&W or .45 ACP. Barrel 5.5" long. Weight 44 oz. Many special features. Built in Austria. Price listed for basic pistol. A number of special order items are offered. Check with importer before a sale. First imported in 1998.

NIB	Exc.	V.G.	Good	Fair	Poor
2000	1600	1250	1000	750	600

WOODWARD, JAMES & SONS
London, England

Prior to WWII, this company produced a variety of boxlock and sidelock shotguns that are regarded as some of the best made. Prospective purchasers should secure a qualified appraisal prior to acquisition.

WURFFLEIN, ANDREW & WILLIAM
Philadelphia, Pennsylvania

Pocket Pistol (Antique)

A .41-caliber percussion single-shot pocket pistol, with 2.5" or 3" barrel, German silver furniture and checkered walnut stock. Lock marked "A. Wurfflein / Phila.". Manufactured during 1850s and 1860s.

Exc.	Fine	V.G.	Good	Fair	Poor
2600	1750	1220	700	200	140

Single-Shot Target Pistol (Antique)

A .22-caliber single-shot pistol, with half octagonal barrels measuring from 8" to 16" in length. Barrel pivots downward for loading and marked "W. Wurfflein Philad'a Pa. U.S.A. Patented June 24th, 1884". Blued, with walnut grips. Also available with detachable shoulder stock, which if present, would add approximately 35 percent to values listed. Manufactured from 1884 to 1890.

Exc.	Fine	V.G.	Good	Fair	Poor
2600	1750	1220	700	200	140

Single-Shot Rifle (Antique)

Single-shot rifle produced in a variety of calibers, with octagonal barrel lengths of 24" to 28". Available with a wide variety of optional features.

Exc.	Fine	V.G.	Good	Fair	Poor
2400	1250	800	350	150	100

Mid-range Model (Antique)

As above, with 28" or 30" half octagonal barrel.

Exc.	Fine	V.G.	Good	Fair	Poor
4250	3000	1970	950	400	280

Model No. 25 (Antique)

Highest grade rifle manufactured by Wurfflein.

Exc.	Fine	V.G.	Good	Fair	Poor
4500	3500	2370	1250	600	420

WYOMING ARMS
Cody, Wyoming

Manufacturer of Model WY-15 match-grade AR-type rifles in various grades and configurations. Each model is guaranteed for 1 MOA or better accuracy with specific match grade ammo.

WY-15 4400

Direct impingement gas system. .223 or .300 Blackout. 1 MOA accuracy.

NIB	Exc.	V.G.	Good	Fair	Poor
2000	1800	1600	—	—	—

WY-15 5500 & 5500 LWT & 5500 Pistol

As above with 16", 18", or 20" barrel in .223, .200, .240, 6.5 Grendel, or .300 Blackout. ¾ MOA accuracy in full-size version, 7 lbs. with 16" barrel. Model WY-15 5500 LWT is a lightweight version with 1 MOA accuracy, 6.3 lbs. with 16" barrel. Pistol version available with 10" barrel.

NIB	Exc.	V.G.	Good	Fair	Poor
2600	2300	2000	—	—	—

WY-15 6600 & 6600 LWT

As above, ½ MOA accuracy in full-size version. Lightweight model also available.

NIB	Exc.	V.G.	Good	Fair	Poor
3200	2900	2500	—	—	—

WY-15 6612

As above chambered 7.62 NATO; 1 MOA accuracy.

NIB	Exc.	V.G.	Good	Fair	Poor
3200	2900	2500	—	—	—

Parker

Single-action semi-auto pistol in .45 ACP or 10mm with 5", 7", or 3 3/8" barrel with premium for long or short barrels. The same model was also later manufactured by LaserAim. Can be difficult to reassemble, deduct value if missing ejector or ejector spring.

Jim Supica photo

NIB	Exc.	V.G.	Good	Fair	Poor
680	450	380	—	—	—

X

XL
Norwich, Connecticut

See—HOPKINS & ALLEN

XPERT
Norwich, Connecticut

See—HOPKINS & ALLEN

Xpert Derringer (Antique)

.22- or .30-caliber spur trigger single-shot pistol, with round barrels 2.25" to 6" in length. Nickel-plated finish, with rosewood grips. Breech-block pivots to left side for loading. Barrel marked "Xpert-Pat. Sep. 23. 1878". Manufactured during 1870s.

Exc.	*Fine*	*V.G.*	*Good*	*Fair*	*Poor*
880	700	550	400	120	80

Xpert Pocket Rifle (Antique)

Similar to derringer, with same size frame fitted with 7.5" barrel. Chambered for .22 cartridge, as well as .30-caliber rimfire. Supplied with wire stock. Values for gun with stock. Produced from about 1870 to 1890s.

Exc.	*Fine*	*V.G.*	*Good*	*Fair*	*Poor*
1480	1150	820	500	150	100

Y

YILDIZ SILAH
Burdur, Turkey

Turkish firearm manufacturer primarily in the market of affordable yet quality shotguns in a variety of configurations

Elegant

Gauge: .410 bore, 3 in. Barrels: 26 in., 28 in., 30 in., with 7mm or 8mm rib. Weight: 4.8-6.0 lbs. Stock: Oil-finish selected walnut from standard through Grades 3 and 5, some pistol grip and others straight English-style. Features: Built of 4140 Steel, with varying degrees of receiver engraving. Manual or automatic safety, extractors, or ejectors, depending on model. Single selective trigger, front bead, full black rubber recoil pad. Models series include: A1, A3, A4, A5, and Special Lux. Includes five Mobil chokes. Manufactured in Turkey and imported/sold through Academy.

NIB	*Exc.*	*V.G.*	*Good*	*Fair*	*Poor*
420	—	—	—	—	—

Z

Z-B RIFLE CO.
Brno, Czechoslovakia

Model ZKW-465 Varmint Rifle

Mauser bolt-action rifle chambered for .22 Hornet cartridge. Has 23" barrel, with three-leaf folding rear sight. Offered standard with double-set triggers. Finish blued, with select walnut checkered stock.

NIB	Exc.	V.G.	Good	Fair	Poor
—	1600	1150	980	800	500

ZANOTTI, FABIO
Brescia, Italy

Model 625

12-gauge to .410 bore boxlock double-barrel shotgun, with automatic ejectors and single-selective trigger. Blued, with checkered walnut stock.

NIB	Exc.	V.G.	Good	Fair	Poor
6500	5200	4700	3500	2500	500

Model 626

As above, engraved with scroll work or hunting scenes.

NIB	Exc.	V.G.	Good	Fair	Poor
7000	5700	5200	4000	2800	500

Giacinto

External hammer boxlock shotgun produced in a variety of gauges, with double triggers.

NIB	Exc.	V.G.	Good	Fair	Poor
6500	5200	4700	3500	2500	500

Maxim

Similar to Model 625 fitted with detachable sidelocks.

NIB	Exc.	V.G.	Good	Fair	Poor
7000	5700	5200	4000	2800	500

Edward

As above, but more intricately engraved.

NIB	Exc.	V.G.	Good	Fair	Poor
12000	9000	6500	4500	3000	1500

Cassiano I

As above, with exhibition grade engraving.

NIB	Exc.	V.G.	Good	Fair	Poor
13000	9000	7000	6000	4000	2000

Cassiano II

As above, with gold inlays.

NIB	Exc.	V.G.	Good	Fair	Poor
14500	12000	9500	7000	5000	2500

Cassiano Executive

Strictly custom-made shotgun produced to client's specifications. Values will vary.

NIB	Exc.	V.G.	Good	Fair	Poor
45000	—	—	—	—	—

ZASTAVA

Former Yugoslavian manufacturer now located in Serbia and a major arms supplier to the world.

Zastava M-70 Semi-Automatic Pistol

This 7.65mm (.32 ACP) caliber pistol was originally designed in 1967 and was modified in 1970 from a short-recoil action to a much more cost effective blowback system. Known in the U.S.A. as the Zastava M-70, it is often referred to as the M 67/70 in Russia, and nicknamed the "Yovanovitch" (a rare, obscure Serbian pistol designed in the 1930s), in the former Soviet Union and Eastern European countries that were one time communist satellites. Utilizing an eight-round magazine, the M-70 was issued to high-ranking Yugoslavian military officers and police during the Cold War, and was originally manufactured by Zavodi Crvena Zastava from 1970 until the beginning of the Balkan Wars of the 1990s. It was sold on the European commercial market during the Combloc era as well. By 2011, it was back in production by the reorganized Zastava Arms of Kragujevac, Serbia. This version is not currently imported to the U.S., however fair quantities of the communist-era variation have been imported at various times. A variation has been catalogued since the 1970s specifying the M-70 in .380 ACP, otherwise known as 9mm Kretek in Serbian. None of these have been seen in the West, and collectors in Europe state that few have ever been seen there, making it a very rare version. The hard rubber grips on the M-70 have a ZCZ circular logo, and all pistols have a bar-type thumb safety on the left rear frame. The pistol is, in essence, a mini Tokarev. Care should be taken not to confuse it with the Zastava M-70A which is a 9mm Luger caliber variant of the full size 7.62x25mm M-57. For M-70 pistols-with the original communist-era box, spare magazine and cleaning brush, add 100 percent to prices below. Engraved examples in various grades normally reap a substantially higher price. A .380 ACP chambering could perhaps double the New-in-Box value, depending on condition.

NIB	Exc.	V.G.	Good	Fair	Poor
1200	580	450	380	250	180

M57A

Single-action semi-auto pistol based on the Soviet TT Tokarev design with external safety. 7.62x25mm Tokarev, 9-round magazine. Add $80 for polished chrome finish.

NIB	Exc.	V.G.	Good	Fair	Poor
400	350	280	—	—	—

M70AA

Similar to above, except in 9mm. Add $80 for chrome.

NIB	Exc.	V.G.	Good	Fair	Poor
400	350	280	—	—	—

CZ999

Alloy frame semi-auto pistol based on CZ 99. 9mm, 15-round magazine, traditional double-action. Add $20 for chrome slide.

NIB	Exc.	V.G.	Good	Fair	Poor
700	650	600	—	—	—

EZ9

Semi-auto 9mm pistol, short recoil, alloy frame, loaded chamber indicator. Compact model EZ9C has the same value.

NIB	Exc.	V.G.	Good	Fair	Poor
700	650	600	—	—	—

ZPAP M70

AK pattern semi-auto rifle, 7.62x39, 16.3" barrel, 7.9 lbs., wood or various color black poly collapsible stock.

NIB	Exc.	V.G.	Good	Fair	Poor
900	800	700	—	—	—

Sniper Rifle M91

Dragunov-style semi-auto rifle, 7.62x54R, 24" barrel, with scope.

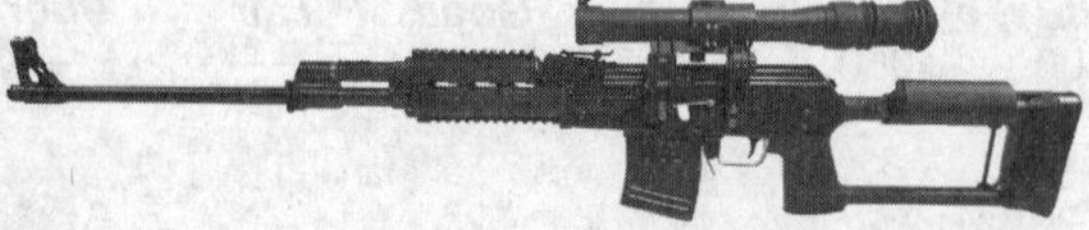

NIB	Exc.	V.G.	Good	Fair	Poor
3000	2650	2250	—	—	—

ZPAP85

AK-pattern semi-auto pistol, 5.56 NATO, 10" barrel, 6.6 lbs.

NIB	Exc.	V.G.	Good	Fair	Poor
750	680	600	—	—	—

ZPAP92

As above, except in 7.62x39mm.

NIB	Exc.	V.G.	Good	Fair	Poor
750	680	600	—	—	—

LK M70

Mauser style bolt action sporting rifle in wide range of popular calibers from .22-250 through .458 Win Mag.

NIB	Exc.	V.G.	Good	Fair	Poor
780	700	620	—	—	—

LK M85

Mini-mauser-style bolt-action sporting rifle in calibers 7.62x39, .223 Rem, or .22-250.

NIB	Exc.	V.G.	Good	Fair	Poor
730	650	580	—	—	—

MP22

Small bore bolt-action rifle in .22 LR.

NIB	Exc.	V.G.	Good	Fair	Poor
430	380	330	—	—	—

ZEHNER, E. WAFFENFABRIK

Suhl, Germany

Zehna

6.35mm semi-automatic pistol, with 2.5" barrel and 5-shot magazine. Slide marked "Zehna DRPA", and caliber on later production models. Blued, with black plastic grips bearing monogram "EZ". Approximately 20,000 made from 1921 to 1927.

NIB	Exc.	V.G.	Good	Fair	Poor
—	400	300	250	180	100

ZEPHYR

Eibar, Spain

Importer—STOEGERS

Woodlander II

12- or 20-gauge boxlock shotgun, with varying barrel lengths, double triggers and extractors. Blued, with walnut stock.

NIB	Exc.	V.G.	Good	Fair	Poor
600	450	400	300	200	100

Uplander

12-, 16-, 20-, 28-gauge or .410 bore sidelock double-barrel shotgun, with varying barrel lengths, double triggers and automatic ejectors. Blued, with walnut stock.

NIB	Exc.	V.G.	Good	Fair	Poor
850	700	500	400	300	150

Upland King

As above in 12- or 16-gauge, with ventilated rib barrels.

NIB	Exc.	V.G.	Good	Fair	Poor
1150	800	700	600	400	250

Vandalia

12-gauge single-barrel trap gun, with 32" Full choked barrel. Blued, with walnut stock.

NIB	Exc.	V.G.	Good	Fair	Poor
750	600	550	450	300	150

Sterlingworth II

Identical to Woodlander, with sidelocks.

NIB	Exc.	V.G.	Good	Fair	Poor
850	700	550	450	300	150

Victor Special

12-gauge boxlock double-barrel shotgun, with 25", 28" or 30" barrels, double triggers and extractors. Blued, with walnut stock.

NIB	Exc.	V.G.	Good	Fair	Poor
520	400	300	250	180	100

Thunderbird

10-gauge Magnum boxlock double-barrel shotgun, with 32" Full choked barrels, double triggers and automatic ejectors. Blued, with walnut stock.

NIB	Exc.	V.G.	Good	Fair	Poor
950	700	600	500	400	200

Honker

10-gauge Magnum single-barrel shotgun, with 36" Full choked and ventilated rib barrel. Blued, with walnut stock.

NIB	Exc.	V.G.	Good	Fair	Poor
600	450	400	300	200	100

ZM WEAPONS
Bernardton, Massachusetts

LR-300 Sport Rifle

Highly modified AR-15 chambered for .223 cartridge. Fitted with 16.25" barrel and true folding stock. Ghost ring rear sight and adjustable post front, with Tritium insert standard. Weight about 7.2 lbs. Introduced in 1997.

NIB	Exc.	V.G.	Good	Fair	Poor
—	1600	1200	950	780	500

ZOLI USA, ANGELO
Brescia, Italy

Slide-Action Shotgun

12-gauge Magnum slide-action shotgun. Produced with a variety of barrel lengths, with detachable choke tubes. Blued, with walnut stock.

NIB	Exc.	V.G.	Good	Fair	Poor
400	300	250	200	150	100

Diano I

12-, 20-gauge or .410 bore single-shot folding barrel shotgun. Produced in a variety of barrel lengths. Blued, with walnut stock.

NIB	Exc.	V.G.	Good	Fair	Poor
180	100	90	80	60	40

Diano II

As above, with bottom lever instead of top release lever.

NIB	Exc.	V.G.	Good	Fair	Poor
180	100	90	80	60	40

Apache

12-gauge Magnum lever-action shotgun, with 20" barrel. Fitted with detachable choke tubes. Blued, with walnut stock.

NIB	Exc.	V.G.	Good	Fair	Poor
500	400	350	300	250	150

Quail Special

.410 Magnum bore double-barrel shotgun, with 28" barrels and single trigger. Blued, with walnut stock.

NIB	Exc.	V.G.	Good	Fair	Poor
320	200	150	120	100	80

Falcon II

As above, with 26" or 28" barrels and double triggers.

NIB	Exc.	V.G.	Good	Fair	Poor
320	200	150	120	100	80

Pheasant

12-gauge Magnum double-barrel shotgun, with 28" barrels, single trigger and automatic ejectors. Blued, with walnut stock.

NIB	Exc.	V.G.	Good	Fair	Poor
450	350	300	250	200	150

Classic

As above, with 26" to 30" barrels fitted with detachable choke tubes, single-selective trigger and automatic ejectors. Blued, with walnut stock.

NIB	Exc.	V.G.	Good	Fair	Poor
850	700	600	500	300	200

Snipe

.410 bore over/under shotgun, with 26" or 28" barrels and single trigger.

NIB	Exc.	V.G.	Good	Fair	Poor
400	300	200	180	150	100

Dove

Similar to above.

NIB	Exc.	V.G.	Good	Fair	Poor
400	300	200	180	150	100

Texas

12-, 20-gauge or .410 bore over/under shotgun, with 26" or 28" barrels, double triggers and bottom barrel release lever.

NIB	Exc.	V.G.	Good	Fair	Poor
350	250	200	150	100	80

Field Special

12- or 20-gauge Magnum double-barrel shotgun. Produced in a variety of barrel lengths. Single trigger and extractors. Blued, with walnut stock.

NIB	Exc.	V.G.	Good	Fair	Poor
550	400	300	250	200	100

Pigeon Model

As above, but more finely finished.

NIB	Exc.	V.G.	Good	Fair	Poor
550	400	300	250	200	100

Standard Model

Similar to above in 12- and 20-gauge only.

NIB	Exc.	V.G.	Good	Fair	Poor
500	400	300	250	200	100

Special Model

As above, with detachable choke tubes and single-selective trigger.

NIB	Exc.	V.G.	Good	Fair	Poor
600	450	300	250	200	100

Deluxe Model

As above, but engraved with better quality walnut.

NIB	Exc.	V.G.	Good	Fair	Poor
800	600	500	400	300	150

Presentation Model

As above, with false sidelocks and finely figured walnut stock.

NIB	Exc.	V.G.	Good	Fair	Poor
950	700	600	450	350	200

St. George's Target

12-gauge over/under shotgun trap or skeet bore, with various barrel lengths, single-selective trigger and automatic ejectors. Blued, with walnut stock.

NIB	Exc.	V.G.	Good	Fair	Poor
1200	900	700	600	550	250

St. George Competition

12-gauge single-barrel gun, with extra set of over/under barrels.

NIB	Exc.	V.G.	Good	Fair	Poor
1950	1600	1200	950	500	300

Express Rifle

.30-06, 7x65Rmm or 9.3x74Rmm over/under double-barrel rifle, with single triggers and automatic ejectors. Blued, with walnut stock.

NIB	Exc.	V.G.	Good	Fair	Poor
4250	3500	2500	1750	1200	600

Express EM

As above, but more finely finished.

NIB	Exc.	V.G.	Good	Fair	Poor
5500	4000	3000	1500	1000	750

Savana E

As above, with double triggers.

NIB	Exc.	V.G.	Good	Fair	Poor
6500	5250	4500	3500	2750	1500

Savana Deluxe

As above, engraved with hunting scenes.

NIB	Exc.	V.G.	Good	Fair	Poor
8000	7000	6000	4750	3500	2000

AZ 1900C

.243, .270, 6.5x55mm, .308 or .30-06 bolt-action rifle, with 24" barrel and open sights. Blued, with walnut stock.

NIB	Exc.	V.G.	Good	Fair	Poor
850	700	500	400	300	150

AZ 1900M

Same as above, with Bell & Carlson composite stock.

NIB	Exc.	V.G.	Good	Fair	Poor
750	600	450	350	280	200

AZ 1900 Deluxe

As above, but more finely finished.

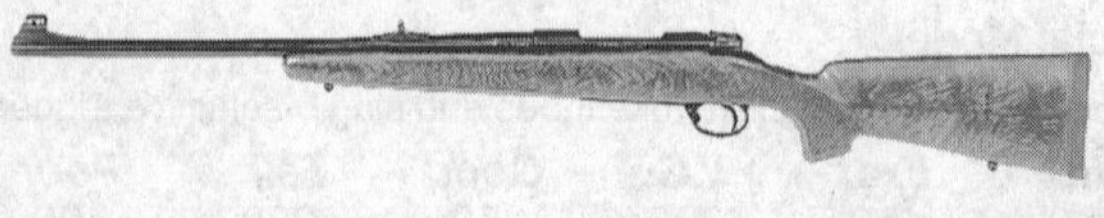

NIB	Exc.	V.G.	Good	Fair	Poor
1100	800	650	500	400	200

AZ 1900 Super Deluxe

As above, engraved with finely figured walnut stock.

NIB	Exc.	V.G.	Good	Fair	Poor
1500	1000	800	600	450	250

Patricia Model

As above in .410 Magnum bore, with 28" ventilated rib barrels, various chokes, single-selective trigger and automatic ejectors. Engraved blued, with finely figured walnut stock.

NIB	Exc.	V.G.	Good	Fair	Poor
1500	1100	950	750	650	400

Condor

.30-06 or .308 and 12-gauge over/under combination shotgun/rifle, with double triggers, extractors and sling swivels. Blued, with walnut stock.

NIB	Exc.	V.G.	Good	Fair	Poor
1500	1050	850	700	500	300

Airone

As above, with false sidelocks.

NIB	Exc.	V.G.	Good	Fair	Poor
1650	1250	1000	800	600	300

Leopard Express

.30-06, .308, 7x65Rmm or .375 H&H over/under double-barrel rifle, with 24" barrels. Express sights, double triggers and extractors. Blued, with walnut stock.

NIB	Exc.	V.G.	Good	Fair	Poor
1750	1400	1000	800	600	300

ZOLI, ANTONIO

Brescia, Italy

Silver Hawk

12- or 20-gauge boxlock double-barrel shotgun. Produced in a variety of barrel lengths and chokes, with double trigger. Engraved blued, with walnut stock.

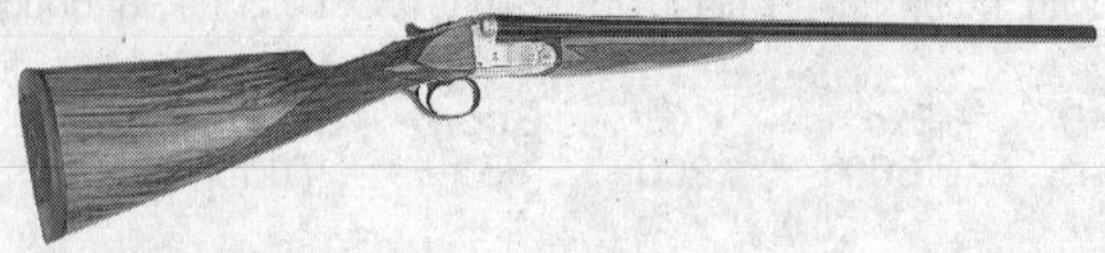

NIB	Exc.	V.G.	Good	Fair	Poor
—	1020	900	850	600	450

Ariete M2

12-gauge boxlock double-barrel shotgun, with 26" or 28" barrels, non-selective single trigger and automatic ejectors. Engraved blued, with walnut stock.

NIB	Exc.	V.G.	Good	Fair	Poor
—	1150	1000	850	700	350

Empire

As above in 12- or 20-gauge, with 27" or 28" barrels. Engraved French case-hardened blued, with walnut stock.

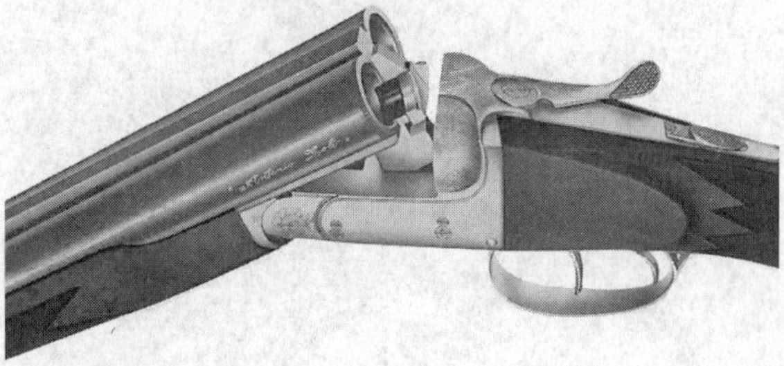

NIB	Exc.	V.G.	Good	Fair	Poor
—	2300	1950	1400	1250	400

Volcano Record

12-gauge sidelock double-barrel shotgun, with 28" barrels. Available in a variety of chokes, single-selective trigger and automatic ejectors. Engraved French case-hardened blued, with walnut stock.

NIB	Exc.	V.G.	Good	Fair	Poor
—	7000	6000	5000	4000	500

Volcano Record ELM

Strictly custom-ordered shotgun produced to purchaser's specifications. Value speculative.

NIB	Exc.	V.G.	Good	Fair	Poor
—	16000	13500	10500	8500	500

Silver Snipe

12- or 20-gauge over/under shotgun. Produced with varying lengths, ventilated rib barrels, single trigger and extractors. Engraved blued, with walnut stock.

NIB	Exc.	V.G.	Good	Fair	Poor
—	600	450	400	320	280

Golden Snipe

As above more finely finished. Fitted with automatic ejectors.

NIB	Exc.	V.G.	Good	Fair	Poor
—	650	500	450	350	300

Delfino

As above in 12- or 20-gauge Magnum, with 26" or 28" ventilated rib barrels, non-selective single trigger and automatic ejectors. Engraved blued, with walnut stock.

NIB	Exc.	V.G.	Good	Fair	Poor
—	580	420	320	280	250

Ritmo Hunting Gun

As above in 12-gauge Magnum, with 26" or 28" separated ventilated rib barrels, single-selective trigger and automatic ejectors. Engraved blued, with walnut stock.

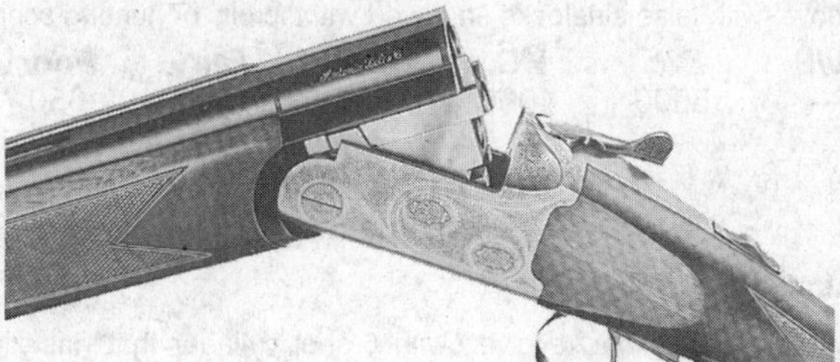

NIB	Exc.	V.G.	Good	Fair	Poor
—	650	500	450	400	350

Condor Model

As above in 12-gauge, with 28" skeet bored barrels. Wide competition rib, single-selective trigger and automatic ejectors. Engraved French case-hardened blued, with walnut stock.

NIB	Exc.	V.G.	Good	Fair	Poor
—	1100	800	650	500	400

Angel Model

As above in field grade version.

NIB	Exc.	V.G.	Good	Fair	Poor
—	1100	800	600	500	400

Ritmo Pigeon Grade IV

As above, with 28" separated ventilated rib barrels, single-selective trigger, automatic ejectors and extensively engraved. French case-hardened blued, with finely figured walnut stock.

NIB	Exc.	V.G.	Good	Fair	Poor
—	2250	1600	1200	800	600

Model 208 Target

As above, with 28" or 30" trap or skeet bored barrels. Fitted with a wide ventilated rib.

NIB	Exc.	V.G.	Good	Fair	Poor
—	1200	850	700	600	500

Model 308 Target

As above, but more finely finished.

NIB	Exc.	V.G.	Good	Fair	Poor
—	1500	1100	850	700	500

Combinato

.222 or .243 and 12- or 20-gauge over/under combination rifle/shotgun, with engraved boxlock-action, double triggers and folding rear sight. French case-hardened blued, with walnut stock.

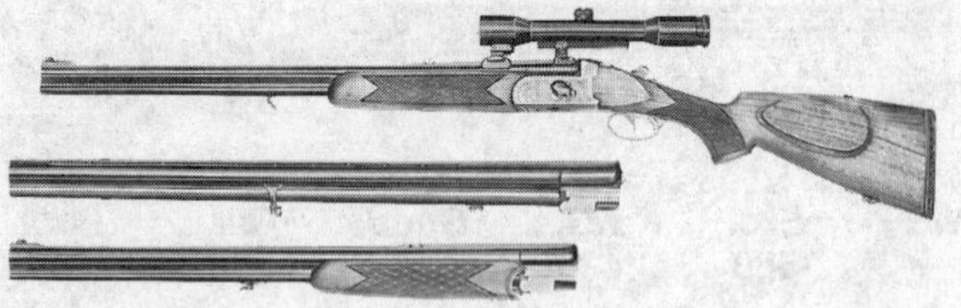

NIB	Exc.	V.G.	Good	Fair	Poor
—	2500	1700	1250	950	500

Safari Deluxe

As above, with false sidelocks engraved with scrolls or hunting scenes.

NIB	Exc.	V.G.	Good	Fair	Poor
—	5000	4000	2850	1500	650

ZULAICA, M.

Eibar, Spain

Zulaica

Solid-frame .22-caliber revolver, with 6-shot cylinder that has zigzag grooves on its exterior surface. Fired by an external hammer. Frame is hollow, with a rod inside of it that connects to breech-block. Serrated cocking piece connected to this rod that is found at top rear of frame. When fired, cartridge case blows from cylinder and activates breech-block similar to a semi-automatic pistol.

NIB	Exc.	V.G.	Good	Fair	Poor
—	1000	800	600	350	250

ROYAL

Royal was applied to a number of pistols produced by this company as listed.

Royal

6.35mm or 7.65mm semi-automatic pistol. Normally marked on slide "Automatic Pistol 6.35 Royal" or "Automatic Pistol 7.65 Royal".

NIB	Exc.	V.G.	Good	Fair	Poor
—	300	180	100	80	50

7.65mm

As above in 7.65mm caliber, with 5.5" barrel and 12-shot magazine.

NIB	Exc.	V.G.	Good	Fair	Poor
—	320	200	120	100	80

6.35mm

Rather poor copy of Mauser Model C/96 semi-automatic pistol, with fixed lockwork.

NIB	Exc.	V.G.	Good	Fair	Poor
—	900	700	500	300	150

Vincitor

6.35mm or 7.65mm caliber semi-automatic pistol. Patterned after Model 1906 Browning. Slide marked "SA Royal Vincitor". Blued, with plastic grips.

NIB	Exc.	V.G.	Good	Fair	Poor
—	300	180	100	80	50

MODEL INDEX

BROWNING ARMS CO.

BROWN MANUFACTURING CO.

BROWN PRECISION, INC.

BROWN PRODUCTS, ED

C

CZ - STRAKONICE

D

DAEWOO

DAISY

DAKIN GUN CO.

DAKOTA ARMS, INC.

DALY, CHARLES

DAN ARMS OF AMERICA

DANIEL DEFENSE

G

I

MOUNTAIN ARMS

MOUNTAIN RIFLES, INC.

MUGICA, JOSE ... 909

MURFREESBORO ARMORY ... 909

MURPHY & O'CONNELL

MURRAY, J. P.

MUSGRAVE

MUSKETEER RIFLES

N

NATIONAL ARMS CO.

NAVY ARMS COMPANY

O

RENETTE, GASTINNE

REPUBLIC ARMS, INC.

RETAY

RETOLAZA HERMANOS

REUNIES

REUTH, F.

REXIO DE ARMAS (COMANCHE)

R. G. INDUSTRIES

RHEINMETALL

RHODE ISLAND ARMS CO.

RICHLAND ARMS CO.

RICHMOND ARMORY

RIEDL RIFLE CO.

RIGBY, JOHN & CO., LTD.

RIGDON, ANSLEY & CO.

RIPOMANTI, GUY

RIVERSIDE ARMS CO.

RIZZINI, BATTISTA

RIZZINI, FRATELLI

ROBAR AND DE KIRKHAVE

ROBAR COMPANIES

ROBBINS & LAWRENCE

ROBERTS DEFENSE

S

SUNDANCE INDUSTRIES, INC.

U